VideoHound's GOLDEN MOVIE RETRIEVER

Also from Visible Ink Press:

Now that you've read *VideoHound's Golden Movie Retriever®*, you're probably in the mood for some more *VideoHound* entertainment titles. Are you in luck! Here's a list of other *VideoHound* titles that can be found at quality bookstores everywhere.

VideoHound's Complete Guide to Cult Flicks and Trash Pics

VideoHound's Sci-Fi Experience: Your Quantum Guide to the Video Universe

VideoHound's Family Video Guide, Second Edition

The VideoHound & All-Movie Guide StarGazer

VideoHound's Movie LaughLines: Quips, Quotes, and Clever Comebacks

VideoHound's Idiot's Delight: The 100 Dumbest Movies of All Time

Toxic Fame: Celebrities Speak on Stardom

VideoHound's GOLDEN MOVIE RETRIEVER

Detroit New York Toronto London

VideoHound®'s Golden Movie Retriever™ 1997

Published by Visible Ink Press®, a division of Gale Research, 835 Penobscot Building, Detroit, MI 48226-4094

ISBN 0-7876-0780-0

Printed in the United States of America

10 9 8 7 6 5 4 3 2 1

Credits

Editors/Casting:
Martin Connors
James Craddock

Editor No More:
Julia Furtaw

Contributing Editors:
Michelle Banks
Kelly M. Cross
Beth A. Fhaner
Christopher P. Scanlon
Terri Schell
Carol Schwartz
Devra M. Sladics
Christine Tomassini
Hilary Weber

Contributors:
Martin Craddock
John Miller
Matthew Totsky

Digital Effects:
Donald Dillaman

Titles and Opticals:
Michael Boyd, Atlis Publishing Services, Inc.

Design Poobah:
Cynthia Baldwin

Design FX:
Mary Krzewinski

Frontmatter Technician:
Marco Di Vita, The Graphix Group

Illustrator:
Steffan Duerr

Key Grips:
Mary Beth Trimper
Dorothy Maki
Evi Seoud
Shanna Heilveil
Wendy Blurton

Assistant to Mr. Hound:
Jane P. Connors

KopyKat:
Sue Stefani

Radio Transmission:
Martin BanDyke

Mr. Hound's Personal Groomer:
Robert Ruffer

Hype:
Jenny Sweetland
Kamela Torvinen

Marketing Propogandist:
Betsy Rovegno

Contents

Introduction

Hey look. We've changed. Some things are different. It had to happen sooner or later. You hang around those Hollywood movie types long enough, eventually you get the urge to make improvements in your appearance. A nip here, a tuck there. Perhaps a little work around the jowls. Maybe pin the ears. Declaw? I don't think so. Remove some of that pesky extra poundage? Sure, as long as it doesn't require exercise. Vanity? Egoism run rampant? A shallow desire to be loved not for our soul, but our superficial physical appearance? You betcha.

The changes to the 1997 edition of *VideoHound's Golden Movie Retriever* were made for the purest of reasons; to ensure the ease and comfort of the people who depend on the *Hound* for entertainment, bar bet answers, and a successful trip to the video store—you. Yes, the *Hound* has once again taken that long walk down self-improvement avenue. Tightened some things. Made others easier to use. Replaced whole parts! Even added stuff! Only the reliability and attitude remain intact.

Within the reviews, you'll notice, perhaps, that some of the most useful information now appears right after the title—the ever-important bone ratings, MPAA rating, release year, and alternate titles. People with failing eyesight will find this much easier to read. We tested it on Bryan the student co-op and he could make out certain patterns while wearing very dark sunglasses in a poorly-lit room. Moments like that make you want to shout, "Eureka!" Information on alternate formats such as Beta or laserdisc have joined the run time, color/black and white symbols, and foreign codes just in front of the cast listings. And the cast listings, not content to rest on their laurels, now include cinematographers. And yes, pricing information has bitten the dust. Because video prices frequently fluctuate and a single video may be available at a whole range of price points, we've eliminated that information, and will devote the space saved to extra long introductions. The distributor information is still there, and a call to the proper distributor will likely reveal current pricing.

Now let's talk about indexes, which continue to grow, flex, and change. The biggest change you'll notice is the combination of some smaller indexes. The Laserdisc/CD-I and Closed Caption indexes have combined with information on Beta, 8mm, and letterbox availability to become the Alternate Formats Index (betcha didn't see that one comin'). The Series Index, which provides information on great screen partnerships and recurring characters, has been absorbed into the Kibbles Index, where it will live in peaceful harmony with listings of stage and literary adaptations, important producers, and quality checks like four-bone classics and **Woofs**.

Can't seem to quench that obsessive thirst for entertainment information with *VideoHound* alone? Why not? Okay, you have your reasons, and, most likely, a PC. So in this edition we proudly unveil the heretofore never attempted Web Site Guide, the first of its kind in a "Major Video Guide." It contains information on web sites devoted to your favorite actors, actresses, directors, and directresses, as well as movie home pages, filmmaker resources, studio info, and cult movie resources. General information citations contain URLs (kinda like the site's address) and text to help you decide if a site is worth the connect time. Sites devoted to celebrities or movies contain only URL addresses because the headings are pretty much self-explanatory. To make room for the Web Site Guide we've removed the Music Video Guide and are storing it in a glass jar in the office. Perhaps someday we'll do a full-fledged music video guide, particularly if you, the loyal reader/user/all-round nice person write in and tell us to do one. Another newcomer is the Cinematographer Index, which looks like the rest of the cast-type indexes and is devoted to those previously overlooked artisans who are responsible for a movie's "look," the directors of photography. Now for the first time you can "look" up Jan DeBont, Haskell Wexler, Gordon Parks, or any other cinematographer. Since many of these folks, including Barry Sonnenfeld and DeBont, tend to graduate to director rank, their camera work is essential to understanding their overall body of work.

We've also relocated the indexes, condensing some of them onto a tiny microchip located in the spine of the book. Don't look, you won't be able to see it. Drop the book in a hot tub, then you'll see it. In response to a serious survey conducted by the team of Craddock, Craddock, and Craddock (Slogan: We've got stamps, and we're not afraid to use 'em) of our loyal audience, we were left with the impression that many of our readers wanted us to send them money and that it would be nice if we put all of the indexes in the back of the book. So, with the exception of the Alternate Titles Index, that's where we put 'em. Alternate Titles stays up front so that you don't have to wander too far from the entries to find a flick that has a different name than you thought it did.

But hey, enough about us. How've you been? How was your summer? Did you watch a lot of movies? We still want to hear from you. That way next year's introduction will be easier to write. Let us know what you think of the changes. Could we still do more? Many of you have asked if we could list movies that aren't yet on video. Well, we have a hard enough time finding room for the ones that *are* on video, but that brings up a good topic of conversation. What are your favorite movies that aren't yet available on video? Even though more movies are being released on video or laserdisc every day, many more have escaped the careful eyes of the people who hunt through vaults looking for gems to release to an unsuspecting public. We'll make it a crusade. Maybe not as urgent as the work of the Film Preservation Society, but a crusade nonetheless. We must rise up against our video oppressors and demand the liberation of certain films onto video. Or DVD. Whatever. There's plenty of fine cinematic fare that hasn't seen the light of harsh video store neon. We can change that. Well, we can discuss and debate it anyway, and maybe appoint a committee to look into it and report back on it. And then we'll do a feasibility study. And if we eventually make our demands known within these pages, maybe we can persuade or convince the studios to heed our requests. After all, it was *VideoHound* that demanded the release of Disney's Snow White and the Seven Dwarfs. But the evil queen wouldn't let them go! A scant four years later, viola! (Or "Eureka!" if you will) it came out on video. So we have power where it counts. Tell us your video dreams. But don't be too explicit.

First cosmetic changes, then megalomania! What's next? Endlessly talking about ourselves? Referring to ourselves in the plural third person? Hosting a talk show? Critics Who Think Joe Piscopo is Funny...On the next *VideoHound!* Nah, this gig is pretty sweet. If Ricki Lake promises not to make any more movies, we promise to stay out of the talk show biz. Well, back to the tough job of reviewing videos. Rough life, but a *VideoHound*'s work is never done. Oh, and a memo to Chuck in Rochester: The *Hound* will find you.

Using VideoHound

Alphabetization

Titles are arranged on a word-by-word basis, including articles and prepositions. Leading articles (*A, An, The*) are ignored in English-language titles. The equivalent foreign articles are not ignored, however: *The Abyss* appears under "A" while *Les Miserables* appears under "L." **Other points to keep in mind:**

- Acronyms appear alphabetically as if regular words. For example *C.H.U.D.* is alphabetized as "Chud"; *M*A*S*H* as "Mash."
- Common abbreviations in titles file as if they are spelled out, so *St. Elmo's Fire* will be found under "Saint Elmo's Fire" and *Mr. Holland's Opus* will be alphabetized as "Mister Holland's Opus."
- Proper Names in titles are alphabetized beginning with the individual's first name; for instance, *Monty Python's The Meaning of Life* is under "M;" *Eddie Murphy: Raw* under "E."
- Titles with numbers (*2001: A Space Odyssey*) are alphabetized as if the number was spelled out under the appropriate letter, in this case "Two Thousand One." When numeric titles gather in close proximity to each other (*2000 Year Old Man, 2001, 2069: A Sex Odyssey*), the titles will be arranged in a low (*2000*) to high (*2069*) numeric sequence.

Indexes

Alternate Title Index A number of videos, particularly older or B-type releases, may have variant titles. Alternate titles are listed alphabetically and refer the reader to the title under which the entry is listed. The alternate titles are also noted within the review.

Category Index Subject categories ranging from the orthodox to slightly eccentric permit you to video sleuth from broad type to significant themes to signature scenes. The mix, arranged alphabetically by category, includes hundreds of traditional film genres and sub-genres as well as a feast of *VideoHound* exclusives. Integrated into the index are cross references, while preceding the index is a list of definitions. **A tipped triangle indicates a movie rated three bones or above.**

Kibbles and Series Index Not your everyday categories, Kibbles span the literary side of movie-making (adapted from a play, Hemingway on video) and point out key producers and special effects masters. Yearly box-office winners (that are now on video) since 1939 are listed, along with classic movies, four-bone delights, trash films, modern Shakespeare, Disney fare, and of course, bottom of the barrel *Woof!* features, some of which are terrible enough to provide an amusing evening.

The index formerly known as Series, now combined with Kibbles, provides listings of major movie series, ranging from James Bond to National Lampoon to Indiana Jones. Recurring cinematic collaborations and partnerships of note are also listed, including Hope & Crosby, Abbott & Costello, De Niro & Scorsese, and Harrelson & Snipes. A complete list of the categories precedes the index. **As in the Category Index, tipped triangles indicate quality views.**

Awards Index The Awards Index lists films honored (or in some cases dishonored) by 20 national and international award bodies, representing some 90 categories of competition. This information is also contained in the review following the credits. **Only features available on video and reviewed in the main section are listed in this index; movies not yet released on video are not covered.**

As award-winning films find their way to video, they will be added to the review section and covered in this index. Awards listed include the Academy Awards; Australia Film Institute; British Academy of Film and Television Arts; Cannes Film Festival; French Cesar; Canadian Genie; Golden Globe; Directors Guild of America; Edgar Allan Poe Awards; Independent Spirit; Montreal Film Festival; and the MTV Awards.

Foreign Film Index Here the *Hound* classifies movies by the country/countries of record in which the feature was financed (but not necessarily where they were filmed). Since the producers of a specific film may hail from more than one country, some videos will be listed under more than one country. **The foreign codes also appear in the review immediately following the color or black and white designation. A**

tipped triangle following the title indicates a three bone or above endeavor.

Cast/Director Indexes The Cast Index provides full videographies for all actors and actresses listed in *VideoHound* with more than one movie on their resume. the Director Index lists the works of any director that made it to video and to *VideoHound*. Although listed in a first name, last name sequence, the names are alphabetized by last name. Film titles, complete with initial year of release, are arranged in chronological order.

Writer Index Scriptwriters and script doctors are listed with their vital works. Names are arranged alphabetically by last name. Works are arranged chronologically.

☆NEW☆ Cinematographer Index Directors of Photography are listed alphabetically by last name, along with their work, which is arranged chronologically. Cinematography is often a starting point for feature directors.

Composer Index Videographies of movie music composers, arrangers, lyricists, and so on are listed. Arranged alphabetically by last name.

Song Title Index Alphabetic list of songs performed during the course of a cinematic musical. Title of the movie in which the song was performed follows the song title.

☆NEW☆ Alternate Formats Index The Laserdisc/CD-I and Closed Captioned Indexes, along with Beta, 8mm, and Letterbox information, have been combined into one index listing the various formats in which you can find and purchase your favorite flicks.

Distributor Guide Each video review has at least one and as many as three distributor codes. In the reviews, these are located at the bottom of the review. The full address and phone, toll-free, and fax numbers of the distributors listed can be found in the *Distributor Guide*. **A caution: a small number of distributors adhere to a nomadic life-style that includes frequent address changes. A tiny minority on the list in any given year will also go out of business. An extra caution: Studio distributors do not sell to the general public, they generally act as wholesalers, selling only to retail outlets.** Up to three distributors are listed in order to give you more choice. A Distributor List, preceding the Guide, provides an alphabetical list of the distributor codes which will refer the reader to the proper distributor.

In the main section, those reviews with the code *OM* are on moratorium (distributed at one time, though not currently). Since a title enjoying such status was once distributed, it may well linger on your local video store shelf. When the distributor is not known, the code *NO* appears. For new releases to the theater that have not yet made it to video (but likely will in the coming year), the code *NYR* (not yet released) appears.

☆NEW☆ Web Site Guide Replaces the Music Video Guide. Lists Internet web sites for popular actors, actresses and directors, studio movie sites, general entertainment information, filmmaker resources, and video outlets, as well as sites for cult movie information. Actor and movie sites list the URLs after the main citation. The more popular the personality, the more URLs. Sites with more generalized information contain text after the URL to help you decide if they are worth a visit.

Sample Review

Each *VideoHound* review contains up to 18 items, ranging from title to the review to awards received to the distributor code. The information in these reviews is designed to help you choose a video you'll like, increase your enjoyment of a movie as you watch (especially by answering that nagging question of "What else have I seen that guy in?"), and increase your knowledge of movie trivia.

1	Title
2	One-to-four bone rating (or *Woof!*)
3	Alternate Title (we made this up)
4	Year released
5	MPAA Rating
6	Description/review
7	Songs (we made these up, too)
8	Length (in minutes)
9	Black and White (B) or Color (C)
10	Format (VHS, Beta, LV-Laserdisc, or 8mm)
11	Country produced in (made it up)
12	Cast (V: indicates voiceovers; also includes cameos)
13	Director
14	Writers
15	Cinematography
16	Composers/Lyricists
17	Awards and Nominations
18	Distributor code

1 Braveheart 2 [3½ bones] **3** Men in Skirts **4 1995 5 (R) 6** Producer-director-star Gibson does it all in this bold, ferocious, reasonably accurate epic about the passion and cost of freedom. Charismatic 13th century Scottish folk hero William Wallace leads his desperate and outnumbered clansmen in revolt against British oppression. Sweeping, meticulous battle scenes fit surprisingly well with moments of stirring romance and snappy wit. Among the mostly unknown (in the States, anyway) cast, Marceau and McCormack are elegant as Wallace's lady loves, and McGoohan is positively hateful as King Edward I. Gory and excessively violent (as medieval warfare tends to be) and a bit too long (as historical epics tend to be), but rewarding entertainment for those who stick it out—where else can you see the king's army get mooned en masse? Script was based on 300 pages of rhyming verse attributed to a blind poet known as Blind Hally. Gibson put up $15 million of his own money to complete the film. **7** Scotland Rules; Blue Moon; Got a Sword in My Eye. **8 178m 9 C 10 VHS, Beta. 11** *GB* **12** Mel Gibson, Sophie Marceau, Patrick McGoohan, Catherine McCormack, Brendan Gleeson, James Cosmo, David O'Hara, Angus McFadyen, Peter Hanly; **13 D:** Mel Gibson; **14 W:** Randall Wallace; **15 C:** John Toll; **16 M:** James Horner. **17** Academy Awards '95: Best Cinematography, Best Director (Gibson), Best Makeup, Best Picture; British Academy Awards '95: Best Cinematography; Golden Globe Awards '96: Best Director (Gibson); MTV Movie Awards '96: Best Action Sequence; Writers Guild of America '95: Best Original Screenplay; Nominations: Academy Awards '95: Best Costume Design, Best Film Editing, Best Screenplay, Best Sound, Best Score; British Academy Awards '95: Best Director (Gibson), Best Score; Directors Guild of America Awards '95: Best Director (Gibson); Golden Globe Awards '96: Best Film—Drama, Best Screenplay, Best Score, MTV Movie Awards '96: Best Film, Best Male Performance (Gibson), Most Desirable Male (Gibson). **18** *PAR*

Mail Order Video Sources

Time Warner Viewer's Edge has assured us that they can provide any video listed in VideoHound's Golden Movie Retriever. You can contact them at 1-800-241-7535. Here are some additional mail-order sources to help you in your quest for that elusive video:

Thomas Video
122 S. Main St.
Clawson, MI 48017
(810)280–2833

Video Vision
Attn: Chris Hendlin
4603 Bloominton Ave.
Minneapolis, MN 55407
(612)729–6491

Movies Unlimited
(800)4–MOVIES
located in Philadelphia

Cape Copy Center
631 Main St.
Hyannis, MA 02601
(508)775–6500

Video Oyster
145 W. 12th St.
New York, NY 10011
(212)989–3300
fax: (212)989–3533
e–mail: video@VideoOyster.com

Facets Video
(800)331–6197
located in Chicago

Video Vault
(800)VAULT66
located in Alexandria, VA

A Million and One World–Wide Videos
(800)849–7309
fax: (800)849–0873

Alternate Title Index

The **Alternate Title Index** provides variant and foreign titles for movies with more than one name. Titles are listed in alphabetical order, followed by a cross-reference to the appropriate entry in the main video review section. If you don't find a movie you're looking for in the main section, this is the best place to look next.

Ami de Mon Ami *See* Boyfriends & Girlfriends (1988)
Amityville 3-D *See* Amityville 3: The Demon (1983)
The Amityville Horror: The Evil Escapes, Part 4 *See* Amityville 4 (1989)
Amok *See* Schizo (1977)
The Amorous General *See* Waltz of the Toreadors (1962)
The Amorous Sex *See* Sweet Beat (1962)
Amour de Poche *See* Girl in His Pocket (1957)
Amy Fisher: My Story *See* Lethal Lolita—Amy Fisher: My Story (1992)
And Comes the Dawn...But Colored Red *See* Web of the Spider (1970)
And Once Upon a Love *See* Fantasies (1973)
And Then There Were None *See* Ten Little Indians (1975)
And Woman...Was Created *See* And God Created Woman (1957)
Anderson's Angels *See* Chesty Anderson USN (1976)
Andrews' Raiders *See* The Great Locomotive Chase (1956)
Andy Colby's Incredibly Awesome Adventure *See* Andy and the Airwave Rangers (1989)
Angel in Red *See* Uncaged (1991)
Angel of Vengeance *See* Ms. 45 (1981)
Angel of Vengeance *See* WarCat (1988)
An Angel Passed Over Brooklyn *See* The Man Who Wagged His Tail (1957)
Angel Street *See* Gaslight (1939)
Angels for Kicks *See* Wild Riders (1971)
Anglagard *See* House of Angels (1992)
Animal House *See* National Lampoon's Animal House (1978)
Anita—Tanze des Lasters *See* Anita, Dances of Vice (1987)
Anne of Green Gables: The Sequel *See* Anne of Avonlea (1987)
Annie's Coming Out *See* A Test of Love (1984)
The Antichrist *See* The Tempter (1974)
L'Anticristo *See* The Tempter (1974)
Antinea, l'Amante Della Citta Sepolta *See* Journey Beneath the Desert (1961)
The Anxious Years *See* Dark Journey (1937)
Any Number Can Win *See* Melodie en Sous-Sol (1963)
Anyone for Venice? *See* The Honey Pot (1967)
Anything for Love *See* 11 Harrowhouse (1974)
Apocalipsis Canibal *See* Night of the Zombies (1983)
Apres l'Amour *See* Love After Love (1994)
Apu Sansat *See* The World of Apu (1959)
Apur Sansar *See* The World of Apu (1959)
The Aqua Sex *See* The Mermaids of Tiburon (1962)
Arctic Heat *See* Born American (1986)
Are You Dying Young Man? *See* Beast in the Cellar (1970)
The Arena *See* Naked Warriors (1973)
Arizona Ripper *See* Terror at London Bridge (1985)
Armored Attack *See* The North Star (1943)
Army Mystery *See* Criminals Within (1941)
Arthur the King *See* Merlin and the Sword (1985)
Artist Nude Secrets *See* Artist's Studio Secrets (1964)
Ascenseur Pour L'Echafaud *See* Frantic (1958)
Ascent to Heaven *See* Mexican Bus Ride (1951)
Ashanti *See* Ashanti, Land of No Mercy (1979)
The Assassination Team *See* Wardogs (1987)
Assault Force *See* ffolkes (1980)
Assault on Paradise *See* Maniac (1977)
Assignment: Istanbul *See* The Castle of Fu Manchu (1968)
Assignment: Kill Castro *See* The Mercenaries (1980)
Asylum Erotica *See* Slaughter Hotel (1971)
Asylum of the Insane *See* Flesh and Blood Show (1973)
At First Sight *See* Love at First Sight (1976)
At the Villa Rose *See* House of Mystery (1941)
Atlantic City U.S.A. *See* Atlantic City (1981)
The Atlantis Interceptors *See* Raiders of Atlantis (1983)
Atlas Against the Cyclops *See* Atlas in the Land of the Cyclops (1961)
Atoll K *See* Utopia (1951)
Atomic Rocketship *See* Flash Gordon: Rocketship (1936)
Ator the Invincible *See* Blade Master (1984)
Attack of the 5 Ft. 2 Women *See* National Lampoon's Attack of the 5 Ft. 2 Women (1994)
Attack of the Monsters *See* Gamera vs. Guiron (1969)
Attack of the Phantoms *See* KISS Meets the Phantom of the Park (1978)
Attack of the Rebel Girls *See* Assault of the Rebel Girls (1959)
Attention! Une Femme Peut en Cacher une Autre *See* My Other Husband (1985)
Au-Dela des Grilles *See* The Walls of Malapaga (1949)
L'Auberge Rouge *See* The Red Inn (1951)
Aura *See* The Witch (1966)
Austerlitz *See* The Battle of Austerlitz (1960)
The Avengers *See* The Day Will Dawn (1942)
Avenging Godfather *See* Avenging Disco Godfather (1976)
L'Aventure Sauvage *See* Trap (1966)
Avonlea *See* Tales from Avonlea, Vol. 1: The Journey Begins (1990)
A.W.O.L. *See* Lionheart (1990)
Az en XX. Szazadom *See* My Twentieth Century (1990)
Babe, the Gallant Pig *See* Babe (1995)
Babes Ahoy *See* Going Overboard (1989)
Babes in Toyland *See* March of the Wooden Soldiers (1934)
Baby Blood *See* The Evil Within (1994)
The Baby Vanishes *See* Broadway Limited (1941)
Bachelor Girl Apartment *See* Any Wednesday (1966)
Bachelor Knight *See* The Bachelor and the Bobby-Soxer (1947)
Backwoods Massacre *See* Midnight (1981)
Bad Boyz *See* Valley Girl (1983)
Bad Girl *See* Teenage Bad Girl (1959)
Bad Girls *See* Delinquent School Girls (1984)
Bad Girls *See* Whore 2 (1994)
Bad Man of Harlem *See* Harlem on the Prairie (1938)
Badkonake Sefid *See* The White Balloon (1995)
The Bailiff *See* Sansho the Bailiff (1954)
Baisers Voles *See* Stolen Kisses (1968)
The Bait *See* L'Appat (1994)
The Baited Trap *See* The Trap (1959)
Bakushu *See* Early Summer (1951)
The Banana Monster *See* Schlock (1973)
Bande a Part *See* Band of Outsiders (1964)
The Bandit *See* Crossfire (1967)
Banditi a Orgosolo *See* Bandits of Orgosolo (1961)
Bang Bang *See* Bang Bang Kid (1967)
Bangiku *See* Late Chrysanthemums (1954)
The Bank Detective *See* The Bank Dick (1940)
Banner in the Sky *See* Third Man on the Mountain (1959)
The Bar Sinister *See* It's a Dog's Life (1955)
Barbados Quest *See* Murder on Approval (1956)
Barbarella, Queen of the Galaxy *See* Barbarella (1968)
The Barbarians and Co. *See* The Barbarians (1987)
The Barbaric Beast of Boggy Creek, Part II *See* Boggy Creek II (1983)
Bargain Basement *See* Department Store (1935)
Baron Blood *See* Torture Chamber of Baron Blood (1972)
Batman: The Animated Movie *See* Batman: Mask of the Phantasm (1993)
Batmen of Africa *See* Darkest Africa (1936)
Battle Beyond the Stars *See* The Green Slime (1968)
The Battle for Anzio *See* Anzio (1968)
Battle of the Astros *See* Godzilla vs. Monster Zero (1968)
The Battle of the Mareth Line *See* Battleforce (1978)
The Battle of the River Plate *See* Pursuit of the Graf Spee (1957)
Battle Stripe *See* The Men (1950)
Battletruck *See* Warlords of the 21st Century (1982)
The Battling Bellhop *See* Kid Galahad (1937)
Battling Hoofer *See* Something to Sing About (1936)
Bawang Bie Ji *See* Farewell My Concubine (1993)
Bay of Blood *See* Twitch of the Death Nerve (1971)
The Bay of Saint Michel *See* Pattern for Plunder (1962)
Bayou *See* Poor White Trash (1957)
Be Beautiful but Shut Up *See* Just Another Pretty Face (1958)
Be My Valentine, Or Else... *See* Hospital Massacre (1981)
Be Roringen *See* The Touch (1971)
The Beans of Egypt, Maine *See* Forbidden Choices (1994)
The Bear Hunt *See* Bare Hunt (1963)
The Beast Must Die *See* Black Werewolf (1975)
The Beast of War *See* The Beast (1988)
Beasts *See* Twilight People (1972)
Beatlemania *See* Beatlemania! The Movie (1981)
Beatsville *See* The Rebel Set (1959)
Beautiful But Dangerous *See* She Couldn't Say No (1952)
Beautiful But Deadly *See* The Don is Dead (1973)
A Beautiful Place to Kill *See* Paranoia (1969)
Beethoven's Great Love *See* Beethoven (1936)
Beggars' Opera *See* The Threepenny Opera (1931)
The Beginners *See* The First Time (1969)
The Beginners Three *See* The First Time (1969)
Behind Enemy Lines *See* The P.O.W. Escape (1986)
Behind Locked Doors *See* Human Gorilla (1948)
Behind the Blue *See* L'Enfant d'Eau (1995)
Behind the Iron Mask *See* The Fifth Musketeer (1979)
Bells *See* Murder by Phone (1982)
The Beloved *See* Restless (1972)
Berry Gordy's The Last Dragon *See* The Last Dragon (1985)
Bethune, The Making of a Hero *See* Dr. Bethune (1990)
Betrayal *See* Trahir (1993)
Between Us *See* Entre-Nous (1983)
Beware! The Blob *See* Son of Blob (1972)
Bewitching Scatterbrain *See* Ravishing Idiot (1964)
The Beyond *See* Seven Doors of Death (1982)
Beyond Bedlam *See* Nightscare (1993)
Beyond Justice *See* Guardian Angel (1994)
Beyond Obsession *See* Beyond the Door (1975)
Beyond the Fog *See* Tower of Evil (1972)
Beyond the Living *See* Hospital of Terror (1978)
Beyond the Living Dead *See* The Hanging Woman (1972)
Beyond the Rising Moon *See* Star Quest (1989)
Bez Konca *See* No End (1984)
Bez Znieczulenia *See* Without Anesthesia (1978)
The Big Bankroll *See* The King of the Roaring '20s: The Story of Arnold Rothstein (1961)
The Big Boss *See* Fists of Fury (1973)
The Big Day *See* Jour de Fete (1948)
Big Deal at Dodge City *See* A Big Hand for the Little Lady (1966)
Big Duel in the North *See* Godzilla vs. the Sea Monster (1966)
Big Enough and Old Enough *See* Savages from Hell (1968)
The Big Heart *See* Miracle on 34th Street (1947)
The Big Lobby *See* Rosebud Beach Hotel (1985)
The Big Payoff *See* Win, Place, or Steal (1972)
Big Time Operators *See* The Smallest Show on Earth (1957)
The Biggest Right on Earth *See* Ghidrah the Three Headed Monster (1965)
Biggles: Adventures in Time *See* Biggles (1985)
Bijo to Ekitainigen *See* H-Man (1959)
Bikini Genie *See* Wildest Dreams (1990)
Billy the Kid's Fighting Pals *See* Trigger Men (1941)
Bio-Force I *See* Mutant Species (1995)
Birds of a Feather *See* The Birdcage (1995)
Birds of Prey *See* Beaks: The Movie (1987)
Birthmark *See* The Omen (1976)
Birumano Tategoto *See* The Burmese Harp (1956)
The Bitch *See* La Chienne (1931)
Bittere Ernte *See* Angry Harvest (1985)
Black Angels *See* Black Bikers from Hell (1970)
Black Arrow Strikes *See* Black Arrow (1948)

The Black Book *See* Reign of Terror (1949)
The Black Bounty Killer *See* Boss (1974)
The Black Buccaneer *See* The Black Pirate (1926)
Black Eliminator *See* Kill Factor (1978)
Black Flowers for the Bride *See* Something for Everyone (1970)
Black Frankenstein *See* Blackenstein (1973)
Black Gauntlet *See* Black Starlet (1974)
Black Jack *See* Captain Blackjack (1951)
Black Love, White Love *See* Sweet Love, Bitter (1967)
Black Rider *See* Joshua (1976)
Black Rose of Harlem *See* Machine Gun Blues (1995)
Black Valor *See* Savage! (1973)
Blade of Steel *See* The Far Pavilions (1984)
Blake Edwards' Son of the Pink Panther *See* Son of the Pink Panther (1993)
Blast-Off *See* Those Fantastic Flying Fools (1967)
Blazing Arrows *See* Fighting Caravans (1931)
Blazing Magnums *See* Strange Shadows in an Empty Room (1976)
Bless 'Em All *See* The Act (1982)
Blind Alley *See* Perfect Strangers (1984)
The Blind Dead *See* Tombs of the Blind Dead (1972)
Blind Man's Bluff *See* Cauldron of Blood (1967)
Blind Terror *See* See No Evil (1971)
Blonde Bombshell *See* Bombshell (1933)
The Blonde From Peking *See* The Peking Blond (1968)
A Blonde in Love *See* Loves of a Blonde (1965)
Blondie Has Servant Trouble *See* Blondie Has Trouble (1940)
Blood and Sand *See* Sand and Blood (1987)
Blood Bath *See* Track of the Vampire (1966)
Blood Beast from Outer Space *See* Night Caller from Outer Space (1966)
Blood Brides *See* Hatchet for the Honeymoon (1970)
The Blood Brother *See* Texas Pioneers (1932)
Blood Castle *See* The Blood Spattered Bride (1972)
Blood Ceremony *See* The Legend of Blood Castle (1972)
Blood Couple *See* Black Vampire (1973)
Blood Creature *See* Terror Is a Man (1959)
The Blood Crowd *See* The McMasters (1970)
The Blood Cult of Shangri-La *See* The Thirsty Dead (1974)
Blood Demon *See* The Torture Chamber of Dr. Sadism (1969)
Blood Doctor *See* Mad Doctor of Blood Island (1969)
The Blood Drinkers *See* The Vampire People (1966)
Blood Feast *See* Night of a Thousand Cats (1972)
Blood Fiend *See* Theatre of Death (1967)
Blood for Dracula *See* Andy Warhol's Dracula (1974)
Blood Hunger *See* Vampyres (1974)
Blood is My Heritage *See* Blood of Dracula (1957)
Blood Mad *See* The Glove (1978)
Blood Money *See* The Killer's Edge (1990)
Blood Moon *See* The Werewolf vs. the Vampire Woman (1970)
Blood Oath *See* Prisoners of the Sun (1991)
Blood of Frankenstein *See* Dracula vs. Frankenstein (1971)
Blood of Fu Manchu *See* Kiss and Kill (1968)
Blood of the Man Devil *See* House of the Black Death (1965)
Blood of the Undead *See* Schizo (1977)
Blood On His Lips *See* Hideous Sun Demon (1959)
The Blood Seekers *See* Cain's Cutthroats (1971)
Blood Splash *See* Nightmare (1982)
The Blood Suckers *See* Alien Massacre (1967)
The Blood Suckers *See* Dr. Terror's House of Horrors (1965)
Blood Thirst *See* Salem's Lot (1979)
Bloodline *See* Sidney Sheldon's Bloodline (1979)
Bloodsilver *See* Beyond the Law (1968)
The Bloody Bushido Blade *See* The Bushido Blade (1980)
Bloody Pom Poms *See* Cheerleader Camp (1988)
Bloomfield *See* The Hero (1971)
The Blow-Out *See* La Grande Bouffe (1973)

Blue *See* Trois Couleurs: Bleu (1993)
Blue and the Gold *See* The Annapolis Story (1955)
Blue Heat *See* The Last of the Finest (1990)
Blue Manhattan *See* Hi, Mom! (1970)
Blue Sierra *See* Courage of Lassie (1946)
Blues for Lovers *See* Ballad in Blue (1966)
Blues La-Chofesh Ha-Godol *See* Late Summer Blues (1987)
Blunt *See* The 4th Man (1979)
The Boat *See* Das Boot (1981)
Boca a Boca *See* Mouth to Mouth (1995)
Bodas de Sangre *See* Blood Wedding (1981)
The Body Stealers *See* Invasion of the Body Stealers (1969)
The Bodyguards *See* La Scorta (1994)
Bogus Bandits *See* The Devil's Brother (1933)
Bohemian Life *See* La Vie de Boheme (1993)
The Bold Cavalier *See* The Bold Caballero (1936)
Bolero: An Adventure in Ecstasy *See* Bolero (1984)
Bombsight Stolen *See* Cottage to Let (1941)
Bordello of Blood *See* Tales from the Crypt Presents Bordello of Blood (1996)
Border Heat *See* Deadly Stranger (1988)
Born Natturunnar *See* Children of Nature (1991)
Born to Kill *See* Cockfighter (1974)
Bosambo *See* Sanders of the River (1935)
Boss Nigger *See* Boss (1974)
Boudu Sauve des Eaux *See* Boudu Saved from Drowning (1932)
Bound by Honor *See* Blood In...Blood Out: Bound by Honor (1993)
Bourbon St. Shadows *See* The Invisible Avenger (1958)
A Bout de Souffle *See* Breathless (1959)
The Boxer *See* Counter Punch (1971)
The Boyfriend School *See* Don't Tell Her It's Me (1990)
Boyichi and the Supermonster *See* Gamera vs. Gaos (1967)
The Boys from Brooklyn *See* Bela Lugosi Meets a Brooklyn Gorilla (1952)
The Brain Machine *See* Mind Warp (1972)
The Brainsnatchers *See* The Man Who Lived Again (1936)
Brainwash *See* Circle of Power (1983)
Bram Stoker's Burial of the Rats *See* Burial of the Rats (1995)
Branded *See* Bad Boy (1939)
Brandy Ashore *See* Green Grow the Rushes (1951)
The Brave and the Beautiful *See* The Magnificent Matador (1955)
The Brave Young Men of Weinberg *See* Up the Academy (1980)
Break In *See* Loophole (1983)
Breakdance *See* Breakin' (1984)
Breakdance 2: Electric Boogaloo *See* Breakin' 2: Electric Boogaloo (1984)
The Breakup *See* La Rupture (1970)
Brenn, Hexe, Brenn *See* Mark of the Devil (1969)
Brennendes Geheimnis *See* Burning Secret (1989)
Bride of the Atom *See* Bride of the Monster (1956)
The Bride of the Lake *See* Lily of Killarney (1934)
Brides of Blood *See* Brides of the Beast (1968)
Bridge Across Time *See* Terror at London Bridge (1985)
Broken Hearts and Noses *See* Crimewave (1985)
Bronenosets Potemkin *See* The Battleship Potemkin (1925)
Bronx Warriors *See* 1990: The Bronx Warriors (1983)
Brothel 8 *See* Sandakan No. 8 (1974)
Brotherhood of the Yakuza *See* The Yakuza (1975)
Bruce Brown's The Endless Summer 2 *See* The Endless Summer 2 (1994)
Bruce Lee's Game of Death *See* Game of Death (1979)
The Brute *See* El Bruto (1952)
Brutti, Sporchi, e Cattivi *See* Down & Dirty (1976)
Buck Rogers *See* Destination Saturn (1939)
Buckaroo Banzai *See* The Adventures of Buckaroo Banzai Across the Eighth Dimension (1984)
Bud Abbott and Lou Costello in Hollywood *See* Abbott and Costello in Hollywood (1945)
Budding Love *See* L'Amour en Herbe (1977)

The Buddy Factor *See* Swimming with Sharks (1994)
Build My Gallows High *See* Out of the Past (1947)
A Bullet from God *See* God's Gun (1975)
Bullfighter *See* Torero (1956)
Bump in the Night *See* The Final Terror (1983)
The Bunny Caper *See* Games Girls Play (1975)
The Burden of Proof *See* Scott Turow's The Burden of Proof (1992)
Buried on Sunday *See* Northern Extremes (1993)
Burn Out *See* Journey into Fear (1974)
Burn, Witch, Burn *See* Mark of the Devil (1969)
Burning Cross *See* The Klansman (1974)
Burning Hearts *See* Kolberg (1945)
The Burning Man *See* Dangerous Summer (1982)
Bushwhacked *See* French Twist (1995)
The Butcher *See* Le Boucher (1969)
The Butcher *See* Psycho from Texas (1983)
Butcher Baker (Nightmare Maker) *See* Night Warning (1982)
The Butterfly Revolution *See* Summer Camp Nightmare (1986)
Bvongiorno, Elefante *See* Pardon My Trunk (1952)
By Hook or By Crook *See* I Dood It (1943)
By Rocket to the Moon *See* Woman in the Moon (1929)
Cabiria *See* Nights of Cabiria (1957)
Caccia Ai Violenti *See* One Step to Hell (1968)
Caccia alla Volpe *See* After the Fox (1966)
Cactus Jack *See* The Villain (1979)
Cafe of the Seven Sinners *See* Seven Sinners (1940)
The Cage *See* My Sister, My Love (1978)
Caged Females *See* Caged Heat (1974)
Caged Heart *See* L'Addition (1985)
Cain's Way *See* Cain's Cutthroats (1971)
Calhoun *See* Nightstick (1987)
The California Dolls *See* ...All the Marbles (1981)
California Holiday *See* Spinout (1966)
California Hot Wax *See* The Bikini Car Wash Company (1990)
California in 1878 *See* Fighting Thru (1930)
California Man *See* Encino Man (1992)
The Californian *See* The Gentleman from California (1937)
Call Harry Crown *See* 99 & 44/100 Dead (1974)
Call it Murder *See* Midnight (1934)
Call of the Savage *See* Savage Fury (1933)
Call the Cops *See* Find the Lady (1975)
The Calling *See* Murder by Phone (1982)
Calling Northside 777 *See* Call Northside 777 (1948)
Campanadas a Medianoche *See* Chimes at Midnight (1967)
Camper John *See* Gentle Savage (1973)
Campsite Massacre *See* The Final Terror (1983)
Canicule *See* Dog Day (1983)
Cannibal Orgy, or the Maddest Story Ever Told *See* Spider Baby (1964)
Cannibals in the City *See* Invasion of the Flesh Hunters (1982)
Cannibals in the Streets *See* Invasion of the Flesh Hunters (1982)
Capitaine Morgan *See* Morgan the Pirate (1960)
Capitalismo Salvaje *See* Savage Capitalism (1993)
Captain Mephisto and the Transformation Machine *See* Manhunt of Mystery Island (1945)
Captain Midnight *See* On the Air Live with Captain Midnight (1979)
Captain Yankee *See* Jungle Raiders (1985)
Captive Women 3: Sweet Sugar *See* Sweet Sugar (1972)
Caravans West *See* Wagon Wheels (1934)
The Card *See* The Promoter (1952)
Cardigan's Last Case *See* State's Attorney (1931)
Care of the Spitfire Grill *See* The Spitfire Grill (1995)
Carlo Collodi's Pinocchio *See* The Adventures of Pinocchio (1996)
Carnage *See* Twitch of the Death Nerve (1971)
Carnival of Fools *See* Death Wish Club (1983)
Carnival of Thieves *See* Caper of the Golden Bulls (1967)
Carquake *See* Cannonball (1976)
Carry On Follow That Camel *See* Follow That Camel (1967)

The Cars That Eat People *See* The Cars That Ate Paris (1974)
Cartagine in Fiamme *See* Carthage in Flames (1960)
Cartes sur Table *See* Attack of the Robots (1966)
Carthage en Flammes *See* Carthage in Flames (1960)
The Case of Jonathan Drew *See* The Lodger (1926)
The Case of the Hillside Stranglers *See* The Hillside Strangler (1989)
Case of the Missing Switchboard Operator *See* The Love Affair, or The Case of the Missing Switchboard Operator (1967)
Cash *See* If I Were Rich (1933)
Cassanova and Co. *See* Sex on the Run (1978)
Castle in the Sky *See* Yidl Mitn Fidl (1936)
Castle of Doom *See* Vampyr (1931)
Castle of Terror *See* Castle of Blood (1964)
Castle of Terror *See* The Virgin of Nuremberg (1965)
The Castle of the Spider's Web *See* Throne of Blood (1957)
Castle of the Walking Dead *See* The Torture Chamber of Dr. Sadism (1969)
The Cat *See* Le Chat (1975)
C.A.T. Squad *See* Stalking Danger (1986)
C.A.T. Squad: Python Wolf *See* Python Wolf (1988)
Catacombs *See* Curse 4: The Ultimate Sacrifice (1990)
Catastrophe 1999 *See* Last Days of Planet Earth (1974)
Catchfire *See* Backtrack (1989)
Catholic Boys *See* Heaven Help Us (1985)
Cathy Tippel *See* Keetje Tippel (1975)
Cauchemares *See* Cathy's Curse (1977)
Cavalleria Commandos *See* Cavalry Command (1963)
The Cave Dwellers *See* One Million B.C. (1940)
Cave Man *See* One Million B.C. (1940)
Cavegirl *See* Cave Girl (1985)
C.C. & Company *See* Chrome Hearts (1970)
Cell Block Girls *See* Women's Prison Escape (19??)
Cemetary Girls *See* The Vampire Hookers (1978)
Cemetary Girls *See* The Velvet Vampire (1971)
Cento Dollari D'Odio *See* Uncle Tom's Cabin (1969)
Ceremonia Sangrienta *See* The Legend of Blood Castle (1972)
A Certain Mr. Scratch *See* The Devil & Daniel Webster (1941)
Cet Obscur Objet Du Desir *See* That Obscure Object of Desire (1977)
Chaingang Girls *See* Sweet Sugar (1972)
The Challenge *See* It Takes a Thief (1959)
Chamber of Fear *See* The Fear Chamber (1968)
Champ d'Honneur *See* Field of Honor (1987)
Champion Charlie *See* The Champion/His New Job (1915)
Changes *See* Danielle Steel's Changes (1991)
Chaos-Kaos *See* Kaos (1985)
Charlie's Ghost Story *See* Charlie's Ghost: The Secret of Coronado (1994)
Charterhouse at Parma *See* La Chartreuse de Parme (1948)
Chastnaya Zhizn *See* Private Life (1982)
The Chautauqua *See* The Trouble with Girls (and How To Get Into It) (1969)
Che? *See* Diary of Forbidden Dreams (1973)
Cheaters *See* Tricheurs (1984)
Chernobyl: The Final Warning *See* Final Warning (1990)
Chevy Van *See* The Van (1977)
The Chief Wants No Survivors *See* No Survivors, Please (1963)
Chikamatsu Monogatari *See* The Crucified Lovers (1954)
Chikyu Boelgun *See* The Mysterians (1958)
The Child *See* Kill and Go Hide (1976)
Child of Satan *See* To the Devil, A Daughter (1976)
Child of the Night *See* What the Peeper Saw (1972)
Childish Things *See* Confessions of Tom Harris (1972)
Children of the Dust *See* A Good Day to Die (1995)
China 9, Liberty 37 *See* Gunfire (1978)
Chinchero *See* The Last Movie (1971)
Christmas Evil *See* Terror in Toyland (1985)
A Christmas Memory *See* ABC Stage 67: Truman Capote's A Christmas Memory (1966)
The Christmas Tree *See* When Wolves Cry (1969)
Christmas Vacation *See* National Lampoon's Christmas Vacation (1989)
Chuck Norris vs. the Karate Cop *See* Slaughter in San Francisco (1981)
Chungon Satluk Linggei *See* Organized Crime & Triad Bureau (1993)
Ciao! Manhattan *See* Edie in Ciao! Manhattan (1972)
Cica Tomina Koliba *See* Uncle Tom's Cabin (1969)
The Circle *See* The Vicious Circle (1957)
The Circle *See* Woman in Brown (1948)
Circuitry Man 2 *See* Plughead Rewired: Circuitry Man 2 (1994)
Citadel of Crime *See* Wheel of Fortune (1941)
Citizen's Band *See* FM (1978)
The City Jungle *See* The Young Philadelphians (1959)
The City of the Dead *See* Horror Hotel (1960)
City of the Living Dead *See* Gates of Hell (1983)
The Clairvoyant *See* The Evil Mind (1934)
The Clairvoyant *See* Killing Hour (1984)
The Clansman *See* The Birth of a Nation (1915)
Class of '86 *See* National Lampoon's Class of '86 (1986)
Class Reunion *See* National Lampoon's Class Reunion (1982)
Claude *See* The Two of Us (1968)
Clean Slate *See* Coup de Torchon (1981)
Cleo de 5 a 7 *See* Cleo from 5 to 7 (1961)
Clickety Clack *See* Dodes 'ka-den (1970)
Clinton & Nadine *See* Blood Money: The Story of Clinton and Nadine (1988)
Clive Barker's Lord of Illusions *See* Lord of Illusions (1995)
The Closest of Kin *See* All the Lovin' Kinfolk (1989)
Club Dead *See* Terror at Red Wolf Inn (1972)
Coast of Terror *See* Summer City (1977)
Coastwatcher *See* The Last Warrior (1989)
Cobweb Castle *See* Throne of Blood (1957)
Code Name: Operation Crossbow *See* Operation Crossbow (1965)
Code Name: Trixie *See* The Crazies (1973)
Code 645 *See* G-Men Never Forget (1948)
Codename: The Soldier *See* The Soldier (1982)
Coffin of Terror *See* Castle of Blood (1964)
Colin Nutley's House of Angels *See* House of Angels (1992)
Collision Course *See* The Bamboo Saucer (1968)
Colonel Blimp *See* The Life and Death of Colonel Blimp (1943)
Colorado Ranger *See* Guns of Justice (1950)
Come Back to Me *See* Doll Face (1946)
Come Dance with Me *See* Voulez-Vous Danser Avec Moi? (1959)
Come 'n' Get It *See* Lunch Wagon (1981)
Coming Attractions *See* Loose Shoes (1980)
Comizi d'Amore *See* Love Meetings (1964)
Communion *See* Alice Sweet Alice (1976)
Como Agua para Chocolate *See* Like Water for Chocolate (1993)
Como Era Gostoso O Meu Frances *See* How Tasty Was My Little Frenchman (1971)
The Company of Strangers *See* Strangers in Good Company (1991)
Computer Killers *See* Horror Hospital (1973)
The Con Man *See* The Con Artists (1980)
Concerto *See* I've Always Loved You (1946)
Confesion a Laura *See* Confessing to Laura (1990)
Confession *See* Repentance (1987)
The Confession *See* Quick, Let's Get Married (1971)
Confessions of A Peeping John *See* Hi, Mom! (1970)
Confidential Report *See* Mr. Arkadin (1955)
Conflagration *See* Enjo (1958)
The Conflict *See* Catholics (1973)
The Conspiracy *See* Le Complot (1973)
Contamination *See* Alien Contamination (1981)
Conte D'Hiver *See* A Tale of Winter (1992)
Continuavamo A Chiamarlo Trinita *See* Trinity is Still My Name (1975)
Contra el Viento *See* Against the Wind (1990)
Convention City *See* Sons of the Desert (1933)
Coonskin *See* Streetfight (1975)
Cop Killers *See* Corrupt (1984)
Cop Tips Waitress $2 Million *See* It Could Happen to You (1994)
A Corps Perdu *See* Straight for the Heart (1988)
The Corpse *See* Crucible of Horror (1969)
A Corpse Hangs in the Web *See* Horrors of Spider Island (1959)
The Cosmic Man Appears in Tokyo *See* Warning from Space (1956)
Cosmo 2000: Planet Without a Name *See* Cosmos: War of the Planets (1980)
Count Dracula and His Vampire Bride *See* The Satanic Rites of Dracula (1973)
Count Dracula's Great Love *See* Dracula's Great Love (1972)
Country Music *See* Las Vegas Hillbillys (1966)
Country Music Daughter *See* Nashville Girl (1976)
Coup de Foudre *See* Entre-Nous (1983)
Coup de Tete *See* Hothead (1978)
Courage *See* Raw Courage (1984)
The Courage of Kavik, the Wolf Dog *See* Kavik the Wolf Dog (1984)
Court Martial *See* Carrington, V.C. (1954)
The Courtneys of Curzon Street *See* The Courtney Affair (1947)
Crack *See* Strike Force (1975)
Cradle of Crime *See* Dead End (1937)
Crash of Silence *See* Mandy (1953)
The Crawling Monster *See* Creeping Terror (1964)
Crazy for You *See* Vision Quest (1985)
Crazy Horse *See* Friends, Lovers & Lunatics (1989)
Crazy House *See* Night of the Laughing Dead (1975)
Crazy Jack and the Boy *See* Silence (1973)
Crazy Joe *See* Dead Center (1994)
Crazy Streets *See* Forever, Lulu (1987)
Created to Kill *See* Embryo (1976)
The Creature Wasn't Nice *See* Spaceship (1981)
Creatures *See* From Beyond the Grave (1973)
Creatures of the Prehistoric Planet *See* Horror of the Blood Monsters (1970)
Creatures of the Red Planet *See* Horror of the Blood Monsters (1970)
The Creature's Revenge *See* Brain of Blood (1971)
The Creeper *See* Dark Side of Midnight (1986)
The Creeper *See* Rituals (1979)
The Creepers *See* Assault (1970)
The Creepers *See* Island of Terror (1966)
The Creeping Unknown *See* The Quatermass Experiment (1956)
Creeps *See* Bloody Birthday (1980)
Cria Cuervos *See* Cria (1976)
The Cricket *See* La Cicada (1983)
Crime Boss *See* New Mafia Boss (1972)
Crime et Chatiment *See* Crime and Punishment (1935)
Crimes in the Wax Museum *See* Nightmare in Wax (1969)
Crimes, Inc. *See* Gangs, Inc. (1941)
The Crimes of Dr. Mabuse *See* Testament of Dr. Mabuse (1962)
The Criminal *See* The Concrete Jungle (1982)
The Crimson Altar *See* The Crimson Cult (1968)
Crimson Executioner *See* The Bloody Pit of Horror (1965)
The Crimson Ghost *See* Cyclotrode "X" (1946)
Crooks in Clover *See* Penthouse (1933)
Crossed Swords *See* The Prince and the Pauper (1978)
Crossing the Line *See* The Big Man: Crossing the Line (1991)
The Crown Caper *See* The Thomas Crown Affair (1968)
Cruel Swamp *See* Swamp Women (1955)
The Cry *See* Il Grido (1957)
Crying Out Loud *See* Cotton Queen (1937)
Crypt of Dark Secrets *See* Mardi Gras Massacre (1978)
C.S. Lewis Through the Shadowlands *See* Shadowlands (1985)

Csillagosok, Katonak *See* The Red and the White (1968)
Cuba Crossing *See* The Mercenaries (1980)
Cuban Rebel Girls *See* Assault of the Rebel Girls (1959)
Cult of the Dead *See* The Snake People (1968)
Cupid in the Rough *See* Aggie Appleby, Maker of Men (1933)
Curley and His Gang in the Haunted Mansion *See* Who Killed Doc Robbin? (1948)
Curse of Dark Shadows *See* Night of Dark Shadows (1971)
The Curse of Demon Mountain *See* Shadow of Chikara (1977)
The Curse of Dracula *See* Return of Dracula (1958)
Curse of Melissa *See* The Touch of Satan (1970)
Curse of the Blood-Ghouls *See* The Slaughter of the Vampires (1962)
Curse of the Crimson Altar *See* The Crimson Cult (1968)
The Curse of the Dragon *See* Bruce Lee: Curse of the Dragon (1993)
Curse of the Living Dead *See* Kill, Baby, Kill (1966)
Curse of the Mushroom People *See* Attack of the Mushroom People (1963)
Curses of the Ghouls *See* The Slaughter of the Vampires (1962)
Cutter and Bone *See* Cutter's Way (1981)
Cybele *See* Sundays & Cybele (1962)
Cyber-Chic *See* Robo-Chic (1989)
Cyberjack *See* Virtual Assassin (1995)
Cyborg Cop 2 *See* Cyborg Soldier (1994)
Czlowiek z Zelaza *See* Man of Iron (1981)
Da Bancarella a Bancarotta *See* Peddlin' in Society (1947)
Daddy *See* Danielle Steel's "Daddy" (1992)
Daddy's Deadly Darling *See* Pigs (1973)
Dagboek Van Een Oude Dwaas *See* Diary of a Mad Old Man (1988)
Dagora *See* Dagora, the Space Monster (1965)
Dai Koesu Yongkari *See* Yongkari Monster of the Deep (1967)
Daibosatsu Toge *See* Sword of Doom (1967)
Daikaiju Baran *See* Varan the Unbelievable (1961)
Daikaiju Gamera *See* Gamera, the Invincible (1966)
Daikyoju Gappa *See* Gappa the Trifibian Monster (1967)
Dalle Ardenne All'Inferno *See* Dirty Heroes (1971)
Dance of the Dwarfs *See* Jungle Heat (1984)
Dance of the Vampires *See* The Fearless Vampire Killers (1967)
Danger Rides the Range *See* Three Texas Steers (1939)
Dangerous Charter *See* Creeping Terror (1964)
Dangerous Female *See* The Maltese Falcon (1931)
A Dangerous Friend *See* The Todd Killings (1971)
Dangerous Kiss *See* True Crime (1995)
Dangerous Love Affairs *See* Dangerous Liaisons (1960)
Danielle Steel's Fine Things *See* Fine Things (1990)
Danny Travis *See* The Last Word (1980)
Dans la Ville Blanche *See* In the White City (1983)
Dans les Griffes du Maniaque *See* The Diabolical Dr. Z (1965)
Danza Macabra *See* Castle of Blood (1964)
Daoma Zei *See* The Horse Thief (1987)
Dark Angel *See* I Come in Peace (1990)
The Dark Avenger *See* The Warriors (1955)
Dark Eyes *See* Demon Rage (1982)
Dark Eyes of London *See* Dead Eyes of London (1961)
Dark Eyes of London *See* The Human Monster (1939)
Dark Sands *See* Jericho (1938)
D'Artagnan *See* The Three Musketeers (1916)
Das Bildness des Dorian Gray *See* Dorian Gray (1970)
Das Blaue Licht *See* The Blue Light (1932)
Das Phantom von Soho *See* The Phantom of Soho (1964)
Das Schlangenei *See* The Serpent's Egg (1978)
Das Schloss *See* The Castle (1968)
Das Ungeheuer von London City *See* The Monster of London City (1964)
Das Versprechen *See* The Promise (1995)
Dashiell Hammett's The Dain Curse *See* The Dain Curse (1978)
The Daughter of Frankenstein *See* Lady Frankenstein (1972)
David Lynch's Hotel Room *See* Hotel Room (1993)
Day of the Woman *See* I Spit on Your Grave (1977)
The Day the Hot Line Got Hot *See* The Hot Line (1969)
The Day the Screaming Stopped *See* The Comeback (1977)
The Day They Gave the Babies Away *See* All Mine to Give (1956)
A Day to Remember *See* Two Bits (1996)
Daybreak *See* Le Jour Se Leve (1939)
De Aanslag *See* The Assault (1986)
De Eso No Se Habla *See* I Don't Want to Talk About It (1994)
De la Part des Copains *See* Cold Sweat (1974)
De Sable et de Sang *See* Sand and Blood (1987)
De Stilte Rond Christine M *See* Question of Silence (1983)
De Wisselwachter *See* The Pointsman (1986)
Dead Aim *See* Born in America (1990)
Dead Drop *See* Chain Reaction (1996)
Dead Kids *See* Strange Behavior (1981)
Dead of Night *See* Deathdream (1972)
Dead on Course *See* Wings of Danger (1952)
Dead or Alive *See* A Minute to Pray, A Second to Die (1967)
Dead or Alive *See* The Tracker (1988)
Dead People *See* Messiah of Evil (1974)
Dead Tired *See* Grosse Fatigue (1994)
Deadlocked: Escape from Zone 14 *See* Deadlock 2 (1994)
Deadly Companion *See* The Double Negative (1980)
Deadly Desire *See* Maybe I'll Be Home in the Spring (1970)
Deadly Desires *See* Home for the Holidays (1972)
Deadly Encounter *See* The Meal (1975)
Deadly is the Female *See* Gun Crazy (1949)
The Deadly Rays From Mars *See* Flash Gordon: Mars Attacks the World (1938)
Deadly Rivals *See* Rivals (1972)
The Deadly Spawn *See* Return of the Aliens: The Deadly Spawn (1983)
Deadly Sting *See* Evil Spawn (1987)
The Deadly Three *See* Enter the Dragon (1973)
The Deadly Tower *See* Sniper (1975)
Deadly Treasure of the Piranha *See* Killer Fish (1979)
Dear Diary *See* Caro Diario (1993)
Dear Inspector *See* Dear Detective (1977)
Death and the Green Slime *See* The Green Slime (1968)
Death Bite *See* Spasms (1982)
Death Collector *See* Family Enforcer (1976)
Death Corps *See* Shock Waves (1977)
Death Dimension *See* Kill Factor (1978)
Death From Outer Space *See* The Day the Sky Exploded (1957)
Death Game *See* Seducers (1977)
Death House *See* Silent Night, Bloody Night (1973)
Death of a Hooker *See* Who Killed Mary What's 'Er Name? (1971)
Death of Her Innocence *See* Our Time (1974)
Death Ride to Osaka *See* Girls of the White Orchid (1985)
Death Scream *See* The Deadly Trap (1971)
Death Train *See* Detonator (1993)
Death Trap *See* Eaten Alive (1976)
Death Vengeance *See* Fighting Back (1982)
The Death Wheelers *See* Psychomania (1973)
Deathstalker 3: The Warriors From Hell *See* Deathstalker 3 (1989)
Debajo del Mundo *See* Under the Earth (1986)
The Debt *See* Veronico Cruz (1987)
Decoy for Terror *See* Playgirl Killer (1966)
Dedee *See* Dedee d'Anvers (1949)
Dellamorte Delamore *See* Cemetery Man (1995)
Delta Pi *See* Mugsy's Girls (1985)
Dem Khann's Zindl *See* The Cantor's Son (1937)
Demanty Noci *See* Diamonds of the Night (1964)
Dementia *See* Daughter of Horror (1955)
Demolition Day *See* Captain Nuke and the Bomber Boys (1995)
Demon *See* God Told Me To (1976)
The Demon *See* Onibaba (1964)
Demon Keeper *See* Tales from the Crypt Presents Demon Knight (1994)
Demon Knight *See* Tales from the Crypt Presents Demon Knight (1994)
Demon Master *See* Craze (1974)
The Demon Planet *See* Planet of the Vampires (1965)
Demoni *See* Demons (1986)
Demonios En El Jardin *See* Demons in the Garden (1982)
The Deputy *See* El Diputado (1978)
Der Amerikanische Soldat *See* The American Soldier (1970)
Der Bewegte Mann *See* Maybe...Maybe Not (1994)
Der Blaue Engel *See* The Blue Angel (1930)
Der Chef Wuenscht Keine Zeugen *See* No Survivors, Please (1963)
Der Fluch Der Gruenen Augen *See* Cave of the Living Dead (1965)
Der Fussgaenger *See* The Pedestrian (1973)
Der Hauptmann von Koepenick *See* The Captain from Koepenick (1956)
Der Henker Von London *See* The Mad Executioners (1965)
Der Himmel Uber Berlin *See* Wings of Desire (1988)
Der Joker *See* Lethal Obsession (1987)
Der Kongress Tanzt *See* Congress Dances (1931)
Der Letzte Mann *See* The Last Laugh (1924)
Der Morder Dimitri Karamasoff *See* The Brothers Karamazov (1958)
Der Prozess *See* The Trial (1963)
Der Schweigende Stern *See* First Spaceship on Venus (1960)
Der Todesspringer *See* The Jumper (1985)
Der Verlone *See* The Lost One (1951)
Der Vilner Shtot Khazn *See* Overture to Glory (1940)
Deranged *See* Idaho Transfer (1973)
Des Enfants Gates *See* Spoiled Children (1977)
Desert Patrol *See* Sea of Sand (1958)
The Deserter *See* Ride to Glory (1971)
Desperate Siege *See* Rawhide (1950)
The Destroyers *See* Devastator (1985)
Destruction, Inc. *See* Just for the Hell of It (1968)
Det Sjunde Inseglet *See* The Seventh Seal (1956)
Det Stora Aventyret *See* The Great Adventure (1953)
Detective Geronimo *See* The Mad Bomber (1972)
The Detective Kid *See* The Gumshoe Kid (1989)
Deutschland im Herbst *See* Germany in Autumn (1978)
The Devil and the Nun *See* Mother Joan of the Angels (1960)
The Devil Walks at Midnight *See* The Devil's Nightmare (1971)
The Devil Within Her *See* I Don't Want to Be Born (1975)
The Devil Woman *See* Onibaba (1964)
The Devil's Bride *See* Velnio Nuotaka (1975)
Devil's Doll *See* The Devil's Hand (1961)
The Devil's Envoys *See* Les Visiteurs du Soir (1942)
Devil's Express *See* Gang Wars (1975)
The Devil's Men *See* Land of the Minotaur (1977)
Devil's Odds *See* The Wild Pair (1987)
The Devil's Plot *See* Counterblast (1948)
The Devil's Undead *See* Nothing But the Night (1972)
The Devil's Weed *See* Wild Weed (1949)
The Diabolical Dr. Mabuse *See* The Thousand Eyes of Dr. Mabuse (1960)
Diabolik *See* Danger: Diabolik (1968)
Diaboliquement Votre *See* Diabolically Yours (1967)
Dial 999 *See* The Way Out (1956)
Diamond Alley *See* Little Ladies of the Night (1977)
Diamond Earrings *See* The Earrings of Madame De... (1954)
Diamond Skulls *See* Dark Obsession (1990)
Diamonds and Crime *See* Hi Diddle Diddle (1943)
Diario Segreto Di Un Carcere Femminele *See* Women in Cell Block 7 (1977)
Diary of Oharu *See* Life of Oharu (1952)

Dick Tracy Meets Karloff *See* Dick Tracy Meets Gruesome (1947)
Dick Tracy's Amazing Adventure *See* Dick Tracy Meets Gruesome (1947)
Die, Beautiful Marianne *See* Die Screaming, Marianne (1973)
Die Bitteren Traenen der Petra von Kant *See* The Bitter Tears of Petra von Kant (1972)
Die Blechtrommel *See* The Tin Drum (1979)
Die Brucke *See* The Bridge (1959)
Die Buechse Der Pandora *See* Pandora's Box (1928)
Die Dreigroschenoper *See* The Three Penny Opera (1962)
Die Dreigroschenoper *See* The Threepenny Opera (1931)
Die Ehe Der Maria Braun *See* The Marriage of Maria Braun (1979)
Die Flambierte Frau *See* A Woman in Flames (1984)
Die Folterkammer des Dr. Fu Manchu *See* The Castle of Fu Manchu (1968)
Die Hard 3 *See* Die Hard: With a Vengeance (1995)
Die Holle von Macao *See* The Corrupt Ones (1967)
Die Holle von Manitoba *See* A Place Called Glory (1966)
Die Nibelungen *See* Kriemhilde's Revenge (1924)
Die Regenschirme Von Cherbourg *See* Umbrellas of Cherbourg (1964)
Die Schlangengrube und das Pendel *See* The Torture Chamber of Dr. Sadism (1969)
Die Sehns Ucht Der Veronika Voss *See* Veronika Voss (1982)
Die Toten Augen von London *See* Dead Eyes of London (1961)
Die Unsichtbaren Krallen des Dr. Mabuse *See* The Invisible Dr. Mabuse (1962)
Die Verlorene Ehre Der Katharina Blum *See* The Lost Honor of Katharina Blum (1975)
Die Xue Shuang Xiong *See* The Killer (1990)
Dio Mio, Come Sono Caduta in Basso *See* Till Marriage Do Us Part (1974)
A Dirty Knight's Work *See* Choice of Weapons (1976)
Dirty Mary *See* A Very Curious Girl (1969)
Disaster at Valdez *See* Dead Ahead: The Exxon Valdez Disaster (1992)
Disco Godfather *See* Avenging Disco Godfather (1976)
The Discreet *See* La Discrete (1990)
Disney's Blank Check *See* Blank Check (1993)
Dispara *See* Outrage (1993)
Disparen a Matar *See* Shoot to Kill (1990)
Distant Cousins *See* Desperate Motives (1992)
Dites-Lui Que Je L'Aime *See* This Sweet Sickness (1977)
Divertimento *See* La Belle Noiseuse (1990)
Divine Obsession *See* Dangerous Obsession (1988)
Divorzio All'Italiana *See* Divorce—Italian Style (1962)
Djavulens Oga *See* The Devil's Eye (1960)
Do You Want to Dance with Me? *See* Voulez-Vous Danser Avec Moi? (1959)
Docteur M. *See* Club Extinction (1989)
Docteur Popaul *See* High Heels (1972)
Dr. Black and Mr. White *See* Dr. Black, Mr. Hyde (1976)
The Doctor from Seven Dials *See* Corridors of Blood (1958)
Doctor Gore *See* The Body Shop (1972)
Dr. Jekyll y el Hombre Lobo *See* Dr. Jekyll and the Wolfman (1971)
Dr. Maniac *See* The Man Who Lived Again (1936)
Doctor Maniac *See* House of the Living Dead (1973)
Doctor of Doom *See* Wrestling Women vs. the Aztec Ape (1962)
Dr. Terror's Gallery of Horrors *See* Alien Massacre (1967)
Doctors Wear Scarlet *See* The Bloodsuckers (1970)
A Dog, a Mouse, and a Sputnik *See* Sputnik (1961)
Dog Soldiers *See* Who'll Stop the Rain? (1978)
Doin' It *See* The First Time (1969)
Doin' It *See* First Time (1982)
Doing Life *See* Truth or Die (1986)
Doing Time *See* Porridge (1991)
Doktor Mabuse der Spieler *See* Dr. Mabuse, Parts 1 & 2 (1922)
Dolwyn *See* The Last Days of Dolwyn (1949)
Dom Za Vesanje *See* Time of the Gypsies (1990)
The Domino Killings *See* The Domino Principle (1977)
Don Juan *See* Private Life of Don Juan (1934)
Don Juan, Mi Querido Fantasma *See* Don Juan, My Love (1990)
Dona Flor e Seus Dois Maridos *See* Dona Flor and Her Two Husbands (1978)
Dona Herlinda y Su Hijo *See* Dona Herlinda & Her Son (1986)
Donato and Daughter *See* Dead to Rights (1993)
Don't Fence Me In *See* Western Double Feature 4: Rogers & Evans (194?)
Don't Look Now, We've Been Shot At *See* La Grande Vadrouille (1966)
The Doomsday Machine *See* Escape from Planet Earth (1967)
The Door With Seven Locks *See* Chamber of Horrors (1940)
Doppelganger *See* Journey to the Far Side of the Sun (1969)
The Double *See* Kagemusha (1980)
Double Down *See* Stacy's Knights (1983)
Double Hit *See* The Arab Conspiracy (1976)
Double Possession *See* Black Vampire (1973)
Double Trouble *See* No Deposit, No Return (1976)
Douce Violence *See* Sweet Ecstasy (1962)
Down Went McGinty *See* The Great McGinty (1940)
Dracula *See* Bram Stoker's Dracula (1992)
Dracula *See* The Horror of Dracula (1958)
Dracula Contra Frankenstein *See* Dracula vs. Frankenstein (1971)
Dracula in the Castle of Blood *See* Web of the Spider (1970)
Dracula Pere et Fils *See* Dracula & Son (1976)
Dracula Saga *See* The Saga of the Draculas (1972)
Dracula: The Bloodline Continues... *See* The Saga of the Draculas (1972)
Dracula vs. Frankenstein *See* The Screaming Dead (1972)
Dracula's Castle *See* Blood of Dracula's Castle (1969)
Dracula's Dog *See* Zoltan...Hound of Dracula (1978)
Dracula's Virgin Lovers *See* Dracula's Great Love (1972)
Dragon Chow *See* Drachenfutter (1987)
Dragon Lady *See* G.I. Executioner (1971)
Dragonfly *See* One Summer Love (1976)
Dragon's Food *See* Drachenfutter (1987)
Draws *See* American Tickler (1976)
The Dreaded Persuasion *See* The Narcotics Story (1958)
Dream Slayer *See* Blood Song (1982)
Dreams *See* Akira Kurosawa's Dreams (1990)
Dreamworld *See* Covergirl (1983)
Dripping Deep Red *See* Deep Red: Hatchet Murders (1975)
Drivers to Hell *See* Wild Ones on Wheels (1962)
Drole de Drama *See* Bizarre Bizarre (1939)
The Drum *See* Drums (1938)
Du Rififi Chez les Hommes *See* Rififi (1954)
Duck, You Sucker *See* A Fistful of Dynamite (1972)
The Duckweed Story *See* Drifting Weeds (1959)
Due Notti Con Cleopatra *See* Two Nights with Cleopatra (1954)
Due Occhi Diabolici *See* Two Evil Eyes (1990)
Duel of the Gargantuas *See* War of the Gargantuas (1970)
Duel of the Space Monsters *See* Frankenstein Meets the Space Monster (1965)
Duello Nel Texas *See* Gun Fight at Red Sands (1963)
Dumb Dicks *See* Detective School Dropouts (1985)
Dumbo Drop *See* Operation Dumbo Drop (1995)
Dungeons and Dragons *See* Mazes and Monsters (1982)
Duvar *See* The Wall (1983)
Dynamite Women *See* The Great Texas Dynamite Chase (1976)
Dyrygent *See* The Conductor (1980)
Each Man For Himself *See* The Ruthless Four (1970)
Each One For Himself *See* The Ruthless Four (1970)
The Eagle with Two Heads *See* The Eagle Has Two Heads (1948)
Earth Defense Forces *See* The Mysterians (1958)
The Earth Will Tremble *See* La Terra Trema (1948)
East of Shanghai *See* Rich and Strange (1932)
East of the Bowery *See* Follow the Leader (1944)
East of the Rising Sun *See* Malaya (1949)
Easy Go *See* Free and Easy (1930)
Eaten Alive by Cannibals *See* Emerald Jungle (1980)
Ebirah, Terror of the Deep *See* Godzilla vs. the Sea Monster (1966)
Eboli *See* Christ Stopped at Eboli (1979)
Edgar Allan Poe's Conqueror Worm *See* The Conqueror Worm (1968)
Edgar Allen Poe's The Oblong Box *See* The Oblong Box (1969)
The Edge of Hell *See* Rock 'n' Roll Nightmare (1985)
Edipo Re *See* Oedipus Rex (1967)
Ein Mann wie Eva *See* A Man Like Eva (1983)
Ein Toter Hing im Netz *See* Horrors of Spider Island (1959)
Eine Liebe in Deutschland *See* A Love in Germany (1984)
Einer Frisst den Anderen *See* Dog Eat Dog (1964)
Ekstase *See* Ecstasy (1933)
El Ataud Del Coffin *See* The Vampire's Coffin (1958)
El Ataud Del Vampiro *See* The Vampire's Coffin (1958)
El Buque Maldito *See* Horror of the Zombies (1974)
El Cazador de la Muerte *See* Deathstalker (1983)
El Cobra *See* The Cobra (1968)
El Coleccionista de Cadaveres *See* Cauldron of Blood (1967)
El Dedo En El Gatillo *See* Finger on the Trigger (1965)
El Espiritu de la Colmena *See* Spirit of the Beehive (1973)
El Grito de la Muerte *See* The Living Coffin (1958)
El la Nave Va *See* And the Ship Sails On (1983)
El Lazarillo de Tormes *See* Lazarillo (1959)
El Mariachi 2 *See* Desperado (1995)
El Mas Fabulosi Golpe del Far West *See* The Boldest Job in the West (1971)
El Rapto de las Sabinas *See* The Rape of the Sabines (1961)
El Retorno de la Walpurgis *See* Curse of the Devil (1973)
El Robot Humano *See* The Robot vs. the Aztec Mummy (1959)
El Rublo de las dos Caras *See* The Hot Line (1969)
El Sonido de la Muerte *See* Sound of Horror (1964)
El Tesoro del Amazones *See* The Treasure of the Amazon (1984)
El Verano de la Senora Forbes *See* The Summer of Miss Forbes (1988)
Electric Boogaloo "Breakin' 2" *See* Breakin' 2: Electric Boogaloo (1984)
The Electric Monster *See* The Electronic Monster (1957)
Elena et les Hommes *See* Elena and Her Men (1956)
Elevator to the Gallows *See* Frantic (1958)
Elisa, My Life *See* Elisa, Vida Mia (1977)
Elisa, My Love *See* Elisa, Vida Mia (1977)
Emergency Landing *See* Robot Pilot (1941)
Emil Und Die Detektive *See* Emil and the Detectives (1964)
Emma Mae *See* Black Sister's Revenge (1976)
The Emperor of Peru *See* The Odyssey of the Pacific (1982)
Empire of Passion *See* In the Realm of Passion (1980)
The Empress Yang Kwei Fei *See* Princess Yang Kwei Fei (1955)

En Compagnie d'Antonin Artaud *See* My Life and Times with Antonin Artaud (1993)
En Effeuillant la Marguerite *See* Mademoiselle Striptease (1957)
En Enda Natt *See* Only One Night (1942)
En Kvinnas Ansikte *See* A Woman's Face (1938)
En Lekiton i Karlek *See* Lesson in Love (1954)
End of the Rainbow *See* Northwest Outpost (1947)
End of the World *See* Panic in the Year Zero! (1962)
End of the World (in Our Usual Bed in a Night Full of Rain) *See* A Night Full of Rain (1978)
Enemies of the Public *See* Public Enemy (1931)
Enemy from Space *See* Quatermass 2 (1957)
Enemy Round-Up *See* Hillbilly Blitzkrieg (1942)
The Engagement *See* Fiances (1963)
The Enigma of Kaspar Hauser *See* Every Man for Himself & God Against All (1975)
Enormous Changes at the Last Minute *See* Enormous Changes (1983)
Enormous Changes at the Last Minute *See* Trumps (1983)
Ensayo de un Crimen *See* The Criminal Life of Archibaldo de la Cruz (1955)
Entebbe: Operation Thunderbolt *See* Operation Thunderbolt (1977)
Entre Tinieblas *See* Dark Habits (1984)
Episoda Del Mare *See* La Terra Trema (1948)
Ercole al Centro Della Terra *See* Hercules in the Haunted World (1964)
Ercole Alla Conquista di Atlantide *See* Hercules and the Captive Women (1963)
Ercole Contro Molock *See* Conquest of Mycene (1963)
Ercole e la Regina de Lidia *See* Hercules Unchained (1959)
Erik the Conqueror *See* The Invaders (1963)
Ernest Hemingway's the Killers *See* The Killers (1964)
Escapade *See* Utopia (1951)
Escape from the Dark *See* The Littlest Horse Thieves (1976)
Escape If You Can *See* St. Benny the Dip (1951)
The Escape of Megagodzilla *See* Terror of Mechagodzilla (1978)
Escape Route *See* I'll Get You (1953)
Escape to Freedom *See* Judgment in Berlin (1988)
Escapement *See* The Electronic Monster (1957)
Escort Girl *See* Half Moon Street (1986)
The Escorts *See* La Scorta (1994)
Espiritismo *See* Spiritism (1961)
Et Dieu Crea la Femme *See* And God Created Woman (1957)
Et Mourir de Plaisir *See* Blood and Roses (1961)
Etat de Siege *See* State of Siege (1973)
European Vacation *See* National Lampoon's European Vacation (1985)
Every Day's a Holiday *See* Seaside Swingers (1965)
Every Home Should Have One *See* Think Dirty (1970)
Every Man For Himself *See* The Ruthless Four (1970)
Every Woman's Man *See* The Prizefighter and the Lady (1933)
Everybody's Cheering *See* Take Me Out to the Ball Game (1949)
Evil Angels *See* A Cry in the Dark (1988)
Evil Dead 3 *See* Army of Darkness (1992)
Evil Eden *See* Death in the Garden (1956)
Evil in the Swamp *See* All the Kind Strangers (1974)
Ewiger Walzer *See* The Eternal Waltz (1954)
Except For Me and Thee *See* Friendly Persuasion (1956)
Expedition Moon *See* Rocketship X-M (1950)
Exploring the Kinsey Report *See* One Plus One (1961)
Expose *See* The House on Straw Hill (1976)
Exquisite Tenderness *See* The Surgeon (1994)
Extase *See* Ecstasy (1933)
Extenuating Circumstances *See* Circonstances Attenuantes (1936)
Extreme Close-Up *See* Sex Through a Window (1972)
An Eye for an Eye *See* Psychopath (1973)
An Eye for an Eye *See* Talion (1966)
Eyes of Hell *See* The Mask (1961)
Eyes Without a Face *See* The Horror Chamber of Dr. Faustus (1959)
Eyewitness *See* Sudden Terror (1970)
Fabula de la Bella Palomera *See* The Fable of the Beautiful Pigeon Fancier (1988)
The Fabulous Baron Munchausen *See* The Original Fabulous Adventures of Baron Munchausen (1961)
Face of a Stranger *See* The Promise (1978)
Face the Music *See* Black Glove (1954)
The Faceless Monsters *See* Nightmare Castle (1965)
Fairytales *See* Fairy Tales (1976)
Fakebook *See* American Blue Note (1989)
Falcon's Gold *See* Robbers of the Sacred Mountain (1983)
Fall Break *See* The Mutilator (1985)
The Fall Guy *See* What's Up Front (1963)
The Fall of the House of Usher *See* La Chute de la Maison Usher (1928)
Falltime *See* Fall Time (1994)
False Face *See* Scalpel (1976)
False Faces *See* Let 'Em Have It (1935)
Falstaff *See* Chimes at Midnight (1967)
Fanatic *See* Die! Die! My Darling! (1965)
The Fanatic *See* The Last Horror Film (1982)
Fangelse *See* Devil's Wanton (1949)
Fanny by Gaslight *See* Man of Evil (1948)
Fanny Och Alexander *See* Fanny and Alexander (1983)
Fan's Video *See* Otaku no Video (1991)
The Far Country *See* Nevil Shute's The Far Country (1985)
Farewell, Friend *See* Honor Among Thieves (1968)
Farewell, My Love *See* Murder, My Sweet (1944)
Farinelli Il Castrato *See* Farinelli (1994)
Farinelli the Castrato *See* Farinelli (1994)
The Farm *See* The Curse (1987)
Farm Girl *See* The Farmer's Other Daughter (1965)
Farm of the Year *See* Miles from Home (1988)
Fashions *See* Fashions of 1934 (1934)
Fast Fortune *See* 11 Harrowhouse (1974)
Fatal Assassin *See* African Rage (1978)
Fatal Woman *See* Femme Fatale (1990)
The Father *See* Baba (1973)
Father & Son: Dangerous Relations *See* Dangerous Relations (1993)
Father Brown *See* The Detective (1954)
Father Damien: The Leper Priest *See* Damien: The Leper Priest (1980)
The Father Kino Story *See* Mission to Glory (1980)
Father Master *See* Padre Padrone (1977)
Father, Son and the Mistress *See* For Richer, For Poorer (1992)
Faustrecht der Freiheit *See* Fox and His Friends (1975)
Fear *See* Night Creature (1979)
The Fear *See* Gates of Hell (1983)
Fear Eats the Soul *See* Ali: Fear Eats the Soul (1974)
Fear in the City of the Living Dead *See* Gates of Hell (1983)
Fear in the Night *See* Dynasty of Fear (1972)
Feast of Flesh *See* Blood Feast (1963)
Federico Fellini's 8 1/2 *See* 8 1/2 (1963)
Federico Fellini's Intervista *See* Intervista (1987)
Feel the Heat *See* Catch the Heat (1987)
Female *See* The Violent Years (1956)
The Female Butcher *See* The Legend of Blood Castle (1972)
A Few Days in the Life of I.I. Oblomov *See* Oblomov (1981)
The Fiend with the Atomic Brain *See* Blood of Ghastly Horror (1972)
The Fiend with the Electronic Brain *See* Blood of Ghastly Horror (1972)
Fiendish Ghouls *See* Mania (1960)
Fierce *See* Fighting Mad (1977)
The Fifth Chair *See* It's in the Bag (1945)
The Fighting Phantom *See* The Mysterious Rider (1933)
The Fighting Pimpernel *See* The Elusive Pimpernel (1950)
The Fighting Seventh *See* Little Big Horn (1951)
Film d'Amore et d'Anarchia *See* Love and Anarchy (1973)
Filofax *See* Taking Care of Business (1990)
The Final Crash *See* Steelyard Blues (1973)
Finally, Sunday *See* Confidentially Yours (1983)
Fine and Dandy *See* The West Point Story (1950)
Fire Festival *See* Himatsuri (1985)
Fire in Eden *See* Tusks (1989)
The First and the Last *See* 21 Days (1937)
The First Great Train Robbery *See* The Great Train Robbery (1979)
The First Hello *See* High Country (1981)
The First of the Few *See* Spitfire (1942)
The First Rebel *See* Allegheny Uprising (1939)
The First Time *See* The Fighter (1952)
First Woman Into Space *See* Space Monster (1964)
A Fist Full of Chopsticks *See* They Call Me Bruce? (1982)
Fist of Fury *See* Chinese Connection (1973)
Fist Right of Freedom *See* Fox and His Friends (1975)
Five Bloody Days to Tombstone *See* Gun Riders (1969)
Five Bloody Graves *See* Gun Riders (1969)
The Five Day Lover *See* Time Out for Love (1961)
Five Days *See* Paid to Kill (1954)
Five Minutes to Live *See* Door to Door Maniac (1961)
Five Women Around Utamaro *See* Utamaro and His Five Women (1946)
Fixing the Shadow *See* Beyond the Law (1992)
The Flame of Torment *See* Enjo (1958)
Flash Gordon's Trip to Mars *See* Flash Gordon: Mars Attacks the World (1938)
Flatbed Annie *See* Flatbed Annie and Sweetiepie: Lady Truckers (1979)
The Flesh and the Fiends *See* Mania (1960)
The Flesh Creatures *See* Horror of the Blood Monsters (1970)
Flesh Creatures of the Red Planet *See* Horror of the Blood Monsters (1970)
Flesh for Frankenstein *See* Andy Warhol's Frankenstein (1974)
The Flight *See* The Taking of Flight 847: The Uli Derickson Story (1988)
The Flight of the White Stallions *See* The Miracle of the White Stallions (1963)
Flipper and the Pirates *See* Flipper's New Adventure (1964)
Floating Weeds *See* Drifting Weeds (1959)
Flying Aces *See* The Flying Deuces (1939)
Fog *See* A Study in Terror (1966)
Folies Bourgeoises *See* Twist (1976)
The Folks at Red Wolf Inn *See* Terror at Red Wolf Inn (1972)
Follow That Bird *See* Sesame Street Presents: Follow That Bird (1985)
Follow the Hunter *See* Fangs of the Wild (1954)
Follow Your Dreams *See* Independence Day (1983)
Fontane Effi Briest *See* Effi Briest (1974)
For a Few Bullets More *See* Any Gun Can Play (1967)
For Better or For Worse *See* Honeymoon Academy (1990)
For Love or Money *See* If I Were Rich (1933)
For Men Only *See* Tall Lie (1953)
For We Too Do Not Forgive *See* Death is Called Engelchen (1963)
Forbidden Alliance *See* The Barretts of Wimpole Street (1934)
Forbidden Love *See* Freaks (1932)
Forbidden Paradise *See* Hurricane (1979)
Forbidden Passions *See* The Sensuous Teenager (1970)
Forbidden Son *See* Bulldance (1988)
The Forbin Project *See* Colossus: The Forbin Project (1970)
Forbrydelsens Element *See* The Element of Crime (1984)
Ford Fairlane *See* The Adventures of Ford Fairlane (1990)
The Forest Primeval *See* The Final Terror (1983)
Forgotten Prisoners: The Amnesty Files *See* Forgotten Prisoners (1990)

The Forsyte Saga *See* That Forsyte Woman (1950)
Fortune in Diamonds *See* The Adventurers (1951)
47 Samurai *See* 47 Ronin, Part 1 (1942)
Forward March *See* Doughboys (1930)
The Four Just Men *See* The Secret Four (1940)
A Fourth for Marriage *See* What's Up Front (1963)
4...3...2...1...Morte *See* Mission Stardust (1968)
F.P. 1 Antwortet Nicht *See* F.P. 1 Doesn't Answer (1933)
Fra Diavolo *See* The Devil's Brother (1933)
Frage 7 *See* Question 7 (1963)
Frameup *See* Jon Jost's Frameup (1993)
Francis *See* Francis the Talking Mule (1949)
Frankenstein *See* Mary Shelley's Frankenstein (1994)
Frankenstein '88 *See* The Vindicator (1985)
Frankenstein Meets the Spacemen *See* Frankenstein Meets the Space Monster (1965)
Frasier the Lovable Lion *See* Frasier the Sensuous Lion (1973)
Fraternally Yours *See* Sons of the Desert (1933)
The Freak From Suckweasel Mountain *See* Geek Maggot Bingo (1983)
Freddie as F.R.O.7 *See* Freddie the Frog (1992)
Free to Live *See* Holiday (1938)
Freefall *See* Firefall (1994)
The Freeze Bomb *See* Kill Factor (1978)
Frenzy *See* Torment (1944)
Fresa y Chocolate *See* Strawberry and Chocolate (1993)
Fresh Bait *See* L'Appat (1994)
Freylekhe Kabtsonim *See* The Jolly Paupers (1938)
Friend of the Family *See* Elke (1995)
The Fright *See* Visiting Hours (1982)
The Frightened Lady *See* The Case of the Frightened Lady (1939)
Frightmare 2 *See* Frightmare (1974)
Friz Freleng's Looney Looney Looney Bugs Bunny Movie *See* Looney Looney Looney Bugs Bunny Movie (1981)
The Frog Prince *See* The French Lesson (1986)
From a Whisper to a Scream *See* The Offspring (1987)
From Broadway to Cheyenne *See* Broadway to Cheyenne (1932)
From the Mixed-Up Files of Mrs. Basil E. Frankweiler *See* The Hideaways (1973)
Fruhlingssinfonie *See* Spring Symphony (1986)
The Fruit Machine *See* Wonderland (1988)
F.T.W. *See* The Last Ride (1994)
Fukkatsu no Hi *See* Virus (1982)
The Fulfillment of Mary Gray *See* Fulfillment (1989)
The Fun House *See* Last House on Dead End Street (1977)
Fun Loving *See* Quackser Fortune Has a Cousin in the Bronx (1970)
Fungus of Terror *See* Attack of the Mushroom People (1963)
Fuoco Fatuo *See* The Fire Within (1964)
Furankenshutain No Kaijusanda Tai Gailah *See* War of the Gargantuas (1970)
The Further Adventures of Ma and Pa Kettle *See* Ma and Pa Kettle (1949)
Fury of Samson *See* The Fury of Hercules (1961)
Fury of the Succubus *See* Demon Rage (1982)
Fury of the Vikings *See* The Invaders (1963)
Future Cop *See* Trancers (1984)
Gallery of Horror *See* Alien Massacre (1967)
Gambara vs. Barugon *See* Gamera vs. Barugon (1966)
Gamblin' Man *See* Cockfighter (1974)
Game of Survival *See* Tenement (1985)
Gamera *See* Gamera, the Invincible (1966)
Gamera Tai Barugon *See* Gamera vs. Barugon (1966)
Gamera Tai Gaos *See* Gamera vs. Gaos (1967)
Gamera Tai Guiron *See* Gamera vs. Guiron (1969)
Gamera Tai Shinkai Kaiju Jigara *See* Gamera vs. Zigra (1971)
Gamera Tai Uchukaiju Bairasu *See* Destroy All Planets (1968)
Gamera Tai Viras *See* Destroy All Planets (1968)
Gamera vs. Gyaos *See* Gamera vs. Gaos (1967)
Gamera Vs. Outer Space Monster Viras *See* Destroy All Planets (1968)
Gamera vs. the Deep Sea Monster Zigra *See* Gamera vs. Zigra (1971)
Gamera Vs. Viras *See* Destroy All Planets (1968)
Gamma Sango Uchu Daisakusen *See* The Green Slime (1968)
Gamma 693 *See* The Chilling (1989)
Gamma 693 *See* Night of the Zombies (1981)
Gammera *See* Gamera, the Invincible (1966)
Gang War *See* Odd Man Out (1947)
Gangs of Sonora *See* Western Double Feature 6: Rogers & Trigger (1950)
Ganja and Hess *See* Black Vampire (1973)
The Gardener *See* Seeds of Evil (1976)
The Gargon Terror *See* Teenagers from Outer Space (1959)
Garou Garou le Passe Muraille *See* Mr. Peek-A-Boo (1950)
Gas-s-s-s... or, It May Become Necessary to Destroy the World in Order to Save It *See* Gas-s-s-s! (1970)
Gasu Ningen Daiichigo *See* The Human Vapor (1968)
A Gathering of Old Men *See* Murder on the Bayou (1991)
Gatto Rossi In Un Labirinto Do Vetro *See* Eyeball (1978)
The Gay Divorce *See* The Gay Divorcee (1934)
The Gay Mrs. Trexel *See* Susan and God (1940)
The Gaze of Ulysses *See* Ulysses' Gaze (1995)
Gazon Maudit *See* French Twist (1995)
Gebroken Spiegels *See* Broken Mirrors (1985)
Geheimecode Wildganse *See* Codename: Wildgeese (1984)
A Gentle Creature *See* A Gentle Woman (1969)
Georgia's Friends *See* Four Friends (1981)
Gestapo *See* Night Train to Munich (1940)
Get Down and Boogie *See* Darktown Strutters (1974)
Get Well Soon *See* Visiting Hours (1982)
Getting Even *See* Utilities (1983)
Gharbar *See* The Householder (1963)
Ghare Baire *See* The Home and the World (1984)
Ghidora, The Three-Headed Monster *See* Ghidrah the Three Headed Monster (1965)
Ghidorah Sandai Kaiju Chikyu Saidai No Kessan *See* Ghidrah the Three Headed Monster (1965)
Ghidrah *See* Ghidrah the Three Headed Monster (1965)
The Ghost Creeps *See* Boys of the City (1940)
The Ghost of John Holling *See* Mystery Liner (1934)
The Ghost Steps Out *See* The Time of Their Lives (1946)
Ghost Story *See* Madhouse Mansion (1974)
The Ghoul in School *See* Werewolf in a Girl's Dormitory (1961)
The Giant Leeches *See* Attack of the Giant Leeches (1959)
Gigantis, the Fire Monster *See* Godzilla Raids Again (1959)
Gilbert Grape *See* What's Eating Gilbert Grape (1993)
Gill Woman *See* Voyage to the Planet of Prehistoric Women (1968)
Gill Women of Venus *See* Voyage to the Planet of Prehistoric Women (1968)
Gingerbread House *See* Who Slew Auntie Roo? (1971)
Gion Bayashi *See* A Geisha (1953)
Gion Festival Music *See* A Geisha (1953)
Girl in Pawn *See* Little Miss Marker (1934)
Girl in the Leather Suit *See* Hell's Belles (1969)
Girl in the Moon *See* Woman in the Moon (1929)
Girl in the Park *See* Sanctuary of Fear (1979)
Girl in the Street *See* London Melody (1937)
The Girl Was Young *See* Young and Innocent (1937)
The Girl You Want *See* Boys (1995)
The Girls *See* Les Bonnes Femmes (1960)
Girls For Rent *See* I Spit on Your Corpse (1974)
Girls in Uniform *See* Maedchen in Uniform (1931)
Giro City *See* And Nothing But the Truth (1982)
Giu la Testa *See* A Fistful of Dynamite (1972)
Giulietta Degli Spiriti *See* Juliet of the Spirits (1965)
Gladiatorerna *See* The Gladiators (1970)
The Glass Cage *See* Glass Tomb (1955)
Gli Indifferenti *See* Time of Indifference (1964)
Gli Invasori *See* The Invaders (1963)
Glorious Sacrifice *See* The Glory Trail (1936)
Glory at Sea *See* The Gift Horse (1952)
The Glove: Lethal Terminator *See* The Glove (1978)
Glump *See* Please Don't Eat My Mother (1972)
G'mar Giviya *See* Cup Final (1992)
Gnaw: Food of the Gods 2 *See* Food of the Gods: Part 2 (1988)
A Gnome Named Gnorm *See* The Adventures of a Gnome Named Gnorm (1993)
Go and See *See* Come and See (1985)
The Goat *See* La Chevre (1981)
God's Gift *See* Wend Kuuni (1982)
Godzilla Fights the Giant Moth *See* Godzilla vs. Mothra (1964)
Godzilla Versus the Bionic Monster *See* Godzilla vs. the Cosmic Monster (1974)
Godzilla vs. Gigan *See* Godzilla on Monster Island (1972)
Godzilla vs. Hedora *See* Godzilla vs. the Smog Monster (1972)
Godzilla vs. Mechagodzilla *See* Godzilla vs. the Cosmic Monster (1974)
Godzilla vs. the Giant Moth *See* Godzilla vs. Mothra (1964)
Godzilla vs. the Thing *See* Godzilla vs. Mothra (1964)
Godzilla's Counter Attack *See* Godzilla Raids Again (1959)
Going Ape *See* Where's Poppa? (1970)
Gojira *See* Godzilla, King of the Monsters (1956)
Gojira no Musuko *See* Son of Godzilla (1966)
Gojira Tai Hedora *See* Godzilla vs. the Smog Monster (1972)
Gojira Tai Megaro *See* Godzilla vs. Megalon (1976)
Gojira Tai Meka-Gojira *See* Godzilla vs. the Cosmic Monster (1974)
Goke, Body Snatcher from Hell *See* Body Snatcher from Hell (1969)
Goke the Vampire *See* Body Snatcher from Hell (1969)
Gokiburi *See* Twilight of the Cockroaches (1990)
Golden Hands of Kurigal *See* Federal Agents vs. Underworld, Inc. (1949)
The Golden Heist *See* Inside Out (1975)
The Golden Hour *See* Pot O' Gold (1941)
Golden Ivory *See* White Huntress (1957)
Golden Marie *See* Casque d'Or (1952)
The Golden Trail *See* Riders of the Whistling Skull (1937)
Goldy 3 *See* The Magic of the Golden Bear: Goldy 3 (1994)
Goliat Contra Los Gigantes *See* Goliath Against the Giants (1963)
Goliath and the Giants *See* Goliath Against the Giants (1963)
Goliath and the Golden City *See* Samson and the 7 Miracles of the World (1962)
Goliath Contro I Giganti *See* Goliath Against the Giants (1963)
Gomar the Human Gorilla *See* Night of the Bloody Apes (1968)
The Good Girls *See* Les Bonnes Femmes (1960)
Good Luck, Miss Wyckoff *See* The Shaming (1971)
A Good Marriage *See* Le Beau Mariage (1982)
Good Morning Babilonia *See* Good Morning, Babylon (1987)
A Good Time, A Bad Girl *See* Good Time with a Bad Girl (1967)
Good to Go *See* Short Fuse (1988)
Goodbye Bruce Lee: His Last Game of Death *See* Game of Death (1979)
Goodbye, Children *See* Au Revoir Les Enfants (1987)
Goodbye Gemini *See* Twinsanity (1970)
Goodbye to the Hill *See* Paddy (1970)
Gordon il Pirata Nero *See* The Black Pirate (1926)
Gorilla *See* Nabonga (1944)
Gosta Berling's Saga *See* The Atonement of Gosta Berling (1924)

Gotter der Pest *See* Gods of the Plague (1969)
Grace Under Pressure *See* Something to Talk About (1995)
The Grail *See* Lancelot of the Lake (1974)
Gran Amore del Conde Dracula *See* Dracula's Great Love (1972)
The Grand Highway *See* Le Grand Chemin (1987)
The Grand Maneuvers *See* Les Grandes Manoeuvres (1955)
The Grass is Singing *See* Killing Heat (1984)
The Grasshopper *See* The Passing of Evil (1970)
Grave Desires *See* Brides of the Beast (1968)
Grave Robbers from Outer Space *See* Plan 9 from Outer Space (1956)
Graveyard Tramps *See* Invasion of the Bee Girls (1973)
The Great Adventure *See* The Adventurers (1951)
Great American Bugs Bunny-Road Runner Chase *See* The Bugs Bunny/Road Runner Movie (1979)
The Great Balloon Adventure *See* Olly Olly Oxen Free (1978)
The Great Day *See* A Special Day (1977)
Great Friends *See* Grandes Amigos (197?)
The Great Georgia Bank Hoax *See* Great Bank Hoax (1978)
The Great Lester Boggs *See* Hootch Country Boys (1975)
The Great Manhunt *See* The Doolins of Oklahoma (1949)
Great Monster Yongkari *See* Yongkari Monster of the Deep (1967)
The Great Schnozzle *See* Palooka (1934)
The Great Spy Mission *See* Operation Crossbow (1965)
The Great Wall is a Great Wall *See* A Great Wall (1986)
The Greatest Battle *See* Battleforce (1978)
The Greatest Battle on Earth *See* Ghidrah the Three Headed Monster (1965)
The Greatest Love *See* Europa '51 (1952)
The Greeks Had a Word for Them *See* Three Broadway Girls (1932)
The Green Carnation *See* The Trials of Oscar Wilde (1960)
Green Monkey *See* Blue Monkey (1987)
The Green Ray *See* Summer (1986)
Greta the Mad Butcher *See* Ilsa, the Wicked Warden (1978)
Grey Matter *See* Mind Warp (1972)
Gridlock *See* Great American Traffic Jam (1980)
Grijpstra and de Gier *See* Fatal Error (1983)
Grine Felder *See* Green Fields (1937)
Gringo *See* Gun Fight at Red Sands (1963)
The Grip of the Strangler *See* The Haunted Strangler (1958)
Gruner Felder *See* Green Fields (1937)
Gruppo di Famiglia in un Interno *See* Conversation Piece (1975)
Guardian of the Wilderness *See* Mountain Man (1977)
Guilty Assignment *See* Big Town (1947)
Gun Man from Bodie *See* Gunman from Bodie (1941)
Gun Moll *See* Get Rita (1975)
Gun Moll *See* Jigsaw (1949)
Guney's The Wall *See* The Wall (1983)
Gunpoint *See* At Gunpoint (1955)
Guns in the Afternoon *See* Ride the High Country (1962)
Guns, Sin and Bathtub Gin *See* Lady in Red (1979)
Gwendoline *See* The Perils of Gwendoline (1984)
Gycklarnas Afton *See* Sawdust & Tinsel (1953)
Haakon Haakonsen *See* Shipwrecked (1990)
Hab Og Karlighed *See* Twist & Shout (1984)
Habricha el Hashemesh *See* Escape to the Sun (1972)
Hadaka No Shima *See* The Island (1961)
Hail to the Chief *See* Hail (1973)
Half Slave, Half Free 2 *See* Charlotte Forten's Mission: Experiment in Freedom (1985)
Hallelujah, I'm a Tramp *See* Hallelujah, I'm a Bum (1933)
Hallucination Generation *See* Hallucination (1967)
Ham Ham *See* Jamon, Jamon (1993)
Ha'Matarah Tiran *See* Sinai Commandos (1968)
The Hammond Mystery *See* The Undying Monster (1942)
Hand of Night *See* Beast of Morocco (1966)
Handgun *See* Deep in the Heart (1983)
Handle With Care *See* Citizens Band (1977)
Hands of a Killer *See* Planets Against Us (1961)
The Hands of Orlac *See* Mad Love (1935)
Hands of the Strangler *See* The Hands of Orlac (1960)
Hands Off the Loot *See* Grisbi (1953)
Handsome Serge *See* Le Beau Serge (1958)
The Hangover *See* The Female Jungle (1956)
Hans Christian Andersen's Thumbelina *See* Thumbelina (1994)
Happiness *See* Le Bonheur (1965)
Happy Go Lucky *See* Hallelujah, I'm a Bum (1933)
Happy Mother's Day, Love, George *See* Run, Stranger, Run (1973)
The Happy New Year Caper *See* Happy New Year (1974)
Happy Times *See* The Inspector General (1949)
Hard Driver *See* The Last American Hero (1973)
Hard Stick *See* A Real American Hero (1978)
The Hardcore Life *See* Hardcore (1979)
Harem Holiday *See* Harum Scarum (1965)
Harlem Hot Shot *See* The Black King (1932)
Harlequin *See* Dark Forces (1983)
Harold Robbins' The Betsy *See* The Betsy (1978)
Harp of Burma *See* The Burmese Harp (1956)
Harrison Bergeron *See* Kurt Vonnegut's Harrison Bergeron (1995)
Harry Black *See* Harry Black and the Tiger (1958)
Harry Tracy—Desperado *See* Harry Tracy (1983)
Harry's Machine *See* Hollywood Harry (1986)
Hasta Clerto Punto *See* Up to a Certain Point (1983)
The Hatchet Murders *See* Deep Red: Hatchet Murders (1975)
Hatred *See* Hate (1995)
The Haunted and the Hunted *See* Dementia 13 (1963)
The Haunting of Hamilton High *See* Hello Mary Lou: Prom Night 2 (1987)
The Haunting of Julia *See* Full Circle (1977)
Haus Der Tausend Freuden *See* The House of 1000 Dolls (1967)
Haxan *See* Witchcraft Through the Ages (1922)
He Lived to Kill *See* Night of Terror (1933)
He Loved an Actress *See* Mad About Money (1930)
He or She *See* Glen or Glenda: Confessions of Ed Wood (1953)
He, She or It *See* The Doll (1962)
Head On *See* Fatal Attraction (1980)
Head Over Heels *See* Chilly Scenes of Winter (1979)
The Head That Wouldn't Die *See* The Brain That Wouldn't Die (1963)
A Heart in Winter *See* Un Coeur en Hiver (1993)
The Heart of New York *See* Hallelujah, I'm a Bum (1933)
Heartbeat *See* Danielle Steel's Heartbeat (1993)
Heartbeat *See* Le Schpountz (1938)
Hearts and Minds *See* Master Touch (1974)
Heartstone *See* Demonstone (1989)
Heavenly Pursuits *See* The Gospel According to Vic (1987)
Hector Servadac's Ark *See* On the Comet (1968)
Hei Ma *See* A Mongolian Tale (1994)
The Heir to Genghis Khan *See* Storm Over Asia (1928)
The Heist *See* Dollars (1971)
Heldorado *See* Helldorado (1946)
Hell Bent for Glory *See* Lafayette Escadrille (1958)
Hell Fire *See* They (1977)
Hell in Normandy *See* Special Forces (1968)
Hell of the Living Dead *See* Night of the Zombies (1983)
Hell to Macao *See* The Corrupt Ones (1967)
Hellborn *See* The Sinister Urge (1960)
Hellcamp *See* Opposing Force (1987)
Hellfire *See* Primal Scream (1987)
Hellfire on Ice, Part 2: Escape from Hell *See* Escape from Hell (1989)
Hello Elephant *See* Pardon My Trunk (1952)
Hellraiser 2 *See* Hellbound: Hellraiser 2 (1988)
Her Mad Night *See* Held for Murder (1932)
Hercules and the Conquest of Atlantis *See* Hercules and the Captive Women (1963)
Hercules and the Haunted Women *See* Hercules and the Captive Women (1963)
Hercules and the Hydra *See* The Loves of Hercules (1960)
Hercules Goes Bananas *See* Hercules in New York (1970)
Hercules: The Movie *See* Hercules in New York (1970)
Here Come the Tigers *See* Manny's Orphans (1978)
Here Is a Man *See* The Devil & Daniel Webster (1941)
Here Lies Love *See* Second Woman (1951)
Here We Go Again *See* Pride of the Bowery (1941)
The Hero of Pine Ridge *See* Yodelin' Kid From Pine Ridge (1937)
Heroes Die Hard *See* Mr. Kingstreet's War (1971)
Herzbube *See* King, Queen, Knave (1972)
The Heterosexuals *See* Les Biches (1968)
Hets *See* Torment (1944)
Hex *See* The Shrieking (1973)
Hidden Face *See* Jail Bait (1954)
The Hidden Room of 1,000 Horrors *See* The Tell-Tale Heart (1962)
Hidden Vision *See* Night Eyes (1990)
Hide and Shriek *See* American Gothic (1988)
Hifazaat *See* In Custody (1994)
High Rolling *See* High Rolling in a Hot Corvette (1977)
The Highest Bidder *See* Woman Hunt (1972)
Highlander 3: The Magician *See* Highlander: The Final Dimension (1994)
Highlander 3: The Sorcerer *See* Highlander: The Final Dimension (1994)
Highway to Hell *See* Running Hot (1983)
Him *See* Only You (1994)
The Hindu *See* Sabaka (1955)
His Other Woman *See* Desk Set (1957)
Histoires Extraordinaires *See* Spirits of the Dead (1968)
Hitler's Gold *See* Inside Out (1975)
Hitman *See* American Commandos (1984)
HMS Defiant *See* Damn the Defiant (1962)
Hol Volt, Hol Nem Volt *See* A Hungarian Fairy Tale (1987)
Holiday *See* Jour de Fete (1948)
Hollow Point *See* The Wild Pair (1987)
Hollow Triumph *See* The Scar (1948)
Hollyweird *See* Flicks (1985)
Hollywood Cowboy *See* Hearts of the West (1975)
Hollywood Hoodlum *See* Hollywood Mystery (1934)
The Hollywood Strangler *See* Don't Answer the Phone (1980)
Hollywood Stunt Man *See* Movie Stuntmen (1953)
Hollywood Thrillmakers *See* Movie Stuntmen (1953)
Holocaust 2000 *See* The Chosen (1977)
Holy Terror *See* Alice Sweet Alice (1976)
Hombre Mirando Al Sudeste *See* Man Facing Southeast (1986)
Home Front *See* Morgan Stewart's Coming Home (1987)
Home In Oklahoma *See* Big Show (1937)
Home is Where the Heart Is *See* Square Dance (1987)
Home on the Range *See* Western Double Feature 2: Wayne & Hale (198?)
L'Homme du Minnesota *See* Minnesota Clay (1965)
L'Homme Qui Aimait les Femmes *See* The Man Who Loved Women (1977)
Honeymoon in Bali *See* My Love For Yours (1939)
Honeymoon of Fear *See* Dynasty of Fear (1972)
The Honeymooners: The Lost Episodes *See* Honeymooners Hidden Episodes, Vol. 1 (1953)
The Honorary Consul *See* Beyond the Limit (1983)
Honour Among Thieves *See* Grisbi (1953)
Hoodlum Girls *See* Youth Aflame (1959)
The Hooker Cult Murders *See* The Pyx (1973)
Hopalong Cassidy Enters *See* Hopalong Cassidy (1935)
The Hopeless Ones *See* The Round Up (1966)

A Hora Da Estrela *See* The Hour of the Star (1985)
The Horrible House on the Hill *See* Devil Times Five (1974)
The Horrible Mill Women *See* Mill of the Stone Women (1960)
Horror Castle *See* The Virgin of Nuremberg (1965)
Horror Convention *See* Nightmare in Blood (1975)
Horror Creatures of the Prehistoric Planet *See* Horror of the Blood Monsters (1970)
Horror High *See* Twisted Brain (1974)
Horror Hotel Massacre *See* Eaten Alive (1976)
Horror in the Midnight Sun *See* Invasion of the Animal People (1962)
Horror Maniacs *See* The Greed of William Hart (1948)
Horror of the Stone Women *See* Mill of the Stone Women (1960)
Horror on Snape Island *See* Tower of Evil (1972)
Horse, My Horse *See* The Horse (1982)
A Horse Named Comanche *See* Tonka (1958)
Horsie *See* Queen for a Day (1951)
Hostage *See* Savage Attraction (1983)
Hostage: Dallas *See* Getting Even (1986)
Hostage: The Christine Maresch Story *See* Savage Attraction (1983)
Hot and Cold *See* Weekend at Bernie's (1989)
Hot Car Girl *See* Hot Rod Girl (1956)
Hot Lead *See* Run of the Arrow (1956)
The Hot One *See* Corvette Summer (1978)
Hot Seat *See* The Chair (1987)
Hot Spot *See* I Wake Up Screaming (1941)
Hot Sweat *See* Keetje Tippel (1975)
Hotel Sorrento *See* Sorrento Beach (1995)
The Houghland Murder Case *See* Murder by Television (1935)
The Hounds of Zaroff *See* The Most Dangerous Game (1932)
Hour of Glory *See* The Small Back Room (1949)
The Hour of the Pig *See* The Advocate (1993)
House 3 *See* The Horror Show (1989)
House by the Lake *See* Death Weekend (1976)
House in Nightmare Park *See* Night of the Laughing Dead (1975)
House of Crazies *See* Asylum (1972)
House of Doom *See* The Black Cat (1934)
House of Evil *See* Dance of Death (1968)
House of Evil *See* The House on Sorority Row (1983)
The House of Exorcism *See* Lisa and the Devil (1975)
House of Fear *See* Fearmaker (1989)
House of Fright *See* The Two Faces of Dr. Jekyll (1960)
House of Insane Women *See* Exorcism's Daughter (1974)
House of Mortal Sin *See* The Confessional (1975)
House of Mystery *See* Night Monster (1942)
House of Pleasure *See* Le Plaisir (1952)
House of Terror *See* Face of the Screaming Werewolf (1959)
House of the Dark Stairway *See* A Blade in the Dark (1983)
House of Usher *See* The Fall of the House of Usher (1960)
The House Where Death Lives *See* Delusion (1984)
The House Where Hell Froze Over *See* Keep My Grave Open (1980)
House Without Windows *See* Seven Alone (1975)
How Is It Going? *See* Comment Ca Va? (1976)
How Long Can You Fall? *See* Till Marriage Do Us Part (1974)
How Sleep the Brave *See* Once Upon a Time in Vietnam (198?)
How to Irritate People *See* John Cleese on How to Irritate People (1968)
How To Steal a Diamond in Four Easy Lessons *See* The Hot Rock (1970)
Howard Beach: Making the Case for Murder *See* Skin (1989)
Huang Tudi *See* Yellow Earth (1989)
Huggers *See* Crazy Moon (1987)
The Human Beast *See* La Bete Humaine (1938)
The Human Tornado *See* Dolemite 2: Human Tornado (1976)
Hunchback *See* The Hunchback of Notre Dame (1982)
Hungry Pets *See* Please Don't Eat My Mother (1972)
Hungry Wives *See* Season of the Witch (1973)
Hunt to Kill *See* The White Buffalo (1977)
The Hunted *See* Touch Me Not (1974)
Hunter of the Apocalypse *See* The Last Hunter (1980)
Hunters Are For Killing *See* Hard Frame (1970)
Huozhe *See* To Live (1994)
Hustler Squad *See* The Doll Squad (1973)
I Accuse *See* J'Accuse (1937)
I Am a Fugitive From the Chain Gang *See* I Am a Fugitive from a Chain Gang (1932)
I Bambini Ci Guardano *See* The Children Are Watching Us (1944)
I Became a Criminal *See* They Made Me a Criminal (1939)
I Call First *See* Who's That Knocking at My Door? (1968)
I Can Make You Love Me: The Stalking of Laura Black *See* Stalking Laura (1993)
I Changed My Sex *See* Glen or Glenda: Confessions of Ed Wood (1953)
I Cinque Della Vendetta *See* Five Giants from Texas (1966)
I Coltelli Del Vendicatore *See* Viking Massacre (1965)
I Corpi Presentano Tracce Di Violenza Carnale *See* Torso (1973)
I Crossed the Line *See* The Black Klansman (1966)
I Fidanzati *See* Fiances (1963)
I Giorni Dell'Inferno *See* Days of Hell (1984)
I Hate Your Guts *See* Shame (1961)
I Have a New Master *See* Passion for Life (1948)
I Have Lived *See* After Midnight (1933)
I Led Two Lives *See* Glen or Glenda: Confessions of Ed Wood (1953)
I Love a Man in Uniform *See* A Man in Uniform (1993)
I Love to Kill *See* Impulse (1974)
I Married Too Young *See* Married Too Young (1962)
I Nuovi Barbari *See* Warriors of the Wasteland (1983)
I Pianeti Contro di Noi *See* Planets Against Us (1961)
I Skiachtra *See* The Enchantress (1985)
I Tre Volti della Paura *See* Black Sabbath (1964)
I, Vampiri *See* The Devil's Commandment (1956)
I Want Her Dead *See* W (1974)
I Was a Teenage Boy *See* Something Special (1986)
I Was a Teenage Teenager *See* Clueless (1995)
I You She He *See* Je Tu Il Elle (1974)
Ich und Er *See* Me and Him (1989)
Ici et Ailleurs *See* Here and Elsewhere (197?)
Identikit *See* Driver's Seat (1973)
Idi i Smotri *See* Come and See (1985)
The Idiot *See* L'Idiot (1946)
Ieri, Oggi E Domani *See* Yesterday, Today and Tomorrow (1964)
If He Hollers, Let Him Go *See* Dead Right (1968)
If You Can't Say It, Just See It *See* Whore (1991)
If You Feel Like Singing *See* Summer Stock (1950)
Ike: The War Years *See* Ike (1979)
Il Bidone *See* The Swindle (1955)
Il Buco *See* Night Watch (1972)
Il Castello de Morti Vivi *See* Castle of the Living Dead (1964)
Il Cobra *See* The Cobra (1968)
Il Conformist *See* The Conformist (1971)
Il Crudeli *See* Hellbenders (1967)
Il Diario di una Cameriera *See* Diary of a Chambermaid (1964)
Il Diavolo in Corpo *See* Devil in the Flesh (1987)
Il Dio Chiamato a Dorian *See* Dorian Gray (1970)
Il Disprezzo *See* Contempt (1964)
Il Figlio del Capitano Blood *See* Son of Captain Blood (1962)
Il Fiume Del Grande Caimano *See* The Great Alligator (1981)
Il Generale Della-Rovere *See* Generale Della Rovere (1960)
Il Giardino Del Finzi-Contini *See* The Garden of the Finzi-Continis (1971)
Il Gigante Di Metropolis *See* The Giant of Metropolis (1961)
Il Giorno e L'Ora *See* The Day and the Hour (1963)
Il Gladiatore Di Roma *See* Gladiator of Rome (1963)
Il Gladiatore Invincible *See* The Invincible Gladiator (1963)
Il Ladro Di Bagdad *See* Thief of Baghdad (1961)
Il Ladro di Bambini *See* The Stolen Children (1992)
Il Lago di Satana *See* The She-Beast (1965)
Il Mio Nome e Nessuno *See* My Name is Nobody (1974)
Il Mondo Di Yor *See* Yor, the Hunter from the Future (1983)
Il Montagna di Dio Cannibale *See* Slave of the Cannibal God (1979)
Il Mulino Delle Donne di Pietra *See* Mill of the Stone Women (1960)
Il Natale Che Quasi Non Fu *See* The Christmas That Almost Wasn't (1966)
Il Pianeta Degli Uomini Spenti *See* Battle of the Worlds (1961)
Il Portiere de Notte *See* The Night Porter (1974)
Il Postino *See* The Postman (1994)
Il Processo *See* The Trial (1963)
Il Re Dei Criminali *See* Superargo (1967)
Il Roso Segmo Della Pollias *See* Hatchet for the Honeymoon (1970)
Il Sicario *See* The Hit Man (1961)
Il Sigillo de Pechino *See* The Corrupt Ones (1967)
Il Terror Dei Baraberi *See* Goliath and the Barbarians (1960)
Il Tigre *See* Tiger and the Pussycat (1967)
Il Treno *See* The Train (1965)
Il Vangelo Secondo Matteo *See* The Gospel According to St. Matthew (1964)
Ill Met By Moonlight *See* Night Ambush (1957)
Illicit Interlude *See* Summer Interlude (1950)
Illuminacja *See* Illumination (1973)
Ilsa, the Absolute Power *See* Ilsa, the Wicked Warden (1978)
Ilya Mourometz *See* Sword & the Dragon (1956)
Im Stahlnetz Des Dr. Mabuse *See* The Return of Dr. Mabuse (1961)
Immediate Disaster *See* The Stranger from Venus (1954)
The Important Story of Alcoholism *See* One Too Many (1951)
Impossible Object *See* The Story of a Love Story (1973)
In a Year with 13 Moons *See* In a Year of 13 Moons (1978)
In Bed with Madonna *See* Truth or Dare (1991)
In Einem Jahr Mit 13 Monden *See* In a Year of 13 Moons (1978)
In Fashion *See* A la Mode (1994)
In Love *See* Falling in Love Again (1980)
In Old Oklahoma *See* War of the Wildcats (1943)
In the Bleak Midwinter *See* A Midwinter's Tale (1995)
In the Devil's Garden *See* Assault (1970)
In the Grip of the Spider *See* Web of the Spider (1970)
In the Woods *See* Rashomon (1951)
In Weiter Ferne, So Nah! *See* Faraway, So Close! (1993)
Incense For the Damned *See* The Bloodsuckers (1970)
Incident at Victoria Falls *See* Sherlock Holmes and the Incident at Victoria Falls (1991)
The Incredible Invasion *See* The Sinister Invasion (1968)
The Incredible Praying Mantis *See* The Deadly Mantis (1957)
The Incredible Torture Show *See* Bloodsucking Freaks (1975)
The Incredibly Strange Creatures *See* Incredibly Strange Creatures Who Stopped Living and Became Mixed-Up Zombies (1963)
An Indian in the City *See* Little Indian, Big City (1995)
Indian Love Call *See* Rose Marie (1936)
Indiscretion *See* Christmas in Connecticut (1945)

Indiscretion *See* Indiscretion of an American Wife (1954)
The Infernal Idol *See* Craze (1974)
Infested *See* Ticks (1993)
The Infra Superman *See* Infra-Man (1976)
Inn of the Frightened People *See* Revenge (1971)
Innocence is Bliss *See* Miss Grant Takes Richmond (1949)
The Innocent and the Damned *See* Girls' Town (1959)
The Insect *See* The Insect Woman (1963)
Inseminoid *See* Horror Planet (1980)
L'Insoumis *See* Fight for Us (1989)
Interlude *See* Intermezzo (1936)
Intermezzo: A Love Story *See* Intermezzo (1939)
The Intruder *See* Shame (1961)
The Invader *See* Old Spanish Custom (1936)
The Invaders *See* The Forty-Ninth Parallel (1941)
Invasion Earth 2150 A.D. *See* Daleks—Invasion Earth 2150 A.D. (1966)
Invasion Force *See* Hangar 18 (1980)
Invasion from Inner Earth *See* They (1977)
Invasion of Planet X *See* Godzilla vs. Monster Zero (1968)
Invasion of the Astro-Monsters *See* Godzilla vs. Monster Zero (1968)
Invasion of the Astros *See* Godzilla vs. Monster Zero (1968)
Invasion of the Flying Saucers *See* Earth vs. the Flying Saucers (1956)
Invasion of the Zombies *See* Horror of Party Beach (1964)
An Investigation of Murder *See* The Laughing Policeman (1974)
The Invisible Horror *See* The Invisible Dr. Mabuse (1962)
Io Speriamo Che Me La Cavo *See* Ciao, Professore! (1994)
Iron Hand *See* Goetz von Berlichingen (1980)
The Iron Hand *See* Chinese Connection (1973)
The Iron Kiss *See* Naked Kiss (1964)
Irving Berlin's Alexander's Ragtime Band *See* Alexander's Ragtime Band (1938)
Irving Berlin's Second Fiddle *See* Second Fiddle (1939)
Island of Monte Cristo *See* Sword of Venus (1953)
Island of the Burning Damned *See* Island of the Burning Doomed (1967)
Island of the Fishmen *See* Screamers (1980)
Island of the Living Horror *See* Brides of the Beast (1968)
Isle of Lost Women *See* 99 Women (1969)
Isle of the Living Dead *See* The Snake People (1968)
Isle of the Snake People *See* The Snake People (1968)
Isn't Life A Bitch? *See* La Chienne (1931)
Istanbul, Keep Your Eyes Open *See* Istanbul (1990)
It Comes Up Murder *See* The Honey Pot (1967)
It Happened at Lakewood Manor *See* Ants (1977)
It Happened in Paris *See* The Lady in Question (1940)
It Happened One Summer *See* State Fair (1945)
It Hurts Only When I Laugh *See* Only When I Laugh (1981)
It Lives By Night *See* The Bat People (1974)
It Only Take Five Minutes *See* Five Minutes to Love (1963)
It Runs in the Family *See* My Summer Story (1994)
It Stalked the Ocean Floor *See* Monster from the Ocean Floor (1954)
It! The Vampire From Beyond Space *See* It! The Terror from Beyond Space (1958)
It Won't Rub Off, Baby *See* Sweet Love, Bitter (1967)
The Italian Connection *See* Hired to Kill (1973)
The Italian Connection *See* Manhunt (1973)
It's Hot in Hell *See* Un Singe en Hiver (1962)
It's Hot in Paradise *See* Horrors of Spider Island (1959)
It's My Life *See* My Life to Live (1962)
It's Only Money *See* Double Dynamite (1951)
Ivan's Childhood *See* My Name is Ivan (1962)
Jack London's Klondike Fever *See* Klondike Fever (1979)
Jackals *See* American Justice (1986)
Jackie Chan's Police Story *See* Jackie Chan's Police Force (1985)
Jack's Wife *See* Season of the Witch (1973)
Jacqueline Susann's Once is Not Enough *See* Once is Not Enough (1975)
Jacquot de Nantes *See* Jacquot (1991)
J'ai Pas Sommeil *See* I Can't Sleep (1993)
Jail Birds *See* Pardon Us (1931)
Jailbirds' Vacation *See* Les Grandes Gueules (1965)
James A. Michener's Texas *See* Texas (1994)
James Clavell's Shogun *See* Shogun (1980)
The Janitor *See* Eyewitness (1981)
Japan Sinks *See* Tidal Wave (1975)
Jatszani Kell *See* Lily in Love (1985)
Jaws 3-D *See* Jaws 3 (1983)
Jayne Mansfield: A Symbol of the '50s *See* The Jayne Mansfield Story (1980)
J.C. *See* Iron Horsemen (1971)
Je Vous Salue Marie *See* Hail Mary (1985)
Jealousy *See* L'Enfer (1993)
Jean de Florette 2 *See* Manon of the Spring (1987)
Jeder Fur Sich Und Gott Gegen Alle *See* Every Man for Himself & God Against All (1975)
Jekyll's Inferno *See* The Two Faces of Dr. Jekyll (1960)
Jennie *See* Portrait of Jennie (1948)
Jennifer (The Snake Goddess) *See* Jennifer (1978)
The Jester *See* Der Purimshpiler (1937)
Jesus de Montreal *See* Jesus of Montreal (1989)
Jeu de Massacre *See* The Killing Game (1967)
Jew Suss *See* Power (1934)
The Jewish Jester *See* Der Purimshpiler (1937)
The Jezebels *See* Switchblade Sisters (1975)
Jigokumen *See* Gate of Hell (1954)
Jim Buck *See* Portrait of a Hitman (1977)
Job Lazadasa *See* The Revolt of Job (1984)
Joe Palooka *See* Palooka (1934)
John Carpenter Presents Body Bags *See* Body Bags (1993)
John Carpenter's Escape from L.A. *See* Escape from L.A. (1996)
John Le Carre's A Perfect Spy *See* A Perfect Spy (1988)
John Travis, Solar Survivor *See* Omega Cop (1990)
Johnnie Mae Gibson: FBI *See* Johnnie Gibson F.B.I. (1987)
Johnny Vagabond *See* Johnny Come Lately (1943)
Johnny Zombie *See* My Boyfriend's Back (1993)
A Joke of Destiny *See* A Joke of Destiny, Lying in Wait Around the Corner Like a Bandit (1984)
Joker's Wild *See* Body Trouble (1992)
Jonas—Qui Aura 25 Ans en l'an 2000 *See* Jonah Who Will Be 25 in the Year 2000 (1976)
Joseph Sold by His Brothers *See* Joseph & His Brethren (1960)
Journey into Autumn *See* Dreams (1955)
Journey of the Hyena *See* Touki Bouki (1973)
J.R. *See* Who's That Knocking at My Door? (1968)
A Judgement in Stone *See* The Housekeeper (1986)
A Judgment in Stone *See* La Ceremonie (1995)
Jules et Jim *See* Jules and Jim (1962)
Jules Verne's Rocket to the Moon *See* Those Fantastic Flying Fools (1967)
Julie Darling *See* Daughter of Death (1982)
July Pork Bellies *See* For Pete's Sake (1974)
Jumbo *See* Billy Rose's Jumbo (1962)
Jungfrukallan *See* The Virgin Spring (1959)
The Jungle Book *See* Rudyard Kipling's The Jungle Book (1994)
Jungle Gold *See* Perils of the Darkest Jungle (1944)
Jungle Woman *See* Nabonga (1944)
Juninatten *See* June Night (1940)
Jury Duty *See* The Great American Sex Scandal (1994)
Just Another Day at the Races *See* Win, Place, or Steal (1972)
Just Ask for Diamond *See* Diamond's Edge (1988)
Just in Time *See* Only You (1994)
Justice Rides Again *See* Destry Rides Again (1939)
Jutai *See* Traffic Jam (1991)
Kaiju Daisenso *See* Godzilla vs. Monster Zero (1968)
Kaiju Soshingeki *See* Destroy All Monsters (1968)
Kaitei Daisenso *See* Terror Beneath the Sea (1966)
Kakushi Toride No San Akunin *See* The Hidden Fortress (1958)
Kaleidoscope *See* Danielle Steel's Kaleidoscope (1992)
Kamakazi *See* Attack Squadron (197?)
Karamazov *See* The Brothers Karamazov (1958)
Karate Cop *See* Slaughter in San Francisco (1981)
Katie's Passion *See* Keetje Tippel (1975)
The Kent Chronicles *See* The Bastard (1978)
Kettle Creek *See* Mountain Justice (1930)
The Key *See* Odd Obsession (1960)
Key West Crossing *See* The Mercenaries (1980)
KGOD *See* Pray TV (1980)
Kid Auto Races at Venice *See* Kid's Auto Race/Mabel's Married Life (1915)
The Kidnap of Mary Lou *See* Almost Human (1979)
Kill Castro *See* The Mercenaries (1980)
Killbots *See* Chopping Mall (1986)
Killer *See* Bulletproof Heart (1995)
Killer Bait *See* Too Late for Tears (1949)
Killer Bats *See* The Devil Bat (1941)
The Killer Behind the Mask *See* Savage Weekend (1980)
Killer Grizzly *See* Grizzly (1976)
Killer of Killers *See* The Mechanic (1972)
Killer With a Label *See* One Too Many (1951)
The Killers *See* Pigs (1973)
Killers of the Wild *See* Children of the Wild (1937)
The Killing Box *See* The Ghost Brigade (1993)
Kimono No Kiroku *See* I Live in Fear (1955)
Kin Folk *See* All the Lovin' Kinfolk (1989)
Kinfolk *See* All the Lovin' Kinfolk (1989)
King Cobra *See* Jaws of Satan (1981)
King Gun *See* The Gatling Gun (1972)
King Kong Tai Godzilla *See* King Kong vs. Godzilla (1963)
King of Africa *See* One Step to Hell (1968)
The King of Criminals *See* Superargo (1967)
King of the Jungleland *See* Darkest Africa (1936)
Kings Ransom *See* Devastator (1985)
Kisenga, Man of Africa *See* Men of Two Worlds (1946)
A Kiss from Eddie *See* The Arousers (1970)
Kiss My Butterfly *See* I Love You, Alice B. Toklas! (1968)
Kiss of Evil *See* Kiss of the Vampire (1962)
KKK *See* The Klansman (1974)
The Knack...and How to Get It *See* The Knack (1965)
Knives of the Avenger *See* Viking Massacre (1965)
The Knock-Out Cop *See* Flatfoot (1978)
Koks I Kulissen *See* Ladies on the Rocks (1983)
Komissar *See* Commissar (1968)
Koneko Monogatari *See* The Adventures of Milo & Otis (1989)
Konjiki Yasha *See* Golden Demon (1953)
Kootenai Brown *See* Showdown at Williams Creek (1991)
Kopek and Broom *See* Find the Lady (1975)
Krasnaya Palatka *See* Red Tent (1969)
Kronos *See* Captain Kronos: Vampire Hunter (1974)
Kumonosujo, Kumonosu-djo *See* Throne of Blood (1957)
Kung Fu Master *See* Le Petit Amour (1987)
Kunisada Chuji *See* The Gambling Samurai (1960)
Kuroi Ame *See* Black Rain (1988)
Kvinn odrom *See* Dreams (1955)
Kvinnors Vantan *See* Secrets of Women (1952)
Kyuketsuki Gokemidoro *See* Body Snatcher from Hell (1969)
La Banda J.&S. Cronaca Criminale del Far West *See* Sonny and Jed (1973)
La Beaute du Diable *See* Beauty and the Devil (1950)
La Belle et Laete *See* Beauty and the Beast (1946)
La Bestia Uccide a Sangue Freddo *See* Slaughter Hotel (1971)
La Cabeza Viviente *See* The Living Head (1959)
La Camara Del Terror *See* The Fear Chamber (1968)

La Casa Con La Scala Nel Buio *See* A Blade in the Dark (1983)
La Casa Del Terror *See* Face of the Screaming Werewolf (1959)
La Casa Dell' Exorcismo *See* Lisa and the Devil (1975)
La Casa Embrujada *See* The Curse of the Crying Woman (1961)
La Casa Nel Parco *See* House on the Edge of the Park (1984)
La Case de L'Oncle Tom *See* Uncle Tom's Cabin (1969)
La Caza *See* The Hunt (1967)
La Chambre Verte *See* The Green Room (1978)
La Chasse aux Papillons *See* Chasing Butterflies (1994)
La Chiesa *See* The Church (1990)
La Ciociara *See* Two Women (1961)
La Cite des Enfants Perdus *See* The City of Lost Children (1995)
La Ciudad y los Perros *See* The City and the Dogs (1985)
La Commare Secca *See* The Grim Reaper (1962)
La Comtesse Perverse *See* The Perverse Countess (1973)
La Decima Vittima *See* 10th Victim (1965)
La Dentielliere *See* The Lacemaker (1977)
La Diagonale du Fou *See* Dangerous Moves (1984)
La Dixieme Victime *See* 10th Victim (1965)
La Donna E Donna *See* A Woman is a Woman (1960)
La Double Vie de Veronique *See* The Double Life of Veronique (1991)
La Dueda Interna *See* Veronico Cruz (1987)
La Famiglia *See* The Family (1987)
La Femme d'a Cote *See* The Woman Next Door (1981)
La Femme De Mon Pote *See* My Best Friend's Girl (1984)
La Femme du Boulanger *See* The Baker's Wife (1933)
La Femme Mariee *See* A Married Woman (1965)
La Fiancee du Pirate *See* A Very Curious Girl (1969)
La Figlia di Frankenstein *See* Lady Frankenstein (1972)
La Fille Du Puisatier *See* Well-Digger's Daughter (1946)
La Flor de My Secreto *See* The Flower of My Secret (1995)
La Folle des Grandeurs *See* Delusions of Grandeur (1976)
La Francaise et L'Amour *See* Love and the Frenchwoman (1960)
La Furia Di Ercole *See* The Fury of Hercules (1961)
La Gifle *See* The Slap (1976)
La Gloire de Mon Pere *See* My Father's Glory (1991)
La Grande Guerre *See* The Great War (1959)
La Grieta *See* Endless Descent (1990)
La Haine *See* Hate (1995)
La Historia Oficial *See* The Official Story (1985)
La Horriplante Bestia Humana *See* Night of the Bloody Apes (1968)
La Illusion en Travnia *See* The Illusion Travels by Streetcar (1953)
La Invasion de Los Vampiros *See* Invasion of the Vampires (1961)
La Isla Del Tersoro *See* Treasure Island (1972)
La Joven *See* The Young One (1961)
La Kermesse Heroique *See* Carnival in Flanders (1935)
La Legge *See* Where the Hot Wind Blows (1959)
La Ley del Deseo *See* Law of Desire (1986)
La Linea Del Cielo *See* Skyline (1984)
La Loi *See* Where the Hot Wind Blows (1959)
La Lune Dans le Caniveau *See* Moon in the Gutter (1983)
La Macchina Ammazzacattivi *See* Machine to Kill Bad People (1948)
La Mala Ordina *See* Manhunt (1973)
La Maldicion de a Llorona *See* The Curse of the Crying Woman (1961)
La Maldicion de la Momia Azteca *See* The Curse of the Aztec Mummy (1959)
La Marca del Muerto *See* Creature of the Walking Dead (1960)
La Mariee Etait en Noir *See* The Bride Wore Black (1968)
La Mitad del Cielo *See* Half of Heaven (1986)
La Momia Azteca Contra el Robot Humano *See* The Robot vs. the Aztec Mummy (1959)
La Mort en Ce Jardin *See* Death in the Garden (1956)
La Morte Vestita di Dollar *See* Dog Eat Dog (1964)
La Morte Viene Dalla Spazio *See* The Day the Sky Exploded (1957)
La Motocyclette *See* The Girl on a Motorcycle (1968)
La Muerte Viviente *See* The Snake People (1968)
La Nipote del Vampiro *See* Fangs of the Living Dead (1968)
La Noche de Los Mil Gatos *See* Night of a Thousand Cats (1972)
La Noche dell Terror Ciego *See* Tombs of the Blind Dead (1972)
La Noia: L'Ennui Et Sa Diversion, L'Erotisme *See* Empty Canvas (1964)
La Notte Che Evelyn Usca Dalla Tomba *See* The Night Evelyn Came Out of the Grave (1971)
La Notte di San Lorenzo *See* The Night of the Shooting Stars (1982)
La Novia Esangentada *See* The Blood Spattered Bride (1972)
La Nuit Americaine *See* Day for Night (1973)
La Nuit de Generaux *See* Night of the Generals (1967)
La Nuit Des Espions *See* Double Agents (1959)
La Passante du Sans Souci *See* La Passante (1983)
La Passion Beatrice *See* Beatrice (1988)
La Permission *See* The Story of a Three Day Pass (1968)
La Planete Sauvage *See* Fantastic Planet (1973)
La Polizia vuole Giustizia *See* Violent Professionals (1973)
La Poupee *See* The Doll (1962)
La Prise de Pouvoir Par Louis XIV *See* The Rise of Louis XIV (1966)
La Provinciale *See* The Wayward Wife (1952)
La Puppa del Gangster *See* Get Rita (1975)
La Reine Margot *See* Queen Margot (1994)
La Romana *See* A Woman of Rome (1956)
La Ruee Des Vikings *See* The Invaders (1963)
La Spada del Cid *See* The Sword of El Cid (1962)
La Spina Dorsale del Diavolo *See* Ride to Glory (1971)
L.A. Streetfighters *See* Ninja Turf (1986)
La Strega in Amore *See* The Witch (1966)
La Tatiche de Ercole *See* Hercules (1958)
La Tragedia di un Uomo Ridicolo *See* The Tragedy of a Ridiculous Man (1981)
La Vendetta De Ercole *See* Goliath and the Dragon (1961)
La Vergine de Norimberga *See* The Virgin of Nuremberg (1965)
La Victoire en Chantant *See* Black and White in Color (1976)
La Vie Devant Soi *See* Madame Rosa (1977)
La Vie est Rien d'Autre *See* Life and Nothing But (1989)
La Vie Est Une Longue Fleuve Tranquille *See* Life Is a Long Quiet River (1988)
La Vie Privee *See* A Very Private Affair (1962)
La Vieille qui Marchait dans la Mer *See* The Old Lady Who Walked in the Sea (1991)
Laberinto de Pasiones *See* Labyrinth of Passion (1982)
Labyrinth *See* A Reflection of Fear (1972)
Ladies of the Park *See* The Ladies of the Bois de Bologne (1944)
Ladri di Biciclette *See* The Bicycle Thief (1948)
Ladri di Saponette *See* The Icicle Thief (1989)
Lady Beware *See* 13th Guest (1932)
The Lady Dances *See* The Merry Widow (1934)
The Lady Dracula *See* Lemora, Lady Dracula (1973)
Lady Hamilton *See* That Hamilton Woman (1941)
Lady in the Fog *See* Scotland Yard Inspector (1952)
Lady Jane Grey *See* Nine Days a Queen (1934)
The Lady Killers *See* The Ladykillers (1955)
Lady of Deceit *See* Born to Kill (1947)
Lady of the Shadows *See* The Terror (1963)
L'Aigle a Deux Tetes *See* The Eagle Has Two Heads (1948)
L'Albero Degli Zoccoli *See* The Tree of Wooden Clogs (1978)
L'Amant *See* The Lover (1992)
L'Amant de Lady Chatterley *See* Lady Chatterley's Lover (1955)
The Lament of the Path *See* Pather Panchali (1954)
L'Amour en Fuite *See* Love on the Run (1978)
The Lamp *See* The Outing (1987)
Lancelot and Guinevere *See* Sword of Lancelot (1963)
Lancelot Du Lac *See* Lancelot of the Lake (1974)
Landru *See* Bluebeard (1963)
The Lane Frost Story *See* 8 Seconds (1994)
L'Anee Derniere a Marienbad *See* Last Year at Marienbad (1961)
The Langoliers *See* Stephen King's The Langoliers (1995)
Larceny Lane *See* Blonde Crazy (1931)
Larsen, Wolf of the Seven Seas *See* The Legend of the Sea Wolf (1958)
Las Vegas Strip War *See* The Vegas Strip Wars (1984)
Lashou Shentan *See* Hard-Boiled (1992)
Lasky Jedne Plavovlasky *See* Loves of a Blonde (1965)
L'Associe *See* The Associate (1982)
The Last Adventure *See* Les Aventuriers (1977)
The Last Adventurers *See* Down to the Sea in Ships (1922)
The Last Battle *See* Le Dernier Combat (1984)
Last Chance For a Born Loser *See* Stateline Motel (1975)
The Last Days of Man on Earth *See* The Final Programme (1973)
The Last Days of Sodom and Gomorrah *See* Sodom and Gomorrah (1962)
The Last Elephant *See* Ivory Hunters (1990)
The Last Frontier *See* Savage Wilderness (1955)
The Last Great Treasure *See* Mother Lode (1982)
Last House on the Left, Part 2 *See* Twitch of the Death Nerve (1971)
Last Message From Saigon *See* Operation C.I.A. (1965)
Last of the Cowboys *See* Great Smokey Roadblock (1976)
The Last Outpost *See* Cavalry Charge (1951)
The Last Page *See* Man Bait (1952)
Last Rites *See* Dracula's Last Rites (1979)
The Last Victim *See* Forced Entry (1975)
The Last Warrior *See* The Final Executioner (1983)
The Last Will of Dr. Mabuse *See* Testament of Dr. Mabuse (1962)
The Late Edwina Black *See* The Obsessed (1951)
Latin Love *See* Greek Street (1930)
Latin Quarter *See* Frenzy (1946)
Laughterhouse *See* Singleton's Pluck (1984)
The Law *See* Tilai (1990)
The Law *See* Where the Hot Wind Blows (1959)
Law Breakers *See* Les Assassins de L'Ordre (1971)
Lawnmower Man 2: Jobe's War *See* Lawnmower Man 2: Beyond Cyberspace (1995)
Lazy Bones *See* Hallelujah, I'm a Bum (1933)
Le Blonde de Pekin *See* The Peking Blond (1968)
Le Caporal Epingle *See* The Elusive Corporal (1962)
Le Carrosse D'Or *See* The Golden Coach (1952)
Le Cerveau *See* The Brain (1969)
Le Charme Discret de la Bourgeoisie *See* The Discreet Charm of the Bourgeoisie (1972)
Le Chateau de Ma Mere *See* My Mother's Castle (1991)
Le Cheval D'Orgeuil *See* The Horse of Pride (1980)
Le Ciel et le Boue *See* The Sky Above, the Mud Below (1961)
Le Confessionnal *See* The Confessional (1995)
Le Corniauds *See* The Sucker (1965)
Le Cri du Hibou *See* The Cry of the Owl (1992)
Le Crime de Monsieur Lange *See* The Crime of Monsieur Lange (1936)

Le Danger Vient de l'Escape *See* The Day the Sky Exploded (1957)
Le Declin De L'Empire Americain *See* The Decline of the American Empire (1986)
Le Dejeuner Sur l'Herbe *See* Picnic on the Grass (1959)
Le Dernier Metro *See* The Last Metro (1980)
Le Desert des Tartares *See* The Desert of the Tartars (1976)
Le Diable au Corps *See* Devil in the Flesh (1946)
Le Distrait *See* The Daydreamer (1975)
Le Docteur Petiot *See* Dr. Petiot (1990)
Le Fantome de la Liberte *See* Phantom of Liberty (1968)
Le Feu Follet *See* The Fire Within (1964)
Le Fils du Requin *See* The Son of the Shark (1993)
Le Fils Prefere *See* The Favorite Son (1994)
Le Fruit Defendu *See* Forbidden Fruit (1952)
Le Geant de la Vallee Das Rois *See* Son of Samson (1962)
Le Gentleman D'epsom *See* Duke of the Derby (1962)
Le Graal *See* Lancelot of the Lake (1974)
Le Grand Bleu *See* The Big Blue (1988)
Le Grand Blond Avec Une Chassure Noire *See* The Tall Blond Man with One Black Shoe (1972)
Le Grand Meaulnes *See* The Wanderer (1967)
Le Huitieme Jour *See* The Eighth Day (1995)
Le Hussard sur le Toit *See* The Horseman on the Roof (1995)
Le Jour et L'Heure *See* The Day and the Hour (1963)
Le Journal d'un Cure de Campagne *See* Diary of a Country Priest (1950)
Le Journal d'une Femme de Chambre *See* Diary of a Chambermaid (1964)
Le Juge et L'assassin *See* The Judge and the Assassin (1975)
Le Locataire *See* The Tenant (1976)
Le Maitre de Musique *See* The Music Teacher (1988)
Le Mepris *See* Contempt (1964)
Le Meraviglie Di Aladino *See* The Wonders of Aladdin (1961)
Le Mur *See* The Wall (1983)
Le Mura di Malapaga *See* The Walls of Malapaga (1949)
Le Neveu de Beethoven *See* Beethoven's Nephew (1988)
Le Notti di Cabiria *See* Nights of Cabiria (1957)
Le Pays Bleu *See* Blue Country (1977)
Le Peau Douce *See* The Soft Skin (1964)
Le Petit Monde de Don Camillo *See* Little World of Don Camillo (1951)
Le Plus Vieux Metier du Monde *See* Oldest Profession (1967)
Le Proces *See* The Trial (1963)
Le Rayon Vert *See* Summer (1986)
Le Regle du Jeu *See* The Rules of the Game (1939)
Le Retour de Martin Guerre *See* The Return of Martin Guerre (1983)
Le Roi de Coeur *See* The King of Hearts (1966)
Le Rouble a Deux Faces *See* The Hot Line (1969)
Le Rouge aux Levres *See* Daughters of Darkness (1971)
Le Rouge et le Noir *See* The Red and the Black (1957)
Le Salaire De La Peur *See* Wages of Fear (1955)
Le Sang d'un Poete *See* The Blood of a Poet (1930)
le Sant de l'Ange *See* Cobra (1971)
Le Sauvage *See* Lovers Like Us (1975)
Le Train *See* The Train (1965)
Le Trou *See* Night Watch (1972)
Le Vieil Homme Et L'Enfant *See* The Two of Us (1968)
Le Voleur De Bagdad *See* Thief of Baghdad (1961)
Leader of the Pack *See* Unholy Rollers (1972)
Lebenszeichen *See* Signs of Life (1968)
L'eclisse *See* The Eclipse (1966)
L'Ecole Buissonniere *See* Passion for Life (1948)
Legacy of Blood *See* Blood Legacy (1973)
The Legacy of Maggie Walsh *See* The Legacy (1979)
The Legend *See* James Dean (1976)
Legend in Leotards *See* Return of Captain Invincible (1983)
Legend of Cougar Canyon *See* The Secret of Navajo Cave (1976)
The Legend of Gosta Berling *See* The Atonement of Gosta Berling (1924)
The Legend of Machine Gun Kelly *See* Melvin Purvis: G-Man (1974)
Legend of the Bayou *See* Eaten Alive (1976)
Legend of the Seven Golden Vampires *See* The 7 Brothers Meet Dracula (1973)
Legend of Witch Hollow *See* The Witchmaker (1969)
Legenda Del Rudio Malese *See* Jungle Raiders (1985)
Legenda Suramskoi Kreposti *See* The Legend of Suram Fortress (1985)
The Legendary Curse of Lemora *See* Lemora, Lady Dracula (1973)
Legion of the Damned *See* Battle of the Commandos (1971)
L'Enfant Sauvage *See* The Wild Child (1970)
Leon *See* The Professional (1994)
Leona Helmsley: The Queen of Mean *See* The Queen of Mean (1990)
Lepassager de la Pluie *See* Rider on the Rain (1970)
L'Eredita Ferramonti *See* The Inheritance (1976)
Les Amities Particulieres *See* This Special Friendship (1967)
Les Bas Fonds *See* The Lower Depths (1936)
Les Belles de Nuit *See* Beauties of the Night (1952)
Les Choses De La Vie *See* The Things of Life (1970)
Les Corrompus *See* The Corrupt Ones (1967)
Les Cousins *See* The Cousins (1959)
Les Dames du Bois de Bologne *See* The Ladies of the Bois de Bologne (1944)
Les Deux Anglaises et le Continent *See* Two English Girls (1972)
Les Deux Rivales *See* Time of Indifference (1964)
Les Diabolique *See* Diabolique (1955)
Les Dimanches de Ville d'Arvay *See* Sundays & Cybele (1962)
Les Enfants du Paradise *See* Children of Paradise (1944)
Les Felins *See* Joy House (1964)
Les Gaspards *See* The Holes (1972)
Les Grandes Gueules *See* Jailbird's Vacation (1965)
Les Grandes Personnes *See* Time Out for Love (1961)
Les Innocents aux Mains Sales *See* Dirty Hands (1976)
Les Jeux Interdits *See* Forbidden Games (1952)
Les Liaisons Dangereuses *See* Dangerous Liaisons (1960)
Les Liens de Sang *See* Blood Relatives (1977)
Les Louves *See* Letters to an Unknown Lover (1984)
Les Mille Et Une Nuits *See* The Wonders of Aladdin (1961)
Les Mongols *See* The Mongols (1960)
Les Noces de Papier *See* A Paper Wedding (1989)
Les Nuits De La Pleine *See* Full Moon in Paris (1984)
Les Orgueilleux *See* The Proud Ones (1953)
Les Parapluies De Cherbourg *See* Umbrellas of Cherbourg (1964)
Les Parents Terribles *See* The Storm Within (1948)
Les Quartre Cents Coups *See* The 400 Blows (1959)
Les Ripoux *See* My New Partner (1984)
Les Roseaux Sauvages *See* Wild Reeds (1994)
Les Somnambules *See* Mon Oncle D'Amerique (1980)
Les Vacances de Monsieur Hulot *See* Mr. Hulot's Holiday (1953)
Les Valseuses *See* Going Places (1974)
Les Yeux Noirs *See* Dark Eyes (1987)
Les Yeux Sans Visage *See* The Horror Chamber of Dr. Faustus (1959)
Lesbian Twins *See* The Virgin Witch (1970)
L'Ete Meurtrier *See* One Deadly Summer (1983)
L'Ete Prochain *See* Next Summer (1984)
L'Eternel Retour *See* Eternal Return (1943)
Lethal *See* The KGB: The Secret War (1986)
A Letter to Mama *See* A Brivele der Mamen (1938)
A Letter to Mother *See* A Brivele der Mamen (1938)
Letyat Zhuravit *See* The Cranes are Flying (1957)
L'Evangile Selon Saint-Matthieu *See* The Gospel According to St. Matthew (1964)
L'Histoire d'Adele H. *See* Story of Adele H. (1975)
L'Homme de Rio *See* That Man from Rio (1964)
L'Hypothese du Tableau Vole *See* The Hypothesis of the Stolen Painting (1978)
Libido *See* The Sensuous Teenager (1970)
Licensed to Kill *See* Second Best Secret Agent in the Whole Wide World (1965)
The Life and Adventures of Nicholas Nickleby *See* Nicholas Nickleby (1946)
The Life and Loves of Beethoven *See* Beethoven (1936)
Life at Stake *See* The Key Man (1957)
Life in the Food Chain *See* Age Isn't Everything (1991)
Life is Rosy *See* La Vie est Belle (1987)
Life of Brian *See* Monty Python's Life of Brian (1979)
The Life of Jack London *See* Jack London (1944)
Lifesavers *See* Mixed Nuts (1994)
The Light Fantastic *See* Love Is Better Than Ever (1952)
Lights of Variety *See* Variety Lights (1951)
Like a Crow on a June Bug *See* Sixteen (1972)
Like Father, Like Son *See* The Executioner (1978)
Lila *See* Mantis in Lace (1968)
Lilacs in the Spring *See* Let's Make Up (1955)
L'Inafferrabile Invincible *See* Mr. Superinvisible (1973)
Lincoln *See* Gore Vidal's Lincoln (1988)
L'Innocente *See* The Innocent (1976)
The Lion's Den *See* La Boca del Lobo (1989)
L'Isola Degli Uomini Pesce *See* Screamers (1980)
The Little Martyr *See* The Children Are Watching Us (1944)
The Little Mermaid *See* La Petite Sirene (1980)
Little Mother *See* Mamele (1938)
Little Pal *See* Healer (1936)
Little Panda *See* The Amazing Panda Adventure (1995)
The Little Sister *See* The Tender Age (1984)
Live a Little, Steal a Lot *See* Murph the Surf (1975)
Live Bait *See* L'Appat (1994)
Live to Love *See* The Devil's Hand (1961)
The Liver Eaters *See* Spider Baby (1964)
Ljubarni Slucaj *See* The Love Affair, or The Case of the Missing Switchboard Operator (1967)
Lo Chiamavano Trinita *See* They Call Me Trinity (1972)
Lo Que Vendra *See* Times to Come (1981)
Lo Sbarco di Anzio *See* Anzio (1968)
Lo Scatenato *See* Catch as Catch Can (1968)
Lo Sceicco Bianco *See* The White Sheik (1952)
Lo Spettro *See* The Ghost (1963)
Lo Strano Vizio Della Signora Wardh *See* The Next Victim (1971)
Lo Zio Indegno *See* The Sleazy Uncle (1989)
Loaded Weapon 1 *See* National Lampoon's Loaded Weapon 1 (1993)
Lock Your Doors *See* The Ape Man (1943)
The Lodger: A Case of London Fog *See* The Lodger (1926)
L'Oeuvre au Noir *See* The Abyss (1989)
The Lone Troubador *See* Two-Gun Troubador (1937)
The Lonely Hearts Killers *See* Honeymoon Killers (1970)
Lonely Man *See* Gun Riders (1969)
The Loner *See* Ruckus (1981)
The Long Arm *See* The Third Key (1957)
The Long, Dark Night *See* The Pack (1977)
Long John Silver Returns to Treasure Island *See* Long John Silver (1953)
The Long Ride *See* Brady's Escape (1984)
The Long Shot *See* African Rage (1978)
Look Down and Die *See* Steel (1980)
The Look of Ulysses *See* Ulysses' Gaze (1995)
Loonies On Broadway *See* Zombies on Broadway (1944)
Loose Joints *See* Flicks (1985)
Looters *See* Trespass (1992)

L'Opera De Quat'Sous *See* The Threepenny Opera (1931)
Lorca and the Outlaws *See* Starship (1987)
Lords of Treason *See* Secret Honor (1985)
L'Oro Di Napoli *See* The Gold of Naples (1954)
L'Orribile Segreto Del Dr. Hichcock *See* The Horrible Dr. Hichcock (1962)
Los Ambiciosos *See* Fever Mounts at El Pao (1959)
Los Despiadados *See* Hellbenders (1967)
Los Ojos Azules de la Muneca Rota *See* House of Psychotic Women (1973)
Los Santos Inocentes *See* The Holy Innocents (1984)
Loser Take All *See* Strike It Rich (1990)
The Lost Glory of Troy *See* The Avenger (1962)
The Lost Illusion *See* The Fallen Idol (1949)
Lost Island of Kioga *See* Hawk of the Wilderness (1938)
Lost Women *See* Mesa of Lost Women (1952)
Lost Women of Zarpa *See* Mesa of Lost Women (1952)
The Loudest Whisper *See* The Children's Hour (1961)
Louis L'Amour's Conagher *See* Conagher (1991)
Louis L'Amour's "The Shadow Riders" *See* The Shadow Riders (1982)
Love and Hate: The Story of Colin and Joanne Thatcher *See* Love and Hate: A Marriage Made in Hell (1990)
The Love Cage *See* Joy House (1964)
Love Eternal *See* Eternal Return (1943)
The Love Factor *See* Alien Women (1969)
Love in Las Vegas *See* Viva Las Vegas (1963)
Love is Blind *See* Love at First Sight (1976)
The Love Maniac *See* Blood of Ghastly Horror (1972)
Love, the Magician *See* El Amor Brujo (1986)
Love Trap *See* Curse of the Black Widow (1977)
Love You to Death *See* Deadly Illusion (1987)
Lover of the Great Bear *See* Smugglers (1975)
Lover, Wife *See* Wifemistress (1979)
Lovers From Beyond the Tomb *See* Nightmare Castle (1965)
Lovers Must Learn *See* Rome Adventure (1962)
The Lovers of Montparnasse *See* Modigliani (1958)
Loves of a Scoundrel *See* Death of a Scoundrel (1956)
The Loves of Isadora *See* Isadora (1968)
The Loyal 47 Ronin *See* 47 Ronin, Part 1 (1942)
L'Ucello dalle Plume di Cristallo *See* The Bird with the Crystal Plumage (1970)
Luci Del Varieta *See* Variety Lights (1951)
The Lucifer Project *See* Barracuda (1978)
Lucky Boots *See* Gun Play (1936)
Lucky 13 *See* Running Hot (1983)
The Lullaby *See* The Sin of Madelon Claudet (1931)
L'Ultimo Uomo Della Terra *See* The Last Man on Earth (1964)
Lunch on the Grass *See* Picnic on the Grass (1959)
Lunch Wagon Girls *See* Lunch Wagon (1981)
L'Une Chante L'Autre Pas *See* One Sings, the Other Doesn't (1977)
L'Uomo Dalle Due Ombre *See* Cold Sweat (1974)
L'Uomo di Rio *See* That Man from Rio (1964)
Lust och Fagring Stor *See* All Things Fair (1995)
Lust of the Vampires *See* The Devil's Commandment (1956)
Lycanthropus *See* Werewolf in a Girl's Dormitory (1961)
M. Hire *See* Monsieur Hire (1989)
Ma and Pa Kettle Go to Paris *See* Ma and Pa Kettle on Vacation (1953)
Ma Nuit Chez Maud *See* My Night at Maud's (1969)
Macabra *See* Demonoid, Messenger of Death (1981)
Macabre Serenade *See* Dance of Death (1968)
Maccheroni *See* Macaroni (1985)
Maciste Alla Corte Del Gran Khan *See* Samson and the 7 Miracles of the World (1962)
Maciste at the Court of the Great Khan *See* Samson and the 7 Miracles of the World (1962)
Maciste la Regina di Samar *See* Hercules Against the Moon Men (1964)
Maciste, L'Eroe Piu Grande Del Mondo *See* Goliath and the Sins of Babylon (1964)
Maciste Nella Terra dei Ciclopi *See* Atlas in the Land of the Cyclops (1961)
Mad Dog *See* Mad Dog Morgan (1976)
The Mad Hatter *See* Breakfast in Hollywood (1946)
Mad Magazine's Up the Academy *See* Up the Academy (1980)
Mad Trapper of the Yukon *See* Challenge To Be Free (1976)
Mad Wednesday *See* The Sin of Harold Diddlebock (1947)
Madagascar Landing *See* Alfred Hitchcock's Aventure Malgache (1944)
Madame De *See* The Earrings of Madame De... (1954)
Madame Frankenstein *See* Lady Frankenstein (1972)
Mademoiselle France *See* Reunion in France (1942)
Madmen of Mandoras *See* They Saved Hitler's Brain (1964)
Madonna Truth or Dare *See* Truth or Dare (1991)
Mafia Junction *See* Super Bitch (1989)
The Mafu Cage *See* My Sister, My Love (1978)
The Magnificent One *See* Le Magnifique (1976)
The Magnificent Seven *See* Seven Samurai (1954)
The Magnificent Showman *See* Circus World (1964)
Making It *See* Going Places (1974)
Mako: The Jaws of Death *See* Jaws of Death (1976)
Malenka, the Vampire *See* Fangs of the Living Dead (1968)
Malenkaya Vera *See* Little Vera (1988)
Malice in Wonderland *See* The Rumor Mill (1986)
Malizia *See* Malicious (1974)
Man and His Mate *See* One Million B.C. (1940)
A Man Betrayed *See* Wheel of Fortune (1941)
Man-Eater *See* Shark! (1968)
The Man From C.O.T.T.O.N., Purlie Victorious *See* Gone are the Days (1963)
Man from Music Mountain *See* Texas Legionnaires (1943)
The Man From Nevada *See* The Nevadan (1950)
Man in a Cocked Hat *See* Carlton Browne of the F.O. (1959)
A Man in Mommy's Bed *See* With Six You Get Eggroll (1968)
The Man in Possession *See* Personal Property (1937)
Man in the Middle *See* 48 Hours to Live (1960)
Man Looking Southeast *See* Man Facing Southeast (1986)
Man of Bronze *See* Jim Thorpe: All American (1951)
Man of the Frontier *See* Red River Valley (1936)
Man of the Hour *See* Colonel Effingham's Raid (1945)
Man on the Move *See* Jigsaw (1971)
The Man Who Changed His Mind *See* The Man Who Lived Again (1936)
The Man Who Watched Trains Go By *See* Paris Express (1953)
The Man With The Deadly Lens *See* Wrong is Right (1982)
The Man with the Green Carnation *See* The Trials of Oscar Wilde (1960)
The Man with the Synthetic Brain *See* Blood of Ghastly Horror (1972)
The Man With the X-Ray Eyes *See* X: The Man with X-Ray Eyes (1963)
The Man with the Yellow Eyes *See* Planets Against Us (1961)
The Man with Thirty Sons *See* The Magnificent Yankee (1950)
Manhattan Project: The Deadly Game *See* The Manhattan Project (1986)
Manhunt in the Dakotas *See* Midnight Murders (1991)
The Maniacs Are Loose *See* The Thrill Killers (1965)
Manifesto *See* A Night of Love (1987)
Manon des Sources *See* Manon of the Spring (1987)
The Manster—Half Man, Half Monster *See* The Manster (1959)
Marching Along *See* Stars and Stripes Forever (1952)
Margaret Bourke-White *See* Double Exposure: The Story of Margaret Bourke-White (1989)
Maria Marten *See* Murder in the Old Red Barn (1936)
Marie Walewska *See* Conquest (1937)
Marijuana the Devil's Weed *See* Wild Weed (1949)
Marijuana: The Devil's Weed *See* Marihuana (1936)
Marilyn *See* Roadhouse Girl (1953)
Marine Issue *See* Instant Justice (1986)
Mark of Terror *See* Drums of Jeopardy (1931)
Mark of the Avenger *See* The Mysterious Rider (1938)
Mark of the Claw *See* Dick Tracy's Dilemma (1947)
Mark of the Vampire *See* The Vampire (1957)
Mark Twain *See* The Adventures of Mark Twain (1985)
Married in Haste *See* Consolation Marriage (1931)
Mars Invades Puerto Rico *See* Frankenstein Meets the Space Monster (1965)
The Marseille Contract *See* The Destructors (1974)
Marshal of Heldorado *See* Blazing Guns (1950)
Martin Lawrence You So Crazy *See* You So Crazy (1994)
Marusa No Onna *See* A Taxing Woman (1987)
Marusa No Onna II *See* A Taxing Woman's Return (1988)
The Marvelous Visit *See* La Merveilleuse Visite (1974)
The Marx Brothers at the Circus *See* At the Circus (1939)
Masculin Feminin *See* Masculine Feminine (1966)
Mask of Dust *See* Race for Life (1955)
Mask of Fury *See* First Yank into Tokyo (1945)
Massacre at Fort Holman *See* A Reason to Live, A Reason to Die (1973)
Massacre Hill *See* Eureka Stockade (1949)
Massacre Mafia Style *See* The Executioner (1978)
The Master *See* Master Ninja (1978)
Master Dolorosa *See* The Torture of Silence (1917)
Master of Lassie *See* The Hills of Home (1948)
Matango *See* Attack of the Mushroom People (1963)
The Mating of the Sabine Women *See* The Rape of the Sabines (1961)
Matka Joanna Od Aniolow *See* Mother Joan of the Angels (1960)
Matt Riker *See* Mutant Hunt (1987)
Mauri *See* Big Mo (1973)
Max, My Love *See* Max, Mon Amour (1986)
The Mayfair Bank Caper *See* The Big Scam (1979)
Mazel Tov Ou le Mariage *See* Marry Me, Marry Me (1969)
McKlusky *See* White Lightning (1973)
The McMasters...Tougher Than the West Itself *See* The McMasters (1970)
Meachorei Hasoragim *See* Beyond the Walls (1984)
The Medicine Hat Stallion *See* Peter Lundy and the Medicine Hat Stallion (1977)
Meet Miss Marple *See* Murder She Said (1962)
Meet the Applegates *See* The Applegates (1989)
Meet Whiplash Willie *See* The Fortune Cookie (1966)
The Meetings of Anna *See* Les Rendez-vous D'Anna (1978)
Mekagojira No Gyakushu *See* Terror of Mechagodzilla (1978)
Melody of Youth *See* They Shall Have Music (1939)
Men in Tights *See* Robin Hood: Men in Tights (1993)
Men of Steel *See* Steel (1980)
The Mercenaries *See* Dark of the Sun (1968)
Mery per Sempre *See* Forever Mary (1989)
The Message *See* Mohammed: Messenger of God (1977)
Messer Im Kopf *See* Knife in the Head (1978)
Metempsycose *See* Tomb of Torture (1965)
Metisse *See* Cafe au Lait (1994)
Meurtre en 45 Tours *See* Murder at 45 R.P.M. (1965)
Mickey Spillane's Margin for Murder *See* Margin for Murder (1981)
Microscopia *See* Fantastic Voyage (1966)

Midnight at Madame Tussaud's *See* Midnight at the Wax Museum (1936)
Midnight Heat *See* Sunset Heat (1992)
The Mighty Ducks 2 *See* D2: The Mighty Ducks (1994)
The Mighty Peking Man *See* Goliathon (1979)
The Mighty Thunder *See* Tundra (1936)
The Mighty Ursus *See* Ursus in the Valley of the Lions (1962)
Mignonne *See* Your Turn Darling (1963)
Mikan No Taikyoku *See* The Go-Masters (1982)
Mike Leigh's Naked *See* Naked (1993)
Mikres Aphrodites *See* Young Aphrodites (1963)
Milagro en Roma *See* Miracle in Rome (1988)
Milczaca Gwiazda *See* First Spaceship on Venus (1960)
Mile a Minute Love *See* Roaring Speedboats (1937)
Milou en Mai *See* May Fools (1990)
Milou in May *See* May Fools (1990)
Mind Games *See* The Agency (1981)
Mind Ripper *See* Wes Craven Presents Mind Ripper (1995)
Mindwarp: An Infinity of Terror *See* Galaxy of Terror (1981)
The Miracle of Fatima *See* Miracle of Our Lady of Fatima (1952)
Miracle of Life *See* Our Daily Bread (1934)
Miracolo a Milano *See* Miracle in Milan (1951)
Miss Europe *See* Prix de Beaute (1930)
Miss Muette *See* The Diabolical Dr. Z (1965)
Mrs. Parker and the Round Table *See* Mrs. Parker and the Vicious Circle (1994)
Mr. Ashton was Indiscreet *See* The Senator was Indiscreet (1947)
Mr. Bug Goes to Town *See* Hoppity Goes to Town (1941)
Mr. Celebrity *See* Turf Boy (1942)
Mr. Forbush and the Penguins *See* Cry of the Penguins (1971)
Mr. Fox of Venice *See* The Honey Pot (1967)
Mr. Invisible *See* Mr. Superinvisible (1973)
Mr. Quilp *See* The Old Curiosity Shop (1975)
Mr. Sebastian *See* Sebastian (1968)
Mister V *See* Pimpernel Smith (1942)
Mr. Wrong *See* Dark of the Night (1985)
Misterios del Ultratumba *See* Black Pit of Dr. M (1947)
Mit Eva Fing Die Sunde An *See* The Bellboy and the Playgirls (1962)
Mitt Liv Som Hund *See* My Life as a Dog (1985)
The Model Killer *See* The Hollywood Strangler Meets the Skid Row Slasher (1979)
Model Massacre *See* Color Me Blood Red (1964)
A Modern Bluebeard *See* Boom in the Moon (1946)
A Modern Hero *See* Knute Rockne: All American (1940)
Modigliani of Montparnasse *See* Modigliani (1958)
Mogliamante *See* Wifemistress (1979)
The Mogul *See* Ratings Game (1984)
Molly Louvain *See* The Strange Love of Molly Louvain (1932)
Mondo Pazzo *See* Mondo Cane 2 (1964)
A Monkey in Winter *See* Un Singe en Hiver (1962)
Monkey Shines: An Experiment in Fear *See* Monkey Shines (1988)
Monsieur Hulot's Holiday *See* Mr. Hulot's Holiday (1953)
Monster *See* Humanoids from the Deep (1980)
The Monster Baran *See* Varan the Unbelievable (1961)
Monster from a Prehistoric Planet *See* Gappa the Trifibian Monster (1967)
Monster Maker *See* Monster from the Ocean Floor (1954)
Monster of Monsters *See* Ghidrah the Three Headed Monster (1965)
Monster of Terror *See* Die, Monster, Die! (1965)
The Monster Show *See* Freaks (1932)
The Monster Walked *See* The Monster Walks (1932)
The Monster with Green Eyes *See* Planets Against Us (1961)
Monster Yongkari *See* Yongkari Monster of the Deep (1967)
Monster Zero *See* Godzilla vs. Monster Zero (1968)
The Monsters Are Loose *See* The Thrill Killers (1965)
Monsters From the Moon *See* Robot Monster (1953)
Monsters from the Unknown Planet *See* Terror of Mechagodzilla (1978)
Monstrosity *See* The Atomic Brain (1964)
Montana Justice *See* Man from Montana (1941)
Monte Carlo or Bust *See* Those Daring Young Men in Their Jaunty Jalopies (1969)
Montenegro—Or Pigs and Pearls *See* Montenegro (1981)
Montparnasse 19 *See* Modigliani (1958)
Morgan: A Suitable Case for Treatment *See* Morgan! (1966)
Morgan il Pirata *See* Morgan the Pirate (1960)
Morgen Grauen *See* Time Troopers (1989)
The Mormon Peril *See* Trapped by the Mormons (1922)
Morning Terror *See* Time Troopers (1989)
Mortal Sins *See* Dangerous Obsession (1988)
Morte a Venezia *See* Death in Venice (1971)
Morton of the Mounted *See* Timber Terrors (1935)
Moscow Distrusts Tears *See* Moscow Does Not Believe in Tears (1980)
Moscow Nights *See* I Stand Condemned (1936)
Moskwa Sljesam Nje Jerit *See* Moscow Does Not Believe in Tears (1980)
The Most Desired Man *See* Maybe...Maybe Not (1994)
Mosura Tai Goira *See* Godzilla vs. Mothra (1964)
Motel *See* Pink Motel (1982)
Motel Vacancy *See* Talking Walls (1985)
Mother Goose A Go-Go *See* The Unkissed Bride (1966)
Mother Riley Meets the Vampire *See* My Son, the Vampire (1952)
Mothra vs. Godzilla *See* Godzilla vs. Mothra (1964)
Mountain of Cannibal Gods *See* Slave of the Cannibal God (1979)
Movie Struck *See* Pick a Star (1937)
The Moving Target *See* Harper (1966)
Mud *See* The Stick-Up (1977)
Muhomatsu no Issho *See* Rikisha-Man (1958)
Mujeres al Borde de un Ataque de Nervios *See* Women on the Verge of a Nervous Breakdown (1988)
Mumsy, Nanny, Sonny, and Girly *See* Girly (1970)
Munkbrogreven *See* The Count of the Old Town (1934)
Murder by Mail *See* Schizoid (1980)
Murder by Proxy *See* Blackout (1954)
The Murder in Thorton Square *See* Gaslight (1944)
Murder, Inc. *See* The Enforcer (1951)
Murder on Diamond Row *See* The Squeaker (1937)
Murder One *See* Death Sentence (1974)
The Murderer Dmitri Karamazov *See* The Brothers Karamazov (1958)
Muriel, Or the Time of Return *See* Muriel (1963)
Muriel, Ou le Temps d'Un Retour *See* Muriel (1963)
The Murri Affair *See* La Grande Bourgeoise (1974)
Music in Darkness *See* Night Is My Future (1947)
Mussolini: The Decline and Fall of Il Duce *See* Mussolini & I (1985)
Mutant *See* Forbidden World (1982)
The Mutation *See* The Freakmaker (1973)
Mutations *See* The Freakmaker (1973)
The Mutilator *See* The Dark (1979)
The Mutineers *See* Pirate Ship (1949)
Mutter Kusters Fahrt Zum Himmel *See* Mother Kusters Goes to Heaven (1976)
My Brother, the Outlaw *See* My Outlaw Brother (1951)
My Crazy Life *See* Mi Vida Loca (1994)
My Darling Shiksa *See* Over the Brooklyn Bridge (1983)
My Father, My Master *See* Padre Padrone (1977)
My Favourite Year *See* My Favorite Year (1982)
My Girlfriend's Boyfriend *See* Boyfriends & Girlfriends (1988)
My Gun is Jammed *See* Bare Hunt (1963)
My Hero *See* A Southern Yankee (1948)
My Love Letters *See* Love Letters (1983)
My Name is John *See* The Legend of Hillbilly John (1973)
My Night with Maud *See* My Night at Maud's (1969)
My Posse Don't Do Homework *See* Dangerous Minds (1995)
My Son Alone *See* American Empire (1942)
My Teenage Daughter *See* Teenage Bad Girl (1959)
My Uncle *See* Mon Oncle (1958)
My Uncle, Mr. Hulot *See* Mon Oncle (1958)
Mystere Alexina *See* The Mystery of Alexina (1986)
Mysterious Invader *See* The Astounding She-Monster (1958)
The Mysterious Satellite *See* Warning from Space (1956)
The Mystery of Kaspar Hauser *See* Every Man for Himself & God Against All (1975)
Mystery of the Black Jungle *See* The Black Devils of Kali (1955)
The Mystery of the Marie Celeste *See* The Mystery of the Mary Celeste (1937)
Mystique *See* Circle of Power (1983)
Na Komete *See* On the Comet (1968)
Nagooa *See* Drifting (1982)
The Naked Goddess *See* The Devil's Hand (1961)
Naked Island *See* The Island (1961)
The Naked Night *See* Sawdust & Tinsel (1953)
Naked Space *See* Spaceship (1981)
The Naked Temptress *See* The Naked Witch (1964)
Naked Under Leather *See* The Girl on a Motorcycle (1968)
The Naked Weekend *See* Circle of Power (1983)
Naked Youth *See* The Cruel Story of Youth (1960)
Nankai No Kai Ketto *See* Godzilla vs. the Sea Monster (1966)
Nara Livet *See* Brink of Life (1957)
Narayama-Bushi-Ko *See* The Ballad of Narayama (1983)
Nathaniel Hawthorne's "Twice Told Tales" *See* Twice-Told Tales (1963)
Nattvardsgaesterna *See* The Winter Light (1962)
Nature's Mistakes *See* Freaks (1932)
The Navy Steps Out *See* A Girl, a Guy and a Gob (1941)
Neat and Tidy *See* Adventures Beyond Belief (1987)
Necromancy *See* The Witching (1972)
Ned Blessing: The Story of My Life and Times *See* Lone Justice 2 (1993)
Ned Kelly, Outlaw *See* Ned Kelly (1970)
Neil Simon's Biloxi Blues *See* Biloxi Blues (1988)
Neil Simon's Brighton Beach Memoirs *See* Brighton Beach Memoirs (1986)
Neil Simon's Broadway Bound *See* Broadway Bound (1992)
Neil Simon's Lost in Yonkers *See* Lost in Yonkers (1993)
Neil Simon's The Slugger's Wife *See* The Slugger's Wife (1985)
Nella Stretta M Orsa Del Ragno *See* Web of the Spider (1970)
Nelly and Mr. Arnaud *See* Nelly et Monsieur Arnaud (1995)
The Neptune Disaster *See* Neptune Factor (1973)
Neskolko Dnel iz Zhizni I.I. Oblomov *See* Oblomov (1981)
Nevada Heat *See* Fake Out (1982)
Never Cry Devil *See* Night Visitor (1989)
Never Give an Inch *See* Sometimes a Great Notion (1971)
The New Adventures of Don Juan *See* Adventures of Don Juan (1949)
New Adventures of Tarzan *See* Tarzan and the Green Goddess (1938)
The New Barbarians *See* Warriors of the Wasteland (1983)
New Girl in Town *See* Nashville Girl (1976)
New Wave *See* Nouvelle Vague (1990)
New Wine *See* Melody Master (1941)
The Newcomers *See* The Wild Country (1971)
The Next Man *See* The Arab Conspiracy (1976)
Nicholas Nickleby *See* The Life and Adventures of Nicholas Nickleby (1981)

The Niece of the Vampire *See* Fangs of the Living Dead (1968)
Niewinni Czarodzieje *See* Innocent Sorcerers (1960)
Night Beauties *See* Beauties of the Night (1952)
The Night Caller *See* Night Caller from Outer Space (1966)
Night Comes Too Soon *See* The Ghost of Rashmon Hall (1947)
Night Encounter *See* Double Agents (1959)
Night Hair Child *See* What the Peeper Saw (1972)
Night Legs *See* Fright (1971)
The Night of San Lorenzo *See* The Night of the Shooting Stars (1982)
Night of the Beast *See* House of the Black Death (1965)
Night of the Big Heat *See* Island of the Burning Doomed (1967)
Night of the Bloodsuckers *See* The Vampire Hookers (1978)
Night of the Claw *See* Island Claw (1980)
Night of the Dark Full Moon *See* Silent Night, Bloody Night (1973)
Night of the Demon *See* Curse of the Demon (1957)
Night of the Demon *See* The Touch of Satan (1970)
Night of the Doomed *See* Nightmare Castle (1965)
Night of the Eagle *See* Burn Witch, Burn! (1962)
Night of the Flesh Eaters *See* Night of the Living Dead (1968)
Night of the Seagulls *See* Night of the Death Cult (1975)
Night of the Silicates *See* Island of Terror (1966)
Night of the Wehrmacht Zombies *See* Night of the Zombies (1981)
Night Scare *See* Nightscare (1993)
Night Shadows *See* Mutant (1983)
The Night They Invented Striptease *See* The Night They Raided Minsky's (1969)
Night Train *See* Night Train to Munich (1940)
Night Walk *See* Deathdream (1972)
Night Watch *See* Detonator 2: Night Watch (1995)
Nightingale *See* The Young Nurses (1973)
A Nightingale Sang in Berkeley Square *See* The Big Scam (1979)
Nightmare *See* City of the Walking Dead (1983)
Nightmare *See* Nightmare in Badham County (1976)
Nightmare at Shadow Woods *See* Blood Rage (1987)
Nightmare City *See* City of the Walking Dead (1983)
Nightmare House *See* Scream, Baby, Scream (1969)
Nightmare Island *See* The Slayer (1982)
Nightmare Maker *See* Night Warning (1982)
Nightmare on Elm Street 6: Freddy's Dead *See* Freddy's Dead: The Final Nightmare (1991)
Nightriders *See* Western Double Feature 2: Wayne & Hale (198?)
Nights in a Harem *See* Son of Sinbad (1955)
Nijushi No Hitomi *See* Twenty-Four Eyes (1954)
1990 I Guerrieri del Bronx *See* 1990: The Bronx Warriors (1983)
1999—Nen No Natsu Yasumi *See* Summer Vacation: 1999 (1988)
Ningen No Joken *See* The Human Condition: Road to Eternity (1959)
Ninja Dragons *See* Magic Kid (1992)
Nippon Chiubotsu *See* Tidal Wave (1975)
Nippon Konchuki *See* The Insect Woman (1963)
No Fear *See* Fear (1996)
No Greater Love *See* The Human Condition: Road to Eternity (1959)
No Knife *See* The Frisco Kid (1979)
No Man's Land *See* No Man's Range (1935)
No Place Like Homicide *See* What a Carve-Up! (1962)
The No-Tell Hotel *See* Rosebud Beach Hotel (1985)
No Worries *See* Clueless (1995)
Nobi *See* Fires on the Plain (1959)
Noce In Galilee *See* A Wedding in Galilee (1987)
Nocturna, Granddaughter of Dracula *See* Nocturna (1979)
Norman Rockwell's Breaking Home Ties *See* Breaking Home Ties (1987)
North Sea Hijack *See* ffolkes (1980)
The Northfield Cemetery Massacre *See* Northville Cemetery Massacre (1976)
Northwest Frontier *See* Flame Over India (1960)
Nosferatu, A Symphony of Horror *See* Nosferatu (1922)
Nosferatu, A Symphony of Terror *See* Nosferatu (1922)
Nosferatu, Eine Symphonie des Grauens *See* Nosferatu (1922)
Nosferatu, The Vampire *See* Nosferatu (1922)
Nostradamus No Daiyogen *See* Last Days of Planet Earth (1974)
Not Against the Flesh *See* Vampyr (1931)
Not Quite Jerusalem *See* Not Quite Paradise (1986)
Not Wanted *See* Streets of Sin (1949)
Nothing in Order *See* All Screwed Up (1974)
Nowhere to Hide *See* Fatal Chase (1977)
Noz w Wodzie *See* Knife in the Water (1962)
Nuclear Run *See* Chain Reaction (1980)
Nuclear Terror *See* Golden Rendezvous (1977)
Nude in His Pocket *See* Girl in His Pocket (1957)
Nuit et Jour *See* Night and Day (1991)
Nuiyan, Seisap *See* Summer Snow (1994)
Number Two *See* Numero Deux (1975)
Numbered Days *See* Cycle Psycho (1972)
Nuovo Cinema Paradiso *See* Cinema Paradiso (1988)
Nurse Sherri *See* Hospital of Terror (1978)
The Nutcracker *See* George Balanchine's The Nutcracker (1993)
Nybyggarna *See* The New Land (1973)
Nyoka and the Lost Secrets of Hippocrates *See* Nyoka and the Tigermen (1942)
Obch Od Na Korze *See* The Shop on Main Street (1965)
Oblivion 2 *See* Backlash: Oblivion 2 (1995)
Obsession *See* The Hidden Room (1949)
Occhi Senza Volto *See* The Horror Chamber of Dr. Faustus (1959)
Oci Ciornie *See* Dark Eyes (1987)
October *See* Ten Days That Shook the World (1927)
Odio le Bionde *See* I Hate Blondes (1983)
Of a Thousand Delights *See* Sandra of a Thousand Delights (1965)
Office Party *See* Hostile Takeover (1988)
The Official History *See* The Official Story (1985)
The Official Version *See* The Official Story (1985)
Oh, Charlie *See* Hold That Ghost (1941)
Oh Woe is Me *See* Helas Pour Moi (1994)
Okasan *See* Mother (1952)
The Old and the New *See* The General Line (1929)
The Old Corral *See* Song of the Gringo (1936)
Old Greatheart *See* Way Back Home (1932)
Old Heidelberg *See* The Student Prince in Old Heidelberg (1927)
The Old Man and the Boy *See* The Two of Us (1968)
Old Mother Riley Meets the Vampire *See* My Son, the Vampire (1952)
Old Shatterhand *See* Apaches Last Battle (1964)
Olelkezo Tekintetek *See* Another Way (1982)
Omar Mukhtar *See* Lion of the Desert (1981)
The Omen 3 *See* The Final Conflict (1981)
On the Great White Trail *See* Renfrew on the Great White Trail (1938)
On the Road Again *See* Honeysuckle Rose (1980)
Once Upon a Texas Train *See* Texas Guns (1990)
Once Upon a Time There Was a Country *See* Underground (1995)
One Born Every Minute *See* Flim-Flam Man (1967)
One Cup of Coffee *See* Pastime (1991)
One For All *See* The President's Mystery (1936)
One for Sorrow, Two for Joy *See* Signs of Life (1989)
One Horse Town *See* Small Town Girl (1953)
One Hundred Percent Pure *See* The Girl from Missouri (1934)
One-Man Mutiny *See* The Court Martial of Billy Mitchell (1955)
One Plus One *See* Sympathy for the Devil (1970)
Onkel Toms Hutte *See* Uncle Tom's Cabin (1969)
Only the French Can! *See* French Can-Can (1955)
Onna Ga Kaidan O Agaru Toki *See* When a Woman Ascends the Stairs (1960)
Oopsie Poopsie *See* Get Rita (1975)
Operacione Paura *See* Kill, Baby, Kill (1966)
Operation Cicero *See* Five Fingers (1952)
Operation Kid Brother *See* Secret Agent 00 (1967)
Operation Overthrow *See* Power Play (1981)
Operation Serpent *See* Fer-De-Lance (1974)
Operation Undercover *See* Report to the Commissioner (1974)
Operazione Goldman *See* Lightning Bolt (1967)
Opium Connection *See* The Poppy Is Also a Flower (1966)
The Oracle *See* The Horse's Mouth (1958)
Orazi e Curiazi *See* Duel of Champions (1961)
Orca—Killer Whale *See* Orca (1977)
Order of Death *See* Corrupt (1984)
Orfeu Negro *See* Black Orpheus (1958)
Orgasmo *See* Paranoia (1969)
Orkobefogadas *See* Adoption (1975)
Orloff Against the Invisible Man *See* The Invisible Dead (1970)
Orphee *See* Orpheus (1949)
Oru Kaiju Daishingeki *See* Godzilla's Revenge (1969)
Osenny Marafon *See* Autumn Marathon (1979)
Other People's Business *See* Way Back Home (1932)
The Other Side of Paradise *See* Foxtrot (1976)
Otto E Mezzo *See* 8 1/2 (1963)
Our Daily Bread *See* City Girl (1930)
Our Girl Friday *See* The Adventures of Sadie (1955)
Ourselves Alone *See* River of Unrest (1937)
Out of Rosenheim *See* Bagdad Cafe (1988)
Out of the Darkness *See* Night Creature (1979)
Out of the Darkness *See* Teenage Caveman (1958)
Out of the Night *See* Strange Illusion (1945)
Out of the Shadow *See* Murder on the Campus (1952)
Out on Probation *See* Daddy-O (1959)
The Outcast *See* Man in the Saddle (1951)
The Outcry *See* Il Grido (1957)
Outer Reach *See* Spaced Out (1980)
Outlaw Gun *See* A Minute to Pray, A Second to Die (1967)
Outomlionnye Solntsem *See* Burnt by the Sun (1994)
Outside In *See* Red, White & Busted (1975)
The Outsider *See* Fatal Error (1983)
The Outsider *See* The Guinea Pig (1948)
Outsider in Amsterdam *See* Fatal Error (1983)
The Outsiders *See* Band of Outsiders (1964)
Over Her Dead Body *See* Enid Is Sleeping (1990)
The Pace That Kills *See* Cocaine Fiends (1936)
Palomino *See* Danielle Steel's Palomino (1991)
Pamela Principle 2 *See* Seduce Me: Pamela Principle 2 (1994)
Pane e Cioccolata *See* Bread and Chocolate (1974)
Panga *See* Curse 3: Blood Sacrifice (1990)
Panic *See* Panique (1947)
Panic at Lakewood Manor *See* Ants (1977)
Panic on the Trans-Siberian Express *See* Horror Express (1972)
Panico en el Transiberiano *See* Horror Express (1972)
Panny z Wilka *See* Maids of Wilko (1979)
Paoda Shuang Deng *See* Red Firecracker, Green Firecracker (1993)
Paper Bullets *See* Gangs, Inc. (1941)
The Parasite Murders *See* They Came from Within (1975)
Pardon Me, Your Teeth are in My Neck *See* The Fearless Vampire Killers (1967)
Paris Brule-t-il? *See* Is Paris Burning? (1968)
Paris Does Strange Things *See* Elena and Her Men (1956)
Paris is Ours *See* Paris Belongs to Us (1960)
Paris Nous Appartient *See* Paris Belongs to Us (1960)
Paris Qui Dort *See* The Crazy Ray (1922)
Paris vu Par *See* Six in Paris (1968)
Park Plaza *See* Norman Conquest (1953)
Paroxismus *See* Venus in Furs (1970)
Parts: The Clonus Horror *See* The Clonus Horror (1979)
Party Girls *See* Party Incorporated (1989)

Pasqualino Settebellezze *See* Seven Beauties (1976)
Pasqualino: Seven Beauties *See* Seven Beauties (1976)
Passages from "Finnegans Wake" *See* Finnegan's Wake (1963)
Passages from James Joyce's "Finnegans Wake" *See* Finnegan's Wake (1963)
The Passerby *See* La Passante (1983)
The Passion Flower Hotel *See* Boarding School (1983)
Passion Play *See* Love Letters (1983)
Passione d'Amore *See* Passion of Love (1982)
Passions *See* The Passing of Evil (1970)
Passport to Shame *See* Room 43 (1958)
The Patsy *See* L'Addition (1985)
Patterns of Power *See* Patterns (1956)
Patton: A Salute to a Rebel *See* Patton (1970)
Patton—Lust for Glory *See* Patton (1970)
Pauline a la Plage *See* Pauline at the Beach (1983)
Paura Nella Citta Dei Morti Viventi *See* Gates of Hell (1983)
The Peace Game *See* The Gladiators (1970)
Peacemaker *See* The Ambassador (1984)
Peau d'Ane *See* Donkey Skin (1970)
The Peking Medallion *See* The Corrupt Ones (1967)
Penn of Pennsylvania *See* The Courageous Mr. Penn (1941)
People Toys *See* Devil Times Five (1974)
People's Enemy *See* Prison Train (1938)
Pepi, Luci, Bom y Otras Chicas del Monton *See* Pepi, Luci, Bom and Other Girls on the Heap (1980)
Percy's Progress *See* It's Not the Size That Counts (1974)
Peril en la Demeure *See* Peril (1985)
Perils from Planet Mongo *See* Flash Gordon: Rocketship (1936)
The Perils of Gwendoline in the Land of the Yik-Yak *See* The Perils of Gwendoline (1984)
Perils of Nyoka *See* Nyoka and the Tigermen (1942)
Persecution *See* The Graveyard (1974)
Persecution and Assassination of Jean-Paul Marat as Performed by the Inmates of the Asylum of Charenton Under the Direction of the Marquis De Sade *See* Marat/Sade (1966)
Perseus the Invincible *See* Medusa Against the Son of Hercules (1962)
Peter Rabbit and Tales of Beatrix Potter *See* Tales of Beatrix Potter (1971)
Petersen *See* Jock Petersen (1974)
Petroleum Girls *See* Legend of Frenchie King (1971)
Phantom Fiend *See* The Return of Dr. Mabuse (1961)
The Phantom of Terror *See* The Bird with the Crystal Plumage (1970)
Phantom of the Air *See* The Phantom Broadcast (1933)
Phantom of the Plains *See* Western Double Feature 7: Wild Bill & Crabbe (1945)
The Phantom Ship *See* The Mystery of the Mary Celeste (1937)
Phar Lap: Heart of a Nation *See* Phar Lap (1984)
Phenomena *See* Creepers (1985)
Philo Vance Returns *See* Infamous Crimes (1947)
Phoebe *See* Zelly & Me (1988)
The Phoenix *See* War of the Wizards (1981)
Pickup on 101 *See* Where the Eagle Flies (1972)
Pigsty *See* Porcile (1969)
Pilgrimage to Rome *See* L'Anne Sainte (1978)
The Pilot *See* Danger in the Skies (1979)
Pinball Pick-Up *See* Pick-Up Summer (1979)
Pinball Summer *See* Pick-Up Summer (1979)
Pinocchio *See* The Adventures of Pinocchio (1996)
Pioneers *See* Pioneer Woman (1973)
Pippi Langstrump Pa de Sju Haven *See* Pippi in the South Seas (1974)
Piranha 2: Flying Killers *See* Piranha 2: The Spawning (1982)
Pirate's Fiancee *See* A Very Curious Girl (1969)
Pirate's Harbor *See* Haunted Harbor (1944)
The Pizza Connection *See* The Sicilian Connection (1985)
The Plains of Heaven *See* Panic Station (1982)
Planet of Horrors *See* Galaxy of Terror (1981)
Planet of the Lifeless Men *See* Battle of the Worlds (1961)
The Plants Are Watching *See* The Kirlian Witness (1978)
Players *See* The Club (1981)
Playgirl Gang *See* Switchblade Sisters (1975)
The Playgirls and the Bellboy *See* The Bellboy and the Playgirls (1962)
Playing for Keeps *See* Lily in Love (1985)
Please! Mr. Balzac *See* Mademoiselle Striptease (1957)
Plein Sud *See* Heat of Desire (1984)
Pluck of the Irish *See* Great Guy (1936)
Po Dezju *See* Before the Rain (1994)
Pocomania *See* The Devil's Daughter (1939)
Poe's Tales of Terror *See* Tales of Terror (1962)
Poisoned by Love: The Kern County Murders *See* Murder So Sweet (1993)
Pokayaniye *See* Repentance (1987)
Police Connection *See* The Mad Bomber (1972)
Police Force *See* Jackie Chan's Police Force (1985)
The Police Story *See* Jackie Chan's Police Force (1985)
Poncomania *See* The Devil's Daughter (1939)
Pony Express *See* Peter Lundy and the Medicine Hat Stallion (1977)
Pookie *See* The Sterile Cuckoo (1969)
Poopsie *See* Get Rita (1975)
Poor Albert and Little Annie *See* I Dismember Mama (1974)
The Poor Outlaws *See* The Round Up (1966)
The Pope Must Die *See* The Pope Must Diet (1991)
Popiol i Diament *See* Ashes and Diamonds (1958)
Poppies Are Also Flowers *See* The Poppy Is Also a Flower (1966)
Porte Aperte *See* Open Doors (1989)
Portrait of a Woman, Nude *See* Nudo di Donna (1983)
Portrait of Alison *See* Postmark for Danger (1956)
Portrait of Maria *See* Maria Candelaria (1946)
Potemkin *See* The Battleship Potemkin (1925)
Practice Makes Perfect *See* Le Cavaleur (1978)
Prairie Outlaws *See* Wild West (1946)
Prairie Rustlers *See* Western Double Feature 7: Wild Bill & Crabbe (1945)
Pratldwandi *See* The Adversary (1971)
The Prehistoric Sound *See* Sound of Horror (1964)
Prehistoric World *See* Teenage Caveman (1958)
Prenom: Carmen *See* First Name: Carmen (1983)
Preparez Vous Mouchoirs *See* Get Out Your Handkerchiefs (1978)
Preppies *See* Making the Grade (1984)
The President's Women *See* Foreplay (1975)
Pret-a-Porter *See* Ready to Wear (1994)
Pride of Kentucky *See* The Story of Seabiscuit (1949)
Priority Red One *See* Delta Force Commando 2 (1990)
Prison *See* Devil's Wanton (1949)
The Prisoner *See* Cold Room (1984)
The Private Life of Paul Joseph Goebbels *See* Enemy of Women (1944)
The Private Lives of Elizabeth and Essex *See* Elizabeth, the Queen (1968)
Private Snuffy Smith *See* Snuffy Smith, Yard Bird (1942)
The Private Wore Skirts *See* Never Wave at a WAC (1952)
Profession: Reporter *See* The Passenger (1975)
The Profile of Terror *See* The Sadist (1963)
Profumo di Donna *See* The Scent of a Woman (1975)
Profundo Rosso *See* Deep Red: Hatchet Murders (1975)
Project Shadowchaser 2 *See* Night Siege Project: Shadowchaser 2 (1994)
Prom Night 2 *See* Hello Mary Lou: Prom Night 2 (1987)
Promise Her Anything *See* Promises! Promises! (1963)
Prophecies of Nostradamus *See* Last Days of Planet Earth (1974)
A Proposito Luciano *See* Lucky Luciano (1974)
The Protectors, Book One *See* Angel of H.E.A.T. (1982)
Proud, Damned, and Dead *See* The Proud and the Damned (1972)
Przesluchanie *See* The Interrogation (1982)
Psycho a Go Go! *See* Blood of Ghastly Horror (1972)
Psycho-Circus *See* Circus of Fear (1967)
Psycho Killers *See* Mania (1960)
Psycho Puppet *See* Delirium (1977)
Psycho Sisters *See* The Sibling (1972)
Psychotic *See* Driver's Seat (1973)
Ptang, Yang, Kipperbang *See* Kipperbang (1982)
Public Be Damned *See* The World Gone Mad (1933)
The Public Be Hanged *See* The World Gone Mad (1933)
Puo Una Morta Rivivere Per Amore? *See* Venus in Furs (1970)
The Purim Player *See* Der Purimshpiler (1937)
Purple Death from Outer Space *See* Flash Gordon Conquers the Universe (1940)
The Purple Riders *See* Purple Vigilantes (1938)
Pursuit *See* Apache Blood (1975)
Putyovka V Zhizn *See* The Road to Life (1931)
Q Planes *See* Clouds Over Europe (1939)
Qiuyue *See* Autumn Moon (1992)
Quai des Orfevres *See* Jenny Lamour (1947)
Quando De Donne Avevando La Coda *See* When Women Had Tails (1970)
Que He Hecho Yo Para Merecer Esto!? *See* What Have I Done to Deserve This? (1985)
Que La Bete Meure *See* This Man Must Die (1970)
Queen of Blood *See* Planet of Blood (1966)
Queen of Broadway *See* Kid Dynamite (1943)
Queen of the Cannibals *See* Doctor Butcher M.D. (1980)
Queen of the Gorillas *See* The Bride & the Beast (1958)
The Queen's Husband *See* The Royal Bed (1931)
Quei Temerari Sulle Loro Pazze, Scatenate, Scalcinate Carriole *See* Those Daring Young Men in Their Jaunty Jalopies (1969)
Quella Villa Accanto Al Cimitero *See* The House by the Cemetery (1983)
Quelqu' Un Derriere la Porte *See* Someone Behind the Door (1971)
Quemimada! *See* Burn! (1970)
The Quest *See* The Longest Drive (1976)
Quien Sabe? *See* A Bullet for the General (1968)
A Quiet Little Neighborhood, A Perfect Little Murder *See* A Perfect Little Murder (1990)
A Quiet Place to Kill *See* Paranoia (1969)
Quoi De Neuf, Pussycat? *See* What's New Pussycat? (1965)
Race for the Yankee Zephyr *See* Treasure of the Yankee Zephyr (1983)
The Radical *See* Katherine (1975)
Radio Ranch *See* The Phantom Empire (1935)
Radon *See* Rodan (1956)
Radon the Flying Monster *See* Rodan (1956)
Rafferty and the Highway Hustlers *See* Rafferty & the Gold Dust Twins (1975)
Rage *See* Rabid (1977)
Rage of the Buccaneers *See* The Black Pirate (1926)
Ragewar *See* Dungeonmaster (1983)
Ragged Angels *See* They Shall Have Music (1939)
The Raging Moon *See* Long Ago Tomorrow (1971)
Raging Waters *See* The Green Promise (1949)
Rags to Riches *See* Callie and Son (1981)
Raiders of the Doomed Kingdom *See* After the Fall of Saigon (1988)
Rainbow on the River *See* It Happened in New Orleans (1936)
Raise Ravens *See* Cria (1976)
Ramblin' Man *See* The Concrete Cowboys (1979)
Ramrodders *See* The Ramrodder (1969)
The Ranger, the Cook and a Hole in the Sky *See* Hole in the Sky (1995)
Ransom *See* Maniac (1977)
Rape of Innocence *See* Dupont Lajoie (1974)
The Rape of Richard Beck *See* Broken Badge (1985)
Rape Squad *See* Act of Vengeance (1974)
Rasputin: The Mad Monk *See* Rasputin and the Empress (1932)
The Rats *See* Deadly Eyes (1982)

The Raven *See* Le Corbeau (1943)
RE: Lucky Luciano *See* Lucky Luciano (1974)
The Reader *See* La Lectrice (1988)
The Rebel *See* The Bushwackers (1952)
Rebel of the Road *See* Hot Rod (1979)
Rebel with a Cause *See* The Loneliness of the Long Distance Runner (1962)
Rece do Gory *See* Hands Up (1981)
Record of a Living Being *See* I Live in Fear (1955)
Red *See* Trois Couleurs: Rouge (1994)
Red Dragon *See* Code Name Alpha (1967)
Red Dragon *See* Manhunter (1986)
The Red Hangman *See* The Bloody Pit of Horror (1965)
The Red Head *See* Poil de Carotte (1931)
Red Hot Tires *See* Racing Luck (1935)
Red Hot Wheels *See* To Please a Lady (1950)
Red on Red *See* Scarred (1984)
The Red Tide *See* Blood Tide (1982)
Redneck County *See* Hootch Country Boys (1975)
Reflections on a Crime *See* Reflections in the Dark (1994)
The Refugee *See* Three Faces West (1940)
Rehearsal for a Crime *See* The Criminal Life of Archibaldo de la Cruz (1955)
Rejuvenatrix *See* The Rejuvenator (1988)
Rekopis Znaleziony W Saragossie *See* The Saragossa Manuscript (1965)
The Remarkable Mr. Kipps *See* Kipps (1941)
Remembrance of Love *See* Holocaust Survivors...Remembrance of Love (1983)
Remorques *See* Stormy Waters (1941)
Renegade Girls *See* Caged Heat (1974)
Renfrew of the Royal Mounted on the Great White Trail *See* Renfrew on the Great White Trail (1938)
Reprieved *See* Sing Sing Nights (1935)
Requiem fur Dominic *See* Requiem for Dominic (1991)
The Rescue *See* Let's Get Harry (1987)
The Resurrection Syndicate *See* Nothing But the Night (1972)
Retaliator *See* Programmed to Kill (1986)
Retik, the Moon Menace *See* Radar Men from the Moon (1952)
Return from the Past *See* Alien Massacre (1967)
The Return of Maxwell Smart *See* The Nude Bomb (1980)
The Return of Mr. H. *See* They Saved Hitler's Brain (1964)
Return of the Blind Dead *See* Return of the Evil Dead (1975)
The Return of the Giant Monsters *See* Gamera vs. Gaos (1967)
Return of the Living Dead *See* Messiah of Evil (1974)
Return of the Magnificent Seven *See* Return of the Seven (1966)
Return of the Zombies *See* The Hanging Woman (1972)
Reunion *See* Reunion in France (1942)
Revenge *See* Blood Feud (1979)
The Revenge of Dracula *See* Dracula vs. Frankenstein (1971)
The Revenge of Milady *See* The Four Musketeers (1975)
The Revenge of the Blood Beast *See* The She-Beast (1965)
Revenge of the Dead *See* Night of the Ghouls (1959)
Revenge of the Innocents *See* South Bronx Heroes (1985)
Revenge of the Living Dead *See* Children Shouldn't Play with Dead Things (1972)
Revenge of the Screaming Dead *See* Messiah of Evil (1974)
Revenge Squad *See* Hit & Run (1982)
Rhodes of Africa *See* Rhodes (1936)
Rhosyn A Rhith *See* Coming Up Roses (1987)
Rhythm on the Ranch *See* Rootin' Tootin' Rhythm (1938)
Rich, Young, and Deadly *See* Platinum High School (1960)
Riches and Romance *See* Amazing Adventure (1937)
The Richest Man in the World: The Story of Aristotle Onassis *See* Onassis (1988)
Richie *See* The Death of Richie (1976)
Rickshaw Man *See* Rikisha-Man (1958)
Ride a Dark Horse *See* Man & Boy (1971)
Riders *See* Guerilla Brigade (1939)
Riffraff *See* Riff Raff (1935)
The Right Man *See* Her First Romance (1940)
Ripped Off *See* Counter Punch (1971)
Risate de Gioia *See* Passionate Thief (1960)
The Rise of Catherine the Great *See* Catherine the Great (1934)
The Rise of Helga *See* Susan Lenox: Her Fall and Rise (1931)
Rising to Fame *See* Susan Lenox: Her Fall and Rise (1931)
Riso Amaro *See* Bitter Rice (1949)
Riten *See* The Rite (1969)
Rites of Summer *See* White Water Summer (1987)
The Ritual *See* The Rite (1969)
The Road *See* La Strada (1954)
Road to Avonlea *See* Tales from Avonlea, Vol. 1: The Journey Begins (1990)
The Road to Frisco *See* They Drive by Night (1940)
Roaring Timber *See* Come and Get It (1936)
Rob Roy *See* Rob Roy—The Highland Rogue (1953)
Robert A. Heinlein's The Puppet Masters *See* The Puppet Masters (1994)
Robinson Crusoeland *See* Utopia (1951)
Rocco et Ses Freres *See* Rocco and His Brothers (1960)
Rocket to the Moon *See* Cat Women of the Moon (1953)
Rocky Mountain Mystery *See* The Fighting Westerner (1935)
Roger Corman Presents: Black Scorpion *See* Black Scorpion (1995)
Roger Corman Presents Burial of the Rats *See* Burial of the Rats (1995)
Roger Corman Presents: Suspect Device *See* Suspect Device (1995)
Roger Corman's Frankenstein Unbound *See* Frankenstein Unbound (1990)
Roma *See* Fellini's Roma (1972)
Roma, Citta Aperta *See* Open City (1945)
Romance and Riches *See* Amazing Adventure (1937)
Romance da Empregada *See* The Story of Fausta (1988)
Romauld et Juliet *See* Mama, There's a Man in Your Bed (1989)
Rome, Open City *See* Open City (1945)
Romeo in Pyjamas *See* Parlor, Bedroom and Bath (1931)
Romeo, Julia a Tma *See* Sweet Light in a Dark Room (1960)
Romeo, Juliet and Darkness *See* Sweet Light in a Dark Room (1960)
Rommel—Desert Fox *See* The Desert Fox (1951)
Rona Jaffe's Mazes and Monsters *See* Mazes and Monsters (1982)
The Rook *See* Something for Everyone (1970)
Rookies *See* Buck Privates (1941)
Rookies Come Home *See* Buck Privates Come Home (1947)
The Rose and the Sword *See* Flesh and Blood (1985)
Rosemary's Killer *See* The Prowler (1981)
The Rotten Apple *See* Five Minutes to Love (1963)
Rouge Baiser *See* Red Kiss (1985)
Rough Company *See* The Violent Men (1955)
Rough Treatment *See* Without Anesthesia (1978)
Ruby Cairo *See* Deception (1992)
Rudyard Kipling's Jungle Book *See* The Jungle Book (1942)
Rue Cases Negres *See* Sugar Cane Alley (1983)
Rules of Obsession *See* A Passion to Kill (1994)
Rumpo Kid *See* Carry On Cowboy (1966)
Run, Simon, Run *See* Savage Run (1970)
The Runaways *See* South Bronx Heroes (1985)
Russicum *See* Third Solution (1989)
Rustler's Roundup *See* Rustler's Hideout (1944)
The Rutles *See* All You Need Is Cash (1978)
The Saboteur *See* Morituri (1965)
Saboteur: Code Name Morituri *See* Morituri (1965)
The Sabre and the Arrow *See* Last of the Comanches (1952)
Sabrina Fair *See* Sabrina (1954)
Sacco e Vanzetti *See* Sacco & Vanzetti (1971)
Sadko *See* The Magic Voyage of Sinbad (1952)
The Saga of Dracula *See* The Saga of the Draculas (1972)
The Saga of Gosta Berling *See* The Atonement of Gosta Berling (1924)
The Saga of the Road *See* Pather Panchali (1954)
Saikaku Ichidai Onna *See* Life of Oharu (1952)
St. Martin's Lane *See* Sidewalks of London (1940)
Sakima and the Masked Marvel *See* The Masked Marvel (1943)
The Salamander *See* La Salamandre (1971)
Salerno Beachhead *See* A Walk in the Sun (1946)
The Salute of the Jugger *See* The Blood of Heroes (1989)
Salvation! Have You Said Your Prayers Today? *See* Salvation! (1987)
Sam Cooper's Gold *See* The Ruthless Four (1970)
Sam Marlowe, Private Eye *See* The Man with Bogart's Face (1980)
Sanda Tai Gailah *See* War of the Gargantuas (1970)
Sandakan House 8 *See* Sandakan No. 8 (1974)
Sandkings *See* The Outer Limits: Sandkings (1995)
The Sandpit Generals *See* Defiant (1970)
Sandra *See* Sandra of a Thousand Delights (1965)
Sans Toit Ni Loi *See* Vagabond (1985)
Sansho Dayu *See* Sansho the Bailiff (1954)
Santa Claus Defeats the Aliens *See* Santa Claus Conquers the Martians (1964)
Santo en el Museo de Cera *See* Samson in the Wax Museum (1963)
Santo in the Wax Museum *See* Samson in the Wax Museum (1963)
Satanic Mechanic *See* Perfect Killer (1977)
Satan's Claw *See* The Blood on Satan's Claw (1971)
Satan's Daughters *See* Vampyres (1974)
Satan's Dog *See* Play Dead (1981)
Satan's Mistress *See* Demon Rage (1982)
Satan's Satellites *See* Zombies of the Stratosphere (1952)
Satan's Skin *See* The Blood on Satan's Claw (1971)
Satansbraten *See* Satan's Brew (1976)
Satellite of Blood *See* First Man into Space (1959)
Satin Vengeance *See* Naked Vengeance (1985)
Saturday Island *See* Island of Desire (1952)
Satyricon *See* Fellini Satyricon (1969)
Saul e David *See* Saul and David (1968)
The Savage *See* Lovers Like Us (1975)
Savage Abduction *See* Cycle Psycho (1972)
Savage Apocalypse *See* Invasion of the Flesh Hunters (1982)
Savage Beasts *See* The Wild Beasts (1985)
Savage Nights *See* Les Nuits Fauves (1992)
The Savage State *See* L'Etat Sauvage (1978)
Sayat Nova *See* The Color of Pomegranates (1969)
Scaramouche *See* Loves & Times of Scaramouche (1976)
Scared Stiff *See* Treasure of Fear (1945)
The Scaremaker *See* Girls Night Out (1983)
Scarface: The Shame of a Nation *See* Scarface (1931)
Scarlet Buccaneer *See* Swashbuckler (1976)
The Scarlet Buccaneer *See* Swashbuckler (1984)
Scherben *See* Shattered (1921)
Schloss Vogelod *See* The Haunted Castle (1921)
The School That Ate My Brain *See* Zombie High (1987)
The Scotland Yard Mystery *See* The Living Dead (1936)
Scoundrel in White *See* High Heels (1972)
Scream *See* The Night God Screamed (198?)
Scream and Die *See* The House that Vanished (1973)
Scream Free! *See* Free Grass (1969)
Screwface *See* Marked for Death (1990)
Scrooge *See* A Christmas Carol (1951)
Scum of the Earth *See* Poor White Trash 2 (1975)
Search for the Mother Lode *See* Mother Lode (1982)
Searchers of the Voodoo Mountain *See* Warriors of the Apocalypse (1985)

Season of Dreams *See* Stacking (1987)
Second Chances *See* Probation (1932)
The Second Coming *See* Messiah of Evil (1974)
Seconds to Live *See* Viva Knievel (1977)
Secret File: Hollywood *See* Secret File of Hollywood (1962)
Secret Honor: A Political Myth *See* Secret Honor (1985)
Secret Honor: The Last Testament of Richard M. Nixon *See* Secret Honor (1985)
The Secret of Dr. Mabuse *See* The Thousand Eyes of Dr. Mabuse (1960)
The Secret of Dorian Gray *See* Dorian Gray (1970)
Secret Paper WB1 *See* Geheimakte WB1 (1942)
The Secret Stranger *See* Rough Riding Rangers (1935)
Secret Weapon *See* Sherlock Holmes and the Secret Weapon (1942)
Secrets of the Red Bedroom *See* Secret Weapons (1985)
Sedotta e Abbandonata *See* Seduced and Abandoned (1964)
The Seductress *See* The Teacher (1974)
Seed of Innocence *See* Teen Mothers (1980)
Seed of Terror *See* Grave of the Vampire (1972)
The Seekers *See* Land of Fury (1955)
Seishun Zanoku Monogatari *See* The Cruel Story of Youth (1960)
Sengoku Gunto-Den *See* Saga of the Vagabond (1959)
Senior Trip *See* National Lampoon's Senior Trip (1995)
Sensations *See* Sensations of 1945 (1944)
Sensuous Vampires *See* The Vampire Hookers (1978)
Separate Beds *See* The Wheeler Dealers (1963)
Sept Fois Femme *See* Woman Times Seven (1967)
Sergeant Steiner *See* Breakthrough (1978)
The Serpent *See* Night Flight from Moscow (1973)
Seryozha *See* A Summer to Remember (1961)
Sette Volte Donna *See* Woman Times Seven (1967)
Seven Bad Men *See* Rage at Dawn (1955)
Seven Different Ways *See* Quick, Let's Get Married (1971)
Seven Graves for Rogan *See* Time to Die (1983)
Seven Sisters *See* The House on Sorority Row (1983)
The Sex of the Stars *See* Le Sexe des Etoiles (1993)
Sex Play *See* Games Girls Play (1975)
The Sex Racketeers *See* Man of Violence (1971)
The Shadow Versus the Thousand Eyes of Dr. Mabuse *See* The Thousand Eyes of Dr. Mabuse (1960)
The Shadow Warrior *See* Kagemusha (1980)
Shadows in an Empty Room *See* Strange Shadows in an Empty Room (1976)
Shadows of Our Ancestors *See* Shadows of Forgotten Ancestors (1964)
Shadows of Our Forgotten Ancestors *See* Shadows of Forgotten Ancestors (1964)
Shadows of the Peacock *See* Echoes of Paradise (1986)
Shalimar *See* Deadly Thief (1978)
Shame of the Sabine Women *See* The Rape of the Sabines (1961)
Shark Reef *See* She Gods of Shark Reef (1956)
Shatter *See* Call Him Mr. Shatter (1974)
Shatterhand *See* Apaches Last Battle (1964)
She Demons of the Swamp *See* Attack of the Giant Leeches (1959)
She Devil *See* Drums O'Voodoo (1934)
She Drives Me Crazy *See* Friends, Lovers & Lunatics (1989)
She Got What She Asked For *See* Yesterday, Today and Tomorrow (1964)
She Knew No Other Way *See* Last Resort (1986)
She Monster of the Night *See* Frankenstein's Daughter (1958)
She Shoulda Said No *See* Wild Weed (1949)
Sheba *See* The Graveyard (1974)
She'll Be Sweet *See* Magee and the Lady (1978)
Shenanigans *See* Great Bank Hoax (1978)
Sheriff of Wichita *See* Western Double Feature 4: Rogers & Evans (194?)
Sherlock Holmes *See* The Adventures of Sherlock Holmes (1939)
Sherlock Holmes and the Prince of Crime *See* Hands of a Murderer (1990)
Sherlock Holmes and the Scarlet Claw *See* Scarlet Claw (1944)
Sherlock Holmes and the Spider Woman *See* Spider Woman (1944)
Sherlock Holmes and the Woman in Green *See* The Woman in Green (1945)
Sherlock Holmes Grosster Fall *See* A Study in Terror (1966)
Sherlock Holmes in The Hound of London *See* The Hound of London (1993)
Sherlock Holmes Und Das Halsband des Todes *See* Sherlock Holmes and the Deadly Necklace (1962)
Shichinin No Samurai *See* Seven Samurai (1954)
Shinju Ten No Amijima *See* Double Suicide (1969)
The Ship was Loaded *See* Carry On Admiral (1957)
Shivers *See* They Came from Within (1975)
Shizuka Naru Ketto *See* A Quiet Duel (1949)
Shock *See* Beyond the Door 2 (1979)
Shocked *See* Mesmerized (1984)
Shockwave *See* The Arrival (1996)
Shogun Island *See* Raw Force (1981)
Shoot the Pianist *See* Shoot the Piano Player (1962)
The Shop on High Street *See* The Shop on Main Street (1965)
Shuban *See* Scandal (1950)
The Shuttered Room *See* Blood Island (1968)
Sidney Sheldon's Windmills of the Gods *See* Windmills of the Gods (1988)
Siegfried's Death *See* Siegfried (1924)
Siegfrieds Tod *See* Siegfried (1924)
Signe Charlotte *See* Sincerely Charlotte (1986)
Significant Other *See* When a Man Loves a Woman (1994)
A Silent Duel *See* A Quiet Duel (1949)
The Silent Flute *See* Circle of Iron (1978)
Silent Night, Evil Night *See* Black Christmas (1975)
Silken Skin *See* The Soft Skin (1964)
Silver Blaze *See* Murder at the Baskervilles (1937)
The Silver Brumby *See* The Silver Stallion: King of the Wild Brumbies (1993)
Silver Devil *See* Wild Horse (1931)
The Sin *See* The Shaming (1971)
Sinai Commandos: The Story of the Six Day War *See* Sinai Commandos (1968)
The Singing Musketeer *See* The Three Musketeers (1939)
Sinister House *See* Who Killed Doc Robbin? (1948)
Sisters *See* Some Girls (1988)
Sitting Bull's History Lesson *See* Buffalo Bill & the Indians (1976)
The Sixth of June *See* D-Day, the Sixth of June (1956)
Sizzle Beach U.S.A. *See* Malibu Hot Summer (1974)
Skate! *See* Blades of Courage (1988)
Ski Lift to Death *See* Snowblind (1978)
Skipper *See* The Todd Killings (1971)
Skyggen Af Emma *See* Emma's Shadow (1988)
The Slammer *See* Short Eyes (1979)
The Slasher *See* Cosh Boy (1961)
Slasher in the House *See* Home Sweet Home (1980)
The Slaughterers *See* Invasion of the Flesh Hunters (1982)
Slave Girls *See* Prehistoric Women (1950)
Slaves of the Invisible Monster *See* The Invisible Monster (1950)
Slay It Again, Sam *See* Codename: Foxfire (1985)
Slip Slide Adventures *See* Water Babies (1979)
Small Town Massacre *See* Strange Behavior (1981)
Smart Alec *See* Movie Maker (1986)
Smokey and the Bandit Ride Again *See* Smokey and the Bandit, Part 2 (1980)
Smorgasbord *See* Cracking Up (1983)
Smultron-Stallet *See* Wild Strawberries (1957)
Snake Eyes *See* Dangerous Game (1993)
Snow White and the Three Clowns *See* Snow White and the Three Stooges (1961)
Snuffy Smith *See* Snuffy Smith, Yard Bird (1942)
So Evil, My Sister *See* The Sibling (1972)
Sodome et Gomorrhe *See* Sodom and Gomorrah (1962)
Soldier Duroc *See* Soldat Duroc...Ca Va Etre Ta Fete! (196?)
Soldier in Skirts *See* Triple Echo (1977)
The Soldier Who Declared Peace *See* Tribes (1970)
The Soldiers *See* Les Carabiniers (1963)
Solomon Northrup's Odyssey *See* Half Slave, Half Free (1985)
Sombra, the Spider Woman *See* The Black Widow (1947)
Some Like It Cool *See* Sex on the Run (1978)
Someone is Killing the Great Chefs of Europe *See* Who Is Killing the Great Chefs of Europe? (1978)
Someone's Killing the World's Greatest Models *See* She's Dressed to Kill (1979)
Something is Out There *See* Day of the Animals (1977)
Something Like the Truth *See* The Offence (1973)
Something to Hide *See* Shattered (1972)
Something Waits in the Dark *See* Screamers (1980)
Somewhere in France *See* The Foreman Went to France (1942)
Sommarlek *See* Summer Interlude (1950)
Sommarnattens Leende *See* Smiles of a Summer Night (1955)
Son of My Life *See* Hijazo de Mi Vidaza (197?)
The Song of the Road *See* Pather Panchali (1954)
Song of the Sierra *See* Springtime in the Sierras (1947)
Sons of the Legion *See* Sons of the Desert (1933)
Sons of the Musketeers *See* At Sword's Point (1951)
Sophie's Place *See* Crooks & Coronets (1969)
Soul *See* Earth (1930)
Sound From a Million Years Ago *See* Sound of Horror (1964)
Sound of Fury *See* Try and Get Me (1950)
Soup to Nuts *See* Waitress (1981)
Sous le Soleil de Satan *See* Under Satan's Sun (1987)
Sous les Toits de Paris *See* Under the Roofs of Paris (1929)
South of Panama *See* Panama Menace (1941)
South Sea Woman *See* Pearl of the South Pacific (1955)
Southwest to Sonora *See* The Appaloosa (1966)
Space 2074 *See* Star Quest (1989)
The Space Amoeba *See* Yog, Monster from Space (1971)
Space Avenger *See* Alien Space Avenger (1991)
Space Invasion from Lapland *See* Invasion of the Animal People (1962)
Space Invasion of Lapland *See* Invasion of the Animal People (1962)
Space Men *See* Assignment Outer Space (1961)
Space Men Appear in Tokyo *See* Warning from Space (1956)
Space Mission of the Lost Planet *See* Horror of the Blood Monsters (1970)
Space Monster Dagora *See* Dagora, the Space Monster (1965)
Space Mutants *See* Planet of the Vampires (1965)
Space Soldiers *See* Flash Gordon: Rocketship (1936)
Spaceship to the Unknown *See* Flash Gordon: Rocketship (1936)
Spara Forte, Piu Forte...Non Capisco *See* Shoot Loud, Louder, I Don't Understand! (1966)
The Specter of Freedom *See* Phantom of Liberty (1968)
Speed Brent Wins *See* Breed of the Border (1933)
The Spell of Amy Nugent *See* Spellbound (1941)
Spell of the Hypnotist *See* Fright (1956)
Spettri *See* Specters (1987)
The Spider *See* Earth vs. the Spider (1958)
Spider Baby, or the Maddest Story Ever Told *See* Spider Baby (1964)
Spider-Man *See* The Amazing Spider-Man (1977)
Spies-A-Go-Go *See* Nasty Rabbit (1964)
Spies, Lies, and Alibis *See* Code Name: Chaos (1990)

Spinal Tap *See* This Is Spinal Tap (1984)
Spione *See* Spies (1928)
Spirit of Tattoo *See* Irezumi (1983)
Spirit of the Dead *See* The Asphyx (1972)
Spirit of the People *See* Abe Lincoln in Illinois (1940)
The Spiritualist *See* The Amazing Mr. X (1948)
Spivs *See* I Vitelloni (1953)
The Split *See* The Manster (1959)
The Spooky Movie Show *See* The Mask (1961)
Spoorloos *See* The Vanishing (1988)
Spot *See* Dog Pound Shuffle (1975)
Spotswood *See* The Efficiency Expert (1992)
Spymaker *See* Spymaker: The Secret Life of Ian Fleming (1990)
Squadron of Doom *See* Ace Drummond (1936)
Stacey and Her Gangbusters *See* Stacey (1973)
Stakeout 2 *See* Another Stakeout (1993)
The Stand *See* Stephen King's The Stand (1994)
Stand and Deliver *See* Bowery Blitzkrieg (1941)
Stand Easy *See* Goon Movie (1953)
Stanno Tutti Bene *See* Everybody's Fine (1990)
Star *See* Danielle Steel's Star (1993)
Star Child *See* Space Raiders (1983)
The Star Man *See* The Star Maker (1995)
Stardust *See* Mad About Money (1930)
Starlight Slaughter *See* Eaten Alive (1976)
The Statutory Affair *See* Lola (1969)
Stella Star *See* Star Crash (1978)
Stepfather *See* Beau Pere (1981)
Stephen King's Graveyard Shift *See* Graveyard Shift (1990)
Stephen King's Silver Bullet *See* Silver Bullet (1985)
Stephen King's Sleepwalkers *See* Sleepwalkers (1992)
Still Smokin' *See* Cheech and Chong: Still Smokin' (1983)
Stolen Hearts *See* Two If by Sea (1995)
Storia de Ragazzi e di Ragazze *See* The Story of Boys & Girls (1991)
Stormy Crossing *See* Black Tide (1958)
Story of a Marriage *See* On Valentine's Day (1986)
The Story of an Artist's Studio Secrets *See* Artist's Studio Secrets (1964)
The Story of Gosta Berling *See* The Atonement of Gosta Berling (1924)
The Story of Joseph and His Brethren *See* Joseph & His Brethren (1960)
The Story of Robin Hood *See* The Story of Robin Hood & His Merrie Men (1952)
A Story of the Cruelties of Youth *See* The Cruel Story of Youth (1960)
The Story Without A Name *See* Without Warning (1952)
Straight Jacket *See* Dark Sanity (1982)
Straight on Till Morning *See* Dressed for Death (1974)
Strange Adventure *See* Wayne Murder Case (1938)
The Strange Adventure of David Gray *See* Vampyr (1931)
The Strange Case of Madeleine *See* Madeleine (1950)
Strange Deception *See* The Accused (1948)
Strange Incident *See* The Ox-Bow Incident (1943)
Strange Interval *See* Strange Interlude (1932)
Strange Journey *See* Fantastic Voyage (1966)
The Strange Ones *See* Les Enfants Terrible (1950)
The Strange World of Planet X *See* The Cosmic Monsters (1958)
The Stranger *See* Shame (1961)
Stranger in Our House *See* Summer of Fear (1978)
Stranger in the House *See* Black Christmas (1975)
A Stranger Walked In *See* Love from a Stranger (1947)
Strangler's Morgue *See* The Crimes of Stephen Hawke (1936)
Street Gang *See* Vigilante (1983)
Street Legal *See* The Last of the Finest (1990)
Street Love *See* Scarred (1984)
Street of Shadows *See* The Shadow Man (1953)
Streets of Laredo *See* Larry McMurtry's Streets of Laredo (1995)
Streets of New York *See* The Abe Lincoln of Ninth Avenue (1939)
Strictly Confidential *See* Broadway Bill (1934)
Strictly for Pleasure *See* Perfect Furlough (1959)
Striking Back *See* Search and Destroy (1981)
Strip Poker *See* The Big Switch (1970)
Striptease Lady *See* Lady of Burlesque (1943)
Struktura Krysztalu *See* The Structure of Crystals (1969)
The Stu Erwin Show *See* The Trouble with Father (1950)
Student Body *See* Getting In (1994)
Subida Al Cielo *See* Mexican Bus Ride (1951)
The Submersion of Japan *See* Tidal Wave (1975)
Subspecies 2 *See* Bloodstone: Subspecies 2 (1992)
Subspecies 3 *See* Bloodlust: Subspecies 3 (1993)
Succubus *See* The Devil's Nightmare (1971)
Such Men are Dangerous *See* The Racers (1955)
Suicide Run *See* Too Late the Hero (1970)
Suicide Squadron *See* Dangerous Moonlight (1941)
A Suitable Case for Treatment *See* Morgan! (1966)
The Sullivans *See* The Fighting Sullivans (1942)
Sult *See* Hunger (1966)
Summer Madness *See* Summertime (1955)
Summer Manoeuvers *See* Les Grandes Manoeuvres (1955)
Summer of Innocence *See* Big Wednesday (1978)
Summer with Monika *See* Monika (1952)
Summerplay *See* Summer Interlude (1950)
Summertime Killer *See* Ricco (1974)
Sumurun *See* One Arabian Night (1921)
The Sun Demon *See* Hideous Sun Demon (1959)
Suna No Onna *See* Woman in the Dunes (1964)
Sunburst *See* Slashed Dreams (1974)
Sunless *See* Sans Soleil (1982)
Sunrise—A Song of Two Humans *See* Sunrise (1927)
Sunset of a Clown *See* Sawdust & Tinsel (1953)
Super Dragon *See* Secret Agent Super Dragon (1966)
Super Fly T.N.T. *See* Superfly T.N.T. (1973)
The Super Inframan *See* Infra-Man (1976)
Superargo the Giant *See* Superargo (1967)
Superfantagenio *See* Aladdin (1986)
Superman and the Strange People *See* Superman & the Mole Men (1951)
Supersnooper *See* Super Fuzz (1981)
Surf 2: The End of the Trilogy *See* Surf 2 (1984)
Surf Warriors *See* Surf Ninjas (1993)
Suspected Alibi *See* Suspended Alibi (1956)
Swamp Diamonds *See* Swamp Women (1955)
Sweeney Todd: The Demon Barber of Fleet Street *See* Demon Barber of Fleet Street (1936)
Sweet Candy *See* Candy Stripe Nurses (1974)
Sweet Dirty Tony *See* The Mercenaries (1980)
Sweet Kill *See* The Arousers (1970)
Sweet Revenge *See* Code of Honor (1984)
Sweet Smell of Woman *See* The Scent of a Woman (1975)
Sweet Violence *See* Sweet Ecstasy (1962)
Sweetheart! *See* Canada's Sweetheart: The Saga of Hal C. Banks (1985)
Swept Away...By an Unusual Destiny in the Blue Sea of August *See* Swept Away... (1975)
Swing it Buddy *See* Swing It, Professor (1937)
Swing, Teacher, Swing *See* College Swing (1938)
Switchboard Operator *See* The Love Affair, or The Case of the Missing Switchboard Operator (1967)
Swordkill *See* Ghostwarrior (1986)
Swords of Blood *See* Cartouche (1962)
Sylvia and the Ghost *See* Sylvia and the Phantom (1945)
Symphony of Love *See* Ecstasy (1933)
Szegenylegenyek Nehezeletuck *See* The Round Up (1966)
T & A Academy *See* H.O.T.S. (1979)
T & A Academy 2 *See* Gimme an F (1985)
Tacones Lejanos *See* High Heels (1991)
Tainted Money *See* Show Them No Mercy (1935)
A Tale of Africa *See* Green Horizon (1983)
Tale of the Cock *See* Confessions of Tom Harris (1972)
A Talent for Loving *See* Gun Crazy (1969)
Tales from the Crypt II *See* Vault of Horror (1973)
Tales of the City *See* Armistead Maupin's Tales of the City (1993)
Tangled Trails *See* Sands of Sacrifice (1921)
Tanner: A Political Fable *See* Tanner '88 (1988)
Target: Embassy *See* Embassy (1972)
Target in the Sun *See* The Man Who Would Not Die (1975)
Target of an Assassin *See* African Rage (1978)
Tartu *See* The Adventures of Tartu (1943)
Taste of Fear *See* Scream of Fear (1961)
Tears in Florence *See* Traenen in Florenz (1984)
Teen Kanya *See* Two Daughters (1961)
Teenage Monster *See* Meteor Monster (1957)
The Teenage Psycho Meets Bloody Mary *See* Incredibly Strange Creatures Who Stopped Living and Became Mixed-Up Zombies (1963)
Tell It To the Marines *See* Here Come the Marines (1952)
Tell Your Children *See* Reefer Madness (1938)
Tema *See* The Theme (1979)
Tempo di Uccidere *See* Time to Kill (1989)
The Tenderfoot *See* Bushwhacked (1995)
Tenderfoots *See* Bushwhacked (1995)
Tendre Poulet *See* Dear Detective (1977)
Tenebrae *See* Unsane (1982)
Tengoku To Jigoku *See* High & Low (1962)
Tenue de Soiree *See* Menage (1986)
Terminal Station Indiscretion *See* Indiscretion of an American Wife (1954)
Terminus Station *See* Indiscretion of an American Wife (1954)
Terra em Transe *See* Earth Entranced (1966)
Terreur dans l'Espace *See* Planet of the Vampires (1965)
Terror Castle *See* The Virgin of Nuremberg (1965)
Terror Eyes *See* Night School (1981)
Terror From the Sun *See* Hideous Sun Demon (1959)
Terror Hospital *See* Hospital of Terror (1978)
Terror House *See* The Night Has Eyes (1942)
Terror House *See* Terror at Red Wolf Inn (1972)
Terror in Space *See* Planet of the Vampires (1965)
Terror in the Midnight Sun *See* Invasion of the Animal People (1962)
Terror of Sheba *See* The Graveyard (1974)
The Terror Strikes *See* The War of the Colossal Beast (1958)
Terror under the House *See* Revenge (1971)
The Testament of Dr. Mabuse *See* Das Testament des Dr. Mabuse (1933)
Texas Desperadoes *See* Drift Fence (1936)
Texas in Flames *See* She Came to the Valley (1977)
Texas Road Agent *See* Road Agent (1926)
Texas Serenade *See* Old Corral (1936)
Teyve der Milkhiker *See* Tevye (1939)
That Man Mr. Jones *See* The Fuller Brush Man (1948)
That Others May Live *See* Border Street (1948)
That They May Live *See* J'Accuse (1937)
That's the Way of the World *See* Shining Star (1975)
Therese Und Isabell *See* Therese & Isabelle (1968)
These Dangerous Years *See* Dangerous Youth (1958)
These Foolish Things *See* Daddy Nostalgia (1990)
They *See* They Watch (1993)
They Call Me Hallelujah *See* Guns for Dollars (1973)
They Don't Wear Pajamas at Rosie's *See* The First Time (1969)
They Loved Life *See* Kanal (1956)
They Made Me a Fugitive *See* They Made Me a Criminal (1939)
They Passed This Way *See* Four Faces West (1948)
They're Coming to Get You *See* Dracula vs. Frankenstein (1971)
Thin Air *See* Invasion of the Body Stealers (1969)
The Thing From Another World *See* The Thing (1951)
Thirst *See* Three Strange Loves (1949)
The Thirteen Chairs *See* 12 Plus 1 (1970)
The Thirty-Sixth Chamber *See* Master Killer (1984)
Thomas Crown and Company *See* The Thomas Crown Affair (1968)
Thoroughbred *See* Run for the Roses (1978)
Those Were the Happy Times *See* Star! (1968)

Thou Shall Not Kill *See* Avenging Conscience (1914)
Thou Shalt Honour Thy Wife *See* Master of the House (1925)
Three Bad Men in the Hidden Fortress *See* The Hidden Fortress (1958)
Three Colors: Blue *See* Trois Couleurs: Bleu (1993)
Three Colors: Red *See* Trois Couleurs: Rouge (1994)
Three Colors: White *See* Trois Couleurs: Blanc (1994)
Three Crazy Legionnaires *See* Three Legionnaires (1937)
Three For the Money *See* Win, Place, or Steal (1972)
Three Rascals in the Hidden Fortress *See* The Hidden Fortress (1958)
Three Steps to the Gallows *See* White Fire (1953)
The Three Stooges Go Around the World in a Daze *See* Around the World in a Daze (1963)
The Threepenny Opera *See* Mack the Knife (1989)
Through the Looking Glass *See* The Velvet Vampire (1971)
Thunder *See* Thunder Warrior (1985)
Thunder Mountain *See* Shadow of Chikara (1977)
Thunder on the Trail *See* Thundering Trail (1951)
Thursday the 12th *See* Pandemonium (1982)
Tianguo Niezi *See* The Day the Sun Turned Cold (1994)
Tidal Wave *See* Portrait of Jennie (1948)
Tierra Bru Tal *See* Savage Guns (1968)
The Tiger *See* Tiger Warsaw (1987)
Tiger in the Sky *See* The McConnell Story (1955)
Tiger of Bengal *See* Journey to the Lost City (1958)
The Tiger Woman *See* Perils of the Darkest Jungle (1944)
Tigers Don't Cry *See* African Rage (1978)
Tight Little Island *See* Whiskey Galore (1948)
Til Dawn Do Us Part *See* Dressed for Death (1974)
Tim Burton's The Nightmare Before Christmas *See* The Nightmare Before Christmas (1993)
Timber Tramps *See* The Big Push (1975)
Time Flyers *See* The Blue Yonder (1986)
A Time For Caring *See* Generation (1969)
The Time of Return *See* Muriel (1963)
Time of the Beast *See* Mutator (1990)
Time Raiders *See* Warriors of the Apocalypse (1985)
Time Trap *See* The Time Travelers (1964)
Time Warp Terror *See* Bloody New Year (1987)
Timeslip *See* The Atomic Man (1956)
Timewarp *See* Day Time Ended (1980)
Tini Zabutykh Predkiv *See* Shadows of Forgotten Ancestors (1964)
Tintorera *See* Tintorera...Tiger Shark (1978)
Tintorera...Bloody Waters *See* Tintorera...Tiger Shark (1978)
Tirez sur le Pianiste *See* Shoot the Piano Player (1962)
Titan Find *See* Creature (1985)
To Be a Man *See* Cry of Battle (1963)
To Catch a Spy *See* Catch Me a Spy (1971)
To Die For *See* Heaven's a Drag (1994)
To Elvis, With Love *See* Touched by Love (1980)
To Have and to Hold *See* When a Man Loves a Woman (1994)
To Live *See* Ikiru (1952)
To Love a Vampire *See* Lust for a Vampire (1971)
To Vlemma Tou Odyssea *See* Ulysses' Gaze (1995)
Today We Live *See* The Day and the Hour (1963)
A Toi De Faire *See* Your Turn Darling (1963)
Tomb of the Cat *See* Tomb of Ligeia (1964)
Tomb of the Living Dead *See* Mad Doctor of Blood Island (1969)
The Tommyknockers *See* Stephen King's The Tommyknockers (1993)
The Tomorrow Man *See* 984: Prisoner of the Future (1984)
Ton Kero Ton Hellinon *See* When the Greeks (1981)
Tong Nien Wang Shi *See* A Time to Live and a Time to Die (1985)
Too Many Chefs *See* Who Is Killing the Great Chefs of Europe? (1978)
Topio Stin Omichli *See* Landscape in the Mist (1988)
Torment *See* L'Enfer (1993)
Torture Zone *See* The Fear Chamber (1968)
Toto the Hero *See* Toto le Heros (1991)
The Touch of Melissa *See* The Touch of Satan (1970)
Touchez Pas Au Grisbi *See* Grisbi (1953)
Tower of Terror *See* Assault (1970)
Tower of Terror *See* Hard to Die (1990)
A Town Called Bastard *See* A Town Called Hell (1972)
The Town That Cried Terror *See* Maniac (1977)
T.R. Sloane *See* Death Ray 2000 (1981)
Trackers *See* Space Rage (1986)
Trail of the Royal Mounted *See* Mystery Trooper (1932)
Train of Terror *See* Terror Train (1980)
Train 2419 *See* The Return of Casey Jones (1934)
Traitement de Choc *See* Shock Treatment (1981)
Trancers *See* Future Cop (1976)
Transport Z Raje *See* Transport from Paradise (1965)
The Transvestite *See* Glen or Glenda: Confessions of Ed Wood (1953)
Tras el Cristal *See* In a Glass Cage (1986)
Trauma *See* Dario Argento's Trauma (1993)
Travels with Anita *See* Lovers and Liars (1981)
The Tree of Hands *See* Innocent Victim (1990)
Tree of Liberty *See* The Howards of Virginia (1940)
Trial by Combat *See* Choice of Weapons (1976)
Trick of the Eye *See* Primal Secrets (1994)
Trigger, Jr. *See* Western Double Feature 6: Rogers & Trigger (1950)
A Trip with Anita *See* Lovers and Liars (1981)
Triple Trouble *See* Kentucky Kernels (1934)
Tristan and Isolde *See* Lovespell (1979)
Trois Hommes et un Couffin *See* Three Men and a Cradle (1985)
The Trollenberg Terror *See* The Crawling Eye (1958)
Tromba *See* Tromba, the Tiger Man (1952)
Trop Belle Pour Toi *See* Too Beautiful for You (1988)
Trop Jolie pour Etre Honette *See* Too Pretty to Be Honest (1972)
Tropicana *See* The Heat's On (1943)
Trottie True *See* The Gay Lady (1949)
Trouble at 16 *See* Platinum High School (1960)
Trouble Chaser *See* Li'l Abner (1940)
The Trout *See* La Truite (1983)
Truman Capote's A Christmas Memory *See* ABC Stage 67: Truman Capote's A Christmas Memory (1966)
Truman Capote's The Glass House *See* The Glass House (1972)
Try and Find It *See* Hi Diddle Diddle (1943)
Tsarskaya Nevesta *See* The Tsar's Bride (1966)
Tsubaki Sanjuro *See* Sanjuro (1962)
Tsvet Granata *See* The Color of Pomegranates (1969)
Tudor Rose *See* Nine Days a Queen (1934)
Tueur de Ch Icago *See* Scarface Mob (1962)
Tulitkkutehtaan Tytto *See* The Match Factory Girl (1990)
The Tunnel *See* Transatlantic Tunnel (1935)
Turkey Shoot *See* Escape 2000 (1981)
Turn Your Pony Around *See* Mortal Danger (1994)
Turtle Beach *See* The Killing Beach (1992)
Twelve Miles Out *See* Second Woman (1951)
Twenty-One Days Together *See* 21 Days (1937)
Twice Bitten *See* The Vampire Hookers (1978)
Twilight of the Dead *See* Gates of Hell (1983)
Twinkle, Twinkle, Killer Kane *See* The Ninth Configuration (1979)
Twinky *See* Lola (1969)
Twisted *See* Medusa (1974)
The Twisted Road *See* They Live by Night (1949)
2 Cries in the Night *See* Funeral Home (1982)
Two Guys Talkin' About Girls *See* At First Sight (1995)
Two Minds for Murder *See* Someone Behind the Door (1971)
2002: The Rape of Eden *See* Bounty Hunter 2002 (1994)
Two Weeks in September *See* A Coeur Joie (1967)
Tystnaden *See* The Silence (1963)
U-238 and the Witch Doctor *See* Jungle Drums of Africa (1953)
Uccellacci e Uccellini *See* The Hawks & the Sparrows (1967)
Uccidero Un Uomo *See* This Man Must Die (1970)
Uchu Daikaiiju Dogora *See* Dagora, the Space Monster (1965)
Uchudai Dogora *See* Dagora, the Space Monster (1965)
Uchujin Tokyo Ni Arawaru *See* Warning from Space (1956)
Ugetsu Monogatari *See* Ugetsu (1953)
Ukigusa *See* Drifting Weeds (1959)
Ulica Graniczna *See* Border Street (1948)
Ulisse *See* Ulysses (1955)
The Ultimate Chase *See* The Ultimate Thrill (1974)
Ultimate Desires *See* Beyond the Silhouette (1990)
The Ultimate Solution of Grace Quigley *See* Grace Quigley (1984)
Ultimi Giorni di Pompeii *See* The Last Days of Pompeii (1960)
The Umbrella Woman *See* The Good Wife (1986)
Un Amour De Swann *See* Swann in Love (1984)
Un Amour En Allemagne *See* A Love in Germany (1984)
Un Angelo e Sceso a Brooklyn *See* The Man Who Wagged His Tail (1957)
Un Arma de Dos Filos *See* Shark! (1968)
Un Autre Homme, Une Autre Chance *See* Another Man, Another Chance (1977)
Un Chapeau de Paille d'Italie *See* Italian Straw Hat (1927)
Un Complicato Intrigo Di Donne, Vicoli E Delitti *See* Camorra: The Naples Connection (1985)
Un Condamne a Mort s'est Echappe *See* A Man Escaped (1957)
Un, Deux, Trois, Quatre! *See* Black Tights (1960)
Un Dimanche a la Campagne *See* A Sunday in the Country (1984)
Un Elephant a Trompe Enormement *See* Pardon Mon Affaire (1976)
Un Grand Amour de Beethoven *See* Beethoven (1936)
Un Homme Amoureux *See* A Man in Love (1987)
Un Homme Est Mort *See* The Outside Man (1973)
Un Homme et Un Femme *See* A Man and a Woman (1966)
Un Homme Et Une Femme: Vingt Ans Deja *See* A Man and a Woman: 20 Years Later (1986)
Un Indien dans la Ville *See* Little Indian, Big City (1995)
Un Minuto Per Pregare, Un Istante Per Morire *See* A Minute to Pray, A Second to Die (1967)
Un Senor Muy Viejo Con Unas Alas Enormes *See* A Very Old Man with Enormous Wings (1988)
Un Trem Para as Estrelas *See* Subway to the Stars (1987)
Un Uomo da Rispettare *See* Master Touch (1974)
Un Zoo, La Nuit *See* Night Zoo (1987)
Una Bruja Sin Escoba *See* A Witch Without a Broom (1968)
Una Giornata Speciale *See* A Special Day (1977)
Una Hacka Para la Luna de Miel *See* Hatchet for the Honeymoon (1970)
Una Pura Formalita *See* A Pure Formality (1994)
Una Ragione Per Vivere e Una Per Morire *See* A Reason to Live, A Reason to Die (1973)
Unakrsna Vatra *See* Operation Cross Eagles (1969)
Uncle Harry *See* The Strange Affair of Uncle Harry (1945)
Uncle Silas *See* Inheritance (1947)
Unconventional Linda *See* Holiday (1938)
Under California Skies *See* Under California Stars (1948)
Under the Clock *See* The Clock (1945)
Under the Olive Trees *See* Through the Olive Trees (1994)
Under the Sun of Satan *See* Under Satan's Sun (1987)
Underground *See* The Lower Depths (1936)
An Underwater Odyssey *See* Neptune Factor (1973)
Underworld *See* Transmutations (1985)

Underworld After Dark *See* Big Town After Dark (1947)
Une Affaire de Femmes *See* The Story of Women (1988)
Une Femme a sa Fentre *See* A Woman at Her Window (1977)
Une Femme Douce *See* A Gentle Woman (1969)
Une Femme Est Une Femme *See* A Woman is a Woman (1960)
Une Femme ou Deux *See* One Woman or Two (1985)
Une Histoire Simple *See* A Simple Story (1979)
Une Partie de Campagne *See* A Day in the Country (1946)
Une Pure Formalite *See* A Pure Formality (1994)
Unknown Satellite Over Tokyo *See* Warning from Space (1956)
Untel Pere et Fils *See* Heart of a Nation (1943)
The Unvanquished *See* Aparajito (1958)
Uomo Dalla Pelle Dura *See* Counter Punch (1971)
L'Uomo delle Stelle *See* The Star Maker (1995)
Up in the Cellar *See* Three in the Cellar (1970)
Up the Chastity Belt *See* Naughty Knights (1971)
Up to a Point *See* Up to a Certain Point (1983)
The Upstate Murders *See* Savage Weekend (1980)
Urga *See* Close to Eden (1990)
Ursus *See* Ursus in the Valley of the Lions (1962)
The Usual Unidentified Thieves *See* Big Deal on Madonna Street (1958)
Utamaro O Meguru Gonin No Onna *See* Utamaro and His Five Women (1946)
Utvandrarna *See* The Emigrants (1972)
Vacation *See* National Lampoon's Vacation (1983)
Vagabond Violinist *See* Broken Melody (1934)
Vaghe Stelle Dell'Orsa *See* Sandra of a Thousand Delights (1965)
Valborgmassoafton *See* Walpurgis Night (1941)
The Valdez Horses *See* Chino (1975)
Valdez the Half Breed *See* Chino (1975)
Valley of Fear *See* Sherlock Holmes and the Deadly Necklace (1962)
Valley of the Swords *See* The Castilian (1963)
The Vampire *See* Vampyr (1931)
The Vampire and the Robot *See* My Son, the Vampire (1952)
The Vampire-Beast Craves Blood *See* Blood Beast Terror (1967)
Vampire Men of the Lost Planet *See* Horror of the Blood Monsters (1970)
Vampire Over London *See* My Son, the Vampire (1952)
The Vampire's Niece *See* Fangs of the Living Dead (1968)
Vampire's Night Orgy *See* Orgy of the Vampires (1973)
Vampyr, Der Traum Des David Gray *See* Vampyr (1931)
Vampyr, Ou L'Etrang e Aventure De David Gray *See* Vampyr (1931)
Vampyres, Daughters of Dracula *See* Vampyres (1974)
The Varrow Mission *See* Teen Alien (1988)
Vasectomy *See* Vasectomy: A Delicate Matter (1986)
The Veil *See* Haunts (1977)
Velvet House *See* Crucible of Horror (1969)
Vendetta: Secrets of a Mafia Bride *See* A Family Matter (1991)
Vengeance *See* The Brain (1962)
Vengeance: The Story of Tony Cimo *See* Vengeance (1989)
Venus in Peltz *See* Venus in Furs (1970)
The Venusian *See* The Stranger from Venus (1954)
Vesnicko Ma Strediskova *See* My Sweet Little Village (1986)
Vessel of Wrath *See* Beachcomber (1938)
The Veteran *See* Deathdream (1972)
The Vicious Circle *See* Woman in Brown (1948)
Victims of the Beyond *See* Sucker Money (1934)
Vindicator *See* Wheels of Fire (1984)
Violence et Passion *See* Conversation Piece (1975)
Violent Journey *See* The Fool Killer (1965)
Violent Midnight *See* Psychomania (1963)
Violent Rage *See* Fearmaker (1989)
Violent Streets *See* Thief (1981)
Violette Noziere *See* Violette (1978)
Virgin Hunters *See* Test Tube Teens from the Year 2000 (1993)
The Virtuous Tramps *See* The Devil's Brother (1933)
Virus *See* Invasion of the Flesh Hunters (1982)
Viskingar Och Rop *See* Cries and Whispers (1972)
Vita Privata *See* A Very Private Affair (1962)
Vitelloni *See* I Vitelloni (1953)
Vivement Dimanche! *See* Confidentially Yours (1983)
Viviamo Oggi *See* The Day and the Hour (1963)
Vivre Savie *See* My Life to Live (1962)
Vogues *See* Vogues of 1938 (1937)
Voodoo Blood Bath *See* I Eat Your Skin (1964)
Vortex *See* Day Time Ended (1980)
Voyage Beyond the Sun *See* Space Monster (1964)
Voyage to a Prehistoric Planet *See* Voyage to the Prehistoric Planet (1965)
Vredens Dag *See* Day of Wrath (1943)
Vulcan, Son of Jupiter *See* Vulcan God of Fire (1962)
Vzlomschik *See* Burglar (1987)
Wages of Fear *See* Sorcerer (1977)
Waiting Women *See* Secrets of Women (1952)
Waldo Warren: Private Dick Without a Brain *See* Maximum Thrust (1988)
The Wandering Kid *See* Urotsukidoj 1: Legend of the Overfiend (1993)
Wannseekonferenz *See* The Wannsee Conference (1984)
Want a Ride, Little Girl? *See* Impulse (1974)
Wanted Women *See* Jessie's Girls (1975)
The Wanton Contessa *See* Senso (1954)
War Between the Planets *See* Planet on the Prowl (1965)
War Games *See* Suppose They Gave a War and Nobody Came? (1970)
The War of the Monsters *See* Gamera vs. Barugon (1966)
War of the Planets *See* Cosmos: War of the Planets (1980)
War Shock *See* Battle Shock (1956)
Ward 13 *See* Hospital Massacre (1981)
Warlock *See* Skullduggery (1979)
The Warm-Blooded Spy *See* Ravishing Idiot (1964)
Warnung Vor Einer Helligen Nutte *See* Beware of a Holy Whore (1970)
Warrior's Rest *See* Le Repos du Guerrier (1962)
Warum Lauft Herr R Amok? *See* Why Does Herr R. Run Amok? (1969)
Washington, B.C. *See* Hail (1973)
Water Child *See* L'Enfant d'Eau (1995)
Water Cyborgs *See* Terror Beneath the Sea (1966)
The Watts Monster *See* Dr. Black, Mr. Hyde (1976)
The Way Ahead *See* Immortal Battalion (1944)
The Way of Life *See* They Call It Sin (1932)
Ways of Love *See* The Miracle (1948)
We Will All Meet in Paradise *See* Pardon Mon Affaire, Too! (1977)
Wedding Bells *See* Royal Wedding (1951)
Wedding Breakfast *See* The Catered Affair (1956)
Wednesday's Child *See* Family Life (1971)
Weekend Babysitter *See* Weekend with the Babysitter (1970)
Welcome Home Brother Charles *See* Soul Vengeance (1975)
Welcome to Oblivion *See* Ultra Warrior (1992)
The Well-Made Marriage *See* Le Beau Mariage (1982)
Wendy Cracked a Walnut *See* ...Almost (1990)
We're in the Army Now *See* Pack Up Your Troubles (1932)
The Werewolf and the Yeti *See* Night of the Howling Beast (1975)
What? *See* Diary of Forbidden Dreams (1973)
What a Chassis! *See* Belle Americaine (1961)
What a Man *See* Never Give a Sucker an Even Break (1941)
What Changed Charley Farthing *See* Bananas Boat (1978)
What Lola Wants *See* Damn Yankees (1958)
The Wheelchair *See* El Cochecito (1960)
Wheels of Terror *See* The Misfit Brigade (1987)
When Knighthood Was in Flower *See* The Sword & the Rose (1953)
When Michael Calls *See* Shattered Silence (1971)
When the Girls Meet the Boys *See* Girl Crazy (1943)
When Youth Conspires *See* Old Swimmin' Hole (1940)
Where the Hell's the Gold? *See* Dynamite and Gold (1988)
Where the River Bends *See* Bend of the River (1952)
While Plucking the Daisy *See* Mademoiselle Striptease (1957)
The Whipping Boy *See* Prince Brat and the Whipping Boy (1995)
White *See* Trois Couleurs: Blanc (1994)
White Paws *See* Pattes Blanches (1949)
White Trash on Moonshine Mountain *See* Moonshine Mountain (1964)
A White White Boy *See* The Mirror (1975)
Who? *See* Roboman (1975)
Who Dares Wins *See* The Final Option (1982)
Who Fears the Devil *See* The Legend of Hillbilly John (1973)
Who Is Killing the Stuntman *See* Stunts (1977)
Who Murdered Joy Morgan? *See* Killjoy (1981)
Who Shot Patakango? *See* Who Shot Pat? (1992)
Whoever Slew Auntie Roo? *See* Who Slew Auntie Roo? (1971)
Why Not? *See* Eijanaika (1981)
Wide-Eyed and Legless *See* The Wedding Gift (1993)
The Widow and the Gigolo *See* Roman Spring of Mrs. Stone (1961)
Wild Beds *See* Tigers in Lipstick (1980)
Wild Drifters *See* Cockfighter (1974)
Wild Flower *See* Fiorile (1993)
Wild Flower *See* Flor Silvestre (1958)
Wild For Kicks *See* Beat Girl (1960)
Wild Geese *See* Mistress (1953)
Wild Horses of Fire *See* Shadows of Forgotten Ancestors (1964)
Wild Oats *See* The Errors of Youth (1978)
The Wild Pack *See* Defiant (1970)
The Wild Side *See* Suburbia (1983)
Wild Youth *See* Naked Youth (1959)
Wildcat *See* Great Scout & Cathouse Thursday (1976)
Wilderness Family, Part 2 *See* Further Adventures of the Wilderness Family, Part 2 (1977)
Willy Milly *See* Something Special (1986)
Wilt *See* The Misadventures of Mr. Wilt (1990)
The Wind Bloweth Where it Listeth *See* A Man Escaped (1957)
A Window in London *See* Lady in Distress (1939)
A Window to the Sky *See* The Other Side of the Mountain (1975)
Wings of the Apache *See* Fire Birds (1990)
Winter Rates *See* Out of Season (1975)
The Wistful Widow *See* The Wistful Widow of Wagon Gap (1947)
The Witch *See* Superstition (1982)
Witch Doctor *See* Men of Two Worlds (1946)
The Witches of Salem *See* The Crucible (1957)
Witchfinder General *See* The Conqueror Worm (1968)
Witchkill *See* The Witchmaker (1969)
Witch's Curse *See* Maciste in Hell (1960)
With Words and Music *See* The Girl Said No (1937)
Wit's End *See* G.I. Executioner (1971)
The Wizard of Mars *See* Horrors of the Red Planet (1964)
Wo Die Grunen Ameisen Traumen *See* Where the Green Ants Dream (1984)
Wolf Larsen *See* The Legend of the Sea Wolf (1958)
Woman Alone *See* Sabotage (1936)
A Woman Destroyed *See* Smash-Up: The Story of a Woman (1947)
Woman, Forty *See* Summer Snow (1994)
The Woman in His House *See* The Animal Kingdom (1932)
Woman of Antwerp *See* Dedee d'Anvers (1949)
Woman of Dolwyn *See* The Last Days of Dolwyn (1949)
Woman of Osaka *See* Osaka Elegy (1936)

Videos A-Z

A la Mode 🦴🦴½ *In Fashion* **1994 (R)** It's Paris in the '60s as shy 17-year-old orphan Fausto (Higelin) is apprenticed to fatherly Jewish tailor Mietek (Yanne). But Fausto is transfixed by lovely mechanic Tonie (Darel) and decides what he really wants (besides the girl) is to design women's fashions. Very frothy coming-of-age tale, anchored by Yanne's veteran charm. Based on the novel "Fausto" by Richard Morgieve. French with subtitles. **89m/C VHS, LV.** *FR* Ken Higelin, Jean Yanne, Florence Darel, Francois Hautesserre; ***D:*** Remy Duchemin; ***W:*** Remy Duchemin, Richard Morgieve; ***M:*** Denis Barbier. *MAX*

A Nos Amours 🦴🦴🦴 **1984 (R)** Craving the attention she is denied at home, a young French girl searches for love and affection from numerous boyfriends in hopes of eradicating her unhappy home. Occasional lapses in quality and slow pacing hamper an otherwise excellent effort. The characterization of the girl Suzanne is especially memorable. In French with English subtitles. **99m/C VHS, Beta, LV.** *FR* Sandrine Bonnaire, Dominique Besnehard, Maurice Pialat, Evelyne Ker; ***D:*** Maurice Pialat. *COL, INJ*

A Nous la Liberte 🦴🦴🦴🦴 **1931** Two tramps encounter industrialization and automation, making one into a wealthy leader, the other into a nature-loving iconoclast. A poignant, fantastical masterpiece by Clair, made before he migrated to Hollywood. Though the view of automation may be dated, it influenced such films as Chaplin's "Modern Times." In French with English subtitles. **87m/B VHS, Beta, 8mm.** *FR* Henri Marchand, Raymond Cordy, Rolla France, Paul Olivier, Jacques Shelly, Andre Michaud; ***D:*** Rene Clair; ***W:*** Rene Clair; ***C:*** Georges Perinal. National Board of Review Awards '32: 5 Best Foreign Films of the Year; Nominations: Academy Awards '32: Best Interior Decoration. *INJ, NOS, MRV*

Aaron Loves Angela 🦴🦴 **1975 (R)** Puerto Rican girl falls in love with a black teen amidst the harsh realities of the Harlem ghetto. "Romeo and Juliet" meets "West Side Story" in a cliched comedy drama. **99m/C VHS, Beta.** Kevin Hooks, Irene Cara, Moses Gunn, Robert Hooks, Jose Feliciano; ***D:*** Gordon Parks Jr.; ***M:*** Jose Feliciano. *COL*

Abbott and Costello Go to Mars 🦴½ **1953** Poor parody of sci-fi films finds the frantic duo aboard a rocket ship and accidentally heading off into outer space. They don't land on Mars, but Venus, which is populated by lots of pretty women and no men. Even this duo looks good to the ladies. Cheapie production and uninspired buffoonery. **77m/B VHS.** Bud Abbott, Lou Costello, Mari Blanchard, Robert Paige, Martha Hyer, Horace McMahon, Jack Kruschen, Anita Ekberg; ***D:*** Charles Lamont; ***W:*** John Grant, D.D. Beauchamp. *MCA*

Abbott and Costello in Hollywood 🦴🦴 *Bud Abbott and Lou Costello In Hollywood* **1945** Bud and Lou appear as a barber and porter of a high class tonsorial parlor in Hollywood. A rather sarcastic look at backstage Hollywood, Abbott & Costello style. Ball makes a guest appearance. **111m/B VHS, Beta.** Bud Abbott, Lou Costello, Frances Rafferty, Warner Anderson, Lucille Ball; ***D:*** Sylvan Simon; ***M:*** George Bassman. *MGM, CCB*

Abbott and Costello in the Foreign Legion 🦴🦴½ **1950** Fight promoters Jonesy and Max trail their runaway fighter to Algiers where they're tricked into joining the French Foreign Legion. They have to cope with a sadistic sargeant, a sexy spy, and still find their man. Most amusement comes from Lou's wild desert mirages. **80m/B VHS.** Bud Abbott, Lou Costello, Walter Slezak, Patricia Medina, Douglass Dumbrille, Leon Belasco, Marc Lawrence, Tor Johnson; ***D:*** Charles Lamont; ***W:*** John Grant, Martin Ragaway, Leonard Stern. *MCA*

Abbott and Costello Meet Captain Kidd 🦴🦴 **1952** With pirates led by Captain Kidd on their trail, Abbott and Costello follow a treasure map. Bland A&C swashbuckler spoof with a disinterested Laughton impersonating the Kidd. One of the duo's few color films. **70m/C VHS, Beta, LV.** Bud Abbott, Lou Costello, Charles Laughton, Hillary Brooke, Fran Warren, Bill Shirley, Leif Erickson; ***D:*** Charles Lamont. *NOS*

Abbott and Costello Meet Dr. Jekyll and Mr. Hyde 🦴🦴 **1952** Abbott and Costello take on evil Dr. Jekyll, who has transformed himself into Mr. Hyde, and is terrorizing London. A lame attempt at recapturing the success of "Abbott and Costello Meet Frankenstein." **77m/B VHS, Beta.** Bud Abbott, Lou Costello, Boris Karloff, Craig Stevens, Helen Westcott, Reginald Denny; ***D:*** Charles Lamont. *MCA*

Abbott and Costello Meet Frankenstein 🦴🦴🦴 *Abbott and Costello Meet the Ghosts* **1948** Big-budget A&C classic is one of their best efforts and was rewarded handsomely at the box office. Two unsuspecting baggage clerks deliver a crate containing the last but not quite dead remains of Dracula and Dr. Frankenstein's monster to a wax museum. The fiends are revived, wreaking havoc with the clerks. Chaney makes a special appearance to warn the boys that trouble looms. Last film to use the Universal creature pioneered by Karloff in 1931. **83m/B VHS, Beta, LV.** Bud Abbott, Lou Costello, Lon Chaney Jr., Bela Lugosi, Glenn Strange, Lenore Aubert, Jane Randolph; ***D:*** Charles T. Barton; ***V:*** Vincent Price. *MCA*

Abbott and Costello Meet the Invisible Man 🦴🦴🦴 **1951** Abbott and Costello play newly-graduated detectives who take on the murder case of a boxer (Franz) accused of killing his manager. Using a serum that makes people invisible, the boxer helps Costello in a prizefight that will frame the real killers, who killed the manager because the boxer refused to throw a fight. Great special effects and hilarious gags make this one of the best from the crazy duo. **82m/B VHS.** Bud Abbott, Lou Costello, Nancy Guild, Adele Jergens, Sheldon Leonard, William Frawley, Gavin Muir, Arthur Franz, Fred Rinaldo, John Grant; ***D:*** Charles Lamont; ***W:*** Robert Lees; ***C:*** George Robinson. *MCA*

Abbott and Costello Meet the Keystone Kops 🦴🦴½ **1954** It's 1912 and the boys are bilked into buying a fake movie studio by a clever con man. When they find out they've been tricked, the duo head to Hollywood to track him down and find out the crook is trying to cheat Sennett's film company. Sennett himself trained A&C and the new Keystone Kops in their recreations of his silent screen routines. Good final chase sequence but the earlier work is tired. **79m/B VHS.** Bud Abbott, Lou Costello, Fred Clark, Lynn Bari, Mack Sennett, Maxie "Slapsie" Rosenbloom, Frank Wilcox, Harold Goodwin; ***D:*** Charles Lamont; ***W:*** John Grant; ***M:*** Henry Mancini. *MCA*

Abbott and Costello Meet the Killer, Boris Karloff 🦴🦴 **1949** Unremarkable Abbott and Costello murder mystery. Karloff plays a psychic who tries to frame Lou for murder. Pleasant enough but not one of their best. **84m/B VHS, Beta, LV.** Bud Abbott, Lou Costello, Boris Karloff, Lenore Aubert, Gar Moore, Donna Martell, Alan Mowbray, James Flavin, Roland Winters; ***D:*** Charles T. Barton. *MCA*

Abbott and Costello Meet the Mummy 🦴🦴½ **1955** Okay comedy from the duo has them stranded in Egypt with a valuable medallion which will lead to secret treasure and the mummy who guards the tomb. The last of the films the twosome made for Universal. **90m/B VHS.** Bud Abbott, Lou Costello, Marie Windsor, Michael Ansara, Dan Seymour, Kurt Katch, Richard Deacon, Mel Welles, Edwin Parker; ***D:*** Charles Lamont; ***W:*** John Grant. *MCA, FCT*

ABC Stage 67: Truman Capote's A Christmas Memory *Truman Capote's A Christmas Memory; A Christmas Memory* **1966** A television drama special narrated by Capote about his remembered childhood experience of baking dozens of fruitcakes for friends at Christmas with his elderly distant cousin, Miss Sook Faulk (Page). She is quiet, lovely and true in this sensitive portrait of why we give and what we have to be thankful for. Adapted from a Capote short story by Capote and Eleanor Perry. **51m/B VHS, Beta, 8mm.** Geraldine Page, Donnie Melvin; ***D:*** Frank Perry. *MOV, VYY*

ABC's of Love & Sex, Australia Style 🦴 **1986** An Australian-made sex-education parody. **87m/C VHS, Beta.** *AU* Brigittia Almsrom, Rettima Borer, Ian Broadbent. *ACA*

Abducted 🦴½ **1986 (PG)** A woman jogger is abducted by a crazed mountain man in the Canadian Rockies. Weird and unbelievably tedious film is nevertheless highlighted by some spectacular wilderness footage of the Vancouver area, a travelogue bonus for those in the mood. **87m/C VHS, Beta.** *CA* Dan Haggerty, Roberta Weiss, Lawrence King Phillips; ***D:*** Boon Collins. *PSM*

Abducted 2: The Reunion 🦴½ **1994 (R)** Three girlfriends decide to go camping for their reunion trip. Oops—psycho mountain man alert! **91m/C VHS.** Dan Haggerty, Jan-Michael Vincent, Donna Jason, Raquel Bianca, Debbie Rochon, Lawrence King; ***D:*** Boon Collins. *AVI*

Abduction 🦴½ **1975 (R)** Exploitative account of the Patty Hearst kidnapping, loosely adapted from the Harrison James novel written before the kidnapping. A young woman from a wealthy capitalist family is kidnapped by black radicals and held for an unusual ransom. Oh, and she tangles with lesbians, too. **100m/C VHS, Beta.** Judith-Marie Bergan, David Pendleton, Gregory Rozakis, Leif Erickson, Dorothy Malone, Lawrence Tierney; ***D:*** Joseph Zito. *MED*

The Abduction of Allison Tate 🦴½ **1992 (R)** Rich developer takes land belonging to a group of Native Americans. Three young tribe members retaliate by kidnapping the developer's daughter. But when their plans go awry and one of the trio is killed, Allison finds herself sympathizing more with them than with her father's ambitions. **95m/C VHS.** Leslie Hope, Bernie White; ***D:*** Paul Leder. *NO*

The Abduction of Kari Swenson 🦴½ **1987** An account of the true-life (it really happened) kidnapping of Olympic biathalon hopeful Swensen by a pair of mischievous Montana mountain men with matrimony in mind. The movie details the abduction of Swenson by the scruffy father and son duo and the massive manhunt. As the put-upon Kari, Pollan exceeds script expectations in this made-for-television exercise in stress avoidance. **100m/C VHS.** Joe Don Baker, M. Emmet Walsh, Ronny Cox, Michael Bowen, Geoffrey Blake, Dorothy Fielding, Tracy Pollan; ***D:*** Stephen Gyllenhaal. *VMK*

Abduction of St. Anne 🦴🦴 **1975** An almost interesting made-for-television mystical thriller about a detective and a bishop trying to track down a gangster's daughter, who may have nifty supernatural healing powers the Church would be very interested in having documented. **78m/C VHS, Beta.** Robert Wagner, E.G. Marshall, William Windom, Lloyd Nolan; ***D:*** Harry Falk; ***M:*** George Duning. *WOV, GKK*

The Abductors 🦴 **1972 (R)** Caffaro's super-agent takes on international white slavery, a worthy target for any exploitation effort. While the novelty is a tough and intelligent on-screen heroine, sufficient sleaze and violence bring it all down to the proper level of swampland video. Sequel to the never-to-be-forgotten "Ginger." **90m/C VHS, Beta.** Cheri Caffaro, William Grannell, Richard Smedley, Patrick Wright, Jennifer Brooks; ***D:*** Don Schain. *MON*

Abdulla the Great 🦴🦴 *Abdullah's Harem* **1956** A dissolute Middle Eastern monarch falls for a model, who spurns him for an army officer. While distracted by these royal shenanigans, the king is blissfully unaware of his subjects' disaffection—until they revolt. Dares to lampoon Egypt's dead King Farouk, going against conventional Hollywood wisdom ("Farouk in film is box office poison"). **89m/C VHS, Beta.** *GB* Gregory Ratoff, Kay Kendall, Sydney Chaplin; ***D:*** Gregory Ratoff. *VYY*

Abe Lincoln in Illinois 🦴🦴🦴🦴 *Spirit of the People* **1940** Massey considered this not only his finest film but a part he was "born to play." Correct on both counts, this Hollywood biography follows Lincoln from his log cabin days to his departure for the White House. The Lincoln-Douglass debate scene and Massey's post-presidential election farewell to the citizens of Illinois are nothing short of brilliant. Written by Sherwood from his Pulitzer-Prize winning play. Contrasted with the well-known "Young Mr. Lincoln" (Henry Fonda), its relative anonymity is perplexing. **110m/B VHS, Beta.** Raymond Massey, Gene Lockhart, Ruth Gordon, Mary Howard, Dorothy Tree, Harvey Stephens, Minor Watson, Alan Baxter, Howard da Silva, Maurice Murphy, Clem Bevans, Herbert Rudley; ***D:*** John Cromwell; ***W:*** Robert Sherwood; ***C:*** James Wong Howe. Nominations: Academy Awards '40: Best Actor (Massey), Best Black and White Cinematography. *MED, TTC*

The Abe Lincoln of Ninth Avenue 🦴🦴½ *Streets of New York* **1939** All-American tale of a poor young man making good in New York. His role model is Abraham Lincoln. Cooper is exceptional, supported by effective performances by the rest of the cast. **68m/B VHS, Beta, 8mm.** Jackie Cooper, Martin Spelling, Marjorie Reynolds, Dick Purcell, George Cleveland, George Irving; ***D:*** William Nigh. *VYY*

Abigail's Party 🦴🦴 **1977** Steadman plays the hostess for a very ill-fated dinner party, especially when she realizes her husband has just died on her new carpet. Made for British television. **105m/C VHS.** *GB* Alison Steadman; ***D:*** Mike Leigh. *WBF, BTV*

Abilene Town 🦴🦴🦴 **1946** In a post-Civil War Kansas town far from the freeway, Scott is the tough marshal trying to calm the conflict between cattlemen and homesteaders. He also finds time to participate in a romantic triangle with dance hall vixen Dvorak and heart-of-gold Fleming. Snappy pace keeps it interesting. Based on a novel by Ernest Haycox. **90m/B VHS, Beta.** Randolph Scott, Ann Dvorak, Edgar Buchanan, Rhonda Fleming, Lloyd Bridges; ***D:*** Edwin L. Marin. *MRV, NOS, PSM*

The Abominable Dr. Phibes 🦴🦴🦴 **1971 (PG)** After being disfigured in a freak car accident that killed his wife, an evil genius decides that the members of a surgical team let his wife die and shall each perish by a different biblical plague. High camp with the veteran cast in top form. **90m/C VHS, Beta, LV.** *GB* Vincent Price, Joseph Cotten, Hugh Griffith, Terry-Thomas, Virginia North, Susan Travers, Alex Scott, Caroline Munro; ***D:*** Robert Fuest. *VES, LIV, ORI*

The Abomination 🦴 **1988 (R)** After a 5,000-year-old creature possesses him during a nightmare, a boy goes on an eye-gouging frenzy. Only the audience gets hurt. **100m/C VHS, Beta.** Van Connery, Victoria Chaney, Gaye Bottoms, Suzy Meyer, Jude Johnson, Blue Thompson, Scott Davis; ***D:*** Max Raven. *DMP*

About Last Night... 🦴🦴🦴 **1986 (R)** Semi-realistic comedy-drama which explores the ups and downs of one couple's relationship. Mostly quality performances, especially Perkins and Belushi as friends of the young lovers. Based on David Mamet's play "Sexual Perversity in Chicago," but considerably softened so that more people would buy tickets at the box office, the film acts as a historical view of contemporary mating rituals before the onset of the AIDS crisis. **113m/C VHS, Beta, LV.** Rob Lowe, Demi Moore, Elizabeth Perkins, James Belushi, George DiCenzo, Robin Thomas, Michael Alldredge; ***D:*** Edward Zwick; ***W:*** Tim Kazurinsky, Denise DeClue; ***M:*** Miles Goodman. *COL*

Above and Beyond 🦴🦴🦴 **1953** Good performance by Taylor as Col. Paul Tibbets, the man who piloted the Enola Gay, which dropped the atomic bomb on Hiroshima. Focuses on the secrecy of the mission and the strain this puts on Tibbets marriage. Exciting action sequences of the mission itself. **122m/B VHS.** Robert Taylor, Eleanor Parker, James Whitmore, Larry Keating, Larry Gates, Robert Burton, Jim Backus; ***D:*** Melvin Frank, Norman Panama; ***W:*** Melvin Frank, Norman Panama, Beirne Lay Jr. *MGM*

Above Suspicion 🦴🦴🦴 **1943** MacMurray and Crawford are American honeymooners (poor Fred!) asked to assist an international intelligence organization. They engage the Nazis in a tense battle of wits. Well-made and engaging. **91m/B VHS.** Joan Crawford, Fred MacMurray, Conrad Veidt, Basil Rathbone, Reginald Owen; ***D:*** Richard Thorpe. *MGM*

Above Suspicion 🦴🦴 **1995 (R)** Dempsey Cain (Reeve) seems to be the perfect cop, as well as a loving husband and father and a mentor to his younger brother. But when Cain is paralyzed by a drug dealer's bullet, he begins to notice just how close his wife (Cattrall) and brother (Kerr) are. There's adultery, there's murder, and there's the cop who just may be a cold-blooded killer. Unnervingly, Reeve plays a paraplegic in the last movie he made before his own paralyzing riding accident. Made for cable. **92m/C VHS.** Christopher Reeve, Kim Cattrall, Joe Mantegna, Edward Kerr; ***D:*** Steven Schachter. *HBO*

Above the Law 🦴🦴 **1988 (R)** In his debut, Seagal does his wooden best to portray a tough Chicago police detective planning an enormous drug bust of one of the biggest felons in the state. Unfortunately, the FBI has ordered him to back off and find another bust. The reasons are almost as complex as Seagal's character, and like most details of the flick, stupid. However, people don't watch these movies for the acting or the plot, but for the fight scenes, which are well-choreographed and violent. Watch it with someone you love. **99m/C VHS, Beta, LV, 8mm.** Steven Seagal, Pam Grier, Henry Silva, Sharon Stone, Ron Dean, Daniel Faraldo; ***D:*** Andrew Davis; ***W:*** Andrew Davis, Steven Pressfield; ***C:*** Robert Steadman. *WAR, TLF*

Above the Rim 🦴🦴½ **1994 (R)** Vulgar, violent hoopster drama about a fiercely competitive inner-city playground game. Kyle-Lee Watson (Martin), a self-involved high school star raised by a saintly single mom (Pinkins), is torn between the lure of the streets and his college recruiting chances. His odds aren't made any easier by homeboy hustler Birdie (Shakur), who wants to improve his chances of making money on the local games by making sure Watson plays for his team. Energetic b-ball sequences, strong performances lose impact amid formulaic melodrama and the usual obscenities. Debut for director Pollack. **97m/C VHS, LV.** Duane Martin, Tupac Shakur, Leon, Marlon Wayans, Tonya Pinkins, Bernie Mac; ***D:*** Jeff Pollack; ***W:*** Jeff Pollack, Barry Michael Cooper; ***M:*** Marcus Miller. Nominations: MTV Movie Awards '95: Best Song ("Regulate"). *NLC*

Above Us the Waves 🦴🦴🦴 **1956** During WWII, the British navy immobilizes a huge German battleship off the coast of Norway. Effectively dramatizes the British naval preparations for what seemed a suicidal mission: using midget submarines to plant underwater explosives on the hull of the German vessel and detonating them before the Germans could detect the danger. **92m/C VHS.** *GB* John Mills, John Gregson, Donald Sinden, James Robertson Justice, Michael Medwin, James Kenney, O.E. Hasse, Thomas Heathcote, Lee Patterson, Theodore Bikel, Lyndon Brook, Anthony Newley; ***D:*** Ralph Thomas. *REP*

Abraham 🦴🦴½ **1994** Made for cable Biblical epic chronicling the Old Testament story of humble shepherd Abraham (Harris), who's commanded by God to lead his family into the promised land of Canaan. Among his family's many trials will be God's command that Abraham sacrifice his son Isaac as a test of faith and obedience. Filmed on location in

Morocco with a commanding performance by Harris that somewhat redeems the film's dullness. **?m/C VHS.** Richard Harris, Barbara Hershey, Maximilian Schell, Vittorio Gassman, Caroline Rosi, Gottfried John, Kevin McNally; ***D:*** Joseph Sargent. *TTC*

Abraham Lincoln ⅋⅋½ **1930** Griffith's first talking movie takes Abraham Lincoln from his birth through his assassination. This restored version includes the original slavery sequences which were believed to be lost, but obviously were not. Musical score included. **97m/B VHS, Beta, LV.** Walter Huston, Una Merkel, Kay Hammond, E. Alyn Warren, Hobart Bosworth, Fred Warren, Henry B. Walthall, Russell Simpson; ***D:*** D.W. Griffith; ***C:*** Karl Struss. *NOS, MRV, CCB*

Abraxas: Guardian of the Universe ⅋½ **1990 (R)** Good space cop versus bad space cop with an ecological twist. Good-guy Abraxas (Ventura) has the task of stopping planets from destroying their environments and fighting senseless wars. His ex-partner Secundas (Ole-Thorsen) has his own mission, seeking an anti-life power which could destroy the universe. They decide to fight it out, using Earth as the battleground. Also available in an edited PG-13 version. **90m/C VHS.** Jesse Ventura, Sven Ole-Thorsen; ***Cameos:*** James Belushi. *PSM*

Abroad with Two Yanks ⅋⅋ **1944** Two Marine buddies on furlough exhibit slapstick tendencies while competing for the same girl. Along the way a big chase ensues with the two soldiers in drag. Typical wartime shenanigans likely to incite only weak chuckling or inspired snoozing. **81m/B VHS, Beta.** William Bendix, Dennis O'Keefe, Helen Walker, John Loder, George Cleveland, Janet Lambert, James Flavin, Arthur Hunnicutt; ***D:*** Allan Dwan. *LIV*

Absence of Malice ⅋⅋½ **1981 (PG)** High-minded story about the harm that the news media can inflict. Field is the earnest reporter who, after being fed some facts by an unscrupulous federal investigator, writes a story implicating Newman in a murder he didn't commit. Field hides behind journalistic confidentiality privilege to put off the outraged Newman, who loses a friend to suicide during the debacle. Interesting performances by Field and Newman. **116m/C VHS, Beta, LV.** Paul Newman, Sally Field, Bob Balaban, Melinda Dillon, Luther Adler, Barry Primus, Josef Sommer, John Harkins, Don Hood, Wilford Brimley; ***D:*** Sydney Pollack; ***W:*** Kurt Luedtke; ***C:*** Owen Roizman; ***M:*** Dave Grusin. Nominations: Academy Awards '81: Best Actor (Newman), Best Original Screenplay, Best Supporting Actress (Dillon). *COL*

The Absent-Minded Professor ⅋⅋⅋½ **1961** Classic dumb Disney fantasy of the era. A professor accidentally invents an anti-gravity substance called flubber, causing inanimate objects and people to become airborne. Great sequence of the losing school basketball team taking advantage of flubber during a game. MacMurray is convincing as the absent-minded genius in this newly colored version. Followed by "Son of Flubber." **97m/C VHS, Beta, LV.** Fred MacMurray, Nancy Olson, Keenan Wynn, Tommy Kirk, Leon Ames, Ed Wynn; ***D:*** Robert Stevenson; ***C:*** Edward Colman; ***M:*** George Bruns. Nominations: Academy Awards '61: Best Art Direction/Set Decoration (B & W), Best Black and White Cinematography. *DIS, BTV*

Absent Without Leave ⅋⅋½ **1995** Ed (McLachlan) marries his pregnant girlfriend Daisy (Hobbs) in 1942 before joining the army. When Daisy miscarries, Ed pledges to take her home even though it means leaving the army wihout permission. As the newleyweds travel across the New Zealand countryside, they struggle with the new demands of their relationship. **104m/C VHS.** *NZ* Craig McLachlan, Katrina Hobbs; ***D:*** John Laing. *LEO*

Absolute Beginners ⅋⅋ **1986 (PG)** Fervently stylish camp musical exploring the lives of British teenagers in the 1950s never quite gets untracked, although MTV video moments fill out a spare plot line. Based on a novel by Colin MacInnes. ♫Absolute Beginners; That's Motivation; Volare; Killer Blow; Have You Ever Been Blue?; Quiet Life; Having It All; Selling Out; Va Va Voom. **107m/C VHS, Beta, LV.** *GB* David Bowie, Ray Davies, James Fox, Eddie O'Connell, Patsy Kensit, Anita Morris, Sade Adu; ***D:*** Julien Temple; ***W:*** Richard Burridge, Don MacPherson. *NO*

Absolution ⅋⅋ **1981 (R)** Two English boys trapped in a Catholic boarding school conspire to drive a tyrannical priest over the edge of sanity. As a result, bad things (including murder) occur. Burton is interesting in sadistic character study. Not released in the U.S. until 1988 following Burton's death, maybe due to something written in the will. **105m/C VHS, Beta, LV.** *GB* Richard Burton, Dominic Guard, Dai Bradley, Andrew Keir, Billy Connolly, Willoughby Gray; ***D:*** Anthony Page. *SIM, TWE, FCT*

The Abyss ⅋⅋⅋ *L'Oeuvre au Noir* **1989 (PG-13)** Underwater sci-fi adventure about a team of oil-drilling divers pressed into service by the navy to locate and disarm an inoperative nuclear submarine. A high-tech thriller with fab footage underwater and pulsating score. The laserdisc version contains 27 extra minutes of footage. **140m/C VHS, Beta, LV.** Ed Harris, Mary Elizabeth Mastrantonio, Todd Graff, Michael Biehn, John Bedford Lloyd, J.C. Quinn, Leo Burmester, Kidd Brewer Jr., Kimberly Scott, Adam Nelson, George Robert Kirk, Chris Elliott, Jimmie Ray Weeks; ***D:*** James Cameron; ***W:*** James Cameron; ***C:*** Mikael Salomon; ***M:*** Alan Silvestri. Academy Awards '89: Best Visual Effects; Nominations: Academy Awards '89: Best Cinematography, Best Sound. *FXV*

Accatone! ⅋⅋⅋ **1961** Accatone (Citti), a failure as a pimp, tries his luck as a thief. Hailed as a return to Italian neo-realism, this is a gritty, despairing, and dark look at the lives of the street people of Rome. Pasolini's first outing, adapted by the director from his novel, "A Violent Life." Pasolini served as mentor to Bernardo Bertolucci, listed in the credits as an assistant director. **116m/B VHS.** *IT* Franco Citti, Franca Pasut, Roberto Scaringelli, Adele Cambria, Paolo Guidi, Silvana Corsini; ***D:*** Pier Paolo Pasolini; ***C:*** Tonino Delli Colli. *WBF, APD, INJ*

Acceptable Risks ⅋½ **1986 (R)** Toxic disaster strikes when a plant manager is ordered to cut costs and sacrifice safety at the Citichem plant. Predictable plot stars Dennehy as the plant manager who risks all and fights politicians to reinstate the safety standards. Meanwhile, Tyson is the city manager who tries to warn the town of a possible chemical accident that could have devastating effects on the community. Made for television drama that shamelessly preys on audience fears. **97m/C VHS, Beta.** Brian Dennehy, Cicely Tyson, Kenneth McMillan, Christine Ebersole, Beah Richards, Richard Gilliland; ***D:*** Rick Wallace. *PSM*

Access Code ⅋ **1984** Government agents attempt to uncover a private organization that has gained control of nuclear weapons for the purpose of world domination. A ragged patchwork of disconnected scenes meant to test the virtue of patience. **90m/C VHS, Beta.** Martin Landau, Michael Ansara, MacDonald Carey; ***D:*** Mark Sobel. *PSM*

Accident ⅋⅋½ **1967** A tangled web of guilt, remorse, humor and thwarted sexuality is unravelled against the background of the English countryside in this complex story of an Oxford love triangle. An inside view of English repression at the university level adapted for the screen by Pinter from the novel by Nicholas Mosley. Long-winded but occasionally engrossing character study with interesting performances. **100m/C VHS, Beta.** *GB* Dirk Bogarde, Michael York, Stanley Baker, Jacqueline Sassard, Delphine Seyrig, Alexander Knox, Vivien Merchant, Freddie Jones, Harold Pinter; ***D:*** Joseph Losey; ***W:*** Harold Pinter. Cannes Film Festival '67: Grand Jury Prize; National Board of Review Awards '67: 10 Best Films of the Year. *NO*

Accident ⅋½ **1983** Skate for your life. A hockey game turns into a nightmare when the roof over the arena collapses under the weight of too much ice and snow. One of the few hockey disaster films. **104m/C VHS, Beta.** Terence Kelly, Fiona Reid, Frank Perry; ***D:*** Donald Britlain. *TWE*

Accidental Meeting ⅋⅋½ **1993 (R)** A female version of "Strangers on a Train." Two women meet because of an auto accident and wind up talking about their lives. The main topic is man trouble and both "jokingly" plot to murder each other's man. Only, one woman does the deed and the other soon finds herself on the murderess' hit list. **91m/C VHS, Beta.** Linda Gray, Linda Purl, Leigh McCloskey, David Hayward, Ernie Lively, Kent McCord; ***D:*** Michael Zinberg; ***W:*** Pete Best, Christopher Horner. *PAR*

The Accidental Tourist ⅋⅋⅋½ **1988 (PG)** A bittersweet and subtle story, adapted faithfully from Anne Tyler's novel, of an introverted, grieving man who learns to love again after meeting an unconventional woman. After his son's death and subsequent separation from wife Turner, Macon Leary (Hurt) avoids emotional confrontation, burying himself in routines with the aid of his obsessive-compulsive siblings. Kooky dog-trainer Muriel Pritchett (an exuberant Davis) wins his attention, but not without struggle. Hurt effectively uses small gestures to describe Macon's emotional journey, while Davis grabs hearts with her open performance. Outstanding supporting cast. **121m/C VHS, Beta, LV, 8mm.** William Hurt, Geena Davis, Kathleen Turner, Ed Begley Jr., David Ogden Stiers, Bill Pullman, Amy Wright; ***D:*** Lawrence Kasdan; ***W:*** Lawrence Kasdan; ***C:*** John Bailey; ***M:*** John Williams. Academy Awards '88: Best Supporting Actress (Davis); New York Film Critics Awards '88: Best Film; Nominations: Academy Awards '88: Best Adapted Screenplay, Best Picture, Best Original Score. *WAR, BTV*

Accidents ⅋½ **1989 (R)** A scientist discovers that his invention has been stolen and is going to be used to cause worldwide havoc. He becomes concerned and spends the remainder of the movie trying to relieve himself of anxiety. **90m/C VHS, Beta.** Edward Albert, Leigh Taylor-Young, Jon Cypher; ***D:*** Gideon Amir. *TWE*

The Accompanist ⅋⅋½ **1993 (PG)** Centers around a Parisian diva Irene's (Safonova) relationship with her talented pianist Sophie (Romane Bohringer), amidst the clamor of WWII Europe. Sophie impresses Irene with her musical abilities, and takes on additional work as her housekeeper. Meanwhile, Charles (Richard Bohringer), Irene's husband, schmoozes with the Nazis to line his own pockets while she helps the war effort by having an affair with a member of the resistance (Labarthe). Unfortunately, Sophie starts to resent living in Irene's shadow. Adapted from the novel by Nina Berberouva. The Bohringers are father and daughter. French with subtitles. **111m/C VHS.** *FR* Elena Safonova, Romane Bohringer, Richard Bohringer, Samuel Labarthe, Nelly Borgeaud, Julien Rassam; ***D:*** Claude Miller; ***W:*** Claude Miller, Luc Beraud; ***M:*** Alain Jomy. *COL*

Accomplice ⅋½ **1946** Plodding whodunit with Arlen as a shy, bookish private eye hired by his old flame to locate her missing husband. His investigations uncover several murders and long after the viewers have put 2 + 2 together, the P.I. smells a rat. The missing husband was a ruse to divert him from the real scam-a bank heist. Painfully low-level excitement. **66m/B VHS.** Richard Arlen, Veda Ann Borg, Tom Dugan, Francis Ford; ***D:*** Walter Colmes. *NOS*

Accused ⅋⅋½ **1936** Married dancers Fairbanks and Del Rio are working in a Parisian revue when the show's sultry leading lady (Desmond) makes a pass at Fairbanks. Though he's turned her down, through a series of misunderstandings Del Rio believes the worst and the two women get into a vicious argument. When the star is found dead guess who gets the blame? Del Rio is lovely, Desmond is spiteful, and Fairbanks serves as a fine object of two women's affections. **83m/B VHS.** *GB* Douglas Fairbanks Jr., Dolores Del Rio, Florence Desmond, Basil Sydney, Athole Stewart, Esme Percy, Googie Withers, Cecil Humphreys; ***D:*** Thornton Freeland. *HCV*

The Accused ⅋⅋½ *Strange Deception* **1948** Young is cast against character in this story of a college professor who is assaulted by one of her students and kills him in self-defense. A courtroom drama ensues, where Young is defended by the dead man's guardian. Film noir with nice ensemble performance. **101m/B VHS, Beta.** Loretta Young, Robert Cummings, Wendell Corey, Sam Jaffe, Douglas Dick, Sara Allgood, Ann Doran; ***D:*** William Dieterle; ***C:*** Milton Krasner. *PAR*

The Accused ꝏꝏꝏ **1988 (R)** Provocative treatment of a true story involving a young woman gang raped in a bar while onlookers cheer. McGillis is the assistant district attorney who takes on the case and must contend with the victim's questionable past and a powerful lawyer hired by a wealthy defendant's parents. As the victim with a past, Foster gives an Oscar-winning performance that won raves for its strength and complexity. **110m/C VHS, Beta, LV, 8mm.** Jodie Foster, Kelly McGillis, Bernie Coulson, Leo Rossi, Ann Hearn, Carmen Argenziano, Steve Antin, Tom O'Brien, Peter Van Norden, Woody Brown; ***D:*** Jonathan Kaplan; ***W:*** Tom Topor; ***C:*** Ralf Bode; ***M:*** Brad Fiedel. Academy Awards '88: Best Actress (Foster); Golden Globe Awards '89: Best Actress—Drama (Foster); National Board of Review Awards '88: Best Actress (Foster). *PAR, FCT, BTV*

Ace Crawford, Private Eye ꝏꝏ **19??** Bumbling private eye struggles with confusing murder and somehow manages to solve the case. **71m/C VHS.** Tim Conway, Billy Barty, Bill Henderson. *MCG*

Ace Drummond ꝏꝏ *Squadron of Doom* **1936** The complete 13-chapter serial about a murder organization that tries to stop several countries from forming a worldwide clipper ship air service and government troubleshooter Ace Drummond who's out to stop them. **260m/B VHS, Beta.** John "Dusty" King, Jean Rogers, Noah Beery Jr.; ***D:*** Ford Beebe. *GPV, HHT, VCN*

Ace High ꝏ½ **1968** Spaghetti western about a ruthless outlaw named Cat Stevens trying to save himself from the noose. Patterned after the famous Sergio Leone-Clint Eastwood westerns, with less of a budget and more camp tendencies. **120m/C VHS, Beta.** *IT* Eli Wallach, Terence Hill, Bud Spencer, Brock Peters, Kevin McCarthy; ***D:*** Giuseppe Colizzi. *PAR, FCT*

Ace of Aces ꝏꝏ **1933** An American sculptor is reviled, particularly by his girlfriend, when he does not join fellows in enlisting in what becomes WWI. Out to prove he's not lacking testosterone, he becomes a pilot in France, but is embittered by his experiences. Dated but well-acted war melodrama. **77m/B VHS, Beta.** Richard Dix, Elizabeth Allan, Theodore Newton, Ralph Bellamy, Joseph Sawyer, Frank Conroy, William Cagney; ***D:*** J. Walter Ruben; ***M:*** Max Steiner. *TTC*

Ace of Hearts ꝏ **1985** A seedy story about a rich guy in the South Pacific who pays heavily to have himself killed. **90m/C VHS, Beta.** Mickey Rooney, Chris Robinson, Pilar Velasquez. *VCD*

Ace Ventura: Pet Detective ꝏꝏ **1993 (PG-13)** Shamelessly silly comedy casts human cartoon Carrey, he of the rubber limbs and spasmodic facial muscles, as Ace, the guy who'll find missing pets, big or small. When the Miami Dolphins' mascot Snowflake is kidnapped, he abandons his search for an albino pigeon to save the lost dolphin just in time for the Super Bowl. This is brain candy, running full throttle with juvenile humor, some charm, and the hyper-energetic Carrey, not to mention Young as the police chief with a secret. Critically trashed box office smash catapulted Carrey into nearly instant stardom after seven seasons as the geeky white guy on "In Living Color." **87m/C VHS, LV, 8mm.** Jim Carrey, Dan Marino, Courteney Cox, Sean Young, Tone Loc; ***D:*** Tom Shadyac; ***W:*** Jim Carrey, Tom Shadyac, Jack Bernstein; ***M:*** Ira Newborn. Blockbuster Entertainment Awards '95: Male Newcomer, Video (Carrey), Comedy Actor, Video (Carrey); Nominations: MTV Movie Awards '94: Best Comedic Performance (Carrey). *WAR*

Ace Ventura: When Nature Calls ꝏꝏ *Ace Ventura Goes to Africa* **1995 (PG-13)** Ace is back on the case as the pet dick (Carrey) ventures to Africa to restore peace among rival tribes by finding an albino bat that's M.I.A. Plot is secondary, however, to multi-million dollar man Carrey's outrageous brand of physical comedy combined with his unique ability to deliver junior high level lines with pseudo-suave savoir-faire. Contains only a handful of outstanding gags, the best with Ace and a mechanical rhino. Mainly for Carrey aficionados (of which there are many) and original "Ace" fans—the low-brow humor runs a bit thin by the end. **94m/C VHS, LV.** Jim Carrey, Ian McNeice, Simon Callow, Maynard Eziashi, Bob Gunton, Sophie Okonedo, Tommy Davidson; ***D:*** Steve Oedekerk; ***W:*** Steve Oedekerk; ***C:*** Donald E. Thorin; ***M:*** Robert Folk. MTV Movie Awards '96: Best Male Performance (Carrey), Best Comedic Performance (Carrey); Nominations: MTV Movie Awards '96: Best Kiss (Jim Carrey/Sophie Okonedo). *WAR*

Aces and Eights ꝏꝏ½ **1936** Gambler McCoy catches a fellow cardsharp cheating and the marshal runs the varmit out of town. When the cheater is murdered, the lawman suspects McCoy, who sets out to prove his innocence. Title refers to the "death hand" held by Wild Bill Hickok, killed while playing poker. Film opens with a shot of Hickok and a speech about gambler's luck. **62m/B VHS.** Tim McCoy, Jimmy Aubrey, Luana Walters, Wheeler Oakman, Earle Hodgins, Frank Glennon, Rex Lease, Charles Stevens, Joseph Girard, John Merton; ***D:*** Sam Newfield. *NOS, DVT, RXM*

Aces: Iron Eagle 3 ꝏꝏ **1992 (R)** Colonel "Chappy" Sinclair returns once again in this air adventure. He's been keeping busy flying in air shows when he stumbles across the nefarious activities of a Peruvian drug baron working out of a remote village. Sinclair recruits a team of maverick air circus pilots and they "borrow" a fleet of WWII vintage aircraft to raid the village, coming up against a fellow Air Force officer who turns out to be another villain. Lots of action and a stalwart cast. **98m/C VHS, LV.** Louis Gossett Jr., Rachel McLish, Paul Freeman, Horst Buchholz, Christopher Cazenove, Sonny Chiba, Fred Dalton Thompson, Mitchell Ryan, Robert Estes, J.E. Freeman; ***D:*** John Glen. *COL*

Aces Wild ꝏ½ **1937** Another poker title. Outlaws menace an honest newspaper until the lawmen show up and send them on their way. **62m/B VHS, Beta, LV.** Harry Carey Sr., Gertrude Messinger, Edward Cassidy, Roger Williams; ***D:*** Harry Fraser. *NO*

The Acid Eaters ꝏ **1967** Straight-laced desk jockeys spend their weekends exploring the realm of the senses. Includes nudity. **62m/C VHS.** Buck Kartalian, Pat Barringer; ***D:*** B. Ron Elliott; ***W:*** B. Ron Elliott, Carl Monson; ***M:*** Billy Allen. *SMW, TPV*

Acla's Descent into Floristella ꝏꝏ *Acla* **1987** Twelve-year-old Acla (Cusimano) is sold by his father to work underground in the sulfur mines for eight years. Repeatedly beaten by his owner, Acla runs away, but there are dire consequences for him and his family. Set in 1930s Sicily. Italian with subtitles. **86m/C VHS.** *IT* Francesco Cusimano, Tony Sperandeo; ***D:*** Aurelio Grimaldi; ***W:*** Aurelio Grimaldi; ***C:*** Maurizio Calvesi; ***M:*** Dario Lucantoni. *FCT*

Acorn People ꝏꝏ **1982** An unemployed teacher takes a summer job at a camp for handicapped children and learns sensitivity. Made-for-television weeper adapted by Tewkesbury from the book by Ron Jones. **97m/C VHS, Beta.** Ted Bessell, Cloris Leachman, LeVar Burton, Dolph Sweet, Cheryl Anderson; ***D:*** Joan Tewkesbury. *TLF*

Acqua e Sapone ꝏ½ **1983 (PG)** A young innocent model goes to Rome under the watchful eyes of an appointed priest-chaperon, but finds love, fun and other sinful things. Sudsy/romantic comedy. **100m/C VHS, Beta.** *IT* Carlo Verdone, Natasha Hovey, Florinda Bolkan, Elena Bolkan; ***D:*** Carlo Verdone. *INJ*

Across 110th Street ꝏꝏ **1972 (R)** Gritty, violent cop thriller in the blaxploitation genre. Both the Mafia and the cops hunt down three black hoods who, in a display of extremely bad judgement, knocked over a mob-controlled bank while disguised as police. Lots of bullets create buckets of blood. Filmed on location in Harlem. **102m/C VHS, Beta.** Anthony Quinn, Yaphet Kotto, Anthony (Tony) Franciosa, Paul Benjamin, Ed Bernard, Antonio Fargas, Tim O'Connor, Lewis Gilbert, Richard Ward; ***D:*** Barry Shear; ***W:*** Luther Davis; ***C:*** Jack Priestley. *MGM, FOX*

Across the Bridge ꝏꝏ½ **1957** A man on the run from Scotland Yard for stealing a fortune flees to Mexico, in the process killing a man and assuming his identity. An ironic twist and his love for a dog seal his final destiny. Steiger's psychological study as the fugitive is compelling. Based on a novel by Graham Greene. **103m/B VHS, Beta.** *GB* Rod Steiger, David Knight, Marla Landi, Noel William, Bernard Lee; ***D:*** Ken Annakin; ***M:*** James Bernard. *LCA*

Across the Great Divide ꝏꝏ½ **1976 (G)** Two orphans must cross the rugged snow-covered Rocky Mountains in 1876 in order to claim their inheritance—a 400-acre plot of land in Salem, Oregon. Pleasant coming-of-age tale with majestic scenery. **102m/C VHS, Beta.** Robert F. Logan, George Flower, Heather Rattray, Mark Hall; ***D:*** Stewart Raffill; ***W:*** Stewart Raffill; ***M:*** Angelo Badalamenti. *MED, VTR*

Across the Moon ꝏꝏ **1994 (R)** A road trip to the desert takes Carmen and Kathy away from their incarcerated boyfriends but into troubles with cowboys and prospectors. **88m/C VHS.** Elizabeth Pena, Christina Applegate, Tony Fields, Peter Berg, James Remar, Michael McKean, Burgess Meredith, Jack Nance; ***D:*** Lisa Gottlieb; ***C:*** Andrzej Sekula; ***M:*** Christopher Tyng, Exene Cervenka. *HMD*

Across the Pacific ꝏꝏꝏ½ **1942** Classic Bogie/Huston vehicle made on the heels of "The Maltese Falcon." Bogie is an American Army officer booted out of the service on false charges of treason. When no other military will accept him, he sails to China (via the Panama Canal) to offer his services to Chiang Kai-Shek. On board, he meets a variety of seedy characters who plan to blow up the canal. Huston again capitalizes on the counterpoint between the rotundly acerbic Greenstreet, who plays a spy, and stiff-lipped Bogart, who's wooing Astor. Great Bogie moments and fine direction make this an adventure classic. When he departed for the service just prior to filming the final scenes, Huston turned over direction to Vincent Sherman. Also available colorized. **97m/B VHS.** Humphrey Bogart, Mary Astor, Sydney Greenstreet, Charles Halton, Victor Sen Yung, Roland Got, Keye Luke, Richard Loo; ***D:*** John Huston. *MGM, FCT*

Across the Plains ꝏ½ **1939** Predictable oater about two brothers who are raised separately after their parents are murdered by outlaws. One is brought up by Indians, the other by the outlaws responsible for wiping out the folks, who tell the boy that Indians did in his ma and pa. Eventually the brothers meet and fight. Odds favor the good one winning, aided by Indian pals. **59m/B VHS, Beta.** Jack Randall, Frank Yaconelli, Joyce Bryant, Hal Price, Dennis Moore, Glenn Strange, Bud Osborne; ***D:*** Spencer Gordon Bennet. *NOS, GPV, DVT*

Across the Tracks ꝏꝏ **1989 (PG-13)** Two brothers, one a juvie-home rebel, the other a straight-A jock, are at odds when the black sheep is pressured into selling drugs. In an attempt to save his brother from a life of crime, the saintly one convinces his brother to join him on the school track team, and the brothers are forced to face off in a big meet. Fairly realistic good guy/bad guy who's really a good guy teen drama. Also available in an "R" rated version. **101m/C VHS.** Rick Schroder, Brad Pitt, Carrie Snodgress; ***D:*** Sandy Tung; ***W:*** Sandy Tung; ***M:*** Joel Goldsmith. *ACA*

Across the Wide Missouri ꝏꝏ½ **1951** Pioneer epic stars Gable as a rugged fur trapper who marries an Indian woman (Marques) so he can trap beaver pelts on her people's rich land. On the journey to the Indian territory however, the trapper truly falls in love with his bride. Superior historical drama is marred slightly by the use of narration (provided by Howard Keel). Look for lively performances from Menjou as a French tippler and Naish as the quirky Indian Chief. Beautiful scenery filmed in the spectacular Rocky Mountains. **78m/C VHS, Beta.** Clark Gable, Ricardo Montalban, John Hodiak, Adolphe Menjou, Maria Elena Marques, J. Carrol Naish, Jack Holt, Alan Napier; ***D:*** William A. Wellman; ***C:*** William Mellor. *MGM, CCB*

The Act 🦴🦴 *Bless 'Em All* **1982 (R)** A muddled satire about political double dealing and union corruption further muddled by a twangy musical score manufactured by folksy Sebastian. **90m/C VHS, Beta.** Jill St. John, Eddie Albert, Pat Hingle, Robert Ginty, Sarah Langenfeld, Nicolas Surovy; ***D:*** Sig Shore; ***M:*** John Sebastian. *VES*

Act of Aggression 🦴🦴 **1973 (R)** When a Parisian man finds his wife and daughter murdered at a summer resort, he takes the law into his own hands, with predictable results. **100m/C VHS, Beta.** *FR* Jean-Louis Trintignant, Catherine Deneuve, Claude Brasseur. *FCT*

Act of Passion: The Lost Honor of Kathryn Beck 🦴🦴½ **1983** A woman meets a man at a party and has the proverbial one-night stand. Her privacy is shattered when she discovers that he's a terrorist under surveillance by the police and press. Strong performances by Thomas and Kristofferson help turn this into an interesting American television remake of the German "Lost Honor of Katharina Blum," based loosely on a novel by Heinrich Boll. **100m/C VHS, Beta.** Marlo Thomas, Kris Kristofferson, George Dzundza, Jon DeVries; ***D:*** Simon Langton. *VMK*

Act of Piracy 🦴½ **1989 (R)** A bankrupt contractor reunites with his estranged wife to track down the brutal terrorists who have kidnapped their son. **105m/C VHS, Beta, LV.** Ray Sharkey, Gary Busey. *WAR*

Act of Vengeance 🦴🦴 *Rape Squad* **1974 (R)** A group of women band together to hunt down and exact revenge on the man who raped them. Exploitative action-filled thriller. **90m/C VHS, Beta.** Jo Ann Harris, Peter Brown, Jennifer Lee, Lisa Moore, Connie Strickland, Pat Estrin; ***D:*** Bob Kelljan. *NO*

Act of Vengeance 🦴🦴½ **1986** Drama about Jock Yablonski, a United Mine Workers official who challenged the president, Tony Boyle. Made for cable, based on fact, showing the events that led up to the murder of Yablonski and his family. Intriguing story lacking cinematic drive. **97m/C VHS, Beta.** Charles Bronson, Ellen Burstyn, Wilford Brimley, Hoyt Axton, Robert Schenkkan, Ellen Barkin, Keanu Reeves; ***D:*** John MacKenzie; ***W:*** Scott Spencer. *NO*

Acting on Impulse 🦴🦴 **1993 (R)** Impulsive, troublemaking movie star (Fiorentino) becomes a murder suspect when her producer is killed. This doesn't slow her down. She checks into a hotel with a major party attitude and manages to seduce a conservative businessman (Howell) and his junior exec (Allen) into helping her forget her troubles. And then the businessman's fiance turns up dead. Any connection? Made for cable television. **94m/C VHS.** Linda Fiorentino, C. Thomas Howell, Nancy Allen, Adam Ant. *ACA*

Action for Slander 🦴🦴½ **1938** A British army officer sporting the typical stiff upper lip is accused of cheating during a card game, and the slander mars his reputation until the case is taken to court. Dryly earnest and honest in its depiction of class differences in pre-war England. Based on a novel by Mary Borden. **84m/B VHS, Beta, 8mm.** *GB* Clive Brook, Ann Todd, Margaretta Scott, Ronald Squire, Francis L. Sullivan, Felix Aylmer, Googie Withers; ***D:*** Tim Whelan. *VYY*

Action in Arabia 🦴🦴 **1944** A newsman uncovers a Nazi plot to turn the Arabs against the Allies while investigating a colleague's murder in Damascus. The desert teems with spies, double agents, and sheiks as suave Sanders goes about his investigative business. Quintessential wartime B-movie. **75m/B VHS, Beta.** George Sanders, Virginia Bruce, Lenore Aubert, Gene Lockhart, Robert Armstrong, H.B. Warner, Alan Napier, Michael Ansara; ***D:*** Leonide Moguy. *TTC*

Action in the North Atlantic 🦴🦴 **1943** Massey and Bogart are the captain and first mate of a Merchant Marine vessel running the lone supply route to the Soviet Union. Eventually they wind up locking horns with a Nazi U-boat. Plenty of action and strenuous flag waving in this propagandorama. Gordon fans won't want to miss her as Massey's wife. Also available colorized. **126m/B VHS.** Humphrey Bogart, Raymond Massey, Alan Hale, Julie Bishop, Ruth Gordon, Sam Levene, Dane Clark; ***D:*** Lloyd Bacon. Nominations: Academy Awards '43: Best Story. *MGM, FCT*

Action Jackson 🦴🦴 **1988 (R)** Power-hungry auto tycoon Nelson tries to frame rebellious black police sergeant Weathers for murder. Being a graduate of Harvard and a tough guy, the cop doesn't go for it. Nelson eats up the screen as the heavy with no redeeming qualities, while Weathers is tongue-in-cheek as the resourceful good guy who keeps running afoul of the law in spite of his best efforts. Lots of action, violence, and a few sexy women help cover the plot's lack of common sense. **96m/C VHS, Beta, LV.** Carl Weathers, Vanity, Craig T. Nelson, Sharon Stone; ***D:*** Craig R. Baxley; ***W:*** Robert Reneau; ***M:*** Herbie Hancock, Michael Kamen. *ORI, WAR*

Action U.S.A. 🦴½ **1989** A young woman witnesses the murder of her boyfriend by gangsters, who then pursue her to make sure she will never tell what she saw. Throughout Texas she rambles with the mob sniffing at her heels, grateful for the opportunity to participate in numerous stunts and car crashes. **90m/C VHS, Beta.** Barri Murphy, Greg Cummins, William Knight, William Smith, Cameron Mitchell; ***D:*** John Stewart; ***W:*** David Reskin. *IMP*

Actor: The Paul Muni Story 🦴🦴 **1978** Musical biography of actor Paul Muni, from his beginnings as a traveling actor in Hungary to his New York theatre and movie career. **105m/C VHS, Beta.** Herschel Bernardi, Georgia Brown, Harold Gould. *LIV*

Actors and Sin 🦴🦴½ **1952** Two-part film casting a critical eye toward actors and Hollywood. "Actor's Blood" is the melodramatic story of Shakespearean actor Robinson and his unhappy actress daughter. She commits suicide and he sets out to prove it was murder. Heavy going. Lighter and more entertaining is "Woman of Sin," which relates a Hollywood satire involving a theatrical agent and his newest client, a precocious nine-year-old. **82m/B VHS, LV.** Edward G. Robinson, Eddie Albert, Marsha Hunt, Alan Reed, Dan O'Herlihy, Tracey Roberts; ***D:*** Lee Garmes, Ben Hecht. *COL*

An Actor's Revenge 🦴🦴 *Yukinojo Henge* **1963** In the early 19th century, a female impersonator in a Kabuki troupe takes revenge on the three men who killed his parents. Fascinating study of opposites—male/female, stage/life, love/hate. In Japanese with English subtitles. **110m/C VHS.** *JP* Kazuo Hasegawa, Fujiko Yamamoto, Ayako Wakao, Ganjiro Nakamura; ***D:*** Kon Ichikawa; ***W:*** Teinosuke Kinugasa, Daisuke Ito, Natto Wada; ***M:*** Yashushi Akutagawa. *NYF, ING*

Adam 🦴🦴🦴½ **1983** Television docu-drama based on a tragic, true story. John and Reve Williams (Travanti and Williams) desperately search for their 6-year-old son abducted during an outing. During their long search and struggle, they lobby Congress for use of the FBI's crime computer. Eventually their efforts led to the creation of the Missing Children's Bureau. Sensitive, compelling performances by Travanti and Williams as the agonized, courageous parents. **100m/C VHS, Beta.** Daniel J. Travanti, JoBeth Williams, Martha Scott, Richard Masur, Paul Regina, Mason Adams; ***D:*** Michael Tuchner. *NO*

Adam at 6 a.m. 🦴🦴 **1970 (PG)** Douglas is a young college professor who decides to spend a summer laboring in Missouri, where life, he thinks, is simpler. Of course, he learns that life in the boonies has its own set of problems, but unfortunately it takes him the entire movie before he catches the drift. **100m/C VHS, Beta.** Michael Douglas, Lee Purcell, Joe Don Baker, Charles Aidman, Marge Redmond, Louise Latham, Grayson Hall, Dana Elcar, Meg Foster, Richard Derr, Anne Gwynne; ***D:*** Robert Scheerer. *FOX*

Adam Had Four Sons 🦴🦴½ **1941** Satisfying character study involving the typical turn-of-the-century family nearly consumed by love, jealousy, and hatred. In the early part of the century, a goodly governess (Bergman in her second U.S. film) watches sympathetically over four sons of an American businessman after their mother dies. Economic necessity separates Bergman from the family for several years. Upon her return, she tangles with scheming bride-to-be Hayward, a bad girl intent on dividing and conquering the family before walking down the aisle with one of the sons. Based on a novel by Charles Bonner. **81m/B VHS, Beta.** Ingrid Bergman, Warner Baxter, Susan Hayward, Fay Wray, Richard Denning, June Lockhart, Robert Shaw; ***D:*** Gregory Ratoff. *COL*

Adam's Rib 🦴🦴🦴🦴 **1950** Classic war between the sexes cast Tracy and Hepburn as married attorneys on opposite sides of the courtroom in the trial of blonde bombshell Holliday, charged with attempted murder of the lover of her philandering husband. The battle in the courtroom soon takes its toll at home as the couple is increasingly unable to leave their work at the office. Sharp, snappy dialogue by Gordon and Kanin with superb direction by Cukor. Perhaps the best of the nine movies pairing Tracy and Hepburn. Also available colorized. **101m/B VHS, Beta, LV.** Spencer Tracy, Katharine Hepburn, Judy Holliday, Tom Ewell, David Wayne, Jean Hagen, Hope Emerson, Polly Moran, Marvin Kaplan, Paula Raymond, Tommy Noonan; ***D:*** George Cukor; ***W:*** Garson Kanin, Ruth Gordon; ***M:*** Miklos Rozsa. Nominations: Academy Awards '50: Best Story & Screenplay. *MGM, HMV*

The Addams Family **1964** The positively ooky family, based on the characters created by cartoonist Charles Addams, appear in the original, uncut television episodes. Two episodes per tape. This volume includes "The Addams Family Goes to School" and "Morticia and the Psychiatrist." **50m/B VHS.** John Astin, Carolyn Jones, Jackie Coogan, Ted Cassidy, Blossom Rock, Ken Weatherwax, Lisa Loring, Felix Silla. *WOV, MOV*

The Addams Family 🦴🦴 **1991 (PG-13)** Everybody's favorite family of ghouls hits the big screen, but something is lost in the translation. An imposter claiming to be long-lost Uncle Fester (Lloyd), who says he was in the Bermuda Triangle for 25 years, shows up at the Addams' home to complete a dastardly deed—raid the family's immense fortune. Although Fester's plan is foiled, a series of plot twists highlight the ghoulish family's eccentricities. Darkly humorous but eventually disappointing: Julia, Huston, and Ricci are great in their roles and the sets look good, but the plot is thin. Much closer to the original comic strip by Charles Addams than the popular TV show ever was. **102m/C VHS, Beta, LV.** Anjelica Huston, Raul Julia, Christopher Lloyd, Dan Hedaya, Elizabeth Wilson, Judith Malina, Carel Struycken, Dana Ivey, Paul Benedict, Christina Ricci, Jimmy Workman, Christopher Hart, John Franklin; ***Cameos:*** Marc Shaiman; ***D:*** Barry Sonnenfeld; ***W:*** Caroline Thompson, Larry Thompson; ***C:*** Owen Roizman; ***M:*** Marc Shaiman. Golden Raspberry Awards '91: Worst Song ("Addams Groove"); Nominations: Academy Awards '91: Best Costume Design. *PAR*

Addams Family Values 🦴🦴½ **1993 (PG-13)** The creepy Addams' are back, but this time they leave the dark confines of the mansion to meet the "real" world. New baby Pubert causes homicidal jealousy in sibs Wednesday and Pugsley, causing Mom and Dad to hire a gold-digging, serial-killing nanny (Cusack) with designs on Uncle Fester to watch over the tot. A step above its predecessor, chock full of black humor, sub-plots, and one-liners. Cusack fits right in with an outrageously over the top performance and Ricci nearly steals the show again as the deadpan Wednesday. **93m/C VHS, Beta, LV.** Anjelica Huston, Raul Julia, Christopher Lloyd, Joan Cusack, Carol Kane, Christina Ricci, Jimmy Workman, Kaitlyn Hooper, Kristen Hooper, Carel Struycken, David Krumholtz, Christopher Hart, Dana Ivey, Peter MacNicol, Christine Baranski, Mercedes McNab; ***D:*** Barry Sonnenfeld; ***W:*** Paul Rudnick; ***M:*** Marc Shaiman. Golden Raspberry Awards '93: Worst Song ("WHOOMP! There It Is"); Nominations: Academy Awards '93: Best Art Direction/Set Decoration; Golden Globe Awards '94: Best Actress—Musical/Comedy (Huston). *PAR*

The Addiction 🦴🦴½ **1995 (R)** Ph.D. candidate Kathleen Conklin (Taylor, in a haunting performance) gets bitten by more than the philosophy bug while attending university in Manhattan. When attacked by a female vampire (Sciorra), Kathleen quickly becomes driven by a ferocious blood need, beginning with an attack that parallels drug addiction when she stabs a derelict with a hypodermic needle and injects his blood into her own veins. Bitingly pretentious, themes experiment with the philosophy of Kirkegaard, Nietzche, and Sarte, and exploitative glimpses of the Holocaust and the My Lai massacre attempt to connect Kathleen's struggle to resist evil to historical atrocities. **82m/B VHS.** Lili Taylor, Christopher Walken, Annabella Sciorra, Edie Falco, Paul Calderone, Fredro Star, Kathryn Erbe, Michael Imperioli; ***D:*** Abel Ferrara; ***W:*** Nicholas St. John; ***M:*** Joe Delia. Nominations: Independent Spirit Awards '96: Best Actress (Taylor), Best Film. *PGV*

Adios Amigo 🦴🦴 **1975 (PG)** Offbeat western comedy has ad-libbing Pryor hustling as a perennially inept con man. Script and direction (both provided by Williamson) are not up to Pryor's level, although excessive violence and vulgarity are avoided in a boring attempt to provide good clean family fare. **87m/C VHS, LV.** Fred Williamson, Richard Pryor, Thalmus Rasulala, James Brown, Robert Philip, Mike Henry; ***D:*** Fred Williamson; ***W:*** Fred Williamson. *SIM, VMK*

Adios Gringo 🦴½ **1965** Routine oater in which a young rancher is swindled in a cattle deal and forced to kill in self defense. **?m/C VHS.** Montgomery Wood, Evelyn Stewart. *SNC*

Adios, Hombre 🦴 **1968** An innocent man who was imprisoned for murder escapes from prison and seeks revenge. You'll be saying adios as well. **90m/C VHS, Beta.** *IT* Craig Hill, Giulia Rubini; ***D:*** Mario Caiano. *UNI*

The Adjuster 🦴🦴½ **1991 (R)** Critics either loved or hated this strange film. Insurance adjuster Noah Render's clients look to him for all sorts of comfort, so much so that his own identity becomes a blurred reflection of their tragedies. Wife Hera is a film censor who secretly tapes the pornographic videos she watches at work. Their carefully organized lives are invaded by Bubba and Mimi, a wealthy couple who pass themselves off as filmmakers who want to use the Render house as a movie set. They are instead looking to involve the Renders in their latest and most elaborate erotic fantasy. Lots of symbolism, but little substance. **102m/C VHS.** *CA* Elias Koteas, Arsinee Khanjian, Maury Chaykin, Gabrielle Rose, David Hemblen, Jennifer Dale, Don McKellar, Raoul Trujillo; ***D:*** Atom Egoyan; ***W:*** Atom Egoyan; ***C:*** Paul Sarossy; ***M:*** Mychael Danna. Toronto-City Award '91: Best Canadian Feature Film. *ORI*

The Admiral Was a Lady 🦴🦴 **1950** Four ex-GIs try to get by in life without going to work. Hendrix walks into their lives as a winning ex-Wave gifted with a knack for repartee who is disgusted by their collective lack of ambition. Nevertheless, she is pursued by the zany quartet with predictable results. **87m/B VHS, Beta.** Edmond O'Brien, Wanda Hendrix, Rudy Vallee, Steve Brodie; ***D:*** Albert Rogell. *NOS, FRH, VHE*

Adomas Nori Buti Zmogumi 🦴🦴 *Adam Wants to Be a Man* **1959** Soviet Lithuanian feature in its original form, with dialogue in Lithuanian. A young worker scrapes together money for a ticket to Buenos Aires, but the money is stolen by the manager of the travel office. **90m/B VHS.** *RU LI* ***D:*** V. Zhalakyavichus. *IHF*

Adoption 🦴🦴🦴 *Orkobefogadas* **1975** The third of Meszaros's trilogy, involving a middle-aged Hungarian woman who longs for a child and instead forms a deep friendship with a 19-year-old orphan. In Hungarian with English subtitles. **89m/B VHS, Beta.** *HU* ***D:*** Marta Meszaros. Berlin International Film Festival '75: Golden Berlin Bear. *KIV, INJ*

The Adorable Cheat 🦴🦴 **1928** A low-budget, late-silent melodrama about a young woman who tries to get involved in the family business, despite her father's refusal of her help. Once in the business, she finds love. **76m/B VHS, Beta, 8mm.** Lila Lee, Cornelius Keefe, Burr McIntosh; ***D:*** Burton King. *GPV, VYY*

Adorable Julia 🦴🦴 **1962** When an actress takes on a lover many years younger than herself, the laughs begin to fly in this sex comedy based on W. Somerset Maugham's novel. **97m/C VHS.** *FR* Lilli Palmer, Charles Boyer; ***D:*** Alfred Weidenmann. *FCT, VEC*

Adrift 🦴🦴½ **1993** Yet another couple-in-terror-from-psychos-on-the-high-seas flick. Katie and Guy Nast (Jackson and Welsh) are on an anniversary sailing adventure intended to shore up their shaky marriage. They discover a boat adrift with two survivors (Greenwood and Rowan) who have a suspicious story but they help them nonetheless. Big mistake. Made for television. **92m/C VHS.** Kate Jackson, Kenneth Welsh, Bruce Greenwood, Kelly Rowan; ***D:*** Christian Duguay. *WOV*

The Adultress 🦴 **1977 (R)** When a husband and wife cannot satisfy their desire to have a family, they hire a young man to help them in this dumb made-for-television melodrama. **85m/C VHS, Beta.** Tyne Daly, Eric (Hans Gudegast) Braeden, Gregory Morton; ***D:*** Norbert Meisel. *NO*

Adventure 🦴🦴 **1945** Gable's first postwar film has him as a roughneck sailor romancing a shy and reserved librarian (Garson). Dull and disappointing—both stars deserve better. However, there is a touching scene of Gable with newborn child that might be of interest to some. Based on the novel by Clyde Brion Davis. **130m/B VHS.** Clark Gable, Greer Garson, Joan Blondell, Thomas Mitchell, Tom Tully, John Qualen, Richard Haydn, Lina Romay; ***D:*** Victor Fleming; ***W:*** Vincent Lawrence, Frederick Hazlitt Brennan; ***C:*** Joseph Ruttenberg. *MGM*

Adventure Island 🦴½ **1947** En route to Australia, a small ship stops at a remote island for supplies. The crew is greeted by a crazed, tyrannical leader who makes their lives difficult. Dull low-budget remake of 1937's "Ebb Tide." **66m/C VHS, Beta.** Rory Calhoun, Rhonda Fleming, Paul Kelly, John Abbott; ***D:*** Sam Newfield. *SNC*

Adventure of the Action Hunters 🦴 **1987 (PG)** A dying sailor leaves a tourist couple a message leading to a treasure, and they vie for it along with gangsters, mercenaries and other unsavory types. **81m/C VHS, Beta.** Ronald Hunter, Sean Murphy, Joe Cimino; ***D:*** Lee Bonner. *NO*

The Adventurer 🦴🦴½ **1917** An escaped convict saves two wealthy women from death. They mistake him for a gallant sportsman and bring him home. Early Chaplin silent with music track. **20m/B VHS, Beta.** Charlie Chaplin, Charles Halton; ***D:*** Charlie Chaplin. *CAB*

The Adventurers 🦴🦴 *Fortune in Diamonds; The Great Adventure* **1951** At the turn of the century, two Boers and an English officer set out to recover stolen jewels hidden in the jungles of South Africa. On the way, greed and anger take their toll a la "The Treasure of Sierra Madre," only on a less convincing scale. **82m/B VHS, Beta.** *GB* Dennis Price, Jack Hawkins, Siobhan McKenna, Peter Hammond, Bernard Lee; ***D:*** David MacDonald. *NOS*

The Adventurers *Woof!* **1970 (R)** Sleazy Harold Robbins novel retains its trashy aura on film. Unfortunately, this turkey is also long and boring. Set in South America, it tells the tale of a rich playboy who uses and destroys everyone who crosses his path. His vileness results from having seen his mother murdered by outlaws, but his obsession is to avenge his father's murder. Blood, gore, revolutions, and exploitive sex follow him everywhere. Watch and be amazed at the big-name stars who signed on for this one. **171m/C VHS.** Candice Bergen, Olivia de Havilland, Bekim Fehmiu, Charles Aznavour, Alan Badel, Ernest Borgnine, Leigh Taylor-Young, Fernando Rey, Thommy Berggren, John Ireland, Sydney Tafler, Rossano Brazzi, Anna Moffo, Christian Roberts, Yorgo Voyagis, Angela Scoular, Yolande Donlan, Ferdinand "Ferdy" Mayne, Jaclyn Smith, Peter Graves, Roberta Haynes; ***D:*** Lewis Gilbert. *PAR*

Adventures Beyond Belief 🦴 *Neat and Tidy* **1987** An irreverent motorcyclist is chased across Europe for a murder he didn't commit. Firmly within the boundaries of belief. **95m/C VHS, Beta.** Elke Sommer, Jill Whitlow, Graham Stark, Stella Stevens, Larry Storch, Thick Wilson, Skyler Cole, Edie Adams, John Astin; ***D:*** Marcus Thompson. *NO*

Adventures in Babysitting 🦴🦴½ **1987 (PG-13)** Pleasant comedy has its moments when a babysitter and her charges leave peaceful suburbia for downtown Chicago to rescue a friend in trouble. After a flat tire strands them on the freeway, trouble takes on a new meaning. Shue is charming as the hapless sitter, unexpectedly dateless, who finds herself doing a lot more than just watching the kids. Ludicrous at times, but still fun to watch. **102m/C VHS, Beta, LV, 8mm.** Elisabeth Shue, Keith Coogan, Maia Brewton, Anthony Rapp, Calvin Levels, Vincent D'Onofrio, Penelope Ann Miller, George Newbern, John Ford Noonan, Lolita Davidovich, Albert Collins; ***D:*** Chris Columbus; ***W:*** David Simkins; ***M:*** Michael Kamen. *TOU*

Adventures in Dinosaur City 🦴🦴 **1992 (PG)** Expect to see lots of movies riding on the coattails of the dino mania sweeping the land. Some will be good, others will not. "Adventures" falls into the latter category. Modern-day pre-teen siblings are transported back in time to the stone age. There they meet their favorite TV characters (they're dinosaurs) and help them solve prehistoric crimes. Family film may amuse kids, but adults should stick to "Jurassic Park." **88m/C VHS, LV.** Omri Katz, Shawn Hoffman, Tiffanie Poston, Pete Koch, Megan Hughes, Tony Doyle, Mimi Maynard; ***D:*** Brett Thompson; ***W:*** Willie Baronet, Lisa Morton; ***M:*** Fredric Teetsel. *REP*

Adventures in Spying 🦴🦴 **1992 (PG-13)** Brian McNichols is just trying to enjoy his summer vacation when he discovers that a notorious drug lord is living in his neighborhood. After realizing there is a $50,000 reward for his capture, he enlists the help of his friend (Schoelen) to get the man's picture for the police. Action-packed film is geared towards the junior high set, but relies too heavily on coincidence and other plot connivances to compete with espionage flicks directed at an older market. **92m/C VHS.** Jill Schoelen, Bernie Coulson, Seymour Cassel, G. Gordon Liddy, Michael Emil; ***D:*** Hil Covington; ***W:*** Hil Covington; ***M:*** James Stemple. *NLC*

The Adventures of a Gnome Named Gnorm 🦴🦴½ *A Gnome Named Gnorm* **1993 (PG)** Silly cop caper finds LAPD detective Casey (Hall) stuck with a very strange new partner—a bark-wearing gnome named Gnorm. The two team up to go after a diamond smuggling ring. The special-effects creature may hold the kiddies interest. **86m/C VHS.** Anthony Michael Hall, Jerry Orbach, Claudia Christian; ***D:*** Stan Winston. *PGV*

Adventures of a Private Eye 🦴 **1987** A self-mocking British detective farce about an inept private eye who takes his time tracking down a beautiful girl's blackmailer, bedding down with all the women he meets along the way. **96m/C VHS, Beta.** *GB* Christopher Neil, Suzy Kendall, Irene Handl; ***D:*** Stanley Long. *ACA*

Adventures of a Taxi Driver *Woof!* **1976** Cabbie finds sex, crime, sex, adventure and sex on the road in this off-duty comedy. **89m/C VHS, Beta.** *GB* Barry Evans, Judy Geeson, Adrienne Posta, Diana Dors, Liz Fraser; ***D:*** Stanley Long. *ACA*

The Adventures of Baron Munchausen 🦴🦴🦴½ **1989 (PG)** From the director of "Time Bandits," "Brazil," and "The Fisher King" comes an ambitious, imaginative, chaotic, and under-appreciated marvel based on the tall (and often confused) tales of the Baron. Munchausen encounters the King of the Moon, Venus, and other odd and fascinating characters during what might be described as an circular narrative in which flashbacks dovetail into the present and place is never quite what it seems. Wonderful special effects and visually stunning sets occasionally dwarf the actors and prove what Gilliam can do with a big budget. **126m/C VHS, Beta, LV, 8mm.** John Neville, Eric Idle, Sarah Polley, Valentina Cortese, Oliver Reed, Uma Thurman, Sting, Jonathan Pryce, Bill Paterson, Peter Jeffrey, Alison Steadman, Charles McKeown, Dennis Winston, Jack Purvis; ***Cameos:*** Robin Williams; ***D:*** Terry Gilliam; ***W:*** Terry Gilliam; ***C:*** Giuseppe Rotunno; ***M:*** Michael Kamen. Nominations: Academy Awards '89: Best Costume Design, Best Makeup. *COL, CRC*

The Adventures of Buckaroo Banzai Across the Eighth Dimension 🦴🦴🦴 *Buckaroo Banzai* **1984 (PG)** A man of many talents, Buckaroo Banzai (Weller) travels through the eighth dimension in a jet-propelled Ford Fiesta to battle Planet 10 aliens led by the evil Lithgow. Buckaroo incorporates his vast knowledge of medicine, science, music, racing, and foreign relations to his advantage. Offbeat and often humorous cult sci-fi trip. **100m/C VHS, Beta, LV.** Peter Weller, Ellen Barkin, Jeff Goldblum, Christopher Lloyd, John Lithgow, Lewis Smith, Rosalind Cash, Robert Ito, Pepe Serna, Vincent Schiavelli, Dan Hedaya, Yakov Smirnoff, Jamie Lee Curtis; ***D:*** W.D. Richter; ***C:*** Fred W. Koenekamp; ***M:*** Michael Boddicker. *VES, LIV*

The Adventures of Bullwhip Griffin 🦴🦴½ **1966** A rowdy, family-oriented comedy-adventure set during the California Gold Rush. Light Disney farce catches Russell at the tail end of his teenage star days. Pleshette and McDowall embark upon an ocean trip from Boston to San Francisco to find her brother, Russell, who's out west digging for gold. Assorted comedic adventures take place. **110m/C VHS, Beta.** Roddy McDowall, Suzanne Pleshette, Karl Malden, Harry Guardino, Kurt Russell; ***D:*** James Neilson; ***C:*** Edward Colman; ***M:*** George Bruns. *DIS*

Adventures of Captain Fabian 🦴½ **1951** When the captain of the "China Sea" learns that a beautiful woman has been falsely imprisoned, he comes to her rescue. Not one of Flynn's better swashbucklers, with typically low-quality Republic production. **100m/B VHS, Beta.** Errol Flynn, Vincent Price, Agnes Moorehead, Micheline Presle; ***D:*** William Marshall. *NO*

The Adventures of Captain Marvel 🦴🦴½ **1941** A 12-episode cliff-hanging serial based on the comic book character. Details the adventures of klutzy Billy Batson, who transforms into superhero Captain Marvel by speaking the magic word, "Shazam!" **240m/B VHS, LV.** Tom Tyler, Frank "Junior" Coghlan, Louise Currie; ***D:*** William Witney. *VCN, REP, MLB*

Adventures of Don Juan 🦴🦴🦴½ *The New Adventures of Don Juan* **1949** Flynn's last spectacular epic features elegant costuming and loads of action. Don Juan saves Queen Margaret from her evil first minister. He then swashbuckles his way across Spain and England in an effort to win her heart. Grand, large-scale fun and adventure with Flynn at his self-mocking best. Special laserdisc edition includes the original trailer. **111m/C VHS, Beta, LV.** Errol Flynn, Viveca Lindfors, Robert Douglas, Romney Brent, Alan Hale, Raymond Burr, Aubrey Mather, Ann Rutherford; ***D:*** Vincent Sherman; ***M:*** Max Steiner. Academy Awards '49: Best Costume Design (Color); Nominations: Academy Awards '49: Best Art Direction/Set Decoration (Color). *MGM, MLB*

Adventures of Eliza Fraser 🦴½ **1976** A young shipwrecked couple move from bawdy pleasures to cannibalism after being captured by aborigines. **114m/C VHS, Beta, LV.** Susannah York, Trevor Howard, Leon Lissek, Abigail, Noel Ferrier, Carole Skinner; ***D:*** Tim Burstall. *NWV*

The Adventures of Ford Fairlane *Woof! Ford Fairlane* **1990 (R)** The Diceman plays an unusual detective specializing in rock 'n' roll cases. When a heavy metal singer dies on stage, he takes the case in his own inimitable fashion, pursuing buxom gals, sleazy record executives and even his ex-wife. Not surprisingly, many of his stand-up bits are worked into the movie. Clay, the ever-so-controversial comic in his first (and likely last) starring role haplessly sneers his way through this rock 'n roll dud of a comedy thriller. A quick effort to cash in on Clay's fading star. Forget about it. **101m/C VHS, Beta, LV.** Andrew Dice Clay, Wayne Newton, Priscilla Presley, Morris Day, Lauren Holly, Maddie Corman, Gilbert Gottfried, David Patrick Kelly, Brandon Call, Robert Englund, Ed O'Neill, Sheila E, Kari Wuhrer, Tone Loc; ***D:*** Renny Harlin; ***W:*** David Arnott, Daniel Waters, James Cappe. Golden Raspberry Awards '90: Worst Picture, Worst Actor (Clay), Worst Screenplay. *FXV*

The Adventures of Frank and Jesse James **1948** The bad brothers of the Wild West are trying to make good for rip-offs committed in their names, so they're hoping to hit pay-dirt with a silver mine. A 13-episode serial on two cassettes. **180m/B VHS.** Steve Darrell, Clayton Moore, Noel Neill, Stanley Andrews; ***D:*** Yakima Canutt. *REP, MOV*

The Adventures of Frontier Fremont 🦴🦴 **1975** A rough and tumble story of a man who leaves the city, grows a beard, and makes the wilderness his home (and the animals his friends). Mountain life, that's the life for me. Almost indistinguishable from Haggerty's "Grizzly Adams," with the usual redeeming panoramic shots of majestic mountains. **95m/C VHS, Beta.** Dan Haggerty, Denver Pyle; ***D:*** Richard Friedenberg. *NO*

The Adventures of Gallant Bess 🦴🦴 **1948** The time-honored story of a rodeo man torn between his girl and his talented horse (the Bess of the title). **73m/C VHS.** Cameron Mitchell, Audrey Long, Fuzzy Knight, James Millican; ***D:*** Lew (Louis Friedlander) Landers. *HEG*

The Adventures of Hairbreadth Harry **192?** Three short spoofs of the early melodramas cranked out by the movie industry. Includes "Sawdust Baby," "Fearless Harry," and "Rudolph's Revenge." **65m/B VHS, Beta.** Billy West. *GPV*

The Adventures of Huck Finn 🦴🦴🦴 **1993 (PG)** Decent Disney attempt at adapting an American favorite by Mark Twain. Mischievious Huck and runaway slave Jim travel down the muddy Mississippi, working on life and friendship and getting into all sorts of adventures in the pre-Civil War era. Fast-paced and amusing with good performances by Wood (in the title role) and Broadway trained Vance (as Jim). Racial epithets and minstrel show dialect have been eliminated in this version. Some material, including Jim's close call with a lynch mob and Huck's drunken, brutal father may be too strong for immature children. **108m/C VHS, Beta, LV.** Elijah Wood, Courtney B. Vance, Robbie Coltrane, Jason Robards Jr., Ron Perlman, Dana Ivey, Anne Heche, James Gammon, Paxton Whitehead, Tom Aldredge, Curtis Armstrong, Mary Louise Wilson, Frances Conroy; ***D:*** Stephen Sommers; ***W:*** Stephen Sommers; ***C:*** Janusz Kaminski; ***M:*** Bill Conti. *DIS, BTV*

The Adventures of Huckleberry Finn 🦴🦴🦴 **1939** Mark Twain's classic story about a boy who runs away and travels down the Mississippi on a raft, accompanied by a runaway slave, is done over in MGM-style. Rooney is understated as Huck (quite a feat), while the production occasionally floats aimlessly down the Mississippi. An entertaining follow-up to "The Adventures of Tom Sawyer." **89m/B VHS, Beta.** Mickey Rooney, Lynne Carver, Rex Ingram, William Frawley, Walter Connolly; ***D:*** Richard Thorpe. *MGM, HMV*

The Adventures of Huckleberry Finn 🦴🦴½ **1960** A lively adaptation of the Twain saga in which Huck and runaway slave Jim raft down the Missisippi in search of freedom and adventure. Miscasting of Hodges as Huck hampers the proceedings, but Randall shines as the treacherous King. Strong supporting cast includes Keaton as a lion-tamer and boxing champ Moore as Jim. **107m/C VHS, Beta.** Tony Randall, Eddie Hodges, Archie Moore, Patty McCormack, Neville Brand, Mickey Shaughnessy, Judy Canova, Andy Devine, Sherry Jackson, Buster Keaton, Finlay Currie, Josephine Hutchinson, Parley Baer, John Carradine, Royal Dano, Sterling Holloway, Harry Dean Stanton; ***D:*** Michael Curtiz. *MGM, FCT*

The Adventures of Huckleberry Finn 🦴🦴 **1978** The classic adventure by Mark Twain of an orphan boy and a runaway slave done again as a TV movie and starring "F-Troop" regulars Tucker and Storch. Lacks the production values of earlier versions. **100m/C VHS, Beta.** Forrest Tucker, Larry Storch, Kurt Ida, Mike Mazurki, Brock Peters; ***D:*** Jack B. Hively. *NO*

The Adventures of Huckleberry Finn 🦴🦴½ **1985** An adaptation of the Mark Twain story about the adventures encountered by Huckleberry Finn and a runaway slave as they travel down the Mississippi River. Top-notch cast makes this an entertaining version. Originally made for television in a much longer version for PBS's "American Playhouse." **121m/C VHS, Beta.** Sada Thompson, Lillian Gish, Richard Kiley, Jim Dale, Barnard Hughes, Patrick Day, Frederic Forrest, Geraldine Page, Butterfly McQueen, Samm-Art Williams; ***D:*** Peter H. Hunt. *MCA, MON*

The Adventures of Ichabod and Mr. Toad 🦴🦴🦴½ **1949** Disney's wonderfully animated versions of Kenneth Grahame's "The Wind in the Willows" and "The Legend of Sleepy Hollow" by Washington Irving. Rathbone narrates the story of Mr. Toad, who suffers from arrogance and eventually must defend himself in court after being charged with driving a stolen vehicle (Disney did take liberties with the story). Crosby provides all the voices for "Ichabod," which features one of the all-time great animated sequences—Ichabod riding in a frenzy through the forest while being pursued by the headless horseman. A treat for all ages. **68m/C VHS, LV.** ***D:*** Clyde Geronomi, James Algar; ***V:*** Jack Kinney, Bing Crosby. *DIS, WTA*

Adventures of Kit Carson **1951** Television western, which ran from 1951-1955, set in the 1880s about the famed frontiersman who kept the peace with the help of Mexican sidekick El Toro. Two episodes per tape. **50m/C VHS, Beta.** Bill Williams, John Hamilton, Don Diamond. *MOV, MVC*

The Adventures of Marco Polo 🦴🦴½ **1938** Lavish Hollywood production based on the exploits of 13th-century Venetian explorer Marco Polo (Cooper). He becomes the first white man to record his visit to the Eastern court of Kublai Khan, where he falls for a beautiful princess also desired by the evil Rathbone. Lots of action, though its hard to picture the laconic Cooper in the title role. **100m/B VHS.** Gary Cooper, Sigrid Gurie, Basil Rathbone, Ernest Truex, George Barbier, Binnie Barnes, Alan Hale, H.B. Warner; ***D:*** Archie Mayo; ***W:*** Robert Sherwood; ***M:*** Hugo Friedhofer. *FCT*

The Adventures of Mark Twain 🦴🦴🦴 **1944** March stars as Mark Twain, the nom de plume of Samuel Clemens, the beloved humorist and writer. His travels and adventures along the Mississippi and on to the California gold rush would later result in the books and stories which would make him so well-known. March attains a quiet nobility as he goes from young man to old sage, along with Smith, who plays Olivia, Twain's beloved wife. **130m/B VHS, Beta.** Fredric March, Alexis Smith, Donald Crisp, Alan Hale, Sir C. Aubrey Smith, John Carradine, William Henry, Robert Barrat, Walter Hampden, Percy Kilbride; ***D:*** Irving Rapper; ***W:*** Alan LeMay, Harry Chandlee; ***M:*** Max Steiner. Nominations: Academy Awards '44: Best Interior Decoration, Best Special Effects, Best Score. *MGM, FCT, BTV*

The Adventures of Mark Twain 🦴🦴🦴 *Mark Twain* **1985 (G)** A clay-animated fantasy based on, and radically departing from, the life and work of Mark Twain. Story begins with Twain flying into outer space in a blimp with stowaways Huck Finn, Tom Sawyer and Becky Thatcher and takes off from there. Above average entertainment for kids and their folks. **86m/C VHS, Beta, LV.** ***D:*** Will Vinton; ***W:*** Susan Shadburne; ***V:*** James Whitmore, Chris Ritchie, Gary Krug, Michele Mariana. *BAR*

The Adventures of Milo & Otis 🦴🦴🦴 *Koneko Monogatari; The Adventures of Chatran* **1989 (G)** Delightful Japanese children's film about a farm-dwelling dog and cat and their odyssey after the cat is accidentally swept away on a river. Notable since no humans appear in the film. A record-breaking success in its homeland. Well received by U.S. children. Narrated by Moore. **89m/C VHS, Beta, LV.** *JP* ***D:*** Masanori Hata; ***W:*** Mark Saltzman; ***M:*** Michael Boddicker. *COL, RDG, HMV*

The Adventures of Nellie Bly 𝓑 **1981** Made for television "Classics Illustrated" story of Nellie Bly, a strong-willed female reporter doing her best to expose wrongdoings in the late 19th century. A decent performance by Purl is overshadowed by the general lack of direction. **100m/C VHS, Beta.** Linda Purl, Gene Barry, John Randolph, Raymond Buktenica, J.D. Cannon, Elayne Heilveil, Cliff Osmond; ***D:*** Henning Schellerup. *NO*

The Adventures of Ozzie & Harriet 195? Each volume in this 12-set series contains 4 episodes of the Nelsons' hit TV show from 1953-1964. Vol. 1 features 17-year-old Mary Tyler Moore doing the commercials. Vol. 2 features Mamie Van Doren as the housemother of Ricky's fraternity (some housemother!). The program was the prototype of family sitcoms. Original commercials included. Tapes are available for purchase individually. **56m/B VHS.** Ozzie Nelson, Harriet Hilliard Nelson, Ricky Nelson, David Nelson; ***D:*** Ozzie Nelson. *MOV*

The Adventures of Picasso 𝓑𝓑 **1980** A Swedish satire on the life of Picasso, dubbed in English. Don't look for art or facts here, or, for that matter, many laughs. **88m/C VHS, Beta.** *SW* Gosta Ekman, Lena Nyman, Hans Alfredson, Margareta Krook, Bernard Cribbins, Wilfrid Brambell; ***D:*** Tage Danielsson. *NO*

The Adventures of Pinocchio 𝓑𝓑½ *Pinocchio; Carlo Collodi's Pinocchio* **1996 (G)** Live-action version of Carlo Collodi's story about woodcarver Gepetto (Landau) who carves himself a puppet son (Thomas) who longs to be a real boy. Story differs from the Disney cartoon version in that it's a little darker and the cat, the fox, and the cricket have larger roles. Jim Henson's Craeture Shop provided the animatronic magic to bring Pinocchio to life. His head alone was jammed with wiring and 18 tiny motors to give the "boy" a full range of facial expressions. It took as many as five puppeteers at a time to animate the character. So lifelike was the puppet that some of the crew actually spoke to it as they did other actors. **?m/C VHS.** Martin Landau, Jonathan Taylor Thomas, Rob Schneider, Bebe Neuwirth, Udo Kier; ***D:*** Steven Barron; ***W:*** Steven Barron, Tom Benedek, Sherry Mills. *NLC*

The Adventures of Priscilla, Queen of the Desert 𝓑𝓑𝓑 **1994 (R)** Quirky down-under musical-comedy follows two drag queens and a transsexual across the Australian Outback on their way to a gig in a small resort town. They make the drive in a pink bus nicknamed Priscilla. Along the way they encounter, and perform for, the usual unusual assortment of local characters. Scenes depicting homophobic natives play out as expected. Finest moments occur on the bus or onstage (all hail ABBA). Strong performances, especially by usually macho Stamp as the widowed Bernadette, rise above the cliches in what is basically a bitchy, cross-dressing road movie, celebrating drag as art and the nonconformity of its heroes. Costumes (by Lizzy Gardner and Tim Chappel) are a lark, the photography's surreal, and the soundtrack fittingly campy. **102m/C VHS, LV.** *AU* Terence Stamp, Hugo Weaving, Guy Pearce, Bill Hunter, Sarah Chadwick, Mark Holmes, Julia Cortez; ***D:*** Stephan Elliott; ***W:*** Stephan Elliott; ***C:*** Brian J. Breheny; ***M:*** Guy Gross. Academy Awards '94: Best Costume Design; Australian Film Institute '94: Best Costume Design; Nominations: Australian Film Institute '94: Best Actor (Stamp), Best Actor (Weaving), Best Cinematography, Best Director (Elliott), Best Film, Best Screenplay; Golden Globe Awards '95: Best Actor—Musical/Comedy (Stamp), Best Film—Musical/Comedy. *PGV*

Adventures of Red Ryder 𝓑𝓑 **1940** The thrills of the rugged West are presented in this twelve-episode serial. Based on the then-famous comic strip character. **240m/B VHS, Beta.** Donald (Don "Red") Barry, Noah Beery Sr.; ***D:*** William Witney. *MLB*

The Adventures of Rex & Rinty 𝓑𝓑 **1935** An adventure serial in 12 chapters, featuring Rin-Tin-Tin, Jr. **156m/B VHS, Beta.** Kane Richmond, Harry Woods, Smiley Burnette; ***D:*** Ford Beebe, B. Reeves Eason. *NOS, VCN, DVT*

The Adventures of Rin Tin Tin 𝓑𝓑½ **1947** Chronicles the adventures of that crime-fighting dog, Rin-Tin-Tin. **65m/B VHS.** Robert (Bobby) Blake. *CCB*

The Adventures of Robin Hood 𝓑𝓑𝓑𝓑 **1938** Rollicking Technicolor tale of the legendary outlaw, regarded as the swashbuckler standard-bearer. The justice-minded Saxon knight battles the Normans, outwits evil Prince John, and gallantly romances Maid Marian. Grand castle sets and lush forest photography display ample evidence of the huge (in 1938) budget of $2 million plus. Just entering his prime, Flynn enthusiastically performed most of his own stunts, including intricate sword play and advanced tree and wall climbing. His Robin brims with charm and bravura, the enthusiastic protector of poor Saxons everywhere and the undeclared king of Sherwood forest. The rest of the cast likewise attacks with zest: de Havilland, a cold but eventually sympathetic Maid Marian; Rains' dastardly Prince John (the predecessor to Alan Rickman's over-the-top spin as the Sheriff in Costner's remake); and Rathbone's conniving Sir Guy to Robin's band of very merry men. Based on various Robin Hood legends as well as Sir Walter Scott's "Ivanhoe" and the opera "Robin Hood" by De Koven-Smith. Also available in letter-box format. **102m/C VHS, Beta, LV.** Errol Flynn, Olivia de Havilland, Basil Rathbone, Alan Hale, Una O'Connor, Claude Rains, Patric Knowles, Eugene Pallette, Herbert Mundin, Melville Cooper, Ian Hunter, Montagu Love; ***D:*** Michael Curtiz; ***W:*** Norman Reilly Raine, Seton I. Miller; ***M:*** Erich Wolfgang Korngold. Academy Awards '38: Best Film Editing, Best Interior Decoration, Best Original Score; Nominations: Academy Awards '38: Best Picture. *MGM, FOX, CRC*

The Adventures of Robin Hood 1955 Filmed on location in England and starring Greene as the legendary outlaw/hero, with Pleasance as the evil Prince John. Two episodes per tape. Volume 1 features "The Highlander" and "Tables Turned." Additional episodes are available. **60m/C VHS, Beta.** Richard Greene, Donald Pleasence. *MVC, MOV*

The Adventures of Rusty 𝓑𝓑½ **1945** Forties family film series begins with this classic boy-meets-dog story. Danny's dog dies in an accident and his widowed father has just remarried so the kid's feeling pretty bad. Then he meets neglected German Shepherd Rusty, a former police dog with an undeservedly bad rep. Naturally, boy and dog bond and even capture a couple of escaped convicts (and Danny learns to love his stepmom too). **67m/B VHS.** Ted Donaldson, Margaret Lindsay, Conrad Nagel, Gloria Holden; ***D:*** Paul Burnford; ***W:*** Aubrey Wisberg. *COL*

The Adventures of Sadie 𝓑𝓑½ *Our Girl Friday* **1955** Collins is stranded on a desert island with three men, two of whom continuously chase her around. Naturally, she falls for the guy who ignores her. Obvious sex comedy which plays on Collins' scantily-clad physical assets. Based on the novel "The Cautious Amorist" by Norman Lindsay. **87m/C VHS.** *GB* Joan Collins, George Cole, Kenneth More, Robertson Hare, Hermione Gingold, Walter Fitzgerald; ***D:*** Noel Langley; ***W:*** Noel Langley. *NO*

The Adventures of Sherlock Holmes 𝓑𝓑½ *Sherlock Holmes* **1939** The immortal Sherlock Holmes and his assistant Dr. Watson conflict with Scotland Yard as they both race to stop arch-criminal Professor Moriarty. The Yard is put to shame as Holmes, a mere amateur sleuth, uses his brilliant deductive reasoning to save the damsel in distress and to stop Moriarty from stealing the Crown Jewels. Second in the series. **83m/B VHS, Beta.** Basil Rathbone, Nigel Bruce, Ida Lupino, George Zucco, E.E. Clive, Mary Gordon; ***D:*** Alfred Werker; ***W:*** Edwin Blum; ***C:*** Leon Shamroy. *FOX*

The Adventures of Sherlock Holmes: Hound of the Baskervilles 1989 Holmes tackles the mysterious and long-lived curse of the Baskervilles. Made for British television. Fine acting, detailed production. A pleasure. **120m/C VHS.** *GB* Jeremy Brett, Edward Hardwicke. *MPI*

The Adventures of Sherlock Holmes' Smarter Brother 𝓑𝓑𝓑 **1978 (PG)** The unknown brother of the famous Sherlock Holmes takes on some of his brother's more disposable excess cases and makes some hilarious moves. Moments of engaging farce borrowed from the Mel Brooks school of parody (and parts of the Brooks ensemble as well). **91m/C VHS, Beta.** Gene Wilder, Madeline Kahn, Marty Feldman, Dom DeLuise, Leo McKern, Roy Kinnear, John Le Mesurier, Douglas Wilmer, Thorley Walters; ***D:*** Gene Wilder; ***W:*** Gene Wilder. *FOX*

Adventures of Smilin' Jack 1943 WWII flying ace Smilin' Jack Martin comes to life in this action-packed serial. Character from the Zack Mosley comic strip about air force fighting over China. **90m/B VHS, Beta.** Tom Brown, Sidney Toler; ***D:*** Ray Taylor. *SNC, NOS, VAN*

The Adventures of Tartu 𝓑𝓑½ *Tartu* **1943** A British secret agent, sent to blow up a Nazi poison gas factory in Czechoslovakia, poses as a Romanian. One of Donat's lesser films, in the style of "The 39 Steps." **103m/C VHS, Beta.** *GB* Robert Donat, Valerie Hobson, Glynis Johns; ***D:*** Harold Bucquet. *HHT, TIM, VEC*

The Adventures of Tarzan 𝓑𝓑 **1921** The screen's first Tarzan in an exciting jungle thriller. Silent. **153m/B VHS, Beta.** Elmo Lincoln. *VYY, GVV*

The Adventures of the Flying Cadets 𝓑½ **1944** Early aerial war adventure serial in thirteen complete chapters. **169m/B VHS, Beta.** Johnny Downs, Regis Toomey; ***D:*** Ray Taylor, Lewis D. Collins. *VYY, VCN, NOS*

The Adventures of the Masked Phantom 𝓑½ **1938** The adventures of the Masked Phantom. **56m/B VHS, Beta.** Monte Rawlins, Betty Burgess, Larry Mason, Sonny Lamont, Jack Ingram; ***D:*** Charles Abbott. *NOS, VYY, RXM*

The Adventures of the Wilderness Family 𝓑𝓑 **1976 (G)** The story of a modern-day pioneer family who becomes bored with the troubles of city life and heads for life in the wilderness. There, they find trouble in paradise. Family-oriented adventure offering pleasant scenery. Followed by "The Wilderness Family, Part 2." **100m/C VHS, Beta, LV.** Robert F. Logan, Susan Damante Shaw; ***D:*** Stewart Raffill; ***W:*** Stewart Raffill. *MED, VTR*

The Adventures of Tom Sawyer 𝓑𝓑𝓑 **1938** The vintage Hollywood adaptation of the Mark Twain classic, with art direction by William Cameron Menzies. Not a major effort from the Selznick studio, but quite detailed and the best Tom so far. **91m/C VHS, Beta, LV.** Tommy Kelly, Walter Brennan, Victor Jory, May Robson, Victor Kilian, Jackie Moran, Donald Meek, Ann Gillis, Marcia Mae Jones, Clara Blandick, Margaret Hamilton; ***D:*** Norman Taurog; ***C:*** James Wong Howe; ***M:*** Max Steiner. Nominations: Academy Awards '38: Best Interior Decoration. *FOX, FCT, MLB*

The Adventures of Tom Sawyer 𝓑𝓑½ **1973** Tom Sawyer is a mischievous Missouri boy who gets into all kinds of trouble in this white-washed, made for TV adaptation of the Mark Twain classic. **76m/C VHS, Beta.** Jane Wyatt, Buddy Ebsen, Vic Morrow, John McGiver, Josh Albee, Jeff Tyler. *MCA*

The Adventurous Knights *Woof!* **1935** An athlete learns he is the heir to a Transylvanian throne. **60m/B VHS, Beta, LV.** David Sharpe, Mary Kornman, Mickey Daniels, Gertrude Messinger; ***D:*** Edward Roberts. *NO*

The Adversary 𝓑𝓑½ *Pratidwandi* **1971** A young man must quit college because of his father's death. He struggles to find employment in Calcutta but his hardships are magnified by the impersonal society. In Bengali with English subtitles. **110m/C VHS.** *IN* ***D:*** Satyajit Ray; ***W:*** Satyajit Ray. *FCT*

Advise and Consent 𝓑𝓑𝓑 **1962** An interesting political melodrama with a fascinating cast, based upon Allen Drury's novel. The President chooses a candidate for the Secretary of State position which divides the Senate and causes the suicide of a senator. Controversial in its time, though somewhat turgid today. Laughton's last film. **139m/B VHS, Beta.** Don Murray, Charles Laughton, Henry Fonda, Walter Pidgeon, Lew Ayres, Burgess Meredith, Gene Tierney, Franchot Tone, Paul Ford, George Grizzard, Betty White, Peter Lawford, Edward Andrews; ***D:*** Otto Preminger; ***W:*** Wendell Mayes; ***C:*** Sam Leavitt. National Board of Review Awards '62: Best Supporting Actor (Meredith). *WAR, KAR, VTR*

The Advocate ♂♂♂ *The Hour of the Pig* **1993 (R)** Bizarre black comedy about 15th-century Paris lawyer Richard Courtois (Firth) who decides to ply his trade in the country, only to find things stranger than he can imagine. His first case turns out to be defending a pig that's accused of murdering a child. And the pig is owned by beautiful gypsy Samira (Annabi), so the idealistic lawyer can fall in love (or lust). There's religion and superstition, there's power struggles, there's ignorance versus knowledge— things sound very modern indeed. **102m/C VHS, LV.** *GB* Colin Firth, Amina Annabi, Nicol Williamson, Ian Holm, Lysette Anthony, Donald Pleasence, Michael Gough, Harriet Walter, Jim Carter; ***D:*** Leslie Megahey; ***W:*** Leslie Megahey. *MAX, TOU*

Aelita: Queen of Mars ♂♂ **1924** Though the title has blockbuster potential, "Aelita" is a little-known silent Soviet sci-fi flick destined to remain little known. After building a rocket to fly to Mars, a Russian engineer finds its no Martian holiday on the fourth planet from the sun, with the Martians in the midst of a revolution. Silent, with a piano score. **113m/B VHS, LV.** *RU* ***D:*** Yakov Protazanov. *KIV, FCT, SNC*

The Affair ♂♂♂ **1973** Songwriter/polio victim Wood falls in love for the first time with attorney Wagner. Delicate situation handled well by a fine cast in this television movie. **74m/C VHS, Beta.** Natalie Wood, Robert Wagner, Bruce Davison, Kent Smith, Frances Reid, Pat Harrington; ***D:*** Gilbert Cates. *NO*

The Affair ♂♂½ **1995 (R)** It's 1944 in a small English town, where a troop of black American soldiers are billeted prior to the D-Day invasion. Travis (Vance) falls for the married Maggie (Fox)—whose husband, Edward (Hinds), is supposed to be away at sea—and they begin an affair. Unfortunately, Edward arrives home unexpectedly and accuses Travis of raping his wife. If Maggie denies the accusation, she'll lose her home and family but if she confirms it, Travis, according to Army law, will be condemned to death. Made for cable TV. **105m/C VHS.** *GB* Courtney B. Vance, Kerry Fox, Ciaran Hinds, Beatie Edney, Leland Gantt, Bill Nunn, Ned Beatty; ***D:*** Paul Seed; ***W:*** Pablo F. Fenjves, Bryan Goluboff; ***C:*** Ivan Strasburg; ***M:*** Christopher Gunning. *HBO*

An Affair in Mind ♂♂ **1989** British television movie about a professional writer who falls in love with a beautiful woman who tries to convince him to assist her in murdering her husband. **88m/C VHS, Beta.** *GB* Amanda Donohoe, Stephen Dillon, Matthew Marsh, Kean-Laurent Cochot; ***D:*** Michael Baker. *FOX*

Affair in Trinidad ♂♂ **1952** Fun in the tropics as nightclub singer Hayworth enlists the help of brother-in-law Ford to find her husband's murderer. The trail leads to international thieves and espionage in a romantic thriller that reunites the stars of "Gilda." Hayworth sings (with Jo Ann Greer's voice) "I've Been Kissed Before." **98m/B VHS, LV.** Rita Hayworth, Glenn Ford, Alexander Scourby, Torin Thatcher, Valerie Bettis, Steve Geray; ***D:*** Vincent Sherman. Nominations: Academy Awards '52: Best Costume Design (B & W). *COL, CCB*

The Affair of the Pink Pearl ♂½ **1984** The husband-and-wife private investigation team of Tommy and Tuppence must find within 24 hours the culprit who stole a valuable pink pearl. Based on the Agatha Christie series of short stories. Made for British television. **60m/C VHS, Beta.** *GB* James Warwick, Francesca Annis. *TPV*

An Affair to Remember ♂♂½ **1957** McCarey remakes his own "Love Affair," with less success. Nightclub singer Kerr and wealthy bachelor Grant discover love on an ocean liner and agree to meet six months later on top of the Empire State Building to see if their feelings are the same. Not as good as the original, but a winner of a fairy tale just the same. Notable for causing many viewers to sob uncontrollably. "Affair" was gathering dust on store shelves until "Sleepless in Seattle" used it as a plot device and rentals skyrocketed. In 1994 real life couple Warren Beatty and Annette Bening attempted a third "Love Affair" remake. **115m/C VHS, Beta, LV.** Cary Grant, Deborah Kerr, Richard Denning, Cathleen Nesbitt, Neva Patterson, Robert Q. Lewis, Fortunio Bonanova, Matt Moore, Nora Marlowe, Sarah Selby; ***D:*** Leo McCarey; ***W:*** Leo McCarey, Delmer Daves; ***C:*** Milton Krasner; ***M:*** Hugo Friedhofer. Nominations: Academy Awards '57: Best Cinematography, Best Costume Design, Best Song ("An Affair to Remember"), Best Original Score. *FOX*

The Affairs of Annabel ♂♂½ **1938** The first of the popular series of Annabel pictures Lucy made in the late 1930s. Appealing adolescent is zoomed to movie stardom by her press agent's stunts. A behind-the-scenes satire on Hollywood, stars, and agents. **68m/B VHS, Beta, LV.** Lucille Ball, Jack Oakie, Ruth Donnelly, Fritz Feld, Bradley Page; ***D:*** Ben Stoloff. *CCB, IME, MLB*

The Affairs of Dobie Gillis ♂♂½ **1953** Light musical-comedy about a group of college kids and their carefree antics. Complete with big-band tunes, dance numbers, and plenty of collegiate shenanigans, this '50s classic inspired a hit TV series, "The Many Loves of Dobie Gillis." ♫I'm Through with Love; All I Do Is Dream of You; You Can't Do Wrong Doing Right; Those Endearing Young Charms. **72m/B VHS.** Debbie Reynolds, Bobby Van, Barbara Ruick, Bob Fosse, Lurene Tuttle, Hans Conried, Charles Lane; ***D:*** Don Weis; ***W:*** Max Shulman; ***C:*** William Mellor. *MGM*

Afraid of the Dark ♂♂ **1992 (R)** Convoluted psycho-thriller from a child's point of view. Young Lucas is fearful for his blind mother. It seems a vicious slasher has been attacking blind women and Lucas' father, a policeman, has yet to apprehend the criminal. But...Lucas it seems has a problem with reality. With his fantasies and realities mixed, all the people in his life also play entirely different roles. Characters are so detached and unreal that a viewer is prevented from a clear understanding of anything that may, or may not, be going on. Directorial debut of Peploe. **91m/C VHS, LV.** Ben Keyworth, James Fox, Fanny Ardant, Paul McGann, Clare Holman, Robert Stephens; ***D:*** Mark Peploe. *COL, NLC*

Africa Screams ♂♂½ **1949** Abbott and Costello go on an African safari in possession of a secret map. Unheralded independent A&C film is actually quite good in the stupid vein, with lots of jungle slapstick, generally good production values and a supporting cast of familiar comedy faces. **79m/B VHS, Beta, LV.** Lou Costello, Bud Abbott, Shemp Howard, Hillary Brooke, Joe Besser, Clyde Beatty; ***D:*** Charles T. Barton. *KAR, MRV, CNG*

Africa Texas Style ♂♂ **1967** An East African rancher hires an American cowboy and his Navajo sidekick to help run his wild game ranch. Decent family adventure which served as the pilot for the short-lived TV series "Cowboy in Africa." Features lots of wildlife footage and a cameo appearance by Hayley Mills. **109m/C VHS.** Hugh O'Brian, John Mills, Nigel Green, Tom Nardini; ***Cameos:*** Hayley Mills; ***D:*** Andrew Marton; ***M:*** Malcolm Arnold. *REP*

An African Dream ♂½ **1990 (PG)** A period tale about a black man and a white woman fighting against repression in South Africa. **94m/C VHS, Beta, LV.** Kitty Aldridge, John Kani, Dominic Jephcott, John Carson, Richard Haines, Joy Stewart Spence; ***D:*** John Smallcombe. *HMD, IME, FCT*

African Journey **1989** A moving, cross-cultural drama of friendship. A young black American goes to Africa for the summer to be with his divorced father who is working in the diamond mines. There he meets a young black African like himself; they overcome cultural clashes and learn respect for one another. Beautiful scenery, filmed in Africa. Part of the "Wonderworks" series. **174m/C VHS.** Jason Blicker, Pedzisai Sithole. *PME, HMV, BTV*

The African Queen ♂♂♂♂ **1951** After Bible-thumping spinster Hepburn's missionary brother is killed in WWI Africa, hard-drinking, dissolute steamer captain Bogart offers her safe passage. Not satisfied with sanctuary, she persuades him to destroy a German gunboat blocking the British advance. The two spend most of their time battling aquatic obstacles and each other, rather than the Germans. Time alone on a African river turns mistrust and aversion to love, a transition effectively counterpointed by the continuing suspense of their daring mission. Classic war of the sexes script adapted from C.S. Forester's novel makes wonderful use of natural dialogue and humor. Shot on location in Africa. **105m/C VHS, Beta, LV.** Humphrey Bogart, Katharine Hepburn, Robert Morley, Theodore Bikel, Peter Bull, Walter Gotell; ***D:*** John Huston; ***W:*** John Huston, James Agee; ***C:*** Jack Cardiff. Academy Awards '51: Best Actor (Bogart); Nominations: Academy Awards '51: Best Actress (Hepburn), Best Director (Huston), Best Screenplay. *FOX, FCT, TLF*

African Rage ♂♂ *Tigers Don't Cry; The Long Shot; Target of an Assassin; Fatal Assassin* **1978** Little known release about an aging male nurse (yes, Quinn) who discovers he's dying of an incurable disease. With nothing left to lose, he plans the kidnapping of an African leader, hoping that the ransom will support his family. Meanwhile, another man is plotting the same leader's death. Decent performances help move along the improbable plot. **90m/C VHS, Beta.** *SA* Anthony Quinn, John Phillip Law, Simon Sabela, Ken Gampu, Marius Weyers, Sandra Prinsloo; ***D:*** Peter Collinson. *MPI*

Afrita Hanen ♂♂♂ **1947** A rare Egyptian fantasy starring the famous Mid-Eastern actor, Farrid El Atrache. In Arabic with titles. **97m/B VHS, Beta.** Farrid El Atrache. *FCT*

After Dark, My Sweet ♂♂♂ **1990 (R)** A troubled young man in search of a little truth ends up entangled in a kidnapping scheme. Muddled direction is overcome by above average performances and gritty realism. Based on the novel by Jim Thompson. **114m/C VHS, LV.** Jason Patric, Rachel Ward, Bruce Dern, George Dickerson, James Cotton, Corey Carrier, Rocky Giordani; ***D:*** James Foley; ***W:*** Robert Redlin, James Foley; ***M:*** Maurice Jarre. *LIV*

After Darkness ♂ **1985** Slow-moving psycho-suspenser about a man obsessed with trying to remedy his twin brother's schizophrenia. **104m/C VHS, Beta.** *SI GB* John Hurt, Julian Sands, Victoria Abril, Pamela Salem; ***D:*** Dominique Othenin-Girard. *CEL*

After Hours ♂♂♂½ **1985 (R)** An absurd, edgy black comedy that's filled with novel twists and turns and often more disturbing than funny. An isolated uptown New York yuppie (Dunne) takes a late night stroll downtown and meets a sexy woman in an all-night coffee shop. From there he wanders through a series of threatening and surreal misadventures, leading to his pursuit by a vigilante mob stirred by ice cream dealer O'Hara. Something like "Blue Velvet" with more Catholicism and farce. Or similar to "Something Wild" without the high school reunion. Great cameos from the large supporting cast, including Cheech and Chong as burglers. A dark view of a small hell-hole in the Big Apple. **97m/C VHS, Beta, LV.** Griffin Dunne, Rosanna Arquette, John Heard, Teri Garr, Catherine O'Hara, Verna Bloom, Linda Fiorentino, Dick Miller, Bronson Pinchot; ***Cameos:*** Richard "Cheech" Marin, Thomas Chong; ***D:*** Martin Scorsese; ***C:*** Michael Ballhaus; ***M:*** Howard Shore. Cannes Film Festival '86: Best Director (Scorsese); Independent Spirit Awards '86: Best Director (Scorsese), Best Film. *WAR*

After Julius ♂♂ **1978** Twenty years after Julius Grace's death, his memory still hovers over his wife's and daughters' lives. British soap opera moves with glacier-like speed. Adapted from the book by Elizabeth Jane Howard. **150m/C VHS.** *GB* Faith Brook, John Carson, Cyd Hayman; ***D:*** John Glenister. *NO*

After Midnight ♂ *I Have Lived* **1933** An aspiring playwright tries to get his work produced, only to meet with dead ends. Eventually, he hooks up with a talented young actress with whom he finds romance and success. **69m/B VHS, Beta.** Alan Dinehart, Anita Page, Allen Vincent, Gertrude Astor; ***D:*** Richard Thorpe. *SNC*

After Midnight ☠☠ **1989 (R)** Suspended in a central story about an unorthodox professor who preys upon the deepest fears of his students, a trio of terror tales come to life. From the writers of "The Fly II" and "Nightmare on Elm Street, Part IV." Some chills, few thrills. **90m/C VHS, Beta.** Marg Helgenberger, Marc McClure, Alan Rosenberg, Pamela Segall, Nadine Van Der Velde, Ramy Zada, Jillian McWhirter, Billy Ray Sharkey; ***D:*** Jim Wheat. *FOX, MGM*

After Pilkington ☠☠ **1988** British television thriller about an uptight Oxford professor who runs into his bewitching childhood sweetheart after many years. She persuades him to help search for a missing archaeologist. **100m/C VHS, Beta.** *GB* Bob Peck, Miranda Richardson, Barry Foster; ***D:*** Christopher Morahan. *FOX*

After the Fall of New York *Woof!* **1985 (R)** Dim-witted post-apocalyptic tale set in New York after the fall of the "Big Bomb." A man, driven to search for the last normal woman, has reason to believe she is frozen alive and kept in the heart of the city. His mission: locate her, thaw her, engage in extremely limited foreplay with her, and repopulate the planet. A poorly dubbed dating allegory. **95m/C VHS, Beta.** *IT FR* Michael Sopkiw, Valentine Monnier, Anna Kanakis, Roman Geer, Edmund Purdom, George Eastman; ***D:*** Martin Dolman. *VES, LIV*

After the Fall of Saigon ☠ *Raiders of the Doomed Kingdom* **1988** Soldiers in Vietnam go on a killing rampage. Dubbed; country of origin isn't known. **100m/C VHS, Beta.** Danny Aswatep, Peter Ramwa, Rayak Ramnate, Krao Spartacus. *NO*

After the Fox ☠☠ *Caccia alla Volpe* **1966** Sellers is a con artist posing as a film director to carry out a bizarre plan to steal gold from Rome. Features occasional backhand slaps at Hollywood, with Mature turning in a memorable performance as the has-been actor starring in Sellers' movie. Though the screenplay was co-written by Neil Simon, the laughs are marginal. **103m/C VHS, Beta.** *GB IT* Peter Sellers, Victor Mature, Martin Balsam, Britt Ekland; ***D:*** Vittorio De Sica; ***W:*** Neil Simon; ***M:*** Burt Bacharach. *MGM, FOX*

After the Promise ☠☠ **1987** During the Depression, a poor carpenter tries to regain custody of his four sons following the death of his wife. Maudlin television melodrama based on a true story. **100m/C VHS.** Mark Harmon, Diana Scarwid, Rosemary Dunsmore, Donnelly Rhodes, Mark Hildreth, Trey Ames, Richard Billingsley; ***D:*** David Greene; ***M:*** Ralph Burns. *VTR, NWV*

After the Rehearsal ☠☠☠ **1984 (R)** Two actresses, one young, the other at the end of her career, challenge their director with love and abuse. Each questions his right to use them on stage and off. A thoughtful discussion of the meaning and reason for art originally made for Swedish television. Swedish with English subtitles. **72m/C VHS, Beta.** *SW* Erland Josephson, Ingrid Thulin, Lena Olin; ***D:*** Ingmar Bergman; ***W:*** Ingmar Bergman; ***C:*** Sven Nykvist. *COL, INJ*

After the Revolution ☠☠ **1990** A struggling novelist decides to write his next book from the viewpoint of his cat. In Hungarian with English subtitles. **82m/C VHS.** *HU* ***D:*** Andras Szirtes. *FCT*

After the Shock ☠☠ **1990 (PG)** Documentary-like dramatization of the San Francisco-Oakland earthquake of October, 1989 and, of course, its aftermath. Incorporates actual footage of the disaster. Made for cable. **92m/C VHS, Beta.** Yaphet Kotto, Rue McClanahan, Jack Scalia, Scott Valentine; ***D:*** Gary Sherman; ***W:*** Gary Sherman. *PAR*

After the Thin Man ☠☠☠ **1936** Second in a series of six "Thin Man" films, this one finds Nick, Nora and Asta, the lovable terrier, seeking out a murderer from Nora's own blue-blooded relatives. Fast-paced mystery with a witty script and the popular Powell/Loy charm. Sequel to "The Thin Man," followed by "Another Thin Man." **113m/B VHS, Beta.** William Powell, Myrna Loy, James Stewart, Elissa Landi, Joseph Calleia, Jessie Ralph, Alan Marshal; ***D:*** Woodbridge S. Van Dyke. Nominations: Academy Awards '36: Best Screenplay. *MGM*

Afterburn ☠☠☠ **1992 (R)** When Ted, her Air Force pilot husband, is killed in a crash of his F-16 fighter, Janet Harduvel learns the official explanation is pilot error. Convinced that something was wrong with his plane, Janet sets out to investigate, and eventually sue, military contractor General Dynamics. Dern turns in a great performance as the tough widow determined to clear her husband's name. Based on a true story; made for cable television. **103m/C VHS, LV.** Laura Dern, Robert Loggia, Vincent Spano, Michael Rooker, Andy Romano; ***D:*** Robert Markowitz; ***W:*** Elizabeth Chandler. *HBO, FCT*

Aftermath ☠½ **1985** Three astronauts return to Earth and are shocked to discover that the planet has been ravaged by a nuclear war. Quickly they make new plans. **96m/C VHS, Beta.** Steve Barkett, Larry Latham, Lynne Margulies, Sig Haig, Forrest J. Ackerman; ***D:*** Ted V. Mikels. *PSM*

Aftershock ☠½ **1988 (R)** A beautiful alien and a mysterious stranger battle the Earth's repressive, evil government. **90m/C VHS, Beta.** Jay Roberts Jr., Elizabeth Kaitan, Chris Mitchum, Richard Lynch, John Saxon, Russ Tamblyn, Michael Berryman, Chris De Rose, Chuck Jeffreys; ***D:*** Frank Harris. *PSM*

Afterward ☠ **1985** Made-for-British-television horror story about a family that moves into a supposedly haunted house with deadly results. **60m/C VHS, Beta.** *GB* Michael J. Shannon, Kay Harper, John Grillo. *PSM*

Against A Crooked Sky ☠☠ **1975 (G)** A young boy sets out with an elderly trapper to find his sister, who was captured by the Indians. Similiar story to "The Searchers," but no masterpiece. **89m/C VHS, Beta.** Richard Boone, Stewart Peterson, Clint Ritchie, Geoffrey Land, Jewel Blanch; ***D:*** Earl Bellamy. *LIV, VES*

Against All Flags ☠☠☠ **1952** An enjoyable Flynn swashbuckler about a British soldier slashing his way through the Spanish fleet at the turn of the 18th century. Though the story has been told before, tight direction and good performances win out. O'Hara is a tarty eyeful as a hot-tempered pirate moll. **81m/C VHS, Beta, LV.** Errol Flynn, Maureen O'Hara, Anthony Quinn, Mildred Natwick; ***D:*** George Sherman. *BAR, MCA*

Against All Odds ☠☠½ **1984 (R)** An interesting love triangle evolves when an ex-football player, played by Bridges, travels to Mexico to find his good friend's girlfriend. Contains complicated plot, numerous double crosses, sensual love scenes, and a chase scene along Sunset Boulevard. As the good friend sans conscience, Woods stars. A remake of 1947's "Out of the Past." **122m/C VHS, Beta, LV, 8mm.** Jeff Bridges, Rachel Ward, James Woods, Alex Karras, Jane Greer, Richard Widmark, Dorian Harewood, Swoosie Kurtz, Bill McKinney, Saul Rubinek; ***D:*** Taylor Hackford; ***C:*** Donald E. Thorin; ***M:*** Michel Colombier, Larry Carlton. Nominations: Academy Awards '84: Best Song ("Against All Odds (Take a Look at Me Now)"). *COL*

Against the Drunken Cat Paws ☠ **1975** A blind young martial arts student seeks to regain her sight and avenge the death of her father. **94m/C VHS, Beta.** Chia Ling, Ou-Yang Ksiek. *UNI*

Against the Wall ☠☠☠ **1994** Compelling and tense dramatization of the 1971 Attica, New York prison uprising in which 10 guards were held hostage and state troopers and the National Guard killed 29 prisoners before regaining control. Partially fictionalized version of the story told from the viewpoints of a young prison guard (MacLachlan) and a politicized prisoner (Jackson). Filmed at a prison in Clarksville, Tennessee. Made for cable television. **115m/C VHS, LV.** Kyle MacLachlan, Samuel L. Jackson, Clarence Williams III, Frederic Forrest, Harry Dean Stanton, Tom Bower, Philip Bosco, Anne Heche, David Ackroyd; ***D:*** John Frankenheimer; ***W:*** Ron Hutchinson; ***M:*** Gary Chang. *HBO*

Against the Wind ☠☠½ **1948** A motley crew is trained for a mission into Nazi Germany to blow up records and rescue a prisoner. The first half of the film focuses on the group's training, but despite its intensity they win only a pyrrhic victory. A well-done production with solid performances from the cast. **96m/B VHS.** Robert Beatty, Jack Warner, Simone Signoret, Gordon Jackson, Paul Dupuis, Peter Illing; ***D:*** Charles Crichton. *NOS, VEC*

Against the Wind ☠☠ *Contra el Viento* **1990** Juan (Banderas) takes refuge in a remote area of Andalusia in an effort to get away from a mutally obsessive love. But his exile is in vain when his lover appears—his sister (Suarez). Spanish with subtitles. **117m/C VHS.** *SP* Antonio Banderas, Emma Suarez; ***D:*** Paco Perinan. *FCT*

Agatha ☠☠½ **1979 (PG)** A speculative period drama about Agatha Christie's still unexplained disappearance in 1926, and a fictional American reporter's efforts to find her. Beautiful but lackluster mystery. Unfortunately, Hoffman and Redgrave generate few sparks. **98m/C VHS, Beta.** Dustin Hoffman, Vanessa Redgrave, Timothy Dalton, Helen Morse, Tony Britton, Timothy West, Celia Gregory; ***D:*** Michael Apted. Nominations: Academy Awards '79: Best Costume Design. *WAR*

Agatha Christie's Miss Marple **198?** Elderly, proper Jane Marple hardly seems the sort to get involved in murder and mayhem but her prim exterior hides a razor-sharp mind and intuitive understanding of criminal behavior. Two boxed collections. **65m/C VHS.** *GB* Joan Hickson. *VCO, AAE, NEW*

Age Isn't Everything ☠ *Life in the Food Chain* **1991 (R)** An appalling clumsy comedy about a recent college graduate who abruptly becomes an old man while retaining his youthful exterior. He looks the same, but walks slowly and talks with a thick Yiddish accent, get it? The cast just marks time until an inexplicable ending. **91m/C VHS.** Jonathan Silverman, Robert Prosky, Rita Moreno, Paul Sorvino, Rita Karin, Robert Cicchini, Brian Williams, Dee Hoty; ***Cameos:*** Dr. Joyce Brothers, Bella Abzug; ***W:*** Douglas Katz. *VES*

The Age of Innocence ☠☠☠ **1993 (PG)** Magnificently lavish adaptation of Edith Wharton's novel of passion thwarted by convention is visually stunning, but don't expect action since these people kill with a word or gesture. Lead performances are strong though perhaps miscast, with Ryder an exception. Outwardly docile and conventional, she nevertheless holds on to her husband with steely manipulation. Woodward's narration of Wharton's observations helps sort out what goes on behind the proper facades. Although slow, see this one for the beautiful period authenticity, thanks to Scorsese, who obviously labored over the small details. He shows up as a photographer; his parents appear in a scene on a train. **138m/C VHS, LV, 8mm.** Daniel Day-Lewis, Michelle Pfeiffer, Winona Ryder, Richard E. Grant, Alec McCowen, Miriam Margolyes, Sian Phillips, Geraldine Chaplin, Stuart Wilson, Mary Beth Hurt, Michael Gough, Alexis Smith, Jonathan Pryce, Robert Sean Leonard; ***Cameos:*** Martin Scorsese; ***D:*** Martin Scorsese; ***W:*** Jay Cocks, Martin Scorsese; ***C:*** Michael Ballhaus; ***M:*** Elmer Bernstein. Academy Awards '93: Best Costume Design; British Academy Awards '93: Best Supporting Actress (Margolyes); Golden Globe Awards '94: Best Supporting Actress (Ryder); National Board of Review Awards '93: Best Director (Scorsese), Best Supporting Actress (Ryder); Nominations: Academy Awards '93: Best Adapted Screenplay, Best Art Direction/Set Decoration, Best Supporting Actress (Ryder); Directors Guild of America Awards '93: Best Director (Scorsese); Golden Globe Awards '94: Best Actress—Drama (Pfeiffer), Best Director (Scorsese), Best Film—Drama. *COL*

Age Old Friends ☠☠☠½ **1989** Crusty octogenarian Cronyn must choose. His daughter (played by real-life offspring Tandy) wants him to move out of a retirement home and into her house. But he's struggling to keep neighbor and increasingly senile friend Gardenia from slipping into "zombieland." An emotional treat with two fine actors deploying dignity and wit in the battle against old age. Originally adapted for HBO from the Broadway play, "A Month of Sundays" by Bob Larbey. **89m/C VHS, Beta.** Vincent Gardenia, Hume Cronyn, Tandy Cronyn, Esther Rolle, Michelle Scarabelli; ***D:*** Allen Kroeker. *HBO*

The Agency ☠☠ *Mind Games* **1981 (R)** An advertising agency attempts to manipulate public behavior and opinion through the use of subliminal advertising. A good premise is bogged down by a dull script and plodding performances by all concerned.

Based on a Paul Gottlieb novel. **94m/C VHS, Beta.** *CA* Robert Mitchum, Lee Majors, Valerie Perrine, Saul Rubinek, Alexandra Stewart, George Kaczender; ***D:*** George Kaczender; ***M:*** Lewis Furey. *VES, MTX, VTR*

Agent on Ice **1986 (R)** Hockey team is stalked by lawyers. No, wait. An ex-CIA agent is stalked for cover-up purposes by the agency and the mob. One slippery fellow. **96m/C VHS, Beta.** Tom Ormeny, Clifford David, Louis Pastore, Matt Craven; ***D:*** Clark Worswick. *VTR, NWV*

Aggie Appleby, Maker of Men ½ *Cupid in the Rough* **1933** A wimpy society boy transforms himself into a tough guy, all for the love of a dame. Based on a play by Joseph O. Kesselring. Very slight comedy. **73m/B VHS.** Charles Farrell, Wynne Gibson, William Gargan, ZaSu Pitts; ***D:*** Mark Sandrich; ***M:*** Max Steiner. *FCT*

Agnes of God **1985 (PG-13)** Stage to screen translation of John Pielmeier's play loses something in the translation. Coarse chain-smoking psychiatrist Fonda is sent to a convent to investigate whether young nun Tilly is fit to stand trial. Seems that the nun may have given birth to and then strangled her baby, although she denies ever having sexual relations and knows nothing about an infant. Naive Tilly is frightened by probing Fonda, while worldly mother-superior Bancroft is distrusting. Melodramatic stew of Catholicism, religious fervor, and science features generally good performances, although Fonda often seems to be acting (maybe it's the cigarettes). **99m/C VHS, Beta, LV.** Jane Fonda, Anne Bancroft, Meg Tilly, Anne Pitoniak, Winston Reckert, Gratien Gelinas; ***D:*** Norman Jewison; ***W:*** John Pielmeier; ***C:*** Sven Nykvist; ***M:*** Georges Delerue. Golden Globe Awards '86: Best Supporting Actress (Tilly); Nominations: Academy Awards '85: Best Actress (Bancroft), Best Supporting Actress (Tilly), Best Original Score. *COL*

The Agony and the Ecstasy ½ **1965** Big-budget (for 1965 anyway at $12 million) adaptation of the Irving Stone book recounts the conflict between Michelangelo and Pope Julius II after His Holiness directs the artist to paint the Sistine Chapel. Follow the tortured artist through his unpredictable creative process and the hours (it seems literal due to movie length) of painting flat on his back. Heston exudes quiet strength in his sincere interpretation of the genius artist, while Harrison has a fling as the Pope. Slow script is not up to the generally good performances. Disappointing at the box office, but worth a look on the small screen for the sets alone. **136m/C VHS, Beta, LV.** Charlton Heston, Rex Harrison, Harry Andrews, Diane Cilento, Alberto Lupo, Adolfo Celi; ***D:*** Carol Reed; ***W:*** Philip Dunne; ***C:*** Leon Shamroy; ***M:*** Jerry Goldsmith, Alex North. National Board of Review Awards '65: Best Supporting Actor (Andrews); Nominations: Academy Awards '65: Best Art Direction/Set Decoration (Color), Best Color Cinematography, Best Costume Design (Color), Best Sound, Best Original Score. *FOX, IGP*

Agony of Love **1966** An unhappy homemaker rents a nearby apartment to live out her wildest fantasies and bring some excitment into her otherwise dull life. **?m/C VHS.** *SMW, TPV*

Aguirre, the Wrath of God ½ **1972** Herzog at his best, combining brilliant poetic images and an intense narrative dealing with power, irony, and death. Spanish conquistadors in 1590 search for the mythical city of gold in Peru. Instead, they descend into the hell of the jungle. Kinski is fabulous as Aquirre, succumbing to insanity while leading a continually diminishing crew in this compelling, extraordinary drama shot in the jungles of South America. Both English- and German-language versions available. **94m/C VHS.** *GE* Klaus Kinski, Ruy Guerra, Del Negro, Helena Rojo, Cecilia Rivera, Peter Berling, Danny Ades; ***D:*** Werner Herzog; ***W:*** Werner Herzog. National Society of Film Critics Awards '77: Best Cinematography. *NYF, APD, INJ*

Ah, Wilderness! ½ **1935** Delightful tale of a teen boy coming of age in small town America. Watch for the hilarious high school graduation scene. Based on the play by Eugene O'Neill. Remade in 1948 as "Summer Holiday," a musical with Mickey Rooney in the lead. **101m/B VHS.** Wallace Beery, Lionel Barrymore, Aline MacMahon, Eric Linden, Cecilia Parker, Spring Byington, Mickey Rooney, Charley Grapewin, Frank Albertson; ***D:*** Clarence Brown; ***C:*** Clyde De Vinna. *MGM, BTV*

Ain't No Way Back **1989** Two hunters stumble upon a feudin' bunch of moonshiners and must leave their city ways behind if they plan to survive. **90m/C VHS, Beta.** *NO*

Air America **1990 (R)** It's the Vietnam War and the CIA is operating a secret drug smuggling operation in Southeast Asia to finance the effort. Flyboys Gibson and Downey drop opium and glib lines all over Laos. Big-budget Gibson vehicle with sufficient action but lacking much of a story, which was adapted from a book by Christopher Robbins. **113m/C VHS, Beta, LV.** Mel Gibson, Robert Downey Jr., Marshall Bell, Nancy Travis, David Marshall Grant, Tim Thomerson, Lane Smith; ***D:*** Roger Spottiswoode; ***W:*** Richard Rush. *LIV, IME*

Air Force ½ **1943** One of the finest of the WWII movies, Hawks' exciting classic has worn well through the years, in spite of the Japanese propaganda. It follows the hazardous exploits of a Boeing B-17 bomber crew who fight over Pearl Harbor, Manila, and the Coral Sea. Extremely realistic dogfight sequences and powerful, introspective real guy interfacing by the ensemble cast are masterfully combined by Hawks. **124m/B VHS.** John Garfield, John Ridgely, Gig Young, Arthur Kennedy, Charles Drake, Harry Carey Sr., George Tobias; ***D:*** Howard Hawks; ***C:*** James Wong Howe. Academy Awards '43: Best Film Editing; Nominations: Academy Awards '43: Best Black and White Cinematography, Best Original Screenplay. *FOX*

Air Hawk **1984** Australian made for TV release details the adventures of an outback pilot involved with stolen diamonds. **90m/C VHS, Beta.** *AU* Eric Oldfield, Louise Howitt, Ellie MacLure, David Robson, David Baker; ***D:*** David Baker. *VCD*

Air Raid Wardens ½ **1943** Laurel & Hardy play a couple of small-town failures who become the local air raid wardens during WWII. They even manage to make a mess of this but redeem themselves when they overhear a spy plot and save the town's munitions factory from a German spy ring. A so-so effort from the comic duo. **67m/B VHS.** Stan Laurel, Oliver Hardy, Edgar Kennedy, Jacqueline White, Stephen McNally, Russell Hicks, Howard Freeman, Donald Meek, Henry O'Neill; ***D:*** Edward Sedgwick. *MGM*

The Air Up There **1994 (PG)** Assistant basketball coach Jimmy Dolan (Bacon) heads to the African village of Winabi to recruit talented (and tall) Saleh (Maina) to play b-ball in the U.S. But Saleh is next in line to be the tribe's king and doesn't want to leave. Stupid American in foreign country learning from the natives story is lighthearted, but relies heavily on formula—and borders on the stereotypical, though climatic game is a lot of fun. **108m/C VHS, LV.** Kevin Bacon, Charles Gitona Maina, Sean McCann, Dennis Patrick; ***D:*** Paul Michael Glaser; ***W:*** Max Apple; ***M:*** David Newman. *HPH*

Airborne ½ **1993 (PG)** Cool California rollerblade dude gets transplanted to Cincinnati for a school year, and has to prove himself when those good ol' midwestern boys come after him. Nothing short of a skate vehicle appealing largely, if not solely, to the high school contingent. **91m/C VHS, Beta, LV.** Shane McDermott, Seth Green, Brittney Powell, Edie McClurg; ***D:*** Rob Bowman; ***W:*** Bill Apablasa; ***M:*** Stewart Copeland. *WAR*

Airheads ½ **1994 (PG-13)** "Wayne's World" meets "Dog Day Afternoon." Silly farce has three metal heads (Buscemi, Fraser, Sandler) holding a radio station hostage in order to get their demo tape played. Events snowball and they receive instant fame. Cast and crew rich with subversive comedic talents, including Sandler and Farley from "Saturday Night Live." Soundtrack authenticity supplied by White Zombie and The Galatic Cowboys. **81m/C VHS, LV.** Brendan Fraser, Steve Buscemi, Adam Sandler, Chris Farley, Michael McKean, Judd Nelson, Joe Mantegna, Michael Richards, Ernie Hudson, Amy Locane, Nina Siemaszko, John Melendez; ***D:*** Michael Lehmann; ***W:*** Rich Wilkes; ***M:*** Carter Burwell. *FXV*

Airplane! ½ **1980 (PG)** Classic lampoon of disaster flicks is stupid but funny and launched a bevy wanna-be spoofs. A former pilot who's lost both his girl (she's the attendant) and his nerve takes over the controls of a jet when the crew is hit with food poisoning. The passengers become increasingly crazed and ground support more surreal as our hero struggles to land the plane. Clever, fast-paced, and very funny parody mangles every Hollywood cliche within reach. The gags are so furiously paced that when one bombs it's hardly noticeable. Launched Nielsen's second career as a comic actor. And it ain't over till it's over: don't miss the amusing final credits. Followed by "Airplane 2: The Sequel." **88m/C VHS, Beta, LV, 8mm.** Robert Hays, Julie Hagerty, Lloyd Bridges, Peter Graves, Robert Stack, Kareem Abdul-Jabbar, Leslie Nielsen, Stephen Stucker; ***Cameos:*** Ethel Merman, Barbara Billingsley; ***D:*** Jerry Zucker, Jim Abrahams, David Zucker; ***W:*** Jerry Zucker, Jim Abrahams, David Zucker; ***C:*** Joseph Biroc; ***M:*** Elmer Bernstein. Writers Guild of America '80: Best Adapted Screenplay. *PAR*

Airplane 2: The Sequel **1982 (PG)** Not a Zucker, Abrahams and Zucker effort, and sorely missing their slapstick and script finesse. The first passenger space shuttle has taken off for the moon and there's a mad bomber on board. Given the number of stars mugging, it's more of a loveboat in space than a fitting sequel to "Airplane." Nonetheless, some funny laughs and gags. **84m/C VHS, Beta, LV.** Robert Hays, Julie Hagerty, Lloyd Bridges, Raymond Burr, Peter Graves, William Shatner, Sonny Bono, Chuck Connors, Chad Everett, Stephen Stucker, Rip Torn, Ken Finkleman, Sandahl Bergman; ***D:*** Ken Finkleman; ***C:*** Joseph Biroc; ***M:*** Elmer Bernstein. *PAR*

Airport **1970 (G)** Old-fashioned disaster thriller built around an all-star cast, fairly moronic script, and an unavoidable accident during the flight of a passenger airliner. A box-office hit that paved the way for many lesser disaster flicks (including its many sequels) detailing the reactions of the passengers and crew as they cope with impending doom. Considered to be the best of the "Airport" series; adapted from the Arthur Hailey novel. **137m/C VHS, Beta, LV.** Dean Martin, Burt Lancaster, Jean Seberg, Jacqueline Bisset, George Kennedy, Helen Hayes, Van Heflin, Maureen Stapleton, Barry Nelson, Lloyd Nolan; ***D:*** George Seaton; ***W:*** George Seaton; ***C:*** Ernest Laszlo. Academy Awards '70: Best Supporting Actress (Hayes); Golden Globe Awards '71: Best Supporting Actress (Stapleton); Nominations: Academy Awards '70: Best Adapted Screenplay, Best Art Direction/Set Decoration, Best Cinematography, Best Costume Design, Best Film Editing, Best Picture, Best Sound, Best Supporting Actress (Stapleton), Best Original Score. *MCA, BTV*

Airport '75 **1975 (PG)** After a mid-air collision, a jumbo 747 is left pilotless. Airline attendant Black must fly da plane. She does her cross-eyed best in this absurd sequel to "Airport" built around a lesser "all-star cast." Safe on the ground, Heston tries to talk the airline hostess/pilot into landing, while the impatient Kennedy continues to grouse as leader of the foam-ready ground crew. A slick, insincere attempt to find box office magic again (which unfortunately worked, leading to two more sequels). **107m/C VHS, Beta.** Charlton Heston, Karen Black, George Kennedy, Gloria Swanson, Helen Reddy, Sid Caesar, Efrem Zimbalist Jr., Susan Clark, Dana Andrews, Linda Blair, Myrna Loy; ***D:*** Jack Smight. *GKK*

Airport '77 **1977 (PG)** Billionaire Stewart fills his converted passenger jet with priceless art and sets off to Palm Beach for a museum opening, joined by an uninvited gang of hijackers. Twist to this in-flight disaster is that the bad time in the air occurs underwater, a novel (and some might say, desperate) twist to the old panic in the plane we're all gonna die formula. With a cast of familiar faces, some of them stars and some of them just familiar faces, this is yet another sequel to "Airport" and another box-office success, leading to the last of the tired series in 1979. **114m/C VHS, Beta, LV.** Jack Lemmon, James Stewart, Lee Grant, Brenda Vaccaro, Joseph Cotten, Olivia de Havilland, Darren McGavin, Christopher Lee, George Kennedy, Kathleen Quinlan; ***D:*** Jack Smight. Nominations: Academy Awards '77: Best Art Direction/Set Decoration. *MCA*

Akermania, Vol. 1 🦴🦴🦴 **1992** This compilation of director Akerman's shorter works includes "I'm Hungry, I'm Cold," the story of two Belgian girls on the loose in Paris, and "Saute Ma Ville," Akerman's first film. Both are in French with English subtitles. Also included is "Hotel Monterey," a silent experimental film. **89m/C VHS.** *FR* Maria De Medeiros, Pascale Salkin, Chantal Akerman; ***D:*** Chantal Akerman. *WAC, INJ*

Akira 🦴🦴 **1989** Secret government experiments on children with ESP go awry, resulting in an cataclysmic explosion on Tokyo. The city in turn builds itself up into a Megalopolis and the experiments continue. Animated; in Japanese with English subtitles or dubbed. **124m/C VHS, LV.** *JP* ***D:*** Katsuhiro Otomo, Sheldon Renan; ***W:*** Katsuhiro Otomo, Izo Hashimoto; ***C:*** Katsuji Misawa. *WTA, STP, INJ*

Akira Kurosawa's Dreams 🦴🦴½ *Dreams* **1990 (PG)** An anthological lesson regarding the simultaneous loss of humanity and nature that threatens us all from the renowned Japanese director. Although the startling and memorable imagery is still present, Kurosawa's lessons are strangely trite and consequently lack the power that is normally associated with his work. Watch for Scorsese as Van Gogh. With English subtitles. **120m/C VHS, LV.** *JP* Akira Terao, Mitsuko Baisho, Meiko Harada, Chishu Ryu, Hisashi Igawa, Mitsunori Isaki, Toshihiko Nakano, Yoshitaka Zushi, Toshie Negishi, Martin Scorsese; ***D:*** Akira Kurosawa; ***W:*** Akira Kurosawa; ***M:*** Shinichiro Ikebe. *INJ, WAR, FCT*

Al Capone 🦴🦴🦴 **1959** Film noir character study of one of the most colorful gangsters of the Roaring Twenties. Sort of an underworld "How to Succeed in Business." Steiger chews scenes and bullets as they fly by, providing the performance of his career. Plenty of gangland violence and mayhem and splendid cinematography keep the fast-paced period piece sailing. **104m/C VHS, Beta.** Rod Steiger, Fay Spain, Murvyn Vye, Nehemiah Persoff, Martin Balsam, James Gregory, Joe De Santis; ***D:*** Richard Wilson. *FOX, FCT*

Alabama's Ghost 🦴½ **1972 (PG)** Musician steals a dead master magician's secrets, incurring the wrath of the paranormal underworld. **96m/C VHS, Beta.** Christopher Brooks, E. Kerrigan Prescott; ***D:*** Fredric Hobbs. *LIV*

Aladdin 🦴 *Superfantagenio* **1986 (PG)** A comedic Italian modernization of the Aladdin fable. **97m/C VHS, Beta.** *IT* Bud Spencer, Luca Venantini, Janet Agren, Julian Voloshin, Umberto Raho; ***D:*** Bruno Corbucci. *MED*

Aladdin 🦴🦴🦴½ **1992 (G)** Boy meets princess, loses her, finds her, wins her from evil vizier and nasty parrot. Superb animation triumphs over average songs and storyline by capitalizing on Williams' talent for ad-lib with lightning speed genie changes, lots of celebrity spoofs, and even a few pokes at Disney itself. Adults will enjoy the 1,001 impersonations while kids will get a kick out of the big blue genie and the songs, three of which are the late Ashman's legacy. Kane and Salonga are responsible for the singing voices of Aladdin and Jasmine; Gottfried is a riot as the obnoxious parrot sidekick. Be forewarned: small children may be frightened by some of the scarier sequences. ♫A Whole New World; Prince Ali; Friend Like Me; One Jump Ahead; Arabian Nights. **90m/C VHS, Beta, LV.** ***D:*** Ron Clements, John Musker; ***W:*** Ron Clements, John Musker, Ted Elliot, Terry Rossio; ***M:*** Alan Menken, Howard Ashman, Tim Rice; ***V:*** Robin Williams, Scott Weinger, Linda Larkin, Jonathan Freeman, Frank Welker, Gilbert Gottfried, Douglas Seale, Brad Kane, Lea Salonga. Academy Awards '92: Best Song ("A Whole New World"), Best Original Score; Golden Globe Awards '93: Best Song ("A Whole New World"), Best Score; MTV Movie Awards '93: Best Comedic Performance (Williams); Nominations: Academy Awards '92: Best Song ("Friend Like Me"), Best Sound, Best Sound Effects Editing. *DIS, BTV, WTA*

Aladdin and His Wonderful Lamp 🦴🦴½ **1984** The story of Aladdin, a young man who finds a magical oil lamp when he is trapped in a tiny cave. From the "Faerie Tale Theatre" series and director of "Beetlejuice" and "Batman" Tim Burton. **60m/C VHS, Beta.** Valerie Bertinelli, Robert Carradine, Leonard Nimoy, James Earl Jones; ***D:*** Tim Burton. *KUI, FOX, FCT*

Aladdin and the King of Thieves **1996** Second-direct-to-video saga once again features Williams as the voice of the genie (after settling a dispute with Disney). Aladdin's married Jasmine but gets involved with a search for his family. **?m/C VHS.** ***V:*** Robin Williams, Scott Weinger, Jerry Orbach, John Rhys-Davies, Gilbert Gottfried, Linda Larkin. *DIS*

Alakazam the Great! **1961** Japanese animated film about an arrogant monkey who is sent on a mission to learn about life. **84m/C VHS.** ***D:*** Lee Kresel; ***M:*** Les Baxter; ***V:*** Frankie Avalon, Dodie Stevens, Jonathan Winters, Arnold Stang, Sterling Holloway. *CNG*

The Alamo 🦴🦴🦴 **1960** Old-fashioned patriotic battle epic recounts the real events of the 1836 fight for independence in Texas. The usual band of diverse and contentious personalities, including Wayne as a coonskin-capped Davy Crockett, defend a small fort against a very big Mexican raiding party outside of San Antonio. Before meeting mythic death, they fight with each other, learn the meaning of life, and ultimately come to respect each other. Just to make it more entertaining, Avalon sings. Big-budget production features an impeccable musical score by Tiomkin and an impressive 7,000 extras for the Mexican army alone. Wayne reportedly received directorial assistance from John Ford, particularly during the big massacre finale. **161m/C VHS, Beta, LV.** John Wayne, Richard Widmark, Laurence Harvey, Frankie Avalon, Richard Boone, Carlos Arruza, Chill Wills, Veda Ann Borg; ***D:*** John Wayne; ***C:*** William Clothier; ***M:*** Dimitri Tiomkin. Academy Awards '60: Best Sound; Golden Globe Awards '61: Best Score; Nominations: Academy Awards '60: Best Color Cinematography, Best Film Editing, Best Picture, Best Song ("The Green Leaves of Summer"), Best Supporting Actor (Wills), Best Original Score. *MGM, FOX, TLF*

Alamo Bay 🦴🦴½ **1985** A slow-moving but sincere tale of contemporary racism. An angry Vietnam veteran and his red-neck buddies feel threatened by Vietnamese refugees who want to go into the fishing business. Set in Texas, filled with Texas-sized characters, and based on a true Texas story, as interpreted by the French Malle. **99m/C VHS, Beta, LV.** Ed Harris, Ho Nguyen, Amy Madigan, Donald Moffat, Cynthia Carle, Truyen V. Tran, Rudy Young; ***D:*** Louis Malle; ***W:*** Alice Arlen; ***M:*** Ry Cooder. *COL*

The Alamo: Thirteen Days to Glory 🦴🦴 **1987** The legendary Davy Crockett (Keith), Colonel William Travis (Baldwin), and Jim Bowie (Arness) overcome personal differences to unite against the Mexican Army, vowing to hold down the fort or die. It takes a true Texan to fully appreciate the merits of this rather pedestrian retelling of a familiar story, but the battle scenes are pretty heady (although they lose some of their froth on the small screen). If nothing else, the ever-versatile Julia is worth seeing as Santa Anna in this made-for-TV rendering of J. Lon Tinkle's "Thirteen Days to Glory." You may not want to remember the Alamo this way. **180m/C VHS, Beta.** James Arness, Lorne Greene, Alec Baldwin, Brian Keith, Raul Julia; ***D:*** Peter Werner; ***M:*** Peter Bernstein. *FRH*

Alamut Ambush 🦴 **1986** A federal agent is stalked by assassins, and decides to hunt them in return. Sequel to "Cold War Killer." **94m/C VHS, Beta.** *GB* Terence Stamp, Michael Culver; ***D:*** Ken Grieve. *NO*

Alan & Naomi 🦴🦴½ **1992 (PG)** In 1944, 14-year-old Alan Silverman is more concerned with his Brooklyn stickball team than the war raging across Europe. This changes when his upstairs neighbor offers refuge to a French-Jewish mother and her young daughter and he is asked to befriend the girl. Naomi witnessed the brutal death of her father by the Nazis and retreated into a world of her own. Together the two build a sweet, if unlikely, friendship. Fine performances save this average coming of age tale. Based on the novel by Myron Levoy. **95m/C VHS, LV.** Lukas Haas, Vanessa Zaoui, Michael Gross, Amy Aquino, Kevin Connolly, Zohra Lampert; ***D:*** Sterling Van Wagenen; ***W:*** Jordan Horowitz; ***M:*** Dick Hyman. *COL*

Alaska 🦴🦴½ **1996 (PG)** Fourteen-year-old boy (Kartheiser) and his 12-year-old sister (Birch) try to rescue their bush pilot father whose plane has crashed in the wilderness. They also rescue an orphaned polar bear cub that manages to help them out along the way. See this flick if only to enjoy the lush backdrop of Alaska and British Columbia. Director Fraser C. Heston directs dad Charlton, appropriate payback for landing him the role as the infant Moses in "The Ten Commandments." **?m/C VHS.** Thora Birch, Vincent Kartheiser, Dirk Benedict, Charlton Heston; ***D:*** Fraser Heston; ***W:*** Andy Burg, Carol Fuchs. *NYR*

The Alaska Wilderness Adventure 🦴🦴 **1978** The tale of a family struggling for survival in the Arctic wilderness. Baby, it's cold out there. **90m/C VHS, Beta.** *NO*

Alberto Express 🦴🦴½ **1992** Black comedy explores the debts children owe their parents—literally. Alberto's family has a peculiar tradition. It seems that now he's married and about to become a father, he's expected to pay back every cent spent on his own upbringing. Cash poor (and panicky) Alberto hops a train from Paris to Rome and frantically tries to raise the necessary cash by preying, in a series of increasingly bizarre ways, on his fellow passengers before he faces his father once again. In French and Italian with English subtitles. **90m/C VHS.** *FR* Sergio Castellitto, Nino Manfredi, Marie Trintignant, Jeanne Moreau, Michel Aumont, Dominique Pinon, Marco Messeri, Eugenia Marruzzo; ***D:*** Arthur Joffe; ***W:*** Arthur Joffe. *FXL*

Albino *Woof!* **1976 (R)** Albino chief leads African terrorists to murder white settlers, one of whom is an ex-policeman's fiancee. So the ex-cop pursues the bad guys, who are fairly easy to identify (just look for the big group hanging with the albino). Danning, Lee, and Howard only briefly show faces and collect checks. **85m/C VHS, Beta.** Christopher Lee, Trevor Howard, Sybil Danning, Horst Frank, James Faulkner; ***D:*** Jurgen Goslar. *MED*

The Alchemist *Woof!* **1981 (R)** See humans transformed into murderous zombies! A bewitched man seeks revenge upon the evil magician who placed a curse on him, causing him to live like an animal. Painfully routine, with a few chills along the way. Amonte is an alias for Charles Band. Filmed in 1981 and released four years later. **86m/C VHS, Beta.** Robert Ginty, Lucinda Dooling, John Sanderford, Viola Kate Stimpson, Bob Glaudini; ***D:*** James Amonte; ***W:*** Alan J. Adler; ***M:*** Richard Band. *VES, LIV*

Alex 🦴🦴½ **1992** Inspirational story about 15-year-old New Zealand swimmer Alex Archer (Jackson), who is working towards a spot at the 1960 Rome Olympics. But her goal is threatened by an accident and a new rival and Alex struggles to overcome her obstacles with the help of her boyfriend (Picker) and her coach (Heywood). Based on the novel by Tessa Duder. **92m/C VHS, LV.** *AU* Lauren Jackson, Chris Haywood, Josh Picker, Catherine Godbold, Elizabeth Hawthorne; ***D:*** Megan Simpson. *ORI*

Alex in Wonderland 🦴🦴½ **1970 (R)** A semi-autobiographical and satirical look at Hollywood from the standpoint of a young director who's trying to follow up his recent hit (in real life, "Bob & Carol & Ted & Alice") with a picture of some integrity that will keep the mass audience away. The confused plot provides obvious parallels to Fellini (who appears in a cameo) and some sharp, often bitter insights into the Hollywood of the early '60s. Strong performances by Sutherland and Burstyn compensate somewhat for the patience-trying self-indulgent arty whining of the script. **109m/C VHS, Beta.** Donald Sutherland, Ellen Burstyn, Jeanne Moreau, Paul Mazursky; ***Cameos:*** Federico Fellini; ***D:*** Paul Mazursky; ***W:*** Larry Tucker, Paul Mazursky. *MGM, FCT*

Alexander Nevsky ☆☆☆½ **1938** A story of the invasion of Russia in 1241 by the Teutonic Knights of Germany and the defense of the region by good old Prince Nevsky. Eisenstein's first completed project in nearly ten years, it was widely regarded as an artistic disappointment upon release and as pro-war propaganda for the looming conflict with the Nazis. Fabulous Prokofiev score illuminates the classic battle scenes, which used thousands of Russian army regulars. Russian with subtitles. **110m/B VHS, LV.** *RU* Nikolai Cherkassov, N.P. Okholopkov, Al Abrikossov; ***D:*** Sergei Eisenstein; ***M:*** Sergei Prokofiev. National Board of Review Awards '39: 5 Best Foreign Films of the Year. *BMG, MRV, NOS*

Alexander the Great ☆☆½ **1955** A lavish epic about the legendary Greek conqueror of the fourth century B.C., which provides Burton a rare chance at an adventure role. Here we find Alexander is the product of a dysfunctional royal family who hopes to create an idealized world modeled after Greek culture to make up for the love he lacks from daddy. This he does by conquering everything before dying at the age of 33. The great cast helps to overcome the sluggish pacing of the spectacle, while numerous battle scenes featuring loads of spears and arrows are staged effectively. **135m/C VHS, Beta, LV.** Richard Burton, Fredric March, Claire Bloom, Harry Andrews, Peter Cushing, Danielle Darrieux, Helmut Dantine; ***D:*** Robert Rossen; ***C:*** Robert Krasker. *MGM, FCT*

Alexander: The Other Side of Dawn ☆☆ **1977** Tired made-for-television sequel to the television movie "Dawn: Portrait of a Teenage Runaway." A young man turns to prostitution to support himself on the street of Los Angeles. **100m/C VHS.** Leigh McCloskey, Eve Plumb, Earl Holliman, Juliet Mills, Jean Hagen, Lonny Chapman; ***D:*** John Erman. *MOV*

Alexander's Ragtime Band ☆☆☆ *Irving Berlin's Alexander's Ragtime Band* **1938** Energetic musical that spans 1915 to 1938 and has Power and Ameche battling for Faye's affections. Power is a society nabob who takes up ragtime. He puts together a band, naming the group after a piece of music (hence the title), and finds a singer (Faye). Ameche is a struggling composer who brings a Broadway producer to listen to their performance. Faye gets an offer to star in a show and becomes an overnight success. Over the years the trio win and lose success, marry and divorce, and finally end up happy. Corny but charming. ♫Alexander's Ragtime Band; All Alone; Blue Skies; Easter Parade; Everybody's Doin' It; Everybody Step; For Your Country and My Country; Heat Wave; I Can Always Find a Little Sunshine at the YMCA. **105m/B VHS.** Tyrone Power, Alice Faye, Don Ameche, Ethel Merman, Jack Haley, Jean Hersholt, Helen Westley, John Carradine, Paul Hurst, Joe King, Ruth Terry; ***D:*** Henry King; ***W:*** Kathryn Scola, Lamar Trotti; ***M:*** Irving Berlin, Irving Berlin. Academy Awards '38: Best Score; Nominations: Academy Awards '38: Best Film Editing, Best Interior Decoration, Best Picture, Best Song ("Now It Can Be Told"), Best Writing. *FXV*

Alfie ☆☆☆ **1966 (PG)** What's it all about, Alfie? Caine, in his first starring role, plays the British playboy out of control in mod London. Alfie is a despicable, unscrupulous and vile sort of guy who uses woman after woman to fulfill his basic needs and then casts them aside until...tragedy strikes. Though this box office hit was seen as a sophisticated take on current sexual mores upon release, it now seems a dated but engaging comedy, notable chiefly for its performances. From the play by Bill Naughton. The title song "Alfie", sung by Dionne Warwick, was a top ten hit. **113m/C VHS, Beta.** *GB* Michael Caine, Shelley Winters, Millicent Martin, Vivien Merchant, Julia Asher; ***D:*** Lewis Gilbert. Cannes Film Festival '67: Grand Jury Prize; Golden Globe Awards '67: Best Foreign Film; National Board of Review Awards '66: 10 Best Films of the Year, Best Supporting Actress (Merchant); Nominations: Academy Awards '66: Best Actor (Caine), Best Adapted Screenplay, Best Picture, Best Song ("Alfie"), Best Supporting Actress (Merchant). *PAR*

Alfred Hitchcock's Aventure Malgache *Madagascar Landing; Alfred Hitchcock's Bon Voyage & Aventure Malgache* **1944** Hitchcock worked with the Moliere Players on this propaganda piece about the French Resistance. He based this story on the experiences of the actor Clarousse. Working for the Resistance in occupied Madagascar, Clarousse is betrayed and sent to prison by the Vichy government. Rescued by the British he returns to resume his work. In French with English subtitles. **31m/B VHS.** ***D:*** Alfred Hitchcock. *MIL*

Alfred Hitchcock's Bon Voyage *Alfred Hitchcock's Bon Voyage & Aventure Malgache* **1944** One of director Hitchcock's short propaganda pieces filmed as a tribute to the French Resistance. In London an RAF pilot is interrogated by the Free French about his escape from France. He was aided by a Polish agent who was actually working for the Gestapo to learn about the Resistance's movements. Flashbacks show the pilot's adventures from the spy's point-of-view. In French with English subtitles. **26m/B VHS.** John Blythe; ***D:*** Alfred Hitchcock. *MIL*

Alfredo, Alfredo ☆☆ **1972 (R)** Hoffman plays a mild-mannered bank clerk who regrets marrying a sexy woman. Lightweight domestic comedy. In Italian with English subtitles (Hoffman's voice was dubbed). **97m/C VHS.** *IT* Dustin Hoffman, Stefania Sandrelli, Carla Gravina, Clara Colosimo, Daniela Patella, Dulio Del Prete; ***D:*** Pietro Germi. *PAR*

Algiers ☆☆☆ **1938** Nearly a scene-for-scene Americanized remake of the 1937 French "Pepe Le Moko" about a beautiful rich girl (Lamarr) who meets and falls in love with a notorious thief (Boyer, then a leading sex symbol). Pursued by French police and hiding in the underworld-controlled Casbah, Boyer meets up with Lamarr in a tragically fated romance done in the best tradition of Hollywood. Boyer provides a measured performance as Le Moko, while Lamarr is appropriately sultry in her American film debut (which made her a star). Later remade as the semi-musical "Casbah." **96m/B VHS, Beta.** Charles Boyer, Hedy Lamarr, Sigrid Gurie, Gene Lockhart, Joseph Calleia, Alan Hale; ***D:*** John Cromwell; ***C:*** James Wong Howe. Nominations: Academy Awards '38: Best Actor (Boyer), Best Cinematography, Best Interior Decoration, Best Supporting Actor (Lockhart). *CNG, MRV, NOS*

Ali Baba and the Forty Thieves ☆☆½ **1943** Ali Baba and his gang of thieves do battle against Hulogn Khan, leader of the Mongols, to save Baghdad and its citizens from ruin and death. **87m/C VHS.** Jon Hall, Turhan Bey, Maria Montez, Andy Devine, Kurt Katch, Frank Puglia, Fortunio Bonanova, Moroni Olsen, Scotty Beckett; ***D:*** Arthur Lubin; ***W:*** Edmund Hartmann; ***C:*** William Howard Greene. *MCA, FCT*

Ali Baba and the 40 Thieves ☆☆☆ *Ali Baba et les Quarante Voleurs* **1954** French adaptation of the popular novel "A Thousand and One Nights." Servant boy Ali Baba discovers the magic cave holding the stolen treasure of Abdul and his 40 thieves. Shot on location in Morocco. Also available dubbed. **92m/C VHS.** *FR* Samia Gamal, Dieter Borsche, Henri Vilbert; ***D:*** Jacques Becker; ***W:*** Jacques Becker. *FRA, FCT*

Ali: Fear Eats the Soul ☆☆☆ *Fear Eats the Soul* **1974** A widow cleaning woman in her sixties has a love affair with a Moroccan man 30 years her junior. To no one's surprise, both encounter racism and moral hypocrisy in West Germany. Serious melodrama from Fassbinder, who wrote it and appears as the squirmy son-in-law. In German with English subtitles. **68m/C VHS.** *GE* Brigitte Mira, El Hedi Ben Salem, Irm Hermann; ***D:*** Rainer Werner Fassbinder. Nominations: Cannes Film Festival '74: Best Film. *NYF, FCT, INJ*

Alias Billy the Kid ☆☆ **1946** Western adventure with Carson posing as a famous outlaw to find out who's behind the scam involving the Denton City cattle trade. **54m/B VHS.** Sunset Carson. *REP*

Alias John Law ☆ **1935** The Good Guy fights for oil rights against the bad guys. Confused program western with an especially convoluted plot. **54m/B VHS, Beta.** Bob Steele; ***D:*** Robert North Bradbury. *NO*

Alias John Preston ☆½ **1956** Yet another one of those pseudo-psychological to sleep perchance to dream movies. Lee plays a man haunted by dreams in which he's a murderer, and soon starts to question whether his dreams might not imitate life. It's been done before, it's been done since, and it's been done better. **66m/B VHS.** *GB* Betta St. John, Alexander Knox, Christopher Lee, Sandra Dorne, Patrick Holt, Betty Ann Davies, John Longden, Bill Fraser, John Stuart; ***D:*** David MacDonald. *SNC*

Alias, La Gringa ☆☆ **1991** Follows the adventures of La Gringa, a likeable criminal capable of escaping from any Peruvian jail. After being aided in his latest escape by a political prisoner, La Gringa decides to return in disguise to pay back the favor. But the prison is rocked by rioting and La Gringa finds himself in a situation out of his control. Spanish with subtitles. **100m/C VHS.** ***D:*** Alberto Durant. *FCT*

Alice ☆☆ **1986** A twist on the "Alice in Wonderland" tale. Alice witnesses an attempted murder, faints, and awakens in a weird, yet strangely familiar environment. Adapted from the stage production. **80m/C VHS, Beta.** Sophie Barjae, Susannah York, Jean-Pierre Cassel, Paul Nicholas. *ORI, WAR*

Alice ☆☆☆½ **1988** An acclaimed surreal version of Lewis Carroll's already surreal "Alice in Wonderland," with the emphasis on Carroll's obsessiveness. Utilizing animated puppets and a live actor for Alice, Czech director Svankmajer injects grotesque images and black comedy into Wonderland. Not for the kids. **84m/C VHS.** *GB* Kristina Kohoutova; ***D:*** Jan Svankmajer. *ICA, WTA, INJ*

Alice ☆☆☆ **1990 (PG-13)** Farrow is "Alice," a woman plagued with doubts about her lifestyle, her religion, and her happiness. Her perfect children, husband, and apartment don't prevent her backaches, and she turns to an Oriental "herbalist" for aid. She finds his methods unusual and the results of the treatments surprising. Lightweight fairytale of Yuppiedom gone awry. Fine performances, but superficial and pointed story that may leave the viewer looking for more. (Perhaps that's Allen's point.) Farewell performance from charactor actor Luke, unbilled cameo from Judith Ivey, and first time out for Dylan O'Sullivan Farrow, adopted daughter of Allen and Farrow, as Kate. **106m/C VHS, Beta, LV.** Mia Farrow, William Hurt, Joe Mantegna, Keye Luke, Alec Baldwin, Cybill Shepherd, Blythe Danner, Gwen Verdon, Bernadette Peters, Judy Davis, Patrick O'Neal, Julie Kavner, Caroline Aaron, Holland Taylor, Robin Bartlett, David Spielberg, Bob Balaban, Dylan O'Sullivan Farrow, Elle Macpherson; ***D:*** Woody Allen; ***W:*** Woody Allen. National Board of Review Awards '90: Best Actress (Farrow); Nominations: Academy Awards '90: Best Original Screenplay. *ORI, FCT*

Alice Adams ☆☆½ **1935** Based on the classic Booth Tarkington novel about a poor girl from a small Midwestern town who falls in love with a man from the upper level of society. She tries desperately to fit in and nearly alienates her family and friends. The sets may be dated, but the insight on human behavior is timeless. **99m/B VHS, Beta, LV.** Katharine Hepburn, Fred MacMurray, Evelyn Venable, Hattie McDaniel, Fred Stone; ***D:*** George Stevens; ***M:*** Max Steiner. National Board of Review Awards '35: 10 Best Films of the Year; Nominations: Academy Awards '35: Best Actress (Hepburn), Best Picture. *CCB, MED, NOS*

Alice Doesn't Live Here Anymore ☆☆½ **1974 (PG)** Scorsese marries road opera with pseudo-feminist semi-realistic melodrama and produces uneven but interesting results. When Alice's husband dies suddenly, leaving her with their eleven-year-old son, she leaves for California, but finds herself stranded in Phoenix, down to her last few bucks. There she lands a job as a waitress in a diner where she meets kindly rancher Kristofferson. Notable for its female point of view, it was also the basis for the once popular TV show "Alice." Burstyn and Ladd lend key performances, while Kristofferson is typically wooden. **105m/C VHS, Beta, LV.** Ellen Burstyn, Kris Kristofferson, Diane Ladd, Jodie Foster, Harvey Keitel, Vic Tayback, Billy Green Bush; ***D:*** Martin Scorsese; ***W:*** Robert Getchell. Academy Awards '74: Best

Actress (Burstyn); British Academy Awards '75: Best Actress (Burstyn), Best Film, Best Screenplay, Best Supporting Actress (Ladd); Nominations: Academy Awards '74: Best Original Screenplay, Best Supporting Actress (Ladd). *WAR, FCT, BTV*

Alice in the Cities ½ **1974** American and German culture are compared and contrasted in this early Wenders road work about a German journalist in the USA on assignment who suddenly finds himself custodian to a worldly nine-year-old girl abandoned by her mother. Together they return to Germany and search for the girl's grandmother. Along the way they learn about each other, with many distinctive and graceful Wenders moments. **110m/B VHS, Beta.** Ruediger Vogler, Yella Rottlaender, Elisabeth Kreuzer, Edda Kochi; ***D:*** Wim Wenders; ***W:*** Wim Wenders. *FCT, APD, GLV*

Alice in Wonderland ½ **1950** Another version of the Lewis Carroll classic which combines the usage of Lou Bunin's puppets and live action to tell the story. Released independently to cash in on the success of the Disney version. Takes a more adult approach to the story and is worth viewing on its own merits. **83m/C VHS, Beta.** *FR* Carol Marsh, Stephen Murray, Pamela Brown, Felix Aylmer, Ernest Milton; ***D:*** Dallas Bower. *MON, WTA*

Alice in Wonderland **1951 (G)** Classic Disney dream version of Lewis Carroll's famous children's story about a girl who falls down a rabbit hole into a magical world populated by strange creatures. Beautifully animated with some startling images, but served with a strange dispassion warmed by a fine batch of songs. Wynn's Mad Hatter and Holloway's Cheshire Cat are among the treats in store. ♫ Alice in Wonderland; I'm Late; A Very Merry Un-Birthday. **75m/C VHS, Beta, LV.** ***D:*** Clyde Geronomi; ***V:*** Kathryn Beaumont, Ed Wynn, Sterling Holloway, Jerry Colonna, Hamilton Luske, Wilfred Jackson. Nominations: Academy Awards '51: Best Original Score. *DIS, FCT, KUI*

Alice in Wonderland ½ **1982** Musical version of the Lewis Carroll's classic tale performed by the Children's Theatre Company and School. **81m/C VHS, Beta.** Annie Enneking, Solvieg Olsen, Wendy Lehr, Jason McLean, Gary Briggle, Elizabeth Fink. *MCA*

Alice Sweet Alice ½ *Holy Terror; Communion* **1976 (R)** Mediocre, gory who-killed-her, best remembered as the debut of Shields (in a small role). **112m/C VHS, Beta.** Brooke Shields, Linda Miller, Paula Sheppard; ***D:*** Alfred Sole. *REP, MRV, BTV*

Alice Through the Looking Glass **1966** Based on Lewis Carroll's classic adventure. Follows the further adventures of young Alice. After a chess piece comes to life, it convinces Alice that excitement and adventure lie through the looking glass. **72m/C VHS, Beta.** Judi Rolin, Ricardo Montalban, Nanette Fabray, Robert Coote, Agnes Moorehead, Jack Palance, Jimmy Durante, Tom Smothers, Roy Castle, Richard Denning; ***D:*** Alan Handley. *SUE, KAR*

Alice to Nowhere **1986** Concerns a running argument in the Outback over a fortune in gems unknowingly carried by a young woman. Made for Australian television and based on a novel by Evan Green. **210m/C VHS, Beta.** *AU* Rosie Jones, Steve Jacobs, John Waters, Ruth Cracknell; ***D:*** John Power. *PAR*

Alice's Adventures in Wonderland **1972** Musical adaptation of Lewis Carroll's timeless fantasy of a young girl who meets new friends when she falls into a rabbit hole. **96m/C VHS, Beta.** *GB* Fiona Fullerton, Michael Crawford, Ralph Richardson, Flora Robson, Peter Sellers, Robert Helpmann, Dudley Moore, Michael Jayston, Spike Milligan, Michael Hordern; ***D:*** William Sterling; ***W:*** William Sterling; ***C:*** Geoffrey Unsworth; ***M:*** John Barry. *VES*

Alice's Restaurant ½ **1969 (PG)** Based on the popular and funny 20-minute Arlo Guthrie song "Alice's Restaurant Massacre" about a Flower Child during the Last Big War who gets hassled for littering, man. Step back in time and study the issues of the hippie era, including avoiding the draft, dropping out of college, and dealing with the local pigs. Sort of a modern movie in the cinematic ambling genre, in that nothing really happens. **111m/C VHS, Beta.** Arlo Guthrie, James Broderick, Pat Quinn, Geoff Outlaw; ***D:*** Arthur Penn. Nominations: Academy Awards '69: Best Director (Penn). *MVD, MGM*

Alien ½ **1979 (R)** Terse direction, stunning sets and special effects, and a well-seasoned cast save this from being another "Slimy monster from Outerspace" story. Instead it's a grisly roller-coaster of suspense and fear (and a huge box office hit). Intergalactic freighter's crew is invaded by an unstoppable carnivorous alien intent on picking off the crew one by one. While the cast mostly bitches and banters while awaiting the horror of their imminent departure, Weaver is exceptional as Ripley, a self-reliant survivor who goes toe to toe with the Big Ugly. Futuristic, in the belly of the beast visual design creates a vivid sense of claustrophobic doom enhanced further by the ominous score. Oscar-winning special effects include the classic baby alien busting out of the crew guy's chest routine, a rib-splitting ten on the gore meter. Successfully followed by "Aliens" and "Alien 3." **116m/C VHS, Beta, LV.** Tom Skerritt, Sigourney Weaver, Veronica Cartwright, Yaphet Kotto, Harry Dean Stanton, Ian Holm, John Hurt; ***D:*** Ridley Scott; ***W:*** Dan O'Bannon; ***M:*** Jerry Goldsmith. Academy Awards '79: Best Visual Effects; Nominations: Academy Awards '79: Best Art Direction/Set Decoration. *FOX*

Alien 3 **1992 (R)** Picks up where "Aliens" left off as Ripley crash lands on Fiorina 161, a planet that serves as a penal colony for 25 celibate but horny men who smell bad. Ripley is forced to shave her head because of the planet's lice problem, and she sets out to survive on the cold, unfriendly planet until a rescue ship can come for her. Fending off sexual advances from the men, Ripley soon discovers she wasn't the only survivor of the crash—the alien survived too and has somehow implanted her with an alien of her own. Dark and disturbing, filled with religious allegories, and a universe removed from the two earlier Aliens. Intended as the final installment of the series. **135m/C VHS, LV.** Sigourney Weaver, Charles S. Dutton, Charles Dance, Paul McGann, Brian Glover, Ralph Brown, Danny Webb, Christopher John Fields, Holt McCallany, Lance Henriksen; ***D:*** David Fincher; ***M:*** Elliot Goldenthal. Nominations: Academy Awards '92: Best Visual Effects. *FXV*

Alien Contamination *Woof! Contamination* **1981 (R)** Tale of two astronauts who return to Earth from an expedition on Mars carrying some deadly bacterial eggs. Controlled by a Martian intent on conquering the world, the eggs squirt a gloppy juice that makes people explode on contact (a special effect). A cheap and sloppy attempt to cash in on the success of "Alien." Dubbed. **90m/C VHS, Beta.** *IT* Ian McCulloch, Louise Monroe, Martin Mase, Samuel Rauch, Lisa Hahn; ***D:*** Lewis (Luigi Cozzi) Coates; ***W:*** Lewis (Luigi Cozzi) Coates. *NO*

Alien Dead **1985 (R)** The teenage victims of a bizarre meteor crash reincarnate as flesh-eating ghouls anxious for a new supply of human food in this extremely low-budget sleep inducer. **87m/C VHS, Beta.** Buster Crabbe, Linda Lewis, Ray Roberts; ***D:*** Fred Olen Ray. *ACA, GHV*

The Alien Factor ½ **1978 (PG)** Another low-budget crazed critter from outerspace dispatch, this one featuring multiple aliens, one of whom is good, who have the misfortune of crash landing near Baltimore. The grotesque extraterrestrials jolt a small town out of its sleepy state by wreaking havoc (except for the good one, of course). Decent special effects. **82m/C VHS, Beta.** Don Leifert, Tom Griffith, Mary Mertens, Dick Dyszel; ***D:*** Donald M. Dohler. *NO*

Alien from L.A. *Woof!* **1987 (PG)** Awesomely inept comedy about a California girl who unwittingly stumbles onto the famed continent of Atlantis and can't find a yogurt stand. Weakly plotted and acted and filmed. Like, really. **88m/C VHS, Beta, LV.** Kathy Ireland, Thom Mathews, Don Michael Paul, Linda Kerridge, William R. Moses, Richard Haines; ***D:*** Albert Pyun; ***W:*** Albert Pyun, Debra Ricci, Regina Davis; ***C:*** Tom Fraser. *MED*

Alien Intruder **1993 (R)** What happens when an evil demon appears before the soldiers of the future in the guise of a beautiful woman? Futuristic trash B-movie emerges from the depths. **90m/C VHS, LV.** Billy Dee Williams, Tracy Scoggins, Maxwell Caulfield; ***D:*** Ricardo Jacques Gale. *PMH*

Alien Massacre *Woof! Dr. Terror's Gallery of Horrors; Return from the Past; The Blood Suckers; Gallery of Horror* **1967** One of the worst films of all time—five short horror stories about zombies and vampires. Goes by many names—stinks in all of them. **90m/C VHS, Beta.** Lon Chaney Jr., John Carradine, Rochelle Hudson, Roger Gentry, Mitch Evans; ***D:*** David L. Hewitt. *ACA, MRV*

Alien Nation ½ **1988 (R)** A few hundred thousand alien workers land accidentally on Earth and slowly become part of its society, although widely discriminated against. One of the "newcomers" teams with a surly and bigoted human cop to solve a racially motivated murder. An inconsistent and occasionally transparent script looks at race conflicts and includes some humorous parallels with contemporary American life. Basis for the television series. Producer Hurd was also the force behind "The Terminator" and "Aliens." **89m/C VHS, Beta, LV.** James Caan, Mandy Patinkin, Terence Stamp, Kevyn Major Howard, Peter Jason, Jeff Kober, Leslie Bevins; ***D:*** Graham Baker; ***W:*** Rockne S. O'Bannon; ***M:*** Curt Sobel. *FOX*

Alien Nation: Dark Horizon ½ **1994 (PG)** The alien Newcomers have successfully adapted to life on Earth but face continuing dangers when a human-supremacy group develops a virus to wipe them out and an alien infiltrator is plotting to return them to slavery on Tencton. Naturally, it's up to detectives Sykes and Francisco to save the day. Based on the TV series. **90m/C VHS.** Gary Graham, Eric Pierpont, Scott Patterson, Terri Treas, Michelle Scarabelli, Lee Bryant, Sean Six, Lauren Woodland, Ron Fassier, Jeff Marcus; ***D:*** Kenneth Johnson; ***W:*** Diane Frolov, Andrew Schneider; ***M:*** David Kurtz. *FXV*

Alien Predators *Woof!* **1980 (R)** Three friends encounter a malevolent alien in this dull reworking of the plot of "The Andromeda Strain" with laughable special effects tossed in for those outwitted by the script. **92m/C VHS, Beta.** Dennis Christopher, Martin Hewitt, Lynn-Holly Johnson, Luis Prendes; ***D:*** Deran Sarafian. *VTR*

Alien Prey ½ **1983 (R)** Two lesbians are making love when they are unexpectedly devoured by a hungry and indiscreet alien. No safe sex there. Graphic sex, violence, and cannibalism abound. Interesting twist to the old eat 'em and leave 'em genre. **85m/C VHS, Beta.** Barry Stokes, Sally Faulkner; ***D:*** Norman J. Warren. *NO*

Alien Private Eye *Alien P.I* **1987** An extraterrestrial detective searches Los Angeles for a missing magic disk while investigating an intergalactic crime ring. **90m/C VHS.** Nikki Fastinetti; ***D:*** Nik Rubenfeld. *NO*

Alien Seed **1989** Aliens kidnap a woman and impregnate her. Estrada is the government scientist hot on her trail. (How far could a woman carrying alien offspring wander?) **88m/C VHS.** Erik Estrada, Heidi Paine, Steven Blade; ***D:*** Bob James. *AIP*

Alien Space Avenger ½ *Space Avenger* **1991** A spaceship piloted by four alien convicts crash lands in New York City. Stalked by an intergalatic bounty hunter whose job is to kill them, the aliens attack and hide inside human bodies to avoid discovery. It's a race against time as the preservation of the human race depends on the avenger's ability to seek and destroy the alien invaders. Bland ripoff of "Aliens" is reminiscent of old-time "B" sci-fi flicks , with more gore and violence. Shot with the old 3-strip Technicolor method. **88m/C VHS.** Robert Prichard, Mike McClerie, Charity Staley, Gina Mastrogiacomo, Kick Fairbanks Fogg, Angela Nicholas, Marty Roberts, James Gillis; ***D:*** Richard W. Haines; ***W:*** Richard W. Haines, Linwood Sawyer; ***M:*** Richard Fiocca. *AIP*

Alien Terminator 🦴 **1995 (R)** Scientists experimenting with DNA find themselves creating an organism capable of instant regeneration that also likes to nosh on living flesh. To make matters worse, the scientists are trapped in their lab complex, which happens to be located five miles below Los Alamos. **95m/C VHS.** Maria Ford, Kevin Alber, Rodger Halstead, Cassandra Leigh, Emile Levisetti; ***D:*** Dave Payne. *NHO*

Alien Warrior *Woof!* **1985 (R)** An extraterrestrial fights a street pimp to save a crime-ridden Earth neighborhood. Low-brain rip-off of Superman. **92m/C VHS, Beta.** Brett Clark, Pamela Saunders; ***D:*** Edward Hunt. *VES, LIV*

Alien Women 🦴 *Zeta One; The Love Factor* **1969 (R)** A soft-core British science fiction yarn about scantily clad alien babes and the special agent who's trying to uncover their secret. It's all very sketchy, silly and campy, though pleasantly cast with plenty of lovely British actresses. **86m/C VHS, Beta.** *GB* James Robertson Justice, Charles Hawtrey, Robin Hawdon, Anna Gael, Brigitte Skay, Dawn Addams, Valerie Leon, Yutte Stensgaard, Wendy Lingham, Rita Webb, Caroline Hawkins; ***D:*** Michael Cort. *PSM, SNC*

Alienator 🦴 **1989 (R)** In the improbable future, an unstoppable android killer is sent after an intergalactic villain. An intentional "Terminator" rip-off. **93m/C VHS, Beta, LV.** Jan-Michael Vincent, John Phillip Law, Ross Hagen, Dyana Ortelli, Dawn Wildsmith, P.J. Soles, Teagan Clive, Robert Clarke, Leo Gordon, Robert Quarry, Fox Harris, Hoke Howell, Jay Richardson; ***D:*** Fred Olen Ray. *PSM*

Aliens 🦴🦴🦴½ **1986 (R)** The bitch is back, some 50 years later. Popular sequel to "Alien" amounts to non-stop, ravaging combat in space. Contact with a colony on another planet has mysteriously stopped. Fresh from deep space sleep, Ripley and a slew of pulsar-equipped Marines return to confront the mother alien at her nest, which is also inhabited by a whole bunch of the nasty critters spewing for a fight. Something's gotta give, and the Oscar-winning special effects are especially inventive (and messy) in the alien demise department. Dimension (acting biz talk) is given to our hero Ripley, as she discovers maternal instincts lurking within her space suit while looking after a young girl, the lone survivor of the colony. Tension-filled gore blaster. Followed by "Aliens 3." **138m/C VHS, Beta, LV.** Sigourney Weaver, Michael Biehn, Lance Henriksen, Bill Paxton, Paul Reiser, Carrie Henn, Jenette Goldstein; ***D:*** James Cameron; ***W:*** James Cameron, Walter Hill; ***M:*** James Horner. Academy Awards '86: Best Sound Effects Editing, Best Visual Effects; Nominations: Academy Awards '86: Best Actress (Weaver), Best Art Direction/Set Decoration, Best Film Editing, Best Sound, Best Original Score. *FOX*

Aliens Are Coming 🦴½ **1980** A spaceship crash lands on Earth, and its devious denizens begin invading human bodies. TV movie that's a dull echo of "Invasion of the Body Snatchers." **100m/C VHS, Beta.** Tom Mason, Melinda Fee, Max Gail, Eric (Hans Gudegast) Braeden, Matthew Laborteaux; ***D:*** Harvey Hart; ***M:*** William Goldstein. *WOV, GKK*

Aliens from Spaceship Earth 🦴½ **1977** Are strange, celestial forces invading our universe? If they are, is man prepared to defend his planet against threatening aliens of unknown strength? Lame docudrama featuring the Hurdy Gurdy man himself, Donovan. **107m/C VHS, Beta.** Donovan, Lynda Day George; ***D:*** Don Como. *GEM*

Alison's Birthday 🦴🦴 **1979** A teenage girl learns that some of her family and friends are Satan worshipers at a terrifying birthday party. Meanwhile, the ghost of her dad hovers about, asking for more lines. **99m/C VHS, Beta.** *AU* Joanne Samuel, Lou Brown, Bunny Brooke; ***D:*** Ian Coughlan. *NO*

Alive 🦴🦴½ **1993 (R)** Recounts the true-life survival story of a group of Uruguayan rugby players in 1972. After their plane crashes in the remote, snowy Andes (in a spectacular sequence) they're forced to turn to cannibalism during a 10-week struggle to stay alive. Marshall doesn't focus on the gruesome idea, choosing instead to focus on all aspects of their desperate quest for survival. The special effects are stunning, but other parts of the film are never fully realized, including the final scene. Based on the nonfiction book by Piers Paul Read. **127m/C VHS, Beta, LV.** Ethan Hawke, Vincent Spano, Josh Hamilton, Bruce Ramsay, John Haymes Newton, David Kriegel, Kevin Breznahan, Sam Behrens, Illeana Douglas, Jack Noseworthy, Christian Meoli, Jake Carpenter; ***Cameos:*** John Malkovich; ***D:*** Frank Marshall; ***W:*** John Patrick Shanley; ***C:*** Peter James; ***M:*** James Newton Howard. *TOU*

Alive: 20 Years Later **1993** With the release of the big-screen fictional version comes this follow-up documentary with the survivors of the 1972 mountain plane crash telling their own story. **51m/C VHS, Beta, LV.** ***D:*** Jill Fullerton-Smith. *TOU*

All About Eve 🦴🦴🦴🦴 **1950** One of the wittiest (and most cynical) flicks of all time follows aspiring young actress Baxter as she ingratiates herself with a prominent group of theater people so she can become a Broadway star without the usual years of work. The not-so-innocent babe becomes secretary to aging star Davis and ruthlessly uses everyone in her climb to the top, much to Davis' initial disbelief and eventual displeasure. Satirical, darkly funny view of the theater world features exceptional work by Davis, Sanders, and Ritter. Based on "The Wisdom of Eve" by Mary Orr. Later staged as the musical "Applause." **138m/B VHS, Beta, LV.** Bette Davis, Anne Baxter, George Sanders, Celeste Holm, Gary Merrill, Thelma Ritter, Marilyn Monroe, Hugh Marlowe, Gregory Ratoff, Eddie Fisher; ***D:*** Joseph L. Mankiewicz; ***W:*** Joseph L. Mankiewicz; ***C:*** Milton Krasner. Academy Awards '50: Best Director (Mankiewicz), Best Picture, Best Screenplay, Best Sound, Best Supporting Actor (Sanders); Cannes Film Festival '51: Best Actress (Davis), Grand Jury Prize; Directors Guild of America Awards '50: Best Director (Mankiewicz); Golden Globe Awards '51: Best Screenplay; National Board of Review Awards '50: 10 Best Films of the Year; New York Film Critics Awards '50: Best Actress (Davis), Best Director (Mankiewicz), Best Film; Nominations: Academy Awards '26: Best Film Editing; Academy Awards '50: Best Actress (Baxter), Best Actress (Davis), Best Art Direction/Set Decoration (B & W), Best Black and White Cinematography, Best Supporting Actress (Holm, Ritter), Best Original Score. *FOX, BTV, HMV*

All-American Murder 🦴🦴 **1991 (R)** A rebellious young man is enrolled in a typical, all-American college for one last shot at mainstream life. Things start out okay, as he meets an attractive young coed. Hours later, he finds himself accused of her grisly murder. The youth is then given 24 hours to prove his innocence by a canny homicide detective. Average performances highlight this film, which isn't able to rise above the mediocre. **94m/C VHS, Beta, LV.** Christopher Walken, Charlie Schlatter, Josie Bissett, Joanna Cassidy, Richard Kind, Woody Watson, J.C. Quinn, Amy Davis; ***D:*** Anson Williams; ***W:*** Barry Sandler. *PSM*

All Creatures Great and Small 🦴🦴🦴 **1974** Taken from James Herriot's best selling novels, this is a delightful, quiet drama of a veterinarian's apprentice in rural England. Fine performance by Hopkins. Followed by "All Things Bright and Beautiful" and a popular British television series. **92m/C VHS, Beta.** *GB* Simon Ward, Anthony Hopkins, Lisa Harrow, Brian Stirner, Freddie Jones, T.P. McKenna; ***D:*** Claude Whatham. *RDG, FOX, HMV*

All Dogs Go to Heaven 🦴🦴 **1989 (G)** Somewhat heavy-handed animated musical (Reynolds sings) about a gangster dog who is killed by his partner in business. On the way to Heaven, he discovers how to get back to Earth to seek his revenge. When he returns to Earth, he is taken in by a little girl and learns about something he missed in life the first time around: Love. Expertly animated, but the plot may not keep the grown-ups engrossed, and the kids may notice its lack of charm. **85m/C VHS, Beta, LV, 8mm.** ***D:*** Don Bluth; ***W:*** Don Bluth, David A. Weiss; ***M:*** Ralph Burns; ***V:*** Burt Reynolds, Judith Barsi, Dom DeLuise, Vic Tayback, Charles Nelson Reilly, Melba Moore, Candy Devine, Loni Anderson. *MGM, RDG, WTA*

All Dogs Go to Heaven 2 🦴🦴½ **1995 (G)** Animated musical finds lovable scamp Charlie (Sheen) the dog discovering that the afterlife is not all it's cracked up to be and pining for dysfunction aplenty back on earth. He gets his chance when Gabriel's Horn is stolen and Charlie is assigned to retrieve it. Charlie teams up again with old buddy Itchy (Deluise) as the two come down from Dog Heaven to stop the villainous Carface (Borgnine) and demonic cat Red (Hearn). Along the way, Charlie falls in love with sexy Irish Setter Sasha (Easton), and finds a chance for redemption by helping a little boy in trouble. Animation not outstanding, but should keep the attention of small children. **82m/C VHS, LV.** ***D:*** Paul Sabella, Larry Leker; ***W:*** Arne Olsen, Kelly Ward, Mark Young; ***M:*** Mark Watters, Barry Mann, Cynthia Weil; ***V:*** Charlie Sheen, Sheena Easton, Ernest Borgnine, Dom DeLuise, George Hearn, Bebe Neuwirth, Hamilton Camp, Wallace Shawn, Bobby DiCicco, Adam Wylie. *MGM*

All Fall Down 🦴🦴½ **1962** A young man (de Wilde) idolizes his callous older brother (Beatty) until a tragedy forces him to grow up. Saint plays the older woman taken in by the brothers' family, who is seduced and abandoned. When she finds herself pregnant and alone, she commits suicide causing the younger brother, who loved her from afar, to vow to kill his older sibling. A well-acted melodrama. Also available colorized. **111m/B VHS.** Eva Marie Saint, Brandon de Wilde, Warren Beatty, Karl Malden, Angela Lansbury, Constance Ford, Barbara Baxley; ***D:*** John Frankenheimer; ***W:*** William Inge; ***C:*** Lionel Lindon; ***M:*** Alex North. *MGM*

All God's Children 🦴🦴½ **1980** Made for television drama about the controversial forced busing issue and two families who must face it. Top-notch cast is occasionally mislead by meandering script attempting to stay true to a sensitive issue. **100m/C VHS, Beta.** Richard Widmark, Ned Beatty, Ossie Davis, Ruby Dee, Mariclare Costello, George Spell, Trish Van Devere, Ken Swofford; ***D:*** Jerry Thorpe; ***M:*** Billy Goldenberg. *NO*

All I Desire 🦴🦴½ **1953** Estranged wife and mother (Stanwyck) returns to her hometown after fleeing years ago to pursue a stage career. She desires a new beginning with her family, but finds things have changed in her absence. The story examines the will of a strong woman and small town values. Director Sirk disagreed with the happy ending demanded by producers, but the drama is still noteworthy. **80m/B VHS.** Barbara Stanwyck, Richard Carlson, Lyle Bettger, Maureen O'Sullivan; ***D:*** Douglas Sirk; ***W:*** James Gunn, Robert Blees, Carl Guthrie, Gina Kaus; ***M:*** Joseph Gershenson. *MCA*

All I Want for Christmas 🦴🦴 **1991 (G)** Low-budget, sappy holiday tale of a young girl (Birch) who wants to reunite her divorced parents. Determined to fulfill her Christmas wish, Hallie seeks out the Santa Claus at Macy's department store to tell him the one thing she truly wants for Christmas. Birch is charming as are Bacall as her grandmother and Nielsen as Santa but the story is too squishy and bland to be believable. **92m/C VHS, LV.** Thora Birch, Leslie Nielsen, Lauren Bacall, Jamey Sheridan, Harley Jane Kozak, Ethan Randall, Kevin Nealon, Andrea Martin; ***D:*** Ron Lieberman; ***W:*** Richard Kramer, Thom Eberhardt, Neal Israel, Gail Parent; ***C:*** Robbie Greenberg; ***M:*** Bruce Broughton. *PAR*

All in a Night's Work 🦴🦴½ **1961** The founder of a one-man publishing empire is found dead with a smile on his face. His nephew inherits the business and finds himself caught in a series of big and small business misunderstandings. He's also falling in love with the woman he suspects was responsible for his uncle's grin. Nicely paced sex and business comedy with warm performances. **94m/C VHS, Beta.** Dean Martin, Shirley MacLaine, Cliff Robertson, Charlie Ruggles; ***D:*** Joseph Anthony; ***W:*** Sidney Sheldon; ***M:*** Andre Previn. *FOX*

All Mine to Give 🦴🦴½ *The Day They Gave the Babies Away* **1956** Sad saga of a Scottish family of eight who braved frontier hardships, epidemics, and death in the Wisconsin wilderness more than a century ago. Midway through, mom and dad die, leaving the oldest child struggling to keep the family together. A strange, though often effective, combination of pioneer adventures and tearjerking moments that avoids becoming hopelessly soapy due to fine performances. Unless you're pretty weathered, you'll need some hankies. Based on the reminiscences of Dale and Katherine Eunson as detailed in a "Cosmopolitan" magazine article. **102m/C VHS, Beta.** Glynis Johns, Cameron Mitchell, Rex Thompson, Patty McCormack, Ernest Truex, Hope Emerson, Alan Hale Jr., Royal Dano, Reta Shaw, Rita Johnson, Ellen Corby, Jon Provost; ***D:*** Allen Reisner; ***M:*** Max Steiner. *NO*

All My Good Countrymen ♂♂½ *All Good Citizens* **1968** A lyrical, funny film about the eccentric denizens of a small Moravian village soon after the socialization of Czechoslovakia in 1948. Completed during the Soviet invasion of 1968 and immediately banned. In Czech with English subtitles. **115m/C VHS, Beta.** *CZ* Vladimir Mensik, Radoslav Brozobohaty, Pavel Pavlovsky; ***D:*** Vojtech Jasny. Cannes Film Festival '69: Best Director (Jasny); Nominations: Cannes Film Festival '69: Best Film. *FCT*

All My Sons ♂♂♂ **1986** A wealthy family is distraught when their eldest son is listed as missing-in-action during WWII. They must cope with guilt, as well as grief, because the father's business reaped profits from the war. Adapted for television from the acclaimed Arthur Miller play. **122m/C VHS, Beta.** James Whitmore, Aidan Quinn, Joan Allen, Michael Learned; ***D:*** John Power. *MCA*

All Night Long ♂♂♂ **1981 (R)** Offbeat middle-age crisis comedy about a burned-out and recently demoted drugstore executive in L.A. who leaves his wife, takes up with his fourth cousin by marriage, and begins a humorous rebellion, becoming an extremely freelance inventor while joining the drifters, weirdos and thieves of the night. An obscure, sometimes uneven little gem with Hackman in top form and an appealing supporting performance by Streisand. Highlighted by delightful malapropisms and sataric inversion of the usual cliches. **100m/C VHS, Beta.** Gene Hackman, Barbra Streisand, Diane Ladd, Dennis Quaid, Kevin Dobson, William Daniels; ***D:*** Jean-Claude Tramont; ***W:*** W.D. Richter; ***M:*** Ira Newborn. *GKK*

All Night Long/Smile Please **1924** Two classic comedies by the most overlooked of the great silent clowns, both produced by slapstick progenitor Mack Sennett. **66m/B VHS, Beta.** Harry Langdon, Natalie Kingston, Jack Cooper, Alberta Vaughn. *VYY*

All of Me ♂♂½ **1984 (PG)** A wealthy woman (Tomlin) dies and her guru accidentally transfers her soul to the right side of her lawyer's body, a modern version of existential hell. Lawyer Martin indulges in some funny slapstick as he discovers that his late client is waging an internal war for control of his body. Flat and cliched at times, but redeemed by the inspired clowning of Martin and witty Martin/Tomlin repartee. Based on the novel "Me Too" by Ed Davis. **93m/C VHS, Beta, LV.** Steve Martin, Lily Tomlin, Victoria Tennant, Madolyn Smith, Richard Libertini, Dana Elcar, Selma Diamond; ***D:*** Carl Reiner; ***W:*** Phil Alden Robinson. New York Film Critics Awards '84: Best Actor (Martin); National Society of Film Critics Awards '84: Best Actor (Martin). *FCT*

All Over Town ♂♂½ **1937** Two vaudevillians with a trained seal find themselves involved in a murder when they are kidnapped by a gang of thugs. A lesser Olsen and Johnson comedy with scattered funny moments. **52m/B VHS, Beta.** Ole Olsen, Chic Johnson, Mary Howard, Franklin Pangborn, James Finlayson; ***D:*** James W. Horne; ***W:*** Jack Townley, Jerome Chodorov. *NOS, MRV, VYY*

All Quiet on the Western Front ♂♂♂♂ **1930** Extraordinary and realistic anti-war epic based on the novel by Erich Maria Remarque. Seven patriotic German youths go together from school to the battlefields of WWI. They experience the horrors of war first-hand, stuck in the trenches and facing gradual extermination. Centers on experiences of one of the young men, Paul Baumer, who changes from enthusiastic war endorser to battle-weary veteran in an emotionally exact performance by Ayres. Boasts a gigantic budget (for the time) of $1.25 million, and features more than 2,000 extras swarming about battlefields set up on ranchland in California. Relentless anti-war message is emotionally draining and startling with both graphic shots and haunting visual poetry. Extremely controversial in the U.S. and Germany upon release, the original version was 140 minutes long (some versions are available with restored footage) and featured ZaSu Pitts as Ayres mother (later reshot with Mercer replacing her). Remarque, who had fought and been wounded on the Western Front, was eventually forced to leave Germany for the U.S. due to the film's ongoing controversy. **103m/B VHS, Beta, LV.** Lew Ayres, Louis Wolheim, John Wray, Slim Summerville, Russell Gleason, Raymond Griffith, Ben Alexander, Beryl Mercer; ***D:*** Lewis Milestone. Academy Awards '30: Best Director (Milestone), Best Picture; National Board of Review Awards '30: 10 Best Films of the Year; Nominations: Academy Awards '30: Best Cinematography, Best Writing. *MCA, FCT, GLV*

All Quiet on the Western Front ♂♂½ **1979** A big-budget television remake of the 1930 masterpiece starring John Boy. Sensitive German youth Thomas plunges excitedly into WWI and discovers its terror and degradation. Nowhere near the original's quality. **150m/C VHS, Beta, LV.** Richard Thomas, Ernest Borgnine, Donald Pleasence, Patricia Neal; ***D:*** Delbert Mann. *FOX, FCT*

All Screwed Up ♂♂♂ *All in Place; Nothing in Order* **1974** A group of young immigrants come to Milan and try to adjust to city life; they soon find that everything is in its place, but nothing is in order. Wertmuller in a lighter vein than usual. **104m/C VHS, Beta.** *IT* Luigi Diberti, Lina Polito; ***D:*** Lina Wertmuller; ***W:*** Lina Wertmuller. *FOX*

All That Jazz ♂♂♂½ **1979 (R)** Fosse's autobiographical portrait with Scheider fully occupying his best role as the obsessed, pill-popping, chain-smoking choreographer/director dancing simultaneously with love and death. But even while dying, he creates some great dancing. Vivid and imaginative with exact editing, and an eerie footnote to Fosse's similar death almost ten years later. Egocentric and self-indulgent for sure, but that's entertainment. ♫On Broadway; Everything Old is New Again; After You've Gone; There'll Be Some Changes Made; Some of These Days; Bye Bye Love. **120m/C VHS, Beta, LV.** Roy Scheider, Jessica Lange, Ann Reinking, Leland Palmer, Cliff Gorman, Ben Vereen, Erzebet Foldi, John Lithgow, Wallace Shawn, Sandahl Bergman, Nicole Fosse, Keith Gordon, Ben Masters, Theresa Merritt; ***D:*** Bob Fosse; ***C:*** Giuseppe Rotunno; ***M:*** Ralph Burns. Academy Awards '79: Best Art Direction/Set Decoration, Best Costume Design, Best Film Editing, Best Original Score; Cannes Film Festival '80: Best Film; Nominations: Academy Awards '79: Best Actor (Scheider), Best Cinematography, Best Director (Fosse), Best Original Screenplay, Best Picture. *FOX, OM*

All the Brothers Were Valiant ♂♂½ **1953** Brothers Taylor and Granger are New England whaling captains but Granger decides to treasure hunt instead. He finds a priceless cache of black pearls on an island but angers the locals who regard the gems as sacred. When Taylor rescues him, Granger promptly turns his brother's crew into mutineers in order to return to the island and retrieve his prize. Lots of brawling and there's an incidental love story with Blyth desired by both men (she's married Taylor and just happens to be aboard). Last role for Stone. Based on the novel by Ben Ames Williams. **101m/C VHS.** Robert Taylor, Stewart Granger, Ann Blyth, Betta St. John, Keenan Wynn, James Whitmore, Kurt Kasznar, Lewis Stone, Robert Burton, Peter Whitney, John Lupton, Billie Dove; ***D:*** Richard Thorpe; ***W:*** Harry Brown; ***M:*** Miklos Rozsa. *MGM*

All the Kind Strangers ♂♂ *Evil in the Swamp* **1974** Traveling photographer Keach picks up a young hitchhiker and takes him to the boy's home. He discovers six other children there who want him as a father, his alternative being death. He and "Mother" Eggar plot their escape from the dangerous orphans. Made-for-television thriller short on suspense. **72m/C VHS, Beta.** Stacy Keach, Robby Benson, John Savage, Samantha Eggar; ***D:*** Burt Kennedy. *FOX*

All the King's Men ♂♂♂♂ **1949** Grim and graphic classic set in the Depression follows the rise of a Louisiana farm-boy from angry and honest political hopeful to powerful but corrupt governor. Loosely based on the life (and death) of Huey Long and told by a newsman who's followed his career (Ireland). Willy Stark (Crawford, in his break-through role) is the politician who, while appearing to improve the state, rules dictatorially, betraying friends and constituents and proving once again that power corrupts. In her first major role, McCambridge delivers a powerful performance as the cunning political aide. Potent morality play based on the Robert Penn Warren book. **109m/B VHS, Beta, LV.** Broderick Crawford, Mercedes McCambridge, John Ireland, Joanne Dru, John Derek, Anne Seymour, Shepperd Strudwick; ***D:*** Robert Rossen; ***W:*** Robert Rossen; ***C:*** Burnett Guffey. Academy Awards '49: Best Actor (Crawford), Best Picture, Best Supporting Actress (McCambridge); New York Film Critics Awards '49: Best Actor (Crawford), Best Film; Nominations: Academy Awards '49: Best Director (Rossen), Best Film Editing, Best Screenplay, Best Supporting Actor (Ireland). *COL, BTV*

All the Lovin' Kinfolk ♂ *Kin Folk; Kinfolk; The Closest of Kin* **1989 (R)** Two recent Hillbilly High graduates decide to take on the big city, but find themselves in dire situations. For those with time to kill. **80m/C VHS.** Mady Maguire, Jay Scott, Anne Ryan, John Denis, Donna Young; ***D:*** John Hayes. *NO*

...All the Marbles ♂♂ *The California Dolls* **1981 (R)** A manager of two beautiful lady wrestlers has dreams of going to the top. Aldrich's last film, and an atypical one, with awkward pacing and a thin veil of sex exploitation. Falk provides needed grace and humor as the seedy manager, with Young contributing his usual competent bit as a hustling promoter dabbling in criminal activity. One of the few tag-team women wrestling pictures, it builds to a rousing finale match in the "Rocky" tradition, although the shift in tone and mounting cliches effectively body slam the intent. **113m/C VHS, Beta, LV.** Peter Falk, Burt Young, Richard Jaeckel, Vicki Frederick; ***D:*** Robert Aldrich; ***C:*** Joseph Biroc. *MGM, OM*

All the President's Men ♂♂♂½ **1976 (PG)** True story of the Watergate break-in that led to the political scandal of the decade, based on the best-selling book by Washington Post reporters Bob Woodward and Carl Bernstein. Intriguing, terse thriller is a nail-biter even though the ending is no secret. Expertly paced by Pakula with standout performances by Hoffman and Redford as the reporters who slowly uncover and connect the seemingly isolated facts that ultimately lead to criminal indictments of the Nixon Administration. Deep Throat Holbrook and Robards as executive editor Ben Bradlee lend authenticity to the endeavor, a realistic portrayal of the stop and go of journalistic investigations. **135m/C VHS, Beta, LV.** Robert Redford, Dustin Hoffman, Jason Robards Jr., Martin Balsam, Jane Alexander, Hal Holbrook, F. Murray Abraham, Stephen Collins, Lindsay Crouse; ***D:*** Alan J. Pakula; ***W:*** William Goldman; ***C:*** Gordon Willis; ***M:*** David Shire. Academy Awards '76: Best Adapted Screenplay, Best Art Direction/Set Decoration, Best Sound, Best Supporting Actor (Robards); New York Film Critics Awards '76: Best Director (Pakula), Best Film, Best Supporting Actor (Robards); Writers Guild of America '76: Best Adapted Screenplay; Nominations: Academy Awards '76: Best Director (Pakula), Best Film Editing, Best Picture, Best Supporting Actress (Alexander). *WAR, BTV*

All the Right Moves ♂♂½ **1983 (R)** Cruise is the high school football hero hoping for a scholarship so he can vacate pronto the dying Pennsylvania mill town where he grew up. At least he thinks that's what he wants to do. Further mixing up his own mixed feelings are his pushy, ambitious coach (Nelson, doing what he does best), his understanding dad (Cioffi) and supportive girlfriend (Thompson, in a notable early role). Strong performances push the relatively cliched melodrama into field goal range. Cinematographer Chapman's directorial debut. **90m/C VHS, Beta, LV.** Tom Cruise, Lea Thompson, Craig T. Nelson, Christopher Penn; ***D:*** Michael Chapman; ***W:*** Michael Kane; ***C:*** Jan De Bont. *FOX, FXV*

All the Rivers Run **1984** First made-for-cable miniseries. A young Australian girl spends her inheritance on a river boat and becomes the first female river captain in Australian history. Directed by George Miller of "Man from Snowy River" fame. Four parts. **400m/C VHS.** *AU* Sigrid Thornton, John Waters, Diane Craig, Charles Tingwell, Gus Mercurio; ***D:*** George Miller, Pino Amenta. *HBO*

All the Vermeers in New York ☙☙☙½ **1991** A stressed-out Wall Street broker flees to the soothing recesses of the Metropolitan Museum's Vermeer Room. There he meets a beautiful, manipulative French actress dreaming of success in Manhattan. Amidst the opulent art world of New York, the two pursue their relationship to an ultimately tragic end. Jost offers an inside look at the collision of commerce and art and the corrupt underside of New York in this elegant contemporary film. **87m/C VHS, LV.** Emmanuelle Chaulet, Stephen Lack, Grace Phillips, Katherine Bean, Laurel Lee Kiefer, Gracie Mansion, Gordon Joseph Weiss, Roger Ruffin; ***D:*** Jon Jost; ***W:*** Jon Jost. *WAC, INJ*

All the Way, Boys ☙½ **1973 (PG)** Two inept adventurers crash-land a plane in the Andes in the hope of discovering slapstick, but find none. "Trinity" cast up to no good. **105m/C VHS, Beta.** *IT* Terence Hill, Bud Spencer, Cyril Cusack, Michel Antoine; ***D:*** Giuseppe Colizzi. *SUE*

All the Young Men ☙☙☙ **1960** Fairly powerful men-uniting-in-battle story with an interesting cast, highlighted by Poitier in an early role. A tiny marine squadron overrun by the Chinese in the Korean War attempts to resist the numerous attackers. In their spare time, the men confront racial prejudice when a black man (guess who) takes command. **86m/B VHS, Beta.** Alan Ladd, Sidney Poitier, James Darren, Glenn Corbett, Mort Sahl; ***D:*** Hall Bartlett; ***W:*** Hall Bartlett; ***C:*** Daniel F. Fapp. *COL*

All Things Fair ☙☙½ *Lust och Fagring Stor* **1995** Coming of age story set in neutral Sweden in 1943. Fifteen-year-old Stig (Widerberg, the director's son) has just arrived in Malmo to begin classes at his all-male school—a situation filled with sexual curiosity and repression. Stig is attracted to his beautiful teacher Viola (Lagercrantz), whose marriage to alcoholic traveling salesman Frank (von Bronssen) is less than ideal, and the duo begin an affair. Frank not only seems not to care but befriends his wife's youthful lover, although the situation is ripe for tragedy. Excellent performances, sensual air, though somewhat lacking in logical narrative. Swedish with subtitles. **128m/C VHS.** *DK SW* Johan Widerberg, Marika Lagercrantz, Tomas von Bromssen, Bjorn Kjellman, Charles A. Palmer; ***D:*** Bo Widerberg; ***W:*** Bo Widerberg; ***C:*** Morten Bruus. Nominations: Academy Awards '95: Best Foreign Language Film. *NYR*

All This and Heaven Too ☙☙☙ **1940** When a governess arrives at a Parisian aristocrat's home in the 1840s, she causes jealous tension between the husband and his wife. The wife is soon found murdered. Based on Rachel Field's best-seller. **141m/B VHS, Beta.** Charles Boyer, Bette Davis, Barbara O'Neil, Virginia Weidler, Jeffrey Lynn, Helen Westley, Henry Daniell, Harry Davenport; ***D:*** Anatole Litvak; ***M:*** Max Steiner. Nominations: Academy Awards '40: Best Black and White Cinematography, Best Picture, Best Supporting Actress (O'Neil). *MGM*

All Through the Night ☙☙☙ **1942** A very funny spy spoof as well as a thrilling crime story with Bogart playing a gambler who takes on a Nazi spy ring. Features memorable double-talk and a great auction scene that inspired the one with Cary Grant in "North by Northwest." Suspense builds throughout the film as Lorre appears in a sinister role as Pepi and Veidt gives a fine performance as the spymaster. **107m/B VHS.** Humphrey Bogart, Conrad Veidt, Karen Verne, Jane Darwell, Frank McHugh, Peter Lorre, Judith Anderson, William Demarest, Jackie Gleason, Phil Silvers, Barton MacLane, Martin Kosleck; ***D:*** Vincent Sherman. *MGM*

All Tied Up ☙☙½ **1992 (R)** Ladies man Brian (Galligan) thinks he's found true love with Linda (Hatcher) but that doesn't mean he's stopped seeing other women. And when Linda finds out, she breaks it off. So Brian goes over to her house to work things out and gets tied up—literally—by Linda and her girlfriends. Talk about teaching a guy a lesson. **90m/C VHS.** Zach Galligan, Teri Hatcher, Tracy Griffith, Lara Harris; ***D:*** John Mark Robinson; ***W:*** Robert Madero, I. Markie Lane; ***M:*** Bernardo Bonazzi. *COL*

All You Need Is Cash ☙☙☙ *The Rutles* **1978** "The Rutles" star in this parody of The Beatles' legend, from the early days of the "Pre-Fab Four" in Liverpool to their worldwide success. A marvelous pseudo-documentary, originally shown on NBC-TV and with various SNL alumni (including Weiss), that captures the development of the Beatles and '60s rock with devastating effect. Served as the inspiration for "This Is Spinal Tap." **70m/C VHS, Beta, LV.** Eric Idle, Neil Innes, Ricky Fataar, Dan Aykroyd, Gilda Radner, John Belushi, George Harrison, Paul Simon, Mick Jagger, John Halsey; ***D:*** Eric Idle, Gary Weis. *MVD, MLT*

Allan Quatermain and the Lost City of Gold ☙½ **1986 (PG)** While trying to find his brother, Quatermain discovers a lost African civilization, in this weak adaptation of an H. Rider Haggard adventure. An ostensible sequel to the equally shallow "King Solomon's Mines." **100m/C VHS, Beta.** Richard Chamberlain, Sharon Stone, James Earl Jones; ***D:*** Gary Nelson; ***W:*** Gene Quintano, Lee Reynolds. *FHE, MED, VTR*

Allegheny Uprising ☙☙½ *The First Rebel* **1939** Set in 1759, the story of a frontiersman who clashes with a British military commander in order to stop the sale of firearms to Indians. The stars of "Stagecoach" are back on board in this lesser effort. Also available colorized. **81m/B VHS, Beta, LV.** John Wayne, Claire Trevor, George Sanders, Brian Donlevy, Chill Wills, Moroni Olsen; ***D:*** William A. Seiter. *CCB, TTC*

Allegro Non Troppo ☙☙☙ **1976 (PG)** An energetic and bold collection of animated skits set to classical music in this Italian version of Disney's "Fantasia." Watch for the evolution of life set to Ravel's Bolero, or better yet, watch the whole darn movie. Features Nichetti (often referred to as the Italian Woody Allen, particularly by people in Italy) in the non-animated segments, who went on to write, direct, and star (he may have sold concessions in the lobby as well) in "The Icicle Thief." **75m/C VHS, LV.** *IT* Maurizio Nichetti; ***D:*** Bruno Bozzetto. *BMG, IME, INJ*

Alley Cat ☙ **1984 (R)** Woman uses martial arts to fight back against a street gang that attacked her. **82m/C VHS, Beta.** Karin Mani, Robert Torti, Brit Helfer, Michael Wayne, Jon Greene; ***D:*** Edward Victor. *VES, LIV*

Alligator ☙☙☙ **1980 (R)** Dumped down a toilet 12 long years ago, lonely alligator Ramon resides in the city sewers, quietly eating and sleeping. In addition to feasting on the occasional stray human, Ramon devours the animal remains of a chemical plant's experiment involving growth hormones and eventually begins to swell at an enormous rate. Nothing seems to satisfy Ramon's ever-widening appetite: not all the people or all the buildings in the whole town, but he keeps trying, much to the regret of the guilt-ridden cop and lovely scientist who get to know each other while trying to nab the gator. Mediocre special effects are only a distraction in this witty eco-monster take. **94m/C VHS, Beta.** Robert Forster, Lewis Teague, Jack Carter, Henry Silva, Robin Riker, Dean Jagger; ***D:*** Lewis Teague; ***W:*** John Sayles, Frank Ray Perilli. *LIV*

Alligator 2: The Mutation ☙☙ **1990 (PG-13)** Not a sequel to 1980's surprisingly good "Alligator," but a bland rehash with a decent cast. Once again a toxic alligator grows to enormous size and menaces a community. A Donald-Trump-like villain and pro wrestlers (!) bring this up to date, but it's all on the level of a TV disaster movie; even the PG-13 rating is a bit too harsh. **92m/C VHS, LV.** Steve Railsback, Dee Wallace Stone, Joseph Bologna, Woody Brown, Bill Daily, Brock Peters; ***W:*** Curt Allen. *COL, NLC*

Alligator Alley ☙ **1972** When two young divers witness a major drug deal, they become entangled in a web of danger they never expected. **92m/C VHS, Beta.** Steve Alaimo, John Davis Chandler, Willie Pastrano, Jeremy Slate, Cece Stone; ***D:*** William Grefe. *PSM*

Alligator Eyes ☙☙½ **1990 (R)** Stranger wearing trouble like a cheap perfume enters the midst of a vacationing trio of New Yorkers. Their vulnerabilities are exposed by a young hitchhiker sporting a slinky polka dot ensemble and way cool sunglasses who insinuates herself into their vacation plans (not to mention their private lives), before the three realize she's blind and full of manipulative and vindictive tricks, thanks to the usual brutal childhood. Psycho-sexo-logical thriller has some fine performances and a promising beginning, before fizzling into celluloid cotton candy. **101m/C VHS.** Annabelle Larsen, Roger Kabler, Mary McLain, Allen McCullough, John MacKay; ***D:*** John Feldman; ***W:*** John Feldman; ***M:*** Sheila Silver. *ACA*

The Allnighter ☙ **1987 (PG-13)** A college coed searches through the hypersexed beach-party milieu of her senior year for Mr. Right. Bangle Hoffs is directed by her mom, to no avail. **95m/C VHS, Beta.** Susanna Hoffs, John Terlesky, Joan Cusack, Michael Ontkean; ***D:*** Tamar Simon Hoffs; ***M:*** Charles Bernstein. *MCA*

Allonsanfan ☙☙☙½ **1973** Early Taviani, in which a disillusioned Jacobin aristocrat in 1816, after Napoleon has fallen, struggles with his revolutionary ideals and his accustomed lifestyle. Exciting score. In Italian with English subtitles. **115m/C VHS, Beta.** *IT* Marcello Mastroianni, Laura Betti, Renato de Carmine, Lea Massari, Mimsy Farmer, Claudio Cassinelli; ***D:*** Paolo Taviani; ***M:*** Ennio Morricone. *FCT, WBF, INJ*

All's Fair ☙ **1989** Silly and predictable comedy about executives who take on their spouses at weekend war games. An unfortunate waste of a good cast. **89m/C VHS, Beta, LV.** George Segal, Sally Kellerman, Robert Carradine, Jennifer Edwards, Jane Kaczmarek, John Kapelos, Lou Ferrigno; ***D:*** Rocky Lane. *MED*

Almanac of Fall ☙☙ **19??** Set in a claustrophic apartment, where the occupants reveal all their deepest hositilies, fears, and obsessions. In Hungarian with English subtitles. **119m/C VHS.** *HU* Hedi Temessy, Erika Bodnar, Miklos B. Szekely, Pal Hetenyi, Janos Dersi; ***D:*** Bela Tarr; ***W:*** Bela Tarr. *FCT*

...Almost ☙☙ *Wendy Cracked a Walnut* **1990 (PG)** Arquette plays a curiously giddy bookworm with a vivid imagination. When her husband disappears on their anniversary, the man of her dreams shows up to sweep her off her feet. Is he real or is he simply another daydream? Almost a good time. **87m/C VHS, LV.** *AU* Rosanna Arquette, Bruce Spence; ***D:*** Michael Pattinson. *NO*

Almost an Angel ☙½ **1990 (PG)** Another in a recent spat of angels and ghosts assigned back to earth by the head office. A life-long criminal (Hogan) commits a heroic act and finds himself a probationary angel returned to earth to gain permanent angel status. He befriends a wheelchair-bound man, falls in love with the guy's sister, and helps her out at a center for potential juvenile delinquents. Melodramatic and hokey in places, relying too much on Hogan's crocodilian charisma. **98m/C VHS, LV.** Paul Hogan, Linda Kozlowski, Elias Koteas, Doreen Lang, Charlton Heston; ***D:*** John Cornell; ***W:*** Paul Hogan. *PAR*

Almost Angels ☙☙ **1962** Two boys romp in Austria as members of the Vienna Boys Choir. Lesser sentimental Disney effort that stars the actual members of the Choir; not much of a draw for today's Nintendo-jaded young viewers. **85m/C VHS, Beta.** Vincent Winter, Peter Weck, Hans Holt; ***D:*** Steve Previn. *DIS*

Almost Blue ☙½ **1993 (R)** A gigantic, slow-moving, movie cliche. Madsen is a sulky, hard-living sax player going off the deep end because of his wife's death. Walden is the good woman who comes along to save him from himself. Tenor saxman Ernie Watts doubles for Madsen. Do yourself a favor—skip the movie and listen to some good jazz instead. **98m/C VHS, LV.** Michael Madsen, Lynette Walden, Garrett Morris, Gale Mayron, Yaphet Kotto; ***D:*** Keoni Waxman. *LIV*

Almost Dead 🦴🦴½ **1994** Psychiatrist Katherine Roshak's (Doherty) mother committed suicide four years ago and suddenly her corpse is appearing to Katherine. When she visits Mom's grave, Katherine finds an empty coffin. So she teams up with a skeptical cop (Mandylor) to figure out what's going on. Lots of loose ends. **92m/C VHS.** Shannen Doherty, Costas Mandylor, John Diehl, William R. Moses; ***D:*** Ruben Preuss. *MNC*

Almost Human *Woof! The Kidnap of Mary Lou* **1979 (R)** An Italian Mafia gorefest about a second-class don who kidnaps a businessman's daughter, and then has trouble trying to collect a ransom. For aficionados of Italian Mafia gorefests only (check your weapons at the door). **90m/C VHS, Beta.** *IT* Henry Silva, Tomas Milian, Laura Belli; ***D:*** Umberto Lenzi; ***M:*** Ennio Morricone. *PSM*

Almost Partners **1987** Grandpa's ashes are in trouble. His urn and remains have been stolen. Fortunately, his teenage granddaughter and a detective are on the case. From the PBS "Wonderworks" television series. **58m/C VHS.** Paul Sorvino, Royana Black, Mary Wickes; ***D:*** Alan Kingsberg. *PME, HMV, FCT*

An Almost Perfect Affair 🦴🦴 **1979 (PG)** Taxing romantic comedy about an ambitious independent American filmmaker who, after finishing a movie about an executed murderer, travels to the Cannes festival and proceeds to fall in love or lust with the wife of an Italian producer. Numerous inside jokes and capable performances nearly overcome script lethargy. **92m/C VHS, Beta.** Keith Carradine, Monica Vitti, Raf Vallone, Christian de Sica, Dick Anthony Williams; ***D:*** Michael Ritchie; ***W:*** Walter Bernstein; ***M:*** Georges Delerue. *PAR*

Almost Pregnant 🦴🦴½ **1991 (R)** Linda Anderson (Roberts) desperately wants a baby, but her husband, Charlie (Conaway) is unable to get her pregnant. Dead set against artificial insemination, Linda decides to take a lover. Charlie doesn't want to lose her, so he goes along with her idea. Linda falls in love with the new guy; discovers he's had a vasectomy and takes yet another lover while continuing to see the other two guys. Hilarious complications abound in her outrageous quest for a baby. An unrated version containing explicit scenes is also available. **90m/C VHS, LV.** Tanya Roberts, Jeff Conaway, Joan Severance, Dom DeLuise; ***D:*** Michael DeLuise; ***W:*** Fred Stroppel. *COL*

Almost Royal Family 🦴 **1984** All kinds of problems arise when a family inherits an island on the St. Lawrence River embargoed by the United States and Canada. **52m/C VHS, Beta.** Sarah Jessica Parker, John Femia. *WAR*

Almost You 🦴🦴 **1985 (R)** Normal marital conflicts and uncertainties grow exponentially when a wealthy New York City thirty-something couple hires a lovely young nurse to help care for the wife after a car accident. An unsentimental marital comedy with a good cast that still misses. **91m/C VHS, Beta.** Brooke Adams, Griffin Dunne, Karen Young, Marty Watt, Christine Estabrook, Josh Mostel, Laura Dean, Dana Delany, Miguel Pinero, Joe Silver, Suzzy Roche, Spalding Gray; ***D:*** Adam Brooks; ***M:*** Jonathan Elias. *FOX*

Aloha, Bobby and Rose 🦴🦴½ **1974 (PG)** A mechanic and his girlfriend in L.A. become accidentally involved in an attempted robbery and murder and go on the run for Mexico, of course. Semi-satisfying drama in the surf, with fine location photography. **90m/C VHS, Beta.** Paul LeMat, Dianne Hull, Robert Carradine, Tim McIntire, Edward James Olmos, Leigh French; ***D:*** Floyd Mutrux. *MED*

Aloha Summer 🦴🦴 **1988 (PG)** Six surfing teenagers of various ethnic backgrounds learn of love and life in 1959 Hawaii while riding the big wave of impending adulthood, with a splash of Kung Fu thrown in for good measure. Sensitive and bland. **97m/C VHS, Beta, LV.** Chris Makepeace, Lorie Griffin, Don Michael Paul, Sho Kosugi, Yuji Okumoto, Tia Carrere; ***D:*** Tommy Lee Wallace; ***W:*** Robert Benedetto. *WAR, ORI*

Alone Against Rome 🦴½ **1962** A muscle-bound warrior takes on the forces of Rome to avenge himself against a scornful woman. **100m/B VHS, Beta.** *IT* Lang Jeffries, Rossana Podesta, Phillippe LeRoy; ***D:*** Herbert Wise. *SNC*

Alone in the Dark 🦴🦴 **1982 (R)** Slash and dash horror attempt featuring four escaped patients from a mental hospital who decide that they must kill their doctor because they don't like him. Conveniently, a city-wide blackout provides the opportunity, as the good doctor defends home and family against the aging stars intent on chewing up as much scenery as possible. **92m/C VHS, Beta.** Jack Palance, Donald Pleasence, Martin Landau, Dwight Schultz; ***D:*** Jack Sholder. *NLC, COL*

Alone in the Neon Jungle 🦴🦴 **1987** A glamorous big-city police captain is assigned to clean up the most corrupt precinct in town. Pleshette is untypically cast but still manages to make her role believable in a serviceable TV cop drama with more dialogue than action. **90m/C VHS.** Suzanne Pleshette, Danny Aiello, Georg Stanford Brown, Frank Converse, Joe Morton; ***D:*** Georg Stanford Brown. *NLC*

Alone in the T-Shirt Zone 🦴 **1986** A maniacal T-shirt designer lands in a mental institution. **81m/C VHS, Beta.** Michael Barrack, Taylor Gilbert, Bill Barron. *NWV*

Along Came Jones 🦴🦴🦴 **1945** Cowboy Cooper, who can't handle a gun and is saddled with grumpy sidekick Demarest, is the victim of mistaken identity as both the good guys and the bad guys pursue him thinking he is a vicious killer. Young is the woman who rides to his defense. Offbeat and charming western parody based on a novel by Alan le May. **93m/B VHS, Beta.** Gary Cooper, Loretta Young, Dan Duryea, William Demarest; ***D:*** Stuart Heisler; ***W:*** Nunnally Johnson; ***C:*** Milton Krasner. *MGM, FCT*

Along the Great Divide 🦴🦴 **1951** A U.S. marshal and his deputy battle pursuing vigilantes and the untamed frontier to bring a falsely accused murderer to trial (and of course, find the real bad guy). Douglas' first western has the usual horse opera cliches supported by excellent cinematography. **88m/B VHS, Beta.** Kirk Douglas, John Agar, Walter Brennan, Virginia Mayo; ***D:*** Raoul Walsh. *WAR, TLF*

Along the Sundown Trail 🦴½ **1942** Standard western escapades as cowboy G-men round up the villains. **59m/B VHS, Beta.** William Boyd, Art Davis, Lee Powell, Julie Duncan, Kermit Maynard, Charles "Blackie" King; ***D:*** Sam Newfield. *GPV, VCN*

Alpha Beta 🦴🦴½ **1973** A stage production set to film studying the break-up of a marriage, where all the husband and wife have in common is the children. Finney and Roberts efficiently carry the load. **70m/C VHS, Beta.** Albert Finney, Rachel Roberts; ***D:*** Anthony Page. *NO*

The Alpha Incident 🦴½ **1976 (PG)** Time-worn doomsday drama about an alien organism with the potential to destroy all living things. Government works hard to cover up. **86m/C VHS, Beta.** Ralph Meeker, Stafford Morgan, John Goff, Carol Irene Newell, John Alderman; ***D:*** Bill Rebane. *MED*

Alphabet City 🦴🦴 **1984 (R)** A drug kingpin who runs New York's Lower East Side has decided to turn over a new leaf, but first he must survive his last night as a criminal while figuring out a way to pay off his large debts. Very stylish and moody, but light on content and plot. **85m/C VHS, Beta.** Vincent Spano, Michael Winslow, Kate Vernon, Jami Gertz, Zohra Lampert, Raymond Serra, Kenny Marino, Daniel Jordano, Miguel Pinero; ***D:*** Amos Poe; ***W:*** Amos Poe. *FOX*

The Alphabet Murders 🦴🦴 *ABC Murders* **1965** Picture this: Randall playing Agatha Christie's famous Belgian sleuth, Hercule Poirot, and Rutherford—in a cameo—as Miss Marple. As if that wouldn't be enough to make Dame Agatha roll over in her grave, there's plenty of cloying wisecracking and slapsticking throughout. An adaptation of "The ABC Murders" in which Poirot stalks a literate killer who snuffs out his victims in alphabetical order. Hardly a must-see, unless you're hellbent on viewing the entire Randall opus. **90m/B VHS, Beta.** Tony Randall, Anita Ekberg, Robert Morley, Maurice Denham, Guy Rolfe, Sheila Allen; ***Cameos:*** Margaret Rutherford; ***D:*** Frank Tashlin. *MGM, FCT*

Alphaville 🦴🦴🦴 *Alphaville, a Strange Case of Lemmy Caution; Alphaville, Une Etrange Aventure de Lemmy Caution* **1965** Engaging and inimitable Godard attempt at science fiction mystery. P.I. Lemmy Caution searches for a scientist in a city (Paris as you've never seen it before) run by robots and overseen by a dictator. The futuristic techno-conformist society must be upended so that Caution may save the scientist as well as nonconformists everywhere. In French with subtitles. **100m/B VHS, Beta.** *FR* Eddie Constantine, Anna Karina, Akim Tamiroff; ***D:*** Jean-Luc Godard; ***W:*** Jean-Luc Godard. Berlin International Film Festival '65: Golden Berlin Bear. *HMV, SNC, MRV*

Alpine Fire 🦴🦴½ **1989 (R)** Coming of age story about an adolescent girl and her deaf-mute brother living an isolated life in the Swiss Alps. When life on the mountain overwhelms them, they turn to each other for love. Sharply observed with a naturalistic style, elevating the proceedings above mere voyeurism. **119m/C VHS, Beta, LV.** *SI* Thomas Knock, Johanna Lier, Dorothea Moritz, Rolf Illig; ***D:*** Fredi M. Murer. *VES, LIV*

Alsino and the Condor 🦴🦴🦴 **1982 (R)** An acclaimed Nicaraguan drama about a young boy, caught in war-torn Nicaragua between the Somoza government and the Sandinista rebels, who dreams of flying above the human strife. In Spanish with English subtitles. **89m/C VHS, Beta, LV.** *NI* Dean Stockwell, Alan Esquivel; ***D:*** Miguel Littin. Nominations: Academy Awards '82: Best Foreign Language Film. *FCT, INJ, TPV*

Altered States 🦴🦴🦴 **1980 (R)** Obsessed with the task of discovering the inner man, Hurt's ambitious researcher ignores his family while consuming hallucinogenic drugs and floating in an immersion tank. He gets too deep inside, slipping way back through the evolutionary order and becoming a menance in the process. Confusing script based upon Chayefsky's (alias Sidney Aaron) confusing novel is supported by great special effects and the usual self-indulgent and provocative Russell direction. Chayefsky eventually washed his hands of the project after artistic differences with the producers. Others who departed from the film include initial director William Penn and special effects genius John Dykstra (relieved ably by Bran Ferren). Hurt's a solemn hoot in his first starring role. **103m/C VHS, Beta, LV.** William Hurt, Blair Brown, Bob Balaban, Charles Haid, Dori Brenner, Drew Barrymore, Miguel Godreau, John Larroquette; ***D:*** Ken Russell; ***W:*** Paddy Chayefsky; ***C:*** Jordan Cronenweth. Nominations: Academy Awards '80: Best Art Direction/Set Decoration, Best Original Score. *WAR*

Alternative 🦴🦴 **1976** A female magazine editor finds herself unmarried and quite pregnant. She is caught in a tug-of-war between the baby's father and her current lover. Dated liberated woman and career snoozer. **90m/C VHS, Beta.** Wendy Hughes, Peter Adams, Mary Mackie, Carla Hoogeveen, Tony Bonner. *NO*

Alvarez Kelly 🦴🦴½ **1966** Offbeat western with Holden as the Mexican-Irish Kelly who has just sold a herd of cattle to the North during the Civil War. Confederate officer Widmark kidnaps Holden in an effort to have the cattle redirected to the South. Aided by the traditional women in the midst of men intent on double-crossing each other, a fierce hatred develops between the two, erupting into violence. Sleepy performance by Holden is countered by an intensive Widmark. Based on a true Civil War incident, the script occasionally wanders far afield with the cattle, who cleverly heighten the excitement by stampeding. **109m/C VHS, Beta.** William Holden, Richard Widmark, Janice Rule, Patrick O'Neal, Harry Carey Jr.; ***D:*** Edward Dmytryk. *COL, GKK*

Alvin Purple 🦴½ **1973 (R)** Pedestrian comedy about a Mr. Purple, an ordinary Aussie who sells waterbeds and is for some reason constantly being pursued by throngs of sexually insatiable women. Fortunately, he too enjoys sex, even though complications abound. Sexual situations, double entendres, and a script that aims for cleverness (but rarely attains it) somehow made the lust romp a hit in its native Australia, while worldwide it helped establish a market for Down Under cinema. Shot in Melbourne, and followed by "Alvin Rides Again." **97m/C VHS, Beta, LV.** *AU* Graeme Blundell, George Whaley, Ellie MacLure, Jacki Weaver; ***D:*** Tim Burstall; ***W:*** Alan Finney, Alan Hopgood, Tim Burstall. *NWV*

Alvin Rides Again 🦴🦴 **1974** The sexually insatiable Alvin Purple is asked to impersonate an American gangster who was accidentally killed. Another Aussie sex farce from the original writers, who conspire to create a decent sequel to "Alvin Purple," with much of the same cast and crew. **89m/C VHS, Beta.** *AU* Graeme Blundell, Alan Finney, Brionny Behets, Frank Thring Jr., Jeff Ashby, Robin Copping; ***D:*** David Bilcock; ***W:*** Tim Burstall, Alan Finney, Alan Hopgood. *NWV*

Always 🦴🦴🦴 **1985 (R)** Jaglom fictionally documents his own divorce and reconciliation with Patrice Townsend: set in the director's home and starring his friends and family, the film provides comic insight into the dynamics of married/about-to-be-married/and used-to-be-married relationships. Set at a Fourth of July barbecue, this bittersweet romantic comedy is a veritable feast for Jaglom fans, but not everyone will find the director's free-form narrative to their taste. **105m/C VHS, Beta, LV.** Henry Jaglom, Patrice Townsend, Bob Rafelson, Melissa Leo, Andre Gregory, Michael Emil, Joanna Frank, Alan Rachins, Jonathan Kaufer; ***D:*** Henry Jaglom; ***W:*** Henry Jaglom. *VES, LIV*

Always 🦴🦴½ **1989 (PG)** A hotshot pilot (Dreyfuss) meets a fiery end and finds that his spirit is destined to become a guardian angel to the greenhorn fire-fighting flyboy (Johnson) who steals his girl's heart. Warm remake of "A Guy Named Joe," one of Spielberg's favorite movies. Sparks between Dreyfuss and Hunter eventually ignite, but Goodman delivers the most heat. Hepburn makes an appearance as the angel who guides Dreyfuss. An old-fashioned tree-burner romance that includes actual footage of the 1988 Yellowstone fire. **123m/C VHS, Beta, LV.** Holly Hunter, Richard Dreyfuss, John Goodman, Audrey Hepburn, Brad Johnson, Marg Helgenberger, Keith David, Roberts Blossom; ***D:*** Steven Spielberg; ***W:*** Jerry Belson; ***C:*** Mikael Salomon; ***M:*** John Williams. *MCA, FCT*

Amadeus 🦴🦴🦴½ **1984 (PG)** Entertaining adaptation by Shaffer of his play about the intense rivalry between 18th century composers Antonio Salieri and Wolfgang Amadeus Mozart. Abraham's Salieri is a man who desires greatness but is tortured by envy and sorrow. His worst attacks of angst occur when he comes into contact with Hulce's Mozart, an immature, boorish genius who, despite his gifts, remains unaffected and delighted by the beauty he creates while irking the hell out of everyone around him. Terrific period piece filmed on location in Prague; excellent musical score, beautiful sets, nifty billowy costumes, and realistic American accents for the 18th century Europeans. ♫Concert No. 27 for Pianoforte and Orchestra in B Flat Major; Ave Verum Corpus; A Quintet For Strings in E Flat; A Concerto for Clarinet and Orchestra in A Major; Number 39 in E Flat Major; Number 40 in G Minor; Number 41 in C Major. **158m/C VHS, Beta, LV.** F. Murray Abraham, Tom Hulce, Elizabeth Berridge, Simon Callow, Roy Dotrice, Christine Ebersole, Jeffrey Jones, Kenny Baker, Cynthia Nixon, Vincent Schiavelli; ***D:*** Milos Forman; ***W:*** Peter Shaffer. Academy Awards '84: Best Actor (Abraham), Best Adapted Screenplay, Best Art Direction/Set Decoration, Best Costume Design, Best Director (Forman), Best Makeup, Best Picture, Best Sound; Cesar Awards '85: Best Foreign Film; Directors Guild of America Awards '84: Best Director (Forman); Golden Globe Awards '85: Best Actor—Drama (Abraham), Best Director (Forman), Best Film—Drama, Best Screenplay; Los Angeles Film Critics Association Awards '84: Best Director (Forman), Best Film, Best Screenplay; Nominations: Academy Awards '84: Best Actor (Hulce), Best Cinematography, Best Film Editing; Los Angeles Film Critics Association Awards '84: Best Actor (Abraham), Best Director (Forman), Best Screenplay. *REP, GLV, BTV*

Amanda and the Alien 🦴½ **1995 (R)** Dumb cable TV saga finds flaky Californian Amanda (Eggert) taking care of a sex-starved, shaping-changing extraterrestrial (Meneses) while a couple of feds hunt him down. Based on a story by Robert Silverberg. **94m/C VHS.** Alex Meneses, Nicole Eggert, Michael Dorn, Stacy Keach, Michael C. Bendetti; ***D:*** Jon Kroll; ***W:*** Jon Kroll. *REP*

Amarcord 🦴🦴🦴½ **1974 (R)** Semi-autobiographical Fellini fantasy which takes place in the village of Rimini, his birthplace. Focusing on the young Zanin's impressions of his town's colorful slices of life, Fellini takes aim at facism, family life, and religion in 1930's Italy. Visually ripe, delivering a generous, occasionally uneven mix of satire, burlesque, drama, and tragicomedic lyricism. Considered by people in the know as one of Fellini's best films and the topic of meaningful discussions among art film students everywhere. **124m/C VHS.** *IT* Magali Noel, Bruno Zanin, Pupella Maggio, Armando Brancia; ***D:*** Federico Fellini; ***W:*** Federico Fellini, Tonino Guerra; ***M:*** Nino Rota. Academy Awards '74: Best Foreign Language Film; National Board of Review Awards '74: 5 Best Foreign Films of the Year; New York Film Critics Awards '74: Best Director (Fellini), Best Film; Nominations: Academy Awards '75: Best Director (Fellini), Best Original Screenplay. *HMV*

The Amateur 🦴½ **1982 (R)** Computer technologist for the CIA dives into a plot of international intrigue behind the Iron Curtain when he investigates the death of his girlfriend, murdered by terrorists. Confused and ultimately disappointing spy drama cursed with a wooden script written by Littell, based on his novel. **112m/C VHS, Beta.** John Savage, Christopher Plummer, Marthe Keller, Arthur Hill, Ed Lauter; ***D:*** Charles Jarrott; ***W:*** Robert Littell. *FOX*

Amateur 🦴🦴🦴 **1994 (R)** Former nun Huppert, trying to make a living writing pornography, hooks up with an amnesiac (Donovan) who turns out to have a criminal past and a porno actress wife (Lowensohn) who wants him dead. Blackmail plot has oddball characters racing through dark and evocative settings while unfolding a tale loaded with offbeat oppositions and an irresistibly bizarre romantic triangle. Lively and playful without becoming pretentious, Hartley's self-described "action thriller... with one flat tire" evokes his typical deadpan subtle style. **105m/C VHS, LV.** Isabelle Huppert, Martin Donovan, Elina Lowensohn, Damian Young, Chuck Montgomery, David Simonds, Pamela Stewart; ***D:*** Hal Hartley; ***W:*** Hal Hartley; ***M:*** Jeff Taylor, Ned Rifle. *COL*

Amateur Night 🦴 **1985** Sloppy musical comedy about the backstage bickering occuring during the amateur night at a famous nightclub. **91m/C VHS, Beta.** Geoffrey Deuel, Dennis Cole, Allen Kirk. *VES, LIV*

Amazing Adventure 🦴🦴 *Romance and Riches; The Amazing Quest of Ernest Bliss; Riches and Romance* **1937** A millionaire wins a bet when he rises from a chauffeur's position to the executive board room without using his wealth. Though not particularly amazing, lightweight English comedy has Grant working hard to charm over and above the demands of the dated formula, a performance he undertook during a vacation from Hollywood. Adapted from a novel by E. Phillips Oppenheim. **63m/C VHS, Beta.** Cary Grant, Mary Brian, Henry Kendall, Leon M. Lion, Ralph Richardson; ***D:*** Alfred Zeisler. *NOS, BAR, DVT*

The Amazing Colossal Man 🦴🦴 **1957** A standard '50s sci-fi film about atomic radiation. Colonel Manning is exposed to massive doses of plutonium when an experiment backfires (literally). The former good-guy grows to seventy feet and starts taking out his anger on a helpless Las Vegas. Can anything stop his murderous rampages? Followed by "War of the Colossal Beast." **79m/B VHS.** Glenn Langan, Cathy Downs, William Hudson, James Seay, Russ Bender, Lyn Osborn; ***D:*** Bert I. Gordon; ***C:*** Joseph Biroc. *COL, FUS*

The Amazing Dobermans 🦴🦴 **1976 (G)** Family-oriented pooch performance piece featuring Astaire in one of his lesser roles. Ex-con man Astaire and his five trained Dobermans assist an undercover agent in foiling a small-time criminal's gambling and extortion racket. The last in a series that includes "The Daring Dobermans" and "The Doberman Gang." **96m/C VHS, Beta.** Fred Astaire, Barbara Eden, James Franciscus, Jack Carter, Billy Barty; ***D:*** Byron Ross Chudnow; ***M:*** Alan Silvestri. *MED*

Amazing Grace 🦴🦴 **1974** Some righteous mothers led by Moms Mabley go up against corrupt city politics in this extremely dated comedy that was cast with a sense of the absurd. **99m/C VHS.** Moms Mabley, Slappy (Melvin) White, Moses Gunn, Rosalind Cash, Dolph Sweet, Butterfly McQueen, Stepin Fetchit; ***D:*** Stan Lathan. *NO*

Amazing Grace & Chuck 🦴🦴 **1987 (PG)** Perhaps the only anti-war/sports fantasy ever made. After a visit to a Minuteman missile site in Montana, 12-year-old Little Leaguer Chuck learns of the dangers of nuclear arms. He begins a protest by refusing to play until the nations come to a peace agreement. In a sudden surge of social conscience, athletes worldwide put down their equipment and join in droves, starting with pro-basketball star Amazing Grace Smith (Denver Nugget English). Capra-like fantasy has good intentions but ultimately lacks two key elements: coherency and plausibility. **115m/C VHS, Beta, LV.** Jamie Lee Curtis, Gregory Peck, William L. Petersen, Joshua Zuehlke, Alex English; ***D:*** Mike Newell; ***M:*** Elmer Bernstein. *HBO*

The Amazing Howard Hughes 🦴🦴½ **1977** Reveals the full story of the legendary millionaire's life and career, from daring test pilot to inventor to Hollywood film producer to isolated wealthy paranoiac with a germ phobia. Lingers on the rich guy with big problems theme. Big-budget, made for television drama with a nice performance by Jones. **119m/C VHS, Beta.** Tommy Lee Jones, Ed Flanders, James Hampton, Tovah Feldshuh, Lee Purcell; ***D:*** William A. Graham. *FCT*

Amazing Mr. Blunden 🦴🦴½ **1972 (G)** Solid kidvid about two youngsters aided by a ghost who travel back in time to save the lives of two murdered children. Adapted by Jeffries from Antonia Barber's novel, "The Ghosts." **100m/C VHS, Beta.** Laurence Naismith, Lynne Frederick, Garry Miller, Marc Granger, Rosalyn London, Diana Dors; ***D:*** Lionel Jeffries; ***M:*** Elmer Bernstein. *MED*

The Amazing Mr. X 🦴🦴½ *The Spiritualist* **1948** When a woman's husband dies, she tries to contact him via a spiritualist. Things are not as they seem however, and the medium may just be part of an intricate scheme to defraud the woman. **79m/B VHS, Beta.** Turhan Bey, Lynn Bari, Cathy O'Donnell, Richard Carlson, Donald Curtis, Virginia Gregg; ***D:*** Bernard Vorhaus. *NOS, SNC, RXM*

The Amazing Panda Adventure 🦴🦴½ *Little Panda; The Amazing Panda Rescue* **1995 (PG)** Ryan (Slater) is off to China during his spring break to visit dad Michael (Lang), who's working on a project to rescue the dwindling panda population. But there's poacher trouble and Ryan and young translator Ling (Ding) decide to rescue the preserve's panda cub, which has been animal-napped (where's Ace Ventura when you need him). Family fare, with a mixture of totally adorable real and animatronic pandas; filmed in the Sichuan province of China, home to the Wolong Nature Reserve which is famous for its successful breeding of the endangered giant pandas. Slater, in his first starring role, is the younger brother of Christian. **84m/C VHS, LV.** Ryan Slater, Stephen Lang, Yi Ding, Wang Fei; ***D:*** Christopher Cain; ***W:*** Laurice Elehwany, Jeff Rothberg; ***C:*** Jack N. Green; ***M:*** William Ross. *WAR*

The Amazing Spider-Man 🦴🦴 *Spider-Man* **1977** The Marvel Comics superhero's unique powers are put to the test when he comes to the rescue of the government by preventing an evil scientist from blackmailing the government for big bucks. The wall-walking web-slinger has his origins probed (a grad student bit by a radioactive spider develops super-human powers) in his live-action debut, which was made for television and led to a short-lived series. **94m/C VHS, Beta, LV.** Nicholas Hammond, David White, Lisa Eilbacher, Michael Pataki; ***D:*** E.W. Swackhamer. *FOX, IME*

Amazing Stories **1985** From the Steven Spielberg produced television series. "The Mission" sees a WWII tail gunner trapped in an unusual predicament. In "The Wedding Ring," a man gives his wife a strange ring and bizarre situations ensue. Additional episodes available. **70m/C VHS, LV.** Kevin Costner, Casey Siemaszko, Kiefer Sutherland, Danny DeVito, Rhea Perlman; ***D:*** Danny DeVito, Steven Spielberg. *MCA, FCT, MOV*

The Amazing Transparent Man *Woof!* **1960** A mad scientist makes a crook invisible in order to steal the radioactive materials he needs. The crook decides to rob banks instead. Shot at the Texas State Fair for that elusive futuristic look. For Ulmer fans only. **58m/B VHS.** Douglas Kennedy, Marguerite Chapman, James Griffith, Ivan Triesault; ***D:*** Edgar G. Ulmer. *NOS, SNC*

The Amazing Transplant *Woof!* **1970** A sleaze-bag psycho has a "love enhancing" transplant, much to the pleasure of his sexual partners. Much to their and our dismay, however, he then kills them and bores us. **90m/C VHS, Beta.** Juan Fernandez, Linda Southern; ***D:*** Doris Wishman. *TPV*

Amazon 🦴🦴 **1990 (R)** An adventure movie filmed in the Brazilian rainforest with an environmental message. A businessman being chased by the police in the Amazon jungle is rescued by a bush pilot who dreams of mining the Amazon's riches. A Brazilian woman enters the picture and persuades the businessman to help save the rainforest. Portions of the proceeds from the sale of this film go to the Rainforest Action Network. **88m/C VHS, LV.** Kari Vaananen, Robert Davi, Rae Dawn Chong; ***D:*** Mika Kaurismaki. *LIV*

Amazon Jail 🦴 **1985** Scantily clad women go over the wall and promptly get caught by devil worshiping men in the jungle. They should have known better. Redeemed only by lingerie selection. **94m/C VHS, Beta.** Elisabeth Hartmann, Mauricio Do Valle, Sondra Graffi; ***D:*** Oswald De Oliveira. *NO*

Amazon Women on the Moon 🦴🦴 **1987 (R)** A plotless, irreverent media spoof, depicting the programming of a slipshod television station as it crams weird commercials and shorts around a comical '50s' science fiction film. Inconsistent, occasionally funny anthology hangs together very loosely. Produced by Landis, with the usual amount of in-joke cameos and allusions to his other works of art. **85m/C VHS, Beta, LV.** Rosanna Arquette, Steve Guttenberg, Steve Allen, B.B. King, Michelle Pfeiffer, Arsenio Hall, Andrew Dice Clay, Howard Hesseman, Lou Jacobi, Carrie Fisher, Griffin Dunne, Sybil Danning, Henny Youngman, Monique Gabrielle, Paul Bartel, Kelly Preston; ***D:*** John Landis, Joe Dante, Carl Gottlieb, Peter Horton, Robert Weiss; ***W:*** Michael Barrie, Jim Mulholland; ***M:*** Ira Newborn. *MCA*

The Amazons 🦴½ **1984** Goofy made for television drama about a beautiful doctor who discovers an underground organization of Amazon-descended women bent on taking over the world or at least making life hard for men while investigating a Congressman's mysterious death. **100m/C VHS, Beta.** Tamara Dobson, Jack Scalia, Stella Stevens, Madeleine Stowe, Jennifer Warren; ***D:*** Paul Michael Glaser; ***M:*** Basil Poledouris. *NO*

Amazons 🦴 **1986 (R)** Tall, strong women who occasionally wander around nude search for a magical talisman that will overthrow an evil magician. **76m/C VHS, Beta.** Windsor Taylor Randolph, Penelope Reed, Joseph Whipp, Willie Nelson, Danitza Kingsley; ***D:*** Alex Sessa. *MGM*

The Ambassador 🦴🦴½ *Peacemaker* **1984** An American ambassador (Mitchum) is sent to the Middle East to try to solve the area's deep political problems. He quickly becomes the target of terrorist attacks, and is blamed for the nation's unrest. To make matters worse, his wife is having an affair with a PLO leader. The President ignores him, forcing the ambassador to fend for himself. Talk about your bad days. Hudson's last feature. Based on Elmore Leonard's "52 Pickup," and remade a year later under its own title. **97m/C VHS, Beta.** Robert Mitchum, Ellen Burstyn, Rock Hudson, Fabio Testi, Donald Pleasence; ***D:*** J. Lee Thompson. *MGM*

Ambassador Bill 🦴🦴 **1931** An Oklahoma rancher is appointed ambassador to a country in revolt. Rogers, of course, saves the day with his rustic witticisms. Based on the story "Ambassador from the United States" by Vincent Sheean. **68m/B VHS.** Will Rogers, Marguerite Churchill, Greta Nissen; ***D:*** Sam Taylor. *FOX, FCT*

The Ambassador's Daughter 🦴🦴 **1956** The Parisian adventures of an American ambassador's daughter De Havilland and soldier Forsythe, who, unaware of her position, falls in love with her. Faltering comedy is supported by an expert cast (although nearly 40, De Havilland is charming as the young woman) with especially good performances from Menjou and Loy. **102m/C VHS.** Olivia de Havilland, John Forsythe, Myrna Loy, Adolphe Menjou, Edward Arnold, Francis Lederer, Tommy Noonan, Minor Watson; ***D:*** Norman Krasna; ***W:*** Norman Krasna. *MOV*

Amber Waves 🦴🦴½ **1982** Credible made for television drama about a generation-gap conflict between a Midwestern farmer (Weaver) and an irresponsible male model (Russell) who has coasted through life on con and charm. **98m/C VHS, Beta.** Dennis Weaver, Kurt Russell; ***D:*** Joseph Sargent. *TLF*

Ambition 🦴½ **1991 (R)** Scriptwriter/star Phillips gets a bone for chutzpah by taking an unsavory lead role; his character torments a paroled psycho so that the killer will kill again and inspire a true-crime bestseller. The plot looks good on paper, but onscreen it's padded and unconvincing. **99m/C VHS, Beta, LV.** Lou Diamond Phillips, Clancy Brown, Cecilia Peck, Richard Bradford, Willard Pugh, Grace Zabriskie, Katherine Armstrong, John Cullum, Haing S. Ngor; ***D:*** Scott Goldstein; ***W:*** Lou Diamond Phillips; ***M:*** Leonard Rosenman. *FXV, MED, VTR*

The Ambulance 🦴🦴½ **1990 (R)** A New York cartoonist witnesses a mysterious ambulance at work and decides to investigate. His probings uncover a plot to sell the bodies of dying diabetics. A surprisingly good no-money feature from low-budget king Cohen. Includes an appearance by Marvel Comics' Stan Lee as himself. **95m/C VHS, LV.** Eric Roberts, James Earl Jones, Megan Gallagher, Richard Bright, Janine Turner, Eric (Hans Gudegast) Braeden, Red Buttons, Laurene Landon, Jill Gatsby, Nicholas Chinlund; ***D:*** Larry Cohen; ***W:*** Larry Cohen. *COL, EPC*

Ambush at Tomahawk Gap 🦴🦴 **1953** Three released prisoners go in search of hidden loot and tempers rise when the goods don't turn up. Then the Apaches show up. **73m/C VHS, Beta.** John Hodiak, John Derek, David Brian, Maria Elena Marques, Ray Teal; ***D:*** Fred F. Sears. *GKK*

The Ambush Murders 🦴🦴½ **1982** True story of a stalwart white attorney defending a black activist accused of killing two cops. Not the compelling television it could be, but still enjoyable. From Ben Bradlee, Jr.'s novel. **100m/C VHS, Beta.** James Brolin, Dorian Harewood, Alfre Woodard, Louis Giambalvo, John McLiam, Teddy Wilson, Antonio Fargas, Amy Madigan; ***D:*** Steven Hilliard Stern. *FRH, LIV*

Ambush Trail 🦴🦴 **1946** Stranger-in-town Steele metes out justice to help local ranchers while sidekick Saylor leaves 'em laughing. **60m/B VHS.** Bob Steele, Syd Saylor, I. Stanford Jolley, Lorraine Miller, Charles "Blackie" King, Kermit Maynard; ***D:*** Harry Fraser. *NOS, GPV*

The Ambushers *Woof!* **1967** Martin's third Matt Helm farce finds him handling a puzzling case involving the first United States spacecraft. When the craft is hijacked with Rule on board, it's Matt to the rescue, regaining control before unfriendly forces can take it back to Earth. Tired formula seems to have worn Martin out while the remainder of the cast goes to camp. Followed by "The Wrecking Crew." **102m/C VHS, Beta, LV.** Dean Martin, Janice Rule, James Gregory, Albert Salmi, Senta Berger; ***D:*** Henry Levin. *COL*

Amelia Earhart: The Final Flight 🦴🦴½ **1994** Investigates the mysterious disappearance of pioneering aviatrix Amelia Earhart's 1937 flight to become the first pilot to circumnavigate the globe. Earhart (Keaton) and her navigator Fred Noonan (Hauer) disappeared over the Pacific Ocean and their fate has never been determined. Dern plays Earhart's husband, publisher George B. Putnam, who served as Amelia's manager and publicist. Based on the biography by Doris L. Rich. Made for television. **95m/C VHS, LV.** Diane Keaton, Rutger Hauer, Bruce Dern, Paul Guilfoyle, Denis Arndt, David Carpenter, Diana Bellamy; ***D:*** Yves Simoneau; ***W:*** Anna Sandor; ***M:*** George S. Clinton. *TTC*

America 🦴½ **1986 (R)** New York cable station receives worldwide fame when their signal bounces off of the moon. Uninspired piece of fluff from otherwise talented director Downey. **83m/C VHS.** Zack Norman, Tammy Grimes, Michael J. Pollard, Monroe Arnold, Richard Belzer, Liz Torres, Howard Thomashefsky, Laura Ashton, Robert Downey Jr.; ***D:*** Robert Downey. *NO*

America at the Movies 🦴🦴½ **1976** Scenes from more than 80 of the finest American motion pictures fly by in an effort to tell the story of the cinema and provide a portrait of America as it has been seen on screen for half a century. Scenes from "The Birth of a Nation," "Citizen Kane," "Dr. Strangelove," "East of Eden," "The French Connection," and "From Here to Eternity," are among the many included. Some black and white scenes; produced by the American Film Institute. **116m/C VHS, Beta, LV.** John Wayne, Orson Welles, Peter Sellers, James Dean, Gene Hackman, Burt Lancaster, Julie Harris, Deborah Kerr, Al Pacino, Robert De Niro. *COL, IME*

America First 🦴½ **1970** A group of seven travelers try to build an "Eden" with the inhabitants of an Appalachian hollow. **90m/C VHS, Beta.** Michael Kennedy, Walter Keller, Pat Estrin, Lois McGuire. *NO*

America/The Fall of Babylon 🦴🦴🦴 **1924** A double feature containing abridged versions; in "America," a Boston patriot and the daughter of an aristocratic Virginia Tory fall in love during the Revolutionary War; "The Fall of Babylon" is one of the stories in D.W. Griffith's "Intolerance." Silent. **56m/B VHS, Beta.** Neil Hamilton, Lionel Barrymore, Constance Talmadge, Elmer Clifton, Alfred Paget. *CCB*

America 3000 🦴 **1986 (PG-13)** Hundreds of years in the holocaust-torn future, men rebel against a brutal, overpowering race of women, with predictable results. **94m/C VHS, Beta.** Chuck Wagner, Laurene Landon; ***D:*** David Engelbach. *MGM*

The American Angels: Baptism of Blood 🦴 **1989 (R)** Three beautiful young women, each with a personal dream, strive to make it in the world of professional wrestling. Hackneyed plot devices, but those simply watching for the wrestling scenes won't be disappointed. **99m/C VHS, Beta, LV.** Jan MacKenzie, Tray Loren, Mimi Lesseos, Trudy Adams, Patricia Cavoti, Susan Sexton, Jean Kirkland, Jeff Lundy, Lee Marshall; ***D:*** Beverly Sebastian, Ferd Sebastian. *PAR*

American Anthem 🦴 **1986 (PG-13)** A young gymnast must choose between family responsibilities or the parallel bars. Olympic gymnast Gaylord makes his movie debut but doesn't get the gold. Good fare for young tumblers, but that's about it. Followed by two of the films' music videos and tape-ads featuring Max Headroom. **100m/C VHS, Beta, LV.** Mitch Gaylord, Janet Jones, Michelle Phillips, Michael Pataki; ***D:*** Albert Magnoli; ***W:*** Evan P. Archerd, Jeff Benjamin; ***M:*** Alan Silvestri. *ORI, WAR*

American Aristocracy 🦴🦴½ **1917** A silent comic romp in which Fairbanks, an old moneyed dandy, wreaks havoc on an island resort whose clientele is composed of the nouveau well-to-do. **52m/B VHS, Beta.** Douglas Fairbanks Sr., Jewel Carmen, Albert Parker; ***D:*** Lloyd Ingraham. *GPV*

American Autobahn 🦴½ **1984** A low-budget independent actioner about a journalist who discovers an underworld weapons ring that hits the highway in pursuit of him. **90m/C VHS, Beta.** Jan Jalenak, Michael von der Goltz, Jim Jarmusch; ***D:*** Andre Degas. *NO*

American Blue Note ♂♂ *Fakebook* **1989 (PG-13)** Loosely plotted, bittersweet account of a struggling jazz quartet in the early 1960s, as its leader (MacNicol) must decide if their fruitless tours of sleazy bars and weddings are still worth it. The debut of director Toporoff. **96m/C VHS, LV.** Peter MacNicol, Carl Capotorto, Tim Guinee, Bill Christopher-Myers, Jonathan Walker, Charlotte d'Amboise, Louis Guss, Zohra Lampert, Trini Alvarado, Sam Behrens; ***D:*** Ralph Toporoff; ***W:*** Gilbert Girion, Larry Schanker. *COL, BTV*

American Born ♂½ **1989** Murder Inc. returns to the dismay of one idealist who embarks on a battle he doesn't intend to lose. The mob had better look out. **90m/C VHS.** Joey Travolta, Andrew Zeller; ***D:*** Raymond Martino; ***W:*** Raymond Martino. *PMH*

American Boyfriends ♂♂ **1989 (PG-13)** An ostensible sequel to "My American Cousin," in which two Canadian girls go to California and discover innocent romance and friendship. **90m/C VHS, Beta, LV.** *CA* Margaret Langrick, John Wildman, Jason Blicker, Lisa Repo Martell; ***D:*** Sandy Wilson; ***W:*** Sandy Wilson. *LIV*

An American Christmas Carol ♂♂ **1979** Charles Dickens' classic story is retold with limited charm in a made for television effort. This time a greedy American financier (Winkler) learns about the true meaning of Christmas. **98m/C VHS, Beta.** Henry Winkler, David Wayne, Dorian Harewood; ***D:*** Eric Till; ***M:*** Hagood Hardy. *VES, LIV*

American Cinema **1994** Ten-part series covering the roughly 100 years of cinema history through a look at the Hollywood film. Lots of clips and interviews with each part providing an overview of a particular feature of the movie industry from stars to studios to independent filmmakers. Available as a five-tape boxed set or individually. **500m/C VHS.** *FOX*

American Commandos ♂ *Hitman* **1984 (R)** An ex-Green Beret slaughters the junkies who killed his son and raped his wife, and then joins his old buddies for a secret, Rambo-esque mission in Vietnam providing a tired rehash of Vietnam movie cliches. **96m/C VHS, Beta.** Chris Mitchum, John Phillip Law, Franco Guerrero; ***D:*** Bobby Suarez. *LIV*

American Cop ♂½ **1994 (PG-13)** Elmo LaGrange is an ordinary cop taking a vacation, when his layover in the Moscow airport becomes a lesson in mistaken identities. He teams up with the pre-requisite beautiful woman to outwit and outrun the Russian mafia. **91m/C VHS, LV.** Wayne Crawford, Ashley Laurence, Daniel Quinn, William Katt, Olga Vodin, Vlaimir Shpoudeiko, Nickolai Nedovodin; ***D:*** Wayne Crawford; ***W:*** Carlos Brooks. *APX*

American Cyborg: Steel Warrior ♂♂½ **1994 (R)** Basic evil-machine-bent-on-mankind's-destruction movie—with a hero bent on rescuing the world. **95m/C VHS, LV.** Joe Lara, John P. Ryan; ***D:*** Boaz Davidson; ***W:*** Bill Crounse. *CAN*

American Dream ♂♂♂ **1981** A midwestern family leaves the suburbs and moves into a Chicago inner-city neighborhood. Good TV-movie pilot for the short-lived series that was Emmy nominated for direction and writing. **90m/C VHS, Beta.** Stephen Macht, Karen Carlson, John Karlen, Andrea Smith, John Malkovich, John McIntire; ***D:*** Mel Damski; ***M:*** Artie Butler. *UNI*

American Dreamer ♂♂ **1984 (PG)** A housewife wins a trip to Paris as a prize from a mystery writing contest. Silly from a blow on the head, she begins living the fictional life of her favorite literary adventure. Sporadic comedy with a good cast wandering about courtesy of a clumsy screenplay. **105m/C VHS, Beta.** JoBeth Williams, Tom Conti, Giancarlo Giannini, Coral Browne, James Staley; ***D:*** Rick Rosenthal; ***M:*** Lewis Furey. *FOX*

American Eagle ♂½ **1990 (R)** A veteran goes crazy and seeks sadistic, bloody revenge on his war buddies. Now his war buddies are the only ones who can stop him. **92m/C VHS, LV.** Asher Brauner, Robert F. Lyons, Vernon Wells, Kai Baker; ***D:*** Robert J. Smawley. *VMK*

American Empire ♂♂½ *My Son Alone* **1942** Two Civil War heroes struggle to build a cattle empire in Texas and are hampered by rustlers, one of whom was their partner. A fine, veteran cast and a tight script keep things moving, including the cattle. **82m/B VHS, Beta.** Preston Foster, Richard Dix, Frances Gifford, Leo Carrillo; ***D:*** William McGann. *NOS, MRV, DVT*

American Fabulous ♂♂½ **1992** The posthumously released autobiography of an eccentric homosexual who lived life in the fast lane. Jeffrey Strouth performs his monologue from the back seat of a 1957 Cadillac, where the images of small-town America are seen to contrast sharply with his flamboyant style. His grotesque and candid recollections include his alcoholic Elvis-impersonator father, a stint as a teenage prostitute, drag queen friends, and drug addiction in New York. Strouth puts a comic twist on even the most brutal of his memories. He died of AIDS at the age of 33 in 1992. **105m/C VHS.** Jeffrey Strouth; ***D:*** Reno Dakota; ***W:*** Jeffrey Strouth. *FRV, ICA*

American Flyers ♂♂½ **1985 (PG-13)** Two competitive brothers train for a grueling three-day bicycle race in Colorado while tangling with personal drama, including the spector that one of them may have inherited dad's tendency for cerebral aneurisms and is sure to drop dead during a bike race soon. Written by bike movie specialist Tesich ("Breaking Away") with a lot of the usual cliches (the last bike ride, battling bros, eventual understanding), which are gracefully overridden by fine bike-racing photography. Interesting performances, especially Chong as a patient girlfriend and Amos as the trainer. **113m/C VHS, Beta, LV.** Kevin Costner, David Marshall Grant, Rae Dawn Chong, Alexandra Paul, John Amos, Janice Rule, Robert Townsend, Jennifer Grey, Luca Bercovici; ***D:*** John Badham; ***W:*** Steve Tesich; ***M:*** Lee Ritenour, Greg Mathieson. *WAR*

The American Friend ♂♂♂½ **1977** Tribute to the American gangster film helped introduce Wenders to American moviegoers. Young Hamburg picture framer thinks he has a terminal disease and is set up by American expatriate Hopper to become a hired assassin in West Germany. The lure is a promise of quick money that the supposedly dying man can then leave his wife and child. After the first assasination, the two bond. Hopper is the typical Wenders protagonist, a strange man in a strange land looking for a connection. Great, creepy thriller adapted from Patricia Highsmith's novel "Ripley's Game." Fuller and Ray (better known as directors) appear briefly as gangsters. **127m/C VHS, Beta, LV.** *FR GE* Bruno Ganz, Dennis Hopper, Elisabeth Kreuzer, Gerard Blain, Jean Eustache, Samuel Fuller, Nicholas Ray, Wim Wenders; ***D:*** Wim Wenders; ***W:*** Wim Wenders. National Board of Review Awards '77: 5 Best Foreign Films of the Year; Nominations: Cannes Film Festival '77: Best Film. *FCT, GLV, INJ*

American Friends ♂♂ **1991 (PG)** Genteel story masquerades as high comedy. Palin is a fussy middle-aged Oxford classics tutor. On a holiday he meets American Hartley (Booth) and her adopted daughter, Elinor (Alvarado). Both women are immensely attracted to the don (for reasons that are unclear) and follow him back to Oxford, where he's engaged in a battle of succession with his rival Molina. Dismal screenplay lacks logic and urgency, making it difficult to care about the story or the characters. Script is said to have been inspired by an incident in the life of Palin's great-grandfather. If this sounds like your cup of tea, save your time and watch a Merchant Ivory film instead. **95m/C VHS, LV.** *GB* Michael Palin, Connie Booth, Trini Alvarado, Alfred Molina; ***D:*** Tristam Powell; ***W:*** Michael Palin, Tristam Powell; ***M:*** Georges Delerue. *VMK, FCT*

The American Gangster **1992** Documentary look at the beginnings of organized crime and the rise of the gangster in American society. Includes vintage film and photographs. Profiles include Bugsy Siegel, Al Capone, John Dillinger, Pretty Boy Floyd, and Lucky Luciano. **45m/C VHS.** *COL*

American Gigolo ♂♂ **1979 (R)** A Los Angeles loner who sexually services the rich women of Beverly Hills becomes involved with the wife of a California state senator and is then framed for a murder he did not commit. A highly stylized but empty view of seamy low lives marred by a contrived plot, with decent romp in the hay readiness displayed by Gere. **117m/C VHS, Beta, LV.** Richard Gere, Lauren Hutton, Hector Elizondo, Paul Schrader; ***D:*** Paul Schrader; ***W:*** Paul Schrader; ***C:*** John Bailey. *PAR*

American Gothic *Woof! Hide and Shriek* **1988 (R)** Three couples headed for a vacation are instead stranded on an island and captured by a demented family headed by Steiger and De Carlo, a scary enough proposition in itself. Even worse, Ma and Pa have three middle-aged moronic offspring who still dress as children and are intent on killing the thwarted vacationers (who are none too bright themselves) one by bloody one. A stultifying career low for all involved. **89m/C VHS, Beta, LV.** Rod Steiger, Yvonne De Carlo, Michael J. Pollard, Sarah Torgov, Fiona Hutchinson; ***D:*** John Hough. *VMK*

American Graffiti ♂♂♂½ **1973 (PG)** Atmospheric, episodic look at growing up in the innocence of America before the Kennedy assassination and the Vietnam War. It all takes place on one hectic but typical night in the life of a group of recent California high school grads unsure of what the next big step in life is. So they spend their time cruising, listening to Wolfman Jack, and meeting at the drive-in. Slice of '60s life boasts a prudent script, great set design, authentic soundtrack, and consistently fine performances by the young cast. Catapulted Dreyfuss, Ford, and Somers to stardom, branded Lucas a hot directorial commodity with enough leverage to launch "Star Wars," and steered Howard and Williams towards continued age-of-innocence nirvana on "Happy Days." **112m/C VHS, Beta, LV.** Richard Dreyfuss, Ron Howard, Cindy Williams, MacKenzie Phillips, Paul LeMat, Charles Martin Smith, Suzanne Somers, Candy Clark, Harrison Ford, Bo Hopkins, Joe Spano, Kathleen Quinlan, Wolfman Jack; ***D:*** George Lucas; ***W:*** George Lucas, Gloria Katz, Willard Huyck. Golden Globe Awards '74: Best Film—Musical/Comedy; New York Film Critics Awards '73: Best Screenplay; National Society of Film Critics Awards '73: Best Screenplay; Nominations: Academy Awards '73: Best Director (Lucas), Best Film Editing, Best Picture, Best Story & Screenplay, Best Supporting Actress (Clark). *MCA, FCT*

American Heart ♂♂♂½ **1992 (R)** Jack (Bridges) is a suspicious ex-con, newly released from prison, with few prospects and little hope. He also has a teenage son, Nick (Furlong), he barely remembers but who desperately wants to have his father back in his life. Jack is reluctantly persuaded to let Nick stay with him in his cheap hotel where Nick befriends fellow resident, Molly, a teenage hooker, and other castoff street kids. Superb performances by both male leads—Furlong, both yearning and frustrated as he pursues his dream of having a family, and Bridges as the tough parolee, unwilling to open his heart. Hardboiled, poignant, and powerful. **114m/C VHS, LV.** Jeff Bridges, Edward Furlong, Lucinda Jenney, Tracey Kapisky, Don Harvey, Margaret Welsh; ***D:*** Martin Bell; ***W:*** Peter Silverman; ***M:*** James Newton Howard. Independent Spirit Awards '94: Best Actor (Bridges); Nominations: Independent Spirit Awards '94: Best Cinematography, Best First Feature, Best Supporting Actor (Furlong), Best Supporting Actress (Jenney). *LIV, BTV*

An American in Paris ♂♂♂♂ **1951** Lavish, imaginative musical features a sweeping score, and knockout choreography by Kelly. Ex-G.I. Kelly stays on in Paris after the war to study painting, supported in his efforts by rich American Foch, who hopes to acquire a little extra attention. But Kelly loves the lovely Caron, unfortunately engaged to an older gent. Highlight is an astonishing 17-minute ballet which holds the record for longest movie dance number—and one of the most expensive, pegged at over half a million for a month of filming. For his efforts, the dance king won a special Oscar citation. While it sure looks like Paris, most of it was filmed in MGM studios. ♫S'Wonderful; I Got Rhythm; Embraceable You; Love Is Here To Stay; Tra-La-La; I'll Build a Stairway to Paradise; Nice Work If You Can Get It; By Strauss; Concerto in F (3rd Movement). **113m/C VHS, Beta, LV, 8mm.** Gene Kelly, Leslie Caron, Oscar Levant, Nina Foch, Georges Guetary; ***D:*** Vincente Minnelli; ***W:*** Alan Jay Lerner; ***C:*** John Alton; ***M:*** George Gershwin, Ira Gershwin. Academy Awards '51: Best Art Direction/Set Decoration (Color), Best Color Cinematography, Best Costume Design (Color), Best Picture, Best Story & Screenplay, Best Score; Golden Globe Awards '52: Best Film—Musical/Comedy; National Board of Review Awards '51: 10 Best Films of the Year; Nominations: Academy Awards '51: Best Director (Minnelli), Best Film Editing. *MGM, TLF, BTV*

American Justice 🦴🦴 *Jackals* **1986 (R)** Two cops, one of whom looks suspiciously like a Simon of "Simon and Simon" fight political corruption and white slavery near the Mexican border. The chief white slaver bears a full resemblance to the other Simon. Sufficient action but less than original. **96m/C VHS, Beta.** Jameson Parker, Gerald McRaney, Wilford Brimley, Jack Lucarelli; ***D:*** Gary Grillo. *LIV*

American Kickboxer 1 🦴½ **1991 (R)** Barrett stars as B.J. Quinn, a down on his luck kickboxing champion who spends much of his time onscreen aimlessly wandering (apparently searching for the meaning of his life.) Lackluster script and performances will make this one trying —even for kickboxing fans. Barrett is Chuck Norris' former workout partner, bu t there isn't enough action often enough for him to show off his formidable skills. **93m/C VHS, Beta.** John Barrett, Keith Vitali, Brad Morris, Terry Norton, Ted Leplat; ***D:*** Frans Nel; ***W:*** Emil Kolbe; ***M:*** Frank Becker. *CAN*

American Kickboxer 2: To the Death 🦴½ **1993 (R)** Lillian must find a way to get her cop ex-husband and her kickboxer ex-lover to work together to save her kidnapped daughter's life. **91m/C VHS, LV.** Dale "Apollo" Cook, Evan Lurie, Kathy Shower, Ted Markland; ***D:*** Jeno Hodl. *VMK*

American Matchmaker 🦴🦴½ *Amerikaner Shadkhn* **1940** Nat Silver decides to go into the matchmaking business, after his own marriages fail miserably, hoping to experience happiness vicariously. However, he soon begins to realize that one of his clients is a better match for him than the man he chose for her. In Yiddish with English subtitles. **87m/B VHS.** Leo Fuchs, Judith Abarbanel. *ERG*

American Me 🦴🦴🦴 **1992 (R)** Violent and brutal depiction of more than thirty years of gang wars and drugs in East Los Angeles. Santana founded a street as a teenager, but has spent the last 18 years in prison, where he's the boss of the so-called Mexican Mafia, which oversees the drugs, scams, murders, and violence that are an everyday fact of prison life. Released from Folsom, Santana goes back to his old neighborhood and attempts to distance himself from his old life but finds his gang ties are stronger than any other alliance. Unsparing and desolate directorial debut from Olmos. **119m/C VHS, LV.** Edward James Olmos, William Forsythe, Pepe Serna, Danny De La Paz, Evelina Fernandez, Sal Lopez, Daniel Villarreal, Cary-Hiroyuki Tagawa; ***D:*** Edward James Olmos; ***W:*** Floyd Mutrux, Desmond Nakano; ***C:*** Reynaldo Villalobos; ***M:*** Dennis Lambert. *MCA*

American Nightmare 🦴½ **1981** Young man searches for his missing sister against a background of pornography, drug peddling, and prostitution in the slums of a city. The usual titillating squalid urban drama. **85m/C VHS, Beta.** Lawrence S. Day, Lora Staley, Lenore Zann, Michael Ironside, Alexandra Paul; ***D:*** Don McBrearty. *MED*

American Ninja 🦴🦴 *American Warrior* **1985 (R)** American Dudikoff is G.I. Joe, a martial-arts expert stationed in the Philippines who alienates most everyone around him (he's a rebel). Deadly black-belt war begins with Joe confronting the army which is selling stolen weapons to the South American black market. Aided by one faithful pal, Joe uses his head-kicking martial arts skills to stop hundreds of ninja combatants working for the corrupt arms dealer. In his spare time he romances the base chief's daughter. Efficient rib-crunching chop-socky action wrapped in no-brainer plot and performed by nonactors. Cannon epic mercilessly followed by at least three sequels. **96m/C VHS, Beta.** Michael Dudikoff, Guich Koock, Judie Aronson, Steve James; ***D:*** Sam Firstenberg; ***W:*** Gideon Amir; ***M:*** Michael Linn. *MGM*

American Ninja 2: The Confrontation 🦴🦴 **1987 (R)** Soldiers Dudikoff and James are back again using their martial arts skills (in lieu of any acting) to take on a Caribbean drug-lord. Apparently he has been kidnapping Marines and taking them to his island, where he genetically alters them to become fanatical ninja assassins eager to do his dirty work. The script hardly gets in the way of the rib-crunching action, but is an improvement upon Ninja Number One. **90m/C VHS, Beta, LV.** Michael Dudikoff, Steve James, Larry Poindexter, Gary Conway; ***D:*** Sam Firstenberg; ***W:*** Gary Conway, James Booth. *MED, VTR*

American Ninja 3: Blood Hunt *Woof!* **1989 (R)** Second sequel in the American Ninja series. Bradley replaces Dudikoff as the martial arts good guy fighting the martial arts bad guys on a Caribbean island. He's pursued by ex-evangelist Marjoe, who wants to inject him with a nasty virus before unloading the germs to bad buys worldwide. Less ninjitsu; more uninspired martial arts. **90m/C VHS, Beta, LV.** David Bradley, Steve James, Marjoe Gortner, Michele Chan, Calvin Jung; ***D:*** Cedric Sundstrom; ***W:*** Paul DeMielche, Gary Conway; ***M:*** George S. Clinton. *MGM, CAN*

American Ninja 4: The Annihilation *Woof!* **1991 (R)** Dudikoff returns after noticeable absence in last sequel. He should have stayed away from #4—it's a rehash of tired ideas that never gets off the ground. Forget this and see "American Ninja 2: The Confrontation," the best of this series. **99m/C VHS, Beta, LV.** Michael Dudikoff, David Bradley, James Booth, Dwayne Alexandre, Robin Stille, Ken Gampu; ***D:*** Cedric Sundstrom; ***W:*** David Geeves; ***M:*** Nicolas Tenbroek. *CAN*

American Pluck 🦴🦴 **1925** Before he can inherit anything, a playboy millionaire's son must go out into the world and prove he can make his own way. He meets a beautiful princess, who is pursued by a villainous count. Walsh, as the dashing hero, was the younger brother of director Raoul. Silent with original organ music. **91m/B VHS, Beta, 8mm.** George Walsh, Wanda Hawley, Frank Leigh, Sidney De Grey; ***D:*** Richard Stanton. *VYY*

The American President 🦴🦴🦴 **1995 (PG-13)** Widower president Andrew Shepherd (Douglas) decides its time to get back into the dating game. But just what woman wants to find her romance in the public eye? Well, it turns out to be feisty environmental lobbyist Sydney Wade (the ever-charming Bening). But the Prez also has to put up with nasty opponent Bob Rumson (Dreyfuss), who's using their courtship as political fodder, approval ratings, and a nosy press. Glossy fairytale material expertly handled by both cast and director. **114m/C VHS, LV.** Michael Douglas, Annette Bening, Martin Sheen, Michael J. Fox, David Paymer, Samantha Mathis, John Mahoney, Anna Deavere Smith, Nina Siemaszko, Wendie Malick, Shawna Waldron, Richard Dreyfuss; ***D:*** Rob Reiner; ***W:*** Aaron Sorkin; ***C:*** John Seale; ***M:*** Marc Shaiman. Nominations: Academy Awards '95: Best Score; Golden Globe Awards '96: Best Actor—Musical/Comedy (Douglas), Best Actress—Musical/Comedy (Bening), Best Director (Reiner), Best Film—Musical/Comedy, Best Screenplay; Writers Guild of America '95: Best Original Screenplay. *COL*

American Roulette 🦴 **1988 (R)** Garcia is the exiled president of a Latin American country living in London in this thin political thriller. A plot riddled with weaknesses and poor direction make this potentially interesting film dull and lifeless. **102m/C VHS, LV.** *GB AU* Andy Garcia, Kitty Aldridge, Robert Stephens, Al Matthews, Susannah York; ***D:*** Maurice Hatton; ***M:*** Michael Gibbs. *NO*

American Samurai 🦴½ **1992 (R)** Drew is the adopted son of a Japanese samurai, who gives him the family's sacred sword. This gesture angers his stepbrother who gets involved with Japanese gangsters and illegal live-blade fighting, and who also vows revenge on this American upstart. Lots of sword play to go with the chop-socky action. **89m/C VHS, LV.** David Bradley, Mark Dacascos, John Fujioka, Valarie Trapp; ***D:*** Sam Firstenberg; ***W:*** John Corcoran. *WAR, PMS, CAN*

The American Scream 🦴½ **198?** An innocent family vacationing in the mountains stumbles on to a satanic cult. And that can really ruin a vacation. **85m/C VHS, Beta.** Jennifer Darling, Pons Marr, Blackie Cammett, Kimberly Kramer, Jean Sapienza, Kevin Kaye, Matt Borlenghi, James Cooper; ***D:*** Mitchell Linden. *GHV*

American Shaolin: King of the Kickboxers 2 🦴½ **1992 (PG-13)** When Drew gets his butt kicked in a karate tournament he decides to head to China and learn some fight-winning moves from a group of warrior monks. **103m/C VHS.** Reese Madigan, Trent Bushy, Daniel Dae Kim, Billy Chang, Cliff Lenderman, Zhang Shi Yen, Kim Chan, Alice Zhang Hung; ***D:*** Lucas Lowe. *ACA*

The American Soldier 🦴🦴½ *Der Amerikanische Soldat* **1970** Fassbinder's homage to the American gangster film tells the story of Ricky, a charismatic hit man. Ricky always wears a gun in a shoulder holster, sports a fedora and a white double-breasted suit, and drinks Scotch straight from the bottle. He also carries out his assigned murders with complete efficiency and no emotion. In German with English subtitles. **80m/C VHS.** *GE* Karl Scheydt, Elga Sorbas, Jan George; ***D:*** Rainer Werner Fassbinder; ***W:*** Rainer Werner Fassbinder; ***M:*** Peer Raben. *NYF, INJ*

An American Story 🦴🦴½ **1992 (PG)** Earnest but predictable story based on an actual incident. Six WWII vets return to their small Texas town as heroes. But when they find a corrupt mayor and a brutal sheriff running things they decide to campaign to unseat the local politicos, in spite of some dire warnings. Meade (Johnson), their commanding officer in Europe, is the designated leader in the plan but his ambitious wife and father-in-law want him to align himself with the status quo instead. Hallmark Hall of Fame production is enjoyable and better than most made for TV movies, but fails to reach the heights of many other HHF offerings. **97m/C VHS.** Brad Johnson, Kathleen Quinlan, Tom Sizemore, Josef Sommer, Patricia Clarkson, Lisa Blount, G.W. Bailey, John M. Jackson; ***D:*** John Gray; ***W:*** John Gray; ***C:*** Johnny E. Jensen. *REP*

An American Summer 🦴🦴 **1990** A Chicago kid spends a summer with his aunt in beach-rich Los Angeles in this coming-of-age tale filled with '90s teen idols. **100m/C VHS.** Brian Austin Green, Joanna Kerns, Michael Landes. *NO*

An American Tail 🦴🦴½ **1986 (G)** While emigrating to New York in the 1880s, a young Russian mouse (Fievel) is separated from his family. He matures as he learns to live on the Big Apple's dirty boulevards. The bad guys are of course cats. Excellent animation and a high-minded (though sentimental and stereotypical) plot keep it interesting for adults. Produced by Spielberg and the first big hit for the Bluth factory, a collection of expatriate Disney artists. Knowing better than to let a money-making mouse tale languish, Bluth followed with "An American Tale: Fievel Goes West." **81m/C VHS, Beta, LV.** ***D:*** Don Bluth; ***M:*** James Horner; ***V:*** Dom DeLuise, Madeline Kahn, Phillip Glasser, Christopher Plummer, Nehemiah Persoff, Will Ryan, John Finnegan, Cathianne Blore. Nominations: Academy Awards '86: Best Song ("Somewhere Out There"). *MCA, WTA, APD*

An American Tail: Fievel Goes West 🦴🦴 **1991 (G)** Fievel and the Mousekewitz family continue their pursuit of the American dream by heading West, where the intrepid mouse seeks to become a famous lawman while his sister looks to make it big as a dance hall singer. The score is performed by the London Symphony Orchestra. Unfortunately released at the same time as "Beauty and the Beast," "Fievel Goes West" suffers from comparison. Worthwhile viewing for the whole family, but it won't ever reach the heights of "B&B." The laser edition is letterboxed and features chapter stops. **75m/C VHS, Beta, LV.** ***D:*** Phil Nibbelink, Simon Wells; ***W:*** Flint Dille; ***M:*** James Horner; ***V:*** John Cleese, Dom DeLuise,

Phillip Glasser, Amy Irving, Jon Lovitz, Cathy Cavadini, Nehemiah Persoff, Erica Yohn, James Stewart. *MCA, WTA*

American Tickler *Draws* **1976 (R)** A thigh-slappin' (or is it head-whacking?) series of satirical pastiches in the grand style of "Kentucky Fried Movie," only more sophomoric. A tasteless collection of yearning to be funny sketches about American institutions. **77m/C VHS, Beta.** W.P. Dremak, Joan Sumner, Marlow Ferguson, Jeff Alin; ***D:*** Chuck Vincent. *GEM*

American Tiger *American Rickshaw* **1989 (R)** The collegiate hero of "American Tiger" is, like so many college students, framed for murder, and he applies himself to clearing his sullied name. Somewhere during this process, he finds himself in the middle of a battle between good and evil on a football field. About what you'd expect from a supernatural kung-fu teen-action drama. **93m/C VHS.** Mitch Gaylord, Donald Pleasence, Daniel Greene, Victoria Prouty; ***D:*** Martin Dolman. *ACA*

An American Werewolf in London **1981 (R)** Strange, darkly humorous version of the classic man-into-wolf horror tale became a cult hit, but never clicked with most American critics. Two American college students (Naughton and Dunne) backpacking through England are viciously attacked by a werewolf one foggy night. Dunne is killed, but keeps appearing (in progressively decomposed form) before the seriously wounded Naughton, warning him of impending werewolfdom when the moon is full; Dunne advises suicide. Seat-jumping horror and gore, highlighted by intensive metamorphosis sequences orchestrated by Rick Baker, are offset by wry humor, though the shifts in tone don't always work. Great moon songs permeate the soundtrack, including CCR's "Bad Moon Rising" and Van Morrison's "Moondance." **97m/C VHS, Beta, LV.** David Naughton, Griffin Dunne, Jenny Agutter, Frank Oz, Brian Glover, David Schofield; ***D:*** John Landis; ***W:*** John Landis; ***M:*** Elmer Bernstein. Academy Awards '81: Best Makeup. *LIV, VES*

American Yakuza **1994 (R)** FBI agent Nick Davis (Mortensen) is sent to L.A. to infiltrate the American arm of the Yakuza, Japan's dangerous criminal underworld. He rises through the ranks and is adopted into the powerful Tendo family. Now Davis finds himself caught between the FBI, the Yakuza, and the vengeful American mafia. **95m/C VHS.** Viggo Mortensen, Michael Nouri; ***D:*** Frank Cappello; ***W:*** Max Strom, John Allen Nelson. *COL*

Americana ½ **1981 (PG)** A troubled Vietnam vet tries to restore himself by rebuilding a merry-go-round in a small midwestern town, while dealing with opposition from the local residents. Offbeat, often effective post-Nam editorial that was produced and directed in 1973 by Carradine and then shelved. Hershey and Carradine were a couple back then. **90m/C VHS, Beta.** David Carradine, Barbara Hershey, Bruce Carradine, John Blythe Barrymore Jr., Michael Greene; ***D:*** David Carradine; ***W:*** Richard Carr. *VES, LIV*

The Americanization of Emily **1964** A happy-go-lucky American naval officer (Garner) with no appetite for war discovers to his horror that he may be slated to become the first casualty of the Normandy invasion as part of a military PR effort in this black comedy-romance. Meanwhile, he spreads the charisma in an effort to woo and uplift Emily (Andrews), a depressed English woman who has suffered the loss of her husband, father, and brother during the war. A cynical, often funny look at military maneuvers and cultural drift that was adapted by Paddy Chayefsky from William Bradford Huie's novel. Also available colorized. **117m/B VHS, LV.** James Garner, Julie Andrews, Melvyn Douglas, James Coburn, Joyce Grenfell, Keenan Wynn, Judy Carne, Liz Fraser, Edward Binns; ***D:*** Arthur Hiller; ***W:*** Paddy Chayefsky. Nominations: Academy Awards '64: Best Art Direction/Set Decoration (B & W), Best Black and White Cinematography. *MGM*

The Americano ½ **1917** Ever-suave Fairbanks frees a South American politician locked in a dungeon, returns him to political success, and captures the heart of his beautiful daughter. Based on Eugene P. Lyle, Jr.'s "Blaze Derringer." **58m/B VHS, Beta.** Douglas Fairbanks Sr., Alma Rubens, Spottiswoode Aitken, Lillian Langdon, Carl Stockdale, Tom Wilson; ***D:*** John Emerson. *GPV*

Americano **1955** A cowboy travelling to Brazil with a shipment of Brahma bulls discovers the rancher he's delivering them to has been murdered. An odd amalgam of western cliches and a South American setting. **85m/C VHS.** Glenn Ford, Frank Lovejoy, Abbe Lane, Cesar Romero; ***D:*** William Castle. *REP*

The Americano/Variety **1925** The two silent classics in abridged form: "The Americano," (1917) about a soldier-of-fortune who aids a revolt-ridden Caribbean country, and "Variety," (1925) a classic German masterpiece about the career of a trapeze artist . **54m/B VHS, Beta.** Douglas Fairbanks Sr., Emil Jannings; ***D:*** John Emerson, E.A. Dupont. *CCB*

America's Deadliest Home Video **1991** Camp spoof about America's obsession with videotaping everything in sight. Video enthusiast Doug is taken hostage by the Clint Dryer gang who want him to tape their crime spree. Every aspect is only seen through the lens of the video camera. **90m/C VHS.** Danny Bonaduce, Mick Wynhoff, Mollena Williams, Melora Walters; ***D:*** Jack Perez; ***W:*** Jack Perez. *FCT*

America's Dream **1995 (PG-13)** Trilogy of short stories covering black life from 1938 to 1958. In "Long Black Song," based on a short story by Richard Wright, Alabama farmer Silas (Glover) lives with lonely wife Sarah (Tifford), who succumbs to the charms of white travelling salesman, David (Donovan). "The Boy Who Painted Christ Black" is young Aaron (Golden), who gives the drawing to his teacher, Miss Williams (Calloway). But the portrait causes a great deal of controversy in Aaron's 1948 Georgia school, especially for ambitious principal George Du Vaul (Snipes). Based on a story by John Henrich Clarke. The last story is Maya Angelou's "The Reunion," about Chicago jazz pianist Philomena (Toussaint), who encounters her childhood nemesis, Beth Ann (Thompsn), the daughter of the white family who employed her parents as servants. **87m/C VHS.** Danny Glover, Tina Lifford, Tate Donovan, Dan Kamin, Wesley Snipes, Jasmine Guy, Vanessa Bell Calloway, Norman D. Golden II, Timothy Carhart, Yolanda King, Rae'ven Kelly, Lorraine Toussaint, Susanna Thompson, Carl Lumbly, Phyllis Cicero; ***D:*** Bill Duke, Kevin Rodney Sullivan, Paris Barclay; ***W:*** Ron Stacker Thompson, Ashley Tyler; ***C:*** Karl Herrmann; ***M:*** Patrice Rushen. *HBO*

Americathon *Woof!* **1979 (PG)** It is the year 1998 and the United States is almost bankrupt, so President Chet Roosevelt decides to stage a telethon to keep the country from going broke. Interesting satiric premise with a diverse cast, but a poor script and slack pacing spoil all the fun. The soundtrack features music by The Beach Boys and Elvis Costello while the narration is by George Carlin. **85m/C VHS, Beta.** Peter Riegert, John Ritter, Nancy Morgan, Harvey Korman, Fred Willard, Meat Loaf, Elvis Costello, Chief Dan George, Howard Hesseman, Jay Leno; ***Cameos:*** Tommy Lasorda, Peter Marshall; ***D:*** Neal Israel; ***W:*** Monica Johnson; ***M:*** Earl Brown Jr. *ORI, WAR*

Amin: The Rise and Fall *Woof!* **1982** Excessively violent and ultimately pointless dramatization of Idi Amin's eight-year reign of terror in Uganda, which resulted in the deaths of a half million people and the near ruin of a nation. **101m/C VHS, Beta.** Joseph Olita, Geoffrey Keen; ***D:*** Sharad Patel. *EMI*

The Amityville Horror **1979 (R)** Sometimes a house is not a home. Ineffective chiller that became a box-office biggie, based on a supposedly real-life occurrence in Amityville, Long Island. The Lutz family moves into the house of their dreams only to find it full of nightmares. Once the scene of a grisly mass murder, the house takes on a devilish attitude, plunging the family into supernatural terror. Pipes and walls ooze icky stuff, flies manifest in the strangest places, and doors mysteriously slam while exorcist Steiger staggers from room to room in scene-chewing prayer. Based on the Jay Anson book and followed by a number of sequels. **117m/C VHS, Beta, LV.** James Brolin, Margot Kidder, Rod Steiger, Don Stroud, Murray Hamilton, Helen Shaver, Amy Wright; ***D:*** Stuart Rosenberg; ***W:*** Sandor Stern; ***C:*** Fred W. Koenekamp; ***M:*** Lalo Schifrin. Nominations: Academy Awards '79: Best Original Score. *WAR, OM*

Amityville 2: The Possession *Woof!* **1982 (R)** More of a prequel than a sequel to "The Amityville Horror" (1979). Relates the story of the house's early years as a haven for demonic forces intent on driving a father to beat the kids, a mother to prayer, and a brother to lust after his sister (before he murders them all). Young etc. portray an obnoxious family that you're actually glad to see wasted by the possessed son. A stupid, clumsy attempt to cash in on the success of the first film, which was also stupid and clumsy but could at least claim novelty in the bad housing development genre. Followed by "Amityville III: The Demon" in 1983. **110m/C VHS, Beta, LV.** James Olson, Burt Young, Andrew Prine, Moses Gunn, Rutanya Alda; ***D:*** Damiano Damiani; ***M:*** Howard Blake. *SUE*

Amityville 3: The Demon ½ *Amityville 3-D* **1983 (R)** America's worst real-estate value dupes another funky buyer. The infamous Amityville house is once again restless with terror and gore, though supported with even less plot than the usual smidgin. Cynical reporter Roberts moves in while trying to get to the bottom of the story by way of the basement. Courtesy of 3-D technology, monsters sprang at theater patrons but the video version is strictly two-dimensional, forcing the viewer to press his or her face directly onto the television screen in order to derive similar effect. **98m/C VHS, Beta, LV.** Tony Roberts, Tess Harper, Robert Joy, Candy Clark, John Beal, Leora Dana, John Harkins, Lori Loughlin, Meg Ryan; ***D:*** Richard Fleischer; ***W:*** David Ambrose; ***M:*** Howard Blake. *VES, LIV*

Amityville 4 ½ *The Amityville Horror: The Evil Escapes, Part 4* **1989 (R)** It's an unusual case of house-to-house transference as the horror from Amityville continues, now lodged in a Californian residence. The usual good house gone bad story has the place creating a lot of unusual creaks and rattles before deciding to use its inherited powers to attack and possess a little girl. Special effects from Richard Stutsman ("The Lost Boys" and "Jaws"). Made for television. **95m/C VHS.** Patty Duke, Jane Wyatt, Norman Lloyd, Frederic Lehne, Brandy Gold; ***D:*** Sandor Stern; ***M:*** Rick Conrad. *VMK*

Amityville: A New Generation ½ **1993 (R)** And the bad sequels just go on and on and on. Terry is a young photographer who's given an old mirror by a crazy homeless man (tell me why he took it). He shares a loft with three friends and all begin experiencing vivid and terrifying dreams of murder. Seems the mirror is tied to Amityville and its evil legacy and Terry is the designated inheritor. **92m/C VHS, LV.** Ross Partridge, Julia Nickson-Soul, David Naughton, Richard Roundtree, Terry O'Quinn; ***D:*** John Murlowski; ***W:*** Christopher DeFaria, Antonio Toro. *REP*

The Amityville Curse *Woof!* **1990 (R)** The possessed house is yet again purchased by a pathetically uninformed family. The usual ghostly shenanigans occur with low-budget regularity in this fifth film in the series. Never released theatrically, for good reason. **91m/C VHS, LV.** *CA* Kim Coates, Dawna Wightman, Helen Hughes, David Stein, Anthony Dean Rubes, Cassandra Gava, Jan Rubes; ***D:*** Tom Berry. *VTR, VMK*

Amityville 1992: It's About Time **1992 (R)** Time is of the essence in the sixth installment of the Amityville flicks. A vintage clock (from Amityville, of course), causes creepy goings-on in a family's house. Actually a halfway decent horror film with high-grade special effects, and much, much better than previous Amityville sequels, which isn't saying much. **95m/C VHS, LV.** Stephen Macht, Shawn Weatherly, Megan Ward, Damon Martin, Nita Talbot, Dick Miller; ***D:*** Tony Randel. *REP*

Among the Cinders **1983** Sometimes interesting coming of age drama about a sixteen-year-old New Zealand boy who runs away to his grandfather's farm to forget about his friend's accidental death. At the farm, he meets an older woman and compromises his virtue. **103m/C VHS, Beta, LV.** *GE NZ* Paul O'Shea, Derek Hardwick, Rebecca Gibney, Yvonne Lawley, Amanda Jones; ***D:*** Rolf Haedrich. *NWV, VTR*

Amongst Friends ☆☆ **1993 (R)** Three boyhood buddies, Trevor (McGaw), Billy (Lindsey), and Andy (Parlavecchio), from a nice Long Island neighborhood turn to crime out of boredom. Trevor gets busted and goes to prison for two years. Upon getting out, he finds his old cronies still share the taste for crime and general aimlessness but also still want that one big score. Trevor finally agrees to join Andy and Billy in a drug deal but the jealous Billy, who wants Trevor's old girlfriend Laura (Sorvino), plans a double-cross that will affect them all. Filled with cutting attacks on the society that spawns aimless youth. Debut of then 26-year-old writer/director Weiss. **88m/C VHS, LV.** Patrick McGaw, Steve Parlavecchio, Joseph Lindsey, Mira Sorvino, David Stepkin, Michael Artura; ***D:*** Rob Weiss; ***W:*** Rob Weiss; ***C:*** Michael Bonvillain; ***M:*** Mick Jones. *COL*

Amor Bandido ☆☆½ **1979** When cab drivers in Rio are turning up dead, a young prostitute is torn between her detective father and her prime suspect boyfriend. Drama based on a true story. In Portuguese with English subtitles. **95m/C VHS, LV.** *BR* Paulo Gracindo, Cristina Ache, Paulo Guarniero; ***D:*** Bruno Barreto. *FXL, IME, INJ*

Amore ☆☆☆ **1948** Rossellini's tribute to actress Magnani consists of the short films "The Human Voice" and "The Miracle." In "The Human Voice," Magnani is shown alone, speaking to her lover on the telephone. Based on Jean Cocteau's one-act drama. In "The Miracle," she is a simple peasant girl who believes her illegitimate child is acutally the new Messiah. In Italian with English subtitles. **78m/B VHS.** *IT* Anna Magnani; ***D:*** Roberto Rossellini. *FCT, INJ, CVC*

Amore! ☆☆½ **1993 (PG-13)** Wealthy investment banker Saul Schwartz (Scalia) hates his job, his wife, and his life. The only way he loses himself is by watching movies starring Italian matinee idol Rudolfo Carbonera (Hamilton). So Saul gets divorced and decides to change his life—by going to Hollywood and becoming an actor like his debonair idol. With the help of some newfound friends he transforms himself into suave leading man material (under the name of Salvatore Guiliano III) but promptly winds up falling for a writer (Ireland), who couldn't care less. **93m/C VHS, LV.** Jack Scalia, Kathy Ireland, Elliott Gould, George Hamilton, Brenda Epperson, James Doohan, Katherine Helmond, Betsy Russell, Norm Crosby, Frank Gorshin; ***D:*** Lorenzo Doumani; ***W:*** Lorenzo Doumani. *PMH*

The Amorous Adventures of Moll Flanders ☆☆ **1965** An amusing romp set in 18th century England focusing on a poor orphan girl who seeks wealth. Moll plots to get ahead through an advantageous series of romances and marriages. Her plan is ruined when she falls in love and he turns out to be a wanted highwayman, landing her in prison. Not surprisingly, love (and money) conquers all. Based on the novel by Daniel Defoe. Novak tries in this female derivative of "Tom Jones," but this period piece isn't her style. **126m/C VHS.** Kim Novak, Richard Johnson, Angela Lansbury, Vittorio De Sica, Leo McKern, George Sanders, Lilli Palmer; ***D:*** Terence Young; ***C:*** Ted Moore; ***M:*** John Addison. *PAR*

Amos ☆☆½ **1985** Douglas is Amos, an aging baseball coach confined most reluctantly to a nursing home. He's disturbed by recent suspicious events there, his concern causing him to take on Montgomery, the staunch head nurse. Well-acted drama produced by Douglas's son Peter, offering an echo of "One Flew Over the Cuckoo's Nest," which Dad starred in on Broadway and son Michael helped produced as a movie classic. **100m/C VHS.** Kirk Douglas, Elizabeth Montgomery, Dorothy McGuire, Noriyuki "Pat" Morita, James Sloyan, Ray Walston; ***D:*** Michael Tuchner; ***M:*** Georges Delerue. *NO*

Amos and Andrew ☆½ **1993 (PG-13)** Embarrassing attempt at comedy stops short of endorsing the stereotypes it tries to parody. Prizewinning African-American author Andrew Sterling (Jackson) is seen moving into a house on an island previously reserved for the uptight white, and the neighbors call the cops, assuming he's a thief. Chief of police (Coleman) eagerly gets into the act, then exploits drifter Amos (Cage) in a cover-up attempt when he realizes his mistake. Talented cast can't overcome lame jokes and transparent plot that serves as an opportunity to bring black and white together for a "see how much we have in common" bonding session. **96m/C VHS, LV.** Nicolas Cage, Samuel L. Jackson, Michael Lerner, Margaret Colin, Giancarlo Esposito, Dabney Coleman, Bob Balaban, Aimee Graham, Brad Dourif, Chelcie Ross, Jodi Long; ***D:*** E. Max Frye; ***W:*** E. Max Frye; ***M:*** Richard Gibbs. *COL, IME, NLC*

The Amphibian Man ☆☆ **1961** What does a scientist do once he's created a young man with gills? Plunge him in the real world of aqua pura to experience life and love, albeit underwater. Trouble is, the protagonist, who's come to be known as the Sea Devil, takes a dive for a young pretty he's snatched from the jaws of death. A 60's Soviet sci-fi romance originally seen on American television. **96m/C VHS.** *RU* K. Korieniev, M. Virzinskaya; ***D:*** Y. Kasancki. *SNC*

The Amsterdam Connection ☆ **197?** Film company acts as a cover for prostitution and drug smuggling, with the girls acting as international couriers. **90m/C VHS, Beta.** *HK* Chen Shing, Kid Sherrif, Yeung Sze, Jason Pai Piu, Fang Mui San; ***D:*** Fang Mui San, Lo Ke. *NO*

The Amsterdam Kill ☆☆ **1978 (R)** A washed-up ex-agent of the U.S. Drug Enforcement Agency is hired by a desperate U.S. Drug Enforcement Agency to hunt down the kingpin of a narcotics syndicate in Hong Kong. Tedious pace with occasional spells of violence fails to awaken somnambulent Mitchum. Shot on location in Hong Kong. **93m/C VHS, Beta, LV.** *HK* Robert Mitchum, Richard Egan, Keye Luke, Leslie Nielsen, Bradford Dillman; ***D:*** Robert Clouse; ***W:*** Robert Clouse. *GKK*

Amsterdamned ☆☆ **1988 (R)** A crime thriller taking place on the canals of Amsterdam featuring a serial skindiver killer who surfaces periodically to slash and splash. A steely detective fishes for clues. Dubbed. **114m/C VHS, Beta, LV.** *NL* Monique Van De Ven, Huub Stapel; ***D:*** Dick Maas. *VES, LIV*

Amy ☆☆½ **1981 (G)** Set in the early 1900s, the story follows the experiences of a woman after she leaves her well-to-do husband to teach at a school for the deaf and blind. Eventually she organizes a football game between the handicapped kids and the other children in the neighborhood. Good Disney family fare. **100m/C VHS, Beta.** Jenny Agutter, Barry Newman, Kathleen Nolan, Margaret O'Brien, Nanette Fabray, Chris Robinson, Lou Fant; ***D:*** Vincent McEveety; ***M:*** Robert F. Brunner. *DIS*

The Amy Fisher Story ☆☆ **1993** Amy Fisher wishes she looked this good. Perhaps if she did, she could be acting in made-for-television movies like Barrymore instead of providing fodder for them. The ABC account draws from a variety of sources to dramatize the relationship between Amy and her married, ahem, friend, and Amy's subsequent attack on his wife. Although it tries not to take sides, it does include some pretty hot sex scenes which could be why this docudrama garnered the highest ratings of the three network productions released on TV. See also: "Casualties of Love: The 'Long Island Lolita' Story" and "Lethal Lolita—Amy Fisher: My Story." **96m/C VHS.** Drew Barrymore, Anthony John Denison, Harley Jane Kozak, Tom Mason, Laurie Paton, Ken Pogue, Linda Darlow; ***D:*** Andy Tennant; ***W:*** Janet Brownell. *ABC*

Anastasia ☆☆☆½ **1956** Bergman won her second Oscar, and deservedly so, for her classic portrayal of the amnesia victim chosen by Russian expatriate Brynner to impersonate Anastasia, the last surviving member of the Romanoff dynasty. As such, she becomes part of a scam to collect millions of rubles deposited in a foreign bank by her supposed father, the now-dead Czar. But is she just impersonating the princess? Brynner as the scheming White General and Hayes as the Grand Duchess who needs to be convinced turn in fine performances as well. Based on Marcelle Maurette's play. **105m/C VHS, LV.** Ingrid Bergman, Yul Brynner, Helen Hayes, Akim Tamiroff; ***D:*** Anatole Litvak; ***W:*** Arthur Laurents; ***C:*** Jack Hildyard. Academy Awards '56: Best Actress (Bergman); Golden Globe Awards '57: Best Actress—Drama (Bergman); New York Film Critics Awards '56: Best Actress (Bergman); Nominations: Academy Awards '56: Best Original Score. *TCF*

Anastasia: The Mystery of Anna ☆☆½ **1986** Irving stars as Anna Anderson, a woman who claimed to be the Grand Duchess Anastasia, the sole surviving daughter of Russian Czar Nicholas II. A powerful epic reliving her experience of royalty, flight from execution, and struggle to retain her heritage. The story of Anastasia remains as one of the greatest dramatic mysteries of the 20th century. Adapted from the book "Anastasia: The Riddle of Anna Anderson" by Peter Kurth; originally broadcast on cable television. **190m/C VHS, LV.** Amy Irving, Olivia de Havilland, Jan Niklas, Nicolas Surovy, Susan Lucci, Elke Sommer, Edward Fox, Claire Bloom, Omar Sharif, Rex Harrison; ***D:*** Marvin J. Chomsky; ***W:*** James Goldman. *CAF, PBS, FUS*

Anatomy of a Murder ☆☆☆☆ **1959** Considered by many to be the best courtroom drama ever made. Small-town lawyer in northern Michigan faces an explosive case as he defends an army officer who has killed a man he suspects was his philandering wife's rapist. Realistic, cynical portrayal of the court system isn't especially concerned with guilt or innocence, focusing instead on the interplay between the various courtroom characters. Classic performance by Stewart as the down home but brilliant defense lawyer who matches wits with Scott, the sophisticated prosecutor; terse and clever direction by Preminger. Though tame by today's standards, the language used in the courtroom was controversial. Filmed in upper Michigan; based on the bestseller by judge Robert Traver. **161m/B VHS, Beta, LV.** James Stewart, George C. Scott, Arthur O'Connell, Ben Gazzara, Lee Remick, Eve Arden, Orson Bean, Kathryn Grant, Murray Hamilton, Joseph Welch; ***Cameos:*** Duke Ellington; ***D:*** Otto Preminger; ***W:*** Wendell Mayes; ***C:*** Sam Leavitt; ***M:*** Duke Ellington. National Board of Review Awards '59: 10 Best Films of the Year; New York Film Critics Awards '59: Best Actor (Stewart), Best Screenplay; Nominations: Academy Awards '59: Best Actor (Stewart), Best Adapted Screenplay, Best Black and White Cinematography, Best Film Editing, Best Picture, Best Supporting Actor (O'Connell, Scott). *COL*

Anatomy of a Psycho ☆ **1961** A man plans to avenge his gas chambered brother by committing mass murder. Very cheaply and poorly produced. **75m/B VHS, Beta.** Ronnie Burns, Pamela Lincoln, Darrell Howe, Russ Bender; ***D:*** Brooke L. Peters. *SNC*

Anatomy of a Seduction ☆☆ **1979** Television formula melodrama of a middle-aged divorcee's affair with her son's best friend. Age knows no boundaries when it comes to television lust. **100m/C VHS, 8mm.** Susan Flannery, Jameson Parker, Rita Moreno, Ed Nelson, Michael Le Clair; ***D:*** Steven Hilliard Stern; ***M:*** Hagood Hardy. *HBO*

Anatomy of Terror ☆ **1974** A made for television drama about an army vet going bonkers (what? really?) and revealing espionage secrets in his home life. **73m/C VHS, Beta.** Paul Burke, Polly Bergen, Dinsdale Landen, Basil Henson. *LIV*

Anchors Aweigh ☆☆☆ **1945** Snappy big-budget (for then) musical about two horny sailors, one a girl-happy dancer and the other a shy singer. While on leave in Hollywood they return a lost urchin to his sister. The four of them try to infiltrate a movie studio to win an audition for the girl from maestro Iturbi. Kelly's famous dance with Jerry the cartoon Mouse (of "Tom and Jerry" fame) is the second instance of combining live action and animation. The young and handsome Sinatra's easy crooning and Grayson's near operatic soprano are blessed with music and lyrics by Styne and Cahn. Lots of fun, with conductor-pianist Iturbi contributing and Hollywood-style Little Mexico also in the brew. ♫We Hate to Leave; I Fall in Love Too Easily; The Charm of You; The Worry Song; Jalousie; All of a Sudden My Heart Sings; I Begged Her; What Makes the Sun Set?; Waltz Serenade. **139m/C VHS, Beta, LV.** Frank Sinatra, Gene Kelly, Kathryn Grayson, Jose Iturbi, Sharon McManus, Dean Stockwell, Carlos Ramirez, Pamela Britton; ***D:*** George Sidney; ***M:*** Jule Styne, Sammy Cahn. Academy Awards '45: Best Score; Nominations: Academy Awards '45: Best Actor (Kelly), Best Color Cinematography, Best Picture, Best Song ("I Fall in Love Too Easily"). *MGM*

And a Nightingale Sang ☙☙½ **1991** WWII England is the scene of this sweet romance, a sad and humorous tale of a woman who gives everything for the war effort. Stunning recreation of the final days of the Blitzkreig. Originally produced for Masterpiece Theatre. **90m/C VHS.** Joan Plowright, Tom Watt, Phyllis Logan, John Woodvine. *PBS, FUS*

And Baby Makes Six ☙☙½ **1979** An unexpected pregnancy creates new challenges for a couple with grown children. Dewhurst is excellent as usual. Made for television. Followed by "Baby Comes Home." **100m/C VHS, 8mm.** Colleen Dewhurst, Warren Oates, Maggie Cooper, Mildred Dunnock, Timothy Hutton, Allyn Ann McLerie; ***D:*** Waris Hussein; ***W:*** Shelley List. *NO*

And God Created Woman ☙☙½ *And Woman...Was Created; Et Dieu Crea la Femme* **1957 (PG)** Launching pad for Bardot's career as a sex siren, as she flits across the screen in a succession of scanty outfits and hangs out at the St. Tropez beach in what is euphemistically known as a swimsuit while turning up the heat for the males always in attendance. The plot concerns an 18-year-old nymphomaniac who is given a home by a local family with three handsome young sons. A cutting-edge sex film in its time that was boffo at the box office. In French with English subtitles. **93m/C VHS, Beta.** *FR* Brigitte Bardot, Curt Jurgens, Jean-Louis Trintignant, Christian Marquand; ***D:*** Roger Vadim; ***W:*** Roger Vadim. *NO*

And God Created Woman ☙½ **1988 (R)** Loose, dull remake by Vadim of his own 1957 softcore favorite about a free-spirited woman dodging men and the law while yearning for rock and roll stardom. DeMornay is a prisoner who hopes to marry one of the local hunks (Spano) so she can be paroled. They marry, she strips, he frets, while political hopeful Langella smacks his lips in anticipation. Available in an unrated 100-minute version. **98m/C VHS, Beta, LV.** Rebecca DeMornay, Vincent Spano, Frank Langella, Donovan Leitch, Judith Chapman, Thelma Houston; ***D:*** Roger Vadim; ***M:*** Tom Chase, Steve Rucker. *VES, LIV*

And God Said to Cain ☙ **196?** Another Biblically titled western from the prolific Kinski, about a put-upon gunman who must fight for his life. **95m/C VHS, Beta.** Klaus Kinski. *UNI*

...And God Spoke ☙☙ **1994 (R)** Low budget spoof takes on both religion and moviemaking with two schlockmeisters filming a biblical epic. Since the duo have no budget and are basic hacks with pretensions , they have to settle...so Sales plays Moses, "The Incredible Hulk" Ferrigno gets cast as Cain, while Plumb ("Jan" on "The Brady Bunch") does Mrs. Noah. Has some lulls but also covers very recognizable territory. Directorial debut of Borman. **82m/C VHS.** Michael Riley, Stephen Rappaport, Soupy Sales, Lou Ferrigno, Eve Plumb, Andy Dick, R.C. Bates, Fred Kaz, Daniel Tisman; ***D:*** Arthur Borman; ***W:*** Gregory S. Malins, Michael Curtis. *WEA*

And Hope to Die ☙☙½ **1972** Moody, muddled crime drama with a good cast about a fleeing Frenchman who joins a gang of hardened criminals in Canada. They go ahead with their plans to kidnap a retarded girl even though she is already dead. Standard caper film is enhanced by arty camera work and some unusual directorial touches. **95m/C VHS, Beta.** *FR* Robert Ryan, Jean-Louis Trintignant, Aldo Ray, Tisa Farrow; ***D:*** Rene Clement. *NO*

And I Alone Survived ☙☙ **1978** Made-for-television adaptation of the true story of a woman who survives a leisure-plane crash in the Sierra Nevadas and her struggle to get to the village below. Brown does her best to elevate the proceedings above the usual I-hope-I-don't-die cliches. **90m/C VHS, Beta.** Blair Brown, David Ackroyd, Vera Miles, G.D. Spradlin; ***D:*** William A. Graham. *PSM*

And Justice for All ☙☙½ **1979 (R)** Earnest attorney Pacino questions the law and battles for justice in and out of the courtroom. He's hired to defend a detested judge from a rape charge, while dealing with a lost-soul caseload of eccentric and tragedy-prone clients. Overly melodramatic, an odd mix of satire, cynicism, and seemingly sincere drama that hits with a club when a stick will do. Jewison aims for black surrealism, permitting both Pacino and Warden (as a judge losing his sanity) to veer into histrionics, to the detriment of what is essentially a gripping behind-the-scenes story. Excellent cast creates sparks, including Lahti in her film debut. And Baltimore never looked lovelier. **120m/C VHS, Beta, LV, 8mm.** Al Pacino, Jack Warden, Christine Lahti, Thomas G. Waites, Craig T. Nelson, John Forsythe, Lee Strasberg; ***D:*** Norman Jewison; ***W:*** Barry Levinson, Valerie Curtin; ***M:*** Dave Grusin. Nominations: Academy Awards '79: Best Actor (Pacino), Best Original Screenplay. *COL*

And Nothing But the Truth ☙☙½ *Giro City* **1982** A multinational corporation is out to ruin the investigative television report team trying to do a story on the company. **90m/C VHS, Beta.** *GB* Glenda Jackson, Jon Finch, Kenneth Colley, James Donnelly; ***D:*** Karl Francis. *NO*

And Now for Something Completely Different ☙☙☙ **1972 (PG)** A compilation of skits from BBC-television's "Monty Python's Flying Circus" featuring Monty Python's own weird, hilarious brand of humor. Sketches include "The Upper Class Twit of the Year Race," "Hell's Grannies" and "The Townswomen's Guild Reconstruction of Pearl Harbour." A great introduction to Python for the uninitiated, or a chance for the converted to see their favorite sketches again. **89m/C VHS, Beta, LV.** *GB* John Cleese, Michael Palin, Eric Idle, Graham Chapman, Terry Gilliam, Terry Jones; ***D:*** Ian McNaughton; ***W:*** John Cleese, Michael Palin, Graham Chapman, Terry Gilliam, Terry Jones. *COL, TVC*

And Now Miguel ☙☙ **1966** Plodding tale of a young boy who wants to take over as head shepherd of his family's flock. Filmed in New Mexico, but the over-long outdoor shots make it drag a bit in spite of Cardi's competent performance. **95m/C VHS.** Pat Cardi, Michael Ansara, Guy Stockwell, Clu Gulager, Joe De Santis, Pilar Del Rey, Buck Taylor; ***D:*** James B. Clark. *NOS*

And Now My Love ☙☙½ **1974 (PG)** A French couple endeavor to maintain their romance despite interfering socio-economic factors—she's a millionaire and he's an ex-con filmmaker. Keller plays three roles spanning three generations, as Lelouch invests autobiographical details to invent a highly stylized, openly sentimental view of French folks in love with love. Along the way he comments on social mores and changing attitudes through the years. Dubbed in English. **121m/C VHS, Beta.** *FR* Marthe Keller, Andre Dussollier, Carla Gravina; ***D:*** Claude Lelouch; ***W:*** Claude Lelouch. Los Angeles Film Critics Association Awards '75: Best Foreign Film; Nominations: Academy Awards '75: Best Original Screenplay. *COL, INJ, SUE*

And Now the Screaming Starts ☙☙½ **1973 (R)** The young bride-to-be of the lord of a British manor house is greeted by bloody faces at the window, a severed hand, and five corpses. Then Cushing shows up to investigate. Good-looking, sleek production with genuine chills. **87m/C VHS, Beta.** *GB* Peter Cushing, Herbert Lom, Patrick Magee, Ian Ogilvy, Stephanie Beacham, Geoffrey Whitehead, Guy Rolfe; ***D:*** Roy Ward Baker. *PSM, MED*

And Soon the Darkness ☙☙ **1970 (PG)** One of two vacationing young nurses disappears in France where a teenager was once murdered and the search is on. Predictable, ineffective suspenser. **94m/C VHS, Beta.** *GB* Pamela Franklin, Michele Dotrice, Sandor Eles, John Nettleton, Claire Kelly, Hanna-Marie Pravda; ***D:*** Robert Fuest; ***W:*** Brian Clemens. *NO*

And the Band Played On ☙☙☙ **1993 (PG-13)** Randy Shilts' monumental, and controversial, 1987 book on the AIDS epidemic comes to television in an equally controversial made for cable movie. Details the intricate medical research undertaken by doctors in France and the U.S. who fought to isolate and identify the mystery virus despite governmental neglect, red tape, clashing egos, and lack of funding. Various aspects of gay life are shown objectively, without sensationalizing. Celebrity cameos are somewhat distracting though most acquit themselves well. The script went through numerous rewrites; director Spottiswoode reportedly objected to HBO interference at the editing stage. **140m/C VHS, LV.** Matthew Modine, Alan Alda, Ian McKellen, Lily Tomlin, Glenne Headly, Richard Masur, Saul Rubinek, Charles Martin Smith, Patrick Bauchau, Nathalie Baye, Christian Clemenson; ***Cameos:*** Richard Gere, David Clennon, Phil Collins, Alex Courtney, David Dukes, David Marshall Grant, Ronald Guttman, Anjelica Huston, Ken Jenkins, Richard Jenkins, Tcheky Karyo, Swoosie Kurtz, Jack Laufer, Steve Martin, Dakin Matthews, Peter McRobbie, Lawrence Monoson, B.D. Wong, Donal Logue, Jeffrey Nordling, Stephen Spinella; ***D:*** Roger Spottiswoode; ***W:*** Arnold Schulman; ***C:*** Paul Elliott; ***M:*** Carter Burwell. *HBO*

And the Children Shall Lead **1985** A young black girl is moved by the coming of the civil rights movement to her small Mississippi town. Part of the "Wonderworks" series. **60m/C VHS.** Danny Glover, LeVar Burton, Pam Potillo, Denise Nicholas, Andrew Prine; ***D:*** Michael Pressman. *PME, PTB, HMV*

And the Ship Sails On ☙☙☙ *El la Nave Va* **1983 (PG)** On the eve of WWI, a group of devoted opera lovers take a luxury cruise to pay their respects to a recently deceased opera diva. Also on board is a group of fleeing Serbo-Croation freedom fighters. A charming and absurd autumnal homage-to-life by Fellini shot entirely in the studio. **130m/C VHS, Beta, LV.** *IT* Freddie Jones, Barbara Jefford, Janet Suzman, Peter Cellier; ***D:*** Federico Fellini; ***W:*** Federico Fellini, Tonino Guerra. *COL, APD, INJ*

And Then There Were None ☙☙☙½ **1945** An all-star cast makes up the ten colorful guests invited to a secluded estate in England by a mysterious host. What the invitations do not say, however, is the reason they have been specifically chosen to visit—to be murdered, one by one. Cat and mouse classic based on Agatha Christie's book with an entertaining mix of suspense and black comedy. Remade in 1966 and again in 1975 as "Ten Little Indians," but lacking the force and gloss of the original. **97m/C VHS, Beta, LV.** Louis Hayward, Barry Fitzgerald, Walter Huston, Roland Young, Sir C. Aubrey Smith, Judith Anderson, Mischa Auer, June Duprez; ***D:*** Rene Clair. *NOS, VCI*

And Then You Die ☙☙☙ **1988 (R)** An intense crime drama about a Canadian drug lord who amasses a fortune from the cocaine and marijuana trade. His empire is threatened as the Mafia, Hell's Angels, and the police try to bring him down. **115m/C VHS, Beta.** *CA* Kenneth Welsh, R.H. Thomson, Wayne Robson, Tom Harvey, George Bloomfield, Graeme Campbell; ***D:*** Francis Mankiewicz. *VMK*

And You Thought Your Parents Were Weird! ☙☙½ **1991 (PG)** A pair of introverted, whiz kid brothers invent a lovable robot to provide fatherly guidance as well as companionship for their widowed mother. Surprisingly charming, sentimental film is only slightly hampered by low-budget special effects. **92m/C VHS.** Marcia Strassman, Joshua Miller, Edan Gross, John Quade, Sam Behrens, Susan Gibney, Gustav Vintas, Eric Walker; ***D:*** Tony Cookson; ***W:*** Tony Cookson; ***M:*** Randy Miller; ***V:*** Alan Thicke, Richard Libertini. *VMK*

The Anderson Tapes ☙☙☙ **1971 (PG)** Newly released from prison, an ex-con assembles his professional pals and plans the million-dollar robbery of an entire luxury apartment house on NYC's upper east side. Of course, he's unaware that a hoard of law men from federal, state, and local agencies are recording their activities for a wide variety of reasons, though none of the surveillance is coordinated and it has nothing to do with the planned robbery. Based on the novel by Lawrence Sanders, the intricate caper is effectively shaped by Lumet, who skillfully integrates broad satire with suspense. Shot on location in New York City. Walken is The Kid, his first major role. **100m/C VHS, Beta, LV.** Sean Connery, Dyan Cannon, Martin Balsam, Christopher Walken, Alan King, Ralph Meeker, Garrett Morris, Margaret Hamilton; ***D:*** Sidney Lumet; ***W:*** Frank Pierson; ***M:*** Quincy Jones. *GKK, COL*

Andersonville 🦴🦴🦴 **1995** Andersonville was an infamous Confederate prison camp in Georgia that by August, 1864 contained more than 32,000 Union POWs—and was planned to hold 8,000 men. One in four soldiers died in the camp. The story is told through the eyes of Massachusetts Corporal Josiah Day (Emick), who is captured in 1864 and struggles to survive the hellish conditions. The commander of the Andersonville was a deranged German-Swiss captain named Wirz (Triska)—who became the only Civil War soldier to be hanged for war crimes (depictd in "The Andersonville Trial"). The TV miniseries was filmed some 150 miles from the original site. **168m/C VHS.** Jarrod Emick, Frederic Forrest, Ted Marcoux, Jan Triska, Cliff DeYoung, Tom Aldredge, Frederick Coffin, Justin Henry, Kris Kamm, William H. Macy, Gabriel Olds, William Sanderson, Bud Davis, Carmen Argenziano, Peter Murnik; ***D:*** John Frankenheimer; ***W:*** David W. Rintels; ***C:*** Ric Waite; ***M:*** Gary Chang. *TTC*

The Andersonville Trial 🦴🦴🦴½ **1970** Details the atrocities experienced by captured Union soldiers who were held in the Confederacy's notorious Andersonville prison during the American Civil War. Provides an interesting account of the war-crimes trial of the Georgia camp's officials, under whom more than 14,000 prisoners died. Moving, remarkable television drama based on the Pulitzer-honored book by MacKinlay Kantor. **150m/C VHS, Beta, LV.** Martin Sheen, William Shatner, Buddy Ebsen, Jack Cassidy, Richard Basehart, Cameron Mitchell; ***D:*** George C. Scott. *LIV*

Andre 🦴🦴½ **1994 (PG)** More human-animal interaction from the director of "The Man from Snowy River," telling the true story of an orphaned seal that was adopted by the local Maine harbormaster (Carradine) and his family. As they raise their houseguest, the question arises whether Andre should be returned to the wild. It'll remind you of "Free Willy" with an appealing smaller sea mammal and the equally appealing Majorino, as the youngster who befriends Andre. For those who are sticklers for accuracy, Andre is actually portrayed by a sea lion and not a seal. **94m/C VHS, Beta.** Keith Carradine, Tina Majorino, Chelsea Field, Keith Szarabajka, Shane Meier; ***D:*** George Miller; ***W:*** Dana Baratta; ***M:*** Bruce Rowland. *PAR*

Andrei Rublev 🦴🦴🦴🦴 **1966** A 15th-century Russian icon painter must decide whether to record history or participate in it as Tartar invaders make life miserable. During the black and white portion, he becomes involved in a peasant uprising, killing a man in the process. After a bout of pessimism and a vow of silence, he goes forth to create artistic beauty as the screen correspondingly blazes with color. A brilliant historical drama censored by Soviet authorities until 1971. In Russian with English subtitles. **185m/C VHS, LV.** *RU* Anatoli Solonitzin, Ivan Lapikov, Nikolai Grinko, Nikolai Sergueiev; ***D:*** Andrei Tarkovsky; ***W:*** Andrei Tarkovsky, Andrei Konchalovsky. *FXL, NOS, FCT*

Androcles and the Lion 🦴🦴½ **1952** Stage-bound Hollywood version of the George Bernard Shaw story about a tailor in Imperial Rome who saves Christians from a hungry lion he had previously befriended. Sharp dialogue and a plot that's relatively (within the bounds of Hollywood) faithful help a great play become a semi-satisfying cinematic morsel. Harpo Marx was originally cast as Androcles, but was fired by producer Howard Hughes five weeks into the shooting. **105m/B VHS, Beta.** Jean Simmons, Alan Young, Victor Mature, Robert Newton, Maurice Evans; ***D:*** Chester Erskine; ***C:*** Harry Stradling. *COL, SUE*

Android 🦴🦴½ **1982 (PG)** When an android who has been assisting a quirky scientist in space learns that he is about to be permanently retired, he starts to take matters into his own synthetic hands. Combines science fiction, suspense and cloned romance. A must for Kinski fans. **80m/C VHS, Beta, LV.** Klaus Kinski, Don Opper, Brie Howard; ***D:*** Aaron Lipstadt. *MED*

The Android Affair 🦴🦴½ **1995 (PG-13)** Karen Garrett (Kozak) is studying at the Institute for Surgical Research where doctors practice experimental techniques on lifelike androids. Her next patient is William (Dunne), a handsome and charming android with a heart defect, who doesn't want to "die" during Karen's risky surgical procedure. What's worse is Karen finds this 'droid all too humanly appealing and decides to help him escape the Institute. From a story by Isaac Asimov and screenwriter Kletter. **90m/C VHS, LV.** Harley Jane Kozak, Griffin Dunne, Ossie Davis, Saul Rubinek, Peter Outerbridge, Natalie Radford; ***D:*** Richard Kletter; ***W:*** Richard Kletter. *MCA*

The Andromeda Strain 🦴🦴½ **1971 (G)** A satellite falls back to earth carrying a deadly bacteria that must be identified in time to save the population from extermination. The tension inherent in the bestselling Michael Crichton novel is talked down by a boring cast. Also available in letter-box format. **131m/C VHS, Beta, LV.** Arthur Hill, David Wayne, James Olson, Kate Reid, Paula Kelly; ***D:*** Robert Wise. Nominations: Academy Awards '71: Best Art Direction/Set Decoration, Best Film Editing. *MCA*

Andy and the Airwave Rangers 🦴🦴 *Andy Colby's Incredibly Awesome Adventure* **1989** Andy is whisked into the TV!! He finds adventure and excitement—car chases, intergalactic battles, and cartoons. **75m/C VHS, LV.** Dianne Kay, Vince Edwards, Bo Svenson, Richard Thomas, Erik Estrada, Randy Josselyn, Jessica Puscas, Chuck Kovacic; ***D:*** Deborah Brock. *COL*

Andy Griffith Show **1960** Life in Mayberry with smalltown sheriff Andy (Griffith), inept deputy Barney Fife (Knotts), Andy's son Opie (Howard), Aunt Bee (Bavier) and all the other townsfolk in the first of the rural comedy series. Two episodes: "Barney's Sidecar" and "The Darlings Are Coming." Additional episodes are available. **52m/B VHS, Beta.** Andy Griffith, Don Knotts, Ron Howard, Jim Nabors, Frances Bavier, George Lindsey, Howard McNear, Hal Smith, Howard Morris. *MOV*

Andy Hardy Gets Spring Fever 🦴🦴 **1939** Andy falls for a beautiful acting teacher, and then goes into a funk when he finds she's engaged. Judge Hardy and the gang help heal the big wound in his heart. A lesser entry (and the seventh) from the popular series. **88m/B VHS, Beta.** Mickey Rooney, Lewis Stone, Ann Rutherford, Fay Holden, Cecilia Parker, Sara Haden, Helen Gilbert; ***D:*** Woodbridge S. Van Dyke. *MGM*

Andy Hardy Meets Debutante 🦴🦴½ **1940** Seems like there should be an article in that title. Garland's second entry in series, wherein Andy meets and falls foolishly for glamorous debutante Lewis with Betsy's help while family is on visit to New York. Judy/Betsy sings "I'm Nobody's Baby" and "Singing in Rain." Also available with "Love Finds Andy Hardy" on laser disc. **86m/B VHS, Beta, LV.** Mickey Rooney, Judy Garland, Lewis Stone, Ann Rutherford, Fay Holden, Sara Haden, Cecilia Parker, Diana Lewis, Tom Neal; ***D:*** George B. Seitz. *MGM*

Andy Hardy's Double Life 🦴🦴½ **1942** In this entertaining installment from the Andy Hardy series, Andy proposes marriage to two girls at the same time and gets in quite a pickle when they both accept. Williams makes an early screen splash. **91m/B VHS, Beta.** Mickey Rooney, Lewis Stone, Ann Rutherford, Fay Holden, Sara Haden, Cecilia Parker, Esther Williams, William Lundigan, Susan Peters, Robert (Bobby) Blake; ***D:*** George B. Seitz. *MGM, MLB*

Andy Hardy's Private Secretary 🦴🦴 **1941** After Andy fails his high school finals he gets help from a sympathetic faculty member. As the secretary, Grayson makes a good first impression in one of her early screen appearances. The Hardy series was often used as a training ground for new MGM talent. **101m/B VHS, Beta.** Mickey Rooney, Kathryn Grayson, Lewis Stone, Fay Holden, Ian Hunter, Gene Reynolds, Sara Haden; ***D:*** George B. Seitz. *MGM*

Andy Warhol's Bad 🦴🦴🦴 **1977 (R)** In the John Waters' school of "crime is beauty," a Queens housewife struggles to make appointments for both her home electrolysis clinic and her all-female murder-for-hire operation, which specializes in children and pets (who are thrown out of windows and knived, respectively). Her life is further complicated by a boarder (King) who's awaiting the go-ahead for his own assignment, an autistic child unwanted by his mother. One of Warhol's more professional-appearing films, and very funny if your tastes run to the tasteless. **100m/C VHS, Beta, LV.** Perry King, Carroll Baker, Susan Tyrrell, Stefania Cassini; ***D:*** Jed Johnson. *SUE, MLB*

Andy Warhol's Dracula 🦴🦴🦴 *Blood for Dracula; Young Dracula* **1974 (R)** Sex and camp humor, as well as a large dose of blood, highlight Warhol's treatment of the tale. As Dracula can only subsist on the blood of pure, untouched maidens ("were-gins"), gardener Dallesandro rises to the occasion in order to make as many women as he can ineligible for Drac's purposes. Very reminiscent of Warhol's "Frankenstein," but with a bit more spoofery. Look for Roman Polanski in a cameo peek as a pub patron. **106m/C VHS, Beta.** *IT FR* Udo Kier, Arno Juergling, Maxine McKendry, Joe Dallesandro, Vittorio De Sica; ***Cameos:*** Roman Polanski; ***D:*** Paul Morrissey; ***W:*** Paul Morrissey. *TRI, GEM, INJ*

Andy Warhol's Frankenstein 🦴🦴½ *Flesh for Frankenstein* **1974 (R)** A most outrageous parody of Frankenstein, featuring plenty of gore, sex, and bad taste in general. Baron von Frankenstein (Kier) derives sexual satisfaction from his corpses (he delivers a particularly thought-provoking philospohy on life as he lustfully fondles a gall bladder); his wife seeks her pleasure from the monster himself (Dallesandro). Originally made in 3-D, this is one of Warhol's campiest outings. **95m/C VHS, Beta.** *GE FR IT* Udo Kier, Dalia di Lazzaro, Monique Van Vooren, Joe Dallesandro; ***D:*** Paul Morrissey; ***W:*** Paul Morrissey. *TRI, MLB*

Angel 🦴🦴½ **1937** Melodrama finds Maria Barker (Dietrich) the bored wife of British diplomat Sir Frederick (Marshall). So she heads off to Paris to visit a friend and meets the dashing Anthony Halton (Douglas), with whom she has a fling. Too bad Halton's next stop is jolly old England where he runs into an old military chum (Sir Fred, of course). High gloss but no heart. **91m/B VHS.** Marlene Dietrich, Herbert Marshall, Melvyn Douglas, Edward Everett Horton, Laura Hope Crews; ***D:*** Ernst Lubitsch; ***W:*** Guy Bolton, Samson Raphaelson, Russell Medcroft; ***C:*** Charles B(ryant) Lang; ***M:*** Friedrich Hollander. *MCA*

Angel 🦴½ **1984 (R)** Low-budget leerer about a 15-year-old honor student who attends an expensive Los Angeles private school during the day and by night becomes Angel, a streetwise prostitute making a living amid the slime and sleaze of Hollywood Boulevard. But wait, all is not perfect. A psycho is following her, looking for an opportunity. **94m/C VHS, Beta.** Donna Wilkes, Cliff Gorman, Susan Tyrrell, Dick Shawn, Rory Calhoun, John Diehl, Elaine Giftos, Ross Hagen; ***D:*** Robert Vincent O'Neil; ***W:*** Joseph M. Cala. *VTR*

Angel 3: The Final Chapter *Woof!* **1988 (R)** Former hooker Angel hits the streets to save her newly discovered sister from a life of prostitution. Trashy sequel with a better cast to tepid "Avenging Angel," which was the inept 1985 follow-up to 1984's tasteless "Angel." **100m/C VHS, Beta, LV.** Maud Adams, Mitzi Kapture, Richard Roundtree, Mark Blankfield, Kin Shriner, Tawny Fere, Toni Basil; ***D:*** Tom De Simone; ***M:*** Eric Allaman. *VTR, NWV, IME*

Angel and the Badman 🦴🦴🦴 **1947** When notorious gunslinger Wayne is wounded during a shoot-out, a pacifist family takes him in and nurses him back to health. While he's recuperating, the daughter in the family (Russell) falls for him. She begs him not to return to his previous life. But Wayne, though smitten, thinks that a Duke's gotta do what a Duke's gotta do. And that means finding the dirty outlaw (Cabot) who killed his pa. Predictable but nicely done, with a good cast and script. Wayne provides one of his better performances (and also produced). **100m/B VHS, LV.** John Wayne, Gail Russell, Irene Rich, Harry Carey Sr., Bruce Cabot; ***D:*** James Edward Grant; ***W:*** James Edward Grant; ***C:*** Archie Stout. *REP, CNG, MRV*

An Angel at My Table 🦴🦴🦴🦴 **1989 (R)** New Zealand television mini-series chronicling the life of Janet Frame, New Zealand's premiere writer/poet. At once whimsical and tragic, the film tells of how a mischievious, free-spirited young girl was wrongly placed in a mental institution for eight years, yet was ultimately able to cultivate her incredible storytelling gifts, achieving success, fame and happiness. Adapted from three of Frame's novels: "To the Island," "An Angel at My Table," and "The Envoy From Mirror City." Highly acclaimed the world over, winner of over 20 major international awards. **157m/C VHS.** *NZ* Kerry Fox, Alexia Keogh, Karen Fergusson, Iris Churn, K.J. Wilson, Martyn Sanderson; ***D:*** Jane Campion; ***W:*** Laura Jones; ***C:*** Stuart Dryburgh. Chicago Film Critics Awards '91: Best Foreign Film; Independent Spirit Awards '92: Best Foreign Film. *COL, INJ, NLC*

Angel Baby 🦴🦴½ **1961** A mute girl struggles to re-define her faith when she is cured by preacher, but then sees him fail with others. Fine performances all around, notably Reynolds in his screen debut, with cinematography by Haskell Wexler. Adapted from "Jenny Angel" by Elsie Oaks Barber. **97m/B VHS.** George Hamilton, Salome Jens, Mercedes McCambridge, Joan Blondell, Henry Jones, Burt Reynolds; ***D:*** Paul Wendkos, Hubert Cornfield; ***C:*** Haskell Wexler. *NO*

Angel Baby 🦴🦴🦴 **1995** Psychiatric out patients Kate (McKenzie) and Harry (Lynch) fall in love and move in together despite some misgivings from family and the medical bureaucracy. When Kate becomes pregnant, they decide to stop taking their medication so the baby has a better chance of being born healthy. Kate's doctors believe she's not capable of dealing with a child, although she is equally determined to have her baby, while Harry struggles to make a life for all of them. Strong performances and an assured debut by writer/director Rymer. Film won all 7 of the Australian Film Institute Awards for which it was nominated. **104m/C VHS.** *AU* John Lynch, Jacqueline McKenzie, Colin Friels, Deborra-Lee Furness, Robyn Nevin; ***D:*** Michael Rymer; ***W:*** Michael Rymer; ***C:*** Ellery Ryan; ***M:*** John Clifford Ryan. Australian Film Institute '95: Best Actor (Lynch), Best Actress (McKenzie), Best Cinematography, Best Director (Rymer), Best Film, Best Film Editing, Best Original Screenplay. *NYR*

Angel City 🦴🦴½ **1980** A Florida labor camp is the setting for this made-for-TV drama. A family of rural West Virginia migrant workers find themselves trapped inside the camp and exploited by the bossman. Adapted from Patricia Smith's book. **90m/C VHS.** Ralph Waite, Paul Winfield, Jennifer Warren, Jennifer Jason Leigh, Mitchell Ryan; ***D:*** Philip Leacock; ***W:*** James Lee Barrett. *XVC*

Angel City 🦴🦴 **1984** An experimental parody of film mysteries where a detective investigates the nature of visual truth in and about Hollywood. **75m/C VHS, Beta.** Bob Glaudini; ***D:*** Jon Jost. *FCT*

An Angel for Satan 🦴½ **1966** Steele plays a dual role in her last major, Italian horror film. She gives a strong performance as a woman obsessed by the spirit of a statue. In Italian with no subtitles. **?m/C VHS.** *IT* Barbara Steele, Anthony Steffen. *SNC*

Angel Heart 🦴🦴½ **1987 (R)** Exotic, controversial look at murder, voodoo cults, and sex in 1955 New Orleans. Bonet defiantly sheds her image as a young innocent (no more Cosby Show for you, young lady). Rourke is slimy as marginal NYC private eye Angel, hired by the devilish De Niro to track a missing big band singer who violated a "contract." His investigation leads him to the bizarre world of the occult in New Orleans, where the blood drips to a different beat. Visually stimulating, with a provocative sex scene between Bonet and Rourke, captured in both R-rated and unrated versions. Adapted by Parker from "Falling Angel" by William Hjortsberg. **112m/C VHS, Beta, LV.** Mickey Rourke, Robert De Niro, Lisa Bonet, Charlotte Rampling, Michael Higgins, Charles Gordone, Kathleen Wilhoite, Stocker Fountelieu, Brownie McGhee; ***D:*** Alan Parker; ***W:*** Alan Parker; ***M:*** Trevor Jones. *LIV, FCT*

Angel in a Taxi 🦴🦴 **1959** A six-year-old boy in an orphanage decides to choose his own mother, a beautiful ballerina he sees in a magazine, when an ugly couple try to adopt him. Italian film dubbed in English. **89m/B VHS, Beta, 8mm.** *IT* Wera Cecova, Ettore Manni, Vittorio De Sica, Marietto, Gabriele Ferzetti. *VYY, FCT*

Angel of Death *Woof!* **1986 (R)** A small mercenary band of Nazi hunters attempt to track down Josef Mengele in South America. Stupid entry in the minor "let's find the darn Nazi before he really causes trouble" genre. Director Franco is also known as A. Frank Drew White. **92m/C VHS, Beta.** Chris Mitchum, Fernando Rey, Susan Andrews; ***D:*** Jess (Jesus) Franco. *VTR, NWV*

Angel of Destruction 🦴½ **1994 (R)** Undercover cop is assigned to protect controversial rock star from psycho fan. Cop gets killed and cop's sister decides to go after the killer. **80m/C VHS, LV.** Maria Ford, Charlie Spradling; ***D:*** Charles Philip Moore. *NHO*

Angel of Fury 🦴🦴½ **1993 (R)** Rothrock plays the head of security of a computer corporation who must battle terrorists after the company's top-secret computer. And there's no one she can trust. Lots of martial arts action with the competent Rothrock. **91m/C VHS, LV.** Cynthia Rothrock, Christopher Barnes, Peter O'Brien; ***D:*** Ackyl Anwary. *IMP*

Angel of H.E.A.T. *Woof! The Protectors, Book One* **1982 (R)** Porn-star Chambers is Angel, a female super-agent on a mission to save the world from total destruction. Sex and spies abound with trashy nonchalance. **90m/C VHS, Beta, LV.** Marilyn Chambers, Mary Woronov, Steve Johnson; ***D:*** Helen Sanford, Myrl A. Schreibman. *VES*

Angel on My Shoulder 🦴🦴🦴 **1946** A murdered convict makes a deal with the Devil (Rains) and returns to earth for revenge as a respected judge who's been thinning Hell's waiting list. Occupying the good judge, the murderous Muni has significant problems adjusting. Amusing fantasy with Muni in a rare and successful comic role. Co-written by Segall, who scripted "Here Comes Mr. Jordan," in which Rains played an angel. Remade in 1980. **101m/B VHS, Beta.** Paul Muni, Claude Rains, Anne Baxter, Onslow Stevens; ***D:*** Archie Mayo; ***W:*** Harry Segall. *MRV, NOS, HHT*

Angel on My Shoulder 🦴🦴 **1980** A small-time hood wrongfully executed for murder comes back as district attorney. He owes the devil, but he's finding it tough to be evil enough to repay his debt. Okay television remake of the better 1946 film starring Paul Muni. **96m/C VHS, Beta.** Peter Strauss, Richard Kiley, Barbara Hershey, Janis Paige; ***D:*** John Berry; ***M:*** Artie Butler. *SUE*

Angel Square 🦴🦴 **1992** A Canadian production from the director of the acclaimed "Bye Bye Blues." When the father of a neighborhood boy is brutally attacked, the community bands together to search for the culprit. **106m/C VHS.** *CA* Ned Beatty; ***D:*** Anne Wheeler; ***W:*** James DeFelice. *NO*

Angel Town 🦴 **1989 (R)** A foreign exchange student, who happens to be a champion kick-boxer, is forced into combat with LA street gangs. **90m/C VHS, Beta, LV.** Olivier Gruner, Theresa Saldana, Frank Aragon, Tony Valentino, Peter Kwong, Mike Moroff; ***D:*** Eric Karson. *IMP*

Angel Unchained 🦴½ **1970** Typical biker exploitation flick has bikers and hippies joining together to fend off small-town redneck hostility. **92m/C VHS.** Don Stroud, Tyne Daly, Luke Askew, Larry Bishop, Aldo Ray, Bill McKinney; ***D:*** Lee Madden; ***W:*** Jeffrey Alladin Fiskin. *ORI*

Angel with the Trumpet 🦴🦴 **1950** Depressing character study of a woman who marries to please her family, rather than herself. When the Gestapo finds out about her Jewish ancestry, she must make the most important decision of her life. **98m/B VHS.** *GB* Eileen Herlie, Basil Sydney, Norman Wooland, Maria Schell, Olga Edwards, Oskar Werner, Anthony Bushell, Wilfrid Hyde-White; ***D:*** Anthony Bushell. *NOS*

Angela 🦴 **1977** Twisted love story about a young man (Railsback) who jumps the bones of an older woman, unaware that she is the mother he's been separated from for 23 long years. Seems that way back when, the boy was kidnapped by crime boss Huston from mom Loren, an ex-prostitute, who then turned in the boy's dad, who was something of a criminal. Mom thought son was dead, dad vowed revenge from prison, and son went about his unwitting business. It all comes together insipidly, at the expense of the cast and viewer. **91m/C VHS, Beta.** *CA* Sophia Loren, Steve Railsback, John Huston, John Vernon; ***D:*** Boris Sagal; ***M:*** Henry Mancini. *SUE, SIM*

Angela 🦴🦴 **1994** Exceedingly mystical film focuses on religiously obsessed 10-year-old Angela (Rhyne), who tells her 6-year-old sister Ellie (Blythe) that unless they are very good the Devil will come to take them away. Meanwhile, she tries to cope with volatile family relationships, including their unstable mother. Good performances in a sometimes sluggish and abstract drama. **105m/C VHS.** Miranda Stuart Rhyne, Charlotte Blythe, Anna Thomson, John Ventimiglia, Vincent Gallo; ***D:*** Rebecca Miller; ***W:*** Rebecca Miller; ***M:*** Michael Rohatyn. Sundance Film Festival '95: Best Cinematography, Filmmakers Trophy. *NYR*

Angele 🦴🦴🦴 **1934** A lovely, naive country girl is lured to the city by a cunning pimp who knows that she wants to escape her oppressive father. With her illegitimate baby, she's discovered in a whorehouse and taken in disgrace back home to dad, who promptly locks her in the barn. One special guy, however, appreciates her purity and plots to rescue her. What he lacks in material resources he makes up for in character. An overlong but moving story of lost innocence and intolerence. In French with English subtitles. Based on the novel "Un de Baumugnes" by Jean Giono. **130m/B VHS.** *FR* Orane Demazis, Fernandel, Henri Poupon, Edouard Delmont; ***D:*** Marcel Pagnol. *INT, INJ*

Angelo My Love 🦴🦴🦴 **1983 (R)** Compassionate docudrama about New York's modern gypsy community. Follows the adventures of 12-year-old Angelo Evans, the streetwise son of a fortune teller, who, with a fresh view, explores the ups and downs of his family's life. Duvall financed the effort and cast non-professional actors in this charming tale of reality and fairy-tale. **91m/C VHS, Beta, LV.** Angelo Evans, Michael Evans, Steve "Patalay" Tsiginoff, Cathy Kitchen, Millie Tsiginoff; ***D:*** Robert Duvall; ***M:*** Michael Kamen. *COL*

Angels and Insects 🦴🦴🦴 **1995 (R)** Very strange Victorian-era romantic drama is definitely an acquired taste. The mysteries of nature are nothing compared to the mysteries of human life as naturalist William Adamson (Rylance) comes to discover when he takes up a position at the home of amateur insect collector, Sir Harald Alabaster (Kemp). He falls in love and quickly marries blondly beautiful Eugenia (Kensit), whose outward propriety hides a sensual nature and some decadent family secrets. Based on A.S. Byatt's novella "Morpho Eugenia." Take particular note of the costumes by Paul Brown, which mimic the exoticness of insects. **116m/C VHS.** *GB* Mark Rylance, Patsy Kensit, Kristin Scott Thomas, Jeremy Kemp, Douglas Henshall, Chris Larkin, Annette Badland, Anna Massey, Saskia Wickham; ***D:*** Philip Haas; ***W:*** Belinda Haas, Philip Haas; ***C:*** Bernard Zitzermann; ***M:*** Alexander Balanescu. *HMK*

Angel's Brigade 🦴🦴 **1979 (PG)** Seven models get together to stop a big drug operation. Drive-in vigilante movie fare fit for a rainy night. **97m/C VHS, Beta.** Jack Palance, Peter Lawford, Jim Backus, Arthur Godfrey; ***D:*** Greydon Clark; ***W:*** Greydon Clark. *LIV*

Angels Die Hard 1984 (R) Novel biker story with the cyclists as the good guys intent on helping a town during a mining disaster. Grizzly Adams makes an early film appearance. **86m/C VHS, Beta, LV.** Tom Baker, R.G. Armstrong, Dan Haggerty, William Smith; ***D:*** Richard Compton. *NWV*

Angels from Hell 1968 Early application in the nutso 'Nam returnee genre. Disillusioned Vietnam veteran forms a massive biker gang for the sole purpose of wreaking havoc upon the Man, the Establishment and anyone else responsible for sending him off to war. The big gang invades a town, with predictably bloody results. Sort of a follow-up to "Hell's Angels on Wheels." **86m/C VHS.** Tom Stern, Arlene Martel, Ted Markland, Stephen Oliver, Paul Bertoya, James Murphy, Jack Starrett, Pepper Martin, Luana Talltree; ***D:*** Bruce Kessler. *NO*

Angels Hard as They Come 1971 (R) Opposing Hell's Angels leaders clash in a hippie-populated ghost town. A semi-satiric spoof of the biker genre's cliches features an early Glenn appearance and Busey's film debut. **86m/C VHS, Beta.** Gary Busey, Scott Glenn, James Iglehart, Gary Littlejohn, Sharon Peckinpah; ***D:*** Joe Viola; ***W:*** Jonathan Demme. *SUE*

Angels in the Outfield 1951 Enjoyable comedy fantasy about the lowly Pittsburgh Pirates who get a little celestial help in their race for the pennant. Great performances all around, especially Douglas as the gruff manager of the losing baseball team. Based on a story by Richard Conlin. **102m/C VHS.** Paul Douglas, Janet Leigh, Keenan Wynn, Donna Corcoran, Lewis Stone, Spring Byington, Bruce (Herman Brix) Bennett, Marvin Kaplan, Ellen Corby, Jeff Richards; ***D:*** Clarence Brown; ***W:*** Dorothy Kingsley, George Wells; ***C:*** Paul Vogel. *MGM*

Angels in the Outfield ½ 1994 (PG) Remake of the 1951 fantasy about a lowly baseball team who, along with some heavenly animated help find themselves on a winning streak. The new lineup includes Glover as manager of the hapless California Angels, Danza as a washed-up pitcher, and Lloyd as captain of the celestial spirits. Gordon-Levitt plays the foster child who believes he'll get his family back together if the Angels win the pennant. Familar ground still yields good, heartfelt family fare. Oakland A's third baseman Carney Lansford served as technical advisor, molding actors into fair semblance of baseball team. **105m/C VHS.** Danny Glover, Tony Danza, Christopher Lloyd, Brenda Fricker, Ben Johnson, Joseph Gordon-Levitt, Jay O. Sanders; ***D:*** William Dear; ***W:*** Holly Goldberg Sloan. *DIS*

Angels of the City 1989 What's a girl got to do to join a sorority? A house prank turns vicious when two coeds take a walk on the wild side and accidentally observe a murder, making them the next targets. Credible exploitation effort, if that's not an oxymoron. **90m/C VHS, Beta.** Lawrence-Hilton Jacobs, Cynthia Cheston, Kelly Galindo, Sandy Gershman; ***D:*** Lawrence-Hilton Jacobs; ***W:*** Lawrence-Hilton Jacobs, Raymond Martino, Joseph Merhi. *PMH*

Angels One Five 1954 A worm's-eye view of British air power in WWII. What little "excitement" there is, is generated by flashing lights, plotting maps and status boards. Hawkins and Denison are the only bright spots. **97m/B VHS.** Jack Hawkins, Michael Denison, Dulcie Gray, John Gregson, Cyril Raymond, Veronica Hurst, Geoffrey Keen, Vida Hope. *NOS*

Angels Over Broadway 1940 Slick, fast-paced black comedy about con man Fairbanks, who plans to hustle suicidal thief Qualen during a poker game, but has a change of heart. With the help of call-girl Hayworth and drunken playwright Mitchell, he helps Qualen turn his life around. Ahead of its time with an offbeat morality, but a delight in the '90s. **80m/B VHS, Beta, LV.** Douglas Fairbanks Jr., Rita Hayworth, Thomas Mitchell, John Qualen, George Watts; ***D:*** Ben Hecht, Lee Garmes; ***C:*** Lee Garmes. Nominations: Academy Awards '40: Best Original Screenplay. *FCT, COL*

Angels' Wild Women *Woof!* 1972 From the man who brought you "Dracula vs. Frankenstein" comes an amalgamation of hippies, motorcycle dudes, evil desert gurus and precious little plot. **85m/C VHS.** Kent Taylor, Regina Carrol, Ross Hagen, Maggie Bemby, Vicki Volante; ***D:*** Al Adamson. *NO*

Angels with Dirty Faces 1938 Rousing classic with memorable Cagney twitches and the famous long walk from the cell to the chair. Two young hoods grow up on NYC's lower East Side with diverse results—one enters the priesthood and the other opts for crime and prison. Upon release from the pen, famed gangster Cagney sets up shop in the old neighborhood, where Father O'Brien tries to keep a group of young toughs (the Dead End Kids) from following in his footsteps. Bogart's his unscrupulous lawyer and Bancroft a crime boss intent on double-crossing Cagney. Reportedly they were blasting real bullets during the big shootout, no doubt helping Cagney's intensity. Adapted from a story by Rowland Brown. **97m/B VHS, Beta, LV.** James Cagney, Pat O'Brien, Humphrey Bogart, Ann Sheridan, George Bancroft, Billy Halop, Leo Gorcey, Huntz Hall, Bobby Jordan, Dan Jesse, Gabriel Dell, J. Frank Burke, William Tracy, Bernard Punsley; ***D:*** Michael Curtiz; ***W:*** John Wexley, Warren Duff; ***M:*** Max Steiner. New York Film Critics Awards '38: Best Actor (Cagney); Nominations: Academy Awards '38: Best Actor (Cagney), Best Director (Curtiz), Best Story. *MGM, FOX, MLB*

Angie 1994 (R) Brassy Angie finds herself pregnant and unmarried. Tired of the advice and criticism she receives from her close knit neighborhood she strikes out of Brooklyn to find a new life for herself. Average "woman's movie" wrought with messages of pregnancy, childbirth, friendship, love, and family has far too much going on and relies too heavily on formula soap. Davis, in what could have been a juicy (read "Oscar") role is strong, but her performance is drowned by all the melodrama. Madonna was originally cast as Angie, but was bounced when the filming of "Snake Eyes" conflicted. Adapted from the book "Angie, I Says" by Avra Wing. **108m/C VHS, LV.** Geena Davis, Aida Turturro, Stephen Rea, Philip Bosco, James Gandolfini, Jenny O'Hara; ***D:*** Martha Coolidge; ***W:*** Todd Graff. *HPH*

AngKor: Cambodia Express 1981 An American journalist travels back to Vietnam to search for his long lost love. **96m/C VHS, Beta.** Robert Walker Jr., Christopher George; ***D:*** Lek Kitiparaporn. *VES, LIV*

Angry Harvest *Bittere Ernte* 1985 During the WWII German occupation of Poland, a gentile farmer shelters a young Jewish woman on the run, and a serious, ultimately interdependent relationship forms. Acclaimed; Holland's first film since her native Poland's martial law imposition made her an exile to Sweden. In German with English subtitles. Contains nudity and violence. **102m/C VHS, Beta.** *GE* Armin Mueller-Stahl, Elisabeth Trissenaar, Wojciech Pszoniak, Margit Carstensen, Kurt Raab, Kathe Jaenicke, Hans Beerhenke, Isa Haller; ***D:*** Agnieszka Holland; ***W:*** Agnieszka Holland. Montreal World Film Festival '85: Best Actor (Mueller-Stahl); Nominations: Academy Awards '85: Best Foreign Language Film. *FCT, GLV, INJ*

Angry Joe Bass 1976 Contemporary Native American Joe Bass faces government officials who continually usurp his fishing rights. Something like "Billy Jack" without the intelligence. **82m/C VHS, Beta.** Henry Bal, Molly Mershon; ***D:*** Thomas G. Reeves. *NO*

The Angry Red Planet 1959 An unintentionally amusing sci-fi adventure about astronauts on Mars fighting off aliens and giant, ship-swallowing amoebas. Filmed using bizarre "Cinemagic" process, which turns almost everything pink. Wild effects have earned the film cult status. **83m/C VHS, Beta.** Gerald Mohr, Les Tremayne, Jack Kruschen; ***D:*** Ib Melchior. *NO*

Anguish ½ 1988 (R) Well-done horror thriller about a lunatic who, inspired to duplicate the actions of an eyeball-obsessed killer in a popular film, murders a movie audience as they watch the movie. Violence and gore abound. **85m/C VHS, Beta, LV.** *SP* Zelda Rubinstein, Michael Lerner, Talia Paul, Clara Pastor; ***D:*** Bigas Luna; ***W:*** Bigas Luna; ***M:*** J.M. Pagan. *FOX*

Angus 1995 (PG-13) Dull teen comedy about self-esteem revolves around the overweight Angus (Talbert), a friendly kid tormented by the usual school bullies. His best bud is twerp Troy (Owen), who tries to help Angus out with his crush on cute blonde Melissa (Ariana). There's even a schmaltzy prom scene. The profanity, though mild, and the boys sexual interests make this questionable for the pre-teen audience that could actually enjoy it. **87m/C VHS.** Charlie Talbert, Kathy Bates, George C. Scott, Chris Owen, Ariana Richards, Lawrence Pressman, Rita Moreno, James Van Der Beek, Anna Thompson; ***D:*** Patrick Read Johnson; ***W:*** Jill Gordon; ***C:*** Alexander Grusynski; ***M:*** David E. Russo. *TTC*

Animal Behavior 1989 (PG) An animal researcher and a music professor fall in love on a college campus. Bowen's (she actually released it under the alias Riley H. Anne) comedy was filmed in 1985 and edited/shelved for over 4 years, with good reason. **79m/C VHS, Beta, LV.** Karen Allen, Armand Assante, Holly Hunter, Josh Mostel, Richard Libertini; ***D:*** Jenny Bowen; ***W:*** Susan Rice; ***M:*** Cliff Eidelman. *HBO*

Animal Called Man 1987 Two crooked buddies join a big western gang in pillaging a small town and get in too deep. **83m/C VHS, Beta.** Vassilli Karis, Craig Hill. *TWE*

Animal Crackers ½ 1930 (G) The second and possibly the funniest of the thirteen Marx Brothers films, "Animal Crackers" is a screen classic. Groucho is a guest at the house of wealthy matron Margaret Dumont and he, along with Zeppo, Chico, and Harpo, destroy the tranquility of the estate. Complete with the Harry Ruby music score—including Groucho's "Hooray for Captain Spaulding" with more quotable lines than any other Marx Brothers film: "One morning I shot an elephant in my pajamas. How he got into my pajamas, I'll never know." Based on a play by George S. Kaufman. **98m/B VHS, Beta, LV.** Groucho Marx, Chico Marx, Harpo Marx, Zeppo Marx, Lillian Roth, Margaret Dumont, Louis Sorin, Hal Thompson, Robert Greig; ***D:*** Victor Heerman; ***W:*** Morrie Ryskind. *MCA, FCT*

Animal Farm 1955 An animated version of George Orwell's classic political satire about a barnyard full of animals who parallel the growth of totalitarian dictatorships. Not entirely successful, but probably best translation of Orwell to film. **73m/C VHS, Beta, LV, 8mm.** ***D:*** John Halas, Joy Batchelor; ***V:*** Maurice Denham, Gordon Heath. *VYY, KUI, VTR*

Animal Instincts 1992 (R) A woman takes a prescription drug that makes her a nymphomaniac, and her police officer husband discovers that he's turned on by videotaping her in bed with other men and women. One of the many in her constant stream of lovers is a politician whose campaign is based on shutting down all the town's sex clubs. Another in the string of sexual thrillers riding on the coattails of "Basic Instinct." **94m/C VHS.** Maxwell Caulfield, Jan-Michael Vincent, Mitch Gaylord, Shannon Whirry, Delia Sheppard, John Saxon, David Carradine; ***D:*** Alexander Gregory Hippolyte. *ACA*

Animal Instincts 2 1994 (R) Joanna leaves her overbearing husband and moves into a supposedly quiet community. Neighbor Steve is a security expert—and a voyeur. He's hidden a camera in Joanna's bedroom but she knows he's watching. **92m/C VHS, Beta, LV.** Shannon Whirry, Woody Brown, Elizabeth Sandifer, Al Sapienza; ***D:*** Alexander Gregory Hippolyte. *ACA*

Animal Instincts 3: The Seductress ½ 1995 (R) Woman finds a new kind of sexual excitement when she gets involved with a blind rock music promoter. The unrated version contains 12 more minutes of footage. **92m/C VHS.** Weny Schumacher, James Mathew; ***D:*** Alexander Gregory Hippolyte. *APX*

The Animal Kingdom ☙☙☙ *The Woman in His House* **1932** A romantic triangle develops when Howard, married to Loy, has an affair with Harding. The problem is Harding acts more like a wife and Loy a mistress. Intelligently written and directed, with a marvelous performance from veteran character actor Gargan. **95m/B VHS.** Ann Harding, Leslie Howard, Myrna Loy, Neil Hamilton, William Gargan, Henry Stephenson, Ilka Chase; ***D:*** Edward H. Griffith; ***W:*** Horace Jackson. *FCT, HEG*

Anita, Dances of Vice ☙☙ *Anita—Tanze des Lasters* **1987** German avant-garde film celebrates Anita Berber, the "most scandalous woman in 1920s Berlin." Berber was openly bisexual, used drugs, and danced nude in public. In von Praunheim's film, she rises from the dead and creates yet more scandal. **85m/C VHS, Beta.** *GE* Lotti Huber, Ina Blum, Mikhael Honesseau; ***D:*** Rosa von Praunheim. *ICA, GLV, INJ*

The Ann Jillian Story ☙½ **1988** Jillian stars as herself in this television melodrama recounting her battle with breast cancer. Several musical numbers are included. **96m/C VHS, Beta.** Ann Jillian, Tony LoBianco, Viveca Lindfors, Leighton Bewley; ***D:*** Corey Allen. *NO*

Ann Vickers ☙☙½ **1933** A dashing young army captain wins over the heart of a dedicated social worker. Okay adaptation of a Sinclair Lewis novel, with Dunne suffering more than usual. **76m/B VHS, Beta.** Irene Dunne, Walter Huston, Bruce Cabot, Conrad Nagel, Edna May Oliver; ***D:*** John Cromwell; ***M:*** Max Steiner. *TTC*

Anna ☙☙ **1951** Novitiate nun Anna (Mangano) is forced to confront her sordid past (as a nightclub entertainer), and her love for two very different men, when her seriously injured former fiancee is brought to the hospital where she is a nurse. Anna must finally deal with her feelings and decide which path her life will take. Dubbed in English. **111m/B VHS.** *IT* Silvana Mangano, Raf Vallone, Vittorio Gassman; ***D:*** Alberto Lattuada; ***C:*** Otello Martelli; ***M:*** Nino Rota. *FCT*

Anna ☙☙☙ **1987 (PG-13)** Age, envy, and the theatrical world receive their due in an uneven but engrossing drama about aging Czech film star Anna, making a sad living in New York doing commercials and trying for off-Broadway roles. She takes in Krystyna, a young Czech peasant girl who eventually rockets to model stardom. Modern, strongly acted "All About Eve" with a story partially based on a real Polish actress. Kirkland drew quite a bit of flak for shamelessly self-promoting for the Oscar. She still lost. **101m/C VHS, Beta, LV.** Sally Kirkland, Paulina Porizkova, Robert Fields, Stefan Schnabel, Larry Pine, Ruth Maleczech; ***D:*** Yurek Bogayevicz; ***W:*** Yurek Bogayevicz, Agnieszka Holland; ***M:*** Greg Hawkes. Golden Globe Awards '88: Best Actress—Drama (Kirkland); Independent Spirit Awards '88: Best Actress (Kirkland); Los Angeles Film Critics Association Awards '87: Best Actress (Kirkland); Nominations: Academy Awards '87: Best Actress (Kirkland). *VES, LIV*

Anna and the King of Siam ☙☙☙½ **1946** Splendid adaptation, from the book by Margaret Landon, about the true life adventures of 33-year-old English widow Anna Leonowens. In 1862 Anna and her son travelled to the exotic kingdom of Siam to educate the harem and children of the king. Dunne is splendid as the strong-willed governess as is Harrison (in his first American film) as the authoritarian eastern ruler. Remade as the musical "The King and I." **128m/B VHS.** Irene Dunne, Rex Harrison, Linda Darnell, Lee J. Cobb, Gale Sondergaard, Mikhail Rasumny, Dennis Hoey, Richard Lyon, John Abbott; ***D:*** John Cromwell; ***W:*** Sally Benson, Talbot Jennings; ***C:*** Arthur C. Miller; ***M:*** Bernard Herrmann. Academy Awards '46: Best Art Direction/Set Decoration, Best Black and White Cinematography. *FXV*

Anna Christie ☙☙☙½ **1923** Silent production of Eugene O'Neill's play that even he liked. A young girl is sent away by her father, a seaman, and finds her way to Chicago, where she becomes a prostitute. Later she visits her father's barge and falls for a sailor. She shares her past life story, hoping they will understand. This film was acclaimed when it was released, and still remains a touching work of art. Remade in 1930. **75m/B VHS, Beta.** Blanche Sweet, George F. Marion Sr., William Russell, Eugenie Besserer, Chester Conklin, George Siegmann, Victor Potel, Fred Kohler Sr.; ***D:*** John Wray. *GPV, FCT*

Anna Christie ☙☙½ **1930** Garbo is the ex-prostitute who finds love with sailor Bickford. Bickford is unaware of his lover's tarnished past and she does her best to keep it that way. Garbo's first sound effort was advertised with the slogan "Garbo Talks." Adapted from the classic Eugene O'Neill play, the film is a slow but rewarding romantic drama. **90m/B VHS, Beta.** Greta Garbo, Marie Dressler, Charles Bickford, George F. Marion Sr.; ***D:*** Clarence Brown; ***C:*** William H. Daniels. Nominations: Academy Awards '30: Best Actress (Garbo), Best Cinematography, Best Director (Brown). *MGM*

Anna Karenina ☙☙☙½ **1935** Cinematic Tolstoy with Garbo as the sad, moody Anna willing to give up everything to be near Vronsky (March), the cavalry officer she's obsessed with. A classic Garbo vehicle with March and Rathbone providing excellent support. Interestingly, a remake of the Garbo and John Gilbert silent, "Love." **85m/B VHS, Beta.** Greta Garbo, Fredric March, Freddie Bartholomew, Maureen O'Sullivan, May Robson, Basil Rathbone, Reginald Owen, Reginald Denny; ***D:*** Clarence Brown; ***C:*** William H. Daniels. New York Film Critics Awards '35: Best Actress (Garbo). *NOS, MGM, HEG*

Anna Karenina ☙☙½ **1948** Stiff version of Tolstoy's passionate story of illicit love between a married woman and a military officer. In spite of exquisite costumes, and Leigh and Richardson as leads, still tedious. **123m/C VHS, LV.** *GB* Vivien Leigh, Ralph Richardson, Kieron Moore; ***D:*** Julien Duvivier. *GKK, FCT, MRV*

Anna Karenina ☙☙½ **1985 (PG)** Made for television version of Tolstoy's novel of betrayal, intrigue, and forbidden love. Anna, defying all social practices of the time, falls into the arms of a dashing count. Features an excellent performance from Paul "A Man For All Seasons" Scofield. **96m/C VHS, Beta, LV.** Jacqueline Bisset, Christopher Reeve, Paul Scofield, Ian Ogilvy, Anna Massey, Judi Bowker; ***D:*** Simon Langton. *VES*

Anna to the Infinite Power ☙☙½ **1984** Sci fi based on the book of the same name follows a young girl with telepathic powers. When the girl discovers that she has sisters as the result of a strange scientific experiment, she sets out to find them, drawing on her own inner strength. **101m/C VHS, Beta.** Dina Merrill, Martha Byrne, Mark Patton; ***D:*** Robert Wiemer. *COL*

Annabel Takes a Tour/Maid's Night Out **1938** A delightful comedy double feature. In "Annabel Takes a Tour," a fading movie star falls in love with a writer while on a tour to boost her career, and in "Maids Night Out," an heiress and a millionaire fall in love. **131m/B VHS, Beta.** Lucille Ball, Jack Oakie, Ruth Donnelly, Joan Fontaine, Allan "Rocky" Lane, Hedda Hopper, Alice White; ***D:*** Lew (Louis Friedlander) Landers. *MLB, TTC*

Annapolis ☙ **1928** Life's in the pink for two guys at the U.S. naval academy until jealousy rears its loathsome head when they fall for the same gal. Just when it's beginning to look like love and honor is an either-or proposition, the lovelorn rivals find that although love transcends all, a guy's gotta do what a guy's gotta do, even if it means sticking up for his romantic nemesis. Lots of sub-par male bonding. **63m/B VHS, Beta.** Johnny Mack Brown, Hugh Allan, Hobart Bosworth, William "Billy" Bakewell, Charlotte Walker, Jeanette Loff; ***D:*** Christy Cabanne. *GPV, FCT*

The Annapolis Story ☙½ *Blue and the Gold* **1955** Cliche-ridden WWII drama about two naval cadets romancing the same lucky girl. Low-rent time for director Siegel which wastes a decent cast. **81m/C VHS, Beta.** John Derek, Kevin McCarthy, Diana Lynn, Pat Dooley, L.Q. Jones; ***D:*** Donald Siegel. *FOX*

Anne of Avonlea ☙☙☙½ *Anne of Green Gables: The Sequel* **1987** Equally excellent mini-series sequel to "Anne of Green Gables" in which the romantic heroine grows up and discovers romance. The same cast returns and Sullivan continues his tradition of lavish filming on Prince Edward Island and beautiful costumes. Based on the characters from L.M. Montgomery's classic novels "Anne of Avonlea," "Anne of the Island," and "Anne of Windy Poplars." CBC, PBS, and Disney worked together on this WonderWorks production. On two tapes. **224m/C VHS, Beta, LV.** *CA* Megan Follows, Colleen Dewhurst, Wendy Hiller, Frank Converse, Patricia Hamilton, Schuyler Grant, Jonathan Crombie, Rosemary Dunsmore; ***D:*** Kevin Sullivan; ***W:*** Kevin Sullivan; ***M:*** Hagood Hardy. *KUI, TOU, DIS*

Anne of Green Gables ☙☙☙ **1934** A lonely Canadian couple adopts an orphan who keeps them on their toes with her animated imagination, and wins a permanent place in their hearts. Warm (but loose) adaptation of Lucy Maud Montgomery's popular novel is entertaining although 1985 remake is far superior. Followed by "Anne of Windy Poplars." **79m/B VHS, Beta.** Anne Shirley, Tom Brown, O.P. Heggie; ***D:*** George Nicholls Jr.; ***M:*** Max Steiner. *TTC*

Anne of Green Gables ☙☙☙½ **1985** Splendid production of the famous Lucy Maud Montgomery classic about a young orphan girl growing to young adulthood with the help of a crusty brother and sister duo. The characters come to life under Sullivan's direction, and the movie is enhanced by the beautiful Prince Edward Island scenery and wonderful costumes. One of the few instances where an adaptation lives up to (if not exceeds) the quality of the original novel. A WonderWorks presentation that was made with the cooperation of the Disney channel, CBC, and PBS. Followed by "Anne of Avonlea." On two tapes. **197m/C VHS, Beta, LV.** *CA* Megan Follows, Colleen Dewhurst, Richard Farnsworth, Patricia Hamilton, Schuyler Grant, Jonathan Crombie, Marilyn Lightstone, Charmion King, Rosemary Radcliffe, Jackie Burroughs; ***D:*** Kevin Sullivan; ***W:*** Kevin Sullivan, Joe Weisenfeld; ***M:*** Hagood Hardy. *KUI, TOU, IGP*

Anne of the Thousand Days ☙☙☙½ **1969 (PG)** Lavish re-telling of the life and loves of Henry the VIII. Henry tosses aside his current wife for the young and devastatingly beautiful Anne Boleyn. Burton's performance of the amoral king garnered him an Oscar nomination. Watch for Elizabeth Taylor as a masked courtesan at the costume ball. **145m/C VHS.** Richard Burton, Genevieve Bujold, Irene Papas, Anthony Quayle, John Colicos, Michael Hordern; ***D:*** Charles Jarrott; ***M:*** Georges Delerue. Academy Awards '69: Best Costume Design; Directors Guild of America Awards '70: Best Director (Jarrott); Golden Globe Awards '70: Best Actress—Drama (Bujold), Best Director (Jarrott), Best Film—Drama, Best Screenplay; Nominations: Academy Awards '69: Best Actor (Burton), Best Actress (Bujold), Best Adapted Screenplay, Best Art Direction/Set Decoration, Best Cinematography, Best Picture, Best Sound, Best Supporting Actor (Quayle), Best Original Score. *MCA*

Annie ☙☙ **1982 (PG)** Stagy big-budget adaption of the Broadway musical, which was an adaptation of the comic strip. A major financial disaster upon release, still it's an entertaining enterprise curiously directed by Huston and engagingly acted by Finney and Quinn. ♫Tomorrow; It's the Hard Knock Life; Maybe; I Think I'm Gonna Like It Here; Little Girls; We Got Annie; Let's Go to the Movies; You're Never Fully Dressed Without a Smile; Easy Street. **128m/C VHS, Beta, LV, 8mm.** Aileen Quinn, Carol Burnett, Albert Finney, Bernadette Peters, Ann Reinking, Tim Curry; ***D:*** John Huston; ***W:*** Thomas Meehan; ***M:*** Ralph Burns. Golden Raspberry Awards '82: Worst Supporting Actress (Quinn); Nominations: Academy Awards '82: Best Art Direction/Set Decoration, Best Original Score. *COL, FCT, MLT*

Annie: A Royal Adventure ☙☙½ **1995** TV sequel to "Annie" finds the red-haired heroine (Johnson) traveling to England with her Daddy Warbucks (Hearn), who's about to be knighted in London. But the evil Lady Edwina Hogbottom (played to a high-camp hilt by Collins) has a plan to blow up Buckingham Palace and take over as queen. Naturally, it's up to Annie to defeat her and have a happy ending. **92m/C VHS.** Ashley Johnson, George Hearn, Joan Collins, Emily Ann Lloyd, Camilla Bell, Ian McDiarmid. *COL*

Annie Hall ☙☙☙☙ **1977 (PG)** Acclaimed coming-of-cinematic-age film for Allen is based in part on his own life. His love affair with Hall/Keaton is chronicled as an episodic, wistful comedy commenting on family, love, loneliness, communicating, maturity, driving, city life, careers, and various other topics. Abounds with classic scenes, including future star Goldblum and his mantra at a cocktail party; Allen and the lobster pot; and Allen, Keaton, a bathroom, a tennis racket, and a spider. The film operates on many levels, as does Keaton's wardrobe, which started a major fashion trend. Don't blink or you'll miss several future stars in bit parts. Expertly shot by Gordon Willis. **94m/C VHS, Beta, LV.** Woody Allen, Diane Keaton, Tony Roberts, Paul Simon, Shelley Duvall, Carol Kane, Colleen Dewhurst, Christopher Walken, Janet Margolin, John Glover, Jeff Goldblum, Sigourney Weaver, Marshall McLuhan, Beverly D'Angelo, Shelley Hack; ***D:*** Woody Allen; ***W:*** Woody Allen, Marshall Brickman; ***C:*** Gordon Willis. Academy Awards '77: Best Actress (Keaton), Best Director (Allen), Best Original Screenplay, Best Picture; British Academy Awards '77: Best Actress (Keaton), Best Director (Allen), Best Film, Best Screenplay; Directors Guild of America Awards '77: Best Director (Allen); Golden Globe Awards '78: Best Actress—Musical/Comedy (Keaton); Los Angeles Film Critics Association Awards '77: Best Screenplay; National Board of Review Awards '77: 10 Best Films of the Year, Best Supporting Actress (Keaton); National Society of Film Critics Awards '77: Best Actress (Keaton), Best Film, Best Screenplay; Writers Guild of America '77: Best Original Screenplay; Nominations: Academy Awards '77: Best Actor (Allen). *MGM, FOX, CRC*

Annie O 🦴🦴½ **1995 (PG)** 15-year-old girl runs into problems when she joins the boys' basketball team. Her teammates are jealous and so are her brother and boyfriend. **93m/C VHS.** Coco Yares, Chad Willet, Robert Stewart; ***D:*** Michael McClary. *HMK*

Annie Oakley 🦴🦴🦴 **1935** Energetic biographical drama based on the life and legend of sharpshooter Annie Oakley and her on-off relationship with Wild Bill Hickok. Stanwyck makes a great Oakley. Later musicalized as "Annie Get Your Gun." **90m/B VHS, Beta.** Barbara Stanwyck, Preston Foster, Melvyn Douglas, Pert Kelton, Andy Clyde; ***D:*** George Stevens. *MED, NOS, TTC*

Annie Oakley **1985** This biography of the acclaimed shooting star covers her career from age 15 to retirement, including some actual silent footage of Miss Oakley filmed by Thomas Edison in 1923. Made for television. From the "Tall Tales & Legends" series by Shelley Duvall. **52m/C VHS, Beta.** Jamie Lee Curtis, Cliff DeYoung, Brian Dennehy; ***D:*** Michael Lindsay-Hogg. *FOX*

The Annihilators *Woof!* **1985 (R)** A group of Vietnam vets band together in an extremely violent manner to protect their small town from a gang of thugs. **87m/C VHS, Beta.** Gerrit Graham, Lawrence-Hilton Jacobs, Paul Koslo, Christopher Stone, Andy Wood, Sid Conrad, Dennis Redfield; ***D:*** Charles E. Sellier. *NWV, VTR*

The Anniversary 🦴🦴 **1968** One-eyed monster mom Mrs. Taggart (Bette at her baddest) gives new meaning to the word "possessive." Thoroughly cowing her three grown sons, she manages to get them to come home each year on the wedding anniversary to the husband she despised. Only this time, the trio tell her they're going to live their own lives. Hah—not if mom has anything to do with it. Based on the play by Bill MacIlwraith. **93m/C VHS.** *GB* Bette Davis, Jack Hedley, James Cossins, Christian Roberts, Sheila Hancock, Elaine Taylor; ***D:*** Roy Ward Baker; ***W:*** Jimmy Sangster; ***C:*** Henry Waxman; ***M:*** Philip Martell. *FXV*

Another Chance 🦴🦴 **1988 (R)** Girl-crazy bachelor is returned from heaven for a second chance and has to choose between a "bad" girl and a "good" girl. What a choice! **99m/C VHS, LV.** Bruce Greenwood, Frank Annese, Jeff East, Anne Ramsey, Barbara Edwards; ***D:*** Jerry Vint. *REP*

Another Country 🦴🦴½ **1984** Julian Mitchell's adaptation of his play about the true story of two English boarding school friends who wind up as spies for the Soviet Union. Based on the lives of Guy Burgess and Donald MacLean, whose youth is rather fancifully depicted in this loving recreation of 1930s English life. Although the film is inferior to the award-winning play, director Kanievska manages to transform a piece into a solid film, and Everett's performance as Burgess is outstanding. **90m/C VHS, Beta, LV.** *GB* Rupert Everett, Colin Firth, Michael Jenn, Robert Addie, Anna Massey, Betsy Brantley, Rupert Wainwright, Cary Elwes; ***D:*** Marek Kanievska. Nominations: Cannes Film Festival '84: Best Film. *SUE*

Another 48 Hrs. 🦴½ **1990 (R)** Continuing chemistry between Nolte and Murphy is one of the few worthwhile items in this stodgy rehash. Any innovation by Murphy seems lost, the story is redundant of any other cop thriller, and violence and car chases abound. Pointlessly energetic and occasionally fun for only the true devotee. **98m/C VHS, Beta, LV, 8mm.** Eddie Murphy, Nick Nolte, Brion James, Kevin Tighe, Bernie Casey, David Anthony Marshall, Ed O'Ross; ***D:*** Walter Hill; ***W:*** Jeb Stuart; ***M:*** James Horner. *PAR*

Another Man, Another Chance 🦴🦴 *Un Autre Homme, Une Autre Chance* **1977 (PG)** Remake of Lelouch's "A Man and a Woman," set in the turn-of-the-century American West, pales by comparison to the original. Slow-moving tale casts widow Bujold and widower Caan as lovers. **132m/C VHS, Beta.** *FR* James Caan, Genevieve Bujold, Francis Huster, Jennifer Warren, Susan Tyrrell; ***D:*** Claude Lelouch; ***W:*** Claude Lelouch. *NO*

Another Pair of Aces: Three of a Kind 🦴🦴🦴 **1991** Nelson and Kristofferson team up to clear the name of Torn, a Texas Ranger accused of murder. Made for television; some scenes deemed too racy for TV were added to the video version. Sequel to "A Pair of Aces." **93m/C VHS.** Willie Nelson, Kris Kristofferson, Joan Severance, Rip Torn, Dan Kamin, Ken Farmer; ***D:*** Bill Bixby. *VMK*

Another Stakeout 🦴🦴½ *Stakeout 2* **1993 (PG-13)** Sequel six years after the original finds Dreyfuss and Estevez partnered again for another stakeout, this time to keep an eye on Moriarty, a reluctant witness against the Mob. The two spying detectives find themselves in an upscale neighborhood where blending in is a hard thing to do. O'Donnell is a breath of fresh air as a wisecracking assistant district attorney. Stowe briefly reprises her role as Dreyfuss' girlfriend. Writer Kouf reportedly had difficulty penning the script, surprising since there isn't much new here. **109m/C VHS, LV.** Richard Dreyfuss, Emilio Estevez, Rosie O'Donnell, Cathy Moriarty, Madeleine Stowe, John Rubinstein, Marcia Strassman, Dennis Farina, Miguel Ferrer; ***D:*** John Badham; ***W:*** Jim Kouf; ***C:*** Roy Wagner. *TOU*

Another Thin Man 🦴🦴½ **1939** Powell and Loy team up for the third in the delightful "Thin Man" series. Slightly weaker series entry takes its time, but has both Powell and Loy providing stylish performances. Nick Jr. is also introduced as the newest member of the sleuthing team. Sequel to "After the Thin Man;" followed by "Shadow of the Thin Man." **105m/B VHS.** William Powell, Myrna Loy, Virginia Grey, Otto Kruger, Sir C. Aubrey Smith, Ruth Hussey; ***D:*** Woodbridge S. Van Dyke. *MGM*

Another Time, Another Place 🦴🦴 **1958** Sappy melodrama about an American journalist who suffers an emotional meltdown when her married British lover is killed during WWII. So she heads for Cornwall to console the widow and family. **98m/B VHS, Beta.** *GB* Lana Turner, Barry Sullivan, Glynis Johns, Sean Connery, Terence Longdon; ***D:*** Lewis Allen; ***C:*** Jack Hildyard. *BAR, PAR*

Another Time, Another Place 🦴🦴🦴 **1983 (R)** Bored young Scottish housewife married to an older fella falls in love with an Italian prisoner-of-war who works on her farm during WWII. Occasionally quirky, always finely crafted view of wartime Britain and the little-known life of POWs in England. **101m/C VHS, Beta, LV.** *GB* Phyllis Logan, Giovanni Mauriello, Gian Luca Favilla, Paul Young, Tom Watson; ***D:*** Michael Radford; ***C:*** Roger Deakins. *SUE*

Another Way 🦴🦴🦴 *Olelkezo Tekintetek* **1982** The director of 1971's much-lauded "Love" sets this politically charged love story in Hungary in 1958. Opening with a view of a female corpse, the story flashes backward to look at the woman's journalistic career and her relationship with a women colleague. Candid love scenes between women in Hungary of 1958, considered a cinematic novelty in many places outside Hungary. In Hungarian with English subtitles. **100m/C VHS, Beta.** *HU* Jadwiga Jankowska Cieslak, Grazyna Szapolowska, Josef Kroner, Hernadi Judit, Andorai Peter; ***D:*** Karoly Makk. Cannes Film Festival '82: Best Actress (Cieslak); Nominations: Cannes Film Festival '82: Best Film. *EVD, FCT, INJ*

Another Woman 🦴🦴🦴 **1988 (PG)** The study of an intellectual woman whose life is changed when she begins to eavesdrop. What she hears provokes her to examine every relationship in her life, finding things quite different than she had believed. Heavy going, with Rowlands effective as a woman coping with an entirely new vision of herself. Farrow plays the catalyst. Although Allen's comedies are more popular than his dramas, this one deserves a look. **81m/C VHS, Beta, LV.** Gena Rowlands, Gene Hackman, Mia Farrow, Ian Holm, Betty Buckley, Martha Plimpton, Blythe Danner, Harris Yulin, Sandy Dennis, David Ogden Stiers, John Houseman, Philip Bosco, Frances Conroy, Kenneth Welsh, Michael Kirby; ***D:*** Woody Allen; ***W:*** Woody Allen; ***C:*** Sven Nykvist. *ORI*

Another You 🦴 **1991 (R)** Con man Wilder takes pathological liar Pryor under his care and decides to use his talents to his fullest advantage. Posing as successful businessmen, the duo initiate a scam so complicated that they may end up being double-crossed or worse yet, dead! Can the pair see their plan through without losing their lives? Sad to see how far these two gifted comedians have fallen. Their collaboration is tired and the movie generally dreadful. **98m/C VHS, LV, 8mm.** Richard Pryor, Gene Wilder, Mercedes Ruehl, Vanessa Williams, Stephen Lang, Kevin Pollak; ***D:*** Maurice Phillips. *COL*

Antarctica 🦴🦴 **1984** Due to unfortunate circumstances, a group of scientists must leave their pack of huskies behind on a frozen glacier in the Antarctic. The film focuses on the dogs' subsequent struggle for survival. Dubbed. **112m/C VHS, Beta.** *JP* Ken Takakura, Masako Natsume, Keiko Oginome; ***D:*** Koreyoshi Kurahara; ***M:*** Vangelis. *FOX*

Anthony Adverse 🦴🦴½ **1936** March is a young man in the 19th century who searches for manhood across America and Mexico. He grows slowly as he battles foes, struggles against adversity and returns home to find his lover in this romantic swashbuckler. A star-studded cast, lush costuming, and an energetic musical score. Highly acclaimed in its time, but now seems dated. Based on the novel by Hervey Allen. **141m/B VHS, Beta.** Fredric March, Olivia de Havilland, Anita Louise, Gale Sondergaard, Claude Rains, Louis Hayward, Scotty Beckett; ***D:*** Mervyn LeRoy; ***C:*** Gaetano Antonio "Tony" Gaudio. Academy Awards '36: Best Cinematography, Best Film Editing, Best Supporting Actress (Sondergaard), Best Score; Nominations: Academy Awards '36: Best Interior Decoration, Best Picture. *MGM, BTV, FHE*

Antonia and Jane 🦴🦴🦴 **1991 (R)** Enjoyable film tells the story of a longstanding, heavily tested friendship between two women. From the very beginning, they are a study in contrasts—Jane as rather plain, frumpy, and insecure; Antonia as glamorous, elegant, and successful. Both believe that each other's lives are more interesting and exciting than their own. Kidron, who directed this smart witty comedy for British television, offers an honest look into the often complex world of adult friendships. **75m/C VHS, Beta.** *GB* Imelda Staunton, Saskia Reeves, Patricia Leventon, Alfred Hoffman, Maria Charles, John Bennett, Richard Hope, Alfred Marks, Lila Kaye, Bill Nighy, Brenda Bruce; ***D:*** Beeban Kidron; ***W:*** Marcy Kahan; ***M:*** Rachel Portman. *PAR*

Antonia's Line 🦴🦴½ **1995 (R)** 90-year-old Antonia (Van Ammelrooy) has decided that she is going to die today and so begins a 50-year-long flashback of her nonconformist life in a Dutch village. Her lesbian daughter Danielle (Dottermans) wants a child without bothering about a husband and Antonia obliging arranges a brief interlude that produces child prodigy Therese (Van Overloop), who eventually has her own daughter, Sarah (Ravesteijn). Lots of female bonding (the male characters are mostly on the periphery of the action) and a certain magic realism abound. Dutch with subtitles. **93m/C VHS.** *NL* Willeke Van Ammelrooy, Els Dottermans, Veerle Van Overloop, Thyrza Ravesteijn, Jan Decleir, Mil Seghers, Jan Steen, Marina De Graaf; ***D:*** Marleen Gorris; ***W:*** Marleen Gorris; ***C:*** Willy Stassen; ***M:*** Ilona Seckaz. Academy Awards '95: Best Foreign Language Film. *BMG*

Antonio ☙☙ **1973** A Texas millionaire on the run from his wife and her divorce lawyer alights in a small Chilean village and turns it upside down. **89m/C VHS, Beta.** Larry Hagman, Trini Lopez, Noemi Guerrero, Pedro Becker; ***D:*** Claudio Guzman. *HEG*

Antonio Das Mortes ☙☙½ **1968** Antonio is a savage mercenary hired to kill rebels against the Brazilian government. Belatedly he realizes he sympathizes with the targets and turns his guns the other way for an incredible shootout finale. A visually lavish poltical polemic, espousing revolutionary guerrilla action within the format of a South American western. In Portuguese with English subtitles. **100m/C VHS.** *BR* Mauricio Do Valle, Odete Lara; ***D:*** Glauce Rocha; ***W:*** Glauce Rocha. Nominations: Cannes Film Festival '69: Best Film. *FCT, INJ*

Antony and Cleopatra ☙☙ **1973 (PG)** Heston wrote, directed, and starred in this long, dry adaptation of the Shakespeare play that centers on the torrid romance between Mark Antony and Cleopatra. **150m/C VHS, Beta.** Charlton Heston, Hildegarde Neil, Fernando Rey, Eric Porter; ***D:*** Charlton Heston. *SUE*

Ants ☙½ *Panic at Lakewood Manor; It Happened at Lakewood Manor* **1977** A mad bug parable for the planet-obsessed 90s. Insecticide-infected ants turn militant and check into a local hotel to vent their chemically induced foul mood on the unsuspecting clientele. The guest register includes a gaggle of celebrities who probably wish they'd signed on the Love Boat instead. Made for television (an ant farm would probably be just too horrible on the big screen). **100m/C VHS, Beta.** Suzanne Somers, Robert Foxworth, Myrna Loy, Lynda Day George, Gerald Gordon, Bernie Casey, Barry Van Dyke, Karen Lamm, Anita Gillette, Moosie Drier, Steve Franken, Brian Dennehy, Bruce French, Stacy Keach, Rene Enriquez, James Storm; ***D:*** Robert Scheerer. *LIV*

Any Gun Can Play ☙ *For a Few Bullets More* **1967** Typical spaghetti western. Three men (banker, thief, and bounty hunter) compete for a treasure of gold while wandering about the Spanish countryside. **103m/C VHS.** *IT SP* Edd Byrnes, Gilbert Roland, George Hilton, Kareen O'Hara, Pedro Sanchez, Gerard Herter; ***D:*** Enzo G. Castellari. *HHE*

Any Man's Death ☙☙ **1990 (R)** Savage is a globe-trotting reporter on the trail of a worldwide conspiracy who accidentally uncovers a Nazi war criminal in Africa. Well-meaning but confused tale. **105m/C VHS, Beta, LV.** John Savage, William Hickey, Mia Sara, Ernest Borgnine, Michael Lerner; ***D:*** Tom Clegg. *PSM*

Any Number Can Play ☙☙½ **1949** Fast-moving drama about an ailing gambler who faces a series of crises. Gable gives a commanding performance as the noble dice-roller. Based on the novel by Edward Harris Heath. **102m/B VHS.** Clark Gable, Alexis Smith, Wendell Corey, Audrey Totter, Frank Morgan, Mary Astor, Lewis Stone, Barry Sullivan; ***D:*** Mervyn LeRoy; ***W:*** Richard Brooks. *MGM*

Any Wednesday ☙☙½ *Bachelor Girl Apartment* **1966** Okay sex farce about powerful industrialist Robards' use of his mistress's apartment as a tax write-off. When a young company executive learns of the "company" apartment, he meets Robards' nonchalant wife for a tryst of their own. Based on Muriel Resnik's Broadway play; similar to the 1960 "The Apartment." **110m/C VHS, Beta.** Jane Fonda, Jason Robards Jr., Dean Jones, Rosemary Murphy; ***D:*** Robert Ellis Miller; ***W:*** Julius J. Epstein, Philip C. Epstein; ***M:*** George Duning. *WAR*

Any Which Way You Can ☙☙ **1980 (PG)** Bad brawler Philo Beddoe and his buddy Clyde, the orangutan, are back again in the sequel to "Every Which Way But Loose." This time Philo is tempted to take part in a big bout for a large cash prize. Clyde steals scenes, brightening up the no-brainer story. **116m/C VHS, Beta, LV.** Clint Eastwood, Sondra Locke, Ruth Gordon, Harry Guardino; ***D:*** Buddy Van Horn. *WAR*

Anything for a Thrill ☙ **1937** Two kids save a cameraman's career, make friends with a millionairess, and foil some crooks. **59m/B VHS.** Frankie Darro, Kane Richmond; ***D:*** Leslie Goodwins. *NOS, DVT, HEG*

Anything for Love ☙½ **1993** Teen musician is the object of a school bully's rage so he decides to dress up as a girl to escape the guy's fists. **90m/C VHS.** Corey Haim. *VMK*

Anzacs: The War Down Under ☙☙☙ **1985** Well-made Australian TV miniseries about the Australian & New Zealand Army Corps during WWI. Follows the men from the time they enlist to the campaigns in Gallipoli and France. **165m/C VHS, Beta.** *AU* Paul Hogan, Andrew Clarke, Jon Blake, Megan Williams; ***D:*** George Miller. *CEL*

Anzio ☙☙ *The Battle for Anzio; Lo Sbarco di Anzio* **1968** The historic Allied invasion of Italy during WWII as seen through the eyes of American war correspondent Mitchum. Fine cast waits endlessly to leave the beach, though big battle scenes are effectively rendered. Based on the book by Wynford Vaughan Thomas. **117m/C VHS, Beta.** Robert Mitchum, Peter Falk, Arthur Kennedy, Robert Ryan, Earl Holliman, Mark Damon, Reni Santoni, Patrick Magee; ***D:*** Edward Dmytryk. *NO*

Apache ☙☙½ **1954** Lancaster is the only Indian in Geronimo's outfit who refuses to surrender in this chronicle of a bitter battle between the Indians and the U.S. cavalry in the struggle for the West. First western for Aldrich is a thoughtful piece for its time that had the original tragic ending reshot (against Aldrich's wishes) to make it more happy. Adapted from "Bronco Apache" by Paul I. Wellman. **91m/C VHS, Beta.** Burt Lancaster, John McIntire, Jean Peters; ***D:*** Robert Aldrich; ***C:*** Ernest Laszlo. *MGM, FOX, FCT*

Apache Blood ☙½ *Pursuit* **1975 (R)** An Indian Brave, the lone survivor of an Indian massacre by the U.S. Army, squares off with a cavalry scout in the forbidding desert. **92m/C VHS.** Ray Danton, DeWitt Lee, Troy Neighbors, Diane Taylor, Eva Kovacs, Jason Clark; ***D:*** Thomas Quillen. *PSM*

Apache Chief ☙ **1950** Two Apache tribe leaders, one good, the other evil clash. Ultimately, and perhaps predictably, they face each other in hand-to-hand combat and peace prevails. **60m/B VHS, Beta, LV.** Alan Curtis, Tom Neal, Russell Hayden, Carol Thurston; ***D:*** Frank McDonald. *NO*

Apache Kid's Escape ☙ **1930** The Apache Kid leads the cavalry on a wild chase across the plains in this saga of the old west. **60m/B VHS, Beta.** Jack Perrin, Buzz Barton. *NOS, DVT, RXM*

Apache Rose ☙☙ **1947** Gambling boat owner plots to gain control of oil found on Vegas Ranch. Roy and Dale oppose the idea. First of the series in color; the original, unedited version of the film. **75m/B VHS, Beta, LV.** Roy Rogers, Dale Evans, Olin Howlin, George Meeker; ***D:*** William Witney. *FOX, NOS, VCN*

Apache Uprising ☙½ **1966** A standard western with Calhoun as the lawman up against gunfighters and stagecoach robbers as well as the usual Indians. **60m/C VHS.** Rory Calhoun, Corinne Calvet, DeForest Kelley, John Russell, Lon Chaney Jr., Gene Evans, Richard Arlen, Robert Harris, Arthur Hunnicutt, Jean Parker, Johnny Mack Brown; ***D:*** R.G. Springsteen. *PAR*

Apache Woman ☙½ **1955** Bridges stars as a government agent sent to investigate some crimes committed by a group of Apache Indians. As he tries to calm the townspeople, Bridges discovers that the group is made up of white people led by an educated half-breed. He instigates the help of the half-breed's sister (and also Bridges' love interest) to stop the gang. Some good action, but lots of dull spots. **82m/C VHS.** Lloyd Bridges, Joan Taylor, Lance Fuller, Morgan Jones, Paul Birch, Jonathan Haze, Paul Dubov, Lou Place; ***D:*** Roger Corman. *COL, FCT*

Apaches Last Battle ☙☙ *Old Shatterhand; Shatterhand* **1964** A boundary scout discovers the ward of an Apache chief has been framed for murder by a cavalry officer who wants to start an Indian war in this exciting Euro western. **?m/C VHS.** Lex Barker, Guy Madison, Pierre Brice. *SNC*

Aparajito ☙☙☙½ *The Unvanquished* **1958** The second of the Apu trilogy, about a boy growing up in India, after "Pather Panchali," and before "The World of Apu." Apu is brought to Benares and his education seriously begins. The work of a master; in Bengali with English subtitles. **108m/B VHS, Beta.** *IN* Pinaki Sen Gupta, Karuna Banerjee, Kanu Banerjee, Ramani Sen Gupta; ***D:*** Satyajit Ray. National Board of Review Awards '59: 5 Best Foreign Films of the Year; Venice Film Festival '57: Best Film. *FCT, MRV, TIM*

Apart from Hugh ☙☙ **1994** Collin and Hugh have been living together for a year and to celebrate the occasion, Hugh decides to plan an anniversary party. Unfortunately, Collin hasn't told Hugh he's having second thoughts about their relationship. Directorial debut of FitzGerald. **87m/B VHS.** ***D:*** Jon FitzGerald. *WBF*

The Apartment ☙☙☙½ **1960** A lowly insurance clerk tries to climb the corporate ladder by "loaning" his apartment out to executives having affairs. Problems arise, however, when he unwittingly falls for the most recent girlfriend of the boss. Highly acclaimed social satire. **125m/B VHS, Beta, LV.** Jack Lemmon, Shirley MacLaine, Fred MacMurray, Ray Walston, Jack Kruschen, Joan Shawlee, Edie Adams, Hope Holiday, David Lewis; ***D:*** Billy Wilder; ***W:*** I.A.L. Diamond, Billy Wilder; ***C:*** Joseph LaShelle. Academy Awards '60: Best Art Direction/Set Decoration (B & W), Best Director (Wilder), Best Film Editing, Best Picture, Best Story & Screenplay; British Academy Awards '60: Best Actor (Lemmon), Best Actress (MacLaine), Best Film; Directors Guild of America Awards '60: Best Director (Wilder); Golden Globe Awards '61: Best Actor—Musical/Comedy (Lemmon), Best Actress—Musical/Comedy (MacLaine), Best Film—Musical/Comedy; National Board of Review Awards '60: 10 Best Films of the Year; New York Film Critics Awards '60: Best Director (Wilder), Best Film, Best Screenplay; Nominations: Academy Awards '60: Best Actor (Lemmon), Best Actress (MacLaine), Best Black and White Cinematography, Best Sound, Best Supporting Actor (Kruschen). *MGM, BTV*

Apartment Zero ☙☙☙½ **1988 (R)** A decidedly weird, deranged psychological drama about the parasite/host-type relationship between two roommates in downtown Buenos Aires: one, an obsessive British movie nut, the other, a sexually mesmerizing stud who turns out to be a cold-blooded psycho. **124m/C VHS, Beta, LV.** *GB* Hart Bochner, Colin Firth, Fabrizio Bentivoglio, Liz Smith; ***D:*** Martin Donovan; ***W:*** Martin Donovan, David Koepp. *ACA, FCT, IME*

The Ape ☙☙ **1940** When his daughter dies of a crippling disease, Karloff becomes fixated with the mission to cure paralysis. Obviously distraught, he begins donning the hide of an escaped circus ape whose spinal fluid is the key to the serum. Hide-bedecked, he slays unknowing townspeople to tap them of their spinal fluid and cure his latest patient. **62m/B VHS, Beta.** Boris Karloff, Maris Wrixon, Henry Hall, Gertrude Hoffman; ***D:*** William Nigh. *NOS, SNC, VYY*

A*P*E* *Woof!* **1976 (PG)** A*P*E* is thirty-six feet tall and ten tons of animal fury who destroys anything that comes between him and the actress he loves. Cheap rip-off of Kong. **87m/C VHS, Beta.** Rod Arrants, Joanna DeVarona, Alex Nicol; ***D:*** Paul Leder. *NWV*

The Ape Man ☙☙ *Lock Your Doors* **1943** With the aid of a secret potion, a scientist turns himself into a murderous ape. The only way to regain his human side is to ingest human spinal fluid. Undoubtedly inspired by Boris Karloff's 1940 film, "The Ape." **64m/B VHS, Beta.** Wallace Ford, Bela Lugosi; ***D:*** William Beaudine. *NOS, MRV, SNC*

A.P.E.X. ☙☙ **1994 (R)** Nicholas Sinclair (Keats), a researcher from 2073, time travels back to 1973 to retrieve a faulty robot probe called A.P.E.X. (Advanced Prototype Extermination Unit). Unwittingly he has been infected with a mysterious virus and when he returns it's to a version of his own time where humans are dying from the virus and robots are sent to eradicate the few survivors. It also seems Sinclair is now a guerilla in an anti-robot army. Yes, it sounds like "The Terminator" but the action moves and though the budget is limited the special effects are still impressive. **103m/C VHS, LV.** Richard Keats, Mitchell

Cox, Lisa Ann Russell, Marcus Aurelius, Adam Lawson; ***D:*** Phillip J. Roth; ***W:*** Phillip J. Roth, Ronald Schmidt; ***M:*** Jim Goodwin. *REP*

Apocalypse Now 🦴🦴🦴🦴 **1979 (R)** Coppola's $40 million epic vision of the Vietnam War was inspired by Joseph Conrad's novella "Heart of Darkness," and continues to be the subject of debate. Disillusioned Army captain Sheen travels upriver into Cambodia to assassinate overweight renegade colonel Brando. His trip is punctuated by surrealistic battles and a terrifying descent into a land where human rationality seems to have slipped away. Considered by some to be the definitive picture of war in its overall depiction of chaos and primal bloodletting; by others, over-wrought and unrealistic. May not translate as well to the small screen, yet worth seeing if for nothing more than Duvall's ten minutes of scenery chewing as a battle-obsessed major ("I love the smell of napalm in the morning!"), a study in manic machismo. Stunning photography by Vittorio Storaro, awe-inspiring battle scenes, and effective soundtrack montage. Both Sheen and Coppola suffered emotional breakdowns during the prolonged filming, and that's a very young Fishburne in his major film debut. Available in widescreen format on laserdisc and in a remastered version in letterbox on VHS with a remixed soundtrack that features Dolby Surround stereo. In 1991 a documentary detailing the making of the film, "Hearts of Darkness: A Filmmaker's Apocalypse," was released. **153m/C VHS, Beta, LV, CD-I.** Marlon Brando, Martin Sheen, Robert Duvall, Frederic Forrest, Sam Bottoms, Scott Glenn, Albert Hall, Laurence "Larry" Fishburne, Harrison Ford, G.D. Spradlin, Dennis Hopper, Colleen Camp, Tom Mason; ***D:*** Francis Ford Coppola; ***W:*** Francis Ford Coppola, John Milius; ***M:*** Carmine Coppola. Academy Awards '79: Best Cinematography, Best Sound; British Academy Awards '79: Best Director (Coppola), Best Supporting Actor (Duvall); Golden Globe Awards '80: Best Director (Coppola), Best Supporting Actor (Duvall), Best Score; National Board of Review Awards '79: 10 Best Films of the Year; National Society of Film Critics Awards '79: Best Supporting Actor (Forrest); Nominations: Academy Awards '79: Best Adapted Screenplay, Best Art Direction/Set Decoration, Best Director (Coppola), Best Film Editing, Best Picture, Best Supporting Actor (Duvall). *PAR*

Apollo 13 🦴🦴🦴½ **1995 (PG)** Realistic big-budget reenactment of the 1970 Apollo lunar mission that ran into a "problem" 205,000 miles from home reunites Hanks and Sinese from "F. Gump" and Howard and Hanks from "Splash." And an enjoyable reunion it is. Explosion in one of two oxygen tanks helping power the spacecraft leaves the three astronauts (lead by Hanks) tumbling through space. With the electrical system kaput and oxygen running low, the men seek refuge in the Lunar Excursion Module. Since it's based on the real event and the outcome is known, director Howard concentrates on the personalities and the details of the seven-day adventure at Mission Control and in space, in the process delivering the dramatic payload. Weightless shots are the real deal as crew filmed for ten days and made 600 parabolic loops in a KC-135 jet, NASA's "Vomit Comet," the long plunge creating 25 seconds of weightlessness. Special effects (by James Cameron's Digital Domain) and set design do the rest; no NASA footage is used, though original TV footage is used to dramatic effect. Script, with an uncredited rewrite by John Sayles, is based on the 1994 book, "Lost Moon," written by 13's Jim Lovell (who has a cameo as the Navy captain welcoming the astronauts aboard the recovery ship), while Apollo 15 commander David Scott served as a consultant. **140m/C VHS, LV.** Tom Hanks, Kevin Bacon, Bill Paxton, Gary Sinise, Ed Harris, Kathleen Quinlan, Brett Cullen, Emily Ann Lloyd, Miko Hughes, Max Elliott Slade, Jean Speegle Howard, Tracy Reiner, Michelle Little, David Andrews, Mary Kate Schellhardt; ***D:*** Ron Howard; ***W:*** William Broyles Jr., Al Reinert; ***C:*** Dean Cundey; ***M:*** James Horner. Academy Awards '95: Best Film Editing, Best Sound; Directors Guild of America Awards '96: Best Director (Howard); Screen Actors Guild Award '95: Best Supporting Actor (Harris), Cast; Blockbuster Entertainment Awards '96: Drama Actor, Theatrical (Hanks); Nominations: Academy Awards '95: Best Adapted Screenplay, Best Art Direction/Set Decoration, Best Picture, Best Supporting Actor (Harris), Best Supporting Actress (Quinlan), Best Score; British Academy Awards '95: Best Cinematography; Golden Globe Awards '96: Best Director (Howard), Best Film—Drama, Best Supporting Actor (Harris), Best Supporting Actress (Quinlan); Writers Guild of America '95: Best Adapted Screenplay. *MCA*

Apology 🦴🦴 **1986** A psychotic killer stalks Warren, an experimental artist, in Manhattan while a detective stalks the killer. Made for cable, so expect a little more sex and violence than network TV movies. Written by Medoff, author of "Children of a Lesser God." **98m/C VHS.** Lesley Ann Warren, Peter Weller, John Glover, George Loros, Jimmie Ray Weeks, Christopher Noth, Harvey Fierstein; ***D:*** Robert Bierman; ***W:*** Mark Medoff; ***M:*** Maurice Jarre. *NO*

The Appaloosa 🦴🦴½ *Southwest to Sonora* **1966** A lamenting loner who decides to begin anew by breeding Appaloosas is ripped off by a desperate woman who steals his horse in order to get away from her abusive amour. Brando falls in love with the girl and the two amazingly survive a wealth of obstacles in their battle against Mexican bandits. **99m/C VHS, Beta, LV.** Marlon Brando, Anjanette Comer, John Saxon; ***D:*** Sidney J. Furie; ***W:*** James Bridges; ***C:*** Russell Metty. *MCA*

Applause 🦴🦴🦴 **1929** Morgan plays a down-and-out burlesque star trying to protect her fresh from the convent daughter. Definitely dated, but a marvelous performance by Morgan. Film buffs will appreciate this early talkie. **78m/B VHS.** Helen Morgan, Joan Peers, Fuller Mellish Jr., Henry Wadsworth, Dorothy Cumming; ***D:*** Rouben Mamoulian. *PAR*

The Apple 🦴½ **1980 (PG)** Futuristic musical filmed in Berlin that features a young, innocent, folk-singing couple who nearly become victims of the evil, glitzy record producer who tries to recruit the couple into a life of sex and drugs. **90m/C VHS, Beta.** Catherine Mary Stewart, Alan Love, Grace Kennedy, Joss Ackland; ***D:*** Menahem Golan. *NO*

The Apple Dumpling Gang 🦴🦴 **1975 (G)** Three frisky kids strike it rich and trigger the wildest bank robbery in the gold-mad West. Unmistakably Disney, a familial subplot and a wacky duo are provided. Mediocre yet superior to its sequel, "The Apple Dumpling Gang Rides Again." **100m/C VHS, Beta.** Bill Bixby, Susan Clark, Don Knotts, Tim Conway, David Wayne, Slim Pickens, Harry (Henry) Morgan; ***D:*** Norman Tokar; ***M:*** Buddy Baker. *DIS*

The Apple Dumpling Gang Rides Again 🦴🦴 **1979 (G)** Two lovable hombres terrorize the West in their bungling attempt to go straight. Fans of Conway or Knotts may appreciate this sequel to Disney's "The Apple Dumpling Gang." **88m/C VHS, Beta.** Tim Conway, Don Knotts, Tim Matheson, Kenneth Mars, Harry (Henry) Morgan, Jack Elam; ***D:*** Vincent McEveety; ***M:*** Buddy Baker. *DIS*

The Applegates 🦴🦴½ *Meet the Applegates* **1989 (R)** Ecologically correct Amazonian beetles are more than a little miffed about the slash-and-burn tactics in their home and decide to establish a kinder, gentler habitat. Bug Begley and his brood transform themselves into average Americans, but then don't want to leave their decadent life: even insects aren't immune to the lure of sex, drugs, and cable shopping networks. Imaginative, often quite funny one-joke flick should've been shorter. Fits quite well as a double feature with Lehmann's earlier "Heathers." **90m/C VHS, Beta, LV.** Ed Begley Jr., Stockard Channing, Dabney Coleman, Cami Cooper, Bobby Jacoby, Glenn Shadix, Susan Barnes, Adam Biesk, Savannah Smith Boucher; ***D:*** Michael Lehmann; ***W:*** Michael Lehmann, Redbeard Simmons. *MED, FOX, VTR*

The Appointment *Woof!* **1982** A supernatural force enters the bodies and minds of people and suddenly everyone begins going crazy. **90m/C VHS, Beta, 8mm.** Edward Woodward, Jane Merrow; ***D:*** Lindsey C. Vickers; ***C:*** Carlo DiPalma. *NO*

Appointment in Honduras 🦴🦴 **1953** An adventurer goes on a dangerous trek through the Central American jungles to deliver funds to the Honduran President. **79m/C VHS, Beta.** Glenn Ford, Ann Sheridan, Zachary Scott; ***D:*** Jacques Tourneur. *NO*

Appointment with Crime 🦴🦴½ **1945** After serving a prison sentence, an ex-con sets out to avenge himself against the colleagues who double crossed him. Well done, highlighted by superior characterizations. Based on the story by Michael Leighton. **91m/B VHS, Beta.** *GB* William Hartnell, Raymond Lovell, Robert Beatty, Herbert Lom, Joyce Howard, Alan Wheatley, Cyril Smith; ***D:*** John Harlow; ***W:*** John Harlow. *SNC*

Appointment with Death 🦴½ **1988 (PG)** Disappointing Agatha Christie mystery with Hercule Poirot solving the murder of a shrewish widow in 1937 Palestine. **103m/C VHS, Beta, LV.** Peter Ustinov, Lauren Bacall, Carrie Fisher, John Gielgud, Piper Laurie, Hayley Mills, Jenny Seagrove, David Soul; ***D:*** Michael Winner; ***W:*** Anthony Shaffer, Peter Buckman, Michael Winner; ***M:*** Pino Donaggio. *WAR, FCT*

Appointment with Fear 🦴 **1985 (R)** A tough detective investigates a murder and all of the clues lead him mysteriously to a comatose asylum inmate. **95m/C VHS, Beta, LV.** Michael Wyle, Michelle Little, Garrick Dowhen; ***D:*** Alan Smithee. *LIV*

Apprentice to Murder 🦴🦴 **1988 (PG-13)** A small Pennsylvania Dutch town is shaken by a series of murders, thought to be associated with a bizarre local mystic and healer. Based on a true story, sort of. **97m/C VHS, Beta, LV.** Donald Sutherland, Mia Sara, Chad Lowe, Eddie Jones; ***D:*** Ralph L. Thomas; ***W:*** Allan Scott, Wesley Moore. *VTR, NWV, HHE*

The Apprenticeship of Duddy Kravitz 🦴🦴🦴½ **1974 (PG)** Young Jewish man in Montreal circa 1948 is driven by an insatiable need to be the "somebody" everyone has always told him he will be. A series of get-rich-quick schemes backfire in different ways, and he becomes most successful at driving people away. Young Dreyfuss is at his best. Made in Canada with thoughtful detail, and great cameo performances. Script by Richler, from his novel. **121m/C VHS, Beta.** *CA* Richard Dreyfuss, Randy Quaid, Denholm Elliott, Jack Warden, Micheline Lanctot, Joe Silver; ***D:*** Ted Kotcheff; ***W:*** Mordecai Richler, Lionel Chetwynd. Berlin International Film Festival '74: Golden Berlin Bear; Writers Guild of America '74: Best Adapted Screenplay; Nominations: Academy Awards '74: Best Adapted Screenplay. *PAR*

April Fool 🦴🦴½ **1926** A man makes a fortune in the umbrella business and then discovers his daughter has fallen in love with the son of a nouveaux riche neighbor, resulting in all sorts of complications. **63m/B VHS.** Alexander Carr, Mary Alden, Raymond Keane, Snitz Edwards; ***D:*** Nat Ross; ***W:*** Zion Myers. *GPV, FCT*

April Fools 🦴🦴 **1969 (PG)** A bored stockbroker falls in love with a beautiful woman who turns out to be married to his boss. **95m/C VHS, Beta.** Jack Lemmon, Catherine Deneuve, Sally Kellerman, Peter Lawford, Charles Boyer, Myrna Loy, Harvey Korman; ***D:*** Stuart Rosenberg; ***M:*** Marvin Hamlisch. *FOX*

April Fool's Day 🦴 **1986 (R)** Rich girl Foreman invites eight college friends to spend the April Fool's weekend with her at her family's isolated island mansion. Everyone is subjected to an endless series of practical jokes when things apparently turn deadly and several of the kids begin disappearing. Lame spoof of "Friday the 13th" and other teenagers-in-peril slasher films. **90m/C VHS, Beta, LV.** Deborah Foreman, Jay Baker, Pat Barlow, Lloyd Berry, Deborah Goodrich, Ken Olandt, Griffin O'Neal, Tom Heaton, Mike Nomad, Leah K. Pinsent, Clayton Rohner, Amy Steel, Thomas F. Wilson; ***D:*** Fred Walton; ***W:*** Danilo Bach; ***M:*** Charles Bernstein. *PAR*

April In Paris 🦴🦴 **1952** Dynamite Jackson (Day), a chorus girl accidentally sent by the State Department to perform in Paris, meets S. Winthrop Putnam (Bolger), a timid fellow trapped in an unpleasant marriage. They eventually sing and dance their way to warm feelings as they begin a lifelong romance and live happily ever after. **100m/C VHS.** Doris Day, Ray Bolger, Claude Dauphin, Eve Miller, George Givot, Paul Harvey; ***D:*** David Butler; ***W:*** Jack Rose, Melville Shavelson. *WAR, CCB, MVD*

The Arab Conspiracy *The Next Man; Double Hit* **1976 (R)** Sharpe plays a hit-woman conspiring with assassins from all over the world to kill Arab leaders. One problem—she falls in love with Saudi Arabian ambassador Connery as he tries to gain peace with Palestine. **108m/C VHS.** Sean Connery, Cornelia Sharpe, Albert Paulsen, Adolfo Celi, Charles Cioffi; ***D:*** Richard Sarafian; ***W:*** Alan R. Trustman; ***C:*** Michael Chapman; ***M:*** Michael Kamen. *SIM, QVD*

Arabesque ½ **1966** A college professor is drawn into international espionage by a beautiful woman and a plot to assassinate an Arab prince. Stylish and fast moving. From the novel "The Cipher" by Gordon Cotler. **105m/C VHS, Beta.** Gregory Peck, Sophia Loren, George Coulouris; ***D:*** Stanley Donen; ***M:*** Henry Mancini. *MCA, FCT*

Arabian Nights **1942** Two brothers fight for the throne of Turkey and the affection of the sultry dancing girl Scheherazade. Enchanting costumes and lavish sets augment the fantasy atmosphere. **87m/C VHS.** Jon Hall, Maria Montez, Sabu, Leif Erickson, Edgar Barrier, Richard Lane, Turhan Bey; ***D:*** John Rawlins; ***W:*** Michael Hogan; ***C:*** Milton Krasner. *MCA, FCT*

Arabian Nights **1974** The third of Pasolini's epic, explicit adaptations of classic portmanteau, featuring ten of the old Scheherazade favorites adorned by beautiful photography, explicit sex scenes and homoeroticism. In Italian with English subtitles; available dubbed. **130m/C VHS, Beta, LV.** *IT* Ninetto Davoli, Franco Merli, Ines Pellegrini, Luigina Rocchi; ***D:*** Pier Paolo Pasolini; ***M:*** Ennio Morricone. *WBF, INJ, APD*

Arachnophobia ½ **1990 (PG-13)** Big-budget big-bug horror story has a few funny moments as lots and lots of spiders wreak havoc in a white picket fence community somewhere off the beaten track. Lethal South American spider makes a trek to sunny California, meets up with local spiders, and rapidly multiplies. Utterly arachnophobic (read: totally scared of spiders) town doctor Daniels pairs with gung-ho exterminator Goodman to try and track down the culprits. The script's a bit yawn-inspiring but the cast and effects will keep you from dozing off. Directorial debut for Marshall, a longtime friend and producer for Spielberg. **109m/C VHS, Beta, LV.** Jeff Daniels, John Goodman, Harley Jane Kozak, Julian Sands, Roy Brocksmith, Stuart Pankin, Brian McNamara, Mark L. Taylor, Henry Jones, Peter Jason, James Handy; ***D:*** Frank Marshall; ***W:*** Wesley Strick, Don Jakoby; ***C:*** Mikael Salomon; ***M:*** Trevor Jones. *HPH*

Arcade ½ **1993 (R)** All the kids in town are desperate to play the new virtual reality game Arcade, only the game is just a little too real. Seems it can transport you into another world with its stunning graphics and sound effects but you really put your life on the line. Only Alex (Ward) worries when kids start to disappear and she decides to battle the game for their lives. **85m/C VHS, Beta.** Megan Ward, Peter Billingsley, John de Lancie, Sharon Farrell, Seth Green, Humberto Ortiz, Jonathan Fuller, Norbert Weisser; ***D:*** Albert Pyun; ***W:*** David S. Goyer; ***M:*** Alan Howarth. *PAR*

Arcadia of My Youth **1982** In the 30th century the evil Illumidus Empire has conquered Earth and only the heroic Captain Harlock and his friends can battle their tyranny. Based on Matsumoto Leiji's comic book series. Draws parallels to the post-WWII occupation of Japan. Animated; in Japanese with English subtitles. **130m/C VHS.** *JP ANI, WTA*

Arch of Triumph **1948** In Paris, an Austrian refugee doctor falls in love just before the Nazis enter the city. Big-budget box-office loser featuring fine cast but sluggish pace. Based on the Erich Maria Remarque novel and remade for television. **120m/B VHS.** Ingrid Bergman, Charles Boyer, Charles Laughton, Louis Calhern; ***D:*** Lewis Milestone; ***W:*** Harry Brown, Lewis Milestone; ***C:*** Russell Metty. *REP*

Arch of Triumph ½ **1985** A refugee doctor falls in love with a mystery woman as the Nazis enter Paris. Made for television remake of the 1948 film. **95m/C VHS.** Anthony Hopkins, Lesley-Anne Down, Donald Pleasence, Frank Finlay; ***D:*** Waris Hussein; ***W:*** Charles Israel; ***M:*** Georges Delerue. *FCT*

Archer: The Fugitive from the Empire **1981** A young warrior battles the forces of evil in this television movie. Lots of strange names to learn even if you already know who's going to win the final battle. **97m/C VHS, Beta.** Lane Caudell, Belinda Bauer, George Kennedy, Victor Campos, Kabir Bedi, George Innes, Marc Alaimo, Allen Rich, John Hancock, Priscilla Pointer, Sharon Barr; ***D:*** Nick Corea. *MCA*

Archer's Adventure ½ **1985** An Australian family film based on a true story. A horsetrainer's young apprentice delivers a prize racehorse to Melbourne, through 600 miles of tough frontier, devious bush rangers, and disaster. **120m/C VHS, Beta.** *AU* Brett Climo, Nicole Kidman; ***D:*** Denny Lawrence. *NWV, VTR, TVC*

Arctic Blue ½ **1993 (R)** Alaskan biologist Walsh gets stuck being the local lawman when he's the only one willing to escort Hauer, a homicidal trapper, to a Fairbanks jail. But nothing's that easy—their plane crashes atop a glacier and the duo must battle each other and the elements to survive, while Hauer's brutal partners hunt Walsh. **95m/C VHS, LV.** Dylan Walsh, Rutger Hauer, Richard Bradford; ***D:*** Peter Masterson; ***W:*** Ross LaManna. *COL*

Are Parents People? **1925** Lighthearted silent comedy about a young girl's successful attempts to reunite her feuding parents. It all begins as she runs away and spends the night in the office of a doctor she has grown to like. After a frantic night of searching, her parents are reunited through their love for her. **60m/B VHS.** Betty Bronson, Adolphe Menjou, Florence Vidor. *GPV, PAR*

Are You in the House Alone? **1978** Made for television adaptation of Richard Peck's award-winning novel. Story of a high school coed who becomes the target of a terror campaign. **100m/C VHS, Beta.** Blythe Danner, Kathleen Beller, Tony Bill, Scott Colomby; ***D:*** Walter Grauman; ***M:*** Charles Bernstein. *WOV, GKK*

Are You Lonesome Tonight ½ **1992 (PG-13)** Suspense thriller casts Seymour as a wealthy socialite who discovers her husband is having an affair with a phone-sex girl. His sudden and mysterious disapppearance forces her to hire a private detective (Stevenson) to track him down, with only the taped conversations as clues. Average made for cable television fare. **91m/C VHS, Beta.** Jane Seymour, Parker Stevenson, Beth Broderick, Joel Brooks, Robert Pine; ***D:*** E.W. Swackhamer; ***W:*** Wesley Moore. *PAR*

Arena **1989 (PG-13)** Remember old boxing melodramas about good-natured palookas, slimy opponents, gangsters and dames? This puts those cliches in a garish sci-fi setting, with handsome Steve Armstrong battling ETs and the astro-mob to be the first human pugilistic champ in decades. A really cute idea (from the screenwriters of "The Rocketeer"), but it conks out at the halfway point. Worth a look for buffs. **97m/C VHS, LV.** *IT* Paul Satterfield, Claudia Christian, Hamilton Camp, Marc Alaimo, Armin Shimerman, Shari Shattuck, Jack Carter; ***D:*** Peter Manoogian; ***W:*** Danny Bilson, Paul DeMeo; ***M:*** Richard Band. *COL*

Aria **1988 (R)** Ten directors were given carte blanche to interpret ten arias from well-known operas. Henry and D'Angelo star in Julien Temple's rendition of Verdi's "Rigoletto." In Fonda's film debut, she and her lover travel to Las Vegas and eventually kill themselves in the bathtub, just like "Romeo & Juliet." Jarman's piece (a highlight) shows an aged operatic star at her last performance remembering an early love affair. "I Pagliacci" is the one aria in which the director took his interpretation in a straightforward manner. **90m/C VHS, Beta.** *GB* Theresa Russell, Anita Morris, Bridget Fonda, Beverly D'Angelo, Buck Henry, John Hurt; ***D:*** Ken Russell, Charles Sturridge, Robert Altman, Bill Bryden, Jean-Luc Godard, Bruce Beresford, Nicolas Roeg, Franc Roddam, Derek Jarman, Julien Temple. *ACA, FCT, LTY*

Ariel **1989** Refreshing, offbeat Finnish comedy by highly praised newcomer Kaurismaki. Hoping to find work in Southern Finland, an out-of-work miner from Northern Finland (Pajala) jets off in his white Cadillac convertible given to him in a cafe by a friend, who promptly shoots himself. There's no linear progression toward a happy ending, although antiheroic subject does find employment and romances a meter maid. Mostly, though, he's one of those it's hell being me guys who wouldn't have any luck if it weren't for bad luck. Strange slice-of-life sporting film noir tendencies, although essentially anti-stylistic. **74m/C VHS.** *FI* Susanna Haavisto, Turo Pajala, Matti Pellonpaa; ***D:*** Aki Kaurismaki; ***W:*** Aki Kaurismaki. National Society of Film Critics Awards '90: Best Foreign Film. *KIV, FCT, INJ*

The Aristocats **1970** Typically entertaining Disney animated story about pampered pussy Duchess (Gabor) and her three kittens, who are left a fortune in their mistress' will. The fortune goes to the butler if the cats don't survive, so he dumps them in the country hoping they won't find their way home. The cats are aided by tough alley denizen O'Malley (Harris)—it's kind of the feline version of "Lady and the Tramp." Maurice Chevalier sings the title tune. **78m/C VHS.** ***D:*** Wolfgang Reitherman; ***M:*** George Bruns; ***V:*** Eva Gabor, Phil Harris, Sterling Holloway, Roddy Maude-Roxby, Bill Thompson, Hermione Baddeley, Carol Shelley, Pat Buttram, Nancy Kulp, Paul Winchell. *DIS*

Arizona ½ **1940** Arthur is a hellion in wild 1860 Tucson who falls for the wandering Holden. He's headed for California and she can't keep him in town so Arthur throws herself into business by establishing a freight line. Only warring Apaches try to burn her out and Holden rides in to save the day (with the cavalry and a stampeding cattle herd). Holden's first western is lively but long. **121m/B VHS.** Jean Arthur, William Holden, Warren William, Porter Hall, Paul Harvey, George Chandler, Regis Toomey, Edgar Buchanan; ***D:*** Wesley Ruggles; ***W:*** Claude Binyon; ***M:*** Victor Young. *COL*

Arizona ½ **1986** A group of illegal aliens struggle for survival after they cross the border into the harsh desert. **94m/C VHS, Beta.** *MX* Roberto "Flaco" Guzman, Juan Valentin. *MED*

Arizona Badman ½ **1935** There is a bad man in Arizona, and he must be gotten rid of. **60m/B VHS, Beta.** Reb Russell; ***D:*** S. Roy Luby. *NOS, DVT*

Arizona Bound **1941** Mesa City is infested with a villain and our "Rough Rider" trio must rid the town of him. **57m/B VHS, Beta.** Buck Jones, Tim McCoy, Raymond Hatton, Dennis Moore, Luana Walters; ***D:*** Spencer Gordon Bennet. *NOS, VCN, DVT*

Arizona Bushwackers ½ **1967** Routine western that has Confederate spy Keel taking job as sheriff in small Arizona town. Once there, he has to straighten out a few bad guys who have been selling weapons to the Apaches. Notable for presence of old western-movie veterans Ireland, Donlevy, Brady, and MacLane. Based on a story by Steve Fisher. **87m/C VHS, LV.** Howard Keel, Yvonne De Carlo, John Ireland, Marilyn Maxwell, Scott Brady, Brian Donlevy, Barton MacLane; ***D:*** Lesley Selander. *PAR*

Arizona Cowboy **1949** An ex-G.I., now the rodeo's big attraction, gets involved in a robbery. **57m/B VHS, Beta.** Rex Allen, Gordon Jones, Roy Barcroft; ***D:*** R.G. Springsteen. *DVT*

Arizona Days ½ **1937** Cowboys join a minstrel group and rescue the show when a group of toughs try to break it up. **56m/B VHS, Beta.** Tex Ritter, Eleanor Stewart, Syd Saylor, Snub Pollard; ***D:*** John English. *NOS, VCI, VDM*

Arizona Dream **1994 (R)** Alex (Depp) is a New York drifter who gets stuck working for his uncle's (Lewis) car dealership in a small Arizona town. He meets an eccentric older woman (Dunaway) with a homemade plane and some dreams of her own. Tends toward the surreal and confusing. **119m/C VHS.** Johnny Depp, Faye Dunaway, Jerry Lewis, Lili

Taylor, Paulina Porizkova, Tricia Leigh Fisher, Vincent Gallo; ***D:*** Emir Kusturica; ***W:*** Emir Kusturica, David Atkins. *WAR*

Arizona Gangbusters **1940** Below-average oater has real-life cowboy McCoy fighting city hall in order to fight other baddies. Newfield directed under the pseudonym "Peter Stewart." **57m/B VHS.** Tim McCoy, Pauline Hadden, Forrest Taylor, Julian Rivero, Curly Dresden; ***D:*** Sam Newfield. *DVT, HEG*

Arizona Gunfighter **1937** A young cowhand seeks revenge against the man who murdered his father in this western. **60m/B VHS, Beta.** Bob Steele, Ted Adams; ***D:*** Sam Newfield. *NOS, DVT*

Arizona Heat **1987 (R)** A violent cop is teamed up with a tough, but tender female cop in this all-too-familiar tale of two cops chasing a cop killer. **91m/C VHS.** Michael Parks, Denise Crosby, Hugh Farrington; ***D:*** John G. Thomas. *REP*

Arizona Kid **1939** Another sagebrush saga featuring Roy in singin' and fightin' action. **54m/B VHS, Beta.** Roy Rogers; ***D:*** Joseph Kane. *NOS, DVT, TIM*

Arizona Mahoney **1936** Weird mixture of circus adventure and serious western doesn't work too well. Confused film with farfetched reasons for having the paths of circus performers and cowboys cross. Based on a Zane Grey novel. **58m/B VHS.** Joe Cook, Robert Cummings, June Martel, Marjorie Gateson, John Miljan, James Mason; ***D:*** James Hogan; ***W:*** Robert Yost, Stuart Anthony. *MOV*

Arizona Raiders **1965** Arizona rangers hunt down killers who have been terrorizing the territory. **88m/C VHS, Beta.** Audie Murphy, Buster Crabbe, Gloria Talbott; ***D:*** William Witney. *NOS, VCI, VCN*

Arizona Roundup ½ **1942** Good vs. bad amid tumbleweed, bleached-white chaps, bloodless shoot-outs and happy endings. **54m/B VHS, Beta.** Tom Keene, Sugar Dawn, Jack Ingram; ***D:*** Robert Emmett Tansey. *NOS, VDM*

Arizona Stagecoach **1942** The Range Busters set out to bust a notorious, guiltless, devil-may-care outlaw gang. **58m/B VHS, Beta.** Ray Corrigan, Max Terhune, Kermit Maynard, Charles "Blackie" King, John "Dusty" King; ***D:*** S. Roy Luby. *NOS*

Arizona Terror ½ **1931** Our hero is on a quest for vengeance, seeking the posse that killed his partner. **64m/B VHS, Beta.** Ken Maynard. *VCN*

Arizona Whirlwind **1944** Our intrepid heroes must battle torrents of gunfire in order to prevent a stage hold-up in this western saga. **59m/B VHS, Beta.** Ken Maynard, Hoot Gibson, Bob Steele. *NOS, DVT*

Ark of the Sun God **1982** Another adventurer battles the Nazis and nutsies for a 2000-year-old ark buried in the Sahara. **95m/C VHS, Beta.** David Warbeck, John Steiner, Susie Sudlow, Alan Collins, Riccardo Palacio; ***D:*** Anthony (Antonio Margheriti) Dawson. *TWE*

Armageddon: The Final Challenge ½ **1994** After a nuclear holocaust, evil forces rule the Earth in the guise of "The Future Bank." They send out Fear-Permutator Clones to keep order and kill undesirables but naturally there's a rebel ready to do battle. **?m/C VHS.** Todd Jensen, Graham Clarke, Tony Caprari, Joanna Rowlands; ***D:*** Michael Garcia; ***W:*** George Garcia, Michael Garcia; ***M:*** Johan Lass.

Armed and Dangerous **1986 (PG-13)** Candy and Levy are incompetent security guards assigned to a do-nothing job. Things get spiced up when a mobster tries to run a crime ring under their nose. Candy catches on and winds up in a full-fledged chase. Not as funny as it sounds, though occasionally has moments of genuine comedy. **88m/C VHS, Beta, LV.** John Candy, Eugene Levy, Kenneth McMillan, Brion James, Robert Loggia, Meg Ryan, Don Stroud, Jonathan Banks, Steve Railsback, Bruce Kirby, Tony Burton, Larry Hankin, Judy Landers, David Wohl; ***D:*** Mark L. Lester; ***W:*** Harold Ramis, Peter Torokvei, James Keach, Brian Grazer. *COL*

Armed for Action **1992** Routine action thriller casts Estevez as Sgt. Phil Towers who gets more than he bargained for when his prisoner, Mafia hitman David Montel, escapes while en route from New York to Los Angeles. When he finally catches up with them, Towers leads a small army of locals on a brutal assault. **88m/C VHS.** Joe Estevez, Rocky Patterson, Barri Murphy, David Harrod, J. Scott Guy; ***D:*** Shane Spaulding. *AIP*

Armed Response **1986 (R)** Carradine leads a group of mercenaries in a battle against Chinatown mobsters. They race to locate a priceless jade statue before it can fall into the wrong hands. **86m/C VHS, Beta, LV.** David Carradine, Lee Van Cleef, Mako, Lois Hamilton, Ross Hagen, Brent Huff; ***D:*** Fred Olen Ray. *NO*

Armistead Maupin's Tales of the City ½ *Tales of the City* **1993** Carefree '70s San Francisco is the setting for the interconnected stories of the inhabitants of 28 Barbary Lane. There's mysterious landlady Mrs. Madrigal (Dukakis); free-spirit Mona Ramsey (Webb); her gay roomie, Michael "Mouse" Tolliver (D'Amico); hetero lawyer-turned-waiter Brian (Gross); nerdy, secretive Norman (DeSantis); and the naively sweet Mary Ann Singleton (Linney). Definite time-warp factor in this pre-AIDS depiction of sex and drugs, but also the timeless search for love and happiness. Maupin first wrote the stories as an ongoing serial for the *San Francisco Chronicle* and they were later turned into 6 novels. Made for British TV. **360m/C VHS.** *GB* Olympia Dukakis, Donald Moffat, Chloe Webb, Laura Linney, Marcus D'Amico, Paul Gross, Stanley DeSantis, Bill Campbell, Cynda Williams, Barbara Garrick, Thomas Gibson, Nina Foch, Paul Dooley, Belita Morena; ***Cameos:*** Karen Black, Edie Adams, Michael Jeter, Ian McKellen, Rod Steiger, Paul Bartel; ***D:*** Alastair Reid; ***W:*** Richard Kramer. *PGV*

Armored Car Robbery **1950** Talman and his buddies plot to rob an armored car but are foiled by McGraw and his crimefighters. Surprisingly good B-crime drama. **68m/B VHS.** Charles McGraw, Adele Jergens, William Talman, Steve Brodie; ***D:*** Richard Fleischer. *NO*

Armored Command ½ **1961** A beautiful German spy infiltrates an American outpost during the Battle of the Bulge. Tepid WWII fare made too long after the fact. **105m/B VHS, Beta.** Burt Reynolds, Tina Louise, Howard Keel, Earl Holliman, Warner Anderson, Carleton Young; ***D:*** Byron Haskin. *FOX, FCT*

The Armour of God **1986** Chan plays an adventurous thief who steals and sells pieces of a prized medieval armour set to collectors. When a criminal gang kidnaps his girl to get the entire set, Chan must come up with some spectacular saves of both the armour and the girl. In Cantonese with English subtitles. **100m/C VHS.** *CH* Jackie Chan; ***D:*** Jackie Chan. *FCT*

Army Brats ½ **1984** In this Dutch film a military family goes bloodily and comically to war with itself. Even in a welfare state, parents can't control their wee ones. **105m/C VHS, Beta.** *NL* Akkemay, Frank Schaafsma, Peter Faber; ***D:*** Ruud Van Hemert. *WAR*

Army of Darkness *Evil Dead 3* **1992 (R)** Campbell returns for a third "Evil Dead" round as the square-jawed, none too bright hero, Ash in this comic book extravaganza. He finds himself hurled back to the 14th-century through the powers of an evil book. There he romances a babe, fights an army of skeletons, and generally causes all those Dark Age knights a lot of grief, as he tries to get back to his own time. Raimi's technical exuberance is apparent and, as usual, the horror is graphic but still tongue-in-cheek. **77m/C VHS, Beta, LV.** Bruce Campbell, Embeth Davidtz, Marcus Gilbert, Ian Abercrombie, Richard Grove, Michael Earl Reid, Tim Quill, Patricia Tallman, Theodore (Ted) Raimi, Ivan Raimi; ***Cameos:*** Bridget Fonda; ***D:*** Sam Raimi; ***W:*** Ivan Raimi, Sam Raimi; ***M:*** Danny Elfman, Joseph Lo Duca. *MCA, FCT*

Army of One ½ **1994 (R)** Santee (Lundgren) and his pal are hauling stolen cars across the desert when a cop pulls them over. Soon there's two dead bodies and Santee's in big trouble. An unrated version is also available. **102m/C VHS, LV.** Dolph Lundgren, George Segal, Kristian Alfonso, Geoffrey Lewis, Michelle Phillips; ***D:*** Vic Armstrong; ***W:*** Steven Pressfield, Joel Goldsmith. *LIV*

Arnold ½ **1973 (PG)** Outrageous black comedy involving a woman who marries a cadaver to gain his large inheritance. Lots of bizarre and creative deaths in this horror spoof. Unusual wedding scene is a must-see. **96m/C VHS, Beta.** Stella Stevens, Roddy McDowall, Elsa Lanchester, Victor Buono, Bernard Fox, Farley Granger, Shani Wallis; ***D:*** Georg Fenady; ***W:*** Jameson Brewer; ***M:*** George Duning. *LIV*

Around the World ½ **1943** Kyser leads a USO-like tour to entertain troops. Interesting only in a historical sense. ♫Doodle-Ee-Doo; He's Got a Secret Weapon; Candlelight and Wine; Great News in the Making; They Chopped Down the Old Apple Tree; A Moke from Shamokin. **80m/B VHS, Beta.** Kay Kyser, Ish Kabibble, Ginny Simms, Joan Davis, Mischa Auer; ***D:*** Allan Dwan. *TTC*

Around the World in 80 Days **1956 (G)** Niven is the unflappable Victorian Englishman who wagers that he can circumnavigate the earth in four-score days. With his faithful manservant Cantinflas they set off on a spectacular journey. A perpetual favorite providing ample entertainment. Star-gazers will particularly enjoy the more than 40 cameo appearances by many of Hollywood's biggest names. Adapted from the novel by Jules Verne. **178m/C VHS, Beta, LV.** David Niven, Shirley MacLaine, Cantinflas, Robert Newton, Charles Boyer, Joe E. Brown, Martine Carol, John Carradine, Charles Coburn, Ronald Colman; ***Cameos:*** Melville Cooper, Noel Coward, Andy Devine, Reginald Denny, Fernandel, Marlene Dietrich, Hermione Gingold, Cedric Hardwicke, Trevor Howard, Glynis Johns, Buster Keaton, Evelyn Keyes, Peter Lorre, Mike Mazurki, Victor McLaglen, John Mills, Robert Morley, Jack Oakie, George Raft, Cesar Romero, Gilbert Roland, Red Skelton, Frank Sinatra, Ava Gardner; ***D:*** Michael Anderson Sr.; ***W:*** James Poe, John Farrow, S.J. Perelman; ***C:*** Lionel Lindon; ***M:*** Victor Young. Academy Awards '56: Best Adapted Screenplay, Best Color Cinematography, Best Film Editing, Best Picture, Best Original Score; Golden Globe Awards '57: Best Actor—Musical/Comedy (Cantinflas), Best Film—Drama; National Board of Review Awards '56: 10 Best Films of the Year; New York Film Critics Awards '56: Best Film, Best Screenplay; Nominations: Academy Awards '56: Best Art Direction/Set Decoration (Color), Best Costume Design (Color), Best Director (Anderson). *WAR, BTV, HMV*

Around the World in 80 Days ½ **1989** TV adaptation of the Jules Verne adventure novel that finds Victorian gentleman Phineas Fogg (Brosnan) wagering that he can circle the globe in 80 days. He's pursued by private detective Fix (Ustinov), who suspects him of a daring bank robbery, and faces many trials and much excitement along the way. On 2 cassettes. **270m/C VHS.** Pierce Brosnan, Peter Ustinov, Eric Idle, Arielle Dombasle, Henry Gibson, John Hillerman, Jack Klugman, Christopher Lee, Patrick Macnee, Roddy McDowall, Darren McGavin, John Mills, Robert Morley, Lee Remick, Pernell Roberts, James B. Sikking, Jill St. John, Robert Wagner, Julia Nickson-Soul; ***D:*** Buzz Kulick. *BFV*

Around the World in 80 Ways ½ **1986 (R)** Sometimes clever, sometimes crude Australian comedy about an aging man rescued from a nursing home and taken on a phony trip around the world by his sons. Odd, but genuinely funny at times. **90m/C VHS, LV.** *AU* Philip Quast, Alan Penney, Diana Davidson, Kelly Dingwall, Gosia Dobrowolska; ***D:*** Stephen MacLean; ***W:*** Stephen MacLean, Paul Leadon; ***M:*** Chris Neal. *SUE, NLC, WTA*

Around the World in a Daze ½ *The Three Stooges Go Around the World in a Daze* **1963** The Stooges are servants for Phileas Fogg's great-grandson, who has decided to repeat his ancestor's famous feat. Mayhem ensues when the three help out in their usual efficient, competent way. **93m/B VHS.** Moe Howard, Larry Fine, Joe DeRita, Jay Sheffield; ***D:*** Norman Maurer. *COL*

Around the World Under the Sea 🦴🦴 **1965** Bunch of men and one woman scientist plunge under the ocean in an experiment to predict earthquakes. They plant earthquake detectors along the ocean floor and discover the causes of tidal waves. They have men-women battles. They see big sea critters. **111m/C VHS, Beta.** David McCallum, Shirley Eaton, Gary Merrill, Keenan Wynn, Brian Kelly, Lloyd Bridges; ***D:*** Andrew Marton. *MGM*

Aroused 🦴 **1966** Hollister is an apparently dedicated policeman who commits a number of blunders in the pursuit of a serial killer, including leaving his wife with the sociopath while he cavorts with the prostitute assigned to his protection. Director Holden's psychothriller was gorily ahead of its time. Includes heart-stopping castration sequence. **78m/B VHS.** Janine Lenon, Steve Hollister, Fleurette Carter, Joanna Mills, Tony Palladino, Ted Gelanza; ***D:*** Anton Holden. *SMW, TPV*

The Arousers 🦴🦴½ *Sweet Kill; A Kiss from Eddie* **1970 (R)** Cult item starring hunk Hunter as a handsome California psycho. Tab travels the coast searching for a woman he is able to make love to; those who fail to arouse him come to tragic, climactic ends. Definitely underground and moderately interesting. **85m/C VHS, Beta.** Tab Hunter, Nadyne Turney, Roberta Collins, Isabel Jewell, John Aprea, Angel Fox; ***D:*** Curtis Hanson. *SUE*

The Arrangement 🦴½ **1969 (R)** Veteran advertising executive Douglas attempts suicide and then sets out to search for the meaning of life. Along the way he attempts to patch up his "arrangements" with his wife, his mistress and his father. Forced, slow, and self-conscious, though well acted. Adapted by Kazan from the director's own novel. **126m/C VHS, Beta.** Kirk Douglas, Faye Dunaway, Deborah Kerr, Richard Boone, Hume Cronyn, Elia Kazan; ***D:*** Elia Kazan; ***C:*** Robert L. Surtees; ***M:*** David Amram. *WAR*

Arrest Bulldog Drummond 🦴🦴 **1938** Captain Drummond is accused of killing the inventor of a futuristic detonator machine and must track down the real killers. Part of the "Bulldog Drummond" series. **57m/B VHS, Beta.** John Howard, Heather Angel, George Zucco, H.B. Warner, E.E. Clive, Reginald Denny, John Sutton; ***D:*** James Hogan. *PAR, RXM, SNC*

The Arrival 🦴 **1990 (R)** An never-seen alien parasite turns an old man into a vampiric young stud after female blood. Plot and characterizations never do arrive. Horror director Stuart Gordon cameos as a hairy biker. **107m/C VHS, LV.** John Saxon, Joseph Culp, Robert Sampson, Michael J. Pollard; ***Cameos:*** David Schmoeller; ***D:*** David Schmoeller; ***W:*** David Schmoeller; ***M:*** Richard Band. *PSM*

The Arrival 🦴🦴½ *Shockwave* **1996 (PG-13)** Radio astronomer Zane (Sheen) picks up a message from deep space and discovers a planned alien invasion. When he brings evidence of such to his boss Gordian (Silver) he finds himself on the run from both government operatives and morphing aliens. Starts off slow, but an intelligent script and premise makes this is a grade above cheesy. The aliens, with their kooky flaps of skin and back bending knees are fun to watch. Directorial debut for Twohy. **109m/C VHS.** Charlie Sheen, Ron Silver, Lindsay Crouse, Teri Polo; ***D:*** David N. Twohy; ***W:*** David N. Twohy; ***C:*** Hiro Narita; ***M:*** Arthur Kempel. *NYR*

Arrivederci, Baby! 🦴 **1966** An unfunny sex comedy with Curtis as a modern Bluebeard who weds rich women and kills them for their money. His last mate plans to turn the tables and kill him first. **100m/C VHS.** Tony Curtis, Rosanna Schiaffino, Lionel Jeffries, Zsa Zsa Gabor, Nancy Kwan, Fenella Fielding, Anna Quayle, Warren Mitchell, Mischa Auer; ***D:*** Ken Hughes; ***W:*** Ken Hughes. *PAR*

Arrowhead 🦴🦴½ **1953** A long-running argument between a tough Cavalry scout and an Apache chief pits the cowboys against the Indians in this western fantasy. The personal battles that become all-out wars turn back to fist-fights before the matter is finally settled. **105m/C VHS, Beta, LV.** Charlton Heston, Jack Palance, Katy Jurado, Brian Keith, Milburn Stone; ***D:*** Charles Marquis Warren; ***C:*** Ray Rennahan. *PAR*

Arrowsmith 🦴🦴½ **1931** A small-town medical researcher battles his conscience as he juggles his selfish and unselfish motivations for the work he does. He travels to the West Indies to confront the issues of his life and come to terms with himself once and for all. A talented cast takes their time. Based on the classic Sinclair Lewis novel. Two edited versions available (99 and 89 minutes), both of which delete much of Loy. **95m/B VHS, Beta.** Ronald Colman, Helen Hayes, Myrna Loy; ***D:*** John Ford. Nominations: Academy Awards '32: Best Adapted Screenplay, Best Cinematography, Best Interior Decoration, Best Picture. *SUE*

Arsenal 🦴🦴🦴 **1929** Classic Russian propagandist drama about strikes affecting the Russian home front during WWI, marking Dovzhenko's first great achievement in the realm of Eisenstein and Pudovkin. Silent. **70m/B VHS, Beta.** *RU* Semyon Svashenko; ***D:*** Alexander Dovzhenko. *NOS, MRV, IHF*

The Arsenal Stadium Mystery 🦴🦴½ **1939** Inspector Banks of Scotland Yard tracks down the killer of a football star in this clever but unassuming murder mystery. **85m/B VHS.** *GB* Leslie Banks, Greta Gynt, Ian MacLean, Liane Linden, Anthony Bushell, Esmond Knight; ***D:*** Thorold Dickinson. *SNC*

Arsenic and Old Lace 🦴🦴🦴½ **1944** Set-bound but energetic adaptation of the classic Joseph Kesselring play. Easy-going drama critic Grant is caught in a sticky situation when he learns of his aunts' favorite pastime. Apparently the kind, sweet, lonely spinsters lure gentlemen to the house and serve them elderberry wine with a touch of arsenic, then they bury the bodies in the cellar—a cellar which also serves as the Panama Canal for Grant's cousin (who thinks he's Theodore Roosevelt). Massey and Lorre excel in their sinister roles. One of the best madcap black comedies of all time—a must-see. Shot in 1941 and released a wee bit later. Available colorized. **158m/B VHS, Beta, LV.** Cary Grant, Josephine Hull, Jean Adair, Raymond Massey, Jack Carson, Priscilla Lane, John Alexander, Edward Everett Horton, John Ridgely, James Gleason, Peter Lorre; ***D:*** Frank Capra; ***W:*** Julius J. Epstein, Philip C. Epstein; ***M:*** Max Steiner. *MGM, FOX, HMV*

Art for Teachers of Children 🦴🦴 **1995** Autobiographical account of 14-year-old Jennifer (McDonnell) who becomes a model for married photographer John (Hannah), who's also her boarding school dorm advisor. He's well-known for his nude portraits of young women as well as his affairs with his models and Jennifer's both confused and excited by her emerging sexuality as she and John become lovers. Remarkably detached considering the provocative subject matter. **82m/B VHS.** Caitlin Grace McDonnell, Duncan Hannah, Coles Burroughs, Bryan Keane; ***D:*** Jennifer Montgomery; ***W:*** Jennifer Montgomery; ***C:*** Jennifer Montgomery. *ZGI*

The Art of Crime 🦴🦴½ **1975** A gypsy/detective is drawn into a homicide case when one of his fellow antique dealers is charged with murder. Maintains an atmospheric edge over others of the crime art genre. A pilot for a prospective television series based on the novel "Gypsy in Amber." **72m/C VHS.** Ron Leibman, Jose Ferrer, David Hedison, Jill Clayburgh; ***D:*** Richard Irving; ***W:*** Bill Davidson, Martin Smith. *MOV*

The Art of Dying 🦴🦴🦴 **1990** A loony videophile decides to start staging productions of his all-time favorite scenes. Trouble is, his idea of a fabulous film moment calls for lots of blood and bile as he lures teenage runaways to his casting couch. Director Hauser stars as the cop who's none too impressed with the cinematic remakes, while cult favorite Pollard is his partner. If you like a little atmosphere and psychological depth in your slashers, you'll find this to be the stuff that populates film noir nightmares. **90m/C VHS, LV.** Wings Hauser, Michael J. Pollard, Sarah Douglas, Kathleen Kinmont, Sydney Lassick; ***D:*** Wings Hauser. *PMH*

Arthur 🦴🦴🦴 **1981 (PG)** Spoiled, alcoholic billionaire Moore stands to lose everything he owns when he falls in love with a waitress. He must choose between wealth and a planned marriage, or poverty and love. Surprisingly funny, with an Oscar for Gielgud as Moore's valet, and great performance from Minnelli. Arguably the best role Moore's ever had, and he makes the most of it, taking the one-joke premise to a nomination for Oscar actor. ♫Arthur's Theme; Blue Moon; If You Knew Susie; Santa Claus is Coming to Town. **97m/C VHS, Beta, LV, 8mm.** Dudley Moore, Liza Minnelli, John Gielgud, Geraldine Fitzgerald, Stephen Elliott, Jill Eikenberry, Lou Jacobi; ***D:*** Steve Gordon; ***M:*** Burt Bacharach. Academy Awards '81: Best Song ("Arthur's Theme"), Best Supporting Actor (Gielgud); Los Angeles Film Critics Association Awards '81: Best Supporting Actor (Gielgud); New York Film Critics Awards '81: Best Supporting Actor (Gielgud); Writers Guild of America '81: Best Original Screenplay; Nominations: Academy Awards '81: Best Actor (Moore), Best Original Screenplay. *WAR, FCT, BTV*

Arthur 2: On the Rocks 🦴½ **1988 (PG)** When Arthur finally marries his sweetheart, it may not be "happily ever after" because the father of the girl he didn't marry is out for revenge. When Arthur discovers that he is suddenly penniless, a bit of laughter is the cure for the blues and also serves well when the liquor runs out. A disappointing sequel with few laughs. **113m/C VHS, Beta, LV, 8mm.** Dudley Moore, Liza Minnelli, John Gielgud, Geraldine Fitzgerald, Stephen Elliott, Ted Ross, Barney Martin, Jack Gilford; ***D:*** Bud Yorkin; ***W:*** Andy Breckman; ***C:*** Stephen Burum; ***M:*** Burt Bacharach. Golden Raspberry Awards '87: Worst Actress (Minnelli). *WAR, FCT*

Arthur's Hallowed Ground 🦴 **1984** A cricket field caretaker battles the board of directors over the fate of his favorite plot of sod. **75m/C VHS, Beta.** Jimmy Jewel, Jean Bolt, Michael Elphick; ***D:*** Frederick A. (Freddie) Young. *MGM*

Article 99 🦴🦴 **1992 (R)** Doctors in a Kansas City Veteran's Administration hospital try to heal patients while putting up with bureaucratic red tape and a stingy administrator. When rogue physician Sturgess (Liotta) is dismissed, the patients hold a siege. Sort of son of "M.A.S.H." (Big Daddy Sutherland did Hawkeye) that gets its title from a fictional rule that says veterans can be treated only for conditions related to military service. Erstwhile cast labors to combine comedic and dramatic intentions of script. **100m/C VHS, LV.** Ray Liotta, Kiefer Sutherland, Forest Whitaker, Lea Thompson, John C. McGinley, John Mahoney, Keith David, Kathy Baker, Eli Wallach, Noble Willingham, Julie Bovasso, Troy Evans, Lynne Thigpen, Jeffrey Tambor, Rutanya Alda; ***D:*** Howard Deutch; ***W:*** Ron Cutler; ***M:*** Danny Elfman. *ORI*

Artists and Models 🦴🦴½ **1955** Martin is a struggling comic book artist and Lewis his idiot roommate. The pair become mixed up in both romance and intrigue when Lewis begins talking in his sleep about spys and such. One of the duo's more pleasant cinematic outings. ♫Inamorata; Lucky Song; You Look So Familiar; Why You Pretend. **109m/C VHS.** Dean Martin, Jerry Lewis, Shirley MacLaine, Dorothy Malone, Eddie Mayehoff, Eva Gabor, Anita Ekberg, George Winslow, Jack Elam, Herbert Rudley, Nick Castle; ***D:*** Frank Tashlin; ***W:*** Frank Tashlin, Hal Kanter, Herbert Baker; ***C:*** Daniel F. Fapp. *PAR, MLB*

Artist's Studio Secrets 🦴 *The Story of an Artist's Studio Secrets; Artist Nude Secrets* **1964** An artist from Greenwich Village only gets aroused by clothed models, so his wife jealously arranges for him to only work with nude women. **78m/B VHS, Beta.** *VDM, TPV*

As Good as Dead 🦴🦴½ **1995 (PG-13)** A young woman allows her sick friend to assume her identity but when her friend is murdered, she realizes the killer was really after her. **88m/C VHS, Beta.** Crystal Bernard, Traci Lords, Judge Reinhold; ***D:*** Larry Cohen; ***W:*** Larry Cohen. *PAR*

As If It Were Raining 🦴🦴 **1963** Constantine gets involved in an embezzlement scheme in Spain in this espionage thriller. **85m/C VHS.** *FR* Eddie Constantine, Henri Cogan, Elisa Montes, Jose Nieto, Silvia Solar; ***D:*** Jose Monter. *SNC*

As Is ☆½ **1985** Two gay New Yorkers deal with a troubled romance and AIDS. A cable television adaptation from the William M. Hoffman play. **86m/C VHS, Beta.** Jonathan Hadary, Robert Carradine; ***D:*** Michael Lindsay-Hogg. *ORI, WAR*

As Summers Die ☆☆ **1986** Louisiana attorney Glenn fights in the late 1950s to protect the rights of a black family, against the wishes of a powerful local clan. Glenn finds support in surprising places, though. From Winston Groom's acclaimed novel. A cable television movie. **100m/C VHS, Beta.** Scott Glenn, Jamie Lee Curtis, Penny Fuller, Bette Davis, John Randolph, Beah Richards, Ron O'Neal, John McIntire; ***D:*** Jean-Claude Tramont. *CNG*

As You Desire Me ☆☆☆ **1932** Garbo plays an amnesia victim who returns to a husband she doesn't even remember after an abusive relationship with a novelist. An interesting, if not down-right bizarre movie, due to the pairing of the great Garbo and the intriguing von Stroheim. An adaption of Luigi Pirandello's play. **71m/B VHS, Beta.** Greta Garbo, Melvyn Douglas, Erich von Stroheim, Owen Moore, Hedda Hopper; ***D:*** George Fitzmaurice. *MGM, FCT*

As You Like It ☆☆½ **1936** A Duke's banished daughter poses as a man to win the attentions of one of her father's attendants in this highly stylized Shakespearean comedy adapted by J.M. Barrie and Robert Cullen. Early Shakespearean Olivier. **96m/B VHS, Beta, LV.** *GB* Elisabeth Bergner, Laurence Olivier, Henry Ainley, Felix Aylmer; ***D:*** Paul Czinner; ***W:*** J.M. Barrie, Robert Cullen. *NOS, MRV, VYY*

As You Were ☆ **1951** A girl with a photographic memory enlists in the Army, becoming both a nuisance and comedic victim to her sergeant. **57m/B VHS, Beta, LV.** Joseph Sawyer, William Tracy, Sondra Rogers, Joan Vohs. *NO*

As Young As You Feel ☆☆☆ **1951** A 65-year-old man is forced to retire from his job. He poses as the head of the conglomerate and convinces them to repeal their retirement policy. He then gains national publicity when he makes a speech about the dignity of man. Watch for Monroe as the boss's secretary. Fine comic performances enhance the script; based on a story by Chayefsky. **77m/C VHS.** Monty Woolley, Thelma Ritter, David Wayne, Jean Peters, Constance Bennett, Marilyn Monroe, Allyn Joslyn, Albert Dekker, Clinton Sundberg, Minor Watson; ***D:*** Harmon Jones; ***W:*** Paddy Chayefsky. *FXV*

The Ascent ☆☆½ **1994 (PG)** Based on the true story of Franco (Spano), a WWII Italian POW who's held in a camp in Africa. The prisoners enjoy making fun of the camp commander (Cross), who consistently fails at his attempts to climb the 15,500 peak of Mt. Kenya. Meanwhile, Franco decides to escape and climb the mountain himself—with the commander right behind. Beware if you suffer from vertigo. **96m/C VHS.** Vincent Spano, Ben Cross, Tony LoBianco, Rachel Ward; ***D:*** Donald Shebib. *CAF*

Ash Wednesday ☆ **1973 (R)** Taylor endures the pain of cosmetic surgery in an effort to rescue her floundering union with Fonda. Another undistinguished performance by Liz. Fonda is especially slimy as the philandering husband, but only appears in the latter stages of the film. **99m/C VHS.** Elizabeth Taylor, Henry Fonda, Helmut Berger, Keith Baxter, Margaret Blye, Maurice Teynac, Monique Van Vooren; ***D:*** Larry Peerce; ***M:*** Maurice Jarre. *PAR, FCT, CCB*

Ashanti, Land of No Mercy ☆☆ *Ashanti* **1979** Caine of the week movie with Michael portraying a doctor acting as a missionary in South Africa who finds himself alone in a battle to rescue his wife from a band of slave traders. The chase spans many Middle Eastern countries and begins to look bleak for our man. Talented cast and promising plot are undone by slow pace. Based on the novel "Ebano" by Alberto Vasquez-Figueroa. **117m/C VHS, Beta.** Michael Caine, Omar Sharif, Peter Ustinov, Rex Harrison, William Holden, Beverly Johnson; ***D:*** Richard Fleischer. *TWE*

Ashes and Diamonds ☆☆☆½ *Popiol i Diament* **1958** In the closing days of WWII, a Polish resistance fighter assassinates the wrong man, tries to find love with the right women, and questions the meaning of struggle. A seminal Eastern European masterpiece that defined a generation of pre-solidarity Poles. Available in Polish with English subtitles or dubbed into English. The last installment of the trilogy that includes "A Generation" and "Kanal" and based on a novel by Jerzy Andrzewski. **105m/B VHS, Beta, LV.** *PL* Zbigniew Cybulski, Eva Krzyzewska, Adam Pawlikowski, Bogumil Kobiela, Waclaw Zastrzezynski; ***D:*** Andrzej Wajda. Venice Film Festival '59: International Critics Award. *ING, SUE, MRV*

Ashes and Embers ☆☆ **1982** A black Vietnam vet in Los Angeles has trouble fitting into society, eventually running afoul of the police. Ethiopian-born director Gerima endows vital subject matter with a properly alienated mood. **120m/C VHS.** John Anderson, Evelyn Blackwell; ***D:*** Haile Gerima. *FCT*

Ashik Kerib ☆☆☆ **1988** Ashik Kerib is a wandering minstrel who is rejected by a rich merchant as his daughter's suitor. He then journeys for 1,000 days trying to earn enough money to marry his beloved. Along the way he's imprisoned by an evil sultan and rides a flying horse, among other adventures. Wonderful use of exotic makeup and costumes highlight this Arabian Nights tale. Adapted from a story by Mikhail Lermontov. Paradjanov's last film. In Russian with English subtitles. **75m/C VHS.** *RU* Yiur Mgoyan, Veronkia Metonidze, Levan Natroshvili, Sofiko Chiaureli; ***D:*** Dodo Abashidze, Sergei Paradjanov; ***W:*** Giya Badridze; ***M:*** Djavashir Kuliev. *KIV, FCT*

Ask Any Girl ☆☆½ **1959** Lighthearted fluff about a small-town girl who moves to Manhattan. MacLaine plays the bright Meg who gets a job at an ad agency and decides to set her sights on marrying her boss (Young). She asks his older brother's (Niven) help in her quest and the inevitable happens. **101m/C VHS.** Shirley MacLaine, David Niven, Gig Young, Rod Taylor, Jim Backus, Claire Kelly, Elisabeth Fraser; ***D:*** Charles Walters. British Academy Awards '59: Best Actress (MacLaine). *MGM, MOV*

Aspen Extreme ☆ **1993 (PG-13)** Former Aspen ski instructor writes and directs a movie on (what else?) ski instructors in (where?) Aspen! Long on ski shots and short on plot, this movie never leaves the bunny hill. Two Detroiters leave Motown for Snowtown to pursue a life on the slopes. T.J (Gross) soon has his hands full with two beautiful women (Polo and Hughes) who encourage his dream of becoming a writer. His friend Dexter (Berg), however, acquires a few bad habits, and the whole movie just goes downhill from there. **128m/C VHS, Beta, LV.** Paul Gross, Peter Berg, Finola Hughes, Teri Polo, Martin Kemp, Nicolette Scorsese, William Russ; ***D:*** Patrick Hasburgh; ***W:*** Patrick Hasburgh; ***M:*** Michael Convertino. *HPH, TOU*

The Asphalt Jungle ☆☆☆☆ **1950** An aging criminal emerges from his forced retirement (prison) and assembles the old gang for one final heist. A very realistic storyline and a superb cast make this one of the best crime films ever made. Highly acclaimed; based on the work of W.R. Burnett. **112m/B VHS, Beta, LV.** Sterling Hayden, Louis Calhern, Jean Hagen, James Whitmore, Sam Jaffe, John McIntire, Marc Lawrence, Barry Kelley, Anthony Caruso, Teresa Celli, Marilyn Monroe; ***D:*** John Huston; ***W:*** Ben Maddow; ***M:*** Miklos Rozsa. Edgar Allan Poe Awards '50: Best Screenplay; National Board of Review Awards '50: 10 Best Films of the Year, Best Director (Huston); Nominations: Academy Awards '50: Best Black and White Cinematography, Best Director (Huston), Best Screenplay, Best Supporting Actor (Jaffe). *MGM*

The Asphyx ☆☆☆ *Spirit of the Dead* **1972 (PG)** Nineteenth century doctor Stephens is studying death when he discovers The Asphyx, an aura that surrounds a person just before they die. Stephens delves deeper into his research and finds the keys to immortality. However, his irresponsibility in unleashing the obscure supernatural power on the world brings a swarm of unforeseen and irreversible troubles. High-class sci fi. **98m/C VHS, Beta.** *GB* Robert Stephens, Robert Powell, Jane Lapotaire, Alex Scott, Ralph Arliss, Fiona Walker, John Lawrence; ***D:*** Peter Newbrook; ***C:*** Frederick A. (Freddie) Young. *MED*

Assassin ☆ **1979** Athletic karate fighter poses as an underworld figure and infiltrates the largest gang in Japan where he is hired as a hit man. **86m/C VHS, Beta.** Sonny Chiba. *FOX*

Assassin ☆☆ **1986 (PG-13)** Made for TV drama about a mad scientist who creates a bionic killer for a bizarre plot to take over the world. He programs the cyborg to assassinate the President and other key people to help carry out his plan. A retired CIA operative emerges to stop the scientist by trying to destroy the robot. **94m/C VHS, Beta.** Robert Conrad, Karen Austin, Richard Young, Jonathan Banks, Robert Webber; ***D:*** Sandor Stern. *ACA*

Assassin ☆☆ **1989 (R)** Fairly lame thriller about a CIA agent protecting a Senator who falls under suspicion when his charge is shot by an assassin. In investigating the killing the agent discovers the usual governmental conspiracy. **92m/C VHS, Beta, LV.** Steve Railsback, Nicholas Guest, Xander Berkeley, Elpidia Carrillo; ***D:*** Jon Hess. *NO*

Assassin of Youth ☆½ **1935** Girl is introduced to marijuana and soon becomes involved in "the thrills of wild parties," and the horrors of the "killer weed." Camp diversion. **70m/B VHS, Beta.** Luana Walters, Arthur Gardner; ***D:*** Elmer Clifton. *SNC, NOS, DVT*

Assassination ☆ **1987 (R)** A serious threat has been made to First Lady Ireland and no one is taking it lightly. Secret Service agent Bronson has been called as Ireland's personal bodyguard and suddenly they are both the target of terrorist attacks. Strangely though, the attacks seem to be directed from inside the White House. Bronson as you've seen him many times before. **93m/C VHS, Beta, LV.** Charles Bronson, Jill Ireland, Stephen Elliott, Michael Ansara; ***D:*** Peter Hunt. *MED, VTR*

The Assassination Bureau ☆☆☆ **1969** Set in Victorian-era London, this amusing farce concerns a society of international assassins led by the charming Reed. Rigg is an intrepid reporter who pays Reed to have his own organization try to kill him. Reed in turn will try to get them first. A cross-European chase ends in a battle aboard a Zeppelin. Tongue-in-cheek whimsey with a fine cast. Based on a short story by Jack London. **106m/C VHS, LV.** *GB* Oliver Reed, Diana Rigg, Telly Savalas, Curt Jurgens, Philippe Noiret, Warren Mitchell, Beryl Reid, Clive Revill, Kenneth Griffith, Vernon Dobtcheff, Annabella Incontrera; ***D:*** Basil Dearden; ***C:*** Geoffrey Unsworth. *PAR*

Assassination of Trotsky ☆☆ **1972** Middling attempt to dramatize the last days of the Russian Revolutionary leader in Mexico before he's done in with an ice pick. **113m/C VHS, Beta, LV.** *FR GB IT* Richard Burton, Alain Delon, Romy Schneider, Valentina Cortese, Jean Desailly; ***D:*** Joseph Losey; ***C:*** Pasqualino de Santis. *REP, FCT, INJ*

The Assassination Run ☆ **1984** A retired British spy is involved against his will in an intricate plot of terrorism, counter-terrorism and espionage. **111m/C VHS, Beta.** *GB* Malcolm Stoddard, Mary Tamm; ***D:*** Ken Hannam. *FOX*

Assassins ☆☆½ **1995 (R)** Stallone gets to play elder statesman in the very deadly rivalry between two contract killers. Robert Rath (Stallone) is the man—number one with a bullet—whose reputation has caught up with him. Hot-headed Miguel Bain (the ever-smoldering Banderas) wants to off Rath and assume the position of top hitman. Caught in the middle of this macho posturing is surveillance expert—and potential murderee—Electra (Moore). It's Stallone to the rescue but his character pays more attention to Pearl, Electra's pampered Persian cat than to the lovely lady herself. But then romance isn't what this film is about—and director Donner does know his action. **132m/C VHS.** Sylvester Stallone, Antonio Banderas, Julianne Moore, Anatoly Davydov; ***D:*** Richard Donner; ***W:*** Brian Helgeland, Andy Wachowski, Larry Wachowski; ***C:*** Vilmos Zsigmond; ***M:*** Mark Mancina. Nominations: Golden Raspberry Awards '95: Worst Actor (Stallone). *WAR*

Assault ☆½ *In the Devil's Garden; Tower of Terror; The Creepers* **1970** Violent sex murders in a girl's school have the police baffled. The school's pretty art teacher offers to act as bait in order to catch the murderer. **89m/C VHS, Beta.** *GB* Suzy Kendall, Frank Finlay, Freddie Jones, James Laurenson, Lesley-Anne Down, Tony Beckley; ***D:*** Sidney Hayers. *SUE*

The Assault ☆☆☆½ *De Aanslag* **1986 (PG)** Powerful and disturbing drama about a Dutch boy who witnesses the arbitrary murder of his family by Nazis. The memory tortures him and leaves him empty as he matures. Years later he meets other victims and also the perpetrators of the incident, each of them changed forever by it. Thought-provoking consideration of WWII and the horrors of living in Nazi Germany from many points of view. Based on a novel by Harry Mulisch. Dutch language dubbed into English. **149m/C VHS, Beta.** *NL* Derek De Lint, Marc Van Uchelen, Monique Van De Ven; ***D:*** Fons Rademakers. Academy Awards '86: Best Foreign Language Film; Golden Globe Awards '87: Best Foreign Film. *MGM, INJ, SWC*

Assault and Matrimony ☆½ **1987** Real-life married people Tucker and Eikenberry play a married couple fighting tooth and nail. Lots of slapstick and general nonsense. Television film based on James Anderson's novel. **100m/C VHS, Beta, LV.** John Hillerman, Michelle Phillips, Joe Cortese, Michael Tucker, Jill Eikenberry; ***D:*** James Frawley. *VMK*

Assault at West Point: The Court-Martial of Johnson Whittaker ☆☆½ **1994 (PG-13)** In 1880, Johnson C. Whittaker, a black West Point cadet, is found beaten, mutilated, and tied to his bed. Instead of seeking his attackers, the Academy sets up a court martial to expel Whittaker, claiming he faked his own attack. Clashes also ignite between Whittaker's defense counsel—white abolitionist lawyer Chamberlain, whose own racism is thinly disguised, and black lawyer Greener, who originally encouraged Whittaker to enroll at the Point. Interesting case but a shallow production. Based on a true story and adapted from the book by John Marszalek. Made for television. **98m/C VHS.** Seth Gilliam, Samuel L. Jackson, Sam Waterston, John Glover, Al Freeman Jr.; ***D:*** Harry Moses; ***W:*** Harry Moses; ***M:*** Terence Blanchard. *REP*

Assault of the Killer Bimbos ☆½ **1988 (R)** A show girl gets framed for the murder of her boss and takes off for the border with a couple of girlfriends. On the way they get pursued by the expected dumb cops and meet up with horny, clean-cut hunks. In Mexico they encounter the villain and extract comic vengeance. Watchable mainly due to the likable female leads and pleasant, lightly camp execution, although it might prove too tame for most of its target audience. **85m/C Beta.** Patti Astor, Christina Whitaker, Elizabeth Kaitan, Griffin O'Neal, Nick Cassavetes, Clayton Landey, Eddie Deezen, Arell Blanton, David Marsh, Tammara Souza, Jamie Bozian, Mike Muscat, Jeffrey Orman, John Quern; ***D:*** Patti Astor; ***W:*** Patti Astor, Anita Rosenberg; ***C:*** Thomas Callaway; ***M:*** Fred Lapides, Marc Ellis. *AFE*

Assault of the Party Nerds ☆ **1989 (R)** Nerds throw a wild party to try and attract new members to their fraternity, while a jock frat plots against them. Sound familiar? Little more than a ripoff of "Revenge of the Nerds" made especially for video. **82m/C VHS, Beta.** Linnea Quigley, Troy Donahue, Richard Gabai, C. Paul Demsey, Marc Silverberg, Robert Mann, Richard Rifkin, Deborah Roush; ***D:*** Richard Gabai. *PSM*

Assault of the Party Nerds 2: Heavy Petting Detective ☆ **1995** Detective tries to save a beauty from her scheming husband. **87m/C VHS.** Linnea Quigley, Richard Gabai, Michelle (McClellan) Bauer, Arte Johnson, Burt Ward. *VCI*

Assault of the Rebel Girls ☆½ *Cuban Rebel Girls; Attack of the Rebel Girls* **1959** A reporter gets involved with smuggling in Castro's Cuba. Flynn's last film, saving the worst for last. **66m/B VHS, Beta.** Errol Flynn, Beverly Aadland, John McKay, Jackie Jackler, Marie Edmund; ***D:*** Barry Mahon; ***W:*** Errol Flynn. *MED*

Assault on a Queen ☆ **1966** Stupid Sinatra vehicle about a group of con men who plot together to rob the Queen Mary on one of her trips. Their attack vessel is a renovated WWII German U-boat. The producers tried to capitalize on the popularity of "Ocean's Eleven," but they didn't even come close. Based on a novel by Jack Finney. **106m/C VHS.** Frank Sinatra, Virna Lisi, Anthony (Tony) Franciosa, Richard Conte, Reginald Denny; ***D:*** Jack Donohue; ***W:*** Rod Serling; ***C:*** William H. Daniels. *PAR*

Assault on Agathon ☆☆ **1975 (PG)** Amid the scenic Greek isles, an "executed" WWII guerilla leader returns to lead a revolution, and bloodshed and bombings ensue. **95m/C VHS, Beta.** *GB IT* Nina Van Pallandt, Marianne Faithfull, John Woodvine, Nico Minardos; ***D:*** Laslo Benedek. *GEM, MRV, PSM*

Assault on Precinct 13 ☆☆☆ **1976** Urban horror invades LA. A sleepy police station in Los Angeles is suddenly under siege from a violent youth gang. Paranoia abounds as the police are attacked from all sides and can see no way out. Carpenter's musical score adds much to the setting of this unique police exploitation story that somehow stands as Carpenter's adaptation of Howard Hawks' "Rio Bravo." Semi-acclaimed and very gripping. **91m/C VHS, Beta, LV.** Austin Stoker, Darwin Joston, Martin West, Tony Burton, Nancy Loomis, Kim Richards, Henry Brandon; ***D:*** John Carpenter; ***W:*** John Carpenter; ***M:*** John Carpenter. *MED*

Assault with a Deadly Weapon ☆ **1982** When the police budget is cutback, crime runs rampant in an unnamed American city. **86m/C VHS, Beta.** Sandra Foley, Richard Holliday, Lamont Jackson; ***D:*** Arthur Kennedy. *LIV*

The Assignment ☆☆ **1978** The assassination of a high-ranking officer in an uneasy Latin American nation spurs violence and political instability. A Swedish diplomat is assigned the tremendous task of restoring peace and stability between the political factions. **92m/C VHS, Beta.** *SW* Christopher Plummer, Thomas Hellberg, Carolyn Seymour, Fernando Rey; ***D:*** Mats Arehn. *NWV*

Assignment Outer Space ☆ *Space Men* **1961** A giant spaceship with bytes for brains is on a collision course with Earth. A team of astronauts is sent to save the world from certain peril. Seems they take the task lightly, though, and their mission (and hence the plot) revolves more around saving sexy sultress Farinon from certain celibacy. If you're into stultifying Italian space operas with a gratuitous sex sub-plot then look up this assignment, but don't say we didn't warn you. Narrated by Jack Wallace; director Margheriti is also known as Anthony Dawson, not to be confused with the actor of the same name. **79m/B VHS.** *IT* Rik von Nutter, Gabriella Farinon, Archie Savage, Dave Montresor, Alan Dijon; ***D:*** Anthony (Antonio Margheriti) Dawson. *NOS, SNC*

Assignment Skybolt ☆½ **198?** When terrorists get their hands on a hydrogen bomb, a special mission is detached to stop them before they start WWIII. **109m/C VHS, Beta.** ***D:*** Greg Tallas. *BFV*

The Assisi Underground ☆☆ **1984** True but boringly told story of how the Catholic Church helped to save several hundred Italian Jews from being executed by the Nazis during the 1943 German occupation of Italy. Edited from 178 minutes, a good-will gesture from the producers. **115m/C VHS, Beta.** James Mason, Ben Cross, Maximilian Schell, Irene Papas; ***D:*** Alexander Ramati; ***M:*** Pino Donaggio. *MGM, IGP*

The Associate ☆☆ *L'Associe* **1982 (R)** A French farce about a penniless financial consultant who invents a fictitious partner in order to get his business rolling. English subtitles. **93m/C VHS, Beta.** *FR* Michel Serrault, Claudine Auger, Catherine Alric, Julien Pardot; ***D:*** Rene Gainville; ***W:*** Jean-Claude Carriere. *SUE*

The Association ☆½ **198?** A man and a woman go undercover to bust an international white slavery ring. **92m/C VHS, Beta.** *TW* Carter Huang, Angela Mao; ***D:*** Cheung Wo Chang. *NO*

Assunta Spina ☆☆ **1915** A very early, very rare Italian epic about ancient Rome, the prototype for the Italian silent epics to come. **70m/B VHS, Beta.** *IT FCT*

The Astounding She-Monster *Woof!* *Mysterious Invader* **1958** How can you not love a movie with a title like this? A bad script and snail-paced plot are a good start. A geologist wanting only to be left alone with his rocks survives a brush with the kidnappers of a wealthy heiress only to happen upon an alien spacecraft that's crashed nearby. At the helm is a very tall, high-heeled fem-alien in an obligatory skin-tight space outfit. Excellent, our rock jock thinks, but it seems she kills with the slightest touch. For connoisseurs of truly bad movies. **60m/B VHS.** Robert Clarke, Kenne Duncan, Marilyn Harvey, Jeanne Tatum, Shirley Kilpatrick, Ewing Miles Brown; ***D:*** Ronnie Ashcroft. *SNC, MRV, CNM*

The Astro-Zombies *Woof!* **1967** A contender as one of the worst movies of all time. Carradine plays a mad scientist creating zombies who eat people's guts. Cult favorite Satana stars. Co-written and co-produced by Rogers of "M*A*S*H" fame. **83m/C VHS, Beta.** Tura Satana, Wendell Corey, John Carradine, Tom Pace, Joan Patrick, Rafael Campos; ***D:*** Ted V. Mikels; ***W:*** Ted V. Mikels, Wayne Rogers. *NO*

Asylum ☆☆½ *House of Crazies* **1972 (PG)** Four strange and chilling stories weave together in this film. A murderer's victim seeks retribution. A tailor seems to be collecting his bills. A man who makes voodoo dolls...only to become one later on. A woman plagued by a double. A doctor visiting the asylum tells each tale. Horrifying and grotesque, not as humorless as American horror films. **100m/C VHS, Beta, LV.** *GB* Peter Cushing, Herbert Lom, Britt Ekland, Barbara Parkins, Patrick Magee, Barry Morse; ***D:*** Roy Ward Baker. *PSM, MED*

Asylum of Satan ☆ **1972** A beautiful concert pianist is savagely tortured by a madman in the Asylum of Satan. Filmed on location in Louisville, Kentucky. **87m/C VHS, Beta.** Charles Kissinger, Carla Borelli, Nick Jolly, Sherry Steiner; ***D:*** William Girdler; ***W:*** William Girdler. *VCI*

At Close Range ☆☆☆ **1986 (R)** Based on the true story of Bruce Johnston Sr. and Jr. in Brandywine River Valley, Pennsylvania. Father, Walken, tempts his teen-aged son, Penn, into pursuing criminal activities with talk of excitement and high living. Penn soon learns that his father is extremely dangerous and a bit unstable, but he's still fascinated by his wealth and power. Sometimes overbearing and depressing, but good acting and fancy camera work. A young cast of stars includes Masterson as the girl Penn tries to impress. Features Madonna's "Live to Tell." **115m/C VHS, Beta, LV.** Sean Penn, Christopher Walken, Christopher Penn, Mary Stuart Masterson, Crispin Glover, Kiefer Sutherland, Candy Clark, Tracey Walter, Millie Perkins, Alan Autry, David Strathairn, Eileen Ryan; ***D:*** James Foley; ***W:*** Nicholas Kazan; ***C:*** Juan Ruiz-Anchia; ***M:*** Patrick Leonard. *VES, LIV*

At First Sight ☆½ *Two Guys Talkin' About Girls* **1995 (R)** Yakky pedestrian comedy about schleppy Lenny (Silverman) and his best friend, macho Joey (Cortese), trying to help each other out with their romantic crises. Lenny meets cute when he picks up Rhonda (Smith) at the planetarium while Joey beds a string of girls, all of whom are named Cindy, in an effort to get over the first Cindy who broke his heart. It's been done before—and better. **90m/C VHS.** Jonathan Silverman, Dan Cortese, Allison Smith, Monte Markham, Kathleen Freeman; ***D:*** Steven Pearl; ***W:*** Ken Copel; ***C:*** Glenn Kershaw; ***M:*** Richard Gibbs. *VMK*

At Gunpoint ☆☆ *Gunpoint* **1955** A store owner becomes the town hero when, by accident, he shoots and kills a bank robber. **81m/C VHS, Beta.** Fred MacMurray, Dorothy Malone, John Qualen, Walter Brennan; ***D:*** Alfred Werker; ***C:*** Ellsworth Fredericks. *REP, HHE*

At Gunpoint ☆½ **1990** A no-account bank robber spends his six year stint in the slammer plotting his revenge. Having gone thoroughly stircrazy, the vengeful criminal stalks the lawman who put him away, like so many vengeful criminals before him. Run of the mill addition to big list of bad-guy-hunting-for-revenge flicks. **90m/C VHS.** Frank Kanig, Tain Bodkin, Scott Claflin; ***D:*** Steven Harris; ***W:*** Steven Harris. *CAF*

At Home with the Webbers ꝏꝏ **1994** **(R)** Gerald, Emma, Johnny, and Miranda Webber win a contest to star in a cable TV series about their lives. What they don't expect is that the series will become a hit or that all the family idosyncrasies will be exaggerated by stardom (the manipulative TV producer doesn't help). Over-the-top comedy requires tolerance but does have some amusing performances. **109m/C VHS, LV.** Jeffrey Tambor, Rita Taggart, Jennifer Tilly, David Arquette, Robby Benson, Brian Bloom, Caroline Goodall; ***D:*** Brad Marlowe; ***W:*** Brad Marlowe. *LIV*

At Midnight, I'll Take Your Soul ꝏ **1963** South American import about an evil gravedigger named Coffin Joe (Marins), who wanders the streets of his hometown in order to meet a desirable woman. His mission is to sire a son to continue his legacy. A study in psycho-sexual horror, this makes "Apocalypse Now" look like a beach party. In Spanish with English subtitles. **?m/B VHS.** *BR* Jose Mojica Marins; ***D:*** Jose Mojica Marins. *SMW, FCT, TPV*

At Play in the Fields of the Lord ꝏꝏꝏ **1991 (R)** A thoughtful epic that never quite lives up to its own self-importance—or length. Two yankee missionary couples try to evangelize a fearsome tribe of Brazilian rain-forest dwellers. One of the Christian families suffers a crisis of faith that's well-acted but not as powerful as a co-plot regarding a modern American Indian (Berenger) who joins the jungle natives with calamitous results. Based on the novel by Peter Matthiessen. **186m/C VHS, Beta, LV.** Tom Berenger, Aidan Quinn, Kathy Bates, John Lithgow, Daryl Hannah, Tom Waits, Stenio Garcia, Nelson Xavier, Jose Dumont, Niilo Kivirinta; ***D:*** Hector Babenco; ***W:*** Hector Babenco, Jean-Claude Carriere; ***M:*** Zbigniew Preisner. *MCA*

At Sword's Point ꝏꝏ *Sons of the Musketeers* **1951** Adventure tale based on Alexandre Dumas' "The Three Musketeers," wherein the sons of the musketeers vie to save their queen from the evil plots of Duke Douglas. **81m/C VHS, Beta, LV.** Cornel Wilde, Maureen O'Hara, Robert Douglas, Dan O'Herlihy, Alan Hale Jr., Blanche Yurka; ***D:*** Lewis Allen. *MED, TTC, FCT*

At the Circus ꝏꝏ½ *The Marx Brothers at the Circus* **1939** Marx Brothers invade the circus to save it from bankruptcy and cause their usual comic insanity, though they've done it better before. Beginning of the end for the Marxes, a step down in quality from their classic work, though frequently darn funny. ♫Lydia the Tattooed Lady; Step Up and Take a Bow; Two Blind Loves; Blue Moon. **87m/B VHS, Beta, LV.** Groucho Marx, Chico Marx, Harpo Marx, Margaret Dumont, Kenny L. Baker, Florence Rice, Eve Arden, Nat Pendleton, Fritz Feld; ***D:*** Edward Buzzell. *MGM*

At the Earth's Core ꝏꝏ **1976 (PG)** A Victorian scientist invents a giant burrowing machine, which he and his crew use to dig deeply into the Earth. To their surprise, they discover a lost world of subhuman creatures and prehistoric monsters. Based on Edgar Rice Burrough's novels. **90m/C VHS, Beta.** *GB* Doug McClure, Peter Cushing, Caroline Munro, Cy Grant, Godfrey James, Keith Barron; ***D:*** Kevin Connor. *WAR, OM*

At War with the Army ꝏꝏ **1950** Serviceable comedy from Martin and Lewis in their first starring appearance, as the recruits get mixed up in all kinds of wild situations at their army base. Based on the play by James Allardice. **93m/B VHS, Beta.** Dean Martin, Jerry Lewis, Polly Bergen, Mike Kellin; ***D:*** Hal Walker. *NOS, MRV, CAB*

Atalia ꝏꝏ **1985** Relates the love between Atalia, a war widow, and the younger man she loves. The problem stems from the fact that she lives in a Kibbutz, and the lifestyle contradicts sharply from that of her beliefs in love, forcing her to eventually make a momentous decision. **90m/C VHS.** Michal Bat-Adam, Yftach Katzur, Dan Toren; ***D:*** Akiva Tevet. *ERG*

Athena ꝏꝏ½ **1954** Two sisters (Powell and Reynolds) from an eccentric, health-faddist family fall in love with their opposites. Purdom is the stuffy Boston lawyer who goes off with Powell and Reynolds entices a TV crooner (Damone). Routine romance with routine songs. Reeves, who would become a star as a movie muscleman, appears in a brief role. ♫Love Can Change the Stars; The Girl Next Door; Imagine; Venezia; Chacun le Sait; I Never Felt Better; Vocalize. **96m/C VHS.** Jane Powell, Debbie Reynolds, Edmund Purdom, Vic Damone, Louis Calhern, Evelyn Varden, Linda Christian, Virginia Gibson, Nancy Kilgas, Dolores Starr, Jane Fischer, Cecile Rogers, Steve Reeves; ***D:*** Richard Thorpe; ***W:*** William Ludwig, Leonard Spigelgass; ***M:*** Hugh Martin, Ralph Blane. *MGM*

Atlantic City ꝏꝏꝏ½ *Atlantic City U.S.A* **1981** **(R)** A small-time, aging Mafia hood falls in love with a young clam bar waitress, and they share the spoils of a big score against the backdrop of Atlantic City. Wonderful character study that becomes something more, a piercing declaration about a city's transformation and the effect on the people who live there. Lancaster, in a sterling performance, personifies the city, both of them fading with time. **104m/C VHS, Beta, LV.** *FR CA* Burt Lancaster, Susan Sarandon, Kate Reid, Michel Piccoli, Hollis McLaren; ***D:*** Louis Malle. British Academy Awards '81: Best Actor (Lancaster), Best Director (Malle); Los Angeles Film Critics Association Awards '81: Best Actor (Lancaster), Best Film, Best Screenplay; New York Film Critics Awards '81: Best Actor (Lancaster), Best Screenplay; National Society of Film Critics Awards '81: Best Actor (Lancaster), Best Director (Malle), Best Film, Best Screenplay; Nominations: Academy Awards '81: Best Actor (Lancaster), Best Actress (Sarandon), Best Director (Malle), Best Original Screenplay, Best Picture. *PAR*

Atlantis, the Lost Continent ꝏ **1961** If anything could sink the fabled lost continent of Atlantis it's this cheap fantasy flick. A greek sailor saves a princess and takes her back to her Atlantis home where he's promptly enslaved by the island's evil ruler. But this hero won't put up with any nonsense so he leads his fellow slaves in a revolt and gains his freedom before sinking both evil ruler and island (using atomic power no less!). **90m/C VHS.** Anthony Hall, Joyce Taylor, John Dall, Bill Smith, Edward Platt, Frank De Kova; ***D:*** George Pal. *MGM, FCT*

Atlas ꝏ **1960** The mighty Atlas takes on massive armies, one of which includes director Corman, in a bid to win the hand of a princess. About as cheap as they come, although it is one of the few Sword & Sandal epics that isn't dubbed. **84m/C VHS.** Michael Forest, Frank Wolff, Barboura Morris, Walter Maslow; ***D:*** Roger Corman; ***W:*** Charles B. Griffith. *DVT, SNC, HEG*

Atlas in the Land of the Cyclops *Woof! Atlas Against the Cyclops; Maciste Nella Terra dei Ciclopi* **1961** Atlas takes on a hideous one-eyed monster to save a baby from an evil queen. Not a divorce custody drama. **100m/C VHS.** *IT* Mitchell Gordon, Chelo Alonso, Vira Silenti; ***D:*** Antonio Leonuiola. *SNC*

Atom Age Vampire *Woof!* **1961** Mad scientist doing research on Japanese nuclear bomb victims falls in love with a woman disfigured in an auto crash. To remove her scars, he treats her with a formula derived from the glands of freshly killed women. English dubbed. Not among the best of its kind (a low-rent district if ever there was one), but entertaining in a mischievous, boy-is-this-a-stupid-film sort of way. **71m/B VHS, Beta.** *IT* Alberto Lupo, Susanne Loret, Sergio Fantoni; ***D:*** Albert Magnoli. *SNC, NOS, VYY*

Atomic Attack ꝏ **1950** Nuclear bomb is dropped on New York City and a family living 50 miles away must escape. Gentlemen, start your engines. **50m/B VHS.** Walter Matthau. *IHF*

The Atomic Brain *Woof! Monstrosity* **1964** An old woman hires a doctor to transplant her brain into the body of a beautiful young girl. Of the three girls who are abducted, two become homicidal zombies and the third starts to act catty when she is given a feline brain. A must-see for bad-brain movie fans. **72m/B VHS.** Frank Gerstle, Erika Peters, Judy Bamber, Marjorie Eaton, Frank Fowler, Margie Fisco; ***D:*** Joseph Mascelli. *NOS, SNC*

The Atomic Cafe ꝏꝏꝏ **1982** A chillingly humorous compilation of newsreels and government films of the 1940's and 1950's that show America's preoccupation with the A-Bomb. Some sequences are in black and white. Includes the infamous training film "Duck and Cover," which tells us what to do in the event of an actual bombing. **92m/C VHS, Beta.** ***D:*** Kevin Rafferty. *NO*

The Atomic City ꝏꝏ½ **1952** Barry plays a nuclear physicist at Los Alamos whose son is kidnapped by terrorists who want his bomb-making formulas. The bad guys hide out in the nearby mountains which at least makes for some pleasant scenery in this average thriller. **84m/B VHS.** Gene Barry, Lee Aaker, Michael Moore, Lydia Clarke, Nancy Gates, Milburn Stone; ***D:*** Jerry Hopper. Nominations: Academy Awards '52: Best Story & Screenplay. *PAR*

The Atomic Kid ꝏ½ **1954** A man survives an atomic blast because of a peanut butter sandwich he was eating. As a result, he himself becomes radioactive and discovers that he has acquired some strange new powers which get him into what pass for hilarious predicaments. **86m/B VHS.** Mickey Rooney, Robert Strauss, Elaine Davis, Bill Goodwin; ***D:*** Leslie Martinson; ***W:*** Blake Edwards; ***M:*** Van Alexander. *REP*

The Atomic Man ꝏ½ *Timeslip* **1956** Owing to radioactive experimentation, a scientist exists for a short time in the future. Once there, both good and evil forces want to use him for their own purposes. **78m/B VHS.** *GB* Gene Nelson, Faith Domergue, Joseph Tomelty, Peter Arne; ***D:*** Ken Hughes. *NOS, SNC*

Atomic Submarine ꝏꝏ **1959** Futuristic sci fi plots government agents against alien invaders. The battle, however, takes place in the ocean beneath the Arctic and is headed by an atomic-powered submarine clashing with a special alien underwater saucer. We all live on the atomic submarine: fun for devotees. **80m/C VHS, Beta.** Arthur Franz, Dick Foran, Bob Steele, Brett Halsey, Joi Lansing, Tom Conway, Paul Dubov; ***D:*** Spencer Gordon Bennet; ***W:*** Orville H. Hampton; ***C:*** Gilbert Warrenton. *SNC*

The Atonement of Gosta Berling ꝏꝏꝏ *Gosta Berling's Saga; The Legend of Gosta Berling; The Story of Gosta Berling; The Saga of Gosta Berling* **1924** A priest, forced to leave the priesthood because of his drinking, falls in love with a young married woman. Garbo shines in the first role which brought her critical acclaim; Hanson's performance also makes this a memorable drama. Adapted from the novel by Selma Lagerlof. **91m/B VHS.** *SW* Lars Hanson, Greta Garbo, Ellen Cederstrom, Mona Martenson, Jenny Hasselquist, Gerda Lundequist; ***D:*** Mauritz Stiller. *VYY, MRV, DVT*

Ator the Fighting Eagle *Woof!* **1983 (PG)** Styled after "Conan The Barbarian" this mythical action fantasy stars O'Keeffe as Ator, son of Thorn. Ator must put an end to the tragic Dynasty of the Spiders, thereby fulfilling the legend of his family at the expense of the viewer. Goofy low-budget sword and sandal stuff. Followed by "The Blade Master." **98m/C VHS, Beta.** *IT* Miles O'Keeffe, Sabrina Siani, Ritza Brown, Edmund Purdom, Laura Gemser; ***D:*** David Hills. *NO*

Attack Force Z ꝏꝏ **1984** An elite corps of Australian military is Force Z. Volunteers are chosen for a dangerous mission: find the plane that crashed somewhere in the South Pacific and rescue the defecting Japanese government official on board, all before the end of WWII and the feature. Talented cast is effectively directed in low-key adventure featuring young Gibson. **84m/C VHS, Beta.** *AU* Sam Neill, Chris Haywood, Mel Gibson, John Phillip Law, John Waters; ***D:*** Tim Burstall. *MCG, MTX*

Attack of the Beast Creatures *Woof!* **1985** The survivors of a wrecked ocean liner are stranded on a desert island overrun by savage creatures. This makes them anxious. **82m/C VHS, Beta.** Robert Nolfi, Robert Langyel, Julia Rust, Lisa Pak; ***D:*** Michael Stanley. *NO*

Attack of the 50 Foot Woman ½ **1958** A beautiful, abused housewife has a frightening encounter with a giant alien, causing her to grow to an enormous height. Then she goes looking for hubby. Perhaps the all-time classic '50s sci fi, a truly fun movie highlighted by the sexy, 50-foot Hayes in a giant bikini. Has intriguing psychological depth and social commentary done in a suitably cheezy manner. Also available with "House on Haunted Hill" on laser disc. Box B **72m/B VHS, Beta, LV.** Allison Hayes, William Hudson, Roy Gordon; ***D:*** Nathan (Hertz) Juran. *FOX, FCT*

Attack of the 50 Ft. Woman ½ **1993** Campy remake of the 1958 sci-fi cult classic features the statuesque Hannah in the title role. Nancy's a put-upon hausfrau with zero self-esteem thanks to her domineering father (Windom) and loutish hubby (Baldwin). They should have been sweet to her because after an encounter with a flying saucer Nancy starts to grow...and grow...and grow. And then she decides to get some revenge. Made for television. **90m/C VHS, LV.** Daryl Hannah, Daniel Baldwin, William Windom, Frances Fisher, Cristi Conaway, Paul Benedict, Lewis Arquette, Xander Berkeley, Hamilton Camp, Richard Edson, Victoria Haas, O'Neal Compton; ***D:*** Christopher Guest; ***W:*** Joseph Dougherty; ***M:*** Nicholas Pike. *HBO*

Attack of the Giant Leeches *The Giant Leeches; She Demons of the Swamp* **1959** Cheapo Corman fare about giant leeches in a murky swamp who suddenly decide to make human flesh their new food supply. Perturbed inn keeper plays along by forcing his wife and lover into the murk. Leeches frolic. Sometimes tedious, sometimes chilling, always low budget and slimy. Although the special effects aren't top notch, this might be a fine choice for a late night scare/laugh. **62m/B VHS.** Ken Clark, Yvette Vickers, Gene Roth, Bruno Ve Sota, Michael Emmet; ***D:*** Bernard L. Kowalski; ***W:*** Leo Gordon; ***C:*** John M. Nickolaus Jr. *VYY, SNC, NOS*

Attack of the Killer Refrigerator *Woof!* **1990** Chiller featuring a group of sleazy college students having a wild party. In the process, they abuse a hapless refrigerator. Fed up, the vengeful appliance goes on a rampage of murder and destruction. Certain to make you view kitchen appliances in a new light. Planned sequels in the newfound kitchen-utility horror genre include "Refrigerator II: Brutally Defrosted" and "Bloody, Bloody Coffee Maker." **?m/C VHS.** *BFA*

Attack of the Killer Tomatoes *Woof!* **1977 (PG)** Candidate for worst film ever made, deliberate category. Horror spoof that defined "low budget" stars several thousand ordinary tomatoes that suddenly turn savage and begin attacking people. No sci-fi cliche remains untouched in this dumb parody. A few musical numbers are performed in lieu of an actual plot. Followed by "Return of the Killer Tomatoes." Originally released at 87 minutes. **100m/C VHS.** George Wilson, Jack Riley, Rock Peace, Eric Christmas; ***D:*** John DeBello; ***W:*** John DeBello. *TOU*

Attack of the Mayan Mummy *Woof!* **1963** A greedy doctor gets his patient to channel her former self so that she can show him where to find an ancient tomb that is filled with treasure. Good idea. **77m/B VHS.** *MX* Richard Webb, Nina Knight, Norman Burton, Steve Conte; ***D:*** Jerry Warren. *NOS, LOO, SNC*

Attack of the Mushroom People *Matango; Fungus of Terror; Curse of the Mushroom People* **1963** Secluded island is the site where people eating mysterious mushrooms have been turning into oversized, killer 'shrooms' themselves. Trouble is, the only witness to this madness has gone insane. Will anyone believe him before it's too late? **70m/B VHS.** *JP* Akira Kubo, Kenji Sahara, Yoshio Tsuchiya, Hiroshi Koizumi, Kumi Mizuno, Miki Yashiro; ***D:*** Inoshiro Honda. *SMW*

Attack of the Robots ½ *Cartes sur Table* **1966** Silly spy spoof about powerful government officials who are being killed off by a mad scientist's robots. Interpol agent Lemmy Caution comes to the rescue. **88m/B VHS, Beta.** *FR SP* Eddie Constantine, Fernando Rey; ***D:*** Jess (Jesus) Franco; ***W:*** Jean-Claude Carriere. *VYY*

Attack of the 60-Foot Centerfold ½ **1995 (R)** Angel Grace wants to be Centerfold of the Year so badly that she gets a doctor to enhance her endowments even more through a mystery formula. Only there's a little complication. Cheesy, with pretty women and no discernable acting (and a spoof of that '58 gem "Attack of the 50 Ft. Woman"). **83m/C VHS.** J.J. North, Tammy Parks, John Lazar; ***Cameos:*** Russ Tamblyn, Michelle (McClellan) Bauer; ***D:*** Fred Olen Ray. *NHO*

Attack of the Swamp Creature *Woof!* **1975** A deranged scientist transforms himself into a swamp critter and terrorizes a small town. **96m/C VHS, Beta.** Frank Crowell, David Robertson; ***D:*** Arnold Stevens. *LIV*

Attack Squadron ½ *Kamakazi* **197?** Story of Japan's suicidal WWII pilots. **105m/C VHS, Beta.** *JP* *NO*

The Attic ½ **1980 (R)** Psycho-drama about an overbearing invalid father and his insecure and unmarried daughter. The girl learns to escape her unhappy life by hiding in the attic. Not horrifying, but a clear analytical look into the game of control. **92m/C VHS, Beta.** Carrie Snodgress, Ray Milland, Rosemary Murphy, Ruth Cox, Francis Bay, Marjorie Eaton; ***D:*** George Edwards. *FOX*

The Attic: The Hiding of Anne Frank ½ **1988** Steenburgen is wonderful in the true story of Miep Gies, the Dutch woman who hid Otto Frank, her employer, and his family from the Nazis. Unusual because it is told from Gies' perspective, rather than from the more familiar Anne Frank story. Based on Gies' book, "Anne Frank Remembered." Made for television. **95m/C VHS, LV.** Mary Steenburgen, Paul Scofield, Huub Stapel, Eleanor Bron, Miriam Karlin, Lisa Jacobs, Ronald Pickup; ***D:*** John Erman; ***W:*** William Hanley; ***M:*** Richard Rodney Bennett. *CAF*

Attica **1980** Tense made for television depiction of the infamous Attica prison takeover in 1971 and the subsequent bloodbath as state troops were called in. Although edited due to the searing commentary by Nelson Rockefeller, it remains powerful and thought-provoking. Adapted from the Tom Wicker bestseller "A Time to Die." **97m/C VHS, Beta.** George Grizzard, Charles Durning, Anthony Zerbe, Roger E. Mosley; ***D:*** Marvin J. Chomsky. *SUE, NLC*

Au Revoir Les Enfants *Goodbye, Children* **1987 (PG)** During the Nazi occupation of France in the 1940s, the headmaster of a Catholic boarding school hides three Jewish boys among the other students by altering their names and identities. Two of the students, Julien (Manesse) and Jean (Fejto), form a friendship that ends tragically when Jean and the other boys are discovered and taken away by the Gestapo. Compelling and emotionally wrenching coming of age tale based on an incident from director Malle's childhood is considered to be his best film to date and quite possibly the best he will ever make. In French with English subtitles. Other 1987 movies with similar themes are "Hope and Glory" and "Empire of the Sun." **104m/C VHS, Beta, LV.** *FR* Gaspard Manesse, Raphael Fejto, Francine Racette, Stanislas Carre de Malberg, Philippe Morier-Genoud, Francois Berleand, Peter Fitz, Francois Negret, Irene Jacob; ***D:*** Louis Malle; ***W:*** Louis Malle; ***M:*** Franz Schubert, Camille Saint-Saens. British Academy Awards '88: Best Director (Malle); Cesar Awards '88: Best Art Direction/Set Decoration, Best Cinematography, Best Director (Malle), Best Film, Best Sound, Best Writing; Los Angeles Film Critics Association Awards '87: Best Foreign Film; Venice Film Festival '87: Best Film; Nominations: Academy Awards '87: Best Foreign Language Film, Best Original Screenplay. *INJ, ORI, FCT*

Audrey Rose **1977 (PG)** Parents of a young girl are terrified when their darling daughter is having dreadful dreams. Mysterious friend Hopkins cements their fears when he declares that his dead daughter has been reincarnated in their child. The nightmares continue suggesting that none other than Lucifer could be at work. Good cast is hampered by slow-moving take-off on "The Exorcist" with a weak staged ending. Adapted by DeFelitta from his novel. **113m/C VHS, Beta.** Marsha Mason, Anthony Hopkins, John Beck, John Hillerman; ***D:*** Robert Wise; ***W:*** Frank de Felitta. *MGM*

August ½ **1995 (PG)** Yet another version of Chekov's "Uncle Vanya," this time transported to 1890s Wales. Hopkins (who makes his directorial debut and composed the score) stars as Ieuan Davies, a bitter drinker who manages the estate of brother-in-law Alexander Blathwaite (Phillips). Blathwaite arrives for his annual summer stay with unhappy, young second wife Helen (Burton), who's the object of desire for both Ieuan and the local doctor, Michael Lloyd (Grainger). It's a perfectedly adequate rendition but offers little new except a change of scenery. **93m/C VHS.** *GB* Anthony Hopkins, Kate Burton, Leslie Phillips, Gawn Grainger, Rhian Morgan, Hugh Lloyd, Rhoda Lewis, Menna Tussler; ***D:*** Anthony Hopkins; ***W:*** Julian Mitchell; ***C:*** Robin Vidgeon; ***M:*** Anthony Hopkins. *NYR*

Augustin **1995** Very short comedy about aspiring actor Augustin (Sibertin-Blanc), who may just get his break when he hears about a part for a room-service waiter and prepares himself rigorously by actually getting a job in a Paris hotel. Pathetically earnest and dignified, at the actual audition he bewilders actor Lhermitte, when instead of just reading the scene, Augustin proceeds to act it out in detail. Very slight but charming thanks to a deadpan performance by Sibertin-Blanc (who's also director Fontaine's brother). French with subtitles. **61m/C VHS.** *FR* Jean-Chretien Sibertin-Blanc, Thierry Lhermitte; ***D:*** Anne Fontaine; ***W:*** Anne Fontaine; ***C:*** Jean-Marie Dreujou. *KIV*

Augustine of Hippo *Agostino di Ippona* **1972** One of Rossellini's later historical epics, depicting the last years of St. Augustine and how they exemplify the growing conflicts between Church and State, Christian ethic and societal necessity. In Italian with subtitles. **120m/C VHS, Beta.** *IT* ***D:*** Roberto Rossellini. *FCT*

Auntie *Woof!* **1980 (R)** Entertainer must dress and act like his madam aunt who has died, in order to fool her former employees in a house of prostitution. **85m/C VHS, Beta.** *NO*

Auntie Lee's Meat Pies ½ **1992 (R)** Auntie Lee's meat pie business is booming thanks to her five beautiful nieces. They help keep their aunt supplied with the secret ingredient—gorgeous young men! Four Playboy Playmates are featured in this cannibalistic horror comedy. **100m/C VHS, LV.** Karen Black, Noriyuki "Pat" Morita, Pat Paulsen, Huntz Hall, Michael Berryman, David Parry, Stephen Quadros; ***D:*** Joseph F. Robertson. *COL*

Auntie Mame **1958** A young boy is brought up by his only surviving relative—flamboyant and eccentric Auntie Mame. Mame is positive that "life is a banquet and most poor suckers are starving to death." Based on the Patrick Dennis novel about his life with "Auntie Mame." Part of the "A Night at the Movies" series, this tape simulates a 1958 movie evening, with a Road Runner cartoon, "Hook, Line and Stinker," a newsreel and coming attractions for "No Time for Sergeants" and "Chase a Crooked Shadow." **161m/C VHS, Beta, LV.** Rosalind Russell, Patric Knowles, Roger Smith, Peggy Cass, Forrest Tucker, Coral Browne; ***D:*** Morton DaCosta; ***W:*** Betty Comden, Adolph Green; ***C:*** Harry Stradling. Golden Globe Awards '59: Best Actress—Musical/Comedy (Russell); Nominations: Academy Awards '58: Best Actress (Russell), Best Art Direction/Set Decoration, Best Color Cinematography, Best Film Editing, Best Picture, Best Supporting Actress (Cass). *WAR*

The Aurora Encounter **1985 (PG)** Aliens surreptitiously infiltrate a small town in 1897, and spread benevolence everywhere. Family fare. **90m/C VHS, Beta.** Jack Elam, Peter Brown, Carol Bagdasarian, Dottie West, George "Spanky" McFarland; ***D:*** Jim McCullough. *NWV, VTR, HHE*

Author! Author! ½ **1982 (PG)** Sweet, likable comedy about playwright Pacino who is about to taste success with his first big hit. Suddenly his wife walks out, leaving him to care for her four children and his own son. His views shift as he begins to worry about, among other things, who will watch the obnoxious kids on opening night. **100m/C VHS, Beta.** Al Pacino, Tuesday Weld, Dyan Cannon, Alan King, Andre Gregory; ***D:*** Arthur Hiller; ***W:*** Israel Horovitz; ***M:*** Dave Grusin. *FOX*

Autobiography of a Princess 🦴🦴 **1975** A brief character study shot by Merchant-Ivory in six days. An East Indian princess, living in self-enforced exile in London, invites her father's former tutor to tea. They watch old movie footage of royal India together and dream of a happier past. **59m/C VHS, LV.** James Mason, Madhur Jaffrey; ***D:*** James Ivory; ***W:*** Ruth Prawer Jhabvala. *FCT, INJ, LUM*

The Autobiography of Miss Jane Pittman 🦴🦴🦴½ **1974** The history of blacks in the South is seen through the eyes of a 110-year-old former slave. From the Civil War through the Civil Rights movement, Miss Pittman relates every piece of black history, allowing the viewer to experience the injustices. Tyson is spectacular in moving, highly acclaimed television drama. Received nine Emmy awards; adapted by Tracy Keenan Wynn from the novel by Ernest J. Gaines. **110m/C VHS, Beta.** Cicely Tyson, Odetta, Joseph Tremice, Richard Dysart, Michael Murphy, Katherine Helmond; ***D:*** John Korty. *PSM*

Automatic 🦴½ **1994 (R)** Renegade RobGen Industries android Gruner saves Ashbrook from the loathsome sexual advances of the boss but kills the scum in the process. So the duo are targeted for death by company head Glover with killers, lead by Kober, sent to do the mopping up. **90m/C VHS, LV.** Olivier Gruner, Daphne Ashbrook, John Glover, Jeff Kober, Dennis Lipscomb; ***D:*** John Murlowski; ***W:*** Susan Lambert, Patrick Highsmith. *REP*

Autopsy 🦴½ **1978 (R)** Rash of unexplainable, spontaneous suicides cause a college student to become emotionally upset. **89m/C VHS, Beta.** *IT* Mimsy Farmer, Barry Primus, Angela Goodwin, Ray Lovelock; ***D:*** Armando Crispino; ***M:*** Ennio Morricone. *MPI, PSM*

Autopsy 🦴 **197?** A young gold-digger and a millionaire marry, and then cheat on each other, provoking blackmail and murder. **90m/C VHS, Beta.** Fernando Rey, Gloria Grahame, Christian Hay. *NO*

Autopsy 🦴½ **1986** A war correspondent in Vietnam discovers the gruesome secret behind the doctors' autopsy methods at a military hospital. **90m/C VHS, Beta.** *NO*

Autopsy of a Ghost 🦴½ **1967** Comedy/horror film stars Rathbone as a ghost and Mitchell as a mad scientist. Notable as Rathbone's last screen appearance. In Spanish with no subtitles. **?m/C VHS.** *SP* Basil Rathbone, John Carradine, Cameron Mitchell. *SNC*

An Autumn Afternoon 🦴🦴🦴½ **1962** Ozu's final film is a beautiful expression of his talent. In postwar Tokyo, an aging widower loses his only daughter to marriage and begins a life of loneliness. A heart-wrenching tale of relationships and loss. In Japanese with English subtitles. **112m/C VHS.** *JP* Chishu Ryu, Shima Iwashita, Shin-Ichiro Mikami, Mariko Okada, Keiji Sada; ***D:*** Yasujiro Ozu; ***W:*** Yasujiro Ozu. *NYF, INJ*

Autumn Born 🦴½ **1979 (R)** Young heiress is abducted by her guardian and imprisoned while she's taught to obey his will. Ill-fated ex-Playmate Dorothy Stratton's first film. **76m/C VHS, Beta.** Dorothy Stratten. *NO*

Autumn Leaves 🦴🦴½ **1956** Crawford plays a middle-aged typist grasping at her last chance for love. She marries a younger man who's been romancing her, then finds him more and more unstable and violent. Weak story material that could turn melodramatic and tawdry, but doesn't because of Crawford's strength. **108m/B VHS, Beta.** Cliff Robertson, Joan Crawford, Vera Miles, Lorne Greene; ***D:*** Robert Aldrich; ***W:*** Robert Blees; ***C:*** Charles B(ryant) Lang. Berlin International Film Festival '56: Best Director (Aldrich). *GKK*

Autumn Marathon 🦴🦴½ *Osenny Marafon* **1979** To say that this is one of the better Russian movies of the past three decades is sort of faint praise, given the state of Soviet cinema. Written by playwright Volodin, it's just another paint-by-number version of the philandering man who's really an OK Joe who loves his kids comedy. In Russian with English subtitles. **100m/C VHS.** *RU* Oleg Basilashvili, Natalia Gundareva, Marina Neyelova; ***D:*** Georgi Daniela; ***W:*** Alexander Volodin. *KIV, AUD*

Autumn Moon 🦴🦴 *Qiuyue* **1992** Young Japanese tourist (Nagase) travels to Hong Kong to enjoy some sexual fun but instead he befriends a 15-year-old girl (Wai), who's afraid of her family's impending emigration to Canada. Not much happens but the Hong Kong setting is eye-catching. English and Cantonese with subtitles. **108m/C VHS.** *HK* Masatoshi Nagase, Li Pui Wai; ***D:*** Clara Law. *ICA*

Autumn Sonata 🦴🦴🦴 **1978** Nordic family strife as famed concert pianist Bergman is reunited with a daughter she has not seen in years. Bergman's other daughter suffers from a degenerative nerve disease and had been institutionalized until her sister brought her home. Now the three women settle old scores, and balance the needs of their family. Excellent performance by Bergman in her last feature film. **97m/C VHS, Beta, LV.** *SW* Ingrid Bergman, Liv Ullmann, Halvar Bjork, Lena Nyman, Gunnar Bjornstrand; ***D:*** Ingmar Bergman; ***W:*** Ingmar Bergman; ***C:*** Sven Nykvist. Golden Globe Awards '79: Best Foreign Film; National Board of Review Awards '78: 5 Best Foreign Films of the Year, Best Actress (Bergman), Best Director (Bergman); National Society of Film Critics Awards '78: Best Actress (Bergman); Nominations: Academy Awards '78: Best Actress (Bergman), Best Original Screenplay. *FOX*

Avalanche 🦴½ **1978 (PG)** Disasterama as vacationers at a new winter ski resort find themselves at the mercy of a monster avalanche leaving a so-called path of terror and destruction in its wake. Talented cast is buried by weak material, producing a snowbound adventure yawn. **91m/C VHS, Beta.** Rock Hudson, Mia Farrow, Robert Forster, Rick Moses; ***D:*** Corey Allen; ***W:*** Corey Allen. *SUE*

Avalanche Express 🦴 **1979 (PG)** Marvin is a CIA agent who uses a defector (Shaw) to lure a scientist (Schell), specializing in biological warfare, aboard a European train. Marvin wants to eliminate Schell but all plans go awry when the snow begins to fall. Ineffective thriller. Director Robson's and actor Shaw's last film—much of Shaw's dialogue was dubbed due to his death before the film's soundtrack was completed. Based on a novel by Colin Forbes. **89m/C VHS.** Lee Marvin, Robert Shaw, Maximilian Schell, Linda Evans, Mike Connors, Joe Namath, Horst Buchholz, David Hess; ***D:*** Mark Robson; ***W:*** Abraham Polonsky; ***C:*** Jack Cardiff. *WAR*

Avalon 🦴🦴🦴 **1990 (PG)** Powerful but quiet portrait of the break-up of the family unit as seen from the perspective of a Russian family settled in Baltimore at the close of WWII. Initally, the family is unified in their goals, ideologies and social lives. Gradually, all of this disintegrates; members move to the suburbs and television replaces conversation at holiday gatherings. Levinson based his film on experiences within his own family of Russian Jewish immigrants. **126m/C VHS, Beta, LV, 8mm.** Armin Mueller-Stahl, Aidan Quinn, Elizabeth Perkins, Joan Plowright, Lou Jacobi, Leo Fuchs, Eve Gordon, Kevin Pollak, Israel Rubinek, Elijah Wood, Grant Gelt, Bernard Hiller; ***D:*** Barry Levinson; ***W:*** Barry Levinson; ***C:*** Allen Daviau; ***M:*** Randy Newman. Writers Guild of America '90: Best Original Screenplay; Nominations: Academy Awards '90: Best Cinematography, Best Costume Design, Best Original Screenplay, Best Original Score. *COL, FCT*

Avanti! 🦴🦴½ **1972 (R)** Stuffy businessman Wendell Armbruster (Lemmon) heads to Italy to claim his father's body when the old man dies while on vacation. Then he discovers dad has been visiting his mistress lo these many years. While trying to get through mountains of red tape, Wendell finds himself romancing the woman's daughter (Mills). Too long but still amusing. **144m/C VHS.** Jack Lemmon, Juliet Mills, Clive Revill, Edward Andrews, Gianfranco Barra, Franco Angrisano; ***D:*** Billy Wilder; ***W:*** I.A.L. Diamond, Billy Wilder. *MCA*

Ava's Magical Adventure 🦴🦴½ **1994 (PG)** Ten-year-old Eddie decides to take Ava on a little adventure. Too bad she's a 2-ton elephant he's stolen from the circus. Based on the Mark Twain story "The Stolen White Elephant." **97m/C VHS, LV.** Timothy Bottoms, Georg Stanford Brown, Patrick Dempsey, Priscilla Barnes, David Lander, Kaye Ballard, Remi Ryan; ***D:*** Patrick Dempsey, Rocky Parker; ***W:*** Susan D. Nimm; ***M:*** Mark Holden. *PSM*

The Avenger 🦴🦴½ **1960** The story of a criminal who cuts off the heads of people and mails them off makes for a shocker. Graphic violence will appeal to those who like a good mail-order gorefest and are not employed by the post office. **102m/B VHS.** *GE* Ingrid van Bergen, Heinz Drache, Ina Duscha, Mario Litto, Klaus Kinski; ***D:*** Karl Anton. *SNC*

The Avenger 🦴 *The Lost Glory of Troy* **1962** This time muscleman Reeves plays Aeneas and leads the Trojans in battle against the Greeks. It's supposedly an adaptation of "The Aeneid" by Virgil. **108m/C VHS.** *FR IT* Steve Reeves, Giacomo "Jack" Rossi-Stuart, Carla Marlier, Gianni "John" Garko, Liana Orfei; ***D:*** Giorgio Rivalta. *SNC, NOS, VYY*

Avenging Angel *Woof!* **1985 (R)** Law student Molly "Angel" Stewart is back on the streets to retaliate against the men who killed the policeman who saved her from a life of prostitution. Worthless sequel to 1984's "Angel," exploiting the original's exploitative intent. Followed listlessly by "Angel III: The Final Chapter." **94m/C VHS, Beta, LV.** Betsy Russell, Rory Calhoun, Susan Tyrrell, Ossie Davis, Barry Pearl, Ross Hagen, Karin Mani, Robert Tessier; ***D:*** Robert Vincent O'Neil; ***W:*** Joseph M. Cala; ***M:*** Paul Antonelli. *NWV, VTR*

The Avenging Angel 🦴🦴½ **1995** Unusual take on religion and western justice. Brigham Young (Heston) and his Mormon sect have established themselves in Utah—with the aid of some sharpshooting vigilantes, including Berenger. When an assassination attempt is made on Young's life, Berenger finds he's stumbled into an ever-widening church conspiracy that threatens to consume him. Based on the novel by Gary Stewart. **100m/C VHS.** Tom Berenger, Charlton Heston, James Coburn, Kevin Tighe, Jeffrey Jones, Tom Bower, Joanna Miles; ***D:*** Craig R. Baxley; ***W:*** Dennis Nemec. *TTC*

Avenging Conscience 🦴🦴 *Thou Shall Not Kill* **1914** An early eerie horror film, based on tales of Edgar Allan Poe. D.W. Griffith's first large-scale feature. Silent. **78m/B VHS, Beta.** Henry B. Walthall, Blanche Sweet; ***D:*** D.W. Griffith. *GPV, VYY, LSV*

Avenging Disco Godfather 🦴½ *Avenging Godfather; Disco Godfather* **1976 (R)** Moore parodies the "Godfather" and martial arts movies. **99m/C VHS, Beta.** Rudy Ray Moore, Lady Reed, Carol Speed, Jimmy Lynch; ***D:*** Rudy Ray Moore. *XVC*

Avenging Force 🦴🦴 **1986 (R)** Okay actioner about retired CIA agent Dudikoff returning to the force to help colleague James run for political office. A group of right-wing terrorists called "Pentangle" threatens James, so Dudikoff adds his name to their wanted list. Conflict leads to a forest manhunt where the avenging force does its avenging. **104m/C VHS, Beta, LV.** Michael Dudikoff, Steve James, John P. Ryan; ***D:*** Sam Firstenberg; ***W:*** Mercer Ellington, James Booth; ***M:*** George S. Clinton. *MED, VTR*

The Avenging Hand 🦴½ **1943** Leaden suspense story about a hotel filled with thieves all searching for stolen loot. **56m/B VHS.** Noah Beery Jr., Kathleen Kelly, Louis Borell, James Harcourt, Charles Oliver, Reginald Long; ***D:*** Victor Hanbury. *HCV*

The Average Woman 🦴🦴 **1924** Gritty journalist consults plain Jane for "Modern Woman" story and finds a major rewrite in order when he falls with a thud for Miss Jane. **52m/B VHS, Beta.** Pauline Garon, David Powell, Burr McIntosh, Harrison Ford, De Sacia Mooers; ***D:*** Christy Cabanne. *GPV, GVV*

The Aviator 🦴🦴 **1985 (PG)** Pilot Reeve, haunted by the memory of a fatal crash, tries to find a new line of work. Large sums of money persuade him to transport spoiled Arquette to Washington. When the biplane crashes in the mountain wilderness, the two fall in love between scavenging for food and fighting wild animals. From the director of "Man From Snowy River." **98m/C VHS, Beta.** Christopher Reeve, Rosanna Arquette, Jack Warden, Tyne Daly, Marcia Strassman, Sam Wanamaker, Scott Wilson; ***D:*** George Miller; ***W:*** Marc Norman. *MGM*

The Awakening ☠½ **1980 (R)** An archeologist discovers the tomb of a murderous queen, but upon opening the coffin, the mummy's spirit is transferred to his baby daughter, born at that instant. They call that bad luck. **101m/C VHS, Beta.** Charlton Heston, Susannah York, Stephanie Zimbalist; ***D:*** Mike Newell; ***W:*** Allan Scott, Chris Bryant; ***C:*** Jack Cardiff; ***M:*** Claude Bolling. *WAR*

Awakening of Candra *Woof!* **1981** Based on a real 1975 incident, a young couple honeymooning in the mountains is assaulted by a lunatic fisherman. The psycho kills the husband and rapes the girl, then he brainwashes poor Candra into thinking it was all an accident. Intense subject matter should be horrifying, but falls short of the mark in this television flop. **96m/C VHS, Beta.** Blanche Baker, Cliff DeYoung, Richard Jaeckel; ***D:*** Paul Wendkos. *GEM*

Awakenings ☠☠☠½ **1990 (PG-13)** Marshall's first dramatic effort is based on the true story of Dr. Oliver Sacks, from his book of the same title. It details his experimentation with the drug L-dopa which inspired the "awakening" of a number of catatonic patients, some of whom had been "sleeping" for as long as thirty years. Occasionally over-sentimental, but still providing a poignant look at both the patients—who find themselves confronted with lost opportunities and faded youth—and at Sacks, who must watch their exquisite suffering as they slip away. De Niro's performance as the youngest of the group is heart-rending, while Williams offers a subdued, moving performance as the doctor. **120m/C VHS, Beta, LV, 8mm.** Robin Williams, Robert De Niro, John Heard, Julie Kavner, Penelope Ann Miller, Max von Sydow, Anne Meara; ***D:*** Penny Marshall; ***W:*** Steven Zaillian; ***M:*** Randy Newman. National Board of Review Awards '90: Best Actor (De Niro), Best Actor (Williams); Nominations: Academy Awards '90: Best Actor (De Niro), Best Adapted Screenplay, Best Picture. *COL, FCT*

Awakenings of the Beast ☠ **1968** Documents the protracted sufferings of an LSD drug user who is beset with hallucinatory visions and is prone to fits of frenzied violence. In Spanish with English subtitles. **?m/C VHS.** *BR* Jose Mojica Marins; ***D:*** Jose Mojica Marins. *SMW, FCT*

Away All Boats ☠☠½ **1956** The true story of one Captain Hawks, who led a crew of misfits to victory in WWII Pacific aboard transport USS Belinda. Battle scenes are well done; look for early (and brief) appearance by young Clint Eastwood. **114m/B VHS, Beta.** Jeff Chandler, George Nader, Richard Boone, Julie Adams, Keith Andes, Lex Barker; ***D:*** Joseph Pevney. *MCA*

The Awful Dr. Orlof ☠ **1962** Set in a bygone era, Dr. Orlof (Vernon) is a retired prison physician who needs unblemished skin to remedy the horrible disfigurement of his daughter Melissa (Lorys), ravaged by fire. He abducts promising young women candidates with the help of his blind zombie henchman Morpho (Valle), who simply cannot be trusted with a scalpel. After several surgical mishaps, they kidnap the perfect specimen, a woman who bears an uncanny resemblance to Melissa. Unfortunately, she is engaged to suspicious police Inspector Tanner (San Martin). French version with English subtitles that includes more explicit gore is also available. **86m/B VHS.** Howard Vernon, Diana Lorys, Frank Wolff, Riccardo Valle, Conrado San Martin; ***D:*** Jess (Jesus) Franco; ***M:*** Jose Pagan, Antonio Ramirez Angel. *SMW, VSM, TPV*

The Awful Truth ☠☠☠☠ **1937** Classic screwball comedy. Young couple discards their marriage made in heaven and go their separate ways in search of happiness. Meticulously sabotaging each others' new relationships, they discover they really were made for each other. First on-screen pairing for Grant and Dunne: Grant is at his most charming with dead-on comic timing while Dunne is brilliant as his needling ex. The scene where Dunne poses as Grant's prodigal fan-dancing sister who pays a surprise cocktail-hour visit to the family of his stuffy, upper-class bride-to-be is among the most memorable screwball vignettes of all time. And don't miss the custody battle they have over the family dog (Asta of "The Thin Man" fame). Based on Arthur Richman's play. Preceded by 1925 and 1929 versions; remade in 1953 as "Let's Do it Again." **92m/B VHS, Beta, LV.** Irene Dunne, Cary Grant, Ralph Bellamy, Alexander D'Arcy, Cecil Cunningham, Molly Lamont, Esther Dale, Joyce Compton, Robert Allen, Robert Warwick, Mary Forbes; ***D:*** Leo McCarey; ***W:*** Vina Delmar. Academy Awards '37: Best Director (McCarey); Nominations: Academy Awards '37: Best Actress (Dunne), Best Film Editing, Best Picture, Best Screenplay, Best Supporting Actor (Bellamy). *MLB, BTV, COL*

An Awfully Big Adventure ☠☠ **1994 (R)** Coming-of-age saga set in postwar Liverpool around a provincial reperatory company. Stage-struck 16-year-old Stella (Cates) gets work as a company apprentice, immediately getting a crush on arch, callous theater manager Meredith Potter (a deliciously nasty Grant), who enjoys degrading everyone around him. The company's chance for success rests on a production of "Peter Pan," with visiting actor P.L. O'Hara (dashing Rickman), who immediately seduces Stella and has more than a few secrets of his own. Theatrically exaggerated; based on the novel by Beryl Bainbridge. **113m/C VHS, LV.** *GB* Georgina Cates, Hugh Grant, Alan Rickman, Peter Firth, Alun Armstrong, Prunella Scales, Rita Tushingham, Alan Cox, Edward Petherbridge, Nicola Pagett, Carol Drinkwater, Clive Merrison, Gerard McSorley; ***D:*** Mike Newell; ***W:*** Charles Wood; ***C:*** Dick Pope; ***M:*** Richard Hartley. *NLC*

Ay, Carmela! ☠☠☠ **1990** During the Spanish Civil War, two vaudevillians with strong anti-Franco views are captured by Franco forces and sentenced to execution. They are reprieved when a theater-loving Lieutenant offers to spare their lives if they will entertain the troops. Clever and entertaining farce, with poignant undertones. **105m/C VHS.** *SP IT* Carmen Maura, Andres Pajares, Gabino Diego, Maurizio De Razza, Miguel Rellan, Edward Zentara, Jose Sancho, Antonio Fuentes; ***D:*** Carlos Saura; ***W:*** Rafael Azcona. *HBO, INJ*

Baba ☠☠☠ *The Father* **1973** A poor boatman agrees to be the fall guy in a murder in exchange for the actual murderer supporting his family. But after 24 years in prison, the boatman finds all his sacrificing has been in vain. His daughter has become a prostitute and his son is working as one of the murderer's henchman. In Turkish with English subtitles. **95m/C VHS.** *TU* ***D:*** Yilmaz Guney. *FCT, HEG*

Babar: The Movie ☠☠½ **1988 (G)** The lovable Babar, king of the elephants, must devise a plan to outwit an angry hoard of attacking rhinos. Based on the characters of Jean and Laurent de Brunhoff. **75m/C VHS, Beta, LV, 8mm.** *CA FR* ***D:*** Alan Bunce; ***W:*** Alan Bunce, John deKlein; ***V:*** Gavin Magrath, Gordon Pinsent, Sarah Polley, Chris Wiggins, Elizabeth Hanna. *FHE, IME, WTA*

Babe! ☠☠☠½ **1975** A fine television movie about the life of one of America's most famous woman athletes, Babe Didrickson. Adapted by Joanna Lee from Didrickson's autobiography, "The Life I've Led." The movie was nominated for Outstanding Special of 1975-76 and Clark won an Emmy for her work. **120m/C VHS.** Susan Clark, Alex Karras, Slim Pickens, Jeanette Nolan, Ellen Geer, Ford Rainey; ***D:*** Buzz Kulik; ***M:*** Jerry Goldsmith. *NO*

The Babe ☠☠½ **1992 (PG)** Follows the life of legendary baseball player Babe Ruth, portrayed as a sloppy drunkard whose appetites for food, drink, and sex were as large as he was. Alvarado and McGillis do well as the Babe's first and second wives, but this is Goodman's show from start to finish. He's excellent as Ruth, and looks the part, but his fine performance can't make up for a lackluster script filled with holes. **115m/C VHS, LV.** John Goodman, Kelly McGillis, Trini Alvarado, Bruce Boxleitner, Peter Donat, J.C. Quinn, Richard Tyson, James Cromwell, Joe Ragno, Bernard Kates, Michael McGrady, Stephen Caffrey; ***D:*** Arthur Hiller; ***W:*** John Fusco; ***C:*** Haskell Wexler; ***M:*** Elmer Bernstein. *MCA*

Babe ☠☠☠½ *Babe, the Gallant Pig* **1995 (G)** Totally charming fable has intelligent piglet Babe being raised by matriarch sheepdog Fly, and learning the art of sheep herding along with his new canine brothers. Farmer Hoggett (Cromwell), Babe's owner by virtue of a winning raffle ticket, sees that he's more than just a ham, and enters them in the world sheepdog herding championship. Whimsy that never crosses the line into treacle. Four different special effects houses were used to make the barnyard animals talk and walk. Filmed on location in Australia; based on Dick King-Smith's book "The Sheep-Pig." **91m/C VHS, LV.** *AU* James Cromwell, Magna Szubanski; ***D:*** Chris Noonan; ***W:*** Chris Noonan, George Miller; ***C:*** Andrew Lesnie; ***M:*** Nigel Westlake; ***V:*** Christine Cavanaugh, Miriam Margolyes, Danny Mann, Hugo Weaving. Academy Awards '95: Best Visual Effects; Golden Globe Awards '96: Best Film—Musical/Comedy; National Society of Film Critics Awards '95: Best Film; Nominations: Academy Awards '95: Best Adapted Screenplay, Best Art Direction/Set Decoration, Best Director (Noonan), Best Film Editing, Best Picture, Best Supporting Actor (Cromwell); Writers Guild of America '95: Best Adapted Screenplay. *MCA*

Babe Ruth Story ☠☠ **1948** An overly sentimental biography about the famed baseball slugger. Bendix is miscast as the Bambino, but the actual film clips of the Babe are of interest. A movie to be watched during those infrequent bouts of sloppy baseball mysticism. **107m/B VHS, Beta.** William Bendix, Claire Trevor, Charles Bickford, William Frawley, Sam Levene, Gertrude Niesen; ***D:*** Roy Del Ruth. *FOX*

Babes in Arms ☠½ **1939** The children of several vaudeville performers team up to put on a show to raise money for their financially impoverished parents. Loosely adapted from the Rodgers and Hart Broadway musical of the same name; features some of their songs as well as new additions. ♫Babes in Arms; I Cried for You; Good Morning; You Are My Lucky Star; Broadway Rhythm; Where or When; Daddy Was a Minstrel Man; I'm Just Wild About Harry; God's Country. **91m/B VHS, Beta, LV.** Judy Garland, Mickey Rooney, Charles Winninger, Guy Kibbee, June Preisser; ***D:*** Busby Berkeley; ***M:*** George Bassman, Richard Rodgers, Lorenz Hart. Nominations: Academy Awards '39: Best Actor (Rooney), Best Score. *MGM*

Babes in Toyland ☠☠ **1961** A lavish Disney production of Victor Herbert's timeless operetta, with Toyland being menaced by the evil Barnaby and his Bogeymen. Yes, Annette had a life after Mickey Mouse and before the peanut butter commercials. Somewhat charming, although the roles of the lovers seem a stretch for both Funicello and Kirk. But the flick does sport an amusing turn by Wynn. **105m/C VHS, Beta.** Annette Funicello, Ray Bolger, Tommy Sands, Ed Wynn, Tommy Kirk; ***D:*** Jack Donohue; ***C:*** Edward Colman; ***M:*** George Bruns. Nominations: Academy Awards '61: Best Original Score. *DIS*

Babes in Toyland ☠½ **1986** Young girl must save Toyland from the clutches of the evil Barnaby and his monster minions. Bland TV remake of the classic doesn't approach the original. **96m/C VHS, LV.** Drew Barrymore, Noriyuki "Pat" Morita, Richard Mulligan, Eileen Brennan, Keanu Reeves, Jill Schoelen, Googy Gress; ***D:*** Clive Donner; ***M:*** Leslie Bricusse. *ORI*

Babes on Broadway ☠☠½ **1941** Mickey and Judy put on a show to raise money for a settlement house. Nearly the best of the Garland-Rooney series, with imaginative numbers staged by Berkeley. ♫Babes on Broadway; Anything Can Happen in New York; How About You?; Hoe Down; Chin Up! Cheerio! Carry On!; Mama Yo Quiero; F.D.R. Jones; Waiting for the Robert E. Lee. **118m/B VHS, Beta, LV.** Mickey Rooney, Judy Garland, Fay Bainter, Richard Quine, Virginia Weidler, Ray Macdonald, Busby Berkeley; ***D:*** Busby Berkeley; ***M:*** George Bassman. Nominations: Academy Awards '42: Best Song ("How About You?"). *MGM*

Babette's Feast ☠☠☠½ **1987** A simple, moving pageant-of-life fable. A group of religiously zealous villagers are taught love and forgiveness through a lavish banquet prepared by one of their housemaids, who turns out to be a world-class chef. Adapted from a tale by Isak Dinesen. In French and

Danish with English subtitles. **102m/C VHS, Beta, LV.** *DK FR* Stephane Audran, Bibi Andersson, Bodil Kjer, Birgitte Federspiel, Jean-Philippe LaFont, Ebbe Rode, Jarl Kulle; ***D:*** Gabriel Axel; ***W:*** Gabriel Axel. Academy Awards '87: Best Foreign Language Film; British Academy Awards '88: Best Foreign Film. *ORI, FCT, APD*

The Baby ☆☆ **1972 (PG)** Bizarre story of a social worker who resorts to swinging an ax to cut the apron strings of "baby," a retarded man-child, from his over-protective and insane (bad combination) mother and sisters. Low-budget production looks and feels like a low-budget production, but any movie featuring a grown man wandering about in diapers can't be all bad. **85m/C VHS, Beta.** Anjanette Comer, Ruth Roman, Marianna Hill, Suzanne Zenor, David Manzy, Michael Pataki; ***D:*** Ted Post. *NO*

The Baby and the Battleship ☆☆½ **1956** The old baby out of (on the?) water plot. While on liberty in Italy, a sailor, after a series of complications, becomes custodian of a baby and attempts to hide the tyke aboard his battleship (hence the title). More complications ensue. Some funny moments. Great cast. **96m/C VHS.** *GB* John Mills, Richard Attenborough, Andre Morell, Bryan Forbes, Lisa Gastoni, Michael Hordern, Lionel Jeffries, Gordon Jackson, John Le Mesurier; ***D:*** Jay Lewis. *NOS, MOV, VEC*

Baby Boom ☆☆½ **1987 (PG)** When a hard-charging female executive becomes the reluctant mother of a baby girl (a gift from a long-lost relative), she adjusts with great difficulty to motherhood and life outside the rat race and New York City (and Sam Shepard as the love interest). A fairly harmless collection of cliches bolstered by Keaton's usual nervous performance as a power-suited yuppie ad queen saddled with a noncareer-enhancing baby, moving from manic yuppie ad maven to jelly-packing Vermont store-owner/mom. To best appreciate flick, see it with a bevy of five- and six-year-olds (a good age for applauding the havoc that a baby creates). **103m/C VHS, Beta, LV.** Diane Keaton, Sam Shepard, Harold Ramis, Sam Wanamaker, James Spader, Pat Hingle, Mary Gross, Victoria Jackson, Paxton Whitehead, Annie Golden, Dori Brenner, Robin Bartlett, Christopher Noth, Britt Leach; ***D:*** Charles Shyer; ***W:*** Charles Shyer, Nancy Meyers; ***M:*** Bill Conti. *MGM, FCT, FOX*

Baby Cart 1: Lend a Child...Lend an Arm ☆ **1972** First in a series of six from the sword-wielding samurai genre. Chronicles the events leading up to a samurai warrior's (Wakayama) expulsion from his native village along with his infant son (Tomikawa). Father's intense rivalry with the evil Shogun whom he was ousted by becomes an epic struggle of good vs. evil. The adorable little "Lone Cub" provides an effective counterpoint for Dad's sideline excursion into a local brothel. In Japanese with English subtitles in a letterbox format. **83m/C VHS.** *JP* Tomisaburo Wakayama, Akihiro Tomikawa; ***D:*** Kenji Misumi. *VSM*

Baby Cart 4: Heart of a Parent...Heart of a Child ☆ **1972** Fourth in a series of six. A man (Wakayama) pushes his son (Tomikawa) across Japan in a baby cart loaded with deadly accessories including built-in guns and switchblades. Copious amounts of bloodshed. In Japanese with English subtitles in a letterbox format. **80m/C VHS.** *JP* Tomisaburo Wakayama, Akihiro Tomikawa; ***D:*** Buichi Sato. *VSM*

Baby Cart at the River Styx ☆ **1972** Second of six parts in the "Kozure Ohkami" ("Sword of Vengeance") series about a man who wheels his motherless infant through the Chinese countryside in a baby cart armed with secret weapons, plotting his revenge on the warlord who expelled him. This one features the intro of Sayka and her fellow female assassins. Subtitled in English. **80m/C VHS.** *JP* Tomisaburo Wakayama, Akihiro Tomikawa; ***D:*** Kenji Misumi. *VSM*

Baby Cart to Hades ☆ **1972** The third "Kozure Ohkami" ("Sword of Vengeance") film once again finds samurai Itto Ogami and his son Diagoro embroiled in a power struggle between a regional landlord and a governor in feudal Japan. Subtitled in English. **88m/C VHS.** *JP* Tomisaburo Wakayama, Akihiro Tomikawa; ***D:*** Kenji Misumi. *VSM*

Baby Doll ☆☆☆ **1956** Suggestive sex at its best, revolving around the love of cotton in Mississippi. Nubile Baker is married to slow-witted Malden, who runs a cotton gin. His torching of Wallach's cotton gin begins a cycle of sexual innuendo and tension, brought to exhilarating life on screen, without a single filmed kiss. Performers and sets ooze during the steamy exhibition, which was considered highly erotic when released. Excellent performances from entire cast, with expert pacing by director Kazan. Screenplay is based on Tennessee Williams' "27 Wagons Full of Cotton." **115m/B VHS, Beta.** Eli Wallach, Carroll Baker, Karl Malden, Mildred Dunnock, Rip Torn; ***D:*** Elia Kazan; ***W:*** Tennessee Williams; ***C:*** Boris Kaufman. Golden Globe Awards '57: Best Director (Kazan); Nominations: Academy Awards '56: Best Actress (Baker), Best Adapted Screenplay, Best Black and White Cinematography, Best Supporting Actress (Dunnock). *WAR, FCT*

The Baby Doll Murders ☆☆ **1992 (R)** Someone in L.A. is killing beautiful young women and then leaving a broken baby doll at the scene of the crime. The gruesome murderer manages to elude everyone, until Detective Benz discovers a link between the victims and a pattern begins to form. He also discovers that his partner's wife is going to be the next victim unless he can stop this ruthless serial killer from striking again. **90m/C VHS.** Jeff Kober, Melanie Smith, John Saxon, Tom Hodges; ***D:*** Paul Leder; ***W:*** Paul Leder. *REP*

Baby Face ☆☆ **1933** A small town girl moves to the city when her father dies. There she gets a job at a bank and sleeps her way to the top of the business world, discarding used men left and right. The Hays Office was extremely upset with the then risque material and forced Warner to trim the first cut. **70m/B VHS, Beta.** Barbara Stanwyck, George Brent, Donald Cook, John Wayne, Henry Kolker, Margaret Lindsay, Douglass Dumbrille, James Murray; ***D:*** Alfred E. Green. *MGM, FCT*

Baby Face Harry Langdon ☆☆½ **1926** Two silent shorts by the limpid-eyed comedian: "Saturday Afternoon" (1926), and "Lucky Stars" (1925). **60m/B VHS, Beta, 8mm.** Harry Langdon, Alice Ward, Natalie Kingston, Vernon Dent, Harry Edwards; ***D:*** Harry Edwards; ***W:*** Frank Capra, Arthur Ripley. *VYY*

Baby Face Morgan ☆☆ **1942** Poor comedy about gangsters who attempt to take advantage of the FBI's preoccupation with saboteurs and spies by muscling in on an insurance firm. **60m/B VHS.** Mary Carlisle, Richard Cromwell, Robert Armstrong, Chick Chandler, Charles Judels, Warren Hymer, Vince Barnett, Ralf Harolde; ***D:*** Arthur Dreifuss. *SNC*

Baby Girl Scott ☆☆½ **1987** Hurt and Lithgow play the parents of an extremely premature infant who is being kept alive by technology. They make a heartrending decision and then must battle doctors and the system to let their daughter die with dignity. Made for television. **97m/C VHS.** John Lithgow, Mary Beth Hurt, Linda Kelsey; ***D:*** John Korty. *LIV*

Baby It's You ☆☆☆ **1982 (R)** In New Jersey in the '60s, the relationship between a smart, attractive Jewish girl who yearns to be an actress and a street-smart Catholic Italian boy puzzles their family and friends. It all works due to Arquette's strong acting and Sayles' script, which explores adolescent dreams, the transition to adulthood, class differences, and the late 1960s with insight and humor. Interesting period soundtrack (Woolly Bully and, for some reason, Bruce Springsteen) helps propel the film, a commercial job which helped finance Sayles' more independent ventures. **105m/C VHS, Beta, LV.** Rosanna Arquette, Vincent Spano, Jack Davidson, Joanna Merlin, Nick Ferrari, Leora Dana, Robert Downey Jr., Tracy Pollan, Matthew Modine; ***D:*** John Sayles; ***W:*** John Sayles; ***C:*** Michael Ballhaus. *PAR*

Baby Love *Woof!* **1969 (R)** A softcore fluff-fest about a trollop seducing a doctor's family. The doctor may or may not be her father. Hayden tantalizes the doctor, the doctor's son, and the doctor's wife, as well as the neighbors, leaving only those in adjoining communities untouched. Based on the novel by Tina Chad Christian. **98m/C VHS, Beta.** *GB* Ann Lynn, Keith Barron, Linda Hayden, Derek Lamden, Diana Dors, Patience Collier; ***D:*** Alastair Reid. *NLC*

Baby Love *Woof!* **1983** Nerds get revenge against the freshmen who run the local frat house. **80m/C VHS, Beta.** *MGM*

The Baby Maker ☆☆ **1970 (R)** A couple who cannot have children because the wife is sterile decides to hire a woman to have a child for them. However, the relationship between the husband and the surrogate progresses beyond what either of them wanted. Hershey stars as the free-love surrogate mama (just before she underwent the supreme 60s transformation into Barbara Seagull) and Bridges makes his directorial debut. Flick is interesting as a combo critique/exploitation of those wild and groovy 1960s. **109m/C VHS.** Barbara Hershey, Collin Wilcox-Horne, Sam Groom, Scott Glenn, Jeannie Berlin; ***D:*** James Bridges; ***W:*** James Bridges. Nominations: Academy Awards '70: Best Original Score. *WAR*

Baby of the Bride ☆☆½ **1991** Follow-up to "Children of the Bride," has McClanahan settling into wedded bliss with younger husband Shackleford when she discovers she's pregnant. Not only is she unsure about wanting to be a mom again at her age but then grown—and single—daughter McNichol announces she is also pregnant. The sheer silliness of this made-for-television fare makes it fun to watch. **93m/C VHS.** Rue McClanahan, Ted Shackleford, Kristy McNichol, John Wesley Shipp, Anne Bobby, Conor O'Farrell; ***D:*** Bill Bixby; ***W:*** Bart Baker. *TTC*

Baby on Board ☆☆ **1992 (PG)** Kane plays the wife of a Mafia bookkeeper who is accidentally killed in a gangland murder. Out for revenge, she tracks her husband's killer to JFK airport with her four-year old daughter in tow. Just as she pulls the loaded gun from her purse and takes aim, a pickpocket snatches her purse, accidentally firing the gun. Now she's on the run and she jumps into the first cab she can find, driven by Reinhold. New York City is turned upside down as mother, daughter, and cabbie try to elude the mob in this funny but predictable comedy. **90m/C VHS, Beta, LV.** Carol Kane, Judge Reinhold, Geza Kovacs, Errol Slue, Alex Stapley, Holly Stapley; ***D:*** Francis Schaeffer. *PSM*

Baby ... Secret of the Lost Legend ☆☆ **1985 (PG)** A sportswriter and his paleontologist wife risk their lives to reunite a hatching brontosaurus with its mother in the African jungle. Although this Disney film is not lewd in any sense, beware of several scenes displaying frontal nudity and some violence. **95m/C VHS, Beta, LV.** William Katt, Sean Young, Patrick McGoohan, Julian Fellowes; ***D:*** Bill W.L. Norton. *TOU*

The Baby-Sitters Club ☆☆½ **1995 (PG)** Centering on the summer vacation of seven enterprising Connecticut 13-year-olds and their teen trials with parents, boys, and babysitting, this film is sure to hit home with a crowd that is rarely featured, preteen girls. Director Mayron claims, "It's the 'Mystic Pizza' of their age." Young girls and girls young at heart should enjoy this touching look at the fragile years of our youth, leaving baby dolls behind and heading towards dating. Based on the best-selling book series by Ann Martin. Fisk, who plays club leader Kristy, is the daughter of actress Sissy Spacek and director Jack Fisk. **92m/C VHS, LV.** Scuyler Fisk, Bre Blair, Rachel Leigh Cook, Larisa Oleynik, Tricia Joe, Stacey Linn Ransower, Zelda Harris, Brooke Adams, Peter Horton, Bruce Davison, Ellen Burstyn, Austin O'Brien, Aaron Michael Metchik; ***D:*** Melanie Mayron; ***W:*** Dalene Young; ***C:*** Willy Kurant; ***M:*** David Michael Frank. *COL*

Baby Snakes: The Complete Version **1979** Concert footage of Zappa is interspersed with clay animation by Bruce Bickford. **166m/C VHS, Beta.** Frank Zappa; ***D:*** Frank Zappa. *MVD*

Baby, Take a Bow ☆☆ **1934 (PG)** Temple's first starring role. As a cheerful Pollyanna-type she helps her father, falsely accused of theft, by finding the true thief. **76m/B VHS, Beta.** Shirley Temple,

James Dunn, Claire Trevor, Alan Dinehart; ***D:*** Harry Lachman. *FXV*

Baby, the Rain Must Fall 🦴🦴 **1964** A rockabilly singer, paroled from prison after serving time for a knifing, returns home to his wife and daughter, but his outbursts of violence make the reunion difficult. Unsentimental with realistic performances, but script is weak (although written by Foote, based on his play, "The Traveling Lady"). Theme song was a Top 40 hit. **100m/B VHS, Beta, LV.** Steve McQueen, Lee Remick, Don Murray; ***D:*** Robert Mulligan; ***W:*** Horton Foote; ***C:*** Ernest Laszlo; ***M:*** Elmer Bernstein. *COL, MOV*

Babycakes 🦴🦴½ **1989** A marshmellow romance between an overweight mortuary attendant who decides to follow her heart when she falls for a hunky ice skater. Can she make him appreciate her inner beauty instead of just her not-the-normal-beauty-standard outward appearance? (Happy ending guaranteed.) A made for television remake of the darker German film "Sugarbaby." **94m/C VHS.** Ricki Lake, Craig Sheffer, Paul Benedict, Betty Buckley, John Karlen, Nada Despotovich; ***D:*** Paul Schneider. *TTC*

Babyfever 🦴🦴½ **1994 (R)** Women gather at a baby shower and tell stories about motherhood and related topics. May be viewed as a babblefest with video accompaniment or as an overdue cinematic exploration of a fairly important aspect of life (where would we be without mom?). That said, pace of the comedy drama is less than feverish, although director Jaglom captures the essence of the stories without disturbing their flow. Foyt, Jaglom's wife and co-screenwriter, makes her acting debut. **110m/C VHS.** Matt Salinger, Eric Roberts, Frances Fisher, Victoria Foyt, Zack Norman, Dinah Lenney, Elaine Kagan; ***D:*** Henry Jaglom; ***W:*** Victoria Foyt, Henry Jaglom. *FXL*

The Babylon Story from "Intolerance" 🦴🦴🦴½ **1916** Lavishly produced vignette from Griffith's film "Intolerance" as it was released on its own in 1919, in order to recoup the studio losses incurred by that grandest of cinematic follies. Silent with organ score, tinted color. **25m/C VHS, Beta.** Constance Talmadge, Alfred Paget; ***D:*** D.W. Griffith. *VYY*

Baby's Day Out 🦴🦴½ **1994 (PG)** Poor man's "Home Alone" refits tired Hughes formula using little tiny baby for original spin. Adorable Baby Bink crawls his way onto the city streets, much to his frantic mother's dismay, and unwittingly outsmarts his would-be kidnappers. As in "HA I and II," the bad guys fall victim to all sorts of cataclysmic Looney Tunes violence. Small kids will get a kick out of this one. Particular problem for the moviemakers was that the nine-month old Worton twins were past the year mark by the end of the shoot, a world of difference in infantdom. Blue screens and out-of-sequence shooting were used to overcome the developmental gap. **99m/C VHS.** Adam Worton, Jacob Worton, Joe Mantegna, Lara Flynn Boyle, Joe Pantoliano, Fred Dalton Thompson, John Neville, Brian Haley, Matthew Glave; ***D:*** Patrick Read Johnson; ***W:*** John Hughes; ***M:*** Bruce Broughton. *FXV*

The Babysitter 🦴🦴 **1980** A family hires the mysterious but ingratiating Johanna (Zimbalist) as live-in help without checking on her references (who'd all checked out). The babysitter is the answer to all their problems—Mom's an alcoholic, Dad's a workaholic, and their daughter's just plain maladjusted—but once Johanna's gained their trust (or, in Dad's case, lust), she sets out to manipulate and exploit the family for her own psychotic purposes. Houseman plays the nosy neighbor who's on to her evil plan. Fair made-for-TV treatment of a common suspense plot. **96m/C VHS, Beta, LV.** William Shatner, Patty Duke, Stephanie Zimbalist, Quinn Cummings, John Houseman, David Wallace; ***D:*** Peter Medak. *NO*

The Babysitter 🦴🦴½ **1995 (R)** All-American teen Jennifer (Silverstone) becomes the unexpected object of desire for family man Harry (Walsh), whose wife Dolly (Garlington) is fantasizing about having an affair with a neighbor (Segal). But then Jennifer's boyfriend (London) gets caught up in a malicious prank that turns bad for everyone involved. Based on a short story by Robert Coover. **90m/C VHS, LV.** Alicia Silverstone, Jeremy London, J.T. Walsh, Lee Garlington, Nicky Katt, Lois Chiles, George Segal; ***D:*** Guy Ferland; ***W:*** Guy Ferland; ***M:*** Loek Dikker. *REP*

The Bacchantes 🦴🦴 **1963** Poorly dubbed account of a ballerina, her life and loves. Based on the play by Euripides. **100m/B VHS.** *IT* Taina Elg, Pierre Brice, Alessandra Panaro, Alberto Lupo, Akim Tamiroff; ***D:*** Giorgio Ferroni. *FCT*

Bach: Mass in B Minor **199?** Features Bach scholar Helmuth Rilling, soprano Arleen Auger, alto Anne Sophie von Otter, tenor Aldo Baldin, tenor Aldo Baldin, Gachinger Kantorei, and Bach-Collegium Stuttgart as they perform the Johann Sebastian Bach classic at the International Bach Festival in Stuttgart, Germany. **m/C VHS.** *PRS*

The Bachelor 🦴🦴🦴 **1993** Beautiful, seductive period drama about a shy and solitary physician who is forced into a new life when a family tragedy changes everything he once took for granted. Richardson and Carradine give brilliant performances in this provocative story of one man's sexual awakening. Based on a novel by Arthur Schnitzler. **105m/C VHS.** Keith Carradine, Miranda Richardson, Mari Torocsik, Max von Sydow, Kristin Scott Thomas, Sarah-Jane Fenton, Franco Diogene; ***D:*** Roberto Faenza; ***W:*** Roberto Faenza, Ennio de Concini, Hugh Fleetwood; ***M:*** Ennio Morricone. *TRI*

The Bachelor and the Bobby-Soxer 🦴🦴🦴 *Bachelor Knight* **1947** Playboy Grant is brought before Judge Loy for disturbing the peace and sentenced to court her teen-age sister Temple. Cruel and unusual punishment? Maybe, but the wise Judge hopes that the dates will help Temple over her crush on handsome Grant. Instead, Loy and Grant fall for each other. **95m/B VHS, Beta, LV.** Cary Grant, Myrna Loy, Shirley Temple, Rudy Vallee, Harry Davenport, Ray Collins, Veda Ann Borg; ***D:*** Irving Reis; ***W:*** Sidney Sheldon. Academy Awards '47: Best Original Screenplay. *CCB, MED, MLB*

Bachelor Apartment 🦴🦴½ **1931** Once at the leading edge of the bachelor on the loose genre, this one's hopelessly dated. The scandalous womanizing of a wealthy thirties Lothario just doesn't have the same impact on the men just don't understand generation. Nevertheless, as vintage if-the-walls-could-talk fluff, it's good for a giggle. **77m/B VHS.** Lowell Sherman, Irene Dunne, Norman Kerry, Claudia Dell, Noel Francis, Charles Coleman; ***D:*** Lowell Sherman. *TTC, FCT*

Bachelor Bait 🦴½ **1934** A marriage license clerk who's tired of just handing out licenses opens a matrimonial service for men. **75m/B VHS, Beta.** Stuart Erwin, Rochelle Hudson, Pert Kelton, Richard "Skeets" Gallagher; ***M:*** Max Steiner. *CCB*

Bachelor in Paradise 🦴🦴½ **1969** Silly tale starring Hope as a writer of books to the lovelorn who decides to do firsthand research on the sexual goings-on of a suburban California community. All the married ladies find him charming (much to their husbands' disgust) and the lone single woman, Turner, isn't single by the end of the movie. **109m/C VHS.** Bob Hope, Lana Turner, Janis Paige, Jim Hutton, Paula Prentiss, Don Porter, Virginia Grey, Agnes Moorehead, John McGiver; ***D:*** Jack Arnold; ***W:*** Hal Kanter, Valentine Davies; ***M:*** Henry Mancini. Nominations: Academy Awards '61: Best Song ("Bachelor in Paradise"). *MGM, FCT*

Bachelor Mother 🦴🦴🦴 **1939** A single salesgirl causes a scandal when she finds an abandoned baby and is convinced by her boss to adopt the child. Smart, witty comedy with nice performance by Rogers. **82m/B VHS, Beta, LV.** Ginger Rogers, David Niven, Charles Coburn; ***D:*** Garson Kanin. Nominations: Academy Awards '39: Best Story. *CCB, MED, FCT*

Bachelor of Hearts 🦴½ **1958** Sophomoric British comedy set at Cambridge University, with a German exchange student whose difficulty with English brings him to date several women in one evening. Notable for horror fans as the debut of femme fright fave Barbara Steele. **94m/C VHS.** *GB* Hardy Kruger, Sylvia Syms, Ronald Lewis; ***D:*** Wolf Rilla; ***W:*** Frederic Raphael, Leslie Bricusse. *NOS*

Bachelor Party 🦴🦴 **1984 (R)** He's silly, cute, and poor. She's intelligent, beautiful, and rich. It must be a marriage made in heaven, because no one in their right mind would put these two together. All is basically well, except that her parents hate him and his friends dislike her. Things are calm until right before the big event, when bride-to-be Kitaen objects to Hank's traditional pre-nuptial partying. Light and semi-entertaining with scattered laughs. **105m/C VHS, Beta, LV.** Tom Hanks, Tawny Kitaen, Adrian Zmed, George Grizzard, Robert Prescott, William Tepper, Wendie Jo Sperber, Barry Diamond, Michael Dudikoff, Deborah Harmon, John Bloom, Toni Alessandra, Monique Gabrielle, Angela Aames, Rosanne Katon; ***D:*** Neal Israel; ***W:*** Pat Proft; ***M:*** Robert Folk. *FXV, FOX*

Back Door to Heaven 🦴🦴🦴½ **1939** Traces the path of a young boy who is born into a poor family and the reasons for his turning to a life of crime. A grim and powerful drama with many convincing performances. **85m/B VHS.** Wallace Ford, Aline MacMahon, Stuart Erwin, Patricia Ellis, Kent Smith, Van Heflin, Jimmy Lydon; ***D:*** William K. Howard. *NOS, MOV*

Back from Eternity 🦴🦴 **1956** Eleven survivors of a plane crash are stranded in a headhunter region of South America's jungle. Remake of "Five Came Back" (1939), which was also directed by Farrow. **97m/B VHS, Beta, LV.** Robert Ryan, Rod Steiger, Anita Ekberg, Phyllis Kirk, Keith Andes, Gene Barry; ***D:*** John Farrow; ***C:*** William Mellor. *NO*

Back Home 🦴🦴½ **1990** A family reunion movie with pure Disney sentiment. A 12-year-old English girl, who has been living in America during WWII, is reunited with her family in postwar England. Made for cable television. **103m/C VHS.** Hayley Carr, Hayley Mills, Jean Anderson, Rupert Frazer, Brenda Bruce, Adam Stevenson, George Clark; ***D:*** Piers Haggard. *DIS*

Back in Action 🦴½ **1994 (R)** Veteran LA detective Rossi (Piper) is out to bust the ruthless drug gang who gunned down his partner. But he's got company—martial-arts expert Billy (Blanks) whose young sister has fallen prey to the same gang. So the two action junkies reluctantly team up to cause some major damage. **93m/C VHS, LV.** Roddy Piper, Billy Blanks, Bobbie Phillips, Matt Birman, Nigel Bennett, Damon D'Oliveira, Kai Soremekun; ***D:*** Paul Ziller, Steve DiMarco; ***W:*** Karl Schiffman. *MCA*

Back in the USSR 🦴½ **1992 (R)** Danger follows two lovers caught up in the Moscow underworld. When young American touring Russia unwittingly gets involved with a beautiful art thief. Lots of fast-paced action in an otherwise muddled film. The first American film shot entirely on location in Moscow. **87m/C VHS.** Frank Whaley, Natalia Negoda, Roman Polanski, Claudia Robinson, Dey Young, Andrew Divoff, Brian Blessed, Ravil Issyanov; ***D:*** Deran Sarafian; ***C:*** Yuri Neyman. *FXV*

Back Roads 🦴🦴 **1981 (R)** Southern hooker meets a down-on-his-luck boxer and both head out for a better life in California, finding love along the way. Ritt road trip lacks any comedic rhythm and survives on Field and Jones working to entertain. **94m/C VHS, Beta.** Sally Field, Tommy Lee Jones, David Keith; ***D:*** Martin Ritt; ***W:*** Gary De Vore; ***C:*** John A. Alonzo; ***M:*** Henry Mancini. *FOX*

Back Street 🦴🦴 **1961** The forbidden affair between a married man and a beautiful fashion designer carries on through many anxious years to a tragic end. The lavish third film version of the Fannie Hurst novel. **107m/C VHS, Beta.** Susan Hayward, John Gavin, Vera Miles; ***D:*** David Miller; ***C:*** William H. Daniels. Nominations: Academy Awards '61: Best Costume Design (Color). *MCA, MLB*

Back to Back 🦴 **1990 (R)** A beautiful young vigilante embarks on a rampage to clear her family's name and make her town's redneck crooks pay for their crimes. Never released in theaters. **95m/C VHS, Beta.** Bill Paxton, Todd Field, Apollonia, Luke Askew, Ben Johnson, David Michael-Standing, Susan Anspach, Sal Landi; ***D:*** John Kincade. *MGM*

Back to Bataan ☙☙½ **1945** Colonel forms guerrilla army to raid Japanese in the Philippines and to help Americans landing on Leyte. Also available in a colorized version. **95m/B VHS, Beta, LV.** John Wayne, Anthony Quinn, Beulah Bondi, Fely Franquelli, Richard Loo, Philip Ahn, Lawrence Tierney; ***D:*** Edward Dmytryk. *TTC*

Back to Hannibal: The Return of Tom Sawyer and Huckleberry Finn ☙☙½ **1990** Mark Twain's characters Tom Sawyer and Huckleberry Finn are reunited as adults to solve a murder mystery. Tom is a lawyer, Finn a newspaper man, and it's Becky Thatcher's husband who's been murdered. Did a freed slave really commit the crime? Made for television. **92m/C VHS.** Raphael Sbarge, Mitchell Anderson, Megan Follows, William Windom, Ned Beatty, Paul Winfield; ***D:*** Paul Krasny; ***M:*** Lee Holdridge. *DIS*

Back to School ☙☙½ **1986 (PG-13)** Dangerfield plays an obnoxious millionaire who enrolls in college to help his wimpy son, Gordon, achieve campus stardom. His motto seems to be "if you can't buy it, it can't be had." At first, his antics embarrass his shy son, but soon everyone is clamoring to be seen with the pair as Gordon develops his own self confidence. **96m/C VHS, Beta, LV.** Rodney Dangerfield, Keith Gordon, Robert Downey Jr., Sally Kellerman, Burt Young, Paxton Whitehead, Adrienne Barbeau, M. Emmet Walsh, Severn Darden, Ned Beatty, Sam Kinison, Kurt Vonnegut Jr., Robert Picardo, Terry Farrell, Edie McClurg, Jason Hervey; ***D:*** Alan Metter; ***W:*** Will Aldis, Steven Kampmann, Harold Ramis, Peter Torokvei; ***M:*** Danny Elfman. *NO*

Back to the Beach ☙½ **1987 (PG)** Frankie and Annette return to the beach as self-parodying, middle-aged parents with rebellious kids, and the usual run of sun-bleached, lover's tiff comedy ensues. Plenty of songs and guest appearances from television past. Tries to bring back that surf, sun, and sand feel of the orignal "Beach Party" movies, but fails. ♫Absolute Perfection; California Sun; Catch a Ride; Jamaica Sky; Papa-Oom-Mow-Mow; Sign of Love; Sun, Sun, Sun, Sun, Sun; Surfin' Bird; Wooly Bully. **92m/C VHS, Beta, LV.** Frankie Avalon, Annette Funicello, Connie Stevens, Jerry Mathers, Bob Denver, Barbara Billingsley, Tony Dow, Paul (Pee Wee Herman) Reubens, Edd Byrnes, Dick Dale, Don Adams, Lori Loughlin; ***D:*** Lyndall Hobbs; ***C:*** Bruce Surtees; ***M:*** Stephen Dorff. *PAR*

Back to the Future ☙☙☙ **1985 (PG)** When neighborhood mad scientist Doc Brown constructs a time machine from a DeLorean, his youthful companion Marty accidentally transports himself to 1955. There, Marty must do everything he can to bring his parents together, elude the local bully, and get back...to the future. Solid fast-paced entertainment is even better due to Lloyd's inspired performance as the loony Doc while Fox is perfect as the boy completely out of his element. Soundtrack features Huey Lewis and the News. Followed by two sequels. **116m/C VHS, Beta, LV.** Michael J. Fox, Christopher Lloyd, Lea Thompson, Crispin Glover, Wendie Jo Sperber, Marc McClure, Thomas F. Wilson, James Tolkan, Casey Siemaszko, Billy Zane, George DiCenzo, Courtney Gains, Claudia Wells, Jason Hervey, Harry Waters Jr., Maia Brewton, J.J. Cohen; ***Cameos:*** Huey Lewis; ***D:*** Robert Zemeckis; ***W:*** Robert Zemeckis, Bob Gale; ***C:*** Dean Cundey; ***M:*** Alan Silvestri. People's Choice Awards '86: Best Film; Nominations: Academy Awards '85: Best Original Screenplay, Best Song ("The Power of Love"), Best Sound. *MCA, FCT, TLF*

Back to the Future, Part 2 ☙☙½ **1989 (PG)** Taking up exactly where Part 1 left off, Doc Brown and Marty time-hop into the future (2015 to be exact) to save Marty's kids, then find themselves returning to 1955 to retrieve a sports almanac that causes havoc for the McFly family. Clever editing allows for Marty Part 2 to see Marty Part 1 at the school dance. Most of the cast returns, although Glover appears only in cuts from the original and Shue steps in as girlfriend Jennifer. Not up to the original, but still satisfying. Cliffhanger ending sets up Part 3, which was shot simultaneously with this. **107m/C VHS, Beta, LV.** Michael J. Fox, Christopher Lloyd, Lea Thompson, Thomas F. Wilson, Harry Waters Jr., Charles Fleischer, Joe Flaherty, Elisabeth Shue, James Tolkan, Casey Siemaszko, Jeffrey Weissman, Flea, Billy Zane, J.J. Cohen, Darlene Vogel, Jason Scott Lee, Crispin Glover, Ricky Dean Logan; ***D:*** Robert Zemeckis; ***W:*** Robert Zemeckis, Bob Gale; ***C:*** Dean Cundey; ***M:*** Alan Silvestri. *MCA*

Back to the Future, Part 3 ☙☙☙ **1990 (PG)** Picks up where Part 2 climaxed a la cliffhanger. Stuck in 1955, time-traveling hero Marty frantically searches for Doc Part 1 so he can return to 1985. Instead, he finds himself in the Wild West circa 1885, trying to save Doc's life. Plot is related to earlier BTTFs, so first time viewers might be confused. For those who've seen previous incarnations, the clever interconnections are really nifty. Nearly matches the original for excitement and offers some snazzy new special effects. Supposedly the last installment, though don't be surprised if another sequel follows. The complete trilogy is available as a boxed set. **118m/C VHS, Beta, LV.** Michael J. Fox, Christopher Lloyd, Mary Steenburgen, Thomas F. Wilson, Lea Thompson, Elisabeth Shue, Matt Clark, Richard Dysart, Pat Buttram, Harry Carey Jr., Dub Taylor, James Tolkan, Marc McClure, Wendie Jo Sperber, J.J. Cohen, Ricky Dean Logan, Jeffrey Weissman; ***D:*** Robert Zemeckis; ***W:*** Robert Zemeckis, Bob Gale; ***C:*** Dean Cundey; ***M:*** Alan Silvestri. *MCA*

Back to the Wall ☙☙ **1956** Moreau is an adulturous wife whose web of deceit results in a suspenseful tale of murder and blackmail. **94m/B VHS.** *FR* Jeanne Moreau, Gerard Oury, Claire Maurier; ***D:*** Edouard Molinaro. *FCT, INJ*

Backbeat ☙☙☙ **1994 (R)** Backed by the beat of early Beatle tunes as rendered by some of today's top alternative musicians, the debut for director Softley explores the Fab Four's beginnings in Hamburg's underground music scene. Storyline is driven by the complications of a romantic triangle between John Lennon, Astrid Kirchherr (the photographer who came up with the band's signature look) and Stu Sutcliffe, Lennon's best friend and the original bass player for the Beatles. Hart's dead-on as Lennon, playing him a second time (check out "The Hours and Times"). Energetic and enjoyable, particularly when the Was-produced music takes center stage. **100m/C VHS, LV.** *GB* Stephen Dorff, Sheryl Lee, Ian Hart, Gary Bakewell, Chris O'Neill, Scot Williams, Kai Wiesinger, Jennifer Ehle; ***D:*** Iain Softley; ***W:*** Michael Thomas, Stephen Ward, Iain Softley; ***M:*** Don Was. *PGV*

Backdraft ☙☙½ **1991 (R)** High action story of Chicago firemen has some of the most stupendous incendiary special effects ever filmed. But then there's that plot, B-movie hokum about a mystery arsonist torching strategic parts of the community with the finesse of an expert and a brother-against-brother conflict. Straight-forward performances from most of the cast in spite of the weak storyline. Writer Widen wrote from experience—he used to be a fireman; real-life Chicago firefighters were reportedly very happy with the realistic and intense fire scenes. Forget the plot and just watch the fires. Also available in a letterboxed version. **135m/C VHS, Beta, LV.** Kurt Russell, William Baldwin, Robert De Niro, Donald Sutherland, Jennifer Jason Leigh, Scott Glenn, Rebecca DeMornay, Jason Gedrick, J.T. Walsh, Tony Mockus Sr., Clint Howard, David Crosby; ***D:*** Ron Howard; ***W:*** Gregory Widen; ***C:*** Mikael Salomon; ***M:*** Hans Zimmer. Nominations: Academy Awards '91: Best Sound, Best Visual Effects. *MCA*

Backfield in Motion ☙☙½ **1991** Silly but harmless comedy about a widowed mom who tries to get closer to her high-schooler son by organizing a mother-son football game. But it's the boys' football coach who really wants to get close—to mom. Made for television movie debut of both Arnolds. **95m/C VHS, Beta.** Roseanne, Tom Arnold, Colleen Camp, Conchata Ferrell, Johnny Galecki, Kevin Scannell; ***D:*** Richard Michaels. *TTC*

Backfire ☙☙ **1922** If you're gonna rob a bank, you shouldn't let anyone hear you plan it, and if you're not gonna rob a bank, you shouldn't let anyone hear you plan one. This vintage "Lightning" Carson crime western has Carson and friend suspected of bank robbery because someone heard them planning one. The sheriff follows their every footstep as they search for the real perpetrators. **56m/B VHS, Beta.** Jack Hoxie, George Sowards, Lew Meehan, Florence Gilbert; ***D:*** Alan James. *GPV*

Backfire ☙☙ **1988 (R)** A mysterious stranger enters the lives of a disturbed 'Nam vet and his discontented wife, setting a pattern of murder and double-cross in motion. **90m/C VHS, Beta, LV.** Karen Allen, Keith Carradine, Jeff Fahey, Bernie Casey, Dinah Manoff, Dean Paul Martin; ***D:*** Gilbert Cates; ***W:*** Larry Brand; ***M:*** David Shire. *VMK*

Backfire! ☙½ **1994 (PG-13)** Silly spoof finds Jeremy (Mosby) wanting to join New York City's all-female fire brigade who are trying to stop an arsonist from blowing up the city's toilets. Mitchum is the fire marshal and Ireland the mayor's charming assistant. **88m/C VHS.** Josh Mosby, Kathy Ireland, Robert Mitchum, Shelley Winters; ***D:*** A. Dean Bell. *APX*

Background to Danger ☙☙☙ **1943** A suspenseful WWII actioner about American agent Raft who travels to Turkey to receive secret documents from the soon-to-be-murdered Massen. Greenstreet is the Nazi master spy who also wants the documents as do Russian spies, Lorre and Marshall. Somewhat confusing plot but fast-paced. Based on the thriller "Uncommon Danger" by Eric Ambler. This film was Warner Brothers' follow-up to "Casablanca" with Raft in the Bogie role he had turned down in that cinema classic. **80m/B VHS.** George Raft, Sydney Greenstreet, Peter Lorre, Brenda Marshall, Osa Massen, Turhan Bey, Kurt Katch; ***D:*** Raoul Walsh. *MGM, MOV*

Backlash ☙☙½ **1986 (R)** An aborigine barmaid is raped. When her assailant turns up dead, she's charged with murder and winds up in the custody of two police officers on a trip across the outback. Holes in the plot undermine this interesting, although graphic, drama with racial overtones. **88m/C VHS, Beta.** *AU* David Argue, Gia Carides, Lydia Miller, Brian Syron, Anne Smith; ***D:*** Bill Bennett; ***W:*** Bill Bennett; ***M:*** Michael Atkinson, Michael Spicer. *MCG*

Backlash: Oblivion 2 ☙☙½ *Oblivion 2* **1995 (PG-13)** Galactic supervillainess Lash stakes her claim to a rare derconium mine on the remote space outpost of Oblivion. Will cave monsters thwart her evil plan before space cowboys come to the town's rescue? **82m/C VHS, LV.** Andrew Divoff, Meg Foster, Isaac Hayes, Julie Newmar, Carel Struycken, George Takei, Musetta Vander, Jimmie F. Skaggs, Irwin Keyes, Maxwell Caulfield; ***D:*** Sam Irvin; ***W:*** Peter David; ***M:*** Pino Donaggio. *FLL*

Backstab ☙☙½ **1990 (R)** A spellbinding tale of work, lust, and murder. Architect Brolin finds himself unable to get over the death of his wife, until a seductive and mysterious woman helps him over his grief. They spend the night together, engulfed in passion, but in the morning he wakes to find himself sleeping with the corpse of his boss. Only the first twist in this intriguing thriller. **91m/C VHS, LV.** James Brolin, Meg Foster, Isabelle Truchon; ***D:*** Jim Kaufman. *MED, VTR*

Backstairs ☙☙ **1921** An obscure German silent film about urban degradation and familial strife. **44m/B VHS, Beta.** *GE* Henny Porten, Fritz Kortner, William Dieterle; ***D:*** Leopold Jessner. *INJ, NOS, DVT*

Backstreet Dreams ☙☙ **1990 (R)** The young parents of an autistic child find themselves torn apart due to their feelings of guilt. The father has an affair with a specialist hired to help the boy, causing further strife. Interesting story possibilities never get far. **104m/C VHS, LV.** Brooke Shields, Jason O'Malley, Sherilyn Fenn, Tony Fields, Burt Young, Anthony (Tony) Franciosa, Nick Cassavetes, Ray "Boom Boom" Mancini; ***D:*** Rupert Hitzig; ***M:*** Bill Conti. *VMK*

Backstreet Justice ☙☙½ **1993 (R)** Pittsburgh PI Keri Finnegan (Kozlowski) is investigating a series of murders in her neighborhood when she uncovers ties to police corruption dating back 30 years. This doesn't make her popular since it involves her dead cop father and a number of old friends (and enemies). Kozlowski is appropriately feisty and the plot twists will hold your attention. **91m/C VHS, LV.** Linda Kozlowski, Hector Elizondo, John Shea, Paul Sorvino, Viveca Lindfors, Tammy Grimes; ***D:*** Chris McIntyre; ***W:*** Chris McIntyre. *PSM*

Backtrack *Catchfire* **1989 (R)** Foster co-stars in this thriller about an artist who accidentally witnesses a mob hit. The mob puts a hitman (Hopper) on her trail, and after studying her background and listening to audio tapes she recorded, he finds himself falling in love. Originally intended for a theatrical release, it hit the European screens in a different cut as "Catchfire;" Hopper restored his original version and it was released on cable TV in the U.S . **102m/C VHS.** Dennis Hopper, Jodie Foster, Dean Stockwell, Vincent Price, John Turturro, Fred Ward, G. Anthony Sirico, Julie Adams, Frank Gio, Sy Richardson, Helena Kallianiotes, Bob Dylan; ***Cameos:*** Charlie Sheen, Joe Pesci; ***D:*** Dennis Hopper; ***W:*** Ann Louise Bardach; ***M:*** Michel Colombier. *LIV*

Backwoods **1987 (R)** Two campers wish they had never encountered a mountain man when he begins to stalk them with murder in mind. **90m/C VHS, Beta.** Jack O'Hara, Dick Kreusser, Brad Armacot; ***D:*** Dean Crow. *NO*

The Bad and the Beautiful ½ **1952** The story of a Hollywood producer, told from the eyes of an actress, a writer, and a director. Featuring what some consider Turner's best performance ever. Winner of five Oscars, a splendid drama. **118m/B VHS, LV.** Kirk Douglas, Lana Turner, Dick Powell, Gloria Grahame, Barry Sullivan, Walter Pidgeon, Gilbert Roland; ***D:*** Vincente Minnelli; ***C:*** Robert L. Surtees. Academy Awards '52: Best Art Direction/Set Decoration (B & W), Best Black and White Cinematography, Best Costume Design (B & W), Best Screenplay, Best Supporting Actress (Grahame); Nominations: Academy Awards '52: Best Actor (Douglas). *MGM, BTV*

Bad Attitude **1993 (R)** Leon is a narcotics officer on a mission to restore his badge after his careless pistol work gets him booted off the force. The quick-tempered cop relentlessly pursues druglord Finque with the help of an open-minded preacher (De Veaux) and his sexy, streetwise assistant (Lim). **87m/C VHS.** Leon, Gina Lim, Nathaniel DeVeaux, Susan Finque; ***D:*** Bill Cummings. *XVC*

Bad Behavior ½ **1992 (R)** Unscripted character-driven drama. Gerry and Ellie McAllister are an Irish couple living in North London. He's tired of working for the local planning commission, she's bored being just a mum at home, and both are still a little uneasy living in England. When they decide to remodel the family bath, the unexpected problems lead to an emotional shakeup. Don't expect a lot of drama, the film works only if you accept the decency of the characters and the small moments of recognizable daily life. Director Blair wrote a basic script outline and had the actors improvise their dialogue, in character, over a long rehearsal period to develop their roles. **103m/C VHS.** *GB* Stephen Rea, Sinead Cusack, Philip Jackson, Clare Higgins, Phil Daniels, Saira Todd; ***D:*** Les Blair; ***M:*** John Altman. *VMK*

Bad Blood **1987** The true story of Stan Graham, who went on a killing spree in the New Zealand bush when his farm was foreclosed and his life ruined. **104m/C VHS, Beta.** *NZ* Jack Thompson, Carol Burns, Dennis Lill; ***D:*** Mike Newell. *ACA*

Bad Blood ½ **1994 (R)** Travis Blackstone (Lamas) will use any methods to protect his brother Franklin, who's targeted for death by a ruthless drug lord. Lots of action and violence. **90m/C VHS, LV.** Lorenzo Lamas, Hank Cheyne, Frankie Thorn, Kimberley Kates, Joe Son; ***D:*** Tibor Takacs. *WEA, LIV*

Bad Boy ½ *Branded* **1939** A country boy goes to the big city, and succumbs to urban evils and temptations, but is eventually saved by motherly love. **60m/B VHS, Beta, LV.** Johnny Downs, Helen MacKellar, Rosalind Keith, Holmes Herbert; ***D:*** Kurt Neumann. *NO*

Bad Boy Bubby **1993** Bizarre black comedy about the extremely maladjusted Bubby (Hope), who becomes a pop culture phenomena. The 35-year-old childlike Bubby has been keep a virtual prisoner by his monstrous mom, who has told him the world outside is filled with poisonous gas. Wondering how his cat survived, Bubby wraps it in plastic wrap and is puzzled when it dies. Still, this gives Bubby an idea—he wraps mom in plastic and escapes outside, where he's soon adopted by a struggling rock band that writes a cult song hit about his experiences. It's even stranger than it sounds. **114m/C VHS.** *IT AU* Nicholas Hope, Claire Benito, Carmel Johnson, Ralph Cotterill, Norman Kaye, Paul Philpot, Graham Duckett, Bridget Walters; ***D:*** Rolf de Heer; ***W:*** Rolf de Heer; ***M:*** Graham Tardiff. Australian Film Institute '94: Best Actor (Hope), Best Director (de Heer), Best Film Editing, Best Original Screenplay; Nominations: Australian Film Institute '94: Best Cinematography, Best Film. *NYR*

Bad Boys **1983 (R)** When a gang member's little brother is killed in a rumble, the teen responsible (Penn, who else?) goes to a reformatory, where he quickly (though somewhat reluctantly) takes charge. Meanwhile, on the outside, his rival attacks Penn's girlfriend (Sheedy, in her feature film debut) in retaliation, is incarcerated, and ends up vying with Penn for control of the cell block. Backed into a corner by their mutual hatred and escalating peer pressure, the two are pushed over the brink into a final and shattering confrontation. Not as violent as it could be, to its credit; attempts to communicate a message. **104m/C VHS, Beta, LV.** Sean Penn, Esai Morales, Reni Santoni, Jim Moody, Eric Gurry, Ally Sheedy, Clancy Brown; ***D:*** Rick Rosenthal; ***C:*** Donald E. Thorin; ***M:*** Bill Conti. *REP*

Bad Boys ½ **1995 (R)** And you thought the old buddy-cop formula was played out. Well, Hollywood sticks with what works, and pairing the two television personalities definitely works at the minimalist level required. Mike (Smith) and Marcus (Lawrence) are Miami cops who must track down $100 million dollars worth of heroin stolen from their evidence room before internal affairs shuts down the precinct. The case leads them to a vicious thief and a beautiful female witness to his murderous handiwork. Plot lacks depth, but high energy and dazzling action sequences keep things moving. Loud adventure is made louder still by cranking soundtrack. Satisfying addition to the odd-couple cops genre with potential to spawn a "Lethal Weapon"-type franchise. Feature film debut for director Bay. **118m/C VHS, LV.** Martin Lawrence, Will Smith, Tcheky Karyo, Tea Leoni, Theresa Randle, Marg Helgenberger, Joe Pantoliano; ***D:*** Michael Bay; ***W:*** Michael Barrie, Jim Mulholland; ***C:*** Howard Atherton. Blockbuster Entertainment Awards '96: Male Newcomer, Theatrical (Smith); Nominations: MTV Movie Awards '96: Best On-Screen Duo (Martin Lawrence/Will Smith), Best Action Sequence. *COL*

Bad Bunch **1976** A white liberal living in Watts tries to befriend a ruthless black street gang, but is unsuccessful. **82m/C VHS, Beta.** Greydon Clark, Tom Johnigam, Pamela Corbett, Jacqulin Cole, Aldo Ray, Jock Mahoney; ***D:*** Greydon Clark. *VCI*

B.A.D. Cats **1980** Two members of a police burglary auto detail team chase after a group of car thieves who are planning a million-dollar gold heist. **74m/C VHS, Beta, LV.** Asher Brauner, Michelle Pfeiffer, Vic Morrow, Jimmie Walker, Steve Hanks, LaWanda Page; ***D:*** Bernard L. Kowalski. *ORI*

Bad Channels **1992 (R)** Radio goes awry when female listeners of station KDUL are shrunk and put into speciman jars by a way-out disc jockey and a visiting alien, who plans to take the women back to his planet. Mildly amusing comedy features ex-MTV VJ Quinn and score by Blue Oyster Cult. Also available with Spanish subtitles. **88m/C VHS, Beta.** Paul Hipp, Martha Quinn, Aaron Lustig, Ian Patrick Williams, Charlie Spradling, Tim Thomerson; ***D:*** Ted Nicolaou; ***W:*** Jackson Barr. *PAR*

Bad Charleston Charlie *Woof!* **1973 (PG)** Dud of a gangster comedy with terrible acting. A comedy? **91m/C VHS.** Ross Hagen, John Carradine; ***D:*** Ivan Nagy. *NO*

Bad Company ½ **1972 (PG)** Thoughtful study of two very different Civil War draft dodgers roaming the Western frontier and eventually turning to a fruitless life of crime. Both the cast and script are wonderful in an entertaining film that hasn't been given the attention it's due. **94m/C VHS, Beta, LV.** Jeff Bridges, Barry Brown, Jim Davis, John Savage; ***D:*** Robert Benton; ***W:*** Robert Benton, David Newman; ***C:*** Gordon Willis. *PAR*

Bad Company **1994 (R)** Cynical thriller pits the bad against the worst. Vic Grimes (Langella) and Margaret Wells (Barkin) run a company of former secret agents who specialize in corporate dirty work. Nelson Crowe (Fishburne) is an ex-CIA agent who's their latest recruit. But maybe he's not so ex and maybe Margaret doesn't like sharing power and maybe the cold-blooded duo will get together to make some changes. Everything is stylish, including the leads, but there's a definite chill in the air. **118m/C VHS, LV.** Ellen Barkin, Laurence "Larry" Fishburne, Frank Langella, Michael Beach, Gia Carides, David Ogden Stiers, Spalding Gray, James Hong, Daniel Hugh-Kelly; ***D:*** Damian Harris; ***W:*** Ross Thomas; ***C:*** Jack N. Green; ***M:*** Carter Burwell. *TOU*

Bad Day at Black Rock ½ **1954** Story of a one-armed man uncovering a secret in a Western town. Wonderful performances from all concerned, especially Borgnine. Fine photography, shot using the new Cinemascope technique. Based on the novel by Howard Breslin. **81m/C VHS, LV.** Spencer Tracy, Robert Ryan, Anne Francis, Dean Jagger, Walter Brennan, John Ericson, Ernest Borgnine, Lee Marvin; ***D:*** John Sturges; ***C:*** William Mellor; ***M:*** Andre Previn. Cannes Film Festival '55: Best Actor (Tracy); Nominations: Academy Awards '54: Best Actor (Tracy), Best Director (Sturges). *MGM, CRC, FCT*

Bad Dreams ½ **1988 (R)** The only surviving member of a suicidal religious cult from the '60s awakens in 1988 from a coma. She is pursued by the living-dead cult leader, who seeks to ensure that she lives up (so to speak) to the cult's pact. Blood begins flowing as her fellow therapy group members begin dying, but the only bad dreams you'd get from this flick would be over the money lost on the video rental. **84m/C VHS, Beta, LV.** Bruce Abbott, Jennifer Rubin, Richard Lynch, Harris Yulin, Dean Cameron, Elizabeth Daily, Susan Ruttan, Charles Fleischer; ***D:*** Andrew Fleming; ***W:*** Andrew Fleming, Steven E. de Souza; ***M:*** Jay Michael Ferguson. *FOX*

Bad Georgia Road ½ **1977 (R)** A New Yorker inherits a moonshine operation from her uncle, and fights off the syndicate for its profits. **85m/C VHS, Beta.** Gary Lockwood, Carol Lynley, Royal Dano, John Wheeler, John Kerry; ***D:*** John Broderick. *VCI*

Bad Girls ½ **1994 (R)** Latest in the current western craze turns the tables as women take their turns being the gunslingers. Four hooker chums hastily flee town after one kills a nasty customer—only to find the bank where their cash was stashed was robbed by baddies Loggia and Russo. Wearing stylish duds and with each hair perfectly in place the beauties manage to recover their loot. Unexciting script leaves a lot to be desired, but a strong performance from Stowe makes this nearly worthwhile. Lots of off-set drama with original director Tamra Davis fired, and the actresses reportedly having a less-than-bonding experience. **99m/C VHS, LV.** Andie MacDowell, Madeleine Stowe, Mary Stuart Masterson, Drew Barrymore, James Russo, Dermot Mulroney, Robert Loggia, James LeGros; ***D:*** Jonathan Kaplan; ***W:*** Ken Friedman, Yolande Finch; ***M:*** Jerry Goldsmith. *FXV*

Bad Girls Do Cry *Woof!* **1954** Unbelievably bad exploitation film. Idiotic plot with long scenes of girls stripping down to their undies. Although an American film, the voice track was dubbed in later. **?m/C VHS.** Bill Page, Misty Ayers, Heather English, Ben Frommer. *SNC, TPV*

Bad Girls Dormitory **1984 (R)** At the New York Female Juvenile Reformatory, suicide seems a painless and welcome escape. Utilizes standard genre identifiers, including rape, drugs, soapy showers, bad docs, and desperate young women trapped in a web of frustration and desire. Cheap and mindless titillation. **95m/C VHS, Beta.** Carey Zuris, Teresa Farley; ***D:*** Tim Kincaid. *AHV*

Bad Girls from Mars *Woof!* **1990 (R)** "B" movie sleaze-o-rama in which everyone is murdered, either before, after, or during sex, just like in real life. When the director of the film within this film hires an actress who is, shall we say, popular, to be the heroine of his latest sci-fier, the fun, slim as it is, begins. **86m/C VHS.** Edy Williams, Brinke Stevens, Jay Richardson, Oliver Darrow; ***D:*** Fred Olen Ray; ***W:*** Sherman Scott, Mark Thomas McGee. *VMK*

Bad Girls Go to Hell *Woof!* **1965** From the sultana of sleaze, Wishman, comes this winning entry into Joe Bob Briggs' "Sleaziest Movies in the History of the World" series. A ditsy-but-sexy housewife accidentally commits murder and what follows is a plethora of perversion involving hirsute men and gender-bending women who are hell-bent on showing her how hot it is where bad girls go. **98m/B VHS.** ***D:*** Doris Wishman; ***W:*** Doris Wishman. *VTR*

Bad Girls in the Movies 🦴 **1986** A compilation of film clips depicting sleazy, criminal, female characters from women's prison films and other seedy sub-genres. **56m/C VHS, Beta.** David Carradine, Gene Autry, Yvonne De Carlo. *LIV*

Bad Guys 🦴🦴 **1979** A goulash western about the outlaw days of Hungary in the 1860s. A gang of bandits terrorizes the Transdanubian countryside. In Hungarian with English subtitles. For those seeking the Eastern European Wild West experience. **93m/C VHS.** *HU* Janos Derzsi, Djoko Rosic, Mari Kiss, Gyorgy Dorner, Laszlo Szabo, Miklos Benedek; ***D:*** Gyorgy Szomjas. *EVD, FCT, INJ*

Bad Guys 🦴 **1986 (PG)** An inane comedy about two ridiculous policemen who decide to take the wrestling world by storm after being kicked off the police force. Featuring scenes with many of the world's most popular wrestlers. **86m/C VHS.** Adam Baldwin, Mike Jolly, Michelle Nicastro, Ruth Buzzi, James Booth, Gene LeBell, Norman Burton; ***D:*** Joel Silberg; ***M:*** William Goldstein. *LIV*

Bad Influence 🦴½ **1990 (R)** A lackluster effort in the evil-doppelganger school of psychological mystery, where a befuddled young executive (Spader) is led into the seamier side of life by a mysterious stranger (Lowe). **99m/C VHS, Beta, LV.** Rob Lowe, James Spader, Lisa Zane, Christian Clemenson, Kathleen Wilhoite; ***D:*** Curtis Hanson; ***M:*** Trevor Jones. *COL*

Bad Jim 🦴½ **1989 (PG)** A cowpoke buys Billy the Kid's horse and, upon riding it, becomes an incorrigible outlaw himself. First feature film for Hollywood legend Clark Gable's son. **110m/C VHS, Beta, LV.** James Brolin, Richard Roundtree, John Clark Gable, Harry Carey Jr., Ty Hardin, Pepe Serna, Rory Calhoun; ***D:*** Clyde Ware. *COL*

Bad Lands 🦴🦴½ **1939** A small cowboy posse finds themselves trapped by a band of Apache Indians in the Arizona desert. A remake of "The Lost Patrol." **70m/B VHS, Beta.** Robert Barrat, Guinn "Big Boy" Williams, Douglas Walton, Andy Clyde, Addison Richards, Robert Coote, Paul Hurst, Noah Beery Jr.; ***D:*** Lew (Louis Friedlander) Landers. *TTC*

Bad Lieutenant 🦴🦴🦴 **1992 (NC-17)** Social chaos and degeneration characterize story as well as nameless loner lieutenant Keitel, who is as corrupt as they come. Assigned to a case involving a raped nun, he's confronted by his own lagging Catholic beliefs and the need for saving grace. From cult filmmaker Ferrara ("Ms. 45") and filled with violence, drugs, and grotesque sexual situations. Tense, over-the-top, urban drama is not intended for seekers of the subtle. Rent it with "Reservoir Dogs" and prepare yourself for a long tense evening of top-rated Keitel and screen-splitting violence. "R" rated version is also available at 91 minutes. **98m/C VHS, LV.** Harvey Keitel, Brian McElroy, Frankie Acciario, Peggy Gormley, Stella Keitel, Victor Argo, Paul Calderone, Leonard Thomas, Frankie Thorn; ***D:*** Abel Ferrara; ***W:*** Zoe Tamerlaine Lund, Abel Ferrara; ***M:*** Joe Delia. Independent Spirit Awards '93: Best Actor (Keitel). *LIV, FCT*

Bad Love 🦴🦴½ **1995 (R)** Unlucky Eloise (Gridley) stays true to nature when she falls for loser Lenny (Sizemore), who decides the big score lies with robbing the fading movie star (O'Neill) Eloise works for. Naturally, things go badly. Slick production for anyone who likes fringe romances. **93m/C VHS.** Tom Sizemore, Pamela Gidley, Debi Mazar, Jennifer O'Neill, Margaux Hemingway, Richard Edson, Seymour Cassel; ***D:*** Jill Goldman. *APX*

Bad Man of Deadwood 🦴 **1941** A man-with-a-past joins a circus as a sharp-shooter, and is threatened with disclosure. **54m/B VHS, Beta.** Roy Rogers, George "Gabby" Hayes. *DVT, NOS, RXM*

Bad Manners 🦴 **1984 (R)** When an orphan is adopted by a wealthy but entirely selfish couple, a group of his orphan friends try to free him from his new home and lifestyle. **85m/C VHS, Beta.** Martin Mull, Karen Black, Anne DeSalvo, Murphy Dunne, Pamela Segall, Edy Williams, Susan Ruttan, Richard Deacon; ***D:*** Bobby Houston. *VTR*

Bad Man's River 🦴🦴 **1972** A Mexican revolutionary leader hires a gang of outlaws to blow up an arsenal used by the Mexican Army. **92m/C VHS, Beta.** *IT SP* Lee Van Cleef, James Mason, Gina Lollobrigida; ***D:*** Gene Martin; ***W:*** Philip Yordan. *NO*

Bad Medicine *Woof!* **1985 (PG-13)** A youth who doesn't want to be a doctor is accepted by a highly questionable Latin American school of medicine. Remember that it was for medical students like these that the U.S. liberated Grenada. **97m/C VHS, Beta.** Steve Guttenberg, Alan Arkin, Julie Hagerty, Bill Macy, Curtis Armstrong, Julie Kavner, Joe Grifasi, Robert Romanus, Taylor Negron, Gilbert Gottfried; ***D:*** Harvey Miller; ***W:*** Harvey Miller. *FOX*

Bad Men of the Border 🦴½ **1945** Routine oater has Kirby posing as a bandit in order to infiltrate an outlaw band passing counterfeit money. He rounds up the bad guys and finds time to romance Armida too. **56m/B VHS.** Kirby Grant, Fuzzy Knight, Armida, John Eldridge, Francis McDonald; ***D:*** Wallace Fox; ***W:*** Adele Buffington. *MOV*

The Bad News Bears 🦴🦴🦴 **1976 (PG)** Family comedy about a misfit Little League team that gets whipped into shape by a cranky, sloppy, beer-drinking coach who recruits a female pitcher. O'Neal and Matthau are top-notch. The kids' language is rather adult, and very titillating for younger viewers. Spawned two sequels and a television series. **102m/C VHS, Beta, LV, 8mm.** Walter Matthau, Tatum O'Neal, Vic Morrow, Joyce Van Patten, Jackie Earle Haley; ***D:*** Michael Ritchie; ***C:*** John A. Alonzo. Writers Guild of America '76: Best Original Screenplay. *PAR*

The Bad News Bears Go to Japan 🦴 **1978 (PG)** The second sequel, in which the famed Little League team goes to the Little League World Series in Tokyo. Comic adventure features Curtis as a talent agent out to exploit the team's fame. **102m/C VHS, Beta, LV.** Tony Curtis, Jackie Earle Haley, Tomisaburo Wakayama, George Wyner; ***D:*** John Berry. *PAR*

The Bad News Bears in Breaking Training 🦴½ **1977 (PG)** With a chance to take on the Houston Toros for a shot at the little league baseball Japanese champs, the Bears devise a way to get to Texas to play at the famed Astrodome. Disappointing sequel to "The Bad News Bears"; followed by "The Bad News Bears Go to Japan" (1978). **105m/C VHS, Beta, LV.** William Devane, Clifton James, Jackie Earle Haley, Jimmy Baio; ***D:*** Michael Pressman; ***W:*** Paul Brickman. *PAR*

Bad Ronald 🦴🦴🦴 **1974** No, not a political biography of Ronald Reagan... Fascinating thriller about a disturbed teenager who kills a friend after being harassed repeatedly. The plot thickens after the boy's mother dies, and he is forced to hide out in a secret room when an unsuspecting family with three daughters moves into his house. The story is accurately recreated from the novel by John Holbrook Vance. **78m/C VHS.** Scott Jacoby, Pippa Scott, John Larch, Dabney Coleman, Kim Hunter, John Fiedler; ***D:*** Buzz Kulik. *LIV*

The Bad Seed 🦴🦴½ **1956** A mother makes the tortuous discovery that her cherubic eight-year-old daughter harbors an innate desire to kill. Based on Maxwell Anderson's powerful Broadway stage play. Remade for television in 1985. **129m/B VHS, Beta.** Patty McCormack, Nancy Kelly, Eileen Heckart, Henry Jones, Evelyn Varden, Paul Fix; ***D:*** Mervyn LeRoy; ***M:*** Alex North. Golden Globe Awards '57: Best Supporting Actress (Heckart); Nominations: Academy Awards '56: Best Actress (Kelly), Best Black and White Cinematography, Best Supporting Actress (Heckart, McCormack). *WAR*

The Bad Seed 🦴🦴 **1985** Television remake of the movie with the same name. Story about a sadistic little child who kills for her own evil purposes. Acting is not up to par with previous version. **100m/C VHS.** Blair Brown, Lynn Redgrave, David Carradine, Richard Kiley, David Ogden Stiers, Carrie Wells; ***D:*** Paul Wendkos. *NO*

The Bad Sleep Well 🦴🦴🦴½ **1960** Japanese variation of the 1940 Warner Brothers crime dramas. A tale about corruption in the corporate world as seen through the eyes of a rising executive. **135m/B VHS, Beta.** *JP* Toshiro Mifune, Masayuki Kato, Masayuki Mori, Takashi Shimura, Akira Nishimura; ***D:*** Akira Kurosawa. *COL, APD, INJ*

Bad Taste 🦴🦴🦴 **1988** A definite pleaser for the person who enjoys watching starving aliens devour the average, everyday human being. Alien fast-food manufacturers come to earth in hopes of harvesting all of mankind. The earth's fate lies in the hands of the government who must stop these rampaging creatures before the whole human race is gobbled up. Terrific make-up jobs on the aliens add the final touch to this gory, yet humorous cult horror flick. **90m/C VHS, LV.** *NZ* Peter Jackson, Pete O'Herne, Mike Minett, Terry Potter, Craig Smith, Doug Wren, Dean Lawrie; ***D:*** Peter Jackson. *FCT*

Badge of the Assassin 🦴🦴 **1985** A television movie based on the true story of a New York assistant DA who directed a campaign to catch a pair of cop-killers from the '70s. **96m/C VHS, Beta, LV.** James Woods, Yaphet Kotto, Alex Rocco, David Harris, Pam Grier, Steven Keats, Richard Bradford, Rae Dawn Chong; ***D:*** Mel Damski. *VMK*

Badge 373 🦴½ **1973 (R)** In the vein of "The French Connection," a New York cop is suspended and decides to battle crime his own way. **116m/C VHS, Beta.** Robert Duvall, Verna Bloom, Eddie Egan; ***D:*** Howard W. Koch. *PAR*

The Badlanders 🦴🦴🦴 **1958** A western remake of the crime drama "The Asphalt Jungle." Ladd and Borgnine plan a gold robbery against Smith, who cheated them out of their share in a gold mine. Cross and double-cross follow the partners as does romance. **85m/C VHS.** Alan Ladd, Ernest Borgnine, Kent Smith, Katy Jurado, Claire Kelly, Nehemiah Persoff, Adam Williams; ***D:*** Delmer Daves. *MGM*

Badlands 🦴🦴🦴½ **1974 (PG)** Based loosely on the Charlie Starkweather murders of the 1950s, this impressive debut by director Malick recounts a slow-thinking, unhinged misfit's killing spree across the midwestern plains, accompanied by a starry-eyed 15-year-old schoolgirl. Sheen and Spacek are a disturbingly numb, apathetic, and icy duo. **94m/C VHS, Beta, LV.** Martin Sheen, Sissy Spacek, Warren Oates; ***D:*** Terence Malick; ***W:*** Terence Malick. *WAR*

Badman's Territory 🦴🦴🦴 **1946** A straight-shooting marshal has to deal with such notorious outlaws as the James and Dalton boys in a territory outside of government control. **79m/B VHS, Beta.** Randolph Scott, Ann Richards, George "Gabby" Hayes, Steve Brodie; ***D:*** Tim Whelan. *TTC*

Badmen of Nevada 🦴½ **1933** Badmen roam Nevada in the early days before law and order. **57m/B VHS, Beta.** Kent Taylor, Gail Patrick. *VCN*

Baffled 🦴🦴½ **1972** Nimoy is a race car driver who has visions of people in danger. He must convince an ESP expert (Hampshire) of the credibility of his vision, and then try to save the lives of the people seen with his sixth sense. Made for television. **90m/C VHS.** Leonard Nimoy, Susan Hampshire, Vera Miles, Rachel

Roberts, Jewel Blanch, Christopher Benjamin; *D:* Philip Leacock. *FOX*

Bagdad Cafe ☙☙☙ *Out of Rosenheim* **1988 (PG)** A large German woman, played by Sagebrecht, finds herself stranded in the Mojave desert after her husband dumps her on the side of the highway. She encounters a rundown cafe where she becomes involved with the off-beat residents. A hilarious story in which the strange people and the absurdity of their situations are treated kindly and not made to seem ridiculous. Spawned a short-lived TV series with Whoopi Goldberg. **91m/C VHS, Beta.** *GE* Marianne Sagebrecht, CCH Pounder, Jack Palance, Christine Kaufmann, Monica Calhoun, Darron Flagg; *D:* Percy Adlon; *W:* Percy Adlon, Eleonore Adlon; *M:* Bob Telson. Cesar Awards '89: Best Foreign Film; Nominations: Academy Awards '88: Best Song ("Calling You"). *FCT, VTR*

Bahama Passage ☙☙½ **1942** Trite story of one lady's efforts to win the affection of a macho Bahamas stud. **83m/C VHS.** Madeleine Carroll, Sterling Hayden, Flora Robson, Leo G. Carroll; *D:* Edward H. Griffith. *PAR, MLB*

Bail Jumper ☙☙ **1989** A story of love and commitment against incredible odds; some of which happen to be a swarm of locusts, a tornado, and falling meteorites. Joe and Elaine are small-time hoods escaping their dreary lives in Murky Springs Missouri by heading for that great bastion of idyllism and idealism—New York City. But even as the world starts to crumble around them, get the message that love prevails. **96m/C VHS, Beta.** Eszter Balint, B.J. Spalding, Tony Askin, Joie Lee; *D:* Christian Faber. *FXL*

Bail Out ☙ **1990 (R)** Three bounty hunters, armed to the teeth, run a car-trashing police gauntlet so they may capture a valuable crook. **88m/C VHS, Beta, LV.** David Hasselhoff, Linda Blair, John Vernon, Tom Rosales, Charlie Brill; *D:* Max Kleven. *VES, LIV*

Bail Out at 43,000 ☙☙ **1957** Movie about the lifestyles and love affairs of your average, everyday parachutist. **80m/B VHS.** John Payne, Karen Steele, Paul Kelly; *D:* Francis D. Lyon; *W:* Paul Monash. *MGM*

Baja ☙☙ **1995 (R)** Bebe (Ringwald) hides out in Baja with her beau Alex (Logue) after a drug deal goes bad. They hold up in a sleazy motel while Bebe waits for dad, John (Bernsen), to bail her out. But instead, John persuades estranged hubby Michael (Nickles) to track down the runaways and Michael finds out that hitman Tom (Henriksen) is hunting for Alex. Must be the desert heat causing all the ensuing commotion. **92m/C VHS, LV.** Molly Ringwald, Lance Henriksen, Michael A. Nickles, Donal Logue, Corbin Bernsen; *D:* Kurt Voss; *W:* Kurt Voss; *C:* Denis Maloney; *M:* Reg Powell. *REP*

Baja Oklahoma ☙ **1987** A made-for-cable-television film about a country barmaid with dreams of being a country singer. Songs by Willie Nelson, Emmylou Harris and Billy Vera. **97m/C VHS, Beta, LV.** Lesley Ann Warren, Peter Coyote, Swoosie Kurtz, Willie Nelson, Julia Roberts; *D:* Bobby Roth; *W:* Bobby Roth. *WAR, ORI*

Baker's Hawk ☙☙ **1976** A young boy befriends a red-tailed hawk and learns the meaning of family and caring. **98m/C VHS, Beta.** Clint Walker, Diane Baker, Burl Ives; *D:* Lyman Dayton. *HHE*

The Baker's Wife ☙☙☙½ *La Femme du Boulanger* **1933** There's a new baker in town, and he brings with him to the small French village an array of tantalizing breads, as well as a discontented wife. When she runs off with a shepherd, her loyal and naive husband refuses to acknowledge her infidelity; however, in his loneliness, the baker can't bake, so the townspeople scheme to bring his wife back. Panned as overly cute Marcel Pagnol peasant glorification, and hailed as a visual poem full of wit; you decide. In French with subtitles. Also available for French students without subtitles; a French script booklet is also available. **101m/B VHS, Beta.** *FR* Raimu, Ginette LeClerc, Charles Moulton, Charpin, Robert Vattier; *D:* Marcel Pagnol. National Board of Review Awards '40: 5 Best Foreign Films of the Year; New York Film Critics Awards '40: Best Foreign Film. *INT, MRV, DVT*

Bakery/Grocery Clerk ☙☙ **1921** A package of shorts featuring crazy comedian Larry Semon, getting tangled up in mayhem and molasses. Silent with piano score. **55m/B VHS, Beta.** Larry Semon, Oliver Hardy, Lucille Carlisle; *D:* Larry Semon. *CCB*

Balalaika ☙☙ **1939** Rather dull operetta about the Russian revolution with Eddy playing a Russian prince. Eddy masquerades as a member of the proletariat in order to romance Massey, who was expected to become the next Garbo. Didn't happen, though. Eddy's rendition of "Stille Nacht" ("Silent Night") is highlight of film. Based on the operetta by Eric Maschwitz, George Ponford, and Bernard Gruen. **102m/B VHS.** Nelson Eddy, Ilona Massey, Charlie Ruggles, Frank Morgan, Lionel Atwill, Sir C. Aubrey Smith, Joyce Compton; *D:* Reinhold Schunzel; *W:* Leon Gordon, Charles Bennett, Jacques Deval; *C:* Karl Freund. *MGM*

Balboa *Woof!* **1982** Set on sun-baked Balboa Island, this is a melodramatic tale of high-class power, jealousy, and intrigue. Never-aired pilot for a television mini-series, in the night-time soap tradition (even features Steve Kanaly from TV's "Dallas"). Special appearance by Cassandra Peterson, also known as horror hostess Elvira; and if that interests you, look for Sonny Bono, as well. **92m/C VHS, Beta.** Tony Curtis, Carol Lynley, Chuck Connors, Sonny Bono, Steve Kanaly, Jennifer Chase, Lupita Ferrer, Martine Beswick, Henry Jones, Cassandra Peterson; *D:* James Polakof. *VES, LIV*

The Balcony ☙☙☙ **1963** A film version of the great Jean Genet play about a surreal brothel, located in an unnamed, revolution-torn city, where its powerful patrons act out their fantasies. Scathing and rude. **87m/B VHS, Beta, LV.** Peter Falk, Shelley Winters, Lee Grant, Kent Smith, Peter Brocco, Ruby Dee, Jeff Corey, Leonard Nimoy, Joyce Jameson; *D:* Joseph Strick. Nominations: Academy Awards '63: Best Black and White Cinematography. *MFV, INJ*

Ball of Fire ☙☙☙ **1941** A gang moll hides out with a group of mundane professors, trying to avoid her loathsome boyfriend. The professors are busy compiling an encyclopedia and Stanwyck helps them with their section on slang in the English language. Cooper has his hands full when he falls for this damsel in distress and must fight the gangsters to keep her. Stanwyck takes a personal liking to naive Cooper and resolves to teach him more than just slang. **111m/B VHS, Beta, LV.** Gary Cooper, Barbara Stanwyck, Dana Andrews, Gene Krupa, Oscar Homolka, Dan Duryea, S.Z. Sakall, Henry Travers; *D:* Howard Hawks; *W:* Billy Wilder, Charles Brackett; *C:* Gregg Toland. Nominations: Academy Awards '41: Best Actress (Stanwyck), Best Sound, Best Story, Best Original Score. *SUE*

Ballad in Blue ☙☙ *Blues for Lovers* **1966** Real life story of Ray Charles and a blind child. Tearjerker also includes some of Charles' hit songs. ♫I Got a Woman; What'd I Say?. **89m/B VHS, Beta.** *GB* Ray Charles, Tom Bell, Mary Peach, Dawn Addams, Piers Bishop, Betty McDowall; *D:* Paul Henreid. *LIV*

Ballad of a Gunfighter ☙ **1964** A feud between two outlaws reaches the boiling point when they both fall in love with the same woman. **84m/C VHS, Beta.** Marty Robbins, Bob Barron, Joyce Redd, Nestor Paiva, Laurette Luez; *D:* Bill Ward. *FHE, PSM*

Ballad of a Soldier ☙☙☙½ **1960** As a reward for demolishing two German tanks, a nineteen-year-old Russian soldier receives a six-day pass so he can see his mother; however, he meets another woman. Well directed and photographed, while avoiding propaganda. **88m/B VHS, Beta.** *RU* Vladimir Ivashov, Shanna Prokhorenko; *D:* Grigori Chukrai. British Academy Awards '61: Best Film; Nominations: Academy Awards '61: Best Story & Screenplay. *VYY, NOS, HHT*

Ballad of Cable Hogue ☙☙☙ **1970 (R)** A prospector, who had been left to die in the desert by his double-crossing partners, finds a waterhole. A surprise awaits his former friends when they visit the remote well. Not the usual violent Peckinpah horse drama, but a tongue-in-cheek comedy romance mixed with tragedy. Obviously offbeat and worth a peek. **122m/C VHS, Beta, LV.** Jason Robards Jr., Stella Stevens, David Warner, L.Q. Jones, Strother Martin, Slim Pickens; *D:* Sam Peckinpah; *C:* Lucien Ballard; *M:* Jerry Goldsmith. *WAR*

Ballad of Gregorio Cortez ☙☙☙ **1983 (PG)** Tragic story based on one of the most famous manhunts in Texas history. A Mexican cowhand kills a Texas sheriff in self-defense and tries to elude the law, all because of a misunderstanding of the Spanish language. Olmos turns in a fine performance as Cortez. **105m/C VHS, Beta, LV.** Edward James Olmos, James Gammon, Tom Bower, Alan Vint, Barry Corbin, Rosana De Soto, Bruce McGill, Brion James, Pepe Serna, William Sanderson; *D:* Robert M. Young; *W:* Robert M. Young; *C:* Reynaldo Villalobos. *SUE, INJ, NLC*

The Ballad of Little Jo ☙☙½ **1993 (R)** Inspired by a true story set during the 1866 gold rush. Easterner Josephine Monaghan is cast out of her wealthy family after she has a baby out of wedlock. Heading west, she passes herself off as a man—Little Jo—in an attempt to forestall harrasssment. Solemn and overly-earnest attempt by Greenwald to demystify the old west and bring a feminist viewpoint to a familiar saga. **110m/C VHS.** Suzy Amis, Bo Hopkins, Ian McKellen, Carrie Snodgress, David Chung, Rene Auberjonois, Heather Graham, Anthony Heald, Sam Robards, Ruth Maleczech; *D:* Maggie Greenwald; *W:* Maggie Greenwald; *M:* David Mansfield. Nominations: Independent Spirit Awards '94: Best Actress (Amis). *COL*

The Ballad of Narayama ☙☙☙☙ *Narayama-Bushi-Ko* **1983** Director Imamura's subtle and vastly moving story takes place a vague century ago. In compliance with village law designed to control population among the poverty-stricken peasants, a healthy seventy-year-old woman must submit to solitary starvation atop a nearby mountain. We follow her as she sets into motion the final influence she will have in the lives of her children and grandchildren, a situation described with detachment and without imposing a tragic perspective. In Japanese with English subtitles. **129m/C VHS.** *JP* Ken Ogata, Sumiko Sakamota, Takejo Aki, Tonpei Hidari, Shoichi Ozawa; *D:* Shohei Imamura; *W:* Shohei Imamura. Cannes Film Festival '83: Best Film. *HMV, FCT, KIV*

The Ballad of Paul Bunyan **1972** The good-humored, legendary American giant is pitted against a powerful lumber camp boss who likes to pick on the little guy. **30m/C VHS.** *D:* Arthur Rankin Jr., Jules Bass. *VTR, PSM*

The Ballad of the Sad Cafe ☙☙½ **1991 (PG-13)** Unusual love story set in a small Southern town during the Depression. The everday lives of its townspeople are suddenly transformed when a distant relation of the town's outcast (Redgrave) unexpectedly shows up. A moving story that tries to portray both sides of love and its power to enhance and destroy simultaneously. Emotion never seems to come to life in a movie that's nice to watch, but is ultimately disappointing. Adapted from the play by Edward Albee, which was based on the critically acclaimed novella by Carson McCullers. A British/U.S. co-production. **100m/C VHS, LV.** *GB* Vanessa Redgrave, Keith Carradine, Cork Hubbert, Rod Steiger, Austin Pendleton, Beth Dixon, Lanny Flaherty, Mert Hatfield, Earl Hindman, Anne Pitoniak; *D:* Simon Callow; *W:* Michael Hirst; *C:* Walter Lassally; *M:* Richard Robbins. *NO*

Ballbuster **19??** Cops take on gangs in an all-out high-stakes battle to win back the streets. **100m/C VHS.** Ivan Rogers, Bonnie Paine, W. Randolph Galvin, Bill Shirk, Brenda Banet; *D:* Eddie Beverly Jr.; *W:* Eddie Beverly Jr. *XVC*

Ballet Shoes ☙☙½ **19??** The classic children's tale of three sisters living a very sheltered life with their guardian Sylvia, who is working to support all four of them. A story of hope and possibilities. From the BBC Television network. **120m/C VHS.** *GB VCO, HMV*

Ballistic ☙½ **1994 (R)** L.A. cop Jesse Gavin (Holden) gets in trouble when the government witness she's supposed to be protecting gets murdered. So she teams up with her ex-con father and her boyfriend to track the mobster responsible for the hit. **86m/C VHS, LV.** Marjean Holden, Richard Roundtree,

Sam Jones, Joel Beeson, Charles Napier; *D:* Kim Bass. *IMP, IME*

The Balloonatic/One Week **1923** "The Balloonatic" (1923) features Keaton in several misadventures. In "One Week" (1920), Keaton and his new bride, Seely, receive a new home as a wedding gift—the kind you have to assemble yourself. Silent. **48m/B VHS, Beta.** Buster Keaton, Phyllis Haver, Sybil Seely; *D:* Buster Keaton. *CCB*

Baltic Deputy 🦴🦴🦴½ **1937** An early forerunner of Soviet historic realism, where an aging intellectual deals with post-revolution Soviet life. In Russian with subtitles. **95m/B VHS, Beta.** *RU* Nikolai Cherkassov; *D:* Yosif Heifitz. National Board of Review Awards '37: 10 Best Films of the Year. *FCT, IHF*

The Baltimore Bullet 🦴🦴 **1980 (PG)** Two men make their living traveling through the country as pool hustlers, bilking would-be pool sharks. Features ten of the greatest pool players in the world. **103m/C VHS, Beta.** James Coburn, Omar Sharif, Bruce Boxleitner, Ronee Blakley, Jack O'Halloran; *D:* Robert Ellis Miller; *W:* Robert Vincent O'Neil, John F. Brascia. *SUE, NLC*

Balto 🦴🦴½ **1995 (G)** Animated adventure, based on a true story, of a half-husky, half-wolf sled dog, Balto, who faces overwhelming odds to bring life-saving medicine to Nome, Alsaka. It's 1925, there's a diptheria epidemic, and Balto is the lead team dog on the final leg of the race to get the serum to Nome in time. Balto and the rest of the team dogs became instant heroes and even journeyed to Hollywood to star in their own silent film "Balto's Race to Nome." **78m/C VHS, LV.** *D:* Simon Wells; *W:* Cliff Ruby, Elana Lesser, David Steven Cohen, Roger S.H. Schulman; *M:* James Horner; *V:* Kevin Bacon, Bob Hoskins, Bridget Fonda, Jim Cummings, Phil Collins, Juliette Brewer, Danny Mann, Miriam Margolyes. *MCA*

Bambi 🦴🦴🦴🦴 **1942 (G)** A true Disney classic, detailing the often harsh education of a newborn deer and his friends in the forest. Proves that Disney animation was—and still is—the best to be found. Thumper still steals the show and the music is delightful, including "Let's Sing a Gay Little Spring Song," "Love is a Song," "Little April Shower," "The Thumper Song," and "Twitterpated." Stands as one of the greatest children's films of all time; a genuine perennial from generation to generation. Based very loosely on the book by Felix Salten. **69m/C VHS, Beta, LV.** *D:* David Hand; *W:* Larry Morey; *M:* Frank Churchill, Edward Plumb; *V:* Bobby Stewart, Peter Behn, Stan Alexander, Cammie King, Donnie Dunagan, Hardie Albright, John Sutherland, Tim Davis, Sam Edwards, Sterling Holloway, Ann Gillis, Perce Pearce. Nominations: Academy Awards '42: Best Song ("Love Is a Song"), Best Sound, Best Original Score. *DIS, APD, RDG*

The Bamboo Saucer 🦴½ *Collision Course* **1968** Russian and American scientists race to find a U.F.O. in Red China. **103m/C VHS.** Dan Duryea, John Ericson, Lois Nettleton, Nan Leslie; *D:* Frank Telford. *REP*

Bananas 🦴🦴🦴 **1971 (PG-13)** Intermittently hilarious pre-"Annie Hall" Allen fare is full of the director's signature angst-ridden philosophical comedy. A frustrated product tester from New York runs off to South America, where he volunteers his support to the revolutionary force of a shaky Latin-American dictatorship and winds up the leader. Don't miss cameos by Stallone and Garfield. Witty score contributes much. **82m/C VHS, Beta, LV.** Woody Allen, Louise Lasser, Carlos Montalban, Howard Cosell, Charlotte Rae, Conrad Bain; *Cameos:* Sylvester Stallone, Allen (Goorwitz) Garfield; *D:* Woody Allen; *W:* Woody Allen; *M:* Marvin Hamlisch. *MGM, FCT, FOX*

Bananas Boat *Woof! What Changed Charley Farthing* **1978** A captain takes a man and his daughter away from the collapsing government of their banana republic. The cast and director take a few risks but fail in this would-be comedy. **91m/C VHS.** *GB* Doug McClure, Hayley Mills, Lionel Jeffries, Dilys Hamlett, Warren Mitchell; *D:* Sidney Hayers. *VCI*

Band of Angels 🦴🦴½ **1957** Orphaned Amantha (De Carlo) learns she has African-American blood and since it's the pre-Civil War era she promptly winds up on the auction block. She becomes both the property and the mistress of mysterious New Orleans landowner Hamish Bond (Gable). Then the Civil War comes along bringing threats and revelations. De Carlo looks properly sultry but this is a weak attempt at costume drama. Based on the novel by Robert Penn Warren. **127m/C VHS.** Clark Gable, Yvonne De Carlo, Sidney Poitier, Efrem Zimbalist Jr., Rex Reason, Patric Knowles, Torin Thatcher, Andrea King, Ray Teal; *D:* Raoul Walsh; *W:* John Twist, Ivan Goff; *M:* Max Steiner. *WAR, MOV*

Band of Outsiders 🦴🦴½ *Bande a Part; The Outsiders* **1964** A woman hires a pair of petty criminals to rip off her aunt; Godard vehicle for exposuing self-reflexive comments on modern film culture. In French with English subtitles. **97m/B VHS, Beta.** *FR* Sami Frey, Anna Karina, Claude Brasseur, Louisa Colpeyn; *D:* Jean-Luc Godard; *W:* Jean-Luc Godard. *INJ, NOS, MRV*

Band of the Hand 🦴 **1986 (R)** A "Miami Vice" type melodrama about five convicts who are trained to become an unstoppable police unit. The first feature film by Glaser, last seen as Starsky in "Starsky & Hutch." **109m/C VHS, Beta, LV.** Stephen Lang, Michael Carmine, Lauren Holly, Leon Robinson; *D:* Paul Michael Glaser; *W:* Jack Baran, Leo Garen. *NO*

The Band Wagon 🦴🦴🦴 **1953** A Hollywood song-and-dance man finds trouble when he is persuaded to star in a Broadway musical. Charisse has been called Astaire's most perfect partner, perhaps by those who haven't seen Rogers. ♫That's Entertainment; Dancing in the Dark; By Myself; A Shine On Your Shoes; Something to Remember You By; High and Low; I Love Louisa; New Sun in the Sky; I Guess I'll Have to Change My Plan. **112m/C VHS, Beta, LV.** Fred Astaire, Cyd Charisse, Oscar Levant, Nanette Fabray, Jack Buchanan, Bobby Watson; *D:* Vincente Minnelli; *W:* Betty Comden; *M:* Arthur Schwartz, Howard Dietz. Nominations: Academy Awards '53: Best Costume Design (Color), Best Story & Screenplay, Best Original Score, Best Original Score. *MGM, FCT*

Bandit King of Texas 🦴🦴½ **1949** A varmint is swindling unsuspecting settlers in a land scheme and then robbing and murdering them when they go to visit their supposed property. Rocky and friends come to the rescue. **60m/B VHS.** Allan "Rocky" Lane, Eddy Waller, Helene Stanley, Robert Bice, Harry Lauter, Jim Nolan, John Hamilton, Lane Bradford; *D:* Fred Brannon; *W:* Olive Cooper. *GPV*

Bandit Queen 🦴½ **1951** Spanish girl forms a band to stop seizure of Spanish possessions by lawless Californians. **71m/B VHS, Beta.** Barbara Britton, Willard Parker, Philip Reed, Jack Perrin; *D:* William (Lester Williams) Berke. *RXM*

Bandit Queen 🦴🦴 **1994** Phoolan Devi (Biswas) is a female Robin Hood in modern-day India. A lower-caste woman, Devi is sold into marriage at 11, brutalized by her husband (and many others throughout the film), and eventually winds up with a equally brutal group of hill bandits. Only this time around, Devi takes action by aiding the group in robbing, kidnapping (and murdering) the rich and higher castes. Devi surrendered to authorities in 1983 and spent 11 years in jail. Based on screenwriter Sen's biography "India's Bandit Queen: The True Story of Phoolan Devi" and Devi's diaries. In Hindi with subtitles. **119m/C VHS, LV.** *GB IN* Seema Biswas, Nirmal Pandey, Manoj Bajpai, Raghubir Yadav, Rajesh Vivek, Govind Namdeo; *D:* Shekhar Kapur; *W:* Mala Sen; *C:* Ashok Mehta. *HMK*

Bandits 🦴½ **1973** Three cowboys team up with a band of Mexican outlaws to fight a Mexican traitor. **83m/C VHS, Beta.** Robert Conrad, Jan-Michael Vincent, Roy Jenson; *D:* Robert Conrad, Alfredo Zacharias. *UNI*

Bandits 🦴🦴½ **1986** Simon Verini (Yanne), a sophisticated fence, is given the loot from a 10 million dollar Cartier heist to exchange for cash by Mozart (Bruel) the leader of the thieves. But two of Mozart's gang want to keep the jewels instead and kidnap Verini's wife as ransom. She's killed, even after he returns the goods, and Verini is then framed for the theft and spends 10 years in prison. He's sent his daughter Marie-Sophie to a Swiss boarding school and upon his release works to both establish a relationship with her and to find those responsible for his wife's death. Director Lelouch's wife portrays the adult Marie-Sophie. In French with English subtitles. **98m/C VHS.** *FR* Jean Yanne, Marie-Sophie L(elouch), Patrick Bruel, Charles Gerard, Corinne Marchand, Christine Barbelivien; *D:* Claude Lelouch; *W:* Pierre Uytterhoeven, Claude Lelouch. *FXL, FCT*

Bandits of Orgosolo 🦴🦴½ *Banditi a Orgosolo* **1961** An acclaimed, patient drama about a Sardinian shepherd who shelters a band of thieves from the police. When one of the cops is killed the shepherd panics and flees into the hills for survival. Dubbed in English. **98m/B VHS, Beta.** *IT* Michele Cossu, Peppeddu Cuccu; *D:* Vittorio de Seta. *NOS, FCT, VYY*

Bandolero! 🦴🦴½ **1968 (PG)** In Texas, Stewart and Martin are two fugitive brothers who run into trouble with their Mexican counterparts. **106m/C VHS, Beta.** James Stewart, Raquel Welch, Dean Martin, George Kennedy, Will Geer, Harry Carey Jr., Andrew Prine; *D:* Andrew V. McLaglen; *C:* William Clothier; *M:* Jerry Goldsmith. *FOX*

Bang Bang Kid 🦴🦴 *Bang Bang* **1967 (G)** A western spoof about a klutzy gunfighter defending a town from outlaws. **78m/C VHS, Beta.** Tom Bosley, Guy Madison, Sandra Milo; *D:* Stanley Prager. *NO*

Bang the Drum Slowly 🦴🦴 **1956** The original television adaptation of a Mark Harris novel about baseball. A ball player stricken by a terminal illness strikes an unlikely friendship with a teammate. Interesting role for an actor (Newman) who claims to have been driven to acting by running away from the sporting goods business. **60m/B VHS.** Paul Newman, George Peppard, Albert Salmi. *NOS, WKV*

Bang the Drum Slowly 🦴🦴🦴 **1973 (PG)** The touching story of a major league catcher who discovers that he is dying of Hodgkins disease and wants to play just one more season. De Niro is the weakening baseball player and Moriarty is the friend who helps him see it through. Based on a novel by Mark Harris. **97m/C VHS, Beta, LV.** Robert De Niro, Michael Moriarty, Vincent Gardenia, Phil Foster, Ann Wedgeworth, Heather MacRae, Selma Diamond, Danny Aiello; *D:* John Hancock. National Board of Review Awards '73: 10 Best Films of the Year; New York Film Critics Awards '73: Best Supporting Actor (De Niro); Nominations: Academy Awards '73: Best Supporting Actor (Gardenia). *PAR, FCT*

The Bank Dick 🦴🦴🦴🦴 *The Bank Detective* **1940** Fields wrote the screenplay (using an alias) and stars in this zany comedy about a man who accidentally trips a bank robber and winds up as a guard. Fields' last major role is a classic, a worthy end to his great career. Side two of the laserdisc is in CAV format, which allows single frame access to the frenetic cops and robbers chase sequence. **73m/B VHS, Beta, LV.** W.C. Fields, Cora Witherspoon, Una Merkel, Evelyn Del Rio, Jack Norton, Jessie Ralph, Franklin Pangborn, Shemp Howard, Grady Sutton, Russell Hicks, Richard Purcell, Reed Hadley; *D:* Eddie Cline; *W:* W.C. Fields; *C:* Milton Krasner. *MCA*

Bank Robber 🦴🦴 **1993 (R)** Billy (Dempsey) is a thief who will retire after one final bank heist, if only he hadn't forgotten to break that surveillance camera. Holed up in a New York hotel he's subjected to extortion schemes and finds himself a new outlaw celebrity to newshounds. Bonet is a sweet hooker who falls in love with him. Satire on crooks and fame is too mild-mannered for its own good but not without charm. Directorial debut of Mead. Unedited NC-17 version also available. **94m/C VHS, LV.** Patrick Dempsey, Lisa Bonet, Olivia D'Abo, James Garde, Forest Whitaker, Judge Reinhold, Michael Jeter, Joe Alaskey, John Chappoulis; *D:* Nick Mead; *W:* Nick Mead; *M:* Stewart Copeland. *LIV*

Bank Shot 🦴🦴🦴 **1974** Hilarious comedy about a criminal who plans to rob a bank by stealing the entire building. Based on the novel by Donald Westlake, and the sequel to "The Hot Rock." **83m/C**

VHS. George C. Scott, Joanna Cassidy, Sorrell Booke, G. Wood, Clifton James, Bob Balaban, Bibi Osterwald; ***D:*** Gower Champion; ***W:*** Wendell Mayes; ***C:*** Harry Stradling Jr. *NO*

The Banker 🦴🦴 **1989 (R)** A cop, played by Forster, suspects a wealthy, highly influential banker of brutal serial killings. **90m/C VHS, Beta, LV.** Robert Forster, Jeff Conaway, Leif Garrett, Duncan Regehr, Shanna Reed, Deborah Richter, Richard Roundtree, Teri Weigel, E.J. Peaker; ***D:*** William Webb. *NO*

Banzai Runner 🦴🦴 **1986** A cop whose brother was killed in an exclusive desert-highway race decides to avenge by joining the race himself.. **88m/C VHS, Beta.** Dean Stockwell, John Shepherd, Charles Dierkop; ***D:*** John G. Thomas; ***M:*** Joel Goldsmith. *VMK*

Bar Girls 🦴🦴 **1995 (R)** Mating rituals, set in L.A. wateringhole "The Girl Bar," finds usually tough cookie Loretta (Wolfe) spotting new face Rachael (D'Agostino) and deciding she likes what she sees. There's various mind games as they chart a rocky course to true love—with jealousy, possessiveness, and past romance all playing their parts. Hoffman adapted from her play and the staginess remains; film debut for director Giovanni. **95m/C VHS, LV.** Nancy Allison Wolfe, Liza D'Agostino, Justine Slater, Paula Sorge, Camila Griggs, Pam Raines; ***D:*** Marita Giovanni; ***W:*** Lauran Hoffman; ***C:*** Michael Ferris. *ORI*

Bar-20 🦴½ **1943** Stage hold-ups and jewel robberies abound in this Hopalong Cassidy western. **54m/B VHS, Beta.** George Reeves, Douglas Fowley, William Boyd, Andy Clyde, Robert Mitchum, Victor Jory; ***D:*** Lesley Selander. *NOS, MRV, GVV*

Barabbas 🦴🦴½ **1962** Barabbas, a thief and murderer, is freed by Pontius Pilate in place of Jesus. He is haunted by this event for the rest of his life. Excellent acting, little melodrama, lavish production make for fine viewing. Based on the novel by Lagerkvist. **144m/C VHS, Beta, LV.** Anthony Quinn, Silvana Mangano, Arthur Kennedy, Jack Palance, Ernest Borgnine, Katy Jurado; ***D:*** Richard Fleischer. National Board of Review Awards '62: 5 Best Foreign Films of the Year. *COL*

Baraka 🦴🦴🦴 **1993** Time-lapse photography transforms a fascinating array of scenic panoramas into a thought-provoking experience. No dialogue, but the captivating visuals, shot in 24 countries, are a feast for the eyes. Points of interest include Iguacu Falls in Argentina, Ayers Rock in Australia, the temples of Angkor Wat in Cambodia, and the Grand Canyon. Also tours Auschwitz and the streets of Calcutta, in an effort to warn the viewer of the planet's fragility. Filmed in 70mm. **96m/C VHS, LV.** ***D:*** Ron Fricke; ***W:*** Ron Fricke, Mark Magidson, Bob Green; ***C:*** Ron Fricke; ***M:*** Michael Stearns. *MPI*

Barb Wire 🦴🦴 **1996 (R)** "Don't call me babe!" That'll be difficult when the figure in question is Anderson Lee's big-screen take on Dark Horse comic book heroine Barb Wire. Barb runs the sleazy Hammerhead Bar & Grille in Steel Harbor, the only neutral city in an America torn by a second civil war, and reluctantly agrees to aid hunky resistance leader Axel (Morrison) on a dangerous peace mission. Pambo gives Stallone a fight for the action title—fetching in high heels and black leather—with lots of fire power and a take-no-prisoners attitude. Plot's secondary to pulchritude but, unfortunately, the movie's just not a lotta fun. **98m/C VHS, LV.** Pamela Anderson Lee, Temuera Morrison, Jack Noseworthy, Victoria Rowell, Xander Berkeley, Udo Kier, Steve Railsback, Clint Howard, Tony Bill; ***D:*** David Hogan; ***W:*** Ilene Chaiken, Chuck Pfarrer; ***C:*** Rick Bota; ***M:*** Michel Colombier. *PGV*

Barbarella 🦴🦴½ *Barbarella, Queen of the Galaxy* **1968 (PG)** Based on the popular French sci-fi comic strip drawn by Jean-Claude Forest, this cult classic details the bizarre adventures of a space nymphette (Fonda) encountering fantastic creatures and super beings. You'll see sides of Fonda you never saw before (not even in the workout videos). Notorious in its day; rather silly, dated camp now. Don't miss the elbow-sex scene. Terry Southern contributed to the script. **98m/C VHS, Beta, LV.** *FR IT* Jane Fonda, John Phillip Law, David Hemmings, Marcel Marceau, Anita Pallenberg, Milo O'Shea; ***D:*** Roger Vadim; ***W:*** Terry Southern; ***C:*** Claude Renoir; ***M:*** Charles Fox. *FUS, PAR*

Barbarian and the Geisha 🦴🦴 **1958** The first US diplomat in Japan undergoes culture shock as well as a passionate love affair with a geisha, circa 1856. **104m/C VHS, Beta.** John Wayne, Eiko Ando, Sam Jaffe, So Yamamura; ***D:*** John Huston; ***M:*** Hugo Friedhofer. *FOX*

Barbarian Queen 🦴 **1985 (R)** Female warriors led by beauteous babe seek revenge for the capture of their men in this sword-and-sorcery epic. Low-budget rip-off "Conan the Barbarian" is laughable. Also available in an unrated version. Followed by "Barbarian Queen 2: The Empress Strikes Back." **71m/C VHS, Beta, LV.** *IT* Lana Clarkson, Frank Zagarino, Katt Shea Ruben, Dawn Dunlap, Susana Traverso; ***D:*** Hector Olivera. *VES, LIV*

Barbarian Queen 2: The Empress Strikes Back 🦴 **1989 (R)** Apparently one movie wasn't enough to tell the beautiful Princess Athalia's story. This time she fights her evil brother Ankaris. He throws her in prison, she escapes, joins a band of female rebels, and leads them into battle. No better than the first attempt. **87m/C VHS.** *IT* Lana Clarkson, Greg Wrangler, Rebecca Wood, Elizabeth Jaegen, Roger Cundy; ***D:*** Joe Finley. *LIV*

The Barbarians 🦴 *The Barbarians and Co* **1987 (R)** Two bodybuilder siblings in animal skins battle wizards and warlords in this dumb-but-fun U.S./Italian co-production. **88m/C VHS, Beta, LV.** *IT* David Paul, Peter Paul, Richard Lynch, Eva LaRue, Virginia Bryant, Sheeba Alahani, Michael Berryman; ***D:*** Ruggero Deodato; ***M:*** Pino Donaggio. *MED, VTR*

Barbarians at the Gate 🦴🦴🦴½ **1993 (R)** In the "greed is good" financial climate of the 80's, this made-for-cable movie chronicles the $25 billion dollar battle in 1988 for RJR Nabisco, which at the time was working on developing a "smokeless cigarette." Garner is CEO F. Ross Johnson, who is confident that their "smokeless cigarette" will boost the stock's value—until he gets the test-marketing results. Unwilling to risk the product's failure, Johnson decides to buy the company and is challenged by master dealer Kravis (Pryce). Fascinating social commentary on the nastiest mega-deal in history. Based on the book by Bryan Burrough and John Helyar. **107m/C VHS.** James Garner, Jonathan Pryce, Peter Riegert, Joanna Cassidy, Fred Dalton Thompson, Leilani Sarelle Ferrer, Matt Clark, Jeffrey DeMunn; ***D:*** Glenn Jordan; ***W:*** Larry Gelbart; ***M:*** Richard Gibbs. Golden Globe Awards '94: Best Movie/Miniseries. *HBO, FCT, BTV*

Barbarosa 🦴🦴🦴 **1982 (PG)** Offbeat western about an aging, legendary outlaw constantly on the lam who reluctantly befriends a naive farmboy and teaches him survival skills. Nelson and Busey are a great team, solidly directed. Lovely Rio Grande scenery. **90m/C VHS, Beta, LV.** Willie Nelson, Gilbert Roland, Gary Busey, Isela Vega; ***D:*** Fred Schepisi; ***M:*** Bruce Smeaton. *FOX*

Barbary Coast 🦴🦴🦴 **1935** A ruthless club owner tries to win the love of a young girl by building her into a star attraction during San Francisco's gold rush days. **90m/B VHS, Beta, LV.** Edward G. Robinson, Walter Brennan, Brian Donlevy, Joel McCrea, Donald Meek, David Niven, Miriam Hopkins; ***D:*** Howard Hawks. Nominations: Academy Awards '35: Best Cinematography. *NO*

The Barbary Coast 🦴🦴 **1974** A turn-of-the-century detective sleuths the streets of San Francisco in this average made-for-television movie. **100m/C VHS.** William Shatner, Dennis Cole, Lynda Day George, John Vernon, Charles Aidman, Michael Ansara, Neville Brand, Bill Bixby; ***D:*** Bill Bixby. *SUE, ORI*

The Barber Shop 🦴🦴🦴 **1933** Fields portrays the bumbling, carefree barber Cornelius O'Hare, purveyor of village gossip and problem solver. Havoc begins when a gangster enters the shop and demands that Cornelius change his appearance. **21m/B VHS, Beta.** W.C. Fields, Elise Cavanna, Harry Watson, Dagmar Oakland, Frank Yaconelli. *CCB*

Barcelona 🦴🦴🦴 **1994 (PG-13)** Old-fashioned talkfest about two neurotic Americans experiencing sibling rivalry in Spain. Serious Ted (Nichols) is an American sales rep, posted to Barcelona, who can't quite get into the city's pleasure-loving rhythm. This is not a problem for Ted's cousin Fred (Eigeman), an obnoxious naval officer, with whom Ted has had a rivalry dating back to their boyhood. Set in the 1980s, the two must also deal with anti-Americanism, which leads both to violence and romantic developments. Tart dialogue, thoughtful performances, and exotic locales prove enticing in low-budget sleeper that effectively mixes drama and dry comedy. Watch for Eigeman in Tom Cruise's uniform from "A Few Good Men." **102m/C VHS, LV.** Taylor Nichols, Christopher Eigeman, Tushka Bergen, Mira Sorvino, Pep Munne, Francis Creighton, Thomas Gibson, Jack Gilpin, Nuria Badia, Hellena Schmied; ***D:*** Whit Stillman; ***W:*** Whit Stillman; ***M:*** Tom Judson, Mark Suozzo. Independent Spirit Awards '95: Best Cinematography. *NLC, TTC, IME*

The Barcelona Kill 🦴½ **1977** When a journalist and her boyfriend get in too deep with the Barcelona mob, their troubles begin. **86m/C VHS, Beta.** Linda Hayden, John Astin, Simon Andrew, Maximo Valverde; ***D:*** Jose Antonio De La Loma. *NO*

Bare Essentials 🦴 **1991 (PG)** Made for TV yuppie Club Med nightmare in which a high-strung couple from New York find themselves marooned on a desert isle with only two other inhabitants. With no cellular telephoning ability and an absence of large-ticket consumer goods to purchase, the two turn their reluctant sights on each other, focusing on the bare essentials, as it were. Great soul-searching scenes for the inarticulate. **94m/C VHS.** Gregory Harrison, Lisa Hartman Black, Mark Linn-Baker, Charlotte Lewis; ***D:*** Martha Coolidge. *REP*

Bare Hunt 🦴 *My Gun is Jammed; The Bear Hunt* **1963** Detective Max T. Unimportant is dragged into the underground world of prospective nude actresses in this supposedly funny "nudie." **69m/B VHS, Beta.** *VDM, TPV*

Bare Knees 🦴🦴 **1928** A woman causes a scandal in her family when she arrives at her sister's birthday party with bare knees, cigarettes, and other flapper items. The quintessential flapper movie. **61m/B VHS, Beta.** Virginia Lee Corbin, Donald Keith, Jane Winton, Johnnie Walker, Forrest Stanley, Maude Fulton; ***D:*** Erle C. Kenton. *GPV*

Bare Knuckles 🦴 **1977 (R)** The adventures of a low-rent bounty hunter. **90m/C VHS, Beta.** Robert Viharo, Sherry Jackson, Michael Heit, Gloria Hendry, John Daniels; ***D:*** Don Edmunds. *TWE*

The Barefoot Contessa 🦴🦴🦴 **1954** The story, told in flashback, of a Spanish dancer's rise to Hollywood stardom, as witnessed by a cynical director. Shallow Hollywood self-examination. **128m/C VHS, Beta.** Ava Gardner, Humphrey Bogart, Edmond O'Brien, Valentina Cortese, Rossano Brazzi; ***D:*** Joseph L. Mankiewicz; ***W:*** Joseph L. Mankiewicz; ***C:*** Jack Cardiff. Academy Awards '54: Best Supporting Actor (O'Brien); Golden Globe Awards '55: Best Supporting Actor (O'Brien); Nominations: Academy Awards '54: Best Story & Screenplay. *MGM, FOX, FCT*

The Barefoot Executive 🦴🦴 **1971** A mailroom boy who works for a national television network finds a chimpanzee that can pick hit shows in this Disney family comedy. **92m/C VHS, Beta.** Kurt Russell, John Ritter, Harry (Henry) Morgan, Wally Cox, Heather North, Joe Flynn; ***D:*** Robert Butler; ***M:*** Robert F. Brunner. *DIS, OM*

Barefoot in Athens 🦴🦴 **1966** Television presentation from "George Schaefer's Showcase Theatre" chronicles the last years of the philosopher Socrates who, barefoot and unkempt, an embarrassment to his wife, and a dangerous critic to the corrupt Athenian leaders, nevertheless believes that democracy and truth are all-important in his city. **76m/C VHS, Beta.** Peter Ustinov, Geraldine Page, Anthony Quayle; ***D:*** George Schaefer. *FHS*

Barefoot in the Park **1967** Neil Simon's Broadway hit translates well to screen. A newly wedded bride (Fonda) tries to get her husband (Redford, reprising his Broadway role) to loosen up and be as free-spirited as she is. **106m/C VHS, Beta, LV.** Robert Redford, Jane Fonda, Charles Boyer, Mildred Natwick; ***D:*** Gene Saks; ***W:*** Neil Simon; ***C:*** Joseph LaShelle. Nominations: Academy Awards '67: Best Supporting Actress (Natwick). *PAR*

Barfly **1987 (R)** Bukowski's semi-autobiographical screenplay is the story of a talented writer who chooses to spend his time as a lonely barfly, hiding his literary abilities behind glasses of liquor. Dunaway's character is right on target as the fellow alcoholic. **100m/C VHS, Beta, LV, 8mm.** Mickey Rourke, Faye Dunaway, Alice Krige, Frank Stallone, J.C. Quinn, Jack Nance; ***D:*** Barbet Schroeder; ***W:*** Charles Bukowski. *WAR, FCT*

The Bargain ½ **1915** Hart's first feature, in which he portrays a bandit desperately trying to go straight. Original titles with musical score. **50m/B VHS, Beta.** William S. Hart. *NOS, GPV, DVT*

Baritone **1985** Concerned Polish drama about a prominent opera singer who promises to deliver a grand concert upon returning to his small town, only to lose his voice just before the show is to start. Proof positive that the opera ain't over 'til the fat lady sings. **100m/C VHS.** *PL* Zbigniew Zapassiewicz; ***D:*** Janusz Zaorski. *FCT*

Barjo **1993** In a bland and isolated French suburb lives willful housewife Fanfan (Bouchet) with her older businessman husband Charles (Bohringer) and her eccentric twin brother Barjo (Girardot). Barjo is obsessed with lists and extraterrestrials and his sister's affair with their next-door neighbor, which he likes to spy on. Her husband naturally begins to go crazy. Deadpan satire based on the novel "Confessions of a Crap Artist" by Philip K. Dick. The post-WWII American setting of the novel makes a decidedly uneasy transistion to contemporary French life. In French with English subtitles. **85m/C VHS.** *FR* Anne Brochet, Hippolyte Girardot, Richard Bohringer, Consuelo de Haviland, Renaud Danner, Nathalie Boutefeu; ***D:*** Jerome Boivin; ***W:*** Jerome Boivin, Jacques Audiard; ***M:*** Hugues Le-Bars. *FXL*

The Barkleys of Broadway **1949** The famous dancing team's last film together; they play a quarreling husband/wife showbiz team. ♫They Can't Take That Away From Me; The Sabre Dance; Swing Trot; Manhattan Downbeat; A Weekend in the Country; My One and Only Highland Fling; You'd Be Hard to Replace; Bouncin' the Blues; Shoes With Wings On. **109m/C VHS, Beta, LV.** Fred Astaire, Ginger Rogers, Gale Robbins, Oscar Levant, Jacques Francois, Billie Burke; ***D:*** Charles Walters; ***W:*** Adolph Green, Betty Comden; ***C:*** Harry Stradling; ***M:*** Ira Gershwin, Harry Warren. Nominations: Academy Awards '49: Best Color Cinematography. *MGM*

Barn of the Naked Dead *Woof!* **1973** Prine plays a sicko who tortures women while his radioactive monster dad terrorizes the Nevada desert. Rudolph's first film, directed under the pseudonym Gerald Comier. Also on video as "Terror Circus" and "Nightmare Circus." **86m/C VHS.** Andrew Prine, Manuella Thiess, Sherry Alberoni, Gylian Roland, Al Cormier, Jennifer Ashley; ***D:*** Alan Rudolph. *NO*

Barnaby and Me **1977** Australian star Barnaby the Koala Bear joins an international con-man in this romantic adventure. The mob is chasing the con-man when he meets and falls for a lovely young woman and her daughter. **90m/C VHS, Beta.** *AU* Sid Caesar, Juliet Mills, Sally Boyden; ***D:*** Norman Panama. *ACA*

Barnum ½ **1986** P.T. Barnum's life is focused upon in this biography about the man who helped to form "The Greatest Show On Earth." **100m/C VHS, Beta, LV.** Burt Lancaster, Hanna Schygulla, Jenny Lind, John Roney; ***D:*** Lee Philips. *ACA*

The Baron ½ **1988** Vengeance is the name of the game when an underworld boss gets stiffed on a deal. Fast-paced no-brainer street drama. **88m/C VHS.** Calvin Lockhart, Charles McGregor, Joan Blondell, Richard Lynch, Marlene Clark; ***D:*** Philip Fently. *NO*

The Baron and the Kid **1984** A pool shark finds out that his opponent at a charity exhibition game is his long-lost son. Based on Johnny Cash's song. Made for TV. **100m/C VHS, Beta.** Johnny Cash, Darren McGavin, June Carter Cash, Richard Roundtree; ***D:*** Gary Nelson; ***M:*** Brad Fiedel. *FOX*

Baron Munchausen **1943** The German film studio UFA celebrated its 25th anniversary with this lavish version of the Baron Munchausen legend, starring a cast of top-name German performers at the height of the Third Reich. Filmed in Agfacolor; available in English subtitled or dubbed versions. **120m/C VHS, Beta.** *GE* Hans Albers, Kaethe Kaack, Hermann Speelmanns, Leo Slezak; ***D:*** Josef von Baky. *INJ, VCD, GLV*

Baron of Arizona **1951** Land office clerk almost succeeds in convincing the U.S. that he owned the state of Arizona. **99m/B VHS, Beta.** Vincent Price, Ellen Drew, Beulah Bondi, Reed Hadley, Vladimir Sokoloff; ***D:*** Samuel Fuller; ***W:*** Samuel Fuller; ***C:*** James Wong Howe. *RXM*

Barracuda *Woof! The Lucifer Project* **1978 (R)** Lots of innocent swimmers are being eaten by crazed killer barracudas. **90m/C VHS, Beta.** Wayne Crawford, Jason Evers, Roberta Leighton; ***D:*** Harry Kerwin. *NO*

The Barretts of Wimpole Street *Forbidden Alliance* **1934** The moving, almost disturbing, account of poetess Elizabeth Barrett, an invalid confined to her bed, with only her poetry and her dog to keep her company. She is wooed by poet Robert Browning, in whose arms she finds true happiness and a miraculous recovery. Multi-faceted drama expertly played by all. **110m/B VHS, LV.** Fredric March, Norma Shearer, Charles Laughton, Maureen O'Sullivan, Katherine Alexander, Una O'Connor, Ian Wolfe; ***D:*** Sidney Franklin; ***C:*** William H. Daniels. Nominations: Academy Awards '34: Best Actress (Shearer), Best Picture. *MGM, CCB*

Barry Lyndon ½ **1975 (PG)** Ravishing adaptation of the classic Thackeray novel about the adventures of an Irish gambler moving from innocence to self-destructive arrogance in the aristocracy of 18th Century England. Visually opulent. Kubrick received excellent performances from all his actors, and a stunning display of history, but the end result still overwhelms. O'Neal has seldom been better. **185m/C VHS, Beta, LV.** Ryan O'Neal, Marisa Berenson, Patrick Magee, Hardy Kruger, Guy Hamilton; ***D:*** Stanley Kubrick. Academy Awards '75: Best Art Direction/Set Decoration, Best Cinematography, Best Costume Design, Best Original Score; British Academy Awards '75: Best Director (Kubrick); Los Angeles Film Critics Association Awards '75: Best Cinematography; National Board of Review Awards '75: 10 Best Films of the Year, Best Director (Kubrick); Nominations: Academy Awards '75: Best Adapted Screenplay, Best Director (Kubrick), Best Picture. *WAR*

Barry McKenzie Holds His Own **1974** In this sequel to "The Adventures of Barry McKenzie," we find that after a young man's aunt is mistaken for the Queen of England, two emissaries of Count Plasma of Transylvania kidnap her to use as a Plasma tourist attraction. Based on the 'Private Eye' comic strip, this crude Australian film is as disappointing as the first of the Barry McKenzie stories. **93m/C VHS, Beta.** *AU* Barry Humphries, Barry Crocker, Donald Pleasence; ***D:*** Bruce Beresford; ***W:*** Barry Humphries, Bruce Beresford. *NO*

Bartleby ½ **1970** A new version of the classic Herman Melville short story. McEnery is Bartleby the clerk, who refuses to leave his job even after he's fired; Scofield is his frustrated boss. **79m/C VHS, LV.** Paul Scofield, John McEnery, Colin Jeavons, Thorley Walters; ***D:*** Anthony Friedman; ***W:*** Rodney Carr-Smith. *WST, TVC*

Barton Fink **1991 (R)** This eerie comic nightmare comes laden with awards (including the Palme D'Or from Cannes) but only really works if you care about the time and place. Fink is a trendy New York playwright staying in a seedy Hollywood hotel in the 1940s, straining to write a simple B-movie script. Macabre events, both real and imagined, compound his writer's block. Superb set design from Dennis Gassner complements an unforgettable cast of grotesques. **116m/C VHS.** John Turturro, John Goodman, Judy Davis, Michael Lerner, John Mahoney, Tony Shalhoub, Jon Polito, Steve Buscemi, David Warrilow, Richard Portnow, Christopher Murney; ***D:*** Joel Coen; ***W:*** Joel Coen, Ethan Coen; ***C:*** Roger Deakins; ***M:*** Carter Burwell. Cannes Film Festival '91: Best Actor (Turturro), Best Director (Coen), Best Film; Los Angeles Film Critics Association Awards '91: Best Cinematography, Best Supporting Actor (Lerner); National Society of Film Critics Awards '91: Best Cinematography; Nominations: Academy Awards '91: Best Art Direction/Set Decoration, Best Costume Design, Best Supporting Actor (Lerner). *FXV, CCB*

Baseball **1994** Ken Burns' follow-up to "The Civil War" is an equally epic history of the great American pastime, spanning 150 years. 9 tapes released in a collector's edition or individually. **1080m/C VHS.** ***D:*** Ken Burns. *TTC, PBS, PAP*

Based on an Untrue Story ½ **1993** Campy spoof of popular "true story" television docudramas in which powerful Satin Chau (Fairchild), a perfume mogul, loses her sense of smell. Satin leaves her mentor Varda (Cannon) to discovery herself but finds that only her two separated-at-birth sisters, Velour (Lake) and Corduroy (Jackson), hold the secrets to the past. It's hard to spoof a genre that's become a cliche but this television movie does its best. **90m/C VHS.** Morgan Fairchild, Dyan Cannon, Victoria Jackson, Ricki Lake, Harvey Korman, Robert Goulet, Dan Hedaya; ***D:*** Jim Drake. *FXV*

The Bashful Bachelor **1942** Yokel joker Abner trades his delivery car for a race horse, hoping to win a big race. **78m/B VHS.** Chester Lauck, Norris Goff, ZaSu Pitts, Grady Sutton, Louise Currie, Irving Bacon, Earle Hodgins, Benny Rubin; ***D:*** Malcolm St. Clair. *NOS, RXM*

Basic Instinct ½ **1992 (R)** Controversial thriller had tongues wagging months before its theatrical release. Burnt-out detective Douglas falls for beautiful, manipulative murder suspect Stone, perfectly cast as a bisexual ice queen who may or may not have done the deed. Noted for highly erotic sex scenes and an expensive (3 million bucks) script; ultimately the predictable plot is disappointing. Gay activists tried to interrupt filming because they objected to the depiction of Stone's character but only succeeded in generating more free publicity. The American release was edited to avoid an "NC-17" rating, but an uncut, unrated video version is also available. **123m/C VHS, Beta.** Michael Douglas, Sharon Stone, George Dzundza, Jeanne Tripplehorn, Denis Arndt, Leilani Sarelle Ferrer, Bruce A. Young, Chelcie Ross, Dorothy Malone, Wayne Knight, Stephen Tobolowsky; ***D:*** Paul Verhoeven; ***W:*** Joe Eszterhas; ***C:*** Jan De Bont; ***M:*** Jerry Goldsmith. MTV Movie Awards '93: Best Female Performance (Stone), Most Desirable Female (Stone); Nominations: Academy Awards '92: Best Film Editing, Best Original Score. *LIV, PMS*

Basic Training *Woof!* **1986 (R)** Three sexy ladies wiggle into the Pentagon in their efforts to clean up the government. **85m/C VHS, Beta.** Ann Dusenberry, Rhonda Shear, Angela Aames, Walter Gotell; ***D:*** Andrew Sugarman. *LIV, VES*

Basileus Quartet **1982** The replacement for a violinist in a well-established quartet creates emotional havoc. Beautiful music, excellent and evocative photography. **118m/C VHS, LV.** *FR IT* Pierre Malet, Hector Alterio, Omero Antonutti, Michel Vitold, Alain Cuny, Gabriele Ferzetti, Elisabeth Kreuzer; ***D:*** Fabio Carpi. *TPV*

Basket Case **1982** A gory horror film about a pair of Siamese twins—one normal, the other gruesomely deformed. The pair is surgically separated at birth, and the evil disfigured twin is tossed in the garbage. Fraternal ties being what they are, the normal brother retrieves his twin—essentially a head atop shoulders—and totes him around in a basket (he ain't heavy). Together they begin twisted and deadly revenge, with the brother-in-a-basket in charge. Very entertaining, if you like this sort of thing. Followed by two sequels, if you just can't get enough. **89m/C VHS, Beta, LV.** Kevin Van Hentenryck, Terri Susan Smith, Beverly Bonner; ***D:*** Frank Henenlotter. *MED*

Basket Case 2 ½ **1990 (R)** Surgically separated teenage mutant brothers Duane and Belial are back! This time they've found happiness in a "special" family—until they're plagued by the paparazzi. Higher production values make this sequel slicker than its low-budget predecessor, but it somehow lacks the same charm. **90m/C VHS, Beta, LV.** Kevin Van Hentenryck, Annie Ross, Kathryn Meisle, Heather Rattray, Jason Evers, Ted Sorel, Matt Mitler; ***D:*** Frank Henenlotter; ***W:*** Frank Henenlotter; ***M:*** Joe Renzetti. *VTR, IME, SGE*

Basket Case 3: The Progeny ½ **1992 (R)** In this sequel to the cult horror hits "Basket Case" and "Basket Case 2," Belial is back and this time he's about to discover the perils of parenthood as the mutant Mrs. Belial delivers a litter of bouncing mini-monsters. Everything is fine until the police kidnap the little creatures and chaos breaks out as Belial goes on a shocking rampage in his newly created mechanical body. Weird special effects make this a cult favorite for fans of the truly outrageous. **90m/C VHS.** Annie Ross, Kevin Van Hentenryck, Gil Roper, Tina Louise Hilbert, Dan Biggers, Jim O'Doherty; ***D:*** Frank Henenlotter; ***W:*** Robert Martin, Frank Henenlotter; ***M:*** Joe Renzetti. *MCA, SGE*

The Basketball Diaries **1994 (R)** Disappointing adaptation of undeground writer/musician Jim Carroll's 1978 cult memoirs, with DiCaprio starring as the teen athlete whose life spirals into drug addiction and hustling on the New York streets. Carroll and friends Mickey (Wahlberg), Neutron (McGaw), and Pedro (Madio), form the heart of St. Vitus' hot hoopster team. But the defiant quartet really get their kicks from drugs, dares, and petty crime—leading to an ever-downward turn. The book takes place in the '60s but the film can't make up its mind what the decade is, although DiCaprio (and Wahlberg) are particularly effective in a self-conscious first effort from Kalvert. **102m/C VHS.** Leonardo DiCaprio, Mark Wahlberg, Patrick McGaw, James Madio, Bruno Kirby, Ernie Hudson, Lorraine Bracco, Juliette Lewis, Josh Mostel, Michael Rapaport, Michael Imperioli; ***Cameos:*** Jim Carroll; ***D:*** Scott Kalvert; ***W:*** Bryan Goluboff; ***C:*** David Phillips; ***M:*** Graeme Revell. *PGV*

The Bastard ½ *The Kent Chronicles* **1978** Dashing (but alas, illegitimate) nobleman roams Europe on futile, Roots-like search, then settles for America during the Revolutionary War in this long-winded television adaptation of John Jakes' equally cumbersome bestseller (part of his popular Bicentennial series). Stevens stars, along with many supporting performers merely keeping active. Followed by "The Rebels" and "The Seekers." **189m/C VHS.** Andrew Stevens, Tom Bosley, Kim Cattrall, Buddy Ebsen, Lorne Greene, Olivia Hussey, Cameron Mitchell, Harry (Henry) Morgan, Patricia Neal, Eleanor Parker, Donald Pleasence, William Shatner, Barry Sullivan, Noah Beery Jr., William Daniels, Keenan Wynn; ***D:*** Lee H. Katzin; ***M:*** John Addison. *MCA*

The Bat **1926** A bat-obsessed killer stalks the halls of a spooky mansion in this early film version of the Mary Roberts Rinehart novel. **81m/B VHS, Beta.** Andre de Beranger, Charles Herzinger, Emily Fitzroy, Louise Fazenda, Arthur Houseman, Robert McKim, Jack Pickford, Jewel Carmen; ***D:*** Roland West; ***W:*** Roland West. *SNC, FUS*

The Bat **1959** A great plot centering around a murderer called the Bat, who kills hapless victims by ripping out their throats when he isn't busy searching for a million dollars worth of securities stashed in the old house he is living in. Adapted from the novel by Mary Roberts Rinehart. **80m/B VHS, Beta.** Vincent Price, Agnes Moorehead, Gavin Gordon, John Sutton, Lenita Lane, Darla Hood; ***D:*** Crane Wilbur. *NOS, SNC, DVT*

The Bat People *It Lives By Night* **1974 (R)** Less-than-gripping horror flick in which Dr. John Bech is bitten by a bat while on his honeymoon. He then becomes a sadistic bat creature, compelled to kill anyone who stumbles across his path. The gory special effects make for a great movie if you've ever been bitten by that sort of thing. **95m/C VHS, Beta.** Stewart Moss, Marianne McAndrew, Michael Pataki, Paul Carr; ***D:*** Jerry Jameson. *HBO*

Bat 21 **1988 (R)** Hackman, an American officer, is stranded in the wilds of Vietnam alone after his plane is shot down. He must rely on himself and Glover, with whom he has radio contact, to get him out. Glover and Hackman give solid performances in this otherwise average film. **112m/C VHS, Beta, LV.** Gene Hackman, Danny Glover, Jerry Reed, David Marshall Grant, Clayton Rohner, Erich Anderson, Joe Dorsey; ***D:*** Peter Markle; ***W:*** Marc Norman, William C. Anderson. *MED, VTR*

The Bat Whispers ½ **1930** A masked madman is stalking the halls of a creepy mansion; eerie tale that culminates in an appeal to the audience to keep the plot under wraps. Unusually crafted film for its early era. Comic mystery based on the novel and play by Mary Roberts Rinehart and Avery Hopwood. **82m/B VHS, LV.** Chester Morris, Chance Ward, Richard Tucker, Wilson Benge, DeWitt Jennings, Una Merkel, Spencer Charters; ***D:*** Roland West; ***W:*** Roland West. *NOS, DVT, MLB*

Bataan ½ **1943** A rugged war-time combat drama following the true story of a small platoon in the Philippines endeavoring to blow up a pivotal Japanese bridge. Also available in a colorized version. **115m/B VHS, Beta.** Robert Taylor, George Murphy, Thomas Mitchell, Desi Arnaz Sr., Lee Bowman, Lloyd Nolan, Robert Walker; ***D:*** Tay Garnett. *MGM, TLF*

Bathing Beauty ½ **1944** This musical stars Skelton as a pop music composer with the hots for college swim teacher Williams. Rathbone is a music executive who sees the romance as a threat to Skelton's career and to his own profit margin. Full of aquatic ballet, Skelton's shtick, and wonderful original melodies. The first film in which Williams received star billing. ♫I Cried for You; Bim, Bam, Boom; Tico-Tico; I'll Take the High Note; Loch Lomond; By the Waters of Minnetonka; Magic is the Moonlight; Trumpet Blues; Hora Staccato. **101m/C VHS, LV.** Red Skelton, Esther Williams, Basil Rathbone, Bill Goodwin, Jean Porter, Carlos Ramirez, Donald Meek, Ethel Smith, Helen Forrest; ***D:*** George Sidney; ***C:*** Harry Stradling; ***M:*** Xavier Cugat. *MGM, TTC, FCT*

Batman ½ **1966** Holy television camp, Batman! Will the caped crusader win the Bat-tle against the combined forces of the Joker, the Riddler, the Penguin, and Catwoman? Will Batman and Robin save the United World Security Council from dehydration? Will the Bat genius ever figure out that Russian journalist Miss Kitka and Catwoman are one and the same? Biff! Thwack! Socko! Not to be confused with the Michael Keaton version of the Dark Knight, this is the pot-bellied Adam West Batman, teeming with Bat satire and made especially for the big screen. **104m/C VHS, Beta, LV.** Burt Ward, Adam West, Burgess Meredith, Cesar Romero, Frank Gorshin, Lee Meriwether; ***D:*** Leslie Martinson. *FOX*

Batman ½ **1989 (PG-13)** The blockbuster fantasy epic that renewed Hollywood's faith in media blitzing. The Caped Crusader is back in Gotham City, where even the criminals are afraid to walk the streets alone. There's a new breed of criminal in Gotham, led by the infamous Joker. Their random attacks via acid-based make-up are just the beginning. Keaton is surprisingly good as the dual personality hero though Nicholson steals the show. Marvelously designed and shot. Much better on the big screen. Followed in 1992 by "Batman Returns." **126m/C VHS, Beta, LV, 8mm.** Michael Keaton, Jack Nicholson, Kim Basinger, Robert Wuhl, Tracey Walter, Billy Dee Williams, Pat Hingle, Michael Gough, Jack Palance, Jerry Hall; ***D:*** Tim Burton; ***W:*** Sam Hamm, Warren Skaaren; ***M:*** Danny Elfman, Prince. Academy Awards '89: Best Art Direction/Set Decoration; People's Choice Awards '90: Best Film—Drama. *FOX, WAR*

Batman Forever **1995 (PG-13)** Holy franchise, Batman! Third-time actioner considerably lightens up Tim Burton's dark vision for a more family-oriented Caped Crusader (now played by Kilmer, who fills out lip requirement nicely). The Boy Wonder also makes a first-time appearance in the bulked-up form of O'Donnell, a street-smart Robin with revenge on his mind. Naturally, the villains still steal the show in the personas of maniacal Carrey (the Riddler) and the sartorially splendid Jones as Harvey "Two-Face" Dent. Rounding out this charismatic cast is Kidman's slinky psychologist Chase Meridian, who's eager to find the man inside the bat (and who can blame her). Lots of splashy toys for the boys and awe-inspiring sets to show you where the money went. A Gotham City gas that did $53 million at it's opening weekend box office—breaking the "Jurassic Park" record, testimony to the power of aggressive marketing. **121m/C VHS, LV.** Val Kilmer, Tommy Lee Jones, Jim Carrey, Chris O'Donnell, Nicole Kidman, Drew Barrymore, Debi Mazar, Michael Gough, Pat Hingle; ***D:*** Joel Schumacher; ***W:*** Janet Scott Batchler, Akiva Goldsman, Lee Batchler; ***C:*** Stephen Goldblatt; ***M:*** Elliot Goldenthal. Blockbuster Entertainment Awards '96: Action Actress, Theatrical (Kidman); Nominations: Academy Awards '95: Best Cinematography, Best Sound; Golden Globe Awards '96: Best Song ("Hold Me, Thrill Me, Kiss Me, Kill Me"); MTV Movie Awards '96: Most Desirable Male (Kilmer), Best Villain (Carrey, Jones), Best Song ("Kiss from a Rose", "Hold Me, Thrill Me, Kiss Me, Kill Me"). *WAR*

Batman: Mask of the Phantasm ½ *Batman: The Animated Movie* **1993 (PG)** Based on the Fox television series with the animated Batman fending off old enemy the Joker, new enemy the Phantasm, and dreaming of his lost first love. Cartoon film noir set in the 1940's but filled with '90s sarcasm. Complicated storyline with a stylish dark look may be lost on the kiddies but adults will stay awake. **77m/C VHS, LV.** ***D:*** Eric Radomski, Bruce W. Timm; ***W:*** Michael Reeves, Alan Burnett, Paul Dini, Martin Pako; ***M:*** Shirley Walker; ***V:*** Kevin Conroy, Dana Delany, Mark Hamill, Stacy Keach, Hart Bochner, Abe Vigoda, Efrem Zimbalist Jr., Dick Miller. *WAR*

Batman Returns ½ **1992 (PG-13)** More of the same from director Burton, with Batman more of a supporting role overshadowed by provocative villains. DeVito is the cruely misshapen Penguin who seeks to rule over Gotham City; Pfeiffer is the exotic and dangerous Catwoman— who has more than a passing purr-sonal interest in Batman; Walken is the maniacal tycoon Max Shreck. Pfeiffer fares best in her wickedly sexy role and second-skin costume (complete with bullwhip). Plot is secondary to special effects and nightmarish settings. Despite a big budget, this grandiose sequel is of the love it or leave it variety. **126m/C VHS.** Michael Keaton, Danny DeVito, Michelle Pfeiffer, Christopher Walken, Michael Gough, Michael Murphy, Cristi Conaway, Pat Hingle, Vincent Schiavelli, Jan Hooks, Paul (Pee Wee Herman) Reubens, Andrew Bryniarski; ***D:*** Tim Burton; ***W:*** Daniel Waters; ***M:*** Danny Elfman. Nominations: Academy Awards '92: Best Makeup, Best Visual Effects. *WAR*

batteries not included** ½ **1987 (PG)** As a real estate developer fights to demolish a New York tenement, the five remaining residents are aided by tiny metal visitors from outer space in their struggle to save their home. Each resident gains a renewed sense of life in this sentimental, wholesome family film produced by Spielberg. Cronyn and Tandy keep the schmaltz from getting out of hand. Neat little space critters. **107m/C VHS, Beta, LV.** Hume Cronyn, Jessica Tandy, Frank McRae, Michael Carmine, Elizabeth Pena, Dennis Boutsikaris; ***D: Matthew Robbins; ***W:*** Matthew Robbins, Brad Bird, Brent Maddock, S.S. Wilson; ***M:*** James Horner. *MCA*

Battle Beneath the Earth **1968** The commies try to undermine democracy once again when American scientists discover a Chinese plot to invade the U.S. via a series of underground tunnels. Perhaps a tad jingoistic. **112m/C VHS, Beta.** *GB* Kerwin Mathews, Peter Arne, Viviane Ventura, Robert Ayres; ***D:*** Montgomery Tully. *MGM*

Battle Beyond the Stars 🦴🦴½ **1980** **(PG)** The planet Akir must be defended against alien rapscallions in this intergalactic Corman creation. Sayles authored the screenplay and co-authored the story on which it was based. **105m/C VHS, Beta, LV.** Richard Thomas, Robert Vaughn, George Peppard, Sybil Danning, Sam Jaffe, John Saxon, Darlanne Fluegel; ***D:*** Jimmy T. Murakami; ***W:*** John Sayles; ***M:*** James Horner. *VES, LIV*

Battle Beyond the Sun 🦴🦴 **1963** Former Russian movie "Nebo Zowet" is Americanized. Everyone is trying to send a mission to Mars. Roger Corman was the producer, Thomas Colchart is a pseudonym for Francis Ford Coppola. **75m/C VHS.** Edd Perry, Arla Powell, Bruce Hunter, Andy Stewart; ***D:*** Francis Ford Coppola; ***M:*** Les Baxter. *NOS, SNC*

Battle Circus 🦴½ **1953** Sappy drama casts Bogart as a surgeon at a M*A*S*H unit during the Korean War. Allyson is a combat nurse who finds love amongst the harsh reality of a war zone. Bogart was badly miscast and his performance proves it. Weak script and uninspired performances don't help this depressing story. **90m/B VHS.** Humphrey Bogart, June Allyson, Keenan Wynn, Robert Keith, William Campbell; ***D:*** Richard Brooks; ***W:*** Richard Brooks; ***C:*** John Alton. *MGM*

Battle Cry 🦴🦴🦴 **1955** A group of U.S. Marines train, romance, and enter battle in WWII. Based on the novel by Leon Uris. Part of the "A Night at the Movies" series, this tape simulates a 1955 movie evening, with a cartoon, "Speedy Gonzales," a newsreel, and coming attractions for "Mr. Roberts" and "East of Eden." **169m/C VHS, Beta, LV.** Van Heflin, Aldo Ray, Mona Freeman, Tab Hunter, Dorothy Malone, Anne Francis, James Whitmore, Raymond Massey; ***D:*** Raoul Walsh. Nominations: Academy Awards '55: Best Original Score. *WAR*

Battle for the Planet of the Apes 🦴🦴 **1973 (G)** A tribe of human atomic bomb mutations are out to make life miserable for the peaceful ape tribe. The story is told primarily in flashback with the opening and closing sequences taking place in the year 2670 A.D. Final chapter in the five-movie simian saga. **96m/C VHS, Beta.** Roddy McDowall, Lew Ayres, John Huston, Paul Williams, Claude Akins, Severn Darden, Natalie Trundy; ***D:*** J. Lee Thompson; ***W:*** John W. Corrington, Joyce H. Corrington. *FOX*

Battle Hell 🦴🦴 *Yangtse Incident* **1956** The true story of how a British ship was attacked by the Chinese Peoples Liberation Army on the Yangtze River in 1949. **112m/B VHS, Beta.** *GB* Richard Todd, Akim Tamiroff, Keye Luke; ***D:*** Michael Anderson Sr. *NO*

Battle Hymn 🦴🦴½ **1957** After accidentally bombing an orphanage as a WWII fighter pilot, Dean Hess (Hudson) becomes a minister. He returns to the Air Force in 1950 to train Korean pilots in Seoul and winds up building a home for the local orphans. True story on which the real Hess served as technical advisor. **109m/C VHS.** Rock Hudson, Dan Duryea, Martha Hyer, Anna Kashfi, Don DeFore, Jock Mahoney, Carl Benton Reid, Alan Hale Jr., Richard Loo, Philip Ahn; ***D:*** Douglas Sirk; ***W:*** Charles Grayson, Vincent B. Evans; ***C:*** Russell Metty; ***M:*** Frank Skinner. *MCA*

The Battle of Algiers 🦴🦴🦴½ **1966** Famous, powerful, award-winning film depicting the uprisings against French Colonial rule in 1954 Algiers. A seminal documentary-style film which makes most political films seem ineffectual by comparison in its use of non-professional actors, gritty photography, realistic violence, and a boldly propagandistic sense of social outrage. **123m/B VHS, Beta, LV.** *AL IT* Yacef Saadi, Jean Martin, Brahim Haggiag, Tommaso Neri, Samia Kerbash, Fawzia el Kader, Michele Kerbash, Mohamed Ben Kassen; ***D:*** Gillo Pontecorvo; ***W:*** Franco Solinas; ***M:*** Ennio Morricone. Venice Film Festival '66: Best Film; Nominations: Academy Awards '66: Best Foreign Language Film; Academy Awards '68: Best Director (Pontecorvo), Best Story & Screenplay. *INJ, IHF, TPV*

The Battle of Austerlitz 🦴🦴 *Austerlitz* **1960 (PG)** Ambitious but numbing costume drama about the events leading up to the epic battle between Napoleon and the overwhelming forces of the Czar and the Austrian Emperor at Austerlitz. Napoleon won. Film has been drastically cut from original 166 minute release. Watch director Gance's silent version, "Napoleon," for a truly epic experience. **123m/C VHS.** *FR IT YU* Claudia Cardinale, Martine Carol, Leslie Caron, Vittorio De Sica, Jean Marais, Ettore Manni, Jack Palance, Orson Welles; ***D:*** Abel Gance. *LIV, TPV*

The Battle of Blood Island 🦴 **1960** Two G.I.s, one Christian and one Jewish, face death at the hands of the Japanese during WWII. Still, they bicker incessantly before finally pulling together to save themselves. **64m/B VHS, Beta.** Richard Devon, Ron Kennedy; ***D:*** Joel Rapp. *NOS, SNC*

Battle of Britain 🦴🦴½ **1969 (G)** A powerful retelling of the most dramatic aerial combat battle of WWII, showing how the understaffed Royal Air Force held off the might of the German Luftwaffe. **132m/C VHS, Beta, LV.** Michael Caine, Laurence Olivier, Trevor Howard, Kenneth More, Christopher Plummer, Robert Shaw, Susannah York, Ralph Richardson, Curt Jurgens, Michael Redgrave, Nigel Patrick, Edward Fox; ***D:*** Guy Hamilton; ***C:*** Frederick A. (Freddie) Young. *MGM, FOX*

Battle of China **1944** A look at the people, culture, and industry of China, and Japan's total commitment to conquer the country during WWII, through authentic newsreel footage. **67m/B VHS, Beta.** ***D:*** Frank Capra. *MPI, MRV, HHT*

The Battle of El Alamein 🦴🦴 **1968** Action filled movie about the alliance of Italy and Germany in a war against the British, set in a North African desert in the year 1942. **105m/C VHS, Beta.** *IT FR* Frederick Stafford, Ettore Manni, Robert Hossein, Michael Rennie, George Hilton, Ira Furstenberg; ***D:*** Calvin Jackson Padget. *CNG, MRV, GEM*

Battle of Elderbush Gulch **1913** An ancient pioneering western short famous for innocently employing the now-established cliches of bad guy, good guy, and helpless frontier heroine. One of Gish's first films. **22m/B VHS, Beta.** Lillian Gish; ***D:*** D.W. Griffith. *VCN, PYR, GVV*

Battle of Neretva 🦴🦴 **1969** During WWII, Yugoslav partisans are facing German and Italian troops and local Chetniks as they battle for freedom. Big budget war film lost continuity with U.S. cut. **106m/C VHS.** *YU* Yul Brynner, Curt Jurgens, Orson Welles, Hardy Kruger, Franco Nero, Sergei Bondarchuk; ***D:*** Veljko Bulajic. Nominations: Academy Awards '69: Best Foreign Language Film. *INJ, REP*

The Battle of Russia **1944** Hitler's forces are victorious in Moscow and Leningrad but are thoroughly defeated at the battle of Stalingrad. Authentic newsreel footage. **83m/B VHS, Beta.** ***D:*** Frank Capra. *HHT, MRV, CCB*

The Battle of San Pietro **1944** John Huston's powerful documentary about the famous battle in Italy's Liri Valley, stressing the number of losses sustained in taking this military objective. The film was almost suppressed by the U.S. government, because it was considered to be too strong for general release. **43m/B VHS, Beta.** John Huston. *IHF, WFV, FUS*

Battle of the Bulge 🦴🦴 **1965** A recreation of the famous offensive by Nazi Panzer troops on the Belgian front during 1944-45, an assault that could have changed the course of WWII. **141m/C VHS, Beta, LV.** Henry Fonda, Robert Shaw, Robert Ryan, Dana Andrews, Telly Savalas, Ty Hardin, Pier Angeli, George Montgomery, Charles Bronson; ***D:*** Ken Annakin; ***W:*** Philip Yordan; ***C:*** Jack Hildyard. *WAR*

Battle of the Bullies *Woof!* **1985** A made-for-television special about an unsalvageable nerd who plots a high-tech revenge upon a slew of high school bullies. **45m/C VHS, Beta.** Manny Jacobs, Christopher Barnes, Sarah Inglis. *NWV*

Battle of the Commandos 🦴 *Legion of the Damned* **1971** A tough Army colonel leads a group of convicts on a dangerous mission to destroy a German-built cannon before it's used against the Allied Forces. **94m/C VHS.** *IT* Jack Palance, Curt Jurgens, Thomas Hunter, Robert Hunter; ***D:*** Umberto Lenzi. *REP*

Battle of the Eagles 🦴½ **1981** Follows the true adventures of the "Partisan Squadron," the courageous airmen known as the "Knights of the Sky" during WWII in Yugoslavia. **102m/C VHS, Beta.** Bekim Fehmiu, George Taylor, Gloria Samara, Frank Phillips; ***D:*** Tom Raymonth. *NO*

The Battle of the Japan Sea 🦴🦴 **1970 (G)** A Japanese epic, dubbed in English, centering around the historic WWII battle between Japan and Russia. **120m/C VHS, Beta.** *JP* Toshiro Mifune. *VCD*

The Battle of the Sexes 🦴🦴🦴 **1960** Sophisticated British comedy has mild-mannered Sellers trying to prevent a business takeover by the brash American Cummings. A good supporting cast and the impeccable Sellers make this one unique. Adapted from the James Thurber short story "The Catbird Seat." **88m/B VHS, Beta.** *GB* Peter Sellers, Robert Morley, Constance Cummings, Jameson Clark; ***D:*** Charles Crichton. *MRV*

Battle of the Worlds 🦴 *Il Pianeta Degli Uomini Spenti; Planet of the Lifeless Men* **1961** Typical low-budget science fiction. A scientist tries to stop an alien planet from destroying the Earth. Even an aging Rains can't help this one. Poorly dubbed in English. **84m/C VHS.** *IT* Claude Rains, Maya Brent, Bill Carter, Marina Orsini, Jacqueline Derval; ***D:*** Anthony (Antonio Margheriti) Dawson. *SNC, MRV*

Battle of Valiant 🦴 **1963** Thundering hordes of invading barbarians trample the splendor of ancient Rome beneath their grimy sandals. **90m/C VHS, Beta.** Gordon Mitchell, Ursula Davis, Massimo Serato; ***D:*** John Gentil. *NO*

Battle Shock 🦴½ *A Woman's Devotion; War Shock* **1956** Painter is accused of murdering a cantina waitress while on his honeymoon in Mexico. **88m/C VHS.** Ralph Meeker, Janice Rule, Paul Henreid; ***D:*** Paul Henreid; ***M:*** Les Baxter. *REP*

Battleforce 🦴 *The Battle of the Mareth Line; The Greatest Battle* **1978** Exciting battle scenes lose their power in the confusion of this mixed-up WWII film about Rommel's last days. Dubbed sequences, news-reel vignettes and surprise performances by big name stars are incomprehensibly glued together. **97m/C VHS, Beta.** *GE YU* Henry Fonda, Stacy Keach, Helmut Berger, Samantha Eggar, Giuliano Gemma, John Huston; ***D:*** Umberto Lenzi. *QVD, TLF*

Battleground 🦴🦴🦴 **1949** A tightly-conceived post-WWII character drama, following a platoon of American soldiers through the Battle of the Bulge. Available in a Colorized version. **118m/B VHS, Beta, LV.** Van Johnson, John Hodiak, James Whitmore, George Murphy, Ricardo Montalban, Marshall Thompson, Jerome Courtland, Don Taylor, Bruce Cowling, Leon Ames, Douglas Fowley, Richard Jaeckel, Scotty Beckett; ***D:*** William A. Wellman; ***W:*** Robert Pirosh; ***C:*** Paul Vogel. Academy Awards '49: Best Black and White Cinematography, Best Story & Screenplay; Golden Globe Awards '50: Best Screenplay, Best Supporting Actor (Whitmore); Nominations: Academy Awards '49: Best Director (Wellman), Best Film Editing, Best Picture, Best Supporting Actor (Whitmore). *MGM*

The Battleship Potemkin 🦴🦴🦴🦴 *Potemkin; Bronenosets Potemkin* **1925** Eisenstein's best work documents mutiny aboard the Russian battleship Potemkin in 1905 which led to a civilian uprising against the Czar in Odessa, and the resulting crackdown by troops loyal to the Czar. Beautiful cinematography, especially the use of montage sequences, changed filmmaking. In particular, a horrifying sequence depicting the slaughter of civilians on an Odessa beach by soldiers coming down the stairs leading to it is exceptional; many movies pay homage to this scene including "The Untouchables" and "Love and Death." Viewers should overlook obvious Marxist overtones and see this film for what it is: a masterpiece. **71m/B VHS, Beta, LV.** *RU* Alexander Antonov, Vladimir Barsky, Grigori Alexandrov, Mikhail Gomorov, Sergei Eisenstein; ***D:*** Sergei Eisenstein; ***M:*** Eric Allaman. *REP, MRV, NOS*

Battlestar Galactica ½ **1978 (PG)** Plot episode of the sci-fi television series which was later released in the theaters. The crew of the spaceship Galactica must battle their robot enemies in an attempt to reach Earth. Contains special effects designed by John "Star Wars" Dykstra. Individual episodes of the series are also available. **125m/C VHS, Beta, LV.** Lorne Greene, Dirk Benedict, Karen Jensen, Jane Seymour, Patrick Macnee, Terry Carter, John Colicos, Richard A. Colla, Laurette Spang, Richard Hatch; ***D:*** Richard A. Colla. *MCA, MOV*

Battling Bunyon ½ **1924** A wily youngster becomes a comedy boxer for profit, and eventually gets fed up and battles the champ. Silent. **71m/B VHS, Beta.** Chester Conklin, Wesley Barry, Mollie Malone, Jackie Fields. *GPV, VYY*

Battling Butler ½ **1926** Rich young Keaton tries to impress a young lady by impersonating a boxer. All goes well until he has to fight the real thing. Mostly charming if uneven; one of Keaton's more unusual efforts, thought to be somewhat autobiographical. Silent. **70m/B VHS.** Buster Keaton, Sally O'Neil, Snitz Edwards, Francis McDonald, Mary O'Brien, Tom Wilson, Walter James; ***D:*** Buster Keaton. *NO*

Battling for Baby **1992** It's the war of the Grandmas. New mother Katherine decides to return to work and both her mother and mother-in-law want to look after the little tyke. Silly made-for-TV fluff. **93m/C VHS.** Courteney Cox, Suzanne Pleshette, Debbie Reynolds, John Terlesky, Doug McClure, Leigh Lawson, Mary Jo Catlett; ***D:*** Art Wolff; ***W:*** Walter Lockwood, Nancy Silvers. *TTC*

Battling Marshal ½ **1948** Fast-moving action western starring Carson. **52m/B VHS, Beta.** Sunset Carson, Lee Roberts; ***D:*** Oliver Drake. *VCN*

Battling Orioles **1924** The once scrappy baseball team is now a bunch of grumpy old men, that is until Glenn whips them into shape. Silent. **58m/B VHS, Beta, 8mm.** Glenn Tryon, Blanche Mehaffey, Noah Young; ***D:*** Ted Wilde, Fred Guiol. *GVV*

Battling Outlaws ½ **194?** Western featuring the American cowboy Bob Steele. **64m/B VHS, Beta.** Bob Steele. *NOS, VCN*

Battling with Buffalo Bill **1931** Twelve episodes of the vintage serial concerning the exploits of the legendary Indian fighter. **180m/B VHS, Beta.** Tom Tyler, Rex Bell, Franklyn Farnum. *VCN*

The Bawdy Adventures of Tom Jones ½ **1976 (R)** An exploitive extension of the Fielding novel about the philandering English lad, with plenty of soft-core skin and lewdness. **89m/C VHS, Beta.** *GB* Joan Collins, Trevor Howard, Terry-Thomas, Arthur Lowe, Murray Melvin; ***D:*** Cliff Owen. *MCA*

Baxter ½ **1989** A bull terrier lives his life with three different sets of masters. He examines all of humankind's worst faults and the viewer quickly realizes that Baxter's life depends on his refusal to obey like a good dog should. Based on the novel by Ken Greenhall. Funny, sometimes erotic, quirky comedy. In French with English subtitles. **82m/C VHS, LV.** *FR* Lisa Delamare, Jean Mercure, Jacques Spiesser, Catherine Ferran, Jean-Paul Roussillon, Sabrina Leurquin; ***D:*** Jerome Boivin; ***W:*** Jerome Boivin, Jacques Audiard; ***M:*** Marc Hillman, Patrick Roffe. *FXL, PMS*

The Bay Boy ½ **1985 (R)** Set in the 1930s in Nova Scotia, this period piece captures the coming-of-age of a rural teenage boy. Young Sutherland's adolescent angst becomes a more difficult struggle when he witnesses a murder, and is tormented by the secret. **107m/C VHS, Beta, LV.** *CA* Liv Ullmann, Kiefer Sutherland, Peter Donat, Matthieu Carriere, Joe MacPherson, Isabelle Mejias, Alan Scarfe, Chris Wiggins, Leah K. Pinsent; ***D:*** Daniel Petrie; ***M:*** Claude Bolling. Genie Awards '85: Best Film, Best Supporting Actor (Scarfe). *ORI*

Bayou Romance **1986** Painter inherits a Louisiana plantation, moves in, and falls in love with a young gypsy. **90m/C Beta.** Annie Potts, Michael Ansara, Barbara Horan. *PSM*

Baywatch the Movie: Forbidden Paradise ½ **1995 (PG)** The "Baywatch" babes and their fellow lifesaving hunks-in-trunks head off to Hawaii to study the latest search and rescue techniques from the state's premier lifeguard team. **90m/C VHS.** David Hasselhoff, Pamela Anderson Lee, Alexandra Paul, Yasmine Bleeth, David Charvet, Gregory Alan-Williams, Jeremy Jackson; ***D:*** Douglas Schwartz. *LIV*

Be My Valentine, Charlie Brown **1975** The Peanuts gang endures the follies of the heart on St. Valentine's Day. Animated. **30m/C VHS, Beta.** ***D:*** Phil Roman. *MED, WTA*

Beach Babes from Beyond Infinity **1993 (R)** "HOT. TAN. ALIEN." Three words that would send shivers through the body of any red-blooded American boy. And as if alien silicone isn't enough to draw a crowd, this piece of fluff also features the relatives of big name stars hoping to cash in on the family name. Typical Hollywood cheese and sleaze should be fun for those who still can't get this kind of quality entertainment on cable. **78m/C VHS.** Joe Estevez, Don Swayze, Joey Travolta, Burt Ward, Jacqueline Stallone, Linnea Quigley, Sara Bellomo, Tamara Landry, Nicole Posey; ***D:*** Ellen Cabot. *PAR*

Beach Blanket Bingo **1965** Fifth entry in the "Beach Party" series (after "Pajama Party") is by far the best and has achieved near-cult status. Both Funicello and Avalon are back, but this time a very young Evans catches Avalon's eye. Throw in a mermaid, some moon-doggies, skydiving, sizzling beach parties, and plenty of nostalgic golly-gee-whiz fun and you have the classic '60s beach movie. Totally implausible, but that's half the fun when the sun-worshipping teens become involved in a kidnapping and occasionally break into song. Followed by "How to Stuff a Wild Bikini." ♫Beach Blanket Bingo; The Cycle Set; Fly Boy; The Good Times; I Am My Ideal; I Think You Think; It Only Hurts When I Cry; New Love; You'll Never Change Him. **96m/C VHS, Beta, LV.** Frankie Avalon, Annette Funicello, Linda Evans, Don Rickles, Buster Keaton, Paul Lynde, Harvey Lembeck, Deborah Walley, John Ashley, Jody McCrea, Marta Kristen, Timothy Carey, Earl Wilson, Bobbi Shaw; ***D:*** William Asher; ***W:*** William Asher, Sher Townsend, Leo Townsend; ***M:*** Les Baxter. *NO*

Beach Girls **1982 (R)** Three voluptuous coeds intend to re-educate a bookish young man and the owner of a beach house. **91m/C VHS, Beta, LV.** Debra Blee, Val Kline, Jeana Tomasina, Adam Roarke; ***D:*** Patrice Townsend. *PAR*

The Beach Girls and the Monster **1965** Here's one on the cutting edge of genre bending: while it meticulously maintains the philosophical depth and production values of sixties beach bimbo fare, it manages to graft successfully with the heinous critter from the sea genre to produce a hybrid horror with acres o'flesh. **70m/B VHS.** Jon Hall, Sue Casey, Walker Edmiston; ***D:*** Jon Hall; ***M:*** Frank Sinatra Jr. *SNC*

Beach House **1982** In this boring comedy, adolescents frolic on the beach, get inebriated, and listen to rock 'n' roll. **76m/C VHS, Beta.** Kathy McNeil, Richard Duggan, Ileana Seidel, John Cosola, Spence Waugh, Paul Anderson, John A. Gallagher; ***W:*** Marino Amaruso. *NO*

Beach Party **1963** Started the "Beach Party" series with the classic Funicello/Avalon combo. Scientist Cummings studying the mating habits of teenagers intrudes on a group of surfers, beach bums, and bikers, to his lasting regret. Typical beach party bingo, with sand, swimsuits, singing, dancing, and bare minimum in way of a plot. Followed by "Muscle Beach Party." ♫Beach Party; Don't Stop Now; Promise Me Anything; Secret Surfin' Spot; Surfin' and a-Swingin'; Treat Him Nicely. **101m/C VHS, Beta.** Frankie Avalon, Annette Funicello, Harvey Lembeck, Robert Cummings, Dorothy Malone, Morey Amsterdam, Jody McCrea, John Ashley, Candy Johnson, Dolores Wells, Yvette Vickers, Eva Six; ***D:*** William Asher; ***W:*** Lou Rusoff; ***M:*** Les Baxter. *NO*

Beachcomber *Vessel of Wrath* **1938** Comedy set in the Dutch East Indies about a shiftless beachcomber (Laughton) who falls in love with a missionary's prim sister (Lanchester), as she attempts to reform him. The real-life couple of Laughton and Lanchester are their usual pleasure to watch. Remade in 1954. Story by W. Somerset Maugham. **88m/B VHS, Beta.** *GB* Charles Laughton, Elsa Lanchester, Robert Newton, Tyrone Guthrie; ***D:*** Erich Pommer. *NOS, MRV, DVT*

Beaches ½ **1988 (PG-13)** Based on the novel by Iris Rainer Dart about two girls whose friendship survived the test of time. The friendship is renewed once more when one of the now middle-aged women learns that she is dying slowly of a fatal disease. **123m/C VHS, Beta, LV, 8mm.** Bette Midler, Barbara Hershey, John Heard, Spalding Gray, Lainie Kazan, James Read, Mayim Bialik; ***D:*** Garry Marshall; ***W:*** Mary Agnes Donoghue; ***C:*** Dante Spinotti; ***M:*** Georges Delerue. Nominations: Academy Awards '88: Best Art Direction/Set Decoration. *TOU, JCF*

Beaks: The Movie *Woof! Birds of Prey* **1987 (R)** Two television reporters try to figure out why birds of prey are suddenly attacking humans. Owes nothing to Hitchcock's "The Birds." **86m/C VHS, Beta.** Christopher Atkins, Michelle Johnson; ***D:*** Rene Cardona Jr. *LIV*

Beanstalk ½ **1994 (PG)** Modern-day version of the fairytale finds young Jack Taylor (Daniels) scheming to make it big to help his hardworking single mom. He meets up with a wacky scientist (Kidder), who gives Jack some recently discovered seeds that naturally grow into an enormous beanstalk. And what does Jack find when he climbs the beanstalk—why an entire family of silly giants. **80m/C VHS, Beta.** J.D. Daniels, Margot Kidder, Richard Moll, Amy Stock-Poynton, Patrick Renna, Richard Paul, David Naughton, Stuart Pankin, Cathy McAuley; ***D:*** Michael Paul Davis; ***W:*** Michael Paul Davis; ***M:*** Kevin Bassinson. *PAR*

The Bear **1989 (PG)** Breathtaking, effortlessly entertaining family film about an orphaned bear cub tagging after a grown male and dealing with hunters. The narrative is essentially from the cub's point of view, with very little dialogue. A huge moneymaker in Europe. Based on a novel by James Oliver Curwood. **92m/C VHS, Beta, LV.** *FR* Jack Wallace, Tcheky Karyo, Andre Lacombe; ***D:*** Jean-Jacques Annaud; ***W:*** Gerard Brach, Michael Kane; ***C:*** Philippe Rousselot; ***M:*** Bill Conti. Nominations: Academy Awards '89: Best Film Editing. *COL, RDG, HMV*

Bear Island ½ **1980 (PG)** Group of secret agents cleverly disguising themselves as U.N. weather researchers converge upon Bear Island in search of a Nazi U-Boat. Looks like rain. **118m/C VHS, Beta.** Donald Sutherland, Richard Widmark, Barbara Parkins, Vanessa Redgrave, Christopher Lee, Lloyd Bridges; ***D:*** Don Sharp. *NO*

The Bears & I **1974 (G)** A young Vietnam vet helps Indians regain their land rights while raising three bear cubs. Beautiful photography in this Disney production. **89m/C VHS.** Patrick Wayne, Chief Dan George, Andrew Duggan, Michael Ansara; ***D:*** Bernard McEveety; ***M:*** Buddy Baker. *DIS*

The Beast ½ *The Beast of War* **1988 (R)** Violent and cliche-driven war drama notable for its novel twist: wild Russian tank officer becomes lost in the Afghanistan wilderness while being tracked by Afghan rebels with revenge in mind. Filmed in the Israel desert and adapted by William Mastrosimone from his play. **93m/C VHS, Beta.** George Dzundza, Jason Patric, Steven Bauer, Stephen Baldwin, Don Harvey, Kabir Bedi, Erik Avari, Haim Gerafi; ***D:*** Kevin Reynolds; ***W:*** William Mastrosimone; ***M:*** Mark Isham. *COL*

The Beast from Haunted Cave **1960** Gold thieves hiding in a wilderness cabin encounter a spiderlike monster. Surprisingly good performances from Sinatra (Frank's nephew) and Carol. Produced by Gene Corman, Roger's brother. **64m/B VHS.** Michael Forest, Sheila Carol, Frank Wolff, Richard Sinatra, Wally Campo; ***D:*** Monte Hellman; ***W:*** Charles B. Griffith. *DVT, MRV, SNC*

The Beast from 20,000 Fathoms 🦴🦴½ **1953** Atomic testing defrosts a giant dinosaur in the Arctic; the hungry monster proceeds onwards to its former breeding grounds, now New York City. Oft-imitated saurian-on-the-loose formula is still fun, brought to life by Ray Harryhausen special effects. Based loosely on the Ray Bradbury story "The Foghorn." **80m/B VHS, Beta, LV.** Paul Christian, Paula Raymond, Cecil Kellaway, Kenneth Tobey, Donald Woods, Lee Van Cleef, Steve Brodie, Mary Hill; ***D:*** Eugene Lourie; ***W:*** Fred Freiberger, Louis Morheim. *WAR, FCT, MLB*

Beast in the Cellar 🦴½ *Are You Dying Young Man?* **1970 (R)** Every family has something to hide, and in the case of two spinster sisters, it's their murderous inhuman brother, whom they keep chained in the cellar. Like all brothers, however, the "beast" rebels against his sisters' bossiness and escapes to terrorize their peaceful English countryside. The sisters' (Reid and Robson) performances aren't bad, but rest of effort is fairly disappointing. **85m/C VHS, Beta.** *GB* Beryl Reid, Flora Robson, T.P. McKenna; ***D:*** James Kelly. *NO*

Beast of Morocco 🦴🦴 *Hand of Night* **1966** Interesting vampire film about a Morrocan vampire princess who sets her sights on seducing a noted archaeologist. Of course his girlfriend ends up being abducted by the vampire's servant. **88m/C VHS.** *GB* William Sylvester, Alizia Gur, Terence de Marney. *SNC*

Beast of the Yellow Night *Woof!* **1970 (R)** A dying soldier sells his soul to Satan at the close of WWII. Years later, existing without aging, he periodically turns into a cannibal monster. Although the first half is tedious, the monster turns things around when he finally shows up. Decent gore effects. **87m/C VHS, Beta.** *PH* John Ashley, Mary Wilcox, Eddie Garcia, Vic Diaz; ***D:*** Eddie Romero. *NOS, VCI, INC*

The Beast of Yucca Flats *Woof!* **1961** A really cheap, quasi-nuclear protest film. A Russian scientist is chased by communist agents into a nuclear testing area and is caught in an atomic blast. As a result, he turns into a club-weilding monster. Voice over narration is used in lieu of dialogue as that process proved too expensive. **53m/B VHS.** Tor Johnson, Douglas Mellor, Larry Aten, Barbara Francis; ***D:*** Coleman Francis; ***W:*** Coleman Francis. *SNC, CNM, MLB*

The Beast that Killed Women 🦴🦴½ **1965** Colonists at a sunny Florida nudist camp have their beach party interrupted by an escaped gorilla. Director Mahon, in his first color effort, stretches this panicky moment into an hour of fleshy fun and games. **60m/C VHS.** ***D:*** Barry Mahon. *SMW, TPV*

The Beast with Five Fingers 🦴🦴½ **1946** After a pianist mysteriously dies and leaves his fortune to his private nurse, the occupants of his villa are terrorized by a creature that turns out to be the pianist's hand which was severed by his personal secretary (Lorre). Lorre is also terrorized by hallucinations of the hand, and no matter what he does to stop it (nail it to a desk, throw it in the fire, etc.), nothing can keep the hand from carrying out its mission. A creepy thriller with inventive shots of the severed hand. **88m/B VHS.** Robert Alda, Andrea King, Peter Lorre, Victor Francen, J. Carrol Naish, Charles Dingle; ***D:*** Robert Florey; ***M:*** Max Steiner. *MGM*

The Beast Within 🦴🦴 **1982 (R)** Young woman has the misfortune of being raped by an unseen creature in a Mississippi swamp. Seventeen years later, her son conceived from that hellish union begins to act quite strange, developing a penchant for shedding his skin before turning into an insect-like critter with a cannibalistic appetite. First film to use the air "bladder" type of prosthetic make-up popularized in later, and generally better, horror films. Contains some choice cuts in photo editing: the juxtaposition of hamburger and human "dead meat" is witty. Based on Edward Levy's 1981 novel. **98m/C VHS, Beta.** Ronny Cox, Bibi Besch, L.Q. Jones, Paul Clemens, Don Gordon; ***D:*** Philippe Mora; ***W:*** Tom Holland; ***M:*** Les Baxter. *MGM*

Beastmaster 🦴🦴 **1982 (PG)** Adventure set in a wild and primitive world. The Beastmaster is involved in a life-and-death struggle with overwhelming forces of evil. Campy neanderthal flesh flick. **119m/C VHS, Beta, LV.** Marc Singer, Tanya Roberts, Rip Torn, John Amos, Josh Milrad, Billy Jacoby; ***D:*** Don A. Coscarelli; ***W:*** Don A. Coscarelli; ***C:*** John Alcott. *MGM*

Beastmaster 2: Through the Portal of Time 🦴½ **1991 (PG-13)** This time the laughs are intentional as the Beastmaster follows an evil monarch through a dimensional gate to modern-day L.A., where the shopping is better for both trendy clothes and weapons. Fun for genre fans, with a behind-the-scenes featurette on the tape. **107m/C VHS, LV.** Marc Singer, Kari Wuhrer, Sarah Douglas, Wings Hauser, James Avery, Robert Fieldsteel, Arthur Malet, Robert Z'Dar, Michael Berryman; ***D:*** Sylvio Tabet; ***M:*** Robert Folk. *REP*

Beastmaster 3: The Eye of Braxus 🦴🦴½ **1995 (PG)** Heroic hunk Dar the Beastmaster (Singer) returns to battle evil. Lord Agon (Warner) needs to obtain a jeweled eye that will bring the demon Braxus back to life—and he'll stop at nothing, including kidnapping Dar's brother King Tal (Van Dien), to reach his terrifying goal. But Dar isn't alone—he's got the bewitching sorceress Morgana (Down), tempting warrioress Shada (Hess), and loyal advisor Seth (Todd) to help him out. **92m/C VHS, LV.** Marc Singer, David Warner, Lesley-Anne Down, Tony Todd, Caspar Van Dien, Keith Coulouris, Sandra Hess, Patrick Kilpatrick; ***D:*** Gabrielle Beaumont; ***W:*** David Wise; ***C:*** Barbara Claman; ***M:*** Jan Hammer. *MCA*

Beasts 🦴 **1983** A young couple's plans for a romantic weekend in the Rockies are slightly changed when the pair are savagely attacked by wild beasts. **92m/C VHS, Beta.** Tom Babson, Kathy Christopher, Vern Potter. *PSM*

The Beat 🦴 **1988** Unrealistic film about a bookish new kid who intercedes in the tension between two rival street gangs, changing their lives in his literary way. **101m/C VHS, Beta, LV.** John Savage, Kara Glover, Paul Dillon, David Jacobson, William McNamara; ***D:*** Peter Mones; ***W:*** Peter Mones; ***M:*** Carter Burwell. *LIV, VES*

Beat Girl 🦴🦴 *Wild For Kicks* **1960** An architect's rebellious teenage daughter sinks to the bottom and gets involved in murder along the way. **85m/B VHS.** *GB* David Farrar, Noelle Adam, Christopher Lee, Gillian Hills, Shirley Anne Field, Oliver Reed; ***D:*** Edmond T. Greville; ***M:*** John Barry. *SNC, FCT, HEG*

Beat Street 🦴🦴½ **1984 (PG)** Intended as a quick cash-in on the break dancing trend, this essentially plotless musical features kids trying to break into local show biz with their rapping and dancing skills. Features the music of Afrika Bambaata and the Soul Sonic Force, Grand Master Melle Mel and the Furious Five, and others. ♫Beat Street Breakdown; Baptize the Beat; Stranger in a Strange Land; Beat Street Strut; Us Girls; This Could Be the Night; Breakers Revenge; Tu Carino (Carmen's Theme); Frantic Situation. **106m/C VHS, Beta, LV.** Rae Dawn Chong, Leon Grant, Saundra Santiago, Guy Davis, Jon Chardiet, Duane Jones, Kadeem Hardison; ***D:*** Stan Lathan; ***W:*** Andrew Davis. *VES, LIV*

Beat the Devil 🦴🦴🦴 **1953** Each person on a slow boat to Africa has a scheme to beat the other passengers to the uranium-rich land that they all hope to claim. An unusual black comedy which didn't fare well when released, but over the years has come to be the epitome of spy-spoofs. **89m/C VHS, Beta, LV.** Humphrey Bogart, Gina Lollobrigida, Peter Lorre, Robert Morley, Jennifer Jones; ***D:*** John Huston; ***C:*** Oswald Morris. *MRV, NOS, COL*

Beatlemania! The Movie 🦴 *Beatlemania* **1981** Boring look at the Fab Four. Not the real Beatles, but impersonators who do a very inadequate job. Based on the equally disappointing stage show. **86m/C VHS, Beta, LV.** Mitch Weissman, Ralph Castelli, David Leon, Tom Teeley; ***D:*** Joseph Manduke. *IME*

The Beatniks 🦴 **1960** Story about the dark secrets of the beat generation in which a man is promised fame and fortune by an agent, but his dreams are dashed when his friend commits murder. A big waste of time. **78m/B VHS.** Tony Travis, Peter Breck, Karen Kadler, Joyce Terry; ***D:*** Paul Frees. *SNC, TPV*

Beatrice 🦴🦴🦴½ *La Passion Beatrice* **1988 (R)** In France during the Middle Ages, a barbaric soldier of the Hundred Years' War returns to his estate that his daughter has maintained, only to brutalize and abuse her. In French with English subtitles. **132m/C VHS, Beta, LV.** *FR* Julie Delpy, Barnard Pierre Donnadieu, Nils Tavernier; ***D:*** Bertrand Tavernier; ***W:*** Colo Tavernier O'Hagan; ***M:*** Lili Boulanger. Cesar Awards '88: Best Costume Design. *NO*

Beau Brummel 🦴🦴½ **1924** The famous silent adaptation of the Clyde Fitch play about an ambitious English dandy's rise and fall. **80m/B VHS, Beta.** John Barrymore, Mary Astor, Willard Louis, Irene Rich, Carmel Myers, Alec B. Francis, William Humphreys; ***D:*** Harry Beaumont. *NOS, HHT, VYY*

Beau Brummel 🦴🦴🦴 **1954** Lavish production casts Granger in the role of the rags-to-riches dandy and chief adviser to the Prince of Wales. Born into a life of poverty, George Bryan Brummel uses wit and intelligence to meet the vain Prince and ingratiate himself to the future king (George IV). He also manages to catch the eye of Taylor, who falls in love with him. Outstanding period piece cinematography, sets, and costumes. Shot on location in England's beautiful countryside, many of the interior shots are from a 15th-century mansion, Ockwell Manor, located near Windsor Castle. Remake of the 1924 silent film starring John Barrymore. Based on the play by Clyde Fitch. **113m/C VHS.** Stewart Granger, Elizabeth Taylor, Peter Ustinov, Robert Morley, James Donald, James Hayter, Rosemary Harris, Paul Rogers, Noel Willman, Peter Dyneley, Charles Carson; ***D:*** Curtis Bernhardt; ***W:*** Karl Tunberg; ***C:*** Oswald Morris. *MGM*

Beau Geste 🦴🦴🦴½ **1939** The classic Hollywood adventure film based on the Percival Christopher Wren story about three brothers who join the Foreign Legion after nobly claiming responsibility for a jewel theft they didn't commit. Once enlisted, they must face desert wars and the most despicable commanding officer ever, before clearing their family name. A rousing, much-copied epic. **114m/B VHS, Beta.** Gary Cooper, Ray Milland, Robert Preston, Brian Donlevy, Donald O'Connor, J. Carrol Naish, Susan Hayward, James Stephenson; ***D:*** William A. Wellman. Nominations: Academy Awards '39: Best Interior Decoration, Best Supporting Actor (Donlevy). *MCA*

Beau Pere 🦴🦴🦴 *Stepfather* **1981** Bittersweet satiric romp from Blier about the war zone of modern romance, wherein a 30-year-old widower falls madly in love with his 14-year-old stepdaughter. Sharp-edged and daring. In French with subtitles. **125m/C VHS, Beta.** *FR* Patrick Dewaere, Nathalie Baye, Ariel Besse, Maurice Ronet; ***D:*** Bertrand Blier; ***W:*** Bertrand Blier. Nominations: Cannes Film Festival '81: Best Film. *MED, INJ*

Beau Revel 🦴🦴🦴½ **1921** Critically acclaimed romantic drama of the silent era. A passionate dancing girl played by Vidor, one of the twenties' more prolific romantic leads (and erstwhile wife of director King Vidor) is the object of romantic interest of a father and son, which leaves the threesome lovelorn, suicidal, and emotionally scarred. You might recognize Stone from his later role as Judge Hardy in the MGM "Hardy Family" series. **70m/B VHS, Beta.** Lewis Stone, Florence Vidor, Lloyd Hughes, Katherine Kirkham, William Conklin; ***D:*** John Wray. *GPV, FCT*

Beauties of the Night 🦴🦴 *Night Beauties; Les Belles de Nuit* **1952** Dreamy fantasy finds a shy music teacher (Philipe) escaping from his boring life into romantic adventures with beautiful women. But his dreams slowly turn nightmarish and he's forced to deal with reality—and real love. French with subtitles. **89m/B VHS.** *FR* Gerard Philipe, Gina Lollobrigida, Martine Carol, Magali Vendeuil, Paolo Stoppa, Raymond Bussieres, Raymond Cordy; ***D:*** Rene Clair; ***W:*** Rene Clair; ***C:*** Armand Thirard; ***M:*** Georges Van Parys. *WBF*

The Beautiful Blonde from Bashful Bend ☆☆½ **1949** Charming comedy-western gets better with age. Grable is the pistol packing mama mistaken for the new school teacher. Fun performances by all, especially Herbert. **77m/C VHS, LV.** Betty Grable, Cesar Romero, Rudy Vallee, Olga San Juan, Hugh Herbert, Porter Hall, Sterling Holloway, El Brendel; ***D:*** Preston Sturges. *FOX*

Beautiful Dreamers ☆½ **1992 (PG-13)** Maurice Bucke is a young Canadian physician who runs the London Insane Asylum. After a chance meeting with poet Walt Whitman, both men discover their mutual outrage for current treatment of the mentally ill. Bucke persuades Whitman to visit his asylum in order to try Whitman's theory of human compassion on the asylum's inmates. However, Bucke runs into opposition from the local townspeople, scandalized by Whitman's radical reputation. Fairly humdrum with a larger-than-life performance by Torn as Whitman. Based on Whitman's visit to Canada in 1880. **108m/C VHS, LV.** *CA* Rip Torn, Colm Feore, Wendel Meldrum, Sheila McCarthy, Colin Fox; ***D:*** John Kent Harrison; ***W:*** John Kent Harrison. *HMD, FCT*

Beautiful Girls ☆☆½ **1996 (R)** Easy-going film highlights the differences between men, women, and relationships. A 10-year high school reunion brings together buddies Tommy (Dillon), Kev (Perlich), Paul (Rappaport), Mo (Emmerich), and Willie (Hutton). They ice-fish, drink, and talk about women (about whom they haven't a clue). All are smitten by Andera (Thurman), the gorgeous visiting cousin of another friend, and Willie becomes intrigued by Marty (Portman), his precociously tantalizing 13-year-old neighbor. They try to work on growing up. Good ensemble work, with O'Donnell's tirade about fake femininity particularly amusing. The Afghan Whigs are featured as the bar band. **110m/C VHS.** Matt Dillon, Timothy Hutton, Michael Rapaport, Max Perlich, Noah Emmerich, Lauren Holly, Uma Thurman, Natalie Portman, Mira Sorvino, Martha Plimpton, Rosie O'Donnell, Annabeth Gish, Pruitt Taylor Vince, Sam Robards, David Arquette, Anne Bobby, Richard Bright; ***D:*** Ted Demme; ***W:*** Scott Rosenberg; ***C:*** Adam Kimmel; ***M:*** David A. Stewart. *NYR*

The Beautiful, the Bloody and the Bare ☆ **1969** Sordid screamer in the Herschell Gordon Lewis tradition. Set in New York City in the sixties, a depraved artist kills the nude models who pose for him. **?m/C VHS.** *MOV*

Beauty and the Beast ☆☆☆☆ *La Belle et Laete* **1946** The classic medieval fairy tale is brought to life on the big screen for the first time. Beauty takes the place of her father after he is sentenced to die by the horrible Beast and falls in love with him. Cocteau uses the story's themes and famous set-pieces to create a cohesive and captivating surreal hymn to romantic love that is still the definitive version of B&B. In French with subtitles. **90m/B VHS, Beta, LV.** *FR* Jean Marais, Josette Day, Marcel Andre, Mila Parely, Nane Germon, Michel Auclair, Georges Auric; ***D:*** Jean Cocteau. *INJ, SUE, MLB*

Beauty and the Beast **1983** From "Faerie Tale Theatre" comes the story of a Beauty who befriends a Beast and learns a lesson about physical appearance and true love. **60m/C VHS, Beta, LV.** Susan Sarandon, Anjelica Huston, Klaus Kinski, Stephen Elliott; ***D:*** Roger Vadim. *WTA, FOX, FCT*

Beauty and the Beast ☆☆☆☆ **1991 (G)** Wonderful Disney musical combines superb animation, splendid characters, and lively songs about a beautiful girl, Belle, and the fearsome and disagreeable Beast. Supporting cast includes the castle servants (a delightful bunch of household objects). Notable as the first animated feature to be nominated for the Best Picture Oscar. Destined to become a classic. The deluxe video version features a work-in-progress rough film cut, a compact disc of the soundtrack, a lithograph depicting a scene from the film, and an illustrated book. ♫Beauty and the Beast; Belle; Something There; Be Our Guest. **84m/C VHS, LV.** ***D:*** Kirk Wise, Gary Trousdale; ***M:*** Alan Menken, Howard Ashman; ***V:*** Paige O'Hara, Robby Benson, Rex Everhart, Richard White, Jesse Corti, Angela Lansbury, Jerry Orbach, David Ogden Stiers, Bradley Michael Pierce, Jo Anne Worley, Kimmy Robertson. Academy Awards '91: Best Song ("Beauty and the Beast"), Best Score; Golden Globe Awards '92: Best Film—Musical/Comedy; Nominations: Academy Awards '91: Best Picture, Best Song ("Belle", "Be Our Guest"), Best Sound. *DIS, OM*

Beauty and the Beast, Episode 1: Once Upon a Time in New York **1987** When socialite attorney Catherine Chandler is brutally attacked in New York, Vincent, a mysterious man/beast, rescues and befriends her, taking her to his fantastical subterranean world. Pilot for the popular television series. Additional episodes are available. **48m/C VHS, LV.** Ron Perlman, Linda Hamilton, Roy Dotrice, Ray Wise. *REP, MOV*

Beauty and the Beast: Though Lovers Be Lost **1989** The love affair of Vincent and Catherine takes a tragic turn when she is kidnapped by a crime lord. Feature-length drama from the television series. **90m/C VHS, LV.** Linda Hamilton, Ron Perlman. *REP*

Beauty and the Devil ☆☆ *La Beaute du Diable* **1950** Ambitious retelling of the Faust legend finds old Faust (Simon) willing to sell his soul to the Devil, courtesy of his agent Mephistopheles (Philipe), in return for youth and beauty to pursue the beautiful woman he loves. Clair has his actors trade roles midway through as Faust makes his bargain. French with subtitles. **97m/B VHS.** *FR* Michel Simon, Gerard Philipe, Simone Valere, Raymond Cordy, Gaston Modot, Paolo Stoppa, Nicole Besnard; ***D:*** Rene Clair; ***W:*** Rene Clair, Armand Salacrou; ***C:*** Michel Kelber; ***M:*** Roman Vlad. *WBF*

Beauty for the Asking ☆ **1939** It sounds like a workable Lucille Ball vehicle—a beautician develops a bestselling skin cream—and even the title sounds like something you'd like to love Lucy in. But somehow the numerous plot implausibilities managed to get by the story's five writers, and the idea of a jilted woman making millions while being financed by her ex's wife just doesn't fly (perhaps it was an idea ahead of its time). Die-hard Lucy fans may find this interesting. **68m/B VHS.** Lucille Ball, Patric Knowles, Donald Woods, Frieda Inescort, Frances Mercer; ***D:*** Glenn Tryon. *TTC, FCT*

Beauty on the Beach ☆ **196?** A comedy about a mad psychologist, his bizarre experiments with women, and his eventual descent into insanity. In Italian with English subtitles. **90m/C VHS, Beta.** *IT* Valeria Fabrizi. *NO*

Beauty School ☆ **1993 (R)** The promise of an advertising contract pits the owners of rival beauty schools against each other. **95m/C VHS, LV.** Sylvia Kristel, Kevin Bernhardt, Kimberly Taylor, Jane Hamilton; ***D:*** Ernest G. Sauer; ***W:*** Mike MacDonald, Merrill Friedman; ***M:*** Jonathan Hannah. *IMP*

Bebe's Kids ☆☆½ **1992 (PG-13)** When ladies' man Robin falls for the lovely Jamika, he gets some unexpected surprises when he takes her out on a first date to an amusement park—and she brings along four kids. Animated comedy takes some funny pot-shots at both black and white culture and Disneyland. The children are amusing, especially baby PeeWee, a tot with chronically dirty diapers and Tone Loc's gravelly voice. Based on characters created by the late comedian Robin Harris. The video includes the seven-minute animated short "Itsy Bitsy Spider." **74m/C VHS, Beta, LV.** ***D:*** Bruce Smith; ***W:*** Reginald Hudlin; ***M:*** John Barnes; ***V:*** Faizon Love, Vanessa Bell Calloway, Wayne Collins, Jonell Green; Marques Houston, Tone Loc, Nell Carter, Myra J. *PAR, WTA*

Because of the Cats ☆½ **1974** Police inspector uncovers an evil cult within his seaside village while investigating a bizarre rape and burglary. **90m/C VHS, Beta.** Bryan Marshall, Alexandra Stewart, Alex Van Rooyen, Sylvia Kristel, Sebastian Graham Jones; ***D:*** Fons Rademakers. *PSM*

Because You're Mine ☆☆ **1952** Lanza plays an opera star who is drafted and falls in love with Morrow, his top sergeant's sister. Plenty of singing—maybe too much at times, but Lanza's fans will enjoy it nonetheless. ♫All the Things You Are; Because You're Mine; Be My Love; Granada; Lee-Ah-Loo; The Lord's Prayer; The Song Angels Sing; You Do Something to Me. **103m/C VHS.** Mario Lanza, James Whitmore, Doretta Morrow, Dean Miller, Rita (Paula) Corday, Jeff Donnell, Spring Byington; ***D:*** Alexander Hall. Nominations: Academy Awards '52: Best Song ("Because You're Mine"). *MGM*

Becket ☆☆☆ **1964** Adaptation of Jean Anouilh's play about the tumultuous friendship between Henry II of England and the Archbishop of Canterbury Thomas Becket. Becket views his position in the church of little relation to the sexual and emotional needs of a man, until he becomes archbishop. His growing concern for religion and his shrinking need of Henry as friend and confidant eventually cause the demise of the friendship and the resulting tragedy. Flawless acting from every cast member, and finely detailed artistic direction make up for the occasional slow moment. **148m/C VHS, Beta, LV.** Richard Burton, Peter O'Toole, John Gielgud, Donald Wolfit; ***D:*** Peter Glenville; ***W:*** Edward Anhalt; ***C:*** Geoffrey Unsworth. Academy Awards '64: Best Adapted Screenplay; Golden Globe Awards '65: Best Actor—Drama (O'Toole), Best Film—Drama; National Board of Review Awards '64: 10 Best Films of the Year; Nominations: Academy Awards '64: Best Actor (Burton), Best Actor (O'Toole), Best Art Direction/Set Decoration (Color), Best Color Cinematography, Best Costume Design (Color), Best Director (Glenville), Best Film Editing, Best Picture, Best Sound, Best Supporting Actor (Gielgud), Best Original Score. *MPI, TVC*

Becky Sharp ☆☆½ **1935** This premiere Technicolor film tells the story of Becky Sharp, a wicked woman who finally performs one good deed. **83m/C VHS, Beta.** Miriam Hopkins, Frances Dee, Cedric Hardwicke, Billie Burke, Nigel Bruce, Pat Nixon; ***D:*** Rouben Mamoulian; ***C:*** Ray Rennahan. Nominations: Academy Awards '35: Best Actress (Hopkins). *NOS, MRV, HEG*

Becoming Colette ☆☆ **1992 (R)** Tedious flashbacking bio of French writer Colette, from her innocent days in the country to her (bad) marriage to writer/publisher Willy and on and on to her own growing career as a writer. She begins writing stories, using an alter-ego character, Claudine, which detail her sexual escapades. Lots of naked flesh but little passion. A postscript notes that Colette wrote "Gigi" and was the first woman to receive the French Legion of Honor. **97m/C VHS.** Mathilda May, Klaus Maria Brandauer, Virginia Madsen, Paul Rhys, Jean-Pierre Aumont, John van Dreelen, Lucienne Hamon; ***D:*** Danny Huston; ***W:*** Ruth Graham; ***M:*** John Scott. *ACA*

Bed & Breakfast ☆☆½ **1992 (PG-13)** Three generations of women lead quiet lives while running a failing Nantucket bed and breakfast. When a mystery man washes up on their beach, he charms them all, but it seems that he has a past that could endanger everyone. Lightweight final role for Dewhurst, though she provides some sparks as the strong and loving matriarch. Gentle romantic comedy skims the surface, but is still enjoyable. **97m/C VHS, LV.** Roger Moore, Talia Shire, Colleen Dewhurst, Nina Siemaszko, Ford Rainey, Stephen Root, Jamie Walters, Victor Slezak; ***D:*** Robert Ellis Miller; ***W:*** Cindy Myers; ***M:*** David Shire. *HMD*

Bed and Sofa ☆☆☆½ **1927** Adultery, abortion, and women's rights are brought about by a housing shortage which forces a man to move in with a married friend. Famous, ground-breaking Russian silent. **73m/B VHS, Beta.** *RU* Nikolai Batalov, Vladimar Fogel; ***D:*** Abram Room. *INJ, IHF*

Bed of Roses ☆☆½ *Amelia and the King of Plants* **1995 (PG)** Wistful romance finds workaholic investment banker Lisa Walker (Masterson) receiving lavish floral tributes from an unknown admirer. When Lisa tracks her giver down, it turns out to be lovestruck widowed florist Lewis Farrell (Slater), who noticed Lisa crying through her apartment window and sent the flowers to cheer her up. Best friend Kim (Seagall) urges Lisa to go for Lewis but a problematic past has Lisa distrusting her emotions and their romantic path has a few bumps (easily overcome). Appealing leads, lots of cliches. Goldenberg's debut.

88m/C VHS, LV. Christian Slater, Mary Stuart Masterson, Pamela Segall, Josh Brolin, Ally Walker, Debra Monk; ***D:*** Michael Goldenberg; ***W:*** Michael Goldenberg; ***C:*** Adam Kimmel; ***M:*** Michael Convertino. *NLC*

Bedazzled **1968 (PG)** In the process of hanging himself, Stanley, a short-order cook is approached by the devil with an offer: seven wishes in exchange for his soul. Each of Stanley's wishes is granted with surprising consequences. Cult comedy is a sometimes uneven, but thoroughly entertaining and funny retelling of the Faustian story. **107m/C VHS, Beta, LV.** *GB* Dudley Moore, Peter Cook, Eleanor Bron, Michael Bates, Raquel Welch; ***D:*** Stanley Donen; ***W:*** Dudley Moore, Peter Cook; ***M:*** Dudley Moore. *FOX*

Bedford Incident ½ **1965** The U.S.S. Bedford discovers an unidentified submarine in North Atlantic waters. The Bedford's commander drives his crew to the point of exhaustion as they find themselves the center of a fateful controversy. **102m/B VHS, Beta, LV.** Richard Widmark, Sidney Poitier, James MacArthur, Martin Balsam, Wally Cox, Donald Sutherland, Eric Portman; ***D:*** James B. Harris. *COL, IME*

Bedknobs and Broomsticks ½ **1971 (G)** A novice witch and three cockney waifs ride a magic bedstead and stop the Nazis from invading England during WWII. Celebrated for its animated art. **117m/C VHS, Beta, LV.** Angela Lansbury, Roddy McDowall, David Tomlinson, Bruce Forsyth, Sam Jaffe; ***D:*** Robert Stevenson. Academy Awards '71: Best Visual Effects; Nominations: Academy Awards '71: Best Art Direction/Set Decoration, Best Costume Design, Best Song ("The Age of Not Believing"), Best Original Score. *DIS, WTA*

Bedlam **1945** Creeper set in the famed asylum in 18th-century London. A woman, wrongfully committed, tries to stop the evil doings of the chief (Karloff) of Bedlam, and endangers herself. Fine horror film co-written by producer Lewton. **79m/B VHS, Beta, LV.** Jason Robards Sr., Ian Wolfe, Glenn Vernon, Boris Karloff, Anna Lee, Billy House, Richard Fraser; ***D:*** Mark Robson. *TTC, MED, FCT*

Bedroom Eyes **1986 (R)** A successful businessman becomes a voyeur by returning nightly to a beautiful woman's window, until she is killed and he is the prime suspect. Part comic, part disappointing thriller. **90m/C VHS, Beta, LV.** Kenneth Gilman, Dayle Haddon, Christine Cattall; ***D:*** William Fruet. *FOX*

Bedroom Eyes 2 **1989 (R)** After discovering his wife has had an affair, a stockbroker takes a lover. When she turns up dead, he and his wife become murder suspects. Provides some suspenseful moments. **85m/C VHS, LV.** Wings Hauser, Kathy Shower, Linda Blair, Jane Hamilton, Jennifer Delora; ***D:*** Chuck Vincent. *VMK, IME*

The Bedroom Window ½ **1987 (R)** Guttenberg is having an illicit affair with his boss' wife (Huppert), who witnesses an assault on another woman (McGovern) from the bedroom window. To keep the affair secret Guttenberg reports the crime, but since it is secondhand, the account is flawed and he becomes a suspect. Semi-tight thriller reminiscent of Hitchcock mysteries isn't always believable, but is otherwise interesting. **113m/C VHS, Beta, LV.** Steve Guttenberg, Elizabeth McGovern, Isabelle Huppert, Wallace Shawn, Paul Shenar, Carl Lumbly, Frederick Coffin, Brad Greenquist; ***D:*** Curtis Hanson; ***W:*** Curtis Hanson; ***M:*** Patrick Gleeson, Michael Shrieve, Felix Mendelessohn. *FHE, VES, LIV*

Bedtime for Bonzo ½ **1951** A professor adopts a chimp to prove that environment, not hereditary, determines a child's future. Fun, lighthearted comedy that stars a future president. Followed by "Bonzo Goes to College." **83m/B VHS, Beta.** Ronald Reagan, Diana Lynn, Walter Slezak, Jesse White, Bonzo the Chimp; ***D:*** Fred de Cordova. *MCA, FCT*

Bedtime Story **1963** Two con artists attempt to fleece an apparently wealthy woman and each other on the French Riviera. Re-made in 1988 as "Dirty Rotten Scoundrels." One of Brando's thankfully few forays into comedy. **99m/C VHS, Beta.** Marlon Brando, David Niven, Shirley Jones, Dody Goodman, Marie Windsor; ***D:*** Ralph Levy. *MCA*

Beer **1985 (R)** A female advertising executive devises a dangerous sexist campaign for a cheap beer, and both the beer and its nickname become nationwide obsessions. Not especially amusing. **83m/C VHS, Beta.** Loretta Swit, Rip Torn, Dick Shawn, David Alan Grier, William Russ, Kenneth Mars, Peter Michael Goetz; ***D:*** Patrick Kelly; ***M:*** Bill Conti. *NO*

The Bees *Woof!* **1978 (PG)** Sting of a poor movie is painful. A strain of bees have ransacked South America and are threatening the rest of the world. The buzz is that no one is safe. Cheap rip-off of "The Swarm," which is saying something. **93m/C VHS, Beta.** John Saxon, John Carradine, Angel Tompkins, Claudio Brook, Alicia Encinas; ***D:*** Alfredo Zacharias. *WAR*

Beethoven *Beethoven's Great Love; The Life and Loves of Beethoven; Un Grand Amour de Beethoven* **1936** Startling biography of the musical genius, filled with opulent, impressionistic visuals. **116m/B VHS.** *FR* Harry Baur, Jean-Louis Barrault, Marcel Dalio; ***W:*** Abel Gance. *CVC, INJ, TPV*

Beethoven ½ **1992 (PG)** Adorable St. Bernard puppy escapes from dognappers and wanders into the home of the Newtons, who, over dad's objections, adopt him. Beethoven grows into a huge, slobbering dog who sorely tries dad's patience. To make matters worse, two sets of villains also wreak havoc on the Newton's lives. Evil veterinarian Dr. Varnick plots to steal Beethoven for lab experiments, and yuppie couple Brad and Brie plot to take over the family business. Enjoyable cast, particularly Grodin as dad and Chris as Beethoven enable this movie to please more than the milk and cookies set. Followed by "Beethoven's 2nd." **89m/C VHS, LV.** Charles Grodin, Bonnie Hunt, Dean Jones, Oliver Platt, Stanley Tucci, Nicholle Tom, Christopher Castile, Sarah Rose Karr, David Duchovny, Patricia Heaton, Laurel Cronin; ***D:*** Brian Levant; ***W:*** John Hughes, Amy Holden Jones. *MCA, FCT*

Beethoven Lives Upstairs ½ **1992** In 19th century Vienna 10 year-old Christoph's life is turned upside-down when the family's eccentric new tenant turns out to be composer Ludwig Van Beethoven. In time, Christoph comes to appreciate the beauty of the music and the tragedy of the composer's deafness. Features more than 25 excerpts of Beethoven's works. **52m/C VHS.** Neil Munro, Illya Woloshyn, Fiona Reid, Paul Soles, Sheila McCarthy, Albert Schultz; ***D:*** David Devine; ***W:*** Heather Conkie. *BMG, MVD*

Beethoven's Nephew ½ *Le Neveu de Beethoven* **1988** A tepid pseudo-historical farce about Beethoven's strange obsession with his only nephew. Directed by erstwhile Warhol collaborator Morrissey. **103m/C VHS, Beta, LV.** *FR* Wolfgang Reichmann, Ditmar Prinz, Jane Birkin, Nathalie Baye; ***D:*** Paul Morrissey; ***W:*** Paul Morrissey, Matthieu Carriere. *NWV, VTR*

Beethoven's 2nd ½ **1993 (PG)** Sequel has awwww factor going for it as new daddy Beethoven slobbers over four adorable and appealing St. Bernard pups and his new love Missy. Same basic evil subplot as the first, with wicked kidnappers replacing evil vet. During the upheaval, the Newtons take care of the little yapping troublemakers, providing the backdrop for endless puppy mischief and exasperation on Grodin's part. Silly subplots and too many human moments tend to drag, but the kids will find the laughs (albeit stupid ones). **87m/C VHS, LV.** Charles Grodin, Bonnie Hunt, Nicholle Tom, Christopher Castile, Sarah Rose Karr, Debi Mazar, Christopher Penn, Ashley Hamilton; ***D:*** Rod Daniel; ***W:*** Len Blum; ***M:*** Randy Edelman. Nominations: Academy Awards '93: Best Song ("The Day I Fall in Love"); Golden Globe Awards '94: Best Song ("The Day I Fall in Love"). *MCA*

Beetlejuice ½ **1988 (PG)** The after-life is confusing for a pair of ultra-nice novice ghosts who are faced with chasing an obnoxious family of post-modern art lovers who move into their house. Then they hear of a poltergeist who promises to rid the house of all trespassers for a price. Things go from bad to impossible when the maniacal Keaton (as the demonic "Betelgeuse") works his magic. The calypso scene is priceless. A cheesy, funny, surreal farce of life after death with inventive set designs popping continual surprises. Ryder is striking as the misunderstood teen with a death complex, while O'Hara is hilarious as the yuppie art poseur. **92m/C VHS, Beta, LV, 8mm.** Michael Keaton, Geena Davis, Alec Baldwin, Sylvia Sidney, Catherine O'Hara, Winona Ryder, Jeffrey Jones, Dick Cavett; ***D:*** Tim Burton; ***W:*** Michael McDowell, Warren Skaaren; ***M:*** Danny Elfman. Academy Awards '88: Best Makeup; National Society of Film Critics Awards '88: Best Actor (Keaton). *WAR, FCT, TLF*

Before and After ½ **1995 (PG-13)** Disjointed drama depicts well-off suburban couple, Carolyn (Streep) and Ben (Neeson), who are thrown into chaos when their teenaged son Jacob (Furlong) is accused of murdering his girlfriend. Upon notification by the police that his son is the prime suspect and on the lam, Ben finds what seems to be bloody evidence in the family's car, which he destroys. The story loses steam from there. Based on the novel by Rosellen Brown, the focus is on the effect the death has on this picture book Massachusetts family. Neeson and Streep fall short of usually deliverable goods and director Schroeder takes the middle-of-the-road sentimental approach. **107m/C VHS.** Meryl Streep, Liam Neeson, Edward Furlong, Alfred Molina, John Heard, Julia Weldon, Daniel von Bargen, John Heard, Ann Magnuson, Alison Folland, Kaiulani Lee; ***D:*** Barbet Schroeder; ***W:*** Ted Tally; ***C:*** Luciano Tovoli; ***M:*** Howard Shore. *NYR*

Before I Hang **1940** When a doctor invents a youth serum from the blood of a murderer, he'll stop at nothing to keep his secret. Karloff himself stands the test of time, and is satisfying as the mad scientist, giving this horror flick its appeal. **60m/B VHS, Beta.** Boris Karloff, Evelyn Keyes, Bruce (Herman Brix) Bennett, Edward Van Sloan; ***D:*** Nick Grinde. *COL*

Before Morning ½ **1933** Police officer poses as a blackmailer to find out which of the two women in the murder victim's life are guilty. **68m/B VHS, Beta, LV.** Leo Carrillo, Lora Baxter, Taylor Holmes. *NO*

Before Sunrise ½ **1994 (R)** Light, "getting-to-know-you," romance unfolds as two twenty-somethings share an unlikely 14-hour date. Gen-Xer Jesse (Hawke) and French beauty (Delpy) meet on the Eurail and he convinces her to join him in exploring Vienna and their mutual attraction before he heads back to the States in the morning. The two exchange life experiences and philosophies in the typical Linklater conversational fashion, but the film strays from the comical accounts of earlier works "Slacker" and "Dazed and Confused". Cinematographer Daniel captures the Old World with finesse, especially in the inevitable "first kiss" atop the Ferris wheel made famous in Orson Welles' "The Third Man". **101m/C VHS, LV.** Ethan Hawke, Julie Delpy; ***D:*** Richard Linklater; ***W:*** Richard Linklater, Kim Krizan; ***C:*** Lee Daniel. Berlin International Film Festival '94: Best Director (Linklater); Nominations: MTV Movie Awards '95: Best Kiss (Ethan Hawke/Julie Delpy). *COL*

Before the Rain *Po Dezju* **1994** War-torn Macedonia is the backdrop for Manchevski's first film (and first made in the newly declared republic of Macedonia). Powerful circular narrative joins three stories about the freedom of love and the pervasiveness of violence. "Words" finds young Macedonian monk Kiril (Colin) distracted from his spiritual duties by young Albanian Muslim Zamira (Mitevska), who takes refuge in his monastery. In "Faces," pregnant picture editor Anne (Cartlidge) is torn between her estranged husband and her lover, Aleksander (Serbedzija), a London-based war photographer who left his native Macedonia years before. "Pictures" finds Aleksandar returning to his old village—now torn by ethnic strife. In Macedonian, Albanian, and English, with subtitles. **120m/C VHS.** *GB FR MA* Rade Serbedzija, Katrin Cartlidge, Gregoire Colin, Labina Mitevska; ***D:*** Milcho Manchevski; ***W:*** Milcho Manchevski; ***C:*** Manuel Teran; ***M:*** Anastasia. Independent Spirit Awards '96: Best Foreign Film; Venice Film Festival '94: Golden Lion; Nominations: Academy Awards '94: Best Foreign Language Film. *PGV*

Before the Revolution ☠☠ **1965** One of Bertolucci's first films. Love and politics are mixed when the young Fabrizio, who is dabbling in communism, is also flirting with his young aunt. Striking and powerful film that has yet to lose its effect despite the times. Italian with subtitles. **115m/C VHS.** *IT* Francesco Barilli, Adrianna Asti, Alain Midgette, Morando Morandini, Domenico Alpi; ***D:*** Bernardo Bertolucci; ***W:*** Bernardo Bertolucci; ***M:*** Ennio Morricone, Gato Barbieri. *NYF, INJ*

Beggars in Ermine ☠☠ **1934** A handicapped, impoverished man organizes all the beggars in the world into a successful corporation. Unusual performance from Atwill. **70m/B VHS, Beta.** Lionel Atwill, Henry B. Walthall, Betty Furness, Jameson Thomas, James Bush, Astrid Allwyn, George "Gabby" Hayes; ***D:*** Phil Rosen. *VYY, SNC*

Beginning of the End ☠½ **1957** Produced the same year as "The Deadly Mantis," Gordon's effort adds to 1957's harvest of bugs on a rampage "B"-graders. Giant, radiation-spawned grasshoppers attack Chicago causing Graves to come to the rescue. Easily the best giant grasshopper movie ever made. **73m/B VHS.** Peggy Castle, Peter Graves, Morris Ankrum, Richard Benedict, James Seay; ***D:*** Bert I. Gordon. *NO*

The Beguiled ☠☠☠ **1970 (R)** During the Civil War a wounded Union soldier is taken in by the women at a girl's school in the South. He manages to seduce both a student and a teacher, and jealousy and revenge ensue. Decidedly weird psychological melodrama from action vets Siegel and Eastwood. **109m/C VHS, Beta, LV.** Clint Eastwood, Geraldine Page, Elizabeth Hartman, Jo Ann Harris; ***D:*** Donald Siegel; ***C:*** Bruce Surtees; ***M:*** Lalo Schifrin. *MCA*

Behave Yourself! ☠½ **1952** A married couple adopts a dog who may be the key for a million-dollar hijacking setup by a gang of hoodlums. **81m/B VHS, Beta.** Shelley Winters, Farley Granger, William Demarest, Lon Chaney Jr., Hans Conried, Elisha Cook Jr., Francis L. Sullivan; ***D:*** George Beck. *NOS*

Behind Enemy Lines ☠½ **1985 (R)** Special Forces soldier goes on a special mission to eliminate a possible Nazi spy. Made for television. **83m/C VHS, Beta.** Hal Holbrook, Ray Sharkey, David McCallum, Tom Isbell, Anne Twomey, Robert Patrick; ***D:*** Sheldon Larry. *MED*

Behind Locked Doors ☠☠½ **1948** A journalist fakes mental illness to have himself committed to an asylum, where he believes a crooked judge is in hiding. A superior "B" mystery/suspense feature, with some tense moments. **61m/B VHS.** Lucille Bremer, Richard Carlson, Tor Johnson, Douglas Fowley, Herbert Heyes, Ralf Harolde; ***D:*** Budd Boetticher. *VDM*

Behind Office Doors ☠☠ **1931** Astor stars as the secretarial "power behind the throne" in this look at who really wields power in an office. Her boss takes her for granted until things go wrong. **82m/B VHS.** Mary Astor, Robert Ames, Ricardo Cortez, Charles Sellon; ***D:*** Melville Brown. *NOS, HEG*

Behind Prison Walls ☠☠ *Youth Takes a Hand* **1943** A steel tycoon and his son are sent to prison, and the son tries to convert his dad to socialism. A fun, light hearted film, the last for veteran Tully. **64m/B VHS.** Alan Baxter, Gertrude Michael, Tully Marshall, Edwin Maxwell, Jacqueline Dalya, Matt Willis; ***D:*** Steve Sekely. *SNC*

Behind the Front ☠☠½ **1926** Two friends tumble in and out of trouble in this comic Army film. One of the most profitable films of the late twenties. **60m/B VHS.** Wallace Beery, Raymond Hatton, Richard Arlen, Mary Brian, Chester Conklin; ***D:*** Edward Sutherland. *GPV*

Behind the Mask ☠☠½ **1946** Lamont Cranston, better known as do-gooder "The Shadow," finds himself accused of murdering a blackmailing newspaper reporter. Based on the radio serial. **68m/C VHS.** Kane Richmond, Barbara Read, George Chandler, Dorothea Kent, Robert Shayne, June Clyde; ***D:*** Phil Karlson. *GPV, ADL*

Behind the Rising Sun ☠☠½ **1943** A Japanese publisher's political views clash with those of his American-educated son in 1930s Japan. Well done despite pre-war propaganda themes. **88m/B VHS, Beta.** Tom Neal, J. Carrol Naish, Robert Ryan, Mike Mazurki, Margo, Gloria Holden, Don Douglas; ***D:*** Edward Dmytryk. *NO*

Behold a Pale Horse ☠☠½ **1964** A Spanish police captain attempts to dupe Peck into believing that his mother is dying and he must visit her on her deathbed. Loyalist Spaniard Peck becomes privy to the plot against him, but goes to Spain anyway in this post Spanish Civil War film. **118m/B VHS, Beta.** Gregory Peck, Anthony Quinn, Omar Sharif, Mildred Dunnock; ***D:*** Fred Zinnemann; ***M:*** Maurice Jarre. *GKK*

The Being ☠ **1983 (R)** People in Idaho are terrorized by a freak who became abnormal after radiation was disposed in the local dump. Another dull monster-created-by-nuclear-waste non-event. Of limited interest is Buzzi. However, you'd be more entertained (read: amused) by Troma's "The Toxic Avenger," which takes itself much (much!) less seriously. **82m/C VHS, Beta.** Ruth Buzzi, Martin Landau, Jose Ferrer; ***D:*** Jackie Kong. *NO*

Being at Home with Claude ☠☠ **1992** Yves (Godin) is a 22-year-old Montreal hustler being interrogated by a nameless inspector (Dupuis) for the murder of his lover, Claude (Pichette). Yves has admitted his guilt but the inspector wants to reconstruct the event and determine a motive. Lots of black-and-white flashbacks as Yves dwells on his work and his psychologically love-death relationship with Claude. Rather pretentious and long-winded. Based on the play by Rene-Daniel DuBois. In French with English subtitles. **86m/C VHS.** *CA* Roy Dupuis, Jacques Godin, Jean-Francois Pichette, Gaston Lepage; ***D:*** Johanne Boisvert; ***W:*** Jean Boudin. *ACA, FCT*

Being Human ☠☠½ **1994 (PG-13)** Ambitious comedy drama promises more than it delivers, and shackles Williams in the process. Hector (Williams) is a regular guy continuously reincarnated throughout the millennia. He plays a caveman, a Roman slave, a Middle Ages nomad, a crew member on a 17th century new world voyage, and a modern New Yorker in separate vignettes that echo and/or extend the main themes of family, identity, and random fate. But he manages to emerge from each sketch as an unassuming everyman who never learns his lesson. One of Williams' periodic chancy ventures away from his comedic roots occasionally strikes gold, but often seems overly restrained. **122m/C VHS, LV.** Robin Williams, John Turturro, Anna Galiena, Vincent D'Onofrio, Hector Elizondo, Lorraine Bracco, Lindsay Crouse, Kelly Hunter, William H. Macy, Grace Mahlaba, Theresa Russell, Charles Miller, Helen Miller; ***D:*** Bill Forsyth; ***W:*** Bill Forsyth; ***M:*** Michael Gibbs. *WAR*

Being There ☠☠☠½ **1979 (PG)** A feeble-minded gardener, whose entire knowledge of life comes from watching television, is sent out into the real world when his employer dies. Equipped with his prize possession, his remote control unit, the gardener unwittingly enters the world of politics and is welcomed as a mysterious sage. Sellers is wonderful in this satiric treat adapted by Jerzy Kosinski from his novel. **130m/C VHS, Beta, LV.** Peter Sellers, Shirley MacLaine, Melvyn Douglas, Jack Warden, Richard Dysart, Richard Basehart; ***D:*** Hal Ashby; ***C:*** Caleb Deschanel. Academy Awards '79: Best Supporting Actor (Douglas); British Academy Awards '90: Best Screenplay; Golden Globe Awards '80: Best Actor—Musical/Comedy (Sellers), Best Supporting Actor (Douglas); National Board of Review Awards '79: 10 Best Films of the Year, Best Actor (Sellers); National Society of Film Critics Awards '79: Best Cinematography; Writers Guild of America '79: Best Adapted Screenplay; Nominations: Academy Awards '79: Best Actor (Sellers); Cannes Film Festival '80: Best Film. *FOX, FCT, WAR*

Being Two Isn't Easy ☠☠½ **1962** Director Ichikawa shows the world through the eyes of a two-year-old as a young couple struggle to raise their son. In Japanese with English subtitles. **88m/C VHS.** *JP* Fujiko Yamamoto, Eiji Funakoshi; ***D:*** Kon Ichikawa. *HMV, FCT*

Bela Lugosi Meets a Brooklyn Gorilla *Woof! The Boys from Brooklyn* **1952** Two men who look like Dean Martin and Jerry Lewis (but aren't) get lost in the jungle, where they meet mad scientist Lugosi. Worse than it sounds. Real Jerry sued for unflattering imitation. **74m/B VHS, Beta.** Bela Lugosi, Duke Mitchell, Sammy Petrillo; ***D:*** William Beaudine. *NOS, SNC, AOV*

Bela Lugosi Scrapbook ☠½ **197?** A compilation of Lugosi appearances, outtakes, flubs, and trailers. **60m/B VHS, Beta.** Bela Lugosi. *DVT, RXM*

Belfast Assassin ☠ **1984** A British anti-terrorist agent goes undercover in Ireland to find an IRA assassin who shot a British cabinet minister. **130m/C VHS, Beta.** Derek Thompson, Ray Lonnen. *PSM*

The Believers ☠☠½ **1987 (R)** Tense horror mystery set in New York city about a series of gruesome, unexplained murders. A widowed police psychologist investigating the deaths unwittingly discovers a powerful Santeria cult that believes in the sacrifice of children. Without warning he is drawn into the circle of the "Believers" and must free himself before his own son is the next sacrifice. Gripping (and grim), unrelenting horror. **114m/C VHS, Beta, LV.** Martin Sheen, Helen Shaver, Malick Bowens, Harris Yulin, Robert Loggia, Jimmy Smits, Richard Masur, Harley Cross, Elizabeth Wilson, Lee Richardson; ***D:*** John Schlesinger; ***W:*** Mark Frost; ***M:*** J. Peter Robinson. *HBO*

Belizaire the Cajun ☠☠½ **1986 (PG)** 19th-century Louisiana love story. White prejudice against the Cajuns is rampant and violent, but that doesn't stop sexy faith healer Assante from falling in love with the inaccessible Cajun wife (Youngs) of a rich local. Made with care on a tight budget. Worthwhile, though uneven. **103m/C VHS, Beta.** Armand Assante, Gail Youngs, Will Patton, Stephen McHattie, Michael Schoeffling, Robert Duvall, Nancy Barrett; ***D:*** Glen Pitre; ***W:*** Glen Pitre; ***M:*** Michael Doucet, Howard Shore. *FOX*

Bell, Book and Candle ☠☠½ **1958** A young witch makes up her mind to refrain from using her powers. When an interesting man moves into her building, she forgets her decision and enchants him with a love spell. **106m/C VHS, Beta, LV.** James Stewart, Kim Novak, Jack Lemmon, Elsa Lanchester, Ernie Kovacs, Hermione Gingold; ***D:*** Richard Quine; ***W:*** Daniel Taradash; ***C:*** James Wong Howe; ***M:*** George Duning. Nominations: Academy Awards '58: Best Art Direction/Set Decoration, Best Costume Design. *COL, FCT, MLB*

Bell Diamond ☠☠ **1981** A study by the experimental filmmaker of a Vietnam vet surviving in a bankrupt mining town. Created without a script using non-professional actors. **96m/C VHS, Beta.** ***D:*** Jon Jost. *FCT*

Bell from Hell ☠☠ **1974** A tale of insanity and revenge, wherein a young man, institutionalized since his mother's death, plots to kill his aunt and three cousins. **80m/C VHS, Beta.** Viveca Lindfors, Renaud Verley, Alfredo Mayo; ***D:*** Claudio Guerin Hill. *UNI*

The Bell Jar ☠½ **1979 (R)** Based on poet Sylvia Plath's acclaimed semi-autobiographical novel, this is the story of a young woman who becomes the victim of mental illness. Not for the easily depressed and a disjointed and disappointing adaptation of Plath's work. **113m/C VHS, Beta.** Marilyn Hassett, Julie Harris, Barbara Barrie, Anne Bancroft, Robert Klein, Anne Jackson; ***D:*** Larry Peerce. *VES*

Bell Ringer of Antigua ☠☠ **1946** Inspirational story by Royer, one of Hollywood's pioneering women. Shot on location in Guatemala. **?m/C VHS.** ***D:*** Fanchon Royer; ***W:*** Fanchon Royer. *LOO*

Bellamy ☠ **1980** Murderous madman massacres masseuses, and Bellamy is the cop out to get him. **92m/C VHS, Beta.** John Stanton, Timothy Elston, Sally Conabere; ***D:*** Colin Eggleston, Pino Amenta. *NO*

The Bellboy ☠☠½ **1960** Lewis makes his directorial debut in this plotless but clever outing. He also stars as the eponymous character, a bellboy at Miami's Fountainbleau Hotel. Cameos from Berle and

Winchell are highlights. **72m/B VHS, Beta, LV.** Jerry Lewis, Alex Gerry, Bob Clayton, Sonny Sands; ***Cameos:*** Milton Berle, Walter Winchell; ***D:*** Jerry Lewis; ***W:*** Jerry Lewis. *LIV*

The Bellboy and the Playgirls *Woof! The Playgirls and the Bellboy; Mit Eva Fing Die Sunde An* **1962** Early Coppola effort adds new film footage to a 1958 German movie. Stars Playboy playmate June "The Body" Wilkinson, with other centerfolds of the time. **93m/C VHS.** June Wilkinson; ***D:*** Francis Ford Coppola; ***W:*** Francis Ford Coppola. *NO*

Belle Americaine 𝓑𝓑 *What a Chassis!* **1961** Title refers to the Cadillac car young Parisian factory worker Dhery buys at a suspiciously bargain price. Naturally, his deal is too good to be true and trouble follows. Dubbed in English. **97m/C VHS.** *FR* Robert Dhery, Louis de Funes, Collette Brosset, Alfred Adam, Bernard Lavelette, Annie Ducaux; ***D:*** Robert Dhery; ***W:*** Robert Dhery, Alfred Adam, Pierre Tchernia; ***C:*** Ghislan Cloquet; ***M:*** Gerard Calvi. *FCT*

Belle de Jour 𝓑𝓑𝓑½ **1967 (R)** Based on Joseph Kessel's novel, one of director Bunuel's best movies has all his characteristic nuances: the hypocrisy of our society; eroticism; anti-religion. Deneuve plays Severine, a chic, frigid Parisian newlywed, who decides to become a daytime prostitute, unbeknownst to her husband. Bunuel blends reality with fantasy, and the viewer is never sure which is which in this finely crafted movie. French with subtitles. **100m/C VHS, LV.** *FR* Catherine Deneuve, Jean Sorel, Genevieve Page, Michel Piccoli, Francesco Rabal, Pierre Clementi, Georges Marchal, Francoise Fabian; ***D:*** Luis Bunuel; ***W:*** Luis Bunuel, Jean-Claude Carriere. Venice Film Festival '67: CINE Golden Eagle. *TOU*

Belle Epoque 𝓑𝓑𝓑 *The Age of Beauty* **1992 (R)** Young army deserter Fernando (Sanz) embarks on a personal voyage of discovery when he meets Manolo (Gomez), an eccentric old man, and father to four beautiful daughters. Fernando can't believe his luck—and the sisters share his interest, resulting in an amusing round of musical beds. Lighthearted romp set in 1930's Spain with a terrific screenplay that tastefully handles the material without stooping to the obvious leering possibilities. In addition to Oscar, won 9 Spanish Goyas, including best picture, director, actress (Gil), and screenplay. Spanish with English subtitles or dubbed. **108m/C VHS, LV.** *SP* Jorge Sanz, Fernando Gomez, Ariadna Gil, Maribel Verdu, Penelope Cruz, Miriam Diaz-Aroca, Mary Carmen Ramirez, Michel Galabru, Gabino Diego; ***D:*** Fernando Trueba; ***W:*** Rafael Azcona. Academy Awards '93: Best Foreign Language Film. *COL*

The Belle of New York 𝓑𝓑 **1952** A turn-of-the-century bachelor falls in love with a Salvation Army missionary in this standard musical. ♫Naughty But Nice; Baby Doll; Oops; I Wanna Be a Dancin' Man; Seeing's Believing; Bachelor's Dinner Song; When I'm Out With the Belle of New York; Let a Little Love Come In. **82m/C VHS, Beta.** Fred Astaire, Vera-Ellen, Marjorie Main, Keenan Wynn, Alice Pearce, Gale Robbins, Clinton Sundberg; ***D:*** Charles Walters. *MGM, FHE*

Belle of the Nineties 𝓑𝓑½ **1934** West struts as a 1890s singer who gets involved with a boxer. Her trademark sexual innuendos were already being censored but such lines as "It's better to be looked over than overlooked," done in West style, get the point across. **73m/B VHS.** Mae West, Roger Pryor, Johnny Mack Brown, John Miljan, Katherine DeMille, Harry Woods, Edward Gargan; ***D:*** Leo McCarey; ***W:*** Mae West; ***C:*** Karl Struss. *MCA, BTV*

Belle Starr 𝓑½ **1979** The career of Wild West outlaw Belle Starr is chronicled in this strange western pastiche about lawlessness and sexual agression. Wertmuller directed under the pseudonym Nathan Wich. Dubbed in English. **90m/C VHS, Beta.** *IT* Elsa Martinelli, Robert Wood, George Eastman, Dan Harrison; ***D:*** Lina Wertmuller. *FCT*

The Belles of St. Trinian's 𝓑𝓑𝓑 **1953** Sim is priceless in a dual role as the eccentric headmistress of a chaotic, bankrupt girls' school and her bookie twin brother who scheme the school into financial security. The first in a series of movies based on a popular British cartoon by Ronald Searles about a girls' school and its mischievous students. Followed by "Blue Murder at St. Trinian's," "The Pure Hell of St. Trinian's," and "The Great St. Trinian's Train Robbery." **86m/B VHS, Beta.** *GB* Alastair Sim, Joyce Grenfell, Hermione Baddeley, George Cole, Eric Pohlmann, Renee Houston, Beryl Reid; ***D:*** Frank Launder; ***M:*** Malcolm Arnold. *REP*

Bellhop/The Noon Whistle **1922** Two comedic shorts back to back, separately featuring the famous comics Laurel and Hardy. **46m/B VHS, Beta.** Stan Laurel, Oliver Hardy. *CCB*

Bellissima 𝓑𝓑𝓑 **1951** A woman living in an Italian tenement has unrealistic goals for her plain but endearing daughter when a famous director begins casting a role designed for a child. The mother's maternal fury and collision with reality highlight a poignant film. Italian with subtitles. **130m/B VHS.** *IT* Anna Magnani; ***D:*** Luchino Visconti; ***W:*** Luchino Visconti, Cesare Zavattini, Francesco Rosi, Suso Cecchi D'Amico. *CIG, APD*

Bellissimo: Images of the Italian Cinema **1987** A panoramic film history of Italian cinema, featuring film clips, behind-the-scenes footage and interviews with the industry's leading figures. Clips from "Open City," "Divorce Italian Style," "8 1/2," and "Seven Beauties" are included. In English, and Italian with subtitles. **110m/C VHS, Beta.** *IT* Sophia Loren, Marcello Mastroianni, Bernardo Bertolucci, Dino de Laurentiis, Marco Ferreri, Roberto Rossellini, Vittorio De Sica, Pier Paolo Pasolini, Franco Zeffirelli, Federico Fellini, Lina Wertmuller, Monica Vitti, Giancarlo Giannini, Anna Magnani; ***D:*** Gianfranco Mingozzi. *WBF, FCT, INJ*

Bellman and True 𝓑𝓑½ **1988 (R)** Rewarding, but sometimes tedious character study of a mild mannered computer whiz who teams with a gang of bank robbers. Fine performances, especially subtle dangerous gang characters. **112m/C VHS, Beta.** *GB* Bernard Hill, Kieran O'Brien, Richard Hope, Frances Tomelty, Derek Newark, John Kavanagh, Ken Bones; ***D:*** Richard Loncraine; ***M:*** Colin Towns. *MGM, CAN, VES*

Bells are Ringing 𝓑𝓑𝓑 **1960** A girl who works for a telephone answering service can't help but take an interest in the lives of the clients, especially a playwright with an inferiority complex. Based on Adolph Green and Betty Comden's Broadway musical. Special letterboxed edition along with the original trailer available on laserdisc format. ♫Just in Time; The Party's Over; It's a Perfect Relationship; Do It Yourself; It's a Simple Little System; Better Than a Dream; I Met a Girl; Drop That Name; I'm Going Back. **126m/C VHS, Beta, LV.** Judy Holliday, Dean Martin, Fred Clark, Eddie Foy Jr., Jean Stapleton; ***D:*** Vincente Minnelli; ***W:*** Betty Comden, Adolph Green; ***C:*** Milton Krasner; ***M:*** Andre Previn. Nominations: Academy Awards '60: Best Original Score. *MGM*

Bells of Coronado 𝓑𝓑 **1950** Rogers and Evans team up to expose the murderer of the owner of a profitable uranium mine. A gang of smugglers trying to trade the ore to foreign powers is thwarted. The usual thin storyline, but filled with action and riding stunts. **67m/B VHS.** Roy Rogers, Dale Evans, Pat Brady, Grant Withers; ***D:*** William Witney. *REP*

Bells of Death 𝓑½ **1990** A young martial arts student infiltrates the gang that killed his family and kidnapped his sister, finishing them off one by one. **91m/C VHS.** Chun Ping, Chang Yi, Chao Hsin Yen; ***D:*** Yueh Fung. *HMD*

Bells of Rosarita 𝓑𝓑½ **1945** Roy helps foil an evil plan to swindle Evans out of the circus she inherited. All-star western cast under the big top. **54m/B VHS, Beta.** Roy Rogers, Dale Evans, George "Gabby" Hayes, Sunset Carson, Adele Mara, Grant Withers, Roy Barcroft, Addison Richards; ***D:*** Frank McDonald. *NOS, MRV, VCN*

The Bells of St. Mary's 𝓑𝓑𝓑½ **1945** An easy-going priest finds himself in a subtle battle of wits with the Mother Superior over how the children of St. Mary's school should be raised. It's the sequel to "Going My Way." Songs include the title tune and "Aren't You Glad You're You?" Also available in a colorized version. **126m/B VHS, Beta, LV.** Bing Crosby, Ingrid Bergman, Henry Travers; ***D:*** Leo McCarey; ***C:*** George Barnes. Academy Awards '45: Best Sound; Golden Globe Awards '46: Best Actress—Drama (Bergman); New York Film Critics Awards '45: Best Actress (Bergman); Nominations: Academy Awards '44: Best Actress (Bergman); Academy Awards '45: Best Actor (Crosby), Best Director (McCarey), Best Film Editing, Best Picture, Best Song ("Aren't You Glad You're You"), Best Original Score. *REP, IGP*

Bells of San Angelo 𝓑 **1947** Roy foils thieves' attempts to steal a girl's inherited ranch. **54m/C VHS, Beta.** Roy Rogers, Dale Evans; ***D:*** William Witney. *NOS, DVT, TIM*

Bells of San Fernando 𝓑 **1947** An Irish seaman wanders into California during early Spanish rule and confronts a cruel overseer in this lackluster Western drama. Scripted by "Cisco Kid" Renaldo. **75m/B VHS.** Donald Woods, Gloria Warren, Byron Foulger; ***D:*** Terry Morse; ***W:*** Jack DeWitt, Duncan Renaldo. *MOV*

The Belly of an Architect 𝓑𝓑𝓑½ **1991 (R)** A thespian feast for the larger-than-life Dennehy as blustering American architect whose personal life and health both crumble as he obsesssively readies an exhibition in Rome. A multi-tiered, carefully composed tragicomedy from the ideosyncratic filmmaker Greenaway, probably his most accessible work for general audiences. **119m/C VHS, LV.** *GB IT* Brian Dennehy, Chloe Webb, Lambert Wilson; ***D:*** Peter Greenaway; ***W:*** Peter Greenaway. *NO*

Beloved Enemy 𝓑𝓑𝓑 **1936** A romantic tragedy set in Civil War-torn Ireland in the 1920s. A rebel leader and a proper English lady struggle to overcome the war's interference with their burgeoning relationship. **86m/B VHS, Beta.** David Niven, Merle Oberon, Brian Aherne, Karen Morley, Donald Crisp; ***D:*** H.C. Potter; ***C:*** Gregg Toland. *NOS, CAB*

Beloved Infidel 𝓑𝓑½ **1959** Sudsy, lavish romancer, based on the book by gossip queen Sheila Graham, about her brief romance with novelist F. Scott Fitzgerald. Fitzgerald (a badly miscast Peck) was in Hollywood trying to write screenplays when he meets young, English, aspiring writer Graham (an equally miscast Kerr). She becomes his mistress, putting up with Fitzgerald's drinking and insults, while he interferes with her career. Story is slanted towards Graham nobly trying to rescue Fitzgerald from himself (he did actually die from a heart attack while with Graham). **123m/C VHS.** Gregory Peck, Deborah Kerr, Eddie Albert, Philip Ober, Herbert Rudley, John Sutton, Karin Booth; ***D:*** Henry King; ***W:*** Sy Bartlett; ***C:*** Leon Shamroy; ***M:*** Franz Waxman. *FXV*

The Beloved Rogue 𝓑𝓑𝓑 **1927** Crosland—who gained a reputation for innovation, having directed "Don Juan" the previous year (noted for the debut of synchronized music), and "The Jazz Singer" the following year (noted for the first talkie bits)—mounted this well-designed and special effect-laden medieval costumer. Barrymore is in high profile as a swashbuckling caricature of French poet Francois Villon, who battles mightily (and verbally) with Louis XI (played by Veidt, in his first US film). Marked by the excesses typical of Barrymore's prestige days, it flouts history, taking generous poetic license when the facts ain't fab enough. In short, it's great entertainment. **110m/B VHS, Beta, LV.** John Barrymore, Conrad Veidt, Marceline Day, Henry Victor, Mack Swain, Slim Summerville; ***D:*** Alan Crosland. *GPV, FCT, CRC*

Below the Belt 𝓑𝓑 **1980 (R)** Almost interesting tale of street-smart woman from New York City who becomes part of the blue-collar "circus" of lady wrestlers. Ex-wrestling champ Burke plays herself. **98m/C VHS, Beta.** Regina Baff, Mildred Burke, John C. Becher; ***D:*** Robert Fowler. *TPV*

Below the Border 𝓑½ **1942** The Rough Riders go undercover to straighten out some cattle rustlers. **57m/B VHS, Beta.** Buck Jones, Tim McCoy, Raymond Hatton, Linda Brent, Roy Barcroft, Charles "Blackie" King; ***D:*** Howard Bretherton. *NOS, DVT, VDM*

Below the Deadline 𝓑𝓑 **1929** A man framed for embezzlement is set free and allowed to clear his name by a sympathetic detective. **79m/B VHS.** Frank Leigh, Barbara Worth, Arthur Rankin, Walter Merrill; ***D:*** J.P. McGowan. *SNC, VYY*

The Belstone Fox 1973 Orphaned fox goes into hiding, and is hunted by the hound he has befriended and his former owner. **103m/C VHS, Beta.** Eric Porter, Rachel Roberts, Jeremy Kemp; ***D:*** James Hill. *SUE*

Ben ½ **1972 (PG)** Sequel to "Willard" finds police Detective Kirtland still on the hunt for a killer rat pack led by Ben, king of the rodents. Title song by young Michael Jackson hit the top of the charts. **95m/C VHS, Beta, LV.** Joseph Campanella, Lee Montgomery, Arthur O'Connell, Rosemary Murphy, Meredith Baxter; ***D:*** Phil Karlson; ***C:*** Russell Metty. Golden Globe Awards '73: Best Song ("Ben"); Nominations: Academy Awards '72: Best Song ("Ben"). *PSM, PAR*

Ben-Hur **1926** Second film version of the renowned story of Jewish and Christian divisiveness in the time of Jesus. Battle scenes and chariot races still look good, in spite of age. Problems lingered on the set and at a cost of over $4,000,000 it was the most expensive film of its time and took years to finish. A hit at the box office, it still stands as the all-time silent classic. In 1931, a shortened version was released. Based on the novel by Lewis Wallace. **148m/B VHS, Beta, LV.** Ramon Novarro, Francis X. Bushman, May McAvoy, Betty Bronson, Claire McDowell, Carmel Myers, Nigel de Brulier, Ferdinand P. Earle; ***D:*** Fred Niblo; ***C:*** Clyde De Vinna. *MGM*

Ben-Hur **1959** The third film version of the Lew Wallace classic stars Heston in the role of a Palestinian Jew battling the Roman empire at the time of Christ. Won a record 11 Oscars. The breathtaking chariot race is still one of the best screen races today. Perhaps one of the greatest pictures of all time. Also available in letterbox format. **212m/C VHS, Beta, LV.** Charlton Heston, Jack Hawkins, Stephen Boyd, Haya Harareet, Hugh Griffith, Martha Scott, Sam Jaffe, Cathy O'Donnell, Finlay Currie; ***D:*** William Wyler; ***W:*** Karl Tunberg; ***C:*** Robert L. Surtees; ***M:*** Miklos Rozsa. Academy Awards '59: Best Actor (Heston), Best Art Direction/Set Decoration (Color), Best Color Cinematography, Best Costume Design (Color), Best Director (Wyler), Best Film Editing, Best Picture, Best Sound, Best Special Effects, Best Supporting Actor (Griffith), Best Original Score; British Academy Awards '59: Best Film; Directors Guild of America Awards '59: Best Director (Wyler); Golden Globe Awards '60: Best Director (Wyler), Best Film—Drama, Best Supporting Actor (Boyd); Nominations: Academy Awards '59: Best Adapted Screenplay. *MGM, APD, BTV*

Ben Turpin: An Eye for an Eye **1924** Two silent Ben Turpin comedies: "He Looked Crooked, or Why Ben Bolted" (1917) and "Ten Dollars or Ten Days" (1924). **77m/B VHS, Beta, 8mm.** Ben Turpin, Harry Gribbon. *VYY*

Bend of the River *Where the River Bends* **1952** A haunted, hardened guide leads a wagon train through Oregon territory, pitting himself against Indians, the wilderness and a former comrade-turned-hijacker. **91m/C VHS, Beta.** James Stewart, Arthur Kennedy, Rock Hudson, Harry (Henry) Morgan, Royal Dano; ***D:*** Anthony Mann. *MCA*

Beneath Arizona Skies/Paradise Canyon ½ **1935** A package of John Wayne westerns filled with lots of rumble tumble action. **109m/B VHS, Beta.** John Wayne. *REP*

Beneath the Planet of the Apes ½ **1970 (G)** In the first sequel, another Earth astronaut passes through the same warp and follows the same paths as Taylor, through Ape City and to the ruins of bomb-blasted New York's subway system, where warhead-worshipping human mutants are found. The strain of sequelling shows instantly, and gets worse through the next three films; followed by "Escape from the Planet of the Apes." **108m/C VHS, Beta, LV.** Charlton Heston, James Franciscus, Kim Hunter, Maurice Evans, James Gregory, Natalie Trundy, Jeff Corey, Linda Harrison, Victor Buono; ***D:*** Ted Post; ***C:*** Milton Krasner. *FOX, FUS*

Beneath the 12-Mile Reef **1953** Two rival groups of divers compete for sponge beds off the Florida coast. Lightweight entertainment notable for underwater photography and early Cinemascope production, as well as Moore in a bathing suit. **102m/C VHS, Beta, LV.** Robert Wagner, Terry Moore, Gilbert Roland, Richard Boone, Peter Graves, J. Carrol Naish; ***D:*** Robert D. Webb. Nominations: Academy Awards '53: Best Color Cinematography. *NOS, FCT, GEM*

Beneath the Valley of the Ultra-Vixens **1979** Sex comedy retread directed by the man with an obsession for big. Scripted by Roger Ebert, who also scripted the cult classic "Beyond the Valley of the Dolls." Explicit nudity. **90m/C VHS.** Francesca "Kitten" Natividad, Ann Marie, Ken Kerr, Stuart Lancaster; ***D:*** Russ Meyer; ***W:*** Roger Ebert. *RMF*

Benefit of the Doubt **1993 (R)** Ex-con Sutherland, released from prison after 22 years, attempts to repaint his family a la Norman Rockwell. Grown-up daughter Irving, who testified against him in her mother's murder, wants to put a crimp in those plans since daddy's new vision of family fondness frankly makes her stomach turn. Aside from the sexual shenanigans, and the haunting Monument Valley backdrop, an extended chase scene would seem to be the film's only hope of salvation. Unfortunately, it fails to deliver, being both implausible and boring. Based on a story by Michael Lieber. **92m/C VHS, Beta.** Donald Sutherland, Amy Irving, Christopher McDonald, Rider Strong, Graham Greene, Theodore Bikel, Gisele Kovach, Ferdinand "Ferdy" Mayne; ***D:*** Jonathan Heap; ***W:*** Jeffrey Polman, Christopher Keyser; ***M:*** Hummie Mann. *PAR*

The Beniker Gang ½ **1983 (G)** Five orphans, supported by the eldest who writes a syndicated advice column, work together as a family. A made-for-television film. **87m/C VHS, Beta.** Andrew McCarthy, Jennie Dundas, Danny Pintauro, Charlie Fields; ***D:*** Ken Kwapis. *WAR*

Benji **1974 (G)** In the loveable mutt's first feature-length movie, he falls in love with a female named Tiffany, and saves two young children from kidnappers. Kiddie classic that was a box office hit when first released. Followed by "For the Love of Benji." **87m/C VHS, Beta.** Benji, Peter Breck, Christopher Connelly, Patsy Garrett, Deborah Walley, Cynthia Smith; ***D:*** Joe Camp; ***W:*** Joe Camp; ***M:*** Euel Box. Golden Globe Awards '75: Best Song ("I Feel Love"); Nominations: Academy Awards '74: Best Song ("Benji's Theme (I Feel Love)"). *VES, FCT, APD*

Benji the Hunted ½ **1987 (G)** The heroic canine, shipwrecked off the Oregon coast, discovers a litter of orphaned cougar cubs, and battles terrain and predators to bring them to safety. **89m/C VHS, Beta, LV.** Benji, Red Steagall, Frank Inn; ***D:*** Joe Camp; ***W:*** Joe Camp; ***M:*** Euel Box. *DIS*

Benji's Very Own Christmas Story **1983** Benji and his friends go on a magic trip and meet Kris Kringle and learn how Christmas is celebrated around the world. Also included: "The Phenomenon of Benji," a documentary about Benji's odyssey from the animal shelter to international stardom. **60m/C VHS, Beta.** *BFV*

Benny & Joon ½ **1993 (PG)** Depending on your tolerance for cute eccentrics and whimsy this will either charm you with sweetness or send you into sugar shock. Masterson is Joon, a mentally disturbed young woman who paints and has a habit of setting fires. She lives with overprotective brother Benny (Quinn). Sam (Depp) is the outsider who charms Joon, a dyslexic loner who impersonates his heroes Charlie Chaplin and Buster Keaton with eery accuracy. Depp is particularly fine with the physical demands of his role, but the film's easy dismissal of Joon's mental illness is a serious flaw. The laserdisc version is letterboxed. **98m/C VHS, Beta, LV.** Johnny Depp, Mary Stuart Masterson, Aidan Quinn, Julianne Moore, Oliver Platt, CCH Pounder, Dan Hedaya, Joe Grifasi, William H. Macy, Eileen Ryan; ***D:*** Jeremiah S. Chechik; ***W:*** Barry Berman; ***M:*** Rachel Portman. Nominations: Golden Globe Awards '94: Best Actor—Musical/Comedy (Depp); MTV Movie Awards '94: Best On-Screen Duo (Johnny Depp/Mary Stuart Masterson), Best Comedic Performance (Depp), Best Song ("I'm Gonna Be 500 Miles"). *MGM*

The Benny Goodman Story **1955** The life and music of Swing Era bandleader Benny Goodman is recounted in this popular bio-pic. Covering Benny's career from his child prodigy days to his monumental 1938 Carnegie Hall Jazz Concert, the movie's soggy plot machinations are redeemed by a non-stop music track featuring the real Benny and an all-star lineup. ♫Don't Be That Way; Memories of You; Sing, Sing, Sing; Slipped Disc. **116m/C VHS, Beta.** Steve Allen, Donna Reed, Gene Krupa, Lionel Hampton, Kid Ory, Ben Pollack, Harry James, Stan Getz, Teddy Wilson, Martha Tilton; ***D:*** Valentine Davies; ***M:*** Henry Mancini. *MCA, FCT*

Benny Hill's Crazy World **1974** The British comedian delivers some of his best material with the help of "Hill's Angels." **55m/C VHS, Beta.** *GB* Benny Hill. *HBO*

Beretta's Island **1992 (R)** When Interpol operative Beretta comes out of retirement to track his friend's killer, the chase leads him to back to his homeland of Sardinia, which has been overrun by drugs. **97m/C VHS.** Franco Columbu, Ken Kercheval; ***Cameos:*** Arnold Schwarzenegger. *LIV*

Bergonzi Hand **1970** Drama about two art scoundrels who are astonished when an immigrant admits to painting a forged "Bergonzi." **62m/C VHS, Beta.** Keith Mitchell, Gordon Jackson, Martin Miller. *VYY*

The Berlin Affair **1985 (R)** A sordid tale from "The Night Porter" director about a Japanese woman seducing various parties in pre-WWII Germany. **97m/C VHS, Beta.** *IT GE* Mio Takaki, Gudrun Landgrebe, Kevin McNally; ***D:*** Liliana Cavani; ***M:*** Pino Donaggio. *MGM, INJ*

Berlin Alexanderplatz ½ **1980** Fassbinder's 15 1/2-hour epic follows the life, death, and resurrection of Franz Biberkof, a former transit worker who has just finished a lengthy prison term and must learn to adjust in the harsh social atmosphere of Berlin in the 1920s. Melodramatic parable with Biblical overtones considered by some to be a masterpiece. Based on the novel by Alfred Doblin; originally aired as a miniseries on German television. On eight tapes. **930m/C VHS, Beta.** *GE* Gunter Lamprecht, Hanna Schygulla, Barbara Sukowa, Gottfried John, Elisabeth Trissenaar, Brigitte Mira, Karin Baal, Ivan Desny; ***D:*** Rainer Werner Fassbinder. *FCT, MGM*

Berlin Blues **1989 (PG-13)** A nightclub singer is torn between two men. **90m/C VHS, LV.** Julia Migenes-Johnson, Keith Baxter; ***D:*** Richardo Franco. *CAN*

The Berlin Conspiracy **1991 (R)** Espionage/action potboiler does an imaginative job of setting its action against the fall of the Berlin Wall and the end of the Cold War. A CIA agent forms a shaky alliance with his East German spymaster rival to prevent germ warfare technology from falling into terrorist hands. **83m/C VHS, LV.** Marc Singer, Mary Crosby, Stephen Davies, Richard Leparmentier, Terence Henry; ***D:*** Terence H. Winkless. *COL*

Berlin Express ½ **1948** Battle of wits ensues between the Allies and the Nazis who are seeking to keep Germans divided in post-WWII Germany. Espionage and intrigue factor heavily. **86m/B VHS, Beta, LV.** Robert Ryan, Merle Oberon, Paul Lukas, Charles Korvin; ***D:*** Jacques Tourneur. *MED, TTC, FCT*

Berlin Tunnel 21 ½ **1981** Based on the novel by Donald Lindquist, five American soldiers attempt a daring Cold War rescue of a beautiful German girl. The plan is to construct a tunnel under the Berlin Wall. A better-than-average film that was made for television. **150m/C VHS, Beta.** Richard Thomas, Jose Ferrer, Horst Buchholz; ***D:*** Richard Michaels. *NO*

Bernadette ½ **1990** A French-made version of the legend of St. Bernadette, who endured persecution after claiming to have seen the Virgin Mary. Beautiful in its simplicity, but overly long. **120m/C VHS, Beta.** *FR* Sydney Penny, Roland LeSaffre, Michele Simonnet, Bernard Dheran, Arlette Didier; ***D:*** Jean Delannoy. *IGP*

Bernard and the Genie ½ **199? (G)** It seems Bernard Bottle is not going to have a happy Christmas—he's been fired from his job and his girlfriend has left him. But things take a turn for the better when he discovers an antique lamp and its resident Genie. But with the Genie granting his every wish, Bernard's sudden wealth is causing some suspicions among both his greedy ex-employer and the police. Meanwhile, the Genie discovers the delights of modern-day England and poses as a department store Santa to truly fulfill a child's Christmas wish. Amusing family fare. **70m/C VHS.** *GB* Alan Cumming, Lenny Henry, Rowan Atkinson; ***D:*** Paul Weiland. *FOX, BTV, VCO*

Berserk! ½ **1967** A seedy traveling circus is beset by a series of murders. Not heralded as one of Crawford's best pieces. **95m/C VHS, Beta.** Joan Crawford, Diana Dors, Judy Geeson, Ty Hardin; ***D:*** James O'Connolly. *COL*

Berserker **1987 (R)** Six camping college students are attacked by a bloodthirsty psychotic out of a Nordic myth, who takes the shape of a badder-than-the-average bear. **85m/C VHS, Beta.** Joseph Alan Johnson, Valerie Sheldon, Greg Dawson; ***D:*** Jef Richard. *PSM*

Bert Rigby, You're a Fool ½ **1989 (R)** A starstruck British coal miner finds his way to Hollywood singing old showtunes, only to be rebuffed by a cynical industry. Available with Spanish subtitles. **94m/C VHS, Beta, LV.** Robert Lindsay, Robbie Coltrane, Jackie Gayle, Bruno Kirby, Cathryn Bradshaw, Corbin Bernsen, Anne Bancroft; ***D:*** Carl Reiner; ***W:*** Carl Reiner; ***M:*** Ralph Burns. *WAR, MVD*

Best Buns on the Beach *Woof!* **1987** Sexploitation movie about 10 beautiful girls in a bikini contest, that ends up with them going topless. Ridiculous plot, for mature (??) audiences. **60m/C VHS, LV.** *IME*

The Best Christmas Pageant Ever **1986** The meanest kids in town just decided to participate in the town's Christmas pageant and something special happens when the curtain finally goes up. **60m/C VHS.** Dennis Weaver, Karen Grassle. *RHV*

Best Defense **1984 (R)** A U.S. Army tank operator is sent to Kuwait to test a new state-of-the-art tank in a combat situation. Although the cast is popular, the movie as a whole is not funny and the story frequently is hard to follow. **94m/C VHS, Beta, LV.** Dudley Moore, Eddie Murphy, Kate Capshaw, George Dzundza, Helen Shaver; ***D:*** Willard Huyck; ***W:*** Willard Huyck, Gloria Katz. *PAR*

Best Enemies ½ **1986** An English film about a man suffering the trials of the 1960s, including Vietnam, and how it affects his relationships with his friends and wife. **96m/C VHS, Beta.** *GB* Sigrid Thornton, Paul Williams, Judy Morris, Brandon Burke; ***D:*** David Baker. *ACA*

Best Foot Forward ½ **1943** Vintage musical about a movie star who agrees to accompany a young cadet to a military ball. Based on the popular Broadway show. The film debuts of Walker, Allyson, and DeHaven. ♫Buckle Down, Winsocki; The Three B's (Barrelhouse, Boogie Woogie, and the Blues); Alive and Kicking; Two O'Clock Jump; Ev'ry Time; Three Men on a Date; Wish I May; Shady Lady; My First Promise. **95m/C VHS, Beta.** Lucille Ball, June Allyson, Tommy Dix, Nancy Walker, Virginia Weidler, Gloria De Haven, William Gaxton, Harry James; ***D:*** Edward Buzzell; ***W:*** Irving Brecher; ***M:*** George Bassman. *MGM*

Best Friends **1982 (PG)** A pair of screenwriters decide to marry after years of living and working together. Story based on the lives of screenwriters Barry Levinson and Valerie Curtin. **109m/C VHS, Beta, LV.** Goldie Hawn, Burt Reynolds, Jessica Tandy, Barnard Hughes, Audra Lindley, Keenan Wynn, Ron Silver; ***D:*** Norman Jewison; ***W:*** Valerie Curtin, Barry Levinson. Nominations: Academy Awards '82: Best Song ("How Do You Keep the Music Playing?"). *WAR*

The Best Intentions ½ **1992** Ingmar Bergman wrote the screenplay chronicling the early years of the stormy relationship of his parents. Set in Sweden at the turn of the century, the film focuses on the class differences that divide his mother and father, while portrayal of little Bergy is limited to a bundle under his mother's maternity dress. Inspired performances and directing illuminates the emotionally complex relationship, revealing truths about the universal human condition along the way. Six-hour version was shot for television in Europe and Japan. Director August and actress August met and married during filming. In Swedish with English subtitles. **182m/C VHS.** *SW* Samuel Froler, Pernilla August, Max von Sydow, Ghita Norby, Mona Malm, Lena Endre, Bjorn Kjellman; ***D:*** Bille August; ***W:*** Ingmar Bergman. Cannes Film Festival '92: Best Actress (August), Best Film. *ACA, FCT*

Best Kept Secrets ½ **1988** A feisty woman discovers corruption and blackmail in the police department where her husband is an officer. **104m/C VHS, Beta.** Patty Duke, Frederic Forrest, Peter Coyote; ***D:*** Jerrold Freedman. *VMK*

Best Legs in the 8th Grade **1984** A handsome attorney bumps into the gorgeous homeroom angel who had ignored his nebbishly dull countenance in grade school. Lightweight made for TV comedy. **60m/C VHS, Beta.** Tim Matheson, James Belushi, Annette O'Toole, Kathryn Harrold; ***D:*** Tom Patchett. *NO*

The Best Little Girl in the World **1981** Exceptional made for TV tale of an apparently perfect teenager suffering from anorexia. Slow starvation is her only cry for help. Fine performances from Durning and Saint. **96m/C VHS, Beta.** Charles Durning, Eva Marie Saint, Jennifer Jason Leigh, Melanie Mayron, Viveca Lindfors, Jason Miller, David Spielberg, Lisa Pelikan, Ally Sheedy; ***D:*** Sam O'Steen; ***M:*** Billy Goldenberg. *NO*

The Best Little Whorehouse in Texas **1982 (R)** Parton is the buxom owner of The Chicken Ranch, a house of ill-repute that may be closed down unless Sheriff-boyfriend Reynolds can think of a way out. Strong performances don't quite make up for the erratically comic script. Based on the long-running Broadway musical, in turn based on a story by Larry McMurtry. Available in a letterboxed edition on laserdisc. **115m/C VHS, Beta, LV.** Dolly Parton, Burt Reynolds, Dom DeLuise, Charles Durning, Jim Nabors, Lois Nettleton; ***D:*** Colin Higgins. Nominations: Academy Awards '82: Best Supporting Actor (Durning). *MCA, FCT*

The Best Man ½ **1964** An incisive, darkly satiric political tract, based on Gore Vidal's play, about two presidential contenders who vie for the endorsement of the aging ex-president, and trample political ethics in the process. **104m/B VHS, Beta.** Henry Fonda, Cliff Robertson, Lee Tracy, Margaret Leighton, Edie Adams, Kevin McCarthy, Ann Sothern, Gene Raymond, Shelley Berman, Mahalia Jackson; ***D:*** Franklin J. Schaffner; ***W:*** Gore Vidal; ***C:*** Haskell Wexler. Nominations: Academy Awards '64: Best Supporting Actor (Tracy). *MGM*

The Best of Abbott & Costello Live **1954** A compilation of vintage live-television routines by the duo, naturally including "Who's on First," along with their other celebrated bits. **58m/B VHS, Beta.** Bud Abbott, Lou Costello, George Raft, Charles Laughton. *WAR*

The Best of Bogart **1943** A two-cassette gift pack of the Bogie classics "The Maltese Falcon" and "Casablanca." **204m/B VHS, Beta.** Humphrey Bogart, Ingrid Bergman, Mary Astor, Sydney Greenstreet. *MGM*

Best of Bugs Bunny & Friends **1940** This collection includes classics from great cartoon stars Bugs Bunny, Daffy Duck, Tweetie Pie and Porky Pig. Includes "Duck Soup to Nuts," "A Feud There Was" and "Tweetie Pie." **53m/C VHS, Beta.** ***D:*** Isadore "Friz" Freleng, Chuck Jones, Robert McKimson. Academy Awards '47: Best Animated Short Film ("Tweetie Pie"). *MGM*

The Best of Chaplin **1918** Three Chaplin comedies when he worked with Mutual. Includes "The Rink," "One A.M.," and "The Floorwalker." **60m/B VHS.** Charlie Chaplin; ***D:*** Charlie Chaplin. *MVC, VRS*

The Best of Cracker Mysteries **1993** Coltrane stars as brilliant-but-abrasive forensic psychologist Dr. Eddie Fitzgerald. His insatiable desires for smoking, drinking, and gambling have blown apart his marriage and caused him grief at work. But Fitz's brilliant at "cracking" cases by reading clues to nail wrongdoers. In these three episodes a murder suspect, claiming to have amnesia, may be a serial killer; a loan shark gets murdered and it seems a recently paroled hijacker and his girlfriend are involved; and a teen suicide turns out to be murder. On 3 cassettes. **350m/C VHS.** *GB* Robbie Coltrane, Andrew Tiernan, Susan Lynch, Christopher Eccleston, Beryl Reid, Adrian Dunbar, Barbara Flynn; ***W:*** Jimmy McGovern. *PBS, AAE, TVC*

Best of Eddie Murphy ½ **1989** A compilation of Murphy's funniest bits from his three seasons on "Saturday Night Live," including appearances as Stevie Wonder, Buckwheat, Bill Cosby and Little Richard. **78m/C VHS, Beta.** Eddie Murphy, Joe Piscopo, Robin Duke, Tim Kazurinsky, Mary Gross, Gary Kroeger, Brad Hall, Julia Louis-Dreyfus. *PAR*

Best of Ernie Kovacs **1956** A compilation of some of the best moments from Ernie Kovacs' television programs that features such memorable characters as Percy Dovetonsils and the Nairobi Trio. **60m/B VHS, Beta.** Ernie Kovacs, Edie Adams, Ernie Hatrak, Bill Wendell, Peter Hanley. *WST, DVT, TVC*

The Best of Everything **1959** Trashy sexist soap opera about women seeking success and love in the publishing world of N.Y.C. Several stories take place, the best being Crawford's hard-nosed editor who's having an affair with a married man. Look for Evans as a philandering playboy (he went on to become the producer of "Chinatown," among others.) Based on the novel by Rona Jaffe. **121m/C VHS.** Hope Lange, Stephen Boyd, Suzy Parker, Diane Baker, Martha Hyer, Joan Crawford, Brian Aherne, Robert Evans, Louis Jourdan; ***D:*** Jean Negulesco; ***W:*** Edith Sommer, Mann Rubin; ***C:*** William Mellor; ***M:*** Alfred Newman. *FXV*

The Best of John Candy on SCTV **198?** Some of Candy's most memorable characters, including Johnny LaRue, Yosh Schmenge, and the grown up Theodore "Beaver" Cleaver, are featured on this compilation of his years on SCTV (Second City Television). **62m/C VHS, LV.** John Candy, Eugene Levy, Rick Moranis, Catherine O'Hara, Harold Ramis, Martin Short. *COL*

The Best of Lovejoy Mysteries **1993** Four-tape series features the best adventures of irrepressible (if untrustworthy) antiques dealer Lovejoy (McShane). What he usually discovers are forgeries, dirty dealing, and other assorted mayhem. Based on the mysteries by Jonathan Gash; made for British TV. **200m/C VHS.** *GB* Ian McShane, Phyllis Logan, Dudley Sutton, Chris Jury. *TVC, AAE*

The Best of Soap: Jessica's Wonderful Life **197?** From the camp TV sitcom comes this take-off on "It's a Wonderful Life." Jessica Tate (Helmond) finds herself at the stairway to heaven, pleading with an angel (Arthur) to return to aid her very dysfunctional family. **70m/C VHS.** Katherine Helmond, Beatrice Arthur, Robert Mandan, Cathryn Damon, Richard Mulligan, Billy Crystal. *REP*

The Best of Soap: Who Killed Peter? **1977** From the outrageous comedy TV series, featuring the eccentric and rich Tate family and the equally eccentric, but working-class, Campbell family. When Jessica Tate (Helmond) is convicted of murdering her tennis pro, brother-in-law Burt (Mulligan) decides to investigate. Crystal gained attention as gay son Jodie Dallas. **72m/C VHS.** Katherine Helmond, Richard Mulligan, Diana Canova, Robert Urich, Robert Mandan, Ted Wass, Billy Crystal, Robert Guillaume. *REP*

Best of the Badmen ½ **1950** A whole bunch of outlaws, although seemingly quite nice, are brought together by an ex-Union general who is being framed. Too much talk, not enough action. **84m/B VHS, Beta.** Robert Ryan, Claire Trevor, Jack

Buetel, Robert Preston, Walter Brennan, Bruce Cabot, John Archer, Lawrence Tierney; **D:** William D. Russell. *TTC*

Best of the Best ☆½ **1989 (PG-13)** An interracial kick-boxing team strives to win a world championship. **95m/C VHS, Beta, LV.** Eric Roberts, Sally Kirkland, Christopher Penn, Phillip Rhee, James Earl Jones, John P. Ryan, John Dye, David Agresta, Tom Everett, Louise Fletcher, Simon Rhee; **D:** Robert Radler. *COL*

Best of the Best 2 ☆½ **1993 (R)** The Coliseum is a notorious martial-arts venue owned by the champion fighter Brackus and his manager Weldon. No rules death matches are the norm and when their friend is killed Tommy and Alex set up a grudge match with Brackus. **100m/C VHS, LV.** Eric Roberts, Phillip Rhee, Christopher Penn, Ralph Moeller, Wayne Newton, Edan Gross, Sonny Landham, Meg Foster, Simon Rhee, Claire Stansfield, Betty Carvalho; **D:** Robert Radler; **W:** John Allen Nelson, Max Strom; **M:** David Michael Frank. *FXV*

Best of the Best 3: No Turning Back ☆☆ **1995 (R)** Tommy Lee (Rhee) discovers a band of racist vigilantes are trying to take over the rural community of Liberty, where his sister lives. But with the help of the sheriff (McDonald) and the school teacher (Gershon), Tommy is going to fight back. **102m/C VHS, LV.** Phillip Rhee, Gina Gershon, Christopher McDonald; **D:** Phillip Rhee. *TOU*

The Best of the Kenny Everett Video Show **1981** Scenes from the popular British late-night television show combining new wave rock music, outrageous dancing and innovative video special effects. **104m/C VHS, Beta.** Kenny Everett. *NO*

The Best of the Kids in the Hall **1993** Features some of the best clips of the hot Canadian comedy ensemble "The Kids in the Hall." Executive producer Lorne Michaels is best known for producing "Saturday Night Live." **120m/C VHS.** *CA* Dave Foley, Bruce McCulloch, Kevin McDonald, Mark McKinney, Scott Thompson. *COL*

The Best of the Two Ronnies **197?** A selection of skits from the well-loved BBC comedy series. **45m/C VHS, Beta.** *GB* Ronnie Barker, Ronnie Corbett. *FOX*

The Best of Times ☆☆ **1986 (PG)** Slim story of two grown men who attempt to redress the failures of the past by reenacting a football game they lost in high school due to a single flubbed pass. With this cast, it should have been better. **105m/C VHS, Beta, LV, 8mm.** Robin Williams, Kurt Russell, M. Emmet Walsh, Pamela Reed, Holly Palance, Donald Moffat, Margaret Whitton, Kirk Cameron; **D:** Roger Spottiswoode; **W:** Ron Shelton. *SUE, NLC*

Best of W.C. Fields **1933** Three of W.C. Field's Mack Sennett shorts are presented in their complete, uncut form: "The Dentist," "The Fatal Glass of Beer," and "The Golf Specialist." **58m/B VHS.** W.C. Fields, Elise Cavanna. *REP*

Best Revenge ☆☆ **1983 (R)** Two aging hippies engage in a Moroccan drug deal in order to free a kidnapped friend from a sleazy gangster. They get caught by the police, but escape, searching for the engineers of the frame-up. **92m/C VHS, Beta.** John Heard, Levon Helm, Alberta Watson, John Rhys-Davies, Moses Znaimer; **D:** John Trent; **M:** Keith Emerson. *ORI, WAR*

Best Seller ☆☆☆ **1987 (R)** Interesting, subtext-laden thriller about a cop/bestselling author with writer's block, and the strange symbiotic relationship he forms with a slick hired killer, who wants his own story written. Dennehy is convincing as the jaded cop, and is paired well with the psychotic Woods. **112m/C VHS, Beta, LV.** James Woods, Brian Dennehy, Victoria Tennant, Paul Shenar, Seymour Cassel, Allison Balson, George Coe, Anne Pitoniak; **D:** John Flynn; **W:** Larry Cohen; **M:** Jay Michael Ferguson. *VES*

The Best Way ☆☆½ **1982** Two summer camp counselors discover they might be gay and desirous of each other. Miller's first film; in French with English subtitles. **85m/C VHS, Beta.** *FR* Patrick Dewaere, Patrick Bouchitey, Christine Pascal, Claude Piepiu; **D:** Claude Miller. *FCT*

The Best Years of Our Lives ☆☆☆☆ **1946** Three WWII vets return home to try to pick up the threads of their lives. A film that represented a large chunk of American society and helped it readjust to the modern postwar ambience is now considered an American classic. Supporting actor Russell, an actual veteran, holds a record for winning two Oscars for a single role. In addition to his Best Supporting Actor award, Russell was given a special Oscar for bringing hope and courage to fellow veterans. Based on the novella by MacKinlay Kantor. Remade for television as "Returning Home" in 1975. **170m/B VHS, Beta, LV.** Fredric March, Myrna Loy, Teresa Wright, Dana Andrews, Virginia Mayo, Harold Russell, Hoagy Carmichael, Gladys George, Roman Bohnen, Steve Cochran, Charles Halton; **D:** William Wyler; **W:** Robert Sherwood; **C:** Gregg Toland; **M:** Hugo Friedhofer. Academy Awards '46: Best Actor (March), Best Director (Wyler), Best Film Editing, Best Picture, Best Screenplay, Best Supporting Actor (Russell), Best Original Score; British Academy Awards '47: Best Film; Golden Globe Awards '47: Best Film—Drama; National Board of Review Awards '46: 10 Best Films of the Year, Best Director (Wyler); Nominations: Academy Awards '46: Best Sound. *HBO, SUE, FCT*

Bethune ☆☆½ **1977** The life story of a Canadian doctor who started a practice in Communist China. **88m/C VHS, Beta.** Donald Sutherland, Kate Nelligan, David Gardner, James Hong; **D:** Eric Till. *TWE*

Betrayal ☆ **1974** Psycho-thriller pits an unhappy widow against her seemingly innocent hired companion. Seems this girl has a boyfriend who has a plan to murder the lonely lady for her money. Routine and predictable. **78m/C VHS.** Amanda Blake, Dick Haymes, Tisha Sterling, Sam Groom; **D:** Gordon Hessler; **M:** Ernest Gold. *JEF*

Betrayal ☆½ **1978** Telefilm based on the book by Lucy Freeman and Julie Roy about a historic malpractice case involving a psychiatrist and one of his female patients. The doctor convinced the female patient that sex with him would serve as therapy. **95m/C VHS, Beta.** Lesley Ann Warren, Rip Torn, Ron Silver, Richard Masur, Stephen Elliott, John Hillerman, Peggy Ann Garner; **D:** Paul Wendkos. *NO*

Betrayal ☆☆½ **1983 (R)** An unusual adult drama, beginning at the end of a seven-year adulterous affair and working its way back in time to finally end at the start of the betrayal of a husband by his wife and his best friend. Kingsley and Irons make Pinter's adaptation of his own play work. **95m/C VHS, Beta.** *GB* Ben Kingsley, Patricia Hodge, Jeremy Irons; **D:** David Jones; **W:** Harold Pinter. Nominations: Academy Awards '83: Best Adapted Screenplay. *FOX*

Betrayal from the East ☆☆ **1944** A carnival barker saves the Panama Canal from the vicious Japanese war machine in this rather silly wartime drama. **82m/B VHS, Beta.** Lee Tracy, Nancy Kelly, Richard Loo, Abner Biberman, Regis Toomey, Philip Ahn, Addison Richards, Victor Sen Yung, Drew Pearson; **D:** William (Lester Williams) Berke. *TTC*

Betrayal of the Dove ☆☆ **1992 (R)** Slater stars as a divorced woman set-up on a blind date by best friend Le Brock. Zane is the dashing doctor who sweeps Slater off her feet but things are never quite what they seem. He may not be Mr. Right and the best friend has her own hidden agenda. **93m/C VHS.** Helen Slater, Kelly Le Brock, Billy Zane, Alan Thicke, Harvey Korman, Stuart Pankin, David Lander; **D:** Strathford Hamilton; **W:** Robby Benson. *PSM*

Betrayed ☆☆☆ **1954** Bombshell Turner and strongman Gable star in this story of WWII intrigue. Suspected of being a Nazi informer, Turner is sent back to Holland for a last chance at redemption. Her cover as a sultry nightclub performer has the Nazis drooling and ogling (can you spell h-o-t?), but her act may be blown by an informant. Can luscious Lana get out of this one intact? **107m/C VHS, Beta.** Clark Gable, Lana Turner, Victor Mature, Louis Calhern, O.E. Hasse, Wilfrid Hyde-White, Ian Carmichael, Niall MacGinnis, Nora Swinburne, Roland Culver; **D:** Gottfried Reinhardt; **C:** Frederick A. (Freddie) Young. *MGM, CCB*

Betrayed ☆☆ **1988 (R)** A rabid political film, dealing with an implausible FBI agent infiltrating a white supremacist organization via her love affair with a handsome farmer who turns out to be a murderous racist. Winger is memorable in her role as the FBI agent, despite the film's limitations, and admirers of Costa-Gavras's directorial work and political stances will want to see how the director botched this one. **112m/C VHS, Beta, LV.** Tom Berenger, Debra Winger, John Mahoney, John Heard, Albert Hall, Jeffrey DeMunn; **D:** Constantin Costa-Gavras; **W:** Joe Eszterhas. *MGM*

The Betsy ☆☆ *Harold Robbins' The Betsy* **1978 (R)** A story of romance, money, power, and mystery centering around the wealthy Hardeman family and their automobile manufacturing business. Loosely patterned after the life of Henry Ford as portrayed in the Harold Robbins' pulp-tome. Olivier is the redeeming feature. **132m/C VHS, Beta.** Laurence Olivier, Kathleen Beller, Robert Duvall, Lesley-Anne Down, Edward Herrmann, Tommy Lee Jones, Katharine Ross, Jane Alexander; **D:** Daniel Petrie; **W:** William Bast, Walter Bernstein; **M:** John Barry. *FOX*

Betsy's Wedding ☆☆½ **1990 (R)** Betsy wants a simple wedding, but her father has other, grander ideas. Then there's the problem of paying for it, which Dad tries to take care of in a not-so-typical manner. Alda at his hilarious best. **94m/C VHS, Beta, LV.** Alan Alda, Joey Bishop, Madeline Kahn, Molly Ringwald, Catherine O'Hara, Joe Pesci, Ally Sheedy, Burt Young, Anthony LaPaglia, Julie Bovasso, Nicolas Coster, Bibi Besch, Dylan Walsh; **D:** Alan Alda; **W:** Alan Alda; **M:** Bruce Broughton. *TOU*

Better Late Than Never ☆☆ **1979** Fun television tale of senior citizens in revolt at an old-age home. Fine characters portrayed by some of the best in the business. **100m/C VHS.** Harold Gould, Tyne Daly, Strother Martin, Harry (Henry) Morgan, Victor Buono, George Gobel, Lou Jacobi, Donald Pleasence, Larry Storch; **D:** Richard Crenna; **M:** Charles Fox. *FOX*

Better Late Than Never ☆½ **1983** Two penniless old fools vie for the acceptance of a bratty 10-year-old millionairess, who must choose one as her guardian. Niven's last film. **95m/C VHS, Beta.** David Niven, Art Carney, Maggie Smith, Kimberly Partridge, Catherine Hicks, Melissa Prophet; **D:** Bryan Forbes; **M:** Henry Mancini. *FOX*

Better Off Dead ☆☆½ **1985 (PG)** A compulsive teenager's girlfriend leaves him and he decides to end it all. After several abortive attempts, he decides instead to out-ski his ex-girlfriend's obnoxious new boyfriend. Uneven but funny. **97m/C VHS, Beta, LV.** John Cusack, Curtis Armstrong, Diane Franklin, Kim Darby, David Ogden Stiers, Dan Schneider, Amanda Wyss, Taylor Negron, Vincent Schiavelli, Demian Slade, Scooter Stevens; **D:** Steve Holland; **W:** Steve Holland; **M:** Rupert Hine. *FOX*

Better Off Dead ☆☆½ **1994** Preachy, manipulative TV movie redeemed by good performances. Kit (Winningham) is an unrepentant white-trash thief who kills a black police officer and is sentenced to death. Daisy is the ambitious black district attorney who prosecuted the case but comes to doubt the wisdom of the death penalty and slowly begins to try to help Kit. **?m/C VHS.** Mare Winningham, Tyra Ferrell; **D:** M. Neema Barnette; **W:** Marlane X. Meyer. *TTC*

A Better Tomorrow ☆½ *Yingxiong Bense* **1986** Gangster movie with the requisite bloodletting and male bonding. Film captured a big box-office. In Cantonese with English subtitles. **95m/C VHS.** *CH* Chow Yung Fat, Leslie Cheung, Ti Lung; **D:** John Woo. *REP, FCT*

A Better Tomorrow, Part 2 ☆½ **1988** A smooth-talking gangster, who was killed in Part I, returns in Part II as the dead man's twin brother (unmentioned in Part I). He teams up with a cop and a reformed gangster to fight the forces of evil. In Cantonese with English subtitles. **100m/C VHS.** *CH* Chow Yung Fat, Leslie Cheung; **D:** John Woo. *FCT*

Betty ☙☙ **1992** Sulky, drunken Betty (Trintignant) is doing her best to destroy her bourgeois life, escaping from her marriage into adultery and debasement. She meets the concerned middle-aged widow Laure (Audran), who inexplicably takes her to her hotel room, cleans her up, and spends the remainder of the movie as Betty's sounding-board. Betty's passive personality offers little to explain her appeal to either Laure or the viewer. Based on the novel by Georges Simenon. French with subtitles. **103m/C VHS.** *FR* Marie Trintignant, Stephane Audran, Jean-Francoise Garreau, Yves Lambrecht, Christiane Minazolli, Pierre Vernier; ***D:*** Claude Chabrol; ***W:*** Claude Chabrol; ***M:*** Matthieu Chabrol. *NYF*

Betty Blue ☙☙☙ **1986 (R)** A vivid, intensely erotic film about two young French lovers and how their inordinately strong passion for each other destroys them, leading to poverty, violence, and insanity. English subtitles. From the director of "Diva." Based on the novel "37.2 Le Matin" by Philippe Djian. **121m/C VHS, Beta, LV.** *FR* Beatrice Dalle, Jean-Hugues Anglade, Gerard Darmon, Consuelo de Haviland, Clementine Celarie, Jacques Mathou, Vincent Lindon; ***D:*** Jean-Jacques Beineix; ***W:*** Jean-Jacques Beineix; ***M:*** Gabriel Yared. Nominations: Academy Awards '86: Best Foreign Language Film; Cesar Awards '86: Best Actor (Anglade). *FOX, INJ*

Between Fighting Men ☙½ **1932** The orphaned daughter of a shepherd is adopted by the cowpoke who caused her father's death. The cowpoke's sons fall in love with, and compete for, the love of the girl. **62m/B VHS.** Ken Maynard, Ruth Hall, Josephine Dunn, Wallace MacDonald; ***D:*** Forrest Sheldon. *NOS, DVT*

Between Friends ☙☙½ **1983** Two women with only their respective divorces in common, meet and become fast friends. The rapport between Burnett and Taylor makes for a touching drama. Adapted for cable television from the book "Nobody Makes Me Cry," by Shelley List, one of the producers. **105m/C VHS, Beta.** Elizabeth Taylor, Carol Burnett; ***D:*** Lou Antonio; ***M:*** James Horner. *VES*

Between God, the Devil & a Winchester ☙ **1972** Violent western with plenty of shooting and dust. Lots of cowboys are hot on the trail of some stolen loot from a church but apparently God isn't on their side since the majority bite the dust and become a snack for the vultures. **98m/C VHS, Beta.** Gilbert Roland, Richard Harrison; ***D:*** Dario Silvester. *UNI*

Between Heaven and Earth ☙☙ **1993** Maria (Maura) is an ambitious television journalist, prone to surreal dreams, who becomes pregnant after a one-night stand. After witnessing a violent protest, Maria becomes convinced that she can communicate with her unborn baby and that the child is unwilling to be born into such a violent world. So Maria must try to convince her baby otherwise. In French with English subtitles. **80m/C VHS.** *BE FR SP* Carmen Maura, Jean-Pierre Cassel, Didier Bezace, Samuel Mussen, Andre Delvaux; ***D:*** Marion Hansel; ***W:*** Marion Hansel. *FCT*

Between Heaven and Hell ☙☙☙ **1956** Prejudiced Southern gentleman Wagner finds how wrong his misconceptions are, as he attempts to survive WWII on a Pacific Island. Ebsen is exceptional, making this rather simplistic story a meaningful classic. **94m/C VHS.** Robert Wagner, Terry Moore, Broderick Crawford, Buddy Ebsen, Robert Keith, Brad Dexter, Mark Damon, Kenneth Clark, Harvey Lembeck, Frank Gorshin, Scatman Crothers; ***D:*** Richard Fleischer. Nominations: Academy Awards '56: Best Original Score. *FXV*

Between Men ☙☙ **1935** A father kills a man he believes killed his son and flees. Later in life, the son meets his father. For father and son, this causes some major concern. **59m/B VHS, Beta.** Johnny Mack Brown, Beth Marion, William Farnum, Earl Dwire, Lloyd Ingraham, Milburn Morante; ***D:*** Robert North Bradbury. *NOS, DVT, GPV*

Between the Lines ☙☙☙½ **1977 (R)** A witty, wonderfully realized ensemble comedy about the staff of a radical post-'60s newspaper always on the brink of folding, and its eventual sell-out. **101m/C VHS, Beta.** John Heard, Lindsay Crouse, Jeff Goldblum, Jill Eikenberry, Stephen Collins, Lewis J. Stadlen, Michael J. Pollard, Marilu Henner, Bruno Kirby; ***D:*** Joan Micklin Silver; ***W:*** Fred Barron; ***M:*** Michael Kamen. *VES*

Between Two Women ☙☙ **1986** A television movie about a wife's rocky relationship with her bossy mother-in-law, until the latter has a stroke and needs care. Dewhurst won an Emmy for her portrayal of the mother-in-law. **95m/C VHS, Beta.** Farrah Fawcett, Michael Nouri, Colleen Dewhurst, Steven Hill, Bridgette Anderson, Danny Corkill; ***D:*** Jon Avnet. *WAR*

Between Wars ☙☙ **1974** Young doctor in Australia's Medical Corps encounters conflict when he tries to introduce Freud's principles into his work. **97m/C VHS, Beta.** *AU* Corin Redgrave, Arthur Dignam, Judy Morris, Patricia Leehy, Gunter Meisner; ***D:*** Michael Thornhill. *NO*

Beulah Land ☙½ **1980** A television mini-series about 45 years in the lives of a Southern family, including the Civil War. Based on the novels "Beulah Land" and "Look Away, Beulah Land" by Lonnie Coleman. **267m/C VHS, Beta, LV.** Lesley Ann Warren, Michael Sarrazin, Don Johnson, Meredith Baxter, Dorian Harewood, Eddie Albert, Hope Lange, Paul Rudd; ***D:*** Virgil W. Vogel, Harry Falk. *COL, TVC*

The Beverly Hillbillies **1962** The successful sitcom series, which ran from 1962-1971, features Jed Clampett and his Ozark clan striking oil, getting rich, and heading for the good life in California. Two episodes per tape. **51m/B VHS.** Buddy Ebsen, Irene Ryan, Donna Douglas, Max Baer Jr., Nancy Kulp, Raymond Bailey, Phil Silvers; ***Cameos:*** John Wayne. *FXV, MOV*

The Beverly Hillbillies ☙☙½ **1993 (PG)** Big-screen transfer of the long-running TV show may appeal to fans. Ozark mountaineer Jed Clampett discovers oil, becomes an instant billionaire, and packs his backwoods clan off to the good life in California. Minimal plot finds dim-bulb nephew Jethro and daughter Elly May looking for a bride for Jed. Not that any of it matters. Everyone does fine by their impersonations, particularly Varney as the good-hearted Jed and Leachman as stubborn Granny. Ebsen, the original Jed, reprises another of his TV roles, detective Barnaby Jones. And yes, the familiar strains of the "Ballad of Jed Clampett" by Jerry Scoggins starts this one off, too. **93m/C VHS, LV.** Jim Varney, Erika Eleniak, Diedrich Bader, Cloris Leachman, Dabney Coleman, Lily Tomlin, Lea Thompson, Rob Schneider, Linda Carlson, Penny Fuller, Kevin Connolly; ***Cameos:*** Buddy Ebsen, Zsa Zsa Gabor, Dolly Parton; ***D:*** Penelope Spheeris; ***W:*** Larry Konner, Mark Rosenthal, Jim Fisher, Jim Staahl; ***M:*** Lalo Schifrin. *FXV*

Beverly Hills Bodysnatchers ☙½ **1989 (R)** A mad scientist and a greedy mortician plot to get rich, but their plan backfires when they bring a Mafia godfather back to life and he terrorizes Beverly Hills. **85m/C VHS, LV.** Vic Tayback, Frank Gorshin, Brooke Bundy, Seth Jaffe, Art Metrano; ***D:*** Jon Mostow. *IME*

Beverly Hills Brats ☙ **1989 (PG-13)** A spoiled, rich Hollywood brat hires a loser to kidnap him, in order to gain his parents' attention, only to have both of them kidnapped by real crooks. **90m/C VHS, Beta, LV.** Martin Sheen, Burt Young, Peter Billingsley, Terry Moore; ***D:*** Dimitri Sotirakis; ***M:*** Barry Goldberg. *LIV, IME, VTR*

Beverly Hills Cop ☙☙½ **1984 (R)** When a close friend of smooth-talking Detroit cop Axle Foley is brutally murdered in L.A., he traces the murderer to the posh streets of Beverly Hills. There he must stay on his toes to keep one step ahead of the killer and two steps ahead of the law. Better than average Murphy vehicle. **105m/C VHS, Beta, LV, 8mm.** Eddie Murphy, Judge Reinhold, John Ashton, Lisa Eilbacher, Ronny Cox, Steven Berkoff, James Russo, Jonathan Banks, Stephen Elliott, Bronson Pinchot, Paul Reiser, Damon Wayans, Rick Overton; ***D:*** Martin Brest; ***W:*** Danilo Bach, Dan Petrie Jr.; ***C:*** Bruce Surtees; ***M:*** Harold Faltermeyer. People's Choice Awards '85: Best Film; Nominations: Academy Awards '84: Best Original Screenplay. *PAR*

Beverly Hills Cop 2 ☙½ **1987 (R)** The highly successful sequel to the first profitable comedy, with essentially the same plot, this time deals with Foley infiltrating a band of international munitions smugglers. **103m/C VHS, Beta, LV, 8mm.** Eddie Murphy, Judge Reinhold, Juergen Prochnow, Ronny Cox, John Ashton, Brigitte Nielsen, Allen (Goorwitz) Garfield, Paul Reiser, Dean Stockwell; ***D:*** Tony Scott; ***W:*** Larry Ferguson, Warren Skaaren; ***M:*** Harold Faltermeyer. Golden Raspberry Awards '87: Worst Song ("I Want Your Sex"); Nominations: Academy Awards '87: Best Song ("Shakedown"). *PAR*

Beverly Hills Cop 3 ☙½ **1994 (R)** Yes, Detroit cop Axel Foley (Murphy) just happens to find another case that takes him back to his friends on the Beverly Hills PD. This time he uncovers a criminal network fronting WonderWorld, an amusement park with a squeaky-clean image. Fast-paced action, lots of gunplay, and Eddie wisecracks his way through the slow spots. Reinhold returns as the still impossibly naive Rosewood, with Bronson briefly reprising his role as Serge of the undeterminable accent. Critically panned box office disappointment relies too heavily on formula and is another disappointing followup. **105m/C VHS, Beta.** Eddie Murphy, Judge Reinhold, Hector Elizondo, Timothy Carhart, Stephen McHattie, Theresa Randle, John Saxon, Alan Young, Bronson Pinchot; ***Cameos:*** Al Green, Gil Hill; ***D:*** John Landis; ***W:*** Steven E. de Souza; ***M:*** Nile Rodgers. *PAR*

Beverly Hills Knockouts **1989** A bevy of beautiful boxers pummel each other with both fists. **60m/C VHS, Beta.** *CEL*

Beverly Hills Madam ☙ **1986 (PG-13)** In this routine plot, a stable of elite call girls struggle with their lifestyle and their madam, played by Dunaway. Made for television. **97m/C VHS, Beta, LV.** Faye Dunaway, Louis Jourdan, Donna Dixon, Robin Givens, Marshall Colt, Melody Anderson, Terry Farrell; ***D:*** Harvey Hart. *ORI*

Beverly Hills 90210 **1990** In the pilot episode for the immensely popular series, the world is introduced to the exciting teens who wander the halls of West Beverly High. Join Brandon and Brenda Walsh as they move from Minneapolis to Beverly Hills and experience all the trials and tribulations that come with the new zip code. Includes 25 minutes of previously unseen footage. **90m/C VHS, LV.** Jason Priestley, Shannen Doherty, Jennie Garth, Brian Austin Green, Tori Spelling, Ian Ziering, Gabrielle Carteris. *WOV, MOV*

Beverly Hills 90210: The Graduation **1993** The 1993 end-of-the-season episode of the hit TV series finds the group finally getting out of Beverly Hills High. As they graduate the friends share plans for the summer (and the future) and you'll see lots of flashbacks as well as their final graduation prank. Includes interviews with the cast and music videos from the series soundtrack. **90m/C VHS.** Jason Priestley, Shannen Doherty, Luke Perry, Jennie Garth, Brian Austin Green, Tori Spelling, Ian Ziering, Gabrielle Carteris. *WOV*

Beverly Hills Vamp ☙☙ **1988 (R)** A madame and her girls are really female vampires with a penchant for hot-blooded men. **88m/C VHS, Beta.** Britt Ekland, Eddie Deezen, Debra Lamb; ***D:*** Fred Olen Ray. *VMK*

Beware ☙½ **1946** A black singer saves a college from bankruptcy and makes off with the gym teacher. The photography may be a bit harsh, but the all-black cast made this a pioneering but impressive film. **64m/B VHS.** Louis Jordan, Frank Wilson, Emory Richardson, Valerie Black, Milton Woods; ***D:*** Bud Pollard. *NOS, RXM*

Beware! Children at Play *Woof!* **1995 (R)** Cult leader kidnaps kids and introduces them to cannibalism. Bleech! As if this didn't sound grim enough, there's also an unrated version. **90m/C VHS.** *TTV*

Beware, My Lovely ☙☙½ **1952** Taut chiller. Lonely widow Lupino hires a new handy-man. He's great with screen doors and storm windows, but has a problem with sharp tools. Intense and gripping with fine performances. **77m/B VHS, LV.** Ida Lupino, Robert Ryan, Taylor Holmes, O.Z. Whitehead, Barbara Whiting, Dee Pollock; ***D:*** Harry Horner. *REP*

Beware of a Holy Whore ℒℒ *Warnung Vor Einer Heiligen Nutte* **1970** German film crew sits around a Spanish resort—complaining, drinking, and making love—as they wait for financial support from Bonn. Provocative and self-indulgently honest look at filmmaking. Filmed on location in Sorrento, Italy; German with subtitles. **103m/C VHS.** *GE* Lou Castel, Eddie Constantine, Hanna Schygulla, Marquard Bohm, Ulli Lommel, Margarethe von Trotta, Kurt Raab, Ingrid Caven, Werner Schroeter, Rainer Werner Fassbinder; ***D:*** Rainer Werner Fassbinder; ***W:*** Rainer Werner Fassbinder; ***C:*** Michael Ballhaus; ***M:*** Peer Raben. *ORI*

Beware of Pity ℒℒ ½ **1946** A crippled baroness thinks she's found true love with a military officer, but it turns out his marriage proposal grew out of pity for her, not passion. A quality but somber British-made historical drama, based on a novel by Stefan Zweig. **105m/B VHS.** Lilli Palmer, Albert Lieven, Cedric Hardwicke, Gladys Cooper, Ernest Thesiger, Freda Jackson; ***D:*** Maurice Elvey. *NOS*

Bewitched **1985** A made-for-British-television horror story about an elderly couple ostensibly plagued by the witch-like conniving of a dead woman. **60m/C VHS, Beta.** *GB* Eileen Atkins, Alfred Lynch; ***D:*** Edmund Oboler. *PSM*

Beyond a Reasonable Doubt ℒℒ **1956** In order to get a behind-the-scenes glimpse at the judicial system, a man plays the guilty party to a murder. Alas, when he tries to vindicate himself, he is the victim of his own folly. Not as interesting as it sounds on paper. **80m/B VHS.** Dana Andrews, Joan Fontaine, Sidney Blackmer, Philip Bourneuf, Barbara Nichols, Shepperd Strudwick, Arthur Franz, Edward Binns; ***D:*** Fritz Lang; ***W:*** Douglas S. Morrow. *NO*

Beyond Atlantis *Woof!* **1973 (PG)** An ancient underwater tribe is discovered when it kidnaps landlubbin' women with which to mate. **91m/C VHS, Beta.** *PH* John Ashley, Patrick Wayne, George Nader; ***D:*** Eddie Romero. *VCI*

Beyond Darkness ℒ ½ **1992 (R)** When Peter and his family move into their New England home they are immediately beset by some unknown terror. With the help of Father George, Peter learns his house was built upon the graves of twenty witches burned for heresy. The witches have decided to seek revenge by kidnapping Peter's young son and sacrificing him to an evil demon. Can Peter destroy the evil spirits before they destroy his son? **111m/C VHS, LV.** Gene Le Brock, David Brandon, Barbara Bingham, Michael Stephenson, Stephen Brown; ***D:*** Clyde Anderson. *IMP*

Beyond Desire ℒℒ ½ **1994 (R)** Con released after 14 years in prison gets picked up by a corvette-driving Las Vegas prostitute but more than sex is on both their minds. **87m/C VHS.** William Forsythe, Kari Wuhrer, Leo Rossi, Sharon Farrell; ***D:*** Dominique Othenin-Girard. *LIV*

Beyond Dream's Door ℒ **1988** A young, All-American college student's childhood nightmares come back to haunt him, making dreams a horrifying reality. **86m/C VHS, Beta.** Nick Baldasare, Rick Kesler, Susan Pinsky, Norm Singer; ***D:*** Jay Woelfel. *NO*

Beyond Erotica **1979** After being cut out of his father's will, a sadistic young man takes out his rage on his mother and a peasant girl. **90m/C VHS.** David Hemmings, Alida Valli, Andrea Rau. *PSM*

Beyond Evil *Woof!* **1980 (R)** Relatively dimwitted newlywed couple moves into an old island mansion despite rumors that the house is haunted. Sure enough, wife George becomes possessed by the vengeful spirit of a woman murdered 200 years earlier, and a reign of pointless terror begins. Poor rip-off of hybrid Amityville/Exorcist paranormality. **98m/C VHS, Beta.** John Saxon, Lynda Day George, Michael Dante, Mario Milano; ***D:*** Herb Freed; ***W:*** Herb Freed; ***M:*** Pino Donaggio. *MED*

Beyond Fear ℒℒ ½ **1975** Compelling drama about a man forced to aid a gang in robbery while they hold his wife and son captive. **92m/C VHS, Beta.** Michael Boquet. *PSM*

Beyond Fear ℒℒ ½ **1993 (R)** Tipper Taylor (Lesseos) is a wilderness tour guide who's also a martial arts expert. This is going to come in handy when her tour group is stalked by two men who are after a videotape innocently filmed by someone in Tipper's group. It seems the tape shows the men committing a murder. **84m/C VHS.** Mimi Lesseos. *MNC*

Beyond Forgiveness ℒℒ ½ **1994 (R)** Basic maverick cop goes after his brother's killers and winds up involved in an international black market in transplantable human organs. **95m/C VHS, LV.** Thomas Ian Griffith, Rutger Hauer, John Rhys-Davies; ***D:*** Bob Misiorowski; ***W:*** Charles Cohen. *REP*

Beyond Innocence ℒ **1987** A 17-year-old lusts after a mature married woman. Ostensibly based on Raymond Radiguet's "Devil in the Flesh." **87m/C VHS, Beta.** Keith Smith, Katia Caballero, John Morris; ***D:*** Scott Murray. *NO*

Beyond Justice ℒℒ **1992 (PG-13)** High action-adventure with the prolific Hauer starring as an ex-CIA agent who is hired to rescue the kidnapped son of a beautiful executive. **113m/C VHS, LV.** Rutger Hauer, Carol Alt, Omar Sharif, Elliott Gould; ***M:*** Ennio Morricone. *VMK*

Beyond Obsession ℒℒ **1982** The strange relationship between a political prisioner, his daughter, and her obsession with a mysterious American is provocatively explored. **116m/C VHS.** *IT* Marcello Mastroianni, Elenora Giorgi, Tom Berenger, Michel Piccoli; ***D:*** Liliana Cavani. *FCT*

Beyond Rangoon ℒℒ ½ **1995 (R)** Sisters Laura (Arquette) and Andy (McDormand) Bowman travel to Burma to unwind, only to have political unrest and a repressive regime spoil the holiday. Dr. Laura (yeah, right) loses her passport and must flee from trigger-happy soldiers with a political dissident (Ko, a real-life exiled Burmese activist) who befriends her. The search for her passport soon becomes a imperiled trek of survival and self-discovery. Tense, well-crafted action sequences hint at a potential for excitement and intrigue; too bad Arquette isn't the least bit convincing. Filmed in Malaysia. **100m/C VHS, LV.** Patricia Arquette, Frances McDormand, Spalding Gray, U Aung Ko, Victor Slezak; ***D:*** John Boorman; ***W:*** Alex Lasker, Bill Rubenstein; ***C:*** John Seale; ***M:*** Hans Zimmer. *COL*

Beyond Reason ℒ **1977** A psychologist uses unorthodox methods by treating the criminally insane with dignity and respect. **88m/C VHS, Beta.** Telly Savalas, Laura Johnson, Diana Muldaur, Marvin Laird, Priscilla Barnes; ***D:*** Telly Savalas. *MED*

Beyond Reasonable Doubt ℒℒ ½ **1980** Chilling true-life murder mystery which shattered the peaceful quiet of a small New Zealand town and eventually divided the country. An innocent farmer (Hargreaves) was convicted of a grisly double murder based on evidence planted by a local cop (Hemmings, in a superb role). It wasn't until Yallop's book questioned the facts of the case that it was reopened. Yallop also wrote the screenplay. **127m/C VHS, Beta.** *NZ* David Hemmings, John Hargreaves, Martyn Sanderson, Grant Tilly, Diana Rowan, Ian Watkin; ***D:*** John Laing; ***W:*** David Yallop. *NO*

Beyond the Bermuda Triangle ℒ ½ **1975** Unfortunate and flat television flick. Businessman MacMurray, now retired, doesn't have enough to do. He begins an investigation of the mysterious geometric island area when his friends and fiancee disappear. Silly. **78m/C VHS.** Fred MacMurray, Sam Groom, Donna Mills, Suzanne Reed, Dana Plato, Woody Woodbury; ***D:*** William A. Graham. *NO*

Beyond the Call of Duty ℒ ½ **1992 (R)** Renegade U.S. Army Commander Len Jordan (Vincent) is after a particularly deadly Vietcong enemy. Aided by the head of a special forces naval unit he tracks his quarry through the notorious Mekong River Delta. But Jordan's mission may be hindered, both personally and professionally, by a beautiful American journalist after a hot story. **92m/C VHS, LV.** Jan-Michael Vincent, Eb Lottimer, Jillian McWhirter; ***D:*** Cirio H. Santiago. *NHO*

Beyond the Carribean ℒℒ **1936** Bizarre jungle thriller featuring voodoo and native crucifixion. Also known as "Manhunters of the Carribean." **56m/B VHS.** Andre Roosevelt. *SNC*

Beyond the Door *Woof! Beyond Obsession* **1975 (R)** San Francisco woman finds herself pregnant with a demonic child. One of the first "Exorcist" rip-offs; skip this one and go right to the sequel, "Beyond the Door 2." In Italian; dubbed. **97m/C VHS, Beta, LV.** *IT* Juliet Mills, Richard Johnson, David Colin Jr.; ***D:*** Oliver Hellman. *MED, COL*

Beyond the Door 2 ℒℒ ½ *Shock* **1979 (R)** Better treatment of the possession theme, but this time the door is to the home of a new family: Colin (from the original) plays a boy possessed by his dead father, who seeks revenge on his widow and her new husband. Director Bava's last feature. **90m/C VHS, Beta.** *IT* John Steiner, Daria Nicolodi, David Colin Jr., Ivan Rassimov; ***D:*** Mario Bava; ***W:*** Lamberto Bava, Franco Barbieri. *MED*

Beyond the Door 3 *Woof!* **1991 (R)** Fool American students in Yugoslavia board a hellish locomotive which speeds them toward a satanic ritual. Demonic disaster-movie stuff (with poor miniatures) isn't as effective as the on-location filming; Serbian scenery and crazed peasants impart an eerie pagan aura. What this has to do with earlier "Beyond the Door" movies only the marketing boys can say. Some dialogue in Serbo-Croat with English subtitles. **94m/C VHS, LV.** Mary Kohnert, Sarah Conway Ciminera, William Geiger, Renee Rancourt, Alex Vitale, Victoria Zinny, Savina Gersak, Bo Svenson; ***D:*** Jeff Kwitny. *COL*

Beyond the Forest ℒ ½ **1949** Camp diva Davis, in her last role for Warner Bros., really turns on the histrionics as a big-city gal married to a small-town guy (Cotten) and bored out of her mind. Although the most memorable line, "What a dump," has become larger-than-life, the film itself is rather small and muddled (interestingly, Vidor directed "The Fountainhead" the same year.) A trashy melodrama full of ennui, envy, unwanted pregnancy, and murder, it's definitely high on camp and low on art. **96m/B VHS.** Bette Davis, Joseph Cotten, David Brian, Ruth Roman, Minor Watson, Regis Toomey; ***D:*** King Vidor; ***C:*** Robert Burks; ***M:*** Max Steiner. Nominations: Academy Awards '49: Best Original Score. *MGM, FCT*

Beyond the Law ℒℒ *Bloodsilver; Al Di La Della Legge* **1968** Spaghetti western with Van Cleef as the too smart bad guy. He becomes sheriff, picks up the stack of silver at the depot, and disappears. Humorous and clever, with fine location photography. **91m/C VHS.** *IT* Lee Van Cleef, Antonio Sabato, Lionel Stander, Bud Spencer, Gordon Mitchell, Ann Smyrner; ***D:*** Giorgio Stegani. *IMP, QVD*

Beyond the Law ℒ ½ *Fixing the Shadow* **1992 (R)** Ex-undercover cop Danny Saxon (Sheen) is recruited by the FBI to infiltrate a biker gang involved in drugs and gun smuggling. But Saxon finds himself drawn too close into the unconventional biker lifestyle and into an uneasy friendship with leader Blood (Madsen). Clumsy and exploitative. **101m/C VHS, LV.** Charlie Sheen, Michael Madsen, Linda Fiorentino, Courtney B. Vance, Leon Rippy, Rip Torn; ***D:*** Larry Ferguson; ***W:*** Larry Ferguson; ***M:*** John D'Andrea, Cory Lerios. *LIV*

Beyond the Limit ℒℒ ½ *The Honorary Consul* **1983 (R)** The story of an intense and darkly ominous love triangle which takes place in the South American coastal city of Corrientes. Based on Graham Greene's novel "The Honorary Consul." **103m/C VHS, Beta.** Michael Caine, Richard Gere, Bob Hoskins, Elpidia Carrillo; ***D:*** John MacKenzie; ***W:*** Christopher Hampton; ***C:*** Phil Meheux. *PAR*

Beyond the Next Mountain ℒ **1987 (PG)** A missionary in China attempts to convert all those he meets. Thin plot and marginal acting will likely make viewers fall asleep. **97m/C VHS, Beta.** Alberto Isaac, Jon Lormer, Bennett Ohta, Richard Lineback, Edward Ashley, Barry Foster; ***D:*** James F. Collier, Rolf Forsberg. *NO*

Beyond the Poseidon Adventure **1979 (PG)** A sequel to the 1972 film in which salvage teams and ruthless looting vandals compete for access to the sunken ocean liner. Sinking ships should be abandoned. **115m/C VHS, Beta.** Michael Caine, Sally Field, Telly Savalas, Peter Boyle, Jack Warden, Slim Pickens, Shirley Knight, Shirley Jones, Karl Malden, Mark Harmon; ***D:*** Irwin Allen; ***C:*** Joseph Biroc. *WAR*

Beyond the Rockies ½ **1932** Keene and a group of cowboys battle cattle rustlers in this action-packed sagebrush saga. Solid script with good direction by Allen. **55m/B VHS.** Tom Keene, Rochelle Hudson, Ernie Adams, Julian Rivero, Hank Bell, Tom London; ***D:*** Fred Allen; ***W:*** John P. McCarthy. *MOV*

Beyond the Silhouette *Ultimate Desires* **1990** It starts out as another sleazy video sex thriller, as the lawyer heroine discovers her sensuality and poses a lot in her underclothes. Then in the third act it become a hyper-paranoid political-conspiracy assassination-o-rama. Pretty weird junk. **90m/C VHS, Beta.** *CA* Tracy Scoggins, Marc Singer, Brion James; ***D:*** Lloyd A. Simanol. *NO*

Beyond the Stars **1989** A sci-fi adventure directed by the author of "Cocoon," wherein a whiz-kid investigates the NASA cover-up of a deadly accident that occurred on the moon during the Apollo 11 landing. Unfortunately, the interesting cast can't make up for the script. **94m/C VHS, Beta, LV.** Martin Sheen, Christian Slater, Olivia D'Abo, F. Murray Abraham, Robert Foxworth, Sharon Stone; ***D:*** David Saperstein. *LIV*

Beyond the Time Barrier ½ **1960** Air Force test pilot gets more than he bargained for when his high speed plane carries him into the future. There he sees the ravages of an upcoming plague, to which he must return. **75m/B VHS, Beta.** Robert Clarke, Darlene Tompkins, Arianne Arden, Vladimir Sokoloff; ***D:*** Edgar G. Ulmer. *SNC, CNM*

Beyond the Trail **1926** One of Bill Patton's most entertaining and funny films. In this comedic Western adventure he must face Black Mike and his gang and rescue Mary from their clutches. **50m/C VHS.** Bill Patton, Sheldon Lewis, Stuart Holmes, Eric Wayne, Janet Dawn, Clara Horton, James F. Fulton; ***D:*** Al(bert) Herman. *GPV*

Beyond the Valley of the Dolls ½ **1970 (NC-17)** Sleazy, spirited nonsequel to "Valley of the Dolls." Meyer ("Faster, Pussycat! Kill! Kill!") directed this Hollywood parody ("BVD," as it came to be known) about an all-girl rock combo and their search for stardom. Labeled the first "exploitation horror camp musical"—how can you pass that up? Screenplay by film critic Ebert, from an original story by Ebert and Meyer. Mondo trasho. **109m/C VHS, Beta, LV.** Edy Williams, Dolly Reed; ***D:*** Russ Meyer; ***W:*** Roger Ebert. *FXV, BTV*

Beyond the Walls ½ *Meachorei Hasoragim* **1984 (R)** The opposing factions of a hellish Israeli prison unite to beat the system. Brutal with good characterizations. Available in both subtitled and dubbed versions. **104m/C VHS, Beta.** *IS* Arnon Zadok, Muhamad Bakri; ***D:*** Uri Barbash; ***W:*** Benny Barbash. Venice Film Festival '85: Best Film; Nominations: Academy Awards '84: Best Foreign Language Film. *WAR, INJ*

Beyond Therapy ½ **1986 (R)** A satire on modern psychotherapy, from the play by Christopher Durang, about a confused, crazily neurotic couple and their respective, and not any saner, analysts. Unfortunately, comes off as disjointed and confused. **93m/C VHS, Beta.** Jeff Goldblum, Tom Conti, Julie Hagerty, Glenda Jackson, Christopher Guest; ***D:*** Robert Altman; ***W:*** Robert Altman. *VTR, NWV*

Beyond Tomorrow **1940** Young romance is guided from the spirit world during the Christmas season, as two "ghosts" come back to help young lovers. **84m/B VHS, Beta.** Richard Carlson, Sir C. Aubrey Smith, Jean Parker, Charles Winninger, Harry Carey Sr., Maria Ouspenskaya, Rod La Rocque; ***D:*** Edward Sutherland. *SNC, NOS, DVT*

Bhaji on the Beach ½ **1994 (R)** Amusing comedy-drama about a group of Indian women who organize a bus outing from Birmingham to the seaside resort town of Blackpool. They range from sari-clad elders to feminist Gen Xers and a couple of teenagers looking for romance. There's bonding and gossiping and secrets galore before the story is tidily wrapped up. **100m/C VHS.** *GB* Kim Vithana, Jimmi Harkishin, Sarita Khajuria, Mo Sesay, Lalita Ahmed, Shaheen Khan; ***D:*** Gurinder Chadha; ***W:*** Meera Syal; ***C:*** John Kenway; ***M:*** John Altman, Craig Preuss. *COL*

Bhowani Junction **1956** A half-Indian, half-English woman is torn between her country and the British officer she loves in post-colonial India. Great cinematography. Based on a book by John Masters. **110m/C VHS, LV.** Ava Gardner, Stewart Granger, Bill Travers, Abraham Sofaer, Francis Matthews, Marne Maitland, Peter Illing, Edward Chapman, Freda Jackson, Lionel Jeffries; ***D:*** George Cukor; ***C:*** Frederick A. (Freddie) Young; ***M:*** Miklos Rozsa. *MGM*

The Bible...In the Beginning **1966** The book of Genesis is dramatized, including the stories of Adam and Eve, Cain and Abel, and Noah and the flood. **155m/C VHS, Beta, LV.** *IT* George C. Scott, Richard Harris, Stephen Boyd, John Huston, Peter O'Toole, Franco Nero, Ava Gardner; ***D:*** John Huston; ***C:*** Giuseppe Rotunno. National Board of Review Awards '66: 10 Best Films of the Year. *FOX*

The Bicycle Thief *Ladri di Biciclette* **1948** A world classic and indisputable masterpiece about an Italian workman who finds a job, only to have the bike he needs for work stolen; he and his son search Rome for it. A simple story that seems to contain the whole of human experience, and the masterpiece of Italian neo-realism. Based on the book by Luigi Bartolini. In Italian with English subtitles. **90m/B VHS, Beta, LV.** *IT* Lamberto Maggiorani, Lianella Carell, Enzo Staiola, Elena Altieri, Vittorio Antonucci, Gino Saltamerenda, Fausto Guerzoni; ***D:*** Vittorio De Sica; ***W:*** Cesare Zavattini. Academy Awards '49: Best Foreign Language Film; British Academy Awards '49: Best Film; Golden Globe Awards '50: Best Foreign Film; National Board of Review Awards '49: 5 Best Foreign Films of the Year, Best Director (De Sica); Nominations: Academy Awards '49: Best Screenplay. *INJ, NOS, MRV*

Big ½ **1988 (PG)** A 13-year-old boy makes a wish at a carnival fortune-teller to be "big." When he wakes up the next morning he finds that he suddenly won't fit into his clothes and his mother doesn't recognize him. Until he finds a cure, he must learn to live in the adult world—complete with job, apartment, and romance. Perkins is wonderful as a warming cynic while Hanks is totally believable as the little boy inside a man's body. Marshall directs with authority and the whole thing clicks from the beginning. **98m/C VHS, Beta, LV.** Tom Hanks, Elizabeth Perkins, John Heard, Robert Loggia, Jared Rushton, David Moscow, Jon Lovitz, Mercedes Ruehl; ***D:*** Penny Marshall; ***W:*** Gary Ross; ***M:*** Howard Shore. Golden Globe Awards '89: Best Actor—Musical/Comedy (Hanks); Los Angeles Film Critics Association Awards '88: Best Actor (Hanks); People's Choice Awards '89: Best Film—Musical/Comedy; Nominations: Academy Awards '88: Best Actor (Hanks), Best Original Screenplay. *FOX, HMV*

Big Bad John ½ **1990 (PG-13)** Some good ol' boys ride around in trucks as they get into a variety of shootouts. The soundtrack includes music by Willie Nelson, The Charlie Daniels Band, and others. **91m/C VHS, Beta, LV.** Jimmy Dean, Ned Beatty, Jack Elam, Bo Hopkins, Romy Windsor, Doug English. *IME*

Big Bad Mama ½ **1974 (R)** Tough and sexy machine-gun toting mother moves her two nubile daughters out of Texas during the Depression, and they all turn to robbing banks as a means of support while creating sharp testosterone increases among the local men. "Wild Palm" Dickinson has notable nude scene with Captain Kirk. "Big Bad Mama 2" arrived some 13 years later. **83m/C VHS, Beta.** Angie Dickinson, William Shatner, Tom Skerritt, Susan Sennett, Robbie Lee, Sally Kirkland, Noble Willingham, Royal Dano, Dick Miller; ***D:*** Steve Carver; ***W:*** William W. Norton Sr. *NO*

Big Bad Mama 2 ½ **1987 (R)** Belated Depression-era sequel to the 1974 Roger Corman gangster film, where the pistol-packin' matriarch battles a crooked politician with the help of her two daughters. **85m/C VHS, Beta.** Angie Dickinson, Robert Culp, Danielle Brisebois, Julie McCullough; ***D:*** Jim Wynorski; ***W:*** Jim Wynorski, R.J. Robertson. *MGM*

The Big Bet **1985 (R)** High school sex comedy about a guy who is challenged by the school bully to get the gorgeous new girl into bed. Energetic romp is for adults. **90m/C VHS, Beta.** Sylvia Kristel, Kimberly Evenson, Ron Thomas; ***D:*** Bert I. Gordon. *NO*

The Big Bird Cage *Women's Penitentiary 2* **1972 (R)** Prison spoof sequel to "The Big Doll House." Horny females incarcerated in a rural jail decide to defy their homosexual guards and plan an escape. They are aided by revolutionaries led by a Brooklynese expatriate and his lover. **93m/C VHS, Beta.** Pam Grier, Sid Haig, Anitra Ford, Candice Roman, Teda Bracci, Carol Speed, Karen McKevic; ***D:*** Jack Hill. *WAR*

The Big Blue ½ *Le Grand Bleu* **1988 (PG)** Vapid, semi-true tale about competing free-divers, who descend deep into the big blue without the aid of any kind of breathing apparatus. Arquette is the ditz who makes them come up for air. **122m/C VHS, Beta, LV.** Rosanna Arquette, Jean Reno, Jean-Marc Barr, Paul Shenar, Sergio Castellitto, Marc Duret, Griffin Dunne; ***D:*** Luc Besson; ***W:*** Luc Besson; ***M:*** Bill Conti. Cesar Awards '89: Best Sound, Best Score. *COL*

Big Bluff *Worthy Deceivers* **1955** Disappointing result from an interesting premise; fatally ill woman finds love, but when she surprisingly recovers, her new husband decides to help her back along the path to death. Uneven and melodramatic. **70m/B VHS.** *SI* John Bromfield, Martha Vickers, Robert Hutton, Rosemary Bowe; ***D:*** W. Lee Wilder. *NOS, MOV, HEG*

Big Boss ½ **1977 (R)** A hoodlum climbs to the top of a crime syndicate. An Italian film previously titled "Mr. Scarface." **90m/C Beta.** *IT* Jack Palance, Edmund Purdom, Al Cliver, Harry Baer, Gisela Hahn. *NO*

The Big Braodcast of 1938 ½ **1938** Fields is the owner of an ocean liner which he enters in a race. Supposedly, the ship can convert the electricity from radio broadcasts into power for the propellers. No, it doesn't make sense, as it's just an excuse for various radio stars to show off their routines in the ship's entertainment room. Hope, in his first feature, gets to sing his Oscar-winning signature tune "Thanks for the Memories." **94m/B VHS.** W.C. Fields, Martha Raye, Dorothy Lamour, Shirley Ross, Russell Hicks, Bob Hope, Ben Blue, Leif Erickson; ***D:*** Mitchell Leisen; ***W:*** Walter DeLeon, Francis Martin. Academy Awards '38: Best Song ("Thanks for the Memories"). *MCA*

The Big Brawl ½ **1980 (R)** Chicago gangster recruits a martial arts expert to fight in a free-for-all match in Texas. **95m/C VHS, Beta.** Jackie Chan, Jose Ferrer, Mako, Rosalind Chao; ***D:*** Robert Clouse; ***W:*** Robert Clouse; ***M:*** Lalo Schifrin. *WAR*

Big Bully **1995 (PG)** David Leary (Moranis) is an aspiring novelist who moves back to the town where he was picked on as a kid. His son immediately starts bullying a smaller child, whose father happens to be Roscoe "Fang" Bigger (Arnold), David's former tormentor. The timid hen-pecked Roscoe's sadistic streak is awakened with the reappearance of his old prey, leading to a barrage of wet willies and indian burns. The slapstick quickly escalates to danger before all is tied up in a syrupy sweet ending. With Moranis playing the nerdy bespectacled underdog and Arnold playing the loud obnoxious guy (although that might not be acting), it may be time to call the typecasting cops. Don Knotts (looking very un-Barney-like) makes an appearance as the high school principal. **93m/C VHS.** Tom Arnold, Rick Moranis, Julianne Phillips, Don Knotts, Carol Kane, Jeffrey Tambor, Curtis Armstrong, Faith Prince, Tony Pierce, Blake Bashoff; ***D:*** Steve Miner; ***W:*** Mark Steven Johnson; ***C:*** Daryn Okada; ***M:*** David Newman. *WAR*

The Big Bus **1976 (PG)** The wild adventures of the world's first nuclear-powered bus as it makes its maiden voyage from New York to Denver. Clumsy disaster-movie parody. **88m/C VHS, Beta.** Joseph Bologna, Stockard Channing, Ned Beatty, Ruth Gordon, Larry Hagman, John Beck, Jose Ferrer, Lynn Redgrave, Sally Kellerman, Stuart Margolin, Richard Mulligan, Howard Hesseman, Richard B. Shull; ***D:*** James Frawley; ***W:*** Lawrence J. Cohen; ***C:*** Harry Stradling Jr.; ***M:*** David Shire. *PAR*

Big Business **1988 (PG)** Strained high-concept comedy about two sets of identical twins, each played by Tomlin and Midler, mismatched at birth by a near-sighted country nurse. The city set of twins intends to buy out the factory where the country set of twins work. So the country twins march up to the big city to stop the sale and destruction of their beloved home. Both set of twins stay in the Plaza Hotel and zany consequences ensue. Essentially a one-joke outing with some funny moments, but talented comediennes Midler and Tomlin are somewhat wasted. Great technical effects. **98m/C VHS, Beta, LV, 8mm.** Bette Midler, Lily Tomlin, Fred Ward, Edward Herrmann, Michele Placido, Barry Primus, Michael Gross, Mary Gross, Daniel Gerroll, Roy Brocksmith; ***D:*** Jim Abrahams; ***C:*** Dean Cundey. *TOU*

Big Business Girl **1931** Less than remarkable comedy starring Young as a corporate climber who must dodge her boss' advances and save her troubled marriage when her jazz singer husband is called away to perform in Paris. Based on a story by Patricia Reilly and Harold N. Swanson. **72m/B VHS.** Loretta Young, Frank Albertson, Ricardo Cortez, Joan Blondell, Dorothy Christy; ***D:*** William A. Seiter; ***W:*** Robert Lord. *MGM*

The Big Bust Out *Woof!* **1973 (R)** Several female convicts escape from prison only to be sold into slavery and face additional torture. Nothing redeeming about this exploitative film. **75m/C VHS, Beta.** Vonetta McGee, Monica Taylor, Linda Fox, Karen Carter, Gordon Mitchell; ***D:*** Karen Carter. *SUE*

Big Calibre **1935** A rancher is inches away from being lynched for his dad's murder before he is found to be innocent. **59m/B VHS, Beta.** Bob Steele, Bill Quinn, Earl Dwire, Peggy Campbell, John Elliott, Georgia O'Dell; ***D:*** Robert North Bradbury. *SNC, DVT, HEG*

The Big Cat **1949** Mountain valley in Utah is ravaged by a cougar, while two ranchers fuss and feud. Big cat, bickering, help make okay adventure. **75m/C VHS, Beta.** Lon McCallister, Peggy Ann Garner, Preston Foster, Forrest Tucker; ***D:*** Phil Karlson; ***C:*** William Howard Greene. *NOS, MRV, DVT*

Big Chase **1954** A rookie cop chases down a mob of payroll thieves in this early action film. **60m/B VHS, Beta, LV.** Glenn Langan, Adele Jergens, Lon Chaney Jr., Jim Davis. *NO*

The Big Chill ½ **1983 (R)** Seven former '60s radicals, now coming upon middle age and middle class affluence, reunite on the occasion of an eighth friend's suicide and use the occasion to reexamine their past relationships and commitments. A beautifully acted, immensely enjoyable ballad to both the counter-culture and its Yuppie descendants. Great period music. Kevin Costner is the dead man whose scenes never made it to the big screen. **108m/C VHS, Beta, LV, 8mm.** Tom Berenger, Glenn Close, Jeff Goldblum, William Hurt, Kevin Kline, Mary Kay Place, Meg Tilly, JoBeth Williams; ***D:*** Lawrence Kasdan; ***W:*** Lawrence Kasdan, Barbara Benedek; ***C:*** John Bailey. Writers Guild of America '83: Best Original Screenplay; Nominations: Academy Awards '83: Best Original Screenplay, Best Picture, Best Supporting Actress (Close). *COL, CRC*

Big Combo **1955** A gangster's ex-girlfriend helps a cop to smash a crime syndicate. Focuses on the relationship between Wilde's cop and the gangster Conte in an effective film noir, with some scenes of torture that were ahead of their time. **87m/B VHS, Beta.** Cornel Wilde, Richard Conte, Jean Wallace, Brian Donlevy, Earl Holliman, Lee Van Cleef, Helen Walker; ***D:*** Joseph H. Lewis; ***W:*** Philip Yordan; ***C:*** John Alton. *PSM*

The Big Country ½ **1958 (R)** Ex-sea captain Peck heads west to marry fiance Baker and live on her father's (Bickford) ranch. Peck immediately clashes with ranch foreman Heston and finds out there's a vicious feud with neighbor Ives. Then Peck decides he and Baker aren't meant to be and he falls for schoolmarm Simmons instead. It's too long but if you like sprawling western sagas, this one has its moments. **168m/C VHS, Beta.** Gregory Peck, Charlton Heston, Burl Ives, Jean Simmons, Carroll Baker, Chuck Connors; ***D:*** William Wyler. Academy Awards '58: Best Supporting Actor (Ives); Golden Globe Awards '59: Best Supporting Actor (Ives); Nominations: Academy Awards '58: Best Original Score. *MGM, BTV*

The Big Crimewave **1986** A cast of unknowns in a comedy about a loner who takes a bus to Kansas City (Kansas City?) to become a screenwriter, with comic adventures along the way. A feast of jabs at genre films. **80m/C VHS, Beta.** *CA* John Paizs, Eva Covacs, Darrel Baran; ***D:*** John Paizs. *HHE*

Big Deadly Game ½ **1954** A vacationing American gets caught up in a complicated espionage plot by helping a mysterious wartime buddy. **63m/B VHS, Beta, LV.** Lloyd Bridges, Simone Silva, Finlay Currie. *NO*

Big Deal on Madonna Street ½ *The Usual Unidentified Thieves* **1958** A band of inept crooks plan to make themselves very rich when they attempt to rob a jewelry store. Their elaborate plans cause numerous (and hilarious) disasters. In Italian with English subtitles. Remade as "Crackers." **90m/B VHS, Beta.** *IT* Marcello Mastroianni, Vittorio Gassman, Claudia Cardinale; ***D:*** Mario Monicelli. Nominations: Academy Awards '58: Best Foreign Language Film. *INJ, CVC, MRV*

The Big Dis **1989** An interracial comedy about a young black soldier on a weekend pass who's looking for a willing sexual partner. His confidence is shattered when 12 possibilities turn him down. Feature debut of Eriksen and O'Brien. **88m/B VHS.** ***D:*** Gordon Eriksen, John O'Brien. *FCT, ICA*

The Big Doll House *Women's Penitentiary 1; Women in Cages* **1971 (R)** Roger Corman-produced prison drama about a group of tormented female convicts who decide to break out. Features vintage Grier, and a caliber of women's-prison sleaziness that isn't equalled in today's films. **93m/C VHS, Beta.** Judy Brown, Roberta Collins, Pam Grier, Brooke Mills, Pat Woodell, Sid Haig, Christianne Schmidtmer, Kathryn Loder; ***D:*** Jack Hill; ***M:*** Les Baxter. *SUE, NLC*

The Big Easy ½ **1987 (R)** A terrific thriller. A slick New Orleans detective uncovers a heroin-based mob war while romancing the uptight assistant DA who's investigating corruption on the police force. An easy, Cajun-flavored mystery, a fast-moving action-comedy, a very sexy romance, and a serious exploration of the dynamics of corruption. **101m/C VHS, Beta, LV.** Dennis Quaid, Ellen Barkin, Ned Beatty, John Goodman, Ebbe Roe Smith, Charles Ludlam, Lisa Jane Persky, Tom O'Brien, Grace Zabriskie; ***D:*** Jim McBride; ***W:*** Dan Petrie Jr.; ***M:*** Brad Fiedel. Independent Spirit Awards '88: Best Actor (Quaid). *HBO, FCT*

The Big Fix **1978 (PG)** Private investigator Moses Wine finds himself in an ironic situation: searching for a fugitive alongside whom he'd protested in the 60s. Based on a Roger Simon novel. **108m/C VHS, Beta.** Richard Dreyfuss, Susan Anspach, Bonnie Bedelia, John Lithgow, F. Murray Abraham, Fritz Weaver, Mandy Patinkin; ***D:*** Jeremy Paul Kagan; ***M:*** Bill Conti. *MCA*

Big Foot *Woof!* **1972** Even genre devotees will be disappointed with this one. Sasquatch, who has procreation on his mind, searches rather half-heartedly for a human mate. A horror flick that forgot to include the horror. **92m/C VHS, Beta.** Chris Mitchum, Joi Lansing, John Carradine, John Mitchum; ***D:*** Bob Slatzer. *NO*

The Big Gag **1987 (R)** An international group of comedians travel the world and pull gags on people. Lame. **84m/C VHS, Beta.** *TWE, HHE*

Big Girls Don't Cry...They Get Even ½ **1992 (PG)** A teenage girl decides to run away from home after she's driven crazy by her eccentric new stepfamily. Comic confusion ensues as various family members set out to find her. Hackneyed script and annoying characters hinder this comedy. **98m/C VHS, LV.** Hillary Wolf, Griffin Dunne, Margaret Whitton, David Strathairn, Ben Savage, Adrienne Shelly, Patricia Kalember; ***D:*** Joan Micklin Silver. *COL, NLC*

The Big Grab ½ **1963** A dark big caper thriller about a couple of aging French thugs determined to rip off a casino at Cannes. In French with English subtitles. Also called "Any Number Can Win." **118m/B VHS, Beta.** *FR* Jean Gabin, Alain Delon, Viviane Romance, Maurice Biraud, Carla Marlier; ***D:*** Henri Verneuil. *FCT*

The Big Green ½ **1995 (PG)** British teacher Anna Montgomery (D'Abo) blows into a small Texas town determined to give the deprived kiddies a boost of self-esteem. With help from the town sheriff (Guttenberg), Anna organizes a soccer team that's supposed to give the kids a reason to live. Problems abound when the star player disappears just before the face-off with the biggest, nastiest team in the league. Sound familiar? This is the soccer version of "The Bad News Bears," "The Little Giants," and "The Mighty Ducks." The formula is less successful in this case, but some mildly amusing moments and a few fresh performances from the kids offer minor bright spots in this tired scenario. **100m/C VHS, LV.** Olivia D'Abo, Steve Guttenberg, Jay O. Sanders, John Terry, Chauncey Leopardi, Patrick Renna, Billy L. Sullivan, Yareli Arizmendi, Bug Hall; ***D:*** Holly Goldberg Sloan; ***W:*** Holly Goldberg Sloan; ***C:*** Ralf Bode; ***M:*** Randy Edelman. *TOU*

A Big Hand for the Little Lady ½ *Big Deal at Dodge City* **1966** Fonda and Woodward, playing two West-headed country bumpkins, get involved in a card game in Laredo against high rollers Robards and McCarthy. Fonda risks their savings, finds himself stuck with a losing hand, and has a bit of heart trouble; that's where the little lady comes in. Fine performances and a nifty twist ending don't entirely compensate for the overly-padded script (which evolved from a 48-minute TV play drafted by Sydney Carroll). **95m/C VHS, Beta.** Henry Fonda, Joanne Woodward, Jason Robards Jr., Charles Bickford, Burgess Meredith, Kevin McCarthy; ***D:*** Fielder Cook; ***C:*** Lee Garmes. *WAR, FCT*

The Big Hangover **1950** Odd story about a man whose allergy to alcohol makes him drunk at the most inopportune moments. Johnson stars as the attorney with the peculiar problem and Taylor plays the boss' daughter who helps him overcome the allergy. Good supporting cast can't help this otherwise boring and predictable film. **82m/B VHS.** Van Johnson, Elizabeth Taylor, Percy Waram, Fay Holden, Leon Ames, Edgar Buchanan, Selena Royle, Gene Lockhart; ***D:*** Norman Krasna; ***W:*** Norman Krasna. *MGM*

The Big Heat ½ **1953** When detective Ford's wife (played by Jocelyn Brando, sister of Marlon) is killed in an explosion meant for him, he pursues the gangsters behind it and uncovers a police scandal. His appetite is whetted after this discovery and he pursues the criminals even more vigorously with the help of gangster moll Gloria Grahame. Definitive film noir. **90m/B VHS, Beta, LV.** Glenn Ford, Lee Marvin, Gloria Grahame, Jocelyn Brando, Alexander Scourby, Carolyn Jones; ***D:*** Fritz Lang; ***C:*** Charles B(ryant) Lang. Edgar Allan Poe Awards '53: Best Screenplay. *COL*

The Big House **1930** Prison melodrama at its best follows top con Beery as he plans a big breakout—and is betrayed. Life in the pen is depicted as brutal and futile, with sadistic guards and a hapless warden. Spawned numerous imitators. **80m/B VHS.** Wallace Beery, Chester Morris, Robert Montgomery, Lewis Stone, Leila Hyams, George F. Marion Sr., Karl Dane, DeWitt Jennings; ***D:*** George Hill; ***W:*** Frances Marion. *MGM*

The Big Hurt ½ **1987 (R)** A reporter investigating a bizarre double murder discovers a secret government agency involved in torture and mind-control. **90m/C VHS, Beta, LV.** *AU* David Bradshaw, Lian Lunson, Simon Chilvers, Nick Wateres; ***D:*** Barry Peak. *NO*

Big Jake 🦴🦴 **1971 (PG)** An aging Texas cattle man who has outlived his time swings into action when outlaws kidnap his grandson and wound his son. He returns to his estranged family to help them in the search for Little Jake. O'Hara is once again paired up with Wayne and the chemistry is still there. **90m/C VHS, Beta, LV.** John Wayne, Richard Boone, Maureen O'Hara, Patrick Wayne, Chris Mitchum, Bobby Vinton; ***D:*** George Sherman; ***C:*** William Clothier; ***M:*** Elmer Bernstein. *FOX*

Big Jim McLain 🦴🦴 **1952** Wayne and Arness are federal agents working on behalf of the House Un-American Activities Committee to eliminate communist terrorism in Hawaii. And there's a suspicious psychiatrist, too: Wayne falls for a babe whose boss is a shrink who doesn't quite seem on the level. Definitely not a highpoint in the Duke's career. **90m/C VHS, LV.** John Wayne, Nancy Olson, James Arness, Veda Ann Borg; ***D:*** Edward Ludwig; ***C:*** Archie Stout. *WAR, FCT*

The Big Knife 🦴🦴🦴 **1955** Palance plays a Hollywood superstar who refuses to renew his studio contract, which enrages studio boss Steiger. It seems Steiger knows a very damaging secret about the star and is willing to go to any lengths to have Palance re-sign or wind up destroying himself. A ruthless, emotional look at fame and power, with excellent performances by all. Based on the play by Clifford Odets. **113m/B LV.** Jack Palance, Rod Steiger, Ida Lupino, Shelley Winters, Wendell Corey, Jean Hagen, Ilka Chase, Everett Sloane, Wesley Addy, Paul Langton; ***D:*** Robert Aldrich; ***C:*** Ernest Laszlo. *FCT*

The Big Lift 🦴🦴½ **1950** Two G.I.'s assigned to the Berlin airlift ally themselves in counter-intelligence when they discover that their mutual girlfriend is a spy. **119m/B VHS, Beta.** Montgomery Clift, Paul Douglas, Cornell Borchers, Bruni Lobel, O.E. Hasse; ***D:*** George Seaton. *NOS, MRV, DVT*

The Big Man: Crossing the Line 🦴🦴🦴 *Crossing the Line* **1991 (R)** Neeson shines as a down on his luck Scottish miner who loses his job during a union strike. Desperate for cash and unable to resolve his bitterness at being unable to support his family, he's enticed by a Glasgow hood to fight in an illegal bare-knuckled boxing match. What follows is an overlong and extremely brutal fight. Good performances from a talented cast overcome a rather preachy script that doesn't disguise its contempt for the Thatcher government, but also allows a glimpse into the tough times that many Brits suffered during the '80s. Based on the novel by William McIlvanney. **93m/C VHS, LV.** *GB* Liam Neeson, Joanne Whalley, Ian Bannen, Billy Connolly, Hugh Grant, Maurice Roeves, Rob Affleck; ***D:*** David Leland; ***W:*** Don MacPherson; ***M:*** Ennio Morricone. *COL*

Big Man on Campus 🦴 **1989 (PG-13)** A modern-day Quasimodo makes his home in an affluent university's belltower. Of course he falls in love with one of the pretty young co-eds and races out of his tower only to be captured by the psychology department. Really, really bad. **102m/C VHS, Beta, LV.** Tom Skerritt, Corey Parker, Allan Katz, Cindy Williams, Melora Hardin, Jessica Harper; ***D:*** Jeremy Paul Kagan. *VES*

Big Meat Eater 🦴🦴 **1985** A musical gore-comedy about extraterrestrials using radioactive butcher's discards for ship fuel. Deliberate camp that is so bad its funny! **81m/C VHS, Beta.** *CA* George Dawson, Big Miller, Andrew Gillies; ***D:*** Chris Windsor. *MED*

Big Mo 🦴🦴 *Mauri* **1973 (G)** True story of the friendship that developed between Cincinnati Royals basketball stars Maurice Stokes and Jack Twyman after a strange paralysis hit Stokes. **110m/C VHS, Beta.** Bernie Casey, Bo Svenson, Stephanie Edwards, Janet MacLachlan; ***D:*** Daniel Mann. *VES*

Big Mouth 🦴 **1967** A dopey fisherman gets ahold of a treasure map and is pursued by cops and gangsters. Standard Lewis fare, with the requisite infantile histrionics; must be French to appreciate. **107m/C VHS, Beta.** Jerry Lewis, Jeannine Riley, Harold J. Stone, Charlie Callas, Buddy Lester, Susan Bay; ***D:*** Jerry Lewis; ***W:*** Jerry Lewis; ***M:*** Harry Betts. *COL*

Big News 🦴🦴 **1929** Based on the play "For Two Cents" by George S. Brooks, this early talkie uses sound to great advantage. Fired for going after a gangster who's a big advertiser (Hardy), reporter Armstrong nevertheless keeps after the crook. When the intrepid reporter pushes too far, murder enters the picture. **75m/B VHS.** Robert Armstrong, Carole Lombard, Tom Kennedy, Warner Richmond, Wade Boteler, Sam Hardy, Lew Ayres; ***D:*** Gregory La Cava. *NOS*

Big Night 🦴🦴½ **1995 (R)** Set in '50s New Jersey, film provides an Old World/New World look at Italian brothers Primo (Shalhoub) and Secondo (Tucci) Pilaggi and their elegant but failing restaurant. Primo is the perfectionist chef who hates compromise while Secondo wants to Americanize the place in an effort to make it a success. (He knows the customer is always right even if they can't appreciate Primo's exquisitely authentic Italian dishes). In order to get attention, Secondo arranges a special night in honor of jazz great Louis Prima, with Primo out to cook the feast of a lifetime—if they can pull it off. Another food film guaranteed to make you hungry. **107m/C VHS.** Tony Shalhoub, Stanley Tucci, Ian Holm, Minnie Driver, Campbell Scott, Isabella Rossellini, Mark Anthony, Allison Janney; ***D:*** Stanley Tucci, Campbell Scott; ***W:*** Stanley Tucci, Joseph Tropiano; ***C:*** Ken Kelsch. Sundance Film Festival '96: Best Screenplay. *NYR*

The Big Parade 🦴🦴🦴🦴 **1925** Wonderful WWI silent, considered to be one of the best war flicks of all time. Gilbert and Adoree are exceptional as lovers torn apart by the conflict. Interesting and thoughtful picture of the trauma and trouble brought to men and their loved ones in wartime. Battle scenes are compelling and intense; Vidor's masterpiece. **141m/B VHS, LV.** John Gilbert, Renee Adoree, Hobart Bosworth, Claire McDowell, Claire Adams, Karl Dane, Tom O'Brien; ***D:*** King Vidor. *MGM*

The Big Picture 🦴🦴½ **1989 (PG-13)** A hilarious, overlooked comedy by and starring a variety of Second City/National Lampoon alumni, about a young filmmaker who is contracted by a big studio, only to see his vision trampled by formula-minded producers, crazed agents, hungry starlets, and every other variety of Hollywood predator. **95m/C VHS, Beta, LV.** Kevin Bacon, Jennifer Jason Leigh, Martin Short, Michael McKean, Emily Longstreth, J.T. Walsh, Eddie Albert, Richard Belzer, John Cleese, June Lockhart, Stephen Collins, Roddy McDowall, Kim Miyori, Teri Hatcher, Dan Schneider, Jason Gould, Tracy Brooks Swope; ***D:*** Christopher Guest; ***W:*** Christopher Guest, Michael McKean, Michael Varhol; ***M:*** David Nichtern. *COL*

The Big Push 🦴½ *Timber Tramps* **1975 (PG)** Motley bunch of Alaskan lumberjacks get together to save a poor widow's logging camp from a pair of greedy mill owners. **98m/C VHS, Beta.** Joseph Cotten, Claude Akins, Cesar Romero, Tab Hunter, Roosevelt Grier, Leon Ames, Stubby Kaye, Patricia Medina; ***D:*** Tay Garnett. *GEM*

Big Red 🦴🦴½ **1962** Set amid the spectacular beauty of Canada's Quebec Province, an orphan boy protects a dog which later saves him from a mountain lion. **89m/C VHS, Beta.** Walter Pidgeon, Gilles Payant; ***D:*** Norman Tokar; ***C:*** Edward Colman. *DIS*

The Big Red One 🦴🦴🦴½ **1980 (PG)** Fuller's harrowing, intense semi-autobiographical account of the U.S. Army's famous First Infantry Division in WWII, the "Big Red One." A rifle squad composed of four very young men, led by the grizzled Marvin, cut a fiery path of conquest from the landing in North Africa to the liberation of the concentration camp at Falkenau, Czechoslovakia. In part a tale of lost innocence, the film scores highest by bringing the raw terror of war down to the individual level. **113m/C VHS, Beta, LV.** Lee Marvin, Robert Carradine, Mark Hamill, Stephane Audran; ***D:*** Samuel Fuller; ***W:*** Samuel Fuller. Nominations: Cannes Film Festival '80: Best Film. *FOX, WAR*

The Big Scam 🦴🦴½ *A Nightingale Sang in Berkeley Square; The Mayfair Bank Caper* **1979** Criminal mastermind Niven recruits ex-con Jordan to pull off a massive bank heist. **102m/C VHS.** Richard Jordan, David Niven, Oliver Tobias, Elke Sommer, Gloria Grahame, Hugh Griffith, Richard Johnson; ***D:*** Ralph Thomas. *SIM*

Big Score 🦴 **1983 (R)** When a policeman is falsely accused and dismissed from the Chicago Police Department, he goes after the men who really stole the money from a drug bust. Script was originally intended to be a Dirty Harry flick; too bad it wasn't. **88m/C VHS, Beta.** Fred Williamson, John Saxon, Richard Roundtree, Nancy Wilson, Ed Lauter, Ron Dean, D'Urville Martin, Michael Dante, Joe Spinell; ***D:*** Fred Williamson. *VES*

Big Shots 🦴 **1987 (PG-13)** Two kids, one naive and white, the other black and streetwise, search for a stolen watch. **91m/C VHS, Beta, LV.** Ricky Busker, Darius McCrary, Robert Joy, Paul Winfield, Robert Prosky, Jerzy Skolimowski; ***D:*** Robert Mandel; ***W:*** Joe Eszterhas; ***M:*** Bruce Broughton. *ORI, WAR*

Big Show 🦴🦴 *Home In Oklahoma* **1937** A western adventure about the making of a western adventure. Autry jangles spurs aplenty in duel role. **54m/B VHS, Beta.** Gene Autry, Smiley Burnette; ***D:*** Mack V. Wright. *NOS, VCN, VDM*

The Big Sky 🦴🦴🦴 **1952** It's 1830, and a rowdy band of fur trappers embark upon a back breaking expedition up the uncharted Missouri River. Based on the A.B. Guthrie Jr. novel, it's an effortlessly enjoyable and level-headed Hawksian American myth, with a streak of gentle gallows humor. Also available colorized. **122m/C VHS, Beta.** Kirk Douglas, Dewey Martin, Arthur Hunnicutt, Elizabeth Threatt, Buddy Baer, Steve Geray, Jim Davis; ***D:*** Howard Hawks. Nominations: Academy Awards '52: Best Black and White Cinematography, Best Supporting Actor (Hunnicutt). *FCT, TTC*

The Big Sleep 🦴🦴🦴🦴 **1946** Private eye Philip Marlowe, hired to protect a young woman from her own indiscretions, falls in love with her older sister while uncovering murders galore. A dense, chaotic thriller that succeeded in defining and setting a standard for its genre. The very best Raymond Chandler on film combining a witty script with great performances, especially from Bogart and Bacall. **114m/B VHS, Beta, LV.** Humphrey Bogart, Lauren Bacall, John Ridgely, Martha Vickers, Louis Jean Heydt, Regis Toomey, Peggy Knudsen, Dorothy Malone, Bob Steele, Elisha Cook Jr.; ***D:*** Howard Hawks; ***W:*** William Faulkner, Jules Furthman, Leigh Brackett; ***M:*** Max Steiner. *MGM, FOX, TLF*

The Big Sleep 🦴🦴 **1978 (R)** A tired remake of the Raymond Chandler potboiler about exhausted Los Angeles private dick Marlowe and his problems in protecting a wild young heiress from her own decadence and mob connections. Mitchum appears to need a rest. **99m/C VHS, Beta, LV.** Robert Mitchum, Sarah Miles, Richard Boone, Candy Clark, Edward Fox, Joan Collins, John Mills, James Stewart, Oliver Reed, Harry Andrews, James Donald, Colin Blakely, Richard Todd; ***D:*** Michael Winner; ***W:*** Michael Winner. *COL*

The Big Slice 🦴½ **1990 (R)** Two would-be crime novelists want to improve their fiction. One masquerades as a cop, the other as a crook, and they infiltrate the underworld from both ends. Clever comedy premise, but vaudeville-level jokes fall flat. **86m/C VHS, LV.** Casey Siemaszko, Leslie Hope, Justin Louis, Heather Locklear, Kenneth Welsh, Nicholas Campbell, Henry Ramer; ***D:*** John Bradshaw; ***W:*** John Bradshaw; ***M:*** Mychael Danna, Jeff Danna. *ACA*

The Big Sombrero 🦴🦴½ **1949** Autry takes a stand against the marriage between an unsuspecting, wealthy Mexican girl and the fortune-seeking bridegroom who wants her land. **77m/C VHS.** Gene Autry, Elena Verdugo, Steve Dunne, George Lewis; ***D:*** Frank McDonald. *NO*

Big Stakes 🦴 **1922** Extremely rare Western feature that has a Texas cowboy falling for a Mexican senorita. Plenty of action as complications ensue. **?m/B VHS.** H.B. Warner, Elinor Fair, Les Bates; ***D:*** Clifford S. Elfelt; ***W:*** Frank Howard Clark. *GVV*

The Big Stampede 🦴🦴 **1932** Twenty-five year old Wayne stars in this action-packed Western that was a remake of "Land Beyond the Law" from Ken Maynard's silent. Based on a story by Marion Jackson. **63m/B VHS.** John Wayne, Noah Beery Sr., Luis Alberni, Berton Churchill, Paul Hurst, Lafe McKee, Frank Ellis, Hank Bell; ***D:*** Tenny Wright; ***W:*** Kurt Kempler. *MGM, GPV*

Big Steal 🦴🦴🦴 **1949** An Army officer recovers a missing payroll and captures the thieves after a tumultuous chase through Mexico. **72m/B VHS, Beta, LV.** Robert Mitchum, William Bendix, Jane Greer, Ramon Novarro, Patric Knowles; ***D:*** Donald Siegel. *MED*

Big Store 🦴🦴½ **1941** Late Marx Brothers in which they are detectives in a large metropolitan department store, foiling a hostile takeover and preventing a murder. Their last MGM effort, with some good moments between the Tony Martin song numbers which include "If It's You" and the immortal "Tenement Symphony." Groucho also leads the "Sing While You Sell" number. **96m/B VHS, Beta.** Groucho Marx, Harpo Marx, Chico Marx, Tony Martin, Margaret Dumont, Virginia Grey, Virginia O'Brien; ***D:*** Charles Riesner; ***M:*** George Bassman. *MGM, CCB*

Big Street 🦴🦴½ **1942** A timid busboy, in love with a disinterested nightclub singer, gets to prove his devotion when she is crippled in a fall. Based on a Damon Runyon story, "Little Pinks." **88m/B VHS, Beta, LV.** Henry Fonda, Lucille Ball, Agnes Moorehead, Louise Beavers, Barton MacLane, Eugene Pallette, Ozzie Nelson; ***D:*** Irving Reis. *MED, TTC*

The Big Sweat 🦴 **1990** Maybe you've heard this one before: a man who has been framed by the mob escapes from prison and heads for Mexico. But first, he's got to get past the mobsters and police who are hot on his trail. And maybe you've seen some of it before: some of the same stock footage appears in Lommel's "Cold Heat." Not surprisingly, this one bypassed theaters and went straight to video. **85m/C VHS, LV.** Robert Z'Dar, Steve Molone, Kevin McBride, William Roebuck, Cheri Caspari, David Rushing, Joanne Watkins, Ken Letner; ***D:*** Ulli Lommel; ***W:*** Max Bolt; ***M:*** John Massari. *AIP*

The Big Switch 🦴½ *Strip Poker* **1970 (R)** Gambler is framed for murder and becomes embroiled in a plot to reinstate an old gangster kingpin. **68m/C VHS, Beta.** Sebastian Breaks, Virginia Wetherell, Erika Raffael; ***D:*** Pete Walker. *NO*

Big Top Pee Wee 🦴🦴 **1988 (PG)** Pee Wee's second feature film following the success of "Pee Wee's Big Adventure." This time Pee Wee owns a farm, has a girlfriend (!) and lives the good life until a weird storm blows a traveling circus onto his property. Cute, but not the manic hilarity the first one was. **86m/C VHS, Beta, LV, 8mm.** Paul (Pee Wee Herman) Reubens, Kris Kristofferson, Susan Tyrrell, Penelope Ann Miller; ***D:*** Randal Kleiser; ***W:*** Paul (Pee Wee Herman) Reubens; ***C:*** Steven Poster; ***M:*** Danny Elfman. *PAR*

Big Town 🦴 *Guilty Assignment* **1947** A newspaper is saved by a new editor who brings integrity to the once scandalous paper. The editor and his reporters also solve a series of murders. Some action, but weak dialogue and direction hold it back. Based on the radio program of the same name. **59m/B VHS.** Philip Reed, Hillary Brooke, Robert Lowery, Byron Barr, Veda Ann Borg, Nana Bryant, Charles Arnt; ***D:*** William C. Thomas. *SNC*

Big Town 🦴🦴 **1987 (R)** A farmboy, lucky with dice, hits Chicago to claim his fortune where he meets floozies, criminals, and other streetlife. Look for Lane's strip number. **109m/C VHS, Beta, LV.** Matt Dillon, Diane Lane, Tommy Lee Jones, Bruce Dern, Tom Skerritt, Lee Grant, Suzy Amis; ***D:*** Ben Bolt; ***C:*** Ralf Bode. *VES, LIV*

Big Town After Dark 🦴🦴 *Underworld After Dark* **1947** Daring journalists search for the bottom-line story on a gang of criminals. They find themselves caught behind the firing lines when the sun goes down. Slightly better than average thriller. **69m/B VHS.** Philip Reed, Hillary Brooke, Richard Travis, Ann Gillis; ***D:*** William C. Thomas. *NOS, SNC, RXM*

Big Trail 🦴🦴🦴 **1930** This pioneering effort in wide-screen cinematography was Wayne's first feature film. A wagon train on the Oregon trail encounters Indians, buffalo, tough terrain, and romantic problems. **110m/B VHS, Beta.** John Wayne, Marguerite Churchill, El Brendel, Tully Marshall, Tyrone Power Sr., Ward Bond, Helen Parrish; ***D:*** Raoul Walsh. *FOX*

Big Trees 🦴🦴🦴 **1952** A ruthless lumberman attempts a takeover of the California Redwood Timberlands that are owned by a group of peaceful homesteaders. **89m/C VHS, Beta.** Kirk Douglas, Patrice Wymore, Eve Miller, Alan Hale Jr., Edgar Buchanan; ***D:*** Felix Feist. *NOS, MRV, DVT*

Big Trouble 🦴🦴 **1986 (R)** An insurance broker endeavors to send his three sons to Yale by conspiring with a crazy couple in a fraud scheme that goes awry in every possible manner. Look for the cameo by screenwriter Bergman as Warren Bogle. **93m/C VHS, Beta, LV.** Alan Arkin, Peter Falk, Beverly D'Angelo, Charles Durning, Robert Stack, Paul Dooley, Valerie Curtin, Richard Libertini; ***Cameos:*** Andrew Bergman; ***D:*** John Cassavetes; ***W:*** Andrew Bergman; ***M:*** Bill Conti. *COL*

Big Trouble in Little China 🦴🦴½ **1986 (PG-13)** A trucker plunges beneath the streets of San Francisco's Chinatown to battle an army of spirits. An uproarious comic-book-film parody with plenty of action and a keen sense of sophomoric sarcasm. **99m/C VHS, Beta, LV.** Kurt Russell, Suzze Pai, Dennis Dun, Kim Cattrall, James Hong, Victor Wong, Kate Burton; ***D:*** John Carpenter; ***W:*** Gary Goldman, W.D. Richter; ***C:*** Dean Cundey; ***M:*** John Carpenter, Alan Howarth. *FXV, FOX*

Big Valley **1968** The western television series's two feature-length episodes: "Explosion," and "Legend of a General." **90m/C VHS, Beta.** Richard Long, Linda Evans, Barbara Stanwyck, Lee Majors. *NO*

Big Wednesday 🦴🦴½ *Summer of Innocence* **1978 (PG)** Three California surfers from the early sixties get back together after the Vietnam war to reminisce about the good old days and take on the big wave. **120m/C VHS, Beta, LV.** Jan-Michael Vincent, Gary Busey, William Katt, Lee Purcell, Patti D'Arbanville; ***D:*** John Milius; ***W:*** John Milius; ***M:*** Basil Poledouris. *WAR*

The Big Wheel 🦴🦴½ **1949** Old story retold fairly well. Rooney is young son determined to travel in his father's tracks as a race car driver, even when dad buys the farm on the oval. Good acting and direction keep this a cut above average. **92m/B VHS.** Mickey Rooney, Thomas Mitchell, Spring Byington, Mary Hatcher, Allen Jenkins, Michael O'Shea; ***D:*** Edward Ludwig. *GPV*

Big Zapper 🦴½ **1973** Violent P.I. Marlowe and masochistic assistant Rock work together in this British comic strip film. **94m/C VHS.** *GB* Linda Marlowe, Gary Hope, Sean Hewitt, Richard Monette, Penny Irving; ***D:*** Lindsay Shonteff. *VCD*

The Bigamist 🦴½ **1953** Have you heard the one about the traveling salesman in this movie? He has one wife in Los Angeles, another in San Francisco, and they inevitably find out about each other. A maudlin soap opera with a do-it-yourself ending, only shows why bigamy was done better as farce in the later "Micki and Maude." **79m/B VHS.** Edmond O'Brien, Joan Fontaine, Ida Lupino, Edmund Gwenn, Jane Darwell, Kenneth Tobey; ***D:*** Ida Lupino. *DVT, NOS, HEG*

Bigfoot: The Unforgettable Encounter 🦴🦴½ **1994 (PG)** Young boy heads off into the woods, comes face to face with Bigfoot, and sets off a media frenzy and a band of ruthless bounty hunters determined to capture his hairy friend. **89m/C VHS.** Zachery Ty Bryan, Matt McCoy, Barbara Willis Sweete, Clint Howard, Rance Howard, David Rasche; ***D:*** Corey Michael Eubanks; ***W:*** Corey Michael Eubanks; ***M:*** Shimon Arama. *REP*

Biggles 🦴🦴 *Biggles: Adventures in Time* **1985 (PG)** Time-travel fantasy in which a young businessman from present-day New York City is inexplicably transferred into the identity of a 1917 WWI flying ace. He suddenly finds himself aboard a fighter plane over Europe during WWI. **100m/C VHS, Beta, LV.** *GB* Neil Dickson, Alex Hyde-White, Peter Cushing; ***D:*** John Hough. *VTR, NWV*

Bikers, Blondes, and Blood **1993** A montage of the sleaze genre's greatest moments including a clip from Jayne Mansfield's "Single Room Furnished." Suitable for dorm keggers, frat parties or any other venue where the audience has supplementary amusements available. Some clips in black and white. **90m/B VHS.** *SMW, TPV*

Bikini Beach 🦴🦴½ **1964** Surfing teenagers of the "Beach Party" series follow up "Muscle Beach Party" with a third fling at the beach and welcome a visitor, British recording star "Potato Bug" (Avalon in a campy dual role). But, golly gee, wealthy Wynn wants to turn their sandy, surfin' shores into a retirement community. What to do? Sing a few songs, dance in your bathing suits, and have fun. Classic early '60s nostalgia is better than the first two efforts; followed by "Pajama Party." ♫Because You're You; Love's a Secret Weapon; Bikini Drag. **100m/C VHS, Beta.** Annette Funicello, Frankie Avalon, Martha Hyer, Harvey Lembeck, Don Rickles, Stevie Wonder, John Ashley, Keenan Wynn, Jody McCrea, Candy Johnson, Danielle Aubry, Meredith MacRae, Dolores Wells, Donna Loren, Timothy Carey; ***D:*** William Asher; ***W:*** William Asher, Leo Townsend, Robert Dillon; ***C:*** Floyd Crosby; ***M:*** Les Baxter. *SUE*

Bikini Bistro 🦴 **1994 (R)** A boring vegetarian cafe gets turned into a gourmet restaurant but, faced with an eviction notice, the female owners decide to increase business by waitressing in bikinis. Also available in an unrated version at 84 minutes. **80m/C VHS.** Marilyn Chambers, Amy Lynn Baxter, Joan Gerardi, Isabelle Fortea, John Altamura, Joseph Pallister; ***D:*** Ernest G. Sauer; ***W:*** Matt Unger. *AVI*

The Bikini Car Wash Company *Woof!* *California Hot Wax* **1990 (R)** Babes in bikinis in Los Angeles. A young man is running his uncle's carwash when he meets a business major who persuades him to let her take over the business for a cut of the profits. She decides that a good gimmick would be to dress all the female employees in the tiniest bikinis possible. The story is of course secondary to the amount of flesh on display. Also available in an unrated version. **87m/C VHS.** Joe Dusic, Neriah Napaul, Suzanne Browne, Kristie Ducati; ***D:*** Ed Hansen. *IMP*

The Bikini Car Wash Company 2 🦴 **1992 (R)** Entrepreneur Melissa and the other lovely ladies of the Bikini Car Wash Co. find themselves a big success, so much so that a greedy businessman wants to buy them out. In order to get money to fight the takeover, the ladies take to the airwaves of a cable-access station. Their new business adventure involves selling sexy lingerie which means the flesh quotient is as great as ever. An unrated version is also available. **?m/C VHS, LV.** Kristie Ducati, Suzanne Browne, Neriah Napaul, Rikki Brando, Greg Raye, Larry De Russy; ***D:*** Gary Orona; ***W:*** Bart B. Gustis; ***M:*** Michael Smith. *IMP*

Bikini Drive-In 🦴½ **1994 (R)** Babe (Rhey) inherits grandad's decrepit drive-in, which is wanted by a mall mogul, but she refuses to sell. So to raise some cash, Rhey stages a B-movie marathon with in-person, bikini-clad scream queens. **85m/C VHS.** Ashlie Rhey, Richard Gabai, Ross Hagen, Sara Bellomo, Steve Barkett, Conrad Brooks; ***D:*** Fred Olen Ray. *AVI*

Bikini Island 🦴 **1991 (R)** Beautiful swimsuit models gather on a remote tropical island for a big photo shoot, each vying to be the next cover girl of the hottest swimsuit magazine. Before long, scantily clad lovelies are turning up dead and full out madness ensues. Will the mystery be solved before they run out of models, or will the magazine have no choice but to grace its cover with a bikinied cadaver? Low-budget trash that has few, if any, redeeming qualities. **85m/C VHS, Beta.** Holly Floria, Alicia Anne, Jackson Robinson, Shannon Stiles, Cyndi Pass, Sherry Johnson; ***D:*** Anthony Markes; ***W:*** Emerson Bixby; ***M:*** Marc David Decker. *PSM*

Bikini Summer 🦴½ **1991** Laughs, music, and skin are the order of the day as two nutty guys and a few beautiful girls form an unlikely friendship on the beach. Konop was Julia Robert's "Pretty Woman" body double. Sort of the 90's version of the old 60's Frankie and Annette beach parties. **90m/C VHS, LV.** David Millburn, Melinda Armstrong, Jason Clow, Shelley Michelle, Alex Smith, Kent Lipham, Kelly Konop, Carmen Santa Maria; ***D:*** Robert Veze; ***W:*** Robert Veze, Nick Stone; ***M:*** John Gonzalez. *PMH*

Bikini Summer 2 **1992 (R)** An eccentric family decides to stage a bikini contest to raise money to help the homeless. **94m/C VHS, LV.** Jeff Conaway, Jessica Hahn, Melinda Armstrong, Avalon Anders; ***D:*** Jeff Conaway; ***M:*** Jim Halfpenny. *PMH*

Bilitis ½ **1977 (R)** A young girl from a private girls' school is initiated into the pleasures of sex and the unexpected demands of love. One of director Hamilton's exploitative meditations on nudity. **95m/C VHS, Beta.** *FR* Patti D'Arbanville, Bernard Giraudeau, Mona Kristensen; ***D:*** David Hamilton. *MED*

Bill **1981** A made-for-television movie based on a true story about a mentally retarded man who sets out to live independently after 44 years in an institution. Rooney gives an affecting performance as Bill and Quaid is strong as the filmmaker who befriends him. Awarded Emmys for Rooney's performance and the well written script. Followed by "Bill: On His Own." **97m/C VHS, Beta.** Mickey Rooney, Dennis Quaid, Largo Woodruff, Harry Goz; ***D:*** Anthony Page. *LIV*

Bill and Coo **1947** An unusual love story with a villian and hero using an all bird cast. **61m/C VHS, Beta, 8mm.** ***D:*** Dean Riesner. *VYY, MRV, NOS*

Bill & Ted's Bogus Journey **1991 (PG)** Big-budget sequel to B & T's first movie has better special effects but about the same quota of laughs. Slain by lookalike robot duplicates from the future, the airhead heroes pass through heaven and hell before tricking the Grim Reaper into bringing them back for a second duel with their heinous terminators. Most excellent closing-credit montage. Nonfans still won't think much of it. **98m/C VHS.** Keanu Reeves, Alex Winter, William Sadler, Joss Ackland, Pam Grier, George Carlin, Amy Stock-Poynton, Hal Landon Jr., Annette Azcuy, Sarah Trigger, Chelcie Ross, Taj Mahal, Roy Brocksmith, William Shatner; ***D:*** Pete Hewitt; ***W:*** Chris Matheson, Edward Solomon; ***M:*** David Newman. *ORI*

Bill & Ted's Excellent Adventure ½ **1989 (PG)** Excellent premise: when the entire future of the world rests on whether or not two '80s dudes pass their history final, Rufus comes to the rescue in his time-travelling telephone booth. Bill and Ted share an adventure through time as they meet and get to know some of history's most important figures. **105m/C VHS, Beta, LV, 8mm.** Keanu Reeves, Alex Winter, George Carlin, Bernie Casey, Dan Shor, Robert Barron, Amy Stock-Poynton, Ted Steedman, Terry Camillieri, Rod Loomis, Al Leong, Tony Camilieri; ***D:*** Stephen Herek; ***W:*** Chris Matheson, Edward Solomon; ***M:*** David Newman. *COL, SUE, NLC*

A Bill of Divorcement ½ **1932** Hepburn's screen debut, as the daughter of a shell-shocked WWI vet, who requires her care after her mother decides to divorce him. Creaky early talker. **76m/B VHS, Beta, LV.** John Barrymore, Katharine Hepburn, Billie Burke, Henry Stephenson, David Manners, Paul Cavanagh, Elizabeth Patterson; ***D:*** George Cukor; ***M:*** Max Steiner. National Board of Review Awards '32: 10 Best Films of the Year. *FOX*

Bill: On His Own **1983** Rooney is again exceptional in this sequel to the Emmy-winning TV movie "Bill." After 44 years in an institution, a mentally retarded man copes more and more successfully with the outside world. Fine supporting cast and direction control the melodramatic potential. **100m/C VHS.** Mickey Rooney, Helen Hunt, Teresa Wright, Dennis Quaid, Largo Woodruff, Paul Leiber, Harry Goz; ***D:*** Anthony Page. *LIV*

Billie ½ **1965** Duke stars as a tomboy athlete who puts the boys' track team to shame. Some amusing but very predictable situations, plus a few songs from Miss Duke. Based on Ronald Alexander's play "Time Out for Ginger." **86m/C VHS, Beta, LV.** Patty Duke, Jim Backus, Jane Greer, Warren Berlinger, Billy DeWolfe, Charles Lane, Dick Sargent, Susan Seaforth Hayes, Ted Bessell, Richard Deacon; ***D:*** Don Weis; ***W:*** Ronald Alexander. *MGM*

The Billion Dollar Hobo ½ **1978 (G)** Poor, unsuspecting heir of a multimillion dollar fortune must duplicate his benefactor's experience as a hobo during the Depression in order to collect his inheritance. Slow-moving family stuff. **96m/C VHS, Beta.** Tim Conway, Will Geer, Eric Weston, Sydney Lassick; ***D:*** Stuart E. McGowan. *FOX*

A Billion for Boris ½ **1990** Boris' TV gives a sneak preview of the future and Boris plans to make some money off of it. Zany comedy in the vein of "Let It Ride." **89m/C VHS, Beta.** Lee Grant, Tim Kazurinsky; ***D:*** Alex Grasshof; ***W:*** Mary Rogers. *IMP*

Billionaire Boys Club ½ **1987** Chilling look at greed in the '80s. Nelson plays Joe Hunt, who gets together with a group of rich, preppie friends to manipulate investments in the commodities markets. When a slick con man (Silver) gets in their way he's murdered to keep their schemes intact. Based on a true story and adapted from the book by Sue Horton. Originally shown on television in two parts, the video version is considerably pared down. **94m/C VHS.** Judd Nelson, Frederic Lehne, Brian McNamara, Raphael Sbarge, John Stockwell, Barry Tubb, Stan Shaw, Jill Schoelen, Ron Silver, James Sloyan, James Karen; ***D:*** Marvin J. Chomsky. *LIV*

Billy Bathgate ½ **1991 (R)** Uneven but well acted drama set in 1935 New York. A street-wise young man decides getting ahead during the Depression means gaining the attention of mobster Dutch Schultz and joining his gang. As Billy becomes the confidant of the racketeer he learns the criminal life is filled with suspicion and violence; in order to stay alive he must rely on every trick he's learned. Willis has a small role as a rival mobster who gets fitted for cement overshoes. Kidman does well as Dutch's girlfriend with Hill fine as the gang's number man. Based on the novel by E.L. Doctorow. **107m/C VHS, Beta, LV.** Dustin Hoffman, Nicole Kidman, Loren Dean, Bruce Willis, Steven Hill, Steve Buscemi, Stanley Tucci, Tim Jerome, Billy Jaye, Katharine Houghton, Mike Starr, John Costelloe, Moira Kelly; ***D:*** Robert Benton; ***W:*** Tom Stoppard; ***M:*** Mark Isham. Nominations: Golden Globe Awards '91: Best Supporting Actress (Kidman). *TOU*

Billy Budd **1962** The classic Melville good-evil allegory adapted to film, dealing with a British warship in the late 1700s, and its struggle between evil master-at-arms and innocent shipmate. Stamp's screen debut as the naive Billy who is tried for the murder of the sadistic first mate. Well directed and acted. **123m/B VHS, Beta, LV.** *GB* Terence Stamp, Peter Ustinov, Robert Ryan, Melvyn Douglas, Paul Rogers, John Neville, Ronald Lewis, David McCallum, John Meillon; ***D:*** Peter Ustinov; ***W:*** Peter Ustinov, Robert Rossen; ***C:*** Robert Krasker. Nominations: Academy Awards '62: Best Supporting Actor (Stamp). *FOX*

Billy Galvin ½ **1986 (PG)** A bullheaded ironworker tries to straighten out the turbulent relationship he has with his rebellious son. **95m/C VHS, Beta.** Karl Malden, Lenny Von Dohlen, Joyce Van Patten, Toni Kalem, Keith Szarabajka, Alan North, Paul Guilfoyle, Barton Heyman; ***D:*** John Gray; ***W:*** John Gray; ***M:*** Joel Rosenbaum. *LIV, VES*

Billy Jack **1971 (PG)** On an Arizona Indian reservation, a half-breed ex-Green Beret with pugnacious martial arts skills (Laughlin) stands between a rural town and a school for runaways. Laughlin stars with his real-life wife Taylor. Features the then-hit song "One Tin Soldier," sung by Coven. The movie and its marketing by Laughlin inspired a "Billy Jack" cult phenomenon. A Spanish-dubbed version of this film is also available. Followed by a sequel in 1974, "Trail of Billy Jack," which bombed. **112m/C VHS, Beta, LV.** Tom Laughlin, Delores Taylor, Clark Howat; ***D:*** Tom Laughlin; ***W:*** Tom Laughlin. *WAR*

Billy Liar **1963** A young Englishman dreams of escaping from his working class family and dead-end job as an undertaker's assistant. Parallels James Thurber's story, "The Secret Life of Walter Mitty." **94m/B VHS, Beta.** *GB* Tom Courtenay, Julie Christie, Finlay Currie; ***D:*** John Schlesinger; ***M:*** Richard Rodney Bennett. *REP*

Billy Madison ½ **1994 (PG-13)** Wealthy slacker Billy (Sandler) must prove to Dad he is capable of running the family hotel business by undertaking the obvious challenge of repeating grades 1-12 in six months. Ponder a few bodily function gags, and you'll have exhausted the humor in this lame attempt at creating a feature-length movie out of what would barely pass as a Saturday Night Live sketch. For only the most diehard fans of Sandler's silly shtick. **90m/C VHS, LV.** Adam Sandler, Darren McGavin, Brigitte Wilson, Bradley Whitford, Josh Mostel, Norm MacDonald, Mark Beltzman, Larry Hankin, Theresa Merritt; ***Cameos:*** Chris Farley, Steve Buscemi; ***D:*** Tamra Davis; ***W:*** Adam Sandler; ***M:*** Randy Edelman. Nominations: MTV Movie Awards '95: Best Comedic Performance (Sandler). *MCA*

Billy: Portrait of a Street Kid **1977** A ghetto youngster tries to pry himself up and out of his bleak surroundings through education, but complications arise when he gets his girlfriend pregnant. **96m/C VHS, Beta.** LeVar Burton, Tina Andrews, Ossie Davis, Michael Constantine; ***D:*** Steven Gethers. *WOV*

Billy Rose's Jumbo *Jumbo* **1962** Better-than-average update of the circus picture. Durante and Raye are terrific, as are the Rodgers and Hart songs. Fun, with lively production numbers in the inimitable Berkeley style. ♫Over and Over Again; Circus on Parade; Why Can't I?; This Can't Be Love; The Most Beautiful Girl in the World; My Romance; Little Girl Blue; What is a Circus; Sawdust, Spangles and Dreams. **125m/C VHS, LV.** Doris Day, Stephen Boyd, Jimmy Durante, Martha Raye, Dean Jagger; ***D:*** Charles Walters; ***W:*** Sidney Sheldon. Nominations: Academy Awards '62: Best Original Score. *MGM*

Billy the Kid ½ **1941** Billy Bonney joins up with a group of outlaws in a Southwest town where he bumps into his old friend Jim Sherwood, now the marshal. Attempting to change his ways, he falls back into the life of a bandit when an outlaw friend is murdered. Although an entertaining western, the story bears no resemblance to the actual last days of Billy the Kid. Based on a story by Howard Emmett Rogers and Bradbury Foote, suggested by the book "The Saga of Billy the Kid" by Walter Noble Burns. **94m/C VHS.** Robert Taylor, Brian Donlevy, Ian Hunter, Mary Howard, Gene Lockhart, Lon Chaney Jr., Guinn "Big Boy" Williams, Cy Kendall, Henry O'Neill, Ted Adams, Frank Puglia, Mitchell Lewis, Dick Curtis, Grant Withers, Joe Yule, Eddie Dunn, Kermit Maynard, Chill Wills, Olive Blakeney, Carl Pitti; ***D:*** David Miller; ***W:*** Gene Fowler Jr.; ***M:*** David Snell. *MGM*

Billy the Kid in Texas ½ **1940** The famed outlaw takes on trouble and makes sure the Texans never forget that he has been there. **52m/B VHS, Beta.** Bob Steele. *NOS, VCN*

Billy the Kid Returns ½ **1938** While trying to clean up a town of its criminal element, Rogers is mistaken for the legendary Billy. Complications ensue. **60m/B VHS, Beta.** Roy Rogers, George "Gabby" Hayes, Smiley Burnette, Lynn (Mary Hart) Roberts; ***D:*** Joseph Kane. *NOS, HHT, VCN*

Billy the Kid Trapped ½ **1942** Billy and his partner are rescued from hanging by an outlaw band. **59m/B VHS.** Buster Crabbe, Al "Fuzzy" St. John, Bud McTaggart, Anne Jeffreys, Glenn Strange; ***D:*** Sam Newfield. *NOS, MRV, DVT*

Billy the Kid Versus Dracula **1966** The title says it all. Dracula travels to the Old West, anxious to put the bite on a pretty lady ranch owner. Her fiance, the legendary outlaw Billy the Kid, steps in to save his girl from becoming a vampire herself. A Carradine camp classic. **95m/C VHS, Beta.** Chuck Courtney, John Carradine, Melinda Plowman, Walter Janovitz, Harry Carey Jr., Roy Barcroft, Virginia Christine, Bing Russell; ***D:*** William Beaudine. *NOS, SUE, VYY*

Billyboy **1979** Coming of age film with the world of boxing as background. Excellent fight scenes. **94m/C VHS, Beta.** Duane Bobrick, Kim Braden. *BFV*

Biloxi Blues ½ *Neil Simon's Biloxi Blues* **1988 (PG-13)** Eugene Morris Jerome has been drafted and sent to boot camp in Biloxi, Mississippi where he encounters a troubled drill sergeant, hostile recruits, and a skillful prostitute. Walken is the drill sergeant from hell. Some good laughs from the ever-wry Broderick. A sequel to Neil Simon's "Brighton Beach Memoirs" and adapted by Simon from his play. Followed by "Broadway Bound." **105m/C VHS, Beta, LV.** Matthew Broderick, Christopher Walken, Casey Siemaszko, Matt Mulhern, Corey Parker, Penelope Ann Miller, Michael Dolan, Park Overall; ***D:*** Mike Nichols; ***W:*** Neil Simon; ***M:*** Georges Delerue. *MCA*

Bim/Dream of the Wild Horses **1952** Two famous French shorts, the first of which is dubbed into English. **110m/B VHS, Beta.** *FR INJ, DVT, GVV*

Bimini Code 🦴 **1984** Two female adventurers accept a dangerous mission where they wind up on Bimini Island in a showdown with the mysterious Madame X. **95m/C VHS, Beta.** Vickie Benson, Krista Richardson, Frank Alexander, Rosanna Simanaitis; ***D:*** Barry Clark. *PSM*

Bingo 🦴🦴½ **1991 (PG)** Mediocre spoof of hero-dog movies. The heroic title mutt roams from Denver to Green Bay in search of his absent-minded master, with numerous absurd adventures en route. Some cute moments, but sometimes Bingo is just lame-o. Good family fare. **90m/C VHS, LV.** Cindy Williams, David Rasche, Robert J. Steinmiller Jr., David French, Kurt Fuller, Joe Guzaldo, Glenn Shadix; ***D:*** Matthew Robbins; ***W:*** Jim Strain; ***M:*** Richard Gibbs. *COL*

Bingo Inferno **1987** A short narrative film about a precocious kid who connives to break his mother of a compulsive Bingo addiction. **13m/C Beta.** *NO*

Bingo Long Traveling All-Stars & Motor Kings 🦴🦴🦴 **1976 (PG)** Set in 1939, this film follows the comedic adventures of a lively group of black ball players who have defected from the old Negro National League. The All-Stars travel the country challenging local white teams. **111m/C VHS, Beta.** Billy Dee Williams, James Earl Jones, Richard Pryor, Stan Shaw; ***D:*** John Badham; ***W:*** Matthew Robbins, Hal Barwood; ***M:*** William Goldstein. *MCA, FCT*

Bio-Dome 🦴 **1996 (PG-13)** Pauly Shore in a hermetically sealed environment separated from the rest of society? Great! Where do I sign? Unfortunately, it's only a movie, and a typically useless one, at that. Shore brings his lame schtick to a scientifically created "perfect environment" that he and his college (yeah, right) buddy Doyle (Baldwin) mistake for a mall and eventually destroy. In Bloom's not-too-auspicious directorial debut, bodily function jokes found in Jim Carrey's wastebasket masquarade as a script, while the supporting cast wanders aimlessly, perhaps pondering a switch in agents. **94m/C VHS, LV.** Pauly Shore, Stephen Baldwin, William Atherton, Henry Gibson, Joey Adams, Teresa Hill, Kylie Minogue, Kevin West, Denise Dowse, Dara Tomanovich; ***D:*** Jason Bloom; ***W:*** Kip Koenig, Scott Marcano; ***C:*** Phedon Papamichael; ***M:*** Andrew Gross. *MGM*

Bio Hazard 🦴 **1985 (R)** A toxic monster needs human flesh to survive and consequently goes on a rampage. **84m/C VHS, Beta.** Angelique Pettyjohn, Carroll Borland, Richard Hench, Aldo Ray; ***D:*** Fred Olen Ray. *MTX*

Biohazard: The Alien Force 🦴½ **1995 (R)** Reptilian mutant, the result of a genetic experiment gone awry, must be hunted down before it can reproduce. Sounds like a rip-off of "Species." **88m/C VHS.** Steve Zurk, Chris Mitchum, Susan Fronsoe, Tom Ferguson, Patrick Moran, John Maynard; ***D:*** Steve Latshaw. *VMK*

The Bionic Woman 🦴🦴 **1975** Sky-diving accident leaves tennis pro Jaimie Somers crippled and near death. Her bionic buddy, Steve Austin, gets his friends to rebuild her and make her better than she was before. The pilot for the television series. **96m/C VHS, Beta.** Lindsay Wagner, Lee Majors, Richard Anderson, Alan Oppenheimer; ***D:*** Richard Moder. *MCA*

The Birch Interval 🦴🦴 **1978 (PG)** A chronicle of a young Amish girl growing up and experiencing adult passions and fears when she visits her kin in their isolated Pennsylvania community. **104m/C VHS, Beta.** Eddie Albert, Rip Torn, Ann Wedgeworth; ***D:*** Delbert Mann; ***W:*** Joanna Crawford. *MED*

Bird 🦴🦴🦴 **1988 (R)** The richly-textured, though sadly one-sided biography of jazz sax great Charlie Parker, from his rise to stardom to his premature death via extended heroin use. A remarkably assured, deeply imagined film from Eastwood that never really shows the Bird's genius of creation. The soundtrack features Parker's own solos re-mastered from original recordings. **160m/C VHS, Beta, LV.** Forest Whitaker, Diane Venora, Michael Zelniker, Samuel E. Wright, Keith David, Michael McGuire, James Handy, Damon Whitaker, Morgan Nagler; ***D:*** Clint Eastwood; ***W:*** Joel Oliansky; ***C:*** Jack N. Green; ***M:*** Lennie Niehaus. Academy Awards '88: Best Sound; Cannes Film Festival '88: Best Actor (Whitaker); Golden Globe Awards '89: Best Director (Eastwood); New York Film Critics Awards '88: Best Supporting Actress (Venora). *MVD, WAR, FCT*

Bird of Paradise 🦴🦴½ **1932** An exotic South Seas romance in which an adventurer is cast onto a remote Polynesian island when his yacht haphazardly sails into a coral reef. There he becomes enamored of an exotic island girl, and nature seems to disapprove. **80m/B VHS, Beta, 8mm.** Joel McCrea, Dolores Del Rio, Lon Chaney Jr.; ***D:*** King Vidor; ***M:*** Max Steiner. *NOS, MRV, VYY*

Bird on a Wire 🦴🦴 **1990 (PG-13)** After suddenly being forced to emerge from a prolonged period under the Witness Protection Program, an ex-hood and his ex-girlfriend are pursued by old enemies. **110m/C VHS, Beta, LV.** Mel Gibson, Goldie Hawn, David Carradine, Bill Duke, Stephen Tobolowsky; ***D:*** John Badham; ***W:*** David Seltzer; ***C:*** Robert Primes; ***M:*** Hans Zimmer. *MCA*

The Bird with the Crystal Plumage 🦴🦴½ *L'Ucello dalle Plume di Cristallo; The Phantom of Terror* **1970 (PG)** An American writer living in Rome witnesses a murder. He becomes involved in the mystery when the alleged murderer is cleared because the woman believed to be his next victim is shown to be a psychopathic murderer. Vintage Argento mayhem. **98m/C VHS, Beta, LV.** *IT* Tony Musante, Suzy Kendall, Eva Renzi; ***D:*** Dario Argento; ***W:*** Dario Argento; ***M:*** Ennio Morricone. *VCI, MRV*

The Birdcage 🦴🦴🦴 *Birds of a Feather* **1995 (R)** Somewhat overlong but well-played remake of "La Cage aux Folles" features Williams suppressing his usual manic schtick to portray Armand, the subdued half of a longtime gay couple living in Miami. His partner is the ever-hysterical-but-loving drag queen Albert (Lane), whose presence provides a distinct challenge when Armand's son Val (Futterman) announces his engagement to the daughter of family values, right-wing senator Kevin Keeley (Hackman). When the Senator and family arrive for dinner, Armand tries to play it straight while Albert opts for a matronly mom impersonation (think Barbara Bush). Highlights include Armand's initial attempts to teach Albert to be butch (walk like John Wayne) and Hackman congoing in drag. **118m/C VHS.** Robin Williams, Nathan Lane, Gene Hackman, Dianne Wiest, Hank Azaria, Dan Futterman, Christine Baranski, Calista Flockhart, Tom McGowan; ***D:*** Mike Nichols; ***W:*** Elaine May; ***C:*** Emmanuel Lubezki. *MGM*

Birdman of Alcatraz 🦴🦴🦴 **1962** Robert Stroud, convicted of two murders and sentenced to life imprisonment on the Island, becomes an internationally accepted authority on birds. Lovingly told, with stunning performance from Lancaster, and exceptionally fine work from the supporting cast. The confinement of Stroud's prison cell makes the film seem claustrophobic and tedious at times, just as the imprisonment must have been. Ritter played Stroud's mother, who never stops trying to get him out of prison. **143m/B VHS.** Burt Lancaster, Karl Malden, Thelma Ritter, Betty Field, Neville Brand, Edmond O'Brien, Hugh Marlowe, Telly Savalas; ***D:*** John Frankenheimer; ***C:*** Burnett Guffey, Robert Krasker; ***M:*** Elmer Bernstein. British Academy Awards '62: Best Actor (Lancaster); Nominations: Academy Awards '62: Best Actor (Lancaster), Best Black and White Cinematography, Best Supporting Actor (Savalas), Best Supporting Actress (Ritter). *COL, FCT*

The Birds 🦴🦴🦴½ **1963 (PG-13)** Hitchcock attempted to top the success of "Psycho" with this terrifying tale of Man versus Nature, in which Nature alights, one by one, on the trees of Bodega Bay to stage a bloody act of revenge upon the civilized world. Only Hitchcock can twist the harmless into the horrific while avoiding the ridiculous; this is perhaps his most brutal film, and one of the cinema's purest, horrifying portraits of apocalypse. Based on a short story by Daphne Du Maurier; screenplay by novelist Evan Hunter (aka Ed McBain). **120m/C VHS, Beta, LV.** Rod Taylor, Tippi Hedren, Jessica Tandy, Veronica Cartwright, Suzanne Pleshette; ***D:*** Alfred Hitchcock; ***C:*** Robert Burks. *MCA*

The Birds 2: Land's End *Woof!* **1994 (R)** Unfortunate rip-off of the Hitchcock fright classic. Killer seagulls begin attacking the inhabitants of east coast Gull Island. Seems they're tired of being oil slick victims. Hedren's the town shopkeeper in a role that's nothing like the one she played in the original. Definitely for the birds—even the director refuses to acknowledge it by officially using the film industry pseudonym "Alan Smithee." Made for TV. **87m/C VHS, LV.** Brad Johnson, Chelsea Field, Tippi Hedren, James Naughton, Jan Rubes, Megan Gallagher; ***D:*** Rick Rosenthal; ***W:*** Jim Wheat, Ken Wheat. *MCA*

Birds & the Bees 🦴🦴 **1956** A millionaire falls in love with an alluring card shark, and then calls it all off when he learns of her profession, only to fall in love with her again when she disguises herself. A remake - and poor shade - of Preston Sturge's 1941 classic "The Lady Eve." **94m/C VHS, Beta.** Mitzi Gaynor, David Niven, George Gobel, Reginald Gardiner, Hans Conried; ***D:*** Norman Taurog; ***W:*** Sidney Sheldon. *BAR*

Birds of Paradise *Woof!* **1984 (R)** Three attractive women who inherit a yacht travel to the Florida Keys to find romance. **90m/C VHS, Beta, LV.** *NO*

Birds of Prey 🦴🦴 **1972** Made-for-television action film pits an ex-WWII army pilot against a group of kidnapping thieves in an airborne chopper chase. **81m/C VHS, Beta.** David Janssen, Ralph Meeker, Elayne Heilveil; ***D:*** William A. Graham. *PSM*

Birds of Prey 🦴 **1985** A tough urban cop stalks a breed of cold, ruthless assassins in a large city. In HiFi. **90m/C VHS, Beta.** *VTR, NWV*

Birdy 🦴🦴🦴½ **1984 (R)** An adaptation of the William Wharton novel about two Philadelphia youths, one with normal interests, the other obsessed with birds, and their eventual involvement in the Vietnam War, wrecking one physically and the other mentally. A hypnotic, evocative film, with a compelling Peter Gabriel soundtrack. **120m/C VHS, Beta, LV.** Matthew Modine, Nicolas Cage, John Harkins, Sandy Baron, Karen Young, Bruno Kirby; ***D:*** Alan Parker; ***W:*** Jack Behr, Sandy Kroopf; ***M:*** Peter Gabriel. Cannes Film Festival '85: Grand Jury Prize. *COL*

Birgitt Haas Must Be Killed 🦴🦴½ **1983** A ruthless secret agent (Noiret) plots to murder a German female terrorist and make it appear that her boyfriend was the killer. Never quite hits the mark, despite novel premise and strong cast. **105m/C VHS, Beta.** Philippe Noiret, Jean Rochefort, Elisabeth Kreuzer; ***D:*** Laurent Heynemann. *GLV*

The Birth of a Nation 🦴🦴🦴🦴 *The Clansman* **1915** Lavish Civil War epic in which Griffith virtually invented the basics of film grammar. Gish and Walthall have some of the most moving scenes ever filmed and the masterful battle choreography brought the art of cinematography to new heights. Griffith's positive attitude toward the KKK notwithstanding, this was the first feature length silent, and it brought credibility to an entire industry. Based on the play "The Clansman" and the book "The Leopard's Spots" by Thomas Dixon, it is still a rouser, and of great historical interest. Silent with music score. Also available in a 124 minute version. **175m/B VHS, LV.** Lillian Gish, Mae Marsh, Henry B. Walthall, Robert "Bobbie" Harron, Wallace Reid, Joseph Henabery, Donald Crisp, Raoul Walsh, Erich von Stroheim, Eugene Pallette; ***D:*** D.W. Griffith. *VYY, MRV, REP*

Birth of the Blues 🦴🦴½ **1941** Songman Crosby starts a band in New Orleans in the midst of the jazz boom. Help from partner Martin and real-life trombonist Teagarden, with comic relief from Eddie "Rochester" Anderson, make for a fun-filled story. Plot is riddled with some unbelievable gangster scenes, but the music and laughs will keep you amused. In B&W with color segments. ♫St. Louis Blues; St. James Infirmary; Melancholy Baby; Birth of the Blues. **76m/B VHS.** Bing Crosby, Mary Martin, Brian Donlevy, Eddie Anderson, J. Carrol Naish, Cecil Kellaway, Warren Hymer, Horace McMahon, Carolyn Lee, Jack Teagarden; ***D:*** Victor Schertzinger; ***W:*** Harry Tugend, Walter DeLeon; ***C:*** William Mellor; ***M:*** Robert Emmett Dolan. Nominations: Academy Awards '41: Best Score. *MCA*

Birthday Boy **1985** A cable comedy about a buffoonish salesman's 30th birthday, on which he takes an ill-fated business trip. Written by Belushi. **33m/C VHS, Beta.** James Belushi; ***D:*** Claude Conrad; ***W:*** James Belushi. *VES, LIV*

The Bishop's Wife **1947** An angel comes down to earth at Christmas to help a young bishop, his wife and his parishioners. Excellent performances by the cast make this an entertaining outing. **109m/B VHS, Beta, LV.** Cary Grant, Loretta Young, David Niven, Monty Woolley, Elsa Lanchester, James Gleason, Gladys Cooper, Regis Toomey; ***D:*** Henry Koster; ***C:*** Gregg Toland. Academy Awards '47: Best Sound; Nominations: Academy Awards '47: Best Director (Koster), Best Film Editing, Best Picture, Best Original Score. *HBO, SUE, FCT*

The Bitch *Woof!* **1978 (R)** High-camp follies are the rule in this lustful continuation of "The Stud" as it follows the erotic adventures of a beautiful divorcee playing sex games for high stakes on the international playgrounds of high society. A collaborative effort by the sisters Collins: written by Jackie, with sister Joan well cast in the title role. **90m/C VHS, Beta.** *GB* Joan Collins, Kenneth Haigh, Michael Coby, Ian Hendry, Carolyn Seymour, Sue Lloyd, John Ratzenberger; ***D:*** Gerry O'Hara. *NO*

Bite the Bullet ½ **1975 (PG)** Moralistic western tells of a grueling 600-mile horse race where the participants reluctantly develop respect for one another. Unheralded upon release and shot in convincing epic style by Harry Stradling, Jr. Excellent cast. **131m/C VHS, Beta, LV.** Gene Hackman, James Coburn, Candice Bergen, Dabney Coleman, Jan-Michael Vincent, Ben Johnson, Ian Bannen, Paul Stewart, Sally Kirkland; ***D:*** Richard Brooks; ***W:*** Richard Brooks; ***C:*** Harry Stradling Jr.; ***M:*** Alex North. Nominations: Academy Awards '75: Best Sound, Best Original Score. *COL*

Bits and Pieces **1977** Crazed mutilating killer strikes fear in the hearts of the city dwellers. **86m/C VHS, Beta.** *TWE*

Bitter Harvest **1981** Emmy-nominated made-for-television movie concerning a dairy farmer frantically trying to discover what is mysteriously killing off his herd. Howard is excellent as the farmer battling the bureaucracy to find the truth. Based on a true story. **98m/C VHS, Beta.** Ron Howard, Art Carney, Tarah Nutter, Richard Dysart, Barry Corbin, Jim Haynie, David Knell; ***D:*** Roger Young. *FRH, LIV*

Bitter Harvest **1993 (R)** Rubin and Kensit are the femme fatales who turn their considerable wiles on the innocent Baldwin. He's more than happy to be their lover but does he want to be their victim as well? **98m/C VHS.** Stephen Baldwin, Patsy Kensit, Jennifer Rubin, Adam Baldwin, M. Emmet Walsh; ***D:*** Duane Clark; ***W:*** Randall Fontana. *PSM*

Bitter Moon **1992 (R)** Polanski effort looks promising, but ultimately disappoints. Bored British couple (Grant and Scott Thomas) meet up with sexual deviants (Coyote and Seigner, aka Mrs. Polanski) on a cruise and learn that passion and cruelty often share the same path to destruction. Masquerades as high class art, but whenever substance is lacking expect a silly, kinky sex scene. Needless to say, there isn't much substance, so erotic mischief abounds. Scott Thomas manages to hold her own, but Coyote is almost embarrassingly over the top. Based on the Pascal Bruckner novel "Lunes de Fiel." **139m/C VHS, LV.** Peter Coyote, Emmanuelle Seigner, Hugh Grant, Kristin Scott Thomas, Victor Banerjee; ***Cameos:*** Stockard Channing; ***D:*** Roman Polanski; ***W:*** Roman Polanski, Gerard Brach, John Brownjohn; ***C:*** Tonino Delli Colli; ***M:*** Vangelis. *COL*

Bitter Rice *Riso Amaro* **1949** Mangano became a star with her sultry performance about survival in postwar Italy. She scrapes by, working in the rice fields of the Po Valley, loved by the down-to-earth Vallone, who provides her with little excitement. Gassman is the rotten-to-the-core thief who meets up with Mangano while he's running from the police. He mistreats her, she steals his money and betrays her friends, and both destroy each other. In Italian with English subtitles. **96m/C VHS.** *IT* Silvana Mangano, Vittorio Gassman, Raf Vallone; ***D:*** Guiseppe de Santis. Nominations: Academy Awards '50: Best Story. *FCT*

Bitter Sweet ½ **1933** Tragic tale of a woman who finally marries the man she loves, only to find that he is a compulsive gambler. Written by Coward, adapted from his operetta. **76m/B VHS.** *GB* Anna Neagle, Fernand Graavey, Esme Percy, Clifford Heatherly, Hugh Williams; ***D:*** Herbert Wilcox; ***W:*** Noel Coward. *NOS, MRV, DVT*

Bitter Sweet **1940** The second version of the Noel Coward operetta, about young romance in 1875 Vienna. Creaky and overrated, but the lush Technicolor and Coward standards help to compensate. ♫Ziguener; I'll See You Again. **94m/C VHS, Beta.** Jeanette MacDonald, Nelson Eddy, George Sanders, Felix Bressart, Ian Hunter, Sig Rumann, Herman Bing, Fay Holden, Curt Bois, Edward Ashley; ***D:*** Woodbridge S. Van Dyke; ***W:*** Lesser Samuels, Noel Coward. Nominations: Academy Awards '40: Best Color Cinematography, Best Interior Decoration. *MGM*

The Bitter Tea of General Yen **1933** Stanwyck arrives in Shanghai to marry a missionary (Gordon) during the threatening days of China's civil war. Unexpectedly swept into the arms of an infamous warlord (Asher), she becomes fascinated, although his attempts to seduce her fail. She even remains with him while his enemies close in. Exotic and poetic, if melodramatic by today's standards. The interracial aspects were considered very daring for their time. Adapted from the book by Grace Zaring Stone. **89m/B VHS.** Barbara Stanwyck, Nils Asther, Gavin Gordon, Walter Connolly, Lucien Littlefield, Toschia Mori, Richard Loo, Clara Blandick; ***D:*** Frank Capra; ***W:*** Edward Paramore. *COL, FCT, BTV*

The Bitter Tears of Petra von Kant ½ *Die Bitteren Traenen der Petra von Kant* **1972** Dark German story of lesbian love, the fashion world, obsession and anger. Claustrophobic settings and slow pace may frustrate some viewers. In German with English subtitles. **124m/C VHS.** *GE* Margit Carstensen, Hanna Schygulla, Irm Hermann, Eva Mattes; ***D:*** Rainer Werner Fassbinder; ***C:*** Michael Ballhaus. *NYF, FCT, INJ*

Bitter Vengeance **1994 (R)** Security guard Jack Westford (Greenwood) pulls off a bank heist with his lover (Hocking) and plans to frame his wife Annie (Madsen) for the crime. Only Annie finds out and sets out to get them before the police get her. Made for cable TV. **90m/C VHS, Beta.** Virginia Madsen, Bruce Greenwood, Kristen Hocking, Eddie Velez, Gordon Jump, Carlos Gomez, Tim Russ; ***D:*** Stuart Cooper; ***W:*** Pablo F. Fenjves. *PAR*

Bittersweet Love ½ **1976 (PG)** Two young people fall in love and marry, only to have the bride's mother and the groom's father confess a 30-year-old affair, disclosing that the two newlyweds are actually half-siblings. **92m/C VHS, Beta.** Lana Turner, Robert Lansing, Celeste Holm, Robert Alda, Meredith Baxter; ***D:*** David Miller. *SUE*

Bix **1990** Based on the brief life of legendary Jazz Age cornetist Leon Bix Beiderbecke, who died at age 28. Story unfolds in flashbacks, through friend Joe Venuti memories of the dissipated genius and the music he created with Hoagy Carmichael, Pee Wee Russell, Paul Whiteman, and others. **100m/C VHS.** *IT* Bryant Weeks, Emile Levisetti, Mark Collver, Sally Groth; ***D:*** Pupi Avati; ***W:*** Pupi Avati, Antonio Avati, Lino Patruno. *RHP*

Bizarre **1987** When a wife escapes her perverse, psychologically threatening marriage, she finds her husband still haunts her literally and figuratively, and plots psychological revenge. Dubbed. **93m/C VHS, Beta.** *IT* Florence Guerin, Luciano Bartoli, Robert Egon Spechtenhauser, Stefano Sabelli. *PSM*

Bizarre Bizarre *Drole de Drama* **1939** A mystery writer is accused of murder and disappears, only to return in disguise to try to clear his name. Along the way, a number of French comedians are introduced with a revue of comedy-farce sketches that include slapstick, burlesque, black humor, and comedy of the absurd. In French with English subtitles. **90m/B VHS, Beta.** *FR* Louis Jouvet, Michel Simon, Francoise Rosay; ***D:*** Marcel Carne. *NOS, HHT, DVT*

The Black Abbot **1963** A mysterious black-hooded figure is seen entering a ruined Abbey tower that leads to a country house with buried treasure. Based on an Edgar Wallace story. **95m/C VHS.** *GE* Joachim Fuchsberger, Dieter Borsche, Gritt Bottcher, Eva Scholtz, Franz Gottlieb; ***D:*** Franz Gottlieb. *SNC*

Black and White as Day and Night **1963** A man's talent for the game of chess becomes a destructive obsession. In German with English subtitles. **?m/C VHS.** Bruno Ganz. *SNC*

Black and White in Color *La Victoire en Chantant* **1976 (PG)** An award-winning satire about a French soldier at an African outpost, who, upon hearing the news of the beginning of WWI, takes it upon himself to attack a neighboring German fort. Calamity ensues. In French, with English subtitles. **100m/C VHS, Beta, LV.** *FR* Jean Carmet, Jacques Dufilho, Catherine Rouvel, Jacques Spiesser, Dora Doll, Jacques Perrin; ***D:*** Jean-Jacques Annaud; ***W:*** George Conchon, Jean-Jacques Annaud; ***M:*** Pierre Bachelet. Academy Awards '76: Best Foreign Language Film. *ORI, WAR, INJ*

Black Arrow *Black Arrow Strikes* **1948** Original adventure film of the famous Robert Louis Stevenson novel. Upon return from 16th century's War of the Roses, a young man must avenge his father's murder by following a trail of clues in the form of black arrows. Well made and fun. **76m/B VHS, Beta.** Louis Hayward, Janet Blair, George Macready, Edgar Buchanan, Paul Cavanagh; ***D:*** Gordon Douglas. *DIS*

The Black Arrow **1984** Exiled bowman returns to England to avenge the injustices of a villainous nobleman. Made-for-cable version of the Robert Louis Stevenson medieval romp is not as well done as the 1948 adaptation. **93m/C VHS, Beta.** Oliver Reed, Benedict Taylor, Georgia Slowe, Stephan Chase, Donald Pleasence; ***D:*** John Hough. *DIS*

Black Beauty **1946** In this adaptation of Anna Sewell's familiar novel, a young girl develops a kindred relationship with an extraordinary horse. **74m/B VHS, Beta.** Mona Freeman, Richard Denning, Evelyn Ankers; ***D:*** Max Nosseck. *CCB, MED, VTR*

Black Beauty **1971 (G)** International remake of the classic horse story by Anna Sewell. **105m/C VHS, Beta, LV.** *GB GE SP* Mark Lester, Walter Slezak; ***D:*** James Hill; ***C:*** Chris Menges; ***M:*** Lionel Bart. *PAR, FCT*

Black Beauty **1994 (G)** Remake of the classic Anna Sewell children's novel about an oft-sold horse whose life has its shares of ups and downs. Timeless tale still brings children and adults to tears. Six-year-old quarterhorse named Justin gives a nuanced portrayal as the Black Beauty, recalling Olivier in "Hamlet." Directorial debut of "Secret Garden" screenwriter Thompson. **88m/C VHS, LV.** Andrew Knott, Sean Bean, David Thewlis, Jim Carter, Alun Armstrong, Eleanor Bron, Peter Cook, Peter Davison, John McEnery, Nicholas Jones; ***D:*** Caroline Thompson; ***W:*** Caroline Thompson. *WAR*

Black Beauty/Courage of Black Beauty **1957** Two feature-length films based on Anna Sewell's novel about the love of a child for a black stallion. "Black Beauty" was first released in 1946; "Courage of Black Beauty" in 1957. Excellent for children who love horses, of course. **145m/C VHS, Beta.** Mona Freeman, Johnny Crawford; ***D:*** Max Nosseck, Harold Schuster. *MED*

Black Belt 🦴 **1992 (R)** A private detective is hired to protect a rock star from a fanatic Vietnam vet. **80m/C VHS.** Don "The Dragon" Wilson, Richard Beymer, Alan Blumenfeld, Matthias Hues; ***D:*** Charles Philip Moore; ***W:*** Charles Philip Moore. *NHO*

Black Belt Jones 🦴 **1974 (R)** Martial arts expert fights the mob to save a school of self-defense in Los Angeles' Watts district. **87m/C VHS, Beta.** Jim Kelly, Gloria Hendry, Scatman Crothers; ***D:*** Robert Clouse. *WAR*

Black Bikers from Hell 🦴½ *Black Angels* **1970 (R)** Black gang-members infiltrate and wreak havoc on their rivals. Who can stop these brutal young men? Cast with real bikers and biker chicks. **87m/C VHS, Beta.** King John III, Des Roberts, Linda Jackson, James Whitworth, James Young-El, Clancy Syrko, Beverly Gardner; ***D:*** Lawrence Merrick; ***W:*** Lawrence Merrick. *TPV, JEF*

Black Bird 🦴🦴 **1975 (PG)** In this satiric "sequel" to "The Maltese Falcon," detective Sam Spade, Jr. searches for the mysterious black falcon statuette that caused his father such trouble. Features appearances by Elisha Cook Jr. and Lee Patrick, who starred in the 1941 classic "The Maltese Falcon" with Humphrey Bogart. **98m/C VHS, Beta.** George Segal, Stephane Audran, Lionel Stander, Lee Patrick, Elisha Cook Jr., Connie Kreski; ***D:*** David Giler. *GKK*

Black Box Affair 🦴½ **1966** An American secret agent must find a black box lost in a B-52 plane crash before it falls into the wrong hands. **95m/C VHS, Beta.** Craig Hill, Teresa Gimpera, Luis Martin, Jorge Rigaud. *NO*

Black Brigade 🦴🦴 **1969** Pryor and Williams star in this low budget movie as leaders of an all-black outfit assigned to a suicide mission behind Nazi lines during WWII. Their force wreaks havoc and earns them the respect of military higher-ups. Lots of action and climactic finish. **90m/C VHS.** Richard Pryor, Billy Dee Williams, Stephen Boyd. *QVD*

Black Caesar 🦴🦴 **1973 (R)** A small-time hood climbs the ladder to be the head of a Harlem crime syndicate. Music by James Brown. Followed by the sequel "Hell Up in Harlem." **92m/C VHS, Beta, LV.** Fred Williamson, Julius W. Harris, Val Avery, Art Lund, Gloria Hendry; ***D:*** Larry Cohen; ***M:*** James Brown. *ORI*

The Black Castle 🦴🦴 **1952** MacNally plays an 18th-century Austrian count whose guests tend to disappear after a visit. This happens to two of Greene's friends and he decides to investigate. Uninspired and melodramatic, not enough horror. Karloff doesn't have enough to do. **81m/B VHS.** Richard Greene, Boris Karloff, Stephen McNally, Rita (Paula) Corday, Lon Chaney Jr., John Hoyt; ***D:*** Nathan (Hertz) Juran. *MCA*

The Black Cat 🦴🦴🦴½ *House of Doom* **1934** The first of the Boris and Bela pairings stands up well years after release. Polished and taut, with fine sets and interesting acting. Confrontation between architect and devil worshipper acts as plot, with strange twists. Worth a look. Also available with "The Raven" (1935) on laserdisc. **65m/B VHS, LV.** Boris Karloff, Bela Lugosi, David Manners, Jacqueline Wells, Lucille Lund, Henry Armetta; ***D:*** Edgar G. Ulmer. *MED, MLB, MCA*

The Black Cat *Woof!* **1981** Spaghetti splattermeister Fulci, best known for his unabashed ripoffs "Zombie" and "Gates of Hell," tones down the gore this time in a vaguely Poe-ish tale of a medium with some marbles loose (Magee) whose kitty provides the temporary habitat for spirits its master calls up. The dreary English village setting and the downright myopic camerawork add up to an oppressive viewing experience. **92m/C VHS.** *IT GB* Patrick Magee, Mimsy Farmer, David Warbeck, Al Cliver, Dagmar Lassander; ***D:*** Lucio Fulci; ***W:*** Lucio Fulci; ***M:*** Pino Donaggio. *MED, RHI*

Black Cat 🦴½ **1990** Filmmakers find lots of action in a haunted house. Chock full of references to the works of spaghetti horror dons Mario Bava and Dario Argento. **?m/C VHS, Beta.** *IT* Caroline Munro, Brett Halsey; ***D:*** Lewis (Luigi Cozzi) Coates; ***W:*** Lewis (Luigi Cozzi) Coates. *COL*

Black Christmas 🦴🦴½ *Silent Night, Evil Night; Stranger in the House* **1975 (R)** A college sorority is besieged by an axe-murderer over the holidays. **98m/C VHS, Beta.** *CA* Olivia Hussey, Keir Dullea, Margot Kidder, John Saxon; ***D:*** Bob (Benjamin) Clark. *WAR*

Black Cobra *Woof!* **1983 (R)** A lesbian exacts revenge for her lover's snake-bite murder by trapping the guilty party with his own snakes. **97m/C VHS, Beta.** Laura Gemser, Jack Palance. *GEM*

The Black Cobra *Woof!* **1987 (R)** After photographing a psychopath in the process of killing someone, a beautiful photographer seeks the help of a tough police sergeant to protect her. The leader of the Black Cobras gang gives chase. **90m/C VHS, Beta.** *IT* Fred Williamson, Karl Landgren, Eva Grimaldi. *TWE*

Black Cobra 2 🦴🦴 **1989 (R)** A mismatched team of investigators tracks a notorious terrorist. They find him holding a school full of children as hostage. **95m/C VHS.** Fred Williamson. *HMD*

Black Cobra 3: The Manila Connection 🦴½ **1990 (R)** Interpol turns to police lieutenant Robert Malone (Williamson) when a team of high-tech weapons thieves threatens the world. Malone attacks like a cyclone on the terrorists' jungle haven. They won't know what hit 'em! **92m/C VHS.** Fred Williamson, Forry Smith, Debra Ward; ***D:*** Don Edwards. *HMD*

The Black Coin **1936** A 15-episode adventure serial about a cursed silver piece from the Middle Ages and the ill luck that has followed its possessors through the years. **316m/B VHS, Beta, LV.** Ralph Graves, Ruth Mix, Dave O'Brien, Matthew Betz. *VYY, NOS, MLB*

Black Devil Doll from Hell 🦴 **1984** This shot-on-video movie deals with a nasty little voodoo doll that likes to kill its owners. **70m/C VHS, Beta.** Shirley Jones, Rickey Roach, Marie Sainvilvs; ***D:*** Chester Turner. *HHT*

The Black Devils of Kali 🦴 *Mystery of the Black Jungle* **1955** Adventurers in the Indian jungle discover a lost race of idol-worshipping primitives. Racist garbage produced near the end of Republic Pictures' existence. Based on a novel by Emillio Salgari. **72m/B VHS.** Lex Barker, Jane Maxwell, Luigi Tosi, Paul Muller; ***D:*** Ralph Murphy. *SNC, MLB*

Black Dragon 🦴 **1974 (R)** Young farm boy moves to the city and teams up with an undercover narcotics agent to infiltrate and destroy the underworld syndicate. **93m/C VHS.** Ron Van Cliff, Jason Rai Pow, Jorge Estraga, Nancy Veronica. *SUN*

The Black Dragons 🦴 **1942** Weird and fairly stupid war drama involving sabotage by the Japanese. Lugosi is the plastic surgeon who deftly cuts and pastes Japanese face parts to permit agents to pass as Americans. Also available colorized. **62m/B VHS, Beta.** Bela Lugosi, Joan Barclay, George Pembroke, Clayton Moore; ***D:*** William Nigh. *VYY, MRV, SNC*

Black Dragon's Revenge 🦴 **1975 (R)** The Black Dragon arrives in Hong Kong to investigate the death of a great kung fu master. **90m/C VHS.** Ron Van Cliff, Charles Bonet, Jason Rai Pow. *SUN*

Black Eagle 🦴🦴 **1988 (R)** Pre-Glasnost, anti-Soviet tale of two high-kicking spies. CIA and KGB agents race to recover innovative equipment in the Mediterranean. **93m/C VHS, Beta, LV.** Bruce Doran, Jean-Claude Van Damme, Sho Kosugi; ***D:*** Eric Karson. *NO*

Black Eliminator 🦴 **197?** A black cop struggles to stop a maniacal secret agent who plans to destroy the world. **84m/C VHS, Beta.** Jim Kelly, George Lazenby, Harold Sakata, Bob Minos, Patch MacKenzie, Aldo Ray. *NO*

Black Eyes 🦴½ **1939** A lowly waiter, working in a Moscow restaurant, manages to overhear a number of stock tips from the wealthy patrons and makes a tidy pile of rubles to improve his daughter's life. The daughter already thinks he's a successful businessman and is disillusioned when she discovers dad's true profession. All comes out right in the end. **72m/B VHS.** *GB* Otto Kruger, Mary Maguire, Walter Rilla, George L. Baxt, Marie Wright; ***D:*** Herbert Brenon. *HCV*

Black Force 🦴🦴 **1975** Brothers who fight crime with violent actions, are called for assistance in the recovery of an African artifact. Originally known as "Force Four." **82m/C VHS, Beta.** Malachi Lee, Warhawk Tanzania, Owen Watson, Judie Soriano; ***D:*** Michael Fink. *NO*

Black Force 2 🦴🦴 **1978 (R)** The brothers are back on the scene in another violent, cartilage-shattering adventure. **90m/C VHS.** Terry Carter, James B. Sikking. *NO*

Black Fox: The Price of Peace 🦴🦴½ **1994** Former plantation owner Reeve and the childhood friend (Todd) he frees from slavery try to forge a new life in 1860s Texas. But there's trouble when an abusive bigot threatens the peace between settlers and Indians when he goes after the wife who left him for a Kiowa warrior. Based on the novel by Matt Braun; made for TV. **90m/C VHS.** Christopher Reeve, Raoul Trujillo, Tony Todd, Chris Wiggins, Cyndy Preston; ***D:*** Steven Hilliard Stern. *CAF*

Black Friday 🦴🦴½ **1940** Karloff is a surgeon who saves the life of his college professor friend (Ridges) by transplanting part of the brain of a gangster (involved in the same car crash) into the man's body. This results in a Jekyll/Hyde complex with the gangster's evil portion taking over and seeking revenge on rival mobster Lugosi. Horror stars Karloff and Lugosi never have any scenes together. **70m/B VHS.** Boris Karloff, Stanley Ridges, Bela Lugosi, Anne Nagel, Anne Gwynne, Paul Fix, Virginia Brissac; ***D:*** Arthur Lubin; ***W:*** Curt Siodmak, Eric Taylor. *MCA*

Black Fury 🦴🦴🦴 **1935** A coal miner's efforts to protest working conditions earn him a beating by the company goons who also kill his friend. He draws national attention to this brutal plight of the workers when he barricades himself inside the mine. Muni's carefully detailed performance adds authenticity to this powerful drama, but it proved too depressing to command a big box office. **95m/B VHS, Beta.** Paul Muni, Barton MacLane, Henry O'Neill, John Qualen, J. Carrol Naish; ***D:*** Michael Curtiz. *FOX*

Black Gestapo *Woof!* **1975 (R)** A black-exploitation film about a vigilante army taking over a Los Angeles ghetto, first to help residents, but later to abuse them. Extremely violent. **89m/C VHS, Beta.** Rod Perry, Charles Robinson, Phil Hoover, Ed Gross. *UNI*

Black Glove 🦴 *Face the Music* **1954** A trumpet star defends himself against charges of murdering a Spanish singer by tracking down the real killer. **84m/B VHS, Beta, LV.** Alex Nicol, Eleanor Summerfield. *NOS*

Black God & White Devil 🦴🦴 **1964** Another Brazilan socio-political commentary by Rocha, an oft-incendiary filmmaker whose left-leaning works are steeped in mysticism, obscure folklore, and powerful images. An impoverished man transforms from a religious zealot to a bandit, his tale underscored by conflict between poor masses and wealthy landowners. Portuguese with subtitles. **102m/C VHS.** *BR* ***D:*** Glauce Rocha. *FCT*

Black Godfather 🦴 **1974 (R)** The grueling story of a hood clawing his way to the top of a drug-selling mob. Features an all-black cast. **90m/C VHS, Beta.** Rod Perry, Damu King, Don Chastain, Jimmy Witherspoon, Diane Summerfield; ***D:*** John Evans. *NO*

Black Gold 🦴🦴 **1936** Oil field suspense thriller by "B" movie king Hopton. **57m/B VHS.** Frankie Darro, Leroy Mason; ***D:*** Russell Hopton. *SNC, VYY*

The Black Hand 🦴🦴🦴 **1950** Kelly plays well against character in this atmospheric turn-of-the-century thriller. The evil society of the Black Hand murders his father, and he seeks revenge. Well-made drama. **93m/B VHS.** Gene Kelly, J. Carrol Naish, Teresa Celli, Marc Lawrence, Frank Puglia; ***D:*** Richard Thorpe; ***C:*** Paul Vogel. *NO*

Black Hand 🦴½ **1976** Unemployed Italian immigrant is drawn into a web of murder and betrayal after he is attacked by an Irish gang. **90m/C VHS, Beta.** Lionel Stander, Mike Placido. *NO*

Black Hills 🦴 **1948** Dull oater with Dean and his sidekick Ates out to avenge the murder of a struggling ranch owner. **60m/B VHS.** Eddie Dean, Roscoe Ates, Shirley Patterson, Terry Frost, Nina Bara, William "Bill" Fawcett; ***D:*** Ray Taylor. *MOV*

The Black Hole 🦴½ **1979 (G)** A high-tech, computerized Disney space adventure dealing with a mad genius who attempts to pilot his craft directly into a black hole. Except for the top quality special effects, a pretty creaky vehicle. **97m/C VHS, Beta, LV.** Maximilian Schell, Anthony Perkins, Ernest Borgnine, Yvette Mimieux, Joseph Bottoms, Robert Forster; ***D:*** Gary Nelson; ***W:*** Gerry Day; ***M:*** John Barry. Nominations: Academy Awards '79: Best Cinematography. *DIS, OM*

Black Ice 🦴🦴 **1992 (R)** After an affair with a popular politician ends violently, Vanessa (Pacula) realizes her boss set up his death—and she's next in line. She finds the nearest taxi and offers the driver plenty of cash if he can quickly get her out of the country. It's going to be the ride of her life. Also available in an unrated version. **90m/C VHS, Beta.** Michael Nouri, Michael Ironside, Joanna Pacula; ***D:*** Neill Fearnley; ***M:*** Amin Bhatia. *PSM*

The Black King 🦴½ *Harlem Hot Shot* **1932** Prejudiced propaganda based on the life of Marcus Garvey, black leader of the '20s, who advocated black superiority and a return to Africa. A black con man takes advantage of fellow blacks by organizing a phony back-to-Africa movement, enriching himself in the process. When one man's girlfriend deserts him for the bogus leader, the jilted one blows the whistle. **70m/B VHS.** A.B. Comethiere, Vivianne Baber, Knolly Mitchell, Dan Michaels, Mike Jackson; ***D:*** Bud Pollard. *FCT, BTV, HEG*

The Black Klansman 🦴 *I Crossed the Line* **1966** A black man masquerades as a white extremist in order to infiltrate the KKK and avenge his daughter's murder. In the interest of racial harmony, he seduces the Klan leader's daughter. As bad as it sounds. **88m/B VHS, Beta.** Richard Gilden, Rima Kutner, Harry Lovejoy; ***D:*** Ted V. Mikels. *UNI*

The Black Lash 🦴 **1952** Two lawmen go undercover to break a silver hijacking gang. **55m/B VHS, Beta.** Lash LaRue, Al "Fuzzy" St. John, Peggy Stewart, Kermit Maynard; ***D:*** Ron Ormond. *NOS, DVT, GPV*

Black Lemons 🦴 **198?** While in prison, a convict is stalked by the Mafia because of what he knows. He eventually spills the beans to the cops, putting himself in unavoidable jeopardy. **93m/C VHS, Beta.** *IT* Peter Carsten, Antonio Sabato, Florinda Bolkan; ***D:*** Camillo Bazzoni. *UNI*

Black Like Me 🦴½ **1964** Based on John Howard Griffin's successful book about how Griffin turned his skin black with a drug and traveled the South to experience prejudice firsthand. Neither the production nor the direction enhance the material. **107m/B VHS, Beta.** James Whitmore, Roscoe Lee Browne, Will Geer, Walter Mason, John Marriott, Clifton James, Dan Priest; ***D:*** Carl Lerner. *RHI, UND, PTB*

Black Limelight 🦴½ **1938** Massey plays a fugitive from justice and Marion the loyal wife who clears her husband of the murder of his mistress. Distracting lead performance by Marion who insists on shouting her lines. Based on the play by Gordon Sherry. **60m/B VHS.** *GB* Raymond Massey, Joan Marion, Walter Hudd, Henry Oscar, Dan Tobin; ***D:*** Paul Stein; ***W:*** Walter Summers. *DVT*

Black Lizard 🦴🦴 **1968** A camp spectacle set in the Japanese underworld. The Lizard is the glamorous queen of Tokyo crime who plots to steal a famous diamond by first kidnapping the owner's daughter. Complications arise when she falls for a detective. The Lizard is played by female impersonator Maruyama. Mishima, who wrote the original drama and the screenplay, has a cameo as an embalmed corpse. Style is all. In Japanese with English subtitles. **112m/C VHS.** *JP* Akihiro Maruyama, Isao Kimura; ***Cameos:*** Yukio Mishima; ***D:*** Kinji Fukasaku; ***W:*** Yukio Mishima. *CCN, INJ*

Black Magic 🦴🦴½ **1949** Cagliostro the magician becomes involved in a plot to supply a double for Marie Antoinette. **105m/B VHS, Beta.** Orson Welles, Akim Tamiroff, Nancy Guild, Raymond Burr; ***D:*** Gregory Ratoff; ***W:*** Charles Bennett. *MED*

Black Magic 🦴🦴½ **1992 (PG-13)** Insomniac Alex, haunted by the nightly appearances of his dead cousin Ross, goes to Ross' hometown to see if he can find a way to make the apparition disappear. On the way, he runs into his cousin's ex-girlfriend Lilian and falls in love. Problem is, Lilian's a witch, maybe. Lightweight made for cable TV fare. **94m/C VHS, LV.** Rachel Ward, Judge Reinhold, Brion James, Anthony LaPaglia; ***D:*** Daniel Taplitz; ***W:*** Daniel Taplitz. *MCA*

Black Magic Terror 🦴 **1979** Jilted by her lover, the old queen of black magic has everybody under her spell. Trouble starts, however, when she turns her back on one of her subjects. **85m/C VHS, Beta.** *JP* Suzanna, W.D. Mochtar, Alan Nuary; ***D:*** L. Sudjio. *TWE*

Black Magic Woman *Woof!* **1991 (R)** An art gallery owner has an affair with a beautiful and exotic woman but starts to get cold feet when he's plagued by inexplicable phenomena. Seems that black magic woman has put a voodoo spell on him. Listless companion to director Warren's "Blood Spell" that gives away the ending, has a wretched script, and poor acting. **91m/C VHS.** Mark Hamill, Amanda Wyss, Apollonia, Abadah Viera, Larry Hankin, Victor Rivers, Bonnie Ebson; ***D:*** Deryn Warren; ***W:*** Gerry Daly; ***M:*** Randy Miller. *VMK*

The Black Maid *Woof!* **1974** A scantily-clad, sassy black maid cleans, cooks, cusses and drives her racist employer to the brink of insanity. **90m/C VHS, Beta.** *IT NO*

The Black Marble 🦴🦴🦴 **1979 (PG)** A beautiful policewoman is paired with a policeman who drinks too much, is divorced, and is ready to retire. Surrounded by urban craziness and corruption, they eventually fall in love. Based on the Joseph Wambaugh novel. **110m/C VHS, Beta.** Paula Prentiss, Harry Dean Stanton, Robert Foxworth, James Woods, Michael Dudikoff, Barbara Babcock, John Hancock, Judy Landers, Anne Ramsey, Christopher Lloyd; ***D:*** Harold Becker; ***M:*** Maurice Jarre. *SUE, NLC*

Black Market Rustlers 🦴½ **1943** The Range Busters are at it again. This time they break up a cattle rustling syndicate. **60m/B VHS, Beta.** Ray Corrigan, Dennis Moore, Max Terhune; ***D:*** S. Roy Luby. *VDM, RXM*

Black Moon Rising 🦴½ **1986 (R)** Based on an idea by John Carpenter ("Halloween"), this film deals with the theft of a new jet-powered car and its involvement in an FBI investigation. Solid performances and steady action enhance this routine effort. **100m/C VHS, Beta, LV.** Tommy Lee Jones, Linda Hamilton, Richard Jaeckel, Robert Vaughn; ***D:*** Harley Cokliss; ***W:*** John Carpenter; ***M:*** Lalo Schifrin. *VTR, NWV*

Black Narcissus 🦴🦴🦴½ **1947** A group of Anglican nuns attempting to found a hospital and school in the Himalayas confront native distrust and human frailties amid beautiful scenery. Adapted from the novel by Rumer Godden. Stunning cinematography. Crucial scenes were cut from the American release by censors. **101m/C VHS, Beta, LV.** *GB* Deborah Kerr, David Farrar, Sabu, Jean Simmons, Kathleen Byron, Flora Robson, Esmond Knight; ***D:*** Michael Powell, Emeric Pressburger; ***C:*** Jack Cardiff. Academy Awards '47: Best Art Direction/Set Decoration (Color), Best Color Cinematography; New York Film Critics Awards '47: Best Actress (Kerr). *MLB*

Black Oak Conspiracy 🦴🦴 **1977 (R)** Based on a true story, this film deals with a mining company conspiracy discovered by an inquisitive stuntman. **92m/C VHS, Beta.** Jesse Vint, Karen Carlson, Albert Salmi, Seymour Cassel, Robert F. Lyons; ***D:*** Bob Kelljan. *NLC*

Black Orchid 🦴🦴½ **1959** A businessman and a crook's widow fall in love and try to persuade their children it can work out. **96m/B VHS, Beta.** Sophia Loren, Anthony Quinn, Ina Balin, Peter Mark Richman, Jimmie Baird; ***D:*** Martin Ritt; ***W:*** Joseph Stefano; ***C:*** Robert Burks. *PAR*

Black Orpheus 🦴🦴🦴½ *Orfeu Negro* **1958** The legend of Orpheus and Eurydice unfolds against the colorful background of the carnival in Rio de Janeiro. In the black section of the city, Orpheus is a street-car conductor and Eurydice, a country girl fleeing from a man sworn to kill her. Dancing, incredible music, and black magic add to the beauty of this film. Based on the play "Orfeu da Conceica." In Portuguese with English subtitles or dubbed. **103m/C VHS, Beta, LV.** *BR FR PT* Breno Mello, Marpessa Dawn, Lea Garcia, Fausto Guerzoni, Lourdes De Oliveira; ***D:*** Marcel Camus; ***C:*** Jean Bourgoin; ***M:*** Antonio Carlos Jobim, Luis Bonfa. Academy Awards '59: Best Foreign Language Film; Cannes Film Festival '59: Best Film; Golden Globe Awards '60: Best Foreign Film. *CVC, FOX, FCT*

Black Panther 🦴½ **1977** True story of psycho-killer Donald Neilson, who murdered heiress Lesley Whittle in England in the 1970s. **90m/C VHS, Beta.** Donald Sumpter, Debbie Farrington; ***D:*** Ian Merrick; ***W:*** Michael Armstrong. *VES, LIV*

The Black Pirate 🦴🦴🦴 *Rage of the Buccaneers; The Black Buccaneer; Gordon il Pirata Nero* **1926** A shipwrecked mariner vows revenge on the pirates who destroyed his father's ship. Quintessential Fairbanks, this film features astounding athletic feats and exciting swordplay. Silent film with music score. Also available in color. **122m/B VHS, Beta, LV.** *IT* Douglas Fairbanks Sr., Donald Crisp, Billie Dove; ***D:*** Albert Parker. *KIV, MRV, REP*

Black Pit of Dr. M 🦴 *Misterios del Ultratumba* **1947** The ghost of a doctor who has been unjustly executed for murder seeks revenge on employees of an insane asylum. The horror is not just confined to the asylum. **90m/B VHS, Beta.** *MX* Gaston Santos, Rafael Bertrand, Mapita Cortes; ***D:*** Fernando Mendez; ***W:*** Raymond Obon. *MAD, SMW*

Black Rain 🦴🦴🦴 *Kuroi Ame* **1988** Erstwhile Ozu assistant Imamura directs this powerful portrait of a post-Hiroshima family five years after the bombing. Tanaka plays a young woman who, having been caught in a shower of black rain (radioactive fallout) on an ill-timed visit to Hiroshima, returns to her village to find herself ostracized by her peers and no longer considered marriage-worthy. Winner of numerous awards (including five Japanese Academy Awards). In Japanese with English subtitles. **123m/B VHS.** *JP* Kazuo Kitamura, Yoshiko Tanaka, Etsuko Ichihara, Shoichi Ozawa, Norihei Miki; ***D:*** Shohei Imamura. *FXL, FCT, INJ*

Black Rain 🦴🦴½ **1989 (R)** Douglas portrays a ruthless American cop chasing a Japanese murder suspect through gang-controlled Tokyo. Loads of action and stunning visuals from the man who brought you "Blade Runner." **125m/C VHS, Beta, LV, 8mm, CD-I.** Michael Douglas, Andy Garcia, Kate Capshaw, Ken Takakura, Yusaku Matsuda, John Spencer, Shigeru Koyama; ***D:*** Ridley Scott; ***W:*** Craig Bolotin, Warren Lewis; ***C:*** Jan De Bont; ***M:*** Hans Zimmer. Nominations: Academy Awards '89: Best Sound. *PAR*

Black Rainbow 🦴🦴🦴 **1991 (R)** Surprisingly good thriller that's relatively unknown, haunted by a menacing mood. Robards and Arquette are a father/daughter duo who perform clairvoyance scams at carnival sideshows. Suddenly, without warning, Arquette's former cons become real: she sees murder victims—before their demise. Quirky sleeper filmed on location in North Carolina. **103m/C VHS, Beta, LV.** Rosanna Arquette, Jason Robards Jr., Tom Hulce, Ron Rosenthal, John Bennes, Linda Pierce, Mark Joy; ***D:*** Mike Hodges; ***W:*** Mike Hodges. *VTR, FXV, MED*

The Black Raven 🦴½ **1943** An action film that combines several plots into one. The Black Raven is an inn that sees more excitement than any other—not the least of which is murder! **64m/B VHS, Beta.** George Zucco, Wanda McKay, Glenn Strange, I. Stanford Jolley; ***D:*** Sam Newfield. *SNC, MLB, RXM*

Black Robe 🦴🦴🦴½ **1991 (R)** In 1634 a young Jesuit priest journeys across the North American wilderness to bring the word of God to Canada's Huron Indians. The winter journey is brutal and perilous and he begins to question his mission after seeing the strength of the Indian's native ways. Stunning cinematography, a good script, and fine acting combine to make this superb. Portrays the Indians in a realistic manner, the only flaw being that Beresford portrays the white culture with very few redeeming qualities and as the only reason for the Indian's downfall. Moore adapted his own novel for the screen. Winner of six Canadian Genie awards in 1991. **101m/C VHS, LV.** *AU CA* Lothaire Bluteau, Aden Young, Sandrine Holt, August Schellenberg, Tantoo Cardinal, Billy Two Rivers, Lawrence Bayne, Harrison Liu; ***D:*** Bruce Beresford; ***W:*** Brian Moore; ***M:*** Georges Delerue. Australian Film Institute '92: Best Cinematography. *VMK, INJ*

The Black Room 🦴🦴🦴 **1935** As an evil count lures victims into his castle of terror, the count's twin brother returns to fulfill an ancient prophecy. Karloff is wonderful in his dual role as the twin brothers. **70m/B Beta, LV.** Boris Karloff, Marian Marsh, Robert Allen, Katherine DeMille, John Buckler, Thurston Hall; ***D:*** Roy William Neill. *GKK, MLB*

The Black Room 🦴 **1982 (R)** Couples are lured to a mysterious mansion where a brother and his sister promise to satisfy their sexual desires. **90m/C VHS, Beta, LV.** Linnea Quigley, Stephen Knight, Cassandra Gaviola, Jim Stathis; ***D:*** Norman Thaddeus Vane. *VES, LIV*

Black Roses 🦴 **1988 (R)** A disgusting band of rockers shows up in a small town, and the local kids start turning into monsters. Coincidence? **90m/C VHS, Beta, LV.** Carmine Appice, Sal Viviano, Carla Ferrigno, Julie Adams, Ken Swofford, John Martin; ***D:*** John Fasano. *IMP*

Black Sabbath 🦴🦴🦴 *I Tre Volti della Paura* **1964** An omnibus horror film with three parts, climaxing with Karloff as a Wurdalak, a vampire who must kill those he loves. Also available with "Black Sunday" on laserdisc. **99m/C VHS, Beta.** *IT* Boris Karloff, Jacqueline Pierreux, Michele Mercier, Lidia Alfonsi, Susy Anderson, Mark Damon, Rika Dialina; ***D:*** Mario Bava; ***M:*** Les Baxter. *SNC*

Black Samurai 🦴 **1977 (R)** When his girlfriend is held hostage, a martial arts warrior will stop at nothing to destroy the organization that abducted her. **84m/C VHS, Beta.** Jim Kelly; ***D:*** Al Adamson. *NO*

The Black Scorpion 🦴½ **1957** Two geologists in Mexico unearth a nest of giant scorpions living in a dead volcano. Eventually one of the oversized arachnids escapes to wreak havoc on Mexico City. **85m/B VHS.** Richard Denning, Mara Corday, Carlos Rivas; ***D:*** Edward Ludwig; ***W:*** Robert Blees. *WAR, MLB, FRG*

Black Scorpion 🦴🦴½ *Roger Corman Presents: Black Scorpion* **1995 (R)** Severance stars as an ex-cop-turned-superhero (the scorpion is her symbol), who dons a mask and fetching (and tight) black vinyl to fight crime and avenge her dad's death. She's got the prerequisite sidekick—an ex-chop shop operator (Morris)—and a supervillain—the asthmatic Breathtaker (Siemaszko) who threatens to annihilate the city with toxic gas. Campy, schlock fun. **?m/C VHS.** Joan Severance, Garrett Morris, Casey Siemaszko, Rick Rossovich; ***D:*** Jonathan Winfrey. *NHO*

Black Shampoo *Woof!* **1976** A black hairdresser on the Sunset Strip fights the mob with a chainsaw. **90m/C VHS, Beta.** John Daniels, Tanya Boyd, Joe Ortiz; ***D:*** Greydon Clark. *VCI*

Black Sheep 🦴½ **1996 (PG-13)** Isn't there a five-day waiting period for remakes? The previously viewed copies of "Tommy Boy" hadn't even hit the sale bin before Spade and Farley went in search of more property to destroy. The twist here? Spade is assigned to keep the oafish brother (not son) of a gubernatorial candidate (not auto parts dealer) out of trouble until after the election (not so he can save the family business). In an effort to provide humor, plot points, and character development, Farley falls out of, off of or onto every prop in sight while Spade smirks. **87m/C VHS, Beta.** Chris Farley, David Spade, Tim Matheson, Christine Ebersole, Gary Busey, Grant Heslov, Timothy Carhart, Bruce McGill; ***D:*** Penelope Spheeris; ***W:*** Fred Wolf; ***C:*** Daryn Okada; ***M:*** William Ross. *PAR*

Black Sister's Revenge 🦴🦴 *Emma Mae* **1976** Poorly selected video title mars this intelligent drama about a young black woman's struggle to adjust to the big city after growing up in the deep South. **100m/C VHS, Beta.** Jerri Hayes, Ernest Williams II, Charles D. Brook III, Eddie Allen; ***D:*** Jamaa Fanaka; ***W:*** Jamaa Fanaka. *UNI*

The Black Six 🦴 **1974 (R)** Six black Vietnam veterans are out to punish the white gang who killed the brother of one of the black men. **91m/C VHS, Beta.** Gene Washington, Carl Eller, Lem Barney, Mercury Morris, Joe "Mean Joe" Greene, Willie Lanier, Rosalind Miles, John Isenbarger, Ben Davidson, Maury Wills; ***D:*** Matt Cimber. *UNI*

Black Snow 🦴½ **1993** The mob is off on a violent search for fifty million bucks in cocaine. **90m/C VHS, LV.** Jane Badler, Peter Sherayko, Julia Montgomery, Randy Brooks; ***D:*** Frank Patterson. *AIP*

The Black Stallion 🦴🦴🦴 **1979 (PG)** A young boy and a wild Arabian Stallion are the only survivors of a shipwreck, and they develop a deep affection for each other. When rescued, they begin training for an important race. Exceptionally beautiful first half. Rooney plays a horse trainer, again. Great for adults and kids. **120m/C VHS, Beta, LV.** Kelly Reno, Mickey Rooney, Teri Garr, Clarence Muse; ***D:*** Carroll Ballard; ***W:*** William D. Wittliff, Melissa Mathison, Jeanne Rosenberg; ***C:*** Caleb Deschanel; ***M:*** Carmine Coppola. Academy Awards '79: Best Sound Effects Editing; Los Angeles Film Critics Association Awards '79: Best Cinematography; National Society of Film Critics Awards '79: Best Cinematography; Nominations: Academy Awards '79: Best Film Editing, Best Supporting Actor (Rooney). *MGM, FOX, TLF*

The Black Stallion Returns 🦴🦴½ **1983 (PG)** Sequel to "The Black Stallion" follows the adventures of young Alec as he travels to the Sahara to search for his beautiful horse, which was stolen by an Arab chieftain. Unfortunately lacks much of the charm that was present in the first film. Adapted from the stories by Walt Farley. **103m/C VHS, Beta, LV.** Kelly Reno, Teri Garr, Vincent Spano; ***D:*** Robert Dalva; ***M:*** Georges Delerue. *FOX*

Black Starlet 🦴½ *Black Gauntlet* **1974 (R)** A girl from the projects of Chicago travels to Hollywood in search of fame. She winds her way through a world of sleaze and drugs in order to make it to the top. **90m/C VHS.** Juanita Brown, Eric Mason, Rockne Tarkington, Damu King, Diane Holden; ***D:*** Chris Munger. *GEM*

Black Sunday 🦴🦴🦴 **1960** Executed one hundred years previously, a witch returns with her vampire servant to do the bidding of Satan. A must see for horror fans; firsts for Steele as star and Bava as director. Also available with "Black Sabbath" on laserdisc. **83m/B VHS.** *IT* Barbara Steele, John Richardson, Ivo Garrani, Andrea Checchi, Arturo Dominici; ***D:*** Mario Bava; ***M:*** Les Baxter. *SNC, MRV, MOV*

Black Sunday 🦴🦴½ **1977 (R)** An Arab terrorist group plots to steal the Goodyear Blimp and load it with explosives. Their intent is to explode it over a Miami Super Bowl game to assassinate the U.S. president and to kill all the fans. Based on Thomas Harris' novel. **143m/C VHS, Beta, LV.** Robert Shaw, Bruce Dern, Marthe Keller, Fritz Weaver, Steven Keats, Michael V. Gazzo, William Daniels; ***D:*** John Frankenheimer; ***W:*** Ernest Lehman; ***C:*** John A. Alonzo; ***M:*** John Williams. *PAR*

The Black Swan 🦴🦴🦴 **1942** Swashbuckling pirate film, based on the novel by Rafael Sabatini, stars Power as James Waring, compatriot of notorious buccanneer Henry Morgan (Cregar). Morgan is pardoned and sent to Jamaica as its new governor—if he can prevent his from associates from continuing their criminal ways. He enlists Waring to help him fight the renegades; meanwhile Waring falls in love with former governor's daughter Margaret (O'Hara). Lots of derring do. **85m/C VHS.** Tyrone Power, Maureen O'Hara, Laird Cregar, Thomas Mitchell, George Sanders, Anthony Quinn, George Zucco, Edward Ashley, Fortunio Bonanova; ***D:*** Henry King; ***W:*** Ben Hecht, Seton I. Miller; ***C:*** Leon Shamroy; ***M:*** Alfred Newman. Academy Awards '42: Best Color Cinematography; Nominations: Academy Awards '42: Best Original Score. *FXV*

Black Terrorist **1985** Terrorists take over a ranch and slay the inhabitants. They keep a young boy alive and the mother tries to rescue him. **81m/C VHS, Beta.** Allan Granville, Vera Jones; ***D:*** Neil Hetherington. *NO*

Black Tide 🦴🦴 *Stormy Crossing* **1958** Suspicions arise that a drowning may have actually been a murder. **69m/C VHS.** John Ireland, Derek Bond. *SNC, VYY*

Black Tights 🦴🦴½ *Un, Deux, Trois, Quatre!* **1960** Chevalier introduces four stories told in dance by Roland Petit's Ballet de Paris company: "The Diamond Crusher," "Cyrano de Bergerac," "A Merry Mourning," and "Carmen." A keeper for dance fans. Shearer's Roxanne in "Cyrano" was her last performance before retirement. **120m/C VHS, Beta.** *FR* Cyd Charisse, Zizi Jeanmarie, Moira Shearer, Dirk Sanders, Roland Petit; ***D:*** Terence Young. *VYY, NOS, VAI*

Black Tower 🦴🦴 **1950** An interesting murder mystery telling the story of a desperately impoverished medical student. **54m/B VHS, Beta.** Peter Cookson, Warren William, Anne Gwynne, Charles Calvert. *VYY*

Black Vampire 🦴½ *Blood Couple; Ganja and Hess; Double Possession* **1973 (R)** Jones plays a professor of African studies who is turned into a vampire by another vampire. He then marries the villain's ex-wife, played by Clark, a veteran of Russ Meyer films. Not much of a story but the acting is actually quite good and there are some creepy moments thanks mainly to an interesting score. **83m/C VHS, Beta.** Duane Jones, Marlene Clark, Bill Gunn, Sam Waymon, Leonard Jackson, Candece Tarpley, Mabel King; ***D:*** Bill Gunn; ***W:*** Bill Gunn. *GEM*

A Black Veil for Lisa 🦴🦴 **1968** A man attempts to exact revenge upon his unfaithful wife, but things go horribly awry. **87m/C VHS.** *IT GE* John Mills, Luciana Paluzzi, Robert Hoffman; ***D:*** Massimo Dallamano. *REP*

The Black Velvet Gown 🦴🦴½ **1992** Riah Millican (McTeer) is a poor miner's widow living in rural 1834 England with her three children. She finds work as a housekeeper to the reclusive Miller (Peck), who agrees to educate her children and even gives Riah the titular gown, which was once his mother's. Now educated out of their working-class, the Millican's lives provide unexpected love and tragedy for all concerned. Based on the novel by Catherine Cookson; made for British TV. **103m/C VHS.** *GB* Janet McTeer, Bob Peck, Geraldine Somerville; ***D:*** Norman Stone. *TVC*

Black Venus *Woof!* **1983 (R)** A soft-core epic, starring the former Miss Bahamas, Josephine Jacqueline Jones, about the 18th-century French aristocracy. Laughably based upon the stories of Balzac. European film dubbed in English. **80m/C VHS, Beta.** Josephine Jacqueline Jones, Emiliano Redondo; ***D:*** Claude Mulot. *MGM*

Black Water 🦴🦴½ **1994** Tennessee fishing trip turns into a nightmare for an innocent man accused of murder. Based on the novel "Minnie" by Hans Werner Kettenbach. **105m/C VHS.** Julian Sands, Stacey Dash, Ned Beatty, Ed Lauter, Denise Crosby, Billy McNamara, Rod Steiger; ***D:*** Nicolas Gessner; ***W:*** Nicolas Gessner, Laird Koeing; ***M:*** Gabriel Yared. *ACA*

Black Water Gold 🦴🦴½ **1969** Television movie about a search for sunken Spanish gold. **75m/C VHS.** Ricardo Montalban, Keir Dullea, Lana Wood, Bradford Dillman, France Nuyen; ***D:*** Alan Landsburg. *NO*

Black Werewolf 🦴🦴 *The Beast Must Die* **1975 (PG)** A millionaire sportsman invites a group of men and women connected with bizarre deaths or the eating of human flesh to spend the cycle of a full moon at his isolated lodge. **93m/C VHS, Beta, LV.** *GB* Peter Cushing, Calvin Lockhart, Charles Gray, Anton Diffring; ***D:*** Paul Annett; ***M:*** Jack Hildyard. *MED, PSM*

The Black Widow *Sombra, the Spider Woman* **1947** A fortune-teller plots to steal scientific secrets and take over the world. Serial in thirteen episodes. **164m/B VHS.** Bruce Edwards, Carol Forman, Anthony Warde; ***D:*** Spencer Gordon Bennet. *VCN, REP, MLB*

Black Widow 🦴🦴🦴 **1987 (R)** A federal agent pursues a beautiful murderess who marries rich men and then kills them, making the deaths look natural. The agent herself becomes involved in the final seduction. The two women are enticing and the locations picturesque. **101m/C VHS, Beta, LV.** Debra Winger, Theresa Russell, Sami Frey, Nicol Williamson, Terry O'Quinn, Dennis Hopper, D.W. Moffett, Lois Smith, Mary Woronov, Rutanya Alda, James Hong, Diane Ladd; ***Cameos:*** David Mamet; ***D:*** Bob Rafelson; ***W:*** Ronald Bass; ***C:*** Conrad Hall; ***M:*** Michael Small. *FOX*

The Black Windmill 🦴🦴½ **1974 (PG)** An English spy is caught between his service and the kidnapping of his family by rival spies. **102m/C VHS, Beta.** Michael Caine, Donald Pleasence, Delphine Seyrig, Clive Revill, Janet Suzman, John Vernon; ***D:*** Donald Siegel. *MCA*

Blackbeard the Pirate 🦴🦴 **1952** The 18th-century buccaneer is given the full-blooded, Hollywood treatment. **99m/C VHS, Beta, LV.** Robert Newton, Linda Darnell, Keith Andes, William Bendix, Richard Egan; ***D:*** Raoul Walsh. *TTC*

Blackbeard's Ghost 🦴🦴 **1967** Disney comedy in which the famed 18th-century pirate's spirit (Ustinov) is summoned to wreak havoc in order to prevent an old family home from being turned into a casino. **107m/C VHS, Beta, LV.** Peter Ustinov, Dean Jones, Suzanne Pleshette, Elsa Lanchester, Richard Deacon; ***D:*** Robert Stevenson; ***C:*** Edward Colman; ***M:*** Robert F. Brunner. *DIS*

Blackbelt 2: Fatal Force 🦴½ **1993 (R)** A man seeks to avenge his brother's murder by going after his killers. **?m/C VHS.** Blake Bahner, Roxanne Baird, Michael Vlastas. *NHO*

Blackboard Jungle 🦴🦴🦴½ **1955** Well-remembered urban drama about an idealistic teacher in a slum area who fights doggedly to connect with his unruly students. Bill Hailey's "Rock Around the Clock" over the opening credits was the first use of rock music in a mainstream feature film. Based on Evan Hunter novel. **101m/B VHS, Beta.** Glenn Ford, Anne Francis, Louis Calhern, Sidney Poitier, Vic Morrow, Richard Kiley, Margaret Hayes, John Hoyt, Warner Anderson; ***D:*** Richard Brooks; ***W:*** Richard Brooks. Nominations: Academy Awards '55: Best Art Direction/Set Decoration (B & W), Best Black and White Cinematography, Best Film Editing, Best Screenplay. *MGM*

Blackenstein *Woof! Black Frankenstein* **1973 (R)** Doctor into nouveau experimentation restores a man's arms and legs. But a jealous assistant gives our man a bogus injection, causing him to become "Blackenstein," a large African American with chip on hulking shoulder who enjoys killing people and otherwise causing big trouble. Ripe blaxploitation. **87m/C VHS, Beta.** John Hart, Ivory Stone, Andrea King, Liz Renay, Joe DiSue; ***D:*** William A. Levey. *MED*

Blackjack 🦴🦴 **1978 (R)** Las Vegas is the scene for action and excitement as the mob puts the hit on tough guy William Smith! **104m/C VHS.** William Smith, Tony Burton, Paris Earl, Damu King, Diane Summerfield, Angela May; ***D:*** John Evans. *TPV*

Blackmail 🦴🦴🦴 **1929** This first sound film for Great Britain and director Hitchcock features an early visualization of some typical Hitchcockian themes. The story follows the police investigation of a murder, and a detective's attempts to keep his girlfriend from being involved. Look for Hitchcock's screen cameo. Made as a silent, this was reworked to become a talkie. **86m/B VHS, Beta, LV.** *GB* Anny Ondra, John Longden, Sara Allgood, Charles Paton, Cyril Ritchard; ***Cameos:*** Alfred Hitchcock; ***D:*** Alfred Hitchcock; ***W:*** Charles Bennett, Alfred Hitchcock. *REP, MRV, NOS*

Blackmail 🦴🦴🦴 **1991 (R)** Familiar story is given new life in this suspenseful movie originally made for cable TV. Blakely is a lonely woman who succumbs to Midkiff's attentions. She doesn't suspect that he's conning her with the help of his lover, Toussaint. Engaging thriller adapted from a short story by Bill Crenshaw. **87m/C VHS, Beta, LV.** Susan Blakely, Dale Midkiff, Beth Toussaint, John Saxon, Mac Davis; ***D:*** Ruben Preuss. *PAR*

Blackout 🦴½ **1950** Blind man recovers his sight and finds that the brother of his girlfriend, once thought dead, is actually alive and well and running a smuggling ring. Routine. **73m/B VHS, Beta.** *GB* Maxwell Reed, Dinah Sheridan, Patric Doonan, Eric Pohlmann; ***D:*** Robert S. Baker. *SNC*

Blackout 🦴🦴 *Murder by Proxy* **1954** A drunken private eye is offered a murder case, and is subsequently framed for the crime. **87m/B VHS, Beta, LV.** Dane Clark, Belinda Lee, Betty Ann Davies; ***D:*** Terence Fisher. *MLB*

Blackout 🦴🦴 **1978 (R)** Four killers terrorize an office building during the 1977 New York electrical blackout. Soon the police enter, confront them, and the fun starts. Comic touches provide some relief from the violence here. **86m/C VHS, Beta.** Jim Mitchum, Robert Carradine, Ray Milland, June Allyson, Jean-Pierre Aumont, Belinda J. Montgomery; ***D:*** Eddy Matalon; ***W:*** Joseph Stefano. *NLC*

Blackout 🦴🦴½ **1985** Made-for-cable-TV thriller. An aging police chief suspects a disfigured amnesiac is responsible for past killings, in spite of the fact that he now leads a subdued family life. **99m/C VHS, Beta.** Richard Widmark, Keith Carradine, Kathleen Quinlan, Michael Beck, Gerald Hiken; ***D:*** Douglas Hickox; ***W:*** David Ambrose. *MED*

Blackout 🦴🦴 **1988 (R)** Strange memories from childhood come back to her as a woman fights for her life. **91m/C VHS, Beta, LV.** Carol Lynley, Gail O'Grady, Michael Keys Hall, Joseph Gian, Joanna Miles; ***D:*** Doug Adams. *NO*

The Blacksmith/The Balloonatic **1923** Two Buster Keaton shorts: "The Blacksmith" (1922) features Buster as the local blacksmith's apprentice who suddenly finds himself in charge. "The Balloonatic" (1923) presents Buster trapped in a runaway hot air balloon. Both films include music score. **57m/B VHS, Beta.** Buster Keaton, Virginia Fox, Phyllis Haver; ***D:*** Buster Keaton. *VYY*

The Blacksmith/The Cops **1922** "The Blacksmith" is a burlesque of Longfellow's famous poem "The Village Blacksmith." In "Cops" Buster tries a new business venture to win his girl's hand. Chaos ensues. Silent comedy at its most adroit. **38m/B VHS, Beta.** Buster Keaton, Virginia Fox. *CCB*

Blacksnake! *Woof!* **1973 (R)** Overheated sex and race tale, set in 1835, finds a British lord travelling to a Caribbean island in search of his brother. What he finds is his sadistic sister-in-law and her evil overseer using violence to keep the slaves in line. **83m/C VHS.** Anouska Hempel, David Warbeck, Percy Herbert, David Prowse; ***D:*** Russ Meyer. *RMF*

Blacula 🦴🦴 **1972 (PG)** The African Prince Mamuwalde stalks the streets of Los Angeles trying to satisfy his insatiable desire for blood. Mildly successful melding of blaxploitation and horror that spawned a sequel, "Scream, Blacula, Scream." **92m/C VHS, Beta, LV.** William Marshall, Thalmus Rasulala, Denise Nicholas, Vonetta McGee; ***D:*** William Crain. *ORI*

Blade 🦴🦴 **1972 (PG)** An honest cop challenges a dirty cover-up in killer-stalked New York. **79m/C VHS, Beta.** Steve Landesburg, John Schuck, Kathryn Walker; ***D:*** Ernie Pintoff. *GEM, MRV*

Blade in Hong Kong 🦴🦴½ **1985** Made-for-TV action outing. Investigator travels to Hong Kong, finds trouble and romance in the underbelly of the city. Pilot for un-sold series. **100m/C VHS.** Terry Lester, Keye Luke, Mike Preston, Jean-Marie Hon, Leslie Nielsen, Nancy Kwan, Anthony Newley, Ellen Regan; ***D:*** Reza Badiyi. *NO*

A Blade in the Dark 🦴🦴 *La Casa Con La Scala Nel Buio; House of the Dark Stairway* **1983** A young man composing a score for a horror film moves into a secluded villa and is inspired and haunted by the mysterious murder he witnesses. **99m/C VHS, Beta.** Andrea Occhipinti, Anny Papa; ***D:*** Lamberto Bava. *VES, LIV*

Blade Master 🦴½ *Ator the Invincible* **1984 (PG)** In this sequel to "Ator the Fighting Eagle," O'Keeffe as Ator is back as the Blade Master. Ator defends his people and his family name in a battle against the "Geometric Nucleus": a primitive bomb. His quest leads him and his small band of men to the castle of knowledge. **92m/C VHS, Beta.** Miles O'Keeffe, Lisa Foster; ***D:*** David Hills. *MED*

Blade of the Ripper *Woof!* **1984** A madman armed with a razor slashes his way through the lovelies of the international jet set. **90m/C VHS, Beta.** George Hilton, Edwige Fenech. *NO*

Blade Runner 🦴🦴🦴½ **1982 (R)** Los Angeles, the 21st century. World-weary cop tracks down a handful of renegade "replicants" (synthetically produced human slaves who, with only days left of life, search madly for some way to extend their prescribed lifetimes). Moody, beautifully photographed, dark thriller with sets from an architect's dream. Based on "Do Androids Dream of Electric Sheep" by Philip K. Dick. Laser edition features restored footage, information about special effects, and production sketches. Director's cut, released at 117 minutes, removes Ford's narration and the last scene of the film, which Scott considered too "up," and inserts several short scenes, including a dream sequence. **122m/C VHS, Beta, LV, 8mm.** Harrison Ford, Rutger Hauer, Sean Young, Daryl Hannah, M. Emmet Walsh, Edward James Olmos, Joe Turkel, Brion James, Joanna Cassidy, William Sanderson; ***D:*** Ridley Scott; ***W:*** Hampton Fancher, David Peoples; ***C:*** Jordan Cronenweth; ***M:*** Vangelis. Los Angeles Film Critics Association Awards '82: Best Cinematography; Nominations: Academy Awards '82: Best Art Direction/Set Decoration. *COL, WAR, CRC*

Blades 🦴 **1989 (R)** Another junk heap from Troma, dealing with the efforts of three golfers who try to stop a maniacal power mower that's been grinding duffers with regularity. **101m/C VHS, Beta, LV.** Robert North, Jeremy Whelan, Victoria Scott, Jon McBride. *MED*

Blades of Courage 🦴🦴 *Skate!* **1988** A made-for-television biography of Olympic skater Lori Larouche. Choreographed by Debbi Wilkes. **98m/C VHS, Beta.** *CA* Lynn Nightingale, Christianne Hirt, Colm Feore, Rosemary Dunsmore; ***D:*** Randy Bradshaw. *ACA*

Bladestorm 🦴 **1986** Ultra-cheapo fantasy/warrior rehash. **87m/C VHS, Beta.** *NO*

Blaise Pascal 🦴🦴🦴½ **1971** Another of Rossellini's later historical portraits, detailing the life and times of the 17th-century philosopher, seen as a man whose scientific ideas conflicted with his own religious beliefs. Made for Italian television. In Italian with subtitles. **131m/C VHS, Beta.** *IT* ***D:*** Roberto Rossellini. *FCT*

Blake of Scotland Yard **1936** Blake, the former Scotland Yard inspector, battles against a villain who has constructed a murderous death ray. Condensed version of the 15 episode serial (originally at 180 minutes). **70m/B VHS, Beta.** Ralph Byrd, Herbert Rawlinson, Joan Barclay, Lloyd Hughes; ***D:*** Robert F. "Bob" Hill. *VYY, DVT, NOS*

Blake's Seven **1978** Freedom-fighter Blake and his crew battle against a totalitarian super-power in this futuristic space adventure series from Great Britain. Created by Terry Nation of "Doctor Who" fame. Each volume contains two episodes and is available individually. **105m/C VHS.** *GB* Gareth Thomas, Sally Knyvette, Paul Darrow, Michael Keating, David Jackson, Jan Chappell; ***D:*** Michael E. Briant, Vere Lorrimer. *VCO, TVC, MOV*

Blame It on Rio 🦴🦴 **1984 (R)** A middle-aged man has a ridiculous fling with his best friend's daughter while on vacation with them in Rio de Janeiro. Caine and Johnson are amusing, but the script is somewhat weak. Remake of the French film "One Wild Moment." **90m/C VHS, Beta, LV.** Michael Caine, Joseph Bologna, Demi Moore, Michelle Johnson, Valerie Harper; ***D:*** Stanley Donen; ***W:*** Charlie Peters, Larry Gelbart. *VES, LIV*

Blame It on the Bellboy 🦴🦴½ **1992 (PG-13)** Wild farce set in Venice about a hotel bellboy who confuses three similarly named visitors—sending the wrong ones to meet corporate bigwigs, date women, or even kill. The brisk pace loses it towards the end and devolves into chase scenes. **79m/C VHS, Beta.** Dudley Moore, Bryan Brown, Richard Griffiths, Andreas

Katsulas, Patsy Kensit, Alison Steadman, Bronson Pinchot, Lindsay Anderson, Penelope Wilton; ***D:*** Mark Herman; ***W:*** Mark Herman; ***M:*** Trevor Jones. *HPH*

Blame It on the Night **1984 (PG-13)** A rock star gets to take care of the military cadet son he never knew after the boy's mother suddenly dies. Mick Jagger helped write the story. Available in VHS and Beta Hi-Fi. **85m/C VHS, Beta.** Nick Mancuso, Byron Thames, Leslie Ackerman, Billy Preston, Merry Clayton; ***D:*** Gene Taft. *FOX*

Blank Check *Disney's Blank Check* **1993 (PG)** Parents may want to verify the whereabouts of their checkbooks after this one. 11-year-old Preston receives a blank check from a mobster on the run, cashes it for a million bucks, and goes on a spending orgy under an assumed name. Where are his parents? Apparently they don't have a problem with a shadowy benefactor taking their son under his wing. Sound familiar? And who thought it would be a good idea to have the little twerp mooning after a comely bank teller? Formula aside, this blatant rip-off of "Home Alone" tries to throw in an ending moral but probably won't fool the kids either. **93m/C VHS, LV.** Brian Bonsall, Miguel Ferrer, Michael Lerner, Tone Loc, Rick Ducommun, Karen Duffy; ***D:*** Rupert Wainwright; ***W:*** Colby Carr, Blake Snyder; ***M:*** Nicholas Pike. *DIS*

Blankman **1994 (PG-13)** Self-appointed superhero (Wayans), who makes up in creativity what he lacks in superpowers, fights crime in his underwear and a cape made from his grandmother's bathrobe. Life is simple, until an ambitious TV reporter (Givens) finds out about him. Silly one-joke premise is carried a little too far; didn't similar "Meteor Man" crash? Gifted comedian Wayans tries, but can't make this guy fly. **96m/C VHS, LV.** Damon Wayans, Robin Givens, David Alan Grier, Jason Alexander, Jon Polito; ***D:*** Mike Binder; ***W:*** Damon Wayans, J.F. Lawton. *COL*

The Blasphemer **1921** A well-crafted, engrossing drama about misfortune that befalls someone who disobeys one of the sacred Commandments. Silent music score. **89m/B VHS, Beta.** *VYY*

Blast-Off Girls **1967** A scuzzball promoter sets out to avenge himself for being blacklisted by the rock 'n' roll industry. He discovers a fresh group, but without corporate backing he can only pay them with groovy clothes and mini-skirted girls. Trouble ensues when they unexpectedly hit the charts and want real money. **83m/C VHS.** Ray Sager, Dan Conway; ***D:*** Herschell Gordon Lewis. *MOV, SMW*

Blastfighter *Woof!* **1985 (R)** After local hoodlums kill his daughter, an ex-con cop goes on a spree of violence and revenge. Director Bava uses the pseudonym "John Old, Jr.," as his father Mario Bava occasionally credited himself as John Old. Italian film shot in Atlanta. **93m/C VHS, Beta.** *IT* Michael Sopkiw, Valerie Blake, George Eastman; ***D:*** Lamberto Bava. *VES, LIV*

Blaze ½ **1989 (R)** The true story of Louisiana governor Earl Long who became involved with a stripper, Blaze Starr, causing a political scandal of major proportions. Robust, good-humored bio-pic featuring a fine character turn by Newman. **117m/C VHS, Beta, LV.** Paul Newman, Lolita Davidovich, Jerry Hardin, Robert Wuhl, Gailard Sartain, Jeffrey DeMunn, Richard Jenkins, Garland Bunting; ***D:*** Ron Shelton; ***W:*** Ron Shelton; ***C:*** Haskell Wexler. Nominations: Academy Awards '89: Best Cinematography. *TOU*

Blazing Guns *Marshal of Heldorado* **1950** A marshal, masquerading inexplicably as a tenderfoot, enters a lawless town and is immediately hired as a deputy. **54m/B VHS, Beta, LV.** Raymond Hatton, Russell Hayden, Fuzzy Knight, Julie Adams. *NOS, HEG*

Blazing Saddles ½ **1974 (R)** Wild, wacky spoof by Brooks of every cliche in the western film genre. Little is Black Bart, a convict offered a reprieve if he will become a sheriff and clean up a nasty frontier town; the previous recipients of this honor have all swiftly ended up in shallow graves. A crazy, silly film with a cast full of lovable loonies including comedy greats Wilder, Kahn, and Korman. Watch for the Count Basie Orchestra. A group writing effort, based on an original story by Bergman. Was the most-viewed movie in its first year of release on HBO cable. **90m/C VHS, Beta, LV.** Cleavon Little, Harvey Korman, Madeline Kahn, Gene Wilder, Mel Brooks, John Hillerman, Alex Karras, Dom DeLuise, Liam Dunn; ***D:*** Mel Brooks; ***W:*** Mel Brooks, Norman Steinberg, Andrew Bergman, Richard Pryor; ***C:*** Joseph Biroc; ***M:*** John Morris. Writers Guild of America '74: Best Original Screenplay; Nominations: Academy Awards '74: Best Film Editing, Best Song ("Blazing Saddles"), Best Supporting Actress (Kahn). *WAR*

Blazing Stewardesses *Woof!* **1975 (R)** The Hound salutes the distributor for truth in advertising, as they stamped this as one of the world's worst videos. Lusty, busty stewardesses relax at a western guest ranch under siege from hooded riders and the aging gags of the Ritz Brothers. **95m/C VHS.** Yvonne De Carlo, Bob Livingston, Donald (Don "Red") Barry, Regina Carrol; ***Cameos:*** The Ritz Brothers; ***D:*** Al Adamson. *NO*

Bleak House ½ **1985** The British television mini-series adaptation of the Charles Dickens tome about an interminable lawsuit and the decadent, criminal ruling class of 19th-century England. On three tapes. **391m/C VHS, Beta.** *GB* Denholm Elliott, Diana Rigg, Philip Franks, Peter Vaughan, T.P. McKenna; ***D:*** Ross Devenish; ***M:*** Geoffrey Burgon. *FOX, SIG, TVC*

Bless the Beasts and Children ½ **1971 (PG)** A group of six teenage boys at a summer camp attempt to save a herd of buffalo from slaughter at a national preserve. Treacly Kramer backwater. Based on the novel by Glendon Swarthout. **109m/C VHS, Beta.** Billy Mumy, Barry Robins, Miles Chapin, Darel Glaser, Bob Kramer, Ken Swofford, Jesse White; ***D:*** Stanley Kramer; ***M:*** Perry Botkin. Nominations: Academy Awards '71: Best Song ("Bless the Beasts and the Children"). *COL*

Blessed Event **1932** Fast-moving, entertaining film about a Broadway gossip columnist with a poison pen. Tracy has the role of a lifetime as a Walter Winchell prototype who thinks no one is exempt from his juicy column. Powell makes film debut as a crooner after a brief career as a band singer. Based on a play by Manuel Seff and Forrest Wilson. **77m/B VHS.** Lee Tracy, Mary Brian, Dick Powell, Allen Jenkins, Ruth Donnelly, Emma Dunn, Walter Miller, Tom Dugan, Isabel Jewell; ***D:*** Roy Del Ruth; ***W:*** Howard J. Green. *MGM*

Blessing **1994** It's an unhappy time down on the Wisconsin dairy farm in this tale of family life. Embittered patriarch Jack (Griffis) can barely make a go of it and takes his frustrations out by beating his cows and climbing to the top of the silo. Despairing wife Arlene (Glynn) enters newspaper lotteries and collects religious statues while daughter Randi (Griffis) keeps delaying leaving the farm because of a nagging sense of responsibility. Claustrophobic atmosphere. **94m/C VHS.** Guy Griffis, Carlin Glynn, Melora Griffis, Gareth Williams, Clovis Siemon; ***D:*** Paul Zehrer; ***W:*** Paul Zehrer; ***C:*** Stephen Kazmierski; ***M:*** Joseph S. DeBeasi. Nominations: Independent Spirit Awards '95: First Screenplay. *LEO*

Blind Ambition ½ **1982** Television mini-series docu-drama traces the career of John Dean, special counsel to President Richard M. Nixon. Focuses on his fractured personal life and touches on virtually all of the Watergate headlines. **95m/C VHS, Beta.** Martin Sheen, Rip Torn. *TLF*

Blind Date ½ **1984 (R)** Blind man agrees to have a visual computer implanted in his brain in order to help the police track down a psychopathic killer. Violent scenes may be disturbing to some. **100m/C VHS, Beta, LV.** Joseph Bottoms, Kirstie Alley, Keir Dullea, James Daughton, Lana Clarkson, Marina Sirtis; ***D:*** Nico Mastorakis; ***W:*** Nico Mastorakis. *VES, LIV*

Blind Date **1987 (PG-13)** A blind date between a workaholic yuppie and a beautiful blonde starts off well, but when she drinks too much at dinner, things get out of hand. In addition to embarrassing her date and destroying the restaurant, she has a jealous ex-boyfriend who must be dealt with. **95m/C VHS, Beta, LV.** Kim Basinger, Bruce Willis, John Larroquette, William Daniels, George Coe, Mark Blum, Phil Hartman, Stephanie Faracy, Alice Hirson, Graham Stark; ***D:*** Blake Edwards; ***C:*** Harry Stradling Jr.; ***M:*** Henry Mancini. *COL*

Blind Faith **1989 (R)** Action and adventure take a turn for the horrific when several men find themselves in captivity. **?m/C VHS.** Eric Gunn, Kevin Yon, Lynne Browne; ***D:*** Dean Wilson; ***W:*** Dean Wilson. *HHE*

Blind Fear ½ **1989 (R)** A blind woman is stalked by three killers in an abandoned country inn. **98m/C VHS, Beta, LV.** Shelley Hack, Jack Langedijk, Kim Coates, Jan Rubes, Heidi von Palleske; ***D:*** Tom Berry; ***W:*** Sergio D. Altieri. *ACA*

Blind Fists of Bruce ½ **197?** A rich, idle young man learns the techniques of kung fu from a former warrior. **92m/C VHS, Beta.** Bruce Li; ***D:*** Kam Bo. *NO*

Blind Fools ½ **1940** A scathing indictment of children neglected by ambitious parents. **66m/B VHS, Beta, LV.** Herbert Rawlinson, Claire Whitney, Russell Hicks, Miriam Battista. *NO*

Blind Fury ½ **1990 (R)** A blind Vietnam vet enlists the aid of a Zen master and a sharpshooter to tackle the Mafia. Hauer works well in the lead, but unfortunately, the movie doesn't. **86m/C VHS, Beta, LV.** Rutger Hauer, Terry O'Quinn, Brandon Call, Lisa Blount, Randall "Tex" Cobb, Noble Willingham, Meg Foster, Sho Kosugi, Nick Cassavetes, Charles Cooper, Rick Overton; ***D:*** Phillip Noyce; ***W:*** Charles Robert Carner; ***M:*** J. Peter Robinson. *COL, FCT*

Blind Husbands ½ **1919** An Austrian officer is attracted to the pretty wife of a dull surgeon. Controversial in its day, this lurid, sumptuous melodrama instigated many stubborn Hollywood myths, including the stereotype of the brusque, jodhpur-clad Prussian officer. This was von Stroheim's first outing as director. **98m/B VHS, Beta.** Erich von Stroheim, Fay Wray; ***D:*** Erich von Stroheim. *VYY, GVV*

Blind Justice **1986** An innocent man is identified as a rapist, and the accusation ruins his life. Made for television. **94m/C VHS, Beta.** Tim Matheson, Lisa Eichhorn, Mimi Kuzyk, Philip Charles MacKenzie, Tom Atkins; ***D:*** Rod Holcomb; ***M:*** Miles Goodman. *FOX*

Blind Justice ½ **1994 (R)** Gunfighter gets blinded in battle and rides into a small town where he's nursed back to health by an attractive lady doctor. While he recovers, he learns the town is trying to protect a cache of government silver from being stolen by bandits. Made for cable TV. **85m/C VHS.** Armand Assante, Elisabeth Shue, Robert Davi; ***D:*** Richard Spence. *HBO*

Blind Man's Bluff **1991 (PG-13)** A blind professor is accused of murdering his neighbor, but as he tries to solve the mystery, evidence points to his ex-girlfriend who may have framed him for the murder. Surprisingly suspenseful made for cable TV movie is hampered by a stock Hollywood ending. **86m/C VHS, Beta.** Robert Urich, Lisa Eilbacher, Patricia Clarkson, Ken Pogue, Ron Perlman; ***D:*** James Quinn; ***W:*** Joel Gross; ***M:*** Richard Bellis. *PAR*

Blind Rage **1978 (R)** When the United States government transports $15 million to the Philippines, five blind kung fu masters want a piece of the action. **81m/C VHS, Beta.** *PH* D'Urville Martin, Leo Fong, Tony Ferrer, Dick Adair, Darnell Garcia, Leila Hermosa, Fred Williamson; ***D:*** Efren C. Pinon. *MGM*

Blind Side ½ **1993 (R)** DeMornay and Silver are a married couple whose Mexican vacation turns into trouble when they get into a hit-and-run accident which they don't report. Back home, they're frightened by the sudden appearance of Hauer, who's also just back from Mexico. They think he's after blackmail but he's really just a run-of-the-mill psycho intrigued by DeMornay, who at least keeps her character in control. Silver and Hauer have a great time chewing scenery. Made for cable television. Also available in an unrated version which run 98 minutes. **92m/C VHS.** Rebecca DeMornay, Ron Silver, Rutger Hauer; ***D:*** Geoff Murphy; ***W:*** John Carlen. *HBO*

Blind Spot ½ **1993** Okay family drama which works because of the performances and not the script. Woodward stars as Nell Harrington, a take-charge U.S. Representative long married to Simon (Weaver). Her troubled, pregnant daughter Phoebe (Linney) is married to Nell's aide Charlie (Diamond).

Charlie is killed and Phoebe injured in a car crash but the real tragedy is when Nell discovers what caused the accident—drugs—and that her daughter is a cocaine addict. Lots of suffering. Made for television. **99m/C VHS.** Joanne Woodward, Laura Linney, Fritz Weaver, Reed Edward Diamond, Cynthia Martells, Patti Yasutake, Patti D'Arbanville; ***D:*** Michael Toshiyuki Uno; ***W:*** Nina Shengold; ***M:*** Patrick Williams. *REP*

Blind Vengeance ½ **1990 (R)** A man whose son was murdered by white supremacists decides to take his own special revenge when they are acquited by the local jury. But this isn't your usual bloodbath, instead he plays psychological games with the men, waiting for them to break. Made for cable television. **93m/C VHS.** Gerald McRaney, Marg Helgenberger, Thalmus Rasulala, Lane Smith, Don Hood, Grand Bush; ***D:*** Lee Philips; ***W:*** Henri Simoun, Curt Allen. *MCA*

Blind Vision ½ **1991** Von Dohlen stars as William Dalton, a mail clerk who is in love with his beautiful neighbor Leanne (Shelton). Suffering from extreme shyness, Dalton can only spy on her through a telephoto lens. Things start to get complicated for him when one of Leanne's boyfriends turns up dead outside her apartment. Soon afterwards, their landlady and a local police detective uncover a shocking sexual secret that forces Dalton into a deadly game of obsession and desire. **92m/C VHS, LV.** Lenny Von Dohlen, Deborah Shelton, Ned Beatty, Robert Vaughn, Louise Fletcher; ***D:*** Shuki Levy. *WOV*

Blind Witness ½ **1989** Routine story about a blind woman who's the only witness to her husband's murder during a robbery. Made for television. **92m/C VHS.** Victoria Principal, Paul LeMat, Stephen Macht, Matt Clark, Tim Choate; ***D:*** Richard A. Colla; ***M:*** Robert Alcivar. *WOV*

Blinded by the Light **1982** Young woman tries to save her brother from attachment to a quasi-religious cult, The Light of Salvation. Real-life brother and sister McNichol team up in this made-for-television drama, one of the earlier examinations of cult behavior. **90m/C VHS, Beta.** Kristy McNichol, Jimmy McNichol, Anne Jackson, Michael McGuire; ***D:*** John Alonzo. *TLF*

Blindfold: Acts of Obsession
1994 (R) Madeline's (Doherty) marriage is boring so she consults therapist Jennings (Nelson). He suggests a number of sexual fantasies Madeline plays out with hubby Woods only to have murder enter the picture. Then Madeline's older sister Chris (Alfonso) is assigned to investigate and lets out lots of family secrets. Shannen in the buff, murder, infidelity, deception, and sex. An unrated version is also available. **93m/C VHS.** Shannen Doherty, Judd Nelson, Michael Woods, Kristian Alfonso, Shell Danielson, Drew Snyder; ***D:*** Lawrence L. Simeone; ***W:*** Lawrence L. Simeone; ***M:*** Shuki Levy. *AVE*

Blindside **1988 (R)** A surveillance hobbyist who owns a motel spies on his tenants until a murder involves him in a big-scale drug war. **98m/C VHS, Beta, LV.** Harvey Keitel, Lori Hallier, Lolita Davidovich, Alan Fawcett, Michael Rudder; ***D:*** Paul Lynch. *NLC*

Blindsided ½ **1993 (PG-13)** A former police officer temporarily loses his sight when he plays the middle man in a bank robbery. Sight improving, he falls for a woman who draws him into another crime. **93m/C VHS, LV.** Jeff Fahey, Mia Sara, Rudy Ramos, Jack Kehler, Ben Gazzara; ***D:*** Tom Donnelly. *MCA*

Blink ½ **1993 (R)** Recent corneal transplants allow blind musician Emma (Stowe) to regain her sight, but until they "settle" what she sees may not register in her mind immediately, a phenomenon the script dubs "retroactive vision." This poses a problem for Chicago cop Quinn when he falls for Emma—the only one who can recognize a sadistic killer. Average thriller has been done better before, but adds two attractive leads, enough suspense, and a unique twist to the typical woman-in-jeopardy tale to keep things interesting. The distorted images in Stowe's blurry vision were created by computer. Stowe also learned fiddle for her place as the fictional member of the real-life Irish-American band, The Drovers. **106m/C VHS, LV.** Madeleine Stowe, Aidan Quinn, Laurie Metcalf, James Remar, Bruce A. Young, Peter Friedman, Paul Dillon, Michael Kirkpatrick; ***D:*** Michael Apted; ***W:*** Dana Stevens; ***C:*** Dante Spinotti; ***M:*** Brad Fiedel. *NLC*

Blink of an Eye ½ **1992 (R)** Special agent Sam Browning (Pare) must use his psychic powers and military skills against the terrorists who have kidnapped the CIA director's daughter. **90m/C VHS, LV.** Michael Pare. *VMK*

Bliss ½ **1985 (R)** A savage, surreal Australian comedy about an advertising executive who dies suddenly for a few minutes, and upon his awakening he finds the world maniacally, bizarrely changed. Based on the Peter Carey novel, and one of the most inspired absurdist films of the decade. **112m/C VHS, Beta, LV.** *AU* Barry Otto, Lynette Curran, Helen Jones; ***D:*** Ray Lawrence; ***W:*** Peter Carey. Australian Film Institute '85: Best Film. *NWV, VTR*

The Bliss of Mrs. Blossom
1968 Three's a crowd in this light-hearted romp through the machinations of a brassiere manufacturer (Attenborough) and his neglected wife (MacLaine). Mrs. Blossom finds sewing machine repairman Booth so appetizing that she hides him in the attic of the Blossom home. He reads books and redecorates, until, several plot twists later, Attenborough discovers the truth. Witty and wise, with fine supporting cast and excellent pacing. **93m/C LV.** *GB* Shirley MacLaine, Richard Attenborough, James Booth, Freddie Jones, John Cleese; ***D:*** Joseph McGrath. *PAR, MOV*

Blithe Spirit ½ **1945** Charming and funny adaptation of Coward's famed stage play. A man re-marries and finds his long-dead wife is unhappy enough about it to come back and haunt him. Clever supporting cast, with Rutherford exceptional as the medium. Received Oscar for its Special Effects. **96m/C VHS.** *GB* Rex Harrison, Constance Cummings, Kay Hammond, Margaret Rutherford, Hugh Wakefield, Joyce Carey; ***D:*** David Lean. Academy Awards '46: Best Special Effects. *MLB*

The Blob ½ **1958** Sci fi thriller about a small town's fight against a slimy jello invader from space. Slightly rebellious McQueen (in his first starring role) redeems himself when he saves the town with quick action. Low-budget, horror/teen-fantasy became a camp classic. Other names considered included "The Glob," "The Glob that Girdled the Globe," "The Meteorite Monster," "The Molten Meteorite," and "The Night of the Creeping Dead." Followed by a worthless sequel in 1972, "Son of Blob" and a worthwhile remake in 1988. Laserdisc contains an additional fifteen minutes of McQueen interviews and the trailers for both the original and the 1988 remake. **83m/C VHS, Beta, LV.** Steve McQueen, Aneta Corsaut, Olin Howlin, Earl Rowe; ***D:*** Irvin S. Yeaworth Jr.; ***C:*** Thomas E. Spalding. *COL, GEM, MLB*

The Blob **1988 (R)** A hi-tech remake of the 1958 camp classic about a small town beset by a fast-growing, man-eating mound of glop shot into space by scientists, irradiated into an unnatural being, and then returned to earth. Well-developed characters make this an excellent tribute to the first film. **92m/C VHS, Beta, LV.** Kevin Dillon, Candy Clark, Joe Seneca, Shawnee Smith, Donovan Leitch, Jeffrey DeMunn, Ricky Paull Goldin; ***D:*** Chuck Russell; ***W:*** Frank Darabont, Chuck Russell. *COL*

Block-heads **1938** Twenty years after the end of WWI, soldier Stan is found, still in his foxhole, and brought back to America, where he moves in with old pal Ollie. Also includes a 1934 Charley Chase short "I'll Take Vanilla." **75m/B VHS, Beta.** Stan Laurel, Oliver Hardy, Billy Gilbert, Patricia Ellis, James Finlayson, Charley Chase; ***D:*** John Blystone. *CCB, MED, MLB*

Blockhouse *Woof!* **1973** Four men are entombed in a subterranean stronghold for six years after the D-Day invasion of Normandy. Encourages claustrophobic feeling in viewer. Based on Jean Paul Cleberts' novel "Le Blockhaus." **88m/C VHS, Beta.** *GB* Peter Sellers, Charles Aznavour, Per Oscarsson, Peter Vaughan, Leon Lissek, Alfred Lynch, Jeremy Kemp; ***D:*** Clive Rees. *NO*

Blonde Blackmailer **1958** Boring story about an innocent man who serves time for the murder of a female blackmailer. When he's released, he searches for the real killer. **69m/B VHS.** *GB* Richard Arlen, Susan Shaw, Vincent Ball, Constance Leigh; ***D:*** Charles Deane; ***W:*** Charles Deane. *RXM*

Blonde Cobra/The Doctor's Dream
1984 Here are two short films by Ken Jacobs: Underground film star Jack Smith reminisces about his career in "Blonde Cobra" and a country doctor saves the life of a little girl in "Doctor's Dream." **57m/C VHS, Beta.** *NO*

Blonde Crazy ½ *Larceny Lane* **1931** A charming grifter hooks up with a gorgeous blonde as he works the territory of a big wheel criminal. Escapist fare, with fun performances from Cagney and Blondell. **81m/B VHS.** James Cagney, Joan Blondell, Louis Calhern, Ray Milland, Nat Pendleton; ***D:*** Roy Del Ruth. *MGM*

Blonde in Black Leather ½ **1977** A bored Italian housewife takes up with a leather-clad lady biker, and together they cavort about. **88m/C VHS, Beta.** Claudia Cardinale, Monica Vitti; ***D:*** Carlo DiPalma. *NLC*

Blonde Savage **1947** Charting African territories, an adventurer encounters a white jungle queen swinging amongst the vines. Essentially a cheap, distaff "Tarzan." **62m/B VHS, Beta.** Leif Erickson, Gale Sherwood, Veda Ann Borg, Douglass Dumbrille, Frank Jenks, Matt Willis, Ernest Whitman; ***D:*** Steve Sekely. *SNC*

Blonde Venus ½ **1932** A German cafe singer marries an Englishman, but their marriage hits the skids when he contracts radiation poisoning and she gets a nightclub job to pay the bills. Sternberg's and Dietrich's fourth film together, and characteristically beautiful, though terribly strange. Dietrich's cabaret number "Hot Voodoo," in a gorilla suit and blonde afro, attains new heights in early Hollywood surrealism. **94m/B VHS, Beta.** Marlene Dietrich, Herbert Marshall, Cary Grant, Dickie Moore, Hattie McDaniel, Sidney Toler; ***D:*** Josef von Sternberg. *MCA*

Blondes Have More Guns **1995 (R)** Very dumb detective Harry Bates (McGaharin) is investigating a chainsaw murder and falls for the mysterious Montana (Key), who's possibly a serial killer, or maybe it's her half-sister, Dakota (Lusiak). Spoof of "Basic Instinct" and others of that ilk, done in the usual Troma fashion. **90m/C VHS.** Michael McGaharin, Elizabeth Key, Gloria Lusiak, Richard Neil; ***D:*** George Merriweather. *TTV*

Blondie ½ **1938** Chic Young's famous comic strip debuted on the big screen with Singleton in the title role, Lake as the bumbling Dagwood, and Simms as Baby Dumpling (son Alexander, when he grows up). The couple are about to celebrate their 5th wedding anniversary when Dagwood loses his job and Blondie suspects him of infidelity. The series eventually contained 28 films. **68m/B VHS.** Penny Singleton, Arthur Lake, Larry Simms, Gene Lockhart, Ann Doran, Jonathan Hale, Gordon Oliver, Stanley Andrews; ***D:*** Frank Strayer; ***W:*** Richard Flournoy. *MOV*

Blondie Has Trouble ½ *Blondie Has Servant Trouble* **1940** Mr. Dithers has a property he just can't sell because of rumors that the house is haunted. So he offers to let the Bumsteads stay in it to prove that the rumors are false. The Bumsteads also find the creepy mansion comes complete with two equally creepy servants. 6th film in the series. **70m/B VHS.** Penny Singleton, Arthur Lake, Larry Simms, Danny Mummert, Jonathan Hale, Arthur Hohl, Esther Dale, Irving Bacon; ***D:*** Frank Strayer; ***W:*** Richard Flournoy. *MOV*

Blondie Hits the Jackpot ½ **1949** Dagwood is fired for the umpteenth time after he makes a mistake in a construction deal and tries frantically to get his job back. Meanwhile, Blondie wins the big prize on a radio quiz show. The 26th film in the series. **66m/B VHS.** Penny Singleton, Arthur Lake, Larry Simms, Marjorie Kent, Jerome Cowan, Lloyd Corrigan,

Danny Mummert, James Flavin; ***D:*** Edward L. Bernds; ***W:*** Jack Henley. *MOV*

Blondie in Society 🦴½ **1941** A weak entry (the ninth) in the comedic series. Dagwood brings home a pedigreed Great Dane and Blondie decides to enter the pooch in the local dog show. Then an important client of Dagwood's decides he wants the dog. **77m/B VHS.** Penny Singleton, Arthur Lake, Larry Simms, William Frawley, Edgar Kennedy, Jonathan Hale, Danny Mummert, Chick Chandler; ***D:*** Frank Strayer; ***W:*** Karen De Wolf. *MOV*

Blondie Knows Best 🦴½ **1946** Dagwood impersonates his boss, Mr. Dithers, and causes all sorts of problems. Howard, one of the Three Stooges, has a cameo as a myopic process-server. The 18th film in the series. **66m/B VHS.** Penny Singleton, Arthur Lake, Larry Simms, Marjorie Kent, Jonathan Hale, Steve Geray, Jerome Cowan, Danny Mummert; ***Cameos:*** Shemp Howard; ***D:*** Abby Berlin; ***W:*** Edward L. Bernds, Al Martin. *MOV*

Blondie Takes a Vacation 🦴🦴½ **1939** Third in the series of fluff films adapted from Chic Young's comic strip. After the Bumstead family is snubbed at a snobby mountain resort they move to a friendlier nearby hotel where they try to help out the owners who are in danger of losing their investment. Baby Dumpling does his bit by unleashing a skunk in the ventilation system of the competing hotel. **68m/B VHS.** Penny Singleton, Arthur Lake, Larry Simms, Danny Mummert, Donald Meek, Donald MacBride, Thomas Ross, Robert Wilcox, Irving Bacon; ***D:*** Frank Strayer; ***W:*** Richard Flournoy. *MOV*

Blondie's Blessed Event 🦴🦴½ **1942** Cookie is born, causing even more chaos in the Bumstead household. Meanwhile, Dagwood gets into trouble at work when he hires a cynical playwright to write an important speech for him. 11th entry in series. **69m/B VHS.** Penny Singleton, Arthur Lake, Larry Simms, Norma Jean Wayne, Jonathan Hale, Danny Mummert, Hans Conried, Irving Bacon, Stanley Brown, Mary Wickes, Paul Harvey, Arthur O'Connell; ***D:*** Frank Strayer; ***W:*** Richard Flournoy, Karen De Wolf, Connie Lee. *MOV*

Blood Alley 🦴🦴 **1955** A seasoned Merchant Marine captain takes on a cargo of refugee Chinese to smuggle through enemy territory. Middling, mid-career Wayne vehicle. **115m/C VHS, Beta, LV.** John Wayne, Lauren Bacall, Paul Fix, Joy Kim, Berry Kroeger, Mike Mazurki, Anita Ekberg; ***D:*** William A. Wellman; ***C:*** William Clothier. *WAR, FCT*

Blood and Black Lace 🦴 **1964** Beautiful models are being brutally murdered and an inspector is assigned to the case, but not before more gruesome killings occur. Bava is, as usual, violent and suspenseful. Horror fans will enjoy this flick. **90m/C VHS, Beta.** *IT FR GE* Cameron Mitchell, Eva Bartok, Mary Arden; ***D:*** Mario Bava. *MED*

Blood & Concrete: A Love Story 🦴🦴 **1990 (R)** Bizarre, violent and stylish film-noir spoof, definitely not for all tastes. The innocent hero gets drawn into a maelstrom of intrigue over a killer aphrodisiac drug. Beals, an addicted punk rocker, gets to perform a few songs. **97m/C VHS, LV.** Billy Zane, Jennifer Beals, Darren McGavin; ***D:*** Jeff Reiner; ***W:*** Jeff Reiner. *COL*

Blood and Guns 🦴½ **1979 (R)** Romance, revenge, and action abound in post-revolutionary Mexico. **96m/C VHS, Beta.** Orson Welles, Tomas Milian, John Steiner; ***D:*** Giulio Petroni. *MRV*

Blood and Roses 🦴🦴 *Et Mourir de Plaisir* **1961** A girl who is obsessed with her family's vampire background becomes posessed by a vampire and commits numerous murders. The photography is good, but the plot is hazy and only effective in certain parts. Based on the book "Carmilla" by Sheridan LeFanu. Later remade as "The Vampire Lovers" and "The Blood-Spattered Bride." **74m/C VHS.** Mel Ferrer, Elsa Martinelli, Annette Vadim, Marc Allegret; ***D:*** Roger Vadim; ***W:*** Roger Vadim. *PAR*

Blood and Sand 🦴🦴½ **1922** Vintage romance based on Vicente Blasco Ibanez's novel about the tragic rise and fall of a matador, and the women in his life. The film that made Valentino a star. Remade in 1941. Silent. **87m/B VHS, Beta.** Rudolph Valentino, Nita Naldi, Lila Lee, Walter Long; ***D:*** Fred Niblo. *REP, NOS, CAB*

Blood and Sand 🦴🦴🦴 **1941** Director Mamoulian "painted" this picture in the new technicolor technique, which makes it a veritable explosion of color and spectacle. Power is the matador who becomes famous and then falls when he is torn between two women, forsaking his first love, bullfighting. Based on the novel "Sangre y Arena" by Vicente Blasco Ibanez. This movie catapulted Hayworth to stardom, primarily for her dancing, but also for her sexiness and seductiveness (and of course, her acting). Remake of the 1922 silent classic; remade again in 1989. **123m/C VHS, Beta, LV.** Tyrone Power, Linda Darnell, Rita Hayworth, Alla Nazimova, Anthony Quinn, J. Carrol Naish, John Carradine, George Reeves; ***D:*** Rouben Mamoulian; ***W:*** Jo Swerling; ***C:*** Ernest Palmer, Ray Rennahan; ***M:*** Alfred Newman. Academy Awards '41: Best Color Cinematography; Nominations: Academy Awards '41: Best Interior Decoration. *FXV*

Blood and Sand 🦴🦴 **1989 (R)** A bullfighter on the verge of super-stardom risks it all when he falls under the spell of a sexy, seductive woman. Will she destroy his one opportunity for fame? Interesting for people who actually enjoy watching the "sport" of bullfighting. Originally made in 1922 and remade in 1941. **96m/C VHS, LV.** Christopher Rydell, Sharon Stone, Ana Torrent, Jose-Luis De Villalonga, Simon Andrew; ***D:*** Javier Elorrieta. *VMK*

Blood and Sand/Son of the Sheik **1926** A double feature containing two abridged versions; in "Blood and Sand," an idolized matador meets another woman just before his wedding; in "Son of the Sheik," a man believes he has been betrayed by a dancing girl, and he abducts her to seek revenge. Silent. **56m/B VHS, Beta.** Rudolph Valentino, Lila Lee, Vilma Banky. *CCB*

Blood and Steel **1925** The railroad tycoon's daughter and the construction foreman wind up together on an exciting train ride. Silent. **?m/B VHS, Beta, 8mm.** Helen Holmes, William Desmond; ***D:*** J.P. McGowan. *GVV*

Blood at Sundown 🦴½ **1988** Routine oater where man returns home after the Civil War to find his wife kidnapped by a group of Mexican outlaws who have also taken over his village. **92m/C VHS, Beta.** Giuliano Gemma, Hally Hamond, Nieves Navarro, Antonio Casas, Fernando Sancho, Pajarito, George Martin; ***D:*** Duccio Tessari. *IMP*

Blood Beach *Woof!* **1981 (R)** A group of teenagers are devoured by menacing sand, which keeps people from getting to the water by swallowing them whole. Weak parody with some humorous moments; more silly than scary. **92m/C VHS, Beta.** David Huffman, Marianna Hill, John Saxon, Burt Young, Otis Young; ***D:*** Jeffrey Bloom; ***W:*** Jeffrey Bloom. *MED*

Blood Beast Terror 🦴½ *The Vampire-Beast Craves Blood* **1967** An entomologist transforms his own daughter into a Deathshead Moth and she proceeds to terrorize and drink innocent victims' blood. **81m/C VHS, Beta.** *GB* Peter Cushing, Robert Flemyng, Wanda Ventham, Vanessa Howard; ***D:*** Vernon Sewell. *MON*

Blood Bride 🦴½ **19??** A lonely young woman finally finds happiness with her new husband but her world comes crashing about her with soul-mangling ferocity when she discovers he is actually a bloodthirsty maniac. **90m/C VHS, Beta.** Ellen Barber, Philip English. *NO*

Blood Brothers 🦴🦴 **1974 (R)** A young man who dreams of becoming a lawyer is disturbed when he discovers that his family has mafia ties. **148m/C VHS, Beta.** *IT* Claudia Cardinale, Franco Nero, Lina Polito; ***D:*** Pasquale Squitieri. *NO*

Blood Brothers **1977** James Grizzly Adams, who lives in the mountains of the American wilderness, relives the story of how he met his Indian blood brother, Nakuma. Beautiful scenery. **50m/C VHS, Beta.** Dan Haggerty, Denver Pyle, Don Shanks. *MCG*

Blood Clan 🦴½ **1991 (R)** Based on the true story of Katy Bane, daughter of notorious Scottish cult leader, Sawney Bane, in whose lair were found the remains of over 1000 killed and cannibalized followers. When found, Bane's entire family was sentenced to death with the exception of Katy, who left to make a new start in Canada. When a rash of mysterious deaths break out in Katy's new home, she must defend herself from rumors that her father's murderous cult is resurfacing. **91m/C VHS.** Gordon Pinsent, Michelle Little, Robert Wisden; ***D:*** Charles Wilkinson. *FXL*

Blood Cult 🦴 **1985** A bizarre series of murder-mutilations take place on a small midwestern campus. Contains graphic violence that is not for the squeamish. This film was created especially for the home video market. **92m/C VHS, Beta.** Chuck Ellis, Julie Andelman, Jim Vance, Joe Hardt; ***D:*** Christopher Lewis. *VCI*

Blood Debts **1983** A father is out for revenge after he saves his daughter from some hunters who raped her and also killed her boyfriend. **91m/C VHS, Beta.** Richard Harrison, Mike Manty, Jim Gaines, Anne Jackson, Anne Milhench; ***D:*** Teddy Page. *NO*

Blood Diner *Woof!* **1987** Two spirit-possessed, diner-owning brothers kill countless young girls for demonic rituals, and serve their corpses as gourmet food in their restaurant. Some funny moments mixed in with the requisite gore. Cult potential. **88m/C VHS, Beta.** Rick Burks, Carl Crew; ***D:*** Jackie Kong. *VES, LIV*

Blood Feast 🦴 *Feast of Flesh* **1963** The first of Lewis' gore-fests, in which a demented caterer butchers hapless young women to splice them together in order to bring back an Egyptian goddess. Dated, campy, and gross; reportedly shot in four days (it shows). **70m/C VHS, Beta.** Connie Mason, Thomas Wood, Malcolm Arnold; ***D:*** Herschell Gordon Lewis. *VTR, FCT*

Blood Feud 🦴🦴 *Revenge* **1979 (R)** In Italy preceding Europe's entry into WWII, a young widow is in mourning over the brutal murder of her husband by the Sicilian Mafia. In the meantime she must contend with the rivalry between Mastroianni as a lawyer and Giannini as a small-time crook both vying for her affections. Dubbed. **112m/C VHS, Beta.** *IT* Sophia Loren, Marcello Mastroianni, Giancarlo Giannini; ***D:*** Lina Wertmuller; ***W:*** Lina Wertmuller. *FOX*

Blood for a Silver Dollar 🦴½ **1966** Action-filled western, littered with murder, revenge and romance. **98m/C VHS, Beta.** Montgomery Wood, Evelyn Stewart. *VYY*

Blood for Blood 🦴½ **1995 (R)** Cop must take up the martial arts skills he learned in childhood in order to protect his family from assassination. **93m/C VHS, LV.** Lorenzo Lamas, James Lew, Mako, Eric Pierpont, James Shigeta, James Callahan; ***D:*** John Weidner; ***M:*** Joel Goldsmith. *LIV*

Blood Freak *Woof!* **1972** An absolutely insane anti-drug, Christian splatter film. A Floridian biker is introduced to drugs by a young woman and eventually turns into a poultry-monster who drinks the blood of junkies. Narrated by a chain smoker who has a coughing fit. Don't miss it. **86m/C VHS, Beta.** Steve Hawkes, Dana Culliver, Randy Grinter Jr., Tina Anderson, Heather Hughes; ***D:*** Steve Hawkes, Brad Grinter. *NO*

Blood Frenzy 🦴 **1987** Psychologist's patients take a therapeutic trip to the desert. The sun and heat take their toll, and everyone gets violent. This kind of therapy we don't need, and the movie's a waste, as well. Made for video. Loring was Wednesday on TV's "The Addams Family." **90m/C VHS, Beta.** John Montero, Lisa Loring, Hank Garrett, Wendy MacDonald; ***D:*** Hal Freeman. *NO*

Blood Games *Woof!* **1990 (R)** Buxom baseball team bats 1000 against the home team and the winning babes find out just how poor losers can be. Diamonds aren't always a girl's best friend. **90m/C VHS, LV.** Gregory Cummings, Laura Albert, Shelly Abblett, Luke Shay, Ross Hagen; ***D:*** Tanya Rosenberg. *COL*

Blood Hook ☠½ **1986** A self-parodying teenage-slasher film about kids running into a backwoods fishing tournament while on vacation, complete with ghouls, cannibalism and grotesquerie. **85m/C VHS, Beta.** Mark Jacobs, Lisa Todd, Patrick Danz; ***D:*** James Mallon. *PSM, PAR*

Blood Horse ☠☠½ **1994** Reeve and Todd maintain an uneasy peace with the local Native Americans until vigilantes attack the tribe. **90m/C VHS.** Christopher Reeve, Raoul Trujillo, Tony Todd; ***D:*** Steven Hilliard Stern. *CAF*

Blood In...Blood Out: Bound by Honor ☠½ *Bound by Honor* **1993 (R)** Three-hour epic about Chicano gang culture focuses on three buddies whose lives evolve into a drug-addicted artist, a narc, and a prison regular. Written by acclaimed poet Baca, the film touches on issues such as poverty, racism, drugs, and violence as they pertain to Hispanic life. Unfortunately, the extreme violence (shootings, stabbings, and garrotings) completely overwhelms the rest of the story. Contains profanity, nudity, and sexual innuendo. Based on a story by Ross Thomas. **180m/C VHS, Beta, LV.** Damian Chapa, Jesse Borrego, Benjamin Bratt, Enrique Castillo, Victor Rivers, Delroy Lindo, Tom Towles; ***D:*** Taylor Hackford; ***W:*** Floyd Mutrux, Jimmy Santiago Baca, Jeremy Iacone; ***M:*** Bill Conti. *HPH, TOU*

Blood Island ☠☠ *The Shuttered Room* **1968** A couple inherits an old house on a remote New England island where the woman grew up. They discover that this old house needs more than a paint job to make it livable; seems there's something evil in them there walls. Based on an H.P. Lovecraft story. Greene, who's best known for later directing "Godspell," and the solid cast fail to animate the inert script. **100m/C VHS.** *GB* Gig Young, Carol Lynley, Oliver Reed, Flora Robson; ***D:*** David Greene. *ACE*

Blood Lake *Woof!* **1987** A psychotic killer stalks teenagers, to the detriment of all. **90m/C VHS.** *VCI*

Blood Legacy ☠☠ *Legacy of Blood* **1973 (R)** Four heirs must survive a night in a lonely country estate to collect their money; what do you think happens? Average treatment of the haunted house theme. **77m/C VHS, Beta.** John Carradine, John Russell, Faith Domergue, Merry Anders; ***D:*** Carl Monson. *CNG, MRV, GEM*

Blood Lust ☠ **198?** Dr. Jekyll returns to London to wreak havoc upon the human race. **90m/C VHS, Beta.** *NO*

Blood Mania ☠ **1970 (R)** A retired surgeon's daughter decides to murder her father to collect her inheritance prematurely, but soon learns that crime doesn't pay as well as medicine. Low-budget, low-interest flick. **90m/C VHS, Beta.** Peter Carpenter, Maria de Aragon, Alex Rocco; ***D:*** Robert Vincent O'Neil. *NO*

Blood Money ☠½ **1980 (PG)** A dying ex-criminal returns to Australia to redeem his name and die with dignity. **64m/C VHS, Beta.** *AU* Bryan Brown, John Flaus, Chrissie James; ***D:*** Christopher Fitchett. *NO*

Blood Money: The Story of Clinton and Nadine ☠☠½ *Clinton & Nadine* **1988** A confusing action/thriller with a good cast. Garcia is a small-time exotic bird smuggler whose gun-running brother has been murdered. He uses high-class hooker Barkin to get close to his brother's contacts, who turn out to be running guns to the Nicaraguan contras and involved in a dangerous government conspiracy. Made for cable television. **95m/C VHS, Beta.** Andy Garcia, Ellen Barkin, Morgan Freeman; ***D:*** Jerry Schatzberg. *FCT*

The Blood of a Poet *Le Sang d'un Poete* **1930** Cocteau's first film, a practically formless piece of poetic cinema, detailing all manner of surreal events occurring in the instant a chimney falls. In French with English subtitles. **55m/B VHS, Beta.** Jean Cocteau; ***D:*** Jean Cocteau; ***C:*** Georges Perinal. National Board of Review Awards '33: 10 Best Films of the Year. *VYY, MRV, HHT*

Blood of Dracula ☠½ *Blood is My Heritage* **1957** They don't make 1950s rock'n'roll girls' school vampire movies like this anymore, for which we may be grateful. Hypnotism, an amulet, and a greasepaint makeup job turn a shy female student into a bloodsucker. **71m/B VHS.** Sandra Harrison, Louise Lewis, Gail Ganley, Jerry Blaine, Heather Ames, Malcolm Atterbury; ***D:*** Herbert L. Strock. *COL, MLB*

Blood of Dracula's Castle ☠☠ *Dracula's Castle* **1969** Couple inherits an allegedly deserted castle but upon moving in, discover Mr. and Mrs. Dracula have settled there. The vampires keep young women chained in the dungeon for continual blood supply. Also present are a hunchback and a werewolf. Awesome Adamson production is highlighted by the presence of the gorgeous Volante. Early cinematography effort by the renowned Laslo Kovacs. **84m/C VHS, Beta.** John Carradine, Alexander D'Arcy, Paula Raymond, Ray Young, Vicki Volante, Robert Dix, John Cardos; ***D:*** Jean Hewitt, Al Adamson. *NO*

Blood of Ghastly Horror *Woof! The Fiend with the Atomic Brain; Psycho a Go Go!; The Love Maniac; The Man with the Synthetic Brain; The Fiend with the Electronic Brain* **1972** A young man thinks he has a new lease on life when he is the happy recipient of a brain transplant, but his dreams are destroyed when he evolves into a rampaging killer. This movie is so awful it hides behind numerous but rather creative aliases. **87m/C VHS.** John Carradine, Kent Taylor, Tommy Kirk, Regina Carrol; ***D:*** Al Adamson. *MOV*

The Blood of Heroes ☠☠ *The Salute of the Jugger* **1989 (R)** A post-apocalyptic action flick detailing the adventures of a battered team of "juggers," warriors who challenge small village teams to a brutal sport (involving dogs' heads on sticks) that's a cross between jousting and football. **97m/C VHS, Beta, LV.** Rutger Hauer, Joan Chen, Vincent D'Onofrio, Anna Katarina; ***D:*** David Peoples; ***W:*** David Peoples; ***M:*** Todd Boekelheide. *HBO*

Blood of Jesus ☠☠ **1941** A sinful husband accidentally shoots his newly-baptized wife, causing an uproar in their rural town. Williams later starred as Andy on the "Amos 'n' Andy" television series. **50m/C VHS.** Spencer Williams Jr., Kathryn Craviness; ***D:*** Spencer Williams Jr.; ***W:*** Spencer Williams Jr. *FCT, HEG, BTV*

The Blood of Others ☠ **1984** A driveling adaptation of the Simone de Beauvoir novel about a young French woman at the outbreak of WWII torn between her absent boyfriend in the Resistance and a kind, wealthy German. Made for French television, it stars Jodie Foster and Michael Ontkean as the Gallic pair. **130m/C VHS, Beta.** *FR* Jodie Foster, Sam Neill, Michael Ontkean, Stephane Audran, Lambert Wilson, John Vernon, Kate Reid, Jean-Pierre Aumont; ***D:*** Claude Chabrol; ***W:*** Brian Moore. *PSM*

Blood of the Hunter ☠☠½ **1994 (PG-13)** Psycho-killer holds postman's wife captive in a remote cabin in the Canadian wilderness. Turns out hubby and psycho share a mysterious past. **92m/C VHS.** Michael Biehn, Alexandra Vandernoot, Gabriel Arcand; ***D:*** Gilles Carle. *VMK, FCT*

Blood of the Vampire ☠½ **1958** A Transylvanian doctor is executed for being a vampire and his hunchbacked assistant brings him back to life. **84m/C VHS, Beta.** *GB* Donald Wolfit, Vincent Ball, Barbara Shelley, Victor Maddern; ***D:*** Henry Cass; ***W:*** Jimmy Sangster. *MPI, MLB*

The Blood on Satan's Claw ☠☠☠ *Satan's Skin; Satan's Claw* **1971** Graphic tale centering on the Devil himself. Townspeople in an English village circa 1670 find the spirit of Satan taking over their children, who begin to practice witchcraft. Well made with lots of attention to period details. Not for the faint-hearted. **90m/C VHS, Beta.** *GB* Patrick Wymark, Linda Hayden, Barry Andrews, Michele Dotrice; ***D:*** Piers Haggard. *MGM, FCT*

Blood on the Badge ☠½ **1992** Illegal arms have been stolen from a military arsenal and fall into the hands of Libyan Nationalists who begin a terrorist campaign. Detective Neal Farrow is assigned to stop them. **92m/C VHS.** Ramon Estevez, David Harrod, Rocky Patterson, Desiree Laforge, Dean Nolen, Melissa Deleon, Todd Everett; ***D:*** Bret McCormick. *AIP*

Blood on the Moon ☠☠½ **1948** Well-acted film about a cowboy's involvement in a friend's underhanded schemes. Based on a Luke Short novel, this dark film revolves around a western land dispute between cattlemen and homesteaders. **88m/B VHS, Beta, LV.** Robert Mitchum, Robert Preston, Walter Brennan, Barbara Bel Geddes; ***D:*** Robert Wise. *MED, TTC*

Blood on the Mountain **1988** After escaping from prison, Jim plots revenge against his accomplice, only to kill an innocent man instead. **71m/C VHS.** Stracker Edwards, Tim Jones, Paula Preston, Cliff Turknett, Rich Jury; ***D:*** Donald W. Thompson.

Blood on the Sun ☠☠½ **1945** Newspaperman in Japan uncovers plans for world dominance as propaganda, violence, and intrigue combine in this action-adventure. Also available colorized. **98m/B VHS, LV.** James Cagney, Sylvia Sidney, Robert Armstrong, Wallace Ford; ***D:*** Frank Lloyd; ***M:*** Miklos Rozsa. Academy Awards '45: Best Interior Decoration. *NOS, MRV, HHT*

Blood Orgy of the She-Devils *Woof!* **1974 (PG)** Exploitative gore nonsense about female demons, beautiful witches, and satanic worship. Some movies waste all their creative efforts on their titles. **73m/C VHS, Beta.** Lila Zaborin, Tom Pace, Leslie McRae, Ray Myles. *NO*

Blood Rage *Woof! Nightmare at Shadow Woods* **1987 (R)** A maniacal twin goes on a murderous rampage through his brother's neighborhood. AKA "Nightmare at Shadow Woods." Only for die-hard "Mary Hartman" fans. **87m/C VHS, Beta.** Louise Lasser, Mike Soper; ***D:*** John Grissmer; ***M:*** Richard Einhorn. *PSM*

Blood Red ☠½ **1988 (R)** In 1895 Northern California, an Italian immigrant and his family give bloody battle to a powerful industrialist who wants their land in wine-growing country. Watch for the scenes involving veteran Roberts and his then-newcomer sister, pretty woman Julia. **91m/C VHS, Beta, LV, 8mm.** Eric Roberts, Dennis Hopper, Giancarlo Giannini, Burt Young, Carlin Glynn, Lara Harris, Susan Anspach, Julia Roberts, Elias Koteas, Frank Campanella, Aldo Ray, Horton Foote Jr.; ***D:*** Peter Masterson; ***W:*** Ron Cutler. *COL, SUE*

Blood Relations ☠½ **1987 (R)** A woman is introduced to her fiance's family only to find out that they, as well as her fiance, are murdering, perverted weirdos competing for an inheritance. **88m/C VHS, Beta, LV.** *CA* Jan Rubes, Ray Walston, Lydie Denier, Kevin Hicks, Lynne Adams; ***D:*** Graeme Campbell. *SUE, NLC*

Blood Relatives ☠ *Les Liens de Sang* **1977** Langlois admits she saw her brother kill her cousin, with whom he had been carrying on an incestuous relationship. But the discovery of the dead girl's diary by police inspector Sutherland reveals many more layers of intrigue than were initially evident. Based on a novel by Ed McBain. The French actors have been dubbed into English. **94m/C VHS.** *CA* Lisa Langlois, Donald Sutherland, Stephane Audran, David Hemmings, Donald Pleasence, Laurent Malet, Micheline Lanctot, Aude Landry; ***D:*** Claude Chabrol; ***W:*** Claude Chabrol. *NO*

Blood Ring ☠½ **1993** When Sue's boxer husband goes missing she enlists old friend Max to help find him. They uncover a gambling ring run by drug lords where the kickboxing matches are to the death. Naturally, Max decides to use his expert kickboxing skills to get a violent revenge. **90m/C VHS.** Dale "Apollo" Cook, Andrea Lamatsch, Don Nakaya Neilsen, Steve Tartalia; ***D:*** Irvin Johnson; ***W:*** Ron Davies. *AIP*

Blood Salvage ☠ **1990 (R)** A crazy junkman kidnaps beautiful girls, selling their organs to the highest bidder. He meets his match when a potential target refuses to become a victim in spite of her wheelchair. Interesting plot twists keep this Grade B thriller above average. **90m/C VHS, Beta, LV.** Evander Holyfield, Lori Birdsong, Danny Nelson, John Saxon, Ray Walston; ***D:*** Tucker Johnson. *TTC*

Blood Screams *Woof!* **1988 (R)** Nosy people drop in on an old town in Mexico and attempt to uncover the secrets hidden there, but bizarre entities throw out the unwelcome mat and terrorize them. Lots of blood and screaming. **75m/C VHS, Beta.** Ran Sands, James Garnett. *WAR*

Blood Simple 🦴🦴🦴½ **1985 (R)** A jealous husband hires a sleazy private eye to murder his adulterous wife and her lover. A dark, intricate, morbid morality tale that deviates imaginatively from the standard murder mystery thriller. First film scripted by the Coen brothers. **96m/C VHS, Beta, LV.** John Getz, M. Emmet Walsh, Dan Hedaya, Frances McDormand; ***D:*** Joel Coen; ***W:*** Ethan Coen, Joel Coen; ***M:*** Carter Burwell. Independent Spirit Awards '86: Best Actor (Walsh), Best Director (Coen). *MCA*

Blood Sisters *Woof!* **1986 (R)** Sorority babes intend to spend a giggle-strewn night in a haunted house but end up decapitated, butchered, and cannibalized. **85m/C VHS, Beta.** Amy Brentano, Marla MacHart, Brigete Cossu, Randy Mooers; ***D:*** Roberta Findlay. *COL*

Blood Song 🦴 *Dream Slayer* **1982** A patient (yester-decade teen throb Frankie Avalon) escapes into the night from a mental institution after murdering an attendant. He takes his only possession with him, a carved wooden flute. A young woman sees him burying his latest victim, and now he's on a hunt to play his "blood song" for her. Pretty bad, but fun to see Avalon play a less-than-squeaky-clean role. **90m/C VHS, Beta.** Frankie Avalon, Donna Wilkes, Richard Jaeckel, Dane Clark, Antoinette Bower; ***D:*** Alan J. Levi. *NO*

The Blood Spattered Bride 🦴 *Blood Castle; La Novia Esangentada* **1972** Newlywed couple honeymoons in a remote castle in southern Spain. They are visited by a mysterious young woman who begins to influence the bride in the ways of lesbian bloodsucking. Okay '70s Euro-eroti-horror based on LeFanu's "Carmilla." **82m/C VHS, Beta.** *SP* Simon Andrew, Maribel Martin, Alexandra Bastedo, Dean Selmier, Rosa Ma Rodriguez, Montserrat Julio; ***D:*** Vicente Aranda. *MPI*

Blood Thirst 🦴🦴 **1965** Obscure horror film about a woman who stays young by indulging in ritual killings and strange experiments. **?m/C VHS.** Robert Winston, Yvonne Nielson. *SNC*

Blood Tide 🦴 *The Red Tide* **1982 (R)** A disgusting, flesh-eating monster disrupts a couple's vacation in the Greek isles. Beautiful scenery, good cast, bad movie. **82m/C VHS, Beta.** James Earl Jones, Jose Ferrer; ***D:*** Richard Jeffries; ***W:*** Nico Mastorakis. *NO*

Blood Ties 🦴½ **1987** An American naval engineer in Sicily gets involved with the Mob in order to save his father's life. **98m/C VHS, Beta.** *IT* Brad Davis, Tony LoBianco, Vincent Spano, Barbara DeRossi, Maria Conchita Alonso; ***D:*** Giacomo Battiato. *TWE*

Blood Ties 🦴🦴½ **1992** Reporter Harry Martin belongs to an unusual family—modern-day vampires (who prefer to be known as Carpathian-Americans). But they have an age-old problem with a band of fanatical vampire hunters. This time around you'll root for the bloodsuckers. Made for television. **90m/C VHS.** Harley Venton, Patrick Bauchau, Kim Johnston-Ulrich, Michelle Johnson, Jason London, Bo Hopkins, Grace Zabriskie; ***D:*** Jim McBride; ***W:*** Richard Shapiro. *NHO*

Blood Tracks 🦴½ **1986** A woman kills her abusive husband, then hides out in the mountains with her kids until they turn into cannibalistic savages. Years later, people show up to shoot a music video. Blood runs in buckets. **82m/C Beta.** Jeff Harding, Michael Fitzpatrick, Naomi Kaneda; ***D:*** Mike Jackson. *NO*

Blood Vows: The Story of a Mafia Wife 🦴🦴 **1987** TV's Laura Ingalls (Gilbert) leaps from the prairie to modern-day mafia in this warped Cinderella story. She meets the man of her dreams, whom she slowly finds is her worst nightmare as she becomes trapped within the confines of her new-found "family." Made for television soaper is way over the top in terms of melodrama. **100m/C VHS.** Melissa Gilbert, Joe Penny, Eileen Brennan, Talia Shire, Anthony (Tony) Franciosa; ***D:*** Paul Wendkos; ***M:*** William Goldstein. *FRH*

Blood Voyage *Woof!* **1977 (R)** A crewman aboard a pleasure yacht must find out who is killing off his passengers one by one. **80m/C VHS, Beta.** Jonathon Lippe, Laurie Rose, Midori, Mara Modair; ***D:*** Frank Mitchell. *NO*

Blood Warriors 🦴½ **1993** An ex-Marine finds out a old buddy is leading a private army of mercenaries. When he refuses to join up their friendship turns violent. **93m/C VHS, LV.** David Bradley, Frank Zagarino; ***D:*** Sam Firstenberg. *IMP, IME*

Blood Wedding 🦴🦴🦴 *Bodas de Sangre* **1981** A wonderfully passionate dance film from Saura and choreographed by Gades, based on the play by famed author Federico Garcia Lorca. A young bride runs off with her married lover on her wedding day and her jilted husband comes after them. If you like flamenco, there are two more: "Carmen" and "El Amor Brujo." In Spanish with English subtitles. **71m/C VHS, Beta.** *SP* Antonio Gades, Christina Hoyos, Marisol, Carmen Villena; ***D:*** Carlos Saura. *XVC, CTH, MED*

Bloodbath **19??** Drugs, sex and terrorism—Hopper is typecast as an American degenerate who, along with his expatriate friends, is persecuted by local religious cults who need sacrifices. **89m/C VHS, Beta.** Dennis Hopper, Carroll Baker, Richard Todd, Faith Brook, Win Wells; ***D:*** Silvio Narizzano. *GHV, HHE*

Bloodbath at the House of Death 🦴🦴 **1985** Price and his compatriots fight a team of mad scientists in this parody of popular horror films. Fun to see Price spoofing his own genre; die-hard horror camp fans will be satisfied. Best line: "Wanna fork?" **92m/C VHS, Beta.** *GB* Kenny Everett, Pamela Stephenson, Vincent Price, Gareth Hunt; ***D:*** Ray Cameron. *MED*

Bloodbath in Psycho Town 🦴 **1989 (R)** A film crew is marked for death by a hooded man when it enters a remote little village. **87m/C VHS.** Ron Arragon, Donna Baltron, Dave Elliott; ***D:*** Allessandro DeGaetano; ***W:*** Allessandro DeGaetano. *NO*

Bloodbeat 🦴 **1985** A supernatural being terrorizes a family as they gather at their country home to celebrate Christmas. **84m/C VHS, Beta.** Helen Benton, Terry Brown, Claudia Peyton; ***D:*** Fabrice A. Zaphiratos. *TWE*

Bloodbrothers 🦴🦴½ **1978 (R)** Portrayal of working-class Italian men's lives—if that's possible without the benefit of Italian writers, producers, or director. Still, lots of cussing and general intensity, as Gere's character struggles between staying in the family construction business and doing what he wants to do—work with children. Re-cut for television and re-titled "A Father's Love." **120m/C VHS.** Richard Gere, Paul Sorvino, Tony LoBianco, Kenneth McMillan, Marilu Henner, Danny Aiello, Lelia Goldoni, Yvonne Wilder; ***D:*** Robert Mulligan; ***C:*** Robert L. Surtees; ***M:*** Elmer Bernstein. Nominations: Academy Awards '78: Best Adapted Screenplay. *WAR*

Bloodfight 🦴 **1990 (PG-13)** Exciting kick-boxing and martial arts tournament turns sour when champ offends the sense of honor of the master. Now the champ must battle the master, and only one will remain standing! **?m/C VHS.** Bolo Yeung. *IMP*

Bloodfist 🦴🦴 **1989 (R)** A kickboxer tears through Manila searching for his brother's killer. A Roger Corman production. **85m/C VHS, Beta.** Don "The Dragon" Wilson, Rob Kaman, Billy Blanks, Kris Aguilar, Riley Bowman, Michael Shaner; ***D:*** Terence H. Winkless. *MGM*

Bloodfist 2 🦴🦴½ **1990 (R)** Six of the world's toughest martial artists find themselves kidnapped and forced to do the bidding of the evil Su. The mysterious recluse stages a series of incredible fights between the experts and his own army of drugged warriors. **85m/C VHS, Beta.** Don "The Dragon" Wilson, Maurice Smith, James Warring, Timothy Baker, Richard Hill, Rina Reyes; ***D:*** Andy Blumenthal. *MGM*

Bloodfist 3: Forced to Fight 🦴½ **1992 (R)** Just as long as nobody's forced to watch, real-life world champion kickboxer Wilson thrashes his way through another showdown-at-the-arena plot. Better-than-average fight choreography. **90m/C VHS.** Don "The Dragon" Wilson, Richard Roundtree, Laura Stockman, Richard Paul, Rick Dean, Peter "Sugarfoot" Cunningham; ***D:*** Oley Sassone; ***W:*** Allison Burnett; ***M:*** Nigel Holton. *NHO*

Bloodfist 4: Die Trying 🦴½ **1992 (R)** To rescue his daughter, a fighter must do battle with the FBI, the CIA, and an international arms cartel. **86m/C VHS, LV.** Don "The Dragon" Wilson, Catya Sassoon, Amanda Wyss, James Tolkan, Liz Torres; ***D:*** Paul Ziller. *NHO*

Bloodfist 5: Human Target 🦴½ **1993 (R)** When undercover FBI agent Jim Roth (Wilson) attempts to unravel an international arms deal he's found out and left for dead. He comes to with no memory only to find himself caught between the arms dealers and the FBI, who think he's turned double-agent. Both sides want Roth dead. **?m/C VHS.** Don "The Dragon" Wilson, Denice Duff, Yuji Okumoto, Don Stark, Danny Lopez, Steve James, Michael Yama; ***D:*** Jeff Yonis; ***W:*** Jeff Yonis. *NHO*

Bloodfist 6: Ground Zero 🦴½ **1994 (R)** Nick Corrigan (Wilson) must battle terrorists who have a nuclear missile aimed at New York City. **86m/C VHS, LV.** Don "The Dragon" Wilson, Cat Sasson, Steve Garvey; ***D:*** Rick Jacobson. *NHO*

Bloodhounds of Broadway 🦴🦴½ **1989 (PG)** A musical tribute to Damon Runyon, detailing the cliched adventures of an assortment of jazz-age crooks, flappers, chanteuses, and losers. **90m/C VHS, Beta, LV.** Madonna, Rutger Hauer, Randy Quaid, Matt Dillon, Jennifer Grey, Julie Hagerty, Esai Morales, Anita Morris, Josef Sommer, William S. Burroughs, Ethan Phillips, Stephen McHattie, Dinah Manoff, Googy Gress, Tony Azito, Tony Longo, Madeleine Potter; ***D:*** Howard Brookner; ***W:*** Howard Brookner, Colman DeKay; ***M:*** Jonathan Sheffer. *COL*

Bloodknot 🦴🦴 **1995 (R)** The Reaves' are devastated when their son Martin is killed in a military accident. So they're an easy target when Kaye (Vernon) shows up, claiming to be Martin's girlfriend. Mom Evelyn (Kidder) and brother Tom (Dempsey) are only too eager to welcome Kaye into the family but it wouldn't be a thriller if devious Kaye didn't have some deadly ulterior motives. Made for cable TV. **98m/C VHS, Beta.** Patrick Dempsey, Kate Vernon, Margot Kidder, Craig Sheffer; ***D:*** Jorge Montesi; ***W:*** Randy Kornfield; ***C:*** Philip Linzey; ***M:*** Ian Thomas. *PAR*

Bloodlink 🦴½ **1986 (R)** A well-to-do doctor has a recurring nightmare about killing an elderly woman. This prompts him to explore his past, discovering that he was separated at birth from a twin brother. Naturally, only by searching frantically for his long-lost sibling can the good doctor hope to solve the mystery of the recurring nightmare. A somnolent tale indeed. **98m/C VHS, Beta.** Michael Moriarty, Penelope Milford, Geraldine Fitzgerald, Cameron Mitchell, Sarah Langenfeld; ***D:*** Alberto De Martino. *SUE, VTR*

Bloodlust 🦴 **1959** More teenagers fall prey to yet another mad scientist, who stores their dead bodies in glass tanks. Low-budget ripoff of "The Most Dangerous Game" and other such films. A must for Mike Brady (Robert Reed) fans though. **89m/B VHS.** Wilton Graff, June Kennedy, Robert Reed, Lilyan Chauvin; ***D:*** Ralph Brooke; ***W:*** Ralph Brooke. *SNC, NOS*

Bloodlust: Subspecies 3 🦴½ *Subspecies 3* **1993 (R)** Equally gory followup to "Bloodstone: Subspecies 2." Sadistic vampire Radu is still battling for Michelle's soul, this time against Michelle's sister Becky, aided by his disgusting Mummy and the demonic Subspecies. Castle Vladislas is awash is blood and Becky discovers more than Michelle's fate is at risk. **83m/C VHS, Beta, LV.** Anders Hove, Kevin Blair, Denice Duff, Pamela Gordon, Ion Haiduc, Michael DellaFemina; ***D:*** Ted Nicolaou; ***W:*** Ted Nicolaou. *PAR*

Bloodmatch 🦴 **1991 (R)** A whodunit, martial-arts-style: the "sleuth" kidnaps all the suspects in a corruption case and kickboxes each to death until somebody confesses. Not exactly Agatha Christie, and artsy camera moves fail to exploit the fancy footwork. **85m/C VHS, LV.** Thom Mathews, Michel Qissi, Benny "The Jet" Urquidez, Marianne Taylor, Hope Marie Carlton, Dale Jacoby, Thunder Wolf, Vincent Klyn, Peter "Sugarfoot" Cunningham, Hector Pena; ***D:*** Albert Pyun; ***W:*** K. Mannah; ***M:*** Tony Riparetti. *HBO*

Bloodmoon *Woof!* **1990** The setting is Australia but the sleazy story's all too familiar: an insane killer employs knives and other sharp objects to prevent sex-crazed students from getting past third base. **104m/C VHS, Beta, LV.** *AU* Leon Lissek, Christine Amor, Ian Patrick Williams, Helen Thomson, Hazel Howson, Craig Cronin, Anya Molina; ***D:*** Alec Mills; ***W:*** Richard Brennan; ***M:*** Brian May. *LIV*

Bloodshed 🦴 **1983 (R)** A psychotic harbors a girl's dead body, and systematically kills anyone who discovers his secret. **88m/C VHS, Beta.** Laslo Papas, Beverly Ross; ***D:*** Richard Cassidy. *NO*

Bloodspell 🦴 **1987 (R)** A student with an evil power unleashes it on those who cross his path. **87m/C VHS, Beta.** Anthony Jenkins, Aaron Teich, Alexandra Kennedy, John Reno; ***D:*** Deryn Warren. *MCG*

Bloodsport 🦴½ **1988 (R)** American soldier Van Damme endeavors to win the deadly Kumite, an outlawed martial arts competition in Hong Kong. Lots of kick-boxing action and the sound of bones cracking. **92m/C VHS, Beta, LV.** Jean-Claude Van Damme, Leah Ayres, Roy Chiao, Donald Gibb, Bolo Yeung, Norman Burton, Forest Whitaker; ***D:*** Newton Arnold; ***W:*** Christopher Cosby. *WAR, TLF*

Bloodsport 2: The Next Kumite 🦴½ **1995 (R)** Old-fashioned kickfest has Alex (Bernhardt) stealing antiquities in Thailand. He's left to take the fall by his partner in the theft of an ancient sword belonging to powerful businessman Leung (Morita) and is sent to a prison where sadistic head guard Demon (Han) takes an instant dislike to him. Alex learns about a sacred fighting competition, the Kumite, from wise prison sage Sun (Hong) and naturally, once Alex manages to get into the contest, his opponent is—you guessed it—Demon. **?m/C VHS.** Daniel Bernhardt, Ong Soo Han, Noriyuki "Pat" Morita, James Hong; ***D:*** Alan Mehrez. *NYR*

Bloodstalkers *Woof!* **1976** Two vacationers in Florida meet up with a band of slaughtering, swamp-based lunatics. **91m/C VHS, Beta.** Kenny Miller, Celea Ann Cole, Jerry Albert; ***D:*** Robert W. Morgan. *VMK*

Bloodstone 🦴🦴 **1988 (PG-13)** A couple honeymooning in the Middle East unexpectedly become involved in a jewel heist when they discover a valuable ruby amongst their luggage. Non-stop action and humor. **90m/C VHS, Beta.** Charlie Brill, Christopher Neame, Jack Kehler, Brett Stimely; ***D:*** Dwight Little; ***W:*** Nico Mastorakis, Curt Allen. *MCG*

Bloodstone: Subspecies 2 🦴½ *Subspecies 2* **1992 (R)** A gory sequel to "Subspecies" finds Radu the vampire pursuing the luscious Michelle. Radu gets some help from his ghoulish mother and yucky demonic spawn. Filmed on location in Romania. **107m/C VHS, LV.** Anders Hove, Denice Duff, Kevin Blair, Michael Denish, Pamela Gordon, Ion Haiduc; ***D:*** Ted Nicolaou; ***W:*** Ted Nicolaou. *PAR*

The Bloodsuckers 🦴🦴 *Incense For the Damned; Doctors Wear Scarlet* **1970** A British horror tale set on a Greek Island. An Oxford don is seduced into an ancient vampire cult. Director Michael Burrowes replaces Hartford-Davis in the credits due to a dispute over post-production editing. **90m/C VHS, Beta.** *GB* Patrick Macnee, Peter Cushing, Patrick Mower, Edward Woodward; ***D:*** Robert Hartford-Davis. *SNC*

Bloodsuckers from Outer Space *Woof!* **1983** Via an alien invasion, Texas farmers becoming bloodsucking zombies. **80m/C VHS, Beta.** Thom Meyer, Laura Ellis, Billie Keller, Kim Braden; ***D:*** Glenn Coburn. *ORI, WAR*

Bloodsucking Freaks *Woof! The Incredible Torture Show* **1975 (R)** Virtually plotless Troma gagfest full of torture, cannibalistic dwarfs, and similar debaucheries, all played out on a Soho Grand Guignol stage (horror shows that allegedly contained real torture and death). Features "The Caged Sexoids," if that tells you anything (a cage of naked cannibal women tended by a dwarf). Not to mention the woman who has her brain sucked out through a straw. Filmed in "Ghoulovision" and originally rated X. Intolerable for most. **89m/C VHS, Beta.** Seamus O'Brian, Niles McMaster; ***D:*** Joel M. Reed. *VES*

Bloodsucking Pharoahs of Pittsburgh *Woof!* **1990 (R)** Pittsburgh is plagued by crazed cannibals who think eternal life is in Pennsylvania. Two detectives on the case are mystified. **89m/C VHS, Beta.** Jake Dengel, Joe Sharkey, Suzanne Fletcher, Beverly Penberthy, Shawn Elliott, Pat Logan, Jane Hamilton; ***D:*** Alan Smithee; ***W:*** Dean Tschetter. *PAR, FCT*

Bloody Avenger 🦴 **198?** A trio of detectives search for a murderer in the streets of Philadelphia. **100m/C VHS, Beta.** Jack Palance, George Eastman, Jenny Tamburi; ***D:*** Al Bradley. *VMK*

Bloody Birthday 🦴½ *Creeps* **1980 (R)** Three youngsters, bound together by their eerie birth during an eclipse (you know what that means), kill everyone around them that ever gave them problems. Typical "and the fun continues" ending; standard fare. **92m/C VHS, Beta.** Susan Strasberg, Jose Ferrer, Lori Lethin, Melinda Cordell, Joe Penny, Ellen Geer, Julie Brown, Michael Dudikoff, Billy Jacoby; ***D:*** Edward Hunt. *PSM*

The Bloody Brood *Woof!* **1959** Really bad flick about a drug-dealing beatnik gang who commit nasty crimes, like feeding messenger boys hamburgers filled with ground glass. Yuck. **80m/C VHS.** *CA* Jack Betts, Barbara Lord, Peter Falk, Robert Christie; ***D:*** Julian Hoffman. *SNC, TPV*

The Bloody Fight 🦴 **197?** Two young people learn the cost of courage and the high price of justice when they avenge a murderer. **90m/C VHS, Beta.** Alan Tang, Yu In Yin, Tan Chin, Pai Ying, Lui Ran In; ***D:*** N.G. Tien Tsu. *NO*

Bloody Mama 🦴🦴½ **1970 (R)** Corman's violent, trashy story of the infamous Barker Gang of the 30s, led by the bloodthirsty and sex-crazed Ma Barker (Winters, can't you just picture it?) and backed by her four perverted sons. De Niro is the space cadet sibling, Walden the homosexual ex-con, Stroud the sadistic mama lover, and Kimbrough the lady killer. They're joined by Walden's prison lover, Dern, who also has a thing for Ma Barker. Winters is a riot in this perverse stew of crime, violence, and, of course, sentimental blood bonding (the family that slays together, stays together). First of the Corman-produced (and sometimes directed) mama movies, followed by "Big Bad Mama" and "Crazy Mama." **90m/C VHS, Beta, LV.** Shelley Winters, Robert De Niro, Don Stroud, Pat Hingle, Bruce Dern, Diane Varsi, Robert Walden, Clinton Kimbrough, Scatman Crothers; ***D:*** Roger Corman; ***C:*** John A. Alonzo. *VES, LIV*

Bloody Moon *Woof!* **1983** Tourists are being brutally attacked and murdered during a small Spanish village's Festival of the Moon. **84m/C VHS, Beta.** Olivia Pascal, Christopher Brugger; ***D:*** Jess (Jesus) Franco. *TWE*

Bloody New Year 🦴 *Time Warp Terror* **1987 (R)** Corpses stalk the living as a group of teens happen upon an impromptu New Year's Eve party on a deserted island. Auld acquaintance shouldn't be forgot, just this flick. **90m/C VHS, Beta.** ***D:*** Norman J. Warren. *ACA*

The Bloody Pit of Horror 🦴½ *Crimson Executioner; The Red Hangman* **1965** While wife Jayne Mansfield was in Italy filming "Primitive Love," bodybuilder Hargitay starred in this sado-horror epic. He owns a castle that is visited by a group of models for a special shoot. While in the dungeon, Hargitay becomes possessed by the castle's former owner, a sadist, and begins torturing the models. Supposedly based on the writings of the Marquis de Sade. **87m/B VHS.** *IT* Mickey Hargitay, Louise Barrett, Walter Brandi, Moa Thai, Ralph Zucker, Albert Gordon; ***D:*** Max (Massimo Pupillo) Hunter. *SNC*

Bloody Trail 🦴 **1972** A Union soldier who chooses the recently pummeled South as the venue for postwar R-and-R is, for some reason, pursued by Confederates. And his good ol' boy pursuers don't have a sudden change of heart when he teams up with a former slave. Lots of violence and nudity; little plot and entertainment. **91m/C VHS.** Paul Harper, Rance Howard, John Mitchum; ***D:*** Richard Robinson. *ACA*

The Bloody Vampire 🦴½ **1962** Atmospheric and chilling Mexican vampire film. Sequel to "Invasion of the Vampires." **?m/C VHS.** *MX* Carlos Agosti. *SNC*

Bloody Wednesday 🦴🦴½ **1987** It's sanity check-out time when a hotel caretaker is driven mad by tormentors...or is he driving himself mad? What is it about vacant hotels that make men lose their minds? If you can remove "The Shining" from yours, this flick's worthwhile. **89m/C VHS, Beta.** Raymond Elmendorf, Pamela Baker, Navarre Perry; ***D:*** Mark Gilhuis; ***W:*** Philip Yordan; ***M:*** Al Sendry. *PSM*

Blossoms in the Dust 🦴🦴 **1941** The true story of Edna Gladney is told as she starts the Texas Children's Home and Aid Society of Fort Worth. Major league Garson tear-jerker. **100m/B VHS, Beta.** Greer Garson, Walter Pidgeon, Felix Bressart, Marsha Hunt, Fay Holden, Samuel S. Hinds, Kathleen Howard; ***D:*** Mervyn LeRoy. Academy Awards '41: Best Interior Decoration; Nominations: Academy Awards '41: Best Actress (Garson), Best Color Cinematography, Best Picture. *MGM*

The Blot 🦴🦴 **1921** A story about a poorly paid professor and his family, whose lifestyle contrasts with that of an affluent neighbor, a butcher. **55m/B VHS, Beta.** Louis Calhern, Claire Windsor; ***D:*** Lois Weber. *GPV, GVV, DVT*

Blow Out 🦴🦴🦴 **1981 (R)** When a prominent senator is killed in a car crash, a sound effects engineer becomes involved in political intrigue as he tries to expose a conspiracy with the evidence he has gathered. An intricate mystery and homage to Antonioni's "Blow-Up." **108m/C VHS, Beta, LV.** John Travolta, Nancy Allen, John Lithgow, Dennis Franz; ***D:*** Brian DePalma; ***W:*** Brian DePalma; ***C:*** Vilmos Zsigmond; ***M:*** Pino Donaggio. *WAR, OM*

Blow-Up 🦴🦴🦴½ **1966** A young London photographer takes some pictures of a couple in the park and finds out he may have recorded evidence of a murder. Though marred by badly dated 1960s modishness, this is Antonioni's most accessible film, a sophisticated treatise on perception and the film-consumer-as-voyeur, brilliantly assembled and wrought. **111m/C VHS, Beta, LV.** *GB IT* David Hemmings, Vanessa Redgrave, Sarah Miles, Jane Birkin, Veruschka; ***D:*** Michelangelo Antonioni; ***W:*** Tonino Guerra, Michelangelo Antonioni; ***C:*** Carlo DiPalma; ***M:*** Herbie Hancock. Cannes Film Festival '67: Best Film; National Society of Film Critics Awards '66: Best Director (Antonioni), Best Film; Nominations: Academy Awards '66: Best Director (Antonioni), Best Story & Screenplay. *MGM, FCT, INJ*

Blowing Wild 🦴½ **1954** Filmed in Mexico, this Quinn-Stanwyck-Cooper love triangle, set in the early thirties, speaks of lust and vengeance, rashness and greed. Stanwyck, married to oil tycoon Quinn, lusts after one-time lover wildcatter Cooper. **92m/B VHS, LV.** Gary Cooper, Barbara Stanwyck, Anthony Quinn, Ruth Roman, Ward Bond; ***D:*** Hugo Fregonese; ***W:*** Philip Yordan. *REP, FCT*

Blown Away 🦴 **1990 (R)** A mafia wife goes up against her husband in order to retrieve her kidnapped child. **92m/C VHS, Beta.** Loni Anderson, John Heard, James Naughton; ***D:*** Michael Miller. *ACA*

Blown Away 🦴½ **1993 (R)** Haim and Feldman are brothers working at a ski resort where Haim falls for rich teenager Eggert. She's a young femme fatale who manages to get Haim all hot and bothered but she's actually using the unsuspecting dupe in a murder plot. Also available in an unrated version at 93 minutes. **91m/C VHS, LV.** Nicole Eggert, Corey Haim, Corey Feldman. *LIV*

Blown Away 🦴🦴 **1994 (R)** Boston Irish bomb-squad cop Jimmy Dove (Bridges) is after former compatriot Ryan Gaerity (Jones), an Irish radical who's taken his bombing expertise onto Jimmy's new turf. Meanwhile, Jimmy wants to keep his unsavory past from unsuspecting wife Amis. Real life dad Lloyd plays Jeff's uncle. While Jones seems adequately obsessed with making things go boom and Bridges significantly concerned that they don't, thriller moves on predictable path toward explosive climax. Special effects create the suspense, as everyday objects become lethal in Gaerity's knowledgeable hands. The final explosion was more than even the special effects coordinator desired—windows were unintentionally blown out in nearby buildings. **121m/C VHS, LV.** Jeff Bridges, Tommy Lee Jones, Suzy Amis, Lloyd Bridges, Forest Whitaker; ***D:*** Stephen Hopkins; ***W:*** Joe Batteer, John Rice; ***C:*** Gregory McClatchy. Nominations: MTV Movie Awards '95: Best Villain (Jones), Best Action Sequence. *MGM*

Blue 🦴 **1968** A dull western about an American boy (Stamp) raised by Mexicans who doesn't trust another living soul until he finds himself face to face with his former gang, led by his adoptive father (Montalban). **113m/C VHS.** Terence Stamp, Joanna Pettet, Karl Malden, Ricardo Montalban, Joe De Santis, Sally Kirkland; ***D:*** Silvio Narizzano; ***W:*** Ronald M. Cohen; ***M:*** Manos Hadjidakis. *PAR*

Blue 🦴🦴 **1993 (R)** Meditation/memoir of director Jarman's deteriorating AIDS condition consists of narration and a soundtrack set against an unvaried blue screen. Jarman ponders the associations with the color blue (sky, ocean, blindness, heaven, eternity) and his own physical problems, alternately expressed with dreamy vagueness or incendiary contempt. Limited in appeal, depending highly on boredom tolerance and ability to suspend visual expectations. **76m/C VHS.** *GB* ***D:*** Derek Jarman; ***W:*** Derek Jarman; ***M:*** Simon Fisher Turner. *KIV*

The Blue and the Gray 🦴🦴 **1985** Epic television mini-series about love and hate inflamed by the Civil War. Keach plays a Pinkerton's secret service agent in this loosely based historical romance. The uncut version is available on three cassettes; the 295 minute version is on two cassettes. **398m/C VHS, Beta, LV.** Gregory Peck, Lloyd Bridges, Colleen Dewhurst, Stacy Keach, John Hammond, Sterling Hayden, Warren Oates; ***D:*** Andrew V. McLaglen; ***M:*** Bruce Broughton. *COL, TVC, FCT*

The Blue Angel 🦴🦴🦴🦴 *Der Blaue Engel* **1930** Tale of a man stripped of his dignity. A film classic filled with sensuality and decay, which made Dietrich a European star and led to her discovery in Hollywood. When a repressed professor (Jannings) goes to a nightclub hoping to catch some of his students in the wrong, he's taken by Lola, the sultry singer portrayed by Dietrich. After spending the night with her, losing his job, and then marrying her, he goes on tour with the troupe, peddling indiscreet photos of his wife. Versions were shot in both German and English, with the German version sporting English subtitles. ♫Falling in Love Again; They Call Me Wicked Lola. **90m/B VHS, Beta, 8mm.** *GE* Marlene Dietrich, Emil Jannings, Kurt Gerron, Rosa Valetti, Hans Albers; ***D:*** Josef von Sternberg; ***W:*** Karl Vollmoller, Robert Liebmann, Carl Zuckmayer; ***M:*** Friedrich Hollander. *NOS, FCT, BAR*

The Blue Bird 🦴🦴🦴 **1940 (G)** A weird, dark fantasy about two children who search for the blue bird of happiness in various fantasy lands, but find it eventually at home. Overlooked and impressively fatalistic. **98m/C VHS, Beta.** Shirley Temple, Gale Sondergaard, John Russell, Eddie Collins, Nigel Bruce, Jessie Ralph, Spring Byington, Sybil Jason; ***D:*** Walter Lang; ***C:*** Arthur C. Miller. Nominations: Academy Awards '40: Best Color Cinematography. *FXV, MLB*

Blue Blazes Rawden **1918** Hart plays a lumberjack who gains control of a local saloon after shooting its villainous proprietor. **?m/B VHS, Beta, 8mm.** William S. Hart. *GPV, GVV*

Blue Blood 🦴 **1973** A demonic butler inflicts nightmares upon a family to gain possession of its mansion. **90m/C VHS, Beta.** *GB* Oliver Reed, Derek Jacobi, Fiona Lewis; ***D:*** Andrew Sinclair. *NO*

Blue Canadian Rockies 🦴½ **1952** Autry's employer sends him to Canada to discourage his daughter from marrying a fortune hunter. The daughter has turned the place into a dude ranch and wild game preserve. When Autry arrives, he encounters some mysterious killings. **58m/B VHS, Beta.** Gene Autry, Pat Buttram, Gail Davis, Ross Ford, Tom London; ***D:*** George Archainbaud. *CCB*

Blue Chips 🦴🦴½ **1994 (PG-13)** Nolte does Bobby Knight in this saga of Western U basketball coach Pete Bell, suffering through his first losing season. What follows is a tug of war between rich alumni who want to win at any cost and his ethics as he recruits for a new season. Larger than life hoopster O'Neal's film debut. McDonnell and Woodard are merely afterthoughts, but look for cameos from many real life b-ballers, including Dick Vitale and Larry Bird. Average script is bolstered by exciting game footage, shot during real games for authenticity. **108m/C VHS, Beta, LV.** Nick Nolte, Shaquille O'Neal, Mary McDonnell, Ed O'Neill, J.T. Walsh, Alfre Woodard; ***Cameos:*** Larry Bird, Bobby Knight, Rick Pitino; ***D:*** William Friedkin; ***W:*** Ron Shelton; ***M:*** Nile Rodgers, Jeff Beck, Jed Leiber. *PAR*

Blue City 🦴½ **1986 (R)** A young man returns to his Florida hometown to find his father murdered, and subsequently vows to solve and avenge the matter. Based on a Ross MacDonald thriller. **83m/C VHS, Beta, LV.** Judd Nelson, Ally Sheedy, Paul Winfield, Anita Morris, David Caruso, Julie Carmen, Scott Wilson; ***D:*** Michelle Manning; ***W:*** Walter Hill, Lukas Heller; ***M:*** Ry Cooder. *PAR*

Blue Collar 🦴🦴🦴 **1978 (R)** An auto assembly line worker, tired of the poverty of his life, hatches a plan to rob his own union. A study of the working class and the robbing of the human spirit. **114m/C VHS, Beta, LV.** Richard Pryor, Harvey Keitel, Yaphet Kotto, Ed Begley Jr.; ***D:*** Paul Schrader; ***W:*** Paul Schrader, Leonard Schrader; ***M:*** Jack Nitzsche. *MCA, FCT*

Blue Country 🦴🦴½ *Le Pays Bleu* **1977 (PG)** A joyful romantic comedy about a pair of free souls who leave their stagnant lives behind to seek out a more idyllic existence. Subtitled in English. **104m/C VHS, Beta.** *FR* Brigitte Fossey, Jacques Sernas; ***M:*** Gerard Anfosso. *COL*

The Blue Dahlia 🦴🦴🦴½ **1946** Classic film noir finds Navy vet Johnny Morrison (Ladd) returning home to discover his wife Helen (Dowling) has been keeping the home fires burning—with Eddie Harwood (Da Silva), owner of the Blue Dahlia nightclub. After a nasty fight, Johnny takes off and is picked up by sultry blonde Joyce (Lake). The next day Johnny discovers he's wanted by the cops for the murder of his wife and decides to hide out until he can find the real killer, with Joyce's help. Very stylish and fast-paced with excellent performances; Chandler's first original screenplay. **100m/B VHS.** Alan Ladd, Veronica Lake, William Bendix, Howard da Silva, Doris Dowling, Tom Powers, Hugh Beaumont, Howard Freeman, Don Costello; ***D:*** George Marshall; ***W:*** Raymond Chandler; ***C:*** Lionel Lindon; ***M:*** Victor Young. *MCA*

Blue De Ville 🦴🦴 **1986 (PG)** Two young women buy a '59 Cadillac and journey from St. Louis to New Mexico, having adventures on the way. The rambling, free-spirited movie was a pilot for a prospective series that never set sail—but when "Thelma & Louise" hit big this superficially similar item was hauled out on video. **96m/C VHS.** Jennifer Runyon, Kimberly Pistone, Mark Thomas Miller, Alan Autry, Robert Prescott; ***D:*** Jim Johnston. *VMK*

Blue Desert 🦴🦴🦴 **1991 (R)** Cox is strong in her performance as Lisa Roberts, a comic book artist who leaves New York City for small town Arizona life after surviving a traumatic rape. Once there, she's befriended by Sheffer and Sweeney, a local cop. Battersby does a good job of keeping the suspense level high (in his directorial debut) as Cox finds that there's danger in small towns, too. Fine performances keep this slightly above average. **98m/C VHS.** D.B. Sweeney, Courteney Cox, Craig Sheffer, Philip Baker Hall, Sandy Ward; ***D:*** Bradley Battersby; ***W:*** Bradley Battersby, Arthur Collis; ***M:*** Jerry Goldsmith. *ACA*

Blue Fin 🦴🦴 **1978 (PG)** When their tuna boat is shipwrecked, and the crew disabled, a young boy and his father learn lessons of love and courage as the son tries to save the ship. **93m/C VHS, Beta.** *AU* Hardy Kruger, Greg Rowe; ***D:*** Carl Schultz. *SUE*

Blue Fire Lady 🦴🦴 **1978** The heartwarming story of a young girl and her love of horses which endures even her father's disapproval. Good family fare. **96m/C VHS, Beta.** Cathryn Harrison, Mark Holden, Peter Cummins. *MED*

Blue Flame 🦴🦴 **1993 (R)** Vigilante cop is hired to track down two humanoid aliens who have escaped captivity in futuristic L.A. They evade him by time-traveling through alternate realities, infiltrating the cop's mind, and using his fantasies against him. **88m/C VHS.** Brian Wimmer, Ian Buchanan, Kerri Green, Cecilia Peck, Jad Mager; ***D:*** Cassian Elwes; ***W:*** Cassian Elwes. *COL*

Blue Hawaii 🦴🦴 **1962** A soldier, returning to his Hawaiian home, defies his parents by taking a job with a tourist agency. Presley sings "Can't Help Falling in Love." For Elvis fans. **101m/C VHS, Beta, LV.** Elvis Presley, Angela Lansbury, Joan Blackman, Roland Winters, Iris Adrian, John Archer, Steve Brodie; ***D:*** Norman Taurog; ***W:*** Hal Kanter. *FOX, MVD*

Blue Heaven 🦴 **1984** A couple struggles through problems with their marriage and alcohol abuse. **100m/C VHS, Beta.** Leslie Denniston, James Eckhouse; ***D:*** Kathleen Dowdey. *VES, LIV*

The Blue Hour 🦴🦴 **1991** Theo is a Berlin hustler whose business is so good he can pick his clients. Marie, his next-door neighbor, lives with her boyfriend Paul until he just walks out one day. Marie is shattered and refuses to leave her apartment until Theo takes an interest in her plight. Just when it seems that the improbable couple could find true love, Paul comes back. In German with English subtitles. **87m/C VHS.** *GE* Andreas Herder, Dina Leipzig, Cyrill Rey-Coquais; ***D:*** Marcel Gisler. *WBF, FCT*

Blue Ice 🦴🦴½ **1992 (R)** Harry Anders (Caine) is an ex-spy with an eye for the ladies and a loyalty to his friends. When his friends start winding up dead, Harry decides to investigate—a very dangerous decision, especially when a mysterious woman (Young) takes an interest. Made for cable television. **96m/C VHS, LV.** Michael Caine, Sean Young, Ian Bannen, Bob Hoskins; ***D:*** Russell Mulcahy; ***W:*** Ron Hutchinson; ***M:*** Michael Kamen. *HBO*

Blue Iguana 🦴🦴 **1988 (R)** An inept bounty hunter travels south of the border to recover millions from a crooked South American bank, and meets up with sexy women, murderous thugs, and corruption. **88m/C VHS, Beta, LV.** Dylan McDermott, Jessica Harper, James Russo, Dean Stockwell, Pamela Gidley, Tovah Feldshuh; ***D:*** John Lafia. *PAR*

Blue In the Face 🦴🦴½ **1995 (R)** Wang and Auster's immediate follow-up to "Smoke," shot in five days, recycles the same Brooklyn cigar shop setting and contains a dozen fast-paced, loosely scripted or wholly improvised scenes that they couldn't cram into "Smoke," led by Reed's deadpan riff on eyewear, New York, and smoking. The action again centers around Auggie (Keitel), the shop manager, who hangs out with the mostly eccentric, and sometimes famous clientele. Jarmusch idly waxes philosophic on smoking technique, while puffing on what he claims is his last. Scenes are woven together with videotaped interviews from actual Brooklyn residents, creating a tribute to life in the borough with a documentary feel. Improv lovers will enjoy watching what sometimes seems more like outtakes than finished performances. **83m/C VHS, LV.** Harvey Keitel, Lou Reed, Michael J. Fox, Roseanne, Jim Jarmusch, Lily Tomlin, Mel Gorham, Jared Harris, Giancarlo Esposito, Victor Argo, Madonna, Keith David, Mira Sorvino; ***D:*** Wayne Wang, Paul Auster; ***W:*** Wayne Wang, Paul Auster. *TOU*

Blue Jeans ½ **1978** A young French boy experiences sexual awakening and humiliation in a British school. In French with English subtitles. **80m/C VHS, Beta.** *FR* ***D:*** Hugues des Roziers. *FCT*

Blue Jeans and Dynamite **198?** A stuntman is hired to lift the "Golden Mask of the Duct Tomb" and is followed on land, water, and air. Great chase scenes and action-filled finale. **90m/C VHS.** Robert Vaughn, Simon Andrew, Katia Kristine. *NO*

The Blue Kite **1993** Fifteen years of political and cultural upheaval in China is shown through the eyes of young troublemaker Tietou, who certainly earns his nickname of "Iron Head" after his 1954 birth. Soon his father is sent to a labor reform camp and his mother remarries—only to be faced with more struggles as the years go by. The kite is Tietou's cherished toy, which keeps getting lost or destroyed but is always being rebuilt, offering one token of hope. Chinese with subtitles. **138m/C VHS.** *CH* Lu Liping, Zhang Wenyao, Pu Quanxin; ***D:*** Tian Zhuangzhuang; ***W:*** Xiao Mao. Nominations: Independent Spirit Awards '95: Best Foreign Language Film. *KIV*

The Blue Knight ½ **1975** Kennedy brings energy and care to this basically standard story. Policeman waiting for retirement searches for his partner's killer. Unexceptional treatment made palatable by actors. Made for television movie. **72m/C VHS.** George Kennedy, Alex Rocco, Glynn Turman, Verna Bloom, Michael Margotta, Seth Arnold; ***D:*** J. Lee Thompson. *LIV*

The Blue Lagoon *Woof!* **1980 (R)** Useless remake of 1949 film of the same name. An adolescent boy and girl marooned on a desert isle discover love (read: sex) without the restraints of society. Not too explicit, but nonetheless intellectually offensive. Gorgeous photography of island paradise is wasted on this Shields vehicle. **105m/C VHS, Beta, LV.** Brooke Shields, Christopher Atkins, Leo McKern, William Daniels; ***D:*** Randal Kleiser; ***C:*** Nestor Almendros; ***M:*** Basil Poledouris. Golden Raspberry Awards '80: Worst Actress (Shields); Nominations: Academy Awards '80: Best Cinematography. *COL*

The Blue Lamp **1949** Action-adventure fans familiar with the hoary plot where a cop must avenge the wrongful death of his partner will appreciate this suspenseful British detective effort. It's one of the very first in the genre to explore buddy cop revenge in a very British sort of way. Also sports a concluding chase scene which has stood the test of time. Led to the long-running British TV series "Dixon of Dock Green." **84m/B VHS.** *GB* Dirk Bogarde, Jimmy Hanley, Jack Warner, Bernard Lee, Robert Flemyng, Patric Doonan, Bruce Seton, Frederick Piper, Betty Ann Davies, Peggy Evans; ***D:*** Basil Dearden. British Academy Awards '50: Best Film. *FCT*

The Blue Light *Das Blaue Licht* **1932** Fairy-tale love story, based on an Italian fable about a mysterious woman, thought to be a witch, and a painter. Riefenstahl's first film which brought her to the attention of Adolf Hitler, who requested she make films glorifying the Nazi Party. In German with English subtitles. **77m/B VHS, Beta.** *GE* Leni Riefenstahl, Matthias Wieman, Max Holsboer; ***D:*** Leni Riefenstahl; ***W:*** Leni Riefenstahl. *VYY, MRV, FCT*

The Blue Lightning ½ **1986** Investigator Elliott travels to Australia to retrieve the priceless Blue Lightening gem. He must fight the crime lord in his Aussie encampment. Nice scenery, but unexceptional television story. **95m/C VHS.** Sam Elliott, Rebecca Gilling, Robert Culp, John Meillon, Robert Coleby, Max Phipps; ***D:*** Lee Philips. *FRH*

The Blue Max ½ **1966** During WWI a young German, fresh out of aviation training school, competes for the coveted "Blue Max" flying award with other members of a squadron of seasoned flyers from aristocratic backgrounds. Based on a novel by Jack D. Hunter. **155m/C VHS, Beta, LV.** George Peppard, James Mason, Ursula Andress; ***D:*** John Guillermin; ***M:*** Jerry Goldsmith. *FOX*

Blue Money **1984** A wild, comedic caper film about a cab-driving nightclub impressionist who absconds with a briefcase packed with cash and is pursued by everyone, even the I.R.A. Originally made for British television. **82m/C VHS, Beta.** *GB* Tim Curry, Dabby Bishop, Billy Connolly, Frances Tomelty; ***D:*** Colin Bucksey. *NO*

Blue Monkey *Green Monkey* **1987 (R)** A mysterious alien plant impregnates a man, who gives birth to a huge, man-eating insect larva. It subsequently grows up into a giant bug, and roams around a quarantined hospital looking for patients to eat. What made you think it had anything to do with monkeys? **97m/C VHS, Beta.** Steve Railsback, Susan Anspach, Gwynyth Walsh, John Vernon, Joe Flaherty; ***D:*** William Fruet. *COL*

Blue Movies *Woof!* **1988 (R)** A couple of jerks try their hand at making porn films with predictable results. **92m/C VHS, Beta.** Larry Linville, Lucinda Crosby, Steve Levitt, Darien Mathias, Larry Poindexter; ***D:*** Paul Koval. *ACA*

Blue Murder at St. Trinian's **1956** The second of the madcap British comedy series (based on cartoons by Ronald Searle) about an incredibly ferocious pack of schoolgirls. This time they travel to the European continent and make life miserable for a jewel thief. Highlight: fantasy sequence in ancient Rome showing the girls thrown to the lions—and scaring the lions. **86m/B VHS.** *GB* Joyce Grenfell, Terry-Thomas, George Cole, Alastair Sim, Lionel Jeffries, Thorley Walters; ***D:*** Frank Launder; ***M:*** Malcolm Arnold. *VYY, VDM, FUS*

Blue Paradise *Woof!* **1986** A depiction of Adam and Eve as they peruse the primal landscape and each other. **90m/C VHS, Beta.** Mark Gregory, Andrea Goldman. *TWE, MLB*

Blue Ribbon Babes *Woof!* **1986** A filmed record of a female athletic competition in Florida, featuring wet T-shirt contests, mud wrestling, and powder-puff boxing. **60m/C VHS, Beta.** *AHV*

Blue River ½ **1995 (PG-13)** Flashbacks highlight this saga of a troubled family. Successful doctor Edward Sellers (McDonough) is dismayed when his derelict older brother Lawrence (O'Connell), whom he hasn't seen in 15 years, suddenly appears on his doorstep. A gifted teenager, Lawrence once built his world around science and logic after their father deserted the family but his only purpose turns out to be getting even with everyone he feels has betrayed him. Young Edward (Stahl) tried to be the "good" son, while Mom (Dey) retreated into religion and an affair with self-righteously nasty school principal Henry Howland (Elliott). TV adaptation of the novel by Ethan Canin. **90m/C VHS.** Jerry O'Connell, Nick Stahl, Susan Dey, Sam Elliott, Neal McDonough, Jean Marie Barnwell, Patrick Renna; ***D:*** Larry Elikann; ***W:*** Maria Nation; ***C:*** Eric Van Haren Noman; ***M:*** Lawrence Shragge. *HMK*

Blue Skies **1946** Former dancer turned radio personality Astaire flashes back to his friendship with singer Crosby and the gal (Caulfield) that came between them. Flimsy plot is just an excuse for some 20 Irving Berlin songs and Astaire's split-screen dance number, "Puttin' on the Ritz." ♫ All By Myself; Always; Any Bonds Today?; Blue Skies; A Couple of Song and Dance Men; Everybody Step; Getting Nowhere; Heat Wave; I'll See You in C-U-B-A. **104m/C VHS, LV.** Fred Astaire, Bing Crosby, Joan Caulfield, Billy DeWolfe, Olga San Juan, Frank Faylen; ***D:*** Stuart Heisler; ***W:*** Arthur Sheekman; ***C:*** Charles B(ryant) Lang. *MCA*

Blue Skies Again ½ **1983 (PG)** Spunky young woman determined to play major league baseball locks horns with the chauvinistic owner and the gruff manager of her favorite team. **91m/C VHS, Beta.** Robyn Barto, Harry Hamlin, Mimi Rogers, Kenneth McMillan, Dana Elcar, Andy Garcia; ***D:*** Richard Michaels. *WAR*

Blue Sky **1991 (PG-13)** Carly Marshall (Lange) is an irrepressible beauty, long married to adoring but uptight military scientist Hank (Jones). Things are barely in control when they're stationed in Hawaii but after Hank's transfer to a backwater base in Alabama, Carly's emotional mood swings go wildly out of control. Hell truly breaks loose when Carly attracts the attention of the camp's commander (Boothe), who's only too willing to take advantage. Set in 1962, a nuclear radiation subplot (Hank's new project) proves a minor distraction. Exceptional performance by Lange with Jones providing a quiet counterpoint as a man still deeply in love with his disturbed wife. Director Richardson's final film. Release date was delayed to 1994 due to Orion's financial problems. **101m/C VHS, LV.** Jessica Lange, Tommy Lee Jones, Powers Boothe, Carrie Snodgress, Amy Locane, Chris O'Donnell, Mitchell Ryan, Dale Dye; ***D:*** Tony Richardson; ***W:*** Jerry Leichtling, Arlene Sarner, Rama Laurie Stagner; ***M:*** Jack Nitzsche. Academy Awards '94: Best Actress (Lange); Golden Globe Awards '95: Best Actress—Drama (Lange); Los Angeles Film Critics Association Awards '94: Best Actress (Lange); Nominations: Screen Actors Guild Award '94: Best Actress (Lange). *ORI*

Blue Steel **1934** A young Wayne saves a town from financial ruin by leading the citizens to a gold strike. Also available with "Man From Utah" on Laser Disc. **59m/B VHS, Beta, LV.** John Wayne, George "Gabby" Hayes; ***D:*** Robert North Bradbury. *COL, NOS, MRV*

Blue Steel **1990 (R)** Director Bigelow's much-heralded, proto-feminist cop thriller. A serious female rookie's gun falls into the hands of a Wall Street psycho who begins a killing spree. Action film made silly with over-anxious sub-text and patriarchy-directed rage. **102m/C VHS, Beta, LV, 8mm.** Jamie Lee Curtis, Ron Silver, Clancy Brown, Louise Fletcher, Philip Bosco, Elizabeth Pena, Tom Sizemore; ***D:*** Kathryn Bigelow; ***W:*** Kathryn Bigelow, Eric Red; ***M:*** Brad Fiedel. *MGM*

Blue Sunshine ½ **1978 (R)** A certain brand of L.S.D. called Blue Sunshine starts to make its victims go insane. **94m/C VHS, Beta.** Zalman King, Deborah Winters, Mark Goddard, Robert Walden, Charles Siebert, Ann Cooper, Ray Young, Alice Ghostley; ***D:*** Jeff Lieberman; ***W:*** Jeff Lieberman. *VES*

Blue Thunder ½ **1983 (R)** Police helicopter pilot Scheider is chosen to test an experimental high-tech chopper that can see through walls, record a whisper, and level a city block. Seems anti-terrorist supercopter is needed to ensure security during 1984 Olympics. Bothered by Vietnam flashbacks, Scheider then battles wacky McDowell in the skies over L.A. High-techy police drama with satisfying aerial combat scenes nearly crashes with storyline. **110m/C VHS, Beta, LV.** Roy Scheider, Daniel Stern, Malcolm McDowell, Candy Clark, Warren Oates; ***D:*** John Badham; ***W:*** Dan O'Bannon, Don Jakoby; ***C:*** John A. Alonzo. Nominations: Academy Awards '83: Best Film Editing. *COL*

Blue Tiger **1994 (R)** Gina Hayes (Madsen) is shopping with her young son when a masked gunman enters the store and opens fire. When Gina realizes her son has been killed she becomes obsessed with finding the assailant. Her one clue—a blue tiger tattoo. **88m/C VHS, LV.** Virginia Madsen, Toru Nakamura, Harry Dean Stanton; ***D:*** Norberto Barba; ***W:*** Joel Soisson. *COL*

Blue Tornado **1990 (PG-13)** An eerie bright light, emitted from a mountain, makes supersonic jets disappear into thin air. A beautiful researcher and a cocky pilot set out to solve the mystery. Better-than-average aerial sequences don't make up for goofy story and ludicrous dialogue. **96m/C VHS.** Dirk Benedict, Patsy Kensit, Ted McGinley, David Warner; ***D:*** Tony B. Dobb. *VMK*

Blue Velvet **1986 (R)** Disturbing, unique exploration of the dark side of American suburbia, involving an innocent college youth who discovers a severed ear in an empty lot, and is thrust into a turmoil of depravity, murder, and sexual deviance. Brutal, grotesque, and unmistakably Lynch; an immaculately made, fiercely imagined film that is unlike any other. Mood is enhanced by the Badalamenti soundtrack. Graced by splashes of Lynchian humor, most notably the movie's lumber theme. Hopper is riveting as the chief sadistic nutcase and Twin Peaks' MacLachlan is a study in loss of innocence. Cinematography by Frederick Elmes. **121m/C VHS, Beta, LV.** Kyle MacLachlan, Isabella Rossellini, Dennis Hopper, Laura Dern, Hope Lange, Jack Nance, Dean Stockwell, George Dickerson, Brad Dourif; ***D:*** David Lynch; ***W:*** David Lynch; ***C:*** Frederick Elmes; ***M:*** Angelo Badalamenti. Independent Spirit Awards '87: Best Actress (Rossellini); Los Angeles Film Critics Association Awards '86: Best Director (Lynch), Best Supporting Actor (Hopper); National Society of Film Critics Awards '86: Best Cinematography, Best Director (Lynch), Best Film, Best Supporting Actor (Hopper); Nominations: Academy Awards '86: Best Director (Lynch). *WAR*

The Blue Yonder ✗½ *Time Flyers* **1986** In this made-for-video feature, a young boy travels back in time to meet the grandfather he never knew, risking historical integrity. **89m/C VHS, Beta.** Art Carney, Peter Coyote, Huckleberry Fox; ***D:*** Mark Rosman. *DIS*

Bluebeard ✗✗½ **1944** Tormented painter with a psychopathic urge to strangle his models is the basis for this effective, low-budget film. One of Carradine's best vehicles. **73m/B VHS, Beta.** John Carradine, Jean Parker, Nils Asther; ***D:*** Edgar G. Ulmer. *NOS, MRV, SNC*

Bluebeard ✗✗✗ *Landru* **1963** French biography of Henri-Desire Landru, who seduced and murdered eleven women and was subsequently beheaded. Dubbed into English. **108m/C VHS, Beta.** *FR* Charles Denner, Danielle Darrieux, Michele Morgan, Hildegarde Neff; ***D:*** Claude Chabrol. *NLC*

Bluebeard ✗½ **1972 (R)** Lady killer Burton knocks off series of beautiful wives in soporific remake of the infamous story. **128m/C VHS.** Richard Burton, Raquel Welch, Joey Heatherton, Nathalie Delon, Virna Lisi, Sybil Danning; ***D:*** Edward Dmytryk; ***M:*** Ennio Morricone. *LIV*

Bluebeard's Eighth Wife ✗✗ **1938** Problematic comedy set on the French Riviera about a spoiled millionaire (Cooper) who's been married seven times and wants to go for eight with Colbert, the daughter of a destitute aristocrat. Good for a few laughs, but Coop seemed out of place in his role. Based on the play by Alfred Savoir, American version by Charlton Andrews. **86m/B VHS.** Claudette Colbert, Gary Cooper, David Niven, Edward Everett Horton, Elizabeth Patterson, Herman Bing, William Hymer, Franklin Pangborn; ***D:*** Ernst Lubitsch; ***W:*** Charles Brackett, Billy Wilder. *MCA*

Blueberry Hill ✗½ **1988 (R)** While her mother struggles with the grief over husband's death, a young girl in a small town learns about life, music, and her late father from a jazz singer. Good soundtrack. **93m/C VHS, Beta.** Jennifer Rubin, Carrie Snodgress, Margaret Avery; ***D:*** Strathford Hamilton. *FOX*

The Blues Brothers ✗✗½ **1980 (R)** As an excuse to run rampant on the city of Chicago, Jake and Elwood Blues attempt to raise $5,000 for their childhood orphanage by putting their old band back together. Good music, and lots of cameos. **133m/C VHS, Beta, LV.** John Belushi, Dan Aykroyd, James Brown, Cab Calloway, Ray Charles, Henry Gibson, Aretha Franklin, Carrie Fisher, John Candy; ***Cameos:*** Frank Oz, Steven Spielberg, Twiggy, Paul (Pee Wee Herman) Reubens, Steve Lawrence, John Lee Hooker; ***D:*** John Landis; ***W:*** Dan Aykroyd, John Landis; ***M:*** Ira Newborn. *MCA*

Blues Busters ✗✗½ **1950** Another entry in the "Bowery Boys" series. When Sach emerges from a tonsillectomy with the velvety voice of a crooner, Slip cashes in by turning Louie's Sweet Shop into a nightclub, the better to showcase his buddy's talents. Sach's singing voice provided by John Lorenz. **68m/B VHS.** Leo Gorcey, Huntz Hall, Adele Jergens, Gabriel Dell, Craig Stevens, Phyllis Coates, Bernard Gorcey, David Gorcey; ***D:*** William Beaudine. *WAR*

Bluffing It ✗✗ **1987** A made-for-television movie about an older man who has been disguising his illiteracy for years. **120m/C VHS.** Dennis Weaver, Janet Carroll, Michelle Little, Robert Sean Leonard, Cleavant Derricks, Victoria Wauchope; ***D:*** James Sadwith; ***M:*** Brad Fiedel. *NO*

The Blum Affair ✗✗ **1948** In post-WWI Germany, a Jewish man is framed for the murder of an accountant and uncovers in his capture and prosecution a rat's nest of corruption and anti-Semitism. In German with English subtitles. **109m/B VHS, Beta.** *GE* Hans-Christian Blech, Gisela Trowe, Kurt Ehrhardt, Paul Bildt, Klaus Becker; ***D:*** Erich Engel. *NOS, FCT, APD*

Blume in Love ✗✗✗ **1973 (R)** An ironic comedy/drama about a man who falls hopelessly in love with his ex-wife who divorced him for cheating on her while they were married. **115m/C VHS, Beta.** George Segal, Susan Anspach, Kris Kristofferson, Shelley Winters, Marsha Mason; ***D:*** Paul Mazursky; ***W:*** Paul Mazursky; ***C:*** Bruce Surtees; ***M:*** Bill Conti. *WAR*

BMX Bandits ✗✗ **1983** Three adventurous Aussie teens put their BMX skills to the test when they witness a crime and are pursued by the criminals. Much big air. **92m/C VHS.** Nicole Kidman, David Argue, John Ley, Angelo D'Angelo; ***D:*** Brian Trenchard-Smith; ***W:*** Patrick Edgeworth. *IMP*

Boarding House ✗ **1983 (R)** Residents of a boardinghouse discover sinister doings in the basement. It does not occur to any of them to move to another house. **90m/C VHS, Beta.** Hank Adly, Kalassu, Alexandra Day; ***D:*** John Wintergate. *MRV*

Boarding School ✗✗ *The Passion Flower Hotel* **1983 (R)** Basic teen sex comedy about students at a proper Swiss boarding school for girls who devise a plan to seduce the boys at a nearby school by posing as prostitutes. Kinski stars as the American girl who masterminds the caper. **100m/C VHS, Beta.** *GE* Nastassia Kinski; ***D:*** Andre Farwagi. *VES, LIV*

Boardinghouse Blues ✗✗ **1948** A show-biz musical centered around a boarding house with tenant troubles. It's an excuse for popular black entertainers of the day to perform, including Lucky Millinder, Bull Moose Jackson, Una Mae Carlisle, and Stumpy and Stumpy. **90m/C VHS.** Dusty Fletcher, Moms Mabley; ***D:*** Josh Binney. *FCT, RXM*

The Boat is Full ✗✗✗ **1981** A group of refugees pose as a family in order to escape from Nazi Germany as they seek asylum in Switzerland. Available in German with English subtitles or dubbed into English. **104m/C VHS, Beta.** *SI* Tina Engel, Curt Bois, Renate Steiger, Mathias Gnaedinger; ***D:*** Markus Imhoof. Berlin International Film Festival '81: Best Director (Imhoof); Nominations: Academy Awards '81: Best Foreign Language Film. *SUE, GLV, JCF*

The Boatniks ✗✗½ **1970 (G)** An accident-prone Coast Guard ensign finds himself in charge of the "Times Square" of waterways: Newport Harbor. Adding to his already "titanic" problems is a gang of ocean-going jewel thieves who won't give up the ship! **99m/C VHS, Beta.** Robert Morse, Stefanie Powers, Phil Silvers, Norman Fell, Wally Cox, Don Ameche; ***D:*** Norman Tokar; ***M:*** Robert F. Brunner. *DIS*

Bob & Carol & Ted & Alice ✗✗½ **1969 (R)** Two California couples have attended a trendy therapy session and, in an attempt to be more in touch with sexuality, resort to applauding one another's extramarital affairs and swinging. Wacky and well-written, this is a farce on free love and psychospeak. Mazursky's directorial debut. **104m/C VHS, Beta, LV.** Natalie Wood, Robert Culp, Dyan Cannon, Elliott Gould; ***D:*** Paul Mazursky; ***W:*** Paul Mazursky, Larry Tucker; ***C:*** Charles B(ryant) Lang; ***M:*** Quincy Jones. New York Film Critics Awards '69: Best Screenplay, Best Supporting Actress (Cannon); Writers Guild of America '69: Best Original Screenplay; Nominations: Academy Awards '69: Best Cinematography, Best Story & Screenplay, Best Supporting Actor (Gould), Best Supporting Actress (Cannon). *GKK*

Bob Dylan: Don't Look Back ✗✗✗ **1991** A famous documentary about Bob Dylan at the beginning of his career: on the road, in performance and during private moments. From the director of "Monterey Pop." **95m/B VHS, Beta, LV.** Bob Dylan, Joan Baez, Donovan; ***D:*** D.A. Pennebaker. *WRV, MVD, PAR*

Bob le Flambeur ✗✗✗ **1955** Wonderful film noir of a compulsive gambler who decides to take a final fling by robbing the casino at Deauville. In French, subtitled in English. English title is "Bob the Gambler." **106m/B VHS, Beta, LV.** *FR* Roger Duchesne, Isabel Corey, Daniel Cauchy; ***D:*** Jean-Pierre Melville. *COL, ING, CVC*

Bob Roberts ✗✗✗ **1992 (R)** Pseudo-documentary satire about a 1990 Pennsylvania senatorial race between Robbins' right-wing folk singer/entrepreneur versus Vidal's aging liberal incumbent. Roberts seems like a gee-whiz kinda guy but he'll stop at nothing to get elected and he knows a lot about political dirty tricks and, even more important, manipulating the media to get what he wants. Robbins directorial debut turned out to be very timely in view of the 1992 presidential campaign. Features a number of cameos. Line to remember: "Vote first. Ask questions later." **105m/C VHS, LV.** Tim Robbins, Giancarlo Esposito, Ray Wise, Rebecca Jenkins, Harry J. Lennix, John Ottavino, Robert Stanton, Alan Rickman, Gore Vidal, Brian Doyle-Murray, Anita Gillette, David Strathairn; ***Cameos:*** Susan Sarandon, James Spader, John Cusack, Fred Ward, Pamela Reed; ***D:*** Tim Robbins; ***W:*** Tim Robbins; ***M:*** David Robbins. *LIV, BTV*

Bobbie Jo and the Outlaw ✗½ **1976 (R)** Wonderwoman Carter is a bored carhop who yearns to be a country singer. She becomes involved with Marjoe, who fancies himself as a contemporary Billy the Kid. Together, they do their Bonnie and Clyde thing, to a significantly lesser dramatic effect than the original, though a glut of violence keeps the bodies dropping. **89m/C VHS, Beta.** Lynda Carter, Marjoe Gortner, Jesse Vint; ***D:*** Mark L. Lester. *VES, LIV*

Bobby Deerfield ✗✗ **1977 (PG)** Cold-blooded Grand Prix driver comes face to face with death each time he races, but finally learns the meaning of life when he falls in love with a critically ill woman. Even with race cars, soap opera stalls. **124m/C VHS, Beta.** Al Pacino, Marthe Keller, Anny Duperey, Romolo Valli; ***D:*** Sydney Pollack; ***W:*** Alvin Sargent; ***M:*** Dave Grusin. *WAR*

Bobo ✗½ **1967** Lousy bullfighter tries to lure a gorgeous woman into romance. Filmed in Spain and Italy. **103m/C VHS, Beta, LV.** *GB* Peter Sellers, Britt Ekland, Rossano Brazzi, Adolfo Celi; ***D:*** Robert Parrish. *WAR, FCT*

Boca ✗✗ **1994 (R)** American journalist Chong arrives in Rio during Carnival to investigate a story about random killings throughout the Brazilian streets. She gets stonewalled asking questions, until she meets an up-from-poverty crimelord named Boca De Ouro. Now, our noisy journalist may learn too much to keep her alive. Filmed in Rio de Janiero. **92m/C VHS.** Rae Dawn Chong, Martin Kemp, Tarcisio Meira, Martin Sheen; ***D:*** Sandra Werneck, Walter Avancini; ***W:*** Ed Silverstein. *REP*

Boccaccio '70 ✗✗ **1962** Three short bawdy/comedy/pageant-of-life films inspired by "The Decameron," each pertaining to ironically twisted sexual politics in middle class life. A fourth story, "Renzo and Luciana," by Mario Monicelli, has been cut. Dubbed. **145m/C VHS, Beta.** *IT* Anita Ekberg, Romy Schneider, Tomas Milian, Sophia Loren; ***D:*** Vittorio De Sica, Luchino Visconti, Federico Fellini; ***W:*** Federico Fellini; ***M:*** Nino Rota. *FCT*

Bodies, Rest & Motion ✗✗ **1993 (R)** Stagnant twentysomething movie in which four young people basically do nothing in the sun-baked town of Enfield, Arizona. Similar to the movie "Singles," but without the Seattle grunge scene. The title's reference to Newton is fitting: "A body in rest or motion remains in that state unless acted upon by an outside force." Appealing cast is wasted in listless film that's content to just drift along. Based on the play by Roger Hedden. **94m/C VHS, LV.** Phoebe Cates, Bridget Fonda, Tim Roth, Eric Stoltz, Scott Johnson, Scott Frederick; ***D:*** Michael Steinberg; ***W:*** Roger Hedden; ***M:*** Michael Convertino. *NLC, BTV*

Bodily Harm ✗✗ **1995 (R)** By-the-numbers neo-noir features Fiorentino as Vegas detective Rita Cates, who's investigating the murders of two women with ties to ex-cop Sam McKeon (Baldwin), not incidentally Rita's former lover. She rekindles their lust but then begins to have second thoughts about Sam's innocence. Unconvincing despite the expert cast. **91m/C VHS.** Linda Fiorentino, Daniel Baldwin, Greg Henry, Bill Smitrovich, Troy Evans, Joe Regalbuto, Millie Perkins, Todd Susman, Shannon Kenny; ***D:*** James Lemmo; ***W:*** James Lemmo, Joseph Whaley, Ronda Barendse; ***M:*** Robert Sprayberry. *AVE*

Body and Soul ✗✗ **1924** The first screen appearance of Robeson has him cast in a dual role as a conniving preacher and his good brother. The preacher preys on the heroine, making her life a misery. Objections by censors to the preacher's character caused him to be redeemed and become worthy of the heroine's love. **?m/B VHS.** Paul Robeson, Julia Theresa Russell, Mercedes Gilbert; ***D:*** Oscar Micheaux. *FCT*

Body and Soul ✂✂✂½ *An Affair of the Heart* **1947** A young boxer fights his way unscrupulously to the top. Vintage '40s boxing film that defines the genre. Remade in 1981. **104m/B VHS, LV.** John Garfield, Lilli Palmer, Hazel Brooks, Anne Revere, William Conrad, Canada Lee; ***D:*** Robert Rossen; ***W:*** Abraham Polonsky; ***C:*** James Wong Howe. Academy Awards '47: Best Film Editing; Nominations: Academy Awards '47: Best Actor (Garfield), Best Original Screenplay. *REP*

Body & Soul ✂✂½ **1981 (R)** Interesting remake of 1947 gem about a boxer who loses his perspective in the world of fame, fast cars, and women. **109m/C VHS, Beta.** Leon Isaac Kennedy, Jayne Kennedy, Peter Lawford, Muhammad Ali, Perry Lang; ***D:*** George Bowers. *MGM*

Body Bags ✂✂½ *John Carpenter Presents Body Bags* **1993 (R)** Three gory, though humorous, made for cable stories hosted by horrormeister Carpenter as your friendly local coroner. "The Gas Station" finds the young female overnight attendent menaced by a psycho. "Hair" is about a balding yuppie who'll do anything for a full head of hair. Then he meets the sinister Dr. Lock and his magical new-hair growth treatment. The grisly "Eye" concerns a ballplayer who loses the aforementioned appendage and finds that his transplanted eyeball, taken from an executed serial killer, is subject to ghastly visions. Several fellow horror directors have cameos. **95m/C VHS, LV.** Alex Datcher, Robert Carradine, Stacy Keach, David Warner, Mark Hamill, Twiggy, John Agar, Deborah Harry, Sheena Easton, David Naughton, John Carpenter; ***Cameos:*** Wes Craven, Sam Raimi, Roger Corman, Tobe Hooper; ***D:*** Tobe Hooper, John Carpenter; ***W:*** Billy Brown, Dan Angel; ***M:*** John Carpenter, Jim Lang. *REP*

Body Beat ✂✂ **1988 (PG)** Wild jazz and rock dancers are integrated into a previously classical ballet academy. While the students become fast friends, the teachers break off into two rival factions. **90m/C VHS, Beta.** Tony Fields, Galyn Gorg, Scott Grossman, Eliska Krupka. *VMK*

The Body Beneath *Woof!* **1970** A living-dead ghoul survives on the blood of innocents and is still preying on victims today. **85m/C VHS, Beta.** Gavin Reed, Jackie Skarvellis, Susan Heard, Colin Gordon; ***D:*** Andy Milligan. *NO*

Body Chemistry ✂ **1990 (R)** A married sexual-behavior researcher starts up a passionate affair with his lab partner. When he tries to end the relationship, his female associate becomes psychotic. You've seen it all before in "Fatal Attraction." And you'll see it again in "Body Chemistry 2." **84m/C VHS, Beta, LV.** Marc Singer, Mary Crosby, Lisa Pescia, Joseph Campanella, David Kagen; ***D:*** Kristine Peterson; ***W:*** Jackson Barr, Thom Babbes; ***C:*** Phedon Papamichael. *COL*

Body Chemistry 2: Voice of a Stranger ✂½ **1991 (R)** An ex-cop (Harrison) obsessed with violent sex gets involved with a talk-radio psychologist (Pescia) whose advice could prove deadly in this erotic sequel. **84m/C VHS, LV.** Gregory Harrison, Lisa Pescia, Morton Downey Jr., Robin Riker; ***D:*** Adam Simon. *COL*

Body Chemistry 3: Point of Seduction ✂✂ **1993 (R)** TV producer Alan Clay (Stevens) finds himself caught in a business and sexual triangle when he okays the making of a movie about the life of a TV sex therapist (Shattuck). Seems the lady's lovers have a nasty habit of getting murdered which doesn't prevent Clay from getting personally involved. His actress wife (Fairchild), who wants to star in the movie, is not pleased. Lives up to its title. **90m/C VHS, LV.** Andrew Stevens, Morgan Fairchild, Shari Shattuck; ***D:*** Jim Wynorski. *NHO*

Body Chemistry 4: Full Exposure ✂½ **1995 (R)** When sex psychologist Claire Archer is accused of murder she hires Simon Mitchell, the best criminal defense attorney around. But Simon becomes just a little too closely involved with his possibly psycho client and it could cost him not only his career and marriage but his life. Also available unrated. **89m/C VHS, LV.** Shannon Tweed, Larry Poindexter. *NHO*

Body Count ✂½ **1987** A weird and wealthy family will stop at nothing, including murder and cannibalism, to enhance their fortune. Rather than bodies, count the minutes 'til the movie's over. Also titled "The 11th Commandment." **90m/C VHS, Beta.** Marilyn Hassett, Dick Sargent, Steven Ford, Greg Mullavey, Thomas Ryan, Bernie White; ***D:*** Paul Leder. *MCG*

Body Count ✂½ **1995 (R)** Professional killer Makoto (Chiba) and his female partner (Nielsen) seek revenge on the New Orleans cops who set them up. Opposing them are special crime unit partners, Eddie Cook (Davi) and Vinnie Rizzo (Bauer). Lots of shootouts and macho bravado. **93m/C VHS, LV.** Sonny Chiba, Brigitte Nielsen, Robert Davi, Steven Bauer; ***D:*** Talun Hsu. *APX*

Body Double ✂✂✂ **1984 (R)** A voyeuristic unemployed actor peeps on a neighbor's nightly disrobing and sees more than he wants to. A grisly murder leads him into an obsessive quest through the world of pornographic films. **114m/C VHS, Beta, LV.** Craig Wasson, Melanie Griffith, Greg Henry, Deborah Shelton, Guy Boyd, Dennis Franz, David Haskell, Rebecca Stanley, Barbara Crampton; ***D:*** Brian DePalma; ***W:*** Brian DePalma, Robert J. Avrech; ***C:*** Stephen Burum; ***M:*** Pino Donaggio. National Society of Film Critics Awards '84: Best Supporting Actress (Griffith). *COL*

Body Heat ✂✂✂½ **1981 (R)** During a Florida heat wave, a none-too-bright lawyer becomes involved in a steamy love affair with a mysterious woman and then in a plot to kill her husband. Hurt and Turner (in her film debut) became stars under Kasdan's direction (the three would reunite for "The Accidental Tourist"). Hot love scenes supplement a twisting mystery with a suprise ending. Rourke's arsonist and Danson's soft shoe shouldn't be missed. **113m/C VHS, Beta, LV.** William Hurt, Kathleen Turner, Richard Crenna, Ted Danson, Mickey Rourke; ***D:*** Lawrence Kasdan; ***W:*** Lawrence Kasdan; ***M:*** John Barry. *WAR*

The Body in the Library ✂½ *Agatha Christie's Miss Marple: The Body In the Library* **1987** A British television-produced Miss Marple mystery, based on Agatha Christie's 1942 novel, involving the septuagenarian detective investigating the murder of a young woman in a wealthy British mansion. **155m/C VHS, Beta.** *GB* Joan Hickson; ***D:*** Silvio Narizzano. *FOX, HMV, VCO*

Body Language ✂✂ **1992 (R)** A successful businesswoman, with a man problem, hires a super secretary with answers to all life's questions—and a deadly agenda all her own. **93m/C VHS, Beta.** Heather Locklear, Linda Purl, Edward Albert, James Acheson; ***D:*** Arthur Seidelman; ***W:*** Dan Gurskis, Brian Ross. *PAR*

Body Language ✂✂½ **1995 (R)** Criminal defense attorney Gavin St. Claire (Berenger) falls for a topless dancer (Schanz), which leads him into all sorts of trouble, including murder. **95m/C VHS.** Tom Berenger, Heidi Schanz, Nancy Travis; ***D:*** George Case. *HBO*

Body Melt ✂✂½ **1993** When a crazed doctor unleashes an experimental drug on an unsuspecting town, the residents begin to literally melt away. **82m/C VHS, LV.** *AU* Gerard Kennedy, Andrew Daddo, Ian Smith, Vincent Gil, Regina Gaigalas; ***D:*** Philip Brophy; ***W:*** Philip Brophy, Rod Bishop; ***M:*** Philip Brophy. *PSM*

Body Moves ✂✂ **1990 (PG-13)** Romantic entanglements heat up the competition when two couples enter a steamy dance contest. Not apt to move you. **98m/C VHS, Beta.** *IT* Kirk Rivera, Steve Messina, Dianne Granger, Linsley Allen, Philip Spruce, Nicole Kolman, Susan Gardner; ***D:*** Gerry Lively; ***W:*** Daniel Steel. *PSM*

Body of Evidence *Woof!* **1992 (R)** Bad movie with pretensions takes "Basic Instinct" a step further. Instead of an ice pick and sex, sex itself is used as the weapon in a murder trial featuring Madonna as the defendant, Dafoe as her lawyer, and Mantegna as the prosecutor. The plot is, of course, secondary to the S&M sex scenes with Dafoe which feature hot wax and broken glass. Madonna's lack of performance is the least of the film's problems since everyone seems to have forgotten any acting talent they possess. Director Edel fails to direct—the film even looks bad. "Body" was the subject of another NC-17 ratings flap but this film shouldn't be seen by anybody. An unrated version is also available. **99m/C VHS, Beta, LV.** Madonna, Willem Dafoe, Joe Mantegna, Anne Archer, Michael Forest, Charles Hallahan, Mark Rolston, Richard Riehle, Julianne Moore, Frank Langella, Juergen Prochnow, Stan Shaw; ***D:*** Uli Edel; ***W:*** Brad Mirman; ***M:*** Graeme Revell. Golden Raspberry Awards '93: Worst Actress (Madonna). *MGM*

Body of Influence ✂✂ **1993 (R)** A Beverly Hills psychiatrist gets overly involved with a beautiful female patient. But she not only wants his love—she wants his life. Also available in an unrated version. **96m/C VHS.** Nick Cassavetes, Shannon Whirry, Sandahl Bergman, Don Swayze, Anna Karin, Catherine Parks, Diana Barton, Richard Roundtree; ***D:*** Andrew Garroni; ***W:*** David Schreiber. *ACA*

Body Parts ✂ **1990** For fans of the demented dismemberer niche. Body Parts, a sleazy skin club, loses some of its star talent when the strippers start turning up in cameo video appearances. Seems there's a psycho killer on the loose who videotapes the dismemberment of his stripper-victims. The police decide they've got to meet this guy when he sends them a sample of his work. **90m/C VHS, LV.** Teri Lee, Dick Monda, Johnny Mandel. *NO*

Body Parts ✂✂ **1991 (R)** A crime psychologist loses his arm in an auto accident and receives a transplant from an executed murderer. Does the limb have an evil will of its own? Poorly paced horror goes off the deep end in gore with its third act. Based on the novel "Choice Cuts" by French writers Pierre Boileau and Thomas Narcejac, whose work inspired some of the greatest suspense films. **88m/C VHS, Beta, LV.** Jeff Fahey, Kim Delaney, Lindsay Duncan, Peter Murnik, Brad Dourif, Zakes Mokae, Johnny Walsh, Paul Benevictor; ***D:*** Eric Red; ***W:*** Eric Red, Norman Snider, Larry Gross; ***M:*** Loek Dikker. *PAR*

Body Rock *Woof!* **1984 (PG-13)** Brooklyn breakdancer Lamas deserts his buddies to work at a chic Manhattan nightclub. Watching Lamas as the emcee/breakdancing fool is a hoot. ♫Body Rock; Team Work; Why Do You Want to Break My Heart?; One Thing Leads to Another; Let Your Body Rock; Vanishing Point; Sharpshooter; The Jungle; Deliver. **93m/C VHS, Beta.** Lorenzo Lamas, Vicki Frederick, Cameron Dye, Michelle Nicastro, Ray Sharkey, Grace Zabriskie, Carole Ita White; ***D:*** Marcelo Epstein. *NO*

The Body Shop *Woof! Doctor Gore* **1972** Unorthodox love story in which a man decides to patch up his relationship with his dead wife by piecing together her dismembered body. For lovers only. Under "Doctor Gore" title the film includes an intro by horror director Herschell Gordon Lewis. **91m/C VHS.** Pat Patterson, Jenny Driggers, Roy Mehaffey, Linda Faile, Candy Furr; ***D:*** Pat Patterson. *NO*

Body Shot ✂✂½ **1993 (R)** Celebrity shutterbug Mickey Dane (Patrick) is fingered in the murder of a rock star after it turns out he did a kinky layout for a look-alike. When police find out he had an obsession for the dead woman, he employs his photographic expertise in the search for the real killer. Effective tension-builder with fast-paced chases through the seamy side of Los Angeles. **98m/C VHS, LV.** Robert Patrick, Michelle Johnson; ***D:*** Dimitri Logothetis; ***W:*** Robert Strauss. *TRI*

Body Slam ✂½ **1987 (PG)** A small-time talent monger hits it big with a rock and roll/ professional wrestling tour. Piper's debut; contains some violence and strong language. **100m/C VHS, Beta.** Roddy Piper, Captain Lou Albano, Dirk Benedict, Tanya Roberts, Billy Barty, Charles Nelson Reilly, John Astin, Wild Samoan, Tonga Kid, Barry Gordon; ***D:*** Hal Needham; ***W:*** Steven H. Burkow; ***M:*** John D'Andrea. *SUE, NLC*

The Body Snatcher ✂✂✂½ **1945** Based on Robert Louis Stevenson's story about a grave robber who supplies corpses to research scientists. Set in Edinburgh in the 19th century, this Lewton production is superior. One of Karloff's best vehicles. **77m/B VHS, Beta, LV.** Edith Atwater, Russell Wade, Rita

(Paula) Corday, Boris Karloff, Bela Lugosi, Henry Daniell; ***D:*** Robert Wise. *MED, TTC*

Body Snatcher from Hell ☆½ *Goke, Body Snatcher from Hell; Goke the Vampire; Kyuketsuki Gokemidoro* **1969** An airliner passes through a mysterious cloud and crashes in a desert. One by one, the passengers are turned into vampires. Some interesting special effects. **84m/C VHS.** *JP* Hideo Ko, Teruo Yoshida, Tomomi Sato, Eizo Kitamura, Masay Takahashi, Cathy Horlan, Kazuo Kato, Yuko Kusunoki; ***D:*** Hajime Sato. *SNC*

Body Snatchers ☆☆ **1993 (R)** Yet another version of "Invasion of the Body Snatchers." An innocent family arrive at an Army base which turns out to be infested with pod people. This time around the heroine is angst-ridden teenager Marti (Anwar) and the pods have something to do with a mysterious toxic spill. The 1978 remake was well done; this so-so version takes advantage of the advances in special effects (particularly in Anwar's bathtub scene) and sound technology but is slow-paced with few jolts of terror. **87m/C VHS, LV.** Gabrielle Anwar, Meg Tilly, Terry Kinney, Forest Whitaker, Billy Wirth, R. Lee Ermey; ***D:*** Abel Ferrara; ***W:*** Stuart Gordon, Dennis Paoli, Nicholas St. John; ***C:*** Bojan Bazelli; ***M:*** Joe Delia. *WAR*

Body Trouble ☆½ *Joker's Wild* **1992 (R)** After being attacked by sharks while vacationing in the Caribbean, a man washes ashore in Miami and then somehow makes his way to New York City. There he meets Vera Vin Rouge and her friends Cinnamon, Spice, Paprika, and Johnny Zero, a gangster. Zero decides he doesn't like the man, so he chases him back to the Caribbean. Supposedly this all happens in only one day. Hmmm... **98m/C VHS.** Dick Van Patten, Priscilla Barnes, Frank Gorshin, James Hong, Marty Rackham, Michael Unger, Jonathan Soloman, Brit Helfer, Leigh Clark, Patricia Cardell, Richie Barathy; ***D:*** Bill Milling; ***W:*** Bill Milling. *TRI*

The Body Vanished ☆☆ **1939** Murder mystery featuring a corpse that disappears from the scene of the crime. **?m/C VHS.** *GB* Lewis Wilson, Frances Dubay, Dana Wilson. *SNC*

Body Waves ☆½ **1992 (R)** Beach comedy starring Calvert as a teenager who bets his father that he can raise money on his own. In typical teen movie fashion, he invents a sex cream that drives boys and girls wild. Brain candy featuring lots of skimpy bikinis. **80m/C VHS.** Bill Calvert, Leah Lail, Larry Linville, Dick Miller, Jim Wise; ***D:*** P.J. Pesce. *NHO*

The Bodyguard ☆½ **1976 (R)** The Yakuza, Japan's mafia, and New York's big crime families face off in this martial arts extravaganza. **89m/C VHS, Beta.** Sonny Chiba, Aaron Banks, Bill Louie, Judy Lee; ***D:*** Maurice Sarli. *MED*

The Bodyguard ☆☆ **1992 (R)** Buttoned-down, ex-Secret Service agent turned private bodyguard reluctantly takes on a wildly successful singer/actress as a client. Houston, in her acting debut as the over-indulged diva, doesn't have to stretch too far but acquits herself well. Costner has really bad hair day but easily portrays the tightly wound Frank. Critically trashed, a box office smash, and too long. Originally scripted by producer Kasdan over a decade ago, with Steve McQueen in mind. Predictable romantic melodrama is kept moving by the occasional sharp dialog and a few action pieces. Songs include the smash hit "I Will Always Love You," written and originally performed by Dolly Parton. **130m/C VHS, LV.** Kevin Costner, Whitney Houston, Gary Kemp, Bill Cobbs, Ralph Waite, Tomas Arana, Michele Lamar Richards, Mike Starr, Christopher Birt, DeVaughn Nixon, Charles Keating, Robert Wuhl; ***Cameos:*** Debbie Reynolds; ***D:*** Mick Jackson; ***W:*** Lawrence Kasdan; ***M:*** Alan Silvestri. MTV Movie Awards '93: Best Song ("I Will Always Love You"); Nominations: Academy Awards '92: Best Song ("I Have Nothing"), Best Song ("Run to You"). *WAR, BTV*

Boeing Boeing ☆☆½ **1965** A dated but still amusing sex farce about a bachelor newspaperman (Curtis) in Paris, his three stewardess girlfriends, and the elaborate plots he resorts to in trying to keep them from finding out about each other. When the new Boeing jet makes air travel faster all Curtis' schemes may come crashing down. Ritter is fun as the exasperated housekeeper and Lewis amazingly subdued as Curtis' business rival. **102m/C VHS, LV.** Tony Curtis, Jerry Lewis, Dany Saval, Christianne Schmidtmer, Suzanna Leigh, Thelma Ritter; ***D:*** John Rich; ***W:*** Edward Anhalt. *PAR*

Bog ☆ **1984 (PG)** Boggy beast from the Arctic north awakens to eat people. Scientists mount an anti-monster offensive. **90m/C VHS, Beta.** Gloria De Haven, Marshall Thompson, Leo Gordon, Aldo Ray. *PSM*

Boggy Creek II ☆½ *The Barbaric Beast of Boggy Creek, Part II* **1983 (PG)** The continuing saga of the eight-foot-tall, 300 pound monster from Texarkana. Third in a series of low-budget movies including "The Legend of Boggy Creek" and "Return to Boggy Creek." **93m/C VHS, Beta, LV.** Charles B. Pierce, Cindy Butler, Serene Hedin; ***D:*** Charles B. Pierce; ***W:*** Charles B. Pierce. *MED*

Bogie: The Last Hero **1980** Television biography of Humphrey Bogart, populated by almost-lookalikes who can almost act. **100m/C VHS, Beta.** Kevin J. O'Connor, Kathryn Harrold, Ann Wedgeworth, Patricia Barry, Alfred Ryder, Donald May, Richard Dysart, Arthur Franz; ***D:*** Vincent Sherman; ***M:*** Charles Bernstein. *FRH*

Bohemian Girl ☆☆☆ **1936** The last of Laurel and Hardy's comic operettas finds them as guardians of a young orphan (Hood, famous for her roles in the Our Gang comedies), whom no one realizes is actually a kidnapped princess. **74m/B VHS, Beta.** Stan Laurel, Oliver Hardy, Mae Busch, Darla Hood, Jacqueline Wells, Thelma Todd, James Finlayson; ***D:*** James W. Horne. *MED, CCB*

Boiling Point ☆½ **1932** Lawman proves once again that justice always triumphs. **67m/B VHS, Beta.** Hoot Gibson. *NOS, VCI, DVT*

Boiling Point ☆☆½ **1993 (R)** Darkly-flavored action drama delves into the personalities of its two main characters before setting up a final confrontation. Treasury agent Jimmy Mercer (Snipes) is trying to solve his partner's murder, relentlessly pursuing the murderers in cold and methodical fashion. Sleazy Red Diamond (Hopper), just out of prison, owes the mob and has one week to pay them back. Lawman and crook both come home to women, (Davidovich and Perrine) graduates of the Hollywood school of female martyrdom, selflessly supportive of their men. Grim but cliched. Adapted from the Gerald Petievich novel "Money Men." **93m/C VHS, Beta, LV.** Wesley Snipes, Dennis Hopper, Lolita Davidovich, Viggo Mortensen, Dan Hedaya, Valerie Perrine, Seymour Cassel, Jonathan Banks, Tony LoBianco, Christine Elise, James Tolkan, Paul Gleason; ***D:*** James B. Harris; ***W:*** James B. Harris; ***M:*** Cory Lerios, John D'Andrea. *WAR*

The Bold Caballero ☆½ *The Bold Cavalier* **1936** Rebel chieftain Zorro overthrows oppressive Spanish rule in the days of early California. **69m/B VHS, Beta.** Bob Livingston, Heather Angel, Sig Rumann, Robert Warwick; ***D:*** Wells Root. *NOS, VDM, VCN*

The Boldest Job in the West ☆ *El Mas Fabulosi Golpe del Far West* **1971** Italian western about bankrobbers who meet to divide their spoils. Problem is, the guys with the loot don't show. Dubbed in English. **200m/C VHS, Beta.** *IT* Mark Edwards, Frank Sancho, Carmen Sevilla; ***D:*** Joseph Loman. *NO*

Bolero ☆☆½ **1982** Beginning in 1936, this international epic traces the lives of four families across three continents and five decades, highlighting the music and dance that is central to their lives. **173m/C VHS, Beta.** James Caan, Geraldine Chaplin, Robert Hossein, Nicole Garcia, Jacques Villeret; ***D:*** Claude Lelouch; ***W:*** Claude Lelouch. *VES*

Bolero *Woof! Bolero: An Adventure in Ecstasy* **1984 (R)** What sounds like a wet dream come true is really just a good snooze: Bo Derek plays a beautiful young woman who goes on a trip around the world in hopes of losing her virginity; in Spain, she meets a bullfighter who's willing to oblige. Too bad Bo cannot act as good as she looks. **106m/C VHS, Beta.** Bo Derek, George Kennedy, Andrea Occhipinti, Anna Obregon, Olivia D'Abo; ***D:*** John Derek; ***W:*** John Derek; ***M:*** Peter Bernstein, Elmer Bernstein. Golden Raspberry Awards '84: Worst Picture, Worst Actress (Derek), Worst Director (Derek), Worst Screenplay, Worst New Star (D'Abo). *LIV*

Bomb at 10:10 ☆☆ **1967** An American pilot escapes from a German POW camp and plots to assassinate a camp commandant. **87m/C VHS, Beta.** George Montgomery, Rada Popovic, Peter Banicevic; ***D:*** Charles Damic. *GEM*

Bombardier ☆☆½ **1943** A group of cadet bombardiers discover the realities of war on raids over Japan during WWII. Also available colorized. **99m/B VHS, Beta.** Pat O'Brien, Randolph Scott, Robert Ryan, Eddie Albert, Anne Shirley, Barton MacLane; ***D:*** Richard Wallace. *TTC*

Bombay Talkie ☆☆½ **1970 (PG)** A bored British writer (Kendal) heads to India to gather "experiences" and becomes involved with an Indian movie actor (Kapoor). Early clash-of-cultures film from Merchant Ivory has it's dull spots; the behind-the-scenes look at the Indian film industry is more interesting than the romance. **110m/C VHS, Beta.** *IN* Jennifer Kendal, Shashi Kapoor, Zia Mohyeddin, Aparna Sen; ***D:*** James Ivory; ***W:*** Ruth Prawer Jhabvala. *INJ, SUE, NLC*

Bombs Away! ☆ **1986** An atomic bomb is mistakenly shipped to a seedy war surplus store in Seattle, and causes much chicanery. **90m/C VHS, Beta.** Michael Huddleston, Pat McCormick; ***D:*** Bruce Wilson. *COL, NLC*

Bombshell ☆☆☆ *Blonde Bombshell* **1933** Wry insightful comedy into the Hollywood of the 1930s. Harlow plays a naive young actress manipulated by her adoring press agent. He thwarts her plans until she finally notices and begins to fall in love with him. Brilliant satire with Harlow turning in perhaps the best performance of her short career. **96m/B VHS, Beta.** Jean Harlow, Lee Tracy, Pat O'Brien, Una Merkel, Sir C. Aubrey Smith, Franchot Tone; ***D:*** Victor Fleming. *MGM, BTV, FCT*

Bon Voyage! ☆½ **1962** A family's long-awaited European "dream" vacation turns into a series of comic misadventures in this very Disney, very family, very predictable comedy. **131m/C VHS, Beta, LV.** Fred MacMurray, Jane Wyman, Deborah Walley, Michael Callan, Tommy Kirk, Jessie Royce Landis; ***D:*** James Neilson. Nominations: Academy Awards '62: Best Costume Design (Color), Best Sound. *DIS*

Bon Voyage, Charlie Brown ☆☆☆ **1980 (G)** The "Peanuts" comic strip group becomes exchange students in Europe, led by Charlie Brown, Linus, Peppermint Patty, Marcie, and the irrepressible beagle, Snoopy. **76m/C VHS, Beta, LV.** ***D:*** Bill Melendez, Lee Mendelson; ***W:*** Charles M. Schulz; ***M:*** Ed Bogas; ***V:*** Arrin Skelley, Laura Planting, Casey Carlson, David Anderson, Annalisa Bartolin, Scott Beads. *PAR, WTA*

Bonanza **1964** This western series about the Cartwright clan and their Ponderosa ranch ran on TV from 1959-1973, second only to "Gunsmoke." Additional episodes available. In "The Pure Truth" Hoss escapes from jail after being unjustly accused of robbing the bank. An eccentric recluse comes to his aid. **50m/C VHS.** Lorne Greene, Pernell Roberts, Dan Blocker, Michael Landon, Glenda Farrell. *REP, MOV*

Bonanza: The Return ☆½ **1993 (PG)** In 1905, the children of various members of the Cartwright clan work to see the Ponderosa is safe from an unscrupulous businessman. Lame update of the classic family western series. Made for television. **96m/C VHS, LV.** Michael Landon Jr., Dirk Blocker, Emily Warfield, Alistair MacDougall, Brian Leckner, Dean Stockwell, Ben Johnson, Richard Roundtree, Linda Gray, Jack Elam. *VMK*

The Bone Yard ☆ **1990 (R)** A weird mortuary is the setting for strange goings on when a murder is investigated. **98m/C VHS, Beta.** Ed Nelson, Deborah Rose, Norman Fell, Jim Eustermann, Denise Young, Willie Stratford Jr., Phyllis Diller; ***D:*** James Cummins; ***W:*** James Cummins. *PSM*

The Bonfire of the Vanities ☆½ **1990 (R)** If you liked Tom Wolfe's viciously satirical novel, chances are you won't like this version. If you didn't read the book, you probably still won't like it. Miscast and stripped of the book's gutsy look inside its characters, the film's sole attribute is Vilmos Zsigmond's photography. Hanks is all wrong as wealthy Wall Street trader Sherman McCoy who, lost in the back streets of the Bronx, panics and accidentally kills a young black kid. Willis' drunken journalist/narrator, Griffith's mistress, and Freeman's righteous judge are all awkward and thinly written. If you're still awake, look for F. Murray Abraham's cameo as the Bronx D.A. **126m/C VHS, Beta, LV, 8mm.** Tom Hanks, Melanie Griffith, Bruce Willis, Morgan Freeman, Alan King, Kim Cattrall, Saul Rubinek, Clifton James, Donald Moffat, Richard Libertini, Andre Gregory, Robert Stephens; ***Cameos:*** F. Murray Abraham; ***D:*** Brian DePalma; ***W:*** Michael Cristofer; ***C:*** Vilmos Zsigmond; ***M:*** Dave Grusin. *WAR, FCT*

Bonjour Tristesse 🦴🦴🦴 **1957** An amoral French girl conspires to break up her playboy father's upcoming marriage to her stuffy godmother in order to maintain her decadent freedom. Preminger attempted, unsuccessfully, to use this soaper to catapult Seberg to stardom. Based on the novel by Francoise Sagan. **94m/C VHS, Beta.** *FR* Deborah Kerr, David Niven, Jean Seberg, Mylene Demongeot, Geoffrey Horne, Walter Chiari, Jean Kent; ***D:*** Otto Preminger; ***W:*** Arthur Laurents; ***C:*** Georges Perinal. *COL*

Bonnie & Clyde 🦴🦴🦴½ **1967** Based on the biographies of the violent careers of Bonnie Parker and Clyde Barrow, who roamed the Southwest robbing banks. In the Depression era, when any job, even an illegal one, was cherished, money, greed, and power created an unending cycle of violence and fury. Highly controversial and influential, with pronounced bloodshed that spurred mainstream cinematic proliferation. Established Dunaway as a star; produced by Beatty in one of his best performances. **111m/C VHS, Beta, LV.** Warren Beatty, Faye Dunaway, Michael J. Pollard, Gene Hackman, Estelle Parsons, Denver Pyle, Gene Wilder, Dub Taylor; ***D:*** Arthur Penn; ***W:*** David Newman, Robert Benton; ***C:*** Burnett Guffey. Academy Awards '67: Best Cinematography, Best Supporting Actress (Parsons); National Society of Film Critics Awards '67: Best Screenplay, Best Supporting Actor (Hackman); Nominations: Academy Awards '66: Best Actor (Beatty), Best Actor (Hackman, Pollard), Best Actress (Dunaway), Best Director (Penn), Best Picture, Best Story & Screenplay; Academy Awards '67: Best Costume Design. *WAR, BTV*

Bonnie Prince Charlie 🦴🦴½ **1948** Historical epic opening in 1745 and romanticizing the title pretender to the British throne, who united Scottish clans in a doomed campaign against King George. Talky and rather slow-moving except for stirring battle scenes. A notorious box-office flop in its native Britain, where the original running time was 140 minutes. **135m/C VHS.** *GB* David Niven, Margaret Leighton, Judy Campbell, Jack Hawkins, Morland Graham, Finlay Currie, Elwyn Brook-Jones, John Laurie; ***D:*** Anthony Kimmins. *NOS*

Bonnie Scotland 🦴🦴½ **1935** Laurel & Hardy accidentally join an India-bound Scottish regiment. Laughs aplenty. **81m/B VHS, Beta.** Stan Laurel, Oliver Hardy, James Finlayson, Daphne Pollard, June Lang; ***D:*** James W. Horne. *MGM, MLB*

Bonnie's Kids 🦴½ **1973 (R)** Two sisters become involved in murder, sex, and stolen money. **107m/C VHS, Beta.** Tiffany Bolling, Robin Mattson, Scott Brady, Alex Rocco; ***D:*** Arthur Marks. *NO*

The Boogey Man 🦴🦴 **1980 (R)** Through the reflection in a mirror, a girl witnesses her brother murder their mother's lover. Twenty years later this memory still haunts her; the mirror is now broken, revealing its special powers. Who will be next? Murder menagerie; see footage from this flick mirrored in "The Boogey Man 2." **93m/C VHS, Beta, LV.** John Carradine, Suzanna Love, Ron James; ***D:*** Ulli Lommel. *HHE*

Boogey Man 2 *Woof!* **1983** The story continues; same footage, new director but with Lommel, the director of the original "Boogey Man," co-writing the script and appearing in the film. **90m/C VHS, Beta.** John Carradine, Suzanna Love, Shannah Hall, Ulli Lommel, Sholto Von Douglas; ***D:*** Bruce Starr. *VHE*

Book of Love 🦴🦴 **1991 (PG-13)** "Zany" hijinks as a teenager struggles with friendship, girls, and those all-important hormones when he moves to a new neighborhood in the mid-50's. Average rehash of every 50's movie and TV show cliche in existence. Surprise! There's a classic rock 'n' roll soundtrack. Adapted by Kotzwinkle from his novel "Jack in the Box." **88m/C VHS, LV, 8mm.** Chris Young, Keith Coogan, Aeryk Egan, Josie Bissett, Tricia Leigh Fisher, Danny Nucci, Michael McKean, John Cameron Mitchell, Lewis Arquette; ***D:*** Robert Shaye; ***W:*** William Kotzwinkle; ***M:*** Stanley Clarke. *COL*

Boom in the Moon *Woof! A Modern Bluebeard* **1946** Keaton fares poorly in this sci-fi comedy. He's trapped on a space ship to the moon. Poor production, with uneven direction and acting. **83m/C VHS.** Buster Keaton, Angel Garasa, Virginia Serret, Fernando Soto, Luis Barreiro; ***D:*** Jaime Salvador. *NO*

Boom Town 🦴🦴½ **1940** A lively vintage comedy/drama/romance about two oil-drilling buddies competing amid romantic mix-ups and fortunes gained and lost. **120m/B VHS, Beta.** Clark Gable, Spencer Tracy, Claudette Colbert, Hedy Lamarr, Frank Morgan, Lionel Atwill, Chill Wills, Curt Bois; ***D:*** Jack Conway. Nominations: Academy Awards '40: Best Black and White Cinematography. *MGM, CCB*

Boomerang 🦴🦴🦴 **1947** Film noir based on actual events features the murder of a Connecticut clergyman and the quick arrest of vagrant John Waldron (Kennedy). Prosecuting attorney Henry Harvey (Andrews) is told by his political bosses to get an equally quick conviction to stem public outrage. The evidence seems overwhelming but Harvey begins his own investigation and suddenly switches to the defense to prove Waldron's innocence in dramatic courtroom style. Kazan filmed on location in Bridgeport, CT in a successful semi-documentary style that heightened the tension. **88m/B VHS.** Dana Andrews, Arthur Kennedy, Lee J. Cobb, Jane Wyatt, Cara Williams, Sam Levene, Ed Begley Sr., Karl Malden, Taylor Holmes, Robert Keith; ***D:*** Elia Kazan; ***W:*** Richard Murphy; ***C:*** Norbert Brodine; ***M:*** David Buttolph. *FXV*

Boomerang 🦴½ **1976** A father rescues his wrongly convicted son from prison. Dubbed. **101m/C VHS, Beta.** *IT* Alain Delon, Carla Gravina, Dora Doll; ***D:*** Jose Giovanni. *UNI*

Boomerang 🦴🦴 **1992 (R)** Successful, womanizing marketing exec for a cosmetics company (Murphy) meets his match when he falls for a colleague (Givens) who is as vain and sexually predatory as he is. She treats him the way he treats women (as a sex object), and he's shocked into the arms of a nice girl (Berry). Although it's refreshing to see this sexual role reversal, the typical Murphy-style humor is in play with sexist jokes and a couple of vulgar female characters. Grier and Lawrence are great as Murphy's best friends. Blaustein and Sheffield are the same guys who wrote Murphy's "Coming to America." **118m/C VHS, Beta, LV.** Eddie Murphy, Halle Berry, Robin Givens, David Alan Grier, Martin Lawrence, Grace Jones, Geoffrey Holder, Eartha Kitt, Chris Rock, Tisha Campbell, John Witherspoon, Melvin Van Peebles; ***D:*** Reginald Hudlin; ***W:*** Barry W. Blaustein, David Sheffield. *PAR*

The Boost 🦴½ **1988 (R)** A feverish, messy melodrama about a young couple's spiraling decline from yuppie-ish wealth in a haze of cocaine abuse. **95m/C VHS, Beta, LV.** James Woods, Sean Young, John Kapelos, Steven Hill, Kelle Kerr, John Rothman, Amanda Blake, Grace Zabriskie; ***D:*** Harold Becker; ***W:*** Darryl Ponicsan. *HBO*

Boot Hill 🦴½ **1969 (PG)** Two guys mess with western baddies and wild women in spaghetti oater. **97m/C VHS, Beta.** *IT* Terence Hill, Bud Spencer, Woody Strode, Victor Buono, Lionel Stander; ***D:*** Giuseppe Colizzi. *NO*

Boot Hill Bandits 🦴🦴½ **1942** "Crash" Corrigan fights on the side of right in this classic western as he helps corral Wells Fargo bandits. **58m/B VHS.** Ray Corrigan, John "Dusty" King, Max Terhune, Jean Brooks, John Merton, Glenn Strange; ***D:*** S. Roy Luby. *NOS, HEG*

Boothill Brigade 🦴🦴 **1937** Former footballer Brown rides to the rescue when criminals steal land from homesteaders. **58m/B VHS.** Johnny Mack Brown, Claire Rochelle, Dick Curtis, Horace Murphy, Frank LaRue, Edward Cassidy, Bobby Nelson, Frank Ball, Steve Clark; ***D:*** Sam Newfield. *NOS, MRV*

Bootleg 🦴🦴 **1989** A detective is on a case that leads to crooked politics and espionage. **82m/C VHS.** Ray Meagher; ***D:*** John Prescott. *AIP*

Boots & Saddles 🦴½ **1937** A young English lord wants to sell the ranch he has inherited but Autry is determined to make him a real Westerner. **54m/B VHS, Beta.** Gene Autry, Judith Allen, Smiley Burnette; ***D:*** Joseph Kane. *NOS, MRV, VYY*

Boots Malone 🦴🦴½ **1952** An old down-on-his-luck gambling addict and a young, rich kid fascinated by the sordid atmosphere of the racetrack stumble upon one another and form a symbiotic relationship. All goes well for while, but there'd be no movie unless a collection of obstacles suddenly threatens their success, friendship, and even their lives. A rather melodramatic buddy tale, but Holden and Stewart hold interest. **103m/C VHS.** William Holden, John Stewart, Ed Begley Sr., Harry (Henry) Morgan, Whit Bissell; ***D:*** William Dieterle; ***M:*** Elmer Bernstein. *GKK*

Boots of Destiny 🦴 **1937** Cheap western with Maynard and his sidekick Barnett on the lam and coming to the aid of ranch owner Dell. Based on a story by E. Morton Hough. **59m/B VHS.** Ken Maynard, Claudia Dell, Vince Barnett, Edward Cassidy, Martin Garralaga; ***D:*** Arthur Rosson; ***W:*** Arthur Rosson. *MOV*

Bopha! 🦴🦴🦴 **1993 (PG-13)** Father-son strife set against the anti-apartheid movement. In the Senior township police officer Mikah takes pride in his peaceful community, particularly in light of the growing unrest in the other townships. Son Zweli has become an activist and wife Rosie must be the family peacemaker. Then a prominent freedom movement member is arrested and two officers of the secret police make their sinister appearance. Well-acted; directorial debut of Freeman. Adapted from the play by Percy Mtwa, although the hopeful ending has been changed in the movie. The title, a Zulu word, stands for arrest or detention. Filmed on location in Zimbabwe. **121m/C VHS, Beta, LV.** Danny Glover, Maynard Eziashi, Alfre Woodard, Malcolm McDowell, Marius Weyers, Malick Bowens, Robin Smith, Michael Chinyamurindi, Christopher John Hall, Grace Mahlaba; ***D:*** Morgan Freeman; ***W:*** Brian Bird, John Wierick; ***M:*** James Horner. *PAR*

Bordello 🦴 **1979** A made-for-television western spoof about cowboys and shady ladies. **90m/C VHS, Beta.** Chuck Connors, Michael Conrad, John Ireland, Isela Vega, George Rivero. *PSM*

The Border 🦴🦴🦴 **1982 (R)** A border guard faces corruption and violence within his department and tests his own sense of decency when the infant of a poor Mexican girl is kidnapped. Excellent cast, fine cinematography, unusual Nicholson performance. **107m/C VHS, Beta, LV.** Jack Nicholson, Harvey Keitel, Valerie Perrine, Warren Oates, Elpidia Carrillo; ***D:*** Tony Richardson; ***W:*** Deric Washburn, Walon Green; ***M:*** Ry Cooder. *MCA*

Border Badmen 🦴½ **1945** It's just another tired old western, even if it does appropriate the classic mystery-thriller plot; following the reading of a silver baron's will, someone starts killing off the relatives. **59m/B VHS, Beta.** Buster Crabbe, Lorraine Miller, Charles "Blackie" King, Ray Bennett, Archie Hall, Budd Buster, Bud Osborne; ***D:*** Sam Newfield. *GPV, MRV*

Border Bandits 🦴 **1946** Plodding oater has Brown going after the bad guys. Not only is it a dirty job, but apparently pretty boring. **57m/B VHS.** Johnny Mack Brown, Raymond Hatton, John Merton, Frank LaRue, Steve Clark, Charles Stevens, Bud Osborne; ***D:*** Lambert Hillyer. *DVT, HEG*

Border Caballero 🦴½ **1936** Western star McCoy and lady cowpoke January shoot out the skies in this lackluster McCoy vehicle. Based on a story by Norman S. Hall. **57m/B VHS.** Tim McCoy, Lois January, Ralph Byrd, Ted Adams; ***D:*** Sam Newfield; ***W:*** Joseph O'Donnell. *MOV*

Border Devils **1932** A boy is pursued by a ruthless gang of outlaws, until he is saved by the good guys. **60m/B VHS, Beta, LV.** Harry Carey Sr., Art Mix, George "Gabby" Hayes; ***D:*** William Nigh. *NO*

Border Feud **1947** LaRue endeavors to prevent someone who, by instigating a family feud, will claim large gold mine rights. **54m/B VHS, Beta.** Lash LaRue, Al "Fuzzy" St. John, Bob Duncan; ***D:*** Ray Taylor. *COL*

Border Law ½ **1931** Jones plays a heroic Texas Ranger who goes undercover to find the man who killed his brother. One of Jones' finest outings and far better than most B westerns. **62m/B VHS.** Buck Jones, Lupita Tovar, James Mason, Frank Rice, Glenn Strange; ***D:*** Louis King; ***W:*** Stuart Anthony. *MOV, GVV*

The Border Legion ½ **1940** Sappy retelling of Grey's novel about an outlaw sacrificing himself for a pair of young lovers. This time Rogers is the outlaw with a heart of gold. Originally filmed in 1930 with Jack Holt, Richard Arlen, and Fay Wray. **58m/B VHS.** Roy Rogers, George "Gabby" Hayes, Carol Hughes, Joseph Sawyer, Maude Eburne, Jay Novello; ***D:*** Joseph Kane; ***W:*** Olive Cooper, Louis Stevens. *MOV*

Border Patrol **1943** Another installment in the Hopalong Cassidy series. This time there's a villainous owner of a silvermine to reckon with. A man so low he's abducting hapless Mexicans as they cross the border, forcing them to work his mines. Hoppy is saddled with the task of persuading him that the town ain't big enough for the both of them. Robert Mitchum makes his perfectly-forgettable film debut as one of the bad guys. Not one of the best in the series, but plenty of action. **63m/B VHS.** William Boyd, Andy Clyde, Jay Kirby, Russell Simpson, Claudia Drake, George Reeves, Duncan Renaldo; ***D:*** Lesley Selander. *NOS*

Border Phantom **1937** Steele (whom you might recognize as Canino in "The Big Sleep"), takes on a suave Chinese businessman who heads a mail order business: seems he's smuggling mail-order brides from Mexico in this vintage "B"-grade horse opera. **60m/B VHS.** Bob Steele, Harley Wood, Don Barclay, Karl Hackett, Horace Murphy, Miki Morita; ***D:*** S. Roy Luby. *NOS, MRV, VTR*

Border Radio *Woof!* **1988** A rock singer decides to steal a car and try to outrun some tough thugs hot on his trail. **88m/B VHS.** Chris D, Luana Anders; ***D:*** Allison Anders, Kurt Voss; ***W:*** Allison Anders, Kurt Voss; ***M:*** Dave Alvin. *FCT*

Border Rangers **1950** A man joins the Rangers in order to avenge the murders of his brother and sister-in-law. **57m/B VHS, Beta, LV.** Robert Lowery, Donald (Don "Red") Barry, Lyle Talbot, Pamela Blake; ***D:*** William (Lester Williams) Berke. *NO*

Border Romance ½ **1930** Three Americans have their horses stolen by bandits while riding through Mexico. Trouble with the locals follows in this early sound western. **58m/B VHS, Beta.** Don Terry, Armida, Marjorie Kane. *VYY*

Border Roundup **1941** The "Lone Rider" uncovers a gang of thieving crooks. **57m/B VHS, Beta.** George Houston, Al "Fuzzy" St. John, Dennis Moore; ***D:*** Sam Newfield. *VDM*

Border Saddlemates **1952** A U.S. government agent becomes involved in a crooked deal when he is asked to doctor Canadian silver foxes. **67m/B VHS, Beta.** Rex Allen. *DVT*

Border Shootout **1990 (PG)** A trigger-happy sheriff battles a rich young cattle rustler. **110m/C VHS, Beta.** Glenn Ford, Charlene Tilton, Jeff Kaake, Michael Horse, Russell Todd, Cody Glenn, Sergio Calderon, Michael Ansara; ***D:*** C.T. McIntyre. *TTC*

Border Street ½ *Ulica Graniczna; That Others May Live* **1948** This film shows how a group of Polish Jews fought off the German occupation forces in the Warsaw ghetto. In Polish with English subtitles. **110m/B VHS, Beta.** *PL IHF*

Border Vengeance ½ **1935** Reb is a member of a family of outlaws. He aims to improve himself and steer his family to the straight and narrow trail. **45m/B VHS.** Reb Russell, Mary Jane Carey, Kenneth MacDonald, Hank Bell, Glenn Strange, Norman Feusier, Charles "Slim" Whitaker; ***D:*** Ray Heinz. *GPV*

Border Vigilantes **1941** Hoppy and pals try to rid a town of outlaws that even the vigilantes can't run off. The big surprise comes when they find out who the leader of the outlaws is. **61m/B VHS.** William Boyd, Russell Hayden, Andy Clyde, Victor Jory, Morris Ankrum, Frances Gifford, Ethel Wales, Hal Taliaferro; ***D:*** Derwin Abrahams. *NOS*

Borderline **1950** MacMurray and Trevor play undercover agents trying to infiltrate a Mexican drug ring. With their real identities hidden, they fall for each other and make a run for the border. Although the leads work well together, they're hindered by an occasionally confusing script. Unfortunately, director Seiter never decides whether the material is of a comedic or dramatic nature. **88m/B VHS.** Fred MacMurray, Claire Trevor, Raymond Burr, Roy Roberts, Jose Torvay, Morris Ankrum, Charles Lane, Don Diamond, Nacho Galindo, Pepe Hern, Richard Irving; ***D:*** William A. Seiter. *HEG*

Borderline **1980 (PG)** Bronson is a border patrol guard in pursuit of a murderer in this action flick. Meanwhile, he gets caught up in trying to help an illegal alien and her young child. **106m/C VHS, Beta.** Charles Bronson, Wilford Brimley, Bruno Kirby, Benito Morales, Ed Harris, Kenneth McMillan; ***D:*** Jerrold Freedman. *FOX*

Bordertown Gunfighters ½ **1943** A cowboy breaks up a vicious lottery racket and falls in love in the process. **56m/B VHS, Beta.** Wild Bill Elliott, Anne Jeffreys. *DVT*

Boris and Natasha: The Movie ½ **1992 (PG)** The two inept spies from the classic television cartoon "The Adventures of Rocky and Bullwinkle" star in this mediocre live-action comedy. These nogoodniks are sent by "Fearless Leader" to America and encounter the usual misadventures. For true fun watch the original animated versions. Never released theatrically, it aired for the first time on cable television. **88m/C VHS.** Sally Kellerman, Dave Thomas, Paxton Whitehead, Andrea Martin, Alex Rocco, Larry Cedar, Arye Gross, Christopher Neame, Anthony Newley; ***Cameos:*** John Candy, John Travolta, Charles Martin Smith; ***D:*** Charles Martin Smith. *ACA, NLC*

B.O.R.N. ½ **1988 (R)** Hagen uncovers an underground network of doctors who kill people and sell the body parts and organs. **90m/C VHS, Beta.** Ross Hagen, P.J. Soles, William Smith, Hoke Howell, Russ Tamblyn, Amanda Blake, Clint Howard, Rance Howard, Debra Lamb; ***D:*** Ross Hagen. *PSM*

Born Again **1978** This is the filmed adaptation of Charles Colson's biography of why he became a born again Christian. **110m/C VHS, Beta.** Dean Jones, Anne Francis, Dana Andrews, George Brent; ***D:*** Irving Rapper; ***C:*** Harry Stradling Jr.; ***M:*** Les Baxter. *SUE*

Born American *Arctic Heat* **1986 (R)** Pre-Glasnost flick about teenagers vacationing in Finland who "accidentally" cross the Russian border. There they battle the Red Plague. Melodramatic and heavily politicized. Original release banned in Finland. **95m/C VHS, Beta.** Mike Norris, Steve Durham, David Coburn, Thalmus Rasulala, Albert Salmi; ***D:*** Renny Harlin. *NO*

Born Beautiful ½ **1982** Made for TV. Beautiful young women come to New York, hoping to strike it rich in the world of modeling. At the same time, a still beautiful, but older and overexposed model comes to grips with a change in her career. Well-told, but sugar-coated. **100m/C VHS.** Erin Gray, Ed Marinaro, Polly Bergen, Lori Singer, Ellen Barber, Judith Barcroft, Michael Higgins; ***D:*** Harvey Hart; ***M:*** Brad Fiedel. *WAR*

Born Free **1966** The touching story of a game warden in Kenya and his wife raising Elsa the orphaned lion cub. When the cub reaches maturity, they work to return her to life in the wild. Great family entertainment based on Joy Adamson's book. Theme song became a hit. ♫Born Free. **95m/C VHS, Beta, LV.** Virginia McKenna, Bill Travers; ***D:*** James Hill; ***M:*** John Barry. Academy Awards '66: Best Song ("Born Free"), Best Original Score; National Board of Review Awards '66: 10 Best Films of the Year. *COL, HMV*

Born in America *Dead Aim* **1990** A young orphan is adopted by an undertaker. The boy grows up enveloped by his guardian's business and, when things are slow, works to bring in business himself. **90m/C VHS.** James Westerfield, Glen Lee, Virgil Frye, Venetia Vianello; ***D:*** Jose Antonio Bolanos. *NO*

Born in East L.A. **1987 (R)** Marin brings his Bruce Springsteen-parody song to life as he plays a mistakenly deported illegal alien who struggles to return to the U.S. Suprisingly resolute effort by the usually self-exploiting Mexican-American. Stern is the American expatriate who helps him get back and Lopez is the love interest who stalls him. **85m/C VHS, Beta, LV.** Richard "Cheech" Marin, Daniel Stern, Paul Rodriguez, Jan-Michael Vincent, Kamala Lopez, Tony Plana, Vic Trevino, A. Martinez; ***D:*** Richard "Cheech" Marin. *MCA, FCT*

Born in Flames **1983** An acclaimed futuristic feminist film about women who band together in an effort to gain control of the state owned media. **90m/C VHS.** ***D:*** Lizzie Borden; ***W:*** Lizzie Borden. *ICA*

Born Innocent ½ **1974** As if "The Exorcist" weren't bad enough, Blair is back for more abuse-on-film, this time as a 14-year-old runaway from a dysfunctional family who lands in a reform school for girls. There, she must struggle to be as brutal as her peers in order to survive. Fairly tame by today's standards, but controversial at its made-for-TV premiere, chiefly due to a rape scene involving a broom handle. First trip up the river for Blair. **92m/C VHS, Beta.** Linda Blair, Joanna Miles, Kim Hunter, Richard Jaeckel; ***D:*** Donald Wrye. *NO*

Born Invincible **1976** A Kung Fu master avenges the kick-death of a student by randomly kick-killing suspects. **90m/C VHS, Beta.** Lo Lieh, Carter Wong, Nancy Yan; ***D:*** Joseph Kuo. *GEM*

Born Killer ½ **1989** Teenagers in the woods meet up with murderous escaped convicts. **90m/C VHS, Beta.** Francine Lapensee, Fritz Matthews, Ted Prior, Adam Tucker; ***D:*** Kimberly Casey. *AIP*

Born Losers **1967 (PG)** The original "Billy Jack" film in which the Indian martial arts expert takes on a group of incorrigible bikers bothering some California babes and runs afoul of the law. Classic drive-in fare. **112m/C VHS, Beta, LV.** Tom Laughlin, Elizabeth James, Jeremy Slate, William Wellman Jr., Robert Tessier, Jane Russell; ***D:*** Tom Laughlin; ***W:*** Tom Laughlin. *VES, LIV*

Born of Fire ½ **1987 (R)** A flutist investigating his father's death seeks the Master Musician; his search leads him to the volcanic (and supernatural) mountains of Turkey. **84m/C VHS, Beta, LV.** Peter Firth, Susan Crowley, Stephan Kalipha; ***D:*** Jamil Dehlavi; ***M:*** Colin Towns. *VMK*

Born on the Fourth of July ½ **1989 (R)** A riveting meditation on American life affected by the Vietnam War, based on the real-life, best-selling experiences of Ron Kovic, though some facts are subtly changed. The film follows him as he develops from a naive recruit to an angry, wheelchair-bound paraplegic to an active antiwar protestor. Well-acted and generally lauded; Kovic co-wrote the screenplay and appears as a war veteran in the opening parade sequence. **145m/C VHS, Beta, LV, 8mm.** Tom Cruise, Kyra Sedgwick, Raymond J. Barry, Jerry Levine, Tom Berenger, Willem Dafoe, Frank Whaley, John Getz, Caroline Kava, Bryan Larkin, Abbie Hoffman, Stephen Baldwin, Josh Evans; ***D:*** Oliver Stone; ***W:*** Oliver Stone; ***C:*** Robert Richardson; ***M:*** John Williams. Academy Awards '89: Best Director (Stone), Best Film Editing; Directors Guild of America Awards '89: Best Director (Stone); Golden Globe Awards '90: Best Actor—Drama (Cruise), Best Director (Stone), Best Film—Drama, Best Screenplay; Nominations: Academy Awards '89: Best Actor (Cruise), Best Adapted Screenplay, Best Cinematography, Best Picture, Best Sound, Best Original Score. *MCA, FCT, BTV*

Born Reckless 🦴½ **1959** Van Doren plays a singer working the rodeo circuit who falls for aging rider Richards. Not bad enough to be funny, however, Van Doren shows an incredible lack of talent while singing several tunes. ♫Song of the Rodeo; Born Reckless; A Little Longer; Home Type Girl; Separate the Men from the Boys; Something to Dream About; You, Lovable You. **79m/B VHS.** Mamie Van Doren, Jeff Richards, Arthur Hunnicutt, Carol Ohmart, Donald (Don "Red") Barry, Nacho Galindo; ***D:*** Howard W. Koch. *MOV*

Born to Be Bad 🦴🦴½ **1950** Fontaine, an opportunistic woman who was b-b-born to be b-b-bad, attempts to steal a wealthy business man away from his wife while carrying on an affair with a novelist. Ray's direction (he's best known for "Rebel Without a Cause," filmed five years later) prevents the film from succumbing to standard Hollywood formula. **93m/B VHS, Beta, LV.** Joan Fontaine, Robert Ryan, Zachary Scott, Joan Leslie, Mel Ferrer; ***D:*** Nicholas Ray. *TTC*

Born to Be Wild 🦴🦴 **1938** A pair of truck drivers are commissioned to deliver a shipment of dynamite. The dynamite will be used to destroy a dam, preventing the surrounding land from falling into the hands of unscrupulous land barons. Good action picture thanks to the cast. **66m/B VHS, Beta.** Ralph Byrd, Doris Weston, Ward Bond, Robert Emmett Keane, Bentley Hewlett, Charles Williams; ***D:*** Joseph Kane. *SNC, RXM*

Born to Be Wild 🦴½ **1995 (PG)** Rebellious teenager Rick (Hornoff) befriends Katie, the 3-year-old gorilla his behaviorial scientist mom (Shaver) is studying. When Katie's owner (Boyle) decides she would make a better sideshow attraction than science project, Rick busts her out and they head for the Canadian border. Animal slapstick and bodily function jokes ensue as the chase continues. "Free Willy"-inspired plot and primate hijinks should keep young kids interested, but anyone over the age of nine probably won't be too impressed. **98m/C VHS, LV.** Wil Horneff, Helen Shaver, Peter Boyle, Jean Marie Barnwell, John C. McGinley, Marvin J. McIntyre; ***D:*** John Gray; ***W:*** John Bunzel, Paul Young; ***C:*** Donald M. Morgan. *WAR*

Born to Boogie 🦴🦴 **1972** A concert, a chronicle, and a tribute, "Born To Boogie" is about Marc Bolan and his band T. Rex. The film, which features concert footage from a 1972 concert at the Wembley Empire Pool in London, chronicles the glitter rock era and the next wave of British rock and roll, and pays tribute to Bolan, who died in 1977 just as he was starting a comeback. Ringo Starr and Elton John join T. Rex in the studio for "Children of the Revolution" and "Tutti-Frutti" as well as a psychadelic soiree where Bolan plays acoustic versions of his hits. This film was never released in the United States. **75m/C VHS.** Marc Bolan, Elton John, Ringo Starr; ***D:*** Ringo Starr. *MPI, MVD*

Born to Dance 🦴🦴½ **1936** A quintessential MGM 1930s dance musical, wherein a beautiful dancer gets a sailor and a big break in a show. Great songs by Cole Porter sung in a less than great manner by a gangly Stewart. Powell's first starring vehicle. ♫Love Me Love My Pekinese; I've Got You Under My Skin; Hey Babe Hey; Easy to Love; Rolling Home; Rap Tap on Wood; Entrance of Lucy James; Swingin' the Jinx Away. **108m/B VHS, Beta, LV.** Eleanor Powell, James Stewart, Virginia Bruce, Una Merkel, Frances Langford, Sid Silvers, Raymond Walburn, Reginald Gardiner, Buddy Ebsen; ***D:*** Roy Del Ruth; ***M:*** Cole Porter, Cole Porter. Nominations: Academy Awards '36: Best Song ("I've Got You Under My Skin"). *MGM, MLB*

Born to Kill 🦴🦴🦴 *Lady of Deceit* **1947** A ruthless killer marries a girl for her money. Minor tough-as-nails film noir exemplifying Tierney's stone-faced human-devil film persona. **92m/B VHS, Beta.** Lawrence Tierney, Claire Trevor, Walter Slezak, Elisha Cook Jr.; ***D:*** Robert Wise. *TTC*

Born to Race 🦴 **1988 (R)** In the world of competitive auto racing, a beautiful engineer is kidnapped for her new controversial engine design. **95m/C VHS, Beta.** Joseph Bottoms, George Kennedy, Marc Singer, Marla Heasly; ***D:*** James Fargo. *FOX*

Born to Ride 🦴🦴 **1991 (PG)** A biker rebel joins the Army prior to WWII in order to escape a prison term after a good ol' boy brush with the law. He shuns Army discipline, but proves himself in action as the leader of a scout troup for the Army's motorcycle cavalry brigade. Available with Spanish subtitles. **88m/C VHS, Beta.** John Stamos, John Stockwell, Teri Polo, Kris Kamm; ***D:*** Graham Baker. *WAR*

Born to Run 🦴🦴 **1977** A young Australian boy dreams of restoring his grandfather's rundown horse farm to its former glory. Filmed on location. **87m/C VHS, Beta.** *DVT*

Born to Run 🦴🦴½ **1993** Nicky Donatello (Grieco) is a Brooklyn street drag racer who gets mixed up with the mob while trying to rescue his no-account brother. But he still finds time to fall for an uptown model who also happens to be the mobster's girlfriend. Made for television. **97m/C VHS, LV.** Richard Grieco, Jay Acovone, Shelli Lether, Christian Campbell, Brent Stait, Martin Cummins, Wren Roberts, Joe Cortese; ***D:*** Albert Magnoli; ***W:*** Randall Badat. *FXV*

Born to Win 🦴🦴½ *Addict* **1971 (R)** A New York hairdresser with an expensive drug habit struggles through life in this well made comedy drama. Excellent acting from fine cast, well-paced, and interestingly photographed. Not well received when first released, but worth a look. **90m/C VHS.** George Segal, Karen Black, Paula Prentiss, Hector Elizondo, Robert De Niro, Jay Fletcher; ***D:*** Ivan Passer; ***C:*** Jack Priestley. *QVD, MGM*

Born Wild 🦴🦴½ **1995 (PG)** Documentary filmmaker Christine Shaye (Shields) has just gotten her first important assignment from overbearing boss Dan Walker (Sheen), which is to capture the beauty of Africa. Christine arrives at the South African game preserve of Londolozi where she meets passionate conservationist John Varty (who plays himself). Varty has filmed one leopard family for 12 years but when the mother leopard is killed, he violates his own ethical code when he rescues her two orphaned cubs. **98m/C VHS, LV.** Brooke Shields, Martin Sheen, John Varty, David Keith; ***D:*** Duncan McLachlan; ***W:*** Duncan McLachlan, Andrea Buck. *COL*

Born Yesterday 🦴🦴🦴½ **1950** Ambitious junk dealer Harry Brock is in love with smart but uneducated Billie Dawn. He hires newspaperman Paul Verrall to teach her the finer points of etiquette. During their sessions, they fall in love and Billie realizes how she has been used by Brock. She retaliates against him and gets to deliver that now-famous line: "Do me a favor, drop dead." Based on the Broadway play. **103m/B VHS, Beta, LV.** Judy Holliday, Broderick Crawford, William Holden; ***D:*** George Cukor. Academy Awards '50: Best Actress (Holliday); Golden Globe Awards '51: Best Actress—Musical/Comedy (Holliday); Nominations: Academy Awards '50: Best Costume Design (B & W), Best Director (Cukor), Best Picture, Best Screenplay. *COL, FCT, BTV*

Born Yesterday 🦴🦴 **1993 (PG)** Remake of the 1950 classic suffers in comparison, particularly Griffith, who has the thankless task of surpassing (or even meeting) Judy Holliday's Oscar-winning mark as not-so-dumb blonde Billie Dawn. Her intellectual inadequacies are glaring when she hits the political world of D.C. with obnoxious tycoon boyfriend Goodman. To save face, he hooks her up with a journalist (Johnson) willing to coach her in Savvy 101, a la Eliza Doolittle. What worked well in post-WWII America seems sadly outdated today; stick with the original. **102m/C VHS, Beta, LV.** Melanie Griffith, John Goodman, Don Johnson, Edward Herrmann, Max Perlich, Fred Dalton Thompson, Nora Dunn, Benjamin C. Bradlee, Sally Quinn, Michael Ensign, William Frankfather, Celeste Yarnall, Meg Wittner; ***D:*** Luis Mandoki; ***W:*** Douglas McGrath; ***C:*** Lajos Koltai; ***M:*** George Fenton. *TOU, HPH*

The Borrower 🦴🦴 **1989 (R)** An exiled unstable mutant insect alien serial killer (you know the type) must switch heads with human beings regularly to survive. This colorful, garish gorefest has humor and attitude, but never develops behind the basic grossout situation. **97m/C VHS, LV.** Rae Dawn Chong, Don Gordon, Antonio Fargas, Tom Towles; ***D:*** John McNaughton. *WAR, CAN*

The Borrowers 🦴🦴🦴 **1993** Excellent made for television adaptation of the May Norton childrens classics "The Borrowers" and "The Borrowers Afield." This miniature family (about mouse-size) live beneath the floorboards of an English house and borrow what they need to survive from the normal-sized human inhabitants. Problems come when the teeny family are discovered and must make their way to a new home. Sweet and humorous. On two cassettes. **199m/C VHS.** *GB* Ian Holm, Penelope Wilton, Rebecca Callard; ***D:*** John Henderson; ***W:*** Richard Carpenter. *TTC*

Borsalino 🦴🦴🦴 **1970 (R)** Delon and Belmondo are partners in crime in this seriocomic film about gang warfare in 1930's Marseilles. The costumes, settings, and music perfectly capture the mood of the period. Followed by a sequel "Borsalino and Co." Based on "The Bandits of Marseilles" by Eugene Saccomano. **124m/C VHS.** *FR* Jean-Paul Belmondo, Alain Delon, Michel Bouquet, Catherine Rouvel, Francoise Christophe, Corinne Marchand; ***D:*** Jacques Deray; ***W:*** Jacques Deray, Claude Sautet, Jean-Claude Carriere; ***M:*** Claude Bolling. *PAR*

Bosom Buddies **1980** Sitcom features best friends Hanks and Scolari who, desperate for cheap rent in New York City, dress in drag in order to move into the women-only Susan B. Anthony hotel. Naturally, this causes some confusion in their love lives. Two episodes per tape. **51m/C VHS.** Tom Hanks, Peter Scolari, Donna Dixon, Wendie Jo Sperber, Holland Taylor, Telma Hopkins. *PAR*

Boss 🦴½ *The Black Bounty Killer; Boss Nigger* **1974 (PG)** Blaxploitation western parody with Williamson and Martin as a couple of bounty hunters tearing apart a town to find a fugitive. Relatively non-violent. **87m/C VHS.** Fred Williamson, D'Urville Martin, R.G. Armstrong, William Smith, Carmen Hayworth, Barbara Leigh; ***D:*** Jack Arnold; ***W:*** Fred Williamson. *NO*

Boss Cowboy 🦴 **1935** A cowboy shows who wears the chaps in his family when he kidnaps his girlfriend to prevent her from moving East. **51m/B VHS, Beta.** Buddy Roosevelt, Frances Morris, Sam Pierce, Fay McKenzie, Lafe McKee; ***D:*** Victor Adamson. *GPV*

Boss Foreman *Woof!* **1939** A languorous, entwining comedy of errors about a construction foreman and his misadventures with the mob. **58m/B VHS, Beta.** Henry Armetta. *VYY*

The Boss Is Served 🦴🦴 **196?** A mother (Berger) and three daughters, racked with debt, are forced to take in boarders. The lascivious man and teenage son want to be more than just boarders to the lovely Berger. In Italian with English subtitles. **95m/C VHS, Beta.** *IT* Senta Berger, Maurizio Arena, Bruno Zanin. *NO*

Boss of Big Town 🦴🦴 **1943** Gangsters try to infiltrate the milk industry in this standard crime drama. **65m/B VHS, Beta.** John Litel, Florence Rice, H.B. Warner, Jean Brooks, John Miljan, Mary Gordon, John Maxwell; ***D:*** Arthur Dreifuss. *SNC, RXM*

Boss of Bullion City 🦴½ **1941** A crooked sheriff is exposed by Brown and sidekick Knight in this sagebrush saga. Based on a story by Arthur St. Claire. **61m/B VHS.** Johnny Mack Brown, Fuzzy Knight, Maria Montez, Earle Hodgins, Harry Woods; ***D:*** Ray Taylor; ***W:*** Victor McLeod, Arthur St. Claire. *MOV*

Boss of Rawhide 🦴 **1944** The Texas Rangers fight for law and order in the old west despite odds against them. **60m/B VHS, Beta.** Dave O'Brien, James Newill. *NOS, DVT*

Boss' Son 🦴🦴🦴 **1979** Worthwhile coming-of-age tale about a young man who learns more than he bargained for about life when he goes to work for his father in the family carpet business. Dad feels he should work his way up through the ranks and makes him a delivery man. The young man meets reality head on and must deal with the injustices of the world around him. Independently filmed by director/writer Roth. **97m/C VHS, Beta.** Rita Moreno, James Darren, Asher Brauner, Rudy Solari, Henry Sanders, Richie Havens, Piper Laurie, Elena Verdugo; ***D:*** Bobby Roth; ***W:*** Bobby Roth. *VES, LIV*

The Boss' Wife **1986 (R)** A young stockbroker attempts to fix what's wrong with his life by maneuvering sexually with the boss' wife, and complications set in. **83m/C VHS, Beta.** Daniel Stern, Arielle Dombasle, Christopher Plummer, Martin Mull, Melanie Mayron, Lou Jacobi; ***D:*** Ziggy Steinberg; ***M:*** Bill Conti. *FOX*

The Boston Strangler ½ **1968** Based on Gerold Frank's bestselling factual book about the deranged killer who terrorized Boston for about a year and a half. Traces events from first killing to prosecution. Curtis, going against type, is compelling in title role. **116m/C VHS, Beta.** Tony Curtis, Henry Fonda, George Kennedy, Murray Hamilton, Mike Kellin, George Voskovec, William Hickey, James Brolin, Hurd Hatfield, William Marshall, Jeff Corey, Sally Kellerman; ***D:*** Richard Fleischer; ***W:*** Edward Anhalt. *FOX*

The Bostonians ½ **1984 (PG)** A faith healer's daughter is forced to choose between the affections of a militant suffragette and a young lawyer in 19th Century Boston. Based on Henry James' classic novel. **120m/C VHS, Beta, LV.** Christopher Reeve, Vanessa Redgrave, Madeleine Potter, Jessica Tandy, Nancy Marchand, Wesley Addy, Linda Hunt, Wallace Shawn; ***D:*** James Ivory; ***W:*** Ruth Prawer Jhabvala; ***C:*** Walter Lassally. National Society of Film Critics Awards '84: Best Actress (Redgrave); Nominations: Academy Awards '84: Best Actress (Redgrave), Best Costume Design. *VES, LIV*

Botany Bay **1953** A rousing costumer about a convict ship in the 1700s that, after a trying voyage, lands in Australia, wherein a framed doctor conquers the local plague. From the novel by Charles Nordoff. **99m/C VHS, Beta.** Alan Ladd, James Mason, Patricia Medina, Cedric Hardwicke; ***D:*** John Farrow. *BAR*

Bottle Rocket ½ **1995 (R)** A trio of inexperienced but aspiring criminals attempt to make their mark on the world in suburban Dallas. Newcomers Wilson, who plays the group's ambitious leader Dignan, and Anderson penned this smart ensemble piece first as a 13-minute black and white short. A subsequent showing at the Sundance Film Festival got the attention of producer James L. Brooks ("Broadcast News"). Film got the backing to go feature length with Anderson directing, and deservedly so, with its fresh dialogue and surprising warmth. **95m/C VHS.** Owen C. Wilson, Luke Wilson, Robert Musgrave, Lumi Cavazos, James Caan, Teddy Wilson, Andrew Wilson, Jim Ponds; ***D:*** Wes Anderson; ***W:*** Owen C. Wilson, Wes Anderson; ***C:*** Robert Yeoman; ***M:*** Mark Mothersbaugh. MTV Movie Awards '96: Best New Filmmaker Award (Anderson). *NYR*

Bottoms Up *Woof!* **1987** Three nymphomaniacs seduce a virginal mechanic and turn him into an insatiable womanizer. Skin aplenty. **90m/C VHS, Beta.** Adam Janas, Sparky Abbrams, Kathleen Johnson. *PSM*

Boudu Saved from Drowning ½ *Boudu Sauve des Eaux* **1932** A suicidal tramp completely disrupts the wealthy household of the man that saves him from drowning. A gentle but sardonic farce from the master filmmaker. Remade in 1986 as "Down and Out In Beverly Hills." **87m/B VHS, Beta.** *FR* Michel Simon, Charles Granval, Jean Daste; ***D:*** Jean Renoir. *INT, MRV, DVT*

Boulevard ½ **1994 (R)** Jennefer (Wuhrer) is forced to give her baby up for adoption, after escaping from an abusive husband, and make her way on the city's mean streets. She meets prostitute Ola (Chong), who decides to look after the naif and protect Jennefer from violent pimp Hassan (Phillips). But Ola gets into trouble with tough cop Claren (Henriksen) and soon Jennefer must survive on her own—against both Hassan and her vengeful husband. Woman empowerment, complete with standard cliches. **96m/C VHS, LV.** Kari Wuhrer, Rae Dawn Chong, Lou Diamond Phillips, Lance Henriksen, Joel Bissonnette; ***D:*** Penelope Buitenhuis; ***W:*** Rae Dawn Chong; ***M:*** Ian Thomas. *LIV*

Boulevard Nights **1979 (R)** A young Latino man tries to escape his neighborhood's street-gang violence, while his older brother is sucked into it. Music by Schifrin, known for the "Mission: Impossible" theme. **102m/C VHS, Beta.** Richard Yniguez, Danny De La Paz, Marta DuBois, Carmen Zapata, Victor Millan; ***D:*** Michael Pressman; ***C:*** John Bailey; ***M:*** Lalo Schifrin. *WAR*

Boulevard of Broken Dreams **1988 (PG-13)** Successful Hollywood screenwriter Tom Garfield (Waters) returns to his native Australia to figure out how his life got so screwed up. His estranged wife is living with someone else and his daughter barely remembers him. Affecting look at personal priorities versus success. **95m/C VHS.** *AU* John Waters, Kim Gyngell, Penelope Stewart; ***D:*** Pino Amenta. *ACA*

Bound **1996 (R)** Ex-con Corky (Gershon) is busy fixing up her new apartment after serving five years for robbery. Her next-door neighbors are Caesar (Pantoliano), a neurotic, money-laundering mobster, and his sexy girlfriend, a seemingly dumb brunette named Violet (Tilly). The femme twosome hook up (in and out of bed) and hatch a plan to steal two million freshly-laundered dollars from Caesar, who goes ballistic when he discovers the money gone. It's a flashy—but not substantive—thriller. Directorial debut for the brothers Wachowski. **107m/C VHS.** Gina Gershon, Jennifer Tilly, Joe Pantoliano, John P. Ryan, Barry Kivel, Christopher Meloni, Peter Spellos; ***D:*** Andy Wachowski, Larry Wachowski; ***W:*** Andy Wachowski, Larry Wachowski; ***C:*** Bill Pope; ***M:*** Don Davis. *NYR*

Bound and Gagged: A Love Story **1993 (R)** For some reason, Elizabeth (Saltarelli), who is desperate for a husband, thinks that she might increase her chances of finding one if she kidnaps her friend Leslie (Allen) and goes on a weird wild goose chase through Minnesota with the hostage and her hopeless partner-in-crime, Cliff (Denton). Go figure. **96m/C VHS, LV.** Ginger Lynn Allen, Karen Black, Chris Denton, Elizabeth Saltarelli, Mary Ella Ross, Chris Mulkey; ***D:*** Daniel Appleby; ***W:*** Daniel Appleby; ***M:*** William Murphy. *TRI*

Bound for Glory ½ **1976 (PG)** The award-winning biography of American folk singer Woody Guthrie set against the backdrop of the Depression. Superb portrayal of the spirit and feelings of the period featuring many of his songs encased in the incidents that inspired them. Haskell Wexler's award-winning camera work is superbly expressive. **149m/C VHS, Beta, LV.** David Carradine, Ronny Cox, Melinda Dillon, Randy Quaid; ***D:*** Hal Ashby; ***W:*** Robert Getchell; ***C:*** Haskell Wexler. Academy Awards '76: Best Adapted Score, Best Cinematography; Los Angeles Film Critics Association Awards '76: Best Cinematography; National Board of Review Awards '76: Best Actor (Carradine); National Society of Film Critics Awards '76: Best Cinematography; Nominations: Academy Awards '76: Best Adapted Screenplay, Best Costume Design, Best Film Editing, Best Picture; Cannes Film Festival '77: Best Film. *MGM*

The Bounty **1984 (PG)** A new version of "Mutiny on the Bounty," with emphasis on a more realistic relationship between Fletcher Christian and Captain Bligh—and a more sympathetic portrayal of the captain, too. The sensuality of Christian's relationship with a Tahitian beauty also receives greater importance. **130m/C VHS, Beta, LV.** Mel Gibson, Anthony Hopkins, Laurence Olivier, Edward Fox, Daniel Day-Lewis, Bernard Hill, Philip Davis, Liam Neeson; ***D:*** Roger Donaldson; ***W:*** Robert Bolt; ***M:*** Vangelis. Nominations: Cannes Film Festival '84: Best Film. *VES, LIV*

Bounty Hunter 2002 ½ *2002: The Rape of Eden* **1994** A rogue virus kills most of the world's population and few of those remaining are completely immune. So slave trading in the capture and sale of immune survivors is a lucrative business and a bounty's hunter's last assignment is to bring in a beautiful but deadly woman. **90m/C VHS, LV.** Phil Nordell, Francine Lapensee, Vernon Wells, Jeff Conaway; ***D:*** Sam Auster; ***W:*** Sam Auster. *AIP*

Bounty Hunters **1989 (R)** A man hunts down his friend's killer. **91m/C VHS, Beta.** Robert Ginty, Bo Hopkins, Loeta Waterdown; ***D:*** Robert Ginty. *AIP*

The Bounty Man **1972** A bounty hunter brings an outlaw in, robbing him of his freedom and his girlfriend. **74m/C VHS, Beta.** Clint Walker, Richard Basehart, Margot Kidder, Arthur Hunnicutt, John Ericson, Gene Evans; ***D:*** John Llewellyn Moxey. *FOX*

Bounty Tracker ½ **1993 (R)** Johnny Damone (Lamas) is a bounty-hunter in pursuit of the killer-for-hire who murdered his brother. This personal vendetta leads to an action-packed martial arts showdown between Johnny and his cold-blooded prey. **90m/C VHS, LV.** Lorenzo Lamas, Matthias Hues. *REP*

Bouquet of Barbed Wire ½ **1976** Overlong soaper revolves around a weathly family and their hidden secrets: incest and infidelity. On three tapes. **330m/C VHS.** Frank Finlay, Susan Penhaligon, Deborah Grant, Sheila Allen, James Aubrey; ***D:*** Tom Wharmby. *NO*

The Bourne Identity **1988** Chamberlain stars as an amnesiac trying to piece together the fragments of his memory. Is he U.S. espionage agent Jason Bourne or an international terrorist? Aided by Smith (the kidnap victim who falls in love with her captor), the two traverse Europe trying to escape the spy network out to assassinate the mystery man who knows too little. Exciting adaptation of the Robert Ludlum thriller. Originally a two-part television miniseries. **185m/C VHS.** Richard Chamberlain, Jaclyn Smith, Denholm Elliott, Anthony Quayle, Donald Moffat, Yorgo Voyagis; ***D:*** Roger Young; ***W:*** Carol Sobieski. *WAR, BTV*

Bowery at Midnight ½ **1942** Lugosi plays a man who recycles criminals into zombies that commit crimes for his benefit. Bela and an intense mood can't quite save this pic. **60m/B VHS, Beta.** Bela Lugosi, Tom Neal, Dave O'Brien, Wanda McKay; ***D:*** Wallace Fox. *NOS, MRV, SNC*

Bowery at Midnight/Dick Tracy vs. Cueball **1942** On one tape, the vintage Lugosi grade-C thriller about zombies in the Bowery, and a standard Dick Tracy entry. **125m/B VHS, Beta.** Bela Lugosi, Morgan Conway, Dick Wessel, Skelton Knaggs. *AOV*

Bowery Blitzkrieg *Stand and Deliver* **1941** This lesser "East Side Kids" entry has Gorcey opting to enter the boxing ring rather than turn to crime. Needs more Huntz. **62m/B VHS.** Leo Gorcey, Huntz Hall, Bobby Jordan, Warren Hull, Charlotte Henry, Keye Luke; ***D:*** Wallace Fox. *NOS, VEC, HEG*

Bowery Boys Meet the Monsters **1954** The infamous Bowery Boys display their usual hilarious hijinks in this comedy in which they confront a group of transplant-happy scientists. **65m/C VHS.** Leo Gorcey, Huntz Hall, Bernard Gorcey, Bennie Bartlett, Lloyd Corrigan; ***D:*** Edward L. Bernds. *GPV*

Bowery Buckaroos **1947** The Bowery Boys take their act West in search of gold, meeting up with the usual amounts of goofy characters and hilarious misunderstandings. **66m/B VHS.** Leo Gorcey, Huntz Hall, Bobby Jordan, Gabriel Dell, Billy Benedict, David Gorcey, Julie Briggs, Bernard Gorcey, Chief Yowlachie, Iron Eyes Cody; ***D:*** William Beaudine. *WAR*

Boxcar Bertha ½ **1972 (R)** Scorsese's vivid portrayal of the South during the 1930s' Depression casts Hershey as a woman who winds up in cahoots with an anti-establishment train robber. Based on the book "Sister of the Road" by Boxcar Bertha Thomson. **90m/C VHS, Beta, LV.** Barbara Hershey, David Carradine, John Carradine; ***D:*** Martin Scorsese; ***W:*** John W. Corrington, Joyce H. Corrington. *VES, LIV*

Boxcar Blues **1990** Bird (Coufos) is a down and out fighter who decides to fight "The Man" (Ventura), a bare knuckle fighter who enjoys beating his opponents to death. On the way to the fight, in New Orleans, he meets up with his girl Casey (Langrick), along with some other shady characters, including a truck driving preacher. **96m/C VHS.** Paul Coufos, Margaret Langrick, Jesse Ventura, M. Emmet Walsh, Donny Lalonde; ***D:*** Damian Lee. *VHE, VTR*

The Boxer and Death ☙☙☙ **1963** A new-wave Czech film about a boxer in a Nazi concentration camp who interests the boxing-obsessed commandant in a match. In Czech with subtitles. **120m/B VHS, Beta.** Stefan Kvietik; ***D:*** Peter Solan. *NOS, FCT, DVT*

Boxing Helena ☙☙ **1993 (R)** Highly publicized as the film that cost Basinger almost $9 million in damages, the debut of director/writer Jennifer Lynch (daughter of David) explores the dark side of relationships between men and women. Sands is Dr. Nick Cavanaugh, a surgeon who becomes dangerously obsessed with the beautiful, yet unattainable Helena (Fenn). When she is hit by a car near his home, he performs emergency surgery and amputates her arms and legs, forcing her to be dependent on him. Metaphorically a situation, albeit an extreme one, that mirrors the power struggle in any sexual relationship. Problematic in some aspects, although equally fascinating as it is disturbing. **107m/C VHS, LV.** Julian Sands, Sherilyn Fenn, Bill Paxton, Kurtwood Smith, Betsy Clark, Nicolette Scorsese, Art Garfunkel; ***D:*** Jennifer Lynch; ***W:*** Jennifer Lynch; ***M:*** Graeme Revell. Golden Raspberry Awards '93: Worst Director (Lynch). *ORI*

A Boy and His Dog ☙☙½ **1975 (R)** In the post-holocaust world of 2024, a young man (Johnson) and his telepathic canine (McIntire supplies narration of the dog's thoughts) cohort search for food and sex. They happen upon a community that drafts Johnson to repopulate their largely impotent race; Johnson is at first ready, willing, and able, until he discovers the mechanical methods they mean to employ. Based on a short story by Harlan Ellison. The dog was played by the late Tiger of "The Brady Bunch." **87m/C VHS, Beta, LV.** Don Johnson, Suzanne Benton, Jason Robards Jr., Charles McGraw, Alvy Moore; ***D:*** L.Q. Jones; ***V:*** Tim McIntire. *ICA, MED, MRV*

A Boy Called Hate ☙☙ **1995 (R)** Troubled teen Steve (Caan)—whose nickname is "Hate" after his tattoo—lives with his divorced dad in an L.A. suburb. Steve's on a latenight motorcycle ride, taking potshots at billboards with his trusty handgun, when he stumbles onto what he thinks is an attempted rape. So Steve shoots at the rapist, Richard (Gould), and takes off with would-be victim Cindy (Crider). Turns out Richard is the assistant D.A. and he tells the cops he's been robbed, so the teen duo are now on the run. Familiar tale with some good twists and believable performances. Caan is the son of James (seen in a cameo as the dad). Debut for director Marcus. **98m/C VHS, Beta.** Scott Caan, Missy Crider, Elliott Gould, Adam Beach; ***Cameos:*** James Caan; ***D:*** Mitch Marcus; ***W:*** Mitch Marcus; ***C:*** Paul Holahan. *PAR*

Boy, Did I Get a Wrong Number! ☙ **1966** A real estate agent gets more than he bargained for when he accidentally dials a wrong number. Zany comedy persists as Hope gets entangled in the life of sexy starlet Sommer. **100m/C VHS, Beta.** Bob Hope, Phyllis Diller, Marjorie Lord, Elke Sommer, Cesare Danova; ***D:*** George Marshall. *MGM, FCT*

The Boy Friend ☙☙☙ **1971 (G)** Russell pays tribute to the Busby Berkeley Hollywood musical. Lots of charming dance numbers and clever parody of plot lines in this adaptation of Sandy Wilson's stage play. Fun! ♫The Boy Friend; I Could Be Happy; Won't You Charleston With Me?; Fancy Forgetting; Sur La Plage; A Room in Bloomsbury; Safety in Numbers; It's Never Too Late to Fall in Love; Poor Little Pierette. **135m/C VHS.** *GB* Twiggy, Christopher Gable, Moyra Fraser, Max Adrian, Vladek Sheybal, Georgina Hale, Tommy Tune; ***D:*** Ken Russell; ***W:*** Ken Russell; ***C:*** David Watkin. Golden Globe Awards '72: Best Actress—Musical/Comedy (Twiggy). *MGM*

The Boy God ☙ **1986** Rocco here describes his trials and everyday shenanigans; he the young demi-God, battling evil on a fantasy land. **100m/C VHS, Beta.** Nino Muhlach; ***D:*** Erastheo J. Navda. *VCD*

Boy in Blue ☙½ **1986 (R)** A "Rocky"-esque biography of Canadian speed-rower Ned Hanlan, who set aside lackluster pursuits to turn to rowing. **97m/C VHS, Beta.** *CA* Nicolas Cage, Christopher Plummer, David Naughton; ***D:*** Charles Jarrott; ***W:*** Douglas Bowie. *FOX*

The Boy in the Plastic Bubble ☙☙½ **1976** Well-made, sensitive television drama about a young man born with immunity deficiencies who must grow up in a specially controlled plastic environment. Travolta is endearing as the boy in the bubble. **100m/C VHS, Beta.** John Travolta, Robert Reed, Glynnis O'Connor, Diana Hyland, Ralph Bellamy, Anne Ramsey; ***D:*** Randal Kleiser. *PSM*

Boy Meets Girl ☙☙☙ **1938** Cagney and O'Brien play screenwriters whose every film is a variation on the boy meets girl theme. Trouble is they're running out of ideas and their scripts get increasingly outlandish. A fading cowboy actor is supposed to star in the duo's next film—if they can ever settle down to work. Then they get the idea to feature their friend Wilson's baby in the movie—and guess who becomes a new star. Good satire on moviemaking and movie moguls, which made fine use of the Warner studio back lots, sound stages, and offices. Based on the play by Bella and Samuel Spewack who also wrote the screenplay. **86m/B VHS.** James Cagney, Pat O'Brien, Ralph Bellamy, Dick Foran, Marie Wilson, Frank McHugh, Bruce Lester, Ronald Reagan, Penny Singleton, James Stephenson; ***D:*** Lloyd Bacon; ***W:*** Bella Spewack, Samuel Spewack. *MGM, FCT*

Boy Meets Girl ☙☙☙ **1984** A French Holden Caulfield type character cruises the seamier side of Paris in this acclaimed film. Carax's directoral debut at age 22. In French with English subtitles. **100m/B VHS.** *FR* Denis Lavant, Mireille Perrier; ***D:*** Leos Carax; ***W:*** Jim Brady. *FCT, MGM*

A Boy Named Charlie Brown ☙☙☙ **1970** Charlie Brown enters the National Spelling Bee in New York and makes the final rounds with one other contestant. Based on Charles Schultz's popular comic strip characters from "Peanuts." Music by the Vince Guaraldi trio is, as always, a treat. **86m/C VHS, Beta, LV.** ***D:*** Bill Melendez; ***W:*** Charles M. Schulz; ***M:*** Vince Guaraldi, Rod McKuen. Nominations: Academy Awards '70: Best Original Score. *FOX, WTA*

Boy of Two Worlds ☙½ **1970 (G)** Because he is of a lineage foreign to his late father's town, a boy is exiled to the life of a junior Robinson Crusoe. **103m/C VHS, Beta.** Jimmy Sternman, Edvin Adolphson; ***D:*** Astrid Henning Jensen. *GEM*

Boy Takes Girl ☙☙ **1983** A little girl finds it hard adjusting to life on a farming cooperative during a summer recess. **93m/C VHS, Beta.** Gabi Eldor, Hillel Neeman, Dina Limon; ***D:*** Michal Bat-Adam. *MGM*

Boy! What a Girl ☙☙ **1945** Moore (in drag) is mistaken for a woman, and is fought over by a couple of suitors. **60m/B VHS, Beta.** Tim Moore, Duke Williams, Sheila Guyse, Beth Mays, Elwood Smith; ***D:*** Arthur Leonard. *FCT, GVV, DVT*

The Boy Who Could Fly ☙☙☙ **1986 (PG)** After a plane crash kills his parents, a boy withdraws into a fantasy land where he can fly. The young daughter of a troubled family makes friends with him and the fantasy becomes real. A sweet film for children, charming though melancholy for adults, too. Fine cast, including Savage, Dewhurst, and Bedelia keep this from becoming sappy. **120m/C VHS, Beta, LV.** Lucy Deakins, Jay Underwood, Bonnie Bedelia, Colleen Dewhurst, Fred Savage, Fred Gwynne, Louise Fletcher, Jason Priestley; ***D:*** Nick Castle; ***W:*** Nick Castle; ***C:*** Steven Poster; ***M:*** Bruce Broughton. *WAR, ORI*

The Boy Who Left Home to Find Out About the Shivers **1981** From "Faerie Tale Theatre" comes this tale about a boy who learns about fear. **60m/C VHS, Beta, LV.** Peter MacNicol, Christopher Lee, David Warner, Dana Hill, Frank Zappa; ***D:*** Graeme Clifford; ***V:*** Vincent Price. *FOX*

The Boy Who Loved Trolls **1984** Paul's fantastic dreams come true when he meets Ofoeti, a real, live troll. The only problem is Ofeoti only has a day to live, and Paul must find a way to save him. Aired on PBS as part of the "Wonderworks" series. **58m/C VHS.** Sam Waterston, Susan Anton, Matt Dill; ***D:*** Harvey Laidman. *PME, HMV, FCT*

The Boy with the Green Hair ☙☙☙ **1948** When he hears that his parents were killed in an air raid, a boy's hair turns green. The narrow-minded members of his community suddenly want nothing to do with him and he becomes an outcast. Thought-provoking social commentary. **82m/C VHS, Beta, LV.** Pat O'Brien, Robert Ryan, Barbara Hale, Dean Stockwell; ***D:*** Joseph Losey. *IME*

Boyfriends & Girlfriends ☙☙½ *My Girlfriend's Boyfriend; Ami de Mon Ami* **1988 (PG)** Another one of Rohmer's "Comedies and Proverbs," in which two girls with boyfriends fade in and out of interest with each, casually reshuffling their relationships. Typical, endless-talks-at-cafes Rohmer, the most happily consistent of the aging French New Wave. In French with subtitles. **102m/C VHS, Beta, LV.** *FR* Emmanuelle Chaulet, Sophie Renoir, Eric Viellard, Francois-Eric Gendron; ***D:*** Eric Rohmer; ***W:*** Eric Rohmer. *ORI, INJ*

Boys ☙ *The Girl You Want* **1995 (PG-13)** Seems like only yesterday we saw Haas as that big-eared, doe-eyed Amish kid from "Witness," but now, in this dry love story, he has grown into a big-eared, doe-eyed teenager lusting after older woman Ryder. John (Haas) saves Patty (Ryder) after a riding accident leaves her unconscious near his New England prep school. Immediately taken by her beauty and mystery, John decides to hide her in his dorm room and a romance blossoms between the unlikely pair. But John isn't the only one hiding something. Patty has a terrible secret from her past (gasp!), but when it's finally revealed, you'll be too bored to care. Based on the short story "Twenty Minutes" by James Salter. **89m/C VHS.** Winona Ryder, Lukas Haas, John C. Reilly, William Sage, Skeet Ulrich; ***D:*** Stacy Cochran; ***W:*** Stacy Cochran; ***C:*** Robert Elswit; ***M:*** Stewart Copeland. *NYR*

The Boys from Brazil ☙☙½ **1978 (R)** Based on Ira Levin's novel, a thriller about Dr. Josef Mengele endeavoring to reconstitute the Nazi movement from his Brazilian sanctuary by cloning a brood of boys from Hitler's genes. **123m/C VHS, Beta, LV.** Gregory Peck, James Mason, Laurence Olivier, Uta Hagen, Steve Guttenberg, Denholm Elliott, Lilli Palmer; ***D:*** Franklin J. Schaffner; ***W:*** Heywood Gould; ***M:*** Jerry Goldsmith. National Board of Review Awards '78: Best Actor (Olivier); Nominations: Academy Awards '78: Best Actor (Olivier), Best Film Editing, Best Original Score. *FOX*

The Boys in Company C ☙☙ **1977 (R)** A frank, hard-hitting drama about five naive young men involved in the Vietnam War. **127m/C VHS, Beta, LV.** Stan Shaw, Andrew Stevens, James Canning, Michael Lembeck, Craig Wasson, R. Lee Ermey, James Whitmore Jr., Scott Hylands; ***D:*** Sidney J. Furie; ***W:*** Sidney J. Furie. *COL*

The Boys in the Band ☙☙½ **1970 (R)** A group of gay friends get together one night for a birthday party. A simple premise with a compelling depiction of friendship, expectations, and lifestyle. One of the first serious cinematic presentations to deal with the subject of homosexuality. The film was adapted from Mart Crowley's play using the original cast. **120m/C VHS, Beta, LV.** Frederick Combs, Cliff Gorman, Laurence Luckinbill, Kenneth Nelson, Leonard Frey; ***D:*** William Friedkin; ***W:*** Matt Crowley. *FOX*

Boys Life ☙☙ **1994** Three shorts about gay teenagers coming of age. "Pool Days" has 17-year-old Justin (Weinstein) taking a summer job as a lifeguard at a health spa. Still clueless as to his sexual preferences, Justin is flustered when cruised by a charming male swimmer but it does get him to thinking. "A Friend of Dorothy" finds NYU student Winston (O'Connell) seeking freedom in Greenwich Village as he looks for like-minded friends (and a little romance). "The Disco Years" takes place in California during the Nixon era as casually gay-bashing high-schooler Tom (Nolan) gradually realizes his true nature. **90m/C VHS.** Josh Weinstein, Nick Poletti, Kimberly Flynn, Richard Salamanca, Raoul O'Connell, Kevin McClatchy, Greg Lauren, Anne Zupa, Matt Nolan, Russell Scott Lewis, Gwen Welles, Dennis Christopher; ***D:*** Brian

Sloan, Raoul O'Connell, Robert Lee King; ***W:*** Brian Sloan, Raoul O'Connell, Robert Lee King. *SHV, MOV*

The Boys Next Door ᴙᴙ½ **1985 (R)** Two California lads kill and go nuts during a weekend in Los Angeles. Sheen overacts as a budding psychotic, not an easy thing to do. Apparently is trying to show what a particular lifestyle can lead to. Violent. **90m/C VHS, Beta, LV.** Maxwell Caulfield, Charlie Sheen, Christopher McDonald, Hank Garrett, Patti D'Arbanville, Moon Zappa; ***D:*** Penelope Spheeris; ***W:*** Glen Morgan, James Wong; ***M:*** George S. Clinton. *VTR, NWV*

The Boys Next Door ᴙᴙ½ **1996 (PG)** Gentle comedy/drama, based on Tom Griffin's play, about four mentally disabled men—Norman (Lane), Barry (Leonard), Arnold (Jeter), and Lucien (Vance)—who share a house under the supervision of too-dedicated social worker Jack (Goldwyn). In fact, Jack's devotion is causing enough problems in his marriage to have him consider changing careers, even as each of "the boys" struggle with their daily lives. **?m/C VHS.** Nathan Lane, Tony Goldwyn, Robert Sean Leonard, Michael Jeter, Courtney B. Vance, Mare Winningham, Jenny Robertson, Elizabeth Wilson, Richard Jenkins, Lynne Thigpen; ***D:*** John Erman; ***W:*** William Blinn; ***C:*** Frank Tidy; ***M:*** John Kander. *HMK*

Boys' Night Out ᴙᴙᴙ **1962** Amusing comedy about four businessmen who desperately want to escape the suburban doldrums by setting up an apartment equipped with plaything Novak. Little do they know, but Novak is a sociology student studying the American male, and they are merely her guinea pigs in an experiment beyond their control. Blair, Page, and Gabor provide comic relief. Based on a story by Marvin Worth and Arne Sultan. **113m/C VHS.** Kim Novak, James Garner, Tony Randall, Howard Duff, Janet Blair, Patti Page, Jessie Royce Landis, Oscar Homolka, Zsa Zsa Gabor; ***D:*** Michael Gordon; ***W:*** Ira Wallach. *MGM*

The Boys of St. Vincent ᴙᴙᴙᴙ **1993** Outstanding, and heartbreaking, story of sexual abuse by Catholic clergy that was inspired by actual events. Divided into two segments, the drama begins in 1975 with 10-year-old Kevin Reevey (Morina) living at the St. Vincent orphanage in an eastern Canadian town. The orphanage is run by charismatic and terrifying Brother Lavin (Czerny), who it turns out has a special fondness for "his boy" Kevin. Nor is Brother Lavin alone—a fact eventually revealed by a police investigation, although the matter is hushed up by both the church and the government. Until 15 years later. In 1990, the case is reopened and Lavin, having married and fathered two sons, is returned to face charges. Now the young men must open wounds that have never truly healed and confront their tormentors in a court of law, amidst a blaze of publicity. Czerny gives a truly inspired performance as the self-loathing monster. The emotional agony is excruciating to watch and be forwarned that the depiction of the sexual abuse is unflinching. Made for Canadian TV; on 2 cassettes. **186m/C VHS.** *CA* Henry Czerny, Johnny Morina, Sebastian Spence, Brian Dodd, David Hewlett, Jonathan Lewis, Jeremy Keefe, Phillip Dinn, Brian Dooley, Greg Thomey, Michael Wade, Lise Roy, Timothy Webber, Kristine Demers, Ashley Billard, Sam Grana; ***D:*** John N. Smith; ***W:*** Sam Grana, John N. Smith, Des Walsh; ***C:*** Pierre Letarte; ***M:*** Neil Smolar. Nominations: Independent Spirit Awards '95: Best Foreign Language Film. *NYF*

Boys of the City ᴙᴙ *The Ghost Creeps* **1940** The East Side Kids run amuck in an eerie mansion while trying to solve the murder of a judge. **63m/B VHS, Beta.** Leo Gorcey, Bobby Jordan; ***D:*** Joseph H. Lewis. *NOS, SNC, DVT*

Boys on the Side ᴙᴙ½ **1994 (R)** It's "Thelma & Louise" come to "Terms of Endearment" by way of "Philadelphia". Goldberg is Jane, an unemployed lesbian singer, who connects with Ms. Priss real estate agent Robin (Parker) for a road trip to California. The two become a female version of the Odd Couple as Jane tags Robin as "the whitest woman in America." They stop off to pick up addle-brain friend Holly (Barrymore) who has just knocked her drug-crazed abusive beau in the head with a baseball bat. Holly's accident turns fatal and the threesome are on the run from cops. They bond like crazy glue and become a family as they face two huge setbacks—one's pregnant, another has AIDS. Strong performances by the lead actresses and a cool soundtrack may make up for this often trite movie of the week premise. **117m/C VHS, LV.** James Remar, Anita Gillette, Matthew McConaughey, Whoopi Goldberg, Mary-Louise Parker, Drew Barrymore; ***D:*** Herbert Ross; ***W:*** Don Roos; ***C:*** Donald E. Thorin. *WAR*

Boy's Reformatory ᴙ½ **1939** Brothers are framed. One takes the rap, goes to the title institution, breaks out, and hunts the real bad guys. Creaky and antiquated. **62m/B VHS.** Frankie Darro, Grant Withers, David Durand, Warren McCollum; ***D:*** Howard Bretherton. *NOS, LOO*

Boys Town ᴙᴙᴙ½ **1938** Righteous portrayal of Father Flanagan and the creation of Boys Town, home for juvenile soon-to-be-ex-delinquents. **93m/B VHS, Beta, LV.** Spencer Tracy, Mickey Rooney, Henry Hull, Gene Reynolds, Sidney Miller, Frankie Thomas Jr.; ***D:*** Norman Taurog. Academy Awards '38: Best Actor (Tracy), Best Original Screenplay; Nominations: Academy Awards '38: Best Director (Taurog), Best Picture, Best Screenplay. *MGM, BTV, IGP*

Boyz N the Hood ᴙᴙᴙ½ **1991 (R)** Singleton's debut as a writer and director is an astonishing picture of young black men, four high school students with different backgrounds, aims, and abilities trying to survive Los Angeles gangs and bigotry. Excellent acting throughout, with special nods to Fishburne and Gooding, Jr. Violent outbreaks outside theaters where this ran only proves the urgency of its passionately nonviolent, pro-family message. Hopefully those viewers scared off at the time will give this a chance in the safety of their VCRs. Singleton was the youngest director ever nominated for an Oscar. The laserdisc version includes two extra scenes and an interview with Singleton. **112m/C VHS, Beta, LV, 8mm.** Laurence "Larry" Fishburne, Ice Cube, Cuba Gooding Jr., Nia Long, Morris Chestnut, Tyra Ferrell, Angela Bassett; ***D:*** John Singleton; ***W:*** John Singleton; ***M:*** Stanley Clarke. Chicago Film Critics Awards '91: Most Promising Actor (Ice Cube); MTV Movie Awards '92: Best New Filmmaker Award (Singleton); National Board of Review Awards '91: 10 Best Films of the Year; Nominations: Academy Awards '91: Best Director (Singleton), Best Original Screenplay. *COL, CRC, FCT*

Braddock: Missing in Action 3 ᴙ **1988 (R)** The battle-scarred, high-kicking 'Nam vet battles his way into the jungles once more, this time to rescue his long-lost Vietnamese family. A family effort, Chuck co-wrote the script; his brother directed. **104m/C VHS, Beta, LV.** Chuck Norris, Aki Aleong, Roland Harrah III; ***D:*** Aaron Norris; ***W:*** Chuck Norris, James Bruner. *MED, CCB, VTR*

The Brady Bunch **1969** Relive classic moments with TV's grooviest family—two episodes per tape—including "The Honeymoon," the premiere episode explaining how Mike and his 3 boys get hitched to Carol and her 3 girls. Additional episodes available. **51m/C VHS.** Robert Reed, Florence Henderson, Ann B. Davis, Maureen McCormick, Barry Williams, Eve Plumb, Christopher Knight, Michael Lookinland, Susan Olsen. *PAR*

The Brady Bunch Movie ᴙᴙᴙ **1995 (PG-13)** Grunge and CDs may be the norm in the '90s, but the Bradys still live in the eight-track world of the '70s, where Davy Jones rocks and every day is a sunshine day. Then greedy developer McKean schemes to cash in on Mike and Carol's financial woes. (Hawaii! The Grand Canyon! What were they thinking?) Great ensemble cast capably fills the white platform shoes of the originals—Cole sounds just like Mr. Brady, Cox hilariously channels Jan's tormented middle child angst, and Taylor's self-absorbed Marcia, Marcia, Marcia is dead-on, right down to the frosty pursed lips. Look for neat-o cameos from some original Bradys and most of the Monkees. **88m/C VHS, Beta.** Shelley Long, Gary Cole, Michael McKean, Jean Smart, Henriette Mantel, Christopher Daniel Barnes, Christine Taylor, Paul Sutera, Jennifer Elise Cox, Jesse Lee, Olivia Hack, David Graf, Jack Noseworthy, Shane Conrad, RuPaul; ***Cameos:*** Ann B. Davis, Florence Henderson, Davy Jones, Barry Williams, Christopher Knight, Michael Lookinland, Mickey Dolenz, Peter Tork; ***D:*** Betty Thomas; ***W:*** Bonnie Turner, Terry Turner, Laurice Elehwany, Rick Copp; ***M:*** Guy Moon. Nominations: MTV Movie Awards '95: Best Dance Sequence (The Brady Kids). *PAR*

Brady's Escape ᴙ½ *The Long Ride* **1984** American WWII pilot is shot down in the Hungarian countryside and befriended by Hungarian csikos (cowboys) in this made-for-cable television movie. **92m/C VHS, Beta, LV.** *HU* John Savage, Kelly Reno; ***D:*** Pal Gabor. *CAF*

The Brain ᴙᴙ½ *Vengeance* **1962** A scientist learns that a mind isn't always a terrible thing to waste when he finds himself being manipulated by the brain of a dead man he's trying to keep alive. Remake of "Donovan's Brain" (1953). **83m/B VHS, Beta, LV.** *GB GE* Anne Heywood, Peter Van Eyck, Bernard Lee, Cecil Parker, Jack MacGowran; ***D:*** Freddie Francis. *NOS, SNC*

The Brain ᴙᴙ *Le Cerveau* **1969 (G)** Run of the mill comedy caper has Niven planning to heist millions from a NATO train. The caper begins when lots of other crooks decide to rob the same train. The cast holds this one together. **100m/C VHS.** *FR* David Niven, Jean-Paul Belmondo, Bourvil, Eli Wallach, Silvia Monti, Fernand Valois; ***D:*** Gerard Oury; ***M:*** Georges Delerue. *PAR*

The Brain ᴙ½ **1988 (R)** Dr. Blake, host of a popular TV talk-show, is in league with a power-hungry alien brain. Viewers of his show kill themselves and others in the midst of many special effects. The ratings go down. **94m/C VHS, Beta.** Tom Breznahan, Cyndy Preston, David Gale; ***D:*** Edward Hunt. *LIV*

Brain Damage ᴙᴙ **1988 (R)** A tongue-in-bloody-cheek farce about a brain-sucking parasite. The parasite in question, Aylmer, addicts our dubious hero to the euphoria induced by the blue liquid the parasite injects into his brain, paving the way for the bloody mayhem that follows. Poor shadow of Henenlotter's far-superior "Basket Case." In fact, it even includes an inside-joke cameo by Van Hentenryck, reprising his "Basket Case" character; look for him on the subway. **89m/C VHS, Beta.** Rick Herbst, Gordon MacDonald, Jennifer Lowry; ***Cameos:*** Kevin Van Hentenryck; ***D:*** Frank Henenlotter. *PAR*

Brain Dead ᴙᴙᴙ½ **1989 (R)** Low-budget but brilliantly assembled puzzle-film about a brain surgeon who agrees to perform experimental surgery on a psychotic to retrieve some corporately valuable data—his first mistake, which begins a seemingly endless cycle of nightmares and identity alterations. A mind-blowing sci-fi feast from ex-"Twilight Zone" writer Charles Beaumont. **85m/C VHS, Beta.** Bill Pullman, Bill Paxton, Bud Cort, Patricia Charbonneau, Nicholas Pryor, George Kennedy; ***D:*** Adam Simon. *MGM*

Brain Donors ᴙᴙ½ **1992 (PG)** Goofy, uneven film starring Turturro as a sleazy lawyer trying to take over the Oglethorpe Ballet Company by sweet-talking its aged patronness. He is helped by two eccentric friends, and together the three crack a lot of bad but witty jokes. The film culminates into a hilarious ballet scene featuring someone giving CPR to the ballerina playing the dying swan, an actor in a duck suit, duck hunters, and a pack of hounds. This trio reminds us of second-rate Marx Brothers (or the Three Stooges) but the movie has enough funny moments to be worth a watch. **79m/C VHS, Beta, LV.** John Turturro, Bob Nelson, Mel Smith, Nancy Marchand, John Savident, George de la Pena, Juli Donald, Spike Alexander, Teri Copley; ***D:*** Dennis Dugan; ***W:*** Pat Proft; ***M:*** Ira Newborn. *PAR*

The Brain Eaters ᴙᴙ **1958** A strange ship from inside the Earth invades a small town, and hairy monsters promptly attach themselves to people's necks in a daring bid to control the planet. The imaginative story compensates somewhat for the cheap special effects. Watch for Nimoy before he grew pointed ears. **60m/B VHS.** Edwin Nelson, Alan Frost, Jack Hill, Joanna Lee, Jody Fair, Leonard Nimoy; ***D:*** Bruno Ve Sota. *NOS, CNM*

The Brain from Planet Arous 🦴 **1957** Lassie meets Alien when an evil alien brain appropriates the body of a scientist in order to take over planet Earth. His plans are thwarted, however, by a good alien brain that likewise inhabits the body of the scientist's dog. High camp and misdemeanors. **80m/B VHS, Beta, LV.** John Agar, Joyce Meadows, Robert Fuller, Henry Travis; ***D:*** Nathan (Hertz) Juran. *SNC, CNM, AOV*

Brain of Blood *Woof! The Creature's Revenge* **1971** Deals with a scientist who transplants the brain of a politician into the body of a deformed idiot. The change is minimal. **107m/C VHS, Beta.** Kent Taylor, John Bloom, Regina Carrol, Angelo Rossitto, Grant Williams, Reed Hadley, Vicki Volante, Zandor Vorkov; ***D:*** Al Adamson. *NO*

Brain Smasher...A Love Story 🦴 **1993 (PG-13)** A bouncer and a super model become the targets of a gang of killer ninjas who want the mysterious blood-red lotus the model's been given. Of course they do. What's the lovely Hatcher doing in such a stupid movie? **88m/C VHS, LV.** Andrew Dice Clay, Teri Hatcher; ***D:*** Albert Pyun. *VMK*

The Brain That Wouldn't Die 🦴🦴½ *The Head That Wouldn't Die* **1963** Love is a many-splattered thing when a brilliant surgeon keeps the decapitated head of his fiancee alive after an auto accident while he searches for a suitably stacked body onto which to transplant the head. Absurd and satiric (head talks so much that Doc tapes her/its mouth shut) adding up to major entry in trash film genre; much of the gore was slashed for the video, however. **92m/B VHS, Beta.** Herb Evers, Virginia Leith, Adele Lamont; ***D:*** Joseph Green. *SNC, MRV, FCT*

The Brainiac 🦴½ **1961** Sorcerer sentenced for black magic returns to strike dark deeds upon the descendants of those who judged him. He turns himself into a hideous monster, feeding on his victims' brains and blood. Yuck. **75m/B VHS, Beta.** *MX* Abel Salazar, Ariadne Welter, Mauricio Garces, Rosa Maria Gallardo. *SNC, MRV, HHT*

Brainscan 🦴 **1994 (R)** Teenage loner takes a trip in virtual reality and finds that murder is the first stop. Furlong ("Terminator 2") is the troubled youth whose voyage is led by Smith as Trickster, the Freddy Krueger meets David Bowie tour guide from virtual hell. Langella turns in a straight performance as a local cop hot on the trail. Hard-core horror fans will be disappointed by the lack of on-screen violence, and special effects buffs won't see anything new. Lame effort tries to appeal to a wide audience and is bland as a result. The end is left wide open, so expect a sequel or two or three. **96m/C VHS, LV.** Edward Furlong, Frank Langella, T. Ryder Smith, David Hemblen, Amy Hargreaves, Jamie Marsh, Victor Ertmanis; ***D:*** John Flynn; ***W:*** Andrew Kevin Walker; ***M:*** George S. Clinton. *COL*

Brainstorm 🦴🦴½ **1983 (PG)** Husband-and-wife scientist team invents headphones that can record dreams, thoughts, and fantasies (VCR-style) and then allow other people to experience them by playing back the tape. Their marriage begins to crumble as the husband becomes more and more obsessed with pushing the limits of the technology; things get worse when the government wants to exploit their discovery. Special effects and interesting camerawork punctuate this sci-fi flick. Wood's last film; in fact, she died before production was completed. **106m/C VHS, Beta, LV.** Natalie Wood, Christopher Walken, Cliff Robertson, Louise Fletcher; ***D:*** Douglas Trumbull; ***W:*** Bruce Joel Rubin; ***M:*** James Horner. *MGM*

Brainwaves 🦴🦴 **1982 (R)** A young woman has disturbing flashbacks after her brain is electrically revived following a car accident. Curtis is the demented doctor who jump-starts her. **83m/C VHS, Beta.** Suzanna Love, Tony Curtis, Keir Dullea, Vera Miles; ***D:*** Ulli Lommel; ***W:*** Ulli Lommel. *SUE*

Bram Stoker's Dracula 🦴🦴 *Dracula* **1992 (R)** Coppola's highly charged view of the vampire classic is visually stunning, heavy on eroticism and violence, and weak in plot and performance. Oldman, in a number of amazing transformations, portrays the deadly bloodsucker as a lonely soul determined to reunite with his lost love, the innocent Ryder. Hopkins cheerfully chews the scenery as nemesis Van Helsing, newcomer Frost is fetching, Reeves is lightweight, and Ryder goes way over the top. Musician Waits is great as bug-eating madman Renfield. Filmed entirely on soundstages with beautiful costumes and some amazing visual effects and sets. Laserdisc includes "The Making of Bram Stoker's Dracula." **128m/C VHS, Beta, LV, 8mm.** Gary Oldman, Winona Ryder, Anthony Hopkins, Keanu Reeves, Richard E. Grant, Cary Elwes, Bill Campbell, Sadie Frost, Tom Waits; ***D:*** Francis Ford Coppola; ***W:*** Jim V. Hart; ***C:*** Michael Ballhaus. Academy Awards '92: Best Costume Design, Best Makeup, Best Sound Effects Editing; Nominations: Academy Awards '92: Best Art Direction/Set Decoration. *COL*

The Bramble Bush 🦴🦴½ **1960** Guy (Burton) is a doctor who returns to his New England hometown to care for a dying friend, Larry (Drake). Unfortunately, Guy falls for Larry's wife Mar (Rush) and they have an affair. When Guy pulls the plug on his friend's suffering, suspicious townspeople (who of course know what's going on) wonder just how "merciful" the doctor was really being and he's tried for murder. Tawdry "Peyton Place"-ish soap opera based on the novel by Charles Mergendahl. **104m/C VHS.** Richard Burton, Barbara Rush, Tom Drake, Jack Carson, Angie Dickinson, James Dunn, Henry Jones, Frank Conroy, Carl Benton Reid; ***D:*** Daniel Petrie; ***W:*** Philip Yordan. *WAR*

Brand New Life 🦴 **1972** A childless couple in their 40s are unexpectedly confronted by the wife's first pregnancy. Both have careers and well-ordered lives that promise to be disrupted. **74m/C VHS, Beta.** Cloris Leachman, Martin Balsam, Wilfrid Hyde-White, Mildred Dunnock; ***D:*** Sam O'Steen; ***M:*** Billy Goldenberg. *LCA*

Brand of Fear 🦴½ **1949** Crooning cowpoke Wakely puts down his guitar long enough to chase rustlers off the land of an innocent lady in this average oater. **56m/B VHS.** Jimmy Wakely, Dub Taylor, Gail Davis, Tom London; ***D:*** Oliver Drake; ***W:*** Basil Dickey. *MOV*

Brand of Hate 🦴 **1934** A good cowboy rustles up a gang of rustlers. **61m/B VHS, Beta.** Bob Steele, George "Gabby" Hayes, Lucille Browne, James Flavin; ***D:*** Lewis D. Collins. *NOS, RXM*

Brand of the Outlaws 🦴 **1936** A cowboy becomes an unwitting aid to rustlers in this early western. **56m/B VHS, Beta.** Bob Steele, Margaret Marquis, Virginia True Boardman, Jack Rockwell; ***D:*** Robert North Bradbury. *NOS, DVT*

Branded 🦴🦴½ **1950** Ladd (pre-"Shane") impersonates the long-gone son of rich rancher Bickford, with unusual results. Nicely balanced action and love scenes makes this old Max Brand story a better-than-average western. Filmed in Technicolor. **95m/C VHS, LV.** Alan Ladd, Mona Freeman, Charles Bickford, Joseph Calleia, Milburn Stone; ***D:*** Rudolph Mate. *PAR*

Branded a Bandit **1924** Yakima must avoid the sheriff while tracking down the killers of an old miner so that he can clear himself of the crime. **58m/C VHS.** Yakima Canutt; ***D:*** Paul Hurst. *GPV*

Branded a Coward 🦴 **1935** A man whose parents were killed seeks revenge via his trusty six-shooters. **56m/B VHS, Beta.** Johnny Mack Brown, Billie Seward, Yakima Canutt; ***D:*** Sam Newfield. *NOS, DVT*

Branded Men 🦴🦴 **1931** A couple of oddballs become mixed up in a number of zany, western-type adventures. **60m/B VHS.** Ken Maynard, June Clyde, Irving Bacon, Billy Bletcher, Charles "Blackie" King, Donald Keith; ***D:*** Phil Rosen. *NOS*

Brannigan 🦴🦴½ **1975 (PG)** The Duke stars in the somewhat unfamiliar role of a rough and tumble Chicago police officer. He travels across the Atlantic to arrest a racketeer who has fled the States rather than face a grand jury indictment. Humor and action abound. **111m/C VHS, Beta.** John Wayne, John Vernon, Mel Ferrer, Daniel Pilon, James Booth, Ralph Meeker, Lesley-Anne Down, Richard Attenborough; ***D:*** Douglas Hickox; ***W:*** Michael Butler, William W. Norton Sr. *MGM, FOX*

Brass 🦴½ **1985 (PG)** First post-Archie Bunker role for O'Connor, who plods through this average police drama at a snail's pace, dragging everything else down with him. Made-for-TV pilot for a series that never aired. **94m/C VHS, LV.** Carroll O'Connor, Lois Nettleton, Jimmie Baird, Paul Shenar, Vincent Gardenia, Anita Gillette; ***D:*** Corey Allen. *ORI*

Brass Target 🦴½ **1978 (PG)** Hypothetical thriller about a plot to kill George Patton in the closing days of WWII for the sake of $250 million in Nazi gold stolen by his staff. Interesting cast can't find story. **111m/C VHS, Beta, LV.** Sophia Loren, George Kennedy, Max von Sydow, John Cassavetes, Patrick McGoohan, Robert Vaughn, Bruce Davison, Edward Herrmann, Ed Bishop; ***D:*** John Hough; ***W:*** Alvin Boretz. *MGM*

The Bravados 🦴🦴🦴 **1958** A rough, distressing Western revenge tale, wherein a man is driven to find the four men who murdered his wife. In tracking the perpetrators, Peck realizes that he has been corrupted by his vengeance. **98m/C VHS, Beta.** Gregory Peck, Stephen Boyd, Joan Collins, Albert Salmi, Henry Silva, Lee Van Cleef, George Voskovec, Barry Coe; ***D:*** Henry King; ***W:*** Philip Yordan; ***C:*** Leon Shamroy. National Board of Review Awards '58: Best Supporting Actor (Salmi). *FOX*

The Brave Bunch 🦴½ **1970** A courageous Greek soldier tries to save his men and country during WWII. **110m/C VHS, Beta.** *GR* Peter Funk, John Miller; ***D:*** Costa Carayiannis. *LIV*

The Brave Little Frog 🦴🦴½ **1994 (G)** Tree frog Jonathan, the new amphibian at Rainbow Pond, is having trouble making friends until his pipe music and a friendly female frog help him out. **90m/C VHS.** *HMD*

The Brave One 🦴🦴🦴 **1956** A love story between a Spanish boy and the bull who saves his life. The animal is later carted off to the bullring. Award-winning screenplay by the then-blacklisted Trumbo, as "Robert Rich." **100m/C VHS, Beta, LV.** Michel Ray, Rodolfo Hoyos, Joi Lansing; ***D:*** Irving Rapper; ***W:*** Dalton Trumbo; ***C:*** Jack Cardiff. Academy Awards '56: Best Original Screenplay; Nominations: Academy Awards '56: Best Film Editing. *VCI*

Braveheart **1925** When a Native American adapts to the white man's world, he alienates his own people. He eventually chooses to renounce his love for a white woman, and returns to lead his people. Silent. **62m/B VHS, Beta, 8mm.** Rod La Rocque; ***D:*** Alan Hale. *GVV, FCT*

Braveheart 🦴🦴🦴½ **1995 (R)** Producer-director-star Gibson does it all in this bold, ferocious, reasonably accurate epic about the passion and cost of freedom. Charismatic 13th-century Scottish folk hero William Wallace leads his desperate and outnumbered clansmen in revolt against British oppression. Sweeping, meticulous battle scenes fit suprisingly well with moments of stirring romance and snappy wit. Among the mostly unknown (in the States, anyway) cast, Marceau and McCormack are elegant as Wallace's lady loves, and McGoohan is positively hateful as King Edward I. Gory and excessively violent (as medieval warfare tends to be) and a bit too long (as historical epics tend to be), but rewarding entertainment for those who stick it out—where else can you see the king's army get mooned en masse? Script was based on 300 pages of rhyming verse attributed to a blind poet known as Blind Hally. Gibson put up $15 million of his own money to complete the film. **178m/C VHS, Beta.** Mel Gibson, Sophie Marceau, Patrick McGoohan, Catherine McCormack, Brendan Gleeson, James Cosmo, David O'Hara, Angus McFadyen, Peter Hanly; ***D:*** Mel Gibson; ***W:*** Randall Wallace; ***C:*** John Toll; ***M:*** James Horner. Academy Awards '95: Best Cinematography, Best Director (Gibson), Best Makeup, Best Picture; British Academy Awards '95: Best Cinematography; Golden Globe Awards '96: Best Director (Gibson); MTV Movie Awards '96: Best Action Sequence; Writers Guild of America '95: Best Original Screenplay; Nominations: Academy Awards '95: Best Costume Design, Best Film Editing, Best Screenplay, Best Sound, Best Score; British Academy Awards '95: Best Director (Gibson), Best Score; Directors Guild of America Awards '95: Best Director (Gibson); Golden Globe Awards '96: Best Film—Drama, Best Screenplay, Best Score; MTV Movie

Awards '96: Best Film, Best Male Performance (Gibson), Most Desirable Male (Gibson). *PAR*

Brazil ℒℒℒ½ **1985 (R)** The acclaimed nightmare comedy about an Everyman trying to survive in a surreal paper-choked bureaucratic society. There are copious references to "1984" and "The Trial," fantastic mergings of glorious fantasy and stark reality, and astounding visual design. **131m/C VHS, Beta, LV.** *GB* Jonathan Pryce, Robert De Niro, Michael Palin, Katherine Helmond, Kim Greist, Bob Hoskins, Ian Holm, Peter Vaughan, Ian Richardson; ***D:*** Terry Gilliam; ***W:*** Terry Gilliam, Tom Stoppard; ***M:*** Michael Kamen. Los Angeles Film Critics Association Awards '85: Best Director (Gilliam), Best Film, Best Screenplay; Nominations: Academy Awards '85: Best Art Direction/Set Decoration, Best Original Screenplay. *MCA, FCT*

Breach of Conduct ℒ½ **1994 (PG-13)** Colonel Bill Case (Coyote) is the commander of the Fort Benton, Utah Army base where Helen Lutz's (Thorne-Smith) husband Tom (Verica) has just been transferred. At first there's a mutual attraction between Helen and Case, but then hubby is assigned a mission off base and, when Helen refuses Case's overtures, things turn very nasty. Made for cable TV. **93m/C VHS, LV.** Peter Coyote, Courtney Thorne-Smith, Tom Verica, Beth Toussaint; ***D:*** Tim Matheson; ***W:*** Scott Abbott; ***C:*** Gideon Porath. *MCA*

Breach of Trust ℒℒ½ **1995 (R)** Smalltime crook Casey (Biehn) winds up in big trouble when he steals a computer disc with access codes to millions in drug cartel money. He goes on the lam and meets Madeline (Ferrer), an undercover cop who thinks that some police are on the cartel's payroll. So the daring duo decide to take on the drug lords and the dirty cops. **96m/C VHS, LV.** Michael Biehn, Matt Craven, Leilani Sarelle Ferrer, Miguel Sandoval, Kim Coates, Ed Lauter; ***D:*** Charles Wilkinson; ***W:*** Gordon Basichis, Raul Inglis; ***C:*** Michael Slovis; ***M:*** Graeme Coleman. *REP*

Bread and Chocolate ℒℒℒ *Pane e Cioccolata* **1974** Uneducated Italian immigrant Manfredi works a series of odd jobs in complacently bourgeois Switzerland and tries desperately to fit in and better himself (which he fails utterly to do). Culture clash satire, with an engaging everyman lead. Italian with subtitles. **109m/C VHS.** *IT* Nino Manfredi, Anna Karina, Johnny Dorelli, Paolo Turco; ***D:*** Franco Brusati; ***W:*** Nino Manfredi, Franco Brusati, Iaia Fiastri; ***C:*** Luciano Tovoli; ***M:*** Daniele Patrucchi. New York Film Critics Awards '78: Best Foreign Film. *HTV*

The Break ℒℒ **1995 (PG-13)** Clumsy teen tennis hopeful refuses to give up his dreams even after his dad hires a coach to show him the error of his game. **104m/C VHS.** Martin Sheen, Vincent Van Patten, Ben Jorgensen, Rae Dawn Chong, Valerie Perrine. *VMK*

Break of Hearts ℒℒ½ **1935** Hepburn marries Boyer, who becomes an alcoholic, and then more troubles arise. Very soapy, but well-made. **78m/B VHS, Beta, LV.** Katharine Hepburn, Charles Boyer, Jean Hersholt, John Beal, Sam Hardy; ***D:*** Philip Moeller; ***M:*** Max Steiner. *TTC*

Breakaway ℒ **1995 (R)** Myra (Thompson) decides to get away from her drop-woman job with $300,000 of mob money. Naturally, she's pursued by a hit man (Estevez) and then betrayed by a boyfriend (De Rose), who steals the cash and hides it in the apartment of the other woman he's seeing (Harding). Thompson does fine but to describe Harding's debut performance as wooden is to be very, very kind. **94m/C VHS.** Teri Thompson, Joe Estevez, Chris De Rose, Tonya Harding; ***D:*** Sean Dash; ***W:*** Sean Dash. *NYR*

Breakdown ℒ **1953** A boxer is set up by his girlfriend's father to take the rap for a murder. Lackluster effort. **76m/B VHS, Beta.** Ann Richards, William Bishop, Anne Gwynne, Sheldon Leonard, Wally Cassell, Richard Benedict; ***D:*** Edmond Angelo. *NOS, SNC*

Breaker! Breaker! ℒ **1977 (PG)** Convoy of angry truck drivers launch an assault on the corrupt and sadistic locals of a small Texas town. Goofy entry in "mad or sex-crazed trucker armed with a CB radio" genre. **86m/C VHS, Beta.** Chuck Norris, George Murdock; ***D:*** Don Hulette. *SUE*

Breaker Morant ℒℒℒ½ **1980 (PG)** In 1901 South Africa, three Australian soldiers are put on trial for avenging the murder of several prisoners. Based on a true story which was then turned into a play by Kenneth Ross, this riveting, popular antiwar statement and courtroom drama heralded Australia's film renaissance. Rich performances by Woodward and Waters. **107m/C VHS, Beta, LV, 8mm.** *AU* Edward Woodward, Jack Thompson, John Waters, Bryan Brown; ***D:*** Bruce Beresford; ***W:*** Jonathon Hardy, David Stevens, Bruce Beresford. Australian Film Institute '80: Best Actor (Thompson), Best Film; Nominations: Academy Awards '80: Best Adapted Screenplay; Cannes Film Festival '80: Best Film. *CCB, COL, HMV*

Breakfast at Tiffany's ℒℒℒ½ **1961** Truman Capote's amusing story of an endearingly eccentric New York City playgirl and her shaky romance with a young writer. Hepburn lends Holly Golightly just the right combination of naivete and worldly wisdom with a dash of melancholy. A wonderfully offbeat romance. ♫Moon River. **114m/C VHS, Beta, LV, 8mm.** Audrey Hepburn, George Peppard, Patricia Neal, Buddy Ebsen, Mickey Rooney, Martin Balsam, John McGiver; ***D:*** Blake Edwards; ***W:*** George Axelrod; ***M:*** Henry Mancini. Academy Awards '61: Best Song ("Moon River"), Best Original Score; Nominations: Academy Awards '61: Best Actress (Hepburn), Best Adapted Screenplay, Best Art Direction/Set Decoration (Color). *PAR, FCT*

The Breakfast Club ℒℒℒ **1985 (R)** Five students from different cliques at a Chicago suburban high school spend a day together in detention. Rather well done teenage culture study; these characters delve a little deeper than the standard adult view of adolescent stereotypes. One of John Hughes' best movies. Soundtrack features Simple Minds and Wang Chung. **97m/C VHS, Beta, LV.** Ally Sheedy, Molly Ringwald, Judd Nelson, Emilio Estevez, Anthony Michael Hall, Paul Gleason, John Kapelos; ***D:*** John Hughes; ***W:*** John Hughes; ***M:*** Gary Chang, Keith Forsey. *MCA, FCT*

Breakfast in Hollywood ℒ½ *The Mad Hatter* **1946** Movie about the popular morning radio show of the 1940s hosted by Tom Breneman, a coast-to-coast coffee klatch. **93m/B VHS, Beta.** Tom Breneman, Bonita Granville, Eddie Ryan, Beulah Bondi, Billie Burke, ZaSu Pitts, Hedda Hopper, Spike Jones; ***D:*** Harold Schuster. *NO*

Breakfast in Paris ℒ½ **1981** Two American professionals in Paris, both crushed from past failures in the love department, find each other. **85m/C VHS, Beta.** *AU* Rod Mullinar, Barbara Parkins, Jack Lenoir; ***D:*** John Lamond. *NWV*

Breakheart Pass ℒℒ **1976 (PG)** A governor, his female companion, a band of cavalrymen, and a mysterious man travel on a train through the mountains of Idaho in 1870. The mystery man turns out to be a murderer. Based on a novel by Alistair MacLean. **92m/C VHS, Beta, LV.** Charles Bronson, Ben Johnson, Richard Crenna, Jill Ireland, Charles Durning, Ed Lauter, Archie Moore, Sally Kirkland; ***D:*** Tom Gries; ***M:*** Jerry Goldsmith. *MGM, FOX*

Breakin' ℒℒ *Breakdance* **1984 (PG)** Dance phenomenon break dancing along with the hit songs that accompanied the fad. ♫Tibetan Jam; Heart of the Beat; Breakin...There's No Stopping Us; Street People; Showdown; 99 1/2. **87m/C VHS, Beta, LV.** Lucinda Dickey, Adolfo "Shabba Doo" Quinones, Michael "Boogaloo Shrimp" Chambers, Ben Lokey, Christopher McDonald, Phineas Newborn III; ***D:*** Joel Silberg; ***W:*** Allen N. DeBevoise; ***M:*** Michael Boyd. *MGM*

Breakin' 2: Electric Boogaloo ℒ *Breakdance 2: Electric Boogaloo; Electric Boogaloo "Breakin' 2"* **1984 (PG)** Breakdancers hold a benefit concert to preserve an urban community center. ♫Electric Boogaloo; Radiotron; Action; When I.C.U. **94m/C VHS, Beta, LV.** Lucinda Dickey, Adolfo "Shabba Doo" Quinones, Michael "Boogaloo Shrimp" Chambers, Susie Bono; ***D:*** Sam Firstenberg. *MGM*

Breakin' Through ℒ **1984** The choreographer of a troubled Broadway-bound musical decides to energize his shows with a troupe of street dancers. **73m/C VHS, Beta.** Ben Vereen, Donna McKechnie, Reid Shelton; ***D:*** Peter Medak. *DIS*

Breaking All the Rules ℒ½ **1985 (R)** Comedy about two teenage lovers who find themselves embroiled in a slapdash jewel robbery at an amusement park during the last day of summer break. **91m/C VHS, Beta.** *CA* Carolyn Dunn, Carl Marotte, Thor Bishopric, Rachel Hayward; ***D:*** James Orr; ***W:*** James Orr, Jim Cruickshank. *NWV, VTR*

Breaking Away ℒℒℒ½ **1979 (PG)** A lighthearted coming-of-age drama about a high school graduate's addiction to bicycle racing, whose dreams are tested against the realities of a crucial race. An honest, open look at present Americana with tremendous insight into the minds of average youth; shot on location at Indiana University. Great bike-racing photography. Quaid, Barrie, and Christopher give exceptional performances. Basis for television series. **100m/C VHS, Beta, LV.** Dennis Christopher, Dennis Quaid, Daniel Stern, Jackie Earle Haley, Barbara Barrie, Paul Dooley, Amy Wright; ***D:*** Peter Yates; ***W:*** Steve Tesich. Academy Awards '79: Best Original Screenplay; Golden Globe Awards '80: Best Film—Musical/Comedy; National Board of Review Awards '79: 10 Best Films of the Year, Best Supporting Actor (Dooley); National Society of Film Critics Awards '79: Best Film, Best Screenplay; Writers Guild of America '79: Best Original Screenplay; Nominations: Academy Awards '79: Best Director (Yates), Best Picture, Best Supporting Actress (Barrie), Best Original Score. *FOX, HMV*

Breaking Free ℒℒ½ **1995 (PG)** Teenaged loser forms an unlikely friendship with a bitter gymnast who's been blinded and forced to give up her dreams. **106m/C VHS.** Jeremy London, Gina Philips, Christine Taylor, Megan Gallagher. *AVE*

Breaking Glass ℒℒ½ **1980 (PG)** A "New Wave" musical that gives an insight into the punk record business and at the same time tells of the rags-to-riches life of a punk rock star. **94m/C VHS, Beta.** *GB* Hazel O'Connor, Phil Daniels, Jon Finch, Jonathan Pryce; ***D:*** Brian Gibson. *PAR*

Breaking Home Ties ℒℒ½ *Norman Rockwell's Breaking Home Ties* **1987** Norman Rockwell's illustration is the basis for this coming of age story set in a small Texas town. A young man is eager to be off to college and lessen his family ties but his mother's serious illness may prevent both. Good performances help overcome the sentimentality. Originally made for television. **95m/C VHS.** Jason Robards Jr., Eva Marie Saint, Doug McKeon, Claire Trevor, Erin Gray; ***D:*** John Wilder; ***W:*** John Wilder. *CAF*

Breaking In ℒℒℒ **1989 (R)** A semi-acclaimed comedy about a professional thief who takes a young amateur under his wing and shows him the ropes. Under-estimated Reynolds is especially charming. Witty and innovative script, with intelligent direction from Forsyth. **95m/C VHS, Beta, LV.** Burt Reynolds, Casey Siemaszko, Sheila Kelley, Lorraine Toussaint, Albert Salmi, Harry Carey Jr., Maury Chaykin, Stephen Tobolowsky, David Frishberg; ***D:*** Bill Forsyth; ***W:*** John Sayles; ***M:*** Michael Gibbs. *HBO, WAR*

Breaking Loose ℒ½ **1990 (R)** A surfer is on the run from a vicious motorcycle gang that kidnapped his girlfriend, but turns to fight eventually, board in hand. **88m/C VHS.** Peter Phelps, Vince Martin, Abigail, David Ngcombujarra; ***D:*** Rod Hay. *HMD*

Breaking Point ℒℒ½ **1994 (R)** Ex-cop Dwight Meadows (Busey) retired from the force when he was nearly killed by a scalpel-wielding mass murderer known as "The Surgeon." Now the psycho is back and Meadows returns to active duty, paired with relentless officer Dana Preston (Fluegel), who wants the killer caught—at any cost. Vancouver, British Columbia fills in for the Seattle, Washington setting. **95m/C VHS, LV.** Gary Busey, Darlanne Fluegel, Jeff Griggs, Kim Cattrall; ***D:*** Paul Ziller; ***M:*** Graeme Coleman. *REP*

Breaking the Ice 🦴🦴 **1938** Unlikely mixture of Mennonites and a big city ice skating show. Young man leaves the farm to get a job singing at the rink. Musical numbers abound with backing by Victor Young and his Orchestra. **79m/B VHS, Beta.** Bobby Breen, Charlie Ruggles, Dolores Costello, Billy Gilbert, Margaret Hamilton. Nominations: Academy Awards '38: Best Original Score. *NOS, VYY, DVT*

Breaking the Rules 🦴🦴½ **1992 (PG-13)** Predicatable buddy-road movie with a tearjerking premise and comedic overtones. Rob, Gene, and Phil were best buds growing up in Cleveland but young adulthood has separated them. They are reunited by Phil, who is dying of leukemia, and whose last wish is a cross-country road trip to California so he can appear as a contestant on "Jeopardy." Along the way they meet brassy waitress Mary, who impulsively decides to join them and winds up bringing the trio's shaky friendship back together. Potts does well as the big-haired, big-hearted Mary but the actors must work hard to maintain any dignity given the story's melodrama. **100m/C VHS, LV.** Jason Bateman, C. Thomas Howell, Jonathan Silverman, Annie Potts, Kent Bateman, Shawn Phelan; ***D:*** Neal Israel; ***W:*** Paul Shapiro; ***M:*** David Kitay. *HBO*

Breaking the Waves 🦴🦴🦴 **1995** Sacrificial journey of shy, religious Beth (Watson), who's living in an austere northern Scotland coastal village in the '70s. Bess, who regularly talks to God, marries Jan (Skarsgard), an adventurer working on a North Sea oil rig. It must be a case of opposites attracting but the couple are happy until Jan is paralyzed from the neck down in a rig accident. Beth, who blames herself, begins sleeping around, believing her actions can somehow help Jan, and slides ever deeper into mental instability. Powerful story is divided into seven chapters and an epilogue. **159m/C VHS.** *DK FR* Emily Watson, Stellan Skarsgard, Katrin Cartlidge, Adrian Rawlins, Jean-Marc Barr, Sandra Voe, Udo Kier, Mikkel Gaup; ***D:*** Lars von Trier; ***W:*** Lars von Trier; ***C:*** Robby Muller; ***M:*** Joachim Holbek. Cannes Film Festival '96: Grand Jury Prize. *NYR*

Breaking Up 🦴🦴½ **1978** A woman fights to rediscover her personal identity after her fifteen-year marriage crumbles. Made for television. Emmy nominated. **90m/C VHS, Beta.** Lee Remick, Granville Van Dusen, David Stambaugh; ***D:*** Delbert Mann. *TLF*

Breaking Up Is Hard to Do 🦴 **1979** Six men leave their wives and shack up together on Malibu for a summer of partying and introspection. Made for television; edited down from its original 201 minute length. **96m/C VHS, Beta, LV.** Billy Crystal, Bonnie Franklin, Ted Bessell, Jeff Conaway, Tony Musante, Robert Conrad, Trish Stewart, David Ogden Stiers, George Gaynes; ***D:*** Lou Antonio; ***M:*** Richard Bellis. *VMK*

Breaking with Old Ideas 🦴🦴 **1975** A film made in the waning years of Mao's Cultural Revolution about the construction of a college of workers. In Chinese with subtitles. **126m/C VHS, Beta.** *CH* ***D:*** Li Wen-Hua. *FCT*

Breakout 🦴🦴 **1975 (PG)** The wife of a man imprisoned in Mexico hires a Texas bush pilot (Bronson) to help her husband (Duvall) escape. **96m/C VHS, Beta, LV.** Charles Bronson, Jill Ireland, Robert Duvall, John Huston, Sheree North, Randy Quaid; ***D:*** Tom Gries; ***M:*** Jerry Goldsmith. *COL*

Breakthrough 🦴🦴 *Sergeant Steiner* **1978 (PG)** German soldier, broken at the end of WWII, sets out to negotiate with the Allies. Average at best. **96m/C VHS, Beta.** Richard Burton, Robert Mitchum, Rod Steiger, Michael Parks, Curt Jurgens; ***D:*** Andrew V. McLaglen. *WOV*

Breath of Scandal 🦴🦴 **1960** An American diplomat in Vienna rescues a princess when she is thrown off a horse; he falls for her like a ton o' bricks. Viennese politics complicate things. Based on a play by Molnar. **98m/C VHS.** Sophia Loren, John Gavin, Maurice Chevalier, Angela Lansbury; ***D:*** Michael Curtiz. *PAR, BAR*

Breathing Fire 🦴🦴 **1991 (R)** A Vietnamese teenager and his American brother find out their ex-GI father is behind an armed bank robbery and murder. They join together to protect the only eyewitness—a young girl—against the ruthless gang of criminals and their own father. Lots of kickboxing action for martial arts fans. **86m/C VHS.** Bolo Yeung, Jonathan Ke Quan, Jerry Trimble; ***D:*** Lou Kennedy. *IMP*

Breathing Lessons 🦴🦴🦴 **1994 (PG)** Sweet look at a long-term marriage that renews itself on a road trip. Flighty Maggie and pragmatic Ira have been married for 28 squabbling but loving years. They're driving from their Baltimore home to a funeral in Pennsylvania and the road stops provide some small adventures and a great deal of conversation. Drama rests easily on the capable shoulders of the veteran performers. Based on the novel by Anne Tyler. Made for TV. **98m/C VHS.** James Garner, Joanne Woodward, Paul Winfield, Kathryn Erbe, Joyce Van Patten, Eileen Heckart, Tim Guinee, Henry Jones, Stephi Lineburg, Jean Louisa Kelly, John Considine; ***D:*** John Erman; ***W:*** Robert W. Lenski. *REP*

Breathless 🦴🦴🦴🦴 *A Bout de Souffle* **1959** Godard's first feature catapulted him to the vanguard of French filmmakers. A carefree Parisian crook, who emulates Humphrey Bogart, falls in love with an American girl with tragic results. Wonderful scenes of Parisian life. Established Godard's Brechtian, experimental style. Belmondo's film debut. Mistitled "Breathless" for American release, the film's French title actually means "Out of Breath"; however, the fast-paced, erratic musical score leaves you breathless. French with English subtitles. Remade with Richard Gere in 1983 with far less intensity. **90m/B VHS, Beta.** *FR* Jean-Paul Belmondo, Jean Seberg, Daniel Boulanger, Jean-Pierre Melville, Liliane Robin; ***D:*** Jean-Luc Godard; ***W:*** Jean-Luc Godard. Berlin International Film Festival '60: Best Director (Godard). *NOS, MRV, CVC*

Breathless 🦴🦴 **1983 (R)** Car thief turned cop killer has a torrid love affair with a French student studying in Los Angeles as the police slowly close in. Glossy, smarmy remake of the Godard classic that concentrates on the thin plot rather than any attempt at revitalizing the film syntax. **105m/C VHS, Beta, LV.** Richard Gere, Valerie Kaprisky, Art Metrano, John P. Ryan, Lisa Jane Persky; ***D:*** Jim McBride; ***W:*** Jim McBride, L.M. Kit Carson; ***M:*** Jack Nitzsche. *VES*

A Breed Apart 🦴🦴 **1984 (R)** An on-going battle over a rare eagle's eggs strikes sparks between a reclusive conservationist and a scheming adventurer hired by a billionaire collector. **95m/C VHS, Beta.** Kathleen Turner, Rutger Hauer, Powers Boothe, Donald Pleasence, Brion James, John Dennis Johnston; ***D:*** Philippe Mora. *HMD*

Breed of the Border 🦴 *Speed Brent Wins* **1933** Tough-fisted cowboys must take the law into their own hands. **60m/B VHS, Beta.** Bob Steele, Marion Byron, George "Gabby" Hayes, Ernie Adams; ***D:*** Robert North Bradbury. *NOS, DVT*

Brenda Starr 🦴 **1986 (PG)** Amateurish adaptation of the comic strip by Dale Messick. Shields stars as girl reporter Brenda Starr, who is once again risking her life to get the scoop. She finds herself in the jungles of South America searching for a mad scientist who is creating a rocket fuel that could destroy the world. The most entertaining thing about this film is the costumes designed by Bob Mackie. **94m/C VHS.** Brooke Shields, Timothy Dalton, Tony Peck, Diana Scarwid, Nestor Serrano, Jeffrey Tambor, June Gable, Charles Durning, Eddie Albert, Henry Gibson, Ed Nelson; ***D:*** Robert Ellis Miller; ***W:*** James David Buchanan. *COL*

The Bretts 🦴🦴🦴 **1988** Amusing two-part British miniseries follows the egos and eccentricities of the British theatrical dynasty, the Bretts. Part 1 is set in the '20s and introduces the family heads, Charles (Rodway) and Lydia (Murray), who enjoy performing off-stage almost as well as they enjoy performing on. Also introduced are their five children and loyal (if opinionated) servants. Part 2 follows the family into the 30s with son Edwin (Yelland) having become a film star, actress daughter Martha (Lang) falling for a politician, and son Tom (Winter) continuing to write his gloomy social dramas. Each part is on 6 cassettes. **600m/C VHS.** *GB* Barbara Murray, Norman Rodway, David Yelland, Belinda Lang, George Winter, Janet Maw, Tim Wylton, Bert Parnaby, Lysette Anthony, Clive Francis, Frank Middlemass, John Castle, Hugh Fraser, Patrick Ryecart, Sally Cookson, Billy Boyle; ***W:*** Rosemary Anne Sisson. *SIG, VCO*

Brewster McCloud 🦴🦴🦴½ **1970 (R)** Altman's first picture after M*A*S*H reunites much of the cast and combines fantasy, black comedy, and satire in the story of a young man whose head is in the clouds or at least in the upper reaches of the Houston Astrodome. Brewster (Cort) lives covertly in the Dome and dreams of flying. He also has a guardian angel (Kellerman) who watches over him and may actually be killing people who give him a hard time. Murphy is a cop obsessed with catching the killer. And there's a circus allegory as well. Hard to figure what it all means and offbeat as they come, but for certain tastes, exquisite. **101m/C VHS, Beta, LV.** Bud Cort, Sally Kellerman, Shelley Duvall, Michael Murphy, William Windom, Rene Auberjonois, Stacy Keach, John Schuck, Margaret Hamilton; ***D:*** Robert Altman; ***W:*** Doran William Cannon. *MGM*

Brewster's Millions 🦴🦴½ **1945** If Brewster, an ex-GI, can spend a million dollars in one year, he will inherit a substantially greater fortune. Originally a 1902 novel, this is the fifth of seven film adaptations. **79m/B VHS, Beta.** Dennis O'Keefe, June Havoc, Eddie Anderson, Helen Walker, Gail Patrick, Mischa Auer; ***D:*** Allan Dwan. Nominations: Academy Awards '45: Best Original Score. *MED*

Brewster's Millions 🦴½ **1985 (PG)** An aging minor league baseball player must spend 30 million dollars in order to collect an inheritance of 300 million dollars. He may find that money can't buy happiness. Seventh remake of the story. **101m/C VHS, Beta, LV.** Richard Pryor, John Candy, Lonette McKee, Stephen Collins, Jerry Orbach, Pat Hingle, Tovah Feldshuh, Hume Cronyn, Rick Moranis; ***D:*** Walter Hill; ***W:*** Herschel Weingrod, Timothy Harris; ***M:*** Ry Cooder. *MCA*

Brian's Song 🦴🦴🦴🦴 **1971 (G)** The story of the unique relationship between Gale Sayers, the Chicago Bears' star running back, and his teammate Brian Piccolo. The friendship between the Bears' first interracial roommates ended suddenly when Brian Piccolo lost his life to cancer. Made for television. Incredibly well-received in its time. **74m/C VHS, Beta, LV.** James Caan, Billy Dee Williams, Jack Warden, Shelley Fabares, Judy Pace; ***D:*** Buzz Kulik. *COL*

The Bride 🦴½ **1985 (PG-13)** Re-telling of "The Bride of Frankenstein." Sting's Dr. Frankenstein has much more success in creating his second monster (Beals). She's pretty and intelligent and he may even be falling in love with her. When she begins to gain too much independence, though, the awful truth about her origins comes out. Fans of the two leads will want to see this one, but for a true classic see Elsa Lanchester's bride. **118m/C VHS, Beta, LV.** Sting, Jennifer Beals, Anthony Higgins, David Rappaport, Geraldine Page, Clancy Brown, Phil Daniels, Veruschka; ***D:*** Franc Roddam; ***C:*** Stephen Burum; ***M:*** Maurice Jarre. *FOX*

The Bride & the Beast *Woof!* *Queen of the Gorillas* **1958** While on an African safari honeymoon, a big game hunter's new bride is carried off by a gorilla. Ludicrous jungle tale. **78m/B VHS, Beta.** Charlotte Austin, Lance Fuller, William Justine; ***D:*** Adrian Weiss; ***W:*** Edward D. Wood Jr.; ***M:*** Les Baxter. *AOV*

The Bride Came C.O.D. 🦴🦴 **1941** Rough'n'tough pilot Cagney is hired by a rich Texas oil man to prevent his daughter (the one with the Bette Davis eyes) from marrying cheesy bandleader Carson. The payoff: $10 per pound if she's delivered unwed. What a surprise when Cagney faces the timeworn dilemma of having to choose between love and money. A contemporary issue of "Time" magazine trumpeted: "Screen's most talented tough guy rough-houses one of screen's best dramatic actresses." That tells you right there it's a romantic comedy. Cagney and Davis—a likely pairing, you'd think—are essentially fish out of water, bothered and bewildered by a weak script. **92m/B VHS.** Bette Davis, James Cagney, Stuart Erwin, Jack Carson, George Tobias, Eugene Pallette, William Frawley; ***D:*** William Keighley; ***W:*** Julius J. Epstein, Philip C. Epstein; ***M:*** Max Steiner. *MGM, FCT*

The Bride Is Much Too Beautiful 🦴🦴½ **1958** Bardot, playing a French farm girl, becomes a renowned model. Dubbed. **90m/C VHS, Beta.** *FR* Brigitte Bardot, Louis Jourdan, Micheline Presle, Marcel Amont; ***D:*** Fred Surin. *NOS, FCT, HEG*

The Bride of Frankenstein 🦴🦴🦴🦴 **1935** The classic sequel to the classic original in which Dr. F. seeks to build a mate for his monster. More humor than the first, but also more pathos, including the monster's famous but short-lived friendship with a blind hermit. Lanchester plays both the bride and Mary Shelley in the opening sequence. **75m/B VHS, Beta, LV.** Boris Karloff, Elsa Lanchester, Ernest Thesiger, Colin Clive, Una O'Connor, Valerie Hobson, Dwight Frye, John Carradine, E.E. Clive, O.P. Heggie, Gavin Gordon, Douglas Walton; ***D:*** James Whale. Nominations: Academy Awards '35: Best Sound. *MCA, MLB*

Bride of Killer Nerd 🦴 **1991** Harold Kunkel, left over from the original "Killer Nerd," finds his opposite sex nirvana in the person of Thelma, also a nerd in mind, body, and soul. They relentlessly pursue revenge on the rockers who humiliate them at a campus beer bash. **75m/C VHS.** Toby Radloff, Wayne A. Harold, Heidi Lohr; ***D:*** Mark Steven Bosko. *TEM*

Bride of Re-Animator 🦴🦴½ **1989** Herbert West is back, and this time he not only re-animates life but creates life—sexy female life—in this sequel to the immensely popular "Re-Animator." High camp and blood curdling gore make this a standout in the sequel parade. Available in a R-rated version as well. **99m/C VHS, Beta, LV.** Bruce Abbott, Claude Earl Jones, Fabiana Udenio, Jeffrey Combs, Kathleen Kinmont, David Gale; ***D:*** Brian Yuzna; ***M:*** Richard Band. *LIV*

Bride of the Gorilla 🦴🦴 **1951** Burr travels to the jungle where he finds a wife, a plantation, and a curse in this African twist on the werewolf legend. Chaney is the local policeman on his trail. Burr's physical changes are fun to watch. **76m/B VHS.** Raymond Burr, Barbara Payton, Lon Chaney Jr., Tom Conway, Paul Cavanagh; ***D:*** Curt Siodmak; ***W:*** Curt Siodmak. *NOS, MRV, SNC*

Bride of the Monster *Woof! Bride of the Atom* **1956** Lugosi stars as a mad scientist trying to create a race of giants. Classic Woodian badness. **70m/B VHS, Beta.** Bela Lugosi, Tor Johnson, Loretta King, Tony McCoy; ***D:*** Edward D. Wood Jr. *NOS, SNC, VYY*

The Bride Walks Out 🦴🦴 **1936** Newlywed crisis: a woman with rich taste learns how to adjust to living on her husband's poor salary, but not before she samples the life of the wealthy. Interesting in a sociological sort of way. **81m/B VHS, Beta.** Barbara Stanwyck, Gene Raymond, Robert Young, Ned Sparks, Willie Best, Helen Broderick, Hattie McDaniel; ***D:*** Leigh Jason. *TTC*

The Bride Wore Black 🦴🦴🦴 *La Mariee Etait en Noir* **1968** Truffaut's homage to Hitchcock, complete with Bernard Herrmann score. A young woman exacts brutal revenge on the five men who accidentally killed her husband. Adapted from a novel by Cornell Woolrich. **107m/C VHS, LV.** *FR* Jeanne Moreau, Claude Rich, Jean-Claude Brialy, Michel Bouquet, Michael Lonsdale; ***D:*** Francois Truffaut; ***C:*** Raoul Coutard; ***M:*** Bernard Herrmann. *MGM, MLB, INJ*

The Bride Wore Red 🦴🦴 **1937** Crawford stars as a cabaret singer who masquerades as a socialite in an attempt to break into the upper crust. When a wealthy aristocrat invites her to spend two weeks at a posh resort in Tyrol, Crawford plays her part to the hilt, managing to charm both a rich gentleman and the village postman. Typical "love conquers all" melodrama. **103m/B VHS.** Joan Crawford, Franchot Tone, Robert Young, Billie Burke, Reginald Owen, Lynne Carver, George Zucco; ***D:*** Dorothy Arzner. *MGM*

Brides of Christ 🦴🦴½ **1991** Set in the Australian Santo Spirito Convent during the Vatican II upheaval of the 1960s. Explores the tensions between old and new religious ideas by focusing on novices, older nuns, and the Reverend Mother of the convent as they try to cope with a changing world. TV miniseries. **300m/C VHS.** Brenda Fricker, Sandy Gore, Josephine Byrnes, Lisa Hensley, Naomi Watts, Kym Wilson, Melissa Thomas; ***D:*** Ken Cameron; ***W:*** John Alsop, Sue Smith. *AAE, NEW*

The Brides of Dracula 🦴🦴½ **1960** A young French woman unknowingly frees a vampire. He wreaks havoc, sucking blood and creating more of the undead to carry out his evil deeds. One of the better Hammer vampire films. **86m/C VHS, LV.** *GB* Peter Cushing, Martita Hunt, Yvonne Monlaur, Freda Jackson, David Peel, Mona Washbourne; ***D:*** Terence Fisher. *MCA, FCT*

Brides of the Beast *Woof! Brides of Blood; Grave Desires; Island of the Living Horror* **1968** Filipino radiation monsters get their jollies by eating beautiful young naked women. Newly arrived research scientist and his bride oppose this custom. First in a series of "Blood Island" horrors. **85m/C VHS, Beta.** *PH* John Ashley, Kent Taylor, Beverly Hills, Eva Darren, Mario Montenegro; ***D:*** Eddie Romero, Gerardo (Gerry) De Leon. *NO*

The Brides Wore Blood *Woof!* **1984** Four prospective brides are mysteriously murdered, but one is brought back to life and becomes a vampire's mate. **86m/C VHS, Beta.** *NO*

Brideshead Revisited 🦴🦴🦴 **1981** The acclaimed British miniseries based on the Evelyn Waugh classic about an Edwardian young man who falls under the spell of a wealthy aristocratic family and struggles to retain his integrity and values. On six tapes. **540m/C VHS, Beta.** *GB* Jeremy Irons, Anthony Andrews, Diana Quick, Laurence Olivier, John Gielgud, Claire Bloom, Stephane Audran, Mona Washbourne, John Le Mesurier, Charles Keating; ***D:*** Charles Sturridge, Michael Lindsay-Hogg; ***M:*** Geoffrey Burgon. *MOV, FUS, FCT*

The Bridge 🦴🦴 *Die Brucke* **1959** In 1945, two days before the end of WWII, seven German schoolboys are drafted to defend an unimportant bridge from American tanks. Emotional anti-war film based on the autobiographical novel of Manfred Gregor. German with subtitles. **102m/B VHS.** *GE* Fritz Wepper, Volker Bohnet, Franz Glaubrecht, Karl Michael Balzer, Gunther Hoffman; ***D:*** Bernhard Wicki; ***W:*** Michael Mansfield, Karl-Wilhelm Vivier; ***C:*** Gerd Von Bonen; ***M:*** Hans-Martin Majewski. Nominations: Academy Awards '59: Best Foreign Language Film. *FCT*

The Bridge at Remagen 🦴🦴½ **1969 (PG)** Based on the true story of allied attempts to capture a vital bridge before retreating German troops destroy it. For war-film buffs. **115m/C VHS, Beta.** George Segal, Robert Vaughn, Ben Gazzara, Bradford Dillman, E.G. Marshall; ***D:*** John Guillermin; ***W:*** William Roberts; ***M:*** Elmer Bernstein. *NO*

The Bridge of San Luis Rey 🦴🦴🦴 **1944** A priest investigates the famous bridge collapse in Lima, Peru that left five people dead. Based upon the novel by Thornton Wilder. **89m/B VHS, Beta, LV.** Lynn Bari, Francis Lederer, Louis Calhern, Akim Tamiroff, Donald Woods, Alla Nazimova, Blanche Yurka; ***D:*** Rowland V. Lee. Nominations: Academy Awards '44: Best Original Score. *NWV, IME*

The Bridge on the River Kwai 🦴🦴🦴🦴 **1957** Award-winning adaptation of the Pierre Bouelle novel about the battle of wills between a Japanese POW camp commander and a British colonel over the construction of a rail bridge, and the parallel efforts by escaped prisoner Holden to destroy it. Holden's role was originally cast for Cary Grant. Memorable too for whistling "Colonel Bogey March." Because the writers were blacklisted, Bouelle (who spoke no English) was credited as screenwriter. **161m/C VHS, Beta, LV.** *GB* William Holden, Alec Guinness, Jack Hawkins, Sessue Hayakawa, James Donald, Geoffrey Horne, Andre Morell, Ann Sears; ***D:*** David Lean; ***W:*** Michael Wilson, Carl Foreman; ***C:*** Jack Hildyard; ***M:*** Malcolm Arnold. Academy Awards '57: Best Actor (Guinness), Best Adapted Screenplay, Best Color Cinematography, Best Director (Lean), Best Film Editing, Best Picture, Best Original Score; British Academy Awards '57: Best Actor (Guinness), Best Film, Best Screenplay; Directors Guild of America Awards '57: Best Director (Lean); Golden Globe Awards '58: Best Actor—Drama (Guinness), Best Director (Lean), Best Film—Drama; National Board of Review Awards '57: 10 Best Films of the Year, Best Actor (Guinness), Best Director (Lean), Best Supporting Actor (Hayakawa); Nominations: Academy Awards '57: Best Supporting Actor (Hayakawa). *COL, BTV, HMV*

Bridge to Hell 🦴½ **1987** A group of allied P.O.W.s try to make their way to the American front during WWII in Yugoslavia. A heavily guarded bridge occupied by Nazi troops stands between them and freedom. A special introduction by Michael Dudikoff doing martial arts. **94m/C VHS.** Jeff Connors, Francis Ferre, Andy Forrest, Paky Valente; ***D:*** Umberto Lenzi. *CAN*

The Bridge to Nowhere 🦴🦴 **1986** Five city kids go hunting and back-packing in the New Zealand wilderness, and are hunted by a maniacal backwoodsman. **82m/C VHS, Beta.** *NZ* Bruno Lawrence, Alison Routledge, Margaret Umbers, Philip Gordon; ***D:*** Ian Mune. *NLC*

Bridge to Silence 🦴🦴 **1989** A young hearing-impaired mother's life begins to crumble following the death of her husband in a car crash. Her mother tries to get custody of her daughter and a friend applies romantic pressure. Made for TV melodrama features Matlin in her first television speaking role. **95m/C VHS.** Marlee Matlin, Lee Remick, Josef Sommer, Michael O'Keefe, Allison Silva, Candice Brecker; ***D:*** Karen Arthur. *FRH*

Bridge to Terabithia **1985** An imaginative girl and a young boy learn the joys of friendship in a magic make-believe kingdom called Terabithia. Adapted from the novel by Katherine Paterson. Originally aired by PBS for the "Wonderworks" television series. **58m/C VHS.** Annette O'Toole, Julian Coutts, Julie Beaulieu; ***D:*** Eric Till. *PME, HMV, FCT*

A Bridge Too Far 🦴🦴 **1977 (PG)** A meticulous recreation of one of the most disastrous battles of WWII, the Allied defeat at Arnhem in 1944. Misinformation, adverse conditions, and overconfidence combined to prevent the Allies from capturing six bridges that connected Holland to the German border. **175m/C VHS, Beta, LV.** *GB* Sean Connery, Robert Redford, James Caan, Michael Caine, Elliott Gould, Gene Hackman, Laurence Olivier, Ryan O'Neal, Liv Ullmann, Dirk Bogarde, Hardy Kruger, Arthur Hill, Edward Fox, Anthony Hopkins; ***D:*** Richard Attenborough; ***W:*** William Goldman; ***C:*** Geoffrey Unsworth; ***M:*** John Addison. British Academy Awards '77: Best Supporting Actor (Fox); National Society of Film Critics Awards '77: Best Supporting Actor (Fox). *MGM, FOX*

The Bridges at Toko-Ri 🦴🦴🦴½ **1955** Based on the James A. Michener novel, the rousing war-epic about a lawyer being summoned by the Navy to fly bombing missions during the Korean War. A powerful anti-war statement. **103m/C VHS, Beta, LV.** William Holden, Grace Kelly, Fredric March, Mickey Rooney, Robert Strauss, Earl Holliman, Keiko Awaji, Charles McGraw; ***D:*** Mark Robson; ***W:*** Valentine Davies; ***C:*** Loyal Griggs. Academy Awards '55: Best Special Effects; Nominations: Academy Awards '55: Best Film Editing. *PAR*

The Bridges of Madison County 🦴🦴🦴 **1995 (PG-13)** Robert Kincaid (Eastwood) is on assignment in 1965 Iowa to photograph Madison County's scenic covered bridges. Only problem is he gets lost and stops for directions at Francesca Johnson's (Streep) farmhouse. There's an immediate attraction between the repressed Italian war-bride-turned-farm-wife and the charismatic world traveler, which they act on in four short days. Much of the treacle from Robert James Waller's novel has been fortunately abandoned but the mature romance remains. 64-year-old Eastwood exudes low-key sexiness while Streep (with a light Italian accent) is all earthy warmth. Fans of both book and stars should be pleased, though the leisurely paced film takes too long to get started. **135m/C VHS, LV.** Clint Eastwood, Meryl Streep, Victor Slezak, Annie Corley, Jim Haynie; ***D:*** Clint Eastwood; ***W:*** Richard LaGravenese; ***C:*** Jack N. Green; ***M:*** Lennie Niehaus. Nominations: Academy Awards '95: Best Actress (Streep); Golden Globe Awards '96: Best Actress—Drama (Streep), Best Film—Drama; Screen Actors Guild Award '95: Best Actress (Streep). *WAR*

Brief Encounter 🦴🦴🦴🦴 **1946** Based on Noel Coward's "Still Life" from "Tonight at 8:30," two middle-aged, middle-class people become involved in a short and bittersweet romance in WWII

England. Intensely romantic, underscored with Rachmaninoff's Second Piano Concerto. **86m/B VHS, Beta.** *GB* Celia Johnson, Trevor Howard, Stanley Holloway, Cyril Raymond, Joyce Carey; ***D:*** David Lean; ***W:*** Noel Coward; ***C:*** Robert Krasker. National Board of Review Awards '46: 10 Best Films of the Year; New York Film Critics Awards '46: Best Actress (Johnson); Nominations: Academy Awards '46: Best Actress (Johnson), Best Director (Lean), Best Screenplay. *PAR, INJ, HMV*

A Brief History of Time **1992 (G)** A stunning documentary about physicist Stephen Hawking, the author of the popular book "Brief History of Time." Crippled by Lou Gehrig's Disease, Hawking narrates the film in the computer-synthesized voice he uses to speak. Interviews with family, friends, and colleagues, bring Hawking's scientific theories to light. **85m/C VHS, Beta.** Stephen Hawking; ***D:*** Errol Morris; ***W:*** Stephen Hawking; ***C:*** John Bailey; ***M:*** Philip Glass. Sundance Film Festival '92: Filmmakers Trophy. *PAR, BTV, WSH*

The Brig **1964** A film by Jonas Mekas documenting the Living Theatre's infamous performance of Kenneth H. Brown's experimental play. Designed by Julian Beck. **65m/B VHS, Beta.** Adolfas Mekas, Jim Anderson, Warren Finnerty, Henry Howard, Tom Lillard, James Tiroff, Gene Lipton; ***D:*** John Mekas. Venice Film Festival '64: Best Documentary. *MFV, FCT, TPV*

Brigadoon **1954** The story of a magical, 18th century Scottish village which awakens once every 100 years and the two modern-day vacationers who stumble upon it. Main highlight is the Lerner and Loewe score. ♫Brigadoon; Almost Like Being in Love; I'll Go Home With Bonnie Jean; Wedding Dance; From This Day On; Heather on the Hill; Waitin' For My Dearie; Once in the Highlands. **108m/C VHS, Beta, LV, 8mm.** Gene Kelly, Van Johnson, Cyd Charisse; ***D:*** Vincente Minnelli; ***C:*** Joseph Ruttenberg; ***M:*** Alan Jay Lerner, Frederick Loewe. Nominations: Academy Awards '54: Best Art Direction/Set Decoration (Color), Best Costume Design (Color), Best Sound. *MGM, TLF*

Brigham Young: Frontiersman **1940** Somewhat interesting story about the pioneering Mormons and their founding of Salt Lake City. Under the leadership of Brigham Young (Jagger), they set out across the plains, battling hardships and starvation along the way. An emphasis was placed on the historical rather than the religious in an effort not to scare off moviegoers, but the picture failed at the box office anyway. Based on the story by Louis Bromfield. **114m/C VHS.** Tyrone Power, Linda Darnell, Dean Jagger, Brian Donlevy, John Carradine, Jane Darwell, Jean Rogers, Mary Astor, Vincent Price; ***D:*** Henry Hathaway; ***W:*** Lamar Trotti; ***C:*** Arthur C. Miller. *FXV*

Bright Angel ½ **1991 (R)** Road movie pairs an unconventional team: George wants to visit his aunt to see if she's heard from his mother who ran off with another man; Luey is a free-spirit trying to free her brother from jail. Good performances by Mulroney, Taylor, & Pullman. Ford adapted two of his short stories, "Childern" and "Great Falls" for the gritty and uncompromising script of life in the modern west. **94m/C VHS.** Dermot Mulroney, Lili Taylor, Sam Shepard, Valerie Perrine, Burt Young, Bill Pullman, Benjamin Bratt, Mary Kay Place, Delroy Lindo, Kevin Tighe, Sheila McCarthy; ***D:*** Michael Fields; ***W:*** Richard Ford; ***M:*** Christopher Young. *HBO*

Bright Eyes **1934 (PG)** Shirley Temple stars as an adorable orphan caught between foster parents. Submitted for an MPAA rating when the video was released. Also available colorized. **84m/B VHS, Beta.** Shirley Temple, James Dunn, Lois Wilson, Jane Withers, Judith Allen; ***D:*** David Butler. *FOX, MLT* .

Bright Lights, Big City **1988 (R)** Based on Jay McInerney's popular novel, Fox plays a contemporary yuppie working in Manhattan as a magazine journalist. As his world begins to fall apart, he embarks on an endless cycle of drugs and nightlife. Fox is poorly cast, and his character is hard to care for as he becomes more and more dissolute. Although McInerney wrote his own screenplay, the intellectual abstractness of the novel can't be captured on film. **110m/C VHS, Beta, LV.** Michael J. Fox, Kiefer Sutherland, Phoebe Cates, Frances Sternhagen, Swoosie Kurtz, Tracy Pollan, Jason Robards Jr., John Houseman, Dianne Wiest, Charlie Schlatter, William Hickey; ***D:*** James Bridges; ***C:*** Gordon Willis. *MGM*

Bright Smiler ½ **1985** A made-for-British-television mystery about a writer who retires to her favorite spa and falls into the hands of a malevolent masseuse. **60m/C VHS, Beta.** *GB* Janet Suzman. *PSM*

Brighton Beach Memoirs ½ *Neil Simon's Brighton Beach Memoirs* **1986 (PG-13)** The film adaptation of the popular (and semiautobiographical) Neil Simon play. Poignant comedy/drama about a young Jewish boy's coming of age in Depression-era Brooklyn. Followed by "Biloxi Blues" and "Broadway Bound." **108m/C VHS, Beta, LV.** Blythe Danner, Bob Dishy, Judith Ivey, Jonathan Silverman, Brian Drillinger, Stacey Glick, Lisa Waltz, Jason Alexander; ***D:*** Gene Saks; ***W:*** Neil Simon; ***C:*** John Bailey; ***M:*** Michael Small. *MCA, FCT*

Brighton Rock *Young Scarface* **1947** Sterling performances highlight this seamy look at the British underworld. Attenborough is Pinkie Brown, a small-time hood who ends up committing murder. He manipulates a waitress to get himself off the hook, but things don't go exactly as he plans. Based on the novel by Graham Greene. **92m/B VHS.** *GB* Richard Attenborough, Hermione Baddeley, William Hartnell, Carol Marsh, Nigel Stock, Wylie Watson, Alan Wheatley, George Carney, Reginald Purdell; ***D:*** John Boulting. *DVT, HEG*

Brighton Strangler **1945** An actor who plays a murderer assumes the role of the strangler after suffering from a concussion. Decent psychodrama. **67m/B VHS, Beta.** John Loder, June Duprez, Miles Mander; ***D:*** Max Nosseck. *NO*

The Brighton Strangler/Before Dawn **1945** A mystery double feature: In "The Brighton Strangler," an actor takes his part too seriously as he murders Londoners at night; in "Before Dawn" a brilliant scientist turns to a life of murderous crime. **128m/B VHS, Beta.** John Loder, June Duprez, Miles Mander, Stuart Oland, Dorothy Wilson. *TTC*

Brighty of the Grand Canyon ½ **1967** The spunky donkey Brighty roams across the Grand Canyon in search of adventure. He finds friendship with a gold-digging old prospector who hits pay dirt. **90m/C VHS, Beta.** Joseph Cotten, Pat Conway, Dick Foran, Karl Swenson; ***D:*** Norman Foster. *AHV, KAR*

A Brilliant Disguise ½ **1993 (R)** Sportswriter gets involved with an artist who turns out to have multiple personality disorder and a sinister psychiatrist. Then his friends start to turn up dead but things aren't exactly what they seem. **97m/C VHS, LV.** Lysette Anthony, Anthony John Denison, Corbin Bernsen, Gregory McKinney, Robert Shafer; ***D:*** Nick Vallelonga; ***W:*** Nick Vallelonga. *PSM*

Brimstone & Treacle **1982 (R)** Weird, obsessive psychodrama in which a young rogue (who may or may not be an actual agent of the Devil) infiltrates the home of a staid British family caring for their comatose adult daughter. **85m/C VHS, Beta.** *GB* Sting, Denholm Elliott, Joan Plowright, Suzanna Hamilton; ***D:*** Richard Loncraine; ***W:*** Dennis Potter. Montreal World Film Festival '82: Best Film. *MGM*

Bring Me the Head of Alfredo Garcia **1974 (R)** Peckinpah falters in this poorly paced outing. American piano player on tour in Mexico finds himself entwined with a gang of bloodthirsty bounty hunters. Bloody and confused. **112m/C VHS.** Warren Oates, Isela Vega, Gig Young, Robert Webber, Helmut Dantine, Emilio Fernandez, Kris Kristofferson; ***D:*** Sam Peckinpah; ***W:*** Sam Peckinpah, Gordon Dawson. *MGM*

Bring Me the Vampire **1961** A wealthy baron must endure a night of terror in order to receive an inheritance. **100m/B VHS.** *MX* Maria Eugenia San Martin, Hector Godoy, Joaquin Vargas. *SNC, MOV*

Bringing Up Baby **1938** The quintessential screwball comedy, featuring Hepburn as a giddy socialite with a "baby" leopard, and Grant as the unwitting object of her affections. One ridiculous situation after another adds up to high speed fun. Hepburn looks lovely, the supporting actors are in fine form, and director Hawks manages the perfect balance of control and mayhem. From a story by Hagar Wilde, who helped Nichols with the screenplay. Also available in a colorized version. **103m/B VHS, Beta, LV.** Katharine Hepburn, Cary Grant, May Robson, Charlie Ruggles, Walter Catlett, Fritz Feld, Jonathan Hale, Barry Fitzgerald, Ward Bond; ***D:*** Howard Hawks; ***W:*** Dudley Nichols; ***C:*** Russell Metty. *TTC, HMV, BTV*

Brink of Life ½ *Nara Livet* **1957** Three pregnant women in a hospital maternity ward await the impending births with mixed feelings. Early Bergman; in Swedish with English subtitles. **82m/B VHS, Beta.** *SW* Eva Dahlbeck, Bibi Andersson, Ingrid Thulin, Babro Ornas, Max von Sydow, Erland Josephson, Gunnar Sjoberg; ***D:*** Ingmar Bergman. Cannes Film Festival '58: Best Actress (Dahlbeck), Best Actress (Andersson, Thulin), Best Director (Bergman). *VYY, INJ*

Brink's Job **1978 (PG)** Recreates the "crime of the century," Tony Pino's heist of 2.7 million dollars from a Brink's truck. The action picks up five days before the statute of limitations is about to run out. **103m/C VHS, Beta.** Peter Falk, Peter Boyle, Warren Oates, Gena Rowlands, Paul Sorvino, Sheldon Leonard, Allen (Goorwitz) Garfield; ***D:*** William Friedkin; ***W:*** Walon Green; ***M:*** Richard Rodney Bennett. Nominations: Academy Awards '78: Best Art Direction/Set Decoration. *MCA*

Britannia Hospital ½ **1982 (R)** This is a portrait of a hospital at its most chaotic: the staff threatens to strike, demonstrators surround the hospital, a nosey BBC reporter pursues an anxious professor, and the eagerly-anticipated royal visit degenerates into a total shambles. **111m/C VHS, Beta.** *GB* Malcolm McDowell, Leonard Rossiter, Graham Crowden, Joan Plowright, Mark Hamill, Alan Bates; ***D:*** Lindsay Anderson. Nominations: Cannes Film Festival '82: Best Film. *REP*

British Intelligence ½ **1940** Silly American-made film about British espionage. Boris Karloff plays a butler (who is also a spy) trapped by an agent who visits the home of a British bureaucrat. Half-baked story that doesn't hold up. **62m/B VHS.** Boris Karloff, Margaret Lindsay, Maris Wrixon, Holmes Herbert, Leonard Mudie, Bruce Lester; ***D:*** Terry Morse. *NOS, SNC, MLB*

A Brivele der Mamen *A Letter to Mother; A Letter to Mama* **1938** A Jewish mother does her best to hold her fragile family together, in spite of the ravages of war and poverty. Her travails take her and her family from the Polish Ukraine to New York City. In Yiddish with English subtitles. **90m/C VHS, Beta.** *PL* Berta Gersten, Lucy Gerhman, Misha Gerhman, Edmund Zayenda; ***D:*** Joseph Green. *ERG, INJ*

Broadcast News ½ **1987 (R)** The acclaimed, witty analysis of network news shows, dealing with the three-way romance between a driven career-woman producer, an ace nebbish reporter and a brainless, popular on-screen anchorman. Incisive and funny, though often simply idealistic. **132m/C VHS, Beta, LV.** William Hurt, Albert Brooks, Holly Hunter, Jack Nicholson, Joan Cusack, Robert Prosky, Lois Chiles, Gennie James; ***Cameos:*** John Cusack; ***D:*** James L. Brooks; ***W:*** James L. Brooks; ***C:*** Michael Ballhaus; ***M:*** Bill Conti, Michael Gore. Los Angeles Film Critics Association Awards '87: Best Actress (Hunter); National Board of Review Awards '87: 10 Best Films of the Year, Best Actress (Hunter); Nominations: Academy Awards '87: Best Actor (Hurt), Best Actress (Hunter), Best Cinematography, Best Film Editing, Best Original Screenplay, Best Picture, Best Supporting Actor (Brooks). *FOX*

Broadway Bill *Strictly Confidential* **1934** A man decides to abandon his nagging wife and his job in her family's business for the questionable pleasures of owning a racehorse known as Broadway Bill. This racetrack comedy was also remade by Frank Capra in 1951 as "Riding High." **90m/C VHS, Beta, LV.** Warner Baxter, Myrna Loy, Walter Connolly, Helen Vinson, Margaret Hamilton, Frankie Darro; ***D:*** Frank Capra. *PAR*

Broadway Bound ½ *Neil Simon's Broadway Bound* **1992** The final film in Simon's trilogy (preceded by "Brighton Beach Memoirs" and "Biloxi Blues"). This time the playwright's alter ego, Eugene Morris Jerome, is ready to leave Brooklyn for good, hoping to make it as a comedy writer for a radio show. Meanwhile, his mother decides what to do about his unfaithful father. Made for television. **90m/C VHS.** Jonathan Silverman, Anne Bancroft, Jerry Orbach, Corey Parker, Hume Cronyn, Michele Lee; ***D:*** Paul Bogart; ***W:*** Neil Simon. *ABC*

Broadway Danny Rose ꝏꝏꝏ½ **1984 (PG)** One of Woody Allen's best films, a hilarious, heart-rending anecdotal comedy about a third-rate talent agent involved in one of his client's infidelities. The film magically unfolds as show business veterans swap Danny Rose stories at a delicatessen. Allen's Danny Rose is pathetically lovable. **85m/B VHS, Beta, LV.** Woody Allen, Mia Farrow, Nick Apollo Forte, Sandy Baron, Milton Berle, Howard Cosell; ***D:*** Woody Allen; ***W:*** Woody Allen; ***C:*** Gordon Willis. British Academy Awards '84: Best Original Screenplay; Writers Guild of America '84: Best Original Screenplay; Nominations: Academy Awards '84: Best Director (Allen), Best Original Screenplay. *VES*

The Broadway Drifter ꝏꝏ **1927** A silent Jazz Age drama about a playboy who repents his decadent ways by opening a girls' health school. Complications ensue. **90m/B VHS, Beta, 8mm.** George Walsh, Dorothy Hall, Bigelow Cooper, Arthur Donaldson; ***D:*** Bernard McEveety Sr. *VYY*

Broadway Limited ꝏꝏ *The Baby Vanishes* **1941** Three aspiring actors head for the Great White Way with a baby to use as a prop. Thinking the baby kidnapped, the police make things tough for the trio. McLaglen was wasted on this one, which was apparently made to show off the considerable assets of Woodworth. **75m/B VHS.** Victor McLaglen, Marjorie Woodworth, Dennis O'Keefe, Patsy Kelly, ZaSu Pitts, Leonid Kinskey, George E. Stone; ***D:*** Gordon Douglas. *NOS*

Broadway Melody ꝏꝏ½ **1929** Early musical in which two sisters hope for fame on Broadway, and encounter a wily song and dance man who traps both their hearts. Dated, but still charming, with a lovely score. Considered the great granddaddy of all MGM musicals; followed by three more melodies in 1935, 1937, and 1940. ♫Broadway Melody; Give My Regards to Broadway; Truthful Parson Brown; The Wedding of the Painted Doll; The Boy Friend; You Were Meant For Me; Love Boat; Broadway Babies. **104m/B VHS, Beta.** Bessie Love, Anita Page, Charles King, Jed Prouty, Kenneth Thomson, Edward Dillon, Mary Doran; ***D:*** Harry Beaumont; ***M:*** Nacio Herb Brown, Arthur Freed. Academy Awards '29: Best Picture; Nominations: Academy Awards '29: Best Actress (Love), Best Director (Beaumont). *MGM, BTV*

Broadway Melody of 1936 ꝏꝏꝏ **1935** Exceptional musical comedy with delightful performances from Taylor and Powell. Benny is a headline-hungry columnist who tries to entrap Taylor by using Powell. ♫Broadway Melody; Broadway Rhythm; You Are My Lucky Star; I've Got a Feeling You're Fooling; All I Do Is Dream of You; Sing Before Breakfast; On a Sunday Afternoon. **110m/B VHS, Beta.** Jack Benny, Eleanor Powell, Robert Taylor, Una Merkel, Sid Silvers, Buddy Ebsen; ***D:*** Roy Del Ruth; ***C:*** Charles Rosher; ***M:*** Nacio Herb Brown, Arthur Freed. Nominations: Academy Awards '35: Best Original Screenplay, Best Picture. *MGM, MLB, CCB*

Broadway Melody of 1938 ꝏꝏ½ **1937** Third entry in the melody series lacks the sparkle of "Broadway Melody of 1936" despite the all-star cast. Lots of singing and dancing without much charm. Two bright spots: a young Garland singing the now famous "Dear Mr. Gable" and the always lovely Powell's dance numbers. ♫Broadway Rhythm; Dear Mr. Gable (You Made Me Love You); A New Pair of Shoes; Yours and Mine; I'm Feeling Like a Million; Everybody Sing; Follow in My Footsteps; Your Broadway and My Broadway; Sun Showers. **110m/B VHS, Beta.** Eleanor Powell, Sophie Tucker, George Murphy, Judy Garland, Robert Taylor, Buddy Ebsen, Binnie Barnes; ***D:*** Roy Del Ruth; ***C:*** William H. Daniels; ***M:*** Nacio Herb Brown, Arthur Freed. *MGM*

Broadway Melody of 1940 ꝏꝏ½ **1940** The last entry in the melody series features the only screen teaming of Astaire and Powell. The flimsy plot is just an excuse for a potent series of Cole Porter musical numbers. ♫I Concentrate on You; I've Got My Eye on You; Begin the Beguine; I am the Captain; Please Don't Monkey With Broadway; Between You and Me; Il Bacio. **103m/B VHS, Beta, LV.** Fred Astaire, Eleanor Powell, George Murphy, Frank Morgan, Ian Hunter; ***D:*** Norman Taurog. *MGM, TTC, FCT*

Broadway Rhythm ꝏꝏ½ **1944** A too-long look at Broadway behind-the-scenes. Murphy plays a Broadway producer who hopes to land a Hollywood star for his new show. She rejects his offer in favor of a show being produced by his father. Just a chance to showcase a number of popular vaudeville acts, songs, and the music of Tommy Dorsey and his orchestra. ♫All the Things You Are; That Lucky Fellow; In Other Words; Seventeen; All In Fun; Brazilian Boogie; What Do You Think I Am?; Somebody Loves Me; Milkman Keep Those Bottles Quiet. **111m/C VHS.** George Murphy, Ginny Simms, Charles Winninger, Gloria De Haven, Nancy Walker, Ben Blue, Lena Horne, Eddie Anderson; ***D:*** Roy Del Ruth; ***W:*** Dorothy Kingsley, Harry Clork. *MGM*

Broadway Serenade ꝏꝏ½ **1939** Melodramatic musical in which a songwriter (Ayres) and his wife, singer MacDonald, make career choices that destroy their marriage. ♫Broadway Serenade for the Lonely Heart; High Flyin'; One Look at You; Time Changes Everything; Un Bel Di; No Time to Argue; Italian Street Song; Les Filles de Cadiz; Musical Contract. **114m/B VHS.** Jeanette MacDonald, Lew Ayres, Ian Hunter, Frank Morgan, Wally Vernon, Rita Johnson, Virginia Grey, William Gargan; ***D:*** Robert Z. Leonard; ***W:*** Charles Lederer. *MGM*

Broadway to Cheyenne ꝏ *From Broadway to Cheyenne* **1932** A group of big city gangsters try to take over a small western town but are opposed by heroic cowboys. **53m/B VHS, Beta.** Rex Bell, George "Gabby" Hayes, Marceline Day, Robert Ellis, Alan Bridge, Matthew Betz; ***D:*** Harry Fraser. *GPV, RXM, VDM*

Broken Angel ꝏ½ **1988** Jamie seemed to be such a nice girl, with good looks and great grades—and membership in a notorious street gang. When Jamie disappears, her family discovers her secret activities and dad tries to find his wayward little girl. Melodramatic made for television goo. **94m/C VHS.** William Shatner, Susan Blakely, Erika Eleniak, Roxann Biggs; ***D:*** Richard T. Heffron. *MGM*

Broken Arrow ꝏꝏ½ **1950** A U.S. scout befriends Cochise and the Apaches, and helps settlers and Indians live in peace together in the 1870s. Acclaimed as the first Hollywood film to side with the Indians, and for Chandler's portrayal of Cochise. **93m/C VHS, Beta.** James Stewart, Jeff Chandler, Will Geer, Debra Paget, Basil Ruysdael, Arthur Hunnicutt, Jay Silverheels; ***D:*** Delmer Daves; ***W:*** Albert Maltz; ***C:*** Ernest Palmer. Nominations: Academy Awards '50: Best Color Cinematography, Best Screenplay, Best Supporting Actor (Chandler). *FOX*

Broken Arrow ꝏꝏ **1995 (R)** Air Force pilot Vic Deakins (Travolta) rips off a couple of nuclear weapons during a routine exercise over the Utah desert. Deakins' ex-co-pilot Riley Hale (Slater), with help from spunky park ranger Terry Carmichael (Mathis), sets out to find and retrieve the warheads before the big bang. Hong Kong action king Woo once again tries his hand at the big-budget Hollywood action extravaganza, with mixed results. Triple script whammy of cheesy dialogue, continuity problems, and predictability undercuts, but doesn't obscure, his talent for choreographing mayhem. Travolta plays the All-American Boy as creepily charming psychotic to great effect. **108m/C VHS.** John Travolta, Christian Slater, Samantha Mathis, Delroy Lindo, Bob Gunton, Frank Whaley, Howie Long; ***D:*** John Woo; ***W:*** Graham Yost; ***C:*** Peter Levy; ***M:*** Hans Zimmer. Nominations: MTV Movie Awards '96: Best Villain (Travolta), Best Action Sequence. *FXV*

Broken Badge ꝏꝏꝏ *The Rape of Richard Beck* **1985** Crenna stars as a macho, chauvinistic cop whose attitude towards rape victims changes dramatically after he himself is raped by a couple of thugs. Excellent TV movie. **100m/C VHS.** Richard Crenna, Meredith Baxter, Pat Hingle, Frances Lee McCain, Cotter Smith, George Dzundza, Joanna Kerns; ***D:*** Karen Arthur; ***W:*** James G. Hirsch; ***M:*** Peter Bernstein. *SIM, VTR*

Broken Blossoms ꝏꝏꝏ½ **1919** One of Griffith's most widely acclaimed films, photographed by Billy Bitzer, about a young Chinaman in London's squalid Limehouse district hoping to spread the peaceful philosophy of his Eastern religion. He befriends a pitiful street waif who is mistreated by her brutal father, resulting in tragedy. Silent. Revised edition contains introduction from Gish and a newly-recorded score. **102m/B VHS, Beta, LV.** Lillian Gish, Richard Barthelmess, Donald Crisp; ***D:*** D.W. Griffith. *NOS, MRV, HHT*

The Broken Chain ꝏꝏ½ **1993** In the mid 18th-century Joseph Brant (Schweig), a member of the Mohawk tribe, is sent away to be educated by the British. When he returns, his loyalties are divided between his Native American roots and his English mentor, Sir William Johnson (Brosnan). His boyhood friend Lohaheo (White Shirt) disdains Joseph's white man ways, leading to tragic consequences. Historical background features the French and Indian Wars, the splintering of the Iroquois Confederacy, and the coming of the American Revolution. Filmed on location in Virginia. Made for television. **93m/C VHS.** Eric Schweig, Wes Studi, Buffy Saint Marie, Pierce Brosnan, J.C. White Shirt, Floyd "Red Crow" Westerman, Graham Greene, Elaine Bilstad, Kim Snyder; ***D:*** Lamont Johnson; ***W:*** Earl W. Wallace; ***M:*** Charles Fox. *TTC*

Broken Harvest ꝏꝏ½ **1995** Jimmy O'Leary remembers his youth in rural 1950s Ireland when a poor wheat harvest led to his family's financial demise and a feud between his father (Lane) and neighbor Josie McCarthy (O'Brien) threatened to destroy their lives. The men fought side by side for Ireland's independence, but the friendship dissolved when they took different sides during the ensuing civil war, and fought over Jimmy's mother. Strong performances and the beautiful West Cork and Wicklow location shots provide a nice balance to the uneven narrative. The black and white scenes were actually filmed in the mid-'80s when the independently-financed project was begun. Adapted from O'Callaghan's own story "The Shilling." **101m/C VHS.** *IR* Colin Lane, Niall O'Brien, Marian Quinn, Darren McHugh, Joy Florish, Joe Jeffers, Pete O'Reilly, Michael Crowley; ***D:*** Maurice O'Callaghan; ***W:*** Maurice O'Callaghan; ***C:*** Jack Conroy; ***M:*** Patrick Cassidy. *NYR*

Broken Hearts of Broadway ꝏꝏ **1923** Stories of heartbreak and success along the Great White Way. **85m/B VHS.** Colleen Moore, John Walker, Alice Lake, Tully Marshall, Creighton Hale; ***D:*** Irving Cummings. *GPV*

Broken Lance ꝏꝏꝏ½ **1954** Western remake of "House of Strangers" that details the dissolution of a despotic cattle baron's family. Beautifully photographed. **96m/C VHS, Beta, LV.** Spencer Tracy, Richard Widmark, Robert Wagner, Jean Peters, Katy Jurado, Earl Holliman, Hugh O'Brian, E.G. Marshall; ***D:*** Edward Dmytryk; ***W:*** Philip Yordan. Academy Awards '54: Best Story; Nominations: Academy Awards '54: Best Supporting Actress (Jurado). *FOX*

The Broken Mask ꝏꝏ **1928** A doctor performs remarkable plastic surgery on a patient, but when the patient becomes attracted to his sweetheart, he throws the Hippocratic oath to the wind, and his patient's spiffy new look has got to go. A ground-breaker amid plastic surgery-gone-amok pieces. **58m/B VHS, Beta.** Cullen Landis, Barbara Bedford, Wheeler Oakman, James Marcus; ***D:*** James Hogan. *GPV, FCT*

Broken Melody ꝏ½ *Vagabond Violinist* **1934** An opera singer sent to prison by mistake must escape in order to return to the woman of his dreams. **62m/B VHS.** *GB* John Garrick, Margot Grahame, Merle Oberon, Austin Trevor, Charles Carson, Harry Terry; ***D:*** Bernard Vorhaus. *FCT*

Broken Mirrors ꝏꝏ½ *Gebroken Spiegels* **1985** A disturbing film which intertwines two stories of violence against women: prostitutes go about their daily business in Amsterdam, while a twisted serial killer who imprisons, photographs, and ultimately destroys his victims, draws near. An independently made chiller with staunch feminist agenda. **110m/C** *NL* Lineke Rijxman, Henriette Tol, Edda Barends, Eddie Brugman, Coby Stunnenberg; ***D:*** Marleen Gorris; ***W:*** Marleen Gorris. *ICA*

Broken Strings ✂ **1940** All-black musical in which a concert violinist must come to terms with himself after an auto accident limits the use of his left hand. **50m/B VHS, Beta.** Clarence Muse, Sybil Lewis, William Washington, Matthew "Stymie" Beard; ***D:*** Bernard B. Ray. *VYY, NOS, VCN*

Broken Trust ✂✂ **1993** Erica inherits her fabulously weathy uncle's estate but she has problems knowing who to trust now that she has all this money. Seems her husband is greedy and her sister resentful but just how far will they go to get what Erica has? **85m/C VHS.** Kimberly Foster, Nick Cassavetes, Kathryn Harris, Don Swayze, Edward Albert, Wendy MacDonald; ***D:*** Rafael Portillo. *MNC*

Broken Trust ✂✂½ **1995** Municipal judge Timothy Nash (Selleck) is recruited for a sting operation, designed to ensnare fellow judges, by two slightly-less-than-ethical feds (Atherton and McGovern). When Nash decides he doesn't like what's going on he discovers it's not going to be so easy to get out. Selleck's stoic, McGovern provides attractive ornamentation, and Atherton excels as the smarmy villain. From the novel "Court of Honor" by William P. Wood; made for cable. **90m/C VHS.** Tom Selleck, Elizabeth McGovern, William Atherton, Fritz Weaver, Marsha Mason, Charles Haid, Stanley DeSantis, Cynthia Martells; ***D:*** Geoffrey Sax; ***W:*** Joan Didion, John Gregory Dunne; ***M:*** Richard Horowitz. *TTC*

Broken Vows ✂✂½ **1987** Made for TV thriller with Jones as ghetto priest Father Joseph, who has doubts about his calling. When he gives last rites to a murder victim, he decides to help the victim's girlfriend find his killers. Based on the novel "Where the Dark Secrets Go" by Dorothy Salisbury Davis. **95m/C VHS.** Tommy Lee Jones, Annette O'Toole, M. Emmet Walsh, Milo O'Shea, David Groh, Madeline Sherwood, Jean De Baer, David Strathairn; ***D:*** Jud Taylor. *CAF*

Bronco Billy ✂✂½ **1980 (PG)** Eastwood stars as a New Jersey shoe clerk who decides to fulfill his dream of being a cowboy hero by becoming the proprietor of a rag-tag wild west show. Locke's one-note performance as a spoiled rich girl who joins up is a problem and the film's charm is as ragged as the acts. Good if you want to see Eastwood in something other than a shoot-'em-up. **117m/C VHS, Beta, LV.** Clint Eastwood, Sondra Locke, Bill McKinney, Scatman Crothers, Sam Bottoms, Geoffrey Lewis, Dan Vadis, Sierra Pecheur; ***D:*** Clint Eastwood; ***M:*** Stephen Dorff. *WAR, TLF, RXM*

Bronson Lee, Champion ✂ **1978 (PG)** Kung-fu and karate highlight this action adventure. **81m/C VHS, Beta.** Tadashi Yamashita. *NO*

Bronson's Revenge ✂½ **1979 (R)** Two frontier soldiers face constant danger as they attempt to transport death row prisoners, a large quantity of gold, and a stranded woman across the Rocky Mountains territory. **90m/C VHS.** Robert Hundar, Roy Hill, Emma Cohen. *SUN*

The Bronx Executioner ✂ **1986** Android, robot, and human interests clash in futuristic Manhattan and all martial arts hell breaks loose. Special introduction by martial arts star Michael Dudikoff. **88m/C VHS, Beta.** Rob Robinson, Margie Newton, Chuck Valenti, Gabriel Gori; ***D:*** Bob Collins. *CAN*

A Bronx Tale ✂✂✂ **1993 (R)** Vivid snapshot of a young Italian-American boy growing up in the '60s among neighborhood small-time wiseguys. As a 9-year-old Calogero witnesses mobster Sonny kill a man but doesn't rat to the police, so Sonny takes the kid under his wing. His upright bus-driving father Lorenzo doesn't approve but the kid is drawn to Sonny's apparent glamor and power. At 17, he's gotten both an education in school and on the streets but he needs to make a choice. Good period detail and excellent performances. Palminteri shows both Sonny's charisma and violence and De Niro handles the less-showy father role with finesse. Based on Palminteri's one-man play; De Niro's directorial debut. **122m/C VHS, LV.** Robert De Niro, Chazz Palminteri, Lillo Brancato, Frank Capra, Taral Hicks, Kathrine Narducci, Clem Caserta, Alfred Sauchelli Jr., Frank Pietrangolare; ***Cameos:*** Joe Pesci; ***D:*** Robert De Niro; ***W:*** Chazz Palminteri. *HBO*

The Bronx War ✂✂ **1990 (R)** Rival gangs take to the streets in this film from the director of "Hangin' with the Homeboys." A malicious gang leader tricks his gang into going to war over a girl he wants. Very violent; an unrated version available. **91m/C VHS.** Joseph B. Vasquez, Fabio Urena, Charmaine Cruz, Andre Brown, Marlene Forte, Francis Colon, Miguel Sierra, Kim West; ***D:*** Joseph B. Vasquez. *ACA*

Bronze Buckaroo ✂✂ **1939** Horse opera in which a cowpoke seeks revenge for his pa's death. Commendable performances from the all-black cast and crew. **57m/B VHS.** Herbert Jeffries, Artie Young, Rellie Hardin, Spencer Williams Jr., Clarence Brooks, F.E. Miller; ***D:*** Richard C. Kahn; ***W:*** Richard C. Kahn. *NOS, MRV, TPV*

The Brood ✂✂½ **1979 (R)** Cronenberg's inimitable biological nightmares, involving an experimentally malformed woman who gives birth to murderous demon-children that kill every time she gets angry. Extremely graphic. Not for all tastes. **92m/C VHS, Beta, LV.** *CA* Samantha Eggar, Oliver Reed, Art Hindle, Susan Hogan; ***D:*** David Cronenberg; ***W:*** David Cronenberg; ***M:*** Howard Shore. *SUE*

Broth of a Boy ✂✂½ **1959** A hungry British producer decides to film a birthday party of the oldest man in the world. The old Irishman wants a portion of the profits. Well made and thought provoking. **77m/B VHS.** *IR* Barry Fitzgerald, Harry Brogan, Tony Wright, June Thorburn, Eddie Golden; ***D:*** George Pollock. *NOS, HEG, FCT*

Brother Cadfael ✂✂½ **1994** Four episodic mysteries featuring a 12th-century Welsh soldier-turned-Benedictine monk (Jacobi), combining medieval atmosphere and politics with murder. Adapted from the novels by Ellis Peters. Hungary substitutes for the no-longer green and rural English setting of Shrewsbury. Made for British TV. Tapes available individually or as a boxed set. **300m/C VHS.** *GB* Derek Jacobi, Sean Pertwee, Tara Fitzgerald, Jonathan Firth, Norman Eshley; ***D:*** Graham Theakston. *SIG, TVC*

The Brother from Another Planet ✂✂✂ **1984** A black alien escapes from his home planet and winds up in Harlem, where he's pursued by two alien bounty hunters. Independently made morality fable by John Sayles before he hit the big time; features Sayles in a cameo as an alien bounty hunter. **109m/C VHS, Beta.** Joe Morton, Dee Dee Bridgewater, Ren Woods, Steve James, Maggie Renzi, David Strathairn; ***Cameos:*** John Sayles; ***D:*** John Sayles; ***W:*** John Sayles; ***M:*** Mason Daring. *FOX, FCT*

Brother Future **1991** T.J., a black, streetsmart city kid who thinks school and helping others is all a waste of time gets knocked out in a car accident. As he's lying unconscious, he is transported back in time to a slave auction block in the Old South. There the displaced urbanite is forced to work on a cotton plantation, and watch the stirrings of a slave revolt. T.J. sees the light and realizes how much opportunity he's been wasting in his own life. He comes to just a few moments later, but worlds away from who he was before. Part of the "Wonderworks" series. **110m/C VHS.** Phill Lewis, Frank Converse, Carl Lumbly, Vonetta McGee. *PME, HMV, BTV*

Brother John ✂✂✂ **1970 (PG)** An early look at racial tensions and labor problems. An angel goes back to his hometown in Alabama to see how things are going. **94m/C VHS, Beta.** Sidney Poitier, Will Geer, Bradford Dillman, Beverly Todd, Paul Winfield; ***D:*** James Goldstone; ***M:*** Quincy Jones. *COL, FCT*

Brother Orchid ✂✂✂ **1940** Mobster puts a henchman in charge of his gang while he vacations in Europe. Upon his return, he is deposed and wounded in an assassination attempt. Hiding out in a monastary, he plots to regain control of the gang, leading to fish outta water episodes and a change in his outlook on life. Fine cast fans through farce intelligently. **87m/B VHS, Beta.** Edward G. Robinson, Humphrey Bogart, Ann Sothern, Donald Crisp, Ralph Bellamy, Allen Jenkins, Charles D. Brown, Cecil Kellaway; ***D:*** Lloyd Bacon; ***C:*** Gaetano Antonio "Tony" Gaudio. *MGM, CCB*

Brother Sun, Sister Moon ✂✂½ **1973 (PG)** Post-'60s costume epic depicting the trials of St. Francis of Assisi as he evaluates his beliefs in Catholicism. **120m/C VHS, Beta.** Graham Faulkner, Judi Bowker, Alec Guinness, Leigh Lawson, Kenneth Cranham, Lee Montague, Valentina Cortese; ***D:*** Franco Zeffirelli; ***M:*** Donovan. Nominations: Academy Awards '73: Best Art Direction/Set Decoration. *PAR, APD, TVC*

The Brotherhood ✂✂½ **1968** Two hot-headed brothers in a Mafia syndicate clash over old vs. new methods and the changing of the Family's guard. **96m/C VHS, Beta, LV.** Kirk Douglas, Alex Cord, Irene Papas, Luther Adler, Susan Strasberg, Murray Hamilton; ***D:*** Martin Ritt; ***W:*** Lewis John Carlino; ***C:*** Boris Kaufman; ***M:*** Lalo Schifrin. *PAR*

Brotherhood of Death ✂½ **1976 (R)** Three black Vietnam veterans return to their southern hometown to get even with the Klansmen who slaughtered all of the townspeople. **85m/C VHS, Beta.** Roy Jefferson, Larry Jones, Mike Bass, Le Tari, Haskell V. Anderson; ***D:*** Bill Berry. *MPI*

Brotherhood of Justice ✂✂ **1986** Young men form a secret organization to rid their neighborhood of drug dealers and violence. As their power grows, their propriety weakens, until all are afraid of the "Brotherhood of Justice." Exciting made-for-television feature. **97m/C VHS.** Keanu Reeves, Kiefer Sutherland, Billy Zane, Joe Spano, Darren Dalton, Evan Mirand, Don Michael Paul; ***D:*** Charles Braverman; ***M:*** Brad Fiedel. *VMK, VTR*

The Brotherhood of Satan ✂✂½ **1971 (PG)** In an isolated southern town, a satanic coven persuades children to join in their devil-may-care attitude. Worthwhile. **92m/C VHS, Beta, LV.** Strother Martin, L.Q. Jones, Charles Bateman, Ahna Capri, Charles Robinson, Alvy Moore, Geri Reischi; ***D:*** Bernard McEveety. *GKK, IME*

The Brotherhood of the Rose ✂½ **1989 (PG-13)** Too many twists and turns mar the otherwise mediocre plot of this murky adaption of a book by David (First Blood) Morrell. Strauss and Morse are the C.I.A. agents marked for death and running for their lives after uncovering their boss's (Mitchum) plot of world domination. Though almost every scene takes place in a different country, the movie was in fact filmed entirely in New Zealand. Convoluted and frustratingly difficult to follow. **103m/C VHS.** Robert Mitchum, Peter Strauss, Connie Sellecca, James B. Sikking, David Morse, M. Emmet Walsh, James Hong; ***D:*** Marvin J. Chomsky. *VMK*

Brotherly Love ✂½ **1985** Good twin/bad twin made-for-TV mystery about an escaped psychopath who's out to get his businessman twin brother (Hirsch in both roles). **94m/C VHS, Beta.** Judd Hirsch, Karen Carlson, George Dzundza, Barry Primus, Lori Lethin; ***D:*** Jeff Bleckner. *FOX*

Brothers in Arms ✂✂ **1988 (R)** Savage mountainmen have developed a weird religion that requires them to hunt down and mercilessly massacre human prey. **95m/C VHS, LV.** Todd Allen, Jack Starrett, Dedee Pfeiffer; ***D:*** George J. Bloom III. *REP*

Brothers in Law ✂✂½ **1957** Wry British humor in this tale of a rookie lawyer up against a veteran judge who forces him to sink or swim. **94m/B VHS.** *GB* Richard Attenborough, Ian Carmichael, Terry-Thomas, Miles Malleson, John Le Mesurier; ***D:*** Roy Boulting; ***W:*** Roy Boulting. *NOS*

The Brothers Karamazov ✂✂✂ *Karamazov; The Murderer Dmitri Karamazov; Der Morder Dimitri Karamasoff* **1958** Hollywood adaptation of the classic novel by Dostoyevsky, in which four 19th-Century Russian brothers struggle with their desires for the same beautiful woman and with the father who brutalizes them. Incredible performances from every cast member, especially Cobb. Long and extremely intense, with fine direction from Brooks. Marilyn Monroe tried desperately to get Schell's part. **147m/C VHS, Beta.** Yul Brynner, Claire Bloom, Lee J. Cobb, William Shatner, Maria

Schell, Richard Basehart; *D:* Richard Brooks; *W:* Richard Brooks; *C:* John Alton. Nominations: Academy Awards '58: Best Supporting Actor (Cobb). *MGM, INJ*

Brother's Keeper ♂♂♂ **1992** Filmmakers Berlinger and Sinofsky document the story of the eccentric and reclusive Ward brothers, four bachelor dairy farmers who shared the same two-room shack for more than 60 years in rural New York. When Bill Ward dies, brother Delbert is accused of murder and goes to trial. The film covers a year's span in preparation for the trial and how the media attention changed the Ward's lives. **104m/C VHS, LV.** *D:* Joe Berlinger, Bruce Sinofsky. National Board of Review Awards '92: Best Feature Documentary; New York Film Critics Awards '92: Best Feature Documentary; Sundance Film Festival '92: Audience Award. *FXL, BTV*

Brothers Lionheart ♂♂½ **1985 (G)** The Lion brothers fight for life, love and liberty during the Middle Ages. **120m/C VHS, Beta.** Staffan Gotestam, Lars Soderdahl, Allan Edwall; *D:* Olle Hellbron. *NO*

The Brothers McMullen ♂♂♂ **1994 (R)** Slice of life drama finds three Irish-American brothers suddenly living under the same Long Island roof for the first time since childhood. Eldest brother Jack (Mulcahy) is a stolid high-school basketball coach married to teacher Molly (Britton) who's pressing him to have children. Cynical middle brother Barry (Burns), a writer, has just broken up with free-spirited Ann (McKay), and earnest young Patrick (McGlone) is engaged to Jewish girlfriend Susan (Albert). All three find their romantic relationships, as well as their belief in each other, tested. Generally good performances and dialogue, with Burns proving himself a triple threat as actor/writer/director. **98m/C VHS.** Edward Burns, Jack Mulcahy, Mike McGlone, Connie Britton, Shari Albert, Elizabeth P. McKay, Maxine Bahns, Jennifer Jostyn; *D:* Edward Burns; *W:* Edward Burns; *M:* Seamus Egan. Independent Spirit Awards '96: Best First Feature; Sundance Film Festival '95: Grand Jury Prize. *FXV*

Brothers of the West ♂½ **1937** Cowboy saves his brothers from being lynched by proving the guilt of the real outlaws. **56m/B VHS, Beta.** Tom Tyler, Bob Terry, Lois Wilde, Dorothy Short. *NOS, VCN, DVT*

Brothers O'Toole ♂♂ **1973 (G)** The misadventures of a pair of slick drifters who, by chance, ride into a broken-down mining town in the 1890s. **94m/C VHS, Beta.** John Astin, Steve Carlson, Pat Carroll, Hans Conried, Lee Meriwether; *D:* Richard Erdman. *NO*

The Browning Version ♂♂♂½ **1951** A lonely, unemotional classics instructor at a British boarding school realizes his failure as a teacher and as a husband. From the play by Terrence Rattigan. **89m/B VHS, Beta.** *GB* Michael Redgrave, Jean Kent, Nigel Patrick, Wilfrid Hyde-White, Bill Travers; *D:* Anthony Asquith. Cannes Film Festival '51: Best Actor (Redgrave); National Board of Review Awards '51: 5 Best Foreign Films of the Year. *HMV, MOV, FUS*

The Browning Version ♂♂½ **1994 (R)** Mediocre remake of the Terence Rattigan play, previously filmed in 1951. Austere classics professor (Finney) at prestigious British boys school is disillusioned with both his floundering career and marriage. His emotional chill drives his younger wife (Scacchi) into an affair with a visiting American science teacher (Modine). Unfortunately updated to contemporary times, which can't hide apparent mustiness. Worth seeing for Finney's superb work as the out-of-touch prof. **97m/C VHS, Beta.** Albert Finney, Greta Scacchi, Matthew Modine, Michael Gambon, Julian Sands, Ben Silverstone, Maryam D'Abo; *D:* Mike Figgis; *W:* Ronald Harwood; *M:* Mark Isham. *PAR*

Brubaker ♂♂♂ **1980 (R)** A sanctimonious drama about a reform warden who risks his life to replace brutality and corruption with humanity and integrity in a state prison farm. Powerful prison drama. **131m/C VHS, Beta, LV.** Robert Redford, Jane Alexander, Yaphet Kotto, Murray Hamilton, David Keith, Morgan Freeman, Matt Clark, M. Emmet Walsh, Everett McGill; *D:* Stuart Rosenberg; *W:* W.D. Richter, Arthur Ross; *M:* Lalo Schifrin. Nominations: Academy Awards '80: Best Original Screenplay. *FOX*

Bruce Lee: Curse of the Dragon ♂♂♂ *The Curse of the Dragon* **1993** A behind the scenes look at the continuing mystery surrounding the life and untimely death of the martial arts superstar who died in 1973 at the age of 32. Highlights the spectacular fight sequences from Lee's movies as well as footage from his funeral and an interview with his son Brandon Lee, whose own death in 1993 raised further comment about a Lee family curse. **90m/C VHS, Beta, LV.** *WAR, BTV*

Bruce Lee Fights Back From the Grave ♂ **1976 (R)** Bruce Lee returns from the grave to fight the Black Angel of Death with his feet and to wreak vengeance on the evil ones who brought about his untimely demise. **97m/C VHS, Beta.** Deborah Chaplin, Anthony Bronson; *D:* Umberto Lenzi. *MED*

Bruce Lee's Ways of Kung Fu ♂ **198?** Copious head-kicking film in honor of the long-dead star. Brings together the best from Shaolin: White Crane, Wu-Deng, Dragon-Fist, Kwun-Lun, Eagle Claws, Tiger, and Leopard in a fight against the Dragon. **87m/C VHS, Beta.** Bruce Lei, Philip Cheung, Pearl Lin. *UNI*

Bruce Le's Greatest Revenge ♂ **1980 (R)** Bruce Le, one e. Kung-fu action and martial arts fighting occur when a martial arts student gets involved in a clash between Chinese and a discriminatory European Club. **94m/C VHS, Beta.** Bruce Le. *GEM*

Bruce Li in New Guinea ♂ **1980 (PG)** Bruce Li, i, not ee. The tribe of a remote island worships the legendary Snake Pearl. Two masters of Kung-fu visit the isle and discover they must defend the daughter of the murdered chief against a cruel wizard. **98m/C VHS, Beta.** Bruce Li, Ho Chung Dao, Chen Sing; *D:* C.Y. Yang. *MGI, GEM, MRV*

Bruce Li the Invincible ♂ **1980** Cheng, the Kung-Fu killer, is pursued by the vengeance-minded Bruce. **93m/C VHS.** Bruce Li, Ho Chung Dao, Chen Sing. *MGI, MRV, GEM*

Bruce the Superhero ♂ **1979** Chop-socky action as the coattails-riding Bruce Le takes on the Black Dragon Society. **88m/C VHS, Beta.** Bruce Le. *BFV, MRV*

Bruce's Deadly Fingers ♂ **1980 (R)** Bruce Lee kept a book of deadly finger techniques for kung fu killing. When a vicious gangster kidnaps the Master's ex-girlfriend, one of his followers must rescue her and maintain the book's integrity. **90m/C VHS, Beta.** Bruce Le, Lo Lieh, Chan Wai, Nora Miao, Rose Marie, Yuen Man Chi, Chang Leih, Young Zee, Wuk Ma No Hans. *GEM*

Bruce's Fists of Vengeance ♂ **1984** Le and Lee guard master Bruce Lee's kicking secrets from an evil adversary. **87m/C VHS, Beta.** Bruce Le, Jack Lee, Ken Watanabe, Romano Kristoff, Don Gordon. *GEM*

Brussels Transit ♂♂♂ **1980** The story of a Yiddish family's arrival and adjustment to the new world of Brussels, Belgium, after WWII. In Yiddish with English subtitles. **80m/B VHS.** *D:* Samy Szlingerbaum. *INJ*

Brutal Fury ♂ **1992** Detective Molly Griffin goes undercover at a local high school and discovers a secret female vigilante group, called the "Fury," which goes after the drug dealers and rapists preying on the school's students. Teenagers with an attitude. **97m/C VHS.** Tom Campitelli, Lisa-Gabrielle Greene, Annette Gerbon, Karen Eppers, Jennifer Winder, Alan Arkus; *D:* Frederick P. Watkins. *AIP*

Brutal Glory ♂♂ **1989** Set in New York City in 1918 and based on the true story of the boxer known as "The Real McCoy." Fascinating and detailed history of a period, a champion, and the man who made it happen. **96m/C VHS.** Robert Vaughn, Timothy Brantley, Leah K. Pinsent; *D:* Koos Roets. *NO*

The Brute Man ♂♂ **1946** A young man who had been disfigured by his school mates goes out on a trail of revenge. Hatton is convincing in the title role, as in real life he was afflicted with acromegaly, an ailment that produces an enlargment of the bones in the face, hands, and feet. **62m/B VHS, Beta, LV.** Rondo Hatton, Tom Neal, Jane Adams; *D:* Jean Yarbrough. *AOV, MLB, COL*

The Buccaneer ♂♂ **1958** A swashbuckling version of the adventures of pirate Jean LaFitte and his association with President Andrew Jackson during the War of 1812. Remake of Cecille B. DeMille's 1938 production. **121m/C VHS, Beta, LV.** Yul Brynner, Charlton Heston, Claire Bloom, Inger Stevens, Charles Boyer, Henry Hull, E.G. Marshall, Lorne Greene; *D:* Anthony Quinn; *C:* Loyal Griggs; *M:* Elmer Bernstein. Nominations: Academy Awards '58: Best Costume Design. *BAR, FCT, RXM*

The Buccaneers ♂♂♂ **1995** Lavish adaptation of the Edith Wharton novel follows the adventures of four American girls in 1870s society. Nouveaux riche, the young ladies are unable to crack New York snobbery and, after vivacious Brazilian Conchita (Sorvino) manages to snag Lord Richard (Vibert), the others are encouraged by English governess Laura Testvalley (Lunghi) to try their luck in London. There, Virginia (Elliott), sister Nan (Gugino), their friend Lizzy (Kihlstedt), and Conchita all find hope and heartbreak among the English aristocracy. Wharton's novel was unfinished at her death and, though she left story notes, scripter Wadey concedes to changes. Made for TV. **288m/C VHS.** *GB* Carla Gugino, Mira Sorvino, Alison Elliott, Rya Kihlstedt, Cherie Lunghi, Connie Booth, Mark Tandy, Ronan Vibert, Jenny Agutter, Richard Huw, Greg Wise, James Frain, Michael Kitchen, Sheila Hancock, Rosemary Leach, Elizabeth Ashley, Conchata Ferrell, Peter Michael Goetz, James Rebhorn, E. Katherine Kerr; *D:* Philip Saville; *W:* Maggie Wadey; *C:* Maggie Wadey; *M:* Colin Towns. *FOX*

Buck and the Preacher ♂♂½ **1972 (PG)** A trail guide and a con man preacher join forces to help a wagon train of former slaves who are seeking to homestead out West. Poitier's debut as a director. **102m/C VHS, Beta.** Sidney Poitier, Harry Belafonte, Ruby Dee, Cameron Mitchell, Denny Miller; *D:* Sidney Poitier. *COL*

Buck Privates ♂♂½ *Rookies* **1941** Abbott and Costello star as two dim-witted tie salesmen, running from the law, who become buck privates during WWII. The duo's first great success, and the film that established the formula for each subsequent film. **84m/B VHS, Beta, LV.** Bud Abbott, Lou Costello, Shemp Howard, Lee Bowman, Alan Curtis, The Andrews Sisters; *D:* Arthur Lubin; *C:* Milton Krasner. Nominations: Academy Awards '41: Best Song ("Boogie Woogie Bugle Boy of Company B"), Best Original Score. *MCA*

Buck Privates Come Home ♂♂♂ *Rookies Come Home* **1947** Abbott and Costello return to their "Buck Privates" roles as two soldiers trying to adjust to civilian life after the war. They also try to help a French girl sneak into the United States. Funny antics culminate into a wild chase scene. **77m/B VHS.** Bud Abbott, Lou Costello, Tom Brown, Joan Shawlee, Nat Pendleton, Beverly Simmons, Don Beddoe, Don Porter, Donald MacBride; *D:* Charles T. Barton. *MCA*

Buck Rogers Conquers the Universe ♂♂ **1939** The story of Buck Rogers, written by Phil Nolan in 1928, was the first science fiction story done in the modern super-hero space genre. Many of the "inventions" seen in this movie have actually come into existence—spaceships, ray guns (lasers), anti-gravity belts—a testament to Nolan's almost psychic farsightedness. **91m/B VHS, Beta.** Buster Crabbe, Constance Moore, Jackie Moran; *D:* Ford Beebe, Saul Goodkind. *FOX*

Buck Rogers in the 25th Century ♂♂ **1979 (PG)** An American astronaut, preserved in space for 500 years, is brought back to life by a passing Draconian flagship. Outer space adventures begin when he is accused of being a spy from Earth. Based on the classic movie serial. Made for TV movie that began the popular series. Additional series episodes are available. **90m/C VHS, Beta, LV.** Gil Gerard, Pamela Hensley, Erin Gray, Henry Silva; *D:* Daniel Haller; *V:* Mel Blanc. *MCA, MOV*

A Bucket of Blood 🦴🦴🦴 **1959** Cult favorite Dick Miller stars as a sculptor with a peculiar "talent" for lifelike artwork. Corman fans will see thematic similarities to his subsequent work, "Little Shop of Horrors" (1960). "Bucket of Blood" was made in just five days, while "Little Shop of Horrors" was made in a record breaking two days. Corman horror/spoof noted for its excellent beatnik atmosphere. **66m/B VHS, Beta.** Dick Miller, Barboura Morris, Antony Carbone, Julian Burton, Ed Nelson, Bert Convy; ***D:*** Roger Corman. *NOS, RHI, SNC*

Buckeye and Blue 🦴½ **1987 (PG)** A hero turned outlaw, his 14 year-old female sidekick, and a gang known as the McCoys are all on the lam from the law in this western adventure. **94m/C VHS, Beta.** Robin Lively, Jeffery Osterhage, Rick Gibbs, Will Hannah, Kenneth Jensen, Patrick Johnston, Stuart Rogers, Michael Horse; ***D:*** J.C. Compton. *ACA*

Buckskin 🦴½ **1968** Slowmoving western about a marshall protecting townspeople from a greedy, land-grabbing cattle baron. **98m/C VHS, LV.** Barry Sullivan, Wendell Corey, Joan Caulfield, Lon Chaney Jr., John Russell, Barbara Hale, Barton MacLane, Bill Williams; ***D:*** Michael Moore. *PAR*

Buckskin Frontier 🦴½ **1943** Story is built around Western railroad construction and cattle empires in the 1860s. Cobb tries to stop the railroad from coming through by hiring Jory to do his dirty work. **75m/B VHS, Beta.** Richard Dix, Jane Wyatt, Lee J. Cobb, Albert Dekker, Victor Jory, Lola Lane, Max Baer Sr.; ***D:*** Lesley Selander. *NOS, MRV, GPV*

Bucktown 🦴½ **1975 (R)** A black man who re-opens his murdered brother's bar fights off police corruption and racism in a Southern town. **95m/C VHS, Beta.** Fred Williamson, Pam Grier, Bernie Hamilton, Thalmus Rasulala, Art Lund; ***D:*** Arthur Marks. *ORI*

Bud and Lou 🦴½ **1978** Comedy/drama recounts Abbott & Costello's rise in Hollywood. While the story, based on the book by Bob Thomas, is interesting, the two funnymen in the leads can't pull off the old classic skits. **98m/C VHS, Beta, LV.** Harvey Korman, Buddy Hackett, Michele Lee, Arte Johnson, Robert Reed; ***D:*** Robert C. Thompson. *JTC*

Buddha Assassinator 🦴 **1982** Young Kung-Fu enthusiast challenges a Ming dynasty lord to a duel to the death. **93m/C VHS, Beta.** Hwang Jang Lee, Mang Hai, Lung Fei, Chien Yueh Sheng. *WVE*

Buddy Buddy 🦴🦴½ **1981 (R)** A professional hitman's well-ordered arrangement to knock off a state's witness keeps being interrupted by the suicide attempts of a man in the next hotel room. **96m/C VHS, Beta.** Jack Lemmon, Walter Matthau, Paula Prentiss, Klaus Kinski; ***D:*** Billy Wilder; ***W:*** Billy Wilder, I.A.L. Diamond; ***C:*** Harry Stradling Jr.; ***M:*** Lalo Schifrin. *MGM*

The Buddy Holly Story 🦴🦴🦴½ **1978 (PG)** An acclaimed biography of the famed 1950s pop star, spanning the years from his meteoric career's beginnings in Lubbock to his tragic early death in the now famous plane crash. Busey performs Holly's hits himself. ♫Rock Around the Ollie Vee; That'll Be the Day; Oh, Boy; It's So Easy; Well All Right; Chantilly Lace; Peggy Sue. **113m/C VHS, Beta, LV.** Gary Busey, Don Stroud, Charles Martin Smith, Conrad Janis, William Jordan; ***D:*** Steve Rash; ***M:*** Joe Renzetti. Academy Awards '78: Best Adapted Score; National Society of Film Critics Awards '78: Best Actor (Busey); Nominations: Academy Awards '78: Best Actor (Busey), Best Sound. *COL*

The Buddy System 🦴🦴 **1983 (PG)** A tale of contemporary love and the modern myths that outline the boundaries between lovers and friends. **110m/C VHS, Beta.** Richard Dreyfuss, Susan Sarandon, Jean Stapleton, Nancy Allen, Wil Wheaton, Ed Winter, Keene Curtis; ***D:*** Glenn Jordan; ***W:*** Mary Agnes Donoghue. *FOX*

Buddy's Song 🦴🦴 **1991 (R)** A '60s coming of age tale, only in this case it's the father and not the son who needs to grow up. Dad (Daltrey) is more interested in hanging out with his no-account musician friends than in looking after his family. Although he's not above meddling in his teenage son's musical career, which could be the success his father's never was. Based on the novel by Nigel Hinton who also did the screenplay. British teen idol Hawkes (in his film debut) had a top ten hit song from the film with "The One and Only." **106m/C VHS, LV.** *GB* Roger Daltrey, Chesney Hawkes; ***W:*** Nigel Hinton. *VMK, BTV*

Buffalo Bill 🦴🦴 **1944** A light, fictionalized account of the life and career of Bill Cody, from frontier hunter to showman. **89m/C VHS, Beta.** Joel McCrea, Maureen O'Hara, Linda Darnell, Thomas Mitchell, Edgar Buchanan, Anthony Quinn, Moroni Olsen, Sidney Blackmer; ***D:*** William A. Wellman; ***C:*** Leon Shamroy. *FOX*

Buffalo Bill & the Indians 🦴🦴🦴 *Sitting Bull's History Lesson* **1976 (PG)** A perennially underrated Robert Altman historical pastiche, portraying the famous Wild West character as a charlatan and shameless exemplar of encroaching imperialism. Great all-star cast amid Altman's signature mise-en-scene chaos. **135m/C VHS, Beta.** Paul Newman, Geraldine Chaplin, Joel Grey, Will Sampson, Harvey Keitel, Burt Lancaster, Kevin McCarthy; ***D:*** Robert Altman; ***W:*** Robert Altman, Alan Rudolph; ***M:*** Richard Baskin. *FOX*

Buffalo Bill Rides Again 🦴½ **1947** With an Indian uprising on the horizon, Buffalo Bill is called in. Mr. Bill finds land swindlers pitting natives against ranchers, but there's precious little action or interest here. **68m/C VHS, Beta.** Richard Arlen, Jennifer Holt, Edward Cassidy, Edmund Cobb, Charles Stevens; ***D:*** Bernard B. Ray. *GPV*

Buffalo Girls 🦴🦴½ **1995** Western saga, set in the 1870s, tells of the lifelong friendship between hard-drinking, hard-living Calamity Jane (Huston—who's not exactly any plain Jane) and buxom, soft-hearted madam Dora DuFran (Griffith). Dora's in love (but refuses to marry) rancher Teddy Blue (Byrne) while Calamity has a daughter by Wild Bill Hickok (Elliott) that she gives up for adoption. There's lots of rambling and commiserating over the changing and civilizing of the west and various man trouble. Based on the novel by Larry McMurty; originally a two-part TV miniseries. **180m/C VHS.** Anjelica Huston, Melanie Griffith, Gabriel Byrne, Peter Coyote, Jack Palance, Sam Elliott, Reba McEntire, Floyd "Red Crow" Westerman, Tracey Walter, Russell Means, Charlaine Woodard, John Diehl, Liev Schreiber, Andrew Bicknell, Paul Lazar; ***D:*** Rod Hardy; ***W:*** Cynthia Whitcomb; ***C:*** David Connell; ***M:*** Lee Holdridge. *CAF*

Buffalo Jump 🦴🦴🦴 **1990** An independent woman, working as a lounge singer in Toronto, returns to her home in Alberta when her father dies. To her surprise he has left her the family ranch and, to the surprise of everyone else, she decides to stay and run it. She hires a good-looking local man to help her out and they both discover that they want more than a working relationship. However, the fireworks really start when he proposes a marriage of convenience. Engaging performances and beautiful scenery help raise this romantic tale of opposites above the average. **97m/C VHS.** *CA* Wendy Crewson, Paul Gross, Marion Gilsenan, Kyra Harper, Victoria Snow; ***D:*** Eric Till. *ACA*

Buffalo Rider 🦴½ **1978** An adventure film depicting the real-life experiences of C.J. "Buffalo" Jones who worked to save the American buffalo from extinction. **90m/C VHS, Beta.** Rick Guinn, John Freeman, Pricilla Lauris, George Sager, Rich Scheeland; ***D:*** George Lauris. *NO*

Buffalo Stampede 🦴 **1933** Our heroes are involved in a plot to round up buffalo to sell for meat. **60m/B VHS, Beta.** Randolph Scott, Buster Crabbe, Harry Carey Sr., Noah Beery Sr., Raymond Hatton. *NOS, VCN, MRV*

Buffet Froid 🦴🦴🦴½ **1979** Surreal black comedy about a group of bungling murderers. First rate acting and directing makes this film a hilarious treat. From the director of "Menage." In French with English subtitles. **95m/C VHS, LV.** *FR* Gerard Depardieu, Bernard Blier, Jean Carmet, Genevieve Page, Denise Gence, Carole Bouquet, Jean Benguigui, Michel Serrault; ***D:*** Bertrand Blier; ***W:*** Bertrand Blier. Cesar Awards '80: Best Writing. *INT, INJ, TPV*

Buffy the Vampire Slayer 🦴🦴🦴 **1992 (PG-13)** Funny, near-camp teen genre spoof. Buffy is a typical mall gal concerned with shopping and cheerleading, until the mysterious Sutherland proclaims it her destiny to slay the vampires who have suddenly infested Los Angeles. Like, really. Buffy requires some convincing, but eventually takes up the challenge, fighting off the vamps and their seductive leader Hauer, aided by perpetual guy-in-distress Perry. "Pee Wee" Reubens is unrecognizable and terribly amusing as the vampire king's sinister henchman, engaging in one of the longer death scenes of film history. Check out Cassandra (Wagner), Natalie Wood's daughter. **98m/C VHS, LV.** Kristy Swanson, Donald Sutherland, Luke Perry, Paul (Pee Wee Herman) Reubens, Rutger Hauer, Michele Abrams, Randall Batinkoff, Hilary Swank, Paris Vaughan, David Arquette, Candy Clark, Natasha Gregson Wagner; ***D:*** Fran Rubel Kazui; ***W:*** Joss Whedon; ***M:*** Carter Burwell. *FXV, PMS*

Buford's Beach Bunnies 🦴 **1992 (R)** Harry Buford has made a fortune selling barbecued rabbit sandwiches served by the sexiest waitresses around. Harry wants to leave the business to his son Jeeter—if Jeeter can overcome his overwhelming fear of women. So three of Harry's waitresses decide to show Jeeter a very good time. Lots of pretty girls in not much clothing. **90m/C VHS.** Jim Hanks, Rikki Brando, Monique Parent, Amy Page, Barrett Cooper, Ina Rogers, Charley Rossman, David Robinson; ***D:*** Mark Pirro; ***W:*** Mark Pirro. *IMP*

Bug *Woof!* **1975 (PG)** The city of Riverside is threatened with destruction after a massive earth tremor unleashes a super-race of ten-inch mega-cockroaches that belch fire, eat raw meat, and are virtually impervious to Raid. Produced by gimmick-king William Castle, who wanted to install windshield wiper-like devices under theatre seats that would brush against the patrons' feet as the cockroaches crawled across the screen; unfortunately, the idea was squashed flat. **100m/C VHS, Beta.** Bradford Dillman, Joanna Miles, Richard Gilliland, Jamie Smith-Jackson, Alan Fudge, Jesse Vint, William Castle; ***D:*** Jeannot Szwarc; ***W:*** William Castle; ***C:*** Michel Hugo; ***M:*** Charles Fox. *PAR*

Bugles in the Afternoon 🦴🦴 **1952** Life in the army during Custer's last days, with a love triangle, revenge and the Little Big Horn for added spice. **85m/C VHS.** Ray Milland, Hugh Marlowe, Helena Carter, Forrest Tucker, Barton MacLane, George Reeves; ***D:*** Roy Rowland. *REP, FCT*

Bugs & Daffy: The Wartime Cartoons **1945** A compilation of Daffy and Bugs classics made during WWII, often dominated by propaganda and Axis-baiting. **120m/C VHS, Beta, LV.** ***D:*** Robert McKimson, Chuck Jones, Isadore "Friz" Freleng. *MGM, WTA*

The Bugs Bunny/Road Runner Movie *Great American Bugs Bunny-Road Runner Chase* **1979 (G)** A compilation of classic Warner Brothers cartoons, starring Bugs Bunny, Daffy Duck, Elmer Fudd, the Road Runner, Wile E. Coyote, Porky Pig, and Pepe Le Pew, including some all-new animated sequences. Also available with Spanish dubbing. **98m/C VHS, Beta.** ***D:*** Chuck Jones, Phil Monroe; ***V:*** Mel Blanc. *WAR, WTA, APD*

Bugs Bunny Superstar **1975 (G)** A collection of nine animated classics starring everybody's favorite "wascally wabbitt." Includes fascinating interviews and behind the scenes moments featuring the men and women who brought Bugs to life. **91m/C VHS, LV.** ***D:*** Larry Jackson, Bob Clampett, Tex Avery, Isadore "Friz" Freleng; ***V:*** Mel Blanc. *MGM, WTA*

Bugsy 🦴🦴🦴½ **1991 (R)** Beatty is Benjamin "Bugsy" Siegel, the 40s gangster who built the Flamingo Hotel in Las Vegas when it was still a virtual desert, before it became a gambling mecca. Bening is perfect as Bugsy's moll, Virginia Hill, who inspired him to carry out his dream of building the Flamingo (which was her nickname). Beatty and Bening heat up the screen and their off-screen relationship was no different. Fans anticipated their seemingly imminent marriage almost as much as the release of this movie. Almost nothing mars this film which Toback adapted from a novel by Dean Jennings, "We Only Kill Each Other: The Life and Bad Times of Bugsy Siegel." **135m/C VHS, Beta, LV, 8mm.** Warren Beatty, Annette Bening, Harvey Keitel, Ben Kingsley, Elliott Gould, Joe

Mantegna, Richard Sarafian, Bebe Neuwirth, Wendy Phillips, Robert Beltran, Bill Graham, Lewis Van Bergen, Debrah Farentino; ***D:*** Barry Levinson; ***W:*** James Toback; ***C:*** Allen Daviau; ***M:*** Ennio Morricone. Academy Awards '91: Best Art Direction/Set Decoration, Best Costume Design; Chicago Film Critics Awards '91: Best Supporting Actor (Keitel); Golden Globe Awards '92: Best Film—Drama; Los Angeles Film Critics Association Awards '91: Best Director (Levinson), Best Film, Best Screenplay; National Board of Review Awards '91: 10 Best Films of the Year, Best Actor (Beatty); Nominations: Academy Awards '91: Best Actor (Beatty), Best Cinematography, Best Director (Levinson), Best Original Screenplay, Best Picture, Best Supporting Actor (Keitel, Kingsley), Best Original Score. *COL*

Bugsy Malone 🦴🦴½ **1976 (G)** Delightful musical features an all-children's cast highlighting this spoof of 1930s' gangster movies. **94m/C VHS, Beta, LV.** *GB* Jodie Foster, Scott Baio, Florrie Augger, John Cassisi, Martin Lev; ***D:*** Alan Parker; ***W:*** Alan Parker; ***M:*** Paul Williams. British Academy Awards '76: Best Screenplay; Nominations: Academy Awards '76: Best Original Score; Cannes Film Festival '76: Best Film. *PAR*

Bull Durham 🦴🦴🦴½ **1988 (R)** Lovable American romantic comedy, dealing with a very minor minor-league team and three of its current constituents: an aging baseball groupie that beds one player each season; a cocky, foolish new pitcher; and the older, weary catcher brought in to wise the rookie up. The scene in which Sarandon tries poetry out on the banal rookie is a hoot. Highly acclaimed, the film sears with Sarandon and Costner's love scenes. **107m/C VHS, Beta, LV.** Kevin Costner, Susan Sarandon, Tim Robbins, Trey Wilson, Robert Wuhl, Jenny Robertson; ***D:*** Ron Shelton; ***W:*** Ron Shelton; ***M:*** Michael Convertino. Los Angeles Film Critics Association Awards '88: Best Screenplay; New York Film Critics Awards '88: Best Screenplay; National Society of Film Critics Awards '88: Best Screenplay; Writers Guild of America '88: Best Original Screenplay; Nominations: Academy Awards '88: Best Original Screenplay. *ORI, HMV*

Bull of the West 🦴½ **1989** Cattlemen battle for land in the wide open spaces of the old West. **90m/C VHS.** Charles Bronson, Lee J. Cobb, Brian Keith, George Kennedy, DeForest Kelley, Doug McClure. *NO*

Bulldance 🦴 *Forbidden Son* **1988** At a gymnastic school in Crete, a girl's obsession with Greek mythological ritual leads to murder. **105m/C VHS, Beta.** Lauren Hutton, Cliff DeYoung, Renee Estevez; ***D:*** Zelda Barron. *ACA*

Bulldog Courage 🦴🦴 **1935** Young man is out to avenge his father's murder. **66m/B VHS, Beta.** Tim McCoy, Lois January, Joan Woodbury, John Elliott; ***D:*** Sam Newfield. *NOS, VCN, DVT*

Bulldog Drummond 🦴🦴½ **1929** The Bulldog Drummond character, created by "Sapper" (Herman Cyril McNeile), underwent a number of different incarnations from 20s silents through the 40s, and even occassionally in the 50s and 60s. A suave ex-British officer (a precursor to the glib shaken-not-stirred gentleman-spy variety), Bulldog has been played by the likes of Colman, Ralph Richardson, and Tom Conway, among others. In this, the first installment in the long-standing series, a WWI vet, bored with civilian life, is enlisted by a beautiful woman to help her father in various adventures. **85m/B VHS, Beta, LV.** Ronald Colman, Joan Bennett, Montagu Love; ***D:*** F. Richard Jones. Nominations: Academy Awards '30: Best Actor (Colman), Best Interior Decoration, Best Interior Decoration. *SUE, RXM*

Bulldog Drummond at Bay 🦴 **1937** Drummond searches for a group of foreign agents who are trying to steal the plans for a top-secret warplane. Poor British entry to the "Bulldog Drummond" series. **63m/B VHS.** *GB* John Lodge, Dorothy Mackaill, Victor Jory, Claud Allister, Hugh Miller; ***D:*** Norman Lee. *SNC*

Bulldog Drummond Comes Back 🦴🦴 **1937** Drummond, aided by Colonel Nielson, rescues his fiancee from the hands of desperate kidnappers. **119m/B VHS, Beta.** John Howard, John Barrymore, Louise Campbell, Reginald Denny, Guy Standing; ***D:*** Louis King. *SNC, NOS, DVT*

Bulldog Drummond Escapes 🦴🦴 **1937** Drummond, aided by his side-kick and valet, rescues a beautiful girl from spies. He then falls in love with her. **67m/B VHS, Beta.** Ray Milland, Heather Angel, Reginald Denny, Guy Standing, Porter Hall, E.E. Clive; ***D:*** James Hogan. *SNC, NOS, VYY*

Bulldog Drummond in Africa/Arrest Bulldog Drummond 🦴🦴 **1938** Two mid-series Bulldog Drummond films, with two new villains. **115m/B VHS, Beta.** John Howard, H.B. Warner, George Zucco. *SUE, RXM*

Bulldog Drummond's Bride 🦴🦴 **1939** Ace detective Bulldog Drummond has to interrupt his honeymoon in order to pursue a gang of bank robbers across France and England. The last of the Bulldog Drummond film series. **69m/B VHS, Beta.** John Howard, Heather Angel, H.B. Warner, E.E. Clive, Reginald Denny, Eduardo Ciannelli; ***D:*** James Hogan. *DVT, MRV, RXM*

Bulldog Drummond's Peril 🦴🦴 **1938** Murder and robbery drag the adventurous Drummond away from his wedding and he pursues the villains until they are behind bars. One in the film series. **77m/B VHS, Beta.** John Barrymore, John Howard, Louise Campbell, Reginald Denny, E.E. Clive, Porter Hall; ***D:*** James Hogan. *SNC, RXM, MRV*

Bulldog Drummond's Revenge 🦴🦴½ **1937** Bulldog's "Revenge" was made during the series' heyday and was the second to star Howard as Drummond; Barrymore revels in the character of Inspector Neilson of Scotland Yard, and Denny is Algy. In this typically fast-paced installment, suave sleuth Drummond stalks the master criminal responsible for stealing the formula to an explosive. **55m/B VHS.** John Howard, John Barrymore, Reginald Denny, Louise Campbell, Frank Puglia, Nydia Westman, Lucien Littlefield; ***D:*** Louis King. *SNC, MOV*

Bulldog Drummond's Revenge/Bulldog Drummond's Peril **1938** Once again, Bulldog Drummond becomes entangled with diamond counterfeiters, secret explosives, and other crime and criminals. Two episodes in a series. **118m/B VHS, Beta.** John Howard, John Barrymore, Louise Campbell, Reginald Denny, E.E. Clive, Porter Hall. *SUE*

Bulldog Drummond's Secret Police 🦴🦴 **1939** The 15th Drummond film, adapted from Herman Cyril McNeile's famed detective novels featuring a million-pound treasure stashed in the Drummond manor and the murderous endeavors to retrieve it. **54m/B VHS, Beta.** John Howard, Heather Angel, H.B. Warner, Reginald Denny, E.E. Clive, Leo G. Carroll; ***D:*** James Hogan. *SNC, VYY, RXM*

Bulldog Edition 🦴🦴 **1936** Two newspapers engage in an all-out feud to be number one in the city, even going so far as to employ gangsters for purposes of sabotage. **57m/B VHS, Beta.** Ray Walker, Evalyn Knapp, Regis Toomey, Cy Kendall, Billy Newell, Oscar Apfel, Betty Compson, Robert Warwick; ***D:*** Charles Lamont. *SNC*

Bulldog Jack 🦴🦴🦴 *Alias Bulldog Drummond* **1935** Fine entry in the series has Drummond's colleague battling it out with Richardson, the leader of gang of jewel thieves. **62m/B VHS, Beta.** *GB* Fay Wray, Jack Hulbert, Claude Hulbert, Ralph Richardson, Paul Graetz, Gibb McLaughlin; ***D:*** Walter Forde. *NOS, SNC*

The Bulldozer Brigade 🦴🦴½ **1985** Young friends fight city hall in an effort to save their secret wooded playground from land developers. **86m/C VHS.** *FHE, BTV*

Bullet Code 🦴🦴 **1940** It's quick-shooting shenanigans when O'Brien chases a pack of angry rustlers off his neighbor's land. **56m/B VHS.** George O'Brien, Virginia Vale, Howard Hickman, Harry Woods, Charles "Slim" Whitaker; ***D:*** David Howard; ***W:*** Doris Schroeder. *MOV*

Bullet for Sandoval 🦴🦴 **1970 (PG)** An ex-Confederate renegade loots and pillages the north Mexican countryside on his way to murder the grandfather of the woman he loves. **96m/C VHS, Beta.** *SP IT* Ernest Borgnine, George Hilton; ***D:*** Julio Buchs. *VCI*

A Bullet for the General 🦴 *Quien Sabe?* **1968** An American mercenary joins with rebel forces during the Mexican Revolution. **95m/C VHS, Beta.** *IT* Martine Beswick, Lou Castel, Gian Marie Volonte, Klaus Kinski; ***D:*** Damiano Damiani; ***M:*** Luis Bacalov. *COL, NLC*

A Bullet in the Head 🦴🦴🦴 **1990** Violent (no surprise there) tale of friendship finds Frank (Cheung), Ben (Leung), and Paul (Lee) heading out of 1967 Hong Kong for Saigon, where they hope to make money selling contraband goods in the city. They wind up on the wrong side of the Vietnamese Army, steal a fortune in gold from a local crime lord, and end up the prisoners of the Viet Cong. There's betrayal and death and a final moral reckoning and—did we mention lots and lots of (over-the-top) violence? Chinese with subtitles. **85m/C VHS.** *HK* Tony Leung, Jacky Cheung, Waise Lee; ***D:*** John Woo. *FCT*

A Bullet Is Waiting 🦴🦴 **1954** A diligent sheriff finally catches his man only to be trapped in a blinding snowstorm with the hardened criminal. **83m/C VHS, Beta.** Jean Simmons, Rory Calhoun, Stephen McNally, Brian Aherne; ***D:*** John Farrow. *GKK*

Bulletproof 🦴 **1988 (R)** An unstoppable ex-CIA agent battles to retrieve a high-tech nuclear tank from terrorist hands. **93m/C VHS, Beta, LV.** Gary Busey, Darlanne Fluegel, Henry Silva, Thalmus Rasulala, L.Q. Jones, R.G. Armstrong, Rene Enriquez; ***D:*** Steve Carver; ***W:*** Steve Carver. *COL*

Bulletproof Heart 🦴🦴🦴 *Killer* **1995 (R)** Mick (LaPaglia), a hit man with a severe case of burnout, is assigned to kill Fiona (Rogers), a beautiful socialite who, conveniently, wants to die. Despite being warned by his boss (Boyle) that Fiona has a habit of making men weak, he falls in love and can't bring himself to kill her. First-time director Malone takes great care to establish the noir look and feel, capitalizing on the all-in-one-night timeframe to raise the tension level. LaPaglia and Rogers turn in riveting performances, but can't stop the film from losing momentum when it becomes self-consciously melodramatic near the end. **95m/C VHS, LV.** Anthony LaPaglia, Mimi Rogers, Peter Boyle, Matt Craven, Monika Schnarre, Joseph Maher; ***D:*** Mark Malone; ***W:*** Gordon Melbourne, Mark Malone; ***C:*** Tobias Schliessler; ***M:*** Graeme Coleman. *REP*

Bullets or Ballots 🦴🦴🦴 **1938** Tough New York cop goes undercover to join the mob in order to get the goods on them. Old-fashioned danger and intrigue follow, making for some action-packed thrills. **82m/B VHS, Beta.** Edward G. Robinson, Humphrey Bogart, Barton MacLane, Joan Blondell, Frank McHugh, Louise Beavers; ***D:*** William Keighley; ***C:*** Hal Mohr. *MGM, CCB*

Bullets Over Broadway 🦴🦴🦴½ **1994 (R)** Mediocre playwright David Shayne (Cusack, in the Allen role) talks up the virtues of artistic integrity to his pretentious hothouse contemporaries, then sells out to a gangster who agrees to finance his latest play provided his no-talent, brassy moll (Tilly) gets a part. And it's her hit-man bodyguard's (Palminteri) unexpected artistic touches that redeem Shayne's otherwise lousy work. Wiest as the eccentric diva, Ullman as the aging ingenue, Reiner as the Greenwich Village sage, and Broadbent as the increasingly plump matinee idol lead a collection of delicious, over-the-top performances in this smart and howlingly funny tribute to Jazz Age New York City that showcases Woody at his self-conscious best. **106m/C VHS, LV.** Dianne Wiest, John Cusack, Jennifer Tilly, Rob Reiner, Chazz Palminteri, Tracey Ullman, Mary-Louise Parker, Joe Viterelli, Jack Warden, Jim Broadbent, Harvey Fierstein, Annie-Joe Edwards; ***D:*** Woody Allen; ***W:*** Woody Allen, Douglas McGrath; ***C:*** Carlo DiPalma. Academy Awards '94: Best Supporting Actress (Wiest); Chicago Film Critics Awards '94: Best Supporting Actress (Wiest); Golden Globe Awards '95: Best Supporting Actress (Wiest); Independent Spirit Awards '95: Best Supporting Actor (Palminteri), Best Supporting Actress (Wiest); New York Film Critics Awards '94: Best Supporting Actress (Wiest); National Society of Film Critics Awards '94: Best Supporting Actress (Wiest); Screen Actors Guild Award '94: Best Supporting Actress (Wiest); Nominations: Academy Awards '94: Best Art Direction/Set Decoration, Best Costume Design, Best Director (Allen), Best Original Screenplay, Best Supporting Actor

(Palminteri), Best Supporting Actress (Tilly); Independent Spirit Awards '95: Best Film, Best Screenplay. *MAX*

Bullfighter & the Lady ½ **1950** An American goes to Mexico to learn the fine art of bullfighting in order to impress a beautiful woman. **87m/B VHS, LV.** Robert Stack, Gilbert Roland, Virginia Grey, Katy Jurado; ***D:*** Budd Boetticher. Nominations: Academy Awards '51: Best Story. *REP*

Bullfighters **1945** Stan and Ollie are in hot pursuit of a dangerous criminal which leads them to Mexico where Stan winds up in a bull ring. **61m/B VHS, Beta.** Stan Laurel, Oliver Hardy, Margo Woode, Richard Lane; ***D:*** Malcolm St. Clair. *FOX, MLB*

Bullies *Woof!* **1986 (R)** A woodland-transplanted young man decides to fight back against an ornery mountain clan who have raped his mother, tortured his father, and beat up his girlfriend. Brutal and unpalatable. **96m/C VHS, Beta, LV.** *CA* Janet-Laine Green, Dehl Berti, Stephen Hunter, Jonathan Crombie, Olivia D'Abo; ***D:*** Paul Lynch. *MCA*

Bullitt **1968 (PG)** A detective assigned to protect a star witness for 48 hours senses danger; his worst fears are confirmed when his charge is murdered. Based on the novel, "Mute Witness" by Robert L. Pike, and featuring one of filmdom's most famous car chases. **105m/C VHS, Beta, LV.** Steve McQueen, Robert Vaughn, Jacqueline Bisset, Don Gordon, Robert Duvall, Norman Fell, Simon Oakland; ***D:*** Peter Yates; ***W:*** Alan R. Trustman; ***C:*** William A. Fraker; ***M:*** Lalo Schifrin. Academy Awards '68: Best Film Editing; Edgar Allan Poe Awards '68: Best Screenplay; National Society of Film Critics Awards '68: Best Cinematography; Nominations: Academy Awards '68: Best Sound. *WAR*

Bullseye! ½ **1990 (PG-13)** Knockabout farce is a letdown considering the talents involved. Shady scientists (Moore and Caine) pursue/are pursued by lookalike con-artists (Caine and Moore), who are pursued in turn by international agents. Full of inside jokes and celebrity cameos, but nothing exceptional. **95m/C VHS, LV.** Michael Caine, Roger Moore, Sally Kirkland, Patsy Kensit, Jenny Seagrove, John Cleese, Lee Patterson, Deborah Barrymore, Mark Burns, Deborah Leng, Alexandra Pigg; ***Cameos:*** Lynn Nesbitt, Steffanie Pitt; ***D:*** Michael Winner; ***W:*** Michael Winner, Leslie Bricusse; ***M:*** John Du Prez. *COL*

Bullshot ½ **1983 (PG)** Zany English satire sends up the legendary Bulldog Drummond. In the face of mad professors, hapless heroines, devilish Huns and deadly enemies, our intrepid hero remains distinctly British. **84m/C VHS, Beta.** *GB* Alan Shearman, Diz White, Ron House, Frances Tomelty, Michael Aldridge, Ron Pember, Christopher Good; ***D:*** Dick Clement; ***M:*** John Du Prez. *NO*

Bullwhip **1958** A man falsely accused of murder saves himself from the hangman's noose by agreeing to a shotgun wedding. **80m/C VHS.** Guy Madison, Rhonda Fleming, James Griffith, Peter Adams; ***D:*** Harmon Jones. *REP*

Bummer *Woof!* **1973 (R)** Rock band's wild party turns into tragedy when the bass player goes too far with two groupies. It's a bad scene, man. **90m/C VHS, Beta.** Kipp Whitman, Dennis Burkley, Carol Speed, Connie Strickland; ***D:*** William Allen Castleman. *NO*

Bums **1993** Sergeant Andrew Holloman is a military officer in search of his long lost brother. It turns out his brother was homeless and is now dead at the hands of a skid row killer. Holloman recruits a platoon of other homeless people to help him track the killer but what he discovers is a multimillion conspiracy behind the murders. **94m/C VHS.** Christopher McDonald, Haskell Phillips, Dawn Evans; ***D:*** Andy Galler; ***W:*** Pat Allee, Ben Hurst. *MNC*

Bunco **1983** Two policemen working for the Los Angeles Police Department's Bunco Squad discover a college for con artists complete with tape-recorded lessons and on-the-job training. **60m/C VHS, Beta.** Tom Selleck, Robert Urich, Donna Mills, Will Geer, Arte Johnson, Alan Feinstein. *ORI, WAR*

Bundle of Joy ½ **1956** Salesgirl who saves an infant from falling off the steps of a foundling home is mistaken for the child's mother. Remake of 1939's "Bachelor Mother." ♫Bundle of Joy; I Never Felt This Way Before; Lullaby in Blue; Worry About Tomorrow; All About Love; Someday Soon; What's So Good About Morning?; You're Perfect In Every Department. **98m/C VHS, Beta, LV.** Debbie Reynolds, Eddie Fisher, Adolphe Menjou; ***D:*** Norman Taurog. *NO*

A Bunny's Tale **1985** The story of Gloria Steinem's undercover journey into the Playboy Club as a fledgling journalist. It is here that she discovered her dedication as a feminist. Based on the book by Steinem. **97m/C VHS, Beta.** Kirstie Alley, Cotter Smith, Deborah Van Valkenburgh, Joanna Kerns, Delta Burke, Diana Scarwid; ***D:*** Karen Arthur. *PSM*

Buona Sera, Mrs. Campbell ½ **1968** The lovely Lollobridgida and some fast-paced plot moves are the main highlights of this comedy. Mrs. Campbell convinced her three American WWII lovers that each of them had fathered her daughter. All three have supported mother and child through the years, unbeknowst to each other and their wives. When their 20-year reunion brings them back to Italy, Mrs. Campbell must do some fast-thinking and some quick-stepping to keep everyone happy. **113m/C VHS, LV.** Gina Lollobrigida, Shelley Winters, Phil Silvers, Peter Lawford, Telly Savalas, Lee Grant, Janet Margolin, Marian Moses; ***D:*** Melvin Frank. *MGM*

The 'Burbs ½ **1989 (PG)** A tepid satire about suburbanites suspecting their creepy new neighbors of murderous activities. Well-designed and sharp, but light on story. **101m/C VHS, Beta, LV.** Tom Hanks, Carrie Fisher, Rick Ducommun, Corey Feldman, Brother Theodore, Bruce Dern, Gale Gordon, Courtney Gains; ***D:*** Joe Dante; ***M:*** Jerry Goldsmith. *MCA, CCB*

Burden of Dreams **1982** The landmark documentary chronicling the berserk circumstances behind the scenes of Werner Herzog's epic "Fitzcarraldo." Stuck in the Peruvian jungles, the film crew was subjected to every disaster imaginable while executing Herzog's vision, including disease, horrendous accident, warring local tribes and the megalomaniacal director himself. Considered better than "Fitzcarraldo," although both films discuss a man's obsession. **94m/C VHS, Beta, LV.** Klaus Kinski, Mick Jagger, Jason Robards Jr., Werner Herzog; ***D:*** Les Blank. *TPV, FFM, BTV*

Bureau of Missing Persons ½ **1933** Comedy-drama about big-city bureau of missing persons, in which the hardened Stone is in charge. O'Brien plays a tough cop who is transferred to the bureau and Davis stars as the mystery woman with whom he gets involved. Although fast-paced and intriguing, the film is somewhat confusing and never stays in one direction for very long. **75m/B VHS.** Bette Davis, Lewis Stone, Pat O'Brien, Glenda Farrell, Allen Jenkins, Ruth Donnelly, Hugh Herbert; ***D:*** Roy Del Ruth. *MGM*

Burglar **1987 (R)** A cat burglar moves to the right side of the law when she tries to solve a murder case. Whoopi's always a treat, but this movie's best forgotten; Goldberg's fans should watch "Jumpin' Jack Flash" again instead. Co-star Goldthwait elevates the comedic level a bit. **103m/C VHS, Beta, LV.** Whoopi Goldberg, Bob(cat) Goldthwait, Lesley Ann Warren, John Goodman, G.W. Bailey, James Handy, Anne DeSalvo; ***D:*** Hugh Wilson; ***W:*** Hugh Wilson. *WAR, KIV*

Burglar *Vzlomschik* **1987** Not to be confused with the Whoopi Goldberg vehicle, this Russian film relates a story no less American than apple pie and teenage angst. Senka and would-be punk star Kostya are two neglected and disaffected brothers whose father is a drunken womanizer best known for absentee paternalism. When Howmuch, a serious heavy metalloid, pressures Kostya to steal a synthesizer, brother Senka steps in to steal the Community Center's property himself. In Russian with English subtitles, the solid performances hold their own against the heavy musical content. **89m/C VHS.** *RU* Konstantin Kinchev, Oleg Yelykomov; ***D:*** Valery Orgorodnikov. *FCT, KIV*

Burial Ground **1985** A classically grisly splatter film in which the hungry dead rise and proceed to kill the weekend denizens of an isolated aristocratic mansion. **85m/C VHS, Beta.** Karen Well, Peter Bark; ***D:*** Andrew Bianchi. *VES, LIV*

Burial of the Rats ½ *Roger Corman Presents Burial of the Rats; Bram Stoker's Burial of the Rats* **1995 (R)** Two women bandits kidnap a man and take him to a bloodthirsty cult, lead by Barbeau, who hate men, worship rats, and live by violence. Based on a story by Bram Stoker; made for cable. **85m/C VHS.** Adrienne Barbeau, Maria Ford, Kevin Alber. *NHO*

Buried Alive **1939** A man is sent to prison on trumped up charges. Only the prison nurse believes he is innocent as a crooked politician strives to keep him behind bars. **74m/B Beta.** Beverly Roberts, Robert Wilcox, George Pembroke, Ted Osborn, Paul McVey, Alden Chase; ***D:*** Victor Halperin. *NOS, MRV, LOO*

Buried Alive **1981** Director d'Amato reaps his finest gore-fest to date, incorporating the well-established taxidermist gone loony motif in his repertoire of appalling bad taste. Not for the squeamish, this bloodier-than-thou spaghetti spooker is chock full of necrophilia, cannibalism, and more. **90m/C VHS.** *IT* Kieran Canter, Cinzia Monreale, Franca Stoppi; ***D:*** Joe D'Amato. *NO*

Buried Alive **1989 (R)** Once Ravenscroft Hall was an asylum for the incurably insane. Now, the isolated mansion is a school for troubled teenage girls, run by a charismatic psychiatrist. Captivated by his charm, a young woman joins the staff. Soon, she is tormented by nightmare visions of the long-dead victims of a nameless killer. When the students begin to disappear, she realizes he still lives...and she may be his next victim. Carradine's last role. **97m/C VHS, LV.** Robert Vaughn, Donald Pleasence, Karen Witter, John Carradine, Ginger Lynn Allen; ***D:*** Gerard Kikione. *COL*

Buried Alive ½ **1990 (PG-13)** One of the many horror flicks entitled "Buried Alive," this one is not bad, injecting a bit of levity into the time-worn genre. Schemestress Leigh and her paramour poison her husband. Or so they think, only to discover that he's not quite dead. Made for cable. **93m/C VHS.** Tim Matheson, Jennifer Jason Leigh, William Atherton, Hoyt Axton; ***D:*** Frank Darabont; ***W:*** Mark Patrick Carducci, Jake Clesi; ***M:*** Michel Colombier. *MCA*

Burke & Wills ½ **1985 (PG-13)** A lush, big-budgeted true story of the two men who first crossed Australia on foot, and explored its central region. Popular Australian film. **120m/C VHS, Beta, LV.** *AU* Jack Thompson, Nigel Havers, Greta Scacchi, Ralph Cotterill, Drew Forsythe, Chris Haywood, Matthew Fargher; ***D:*** Graeme Clifford; ***W:*** Michael Thomas; ***M:*** Peter Sculthorpe. *NLC, INJ*

Burlesque of Carmen **1916** A silent pastiche of the Bizet opera, with Charlie as Don Schmose. Interesting early work. **30m/B VHS, Beta.** Charlie Chaplin, Ben Turpin, Edna Purviance; ***D:*** Charlie Chaplin. *NOS, DVT, GVV*

The Burmese Harp *Harp of Burma; Birumano Tategoto* **1956** At the end of WWII, a Japanese soldier is spiritually traumatized and becomes obsessed with burying the masses of war casualties. A searing, acclaimed anti-war statement, in Japanese with English subtitles. Remade by Ichikawa in 1985. **115m/B VHS, Beta, LV.** *JP* Shoji Yasui, Rentaro Mikuni, Tatsuya Mihashi, Tanie Kitabayashi, Yunosuke Ito; ***D:*** Kon Ichikawa. *CVC, INJ, APD*

Burn! ½ *Quemimada!* **1970 (PG)** An Italian-made indictment of imperialist control by guerrilla-filmmaker Pontecorvo, depicting the efforts of a 19th century British ambassador to put down a slave revolt on a Portuguese-run Caribbean island. Great Brando performance. **112m/C VHS, Beta, LV.** *IT* Marlon Brando, Evarist Marquez, Renato Salvatori; ***D:*** Gillo Pontecorvo; ***M:*** Ennio Morricone. *MGM, CRC, FCT*

Burn 'Em Up Barnes **1934** Twelve episodes each depicting the adventures of "Burn'Em Up" Barnes, a racer, and his buddy, Bobbie. **40m/B VHS, Beta.** Frankie Darro, Lola Lane, Jack Mulhall. *SNC, NOS, VCN*

Burn Witch, Burn! 🦴🦴🦴 *Night of the Eagle* **1962** A college professor proudly finds himself rapidly rising in his profession. His pride turns to horror though when he discovers that his success is not due to his own abilities, but to the efforts of his witchcraft practicing wife. Excellent, atmospheric horror with a genuinely suspenseful climax. **87m/B VHS.** *GB* Peter Wyngarde, Janet Blair, Margaret Johnston, Anthony Nicholls, Colin Gordon, Kathleen Byron, Reginald Beckwith, Jessica Dunning; ***D:*** Sidney Hayers; ***W:*** Richard Matheson. *FRG*

Burndown 🦴 **1989 (R)** Victims of a serial killer in a town with a large nuclear reactor are themselves radioactive, which leads the Police Chief and a beautiful reporter to the truth and the hidden conspiracy. **97m/C VHS, Beta, LV.** Cathy Moriarty, Peter Firth; ***D:*** James Allen. *NO*

The Burning 🦴 **1982 (R)** Story of macabre revenge set in the dark woods of a seemingly innocent summer camp. **90m/C VHS, Beta.** Brian Matthews, Leah Ayres, Holly Hunter, Jason Alexander; ***D:*** Tony Maylam. *NO*

The Burning Bed 🦴🦴🦴½ **1985** A made for television dramatic expose (based on a true story) about wife-beating. Fawcett garnered accolades for her performance as the battered wife who couldn't take it anymore. Highly acclaimed and Emmy-nominated. **95m/C VHS, Beta.** Farrah Fawcett, Paul LeMat, Penelope Milford, Richard Masur; ***D:*** Robert Greenwald. *FOX*

The Burning Court 🦴½ **1962** Unusual horror film involving occultism, possession, and family curses. Dubbed into English. Based on a story by John Dickson Carr. **102m/C VHS.** Nadja Tiller, Jean-Claude Brialy, Edith Scob. *SNC*

The Burning Hills 🦴½ **1956** Unexceptional cow flick based on a Louis L'Amour novel. Hunter hides from cattle thieves in a barn and, eventually, in the arms of a half-breed Mexican girl (Wood). Tedious and unsurprising. **94m/C VHS.** Tab Hunter, Natalie Wood, Skip Homeier, Eduard Franz; ***D:*** Stuart Heisler. *WAR, MLB*

Burning Rage 🦴 **1984** A blazing, abandoned coal mine threatens to wreak havoc in the Appalachians. The government sends geologist Mandrell to help prevent a disaster. Made for television. **100m/C VHS, LV.** Barbara Mandrell, Tom Wopat, Bert Remsen, John Pleshette, Carol Kane, Eddie Albert; ***D:*** Gilbert Cates. *VTR*

The Burning Season 🦴🦴🦴 **1994** In one of his last performances, Julia inspires as Chico Mendes, a socialist union leader who fought to protect the homes and land of Brazilian peasants in the western Amazon rain forest. With Mendes' help the peasants form a union and struggle to prevent the building of a road that will provide easy access to forest land for speculators and cattlemen. Naturally, they are violently opposed by corruption-ridden capitalist powers in the government. Julia provides a haunting portrayal of the heroic figure who was assassinated in 1990. Based in part on the book by Andrew Revkin. Filmed on location in Mexico. **123m/C VHS.** Raul Julia, Edward James Olmos, Sonia Braga, Luis Guzman, Nigel Havers, Kamala Dawson, Tomas Milian, Esai Morales, Tony Plana, Carmen Argenziano; ***D:*** John Frankenheimer; ***W:*** William Mastrosimone, Michael Tolkin, Ron Hutchinson; ***M:*** Gary Chang. *WAR*

Burning Secret 🦴🦴 *Brennendes Geheimnis* **1989 (PG)** After WWI, a widow in Austria (Dunaway) meets a baron (Brandauer) who has befriended her son. Mutual seduction ensues but the sparks don't fly. Adapted from Stefan Zweig story. **107m/C VHS, Beta, LV.** *GB* Faye Dunaway, Klaus Maria Brandauer, Ian Richardson, David Eberts; ***D:*** Andrew Birkin; ***W:*** Andrew Birkin; ***M:*** Hans Zimmer. *VES, IME, LIV*

Burning Vengeance **1989** A DEA agent enters the deadly world of drugs and singlehandedly annihilates the drug smugglers and destroys their kingpin. **120m/C VHS, Beta.** *AIP*

The Burns and Allen Show **1950** George and Gracie's classic vaudeville routines are a highlight of this sitcom series, with George the perpetually harried husband to the scatterbrained Gracie. Additional episodes are available. **115m/B VHS, Beta, LV.** Gracie Allen, George Burns. *SHO, COL, MOV*

Burnt by the Sun 🦴🦴🦴 *Outomlionnye Solntsem* **1994 (R)** Masterful evocation of '30's Stalinist Russia, covering a day in the life of Soviet revolutionary hero Serguei (Mikhalkov) and his family, far from the purges and gulags. Enjoying a country existence with wife Moroussia (Dapkounaite) and daughter Nadia (played by Mikhalkov's daughter), his idyll is disturbed by mystery man Dimitri (Menchikov), and Serguei realizes their fates are bound by the difference between their Communist dreams and reality. Symbolism is a little heavy but film delivers emotionally. Russian with subtitles. **134m/C VHS, LV.** *RU FR* Nikita Mikhalkov, Ingeborga Dapkounaite, Oleg Menchikov, Nadia Mikhalkov, Andre Oumansky, Viatcheslav Tikhonov, Svetlana Krioutchkova, Vladimir Ilyine; ***D:*** Nikita Mikhalkov; ***W:*** Nikita Mikhalkov, Rustam Ibragimbekov; ***M:*** Eduard Artemyev. Academy Awards '94: Best Foreign Language Film; Cannes Film Festival '94: Grand Jury Prize; Nominations: British Academy Awards '95: Best Foreign Film. *COL*

Burnt Offerings 🦴🦴 **1976 (PG)** A family rents an old mansion for the summer and they become affected by evil forces that possess the house. Based on the novel by Robert Marasco. **116m/C VHS, Beta.** Oliver Reed, Karen Black, Bette Davis, Burgess Meredith; ***D:*** Dan Curtis; ***W:*** Dan Curtis. *MGM*

Bury Me an Angel 🦴 **1971** A female biker sets out to seek revenge against the men who killed her brother. **85m/C VHS, Beta, LV.** Dixie Peabody, Terry Mace, Clyde Ventura, Dan Haggerty, Stephen Whittaker, Gary Littlejohn; ***D:*** Barbara Peeters. *NWV, HHT*

Bury Me Not On the Lone Prairie 🦴🦴 **1941** When his brother is murdered in cold blood by claim jumpers, mining engineer Brown goes to avenge the dead. Based on a story by Sherman Lowe. **57m/B VHS.** Johnny Mack Brown, Fuzzy Knight, Nell O'Day, Frank O'Connor, Kermit Maynard; ***D:*** Ray Taylor; ***W:*** Sherman Lowe, Victor McLeod. *MOV*

The Bus Is Coming 🦴🦴 **1972** A love story entwined with the problems of blacks in a small town. **95m/C VHS, Beta.** Mike Sims, Stephanie Faulkner, Morgan Jones; ***D:*** Horace Jackson. *NO*

Bus Stop 🦴🦴🦴 *The Wrong Kind of Girl* **1956** Murray plays a naive cowboy who falls in love with Monroe, a barroom singer, and decides to marry her without her permission. Considered by many to be the finest performance by Marilyn Monroe; she sings "That Old Black Magic" in this one. Very funny with good performances by all. Based on the William Inge play. **96m/C VHS, Beta, LV.** Marilyn Monroe, Arthur O'Connell, Hope Lange, Don Murray, Betty Field, Max Casey Adams Showalter, Hans Conried, Eileen Heckart; ***D:*** Joshua Logan; ***W:*** George Axelrod; ***C:*** Milton Krasner. National Board of Review Awards '56: 10 Best Films of the Year; Nominations: Academy Awards '56: Best Supporting Actor (Murray). *FOX*

The Busby Berkeley Disc **1992** A collection of the innovative dance director's work at Warner Bros. studio covering 1933-37. Berkeley was known for his elaborate production numbers, beautiful women, military precision, and kaleidoscopic patterns in such films as "42nd Street," "Footlight Parade," and the "Gold Diggers" series. **176m/B LV.** *MGM*

Bush Mama 🦴🦴 **1976** A hallucinatory film about a black woman on welfare trying to care for her daughter in a Los Angeles ghetto. Street violence varies with fantasy scenes in a loose narrative filled with flashbacks. **100m/C VHS.** ***D:*** Haile Gerima. *FCT*

The Bushbaby 🦴½ **1970** The young Brooks is given a tiny bushbaby while visiting Africa with her father. Because of her pet she misses her ship home and finds herself with former servant Gossett, who agrees to take her to a family friend. Unfortunately, the authorities think he's kidnapped the girl and the two, along with the trouble-causing pet, are pursued by the police. Simple-minded kiddie fare. **100m/C VHS.** Margaret Brooks, Louis Gossett Jr., Donald Houston, Laurence Naismith, Marne Maitland, Geoffrey Bayldon, Jack Gwillim; ***D:*** John Trent. *MGM, FCT*

The Busher 🦴½ **1919** All-American pitcher's romance is interrupted by a gratuitous Mr. Moneybags. Minor-league conflict with little real hardball. **54m/B VHS, Beta.** Charles Ray, Colleen Moore, John Gilbert. *GPV, FCT, GVV*

The Bushido Blade 🦴🦴½ *The Bloody Bushido Blade* **1980** An action-packed samurai thriller of adventure and betrayal set in medieval Japan. **92m/C VHS, Beta.** *JP* Richard Boone, James Earl Jones, Frank Converse; ***D:*** Tom Kotani. *NO*

The Bushwackers 🦴½ *The Rebel* **1952** Ireland plays a veteran of the Confederate army who wishes only to put his violent past behind him. He is forced to reconsider his vow when old-west bullies threaten his family. **70m/B VHS.** Dorothy Malone, John Ireland, Wayne Morris, Lawrence Tierney, Jack Elam, Lon Chaney Sr., Myrna Dell; ***D:*** Rod Amateau. *NOS, LOO, SNC*

Bushwhacked 🦴🦴½ *Tenderfoots; The Tenderfoot* **1995 (PG-13)** Crude, rude, dim-witted, kid-hating Max Grabelski (Stern) is falsely accused of murder and forced to become a fugitive. While not to be confused with Harrison Ford, he is mistaken for the leader of a group of Cub Scouts out on their maiden camping trip and soon finds himself in an unlikely partnership with the boys. Together they encounter everything from grizzly bears to whitewater rapids. Light-hearted, goofy comedy continues Stern's tendency toward kid-intensive, family-oriented fare in the "Rookie of the Year" vein. **85m/C VHS.** Daniel Stern, Jon Polito, Brad Sullivan, Ann Dowd, Anthony Heald, Thomas Wood; ***D:*** Greg Beeman; ***W:*** Tommy Swerdlow, Michael Goldberg, John Jordan, Danny Byers; ***M:*** Bill Conti. *FXV*

A Business Affair 🦴🦴½ **1993 (R)** Kate Swallow (the ravishing Bouquet), the neglected wife of tempermental author Alex Bolton (Pryce), begins an affair with his flamboyant American publisher Vanni Corso (Walken). While the men posture between themselves for her affections, Kate, who has literary aspirations, decides to strike out on her own. Based on the romantic triangle of British writers Barbara Skelton and Cyril Connolly and his publisher George Weidenfeld and taken from Skelton's memoirs "Tears Before Bedtime" and "Weep No More." **102m/C VHS.** Carole Bouquet, Jonathan Pryce, Christopher Walken, Sheila Hancock; ***D:*** Charlotte Brandstrom; ***W:*** William Stadiem; ***C:*** Willy Kurant; ***M:*** Didier Vasseur. *VMK*

Business as Usual 🦴🦴 **1988 (PG)** A meek boutique manager in Liverpool defends a sexually harassed employee, is fired, fights back, and creates a national furor over her rights as a woman. **89m/C VHS, Beta.** Glenda Jackson, Cathy Tyson, John Thaw; ***D:*** Lezli-Ann Barrett; ***W:*** Lezli-Ann Barrett. *WAR*

Busted Up 🦴 **1986 (R)** A young, hard-luck urban street-fighter battles for the sake of his family and neighborhood against local crimelords. **93m/C VHS, Beta.** *CA* Irene Cara, Paul Coufos, Tony Rosato, Stan Shaw, Gordon Judges; ***D:*** Conrad Palmisano; ***M:*** Charles P. Barnett. *MCA*

Buster 🦴🦴½ **1988 (R)** The story of Buster Edwards, the one suspect in the 1963 Great Train Robbery who evaded being captured by police. Collins makes his screen debut as one of Britain's most infamous criminals. Collins also performs on the film's soundtrack, spawning two hit singles, "Two Hearts" and "Groovy Kind of Love." **102m/C VHS, Beta, LV.** *GB* Phil Collins, Julie Walters, Larry Lamb, Stephanie Lawrence, Ellen Beaven, Michael Atwell, Ralph Brown, Christopher Ellison, Sheila Hancock, Martin Jarvis, Anthony Quayle; ***D:*** David Green; ***M:*** Anne Dudley. Nominations: Academy Awards '88: Best Song ("Two Hearts"). *HBO*

Buster and Billie 🦴½ **1974 (R)** Tragedy ensues when a popular high school student falls in love with the class tramp in rural Georgia in 1948. Serious, decently appointed period teen drama. **100m/C VHS, Beta.** Jan-Michael Vincent, Joan Goodfellow, Clifton James, Pamela Sue Martin, Robert Englund; ***D:*** Daniel Petrie. *COL*

Buster Keaton Rides Again/The Railrodder **1965** "The Railrodder" is a silent comedy short that returns Buster Keaton to the type of slapstick he made famous in his legendary 1920's films. "Buster Keaton Rides Again" (in black-and-white) is a documentary-style look at Keaton filmed during the making of "The Railrodder." Besides scenes of Keaton at work, there is also a capsule rundown of his career. **81m/C VHS, Beta, LV.** Buster Keaton. *GPV*

Bustin' Loose **1981 (R)** A fast-talking ex-con reluctantly drives a bus load of misplaced kids and their keeper cross-country. **94m/C VHS, Beta, LV.** Richard Pryor, Cicely Tyson, Robert Christian, George Coe, Bill Quinn; ***D:*** Oz Scott; ***W:*** Richard Pryor, Lonne Elder III. *MCA*

Busting ½ **1974 (R)** Gould and Blake play a pair of slightly off-the-wall L.A. cops. The pair are forced "to bust" local addicts and prostitutes instead of the real crime bosses because much of the police department is on the take. Plenty of comedy and action as well as highly realistic drama. **92m/C VHS.** Elliott Gould, Robert (Bobby) Blake, Allen (Goorwitz) Garfield, Antonio Fargas, Michael Lerner, Sid Haig, Cornelia Sharpe; ***D:*** Peter Hyams; ***W:*** Peter Hyams; ***M:*** Billy Goldenberg. *MGM, MCA*

But Not for Me ½ **1959** Gable stars as a middled-aged entertainment executive who thinks he can forestall maturity by carrying on with his youthful secretary. **105m/B VHS.** Clark Gable, Carroll Baker, Lilli Palmer, Lee J. Cobb, Barry Coe, Thomas Gomez, Charles Lane; ***D:*** Walter Lang; ***W:*** John Michael Hayes; ***C:*** Robert Burks. *PAR*

But Where Is Daniel Wax? **1974** At a class reunion, a doctor and a popular singing star reminisce about their youth and Daniel Wax, their one-time hero. Hebrew with English subtitles. **95m/C VHS, Beta.** Lior Yaeni, Michael Lipkin, Esther Zevko; ***D:*** Avram Heffner. *ERG, INJ*

Butch and Sundance: The Early Days ½ **1979 (PG)** Traces the origins of the famous outlaw duo. It contains the requisite shoot-outs, hold-ups, and escapes. A "prequel" to "Butch Cassidy and the Sundance Kid." **111m/C VHS, Beta.** Tom Berenger, William Katt, John Schuck, Jeff Corey, Jill Eikenberry, Brian Dennehy, Peter Weller; ***D:*** Richard Lester; ***W:*** Allan Burns. Nominations: Academy Awards '79: Best Costume Design. *FOX*

Butch Cassidy and the Sundance Kid **1969 (PG)** Two legendary outlaws at the turn of the century take it on the lam with a beautiful, willing ex-school teacher. With a clever script, humanly fallible characters, and warm, witty dialogue, this film was destined to become a box-office classic. Featured the hit song, "Raindrops Keep Falling on My Head" and renewed the buddy film industry, as Newman and Redford trade insult for insult. Look for the great scene where Newman takes on giant Ted Cassidy in a fist fight. ♫Raindrops Keep Fallin' on My Head; On a Bicycle Built for Joy. **110m/C VHS, Beta, LV.** Paul Newman, Robert Redford, Katharine Ross, Jeff Corey, Strother Martin, Cloris Leachman, Kenneth Mars, Ted Cassidy, Henry Jones, George Furth, Sam Elliott; ***D:*** George Roy Hill; ***W:*** William Goldman; ***C:*** Conrad Hall; ***M:*** Burt Bacharach. Academy Awards '69: Best Cinematography, Best Song ("Raindrops Keep Fallin' on My Head"), Best Story & Screenplay, Best Original Score; British Academy Awards '70: Best Actor (Redford), Best Actress (Ross), Best Director (Hill), Best Film, Best Screenplay; Golden Globe Awards '70: Best Score; Writers Guild of America '69: Best Adapted Screenplay; Nominations: Academy Awards '69: Best Director (Hill), Best Picture, Best Sound. *FXV, OM*

The Butcher's Wife **1991 (PG-13)** Charming tale of a young psychic (Moore) who brings romance to a Greenwich Village neighborhood that never quite gets off the ground. Moore stars as the clairvoyant whose mystical powers bring magic into the lives of everyone around her, including the local psychiatrist (Daniels), who falls under her spell. Talented cast is virtually wasted with a script that is lightweight; excepting Steenburgen and Dzundza who shine. **107m/C VHS, Beta, LV.** Demi Moore, Jeff Daniels, George Dzundza, Frances McDormand, Margaret Colin, Mary Steenburgen, Max Perlich, Miriam Margolyes, Christopher Durang, Diane Salinger; ***D:*** Terry Hughes; ***W:*** Ezra Litwack, Marjorie Schwartz; ***M:*** Michael Gore. *PAR*

Butler's Dilemma **1943** A jewel thief and a playboy both claim the identity of a butler who never existed, with humorous results. **75m/B VHS, Beta.** *GB* Richard Hearne, Francis L. Sullivan, Hermione Gingold, Ian Fleming. *VYY*

Butterfield 8 **1960** A seedy film of the John O'Hara novel about a prostitute that wants to go straight and settle down. Taylor won an Oscar, perhaps because she was ill and had lost in the two previous years in more deserving roles. **108m/C VHS, Beta, LV.** Elizabeth Taylor, Laurence Harvey, Eddie Fisher, Dina Merrill, Mildred Dunnock, Betty Field, Susan Oliver, Kay Medford; ***D:*** Daniel Mann; ***W:*** John Michael Hayes, Charles Schnee; ***C:*** Joseph Ruttenberg. Academy Awards '60: Best Actress (Taylor); Nominations: Academy Awards '60: Best Color Cinematography. *MGM, BTV*

Butterflies **1975** Ria, a middle-aged housewife with two lazy sons, is beginning to feel her age, and like a butterfly, feeling like she has too much to do and not enough time. Then Leonard appears in her life—divorced, lonely and romantic. Made for British television. **60m/C VHS.** *GB VCO*

Butterflies Are Free **1972 (PG)** Fast-paced humor surrounds the Broadway play brought to the big screen. Blind youth Albert is determined to be self-sufficient. A next-door-neighbor actress helps him gain independence from his over-protective mother (Heckart). **109m/C VHS, Beta.** Goldie Hawn, Edward Albert, Eileen Heckart, Michael Glaser; ***D:*** Milton Katselas; ***C:*** Charles B(ryant) Lang; ***M:*** Robert Alcivar. Academy Awards '72: Best Supporting Actress (Heckart); Nominations: Academy Awards '72: Best Cinematography, Best Sound. *GKK*

Butterfly ½ **1982 (R)** Based on James M. Cain's novel about an amoral young woman (Pia, who'd you think?) who uses her beauty and sensual appetite to manipulate the men in her life, including her father. Set in Nevada of the 1930s, father and daughter are drawn into a daring and forbidden love affair by their lust and desperation. **105m/C VHS, Beta, LV.** Pia Zadora, Stacy Keach, Orson Welles, Edward Albert, James Franciscus, Lois Nettleton, Stuart Whitman, June Lockhart, Ed McMahon; ***D:*** Matt Cimber; ***W:*** Matt Cimber; ***M:*** Ennio Morricone. Golden Raspberry Awards '82: Worst Actress (Zadora), Worst Supporting Actor (McMahon), Worst New Star (Zadora). *VES, LIV*

Butterfly Affair ½ **1971 (PG)** Beautiful singer, involved in a scheme to smuggle two million dollars worth of gems, plots to double-cross her partners in crime. **75m/C VHS, Beta.** Claudia Cardinale, Henri Charriere, Stanley Baker; ***D:*** Jean Herman. *NO*

Butterfly Ball **1976** Retelling of the 19th century classic combines the rock music of Roger Glover, live action and animation by Halas and Batchelor. Only for the brain-cell depressed. **85m/C VHS, Beta.** *GB* Twiggy, Ian Gillian, David Coverdale; ***D:*** Tony Klinger. *NO*

Butterfly Kiss **1994** Strange psychodrama/road tale finds drifter Eunice (Plummer) wandering the motorways of northern England. At one service station she meets Miriam (Reeves)—the two, immediately drawn together, make love at Miriam's that night. When Eunice hitches a ride with a trucker next morning, Miriam decides to follow and discovers Eunice with the truck and the driver's dead body. It's soon not the only dead body Miriam encounters as she discovers Eunice is a serial killer—not that this seems to worry Miriam a great deal as she herself gets into the spirit of their crimes. Grim all the way 'round. **85m/C VHS.** *GB* Amanda Plummer, Saskia Reeves, Paul Brown, Des McAleer, Ricky Tomlinson; ***D:*** Michael Winterbottom; ***W:*** Frank Cottrell Boyce; ***C:*** Seamus McGarvey; ***M:*** John Harle. *TRI*

Butterfly Wings *Alas de Mariposa* **1991** The tragedy of a dysfunctional family. Pregnant Carmen longs for a boy to carry on her husband's name but she's afraid to tell her shy six-year-old daughter Ami about the baby. Maybe with reason, since the child's brith triggers a series of nightmarish events. Spanish with subtitles. **105m/C VHS.** *SP* ***D:*** Juanma Bajo Ulloa. *FCT*

Buy & Cell ½ **1989 (R)** A stockbroker attempts to set up a business while serving a prison sentence. An assortment of amusing inmates doesn't help matters much. Fans of Malcolm McDowell will enjoy his performance as the shady warden. **95m/C VHS, LV.** Robert Carradine, Michael Winslow, Malcolm McDowell, Ben Vereen, Lise Cutter, Randall "Tex" Cobb, Roddy Piper; ***D:*** Robert Boris. *NWV*

Buying Time **1989 (R)** Two teenagers are arrested when they try to pry their money away from a dishonest bookie, and the police use their connections to solve a drug-related murder. **97m/C VHS, Beta.** Dean Stockwell, Jeff Schultz, Michael Rudder, Tony De Santis, Leslie Toth, Laura Cruickshank; ***D:*** Mitchell Gabourie. *FOX*

Buzzy Rides the Range **1940** Average "B" western with a kid saving the day. **60m/C VHS.** Robert "Buzzy" Henry, Dave O'Brien. *LOO*

By Dawn's Early Light **1989** Made-for-cable-TV thriller about two Air Force pilots who must decide whether or not to drop the bombs that would begin WWIII. **100m/C VHS, Beta, LV.** Powers Boothe, Rebecca DeMornay, James Earl Jones, Martin Landau, Rip Torn, Darren McGavin; ***D:*** Jack Sholder; ***M:*** Trevor Jones. *HBO*

By Design **1982 (R)** Two cohabiting women want to have a baby, so they embark on a search for the perfect stud. Not one of Astin's better performances. **90m/C VHS, Beta.** *CA* Patty Duke, Sara Botsford; ***D:*** Claude Jutra. *NO*

By Love Possessed ½ **1961** Can a seemingly typical, quiet, New England town stay quiet when Lana Turner is your neighbor? Vintage romantic melodrama about an attorney who is drawn into an affair when he realizes his home life is not all it could be. **115m/C VHS.** Lana Turner, Efrem Zimbalist Jr., Jason Robards Jr., George Hamilton, Thomas Mitchell; ***D:*** John Sturges; ***C:*** Russell Metty; ***M:*** Elmer Bernstein. *MGM*

By the Blood of Others **1973** In a small French town, a psycho holds two women hostage in a farmhouse, and the townspeople try to figure out a solution without getting anyone killed. In French with English subtitles. **90m/C VHS, Beta.** *FR* Mariangela Melato; ***D:*** Marc Simenon. *FCT*

By the Light of the Silvery Moon ½ **1953** The equally old-fashioned sequel to "On Moonlight Bay" finds Day engaged to MacRae, who's just returned from Army service in WWI. He wants to postpone their marriage until he gets financially secure and the waiting causes some jealous misunderstandings (naturally resolved by movie's end). Based on Booth Tarkington's "Penrod" stories. ♫By the Light of the Silvery Moon; I'll Forget You; Your Eyes Have Told Me So; Be My Little Baby Bumble Bee; If You Were the Only Girl in the World; Ain't We Got Fun; King Chanticleer. **101m/C VHS, LV.** Doris Day, Gordon MacRae, Leon Ames, Billy Gray, Rosemary DeCamp, Mary Wickes, Russell Arms, Maria Palmer; ***D:*** David Butler; ***W:*** Robert O'Brien, Irving Elinson; ***M:*** Max Steiner. *WAR, MVD*

By the Sword ½ **1993 (R)** Maximilian Suba (Abraham) is a one-time fencing whiz who has spent the last 25 years in prison for the murder of his mentor during a fencing match. Upon his release, Suba heads back to his old fencing grounds to see what's become of the murdered man's now-grown son and discovers Alexander (Roberts) is as ruthless and ambitious as Suba once was. Incoherent plot leaves both actors and viewers in the dark. **91m/C VHS.** F. Murray Abraham, Eric Roberts, Mia Sara, Christopher Rydell; ***D:*** Jeremy Paul Kagan; ***W:*** John McDonald, James Donadio; ***M:*** Bill Conti. *COL*

Bye, Bye Baby **1988 (R)** Two luscious young women cavort amid lusty Italian men on various Mediterranean beaches. **80m/C VHS, Beta, LV.** *IT* Carol Alt, Brigitte Nielsen, Jason Connery, Luca Barbareschi; ***D:*** Enrico Oldoini; ***M:*** Manuel De Sica. *PSM, PAR*

Bye, Bye, Birdie **1963** Energized and sweet film version of the Broadway musical about a teen rock and roll idol (Pearson doing Elvis) coming to a small town to see one of his fans before he leaves for the army. The film that made Ann-Margret a star. ♫Bye Bye Birdie; The Telephone Hour; How Lovely to be a Woman; Honestly Sincere; One Boy; Put on a Happy Face; Kids; One Last Kiss; A Lot of Livin' to Do. **112m/C VHS, Beta, LV.** Dick Van Dyke, Janet Leigh, Ann-Margret, Paul Lynde, Bobby Rydell, Maureen Stapleton, Ed Sullivan, Trudi Ames; ***D:*** George Sidney; ***W:*** Irving Brecher; ***C:*** Joseph Biroc. Nominations: Academy Awards '63: Best Sound, Best Original Score. *COL*

Bye Bye Blues ½ **1989 (PG)** The lives of the Cooper family are disrupted when the husband is called to service during WWII and is then taken prisoner by the Japanese. In need of money, wife Daisy (Jenkins) joins a local swing band and begins charming all who watch her, especially the band's trombone player (Reilly). A sweet-spirited tale of love, loyalty, and the search for inner strength. Jenkins gives a strong performance as the shy wife who becomes an independent woman during her husband's absence. **110m/C VHS.** *CA* Rebecca Jenkins, Michael Ontkean, Luke Reilly, Stuart Margolin, Robyn Stevan, Kate Reid, Wayne Robson; ***D:*** Anne Wheeler; ***W:*** Anne Wheeler; ***M:*** George Blondheim. Genie Awards '90: Best Actress (Jenkins), Best Supporting Actress (Stevan). *MNC*

Bye Bye Brazil ½ **1979** A changing Brazil is seen through the eyes of four wandering gypsy minstrels participating in a tent show traveling throughout the country. Lots of Brazilian charm. In Portuguese with English subtitles. **115m/C VHS, Beta, LV.** *BR* Jose Wilker, Betty Faria, Fabio Junior, Zaira Zambello; ***D:*** Carlos Diegues; ***W:*** Carlos Diegues. Nominations: Cannes Film Festival '80: Best Film. *FXL, INJ, TPV*

Bye Bye, Love ½ **1994 (PG-13)** Forty-eight hours in the lives of three divorced buddies starts at the local Mickey D's for the biweekly exchange of their kids. The dads don't offer any surprises: Donny (Reiser) still loves his ex, Vic (Quaid) hates his, and Dave (Modine) loves anything in a skirt. Sometimes witty, but just as often sadly poignant, the plot is as shallow as a TV sitcom, with an easy answer for every difficult question about divorce. The three leads are likeable enough, but Garofalo is the gem in an otherwise dull flick. She looks like she's having a blast, stealing scenes with abandon as Vic's blind date from hell. **107m/C VHS, LV.** Matthew Modine, Randy Quaid, Paul Reiser, Rob Reiner, Janeane Garofalo, Ed Flanders, Lindsay Crouse, James Whitworth, Maria Pitillo; ***D:*** Sam Weisman; ***W:*** Gary David Goldberg, Brad Hall; ***M:*** J.A.C. Redford. *FXV*

The C-Man **1949** Customs agent Jagger finds work isn't so dull after all. Murder and theft on an international scale make for a busy week as he follows jewel smugglers from Paris to New York. Docu-style though routine crime story. **75m/B VHS.** Dean Jagger, John Carradine, Harry Landers, Rene Paul; ***D:*** Joseph Lerner. *SNC*

Cabaret ½ **1972 (PG)** Hitler is rising to power, racism and anti-Semitism are growing, and the best place to hide from it all is the cabaret. With dancing girls, androgynous master of ceremonies Grey and American expatriate and singer Minnelli, you can laugh and drink and pretend tomorrow will never come. Minnelli does just that. Face to face with the increasing horrors of Nazism, she persists in the belief that the "show must go on." Based on the John Kander's hit Broadway musical (taken from the Christopher Isherwood stories), the film is impressive, with excellent direction and cinematography. ♫Cabaret; Wilkommen; Mein Herr; Maybe This Time; Two Ladies; Money, Money; Hieraten; Tomorrow Belongs to Me; If You Could See Her. **119m/C VHS, Beta, LV.** Liza Minnelli, Joel Grey, Michael York, Marisa Berenson; ***D:*** Bob Fosse; ***W:*** Jay Presson Allen; ***C:*** Geoffrey Unsworth; ***M:*** Ralph Burns. Academy Awards '72: Best Actress (Minnelli), Best Art Direction/Set Decoration, Best Cinematography, Best Director (Fosse), Best Film Editing, Best Sound, Best Supporting Actor (Grey), Best Score; British Academy Awards '72: Best Actress (Minnelli), Best Director (Fosse), Best Film; Golden Globe Awards '73: Best Actress—Musical/Comedy (Minnelli), Best Film—Musical/Comedy, Best Supporting Actor (Grey); National Society of Film Critics Awards '72: Best Supporting Actor (Grey); Writers Guild of America '72: Best Adapted Screenplay; Nominations: Academy Awards '72: Best Adapted Screenplay, Best Picture. *FOX, BTV, CCB*

Cabeza de Vaca **1990 (R)** In 1528, a Spanish expedition shipwrecks in unknown territory off the Florida coast. Only survivor Cabeza de Vaca is captured by the Iguase Indian tribe and made a slave to their shaman. He's later freed, but leaves with respect for their culture. Spanish soldiers find him and want his help in capturing the natives, but he is outraged by their cruelty and must confront his own people. Strong visual style easily brings the audience deeply into this uncharted world. Based on Cabeza de Vaca's book "Naufragios." Director Echevarria's feature film debut. Spanish and Indian with subtitles. **111m/C VHS.** *MX SP* Juan Diego, Daniel Gimenez Cacho, Roberto Sosa, Carlos Castanon, Gerardo Villarreal, Roberto Cobo, Jose Flores, Ramon Barragan; ***D:*** Nicolas Echevarria; ***W:*** Guillermo Sheridan, Nicolas Echevarria; ***M:*** Mario Lavista. *NHO, FCT*

Cabin Boy *Woof!* **1994 (PG-13)** Obnoxious "fancy lad" Elliott mistakenly boards the wrong boat and becomes the new cabin boy for a ridiculous bunch of mean, smelly sailors. Fish out of water saga is so bad it's — bad, a blundering attempt at parody that's just plain stupid. Surprisingly produced by Tim Burton, this effort will disappoint even diehard fans. Look for Chris' real life dad Bob as the lad's dad; good friend Letterman appears briefly as nasty "Old Salt," but uses the alias Earl Hofert in the final credits. As usual, the acerbic Letterman gets the best line, "Man, oh, man do I hate them fancy lads." We know how you feel Dave. **80m/C VHS, LV.** Chris Elliott, Ann Magnuson, Ritch Brinkley, James Gammon, Brian Doyle-Murray, Russ Tamblyn, Brion James, Ricki Lake, Bob Elliott; ***Cameos:*** David Letterman; ***D:*** Adam Resnick; ***W:*** Adam Resnick; ***M:*** Steve Bartek. *TOU*

The Cabin in the Cotton ½ **1932** Davis stars as a rich, ruthless Southern belle in this dated melodrama about sharecroppers. Barthelmess is cast as a poor sharecropper who is almost brought to ruin when he falls for the sexy Southern vamp. Contains Davis's most famous line, "Ah'd love t'kiss you, but ah jes washed mah hair." **77m/B VHS.** Bette Davis, Richard Barthelmess, Dorothy Jordan, Henry B. Walthall, Tully Marshall; ***D:*** Michael Curtiz; ***W:*** Paul Green. *MGM*

Cabin in the Sky **1943** A poor woman fights to keep her husband's soul out of the devil's clutches. Based on a Broadway show and featuring an all-Black cast. Lively dance numbers and a musical score with contributions from Duke Ellington. Minnelli's first feature film. ♫Cabin in the Sky; Happiness Is Just a Thing Called Joe; Taking a Chance on Love; Life's Full of Consequence; Li'l Black Sheep; Shine; Honey in the Honeycomb. **99m/C VHS, Beta, LV.** Ethel Waters, Eddie Anderson, Lena Horne, Rex Ingram, Louis Armstrong, Duke Ellington; ***D:*** Vincente Minnelli; ***M:*** Duke Ellington, Harold Arlen, E.Y. Harburg, George Bassman. Nominations: Academy Awards '43: Best Song ("Happiness Is a Thing Called Joe"). *MGM, MLB, FHE*

The Cabinet of Dr. Caligari **1919** A pioneering film in the most extreme expressionistic style about a hypnotist in a carnival and a girl-snatching somnambulist. Highly influential in its approach to lighting, composition, design and acting. Much imitated. Silent. **92m/B VHS, Beta, LV.** *GE* Conrad Veidt, Werner Krauss, Lil Dagover; ***D:*** Robert Wiene. *KIV, REP, MRV*

Cabiria ½ **1914** The pioneering Italian epic about a Roman and a slave girl having a love affair in Rome during the Second Punic War. Immense sets and set-pieces; an important influence on Griffith and DeMille. Silent. **123m/B VHS, Beta, 8mm.** *IT* ***D:*** Giovanni Pastrone. *KIV, FCT, INJ*

The Cable Guy ½ **1996 (PG-13)** Carrey's first $20 million paycheck picture finds cable subscriber Broderick in for a comedic nightmare when he accepts the offer of free movie channels. The overeager installer (Carrey, naturally) turns his life upside down. A little darker humor than Carrey fans may be used to, and don't expect any bodily ventriloquism. Carrey (did we mention he's in it?) gets to act with real life people, and it seems to suit him. Director Stiller does a nice job of reining in his more manic impulses when necessary. Broderick holds his own as the reluctant pal. Original scripter Holtz won a Writer's Guild arbitration for sole writing credit from producer-writer Judd Apatow. **95m/C VHS.** Jim Carrey, Matthew Broderick, Leslie Mann, George Segal, Diane Baker, Jack Black, Janeane Garofalo, Andy Dick, Charles Napier; ***D:*** Ben Stiller; ***W:*** Judd Apatow, Lou Holtz Jr.; ***C:*** Robert Brinkmann; ***M:*** John Ottman. *NYR*

Cabo Blanco **1981 (R)** A bartender and a variety of other characters, including an ex-Nazi and a French woman searching for her lover, assemble in Peru after WWII. Nazi Robards controls police chief Rey, while American Bronson runs the local watering hole and eyes French woman Sanda. Hey, this sounds familiar. Everyone shares a common interest: finding a missing treasure of gold, lost in a ship wreck. Remaking "Casablanca" via "The Treasure of Sierra Madre" is never easy. **87m/C VHS, Beta.** Charles Bronson, Jason Robards Jr., Dominique Sanda, Fernando Rey, Gilbert Roland, Simon MacCorkindale; ***D:*** J. Lee Thompson; ***M:*** Jerry Goldsmith. *MED*

Cactus ½ **1986** Melodrama about a young French woman, separated from her husband, who faces the reality of losing her sight after a car accident. She experiences a growing relationship with a blind man and contemplates the thought of risky surgery which may improve her eyesight or cause complete blindness. Countering all that blindness and tangled romance is a camera that pans lush Australian landscapes and humorously focuses on the small telling details of daily life. **95m/C VHS, Beta.** *AU* Isabelle Huppert, Robert Menzies, Monica Maughan, Sheila Florence, Norman Kaye, Banduk Marika; ***D:*** Paul Cox; ***W:*** Norman Kaye, Paul Cox, Bob Ellis; ***M:*** Giovanni Pergolese, Yannis Markopolous, Elsa Davis. *ORI*

Cactus Flower **1969 (PG)** Good cast doesn't quite suffice to make this adaptation of a Broadway hit work. A middle-aged bachelor dentist gets involved with a kookie mistress, refusing to admit his real love for his prim and proper receptionist. Hawn's big leap to stardom. **103m/C VHS, Beta, LV.** Walter Matthau, Goldie Hawn, Ingrid Bergman, Jack Weston, Rick Lenz; ***D:*** Gene Saks; ***C:*** Charles B(ryant) Lang; ***M:*** Quincy Jones. Academy Awards '69: Best Supporting Actress (Hawn); Golden Globe Awards '70: Best Supporting Actress (Hawn). *COL*

Cactus in the Snow ½ **1972** A virginal Army private serving during the Vietnam War era tries to find sex on a 72-hour leave and instead discovers love. Some guys have all the luck. Melodrama never grabs where it ought to. **90m/C VHS, Beta, LV.** Richard Thomas, Mary Layne, Lucille Benson; ***D:*** Martin Zweiback. *NO*

Caddie ½ **1981** Based on an autobiographical story of a woman who leaves her unfaithful husband in 1930s Australia. Struggling to raise her two children, she works as a waitress in a bar where she finds romance with one of the regulars. Average script bolstered by Morse's performance. **107m/C VHS, Beta.** *AU* Helen Morse, Jack Thompson; ***D:*** Donald Crombie. *NO*

The Caddy **1953** Lewis plays frantic caddy prone to slapstick against Martin's smooth professional golfer with a bent toward singing. Mostly a series of Martin and Lewis sketches that frequently land in the rough. Introduces several songs, including a classic Martin and Lewis rendition of "That's Amore." Look for cameos by a host of professional golfers. **95m/C VHS, Beta.** Dean Martin, Jerry Lewis, Donna Reed, Barbara Bates, Joseph Calleia, Marshall Thompson, Fred Clark; ***Cameos:*** Ben Hogan, Sam Snead, Byron Nelson, Julius Boros, Jimmy Thomson, Harry E. Cooper; ***D:*** Norman Taurog; ***W:*** Danny Arnold. Nominations: Academy Awards '53: Best Song ("That's Amore"). *PAR*

Caddyshack ½ **1980 (R)** Inspired performances by Murray and Dangerfield drive this sublimely moronic comedy onto the green. The action takes place at Bushwood Country Club, where caddy O'Keefe is bucking to win the club's college scholarship. Characters involved in various sophomoric set pieces include obnoxious club president Knight, a playboy who is too laid back to keep his score (Chase), a loud, vulgar, and extremely rich golfer (Dangerfield), and Murray as a filthy gopher-hunting groundskeeper. Occasional dry moments are followed by scenes of pure (and tasteless) anarchy, so watch with someone immature. Does for golf what "Major League" tried to do for baseball. **99m/C VHS, Beta, LV.** Chevy Chase, Rodney Dangerfield, Ted Knight, Michael O'Keefe, Bill Murray, Sarah Holcomb, Brian Doyle-Murray; ***D:*** Harold Ramis; ***W:*** Brian Doyle-Murray, Doug Kenney, Harold Ramis. *WAR*

Caddyshack 2 ½ **1988 (PG)** Obligatory sequel to "Caddyshack," minus Bill Murray who wisely avoided further encroachment of gopher holes and director Ramis who opted for the screenwriting chore. Mason is the star of the show as a crude self-made millionaire who tangles with the snobs at the country club. Although it occasionally earns a side-splitting chuckle, "Shack 2" has significantly fewer guffaws than the original, proving once again that funny guys are always undone by lousy scripts and weak direction. **103m/C VHS, Beta, LV, 8mm.** Jackie Mason, Chevy Chase, Dan Aykroyd, Dyan Cannon, Robert Stack, Dina Merrill, Randy Quaid, Jessica Lundy, Jonathan Silverman, Chynna Phillips; ***D:*** Allan Arkush; ***W:*** Harold Ramis, Peter Torokvei; ***C:*** Harry Stradling Jr.; ***M:*** Ira Newborn. Golden Raspberry Awards '88: Worst Supporting Actor (Aykroyd), Worst Song ("Jack Fresh"). *WAR*

Cadence **1989 (PG-13)** The directorial debut of actor Martin Sheen, this fitful melodrama stars son Charlie as an unruly trooper on a 1960s army base. Placed in an all-black stockade for punishment, he bonds with his brother prisoners by defying the hardcase sergeant (played by Sheen the elder). Characters and situations are intriguing but not rendered effectively. Based on the novel "Count a Lonely Cadence" by Gordon Weaver. **97m/C VHS, LV.** Charlie Sheen, Martin Sheen, Laurence "Larry" Fishburne, Michael Beach, Ramon Estevez; ***D:*** Martin Sheen; ***M:*** Georges Delerue. *REP*

Cadillac Girls ½ **1993** Page is a self-destructive teenager who is arrested for car theft. To avoid jail, Page is placed in her single mom's custody and moves to her family's straitlaced hometown in Nova Scotia. Mom isn't exactly good at parenting and Page's adolescent anger extends to putting the moves on mom's potential new beau. **99m/C VHS.** Jennifer Dale, Gregory Harrison, Mia Kirshner. *MNC*

Cadillac Man **1990 (R)** Williams is the quintessential low-life car salesman in this rather disjointed comedy. A lesser comedic talent might have stalled and been abandoned, but Williams manages to drive away despite the flat script and direction. One storyline follows his attempt to sell 12 cars in 12 days or lose his job, while another follows his confrontation with a gun-toting, mad-as-hell cuckolded husband. Williams and Robbins are often close to being funny in a hyperkinetic way, but the situations are dumb enough to rob most of the scenes of their comedy. Watch for a movie-stealing bit by the spunky waitress at the local Chinese restaurant. **95m/C VHS, Beta, LV.** Robin Williams, Tim Robbins, Pamela Reed, Fran Drescher, Zack Norman, Annabella Sciorra, Lori Petty, Paul Guilfoyle; ***D:*** Roger Donaldson; ***W:*** Ken Friedman. *ORI*

Caesar and Cleopatra ½ **1946** Based on the classic George Bernard Shaw play. Caesar meets the beautiful Cleopatra in ancient Egypt and helps her gain control of her life. Remains surprisingly true to Shaw's adaptation, unlike many other historical films of the same era. **135m/C VHS, Beta.** *GB* Claude Rains, Vivien Leigh, Stewart Granger, Flora Robson, Francis L. Sullivan, Cecil Parker; ***D:*** Gabriel Pascal; ***C:*** Robert Krasker. Nominations: Academy Awards '46: Best Interior Decoration. *NO*

Cafe au Lait *Metisse* **1994** Actor/director/writer Kassovitz scores in his debut feature about an interracial menage a trois. Beautiful mulatto Lola (Mauduech) is pregnant but she's not sure by which of her two contrasting lovers (who don't yet know about each other). It could be white, Jewish, easy-going bicycle messenger Felix (Kassovitz) or stuffy, wealthy, black Moslem student Jamal (Kounde). Both men desire the fatherhood role and both move in with Lola to share responsibility. This is not without complications. Generally light and frothy without ignoring racial tensions. French with subtitles. **94m/C VHS.** *FR* Mathieu Kassovitz, Julie Mauduech, Hubert Kounde, Vincent Cassel, Tadek Lokcinski, Jany Holt; ***D:*** Mathieu Kassovitz; ***W:*** Mathieu Kassovitz; ***C:*** Pierre Aim; ***M:*** Marie Daulne, Jean-Louis Daulne. *NYR*

Cafe Express ½ **1983** A con artist (he sells coffee illegally aboard an Italian train) stays one step ahead of the law as he raises money to help his ailing son. As in "Bread and Chocolate," Manfredi is again the put-upon working class hero comedically attempting to find a better way of life in this bittersweet tale. **90m/C VHS, Beta.** *IT* Nino Manfredi, Gigi Reder, Adolfo Celi, Vittorio Mezzogiorno; ***D:*** Nanni Loy. *NO*

Cafe Romeo **1991 (R)** Tale of twenty-something friendships forged in the neighborhood coffeehouse of a heavily Italian community. Lia (Stewart) is a waitress who dreams of becoming a fashion designer, but her marriage to a small time hood holds her back. Crombie, her cousin by marriage, is a dental student confused about his future, but very much in love with Lia. Quiet movie boasts average script that's helped along by strong performances. Originally broadcast on Canadian TV. **93m/C VHS, LV.** *CA* Catherine Mary Stewart, Jonathan Crombie; ***D:*** Rex Bromfield. *REP*

The Cage **1989 (R)** Gangsters enlist a brain-damaged Vietnam vet played by Ferrigno to participate in illegal "cage fights," enclosed wrestling matches fought to the death. Crude and annoying. **101m/C VHS, Beta, LV.** Lou Ferrigno, Reb Brown, Michael Dante, Mike Moroff, Marilyn Tokuda, James Shigeta, Al Ruscio; ***D:*** Hugh Kelley. *ORI*

The Cage **1990** Sent to prison for murdering his girlfriend, Jive has no idea what the pen has in store for him. The inmates stage a mock trial, the defendant is found guilty and the sentence is too horrible to imagine. From a stage play by the San Quentin Drama Workshop and co-starring Hayes, author of "Midnight Express." **90m/C VHS, Beta.** Rick Cluchey, William Hayes; ***D:*** Rick Cluchey; ***W:*** Rick Cluchey. *NO*

Cage 2: The Arena of Death ½ **1994 (R)** Billy Thomas (Ferrigno) is kidnapped by a vicious mobster and forced to battle martial arts experts in a steel cage battle to the death. But his best friend (Brown) plans to infiltrate the show and put a stop to the carnage. **94m/C VHS.** Lou Ferrigno, Reb Brown; ***D:*** Lang Elliott. *PAR*

Caged Fear ½ **1992 (R)** Young Krissie (Cloke) is mistakenly put behind bars in a brutal, high-security prison for a shootout caused by her outlaw husband Tommy (Keith) during their honeymoon. Tommy comes up with an outrageous scheme to rescue her. Not quite as bad as it sounds, but close. **94m/C VHS, LV.** David Keith, Deborah May, Ray Sharkey, Loretta Devine, Karen Black, Kristen Cloke; ***D:*** Bobby Houston; ***W:*** Bobby Houston. *NLC*

Caged Fury **1980 (R)** American women being held captive in Southeast Asia are brainwashed into becoming walking time bombs. Yes, that dame's gonna blow. Made in the Philippines with the best of intentions. **90m/C VHS, Beta.** *PH* Bernadette Williams, Taffee O'Connell, Jennifer Laine; ***D:*** Cirio H. Santiago. *NO*

Caged Fury **1990** Two Los Angeles women allegedly commit sexual crimes and are sent to prison. Cheap, exploitive women's prison rehash. **85m/C VHS, Beta, LV.** Erik Estrada, Richie Barathy, Roxanna Michaels, Paul Smith, James Hong, Greg Cummins; ***D:*** Bill Milling. *COL*

Caged Hearts **1995 (R)** Chicks-behind-bars flick finds Genzel and McClure framed for murder by a shady organization called "The Shield." Cliches abound. **87m/C VHS.** Tane McClure, Carrie Genzel, Taylor Leigh, Nick Wilder; ***D:*** Henri Charr. *PMH*

Caged Heat *Renegade Girls; Caged Females* **1974 (R)** Low-budget babes-behind-bars film touted as the best sexploitation film of the day. Demme's directorial debut is a genre-altering installment in Roger Corman's formulaic cellblock Cinderella cycle. Recycled plot—innocent woman is put behind bars, where she loses some of her innocence—boasts an updated treatment. These babes may wear hot pants and gratuitously bare their midriffs, but they're not brainless bimbos. They're strong individuals who work together to liberate themselves. Reached cult status. Cult diva Steele returned to the big screen after six years to play the wheelchair-ridden prison warden, written specifically for her. **83m/C VHS, LV.** Juanita Brown, Erica Gavin, Roberta Collins, Barbara Steele, Ella Reid, Cheryl "Rainbeaux" Smith; ***D:*** Jonathan Demme; ***W:*** Jonathan Demme. *SUE, NWV*

Caged Heat 2: Stripped of Freedom ½ **1994 (R)** Women-in-prison formula with a princess thrown into the pen following a political coup. CIA agent is sent undercover as an inmate to bust her out. Usual sadistic guards, rape, and revenge scenes. From Roger Corman's direct-to-video factory. **84m/C VHS, LV.** Jewel Shepard, Chanel Akiko Hirai, Pamella D'Pella, Vic Diaz; ***D:*** Cirio H. Santiago. *NHO*

Caged in Paradiso ½ **1989 (R)** A convicted criminal and his wife are dumped onto a remote prisoner's isle to live out their lives. When Cara loses contact with her husband, she must fend for herself. Survival tale boringly told. **90m/C VHS, Beta, LV.** Irene Cara; ***D:*** Michael Snyder. *VMK, IME*

Caged Terror *Woof!* **1972** Two urbanites hit the countryside for a weekend and meet a band of crazy rapists who ravage the wife and set the husband raging with bloodthirsty revenge. Squalid stroll through the ruins. **76m/C VHS, Beta.** Percy Harkness, Elizabeth Suzuki, Leon Morenzie. *NWV*

Caged Women *Women's Penitentiary 4* **1984 (R)** Undercover journalist enters a women's prison and gets the usual eyeful. **97m/C VHS, Beta.** *FR IT* Laura Gemser, Gabriele Tinti, Lorraine De Selle, Maria Romano; ***D:*** Vincent Dawn. *VES, LIV, DMP*

Cahill: United States Marshal **1973 (PG)** The aging Duke in one of his lesser moments, portraying a marshal who comes to the aid of his sons. The boys are mixed up with a gang of outlaws, proving that no matter how good a parent you are, sometimes the kids just lean toward the wayward. Turns out, though, that the boys harbor a grudge against the old man due to years of workaholic neglect. Will Duke see the error of his ways and reconcile with the delinquent boys? Will he catch the outlaw leader? Will he go on to star in other Duke vehicles? **103m/C VHS, Beta, LV.** John Wayne, Gary Grimes, George Kennedy, Neville Brand, Marie Windsor, Harry Carey Jr.; ***D:*** Andrew V. McLaglen; ***M:*** Elmer Bernstein. *WAR, TLF*

The Caine Mutiny **1954** A group of naval officers revolt against a captain they consider mentally unfit. Bogart is masterful as Captain Queeg, obsessed with cleanliness while onboard and later a study in mental meltdown during the court-martial of a crew member who participated in the mutiny. Based on the Pulitzer-winning novel by Herman Wouk, the drama takes a close look at the pressure-filled life aboard ship during WWII. **125m/C VHS, Beta, LV, 8mm.** Humphrey Bogart, Jose Ferrer, Van Johnson, Fred MacMurray, Lee Marvin, Claude Akins, E.G. Marshall, Robert Francis, May Wynn, Tom Tully; ***D:*** Edward Dmytryk; ***W:*** Stanley Roberts; ***M:*** Max Steiner. Nominations: Academy Awards '53: Best Actor (Tully); Academy Awards '54: Best Actor (Bogart), Best Film Editing, Best Picture, Best Screenplay, Best Sound, Best Original Score. *COL, HMV*

The Caine Mutiny Court Martial **1988 (PG)** A young lieutenant is up for a court-martial after taking control of the U.S.S. Caine in the midst of a typhoon. In order to save him, his lawyer must discredit the paranoid Commander Queeg. As the events of the mutiny unfold, it becomes clear that Queeg's obsession with discipline had become a threat to everyone aboard. Good performances, particularly by Bogosian as the lawyer. Based on the Pulitzer Prize-winning novel by Herman Wouk. Made for television. **100m/C VHS, LV.** Jeff Daniels, Eric Bogosian, Brad Davis, Peter Gallagher, Michael Murphy, Kevin J. O'Connor, Daniel H. Jenkins; ***D:*** Robert Altman. *VMK*

Cain's Cutthroats *Cain's Way; The Blood Seekers* **1971 (R)** A former Confederate army captain and a bounty hunting preacher team up to settle the score with soldiers on a gang-raping, murdering spree. **87m/C VHS, Beta.** Scott Brady, John Carradine, Robert Dix. *GHV*

Cairo **1942** War correspondent Young lands in Cairo where he is supposed to pass along classified information to a Nazi spy posing as a Brit. He meets and falls in love with American movie queen thought to be enemy agent (MacDonald) and a race across the desert follows when Young is trapped in a pyramid. Catchy tunes can't save this cheesy WWII spy spoof that marked the end of MacDonald's MGM contract. **101m/B VHS.** Jeanette MacDonald, Robert Young, Ethel Waters, Reginald Owen, Grant Mitchell, Lionel Atwill, Eduardo Ciannelli, Mitchell Lewis; ***D:*** Woodbridge S. Van Dyke; ***W:*** John McClain; ***M:*** Herbert Stothart. *MGM*

Cajon Pass **1988** A group of trains challenges the terrain attempting to go through Cajon Pass into Los Angeles. **60m/C VHS, Beta.** *PEN*

Cal **1984 (R)** A young Catholic man is recruited into the Irish Republican Army. He falls in love with an older Protestant widow, whose husband, a policeman, he helped kill, acting as the get-away driver for his fellow Republicans. Thoughtful and tragic, with excellent performances; set in Northern Ireland. **104m/C VHS, Beta.** *IR* Helen Mirren, John Lynch, Donal McCann, Kitty Gibson, Ray McAnally, John Kavanagh; ***D:*** Pat O'Connor; ***W:*** Bernard MacLaverty; ***M:*** Mark Knopfler. Cannes Film Festival '84: Best Actress (Mirren); Nominations: Cannes Film Festival '84: Best Film. *WAR, FCT, INJ*

Calamity Jane **1953** In one of her best Warner musicals, Day stars as the rip-snortin', guntotin' Calamity Jane of Western lore, in an on-again, off-again romance with Wild Bill Hickok. ♫Secret Love; Just Blew in From the Windy City; The Black Hills of Dakota; The Deadwood Stage (Whip-Crack-Away!). **101m/C VHS, Beta, LV.** Doris Day, Howard Keel, Allyn Ann McLerie; ***D:*** David Butler; ***M:*** Sammy Fain, Paul Francis Webster. Academy Awards '53: Best Song ("Secret Love"); Nominations: Academy Awards '53: Best Sound, Best Original Score. *WAR, FCT*

Calamity Jane ½ **1982** A made-for-television biography of the famous lady crack shot. Alexander is cast as the tough-as-nails woman who considered herself on a par with any man. **96m/C VHS, Beta.** Jane Alexander, Frederic Forrest, Ken Kercheval, Talia Balsam, David Hemmings; ***D:*** James Goldstone. *FOX*

Calendar **1993** A Canadian photographer (Egoyan) is hired to take pictures of ancient Armenian churches for a calendar. His wife (Egoyan's real-life spouse Khanjian) accompanies him, serving as a translator, and they hire a driver (Adamian) who turns out to be an architectural expert. Told in flashback, the film gradually reveals a romantic triangle—with the photographer becoming so caught up in his work that he fails to realize his wife, increasingly drawn to her ethnic heritage, and their driver are having an affair. This romantic puzzle also includes the photographer, having returned to Canada wifeless and apparently seeking a replacement, having dinner with a series of women he's meet through the personals. In English and Armenian. **78m/C VHS.** *CA* Atom Egoyan, Arsinee Khanjian, Ashot Adamian; ***D:*** Atom Egoyan; ***W:*** Atom Egoyan; ***C:*** Norayr Kasper. *KIV*

Calendar Girl ½ **1993 (PG-13)** In 1962 three high-school best friends borrow a convertible and travel from their Nevada homes to Hollywood to meet their pinup idol, Marilyn Monroe. Roy's (Priestley) a rebel, Ned's (Olds, in his film debut) sensitive, and Scott's (O'Connell) just a nice guy. They stay with Roy's Uncle Harvey (Pantoliano), an aspiring actor, and work to meet their dream girl. Which they finally do, in a notably weak sequence which fits in with this notably uninspired film. The three actors at least have enough comradery to make realistic buddies—one of the few true touches in the film. **86m/C VHS, LV, 8mm.** Jason Priestley, Gabriel Olds, Jerry O'Connell, Joe Pantoliano, Stephen Tobolowsky, Kurt Fuller, Steve Railsback, Emily Warfield, Stephanie Anderson; ***Cameos:*** Chubby Checker; ***D:*** John Whitesell; ***W:*** Paul Shapiro; ***M:*** Hans Zimmer. *COL*

Calendar Girl Murders ½ **1984** Minor mystery about the murder of some girlie magazine pinups. Made for television. **104m/C VHS.** Robert Culp, Tom Skerritt, Barbara Parkins, Sharon Stone; ***D:*** William A. Graham; ***M:*** Brad Fiedel. *EDV*

California Casanova *Woof!* **1989 (R)** Mirthless, semi-musical farce about a nerdy stagehand learning to be a great lover to win a beautiful singer's heart who's being blackmailed by a cruel gangster. Nice cast; nobody's home. **94m/C VHS.** Jerry Orbach, Audrey Landers, Tyrone Power Jr., Bryan Genesse, Ken Kercheval, Ted Davis, Joyce Blair; ***D:*** Nathaniel Christian; ***W:*** Nathaniel Christian. *ACA*

California Dreaming **1979 (R)** Nerdy young man heads west to California where he tries to fit in with the local beach crowd. Reminiscent of the popular beach movies of the '60s. **93m/C VHS, Beta.** Dennis Christopher, Tanya Roberts, Glynnis O'Connor, John Calvin, Seymour Cassel; ***D:*** John Hancock. *VES, LIV*

California Girls **1984** Radio station stages a beauty contest and three sexy ladies prove to be tough competition. Features women in little swimsuits, minimal plot, and a soundtrack by the Police, Kool & the Gang, Blondie, Queen, and 10cc. **83m/C VHS, Beta.** Al Music, Mary McKinley, Alicia Allen, Lantz Douglas, Barbara Parks; ***D:*** Rick Wallace. *NO*

California Gold Rush **1981** Hays portrays young aspiring writer, Bret Harte, who, in search of adventure in 1849, arrives in Sutter's Fort and takes on a job at the local sawmill. When gold is found, Sutter's Fort is soon overrun with fortune hunters whose greed, violence and corruption threaten to tear apart the peaceful community. Made for television. **100m/C VHS, Beta.** Robert Hays, John Dehner, Dan Haggerty, Ken Curtis; ***D:*** Jack B. Hively. *NO*

California Joe **1943** California is being eyed by Confederate sympathizers and also by their leader, who wants it for his own plans. Enter California Joe, a Union officer in disguise, who will save the day. Standard western. **55m/B VHS, Beta.** Donald (Don "Red") Barry, Lynn Merrick, Helen Talbot. *DVT*

California Straight Ahead **1925** Denny—whose niche in the twenties was silent action comedies, and who had teamed with director Pollard earlier in the decade to produce "The Leatherpushers" series—stars in this silent actioner which features a cross-country road trip, zoo animals-on-a-rampage, and a car-racing conclusion (sounds like an action formula ahead of its time). Audiences didn't realize until the talkies that the All-American manly man was in fact played by a Brit. For those who revel in trivia, Denny appeared in the 1961 "Batman." **77m/B VHS, Beta.** Reginald Denny, Gertrude Olmsted, Tom Wilson, Lucille Ward, John Steppling; ***D:*** Harry Pollard. *GPV, FCT*

California Suite **1978 (PG)** The posh Beverly Hills Hotel is the setting for four unrelated Neil Simon skits, ranging from a battling husband and wife to feuding friends. Simonized dialogue is crisp and funny. **103m/C VHS, Beta, LV.** Alan Alda, Michael Caine, Bill Cosby, Jane Fonda, Walter Matthau, Richard Pryor, Maggie Smith, Elaine May; ***D:*** Herbert Ross; ***W:*** Neil Simon; ***M:*** Claude Bolling. Academy Awards '78: Best Supporting Actress (Smith); Golden Globe Awards '79: Best Actress—Musical/Comedy (Smith); Nominations: Academy Awards '78: Best Adapted Screenplay, Best Art Direction/Set Decoration. *COL*

Caligari's Cure **1982** Palazzolo's first film is a satiric, non-narrative stab at his Catholic upbringing via German expressionism and modern performance art. **70m/C VHS, Beta.** ***D:*** Tom Palazzolo. *FCT*

Caligula *Woof!* **1980** Infamous, expensive, extremely graphic, and sexually explicit adaptation of the life of the mad Roman emperor, Caligula. Scenes of decapitation, necrophilia, rape, bestiality, and sadomasochism abound. Biggest question is why Gielgud, O'Toole, and McDowell lent their talents to this monumentally abhorred film (not to mention Gore Vidal on the writing end, who didn't want the credit). Adult magazine publisher Bob Guccione coproduced and didn't particularly want to release it. Also available in a censored, "R" rated version. **143m/C VHS, Beta, LV.** *IT* Malcolm McDowell, John Gielgud, Peter O'Toole, Helen Mirren; ***D:*** Tinto Brass; ***W:*** Gore Vidal. *NO*

Call Him Mr. Shatter *Shatter* **1974 (R)** A hired killer stalks a tottering Third World president and becomes embroiled in international political intrigue. **90m/C VHS, Beta.** *GB* Stuart Whitman, Peter Cushing, Anton Diffring; ***D:*** Michael Carreras. *NLC*

Call Me **1988 (R)** Psycho-drama about a lusty young woman who responds positively to an obscene telephone caller until she witnesses him murder another person. Doubt creeps into the relationship. **98m/C VHS, Beta, LV.** Patricia Charbonneau, Patti D'Arbanville, Sam Freed, Boyd Gaines, Stephen McHattie; ***D:*** Sollace Mitchell. *VES*

Call Me Bwana ½ **1963** Pure cornpone with Hope as a bumbling explorer sent with CIA agent Adams to track down a lost American space capsule in deepest Africa. Enemy agents Ekberg and Jeffries try to make things difficult. **103m/C VHS.** Bob Hope, Edie Adams, Anita Ekberg, Lionel Jeffries, Percy Herbert, Paul Carpenter, Orlando Martins; ***D:*** Gordon Douglas; ***W:*** Nate Monaster, Johanna Harwood. *MGM, FCT*

Call Northside 777 ½ *Calling Northside 777* **1948** Chicago reporter Stewart finds himself in the crux of a decade-old murder investigation when he follows up a newspaper ad offering $5,000 for any information leading to the arrest and conviction of a police killer. The cunning reporter discovers police coverups and missing evidence pointing to an imprisoned man's innocence. Powerful performance from Stewart directs this docu-drama based on the real-life story of Chicago's Joe Majczek, unjustly imprisoned for 11 years, and the Pulitzer Prize winning reporter Jim McGuire who, through a clever investigation, found enough evidence to have the case re-opened. **111m/B VHS.** James Stewart, Richard Conte, Lee J. Cobb, Helen Walker, Betty Garde, Moroni Olsen, E.G. Marshall, Howard Smith, John McIntire, Paul Harvey, George Tyne, Michael Chapin, Addison Richards, Richard Rober, Eddie Dunn, Charles Lane, Walter Greaza, William Post Jr., George Melford, Charles Miller, Lionel Stander, Jonathan Hale; ***D:*** Henry Hathaway; ***M:*** Alfred Newman. *FXV*

Call of the Canyon ½ **1942** A crooked agent for a local meat packer won't pay a fair price, so Gene goes off to talk to the head man to set him straight. **71m/B VHS, Beta.** Gene Autry, Smiley Burnette, Ruth Terry, Thurston Hall, Pat Brady; ***D:*** Joseph Santley. *CCB, VCN, GPV*

Call of the Forest ½ **1949** Bobby makes friends with a beautiful wild black stallion which is captured and tamed by his father. The father has found a goldmine, also desired by an villain, and Bobby and his horse must come to his father's aid. Black Diamond (the horse) has the best role. **74m/B VHS.** Robert Lowery, Ken Curtis, Martha Sherrill, Chief Thundercloud, Charles Hughes; ***D:*** John F. Link. *NOS, DVT, VYY*

Call of the Rockies **1944** Action-packed oater in which Carson and Burnette ride across country to save Placer City's mine from crooked townsmen. **54m/B VHS.** Sunset Carson, Smiley Burnette. *REP*

Call of the Wild **1972 (PG)** Jack London's famous story about a man whose survival depends upon his knowledge of the Alaskan wilderness almost comes to life. Filmed in Finland. **105m/C VHS, Beta.** Charlton Heston, Michele Mercier, George Eastman; ***D:*** Ken Annakin. *KUI, SIM, MPI*

Call of the Wild ☠☠½ **1993** Another of Jack London's survival tales is dramatized for television. John Thornton (Schroder) is a rich greenhorn seeking adventure during the 1897 Klondike gold rush. Buck is a German shepherd, sold as a sled dog, who finds adventures of his own in the frozen North until man and dog are united to search for a legendary gold mine. The book is more exciting but the film is more violent. Filmed on location in British Columbia. **97m/C VHS.** Rick Schroder, Gordon Tootoosis, Mia Sara, Duncan Fraser, Richard Newman, Brent Stait. *CAF*

Call Out the Marines ☠☠ **1942** A group of army buddies re-enlist to break up a spy ring. Two of the guys fall in love with the same girl, not realizing that she's one of the spies. McLaglen and Lowe's last comedy together. Mediocre outing isn't redeemed by below average musical numbers. ♫Call Out the Marines; Zana Zaranda; The Light of My Life; Beware; Hands Across the Border. **67m/B VHS, Beta.** Edmund Lowe, Victor McLaglen, Binnie Barnes, Paul Kelly, Dorothy Lovett, Franklin Pangborn; ***D:*** William Hamilton, Frank Ryan. *NO*

Call to Glory ☠☠½ **1984** Pilot for the critically praised television series. An Air Force pilot and his family face turbulent times during the Cuban missile crisis. **96m/C VHS, Beta, LV.** Craig T. Nelson, Cindy Pickett, Gabriel Damon, Keenan Wynn, Elisabeth Shue, G.D. Spradlin. *PAR*

The Caller ☠ **1987 (R)** A strange man enters the house of a lone woman and sets off a long night of suspense and an almost longer evening of inept movie-making. **90m/C VHS, Beta.** Malcolm McDowell, Madolyn Smith; ***D:*** Arthur Seidelman; ***M:*** Richard Band. *TWE*

Callie and Son ☠☠ *Rags to Riches* **1981** Details the sordid story of a waitress who works her way up to become a Dallas socialite and her obsessive relationship with her illegitimate son. Also known as "Rags to Riches." **97m/C VHS, VHS, Beta.** Lindsay Wagner, Dabney Coleman, Jameson Parker, Andrew Prine, James Sloyan, Michelle Pfeiffer; ***D:*** Waris Hussein; ***M:*** Billy Goldenberg. *WAR*

Calling Paul Temple ☠½ **1948** The wealthy patients of a nerve doctor have been dying and a detective is called in to investigate. **92m/B VHS, Beta.** *GB* John Bentley, Dinah Sheridan, Margaretta Scott, Abraham Sofaer, Celia Lipton, Alan Wheatley, Wally Patch; ***D:*** Maclean Rogers. *SNC*

Calling Wild Bill Elliott ☠½ **1943** The crooked territorial governor is exposed by hero Elliott and sidekick Hayes and justice is restored in this typical B-western. Elliott's first film for Republic; he went on to star in 16 Red Ryder films as well as other westerns for the studio. **55m/B VHS.** Wild Bill Elliott, George "Gabby" Hayes, Herbert Heyes, Anne Jeffreys, Fred Kohler Jr., Roy Barcroft, Yakima Canutt; ***D:*** Spencer Gordon Bennet. *REP*

Came a Hot Friday ☠☠ **1985 (PG)** Two cheap conmen arrive in a 1949 southern New Zealand town, run various scams and pursue women. **101m/C VHS, Beta.** *NZ* Peter Bland, Philip Gordon, Billy T. James; ***D:*** Ian Mune. *NLC*

Camel Boy ☠½ **1984** True story of a young Arabian boy who befriends a camel and their treacherous trek across the desert. **78m/C VHS, Beta.** *AU* ***D:*** Yoram Gross; ***V:*** Michael Pate, Ron Haddrick, John Meillon. *VES, LIV, WTA*

Camelot ☠☠ **1967** The long-running Lerner and Loewe Broadway musical about King Arthur, Guinevere, and Lancelot was adapted from T.H. White's book, "The Once and Future King." Redgrave and Nero have chemistry as the illicit lovers, Harris is strong as the king struggling to hold together his dream, but muddled direction undermines the effort. Laserdisc edition contains 28 minutes of previously edited footage, trailers and backstage info. ♫I Wonder What the King is Doing Tonight; The Simple Joys of Maidenhood; Camelot; C'est Moi; The Lusty Month of May; Follow Me; How To Handle a Woman; Then You May Take Me to the Fair; If Ever I Would Leave You. **150m/C VHS, Beta, LV.** Richard Harris, Vanessa Redgrave, David Hemmings, Franco Nero, Lionel Jeffries; ***D:*** Joshua Logan; ***M:*** Frederick Loewe, Alan Jay Lerner. Academy Awards '67: Best Art Direction/Set Decoration, Best Costume Design, Best Score; Golden Globe Awards '68: Best Actor—Musical/Comedy (Harris), Best Song ("If Ever I Should Leave You"), Best Score; Nominations: Academy Awards '67: Best Cinematography, Best Sound. *WAR, RDG, HMV*

Camera Buff ☠☠ *Amator* **1979** Satire on bureaucracy finds a factory worker buying a home-movie camera to film his new baby but becoming obsessed with his new toy. So he begins recording everything he sees—even things the authorities don't want shown. Polish with subtitles. **108m/C VHS.** *PL* Jerzy Stuhr, Malgorzata Zajaczkowska, Ewa Pokas, Krzysztof Zanussi; ***D:*** Krzysztof Kieslowski; ***W:*** Jerzy Stuhr, Krzysztof Kieslowski; ***M:*** Krzysztof Knittel. *NYF*

The Cameraman ☠☠☠☠ **1928** After moving to MGM, Keaton made his first feature with a major studio, giving up the artistic control he had enjoyed in his previous films. Spared from the vilification of studio politics (not the case with later Keaton films) "The Cameraman" enjoyed both critical and popular success. Keaton's inept tintype portrait-maker has a heart that pitter-patters for an MGM office girl. He hopes to impress her by joining the ranks of the newsreel photographers. Fortuitously poised to grab a photo scoop on a Chinese tong war, he is forced to return empty-handed when an organ-grinder's monkey absconds with his firsthand footage. Silent with a musical score. **78m/B VHS, LV.** Buster Keaton, Marceline Day, Harold Goodwin, Harry Gribbon, Sidney Bracy, Edward Brophy, Vernon Dent, William Irving; ***D:*** Edward Sedgwick. *MGM, FCT*

Cameron's Closet ☠½ **1989 (R)** Every child's nightmare comes true. A young boy is convinced that a monster lives in his closet due to his perverse father's psychological tortures. Only this time the monster is real! **86m/C VHS, LV.** Cotter Smith, Mel Harris, Scott Curtis, Chuck McCann, Leigh McCloskey, Kim Lankford, Tab Hunter; ***D:*** Armand Mastroianni; ***W:*** Gary Brandner. *COL*

Camila ☠☠☠ **1984** The true story of the tragic romance between an Argentinean socialite and a Jesuit priest in 1847. The two lovers escape to a small provincial village where they live together as man and wife. Eventually they are recognized and condemned to death. Available in Spanish with English subtitles or dubbed into English. **121m/C VHS, Beta.** *AR SP* Susu Pecoraro, Imanol Arias, Hector Alterio, Elena Tasisto; ***D:*** Maria-Luisa Bemberg. Nominations: Academy Awards '84: Best Foreign Language Film. *COL, SUE, MFI*

Camilla ☠☠½ **1994 (PG-13)** Tandy is delightful in her last starring role as a former violinist on the run with frustrated musician Fonda. Oafish son (Chaykin) and insensitive husband (Koteas) just don't understand, so its time to head to Toronto, site of a fondly, if perhaps incorrectly, remembered triumph. Sort of a May-December female-bonding roadtrip with lots of conversation and comic asides. An inevitably poignant pairing of Tandy and real-life husband Cronyn offers the chance to experience one of America's greatest acting teams one last time. Lack of stereotyping and fairly novel twist on the road movie keep this one on the highway. **91m/C VHS, LV.** Jessica Tandy, Bridget Fonda, Hume Cronyn, Elias Koteas, Maury Chaykin, Graham Greene; ***D:*** Deepa Mehta; ***W:*** Paul Quarrington; ***M:*** Daniel Lanois. *MAX*

Camille ☠☠ **1921** Dying courtesan falls in love with innocent young man in the Dumas classic. Valentino in his prime. **55m/B VHS.** Rudolph Valentino, Alla Nazimova; ***D:*** Fred Niblo. *FCT*

Camille ☠☠☠½ **1936** The classic Alexandre Dumas story about a dying French courtesan falling in love with a shallow young nobleman. A clean, romantic adaptation that somehow escapes the cliches and stands as one of the most telling monuments to Garbo's unique magic and presence on film. **108m/B VHS, Beta.** Greta Garbo, Robert Taylor, Lionel Barrymore, Henry Daniell, Elizabeth Allan, Rex O'Malley, Lenore Ulric, Laura Hope Crews; ***D:*** George Cukor; ***C:*** William H. Daniels. National Board of Review Awards '37: 10 Best Films of the Year; New York Film Critics Awards '37: Best Actress (Garbo); Nominations: Academy Awards '37: Best Actress (Garbo). *MGM*

Camille Claudel ☠☠☠ **1989 (R)** A lushly romantic version of the art world at the turn of the century, when art was exploding in new forms and independence for women was unheard of. Sculptor Claudel's tragic love for art, Auguste Rodin (for whom she modeled), and independence clash, costing her sanity. Very long, it requires an attentive and thoughtful viewing. In French with English subtitles. **149m/C VHS, Beta, LV.** *FR* Isabelle Adjani, Gerard Depardieu, Laurent Grevill, Alain Cuny, Madeleine Robinson, Katrine Boorman; ***D:*** Bruno Nuytten; ***W:*** Bruno Nuytten, Marilyn Goldin; ***M:*** Gabriel Yared. Cesar Awards '89: Best Actress (Adjani), Best Art Direction/Set Decoration, Best Cinematography, Best Costume Design, Best Film; Nominations: Academy Awards '89: Best Actress (Adjani), Best Foreign Language Film. *ORI, IME, INJ*

Camorra: The Naples Connection ☠☠ *Un Complicato Intrigo Di Donne, Vicoli E Delitti* **1985 (R)** A prostitute and an American drug dealer find themselves embroiled in the murders of Neapolitan Mafia heads. Violent, overblown, minor Wertmuller. **94m/C VHS, Beta.** *IT* Harvey Keitel, Angela Molina, Lorraine Bracco, Francesco Rabal; ***D:*** Lina Wertmuller; ***W:*** Lina Wertmuller. *MGM*

Camp Classics #1 **195?** Five corny classics spanning four decades make up this collection: "Mystery of the Leaping Fish" with Douglas Fairbanks, "Foreign Press Awards," "Musical Beauty Shop," "Edsel Commercial," and "Nixon's Checkers Speech." **80m/B VHS, Beta.** Douglas Fairbanks Sr. *WFV*

Camp Cucamonga: How I Spent My Summer Vacation ☠ **1990** Zany antics at summer camp abound when Camp Cucamonga's owner mistakes the new handyman for the camp inspector. Well known stars from TV's "Cheers," "The Jeffersons," "The Wonder Years," and "The Love Boat" are featured in this silly made for television flick. **100m/C VHS.** John Ratzenberger, Sherman Hemsley, Josh Saviano, Danica McKellar, Chad Allen, Dorothy Lyman, Lauren Tewes, G. Gordon Liddy; ***D:*** Roger Duchonwny. *GKK*

Camp Double Feature **1939** Two cautionary anti-pot films, now universally recognized as high camp: "Reefer Madness" and "Marihuana." Both are available individually on video. **120m/B VHS, Beta.** Harley Wood, Hugh McArthur, Paul Ellis, Dave O'Brien, Dorothy Short. *JEF*

Camp Nowhere ☠☠ **1994 (PG)** Video fodder for the juniors in the household as kids turn tables on parents. Instead of trudging off to summer camp for the umpteenth time, a group of upscale kids create their own with the help of laid-off drama teacher Lloyd, who must first con their parents into believing that Camp Nowhere is legit. What follows is that very special summer camp in the Hollywood tradition with lots of junk food, video games galore, and of course, no rules. Camp beserko formula good for a few laughs. **106m/C VHS, LV.** Christopher Lloyd, Wendy Makkena, M. Emmet Walsh, Peter Scolari, Peter Onorati, Ray Baker, Kate Mulgrew, Jonathan Jackson, Romy Walthall, Maryedith Burrell, Tom Wilson, Nathan Cavaleri, Andrew Keegan, Melody Kay; ***D:*** Jonathan Prince; ***W:*** Andrew Kurtzman, Eliot Wald; ***C:*** Sandi Sissel. *TOU*

Campaign in Poland ☠☠ **1940** This documentary chronicles the German invasion of Poland during WWII. **80m/B VHS, Beta.** *NOS, DVT, HEG*

The Campus Corpse ☠ **1977 (PG)** Young man stumbles into deadly college frat hazing and discovers he and rest of cast are utterly devoid of acting ability. **92m/C VHS, Beta.** Charles Martin Smith, Jeff East, Brad Davis; ***D:*** Douglas Curtis. *VES*

Campus Knights ☠ **1929** If you're a serious student of the campus caper film, this is one of the earliest (though not one of the best) of the genre (if such a distinction can be made). The story involves twin brothers—one a tweedy high-browed professor, the other a bon vivant man about town—who wreak fraternal chaos on the quads. **70m/B VHS, Beta.** Raymond McKee, Shirley Palmer, Marie Quillen, Jean Laverty, Sybil Grove; ***D:*** Albert Kelly. *GPV, FCT*

Campus Man 🦴 **1987 (PG)** An entrepreneurial college student markets a beefcake calendar featuring his best friend, until the calendar's sales threaten his friend's amateur athletic status. **94m/C VHS, Beta, LV.** John Dye, Steve Lyon, Kim Delaney, Miles O'Keeffe, Morgan Fairchild, Kathleen Wilhoite; ***D:*** Ron Casden; ***W:*** Geoffrey Baere; ***M:*** James Newton Howard. *PAR*

Can-Can 🦴🦴 **1960** Lackluster screen adaptation of the Cole Porter musical bears little resemblance to the stage version. MacLaine is a cafe owner who goes to court to try and get the "Can-Can," a dance considered risque in gay Paree at the end of the nineteenth century, made legal. Love interest Sinatra happens to be a lawyer. ♫C'est Manifique; Let's Do It; I Love Paris; You Do Something to Me; It's All Right With Me; Live and Let Live; Come Along With Me; Just One of Those Things. **131m/C VHS, Beta, LV.** Frank Sinatra, Shirley MacLaine, Maurice Chevalier, Louis Jourdan, Juliet Prowse, Marcel Dalio, Leon Belasco; ***D:*** Walter Lang; ***C:*** William H. Daniels. Nominations: Academy Awards '60: Best Costume Design (Color), Best Original Score. *FOX, FCT*

Can I Do It...Till I Need Glasses? *Woof!* **1977** More to the point, can you stay awake till the end? Prurient juvenile junk. Brief Williams footage was grafted to this mess during 15 minutes of Mork fame. **72m/C VHS, Beta.** Robin Williams, Roger Behr, Debra Klose, Moose Carlson, Walter Olkewicz; ***D:*** I. Robert Levy. *MED*

Can She Bake a Cherry Pie? 🦴🦴 **1983** Two offbeat characters meet and fall in love in an odd sort of way. Slow-moving and talky but somewhat rewarding. One of Black's better performances. **90m/C VHS, Beta.** Karen Black, Michael Emil, Michael Margotta, Frances Fisher, Martin Frydberg; ***D:*** Henry Jaglom; ***W:*** Henry Jaglom; ***M:*** Karen Black. *PAR, FCT*

Can You Feel Me Dancing? 🦴🦴 **1985** Family-happy lightweight entertainment coproduced by Kent Bateman and starring Bateman progeny Jason and Justine as brother and sister, a novel premise that only a father could love. A blind independence-impaired teenager tries to liberate herself from her overbearing family, and finds the secret to conquering her fears and to standing up for herself when she falls in love. Written by spouse-team Steven and J. Miyoko Hensley. **95m/C VHS.** Jason Bateman, Justine Bateman; ***D:*** Michael Miller; ***W:*** Steven Hensley, J. Miyoko Hensley. *NO*

Can You Hear the Laughter? The Story of Freddie Prinze 🦴🦴 **1979** Heartstring tugging biography of the late Puerto Rican comedian whose troubled life lead to suicide in spite of his apparent success. He was most noted for his starring role in "Chico and the Man." **100m/C VHS, Beta.** Ira Angustain, Kevin Hooks, Randee Heller, Devon Ericson, Julie Carmen, Stephen Elliott; ***D:*** Burt Brinckerhoff. *GEM*

Canada's Sweetheart: The Saga of Hal C. Banks 🦴🦴 *Sweetheart!* **1985** True story of Banks, hired by the Canadian government to break up a strike among the communist-led seaman's union which had put a stranglehold on Canadian commerce, and who was eventually convicted of strong-arm tactics. **115m/C VHS, Beta.** *CA* Maury Chaykin. Toronto-City Award '85: Best Canadian Feature Film. *NO*

Canadian Bacon 🦴½ **1994 (PG)** Regrettably amateurish satire (with some sharp observations) serves as the feature film debut for Moore, who irritated many with "Roger and Me." Title refers to the military code name for a campaign to whip up anti-Canadian hysteria and justify a U.S. invasion of its neighbor to the north. Evil political advisor Pollak convinces well-meaning but inept President Alda that it's just the thing to get the presidential popularity up and those defense industries humming. Ugly Americans abound, at expense of polite Canadians, eh? Filmed in Toronto, which is shown to good advantage. Candy in one of last roles is the superpatriotic sheriff of Niagara Falls, New York. **110m/C VHS.** Alan Alda, Kevin Pollak, John Candy, Rhea Perlman, Rip Torn, Bill Nunn, Kevin J. O'Connor, Steven Wright, G.D. Spradlin; ***Cameos:*** Michael Moore; ***D:*** Michael Moore; ***W:*** Michael Moore; ***C:*** Haskell Wexler; ***M:*** Elmer Bernstein. *PGV*

Canadian Mounties vs. Atomic Invaders 🦴🦴½ **1953** Mountie Don Roberts and undercover agent Kay Conway chase foreign agents and face natural disasters (avalanches and reindeer stampedes) to keep atomic missiles away from Canada and the U.S. Part of "The Cliffhanger Serials" series. 12 chapters. **169m/B VHS.** William Henry, Susan Morrow, Arthur Space. *REP, MOV*

Cancel My Reservation 🦴 **1972 (G)** New York talk show host Hope sets out for a vacation on an Arizona ranch, but winds up in trouble due to a mysterious corpse, a rich rancher, and an enigmatic mystic. Even more muddled than it sounds. Based on the novel "Broken Gun" by Louis L'Amour, with pointless cameos by Crosby, Wayne, and Wilson. **99m/C VHS, Beta.** Bob Hope, Eva Marie Saint, Ralph Bellamy, Anne Archer, Forrest Tucker, Keenan Wynn, Flip Wilson, Noriyuki "Pat" Morita, Chief Dan George; ***Cameos:*** John Wayne, Bing Crosby, Doodles Weaver; ***D:*** Paul Bogart; ***W:*** Arthur Marx; ***C:*** Russell Metty. *COL, FCT*

The Candidate 🦴🦴🦴 **1972 (PG)** Realistic, satirical look at politics and political campaigning. A young, idealistic lawyer is talked into trying for the Senate seat and learns the truth about running for office. Ritchie's other efforts include "Downhill Racer" and "Bad News Bears." **105m/C VHS, Beta, LV.** Robert Redford, Peter Boyle, Don Porter, Allen (Goorwitz) Garfield, Karen Carlson, Melvyn Douglas, Michael Lerner; ***D:*** Michael Ritchie; ***W:*** Jeremy Larner. Academy Awards '72: Best Story & Screenplay; National Board of Review Awards '72: 10 Best Films of the Year; Writers Guild of America '72: Best Original Screenplay; Nominations: Academy Awards '72: Best Sound. *WAR*

Candles at Nine 🦴½ **1944** An innocent showgirl must spend a month in her late uncle's creepy mansion in order to inherit it, much to the malevolent chagrin of the rest of the family who want the place and the loot for themselves. Uninspired. **84m/B VHS, Beta.** *GB* Jessie Matthews, John Stuart, Reginald Purdell; ***D:*** John Harlow. *SNC, VYY, MLB*

Candleshoe 🦴🦴 **1978 (G)** A Los Angeles street urchin poses as an English matron's long lost granddaughter in order to steal a fortune hidden in Candleshoe, her country estate, where Niven butlers. Somewhat slapschticky Disney fare. **101m/C VHS, Beta.** Vivian Pickles, Helen Hayes, David Niven, Jodie Foster, Leo McKern; ***D:*** Norman Tokar. *DIS*

Candy Mountain 🦴🦴 **1987 (R)** Guitar playin' O'Connor roadtrips across America and Canada in search of a legendary guitar maker Yulin. Occasional interest derives from musician cameos from the likes of Buster Poindexter, Dr. John and Redbone. **90m/C VHS.** *FR SI CA* Kevin J. O'Connor, Harris Yulin, Tom Waits, Bulle Ogier, Roberts Blossom; ***Cameos:*** David Johansen, Leon Redbone, Joe Strummer, Rita MacNeil, Laurie Metcalf; ***D:*** Robert Frank; ***W:*** Rudy Wurlitzer. *REP, FCT*

Candy Stripe Nurses 🦴 *Sweet Candy* **1974 (R)** Even hard-core Roger Corman fans might find his final installment in the nursing comedy pentad to be a lethargic exercise in gratuitous "sexual situations." Bet those uniforms don't meet hospital standards. The previous films in the series are: "The Student Nurses," "Private Duty Nurses," "Night Call Nurses," and "The Young Nurses." **80m/C VHS, Beta.** Candice Rialson, Robin Mattson, Maria Rojo, Kimberly Hyde, Dick Miller, Stanley Ralph Ross, Monte Landis, Tom Baker; ***D:*** Allan Holleb. *SUE*

Candy Tangerine Man 🦴 **1975** Respectable businessman leads a double life as loving father and LA pimp. **88m/C VHS, Beta.** John Daniels, Tom Hankerson, Eli Haines, Marva Farmer, George Flower; ***D:*** Matt Cimber. *UNI*

Candyman 🦴🦴 **1992 (R)** This terrifying tale from horror maven Clive Barker is an effective combination of American gothic, academia, and urban squalor. A search for dissertation material leads graduate student Helen Lyle (Madsen) into gang-infested housing. There she encounters the urban myth of Candyman, the son of a former slave who was lynched and is now back with a hook and a vendetta. Filled with the appropriate amount of yucky stuff, yet successfully employs subtle scare tactics and plausible characters. **98m/C VHS, Beta, LV, 8mm.** Virginia Madsen, Tony Todd, Xander Berkeley, Kasi Lemmons, Vanessa Williams, DeJuan Guy, Michael Culkin, Gilbert Lewis, Stanley DeSantis; ***D:*** Bernard Rose; ***W:*** Bernard Rose; ***M:*** Philip Glass. *COL*

Candyman 2: Farewell to the Flesh 🦴 **1994 (R)** Explains the origins of the urban bogeyman called Candyman—the man, the hook and the bees. Rehashes the same old scare tactics from previous and better horror movies and uses cheesy special effects. The sensual background of New Orleans during Mardi Gras can't help this stale sequel. Embrace this "Farewell" from a distance. Based on stories by Clive Barker. **99m/C VHS.** Tony Todd, Kelly Rowan, Veronica Cartwright, Timothy Carhart, William O'Leary, Bill Nunn, Fay Hauser; ***D:*** William Condon; ***W:*** Rand Ravich, Mark Kruger; ***C:*** Tobias Schliessler; ***M:*** Philip Glass. *PGV*

Cannery Row 🦴🦴½ **1982 (PG)** Baseball has-been Nolte lives anonymously among the downtrodden in the seamy part of town and carries on with working girl girlfriend Winger. Based on John Steinbeck's "Cannery Row" and "Sweet Thursday." **120m/C VHS, Beta.** Nick Nolte, Debra Winger, Audra Lindley, M. Emmet Walsh, Frank McRae, James Keane, Sunshine Parker; ***D:*** David S. Ward; ***W:*** David S. Ward; ***C:*** Sven Nykvist; ***M:*** Jack Nitzsche. *MGM*

Cannibal Campout 🦴 **1988** Crazed orphans with eating disorders make square meal of coed babes getting back to nature. **89m/C VHS, Beta.** Carrie Lindell, Richard Marcus, Amy Chludzinski, Jon McBride; ***D:*** Jon McBride, Tom Fisher. *DMP*

Cannibal Women in the Avocado Jungle of Death 🦴🦴½ **1989 (PG-13)** Tongue-in-cheek cult classic features erstwhile playmate Tweed as feminist anthropologist who searches with ditzy student and mucho macho male guide for lost tribe of cannibal women who dine on their mates. Lawton directed under the alias "J.D. Athens." **90m/C VHS, Beta, LV.** Shannon Tweed, Adrienne Barbeau, Karen Mistal, Barry Primus, Bill Maher; ***D:*** J.F. Lawton; ***W:*** J.F. Lawton. *PAR*

Cannon Ball/Eyes Have It **1915** Conklin stars in "The Cannon Ball" (1915), as an explosives expert in the Boom Powder Factory. "The Eyes Have It" (1928), stars Turpin involved in another misunderstanding with wife and mother-in-law. Silent. **41m/B VHS, Beta.** Chester Conklin, Ben Turpin, Georgia O'Dell, Helen Gilmore, Jack Lipson. *CCB*

Cannon Movie Tales: Red Riding Hood 🦴🦴½ **1989 (G)** Bright re-telling of the little girl in red and that nasty wolf. **84m/C VHS.** Craig T. Nelson, Isabella Rossellini; ***D:*** Adam Brooks. *WAR*

Cannon Movie Tales: Sleeping Beauty 🦴🦴½ **1989 (G)** Fairchild stars in this version of the sleeping princess and the evil witch. **90m/C VHS.** Morgan Fairchild, Tracy Welch, Nicholas Clay, Sylvia Miles, Kenny Baker, David Holliday; ***D:*** David Irving. *WAR*

Cannon Movie Tales: The Emperor's New Clothes 🦴🦴½ **1989** Caesar stars in this version of vain despot and the crafty tailors. **85m/C VHS.** Sid Caesar, Robert Morse, Clive Revill; ***D:*** David Irving. *WAR*

Cannonball 🦴🦴 *Carquake* **1976 (PG)** Assorted ruthless people leave patches of rubber across the country competing for grand prize in less than legal auto race. Not top drawer New World but nonetheless a cult fave. Inferior to Bartel's previous cult classic, "Death Race 2000." Most interesting for plethora of cult cameos, including Scorsese, Dante, and grandmaster Corman. **93m/C VHS, Beta.** David Carradine, Bill McKinney, Veronica Hamel, Gerrit Graham, Robert Carradine, Sylvester Stallone, Jonathan Kaplan; ***Cameos:*** Martin Scorsese, Roger Corman, Joe Dante; ***D:*** Paul Bartel; ***W:*** Paul Bartel; ***M:*** David A. Axelrod. *NO*

Cannonball/Dizzy Heights and Daring Hearts **1916** Two classic comedies featuring Conklin, the Keystone Kops, and wacky aeroplanes from the irrepressible Sennett. **71m/B VHS, Beta.** Chester Conklin; ***D:*** Mack Sennett. *VYY*

Cannonball Run 🦴½ **1981 (PG)** So many stars, so little plot. Reynolds and sidekick DeLuise disguise themselves as paramedics to foil cops while they compete in cross-country Cannonball race. Shows no sign of having been directed by an ex-stuntman. One of 1981's top grossers—go figure. Followed by equally languid sequel "Cannonball Run II." **95m/C VHS, Beta, LV.** Burt Reynolds, Farrah Fawcett, Roger Moore, Dom DeLuise, Dean Martin, Sammy Davis Jr., Jack Elam, Adrienne Barbeau, Peter Fonda, Molly Picon, Bert Convy, Jamie Farr; ***D:*** Hal Needham. *VES*

Cannonball Run 2 🦴 **1984 (PG)** More mindless cross-country wheel spinning with gratuitous star cameos. Director Needham apparently subscribes to the two wrongs make a right school of sequels. **109m/C VHS, Beta, LV.** Burt Reynolds, Dom DeLuise, Jamie Farr, Marilu Henner, Shirley MacLaine, Jim Nabors, Frank Sinatra, Sammy Davis Jr., Dean Martin, Telly Savalas, Susan Anton, Catherine Bach, Jack Elam, Sid Caesar, Ricardo Montalban, Charles Nelson Reilly; ***Cameos:*** Henry Silva, Tim Conway, Don Knotts, Molly Picon; ***D:*** Hal Needham; ***W:*** Harvey Miller; ***M:*** Stephen Dorff. *WAR*

The Canon Operation 🦴 **1983** An ostensibly true story about Korean War espionage. **90m/C VHS, Beta.** *VCD*

Can't Buy Me Love 🦴½ **1987 (PG-13)** Unpopular high school nerd Dempsey buys a month of dates with teen babe Peterson for $1000 in order to win friends and influence people. Previously known as "Boy Rents Girl." **94m/C VHS, Beta, LV.** Patrick Dempsey, Amanda Peterson, Dennis Dugan, Courtney Gains; ***D:*** Steve Rash; ***M:*** Robert Folk. *TOU*

Can't Stop the Music *Woof!* **1980 (PG)** Retired model invites friends from Greenwich Village to a party to help the career of her roommate, an aspiring composer. Disco inferno that nearly reaches heights of surreal ineptness. Put it in a time capsule and let the people of the future decide what the heck was going on in the seventies. Features two of the top hits by the Village People. ♫Y.M.C.A.; Macho Man; Give Me a Break; The Sound of the City; Samantha; I'm a Singing Juggler; Sophistication; Liberation; I Love You to Death. **120m/C VHS, Beta.** Valerie Perrine, Bruce Jenner, Steve Guttenberg, Paul Sand, Leigh Taylor-Young, Village People; ***D:*** Nancy Walker; ***W:*** Allan Carr. Golden Raspberry Awards '80: Worst Picture, Worst Screenplay. *REP*

A Canterbury Tale 🦴🦴🦴 **1944** Writer-director team Powell and Pressburger have loosely modeled a retelling of Chaucer's famous tale of a pilgrimage to the cathedral in Canterbury. Set in Nazi-threatened Britain in 1944, the story follows the pilgrimage of three Brits and an American GI to the eponymous cathedral. Strange, effective, worth looking at. The 95-minute American version, with added footage of Kim Hunter, is inferior to the 124-minute original. **124m/B VHS.** *GB* Eric Portman, Sheila Sim, Dennis Price, Esmond Knight, Charles Hawtrey, Hay Petrie; ***D:*** Michael Powell, Emeric Pressburger. *HMV*

The Canterbury Tales 🦴🦴 **1971** Four Chaucer tales, most notably "The Merchant's Tale" and "The Wife of Bath," are recounted by travelers, with director Pasolini as the bawdy poet. Deemed obscene by the Italian courts, it's the second entry in Pasolini's medieval "Trilogy of Life," preceded by "The Decameron" and followed by "The Arabian Nights." In Italian with English subtitles. **109m/C VHS, Beta.** *IT* Laura Betti, Ninetto Davoli, Pier Paolo Pasolini, Hugh Griffith, Josephine Chaplin, Michael Balfour, Jenny Runacre; ***D:*** Pier Paolo Pasolini. Berlin International Film Festival '72: Golden Berlin Bear. *WBF, INJ, APD*

The Canterville Ghost 🦴🦴½ **1944** Laughton, a 300-year old ghost with a yellow streak, is sentenced to spook a castle until he proves he's not afraid of his own shadow. American troops stay at the castle during WWII, and, as luck would have it, soldier Young is distantly related to spunky young keeper of the castle O'Brien, ghost Laughton's descendant. Once Young is acquainted with his cowardly ancestor, he begins to fear a congenital yellow streak, and both struggle to be brave despite themselves. Vaguely derived from an Oscar Wilde tale. **95m/B VHS, Beta.** Charles Laughton, Robert Young, Margaret O'Brien, William Gargan, Reginald Owen, Rags Ragland, Una O'Connor, Peter Lawford, Mike Mazurki; ***D:*** Jules Dassin; ***W:*** Edwin Blum; ***M:*** George Bassman. *MGM*

The Canterville Ghost **1991** During a family's vacation in an old English manor, they run into a ghost who is doomed to haunt the place until he can overcome his fears. Problems start when the family tries to scare him away. From the "Wonderworks" family movie series. **58m/C VHS.** Richard Kiley, Mary Wickes. *PME, FCT*

The Canterville Ghost 🦴🦴½ **1996 (PG)** Stewart is the highlight of this updated TV version of the Oscar Wilde short story. He's the cursed Elizabethan spirit of Sir Simon de Canterville, doomed to haunt the family mansion until a prophecy is fulfilled. But he's not happy with a family of American intruders, until teenager Virginia (Campbell) discovers Sir Simon and realizes she may hold the key to freeing the unhappy ghost. **91m/C VHS.** Patrick Stewart, Neve Campbell, Ed Wiley, Cherie Lunghi, Donald Sinden, Joan Sims, Leslie Phillips, Ciaran Fitzgerald, Daniel Betts, Raymond Pickard; ***D:*** Syd Macartney; ***W:*** Robert Benedetto; ***C:*** Denis Lewiston; ***M:*** Ernest Troost. *HMK*

Cantonen Iron Kung Fu 🦴 **197?** The ten tigers of Quon Tung perfect martial arts skills known as Cantonen Iron Kung Fu. **90m/C VHS, Beta.** Liang Jia Ren; ***D:*** Li Chao. *WVE*

The Cantor's Son 🦴½ *Dem Khann's Zindl* **1937** Real-life story based on Moishe Oysher's life, vaguely influenced by Jolson's "Jazz Singer." Runaway Oysher joins troupe of performers as a youth, travels to the shores of America, and finds fame once his beautiful voice is discovered. Returning to his mother country to celebrate his parents' golden anniversary, he encounters his childhood sweetheart and falls in love, but another woman is written into the plot to complicate matters. Poorly acted, laughable staging. In Yiddish with English subtitles. **90m/B VHS, Beta.** Judith Abarbanel, Florence Weiss, Moishe Oysher, Isadore Cashier; ***D:*** Ilya Motyleff. *ERG, INJ, HEG*

Canvas: The Fine Art of Crime 🦴🦴 **1992 (R)** A ruthless, underhanded art gallery owner recruits a desperate young artist into his art stealing schemes. The artist learns how to steal, but decides he wants out after his burglary partner has a brush with death. The gallery owner, however, wants one last job completed. **94m/C VHS.** Gary Busey, John Rhys-Davies, Vittorio Rossi, Nick Cavaiola, Cary Lawrence; ***D:*** Alain Zaloum. *LIV*

Cape Fear 🦴🦴🦴½ **1961** Former prosecutor turned small-town lawyer Peck and his family are plagued by the sadistic attentions of criminal Mitchum, who just finished a six year sabbatical at the state pen courtesy of prosecutor Peck. Taut and creepy; Mitchum's a consummate psychopath. Based on (and far superior to) John MacDonald's "The Executioners." Don't pass this one up in favor of the Scorsese remake. **106m/B VHS, Beta.** Gregory Peck, Robert Mitchum, Polly Bergen, Martin Balsam, Telly Savalas, Jack Kruschen; ***D:*** J. Lee Thompson; ***C:*** Sam Leavitt. *MCA*

Cape Fear 🦴🦴🦴 **1991 (R)** Scorsese takes on this terrifying tale of brutality and manipulation (previously filmed in 1961) and cranks it up a notch as a paroled convict haunts the lawyer who put him away. Great cast, a rollercoaster of suspense. Note the cameos by Mitchum, Peck, and Balsam, stars of the first version. Original source material was "The Executioners" by John D. MacDonald. Breath-taking rollercoaster of a film. Elmer Bernstein adapted the original score by Bernard Herrmann. **128m/C VHS, LV.** Robert De Niro, Nick Nolte, Jessica Lange, Juliette Lewis, Joe Don Baker, Illeana Douglas, Fred Dalton Thompson; ***Cameos:*** Robert Mitchum, Gregory Peck, Martin Balsam; ***D:*** Martin Scorsese; ***W:*** Wesley Strick; ***M:*** Bernard Herrmann, Elmer Bernstein. Chicago Film Critics Awards '91: Most Promising Actress (Lewis); Nominations: Academy Awards '91: Best Actor (De Niro), Best Supporting Actress (Lewis). *MCA*

Caper of the Golden Bulls 🦴 *Carnival of Thieves* **1967** Former bank robber Boyd is blackmailed into joining a group of safecrackers who plan to assault the Royal Bank of Spain during the annual Santa Maria bull run. More like siesta of the golden bulls. **104m/C VHS, Beta.** Stephen Boyd, Yvette Mimieux, Giovanna Ralli, Walter Slezak, Vito Scotti; ***D:*** Russel Rouse. *NLC*

Capone 🦴🦴½ **1989 (R)** This is the story of the gangster after Elliot Ness put him in a Chicago jail. That didn't stop Capone from running his crime empire until a single FBI agent worked to sent the crime boss to Alcatraz, where his power would be useless. Exuberant performances from Sharkey and Carradine. Made for television. **96m/C VHS, LV.** Ray Sharkey, Keith Carradine, Debrah Farentino. *VMK*

Capricorn One 🦴🦴🦴 **1978 (R)** Astronauts Brolin, Simpson and Waterston follow Mission Controller Holbrook's instructions to fake a Mars landing on a fabricated soundstage when their ship is discovered to be defective. When they find out they're supposed to expire in outer space so that the NASA scam won't become public knowledge, they flee to the desert, while reporter Gould sniffs out the cover up. Based on a pseudonymous novel by Ken Follett. **123m/C VHS, Beta, LV.** Elliott Gould, James Brolin, Brenda Vaccaro, O.J. Simpson, Hal Holbrook, Sam Waterston, Karen Black, Telly Savalas; ***D:*** Peter Hyams; ***W:*** Peter Hyams; ***M:*** Jerry Goldsmith. *FOX*

Captain America **1944** Captain America battles a mad scientist in this fifteen-episode serial based on the comic book character. **240m/B VHS, Beta.** Dick Purcell, Adrian Booth, Lionel Atwill; ***D:*** John English; ***W:*** Elmer Clifton. *VCN, MLB, VTR*

Captain America 🦴½ **1979** Marvel Comic character steps into feature film and flounders. The patriotic superhero son of WWII hero fights bad guy with contraband nuclear weapon. Made for television. Followed the same year with "Captain America II: Death Too Soon." **98m/C VHS, Beta.** Reb Brown, Len Birman, Heather Menzies, Steve Forrest, Robin Mattson, Joseph Ruskin, Michael McManus; ***D:*** Rod Holcomb. *MCA*

Captain America 🦴½ **1989 (PG-13)** Based on the Marvel Comics superhero. It's 1941 and Steve Rogers has just been recruited to join a top secret experimental government program after flunking his army physical. Injected with a serum, Steve becomes super strong, fast, and smart but is matched in all three by an evil Nazi counterpart, Red Skull. The two battle to a WWII standstill and while Red Skull goes on with his evil plots, the next 40 years finds Captain America fast frozen in the Alaskan tundra. Finally, our hero is thawed in time to do a final battle with his evil nemesis. This one is ridiculous even by comic book standards but it may amuse the kids. **103m/C VHS, LV.** Matt Salinger, Scott Paulin, Ronny Cox, Ned Beatty, Darren McGavin, Melinda Dillon; ***D:*** Albert Pyun; ***W:*** Stephen Tolkin. *COL*

Captain America 2: Death Too Soon 🦴 **1979** Terrorists hit America where it hurts, threatening to use age accelerating drug. Sequelized superhero fights chronic crow lines and series dies slow, painful death. Made for television. **98m/C VHS, Beta.** Reb Brown, Connie Sellecca, Len Birman, Christopher Lee, Katherine Justice, Lana Wood, Christopher Carey; ***D:*** Ivan Nagy. *MCA*

Captain Apache 🦴 **1971** Union intelligence officer Van Cleef investigates murder of Indian commissioner and discovers fake Indian war landscam. As clever as the title. **95m/C VHS, Beta.** Lee Van Cleef, Carroll Baker, Stuart Whitman; ***D:*** Alexander Singer; ***W:*** Philip Yordan. *MRV, PSM*

Captain Blackjack 🦴🦴 *Black Jack* **1951** All star cast craps out in wannabe thriller about drug smuggling on the French Riviera. Social butterfly Moorehead directs drug traffic, detective Marshall undercovers as doctor, and Sanders looks bored in a

British sort of way. **90m/B VHS.** *FR* George Sanders, Herbert Marshall, Agnes Moorehead, Patricia Roc, Marcel Dalio; ***D:*** Julien Duvivier. *NO*

Captain Blood ½ **1935** Sabatini adventure story launched then unknown 26-year old Flynn and 19-year old De Havilland to fame in perhaps the best pirate story ever. Exiled into slavery by a tyrannical governor, Irish physician Peter Blood is forced into piracy but ultimately earns a pardon for his swashbuckling ways. Love interest De Havilland would go on to appear in seven more features with Flynn, who took the part Robert Donat declined for health reasons. Cleverly budgeted using ship shots from silents, and miniature sets when possible. First original film score by composer Korngold. Also available colorized. **120m/B VHS, Beta.** Errol Flynn, Olivia de Havilland, Basil Rathbone, J. Carrol Naish, Guy Kibbee, Lionel Atwill; ***D:*** Michael Curtiz; ***C:*** Hal Mohr. Nominations: Academy Awards '35: Best Picture, Best Sound. *MGM, FCT, MLB*

Captain Caution **1940** Young girl throws caution to the wind when dad dies during the War of 1812, assisting young Mature to take over the old man's ship to do battle with the British. Watch for then unknown sailor Ladd. **84m/B VHS, Beta.** Victor Mature, Louise Platt, Bruce Cabot, Alan Ladd, Robert Barrat, Vivienne Osborne; ***D:*** Richard Wallace. Nominations: Academy Awards '40: Best Sound. *MED*

The Captain from Koepenick ½ *Der Hauptmann von Koepenick* **1956** Popular true life comedy about a Berlin cobbler in 1906 who rebels against military bureaucracy by impersonating a Prussian officer and wreaking havoc on his town, arresting authorities and capturing soldiers, only to enjoy folk herodom when his ruse is discovered. Remake of Richard Oswald's 1931 classic. In German with subtitles. **93m/B VHS, Beta.** *GE* Heinz Ruehmann, Hannelore Schroth, Martin Held, Erich Schellow; ***D:*** Helmut Kaeutner. *NOS, FCT*

Captain Horatio Hornblower **1951** A colorful drama about the life and loves of the British sea captain during the Napoleonic wars. Peck is rather out of his element as the courageous, swashbuckling hero (Errol Flynn was originally cast) but there's enough fast-paced derring-do to make this a satisfying saga. Based on the novel by C.S. Forester. **117m/C VHS, Beta, LV.** *GB* Gregory Peck, Virginia Mayo, Robert Beatty, Denis O'Dea, Christopher Lee; ***D:*** Raoul Walsh; ***W:*** Ivan Goff; ***C:*** Guy Green. *WAR*

Captain January ½ **1936 (G)** Crusty old lighthouse keeper rescues little orphan girl with curly hair from drowning and everyone breaks into cutesy song and dance, interrupted only when the authorities try to separate the two. Also available colorized. ♫At the Codfish Ball; Early Bird; The Right Somebody to Love. **81m/B VHS.** Shirley Temple, Guy Kibbee, Buddy Ebsen, Slim Summerville, Jane Darwell, June Lang, George Irving, Si Jenks; ***D:*** David Butler. *FXV*

Captain Kidd ½ **1945** Laughton huffs and puffs and searches for treasure on the high seas, finds himself held captive with rest of cast in anemic swashbuckler. **83m/B VHS, Beta.** Charles Laughton, John Carradine, Randolph Scott, Reginald Owen, Gilbert Roland, Barbara Britton, John Qualen, Sheldon Leonard; ***D:*** Rowland V. Lee; ***C:*** Archie Stout. Nominations: Academy Awards '45: Best Original Score. *MRV, NOS, HHT*

Captain Kronos: Vampire Hunter *Kronos* **1974 (R)** Captain Kronos fences thirsty foes in Hammer horror hybrid. Artsy, atmospheric and atypical, it's written and directed with tongue firmly in cheek by Clemens, who penned many an "Avengers" episode. **91m/C VHS, Beta.** *GB* Horst Janson, John Carson, Caroline Munro, Ian Hendry, Shane Briant, Wanda Ventham; ***D:*** Brian Clemens; ***W:*** Brian Clemens. *PAR*

Captain Newman, M.D. ½ **1963** Three army guys visit stiff shrink Peck during the final months of WWII in VA ward for the mentally disturbed. Much guilt and agonizing, with comic relief courtesy of Curtis. Peck is sub par, the direction flounders and there's something unsettling about quicksilver shifts from pathos to parody. Nonetheless touching with fine performance from Darin as guilt ridden hero. Based on the novel by Leo Rosten. **126m/C VHS, Beta.** Gregory Peck, Bobby Darin, Tony Curtis, Angie Dickinson, Eddie Albert, James Gregory, Jane Withers, Larry Storch, Robert Duvall; ***D:*** David Miller. Nominations: Academy Awards '63: Best Adapted Screenplay, Best Sound, Best Supporting Actor (Darin). *MCA*

Captain Nuke and the Bomber Boys ½ *Demolition Day* **1995 (PG)** Three teenagers, who've stumbled across an atomic bomb, decide to use the device to get school called off. Instead, they wind up with the FBI and a couple of crooks after them. **?m/C VHS.** Joe Mantegna, Martin Sheen, Joe Piscopo, Joanna Pacula, Rod Steiger. *NHO*

Captain Ron ½ **1992 (PG-13)** Harried couple Short and Place inherit a large boat and, with their two smart-mouthed kids, go to the Caribbean to sail the boat back to the U.S. Of course they know nothing about sailing, so they hire Captain Ron (Russell), a one-eyed, Long John Silver-talking boat captain. From there, numerous mishaps occur. Amusing sounding premise sinks like a stone. Russell looks great in his teeny-weeny bikini, and the scenery is beautiful, but that's about it. **104m/C VHS, Beta, LV.** Kurt Russell, Martin Short, Mary Kay Place, Meadow Sisto, Benjamin Salisbury; ***D:*** Thom Eberhardt; ***W:*** Thom Eberhardt. *TOU*

Captain Scarlett ½ **1953** Formulaic swashbuckler has nobleman Greene and highway guy Young fighting nasty French Royalists who've been putting the pressure on impecunious peasants. Runaway Spanish damsel in distress courtesy of Amar. Most novel aspect of the production is that the post-Napoleon French terrain has that vaguely south of the border feel. **75m/C VHS, Beta.** Richard Greene, Leonora Amar, Isobel Del Puerto, Nedrick Young, Manolo Fabregas; ***D:*** Thomas Carr. *NOS, MRV, GEM*

Captain Sinbad ½ **1963** Captain Sinbad must destroy the evil El Kerim, but first he must tackle a many-headed ogre, man-eating fish and crocodiles, a large fist clad in a spiked glove, an invisible monster, and more. To kill the villain, Sinbad must destroy his heart, which is kept in a tower with no entrance. A huge, witty, epic production with lots of special effects. This one is fun. **85m/C VHS.** Guy Williams, Heidi Bruhl, Pedro Armendariz Sr., Abraham Sofaer, Bernie Hamilton, Helmut Schneider; ***D:*** Byron Haskin. *MGM*

Captain Swagger ½ **1925** A man on the brink of thievery experiences some changes that keep him on the right side of the law. **50m/B VHS, Beta.** Rod La Rocque, Sue Carol, Richard Tucker, Victor Potel, Ullrich Haupt; ***D:*** Edward H. Griffith. *GPV*

Captains Courageous **1937** Rich brat Bartholomew takes a dip sans life jacket while leaning over an ocean liner railing to relieve himself of the half dozen ice cream sodas imprudently consumed at sea. Picked up by a Portugese fishing boat, he at first treats his mandatory three month voyage as an unscheduled cab ride, but eventually, through a deepening friendship with crewman Tracy, develops a hitherto unheralded work ethic. The boy's filial bond with Tracy, of course, requires that the seaman meet with watery disaster. Based on the Rudyard Kipling novel. Director Fleming went on to "Gone With the Wind" and "The Wizard of Oz." **116m/B VHS, Beta.** Spencer Tracy, Lionel Barrymore, Freddie Bartholomew, Mickey Rooney, Melvyn Douglas, Charley Grapewin, John Carradine, Bobby Watson, Jack LaRue; ***D:*** Victor Fleming. Academy Awards '37: Best Actor (Tracy); National Board of Review Awards '37: 10 Best Films of the Year; Nominations: Academy Awards '37: Best Film Editing, Best Picture, Best Screenplay. *MGM, BMV, BTV*

Captains of the Clouds ½ **1942** Unabashedly patriotic film starring Cagney as a daredevil, independent Canadian bush pilot who makes his own flying rules. When WWII begins he joins the Royal Canadian Air Force but washes out when he can't follow orders. However, he finds a way to prove himself a hero as a civilian pilot ferrying a bomber to England. Cagney's first Technicolor film. **113m/C VHS.** James Cagney, Dennis (Stanley Morner) Morgan, Brenda Marshall, Alan Hale, George Tobias, Reginald Gardiner, Reginald Denny, Russell Arms, Paul Cavanagh, Charles Halton; ***D:*** Michael Curtiz; ***M:*** Max Steiner. *MGM, FCT*

Captain's Paradise **1953** Golden Fleece captain Guinness chugs between wives in Gibraltar and North Africa, much to the adulation of chief officer Goldner. While Gibraltar's little woman Johnson is homegrown homebody, little woman de Carlo is paint the town red type, allowing Guinness to have cake and eat it too, it seems, except that he's inconveniently positioned in front of a firing squad at movie's start. **89m/B VHS, Beta.** *GB* Alec Guinness, Yvonne De Carlo, Celia Johnson, Miles Malleson, Nicholas Phipps, Ferdinand "Ferdy" Mayne, Sebastian Cabot; ***D:*** Anthony Kimmins; ***M:*** Malcolm Arnold. Nominations: Academy Awards '53: Best Story. *FCT*

The Captain's Table **1960** Former cargo vessel captain Gregson is given luxury liner to command, and fails to revise his cargo captain style to fit new crew and clientele. British cast saves unremarkable script from mediocrity. **90m/C VHS.** *GB* John Gregson, Peggy Cummins, Donald Sinden, Nadia Gray; ***D:*** Jack Lee. *PAR*

Captive ½ **1987 (R)** Spoiled heiress is kidnapped by terrorist trio and brainwashed into anti-establishment Hearst-like creature. **98m/C VHS, Beta.** Oliver Reed, Irina Brook, Xavier DeLuc, Hiro Arai; ***D:*** Paul Mayersberg. *VTR*

Captive Heart **1947** Czech soldier Redgrave assumes the identity of a dead British officer in order to evade Nazis in WWII. Captured and imprisoned in camp reserved for British POWs, his stalagmates think they smell a spy, but he manages to convince them he's an OK Joe. Meanwhile, he's been writing letters home to the little missus, which means he's got a little explaining to do when he's released from prison. Especially fine Redgrave performance. **86m/B VHS, Beta.** *GB* Michael Redgrave, Basil Radford, Jack Warner, Jimmy Hanley, Rachel Kempson, Mervyn Johns; ***D:*** Basil Dearden. *NOS, DVT, VEC*

Captive Hearts **1987 (PG)** Well frayed story holds cast captive in sushi romance. Two American flyers are shot down and taken prisoner in isolated Japanese mountain village, and one is shot by Cupid's arrow. **97m/C VHS, Beta.** Noriyuki "Pat" Morita, Michael Sarrazin, Chris Makepeace; ***D:*** Paul Almond; ***M:*** David Benoit. *MGM, FOX*

A Captive in the Land ½ **1991 (PG)** Routine survival pic pits two strangers against the frozen Arctic tundra. Potapov is a Soviet airman who's too injured to walk when he's discovered by American meteorologist Waterston. When a rescue seems unlikely, the two are forced to try for a trek to civilization. Based on the novel by James Aldridge. **96m/C VHS.** Sam Waterston, Alexander Potapov; ***D:*** John Berry; ***M:*** Bill Conti, Lee Gold. *LIV*

Captive Planet **1978** Bargain basement FX and really atrocious acting hold audience captive in routine earth on the verge of obliteration yarn. **95m/C VHS, Beta.** Sharon Baker, Chris Auram, Anthony Newcastle; ***D:*** Al Bradley. *NO*

Captive Rage **1988 (R)** South American general Reed hijacks planeful of girlies to encourage US to release his son, who's in trouble because he swaps money for white powder. Violence lives up to title, all else disappoints. **99m/C VHS, Beta.** Oliver Reed, Robert Vaughn, Claudia Udy; ***D:*** Cedric Sundstrom. *MCG*

The Captive: The Longest Drive 2 **1976 (PG-13)** Matheson and Russell play two recently reunited brothers in search of their sister, whom they believe is still a captive of the Cheyenne Indians who also raised Russell. Along the way the two come to the aid of a pioneer woman and her young son. This western was actually a brief television series known as "The Quest," and is a continuation of the pilot episode released on video as "The Longest Drive." **80m/C VHS, LV.** Kurt Russell, Tim Matheson. *VMK*

Captive Wild Woman 🦴🦴½ **1943** Mad scientist Dr. Sigmund Walters (Carradine) transforms an ape into the beautiful Paula Depress (Aquanetta), who promptly joins the circus as a mysterious animal trainer. Unfortunately, she falls in love with fellow trainer Fred (Stone), who already has a gal, bringing back the beast in the pretty Paula. Sequelled by "Jungle Captive" and "Jungle Woman." **61m/B VHS.** Acquanetta, John Carradine, Milburn Stone, Evelyn Ankers, Lloyd Corrigan, Vince Barnett, Paul Fix; ***D:*** Edward Dmytryk; ***W:*** Griffin Jay, Henry Sucher. *MCA*

Captives 🦴🦴½ **1994 (R)** Middle-class dentist Rachel Clifford (Ormond), recently separated from her husband, takes a part-time job at a local prison where she becomes attracted to her patient, Cockney charmer Philip Chaney (Roth). He's coming to the end of a 10-year sentence and the lusty duo manage to consummate their relationship during one of Philip's day-releases. Only problem is fellow con Towler (Salmon) notices what's happening and blackmails and threatens Rachel—leading to a violent confrontation. Roth and Ormond click believably as opposites-attract partners though the script has some weak elements. **100m/C VHS.** *GB* Tim Roth, Julia Ormond, Colin Salmon, Keith Allen, Siobhan Redmond, Peter Capaldi, Richard Hawley, Annette Badland, Jeff Nuttal; ***D:*** Angela Pope; ***W:*** Frank Deasy; ***C:*** Remi Adefarasin; ***M:*** Colin Towns. *NYR*

The Capture 🦴🦴🦴 **1950** Above-average story told in flashback has Ayres hiding out in Mexico because he thought he killed an innocent man. He seeks out the widow to question her about him and they wind up marrying. When he finds the real culprit, the man is killed and the evidence points to Ayres. Ayres and Wright are great, as is the native Mexican musical score. **67m/B VHS.** Lew Ayres, Teresa Wright, Victor Jory, Jacqueline White, Jimmy Hunt, Duncan Renaldo, William "Billy" Bakewell; ***D:*** John Sturges. *NOS*

The Capture of Bigfoot 🦴 **1979 (PG)** Barefoot monster tracks footprints around town after 25 years of peace, and evil businessman attempts to capture creature for personal gain. **92m/C VHS, Beta.** Stafford Morgan, Katherine Hopkins, Richard Kennedy, Otis Young, George Flower, John Goff; ***D:*** Bill Rebane. *AHV*

The Capture of Grizzly Adams 🦴½ **1982** Framed for murder, Adams and his ever-faithful companion Ben the bear must not only clear his name but outwit a band of outlaws who are holding his young daughter captive. Made for television. **96m/C VHS.** Dan Haggerty, Chuck Connors, June Lockhart, Kim Darby, Noah Beery Jr., Keenan Wynn. *WOV*

Captured in Chinatown 🦴 **1935** Dog chases bad guys in Chinatown. Bow wow. **53m/B VHS, Beta, LV.** Marion Shilling, Charles Delaney, Philo McCullough, Robert Ellis; ***D:*** Elmer Clifton. *SNC*

Car Crash 🦴 **19??** Organized crime hits stock car racing head on to produce crashing bore. **103m/C VHS.** Joey Travolta, Anna Obregon, Vittorio Mezzogiorno. *NO*

Car 54, Where Are You? **1961** The first situation comedy about police officers ran on television from 1961-1963. Join offbeat New York cops Gunther Toody and Francis Muldoon of the beleaguered 53rd Precinct. Each cassette contains two episodes. Eight cassettes. **50m/B VHS.** Fred Gwynne, Joe E. Ross, Nipsey Russell, Al Lewis; ***D:*** Stanley Prager, Nat Hiken. *REP, FCT, MOV*

Car 54, Where Are You? 🦴 **1994 (PG-13)** Exceedingly lame remake of the exceedingly lame television series, which ran for only two seasons, 1961-63. This time, Toody (Johansen) and Muldoon (McGinley) are protecting a mafia stool pigeon (Piven), while vampy Velma Velour (Drescher) sets her sights on Muldoon. Not many laughs and a waste of a talented cast. Sat on the shelf at Orion for three years (with good reason). **89m/C VHS, LV.** David Johansen, Fran Drescher, Rosie O'Donnell, John C. McGinley, Nipsey Russell, Al Lewis, Daniel Baldwin, Jeremy Piven; ***D:*** Bill Fishman; ***W:*** Ebbe Roe Smith, Erik Tarloff, Peter McCarthy, Peter Crabbe; ***M:*** Bernie Worrell, Pray For Rain. Golden Raspberry Awards '94: Worst Supporting Actress (O'Donnell). *ORI*

Car Trouble 🦴🦴½ **1986 (R)** Young English husband buys new Jaguar and wife's not so minor car trouble causes major marital trouble. Funnybone-tickling pairing of Walters and Charleson. **93m/C VHS, Beta, LV.** *GB* Julie Walters, Ian Charleson; ***D:*** David Green; ***M:*** Meat Loaf. *MCG*

Car Wash 🦴🦴½ **1976 (PG)** L.A. carwash provides a soap-opera setting for disjointed comic bits about owners of dirty cars and people who hose them down for a living. Econo budget and lite plot, but serious comic talent. A sort of disco carwash version of "Grand Hotel." **97m/C VHS, Beta.** Franklin Ajaye, Sully Boyer, Richard Brestoff, George Carlin, Richard Pryor, Melanie Mayron, Ivan Dixon, Antonio Fargas; ***D:*** Michael A. Schultz; ***W:*** Joel Schumacher. Nominations: Cannes Film Festival '77: Best Film. *MCA, FCT*

Caravaggio 🦴🦴🦴 **1986** Controversial biography of the late Renaissance painter famous for his bisexuality, fondness for prostitute models, violence and depravity. Photography by Gabriel Beristain reproduces the artist's visual style. **97m/C VHS, Beta, LV.** *GB* Nigel Terry, Sean Bean, Tilda Swinton; ***D:*** Derek Jarman; ***W:*** Derek Jarman. *TPV, FCT, INJ*

Caravan to Vaccares 🦴 **1974 (PG)** French Duke hires young American to sneak Eastern European scientist into the States, and little suspense ensues. Based on Alistair MacLean novel. **98m/C VHS, Beta.** David Birney, Charlotte Rampling; ***D:*** Geoffrey Reeve. *MED*

The Caravan Trail 🦴🦴 **1946** A cowboy becomes marshal in order to bring to justice those who have stolen land and murdered his friend. This was shot in color, which was rare for the 1940s. **53m/C VHS.** Eddie Dean, Lash LaRue, Emmett Lynn, Jean Carlin, Charles "Blackie" King, Bob Barron, Lloyd Ingraham, Bud Osborne; ***D:*** Robert Emmett Tansey. *NOS, RXM, HEG*

Carbon Copy 🦴🦴 **1981 (PG)** Successful white executive has life turned inside out when his seventeen-year old illegitimate son, who happens to be black, decides it's time to look up dear old dad. Typical comedy-with-a-moral. **92m/C VHS, Beta, LV.** George Segal, Susan St. James, Jack Warden, Paul Winfield, Dick Martin, Vicky Dawson, Tom Poston, Denzel Washington; ***D:*** Michael A. Schultz; ***W:*** Stanley Shapiro; ***M:*** Bill Conti. *COL, SUE*

Cardiac Arrest 🦴 **1974 (PG)** Lunatic eviscerates victims in trolley town. They left their hearts in San Francisco. **95m/C VHS, Beta.** Garry Goodrow, Mike Chan, Max Gail; ***D:*** Murray Mintz. *MED*

The Cardinal 🦴🦴½ **1963** Priestly young Tryon rises through ecclesiastical ranks to become Cardinal, struggling through a plethora of tests of faith, none so taxing as the test of the audience's patience. Had Preminger excised some sixty minutes of footage, he might have had a compelling portrait of faith under fire, but as it stands, the cleric's life is epic confusion. Fine acting, even from Tryon, who later went on to bookish fame, and from Huston who's normally on the other side of the camera. McNamara's final performance. Based on the Henry Morton Robinson novel. **175m/C VHS, Beta, LV.** Tom Tryon, Carol Lynley, Dorothy Gish, Maggie McNamara, Cecil Kellaway, John Huston, John Saxon, Burgess Meredith; ***D:*** Otto Preminger; ***C:*** Leon Shamroy. Golden Globe Awards '64: Best Film—Drama, Best Supporting Actor (Huston); Nominations: Academy Awards '63: Best Art Direction/Set Decoration (Color), Best Color Cinematography, Best Director (Preminger), Best Film Editing, Best Supporting Actor (Huston). *WAR, IME, VTR*

The Care Bears Movie 🦴🦴 **1984 (G)** The Care Bears leave their cloud home in Care-a-lot to try and teach earthlings how to share their feelings of love and caring for each other. **75m/C VHS, Beta.** ***D:*** Arna Selznick; ***V:*** Mickey Rooney, Georgia Engel, Harry Dean Stanton. *LIV, VES, FCT*

The Care Bears Movie 2: A New Generation 🦴🦴 **1986 (G)** Sequel to the sweet adventures of the animated bear family and their new offspring. **77m/C VHS, Beta.** ***D:*** Dale Schott; ***V:*** Maxine Miller, Pam Hyatt, Hadley Key. *COL, WTA*

Career 🦴🦴½ **1959** An overwrought, depressing drama about the trials and tribulations of an actor trying to make it on Broadway. He'll try anything to succeed. Good direction, but so-so acting. **105m/B VHS, LV.** Dean Martin, Anthony (Tony) Franciosa, Shirley MacLaine, Carolyn Jones, Joan Blackman, Robert Middleton, Donna Douglas; ***D:*** Joseph Anthony; ***C:*** Joseph LaShelle. Golden Globe Awards '60: Best Actor—Drama (Franciosa); Nominations: Academy Awards '59: Best Art Direction/Set Decoration (B & W), Best Black and White Cinematography, Best Costume Design (B & W). *PAR*

Career Opportunities 🦴½ **1991 (PG-13)** "Home Alone" clone for teenagers from John Hughes' factory. Whaley is an unsuccessful con-artist who finally gets a job as the night janitor of the local department store. He fools around at company expense until he finds the town's beauty (Connelly) asleep in a dressing room. The pair then play make-believe until its time to thwart some small-time thieves. Unexciting and unrealistic in the worst way; no wonder Candy isn't billed—he probably didn't want to be. **83m/C VHS, LV.** Frank Whaley, Jennifer Connelly, Dermot Mulroney, Kieran Mulroney, John M. Jackson, Jenny O'Hara, Noble Willingham, Barry Corbin, Denise Galik, William Forsythe; ***Cameos:*** John Candy; ***D:*** Bryan Gordon; ***W:*** John Hughes; ***M:*** Thomas Newman. *MCA*

Carefree 🦴🦴🦴 **1938** Dizzy radio singer Rogers can't make up her mind about beau Bellamy, so he sends her to analyst Astaire. Seems she can't even dream a little dream until shrink Astaire prescribes that she ingest some funny food, which causes her to dream she's in love with the Fredman. Au contraire, says he, it's a Freudian thing, and he hypnotically suggests that she really loves Bellamy. The two line up to march down the aisle together, and Fred stops dancing just long enough to realize he's in love with Ginger. A screwball comedy with music. ♫I Used to be Colorblind; The Night is Filled With Music; Change Partners; The Yam. **83m/B VHS, Beta, LV.** Fred Astaire, Ginger Rogers, Ralph Bellamy, Jack Carson, Franklin Pangborn, Hattie McDaniel; ***D:*** Mark Sandrich; ***M:*** Irving Berlin. Nominations: Academy Awards '38: Best Interior Decoration, Best Song ("Change Partners and Dance with Me"), Best Score. *TTC, MED, IME*

Careful 🦴🦴 **1994** Butler-in-training Neale courts Neville in an alpine mountain village where silence is golden, or at least being quiet will lessen the chance of an avalanche. Dig a little deeper and you find incest, repression and other nasty things. Highly individualistic black comedy parodies German Expressionism and Freudian psychology to the point of absurdity, dealing with snow, sex, sleep, spirits, and obsessive/compulsive personality disorders. Third film from Canadian cult director Maddin is awash in vivid primary colors when it suits the scene's mood and employs between-scenes titles in a homage to cinematic antiquity. **100m/C VHS.** Kyle McCulloch, Gosia Dobrowolska, Jackie Burroughs, Sarah Neville, Brent Neale, Paul Cox, Victor Cowie, Michael O'Sullivan, Vince Rimmer, Katya Gardner; ***D:*** Guy Maddin; ***W:*** Guy Maddin, George Toles; ***M:*** John McCulloch. *KIV*

Careful, He Might Hear You 🦴🦴🦴 **1984 (PG)** Abandoned by his father, six-year-old P.S. becomes a pawn between his dead mother's two sisters, one working class and the other wealthy, and his worldview is further overturned by the sudden reappearance of his prodigal father. Set in Depression-era Australia, Schultz's vision is touching and keenly observed, and manages a sort of child's eye sense of proportion. Based on a novel by Sumner Locke Elliott. **113m/C VHS, Beta.** *AU* Nicholas Gledhill, Wendy Hughes, Robyn Nevin, John Hargreaves; ***D:*** Carl Schultz. Australian Film Institute '83: Best Actress (Hughes), Best Film. *FOX*

Caribe 🦴½ **1987** Caribbean travelogue masquerades as spy thriller. Arms smuggling goes awry, and neither voodoo nor bikinied blondes can prevent audience from dozing. Never released theatrically. **96m/C VHS, Beta, LV.** John Savage, Kara Glover, Stephen McHattie, Sam Malkin; ***D:*** Michael Kennedy. *LIV, VES*

The Cariboo Trail ₰₰ **1950** Two prospecting men seek their fortune in British Columbia, the golden West of Canada in the 1890s. But they find themselves opposed by a ruthless rancher and claim-jumpers. Actually filmed in Colorado with excellent cinematography and solid performances from some big names, it's still a run-of-the-mill entry. Made the same year that the Gabby Hayes' show first aired. **80m/C VHS, LV.** Randolph Scott, George "Gabby" Hayes, Bill Williams, Victor Jory; ***D:*** Edwin L. Marin. *FRH, IME*

Carlito's Way ₰₰₰ **1993 (R)** Puerto Rican crime czar Carlito Brigante (Pacino) has just gotten out of jail and wants to go straight. But his drug underworld cohorts don't believe he can do it. Penn (barely recognizable) is great as a sleazy coked-out lawyer who's way out of his league. Remarkably subdued violence given DePalma's previous rep—it's effective without being gratuitous, especially the final shootout set in Grand Central Station. Pacino's performance is equally subdued, with controlled tension and lots of eye contact rather than grandiose emotions. Based on the novels "Carlito's Way" and "After Hours" by Edwin Torres. Pacino and DePalma previously teamed up for "Scarface." **145m/C VHS, LV.** Al Pacino, Sean Penn, Penelope Ann Miller, Luis Guzman, John Leguizamo, Ingrid Rogers, James Rebhorn, Viggo Mortensen, Jorge Porcel, Joseph Siravo, Adrian Pasdar; ***D:*** Brian DePalma; ***W:*** David Koepp; ***C:*** Stephen Burum; ***M:*** Patrick Doyle. Nominations: Golden Globe Awards '94: Best Supporting Actor (Penn), Best Supporting Actress (Miller). *MCA*

Carlton Browne of the F.O. ₰₰½ *Man in a Cocked Hat* **1959** Bumbling Brit diplomat Thomas visits tiny Pacific island of Gallardia, forgotten by the mother country for some fifty years, to insure tenuous international agreement after the island's king dies. Not sterling Sellers but some shining moments. **88m/C VHS, Beta.** *GB* Peter Sellers, Terry-Thomas, Luciana Paluzzi, Ian Bannen; ***D:*** Roy Boulting, Jeffrey Dell; ***W:*** Roy Boulting; ***M:*** John Addison. *FCT*

Carmen ₰₰₰ **1983 (R)** Choreographer casts Carmen and finds life imitates art when he falls under the spell of the hotblooded Latin siren. Bizet's opera lends itself to erotically charged flamenco context. Well acted, impressive scenes including cigarette girls' dance fight and romance between Carmen and Don Jose. In Spanish with English subtitles. **99m/C VHS, Beta.** *SP* Antonio Gades, Laura Del Sol, Paco DeLucia, Christina Hoyos; ***D:*** Carlos Saura. British Academy Awards '84: Best Foreign Film; Nominations: Academy Awards '83: Best Foreign Language Film; Cannes Film Festival '83: Best Film. *CTH, MED, INJ*

Carmen Jones ₰₰₰ **1954** Bizet's tale of fickle femme fatale Carmen heads South with an all black cast and new lyrics by Hammerstein II. Soldier Belafonte falls big time for factory working belle Dandridge during the war, and runs off with miss thang after he kills his C.O. and quits the army. Tired of prettyboy Belafonte, Dandridge's eye wanders upon prize pugilist Escamillo, inspiring ex-soldier beau to wring her throaty little neck. Film debuts of Carroll and Peters. More than a little racist undertone to the direction. Actors' singing is dubbed. ♫Dat's Love; Dere's a Cafe on de Corner; Beat Out Dat Rhythm on a Drum; You Talk Just Like My Maw; Stand Up and Fight; Dis Flower; My Joe. **105m/C VHS, LV.** Dorothy Dandridge, Harry Belafonte, Pearl Bailey, Roy Glenn, Diahann Carroll, Brock Peters; ***D:*** Otto Preminger; ***C:*** Sam Leavitt. Golden Globe Awards '55: Best Film—Musical/Comedy; Nominations: Academy Awards '54: Best Actress (Dandridge), Best Original Score. *FXV*

Carmilla **1989** An adaptation of the Sheridan Le Fanu lesbian vampire tale. From Shelley Duvall's cable television series "Nightmare Classics." **60m/C VHS, Beta.** Meg Tilly, Ione Skye, Roddy McDowall, Roy Dotrice; ***D:*** Gabrielle Beaumont. *NO*

Carnage ₰ **1984** Hungry house consumes inhabitants. **91m/C VHS, Beta.** Leslie Den Dooven, Michael Chiodo, Deeann Veeder; ***D:*** Andy Milligan. *MED*

Carnal Crimes ₰½ **1991 (R)** Well-acted upscale softcore trash about a sensuous woman, ignored by her middle-aged lawyer husband and drawn to a young stud photographer with a shady past and S&M tendencies. Available in a sexy unrated version also. **103m/C VHS.** Martin Hewitt, Linda Carol, Rich Crater, Alex Kubik, Yvette Stefens, Paula Trickey; ***D:*** Alexander Gregory Hippolyte; ***W:*** Jon Robert Samsel; ***M:*** Matthew Ross, Jeff Fishman. *NO*

Carnal Knowledge ₰₰₰ **1971 (R)** Carnal knowledge of the me generation. Three decades in the sex-saturated lives of college buddies Nicholson and Garfunkel, chronicled through girlfriends, affairs and marriages. Controversial upon release, it's not a flattering anatomy of Y chromosome carriers. Originally written as a play. Kane's debut. **96m/C VHS, Beta, LV, 8mm.** Jack Nicholson, Candice Bergen, Art Garfunkel, Ann-Margret, Rita Moreno, Carol Kane; ***D:*** Mike Nichols; ***W:*** Jules Feiffer; ***C:*** Giuseppe Rotunno. Golden Globe Awards '72: Best Supporting Actress (Ann-Margret); Nominations: Academy Awards '71: Best Supporting Actress (Ann-Margret). *SUE, COL, FOX*

Carnival in Flanders ₰₰₰½ *La Kermesse Heroique* **1935** When Spanish invaders enter a small 17th century Flemish village they discover all the men have diappeared. So it's up to the women to save the town from destruction—and they decide to do it by seducing the invaders. Classic French costume farce with a witty script and fine performances. In French with English subtitles. **90m/B VHS, Beta.** *FR* Francoise Rosay, Louis Jouvet, Jean Murat, Andre Aleme, Micheline Cheirel; ***D:*** Jacques Feyder; ***C:*** Harry Stradling. National Board of Review Awards '36: 5 Best Foreign Films of the Year; New York Film Critics Awards '36: Best Foreign Film; Venice Film Festival '36: Best Director (Feyder). *HTV, MRV, HHT*

Carnival Lady ₰ **1933** Silver spooner Vincent is scheduled to tie the knot until little lady-to-be discovers he's a bit out of pocket after the stock market takes a wee dip. Jilted and impecunious, he heads for the big top, where he horns in on the high diver's turf, and it's all downhill from there. **66m/B VHS, Beta.** Patricia "Boots" Mallory, Allen Vincent. *VCN*

Carnival of Blood ₰ **1971 (PG)** Boring talky scenes punctuated by Coney Island murder mayhem followed by more boring talky scenes. Young's debut, not released for five years. The question's not why they delayed release, but why they bothered at all. A carnival of cliches. **80m/C VHS, Beta.** Earle Edgerton, Judith Resnick, Martin Barlosky, John Harris, Burt Young; ***W:*** Leonard Kirtman. *NO*

Carnival of Souls ₰₰₰ **1962** Cult-followed zero budget zombie opera has young Hilligoss and girlfriends take wrong turn off bridge into river. Mysteriously unscathed, Hilligoss rents room and takes job as church organist, but she keeps running into dancing dead people, led by director Harvey. Spooky, very spooky. Laserdisc version offers restored picture quality and a refined audio track, as well as introductory feature on the movie's background. **80m/B VHS, Beta, LV.** Candace Hilligoss, Sidney Berger, Frances Feist, Stan Levitt, Art Ellison, Harold (Herk) Harvey; ***D:*** Harold (Herk) Harvey. *MRV, SNC, NOS*

Carnival Rock ₰½ **1957** Story of love triangular in seedy nightclub. Club owner Stewart loves chanteuse Cabot who loves card playin' Hutton. Who cares? Maybe hard-core Corman devotees. Good tunes from the Platters, the Blockbusters, Bob Luman and David Houston. **80m/B VHS, Beta.** Susan Cabot, Brian Hutton, David J. Stewart, Dick Miller; ***D:*** Roger Corman. *RHI, AOV, FCT*

Carnival Story ₰½ **1954** Yet another melodramatic cliche about love triangular under the big top. German girl joins American-owned carnival and two guys start acting out unbecoming territorial behavior. Filmed in Germany. **94m/C VHS, Beta.** Anne Baxter, Steve Cochran, Lyle Bettger, George Nader; ***D:*** Kurt Neumann. *NOS, GEM, DVT*

The Carnivores ₰₰ **1983** The flesh-eaters of the animal kingdom—bears, lions, tigers, and others—and their survival instincts are the focus of this nature documentary. **90m/C VHS, Beta.** *DIS*

Carnosaur ₰₰ **1993 (R)** Straight from the Corman film factory, this exploitive quickie about dinosaurs harkens back to '50s-style monster epics. Predictable plot with extremely cheap effects. Genetic scientist Dr. Jane Tiptree (Ladd) is hatching diabolic experiments with chickens when things go awry. The experiments result in a bunch of lethal prehistoric creatures wrecking havoc among the community. **82m/C VHS.** Diane Ladd, Raphael Sbarge, Jennifer Runyon, Harrison Page, Clint Howard, Ned Bellamy; ***D:*** Adam Simon; ***W:*** Adam Simon; ***M:*** Nigel Holton. *NHO*

Carnosaur 2 ₰½ **1994 (R)** Technicians investigating a power shortage at a secret military mining facility encounter deadly dinos. Entertaining schlock. **90m/C VHS, LV.** John Savage, Cliff DeYoung, Arabella Holzbog, Ryan Thomas Johnson; ***D:*** Louis Morneau. *NHO*

Carny ₰₰₰ **1980 (R)** Hothead carnival bozo Busey and peacemaker Robertson experience friendship difficulties when runaway Foster rolls in hay with one and then other. Originally conceived as a documentary by "Derby" filmmaker Kaylor, it's a candid, unsavory, behind-the-scenes anatomy. Co-written by "The Band" member Robertson. **102m/C VHS, Beta.** Gary Busey, Robbie Robertson, Jodie Foster, Meg Foster, Kenneth McMillan, Elisha Cook Jr., Craig Wasson; ***D:*** Robert Kaylor; ***W:*** Robbie Robertson, Thomas Baum; ***C:*** Harry Stradling Jr.; ***M:*** Alex North. *FOX, WAR*

Caro Diario ₰₰₰ *Dear Diary* **1993** Three offbeat chapters from director Moretti's own life. "On My Vespa" has the director taking off on a personal tour of Rome, including its cinemas and their influence on him. In "Islands" Moretti and friend Gerardo travel to a series of island communities, including Salina, dominated by only children to whom their parents defer obsessively. "Doctors" finds Moretti experiencing a misdiagnosed medical crisis. Lots of charm and a certain shameless romanticism. Italian with subtitles. **100m/C VHS, LV.** *IT* Renato Carpentieri; ***D:*** Nanni Moretti; ***W:*** Nanni Moretti; ***M:*** Nicola Piovani. Cannes Film Festival '94: Best Director (Moretti). *NLC*

Carolina Skeletons ₰₰ **1992 (R)** As a child in a small southern town Gossett, Jr. watched as his brother was accused of a vicious double murder and quickly tried and executed. Thirty years later, the ex-Green Beret returns home to find the real killer and clear his brother's name. But there are those in the town who will do anything to stop their secrets from being revealed. **94m/C VHS, LV.** Louis Gossett Jr., Bruce Dern, Melissa Leo, Paul Roebling, G.D. Spradlin, Bill Cobbs, Henderson Forsythe, Clifton James; ***D:*** John Erman; ***W:*** Tracy Keenan Wynn; ***M:*** John Morris. *TRI*

Caroline? ₰₰₰ **1990 (PG)** A wealthy young woman is presumed dead in a plane crash. Now 15 years later a stranger appears at the family home claiming to be Caroline—and wanting her inheritance. Is it possible that what she says is true or is it all an elaborate ruse? An especially good performance by Zimbalist. Made for television as a "Hallmark Hall of Fame" presentation. Based on the novel "Father's Arcane Daughter" by E.L. Konigsburg. **100m/C VHS, LV.** Stephanie Zimbalist, Pamela Reed, George Grizzard, Dorothy McGuire, Patricia Neal, Shawn Phelan, Jenny Jacobs; ***D:*** Joseph Sargent; ***M:*** Charles Bernstein. *REP*

Caroline at Midnight ₰₰ **1993 (R)** After a reporter's former girlfriend, Caroline, dies in a mysterious auto accident he winds up falling for her girlfriend Victoria. Then he discovers both women are connected to drug-dealing cops. Good cast in this atmospheric erotic thriller with plenty of puzzles. **92m/C VHS, LV.** Clayton Rohner, Mia Sara, Timothy Daly, Judd Nelson, Virginia Madsen, Zach Galligan; ***D:*** Scott McGinnis. *NHO*

Carousel ₰₰₰ **1956** Much-loved Rodgers & Hammerstein musical based on Ferenc Molnar's play "Liliom" (filmed by Fritz Lang in 1935) about a swaggering carnival barker (MacRae) who tries to change his life after he falls in love with a good woman. Killed while attempting to foil a robbery he was supposed to help commit, he begs his heavenly hosts for the chance to return to the mortal realm just long enough to set things straight with his teenage daughter. Now indisputably a classic, the film lost $2 million when it was released. ♫If I Loved You; Soliloquy; You'll Never Walk Alone; What's the Use of Wond'rin; When I Marry Mister Snow; When the Children Are Asleep; A Real Nice Clambake; Carousel Ballet; Carousel Waltz. **128m/C VHS, Beta, LV.** Gordon MacRae, Shirley Jones, Cameron Mitchell, Gene Lockhart, Barbara Ruick, Robert Rounseville, Richard Deacon, Tor Johnson; ***D:*** Henry King; ***M:*** Richard Rodgers, Oscar Hammerstein. *FOX, RDG, HMV*

The Carpathian Eagle 🦴 **1981** Police wonder why murdered victims have hearts ripped out while audience wonders what weird title has to do with anything. Routine evisceration fest, part of Elvira's Thriller Video. **60m/C VHS, Beta.** Suzanne Danielle, Sian Phillips, Pierce Brosnan, Anthony Valentine; ***D:*** Francis Megahy. *LIV*

The Carpenter 🦴 **1989 (R)** Post-nervous breakdown woman receives nightly visits from guy who builds stuff with wood. Very scary stuff. Also available in slightly longer unrated version. **85m/C VHS, LV.** Wings Hauser, Lynne Adams, Pierce Lenoir, Barbara Ann Jones; ***D:*** David Wellington. *REP*

Carpet of Horror 🦴🦴 **1964** The city of London is terrorized by a small ball emitting poison gas in this schlock horror film. Death results when the ball is rolled into the living rooms of intended victims. **?m/C VHS.** Joachim Berger, Carl Lange, Karin Dor. *SNC*

The Carpetbaggers 🦴🦴 **1964 (PG)** Uncannily Howard Hughesian Peppard wallows in wealth and women in Hollywood in the 1920s and 1930s. Spayed version of the Harold Robbins novel. Ladd's final appearance. Followed by the prequel "Nevada Smith." Introduced by Joan Collins. **150m/C VHS, Beta.** George Peppard, Carroll Baker, Alan Ladd, Elizabeth Ashley, Lew Ayres, Martha Hyer, Martin Balsam, Robert Cummings, Archie Moore, Audrey Totter; ***D:*** Edward Dmytryk; ***W:*** John Michael Hayes; ***M:*** Elmer Bernstein. National Board of Review Awards '64: Best Supporting Actor (Balsam). *PAR*

Carrie 🦴🦴🦴 **1952** In a part turned down by Cary Grant, Olivier plays a married American who self destructs as the woman he loves scales the heights to fame and fortune. The manager of a posh epicurean mecca, Olivier deserts wife Hopkins and steals big bucks from his boss to head east with paramour Jones, a country bumpkin transplanted to Chicago. Once en route to thespian fame in the Big Apple, Jones abandons her erstwhile beau, who crumbles pathetically. Adapted from Theodore Dreiser's "Sister Carrie," it's mega melodrama, but the performances are above reproach. **118m/B VHS, Beta, LV.** Laurence Olivier, Jennifer Jones, Miriam Hopkins, Eddie Albert, Basil Ruysdael, Ray Teal, Barry Kelley, Sara Berner, William Reynolds, Mary Murphy, Charles Halton; ***D:*** William Wyler; ***C:*** Victor Milner. Nominations: Academy Awards '52: Best Art Direction/Set Decoration (B & W), Best Costume Design (B & W). *PAR, FCT*

Carrie 🦴🦴🦴 **1976 (R)** Overprotected by religious fanatic mother Laurie and mocked by the in-crowd, shy, withdrawn high school girl Carrie White is asked to the prom. Realizing she's been made the butt of a joke, she unleashes her considerable telekinetic talents. Travolta, Allen, and Irving are teenagers who get what they deserve. Based on the Stephen King novel. Laserdisc version features the original movie trailer, an interview with screenwriter Lawrence D. Cohen, publicity shots, a study of De Palma's filmmaking techniques, and commentary by film expert Laurent Bouzereau. **98m/C VHS, Beta, LV.** Sissy Spacek, Piper Laurie, John Travolta, William Katt, Amy Irving, Nancy Allen, Edie McClurg, Betty Buckley; ***D:*** Brian DePalma; ***W:*** Lawrence D. Cohen; ***M:*** Pino Donaggio. National Society of Film Critics Awards '76: Best Actress (Spacek); Nominations: Academy Awards '76: Best Actress (Spacek), Best Supporting Actress (Laurie). *MGM, FOX, CRC*

Carried Away 🦴🦴½ *Acts of Love* **1995 (R)** Exposing his middle-aged bod, as well as the myth that he can play only psycho toughs, Hopper, as the Midwestern teacher Joseph, is seduced by a 17-year-old student (Locane) in their small conservative town. Based on Harrison's novel "Farmer," it's a sexually active slice of life with the injured Joseph limping through the care of his dying mother, the fate of the small country school where he teaches and his relationship with longtime lover Rosealee (Amy Irving). Hopper's not the only one playing against type, as Irving turns in a fine performance as the widowed schoolmarm. Director Barreto (and Irving's husband) pushes the envelope with full frontal nudity. **107m/C VHS.** Dennis Hopper, Amy Locane, Gary Busey, Hal Holbrook, Amy Irving, Julie Harris, Christopher Pettiet, Priscilla Pointer, Gail Cronauer; ***D:*** Bruno Barreto; ***W:*** Ed Jones; ***C:*** Declan Quinn; ***M:*** Bruce Broughton. *NYR*

The Carrier 🦴🦴 **1987 (R)** Smalltown Sleepy Rock is ideal family-raising turf until plague mysteriously blights inhabitants, and townspeople are out to exterminate all potential carriers. Silverman is standout as local spiritual leader; well orchestrated crowd scenes. Best park your IQ before watching. Filmed on location in Manchester, Michigan. **99m/C VHS, Beta.** Gregory Fortescue, Steve Dixon, Paul Silverman; ***D:*** Nathan J. White. *NO*

Carrington 🦴🦴½ **1995 (R)** England's artistic Bloomsbury group is examined through the eccentric relationship of artist Dora Carrington (Thompson) and her love for homosexual Lytton Strachey (Pryce), celebrated author of "Eminent Victorians." There's many a menage as the duo live together with Carrington's husband (Waddington), on whom Strachey has a crush, and both their various amours (though Carrington's heart is reserved for Lytton). Film is distractingly divided into titled segments (from 1915 to 1932) and, while Pryce gives a bravura performance, Thompson is merely enigmatic. Based on Michael Holroyd's biography "Lytton Strachey." Hampton's directorial debut. **120m/C VHS, LV.** *FR GB* Emma Thompson, Jonathan Pryce, Steven Waddington, Sam West, Rufus Sewell, Penelope Wilton, Jeremy Northam, Peter Blythe, Janet McTeer, Alex Kingston, Sebastian Harcombe, Richard Clifford; ***D:*** Christopher Hampton; ***W:*** Christopher Hampton; ***C:*** Denis Lenoir; ***M:*** Michael Nyman. Cannes Film Festival '95: Special Jury Prize, Best Actor (Pryce); Nominations: British Academy Awards '95: Best Actor (Pryce), Best Film. *PGV*

Carrington, V.C. 🦴🦴🦴 *Court Martial* **1954** British army major Niven is brought up for a court-martial on embezzlement charges because he arranges, without official permission, to be reimbursed for money owed to him. A former war hero, he decides to defend himself in court, and, once an affair comes to light, his vindictive wife joins the opposition. Good cast, superlative Niven performance. **100m/B VHS, Beta.** *GB* David Niven, Margaret Leighton, Noelle Middleton, Laurence Naismith; ***D:*** Anthony Asquith. *NO*

Carry Me Back 🦴½ **1982** Two brothers carry dead dad back to Australian ranch in order to inherit mucho dinero. **93m/C VHS, Beta.** *AU* Grant Tilly, Kelly Johnson. *LIV*

Carry On Admiral 🦴½ *The Ship was Loaded* **1957** Weak British comedy about two friends who get drunk and decide it would be fun to switch identities. One has an easy job as a public relations exec but the other is supposedly the captain of a ship. His lack of sea knowledge causes wacky catastrophes. Unrelated to the "Carry On" series of comedies. **85m/B VHS.** *GB* David Tomlinson, Brian Reece, Peggy Cummins, Eunice Gayson, A.E. Matthews, Lionel Murton, Joan Sims; ***D:*** Val Guest; ***W:*** Val Guest. *FUS*

Carry On at Your Convenience 🦴½ **1971** Low-brow humor in and around a toilet factory. **86m/C VHS, Beta.** *GB* Sidney James, Kenneth Williams, Charles Hawtrey, Joan Sims, Kenneth Cope; ***D:*** Gerald Thomas. *NO*

Carry On Behind 🦴🦴 **1975** "Carry On" crew heads for archeological dig and find themselves sharing site with holiday caravan. **95m/C VHS, Beta.** *GB* Sidney James, Kenneth Williams, Elke Sommer, Joan Sims; ***D:*** Gerald Thomas. *SUE*

Carry On Camping 🦴½ **1971** Another entry in the silly series finds James and Bresslaw trying to persuade their girlfriends to go on a camping trip to what the men hope is a nudist colony. They don't find nudists but they do find a group of sex-starved schoolgirls. **88m/C VHS.** *GB* Sidney James, Bernard Bresslaw, Kenneth Williams, Joan Sims, Charles Hawtrey, Barbara Windsor; ***D:*** Gerald Thomas; ***W:*** Talbot Rothwell. *TVC*

Carry On Cleo 🦴🦴½ **1965** "Carry On" spoof of Shakespeare's "Antony and Cleopatra." **91m/C VHS, Beta.** *GB* Sidney James, Amanda Barrie, Kenneth Williams, Kenneth Connor, Jim Dale, Charles Hawtrey, Joan Sims; ***D:*** Gerald Thomas. *NO*

Carry On Cowboy 🦴🦴 *Rumpo Kid* **1966** "Carry On" Western parody of "High Noon." **91m/C VHS, Beta.** *GB* Sidney James, Kenneth Williams, Jim Dale. *NO*

Carry On Cruising 🦴 **1962** "Carry On" gang attacks sailing world with low humor and raunchiness. **89m/C VHS, Beta.** Sidney James, Kenneth Williams, Liz Fraser; ***D:*** Gerald Thomas. *NO*

Carry On Dick 🦴🦴 **1975** What made the seemingly endless "Carry On" series of super-low-budget British farces such a hit is a mystery not to be solved. Low production values, scripts that peter out midway, and manifest humor don't normally a classic make; and yet the gang has its following. "Dick," a detective movie spoof, was preceded by some twenty-odd carryings on; suffice it to say that the series, which began in 1958 with "Carry on Sergeant," has not improved with age in subsequent incarnations. **95m/C VHS.** *GB* Sidney James, Joan Sims; ***D:*** Gerald Thomas. *NO*

Carry On Doctor 🦴🦴🦴 **1968** British series continues as characters of questionable competence join the medical profession. Hospital staff gets caught in battle over secret weight loss formula. **95m/C VHS.** *GB* Frankie Howerd, Kenneth Williams, Jim Dale, Barbara Windsor; ***D:*** Gerald Thomas. *PAR*

Carry On Emmanuelle 🦴 **1978** Bedroom diplomat Emmanuelle enters international politics by taking on foreign legion. Part of the British "Carry On" series. **104m/C VHS, Beta.** *GB* Suzanne Danielle, Kenneth O'Connor, Kenneth Williams, Beryl Reid; ***D:*** Gerald Thomas. *NO*

Carry On England 🦴 **1976** Mercifully, the gang didn't carry on much beyond this entry, in which a WWII antiaircraft fleet captain bumbles through the usual pranks and imbroglios. **89m/C VHS.** *GB* Kenneth Connor, Patrick Mower, Judy Geeson; ***D:*** Gerald Thomas. *NO*

Carry On Henry VIII 🦴½ **1971** Slapstick sex humor with Henry marrying the French Marie of Normandie and having to deal with both her addiction to garlic and the fact that she's pregnant by her lover. **88m/C VHS.** *GB* Sidney James, Kenneth Williams, Joan Sims, Charles Hawtrey, Barbara Windsor, Kenneth Connor, Julian Holloway; ***D:*** Gerald Thomas; ***W:*** Talbot Rothwell. *TVC*

Carry On Nurse 🦴🦴 **1959** Men's ward in a British hospital declares war on nurses and the rest of the hospital. The second of the "Carry On" series. **86m/B VHS, Beta.** *GB* Shirley Eaton, Kenneth Connor, Hattie Jacques, Wilfrid Hyde-White; ***D:*** Gerald Thomas. *NOS, VYY, VDM*

Carry On 'Round the Bend 🦴½ **1972** Williams, who played in the original ("Carry On Sergeant"), and Carry On regulars (charpei-mugged James and ever-zaftig Jacques), go 'round the bend in yet another installment of the British spoof. **89m/C VHS.** *GB* Sidney James, Kenneth Williams, Hattie Jacques; ***D:*** Gerald Thomas. *NO*

Carry On Screaming 🦴🦴 **1966** "Carry On" does horror. A pair of goofy detectives trail monsters suspected in kidnapping. **97m/C VHS.** *GB* Harry H. Corbett, Kenneth Williams, Fenella Fielding, Joan Sims,

Charles Hawtrey, Jim Dale, Angela Douglas, Jon Pertwee; ***D:*** Gerald Thomas. *MOV*

The Cars That Ate Paris 🦴🦴🦴 *The Cars That Eat People* **1974 (PG)** Parasitic town in the Parisian (Australia) outback preys on car and body parts generated by deliberate accidents inflicted by wreck-driving wreckless youths. Weir's first film released internationally, about a small Australian town that survives economically via deliberately contriving car accidents and selling the wrecks' scrap parts. A broad, bitter black comedy with some horror touches. **91m/C VHS, Beta.** *AU* Terry Camillieri, Kevin Miles, John Meillon, Melissa Jaffe; ***D:*** Peter Weir; ***W:*** Peter Weir. *COL*

Carson City Kid 🦴½ **1940** Typical western which has Rogers trying to exact revenge on the man who killed his brother. **54m/B VHS, Beta.** Roy Rogers. *NOS, VCN, MED*

Cartel *Woof!* **1990 (R)** O'Keeffe, "B" actor extraordinaire, plays the wrong man to pick on in this rancid dope opera. Hounded by drug lord Stroud and framed for murder, pilot O'Keeffe decides the syndicate has gone too doggone far when they kill his sister. Exploitive and otherwise very bad. **106m/C VHS, LV.** Miles O'Keeffe. *IME*

Carthage in Flames 🦴🦴 *Cartagine in Fiamme; Carthage en Flammes* **1960** A graphic portrayal of the destruction of ancient Carthage in a blood and guts battle for domination of the known world. A tender love story is a welcome aside in this colorful Italian-made epic. **96m/C VHS, Beta.** *IT* Anne Heywood, Jose Suarez, Pierre Brasseur; ***D:*** Carmine Gallone. *NO*

Cartier Affair 🦴 **1984** A beautiful television actress unwittingly falls in love with the man who wants to steal her jewels. Collins designed her own wardrobe. Made for television. **120m/C VHS, Beta.** Joan Collins, David Hasselhoff, Telly Savalas, Ed Lauter, Joe La Due; ***D:*** Rod Holcomb. *ORI, WAR*

Cartouche 🦴🦴🦴 *Swords of Blood* **1962** A swashbuckling action-comedy set in 18th-century France. Belmondo plays a charming thief who takes over a Paris gang, aided by the lovely Cardinale. When he is captured, she sacrifices her life to save him and Belmondo and his cohorts vow to have their revenge. Based on a French legend and a well-acted combination of tragedy, action, and farce. In French with English subtitles. **115m/C VHS.** *FR IT* Jean-Paul Belmondo, Claudia Cardinale, Odile Versois, Philippe Lemaire; ***D:*** Philippe de Broca; ***W:*** Philippe de Broca; ***M:*** Georges Delerue. *FCT, HTV*

Carve Her Name with Pride 🦴🦴½ **1958** The true story of Violette Szabo who at age nineteen became a secret agent with the French Resistance in WWII. **119m/B VHS, Beta.** Virginia McKenna, Paul Scofield. *LCA*

The Cary Grant Collection **1990** Three of Cary Grant's most memorable films: "Father Goose," Oscar-winning script; "Indiscreet" (w/ Ingrid Bergman); and "Operation Petticoat" (Tony Curtis and Grant are quite a team in this military comedy! Some great gags.) **336m/C VHS, Beta.** Cary Grant, Ingrid Bergman, Leslie Caron, Trevor Howard, Tony Curtis, Dina Merrill, Gavin MacLeod, Madlyn Rhue; ***D:*** Ralph Nelson, Stanley Donen, Blake Edwards. *REP*

Casablanca 🦴🦴🦴🦴 **1942 (PG)** Can you see George Raft as Rick? Jack Warner did, but producer Hal Wallis wanted Bogart. Considered by many to be the best film ever made and one of the most quoted movies of all time, it rocketed Bogart from gangster roles to romantic leads as he and Bergman (who never looked lovelier) sizzle on screen. Bogart runs a gin joint in Morocco during the Nazi occupation, and meets up with Bergman, an old flame, but romance and politics do not mix, especially in Nazi-occupied French Morocco. Greenstreet, Lorre, and Rains all create memorable characters, as does Wilson, the piano player to whom Bergman says the oft-misquoted, "Play it, Sam." Without a doubt, the best closing scene ever written; it was scripted on the fly during the end of shooting, and actually shot several ways. Written from an unproduced play. See it in the original black and white. Laserdisc edition features restored imaging and sound and commentary by film historian Ronald Haver about the production, the play it was based on, and the famed evolution of the screenplay on audio track two. 50th Anniversary Edition contains a restored and remastered print, the original 1942 theatrical trailer, a film documentary narrated by Lauren Bacall, and a booklet. **102m/B VHS, Beta, LV, 8mm.** Humphrey Bogart, Ingrid Bergman, Paul Henreid, Claude Rains, Peter Lorre, Sydney Greenstreet, Conrad Veidt, S.Z. Sakall, Dooley Wilson, Marcel Dalio, John Qualen, Helmut Dantine; ***D:*** Michael Curtiz; ***W:*** Julius J. Epstein, Philip C. Epstein, Howard Koch; ***M:*** Max Steiner. Academy Awards '43: Best Director (Curtiz), Best Picture, Best Screenplay; National Board of Review Awards '45: 10 Best Films of the Year; Nominations: Academy Awards '43: Best Actor (Bogart), Best Black and White Cinematography, Best Film Editing, Best Supporting Actor (Rains), Best Original Score. *MGM, FOX, TLF*

Casablanca Express 🦴 **1989** Nazi commandos hijack Churchill's train in this action-adventure drama. **90m/C VHS, Beta.** Glenn Ford, Donald Pleasence, Jason Connery; ***D:*** Sergio Martino. *NO*

Casanova 🦴🦴 **1987 (PG-13)** A comedic romp through the bedrooms of 18th-century Europe with Chamberlain as the legendary lover. Lots of lovely ladies and hammy performances. Made for television. **122m/C VHS, Beta, LV.** Richard Chamberlain, Faye Dunaway, Sylvia Kristel, Ornella Muti, Hanna Schygulla, Sophie Ward, Frank Finlay, Kenneth Colley; ***D:*** Simon Langton; ***W:*** George MacDonald Fraser; ***C:*** Giuseppe Rotunno. *TTC*

Casanova Brown 🦴🦴½ **1944** Lighthearted comedy about a shy English professor (Cooper) who learns that his recent ex-wife (Wright) has had a baby (guess whose). When Cooper learns Wright has decided to give their daughter up for adoption he kidnaps the tyke and attempts fatherhood in a hotel room. When Wright finds out where he is, the twosome (who have really been in love all along) decide to remarry and be a family. Cooper, with baby and surrounded by diapers, makes a comedic sight. Based on the play "The Little Accident" by Floyd Dell and Thomas Mitchell. **94m/B VHS, Beta.** Gary Cooper, Teresa Wright, Frank Morgan, Anita Louise, Patricia Collinge, Edmund Breon, Jill Esmond, Emory Parnell, Isobel Elsom, Mary Treen, Halliwell Hobbes; ***D:*** Sam Wood; ***W:*** Nunnally Johnson; ***M:*** Arthur Lange. Nominations: Academy Awards '44: Best Interior Decoration, Best Sound, Best Score. *MGM, FCT*

Casanova '70 🦴🦴½ **1965** Mastroianni plays a handsome soldier who has a knack for enticing liberated women in this comic rendition of the much-cinematized legendary yarn. Trouble is, he's in the mood only when he believes that he's in imminent danger. In Italian with English subtitles. **113m/C VHS.** *IT* Marcello Mastroianni, Virna Lisi, Michele Mercier, Guido Alberti, Margaret Lee, Bernard Blier, Liana Orfei; ***D:*** Mario Monicelli; ***W:*** Tonino Guerra. Nominations: Academy Awards '65: Best Story & Screenplay. *FOX*

Casanova's Big Night 🦴🦴½ **1954** Classic slapstick comedy stars Hope masquerading as Casanova to test Fontaine's virtue before her marriage to a duke. The all-star cast provides one hilarious scene after another in this dated film. Price has a cameo as the "real" Casanova. Based on a story by Aubrey Wisberg. **85m/C VHS, LV.** Bob Hope, Joan Fontaine, Audrey Dalton, Basil Rathbone, Hugh Marlowe, Vincent Price, John Carradine, Raymond Burr; ***D:*** Norman Z. McLeod; ***W:*** Hal Kanter, Edmund Hartmann; ***C:*** Lionel Lindon. *PAR, CCB*

A Case for Murder 🦴🦴½ **1993 (R)** Jack Hammet has just become the youngest full partner ever at his Chicago law firm, with a knack for winning impossible cases. His next one's a beaut. Seems an envious colleague has gotten himself murdered and his estranged wife is the prime suspect. Jack decides to work with newly-arrived lawyer Kate Weldon but as the two become personally involved, Kate begins to question Jack's ethics. Seems the evidence is more than a little shady and Jack isn't telling all. **94m/C VHS, LV.** Peter Berg, Jennifer Grey, Belinda Bauer; ***D:*** Duncan Gibbins; ***W:*** Duncan Gibbins, Pablo F. Fenjves. *MCA*

A Case of Deadly Force 🦴🦴🦴 **1986** Based on the true story of a black man wrongfully killed by Boston's Tactical Police Force who mistook him for a robber. The police investigation calls it self-defense but the family and the attorney they hire fight to change the verdict. Excellent cast, great dramatic story. Originally made for television. **95m/C VHS, LV.** Richard Crenna, John Shea, Lorraine Toussaint, Frank McCarthy, Tom Isbell; ***D:*** Michael Miller. *CAF*

A Case of Libel 🦴🦴½ **1983** A made for television dramatization based on attorney Louis Nizer's account of Quentin Reynolds' libel suit against columnist Westbrook Pegler. **90m/C VHS, Beta.** Daniel J. Travanti, Ed Asner; ***D:*** Eric Till. *LIV*

Case of the Baby Sitter 🦴 **1947** A private eye investigates jewel thieves posing as nobility. **40m/B VHS, Beta, LV.** Tom Neal, Allen Jenkins, Pamela Blake. *SNC*

The Case of the Frightened Lady 🦴 *The Frightened Lady* **1939** A homicidal family does its collective best to keep its dark past a secret in order to collect some inheritance money. Watch, if you're still awake, for the surprise ending. **80m/B VHS, Beta.** *GB* Marius Goring, Helen Haye, Penelope Dudley Ward, Felix Aylmer, Patrick Barr; ***D:*** George King. *SNC*

The Case of the Lucky Legs 🦴🦴½ **1935** Yes, there was a Perry Mason before Raymond Burr. Erle Stanley Gardner's sleuthing litigator's first appearance was 1934's "The Case of the Howling Dog," which initiated Warner Bros' "A"-grade (but soon-to-be "B"-grade) series. More akin to Nick Charles than to Gardner's character or to his later TV incarnation, the "Lucky Legs" Perry is a high-living, interminably hungover tippler who winces and wisecracks as he unravels the case of the corpse of a crooked con man. William, who left shortly after the series was downgraded to "B" status, plays the esquire; Tobin plays his smart-mouthed secretary, and Ellis is the tomato suspected of murder. **76m/B VHS, Beta.** Warren William, Genevieve Tobin, Patricia Ellis, Lyle Talbot, Allen Jenkins, Barton MacLane, Peggy Shannon, Porter Hall; ***D:*** Archie Mayo. *SNC, RXM*

The Case of the Missing Lady 🦴½ **1983** A famous Arctic explorer asks Tommy and Tuppence to find his missing fiancee. Based on the Christie story. **51m/C VHS, Beta.** *GB* Francesca Annis, James Warwick. *TPV*

The Case of the Mukkinese Battle Horn 🦴🦴 **1956** The cast of Britain's "The Goon Show" takes over in a zany, slapdash featurette-length mystery spoof. **27m/C VHS, Beta, 8mm.** *GB* Peter Sellers, Spike Milligan, Dick Emery; ***M:*** Edwin Astley. *VYY*

Casey at the Bat **1985** From Shelley Duvall's made for cable television "Tall Tales and Legends" series, in which the immortal poem is brought to life. Rousing comedy for the whole family. **52m/C VHS, Beta.** Bill Macy, Hamilton Camp, Elliott Gould, Carol Kane, Howard Cosell; ***D:*** David Steinberg. *FOX*

Casey Jones and Fury (Brave Stallion) **1957** An episode from each of these early adventure series. **60m/B VHS, Beta.** Alan Hale Jr., Peter Graves. *NOS, DVT*

Casey's Shadow 🦴🦴 **1978 (PG)** The eight-year-old son of an impoverished horse trainer raises a quarter horse and enters it in the world's richest horse race. **116m/C VHS, Beta.** Walter Matthau, Alexis Smith, Robert Webber, Murray Hamilton; ***D:*** Martin Ritt; ***C:*** John A. Alonzo. *COL*

Cash McCall 🦴🦴½ **1960** McCall (Garner) is a corporate raider who just loves making money. But problems come in when he falls for the lovely daughter (Wood) of his latest takeover target, failing businessman Jagger. Based on the novel by Cameron Hawley. **116m/C VHS.** James Garner, Natalie Wood, Dean Jagger, Nina Foch, E.G. Marshall, Henry Jones, Otto Kruger, Roland Winters, Parley Baer, Dabbs Greer; ***D:*** Joseph Pevney; ***W:*** Lenore Coffee, Marion Hargrove; ***M:*** Max Steiner. *WAR*

Casino 🦴½ **1980** A made-for-television thriller about back-stabbings and ritzy romance aboard a high-priced gambling liner. **100m/C VHS, Beta.** Mike Connors, Lynda Day George, Bo Hopkins, Gary Burghoff, Joseph Cotten, Robert Reed, Barry Sullivan; ***D:*** Don Chaffey. *PSM*

Casino 🦴🦴🦴 **1995 (R)** Final part of the Scorsese underworld crime trilogy that began with "Mean Streets" and continued in "GoodFellas." Casino boss Sam "Ace" Rothstein (De Niro), his ex-hustler wife Ginger (Stone), and his loose-cannon enforcer pal Nicky (Pesci) are the principals in this lengthy, fictionalized account of how the mob lost Las Vegas in a haze of drugs, sex, coincidence and betrayal. Flashy, intricate, and unflinchingly violent account of mob-run '70s Vegas clicks when exploring the inner workings of a major casino and its hierarchy. Although Stone shines as a hedonistic money chaser, visuals are great and the soundtrack is a killer, story line suffers from deja vu. Pileggi again adapted the screenplay from his own book. **177m/C VHS, LV.** Robert De Niro, Joe Pesci, Sharon Stone, James Woods, Don Rickles, Alan King, Kevin Pollak, L.Q. Jones, Dick Smothers, John Bloom; ***Cameos:*** Frankie Avalon, Steve Allen, Jayne Meadows, Jerry Vale; ***D:*** Martin Scorsese; ***W:*** Nicholas Pileggi, Martin Scorsese; ***C:*** Robert Richardson. Golden Globe Awards '96: Best Actress—Drama (Stone); Nominations: Academy Awards '95: Best Actress (Stone); Golden Globe Awards '96: Best Director (Scorsese); MTV Movie Awards '96: Best Female Performance (Stone), Best Villain (Pesci). *MCA*

Casino Royale 🦴 **1967** The product of five directors, three writers and a mismatched cast of dozens, this virtually plotless spoof of James Bond films can stand as one of the low-water marks for 1960s comedy. And yet, there are some marvelous bits within, scenes of bizarre hilarity. Welles and Sellers literally couldn't stand the sight of one another, and their scenes together were filmed separately, with stand-ins. **130m/C VHS, Beta, LV.** David Niven, Woody Allen, Peter Sellers, Ursula Andress, Orson Welles, Jacqueline Bisset, Deborah Kerr, Peter O'Toole, Jean-Paul Belmondo, Charles Boyer, Joanna Pettet, John Huston, William Holden, George Raft; ***D:*** John Huston, Ken Hughes, Robert Parrish, Val Guest, Joseph McGrath; ***C:*** Jack Hildyard; ***M:*** Burt Bacharach. Nominations: Academy Awards '67: Best Song ("The Look of Love"). *MRV, COL*

Casper 🦴🦴🦴 **1995 (PG)** World's friendliest ghost appears on the big screen with outstanding visual trickery (from Industrial Light and Magic) and a lively, if hokey, story. Evilish Carrigan Crittenden (Moriarty) inherits ghost-infested Whiplash Manor and hires scatterbrained "ghost therapist" Dr. Harvey (Pullman) to get rid of its unwanted occupants. His daughter Kat (Ricci) is soon the object of Casper's friendly attention while the good doc must contend with Casper's mischievous uncles—Stinkie, Fatso, and Stretch. Exec producer Spielberg shows his influence with numerous topical gags and screen references that help amuse the adults while the ghosts work their magic on the kiddies. Silberling's directorial debut; based on the comic-book and television cartoon character created more than 30 years ago. **95m/C VHS, LV.** Christina Ricci, Bill Pullman, Cathy Moriarty, Eric Idle, Amy Brenneman; ***Cameos:*** Don Novello, Rodney Dangerfield, Clint Eastwood, Mel Gibson, Dan Aykroyd; ***D:*** Brad Silberling; ***W:*** Sherri Stoner, Deanna Oliver; ***C:*** Dean Cundey; ***M:*** James Horner; ***V:*** Malachi Pearson, Joe Nipote, Joe Alaskey, Brad Garrett. *MCA*

Casque d'Or 🦴🦴🦴 *Golden Marie* **1952** Crime passionnel in turn-of-the-century Paris as an honest carpenter (Reggiani) gets drawn into the netherworld of pimps and thieves. He's finally driven to murder—all for love of gangster's moll Marie (a very sultry Signoret). French with subtitles. **96m/B VHS.** *FR* Serge Reggiani, Simone Signoret, Claude Dauphin, Raymond Bussieres, Gaston Modot; ***D:*** Jacques Becker; ***W:*** Jacques Becker, Jacques Companeez; ***C:*** Robert Le Febvre; ***M:*** Georges Van Parys. *FCT*

Cass 🦴 **1978** Disenchanted filmmaker returns home to Australia to experiment with alternative lifestyles. **90m/C VHS, Beta.** Michelle Fawden, John Waters, Judy Morris, Peter Carroll. *NO*

Cass Timberlane 🦴🦴½ **1947** Scandalous story of a May-December romance set in a small Midwestern town. Tracy stars as Cass Timberlane, a widowed judge who falls for a voluptuous young girl from the wrong side of the tracks (Turner). They marry and experience problems when she is shunned by his snobbish friends. Good performances, especially from the supporting cast, dominate this fairly predictable film. Based on the novel by Sinclair Lewis. **119m/B VHS.** Spencer Tracy, Lana Turner, Zachary Scott, Tom Drake, Mary Astor, Albert Dekker, Margaret Lindsay, John Litel, Mona Barrie, Josephine Hutchinson, Rose Hobart, Selena Royle; ***Cameos:*** Walter Pidgeon; ***D:*** George Sidney; ***W:*** Donald Ogden Stewart. *MGM*

Cassandra 🦴 **1987 (R)** A fragile young woman has dreams that foretell the future—specifically, a series of grisly murders. **94m/C VHS, Beta, LV.** Shane Briant, Brionny Behets, Tessa Humphries, Kit Taylor, Lee James; ***D:*** Colin Eggleston. *VTR*

The Cassandra Crossing 🦴½ **1976 (R)** A terrorist with the plague causes havoc on a transcontinental luxury train. Turgid adventure filmed in France and Italy. **129m/C VHS, Beta.** *GB* Sophia Loren, Richard Harris, Ava Gardner, Burt Lancaster, Martin Sheen, Ingrid Thulin, Lee Strasberg, John Phillip Law, Lionel Stander, O.J. Simpson, Ann Turkel, Alida Valli; ***D:*** George P. Cosmatos; ***W:*** George P. Cosmatos, Tom Mankiewicz; ***M:*** Jerry Goldsmith. *FOX*

Cassie 🦴 **1987 (R)** Follows the rise of Cassie, a successful country and western singer, and documents all her trials along the way. **75m/C VHS, Beta.** Marilyn Chambers; ***D:*** Godfrey Daniels. *NO*

Cast a Dark Shadow 🦴🦴🦴 **1955** Bogarde is the charmer who decides to reap his reward by marrying and murdering elderly women for their fortunes. But Bogarde meets his match when he plots against his latest intended (Lockwood). Tidy thriller with effective performances. Based on the play "Murder Mistaken" by Janet Green. **82m/B VHS.** *GB* Dirk Bogarde, Margaret Lockwood, Mona Washbourne, Kay Walsh, Kathleen Harrison, Robert Flemyng, Walter Hudd; ***D:*** Lewis Gilbert; ***W:*** John Cresswell. *FCT*

Cast a Deadly Spell 🦴🦴🦴 **1991 (R)** A bubbly, flavorful witch's brew of private-eye and horror cliches, set in a fantasy version of 1948 Los Angeles where sorcery and voodoo abound, but gumshoe Harry P. Lovecraft uses street smarts instead of magic to track down a stolen Necronomicon—and if you know what that is you'll want to watch. Wild creatures and f/x wizardry complement this made-for-cable-TV trick and treat. **93m/C VHS, LV.** Fred Ward, David Warner, Julianne Moore, Clancy Brown, Alexandra Powers; ***D:*** Martin Campbell; ***W:*** Joseph Dougherty, Dave Edison. *HBO, FCT*

Cast a Giant Shadow 🦴🦴 **1966** Follows the career of Col. David "Mickey" Marcus, an American Jew and WWII hero who helped turn Israel's army into a formidable fighting force during the 1947-48 struggle for independence. **142m/C VHS, Beta.** Kirk Douglas, Senta Berger, Angie Dickinson, John Wayne, James Donald, Chaim Topol, Frank Sinatra, Yul Brynner; ***D:*** Melville Shavelson; ***W:*** Melville Shavelson; ***M:*** Elmer Bernstein. *MGM, FCT*

Cast the First Stone 🦴🦴 **1989** Made for TV soaper based on the true story of a former nun who becomes a small town schoolteacher. After being raped, Diane Martin discovers she's pregnant and when she decides to keep the baby the school board dismisses her. The plot centers around her fight to regain her job and dignity—while trying to convince everybody that she doesn't deserve to lose her job simply because she is an unwed mother. Eikenberry gives a strong performance, but it can't carry this lackluster film. **94m/C VHS, LV.** Jill Eikenberry, Richard Masur, Joe Spano, Lew Ayres, Holly Palance; ***D:*** John Korty; ***M:*** Ira Newborn. *COL*

Castaway 🦴🦴½ **1987 (R)** Based on the factual account by Lucy Irvine. The story of Michael Wilmington, who placed an ad for a young woman to spend a year on a Pacific atoll with him, and the battle of the sexes that followed. **118m/C VHS, Beta.** Oliver Reed, Amanda Donohoe, Tony Rickards, Georgina Hale, Frances Barber, Todd Rippon; ***D:*** Nicolas Roeg; ***W:*** Allan Scott; ***M:*** Stanley Myers. *WAR*

The Castaway Cowboy 🦴🦴 **1974 (G)** A shanghaied cowboy becomes partners with a widow when she turns her Hawaiian potato farm into a cattle ranch. Good, clean "family fare." **91m/C VHS, Beta.** James Garner, Robert Culp, Vera Miles; ***D:*** Vincent McEveety; ***M:*** Robert F. Brunner. *DIS, OM*

The Castilian 🦴🦴½ *Valley of the Swords* **1963** Some very odd casting in this historical tale of heroism and swordplay about a Spanish nobleman who leads his followers against the invading Moors and their evil king (Crawford). Based on a 13th century poem. **128m/C VHS.** Cesar Romero, Broderick Crawford, Alida Valli, Frankie Avalon, Espartaco Santoni, Fernando Rey, Jorge Rigaud; ***D:*** Javier Seto; ***W:*** Sidney Pink. *WAR, FCT*

Casting Call **1988** Eighteen would-be Hollywood starlets undress and cavort for the camera, in hopes of getting real film work. **60m/C VHS, Beta.** *AHV*

The Castle 🦴🦴🦴 *Das Schloss* **1968** A man is summoned by the seemingly invisible occupants of a castle to their village. All his efforts to meet with those inhabiting the castle are futile and the task gradually becomes his obsession. Both wonderfully acted and shot, this is a well-executed adaptation of Franz Kafka's novel. **90m/C VHS, Beta.** *GE SI* Maximilian Schell, Cordula Trantow, Trudik Daniel, Helmut Qualtinger; ***D:*** Rudolf Noelte. *NO*

Castle Freak 🦴🦴 **1995 (R)** Italian countess leaves her creepy haunted castle to her American nephew and his family. They find an unwelcome surprise lurking in the cellar. **90m/C VHS, LV.** Jeffrey Combs, Barbara Crampton, Jonathan Fuller, Jessica Dollarhide; ***D:*** Stuart Gordon; ***W:*** Dennis Paoli; ***C:*** Mario Vulpiani; ***M:*** Richard Band. *FLL*

Castle in the Desert 🦴🦴½ **1942** Charlie Chan investigates murder and other strange goings-on in a spooky old castle. One of the last in the series. **62m/B VHS.** Sidney Toler, Arleen Whelan, Richard Derr, Douglass Dumbrille, Henry Daniell, Victor Sen Yung; ***D:*** Harry Lachman. *FOX*

Castle of Blood 🦴🦴 *Castle of Terror; Coffin of Terror; Danza Macabra* **1964** Staying overnight in a haunted castle, a poet is forced to deal with a number of creepy encounters. Cult favorite Steele enhances this atmospheric chiller. Dubbed in English. **85m/B VHS.** *IT FR* Barbara Steele, George Riviere, Margrete Robsahm, Henry Kruger, Montgomery Glenn, Sylvia Sorente; ***D:*** Anthony (Antonio Margheriti) Dawson. *SNC*

The Castle of Cagliostro **1980** An animated Japanese adventure tale featuring a hero named Wolf, who's a thief. Wolf infiltrates the suspicious country of Cagliostro, whose one industry is conterfeiting money, and winds up rescuing a princess. Lots of violence to go with the action. In Japanese with English subtitles. **100m/C VHS.** *JP WTA, STP*

Castle of Evil *Woof!* **1966** Group of heirs gathers on a deserted isle to hear the reading of the will of your basic mad scientist. One by one, they fall victim to a humanoid created by the loony doc in his own image. Inspired moments of unintentional fun. **81m/C VHS.** Scott Brady, Virginia Mayo, Lisa Gaye, David Brian, Hugh Marlowe, William Thourlby, Shelly Morrison; ***D:*** Francis D. Lyon. *REP, FCT*

The Castle of Fu Manchu 🦴 *Assignment: Istanbul; Die Folterkammer des Dr. Fu Manchu* **1968 (PG)** The final chapter in a series starring Lee as the wicked doctor. This time, Lee has developed a gadget which will put the earth into a deep freeze, and at his mercy. To fine tune this contraption, he enlists the help of a gifted scientist by abducting him. However, the helper/hostage has a bad ticker, so Lee must abduct a heart surgeon to save his life, and thus, the freezer project. Most critics felt this was the weakest installment in the series. **92m/C VHS.** *GE SP IT GB* Christopher Lee, Richard Greene, H. Marion Crawford, Tsai Chin, Gunther Stoll, Rosalba (Sara Bay) Neri, Maria Perschy; ***D:*** Jess (Jesus) Franco. *MRV*

Castle of the Creeping Flesh *Woof!* **1968** A surgeon's daughter is brutally murdered. Vowing to bring her back he begins ripping out the organs of innocent people and transplanting them into her body. Has the dubious honor of being one of the few movies to sport actual open heart surgery footage. So bad it's...just bad. **85m/C VHS, Beta.** Adrian Hoven, Janine Reynaud, Howard Vernon; ***D:*** Percy G. Parker. *NO*

Castle of the Living Dead 🦴🦴 *Il Castello de Morti Vivi* **1964** Evil Count Drago's hobbies include mummifying a traveling circus group visiting his castle. Lee is as evil as ever, but be sure to look for Sutherland's screen debut. In a dual role, he plays not only the bumbling inspector, but also a witch, in drag. **90m/B VHS.** *IT FR* Christopher Lee, Gaia Germani, Phillippe LeRoy, Jacques Stanislawsky, Donald Sutherland; ***D:*** Herbert Wise. *SNC, MRV*

Casual Sex? 🦴½ **1988 (R)** Two young women, looking for love and commitment, take a vacation at a posh resort where they are confronted by men with nothing on their minds but sex, be it casual or the more formal black-tie variety. Supposedly an examination of safe sex in a lightly comedic vein, though the comic is too light and the morality too limp. Adapted from the play by Wendy Goldman and Judy Toll. **87m/C VHS, Beta, LV.** Lea Thompson, Victoria Jackson, Stephen Shellan, Jerry Levine, Mary Gross, Andrew Dice Clay; ***D:*** Genevieve Robert. *MCA*

Casualties of Love: The "Long Island Lolita" Story 🦴🦴 **1993 (PG-13)** Told from the Buttafuoco's point of view, Amy Fisher was nothing but a wacko fatally attracted teenager who misunderstood Joey's harmless flirtations and deliberately went after his wife with a gun. The Buttafuocos received $300,000 from CBS to tell their side of the story which features Milano, who resembles Amy not in the least, as the lead. One of three competing network television versions of the sordid story. See also: "The Amy Fisher Story" and "Lethal Lolita—Amy Fisher: My Story." **94m/C VHS.** Jack Scalia, Alyssa Milano, Phyllis Lyons, Jack Kehler, Michael Bowen, J.E. Freeman, Nicky Corello, Lawrence Tierney, Peter Van Norden, Anne DeSalvo; ***D:*** John Herzfeld; ***W:*** John Herzfeld. *COL*

Casualties of War 🦴🦴🦴 **1989 (R)** A Vietnam war morality play about army private Fox in the bush who refuses to let his fellow soldiers and commanding sergeant (Penn) skirt responsibility for the rape and murder of a native woman. Fox achieves his dramatic breakthrough. Based on the true story by Daniel Lang. **120m/C VHS, Beta, LV, 8mm.** Sean Penn, Michael J. Fox, Don Harvey, Thuy Thu Le, John Leguizamo, Sam Robards, John C. Reilly, Erik King; ***D:*** Brian DePalma; ***W:*** David Rabe; ***C:*** Stephen Burum; ***M:*** Ennio Morricone. *COL*

A Casualty of War 🦴🦴½ **1990 (R)** Made-for-TV adaptation of Frederick Forsyth's thriller about modern-day arms smuggling (Libya to Ireland) and espionage. Well-acted, with the exception of Hack. **96m/C VHS.** Shelley Hack, David Threlfall, Richard Hope, Alan Howard, Clarke Peters; ***D:*** Tom Clegg; ***W:*** Frederick Forsyth. *NO*

The Cat 🦴 **1966** A boy and a tamed mountain lion become friends on the run from a murderous poacher. **95m/C VHS, Beta.** Peggy Ann Garner, Roger Perry, Barry Coe; ***D:*** Ellis Kadisan. *COL, NLC*

Cat and Mouse 🦴🦴🦴½ **1978 (PG)** A very unorthodox police inspector is assigned to investigate a millionaire's mysterious death. Who done it? French dialogue with English subtitles. **107m/C VHS, Beta.** *FR* Michele Morgan, Serge Reggiani, Jean-Pierre Aumont; ***D:*** Claude Lelouch. *COL*

The Cat and the Canary 🦴🦴🦴 **1927** A great silent film about the ghost of a madman that wanders nightly through the corridors of an old house. Remade twice, once in 1939 and again in 1979. **70m/B VHS, Beta.** Laura La Plante, Creighton Hale, Tully Marshall, Gertrude Astor; ***D:*** Paul Leni. *NOS, MRV, VYY*

The Cat and the Canary 🦴🦴 **1979 (PG)** A stormy night, a gloomy mansion, and a mysterious will combine to create an atmosphere for murder. An entertaining remake of the 1927 silent film. **96m/C VHS, Beta.** *GB* Carol Lynley, Michael Callan, Wendy Hiller, Olivia Hussey, Daniel Massey, Honor Blackman, Edward Fox, Wilfrid Hyde-White; ***D:*** Radley Metzger. *COL, OM*

The Cat and the Fiddle 🦴🦴🦴 **1934** Lovely Jerome Kern-Oscar Hammerstein operetta in which Novarro plays a struggling composer who forces his affections on MacDonald. She sings in response to his romantic proposals. The final sequence is in color. ♫The Night Was Made for Love; She Didn't Say 'Yes'; A New Love is Old; Try to Forget; One Moment Alone; Don't Ask Us Not To Sing; I Watch the Love Parade; The Breeze Kissed Your Hair; Impressions in a Harlem Flat. **90m/B VHS.** Ramon Novarro, Jeanette MacDonald, Frank Morgan, Charles Butterworth. *MGM*

Cat Ballou 🦴🦴🦴½ **1965** At the turn of the century, a schoolmarm turns outlaw with the help of a drunken gunman. Marvin played Kid Shelleen and his silver-nosed evil twin Tim Strawn in this cheery spoof of westerns. Cole and Kaye sing the narration in a one of a kind Greek chorus. **96m/C VHS, Beta.** Jane Fonda, Lee Marvin, Michael Callan, Dwayne Hickman, Reginald Denny, Nat King Cole, Stubby Kaye; ***D:*** Elliot Silverstein; ***W:*** Frank Pierson. Academy Awards '65: Best Actor (Marvin); Berlin International Film Festival '65: Best Actor (Marvin); British Academy Awards '65: Best Actor (Marvin); Golden Globe Awards '66: Best Actor—Musical/Comedy (Marvin); National Board of Review Awards '65: 10 Best Films of the Year, Best Actor (Marvin); Nominations: Academy Awards '65: Best Adapted Screenplay, Best Film Editing, Best Song ("The Ballad of Cat Ballou"), Best Original Score. *COL, BTV*

Cat Chaser 🦴🦴 **1990** Weller walks listlessly through the role of an ex-soldier in Miami who has an affair with the wife of an exiled—but still lethal—military dictator. Surpisingly low-key, sometimes effective thriller that saves its energy for sex scenes, also available in a less steamy, 90-minute "R" rated version. Based on an Elmore Leonard novel. **97m/C VHS.** Kelly McGillis, Peter Weller, Charles Durning, Frederic Forrest, Tomas Milian, Juan Fernandez; ***D:*** Abel Ferrara; ***W:*** Elmore Leonard, Jim Borrelli; ***M:*** Chick Corea. *VES*

The Cat from Outer Space 🦴🦴 **1978 (G)** An extraterrestrial cat named Jake crashes his spaceship on Earth and leads a group of people on endless escapades. Enjoyable Disney fare. **103m/C VHS, Beta.** Ken Berry, Sandy Duncan, Harry (Henry) Morgan, Roddy McDowall, McLean Stevenson; ***D:*** Norman Tokar. *DIS, OM*

Cat Girl 🦴 **1957** A young bride on her honeymoon finds she has inherited the family curse—she has a psychic link to a ferocious leopard. Numerous murders ensue. Poor production value and a weak script, despite Shelley's fine acting, make this an unworthwhile film. **69m/B VHS.** Barbara Shelley, Robert Ayres, Kay Callard, Paddy Webster; ***D:*** Alfred Shaughnessy. *PAR, COL*

Cat in the Cage 🦴½ **1968** A young man finds many things have changed at home while he was in a mental institution. Dad has remarried, the housekeeper is practicing witchcraft, the chauffeur is after his mistress, and the cat is gone. So where'd that cat go? **96m/C VHS, Beta.** Colleen Camp, Sybil Danning, Mel Novak, Frank De Kova; ***D:*** Tony Zarin Dast. *GHV*

The Cat o' Nine Tails 🦴 **1971 (PG)** A blind detective and a newsman team up to find a sadistic killer. A gory murder mystery. **112m/C VHS, 8mm.** *GE FR IT* Karl Malden, James Franciscus, Catherine Spaak, Cinzia de Carolis, Carlo Alighiero; ***D:*** Dario Argento; ***W:*** Dario Argento; ***M:*** Ennio Morricone. *SIM*

Cat on a Hot Tin Roof 🦴🦴🦴½ **1958** Tennessee Williams' powerful play about greed and deception in a patriarchal Southern family. Big Daddy (Ives) is dying. Members of the family greedily attempt to capture his inheritance, tearing the family apart. Taylor is a sensual wonder as Maggie the Cat, though the more controversial elements of the play were toned down for the film version. Intense, believable performances from Ives and Newman. **108m/C VHS, Beta, LV.** Paul Newman, Burl Ives, Elizabeth Taylor, Jack Carson, Judith Anderson; ***D:*** Richard Brooks; ***W:*** Richard Brooks, James Poe; ***C:*** William H. Daniels. National Board of Review Awards '58: 10 Best Films of the Year; Nominations: Academy Awards '56: Best Director (Brooks); Academy Awards '58: Best Actor (Newman), Best Actress (Taylor), Best Adapted Screenplay, Best Color Cinematography, Best Picture. *MGM, FCT, CCB*

Cat on a Hot Tin Roof 🦴🦴 **1984** In this adaptation of the Tennessee Williams play, fights over the family inheritance tear a family apart. **122m/C VHS, Beta, LV.** Jessica Lange, Tommy Lee Jones, Rip Torn, David Dukes; ***D:*** Jack Hofsiss. *MGM, LIV, VES*

Cat People 🦴🦴🦴 **1942** A young dress designer is the victim of a curse that changes her into a deadly panther who must kill to survive. A classic among the horror genre with unrelenting terror from beginning to end. First horror film from producer Val Lewton. **73m/B VHS, Beta, LV.** Jane Randolph, Elizabeth Russell, Jack Holt, Alan Napier, Simone Simon, Kent Smith, Tom Conway; ***D:*** Jacques Tourneur. *MED, BTV, TTC*

Cat People 🦴🦴½ **1982 (R)** A beautiful young woman learns that she has inherited a strange family trait—she turns into a vicious panther when sexually aroused. The only person with whom she can safely mate is her brother, a victim of the same genetic heritage. Kinski is mesmerizing as the innocent, sensual woman. Remake of the 1942 film. **118m/C VHS, Beta, LV.** Nastassia Kinski, Malcolm McDowell, John Heard, Annette O'Toole, Ruby Dee, Ed Begley Jr., John Larroquette; ***D:*** Paul Schrader; ***W:*** Alan Ormsby; ***C:*** John Bailey. *MCA, FCT*

Cat Women of the Moon 🦴🦴 *Rocket to the Moon* **1953** Scientists land on the moon and encounter an Amazon-like force of skimpily attired female chauvinists. Remade as "Missile to the Moon." Featuring the Hollywood Cover Girls as various cat women. Available in its original 3-D format. **65m/B VHS, Beta.** Sonny Tufts, Victor Jory, Marie Windsor, Bill Phipps, Douglas Fowley, Carol Brewster, Suzanne Alexander, Susan Morrow; ***D:*** Arthur Hilton; ***M:*** Elmer Bernstein. *RHI, SNC, MWP*

Cataclysm 🦴🦴½ **1981 (R)** A swell flick about a sadistic demon who spends his time either finding people willing to join him or killing the people who won't. Also on video as "Satan's Supper." **94m/C VHS, Beta.** Cameron Mitchell, Marc Lawrence, Faith Clift, Charles Moll; ***D:*** Tom McGowan, Greg Tallas, Philip Marshak. *FOX, ACA*

Catacombs 🦴 **1989 (R)** An investigative monk and a beautiful photographer stumble across a mysterious, centuries-old evil power. **112m/C VHS, Beta.** Timothy Van Patten, Laura Schaefer, Ian Abercrombie, Jeremy West; ***D:*** David Schmoeller; ***W:*** C. Courtney Joyner; ***M:*** Pino Donaggio. *TWE*

The Catamount Killing 🦴½ **1974 (PG)** The story of a small town bank manager and his lover. They decide to rob the bank and run for greener pastures only to find their escape befuddled at every turn. **82m/C VHS, Beta.** *GE* Horst Buchholz, Ann Wedgeworth; ***D:*** Krzysztof Zanussi. *NO*

Catch as Catch Can 🦴 *Lo Scatenato* **1968** An Italian male model is comically besieged by animals of every type, making a mess of his life and career. Dubbed. **95m/C VHS, Beta.** *IT* Vittorio Gassman, Martha Hyer, Gila Golan; ***D:*** Franco Indovina; ***M:*** Luis Bacalov. *NLC*

Catch Me a Spy 🦴½ *To Catch a Spy* **1971** A foreign agent attempts to lure an innocent man into becoming part of a swap for an imprisoned Russian spy. **94m/C VHS, Beta.** *GB FR* Kirk Douglas, Tom Courtenay, Trevor Howard, Marlene Jobert, Bernard Blier, Patrick Mower, Bernadette LaFont; ***D:*** Dick Clement; ***W:*** Dick Clement, Ian LaFrenais; ***M:*** Claude Bolling. *PSM*

Catch Me...If You Can 🦴🦴 **1989 (PG)** High school class president Melissa doesn't want to see the school torn down. To raise fast cash, she teams up with a drag racer and the fun begins. **105m/C VHS, LV.** Matt Lattanzi, Loryn Locklin, M. Emmet Walsh, Geoffrey Lewis; ***D:*** Stephen Sommers. *MCG*

Catch the Heat 🦴 *Feel the Heat* **1987 (R)** Alexandra is an undercover narcotics agent sent to infiltrate Steiger's South American drug operation. **90m/C VHS, Beta.** Tiana Alexandra, David Dukes, Rod Steiger; ***D:*** Joel Silberg; ***W:*** Stirling Silliphant; ***M:*** Tom Chase, Steve Rucker. *MED, VTR*

Catch-22 🦴🦴🦴 **1970 (R)** Buck Henry's adaptation of Joseph Heller's black comedy about a group of fliers in the Mediterranean during WWII. A biting anti-war satire portraying the insanity of the situation in both a humorous and disturbing manner. Perhaps too literal to the book's masterfully chaotic structure, causing occasional problems in the "are you following along department?" Arkin heads a fine and colorful cast. **121m/C VHS, Beta, LV.** Alan Arkin, Martin Balsam, Art Garfunkel, Jon Voight, Richard Benjamin, Buck Henry, Bob Newhart, Paula Prentiss, Martin Sheen, Charles Grodin, Anthony Perkins, Orson Welles, Jack Gilford; ***D:*** Mike Nichols; ***W:*** Buck Henry; ***C:*** David Watkin. *PAR*

The Catered Affair 🦴🦴🦴 *Wedding Breakfast* **1956** Davis, anti-typecast as a Bronx housewife, and Borgnine, as her taxi-driving husband, play the determined parents of soon-to-be-wed Reynolds set on giving her away in a style to which she is not accustomed. Based on Paddy Chayefsky's teleplay, the catered affair turns into a familial trial, sharing the true-to-life poignancy that marked "Marty," the Oscar-winning Chayefsky drama of the previous year. **92m/B VHS.** Bette Davis, Ernest Borgnine, Debbie Reynolds, Barry Fitzgerald, Rod Taylor, Robert Simon; ***D:*** Richard Brooks; ***W:*** Gore Vidal; ***C:*** John Alton; ***M:*** Andre Previn. *MGM, FCT, CCB*

Catherine & Co. 🦴½ **1976 (R)** Lonely, penniless girl arrives in Paris and "opens shop" on the streets of Paris. As business booms, she takes a cue from the big corporations and sells stock in herself. **91m/C VHS, Beta.** *FR IT* Jane Birkin, Patrick Dewaere, Jean-Pierre Aumont, Jean-Claude Brialy; ***D:*** Michel Boisrond. *NO*

Catherine the Great 🦴🦴½ *The Rise of Catherine the Great* **1934** Slow but lavish and engrossing British dramatization of the tortured and doomed love affair between Catherine, Empress of Russia, and her irrational, drunken husband Peter. **88m/B VHS, Beta, LV.** *GB* Douglas Fairbanks Jr., Elisabeth Bergner, Flora Robson; ***D:*** Paul Czinner; ***C:*** Georges Perinal. National Board of Review Awards '34: 5 Best Foreign Films of the Year. *SUE, BAR, VYY*

Catholic Hour 🦴🦴 **1960** A dramatized version of the life story of Thomas Frederick Price who co-founded the Maryknoll Missionaries in the early 1900's. **30m/B VHS, Beta.** Edward Cullen, Arthur Gary. *VYY*

Catholics 🦴🦴🦴 *The Conflict* **1973** A sensitive exploration of contemporary mores and changing attitudes within the Roman Catholic church. Sheen is sent by the Pope to Ireland to reform some priests. Based on Brian Moore's short novel and made for television. **86m/C VHS, Beta.** Martin Sheen, Trevor Howard; ***D:*** Jack Gold; ***M:*** Carl Davis. *NO*

Cathy's Curse 🦴 *Cauchemares* **1977** The spirit of her aunt, who died as a child, possesses a young girl in this Canadian-French collaboration. Tries to capitalize on the popularity of "The Exorcist," but falls seriously short. **90m/C VHS, Beta.** *FR CA* Alan Scarfe, Beverly Murray; ***D:*** Eddy Matalon. *NO*

Catlow 🦴🦴½ **1971 (PG-13)** A comedic western with Brynner aiming to steal 2 million dollars in gold from under the nose of his friend, lawman Crenna. Based on the novel by Louis L'Amour. **103m/C VHS.** Yul Brynner, Richard Crenna, Leonard Nimoy, JoAnn Pflug, Jeff Corey, Michael Delano, David Ladd, Bessie Love; ***D:*** Sam Wanamaker; ***W:*** Scot Finch, J.J. Griffith. *MGM*

Cat's Eye 🦴🦴 **1985 (PG-13)** An anthology of three Stephen King short stories connected by a stray cat who wanders through each tale. **94m/C VHS, Beta, LV.** Drew Barrymore, James Woods, Alan King, Robert Hays, Candy Clark, Kenneth McMillan, James Naughton, Charles S. Dutton; ***D:*** Lewis Teague; ***W:*** Stephen King; ***M:*** Alan Silvestri. *FOX, FCT*

Cat's Play 🦴🦴 **1974** A widowed music teacher makes a ceremonial occasion of a weekly dinner with an old flame. Then an old friend from her youth suddenly reappears and begins an affair with the gentleman, causing self-destructive passions to explode. In Hungarian with English subtitles. **115m/C VHS.** *HU* Margit Dayka, Margit Makay, Elma Bulla; ***D:*** Karoly Makk. Nominations: Academy Awards '74: Best Foreign Language Film; Cannes Film Festival '74: Best Film. *CVC, INJ*

Cattle Queen of Montana 🦴🦴½ **1954** Reagan stars as an undercover federal agent investigating livestock rustlings and Indian uprisings. **88m/C VHS, Beta, LV.** Ronald Reagan, Barbara Stanwyck, Jack Elam, Gene Evans, Lance Fuller, Anthony Caruso; ***D:*** Allan Dwan; ***W:*** Robert Blees. *NO*

Caught 🦴🦴🦴 **1949** A woman marries for wealth and security and is desperately unhappy. She runs away and takes a job with a struggling physician, and falls in love with him. Her husband finds her, forcing her to decide between a life of security or love. **90m/B VHS.** James Mason, Barbara Bel Geddes, Robert Ryan, Curt Bois, Natalie Schafer, Art Smith; ***D:*** Max Ophuls; ***C:*** Lee Garmes. *REP*

Caught in the Act 🦴🦴½ **1993 (PG-13)** Scott McNally (Harrison) is an out-of-work actor who teaches acting classes to make a buck. Into one of his classes walks the sultry Rachel (Hope) and they start a hot affair. Then Rachel calls Scott, claiming to be kidnapped, he suddenly finds 10 million dollars in his bank account, and his landlord is murdered. Scott finds himself the pawn in an embezzlement scheme and framed for murder. But this is one role Scott doesn't want and he intends to work with a new script of his own devise. Made for cable television. **93m/C VHS, LV.** Gregory Harrison, Leslie Hope, Patricia Clarkson, Kevin Tighe; ***D:*** Deborah Reinisch; ***W:*** Ken Hixon. *MCA*

Caught in the Draft 🦴🦴🦴 **1941** Hope's funniest role has him as a Hollywood star trying to evade the draft in WW II, but he ends up accidentally enlisting himself. Lamour plays the daughter of a colonel in the Army whom Hope plans to marry, thinking it will get him out of the service. Very funny military comedy and one of Hope's best. Based on a story by Harry Tugend. **82m/B VHS.** Bob Hope, Dorothy Lamour, Lynne Overman, Eddie Bracken, Clarence Kolb, Paul Hurst, Ferike Boros, Irving Bacon; ***D:*** David Butler; ***W:*** Harry Tugend. *MCA, BTV*

Cauldron of Blood 🦴½ *Blind Man's Bluff; El Coleccionista de Cadaveres* **1967 (PG)** Blind sculptor Karloff unwittingly uses human skeletons supplied by his crazed wife Lindfors as the framework of his art pieces. **95m/C VHS.** *SP* Boris Karloff, Viveca Lindfors, Jean-Pierre Aumont, Rosenda Monteros, Ruben Rojo, Dianik Zurakowska; ***D:*** Edward Mann; ***W:*** Edward Mann. *REP, VDC, FCT*

Cause for Alarm 🦴🦴½ **1951** A jealous husband recovering from a heart attack begins to lose his mind. He wrongly accuses his wife of having an affair and attempts to frame her for his own murder. A fast-paced thriller with a nifty surprise ending. **74m/B VHS.** Loretta Young, Barry Sullivan, Bruce Cowling, Margalo Gillmore, Irving Bacon, Carl "Alfalfa" Switzer; ***D:*** Tay Garnett; ***M:*** Andre Previn. *NOS, SNC, MGM*

Cause of Death 🦴½ **1990 (R)** After the accidental death of his brother, Colombian drug lord Manuel Ramirez is lured to L.A. to collect his millions in blood money. **90m/C VHS.** Michael Barak, Sydney Coale Phillips, Daniel Martine; ***D:*** Philip Jones. *VSE*

Cavalcade 🦴🦴🦴 **1933** Traces the lives of the British Marryot family from the death of Queen Victoria, through WWI, the Jazz Age, and the Depression. A wistful adaptation of the hit play by Noel Coward with its touching portrayal of one family trying to weather good times and bad together. **110m/B VHS.** Diana Wynyard, Clive Brook, Herbert Mundin, Una O'Connor, Ursula Jeans, Beryl Mercer, Merle Tottenham, Frank Lawton, John Warburton, Margaret Lindsay, Billy Bevan; ***D:*** Frank Lloyd; ***C:*** Ernest Palmer. Academy Awards '33: Best Director (Lloyd), Best Interior Decoration, Best Picture; Nominations: Academy Awards '33: Best Actress (Wynyard). *FXV, BTV*

Cavalcade of the West 🦴🦴 **1936** Typical western with two brothers, separated by a kidnapping, growing up on opposite sides of the law. Much later they meet, and the question is: will the outlaw be reformed and reunited with his happy family? **70m/B VHS, Beta.** Hoot Gibson, Rex Lease, Marion Shilling, Earl Dwire; ***D:*** Harry Fraser. *GPV, DVT, VCN*

The Cavalier 🦴 **198?** Chinese cavalier faces love, danger and intrigue while deploying martial arts skills. **90m/C VHS, Beta.** Tang Wei, Lung Fei, Yeh Yuen, Tseng Tsao. *UNI*

Cavalier of the West 🦴 **1931** An Army captain is the only negotiating force between the white man and a primitive Indian tribe. **66m/B VHS, Beta, LV.** Harry Carey Sr., Kane Richmond, George "Gabby" Hayes; ***D:*** John P. McCarthy. *NOS*

Cavalry 🦴½ **1936** A Union Army Lieutenant is reunited with his family after the Civil War, bringing them happiness and joy. **60m/B VHS, Beta.** Bob Steele, Frances Grant, Karl Hackett, Hal Price; ***D:*** Robert North Bradbury. *NOS, DVT*

Cavalry Charge 🦴🦴½ *The Last Outpost* **1951** Vance Britton (Reagan) is the captain of a brigade of Confederate troops wreaking havoc on Union outposts. His brother Jeb (Bennett) is a Union soldier sent to the western frontier to take care of the Confederate problem. Vance's former fiance Julie (Fleming) is also living in the territories with her new husband. All three converge when the Union fort, where Julie is living and Jeb is defending, is attacked by Apaches. Brother Vance rides to the rescue. Lots of action. **72m/C VHS.** Ronald Reagan, Bruce (Herman Brix) Bennett, Rhonda Fleming, Noah Beery Jr., Bill Williams, Peter Hanson, Hugh Beaumont, John Ridgely, Lloyd Corrigan, James Burke, Richard Crane, Ewing Mitchell; ***D:*** Lewis R. Foster; ***W:*** Geoffrey Homes, George Worthing Yates, Winston Miller; ***C:*** Loyal Griggs. *IVY*

Cavalry Command 🦴½ *Cavalleria Commandos* **1963** Good will and integrity characterize the U.S. soldiers called into a small village to quiet a guerrilla rebellion. **77m/C VHS, Beta.** John Agar, Richard Arlen, Myron Healey, Alicia Vergel, William Phipps, Eddie Infante; ***D:*** Eddie Romero; ***W:*** Eddie Romero. *RHI*

Cave Girl *Woof! Cavegirl* **1985 (R)** After falling through a time-warp during a high-school field trip, a social pariah makes a hit with a pre-historic honey. Sexist teen exploitation film, with few original ideas and a not-so-hot cast. **85m/C VHS, Beta, LV.** Daniel Roebuck, Cindy Ann Thompson, Saba Moor, Jeff Chayette; ***D:*** David Oliver; ***W:*** David Oliver. *COL*

Cave of the Living Dead *Woof! Der Fluch Der Gruenen Augen* **1965** Mad professor with a past is up to something in a cave under castle. Villagers summon Inspector Doren of Interpol to solve a rash of nasty murders that they've blamed on green-eyed, cave-dwelling vampires. A challenge to watch till the end. Filmed in Sepiatone. **87m/B VHS, Beta.** *GE YU* Adrian Hoven, Erika Remberg, Carl Mohner, Wolfgang Preiss, Karin Field, John Kitzmiller, Akos Von Rathony; ***D:*** Akos Von Rathony. *MSP*

Caveman 🦴🦴 **1981 (PG)** Starr stars in this prehistoric spoof about a group of cavemen banished from different tribes who band together to form a tribe called "The Misfits." **92m/C VHS, Beta.** Ringo Starr, Barbara Bach, John Matuszak, Dennis Quaid, Jack Gilford, Shelley Long, Cork Hubbert; ***D:*** Carl Gottlieb; ***W:*** Carl Gottlieb, Rudy DeLuca; ***M:*** Lalo Schifrin. *MGM, FOX*

CB4: The Movie 🦴½ **1993 (R)** Falling somewhere between a serious attempt and parody, CB4 tries to do both and succeeds at neither. Written in the key of "Wayne's World" by "Saturday Night Live's" Rock, it starts out as a "rockumentary" (please refer to "This is Spinal Tap"), but quickly turns into a sitcom after two gangsta rap friends assume the identity of a local club owner when he is in jail. Hartman, also of SNL, appears as a right-wing city councilman. Chock full of violence, sexism, and profanity tucked into a wandering plot. **83m/C VHS, LV.** Chris Rock, Allen Payne, Deezer D, Phil Hartman, Charlie Murphy, Khandi Alexander, Art Evans, Chris Elliott, Willard

Pugh, Theresa Randle; **D:** Tamra Davis; **W:** Chris Rock, Nelson George, Robert Locash; **M:** John Barnes. *MCA*

Cease Fire ✗✗ **1985 (R)** The story of a troubled Vietnam vet who finds solace in a veterans' therapy group. Adapted from the play by George Fernandez. **97m/C VHS, Beta.** Don Johnson, Robert F. Lyons, Lisa Blount; **D:** David Nutter; **M:** Gary Fry. *CNG*

Ceiling Zero ✗✗✗ **1935** Cagney is an irrepressible pilot who does as he pleases and loves to aggravate his soft-hearted boss O'Brien. He falls for aviatrix Travis and neglects his duties to woo her, which leads to tragedy. Naturally, this sobers Cagney up and he volunteers for a dangerous test flight. Lots of fast-paced action and Cagney is at his swaggering best. Based on a play by Frank Wead, who also wrote the screenplay. Remade in 1941 as "International Squadron." **95m/B VHS.** James Cagney, Pat O'Brien, June Travis, Stuart Erwin, Henry Wadsworth, Isabel Jewell, Barton MacLane; **D:** Howard Hawks; **W:** Frank Wead. *MGM, FCT*

Celebrity ✗½ **1985** In this television film, a tragic childhood secret must be confronted by three friends when one is charged with murder. Based on the Thomas Thompson novel. **313m/C VHS, Beta.** Michael Beck, Ben Masters, Joseph Bottoms; **D:** Paul Wendkos. *NO*

Celeste ✗✗✗ **1981** Adlon (who later made the offbeat comedy "Sugarbaby") directed this longish but finely detailed and beautifully photographed biographical look at French writer Marcel (Remembrance of Things Past) Proust. Based on the memoirs of Proust's housekeeper, Celeste Albaret, an uneducated farmgirl, portraying the woman's devoted relationship ('til death did them part) with the middle-aged, homosexual author. It does so with wit, poignancy, and insight, but is not entirely successful in its attempt to render Proust's verbal literary style into a visual medium. In German with English subtitles. **107m/C VHS.** *GE* Eva Mattes, Jurgen Arndt, Norbert Wartha, Wolf Euba; **D:** Percy Adlon; **W:** Percy Adlon. *NYF, FCT, APD*

Celia: Child Of Terror ✗✗ **1989** Set in the 1950s, this film deals with the awful results of a young girl's inability to handle disappointment. **110m/C VHS, Beta.** Rebecca Smart, Nicholas Eadie, Victoria Longley, Mary-Anne Fahey; **D:** Ann Turner. *NO*

The Cellar ✗½ **1990 (PG-13)** A young boy finds an ancient Comanche monster spirit in the basement of his home. His parents, as usual, don't believe him, so he must battle the monster alone. **90m/C VHS.** Patrick Kilpatrick, Suzanne Savoy, Chris Miller, Ford Rainey; **D:** Kevin S. Tenney. *HMD*

Cellar Dweller *Woof!* **1987** A cartoonist moves into an old house and soon discovers it's haunted by a demonic cartoonist who killed himself thirty years earlier. What a coincidence. Low-budget scare-'em-upper filmed on one set and lit by a floodlamp. **78m/C VHS, Beta, LV.** Pamela Bellwood, Deborah Muldowney, Brian Robbins, Vince Edwards, Jeffrey Combs, Yvonne De Carlo; **D:** John Carl Buechler. *NWV*

The Celluloid Closet ✗✗✗½ **1995 (R)** Terrific documentary on how Hollywood films have depicted homosexual characters, subliminally and otherwise. Working chronologically and in an historical context, beginning with silent films, there are clips from more than 100 films, along with interviews from writers and actors. (Notable is writer Gore Vidal's comments on the gay subtext in 1959's "Ben-Hur"). Based on Vito Russo's 1981 book. **102m/C VHS. D:** Robert Epstein, Jeffrey Friedman; **W:** Armistead Maupin; **C:** Nancy Schreiber; **M:** Carter Burwell. *NYR*

Celtic Pride ✗✗ **1996 (PG-13)** Mike O'Hara (Stern) and Jimmy Flaherty (Aykroyd) are the worst kind of crazy. They're sports nuts. They are so consumed with passion for their beloved Celtics that they kidnap foul-mouthed superstar Lewis Scott (Wayans) of the Utah Jazz before game seven of the NBA finals. If this sounds far fetched, well...it is, unless you have an ESPN junkie in your life. There's not as much court action as you would expect, since most of the story revolves around intermittent trash-talking and escape attempts. If you're a Celtic hater, stick around for the end, when the Boston Garden is demolished using special effects. **90m/C VHS.** Damon Wayans, Daniel Stern, Dan Aykroyd, Gail O'Grady, Adam Hendershott, Paul Guilfoyle, Deion Sanders, Christopher McDonald, Gus Williams, Ted Rooney, Vladimir Cuk; **Cameos:** Bill Walton, Larry Bird; **D:** Tom DeCerchio; **W:** Judd Apatow; **C:** Oliver Wood; **M:** Basil Poledouris. *NYR*

The Cemetery Club ✗✗½ **1993 (PG-13)** Story of three Jewish widows who make weekly visits to their husband's graves while attempting to cope with their lives. Doris (Dukakis) is loyal to the memory of her husband and acts as the moral conscience of the trio. Lucille (Ladd) is a merry widow who wears clothes more suitable for younger women, but she also harbors a painful secret. Esther (Burstyn) struggles with her loneliness until a widowed cab driver begins to woo her. Commendably, the characters are given more dimension than Hollywood usually grants women of a certain age. Based on the play "The Cemetary Club" by Menchell, who also wrote the screenplay. **114m/C VHS, Beta, LV.** Ellen Burstyn, Olympia Dukakis, Diane Ladd, Danny Aiello, Lainie Kazan, Christina Ricci, Bernie Casey, Alan Mason, Sam Schwartz, Jeff Howell, Robert Costanzo, Wallace Shawn, Louis Guss; **D:** Bill Duke; **W:** Ivan Menchell; **C:** Steven Poster; **M:** Elmer Bernstein. *TOU, BTV*

Cemetery High ✗ **1989** Beautiful high school girls decide to lure the local boys into a trap and kill them. **80m/C VHS, Beta.** Debi Thibeault, Karen Nielsen, Lisa Schmidt, Ruth Collins, Simone, Tony Kruk, David Coughlin, Frank Stewart; **D:** Gorman Bechard; **W:** Gorman Bechard, Carmine Capobianco. *UNI, HHE*

Cemetery Man ✗✗ *Dellamorte Delamore* **1995 (R)** Grotesque little saga about zombies and necrophilia set in a small Italian cemetery. Thanks to a weird post-death plague the corpses refuse to stay quietly in their graves, forcing watchman Francisco Dellamorte (Everett) and mute gravedigger Gnaghi (Hadji-Lazaro) to split their heads open. But when Francisco's dead sweetheart (Falchi) rises from her grave, he's a little slow to rebury the still-active corpse. Based on the Italian graphic novel "Dellamorte Dellamore," from the "Dylan Dog" series by Tiziano Sclavi. **100m/C VHS.** *IT* Rupert Everett, Anna Falchi, Francois Hadji-Lazaro; **D:** Michele (Michael) Soavi; **W:** Gianni Romoli; **C:** Mauro Marchetti; **M:** Manuel De Sica. *NYR*

Center of the Web ✗✗ **1992 (R)** John Phillips is a victim of mistaken identity—someone thinks he's a professional hit man. After surviving an apparent mob attempt on his life, Phillips is persuaded by a CIA operative to go along with the deception in order to capture a potential political assassin. At least that's what Phillips is told, but he soon realizes that the deeper he gets into his new role, the deadlier the plot becomes. Davi is one of the best bad guys around and the fast-paced stunts and plot twists make this watchable. **88m/C VHS, LV.** Ted Prior, Robert Davi, Tony Curtis, Charlene Tilton, Bo Hopkins, Charles Napier; **D:** David A. Prior. *AIP*

The Centerfold Girls *Woof!* **1974 (R)** Microscopic storyline involves a deranged man who is determined to kill all the voluptuous young women who have posed nude for a centerfold. **93m/C VHS, Beta.** Andrew Prine, Tiffany Bolling, Aldo Ray, Jeremy Slate, Ray Danton, Francine York; **D:** John Peyser. *MED*

Century ✗✗ **1994 (R)** Ambitious young doctor Paul Reisner (Owen), the son of a prosperous Jewish father (Stephens), gets a position at a London research hospital headed by the charismatic Professor Mandry (Dance). Paul manages to disgrace himself by provoking Mandry and is dismissed but finds out some disturbing information and is determined to discredit his former mentor. Anti-Semitism lurks as does the change from Victorian mores to the challenging dawn of the 20th century. Complex performances are somewhat undermined by the static direction. **112m/C VHS.** *GB* Clive Owen, Charles Dance, Miranda Richardson, Robert Stephens, Joan Hickson, Lena Headey, Neil Stuke; **D:** Stephen Poliakoff; **W:** Stephen Poliakoff; **C:** Witold Stok; **M:** Michael Gibbs. *PGV*

A Century of Women **1994** Three-part look at the lives and accomplishments of American women over the past 100 years, including the changing role of women in the workplace and the home. The documentary segments are interspersed with a fictional story spanning five generations of women who reunite for a weekend. On 3 cassettes. **360m/C VHS.** Teresa Wright, Olympia Dukakis, Justine Bateman, Talia Shire, Madge Sinclair, Jasmine Guy, Brooke Smith. *TTC*

Certain Fury ✗ **1985 (R)** Two timid women go on the lam when they are mistaken for escaped prostitutes who shot up a courthouse. The sooner they get caught, the better. **88m/C VHS, Beta, LV.** Tatum O'Neal, Irene Cara, Peter Fonda, Nicholas Campbell, Moses Gunn; **D:** Stephen Gyllenhaal. *NWV, VTR*

Certain Sacrifice ✗ **1980** Nineteen-year-old Madonna expresses herself in her film debut. Seeking revenge on the man who raped her, she murders him in a strange ritualistic manner underneath the Brooklyn Bridge. Poor is the man whose pleasures depend on the permission of another? **60m/C VHS, Beta.** Madonna, Jeremy Pattnosh, Charles Kurtz; **D:** Stephen Lewicki. *WOV, MVD*

Cesar ✗✗✗✗ **1936** This is the third and most bittersweet part of Pagnol's famed trilogy based on his play depicting the lives and loves of the people of Provence, France. Marius returns after a 20-year absence to his beloved Fanny and his now-grown son, Cesariot. The first two parts of the trilogy are "Marius" and "Fanny" and were directed by Alexander Korda and Marc Allegret respectively. In French with English subtitles. **117m/B VHS, Beta, LV.** *FR* Raimu, Pierre Fresnay, Orane Demazis, Charpin, Andre Fouche, Alida Rauffe; **D:** Marcel Pagnol; **W:** Marcel Pagnol; **M:** Vincent Scotto. *NOS, MRV, INT*

Cesar & Rosalie ✗✗✗ **1972 (PG)** Acclaimed French comedy depicts the love triangle between a beautiful divorcee, her aging live-in companion and a younger man. Engaging portrait of how their relationship evolves over time. In French with English subtitles. **110m/C VHS, Beta, LV.** *FR* Romy Schneider, Yves Montand, Sami Frey, Umberto Orsini; **D:** Claude Sautet. *TPV, INJ*

Cesare Borgia ✗✗ **1923** Veidt stars in this bloodthirsty saga as the ruthless son of Pope Alexander VI who'll let nothing come between him and his desires. **83m/B VHS.** *GE* Conrad Veidt; **D:** Richard Oswald. *FCT*

Chain Gang Killings ✗ **1985** Pair of shackled prisoners, one black, the other white, escape from a truck transporting them to prison. **99m/C VHS, Beta.** Ian Yule, Ken Gampu. *NO*

Chain Gang Women *Woof!* **1972 (R)** Sordid violence. Two escaped convicts plunder, rob, and rape until a victim's husband comes looking for revenge. **85m/C VHS.** Robert Lott, Barbara Mills, Michael Stearns, Linda York; **D:** Lee Frost. *NO*

Chain Lightning ✗✗ **1950** Bogart stars as a bomber pilot who falls in love with a Red Cross worker (Parker) while fighting in Europe in 1943. They lose touch after the war until Bogie goes to work as a test pilot for the same shady airplane manufacturer (Massey) where Parker works. He is given the chance to test a new plane, which has already cost the life of one of his friends. Bogart has more success, along with rekindling the flames of romance. Average script but the flying sequences are well-done. **94m/B VHS.** Humphrey Bogart, Eleanor Parker, Raymond Massey, Richard Whorf; **D:** Stuart Heisler. *MGM*

Chain of Desire ✗✗ **1993** Nightclub inside Manhattan's Chrysler Building is the spot for numerous folk to have lot of meaningless sexual encounters and look at the emptiness of their lives. **107m/C VHS, Beta, LV.** Linda Fiorentino, Elias Koteas, Malcolm McDowell, Grace Zabriskie, Tim Guinee, Assumpta Serna, Patrick Bauchau, Seymour Cassel, Kevin Conroy, Angel Aviles, Holly Marie Combs; **D:** Temistocles Lopez; **W:** Temistocles Lopez; **M:** Nathan Birnbaum. Nominations: Independent Spirit Awards '94: Best Cinematography. *PSM*

Chain Reaction ½ *Nuclear Run* **1980** When a nuclear scientist is exposed to radiation after an accident at an atomic power plant, he must escape to warn the public of the danger. **87m/C VHS, Beta, LV.** Steve Bisley, Ross Thompson; ***D:*** Ian Barry. *NO*

Chain Reaction ½ *Dead Drop* **1996 (PG-13)** Government/scientific conspiracy chase story finds Chicago lab tech Eddie Kasalivich (Reeves) a member of a research team that's discovered the formula for cheap, pollution-free energy. This doesn't sit well with someone since the team's leader is murdered and the lab destroyed in an explosion. Eddie and scientist Lily Sinclair (Weisz) survive, are framed for murder, and pursued by government types as they try to find the conspirators. Davis did "The Fugitive," so he knows his tension-filled chases. Script underwent a significant number of changes before production was finished. **?m/C VHS.** Keanu Reeves, Morgan Freeman, Rachel Weisz, Fred Ward, Brian Cox; ***D:*** Andrew Davis; ***C:*** Frank Tidy. *NYR*

Chained ½ **1934** Crawford and Gable star in this love triangle that somehow never sizzles. Crawford, in love with married businessman Kruger, takes a South American cruise to get away from it all, meets Gable, and of course falls in love. Seems simple enough, but wait! Crawford goes back to New York City and marries Kruger (his wife grants him a divorce) and is miserable. But then Gable shows up, further complicating matters. Choices, choices. Predictable script was not helped by half-hearted performances. **73m/B VHS, Beta.** Joan Crawford, Clark Gable, Otto Kruger, Stuart Erwin, Una O'Connor; ***D:*** Clarence Brown. *MGM, CCB*

Chained for Life *Woof!* **1951** Daisy and Violet Hilton, real life Siamese twins, star in this old-fashioned "freak" show. When a gigolo deserts one twin on their wedding night, the other twin shoots him dead. The twins go on trial and the judge asks the viewer to hand down the verdict. Exploitative and embarrassing to watch. **81m/B VHS, Beta.** Daisy Hilton, Violet Hilton; ***D:*** Harry Fraser. *SNC, NOS, RHI*

Chained Heat **1983 (R)** Seamy tale of the vicious reality of life for women behind bars. Naive Blair is imprisoned again (after another bad jailhouse gig in "Born Innocent") and has usual assortment of negative experiences with domineering prisoners, degenerative guards, and the creepy warden who maintains a prison bachelor pad equipped with hot tub. Needless to say, she grows up in a hurry. Trashifying, archetypal women-in-prison effort that aims to satisfy full range of low-quality audience demands. Sequel to 1982 "Concrete Jungle." **97m/C VHS, Beta, LV.** Linda Blair, Stella Stevens, Sybil Danning, Tamara Dobson, Henry Silva, John Vernon, Nita Talbot, Louisa Moritz; ***D:*** Paul Nicholas. Golden Raspberry Awards '83: Worst Supporting Actress (Danning). *VES*

Chained Heat 2 ½ **1992 (R)** Another sordid tale of women behind bars. Nielsen stars as the psychotic stiletto-heeled warden of an infamous prison, complete with sadistic heroin-smuggling guards. This drug ring also deals in prostitution, which results in two imprisoned sisters (innocent, naturally) being separated from one another. One sister is determined to find true justice. **98m/C VHS, LV.** Brigitte Nielsen, Paul Koslo, Kari Whitman, Kimberley Kates; ***D:*** Lloyd A. Simanol; ***W:*** Chris Hyde. *NLC*

Chains **1989 (R)** A Chicago gangland feud entraps two couples in its web, and the innocents must take care of themselves when the situation goes from bad to worse. **93m/C VHS, LV.** Jimi Jourdan, Michael Dixon, John L. Eves; ***D:*** Roger J. Barski. *IMP*

Chains of Gold **1992 (R)** Kind social worker (Travolta) befriends teen who wants to get out of the crack-dealing gang in which he's involved. He infiltrates the gang and risks his life helping the boy get out. Originally aired on cable television. **95m/C VHS.** John Travolta, Marilu Henner, Bernie Casey, Hector Elizondo, Joey Lawrence; ***D:*** Rod Holcomb; ***M:*** Trevor Jones. *ACA*

The Chair *Hot Seat* **1987 (R)** The penitentiary where an evil superintendent was fried in his own electric chair during an inmate uprising is reopened after two decades. The new warden (Benedict), who used to be a subordinate to the dead man, believes in rigid control of the inmates and locks horns with the big-house shrink (Coco), who on the surface is an intelligent humanitarian, but may have a darker side. This acrimonious dispute takes a back seat, when it appears that the spirit of the late warden has come back to make the inmates pay for his untimely death. **90m/C VHS, LV.** James Coco, Paul Benedict, Stephen Geoffreys, Trini Alvarado, John Bentley; ***D:*** Waldemar Korzeniowsky. *IMP*

The Chalk Garden **1964** A woman with a mysterious past takes on the job of governess for an unruly 14-year-old girl, with unforseen consequences. An excellent adaptation of the Enid Bagnold play although not as suspenseful as the stage production. **106m/C VHS, Beta.** *GB* Deborah Kerr, Hayley Mills, Edith Evans, John Mills, Elizabeth Sellars, Felix Aylmer; ***D:*** Ronald Neame; ***W:*** John Michael Hayes; ***M:*** Malcolm Arnold. National Board of Review Awards '64: 10 Best Films of the Year, Best Supporting Actress (Evans); Nominations: Academy Awards '64: Best Supporting Actress (Evans). *MCA*

The Challenge **1938** Story of the courageous party of explorers who conquered the Matterhorn. Incredible avalanche scenes. **77m/B VHS, Beta.** Luis Trenker, Robert Douglas. *DVT, VYY*

Challenge *Woof!* **1974 (PG)** When his entire family is killed, dad decides to seek revenge with his shotgun. Very bloody and violent and very nearly plotless. **90m/C VHS.** Earl Owensby, William T. Hicks, Katheryn Thompson, Johnny Popwell; ***D:*** Martin Beck. *FOX*

The Challenge ½ **1982 (R)** A contemporary action spectacle which combines modern swordplay with the mysticism and fantasy of ancient Samurai legends. **108m/C VHS, Beta.** Scott Glenn, Toshiro Mifune; ***D:*** John Frankenheimer; ***W:*** John Sayles, Richard Maxwell; ***M:*** Jerry Goldsmith. *FOX*

Challenge of a Lifetime ½ **1985** Marshall stars as a divorcee whose dream is to compete in the Hawaiian Ironman Triathlon. Cult favorite; Woronov has a substantial supporting role. **100m/C VHS.** Penny Marshall, Richard Gilliland, Jonathan Silverman, Mary Woronov, Paul Gleason, Mark Spitz, Cathy Rigby; ***D:*** Russ Mayberry. *TTC, MOV*

Challenge of McKenna **1983** Run-of-the-prairie horse opera has drifter Ireland stumble upon danger and intrigue when he enters a mysterious town. **90m/C VHS.** John Ireland, Robert Woods. *PMH*

Challenge of the Masters **1989** A young Kung-Fu artist wins a new tutor in a contest. Soon he's fighting for a friend to protect his family's honor. **97m/C VHS.** Liu Chia Hui, Liu Chia-Yung, Chen Kuan-Tai, Chiang Yang; ***D:*** Lu Chia-Liang. *HMD*

Challenge the Ninja **198?** One talented fighter defends a town from high-kicking hordes. Lots of kung fu action for martial arts fans. **92m/C VHS, Beta.** Bruce Baron, Pierre Tremblay, Richard Berman, Eric Redner. *TWE*

Challenge To Be Free *Mad Trapper of the Yukon* **1976 (G)** Action adventure geared toward a young audience depicting the struggles of a man being pursued by 12 men and 100 dogs across a thousand miles of frozen wilderness. The last film directed by Garnett, who has a cameo as Marshal McGee. Produced in 1972, the release wasn't until 1976. **90m/C VHS, Beta.** Mike Mazurki, Jimmy Kane; ***Cameos:*** Tay Garnett; ***D:*** Tay Garnett. *MED, VTR*

Challenge to Lassie ½ **1949 (G)** When Lassie's Scottish master dies, the faithful pup remains at his grave. An unsympathetic policeman orders Lassie to leave the premises, inspiring a debate among the townsfolk as to the dog's fate. Based on a true story (although the original hero was a Skye Terrier); remade as "Greyfriar's Bobby." **76m/C VHS, Beta.** Edmund Gwenn, Donald Crisp, Geraldine Brooks, Reginald Owen, Alan Webb, Henry Stephenson, Alan Napier, Sara Allgood; ***D:*** Richard Thorpe; ***M:*** Andre Previn. *MGM, FCT*

Challenge to White Fang ½ **1986 (PG)** A courageous dog prevents a scheming businessman from taking over an old man's gold mine. **89m/C VHS, Beta.** Harry Carey Jr., Franco Nero; ***D:*** Lucio Fulci. *TWE*

The Challengers ½ **1993** Young Mackie wants to join local rock band The Challengers, only to discover their main rule is no girls. So Mackie disguises herself as her male cousin Mac—getting ever more confused as she tries to juggle her dual identities. Then she gets found out. **97m/C VHS.** Gema Zamprogna, Gwynyth Walsh, Eric Christmas, Eric Till; ***W:*** Clive Endersby. *TRI*

Chamber of Horrors ½ *The Door With Seven Locks* **1940** A family is brought together at an English castle to claim a fortune left by an aristocrat. However, there's a catch—seven keys may open the vault with the fortune, or leave the key turner dead. Based on the work by Edgar Wallace. **80m/B VHS, Beta.** *GB* Leslie Banks, Lilli Palmer; ***D:*** Norman Lee. *NOS, MRV, SNC*

Chameleon **1981** A freeform dramatic examination of a day in the life of a Los Angeles pusher. **90m/C VHS, Beta.** Bob Glaudini; ***D:*** Jon Jost. *FCT*

Chameleon **1995 (R)** Undercover agent, who's a master of disguise, has his family murdered by drug cartel head and he seeks revenge. **108m/C VHS.** Anthony LaPaglia, Kevin Pollak, Melora Hardin, Wayne Knight; ***D:*** Michael Pavone; ***W:*** Michael Pavone; ***C:*** Ross Berryman; ***M:*** John Debney. *AVE*

Chameleon Street **1989 (R)** Entertaining fact-based account of William Douglas Street, a Detroit man who successfully impersonated, among others, a Time magazine reporter and a surgeon until he was caught and sent to prison. He escaped and went to Yale, faked his identity as a student, and then returned to Michigan to impersonate a lawyer for the Detroit Human Rights Commission. Harris wrote and directed this insightful look into the man who fooled many people, including the mayor of Detroit, Coleman A. Young, who appears briefly as himself. **95m/C VHS, LV.** Wendell B. Harris Jr., Angela Leslie, Amina Fakir, Paula McGee, Mano Breckenridge, Richard Kiley, Anthony Ennis; ***D:*** Wendell B. Harris Jr.; ***W:*** Wendell B. Harris Jr. Sundance Film Festival '90: Grand Jury Prize. *ACA, FCT*

The Champ **1931** A washed up boxer dreams of making a comeback and receives support from no one but his devoted son. Minor classic most notorious for jerking the tears and soiling the hankies, this was the first of three Beery/Cooper screen teamings. **87m/B VHS, Beta, LV.** Wallace Beery, Jackie Cooper, Irene Rich, Roscoe Ates, Edward Brophy, Hale Hamilton, Jesse Scott, Marcia Mae Jones; ***D:*** King Vidor; ***W:*** Frances Marion. Academy Awards '32: Best Actor (Beery), Best Original Screenplay; Nominations: Academy Awards '32: Best Director (Vidor), Best Picture. *MGM, FCT, BTV*

The Champ ½ **1979 (PG)** An ex-fighter with a weakness for gambling and drinking is forced to return to the ring in an attempt to keep custody of his son. Excessive sentiment may cause cringing. Remake of the 1931 classic. **121m/C VHS, Beta, LV.** Jon Voight, Faye Dunaway, Rick Schroder, Jack Warden, Arthur Hill, Strother Martin, Joan Blondell, Elisha Cook Jr.; ***D:*** Franco Zeffirelli; ***C:*** Fred W. Koenekamp; ***M:*** Dave Grusin. Nominations: Academy Awards '79: Best Original Score. *MGM*

Champagne **1928** A socialite's father fakes bankruptcy to teach his irresponsible daughter a lesson. Early, silent endeavor from Hitchcock is brilliantly photographed. **93m/B VHS.** *GB* Betty Balfour, Gordon Harker, Ferdinand von Alten, Clifford Heatherly, Jack Trevor; ***D:*** Alfred Hitchcock; ***W:*** Alfred Hitchcock. *GPV, MLB, VEC*

Champagne for Breakfast **1935 (R)** Sex comedy follows the fun-filled adventures of "Champagne," a free-spirited beauty living life to the fullest. **69m/B VHS.** Mary Carlisle, Hardie Albright, Joan Marsh, Lila Lee, Sidney Toler, Bradley Page, Emerson Treacy; ***D:*** Melville Brown. *NO*

Champagne for Caesar 🦴🦴🦴 **1950** The laughs keep coming in this comedy about a self-proclaimed genius-on-every-subject who goes on a television quiz show and proceeds to win everything in sight. The program's sponsor, in desperation, hires a femme fatale to distract the contestant before the final program. Wonderful spoof of the game-show industry. **90m/B VHS, Beta, LV.** Ronald Colman, Celeste Holm, Vincent Price, Art Linkletter, Barbara Britton; ***D:*** Richard Whorf. *VCI*

Champion 🦴🦴🦴½ **1949** An ambitious prizefighter alienates the people around him as he desperately fights his way to the top. When he finally reaches his goal, he is forced to question the cost of his success. From a story by Ring Lardner. Certainly one of the best films ever made about boxing, with less sentiment than "Rocky" but concerned with sociological correctness. **99m/B VHS.** Kirk Douglas, Arthur Kennedy, Marilyn Maxwell, Ruth Roman, Lola Albright; ***D:*** Mark Robson. Academy Awards '49: Best Film Editing; Nominations: Academy Awards '49: Best Actor (Douglas), Best Black and White Cinematography, Best Screenplay, Best Supporting Actor (Kennedy), Best Original Score. *REP*

The Champion/His New Job 🦴🦴🦴 *Champion Charlie* **1915** Two classic silent shorts by Chaplin, with music; the first is alternately entitled "Champion Charlie." **53m/B VHS, Beta, 8mm.** Charlie Chaplin, Edna Purviance, Ben Turpin, Gloria Swanson, Mack Swain, "Broncho" Billy Anderson; ***D:*** Charlie Chaplin. *VYY*

Champion Operation 🦴 **1987** Hong Kong heavies pose as police officers. The action follows them from the slums to the red-light district. Lots of martial arts action. **100m/C VHS.** Tong Chun Chung, Yu Ka Hei, Tang Ho Kwong. *MGI*

Champions 🦴🦴 **1984** Moving but cliched story of Bob Champion, a leading jockey who overcame cancer to win England's Grand National Steeplechase. A true story, no less. **113m/C VHS, Beta, LV.** *GB* John Hurt, Gregory Jones, Mick Dillon, Ann Bell, Jan Francis, Peter Barkworth, Edward Woodward, Ben Johnson, Kirstie Alley, Alison Steadman; ***D:*** John Irvin; ***W:*** Evan Jones; ***M:*** Carl Davis. *SUE, NLC*

Chan is Missing 🦴🦴🦴 **1982** Two cab drivers try to find the man who stole their life savings. Wry, low-budget comedy filmed in San Francisco's Chinatown was an art-house smash. The first full-length American film produced exclusively by an Asian-American cast and crew. **80m/B VHS.** Wood Moy, Marc Hayashi, Laureen Chew, Judy Mihei, Peter Wang, Presco Tabios; ***D:*** Wayne Wang; ***W:*** Terrel Seltzer, Isaac Cronin. *NYF, INJ*

Chance 🦴½ **1989** With over a million dollars in diamonds missing, Haggerty and Jacobs throw out all the stops to recover them in this action thriller. **90m/C VHS.** Dan Haggerty, Lawrence-Hilton Jacobs, Addison Randall, Roger Rudd, Charles Gries, Pamela Dixon; ***D:*** Addison Randall, Charles Kanganis. *PMH*

Chances Are 🦴🦴🦴 **1989 (PG)** After her loving husband dies in a chance accident, a pregnant woman remains unmarried, keeping her husband's best friend as her only close male companion. Years later, her now teenage daughter brings a friend home for dinner, but due to an error in heaven, the young man begins to realize that this may not be the first time he and this family have met. A wonderful love-story hampered only minimally by the unbelievable plot. **108m/C VHS, Beta, LV, 8mm.** Cybill Shepherd, Robert Downey Jr., Ryan O'Neal, Mary Stuart Masterson, Josef Sommer, Christopher McDonald, Joe Grifasi, James Noble, Susan Ruttan, Fran Ryan; ***D:*** Emile Ardolino; ***W:*** Perry Howze, Randy Howze; ***M:*** Maurice Jarre. Nominations: Academy Awards '89: Best Song ("After All"). *COL, FCT*

Chandu on the Magic Island 🦴🦴 **1934** Chandu the Magician takes his powers of the occult to the mysterious lost island of Lemuri to battle the evil cult of Ubasti. Sequel to "Chandu the Magician" and just as campy. **67m/B VHS, Beta.** Bela Lugosi, Maria Alba, Clara Kimball Young. *NOS, SNC, VYY*

Chandu the Magician 🦴🦴 **1932** Bad guy searches desperately for the secret of a powerful death ray so he can (surprise!) destroy civilization. Not well received in its day, but makes for great high-camp fun now. One of Lugosi's most melodramatic performances. **70m/B VHS, Beta.** Edmund Lowe, Bela Lugosi, Irene Ware, Henry B. Walthall; ***D:*** William Cameron Menzies, Marcel Varnel; ***C:*** James Wong Howe. *MLB, RXM*

Chanel Solitaire 🦴🦴 **1981 (R)** Uninspiring biography follows the fabulous (simply fabulous) career of dress designer Gabrielle "Coco" Chanel. Ah, go sew something. **124m/C VHS, Beta.** Marie-France Pisier, Rutger Hauer, Timothy Dalton, Karen Black, Brigitte Fossey; ***D:*** George Kaczender. *MED, FCT*

Chang: A Drama of the Wilderness 🦴🦴🦴½ **1927** A farmer and his family has settled a small patch of ground on the edge of the jungle and must struggle for survival against numerous wild animals. The climactic elephant stampede is still thrilling. Shot on location in Siam. **67m/B VHS.** ***D:*** Ernest B. Schoedsack; ***W:*** Merian C. Cooper, Ernest B. Schoedsack. *MIL*

Change of Habit 🦴🦴 **1969 (G)** Three novitiates undertake to learn about the world before becoming full-fledged nuns. While working at a ghetto clinic a young doctor forms a strong, affectionate relationship with one of them. Presley's last feature film. ♫Change of Habit; Let Us Pray; Rubberneckin'. **93m/C VHS, Beta.** Elvis Presley, Mary Tyler Moore, Barbara McNair, Ed Asner, Ruth McDevitt, Regis Toomey; ***D:*** William A. Graham; ***C:*** Russell Metty; ***M:*** Billy Goldenberg. *MCA, GKK*

A Change of Seasons 🦴🦴 **1980 (R)** One of them so-called sophisticated comedies that look at the contemporary relationships and values of middle-class, middle-aged people who should know better. The wife of a college professor learns of her husband's affair with a seductive student and decides to have a fling with a younger man. The situation reaches absurdity when the couples decide to vacation together. **102m/C VHS, Beta.** Shirley MacLaine, Bo Derek, Anthony Hopkins, Michael Brandon, Mary Beth Hurt; ***D:*** Richard Lang; ***W:*** Erich Segal; ***M:*** Henry Mancini. *FOX*

The Changeling 🦴🦴½ **1980 (R)** A music teacher moves into an old house and discovers that a young boy's ghostly spirit is his housemate. The ghost wants revenge against the being that replaced him upon his death. Scary ghost story with some less than logical leaps of script. **114m/C VHS, Beta, LV.** *CA* George C. Scott, Trish Van Devere, John Russell, Melvyn Douglas, Jean Marsh; ***D:*** Peter Medak. Genie Awards '80: Best Film. *VES*

Changes 🦴 **1969 (PG)** A young man leaves home and thumbs across the California coast in order to find himself. On the road again. **103m/C VHS, Beta.** Kent Lane, Michele Carey, Jack Albertson, Marcia Strassman; ***D:*** Hall Bartlett. *PSM*

The Channeler 🦴 **1989** The traditional dopey students probe an old Colorado mine and encounter black-robed, demon whazzits. A spunky cast and nice scenery didn't stop the Hound from switching channels on this one. **90m/C VHS, Beta.** Dan Haggerty, Richard Harrison, Jay Richardson, David Homb, Oliver Darrow, Robin Sims, Charles Solomon; ***D:*** Grant Austin Waldman. *NO*

Chantilly Lace 🦴🦴½ **1993 (R)** Ensemble cast tries hard in this story of modern American women and friendship in the nineties. Val (Eilenberry) gathers a group of seven close friends at her new house in Sundance. Turns out trying to "have it all" is causing some emotional crises to surface, which are explored over the course of a year. Actresses improvised their dialogue from basic character information. Lots of weeping and bonding. Made for cable television. **102m/C VHS.** Jill Eikenberry, Ally Sheedy, Helen Slater, Lindsay Crouse, JoBeth Williams, Martha Plimpton, Talia Shire; ***D:*** Linda Yellen; ***W:*** Linda Yellen, Rosanne Ehrlich; ***M:*** Patrick Seymour. *COL*

Chapayev 🦴🦴🦴 **1934** Striking propagandist drama dealing with the exploits of a legendary Red Army commander during the 1919 battle with the White Russians. Stunning, and carefully choreographed, battle scenes. Adapted from a biographical novel by Dmitri Furmanov. In Russian with English subtitles. **101m/B VHS, Beta.** *RU* Boris Babochkin, Leonid Kmit; ***D:*** Sergei Vasiliev, Gregory Vasiliev. National Board of Review Awards '35: 5 Best Foreign Films of the Year. *VYY, AUD, IHF*

Chaplin 🦴🦴🦴 **1992 (PG-13)** The life and career of "The Little Tramp" is chronicled by director Attenborough and brilliantly portrayed by Downey, Jr, as Chaplin. A flashback format traces his life from its poverty-stricken Dickensian origins in the London slums through his directing and acting career, to his honorary Oscar in 1972. Slow-moving at parts, but captures Chaplin's devotion to his art and also his penchant towards jailbait. In a clever casting choice, Chaplin's own daughter from his fourth marriage to Oona O'Neill, Geraldine Chaplin, plays her own grandmother who goes mad. **135m/C VHS, LV.** Robert Downey Jr., Dan Aykroyd, Geraldine Chaplin, Kevin Dunn, Anthony Hopkins, Milla Jovovich, Moira Kelly, Kevin Kline, Diane Lane, Penelope Ann Miller, Paul Rhys, John Thaw, Marisa Tomei, Nancy Travis, James Woods, David Duchovny, Deborah Maria Moore, Bill Paterson, John Standing, Robert Stephens; ***D:*** Richard Attenborough; ***W:*** Bryan Forbes, William Boyd, William Goldman; ***C:*** Sven Nykvist; ***M:*** John Barry. British Academy Awards '92: Best Actor (Downey); Nominations: Academy Awards '92: Best Actor (Downey), Best Art Direction/Set Decoration, Best Original Score. *LIV, MOV, FCT*

Chaplin: A Character Is Born **1979** The evolution of Chaplin's "Little Tramp" is shown in scenes from his early classics, "The Pawnshop," "The Rink," and "The Immigrant." **40m/B VHS, Beta.** Charlie Chaplin. *NO*

Chaplin Essanay Book 1 **1915** Two of Chaplin's early shorts: "The Tramp" and "The Champion." **51m/B VHS, Beta.** Charlie Chaplin, Edna Purviance, Ben Turpin. *CCB*

The Chaplin Revue **1958** The "Revue," put together by Chaplin in 1958, consists of three of his best shorts: "A Dog's Life" (1918), the WWI comedy "Shoulder Arms" (1918), and "The Pilgrim," in which a convict hides out in a clerical guise (1922). Chaplin added self-composed score, narration, and some documentary on-the-set material. **121m/B VHS, Beta.** Charlie Chaplin, Edna Purviance, Sydney Chaplin, Mack Swain; ***D:*** Charlie Chaplin. *FOX*

Chapter in Her Life 🦴🦴½ **1923** An early silent film by Lois Weber which examines the relationships between an orphaned child and the adults in her life. **87m/B VHS, Beta.** ***D:*** Lois Weber. *GVV*

Chapter Two 🦴🦴 **1979 (PG)** Loosely based on Neil Simon's marriage to Mason and his Broadway hit of the same name. A writer, grief-stricken over the death of his first wife, meets the woman who will become his second. Witty dialogue in first half deteriorates when guilt strikes. **124m/C VHS, Beta, LV.** James Caan, Marsha Mason, Valerie Harper, Joseph Bologna; ***D:*** Robert Moore; ***W:*** Neil Simon. Nominations: Academy Awards '79: Best Actress (Mason). *COL*

Charade 🦴🦴 **1953** Mason and wife Pamela star in this trilogy of love and violence. "Portrait of a Murderer" has a young artist sketching the picture of the man who—unknown to her—has just murdered her girlfriend. "Duel at Dawn" concerns an 1880s Austrian officer who steals a woman from another officer and is then challenged to a duel. "The Midas Touch" revolves around a successful but dissatisfied man who abandons his riches to find the meaning of life. Mason himself had said he hoped "this curiosity" would disappear. **83m/B VHS.** James Mason, Pamela Mason, Scott Forbes, Paul Cavanagh, Bruce Lester, Sean McClory, Vince Barnett; ***D:*** Roy Kellino. *NOS*

Charade 🦴🦴🦴½ **1963** After her husband is murdered, a young woman finds herself on the run from crooks and double agents who want the $250,000 her husband stole during WWII. Hepburn and Grant are charming and sophisticated as usual in this stylish intrigue filmed in Paris. Based on the story "The Unsuspecting Wife" by Marc Behm and Peter Stone. **113m/C VHS, Beta.** Cary Grant, Audrey Hepburn, Walter Matthau, James Coburn, George Kennedy; ***D:*** Stanley

Donen; ***W:*** Peter Stone; ***C:*** Charles B(ryant) Lang; ***M:*** Henry Mancini. British Academy Awards '64: Best Actress (Hepburn); Edgar Allan Poe Awards '63: Best Screenplay; Nominations: Academy Awards '63: Best Song ("Charade"). *CNG, MRV, MCA*

The Charge of the Light Brigade 🦴🦴🦴 **1936 (PG-13)** A British army officer stationed in India deliberately starts the Balaclava charge to even an old score with Surat Khan, who's on the other side. Still an exciting film, though it's hardly historically accurate. De Havilland is along to provide the requisite romance with Flynn. Also available colorized. **115m/B VHS, Beta, LV.** Olivia de Havilland, Errol Flynn, David Niven, Nigel Bruce, Patric Knowles, Donald Crisp, Sir C. Aubrey Smith, J. Carrol Naish, Henry Stephenson, E.E. Clive, Scotty Beckett; ***D:*** Michael Curtiz; ***M:*** Max Steiner. Nominations: Academy Awards '36: Best Sound, Best Original Score. *MGM, FCT, FOX*

The Charge of the Light Brigade 🦴🦴½ **1968 (PG-13)** Political indictment of imperialistic England in this revisionist retelling of the notorious British defeat by the Russians at Balaclava. Battle scenes are secondary to this look at the stupidity of war. Fine cast; notable animation sequences by Richard Williams. **130m/C VHS.** *GB* Trevor Howard, John Gielgud, David Hemmings, Vanessa Redgrave, Harry Andrews, Jill Bennett, Peter Bowles, Mark Burns, Alan Dobie, T.P. McKenna, Corin Redgrave, Norman Rossington, Rachel Kempson, Donald Wolfit; ***D:*** Tony Richardson; ***W:*** Charles Wood; ***C:*** David Watkin; ***M:*** John Addison. *MGM*

Charge of the Model T's 🦴½ **1976 (G)** Comedy about a WWI German spy who tries to infiltrate the U.S. army. **90m/C VHS, Beta.** Louis Nye, John David Carson, Herb Edelman, Carol Bagdasarian, Arte Johnson; ***D:*** Jim McCullough. *SUE*

Chariots of Fire 🦴🦴🦴½ **1981 (PG)** A lush telling of the parallel stories of Harold Abraham and Eric Liddell, English runners who competed in the 1924 Paris Olympics. One was compelled by a hatred of anti-Semitism, the other by the love of God. Outstanding performances by the entire cast. **123m/C VHS, Beta, LV.** *GB* Ben Cross, Ian Charleson, Nigel Havers, Ian Holm, Alice Krige, Brad Davis, Dennis Christopher, Patrick Magee, Cheryl Campbell, John Gielgud, Lindsay Anderson, Nigel Davenport; ***D:*** Hugh Hudson; ***W:*** Colin Welland; ***C:*** David Watkin; ***M:*** Vangelis. Academy Awards '81: Best Costume Design, Best Original Screenplay, Best Picture, Best Score; British Academy Awards '81: Best Film, Best Supporting Actor (Holm); New York Film Critics Awards '81: Best Cinematography; Nominations: Academy Awards '81: Best Director (Hudson), Best Supporting Actor (Holm). *WAR, FCT, BTV*

Charlemagne 🦴🦴½ **1995** British miniseries follows the life of the royal conqueror who civilized western Europe and ruled as emperor from 800-814. On 5 cassettes. **250m/C VHS.** *GB* Christian Brendel, Anna Dupery; ***D:*** Clive Donner. *TVC, ACN*

Charles & Diana: A Palace Divided 🦴🦴½ **1993** Trashy scandalous tale of the disintegration of the fairytale romance and marriage of Prince Charles and Princess Diana. Oxenberg stars as Princess Di, a role she played a decade ago in "The Royal Romance of Charles and Diana," and Rees does a fine job playing the conservative Prince Charles. Although the film covers all of the couple's highly-publicized troubles, it's such a quick superficial treatment that it's often hard to follow. Nonetheless, it's a flashingly inviting look into the privileged House of Windsor. **92m/C VHS.** Roger Rees, Catherine Oxenberg, Benedict Taylor, Tracy Brabin, Amanda Walker, David Quilter, Jane How; ***D:*** John Power. *TTC*

Charles et Lucie 🦴🦴🦴 **1979** A has-been couple are ripped off, pursued, persecuted, and saddled with very bad luck in the South of France. Essentially a character study; semi-acclaimed. In French with subtitles. **96m/C VHS, Beta.** *FR* Daniel Ceccaldi, Ginette Garcin, Jean-Marie Proslier, Samson Fainsilber; ***D:*** Nelly Kaplan. *FCT*

Charleston 🦴🦴🦴 **1926** Renoir's third film, a simple erotic dance fantasy that caused much controversy in its day. Silent, with jazz score and historical introduction. **30m/B VHS, Beta.** Catherine Hessling; ***D:*** Jean Renoir. *FCT*

Charley and the Angel 🦴🦴½ **1973 (G)** Touching story of a man who changes his cold ways with his family when informed by an angel that he hasn't much time to live. Amusing Disney movie set in the Great Depression. **93m/C VHS.** Fred MacMurray, Cloris Leachman, Harry (Henry) Morgan, Kurt Russell, Vincent Van Patten, Kathleen Cody; ***D:*** Vincent McEveety. *DIS, OM*

Charley Chase Festival, Vol. 1 🦴🦴 **1923** Six classic Charley Chase comedies: "At First Sight" (1923), "Fighting Fluid" (1924), "Young Oldfield" (1924), "Ten Minute Egg" (1924), "Stolen Goods" (1924), and "Long Fliv the King" (1926). **70m/B VHS, Beta.** Charley Chase. *VDM*

Charley Varrick 🦴🦴🦴 **1973 (PG)** Matthau, a small-town hood, robs a bank only to find out that one of its depositors is the Mob. Baker's the vicious hit-man assigned the job of getting the loot back. A well-paced, on-the-mark thriller. **111m/C VHS, Beta.** Walter Matthau, Joe Don Baker, Felicia Farr, John Vernon, Sheree North, Norman Fell, Andrew (Andy) Robinson; ***D:*** Donald Siegel; ***M:*** Lalo Schifrin. *MCA*

Charley's Aunt 🦴🦴½ **1925** Amusing Victorian farce in which two young male students convince an older fellow student to dress up as their female chaperon so they can pitch woo to two local lovelies. Fun performances and well-paced direction by Sidney. Based on the Brandon Thomas farce, the movie was remade in 1930, starring Charles Ruggles, and again in 1941, with Jack Benny. **75m/B VHS, Beta.** Sydney Chaplin, Ethel Shannon, Lucien Littlefield, Alec B. Francis; ***D:*** Scott Sidney. *GPV, FCT*

Charlie and the Great Balloon Chase 🦴🦴 **1982** When a grandfather takes his grandson on a cross-country balloon trip, they are hotly pursued by the boy's mother, her stuffy fiance (who wants the boy in military school), the FBI, a reporter, and the Mafia. Made for television. **98m/C VHS, Beta.** Jack Albertson, Adrienne Barbeau, Slim Pickens, Moosie Drier; ***D:*** Larry Elikann. *TLF*

Charlie Boy 🦴½ **1981** The new owner of an ancient African idol enters the world of the supernatural when he casts a death spell on six people. **60m/C VHS, Beta.** Leigh Lawson, Angela Bruce, Marius Goring; ***D:*** Robert M. Young. *LIV*

Charlie Bravo 🦴 **198? (R)** A commando group is commanded to rescue a captured nurse in Vietnam. Dubbed. **94m/C VHS, Beta.** *FR* Bruno Pradal, Karen Verlier, Jean-Francois Poron; ***D:*** Rene Demoulin. *GEM*

A Charlie Brown Celebration **1984** The Peanuts gang in an extended adventure in which Lucy courts Schroeder, Patty goes to obedience school, and Charlie Brown finally kicks the football. **49m/C VHS, Beta.** ***D:*** Bill Melendez. *BAR, WTA*

A Charlie Brown Christmas **1965** Disillusioned by the commercialization of the holiday season, Charlie Brown sets out to find the true meaning of Christmas. **30m/C VHS, Beta.** ***D:*** Bill Melendez. *MED, SHV, FCT*

A Charlie Brown Thanksgiving **1981** The Peanuts gang learns that Thanksgiving is more than just turkey and stuffing in this family favorite. **25m/C VHS, Beta.** ***D:*** Bill Melendez, Phil Roman. *BAR, KAR, WTA*

Charlie Brown's All-Stars **1966** Charlie Brown and the whole Peanuts gang is here to delight young and old alike. **26m/C VHS.** ***D:*** Bill Melendez. *MED, WTA*

Charlie Chan and the Curse of the Dragon Queen 🦴½ **1981 (PG)** The famed Oriental sleuth confronts his old enemy the Dragon Queen, and reveals the true identity of a killer. **97m/C VHS, Beta.** Peter Ustinov, Lee Grant, Angie Dickinson, Richard Hatch, Brian Keith, Roddy McDowall, Michelle Pfeiffer, Rachel Roberts; ***D:*** Clive Donner; ***W:*** David Axelrod, Stanley Burns. *MED*

Charlie Chan at the Opera 🦴🦴🦴 **1936** The great detective investigates an amnesiac opera star (Karloff) who may have committed murder. Considered one of the best of the series. Interesting even to those not familiar with Charlie Chan. **66m/B VHS, LV.** Warner Oland, Boris Karloff, Keye Luke, Charlotte Henry, Thomas Beck, Nedda Harrigan, William Demarest; ***D:*** H. Bruce Humberstone. *FOX*

Charlie Chan at the Wax Museum 🦴½ **1940** Charlie and number one son must find a criminal hiding out in a wax museum. Chills abound when the fugitive heads for the chamber of horrors. **63m/B VHS, LV.** Sidney Toler, Victor Sen Yung, C. Henry Gordon, Marc Lawrence, Joan Valerie, Marguerite Chapman, Ted Osborn, Michael Visaroff; ***D:*** Lynn Shores. *FOX*

The Charlie Chan Collection **194?** "The Secret Service," "Meeting at Midnight," "The Chinese Cat," "The Jade Mask," "The Scarlet Clue," and "The Shanghai Cobra" are included on a four-disc boxed set. **391m/C LV.** *MGM*

Charlie Chan in Paris 🦴🦴½ **1935** Chan scours the city of lights to track down a trio of counterfeiters. Top-notch plot and plenty of suspense will please all. **72m/B VHS, LV.** Warner Oland, Mary Brian, Thomas Beck, Erik Rhodes, John Miljan, Minor Watson, John Qualen, Keye Luke, Henry Kolker; ***D:*** Lewis Seiler. *FOX*

Charlie Chan in Rio 🦴🦴 **1941** Local police call on Chan to help solve a double murder. One of the series' weaker entries but with fine setting and music. **60m/B VHS, LV.** Sidney Toler, Mary Beth Hughes, Cobina Wright Jr., Ted North, Victor Jory, Harold Huber, Victor Sen Yung; ***D:*** Harry Lachman. *FOX*

Charlie Chan in the Secret Service 🦴½ **1944** Toler's Chan is now a government agent who is assigned to find the killer of an inventor. Moreland joins up as Chan's taxi-driving, constantly terrified sidekick. The series moved from 20th-century Fox to low-budget Monogram Pictures with this entry, with an ensuing drop in production quality. **64m/B VHS.** Sidney Toler, Mantan Moreland, Gwen Kenyon, Arthur Loft, Marianne Quon, Lela Tyler, Benson Fong; ***D:*** Phil Rosen. *MGM*

Charlie Chan's Secret 🦴🦴 **1935** Chan must solve the murder of the heir to a huge fortune. A good, logical script with plenty of suspects to keep you guessing. **72m/B VHS.** Warner Oland, Rosina Lawrence, Charles Quigley, Henrietta Crosman, Edward Trevor, Astrid Allwyn; ***D:*** Gordon Wiles. *FOX*

Charlie Chaplin: Night at the Show 🦴🦴🦴 **1915** Chaplin plays two different mugs, both out for a night on the town. Mr. Pest, a sharp-dressed upper-cruster, clings to his disgusting habits, and Mr. Rowdy is his working-class doppleganger. Both obnoxious Chaplins-in-disguise collaborate to wreak havoc on a local theater. Contains original organ score. **?m/B VHS, Beta.** Charlie Chaplin, Edna Purviance; ***D:*** Charlie Chaplin; ***W:*** Charlie Chaplin. *VYY*

Charlie Chaplin: The Early Years, Vol. 1 **1917** This video package includes Chaplin's "The Immigrant," "The Count," and "Easy Street." Silent. **62m/B VHS, LV.** Charlie Chaplin, Edna Purviance, John Rand, Eric Campbell. *REP, FCT, KIV*

Charlie Chaplin: The Early Years, Vol. 2 **1917** This video package includes Chaplin's "The Pawnshop" (1916), "The Adventurer" (1917), and "One A.M." (1916). **61m/B VHS, LV.** Charlie Chaplin, Edna Purviance, Eric Campbell, Albert Austin, Henry Bergman, John Rand. *REP, FCT, KIV*

Charlie Chaplin: The Early Years, Vol. 3 **1916** This video package includes Chaplin's "The Cure" (1916), "The Floorwalker" (1916), and "The Vagabond." **64m/B VHS, LV.** Charlie Chaplin, Edna Purviance, Eric Campbell, Albert Austin. *REP, FCT, KIV*

Charlie Chaplin: The Early Years, Vol. 4 **1916** This video package includes Chaplin's "Behind the Screen," "The Fireman" (1916), and "The Rink" (1916). **63m/B VHS, Beta, LV.** Charlie

Chaplin, Edna Purviance, Eric Campbell, Lloyd Bacon, Albert Austin. *REP, FCT, KIV*

Charlie Chaplin...Our Hero! **1915** Two shorts from 1915 written and directed by Chaplin, "Night at the Show" and "In the Park," as well as a 1914 film, "Hot Finish," in which Charlie plays the villain. **58m/B VHS, Beta, 8mm.** Charlie Chaplin, Edna Purviance, Lloyd Bacon, Mabel Normand, Chester Conklin, Mack Sennett; ***D:*** Charlie Chaplin. *VYY*

Charlie Chaplin's Keystone Comedies #1 **1914** Six one-reelers which Chaplin filmed in 1914, his first movie-making year: "Making a Living," Chaplin's first, in which he plays a villain; "Kid Auto Races," in which Charlie now sports baggy pants, bowler hat and cane; "A Busy Day," featuring Charlie in drag; "Mabel's Married Life;" "Laughing Gas;" and "The New Janitor." Silent with musical score. **59m/B VHS, Beta.** Charlie Chaplin, Mabel Normand, Mack Swain. *VYY, KIV*

Charlie Chaplin's Keystone Comedies #2 **1914** Three hilarious early Chaplin shorts, "His Trysting Place," "Getting Acquainted" and "The Fatal Mallet." Silent with musical score. **60m/B VHS, Beta.** Charlie Chaplin, Mabel Normand, Mack Swain, Mack Sennett. *VYY, KIV*

Charlie Chaplin's Keystone Comedies #3 **1914** Three more vintage early Chaplin shorts: "Caught in a Cabaret," "The Masquerader," and "Between Showers." Silent, includes a musical score. **59m/B VHS, Beta.** Charlie Chaplin, Mack Swain, Mabel Normand, Chester Conklin; ***D:*** Charlie Chaplin. *VYY, KIV*

Charlie Chaplin's Keystone Comedies #4 **1914** Four classic silent shorts featuring Chaplin in 1914, Including "Caught in the Rain (in the Park)," "His Million Dollar Job," "Mabel's Busy Day," and "The Face on the Bar Room Floor." With musical score. **54m/B VHS, Beta, 8mm.** Charlie Chaplin, Mack Swain, Alice Davenport, Fatty Arbuckle, Mabel Normand, Chester Conklin, Slim Summerville, Cecile Arnold, Alice Howell. *VYY, KIV*

Charlie Chaplin's Keystone Comedies #5 **1914** Four classic silent features: "Mabel's Strange Predicament," "The Rounders," "Tango Tangles," and "The Star Border." **57m/B VHS.** Charlie Chaplin; ***D:*** Charlie Chaplin. *VYY, KIV*

Charlie Chase and Ben Turpin **1921** Three silent comedy classics, "All Wet," "Publicity Pays," and "A Clever Dummy." **67m/B VHS, Beta.** Ben Turpin, Charley Chase, Wallace Beery, Juanita Hansen. *VYY*

Charlie Grant's War 🦴🦴 **1980** The true story of a Canadian businessman who hears of Nazi brutality and determines to save European Jews from persecution during the Holocaust. Not among the more distinguished works of its kind. **130m/C VHS, Beta.** *GB* Jan Rubes, R.H. Thomson. *MOV*

Charlie, the Lonesome Cougar 🦴🦴 **1967 (G)** Life for a rugged logger will never be the same after he adopts an orphaned cougar. From the Disney factory. **75m/C VHS, Beta.** Linda Wallace, Jim Wilson, Ron Brown, Brian Russell, Clifford Peterson; ***D:*** Winston Hibler. *DIS*

Charlie's Ghost: The Secret of Coronado 🦴🦴½ *Charlie's Ghost Story* **1994 (PG)** Kid who has trouble fitting in is befriended by the ghost of a Spanish conquistador. **92m/C VHS.** Richard "Cheech" Marin, Trenton Knight, Anthony Edwards, Linda Fiorentino, Daphne Zuniga. *PSM*

Charlotte Forten's Mission: Experiment in Freedom 🦴🦴🦴 *Half Slave, Half Free 2* **1985** Fact-based story, set during the Civil War. A wealthy, educated black woman, determined to prove to President Lincoln that blacks are equal to whites, journeys to a remote island off the coast of Georgia. There she teaches freed slaves to read and write. Part of the "American Playhouse" series on PBS. Preceded by "Solomon Northrup's Odyssey." **120m/C VHS.** Melba Moore, Mary Alice, Ned Beatty, Carla Borelli, Micki Grant, Moses Gunn, Anna Maria Horsford, Bruce McGill, Glynn Turman, Roderick Wimberly; ***D:*** Barry Crane; ***W:*** Samm-Art Williams. *FCT, PTB, XVC*

Charlotte's Web 🦴🦴½ **1979 (G)** E.B. White's classic story of a friendship between a spider and a pig is handled only adequately by Hanna-Barbera studios. Some okay songs. **94m/C VHS, Beta, LV.** ***D:*** Charles A. Nichols; ***V:*** Debbie Reynolds, Agnes Moorehead, Paul Lynde, Henry Gibson. *PAR, FCT, WTA*

Charly 🦴🦴🦴 **1968** A retarded man becomes intelligent after brain surgery, then romances a kindly caseworker before slipping back into retardation. Moving account is well served by leads Robertson and Bloom. Adapted from the Daniel Keyes novel "Flowers for Algernon." **103m/C VHS, Beta, LV.** Cliff Robertson, Claire Bloom, Lilia Skala, Leon Janney, Dick Van Patten, William Dwyer; ***D:*** Ralph Nelson; ***W:*** Stirling Silliphant. Academy Awards '68: Best Actor (Robertson); Golden Globe Awards '69: Best Screenplay; National Board of Review Awards '68: 10 Best Films of the Year, Best Actor (Robertson). *FOX, BTV*

Charm of La Boheme 🦴🦴½ **1936** A vintage German musical based on the Puccini opera. With English subtitles. **90m/B VHS, Beta.** *GE* Jan Kiepura, Martha Eggerth, Paul Kemp; ***D:*** Geza von Bolvary. *NOS, DVT, APD*

The Charmer 🦴🦴½ **1989** Havers stars as Ralph Gorse, a charming but amoral con man who uses any means to get what he wants. This includes using the affection (and money) of an older woman, blackmail, and even murder. Set in the late 30s. Made for British television miniseries on 6 cassettes. **312m/C VHS.** *GB* Nigel Havers, Rosemary Leach, Bernard Hepton, Fiona Fullerton, Abigail McKern, George Baker, Judy Parfitt; ***D:*** Alan Gibson; ***W:*** Allan Prior. *SIG, VCO*

Charro! 🦴 **1969 (G)** Presley in a straight role as a reformed bandit hounded by former gang members. Western fails on nearly all accounts, with Presley hopelessly acting outside the bounds of his talent. Furthermore, he sings only one song. **98m/C VHS.** Elvis Presley, Ina Balin, Victor French, Lynn Kellogg, Barbara Werle, Paul Brinegar, James B. Sikking; ***D:*** Charles Marquis Warren; ***W:*** Charles Marquis Warren; ***M:*** Hugo Montenegro. *WAR*

The Chase 🦴🦴½ **1946** Not realizing that his boss-to-be is a mobster, Cummings takes a job as a chauffeur. Naturally, he falls in love with the gangster's wife (Morgan), and the two plan to elope. Somewhat miffed, the cuckolded mafioso and his bodyguard (Lorre) pursue the elusive couple as they head for Havana. The performances are up to snuff, but the story's as unimaginative as the title, with intermittent bouts of suspense. **86m/B VHS, Beta, LV.** Robert Cummings, Michele Morgan, Peter Lorre, Steve Cochran, Lloyd Corrigan, Jack Holt, Don Wilson; ***D:*** Arthur Ripley; ***W:*** Philip Yordan. *NOS, MRV, SNC*

The Chase 🦴🦴½ **1966** Southern community is undone when rumors circulate of a former member's prison escape and return home. Excellent cast only partially shines. Brando is outstanding as the beleaguered, honorable sheriff, and Duvall makes a splash in the more showy role of a cuckold who fears the escapee is returning home to avenge a childhood incident. Reliable Dickinson also makes the most of her role as Brando's loving wife. Fonda, however, was not yet capable of fashioning complex characterizations, and Redford is under-utilized as the escapee. Adapted from the play by Horton Foote. Notorious conflicts among producer, director, and writer kept it from being a winner. **135m/C VHS, Beta, LV.** Marlon Brando, Robert Redford, Angie Dickinson, E.G. Marshall, Jane Fonda, James Fox, Janice Rule, Robert Duvall, Miriam Hopkins, Martha Hyer; ***D:*** Arthur Penn; ***W:*** Lillian Hellman, Horton Foote; ***M:*** John Barry. *COL*

Chase 🦴½ **1985** A big-city lawyer returns to her small hometown to defend a killer and ends up at odds with the town, including an ex-lover. Routine made for television drama. **104m/C VHS, Beta.** Jennifer O'Neill, Robert Woods, Richard Farnsworth, Michael Parks; ***D:*** Rod Holcomb; ***M:*** Charles Bernstein. *FOX*

The Chase 🦴🦴 **1991 (PG-13)** Routine made for television actioner. An ex-con killer leads a ruthless cop and a TV news team on a wild chase. Loosely based on a true story. **93m/C VHS, LV.** Casey Siemaszko, Ben Johnson, Gerry Bamman, Robert Beltran, Barry Corbin, Ricki Lake, Megan Follows. *VMK*

The Chase 🦴🦴½ **1993 (PG-13)** Heiress Natalie Voss (Swanson) is in the wrong place at the wrong time when she's carjacked by escaped con Jack Hammond (Sheen) who uses a Butterfinger for his weapon. Frantic chases ensues as it turns out that Daddy Voss is a media hungry millionaire and he's followed by not only the cops but the media as well. One-dimensional characters aren't helped by a one-dimensional script, but slick filmmaking and a little charm helps. Skewers the media hype that surrounds crime, taking on news programs that offer immediate coverage and reality based shows with glee. **87m/C VHS, LV.** Kristy Swanson, Charlie Sheen, Josh Mostel, Ray Wise, Henry Rollins, Flea; ***D:*** Adam Rifkin; ***W:*** Adam Rifkin; ***M:*** Richard Gibbs. *FXV*

Chasers 🦴🦴 **1994 (R)** Gruff Navy petty officer Rock Reilly (Berenger) and his conniving partner Eddie Devane (McNamara) are stuck escorting maximum security prisoner Toni Johnson (Eleniak) to a Charleston naval base. Imagine their surprise when Toni turns out to be a beautiful blonde whose one purpose is to escape her jail-sentence for going AWOL. Considering how dumb her jailers are this shouldn't be too difficult. Lots of sneering, leering, and macho posturing. **100m/C VHS, LV.** Tom Berenger, William McNamara, Erika Eleniak; ***Cameos:*** Gary Busey, Crispin Glover, Dean Stockwell, Seymour Cassel, Frederic Forrest, Marilu Henner, Dennis Hopper; ***D:*** Dennis Hopper; ***W:*** Joe Batteer, John Rice, Dan Gilroy; ***M:*** Dwight Yoakam, Pete Anderson. *WAR*

Chasing Butterflies 🦴🦴 *La Chasse aux Papillons* **1994** Society's decline is represented by a once-grand, now-decaying chateau, located in a small French village, and its equally decaying inhabitants. Marie-Agnes, confined to a wheelchair, is attended to by her cousin Solange and sullen maid Valerie. When Marie-Agnes suddenly dies, the greedy relatives descend, as well as untrustworthy antiques dealers, and Japanese businessmen interested in acquiring foreign real estate. The film is also an acquired taste. French with subtitles. **115m/C VHS.** *FR* Thamar Taraschvili, Narda Blanchet, Pierrette Pompom Bailhache, Alexandre Tcherkassoff; ***D:*** Otar Iosseliani; ***W:*** Otar Iosseliani. *NYF, FCT*

Chasing Dreams 🦴½ **1981 (PG)** Sickly melodrama about a farmboy who finds fulfillment as a baseball player. Lame film promoted as Costner baseball vehicle, but the star of "Bull Durham" and "Field of Dreams" appears only briefly in a secondary role. **96m/C VHS, Beta.** David G. Brown, John Fife, Jim Shane, Lisa Kingston, Matt Clark, Kevin Costner; ***D:*** Sean Roche, Therese Conte. *PSM*

Chasing Those Depression Blues **1935** Four '30s comedy shorts: "Money on Your Life," "Dental Follies," "Any Day in Hollywood" and "Art in the Raw." **58m/B VHS, Beta.** Danny Kaye, Pinky Lee, Edgar Kennedy, Ben Turpin. *VYY*

Chato's Land 🦴🦴½ **1971 (PG)** An Indian is tracked by a posse eager to resolve a lawman's death. Conventional violent Bronson vehicle is bolstered by presence of masterful Palance. **100m/C VHS, Beta.** Charles Bronson, Jack Palance, Richard Basehart, James Whitmore, Simon Oakland, Richard Jordan, Ralph Waite, Victor French, Lee Patterson; ***D:*** Michael Winner. *MGM, VTR*

Chattahoochee 🦴🦴½ **1989** A man suffering from post-combat syndrome lands in a horrifying institution. Strong cast, with Oldman fine in the lead, and Hopper memorable in extended cameo. Fact-based film is, unfortunately, rather conventionally rendered. **97m/C VHS, LV.** Gary Oldman, Dennis Hopper, Frances McDormand, Pamela Reed, Ned Beatty, M. Emmet Walsh, William De Acutis, Lee Wilkof, Matt Craven, Gary Klar; ***D:*** Mick Jackson; ***W:*** James Cresson. *HBO, IME, FCT*

Chattanooga Choo Choo 🦴½ **1984 (PG)** A football team owner must restore the Chattanooga Choo Choo and make a 24-hour run from Chattanooga to New York in order to collect one-million dollars left to him in a will. The train never leaves the station. **102m/C VHS, Beta.** Barbara Eden, George Kennedy, Melissa Sue Anderson, Joe Namath, Bridget Hanley, Christopher McDonald, Clu Gulager, Tony Azito; ***D:*** Bruce Bilson. *HBO*

Chatterbox 🦴🦴 **1976** A starlet's life and career are severely altered when her sex organs begin speaking. So why didn't they warn her about movies like this? Plenty of B-queen Rialson on view. Good double bill with "Me and Him." **73m/C VHS, Beta.** Candice Rialson, Larry Gelman, Jean Kean, Perry Bullington; ***D:*** Tom De Simone. *LIV, VES*

The Cheap Detective 🦴🦴🦴 **1978 (PG)** Neil Simon's parody of the "Maltese Falcon" gloriously exploits the resourceful Falk in a Bogart-like role. Vast supporting cast—notable Brennan, DeLuise, and Kahn—equally game for fun in this consistently amusing venture. **92m/C VHS.** Peter Falk, Ann-Margret, Eileen Brennan, Sid Caesar, Stockard Channing, James Coco, Dom DeLuise, Louise Fletcher, John Houseman, Madeline Kahn, Fernando Lamas, Marsha Mason, Phil Silvers, Vic Tayback, Abe Vigoda, Paul Williams, Nicol Williamson; ***D:*** Robert Moore; ***W:*** Neil Simon; ***C:*** John A. Alonzo. *CSM, COL*

Cheap Shots 🦴½ **1991 (PG-13)** Cheap best describes this. Two guys running a sleazy New York State resort motel plot to videotape patrons having sex, but capture an apparent mob murder instead. More of a character study than sexploitation, but who needs these characters? Not a stellar writing/directing debut for Ureles and Stoeffhaas. **90m/C VHS.** Louis Zorich, David Patrick Kelly, Mary Louise Wilson, Michael Twaine, Patience Moore; ***D:*** Jeff Ureles; ***W:*** Jeff Ureles, Jerry Stoeffhaas; ***M:*** Jeff Beal. *HMD*

Cheaper by the Dozen 🦴🦴🦴 **1950** Turn-of-the-century family comedy based on the book by Frank B. Gilbreth, Jr. and Ernestine Gilbreth Carey, which chronicled life in the expansive Gilbreth household—12 children, efficiency expert father Frank (Webb) and psychologist mother Lillian (Loy). Stern dad likes to test his theories on the family (and have everything his own way) while nuturing mom easily manages him as well as their large household. There are various family crises (times twelve) but it's all very heartwarming. Followed by "Belles On Their Toes." **85m/C VHS.** Clifton Webb, Myrna Loy, Jeanne Crain, Edgar Buchanan, Mildred Natwick, Sara Allgood, Betty Lynn, Barbara Bates, Norman Ollestad; ***D:*** Walter Lang; ***W:*** Lamar Trotti; ***C:*** Leon Shamroy; ***M:*** Cyril Mockridge. *FXV*

Cheaper to Keep Her *Woof!* **1980 (R)** Alleged comedy about a private detective hired to track likely alimony dodgers. Loathsome, repellent fare, with Davis hopeless in the lead. **92m/C VHS, Beta.** Mac Davis, Tovah Feldshuh, Jack Gilford, Rose Marie; ***D:*** Ken Annakin; ***W:*** Herschel Weingrod, Timothy Harris. *MED*

The Cheat 🦴🦴🦴 **1915** Ward plays a frivolous socialite heavily indebted to Hayakawa as the Japanese money lender. Hayakawa makes Ward pay with her honor and her flesh by branding her. A dark and captivating drama. Silent with piano score. **55m/B VHS, Beta.** Fannie Ward, Sessue Hayakawa; ***D:*** Cecil B. DeMille. *GPV, KIV*

The Cheaters 🦴 **1976 (R)** A young gambler runs away with his boss's son's girlfriend, and is pursued therein. **91m/C VHS, Beta.** *IT* Dayle Haddon, Luc Merenda, Lino Troisi, Enrico Maria Salerno; ***D:*** Sergio Martino. *PSM*

Cheaters 🦴½ **1984** Two middle class couples are having affairs with each other's spouses. Complications arise when their respective children decide to marry each other. **103m/C VHS, Beta.** Peggy Cass, Jack Kruschen. *NO*

Cheatin' Hearts 🦴🦴½ **1993 (R)** Kirkland is a woman beset by woe: she's about to lose her house, her philandering husband (Brolin) wanders back to town with his latest bimbo in tow, and her daughter's getting married. This should be a good thing, except hubby makes a fool of himself at the wedding and nearly ruins everything. Well, at least local rancher Kristofferson is around to lift a woman's spirits. And yes, there's a (predictably) happy ending. **88m/C VHS, LV.** Sally Kirkland, James Brolin, Kris Kristofferson, Pamela Gidley, Laura Johnson; ***D:*** Rod McCall. *VMK*

Check & Double Check 🦴 **1930** Radio's original Amos 'n' Andy (a couple of black-faced white guys) help solve a lover's triangle in this film version of the popular radio series. Interesting only as a novelty. Duke Ellington's band plays "Old Man Blues" and "Three Little Words." **85m/B VHS, Beta, LV.** Freeman Gosden, Charles Correll, Duke Ellington; ***D:*** Melville Brown; ***M:*** Max Steiner. *NOS, MRV, VYY*

Check Is in the Mail 🦴½ **1985 (R)** Lame comedy about a financier determined to make his home entirely independent from the rat-race of capitalist society. Dependables Dennehy and Archer are wasted. **83m/C VHS, Beta.** Brian Dennehy, Anne Archer, Dick Shawn; ***D:*** Joan Darling. *MED, VTR*

Check Your Guns 🦴🦴 **1948** A crooked judge and a gang of outlaws team up to prey on law-abiding folk and cause headaches for the new sheriff, who's pushing an unsuccessful Old West version of gun control. Nothing really noteworthy here. **55m/B VHS.** Eddie Dean, Roscoe Ates, Nancy Gates, George Chesebro, I. Stanford Jolley, Mikel Conrad, William "Bill" Fawcett; ***D:*** Ray Taylor. *NOS*

The Checkered Flag 🦴 **1963** Lame auto-racing drama about an aging, millionaire race car driver with an alcoholic wife who would like nothing more than to see him dead. She talks a young rookie into helping her dispose of hubby. Plans go awry—with horrifying results. Racing scenes overshadow incredibly weak script and performances. **110m/C VHS.** Joe Morrison, Evelyn King, Charles G. Martin, Peggy Vendig; ***D:*** William Grefe; ***W:*** William Grefe. *SNC*

Checking Out 🦴½ **1989 (R)** Black comedy about a manic hypochondriac who is convinced that his demise will soon occur. You'll pray that he's right. Daniels can't make it work, and supporters Mayron and Magnuson also have little chance in poorly conceived roles. **95m/C VHS, Beta, LV.** Jeff Daniels, Melanie Mayron, Michael Tucker, Kathleen York, Ann Magnuson, Allen Havey, Jo Harvey Allen, Felton Perry, Alan Wolfe; ***D:*** David Leland; ***W:*** Joe Eszterhas; ***M:*** Carter Burwell. *NO*

Cheech and Chong: Still Smokin' 🦴½ *Still Smokin'* **1983 (R)** Not really. More like still trying to make a buck. Veteran marijuana-dazed comedy duo travel to Amsterdam to raise funds for a bankrupt film festival group by hosting a dope-a-thon. Lots of concert footage used in an attempt to hold the slim plot together. Only for serious fans of the dopin' duo. **91m/C VHS, Beta, LV.** Richard "Cheech" Marin, Thomas Chong; ***D:*** Thomas Chong; ***W:*** Richard "Cheech" Marin, Thomas Chong; ***M:*** George S. Clinton. *PAR*

Cheech and Chong: Things Are Tough All Over 🦴🦴 **1982 (R)** Stoner comedy team are hired by two rich Arab brothers (also played by Cheech and Chong in acting stretch) and unwittingly drive a car loaded with money from Chicago to Las Vegas. Tired fourth in the series. **87m/C VHS, Beta.** Richard "Cheech" Marin, Thomas Chong, Shelby Fiddis, Rikki Marin, Evelyn Guerrero, Rip Taylor; ***D:*** Tom Avildsen; ***W:*** Richard "Cheech" Marin, Thomas Chong. *COL*

Cheech and Chong's Next Movie 🦴🦴 **1980 (R)** A pair of messed-up bumblers adventure into a welfare office, massage parlor, nightclub, and flying saucer, while always living in fear of the cops. Kinda funny, like. Sequel to "Up in Smoke." **95m/C VHS, Beta, LV.** Richard "Cheech" Marin, Thomas Chong, Evelyn Guerrero, Edie McClurg, Paul (Pee Wee Herman) Reubens, Phil Hartman; ***D:*** Thomas Chong; ***W:*** Richard "Cheech" Marin, Thomas Chong. *MCA*

Cheech and Chong's Nice Dreams 🦴🦴 **1981 (R)** The spaced-out duo are selling their own "specially mixed" ice cream to make cash and realize their dreams. Third in the series. **97m/C VHS, Beta, LV.** Richard "Cheech" Marin, Thomas Chong, Evelyn Guerrero, Stacy Keach, Paul (Pee Wee Herman) Reubens; ***D:*** Thomas Chong, Timothy Leary; ***W:*** Richard "Cheech" Marin, Thomas Chong; ***M:*** Harry Betts. *COL*

Cheech and Chong's The Corsican Brothers *Woof!* **1984 (PG)** Wretched swashbuckler features the minimally talented duo in a variety of worthless roles. Dumas would vomit in his casket if he knew about this. Fifth in the series. **91m/C VHS, LV.** Richard "Cheech" Marin, Thomas Chong, Roy Dotrice, Rae Dawn Chong, Shelby Fiddis, Rikki Marin, Edie McClurg; ***D:*** Thomas Chong; ***W:*** Richard "Cheech" Marin, Thomas Chong. *LIV*

Cheech and Chong's Up in Smoke 🦴🦴½ **1979 (R)** A pair of free-spirited burn-outs team up for a tongue-in-cheek spoof of sex, drugs, and rock and roll. First and probably the best of the dopey duo's cinematic adventures. A box-office bonanza when released and still a cult favorite. **87m/C VHS, Beta, LV.** Richard "Cheech" Marin, Thomas Chong, Stacy Keach, Tom Skerritt, Edie Adams, Strother Martin, Cheryl "Rainbeaux" Smith; ***D:*** Lou Adler; ***W:*** Richard "Cheech" Marin, Thomas Chong. *PAR*

The Cheerful Fraud 🦴🦴½ **1927** Denny, who appeared in some two hundred-odd films in his career, masquerades as a butler to be near the girl he loves. A fool for love is a cheerful fraud. A zanily romantic silent comedy. **64m/B VHS, Beta.** Reginald Denny, Gertrude Olmsted, Emily Fitzroy, Gertrude Astor; ***D:*** William A. Seiter. *GPV*

Cheering Section *Woof!* **1973 (R)** High school football teams compete for the grand prize—the privilege of ravishing the losing school's cheerleaders. Rah, rah, rah. **84m/C VHS.** Rhonda Foxx, Tom Leindecker, Gregg D'Jah, Patricia Michelle, Jeff Laine; ***D:*** Harry Kerwin. *NO*

Cheerleader Camp *Woof! Bloody Pom Poms* **1988 (R)** Nubile gals are stalked by a psychopath while they cavort semi-clad at summer camp. **89m/C VHS, Beta.** Betsy Russell, Leif Garrett, Lucinda Dickey, Lorie Griffin, George Flower, Teri Weigel, Rebecca Ferratti; ***D:*** John Quinn. *PSM, PAR*

The Cheerleaders *Woof!* **1972 (R)** Dimwitted exploitation effort has the usual suspects—moronic jocks and lamebrained gals—cavorting exuberantly. Followed by "Revenge of the Cheerleaders." **84m/C VHS, Beta, LV.** Stephanie Fondue, Denise Dillaway, Jovita Bush, Debbie Lowe, Sandy Evans; ***D:*** Paul Glickler. *PSM, IME*

Cheerleaders' Wild Weekend *Woof!* **1985 (R)** Group of cheerleaders are held captive by a disgruntled former football star. Pom poms wave. **87m/C VHS, Beta.** Jason Williams, Kristine DeBell; ***D:*** Jeff Werner. *LIV, VES*

Cheers for Miss Bishop 🦴🦴½ **1941** The story of a woman who graduates from college then teaches at the same institution for the next 50 years. Somewhat moving. Based on Bess Streeter Aldrich's novel. **95m/B VHS, Beta.** Martha Scott, William Gargan, Edmund Gwenn, Sterling Holloway, Rosemary DeCamp; ***D:*** Tay Garnett; ***M:*** Edward Ward. Nominations: Academy Awards '41: Best Original Score. *NOS, MRV, VYY*

Cheetah 🦴🦴 **1989 (G)** Two California kids visiting their parents in Kenya embark on the adventure of their lives when, with the help of a young Masai, they adopt and care for an orphaned cheetah. Usual Disney kids and animals story. **80m/C VHS, LV.** Keith Coogan, Lucy Deakins, Collin Mothupi; ***D:*** Jeff Blyth; ***W:*** John Cotter. *DIS*

Cherry Hill High *Woof!* **1976 (R)** Five teen girls compete for former-virgin status. Pass on this one. **92m/C VHS, Beta.** Linda McInerney, Carrie Olsen, Nina Carson, Lynn Hastings, Gloria Upson, Stephanie Lawlor; ***D:*** Alex E. Goiten. *MCA*

Cherry 2000 🦴🦴 **1988 (PG-13)** Futuristic flick concerns a man who short-circuits his sex-toy robots and embarks on a search for replacement parts across treacherous territory, only to meet a real female—Griffith. Offbeat, occasionally funny. **94m/C VHS, Beta, LV.** Melanie Griffith, David Andrews, Ben Johnson, Tim Thomerson, Michael C. Gwynne; ***D:*** Steve DeJarnatt; ***W:*** Michael Almereyda; ***M:*** Basil Poledouris. *ORI*

Chesty Anderson USN 🦴 *Anderson's Angels* **1976** Ultra-lame sexploitation about female naval recruits. Minimal nudity. **90m/C VHS, Beta.** Shari Eubank, Dorri Thompson, Rosanne Katon, Marcie Barkin, Scatman Crothers, Frank Campanella, Fred Willard; ***D:*** Ed Forsyth. *NO*

Cheyenne Autumn 🦴🦴½ **1964** The newly restored version of the ambitious, ultimately hit-and-miss western epic about three hundred Cheyenne Indians who migrate from Oklahoma to their Wyoming homeland in 1878. The cavalry, for once, are not the good guys. Widmark is strong in the lead. Stewart is memorable in his comic cameo as Wyatt Earp. Last film from genre master Ford, capturing the usual rugged panoramas. Based on a true story as told in the Mari Sandoz novel. **156m/C VHS, Beta.** Richard Widmark, Carroll Baker, Karl Malden, Dolores Del Rio, Sal Mineo, Edward G. Robinson, Ricardo Montalban, Gilbert Roland, Arthur Kennedy, John Carradine, Victor Jory, Mike Mazurki, George O'Brien, John Qualen; ***Cameos:*** James Stewart; ***D:*** John Ford; ***C:*** William Clothier; ***M:*** Alex North. Nominations: Academy Awards '64: Best Color Cinematography. *WAR, FCT*

Cheyenne Kid 🦴½ **1933** Determined bronco buster is up against a gang of bad guys. **40m/B VHS, Beta.** Tom Keene, Mary Mason, Roscoe Ates; ***M:*** Max Steiner. *NOS, DVT*

Cheyenne Rides Again 🦴½ **1938** Cheyenne poses as an outlaw to hunt a gang of rustlers. **60m/B VHS, Beta.** Tom Tyler, Lucille Browne, Lon Chaney Jr., Roger Williams, Charles "Slim" Whitaker; ***D:*** Robert F. "Bob" Hill. *NOS, VYY, VCN*

The Cheyenne Social Club 🦴🦴 **1970 (PG)** Stewart inherits a brothel and Fonda helps him operate it. Kelly directs, sort of. Some laughs, but this effort is beneath this trio. **103m/C VHS.** Henry Fonda, James Stewart, Shirley Jones, Sue Ane Langdon, Elaine Devry; ***D:*** Gene Kelly; ***C:*** William Clothier. *WAR*

Cheyenne Takes Over 🦴 **1947** Lash sniffs out the bad guy in the case of a murdered ranch heir. **56m/B VHS, Beta.** Lash LaRue, Al "Fuzzy" St. John, George Chesebro; ***D:*** Ray Taylor. *COL*

Cheyenne Warrior 🦴🦴½ **1994 (PG)** Pregnant young bride Rebecca heads west with a husband who soons winds up dead, leaving her stranded at an isolated trading post. She takes in a wounded Cheyenne warrior, nurses him back to health, and he tries to convince her to let his tribe care for her. Respectable performances if unexciting. **90mm/C VHS, LV.** Kelly Preston, Pato Hoffmann, Bo Hopkins, Dan Haggerty, Charles Powell, Rick Dean, Clint Howard; ***D:*** Mark Griffiths; ***W:*** Michael B. Druxman. *NHO*

Chicago Joe & the Showgirl 🦴🦴 **1990 (R)** A London-based GI befriends a loopy showgirl and helps her in various crimes during WWII. Appealing Lloyd overwhelms Sutherland, who shows only limited acting ability here. Kensit and Pigg are fine in smaller roles. **105m/C VHS, LV.** *GB* Emily Lloyd, Kiefer Sutherland, Patsy Kensit, Keith Allen, Liz Fraser, Alexandra Pigg, Ralph Nossek, Colin Bruce; ***D:*** Bernard Rose; ***M:*** Hans Zimmer. *LIV, IME*

The Chicken Chronicles 🦴 **1977 (PG)** An affluent high school dude longs to get horizontal with his dream girl. Set in the 1960s. First feature film appearance for Guttenberg. **94m/C VHS, Beta.** Phil Silvers, Ed Lauter, Steve Guttenberg, Lisa Reeves, Meredith Baer; ***D:*** Francis Simon. *COL, SUE*

Chiefs 🦴🦴 **1983** A police chief in a Southern town discovers a series of murders concealed by town big wigs. Made for TV film boasts a surprisingly strong cast, but provides otherwise conventional entertainment. **200m/C VHS, Beta.** Charlton Heston, Paul Sorvino, Keith Carradine, Brad Davis, Billy Dee Williams, Wayne Rogers, Stephen Collins, Tess Harper, Victoria Tennant; ***D:*** Jerry London. *VTR, NWV*

Child Bride of Short Creek 🦴🦴½ **1981** A young Korean war veteran returns to his community where polygamy is allowed, to find that his father intends to marry again, this time to a 15-year-old. Conflict ensues. Made for television. Based on an actual event that occurred in the 1950s. **100m/C VHS, Beta.** Diane Lane, Conrad Bain, Christopher Atkins, Kiel Martin, Helen Hunt; ***D:*** Robert Lewis. *PSM*

Child in the Night 🦴🦴 **1990 (R)** A shaken eight-year old boy is a witness to murder in his family, and a psychologist with plenty of her own problems must get him to testify. First film for Wood. Middling TV-movie suspense. **93m/C VHS, Beta.** Tom Skerritt, JoBeth Williams, Darren McGavin, Season Hubley, Elijah Wood; ***D:*** Mike Robe. *TRI*

A Child is Waiting 🦴🦴🦴 **1963** Poignant and provocative story of teachers in an institution for the mentally retarded. Fine performances include Lancaster as the institution's administrator and Garland as a teacher who cares too much for everyone's good. Cassavetes incorporates footage using handicapped children as extras—not entirely seamlessly—providing a sensitive and candid edge. **105m/B VHS, Beta.** Burt Lancaster, Judy Garland, Gena Rowlands, Steven Hill, Bruce Ritchey; ***D:*** John Cassavetes; ***W:*** Abby Mann; ***M:*** Ernest Gold. *MGM*

Child of Darkness, Child of Light 🦴½ **1991 (PG-13)** A priest is sent to investigate two virgin pregnancies and discovers that one child will be a savior and the other the Anti-Christ. Totally mindless brain candy resembling the "Omen" movies and "Rosemary's Baby." Made for cable television. Adapted from James Patterson's book "Virgin." **85m/C VHS, Beta.** Anthony John Denison, Brad Davis, Paxton Whitehead, Claudette Nevins, Sydney Penny, Kristin Datillo, Viveca Lindfors, Sela Ward, Alan Oppenheimer, Eric Christmas; ***D:*** Marina Sargenti; ***W:*** Brian Taggert. *PAR*

Child of Glass 🦴🦴 **1978 (G)** A young boy's family moves into a huge New Orleans mansion, and soon after encounters a young girl's ghost and lost treasure from the Civil War. A Disney made for TV movie. **93m/C VHS, Beta.** Barbara Barrie, Biff McGuire, Anthony Zerbe, Nina Foch, Steve Shaw, Katy Kurtzman, Olivia Barash; ***D:*** John Erman. *DIS*

Child of the Prairie 🦴 **1918** An early Mix film about a young cowboy and his city-loving wife down on their luck in a western town. Silent with music score. **63m/B VHS, Beta, 8mm.** Tom Mix. *VYY*

The Children *Woof!* **1980 (R)** Familiar nuclear leak leads to monster mutants done to a novel (though extremely low-budget) turn: after a school bus passes through radioactive fog, the kiddies inside assume the ability to incinerate whoever they hug. They also assume a certain zombie-like demeanor and sport black fingernails. None of this is noted by their uncaring and less-than-observant parents, many of whom are enticed into a very warm hug. This may be intended as social satire. Not only are the little microwaves extremely dangerous, the only way to kill them is to chop off their hands, leading to a wild limbless finale. **89m/C VHS, Beta.** Martin Shaker, Gale Garnett, Gil Rogers; ***D:*** Max Kalmanowicz. *VES, FCT, RHI*

The Children 🦴🦴½ **1990** Kingsley stars as a middle-aged engineer who finds himself caring for seven children in this touching love story from novelist Edith Wharton. Shot on location in Venice, the cinematography is excellent and the cast is superb, but the film lags in places. A remake of "The Marriage Playground." **90m/C VHS.** *GB GE* Ben Kingsley, Kim Novak, Siri Neal, Geraldine Chaplin, Joe Don Baker, Britt Ekland, Donald Sinden, Karen Black, Robert Stephens, Rupert Graves, Rosemary Leach; ***D:*** Tony Palmer. *HMD*

The Children Are Watching Us 🦴🦴🦴 *The Little Martyr; I Bambini Ci Guardano* **1944** Sobering drama of a family dissolution as seen by a child. Worthy example of Italian neo-realism marks the first collaboration between Zavattini and De Sica. In Italian with subtitles. **92m/B VHS, Beta.** *IT* Luciano de Ambrosis, Isa Pola, Emilio Cigoli; ***D:*** Vittorio De Sica; ***W:*** Cesare Zavattini, Vittorio De Sica. *FCT*

Children in the Crossfire 🦴🦴½ **1984** When youngsters from war-torn Northern Ireland spend a summer in America with children from the Republic of Ireland, both sides find their nationalistic prejudices falling away. But a great challenge awaits them when they return home from their summer of fun. Nicely done drama made for television. **96m/C VHS, LV.** Charles Haid, Karen Valentine, Julia Duffy, David Hoffman; ***D:*** George Schaefer; ***M:*** Brad Fiedel. *LIV, VES*

Children of a Lesser God 🦴🦴🦴½ **1986 (R)** Based upon the play by Mark Medoff, this sensitive, intelligent film deals with an unorthodox speech teacher at a school for the deaf, who falls in love with a beautiful and rebellious ex-student. Inarguably romantic; the original stage production won the Best Play Tony in 1980. Hurt and Matlin reportedly continued their romance off-screen as well. **119m/C VHS, Beta, LV, 8mm.** William Hurt, Marlee Matlin, Piper Laurie, Philip Bosco, E. Katherine Kerr; ***D:*** Randa Haines; ***W:*** Hesper Anderson, Mark Medoff; ***C:*** John Seale; ***M:*** Michael Convertino. Academy Awards '86: Best Actress (Matlin); Golden Globe Awards '87: Best Actress—Drama (Matlin); Nominations: Academy Awards '86: Best Actor (Hurt), Best Adapted Screenplay, Best Picture, Best Supporting Actress (Laurie). *PAR, BTV, JCF*

The Children of An Lac 🦴🦴½ **1980** Three women attempt to rescue hundreds of Vietnamese orphans before Saigon falls to the communists. The film derives from actress Balin's actual wartime experience. Made for television. **100m/C VHS, Beta.** Shirley Jones, Ina Balin, Beulah Quo, Alan Fudge, Ben Piazza, Lee Paul, Kieu Chinh, Vic Diaz. *FRH*

Children of Divorce 🦴½ **1980** Made-for-television drama shows divorce from the children's point of view. Standard fare. **96m/C VHS, Beta.** Barbara Feldon, Lance Kerwin, Stacey Nelkin, Billy Dee Williams; ***D:*** Joanna Lee; ***M:*** Minette Alton. *LIV*

Children of Fury 🦴🦴 **1994 (PG-13)** Fact-based TV movie covers the death of self-proclaimed prophet, Utah polygamist Addam Swapp. His equally fanatical widow and son-in-law bomb a Morman church in retaliation, causing a 13-day siege of his heavily armed home by the FBI. **85m/C VHS.** Ed Begley Jr., Tess Harper, Dennis Franz, Kyle Secor, Paul LeMat; ***D:*** Charles Haid; ***W:*** Rich Husky. *NHO*

Children of Nature 🦴🦴½ *Born Natturunnar* **1991** A 78-year-old man unwillingly enters a nursing home where he meets a long-ago sweetheart. The two fall in love again and decide to escape from the home and return to their childhood village. Sweet love story about late-blooming passions laced with fantasy and humor. Iceland's first Academy Award nomination. In Icelandic with English subtitles. **85m/C VHS.** *IC* Gisli Halldorsson, Sigridur Hagalin, Bruno Ganz; ***D:*** Fridrik Thor Fridriksson; ***W:*** Fridrik Thor Fridriksson, Einar Mar Gudmundsson; ***M:*** Hilmar Orn Hilmarsson. Nominations: Academy Awards '92: Best Foreign Language Film. *FXL, ING*

Children of Paradise 🦴🦴🦴🦴 *Les Enfants du Paradise* **1944** Considered by many to be the greatest film ever made, certainly one of the most beautiful. In the Parisian theatre district of the 1800s an actor falls in love with a seemingly unattainable woman. Although circumstances keep them apart, their love never dies. Produced in France during WWII right under the noses of Nazi occupiers; many of the talent (including the writer, poet Jacques Prevert) were active resistance fighters. Laserdisc version features: interview with director Marcel Carne, production photos, analysis of influences of French painting on the film, and audio essay by film authority Brian Stonehill. In French with English subtitles. **188m/B VHS, LV.** *FR* Jean-Louis Barrault, Arletty, Pierre Brasseur, Maria Casares, Albert Remy, Leon Larive, Marcel Herrand, Pierre Renoir; ***D:*** Marcel Carne; ***W:*** Jacques Prevert; ***M:*** Maurice Thiriet, Joseph Kosma. *HMV, CRC, FCT*

Children of Rage 🦴🦴½ **1975 (PG)** High-minded and long-winded drama dealing with the Israeli/Palestinian war and terrorism from the viewpoint of an Israeli doctor yearning for peace. **106m/C VHS, Beta.** *GB IS* Simon Ward, Cyril Cusack, Helmut Griem, Olga Georges-Picot; ***D:*** Arthur Seidelman; ***W:*** Richard Alfieri. *ACA*

Children of Sanchez 🦴🦴 **1979 (PG)** Mexican man attempts to provide for his family with very little except faith and love. U.S./Mexican production based on Oscar Lewis' novel. **103m/C VHS, Beta.** *MX* Anthony Quinn, Dolores Del Rio, Katy Jurado, Lupita Ferrer; ***D:*** Hall Bartlett; ***W:*** Hall Bartlett; ***M:*** Chuck Mangione. *MON*

Children of the Corn ½ **1984 (R)** Young couple lands in a small Iowa town where children appease a demon by murderously sacrificing adults. Time to move or dispense with some major spankings. Infrequently scary. Another feeble attempt to translate the horror of a Stephen King book to film. **93m/C VHS, Beta, LV.** Peter Horton, Linda Hamilton, R.G. Armstrong, John Franklin, Courtney Gains, Robbie Kiger; ***D:*** Fritz Kiersch; ***M:*** Jonathan Elias. *SUE, VTR*

Children of the Corn 2: The Final Sacrifice ½ **1992 (R)** Reporter working for a tabloid paper gets more than he bargained for when he decides to do a story on the adults murdered in the town of Gatlin, Nebraska. Gatlin's surviving children, who killed their parents in the first film, are now living in a neighboring town and free to kill again. This youthful satanic cult does in authority figures in a number of sacrifical ways, working ever more smartly to create the prime attraction—blood flow. Not based on anything written by Stephen King. **93m/C VHS.** Terence Knox, Paul Scherrer, Rosalind Allen, Christie Clark, Ned Romero, Ryan Bollman, Ted Travelstead; ***D:*** David F. Price; ***W:*** Gilbert Adler, A.L. Katz. *PAR*

Children of the Corn 3: Urban Harvest **1995 (R)** Joshua (Melendez) and younger brother Eli (Cerny) are adopted by a wealthy couple and transplanted from Nebraska to Chicago's suburbia. But when Eli grows a corn patch that resurrects an evil force, only Joshua can stop his reign of terror. Contrived premise but lots of nifty special effects. **103m/C VHS, LV.** Daniel Cerney, Ron Melendez, Mari Morrow, Duke Stroud, Jim Metzler, Nancy Lee Grahn; ***D:*** James D.R. Hickox; ***W:*** Dode Levenson; ***C:*** Gerry Lively; ***M:*** Daniel Licht. *TOU*

Children of the Damned **1963** Six children, who are a sample of what man will evolve to in a million years, are born all around the world with genius IQs, ray-gun eyes, and murderous dispositions. Two investigators bring the children together, and while they are being examined by scientists they escape. The children hide out in a church, but they are doomed because their destiny is to be destroyed to teach a lesson to modern man. A sequel to "Village of the Damned" based loosely on the novel "The Midwich Cuckoos" by John Wyndham. **90m/B VHS, LV.** *GB* Ian Hendry, Alan Badel, Barbara Ferris, Alfred Burke, Sheila Allen, Clive Powell, Frank Summerscales, Mahdu Mathen, Gerald Delsol, Roberta Rex, Franchesca Lee, Harold Goldblatt; ***D:*** Anton Leader; ***W:*** John Briley. *MGM*

Children of the Full Moon **1984** A young couple find themselves lost in a forest that is the home of a family of werewolves. Earns praise only for brevity. Even bad movie aficionados will want to skip this howler. **60m/C VHS, Beta.** *GB* Christopher Cazenove, Celia Gregory, Diana Dors, Jacof Witken, Robert Urquhart; ***D:*** Tom Clegg. *LIV*

Children of the Night ½ **1992 (R)** Allburg seems like a typically quiet small town far removed from any danger—until a vampire is released from an underground crypt and decides to make the town his bloodthirsty target. When a teacher, whose girlfriend is visiting Allburg, learns of the supernatural goings on he decides to investigate, which may be a deadly mistake. **92m/C VHS.** Peter DeLuise, Karen Black, Ami Dolenz; ***D:*** Tony Randel. *COL*

Children of the Wild ½ *Killers of the Wild* **1937** Adventure story about a pack of dogs surviving in the Rocky Mountain wilderness. Splendid scenery and some interesting sequences. **65m/B VHS.** Patsy Moran. *VYY*

The Children of Theatre Street **1977** Absorbing documentary follows three children attending the renowned Kirov Ballet School. A show for all ages that may be especially enjoyed by kids who are interested in ballet. Kelly's last film appearance. **92m/C VHS, Beta.** ***D:*** Robert Dornhelm, Earle Mack. Nominations: Academy Awards '77: Best Feature Documentary. *MVD, PBC, KUL*

The Children of Times Square **1986** A mother pursues her son who has fled home and joined a gang of drug dealers in New York City's seedy Times Square. Ordinary television film despite strong casting of Cassidy and Rollins. **95m/C VHS, Beta.** Joanna Cassidy, Howard E. Rollins Jr., Brandon Douglas, David Ackroyd, Griffin O'Neal, Danny Nucci, Larry B. Scott; ***D:*** Curtis Hanson; ***M:*** Patrick Gleeson. *FRH*

Children Shouldn't Play with Dead Things ½ *Revenge of the Living Dead* **1972** A band of foolhardy hippie filmmakers on an island cemetary skimp on special effects by using witchcraft to revive the dead. The plan works. Soon the crew has an island full of hungry ghouls to contend with. Film strives for yucks, frequently succeeds. A late night fave, sporting some excellent dead rising from their grave scenes as well as a selection of groovy fashions. Screenwriter/star Ormsby went on to write the remake of "Cat People," while director Clark would eventually helm "Porky's." **85m/C VHS, Beta.** Alan Ormsby, Valerie Mamches, Jeff Gillen, Anya Ormsby, Paul Cronin, Jane Daly, Roy Engelman, Robert Philip, Bruce Solomon, Alecs Baird, Seth Sklarey; ***D:*** Bob (Benjamin) Clark; ***W:*** Alan Ormsby, Bob (Benjamin) Clark. *VCI, MPI*

The Children's Hour *The Loudest Whisper* **1961** The teaching careers of two women are ruined when girls begin circulating vicious rumors. Only an occasionally taut drama despite forceful handling of a lesbian theme. Updated version of Lillian Hellman's play (adapted by Hellman) is more explicit, but less suspenseful in spite of excellent performances from the talented cast. Remake of Wyler's own "These Three." **107m/C VHS, LV.** Shirley MacLaine, Audrey Hepburn, James Garner, Miriam Hopkins, Veronica Cartwright, Fay Bainter; ***D:*** William Wyler; ***W:*** John Michael Hayes; ***M:*** Alex North. Nominations: Academy Awards '61: Best Art Direction/Set Decoration (B & W), Best Black and White Cinematography, Best Costume Design (B & W), Best Sound, Best Supporting Actress (Bainter). *MGM, BTV, FCT*

Children's Island **1984** A two-volume saga, sold in one package, about children who, after being shipwrecked on an island during WWII, begin a democratic mini-society. **100m/C VHS, Beta.** *NO*

Child's Christmas in Wales **1988** A film of Dylan Thomas's Christmas story about an old, traditional Christmas in Wales circa 1910. **55m/C VHS, Beta.** Mathonwy Reeves; ***D:*** Don McBrearty. *LIV, VES, HMV*

Child's Play ½ **1988 (R)** A boy discovers that his new doll named Chucky is actually the embodiment of a deranged killer. His initially skeptical mom and a police officer come around after various killings. Exciting, if somewhat moronic, fare, with fine special effects. Followed by "Child's Play 2." **95m/C VHS, Beta, LV.** Catherine Hicks, Alex Vincent, Chris Sarandon, Dinah Manoff, Brad Dourif, Tommy Swerdlow, Jack Colvin; ***D:*** Tom Holland; ***W:*** Don Mancini, John Lafia, Tom Holland; ***M:*** Joe Renzetti. *MGM*

Child's Play 2 *Woof!* **1990 (R)** Chuckie lives. Basic doll-on-a-rampage story, a metaphor for the Reagan years, lives on in the sequel (you remember: somehow guy-doll Chuckie made it past the quality control people with a highly inflammable temper). A little dotty from playing with dolls, young Vincent finds himself fostered by two new parents, and plagued by an obnoxious and very animated doll that fosters ill will toward all. What's worse is the doll is transmigratory, craving the boy's body as his next address. Chef d'effects Kevin Yagher's new toy is bad, real bad, and so are the other part two FX. Little Chuckie's saga, however grows a tad tiresome. A bad example for small children. **84m/C VHS, Beta, LV.** Alex Vincent, Jenny Agutter, Gerrit Graham, Christine Elise, Grace Zabriskie; ***D:*** John Lafia; ***W:*** Don Mancini; ***M:*** Graeme Revell; ***V:*** Brad Dourif. *MCA*

Child's Play 3 **1991 (R)** Possessed doll Chucky returns to life again in search of a new child to control, and luckily finds his old pal (Whalin) at a military school filled with the usual stereotypes. Gory sequel in a mostly awful series. "Don't F—- With the Chuck" was its catch phrase; that should indicate the level of this junk. **89m/C VHS, Beta, LV.** Justin Whalin, Perrey Reeves, Jeremy Sylvers, Peter Haskell, Dakin Matthews, Travis Fine, Dean Jacobson, Matthew Walker, Andrew (Andy) Robinson; ***D:*** Jack Bender; ***W:*** Don Mancini; ***M:*** Cory Lerios, John D'Andrea; ***V:*** Brad Dourif. *MCA*

Chill Factor **1990 (R)** A television reporter for an investigative news show uncovers evidence of an international conspiracy. Plot twists abound. **?m/C VHS.** Paul Williams, Patrick Macnee, Andrew Prine, Carrie Snodgress, Patrick Wayne, Gary Crosby; ***D:*** David L. Stanton. *NO*

Chillers **1988** Travellers waiting for a bus are besieged by carnivorous zombies and voracious vampires. How this is different from the standard bus trip is unclear. **90m/C VHS, Beta.** Jesse Emery, Marjorie Fitzsimmons, Laurie Pennington, Jim Wolfe, David Wohl; ***D:*** Daniel Boyd; ***W:*** Daniel Boyd. *PSM*

The Chilling *Woof!* *Gamma 693* **1989 (R)** Corpses preserved in a deep freeze come alive and plague Kansas City as flesh-chomping zombies. Utterly worthless film doesn't even provide convincing effects. **91m/C VHS.** Linda Blair, Dan Haggerty, Troy Donahue, Jack A. De Rieux, Ron Vincent; ***D:*** Deland Nuse, Jack A. Sunseri. *HMD*

Chilly Scenes of Winter ½ *Head Over Heels* **1979 (PG)** Quirky comedy with a cult following about a man obsessed with regaining the love of a former girlfriend who is now married. He must also deal with an insane mom and various other problems. Strong, subtle performances from Heard and Riegert. Hurt is somewhat less satisfying as the supposedly fascinating woman. Released with a different, inferior ending as "Head Over Heels." Adapted by Joan Micklin Silver from Ann Beattie's first novel. Watch for Beattie's cameo as a waitress. **96m/C VHS, Beta.** John Heard, Mary Beth Hurt, Peter Riegert, Kenneth McMillan, Gloria Grahame, Nora Heflin, Griffin Dunne; ***Cameos:*** Ann Beattie; ***D:*** Joan Micklin Silver; ***W:*** Joan Micklin Silver. *MGM*

Chimes at Midnight *Falstaff; Campanadas a Medianoche* **1967** Classic tragedy—derived by Welles from five Shakespeare plays—about a corpulent blowhard and his friendship with a prince. Crammed with classic sequences, including a battle that is both realistic and funny. The love scene between massive Welles and a nonetheless willing Moreau also manages to be both sad and amusing. Great performances all around, but Welles understandably dominates. The film's few flaws (due to budget problems) are inconsequential before considerable strengths. This one ranks among Welles', and thus the entire cinema's, very best. **115m/B VHS, Beta.** *SP SI* Orson Welles, Jeanne Moreau, Margaret Rutherford, John Gielgud, Marina Vlady, Keith Baxter, Fernando Rey, Norman Rodway; ***D:*** Orson Welles; ***W:*** Orson Welles; ***M:*** Angelo Francesco Lavagnino. *FCT*

China Beach **1988** TV movie/pilot launched the acclaimed series about American military women behind the lines during the chaos of the Vietnam War. Nurse McMurphy has only seven days left on her first tour of duty, and in spite of her hate of the brutality of the war, she has mixed feelings about leaving her friends and her work. A USO singer on a one week tour finds her search for men brings the war too close for comfort. Cherry, a new Red Cross volunteer, shows up at the Beach. Skillfully introduces the viewer to all the characters, their problems and joys, without melodrama or redundancy. **95m/C VHS, Beta.** Dana Delany, Chloe Webb, Robert Picardo, Nan Woods, Michael Boatman, Marg Helgenberger, Tim Ryan, Concetta Tomei, Jeff Kober, Brian Wimmer; ***D:*** Rod Holcomb; ***W:*** John Sacret Young. *WAR*

China Cry ½ **1991 (PG-13)** Based on the true story of Sung Negn Yee who escaped from Communist China to the freedom of Hong Kong in the early '60s. Fine portrayal of the young woman from a privileged background who witnessed some of the atrocities of Mao's government policies. **103m/C VHS.** Julia Nickson-Soul, Russell Wong, James Shigeta, France Nuyen; ***D:*** James F. Collier. *INJ, IGP*

China Gate 🦴🦴🦴 **1957** A band of multi-national troops follows a French officer against a communist stronghold in Indochina. Conventional fare bolstered considerably by director Fuller's flair for action. Weak male leads, but Dickinson shines. **97m/B VHS.** Gene Barry, Angie Dickinson, Nat King Cole, Paul Dubov, Lee Van Cleef, George Givot, Marcel Dalio; ***D:*** Samuel Fuller; ***W:*** Samuel Fuller; ***M:*** Max Steiner. *REP*

China Girl 🦴🦴½ **1987 (R)** An Italian-American boy and a Chinese-American girl romance despite a war between gangs in their respective NYC communities. This often violent drama is enriched by director Ferrara's slick, high-energy approach. **90m/C VHS, Beta, LV.** Richard Panebianco, James Russo, Sari Chang, Russell Wong, David Caruso, Joey Chin; ***D:*** Abel Ferrara; ***W:*** Nicholas St. John; ***M:*** Joe Delia. *VES*

The China Lake Murders 🦴🦴½ **1990 (PG-13)** A made for cable crazy cop on the loose fable in which a serial killer disguised as a highway patrolman practices population control on the inhabitants of a small town in the Mojave desert. Meanwhile the local sheriff (Skerritt), unwittingly befriends the killer-patrolman. **100m/C VHS, Beta.** Tom Skerritt, Michael Parks, Nancy Everhard, Lauren Tewes, Bill McKinney, Lonny Chapman; ***D:*** Alan Metzger; ***W:*** Nevin Schreiner. *MCA*

China Moon 🦴🦴½ **1991 (R)** Convoluted police thriller, set in Florida, about beautiful Rachel (Stowe), who's married to rich-but-abusive Rupert (Dance). Kyle (Harris) is the lonely homicide detective who's besotted by Rachel and conveniently helps her dispose of her murdered husband's body. Kyle's problems increase when his rookie partner (Del Toro) turns out to be smarter than anyone thinks. Good performances but the suspense is only average. **99m/C VHS, LV.** Ed Harris, Madeleine Stowe, Benicio Del Toro, Charles Dance; ***D:*** John Bailey; ***W:*** Roy Carlson; ***M:*** George Fenton. *ORI*

China, My Sorrow 🦴🦴½ **1989** Thirteen-year-old "Little Four Eyes" is sent to a Chinese re-education camp for the crime of playing a love song to a girl. There he befriends another enemy of the revolution and a Buddhist monk who help him maintain his familial traditions and identity. Tragi-comic look at how freedom's spirit survived the Cultural Revolution. In Mandarin and Shanghaiese with English subtitles. **86m/C VHS.** *CH* Guo Yiang Yi, Tieu Quan Nghieu, Vong Han Lai, Chi-Vy Sam, Chang Cheung Siang; ***D:*** Dai Sijie; ***W:*** Dai Sijie, Shan Yuan Zhu; ***M:*** Chen Qi Gang. *CVC, FCT*

China O'Brien 🦴½ **1988 (R)** Gorgeous police officer with martial arts expertise returns home for a little R & R, but finds she has to kick some major butt instead. Violent, dimwitted action drama proves only that cleavage can be macho too. **90m/C VHS.** Cynthia Rothrock, Richard Norton, Patrick Adamson, David Blackwell, Steven Kerby, Robert Tiller, Lainie Watts, Keith Cooke; ***D:*** Robert Clouse; ***M:*** Paul Antonelli. *IMP, BTV*

China O'Brien 2 🦴½ **1989 (R)** The unbreakable China, now a sheriff, battles the standard-issue Vietnam-vet druglord who invades her little town. Made back-to-back with the first film (note that both pics' bad guys have the same gang of henchman!), and in both films Rothrock is basically invincible, so there's no suspense. **85m/C VHS.** Cynthia Rothrock, Richard Norton, Keith Cooke; ***D:*** Robert Clouse. *IMP*

China Seas 🦴🦴🦴 **1935** The captain of a commercial steamship on the China route has to fight off murderous Malay pirates, a spurned woman, and a raging typhoon to reach port safely. Fast-moving romantic action taken from Crosbie Garstin's novel. **89m/B VHS, Beta.** Clark Gable, Jean Harlow, Wallace Beery, Rosalind Russell, Lewis Stone, Sir C. Aubrey Smith, Dudley Digges, Robert Benchley; ***D:*** Tay Garnett. *MGM*

China Sky 🦴🦴 **1944** An American doctor fights alongside Chinese guerillas against the Japanese during WWII. Drama, to its credit, often opts for character conflict instead of warfare, but this makes it merely dull instead of cliched. Adapted from a Pearl S. Buck novel. **78m/B VHS, Beta, LV.** Randolph Scott, Ellen Drew, Ruth Warrick, Anthony Quinn, Carol Thurston, Richard Loo, Philip Ahn; ***D:*** Ray Enright. *TTC*

The China Syndrome 🦴🦴🦴½ **1979 (PG)** A somewhat unstable executive at a nuclear plant uncovers evidence of a concealed accident, takes drastic steps to publicize the incident. Lemmon is excellent as the anxious exec, while Fonda and Douglas are scarcely less distinguished as a sympathetic TV journalist and camera operator, respectively. Tense, prophetic thriller that ironically preceded the Three Mile Island accident by just a few months. Produced by Douglas. **123m/C VHS, Beta, LV.** Jane Fonda, Jack Lemmon, Michael Douglas, Scott Brady, James Hampton, Peter Donat, Wilford Brimley, James Karen; ***D:*** James Bridges; ***W:*** Mike Gray, T.S. Cook, James Bridges. British Academy Awards '79: Best Actor (Lemmon), Best Actress (Fonda); National Board of Review Awards '79: 10 Best Films of the Year; Writers Guild of America '79: Best Original Screenplay; Nominations: Academy Awards '78: Best Actress (Fonda), Best Original Screenplay; Academy Awards '79: Best Actor (Lemmon), Best Art Direction/Set Decoration; Cannes Film Festival '79: Best Film. *COL*

China White **1991 (R)** Violence erupts in the streets of Paris, Amsterdam and Bangkok, when international drug cartels battle over the ownership of China White - premium heroin, its sources and its outlets. Rousing, realistic action. **?m/C VHS.** Billy Drago, Russell Wong, Lisa Schrage, Steven Leigh; ***D:*** Ronny Yu. *IMP*

Chinatown 🦴🦴🦴🦴 **1974 (R)** Private detective finds himself overwhelmed in a scandalous case involving the rich and powerful of Los Angeles. Gripping, atmospheric mystery excels in virtually every aspect, with strong narrative drive and outstanding performances from Nicholson, Dunaway, and Huston. Director Polanski also appears in a suitable unsettling cameo. Fabulous. A sneaky, snaking delight filled with seedy characters and plots-within-plots. Followed more than 15 years later by "The Two Jakes." **131m/C VHS, Beta, LV, 8mm.** Jack Nicholson, Faye Dunaway, John Huston, Diane Ladd, John Hillerman, Burt Young, Perry Lopez, Darrell Zwerling; ***Cameos:*** Roman Polanski; ***D:*** Roman Polanski; ***W:*** Robert Towne; ***C:*** John A. Alonzo; ***M:*** Jerry Goldsmith. Academy Awards '74: Best Original Screenplay; British Academy Awards '74: Best Actor (Nicholson), Best Director (Polanski), Best Screenplay; Edgar Allan Poe Awards '74: Best Screenplay; Golden Globe Awards '75: Best Actor—Drama (Nicholson), Best Director (Polanski), Best Film—Drama, Best Screenplay; National Board of Review Awards '74: 10 Best Films of the Year; New York Film Critics Awards '74: Best Actor (Nicholson); National Society of Film Critics Awards '74: Best Actor (Nicholson); Writers Guild of America '74: Best Original Screenplay; Nominations: Academy Awards '74: Best Actor (Nicholson), Best Actress (Dunaway), Best Art Direction/Set Decoration, Best Cinematography, Best Costume Design, Best Director (Polanski), Best Film Editing, Best Picture, Best Original Score. *PAR*

Chinatown After Dark 🦴 **1931** Ludicrous, inane melodrama about a white girl raised by the Chinese. **50m/B VHS.** Rex Lease, Barbara Kent, Carmel Myers; ***D:*** Stuart Paton. *SNC, NOS, DVT*

Chinatown Connection 🦴 **1990 (R)** For some inexplicable reason, local drug dealers start selling poisoned cocaine. Two renegade cops discover the super-secret organization doing the poisoning, arm themselves heavily, and kill lots of people while putting an end to the poisonings. Violent, foolish film with dull performances. **94m/C VHS.** Bruce Ly, Lee Majors, Pat McCormick, Art Camacho, Susan Frailey, Scott Richards; ***D:*** Jean-Paul Ouellette. *NO*

The Chinatown Kid 🦴 **1978** Tan Tung escapes from Red China on a ship bound for San Francisco. There he becomes involved in a local extortion racket and he'll need all his martial arts skills to overcome the two gangs fighting for power. **115m/C VHS.** Alexander Fu Sheng, Sun Chein, Shirley Yu, Shaw Yin-Yin; ***D:*** Chen Chen. *HMD, FXL*

The Chinatown Murders: Man Against the Mob 🦴🦴 **1992 (R)** A tough cop is up against the Chinese mafia and his own corrupt police force as he tries to stay alive and find some justice. **96m/C VHS.** George Peppard, Charles Haid, Richard Bradford, Ursula Andress. *VMK*

Chinese Boxes 🦴🦴½ **1984** An American man in Berlin is framed in a murder and becomes caught in an international web of crime and intrigue. Low budget but interesting thriller. **87m/C VHS, Beta.** *GE GB* Will Patton, Adelheid Arndt, Robbie Coltrane; ***D:*** Christopher Petit; ***W:*** L.M. Kit Carson. *LIV, VES*

The Chinese Cat 🦴 **1944** Poorly scripted formula mystery has the younger Chan smitten with a girl who needs the elder Chan's detective skills in finding her father's killer. **65m/B VHS.** Sidney Toler, Benson Fong, Mantan Moreland, Weldon Heyburn, Joan Woodbury, Ian Keith, Sam Flint; ***D:*** Phil Rosen. *MGM*

Chinese Connection 🦴🦴½ *Fist of Fury; The Iron Hand* **1973 (R)** A martial arts expert tracks sadistic brutes who slew his instructor. Wild action sequences provide a breathtaking view of Lee's skill. Dubbed. **90m/C VHS, Beta, LV.** *CH* Bruce Lee, James Tien, Robert Baker; ***D:*** Lo Wei. *FOX, MRV, REP*

Chinese Connection 2 🦴🦴 **1984** A martial-arts expert learns that the school where he trained is now run by an unappealing master. Conflict ensues. Bruce Li is not Bruce Lee, but he is fairly good in action portions of this otherwise dull, sloppy venture. **96m/C VHS, Beta.** Bruce Li. *TWE*

Chinese Roulette 🦴🦴½ **1986** A host of unappealing characters convene at a country house for sexual shenanigans and a cruel game masterminded by a sadistic crippled girl. Cold effort from German master Fassbinder. In German with English subtitles. **96m/C VHS, Beta, LV.** *GE* Anna Karina, Margit Carstensen, Ulli Lommel, Brigitte Mira, Macha Meril, Andrea Schober, Volker Spengler; ***D:*** Rainer Werner Fassbinder; ***W:*** Rainer Werner Fassbinder; ***C:*** Michael Ballhaus. *CVC, INJ*

Chinese Web 🦴 **1978** Spiderman adventure in which Spidey becomes entwined in international intrigue and corrupt officials. **95m/C VHS, Beta.** Nicholas Hammond, Robert F. Simon, Rosalind Chao, Ted Danson; ***D:*** Donald McDougall. *FOX*

Chino 🦴🦴 *Valdez the Half Breed; The Valdez Horses* **1975 (PG)** A half-Indian horse rancher struggles to maintain his livelihood in this spaghetti western. Not among Bronson's stronger—that is, more viscerally effective—films. Adapted from Lee Hoffman's novel. **97m/C VHS, Beta.** *IT* Charles Bronson, Jill Ireland, Vincent Van Patten; ***D:*** John Sturges. *MPI, MRV, VTR*

The Chipmunk Adventure 🦴🦴 **1987** The three animated chipmunks, Simon, Theodore and Alvin, get involved with a diamond smuggling ring. Original songs. In HiFi Stereo. **76m/C VHS, Beta, LV.** ***D:*** Janice Karman; ***W:*** Janice Karman, Ross Bagdasarian; ***M:*** Randy Edelman. *ORI, WAR, WTA*

Chips, the War Dog 🦴🦴½ **1990** A WWII Army recruit, who's scared of dogs, is assigned to train a German shepherd for duty. Made for cable television. **90m/C VHS.** Brandon Douglas, Ned Vaughn, Paxton Whitehead, Ellie Cornell, Robert Miranda, William Devane; ***D:*** Ed Kaplan. *DIS*

The Chisholms 🦴🦴½ **1979** If you're into oaters, here's a high fiber six-hour serial: Chisolm (Preston) leads the family as they head west and find trouble with a capital "T" en route from Virginia to Californ-i-a. Originally a network miniseries, it's now a two-cassette rentable; adapted by Evan Hunter from his novel. **300m/C VHS, Beta.** Robert Preston, Rosemary Harris, Brian Keith, Ben Murphy, Charles Frank; ***D:*** Mel Stuart; ***M:*** Elmer Bernstein. *LIV*

Chisum 🦴½ **1970 (G)** Cattle baron faces various conflicts, including a confrontation with Billy the Kid. Lame Wayne vehicle contributes nothing to exhausted western genre. Laserdisc available in widescreen letterbox edition. **111m/C VHS, Beta, LV.** John Wayne, Forrest Tucker, Geoffrey Deuel, Christopher George, Ben Johnson, Bruce Cabot, Patric Knowles, Richard Jaeckel, Glenn Corbett; ***D:*** Andrew V. McLaglen; ***W:*** Andrew J. Fenady; ***C:*** William Clothier. *WAR, TLF*

Chitty Chitty Bang Bang 🦴🦴 **1968 (G)** An eccentric inventor spruces up an old car and, in fantasy, takes his children to a land where the evil rulers have forbidden children. Poor special effects and forgettable score stall effort. Loosely adapted by

Roald Dahl and Hughes from an Ian Fleming story. ♫Chitty Chitty Bang Bang; Hushabye Mountain; Truly Scrumptious; You Two; Toot Sweet; Me Ol' Bamboo; Lovely Lonely Man; Posh; The Roses of Success. **142m/C VHS, Beta, LV.** *GB* Dick Van Dyke, Sally Ann Howes, Lionel Jeffries, Gert Frobe, Anna Quayle, Benny Hill; ***D:*** Ken Hughes; ***W:*** Ken Hughes, Roald Dahl. Nominations: Academy Awards '68: Best Song ("Chitty Chitty Bang Bang"). *FOX, MGM, TLF*

Chloe in the Afternoon 🦴🦴🦴 **1972 (R)** A married man finds himself inexplicably drawn to an ungainly young woman. Sixth of the "Moral Tales" series is typical of director Rohmer's talky approach. Not for all tastes, but rewarding for those who are drawn to this sort of thing. In French with English subtitles. **97m/C VHS, Beta.** *FR* Bernard Verley, Zouzou, Francoise Verley, Daniel Ceccaldi, Malvina Penne, Babette Ferrier, Suze Randall, Marie-Christine Barrault; ***D:*** Eric Rohmer; ***W:*** Eric Rohmer; ***C:*** Nestor Almendros. National Board of Review Awards '72: 5 Best Foreign Films of the Year. *INJ, FCT*

Chocolat 🦴🦴🦴½ **1988 (PG-13)** A woman recalls her childhood spent in French West Africa and the unfulfilled sexual tension between her mother and black servant. Vivid film provides a host of intriguing characters and offers splendid panoramas of rugged desert landscapes. Profound, if somewhat personal filmmaking from novice director Denis. In French with English subtitles. **105m/C VHS, Beta, LV.** Mireille Perrier, Emmet Judson Williamson, Cecile Ducasse, Giulia Boschi, Francois Cluzet, Isaach de Bankole, Kenneth Cranham; ***D:*** Claire Denis; ***W:*** Claire Denis, Jean-Pol Fargeau. *ORI, INJ*

The Chocolate Soldier 🦴 **1941** Dull musical in which an opera star tests his wife's fidelity. Lovers of the musical genre will find that this one has too much talking, not enough singing. Lovers of fine films will realize that more singing would hardly improve things. Based loosely on Molnar's play "The Guardsman." **102m/B VHS.** Nelson Eddy, Rise Stevens, Nigel Bruce, Florence Bates, Dorothy Gilmore, Nydia Westman; ***D:*** Roy Del Ruth; ***C:*** Karl Freund. Nominations: Academy Awards '41: Best Black and White Cinematography, Best Sound, Best Original Score. *MGM*

The Chocolate War 🦴🦴🦴 **1988 (R)** An idealistic student and a hardline headmaster butt heads at a Catholic boys' school over an unofficial candy business in this tense, unsettling drama. Glover is notable in his familiar villain role, and Gordon is effective in his first effort as director. Based on the Robert Cormier novel. **95m/C VHS, Beta, LV.** John Glover, Jenny Wright, Wally Ward, Bud Cort, Ilan Mitchell-Smith, Adam Baldwin; ***D:*** Keith Gordon; ***W:*** Keith Gordon. *MCG*

The Choice 🦴🦴 **1981** A young woman must make the choice between aborting or keeping her baby in this fairly insipid television drama. **96m/C VHS, Beta.** Susan Clark, Jennifer Warren, Mitchell Ryan, Largo Woodruff; ***D:*** David Greene. *LIV*

Choice of Arms 🦴🦴½ **1983** A gangster's rural retirement is undone by a dimwitted criminal in this sometimes gripping drama. Montand and Deneuve are serviceable in undemanding roles of the gangster and his glamorous wife; Depardieu is more impressive as the trouble-making punk. In French with English subtitles. **114m/C VHS, Beta.** *FR* Gerard Depardieu, Catherine Deneuve, Yves Montand; ***D:*** Alain Corneau. *INJ, MED*

Choice of Weapons 🦴🦴 *A Dirty Knight's Work; Trial by Combat* **1976** Ex-cop trying to solve murders focuses on a curious group of 20th-century men who live within a 12th-century fantasy—jousting for sport and chivalrous honor. Offbeat lance thruster notable for incongruity and all-star cast. **88m/C VHS, Beta.** *GB* David Birney, Peter Cushing, Donald Pleasence, Barbara Hershey, John Mills, Margaret Leighton; ***D:*** Kevin Connor; ***W:*** Julian Bond. *NO*

Choices 🦴½ **1981** A hearing-impaired athlete suffers alienation when banned from the football squad. What? Controversial covergirl Moore is a supporting player in this, her first film. **90m/C VHS, Beta.** Paul Carafotes, Victor French, Lelia Goldoni, Val Avery, Dennis Patrick, Demi Moore; ***D:*** Rami Alon. *VHE, HHE, VTR*

Choices 🦴🦴½ **1986** Scott is a 62-year-old man with a lovely second wife (Bisset) and a rebellious grown daughter (Gilbert), who announces she's pregnant and is getting an abortion. Meanwhile, his wife also discovers she's pregnant and wants the child, although Scott is adamantly opposed to raising a second family at his age. Family strife carried by fine performances. Made for television. **95m/C VHS.** George C. Scott, Jacqueline Bisset, Melissa Gilbert; ***D:*** David Lowell Rich. *CAF*

The Choirboys 🦴 **1977 (R)** Thoroughly mediocre production about overbearing L.A. cops and their off-hours handling of job stress. Few of the strong cast emerge unscathed. Based on the Joseph Wambaugh novel. **120m/C VHS, Beta.** Charles Durning, Louis Gossett Jr., Perry King, Clyde Kusatsu, Stephen Macht, Tim McIntire, Randy Quaid, Chuck Sacci, Don Stroud, James Woods, Burt Young, Robert Webber, Barbara Rhoades, Vic Tayback, Blair Brown, Charles Haid, Jim Davis; ***D:*** Robert Aldrich; ***C:*** Joseph Biroc. *MCA*

Choke Canyon 🦴🦴 **1986 (PG)** An environmentalist thwarts the henchmen of an industrialist eager to coverup a nuclear dump in a picturesque canyon. Good intentions do not necessarily make for a good movie. **95m/C VHS, Beta.** Stephen Collins, Bo Svenson, Lance Henriksen; ***D:*** Chuck Bail. *MED*

C.H.O.M.P.S. 🦴½ **1979 (PG)** Comedy in which a youthful inventor and a popular robot guard dog become the target of a business takeover. Harmless but unfunny and unfun. **90m/C VHS, Beta.** Jim Backus, Valerie Bertinelli, Wesley Eure, Conrad Bain, Chuck McCann, Red Buttons; ***D:*** Don Chaffey. *NO*

Choose Me 🦴🦴🦴½ **1984 (R)** Comedy-drama about sad, lonely, and often quirky characters linked to an unlikely L.A. radio sex therapist. Moody, memorable fare features especially strong playing from Bujold as a sexually inexperienced sex therapist and Warren as one of her regular listeners. Typically eccentric fare from director Rudolph. **106m/C VHS, Beta, LV.** Keith Carradine, Genevieve Bujold, Lesley Ann Warren, Rae Dawn Chong, John Larroquette, John Considine; ***D:*** Alan Rudolph; ***W:*** Alan Rudolph. *MED*

Chopper Chicks in Zombietown 🦴🦴 **1991 (R)** Tough but sexy Chopper Chicks show up in that American vacation mecca, Zombietown, for a little rest and relaxation. Little do they know that a mad mortician has designs on turning our hot heroines into mindless zombie slaves. Can the buxom biker babes thwart the evil embalmer before it's too late, or will they abandon their Harleys to shuffle about in search of human flesh? From the Troma Team. **86m/C VHS, LV.** Jamie Rose, Catherine Carlen, Lycia Naff, Vicki Frederick, Kristina Loggia, Martha Quinn, Don Calfa; ***D:*** Dan Hoskins; ***W:*** Dan Hoskins. *COL, NLC*

The Choppers 🦴 **1961** Naw, not a fable about false teeth. Teen punk Hall operates a car theft ring made up of fellow punksters. Rock'n'roll tunes by the Hall-meister include the much-overlooked "Monkey in my Hatband." **66m/B VHS, Beta.** Arch Hall Jr., Marianne Gaba, Robert Paget, Tom Brown, Rex Holman, Bruno Ve Sota; ***D:*** Leigh Jason. *SNC*

Chopping Mall 🦴½ *Killbots* **1986 (R)** A freak electric storm unleashes killer security robots on a band of teens trapped inside the mall. Nobody shops. Premise undone by obscure humor, lack of flair, action, or horror. Updated imitation of the 1973 TV movie "Trapped." **77m/C VHS, Beta.** Paul Bartel, Mary Woronov, Kelli Maroney, Tony O'Dell, Dick Miller, Suzee Slater, Russell Todd, Karrie Emerson; ***D:*** Jim Wynorski; ***W:*** Jim Wynorski. *LIV*

A Chorus Line 🦴🦴 **1985 (PG-13)** A range of performers reveal their insecurities and aspirations while auditioning before a hardnosed director in this adaptation of the popular, overblown Broadway musical. Singing and dancing is rarely rousing. Director Attenborough probably wasn't the right choice for this one. ♫Dance 10, Looks 3; What I Did for Love; At the Ballet; I Can Do That; Let Me Dance For You; I Hope I Get It; Nothing; The Music and the Mirror; And. **118m/C VHS, Beta, LV, 8mm.** Michael Douglas, Audrey Landers, Gregg Burge, Alyson Reed, Janet Jones, Michael Blevins, Terrence Mann, Cameron English, Vicki Frederick, Nicole Fosse, Michelle Johnson; ***D:*** Richard Attenborough; ***W:*** Arnold Schulman; ***M:*** Marvin Hamlisch, Ralph Burns. Nominations: Academy Awards '85: Best Film Editing, Best Song ("Surprise, Surprise"), Best Sound. *SUE, NLC*

A Chorus of Disapproval 🦴½ **1989 (PG)** Adaptation of prolific Alan Ayckbourn's play about a withdrawn, somewhat dimwitted British widower who attempts social interaction by joining community theater, then finds himself embroiled in romantic shenanigans and theatrical intrigue. Irons is fine in the lead, but Hopkins sparkles in the more spectacular role of the musical production's demanding but beleaguered director. Seagrove is impressive as an amoral sexpot. Sharper focus from director Winner would have improved this one, but the film is fun even when it isn't particularly funny. **105m/C VHS, Beta.** *GB* Jeremy Irons, Anthony Hopkins, Jenny Seagrove, Lionel Jeffries, Patsy Kensit, Gareth Hunt, Prunella Scales, Sylvia Syms, Richard Briers, Barbara Ferris; ***D:*** Michael Winner; ***W:*** Michael Winner, Alan Ayckbourn; ***M:*** John Du Prez. *NO*

The Chosen *Woof! Holocaust 2000* **1977 (R)** Executive of a nuclear power facility located in the Sahara Desert realizes that his son is the Anti-Christ bent on the world's destruction. This truly horrible film provides nothing in terms of entertainment. It's rarely even laughably bad. **102m/C VHS, Beta.** Kirk Douglas, Simon Ward, Agostina Belli, Anthony Quayle, Virginia McKenna, Alexander Knox; ***D:*** Alberto De Martino; ***M:*** Ennio Morricone. *FOX, LIV, VES*

The Chosen 🦴🦴🦴 **1981** Set in 1940's Brooklyn about the friendship between two teenagers—Benson, the Hassidic son of a rabbi and Miller, whose father is a Zionist professor. Based on the novel by Chaim Potok. **108m/C VHS.** Robby Benson, Barry Miller, Maximilian Schell, Rod Steiger, Hildy Brooks, Ron Rifkin, Val Avery; ***D:*** Jeremy Paul Kagan; ***M:*** Elmer Bernstein. *FXV*

Christ Stopped at Eboli 🦴🦴🦴🦴 *Eboli* **1979** Subdued work about an anti-Fascist writer exiled to rural Italy in the 1930s. Excellent performances from the lead Volonte and supporting players Papas and Cuny. Slow, contemplative film is probably director Rosi's masterpiece. Adapted from Carlo Levi's book. In Italian with English subtitles. **118m/C VHS, Beta.** *IT FR* Gian Marie Volonte, Irene Papas, Paolo Bonacelli, Francois Simon, Alain Cuny, Lea Massari; ***D:*** Francesco Rosi; ***W:*** Francesco Rosi; ***C:*** Pasqualino de Santis. British Academy Awards '82: Best Foreign Film; National Board of Review Awards '80: 5 Best Foreign Films of the Year. *COL, APD, INJ*

Christabel 🦴🦴 **1989** Condensed version of the BBC mini-series based on the true-life WWII exploits of Christabel Bielenberg, a British woman who battled to save her German husband from the horrors of the Ravensbruck concentration camp. **148m/C VHS, Beta.** *GB* Elizabeth Hurley, Stephen Dillon, Nigel le Vaillant, Geoffrey Palmer; ***W:*** Dennis Potter. *FOX, INJ*

Christian the Lion 🦴🦴½ **1976 (G)** The true story of Christian, a lion cub raised in a London zoo, who is transported to Africa to learn to live with other lions. With the principals from "Born Free." **87m/C VHS, Beta.** *GB* Virginia McKenna, Bill Travers, George Adamson, James Hill; ***D:*** Bill Travers. *UNI*

Christiane F. 🦴🦴🦴 **1982 (R)** Gripping, visually impressive story of a bored German girl's decline into drug use and prostitution. Based on a West German magazine article. Sobering and dismal look at a milieu in which innocence and youth have run amok. The film's impact is only somewhat undermined by poor dubbing. Bowie appears in a concert sequence. **120m/C VHS, Beta.** *GE* Natja Brunkhorst, Thomas Haustein, David Bowie; ***D:*** Uli Edel; ***M:*** David Bowie. *MED, GLV*

Christina 🦴🦴½ **1974 (PG)** Gloomy suspense fare in which a beautiful woman pays a forlorn fellow $25,000 to marry her, then disappears as he begins to actually fall in love with her. His search takes him to various gothic settings. Intriguing, but not really fulfilling. Parkins, however, is appropriately mysterious in the lead. **95m/C VHS, Beta.** *CA* Barbara Parkins, Peter Haskell; ***D:*** Paul Krasny. *MPI*

Christine 🦴🦴½ **1984 (R)** Unassuming teen gains posession of a classic auto equipped with a murderous will. The car more than returns the care and consideration its owner provides it. Are you listening GMC? Based on a novel by Stephen King. **110m/C VHS, Beta, LV, 8mm.** Keith Gordon, John Stockwell, Alexandra Paul, Robert Prosky, Harry Dean Stanton, Kelly Preston; ***D:*** John Carpenter; ***W:*** Bill Phillips; ***C:*** Donald M. Morgan; ***M:*** John Carpenter, Alan Howarth. *COL*

A Christmas Carol 🦴🦴🦴 **1938** An early version of Dickens' classic tale about miser Scrooge, who is instilled with the Christmas spirit after a grim evening with some ghosts. Good playing from Owen as Scrooge and Lockhart as the hapless Bob Cratchit. Scary graveyard sequence too. **70m/B VHS, Beta, LV.** Reginald Owen, Gene Lockhart, Terence Kilburn, Leo G. Carroll, Lynne Carver, Ann Rutherford; ***D:*** Edwin L. Marin. *MGM*

A Christmas Carol 🦴🦴🦴🦴 *Scrooge* **1951** A fine retelling of the classic tale about a penny-pinching holiday hater who learns appreciation of Christmas following a frightful, revealing evening with supernatural visitors. Perhaps the best rendering of the Dickens classic. "And God bless Tiny Tim!" **86m/B VHS, Beta, LV.** *GB* Alastair Sim, Kathleen Harrison, Jack Warner, Michael Hordern, Patrick Macnee, Mervyn Johns, Hermione Baddeley, Clifford Mollison, George Cole, Carol Marsh, Miles Malleson, Ernest Thesiger, Hattie Jacques, Peter Bull, Hugh Dempster; ***D:*** Brian Desmond Hurst; ***W:*** Noel Langley; ***M:*** Richard Addinsell. *MLB, HMV*

A Christmas Carol 🦴🦴 **1954** Musical version of the Dickens' classic about a stingy old man who is visited by three ghosts on Christmas Eve. **54m/B VHS, Beta.** Fredric March, Basil Rathbone, Ray Middleton, Bob Sweeney, Christopher Cook. *CFV*

A Christmas Carol 🦴🦴🦴 **1984 (PG)** Excellent TV adaptation of the Dickens Christmas classic features a memorable Scott as miserly misanthrope Ebenezer Scrooge, who gets a scary look at his life thanks to a Christmas Eve visit from the ghosts of Christmas Past, Present, and Future. Terrific supporting cast; filmed on location in Shrewsbury, England. **100m/C VHS.** *TCF*

The Christmas Coal Mine Miracle 🦴½ **1977** Syrupy made-for-television story about miners struggling for survival in a collapsed mine on Christmas Eve. Also titled "Christmas Miracle in Caulfield, U.S.A." **98m/C VHS, Beta.** Mitchell Ryan, Kurt Russell, Andrew Prine, John Carradine, Barbara Babcock, Melissa Gilbert, Don Porter, Shelby Leverington; ***D:*** Jud Taylor. *FOX*

Christmas Comes to Willow Creek 🦴🦴 **1987** Mutually antagonistic brothers are enlisted to deliver Christmas gifts to an isolated Alaskan community. Can brotherly love be far off? Two leads played together in the rowdy TV series "Dukes of Hazzard." This is hardly an improvement. **96m/C VHS, Beta.** John Schneider, Tom Wopat, Hoyt Axton, Zachary Ansley, Kim Delaney; ***D:*** Richard Lang; ***M:*** Charles Fox. *LIV, FHE*

Christmas in Connecticut 🦴🦴🦴 *Indiscretion* **1945** Lightweight comedy about a housekeeping magazine's successful columnist who isn't quite the expert homemaker she presents herself to be. When a war veteran is invited to her home as part of a publicity gimmick, she must master the ways of housekeeping or reveal her incompetence. Stanwyck is winning in the lead role. Also available in a colorized version. **101m/B VHS, Beta, LV.** Barbara Stanwyck, Reginald Gardiner, Sydney Greenstreet, Dennis (Stanley Morner) Morgan, S.Z. Sakall, Una O'Connor, Robert Shayne, Joyce Compton; ***D:*** Peter Godfrey. *MGM*

Christmas in Connecticut 🦴🦴 **1992** Cannon hosts a weekly television show as America's favorite homemaker/hostess. A local forest ranger (Kristofferson) becomes a hero by saving a little boy's life and her network stages a media event by inviting him to her home for a traditional Christmas dinner. There's only one problem: she can't cook. Schwarzenegger's directorial debut lacks challenge in this fluffy remake. See the original instead. Made for cable television. **93m/C VHS.** Dyan Cannon, Kris Kristofferson, Tony Curtis, Richard Roundtree, Kelly Cinnante, Gene Lithgow, Vivian Bonnell; ***D:*** Arnold Schwarzenegger; ***W:*** Janet Brownell. *TTC*

Christmas in July 🦴🦴🦴½ **1940** A young man goes on a spending spree when he thinks he's won a sweepstakes. Things take a turn for the worse when he finds out that it was all a practical joke. Powell provides a winning performance in this second film from comic master Sturges. **67m/B VHS, Beta, LV.** Dick Powell, Ellen Drew, Raymond Walburn, William Demarest, Franklin Pangborn; ***D:*** Preston Sturges. *MCA, FCT*

The Christmas Kid 🦴½ **1968** A desperado struggles to determine his true identity while stopping in a frontier town. Gunplay ensues. Don't bother with this one. **87m/C VHS.** *SP* Jeffrey Hunter, Louis Hayward, Gustavo Rojo, Perla Cristal, Luis Prendes; ***D:*** Sidney Pink. *NO*

Christmas Lilies of the Field 🦴🦴½ **1984** This made-for-television sequel to "Lilies of the Field" follows an ex-soldier who returns to the church he helped build. This time he sets out to build an orphanage. **98m/C VHS, Beta.** Billy Dee Williams, Maria Schell, Fay Hauser, Judith Piquet; ***D:*** Ralph Nelson. *MPI*

A Christmas Story 🦴🦴🦴 **1983 (PG)** Unlikely but winning comedy of a boy's single-minded obsession to acquire a Red Ryder BB-gun for Christmas. Particularly great sequence involving an impatient department-store Santa. Fun for everyone. Based on "In God We Trust, All Others Pay Cash," an autobiographical story by Shepherd. **95m/C VHS, Beta, LV.** Peter Billingsley, Darren McGavin, Melinda Dillon, Ian Petrella; ***D:*** Bob (Benjamin) Clark; ***W:*** Bob (Benjamin) Clark, Leigh Brown, Jean Shepherd. Genie Awards '84: Best Director (Clark). *MGM*

The Christmas That Almost Wasn't 🦴½ *Il Natale Che Quasi Non Fu* **1966 (G)** Loathsome humbug decides to destroy Christmas forever by removing Santa Claus from the North Pole. Crude Italian-made children's film nonetheless remembered fondly by a generation of kids. ♪The Christmas That Almost Wasn't; Christmas is Coming; Hustle Bustle; I'm Bad; Kids Get All the Breaks; The Name of the Song is Prune; Nothing to do But Wait; Santa Claus; Time For Christmas. **95m/C VHS, Beta.** *IT* Rossano Brazzi, Paul Tripp, Lidia Brazzi, Sonny Fox, Mischa Auer; ***D:*** Rossano Brazzi. *HBO*

A Christmas to Remember 🦴🦴½ **1978 (G)** Depression-era Minnesota farmer who has lost his son in WWI brings his city-bred grandson to the farm for a holiday visit. Somber, occasionally poignant film buoyed by Robards presence, and Saint's as well. Made for television. **96m/C VHS, Beta.** Jason Robards Jr., Eva Marie Saint, Joanne Woodward; ***D:*** George Englund. *NO*

The Christmas Wife 🦴🦴½ **1988** A lonely man pays a woman to be his holiday companion at a mountain retreat. Sturdy performances by Robards and Harris manage to keep this one from going to the dogs. Based on a story by Helen Norris. Made for cable television. **73m/C VHS, Beta.** Jason Robards Jr., Julie Harris, Don Francks, Patricia Hamilton, Deborah Grover, James Eckhouse; ***D:*** David Jones. *HBO*

A Christmas Without Snow 🦴🦴½ **1980** Made-for-television film about a lonely divorced woman finding communal happiness within a local church choir led by a crusty choir master. **96m/C VHS, Beta.** Michael Learned, John Houseman, Ramon Bieri, James Cromwell, Valerie Curtin, Ruth Nelson, Beah Richards, Calvin Levels; ***D:*** John Korty; ***M:*** Ed Bogas. *FOX*

Christopher Columbus 🦴🦴½ **1949** Step-by-step biography of the fifteenth-century explorer, his discovery of America, the fame that first greeted him, and his last days. **103m/C VHS.** *GB* Fredric March, Florence Eldridge, Francis L. Sullivan; ***D:*** David MacDonald. *FCT, IGP, LCA*

Christopher Columbus 🦴🦴½ **1985** The man who explored the New World is shown in all his flawed complexity in this film that takes a contemporary approach to the discoveries and character of Christopher Columbus. Shot on location in Spain, Malta, and the Dominican Republic, the film features an exact replica of Columbus' flagship, the Santa Maria. Originally aired as a six-hour television miniseries. **128m/C VHS.** Gabriel Byrne, Faye Dunaway, Oliver Reed, Max von Sydow, Eli Wallach, Nicol Williamson, Jose Ferrer, Virna Lisi, Raf Vallone; ***D:*** Alberto Lattuada. *WAR*

Christopher Columbus: The Discovery 🦴 **1992 (PG-13)** The 500th anniversary of Columbus' voyage brought this lame excursion in historical biography to the screen briefly. Columbus is portrayed as a swashbuckling adventurer who finally gets the Queen of Spain to agree to finance his voyage of discovery (which primarily consists of discovering a lot of bare-breasted native women). Story is secondary to the banality of the entire production, including the acting. Brando is briefly seen as Torquemada—another film in which he took his substantial paycheck and ran. **120m/C VHS, Beta, LV.** Georges Corraface, Rachel Ward, Tom Selleck, Marlon Brando, Robert Davi, Oliver Cotton, Benicio Del Toro, Catherine Zeta Jones, Matthieu Carriere, Nigel Terry, Branscombe Richmond; ***D:*** John Glen; ***W:*** John Briley, Mario Puzo, Cary Bates; ***M:*** Cliff Eidelman. Golden Raspberry Awards '92: Worst Supporting Actor (Selleck). *WAR*

Christopher Strong 🦴🦴½ **1933** Interesting Hepburn turn as a daredevil aviatrix who falls in love with a married British statesman. **77m/B VHS, Beta, LV.** Katharine Hepburn, Billie Burke, Colin Clive, Helen Chandler; ***D:*** Dorothy Arzner; ***M:*** Max Steiner. *TTC*

Christy **1994** Pilot movie for the TV series finds 19-year-old Christy Huddleston (Martin) leaving her privileged Southern life to teach school in the Great Smoky Mountains. It's 1912 in Cutter Gap, Tennessee and her students are literally dirt poor, with ignorance and supersitition the norm. Christy's inspiration in Miss Alice (Daly), a middle-aged Quaker who runs the mission school. And Christy needs encouragement as she struggles to cope with her new life and responsibilities. Based on the novel by Catherine Marshall, which is a fictional biography of her mother. **90m/C VHS.** Kellie Martin, Tyne Daly, Tess Harper, Randall Batinkoff, Annabelle Price, Stewart Finlay-McLennan; ***D:*** Michael Rhodes; ***M:*** Ron Ramin. *GKK*

Chrome and Hot Leather 🦴½ **1971 (PG)** A Green Beret is out for revenge after vicious bikers kill his fiance. Conventional, tasteless genre fare notable only as Gaye's first film. **91m/C VHS.** William Smith, Tony Young, Michael Haynes, Peter Brown, Marvin Gaye, Michael Stearns, Katherine Baumann, Wes Bishop, Herbert Jeffries; ***D:*** Lee Frost. *ORI*

Chrome Hearts 🦴 *C.C. & Company* **1970 (R)** Rebel biker rescues a buxom gal from a fate worse than death, than vies for control of the gang. Laughable, with Namath hopeless in his film debut. Redeemed only by Ann-Margret in continual disarray. **91m/C VHS, Beta.** Joe Namath, Ann-Margret, William Smith, Jennifer Billingsley, Teda Bracci, Greg Mullavey, Sid Haig, Bruce Glover; ***D:*** Seymour Robbie. *COL, SUE, SIM*

Chrome Soldiers 🦴🦴 **1992** Five Vietnam veterans come together to avenge a friend's murder in a town controlled by drug dealers. Busey, as the murdered man's brother, leads the "Chrome Soldiers" in their battle to expose the killers and end local corruption. **92m/C VHS, Beta.** Gary Busey, Ray Sharkey, William Atherton, Yaphet Kotto, Nicholas Guest, Kim Robillard, Norman Skaggs, D. David Morin; ***D:*** Thomas J. Wright; ***W:*** Nick Randall. *PAR*

The Chronicles of Narnia **1989** Exceptional BBC production of the C.S. Lewis fantasy about four brave children who battle evil in a mythical land where the animals talk and strange creatures roam the countryside. In three volumes; aired on PBS as part of the "Wonderworks" family movie series. **180m/C VHS.** *GB* Barbara Kellerman, Jeffery Perry, Richard Dempsey, Sophie Cook, Jonathan Scott, Sophie Wilcox, David Thwaites, Tom Baker; ***D:*** Alex Kirby. *FCT, PME, TVC*

Chu Chu & the Philly Flash *Woof!* **1981 (PG)** A has-been baseball player and a lame dance teacher meet while hustling the same corner; he sells hot watches, she's a one-woman band. A briefcase full of government secrets soon involves them with the feds, the mob, and a motley collection of back-alley bums. Insipid comedy is actually worse than its title, with Burnett and Arkin both trying too hard. Supporters Warden, Aiello, and Glover don't help either. **102m/C VHS, Beta.** Alan Arkin, Carol Burnett, Jack Warden, Danny Aiello, Ruth Buzzi, Danny Glover, Lou Jacobi; ***D:*** David Lowell Rich; ***W:*** Barbara Dana. *FOX*

Chuck Amuck: The Movie **1991** An in-depth look at legendary animator/director Chuck Jones. **51m/C VHS.** Chuck Jones. *WAR, FCT, WTA*

Chuck Berry: Hail! Hail! Rock 'n' Roll 🦴🦴🦴½ **1987 (PG)** Engaging, energetic portrait of one of rock's founding fathers, via interviews, behind-the-scenes footage and performance clips of Berry at 60. Songs featured: "Johnny B. Goode," "Roll Over Beethoven," "Maybelline," and more. Appearances by Eric Clapton, Etta James, John and Julian Lennon, Roy Orbison, Linda Ronstadt, Bo Diddley and Bruce Springsteen among others. **121m/C VHS, Beta.** Chuck Berry, Eric Clapton, Etta James, Robert Cray, Julian Lennon, Keith Richards, Linda Ronstadt, John Lennon, Roy Orbison, Bo Diddley, Jerry Lee Lewis, Bruce Springsteen, Kareem Abdul-Jabbar; ***D:*** Taylor Hackford. *MCA, MVD, FCT*

C.H.U.D. *Woof!* **1984 (R)** Cannibalistic Humanoid Underground Dwellers are what it's about. Exposed to toxic wastes, a race of flesh-craving, sewer-dwelling monstrosities goes food shopping on the streets of New York. Don't be fooled by the presence of real actors, this one is inexcusable. Followed by a sequel. **90m/C VHS, Beta, LV.** John Heard, Daniel Stern, Christopher Curry, Kim Greist, John Goodman; ***D:*** Douglas Cheek; ***W:*** Shepard Abbott. *VTR, MRV*

C.H.U.D. 2: Bud the Chud *Woof!* **1989 (R)** Asinine teens steal a corpse that is actually a zombie cannibal capable of passing the trait to anyone it bites (but doesn't eat entirely). Graham excels as the kidnapped corpse, but this horror-comedy is consistently repellent. Contains one of Jagger's few film appearances, a situation of no despair. **84m/C VHS, Beta, LV.** Brian Robbins, Bill Calvert, Gerrit Graham, Tricia Leigh Fisher, Bianca Jagger, Robert Vaughn, Larry Cedar; ***D:*** David Irving. *LIV, VES, IME*

Chuka 🦴🦴½ **1967** A gunfighter tries to resolve a conflict between Indians and unlikeable troops while simultaneously romancing the fort's beautiful occupant. Pedestrian western features convincing playing from the always reliable Taylor. **105m/C VHS.** Rod Taylor, Ernest Borgnine, John Mills, Luciana Paluzzi, James Whitmore, Angela Dorian, Louis Hayward, Michael Cole, Hugh Reilly; ***D:*** Gordon Douglas. *PAR, FCT*

A Chump at Oxford 🦴🦴½ **1940** Two street cleaners foil a bank robbery and receive an all-expenses-paid education at Oxford as their reward. This loopy Laurel and Hardy vehicle provides regular amusement in detailing the duo's exploits in Britain. **63m/B VHS, Beta, LV.** Stan Laurel, Oliver Hardy, James Finlayson, Wilfrid Lucas, Peter Cushing, Charlie Hall; ***D:*** Alfred Goulding. *MED, CCB, FCT*

Chungking Express 🦴🦴🦴 **1995 (PG-13)** Director Kar-wai presents two quirky tales of loneliness and love, loosely linked by a snack bar in the tourist section of Hong Kong. Cops and drugs are still a part of the storyline, but this is no chop-socky action movie. Both male protagonists are cops, identified only by their badge numbers, who have recently been dumped by their girlfriends. One has a fixation for canned pineapple and expiration dates, the other talks to the inanimate objects in his apartment. The women they eventually fall for are a blonde-wigged heroin dealer and a shy counter girl who bops to "California Dreaming" after breaking in and cleaning the cop's apartment without his knowledge. Shot commando-style in 23 days during the hiatus of Wong's "Ashes of Time" without permits or professional lighting. The high energy is reflected in the pacing and acting performances. Chosen by Quentin Tarantino as the first release of his Miramax-backed Rolling Thunder imprint. **97m/C VHS.** *HK* Bridget Lin, Takeshi Kaneshiro, Tony Leung, Faye Wong, Valerie Chow, Piggy Chan; ***D:*** Wong Kar-Wai; ***W:*** Wong Kar-Wai; ***C:*** Christopher Doyle, Lau Wai-Keung; ***M:*** Frankie Chan, Roel A. Garcia. *NYR*

The Church 🦴🦴🦴 *La Chiesa* **1990** Italian thrillmeister Argento scripted and produced this ecclesiastical gorefest. A gargoyle-glutted gothic cathedral which happens to stand on the site of a gruesome mass murder is renovated, and the kirk-cleaning turns into a special-effects loaded demonic epiphany. It'll have you muttering your pater noster. Unrated, it's also available in an R-rated version. **110m/C VHS.** *IT* Tomas Arana, Hugh Quarshine, Feodor Chaliapin Jr; ***D:*** Michele (Michael) Soavi; ***W:*** Dario Argento; ***M:*** Keith Emerson. *NO*

Churchill and the Generals 🦴🦴 **1981** The true story of how Winston Churchill led England away from the bleak Dunkirk battle and rallied the Allied generals to a D-Day victory. Based upon Churchill's memoirs. **180m/C VHS, Beta.** Timothy West, Joseph Cotten, Arthur Hill, Eric Porter, Richard Dysart. *PSM*

C.I.A.: Code Name Alexa 🦴½ **1992 (R)** Alexa is the beautiful and deadly protege of Victor, who heads an international crime ring. A CIA agent decides the best way to stop Victor is to turn Alexa against her boss. Lots of action and violence. **93m/C VHS, LV.** Kathleen Kinmont, Lorenzo Lamas, Alex Cord, O.J. Simpson, Stephen Quadros, Pamela Dixon, Michael Smith; ***D:*** Joseph Merhi. *PMH*

C.I.A. 2: Target Alexa 🦴🦴 **1994** When a nuclear guidance system is stolen from a government facility CIA agent Mark Graver (Lamas) reteams with former terrorist Alexa (Kinmont) to retrieve the system from international terrorist Franz Klug (Savage). Complicating things are ex-CIA agent Straker (Ryan), who now heads his own commando army and wants to sell the device to the highest bidder. **90m/C VHS, LV.** Lorenzo Lamas, Kathleen Kinmont, John Savage, John P. Ryan, Pamela Dixon, Larry Manetti; ***D:*** Lorenzo Lamas; ***W:*** Michael January. *PMH*

Ciao Federico! Fellini Directs Satyricon **1969** A documentary of Frederico Fellini's filming of Petronius' "Satyricon." Portrays the Italian filmmaker's larger-than-life directorial approach and relationship with his actors. In English and Italian, with English subtitles. **60m/C VHS, Beta.** Federico Fellini, Martin Potter, Hiram Keller, Roman Polanski, Sharon Tate; ***D:*** Gideon Bachmann. *MFV, INJ, TPV*

Ciao, Professore! 🦴🦴½ *Io Speriamo Che Me La Cavo* **1994 (R)** Okay comedy about conventional teacher Marco Sperelli (Villaggio), from northern Italy, who is mistakenly sent to a ramshackle village school in Naples, populated by poor, wily, unruly students. Both, of course, manage to learn from each other. Humor derived from northern vs. southern Italian culture clash may bypass most viewers although the cast of amateur kid actors provide charm. Italian with subtitles. **91m/C VHS, LV.** *IT* Paolo Villaggio, Isa Danieli, Ciro Esposito; ***D:*** Lina Wertmuller; ***W:*** Leo Benvenuti, Piero De Bernardi, Alessandro Bencivenni, Domenico Saverni, Lina Wertmuller. *MAX*

The Cigarette Girl of Mosselprom 🦴🦴½ **1924** A lowly cigarette girl is thrust into the world of moviemaking in this sharp Russian satire. Silent with orchestral score. **78m/B VHS.** *RU* ***D:*** Yuri Zhelyabuzhsky. *KIV, FCT, INJ*

Cimarron 🦴🦴 **1930** Hopelessly overblown saga of an American frontier family from 1890 to 1915. Hokey, cliched, with only sporadic liveliness. How did this one win an Oscar? An adaptation of Edna Ferber's novel, featuring Dunne in an early major role. Remade in 1960. **130m/B VHS, Beta.** Richard Dix, Irene Dunne, Estelle Taylor, Nance O'Neil, William Collier Jr., Roscoe Ates, George E. Stone, Stanley Fields, Edna May Oliver, Dennis O'Keefe; ***D:*** Wesley Ruggles; ***M:*** Max Steiner. Academy Awards '31: Best Adapted Screenplay, Best Interior Decoration, Best Picture; National Board of Review Awards '31: 10 Best Films of the Year; Nominations: Academy Awards '31: Best Actor (Dix), Best Actress (Dunne), Best Cinematography, Best Director (Ruggles). *MGM, BTV*

Cimarron 🦴🦴½ **1960** Director Mann's remake of the 1931 Academy Award-winning film about frontier life in Oklahoma. This version features Ford as a carefree survivor of the Old West with an extreme case of wanderlust. Schell plays his civilizing wife. Based on Edna Ferber's novel. **140m/C VHS.** Glenn Ford, Maria Schell, Anne Baxter, Arthur O'Connell, Russ Tamblyn, Mercedes McCambridge, Vic Morrow, Robert Keith, Charles McGraw; ***D:*** Anthony Mann; ***W:*** Arnold Schulman; ***M:*** Franz Waxman. *MGM*

The Cincinnati Kid 🦴🦴½ **1965** Cardsharks gather for a major stakes poker game, with some romance on the side. Conventional fare helped along by serviceable performances and some stunning cinematography. Sam Peckinpah was dismissed as director from this one. Guess he took the script with him. **104m/C VHS, Beta, LV.** Steve McQueen, Edward G. Robinson, Ann-Margret, Tuesday Weld, Karl Malden, Joan Blondell, Rip Torn, Jack Weston, Cab Calloway; ***D:*** Norman Jewison; ***W:*** Ring Lardner Jr., Terry Southern; ***M:*** Lalo Schifrin. National Board of Review Awards '65: Best Supporting Actress (Blondell). *MGM*

The Cinder Path 🦴🦴½ **1994** Coming-of-age story begins in 1913 with unassuming Charlie MacFell (Owen) forced to take over the family farm. Charlie (who needs a spine transplant) also goes along with an arranged marriage to local lovely Victoria (Jones), a disaster since she's little more than a well-bred tart and it's her younger sister Nellie (Miles) who's really in love with Charlie anyway. As if Charlie didn't have enough to cope with, he's soon an army soldier as WWI begins and up against vindictive Ginger (Byrne), a former farmhand who resents the monied classes Charlie represents. Based on the novel by Catherine Cookson. **145m/C VHS.** *GB* Lloyd Owen, Catherine Zeta Jones, Maria Miles, Antony Byrne, Tom Bell; ***D:*** Simon Langton; ***W:*** Alan Seymour; ***M:*** Barrington Pheloung. *VCO*

Cinderella 🦴🦴🦴½ **1950** Classic Disney animated fairytale about the slighted beauty who outshines her evil stepsisters at a royal ball, then returns to her grim existence before the handsome prince finds her again. Engaging film, with a wicked stepmother, kindly fairy godmother, and singing mice. ♫Cinderella; Bibbidy-Bobbidi-Boo; So This Is Love; A Dream Is a Wish Your Heart Makes; The Work Song; Oh Sing, Sweet Nightingale. **76m/C VHS, Beta.** ***D:*** Wilfred Jackson; ***V:*** Ilene Woods, William Phipps, Verna Felton, James MacDonald. Venice Film Festival '50: Special Jury Prize; Nominations: Academy Awards '50: Best Song ("Bibbidy-Bobbidi-Boo"), Best Sound, Best Original Score. *DIS*

Cinderella 🦴🦴 **1964** A made-for-television rendition of the fairy tale as scored by Rodgers and Hammerstein. Songs include "The Loveliness of Evening," "Ten Minutes Ago" and "Do I Love You (Because You're Beautiful?)." **83m/C VHS, Beta, LV.** Lesley Ann Warren, Ginger Rogers, Walter Pidgeon, Stuart Damon, Celeste Holm; ***D:*** Charles S. Dubin; ***M:*** Richard Rodgers, Oscar Hammerstein. *FOX, FCT*

Cinderella **1984** From the "Faerie Tale Theatre" comes the classic tale of a poor girl who goes to a ball to meet the man of her dreams, despite her nasty stepmother and stepsisters. **60m/C VHS, Beta, LV.** Jennifer Beals, Jean Stapleton, Matthew Broderick, Eve Arden; ***D:*** Mark Cullingham. *FOX, FCT, HMV*

Cinderella Liberty 🦴🦴🦴 **1973 (R)** Bittersweet romance in which a kindly sailor falls for a brash hooker with a son. Sometimes funny, sometimes moving, with sometimes crude direction overcome by truly compelling performances from Caan and Mason. Story written by Darryl Ponicsan from his novel. **117m/C VHS, Beta.** James Caan, Marsha Mason, Eli Wallach, Kirk Calloway, Burt Young, Bruce Kirby, Dabney Coleman, Sally Kirkland; ***D:*** Mark Rydell; ***W:*** Darryl Ponicsan; ***C:*** Vilmos Zsigmond; ***M:*** John Williams. Golden Globe Awards '74: Best Actress—Drama (Mason); Nominations: Academy Awards '73: Best Actress (Mason), Best Song ("You're So Nice to Be Around"), Best Original Score. *FOX*

Cinderella 2000 🦴🦴 **1978 (R)** Soft-core musical version of the classic fairy tale. It's the year 2047 and sex is outlawed, except by computer. Strains of Sugarman's score, including "Doin' Without" and

"We All Need Love," set the stage for Erhardt's Cinderella to meet her Prince Charming at that conventional single prince romance venue, a sex orgy. Trouble is, it wasn't a shoe Cinderella lost before she fled, and the charming one must interface, as it were, with the local pretenders to the throne in order to find his lost princess. Touching. **86m/C VHS.** Catharine Erhardt, Jay B. Larson, Vaughn Armstrong; ***D:*** Al Adamson; ***M:*** Sparky Sugarman. *NO*

Cinderfella 🦴🦴½ **1960** This twist on the classic children's fairy tale features Lewis as the hapless buffoon guided by his fairy godfather. Somewhat overdone, with extended talking sequences and gratuitous musical interludes. Lewis, though, mugs effectively. **88m/C VHS, Beta.** Jerry Lewis, Ed Wynn, Judith Anderson, Anna Maria Alberghetti, Henry Silva, Count Basie, Robert Hutton; ***D:*** Frank Tashlin; ***W:*** Frank Tashlin. *LIV*

Cinema Paradiso 🦴🦴🦴 *Nuovo Cinema Paradiso* **1988** Memoir of a boy's life working at a movie theatre in small-town Italy after WWII. Film aspires to both majestic sweep and stirring poignancy, but only occasionally hits its target. Still manages to move the viewer, and it features a suitably low-key performance by the masterful Noiret. Autobiographically inspired script written by Tornatore. The version shown in America is approximately a half-hour shorter than the original Italian form. **123m/C VHS, LV, 8mm.** *IT* Philippe Noiret, Jacques Perrin, Salvatore Cascio, Marco Leonardi, Agnes Nano, Leopoldo Trieste; ***D:*** Giuseppe Tornatore; ***W:*** Giuseppe Tornatore; ***M:*** Ennio Morricone. Academy Awards '89: Best Foreign Language Film; British Academy Awards '90: Best Actor (Noiret), Best Foreign Film, Best Original Screenplay, Best Supporting Actor (Cascio); Golden Globe Awards '90: Best Foreign Film. *HBO, APD, INJ*

Cinema Shrapnel **1987** A tour through the wonderful world of screen hype and bad movies, with scenes from terrible trailers, maudlin fundraising shorts, and glitzy movie premieres. **60m/C VHS, Beta.** *NO*

Cinemagic **1985** A compilation of four short horror and science fiction films including "Nightfright," "Dr. Dobermind," "Illegal Alien" and "The Thing in the Basement." **60m/C VHS, Beta.** *MPI*

Circle Canyon 🦴 **1933** In a remote canyon two opposing outlaw gangs battle to the death. **48m/B VHS, Beta.** Buddy Roosevelt. *NO*

Circle Man 🦴 **1987** A made-for-video action drama about the underground sporting phenomenon, bare-knuckle fighting. **90m/C VHS, Beta.** William Sanderson. *ACA*

Circle of Death 🦴½ **1936** Average formula western about a white boy who is raised as an Indian. Later he falls in love with a white girl and leaves the tribe. **55m/B VHS, Beta.** Monte Montana, Yakima Canutt. *NOS, VDM*

Circle of Deceit 🦴🦴½ **1994** SAS officer John Neil (Waterman) is called back into service in Belfast two years after his wife and child were killed by terrorists. His assignment is to assume the identity of recently deceased IRA soldier Jackie O'Connell and learn about an arms shipment headed for Northern Ireland. But can his disguise hold against local IRA commander Liam McAuley (Vaughan)? Made for British TV. **103m/C VHS.** *GB* Dennis Waterman, Peter Vaughan, Derek Jacobi, Clare Higgins; ***W:*** Jean-Claude Carriere. *VCO*

Circle of Fear 🦴½ **1989 (R)** An ex-hitman who worked for the Mob upends the black market for sex and drugs in the Philippines while looking for his daughter who was sold into a sex slave ring. El cheapo exploiter. **90m/C VHS, Beta.** *PH* Patrick Dollaghan, Welsey Pfenning, Joey Aresco, Vernon Wells; ***D:*** Clark Henderson. *MGM*

Circle of Friends 🦴🦴½ **1994 (PG-13)** Nostalgic Irish coming-of-ager focuses on three friends and the trials and tribulations they face when hearts and hormones conflict with a strict Catholic upbringing. Small-town teenager Benny (Driver), overweight and slightly awkward, reunites with her friends at university in Dublin. Benny begins a romance with gentle, doe-eyed Jack Foley (O'Donnell) and endures the humorous but sometimes painful passage from adolescence to womanhood. Sentimental moments can be too sticky-sweet at times, but humor, disappointment, and small triumphs are convincingly portrayed, offering a universal appeal. Adapted from the Maeve Binchy novel. **96m/C VHS.** Chris O'Donnell, Minnie Driver, Geraldine O'Rawe, Saffron Burrows, Colin Firth, Alan Cummings, Aidan Gillen; ***D:*** Pat O'Connor; ***W:*** Andrew Davies; ***M:*** Michael Kamen. *HBO*

Circle of Iron 🦴🦴½ *The Silent Flute* **1978 (R)** Plenty of action and martial arts combat abound in this story of one man's eternal quest for truth. Originally co-written by and intended for Bruce Lee as a rib-crunching vehicle, until he died before production began and was replaced by Kung-Fu Carradine. A cut above most chop-socky actioners. Filmed in Israel. **102m/C VHS, Beta.** *GB* Jeff Cooper, David Carradine, Roddy McDowall, Eli Wallach, Christopher Lee; ***D:*** Richard Moore; ***W:*** Bruce Lee, James Coburn, Stirling Silliphant; ***M:*** Bruce Smeaton. *SUE*

Circle of Love 🦴🦴 **1964** Episodic melodrama drifts from romance to romance in contemporary Paris. A somewhat pretentious remake of Ophuls classic "La Ronde," which was in turn adapted from Arthur Schnitzler's play. Credible performers are undone by Vadim's strained direction. **110m/C VHS, Beta.** *FR* Jane Fonda, Francine Berge, Marie DuBois, Jean-Claude Brialy, Catherine Spaak, Claude Giraud; ***D:*** Roger Vadim; ***W:*** Jean Anouilh. *JEF*

Circle of Power 🦴½ *Brainwash; The Naked Weekend; Mystique* **1983 (R)** Mimieux must cure various business men of their problems (homosexuality, alcoholism and the like) to help them become better executives. Intriguing and somewhat disturbing, supposedly based on a true story. **103m/C VHS.** *GB* Yvette Mimieux, John Considine, Terence Knox, Cindy Pickett, Christopher Allport; ***D:*** Bobby Roth; ***W:*** Stephen F. Bello. *MED*

Circle of Two 🦴🦴 **1980 (PG)** A platonic friendship between an aging artist and a young girl is misunderstood by others. Well, of course they do meet in a porno theater. Pedestrian fare adapted from a story by Marie Therese Baird. **90m/C VHS, Beta.** *CA* Richard Burton, Tatum O'Neal, Kate Reid; ***D:*** Jules Dassin. *VES, VTR*

Circonstances Attenuantes 🦴🦴½ *Extenuating Circumstances* **1936** French classic about a retired judge who moves to the outskirts of Paris with his wife and attempts to convert the locals from disreputable to law-abiding citizens. Also available dubbed. **90m/B VHS.** *FR* Michel Simon, Arletty; ***D:*** Jean Boyer. *FRA, FCT*

Circuitry Man 🦴🦴½ **1990 (R)** Post-apocolyptic saga of future American life as a woman tries to deliver a briefcase full of computer chips to the underground Big Apple. Along the way she runs into Plughead, a humanoid with electrical outlets that allow him to "plug in" to other people's fantasies. Intelligent retelling of a standard tale with an inspired soundtrack by Deborah Holland. Witty and original. **85m/C VHS, LV.** Jim Metzler, Dana Wheeler-Nicholson, Lu Leonard, Vernon Wells, Barbara Alyn Woods, Dennis Christopher; ***D:*** Steven Lovy; ***W:*** Steven Lovy; ***M:*** Deborah Holland. *COL*

Circumstances Unknown 🦴½ **1995 (R)** A jealous killer targets his unhappily married friends for murder. Based on the novel by Jonellen Heckler. **91m/C VHS, Beta.** Judd Nelson, Isabel Glasser; ***D:*** Robert Lewis; ***W:*** Thomas Hood, Emily Shoemaker. *PAR*

Circumstantial Evidence 🦴🦴 **1935** Newspaper reporter (Chandler) goes to extremes for a story and nearly dies as a result. Chandler sets it up to look like he's murdered a colleague, and he's tried and convicted on, you guessed it, circumstantial evidence. The colleague's then supposed to come forward but there's a problem. **69m/B VHS.** Chick Chandler, Shirley Grey, Dorothy Revier, Arthur Vinton; ***D:*** Charles Lamont; ***W:*** Ewart Adamson. *SNC*

The Circus 🦴🦴🦴½ **1919** Classic comedy silent details the tramp's exploits as a member of a traveling circus, including a romance with the bareback rider. Hilarious, less sentimental than most of Chaplin's feature films. Chaplin won a special Academy Award for "versatility and genius in writing, acting, directing and producing" for this one. Outrageous final scenes. **105m/B VHS.** Charlie Chaplin, Merna Kennedy; ***D:*** Charlie Chaplin. Nominations: Academy Awards '28: Best Actor (Chaplin), Best Director (Chaplin). *FOX*

Circus Angel 🦴🦴🦴 **1965** The renowned director of "The Red Balloon" creates a fantasy about a klutzy burglar transformed by a found nightgown into an angel. He begins to serve the dreams and actions of an odd lot of characters. Subtitled in English. **80m/B VHS, Beta.** *FR* Philippe Avron, Mirielle Negre; ***D:*** Albert Lamorisse. *SUE, NLC*

Circus of Fear 🦴½ *Psycho-Circus* **1967** A travelling troupe is stalked by a murderer. The unedited version is occasionally scary. **92m/C VHS, Beta.** *GB GE* Christopher Lee, Leo Genn, Anthony Newlands, Heinz Drache, Eddi Arent, Klaus Kinski, Margaret Lee, Suzy Kendall; ***D:*** John Llewellyn Moxey. *INC, SNC, NOS*

Circus of Horrors 🦴🦴½ **1960** Nip 'n tuck horror about a plastic surgeon who takes over a circus to escape a disfigured patient bent on revenge. The circus is staffed by former patients with new faces who, one by one, fall victim in fine circus style. A bloody one-ring extravaganza. **87m/C VHS, Beta.** *GB* Donald Pleasence, Anton Diffring, Erika Remberg, Yvonne Monlaur, Jane Hylton, Kenneth Griffith; ***D:*** Sidney Hayers; ***W:*** George L. Baxt. *REP*

Circus World 🦴🦴½ *The Magnificent Showman* **1964** A circus boss tries to navigate a reckless, romancing crew through a European tour while searching for aerialist he loved 15 years before and whose daughter he has reared. Too long and too familiar, but nonetheless well done with an excellent finale. **132m/C VHS, Beta, LV.** John Wayne, Rita Hayworth, Claudia Cardinale, Lloyd Nolan, Richard Conte; ***D:*** Henry Hathaway; ***W:*** Ben Hecht, James Edward Grant, Julian Halevy; ***C:*** Jack Hildyard. Golden Globe Awards '65: Best Song ("Circus World"). *NO*

The Cisco Kid **1950** Renaldo is the heroic Cisco, a do-gooder who, with his sidekick Pancho, championed the poor and downtrodden. The first TV series shown in color. Features two episodes: "Quarterhorse" and "The Postmaster." Additional episodes are available. **60m/C VHS.** Duncan Renaldo, Leo Carrillo. *HEG, MOV*

The Cisco Kid 🦴🦴½ **1994** The Cisco Kid and his sidekick Pancho went from O. Henry's short story, to silent movies, talkies, a '50s TV series, and now this made for TV movie. Benito Juarez is leading an uprising to overthrow the French-backed Emperor Maximilian in 1867 Mexico. Cisco's (Smits) supplying the rebels with guns while carrying on romantic escapades (watch for the tango). Meanwhile, true-believer Pancho tries to convince his friend to become a revolutionary. Light-hearted with pedestrian action shots. Filmed on location in Mexico. **96m/C VHS, LV.** Jimmy Smits, Richard "Cheech" Marin, Sadie Frost, Tim Thomerson, Bruce Payne; ***D:*** Luis Valdez; ***W:*** Michael Kane, Luis Valdez. *TTC*

The Citadel 🦴🦴🦴 **1938** From the A.J. Cronin novel, the intelligent and honest Hollywood drama about a young British doctor who is morally corrupted by his move from a poor mining village to a well-off practice treating wealthy hypochondriacs. Somewhat hokey but still consistently entertaining, with Donat fine in the lead. **114m/C VHS, Beta.** *GB* Robert Donat, Rosalind Russell, Rex Harrison, Ralph Richardson, Emlyn Williams, Penelope Dudley Ward; ***D:*** King Vidor; ***C:*** Harry Stradling. National Board of Review Awards '38: 10 Best Films of the Year; New York Film Critics Awards '38: Best Film; Nominations: Academy Awards '38: Best Actor (Donat), Best Director (Vidor), Best Picture, Best Screenplay. *MGM, HMV*

Citizen Cohn 🦴🦴 **1992 (R)** An appallingly fascinating look at a human monster. Told in hallucinatory flashbacks, as he lays dying from AIDS, Roy Cohn is a lawyer and power broker, probably best-remembered as the malevolent sidekick to Communist-hunting Senator Joseph McCarthy. But his contempt also extended to antisemitism and gay-bashing (though Cohn was both homosexual and Jewish), and his past comes, literally, back to haunt him. Woods does an exceptional job in bringing this sociopathic heel to wretched life. Adapted from the biography by Nicholas von Hoffman. Made for cable television. **112m/C VHS, LV.** James Woods, Joe Don Baker, Joseph Bologna, Ed Flanders, Frederic Forrest, Lee Grant, Pat Hingle; ***D:*** Frank Pierson; ***W:*** David Franzoni; ***C:*** Paul Elliott. National Academy of Cable Programming ACE Awards '93: Best Movie/Miniseries, Best Director (Pierson), Best Writing (Franzoni). *HBO, BTV*

Citizen Kane ☙☙☙☙ **1941** Extraordinary film is an American tragedy of a newspaper tycoon (based loosely on William Randolph Hearst) from his humble beginnings to the solitude of his final years. One of the greatest films ever made—a stunning tour-de-force in virtually every aspect, from the fragmented narration to breathtaking, deep-focus cinematography; from a vivid soundtrack to fabulous ensemble acting. Welles was only 25 when he co-wrote, directed, and starred in this masterpiece. Three disc laser edition was reproduced from a superior negative and features liner notes and running commentary from film historian Robert J. Carringer. Watch for Ladd and O'Connell as reporters. **119m/B VHS, Beta, LV, 8mm.** Orson Welles, Joseph Cotten, Everett Sloane, Dorothy Comingore, Ruth Warrick, George Coulouris, Ray Collins, William Alland, Paul Stewart, Erskine Sanford, Agnes Moorehead, Alan Ladd, Gus Schilling, Philip Van Zandt, Harry Shannon, Sonny Bupp, Arthur O'Connell; ***D:*** Orson Welles; ***W:*** Orson Welles, Herman J. Mankiewicz; ***C:*** Gregg Toland; ***M:*** Bernard Herrmann. Academy Awards '41: Best Original Screenplay; National Board of Review Awards '41: 10 Best Films of the Year; New York Film Critics Awards '41: Best Film; Nominations: Academy Awards '41: Best Actor (Welles), Best Black and White Cinematography, Best Director (Welles), Best Film Editing, Best Interior Decoration, Best Picture, Best Sound, Best Original Score. *CRC, FCT, TTC*

Citizen X ☙☙☙ **1995 (R)** Based on the true story of '80's Russian serial killer Andrei Chikatilo (DeMunn) and his 52 victims. Viktor Burakov (Rea) is a beleagured rural forensics expert who is blatantly told by party officials that the Soviet state does not have serial killers—in spite of a rising body count. His only ally is Col. Fetisov (Sutherland), who's adept at political maneuvering, but it takes the duo eight frustrating years to bring the grisly killer to justice. Fine performances highlight a literate script from Robert Cullen's book "The Killer Department." Filmed on location in Budapest, Hungary. Made for cable television. **100m/C VHS.** Stephen Rea, Donald Sutherland, Jeffrey DeMunn, John Wood, Joss Ackland, Max von Sydow, Ralph Nossek, Imelda Staunton; ***D:*** Chris Gerolmo; ***W:*** Chris Gerolmo; ***C:*** Robert Fraisse; ***M:*** Randy Edelman. *HBO*

Citizens Band ☙☙☙ *Handle With Care* **1977 (PG)** Episodic, low-key comedy about people united by their CB use in a midwestern community. Notable performance from Clark as a soft-voiced guide for truckers passing through. Demme's first comedy is characteristically idiosyncratic. **98m/C VHS, Beta.** Paul LeMat, Candy Clark, Ann Wedgeworth, Roberts Blossom, Charles Napier, Marcia Rodd, Bruce McGill, Ed Begley Jr., Alix Elias; ***D:*** Jonathan Demme; ***W:*** Paul Brickman; ***M:*** Bill Conti. National Society of Film Critics Awards '77: Best Supporting Actress (Wedgeworth). *PAR*

The City ☙ **1976** Police desperately search for a psychotic determined to kill a country singer. He shouldn't be too hard to find. Made for television. **78m/C VHS, Beta.** Don Johnson, Robert Forster, Ward Costello, Jimmy Dean, Mark Hamill; ***D:*** Harvey Hart. *WOV*

The City and the Dogs ☙☙☙ *La Ciudad y los Perros* **1985** A brutal, cynical adaptation of Mario Vargas Llosa's novel. A young military recruit rebels against the authority establishments around him. In Spanish with English subtitles. **135m/C VHS, Beta.** *SP* ***D:*** Francisco J. Lombardi Pery. *FCT, INJ*

City Boy ☙☙☙ **1993** At the turn of the century the orphaned Nick makes his way from Chicago to the Pacific Northwest in search of his natural father. He takes a job guarding Limberlost, a valuable old-growth forest, from thieves and is torn between the ideals of two new friends. His mentor Tom sees the forest as timber that will build homes and provide jobs, while Angelica sees the forest as an irreplaceable sanctuary. Filmed on location in Vancouver, British Columbia. Adaptation of "Freckles" by Gene Stratton Porter. **120m/C VHS.** *GB CA* Christian Campbell, James Brolin, Sarah Chalke, Wendel Meldrum, Christopher Bolton; ***D:*** John Kent Harrison; ***W:*** John Kent Harrison. *PME, BTV, HMV*

City for Conquest ☙☙☙ **1940** Two lovers go their separate ways to pursue individual careers. He attempts to become a boxing champ, but is blinded in the ring and ends up selling newspapers. She takes a shot at a dancing career but hooks up with an unscrupulous partner. Will the ill-fated pair find happiness again? **101m/B VHS, Beta.** James Cagney, Ann Sheridan, Frank Craven, Donald Crisp, Arthur Kennedy, Frank McHugh, George Tobias, Anthony Quinn, Blanche Yurka, Elia Kazan, Bob Steele; ***D:*** Anatole Litvak; ***C:*** James Wong Howe; ***M:*** Max Steiner. *MGM, CCB*

City Girl ☙☙½ *Our Daily Bread* **1930** Friedrich Murnau, who directed the silent vampire classic "Nosferatu," was removed from the director's chair before "City Girl" was completed and it shows. But so do the marks of his inimitable camera direction. The story concerns a Minnesota grain grower who visits the Windy City and returns with a waitress as his wife. Frustratingly inconsistent, leading you to wonder what could have been had Murnau remained behind the camera (he died the following year). Silent. **90m/B VHS, Beta.** Charles Farrell, Mary Duncan; ***D:*** F.W. Murnau. *GPV, FCT*

City Hall ☙☙☙ **1995 (R)** Investigating the deaths of a heroic cop, a drug dealer, and six-year old boy in a shoot-out, idealistic deputy mayor Cusack uncovers a web of corruption and deceit in the Big Apple. Pacino excels as charismatic mayor John Pappas by showing the crafty string-puller behind the glossy image of the modern politico. Supporting cast is also strong, including Aiello as a Rodgers and Hammerstein-loving Brooklyn boss, and Fonda as the police union lawyer and standard issue love interest. Screenplay was conceived by Ken Lipper, who was once deputy mayor under Ed Koch, but the involvement of three other scripters causes confusion over what type of picture it's aiming to be. Cash-strapped New York rented its actual city hall out for filming at a price of $50,000. **111m/C VHS, LV.** Al Pacino, John Cusack, Bridget Fonda, Danny Aiello, David Paymer, Martin Landau, Anthony (Tony) Franciosa, Lindsay Duncan, Nestor Serrano, Mel Winkler, Richard Schiff; ***D:*** Harold Becker; ***W:*** Paul Schrader, Nicholas Pileggi, Bo Goldman, Ken Lipper; ***C:*** Michael Seresin; ***M:*** Jerry Goldsmith. *COL*

City Heat ☙☙½ **1984 (PG)** A hardnosed cop and a plucky private eye berate each other while opposing the mob in this overdone comedy. Both Eastwood and Reynolds spoof their screen personas, but the results are only slightly satisfactory. Good back-up, though, from Alexander and Kahn as the dames. Screenplay written by Blake Edwards under the pseudonym Sam O. Brown. **98m/C VHS, Beta, LV.** Clint Eastwood, Burt Reynolds, Jane Alexander, Irene Cara, Madeline Kahn, Richard Roundtree, Rip Torn, Tony Lo-Bianco, William Sanderson; ***D:*** Richard Benjamin; ***W:*** Blake Edwards; ***M:*** Lennie Niehaus. *WAR*

City in Fear ☙☙☙ **1980** Stellar cast lights up a made-for-television drama about a tired newspaper columnist (Janssen) who communicates directly with a murdering psychotic (Rourke), as publisher Vaughn applauds and hypes. Rourke's first role, Janssen's last, and Smithee is actually Jud Taylor. **135m/C VHS, Beta.** David Janssen, Robert Vaughn, Mickey Rourke, William Daniels, Perry King, Susan Sullivan, William Prince; ***D:*** Alan Smithee. *LIV, HHE*

City in Panic ☙ **1986** A detective and radio talk show host try to catch a psychotic mass murderer busy offing homosexuals throughout the city. Violent with no redeeming social qualities. **85m/C VHS, Beta.** Dave Adamson, Ed Chester, Leeann Westegard; ***D:*** Robert Bouvier. *TWE*

City Killer ☙ **1987** A lunatic tries to blackmail the girl he loves into going out on a few dates by committing huge destructive acts of inner-city terrorism (flowers won't do). Made for television. **120m/C VHS, Beta.** Heather Locklear, Gerald McRaney, Terence Knox, Peter Mark Richman, John Harkins; ***D:*** Robert Lewis. *PSM*

City Lights ☙☙☙☙ **1931** Masterpiece that was Chaplin's last silent film. The "Little Tramp" falls in love with a blind flower seller. A series of lucky accidents permits him to get the money she needs for a sight-restoring surgery. One of the most eloquent movies ever filmed, due to Chaplin's keen balance between comedy and tragedy. **86m/B VHS, Beta, LV.** Charlie Chaplin, Virginia Cherrill, Florence Lee, Hank Mann, Harry Myers, Henry Bergman, Jean Harlow; ***D:*** Charlie Chaplin. National Board of Review Awards '31: 10 Best Films of the Year. *FOX*

City Limits ☙ **1985 (PG-13)** In a post-apocalyptic city, gangs of young people on choppers clash. **85m/C VHS, Beta, LV.** John Stockwell, Kim Cattrall, Darrell Larson, Rae Dawn Chong, Robby Benson, James Earl Jones, Jennifer Balgobin; ***D:*** Aaron Lipstadt. *VES, LIV, HHE*

City of Blood ☙☙½ **1988 (R)** A South African doctor is embroiled in mystery with racial overtones when prostitutes are being killed with a spiked club. Packaged as a horror film, this movie actually deals with the questions of South African racial tensions in a sophisticated, ultimately tragic manner. **96m/C VHS, Beta.** *SA* Joe Stewardson, Ian Yule, Susan Coetzer; ***D:*** Darrell Roodt. *NO*

City of Hope ☙☙☙ **1991 (R)** The picture that "Bonfire of the Vanities" wanted to be, an eventful few days in the fictional metropolis of Hudson: an ugly racial incident threatens to snowball, the corrupt mayor pushes a shady real-estate deal, and a botched robbery has profound implications. Some of the subplots resolve too easily, but this cynical, crazy-quilt of urban life is worthy of comparison with "American Graffiti" and "Nashville" as pure Americana. **132m/C VHS, LV, 8mm.** Vincent Spano, Tony LoBianco, Joe Morton, Todd Graff, David Strathairn, Anthony John Denison, Barbara Williams, Angela Bassett, Gloria Foster, Lawrence Tierney, John Sayles, Maggie Renzi, Kevin Tighe, Chris Cooper, Jace Alexander, Frankie Faison, Tom Wright, Michael Mantell, Josh Mostel, Joe Grifasi, Louis Zorich, Gina Gershon, Rose Gregorio, Bill Raymond, Maeve Kinkead, Ray Aranha; ***D:*** John Sayles; ***W:*** John Sayles; ***C:*** Robert Richardson; ***M:*** Mason Daring. Independent Spirit Awards '92: Best Supporting Actor (Strathairn). *COL*

City of Joy ☙☙ **1992 (PG-13)** Disillusioned American heart surgeon Swayze flees to India after losing a patient. In Calcutta he is beaten by a street gang and loses his money and passport, but finds help from a farmer (Puri) who takes him to a nearby clinic in the City of Joy, one of Calcutta's poorest areas. Collins runs the clinic and recruits the reluctant doctor, who undergoes a life-changing transformation. The squalor of Calcutta is shown, but the city's portrayal as a magical place where problems miraculously disappear is unrealistic. Swayze lacks the emotional range for his part, but Collins and Puri are excellent in their roles. Adapted from the book by Dominique Lapierre. **134m/C VHS, LV.** *GB FR* Patrick Swayze, Pauline Collins, Om Puri, Shabana Azmi, Art Malik, Ayesha Dharker, Santu Chowdhury, Imran Badsah Khan, Shyamanand Jalan; ***Cameos:*** Sam Wanamaker; ***D:*** Roland Joffe; ***W:*** Mark Medoff; ***M:*** Ennio Morricone. *COL*

The City of Lost Children ☙☙ *La Cite des Enfants Perdus* **1995 (R)** Weird not-for-the-kiddies fairytale finds crazed inventor Krank (Emilfork) getting his evil one-eyed minions, the appropriately-named Cyclops', to kidnap local children so that he can steal their dreams (because Krank himself is incapable of dreaming). The latest victim is young Denree (Lucien), the adopted brother of sideshow strongman

One (Perlman), who single-mindedly pursues a way to get Denree back—aided by 9-year-old feral child Miette (Vittet) and a band of orphan thieves. Freaks galore with avant-garde designer Jean-Paul Gaultier in charge of costumes. French with subtitles or dubbed. **114m/C VHS, LV.** *FR* Ron Perlman, Daniel Emilfork, Joseph Lucien, Judith Vittet, Dominique Pinon, Jean Claude Dreyfus, Odile Mallet, Genevieve Brunet, Mireille Mosse; ***D:*** Jean-Marie Jeunet, Marc Caro; ***W:*** Jean-Marie Jeunet, Marc Caro, Gilles Adrien; ***C:*** Darius Khondji; ***M:*** Angelo Badalamenti; ***V:*** Jean-Louis Trintignant. Nominations: Cesar Awards '96: Best Art Direction/Set Decoration, Best Cinematography, Best Costume Design, Best Score; Independent Spirit Awards '96: Best Foreign Language Film. *COL*

City of Shadows 🦴🦴 **1986 (R)** Twins separated at birth are reunited by a criminal mind with evil intentions. Double trouble? **97m/C VHS, Beta.** John P. Ryan, Paul Coufos, Tony Rosato; ***D:*** David Mitchell; ***M:*** Tangerine Dream. *VTR, NWV*

City of the Walking Dead 🦴 *Nightmare City; Nightmare* **1983** Eco-misery as a community must contend with prowling, radiation-zapped zombies who enjoy chewing through human flesh. **92m/C VHS.** *IT SP* Mel Ferrer, Hugo Stiglitz, Laura Trotter, Francesco Rabal; ***D:*** Umberto Lenzi. *NO*

City of Women 🦴🦴 **1981 (R)** Visually stunning, but otherwise thin fantasy/drama about a man smothered with women. A journalist wanders through a feminist theme park replete with a roller rink and screening room. Some worthwhile adventures are mixed in with rather dull stretches. Not among the best from either Mastroianni, who is under utilized, or Fellini, who here seems incapable of separating good ideas from bad. Plenty of buxom babes, but otherwise undistinguished. In Italian with English subtitles. **140m/C VHS, Beta.** *IT* Marcello Mastroianni, Ettore Manni, Anna Prucnall, Bernice Stegers; ***D:*** Federico Fellini; ***W:*** Federico Fellini; ***C:*** Giuseppe Rotunno; ***M:*** Luis Bacalov. *NYF, FCT, INJ*

City on Fire *Woof!* **1978 (R)** An arsonist starts a fire that could engulf an entire city. Flaming bore. **101m/C VHS, Beta.** *CA* Barry Newman, Susan Clark, Shelley Winters, Leslie Nielsen, Henry Fonda, Ava Gardner; ***D:*** Alvin Rakoff. *SUE*

City Slickers 🦴🦴🦴 **1991 (PG-13)** Three men with mid-life crises leave New York City for a cattle-ranch vacation that turns into an arduous, character-building stint. Many funny moments supplied by leads Crystal, Stern, and Kirby, but Palance steals the film as a salty, wise cowpoke. Slater is fetching as the lone gal vacationer on the cattle drive. Box office winner notable for a realistic calf birthing scene, one of few in cinema history. From an idea by Crystal, who also produced. Palance stole the show from Oscar ceremonies host Crystal a second time when he accepted his award and suddenly started doing one-arm pushups, startling the audience into laughter. **114m/C VHS, Beta, LV, 8mm.** Billy Crystal, Daniel Stern, Bruno Kirby, Patricia Wettig, Helen Slater, Jack Palance, Noble Willingham, Tracey Walter, Josh Mostel, David Paymer, Bill Henderson, Jeffrey Tambor, Phill Lewis, Kyle Secor, Yeardley Smith, Jayne Meadows; ***D:*** Ron Underwood; ***W:*** Lowell Ganz, Babaloo Mandel; ***C:*** Dean Semler; ***M:*** Marc Shaiman. Academy Awards '91: Best Supporting Actor (Palance); Golden Globe Awards '92: Best Supporting Actor (Palance); MTV Movie Awards '92: Best Comedic Performance (Crystal); People's Choice Awards '92: Best Film—Musical/Comedy. *COL, NLC*

City Slickers 2: The Legend of Curly's Gold 🦴🦴½ **1994 (PG-13)** Mid-life crisis meets the wild west, part deux. Crystal and his fellow urban dudes discover a treasure map in the hat of departed trail boss Curly and decide to go a-huntin'. Palance is back as Curly's seafarin,' equally cantankerous, twin brother. Lovitz occupies the screen as Crystal's ne'er-do-well brother, replacing sidekick Bruno Kirby. A bit of a rehash, formulaic and occasionally straining for a punchline, it's still pretty darn funny, especially when the boys start to improvise. **116m/C VHS, LV.** Billy Crystal, Daniel Stern, Jon Lovitz, Jack Palance, Patricia Wettig, Pruitt Taylor Vince, Bill McKinney, Lindsay Crystal, Noble Willingham, David Paymer, Josh Mostel; ***D:*** Paul Weiland; ***W:*** Billy Crystal, Lowell Ganz, Babaloo Mandel; ***M:*** Marc Shaiman. *COL*

City That Never Sleeps 🦴🦴½ **1953** A Chicago cop must decide whether or not to run off with an entertainer, or continue his life with his family. Decisions, decisions. Moody but dated melodrama that's finely acted and indecisively directed, with good use of dim city lights. Nothing new here. **90m/B VHS.** Gig Young, Mala Powers, Edward Arnold, Paula Raymond, Chill Wills, Marie Windsor; ***D:*** John H. Auer. *REP*

City Without Men 🦴½ **1943** Melodramatic story about a boarding house near a prison where the women tenants await the release of their imprisoned men. Little plot, no suspense. **75m/B VHS.** Linda Darnell, Sara Allgood, Michael Duane, Edgar Buchanan, Leslie Brooks, Glenda Farrell, Margaret Hamilton, Sheldon Leonard; ***D:*** Sidney Salkow. *RXM*

The City's Edge 🦴½ **1983** A young man becomes involved with the mysterious residents of a boarding house on the edge of the ocean. **86m/C VHS, Beta.** *AU MGM*

Civil War Diary *Across Five Aprils* **1990** Too young to go to war, a young man struggles for the survival of his family amidst harsh winters, the devastation of the Civil War and his own personal nightmares. Winner of the International Heritage Award in 1990. Based on the Newberry Award winning young people's novel "Across Five Aprils." **82m/C VHS.** *RHI*

The Civil War, Episode 1: The Cause—1861 🦴🦴🦴🦴 **1990** The blowout PBS hit mini-series, five years in the making by author and filmmaker Ken Burns, is a staggering historical achievement. Episode 1 focuses on the causes of the Civil War from the schism created by Lincoln's election, John Brown's assault on Harper's Ferry, and the firing on Fort Sumpter. Also available as a set for $179.95. **99m/C VHS.** ***D:*** Ken Burns; ***W:*** Ken Burns. *PBS, SIG, CCP*

The Civil War, Episode 2: A Very Bloody Affair—1862 🦴🦴🦴🦴 **1990** Second in the enormously popular PBS series looks at the unexpectedly extreme costs in human life of the War Between the States. **69m/C VHS.** ***D:*** Ken Burns; ***W:*** Ken Burns. *PBS, SIG, CCP*

The Civil War, Episode 3: Forever Free—1862 🦴🦴🦴🦴 **1990** Third volume in the PBS Emmy-nominated mini-series covers Antietam, Robert E. Lee and Stonewall Jackson planning Confederate strategy, and Lincoln's decision to free the slaves. **76m/C VHS.** ***D:*** Ken Burns; ***W:*** Ken Burns. *PBS, SIG, CCP*

The Civil War, Episode 4: Simply Murder—1863 🦴🦴🦴🦴 **1990** Union forces meet disaster at Fredericksburg, and Gen. Lee wins a victory but loses Stonewall Jackson in the fourth episode of the Emmy-nominated PBS mini-series. **62m/C VHS.** ***D:*** Ken Burns; ***W:*** Ken Burns. *PBS, SIG, CCP*

The Civil War, Episode 5: The Universe of Battle—1863 🦴🦴🦴🦴 **1990** Gettysburg, the battleground which claimed 150,000 American lives, is examined in the 5th episode of the Emmy-nominated PBS mini-series. **95m/C VHS.** ***D:*** Ken Burns; ***W:*** Ken Burns. *PBS, SIG, CCP*

The Civil War, Episode 6: Valley of the Shadow of Death—1864 🦴🦴🦴🦴 **1990** Profiles of Grant and Lee are offered, plus Sherman's assault on Atlanta, in this volume from the Emmy-nominated PBS mini-series. **70m/C VHS.** ***D:*** Ken Burns; ***W:*** Ken Burns. *PBS, SIG, CCP*

The Civil War, Episode 7: Most Hallowed Ground—1864 🦴🦴🦴🦴 **1990** The nation re-elects Abraham Lincoln, and the North turns General Lee's mansion into Arlington National Cemetery in this episode of the Emmy-nominated PBS mini-series. **72m/C VHS.** ***D:*** Ken Burns; ***W:*** Ken Burns. *PBS, SIG, CCP*

The Civil War, Episode 8: War is All Hell—1865 🦴🦴🦴🦴 **1990** Sherman marches to the sea and Lee surrenders to Grant in this episode from the Emmy-nominated PBS mini-series. **69m/C VHS.** ***D:*** Ken Burns; ***W:*** Ken Burns. *PBS, SIG, CCP*

The Civil War, Episode 9: The Better Angels of Our Nature—1865 🦴🦴🦴🦴 **1990** In this final episode of the Emmy-nominated PBS mini-series, Lincoln's assasination is examined, and the central characters of the war are summarized. **68m/C VHS.** ***D:*** Ken Burns; ***W:*** Ken Burns. *PBS, SIG, CCP*

Civilization 🦴🦴🦴 **1916** A silent epic about the horrors and immorality of war as envisioned by the ground-breaking film pioneer Ince, who was later murdered. Famous scene involves Christ walking through body-ridden battlefields. **80m/B VHS, Beta.** Howard Hickman, Enid Markey, Lola May; ***D:*** Thomas Ince, Reginald Barker, Raymond B. West. *GPV, VYY, GVV*

Claire of the Moon 🦴🦴 **1992** Famous satirist Claire goes to a women writers retreat in the Pacific Northwest where she's assigned a room with Noel, a solemn sex therapist. Noel's recovering from a disasterous love affair while Claire is promiscuous and unwilling to commit. Inspite of their differences, the two women find themselves drawn together. Too many philosophical debates slow the story down but the gentle romance works well. **102m/C VHS.** Trisha Todd, Karen Trumbo, Faith McDevitt, Damon Craig; ***D:*** Nicole Conn; ***W:*** Nicole Conn; ***M:*** Michael Allen Harrison. *FXL, FCT, BTV*

Claire's Knee 🦴🦴🦴½ **1971** A grown man about to be married goes on a holiday and develops a fixation on a young girl's knee. Another of Rohmer's Moral Tales exploring sexual and erotic obsessions. Lots of talk, little else. You'll either find it fascinating or fail to watch more than 10 minutes. Most, however, consider it a classic. Sophisticated dialogue, lovely visions of summer on Lake Geneva. In French with English subtitles. **105m/C VHS, Beta, LV.** *FR* Jean-Claude Brialy, Aurora Cornu, Beatrice Romand; ***D:*** Eric Rohmer; ***W:*** Eric Rohmer; ***C:*** Nestor Almendros. National Board of Review Awards '71: 5 Best Foreign Films of the Year; National Society of Film Critics Awards '71: Best Film. *INJ, MED, FCT*

Clambake 🦴 **1967** Noxious Elvis vehicle about a rich man's son who wants success on his own terms, so he trades places with a water-skiing teacher. Inane, even in comparison to other Elvis ventures. ♫Clambake; The Girl I Never Loved; Hey, Hey, Hey; Confidence; Who Needs Money?; A House That Has Everything. **98m/C VHS, Beta.** Elvis Presley, Shelley Fabares, Bill Bixby, James Gregory, Gary Merrill, Will Hutchins, Harold Peary; ***D:*** Arthur Nadel. *MGM*

The Clan of the Cave Bear 🦴½ **1986 (R)** A scrawny cavegirl is taken in by Neanderthals after her own parents are killed. Hannah is lifeless as a primitive gamine, and the film is similarly DOA. Ponderous and only unintentionally funny. Based on the popular novel by Jean M. Auel. **100m/C VHS, Beta, LV.** Daryl Hannah, James Remar, Pamela Reed, John Doolittle, Thomas G. Waites; ***D:*** Michael Chapman; ***W:*** John Sayles; ***M:*** Alan Silvestri. Nominations: Academy Awards '86: Best Makeup. *FXV, FOX*

Clara's Heart 🦴 **1988 (PG-13)** A Jamaican maid enriches the lives of her insufferable, bourgeois employers and their particularly repellent son. A kinder, gentler waste of film and Goldberg; sentimental clap-trap which occasionally lapses into comedy. **108m/C VHS, Beta, LV.** Whoopi Goldberg, Michael Ontkean, Kathleen Quinlan, Neil Patrick Harris, Spalding Gray, Beverly Todd, Hattie Winston; ***D:*** Robert Mulligan; ***W:*** Mark Medoff; ***M:*** Dave Grusin. *WAR, FCT*

Clarence 🦴🦴½ **1991 (G)** Clarence, the benevolent angel from the classic "It's a Wonderful Life" is back, risking his wings for a beautiful young woman. Made for cable. **92m/C VHS.** Robert Carradine, Kate Trotter; ***D:*** Eric Till; ***W:*** Lorne Cameron. *REP*

Clarence Darrow 🦴🦴🦴 **1978** Riveting one-man stage performance shot for television and based on Darrow's writings, adapted from the play by Irving Stone. **81m/C VHS, Beta, LV.** Henry Fonda; ***D:*** John Rich. *ALL, KAR, IME*

Clarence, the Cross-eyed Lion 🦴🦴🦴 **1965** Follows the many adventures of a cross-eyed lion and his human compatriots. Great family viewing from the creator of "Flipper." **98m/C VHS.** Marshall Thompson, Betsy Drake, Richard Haydn, Cheryl Miller, Rockne Tarkington, Maurice Marsac; ***D:*** Andrew Marton; ***W:*** Alan Cailou. *MGM, FCT*

Clark & McCullough 🦴🦴½ **1933** The zany duo, a hit in burlesque and night clubs, transferred some of their crazy antics onto film. Their comedy shorts include "Fits in a Fiddle" (1933), "Love and Kisses" (1934), "Alibi Bye Bye" (1935), and a rehearsal of "Mademoiselle from New Rochelle" from "Strike Up the Band" (with George Gershwin on piano). **53m/B VHS, Beta.** Bobby Clark, Paul McCullough, George Gershwin, James Finlayson. *GVV, DVT, VYY*

Clash by Night 🦴🦴🦴½ **1952** A wayward woman marries a fisherman, then beds his best friend. Seamy storyline is exploited to the hilt by master filmmaker Lang. An utterly unflinching melodrama. Early Monroe shines in a supporting role too. Based on the Clifford Odets play. **105m/B VHS.** Barbara Stanwyck, Paul Douglas, Marilyn Monroe, Robert Ryan, J. Carrol Naish; ***D:*** Fritz Lang. *TTC*

Clash of the Ninja 🦴½ **1986** Evil Occidental ninja runs medical smuggling operation. Interpol ninja sets out to stop him. Wild ninja nonsense includes ninja with rotating head and exploding ninja. Dubbed poorly. **90m/C VHS, Beta.** *HK* Paul Torcha, Louis Roth, Eric Neff, Bernie Junker, Joe Redner, Klaus Mutter, Eddie Chan, Max Kwan, Tom Allen, Stanley Tong; ***D:*** Wallace Chan; ***W:*** Kurt Spielberg. *TWE*

Clash of the Titans *Woof!* **1981 (PG)** Mind-numbing fantasy derived from Greek legends about heroic Perseus, who slays the snake-haired Medusa and rescues a semi-clad maiden from the monstrous Kraken. Wooden Hamlin plays Perseus and fares better than more accomplished Olivier and Smith, who seem in need of enemas as they lurch about Mt. Olympus. Only Bloom seems truly godlike in a supporting role. Some good, some wretched special effects from pioneer Harryhausen. **118m/C VHS, Beta, LV.** *GB* Laurence Olivier, Maggie Smith, Claire Bloom, Ursula Andress, Burgess Meredith, Harry Hamlin, Sian Phillips, Judi Bowker; ***D:*** Desmond Davis; ***W:*** Beverley Cross; ***C:*** Ted Moore. *MGM, MLB*

Class 🦴🦴 **1983 (R)** A prep school student discovers that his mother is the lover whom his roommate has bragged about. Lowe is serviceable as the stunned son of sexy Bisset, who woos McCarthy, even in an elevator. Too ludicrous to be enjoyed, but you may watch just to see what happens next. **98m/C VHS, Beta, LV.** Jacqueline Bisset, Rob Lowe, Andrew McCarthy, Cliff Robertson, John Cusack, Stuart Margolin, Casey Siemaszko; ***D:*** Lewis John Carlino; ***M:*** Elmer Bernstein. *VES*

Class Act 🦴🦴½ **1991 (PG-13)** Rappers Kid 'N' Play team up once again in this role reversal comedy. A straight-laced brain and a partying, macho bully find their school records and identifications switched when they enroll in a new high school. This turns out to be good for the character of both young men, as the egghead learns to loosen up and the bully learns what it feels like to be respected for his ideas rather than a fierce reputation. Comedy is very uneven but the duo are energetic and likable. **98m/C VHS, LV.** Christopher Reid, Christopher Martin, Meshach Taylor, Karyn Parsons, Doug E. Doug, Rick Ducommun, Lamont Jackson, Rhea Perlman; ***D:*** Randall Miller; ***M:*** Vassal Benford. *WAR*

Class Action 🦴🦴🦴 **1991 (R)** 1960s versus 1990s ethics clash when a father and daughter, both lawyers, wind up on opposing sides of a litigation against an auto manufacturer. Hackman and Mastrantonio give intense, exciting performances, almost surmounting the melodramatic script. **110m/C VHS, Beta, LV.** Mary Elizabeth Mastrantonio, Gene Hackman, Joanna Merlin, Colin Friels, Laurence "Larry" Fishburne, Donald Moffat, Jan Rubes, Matt Clark, Fred Dalton Thompson, Jonathan Silverman, Dan Hicks; ***D:*** Michael Apted; ***W:*** Samantha Shad, Christopher Ames; ***M:*** James Horner. *FXV*

Class of Fear 🦴½ **1991 (R)** The new kid in school is having a particularly rough time. He's been framed for murdering a teacher and must prove his innocence before he winds up in prison. **105m/C VHS.** Julianne McNamara, Noah Blake. *MOV*

Class of '44 🦴½ **1973 (PG)** The sequel to "Summer of '42" finds insufferable boys becoming insufferable men at military school. Worse than its predecessor, and notable only in that it is Candy's film debut. **95m/C VHS, Beta.** Gary Grimes, Jerry Houser, Oliver Conant, Deborah Winters, William Atherton, Sam Bottoms, John Candy; ***D:*** Paul Bogart; ***M:*** David Shire. *WAR*

The Class of Miss MacMichael 🦴🦴 **1978 (R)** A dedicated instructor inherits and ultimately inspires a class of high school misfits and malcontents. Derivative venture is beneath considerable talents of Jackson. Based on a novel by Sandy Hutson. **95m/C VHS, Beta.** *GB* Glenda Jackson, Oliver Reed, Michael Murphy, Rosalind Cash; ***D:*** Silvio Narizzano; ***W:*** Judd Bernard. *FOX, MED*

Class of 1984 *Woof!* **1982 (R)** Teacher King must face a motley crew of teenagers in the classroom. Ring leader and student psychopath Van Patten leads his groupies on a reign of terror through the high school halls, stopping to gang rape King's wife. Teacher attempts revenge. Bloody and thoughtless update of "Blackboard Jungle." Early Fox appearance. Followed by "Class of 1999." **93m/C VHS, Beta, LV.** *CA* Perry King, Roddy McDowall, Timothy Van Patten, Michael J. Fox, Merrie Lynn Ross, Stefan Arngrim, Al Waxman; ***D:*** Mark L. Lester; ***W:*** Mark L. Lester, Tom Holland; ***M:*** Lalo Schifrin. *VES*

Class of 1999 🦴 **1990 (R)** Freewheeling sci-fi set in the near future where teen gangs terrorize seemingly the entire country. A high school principal determines to enforce law and order by installing human-like robots with rocket launchers for arms. Violent, crude entertainment. Class dismissed. Sequel to "Class of 1984" and available in an unrated version. **98m/C VHS, Beta.** Bradley Gregg, Traci Lind, Malcolm McDowell, Stacy Keach, Patrick Kilpatrick, Pam Grier, John P. Ryan, Darren E. Burrows, Joshua Miller; ***D:*** Mark L. Lester; ***W:*** C. Courtney Joyner. *VES, LIV*

Class of 1999 2: The Substitute 🦴½ **1993 (R)** High school in 1999 is filled with violent gangs who murder at random. Enter substitute teacher John Bolen, who has his own ideas of discipline—leading to an even higher body count. John just doesn't seem human and when a CIA agent starts investigating, school may never be the same. **90m/C VHS, LV.** Sasha Mitchell, Nick Cassavetes, Caitlin Dulany, Jack Knight, Gregory West, Rick Hill; ***D:*** Spiro Razatos; ***W:*** Mark Sevi. *VMK*

Class of Nuke 'Em High 🦴½ **1986 (R)** Team Troma once again experiments with the chemicals, with violent results. Jersey high school becomes a hotbed of mutants and maniacs after a nuclear spill occurs. Good teens Chrissy and Warren succumb, the school blows, life goes on. High camp, low budget, heavy gore. Followed by "Class of Nuke 'Em High Part 2." **84m/C VHS, Beta.** Janelle Brady, Gilbert Brenton, Robert Prichard; ***D:*** Richard W. Haines, Lloyd (Samuel Weil) Kaufman. *MED*

Class of Nuke 'Em High 2: Subhumanoid Meltdown 🦴 **1991 (R)** The Troma team brings us back into the world of the strange. In this adventure, the evil Nukamama Corporation holds secret experiments at their "college" and create sub-humanoids as slave labor, swelling unemployment and wrecking the economy. This does not fare too well with the rest of society, including our heroes Roger the reporter, Professor Holt, and the scantily clad sub-humanoid Victoria. **96m/C VHS, Beta, LV.** Lisa Gaye, Brick Bronsky, Leesa Rowland; ***D:*** Eric Louzil. *VTR, MED, FXV*

Class of Nuke 'Em High 3: The Good, the Bad and the Subhumanoid *Woof!* **1994 (R)** Revisit Tromie the nuclear rodent and the other disaster-prone denizens of Tromaville, USA. Admire the classic good twin vs. evil subhumanoid twin plot as they battle against each other, aided by chicks with guns and tin undergarments. Supposedly inspired by Shakespeare's Comedy of Errors. Tip: stick to the BBC production for your senior thesis. **95m/C VHS.** Brick Bronsky, Lisa Gaye; ***D:*** Eric Louzil; ***W:*** Lloyd (Samuel Weil) Kaufman. *TTV*

Class of '61 🦴🦴½ **1992** 1861, that is, as this class of West Point cadets prepares for the outbreak of war. Three close friends find themselves on opposing sides and with romantic entanglements, as well. Illustrated history, complete with voiceover passages from soldiers' letters, tend to slow the action, although the battles scenes are well done. Made for TV. **95m/C VHS.** Dan Futterman, Clive Owen, Joshua Lucas, Sophie Ward, Laura Linney, Andre Braugher, Len Cariou, Dana Ivey, Scott Burkholder, Niall O'Brien, Christien Anholt, Paul Guilfoyle, Beverly Todd, Ed Wiley, Sue-Ann Leeds; ***D:*** Gregory Hoblit; ***W:*** Jonas McCord; ***C:*** Janusz Kaminski. *MCA*

Class of '63 🦴🦴 **1973** An unfulfilled woman finally discovers the lover she lost nearly ten years ago at her college reunion. Nearly average made for television drama. **74m/C VHS, Beta.** James Brolin, Joan Hackett, Cliff Gorman, Ed Lauter; ***D:*** John Korty. *ORI*

Class Reunion *Woof!* **1987 (X)** Sexual highjinks are the order of the day at a 10-year high school reunion. Insipid softcore effort. It's cheaper just to cut out heads from yearbooks and paste 'em to skin mags torsos. Not to be confused with "National Lampoon's Class Reunion," equally bad but nonetheless distinct. **90m/C VHS, Beta, LV.** Marsha Jordan, Renee Bond, Terry Johnson. *MED*

Class Reunion Massacre *Woof!* **1977 (R)** Typically lame-brained horror about the mysterious deaths of former school jerks who've reconvened for the 10-year reunion. Worthless flick stars someone named Finkbinder. Contains graphic violence that is not for the squeamish. Also titled "The Redeemer." **87m/C VHS, Beta.** T.K. Finkbinder, Damien Knight, Nick Carter. *NO*

Claudia 🦴🦴 **1985 (R)** A wealthy woman who's part of London's high society falls for a lowly musician while trying to escape her dominating husband. Melodramatic meanderings not likely to move you. **88m/C VHS.** Deborah Raffin, Nicholas Ball; ***D:*** Anwar Kawadri. *TTC*

The Claw **1927** A young British profligate goes to Africa to prove his manhood to the woman who rejected him. Silent. **?m/B VHS, Beta, 8mm.** Claire Windsor, Norman Kerry; ***D:*** Sidney Olcott. *GVV*

Claws 🦴 **1977 (PG)** A woodsman, a game commissioner and an Indian band together to stop a grizzly bear who is killing residents of a small Alaskan town. **100m/C VHS, Beta.** Leon Ames, Jason Evers, Anthony Caruso, Glenn Sipes, Carla Layton, Myron Healey; ***D:*** Richard Bansbach, R.E. Pierson. *GEM*

Claws *Woof!* **1985** A lone farmboy is subjected to repeated attacks by feline mutants. Meow, baby. **84m/C VHS, Beta.** Jason Roberts, Brian O'Shaughnessy, Sandra Prinsloo. *NO*

The Clay Pigeon 🦴🦴½ **1949** Seaman comes to in the hospital after a long coma and discovers he's about to be court-martialed for treason and murder. Effective suspense as he goes after the man who incriminated him. **63m/B VHS, Beta.** Bill Williams, Barbara Hale, Richard Loo; ***D:*** Richard Fleischer. *NO*

Clayton County Line 🦴 **198?** Plucky buddies decide to end a cruel sheriff's reign of terror. Derivative and unredeeming. **80m/C VHS.** Kelly Bradish, Vince Csapos, Michael Heinz, Donald Kenney, Kathy Kenney, Gregg Schultz, Dan Quine, Steve Szilagyi, Dean Wilson; ***D:*** Dean Wilson. *NO*

Clean and Sober 𝔅𝔅𝔅½ **1988 (R)** A drug addict hides out at a rehabilitation clinic and actually undergoes treatment. A serious, subtle, and realistic look at the physical/emotional detoxification of an obnoxious, substance-abusing real estate broker; unpredictable and powerful without moralizing. Keaton is fine in unsympathetic lead, with both Baker and Freeman excelling in lesser roles. Not for all tastes, but it's certainly a worthwhile work. Caron, creator of TV's "Moonlighting," debuts here as director. **124m/C VHS, Beta, LV, 8mm.** Michael Keaton, Kathy Baker, Morgan Freeman, M. Emmet Walsh, Claudia Christian, Pat Quinn, Ben Piazza, Brian Benben, Luca Bercovici, Tate Donovan, Henry Judd Baker, Mary Catherine Martin; ***D:*** Glenn Gordon Caron; ***W:*** Tod Carroll; ***C:*** Jan Kiesser. National Society of Film Critics Awards '88: Best Actor (Keaton). *WAR, FCT*

Clean, Shaven 𝔅𝔅 **1993** Schizophrenic Peter Winter (Greene in a stunning performance) is searching bleak Miscou Island, off the New Brunswick coast, for the young daughter his mother put up for adoption after Peter was institutionalized and his wife died. Peter's being tailed by Detective McNally (Albert), who suspects him of a child's murder, and his tenuous hold on reality slowly disintegrates into torment and self-mutilation. Debut for director/writer Kerrigan. **80m/C VHS.** Peter Greene, Robert Albert, Jennifer MacDonald, Megan Owen, Molly Castelloe; ***D:*** Lodge Kerrigan; ***W:*** Lodge Kerrigan; ***C:*** Teodoro Maniaci; ***M:*** Hahn Rowe. Nominations: Independent Spirit Awards '95: Best First Feature. *ORI*

Clean Slate 𝔅𝔅 **1994 (PG-13)** Private-eye Maurice Pogue (Carvey) sustains injuries that cause a rare type of amnesia making every day seem like the first day of his life. As the only witness to a crime, he bumbles through mix-ups with the mob and his job as a bodyguard. Lightweight comedy fare is good for a few yuks but doesn't work as well as the similar "Groundhog Day." Barkley the sight-impaired dog steals nearly every scene he's in. **106m/C VHS, Beta, LV.** Dana Carvey, Valeria Golino, James Earl Jones, Kevin Pollak, Michael Murphy, Michael Gambon, Jayne Brook, Vyto Ruginis, Olivia D'Abo; ***D:*** Mick Jackson; ***W:*** Robert King; ***M:*** Alan Silvestri. *MGM*

Clear and Present Danger 𝔅𝔅½ **1994 (PG-13)** Ford returns for a second go at CIA agent Jack Ryan in the third installment of Tom Clancy's bestselling adventures. With the Cold War over, the U.S. government is the bad guy as Ryan discovers a link between a South American drug cartel and a Presidential advisor. Viewers will also finally get an answer to that nagging question at the end of "Patriot Games:" is it a boy or a girl? Archer's back as Ryan's annoying wife, and Birch and Jones also return. Keep alert for complex plot twists in lieu of tons of action, though there's enough to keep action fans happy. **141m/C VHS, Beta.** Harrison Ford, Anne Archer, James Earl Jones, Willem Dafoe, Thora Birch, Henry Czerny, Harris Yulin, Raymond Cruz, Joaquim de Almeida, Miguel Sandoval, Donald Moffat, Theodore (Ted) Raimi, Dean Jones; ***D:*** Phillip Noyce; ***W:*** Steven Zaillian, Donald Stewart, John Milius. Blockbuster Entertainment Awards '95: Action Actor, Theatrical (Ford); Blockbuster Entertainment Awards '96: Action Actor, Video (Ford); Nominations: Academy Awards '94: Best Sound; MTV Movie Awards '95: Best Action Sequence. *PAR*

Clearcut 𝔅𝔅½ **1992 (R)** Progressive lawyer finds his liberalism and his survival skills tested among modern Canadian Indians, when a militant native resorts to kidnapping the businessman who threatens their land. Well-acted, brutal drama that asks tough questions; it includes what purports to be the first authentic sweat-lodge ceremony ever filmed. **98m/C VHS.** *CA* Graham Greene, Ron Lea, Michael Hogan, Floyd "Red Crow" Westerman, Rebecca Jenkins; ***D:*** Richard Bugajski. *ACA*

Clearing the Range 𝔅½ **1931** Hoot wants the bad guy who knocked off his brother so he poses as a cringing coward in the hopes of uncovering the villain. Eilers is the love interest as well as his real-life wife. **64m/B VHS, Beta.** Hoot Gibson, Sally Eilers, Hooper Atchley; ***D:*** Otto Brower. *NOS, VCN, DVT*

Cleo from 5 to 7 𝔅𝔅𝔅½ *Cleo de 5 a 7* **1961** A singer strolls through Paris for 90 minutes, and reconsiders her life while awaiting the results of medical tests for cancer. Typical documentary-like effort from innovative filmmaker Varda, who constructed the film in real time. Look for a brief appearance of master director Jean-Luc Godard. In French with English subtitles. **90m/B VHS, Beta.** *FR* Corinne Marchand, Antoine Bourseillor, Dorothee Blanck, Michel Legrand, Jean-Claude Brialy, Jean-Luc Godard, Anna Karina, Eddie Constantine, Sami Frey; ***D:*** Agnes Varda; ***W:*** Agnes Varda. *FCT*

Cleo/Leo 𝔅 **1989 (R)** Crude and sexist jerk Leo gets chased into the East River by a gun-toting feminist. Reincarnated, Leo returns as Cleo and endures the same Neanderthal remarks and attitudes that "he" used to dish out. Tasteless, exploitive comedy only cynically explores the sex reversal theme. **94m/C VHS.** Jane Hamilton, Scott Thompson Baker, Kevin Thomas, Alan Naggar, Ginger Lynn Allen; ***D:*** Chuck Vincent. *VTR, MED*

Cleopatra 𝔅𝔅 **1934** Early Hollywood DeMille version of the Egyptian temptress's lust for Marc Antony after Julius Caesar's death. Intermittently interesting extravaganza. Colbert seems to be enjoying herself in the lead role in this hokey, overdone epic. Includes the original theatrical trailer on laser-track 2. Remade in 1963. **100m/B VHS, Beta, LV.** Claudette Colbert, Henry Wilcoxon, Warren William, Gertrude Michael, Joseph Schildkraut, Sir C. Aubrey Smith; ***D:*** Cecil B. DeMille; ***C:*** Victor Milner. Academy Awards '34: Best Cinematography; Nominations: Academy Awards '34: Best Film Editing, Best Picture, Best Sound. *MCA*

Cleopatra 𝔅 **1963** And we thought DeMille's version was extravagant. After the death of Julius Caesar, Cleopatra, Queen of Egypt, becomes infatuated with Mark Antony. Costly four-hour epic functions like a blimp-sized, multi-colored sleeping tablet. Historical characters are utterly dwarfed by the film's massive scope, and audiences are benumbed by a spectacle of crowd scenes and opulent, grotesque interiors. Taylor looks and often acts like a sex bomb ruler, while Harrison has some notion of Caesar's majesty. Burton, however, is hopelessly wooden. Hard to believe this came from director Mankiewicz. **246m/C VHS, Beta, LV.** Elizabeth Taylor, Richard Burton, Rex Harrison, Roddy McDowall, Martin Landau, Pamela Brown, Michael Hordern, Kenneth Haigh, Andrew Keir, Hume Cronyn, Carroll O'Connor; ***D:*** Joseph L. Mankiewicz; ***W:*** Joseph L. Mankiewicz; ***C:*** Leon Shamroy; ***M:*** Alex North. Academy Awards '63: Best Art Direction/Set Decoration (Color), Best Color Cinematography, Best Costume Design (Color), Best Visual Effects; National Board of Review Awards '63: Best Actor (Harrison); Nominations: Academy Awards '63: Best Actor (Harrison), Best Film Editing, Best Picture, Best Sound, Best Original Score. *FOX*

Cleopatra Jones 𝔅𝔅 **1973 (PG)** Lean and lethal government agent with considerable martial arts prowess takes on loathsome drug lords. Dobson is fetching as the lead performer in this fast-paced, violent flick. Followed by "Cleopatra Jones and the Casino of Gold." **89m/C VHS, Beta.** Tamara Dobson, Shelley Winters, Bernie Casey, Brenda Sykes; ***D:*** Jack Starrett. *WAR*

Cleopatra Jones & the Casino of Gold 𝔅𝔅 **1975 (R)** Dobson returns as the lethal, physically imposing federal agent to Hong Kong to take on a powerful druglord in this sequel to "Cleopatra Jones." Watch for sexy Stevens as the Dragon Lady. **96m/C VHS, Beta.** Tamara Dobson, Stella Stevens, Norman Fell; ***D:*** Chuck Bail. *WAR*

The Clergyman's Daughter 𝔅½ **1984** A clergyman's daughter calls upon detectives Tommy and Tuppence to investigate some murders at the family's country house. Made for British television and based on the Agatha Christie story. **60m/C VHS, Beta.** *GB* James Warwick, Francesca Annis. *TPV*

Clerks 𝔅𝔅𝔅 **1994 (R)** "What kind of convenience store do you run here?" Day in the life of a convenience store clerk is an often hilarious lesson in the profane from first time writer/director Smith (who has a cameo as Silent Bob). Twenty-two-year-old Dante Hicks (O'Halloran) is a disaffected New Jersey Quick Stop employee who spends most of his time bored and dealing with borderline crazies. The next-door video store is clerked by his best friend Randal (Anderson), who derives equal delight from tormenting his customers and debating absolutely anything (especially anything sexual). Nothing much actually happens but the very low-budget ($27,575) production has a decidedly scuzzy charm and a cult following. Based on the director's four years of clerking at the Quick Stop and shot on location. **91m/B VHS, LV.** Brian O'Halloran, Jeff Anderson, Marilyn Ghigliotti, Lisa Spoonhauer, Jason Mewes; ***Cameos:*** Kevin Smith; ***D:*** Kevin Smith; ***W:*** Kevin Smith; ***M:*** Scott Angley. Sundance Film Festival '94: Filmmakers Trophy; Nominations: Independent Spirit Awards '95: Best First Feature, Debut Performance (Anderson), First Screenplay. *MAX*

The Client 𝔅𝔅½ **1994 (PG-13)** Another legal thriller from the Grisham factory. Reggie Love (Sarandon) is a troubled attorney hired by 11-year-old Mark (Renfro), who witnessed the suicide of a Mafia attorney and now knows more than he should. Ambitious federal prosecutor Foltrigg's (Jones) willing to risk the boy's life in exchange for career advancement. Lacks the mega-big Hollywood names of "The Firm" and "The Pelican Brief" but gains solid acting in return with Renfro a find in his film debut. No frills, near-faithful adaptation by Schumacher basically travels down the path of least resistance. Filmed on location in Memphis. **121m/C VHS, LV, 8mm.** Susan Sarandon, Tommy Lee Jones, Brad Renfro, Mary-Louise Parker, Anthony LaPaglia, Bradley Whitford, Anthony Edwards, Ossie Davis, Walter Olkewicz, J.T. Walsh, Will Patton, Anthony Heald; ***D:*** Joel Schumacher; ***W:*** Robert Getchell, Akiva Goldsman. British Academy Awards '94: Best Actress (Sarandon); Nominations: Academy Awards '94: Best Actress (Sarandon); Screen Actors Guild Award '94: Best Actress (Sarandon). *WAR*

Cliffhanger 𝔅𝔅𝔅 **1993 (R)** Action-packed thriller. Expert climber Gabe Walker (Stallone) faces his greatest challenge when criminal mastermind Lithgow and his henchman appear on the scene. Turner plays fellow climber and love interest. Lithgow makes a particularly convincing, if not downright chilling, murderous thief. Filmed in the Italian Alps with a budget of $70 million-plus; boasts stunning cinematography and breathtaking footage of the Dolomite mountain range. Harlin's expert pacing and direction combine to produce maximum thrills and suspense. The hit Stallone's been waiting for, placing eighth on the list of top 1993 box office grossers. **113m/C VHS, Beta, LV, 8mm.** Sylvester Stallone, John Lithgow, Michael Rooker, Janine Turner, Rex Linn, Caroline Goodall, Leon, Paul Winfield, Ralph Waite, Craig Fairbrass, Michelle Joyner, Max Perlich; ***D:*** Renny Harlin; ***W:*** Sylvester Stallone, Michael France; ***C:*** Alex Thomson; ***M:*** Trevor Jones. Nominations: Academy Awards '93: Best Sound, Best Sound Effects Editing, Best Visual Effects; MTV Movie Awards '94: Best Action Sequence. *COL, BTV, FCT*

Clifford *Woof!* **1992 (PG)** Short plays a 10-year-old in an effort delayed by Orion's financial crisis. Creepy little Clifford's uncle Martin (Grodin) rues the day he volunteered to babysit his nephew to prove to his girlfriend (Steenburgen) how much he likes kids. Clifford terrorizes Grodin in surprisingly nasty ways when their plans for visiting Dinosaurworld fall through, although Grodin sees to well-deserved revenge. Not just bad in the conventional sense, but bad in a bizarre sort of alien fashion that raises questions about who was controlling the bodies of the producers. To create the effect of Short really being short, other actors stood on boxes and sets were built slightly larger. **90m/C VHS, LV.** Martin Short, Charles Grodin, Mary Steenburgen, Dabney Coleman, Sonia Jackson; ***D:*** Paul Flaherty; ***W:*** Bobby Von Hayes, Jay Dee Rock, Steven Kampmann, Will Aldis; ***M:*** Richard Gibbs. *ORI*

A Climate for Killing 𝔅𝔅½ **1991 (R)** Arizona police are baffled when a woman murdered 16 years earlier is again found dead. Case open? Hunks Bauer and Beck are earnest in leads, and Ross and Sara are foxy. Passable entertainment. **104m/C VHS, Beta, LV.** Steven Bauer, John Beck, Katharine Ross, Mia Sara, John Diehl, Phil Brock, Dedee Pfeiffer, Lu Leonard, Jack

Dodson, Eloy Casados; *D:* J.S. Cardone; *W:* J.S. Cardone; *M:* Robert Folk. *MED*

The Climb 🦴🦴½ **1987 (PG)** German mountain climbers attempt to conquer the Himalayan Nanga Parbat, the world's fifth highest peak. Sometimes compelling film based on 1953 expedition in which only one member succeeded in reaching the summit. **90m/C VHS, Beta, LV.** Bruce Greenwood, James Hurdle, Kenneth Welsh; *D:* Donald Shebib; *W:* Donald Shebib; *M:* Peter Jermyn. *IME*

Clipped Wings 🦴🦴½ **1953** The Bowery Boys are at their best as they inadvertantly join the army while visiting a friend and in the process of their usual bumblings, uncover a Nazi plot. **62m/B VHS.** Leo Gorcey, Huntz Hall, Bernard Gorcey, David Condon, Bennie Bartlett, June Vincent, Mary Treen, Philip Van Zandt, Elaine Riley, Jeanne Dean, Lyle Talbot; *D:* Edward L. Bernds. *WAR*

Cloak and Dagger 🦴🦴 **1946** An American physicist joins the secret service during WWII and infiltrates Nazi territory to release a kidnapped scientist who is being forced to build a nuclear bomb. Disappointing spy show with muted anti-nuclear tone. **106m/B VHS, LV.** Gary Cooper, Lilli Palmer, Robert Alda, James Flavin, Vladimir Sokoloff, J. Edward Bromberg, Marc Lawrence, Ludwig Stossel; *D:* Fritz Lang; *W:* Ring Lardner Jr., Albert Maltz; *M:* Max Steiner. *REP, FCT*

Cloak & Dagger 🦴🦴½ **1984 (PG)** A young boy, last seen befriending E.T., depends upon his imaginary super-friend to help him out when some real-life agents are after his video game. Coleman is particularly fun as both dad and fantasy hero in an interesting family adventure. **101m/C VHS, Beta, LV.** Dabney Coleman, Henry Thomas, Michael Murphy, John McIntire, Jeanette Nolan; *D:* Richard Franklin; *W:* Tom Holland. *MCA*

The Clock 🦴🦴🦴 *Under the Clock* **1945** Appealing romance about an office worker who meets and falls in love with a soldier on two-day leave in New York City. Charismatic Walker and likeable Garland make a fine screen couple, and Wynn is memorable as the drunk. The original theatrical trailer is included on the laserdisc format. **91m/B VHS, LV.** Judy Garland, Robert Walker, James Gleason, Marshall Thompson, Keenan Wynn; *D:* Vincente Minnelli; *M:* George Bassman. *BTV, MGM, FCT*

Clockers 🦴🦴🦴 **1995 (R)** Strike (Phifer), leader of a group of bottom-feeding drug dealers ("clockers"), engages in a power struggle with his boss (Lindo), his do-the-right-thing brother Victor (Washington), and his own conscience. He's also suspected of murder by relentless narcotics cop Rocco Klein (Keitel). Supported by an excellent cast, first-timer Phifer surprises with a fierce and powerful performance. Lindo, in particular, stands out as the paternally evil Rodney. Aggressively edited, with Turturro's performance mostly lost on the cutting room floor. Critically lauded cinematography is marred by the occasional boom shot. Poignant and compelling street drama is based on the Richard Price novel. Lee took over after Scorsese and De Niro dropped out to make "Casino." **128m/C VHS, LV.** Mekhi Phifer, Harvey Keitel, Delroy Lindo, Isaiah Washington, John Turturro, Keith David; *D:* Spike Lee; *W:* Richard Price, Spike Lee; *C:* Malik Hassan Sayeed; *M:* Terence Blanchard. *MCA*

The Clockmaker 🦴🦴🦴½ **1976** Contemplative drama about a clockmaker whose life is shattered when his son is arrested as a political assassin. Tavernier regular Noiret excels in the lead. In French with English subtitles. **105m/C VHS, Beta, LV.** *FR* Philippe Noiret, Jean Rochefort, Jacques Denis, William Sabatier, Christine Pascal; *D:* Bertrand Tavernier. National Board of Review Awards '76: 5 Best Foreign Films of the Year. *FCT, LUM*

Clockwise 🦴🦴½ **1986 (PG)** Monty Python regular Cleese is a teacher preoccupied by punctuality. His neurosis proves his undoing when he falls victim to misadventure while traveling to deliver a speech. Cleese is acceptable, dialogue and story is less so, though sprinkled with a fair amount of humor. **96m/C VHS, LV.** *GB* John Cleese, Penelope Wilton, Alison Steadman, Stephen Moore, Sharon Maiden; *D:* Christopher Morahan; *W:* Michael Frayn; *M:* George Fenton. *REP*

A Clockwork Orange 🦴🦴🦴🦴 **1971 (R)** In the Britain of the near future, a sadistic punk leads a gang on nightly rape and murder sprees, then is captured and becomes the subject of a grim experiment to eradicate his violent tendencies in this extraordinary adaptation of Anthony Burgess's controversial novel. The film is an exhilarating experience, with an outstanding performance by McDowell as the funny, fierce psychopath. Many memorable, disturbing sequences, including a rape conducted while assailant McDowell belts "Singing in the Rain." Truly outstanding, provocative work from master filmmaker Kubrick. **137m/C VHS, Beta, LV.** *GB* Malcolm McDowell, Patrick Magee, Adrienne Corri, Michael Bates, Warren Clarke, Aubrey Morris, James Marcus, Steven Berkoff, David Prowse; *D:* Stanley Kubrick; *W:* Stanley Kubrick. New York Film Critics Awards '71: Best Director (Kubrick), Best Film; Nominations: Academy Awards '71: Best Adapted Screenplay, Best Director (Kubrick), Best Film Editing, Best Picture. *WAR, FCT, FUS*

Clodhopper 🦴🦴 **1917** A farmboy decides to head out for New York where he achieves fame on Broadway for his dance number, the "Clophooper Glide." He stays true to his hometown girl, however, and returns to save his father's farm from financial ruin. **47m/B VHS, Beta.** Charles Ray, Margery Wilson; *D:* Victor Schertzinger. *GPV, CCB, DVT*

The Clones 🦴🦴 **1973 (PG)** A doctor discovers a government experiment engineered to murder him with a perfect clone. **90m/C VHS, Beta.** Michael Greene, Gregory Sierra; *D:* Paul Hunt, Lamar Card. *LIV, HHE*

Clones of Bruce Lee 🦴🦴 **1980 (R)** It's a martial arts free-for-all as bold masters from throughout the world duel for supremacy in the realm of self defense. If you like martial arts movies, you'll probably like this one. If you don't know if you like martial arts movies, find out with one of the actual Bruce Lee's flicks. **87m/C VHS, Beta.** Dragon Lee, Bruce Le, Bruce Lai, Bruce Thai; *D:* Joseph Kong. *MED*

The Clonus Horror 🦴½ *Parts: The Clonus Horror* **1979** A scientist discovers a government plot to clone the population by freezing bodies alive and using their parts in surgery. **90m/C VHS, Beta.** Tim Donnelly, Keenan Wynn, Peter Graves, Dick Sargent, Paulette Breen; *D:* Robert S. Fiveson. *LIV*

Close Encounters of the Third Kind 🦴🦴🦴🦴 **1977 (PG)** Middle-American strangers become involved in the attempts of benevolent aliens to contact earthlings. Despite the sometimes mundane nature of the characters, this Spielberg epic is a stirring achievement. Studded with classic sequences; the ending is an exhilarating experience of special effects and peace-on-earth feelings. Dreyfuss and Dillon excel as friends who are at once bewildered and obsessed by the alien presence, and French filmmaker Truffaut is also strong as the stern, ultimately kind scientist. Laserdisc includes formerly edited scenes, live interviews with Spielberg, special effects man Douglas Trumbull, and composer Williams, publicity materials, and over 1,000 production photos. **152m/C VHS, Beta, LV.** Richard Dreyfuss, Teri Garr, Melinda Dillon, Francois Truffaut, Bob Balaban, Cary Guffey, J. Patrick McNamara; *D:* Steven Spielberg; *W:* Steven Spielberg; *C:* Vilmos Zsigmond; *M:* John Williams. Academy Awards '77: Best Cinematography, Best Sound Effects Editing; National Board of Review Awards '77: 10 Best Films of the Year; Nominations: Academy Awards '77: Best Art Direction/Set Decoration, Best Director (Spielberg), Best Film Editing, Best Sound, Best Supporting Actress (Dillon), Best Original Score. *COL, CRC, FUS*

Close My Eyes 🦴🦴 **1991 (R)** A hot, steamy summer arouses vibrant passions in a brother and sister, and neither marriage nor blood relation can halt the inevitable. **105m/C VHS.** Alan Rickman, Clive Owen, Saskia Reeves; *D:* Stephen Poliakoff. *ACA*

Close to Eden 🦴🦴 *Urga* **1990 (PG)** A peasant couple living in inner Mongolia with their three children are prevented by strict Chinese law from having a fourth. The husband sets out from his village to obtain birth control from the nearby town. While on his way, the farmer (Bayaertu) saves a Russian truck driver (Gostukhin) after he drives into a lake. Sergei is introduced to another way of life when he's taken home by his rescuer to meet the family and becomes accustomed to the tranquility of farm life in the rural Mongolian steppe. Essentially a story about the changes modern civilization can bring to a rural way of life. Filmed in Mongolia. In Russian with English subtitles. **109m/C VHS, Beta.** *RU* Baoyinhexige, Badema, Nikita Mikhalkov; *D:* Nikita Mikhalkov; *W:* Rustam Ibragimbekov; *M:* Eduard Artemyev. Venice Film Festival '91: Best Film; Nominations: Academy Awards '92: Best Foreign Language Film. *PAR, FCT*

Close to Home 🦴🦴 **1986** A runaway fleeing a home life of abuse and neglect befriends a TV journalist doing a story on similar girls. She turns to him for support after she is arrested and returned home. Merely mediocre. **93m/C VHS, Beta.** *CA* Daniel Allman, Jillian Fargey, Anne Petrie; *D:* Rick Beairsto. *TWE*

Closely Watched Trains 🦴🦴🦴½ **1966** A novice train dispatcher attempts to gain sexual experience in German-occupied Czechoslovakia during WWII. Many funny scenes in this film regarded by some as a classic. Based upon the Czech novel by Bohumil Hrabal. In Czech with English subtitles. **89m/B VHS, Beta, LV.** *CZ* Vaclav Neckar, Jitka Bendova, Vladimir Valenta, Josef Somr; *D:* Jiri Menzel; *W:* Jiri Menzel. Academy Awards '67: Best Foreign Language Film. *FXL, INJ, COL*

The Closer 🦴🦴½ **1991 (R)** Aiello is "The Closer," a high-powered salesman whose world is falling apart. Somewhere between the money and the power, he's lost touch with his family and the truly important things in life. Is it too late to get them back? **87m/C VHS, LV.** Danny Aiello, Michael Pare, Joe Cortese, Justine Bateman, Diane Baker, James Karen, Rick Aiello, Michael Lerner; *D:* Dimitri Logothetis; *W:* Robert Keats, Louis LaRusso II; *M:* Al Kasha. *ACA*

Closet Cases of the Nerd Kind **1980** In this comical takeoff on "Close Encounters of the Third Kind," a zany assortment of mortals meet up with extraterrestrials. All of the memorable scenes of the Spielberg film are recreated and spoofed. **12m/C VHS, Beta.** *PYR*

Closet Land 🦴½ **1990 (R)** Severe, stylized political allegory aims high but fails to convincingly distill totalitarian repression into just two characters—a government inquisitor and his captive, a woman subjected to hideous mental and physical torture. Child-molesting emerges as an ill-advised subtheme. A better video on the same subject: "Interrogation," from Poland. **95m/C VHS, Beta, LV.** Madeleine Stowe, Alan Rickman; *D:* Radha Bharadwaj; *W:* Radha Bharadwaj; *M:* Richard Einhorn. *FXV, VTR*

Cloud Dancer 🦴🦴 **1980 (PG)** A self-absorbed acrobat uses and abuses those around him, including his girlfriend. Carradine and O'Neill fail to distinguish themselves in this mediocre film. **107m/C VHS, Beta.** David Carradine, Jennifer O'Neill, Joseph Bottoms, Colleen Camp; *D:* Barry Brown; *W:* William Goodhart. *PSM*

Cloud Waltzing 🦴🦴½ **1987** The screen version of a Harlequin romance about a journalist who arrives in France to interview a vintner and finds romance and danger. Melodrama bolstered by the presence of photogenic Beller. **103m/C VHS, Beta.** Kathleen Beller, Francois-Eric Gendron, Paul Maxwell, Therese Liotard, Claude Gensac, David Baxt; *D:* Gordon Flemyng. *PAR*

The Clouded Yellow 🦴🦴🦴 **1951** Young, lovely, and a little unstable, Sophie Malraux (Simmons) is accused of murdering the handyman who worked for her guardians (Jones and Dresdel). Ex-British Secret Service agent David Somers (Howard), who's in love with Sophie, helps her escape from jail and the two head for Liverpool and a ship to Mexico. But the police (hoping to find the real killer) are hot on their trail. Romantic suspense with good lead pairing. **95m/B VHS.** *GB* Jean Simmons, Trevor Howard, Sonia Dresdel, Barry Jones, Maxwell Reed, Kenneth More, Andre Morell, Geoffrey Keen; *D:* Ralph Thomas; *W:* Eric Ambler; *C:* Geoffrey Unsworth. *HMV*

Clouds Over Europe ☆☆☆ *Q Planes* **1939** A test pilot and a man from Scotland Yard team up to find out why new bomber planes are disappearing. **82m/B VHS, Beta, LV.** Laurence Olivier, Valerie Hobson, Ralph Richardson; ***D:*** Tim Whelan; ***C:*** Harry Stradling. *SUE*

Clown ☆☆½ **1953** A broken-down funny man with a worshipful son obtains one last career opportunity. This "Champ"-derived tearjerker features credible playing from Skelton and Considine as father and son, respectively. **91m/B VHS, Beta.** Red Skelton, Jane Greer, Tim Considine, Steve Forrest; ***D:*** Robert Z. Leonard; ***C:*** Paul Vogel. *MGM*

Clown House ☆ **1988 (R)** Young brothers are stalked in their home by three demonic clowns. **95m/C VHS, Beta, LV.** Nathan Forrest Winters, Brian McHugh, Sam Rockwell, Viletta Skillman, Timothy Enos, Tree; ***D:*** Victor Salva. *COL*

Clown Murders ☆½ **1983** Posh Halloween party is undone when a cruel group fakes a kidnapping to ruin a too-prosperous pal's business deal. Awkward thriller boasts little suspense. Candy plays it straight, mostly, in this one. **94m/C VHS, Beta.** John Candy, Al Waxman, Susan Keller, Lawrence Dane; ***D:*** Martyn Burke. *TWE*

Clowning Around ☆☆½ **1992** Simon, who has lived in foster homes all his life, dreams of becoming a famous circus clown. When he's sent to a new home, his new foster parents think his idea is silly, so he runs away and joins the circus. There he meets Anatole, a European clown has-been who can no longer perform because of injuries. Simon believes Anatole can teach him about clowning, so he follows Anatole to Paris to help make his dream come true. Part of the "Wonderworks" series. **165m/C VHS.** *AU* Clayton Williamson, Jean-Michel Dagory, Ernie Dingo. *PME, HMV, BTV*

Clowning Around 2 ☆☆½ **1993** The continuing story of Sim, whose dream is to become a world-famous clown. Now a member of the Winter Circus in Paris, he is still training with his mentor Anatole. But Sim is dissatisfied and when he befriends Eve, another young clown, he learns an experimental style of clowning which gets them both fired. He first follows Eve to her home in Montreal but then returns to his own home in Australia where he has been left the co-owner of a less-than-successful circus by a former employer. Filmed on location in Paris, France and Perth, Australia. **120m/C VHS.** *AU* Clayton Williamson, Jean-Michel Dagory, Ernie Dingo, Frederique Fouche; ***D:*** George Whaley. *PME, BTV*

The Clowns ☆☆☆½ **1971 (G)** An idiosyncratic documentary about circus clowns. Director Fellini has fashioned an homage that is sincere, entertaining, and personal. Contains some truly poignant sequences. Made for Italian television with English subtitles. **90m/C VHS, Beta.** *IT* ***D:*** Federico Fellini; ***W:*** Federico Fellini; ***M:*** Nino Rota. National Board of Review Awards '71: 5 Best Foreign Films of the Year. *HTV, NOS, MRV*

The Club ☆☆☆ *Players* **1981 (PG)** A soccer coach tries to train and motivate a mediocre squad into one worth playing for—and perhaps even winning—the league cup. Conventional sports story is significantly improved by Thompson's rendering of the coach. **99m/C VHS, Beta.** *AU* Jack Thompson, Graham Kennedy, John Wood, John Howard, Alan Cassell; ***D:*** Bruce Beresford; ***W:*** David Williamson. *ACA*

The Club ☆ **1994 (R)** Typical teens-in-peril flick finds the high school prom held in a mysterious old castle with ghouls out to get the unfortunate seniors. Visuals are decent but frights are tepid. **88m/C VHS, LV.** Kim Coates, Joel Wyner, Andrea Roth, Rino Romano, Zack Ward, Kelli Taylor, Matthew Ferguson; ***D:*** Benton Spencer; ***W:*** Robert Cooper; ***M:*** Paul Zaza. *IMP*

Club Extinction ☆☆½ *Docteur M* **1989 (R)** A near-future thriller in which Berlin is plagued by a wave of suicides. An investigator suspects a spa representative and a media tycoon of being involved. Features a fine international cast, but the film is a lesser venture from prolific master Chabrol. **105m/C VHS, Beta.** *GE* Alan Bates, Andrew McCarthy, Jennifer Beals, Jan Niklas, Hanns Zischler, Benoit Regent, Peter Fitz, Wolfgang Preiss, Isolde Barth; ***D:*** Claude Chabrol. *PSM, FCT*

Club Fed ☆½ **1990 (PG-13)** A rigid prison warden's plot to impose greater discipline is undone by inmate highjinks. Crude laughs and one-dimensional play from a cast of recognizable names and faces. **93m/C VHS, Beta.** Judy Landers, Sherman Hemsley, Karen Black, Burt Young, Rick Schmidt, Allen (Goorwitz) Garfield, Joseph Campanella, Lyle Alzado, Mary Woronov, Debbie Lee Carrington; ***D:*** Nathaniel Christian. *PSM*

Club Havana ☆½ **1946** A benevolent nightclub owner tries to save one of his singers from the depths of despair by reuniting her with her boyfriend. Minor musical with minor musical numbers. ♫Besame Mucho; Tico Tico. **62m/B VHS, Beta.** Tom Neal, Margaret Lindsay, Don Douglas, Isabelita, Dorothy Morris, Ernest Truex; ***D:*** Edgar G. Ulmer. *SNC*

Club Life ☆ **1986 (R)** A hardened biker finds sex, drugs, and violence on the Hollywood streets. What did he expect? Peace, love, and understanding? **93m/C VHS, Beta.** Tony Curtis, Dee Wallace Stone, Tom Parsekian, Michael Parks, Jamie Barrett; ***D:*** Norman Thaddeus Vane. *PSM*

Club Med ☆☆ **1983 (PG)** An insecure comedian and his goofy friend try to make the most of a ski vacation. Perhaps your only chance to see Thicke, Killy, and Coolidge together. **60m/C VHS, Beta.** Alan Thicke, Jim Carrey, Jean-Claude Killy, Rita Coolidge, Ronnie Hawkins; ***D:*** David Mitchell, Bob Giraldi; ***M:*** Peter Bernstein. *AHV*

Club Paradise ☆☆½ **1986 (PG-13)** A Chicago fireman flees the big city for a faltering tropical resort and tries to develop some night life. Somewhat disappointing with Williams largely playing the straight man. Most laughs provided by Martin, particularly when she is assaulted by a shower, and Moranis, who gets lost while windsurfing. **96m/C VHS, Beta, LV.** Robin Williams, Peter O'Toole, Rick Moranis, Andrea Martin, Jimmy Cliff, Brian Doyle-Murray, Twiggy, Eugene Levy, Adolph Caesar, Joanna Cassidy, Mary Gross, Carey Lowell, Robin Duke, Simon Jones; ***D:*** Harold Ramis; ***W:*** Harold Ramis, Brian Doyle-Murray; ***M:*** David Mansfield, Van Dyke Parks. *WAR*

Clue ☆☆½ **1985 (PG)** The popular boardgame's characters must unravel a night of murder at a spooky Victorian mansion. The entire cast seems to be subsisting on sugar, with wild eyes and frantic movements the order of the day. Butler Curry best survives the uneven script and direction. Warren is appealing too. The theatrical version played with three alternative endings, and the video version shows all three successively. **96m/C VHS, Beta, LV.** Lesley Ann Warren, Tim Curry, Martin Mull, Madeline Kahn, Michael McKean, Christopher Lloyd, Eileen Brennan, Howard Hesseman, Lee Ving, Jane Wiedlin, Colleen Camp, Bill Henderson; ***D:*** Jonathan Lynn; ***W:*** Jonathan Lynn, John Landis; ***M:*** John Morris. *PAR*

Clueless ☆☆☆ *I Was a Teenage Teenager; No Worries* **1995 (PG-13)** Watch out "Beverly Hills 90210," here comes Cher. No, not the singer Cher, but ultra-filthy-rich brat Cher, who's out to make over her classmates and teachers, specifically flannel-shirted transfer student Tai (Murphy). Aerosmith vamp Silverstone stars as the teenage manipulator who knows all too well how to spend her trust fund. The only person who can match her wits is disapproving stepbrother Josh (Rudd). (Ah, love.) Loosely based on Jane Austen's "Emma," Heckerling, of "Fast Times at Ridgemont High" fame, knows this territory and directs a bright, surprisingly satirical romp. **113m/C VHS.** Alicia Silverstone, Stacey Dash, Paul Rudd, Brittany Murphy, Donald A. Faison, Julie Brown, Jeremy Sisto, Dan Hedaya, Wallace Shawn, Breckin Meyer, Elisa Donovan, Aida Linares; ***D:*** Amy Heckerling; ***W:*** Amy Heckerling; ***C:*** Bill Pope; ***M:*** David Kitay. MTV Movie Awards '96: Best Female Performance (Silverstone), Most Desirable Female (Silverstone); Blockbuster Entertainment Awards '96: Female Newcomer, Theatrical (Silverstone); Nominations: MTV Movie Awards '96: Best Film, Best Comedic Performance (Silverstone). *PAR*

The Clutching Hand ☆☆ **1936** The Clutching Hand seeks a formula that will turn metal into gold and detective Craig Kennedy is out to prevent him from doing so. A serial in 15 chapters on three cassettes. **268m/B VHS, Beta.** Jack Mulhall, Rex Lease. *SNC, NOS, VDM*

Coach ☆½ **1978 (PG)** Sexy woman is unintentionally hired to coach a high school basketball team and mold rookies into lusty young champions. Low-grade roundball fever. **100m/C VHS, Beta.** Cathy Lee Crosby, Michael Biehn, Keenan Wynn, Sidney Wicks; ***D:*** Bud Townsend. *MED*

Coal Miner's Daughter ☆☆☆ **1980 (PG)** A strong bio of country singer Loretta Lynn, who rose from Appalachian poverty to Nashville riches. Spacek is perfect in the lead, and she even provides acceptable rendering of Lynn's tunes. Band drummer Helm shines as Lynn's father, and Jones is strong as Lynn's downhome husband. Uneven melodrama toward the end, but the film is still a good one. ♫Coal Miner's Daughter; Sweet Dreams of You; I'm a Honky-Tonk Girl; You're Lookin' at Country; One's On the Way; You Ain't Woman Enough to Take My Man; Back in My Baby's Arms. **125m/C VHS, Beta, LV.** Sissy Spacek, Tommy Lee Jones, Levon Helm, Beverly D'Angelo; ***D:*** Michael Apted; ***C:*** Ralf Bode. Academy Awards '80: Best Actress (Spacek); Golden Globe Awards '81: Best Actress—Musical/Comedy (Spacek), Best Film—Musical/Comedy; Los Angeles Film Critics Association Awards '80: Best Actress (Spacek); National Board of Review Awards '80: 10 Best Films of the Year, Best Actress (Spacek); National Society of Film Critics Awards '80: Best Actress (Spacek); Nominations: Academy Awards '80: Best Adapted Screenplay, Best Art Direction/Set Decoration, Best Cinematography, Best Film Editing, Best Picture. *MCA, BTV*

The Coast Patrol ☆☆½ **1925** B. Reeves Eason, responsible for the chariot scene in the silent "Ben Hur" and the action scenes in "The Charge of the Light Brigade," directed Fay in one of her earliest parts, eight years before the role that prompted her to say "I didn't realize that King Kong and I were going to be together for the rest of our lives, and longer... " Much Eason-style high action when smugglers meet the coast patrol. **63m/B VHS, Beta.** Kenneth McDonald, Claire De Lorez, Fay Wray; ***D:*** Bud Barsky. *NOS, GPV, FCT*

Coast to Coast ☆☆ **1980 (PG)** A wacky woman escapes from a mental institution and teams with a pugnacious trucker for a cross-country spree. Ostensibly freewheeling comedy is only occasionally worthwhile despite appropriate playing from leads Cannon and Blake, who deserve better. **95m/C VHS, Beta, LV.** Dyan Cannon, Robert (Bobby) Blake, Quinn Redeker, Michael Lerner, Maxine Stuart, William Lucking; ***D:*** Joseph Sargent; ***M:*** Charles Bernstein. *PAR*

Cobb ☆☆☆ **1994 (R)** Biography of Ty Cobb (Jones), the universally acknowledged "most hated man in baseball" who, near the end of his life, realizes he doesn't want to be remembered in that way. So he hires sportswriter Al Stump (Wuhl) to ghostwrite (read: sugarcoat) his life story. As seen through Stump's eyes, Cobb is an unrelenting, petty, bigoted, hateful, paranoid, drunken, and yet compelling man. They form an uneasy bond as Stump duly records the fiction Cobb is feeding him, secretly deciding to write the truth after the legend's death. Jones is at his scene-chewing, antagonistic best, while Wuhl seems both overwhelmed and overshadowed as the embattled Stump. Shelton has something to say about American hero worship and a celebrity's desire for posterity, but with the focus intent on portraying Cobb's meanness, it's hard to say what. Surprisingly little baseball action for a baseball bio. Based on Stump's "Cobb: A Biography." **128m/C VHS, LV.** Tommy Lee Jones, Robert Wuhl, Lolita Davidovich; ***D:*** Ron Shelton; ***W:*** Ron Shelton. *WAR*

Cobra ☆ **1925** To pay off the debts incurred by his profligate playboyance, Valentino takes a job with an antique dealer, falls for the dealer's secretary and arranges an assignation with the dealer's wife, who is inconveniently killed at the designated rendezvous. Complications abound as Valentino finds himself

Sheik out of luck. Lesser Valentino effort was released a year before the famous heartthrob's untimely death and enjoyed a rather acrid critical reception. Which isn't to say the public didn't flock to see the Italian stallion flare his nostrils. **70m/B VHS, Beta.** Rudolph Valentino, Nita Naldi, Casson Ferguson, Gertrude Olmsted; ***D:*** Joseph Henabery. *VYY, FCT, GPV*

The Cobra 🦴 *Il Cobra; El Cobra* **1968** A tight-lipped U.S. agent ogles a voluptuous siren when not fighting opium smugglers from the Middle East. A must for all admirers of Ekberg. **93m/C VHS.** Dana Andrews, Anita Ekberg; ***D:*** Mario Sequi. *NO*

Cobra 🦴🦴½ *le Sant de l'Ange* **1971** A hired killer destroys most of a mob family and becomes the target of revenge for the lone survivor. Moody thriller boasts an international cast. **93m/C VHS, Beta.** *FR IT* Sterling Hayden, Senta Berger, Jean Yanne; ***D:*** Yves Boisset. *UNI*

Cobra 🦴 **1986 (R)** A cold-blooded cop protects a model from a gang of deranged killers. Low-brow, manipulative action fare void of feeling. Truly exploitive, with little expression from the leads. Highlight is the extended chase sequence. Based on the Paula Gosling novel "Fair Game," which was remade under the book's title (and in a more faithful adaptation) in 1995. **87m/C VHS, Beta, LV.** Sylvester Stallone, Reni Santoni, Brigitte Nielsen, Andrew (Andy) Robinson; ***D:*** George P. Cosmatos; ***W:*** Sylvester Stallone. *WAR*

Cobra Against Ninja 🦴 **1987** Once again, two martial arts experts try to kill each other. Can't be many of these fellas left. **88m/C VHS.** Jimmy Bosco, Paul Branney, Gary Carter, Alan Friss, Alfred Pears; ***D:*** Joseph Lai. *IMP*

The Cobra Strikes 🦴½ **1948** Nosey thief gets more than he bargained for when he works his way through an inventor's studio. Low-budget and unexceptional. **62m/B VHS.** Sheila Ryan, Richard Fraser, Leslie Brooks, Herbert Heyes; ***D:*** Charles F. Reisner. *NOS, MOV, RXM*

Cobra Woman 🦴🦴½ **1944** Technicolor adventure fantasy about the jungle queen (Montez) of a cobra-worshipping cult and her evil twin sister who wants the throne for herself. **70m/C VHS.** Maria Montez, Jon Hall, Sabu, Edgar Barrier, Lois Collier, Lon Chaney Jr.; ***D:*** Robert Siodmak; ***W:*** Richard Brooks; ***C:*** William Howard Greene. *NO*

The Cobweb 🦴🦴 **1955** Shady goings on are uncovered at a psychiatric ward run by a bunch of neurotic administrators. A strong cast, director and producer do not add much to this dull outing. **125m/C LV.** Lauren Bacall, Richard Widmark, Gloria Grahame, Charles Boyer, Lillian Gish, John Kerr, Susan Strasberg, Oscar Levant, Tommy Rettig, Paul Stewart, Adele Jergens, Bert Freed, Sandy Descher, Fay Wray, Virginia Christine; ***D:*** Vincente Minnelli. *MGM*

The Coca-Cola Kid 🦴🦴🦴½ **1984 (R)** A smug sales executive treks to Australia to improve regional sales and becomes embroiled in sexual and professional shenanigans. Roberts is strong in the difficult lead role, and Scacchi is compelling in an awkwardly constructed part. Ambitious satire is somewhat scattershot, with more storylines than it needs. Still, filmmaker Makavejev is usually capable of juggling the entire enterprise. **94m/C VHS, Beta, LV.** *AU* Eric Roberts, Greta Scacchi, Bill Kerr; ***D:*** Dusan Makavejev. *LIV, VES, FCT*

Cocaine Cowboys 🦴½ **1979 (R)** Lame rockers support themselves between gigs by peddling drugs then find out they've run afoul of the mob. Palance is the only worthwhile aspect of this rambling venture produced at Andy Warhol's home. **90m/C VHS, Beta.** Jack Palance, Andy Warhol, Tom Sullivan, Suzanna Love; ***D:*** Ulli Lommel. *MED, OM*

Cocaine Fiends 🦴🦴 *The Pace That Kills* **1936** Drug use leads siblings into a squalid life of addiction, crime, prostitution, and eventually suicide. Ostensibly straight morality tale functions better as loopy camp. Features memorable slang. **74m/B VHS, Beta.** Lois January, Noel Madison; ***D:*** William O'Connor. *SNC, NOS, MED*

Cocaine: One Man's Seduction 🦴🦴½ **1983** Made-for-television film documents one man's degeneration into drug addiction. Weaver snorts convincingly in lead. **97m/C VHS, Beta.** Dennis Weaver, Karen Grassle, Pamela Bellwood, David Ackroyd; ***D:*** Paul Wendkos; ***M:*** Brad Fiedel. *FRH*

Cocaine Wars 🦴 **1986 (R)** An undercover U.S. agent kills dozens while trying to rescue his kidnapped girlfriend from an evil South American drug tycoon. Violent, but otherwise unaffecting. **82m/C VHS, Beta.** John Schneider, Kathryn Witt, Royal Dano; ***D:*** Hector Olivera. *MED, VTR*

Cockeyed Cavaliers 🦴🦴 **1934** Wheeler and Woolsey are stockaded for stealing the Duke's horses and carriage. To escape jail they swap clothes with some drunken royalty. **70m/B VHS, Beta.** Bert Wheeler, Robert Woolsey, Dorothy Lee, Thelma Todd; ***D:*** Mark Sandrich. *CCB*

Cockfighter 🦴🦴🦴 *Gamblin' Man; Born to Kill; Wild Drifters* **1974 (R)** A unique, grim portrait of a cockfighting trainer. Oates, in the lead, provides voiceover narrations, but the film otherwise remains silent until the end. Strong support from Stanton. Interesting, violent fare. **84m/C VHS, Beta.** Warren Oates, Harry Dean Stanton, Richard B. Shull, Troy Donahue, Millie Perkins; ***D:*** Monte Hellman; ***C:*** Nestor Almendros; ***M:*** Michael Franks. *SUE*

Cocktail 🦴🦴½ **1988 (R)** A smug young man finds fame and fortune as a proficient, flashy bartender, charming the ladies with his bottle and glass juggling act. Slick, superficial film boasts a busy soundtrack and serviceable exchanges between male leads Cruise and Brown. There's less chemistry between Cruise and love interest Shue. Filmed in a high-tech rock video style. **103m/C VHS, Beta, LV, 8mm.** Tom Cruise, Bryan Brown, Elisabeth Shue, Lisa Banes, Laurence Luckinbill, Kelly Lynch, Gina Gershon, Ron Dean, Paul Benedict; ***D:*** Roger Donaldson; ***W:*** Heywood Gould; ***C:*** Dean Semler; ***M:*** J. Peter Robinson. Golden Raspberry Awards '88: Worst Picture, Worst Screenplay. *TOU*

The Cocoanuts 🦴🦴½ **1929** In their film debut, the Marx Brothers create their trademark, indescribable mayhem. Stagey, technically crude comedy nonetheless delights with zany, free-for-all exchanges, antics. Includes famous "viaduct" exchange. **96m/B VHS, Beta, LV.** Groucho Marx, Chico Marx, Harpo Marx, Zeppo Marx, Margaret Dumont, Kay Francis, Oscar Shaw, Mary Eaton; ***D:*** Robert Florey, Joseph Santley; ***W:*** George S. Kaufman, Morrie Ryskind; ***M:*** Irving Berlin. *MCA*

Cocoon 🦴🦴🦴 **1985 (PG-13)** Humanist fantasy in which senior citizens discover their fountain of youth is actually a breeding ground for aliens. Heartwarming, one-of-a kind drama showcases elderly greats Ameche, Brimley, Gilford, Cronyn, and Tandy. A commendable, recommendable venture. Based on David Saperstein's novel and followed by "Cocoon: The Return." **117m/C VHS, Beta, LV.** Wilford Brimley, Brian Dennehy, Steve Guttenberg, Don Ameche, Tahnee Welch, Jack Gilford, Hume Cronyn, Jessica Tandy, Gwen Verdon, Maureen Stapleton, Tyrone Power Jr., Barret Oliver, Linda Harrison, Herta Ware, Clint Howard; ***D:*** Ron Howard; ***W:*** Tom Benedek; ***M:*** James Horner. Academy Awards '85: Best Supporting Actor (Ameche), Best Visual Effects. *FOX, FCT, BTV*

Cocoon: The Return 🦴🦴 **1988 (PG)** Old timers who left with aliens in "Cocoon" return to earth and face grave problems. Less compelling sequel misses guiding hand of earlier film's director, Ron Howard. Still, most of cast from the original is on board here, and the film has its moments. **116m/C VHS, Beta, LV.** Don Ameche, Wilford Brimley, Steve Guttenberg, Maureen Stapleton, Hume Cronyn, Jessica Tandy, Gwen Verdon, Jack Gilford, Tahnee Welch, Courteney Cox, Brian Dennehy, Barret Oliver; ***D:*** Daniel Petrie; ***C:*** Tak Fujimoto; ***M:*** James Horner. *FOX*

C.O.D. 🦴 **1983 (PG)** Bosom buddies must develop advertising campaign for brassiere producer or find their careers are bust. Premise milked for all its worth, so you may want to keep abreast of this one. On the other hand, you may not give a hoot. Oh well, tit for tat. **96m/C VHS, Beta.** Chris Lemmon, Olivia Pascal, Jennifer Richards, Corinne Alphen, Teresa Ganzel, Carole Davis; ***D:*** Chuck Vincent; ***W:*** R.J. Marx. *VES, LIV*

Code Name Alpha 🦴🦴 *Red Dragon; A-009 Missione Hong Kong* **1967** You don't have to have a federal case of intelligence to figure out where this FBI story's going and how it's going to get there. Someone's smuggling sophisticated electrical components to the communists, and a team of intelligence agents, including Granger and Schiaffino, hike over to Hong Kong to break up the party. Based on the story "Le Riviere des Trois Jonques" by Georges Godefroy. **89m/C VHS.** *IT GE* Stewart Granger, Rosanna Schiaffino, Harald Juhnke, Paul Klinger, Helga Sommerfeld, Horst Frank; ***D:*** Ernest Hofbauer. *SNC*

Code Name: Chaos 🦴🦴 *Spies, Lies, and Alibis* **1990 (R)** A political spoof featuring a group of renegade spies trying to come up with a get-rich-quick scheme. It involves inventing a global crisis in a small Asian country but the plan comes under the scrutiny of a CIA agent who's not in on the scheme. **96m/C VHS.** Robert Loggia, Diane Ladd, David Warner, Alice Krige, Brian Kerwin; ***D:*** Antony Thomas. *LIV, MOV, LIV*

Code Name: Dancer **1987** A retired spy leaves her peaceful life, husband and family to take care of business in Cuba. Made for television. **93m/C VHS.** Kate Capshaw, Jeroen Krabbe, Gregory Sierra, Cliff DeYoung. *VMK*

Code Name: Diamond Head 🦴 **1977** In Hawaii, a secret agent is assigned to retrieve a deadly chemical that has been hidden by a master of disguises. Made for television. **78m/C VHS, Beta.** Roy Thinnes, France Nuyen, Zulu, Ian McShane; ***D:*** Jeannot Szwarc. *WOV*

Code Name: Emerald 🦴 **1985 (PG)** WWII drama in which an American agent must stop an enemy spy with knowledge of impending D-Day invasion. Conventional TV fare boasts a fine performance by von Sydow, but Stolz is hopelessly miscast as an adult. Perhaps the only film featuring both Buchholz and Berger. First feature film by NBC-TV network. **95m/C VHS, Beta, LV.** Ed Harris, Max von Sydow, Eric Stoltz, Horst Buchholz, Helmut Berger, Cyrielle Claire, Patrick Stewart, Graham Crowden; ***D:*** Jonathan Sanger; ***W:*** Ronald Bass; ***M:*** John Addison. *FOX*

Code Name: Zebra 🦴½ **1984** The Zebra Force helps the cops put bad guys away. When the bad guys get out, they want revenge. The result: lots of violence and action. Wasn't released theatrically. **96m/C VHS, Beta.** Jim Mitchum, Mike Lane, Tim Brown, Joe Dante, Deana Jurgens, Frank Sinatra Jr.; ***D:*** Joe Tornatore. *TWE*

Code of Honor 🦴🦴½ *Sweet Revenge* **1984** A young woman vows revenge on the military commanders who caused her brother's demise. Neatly made psychological thriller is surprisingly good for a TV movie. **105m/C VHS.** Kevin Dobson, Wings Hauser, Alec Baldwin, Merritt Butrick, Kelly McGillis, Alfre Woodard, Savannah Smith, Helen Hunt, Dana Elcar; ***D:*** David Green. *XVC, VTR*

Code of Honor 🦴 **1988** Prominent businessman embarks on mission of revenge when police fail to apprehend his wife's rapist. No surprise here. You either enjoy this sort of thing or you lead a reasonably fulfilling life. **90m/C VHS.** Cameron Mitchell, Mark Sabin. *NO*

Code of Silence 🦴🦴 **1985 (R)** A police loner must contend with both a gang war and police department corruption. Hectic, violent action-drama with some wild stunts. **100m/C VHS, Beta, LV.** Chuck Norris, Henry Silva, Bert Remsen, Molly Hagan, Nathan Davis, Dennis Farina; ***D:*** Andrew Davis; ***W:*** Michael Butler, Mike Gray. *NO*

Code of the Fearless 🦴 **1939** A cowboy wins the heart of a beautiful maiden while bringing evildoers to justice. **56m/B VHS.** Fred Scott, Claire Rochelle, John Merton, Harry Harvey, Walter McGrail, Roger Williams; ***D:*** Raymond K. Johnson. *NOS, DVT*

Codename: Foxfire 🦴🦴 *Slay It Again, Sam* **1985** An attractive secret agent is framed for wrongdoing and must clear her name by tracking the enemy spy lurking within the intelligence network. Always interesting Cassidy is an asset, but this by-the-numbers TV film is otherwise a misappropriation of the term "intelligence" in relation to espionage. **99m/C VHS, Beta.** Joanna Cassidy, John McCook, Sheryl Lee Ralph, Henry Jones, Luke Andreas; ***D:*** Corey Allen. *MCA*

Codename: Icarus ♂♂ **1985** A young mathematical genius, enrolled at a special school for accelerated study uncovers evil government plots to use the students for espionage. Made for British television. **106m/C VHS, Beta.** *GB* Barry Angel, Jack Galloway; ***D:*** Marilyn Fox. *FOX, TVC, VCO*

Codename Kyril ♂♂½ **1991 (R)** Woodward plays a British spy pitted against Soviet assassin Kyril (Charleson) who's been sent to England by the KGB to rout out a double agent. Turns out there's more to it than Kyril knows, and nobody loves an assassin. Based on John Trenhaile's "A Man Called Kyril," the script is slow from the gun, but eventually builds something akin to momentum. Made for cable TV. **115m/C VHS.** Edward Woodward, Ian Charleson, Denholm Elliott, Joss Ackland, Richard E. Grant, Sven-Bertil Taube, Catherine Nielson, John McEnery, Peter Vaughan, James Laurenson; ***D:*** Ian Sharp; ***W:*** John Hopkins. *TTC*

Codename: Terminate ♂½ **1990** Title says it all in this tender exploration of the human condition. Jungle-trained mercenaries grab their guns and go after an American pilot shot down behind enemy lines. **84m/C VHS.** Robert Mason, Jim Gaines. *NO*

Codename: Vengeance ♂ **1987 (R)** A macho fellow tries to stop a killer holding the shah's wife and son hostage. Dated. **97m/C VHS.** Robert Ginty, Cameron Mitchell, Shannon Tweed; ***D:*** David Winters. *VTR, MCG*

Codename: Wildgeese ♂½ *Geheimecode Wildganse* **1984 (R)** The big-name cast of this meandering mercenary macho-rama probably wish they'd been credited under code names; solid histrionics cannot a silly script save. A troop of commandos-for-hire are engaged by the Drug Enforcement Administration to obliterate an opium operation in Asia's infamous Golden Triangle, and much mindless agitation ensues. **101m/C VHS.** *IT GE* Lewis Collins, Lee Van Cleef, Ernest Borgnine, Klaus Kinski, Mimsy Farmer; ***D:*** Anthony (Antonio Margheriti) Dawson. *VTR, NWV*

Cody ♂ **1967** A former bronco buster wants his son to "take it like a man" when the boy's dog dies. Then a mystical goose arrives to mellow the old man. That's really the plot. **82m/C VHS, Beta.** Tony Becker, Terry Evans. *NO*

A Coeur Joie ♂♂ *Two Weeks in September* **1967** Sixties set piece about a gorgeous woman who must choose between her much older lover or her newfound stud. Bardot and U.K. scenery keep this one from sinking entirely. In French with English subtitles. **100m/C VHS, Beta.** *FR* Brigitte Bardot, Laurent Terzieff; ***D:*** Serge Bourguignon. *BAR*

Coffy ♂♂ **1973 (R)** A beautiful woman feigns drug addiction to discover and destroy the evil dealers responsible for her sister's death. Grier is everything in this exploitative flick full of violence and nudity. **91m/C VHS, Beta, LV.** Pam Grier, Booker Bradshaw, Robert DoQui, Allan Arbus; ***D:*** Jack Hill; ***M:*** Roy Ayers. *ORI, FCT*

Cohen and Tate ♂♂ **1988 (R)** Two antagonistic mob hitmen kidnap a 9-year-old who witnessed his parent's recent murder by the mob. In order to survive, the boy begins to play one psycho off the other. **113m/C VHS, Beta, LV.** Roy Scheider, Adam Baldwin, Harley Cross, Cooper Huckabee; ***D:*** Eric Red; ***W:*** Eric Red; ***M:*** Bill Conti. *SUE, NLC*

Cold Blood ♂½ **197? (R)** A small dubbed Dutch film about a pair of kidnap victims who turn the tables on their captors. **90m/C VHS, Beta.** *NL* Rutger Hauer. *SIM*

Cold Comfort ♂♂½ **1990 (R)** A father arranges his teen daughter's romance, but finds his plans going awry in this Canadian thriller. Nominated for several Canadian television awards, including Best Actress, Best Actor, Best Picture and Best Musical Score. **90m/C VHS.** *CA* Margaret Langrick, Maury Chaykin; ***D:*** Vic Sarin. *REP*

Cold Comfort Farm ♂♂♂ **1994 (PG)** Stella Gibbons classic 1932 comedic novel is brought to life in this TV adaptation, which finds London lass Flora Poste (Beckinsdale) trying to take charge of the lives of her very odd country cousins, the Starkadders. The rowdy family and their dilapidated farm are putty in practical Flora's hands as she works to make everybody happy (including herself). Terrific ensemble cast, with a fast pace and wicked humor. **95m/C VHS.** *GB* Kate Beckinsale, Eileen Atkins, Ian McKellen, Sheila Burrell, Rufus Sewell, Maria Miles, Freddie Jones, Ivan Kaye, Miriam Margolyes, Joanna Lumley, Stephen Fry, Christopher Bowen; ***D:*** John Schlesinger; ***W:*** Malcolm Bradbury; ***C:*** Chris Seager; ***M:*** Robert Lockhart. *NYR*

Cold Days ♂♂½ **1966** Four men await execution for their part in the WWII massacre of Jews and Serbs. Their reminiscences and justifications, if any, are examined. Stunning cinematography and unusual theme for 1960s Hungarian political climate. **102m/C VHS.** *HU* ***D:*** Andras Kovacs. *FCT*

Cold Eyes of Fear ♂ **197?** A man and his girlfriend are besieged by a raving convict whom his uncle, a judge, had put away years before. Shades of "Cape Fear" on a low budget. **88m/C VHS, Beta.** Fernando Rey, Frank Wolfe, Karin Schubert; ***D:*** Enzo G. Castellari; ***M:*** Ennio Morricone. *TWE*

Cold Feet ♂♂½ **1984 (PG)** Light romantic comedy about a television director just recovering from a failed marriage and his fall for a lab researcher who just went through a break-up herself. **96m/C VHS, Beta.** Griffin Dunne, Marissa Chibas, Blanche Baker, Mark Cronogue; ***D:*** Bruce Van Dusen. *FOX*

Cold Feet ♂♂½ **1989 (R)** Modern-day western in which a trio of loopy desperados smuggle jewels inside a racehorse's stomach. Quirky comedy offers wild performances from Waits and sex-bomb Kirkland, but could use a few more laughs. Filmed largely on McGuane's ranch. **94m/C VHS, Beta, LV.** Keith Carradine, Tom Waits, Sally Kirkland, Rip Torn, Kathleen York, Bill Pullman, Vincent Schiavelli; ***D:*** Robert Dornhelm; ***W:*** Thomas McGuane, Jim Harrison; ***M:*** Tom Bahler. *LIV*

Cold Front ♂½ **1989 (R)** A hired assassin turned serial killer is hunted by two dedicated cops. **94m/C VHS, Beta, LV.** *CA* Martin Sheen, Michael Ontkean, Beverly D'Angelo, Kim Coates; ***D:*** Allan Goldstein. *HBO*

Cold Heat ♂♂ **1990** When a custody battle rocks a crime boss' world, he pulls out all the stops in the war against his wife. **85m/C VHS, Beta.** John Phillip Law, Britt Ekland, Robert Sacchi, Roy Summerset, Joanne Watkins, Chance Michael Corbitt; ***D:*** Ulli Lommel. *AIP*

Cold Heaven ♂½ **1992 (R)** Alex and Marie Davenport are on vacation when an accident occurs and Alex dies—or does he? The next day his body disappears and his unfaithful wife begins to have paranoid delusions that he is returning to exact retribution for her affair. But these aren't her only visions, for during the past year Marie has also had religious visions she believes are part of a personal battle with God. Harmon does what he can with his role as the alleged corpse but Russell is uncharacteristically whiny and bland. Convoluted story of marriage, death, and spirituality; doesn't pan out on any accounts. Based on a novel by Brian Moore. **103m/C VHS, LV.** Theresa Russell, Mark Harmon, James Russo, Talia Shire, Will Patton, Richard Bradford; ***D:*** Nicolas Roeg; ***W:*** Allan Scott. *HMD, FCT*

Cold Justice ♂♂ **1989 (R)** An ex-prizefighter (Daltrey) and his friends welcome an English priest into their tough southside Chicago neighborhood. The good father seems too good to be true as he befriends the locals—even raising funds for the children's hospital. When the funds never make it to the hospital and the neighborhood begins to experience a number of violent tragedies, the residents decide to take their own revenge. **106m/C VHS, LV.** Dennis Waterman, Roger Daltrey, Penelope Milford, Ron Dean, Bert Rosario; ***D:*** Terry Green; ***W:*** Terry Green. *COL*

Cold Light of Day ♂♂ **1995** Police officer Victor Marek (Grant) is hunting a serial killer of young children in the English countryside—and he'll do anything, including using a young girl as bait. Marek seduces single mother Milena (Baxter) to use her young daughter to set a trap for the killer but can he catch the madman before it's too late? **101m/C VHS.** *GB* Richard E. Grant, Lynsey Baxter, Heathcote Williams; ***D:*** Rudolf Van Den Berg. *PGV*

Cold River ♂♂½ **1981 (PG)** An experienced guide takes his two children on an extended trip through the Adirondacks. For the children, it's a fantasy vacation until their father succumbs to a heart attack in the chilly mountains. "Cold River" is a journey of survival, and an exploration of human relationships. **94m/C VHS, Beta.** Pat Petersen, Richard Jaeckel, Suzanne Weber; ***D:*** Fred G. Sullivan. *FOX*

Cold Room ♂½ *The Prisoner* **1984** College student on vacation with her father in East Berlin discovers the horrors hidden in an antiquated hotel room next to hers. Made for cable television. From the novel by Jeffrey Caine. **95m/C VHS, Beta.** George Segal, Renee Soutendijk, Amanda Pays, Warren Clarke, Anthony Higgins; ***D:*** James Dearden; ***M:*** Michael Nyman. *FOX*

Cold Sassy Tree ♂♂♂½ **1989** Endearing romance of a scandalous May-December marriage as perceived by the younger woman's teenage son. Dunaway and Widmark shine, and small town pettiness is vividly rendered. Adapted from the books by Olive Ann Burns. A superior made-for-cable production. **95m/C VHS.** Faye Dunaway, Richard Widmark, Neil Patrick Harris, Frances Fisher, Lee Garlington, John M. Jackson; ***D:*** Joan Tewkesbury; ***W:*** Joan Tewkesbury; ***M:*** Brad Fiedel. *TTC*

Cold Steel ♂½ **1987 (R)** Standard revenge drama about a hardnosed Los Angeles cop tracking his father's disfigured psycho-killer. Cast includes the always intense Davis, ex-pop star Ant, and screen scorchstress Stone. Still it's predictable, low-grade fare. **91m/C VHS, Beta.** Brad Davis, Jonathan Banks, Adam Ant, Sharon Stone; ***D:*** Dorothy Ann Puzo. *COL*

Cold Steel for Tortuga ♂ **1965** An Italian epic about a mercenary rescuing his woman and his gold from an evil governor. Dubbed. **95m/C VHS, Beta.** *IT* Guy Madison, Rick Battaglia, Ingeborg Schoener; ***D:*** Luigi Capuano. *NO*

Cold Sweat ♂♂ *L'Uomo Dalle Due Ombre; De la Part des Copains* **1974 (PG)** A brutal drug trader takes his ultra-violent revenge after his wife is captured by a drug boss' moronic henchmen. Typical Bronson flick boasts superior supporting cast of Ullmann and Mason. Writing and direction, however, are mediocre. **94m/C VHS, Beta.** *IT FR* Charles Bronson, Jill Ireland, Liv Ullmann, James Mason; ***D:*** Terence Young. *GEM, MRV*

Cold Sweat ♂♂ **1993 (R)** A professional hit man (Cross) is literally haunted by the ghost of his last victim (who happens to be female and usually appears naked), so he decides his next assignment will be his last. A ruthless businessman suspects his very sexy wife (Tweed) has been unfaithful but she has lots of other secrets to hide. **93m/C VHS, Beta.** Ben Cross, Shannon Tweed, Adam Baldwin, Dave Thomas; ***D:*** Gail Harvey; ***W:*** Richard Beattie. *PAR, VTR*

Cold Turkey ♂♂♂ **1971 (PG)** Often witty satire about what happens when an entire town tries to stop smoking for a contest. Van Dyke is fine as the anti-smoking minister; newscasters Bob and Ray are riotous; oldtimer Horton's swansong. Wholesome, somewhat tame fare. **99m/C VHS, Beta, LV.** Dick Van Dyke, Pippa Scott, Tom Poston, Bob Newhart, Vincent Gardenia, Barnard Hughes, Jean Stapleton, Graham Jarvis, Edward Everett Horton; ***D:*** Norman Lear; ***W:*** Norman Lear; ***M:*** Randy Newman. *MGM*

Cold War Killers ♂½ **1986 (PG)** Soviet and British agents vie for control of prized cargo plane recently retrieved from the sea floor. **85m/C VHS, Beta.** *GB* Terence Stamp; ***D:*** William Brayne. *NO*

Coldblooded 🦴½ **1994 (R)** Minor mob flunky (and dim bulb) Cosmo (Priestley) is unwillingly promoted to the position of hit man by his mobster boss. He's tutored by the organization's primo professional (Riegert) and finds out he has a real knack for murder. More sophomoric than satiric and a waste of Riegert's talents; Williams is attractive as Priestley's clueless girlfriend. Directorial debut of Wolodarsky. **92m/C VHS.** Jason Priestley, Peter Riegert, Kimberly Williams, Robert Loggia, Janeane Garofalo, Josh Charles; ***Cameos:*** Talia Balsam, Michael J. Fox; ***D:*** M. Wallace Wolodarsky; ***W:*** M. Wallace Wolodarsky; ***C:*** Robert Yeoman; ***M:*** Steve Bartek. *PGV*

Coldfire 🦴½ **1990** Two rookie cops work to undo the havoc unleashed on the streets of LA because of a deadly new drug sought for its powerful high. Not many surprises here. **90m/C VHS, LV.** Wings Hauser, Kamar Reyes, Robert Viharo, Gary Swanson; ***D:*** Wings Hauser. *PMH*

The Colditz Story 🦴🦴½ **1955** Prisoners of war from the Allied countries join together in an attempt to escape from Colditz, an allegedly escape-proof castle-prison deep within the Third Reich. **93m/B VHS, Beta.** John Mills, Eric Portman, Lionel Jeffries, Bryan Forbes, Ian Carmichael, Anton Diffring; ***D:*** Guy Hamilton. *REP, CNG*

Cole Justice 🦴🦴 **1989** An older man, haunted by the memory of his girlfriend's rape and murder thirty-five years earlier, takes to the streets to protect innocent citizens from lowlife criminals. Somewhat unusual revenge pic filmed in and around Tulsa, Oklahoma. **90m/C VHS, Beta.** Carl Bartholomew, Keith Andrews, Mike Wiles, Nick Zickefoose; ***D:*** Carl Bartholomew. *NO*

The Collector 🦴🦴🦴½ **1965** Compelling adaptation of the John Fowles novel about a withdrawn butterfly collector who decides to add to his collection by kidnapping a beautiful girl he admires. He locks her in his cellar hoping she will fall in love with him. Chilling, unsettling drama with Stamp unnerving, yet sympathetic in lead. **119m/C VHS, Beta, LV.** *GB* Terence Stamp, Samantha Eggar, Maurice Dallimore, Mona Washbourne; ***D:*** William Wyler; ***C:*** Robert Krasker, Robert L. Surtees; ***M:*** Maurice Jarre. Cannes Film Festival '65: Best Actor (Stamp), Best Actress (Eggar); Nominations: Academy Awards '65: Best Actress (Eggar), Best Adapted Screenplay, Best Director (Wyler). *COL*

Collector's Item 🦴🦴🦴 **1989** Two lovers reunite after 16 years and a flurry of memories temporarily rekindles their passion, which comes dangerously close to obsession. Casting of the physically bountiful Antonelli helps this effective erotic drama. **99m/C VHS, Beta.** *IT* Tony Musante, Laura Antonelli, Florinda Bolkan; ***D:*** Giuseppe Patroni Griffi. *NO*

College 🦴🦴🦴½ **1927** A high school valedictorian tries out for every sport in college, hoping to win the girl. Vintage Keaton antics, including disaster as a soda jerk, an attempt to be a track star, and the pole vault through a window to rescue the damsel in distress. **60m/B VHS, Beta, LV.** Buster Keaton, A. Cornwall, Harold Goodwin; ***D:*** James W. Horne; ***M:*** John Muri. *DVT, MRV, CCB*

College Swing 🦴½ *Swing, Teacher, Swing* **1938** Lightweight, lackluster musical about Allen inheriting a small town college which she turns into a hangout for her vaudeville pals. Top cast is basically wasted performing many forgettable songs and familiar routines. Based on an adaptation by Frederick Hazlitt Brennan from a story by Ted Lesser. ♫College Swing; What Did Romeo Say to Juliet?; I Fall In Love With You Every Day; You're a Natural; The Old School Bell; Moments Like This; How D'ja Like to Love Me?; What a Rumba Does to Romance. **86m/B VHS.** George Burns, Gracie Allen, Martha Raye, Bob Hope, Edward Everett Horton, Ben Blue, Betty Grable, Jackie Coogan, John Payne; ***D:*** Raoul Walsh. *MCA, BTV*

Collision Course 🦴 **1989 (PG)** A wise-cracking cop from Detroit teams up with Japan's best detective to nail a ruthless gang leader. Release was delayed until 1992 due to a lawsuit, but it was resolved in time to coordinate the release with Leno's debut as the host of "The Tonight Show." Pretty marginal, but diehard fans of Leno may appreciate it. Filmed on location in Detroit. **99m/C VHS, Beta, LV.** Noriyuki "Pat" Morita, Jay Leno, Chris Sarandon, Al Waxman; ***D:*** Lewis Teague. *HBO*

The Colombian Connection 🦴½ **1991** America's best undercover agent battles a powerful cocaine empire deep in the jungles of the Amazon, where slave labor and political corruption abound. **90m/C VHS, Beta.** Miles O'Keeffe, Henry Silva. *NO*

Colonel Chabert 🦴🦴 **1994** In the 1807 Battle of Eylau, French officer Chabert (Depardieu) is thought dead and stripped of all he possesses. After 10 years of imprisonment, a man shows up in the office of Paris lawyer Derville (Luchini), claiming to be the dead Chabert. His remarried wife (Ardant), now the Countess Ferraud, has used his fortune to bolster the political aspirations of her second husband (Dussolier) and refuses to acknowledge this stranger's claims. Is Chabert a fraud? And what exactly are the motives of all the players? Based on the novel by Honore de Balzac. Directorial debut of Angelo. French with subtitles. **111m/C VHS.** *FR* Gerard Depardieu, Fanny Ardant, Fabrice Luchini, Andre Dussollier; ***D:*** Yves Angelo; ***W:*** Yves Angelo, Jean Cosmos, Veronique Lagrange; ***C:*** Bernard Lutic. Nominations: Cesar Awards '94: Best Actor (Depardieu). *REP*

Colonel Effingham's Raid 🦴🦴½ *Man of the Hour* **1945** A retired army colonel uses military tactics to keep an old historical courthouse open, while defeating some crooked politicians in the process. **70m/B VHS, Beta.** Joan Bennett, Charles Coburn, William Eythe, Donald Meek; ***D:*** Irving Pichel. *NOS, HEG*

Colonel Redl 🦴🦴🦴🦴 **1984 (R)** Absorbing, intricately rendered psychological study of an ambitious officer's rise and fall in pre-WWI Austria. Brandauer is excellent as the vain, insecure homosexual ultimately undone by his own ambition and his superior officer's smug loathing. Muller-Stahl and Landgrebe are particularly distinguished among the supporting players. The second in the Szabo/Brandauer trilogy, after "Mephisto" and before "Hanussen." In German with English subtitles. **114m/C VHS, Beta, LV.** *GE HU* Klaus Maria Brandauer, Armin Mueller-Stahl, Gudrun Landgrebe, Jan Niklas, Hans-Christian Blech, Laszlo Mensaros, Andras Balint; ***D:*** Laszlo Szabo; ***C:*** Lajos Koltai. British Academy Awards '85: Best Foreign Film; Cannes Film Festival '85: Special Jury Prize; Nominations: Academy Awards '85: Best Foreign Language Film. *FCT, GLV, INJ*

Colonel Wolodyjowski 🦴🦴½ **1969** An adaptation of the monumental novels by Henryk Sinkiewicz chronicling the attack on Poland's eastern border by the Turks in 1668. In Polish with English subtitles. **160m/C VHS.** *PL* Tadeusz Loniski, Magdalena Zawadzka, Daniel Olbrychski; ***D:*** Jerzy Hoffman. *FCT*

The Colony 🦴🦴½ **1995 (PG-13)** "The Colony" is a luxurious and exclusive gated community owned by secretive billionaire developer Phillip Denning (Linden). Newest residents, security expert Rick Knowlton (Ritter), wife Leslie (Keller) and their two children, find out things are just too good to be true—and that trying to leave could be the very last thing they'll ever do. **93m/C VHS.** John Ritter, Hal Linden, Mary Page Keller, Marshall Teague, Frank Bonner, Michelle Scarabelli, June Lockhart, Todd Jeffries, Alexandra Picatto, Cody Dorkin; ***D:*** Rob Hedden; ***W:*** Rob Hedden. *MCA*

Color Me Blood Red *Woof! Model Massacre* **1964** Artist decides that the red in his paintings is best rendered with human blood. He even manages to continue his art career—when not busy stabbing and mutilating the unsuspecting citizenry. Short and shoddy. Also known as "Model Massacre." **74m/C VHS, Beta.** Don Joseph, Sandi Conder; ***D:*** Herschell Gordon Lewis. *NO*

Color Me Dead 🦴½ **1969 (R)** A victim of an extremely slow-acting poison frantically spends his final days trying to uncover his killer. Another inferior remake of B-thriller "D.O.A." Rent that one instead. **97m/C VHS.** *AU* Tom Tryon, Carolyn Jones, Rick Jason, Patricia Connolly, Tony Ward; ***D:*** Eddie Davis. *REP*

Color of a Brisk and Leaping Day 🦴🦴 **1995** While living in L.A. at the end of WWII, Chinese-American John Lee (Alexander) learns that the Yosemite Valley Railroad is being scrapped and he becomes determined to save it—in part as a homage to his grandfather who emigrated to work as a railroad laborer. A romantic train fanatic himself, Lee arranges financing from wealthy businessman Pinchot (Diehl) but must make the railroad pay within a year—unlikely as the automobile rapidly takes over as preferred transportation. Well-captures a '40s atmosphere but pacing and dialogue are uneven. **87m/B VHS.** Peter Alexander, Jeri Arrendondo, Henry Gibson, Michael Stipe, John Diehl, David Chung, Diana Larkin, Bok Yun Chon; ***D:*** Christopher Munch; ***W:*** Christopher Munch; ***C:*** Rob Sweeney. Sundance Film Festival '96: Best Cinematography. *NYR*

The Color of Evening 🦴🦴 **1995** Aging painter Landau tries to regain his youth by pursuing his young model Skye, but it's the older Burstyn who really inspires his imagination. **?m/C VHS.** Martin Landau, Ellen Burstyn, Ione Skye.

The Color of Money 🦴🦴🦴½ **1986 (R)** Flashy, gripping drama about former pool hustler Fast Eddie Felsen (Newman) who, after years off the circuit, takes a brilliant but immature pool shark (Cruise) under his wing. Strong performances by Newman as the grizzled veteran, Cruise as the show-boating youth, and Mastrantonio and Shaver as the men's worldly girlfriends. Worthy sequel to "The Hustler." **119m/C VHS, Beta, LV.** Paul Newman, Tom Cruise, Mary Elizabeth Mastrantonio, Helen Shaver, John Turturro, Forest Whitaker; ***D:*** Martin Scorsese; ***W:*** Richard Price; ***C:*** Michael Ballhaus. Academy Awards '86: Best Actor (Newman); National Board of Review Awards '86: Best Actor (Newman); Nominations: Academy Awards '86: Best Adapted Screenplay, Best Art Direction/Set Decoration, Best Supporting Actress (Mastrantonio). *TOU, BTV*

Color of Night 🦴½ **1994 (R)** Psychologist Dr. Bill Capa (Willis) takes over a murdered colleague's therapy group hoping to find out the killer's identity. Then he meets temptress Rose (March) and gets involved in a hot affair, but she's not what she seems—nor is anyone else. Preposterous thriller fails to deliver necessary suspense although the eroticism could spark some interest, particularly in the director's cut, which puts the sex back in the sex scenes between Willis and March (and is 15 minutes longer than the theatrical release). **136m/C VHS.** Bruce Willis, Jane March, Scott Bakula, Ruben Blades, Lesley Ann Warren, Lance Henriksen, Kevin J. O'Connor, Andrew Lowery, Brad Dourif, Eriq La Salle, Jeff Corey, Shirley Knight, Kathleen Wilhoite; ***D:*** Richard Rush; ***W:*** Matthew Chapman, Billy Ray, Richard Rush; ***M:*** Dominic Frontiere. Golden Raspberry Awards '94: Worst Picture; Nominations: Golden Globe Awards '95: Best Song ("The Color of the Night"); Golden Raspberry Awards '94: Worst Actor (Willis). *HPH*

The Color of Pomegranates 🦴🦴🦴 *Sayat Nova; Tsvet Granata* **1969** Paradjanov's depiction of the life of Armenian poet Arutiun Sayadin, known as Sayat Nova, who rises from carpet weaver to court minstrel to archbishop. Eloquent imagery and symbols are derived from Armenian paintings, poetry and history. In Armenian with English subtitles. Also includes "Hagop Hovnatanian," a 12-minute short on the artist. **80m/C VHS.** *RU* Sofiko Chiaureli, M. Aleksanian, V. Galstian; ***D:*** Sergei Paradjanov; ***W:*** Sergei Paradjanov. *CVC, FCT*

The Color Purple 🦴🦴🦴½ **1985 (PG-13)** Celie is a poor black girl who fights for her self-esteem when she is separated from her sister and forced into a brutal marriage. Spanning 1909 to 1947 in a small Georgia town, the movie chronicles the joys, pains, and people in her life. Adaptation of Alice Walker's acclaimed book features strong lead from Goldberg (her screen debut), Glover, Avery, and talk-show host Winfrey (also her film debut). It's hard to see director Spielberg as the most suited for this one, but he acquits himself nicely, avoiding the facileness that sometimes flaws his pics. Brilliant photography by Allen Daviau and musical score by Jones (who co-produced) compliment this strong film. **154m/C VHS,**

Beta, LV. Whoopi Goldberg, Danny Glover, Oprah Winfrey, Margaret Avery, Adolph Caesar, Rae Dawn Chong, Willard Pugh, Akosua Busia; ***D:*** Steven Spielberg; ***C:*** Allen Daviau; ***M:*** Chris Boardman, Quincy Jones. Directors Guild of America Awards '85: Best Director (Spielberg); Golden Globe Awards '86: Best Actress—Drama (Goldberg); National Board of Review Awards '85: 10 Best Films of the Year, Best Actress (Goldberg); Nominations: Academy Awards '85: Best Actress (Goldberg), Best Adapted Screenplay, Best Art Direction/Set Decoration, Best Cinematography, Best Costume Design, Best Makeup, Best Picture, Best Song ("Miss Celie's Blues (Sister)"), Best Supporting Actress (Avery, Winfrey), Best Original Score. *WAR, FCT*

Colorado ☾½ **1940** Roy tries to find his brother, a Union deserter, during the Civil War. **54m/B VHS, Beta.** Roy Rogers, George "Gabby" Hayes, Milburn Stone; ***D:*** Joseph Kane. *NOS, MED, DVT*

Colorado Serenade ☾☾ **1946** Standard oater has Dean, Sharpe and Ates trying to prevent a young outlaw from bullying the local citizenry. Sharpe shows off his athletic prowess, and King provides some laughs. Other than that, it's pretty routine stuff. **68m/C VHS.** Eddie Dean, David Sharpe, Roscoe Ates, Forrest Taylor, Dennis Moore, Warner Richmond, Bob Duncan, Charles "Blackie" King; ***D:*** Robert Emmett Tansey. *NOS, RXM, HEG*

Colorado Sundown ☾ **1952** A conniving brother and sister attempt to cheat a man out of his inheritance. **67m/B VHS.** Rex Allen, Mary Ellen Kay, Slim Pickens, June Vincent, Koko; ***D:*** William Witney. *NOS, DVT*

Colors ☾☾☾½ **1988 (R)** Vivid, realistic cop drama pairs sympathetic veteran Duvall and trigger-tempered rookie Penn on the gang-infested streets of East Los Angeles. Fine play from leads is one of the many assets in this controversial, unsettling depiction of deadly streetlife. Colorful, freewheeling direction from the underrated Hopper. Rattling rap soundtrack too. Additional footage has been added for video release. **120m/C VHS, Beta, LV.** Sean Penn, Robert Duvall, Maria Conchita Alonso, Trinidad Silva, Randi Brooks, Grand Bush, Don Cheadle, Rudy Ramos; ***D:*** Dennis Hopper; ***W:*** Michael Schiffer; ***C:*** Haskell Wexler; ***M:*** Herbie Hancock. *ORI, FCT*

Colossus and the Amazon Queen ☾½ **1964** Idle gladiators are unwillingly recruited for service to Amazons. Doesn't seem like the worst way to make a living. But lead actor Taylor—so notable in comedies, thrillers, and action flicks—is too good for this sort of thing. Dubbed. **94m/C VHS, Beta, 8mm.** *IT* Rod Taylor, Dorian Gray, Ed Fury. *VYY*

Colossus of the Arena ☾☾ **1960** In 4th century Rome, Forest plays a mighty gladiator who uncovers a plot to imprison a beautiful princess. Through an incredible series of feats and combats, he exposes an evil duke as a traitor. **?m/C VHS.** Mark Forest, Scilla Gabel. *SNC*

Colossus: The Forbin Project ☾☾☾ *The Forbin Project* **1970** A computer designed to manage U.S. defense systems teams instead with its Soviet equal and they attempt world domination. Wire-tight, suspenseful film seems at once dated yet timely. Based on the novel by D.F. Jones. **100m/C VHS, Beta.** Eric (Hans Gudegast) Braeden, Susan Clark, Gordon Pinsent, William Schallert, Georg Stanford Brown; ***D:*** Joseph Sargent; ***W:*** James Bridges; ***C:*** Gene Polito; ***M:*** Michel Colombier. *MCA*

Colt Comrades ☾☾ **1943** A bad guy's monopoly on water rights is jeopardized when Boyd and Clyde strike water while drilling for oil. Nothing really notable here, except for Bob (Robert) Mitchum and George ("Superman") Reeves in minor roles. **67m/B VHS.** William Boyd, Andy Clyde, Jay Kirby, George Reeves, Gayle Lord, Earle Hodgins, Victor Jory, Douglas Fowley, Herbert Rawlinson, Robert Mitchum; ***D:*** Lesley Selander. *NOS*

Columbo: Murder By the Book ☾☾½ **1971** The rumpled, cigar-smoking television detective investigates the killing of a mystery writer. Scripted by Bochco of "Hill Street Blues" and "L.A. Law" fame. **79m/C VHS, Beta.** Peter Falk, Jack Cassidy, Rosemary Forsyth, Martin Milner; ***D:*** Steven Spielberg; ***W:*** Steven Bochco. *MCA*

Columbo: Prescription Murder **1967** Falk's debut as the raincoat-clad lieutenant who always has just one more question. In the TV series pilot he investigates the death of a psychiatrist's wife. Rich with subplots. Good mystery fare. **99m/C VHS, Beta.** Peter Falk, Gene Barry, Katherine Justice, William Windom, Nina Foch, Anthony James, Virginia Gregg; ***D:*** Richard Irving; ***W:*** Richard Levinson, William Link. *MCA*

Coma ☾☾☾ **1978 (PG)** A doctor discovers murder and corpse-nabbing at her Boston hospital, defies her male bosses, and determines to find out what's going on before more patients die. Exciting, suspenseful fare, with Bujold impressive in lead. Based on the novel by Robin Cook. **113m/C VHS, Beta, LV.** Genevieve Bujold, Michael Douglas, Elizabeth Ashley, Rip Torn, Richard Widmark, Lois Chiles, Hari Rhodes, Tom Selleck, Ed Harris; ***D:*** Michael Crichton; ***W:*** Michael Crichton; ***M:*** Jerry Goldsmith. *MGM*

Comanche Territory ☾☾ **1950** Western frontiersman Jim Bowie travels to Comanche country and helps the Indians save their land from settlers. Routine oater. Based on a story by Meltzer. **76m/C VHS.** Maureen O'Hara, MacDonald Carey, Will Geer, Charles Drake; ***D:*** George Sherman; ***W:*** Oscar Brodney, Lewis Meltzer. *MCA*

The Comancheros ☾☾☾ **1961** Texas Ranger Wayne and his prisoner fight with the Comancheros, an outlaw gang who is supplying guns and liquor to the dreaded Comanche Indians. Musical score adds flavor. Last film by Curtiz. **108m/C VHS, Beta, LV.** John Wayne, Ina Balin, Stuart Whitman, Nehemiah Persoff, Lee Marvin, Bruce Cabot; ***D:*** Michael Curtiz; ***C:*** William Clothier; ***M:*** Elmer Bernstein. *FOX*

Combat! **1962** Morrow and Jason starred in this gritty series about an Army platoon in Europe during the final years of WWII. In "The Bridge at Chalons" Marvin guest stars as a demolitions expert. Additional episodes available. **50m/B VHS, Beta.** Vic Morrow, Rick Jason, Lee Marvin. *GKK, MOV*

Combat Academy ☾ **1986** Weak comedy about two goofballs sent to a military academy to straighten out, but instead turn the academy on its ear with their antics. Unremarkable. **96m/C VHS, LV.** Keith Gordon, Jamie Farr, Sherman Hemsley, John Ratzenberger, Bernie Kopell, Charles Moll; ***D:*** Neal Israel. *VTR, NWV*

Combat Killers ☾☾ **1980** A WWII Army captain grabs for individual glory on the battlefield, and jeopardizes the lives of his platoon. **96m/C VHS, Beta.** Paul Edwards, Marlene Dauden, Claude Wilson; ***D:*** Ken Loring. *MED*

Combat Shock ☾ *American Nightmares* **1984 (R)** A Vietnam veteran returns home and can't cope with the stresses of modern life, including the lowlifes who have been taking over the streets. So he goes after some scum who have been trying to kill him, succeeds, but things don't end well. Familiar plot handled in a conventional manner. **85m/C VHS, Beta.** Ricky Giovinazzo, Nick Nasta, Veronica Stork; ***D:*** Buddy Giovinazzo. *PSM*

Combination Platter ☾☾½ **1993** Anxious young immigrant Robert (Lau), newly arrived from Hong Kong, becomes a waiter at the Szechuan Inn in Queens, New York, where he gets a crash course in American culture and romance (as well as tipping). Gentle comedy works best with little details that ring true: overheard customer conversations, staff banter, the kitchen scenes. Lau's earnest, but effort feels like a series of small vignettes rather than a complete story. Still, a worthy first effort for the then 24-year-old Chan, who directed on a $250,000 budget, using his parents restaurant after hours for a set. **84m/C VHS.** Jeff Lau, Colleen O'Brien, Lester Chan, Thomas S. Hsiung, David Chung; ***D:*** Tony Chan; ***W:*** Tony Chan, Edwin Baker. Sundance Film Festival '93: Best Screenplay; Nominations: Independent Spirit Awards '94: Best First Feature, Best Screenplay, Best Supporting Actor (Chung). *AVI*

Come Along with Me ☾☾½ **1984** A made-for-television adaptation of Shirley Jackson's unfinished novel about a woman who sells all and leaves her hometown when her husband dies, determined to start a new career as a seer. **60m/C VHS, Beta.** Estelle Parsons, Barbara Baxley, Sylvia Sidney; ***D:*** Joanne Woodward. *MON, KAR*

Come and Get It ☾☾☾ *Roaring Timber* **1936** A classic adaptation of the Edna Ferber novel about a lumber king battling against his son for the love of a woman. Farmer's most important Hollywood role. **99m/B VHS, Beta.** Frances Farmer, Edward Arnold, Joel McCrea, Walter Brennan, Andrea Leeds, Charles Halton; ***D:*** William Wyler, Howard Hawks. Academy Awards '36: Best Supporting Actor (Brennan); Nominations: Academy Awards '36: Best Film Editing. *HBO, SUE, BTV*

Come and See ☾☾☾☾ *Idi i Smotri; Go and See* **1985** Harrowing, unnerving epic which depicts the horrors of war as a boy soldier roams the Russian countryside during the Nazi invasion. Some overwhelming sequences, including tracer-bullets flashing across an open field. War has rarely been rendered in such a vivid, utterly grim manner. Outstanding achievement from Soviet director Klimov. In Russian with English subtitles. **142m/C VHS.** *RU* Alexei Kravchenko, Olga Mironova, Lubomiras Lauciavicus; ***D:*** Elem Klimov. *KIV, .FCT, TPV*

Come Back, Africa ☾☾☾ **1960** A classic documentary about a Zulu family surviving under apartheid in South Africa. **83m/B VHS, Beta.** *MFV, FCT, TPV*

Come Back Little Reba ☾ **1986** A semi-educational film about a young black boy and his lovable aging dog. **60m/C VHS, Beta, LV.** *PAR*

Come Back, Little Sheba ☾☾☾½ **1952** Unsettling drama about a worn-out housewife, her abusive, alcoholic husband and a comely boarder who causes further marital tension. The title refers to the housewife's despairing search for her lost dog. Booth, Lancaster, and Moore are all excellent. Based on the play by William Inge, this film still packs an emotional wallop. **99m/B VHS, Beta, LV.** Burt Lancaster, Shirley Booth, Terry Moore, Richard Jaeckel, Philip Ober, Lisa Golm, Walter Kelley; ***D:*** Daniel Mann; ***C:*** James Wong Howe. Academy Awards '52: Best Actress (Booth); Cannes Film Festival '53: Best Actress (Booth); Golden Globe Awards '53: Best Actress—Drama (Booth); New York Film Critics Awards '52: Best Actress (Booth); Nominations: Academy Awards '52: Best Film Editing, Best Supporting Actress (Moore). *PAR, FCT, BTV*

Come Back to the Five & Dime Jimmy Dean, Jimmy Dean ☾☾☾ **1982 (PG)** Five women convene at a run-down Texas drugstore for a 20-year reunion of a local James Dean fan club. The women recall earlier times and make some stunning revelations. Altman's filming of Ed Graczyk's sometimes funny, sometimes wrenching play proves fine vehicle for the actresses. Cher is probably the most impressive, but Dennis and Black are also memorable. **109m/C VHS, Beta, LV.** Sandy Dennis, Cher, Karen Black, Kathy Bates, Sudie Bond, Marta Heflin; ***D:*** Robert Altman. *SUE*

Come Blow Your Horn ☾☾☾ **1963** Neil Simon's first major Broadway success is a little less successful in its celluloid wrapper, suffering a bit from a familiar script. Sinatra's a playboy who blows his horn all over town, causing his close-knit New York Jewish family to warp a bit. Dad's not keen on his son's pledge of allegiance to the good life, and kid brother Bill would like to be his sibling's understudy in playboyhood. **115m/C VHS, Beta.** Frank Sinatra, Lee J. Cobb, Tony Bill, Molly Picon, Barbara Rush, Jill St. John; ***D:*** Bud Yorkin; ***W:*** Norman Lear; ***C:*** William H. Daniels. Nominations: Academy Awards '63: Best Art Direction/Set Decoration (Color). *PAR*

Come On, Cowboys ☾½ **1937** The Three Mesquiteers rescue an old circus friend from certain death. Part of "The Three Mesquiteers" series. **54m/B VHS, Beta.** Bob Livingston, Ray Corrigan. *MED, DVT*

Come On Danger! ☾☾½ **1932** Keene makes his "B" Western debut, out to avenge the death of his brother and battle an outlaw gang. Haydon is forced into a life of crime in order to save her ranch from villain Ellis and only Texas Ranger Keene can set her free. **60m/B VHS.** Tom Keene, Julie Haydon,

Roscoe Ates, Robert Ellis, Wade Boteler; ***D:*** Robert F. "Bob" Hill; ***W:*** Bennett Cohen. *MOV*

Come On Rangers 🦴 **1938** Also called "Come On Ranger." Rogers and his friends go to Texas to avenge the death of a comrade. **54m/B VHS, Beta.** Roy Rogers, George "Gabby" Hayes. *NOS, DVT, RXM*

Come On Tarzan 🦴½ **1932** Maynard and his trusty horse Tarzan save wild horses from the bad guys who want to turn them into dog food. **60m/B VHS, Beta.** Ken Maynard. *NOS, VDM, DVT*

Come See the Paradise 🦴🦴🦴 **1990 (R)** Jack McGurn (Quaid) takes a job at a movie theatre in Los Angeles' Little Tokyo and falls for owner's daughter Lily (Tomita). They marry, but after the bombing of Pearl Harbor all Japanese-Americans are interned. Told in flashback, the story offers a candid look at the racism implicit in the relocations and the hypocrisy that often lurks beneath the surface of the pursuit of liberty and justice for all. Sometimes melodramatic script indulges a bit too much in the obvious, but the subject is worthwhile, one that has not yet been cast into the vast bin of Hollywood cliches. The cast, apart from Quaid's misguided attempt at seriousness, is excellent. **135m/C VHS, Beta, LV.** Dennis Quaid, Tamlyn Tomita, Sab Shimono, Shizuko Hoshi, Stan Egi, Ronald Yamamoto, Akemi Nishino, Naomi Nakano, Brady Tsurutani, Pruitt Taylor Vince, Joe Lisi; ***D:*** Alan Parker; ***W:*** Alan Parker; ***M:*** Randy Edelman. *FOX, FCT, CCB*

Come September 🦴🦴½ **1961** American business tycoon Robert Talbot (Hudson) maintains a holiday villa on the Italian Riveria. But the only time he uses the place is the month of September, so when Talbot arrives in July he discovers his enterprising major domo Maurice (Slezak) has been managing the place as a hotel the rest of the year. Talbot finds his home filled with tourists and, to make matters worse, discovers his Italian lover Lisa (Lollobrigida) about to get married. Darin and Dee are the film's romantic ingenues and wound up getting married after filming wrapped; his screen debut. **114m/C VHS.** Rock Hudson, Gina Lollobrigida, Sandra Dee, Bobby Darin, Walter Slezak, Joel Grey, Brenda de Banzie; ***D:*** Robert Mulligan; ***W:*** Stanley Shapiro, Maurice Richlin; ***C:*** William H. Daniels; ***M:*** Hans J. Salter. *MCA*

Come to the Stable 🦴🦴🦴 **1949** Warm, delightful story about two French nuns, Young and Holm, who arrive in New England and set about building a children's hospital. Although Catholic in intent, pic demonstrates that faith and tenacity can move mountains. (This film must have been Fox's response to Paramount's "Going My Way" and "The Bells of Saint Mary's.") Based on a story by Clare Boothe Luce. **94m/B VHS.** Loretta Young, Celeste Holm, Hugh Marlowe, Elsa Lanchester, Regis Toomey, Mike Mazurki; ***D:*** Henry Koster; ***W:*** Oscar Millard, Sally Benson; ***C:*** Joseph LaShelle; ***M:*** Cyril Mockridge. Nominations: Academy Awards '49: Best Actress (Young), Best Adapted Screenplay, Best Art Direction/Set Decoration (B & W), Best Black and White Cinematography, Best Supporting Actress (Holm, Lanchester). *FXV*

The Comeback 🦴 *The Day the Screaming Stopped* **1977** A singer attempting a comeback in England finds his wife murdered. **100m/C VHS, Beta.** *GB* Jack Jones, Pamela Stephenson, David Doyle, Bill Owen, Sheila Keith, Richard Johnson; ***D:*** Pete Walker. *ORI*

Comeback 🦴🦴½ **1983** The story of a disillusioned rock star, played by Eric Burdon (the lead singer of the Animals), who gives up his life in the fast lane and tries to go back to his roots. **105m/C VHS, Beta.** Eric Burdon; ***D:*** Christel Bushmann; ***M:*** Eric Burdon. *MGM*

Comeback Kid 🦴🦴 **1980** An ex-big league baseball player is conned into coaching an urban team of smarmy street youths, and falls for their playground supervisor. Made for television. **97m/C VHS, Beta.** John Ritter, Susan Dey; ***D:*** Peter Levin. *SUE, NLC*

The Comedians 🦴🦴½ **1967** Disturbing and powerful drama of political intrigue set against the murderous dictatorship of "Papa Doc" Duvalier. Burton plays the cynical owner of a resort hotel with Taylor as his German mistress. Ustinov is great as he does his usual scene-stealing in his role as a South American ambassador married to Taylor. Excellent cast was somewhat held back by sluggish direction and an uninspired script. Based on the novel of the same name by Graham Greene. **148m/C VHS.** Elizabeth Taylor, Richard Burton, Alec Guinness, Peter Ustinov, Paul Ford, Lillian Gish, Raymond St. Jacques, Zakes Mokae; ***D:*** Peter Glenville; ***W:*** Graham Greene. National Board of Review Awards '67: Best Supporting Actor (Ford). *MGM*

The Comedy of Terrors 🦴🦴🦴 **1964** Comedy in which some deranged undertakers take a hands-on approach to insuring their continued employment. Much fun is supplied by the quartet of Price, Lorre, Karloff, and Rathbone, all veterans of the horror genre. **84m/C VHS, LV.** Vincent Price, Peter Lorre, Boris Karloff, Basil Rathbone, Joe E. Brown, Joyce Jameson; ***D:*** Jacques Tourneur; ***W:*** Richard Matheson; ***C:*** Floyd Crosby; ***M:*** Les Baxter. *MOV*

Comes a Horseman 🦴🦴½ **1978 (PG)** Robards is a cattle baron, attempting to gobble up all the oil-rich land his neighbor owns. Neighbor Fonda has the courage to stand up to him, with the help of a WWII veteran and the local old timer Farnsworth, in this slow-moving but intriguing western drama. **119m/C VHS, Beta.** James Caan, Jane Fonda, Jason Robards Jr., George Grizzard, Richard Farnsworth, Jim Davis, Mark Harmon; ***D:*** Alan J. Pakula; ***W:*** Dennis Lynton Clark; ***C:*** Gordon Willis. National Board of Review Awards '78: 10 Best Films of the Year, Best Supporting Actor (Farnsworth); Nominations: Academy Awards '78: Best Supporting Actor (Farnsworth). *FOX*

Comfort and Joy 🦴🦴🦴½ **1984 (PG)** After his kleptomaniac girlfriend deserts him, a Scottish disc jockey is forced to reevaluate his life. He becomes involved in an underworld battle between two mob-owned local ice cream companies. Another odd comedy gem from Forsyth, who did "Gregory's Girl" and "Local Hero". Music by Dire Straits guitarist Knopfler. **93m/C VHS, Beta.** *GB* Bill Paterson, Eleanor David, C.P. Grogan, Alex Norton, Patrick Malahide, Rikki Fulton, Roberto Berrardi; ***D:*** Bill Forsyth; ***C:*** Chris Menges; ***M:*** Mark Knopfler. National Society of Film Critics Awards '84: Best Cinematography. *MCA*

The Comfort of Strangers 🦴🦴🦴 **1991 (R)** Atmospheric psychological thriller. Mary and Colin (Richardson and Everett), a handsome young British couple, take a Venetian holiday to rediscover the passion in their relationship. Lost in the city, they chance, it seems, upon Robert (Walken), a sort of Virgil in an Italian suit. He later reappears, and, abetted by his wife Caroline (Mirren), gradually leads the couple on an eerie tour of urbane decadence that hints at danger. Psychologically tantalizing and horrifyingly erotic, the movie's based on Ian McEwan's novel. **102m/C VHS, Beta.** Christopher Walken, Natasha Richardson, Rupert Everett, Helen Mirren; ***D:*** Paul Schrader; ***W:*** Harold Pinter; ***C:*** Dante Spinotti; ***M:*** Angelo Badalamenti. *PAR, FCT*

The Comic 🦴🦴🦴 **1969 (PG)** Van Dyke is terrific as a silent screen comedian (a composite of several real-life screen comics) whose ego destroys his career. Recreations of silent films, and the blend of comedy and pathos, are especially effective. **96m/C VHS, Beta, LV.** Dick Van Dyke, Mickey Rooney, Michele Lee, Cornel Wilde, Nina Wayne, Pert Kelton, Jeannine Riley; ***D:*** Carl Reiner; ***W:*** Carl Reiner. *COL*

The Comic 🦴 **1985** In a future police state, a young comedian kills the star and takes his place in the show. His future rises, but who cares? **90m/C VHS, Beta.** Steve Munroe, Bernard Plant, Jeff Pirie; ***D:*** Richard Driscoll. *NO*

Comic Book Kids 🦴½ **1982 (G)** Two youngsters enjoy visiting their friend's comic strip studio, since they have the power to project themselves into the cartoon stories. Viewers will be less impressed. **90m/C VHS, Beta.** Joseph Campanella, Mike Darnell, Robyn Finn, Jim Engelhardt, Fay De Witt. *GEM*

Comic Cabby *Woof!* **1987** A day in the life of an introvert cabby seems to last forever. From "New York City Cab Driver's Joke Book" by Jim Pietsch. **59m/C VHS, Beta.** Bill McLaughlin, Al Lewis. *VES, LIV*

Comin' Round the Mountain 🦴🦴½ **1951** The duo are caught in a Kentucky family feud while seeking a fortune in gold. Funniest bit has backwoods witch Hamilton squaring off with Costello when he refuses to pay for the love potion she's made him. **77m/B VHS.** Bud Abbott, Lou Costello, Dorothy Shay, Kirby Grant, Joseph Sawyer, Margaret Hamilton, Glenn Strange, Guy Wilkerson; ***D:*** Charles Lamont; ***W:*** John Grant, Robert Lees, Fred Rinaldo. *MCA*

Coming Home 🦴🦴🦴½ **1978 (R)** Looks at the effect of the Vietnam War on home front. The wife of a gung-ho Marine officer volunteers as an aide in a Veteran's Hospital, befriends and eventually falls in love with a Vietnam vet, paralyzed from war injuries. His attitudes, pain, and first-hand knowledge of the war force her to re-examine her previously automatic responses. Honest look at the everyday life of disabled veterans, unusual vision of the possibilities of simple friendship between men and women. Fonda and Voight are great; Dern's character suffers from weak scriptwriting late in the film. Critically acclaimed. Compelling score from late '60s music. **130m/C VHS, Beta, LV.** Jane Fonda, Jon Voight, Bruce Dern, Penelope Milford, Robert Carradine, Robert Ginty; ***D:*** Hal Ashby; ***W:*** Robert C. Jones; ***C:*** Haskell Wexler. Academy Awards '78: Best Actor (Voight), Best Actress (Fonda), Best Screenplay; Cannes Film Festival '78: Best Actor (Voight); Golden Globe Awards '79: Best Actor—Drama (Voight), Best Actress—Drama (Fonda); New York Film Critics Awards '78: Best Actor (Voight); Writers Guild of America '78: Best Original Screenplay; Nominations: Academy Awards '78: Best Director (Ashby), Best Film Editing, Best Picture, Best Supporting Actor (Dern), Best Supporting Actress (Milford). *MGM, FOX, FCT*

The Coming of Amos 🦴🦴🦴 **1925** A wonderful send-up of all those Fairbanks-style melodramas, with La Rocque as an Aussie on vacation on the French Riviera falling for and eventually rescuing Goudal, as the Russian princess held captive by the lustful Beery. **60m/B VHS, Beta.** Rod La Rocque, Jetta Goudal, Noah Beery Sr., Florence Vidor; ***D:*** Paul Sloane. *GVV*

Coming Out Alive 🦴🦴½ **1984** Tense thriller about a woman and her hired mercenary who try to rescue her kidnapped son from his estranged father—a radical is involved in an assassination plot. Hylands is especially compelling. **73m/C VHS, Beta.** Helen Shaver, Scott Hylands, Michael Ironside, Monica Parker. *TWE*

Coming Out of the Ice 🦴🦴🦴 **1982 (PG)** Engrossing true story of Victor Herman, an outstanding American athlete who worked in Russia in the 1930s. He was imprisoned in Siberia (for 38 years!) for refusing to renounce his American citizenship. Made for television. **100m/C VHS, Beta.** John Savage, Willie Nelson, Ben Cross, Francesca Annis, Peter Vaughan; ***D:*** Waris Hussein; ***M:*** Maurice Jarre. *FOX*

Coming Through 🦴🦴½ **1990** Writer D.H. Lawrence meets the married Frieda von Richthofer and begins a scandalous affair which intertwines with his own writings, and the life of a young man in the present day. Made for British television production lacks passion. **78m/C VHS.** *GB* Kenneth Branagh, Helen Mirren, Alison Steadman, Philip Martin Brown, Norman Rodway; ***D:*** Peter Barber-Fleming; ***W:*** Alan Plater. *TVC, VCO*

Coming to America 🦴🦴🦴 **1988 (R)** An African prince (Murphy) decides to come to America in search of a suitable bride. He lands in Queens, and quickly finds American women to be more confusing than he imagined. Sometimes overly-cute entertainment relieved by clever costume cameos by Murphy and Hall. Later lawsuit resulted in columnist Art Buchwald being given credit for story. **116m/C VHS, Beta, LV, 8mm.** Eddie Murphy, Arsenio Hall, James Earl Jones, John Amos, Madge Sinclair, Shari Headley, Don Ameche, Louie Anderson, Paul Bates, Allison Dean, Eriq La Salle, Calvin Lockhart, Samuel L. Jackson, Cuba Gooding Jr., Vanessa Bell, Frankie Faison, Vondie Curtis-Hall; ***D:*** John Landis; ***W:*** David Sheffield, Barry W. Blaustein; ***M:*** Nile Rodgers. Nominations: Academy Awards '88: Best Costume Design. *PAR, FCT*

Coming Up Roses ☠☠½ *Rhosyn A Rhith* **1987 (PG)** Pleasant comedy about the residents of a small mining village in the South of Wales who fight to keep their local movie house from being shut down. In Welsh with English subtitles. **95m/C VHS, Beta.** *GB* Dafydd Hywel, Iola Gregory, Olive Michael, Mari Emlyn, Bill Paterson; ***D:*** Stephen Bayly; ***W:*** Ruth Carter; ***M:*** Michael Storey. *FCT, INJ*

Command Decision ☠☠½ **1948** Upon realizing he must send his men on missions-of-no-return to destroy German jet production, Gable's WWII flight commander becomes tactically at odds with his political superior, Pidgeon (who's not keen to have his precision bombing plans placed in an unflattering light). Based on the stage hit by William Wister Haines, it's a late war pic by Wood, who earlier directed such diverse efforts as "A Night at the Opera," "The Devil and Miss Jones," and "Our Town." Vintage war-is-hell actioner. **112m/B VHS.** Clark Gable, Walter Pidgeon, Van Johnson, Brian Donlevy, Charles Bickford, John Hodiak; ***D:*** Sam Wood; ***M:*** Miklos Rozsa. *MGM, FCT*

Commando ☠☠☠ **1985 (R)** An ex-commando leader's daughter is kidnapped in a blackmail scheme to make him depose a South American president. He fights instead, and proceeds to rescue his daughter amid a torrential flow of falling bodies. Violent action spiced with throwaway comic lines. **90m/C VHS, Beta, LV.** Arnold Schwarzenegger, Rae Dawn Chong, Dan Hedaya, Vernon Wells, James Olson, David Patrick Kelly, Alyssa Milano, Bill Duke; ***D:*** Mark L. Lester; ***W:*** Steven E. de Souza; ***M:*** James Horner. *FXV, TLF*

Commando Attack ☠½ **1967** A tough sergeant leads a group of misfit soldiers to blow up a German radio transmitter the day before D-Day. **90m/C VHS, Beta.** Michael Rennie, Monica Randall, Bob Sullivan. *UNI*

Commando Invasion ☠ **1987** When an army captain is accused of murder, he hunts down the man he knows is responsible for the crime. Jungle revenge mayhem is confusing. Set in Viet Nam. **90m/C VHS.** Jim Gaines, Michael James, Gordon Mitchell, Carol Roberts, Pat Vance, Ken Watanabe; ***D:*** John Gale. *NO*

Commando Squad ☠ **1976 (R)** During WWII, soldiers go to battle to prevent the development of a device that re-animates flesh. The script stays dead. **82m/C VHS, Beta.** Chuck Alford, Peter Owen, April Adams; ***D:*** Charles Nizet. *GHV*

Commando Squad ☠ **1987 (R)** Story of drug agents undercover in Mexico, and a female agent who rescues her kidnapped lover. Firepower is wasted, but Shower is a former "Playboy" Playmate of the Year. **90m/C VHS, Beta.** Brian Thompson, William Smith, Kathy Shower, Sid Haig, Robert Quarry, Ross Hagen, Mel Welles, Marie Windsor, Russ Tamblyn; ***D:*** Fred Olen Ray. *TWE*

Commandos ☠½ **1973 (PG)** Commando operation against Rommel's forces in North Africa during WWII. Too much said, not enough action. Also know as "Sullivan's Marauders." **100m/C VHS, Beta.** *GE IT* Lee Van Cleef, Jack Kelly; ***D:*** Armando Crispino. *GEM, MRV, PSM*

Commandos Strike at Dawn ☠☠½ **1943** Norwegian villagers, including Muni, fight the invading Nazis, and eventually help the British Navy battle them over an Arctic supply line. Okay script helped along by veteran actors Muni and Gish. Based on a C.S. Forester story. **100m/B VHS, Beta.** Paul Muni, Lillian Gish, Cedric Hardwicke, Anna Lee, Ray Collins, Robert Coote, Alexander Knox, Rosemary DeCamp; ***D:*** John Farrow; ***W:*** Irwin Shaw; ***C:*** William Mellor. Nominations: Academy Awards '43: Best Original Score. *COL*

Comment Ca Va? ☠☠ *How Is It Going?* **1976** The boss and workers in a Communist publishing house decide to make a simple film about how information is manufactured. But Odette, one of the workers, has some strange ideas about filmmaking. In French with English subtitles. **76m/C VHS.** *FR* Anne-Marie Mieville; ***D:*** Jean-Luc Godard. *FCT*

The Commies are Coming, the Commies are Coming ☠☠ **1957** Cult classic will leave viewers red from laughing in disbelief. Webb narrates this anti-communist movie about the Russians taking over the United States. Filmed in a documentary style, it captures the paranoia of the times. Re-released in 1984, just before the Evil Empire collapsed. **60m/B VHS, Beta.** Jack Webb, Andrew Duggan, Robert Conrad, Jack Kelly, Peter Brown; ***D:*** George Waggner. *RHI*

Commissar ☠☠☠☠ *Komissar* **1968** Before the Soviet Union ended up in the ashcan of history, this film was labeled as "treason" and shelved in Red Russia. Now, even Americans can view the story of a female Soviet soldier who becomes pregnant during the civil war of 1922. The Soviet military has no policy regarding pregnancy, so the woman is dumped on a family of outcast Jews to complete her pregnancy. This film makes the strong statement that women were just as discriminated against in the U.S.S.R. as were many races or creeds, especially Jews. In Russian with English subtitles. Released in the U.S. in 1988. **105m/B VHS.** *RU* Nonna Mordyukova, Rolan Bykov; ***D:*** Alexander Askoldov. *KIV*

The Commitments ☠☠☠ **1991 (R)** Convinced that they can bring soul music to Dublin, a group of working-class youth form a band. High-energy production paints an interesting, unromanticized picture of modern Ireland and refuses to follow standard showbiz cliches, even though its lack of resolution hurts. Honest, whimsical dialog laced with poetic obscenities, delivered by a cast of mostly unknowns. Very successful soundtrack features the music of Wilson Pickett, James Brown, Otis Redding, Aretha Franklin, Percy Sledge, and others, and received a Grammy nomination. Based on the book "The Commitments" by Roddy Doyle, part of a trilogy which includes "The Snapper" and "The Van." **116m/C VHS, Beta, LV.** *IR* Andrew Strong, Bronagh Gallagher, Glen Hansard, Michael Aberne, Dick Massey, Ken McCluskey, Robert Arkins, Dave Finnegan, Johnny Murphy, Angeline Ball, Felim Gormley, Maria Doyle, Colm Meaney; ***D:*** Alan Parker; ***W:*** Dick Clement, Roddy Doyle, Ian LaFrenais. British Academy Awards '91: Best Adapted Screenplay, Best Director (Parker), Best Film; Nominations: Academy Awards '91: Best Film Editing. *FXV, CCB, IME*

Committed ☠½ **1991 (R)** Schlock-meister Levey's latest directorial effort is a step above his earlier "Slumber Party" and "Happy Hooker Goes to Washington," a statement ringing with the faintest of praise. Thinking she's applying for a job at an asylum, a nurse discovers she has committed herself. Try as she may, not even a committed nurse can snake her way out of the pit of madness they call "The Institute." **93m/C VHS.** Jennifer O'Neill, William Windom, Robert Forster, Ron Palillo, Sydney Lassick; ***D:*** William A. Levey. *MED, VTR*

The Committee ☠☠ **1968 (PG)** Comedy film of the seminal comedy troupe "The Committee," specialists in short, punchy satire. Dated, but of interest to comedy buffs. **88m/C VHS, Beta.** Wolfman Jack, Howard Hesseman, Barbara Bosson, Peter Bonerz, Garry Goodrow, Carl Gottlieb; ***D:*** Jack Del. *NO*

Common Bonds ☠☠½ **1991 (PG)** After being put together in an experimental outreach program, two mismatched partners struggle to break free from a system that threatens to destroy them both. **109m/C VHS, Beta.** Rae Dawn Chong, Michael Ironside, Brad Dourif; ***D:*** Allan Goldstein; ***M:*** Graeme Coleman. *ACA*

Common Law Wife ☠ **1963 (R)** Made-for-the-drive-in flick about a man whose common law marriage is threatened by his niece, who wants his money. Murder and mayhem abound when the man's moonshine is poisoned. Cheap and exploitative. **81m/B VHS.** Lacy Kelly, Shugfoot Rainey, Annabelle Lee, Jody Works, Anne MacAdams, George Edgely; ***D:*** Eric Sayers. *SNC*

Common Threads: Stories from the Quilt **1989** The heavily awarded, made-for-cable-TV documentary about the Quilt: an immense 14-acre blanket created by the survivors of AIDS victims as a monument to their loved ones' premature deaths. All proceeds from the sale of this tape go to the NAMES Project Foundation in support of the Quilt and AIDS service providers. **79m/C VHS, Beta, LV.** ***D:*** Robert Epstein, Jeffrey Friedman. Academy Awards '89: Best Feature Documentary. *WAR, HBO, IME*

Communion ☠☠ **1989 (R)** A serious adaptation of the purportedly nonfictional bestseller by Whitley Strieber about his family's abduction by extraterrestrials. Spacey new age story is overlong and hard to swallow. **103m/C VHS, Beta, LV.** Christopher Walken, Lindsay Crouse, Frances Sternhagen, Joel Carlson, Andreas Katsulas, Basil Hoffman; ***D:*** Philippe Mora; ***M:*** Eric Clapton. *NO*

The Companion ☠☠ **1994 (R)** In 2015 romance novelist Gillian Tanner (Harrold) decides to hide out at a remote mountain cabin to get over a broken love affair. For safety's sake, Gillian takes along custom-designed android companion Geoffrey (Greenwood). But then Gillian decides to tinker with Geoffrey's programming, turning him from domestic guardian to devoted lover. Unfortunately, Geoffrey doesn't understand the difference between fantasy and reality and becomes lethally obsessed. **94m/C VHS, LV.** Kathryn Harrold, Bruce Greenwood, Talia Balsam, Brion James, Bryan Cranston, Joely Fisher; ***D:*** Gary Fleder; ***W:*** Ian Seeberg, Valerie Bennett. *MCA*

Company Business ☠½ **1991 (PG-13)** Sam Boyd is a retired CIA agent who's brought back to swap Pyiotr Grushenko (Baryshnikov), a Russian mole in the State Department, for a U-2 pilot being held in Moscow. The swap is to be made in Berlin and also involves two million dollars of what turns out be to Colombian drug money. When things inevitably go wrong (both intelligence agencies would like them out of the way permanently) the two men find they must depend on each other if they want to stay alive. An unimaginative plot wastes a stalwart cast in this old-fashioned spy drama. **104m/C VHS.** Gene Hackman, Mikhail Baryshnikov, Kurtwood Smith, Terry O'Quinn; ***D:*** Nicholas Meyer; ***W:*** Nicholas Meyer. *MGM*

Company Limited ☠☠ **197?** The story of a young Indian sales executive working for a British owned firm, set in contemporary Calcutta. English subtitles. **112m/B VHS, Beta.** *IN CIG*

The Company of Wolves ☠☠☠ **1985 (R)** A young girl on the threshold of womanhood listens to her grandmother tell fairy tales and dreams of a medieval fantasy world inhabited by wolves and werewolves. An adult "Little Red Riding Hood" type comedy heavy on Freudian symbolism. Not really for kids. **95m/C VHS, Beta, LV.** Angela Lansbury, David Warner, Stephen Rea, Tusse Silberg, Sarah Patterson, Brian Glover, Danielle Dax, Graham Crowden, Micha Bergese; ***D:*** Neil Jordan; ***W:*** Neil Jordan, Angela Carter; ***M:*** George Fenton. *VES, LIV*

The Competition ☠☠☠ **1980 (PG)** Two virtuoso pianists meet at an international competition and fall in love. Will they stay together if one of them wins? Can they have a performance career and love too? Is he trying to distract her with sex, so he can win? Dreyfuss and Irving are fine (they practiced for four months to look like they were actually playing the pianos), and Remick's character has some interesting insights into the world of art. **125m/C VHS, Beta, LV.** Richard Dreyfuss, Amy Irving, Lee Remick, Sam Wanamaker, Joseph Cali, Ty Henderson, Priscilla Pointer, James B. Sikking; ***D:*** Joel Oliansky; ***M:*** Lalo Schifrin. Nominations: Academy Awards '80: Best Film Editing, Best Song ("People Alone"). *COL, TVC*

The Compleat Beatles ☠☠☠ **1982** Music, interviews, film clips, animation and live performances make up this "rockumentary" on the Beatles. New interviews are featured, as well as vintage film clips and studio footage with narration by Malcolm McDowell. The first U.S. press conference, legendary Hamburg footage, and an in-depth interview with George Martin are highlights. **120m/C VHS, Beta, LV.** John Lennon, Paul McCartney, Ringo Starr, George Harrison, George Martin, Brian Epstein, Billy Preston, Milt Oken, Bruce Johnston, Roger McGuinn, Mike McCartney, Mick Jagger; ***D:*** Patrick Montgomery. *MVD, MGM*

Complex **1985** Cute tale of a clever dog (aren't they all?) who annoys his swinish, beer-guzzling master by learning how to play chess, speak French, and read Dostoevsky. **12m/C VHS, Beta.** *BFA*

Complex World 🦴½ **1992 (R)** The Heartbreak Hotel is a notorious rock club which may not be around much longer. It seems the young owner's father is an ex-CIA redneck who is running for President and his son's profession is a political liability. Meanwhile, the town's mayor wants to replace the club with a shopping mall. A bomb is planted in the club's basement, terrorists lurk, and a gang of bikers is spoiling for a fight but the crowd at the Heartbreak just rocks on. **81m/C VHS.** Dan Welch, Bob Owczarek, Jay Charbonneau, Tilman Gandy Jr., David P.B. Stephens; ***D:*** James Wolpaw; ***W:*** James Wolpaw. *NO*

Compromising Positions 🦴🦴 **1985 (R)** A philandering dentist is killed on Long Island, and a bored housewife begins to investigate, uncovering scandal after scandal. Black comedy mixed unevenly with mystery makes for unsatisfying brew. However, Ivey is a standout as Sarandon's best friend. Screenplay was written by Susan Isaacs, based on her novel of the same title. **99m/C VHS, Beta, LV.** Susan Sarandon, Raul Julia, Edward Herrmann, Judith Ivey, Mary Beth Hurt, Joe Mantegna, Josh Mostel, Anne DeSalvo; ***D:*** Frank Perry; ***M:*** Brad Fiedel. *PAR*

Compulsion 🦴🦴🦴½ **1959** Artie Strauss (Dillman) is a mother-dominated sadist who, along with submissive friend Judd Steiner (Stockwell), plan and execute a cold-blooded murder. Flamboyant lawyer Jonathan Wilk (brilliantly portrayed by Welles) knows he has no defense so he attacks the system and establishment, seeking to at least save his clients from death. A suspenseful shocker with taut direction and a tight script. Based on the notorious 1924 Leopold and Loeb murder trial, also filmed as "Rope" and "Swoon." **103m/B VHS.** Orson Welles, Bradford Dillman, Dean Stockwell, Diane Varsi, E.G. Marshall, Martin Milner, Richard Anderson, Robert Simon, Edward Binns, Robert Burton, Wilton Graff, Gavin MacLeod; ***D:*** Richard Fleischer; ***W:*** Richard Murphy; ***C:*** William Mellor. *FXV*

Computer Beach Party 🦴 **1988** A couple of surf-head college computer hackers foil their mayor's plans to develop their favorite beach. The title, at least, is original. **97m/C VHS, Beta.** Hank Amigo, Stacey Nemour, Andre Chimene; ***D:*** Gary A. Troy. *VES, LIV*

Computer Wizard 🦴 **1977 (G)** Boy genius builds a powerful electronic device. His intentions are good, but the invention disrupts the town and lands him in big trouble. Not the "Thomas Edison Story." **91m/C VHS, Beta.** Henry Darrow, Kate Woodville, Guy Madison, Marc Gilpin; ***D:*** John Florea. *NO*

The Computer Wore Tennis Shoes 🦴½ **1969 (G)** Disney comedy (strictly for the kids) about a slow-witted college student who turns into a genius after a "shocking" encounter with the campus computer. His new brains give the local gangster headaches. Sequel: "Now You See Him, Now You Don't." **87m/C VHS, Beta.** Kurt Russell, Cesar Romero, Joe Flynn, William Schallert, Alan Hewitt, Richard Bakalayan; ***D:*** Robert Butler; ***M:*** Robert F. Brunner. *DIS, OM*

Comrade X 🦴🦴½ **1940** Gable is an American correspondent in Moscow who is blackmailed into marrying die-hard Communist Lamarr in this comedic spinoff of "Ninotchka." The two stars failed to create any sparks as a love duo, although their previous film "Boom Town" was a hit. Based on a story by Walter Reisch. **87m/B VHS.** Clark Gable, Hedy Lamarr, Oscar Homolka, Felix Bressart, Eve Arden, Sig Rumann, Natasha Lytess, Vladimir Sokoloff; ***D:*** King Vidor; ***W:*** Ben Hecht, Charles Lederer. *MGM*

Comrades in Arms 🦴½ **1991 (R)** When an international drug cartel threatens to take over the world, the United States and Russia must set their differences aside and team up to stop them. **91m/C VHS.** Lyle Alzado, Rick Washburne, John Christian, Lance Henriksen; ***D:*** J. Christian Ingvordsen; ***W:*** J. Christian Ingvordsen. *REP*

The Comrades of Summer 🦴🦴½ **1992 (R)** Mantegna plays big-league baseball coach Sparky Smith, whose fiery temper gets him into big trouble. Out of a job, he discovers the only team willing to take a chance on him happens to be Russian. Sparky finds the players of the Russian National team need a lot of help—and not just with their English. Made for cable television. **90m/C VHS, LV.** Joe Mantegna, Natalia Negoda, Mark Rolston, John Fleck, Eric Allen Kramer, Michael Lerner, Ian Tracey; ***D:*** Tommy Lee Wallace; ***W:*** Robert Rodat; ***M:*** William Olvis. *HBO*

The Con Artists 🦴½ *The Con Man* **1980** After con man Quinn is sprung from prison, he and his protege set up a sting operation against the beautiful Capucine. Not clever or witty enough for the caper to capture interest. **86m/C VHS, Beta.** *IT* Anthony Quinn, Adriano Celentano, Capucine, Corinne Clery; ***D:*** Sergio Corbucci. *HHE*

Con Man 🦴🦴 **1992** Robin Mitchell is a small-time con man on the fringes of London's underworld. He witnesses a brutal mob hit, which means they want him dead, and his girlfriend has decided it's just too dangerous being a part of his life. But Mitchell is convinced his luck will change for the better as he puts together a million-dollar long-shot that could secure him for life—if he survives. **91m/C VHS.** Ian McShane, Gayle Hunnicutt, Keith Barron, Alan Lake, Luan Peters; ***D:*** Francis Megahy. *NO*

Conagher 🦴🦴½ *Louis L'Amour's Conagher* **1991** A lyrical, if poorly plotted Western about a veteran cowboy who takes the whole movie to decide to end up in the arms of the pretty widow lady. Cable-TV adaptation of Louis L'Amour's novel doesn't have much intensity, though Elliott captures his character well. **94m/C VHS, Beta.** Sam Elliott, Katharine Ross, Barry Corbin, Buck Taylor, Dub Taylor, Daniel Quinn, Anndi McAfee, Billy Green Bush, Ken Curtis; ***D:*** Reynaldo Villalobos. *TTC*

Conan the Barbarian 🦴🦴🦴 **1982 (R)** A fine sword and sorcery tale featuring brutality, excellent production values, and a rousing score. Conan's parents are killed and he's enslaved. But hardship makes him strong, so when he is set free he can avenge their murder and retrieve the sword bequeathed him by his father. Sandahl Bergman is great as The Queen of Thieves, and Schwarzenegger maintains an admirable sense of humor throughout. Jones is dandy, as always. Based on the character created by Robert E. Howard. Sequel: "Conan the Destroyer." **115m/C VHS, Beta, LV.** Arnold Schwarzenegger, James Earl Jones, Max von Sydow, Sandahl Bergman, Mako, Ben Davidson, Valerie Quennessen, Cassandra Gaviola, William Smith; ***D:*** John Milius; ***W:*** John Milius, Oliver Stone; ***M:*** Basil Poledouris. *MCA*

Conan the Destroyer 🦴🦴½ **1984 (PG)** Conan is manipulated by Queen Tamaris into searching for a treasure. In return she'll bring Conan's love Valeria back to life. On his trip he meets Jones and Chamberlain, who later give him a hand. Excellent special effects, good humor, camp fun, somewhat silly finale. Sequel to the better "Conan the Barbarian." **101m/C VHS, Beta, LV.** Arnold Schwarzenegger, Grace Jones, Wilt Chamberlain, Sarah Douglas, Mako, Jeff Corey, Olivia D'Abo; ***D:*** Richard Fleischer; ***C:*** Jack Cardiff; ***M:*** Basil Poledouris. Golden Raspberry Awards '84: Worst New Star (D'Abo). *MCA*

Concealed Weapon 🦴½ **1994 (R)** A struggling actor gets the part of a lifetime but then becomes the prime suspect in a brutal crime. **80m/C VHS.** Daryl Haney, Suzanne Wouk, Monica Simpson, Mark Driscoll, Karen Stone; ***D:*** Dave Payne, Milan Zivkovich. *NHO*

The Concentratin' Kid 🦴🦴 **1930** An unusual horse opera sans shootouts and fisticuffs. Hoot's fiancee is kidnapped and taken to the range so that the renegade cowpokes can, uh, benefit from a female perspective on home decorating. Despite being outnumbered, Hoot concentrates and sets the rescue in motion, taking on the gang of rustlers without firing a shot. **54m/B VHS, Beta.** Hoot Gibson, Kathryn Crawford, Duke Lee, Robert E. Homans, James Mason; ***D:*** Arthur Rosson. *GPV*

The Concorde: Airport '79 🦴 *Airport '79* **1979 (PG)** A supersonic film in the "Airport" tradition has the Concorde chased by missiles and fighter aircraft before it crashes in the Alps. Incredibly far-fetched nonsense with an all-star cast doesn't fly. **103m/C VHS, Beta.** Alain Delon, Susan Blakely, Robert Wagner, Sylvia Kristel, John Davidson, Charo, Sybil Danning, Jimmie Walker, Eddie Albert, Bibi Andersson, Monica Lewis, Andrea Marcovicci, Martha Raye, Cicely Tyson, Mercedes McCambridge, George Kennedy, David Warner; ***D:*** David Lowell Rich; ***W:*** Eric Roth; ***M:*** Lalo Schifrin. *MCA*

Concrete Angels 🦴 **1987 (R)** A poignant glimpse at the influence of rock music in its infancy. A group of deprived teens in Toronto form a band and audition to open for the Beatles. Lack of nostalgia is refreshing, but too much of this is amateurish. **97m/C VHS, Beta.** *CA* Joseph Dimambro, Luke McKeehan, Omie Craden, Dean Bosacki. *ACA*

Concrete Beat 🦴½ **1984** A newspaper reporter simultaneously searches for a murderer, tries to win his ex-wife back, and writes front page stories for his editor/ex-father-in-law. Tough assignment. Made for television. **74m/C VHS, Beta.** Kenneth McMillan, John Getz, Darlanne Fluegel, Rhoda Gemignani; ***D:*** Robert Butler. *PSM*

The Concrete Cowboys 🦴½ *Ramblin' Man* **1979** Two bumbling cowboys from Montana come to the metropolis of Nashville and promptly turn detective to foil a blackmail scheme and locate a missing singer. Barbara Mandrell and Roy Acuff play themselves. Silly made-for-TV pilot of short-lived series. **100m/C VHS.** Jerry Reed, Tom Selleck, Morgan Fairchild, Claude Akins, Gene Evans, Roy Acuff, Barbara Mandrell; ***D:*** Burt Kennedy. *FOX, EDV, HHE*

The Concrete Jungle 🦴🦴 *The Criminal* **1982 (R)** After being set up by her no-good boyfriend, Bregman is sent to a correctional facility for drug smuggling. There she must learn to fend for herself (or else). Typical prison for gals fare with cute babes in revealing outfits, a topless riot, the bad warden, and a concerned social worker. Followed by "Chained Heat." **106m/C VHS, Beta.** Tracy Bregman, Jill St. John, Barbara Luna, Peter Brown, Aimee Eccles, Nita Talbot, Sondra Currie; ***D:*** Tom De Simone; ***W:*** Alan J. Adler. *COL*

Condemned to Hell *Woof!* **198?** A tough-as-iron street punk gets thrown into a women's prison, where she must fight for her existence. Low-brow violence galore. **97m/C VHS, Beta.** *IT* Leonor Benedetto. *TWE*

Condemned to Live 🦴🦴 **1935** Mild-mannered doctor Ralph Morgan and his fiancee Maxine Doyle seem like your average early 20th Century Middle-European couple...but the doctor's hunchbacked servant Mischa Auer is a tipoff that this is a horror movie of some sort. Like many men, the doctor has suffered from a vampire curse all his life. And, like many men, he is unaware of his blood-sucking habit, thanks to the concealment efforts of his loyal (hunchback) servant. Doyle discovers her fiance's sanguine secret, but not before she finds out she really loves Gleason, anyway. Answers the question: just how do you jilt a vampire? **68m/B VHS.** Ralph Morgan, Maxine Doyle, Russell Gleason, Pedro de Cordoba, Mischa Auer, Lucy Beaumont, Carl Stockdale; ***D:*** Frank Strayer. *SNC, LSV*

Condition Red 🦴🦴 **1995 (R)** Prison guard Russo's illicit involvement with inmate Williams turns deadly. **?m/C VHS.** James Russo, Cynda Williams; ***D:*** Mika Kaurismaki. *AVI*

Condorman 🦴🦴½ **1981 (PG)** Woody Wilkins, an inventive comic book writer, adopts the identity of his own character, Condorman, in order to help a beautiful Russian spy defect. A Disney film, strictly for the small fry. **90m/C VHS, Beta.** Michael Crawford, Oliver Reed, Barbara Carrera, James Hampton, Jean-Pierre Kalfon, Dana Elcar; ***D:*** Charles Jarrott; ***W:*** Glenn Gordon Caron; ***M:*** Henry Mancini. *DIS*

Conduct Unbecoming 🦴🦴½ **1975 (PG)** Late nineteenth century India is the setting for a trial involving the possible assault of a British officer's wife. Ambitious production based on a British stage play suffers from claustrophobic atmosphere but is greatly redeemed by the first rate cast. **107m/C VHS.** *GB* Michael York, Richard Attenborough, Trevor Howard, Stacy Keach, Christopher Plummer, Susannah York, James Faulkner, Michael Culver, Persis Khambatta; ***D:*** Michael Anderson Sr. *CRV*

The Conductor 🦴🦴 *Dyrygent* **1980** A famous Polish-born conductor (Gielgud) returns to his birthplace after 50 years of living in the U.S. A dying man, he decides to work with a struggling provincial orchestra, much to the dismay of their own conductor. But the conductor finds himself being used in government schemes to take advantage of his return. In English and Polish with subtitles. **101m/C VHS.** *PL* John Gielgud, Krystyna Janda, Andrzej Seweryn, Jan Ciercierski, Tadeusz Czechowski; ***D:*** Andrzej Wajda; ***W:*** Andrzej Kijowski. *NYF, ING*

Coneheads 🦴🦴½ **1993 (PG)** Comedy inspired by once popular characters from "Saturday Night Live" coasts in on the coattails of "Wayne's World." Aykroyd and Curtin reprise their roles as Beldar and Prymaat, the couple from the planet Remulak who are just trying to fit in on Earth. Newman, who created the role of teenage daughter Connie, appears as Beldar's sister, while Burke takes over as Connie (toddler Connie is Aykroyd's daughter, in her film debut). One-joke premise is a decade late and a dime short, though cast of comedy all-stars provides a lift. **86m/C VHS, Beta.** Dan Aykroyd, Jane Curtin, Laraine Newman, Jason Alexander, Michelle Burke, Chris Farley, Michael McKean, Phil Hartman, David Spade, Dave Thomas, Michael Richards, Lisa Jane Persky, Sinbad, Shishir Kurup, Jan Hooks, Chris Rock, Adam Sandler, Julia Sweeney, Danielle Aykroyd; ***D:*** Steven Barron; ***W:*** Dan Aykroyd, Tom Davis, Bonnie Turner, Terry Turner. *PAR, BTV*

Confessing to Laura 🦴🦴 *Confesion a Laura* **1990** Set in Colombia after the 1948 assassination of liberal leader Jorge Elieser Gaitain, which begets a violent civil war. Two people are trapped at Laura's house by the riots—setting up a night of volatile emotion. Spanish with subtitles. **90m/C VHS.** *CL* ***D:*** Jaime Osorio Gomez. *FCT*

The Confession 🦴🦴½ **1920** A priest hears a killer's confession and must protect the oath of confidentiality, even as his own brother is being convicted of the murder. **78m/B VHS.** Henry B. Walthall, Francis McDonald, William H. Clifford, Margaret McWade, Margaret Landis; ***D:*** Bertram Bracken. *GPV*

The Confessional 🦴 *House of Mortal Sin* **1975 (R)** A mad priest unleashes a monster from his confessional to wreak havoc upon the world. Pray for your VCR. **108m/C VHS, Beta.** *GB* Anthony Sharp, Susan Penhaligon, Stephanie Beacham, Norman Eshley, Sheila Keith; ***D:*** Pete Walker. *PSM*

The Confessional 🦴🦴½ *Le Confessionnal* **1995** Ambiguous psychological drama that's, in part, a homage to Alfred Hitchcock's 1952 film "I Confess," which was filmed in the same Quebec City locations. Pierre (Bluteau) returns to Quebec in 1989 for his father's funeral and to reunite with his adoptive brother Marc (Goyette). Marc's mother Rachel (who committed suicide shortly after his birth) refused to name his father, thought to be a priest, perhaps at the church where Hitchcock filmed his movie. Flashbacks depict the rotund director (Burrage) and his assistant (Scott Thomas) and their production. Lots of intriguing visuals, thanks to director Lepage's innovative stage background. French with subtitles. **100m/C VHS.** *CA FR GB* Lothaire Bluteau, Patrick Goyette, Jean-Louis Millette, Kristin Scott Thomas, Ron Burrage, Richard Frechette, Francois Papineau, Marie Gignac; ***D:*** Robert Lepage; ***W:*** Robert Lepage; ***C:*** Alan Dostie; ***M:*** Sacha Puttnam. Genie Awards '95: Best Art Direction/Set Decoration, Best Director (Lepage), Best Film; Nominations: Genie Awards '95: Best Actor (Bluteau). *NYR*

Confessions of a Hit Man 🦴🦴 **1994 (R)** Nephew who stole millions from his mobster uncle must amend his sordid past. **93m/C VHS, LV.** James Remar, Michael Wright, Emily Longstreth; ***D:*** Larry Leahy; ***W:*** Tony Cinciripini, Larry Leahy; ***M:*** Billy Talbot. *HMD*

Confessions of a Police Captain 🦴🦴 **1972 (PG)** A dedicated police captain tries to wipe out the bureaucratic corruption that is infecting his city. Balsam gives a fine performance in a heavy-going tale. **104m/C VHS, Beta.** *IT* Martin Balsam, Franco Nero, Marilu Tolo; ***D:*** Damiano Damiani. *SUE*

Confessions of a Serial Killer 🦴🦴 **1987** True story based on the life of Henry Lee Lucas, one of the nation's most vicious killers. Burns plays Lucas in this grisly account of his most violent murders. Shocking realistic look inside the mind of a serial killer. **85m/C VHS.** Robert Burns, Dennis Hill; ***D:*** Mark Blair. *NHO*

Confessions of a Vice Baron 🦴 **1942** Vice Baron Lombardo makes it big as a drug dealer and flesh peddler, then loses it all when he falls in love. Sleazy exploitation. **70m/B VHS, Beta.** Willy Castello; ***D:*** John Melville. *SNC*

Confessions of Tom Harris 🦴 *Tale of the Cock; Childish Things* **1972 (PG)** Somewhere between all the prize-fighting, leg-breaking for the mob, and jail terms for rape, Tom Harris finds time for a life-changing encounter with love. Based on true story. **90m/C VHS, Beta.** Don Murray, Linda Evans, David Brian, Gary Clarke, Logan Ramsey, Angelique Pettyjohn; ***D:*** John Derek, David Nelson; ***W:*** Don Murray. *NO*

Confidential 🦴🦴½ **1935** A G-man goes under cover to infiltrate a crime ring. Well made and full of action, fun array of character actors. Naish particularly good as nasty killer. **67m/B VHS.** Donald Cook, Evalyn Knapp, Warren Hymer, J. Carrol Naish, Herbert Rawlinson, Morgan Wallace, Kane Richmond, Theodore von Eltz, Reed Howes; ***D:*** Edward L. Cahn. *VYY*

Confidential *Woof!* **1986 (R)** A '40s detective tries to solve a decades-old axe murder, only to disappear himself. Horrible fare from our friends north of the border. **95m/C VHS, Beta.** *CA* Neil Munro, August Schellenberg, Chapelle Jaffe, Tom Butler; ***D:*** Bruce Pittman. *NO*

Confidentially Yours 🦴🦴🦴 *Vivement Dimanche!; Finally, Sunday* **1983 (PG)** Truffaut's homage to Hitchcock, based on Charles Williams' "The Long Saturday Night." A hapless small-town real estate agent is framed for a rash of murders and his secretary, who is secretly in love with him, tries to clear his name. Truffaut's last film is stylish and entertaining. In French with English subtitles. **110m/B VHS, Beta, LV.** *FR* Fanny Ardant, Jean-Louis Trintignant, Philippe Morier-Genoud, Philippe Laudenbach, Caroline Sihol; ***D:*** Francois Truffaut; ***W:*** Suzanne Schiffman; ***C:*** Nestor Almendros; ***M:*** Georges Delerue. *FOX, INJ, HMV*

Conflict 🦴🦴🦴 **1945** Bogart falls for his sister-in-law and asks his wife for a divorce. She refuses, he plots her murder, and thinks up the alibi. When the police fail to notify him of her death, Bogart is forced to report his wife missing. But is she dead? Her guilty husband smells her perfume, sees her walking down the street, and discovers the body is missing from the scene of the crime. Suspenseful thriller also features Greenstreet as a psychologist/family friend who suspects Bogart knows more than he's telling. **86m/B VHS.** Humphrey Bogart, Alexis Smith, Sydney Greenstreet, Rose Hobart, Charles Drake, Grant Mitchell; ***D:*** Curtis Bernhardt. *MGM*

Conflict of Interest 🦴½ **1992 (R)** Gideon (Nelson) is a thug who runs stolen cars, drugs, and women from his heavy-metal club on the wrong side of town. Mickey Flannery (McDonald) is the new cop determined to get Gideon behind bars, especially after Gideon kills Mickey's wife, sets up his son on a phony murder rap, and kidnaps his son's girlfriend. Now it's personal and Mickey will stop at nothing to get his revenge. Over-the-top performance by Nelson will have the viewer hoping he gets it soon and puts the film out of its misery. **88m/C VHS.** Judd Nelson, Christopher McDonald, Alyssa Milano, Dey Young, Gregory Alan Harris; ***D:*** Gary Davis; ***W:*** Gregory Miller, Michael Angeli. *HBO*

The Conformist 🦴🦴🦴🦴 *Il Conformist* **1971 (R)** Character study of young Italian fascist, plagued by homosexual feelings, who must prove his loyalty by killing his old professor. Decadent and engrossing story is brilliantly acted. Based on the novel by Alberto Moravia. **108m/C VHS, Beta, LV.** *IT FR GE* Jean-Louis Trintignant, Stefania Sandrelli, Dominique Sanda, Pierre Clementi, Gastone Moschin, Pasquale Fortunato; ***D:*** Bernardo Bertolucci; ***W:*** Bernardo Bertolucci; ***C:*** Vittorio Storaro; ***M:*** Georges Delerue. National Board of Review Awards '71: 5 Best Foreign Films of the Year; National Society of Film Critics Awards '71: Best Cinematography, Best Director (Bertolucci); Nominations: Academy Awards '71: Best Adapted Screenplay. *INJ, PAR, APD*

Congo 🦴🦴 **1995 (PG-13)** Communications company supervisor jets off to the African jungle along with a primatologist to search for a lost city's priceless diamonds, and to return Amy, a gorilla who communicates with sign language to her natural habitat. Why she would want to return to volcanoes and bloodthirsty mutant gray gorillas is anybody's guess. This appropriately technology-laden adaptation of Michael Crichton's novel delivers all the cliches of the old B-movie jungle flicks, but none of the thrills or fun of other Crichton adaptations. **109m/C VHS, Beta.** Dylan Walsh, Laura Linney, Ernie Hudson, Tim Curry, Grant Heslov, Joe Don Baker; ***D:*** Frank Marshall; ***W:*** John Patrick Shanley; ***C:*** Allen Daviau; ***M:*** Jerry Goldsmith. Nominations: Golden Raspberry Awards '95: Worst Picture. *NYR*

Congress Dances 🦴🦴 *Der Kongress Tanzt* **1931** A rare German musical about a romance in old Vienna. Popular in its day, it was subsequently banned by the Nazis in 1937. In German with English subtitles. **92m/B VHS, Beta.** *GE* Lilian Harvey, Conrad Veidt, Willy Fritsch; ***D:*** Erik Charell. *INJ, NOS, HHT*

A Connecticut Yankee 🦴🦴🦴 **1931** A charming, if somewhat dated, version of the popular Mark Twain story, "A Connecticut Yankee in King Arthur's Court." Rogers is a radio shop owner who dreams his way back to the Knights of the Round Table. Story rewritten to fit Rogers' amiable style and to make then-current wisecracks. Great cast overcomes weak points in the script. **96m/B VHS.** Will Rogers, Myrna Loy, Maureen O'Sullivan, William Farnum; ***D:*** David Butler. *FOX, FCT*

A Connecticut Yankee in King Arthur's Court 🦴🦴½ *A Yankee in King Arthur's Court* **1949** A pleasant version of the famous Mark Twain story about a 20th century man transported to Camelot and mistaken for a dangerous wizard. This was the third film version of the classic, which was later remade as "Unidentified Flying Oddball," a made for television movie and an animated feature. ♫Once and For Always; Busy Doin' Nothin'; If You Stub Your Toe on the Moon; When Is Sometime?; Twixt Myself and Me. **108m/C VHS, Beta, LV.** Bing Crosby, Rhonda Fleming, William Bendix, Cedric Hardwicke, Henry Wilcoxon, Murvyn Vye, Virginia Field; ***D:*** Tay Garnett; ***C:*** Ray Rennahan. *MCA*

A Connecticut Yankee in King Arthur's Court 🦴🦴½ **1989** The Mark Twain classic has had a gender switch in this TV version, with Pulliam as the time-travelling heroine who winds up in the royal court. **100m/C VHS.** Keisha Knight Pulliam, Jean Marsh, Rene Auberjonois, Emma Samms, Whip Hubley, Michael Gross; ***D:*** Mel Damski. *FHE*

The Connection 🦴🦴🦴½ **1961** The Living Theatre's ground-breaking performance of Jack Gelber's play about heroin addicts waiting for their connection to arrive, while a documentary filmmaker hovers nearby with his camera. **105m/B VHS, Beta.** Warren Finnerty, Carl Lee, William Redfield, Roscoe Lee Browne, Garry Goodrow, James Anderson, Jackie McLean; ***D:*** Shirley Clarke. *MFV, FCT*

The Connection 🦴🦴½ **1973** Durning steps in to work a deal between hotel jewel thieves and the insurance company. Complex plot handled deftly by all concerned. Made for television. **74m/C VHS, Beta.**

Charles Durning, Ronny Cox, Dennis Cole, Zohra Lampert, Heather MacRae, Dana Wynter; ***D:*** Tom Gries. *VMK*

The Conqueror *Woof!* **1956** Wayne in pointed helmet and goatee is convincingly miscast as Genghis Khan in this woeful tale of the warlord's early life and involvement with the kidnapped daughter of a powerful enemy. Rife with stilted, unintentionally funny dialogue, Oriental western was very expensive to make (with backing by Howard Hughes), and is now listed in the "Fifty Worst Films of All Time." No matter; it's surreal enough to enable viewer to approximate an out-of-body experience. Even those on the set suffered; filming took place near a nuclear test site in Utah and many members of the cast and crew eventually developed cancer. **111m/C VHS, Beta.** John Wayne, Susan Hayward, William Conrad, Agnes Moorehead, Lee Van Cleef, Pedro Armendariz Sr., Thomas Gomez, John Hoyt; ***D:*** Dick Powell; ***W:*** Oscar Millard; ***C:*** Joseph LaShelle. *MCA*

Conqueror & the Empress *Woof!* **1964** Low-budget tale of English explorers who roust an island prince from his throne, motivating him to engage in inspired blood-letting. **89m/C VHS, Beta.** Guy Madison, Ray Danton, Mario Petri, Alberto Farnese. *NO*

Conqueror of the World *Woof!* **1985** The adventures of a caveman named Bog. Really. Based on the novel by Albert Cavallone. Available in Spanish. **90m/C VHS, Beta.** *NO*

The Conqueror Worm 🦴🦴🦴 *Witchfinder General; Edgar Allan Poe's Conqueror Worm* **1968** Price turns in a fine performance portraying the sinister Matthew Hopkins, a real-life 17th century witchhunter. No "ham" in this low-budget, underrated thriller. The last of three films from director Reeves, who died from an accidental overdose in 1969. Also available with "Tomb of Ligeia" on Laser Disc. **95m/C VHS.** *GB* Vincent Price, Ian Ogilvy, Hilary Dwyer, Rupert Davies, Robert Russell, Patrick Wymark, Wilfrid Brambell; ***D:*** Michael Reeves. *HBO, FCT*

Conquest 🦴🦴🦴 *Marie Walewska* **1937** Garbo, as the Polish countess Marie Walewska, tries to persuade Napoleon (Boyer) to free her native Poland from the Russian Tsar. Garbo, Boyer, and Ouspenskaya are outstanding, while the beautiful costumes and lavish production help, but the script is occasionally weak. A box office flop in the U.S., which ended up costing MGM more than any movie it had made up until that time. **115m/B VHS, Beta.** Greta Garbo, Charles Boyer, Reginald Owen, Alan Marshal, Henry Stephenson, Leif Erickson, May Whitty, Maria Ouspenskaya, Vladimir Sokoloff, Scotty Beckett; ***D:*** Clarence Brown; ***C:*** Karl Freund. *MGM, FCT*

Conquest 🦴½ **1983 (R)** Sword and sorcery tale of two mighty warriors against an evil sorceress who seeks world domination. Excellent score. **92m/C VHS, Beta.** *IT SP MX* Jorge Rivero, Andrea Occhipinti, Violeta Cela, Sabrina Siani; ***D:*** Lucio Fulci; ***M:*** Claudio Simonetti. *MED*

Conquest of Cochise 🦴🦴 **1953** Mediocre oater about a cavalry officer who must stop the war between the Apache and Comanche tribes and a group of Mexicans in the Southwest of the 1850s. **70m/C VHS, Beta.** John Hodiak, Robert Stack, Joy Page; ***D:*** William Castle. *GKK*

Conquest of Mycene 🦴½ *Ercole Contro Molock* **1963** Hercules battles an evil queen and this time he may actually lose! Muscleman mayhem will entertain the kids. **102m/C VHS.** *IT FR* Gordon Scott, Rosalba (Sara Bay) Neri, Jany Clair; ***D:*** Giorgio Ferroni. *SNC*

Conquest of Space 🦴½ **1955** A spaceship sets off to explore Mars in spite of the commander's attempts to sabotage the voyage. He believes the flight is an heretical attempt to reach God. An uneasy mixture of religion and space exploration detracts from the nifty special effects which are the only reason to watch. **81m/C VHS.** Walter Brooke, Eric Fleming, Mickey Shaughnessy, Phil Foster, William Redfield, William Hopper, Benson Fong, Ross Martin; ***D:*** Byron Haskin; ***C:*** Lionel Lindon. *PAR*

Conquest of the Normans 🦴 **1962** During the Norman invasion of England, Oliver is accused of kidnapping the King. To save his life, Oliver must find the true identity of the abductors. With so much plot, there should have been some suspense. **83m/C Beta.** Cameron Mitchell. *AIP*

Conquest of the Planet of the Apes 🦴🦴½ **1972 (PG)** The apes turn the tables on the human Earth population when they lead a revolt against their cruel masters in the distant year of 1990. Sure, there's plenty of cliches—but the story drags you along. The 4th film in the series. Followed by "Battle for the Planet of the Apes." **87m/C VHS, Beta, LV.** Roddy McDowall, Don Murray, Ricardo Montalban, Natalie Trundy, Severn Darden, Hari Rhodes; ***D:*** J. Lee Thompson; ***C:*** Bruce Surtees. *FOX*

Conrack 🦴🦴🦴 **1974 (PG)** The true story of Pat Conroy, who tried to teach a group of illiterate Black children in South Carolina by using common-sense teaching techniques to inspire their interest. Voight is convincing as the earnest teacher. Based on Conroy's novel "The Water Is Wide." **111m/C VHS, Beta.** Jon Voight, Paul Winfield, Madge Sinclair, Hume Cronyn, Martin Ritt; ***D:*** Martin Ritt; ***W:*** Harriet Frank Jr., Irving Ravetch; ***C:*** John A. Alonzo; ***M:*** John Williams. *FOX*

Consenting Adult 🦴🦴½ **1985** Made for television movie about a distressed family coming to terms with a favorite son's homosexuality. Restrained exploration of the controversial subject. Based on Laura Z. Hobson's novel. **100m/C VHS.** Marlo Thomas, Martin Sheen, Barry Tubb, Talia Balsam, Ben Piazza, Corinne Michaels; ***D:*** Gilbert Cates; ***W:*** John McGreevey. *NO*

Consenting Adults 🦴🦴 **1992 (R)** Cookie-cutter thriller capitalizes on popular "psycho-destroys-your-normal-life" theme. Average yuppie couple (Kline and Mastrantonio) are startled and then seduced by the couple moving in next door (Spacey and Miller), who conduct a considerably less-restrained lifestyle. Wife-swapping leads to murder and an innocent man is framed. Plot and characters are underdeveloped yet manage to hold interest through decent performances. **100m/C VHS, Beta, LV.** Kevin Kline, Mary Elizabeth Mastrantonio, Kevin Spacey, Rebecca Miller, Forest Whitaker, E.G. Marshall, Billie Neal; ***D:*** Alan J. Pakula; ***W:*** Matthew Chapman. *HPH, IME*

Consolation Marriage 🦴🦴½ *Married in Haste* **1931** A couple meet and marry after being jilted by others, then must make a choice when their old flames return. Dunne and O'Brien make a charming couple in this early talkie. One of Dunne's early starring roles. **82m/B VHS, Beta.** Irene Dunne, Pat O'Brien, John Halliday, Matt Moore, Myrna Loy, Lester Vail; ***D:*** Paul Sloane. *TTC*

Conspiracy 🦴🦴 **1989 (R)** Defense Secretary William Baine is haunted by a past sexual encounter, and a top secret team moves in to avert any hint of what could become a "sex scandal." Based on a true story. **87m/C VHS, Beta.** James Wilby, Kate Hardie, Glyn Houston; ***D:*** Christopher Barnard. *ACA*

Conspiracy of Hearts 🦴🦴🦴 **1960** A convent of nuns hide Jewish children in 1943 Italy despite threats to their personal safety. Suspenseful tale despite the familiar plot. **113m/B VHS, Beta.** *GB* Lilli Palmer, Yvonne Mitchell, Sylvia Syms, Ronald Lewis; ***D:*** Ralph Thomas. *LCA*

A Conspiracy of Love 🦴 **1987** A made-for-television movie about three generations of a divorce-torn family trying to pull itself back together. Sugary domestic tale tries to be uplifting, succeeds in being cliche-ridden. **93m/C VHS.** Robert Young, Drew Barrymore, Glynnis O'Connor, Elizabeth Wilson, Michael Laurence, John Fujioka, Alan Fawcett; ***D:*** Noel Black. *VTR, NWV*

Conspiracy of Terror 🦴🦴 **1975** Married detectives investigate a series of murders and unearth a grisly cult in a quiet suburb. Standard fare with a few too cute lines concerning the leads' mixed-faith marriage. Made for television pilot. **78m/C VHS.** Michael Constantine, Barbara Rhoades, Mariclare Costello, Roger Perry, David Opatoshu, Logan Ramsey; ***D:*** John Llewellyn Moxey. *LIV*

Conspiracy: The Trial of the Chicago Eight 🦴🦴🦴 **1987** Courtroom drama focuses on the rambunctious trial of the Chicago Eight radicals, charged with inciting a riot at the Democratic National Convention of 1968. Dramatized footage mixed with interviews with the defendants. Imaginative reconstruction of history. **118m/C VHS, Beta.** Peter Boyle, Elliott Gould, Robert Carradine, Martin Sheen, David Clennon, David Kagen, Michael Lembeck, Robert Loggia; ***D:*** Jeremy Paul Kagan. *NO*

Conspirator 🦴🦴½ **1949** Somewhat engrossing drama about a beautiful young girl who discovers that her new husband, a British army officer, is working with the Communists. Elizabeth Taylor stars as the naive American wife and Robert Taylor plays her Russkie agent husband. Although madly in love with his wife, he is given orders to kill her. Picture falls apart at end due to weak script. Based on the novel by Humphrey Slater. **85m/B VHS.** *GB* Robert Taylor, Elizabeth Taylor, Robert Flemyng, Harold Warrender, Honor Blackman, Marjorie Fielding, Thora Hird; ***D:*** Victor Saville; ***W:*** Sally Benson, Gerard Fairlie; ***C:*** Frederick A. (Freddie) Young. *MGM*

Consuming Passions 🦴½ **1988 (R)** A ribald, food-obsessed English comedy about a young idiot who rises within the hierarchy of a chocolate company via murder. You'll never guess what the secret ingredient in his wonderful chocolate is. Based on a play by Michael Palin and Terry Jones (better known as part of the Monty Python troupe), the film is sometimes funny, more often gross, and takes a single joke far beyond its limit. **95m/C VHS, Beta, LV.** *GB* Vanessa Redgrave, Jonathan Pryce, Tyler Butterworth, Freddie Jones, Prunella Scales, Sammi Davis, Thora Hird; ***D:*** Giles Foster; ***W:*** Michael Palin, Andrew Davies. *NO*

Contagion 🦴½ **1987** Innocent real estate agent meets a reclusive, eccentric millionaire who offers him unlimited wealth and beautiful women, but only if he kills someone. Interesting ethical premise loses its philosophic purity. **90m/C VHS, Beta.** *AU* John Doyle, Nicola Bartlett, Roy Barrett, Nathy Gaffney, Pamela Hawksford; ***D:*** Karl Zwicky. *NO*

Contempt 🦴🦴🦴½ *Le Mepris; Il Disprezzo* **1964** A film about the filming of a new version of "The Odyssey," and the rival visions of how to tell the story. Amusing look at the film business features Fritz Lang playing himself, Godard as his assistant. Bardot is pleasant scenery. Adapted from Moravia's "A Ghost at Noon." **102m/C VHS, Beta, LV.** *IT FR* Brigitte Bardot, Jack Palance, Fritz Lang, Georgia Moll, Michel Piccoli; ***D:*** Jean-Luc Godard; ***W:*** Jean-Luc Godard; ***M:*** Georges Delerue. *COL, INJ, SUE*

Continental Divide 🦴🦴 **1981 (PG)** A hard-nosed political columnist takes off for the Colorado Rockies on an "easy assignment"—interviewing a reclusive ornithologist, with whom he instantly falls in love. A city slicker, he first alienates her, but she eventually falls for him, too. But it's not exactly a match made in heaven. Story meanders to a conclusion of sorts. Probably the most normal Belushi ever was on screen. **103m/C VHS, Beta, LV.** John Belushi, Blair Brown, Allen (Goorwitz) Garfield, Carlin Glynn, Val Avery, Tony Ganios, Tim Kazurinsky; ***D:*** Michael Apted; ***W:*** Lawrence Kasdan. *MCA*

Contra Company 🦴 **1988 (R)** A teenage girl and an embittered ex-terrorist narrowly escape from a terrorist-infested region in this confusing film about politics, drugs, and sinister dealings. **110m/C VHS, Beta.** *NO*

Contraband 🦴½ **1986** The leader of a smuggling gang escapes from an ambush in which his brother was murdered. He searches for a haven of safety while his cronies seek brutal revenge. Average crime yarn lacks much excitement. Dubbed into English. **95m/C VHS, Beta.** *IT* Fabio Testi, Ivana Monti; ***D:*** Lucio Fulci. *NO*

Control 🦴½ **1987** Tedious tale of fifteen volunteers for a 20-day fallout shelter habitation experiment who become trapped when a real nuclear emergency occurs. Filmed in Rome. Made for cable TV. **83m/C VHS, Beta.** *IT* Burt Lancaster, Kate Nelligan, Ben

Gazzara, Andrea Ferreol, Lavinia Segurini, Andrea Occhipinti, Cyrielle Claire, Jean Benguigui, Kate Reid, Erland Josephson, Ingrid Thulin; ***D:*** Guiliano Montaldo. *CNG, HBO*

The Conversation ♂♂♂ ½ **1974 (PG)** Hackman plays a surveillance expert increasingly uneasy about his job as he begins to suspect he is an accomplice to murder. Powerful statement about privacy, responsibility and guilt. One of the best movies of the '70s. **113m/C VHS, Beta, LV.** Gene Hackman, John Cazale, Frederic Forrest, Allen (Goorwitz) Garfield, Cindy Williams, Robert Duvall, Teri Garr, Michael Higgins, Elizabeth McRae, Harrison Ford; ***D:*** Francis Ford Coppola; ***W:*** Francis Ford Coppola; ***M:*** David Shire. Cannes Film Festival '74: Best Film; National Board of Review Awards '74: 10 Best Films of the Year, Best Actor (Hackman), Best Director (Coppola); Nominations: Academy Awards '74: Best Original Screenplay, Best Picture, Best Sound. *PAR*

Conversation Piece ♂♂♂ *Violence et Passion; Gruppo di Famiglia in un Interno* **1975 (R)** An aging art historian's life is turned upside down when a Countess and her daughters rent out the penthouse in his estate. Sometimes-talky examination of scholarly pretensions. **112m/C VHS, Beta.** *IT FR* Burt Lancaster, Silvana Mangano, Helmut Berger, Claudia Cardinale; ***D:*** Luchino Visconti; ***C:*** Pasqualino de Santis. *NO*

Convict Cowboy ♂♂ ½ **1995 (R)** Hardbitten professional rodeo cowboy Ry Weston (Voight) killed a man and now works the Montana prison rodeo circuit. Newcomer greenhorn Clay Treyton (Chandler) wants to get out of kitchen duty and decides Ry is the perfect ridin' and ropin' teacher. Only Ry isn't interested in wasting his time (at first). It's a predictable bonding experience in a melodramatic cable movie. **106m/C VHS.** Jon Voight, Kyle Chandler, Ben Gazzara, Marcia Gay Harden, Glenn Plummer, Stephen McHattie; ***D:*** Rod Holcomb. *MGM*

Convicted ♂♂ ½ **1932** Lean thriller about a woman cleared of a murder charge, but only when a second, identical murder occurs while she is jailed. **57m/B VHS, Beta, LV.** Aileen Pringle, Jameson Thomas, Harry Myers, Dorothy Christy, Richard Tucker; ***D:*** Christy Cabanne. *NOS*

Convicted ♂♂ ½ **1986** Solid story of innocent man imprisoned for rape, and his wife's determined efforts to free him. Larroquette does well in unexpected role. Based on a true story. Made for television. **94m/C VHS, Beta.** John Larroquette, Carroll O'Connor, Lindsay Wagner; ***D:*** David Lowell Rich; ***M:*** Stephen Dorff. *TTC*

Convicted: A Mother's Story ♂ **1987** Jillian embezzles cash from her employer, all for the sake of a bum of a boyfriend, and goes to jail. Odd casting hinders a ho-hum plot. Made for television. **95m/C VHS, Beta.** Ann Jillian, Kiel Martin, Fred Savage, Gloria Loring, Christa Denton; ***D:*** Richard T. Heffron; ***M:*** David Shire. *JTC*

Convicts at Large ♂ **1938** An escaped convict steals the clothes of a inept architect. Left with only prison duds, the architect stumbles into the bad side of town and gets involved with the mob. Inane. **58m/B VHS, Beta, LV.** Ralph Forbes, Paula Stone. *NO*

Convoy ♂♂ ½ **1940** Life aboard a convoy ship in the North Sea during WWII. The small cruiser is picked on by a German U-Boat. Will a rescuer appear? Noted for technical production values. **95m/B VHS.** Clive Brook, John Clements, Edward Chapman, Judy Campbell, Edward Rigby, Stewart Granger, Michael Wilding, George Benson; ***D:*** Pen Tennyson. *NOS*

Convoy ♂♂ **1978 (R)** A defiant trucker leads an indestructible truck convoy to Mexico to protect high gasoline prices. Lightweight stuff was inspired by the song "Convoy" by C.W. McCall. **106m/C VHS, Beta.** Kris Kristofferson, Ali MacGraw, Ernest Borgnine, Burt Young, Madge Sinclair, Franklin Ajaye, Cassie Yates; ***D:*** Sam Peckinpah; ***C:*** Harry Stradling Jr. *NO*

Coogan's Bluff ♂♂♂ **1968 (PG)** An Arizona deputy sheriff (Eastwood) travels to New York in order to track down a killer on the loose. First Eastwood/Siegel teaming is tense actioner. The television series "McCloud" was based on this film. **100m/C VHS, Beta, LV.** Clint Eastwood, Lee J. Cobb, Tisha Sterling, Don Stroud, Betty Field, Susan Clark, Tom Tully; ***D:*** Donald Siegel; ***M:*** Lalo Schifrin. *MCA*

The Cook, the Thief, His Wife & Her Lover ♂♂♂ ½ **1990 (R)** An exclusive restaurant houses four disturbing characters. Greenaway's powerful vision of greed, love, and violence may be too strong for some tastes. Available in several different versions: the standard unrated theatrical release, the unrated version in a letterboxed format, an R-rated cut which runs half an hour shorter, and a Spanish-subtitled version. **123m/C VHS.** *GB* Richard Bohringer, Michael Gambon, Helen Mirren, Alan Howard, Tim Roth; ***D:*** Peter Greenaway; ***W:*** Peter Greenaway; ***M:*** Michael Nyman. *VMK*

Cookie ♂♂ ½ **1989 (R)** Light comedy about a Mafia don's daughter trying to smart mouth her way into the mob's good graces. A character-driven vehicle, this plot takes a backseat to casting. Wiest is superb as Falk's moll. **93m/C VHS, Beta, LV, 8mm.** Emily Lloyd, Peter Falk, Dianne Wiest, Jerry Lewis, Brenda Vaccaro, Ricki Lake, Lionel Stander, Michael V. Gazzo, Adrian Pasdar, Bob Gunton, Rockets Redglare, G. Anthony Sirico; ***D:*** Susan Seidelman; ***W:*** Alice Arlen, Nora Ephron; ***M:*** Thomas Newman. *WAR*

Cooking Up Trouble ♂♂ **1944** The crazy trio become foster dads in this "Stooge" type comedy. **?m/C VHS.** Shemp Howard, Billy Gilbert, Maxie "Slapsie" Rosenbloom. *LOO*

Cool As Ice ♂ **1991 (PG)** "Rapper" Vanilla Ice makes his feature film debut as a rebel with an eye for the ladies, who motors into a small, conservative town. Several so-so musical segments. For teenage girls only. **92m/C VHS, Beta, LV.** Vanilla Ice, Kristin Minter, Michael Gross, Sydney Lassick, Dody Goodman, Naomi Campbell, Candy Clark; ***D:*** David Kellogg; ***C:*** Janusz Kaminski; ***M:*** Stanley Clarke. Golden Raspberry Awards '91: Worst New Star (Vanilla Ice). *MCA*

Cool Blue ♂½ **1988 (R)** An unsuccessful painter meets the woman of his dreams, has a brief affair, then tries to locate her in the greater Los Angeles metro area. Good luck. Watch for Penn's cameo. **93m/C VHS, Beta, LV.** Woody Harrelson, Hank Azaria, Ely Pouget, John Diehl; ***Cameos:*** Sean Penn; ***D:*** Mark Mullin, Richard Shepard. *COL*

Cool Change ♂♂ ½ **1986 (PG)** Man and woman from feuding families ally to expose a corrupt conservation movement that threatens cattle herders. **79m/C VHS.** *FHE, BTV*

Cool Hand Luke ♂♂♂ ½ **1967** One of the last great men-in-chains films. A man (Newman) sentenced to sweat out a term on a prison farm refuses to compromise with authority. Martin shines in his supporting role as the oily warden, uttering that now-famous phrase, "What we have here is a failure to communicate." Kennedy's performance as leader of the chain gang won him an Oscar. Based on the novel by Donn Pearce. **126m/C VHS, Beta, LV.** Paul Newman, George Kennedy, J.D. Cannon, Strother Martin, Dennis Hopper, Anthony Zerbe, Lou Antonio, Wayne Rogers, Harry Dean Stanton, Ralph Waite, Joe Don Baker, Richard Davalos, Jo Van Fleet; ***D:*** Stuart Rosenberg; ***W:*** Frank Pierson; ***C:*** Conrad Hall; ***M:*** Lalo Schifrin. Academy Awards '67: Best Supporting Actor (Kennedy); Nominations: Academy Awards '66: Best Adapted Screenplay, Best Original Score; Academy Awards '67: Best Actor (Newman). *WAR, BTV*

Cool It, Baby **1967** A woman's life is ripped apart when she unknowingly appears in a raunchy stag film while under the influence of drugs. **?m/B VHS.** *SMW, TPV*

Cool Mikado ♂♂ **1963** A jazzy modernization of the Gilbert-Sullivan operetta, in which an American soldier is kidnapped by the gangster fiance of the Japanese girl he loves. **81m/C VHS, Beta.** *GB* Stubby Kaye, Frankie Howerd, Dennis Price; ***D:*** Michael Winner. *JEF*

Cool Runnings ♂♂ ½ **1993 (PG)** Bright, slapstick comedy based on the true story of the Jamaican bobsled team's quest to enter the 1988 Winter Olympics in Calgary. Candy is recruited to coach four unlikely athletes who don't quite exemplify the spirit of the Games. He accepts the challenge not only because of its inherent difficulty but because he needs to reconcile himself to past failures as a former sledder. When our heroes leave their sunny training ground for Calgary, their mettle is tested by serious sledders from more frigid climes who pursue the competition with a stern sense of mission. An upbeat story which will appeal to children, its target audience. **98m/C VHS, LV.** Leon, Doug E. Doug, John Candy, Marco Brambilla, Malik Yoba, Rawle Lewis, Raymond J. Barry, Peter Outerbridge, Larry Gilman, Paul Coeur; ***D:*** Jon Turteltaub; ***W:*** Tommy Swerdlow, Lynn Siefert, Michael Goldberg; ***C:*** Phedon Papamichael; ***M:*** Hans Zimmer. *DIS*

The Cool Surface ♂♂ **1992 (R)** Sex and ambition, Hollywood style. Dani, a wannbe actress, and Jarvis, an aspiring screenwriter become lovers. Jarvis turns their hot affair into a sizzling novel and then a script. Dani may have inspired the lead role but that doesn't mean she'll get the part. But it won't be for lack of trying (anything). **88m/C VHS.** Robert Patrick, Teri Hatcher, Matt McCoy, Cyril O'Reilly, Ian Buchanan; ***D:*** Erik Anjou; ***W:*** Erik Anjou; ***M:*** Dave Kopplin. *COL*

Cool World ♂♂ **1992 (PG-13)** Underground cartoonist Jack Deebs enters his own adult cartoon "Cool World," lured by his sex-kitten character "Holli Would," who needs him to leave her animated world and become human. Holli's plan is opposed by the only other human to occupy Cool World, a slick detective whose main job is to prevent noids (humans) and doodles (cartoons) from having sex and destroying the balance between the two existences. A mixture of live-action and wild animation. Director Bakshi's creations are not intended for children but this is less explicit than usual, which may be one of the problems. Little humor and a flat script leave this film too uninvolving. **101m/C VHS, Beta, LV.** Gabriel Byrne, Kim Basinger, Brad Pitt, Michele Abrams, Deidre O'Connell, Carrie Hamilton, Frank Sinatra Jr.; ***D:*** Ralph Bakshi. *PAR, PMS, WTA*

Cooley High ♂♂♂ **1975 (PG)** Black high school students in Chicago go through the rites of passage in their senior year during the '60s. Film is funny, smart and much acclaimed. Great soundtrack featuring Motown hits of the era is a highlight. Sequel to the TV series "What's Happening." **107m/C VHS, LV.** Glynn Turman, Lawrence-Hilton Jacobs, Garrett Morris, Cynthia Davis; ***D:*** Michael A. Schultz; ***W:*** Eric Monte. *ORI, FCT, PTB*

Cooperstown ♂♂ ½ **1993** Harry (Arkin) is a former major-league pitcher who now works as a baseball scout in Florida. He's been angry for 30 years over giving up a home-run pitch that kept his team (the ficitional Chicago Barons) out of the World Series. Harry's feels this error cost him his chance at induction into the Baseball Hall of Fame in Cooperstown, New York, and he's always blamed ex-friend and former catcher Raymond (Greene), who's just had the gall to be elected. Only Raymond's just died—but his ghostly figure visits Harry and urges him to take a road trip not only to the baseball shrine but into his past. Made for cable television. **100m/C VHS.** Alan Arkin, Graham Greene, Hope Lange, Josh Charles, Ed Begley Jr., Maria Pitillo, Ann Wedgeworth, Paul Dooley, Joanna Miles, Charles Haid; ***D:*** Charles Haid; ***W:*** Lee Blessing. *NO*

Cop ♂♂ ½ **1988 (R)** Left by his wife and child, a ruthless and work-obsessed detective goes after a twisted serial killer. Woods' exceptional ability to play sympathetic weirdos is diluted by a script—based on James Ellroys's novel "Blood on the Moon"—that warps the feminist theme, is violent, and depends too heavily on coincidence. **110m/C VHS, Beta, LV.** James Woods, Lesley Ann Warren, Charles Durning, Charles Haid, Raymond J. Barry, Randi Brooks, Annie McEnroe, Victoria Wauchope; ***D:*** James B. Harris; ***W:*** James B. Harris; ***M:*** Michel Colombier. *PAR*

Cop and a Half ♂½ **1993 (PG)** Streetwise 8-year-old (Golden) accidentally witnesses a murder and then bullys police into letting him join the force (for a day) when he withholds key information. Enter his partner for the day—hard-edged detective Reynolds, who claims to hate kids, but who we know will learn to love them. Meanwhile, the outlaw (Sharkey) knows Devon saw him and is trying to silence him permanently. Predictable fantasy may appeal to kids, but will make most adults yawn. One of Sharkey's last roles. **87m/C VHS, LV.** Norman D. Golden II, Burt Reynolds, Ruby Dee, Ray Sharkey, Holland Taylor, Frank Sivero, Marc Macaulay, Rocky Giordani, Sammy Hernandez; ***D:*** Henry Winkler; ***W:*** Arne Olsen; ***M:*** Alan Silvestri. Golden Raspberry Awards '93: Worst Actor (Reynolds). *MCA*

The Cop & the Girl 🦴 **1986** A cop falls for a teenage runaway, ends up on the lam. Confused story overpowered by camera work. Lots of violence and strong language. Dubbed. **94m/C VHS, Beta.** *GE* Juergen Prochnow, Annette Von Klier; ***D:*** Peter Keglevic. *NO*

A Cop for the Killing 🦴🦴 **1994 (R)** Undercover L.A. narcotics squad is about to bust the city's biggest drug lord when their sting operation goes bad and one of the team is brutally murdered. So, squad leader Ray Wiltern (Farentino) decides to get even. **95m/C VHS.** James Farentino, Steven Weber, Charles Haid. *NHO*

Cop in Blue Jeans 🦴 **1978** Undercover cop goes after a mob kingpin in this violent, badly dubbed crime yarn. **92m/C VHS, Beta.** Tomas Milian, Jack Palance, Maria Rosaria Omaggio, Guido Mannari; ***D:*** Bruno Corbucci. *VMK*

Cop-Out 🦴🦴 **1991** A cop is framed. His brother is mad. Teamed up with a sexy lawyer, he exposes the filth that is corrupting the city. Okay melodrama. **102m/C VHS, Beta, LV.** David Buff, Kathryn Luster, Dan Ranger, Reggie DeMorton, Lawrence L. Simeone; ***D:*** Lawrence L. Simeone; ***W:*** Lawrence L. Simeone. *AIP*

Copacabana 🦴🦴 **1947** A shady theatrical agent (Groucho) books a nightclub singer into two shows at the same time at New York's ritzy nightclub. Lots of energy spent trying to enliven a routine script. Also available colorized. ♫Tico Tico; Stranger Things Have Happened; Je Vous Amie; My Heart Was Doing a Bolero; Let's Do the Copacobana; I Haven't Got a Thing to Sell; We've Come to Copa. **91m/B VHS, LV.** Groucho Marx, Carmen Miranda, Steve Cochran, Gloria Jean, Andy Russell, Earl Wilson; ***D:*** Alfred E. Green. *REP, FCT, MLB*

Copkillers *Woof!* **1977 (R)** Two men desperate for an easy way to make money embark on a murderous shooting spree. Mostly blanks. **93m/C VHS, Beta.** Jason Williams, Bill Osco. *TWE*

Copper Canyon 🦴🦴½ **1950** Milland plays a Confederate Army officer who heads West after the Civil War, meets up with Lamarr, and sparks a romance. Good chemistry between the leads in this otherwise standard western. **84m/B VHS.** Ray Milland, Hedy Lamarr, MacDonald Carey, Mona Freeman, Harry Carey Jr., Frank Faylen, Taylor Holmes, Peggy Knudsen; ***D:*** John Farrow. *PAR, FCT*

Copperhead 🦴 **1984 (R)** A group of copperhead snakes attack a family who possess a stolen Incan gold necklace. This one bites. **90m/C VHS, Beta.** Jack Renner, Gretta Ratliff, David Fritts, Cheryl Nickerson. *VCI*

Cops and Robbers 🦴🦴½ **1973 (PG)** Two cops use a Wall Street parade for returning astronauts as a cover for a multi-million dollar heist. Exceptional caper film thanks to the likable leads and genuine suspense. **89m/C VHS.** Joseph Bologna, Dick Ward, Shepperd Strudwick, John P. Ryan, Ellen Holly, Dolph Sweet, Joe Spinell, Cliff Gorman; ***D:*** Aram Avakian; ***W:*** Donald E. Westlake. *MGM, WKV*

Cops and Robbersons 🦴 **1994 (PG)** Bored, dim-witted dad Chase, a TV cop-show junkie, wishes his life had a little more danger and excitement. How lucky for him when hard-nosed cop Palance sets up a command post in his house to stake out the mobster living next door (Davi). Predictable plot isn't funny and drags Chase's bumbling idiot persona on for too long; Wiest and Davi are two bright spots, but their talents are wasted, while Palance does little more than reincarnate his "City Slickers" character. Poor effort for otherwise notable director Ritchie. **93m/C VHS, LV, 8mm.** Chevy Chase, Jack Palance, Dianne Wiest, Robert Davi, Jason James Richter, Fay Masterson, Miko Hughes, Richard Romanus, David Barry Gray; ***D:*** Michael Ritchie; ***W:*** Bernie Somers; ***M:*** William Ross. *COL*

Cops/One Week **1922** Two vintage Keaton shorts, with original organ score. **51m/B VHS, Beta, 8mm.** Buster Keaton; ***D:*** Buster Keaton, Eddie Cline. *VYY*

Copycat 🦴🦴 **1995 (R)** Crowded serial killer genre yields crooner Connick as southern psychopath stuck on murder. Soon he's in jail, advising the police in their hunt for another serial killer who imitates the murders of other infamous serial killers. Agoraphobic, boozing criminal psychologist Helen Hudson (Weaver), still suffering the after effects of an attack by sicko subject Darryl Lee Cullum (Connick), is enlisted to help detective M.J. Monahan (Hunter) catch the homage specialist. Weaver and Hunter bring sparks to the usually testosterone-laden formula, helping mask the preponderance of serial killer cliches and giant holes in the script. Connick's turn as a nut-job killer won't make you forget Anthony Hopkins, or even Frank Sinatra. Exploitative and imitative, and always faithful to the formula. **124m/C VHS.** Sigourney Weaver, Holly Hunter, Dermot Mulroney, Harry Connick Jr., William McNamara, Will Patton, John Rothman; ***D:*** Jon Amiel; ***W:*** Ann Biderman, David Madsen; ***C:*** Laszlo Kovacs; ***M:*** Christopher Young. *WAR*

Coquette 🦴🦴½ **1929** Pickford's first talkie portrays her as a flirtatious flapper from a well-to-do family who falls in love with a poor man her father despises. So much in fact that daddy kills the young man and then commits suicide, leaving his daughter to face the world alone. Pickford and Brown get to share a melodramatic death scene and audiences flocked to hear "America's Sweetheart" speak onscreen. Based on a play by George Abbott and Anne Preston. **75m/B VHS.** Mary Pickford, Johnny Mack Brown, Matt Moore, John St. Polis, Henry Kolker, George Irving, Louise Beavers, William Janney; ***D:*** Sam Taylor; ***C:*** Karl Struss. Academy Awards '29: Best Actress (Pickford). *MGM*

Cord & Dischords/Naughty Nurse 🦴🦴 **1928** Two vintage silent shorts featuring some lesser known slapstick clowns cavorting in blackface. **50m/B VHS, Beta.** Fred Parker, Jack Cooper, Ella MacKenzie, Spencer Williams Jr. *VYY*

Cordelia 🦴🦴 **1987** A dramatization of an actual court case in turn-of-the century Quebec, in which an "overly" vivacious woman is accused of murdering her husband. **115m/C VHS, Beta.** *CA NFB*

Coriolanus, Man without a Country 🦴 **1964** When the Romans begin to abuse their rights, the Plebians call upon the brave and mighty Coriolanus to lead them into battle against their oppressors. Predictable muscle man outing. **?m/C VHS, Beta.** *IT* Gordon Scott, Alberto Lupo, Lilla Brignone. *SNC*

Corleone 🦴 **1979 (R)** Limp tale about two boyhood friends who grow up to fight the evil landowners who dominate Italy. To accomplish this, one becomes a mobster, the other a politician. **115m/C VHS, Beta.** *IT* Claudia Cardinale, Giuliano Gemma; ***D:*** Pasquale Squitieri. Montreal World Film Festival '79: Best Actor (Gemma). *MGM*

The Corn is Green 🦴🦴🦴 **1945** Touching story of a school teacher in a poor Welsh village who eventually sends her pet student to Oxford. Davis makes a fine teacher, though a little young, while the on-site photography provides atmosphere. Based on the play by Emlyn Williams. Remade in 1979. **115m/B VHS, Beta.** Bette Davis, John Dall, Nigel Bruce, Joan Lorring, Arthur Shields, Mildred Dunnock, Rhys Williams, Rosalind Ivan; ***D:*** Irving Rapper; ***M:*** Max Steiner. Nominations: Academy Awards '45: Best Supporting Actor (Dall), Best Supporting Actress (Lorring). *MGM, FCT*

Cornbread, Earl & Me 🦴🦴 **1975 (R)** A high school basketball star from the ghetto is mistaken for a murderer by cops and shot, causing a subsequent furor of protest and racial hatred. Superficial melodrama. **95m/C VHS, Beta.** Moses Gunn, Rosalind Cash, Bernie Casey, Tierre Turner, Madge Sinclair, Keith Wilkes, Antonio Fargas; ***D:*** Joseph Manduke; ***M:*** Donald Byrd. *NO*

Cornered 🦴 **1932** McCoy is a sheriff, chasing bad guys, whose life is saved by Welch. Basically boring. **62m/B VHS.** Tim McCoy, Niles Welch, Raymond Hatton, Noah Beery Sr., Shirley Grey, Walter Long; ***D:*** B. Reeves Eason. *GPV*

Cornered 🦴🦴🦴 **1945** Tough Powell plays an airman released from a German prison camp who pursues a Nazi war criminal to avenge the death of his wife and child. **102m/B VHS, Beta, LV.** Dick Powell, Walter Slezak, Micheline Cheirel, Luther Adler; ***D:*** Edward Dmytryk. *TTC*

Coroner Creek 🦴🦴½ **1948** Scott's fiancee commits suicide during an Indian attack on her stagecoach, and the couple's dowry is stolen. Scott sets out to trace the loot and exact his revenge. A superior production, notable for being one of the first westerns with an adult theme. **89m/B VHS.** Randolph Scott, Marguerite Chapman, George Macready, Sally Eilers, Edgar Buchanan, Wallace Ford, Forrest Tucker; ***D:*** Ray Enright. *NO*

Corporate Affairs 🦴🦴 **1990 (R)** A ruthless business woman climbing her way to the top literally seduces her boss tó death. **92m/C VHS.** Peter Scolari, Mary Crosby, Chris Lemmon, Ken Kercheval; ***D:*** Terence H. Winkless; ***W:*** Terence H. Winkless, Geoffrey Baere. *MGM*

The Corpse Grinders *Woof!* **1971 (R)** Low-budget bad movie classic in which a cardboard corpse-grinding machine makes nasty cat food that makes cats nasty. Sets are cheap, gore effects silly, and cat attacks ridiculous. **73m/C VHS, Beta.** Sean Kenney, Monika Kelly, Sandford Mitchell; ***D:*** Ted V. Mikels; ***W:*** Ted V. Mikels. *NO*

The Corpse Vanishes 🦴🦴½ **1942** Lugosi at his chilling best as a diabolical scientist who snatches young brides and drains their blood in an effort to keep his 70-year-old wife eternally youthful. Not for newlyweds! **64m/B VHS, Beta.** Bela Lugosi, Luana Walters, Tristram Coffin, Elizabeth Russell, Vince Barnett, Joan Barclay, Angelo Rossitto; ***D:*** Wallace Fox. *NOS, MRV, SNC*

Corregidor 🦴🦴 **1943** A love triangle develops between doctors treating the wounded during the WWII battle. A poor propaganda piece which contains only shaky stock footage for its "action" sequences. **73m/B VHS.** Otto Kruger, Elissa Landi, Donald Woods, Rick Vallin, Frank Jenks, Wanda McKay, Ian Keith; ***D:*** William Nigh. *NOS, MOV, HEG*

Corrida Interdite 🦴🦴 **1958** Slow-motion sequences reveal the beauty of the bullfighting ritual without neglecting the deadly nature of the sport. **10m/C VHS, Beta.** *FLI*

The Corridor: Death **1989** Two Americans are involved in a car accident in Israel which triggers a debate on the Jewish perspective of death and the afterlife. Filmed on location at Hadassah Hospital on St. Scopus, Jerusalem. The final part of the trilogy preceded by "The Eighth Day: Circumcision" and "The Journey: Bar Mitzvah." **25m/C VHS, Beta.** *ERG*

Corridors of Blood 🦴🦴½ *The Doctor from Seven Dials* **1958** Karloff is a doctor, in search of a viable anesthetic, who accidently becomes addicted to drugs, then turns to grave robbers to support his habit. Karloff plays usual threatening doctor to perfection. **86m/C VHS, Beta.** *GB* Boris Karloff, Betta St. John, Finlay Currie, Christopher Lee, Francis Matthews, Adrienne Corri, Nigel Green; ***D:*** Robert Day. *MPI*

Corrina, Corrina 🦴🦴½ **1994 (PG)** Newly-widowed jingle-writer Liotta needs someone to care for his withdrawn eight year-old daughter. Enter Whoopi, as housekeeper and eventual love interest. Sweet, nostalgic romance set in the 1950's. Goldberg also found off-screen romance (again), this time with the film's union organizer Lyle Trachtenberg. Last role for Ameche. **115m/C VHS, LV.** Whoopi Goldberg, Ray Liotta, Don Ameche, Tina Majorino, Wendy Crewson, Jenifer Lewis, Larry Miller, Erica Yohn; ***Cameos:*** Anita Baker; ***D:*** Jessie Nelson; ***W:*** Jessie Nelson. *NLC, TTC*

Corrupt 🦴🦴🦴 *Order of Death; Cop Killers* **1984 (PG)** Bad narcotics cop goes after murderer, but mysterious Lydon gets in the way. An acquired taste, best if you appreciate Lydon, better known as Johnny Rotten of the Sex Pistols. **99m/C VHS, Beta.** *IT* Harvey Keitel, John (Johnny Rotten) Lydon, Sylvia Sidney, Nicole Garcia, Leonard Mann; ***D:*** Roberto Faenza; ***M:*** Ennio Morricone. *NO*

The Corrupt Ones 🦴🦴½ *Il Sigillo de Pechino; Die Holle von Macao; Les Corrompus; The Peking Medallion; Hell to Macao* **1967** Everyone's after a photographer who has a medallion that will lead to buried treasure in China. Great characters hampered by pedestrian script. **87m/C VHS, Beta.** Robert Stack, Elke Sommer, Nancy Kwan, Christian Marquand, Werner Peters; ***D:*** James Hill; ***W:*** Brian Clemens. *SUE, NLC*

Corruption *Woof!* **1989 (R)** Mostly soft-porn. Alleged plot: The Mob is interested in having Shea work for them, and makes it worth his while. **80m/C VHS.** Mary McGee, Patrick Shea. *NO*

Corsair 🦴🦴 **1931** Actioner about a gorgeous debutante and a handsome gangster who find themselves caught up with a gang of bootlegging pirates. Todd is always worth watching. **73m/B VHS, Beta.** Chester Morris, Thelma Todd, Frank McHugh, Ned Sparks, Mayo Methot; ***D:*** Roland West. *GPV, RXM, HEG*

The Corsican Brothers 🦴🦴½ **1942** Alexander Dumas' classic about twins who, although separated, remain spiritually tied throughout their various adventures. Fairbanks takes on dual roles in this entertaining swashbuckler. Remade for television in 1984. **111m/B VHS, Beta, LV.** Douglas Fairbanks Jr., Akim Tamiroff, Ruth Warrick, J. Carrol Naish, H.B. Warner, Henry Wilcoxon, Veda Ann Borg; ***D:*** Gregory Ratoff; ***C:*** Harry Stradling. Nominations: Academy Awards '42: Best Original Score. *VTR, LIV*

Corvette Summer 🦴 *The Hot One* **1978 (PG)** After spending a semester restoring a Corvette in his high school shop class, an L.A. student must journey to Las Vegas to recover the car when it is stolen. There he meets a prostitute, falls in love, and steps into the "real world" for the first time. Potts intriguing as the low-life love interest, but she can't save this one. **104m/C VHS, Beta.** Mark Hamill, Annie Potts, Eugene Roche, Kim Milford, Richard McKenzie, William Bryant; ***D:*** Matthew Robbins; ***W:*** Matthew Robbins, Hal Barwood. *MGM*

Cosh Boy *Woof! The Slasher* **1961** Vicious male youths stalk women on the streets of London in this low-budget Jack the Ripper rip-off. **90m/B VHS, Beta.** Joan Collins, James Kennedy. *NO*

The Cosmic Eye 🦴🦴🦴 **1971** Animated tale of three musicians from outer space who come to earth to spread the message of worldwide peace and harmony. A variety of cultural perspectives about the origins and destiny of the Earth are offered. Rather moralizing but the animation is impressive. **71m/C VHS, Beta, LV.** ***D:*** Faith Hubley; ***V:*** Dizzy Gillespie, Maureen Stapleton, Benny Carter. *LTY, WTA, DIS*

The Cosmic Man 🦴½ **1959** An alien arrives on Earth with a message of peace and restraint. He is regarded with suspicion by us nasty Earthlings. Essentially "The Day the Earth Stood Still" without the budget, but interesting nonetheless. **72m/B VHS, Beta.** Bruce (Herman Brix) Bennett, John Carradine, Angela Greene, Paul Langton, Scotty Morrow; ***D:*** Herbert Greene. *SNC*

The Cosmic Monsters 🦴½ *The Strange World of Planet X* **1958** Scientist accidentally pops a hole in the ionosphere during a magnetism experiment. Then huge, mean insects arrive to plague mankind. Coincidence? You figure it out. **75m/B VHS, Beta.** Forrest Tucker, Gaby Andre, Alec Mango, Hugh Latimer, Martin Benson; ***D:*** Gilbert Gunn. *MRV, SNC, MWP*

Cosmic Slop 🦴🦴 **1994 (R)** Three-part anthology. "Space Traders," based on a story by Derrick Bell, finds a fleet of aliens offering to solve all of U.S. society's most pressing social ills if they can have the entire black population in return (for what purpose is never explained). "The First Commandment" features a Catholic priest in a Latino parish who comes up against his parishoners pagan beliefs in Santeria. "Tang," based on a story by Chester Himes, finds a poor, desperately unhappy married couple dreaming about what they'll do with the rifle mysteriously delivered in a flower carton to their door. **87m/C VHS.** Robert Guillaume, Jason Bernard, Nicholas Turturro, Richard Herd, Paula Jai Parker, Chi McBride; ***D:*** Reginald Hudlin, Warrington Hudlin, Kevin Sullivan; ***W:*** Warrington Hudlin, Trey Ellis, Kyle Baker. *HBO*

Cosmo Jones, Crime Smasher 🦴🦴 **1943** Murder mystery based on a forties radio program. **?m/C VHS.** Mantan Moreland, Frank Graham. *SNC*

Cosmos: War of the Planets *Woof! Cosmo 2000: Planet Without a Name; War of the Planets* **1980 (PG)** The ultimate battle for survival is fought in outer space, though not very well and on a small budget. Special effects especially laughable. **90m/C VHS, Beta.** *IT* Katia Christine, West Buchanan, John Richardson, Yanti Somer; ***D:*** Al Bradley. *NO*

Cottage to Let 🦴½ *Bombsight Stolen* **1941** Propaganda thriller about a Nazi plot to kidnap the inventor of a new bombsight. Focused cast struggles with lackluster script. **90m/B VHS, Beta.** *GB* Leslie Banks, Alastair Sim, John Mills, Jeanne de Casalis, Carla Lehmann, George Cole, Michael Wilding, Frank Cellier, Wally Patch, Catherine Lacey; ***D:*** Anthony Asquith. *SNC*

Cotter 🦴 **1972** A Native American rodeo clown feels responsible for a cowboy's death, returns home to reflect on his life. Fair story, best at the small town feeling. **94m/C VHS, Beta.** Don Murray, Carol Lynley, Rip Torn, Sherry Jackson; ***D:*** Paul Stanley. *XVC*

Cotton Candy 🦴🦴 **1982** Follows the faintly interesting trials and tribulations of a high school senior who tries to form a rock band. At first he meets failure, but is ultimately successful with the band and romance. Made for television. Joint script-writing venture by brothers Clint and Ron Howard. **97m/C VHS, Beta.** Charles Martin Smith, Clint Howard, Leslie King; ***D:*** Ron Howard; ***W:*** Clint Howard, Ron Howard. *TLF*

The Cotton Club 🦴🦴🦴 **1984 (R)** With $50 million in his pocket, Francis reaches for an epic and delivers: handsome production, lots of dance, bit of singing, confused plot, uneven performances, tad too long. A musician playing at The Cotton Club falls in love with gangster Dutch Schultz's girlfriend. A black tap dancer falls in love with a member of the chorus line who can pass for white. These two love stories are told against a background of mob violence and music. Excellent performances by Hoskins and Gwynne. ♫Minnie the Moocher; Ill Wind; The Mooch; Ring Dem Bells; Drop Me Off in Harlem; Cotton Club Stomp; Truckin; Mood Indigo; Copper Colored Gal. **121m/C VHS, Beta, LV, 8mm.** Diane Lane, Richard Gere, Gregory Hines, Lonette McKee, Bob Hoskins, Fred Gwynne, James Remar, Nicolas Cage, Lisa Jane Persky, Allen (Goorwitz) Garfield, Gwen Verdon, Joe Dallesandro, Jennifer Grey, Tom Waits, Diane Venora; ***D:*** Francis Ford Coppola; ***W:*** Francis Ford Coppola, William Kennedy, Mario Puzo; ***M:*** John Barry. Nominations: Academy Awards '84: Best Art Direction/Set Decoration, Best Film Editing. *SUE, NLC*

Cotton Comes to Harlem 🦴🦴🦴 **1970 (R)** Cambridge and St. Jacques star as Harlem plainclothes detectives Grave Digger Jones and Coffin Ed Johnson in this successful mix of crime and comedy. They're investigating a suspicious preacher's back-to-Africa scheme which they suspect is a swindle. Directorial debut of Davis. Filmed on location in Harlem, New York. Based on the novel by Chester Himes. Followed by a weak sequel, "Come Back, Charleston Blue." **97m/C VHS.** Godfrey Cambridge, Raymond St. Jacques, Calvin Lockhart, Judy Pace, Redd Foxx, John Anderson, Emily Yancy, J.D. Cannon, Teddy Wilson, Eugene Roche, Cleavon Little, Lou Jacobi; ***D:*** Ossie Davis; ***W:*** Ossie Davis. *MGM*

Cotton Queen 🦴½ *Crying Out Loud* **1937** Romance and light intrigue plague the children of two rival textile mill owners. **80m/B VHS, Beta, 8mm.** Will Fyffe, Stanley Holloway; ***D:*** Bernard Vorhaus. *VYY, FCT*

The Couch Trip 🦴½ **1987 (R)** Aykroyd is an escapee from a mental institution who passes himself off as a radio psychologist and becomes a media sensation. There are a few laughs and some funny characters but for the most part this one falls flat. **98m/C VHS, Beta, LV.** Dan Aykroyd, Walter Matthau, Charles Grodin, Donna Dixon, Richard Romanus, Arye Gross, David Clennon, Mary Gross; ***D:*** Michael Ritchie; ***W:*** Will Aldis, Steven Kampmann; ***M:*** Michel Colombier. *ORI*

Could It Happen Here? 🦴 **198?** A lurid Italian spectacle about a metropolis thrown into a state of chaotic martial law by terrorism. Dubbed. **90m/C VHS, Beta.** *IT* Luc Merenda, Marcella Michelangeli; ***D:*** Massimo Pirri. *NO*

The Count 🦴🦴½ **1916** Chaplin pretends to be the secretary of his boss, who in turn is posing as a count. Silent with musical soundtrack added. **20m/B VHS, Beta.** Charlie Chaplin; ***D:*** Charlie Chaplin. *CAB*

Count/Adventurer **1917** Two Chaplin two-reelers: "The Count (The Phoney Nobleman)" (1916), in which Charlie impersonates a count at the home of Miss Moneybags, and "The Adventurer" (1917), Chaplin's final film for Mutual, in which he plays an escaped convict with the law relentlessly on his trail. Silent with musical score. **52m/B VHS, Beta.** Charlie Chaplin, Eric Campbell, Edna Purviance, Frank Coleman; ***D:*** Charlie Chaplin. *VYY*

Count Dracula 🦴🦴½ **1971 (R)** Passable version of the Dracula legend (based on the novel by Bram Stoker) has Lee as the thirsty count on the prowl for fresh blood. **90m/C VHS.** *SP GE IT* Christopher Lee, Herbert Lom, Klaus Kinski, Frederick Williams, Maria Rohm, Soledad Miranda; ***D:*** Jess (Jesus) Franco. *REP, FCT*

Count Dracula's Great Love 🦴🦴 **1972** European horror superstar Naschy plays Dracula; stylishly done in the Hammer tradition. Considered by many to be Naschy's best horror film. **?m/C VHS.** Paul Naschy. *SNC, SMW*

The Count of Monte Cristo 🦴🦴½ **1912** One of the first full-length features starring popular stage stars of the day. The first truly American feature, it was based on the classic tale of revenge by Alexander Dumas. Silent. Remade many times. Lead actor O'Neill was the father of famed American playwright, Eugene O'Neill, who covered his father's success in this role in his own family drama "Long Day's Journey Into Night." **90m/B VHS, Beta.** James O'Neill; ***D:*** Edwin S. Porter. *NOS, VYY, DVT*

The Count of Monte Cristo 🦴🦴🦴 **1934** A true swashbuckling revenge tale about Edmond Dantes, who unjustly spends years in prison. After escaping, he gains ever so sweet and served quite cold revenge. Adaptation of the Alexandre Dumas classic. **114m/B VHS, Beta.** Robert Donat, Elissa Landi, Louis Calhern, Sidney Blackmer, Irene Hervey, Raymond Walburn, O.P. Heggie; ***D:*** Rowland V. Lee. *CCB, MED, MOV*

The Count of Monte Cristo 🦴🦴½ **1974** The Alexander Dumas classic about an innocent man (Chamberlain) who is imprisoned, escapes, and finds the treasure of Monte Cristo, which he uses to bring down those who wronged him. Good version of the historical costumer. Originally shown in theaters in Europe, but broadcast on television in the U.S. **104m/C VHS, Beta.** *GB* Richard Chamberlain, Kate Nelligan, Donald Pleasence, Alessio Orano, Tony Curtis, Louis Jourdan, Trevor Howard, Taryn Power; ***D:*** David Greene. *LIV, FUS*

The Count of the Old Town 🦴🦴 *Munkbrogreven* **1934** Feisty townsfolk settle the score after a gang of booze smugglers trick them out of their money. Bergman's film debut as a maid swept off her feet by a mysterious young stranger. Adapted from the play "Greven fran Gamla Sta'n" by Arthur and Sigfried Fischer. In Swedish with English subtitles. **90m/B VHS, Beta.** *SW* Edvin Adolphson, Ingrid Bergman, Sigurd Wallen, Valdemar Dahlquist; ***D:*** Edvin Adolphson, Sigurd Wallen; ***W:*** Gosta Stevens. *WAC, INJ*

Count Yorga, Vampire 🦴🦴½ **1970 (PG)** The vampire Count Yorga is practicing his trade in Los Angeles, setting up a coven and conducting seances. Good update of the traditional character, with Quarry suitably solemn and menacing. Followed by "The Return of Count Yorga." Also available with "Cry of the Banshee" on laserdisc. **90m/C VHS, Beta.** Robert Quarry, Roger Perry, Michael Murphy, Michael Macready, Donna Anders, Judith Lang; ***D:*** Bob Kelljan. *NO*

Countdown ½ **1968** Documentary-type fictional look at the first moon mission and its toll on the astronauts and their families. Timely because the U.S. was trying to send a man to the moon in 1968. Interesting as a look at the developing Altman style. **102m/C VHS, Beta.** James Caan, Robert Duvall, Michael Murphy, Ted Knight, Joanna Moore, Barbara Baxley, Charles Aidman, Steve Ihnat, Robert Altman; ***D:*** Robert Altman. *WAR*

Counter Attack ½ **1984** Story of murder and insurance fraud takes place on the back lots of the Hong Kong film industry. As good as these get. **105m/C VHS, Beta.** Bruce Li, Dan Inosanto, John Ladalski, Young Kong; ***D:*** Bruce Li. *WVE*

Counter Measures **198?** A helicopter pilot stumbles on to a bizarre chain of crimes and disasters. **98m/C VHS, Beta.** Monte Markham; ***D:*** Gerban Ceth. *NO*

Counter Punch ½ *Ripped Off; The Boxer; Uomo Dalla Pelle Dura* **1971 (R)** Blake is a boxer framed for the murder of his manager who sets out to clear his name by finding the killers. Fair rendition of a familiar plot. **72m/C VHS, Beta.** *IT* Robert (Bobby) Blake, Ernest Borgnine, Gabriele Ferzetti, Catherine Spaak, Tomas Milian; ***D:*** Franco Prosperi. *SIM, LIV*

Counterblast *The Devil's Plot* **1948** A Nazi spy assumes the role of a British scientist in order to gain classified information for the Fatherland. The trouble begins when he refuses to carry out an order to execute a pretty young assistant. Appealing performances distract from the somewhat confusing plot. **99m/B VHS, Beta.** *GB* Robert Beatty, Mervyn Johns, Nova Pilbeam, Margaretta Scott, Sybilla Binder, Marie Lohr, Karel Stepanek, Alan Wheatley; ***D:*** Paul Stein. *SNC, RXM*

The Counterfeit Traitor ½ **1962** Suspense thriller with Holden playing a double agent in Europe during WWII. Based on the true adventures of Eric Erickson, the top Allied spy of WW II, who was captured by the Gestapo but escaped. **140m/C VHS, Beta.** William Holden, Lilli Palmer, Hugh Griffith, Werner Peters, Eva Dahlbeck; ***D:*** George Seaton; ***W:*** George Seaton; ***C:*** Jean Bourgoin. *PAR*

Counterforce **1987 (R)** A rough group of mercenaries is hired to guard a Mideastern leader being chased by his country's ruling despot. Mild action with predictable story. **98m/C VHS, Beta, LV.** George Rivero, George Kennedy, Andrew Stevens, Isaac Hayes, Louis Jourdan, Kevin Bernhardt, Hugo Stiglitz, Robert Foster, Susana Dosamantes; ***D:*** J. Anthony Loma. *LIV*

A Countess from Hong Kong **1967 (G)** Very bad romantic comedy features impoverished Russian countess Natasha (would you believe Loren is Russian?) stowing away in the luxury liner suite of stuffy American diplomat Ogden Mears (equally miscast Brando). The ship is sailing from Hong Kong to Honolulu and Natasha has until then to persuade Ogden to assist her. Chaplin's final film. **108m/C VHS.** Marlon Brando, Sophia Loren, Sydney Chaplin, Tippi Hedren, Patrick Cargill, Michael Medwin, Oliver Johnston, Margaret Rutherford; ***D:*** Charlie Chaplin; ***W:*** Charlie Chaplin; ***C:*** Arthur Ibbetson; ***M:*** Charlie Chaplin. *MCA*

Country **1984 (PG)** Strong story of a farm family in crisis when the government attempts to foreclose on their land. Good performances all around and an excellent portrayal of the wife by Lange. "The River" and "Places In the Heart," both released in 1984, also dramatized the plight of many American farm families in the early 1980s. **109m/C VHS, Beta, LV.** Jessica Lange, Sam Shepard, Wilford Brimley, Matt Clark, Therese Graham, Levi L. Knebel; ***D:*** Richard Pearce; ***W:*** William D. Wittliff. Nominations: Academy Awards '84: Best Actress (Lange). *TOU*

The Country Diary of an Edwardian Lady ½ **1988** Biographical dramatization of the life of English writer Edith Holden. Chronicles her life from 1877 until her mysterious death. **90m/C VHS.** *GB VCO, BTV*

Country Gentlemen **1936** Vaudeville team, Olsen and Johnson, play fast-talking conmen who sell shares in a worthless oil field to a bunch of WWI veterans. What a surprise when oil is actually found there. Not one of the duo's better performances. **54m/B VHS, Beta.** Ole Olsen, Chic Johnson, Joyce Compton, Lila Lee, Ray Corrigan, Donald Kirke, Pierre Watkin; ***D:*** Ralph Staub. *NOS, MRV, VYY*

Country Girl ½ **1954** In the role that completely de-glamorized her (and won her an Oscar), Kelly plays the wife of alcoholic singer Crosby who tries to make a comeback with the help of director Holden. One of Crosby's four dramatic parts, undoubtedly one of his best. Seaton won an Oscar for his adaptation of the Clifford Odets play. Remade in 1982. ♫The Search is Through; Dissertation on the State of Bliss; It's Mine, It's Yours; The Land Around Us. **104m/B VHS, Beta.** Bing Crosby, Grace Kelly, William Holden, Gene Reynolds, Anthony Ross; ***D:*** George Seaton; ***W:*** George Seaton. Academy Awards '54: Best Actress (Kelly), Best Screenplay; Golden Globe Awards '55: Best Actress—Drama (Kelly); National Board of Review Awards '54: 10 Best Films of the Year, Best Actress (Kelly); Nominations: Academy Awards '54: Best Actor (Crosby), Best Black and White Cinematography, Best Director (Seaton), Best Picture; Academy Awards '56: Best Art Direction/Set Decoration (B & W). *PAR, BTV*

Country Girl **1982** Aging, alcoholic actor is desperate for a comeback. His director blames his fiercely loving wife for the downfall. Poor cable TV remake of 1954 version with Bing Crosby. **137m/C VHS, Beta.** Dick Van Dyke, Faye Dunaway, Ken Howard. *NO*

The Country Kid **1923** A freckle-faced teenager and his two brothers are beset by a wicked uncle out to steal their inheritance. One of Barry's best-remembered films. **60m/B VHS, Beta.** Wesley Barry, "Spec" O'Donnell, Bruce Guerin, Kate Toncray, Helen Jerome Eddy, George Nicholls Jr.; ***D:*** William Beaudine. *NO*

Country Life **1995 (PG-13)** Down Under adaptation of Chekov's "Uncle Vanya," has Blakemore returning to Aussie farm roots after 22-year stint as unsuccessful London theater critic. His bored young wife (Scacchi) upsets the business-as-usual life of her husband's brother-in-law (Hargreaves) and abandoned daughter, Sally (Fox), who is also jealous of the attention paid the beautiful Deborah by both her uncle and longtime crush, Dr. Askey (Neill). Exchanges Chekov's emotional exploration for a light comedy of manners and a message of Australian independence from England. **107m/C VHS, LV.** *AU* Sam Neill, Greta Scacchi, Kerry Fox, John Hargreaves, Googie Withers, Patricia Kennedy, Michael Blakemore; ***D:*** Michael Blakemore; ***W:*** Michael Blakemore; ***C:*** Stephen Windon; ***M:*** Peter Best. *TOU*

Country Lovers, City Lovers ½ **1972** Two adaptations of short stories by South African novelist Nadine Gordimer about interracial love. **121m/C VHS, Beta.** *MGM*

Countryman **1983 (R)** A dope-smuggling woman crashes her plane in Jamaica and is rescued by Countryman, a rasta super hero. Not very good, but at least there's great music by Bob Marley and others. **103m/C VHS, Beta.** Hiram Keller, Kristine Sinclair; ***D:*** Dickie Jobson. *MVD, MED*

County Fair **1920** This early silent film is an adaptation of Neil Burgess' play about life in New England. **60m/B VHS, Beta.** Helen Jerome Eddy, David Butler. *NOS, DVT, HEG*

Coup de Grace ½ **1978** Engaging political satire about a wealthy aristocratic woman in Latvia during the 1919-1920 Civil War, and how she attempts to maintain her lifestyle as German soldiers are housed on her estate. Her unrequited love for a German officer adds to her troubles. In German with English subtitles. Co-written by von Trotta and based on the novel by Marguerite Yourcenar. **96m/B Beta.** *GE FR* Margarethe von Trotta, Matthias Habich, Rudiger Kirschstein, Matthieu Carriere; ***D:*** Volker Schlondorff; ***W:*** Margarethe von Trotta. *COL, APD, GLV*

Coup de Torchon *Clean Slate* **1981** Set in 1938 French West Africa, Noiret plays corrupt police chief Lucien Cordier who is consistently harrassed by his community, particularly by the town pimp. He usually overlooks the pimp's crimes, but when Cordier catches him and a friend shooting at plague victims' bodies floating down the river he decides to murder them in cold blood. Based on the novel "POP 1280" by Jim Thompson. In French with English subtitles. **128m/C VHS.** *FR* Philippe Noiret, Isabelle Huppert, Guy Marchand, Stephane Audran, Eddy Mitchell, Jean-Pierre Marielle; ***D:*** Bertrand Tavernier; ***W:*** Bertrand Tavernier. Nominations: Academy Awards '81: Best Foreign Language Film. *HMV*

Coupe de Ville ½ **1990 (PG-13)** Three brothers are forced by their father to drive mom's birthday present from Detroit to Florida in the summer of '63. Period concerns and music keep it interesting. **98m/C VHS, Beta, LV.** Patrick Dempsey, Daniel Stern, Arye Gross, Joseph Bologna, Alan Arkin, Annabeth Gish, Rita Taggart, James Gammon; ***D:*** Joe Roth; ***W:*** Mike Binder; ***M:*** James Newton Howard. *MCA*

Couples and Robbers **1984** Rich couple and a poor couple are unexpectedly brought together. **29m/C VHS, Beta.** *DCL*

Courage **1986** Based on fact, a television movie about a Hispanic mother in New York City who, motivated by her drug-troubled children, goes undercover and exposes a multimillion-dollar drug ring. Loren is great in a decidedly non-glamorous role. **141m/C VHS, Beta.** Sophia Loren, Billy Dee Williams, Hector Elizondo, Val Avery, Dan Hedaya, Ron Rifkin, Jose Perez; ***D:*** Jeremy Paul Kagan. *VTR, NWV*

Courage Mountain **1989 (PG)** If you're looking for a good sequel to Johanna Spyri's classic "Heidi" this isn't it. Europe is on the brink of WWI when teenage Heidi leaves her beloved mountain for an exclusive boarding school in Italy. Not surprisingly in a war zone, the military takes over and the kids are sent to an orphanage run by nasties (see also "Oliver!"). The girls escape to the mountains and are saved by none other than Sheen as Heidi's pal Peter (who cast the twentysomething Sheen as a teenager? Bad mistake.) Ridiculous sequel to the classic tale will appeal to kids despite what the critics say. **92m/C VHS, Beta, LV.** Juliette Caton, Joanna Clarke, Nicola Stapleton, Charlie Sheen, Jan Rubes, Leslie Caron, Jade Magri, Kathryn Ludlow, Yorgo Voyagis; ***D:*** Christopher Leitch; ***W:*** Weaver Webb; ***M:*** Sylvester Levay. *COL, FCT*

Courage of Black Beauty ½ **1957** Another version of the perennial heart warmer about a boy and his horse. **80m/C VHS, Beta.** Johnny Crawford, Mimi Gibson, John Bryant, Diane Brewster, J. Pat O'Malley; ***D:*** Harold Schuster. *LIV*

Courage of Lassie ½ *Blue Sierra* **1946 (G)** Fourteen-year-old Taylor is the heroine in this girl loves dog tale. In this case, the dog is actually called Bill, not Lassie, in spite of the film's title. Bill is found wounded by Taylor and she nurses him back to health. He proves to be loving, loyal, and useful, so much so that, through a complicated plotline, he winds up in the Army's K-9 division and returns home with the doggie version of shell-shock. Taylor's still there to nurse him back to his old kind self again. **93m/C VHS.** Elizabeth Taylor, Frank Morgan, Tom Drake, Selena Royle, Harry Davenport; ***D:*** Fred M. Wilcox. *MGM*

Courage of Rin Tin Tin **1983** Rusty and his faithful dog Rin Tin Tin help the cavalry soldiers of Fort Apache keep law and order in a small Arizona town. The perennial kid-pleasing German Shepherd comes through again. **90m/C VHS, Beta.** James Brown, Lee Aaker. *MON*

Courage of the North ½ **1935** The Mounties break up a fur-stealing ring with the help of Captain Dog and Dynamite Horse. Bound to set your hair on end. **55m/B VHS, Beta.** John Preston, June Love, William Desmond, Tom London, Jimmy Aubrey. *NO*

Courage Under Fire **1996 (R)** Army Col. Nat Serling (Washington) is a tank commander unexpectedly assigned to review the candidacy of Capt. Karen Emma Walden (Ryan, seen only in flashbacks) to receive the posthumous Medal of Honor for bravery in combat. A Gulf War Medevac pilot, Walden would be the first woman awarded the honor if Serling can figure out the truth from her surviving crew's wildly conflicting reports. Ironically, Serling's dealing with a guilt complex since four members of his unit died in the war under friendly fire. Based on the novel by Duncan, who also did the screenplay; Washington and director Zwick previously worked together on "Glory." **?m/C VHS.** Denzel Washington, Meg Ryan, Matt Damon, Lou Diamond Phillips, Michael Moriarty, Scott Glenn, Bronson Pinchot, Seth Gilliam, Sean Astin, Regina Taylor; ***D:*** Edward Zwick; ***W:*** Patrick Sheane Duncan; ***C:*** Roger Deakins; ***M:*** James Horner. *NYR*

Courageous Avenger ♪ **1935** A sheriff brings a treacherous ore mine foreman to justice. **59m/B VHS, Beta, LV.** Johnny Mack Brown. *MLB*

Courageous Dr. Christian ♪♪ **1940** Dr. Christian is faced with an epidemic of meningitis among the inhabitants of a shanty town. Typical entry in the "Dr. Christian" series. **66m/B VHS, Beta.** Jean Hersholt, Dorothy Lovett, Tom Neal, Robert Baldwin, Maude Eburne; ***D:*** Bernard Vorhaus; ***C:*** John Alton. *NOS, VYY, DVT*

The Courageous Mr. Penn ♪♪ *Penn of Pennsylvania* **1941** Slow-moving British film, outlining the achievements of William Penn, the Quaker founder of Pennsylvania. **79m/B VHS, Beta.** *GB* Clifford Evans, Deborah Kerr, Dennis Arundell, Aubrey Mallalieu, D.J. Williams, O.B. Clarence, Charles Carson, Henry Oscar, J.H. Roberts; ***D:*** Lance Comfort. *NOS, VYY, VEC*

The Courier ♪♪ **1988 (R)** A former drug addict seeks revenge on the dealers who killed his friend. Only thing that saves it are the songs by U2, The Pogues, and Hothouse Flowers. Musical score by Elvis Costello. **85m/C VHS, Beta, LV.** *IR* Gabriel Byrne, Ian Bannen, Padraig O'Loingsigh, Cait O'Riordan, Patrick Bergin; ***D:*** Frank Deasy, Joe Lee; ***M:*** Elvis Costello. *VES, LIV*

Courier of Death ♪ **1984** A courier is embroiled in a mob war/struggle over a locked briefcase with mysterious contents. **77m/C VHS, Beta.** Joey Johnson, Barbara Garrison; ***D:*** Tom Shaw. *VES, LIV*

Court Jester ♪♪♪½ **1956** Swashbuckling comedy stars Danny Kaye as a former circus clown who teams up with a band of outlaws trying to dethrone a tyrant king. Kaye poses as the court jester so he can learn of the evil king's intentions. Filled with more color, more song, and more truly funny lines than any three comedies put together, this is Kaye's best performance. ♫They'll Never Outfox the Fox; Baby, Let Me Take You Dreaming; My Heart Knows a Lovely Song; The Maladjusted Jester. **101m/C VHS, Beta, LV.** Danny Kaye, Glynis Johns, Basil Rathbone, Angela Lansbury, Cecil Parker, John Carradine, Mildred Natwick, Robert Middleton; ***D:*** Norman Panama, Melvin Frank; ***W:*** Norman Panama. *PAR*

The Court Martial of Billy Mitchell ♪♪♪ *One-Man Mutiny* **1955** Terrific courtroom drama depicts the secret trial of Billy Mitchell, head of the Army Air Service in the 1920s, who predicted the role of airpower in subsequent warfare and the danger of war with Japan. Mitchell incurred the wrath of the military by publicly faulting the lack of U.S. preparedness for invasion. Steiger is outstanding as the attorney; Cooper is great as Mitchell. Debut for Montgomery. **100m/C VHS, LV.** Gary Cooper, Charles Bickford, Ralph Bellamy, Rod Steiger, Elizabeth Montgomery, Fred Clark, James Daly, Jack Lord, Peter Graves, Darren McGavin, Robert Simon, Jack Perrin, Charles Dingle; ***D:*** Otto Preminger; ***C:*** Sam Leavitt. Nominations: Academy Awards '55: Best Story & Screenplay. *REP*

The Court Martial of Jackie Robinson ♪♪♪½ **1990 (R)** True story of a little known chapter in the life of the famous athlete. During his stint in the Army, Robinson refused to take a back seat on a bus and subsequently faced the possibility of court martial. Originally made for cable television. **94m/C VHS, Beta.** Andre Braugher, Daniel Stern, Ruby Dee, Stan Shaw, Paul Dooley, Bruce Dern; ***D:*** Larry Peerce; ***W:*** Dennis Lynton Clark. *TTC, FCT*

The Courtesans of Bombay ♪♪♪ **1985** Gritty docudrama, set in Pavanpul, the poverty-stricken brothel section of Bombay, looks at how the impoverished women support themselves through a combination of prostitution and performing. Made for British television. **74m/C VHS, Beta.** *GB* Kareem Samar, Zohra Segal, Saeed Jaffrey; ***D:*** Ismail Merchant, James Ivory, Ruth Prawer Jhabvala. *SUE, INJ, NLC*

Courtin' Wildcats ♪½ **1929** Early Gibson programmer in which he plays a frail eastern college boy who was sent west by his father to toughen up. Once there, he meets Gilbert and ends up marrying her. **56m/B VHS.** Hoot Gibson, Eugenia Gilbert, Monte Montague; ***D:*** Jerome Storm. *GPV*

The Courtney Affair ♪♪½ *The Courtneys of Curzon Street* **1947** An aristocratic young Britisher causes a stir when he marries an Irish maid. As a result, the couple must face terrific social ostracism. Classy soap opera family saga was a big money maker in England. **112m/B VHS.** *GB* Anna Neagle, Michael Wilding, Gladys Young, Michael Medwin, Coral Browne, Jack Watling, Bernard Lee; ***D:*** Herbert Wilcox. *VYY*

Courtship ♪♪♪ **1987** From renowned playwright Horton Foote comes this touching story about a sheltered, upper-crust young girl who shocks her family and friends by eloping with a traveling salesman. Made for television. **84m/C VHS, Beta.** Hallie Foote, William Converse-Roberts, Amanda Plummer, Rochelle Oliver, Michael Higgins; ***D:*** Howard Cummings. *ORI, WAR*

The Courtship of Eddie's Father ♪♪♪ **1962** A clever nine-year-old boy plays matchmaker for his widowed dad in this rewarding family comedy-drama (the inspiration for the TV series). Some plot elements are outdated, but young Howard's performance is terrific; he would later excel at direction. Based on the novel by Mark Toby. **117m/C VHS.** Glenn Ford, Shirley Jones, Stella Stevens, Dina Merrill, Ron Howard, Jerry Van Dyke; ***D:*** Vincente Minnelli; ***W:*** John Gay; ***C:*** Milton Krasner. *MGM, FCT*

The Courtyard ♪♪ **1995 (R)** Jonathan Hoffman (McCarthy) seems to have the perfect life—a great job, great girl, great California apartment. But then his apartment complex is bedeviled by a series of sinister crimes and Jonathan becomes the prime suspect. **103m/C VHS.** Andrew McCarthy, Madchen Amick, Richard "Cheech" Marin. *REP*

Cousin, Cousine ♪♪♪½ **1976 (R)** Pleasant French comedy about distant cousins who meet at a round of family parties, funerals, and weddings and become friends, but their relationship soon becomes more than platonic. Remade in the U.S. in 1989 as "Cousins." In French with English subtitles. **95m/C VHS, Beta, LV.** *FR* Marie-Christine Barrault, Marie-France Pisier, Victor Lanoux, Guy Marchand, Ginette Garcin, Sybil Maas; ***D:*** Jean-Charles Tacchella; ***M:*** Gerard Anfosso. Cesar Awards '76: Best Supporting Actress (Pisier); National Board of Review Awards '76: 5 Best Foreign Films of the Year; Nominations: Academy Awards '76: Best Actress (Barrault), Best Foreign Language Film, Best Original Screenplay. *TPV, IME, FOX*

The Cousins ♪♪♪ *Les Cousins* **1959** Set against the backdrop of Parisian student life, two very different cousins (one twisted, the other saintly) vie for the hand of Mayniel. This country mouse, city mouse adult fable ultimately depicts the survival of the fittest. Chabrol's lovely but sad second directorial effort. **112m/B VHS.** *FR* Jean-Claude Brialy, Gerard Blain, Juliette Mayniel, Claude Cerval, Genevieve Cluny; ***D:*** Claude Chabrol; ***W:*** Claude Chabrol. *PAR*

Cousins ♪♪♪½ **1989 (PG-13)** An American remake of "Cousin, Cousine," in which two distant cousins-by-marriage meet at a wedding and, due to their respective spouses' infidelities, fall into each other's arms. A gentle love story with a humorous and biting look at the foibles of extended families. **110m/C VHS, Beta, LV.** Isabella Rossellini, Sean Young, Ted Danson, William L. Petersen, Norma Aleandro, Lloyd Bridges, Keith Coogan; ***D:*** Joel Schumacher; ***W:*** Stephen Metcalfe; ***C:*** Ralf Bode; ***M:*** Angelo Badalamenti. *PAR, FCT, HMV*

Cover Girl ♪♪♪ **1944** A vintage wartime musical about a girl who must decide between a nightclub career and a future as a cover model. Hayworth is beautiful, Kelly dances like a dream, and Silvers and Arden are hilarious. Cinematography by Rudolph Mate. ♫Cover Girl; Sure Thing; Make Way For Tomorrow; Put Me to the Test; Long Ago and Far Away; That's the Best of All; The Show Must Go On; Who's Complaining?; Poor John. **107m/C VHS, Beta, LV.** Rita Hayworth, Gene Kelly, Phil Silvers, Otto Kruger, Lee Bowman, Jinx Falkenberg, Eve Arden, Edward Brophy, Anita Colby; ***D:*** Charles Vidor; ***M:*** Ira Gershwin, Jerome Kern. Academy Awards '44: Best Score; Nominations: Academy Awards '44: Best Color Cinematography, Best Interior Decoration, Best Song ("Long Ago and Far Away"), Best Sound. *COL*

Cover Girl Models ♪ **1975** An action-packed seventies adventure in which beautiful models are forced to fight for survival. **82m/C VHS, Beta.** Lindsay Bloom, Pat Anderson, John Kramer, Rhonda Leigh Hopkins, Mary Woronov; ***D:*** Cirio H. Santiago. *SUE*

The Cover Girl Murders ♪♪½ **1993 (PG-13)** Six beautiful models have been brought together on a remote island to shoot a magazine's popular swimsuit issue. Each one wants to be the cover model—but someone is willing to kill to get the job. **87m/C VHS, Beta.** Lee Majors, Jennifer O'Neill, Adrian Paul, Beverly Johnson, Vanessa Angel; ***D:*** James A. Contner; ***W:*** Douglas Barr, Bernard Maybeck; ***M:*** Rick Marotta. *PAR*

Cover Me ♪♪ **1995 (R)** When beautiful models turn up dead, L.A. detectives Bobby Colter (Rossovich) and J.J. Davis (Sorvino) discover they were all on the cover of L.A. Erotica magazine. So detective Holly Jacobsen, Colter's girlfriend, (Taylor) goes undercover at the magazine and learns more about the seamy sex underworld than the killer wants her to know. **94m/C VHS, Beta.** Courtney Taylor, Rick Rossovich, Paul Sorvino, Elliott Gould, Corbin Bernsen; ***D:*** Michael Schroeder; ***W:*** Steve Johnson. *PAR*

Cover Story ♪½ **1993** Journalist Matt McKendree falls in love with a mystery woman whose story he's investigating. Too bad she's dead—or is she. **93m/C VHS.** William Wallace, Tuesday Knight, Robert Forster, Christopher McDonald. *AVI*

Cover-Up ♪½ **1991 (R)** Terrorist attacks on U.S. military bases in Israel are just a smokescreen for a greater threat. The below-par actioner stands out only for the hokey religious symbolism in its Good Friday climax. **89m/C VHS, LV.** Dolph Lundgren, Louis Gossett Jr., John Finn; ***D:*** Manny Coto. *LIV, IME*

The Covered Wagon ♪♪½ **1923** Prototypical silent Western began the genre. Wagon train moves cross-country, battling weather and wild Indians. By today's standards, somewhat bucolic and uneventful, but the location photography holds up quite well. Big budget film in its day, and enormously popular. **98m/B VHS, LV.** Warren Kerigan, Lois Wilson, Alan Hale, Ernest Torrence; ***D:*** James Cruze. *PAR*

Covered Wagon Days ♪♪ **1940** The Three Mesquiteers set out after silver smugglers who have framed Rico's brother for murder. **54m/B VHS.** Bob Livingston, Raymond Hatton, Duncan Renaldo, John Merton, Reed Howes; ***D:*** George Sherman. *REP*

Covered Wagon Trails ♪ **1940** Substandard Western has good guy Randall dealing with the shifty cattleman's association and making the West safe for the hardworking locals. Future Frankenstein monster Strange plays the hired muscle. **52m/B VHS.** Jack Randall, Sally Cairns, David Sharpe, Lafe McKee, Budd Buster, Glenn Strange; ***D:*** Raymond K. Johnson; ***W:*** Tom Gibson. *MOV*

Covergirl ♪½ *Dreamworld* **1983 (R)** Wealthy man decides to relieve his boredom by molding a young woman into a supermodel. She finds the glamorous life isn't always what it's cracked up to be. TV-type melodrama. **98m/C VHS, Beta.** *CA* Jeff Conaway, Irena Ferris, Cathie Shirriff, Roberta Leighton, Deborah Wakeham; ***D:*** Jean-Claude Lord. *VTR*

Covert Action ♪½ **1988** A drug kingpin who desires to protect his business tries to frame a captain for a crime he did not commit. **85m/C VHS, Beta.** Rick Washburne, John Christian, Stuart Garrison Day, Amanda Zinsser, Johnny Stumper; ***D:*** J. Christian Ingvordsen. *MCG*

Covert Assassin ♪♪ **1994 (R)** Anti-terrorist specialist is hired by wealthy widow to avenge her husband's murder. Adapted from the novel "Wild Justice" by Wilbur Smith. **114m/C VHS.** Roy Scheider, Sam Wanamaker, Ted McGinley, Christopher Buchholz; ***D:*** Tony Wharmby. *VMK*

Cow Town 1950 A range war results when ranchers begin fencing in their land to prevent cattle rustling. Autry's 72nd film has some good songs and a dependable cast. **70m/B VHS, Beta.** Gene Autry, Gail Davis, Jock Mahoney, Harry Shannon; ***D:*** John English. *CCB*

Coward of the County ½. **1981** A devout pacifist is put to the test when his girlfriend is raped. Good performances by all concerned. Based on the lyrics of Kenny Rogers' hit song of the same name. Made for television. **115m/C VHS, Beta.** Kenny Rogers, Frederic Lehne, Largo Woodruff, Mariclare Costello, Ana Alicia, Noble Willingham; ***D:*** Dick Lowry. *ORI, WAR*

Cowboy ½ **1954** Film chronicling the determination of cattle-herders in the West. **69m/C VHS, Beta, LV.** *RXM*

Cowboy **1958** Western roundup based on the memoirs of tenderfoot-turned-cowpoke Frank Harris. Harris (Lemmon) is a Chicago hotel clerk who meets cattle boss Tom Reece (Ford) who's in the city on business. Losing his money in a poker game, Reece reluctantly accepts a loan from Harris in exchange for a piece of his cattle business. So Harris and Reece hit the dusty trail on a cattle drive that takes them into Mexico where Harris falls in love with Maria (Kashfi), the daughter of a wealthy rancher, and gradually turns from city slicker into hardened trail boss. Good cast, no fuss. From the book "Reminiscences As a Cowboy" by Harris. **92m/C VHS.** Jack Lemmon, Glenn Ford, Anna Kashfi, Brian Donlevy, Dick York, Victor Manuel Mendoza, Richard Jaeckel, King Donovan; ***D:*** Delmer Daves; ***W:*** Edmund H. North; ***C:*** Charles Lawton Jr.; ***M:*** George Duning. *COL*

The Cowboy & the Ballerina **1984** A television movie about an aging rodeo star who falls in love with a petite ballerina defecting from a Russian Dance Company. Good cast makes it watchable. **96m/C VHS, Beta.** Lee Majors, Leslie Wing, Christopher Lloyd, Anjelica Huston, George de la Pena; ***D:*** Jerry Jameson; ***M:*** Bruce Broughton. *PSM*

Cowboy & the Bandit **1935** A cowboy comes to the aid of a widow being victimized by outlaws. **58m/B VHS, Beta.** Rex Lease, Bobby Nelson, William Desmond; ***D:*** Al(bert) Herman. *NOS*

The Cowboy and the Lady ½ **1938** Oberon plays a madcap heiress who is deposited by her politician father on their Florida estate to keep her out of trouble while he seeks the Presidential nomination. She is bored and decides to go to a local rodeo where she meets cowboy Cooper. Both are instantly smitten and marry on impulse. Cooper doesn't know about her wealth and when her father finds out about the marriage he's appalled that his daughter has married beneath her. Since this is a comedy all comes out right in the end. Good cast, weak story. **91m/B VHS.** Gary Cooper, Merle Oberon, Patsy Kelly, Walter Brennan, Fuzzy Knight, Mabel Todd, Henry Kolker, Harry Davenport; ***D:*** H.C. Potter; ***C:*** Gregg Toland. Academy Awards '38: Best Sound; Nominations: Academy Awards '38: Best Song ("The Cowboy and the Lady"), Best Original Score. *FCT, HBO*

Cowboy & the Senorita **1944** A cowboy solves the mystery of a missing girl and wins her lovely cousin. The first film that paired Rogers and Evans, who went on to become a winning team, on and offscreen. **56m/B VHS, Beta.** Roy Rogers, John Hubbard, Dale Evans. *NOS, MRV, DVT*

Cowboy Commandos ½ **1943** Improbable plot has cowboys riding out after Nazi spies, who want to steal valuable ore. **53m/B VHS.** Ray Corrigan, Dennis Moore, Max Terhune, Budd Buster, John Merton; ***D:*** S. Roy Luby. *DVT, RXM, HEG*

Cowboy Counselor **1933** Cowboy Hoot Gibson helps an enchanting girl clear her innocent brother's name. **60m/B VHS, Beta.** Hoot Gibson. *VCI*

Cowboy Millionaire ½ **1935** An Englishwoman comes to an American dude ranch and falls in love with one of the ranch hands. Entertaining Western comedy. **65m/B VHS.** George O'Brien, Evalyn Bostock, Edgar Kennedy, Alden Chase; ***D:*** Eddie Cline. *NOS, DVT, RXM*

The Cowboy Way ½ **1994 (PG-13)** A mess from start to finish made somewhat watchable by cowpoke charm of the leads and one good horse chase. Two rodeo stars (Harrelson and Sutherland) from New Mexico ride into New York City to avenge a buddy's death, with Hudson as a mounted NYC cop who always yearned to be a cowboy. Great premise is overcome by tasteless humor and a patched-up plot shot full of holes. Good for a gander is the 90-foot Times Square billboard of Harrelson's character as a Calvin Klein underwear model, which stopped traffic even in jaded New York. **106m/C VHS, LV.** Woody Harrelson, Kiefer Sutherland, Dylan McDermott, Ernie Hudson, Cara Buono, Marg Helgenberger, Tomas Milian, Joaquin Martinez; ***Cameos:*** Travis Tritt; ***D:*** Gregg Champion; ***W:*** William D. Wittliff, Rob Thompson; ***M:*** David Newman. *MCA*

The Cowboys **1972 (PG)** Wayne stars as a cattle rancher who is forced to hire eleven schoolboys to help him drive his cattle 400 miles to market. Clever script makes this one of Wayne's better Westerns. Carradine's film debut. Inspired the television series. Laserdisc available in widescreen letterbox edition. **128m/C VHS, Beta, LV.** John Wayne, Roscoe Lee Browne, A. Martinez, Bruce Dern, Colleen Dewhurst, Slim Pickens, Robert Carradine, Clay O'Brien; ***D:*** Mark Rydell; ***W:*** Harriet Frank Jr., Irving Ravetch; ***C:*** Robert L. Surtees; ***M:*** John Williams. *WAR, TLF*

Cowboys Don't Cry **1988** When a modern cowboy's wife is killed in an automobile accident, he must change his immature ways and build a solid future with his teenage son or perish in loneliness. **96m/C VHS, Beta.** Rebecca Jenkins, Ron White, Janet-Laine Green. *MCA*

Cowboys from Texas ½ **1939** The Three Mesquiteers bring about a peaceful settlement to a fight between cattlemen and homesteaders. Part of "The Three Mesquiteers" series. **54m/B VHS, Beta.** Bob Livingston, Raymond Hatton, Duncan Renaldo, Carole Landis. *MED*

Cowboys of the Saturday Matinee **1984** The history of B-movie westerns is traced from the beginning of the sound era. **75m/B VHS, Beta.** Gene Autry, Tex Ritter, Roy Rogers. *ORI, FCT, WAR*

Coyote Trails ½ **1935** Standard western adventure has cowboy Tyler helping a damsel in distress. **68m/B VHS, Beta.** Tom Tyler. *NOS, VCN, RXM*

Crack House **1989 (R)** A man seeks revenge for the murder of a relative by drug dealers. Average exploitation flick. **91m/C VHS, Beta, LV.** Jim Brown, Richard Roundtree, Anthony Geary, Angel Tompkins, Greg Gomez Thomsen, Clyde Jones, Cheryl Kay; ***D:*** Michael Fischa. *MGM, WAR*

Crack Shadow Boxers **197?** Through a series of misadventures, Wu Lung and Chu San battle to protect the inhabitants of a small village from the onslaught of relentless bandits. **91m/C VHS, Beta.** *HK* Ku Feng, Chou Li Lung, Han Guo Gai; ***D:*** Weng Yao Hai. *MGI*

Crack-Up ½ **1946** Largely ignored at the time of its release, this tense tale is now regarded as a minor classic of film noir. An art expert suffers a blackout while investigating a possible forgery and must piece together the missing hours to uncover a criminal conspiracy. **70m/B VHS, Beta, LV.** Pat O'Brien, Claire Trevor, Herbert Marshall, Ray Collins, Wallace Ford, Damian O'Flynn, Erskine Sanford; ***D:*** Irving Reis. *TTC*

The Cracker Factory ½ **1979** Wood is impressive as a woman committed to a mental institution who attempts to charm her way out of treatment. Made for television. **90m/C VHS, Beta.** Natalie Wood, Perry King, Shelley Long, Vivian Blaine, Juliet Mills, Peter Haskell; ***D:*** Burt Brinckerhoff; ***M:*** Billy Goldenberg. *NO*

Crackerjack **1994 (R)** Chicago cop Jack Wild (Griffith) agrees to join his brother's family at a vacation resort in the Rocky Mountains. Coincidentally, a team of mercenaries are determined to hijack $50 million in diamonds from the resort and it's up to Jack to stop them. **96m/C VHS, LV.** Thomas Ian Griffith, Nastassia Kinski, Christopher Plummer; ***D:*** Michael Mazo; ***W:*** Jonas Quastel, Michael Bafaro; ***M:*** Peter Allen. *REP*

Crackers **1984 (PG)** The offbeat story of two bumbling thieves who round up a gang of equally inept neighbors and go on the wildest crime spree you have ever seen. A would-be comic remake of "Big Deal on Madonna Street." **92m/C VHS, Beta, LV.** Donald Sutherland, Jack Warden, Sean Penn, Wallace Shawn, Larry Riley, Trinidad Silva, Christine Baranski, Charlaine Woodard, Tasia Valenza; ***D:*** Louis Malle. *MCA*

Cracking Up ½ *Smorgasbord* **1983 (PG)** Accident-prone misfit's mishaps on the road to recovery create chaos for everyone he meets. Lewis plays a dozen characters in this overboard comedy with few laughs. **91m/C VHS, Beta.** Jerry Lewis, Herb Edelman, Foster Brooks, Milton Berle, Sammy Davis Jr., Zane Buzby, Dick Butkus, Buddy Lester; ***D:*** Jerry Lewis. *WAR*

The Crackler **1984** During the '20s, a husband-and-wife private investigation team (Tommy and Tuppence) set out to find a gang of forgers operating in high society circles. Based on a story by Agatha Christie. Made for British television. **60m/C VHS, Beta.** *GB* James Warwick, Francesca Annis. *TPV*

The Cradle Will Fall *Woof!* **1983** A made-for-television adaptation of the pulpy bestselling mystery by Mary Higgins Clark about a woman who cannot convince anyone she witnessed a murder. The cast of "The Guiding Light" appear. Poor script and poor direction do not a thriller make. **103m/C VHS, Beta.** Lauren Hutton, Ben Murphy, James Farentino, Charita Bauer, Peter Simon; ***D:*** John Llewellyn Moxey. *ORI, WAR*

The Craft ½ **1996 (R)** Call it "Heathers" with hexes. Troubled 17-year-old Sarah (Tunney) moves to L.A. and begins her senior year at St. Benedict's Academy. She takes up with three rebels—Nancy (Balk), Bonnie (Campbell), and Rochelle (True)—who like to dabble in witchcraft. Now, with the addition of would-be witch Sarah, these black magic women start slinging spells at their uppity classmates. Works best when concentrating on the girls and their problems, but degenerates into a special effects barrage toward the end. Alas, no one is turned into a newt. **100m/C VHS.** Robin Tunney, Fairuza Balk, Neve Campbell, Rachel True, Skeet Ulrich, Helen Shaver, Cliff DeYoung, Christine Taylor, Assumpta Serna; ***D:*** Andrew Fleming; ***W:*** Andrew Fleming, Peter Filardi; ***C:*** Alexander Grusynski; ***M:*** Graeme Revell. *NYR*

Craig's Wife **1936** A classic soap opera about a pitiful woman driven to total ruin by her desire for social acceptance and material wealth. Russell makes her surprisingly sympathetic. Based on a Pulitzer Prize-winning George Kelly play. Remake of a silent film, was also remade as "Harriet Craig." **75m/B VHS, Beta.** Rosalind Russell, John Boles, Alma Kruger, Jane Darwell, Billie Burke; ***D:*** Dorothy Arzner. *NO*

Crainquebille **1923** The classic satire based on the Anatole France story about a street merchant in Paris unfairly imprisoned and eventually surviving peacefully as a tramp. Silent. **50m/B VHS, Beta.** *FR* Maurice Feraudy; ***D:*** Jacques Feyder. *FCT, GPV*

The Cranes are Flying ½ *Letyat Zhuravit* **1957** When her lover goes off to fight during WWII, a girl is seduced by his cousin. Touching love story is free of politics. Filmed in Russia; English subtitles. **91m/B VHS, Beta, LV.** *RU* Tatyana Samoilova, Alexei Batalov, Vasily Merkuryev, A. Shvorin; ***D:*** Mikhail Kalatozov. Cannes Film Festival '58: Best Film. *IHF, CVC*

Crash **1995 (NC-17)** You can always expect surreal kinkiness from Cronenberg and this film, awarded a Special Jury Prize at Cannes for "daring, originality, and audacity," won't prove the exception. It's "auto" erotica taken to the max, with car crashes and bodily injury turned into fetishes. James (Spader) lands in the hospital after an accident that killed the other driver and injured Helen (Hunter), the man's wife. However, Helen and James' shared experience soon leads to a sexual relationship, which doesn't bother James' wife, Catherine (Unger). Then there's Vaughan (Koteas) and his group, who like to reenact famous auto crashes (like those of James Dean and Jayne Mansfield). Oh yes, there's lots more sex (in various combinations). Based on J.G. Ballard's 1973 cult novel. **98m/C VHS.** *CA* James Spader, Holly Hunter, Elias Koteas, Deborah Unger, Rosanna Arquette, Peter MacNeill; ***D:*** David Cronenberg; ***W:*** David Cronenberg; ***C:*** Peter Suschitzsky; ***M:*** Howard Shore. Cannes Film Festival '96: Special Jury Prize. *NYR*

Crash and Burn ☠½ **1990 (R)** Rebels in a repressive future police state reactivate a huge, long-dormant robot to battle the establishment's army of powerful androids. Special effects by David Allen make the mayhem interesting. **85m/C VHS, Beta, LV.** Ralph Waite, Paul Ganus, Eva LaRue, Bill Moseley, Jack McGee; ***D:*** Charles Band; ***W:*** J.S. Cardone; ***M:*** Richard Band. *PAR*

Crash Dive ☠☠½ **1943** WWII glory film provides comic relief in the form of romance. Second-in-command Power falls hopelessly in love with school teacher Baxter, only to find out later that she is Lt. Commander Andrews' fiance. Once this little tidbit of information is disclosed, the two officers embark on a mission to destroy a Nazi U-Boat responsible for laying mines in the North Atlantic. Fantastic special effects and sound. Based on the story by W.R. Burnett. **105m/B VHS.** Tyrone Power, Anne Baxter, Dana Andrews, James Gleason, May Whitty, Harry (Henry) Morgan, Ben Carter, Frank Conroy, Florence Lake, John Archer, Minor Watson, Kathleen Howard, Stanley Andrews, Thurston Hall, Trudy Marshall; ***D:*** Archie Mayo; ***W:*** Jo Swerling; ***C:*** Leon Shamroy; ***M:*** David Buttolph. Academy Awards '44: Best Special Effects (Sersen). *FXV*

The Crash of Flight 401 ☠½ **1978** A plane, full of recognizable TV stars, crashes in the Florida Everglades. "Airport" for a smaller screen. Based on a real event. Made for televisiion. **97m/C VHS, Beta.** William Shatner, Adrienne Barbeau, Eddie Albert, Brooke Bundy, Christopher Connelly, Lorraine Gary, Ron Glass, Sharon Gless, Brett Halsey, George Maharis, Gerald S. O'Loughlin; ***D:*** Barry Shear. *FRH*

Crashout ☠☠½ **1955** Six men break out of prison in this entertaining melodrama. Bendix plays the gang's leader to nasty perfection. **82m/B VHS.** William Bendix, Gene Evans, Arthur Kennedy, Luther Adler, William Talman, Marshall Thompson, Beverly Michaels; ***D:*** Lewis R. Foster. *REP*

The Crater Lake Monster *Woof!* **1977 (PG)** The dormant egg of a prehistoric creature hatches after a meteor rudely awakens the dozing dino. He's understandably miffed and begins a revenge campaign. Prehistoric yawner. **85m/C VHS, Beta.** Richard Cardella, Glenn Roberts, Mark Siegel, Bob Hyman, Kacey Cobb; ***D:*** William R. Stromberg. *VCI, MRV*

The Craving ☠ **1980 (R)** Naschy returns as El Hombre Lobo for the umpteenth time and once again battles a female vampire (see "Werewolf vs. the Vampire Woman"). Although continental Europe's biggest horror star, this film was such a box office disaster that Naschy went bankrupt. He was then forced to turn to Japan for financing (see "The Human Beasts"). Naschy also directed under a pseudonym. **93m/C VHS, Beta.** *MX* Paul Naschy, Julie Saly; ***D:*** Jack Molina. *VES, LIV*

The Crawlers ☠ **1993 (R)** Illegal radioactive dumping has caused a living, lethal organism to invade in a small western town. Seems the local sheriff and the nuclear plant manager were partners in a toxic dumping scheme that went awry and two teenagers are the only ones willing to expose the truth. More to the point—scary monster attacks woman with artistically enhanced cleavage. **94m/C VHS.** Jason Saucier, Mary Sellers; ***D:*** Martin Newlin; ***W:*** Dan Price, Martin Newlin. *COL*

The Crawling Eye ☠☠ *The Trollenberg Terror* **1958** Hidden in a radioactive fog on a mountaintop, the crawling eye decapitates its victims and returns these humans to Earth to threaten mankind. Average acting, but particularly awful special effects. Based on a British TV series. **87m/B VHS, Beta, LV.** *GB* Forrest Tucker, Laurence Payne, Janet Munro, Jennifer Jayne, Warren Mitchell; ***D:*** Quentin Lawrence; ***W:*** Jimmy Sangster; ***M:*** Stanley Black. *SNC, MRV, MED*

The Crawling Hand *Woof!* **1963** An astronaut's hand takes off without him on an unearthly spree of stranglings. Silly stuff is a hands-down loser. **98m/B VHS, Beta, LV.** Alan Hale Jr., Rod Lauren, Richard Arlen, Peter Breck, Kent Taylor, Arline Judge, Allison Hayes; ***D:*** Herbert L. Strock. *NOS, RHI, GEM*

Crawlspace ☠ **1986 (R)** Beautiful girls lease rooms from a murdering, perverted doctor who spies on them, then kills. You may find Kinski amusing but not terrifying. **86m/C VHS, Beta.** Klaus Kinski, Talia Balsam, Joyce Van Patten, Sally Brown, Barbara Whinnery; ***D:*** David Schmoeller; ***W:*** David Schmoeller; ***M:*** Pino Donaggio. *VES, LIV*

Craze ☠☠ *The Infernal Idol; Demon Master* **1974 (R)** Toungue-in-cheek tale of a crazed antique dealer who slays a number of women as sacrifices to an African idol named Chuku. **96m/C VHS, Beta.** Jack Palance, Diana Dors, Julie Ege, Suzy Kendall, Michael Jayston, Edith Evans, Hugh Griffith, Trevor Howard; ***D:*** Freddie Francis. *MRV*

Crazed *Woof!* **1982** Dull plodder about a psychopath who keeps a dead girl's body in his boarding house and kills all intruders to keep his secret. **88m/C VHS, Beta.** Laslo Papas, Belle Mitchell, Beverly Ross; ***D:*** Richard Cassidy. *TWE*

Crazed Cop ☠ **1988** A man's mind snaps when his wife is found raped and murdered, and nothing will stop him on his quest for revenge. Low budget and violent. **85m/C VHS, Beta.** Ivan Rogers, Sandy Brooke, Rich Sutherlin, Doug Irk, Abdulah the Great; ***D:*** Paul Kyriazi. *UNI*

The Crazies ☠☠ *Code Name: Trixie* **1973 (R)** A poisoned water supply makes the residents of a small town go on a chaotic, murderous rampage. When the army is called into to quell the anarchy, a small war breaks out. Message film about the military is muddled and derivative. **103m/C Beta.** Lane Carroll, W.G. McMillan, Harold W. Jones, Lloyd Hollar, Lynn Lowry; ***D:*** George A. Romero; ***W:*** George A. Romero. *NO*

Crazy Fat Ethel II *Woof!* **1985** A fat, hungry, homicidal female psychopath gets released from the asylum and goes on a cannabilistic rampage. Offensive junk. Sequel to "Criminally Insane." **90m/C VHS, Beta.** Priscilla Alden, Michael Flood, Jane Lambert, Robert Copple; ***D:*** Nick Phillips. *NO*

Crazy for Love ☠☠½ **1952** A village idiot stands to inherit the town inn if he can get a diploma within a year. With English subtitles. **80m/B VHS, Beta.** *FR* Brigitte Bardot, Bourvil, Jane Marken, Nadine Basile. *DVT, INJ, GVV*

Crazy from the Heart ☠☠☠ **1991** Sweet made-for-cable TV tale of a high school principal in a small south Texas town who discovers the romance of her life one weekend with a Mexican janitor. Strong, nuanced performances from Lahti and Blades make this chestnut of a story work beautifully, with able help from supporting actors. **104m/C VHS, Beta, LV.** Christine Lahti, Ruben Blades, Mary Kay Place, Brent Spiner, William Russ, Louise Latham, Tommy Muntz, Robin Lively, Bibi Besch, Kamala Lopez; ***D:*** Thomas Schlamme. *TTC*

Crazy Horse and Custer: "The Untold Story" ☠ **1990 (R)** Long before Little Big Horn, two legendary enemies find themselves trapped together in deadly Blackfoot territory. George Armstrong Custer and Crazy Horse are forced to form a volatile alliance in their life-or- death struggle against the murderous Blackfoot Tribe. History takes a back seat to Hollywood scriptwriting. **120m/C VHS.** Slim Pickens, Wayne Maunder, Mary Ann Mobley, Michael Dante. *NO*

Crazy in Love ☠☠½ **1992** Three generations of women live on an island in the home that has been in their family for years. Hunter is wildly in love with her husband, but misses (and doesn't quite trust) him when he is away on business. Enter Sands, who showers her with affection and fills the void in her life. The supporting cast fleshes out the story nicely and illustrates the reasons behind Hunter's insecurity. Enjoyable romantic comedy doesn't throw out anything heavy. Adapted from the novel by Luanne Rice; made for television. **93m/C VHS, LV.** Holly Hunter, Gena Rowlands, Bill Pullman, Julian Sands, Frances McDormand, Herta Ware, Joannne Baron; ***D:*** Martha Coolidge; ***W:*** Gerald Ayres. National Academy of Cable Programming ACE Awards '93: Best Supporting Actress (Ware). *TTC*

Crazy Mama ☠☠½ **1975 (PG)** Three women go on a crime spree from California to Arkansas, picking up men and having a hoot. Crime and comedy in a campy romp. Set in the 1950s and loaded with period kitsch. **81m/C VHS, Beta.** Cloris Leachman, Stuart Whitman, Ann Sothern, Jim Backus, Linda Purl; ***D:*** Jonathan Demme. *SUE*

Crazy Moon ☠☠½ *Huggers* **1987 (PG-13)** A rich high school nerd falls in love with a deaf girl, and must struggle against his domineering father's and older brother's prejudices. The viewer must struggle against the romantic cliches and heavy-handed message to enjoy a basically tender tale of romance. **89m/C VHS, Beta, LV.** Kiefer Sutherland, Vanessa Vaughan, Peter Spence, Ken Pogue, Eve Napier; ***D:*** Allan Eastman; ***W:*** Tom Berry, Stefan Wodoslowsky; ***M:*** Lou Forestieri. *SUE, NLC*

Crazy People ☠½ **1990 (R)** Advertising exec Emory Leeston (Moore) writes commercials that describe products with complete honesty, and is committed to a mental hospital as a result. He meets a variety of characters at the hospital, including Hannah, with whom he falls in love. Tepid box-office blunder sounds funnier than it is. We give half a bone for the ad slogans, the funniest part of the movie. Our favorite: "Most of our passengers arrive alive" for an airline. **91m/C VHS, Beta, LV.** Dudley Moore, Daryl Hannah, Paul Reiser, Mercedes Ruehl, J.T. Walsh, Ben Hammer, Dick Cusack, Alan North, David Paymer, Danton Stone, Doug Yasuda, Bill Smitrovich, Paul Bates, Floyd Vivino; ***D:*** Tony Bill; ***W:*** Mitch Markowitz; ***M:*** Cliff Eidelman. *PAR*

The Crazy Ray ☠☠☠ *Paris Qui Dort* **1922** The classic silent fantasy about a mad scientist who endeavors to put the whole population of Paris in a trance. Vintage Clair nonsense. **60m/B VHS, Beta.** *FR* Henri Rollan, Albert Prejean, Marcel Vallee, Madeleine Rodrigue; ***D:*** Rene Clair. *SNC, FCT, MRV*

The Crazysitter ☠☠½ **1994 (PG-13)** Edie (D'Angelo), a petty thief recently released from jail, is hired as a sitter to the twins-from-hell. So, she decides to sell the little monsters. **92m/C VHS, LV.** Beverly D'Angelo, Ed Begley Jr., Carol Kane, Phil Hartman, Brady Bluhm, Rachel Duncan; ***Cameos:*** Nell Carter, Steve Landesburg; ***D:*** Michael James McDonald. *NHO*

Creation of Adam ☠☠ **1993** Weirdly mystical Russian drama finds Andrey's marriage in trouble because his wife thinks he's gay. She may be right because during a business meeting, Andrey is drawn to the charasmatic Philip, who, it turns out, is some sort of angelic messenger whose mission seems to be to give Andrey confidence in love. Good performances although the plot lacks coherence and is not helped by the poor subtitling. **93m/C VHS.** *RU* Alexander Strizhenov, Anzhelika Nevolina, Saulus Balandis, Serghei Vinogradov, Irina Metlitshkaya; ***D:*** Yuri Pavlov. *WBF*

The Creation of the Humanoids *Woof!* **1962** Set in the familiar post-holocaust future, this is a tale of humans outnumbered by androids and the resulting struggle for survival. Slow and silly low-budget sets. For some reason, Andy Warhol was reported to love this film. **84m/C VHS, Beta.** Don Megowan, Frances McCann, Erica Elliot, Don Doolittle, Dudley Manlove; ***D:*** Wesley E. Barry. *MRV, SNC*

Creator ☠☠ **1985 (R)** A Frankenstein-like scientist plans to clone a being based on his wife, who died thirty years ago. As his experiments begin to show positive results, his romantic attention turns towards his beautiful lab assistant. O'Toole as the deranged scientist almost saves this one. Based on a novel by Jeremy Leven. **108m/C VHS, Beta, LV.** Peter O'Toole, Mariel Hemingway, Vincent Spano, Virginia Madsen, David Ogden Stiers, John Dehner, Karen Kopins, Jeff Corey; ***D:*** Ivan Passer; ***C:*** Robbie Greenberg. *NO*

Creature 🦴 *Titan Find* **1985 (R)** A two thousand-year-old alien life form is killing off astronauts exploring the planet Titan. "Alien" rip-off has its moments, but not enough of them. Kinski provides some laughs. **97m/C VHS, Beta, LV.** Klaus Kinski, Stan Ivar, Wendy Schaal, Lyman Ward, Annette McCarthy, Diane Salinger; ***D:*** William Malone; ***M:*** Tom Chase, Steve Rucker. *MED*

Creature from Black Lake 🦴 **1976 (PG)** Two anthropology students from Chicago travel to the Louisiana swamps searching for the creature from Black Lake. Predictably, they find him. McClenny, incidentally, is Morgan Fairchild's sister. **95m/C VHS, Beta.** Jack Elam, Dub Taylor, Dennis Fimple, John David Carson, Bill Thurman, Catherine McClenny; ***D:*** Joy Houck Jr. *MRV, VES, LIV*

Creature from the Black Lagoon 🦴🦴🦴 **1954** An anthropological expedition in the Amazon stumbles upon the Gill-Man, a prehistoric humanoid fish monster who takes a fancy to fetching Adams, a coed majoring in "science," but the humans will have none of it. Originally filmed in 3-D, this was one of the first movies to sport top-of-the-line underwater photography and remains one of the most enjoyable monster movies ever made. Gershenson's score became a "Creature Features" standard. Based on a story by Maurice Zimm. Sequels: "Revenge of the Creature" and "The Creature Walks Among Us." **79m/B VHS, Beta, LV.** Richard Carlson, Julie Adams, Richard Denning, Antonio Moreno, Whit Bissell, Nestor Paiva, Ricou Browning; ***D:*** Jack Arnold; ***W:*** Arthur Ross; ***M:*** Hans J. Salter. *MCA, GKK*

Creature from the Haunted Sea 🦴🦴 **1960** Monster movie satire set in Cuba shortly after the revolution and centering around an elaborate plan to loot the Treasury and put the blame on a strange sea monster. Corman comedy is predictably low budget but entertaining. "Wain" is really Robert Towne, winner of an Oscar for screenwriting. Remake of "Naked Paradise." **76m/B VHS, Beta.** Antony Carbone, Betsy Jones-Moreland, Beach Dickerson, Edward Wain, Edmundo Rivera Alvarez, Robert Bean; ***D:*** Roger Corman, Monte Hellman; ***W:*** Charles B. Griffith. *NOS, MRV, SNC*

Creature of Destruction 🦴 **1967** A beautiful young woman is hypnotized and inadvertantly reverted to her past life as a hideous sea monster. Buchanan's remake of his own 1956 production, "The She Creature." **?m/B VHS.** Les Tremayne, Aron Kincaid, Pat Delaney, Neil Fletcher, Ann McAdams; ***D:*** Larry Buchanan. *NO*

Creature of the Walking Dead 🦴½ *La Marca del Muerto* **1960** Scientist brings his grandfather back to life with horrifying results for the cast and the audience. Made cheaply and quickly in Mexico in Mexico in 1960, then released with added footage directed by Warren. **74m/B VHS.** *MX* Rock Madison, Ann Wells, George Todd, Willard Gross, Bruno Ve Sota; ***D:*** Frederic Corte, Jerry Warren. *NOS, MRV, SNC*

The Creature Walks Among Us 🦴½ **1956** Sequel to "Revenge of the Creature" has the Gill-Man once again being captured by scientists for studying purposes. Through an accidental lab fire, the creature's gills are burned off and he undergoes surgery in an attempt to live out of water. Final entry in the Creature series has little magic of the original. Also shot in 3-D. Available on laserdisc as part of a special Encore Edition Double Feature with "Revenge of the Creature." **79m/B VHS, LV.** Jeff Morrow, Rex Reason, Leigh Snowden, Gregg Palmer; ***D:*** John Sherwood; ***W:*** Arthur Ross; ***M:*** Joseph Gershenson. *MCA, FCT*

Creature with the Blue Hand 🦴🦴 **1970** A German horror film based on a passable Edgar Wallace story about a man unjustly convicted of murders actually committed by a lunatic. Dubbed. **92m/C VHS, Beta.** *GE* Klaus Kinski, Harald Leopold, Hermann Leschau, Diana Kerner, Carl Lange, Ilse Page; ***D:*** Alfred Vohrer. *NO*

Creatures the World Forgot *Woof!* **1970** A British-made bomb about two tribes of cavemen warring over power and a cavewoman. No special effects, dinosaurs, or dialogue. **96m/C VHS, Beta.** Julie Ege, Robert John, Tony Bonner, Rosalie Crutchley, Sue Wilson; ***D:*** Don Chaffey; ***W:*** Michael Carreras. *COL, MLB*

The Creeper 🦴🦴 **1948** After experimenting with a variety of serums, a doctor turns into a murderous monster with feline paws. **65m/B VHS, Beta.** Eduardo Ciannelli, Onslow Stevens, June Vincent, Ralph Morgan; ***D:*** Jean Yarbrough. *MLB*

Creepers 🦴🦴½ *Phenomena* **1985 (R)** A young girl talks to bugs and gets them to follow her instructions, which comes in handy when she battles the lunatic who is killing her school chums. Argento weirdness—and graphic gore—may not be for all tastes. **82m/C VHS, Beta.** *IT* Jennifer Connelly, Donald Pleasence, Daria Nicolodi, Elenora Giorgi, Dalia di Lazzaro, Patrick Bauchau, Fiore Argento; ***D:*** Dario Argento; ***W:*** Franco Ferrini, Dario Argento; ***M:*** Simon Boswell. *MED*

The Creeping Flesh 🦴🦴½ **1972 (PG)** A scientist decides he can cure evil by injecting his patients with a serum derived from the blood of an ancient corpse. Some truly chilling moments will get your flesh creeping. **89m/C VHS, Beta, LV.** *GB* Peter Cushing, Christopher Lee, Lorna Heilbron, George Benson; ***D:*** Freddie Francis. *COL, IME, MLB*

Creeping Terror *Woof! The Crawling Monster; Dangerous Charter* **1964** Gigantic alien carpet monster (look for the tennis shoes sticking out underneath) devours slow-moving teenagers. Partially narrated because some of the original soundtrack was lost, with lots of bad acting, a worse script, laughable sets, and a ridiculous monster. Beware of the thermometer scene. **81m/B VHS, Beta.** Vic Savage, Shannon O'Neal, William Thourlby, Louise Lawson, Robin James; ***D:*** John Sherwood. *NO*

Creepozoids 🦴 **1987** In the near future, a monster at an abandoned science complex stalks army deserters hiding out there. Violent nonsense done better by others. **72m/C Beta, LV.** Linnea Quigley, Ken Abraham, Michael Aranda; ***D:*** David DeCoteau. *NO*

Creepshow 🦴🦴½ **1982 (R)** Stephen King's tribute to E.C. Comics, those pulp horror comic books of the 1950s that delighted in grisly, grotesque, and morbid humor, the film tells five horror tales. Features King himself in one segment, as a none-too-bright farmer who unknowingly cultivates a strange, alien-origin moss. With despicable heroes and gory monsters, this is sure to delight all fans of the horror vein. Those easily repulsed by cockroaches beware! **120m/C VHS, Beta, LV.** Hal Holbrook, Adrienne Barbeau, Viveca Lindfors, E.G. Marshall, Stephen King, Leslie Nielsen, Carrie Nye, Fritz Weaver, Ted Danson, Ed Harris; ***D:*** George A. Romero; ***W:*** Stephen King. *WAR*

Creepshow 2 🦴½ **1987 (R)** Romero adapted three Stephen King stories for this horror anthology which presents gruesome looks at a hit-and-run driver, a wooden Indian, and a vacation gone wrong. Gory and childish stuff from two masters of the genre. Look for King as a truck driver. **92m/C VHS, Beta, LV.** Lois Chiles, George Kennedy, Dorothy Lamour, Tom Savini, Domenick John, Frank S. Salsedo, Holt McCallany, David Holbrook, Page Hannah, Daniel Beer, Stephen King; ***D:*** Michael Gornick; ***W:*** George A. Romero. *VTR, NWV*

The Cremators *Woof!* **1972** A meteorite carrying an alien lands at a seaside resort and everyone begins bursting into flames. Low budget effort from the scripter of "It Came from Outer Space." **90m/C VHS, Beta.** Marvin Howard, Maria de Aragon; ***D:*** Harry Essex. *NO*

The Crew 🦴🦴 **1995 (R)** Sometimes it doesn't pay to be a good samaritan—as a boatload of pleasure cruisers discover when they rescue two psychopaths from a burning boat in the Bahamas. **99m/C VHS.** Viggo Mortensen, Jeremy Sisto, Pamela Gidley, Donal Logue, Laura Del Sol, Grace Zabriskie, John Philbin; ***D:*** Carl Colpaert; ***W:*** Carl Colpaert. *LIV*

Cria 🦴🦴🦴 *Cria Cuervos; Raise Ravens* **1976 (PG)** The award-winning story of a 9-year-old girl's struggle for maturity in a hostile adult world. In Spanish with English subtitles. **115m/C VHS, Beta, LV.** *SP* Geraldine Chaplin, Ana Torrent, Conchita Perez; ***D:*** Carlos Saura. Cannes Film Festival '76: Grand Jury Prize; National Board of Review Awards '77: 5 Best Foreign Films of the Year; Nominations: Cannes Film Festival '76: Best Film. *INT, TPV, APD*

Cricket on the Hearth 🦴🦴 **1923** An adaptation of Charles Dickens' short story about a mail carrier and his bride, who find the symbol of good luck, a cricket on the hearth, when they enter their new home. Silent with organ score. **68m/B VHS, Beta.** Paul Gerson, Virginia Brown Faire, Paul Moore, Joan Standing. *CCB*

Cries and Whispers 🦴🦴🦴 *Viskingar Och Rop* **1972 (R)** As a woman dies slowly of tuberculosis, three women care for her: her two sisters, one sexually repressed, the other promiscuous, and her servant. The sisters remember family love and closeness, but are too afraid to look death in the face to aid their sister. Only the servant can touch her in her dying and only the servant believes in God and his will. Beautiful imagery, focused through a nervous camera, which lingers on the meaningless and whisks away from the meaningful. Absolute mastery of cinematic art by Bergman. **91m/C VHS, Beta, LV.** *SW* Harriet Andersson, Ingrid Thulin, Liv Ullmann, Kary Sylway, Erland Josephson, Henning Moritzen; ***D:*** Ingmar Bergman; ***W:*** Ingmar Bergman; ***C:*** Sven Nykvist. Academy Awards '73: Best Cinematography; National Board of Review Awards '73: 5 Best Foreign Films of the Year, Best Director (Bergman); National Society of Film Critics Awards '72: Best Cinematography, Best Screenplay; Nominations: Academy Awards '73: Best Costume Design, Best Director (Bergman), Best Picture, Best Story & Screenplay. *HMV, INJ, WAR*

Crime & Passion 🦴½ **1975 (R)** Two scheming lovers plan to get rich by having the woman marry a multimillionaire and sue for a quick divorce. The multimillionaire is no patsy, however, and seeks a deadly revenge. Three scripts by six writers were combined to create this story. That explains the many problems. **92m/C VHS, Beta.** Omar Sharif, Karen Black, Joseph Bottoms, Bernhard Wicki; ***D:*** Ivan Passer. *VES, LIV*

Crime and Punishment 🦴🦴🦴 **1935** Pared down but well-executed version of the Dostoyevski novel. Lorre is superb as Raskolnikov, who robs and murders an elderly pawnbroker. Believing he has committed the perfect murder, he accepts the invitation of police inspector Porfiry (Arnold) to observe the investigation. Gradually Raskolnikov's conscience begins to overwhelm him as Porfiry slowly works to wring a confession from the killer. Von Sternberg's subdued directorial approach worked well to explore the psychological aspects of guilt, although the melodramatic French film version (released at the same time) scored better with the critics. **88m/B VHS.** Peter Lorre, Edward Arnold, Marian Marsh, Tala Birell, Elisabeth Risdon, Robert Allen, Douglass Dumbrille, Gene Lockhart; ***D:*** Josef von Sternberg; ***W:*** S.K. Lauren, Joseph Anthony. *COL*

Crime and Punishment 🦴🦴🦴🦴 *Crime et Chatiment* **1935** Original French production (preceding the American version by just one week) of Dostoyevski's novel, the tale of a young murderer, his crime, and ultimately, his confession. Generally considered better than the American version, the French throw out all that is not dramatic, keeping the psychology and suspense. Remade in 1958. **110m/B VHS.** Harry Baur, Pierre Blanchar, Madeleine Ozeray, Marcelle Geniat, Lucienne Lemarchand; ***D:*** Pierre Chenal; ***W:*** Marcel Ayme, Chenal, Christian Stengel, Wladimir Strijewski; ***M:*** Arthur Honegger. *FCT*

Crime and Punishment 🦴🦴 **1970** Ponderous, excruciatingly long adaptation of the Dostoyevski classic involving a haunted murderer and the relentless policeman who seeks to prove him guilty. In Russian with English subtitles. **200m/B VHS.** *RU* Georgi Taratorkin, Victoria Fyodorova; ***D:*** Lev Kulijanov; ***W:*** Lev Kulijanov. *INJ, DVT, HEG*

Crime Broker 🦴🦴 **1994** A respected judge (Bisset) decides to experience life on the other side of the bench for a change. So she hooks up with a handsome partner to execute a series of high-profile robberies of bank vaults and museums. Implied sex so don't look for this under erotic thrillers. **93m/C VHS.**

Jacqueline Bisset, Masaya Kato, Gary Day; ***D:*** Ian Barry; ***W:*** Tony Morphett; ***C:*** Dan Burstall; ***M:*** Roger Mason. *APX*

Crime Busters 🦴½ **1978 (PG)** Two guys attempt to pull off a bank heist but accidentally join the Miami police force instead. Hill and Spencer are enjoyable as usual but the film suffers from poor dubbing. Remake of "Two Supercops." **114m/C VHS, Beta.** *IT* Terence Hill, Bud Spencer, Laura Gemser, Luciana Catenacci, David Huddleston; ***D:*** E.B. Clucher. *WAR*

Crime Killer 🦴 **1985** Confusing shenanigans about an explosive ex-CIA agent enlisted by the FBI to battle a brutal crime syndicate shipping guns to nasty Arabs. **90m/C VHS, Beta.** George Pan-Andreas, Leo Morrell, Althan Karras; ***D:*** George Pan-Andreas. *VTR, NWV*

Crime Lords 🦴🦴 **1991 (R)** When a pair of cops are suspended from the force for committing a blunder, they travel to Hong Kong to continue their investigation. Little do they know their sleuthing has drawn then into a confrontation with one of largest crime syndicates in the world. Lots of action, beautiful women, and exotic locations keep this basic buddy plot moving well. **96m/C VHS.** Wayne Crawford, Martin Hewitt, Susan Byun, Mel Castelo, James Hong; ***D:*** Wayne Crawford. *ACA*

The Crime of Dr. Crespi 🦴🦴 **1935** A doctor takes his revenge on a man who is after his girlfriend by injecting him with suspended animation serum. Extremely campy performance from von Stroheim; Frye's biggest role in terms of screen time. **64m/B VHS, Beta.** Erich von Stroheim, Dwight Frye, Paul Guilfoyle, Harriett Russell, John Bohn; ***D:*** John H. Auer. *NOS, SNC, MLB*

Crime of Honor 🦴 **1985** A European executive goes public with his company's corruption, and his family suffers predictable ruin as a result. Based on a true story. **95m/C VHS, Beta.** Maria Schneider, David Suchet; ***D:*** John Goldschmidt. *ACA*

The Crime of Monsieur Lange 🦴🦴🦴 *Le Crime de Monsieur Lange* **1936** Charming French socialist fantasy where workers at a publishing company turn the business into a thriving cooperative while their evil boss is gone. When he returns, worker Lefevre plots to kill him. Rather talky, but humorous. In French with subtitles. French script booklet also available. **90m/B VHS, Beta.** *FR* Rene Lefevre, Jules Berry, Florelle, Sylvia Bataille, Jean Daste, Nadia Sibirskaia; ***D:*** Jean Renoir; ***W:*** Jacques Prevert. *FCT, INT, APD*

Crime of Passion 🦴🦴½ **1957** Stanwyck plays a femme fatale whose ambitions for detective hubby lead to murder. Good performances from Stanwyck, Hayden, and Burr make this an above-average, although outlandish, crime-drama. **85m/B VHS.** Barbara Stanwyck, Sterling Hayden, Raymond Burr, Fay Wray, Royal Dano, Virginia Grey, Dennis Cross, Robert Griffin, Jay Adler, Malcolm Atterbury, S. John Launer; ***D:*** Gerd Oswald; ***W:*** Jo Eisinger. *MGM, FCT*

Crime Story: The Complete Saga **1986** All 42 episodes of the 1986-1988 NBC cops-versus-mobsters series set first in Chicago in 1963, and later in Las Vegas. The series was created by Michael Mann, the executive producer of "Miami Vice." Del Shannon updated the lyrics to his hit "Runaway" for the series theme. Available as a boxed set of ten tapes or individually. **?m/C VHS.** Dennis Farina, Anthony John Denison, Bill Smitrovich, Steve Ryan, Bill Campbell, Paul Butler, Stephen Lang, Darlanne Fluegel. *VTR, MOV*

Crime Zone 🦴🦴½ **1988 (R)** In a totalitarian, repressive, future society, two young lovers try to beat the system and make it on their own. A well-made, if occasionally muddled, low-budget film shot in Peru, of all places. **96m/C VHS.** David Carradine, Peter Nelson, Sherilyn Fenn, Orlando Sacha, Don Manor, Michael Shaner; ***D:*** Luis Llosa; ***W:*** Daryl Haney; ***M:*** Rick Conrad. *MGM*

Crimebusters 🦴½ **1979 (PG)** A man exacts revenge against a government conspiracy that kidnapped his loved ones. **90m/C VHS, Beta.** Henry Silva, Antonio Sabato; ***D:*** Michael Tarantini. *NO*

Crimes & Misdemeanors 🦴🦴🦴 **1989 (PG-13)** One of Allen's most mature films, exploring a whole range of moral ambiguities through the parallel and eventually interlocking stories of a nebbish filmmaker—who agrees to make a profile of a smug Hollywood television comic and then sabotages it—and an esteemed ophthalmologist who is being threatened with exposure by his neurotic mistress. Intriguing mix of drama and comedy few directors could pull off. Look for Daryl Hannah in an unbilled cameo. **104m/C VHS, Beta, LV.** Martin Landau, Woody Allen, Alan Alda, Mia Farrow, Joanna Gleason, Anjelica Huston, Jerry Orbach, Sam Waterston, Claire Bloom, Jenny Nichols, Caroline Aaron; ***Cameos:*** Daryl Hannah, Nora Ephron, Jerry Zaks; ***D:*** Woody Allen; ***W:*** Woody Allen; ***C:*** Sven Nykvist. National Board of Review Awards '89: Best Supporting Actor (Alda); New York Film Critics Awards '89: Best Supporting Actor (Alda); Writers Guild of America '89: Best Original Screenplay; Nominations: Academy Awards '89: Best Director (Allen), Best Original Screenplay, Best Supporting Actor (Landau). *ORI*

Crimes at the Dark House 🦴🦴🦴 **1939** In this campy, melodramatic adaptation of Wilkie Collins's novel "The Woman in White," a man kills his rich wife and puts a disguised mental patient in her place. Later remade using the book's title. **69m/B VHS.** *GB* Tod Slaughter, Hilary Eaves, Sylvia Marriott, Hay Petrie, Geoffrey Wardwell; ***D:*** George King. *NOS, MRV, SNC*

Crimes of Dr. Mabuse 🦴🦴🦴½ **1932** Supernatural horror classic about the evil Dr. Mabuse controlling an underworld empire while confined to an insane asylum. One of the best "mad doctor" movies ever made. Also known as "The Testament of Dr. Mabuse" or "The Last Will of Dr. Mabuse." **120m/B VHS.** *GE* Rudolf Klein-Rogge, Otto Wernicke, Gustav Diesl, Karl Meixner; ***D:*** Fritz Lang. *SNC*

Crimes of Passion 🦴🦴🦴 **1984** Vintage whacked-out Russell, not intended for the kiddies. A business-like fashion designer becomes a kinky prostitute at night. A disturbed street preacher makes her the heroine of his erotic fantasies. A dark terrifying vision of the underground sex world and moral hypocrisy. Sexually explicit and violent, with an extremely black comedic center. Turner's portrayal is honest and believable, Perkins overacts until he nearly gets a nosebleed, but it's all for good effect. Cut for "R" rating to get it in the theatres; this version restores some excised footage. Also available in rated version. **101m/C VHS, Beta, LV.** Kathleen Turner, Anthony Perkins, Annie Potts, John Laughlin, Bruce Davison, Norman Burton; ***D:*** Ken Russell; ***W:*** Barry Sandler; ***M:*** Rick Wakeman. Los Angeles Film Critics Association Awards '84: Best Actress (Turner). *NWV, VTR*

The Crimes of Stephen Hawke 🦴🦴 *Strangler's Morgue* **1936** The world knows Stephen Hawke as a big-hearted money lender. What they don't know is his favorite hobby is breaking peoples' spines. An entertaining thriller set in the 1800s. **65m/B VHS, Beta.** *GB* Tod Slaughter, Marjorie Taylor, D.J. Williams, Eric Portman, Ben Soutten; ***D:*** George King. *SNC, MRV, HEG*

Crimes of the Heart 🦴🦴½ **1986 (PG-13)** Based on Beth Henley's acclaimed play. A few days in the lives of three very strange Southern sisters, one of whom has just been arrested for calmly shooting her husband after he chased her black lover out of town. Spacek as the suicidal sister is a lark. A tart, black comedy that works better as a play than a film. **105m/C VHS, Beta, LV.** Sissy Spacek, Diane Keaton, Jessica Lange, Sam Shepard, Tess Harper, Hurd Hatfield; ***D:*** Bruce Beresford; ***W:*** Beth Henley; ***C:*** Dante Spinotti; ***M:*** Georges Delerue. Golden Globe Awards '87: Best Actress—Musical/Comedy (Spacek); New York Film Critics Awards '86: Best Actress (Spacek); Nominations: Academy Awards '86: Best Actress (Spacek), Best Adapted Screenplay, Best Supporting Actress (Harper). *ORI, WAR*

Crimewave 🦴🦴 *The XYZ Murders; Broken Hearts and Noses* **1985 (PG-13)** Zany spoof about serial killers set in Detroit (director Raimi's hometown). A rhapsody to comic book style, short on plot and long on style. With such credentials you expect more. **83m/C VHS, Beta.** Louise Lasser, Paul Smith, Brion James, Bruce Campbell, Reed Birney, Sheree J. Wilson, Edward R. Pressman, Julius W. Harris; ***D:*** Sam Raimi; ***W:*** Ethan Coen, Joel Coen, Sam Raimi. *NLC*

Criminal Act 🦴½ **1988** A newspaper editor hits the street to prove she's still a tough reporter, but uncovers a dangerous scandal in the process. **94m/C VHS, Beta.** Catherine Bach, Charlene Dallas, Nicholas Guest, John Saxon, Vic Tayback; ***D:*** Mark Byers. *PSM*

Criminal Code 🦴🦴½ **1931** Aging melodrama about a young man who's jailed for killing in self-defense. His life worsens at the hands of a prison warden when the head guy's daughter falls for him. Remade as "Penitentiary" and "Convicted." **98m/B VHS, Beta.** Walter Huston, Phillips Holmes, Boris Karloff, Constance Cummings, Mary Doran, DeWitt Jennings, John Sheehan; ***D:*** Howard Hawks. Nominations: Academy Awards '31: Best Adapted Screenplay. *COL, MLB*

Criminal Court 🦴🦴 **1946** A man accused of murdering his blackmailer hires the real killer as his attorney. Hard to follow, with an interesting premise that turns flat. **63m/B VHS, Beta.** Tom Conway, Martha O'Driscoll, Robert Armstrong, Addison Richards, June Clayworth, Pat Gleason, Steve Brodie; ***D:*** Robert Wise. *NO*

Criminal Hearts 🦴🦴 **1995 (R)** Jilted young woman picks up a hitchhiker/thief who's stolen Mob money and goes on the run after being framed for murder. **92m/C VHS.** Kevin Dillon, Amy Locane, Morgan Fairchild, M. Emmet Walsh; ***D:*** Dave Payne; ***W:*** Dave Payne. *AVE*

Criminal Justice 🦴🦴🦴 **1990 (R)** A black man is accused of a crime by a woman with whom he was involved. Is it justice or revenge? Strong cast in important story. Made for cable TV. **92m/C VHS.** Forest Whitaker, Jennifer Grey, Rosie Perez, Anthony LaPaglia, Tony Todd; ***D:*** Andy Wolk; ***W:*** Andy Wolk. *HBO*

Criminal Law 🦴🦴 **1989 (R)** An ambitious young Boston lawyer gets a man acquitted for murder, only to find out after the trial that the man is guilty and renewing his killing spree. Realizing he's the only one privy to the killer's trust, the lawyer decides to stop him himself. A white-knuckled thriller burdened by a weak script. **113m/C VHS, Beta, LV.** Kevin Bacon, Gary Oldman, Karen Young, Joe Don Baker, Tess Harper; ***D:*** Martin Campbell; ***M:*** Jerry Goldsmith. *HBO, WAR*

The Criminal Life of Archibaldo de la Cruz 🦴🦴🦴 *Ensayo de un Crimen; Rehearsal for a Crime* **1955** Seeing the death of his governess has a lasting effect on a boy. He grows up to be a demented cretin whose failure with women leads him to conspire to kill every one he meets, a task at which he also fails. Hilarious, bitter Bunuelian diatribe. In Spanish with English subtitles. **95m/B VHS, Beta.** *MX SP* Ernesto Alonso, Ariadne Welter, Rita Macedo, Rodolfo Landa, Andrea Palma, Miroslava Stern; ***D:*** Luis Bunuel. *FCT, WBF*

The Criminal Mind 🦴🦴 **1993 (R)** L.A. District Attorney Nick August (Rossi) reunites with his long-lost brother (Cross), whom he discovers is very familiar with the other side of the law. Tied up with the mob, Cross forces his bro to watch a hit and then Rossi winds up the next target for a group of assassins and some corrupt cops. **93m/C VHS.** Ben Cross, Frank Rossi, Tahnee Welch, Lance Henriksen, Joseph Ruskin, Lynn-Holly Johnson; ***D:*** Joseph Vittorie; ***W:*** Sam A. Scribner. *COL*

Criminally Insane 🦴 **1975** Authorities release 250 pounds of cleaver-wielding maniacal fury from the loony bin. She seeks food and human blood. They should have known better. Followed by "Crazy Fat Ethel II." **61m/C VHS, Beta.** Priscilla Alden, Michael Flood; ***D:*** Nick Phillips. *NO*

Criminals Within 🦴 *Army Mystery* **1941** A scientist working on a top secret formula is murdered and a detective tries to nail the spy ring responsible. Very confusing, poor usage of some fine female cast members. **67m/B VHS, Beta.** Eric Linden, Ann Doran, Constance Worth, Donald Curtis, Weldon Heyburn, Ben Alexander; ***D:*** Joseph H. Lewis. *SNC*

The Crimson Cult 🦴 *The Crimson Altar; Curse of the Crimson Altar* **1968 (PG)** Eden and his girlfriend are invited to a mysterious mansion. They discover that Lee is out to enact revenge as his ancestor was burned for witchcraft by Eden's. An all-star horror disaster. Karloff was eighty and confined to a wheelchair. Despite ads claiming this as his last film, he made four more in Mexico. Highlights include the scantily clad Steele in sado-masochistic sequences and a psychedelic party with strippers and body painters. **87m/C VHS.** *GB* Boris Karloff, Christopher Lee, Mark Eden, Barbara Steele, Virginia Wetherell, Michael Gough, Rupert Davies; ***D:*** Vernon Sewell. *MOV*

Crimson Pirate ½ **1952** An 18th-century buccaneer pits his wits and brawn against the might of a ruthless Spanish nobleman. Considered by many to be one of the best swashbucklers, laced with humor and enthusiastically paced. Showcase for Lancaster and Cravat's acrobatic talents. **104m/C VHS, Beta, LV.** *GB* Burt Lancaster, Eva Bartok, Torin Thatcher, Christopher Lee, Nick Cravat; ***D:*** Robert Siodmak. *WAR*

Crimson Romance **1934** Two unemployed American pilots in Europe decide to join the German airforce for want of anything better to do. Conflicts revolve around a warmongering Commandant and his pilot. **70m/B VHS, Beta, 8mm.** Ben Lyon, Sari Maritza, James Bush, Erich von Stroheim, Jason Robards Sr., Herman Bing, Vince Barnett; ***D:*** David Howard. *NOS, VYY, RXM*

Crimson Tide **1995 (R)** Mutiny erupts aboard the submarine USS Alabama as Captain Ramsey (Hackman) and his Executive Officer Hunter (Washington) clash over the validity of orders to launch the sub's missiles. Ramsey, who wants to fire the missiles, and Hunter, who refuses to comply until the message is verified, battle for control of the sub. Suspenseful and well-paced thriller lets Hackman and Washington show off their considerable screen presence, while Bruckheimer, Simpson, and Scott show that they haven't lost any of their trademark big-budget, testosterone-laden flash. Original screenplay went under the knife of a number of script doctors, most notably Quentin Tarantino. **116m/C VHS, LV.** Gene Hackman, Denzel Washington, George Dzundza, Viggo Mortensen, James Gandolfini, Matt Craven, Lillo Brancato, Danny Nucci, Steve Zahn, Rick Schroder, Vanessa Bell Calloway, Rocky Carroll; ***Cameos:*** Jason Robards Jr.; ***D:*** Tony Scott; ***W:*** Michael Schiffer, Richard P. Henrick; ***C:*** Dariusz Wolski; ***M:*** Hans Zimmer. Nominations: Academy Awards '95: Best Film Editing, Best Sound; MTV Movie Awards '96: Best Male Performance (Washington). *TOU*

The Crimson Trail ½ **1935** Buck believes his uncle may be involved in cattle rustling. Lots of action, minimal plot. **56m/B VHS.** Buck Jones, Polly Ann Young, Carl Stockdale, Charles French, Ward Bond, Robert F. (Bob) Kortman, Bud Osborne, Charles Brinley, Robert Walker; ***D:*** Al Raboch; ***W:*** Jack Natteford. *GPV*

Crisis at Central High **1980** A dramatic television recreation of the events leading up to the 1957 integration of Central High in Little Rock, Arkansas. Based on teacher Elizabeth Huckaby's journal. Emmy-nominated performance by Woodward as Huckaby. **120m/C VHS, Beta.** Joanne Woodward, Charles Durning, William Ross, Henderson Forsythe; ***D:*** Lamont Johnson; ***M:*** Billy Goldenberg. *NO*

Criss Cross **1948** A classic grade-B film noir, in which an armored car driver is suckered into a burglary by his ex-wife and her hoodlum husband. Multiple back-stabbings and double-crossings ensue. **98m/B VHS, Beta.** Burt Lancaster, Yvonne De Carlo, Dan Duryea, Stephen McNally, Richard Long, Tony Curtis; ***D:*** Robert Siodmak; ***W:*** Daniel Fuchs; ***M:*** Miklos Rozsa. *MCA*

Crisscross ½ *Alone Together* **1992 (R)** It's 1969 and Tracy Cross is a divorced mom whose ex-husband is a traumatized Vietnam vet who has left her alone to raise their 12 year-old son Chris during some hard times. She works two jobs, as a waitress and, unbeknownst to her son, as a stripper in a local club. When Chris sneaks into the club and sees her act he takes drastic measures to help out—by selling drugs. Film is sluggish and relies too much on voice-overs to explain thoughts but Hawn gives a convincing and restrained performance as the mother. **107m/C VHS, LV.** Goldie Hawn, David Arnott, Arliss Howard, James Gammon, Keith Carradine, J.C. Quinn, Steve Buscemi, Paul Calderone; ***D:*** Chris Menges; ***M:*** Trevor Jones. *MGM*

Critical Condition **1986 (R)** During a blackout, a criminal masquerades as a doctor in a city hospital. Limp comedy embarrassing for Pryor. **99m/C VHS, Beta, LV.** Richard Pryor, Rachel Ticotin, Ruben Blades, Joe Mantegna; ***D:*** Michael Apted; ***C:*** Ralf Bode; ***M:*** Alan Silvestri. *PAR*

Critters ½ **1986 (PG-13)** A gang of furry, razor-toothed aliens escapes from its prison ship to Earth with their bounty hunters right behind them. They make it to a small town in Kansas where they begin to attack anything that moves. Not just a thrill-kill epic, but a sarcastic other-worldly thrill-kill epic. **86m/C VHS, Beta, LV.** Dee Wallace Stone, M. Emmet Walsh, Billy Green Bush, Scott Grimes, Nadine Van Der Velde, Terrence Mann, Billy Zane, Don Opper, Terrence Mann; ***D:*** Stephen Herek; ***W:*** Stephen Herek; ***M:*** David Newman. *COL*

Critters 2: The Main Course **1988 (PG-13)** Sequel to the hit horror-comedy, wherein the voracious alien furballs return in full force to Grovers Bend, Kansas, from eggs planted two years before. Occasionally inspired "Gremlins" rip. **93m/C VHS, Beta, LV.** Scott Grimes, Liane Curtis, Don Opper, Barry Corbin, Terrence Mann; ***D:*** Mick Garris; ***W:*** Mick Garris, David N. Twohy. *COL*

Critters 3 **1991 (PG-13)** The not-so-loveable critters are back, terrorizing the occupants of a tenement building. **86m/C VHS.** Francis Bay, Aimee Brooks, Leonardo DiCaprio, Don Opper; ***D:*** Kristine Peterson; ***W:*** David J. Schow. *COL, NLC*

Critters 4 **1991 (PG-13)** The ghoulish critters are back, and this time a strain of genetically engineered mutant critters (what's the difference?) wants to take over the universe. **94m/C VHS, LV.** Don Opper, Paul Whitthorne, Angela Bassett, Brad Dourif, Terrence Mann; ***D:*** Rupert Harvey; ***W:*** David J. Schow. *NLC, COL*

Crocodile *Woof!* **1981 (R)** Giant crocodile attacks a beach town, killing and devouring dozens of people. The locals sit around trying to figure a way to stop the critter. Special effects include rear-projected croc. Lots of blood but lacking humor of "Alligator." Filmed in Thailand and Korea. **95m/C VHS, Beta.** Nat Puvanai, Tiny Tim; ***D:*** Herman Cohen. *NO*

Crocodile Dundee ½ **1986 (PG-13)** New York reporter Sue Charlton is assigned to the Outback to interview living legend Mike Dundee. When she finally locates the man, she is so taken with him that she brings him back to New York with her. There, the naive Aussie wanders about, amazed at the wonders of the city and unwittingly charming everyone he comes in contact with, from high-society transvestites to street hookers. One of the surprise hits of 1986. **98m/C VHS, Beta, LV, 8mm.** *AU* Paul Hogan, Linda Kozlowski, John Meillon, David Gulpilil, Mark Blum; ***D:*** Peter Faiman; ***W:*** Paul Hogan, John Cornell; ***M:*** Peter Best. Golden Globe Awards '87: Best Actor—Musical/Comedy (Hogan); Nominations: Academy Awards '86: Best Original Screenplay. *PAR*

Crocodile Dundee 2 ½ **1988 (PG)** In this sequel Mike Dundee, the loveable rube, returns to his native Australia looking for new adventure, having "conquered" New York City. He inadvertently gets involved in stopping a gang of crooks active in Australia and New York. Lacks the charm and freshness of the first film. **110m/C VHS, Beta, LV.** Paul Hogan, Linda Kozlowski, Kenneth Welsh, John Meillon, Ernie Dingo, Juan Fernandez, Charles S. Dutton; ***D:*** John Cornell; ***W:*** Paul Hogan; ***M:*** Peter Best. *PAR*

Cromwell ½ **1970 (G)** A lavish British-made spectacle about the conflict between Oliver Cromwell and Charles I, and the British Civil War. History is twisted as Cromwell becomes the liberator of the oppressed. Harris gives a commanding performance and the battle scenes are stunners. **139m/C VHS, Beta, LV.** *GB* Richard Harris, Alec Guinness, Robert Morley, Frank Finlay, Patrick Magee, Timothy Dalton; ***D:*** Ken Hughes; ***W:*** Ken Hughes; ***C:*** Geoffrey Unsworth. Academy Awards '70: Best Costume Design; Nominations: Academy Awards '70: Best Original Score. *COL, TVC*

Cronos **1994 (R)** Stylish Mexican variation of the vampire tale. Aged antiques dealer Jesus Gris (Luppi) comes across the mysterious title object—a 14th century golden egg possessing magical powers to grant eternal life. But can its possessor stand the consequences, which include a developing taste for blood? Another problem is Gris isn't the only one to know about the device. First feature for writer/director del Toro. Spanish with subtitles. **92m/C VHS, LV.** *MX* Federico Luppi, Ron Perlman, Claudio Brook, Tamara Shanath; ***D:*** Guillermo del Toro; ***W:*** Guillermo del Toro; ***M:*** Ian Deardon. *VMK*

The Crooked Circle ½ **1932** More comedy than mystery as slapstick policeman Gleason goes under cover as a swami. Not helped at all by a weak script and poor photography. **68m/B VHS.** Ben Lyon, ZaSu Pitts, James Gleason, C. Henry Gordon, Raymond Hatton, Roscoe Karns; ***D:*** H. Bruce Humberstone. *SNC, NOS*

Crooked Hearts **1991 (R)** Dysfunctional family drama means well but lays it on too thick, as a father/son rivalry threatens to sunder the tight-knit Warrens. Based on a novel by Robert Boswell. **113m/C VHS, Beta, LV.** Peter Coyote, Jennifer Jason Leigh, Peter Berg, Cindy Pickett, Vincent D'Onofrio; ***D:*** Michael Bortman; ***W:*** Michael Bortman. *MGM*

Crooked Trail **1936** A lawman and bad guy become friends. **58m/B VHS, Beta, LV.** Johnny Mack Brown. *NO*

Crooklyn **1994 (PG-13)** Director Lee turns from the life of Malcolm X to the early lives of Generation X in this profile of an African-American middle class family growing up in 1970's Brooklyn. Lee's least politically charged film to date is a joint effort between him and sibs Joie and Cinque, and profiles the only girl in a family of five children coming of age. Tender and real performances from all, especially newcomer Harris, propel the sometimes messy, music-laden trip to nostalgia land. **112m/C VHS, LV.** Alfre Woodard, Delroy Lindo, Zelda Harris, David Patrick Kelly, Carlton Williams, Sharif Rashed, Tse-March Washington, Christopher Knowings, Jose Zuniga, Isaiah Washington, Ivelka Reyes, N. Jeremi Duru, Frances Foster, Norman Matlock, Patriece Nelson, Joie Lee, Vondie Curtis-Hall, Tiasha Reyes, Spike Lee; ***D:*** Spike Lee; ***W:*** Joie Lee, Cinque Lee; ***M:*** Terence Blanchard. *MCA*

Crooks & Coronets ½ *Sophie's Place* **1969 (PG)** Two-bit crooks plot to rob the country estate of an eccentric British dowager. **106m/C VHS, Beta.** *GB* Cesar Romero, Telly Savalas, Warren Oates, Edith Evans; ***D:*** James O'Connolly. *WAR*

The Cross & the Switchblade ½ **1972 (PG)** An idealistic priest tries to bring the message of religion to the members of a vicious street gang. They don't wanna listen. Spanish language version available. **105m/C VHS, Beta.** Pat Boone, Erik Estrada, Jackie Giroux, Jo-Ann Robinson; ***D:*** Don Murray. *VBL*

Cross Country ½ **1983 (R)** Action revolves around the brutal murder of a call girl, with initial suspicion falling on a television advertising director involved with the woman. The story twists and turns from the suspect to investigating detective Ironside without becoming particularly interesting. **95m/C VHS, Beta, LV.** *CA* Richard Beymer, Nina Axelrod, Michael Ironside; ***D:*** Paul Lynch; ***W:*** Logan N. Danforth. *SUE, NLC*

Cross Creek ½ **1983 (PG)** Based on the life of Marjorie Kinnan Rawlings, author of "The Yearling," who, after 10 years as a frustrated reporter/writer, moves to the remote and untamed Everglades. There she meets colorful local characters and receives the inspiration to write numerous best-sellers. Well acted though overtly sentimental at times. **115m/C VHS, Beta.** Mary Steenburgen, Rip Torn, Peter Coyote, Dana Hill, Alfre Woodard, Malcolm McDowell; ***D:*** Martin Ritt; ***C:*** John A. Alonzo. Nominations: Academy Awards '83: Best Costume Design, Best Supporting Actor (Torn), Best Supporting Actress (Woodard), Best Original Score; Cannes Film Festival '83: Best Film. *REP*

Cross Examination 🦴½ **1932** A boy is charged with his father's murder, and a defense attorney struggles to acquit him. **61m/B VHS, Beta, LV.** H.B. Warner, Sally Blane, Sarah Padden. *NO*

Cross Mission 🦴 **1989 (R)** Predictable actioner about a photographer and a soldier who are captured by the enemy. Packed with a bit of ninja, ammo, and occult. **90m/C VHS.** Richard Randall; ***D:*** Al Bradley. *CAN*

Cross My Heart 🦴🦴 **1988 (R)** Light comedy about two single people with complicated, post-divorce lives who go on a date and suffer accordingly. Will true love prevail? **91m/C VHS, Beta.** Martin Short, Annette O'Toole, Paul Reiser, Joanna Kerns; ***D:*** Armyan Bernstein; ***W:*** Armyan Bernstein; ***M:*** Bruce Broughton. *MCA*

Cross My Heart 🦴🦴 **1991** A group of school children conspire to hide the death of one of the group's mothers. This will prevent his placement in the state orphanage. Interesting premise is blandly treated by Fansten. Child actors don't seem realistic, photography is without flair. In French with English subtitles. **?m/C VHS, Beta.** *FR* Sylvain Copans; ***D:*** Jacques Fansten. *FXL*

Cross of Iron 🦴🦴½ **1976 (R)** During WWII, two antagonistic German officers clash over personal ideals as well as strategy in combatting the relentless Russian attack. Followed by "Breakthrough." **120m/C VHS, Beta.** James Coburn, Maximilian Schell, James Mason, David Warner, Senta Berger; ***D:*** Sam Peckinpah; ***W:*** Julius J. Epstein; ***M:*** Ernest Gold. *MED*

Crossbar 🦴🦴 **1979** Aaron Kornylo is determined to reach Olympic qualifications in the high jump despite having only one leg. Inspired by a true story, this program dramatically shows how far determination and work can take a person. **77m/C VHS, Beta.** John Ireland, Brent Carver, Kate Reid; ***D:*** John Trent. *TWE, LCA*

Crosscut 🦴🦴 **1996 (R)** Mob hitman Martin Niconi (Mandylor) makes a mistake that could cost him his life. He escapes to a small logging town but the mob is still on his trail. Now, Niconi's only hope is to get them first. **90m/C VHS, LV.** Costas Mandylor, Megan Gallagher, Casey Sander; ***D:*** Paul Raimondi. *APX*

Crossfire 🦴🦴🦴½ **1947** A Jewish hotel guest is murdered and three soldiers just back from Europe are suspected of the crime. The first Hollywood film that explored racial bigotry. Due to the radical nature of its plot, the director and the producer were eventually black-listed for promoting "un-American" themes. Loosely based on Richard Brooks' "The Brick Foxhole." **86m/B VHS, Beta.** Robert Young, Robert Mitchum, Robert Ryan, Gloria Grahame, Paul Kelly; ***D:*** Edward Dmytryk. Edgar Allan Poe Awards '47: Best Screenplay; National Board of Review Awards '47: 10 Best Films of the Year; Nominations: Academy Awards '46: Best Picture; Academy Awards '47: Best Director (Dmytryk), Best Screenplay, Best Supporting Actor (Ryan), Best Supporting Actress (Grahame). *MED*

Crossfire 🦴 *The Bandit* **1967 (PG)** Two bandits are almost hung in the midst of the Mexican revolution. Released in the U.S. in 1979. **82m/C VHS, Beta.** *MX* Robert Conrad, Jan-Michael Vincent, Manuel Lopez Ochoa, Roy Jenson; ***D:*** Robert Conrad, Alfredo Zacharias. *ACA*

Crossfire **1989 (R)** A rescue team heads to Vietnam to pick up their MIA comrades. With no help from the government and the enemy at every turn, can they possibly succeed? **99m/C VHS, LV.** Richard Norton, Michael Meyer, Daniel Dietrich, Don Pemrick, Eric Hahn, Wren Brown, Steve Young; ***D:*** Anthony Maharaj; ***W:*** Noah Blough. *SUE*

The Crossing 🦴🦴 **1992 (R)** Powerful coming-of-age story in which Meg, a sheltered young woman, falls in love with an ambitious artist named Sam. When he decides to leave their small town to pursue his career, she turns to his best friend for comfort and companionship. However, when Sam unexpectedly returns, Meg is forced to make a choice that could drastically change all of their lives. **92m/C VHS, LV.** *AU* Russell Crowe, Danielle Spencer, Robert Mammone; ***W:*** Ranald Allan; ***M:*** Martin Armiger. *REP*

Crossing Delancey 🦴🦴🦴 **1988 (PG)** Jewish woman (Bozyk), in old world style, plays matchmaker to her independent thirtysomething granddaughter. Charming modern-day New York City fairy tale deftly manipulates cliches and stereotypes. Lovely performance from Irving as the woman whose heart surprises her. Riegert is swell playing the gentle but never wimpy suitor. Perfectly cast Bozyk was a star on the Yiddish vaudeville stage, this is her film debut. Appealing music by the Roches, with Suzzy Roche giving a credible performance as Irving's friend. Adapted for the big screen by Sandler from her play of the same name. **97m/C VHS, Beta, LV, 8mm.** Amy Irving, Reizl Bozyk, Peter Riegert, Jeroen Krabbe, Sylvia Miles, Suzzy Roche, George Martin, John Bedford Lloyd, Rosemary Harris, Amy Wright, Claudia Silver; ***D:*** Joan Micklin Silver; ***W:*** Susan Sandler. *WAR, FCT, JCF*

The Crossing Guard 🦴🦴🦴 **1994 (R)** Nicholson headlines as Freddy Gale, a revenge-minded father who hunts down a drunk driver (Morse), who killed his daughter five years previous. Story focuses on dual emotions of the two men: Gale seeks an end to his grief and rage; Booth attempts to deal with guilt and regret. Writer Penn pairs one-time lovers Nicholson and Huston (playing ex-spouses here) in his sophomore directorial effort with explosive results. Focus is, accordingly, on emotional performances while narrative and directorial finesse take a back seat. **111m/C VHS, LV.** Jack Nicholson, Anjelica Huston, David Morse, Robin Wright, Robbie Robertson, Piper Laurie, Richard Bradford, John Savage, Priscilla Barnes, Kari Wuhrer; ***D:*** Sean Penn; ***W:*** Sean Penn; ***C:*** Vilmos Zsigmond; ***M:*** Jack Nitzsche. Nominations: Golden Globe Awards '96: Best Supporting Actress (Huston); Independent Spirit Awards '96: Best Supporting Actor (Morse); Screen Actors Guild Award '95: Best Supporting Actress (Huston). *TOU*

Crossing the Bridge 🦴🦴 **1992 (R)** An after high-school tale of three buddies and their restless lives as they take their uncertain steps towards adulthood. It's 1975 in Detroit and Mort, Danny, and Tim cling to high-school memories as they pass time on petty jobs, drinking, and cruising across the Ambassador Bridge to check out the Canadian strip joints. Their big moment—for better or worse—comes when they are offered the chance to make a lot of quick cash if they'll smuggle hash from Toronto to Detroit. Directorial debut of Binder. **105m/C VHS, Beta, LV.** Josh Charles, Jason Gedrick, Stephen Baldwin, Cheryl Pollak, Jeffrey Tambor; ***D:*** Mike Binder; ***W:*** Mike Binder. *TOU*

Crossing the Line 🦴 **1990 (R)** Two motocross racers battle it out for the championship. **90m/C VHS, Beta, LV.** Jon Stafford, Rick Hearst, Paul Smith, Cameron Mitchell, Vernon Wells, Colleen Morris, John Saxon; ***D:*** Gary Graver. *COL*

Crossover 🦴½ **1982 (R)** A devoted male nurse works the graveyard shift in the psychiatric ward and neglects his personal life. **96m/C VHS, Beta.** James Coburn, Kate Nelligan; ***D:*** John Guillermin. *VES, LIV*

Crossover Dreams 🦴🦴½ **1985** Actor and musician Blades moves this old story along. Sure that he has at last made the international Big Time, a salsa artist becomes a self-important back-stabber after cutting an album. Great music. Blades's first film. ♫Good For Baby; Liz's Theme; Sin Fe; Todos Vuelven; Libra Timbero; Elegua; Merecumbe; Judy, Part 2; Yiri Yiri Bon. **86m/C VHS, Beta.** Ruben Blades, Shawn Elliott, Elizabeth Pena, Virgilio Marti, Tom Signorelli, Frank Robles, Joel Diamond, Amanda Barber, John Hammil; ***D:*** Leon Ichaso; ***W:*** Ruben Blades, Leon Ichaso, Manuel Arce; ***M:*** Mauricio Smith. *CNG*

Crossroads 🦴🦴½ **1986 (R)** A blues-loving young white man, classically trained at Juilliard, befriends an aging black blues-master. After helping the old man escape from the nursing home, the two hop trains to the South where it's literally a duel with the devil. Fine performances by Macchio, Gertz, and Morton, and a wonderful score. **100m/C VHS, Beta, LV.** Ralph Macchio, Joe Seneca, Jami Gertz, Joe Morton, Robert Judd, Harry Carey Jr.; ***D:*** Walter Hill; ***W:*** John Fusco; ***M:*** Ry Cooder. *COL*

The Crow 🦴🦴½ **1993 (R)** Revenge-fantasy finds Eric Draven (Lee) resurrected on Devil's Night, a year after his death, in order to avenge his own murder and that of his girlfriend. 90% of the scenes are at night, in the rain, or both, and it's not easy to tell what's going on (a blessing considering the violence level). Very dark, but with good performances, particularly from Lee, in his last role before an unfortunate on set accident caused his death. That footage has been destroyed, but use of a stunt double and camera trickery allowed for the movie's completion. Film was dedicated to Lee and his fiance Eliza. Based on the comic strip by James O'Barr. The video release includes Brandon Lee's final interview. **100m/C VHS, LV.** Brandon Lee, Ernie Hudson, Michael Wincott, David Patrick Kelly, Rochelle Davis, Angel David, Michael Massee, Bai Ling, Lawrence Mason, Bill Raymond, Marco Rodriguez, Anna Thomson, Sofia Shinas, Jon Polito, Tony Todd; ***D:*** Alex Proyas; ***W:*** David J. Schow, John Shirley; ***M:*** Graeme Revell. MTV Movie Awards '95: Best Song ("Big Empty"); Nominations: MTV Movie Awards '95: Best Film, Best Male Performance (Lee). *TOU*

The Crow 2: City of Angels 🦴🦴🦴 **1996 (R)** James O'Barr's cult graphic-novel "hero" returns in a new incarnation. It's 8 years later (in film time) and the setting's changed from Detroit to L.A. but the horror remains. Ashe Corbin (Perez) and his young son witness a murder committed by scumbags Curve (Pop) and Judah (Brooks), who promptly drown the onlookers. So the Crow brings back Ashe to avenge his son's death. Also reluctantly involved is Sarah (Kirshner), who retains her role as story narrator but is now a grown-up tattoo artist who falls in love with Ashe (who has trouble believing he's actually dead). The eerie sepia-toned look is created with sodium lighting. **?m/C VHS.** Vincent Perez, Mia Kirshner, Iggy Pop, Richard Brooks, Ian Dury; ***D:*** Tim Pope; ***W:*** David S. Goyer; ***M:*** Graeme Revell. *NYR*

Crow Hollow 🦴🦴 **1952** A Victorian mansion inhabited by three whacko sisters is the site of a murder committed in an attempt to cash in on an inheritance. When a young woman investigates, eyebrows are raised. **69m/B VHS, Beta.** *GB* Donald Houston, Natasha Parry, Nora Nicholson, Esma Cannon, Melissa Stribling; ***D:*** Michael McCarthy. *SNC, RXM*

The Crowd 🦴🦴🦴🦴 **1928** A look at the day-to-day trials of a working-class family set against the backdrop of wealthy society. True-to-life, it's peppered with some happy moments, too. One of the best silent films. Available on laserdisc as a double feature with another '20s classic, "The Wind." **104m/B VHS, Beta, LV.** Eleanor Boardman, James Murray, Bert Roach, Daniel G. Tomlinson, Dell Henderson, Lucy Beaumont; ***D:*** King Vidor. Nominations: Academy Awards '28: Best Director (Vidor). *MGM*

Crows and Sparrows 🦴🦴🦴 *Wuya Yu Maque* **1949** Poor tenants of a Shanghai boardinghouse are about to lose their home when their greedy landlord decides to sell and move to Taiwan. But the advancing Red Army causes a change in plans and they're saved! Sounds politically turgid but isn't, thanks to naturalistic acting and dialog. Completed just before the revolution, the film was censored by the Nationalist Kuomintang government but cuts were restored when the Communists came to power. Mandarin with subtitles. **108m/B VHS.** *CH* Zhao Dan, Wu Yin, Wei Heling, Sun Dao-Lin, Li Tianji, Ouyang Yunzhu; ***D:*** Zheng Junli; ***W:*** Zhao Dan, Zheng Junli; ***C:*** Miao Zhenhua, Hu Zhenhua; ***M:*** Wang Yunjie. *HTV, FCT*

The Crucible 🦴🦴🦴 *The Witches of Salem* **1957** Signoret is outstanding in this version of Arthur Miller's play about the Salem witch trials in 17th-century New England. Miller's depiction of witch hunts was written as a searing commentary on McCarthyism and the anti-communist panic that swept America in the 1950s. Film was made in France because Miller was blacklisted in America and blackballed by Hollywood at the time. In French with English subtitles. **108m/B VHS.** *FR* Simone Signoret, Yves Montand, Mylene Demongeot, Jean Debucourt; ***D:*** Raymond Rouleau; ***W:*** Jean-Paul Sartre. *HTV*

Crucible of Horror *Velvet House; The Corpse* **1969** Chilling story of a terrorized wife, who, along with her daughter, plots to murder her sadistic husband to end his abusive treatment of them. However, he isn't yet ready to die and comes back to drive them mad. **91m/C VHS, Beta.** *GB* Michael Gough, Yvonne Mitchell, Sharon Gurney; ***D:*** Viktors Ritelis. *MGM, FCT*

Crucible of Terror *Woof!* **1972** Mad sculptor covers beautiful models with hot wax, then imprisons them in a mold of bronze. **95m/C VHS, Beta.** Mike Raven, Mary Maude, James Bolam. *PSM, MRV, GEM*

The Crucifer of Blood ½ **1991** A disappointing Sherlock Holmes yarn, made for cable TV. Heston is adequate as the Baker Street sleuth, but the mystery—about two retired British soldiers who share an accursed secret and a vengeful comrade—unreels clumsily in the form of flashbacks that give away most of the puzzle from the start. Interesting only in that Dr. Watson has a love affair, more or less. Adapted from a play (and looking like it) by Paul Giovanni, inspired by Arthur Conan Doyle's "The Sign of Four." **105m/C VHS, Beta.** Charlton Heston, Richard Johnson, Susannah Harker, John Castle, Clive Wood, Simon Callow, Edward Fox; ***D:*** Fraser Heston. *TTC*

The Crucified Lovers ½ *Chikamatsu Monogatari* **1954** A shy scrollmaker falls in love with his master's wife. Excellent Japanese tragedy with fine performances all around. **100m/B VHS.** *JP* Kazuo Hasegawa, Kyoko Kagawa, Yoko Minamida, Eitaro Shindo, Sakae Ozawa; ***D:*** Kenji Mizoguchi. *FCT*

The Crude Oasis ½ **1995 (R)** Shot in 14 days on a $25,000 budget, producer/writer/director Graves' debut is an aggressively moody suspenser. Karen (Taylor) is a neglected, suicidal Kansas housewife who is haunted by dreams of a mystery man. He turns up in the form of Shields, the pump jockey at a local gas station. Obsessed by the stranger, Karen begins following him, leading to situations paralleling her dream. Adept at setting up an atmosphere of small-town menace and constructing a plot with surprising twists and turns, Graves can't quite deliver the payoff required. **82m/C VHS, Beta.** Jennifer Taylor, Aaron Shields, Robert Peterson, Mussef Sibay, Lynn Bieler, Roberta Eaton; ***D:*** Alex Graves; ***W:*** Alex Graves; ***C:*** Steven Quale. *PAR*

Cruel Sea **1953** Well-made documentary-like account of a Royal Navy corvette on convoy duty in the Atlantic during WWII. **121m/B VHS, Beta.** *GB* Jack Hawkins, Stanley Baker, Denholm Elliott, Virginia McKenna; ***D:*** Charles Frend. Nominations: Academy Awards '53: Best Screenplay. *REP, BMV, HMV*

The Cruel Story of Youth *Seishun Zanoku Monogatari; Naked Youth; A Story of the Cruelties of Youth* **1960** A teenage girl and her criminal boyfriend use sex to get money out of rich, middle-aged men in this controversial look at the disillusionment of youth and the breaking of old values and traditions in Japan after WWII. In Japanese with English subtitles. **96m/C VHS.** *JP* Yusuke Kawazu, Miyuki Kuwano, Yoshiko Kuga; ***D:*** Nagisa Oshima; ***W:*** Nagisa Oshima. *NYF*

Cruise into Terror *Woof!* **1978** A sarcophagus brought aboard a pleasure cruise ship unleashes an evil force that slowly starts to kill off the ship's passengers, most of whom likely thought they were on the Love Boat. Made for television. **100m/C VHS, Beta.** Ray Milland, Hugh O'Brian, John Forsythe, Christopher George, Dirk Benedict, Frank Converse, Lynda Day George, Stella Stevens; ***D:*** Bruce Kessler. *PSM*

Cruise Missile **1978** Unique task force is on a mission to keep the world from nuclear holocaust. **100m/C VHS, Beta.** Peter Graves, Curt Jurgens, Michael Dante; ***D:*** Ted V. Mikels. *NO*

Cruisin' High **1975 (R)** Two city street gangs battle it out. **109m/C VHS, Beta.** David Kyle, Kelly Yaegermann, Rhodes Reason. *VES, LIV*

Cruising **1980 (R)** Rookie cop Pacino is deep undercover investigating the bizarre murders of homosexuals in New York's West Village. Sexually explicit but less than suspenseful mystery. Release was sensationalized, with many gay rights groups voicing loud disapproval of the sordid gay characterization, while others feared copy-cat crimes. Excellent NYC cinematography. **102m/C VHS, Beta.** Al Pacino, Paul Sorvino, Karen Allen, Powers Boothe; ***D:*** William Friedkin; ***W:*** William Friedkin; ***M:*** Jack Nitzsche. *WAR*

Crumb ½ **1994 (R)** Countercultural documentary looking at the life of underground cartoonist Robert Crumb—sixties satirist and social misfit who created such drug and sex characters as Fritz the Cat and Mr. Natural. Crumb's extraordinarily dysfunctional family play a significant role, with his mother and two brothers, elder brother Charles and younger brother Max, also interviewed as well as Crumb's friends and current and former wives. The dead abusive father also plays a part. Director Zwigoff spent six years filming his material, and gained wider distribution for his work after taking the Grand Jury prize at Sundance. **119m/C VHS, LV.** ***D:*** Terry Zwigoff. National Society of Film Critics Awards '95: Best Documentary; Sundance Film Festival '95: Best Cinematography, Grand Jury Prize. *COL*

The Crusades ½ **1935** Typical DeMille extravaganza, loosely based on the Third Crusade, which finds Richard the Lionheart (Wilconxon) and the armies of Europe battling Saladin and the Mahommedan horde in order to reclaim Jerusalem. Meanwhile, Richard marries by proxy in order to gain supplies for his men—something that enrages his bride Berengaria (Young). Once he realizes how beautiful she is, Richard tries to win her love. Obviously, not historically accurate and it's all secondary to the battle scenes, anyway. Based on the Harold Lamb book "The Crusade: Iron Men and Saints." **126m/B VHS.** Henry Wilcoxon, Loretta Young, Sir C. Aubrey Smith, Ian Keith, Katherine DeMille, Joseph Schildkraut, Alan Hale, C. Henry Gordon, George Barbier, Lumsden Hare, William Farnum, Hobart Bosworth, Montagu Love, Pedro de Cordoba, Mischa Auer; ***D:*** Cecil B. DeMille; ***W:*** Waldemar Young, Dudley Nichols, Harold Lamb; ***C:*** Victor Milner; ***M:*** Rudolph Kopp. *MCA*

Crush **1993** Christina is a local New Zealand literary critic on her way to interview Colin, a reclusive novelist. Along for the ride is her seductive American friend Lane who manages to crash the car but walk away with hardly a scratch. Christina appears to be dead and Lane abandons her, finding her way to the home Colin shares with his teenage daughter Angela. Lane promptly sets out to seduce Colin, making Angela jealous, (oh, and Christina's not dead after all). Poor script finds the characters actions baffling and why Lane is so wildly attractive is never apparent. **97m/C VHS.** *NZ* Marcia Gay Harden, Donough Rees, William Zappa, Caitlin Bossley; ***D:*** Alison Maclean; ***W:*** Alison Maclean, Anne Kennedy. *FXL, ORI*

The Crush ½ **1993 (R)** Wealthy 14-year-old temptress Silverstone (in her debut) develops an obsessive crush on handsome 28-year-old Elwes, who rents her family's guest house. In an attempt to win his heart, she rewrites his poorly composed magazine articles. This doesn't convince him they should mate for life, so she sabotages his apartment to vent her rage. Sound familiar? The plot's lifted right out of "Fatal Attraction" and Shapiro doesn't offer viewers anything inventively different. He does manage to substitute new methods for the spurned lover to snare her prey. Limp plot would have been exciting if we hadn't seen it so many times before. **89m/C VHS, Beta, LV.** Cary Elwes, Alicia Silverstone, Jennifer Rubin, Kurtwood Smith, Gwynyth Walsh, Amber Benson; ***D:*** Alan Shapiro; ***W:*** Alan Shapiro; ***M:*** Graeme Revell. MTV Movie Awards '94: Breakthrough Performance (Silverstone), Best Villain (Silverstone). *WAR*

Crusoe ½ **1989 (PG-13)** A lushly photographed version of the Daniel Defoe classic. Crusoe is an arrogant slave trader stranded on a desert island populated by unfriendly natives. Themes of prejudice, fear, and choice appear in this never-padded, thoughtful film. Quinn gives an excellent performance as the stranded slave-trader. **94m/C VHS, Beta, LV.** Aidan Quinn, Ade Sapara, Jimmy Nail, Timothy Spall, Colin Bruce, Michael Higgins, Shane Rimmer, Hepburn Grahame; ***D:*** Caleb Deschanel; ***W:*** Walon Green, Christopher Logue; ***M:*** Michael Kamen. *NO*

Cry-Baby **1990 (PG-13)** An homage and spoof of '50s teen-rock melodramas by the doyen of cinematic Bad Taste, involving a terminal bad-boy high schooler who goes with a square blond and starts an inter-class rumble. Musical numbers, throwaway gags and plenty of knee-bending to Elvis, with a weak story supported by offbeat celeb appearances. **85m/C VHS, Beta, LV.** Johnny Depp, Amy Locane, Polly Bergen, Traci Lords, Ricki Lake, Iggy Pop, Susan Tyrrell, Patty Hearst, Kim McGuire, Darren E. Burrows, Troy Donahue, Willem Dafoe, David Nelson, Mink Stole, Joe Dallesandro, Joey Heatherton, Robert Walsh; ***D:*** John Waters; ***W:*** John Waters; ***M:*** Patrick Williams. *MCA*

Cry Danger **1951** A falsely imprisoned man is released from jail, and he searches for those who framed him. **80m/B VHS.** Dick Powell, Rhonda Fleming, William Conrad, Richard Erdman; ***D:*** Robert Parrish; ***C:*** Joseph Biroc. *REP*

A Cry for Love **1980** An amphetamine addict and an alcoholic meet, fall in love, and help each other recover. Based on the best seller by Jill Schary Robinson, "Bedtime Story." **96m/C VHS, Beta.** Susan Blakely, Powers Boothe, Gene Barry, Charles Siebert, Herb Edelman, Fern Fitzgerald, Lainie Kazan; ***D:*** Paul Wendkos. *FRH*

Cry Freedom ½ **1987 (PG)** A romantic look at the short life of South African activist Steven Biko, and his friendship with the white news editor, Donald Woods. The film focuses on Woods' escape from Africa while struggling to bring Biko's message to the world. Based on a true story. **157m/C VHS, Beta, LV.** Kevin Kline, Denzel Washington, Penelope Wilton, Kevin McNally, John Thaw, Timothy West, John Hargreaves, Alec McCowen, Zakes Mokae, Ian Richardson, Juanita Waterman; ***D:*** Richard Attenborough; ***W:*** John Briley; ***M:*** George Fenton, Jonas Gwangwa. Nominations: Academy Awards '87: Best Song ("Cry Freedom"), Best Supporting Actor (Washington), Best Original Score. *MCA, KUI, FCT*

A Cry from the Mountain **1985 (PG)** Heavily religious film about a father and son who go on a kayak trip through Alaska's wilderness so the father can break the news of his impending divorce. A series of events occurs that change their lives, and they meet a mysterious mountain man who relies on his faith in God to get by in the wilderness. Features an appearance by Rev. Billy Graham. **78m/C VHS, Beta, LV.** James Cavan, Wes Parker, Rita Walter, Chris Kidd, Coleen Gray, Jerry Ballew, Allison Argo, Glen Alsworth, Myrna Kidd; ***D:*** James F. Collier. *LIV*

A Cry from the Streets **1957** Drama about the plight of orphan children and dedicated social workers in England. **100m/C VHS.** *GB* Max Bygraves, Barbara Murray, Kathleen Harrison, Colin Petersen; ***D:*** Lewis Gilbert; ***M:*** Larry Adler. *FCT*

A Cry in the Dark ½ *Evil Angels* **1988 (PG-13)** Tight film story of the infamous Australian murder trial of Lindy Chamberlain, who was accused of killing her own baby, mostly because of the intensely adverse public opinion, aroused by vicious press, that surrounded the case. Chamberlain blamed the death on a wild dingo dog. Near-documentary style, with Streep excellent as the religious, unknowable mother. Based on the book "Evil Angels" by John Bryson. This case was also detailed in the film "Who Killed Baby Azaria?" **120m/C VHS, Beta, LV, 8mm.** *AU* Meryl Streep, Sam Neill, Bruce Myles, Charles Tingwell, Nick Tate, Neil Fitzpatrick, Maurice Fields, Lewis Fitz-gerald; ***D:*** Fred Schepisi; ***W:*** Fred Schepisi, Robert Caswell; ***M:*** Bruce Smeaton. Australian Film Institute '89: Best Actor (Neill), Best Actress (Streep), Best Film; Cannes Film Festival '89: Best Actress (Streep); New York Film Critics Awards '88: Best Actress (Streep); Nominations: Academy Awards '88: Best Actress (Streep). *WAR, FCT*

A Cry in the Night ½ **1993 (PG-13)** After Jenny (Higgins Clark) marries an internationally-acclaimed artist, she thinks her life is complete. However, once she and her two daughters move into his country estate, her life takes a tragic turn as she's haunted by the mysterious deaths of her ex-husband and newborn child. King plays the new husband who turns out to have a few psychological quirks of his own. Based on the bestselling novel by Mary Higgins Clark. Actress Higgins Clark is the novelist's daughter. Made for television. **99m/C VHS.** Perry King, Carol Higgins Clark; ***D:*** Robin Spry; ***W:*** Robin Spry. *REP*

A Cry in the Wild ♕♕♕ **1990 (PG)** A 14 year old boy must find his way back to civilization when he's the lone survivor of an airplane crash. Strong acting from Rushton, excellent nature photography make this well-used story work again. **93m/C VHS.** Jared Rushton, Ned Beatty, Pamela Sue Martin, Stephen Meadows; ***D:*** Mark Griffiths; ***W:*** Catherine Cyran. *MGM*

Cry of a Prostitute: Love Kills ♕ **1972 (R)** Former prostitute joins with a professional assassin in an effort to pacify rival gangsters in Italy. **86m/C VHS, Beta.** Henry Silva, Barbara Bouchet; ***D:*** Andrew Bianchi. *PSM*

Cry of Battle ♕♕½ *To Be a Man* **1963** Anxious for the challenges of manhood, a well-heeled young man joins a guerrilla militia in the Philippines. **99m/B VHS, Beta.** Van Heflin, Rita Moreno, James MacArthur; ***D:*** Irving Lerner. *PSM, MRV, FGF*

Cry of the Banshee ♕♕½ **1970 (PG)** Witch-hunter Price and family are tormented by Satanic powers seeking revenge. Superior horror period piece. Also available with "Count Yorga, Vampire" on Laserdisc. **87m/C VHS, Beta.** *GB* Vincent Price, Elisabeth Bergner, Essy Persson, Hugh Griffith, Hilary Dwyer, Sally Geeson, Patrick Mower; ***D:*** Gordon Hessler; ***M:*** Les Baxter. *HBO*

Cry of the Black Wolves ♕ **197?** A trapper wrongly accused of murder saves the life of a bounty hunter hired to capture him. **90m/C VHS, Beta.** Ron Ely, Catherine Conti. *VTR*

Cry of the Innocent ♕♕♕ **1980** An action-packed thriller about a Vietnam veteran who is out to find a group of Irish terrorists that killed his family. **93m/C VHS, Beta.** Cyril Cusack, Alexander Knox, Rod Taylor, Joanna Pettet, Nigel Davenport; ***D:*** Michael O'Herlihy. *NO*

The Cry of the Owl ♕♕ *Le Cri du Hibou* **1992** Robert (Malavoy) has divorced the dreadful Veronique (Thevenet) and struck up a friendship with Juliette (May). He admires the way her life seems so satisfied and orderly but Juliette decides she doesn't like this idea of herself and impulsively drops her swinish fiance Patrick (Penot) and pursues Robert instead. But Robert is only interested in friendship, leading to some very twisted revenge plots. Suspenseful look at what obsessions can drive people to do. Adapted from the novel by Patricia Highsmith. In French with English subtitles. **102m/C VHS.** *FR IT* Christophe MaLavoy, Mathilda May, Virginie Thevenet, Jacques Penot, Jean-Pierre Kalfon, Patrice Kerbrat; ***D:*** Claude Chabrol; ***W:*** Claude Chabrol, Odile Barski; ***M:*** Matthieu Chabrol. *CVC*

Cry of the Penguins ♕♕½ *Mr. Forbush and the Penguins* **1971** Womanizing biologist Forbush (Hurt) heads off on an Antartic expedition to study penguins when his would-be romance with Tara (Mills) comes to naught. Beautiful photography, shallow story. Adapted from the novel "Mr. Forbush and the Penguins" by Graham Billing. Note the similarities with "Never Cry Wolf." **105m/C VHS.** *GB* John Hurt, Hayley Mills, Dudley Sutton, Tony Britton, Thorley Walters, Judy Campbell, Joss Ackland, Nicholas Pennell; ***D:*** Albert T. Viola; ***W:*** Anthony Shaffer; ***M:*** John Addison. *TVC*

Cry of the Werewolf ♕♕ **1944** A beautiful New Orleans gypsy protects her mother's mummified remains by periodically turning into a werewolf and killing people. **63m/B VHS.** Nina Foch, Stephen Crane, Osa Massen, Blanche Yurka, Barton MacLane, Ivan Triesault, John Abbott, Fritz Leiber; ***D:*** Henry Levin. *MOV*

Cry Panic ♕♕ **1974** A man is thrown into a strange series of events after accidentally running down a man on a highway. Made for television. **74m/C VHS, Beta.** John Forsythe, Anne Francis, Earl Holliman, Claudia McNeil, Ralph Meeker; ***D:*** James Goldstone. *PSM*

Cry Terror ♕♕ **1974** Two escaped convicts take two beautiful women hostage hoping to gain their own freedom. Only a quick-thinking undercover police officer can save the girls. Made for television. **71m/C VHS, Beta.** *GB* Bob Hoskins, Susan Hampshire, Gabrielle Drake. *NO*

Cry, the Beloved Country ♕♕♕½ *African Fury* **1951** A black country minister travels to Johannesberg to be with his son after the youth is accused of killing a white man. Through the events of the trial, the horror, oppression, and destruction of South Africa's apartheid system are exposed. Startling and moving, the first entertainment feature set against the backdrop of apartheid. Still trenchant; based on the novel by Alan Paton. **111m/B VHS.** *GB* Canada Lee, Charles Carson, Sidney Poitier, Joyce Carey, Geoffrey Keen; ***D:*** Zoltan Korda; ***C:*** Robert Krasker. *MON, FCT*

Cry, the Beloved Country ♕♕♕ **1995 (PG-13)** Alan Paton's classic South African apartheid novel (first filmed in 1951) depicts a Zulu Christian pastor and a wealthy white farmer finding common ground through personal loss—both of their sons were killed in regional violence. Rural black minister Stephen Kumalo (Jones), travels to Johannesburg only to discover his sister (Kente) is a prostitute, his younger brother John (Dutton) no longer believes in Christianity and his son is in prison for the murder of a white man. That man turns out to be the son of rich farmer James Jarvis (Harris), from Kumalo's own village. Both Jones and Harris turn in wonderfully understated performances in this hopeful tale of potential racial harmony. **112m/C VHS, LV.** *SA* James Earl Jones, Richard Harris, Charles S. Dutton, Leleti Khumalo, Dambisa Kente, Vusi Kunene, Eric Miyeni, Ian Robers; ***D:*** Darrell Roodt; ***W:*** Ronald Atwood; ***C:*** Paul Gilpin; ***M:*** John Barry. Nominations: Screen Actors Guild Award '95: Best Actor (Jones). *TOU*

Cry Uncle ♕½ **1971 (R)** Comic account of a private eye who investigates a blackmailing case involving a film of orgies in which, much to his chagrin, he participated. **85m/C VHS.** Allen (Goorwitz) Garfield, Paul Sorvino, Devin Goldenberg, Madeleine Le Roux; ***D:*** John G. Avildsen; ***W:*** David Odell; ***C:*** John G. Avildsen. *TTV*

Cry Vengeance ♕♕½ **1954** A falsely-imprisoned detective gets out of jail and searches for the people who framed him and killed his family. **83m/B VHS, Beta.** Mark Stevens, Joan Vohs, Martha Hyer, Skip Homeier; ***D:*** Mark Stevens. *REP*

Cry Wolf ♕♕ **1947** Weak mystery thriller places Stanwyck in creepy environs when she goes to claim her inheritance from her late husband's estate. Based on the novel by Marjorie Carleton. **83m/B VHS.** Errol Flynn, Barbara Stanwyck, Richard Basehart, Geraldine Brooks, Jerome Cowan, John Ridgely, Patricia White; ***D:*** Peter Godfrey; ***W:*** Catherine Turney. *MGM*

The Crying Game ♕♕♕½ **1992 (R)** PR lesson in how to launch a small movie into the hypersphere and ensure critical silence on salient characterization. Jordan's gritty drama is on par with his best, a complex blend of violence, love, betrayal, guilt, and redemption and is not about what it seems to be about much of the time. Wonderful performances by all, including Rea as the appealing, conscience-stricken Fergus; Richardson as the cold, violent IRA moll Jude; and Davidson, in a film debut, as the needy, charismatic Dil. Whitaker is terrific in his 15 minutes of intense screen time. Filled with definite surprises and unexpected pleasures. Title is taken from a top-5 British hit of 1964, three versions of which are heard. **112m/C VHS, LV.** *IR* Stephen Rea, Jaye Davidson, Miranda Richardson, Forest Whitaker, Adrian Dunbar, Jim Broadbent, Ralph Brown, Breffini McKenna, Joe Savino, Birdie Sweeney, Andre Bernard; ***D:*** Neil Jordan; ***W:*** Neil Jordan; ***M:*** Anne Dudley. Academy Awards '92: Best Original Screenplay; Australian Film Institute '93: Best Foreign Film; Chicago Film Critics Awards '92: Best Foreign Film; Independent Spirit Awards '93: Best Foreign Film; Los Angeles Film Critics Association Awards '92: Best Foreign Film; New York Film Critics Awards '92: Best Screenplay, Best Supporting Actress (Richardson); Writers Guild of America '92: Best Original Screenplay; Nominations: Academy Awards '92: Best Actor (Rea), Best Director (Jordan), Best Film Editing, Best Picture, Best Supporting Actor (Davidson). *LIV, MOV, BTV*

Crypt of Dark Secrets ♕ **1976 (R)** Vietnam veteran recovering from wounds in the Louisiana swamps encounters a friendly Indian spirit who saves him from death. **100m/C VHS, Beta.** Maureen Chan, Ronald Tanet, Wayne Mack, Herbert G. Jahncke; ***D:*** Jack Weis. *NO*

Crypt of the Living Dead *Woof!* **1973 (PG)** An undead woman from the 13th century makes life miserable for visitors on Vampire Island. **75m/C VHS, Beta.** Andrew Prine, Mark Damon, Teresa Gimpera, Patty Shepard, Francisco (Frank) Brana; ***D:*** Ray Danton. *NO*

Crystal Heart ♕ **1987 (R)** A medically isolated songwriter with an incurable disease falls in love with a lovely rock singer. **103m/C VHS, Beta.** Lee Curreri, Tawny Kitaen, Lloyd Bochner; ***D:*** Gil Bettman; ***M:*** Joel Goldsmith. *VTR, NWV*

Crystalstone ♕♕ **1988 (PG)** A wooden cross leads a pair of orphans on a dangerous search for the legendary Crystalstone. **103m/C VHS, Beta.** Frank Grimes, Kamlesh Gupta, Laura Jane Goodwin, Sydney Bromley; ***D:*** Antonio Pelaez. *MCG*

Cthulhu Mansion *Woof!* **1991 (R)** The oldest-looking juvenile delinquents you've ever seen release evil spirits when they take over a magician's estate. Not very special effects and abominable dialogue; it claims to be based on H.P. Lovecraft stories, but that's a load of dung. **95m/C VHS.** Frank Finlay, Marcia Layton, Brad Fisher, Melanie Shatner, Luis Fernando Alves, Kaethe Cherney, Paul Birchard, Francisco (Frank) Brana; ***D:*** J. Piquer Simon; ***W:*** J. Piquer. Simon. *REP*

Cuba ♕♕♕ **1979 (R)** Cynical, satirical adventure/love story. Mercenary soldier rekindles an old affair during the Castro revolution. Charismatic cast and good direction make for an entertaining, if overlooked, Connery vehicle. **121m/C VHS, Beta.** Sean Connery, Brooke Adams, Jack Weston, Hector Elizondo, Denholm Elliott, Chris Sarandon, Lonette McKee; ***D:*** Richard Lester; ***W:*** Charles Wood; ***C:*** David Watkin. *MGM, FOX*

Cujo ♕♕ **1983 (R)** A rabid dog goes berserk and attacks a mother and her child who are trapped inside a broken-down Pinto. Frighteningly realistic film is based on Stephen King's bestseller. **94m/C VHS, Beta, LV.** Dee Wallace Stone, Daniel Hugh-Kelly, Danny Pintauro, Ed Lauter, Christopher Stone; ***D:*** Lewis Teague; ***C:*** Jan De Bont; ***M:*** Charles Bernstein. *WAR*

Cul de Sac ♕♕♕ **1966** A macabre, psychological thriller set in a dreary castle on a small island off the British coast. Pleasence is an eccentric, middle-aged hermit living acrimoniously with his young, nympho wife (Dorleac) when their home is invaded by two wounded gangsters (Stander and MacGowran), who proceed to hold the couple hostage. MacGowran soon dies of his wounds, leaving Stander and Pleasence to fight it out, encouraged by the luscious Dorleac, who finds her fun where she can. A bleak, sinister film considered one of Polanski's best. **111m/C VHS.** *GB* Donald Pleasence, Francoise Dorleac, Lionel Stander, Jack MacGowran, Jacqueline Bisset; ***D:*** Roman Polanski; ***W:*** Roman Polanski, Gerard Brach. *FCT*

Culpepper Cattle Co. ♕♕½ **1972 (PG)** A young, starry-eyed yokel wants to be a cowboy and gets himself enlisted in a cattle drive, where he learns the harsh reality of the West. **92m/C VHS, Beta.** Gary Grimes, Billy Green Bush, Bo Hopkins, Charles Martin Smith, Geoffrey Lewis; ***D:*** Dick Richards; ***M:*** Jerry Goldsmith. *FOX*

Cult of the Cobra ♕♕ **1955** Mysterious horror film that became minor camp classic. It seems ex-servicemen are being killed by exotic snake-lady Domergue. Cheesy film that can be fun. Based on a story by Jerry Davis. **75m/B VHS.** Faith Domergue, Richard Long, Marshall Thompson, William Reynolds, Jack Kelly, Kathleen Hughes; ***D:*** Francis D. Lyon; ***W:*** Jerry Davis. *MCA*

Cult People ♕½ **1989** Interviews and film clips featuring a host of filmmaking's favorite cult personalities. **60m/C VHS.** Patrick Macnee, Cameron Mitchell, James Karen, Russ Meyer, Curtis Harrington, Waris Hussein, Michael Sarne. *FCT*

Cup Final *G'mar Giviya* **1992** The similarities and contradictions in war and sports, where passions and competition run high, are depicted in this emotional drama. Set in 1982 during Israel's invasion of Lebanon. Cohen is an Israeli soldier passionately interested in the World Cup soccer tournament. When he is taken prisoner by the PLO he discovers his captor Ziad shares his interest in the Italian national team. This common interest brings the two antagonists reluctantly together. In Hebrew and Arabic with English subtitles. **107m/C VHS.** *IS* Moshe Ivgi, Muhamad Bacri, Suheil Haddad; ***D:*** Eran Riklis; ***W:*** Eyal Halfon; ***M:*** Raviv Gazil. *ICA, BTV*

The Cure **1917** Chaplin arrives at a spa to take a rest cure, accompanied by a trunk full of liquor that somehow gets dumped into the water at the resort. Silent with music track. **20m/B VHS, Beta.** Charlie Chaplin, Edna Purviance, Eric Campbell, Albert Austin; ***D:*** Charlie Chaplin. *VYY, GVV, CAB*

The Cure ½ **1995 (PG-13)** Erik (Renfro), the neighborhood bad kid, befriends Dexter (Mazzello), a boy with AIDS. As Dexter's health weakens, Erik decides they must go on a quest for a cure, Huck Finn style, by floating along the Mississippi River to New Orleans. Despite film's preposterous plot, the performances of the two young leads do inspire a level of sentiment. **99m/C VHS, LV.** Brad Renfro, Joseph Mazzello, Annabella Sciorra, Diana Scarwid, Bruce Davison; ***D:*** Peter Horton; ***W:*** Robert Kuhn; ***C:*** Andrew Dintenfass; ***M:*** Dave Grusin. *MCA*

Curfew **1988 (R)** A young woman rushes home so she doesn't break her curfew, only to find two killers with time on their hands waiting for her. Violent. **86m/C VHS, Beta, LV.** John Putch, Kyle Richards, William Wellman Jr., Bert Remsen; ***D:*** Gary Winick. *VTR, NWV*

The Curfew Breakers **1957** Dim teen-exploitation/message-movie finds a pair of community workers investigating the murder of a gas station attendent by a drug-crazed youth. **78m/B VHS.** Regis Toomey, Paul Kelly, Cathy Downs, Marilyn Madison, Sheila Urban; ***D:*** Alex Wells. *SNC, SMW, TPV*

Curiosity Kills ½ **1990 (R)** Young people find more than they bargained for when they begin to investigate the death of a fellow tenant. Tense made-for-cable thriller. **86m/C VHS.** Rae Dawn Chong, C. Thomas Howell, Courteney Cox, Paul Guilfoyle, Jeff Fahey; ***D:*** Colin Bucksey; ***W:*** Joe Batteer, John Rice. *MCA*

The Curious Dr. Humpp **1970** A mad scientist (Barbero) kidnaps exotic dancers and extracts their libidos to preserve his youth. Under the guise of research, he encourages his victims to engage in trysts so that their carnal energies will increase. Everything is hunky dory until a reporter (Bauleo) starts snooping around the laboratory, discovering Dr. Humpp observing multiple couplings via closed-circuit television. Boldly exploitative, the American distributor added about 10 minutes of raunchy hard-core footage of exotic dance routines. **87m/B VHS.** *AR* Ricardo Bauleo, Aldo Barbero; ***D:*** Emilio Vieyra. *SMW, TPV*

Curley **1947** High-spirited youngsters play pranks on their schoolteacher. A part of the Hal Roach Comedy Carnival. **53m/C VHS, Beta.** Larry Olsen, Frances Rafferty, Eilene Janssen, Walter Abel; ***D:*** Bernard Carr. *DVT, NOS, HHT*

Curly Sue **1991 (PG)** Adorable, homeless waif Porter and her scheming, adoptive father Belushi plot to rip off single, career-minded female attorney Lynch in order to take in some extra cash. Trouble is, all three heartstrings are tugged, and the trio develop a warm, caring relationship. A throwback to the Depression era's Shirley Temple formula films met with mixed reviews. Undiscriminating younger audiences should have a good time, though. Available in widescreen format on laserdisc. **102m/C VHS, Beta, LV, 8mm.** James Belushi, Kelly Lynch, Alison Porter, John Getz, Fred Dalton Thompson; ***D:*** John Hughes; ***W:*** John Hughes; ***M:*** Georges Delerue. *WAR, CCB*

Curly Top ½ **1935 (G)** Orphan Temple helps land a husband for her beautiful sister. Along the way, she sings "Animal Crackers in My Soup." Remake of the silent "Daddy Long Legs," which was remade again in 1955. **74m/B VHS, Beta.** Shirley Temple, John Boles, Rochelle Hudson, Jane Darwell, Esther Dale, Arthur Treacher, Rafaela Ottiano; ***D:*** Irving Cummings. *FOX, MLT*

The Curse *The Farm* **1987 (R)** After a meteorite lands near a small farming community and contaminates the area, a young boy tries to prevent residents from turning into slime-oozing mutants. Remake of "Die, Monster, Die." **92m/C VHS, Beta, LV.** Wil Wheaton, Claude Akins, Malcolm Danare, Cooper Huckabee, John Schneider, David Keith, Amy Wheaton, David Chaskin; ***D:*** David Keith; ***W:*** David Chaskin. *MED, IME*

Curse 2: The Bite **1988 (R)** Radiation affected snakes are transformed into deadly vipers whose bites change their unsuspecting victims into horrible creatures. **97m/C VHS, Beta.** Jill Schoelen, J. Eddie Peck, Jamie Farr, Savina Gersak, Bo Svenson; ***D:*** Fred Goodwin. *TWE*

Curse 3: Blood Sacrifice *Panga* **1990 (R)** An African sugar cane plantation becomes host to a horrible nightmare when a voodoo curse is placed on the owners. The monstrous God of the Sea is summoned to avenge the accidental death of a baby, and the hellish journey into insanity begins. **91m/C VHS, LV.** Christopher Lee, Jenilee Harrison, Henry Cele; ***D:*** Sean Barton. *COL*

Curse 4: The Ultimate Sacrifice ½ *Catacombs* **1990 (R)** Beneath the monastery at San Pietro lies buried the beast of the Apocalypse. For 400 years the secret has been kept and then an American priest and a lovely school teacher unwittingly break the seal and unleash the cursed beast upon an unsuspecting world. **84m/C VHS, LV.** Timothy Van Patten, Laura Schaefer, Jeremy West, Ian Abercrombie; ***D:*** David Schmoeller. *COL*

The Curse of Frankenstein ½ **1957** Young Victor Frankenstein reenacts his father's experiments with creating life from the dead resulting in a terrifying, hideous creature. The first in Hammer's Frankenstein series and followed by "Revenge of Frankenstein." From the Shelley story. Make-up by Jack Pierce, who also created the famous make-up for Universal's Frankenstein monster. **83m/C VHS, Beta.** *GB* Peter Cushing, Christopher Lee, Hazel Court, Robert Urquhart, Valerie Gaunt; ***D:*** Terence Fisher; ***W:*** Jimmy Sangster; ***M:*** James Bernard. *WAR, MLB*

The Curse of King Tut's Tomb ½ **1980** Made-for-television movie is set in 1922 where archaeologists have just opened Tutankhamen's tomb. The curse of the boy king is unleashed as tragic events bring the adventurers uncommon gloom. Oh boy. **98m/C VHS, Beta.** Robin Ellis, Harry Andrews, Eva Marie Saint, Raymond Burr, Wendy Hiller; ***D:*** Philip Leacock. *GKK*

Curse of the Alpha Stone *Woof!* **1985** A professor experiments with an ancient formula on a student, creating a babbling maniac who slaughters freshman girls. **90m/C VHS, Beta.** *NO*

The Curse of the Aztec Mummy *Woof! La Maldicion de la Momia Azteca* **1959** A mad scientist schemes to rob a Mayan pyramid of its treasure but the resident mummy will have none of it. Sequel to "Robot vs. the Aztec Mummy" and followed by "Wrestling Women vs. the Aztec Mummy." **65m/B VHS.** *MX* Ramon Gay, Rosita Arenas, Crox Alvarado; ***D:*** Rafael Portillo. *SNC*

Curse of the Aztec Mummy/Robot vs. the Aztec Mummy *Woof!* **1959** Vengeful mummy of an Aztec warrior stalks those who attempt to steal a fabulous treasure. A mad criminal scientist wants the treasure and uses gangsters and a human robot to get what he wants. **130m/B VHS, Beta.** Ramon Gay, Rosita Arenas, Crox Alvarado, Luis Aceves Cantaneda; ***D:*** Rafael Portillo. *HHT*

Curse of the Black Widow *Love Trap* **1977** An investigator follows a trail of brutal murders to the lair of a supernatural gigantic spider in the middle of Los Angeles. Made for television. **100m/C VHS, Beta.** Patty Duke, Anthony (Tony) Franciosa, Donna Mills, June Lockhart, Sid Caesar, Vic Morrow, June Allyson, Roz Kelly, Jeff Corey; ***D:*** Dan Curtis. *NO*

Curse of the Blue Lights *Woof!* **1988 (R)** Mysterious lights begin appearing at the local romantic spot. Little do the young lovers know, it hails the arrival of a ghoul, intent on raising the dead. Also available in an unedited version. Unfortunately, nothing can resurrect this film. **93m/C VHS, Beta.** Brent Ritter; ***D:*** John H. Johnson. *NO*

Curse of the Cat People **1944** A young sensitive girl is guided by the vision of her dead mother. Sequel to "Cat People." Available in a colorized version. **70m/B VHS, Beta, LV.** Simone Simon, Kent Smith, Jane Randolph, Elizabeth Russell, Ann Carter; ***D:*** Robert Wise, Gunther Von Fritsch. *MED, TTC*

The Curse of the Crying Woman ½ *La Maldicion de a Llorona; La Casa Embrujada* **1961** Unknowing descendant of a witch is lured to her aunt's home to perform the act that will revive the monstrous crying woman and renew a reign of evil. **74m/B VHS, Beta.** *MX* Rosita Arenas, Abel Salazar, Rita Macedo. *SNC, HHT*

Curse of the Crystal Eye **1993 (PG-13)** A gunrunner tries to get the treasure of Ali Baba aided by the requisite lovely lady and opposed by your usual bad guys. **90m/C VHS.** Jameson Parker, Cynthia Rhodes, Mike Lane, David Sherwood, Andre Jacobs; ***D:*** Joe Tornatore. *NHO*

Curse of the Demon ½ *Night of the Demon* **1957** A famous psychologist investigates a colleague's mysterious death and enters a world of demonology and the occult, climaxing in a confrontation with a cult's patron demon. Superb thriller based upon the story "Casting the Runes" by M.R. James. **81m/B VHS, Beta, LV.** *GB* Dana Andrews, Peggy Cummins, Niall MacGinnis, Maurice Denham; ***D:*** Jacques Tourneur; ***W:*** Charles Bennett. *GKK, MLB*

Curse of the Devil ½ *El Retorno de la Walpurgis* **1973 (R)** This time Naschy is turned into a werewolf by annoyed gypsies whose ancestors were slain by his. **73m/C VHS.** *MX SP* Paul Naschy, Maria Silva, Patty Shepard, Fay Falcon; ***D:*** Carlos Aured; ***W:*** Paul Naschy. *SNC*

Curse of the Headless Horseman **1972** The headless horseman rides again, bringing terror to all who cross his path! **80m/C VHS.** Don Carrara, Claudia Dean, B.G. Fisher, Margo Dean, Lee Byers, Joe Cody; ***D:*** John Kirkland. *NO*

Curse of the Living Corpse **1964** A millionaire comes back to rotting life to kill his negligent relatives. Scheider's first film. **84m/C VHS, Beta.** Candace Hilligoss, Roy Scheider, Helen Warren, Margot Hartman; ***D:*** Del Tenney. *PSM*

Curse of the Living Dead **1989** Two siblings are forced to eat flesh for eternity after their witch-doctor mother puts a curse on them. **90m/C VHS, Beta.** ***D:*** Lawrence Foldes. *ELV, HHE*

Curse of the Pink Panther **1983 (PG)** Clifton Sleigh, an inept New York City detective played by Wass, is assigned to find the missing Inspector Clouseau. His efforts are complicated by an assortment of gangsters and aristocrats who cross paths with the detective. So-so attempt to keep popular series going after Seller's death. Niven's last film. **110m/C VHS, Beta.** Ted Wass, David Niven, Robert Wagner, Herbert Lom, Joanna Lumley, Capucine, Robert Loggia, Harvey Korman, Leslie Ash, Denise Crosby; ***D:*** Blake Edwards; ***W:*** Blake Edwards; ***M:*** Henry Mancini. *MGM*

Curse of the Queerwolf **1987** A man is bitten on the butt by gay werewolf and transforms into the title character. Filmed in Santa Barbara in 8mm; some funny moments. From the director of "A Polish Vampire in Burbank." **90m/C VHS.** Michael Palazzolo, Kent Butler, Taylor Whitney; ***D:*** Mark Pirro. *HHE*

Curse of the Screaming Dead *Woof!* **1984** An unpredictable zombie yarn. **90m/C VHS, Beta.** *NO*

Curse of the Starving Class 🦴🦴 **1994 (R)** Ineffective adaptation of Sam Shepard's 1977 play exploring family disintegration. Weston (Woods) is the alcoholic, irresponsible patriarch of a decaying farm. His unhappy wife, Ella (Bates), wants to sell out to land speculator Taylor (Quaid) and move to Paris while rebellious teenager Emma (Fiorella) plans to run off to Mexico and sullen older brother Wesley (Thomas) desires to stay and make a go of things. One-dimensional characterizations don't translate well from stage to screen. **102m/C VHS, LV.** James Woods, Kathy Bates, Henry Thomas, Kristin Fiorella, Randy Quaid, Louis Gossett Jr.; ***D:*** Michael McClary; ***W:*** Bruce Beresford. *VMK*

Curse of the Stone Hand *Woof!* **1964** A pair of stone hands causes folks to do suicidal things. A mutation of a Mexican and a Chilean horror film, each purchased and monster-mashed into one by Warren. **72m/B VHS.** *MX* John Carradine, Ernest Walch, Sheila Bon, Katherine Victor, Lloyd Nelson; ***D:*** Jerry Warren. *NOS, LOO*

Curse of the Swamp Creature 🦴 **1966** A mad scientist in the Everglades attempts to create half human/half alligator monsters. In turn, a geologic expeditionary force attempts to stop his experimentation. Low budget thrills courtesy of Larry Buchanan. **80m/C VHS.** John Agar, Francine York, Shirley McLine, Bill Thurman, Jeff Alexander; ***D:*** Larry Buchanan. *MOV, VDM*

The Curse of the Werewolf 🦴🦴½ **1961** Horror film about a 19th-century European werewolf that is renowned for its ferocious departure from the stereotypical portrait of the beast. **91m/C VHS, Beta.** *GB* Oliver Reed, Clifford Evans, Yvonne Romain, Catherine Feller, Anthony Dawson, Michael Ripper; ***D:*** Terence Fisher. *MCA, TLF, MLB*

Curse of the Yellow Snake 🦴🦴 **1963** Voluminous yarn features a running battle over an ancient Chinese artifact, with crazed Chinese cultists running through foggy London streets. **98m/C VHS, Beta.** *GE* Joachim Berger, Werner Peters; ***D:*** Franz Gottlieb. *VYY*

The Cursed Mountain Mystery 🦴½ **1993 (R)** Two petty thieves steal a legendary precious gem rumored to cursed. The immortal warrior supposed to guard the gem lures the crooks to Sher Mountain, where he intends to eliminate them and return the stone to its keeper. **87m/C VHS.** Phillip Avalon, Tom Richards, Joe Bugner; ***D:*** Vince Martin; ***W:*** Denis Whitburn. *COL*

Curtain Up 🦴🦴 **1953** "Little theatre" dramatics and the exasperating temperaments of amateur theatricals are exposed in this adaptation of the play "On Monday Next," by Philip King. **82m/C VHS, Beta.** *GB* Robert Morley, Margaret Rutherford, Olive Sloane; ***D:*** Ralph Smart; ***W:*** Jack Davies; ***M:*** Malcolm Arnold. *LCA*

Curtains *Woof!* **1983 (R)** Director has a clash of wills with a film star that spells "Curtains" for a group of aspiring actresses gathered together at a haunted house for an audition. Hamfest with no thrills, chills, gore, or gratuitous skin. No wonder why director Richard Ciupka hides behind pseudonym Stryker. **90m/C VHS, Beta.** *CA* John Vernon, Samantha Eggar; ***D:*** Jonathan Stryker; ***W:*** Robert Guza Jr. *VES*

Custer's Last Fight 🦴½ **1912** Re-enactment of the American West period when the Sioux and Cheyenne Indian tribes bitterly opposed the white man. Silent. **50m/B VHS, Beta.** ***D:*** Francis Ford. *NOS, DVT, CCP*

Custer's Last Stand 🦴½ **1936** Feature-length version of the Mascot serial recounting the last days of the famous General. **70m/B VHS, Beta.** Frank McGlynn, Rex Lease, Nancy Caseell, Lona Andre, William Farnum, Reed Howes, Jack Mulhall, Josef Swickard, Ruth Mix; ***D:*** Elmer Clifton. *VCN, GPV*

The Custodian 🦴🦴 **1994 (R)** Honest cop must battle corruption of Australian police precinct while dealing with numerous personal problems. Good cast goes a long way in routine story. **110m/C VHS, LV.** *AU* Anthony LaPaglia, Hugo Weaving, Barry Otto, Bill Hunter, Kelly Dingwall, Gosia Dobrowolska, Naomi Watts; ***D:*** John Dingwall. *ACA*

Cut and Run 🦴 **1985 (R)** Two journalists follow a lead to the former South American home of Jim Jones, and are instantly captured by local guerrillas. **87m/C VHS, Beta.** Michael Berryman, Willie Aames, Lisa Blount, Karen Black. *VTR, NWV*

The Cut Throats 🦴 **1989 (R)** Americans stumble upon an isolated Nazi outpost stocked with gold and beautiful women. Exploitation at its worst. **80m/C VHS.** Jay Scott, Joanne Douglas, Jeff Letham, Pat Michaels, Barbara Lane; ***D:*** John Hayes; ***W:*** John Hayes. *TPV*

Cutter's Way 🦴🦴½ *Cutter and Bone* **1981 (R)** An embittered and alcoholic disabled Vietnam vet and his small-time crook/gigolo friend wrestle with justice and morality when the drifter uncovers a murder but declines to get involved. An unusually cynical mystery from the novel by Newton Thorburg. **105m/C VHS, Beta, LV.** Jeff Bridges, John Heard, Lisa Eichhorn, Ann Dusenberry, Stephen Elliott, Nina Van Pallandt, George Dickerson; ***D:*** Ivan Passer; ***M:*** Jack Nitzsche. Edgar Allan Poe Awards '81: Best Screenplay. *MGM*

Cutthroat Island 🦴🦴½ **1995 (PG-13)** Big-budget swashbuckling adventure—long on action and short on plot and character. Female pirate captain Morgan Adams (Davis) is left part of a treasure map by her father and "persuades" educated slave/thief William Shaw (Modine), who has lots of charm and no morals, to assist her. Her scurvy Uncle Dawg (despically well-played by Langella) also has a portion of the map and is willing to let Morgan find the treasure—on Cutthroat Island—before taking it for himself. Director Harlin likes lots of big, noisy explosions (when he doesn't know what else to do) but Davis' exuberance for her pirate queen role is appealing. **123m/C VHS, LV.** Geena Davis, Matthew Modine, Frank Langella, Patrick Malahide, Stan Shaw, Maury Chaykin, Harris Yulin, George Murcell; ***D:*** Renny Harlin; ***W:*** Robert King, Marc Norman; ***C:*** Peter Levy; ***M:*** John Debney. *LIV*

Cutting Class 🦴🦴 **1989 (R)** Murders proliferate in a high school, where a student with a history of mental illness is number one on the suspect list. Tongue-in-cheek mayhem. **91m/C VHS, LV.** Jill Schoelen, Roddy McDowall, Donovan Leitch, Martin Mull, Brad Pitt; ***D:*** Rospo Pallenberg. *REP*

The Cutting Edge 🦴🦴½ **1992 (PG)** Spoiled figure skater's lifelong quest for Olympic gold is seriously hampered by her inability to be nice to her partners. In a final effort to snag the medal she teams up with a cocky guy who thinks the only sport on ice is hockey, but whose own dreams of NHL stardom were cut short by an injury. Saddled with a predictable and thin plot, it sometimes looks and feels like a TV movie. So why bother? Because the chemistry between photogenic leads Kelly and Sweeney is terrific. Add half a bone for the flying sparks and snappy dialogue, sit back, and enjoy. **101m/C VHS, LV.** D.B. Sweeney, Moira Kelly, Roy Dotrice, Terry O'Quinn, Dwier Brown, Rachelle Ottley, Jo Jo Starbuck; ***D:*** Paul Michael Glaser; ***W:*** Tony Gilroy; ***M:*** Patrick Williams. *MGM*

Cyber Bandits 🦴½ **1994 (R)** In a future society, navigator Jack Morris (Kemp) has just sailed a pleasure craft to the island city of Pacifica. His passengers included wealthy Morgan Wells (Hays), whose scientists have developed a deadly virtual reality weapon, and Wells' mistress Rebecca (Paul). Rebecca steals the plans for the weapon and seduces Jack into having the data digitally transferred onto his back in the form of a tattoo. Then Rebecca disappears and Jack finds himself in big trouble. **86m/C VHS, LV.** Martin Kemp, Alexandra Paul, Robert Hays, Adam Ant, Grace Jones; ***D:*** Erik Fleming; ***W:*** James Robinson, Winston Beard. *COL*

Cyber Ninja 🦴🦴½ **1994** Warrior princess Saki is captured by the Dark Overlord, who plans to sacrifice her. It's up to a mercenary to come to her rescue. Lightweight, action-oriented Japanese mix of samurais and science fiction. Dubbed. **80m/C VHS.** *JP* Hanbel Kawai, Hiroki Ida. *FXL*

Cyber-Tracker 🦴½ **1993 (R)** In the judicial system of the future androids hunt down vicious criminals and execute them immediately. When secret service agent Eric Phillips is framed for murder, he's also marked for death. His only chance is to link up with rebels fighting the mechanized monsters. **?m/C VHS, LV.** Don "The Dragon" Wilson, Richard Norton, Joseph Ruskin, Abby Dalton, John Aprea; ***D:*** Richard Pepin. *PMH*

Cyber-Tracker 2 🦴½ **1995 (R)** An international weapons dealer has gotten control of the cybertracker technology and created cyborg lookalikes of secret agent Eric Phillips (Wilson) and his newscaster wife Connie (Foster). When the cyborgs commit murder on live TV, the human duo become fugitives who must expose the real killers. **97m/C VHS.** Don "The Dragon" Wilson, Stacie Foster, Stephen Burton. *PMH*

Cyberzone 🦴½ **1995 (R)** Intergalactic investigator pursues four dangerous androids who are hiding on earth. **95m/C VHS.** Marc Singer, Matthias Hues. *NHO*

Cyborg 🦴 **1989 (R)** In a deathly, dirty, post-holocaust urban world, an able cyborg battles a horde of evil mutant thugs. Poorly-made action flick. **85m/C VHS, Beta, LV.** Jean-Claude Van Damme, Deborah Richter, Vincent Klyn, Dayle Haddon; ***D:*** Albert Pyun; ***W:*** Kitty Chalmers; ***M:*** Kevin Bassinson. *MGM*

Cyborg 2 🦴🦴 **1993 (R)** In the year 2074 cyborgs have replaced humans at all levels. A devious company which manufactures cyborgs decides to get rid of its chief competition by literally killing them off. They plan to inject cyborg Cash Reese (Jolie) with a liquid explosive that will detonate her and everything else in sight. Tech-master Mercy (Palance) clues Cash in and she escapes with the help of the human Colton (Koteas) but they've become prey to a group of ruthless hunters. **99m/C VHS, LV.** Angelina Jolie, Elias Koteas, Jack Palance, Billy Drago. *VMK*

Cyborg 3: The Recycler 🦴🦴 **1995 (R)** Female cyborg has been programmed to become a creator—essentially making mankind useless. **90m/C VHS.** Khrystyne Haje, Zach Galligan, Andrew Bryniarski, Richard Lynch, Malcolm McDowell; ***D:*** Michael Schroeder; ***W:*** Barry Victor, Troy Bolotnick. *AVE*

Cyborg Cop 🦴½ **1993 (R)** DEA agent Phillip (Jenson) is captured during a foreign drug raid and is turned into a half-man, half-machine by mad scientist Kessel (Rhys-Davies), who wants to sell his cyborgs as unstoppable hitmen. Phillip's brother Jack (Bradley) tries to come to his rescue. Lots of stunts and car chases and even a minor romantic subplot with Jack and a tough reporter (Shaw). **97m/C VHS, LV.** David Bradley, John Rhys-Davies, Todd Jensen, Alonna Shaw; ***W:*** Glenn A. Bruce. *VMK*

Cyborg Soldier 🦴🦴½ *Cyborg Cop 2* **1994 (R)** Loose cannon cop Jack Ryan (Bradley) is up against psycho killer Starkraven (Hunter) who gets turned into a new-model cyborg by your basic suspicious government agency. But when the cyborg decides to go on an unplanned human killing spree, Ryan gets to break out the heavy artillery to mow him down. Also available in an unrated version. **96m/C VHS, LV.** David Bradley, Morgan Hunter, Jill Pierce; ***D:*** Sam Firstenberg; ***W:*** Jon Stevens. *NLC*

Cycle Psycho *Woof! Numbered Days; Savage Abduction* **1972 (R)** Serial killer blackmails the businessman whose wife he was contracted to kill into bringing him young girls to slaughter. The businessman hires out the job to sleazy motorcycle gang. **80m/C VHS, Beta.** Joe Turkel, Tom Drake, Stephen Oliver; ***D:*** John Lawrence; ***W:*** John Lawrence. *ACA*

Cycle Vixens *Woof! The Young Cycle Girls* **1979 (R)** Three girls jump on their hogs and head from Colorado to California. Much leather, motor revving and other obligatory motorcycle-trash trimmings. **90m/C VHS.** Loraine Ferris, Daphne Lawrence, Deborah Marcus, Lonnie Pense, Kevin O'Neill, Bee Lechat, Billy Bullet; ***D:*** Peter Perry. *SIM*

Cyclone **1987 (R)** The girlfriend of a murdered scientist must deliver a secretly devised motorcycle into righteous government hands, much to the dismay of evil agents and corrupt officials. Good fun, sparked by a stellar "B" cast. **89m/C VHS, Beta, LV.** Heather Thomas, Jeffrey Combs, Ashley Ferrare, Dar Robinson, Martine Beswick, Robert Quarry, Martin Landau, Huntz Hall, Troy Donahue, Michael Reagan, Dawn Wildsmith, Bruce Fairbairn, Russ Tamblyn; ***D:*** Fred Olen Ray. *COL*

Cyclone Cavalier **1925** A dauntless hero travels through Central America on an adventurous spree. **58m/B VHS, Beta.** Reed Howes; ***D:*** Albert Rogell. *GPV, GVV*

Cyclone of the Saddle **1935** Typical Western about a range war. **53m/B VHS, Beta.** Rex Lease, Bobby Nelson, William Desmond, Yakima Canutt; ***D:*** Elmer Clifton. *NO*

Cyclops **1956** When an expedition party searches throughout Mexico for a woman's long lost fiance, they are shocked when they find out that radiation has turned him into a one-eyed monster. **72m/B VHS, Beta.** Tom Drake, Gloria Talbott, Lon Chaney Jr., James Craig; ***D:*** Bert I. Gordon. *LIV, MLB*

Cyclotrode "X" *The Crimson Ghost* **1946** The Crimson Ghost attempts to kidnap the inventor of the title machine, which would enable him to rule the world. Moore (The Lone Ranger) plays a bad guy. Serial in 12 episodes. Also available in a 93-minute colorized edition. **100m/B VHS, Beta.** Charles Quigley, Linda Stirling, I. Stanford Jolley, Clayton Moore, Kenne Duncan; ***D:*** William Witney, Fred Brannon. *VCN, REP, MLB*

Cyrano de Bergerac **1925** Silent version of Edmond Rostand's novel about romantic Cyrano who fears to reveal his love to Roxanne because he feels his enormous nose makes him unattractive. So, he serves as a surrogate lover by encouraging another man's attentions to her. Color-tinted. **114m/C VHS.** *IT FR* Pierre Magnier, Linda Moglia, Angelo Ferrari; ***D:*** Augusto Genina; ***M:*** Carlo Moser. *KIV*

Cyrano de Bergerac **1950** Edmund Rostand's famous story of a large nosed yet poetic cavalier, who finds himself too ugly to be loved. He bears the pain of his devotion to Roxanne from afar, and helps the handsome but tongue-tied Christian to romance her. Ferrer became famous for this role, which won him an Oscar. Based on Brian Hooke's translation of the play. Also available colorized. **112m/B VHS, LV.** Jose Ferrer, Mala Powers, William Prince, Elena Verdugo, Morris Carnovsky; ***D:*** Michael Gordon; ***W:*** Carl Foreman; ***M:*** Dimitri Tiomkin. Academy Awards '50: Best Actor (Ferrer); Golden Globe Awards '51: Best Actor—Drama (Ferrer); National Board of Review Awards '50: 10 Best Films of the Year. *CNG, MRV, NOS*

Cyrano de Bergerac **1985** Edmond Rostand's gallant poet and swordsman, with the extraordinary nose, is well-portrayed by Jacobi in this Royal Shakespeare Company production. Translated and adapted by Anthony Burgess. **177m/C VHS.** *GB* Derek Jacobi, Sinead Cusack. *TVC, TTC*

Cyrano de Bergerac **1990 (PG)** Depardieu brings to exhilarating life Rostand's well-loved play about the brilliant but grotesque-looking swordsman/poet, afraid of nothing—except declaring his love to the beautiful Roxanne. One of France's costliest modern productions, a multi-award winner for its cast, costumes, music and sets. English subtitles (by Anthony Burgess) are designed to capture the intricate rhymes of the original French dialogue. **135m/C VHS, LV.** *FR* Gerard Depardieu, Jacques Weber, Anne Brochet, Vincent Perez, Roland Bertin, Josiane Stoleru, Phillipe Volter, Philippe Morier-Genoud, Pierre Maguelon; ***D:*** Jean-Paul Rappeneau; ***W:*** Jean-Claude Carriere, Jean-Paul Rappeneau. Academy Awards '90: Best Costume Design; Cannes Film Festival '90: Best Actor (Depardieu); Cesar Awards '91: Best Actor (Depardieu), Best Art Direction/Set Decoration, Best Cinematography, Best Costume Design, Best Director (Rappeneau), Best Film, Best Sound, Best Supporting Actor (Weber), Best Score; Golden Globe Awards '91: Best Foreign Film; Nominations: Academy Awards '90: Best Actor (Depardieu), Best Art Direction/Set Decoration, Best Foreign Language Film, Best Makeup. *ORI, FCT, BTV*

D-Day on Mars **1945** Alien invader the Purple Monster is bent on taking over Earth. Originally a 15-part Republic serial titled "The Purple Monster Strikes." **100m/B VHS.** Dennis Moore, Linda Stirling, Roy Barcroft, James Craven, Bud Geary, Mary Moore; ***D:*** Spencer Gordon Bennet, Fred Brannon. *REP*

D-Day, the Sixth of June *The Sixth of June* **1956** An American soldier has an affair with a Englishwoman weeks before D-Day, where he unhappily finds himself fighting side by side with her husband. Based on the novel by Lionel Shapiro. **106m/C VHS, Beta.** Richard Todd, Dana Wynter, Robert Taylor, Edmond O'Brien, John Williams, Jerry Paris, Richard Stapley; ***D:*** Henry Koster; ***C:*** Lee Garmes. *FXV*

Da ½ **1988 (PG)** A middle-aged man returns to Ireland for his father's funeral. As he sorts out his father's belongings, his father returns as a ghostly presence to chat with him about life, death, and their own relationship. Based on the Hugh Leonard play with Hughes recreating his Tony-award winning role. **102m/C VHS, Beta, LV.** Barnard Hughes, Martin Sheen, William Hickey, Hugh O'Conor; ***D:*** Matt Clark; ***W:*** Hugh Leonard; ***M:*** Elmer Bernstein. *NO*

Dad ½ **1989 (PG)** Hoping to make up for lost time, a busy executive rushes home to take care of his father who has just had a heart attack. What could have easily become sappy is made bittersweet by the convincing performances of Lemmon and Danson. Based on the novel by William Wharton. **117m/C VHS, Beta, LV.** Jack Lemmon, Ted Danson, Ethan Hawke, Olympia Dukakis, Kathy Baker, Zakes Mokae, J.T. Walsh, Kevin Spacey, Chris Lemmon; ***D:*** Gary David Goldberg; ***W:*** Gary David Goldberg; ***M:*** James Horner. National Media Owl Awards '90: First Prize; Nominations: Academy Awards '89: Best Makeup. *MCA*

Daddy Long Legs **1955** Far from the great musicals, but enjoyable. An eccentric millionaire glimpses a French orphan and becomes her anonymous benefactor. Her musing over his identity spawns some surreal (often inexplicable) dance numbers, but love conquers all, even lesser Johnny Mercer songs. From a story by Jean Webster, also done in 1919 with Mary Pickford, 1931 with Janet Gaynor and 1935 with Shirley Temple as "Curly Top." ♫Daddy Long Legs; Something's Got To Give; Sluefoot; Dream; History of the Beat; C-A-T Spells Cat; Welcome Egghead. **126m/C VHS, LV.** Fred Astaire, Leslie Caron, Terry Moore, Thelma Ritter, Fred Clark, Charlotte Austin, Larry Keating; ***D:*** Jean Negulesco; ***C:*** Leon Shamroy; ***M:*** Alex North. Nominations: Academy Awards '55: Best Art Direction/Set Decoration (Color), Best Song ("Something's Gotta Give"), Best Original Score. *FXV, FCT*

Daddy Nostalgia *These Foolish Things* **1990** Birkin plays the estranged daughter of Bogarde, who rushes from her home in England to France to be with her seriously ill father. She must come to terms with her feelings for him just as Bogarde must deal with his own mortality. Wonderful performances, with Bogarde a charming and dominating presence. In French with English subtitles. **105m/C VHS.** *FR* Dirk Bogarde, Jane Birkin, Odette Laure; ***D:*** Bertrand Tavernier; ***W:*** Colo Tavernier O'Hagan; ***M:*** Antoine Duhamel. *FCT*

Daddy-O *Out on Probation* **1959** Drag racer Daddy-O traps the killers of his best friend and lands the blonde bombshell Jana. It might seem bad since it's dated, but, hey, it may have been bad in 1959, too! **74m/B VHS.** Dick Contino, Sandra Giles; ***D:*** Lou Place; ***W:*** David Moessinger. *COL*

Daddy's Boys ½ **1987 (R)** Since farming during the Depression is a rather low-paying endeavor, this family turns to thieving instead. But all-for-one and one-for-all is not the credo for one of the sons who decides to branch out on his own. Produced by Roger Corman. **90m/C VHS, Beta, LV.** Daryl Haney, Laura Burkett, Raymond J. Barry, Dan Shor; ***D:*** Joe Minion; ***W:*** Daryl Haney. *COL*

Daddy's Dyin'...Who's Got the Will? ½ **1990 (PG-13)** Based on the critically acclaimed play, this bittersweet comedy stars Bridges and D'Angelo as two members of the spiteful Turnover clan. When Daddy is on his deathbed, the entire family uses the opportunity to stab each other in the back. Non-stop humor and deep-hearted honesty carries this delightful adaptation quickly from beginning to end. **95m/C VHS, Beta, LV.** Beau Bridges, Beverly D'Angelo, Tess Harper, Judge Reinhold, Amy Wright, Keith Carradine, Patrika Darbo, Molly McClure, Bert Remsen; ***D:*** Jack Fisk; ***W:*** Del Shores; ***M:*** David McHugh. *MGM*

Daddy's Gone A-Hunting **1969 (PG)** It's an eye for an eye, a baby for a baby in this well-done psychological thriller. A happily married woman is stalked by her deranged ex-boyfriend, whose baby she aborted years before. Now he wants the life of her child as just compensation for the loss of his. **108m/C VHS.** Carol White, Paul Burke, Scott Hylands, Rachel Ames, Mala Powers, James B. Sikking; ***D:*** Mark Robson; ***W:*** Larry Cohen; ***C:*** Ernest Laszlo; ***M:*** John Williams. *WAR*

Daens ½ **1992** Looks at the disparity between rich and poor at the turn of the century. Daens, a priest, returns home to Flanders to find desperate poverty among the Flemish-speaking workers of the local textile mill. The French-speaking mill owners are supported by the local Catholic church while Daens believes in the rights of the workers. Decleir makes his priest a complex and troubled man, who must choose between his conscience and social reform and the dictates of his church. Marred by somewhat cardboard villains and a complex political/social situation that isn't adequately explained. Based on the novel by Louis Paul Boon. Flemish and French with English subtitles. **134m/C VHS.** *FR BE NL* Jan Decleir, Gerard Desarthe, Antje De Boeck, Michael Pas, Johan Leysen, Idwig Stephane, Linda Van Dijck, Wim Meuwissen; ***D:*** Stijn Coninx; ***W:*** Francois Chevallier, Stijn Coninx; ***M:*** Dirk Brosse. Nominations: Academy Awards '92: Best Foreign Language Film. *ORI*

Daffy Duck's Movie: Fantastic Island **1983 (G)** A compilation of classic Warner Brothers cartoons, starring Daffy Duck, Speedy Gonzales, Bugs Bunny, Porky Pig, Sylvester, Tweety, Pepe Le Pew, Pirate Sam, Granny, Foghorn Leghorn and the Tasmanian Devil. **78m/C VHS, Beta, LV.** ***D:*** Isadore "Friz" Freleng; ***V:*** Mel Blanc, June Foray, Les Tremayne. *WAR, FCT, WTA*

Daffy Duck's Quackbusters **1989 (G)** Daffy, with help from pals Bugs and Porky, sets up his own "ghostbusting" service. Good compilation of old classics such as "Night of the Living Duck," plus a new feature, "The Duxcorcist." Video is also available in Spanish. **79m/C VHS, Beta, LV.** ***D:*** Greg Ford, Terry Lennon; ***V:*** Mel Blanc. *WAR, FCT, APD*

Dagger Eyes ½ **198?** A political assassin at work is inadvertently captured on film by a photographer. The assassin's mob employers will go to any lengths to destroy the film. Say cheeeeeese! **84m/C VHS, Beta.** Carole Bouquet, Philip Coccioletti, John Steiner; ***D:*** Carlo Vanzina. *NO*

The Dagger of Kamui ½ **1985** Jiro is pursued by minions of the evil Tenkai as he races from Japan to the American Old West and back again. He's trying to avenge the murder of his father and Jiro's only weapon is the mysterious Dagger of Kamui, which holds the secret to a treasure and the future of Japan. In Japanese with English subtitles. **132m/C VHS, LV.** *JP ANI, WTA, CPM*

Dagora, the Space Monster *Woof! Dagora; Space Monster Dagora; Uchudai Dogora; Uchu Daikaiju Dogora* **1965** Giant, slimy, pulsating mass from space lands on Earth and begins eating everything in sight. Scientists join together in a massive effort to destroy the creature. Believe it or not, it's sillier than most of the Japanese sci-fi genre. **80m/C VHS, Beta.** *JP* Yosuke Natsuki, Yoko Fujiyama, Akiko Wakabayashi, Hiroshi Koizumi; ***D:*** Inoshiro Honda; ***W:*** Shinichi Sekizawa; ***C:*** Hajime Koizumi. *VYY*

The Dain Curse ☠☠ *Dashiell Hammett's The Dain Curse* **1978** In 1928, private eye Hamilton Nash must recover stolen diamonds, solve a millionaire's suicide, avoid being murdered, and end a family curse. Based on the novel by Dashiell Hammett. Made-for-television as a 312-minute miniseries. **138m/C VHS, Beta.** James Coburn, Jason Miller, Jean Simmons, Beatrice Straight, Hector Elizondo, Nancy Addison; ***D:*** E.W. Swackhamer. *EHV, MTX, SUE*

Daisy Miller ☠☠½ **1974 (G)** Shepherd portrays the title character in this adaptation of the Henry James novella about a naive young American woman travelling through Europe and getting a taste of the Continent during the late 19th century. Though it is intelligently written and has a good supporting cast, the film seems strangely flat, due in large part to Shepherd's hollow performance. **93m/C VHS, Beta.** Cybill Shepherd, Eileen Brennan, Cloris Leachman, Mildred Natwick; ***D:*** Peter Bogdanovich; ***W:*** Frederic Raphael. National Board of Review Awards '74: 10 Best Films of the Year; Nominations: Academy Awards '74: Best Costume Design. *PAR*

Dakota ☠☠ **1945** Fine cast becomes embroiled in railroad land dispute. In the meantime, love strikes The Duke. Standard Wayne western saga never quite gets on track. **82m/B VHS, LV.** John Wayne, Vera Ralston, Walter Brennan, Ward Bond, Ona Munson; ***D:*** Joseph Kane. *REP*

Dakota ☠☠ **1988 (PG)** A troubled half-breed teenager works for a rancher, romances his daughter, and befriends his crippled 12-year-old son. A well-meaning, but predictable drama. **96m/C VHS, Beta, LV.** Lou Diamond Phillips, Dee Dee Norton, Eli Cummins, Herta Ware; ***D:*** Fred Holmes. *HBO*

Dakota Incident ☠☠ **1956** Decent western about stagecoach passengers travelling through Dakota Territory who must defend themselves against an Indian attack. **88m/C VHS.** Dale Robertson, Ward Bond, Linda Darnell, John Lund; ***D:*** Lewis R. Foster. *REP*

Daleks—Invasion Earth 2150 A.D. ☠☠½ *Invasion Earth 2150 A.D* **1966** A sequel to "Dr. Who and the Daleks," wherein the popular British character endeavors to save the Earth from a robotic threat. **81m/C VHS, Beta.** *GB* Peter Cushing, Andrew Keir, Jill Curzon, Ray Brooks; ***D:*** Gordon Flemyng. *NO*

The Dallas Connection ☠ **1994 (R)** Three of the four scientists working on a satellite weapons system are assassinated by a trio of sexy but lethal females. Now the remaining scientist is under federal protection in Dallas while he continues his work. Lots of T&A. **90m/C VHS.** Julie Strain, Samantha Phillips, Julie K. Smith, Wendy Hamilton; ***D:*** Drew Sidaris. *MNC*

Dalva ☠½ **1995** Dull TV movie finds restless Dalva Northridge (Fawccett) deciding to search for the son she was forced to give up for adoption some 20 years before. But she gets sidetracked juggling two love affairs—with Sam Creekmouth (Boothe), whose Indian heritage is tied to Dalva's family, and alcoholic university professor Michael (Coyote) who wants the Northridge family diaries for his research on the Great Plains. Based on the novel by Jim Harrison. **?m/C VHS.** Farrah Fawcett, Powers Boothe, Peter Coyote, Rod Steiger, Carroll Baker. *NYR*

Dam Busters ☠☠☠½ **1955** Well-done and exciting film details the efforts of British scientists trying to devise a method of destroying a strategic dam in Nazi Germany during WWII. Definitely one of the better in the war movie genre. **119m/B VHS, Beta.** *GB* Michael Redgrave, Richard Todd, Ursula Jeans, Basil Sydney; ***D:*** Michael Anderson Sr. *HMV, CNG*

Damage ☠☠☠ **1992 (R)** The elegant Irons portrays Stephen, a middle-aged, married British politican who has always been completely in control of his life, especially where his feelings are concerned. Then he meets Anna (Binoche), his son's less-than-innocent fiance, and immediately begins an obsessive, wildly sexual affair with her. Stephen should have listened to Anna's warning about herself "Damaged people are dangerous, they know they can survive," because their passion leads to betrayal and tragedy. Binoche is more icon than human being but the film still hypnotizes as an exploration of passion. Based on the novel by Josephine Hart. An unrated version is also available. **111m/C VHS, LV.** *GB FR* Jeremy Irons, Juliette Binoche, Rupert Graves, Miranda Richardson, Ian Bannen, Leslie Caron, Peter Stormare, Gemma Clark, Julian Fellowes; ***D:*** Louis Malle; ***W:*** David Hare; ***M:*** Zbigniew Preisner. British Academy Awards '92: Best Supporting Actress (Richardson); Los Angeles Film Critics Association Awards '92: Best Score; Nominations: Academy Awards '92: Best Supporting Actress (Richardson). *COL, IME, MOV*

Dames ☠☠☠ **1934** A millionaire with fanatically religious beliefs tries to stop the opening of a Broadway show. In the last of the grand budget-breaking spectacles before the "production code" came into being, distinguished choreographer Busby Berkeley took his imagination to the limit: watch for the dancing clothes on an ironing board and dancing girls with puzzle pieces on their backs which form the real Keeler. ♫Dames; I Only Have Eyes For You; When You Were a Smile on Your Mother's Lips and a Twinkle in Your Father's Eye; Try To See It My Way; The Girl at the Ironing Board. **95m/B VHS, Beta, LV.** Dick Powell, Joan Blondell, Ruby Keeler, ZaSu Pitts, Guy Kibbee, Busby Berkeley; ***D:*** Ray Enright; ***W:*** Delmer Daves; ***C:*** George Barnes. *MGM, FOX*

Dames Ahoy ☠ **1930** Three sailors on shore leave try to find the blonde who tricked one of them out of his pay. This is the original silent version with a piano score. **52m/B VHS.** Glenn Tryon, Otis Harlan, Eddie Gribbon, Helen Wright, Gertrude Astor; ***D:*** William James Craft. *GPV, FCT*

Damien: Omen 2 ☠☠ **1978 (R)** Sequel to "The Omen" about Damien, a young boy possessed with mysterious demonic powers, who kills those people who anger him. Followed by "The Final Conflict." **110m/C VHS, Beta, LV.** William Holden, Lee Grant, Lew Ayres, Robert Foxworth, Sylvia Sidney, Lance Henriksen, Jonathan Scott-Taylor; ***D:*** Don Taylor; ***W:*** Mike Hodges; ***M:*** Jerry Goldsmith. *FOX*

Damien: The Leper Priest ☠☠ *Father Damien: The Leper Priest* **1980** True story of a Roman Catholic priest who doomed himself by voluntarily serving on a leper colony one hundred years ago. Somewhat disappointing considering the dramatic material. Originally a vehicle for David Janssen, who died prior to filming. Made for television. **100m/C VHS, Beta.** Ken Howard, Mike Farrell, Wilfrid Hyde-White, William Daniels, David Ogden Stiers; ***D:*** Steven Gethers. *LIV*

Damn the Defiant ☠☠☠ *HMS Defiant* **1962** Adventure abounds when Guinness, as captain of the HMS Defiant during the Napoleonic wars, finds himself up against not only the French but his cruel second-in-command (Bogarde) and a mutinous crew as well. In the end, both a fleet-wide mutiny and a French invasion of England are avoided. Much attention is paid to period detail in this well-crafted film. **101m/C VHS, Beta, LV.** *GB* Alec Guinness, Dirk Bogarde, Maurice Denham, Anthony Quayle; ***D:*** Lewis Gilbert. *COL, FCT*

Damn Yankees ☠☠☠ *What Lola Wants* **1958** Musical feature adapted from the Broadway hit. A baseball fan frustrated by his team's lack of success makes a pact with the devil to become the team's new star. Verdon is dynamite as the devil's accomplice. Great Bob Fosse choreography. ♫Whatever Lola Wants; (You Gotta Have) Heart; Shoeless Joe From Hannibal Mo; Goodbye, Old Girl; A Little Brains, a Little Talent; Who's Got the Pain; Two Lost Souls; There's Something About an Empty Chair; Those Were the Good Old Days. **110m/C VHS, Beta, LV.** Gwen Verdon, Ray Walston, Tab Hunter, Jean Stapleton, Russ Brown; ***D:*** George Abbott, Stanley Donen. Nominations: Academy Awards '58: Best Original Score. *WAR, FCT, HMV*

Damnation Alley ☠½ **1977 (PG)** A warrior, an artist, and a biker jump in tank and set off in search of civilization after Armageddon. They go to Albany instead. So-so attempt to revive the post-nuclear holocaust genre which was more successfully accomplished by the "Mad Max" series. Adapted from Roger Zelazny's novel. **87m/C VHS, Beta.** George Peppard, Jan-Michael Vincent, Paul Winfield, Dominique Sanda, Jackie Earle Haley; ***D:*** Jack Smight; ***W:*** Alan Sharp, Lukas Heller; ***C:*** Harry Stradling Jr.; ***M:*** Jerry Goldsmith. *FOX*

The Damned ☠☠½ **1969 (R)** Depicts the Nazi takeover of a German industrialist family and their descent into greed, lust, and madness. Comes in dubbed or subtitled formats. **146m/C VHS, Beta.** *IT GE* Dirk Bogarde, Ingrid Thulin, Helmut Griem, Charlotte Rampling, Helmut Berger; ***D:*** Luchino Visconti; ***M:*** Maurice Jarre. National Board of Review Awards '69: 5 Best Foreign Films of the Year; Nominations: Academy Awards '69: Best Story & Screenplay. *WAR, APD, INJ*

Damned River ☠½ **1989 (R)** Four friends take a guided tour down Zimbabwe's Zambezi River, only to find midway down that their guide is a murderous psycho. Survival becomes a priority. **93m/C VHS, Beta.** Stephen Shellan, Lisa Aliff, John Terlesky, Marc Poppel, Bradford Bancroft; ***D:*** Michael Schroeder; ***W:*** John Crowther. *FOX*

A Damsel in Distress ☠☠☠ **1937** Astaire falls for an upper-class British girl, whose family wants her to have nothing to do with him. Features memorable songs from the Gershwins. ♫A Foggy Day in Londontown; Nice Work If You Can Get It; Stiff Upper Lip; Put Me to the Test; I Can't Be Bothered Now; The Jolly Tar and the Milkmaid; Things Are Looking Up; Sing of Spring; Ah Che a Voi Perdoni Iddio. **101m/B VHS, Beta, LV.** Fred Astaire, Joan Fontaine, George Burns, Gracie Allen, Ray Noble, Montagu Love, Reginald Gardiner; ***D:*** George Stevens; ***M:*** George Gershwin, George Bassman, Ira Gershwin. Nominations: Academy Awards '37: Best Interior Decoration. *CCB, MED, TTC*

Dan Candy's Law ☠½ *Alien Thunder* **1973** A Canadian mountie becomes a driven hunter, and then desperate prey, when he tries to track down the Indian who killed his partner. **90m/C VHS, Beta.** *CA* Donald Sutherland, Gordon Tootoosis, Chief Dan George, Kevin McCarthy; ***D:*** Claude Fournier; ***M:*** Georges Delerue. *PSM, SIM*

Dance ☠½ **1990** Two ballet dancers struggle to find love amidst the backstage treacheries and demanding schedules of their profession. **90m/C VHS, Beta.** John Revall, Ellen Troy, Carlton Wilborn, Charlene Campbell; ***D:*** Robin Murray. *AIP*

Dance Fools Dance ☠☠☠ **1931** Fast-paced drama has Crawford and Bakewell as a pair of spoiled rich kids who are forced to face poverty when the stock market crashes. He meets up with Gable, who's producing liquor illegally, while she gets a job at a newspaper. When Gable arranges something akin to the St. Valentine's Day Massacre, Bakewell's investigative reporting of the situation produces fatal results. The Hays Office had a problem with Crawford and friends appearing in their underwear. Cast notes: Gable was just starting out at MGM, which is why he was billed sixth; the William Holden here is not THE William Holden, and Edwards went on to provide the voice of Jiminy Cricket in "Pinocchio." **82m/B VHS, Beta.** Joan Crawford, Lester Vail, Cliff Edwards, William "Billy" Bakewell, Clark Gable; ***D:*** Harry Beaumont; ***C:*** Charles Rosher. *MGM, FCT*

Dance, Girl, Dance ☠☠ **1940** The private lives and romances of a wartime nightclub dance troupe. Standard Hollywood potpourri of dance, drama, comedy. ♫Mother, What Do I Do Now?; Jitterbug Bite; Morning Star. **88m/B VHS, Beta, LV.** Maureen O'Hara, Louis Hayward, Lucille Ball, Virginia Field, Ralph Bellamy, Maria Ouspenskaya, Mary Carlisle, Katherine Alexander, Edward Brophy; ***D:*** Dorothy Arzner. *TTC*

The Dance Goes On ☠☠ **1992** After the death of an uncle, Keach and his estranged son Almond reunite at the old Quebec family farm left to them. The father is country-bred and appreciates the property but his Los Angeles-reared son wants to sell for a quick profit. Director Almond cast his own son in the starring role as well as ex-wife Bujold, who plays the ambitious showbiz mother. **104m/C VHS.** James Keach, Matt Almond, Genevieve Bujold, Cary Lawrence; ***D:*** Paul Almond; ***W:*** Paul Almond. *MNC*

Dance Hall ½ **1941** A Pennsylvania dance hall owner is propelled into romantic confusion with the introduction of a sultry blond dancer into his club. **73m/B VHS, Beta.** Cesar Romero, Carole Landis, William Henry, June Storey, Charles Halton; ***D:*** Irving Pichel. *NOS, BAR, HEG*

Dance Hall Racket **1958** A sleazy, stilted expose of dance hall vice featuring a brief appearance by Bruce and his wife, Harlow. **60m/B VHS, Beta.** Lenny Bruce, Honey Harlow; ***D:*** Phil Tucker. *DVT, HEG*

Dance Macabre **1991 (R)** Englund takes on a dual role as a man with a split personality—one of whom is deadly. Jessica, an American ballerina, enrolls in a Russian dance academy and meets mesmerizing choreographer, Anthony. Unfortunately for Jessica she happens to look exactly like Anthony's long-dead lover and he becomes obsessed with her. Also, her fellow dancers are being brutally murdered. Are the events connected? **97m/C VHS, LV.** Robert Englund, Michelle Zeitlin, Marianna Moen, Julene Renee, Alexander Sergeyev; ***D:*** Greydon Clark; ***W:*** Greydon Clark. *COL*

Dance Me Outside ½ **1995 (R)** Native Canadian teens look for some excitement on their Northern Ontario reservation and find themselves cut off from their tradition-bound parents in this slice of life drama. Friends Silas and Blackie plot revenge against a white who murdered a native girl while Silas' sister Illianna comes to visit from Toronto, with her Yuppie lawyer husband, just as her ex-boyfriend returns from a prison stint. Based on the novel by W.P. Kinsella. **91m/C VHS, LV.** *CA* Ryan Black, Adam Beach, Michael Greyeyes, Lisa Lacroix; ***D:*** Bruce McDonald; ***W:*** Bruce McDonald, Don McKellar, John Frizzell. Genie Awards '95: Best Film Editing. *APX*

Dance of Death *Woof! House of Evil; Macabre Serenade* **1968** Just before his death, Karloff agreed to appear in footage for four Mexican cheapies that were practically thrown together (Karloff actually filmed his scenes in Los Angeles). If they had mixed the footage instead of matched it, the flicks couldn't be any worse. This one concerns a lunatic toy-maker whose toys kill and maim his heirs. **89m/C VHS, Beta.** *MX* Boris Karloff, Julissa, Andres Garcia, Jack Hill; ***D:*** Juan Ibanez. *SNC, MPI*

Dance of Death **1984** A girl learns kung fu and kills many warriors by kicking them in the ribs and head. **81m/C VHS, Beta.** Mao Ying, Shih Tien, Shiao Bou-Lo, Chien Pay, Chia Kai, Noh Tikki. *UNI*

Dance of Life ½ **1929** A look at the backstage goings-on at a burlesque theater. A successful entertainer's life goes down the tubes when he hits the bottle. His wife leaves him because of his philandering, but returns when she sees how much he really needs her. One scene of the Ziegfeld Follies uses two-tone Technicolor technology. This was remade twice: as "Swing High, Swing Low" in 1937 and as "When My Baby Smiles at Me" in 1948. Carroll replaced the stage lead, who was said to have no "name recognition"—Barbara Stanwyck. ♫True Blue Lou; King of Jazzmania; Cuddlesome Baby; Flippity Flop; Ladies of the Dance; The Mightiest Matador; Sweet Rosie O'Grady; In the Gloaming; Sam, the Accordion Man. **115m/B VHS.** Nancy Carroll, Hal Skelly, Ralph Theadore, Charles D. Brown, Dorothy Revier, Al "Fuzzy" St. John, Oscar Levant; ***D:*** John Cromwell. *NOS, MLB*

Dance of the Damned **1988 (R)** A case where low-budget isn't synonymous with bomb. Fascinating noir-ish plot concerning a vampire who wants to learn more about the life of his next victim, a deep-thinking stripper, who has lost the will to live it. Surprisingly well-done and acted; above-par for this genre. **83m/C VHS, Beta, LV.** Cyril O'Reilly, Starr Andreeff; ***D:*** Katt Shea Ruben; ***W:*** Katt Shea Ruben, Andy Ruben. *NO*

Dance or Die **1987** Just goes to show that in Las Vegas you can't have your dance and drugs too, because if the Mob doesn't get you, the Feds will. Made for video (though maybe it shouldn't have been made at all). In HiFi Stereo. **90m/C VHS, Beta.** Ray Kieffer, Rebecca Barrington; ***D:*** Richard W. Munchkin. *NO*

Dance with a Stranger ½ **1985 (R)** The engrossing and factual story of Ruth Ellis who gained notoriety as the last woman hanged in Great Britain. This emotional and sometimes violent film mirrors the sensationalism produced in the 1950s. The film follows Ellis's pre-trial life and her perpetual struggle to maintain her independence. Newcomer Richardson portrays the Marilyn Monroe look-alike barmaid. **101m/C VHS, Beta, LV.** *GB* Miranda Richardson, Rupert Everett, Ian Holm, Joanne Whalley; ***D:*** Mike Newell; ***W:*** Shelagh Delaney. Cannes Film Festival '85: Best Film. *VES, LIV*

Dance with Death **1991 (R)** When strippers turn up brutally murdered, a young journalist goes undercover to solve the case. **90m/C VHS, LV.** Maxwell Caulfield, Barbara Alyn Jones, Martin Mull, Drew Snyder, Catya Sassoon; ***D:*** Charles Philip Moore. *HBO*

Dance with Me, Henry ½ **1956** When Lou becomes involved with Bud's gambling debts and the local district attorney turns up dead, Lou's not only wanted by the law, but by the mafia as well. This was the great comedy duo's last picture together and it's clear the pair are not happy about working with each other, even on this mediocre effort. **90m/B VHS.** Bud Abbott, Lou Costello, Gigi Perreau, Rusty Hamer, Mary Wickes, Ted de Corsia; ***D:*** Charles T. Barton. *MGM*

Dance with Us: A Creative Movement Video **199?** Instructs as well as entertains as kids learn coordination through creative dance movements set to music. **25m/C VHS.**

Dancers ½ **1987 (PG)** During the filming of the ballet "Giselle" in Italy, a famous, almost-over-the-hill dancer (Baryshnikov, ten years after his role in "The Turning Point") coaches a young, inexperienced starlet. He hopes to revitalize his life and his dancing. Features dancers from the Baryshnikov-led American Ballet Theatre. **99m/C VHS, Beta, LV.** Mikhail Baryshnikov, Leslie Browne, Julie Kent, Mariangela Melato, Alessandra Ferri, Lynn Seymour, Victor Barbee, Tommy Rall; ***D:*** Herbert Ross; ***M:*** Pino Donaggio. *CTH, WAR, FCT*

Dances with Wolves ½ **1990 (PG-13)** The story of a U.S. Army soldier, circa 1870, whose heroism in battle allows him his pick of posts. His choice, to see the West before it disappears, changes his life. He meets, understands and eventually becomes a member of a Lakota Sioux tribe in the Dakotas. Costner's first directorial attempt proves him a talent of vision and intelligence. This sometimes too objective movie lacks a sense of definitive character, undermining its gorgeous scenery and interesting perspective on the plight of Native Americans. Lovely music and epic proportions. Adapted by Blake from his novel. **181m/C VHS, Beta, LV.** Kevin Costner, Mary McDonnell, Graham Greene, Rodney Grant, Floyd "Red Crow" Westerman, Tantoo Cardinal, Robert Pastorelli, Charles Rocket, Maury Chaykin, Jimmy Herman, Nathan Lee Chasing His Horse, Wes Studi; ***D:*** Kevin Costner; ***W:*** Michael Blake; ***C:*** Dean Semler; ***M:*** John Barry. Academy Awards '90: Best Adapted Screenplay, Best Cinematography, Best Director (Costner), Best Film Editing, Best Picture, Best Sound, Best Score; Directors Guild of America Awards '90: Best Director (Costner); Golden Globe Awards '91: Best Director (Costner), Best Film—Drama, Best Screenplay; National Board of Review Awards '90: 10 Best Films of the Year, Best Director (Costner); Nominations: Academy Awards '90: Best Actor (Costner), Best Art Direction/Set Decoration, Best Costume Design, Best Supporting Actor (Greene), Best Supporting Actress (McDonnell), Best Original Score. *ORI, FCT, IME*

Dancing in the Dark ½ **1986 (PG-13)** An interesting but slow-moving Canadian film about the perfect housewife who learns that after 20 years of devotion to him, her spouse has been unfaithful. Realizing how her life has been wasted she murders her husband and, in the end, suffers a mental breakdown. **93m/C VHS, Beta.** *CA* Martha Henry, Neil Munro, Rosemary Dunsmore, Richard Monette; ***D:*** Leon Marr; ***W:*** Leon Marr; ***M:*** Erik Satie. Genie Awards '87: Best Actress (Henry). *VTR, NWV*

Dancing Lady ½ **1933** Rarely seen film is MGM's answer to "42nd Street," with Crawford as a small-time hoofer trying to break into Broadway. The screen debuts of Astaire and Eddy. ♫Everything I Have Is Yours; Heigh-Ho! The Gang's All Here; Hold Your Man; That's the Rhythm of the Day; My Dancing Lady; Let's Go Bavarian; Hey Young Fella. **93m/B VHS, Beta.** Clark Gable, Joan Crawford, Fred Astaire, Franchot Tone, Nelson Eddy, Ted Healy, Moe Howard, Shemp Howard, Larry Fine; ***D:*** Robert Z. Leonard. *MGM, TTC, FCT*

Dancing Man ½ **1933** A gigolo romances both mother and daughter and winds up implicated in murder as a result. Dismissable. **65m/B VHS, Beta, 8mm.** Judith Allen, Reginald Denny, Natalie Moorhead; ***D:*** Albert Ray. *VYY*

Dancing Mothers ½ **1926** A fast-living woman becomes involved with her mother's roguish boyfriend in this silent film with accompanying musical score. **85m/B VHS, Beta.** Clara Bow, Alice Joyce, Conway Tearle, Donald Keith; ***D:*** Herbert Brenon. *NOS, MRV, DVT*

Dancing Pirate **1936** A Boston dance instructor is kidnapped by pirates and jumps ship in Mexico, where he romances a mayor's daughter. The silly story boasts some Rodgers and Hart tunes, plus the early use of Technicolor, exploited here for all it was worth and then some. ♫Are You My Love?; When You're Dancing the Waltz. **83m/C VHS.** Charles Collins, Frank Morgan, Steffi Duna, Luis Alberni, Victor Varconi, Jack LaRue; ***D:*** Lloyd Corrigan. *NOS, LOO*

The Dancing Princesses **1984** When five naughty princesses wear the soles of their slippers out every night, their father the King must foot the bill. He soon tires of this expense and offers a reward to the person who can discover how this happens. A handsome prince becomes invisible to follow the lovely ladies and discover their secret. From the "Faerie Tale Theatre" series. Made for television. **60m/C VHS, Beta.** Lesley Ann Warren, Peter Weller, Sachi Parker, Roy Dotrice; ***D:*** Peter Medak. *FOX, FCT*

Dancing with Danger ½ **1993 (PG-13)** A private investigator is hired to find out why a taxi dancer's customers all end up dead. Soon the PI's employer is the next victim of a serial killer whose ultimate target is the dancer herself. **90m/C VHS, Beta.** Cheryl Ladd, Ed Marinaro, Miguel Sandoval, Pat Skipper; ***D:*** Stuart Cooper; ***W:*** Elisa Bell. *PAR*

Dandelions **1974** German soft-core flick starring Hauer in an early role as a man jilted by his wife. To make himself feel better he decides to explore the sleazier side of life. Meaningless film evokes no sympathy but some may appreciate the titillation. Dubbed. **92m/C VHS, Beta.** *GE* Rutger Hauer, Dagmar Lassander; ***D:*** Adrian Hoven. *NO*

Dandy in Aspic ½ **1968 (R)** A double-agent is assigned to kill himself in this hard to follow British spy drama. The film is based on Derek Marlowe's novel. Mann died midway through shooting and Harvey finished direction. **107m/C VHS, Beta, LV.** *GB* Laurence Harvey, Tom Courtenay, Lionel Stander, Mia Farrow, Harry Andrews, Peter Cook, Per Oscarsson; ***D:*** Anthony Mann; ***M:*** Quincy Jones. *COL*

Danger Ahead **1940** Newill stars again as Renfrew of the Mounties—this time he tries to rid the north woods of the baddies who are trying to take over. **57m/B VHS.** James Newill, Dorothea Kent, Guy Usher, Dave O'Brien, Bob Terry; ***D:*** Ralph Staub. *DVT, HEG*

Danger: Diabolik *Diabolik* **1968 (PG-13)** A superthief called Diabolik (Law) continuously evades the law while performing his criminal antics. **99m/C VHS.** *IT* John Phillip Law, Marisa Mell, Michel Piccoli, Terry-Thomas; ***D:*** Mario Bava; ***M:*** Ennio Morricone. *PAR*

Danger in the Skies ½ *The Pilot* **1979 (PG)** An alcoholic airline pilot tries to straighten out his life when he nearly loses everything while drinking on the job. Made for cable television. **99m/C VHS, Beta.** Cliff Robertson, Diane Baker, Dana Andrews, Gordon MacRae, Milo O'Shea, Frank Converse, Edward Binns; ***D:*** Cliff Robertson; ***C:*** Walter Lassally. *HHE*

Danger Lights 🦴½ **1930** Depicts the railroads and the railroad men's dedication to each other and their trains. **73m/B VHS, Beta.** Jean Arthur, Louis Wolheim, Robert Armstrong; ***D:*** George B. Seitz. *PEN, MRV, NOS*

Danger Man **1961** British tv series starring McGoohan as NATO agent John Drake. Half-hour episodes were known as "Danger Man" in England, when the series went to 60 minutes the title was changed to "Secret Agent" with the premise remaining the same. Additional episodes available. **30m/B VHS.** *GB* Patrick McGoohan. *MPI, MOV*

Danger of Love 🦴½ **1995 (R)** Married teacher Michael Carlin (Penny) has an affair with seductive colleague Carolyn Warmus (Robertson) but when he's about to end it, his wife is murdered. The detective (Bologna) thinks Michael is guilty but it's Carolyn who's hiding all the secrets. Based on a true story; made for TV. **95m/C VHS.** Joe Penny, Jenny Robertson, Joseph Bologna, Richard Lewis; ***D:*** Joyce Chopra. *VMK*

Danger on the Air 🦴🦴 **1938** A radio program sponsor—a much-despised misogynist—is murdered, and the sound engineer attempts to solve the mystery. Features Cobb in one of his earliest roles; Garrett also directed "Lady in the Morgue" that year. **70m/B VHS, Beta.** Donald Woods, Nan Grey, Berton Churchill, Jed Prouty, William Lundigan, Richard "Skeets" Gallagher, Edward Van Sloan, George Meeker, Lee J. Cobb, Johnny Arthur, Linda Hayes, Louise Stanley; ***D:*** Otis Garrett. *SNC*

Danger Trails 🦴½ **1935** Rehashed western programmer. Features the hero who must save the rancher's honor as well as the ranch, while fighting detestable hombres with the traditional fare as an arsenal. **55m/B VHS.** Guinn "Big Boy" Williams, Marjorie Gordon, Wally Wales, John Elliott, Ace Cain, Edmund Cobb; ***D:*** Robert F. "Bob" Hill. *NOS, DVT, GPV*

Danger UXB 🦴🦴½ **1981** During the 1940 London blitz "Danger UXB" was scrawled wherever there was, or thought to be, an unexploded German bomb. This miniseries covers the exploits of the Royal Engineers whose job it was, with little training and lots of nerve, to defuse the bombs. Based on the memoirs of Major A.B. Hartley of the Royal Engineers. On five cassettes. Made for television. **660m/C VHS.** *GB* Anthony Andrews, Judy Geeson, Maurice Roeves, Kenneth Cranham, Jeremy Sinden, Iain Cuthbertson, George Innes, Norman Chappell, Kenneth Farrington, Gordon Kane, Ken Kitson, Robert Longden, Robert Pugh, Deborah Watling. *SIG, TVC, FUS*

Danger Zone 🦴🦴 **1951** A man is hired to bid for a saxophone at an auction and then has the instrument stolen from him. He discovers it contained stolen jewelry and tries to recover it. **56m/B VHS, Beta, LV.** Hugh Beaumont, Tom Neal, Richard Travis, Virginia Dale. *NO*

Danger Zone *Woof!* **1987 (R)** A low-budget, low-brow flick about an all-female rock band whose bus breaks down in the middle of the desert, leaving the girls to defend themselves against a merciless motorcycle gang. You'll wish this one was a mirage. **90m/C VHS, Beta.** Robert Canada, Jason Williams, Kriss Braxton, Dana Dowell, Jamie Ferreira; ***D:*** Henry Vernon. *NLC*

Danger Zone 2 🦴 **1989 (R)** A pernicious biker is released from prison on a technicality and decides to pay a social call to the undercover cop who set him up. **95m/C VHS.** Jason Williams, Robert Random; ***D:*** Geoffrey G. Bowers; ***W:*** Dulany Ross Clements. *MCG*

Danger Zone 3: Steel Horse War 🦴 **1990 (R)** The "Danger Zone" dude is back and this time he's taken on a bevy of biker-types in a most gruesome battle to make our deserts safe. **91m/C VHS, Beta.** Jason Williams, Robert Random, Barne Suboski, Juanita Ranney, Rusty Cooper, Giles Ashford; ***D:*** Douglas Bronco. *PMR*

Dangerous 🦴🦴½ **1935** Davis won her first Oscar for her rather overdone portrayal of a has-been alcoholic actress reformed by a smitten architect who recognizes her from her days as a star. **72m/B VHS, Beta, LV.** Bette Davis, Franchot Tone, Margaret Lindsay, Alison Skipworth, John Eldridge, Dick Foran; ***D:*** Alfred E. Green. Academy Awards '35: Best Actress (Davis). *MGM, BTV*

The Dangerous 🦴½ **1995 (R)** New Orleans' seamy underworld is the setting for a hot-headed cop (Pare), a mystery man (Davi), and the beauty (Barbieri) they're both interested in. Also available unrated. **96m/C VHS, LV.** Robert Davi, Michael Pare, Paula Barbieri, Elliott Gould, John Savage, Joel Grey; ***D:*** Maria Dante, Rod Hewitt; ***W:*** Rod Hewitt. *ORI*

A Dangerous Age 🦴½ **1957** A young girl, hoping to marry her lover, runs away from boarding school. **?m/C VHS.** Ben Piazza, Ann Pearson. *SNC*

Dangerous Appointment 🦴🦴 **1934** Story of an innocent store clerk accused of theft and attempted murder. **?m/C VHS.** Charles Starrett, Dorothy Wilson. *SNC*

Dangerous Charter 🦴½ **1962** A group of fishermen discover a deserted yacht and man its helm. But their good fortune takes a decided turn for the worst as they become caught in mob-propelled danger. **76m/C VHS, Beta.** Chris Warfield, Sally Fraser, Richard Foote, Peter Foster, Wright King; ***D:*** Robert Gottschalk. *NOS, ACA*

Dangerous Curves 🦴½ **1988 (PG)** Two friends are assigned to deliver a new Porsche to a billionaire's daughter - one of them talks the other into taking a little detour, and the trouble begins. This one went straight to video. **93m/C VHS, Beta.** Robert Stack, Tate Donovan, Danielle von Zerneck, Robert Klein, Elizabeth Ashley, Leslie Nielsen; ***D:*** David Lewis. *VES, LIV*

Dangerous Game 🦴½ **1990 (R)** A computer hacker leads his friends through a department store's security system, only to find they can't get out until morning. They soon discover they are not alone when one of the group turns up dead. **102m/C VHS, Beta, LV.** Miles Buchanan, Sandy Lillingston, Kathryn Walker, John Polson; ***D:*** Stephen Hopkins. *ACD*

Dangerous Game 🦴🦴 *Snake Eyes* **1993 (R)** Abrasive filmmaker Eddie Israel's (Keitel) new movie is about a couple's disintegrating marriage turning violent. Stars Sarah (Madonna) and Francis (Russo) find the on-camera violence spilling over into their tangled private lives while Eddie finds his personal traumas intruding more and more into the fictional material. Very raw movie within a movie features volatile Keitel (who also worked with Ferrera on "Bad Lieutenant") and suitably histrionic Russo; Madonna manages to hold her own in the least showy role, a cinematic first. Eddie's betrayed and bewildered wife is sympathetically portrayed by Ferrara, director Abel's wife. Also available in an unrated version. **107m/C VHS, LV.** Harvey Keitel, James Russo, Madonna, Nancy Ferrara; ***D:*** Abel Ferrara; ***W:*** Nicholas St. John. *MGM*

Dangerous Heart 🦴🦴 **1993 (R)** A crooked undercover cop steals a bundle from a drug dealer and gets himself killed for his troubles. Only the dealer doesn't know where the money is. So he decides to befriend the cop's widow, get romantically involved, and see what she knows. **93m/C VHS, LV.** Timothy Daly, Lauren Holly, Jeffrey Nordling, Alice Carter, Joe Pantoliano; ***D:*** Michael Scott; ***W:*** Patrick Cirillo. *MCA*

Dangerous Holiday 🦴🦴 **1937** A young violin prodigy would rather be just "one of the boys" than be forced to practice all the time. He decides to run away but has everyone in an uproar thinking he's been kidnapped. **54m/B VHS, Beta.** Hedda Hopper, Guinn "Big Boy" Williams, Jack LaRue, Franklin Pangborn, Grady Sutton. *VYY*

Dangerous Hours 🦴🦴 **1919** An anti-communist propaganda film with Hughes as the innocent young college boy who gets duped by the evil Marxists until he realizes the truth of his all-American upbringing. Silent with original organ score. **88m/B VHS, Beta, 8mm.** Lloyd Hughes; ***D:*** Fred Niblo; ***C:*** George Barnes. *VYY, FCT, GPV*

Dangerous Indiscretion 🦴🦴 **1994 (R)** Ad exec finds his girlfriend is actually a woman married to a very powerful man, who's not going to be happy to find out about their liaison. **81m/C VHS.** Joan Severance, C. Thomas Howell, Malcolm McDowell; ***D:*** Richard Kletter; ***W:*** Richard Kletter, Jack Tarpon; ***M:*** Richard Gibbs. *PAR*

Dangerous Liaisons 🦴🦴 *Les Liaisons Dangereuses; Dangerous Love Affairs* **1960** A couple take each other to the brink of destruction via their insatiable desire for extra-marital affairs. Vadim attempted to repeat his success with Brigitte Bardot by featuring wife Annette as a new sex goddess, but lightning didn't strike twice. **111m/B VHS, LV.** *FR IT* Gerard Philipe, Jeanne Moreau, Jeanne Valeri, Annette Vadim, Simone Renant, Jean-Louis Trintignant, Nikolas Vogel; ***D:*** Roger Vadim; ***W:*** Roger Vadim. *INT, APD, INJ*

Dangerous Liaisons 🦴🦴🦴 **1988 (R)** Stylish and absorbing, this adaptation of the Laclos novel and the Christopher Hampton play centers around the relationship of two decadent members of 18th-century French nobility. The two, Close and Malkovich, spend their time testing and manipulating the loves of others. They find love often has a will of its own. Possibly the best of the several versions available. Interesting to comparison-view with director Milos Forman's version of this story, 1989's "Valmont." **120m/C VHS, Beta, LV, 8mm.** John Malkovich, Glenn Close, Michelle Pfeiffer, Uma Thurman, Keanu Reeves, Swoosie Kurtz, Mildred Natwick, Peter Capaldi; ***D:*** Stephen Frears; ***W:*** Christopher Hampton; ***C:*** Philippe Rousselot; ***M:*** George Fenton. Academy Awards '88: Best Adapted Screenplay, Best Art Direction/Set Decoration, Best Costume Design; British Academy Awards '89: Best Adapted Screenplay, Best Supporting Actress (Pfeiffer); Writers Guild of America '88: Best Adapted Screenplay; Nominations: Academy Awards '88: Best Actress (Close), Best Picture, Best Supporting Actress (Pfeiffer), Best Original Score. *WAR, FCT*

Dangerous Life 🦴🦴 **1989** Explosive drama brings to the screen the story of the Philippine uprising. It shows the horrible events that lead to the fall of Marcos and permitted the rise of Corazon Aquino. **163m/C VHS, Beta, LV.** Gary Busey; ***W:*** David Williamson. *NO*

Dangerous Love *Woof!* **1987** Advice to the lovelorn: Avoid this one. Female members of a video dating service are being filmed in a death scene—their own. **87m/C VHS, Beta.** Lawrence Monoson, Brenda Bakke, Peter Marc, Elliott Gould, Anthony Geary; ***D:*** Marty Ollstein. *MED*

A Dangerous Man: Lawrence after Arabia 🦴🦴🦴 **1991** At the 1919 Paris Peace Conference, T.E. Lawrence serves as the liaison to the Hashemite delegation in an effort to have the Allies agree to Arab independence. He finds the diplomatic fields more treacherous than anything he encountered during WWI. Fiennes does well in the difficult role of the reluctant, ambivalent hero. Made for television. **104m/C VHS.** *GB* Ralph Fiennes, Denis Quilley, Alexander Siddig, Nicholas Jones, Roger Hammond, Peter Copley, Paul Freeman, Polly Walker; ***D:*** Christopher Menaul; ***W:*** Tim Rose Price. *PBS*

Dangerous Minds 🦴🦴½ *My Posse Don't Do Homework* **1995 (R)** Based on the autobiography of LouAnne Johnson (Pfeiffer), a 10-year Marine turned inspirational inner-city high school English teacher. Naturally, Johnson has to take on the establishment educational system to fight for her kids. If you can buy Pfeiffer as an ex-jarhead, a tough teacher should be no problem. A subplot romance involving Pfeiffer and Andy Garcia was cut from the film to focus on the teacher/student byplay (which seems a real shame); Elaine May did a uncredited script rewrite. Kinda squishy and surprisingly successful. **99m/C VHS, LV.** Michelle Pfeiffer, George Dzundza, Courtney B. Vance, Robin Bartlett, Renoly Santiago, Lorraine Toussaint; ***Cameos:*** John Neville; ***D:*** John N. Smith; ***W:*** Ronald Bass; ***C:*** Pierre Letarte. Blockbuster Entertainment Awards '96: Drama Actress, Theatrical (Pfeiffer); Nominations: MTV Movie Awards '96: Best Film, Best Female Performance (Pfeiffer), Most Desirable Female (Pfeiffer), Best Song ("Gangsta's Paradise"). *TOU*

Dangerous Mission 🦴½ **1954** A young woman witnesses a mob murder in New York and flees to the Midwest, pursued by killers and the police. Good cast couldn't do much with this one. **75m/B VHS, Beta.** Victor Mature, Piper Laurie, Vincent Price, William Bendix; **D:** Louis King; **W:** W.R. Burnett, Charles Bennett. *MED*

Dangerous Moonlight *Suicide Squadron* **1941** Polish concert pianist becomes a bomber pilot for the British in WWII, though his wife wants him to stay at the piano. Great battle and music sequences; the piece "Warsaw Concerto" became a soundtrack hit. **97m/B VHS, Beta.** *GB* Anton Walbrook, Sally Gray, Derrick DeMarney, Cecil Parker, Percy Parsons, Keneth Kent, Guy Middleton, John Laurie, Frederick Valk; **D:** Brian Desmond Hurst. *TTC*

Dangerous Moves *La Diagonale du Fou* **1984 (PG)** A drama built around the World Chess championship competition between a renowned Russian master and a young, rebellious dissident. The chess game serves as both metaphor and background for the social and political tensions it produces. With English subtitles. **96m/C VHS, Beta, LV.** *SI* Liv Ullmann, Michel Piccoli, Leslie Caron, Alexandre Arbatt; **D:** Richard Dembo; **W:** Richard Dembo. Academy Awards '84: Best Foreign Language Film. *ORI, IME*

Dangerous Obsession *Divine Obsession; Mortal Sins* **1988 (R)** A woman kidnaps the doctor she blames for her boyfriend's death and instead of exacting revenge, she makes him her personal sex slave. In the case of this flick, it's really a fate worse than death. **81m/C VHS.** *IT* Corinne Clery, Brett Halsey; **D:** Lucio Fulci; **M:** Simon Boswell. *AIP*

Dangerous Orphans ½ **1986 (R)** Not completely awful tale of three brothers, orphaned as boys when their father is murdered before their very eyes, and the vendetta they have against the killer. **90m/C VHS, Beta.** *NZ* Peter Stevens, Peter Bland, Ian Mune, Ross Girven, Jennifer Ward-Lealand; **D:** John Laing. *ACA*

Dangerous Passage **1944** A ne'er-do-well inherits 200 grand but gets in trouble before he can collect it. He ends up falling in with assorted misfits aboard a tramp steamer. **60m/B VHS, Beta, 8mm.** Robert Lowery, Phyllis Brooks, Jack LaRue, Victor Kilian; **D:** William (Lester Williams) Berke. *VYY*

Dangerous Passion ½ **1995** Underworld figure gets a promotion from his lethal boss and finds himself in the unenviable position of becoming involved with the ruthless guy's beautiful wife. **94m/C VHS.** Billy Dee Williams, Carl Weathers, Lonette McKee; **D:** Michael Miller. *LIV*

A Dangerous Place ½ **1994 (R)** Teenaged Ethan (Roberts) joins a karate team to prove his older brother's death was not a suicide. But the Scorpion's leader (Feldman) has a definite mean streak. **97m/C VHS, LV.** Ted Jan Roberts, Corey Feldman, Mako, Erin Gray, Dick Van Patten; **D:** Jerry P. Jacobs. *PMH*

Dangerous Prey ½ **1995 (R)** Young woman, looking for adventure while vacationing in Europe, gets more than she bargained for when she gets mixed up with a high-tech training school for female mercenaries. **93m/C VHS.** Shannon Whirry, Ciara Hunter; **D:** Lloyd A. Simanol. *MNC*

Dangerous Pursuit **1989** A woman discovers that a man she slept with years ago is an assassin. Knowing too much, she finds herself next on his hit list. Decent psycho-thriller that was never released theatrically. **95m/C VHS, Beta, LV.** Gregory Harrison, Alexandra Powers, Scott Valentine, Brian Wimmer, Elena Stiteler; **D:** Sandor Stern. *PAR*

Dangerous Relations ½ *Father & Son: Dangerous Relations* **1993 (PG-13)** Made for TV drama with Gossett as a tough convict at the end of 15-year prison sentence whose authority is challenged by young punk prisoner Underwood. Imagine his surprise when the old con realizes the punk is the son he hasn't seen since he started his time behind bars. Things don't improve (well, not at first) when they are paroled into each other's custody. **93m/C VHS.** Louis Gossett Jr., Blair Underwood, Rae Dawn Chong, Clarence Williams III. *ACA*

Dangerous Summer *The Burning Man* **1982** In Australia, an American businessman building a resort is the victim of elaborate arson/murder insurance schemes. **100m/C VHS, Beta.** *AU* Tom Skerritt, James Mason, Ian Gilmour, Wendy Hughes; **D:** Quentin Masters; **W:** David Ambrose. *NO*

Dangerous Touch ½ **1994 (R)** A very charming sociopath seduces a radio host/therapist into a willing, if kinky, sexual relationship. But everything she values is put at risk when he threatens to show an incriminating video tape if she doesn't continue to do as he demands. An unrated version is also available. **101m/C VHS, LV.** Lou Diamond Phillips, Kate Vernon; **D:** Lou Diamond Phillips. *VMK*

Dangerous When Wet **1953** A typical Williams water-musical. A farm girl dreams of fame by swimming the English Channel. One famous number pairs Williams with cartoon characters Tom & Jerry in an underwater frolic. ♫I Got Out of Bed on the Right Side; Ain't Nature Grand; I Like Men; Fifi; In My Wildest Dreams. **96m/C VHS, Beta, LV.** Esther Williams, Fernando Lamas, Charlotte Greenwood, William Demarest, Jack Carson; **D:** Charles Walters; **M:** Arthur Schwartz, Johnny Mercer. *MGM*

A Dangerous Woman **1993 (R)** No, this isn't the femme fatale romance the word "dangerous" suggests. Instead, the eponymous character is a mildly retarded woman, Martha (Winger), whose simplistic view on life places her in ethically compromising positions. When a hunky Irish handyman (Byrne) comes on the scene and seduces both her and the aunt with whom she lives (Hershey), Martha awakens to feelings she has never experienced. Winger's performance is both sensitive and provocative, but is wasted in a film filled with two-dimensional characters, and really, not too much of a point. Adapted from a novel by Mary McGarry Morris. Screenplay by Foner, wife of director Gyllenhaal. **101m/C VHS, LV.** Debra Winger, Barbara Hershey, Gabriel Byrne, David Strathairn, Chloe Webb, John Terry, Jan Hooks, Paul Dooley, Viveka Davis, Richard Riehle, Laurie Metcalf; **D:** Stephen Gyllenhaal; **W:** Naomi Foner; **M:** Carter Burwell. Golden Globe Awards '94: Best Actress—Drama (Winger). *MCA*

Dangerous Youth *These Dangerous Years* **1958** Would-be Liverpool rocker Vaughan is drafted into the army where he becomes a man. He gets into trouble, goes AWOL, but manages to set things right. The Brit version of the troubled-teen exploitation flick. **97m/B VHS.** *GB* Frankie Vaughan, George Baker, Carole Lesley, Jackie Lane, Eddie Byrne, Thora Hird; **D:** Herbert Wilcox; **W:** Jack Trevor Story. *SNC*

Dangerously Close ½ **1986 (R)** A group of anti-crime high school students organize a hall monitoring gang that becomes a group of neo-fascist disciplinarian elite. **96m/C VHS, Beta.** John Stockwell, Carey Lowell, J. Eddie Peck; **D:** Albert Pyun; **C:** Walt Lloyd. *MED*

Daniel ½ **1983 (R)** The children of a couple who were executed for espionage (patterned after the Rosenbergs) struggle with their past in the dissident 1960s. So-so adaptation of E.L. Doctorow's "The Book of Daniel." **130m/C VHS, Beta.** Timothy Hutton, Amanda Plummer, Mandy Patinkin, Lindsay Crouse, Ed Asner, Ellen Barkin; **D:** Sidney Lumet. *PAR*

Daniel and the Towers **199?** Daniel and his friends enjoy making fun of Sam, the man who is building glass towers in Watts, California. But when Daniel must pay for the repairs of a shopkeeper's window, he turns to Sam for help. Sam agrees to fix the windows if Daniel helps him collect glass for the towers. In the process, Sam and Daniel become friends and Sam teaches Daniel valuable lessons about beauty and determination. Although this story is fictional, the glass towers, built by Sam Rodia, really stand in Watts. A viewers' guide is included. Part of the "Wonderworks" series. **58m/C VHS.** Allan Arbus, Michael McKean, Carmen Zapata, Miguel Alamo; **D:** Paul Schneider. *PME, BTV*

Daniel Boone ½ **1934** Daniel Boone guides a party of settlers from North Carolina to the fertile valleys of Kentucky, facing Indians, food shortages and bad weather along the way. O'Brien turns in a fine performance as the early American frontier hero. **75m/B VHS, Beta.** George O'Brien, Heather Angel, John Carradine; **D:** David Howard. *NOS, MRV, VCN*

Daniel Boone: Trail Blazer ½ **1956** Low-budget, though surprisingly well-acted rendition of the frontiersman's heroics, filmed in Mexico. **75m/B VHS.** Bruce (Herman Brix) Bennett, Lon Chaney Jr., Faron Young, Damian O'Flynn, Fred Kohler Jr., Claudio Brook, Kem Dibbs; **D:** Ismael Rodriguez, Albert C. Gannaway; **W:** John Patrick, Tom Hubbard. *NOS, MRV, REP*

Danielle Steel's Changes ½ *Changes* **1991** Ladd is a successful, divorced New York television anchorwoman who turns her life upside-down when she marries an equally successful, widowed Los Angeles surgeon (Nouri). Can they overcome their bicoastal careers to make things work? What do you think. Made for television. **96m/C VHS.** Cheryl Ladd, Michael Nouri, Christopher Gartin, Randee Heller, Charles Frank, James Sloyan, Cynthia Bain; **D:** Charles Jarrott. *CMB, WOV*

Danielle Steel's "Daddy" ½ *Daddy* **1992** Ad exec Oliver Watson (Duffy) is happily married to Sarah (Mulgrew) and living the good life with their three kids—or so he thinks. Then Sarah announces she's leaving and Oliver's left to cope with family crisis as a single parent. A move to a new job in LA finds Oliver falling for an actress (Carter) and wondering if his family can ever be put back together again. Made for television. **95m/C VHS.** Patrick Duffy, Lynda Carter, Kate Mulgrew; **D:** Michael Miller. *CMB, WOV*

Danielle Steel's Heartbeat ½ *Heartbeat* **1993** Shameless soap opera with Draper as Adrian Townsend, an L.A. TV-news producer with a self-involved ad-exec hubby (Kilner) who never wants children because of his own lousy childhood. When Adrian gets preggers the louse dumps her and she's left to weep prettily. That is until lovable divorced dad Bill Grant (Ritter) comes along to dry her eyes. Predictable and glossy adaptation of the Steel best-seller. Made for television. **95m/C VHS.** Polly Draper, John Ritter, Kevin Kilner, Michael Lembeck, Nancy Morgan, Victor Dimattia, Christian Cousins; **D:** Michael Miller; **W:** Jan Worthington. *CMB*

Danielle Steel's Kaleidoscope ½ *Kaleidoscope* **1992** Three sisters are separated in childhood, after the mysterious deaths of their parents. Then a detective is hired to reunite the adult siblings. But Hilary, the eldest, has secrets she doesn't want her sisters to share. Made for television. **96m/C VHS.** Jaclyn Smith, Perry King, Colleen Dewhurst, Donald Moffat; **D:** Jud Taylor. *CMB, WOV*

Danielle Steel's Palomino ½ *Palomino* **1991** Bittersweet romance with Frost as an ambitious photojournalist who gets involved with a headstrong cowboy (Horsley). Their differences drive them apart and tragedy strikes when Frost becomes a paraplegic after a horse-riding accident. This leads her to new goals and the eventual return of her old flame. Between the palomino's blond mane and the equally impressive blond locks of Frost, there's a lot of streaming in the wind hair shots. Horsley's merely tall, dark, and handsome. Made for television. **90m/C VHS.** Lindsay Frost, Lee Horsley, Eva Marie Saint, Rod Taylor, Michelle Greene, Beau Gravitte. *CMB*

Danielle Steel's Star ½ *Star* **1993** Garth is the country girl with big dreams of a singing career but an unhappy love life. She falls for an idealist lawyer (Bierko) but their romance is put on hold by career ambitions. She goes to Hollywood and gets discovered, becoming a singing/acting sensation who's under the thumb of her increasingly obsessed manager, Wass. Meanwhile, Bierko's trapped in a miserable marriage to the wealthy, influential Farrell. Do the true lovers get together? (Take a guess). Although the story spans 15 years and lots of tribulations the young Garth never ages a day. Made for television. **90m/C VHS.** Jennie Garth, Craig Bierko, Ted Wass, Terry Farrell, Penny Fuller, Mitchell Ryan, Jim Haynie; **D:** Michael Miller; **W:** Claire Labine. *CMB*

Danny ☆☆½ **1979 (G)** Charming story of a lonely young girl who receives an injured horse that was no longer fit for the spoiled daughter of the rich owners. **90m/C VHS, Beta.** Rebecca Page, Janet Zarish, Barbara Jean Earhardt, Gloria Maddox, George Luce; ***D:*** Gene Feldman. *MON, WOM, HHE*

Danny Boy ☆½ **1946** Veteran dog, returning from the war, has difficulty adjusting to life back home. Things get worse for him and his young master when Danny Boy is assumed to be shell-shocked and dangerous. One of the few shell-shocked dog stories ever filmed. **67m/B VHS, Beta.** *VYY*

Danny Boy ☆☆☆ **1984 (R)** Takes place in Ireland where a young saxaphonist witnesses a murder and, in an effort to understand it, sets out to find the killer. Thought-provoking film is meant to highlight the continuing struggles in Ireland. **92m/C VHS, Beta.** *IR* Stephen Rea, Veronica Quilligan, Honor Heffernan, Marie Kean, Donal McCann, Ray McAnally; ***D:*** Neil Jordan; ***W:*** Neil Jordan. *COL*

Dante's Inferno ☆☆☆ **1924** Abandon all hope you who watch this film. A one-time friend sends his ruthless capitalist nemesis a copy of Dante's "Inferno," and the man reads the book and dreams he's gone to hell (would that be the dress circle?) A silent film that was controversial in its day: the body-stockinged actors were believed to be nude (which would have made it the first nudie Comedy). **54m/B VHS.** Lawson Butt, Howard Gaye, Ralph Lewis, Pauline Starke, Josef Swickard; ***D:*** Henry Otto. *CNM*

Dante's Inferno: Life of Dante Gabriel Rossetti ☆☆ **1969** The flamboyant life of mid-19th century English Pre-Raphaelite artist/poet Dante Gabriel Rossetti is depicted with the usual Russell flair. The drunken, drug-taking, womanizing Rossetti was part of the leading intellectual group of his age, which included Swinburne, Morris, Ruskin, and Rossetti's sister, the poet Christina Rossetti. **90m/B VHS.** *GB* Oliver Reed; ***D:*** Ken Russell. *INJ, TPV*

Danton ☆☆☆☆ **1982 (PG)** A sweeping account of the reign of terror following the French Revolution. Focuses on the title character (wonderfully portrayed by Depardieu) and is directed with searching parallels to modern-day Poland by that country's premier filmmaker, Andrzej Wajda. Well-done period sets round out a memorable film. In French with English subtitles. **136m/C VHS, Beta, LV.** *PL FR* Gerard Depardieu, Wojciech Pszoniak, Patrice Chereau, Angela Winkler, Boguslaw Linda; ***D:*** Andrzej Wajda; ***W:*** Jean-Claude Carriere, Agnieszka Holland, Boleslaw Michalek, Jacek Gasiorowski, Andrzej Wajda. British Academy Awards '83: Best Foreign Film; Cesar Awards '83: Best Director (Wajda); Montreal World Film Festival '83: Best Actor (Depardieu). *COL, INJ*

Danzon ☆☆☆½ **1991 (PG)** Julia (Rojo), a single, working-class mom escapes the drudgery of her simple existence by going to a Mexico City dance hall every Wednesday. There she loses herself to the movement of the danzon, a dance with Haitian roots, popular in Mexico for over 100 years. When her partner of six years, Carmelo (Rergis), doesn't show up one night, her life is turned upside down. So begins a search for Carmelo—and herself. Quiet and restrained, like the ballroom-style danzon at the center of the plot. Applauded at Cannes. In Spanish with English subtitles. **103m/C VHS.** *SP* Maria Rojo, Carmen Salinas, Blanca Guerra, Tito Vasconcelos, Victor Carpinteiro, Victor Vasconcelos; ***D:*** Maria Novaro; ***W:*** Maria Novaro, Betriz Novaro. *COL, FCT*

Darby O'Gill & the Little People ☆☆☆½ **1959 (G)** Set in Ireland, a roguish old story teller tumbles into a well and visits the land of leprechauns who give him three wishes in order to rearrange his life. When he tries to tell his friends what happened, they think that it is only another one of his stories. A wonderful Disney production (despite its disappointing box-office performance) with wit, charm and an ounce or two of terror. **93m/C VHS, Beta, LV.** Albert Sharpe, Janet Munro, Sean Connery, Estelle Winwood; ***D:*** Robert Stevenson; ***C:*** Winton C. Hoch. *DIS*

Darby's Rangers ☆☆½ *Young Invaders* **1958** WWII pot-boiler with Garner as the leader of a commando team put together for covert operations in North Africa and Italy. Successful battle sequences combine with slow-paced romantic scenes as the soldiers chase women when not chasing the enemy. **122m/B VHS.** James Garner, Jack Warden, Edd Byrnes, Peter Brown, Stuart Whitman, David Janssen, Etchika Choureau, Venetia Stevenson, Torin Thatcher, Joan Elan, Corey Allen, Murray Hamilton; ***D:*** William A. Wellman; ***W:*** Guy Trosper; ***C:*** William Clothier; ***M:*** Max Steiner. *WAR*

Daredevils of the Red Circle **1938** Three young men set out to free a man held prisoner by an escaped convict. A serial in twelve chapters. **195m/B VHS.** Charles Quigley, Bruce (Herman Brix) Bennett, Carole Landis; ***D:*** John English, William Witney. *REP, VCN, MLB*

Daring Danger ☆½ **1932** McCoy is nearly killed in a fight with the villainous Alexander. When he recovers he finds Alexander has joined forces with a rustler (Ellis), so McCoy battles both of them—while his horse goes for help. **58m/B VHS.** Tim McCoy, Richard Alexander, Robert Ellis, Alberta Vaughn, Wallace MacDonald, Murdock McQuarrie, Max Davidson; ***D:*** David Ross Lederman. *GPV*

Daring Dobermans ☆☆ **1973 (PG)** In this sequel to "The Doberman Gang," the barking bankrobbers have a new set of crime-planning masters. A young Indian boy who loves the dogs enters the picture and may thwart their perfect crime. **88m/C VHS, Beta.** Charles Robinson, Tim Considine, David Moses, Claudio Martinez, Joan Caulfield; ***D:*** Byron Ross Chudnow. *FOX*

Daring Game ☆☆ **1968** A group of scuba divers nicknamed the Flying Fish attempt to rescue a woman's husband and daughter from an island dictatorship. Failed series pilot by producer Ivan Tors, better known for "Sea Hunt" and "Flipper." **100m/C VHS, Beta.** Lloyd Bridges, Brock Peters, Michael Ansara, Joan Blackman; ***D:*** Laslo Benedek; ***M:*** George Bruns. *NO*

Dario Argento's Trauma ☆☆ *Trauma* **1993 (R)** When a teenage girl's parents are decapitated, she and an artist friend start following the clues to a psychotic killer known as "The Headhunter." Trademark horror work for Italian cult director Argento with high suspense quotient and equally high gore. An unrated version is also available. **106m/C VHS.** Christopher Rydell, Asia Argento, Laura Johnson, James Russo, Brad Dourif, Frederic Forrest, Piper Laurie; ***D:*** Dario Argento; ***W:*** Ted Klein, Dario Argento. *REP, WOV*

The Dark ☆½ *The Mutilator* **1979 (R)** A supernatural beast commits a string of gruesome murders. **92m/C VHS, Beta.** William Devane, Cathy Lee Crosby, Richard Jaeckel, Keenan Wynn, Vivian Blaine; ***D:*** John Cardos. *MED*

The Dark ☆½ **1994 (R)** Cop and scientist seek a mysterious graveyard creature who holds both the power to heal and destroy. One man wants to kill it, one man wants to save it, and they race to be the first to find it. **90m/C VHS, LV.** Brion James, Jaimz Woolvett, Cynthia Belliveau, Stephen McHattie; ***D:*** Craig Pryce. *IMP*

A Dark Adapted Eye ☆☆☆ **1993** Sinister TV mystery adapted from the psychological thriller by Ruth Rendell (writing as Barbara Vine). In 1951 Vera Hillyard (Imrie) is hung for murdering her younger sister Eden (Ward)—an act that has profound effects on the family, including young niece Faith (Bonham Carter). Long haunted by the "why" of the crime, Faith later begins an investigation into her family's past—and discovers very dark and disturbing secrets dating back to WWII. Title refers to a vision problem caused by remaining in darkness too long. **150m/C VHS.** *GB* Helena Bonham Carter, Celia Imrie, Sophie Ward, Robin Ellis, Ciaran Hinds, Pip Torrens, William Gaminara, Polly Adams, Bernice Stegers, Steven Macintosh, Jason Durr; ***D:*** Tim Fywell; ***W:*** Sandy Welch; ***M:*** David Ferguson. *FOX*

Dark Age ☆☆½ **1988 (R)** An Australian conservationist must track down a rampaging, giant, semi-mythical alligator before it is killed by bounty hunters. Based on the novel (and Aboriginal legend) "Numunwari." **90m/C VHS, Beta, LV.** *AU* John Jarratt, David Gulpilil, Max Phipps, Ray Meagher, Nikki Coghill, Burnam Burnam; ***D:*** Arch Nicholson. *NLC*

The Dark Angel ☆☆☆ **1991** Maud is the young and innocent heiress to a fortune in this gothic mystery of creeping unease. She is intrigued by the romantic portrait of her youthful and unknown Uncle Silas. But her mysterious uncle is no longer the Byronic hero. What secret wickedness does his ravaged face hide? And what about Maud's drug-addicted governess and the brutish young man in the cemetary? Does Uncle Silas just want Maud's fortune or Maud herself? Excellent performances by O'Toole as the decadent uncle and Edney as the innocent-but-not-stupid Maud. Based on the novel "Uncle Silas" by J.S. Le Fanu. Made for British TV. **150m/C VHS.** *GB* Peter O'Toole, Beatie Edney, Jane Lapotaire, Tim Woodward, Alan MacNaughton, Barbara Shelley, Guy Rolfe; ***D:*** Peter Hammond. *FOX, VCO*

Dark Angel: The Ascent ☆½ **1994 (R)** She-devil gets tired of hell and decides to get a look at the world upstairs. She also decides to turn vigilante and dispatch some bad guy souls to her former home. **80m/C VHS, Beta.** Charlotte Stewart, Daniel Markel, Michael C. Mahon, Nicholas Worth, Milton James; ***D:*** Linda Hassani; ***W:*** Matthew Bright; ***M:*** Fuzzbee Morse. *PAR*

Dark August ☆☆ **1976 (PG)** A New Yorker drops out and transplants to rural Vermont, where he accidentally kills a young girl and then suffers numerous horrors as a result of a curse put on him by the girl's grandfather. **87m/C VHS, Beta.** J.J. Barry, Carole Shelyne, Kim Hunter, William Robertson; ***D:*** Martin Goldman. *VES, LIV*

The Dark Backward ☆½ **1991 (R)** A dark, subversive comedy about a garbage man who dreams of making it big in show biz as a stand-up comedian. He's terrible until a third arm starts growing out of his back and the sheer grotesqueness of his situation makes him a temporary star. Caan and Newton are interestingly cast, but young, first-time director Rifkin's foray into David Lynch territory was not well received by critics. **97m/C VHS, LV.** Judd Nelson, Bill Paxton, Wayne Newton, Lara Flynn Boyle, James Caan, Rob Lowe, Claudia Christian; ***D:*** Adam Rifkin; ***W:*** Adam Rifkin. *COL*

Dark Before Dawn ☆½ **1989 (R)** American farmers and Vietnam veterans team up against corrupt government officials and ruthless businessmen in this violent film about the plight of the underdog. **95m/C VHS, Beta, LV.** Doug McClure, Sonny Gibson, Ben Johnson, Billy Drago, Rance Howard, Morgan Woodward, Buck Henry, Jeffery Osterhage, Red Steagall, John Martin, Gary Cooper; ***D:*** Robert Totten. *VES, LIV*

Dark Command ☆☆☆ **1940** The story of Quantrell's Raiders who terrorized the Kansas territory during the Civil War until one man came along to put a stop to it. Colorful and talented cast add depth to the script. Also available colorized. **95m/B VHS, Beta.** John Wayne, Walter Pidgeon, Claire Trevor, Roy Rogers, Marjorie Main, George "Gabby" Hayes; ***D:*** Raoul Walsh. Nominations: Academy Awards '40: Best Interior Decoration, Best Original Score. *REP, FCT*

Dark Corner ☆☆☆ **1946** Gripping, intricate film noir about a detective, already framed once, who may go up the river yet again—this time for the murder of his ex-partner, the guy who framed him the first time. Loyal secretary Ball helps to extricate him from this tangled web. **99m/B VHS, Beta.** Lucille Ball, Mark Stevens, Clifton Webb, William Bendix, Cathy Downs, Reed Hadley, Constance Collier, Kurt Kreuger; ***D:*** Henry Hathaway. *FOX*

The Dark Crystal ☆☆☆ **1982 (PG)** Jen and Kira, two of the last surviving Gelflings, attempt to return a crystal shard (discovered with the help of a sorceress) to the castle where the Dark Crystal lies, guarded by the cruel and evil Skeksis. Designed by Brian Froud. From the creators of the Muppets. **93m/C VHS, Beta, LV.** ***D:*** Jim Henson, Frank Oz; ***W:*** David Odell; ***C:*** Oswald Morris; ***M:*** Trevor Jones; ***V:*** Jim Henson, Frank Oz, Kathryn Mullen, Dave Goelz. *TOU*

The Dark Dancer 🦴½ **1995 (R)** Psychology prof Maggie (Tweed), who authors books on feminine sexual behavior, gets her experience first-hand by working in a strip club. Now, she's also the target of a police investigation. Also available unrated. **?m/C VHS.** Shannon Tweed. *TCE*

The Dark Dealer 🦴🦴 **1995** Three terror tales find the Devil's assistant dealing a deadly game of blackjack to a trio in limbo, with the cards propelling each man into a horrific adventure. Provides some real scares along with effective (if low-budget) special effects. **85m/C VHS.** Mark Fickert, Richard Hull, Vincent Gaskins, Rocky Patterson, Gordon Fox; ***D:*** Tom Alexander. *SDE*

Dark Eyes 🦴🦴🦴½ *Les Yeux Noirs; Oci Ciornie* **1987** An acclaimed Italian film based on a several short stories by Anton Chekov. Mastroianni is a weak-willed Italian, trapped in a marriage of convenience, who falls in love with a mysterious, also married, Russian beauty he meets in a health spa. He embarks on a journey to find her and, perhaps, his lost ideals. Hailed as Mastroianni's consummate performance. In Italian with English subtitles. **118m/C VHS, Beta.** *IT* Marcello Mastroianni, Silvana Mangano, Elena Sofonova, Marthe Keller; ***D:*** Nikita Mikhalkov. Cannes Film Festival '87: Best Actor (Mastroianni); Nominations: Academy Awards '87: Best Actor (Mastroianni). *GHV, FOX*

Dark Forces 🦴🦴 *Harlequin* **1983 (PG)** A faith-healer promises to help a senator's dying son and finds the politician's wife also desires his assistance. This Australian film is uneven and predictable. Though rated "PG," beware of two rather brief, but explicit, nudity scenes. **96m/C VHS, Beta.** *AU* Robert Powell, David Hemmings, Broderick Crawford, Carmen Duncan; ***D:*** Simon Wincer. *MED*

Dark Habits 🦴🦴½ *Entre Tinieblas* **1984** An early Almodovar farce about already-demented nuns in a failing convent trying to raise funds with the help of a nightclub singer who is on the run. Although certainly irreverant, it doesn't quite have the zing of his later work. In Spanish with subtitles. **116m/C VHS, Beta, LV.** *SP* Carmen Maura, Christina Pascual, Julieta Serrano, Marisa Paredes; ***D:*** Pedro Almodovar; ***W:*** Pedro Almodovar. *INJ, CCN, TPV*

The Dark Half 🦴🦴 **1991 (R)** Flawed chiller based on a Stephen King novel. Thad Beaumont's serious novels have been failures, but writing as George Stark, he's had phenomenal success with grisly horror stories. In a publicity stunt Thad kills off and publicly buries George (who doesn't want to stay dead). Soon everyone who's crossed Thad is brutally murdered. Hutton acquits himself well in a change of pace dual role. Otherwise, the psychological thrills are few and the gore is plentiful. Pittsburgh serves as location double for King's usual New England territory. Film's release was delayed due to Orion's bankruptcy problems. **122m/C VHS.** Timothy Hutton, Amy Madigan, Michael Rooker, Julie Harris, Robert Joy, Kent Broadhurst, Beth Grant, Rutanya Alda, Tom Mardirosian, Chelsea Field, Royal Dano; ***D:*** George A. Romero; ***W:*** George A. Romero; ***M:*** Christopher Young. *ORI*

Dark Horse 🦴🦴½ **1992 (PG)** Meyers is a young woman distraught over the death of her mother. She gets into trouble and is assigned to do community service work at a horse farm where she finds herself caring for a prize-winning horse. **98m/C VHS.** Ari Meyers, Mimi Rogers, Ed Begley Jr., Donovan Leitch, Samantha Eggar; ***D:*** David Hemmings. *LIV, MOV, FCT*

The Dark Hour 🦴½ **1936** Two detectives team up to solve a murder in which multiple suspects are involved. Based on Sinclair Gluck's "The Last Trap." **72m/B VHS, Beta.** Ray Walker, Irene Ware, Berton Churchill, Hedda Hopper, Hobart Bosworth, E.E. Clive; ***D:*** Charles Lamont. *NOS, LOO, SNC*

Dark Journey 🦴🦴🦴 *The Anxious Years* **1937** WWI Stockholm is the setting for a love story between a double agent and the head of German Intelligence. Clever, sophisticated production; Leigh is stunning. **82m/B VHS, Beta.** *GB* Vivien Leigh, Conrad Veidt, Joan Gardner, Anthony Bushell, Ursula Jeans; ***D:*** Victor Saville. *NOS, MRV, CAB*

Dark Justice 🦴🦴½ **1991** Judge by day, avenger by night in this actioner created from three episodes of the late-night television series. Judge Nicholas Marshall is disgusted by the criminals sprung on legal loopholes and backroom deals. So he decides to take justice into his own hands. **99m/C VHS.** Ramy Zada, Dick O'Neill, Clayton Prince, Begona Plaza. *WAR*

Dark Mirror 🦴🦴🦴 **1946** A psychologist and a detective struggle to determine which twin sister murdered a prominent physician. Good and evil siblings finely-acted by de Havilland. **85m/B VHS.** Olivia de Havilland, Lew Ayres, Thomas Mitchell, Garry Owen; ***D:*** Robert Siodmak; ***C:*** Milton Krasner. Nominations: Academy Awards '46: Best Story. *REP*

Dark Mountain 🦴½ **1944** A forest ranger rescues his gal from the clutches of a hardened criminal. **56m/B VHS.** Robert Lowery, Ellen Drew, Regis Toomey, Eddie Quillan, Elisha Cook Jr.; ***D:*** William (Lester Williams) Berke, William C. Thomas. *NOS, DVT*

Dark Night of the Scarecrow 🦴🦴½ **1981** Thriller with a moral. Prejudiced townspeople execute a retarded man who was innocently befriended by a young girl. After his death unusual things begin to happen. Slow to start but effective. Made for television. **100m/C VHS, Beta.** Charles Durning, Tanya Crowe, Larry Drake; ***D:*** Frank de Felitta. *FOX, HHE*

Dark Obsession 🦴🦴 *Diamond Skulls* **1990 (R)** Byrne portrays a husband who lives out his dark erotic fantasies with his wife (Donohoe), and is involved in a hit-and-run accident. Driven by guilt, madness slowly begins to take him. Ugly and depressing. Based on a true scandal. Available in an "NC-17" rated version. **97m/C VHS, Beta.** Gabriel Byrne, Amanda Donohoe, Michael Hordern, Judy Parfitt, Douglas Hodge, Sadie Frost, Ian Carmichael; ***D:*** Nick Broomfield; ***W:*** Tim Rose Price; ***M:*** Hans Zimmer. *PSM*

Dark of the Night 🦴🦴½ *Mr. Wrong* **1985** A young woman, new to the city, purchases a used Jaguar and finds she must share it with the car's former owner—a woman murdered inside the Jag. Decent psycho-thriller with some suspenseful and amusing moments. **88m/C VHS, Beta.** *NZ* Heather Bolton, David Letch, Gary Stalker, Michael Haigh, Danny Mulheron, Kate Harcourt; ***D:*** Gaylene Preston; ***W:*** Gaylene Preston, Geoff Murphy, Graham Tetley; ***M:*** Jonathan Crayford. *LIV*

Dark of the Sun 🦴🦴½ *The Mercenaries* **1968 (PG)** Lots of action; routine plot. Taylor is a tough mercenary hired to retrieve a supply of uncut diamonds from a beseiged town in the Congo during the 1950's rebellion. Oh, and if he can help out the town's inhabitants that's okay too. Based on the novel by Wilbur A. Smith. **101m/C VHS.** *GB* Rod Taylor, Jim Brown, Yvette Mimieux, Kenneth More, Peter Carsten, Calvin Lockhart, Andre Morell; ***D:*** Jack Cardiff; ***W:*** Quentin Werty, Adrian Spies; ***M:*** Jacques Loussier. *MGM*

Dark Passage 🦴🦴½ **1947** Bogart plays a convict who escapes from San Quentin to prove he was framed for the murder of his wife. He undergoes plastic surgery and is hidden and aided by Bacall as he tries to find the real killer. Stars can't quite compensate for a far-fetched script and so-so direction. **107m/B VHS, Beta, LV.** Humphrey Bogart, Lauren Bacall, Agnes Moorehead, Bruce (Herman Brix) Bennett, Tom D'Andrea; ***D:*** Delmer Daves. *FOX*

The Dark Past 🦴🦴🦴 **1949** A crazy, escaped convict holds a psychologist and his family hostage, and the two men engage in psychological cat-and-mouse combat. An underrated thriller with off-beat casting. **75m/B VHS, Beta.** William Holden, Lee J. Cobb, Nina Foch, Adele Jergens; ***D:*** Rudolph Mate; ***M:*** George Duning. *COL*

Dark Places 🦴🦴 **1973 (PG)** Masquerading as a hospital administrator, a former mental patient inherits the ruined mansion of a man who had killed his wife and children and died insane. As he lives in the house, the spirit of its former owner seems to overcome him with a need to repeat the crime. Meanwhile, Lee, Collins, and Lom think the nut is hiding money they would like to get their collective hands on. Low-budget but fairly effective. **91m/C VHS, Beta.** *GB* Joan Collins, Christopher Lee, Robert Hardy; ***D:*** Don Sharp. *SUE*

The Dark Power 🦴 **1985** Ex-cowboy LaRue and his trusty whip provide this flick with its only excitement. As sheriff, he must deal with the dead Mexican warriors who rise to wreak havoc when a house is built on their burial ground. **87m/C VHS, Beta.** Lash LaRue, Anna Lane Tatum; ***D:*** Phil Smoot. *NO*

The Dark Ride 🦴½ **1984** Lunatic picks up women with the intention of raping and killing them. Ugly thriller based on the evil deeds of serial murderer Ted Bundy. **83m/C VHS, Beta.** James Luisi, Susan Sullivan, Martin Speer; ***D:*** Jeremy Hoenack. *MED*

Dark Rider **1991** Dark Rider is a mysterious, motorcycle riding hero who comes to the rescue of a small town. Besieged by a gangster who buys up all their land, the townspeople must abandon their homes and indeed, their very dreams. That is until Dark Rider rolls into to town to enact his own unique brand of vengeance. **94m/C VHS.** Joe Estevez, Doug Shanklin, Alicia Kowalski, David Shark, Chuck Williams; ***W:*** Chuck Williams, Bob Ivy. *AIP*

Dark River: A Father's Revenge 🦴🦴 **1990** When his daughter is killed in a toxic waste dump accident, a man begins revenge on the company and its managers. Tense, with important message. **95m/C VHS.** Helen Hunt, Mike Farrell, Tess Harper. *TTC*

Dark Sanity *Woof! Straight Jacket* **1982** Uninvolving attempt at horror has a recently de-institutionalized woman envisioning death and destruction (something you'll wish the film would do) while everyone else just thinks she's losing her marbles. Problem is we don't really care. **89m/C VHS, Beta.** Aldo Ray, Kory Clark, Andy Gwyn, Bobby Holt; ***D:*** Martin Greene. *PSM*

The Dark Secret of Harvest Home 🦴🦴½ **1978** An urban couple confront a pagan cult in the New England town into which they've moved. Based upon the Thomas Tryon novel. Made for television. **118m/C VHS, Beta.** Bette Davis, Rosanna Arquette, David Ackroyd, Rene Auberjonois, Michael O'Keefe; ***D:*** Leonard Penn. *MCA*

Dark Secrets 🦴 **1995 (R)** Society gal goes slumming at underground club that caters to fulfilling sexual fantasies. The unrated version is 99 minutes. **90m/C VHS.** Monique Parent, Julie Strain, Justine Carroll. *APX*

Dark Shadows **1967** "Dark Shadows" had already been on television for about eight months when the character of Barnabas Collins was introduced. This volume serves to familiarize the viewer with characters and situations that were running on the series at that time. These are the first five episodes that feature Barnabas. Original air dates are April 17 to May 1, 1967. Contains both B&W and color episodes. Additional episodes available. **120m/B VHS.** Joan Bennett, Kathryn Leigh Scott, John Karlen, Alexandra Moltke, Jonathan Frid, David Selby, Kate Jackson; ***D:*** John Sedwick. *MPI, MOV*

Dark Shadows: Episode 1 **1991** The short-lived primetime remake of the 1960s camp television classic about eerie Collinwood mansion and the mysterious and tragic Collins family, including cousin Barnabas who happens to be a vampire. The revival featured more explicit sex and violence and a darker tone. In 12 parts. **105m/C VHS.** Ben Cross, Jean Simmons, Roy Thinnes, Barbara Steele, Joanna Going, Lysette Anthony, Michael T. Weiss; ***D:*** Dan Curtis. *MPI, TPV*

Dark Side of Genius 🦴🦴 **1994 (R)** Jennifer (Hughes), a reporter for an L.A. arts weekly, tries to get the story on an artist (Fraser) who's just been paroled after being imprisoned for the murder of his model. Now his lurid new paintings of a sultry nude model hint at some obsessive behavior and Jennifer's reporter instincts may be the death of her. **86m/C VHS, Beta.** Finola Hughes, Brendan Fraser, Glenn Shadix, Moon Zappa, Patrick Richwood, Seymour Cassel; ***D:*** Phedon Papamichael; ***W:*** Fred Stroppel; ***C:*** Phedon Papamichael; ***M:*** Tom Hiel. *PAR*

The Dark Side of Love 🦴½ **1979** A young girl gets involved with the rougher side of New Orleans society, gets pregnant, and realizes how she's been degraded. **94m/C VHS, Beta.** James Stacy, Glynnis O'Connor, Jan Sterling, Mickey Rooney. *GEM*

Dark Side of Midnight 🦴½ *The Creeper* **1986 (R)** A super-detective tracks down a psychopathic killer. **108m/C VHS, Beta.** James Moore, Wes Olsen, Sandy Schemmel, Dave Bowling. *PSM*

Dark Side of the Moon 🦴🦴 **1990 (R)** Members of a space ship sent on a routine mission to the far side of the moon, discover an unknown force that feeds on human emotion and consumes the soul. Lukewarm science fiction/horror. **96m/C VHS, LV.** William Bledsoe, Alan Blumenfeld, John Diehl, Robert Sampson, Wendy MacDonald, Camilla More, Joe Turkel; ***D:*** D.J. Webster. *VMK*

Dark Star 🦴🦴🦴 **1974 (G)** John Carpenter's directorial debut is a low-budget, sci-fi satire which focuses on a group of scientists whose mission is to destroy unstable planets. During their journey, they battle their alien mascot (who closely resembles a walking beach ball), as well as a "sensitive" and intelligent bombing device which starts to question the meaning of its existence. Enjoyable early feature from John "Halloween" Carpenter and Dan "Aliens" O'Bannon. Fun, weird, and unpredictable. **95m/C VHS, Beta, LV.** Dan O'Bannon, Brian Narelle; ***D:*** John Carpenter; ***W:*** Dan O'Bannon, John Carpenter; ***M:*** John Carpenter. *HHT, IME, VCI*

Dark Tide 🦴🦴 **1993 (R)** Erotic action thriller about a pair of deep sea divers whose love life is disturbed when their boat captain becomes sexually fixated on the woman. Also available in an uncut, unrated version. **92m/C VHS, LV.** Brigitte Bako, Richard Tyson, Chris Sarandon. *VMK*

Dark Tower 🦴 **1987 (R)** Decent cast is wasted in yet another inept attempt at horror. An architect is dismayed to learn that an evil force is inhabiting her building and it might just be the ghost of her dearly departed husband. **91m/C VHS, Beta, LV.** Michael Moriarty, Jenny Agutter, Theodore Bikel, Carol Lynley, Anne Lockhart, Kevin McCarthy; ***D:*** Ken Barnett; ***W:*** Robert J. Avrech, Kenneth G. Blackwell. *VTR, IME*

Dark Universe 🦴½ **1993 (R)** An alien terror wants to conquer the Earth and make its inhabitants their new food source. **83m/C VHS, Beta.** Blake Pickett, Cherie Scott, Bently Tittle, John Maynard, Paul Austin Saunders, Tom Ferguson, Steve Barkett, Joe Estevez, Patrick Moran; ***D:*** Steve Latshaw; ***W:*** Patrick Moran. *PSM*

Dark Victory 🦴🦴🦴½ **1939** A spoiled young heiress discovers she is dying from a brain tumor. She attempts to pack a lifetime of parties into a few months, but is rescued by her doctor, with whom she falls in love. Classic final scene with Davis at the top of her form. Bogart plays an Irish stable hand, but not especially well. Also available in a colorized version. **106m/B VHS, Beta, LV.** Bette Davis, George Brent, Geraldine Fitzgerald, Humphrey Bogart, Ronald Reagan, Henry Travers; ***D:*** Edmund Goulding; ***M:*** Max Steiner. Nominations: Academy Awards '39: Best Actress (Davis), Best Picture, Best Original Score. *MGM*

Dark Waters 🦴🦴 **1944** The drowning death of her parents has left a young woman mentally unstable. She returns to her family home in the backwaters of Louisiana with her peculiar aunt and uncle to serve as guardians. It eventually becomes apparent that someone is trying to drive her insane. This one tends to be rather murky and it's not simply due to the plentiful scenes of misty swampland. **93m/B VHS, Beta, LV.** Merle Oberon, Franchot Tone, Thomas Mitchell, Fay Bainter, Elisha Cook Jr., John Qualen, Rex Ingram; ***D:*** Andre de Toth; ***M:*** Miklos Rozsa. *VTR*

The Dark Wind 🦴½ **1991 (R)** The first of Tony Hillerman's popular Native American mysteries comes to the screen in a lame adaptation. Phillips stars as the Navaho cop investigating a murder on a New Mexico Indian reservation. Since the Navaho believe a "dark wind" enters a man's soul when he does evil, expect some "spirited" goings-on as well. **111m/C VHS, LV.** Lou Diamond Phillips; ***D:*** Errol Morris; ***W:*** Eric Bergren. *LIV*

Darker than Amber 🦴🦴 **1970 (R)** John D. MacDonald's houseboat-dwelling detective Travis McGee (Taylor) rescues a girl (Kendall) he's fallen for, and soon discovers that the mugs who thugged her were part of a collection racket. A violent action melodrama upgraded from its original "R" rating. **96m/C VHS.** Rod Taylor, Suzy Kendall, Theodore Bikel, Jane Russell, James Booth, Janet MacLachlan, William Smith, Ahna Capri, Chris Robinson; ***D:*** Robert Clouse. *NO*

Darkest Africa *Batmen of Africa; King of the Jungleland* **1936** Legendary animal trainer Beatty is the hero of this 15 episode cliffhanger serial as he vies with beasts—both animal and human. **270m/B LV.** Clyde Beatty, Manuel King, Elaine Shepard; ***D:*** Joseph Kane, B. Reeves Eason. *REP, MOV*

Darkman 🦴🦴🦴 **1990 (R)** Raimi's disfigured-man-seeks-revenge suspenser is comicbook kitsch cross-pollinated with a strain of gothic horror. Neeson plays a scientist who's on the verge of discovering the key to cloning body parts; brutally attacked by the henchmen of a crooked politico, his lab is destroyed and he's left for dead. Turns out he's not dead—just horribly disfigured and a wee bit chafed—and he stalks his deserving victims from the shadows, using his lab know-how to disguise his rugged bad looks. Exquisitely violent. Montage by Pablo Ferro. **96m/C VHS, Beta, LV.** Liam Neeson, Frances McDormand, Larry Drake, Colin Friels, Nelson Mashita, Jenny Agutter, Rafael H. Robledo; ***D:*** Sam Raimi; ***W:*** Sam Raimi, Ivan Raimi; ***M:*** Danny Elfman. *MCA, CCB*

Darkman 2: The Return of Durant 🦴🦴½ **1994 (R)** The first in a series of direct-to-video adventures about disfigured scientist Peyton "Darkman" Westlake (now played by Vosloo), who's continuing his liquid skin research in the hopes of transforming his grotesque appearance. He finds an ally in scientist David Brinkman but Westlake's nemesis, crime boss Robert G. Durant (Drake), wants the property where Brinkman's lab is located. And what Durant wants, he takes. Sam Raimi, who directed the original film, is one of the series producers. **93m/C VHS, LV.** Arnold Vosloo, Larry Drake, Kim Delaney, Renee O'Connor, Rod Wilson; ***D:*** Bradford May; ***W:*** Steven McKay, Chuck Pfarrer; ***M:*** Randy Miller. *MCA*

Darkman 3: Die Darkman Die 🦴🦴½ **1995 (R)** The second direct-to-video Darkman saga finds Dr. Peyton Westlake (Vosloo) disrupting the drug-dealing activities of underworld boss Peter Rooker (Fahey). The obsessed Rooker is determined to figure out the secret to Darkman's enormous strength, employing the feminine wiles of his mistress, Dr. Bridget Thorne (Fluegel). Then Westlake/Darkman finds himself drawn to Rooker's neglected wife and young daughter. Our hero suffers a lot (as usual) and there's lots of action (as usual). **87m/C VHS, LV.** Arnold Vosloo, Jeff Fahey, Darlanne Fluegel, Nigel Bennett, Roxann Biggs-Dawson; ***D:*** Bradford May; ***W:*** Mike Werb; ***M:*** Randy Miller. *MCA*

Darkroom 🦴½ **1990** An unstable young man devises a scheme to photograph his father in bed with his mistress, and then use the pics to blackmail dear ol' dad. **90m/C VHS.** Jill Pierce, Jeffrey Allen Arbaugh, Sara Lee Wade, Aaron Teich; ***D:*** Terrence O'Hara. *NO*

The Darkside 🦴½ **1987 (R)** In this frightening drama, a young prostitute and an innocent cabbie attempt to escape the clutches of a maniacal film producer with a secret he won't let them reveal. **95m/C VHS.** Tony Galati, Cyndy Preston; ***D:*** Constantino Magnatta. *VMK*

Darktown Strutters 🦴 *Get Down and Boogie* **1974 (PG)** Effort to satirize racial stereotypes is humorless and ineffective. Black female motorcycle gang searches for the kidnapped mother of one of the members. **85m/C VHS, Beta.** Trina Parks, Roger E. Mosley, Shirley Washington; ***D:*** William Witney. *NLC*

Darling 🦴🦴🦴½ **1965** Young amoral model tries to hold boredom at bay by having a number of love affairs. She joins the international jet set and manages to reach the top of European society by marrying a prince. She then learns what an empty life she has. Christie won an Oscar for her portrayal of the disillusioned, cynical young woman. **122m/B VHS, Beta, LV.** *GB* Julie Christie, Dirk Bogarde, Laurence Harvey; ***D:*** John Schlesinger; ***W:*** Frederic Raphael. Academy Awards '65: Best Actress (Christie), Best Costume Design (B & W), Best Story; British Academy Awards '65: Best Actor (Bogarde), Best Actress (Christie), Best Screenplay; Golden Globe Awards '66: Best Foreign Film; National Board of Review Awards '65: 10 Best Films of the Year, Best Actress (Christie), Best Director (Schlesinger); Nominations: Academy Awards '65: Best Director (Schlesinger), Best Picture. *COL, BTV, SUE*

Darling Lili 🦴🦴½ **1970** Big-budget WWI spy comedy/musical with Andrews as a German agent posing as an English music hall performer, who falls in love with squadron leader Hudson and finds she can't betray him. A critical flop when first released, film has its charms though director Edwards did much better for Andrews in "Victor/Victoria." ♫Whistling Away the Dark; The Girl In No Man's Land; Smile Away Each Rainy Day; I'll Give You Three Guesses; Your Good Will Ambassador; Darling Lili; The Little Birds. **136m/C VHS.** Julie Andrews, Rock Hudson, Jeremy Kemp, Jacques Marin, Michael Witney, Vernon Dobtcheff; ***D:*** Blake Edwards; ***W:*** Blake Edwards, William Peter Blatty; ***M:*** Henry Mancini, Johnny Mercer. Golden Globe Awards '71: Best Song ("Whistling Away the Dark"). *PAR*

D.A.R.Y.L. 🦴🦴 **1985 (PG)** The little boy found by the side of the road is too polite, too honest and too smart. His friend explains to him the necessity of imperfection (If you don't want the grown-ups to bother you too much) and he begins to become more like a real little boy. But the American military has a top-secret interest in this child, since he is in fact the combination of a cloned body and a computer brain. More interesting when it's involved with the human beings and less so when it focuses on science. **100m/C VHS, Beta, LV.** Mary Beth Hurt, Michael McKean, Barret Oliver, Colleen Camp, Danny Corkill; ***D:*** Simon Wincer; ***W:*** David Ambrose, Allan Scott; ***M:*** Marvin Hamlisch. *PAR*

Das Boot 🦴🦴🦴🦴 *The Boat* **1981 (R)** Superb detailing of life in a German U-boat during WWII. Intense, claustrophobic atmosphere complemented by nail-biting action provides a realistic portrait of the stressful conditions that were endured on these submarines. Excellent performances, especially from Prochnow. With English subtitles. Originally a 6-hour special made for German television. Also available in a dubbed version. From the novel by Lothar-Guenther Buccheim. **150m/C VHS, Beta, LV.** *GE* Juergen Prochnow, Herbert Gronemeyer, Klaus Wennemann, Hubertus Bengsch, Martin Semmelrogge, Bernd Tauber, Erwin Leder, Martin May; ***D:*** Wolfgang Petersen; ***W:*** Wolfgang Petersen; ***M:*** Klaus Doldinger. Nominations: Academy Awards '82: Best Adapted Screenplay, Best Cinematography, Best Director (Petersen), Best Film Editing, Best Sound. *COL, APD, INJ*

Das Testament des Dr. Mabuse 🦴🦴🦴½ *The Testament of Dr. Mabuse* **1933** The third, and only sound, Mabuse film by Lang. The infamous crime lord/megalomaniac plots the world's destruction from the confines of an asylum cell. In German, with English subtitles. Released as "The Last Will of Dr. Mabuse" in the U.S. in 1943. **122m/B VHS, Beta.** *GE* Rudolf Klein-Rogge, Otto Wernicke, Gustav Diesl, Karl Meixner; ***D:*** Fritz Lang. *SNC, SUE, GLV*

Date Bait 🦴 **1960** When a teen couple decides—much to their parents' chagrin—to elope, they find themselves on a date with danger when their post-nuptuals are plagued by pushers and assorted other bad guys. **71m/B VHS, Beta.** Gary Clarke, Marlo Ryan, Richard Gering, Danny Logan; ***D:*** O'Dale Ireland. *SNC*

Date with an Angel 🦴½ **1987 (PG)** When aspiring musician Knight fishes a beautiful angel out of the swimming pool, he is just trying to rescue her. But the beauty of the angel overwhelms him and he finds himself questioning his upcoming wedding to Cates, a cosmetic mogul's daughter. Sickeningly cute and way too sentimental, though Beart's beauty is other-wordly. **114m/C VHS, Beta, LV.** Emmanuelle Beart, Michael E. Knight, Phoebe Cates, David Dukes, Bibi Besch, Albert Macklin, David Hunt, Michael Goodwin; ***D:*** Tom McLoughlin. *NO*

A Date with Judy **1948** Standard post-war musical dealing with teenage mix-ups in and around a big high school dance. Choreography by Stanley Donen. ♫Cuanto La Gusto; Strictly on the Corny Side; It's a Most Unusual Day; Judaline; I've Got a Date with Judy; I'm Gonna Meet My Mary; Temptation; Mulligatawny. **114m/C VHS, Beta, LV.** Jane Powell, Elizabeth Taylor, Carmen Miranda, Wallace Beery, Robert Stack, Xavier Cugat, Selena Royle, Leon Ames; ***D:*** Richard Thorpe; ***C:*** Robert L. Surtees. *MGM, MLB*

Daughter of Darkness ½ **1989 (R)** A young woman goes to Hungary in search of her family tree, only to discover vampires nestled there. **93m/C VHS.** Mia Sara, Anthony Perkins, Robert Reynolds, Jack Coleman; ***D:*** Stuart Gordon. *VMK*

Daughter of Death *Julie Darling* **1982 (R)** A little mentally off-center since she witnessed the gruesome rape and murder of her mother, a teenage girl doesn't bond well with her new mom when dad remarries. **100m/C VHS.** *CA GE* Anthony (Tony) Franciosa, Isabelle Mejias, Sybil Danning, Cindy Gurling, Paul Hubbard, Benjamin Schmoll; ***D:*** Paul Nicholas. *FCT*

The Daughter of Dr. Jekyll ½ **1957** The doc's daughter believes she may have inherited her father's evil curse when several of the locals are found dead. **71m/B VHS, Beta.** John Agar, Arthur Shields, John Dierkes, Gloria Talbott; ***D:*** Edgar G. Ulmer. *FOX*

Daughter of Don Q ½ **1946** Delores' father is very rich with a huge real estate empire and she is his only heir. Greedy cousin Carlos would like to change that—by killing Delores. Delores must dodge speeding cars, hurling harpoons, and more to escape Carlos' evil plot. Part of "The Cliffhanger Serials" series. **166m/B VHS.** Adrian Booth, Kirk Alyn, Leroy Mason. *REP, MOV*

Daughter of Horror *Dementia* **1955** A young woman finds herself involved with a porcine mobster who resembles her abusive father. Trouble is, Dad's dead, and daughter dearest abetted his departure. Obscure venture into expressionism that was initially banned by the New York State Board of Censors. Shot on a low budget (how low was it? So low that McMahon narrated because shooting with sound was too expensive). The 55 minutes tend to lag, although the film should be intriguing to genre enthusiasts and to fans of things pseudo-Freudian. **60m/B VHS.** Adrienne Barrett, Bruno Ve Sota, Ben Roseman; ***D:*** John Parker; ***W:*** John Parker. *NOS, SNC, MRV*

Daughter of the Dragon **1931** Fu Manchu is again on the prowl, this time sending his daughter to murder Fletcher to avenge the death of his wife and son during China's Boxer Rebellion. Based on a Sax Rohmer story. **70m/B VHS.** Anna May Wong, Warner Oland, Sessue Hayakawa, Bramwell Fletcher, Holmes Herbert; ***D:*** Lloyd Corrigan. *NOS*

Daughter of the Tong **1939** FBI agent gets tong twisted when he tries to put a lid on a smuggling ring headed by a woman (who's beautiful, of course). Something that resembles acting is wasted in a mess of a movie. **56m/B VHS, Beta.** Evelyn Brent, Grant Withers, Dorothy Short, Dave O'Brien; ***D:*** Raymond K. Johnson. *NOS, SNC*

Daughters of Darkness *Le Rouge aux Levres* **1971 (R)** Newlyweds on their way to England stop at a posh French hotel. There they meet a beautiful woman whom the hotel owner swears had been there forty years ago, even though she hasn't aged a bit. When she introduces herself as Countess of Bathory (the woman who bathed in the blood of virgins to stay young) folks begin to wonder. A really superb erotic vampire film charged with sensuality and a sense of dread. **87m/C VHS, Beta.** *BE GE IT FR* Delphine Seyrig, John Karlen, Daniele Ouimet, Andrea Rau, Paul Esser, Georges Jamin, Joris Collet, Fons Rademakers; ***D:*** Harry Kumel. *NO*

Daughters of Satan **1972 (R)** Selleck, in an early role as a virile museum buyer, antagonizes a coven of witches when he purchases a painting. His wife, played by Grant, becomes a target of the witches' revenge and salacious shenanigans ensue. **96m/C VHS, Beta.** Tom Selleck, Barra Grant, Paraluman, Tani Phelps Guthrie; ***D:*** Hollingsworth Morse. *NO*

Daughters of the Dust ½ **1991** Five women of a Gullah family living on the Sea Islands off the Georgia coast in 1902 contemplate moving to the mainland in this emotional tale of change. The Gullah are descendants of West African slaves and their isolation has kept their superstitions and native dialect (a mixture of Western African, Creole, and English) intact. Family bonds and memories are celebrated with a quiet narrative and beautiful cinematography in Dash's feature-film directorial debut. **113m/C VHS.** Cora Lee Day, Barbara O, Alva Rogers, Kaycee Moore, Cheryl Lynn Bruce, Adisa Anderson; ***D:*** Julie Dash; ***W:*** Julie Dash; ***M:*** John Barnes. Sundance Film Festival '91: Best Cinematography. *KIV, FCT, PMS*

Dave **1993 (PG-13)** Regular guy Dave Kovic (Kline) is a dead ringer for the President, launching him into the White House after the prez suffers a stroke in embarrassing circumstances. Seamless comedy prompts lots of hearty laughs and the feel-good faith that despite the overwhelming odds, everything will turn out just fine. Political cameos abound: look for real-life Senators Alan Simpson, Paul Simon, Howard Metzenbaum, Tom Harkin, and Christopher Dodd as well as the commentators from TV's "The McLaughlin Group," and Stone, poking fun at himself on "Larry King Live," as he tries to convince the public there's a conspiracy going on. **110m/C VHS, Beta, LV.** Kevin Kline, Sigourney Weaver, Frank Langella, Kevin Dunn, Ving Rhames, Ben Kingsley, Charles Grodin, Faith Prince, Laura Linney, Bonnie Hunt, Parley Baer, Stefan Gierasch, Anna Deavere Smith, Bonnie Bartlett; ***Cameos:*** Oliver Stone, Arnold Schwarzenegger, Jay Leno, Larry King; ***D:*** Ivan Reitman; ***W:*** Gary Ross; ***M:*** James Newton Howard. Nominations: Academy Awards '93: Best Original Screenplay; Golden Globe Awards '94: Best Actor—Musical/Comedy (Kline), Best Film—Musical/Comedy. *WAR, BTV, FCT*

David ½ **1979** A haunting portrait of the survival of a Jewish teenager in Berlin during the Nazi reign of terror, based on the novel by Joel Koenig. Universally acclaimed, this was the first film about the Holocaust made in Germany by a German Jew. In German with English subtitles. **106m/C VHS, Beta.** *GE* Mario Fischel, Walter Taub, Irene Vrkijan, Torsten Hentes, Eva Mattes; ***D:*** Peter Lilienthal. Berlin International Film Festival '79: Golden Berlin Bear. *KIV, GLV, INJ*

David and Bathsheba **1951** The Bible story comes alive in this lush and colorful Fox production. Peck and Hayward are great together and Peck is properly concerned about the wrath of God over his transgressions. Terrific costumes and special effects, lovely music and a fine supporting cast keep this a notch above other Biblical epics. **116m/C VHS, LV.** Gregory Peck, Susan Hayward, Raymond Massey, Kieron Moore, James Robertson Justice, Jayne Meadows, John Sutton, Dennis Hoey, Francis X. Bushman, George Zucco; ***D:*** Henry King; ***W:*** Philip Dunne; ***C:*** Leon Shamroy. Nominations: Academy Awards '51: Best Art Direction/Set Decoration (Color), Best Color Cinematography, Best Costume Design (Color), Best Story & Screenplay, Best Original Score. *FXV, FOX*

David and Lisa **1962** Director Perry was given an Oscar for this sensitive independently-produced film. Adapted from Theodore Isaac Rubin's true case history novel concerning a young man and woman who fall in love while institutionalized for mental illness. Dullea and Margolin are excellent in the title roles of this sleeper. **94m/B VHS, Beta, LV.** Keir Dullea, Janet Margolin, Howard da Silva, Neva Patterson, Clifton James; ***D:*** Frank Perry. Nominations: Academy Awards '62: Best Adapted Screenplay, Best Director (Perry). *COL, MRV*

David Copperfield **1935** Superior adaptation of Charles Dickens' great novel. An orphan grows to manhood in Victorian England with a wide variety of help and harm. Terrific acting by Bartholomew, Fields, Rathbone, and all the rest. Lavish production, lovingly filmed. **132m/B VHS, Beta, LV.** Lionel Barrymore, W.C. Fields, Freddie Bartholomew, Maureen O'Sullivan, Basil Rathbone, Lewis Stone, Frank Lawton, Madge Evans, Roland Young, Edna May Oliver, Lennox Pawle, Elsa Lanchester, Una O'Connor, Arthur Treacher; ***D:*** George Cukor; ***W:*** Howard Estabrook, Hugh Walpole; ***M:*** Herbert Stothart. National Board of Review Awards '35: 10 Best Films of the Year; Nominations: Academy Awards '35: Best Film Editing; Academy Awards '36: Best Picture. *MGM*

David Copperfield ½ **1970** This British made-for-television production is more faithful to the Dickens classic than any of its predecessors. The added material, however, fails to highlight any one character as had the successful 1935 MGM version. Still, the exceptional (and largely stage-trained) cast do much to redeem the production. **118m/C VHS.** Richard Attenborough, Cyril Cusack, Edith Evans, Pamela Franklin, Susan Hampshire, Wendy Hiller, Ron Moody, Laurence Olivier, Robin Phillips; ***D:*** Delbert Mann; ***M:*** Malcolm Arnold. *FOX, TVC*

David Holzman's Diary **1967** Director McBride helmed this fake underground movie, a legendary put-on focusing on film student pretensions. Holzman is a sincere geek who seeks the meaning of life by filming his own existence in oh-so-chic grainy black and white verite. He learns reality is more important than film. Drolly captures the state of the art in late '60's America. **71m/B VHS, LV.** L.M. Kit Carson; ***D:*** Jim McBride; ***W:*** L.M. Kit Carson, Jim McBride. *FXL*

DaVinci's War **1992 (R)** Frank DaVinci's sister is murdered and he wants revenge. So he hooks up with a professional killer and a bunch of Vietnam vets and gets the firepower he needs to blow the bad guys away. **94m/C VHS.** Joey Travolta, Michael Nouri, Vanity, Richard Foronjy, Branscombe Richmond, Sam Jones, Jack Bannon; ***Cameos:*** Brian Robbins, James Russo; ***D:*** Raymond Martino; ***W:*** Raymond Martino; ***M:*** Jeff Lass. *TRI*

Davy Crockett and the River Pirates ½ **1956 (G)** Another Disney splice and dice of two episodes from the television series, chronicling the further adventures of our frontier hero. Davy meets up with Mike Fink, the King of the Ohio River, and the two engage in a furious keelboat race, and then unite to track down a group of thieves masquerading as Indians and threatening the peace. **81m/C VHS, Beta, LV.** Fess Parker, Buddy Ebsen, Jeff York; ***D:*** Norman Foster; ***M:*** George Bruns. *DIS*

Davy Crockett, King of the Wild Frontier **1955 (PG)** Three episodes of the popular Disney television series are blended together here to present the life and some of the adventures of Davy Crockett. These include his days as an Indian fighter and his gallant stand in defense of the Alamo. Well-done by a splendid cast, the film helped to spread Davy-mania among the children of the 1950s. **93m/C VHS, Beta.** Fess Parker, Buddy Ebsen, Hans Conried, Ray Whiteside, Pat Hogan, William "Billy" Bakewell, Basil Ruysdael, Kenneth Tobey; ***D:*** Norman Foster; ***M:*** George Bruns. *DIS, BTV*

Dawn! **1983** True story of Dawn Fraser, an Olympic champion swimmer and an unfulfilled woman willing to fight for her happiness. **114m/C VHS, Beta.** Bronwyn MacKay-Payne, Tom Richards. *NO*

Dawn Express ½ **1942** Nazi spies infiltrate the U.S. in search of a secret formula designed to enhance the power of gasoline. Another film made to contribute to the war effort that doesn't make much sense. **63m/B VHS, Beta.** Michael Whalen, Anne Nagel, William "Billy" Bakewell, Constance Worth, Hans von Twardowski, Jack Mulhall, George Pembroke, Kenneth Harlan, Robert Frazer; ***D:*** Al(bert) Herman. *SNC*

Dawn of the Dead ½ **1978** Romero's gruesome sequel to his "Night of the Living Dead." A mysterious plague causes the recently dead to rise from their graves and scour the countryside for living flesh. Very violent, gory, graphic, and shocking, yet not without humor. Gives interesting consideration to the violence created by the living humans in their efforts to save themselves. **126m/C VHS, Beta, LV.** David Emge, Ken Foree, Gaylen Ross; ***D:*** George A. Romero; ***W:*** George A. Romero. *REP, FCT*

Dawn of the Mummy *Woof!* **1982** Lousy plot and bad acting—not to mention gore galore—do this one in. A photographer and a bevy of young fashion models travel to Egypt for a special shoot. They unwittingly stumble upon an ancient tomb, teeming with vengeance-minded mummies. **93m/C VHS, Beta.** Brenda King, Barry Sattels, George Peck, Joan Levy; ***D:*** Frank Agrama. *NO*

Dawn on the Great Divide ☠☠½ **1942** Jones' last film before his tragic and untimely death trying to save people from a fire at the Coconut Grove in Boston. Wagon train has to battle not only Indians, but bad guys as well. Plot provides more depth than the usual western fare. **57m/B VHS, Beta.** Buck Jones, Tim McCoy, Raymond Hatton, Mona Barrie, Robert Lowery, Betty Blythe, Jan Wiley, Harry Woods, Roy Barcroft; ***D:*** Howard Bretherton. *NOS, MRV, VCN*

Dawn Patrol ☠☠☠ **1938** Flynn plays a flight commander whose nerves are shot in this story of the British Royal Flying Corps during WWI. The focus is on the effects that the pressures and deaths have on all those concerned. Fine performances from all in this well-done remake of the 1930 film. **103m/B VHS, Beta.** Errol Flynn, David Niven, Basil Rathbone, Donald Crisp, Barry Fitzgerald, Melville Cooper; ***D:*** Edmund Goulding; ***C:*** Gaetano Antonio "Tony" Gaudio; ***M:*** Max Steiner. *FOX, MGM*

Dawn Rider ☠☠ **1935** Formula western has all the right ingredients: Wayne as a cowboy out to get revenge on the gang that murdered his father. Features stuntman Canutt in rare acting role. **60m/B VHS.** John Wayne, Marion Burns, Yakima Canutt; ***D:*** Robert North Bradbury. *COL, REP, MRV*

Dawn Rider/Frontier Horizon **1939** A double feature of two of Wayne's earliest western films. **114m/B VHS, Beta.** John Wayne, Jennifer Jones, Marion Burns; ***D:*** Robert North Bradbury, George Sherman. *REP*

The Dawning ☠☠½ **1988** An Irish revolutionary in the 1920's draws a young woman into his dangerous world of romance, intrigue and death. Howard's last film. Based on the novel "Old Jest" by Jennifer Johnston. **97m/C VHS, LV.** *GB* Anthony Hopkins, Jean Simmons, Trevor Howard, Rebecca Pidgeon, Hugh Grant, Tara MacGowran; ***D:*** Robert Knights. *LIV, PMS*

The Dawson Patrol ☠½ **1978** Royal Canadian Mountie dog-sled race turns into a dramatic battle for survival. **75m/C VHS, Beta.** George R. Robinson, Tim Henry, Neil Dainaro, James B. Douglas; ***D:*** Peter Kelly. *TWE*

The Day After ☠☠☠ **1983** Powerful drama graphically depicts the nuclear bombing of a mid-western city and its after-effects on the survivors. Made for television, and very controversial when first shown, gathering huge ratings and vast media coverage. **122m/C VHS, Beta, LV.** Jason Robards Jr., JoBeth Williams, John Lithgow, Steve Guttenberg, John Cullum; ***D:*** Nicholas Meyer. *PAR*

The Day and the Hour ☠☠½ *Today We Live: Le Jour et L'Heure; Il Giorno e L'Ora; Viviamo Oggi* **1963** A woman becomes accidentally involved in the resistance movement during the Nazi occupation of France in WWII. **110m/C VHS, Beta.** *FR JP* Simone Signoret, Stuart Whitman, Genevieve Page, Michel Piccoli, Reggie Nalder, Pierre Dux, Billy Kearns; ***D:*** Rene Clement; ***M:*** Claude Bolling. *INJ*

A Day at the Races ☠☠☠½ **1937** Though it seems labored at times, the brilliance of the brothers Marx still comes through in this rather weak tale of a patient in a sanitorium who convinces horse doctor Groucho to take on running the place. ♫A Message from the Man in the Moon; On Blue Venetian Waters; Tomorrow is Another Day; All God's Chillun Got Rhythm. **111m/B VHS, Beta, LV.** Groucho Marx, Harpo Marx, Chico Marx, Sig Rumann, Douglass Dumbrille, Margaret Dumont, Allan Jones, Maureen O'Sullivan; ***D:*** Sam Wood; ***C:*** Joseph Ruttenberg; ***M:*** George Bassman. *MGM, CCB*

Day for Night ☠☠☠☠ *La Nuit Americaine* **1973 (PG)** A wryly affectionate look at the profession of moviemaking—its craft, character, and the personalities that interact against the performances commanded by the camera. In French with English subtitles. **116m/C VHS, Beta.** *FR* Jean-Pierre Leaud, Jacqueline Bisset, Jean-Pierre Aumont, Valentina Cortese, Alexandra Stewart, Dani, Nathalie Baye, Francois Truffaut; ***D:*** Francois Truffaut; ***W:*** Suzanne Schiffman, Jean-Louis Richard, Francois Truffaut; ***M:*** Georges Delerue. Academy Awards '73: Best Foreign Language Film; British Academy Awards '73: Best Director (Truffaut), Best Film, Best Supporting Actress (Cortese); National Society of Film Critics Awards '73: Best Director (Truffaut), Best Film, Best Supporting Actress (Cortese); Nominations: Academy Awards '74: Best Director (Truffaut), Best Original Screenplay, Best Supporting Actress (Cortese). *INJ, WAR, APD*

A Day for Thanks on Walton's Mountain ☠☠ **1982** Many of the original television-show cast members returned for this sentimental Thanksgiving reunion on Walton's Mountain. Made for television. **97m/C VHS.** Ralph Waite, Ellen Corby, Judy Norton-Taylor, Eric Scott, Jon Walmsley, Robert Wightman, Mary McDonough, David W. Harper, Kami Cotler, Joe Conley, Ronnie Clair Edwards, Richard Gilliland, Melinda Naud; ***D:*** Harry Harris. *WAR*

A Day in October ☠☠½ **1992 (PG-13)** 1943, Copenhagen, Denmark. There are signs the Jewish population is in danger from occupying Nazi officials and the resistance movement is active. Wounded resistance fighter Sweeney is rescued by the Jewish Sara (Wolf), and their relationship deepens as the realities of WWII change their lives. Based on historical fact, but there's little explanation of the politics or the fierce nationalism and intense loyalty most Danes felt towards their fellow countrymen, a loyalty that ultimately saved most of the Danish Jews from the Holocaust. Good performances, particularly Benzali as Sara's father, help overcome the script weaknesses. Filmed on location in Denmark. **96m/C VHS.** D.B. Sweeney, Kelly Wolf, Tovah Feldshuh, Daniel Benzali, Ole Lemmeke, Kim Romer, Anders Peter Bro, Lars Oluf Larsen; ***D:*** Kenneth Madsen; ***W:*** Damian F. Slattery; ***M:*** Jens Lysdal. *ACA, FOX*

A Day in the Country ☠☠☠½ *Une Partie de Campagne* **1946** The son of the famed painter gives us the moving tale of a young woman's sudden and intense love for a man she meets while on a picnic with her family. Beautifully adapted from a story by Guy de Maupassant. Renowned photographer Henri Cartier-Bresson contributed to the wonderful cinematography. In French with English subtitles. **40m/B VHS, Beta.** *FR* Sylvia Bataille, Georges Darnoux, Jane Marken, Paul Temps; ***D:*** Jean Renoir. *NOS, MRV, DVT*

A Day in the Death of Joe Egg ☠☠☠ **1971 (R)** Based on the Peter Nichols play, an unlikely black comedy about a British couple trying to care for their retarded/autistic child, nearly destroying their marriage in the process. They begin to contemplate euthanasia as a solution. Well-acted, but potentially offensive to some. **106m/C VHS, Beta.** *GB* Alan Bates, Janet Suzman, Elizabeth Robillard, Peter Bowles, Joan Hickson, Sheila Gish; ***D:*** Peter Medak; ***W:*** David Deutsch. *COL*

The Day It Came to Earth *Woof!* **1977 (PG)** Completely silly and unbelievable sci-fi flick has meteor crashing into the watery grave of a mobster. The decomposed corpse is revived by the radiation and plots to take revenge on those who fitted him with cement shoes. **89m/C VHS, Beta.** Roger Manning, Wink Roberts, Bob Ginnaven, Rita Wilson, Delight de Bruine; ***D:*** Harry Z. Thomason. *NO*

The Day My Parents Ran Away ☠☠½ **1993 (PG)** Rebellious 16-year-old gets a tough lesson in responsibility when his parents get tired of his antics and decide to leave home in search of a new life. He finds out things aren't so easy on your own. **95m/C VHS, LV.** Matt Frewer, Bobby Jacoby, Brigid Conley Walsh, Blair Brown, Martin Mull; ***D:*** Martin Nicholson; ***W:*** Handel Glassberg; ***M:*** J. Peter Robinson. *COL, IME*

Day of Atonement ☠☠½ **1993 (R)** It's a war for power between rival druglords when Hanin is released from prison and finds out his son and cousin are battling over turf. Then Walken is dragged into the fracas. Beals is the government agent trying to regain some control of the dangerous situation. **127m/C VHS, LV.** Christopher Walken, Jennifer Beals, Jill Clayburgh, Roger Hanin, Richard Berry. *VMK*

Day of Judgment ☠½ **1981** A mysterious stranger arrives in a town to slaughter those people who violate the Ten Commandments. **101m/C VHS, Beta.** William T. Hicks, Harris Bloodworth, Brownlee Davis; ***D:*** C.D.H. Reynolds. *NO*

Day of the Animals ☠ *Something is Out There* **1977 (PG)** Nature gone wild. It seems a depleted ozone layer has exposed the animals to the sun's radiation, turning Bambi and Bugs into brutal killers. A group of backpackers trek in the Sierras, unaware of the transformation. Far-fetched and silly (we hope). **95m/C VHS.** Christopher George, Leslie Nielsen, Lynda Day George, Richard Jaeckel, Michael Ansara, Ruth Roman, Jon Cedar, Susan Backlinie, Andrew Stevens, Gil Lamb; ***D:*** William Girdler; ***W:*** William W. Norton Sr. *MED*

Day of the Assassin ☠ **1981** A Mideast shah's yacht explodes, sending a huge fortune to the bottom of a murky bay. This sets off a rampage of treasure hunting by a variety of ruthless mercenaries. **94m/C VHS, Beta.** Glenn Ford, Chuck Connors, Richard Roundtree, Henry Silva, Jorge Rivero; ***D:*** Brian Trenchard-Smith. *PSM*

Day of the Cobra ☠½ **1984** A corrupt narcotics bureau official hires an ex-cop to find a heroin kingpin on the back streets of Genoa, Italy. **95m/C VHS, Beta.** *IT* Franco Nero, Sybil Danning, Mario Maranzana, Licinia Lentini, William Berger; ***D:*** Enzo G. Castellari. *MED*

Day of the Dead ☠½ **1985** The third in Romero's trilogy of films about flesh-eating zombies taking over the world. Romero hasn't thought up anything new for the ghouls to do, and the humans are too nasty to care about this time around. For adult audiences. **91m/C VHS, Beta, LV.** Lori Cardillo, Terry Alexander, Joseph Pilato, Jarleth Conroy; ***D:*** George A. Romero; ***W:*** George A. Romero. *MED, IME, VTR*

The Day of the Dolphin ☠☠ **1973 (PG)** Research scientist, after successfully working out a means of teaching dolphins to talk, finds his animals kidnapped; espionage and assassination are involved. Dolphin voices by Henry, who also wrote the screenplay. **104m/C VHS, Beta, LV.** George C. Scott, Trish Van Devere, Paul Sorvino, Fritz Weaver, Jon Korkes, John Dehner, Edward Herrmann, Severn Darden; ***D:*** Mike Nichols; ***W:*** Buck Henry; ***M:*** Georges Delerue; ***V:*** Buck Henry. National Board of Review Awards '73: 10 Best Films of the Year; Nominations: Academy Awards '73: Best Sound. *SUE, NLC*

The Day of the Jackal ☠☠☠½ **1973 (PG)** Frederick Forsyth's best-selling novel of political intrigue is splendidly brought to the screen by Zinnemann. A brilliant and ruthless assassin hired to kill Charles de Gaulle skirts the international intelligence pool, while intuitive police work to stop him. Tense, suspenseful, beautiful location photography. Excellent acting by Fox, Cusack and Britton. **142m/C VHS, Beta, LV.** Edward Fox, Alan Badel, Tony Britton, Derek Jacobi, Cyril Cusack, Olga Georges-Picot; ***D:*** Fred Zinnemann; ***M:*** Georges Delerue. Nominations: Academy Awards '73: Best Film Editing. *MCA*

The Day of the Locust ☠☠☠½ **1975 (R)** Compelling adaptation of Nathaniel West's novel concerning the dark side of 1930s' Hollywood. A no-talent amoral actress's affair with a meek accountant leads to tragedy and destruction. Told from the view of a cynical art director wise to the ways of Hollywood. **140m/C VHS, Beta, LV.** Donald Sutherland, Karen Black, Burgess Meredith, William Atherton, Billy Barty, Bo Hopkins, Richard Dysart, Geraldine Page; ***D:*** John Schlesinger; ***C:*** Conrad Hall; ***M:*** John Barry. National Board of Review Awards '75: 10 Best Films of the Year; Nominations: Academy Awards '75: Best Cinematography, Best Supporting Actor (Meredith). *PAR*

Day of the Maniac 🦴½ **1977 (R)** Psychotic drug addict will stop at nothing to support his growing habit. **89m/C VHS, Beta.** George Hilton, Susan Scott; ***D:*** Sergio Martino. *REP*

Day of the Panther 🦴½ **1988** The Panthers—-the world's most formidable martial artists—-are mighty torqued when panther-Linda is pithed, and they're not known to turn the other cheek. Much chop-socky kicking and shrilling. **86m/C VHS, Beta.** John Stanton, Eddie Stazak; ***D:*** Brian Trenchard-Smith. *CEL*

Day of the Triffids 🦴🦴🦴 **1963** The majority of Earth's population is blinded by a meteor shower which also causes plant spores to mutate into giant carnivores. Well-done adaptation of John Wyndham's science fiction classic. **94m/C VHS, Beta, LV.** Howard Keel, Janet Scott, Nicole Maurey, Kieron Moore, Mervyn Johns, Alison Leggatt, Ewan Roberts, Janina Faye; ***D:*** Freddie Francis, Steve Sekely; ***W:*** Philip Yordan. *MED, MRV, PSM*

Day of Triumph **1954** A dynamic version of the life of Christ as seen through the eyes of the apostles Andrew and Zadok, the leaders of the Zealot underground. **110m/C VHS.** Lee J. Cobb, Robert Wilson, Ralph Freud; ***D:*** Irving Pichel. *REP*

Day of Wrath 🦴🦴🦴🦴 *Vredens Dag* **1943** An involving psychological thriller based on records of witch trials from the early 1600s. An old woman, burned at the stake as a witch, puts a curse on the local parson and his family. Grim and unrelentingly pessimistic, moving from one horrific scene to another, director Dreyer creates a masterpiece of terror. Based on a play by Hans Wiers Jenssen. In Danish with English subtitles. **110m/B VHS.** *DK* Thorkild Roose, Sigrid Neiiendam, Lisbeth Movin, Preben Lerdorff, Anna Svierker; ***D:*** Carl Theodor Dreyer; ***W:*** Carl Theodor Dreyer; ***M:*** Poul Schierbeck. National Board of Review Awards '48: 10 Best Films of the Year. *HTV, NOS, SNC*

Day One 🦴🦴🦴 **1989** Vivid recreation of one of the most turbulent periods of American history—the WWII race to build the atomic bomb. Chronicles the two year top-secret efforts of the Manhattan Project, with General Leslie Groves (Dennehy) having to supervise the project and contain the scientific rivalries. Outstanding cast, with Strathairn notable as physicist J. Robert Oppenheimer. Adapted from "Day One: Before Hiroshima and After" by Peter Wyden. Made for television. **141m/C VHS.** Brian Dennehy, David Strathairn, Michael Tucker, Hume Cronyn, Richard Dysart, Barnard Hughes, Hal Holbrook, David Ogden Stiers, John McMartin; ***D:*** Joseph Sargent; ***W:*** David W. Rintels; ***M:*** Mason Daring. *WOV*

The Day That Shook the World 🦴🦴 **1978 (R)** Slow-moving but intriguing account of events surrounding the assassination of Archduke Ferdinand of Austria that triggered WWI. Garnered an R-rating due to some disturbingly graphic scenes. **111m/C VHS.** Christopher Plummer, Florinda Bolkan, Maximilian Schell; ***D:*** Veljko Bulajic. *NO*

Day the Bookies Wept 🦴🦴 **1939** Decent yarn about cabbies tricked into buying a "racehorse." Turns out she's old as the hills and hooked on alcohol to boot, but they enter her in the big race anyway. **50m/B VHS, Beta.** Betty Grable, Joe Penner, Tom Kennedy, Richard Lane; ***D:*** Leslie Goodwins. *CCB*

The Day the Earth Caught Fire 🦴🦴🦴½ **1961** The earth is knocked out of orbit and sent hurtling toward the sun when nuclear testing is done simultaneously at both the North and South Poles. Realistic and suspenseful, this is one of the best of the sci-fi genre. **95m/B VHS, Beta.** Janet Munro, Edward Judd, Leo McKern; ***D:*** Val Guest; ***W:*** Val Guest, Wolf Mankowitz. British Academy Awards '61: Best Screenplay. *REP, KAR*

The Day the Earth Froze 🦴🦴 **1959** Witch steals the sun because she couldn't have a magical mill that produced grain, salt, and gold. Everything on Earth freezes. Based on a Finnish epic poem. **67m/B VHS.** *FI RU* Nina Anderson, Jon Powers, Ingrid Elhardt, Paul Sorenson; ***D:*** Gregg Sebelious. *SNC*

The Day the Earth Stood Still 🦴🦴🦴½ **1951** A gentle alien lands on Earth to deliver a message of peace and a warning against experimenting with nuclear power. He finds his views echoed by a majority of the population, but not the ones who are in control. In this account based loosely on the story of Christ, Rennie is the visitor backed by the mighty robot Gort. One of the greatest science fiction films of all time. **92m/B VHS, Beta, LV.** Michael Rennie, Patricia Neal, Hugh Marlowe, Sam Jaffe, Frances Bavier, Lock Martin, Billy Gray; ***D:*** Robert Wise; ***W:*** Edmund H. North; ***C:*** Leo Tover; ***M:*** Bernard Herrmann. *FOX, FCT, MLB*

The Day the Sky Exploded 🦴½ *Death From Outer Space; La Morte Viene Dalla Spazio; Le Danger Vient de l'Escape* **1957** Sci-fi disaster drama doesn't live up to the grandiose title, as a runaway rocket ship hits the sun, unleashing an asteroid shower that threatens Earth with tidal waves, earthquakes, heat waves and terrible dialogue. The highlight of this Franco-Italian effort is the cinematography by horror director Mario Bava. **80m/B VHS.** *FR IT* Paul Hubschmid, Madeleine Fischer, Fiorella Mari, Ivo Garrani, Dario Michaelis; ***D:*** Richard Benson. *NOS, FCT*

The Day the Sun Turned Cold 🦴🦴🦴 *Tianguo Niezi* **1994** In an apparent crisis of conscience a young man (Zhong Hua) enters a police station and tries to convince a weary captain (Hu) that his mother (Gowa) murdered his cruel father (Jingwu) 10 years before in order to marry another man. The detective eventually concludes he should investigate the supposed crime, which happened in a remote village, but Zhong Hua's accusations naturally stir up a great deal of resentment and anger. There's lots of questions about guilt, innocence, and motives—on everybody's part. Mandarin with subtitles. **99m/C VHS.** *HK* Siqin Gowa, Tuo Zhong Hua, Wai Zhi, Ma Jingwu, Li Hu; ***D:*** Yim Ho; ***W:*** Yim Ho; ***C:*** Hou Yong; ***M:*** Yoshihide Otomo. *KIV*

The Day the Women Got Even 🦴½ **1980** Four suburban homemakers take up the life of vigilantes to save unsuspecting actresses from a talent agent's blackmail scheme. Made for television. **98m/C VHS, Beta.** JoAnn Pflug, Tina Louise, Georgia Engel, Barbara Rhoades, Julie Hagerty, Ed O'Neill; ***D:*** Burt Brinckerhoff; ***M:*** Brad Fiedel. *TLF*

Day the World Ended 🦴 **1955** The first science fiction film of exploitation director Roger Corman. Five survivors of nuclear holocaust discover a desert ranch house fortress owned by a survivalist (Birch) and his daughter (Nelson). With relatively abundant supplies, they fatuously wallow in false misery until a disfigured visitor, wasting away from radiation, stumbles into their paradise. His mutation into an alien being confronts them with the horror that lurks outside. **79m/B VHS.** Paul Birch, Lori Nelson, Adele Jergens, Raymond Hatton, Paul Dubov, Richard Denning, Mike Connors; ***D:*** Roger Corman; ***W:*** Lou Rusoff. *COL*

Day Time Ended 🦴🦴 *Vortex; Timewarp* **1980** A pair of glowing UFO's streaking across the sky and an alien mechanical device with long menacing appendages are only two of the bizarre phenomena witnessed from a lone house in the desert. Good special effects. Also released as "Time Warp" (1978). **80m/C VHS, Beta, LV.** Chris Mitchum, Jim Davis, Dorothy Malone; ***D:*** John Cardos; ***W:*** David Schmoeller, J. Larry Carroll; ***M:*** Richard Band. *MED, MRV*

The Day Will Dawn 🦴🦴🦴 *The Avengers* **1942** Suspenseful British-made WWII thriller about a reporter and a young Norwegian girl who plot to sabotage a secret Nazi U-boat base near the girl's town. **100m/B VHS, Beta, 8mm.** *GB* Deborah Kerr, Hugh Williams, Griffith Jones, Ralph Richardson, Francis L. Sullivan, Roland Culver, Niall MacGinnis, Finlay Currie, Patricia Medina; ***D:*** Harold French; ***W:*** Terence Rattigan. *VYY*

Day with Conrad Green **1980** Set in 1927, this program presents a somewhat farcical look at a successful Broadway producer as he attempts to cope with a full schedule of personal and business problems on the day of the funeral of his longtime assistant. **60m/C VHS, Beta.** Fred Gwynne. *MTP*

Daybreak 🦴🦴½ **1993 (R)** In the near future America has been decimated by a nameless, sexually transmitted disease (read AIDS parable) and public policy is to quarantine the infected in concentration camp-like prisons. This leads to a quasi-official group of green-shirted thugs roaming the streets and imprisoning or killing anyone they suspect has the disease. A small resistance movement is lead by Torch (Gooding, Jr.), who happens to fall in love with Blue (Kelly), the sister of one of the fascist leaders. Based on Alan Bowne's play "Beirut, Daybreak." Made for cable television. **91m/C VHS.** Cuba Gooding Jr., Moira Kelly, Omar Epps, Martha Plimpton, Alice Drummond, David Eigenberg, John Savage; ***Cameos:*** Phil Hartman; ***D:*** Stephen Tolkin; ***W:*** Stephen Tolkin. *HBO*

The Daydreamer 🦴🦴½ *Absent-Minded; Le Distrait* **1975** Actor/director/writer Richard stars as a bumbling fool let loose in the French corporate world with comical results. In French with subtitles. **90m/C VHS, Beta.** *FR* Pierre Richard, Bernard Blier, Maria Pacome, Marie-Christine Barrault; ***D:*** Pierre Richard; ***W:*** Pierre Richard; ***M:*** Vladimir Cosma. *FCT*

Days and Nights in the Forest 🦴🦴½ **1970** Four men living in Calcutta decide to leave the city for a brief vacation. Each has a different emotional experience which will change him forever, including a brief love affair and finding true romance. In Bengali with English subtitles. **120m/C VHS.** *IN* ***D:*** Satyajit Ray. *FCT*

Days of Glory 🦴🦴½ **1943** Peck's screen debut finds him as a Russian peasant bravely fighting the Nazi blitzkrieg almost single-handedly. **86m/B VHS, Beta.** Tamara Toumanova, Gregory Peck, Alan Reed, Maria Palmer, Lowell Gilmore, Hugo Haas; ***D:*** Jacques Tourneur; ***C:*** Gaetano Antonio "Tony" Gaudio. *TTC*

Days of Heaven 🦴🦴🦴½ **1978 (PG)** Drifter Gere, his younger sister, and a woman he claims is his sister become involved with a Texas sharecropper. Told through the eyes of the younger girl, this is a sweeping vision of the U.S. before WWI. Loss and loneliness, deception, frustration, and anger haunt these people as they struggle to make the land their own. Deservedly awarded an Oscar for breathtaking cinematography. **95m/C VHS, Beta, LV.** Richard Gere, Brooke Adams, Sam Shepard, Linda Manz, Stuart Margolin; ***D:*** Terence Malick; ***W:*** Terence Malick; ***C:*** Nestor Almendros; ***M:*** Ennio Morricone. Academy Awards '78: Best Cinematography; Cannes Film Festival '79: Best Director (Malick); Los Angeles Film Critics Association Awards '78: Best Cinematography; National Board of Review Awards '78: 10 Best Films of the Year; New York Film Critics Awards '78: Best Director (Malick); National Society of Film Critics Awards '78: Best Cinematography, Best Director (Malick), Best Film; Nominations: Academy Awards '78: Best Costume Design, Best Sound, Best Original Score; Cannes Film Festival '79: Best Film. *PAR*

Days of Hell 🦴 *I Giorni Dell'Inferno* **1984** Forgettable tale of four mercenaries who are hired to rescue a doctor and his daughter held captive by guerrillas somewhere in Afghanistan only to find out they're pawns in an even bigger scheme. **90m/C VHS, Beta.** Conrad Nichols, Richard Raymond, Stephen Elliott, Kinako Harada; ***D:*** Anthony Richmond. *NO*

Days of Thrills and Laughter 🦴🦴🦴½ **1961** Delightful compilation of clips from the era of silent films, showcasing the talents of the great comics as well as daring stuntman. **93m/B VHS, Beta.** Buster Keaton, Charlie Chaplin, Harold Lloyd, Stan Laurel, Oliver Hardy, Douglas Fairbanks Sr.; ***D:*** Robert Youngson. *MPI*

Days of Thunder 🦴🦴 **1990 (PG-13)** "Top Gun" in race cars! Cruise follows the same formula he has followed for several years now (with the notable exception of "Born on the Fourth of July.") Cruise and Towne co-wrote the screenplay concerning a young kid bursting with talent and raw energy who must learn to deal with his mentor, his girlfriend, and eventually the bad guy. First film that featured cameras that were actually on the race cars. If you like Cruise or race cars then this is the movie for you. **108m/C VHS, Beta, LV.** Tom Cruise, Robert Duvall, Randy Quaid, Nicole Kidman, Cary Elwes, Michael Rooker, Fred Dalton Thompson, John C. Reilly; *D:* Tony Scott; *W:* Tom Cruise, Robert Towne; *M:* Hans Zimmer. Nominations: Academy Awards '90: Best Sound. *PAR*

Days of Wine and Roses ℒℒ½ **1958** The original "Playhouse 90" television version of J.P. Miller's story which was adapted for the big screen in 1962. An executive on the fast track and his young wife, initially only social drinkers, find themselves degenerating into alcoholism. A well-acted, stirring drama. **89m/B VHS, Beta.** Cliff Robertson, Piper Laurie; *D:* John Frankenheimer. *RHI, MGM, BTV*

Days of Wine and Roses ℒℒℒ½ **1962** A harrowing tale of an alcoholic advertising man who gradually drags his wife down with him into a life of booze. Part of the "A Night at the Movies" series, this tape simulates a 1962 movie evening with a Bugs Bunny cartoon, "Martian Through Georgia," a newsreel, and coming attractions for "Gypsy" and "Rome Adventure." Big screen adaptation of the play originally shown on television. ♫Days of Wine and Roses. **138m/B VHS, Beta, LV.** Jack Lemmon, Lee Remick, Charles Bickford, Jack Klugman, Jack Albertson; *D:* Blake Edwards; *M:* Henry Mancini, Johnny Mercer. Academy Awards '62: Best Song ("Days of Wine and Roses"); Nominations: Academy Awards '62: Best Actor (Lemmon), Best Actress (Remick), Best Art Direction/Set Decoration (B & W), Best Costume Design (B & W). *WAR*

Dayton's Devils ℒℒ **1968** Nielsen is the leader of a motley crew of losers who plan to rob a military base bank in this action-packed heist flick. **107m/C VHS, Beta.** Rory Calhoun, Leslie Nielsen, Lainie Kazan, Eric (Hans Gudegast) Braeden, Georg Stanford Brown; *D:* Jack Shea. *NO*

Dazed and Confused ℒℒℒ **1993 (R)** A day in the life of a bunch of high schoolers should prove to be a trip back in time for those coming of age in the 70's. Eight seniors facing life after high school have one last year long hurrah, as they search for Aerosmith tickets and haze the incoming freshmen. Keen characterization by writer/director Linklater captures the spirit of a generation shaped by Watergate, the Vietnam War, feminism, and marijuana. Groovy soundtrack features Alice Cooper, Deep Purple, KISS, and Foghat. **97m/C VHS, LV.** Jason London, Rory Cochrane, Sasha Jensen, Wiley Wiggins, Michelle Burke, Adam Goldberg, Anthony Rapp, Marissa Ribisi, Parker Posey; *D:* Richard Linklater; *W:* Richard Linklater. *MCA*

D.C. Cab ℒℒ½ **1984 (R)** A rag-tag group of Washington, D.C. cabbies learn a lesson in self-respect in this endearing comedy. Though not without flaws, it's charming all the same. **100m/C VHS, Beta, LV.** Mr. T, Leif Erickson, Adam Baldwin, Charlie Barnett, Irene Cara, Anne DeSalvo, Max Gail, Gloria Gifford, Gary Busey, Jill Schoelen, Marsha Warfield; *D:* Joel Schumacher; *W:* Joel Schumacher, Topper Carew. *MCA*

The Dead ℒℒℒ½ **1987 (PG)** The poignant final film by Huston, based on James Joyce's short story. At a Christmas dinner party in turn-of-the-century Dublin, a man discovers how little he knows about his wife when a song reminds her of a cherished lost love. Beautifully captures the spirit of the story while providing Huston an opportunity to create a last lament on the fickle nature of time and life. **82m/C VHS, Beta, LV.** *GB* Anjelica Huston, Donal McCann, Marie Kean, Donal Donnelly, Dan O'Herlihy, Helen Carroll, Frank Patterson; *D:* John Huston; *C:* Fred Murphy; *M:* Alex North. Independent Spirit Awards '88: Best Director (Huston), Best Supporting Actress (Huston); National Society of Film Critics Awards '87: Best Film; Nominations: Academy Awards '87: Best Adapted Screenplay, Best Costume Design. *LIV, VES, TVC*

Dead Again ℒℒℒ½ **1991 (R)** Branagh's first film since his brilliant debut as the director/star of "Henry V" again proves him a visionary force on and off camera. As the smart L.A. detective hired to discover the identity of a beautiful, but mute woman, he's realistic, clever, tender and cynical. He finds that he's apparently trapped in a nightmarish cycle of murder begun years before. Literate, lovely to look at, suspenseful, with a sense of humor to match its high style. **107m/C VHS, LV.** Kenneth Branagh, Emma Thompson, Andy Garcia, Lois Hall, Richard Easton, Derek Jacobi, Hanna Schygulla, Campbell Scott, Wayne Knight, Christine Ebersole; ***Cameos:*** Robin Williams; *D:* Kenneth Branagh; *W:* Scott Frank; *M:* Patrick Doyle. National Board of Review Awards '91: 10 Best Films of the Year. *PAR, CCB*

Dead Ahead: The Exxon Valdez Disaster ℒℒℒ *Disaster at Valdez* **1992 (PG-13)** Focuses on the first crucial days after the March 24, 1989 oil spill when the Exxon Valdez ran aground off Alaska in Prince William Sound. Portrays the inadequate precautions, incompetence, greed, and petty bureaucracy that made an appalling situation even worse. Lloyd stars as Exxon official Frank Iarossi, in charge of the official cleanup, caught between onsite confusion and corporate bungling while Heard is outraged environmentalist Dan Lawn. News and home videotapes of the actual spill are used to enhance the dramatization. Filmed in Vancouver, British Columbia. Made for cable television. **90m/C VHS.** Christopher Lloyd, John Heard, Rip Torn, Michael Murphy, Don S. Davies, Ken Walsh, Bob Gunton, Mark Metcalf, Paul Guilfoyle, David Morse, Jackson Davies; *D:* Paul Seed; *W:* Michael Baker; *M:* David Ferguson. *IMP*

Dead Aim *Woof!* **1987 (R)** A dud about Soviet spies who introduce even more drugs into New York City, ostensibly to bring about the downfall of the U.S. Obviously a completely far-fetched plot. **91m/C VHS, LV.** Ed Marinaro, Isaac Hayes, Corbin Bernsen; *D:* William Vanderkloot. *LIV, HHE*

Dead Air ℒℒ **1994 (PG-13)** Atmospheric murder mystery finds radio deejay Hines getting calls from a mystery woman who says she knows him well and has kidnapped his new girlfriend. Meanwhile, a woman claiming to be a reporter wants to interview him and things around the radio station start looking decidedly sinister. **91m/C VHS, LV.** Gregory Hines, Debrah Farentino, Gloria Reuben, Beau Starr, Laura Harrington, Michael Harris, W. Earl Brown, Veronica Cartwright; *D:* Fred Walton; *W:* David Amann; *M:* Dana Kaproff. *MCA*

Dead Alive ℒℒ **1993 (R)** This outrageously over-the-top horror flick from New Zealand is a gore aficionado's delight (think "Evil Dead" movies for comparison). Set in 1957 and satirizing the bland times, the "plot" has the mom of a nerdy son getting bitten by an exotic monkey, which promptly turns her into a particularly nasty ghoul. This condition is apparently contagious (except for her son who tries to hide the fact mom is literally a monster) and calls for lots of spurting blood and body parts which take on lives of their own. For those with strong stomachs and senses of humor. **97m/C VHS, LV.** *NZ* Timothy Balme, Elizabeth Moody, Diana Penalver, Ian Watkin; *D:* Peter Jackson; *W:* Peter Jackson. *VMK, FCT*

Dead and Buried ℒℒ½ **1981 (R)** Farentino is the sheriff who can't understand why the victims of some pretty grisly murders seem to be coming back to life. Eerily suspenseful. **95m/C VHS, Beta.** James Farentino, Jack Albertson, Melody Anderson, Lisa Blount, Bill Quinn, Michael Pataki; *D:* Gary Sherman; *W:* Dan O'Bannon. *VES*

Dead as a Doorman ℒ½ **1985** A young writer takes a part-time post as a doorman and becomes the target of a murderous lunatic. **83m/C VHS, Beta.** Bradley Whitford, Sharon Schlarth, Bruce Taylor; *D:* Gary Youngman. *LIV, VES*

Dead Badge ℒℒ½ **1994 (R)** An honest cop is reassigned to a corrupt precinct and becomes targeted for death. **95m/C VHS.** Brian Wimmer, Olympia Dukakis, Yaphet Kotto, M. Emmet Walsh, James B. Sikking, Marta DuBois. *CAF*

Dead Bang ℒℒ½ **1989 (R)** A frustrated cop uncovers a murderous white supremacist conspiracy in L.A. Frankenheimer's deft directorial hand shapes a somewhat conventional cop plot into an effective vehicle for Johnson. **102m/C VHS, Beta, LV, 8mm.** Don Johnson, Bob Balaban, William Forsythe, Penelope Ann Miller, Tim Reid, Frank Military, Michael Higgins, Michael Jeter, Evans Evans, Tate Donovan; *D:* John Frankenheimer; *W:* Robert Foster; *M:* Gary Chang, Michael Kamen. *WAR*

Dead Beat ℒℒ½ **1994 (R)** Teen love and lust—and murder—all set in Albuquerque, New Mexico, circa 1965. Womanizer Kit (Ramsey) will use any tale to score with his dates—and is happy to pass on tips to adoring disciple Rudy (Getty). When Kit meets up with rebellious rich girl Kirsten (Wagner), she demands proof of his love and he confides he once murdered a girl. Kirsten tries to tighten her stranglehold on Kit with this info and force Rudy from his life but Kit's dark side doesn't stay hidden either. **94m/C VHS.** Bruce Ramsay, Natasha Gregson Wagner, Balthazar Getty, Meredith Salenger, Sara Gilbert, Deborah Harry, Max Perlich, Alex Cox; *D:* Adam Dubov; *W:* Adam Dubov. *WEA, LIV*

Dead Boyz Can't Fly ℒℒ **1993 (R)** Disturbing look at urban violence. Dysfunctional punk leads his equally amoral cohorts on a looting spree in a near-empty highrise in revenge against a patronizing businessman. The unrated version contains 10 more minutes of violence. **92m/C VHS.** Delia Sheppard, Sheila Kennedy, Ruth Collins, Mark McCulley, Brad Friedman; *D:* Howard Winters. *NO*

Dead Calm ℒℒℒ **1989 (R)** A taut Australian thriller based on a novel by Charles Williams. A young married couple is yachting on the open seas when they happen upon the lone survivor of a sinking ship. They take him on board only to discover he's a homicidal maniac. Makes for some pretty suspenseful moments that somewhat make up for the weak ending. **97m/C VHS, Beta, LV, 8mm.** *AU* Sam Neill, Billy Zane, Nicole Kidman, Rod Mullinar; *D:* Phillip Noyce; *W:* Terry Hayes; *C:* Dean Semler; *M:* Graeme Revell. *WAR, FCT*

Dead Center ℒℒ *Crazy Joe* **1994 (R)** Street punk gets trained as assassin by secret government agency that frames him for the murder of a U.S. senator. So now he has to stay alive long enough to prove his innocence. **90m/C VHS, LV.** Justin Lazard, Eb Lottimer, Rachel York; *D:* Steve Carver. *VMK*

Dead Certain ℒ **1992 (R)** A "Silence of the Lambs" rip-off. Dourif (again specializing in weirdos) is the jailed serial killer providing tantalizing clues to the identity of a new killer on the loose. **93m/C VHS.** Brad Dourif, Francesco Quinn, Karen Russell, Joel Kaiser; *D:* Anders Palm; *W:* Anders Palm. *HMD*

Dead Cold ℒℒ **1996 (R)** Writer and his wife's second honeymoon at a remote cabin is disturbed by a sinister stranger. But then the writer discovers his wife is not what she seems. **91m/C VHS, LV.** Lysette Anthony, Chris Mulkey, Peter Dobson, Alina Thompson, Michael Champion; *D:* Kurt Anderson; *W:* Richard Brandes. *LIV*

Dead Connection ℒℒ **1994 (R)** Beautiful reporter Bonet is in cahoots with cop Madsen to see justice brought the "phone sex killer" who is terrorizing Los Angeles. **93m/C VHS.** Michael Madsen, Lisa Bonet, Gary Stretch; *D:* Nigel Dick; *W:* Larry Grolin; *M:* Rolfe Kent. *PGV*

The Dead Don't Die ℒ **1975** Unbelievable plot set in the 1930s has Hamilton as a detective trying to prove his brother was wrongly executed for murder. He ultimately clashes with the madman who wants to rule the world with an army of zombies. Perhaps if they had cast Hamilton as Master of the Zombies. Made for television. **74m/C VHS, Beta.** George Hamilton, Ray Milland, Linda Cristal, Ralph Meeker, Joan Blondell, James McEachin; *D:* Curtis Harrington. *WOV, GKK*

Dead Easy ℒℒ **1982** Livin' ain't easy for a Sydney sleaze-club owner, his working-girl girlfriend, and a slandered cop when they're caught between machete-wielding enemy gangs (it seems somebody made the crime boss REALLY mad). The three flee in that quintessential escape vehicle—a two-ton truck—to qualify the effort as an Australian contender for greatest chase scene ever (heavy chassis category). **92m/C VHS, Beta.** *AU* Scott Burgess, Rosemary Paul; *D:* Bert Deling. *MCG*

Dead End ℒℒℒ½ *Cradle of Crime* **1937** Sidney Kingsley play, adapted for the big screen by Lillian Hellman, traces the lives of various inhabitants of the slums on New York's Lower East Side as they try to overcome their surroundings. Gritty drama saved from melodrama status by some genuinely funny moments. Film launched the Dead End Kids. **92m/B VHS, Beta, LV.** Sylvia Sidney, Joel McCrea, Humphrey Bogart, Wendy Barrie, Claire Trevor, Allen Jenkins, Marjorie Main, Leo Gorcey, Charles Halton; ***D:*** William Wyler; ***C:*** Gregg Toland. Nominations: Academy Awards '37: Best Cinematography, Best Interior Decoration, Best Picture, Best Supporting Actress (Trevor). *MGM, SUE, MLB*

Dead End City 🦴½ **1988** Street-wise resident of L.A. organizes fellow citizens into a vigilante force to fight the gangs for control of the city. **88m/C VHS, Beta.** Dennis Cole, Greg Cummins, Christine Lunde, Robert Z'Dar, Darrell Nelson, Alena Downs; ***D:*** Peter Yuval; ***W:*** Michael Bogert. *AIP*

Dead End Drive-In 🦴🦴 **1986 (R)** In a surreal, grim future a man is trapped at a drive-in theater-cum-government-run concentration camp, where those considered to be less than desirable members of society are incarcerated. **92m/C VHS, Beta.** *AU* Ned Manning, Natalie McCurry, Peter Whitford; ***D:*** Brian Trenchard-Smith. *VTR, NWV*

Dead End Street 🦴½ **1983** Young prostitute attempts to change her self-destructive lifestyle. It's not easy. **86m/C VHS, Beta.** *IS* Anat Atzman, Yehoram Gaon. *TWE*

Dead Eyes of London 🦴🦴½ *Dark Eyes of London; Die Toten Augen von London* **1961** Blind old German men are dying to lower their premiums in this geriatric thriller: someone (perhaps the director of the home for the blind?) is killing off the clientele for their insurance money, and a Scotland Yard inspector aims to expose the scam. Relatively early vintage Kinski, it's a remake of the eerie 1939 Lugosi vehicle, "The Human Monster" (originally titled "Dark Eyes of London"), adapted from Edgar Wallace's "The Testament of Gordon Stuart." **95m/B VHS.** *GE* Joachim Fuchsberger, Karin Baal, Dieter Borsche, Ady Berber, Klaus Kinski, Eddi Arent, Wolfgang Lukschy; ***D:*** Alfred Vohrer. *SNC*

Dead for a Dollar 🦴½ **197?** A Colonel, a con man, and a mysterious woman team up in the Old West to search for the two hundred thousand dollars they stole from a local bank. **92m/C VHS, Beta.** John Ireland, George Hilton, Piero Vida, Sandra Milo. *UNI, MOV*

Dead Funny 🦴🦴 **1994 (R)** Vivian (Pena) returns to her Manhattan walk-up to find boyfriend Reggie (McCarthy) dead on her kitchen table, skewered by a Samurai sword. Instead of calling the police, Viv gets gal pal Louise (Turco) to come over to figure out who did Reg in. Instead, they get drunk and discuss Reggie's (who seen in flashbacks) immaturity and penchent for practical jokes. Good performances, twist ending, but situation runs out of steam. **91m/C VHS, LV.** Elizabeth Pena, Andrew McCarthy, Paige Turco, Blanche Baker, Lisa Jane Persky, Michael Mantell; ***D:*** John Feldman; ***W:*** John Feldman; ***M:*** Sheila Silver. *APX*

Dead Girls 🦴 **1990 (R)** A rock group whose lyrics focus on suicide goes on vacation. The members find themselves stalked by a serial killer who decides to take matters out of the musicians' hands and into his own. Graphic violence. **105m/C VHS.** Diana Karanikas, Angela Eads; ***D:*** Dennis Devine. *HHE*

Dead Heat 🦴½ **1988 (R)** Some acting talent and a few funny moments unfortunately don't add up to a fine film, though they do save it from being a complete woofer. In this one even the cops are zombies when one of them is resurrected from the dead to help his partner solve his murder and rid the city of the rest of the undead. **86m/C VHS, Beta, LV.** Joe Piscopo, Treat Williams, Lindsay Frost, Darren McGavin, Vincent Price, Keye Luke, Clare Kirkconnell; ***D:*** Mark Goldblatt; ***W:*** Terry Black; ***M:*** Ernest Troost. *VTR, NWV*

Dead Heat on a Merry-Go-Round 🦴🦴🦴 **1966 (R)** Coburn turns in a great performance as the ex-con who masterminds the heist of an airport safe. Intricately woven plot provides suspense and surprises. The film is also notable for the debut of Ford in a bit part (he has one line as a hotel messenger). **108m/C VHS, Beta.** James Coburn, Camilla Sparv, Aldo Ray, Nina Wayne, Robert Webber, Rose Marie, Todd Armstrong, Marian Moses, Severn Darden, Harrison Ford; ***D:*** Bernard Girard; ***C:*** Lionel Lindon. *COL*

Dead in the Water 🦴½ **1991 (PG-13)** Brown is Charlie Deegan, a big-time lawyer with a rich wife that he'd rather see dead. Charlie and his mistress plot the perfect murder to dispose of his spouse and collect her money. When plans go awry, he ends up as a suspect for the wrong murder in this story of infidelity and greed. **90m/C VHS, Beta.** Bryan Brown, Teri Hatcher, Anne DeSalvo, Veronica Cartwright; ***D:*** Bill Condon; ***W:*** Eleanor Gaver, Robert Seidenberg, Walter Klenhard. *MCA*

Dead Lucky 🦴½ **1960** A novice tries gambling and wins a fortune, but his luck leads him into an entanglement with an assassin, a scam artist, and a beautiful woman. Based on the novel "Lake of Darkness." **91m/B VHS, Beta.** *GB* Vincent Ball, Betty McDowall, John Le Mesurier, Alfred Burke, Michael Ripper; ***D:*** Montgomery Tully. *FCT, VCO*

Dead Man 🦴🦴 **1995 (R)** Depp wanders throughs the 19th-century American west as William Blake, an Ohio accountant who runs afoul of the law. Hooking up with a Native American named Nobody (Farmer), who envisions Blake as the famous English poet, the two try to stay one step ahead of the hired guns and lawmen out to get them. Action is sporadic and pace is all over the road in this offbeat and long-winded western, while Farmer's performance and Jarmusch's polished visuals are high points. **134m/B VHS.** Johnny Depp, Gary Farmer, Lance Henriksen, Michael Wincott, Mili Avital, Crispin Glover, Gabriel Byrne, Iggy Pop, Billy Bob Thornton, Jared Harris, Jimmie Ray Weeks, Mark Bringleson, John Hurt, Alfred Molina, Robert Mitchum; ***D:*** Jim Jarmusch; ***M:*** Neil Young. *NYR*

Dead Man Out 🦴🦴🦴 **1989** Both Glover and Blades turn in exceptional performances in this thought-provoking drama. A convict on Death Row (Blades) goes insane and therefore cannot be executed. The state calls in a psychiatrist (Glover) to review the case and determine whether he can be cured so that the sentence can be carried out. Powerful and riveting morality check. **87m/C VHS, Beta, LV.** Danny Glover, Ruben Blades, Tom Atkins, Larry Block, Sam Jackson, Maria Ricossa; ***D:*** Richard Pearce; ***M:*** Cliff Eidelman. *HBO*

Dead Man Walking 🦴🦴 **1988 (R)** In a post-holocaust future, half the population has been stricken with a deadly plague. Hauser is a mercenary, dying from the disease, who is hired to rescue a young woman who was kidnapped and is being held in the plague zone. **90m/C VHS.** Wings Hauser, Brion James, Pamela Ludwig, Sy Richardson, Leland Crooke, Jeffrey Combs; ***D:*** Gregory Brown; ***W:*** R.J. Marx. *REP*

Dead Man Walking 🦴🦴🦴½ **1995 (R)** True story of a nun whose anti-death penalty beliefs put her in moral crisis with grieving victims when she becomes the spiritual advisor to a death-row murderer. Based on the book by Sister Helen Prejean, Sarandon stars as the nun who develops a relationship of understanding with inmate Poncelet (Penn), unwavering in her Christian beliefs even though Penn's character shows little or no remorse for the two young lovers he was accused of murdering. Penn offers one of the best performances (but worst hairdos) of his career, while writer/director Robbins presents both sides of the death-penalty issue mingled with simple human compassion. **122m/C VHS, LV.** Susan Sarandon, Sean Penn, Robert Prosky, Raymond J. Barry, R. Lee Ermey, Celia Weston, Lois Smith; ***D:*** Tim Robbins; ***W:*** Tim Robbins; ***C:*** Roger Deakins; ***M:*** David Robbins. Academy Awards '95: Best Actress (Sarandon); Independent Spirit Awards '96: Best Actor (Penn); Screen Actors Guild Award '95: Best Actress (Sarandon); Nominations: Academy Awards '95: Best Actor (Penn), Best Director (Robbins), Best Song ("Dead Man Walking"); Independent Spirit Awards '96: Best Supporting Actress (Weston); MTV Movie Awards '96: Best Female Performance (Sarandon); Screen Actors Guild Award '95: Best Actor (Penn). *PGV*

Dead Man's Revenge 🦴🦴½ **1993 (PG-13)** Ruthless railroad mogul Payton McCay (Dern) doesn't let anyone stand in his way—even if it means framing innocent homesteader Hatcher (Ironside) in order to get his land. Hatcher escapes from jail and goes after McCay, trailed by bounty hunter Bodeen (Couloris). But Bodeen's not what he seems and has his own plans on getting even with the villainous McCay. **92m/C VHS, LV.** Bruce Dern, Michael Ironside, Keith Coulouris, Randy Travis; ***D:*** Alan J. Levi; ***W:*** Jim Byrnes, David Chisholm. *MCA*

Dead Mate 🦴 **1988** A woman marries a mortician after a whirlwind romance only to discover that, to her husband, being an undertaker is not just a job, it's a way of life. **93m/C VHS, Beta.** Elizabeth Mannino, David Gregory, Lawrence Bockus, Adam Wahl; ***D:*** Straw Weisman. *PSM*

Dead Men Don't Die 🦴½ **1991 (PG-13)** An anchorman is slain by criminals but resurrected as a shambling voodoo zombie. Few viewers notice the difference in this inoffensive but repetitious farce. The living-dead Gould appears to be having a lot of fun. **94m/C VHS.** Elliott Gould, Melissa Anderson, Mark Moses, Philip Bruns, Jack Betts, Mabel King; ***D:*** Malcolm Marmorstein; ***W:*** Malcolm Marmorstein. *ACA*

Dead Men Don't Wear Plaid 🦴🦴½ **1982 (PG)** Martin is hilarious as a private detective who encounters a bizarre assortment of suspects while trying to find out the truth about a scientist's death. Ingeniously interspliced with clips from old Warner Brothers films. Features Humphrey Bogart, Bette Davis, Alan Ladd, Burt Lancaster, Ava Gardner, Barbara Stanwyck, Ray Milland and others. Its only flaw is that the joke loses momentum by the end of the film. **89m/B VHS, Beta, LV.** Steve Martin, Rachel Ward, Reni Santoni, George Gaynes, Frank McCarthy, Carl Reiner; ***D:*** Carl Reiner; ***W:*** Steve Martin, Carl Reiner; ***C:*** Michael Chapman; ***M:*** Miklos Rozsa. *MCA, FCT, HMV*

Dead Men Walk 🦴🦴 **1943** A decent, albeit low budget, chiller about twin brothers (Zucco in a dual role); one a nice, well-adjusted member of society, the other a vampire who wants to suck his bro's blood. Sibling rivalry with a bite. **65m/B VHS, Beta.** George Zucco, Mary Carlisle, Dwight Frye, Nedrick Young, Al "Fuzzy" St. John; ***D:*** Sam Newfield. *NOS, MRV, SNC*

The Dead Next Door 🦴 **1989** Eerily reminiscent of "Night of the Living Dead." A scientist manufactures a virus which inhabits corpses and multiplies while replacing the former cells with its own. But the newly living corpses need human flesh to survive. In response, the government creates "The Zombie Squad" who do heroic battle with the stiffs. When a bizarre cult whose goal is the eradication of the human race befriend the dead, the battle gets ugly. **84m/C VHS.** Scott Spiegel, Peter Terry; ***W:*** J.R. Bookwalter. *TEM, MOV*

Dead of Night 🦴🦴🦴🦴 **1945** The template for episodic horror films, this suspense classic, set in a remote country house, follows the individual nightmares of five houseguests. Redgrave turns in a chillingly convincing performance as a ventriloquist terrorized by a demonic dummy. Not recommended for light-sleepers. Truly spine-tingling. **102m/B VHS, Beta.** *GB* Michael Redgrave, Sally Ann Howes, Basil Radford, Naunton Wayne, Mervyn Johns, Roland Culver, Googie Withers, Frederick Valk, Antony Baird, Judy Kelly, Miles Malleson, Ralph Michael; ***D:*** Alberto Cavalcanti, Charles Crichton, Basil Dearden, Robert Hamer; ***W:*** T.E.B. Clarke, John Baines, Angus MacPhail; ***M:*** Georges Auric. *REP, RXM, CNG*

Dead of Night 🦴½ **1977** This trilogy features Richard Matheson's tales of the Supernatural: "Second Chance," "Bobby," and "No Such Thing As a Vampire," all served up by your hostess, Elvira. **76m/C VHS, Beta, LV.** Joan Hackett, Ed Begley Jr., Patrick Macnee, Anjanette Comer; ***D:*** Dan Curtis. *LIV*

Dead of Winter 🦴🦴🦴 **1987 (R)** A young actress is suckered into a private screen test for a crippled old director, only to find she is actually being remodeled in the guise of a murdered woman. Edge-of-your-seat suspense as the plot twists. **100m/C VHS, Beta, LV.** Mary Steenburgen, Roddy McDowall, Jan Rubes, Ken Pogue, William Russ; ***D:*** Arthur Penn; ***W:*** Mark Shmuger, Mark Malone; ***M:*** Richard Einhorn. *MGM, FOX*

Dead On ☠½ **1993 (R)** Illicit lovers want to get rid of their inconvenient spouses so they can be together always. But their perfect plan doesn't work out as expected. Also available in an unrated version. **87m/C VHS, LV.** Matt McCoy, Shari Shattuck, David Ackroyd, Tracy Scoggins, Thomas Wagner; ***D:*** Ralph Hemecker; ***W:*** April Wayne. *ORI*

Dead on Sight ☠☠½ **1994 (R)** A college student dreams of a masked man, a knife, a bound woman, and other terrors. Too bad her nightmares match the actions of a serial killer. **96m/C VHS.** Jennifer Beals, Daniel Baldwin, Kurtwood Smith, William H. Macy; ***D:*** Ruben Preuss; ***W:*** Lewis Green; ***M:*** Harry Manfredini. *PAR*

Dead on the Money ☠☠½ **1991** Adequate made for TV suspenser about a woman who believes her lover plots a dire fate for her cousin. But nothing is what it seems here. Confusing, droopy in spots, but fun. **92m/C VHS, Beta.** Corbin Bernsen, Amanda Pays, John Glover, Eleanor Parker, Kevin McCarthy; ***D:*** Mark Cullingham; ***W:*** Gavin Lambert. *TTC*

Dead or Alive ☠½ **1941** Tex and the Texas Rangers pretend to be outlaws in order to join a gang terrorizing a town. **54m/B VHS, Beta.** Tex Ritter, Dave O'Brien, Guy Wilkerson, Charles "Blackie" King, Bud Osborne, Reed Howes; ***D:*** Elmer Clifton. *GPV, RXM, VCN*

Dead Pigeon on Beethoven Street ☠☠½ **1972 (PG)** Sandy (Corbett) is a detective whose partner gets murdered while investigating blackmailers who take compromising pictures of international big-wigs. So Sandy goes undercover and joins the gang. Cheeky paranoia from Fuller. **92m/C VHS.** Glenn Corbett, Christa Lang, Anton Diffring, Alexander D'Arcy; ***D:*** Samuel Fuller; ***W:*** Samuel Fuller. *FCT*

Dead Pit *Woof!* **1989 (R)** Leave this one in the pit it crawled out of. Twenty years ago a mad scientist was killed as a result of horrible experiments he was conducting on mentally ill patients at an asylum. A young woman stumbles across his experiments, awakening him from the dead. **90m/C VHS, Beta.** Jeremy Slate, Steffen Gregory Foster; ***D:*** Brett Leonard. *IMP*

Dead Poets Society ☠☠☠½ **1989 (PG)** An idealistic English teacher inspires a group of boys in a 1950s' prep school to pursue individuality and creative endeavor, resulting in clashes with school and parental authorities. Williams shows he can master the serious roles as well as the comic with his portrayal of the unorthodox educator. Big box office hit occasionally scripted with a heavy hand in order to elevate the message. The ensemble cast is excellent. **128m/C VHS, Beta, LV, 8mm.** Robin Williams, Ethan Hawke, Robert Sean Leonard, Josh Charles, Gale Hansen, Kurtwood Smith, James Waterson, Dylan Kussman, Lara Flynn Boyle, Melora Hardin; ***D:*** Peter Weir; ***W:*** Tom Schulman; ***C:*** John Seale; ***M:*** Maurice Jarre. Academy Awards '89: Best Original Screenplay; British Academy Awards '89: Best Film; Cesar Awards '91: Best Foreign Film; Nominations: Academy Awards '89: Best Actor (Williams), Best Director (Weir), Best Picture. *TOU*

The Dead Pool ☠½ **1988 (R)** Dirty Harry Number Five features a new twist on the sports pool: a list of celebrities is distributed and bets are placed on who will be first to cross the finish line, literally. Unfortunately someone seems to be hedging their bet by offing the celebs themselves. When Harry's name appears on the list, he decides to throw the game. **92m/C VHS, Beta, LV, 8mm.** Clint Eastwood, Liam Neeson, Patricia Clarkson, Evan C. Kim, David Hunt, Michael Currie, Michael Goodwin; ***D:*** Buddy Van Horn; ***M:*** Lalo Schifrin. *WAR, TLF*

Dead Presidents ☠☠½ **1995 (R)** Sophomoric release for the Hughes brothers falls short of impact of "Menace II Society," but not for lack of ambition. Combination coming of age tale, war story, period piece and caper film follows Anthony ("Menace" veteran Tate) from his Bronx neighborhood in 1968 to Vietnam (for "Platoon" adventures in the wilds of Florida) and then back to the 'hood, where his life continues to spiral downward. Desperate to escape, he becomes involved in an armoured car heist to grab some cash (the "dead presidents"). Supported by hard-edged and effective acting, the Hughes continue to develop their control of cinematic imagery, displaying genius for staging violent, confrontational scenes. But the script, based on a story by the brothers, fails to live up to the vision, with characterization and dialogue lagging. Pounding period soundtrack with contributions by Curtis Mayfield, James Brown, and Marvin Gaye keeps things humming. **120m/C VHS, LV.** Larenz Tate, Keith David, Chris Tucker, Freddy Rodriguez, N'Bushe Wright, Bokeem Woodbine, Rose Jackson, Clifton Powell; ***D:*** Albert Hughes, Allen Hughes; ***W:*** Michael Henry Brown; ***C:*** Lisa Rinzler; ***M:*** Danny Elfman. *TOU*

Dead Reckoning ☠☠☠ **1947** Bogart and Prince are two WWII veterans en route to Washington when Prince disappears. Bogart trails Prince to his Southern hometown and discovers he's been murdered. Blackmail and more murders follow as Bogie tries to uncover the truth. Suspenseful with good performances from all, especially Bogart. **100m/B VHS, Beta, LV.** Humphrey Bogart, Lizabeth Scott, Morris Carnovsky, Charles Cane, Wallace Ford, William Prince, Marvin Miller; ***D:*** John Cromwell. *CCB, COL*

Dead Reckoning ☠½ **1989 (R)** A plastic surgeon and his lovely wife embark on a cruise aboard his new luxury yacht. The intrigue begins with a storm, an isolated island, and the discovery that the captain is the wife's former lover. **95m/C VHS, LV.** Cliff Robertson, Susan Blakely, Rick Springfield; ***D:*** Robert Lewis. *MCA*

Dead Right ☠½ *If He Hollers, Let Him Go* **1968** A black man is unjustly put into prison in the Deep South. He manages to escape in order to try and prove his innocence. **111m/C VHS, Beta.** Raymond St. Jacques, Dana Wynter, Kevin McCarthy, Barbara McNair. *PSM*

Dead Ringers ☠☠☠ **1988 (R)** A stunning, unsettling chiller, based loosely on a real case and the bestseller by Bari Wood and Jack Geasland. Irons, in an excellent dual role, is effectively disturbing as the twin gynecologists who descend into madness when they can no longer handle the fame, fortune, drugs, and women in their lives. Acutely upsetting film made all the more so due to its graphic images and basis in fact. **117m/C VHS, Beta, LV.** *CA* Jeremy Irons, Genevieve Bujold, Heidi von Palleske, Shirley Douglas, Stephen Lack; ***D:*** David Cronenberg; ***W:*** Norman Snider, David Cronenberg; ***M:*** Howard Shore. Genie Awards '89: Best Actor (Irons), Best Director (Cronenberg), Best Film; Los Angeles Film Critics Association Awards '88: Best Director (Cronenberg), Best Supporting Actress (Bujold). *CCB, MED, VTR*

Dead Silence **1990 (R)** Screenwriter Cliff Morgan has written a classic film noir screenplay... with the money, it seems all Cliff's problems are solved... or are they? **92m/C VHS.** Clete Keith, Doris Anne Soyka, Joseph Scott, Craig Fleming; ***D:*** Harrison Ellenshaw. *NO*

Dead Sleep ☠☠ **1991 (R)** A nurse discovers that comatose patients at a private clinic have been used as guinea pigs by an overzealous doctor. This minor-league chiller from Down Under is said to have been inspired by an actual medical scandal. **95m/C VHS.** Linda Blair, Tony Bonner; ***D:*** Alec Mills. *VES*

Dead Solid Perfect ☠☠ **1988** Quaid stars as a golf pro whose life on the PGA tour is handicapped by his taste for scotch and his eye for the ladies. Based on the book by Dan Jenkins. **97m/C VHS, Beta.** Randy Quaid, Kathryn Harrold, Jack Warden, Larry Riley, Brett Cullen, Corinne Bohrer; ***D:*** Bobby Roth; ***W:*** Dan Jenkins, Bobby Roth. *WAR, BTV*

Dead Space ☠ **1990 (R)** Dead space lay between the ears of whoever thought we needed this remake of 1982's "Forbidden World." At a lab on a hostile planet an experimental vaccine mutates into a prickly puppet monster who menaces the medicos. Needed: a vaccine against cheapo "Alien" ripoffs. **72m/C VHS, LV.** Marc Singer, Laura Tate, Bryan Cranston, Judith Chapman; ***D:*** Fred Gallo. *COL*

Dead to Rights ☠☠½ *Donato and Daughter* **1993 (R)** TV movie finds veteran LAPD cop Donato (Bronson) on the trail of a serial killer along with his new partner—who's not only his daughter but his superior officer. **90m/C VHS.** Charles Bronson, Dana Delany, Xander Berkeley, Bonnie Bartlett, Jenette Goldstein, Louis Giambalvo; ***D:*** Rod Holcomb. *VMK*

Dead Weekend ☠☠ **1995 (R)** Made for cable sci fier finds Lt. Weed (Baldwin) given the task of finding and destroying a seductively dangerous female alien. Turns out she has the ability to physically change into a number of different women—all of whom attract the willing-and-eager soldier. **82m/C VHS.** Stephen Baldwin, David Rasche, Damian Jones; ***D:*** Amos Poe; ***W:*** Joel Rose. *PAR*

Dead Women in Lingerie *Woof!* **1990 (R)** When beautiful models are turning up dead, a detective is called in to solve the mystery. Perhaps they committed suicide to avoid being in this picture any longer than necessary. Title sounds like the next episode of "Geraldo." **87m/C VHS.** June Lockhart, Lyle Waggoner, John Romo, Jerry Orbach, Maura Tierney; ***D:*** Erika Fox. *NO*

Dead Wrong ☠½ **1983** Undercover agent falls in love with the drug smuggler she's supposed to bring to justice. **93m/C VHS, Beta.** Britt Ekland, Winston Rekert, Jackson Davies. *MED*

Dead Wrong: The John Evans Story ☠½ **1984** The true story of Evans' life of crime and eventual execution in the electric chair, using footage of an interview taped before his death. **45m/C VHS.** *AFC*

Dead Zone ☠☠☠ **1983 (R)** A man gains extraordinary psychic powers following a near-fatal accident. He is forced to decide between seeking absolute seclusion in order to escape his frightening visions, or using his "gift" to save mankind from impending evil. A good adaptation of the Stephen King thriller. **104m/C VHS, Beta, LV.** Christopher Walken, Brooke Adams, Tom Skerritt, Martin Sheen, Herbert Lom, Anthony Zerbe, Colleen Dewhurst; ***D:*** David Cronenberg; ***W:*** Jeffrey Boam; ***M:*** Michael Kamen. *PAR*

Deadbolt ☠☠ **1992 (R)** Divorced med student Marty Hiller (Bateman) desperately needs a roommate and Alec Danz (Baldwin) seems perfect. Soon they're sharing more than the rent, until Danz kills her friends and imprisons her in the apartment (equipped of course with soundproof walls and bulletproof glass—one wonders why she doesn't bang on the floor to gain attention.) Predictable and silly would-be thriller attempts to capitalize on the roommate from hell theme that started with "Single White Female," but isn't nearly as effective. Went straight to video and showed up on network TV several months later. **95m/C VHS, LV.** Justine Bateman, Adam Baldwin, Michelle Scarabelli, Chris Mulkey, Cyndi Pass, Isabelle Truchon; ***D:*** Douglas Jackson. *NLC*

Deadfall ☠☠½ **1993 (R)** Father/son grifters plan an elaborate scam that goes wrong when son Joe (Biehn) inadvertently kills dear old dad (Coburn). When Joe is going through his father's effects he finds out about an unknown twin uncle, who also turns out to be a racketeer. Along with Uncle Lou's mistrustful henchman Eddie (Cage), they plan another con but swindles and vendettas abound. **99m/C VHS, LV.** Michael Biehn, Sarah Trigger, Nicolas Cage, James Coburn, Charlie Sheen, Peter Fonda; ***D:*** Christopher Coppola; ***W:*** Christopher Coppola, David Peoples. *VMK*

The Deadliest Art: The Best of the Martial Arts Films **1990** The masters of bare-handed combat team up in this look at the best of the martial arts movies. Action packed. **?m/C VHS.** Yuen Biao, Jackie Chan, Samo Hung, Kareem Abdul-Jabbar, Sho Kosugi, Bruce Lee, Angela Mao, Cynthia Rothrock; ***D:*** Sandra Weintraub; ***W:*** Sandra Weintraub. *FXV*

Deadline ☠½ **1981** Journalist must find out the truth behind a minor earthquake in Australia. **94m/C VHS, Beta.** Barry Newman, Trisha Noble, Bill Kerr. *WOV*

Deadline ☠☠ **1982** Eerie tale of horror writer's life as it begins to reflect his latest story in this play on the "truth is stranger than fiction" adage. **85m/C VHS, Beta.** Stephen Young, Sharon Masters, Cindy Hinds, Phillip Leonard; ***D:*** Mario Azzopardi. *NO*

Deadline 🦴🦴 **1987 (R)** Walken is a cynical American journalist assigned to cover the warring factions in Beirut. He finds himself becoming more and more involved in the events he's supposed to report when he falls in love with a German nurse who is aiding the rebel forces. Tense, though sometimes murky drama. **110m/C VHS, Beta, LV.** *GE* Christopher Walken, Hywel Bennett, Marita Marschall; ***D:*** Nathaniel Gutman. *VTR*

Deadline Assault 🦴½ *Act of Violence* **1990 (R)** Kate McSweeny is a beautiful young reporter who is brutally attacked and raped by a gang of savage youths. Kate must now face the unsettling facts; they're still on the streets and they may be stalking her again. **90m/C VHS.** Elizabeth Montgomery, James Sloyan, Sean Frye, Biff McGuire, Michael Goodwin, Linden Chiles; ***D:*** Paul Wendkos. *ELV, HHE*

Deadline at Dawn 🦴🦴 **1946** Hayward is an aspiring actress who tries to help a sailor (Williams) prove that he is innocent of murder. Based on a novel by Cornell Woolrich. **82m/B VHS, Beta.** Bill Williams, Susan Hayward, Lola Lane, Paul Lukas, Joseph Calleia; ***D:*** Harold Clurman; ***W:*** Clifford Odets. *MLB, TTC*

Deadline Auto Theft 🦴 **1983** A fun lovin' guy drives fast cars and meets beautiful women. Nudge, nudge, wink, wink. **90m/C VHS, Beta.** H.B. Halicki, Hoyt Axton, Marion Busia, George Cole, Judi Gibbs, Lang Jeffries Jr.; ***D:*** H.B. Halicki. *IMP*

Deadlock 🦴🦴½ **1991 (R)** Hauer and Rogers star as inmates in a prison of the future. This prison has no walls, no fences and no guards - and no one EVER escapes. Each prisoner wears an explosive collar that is tuned to the same frequency as one of the other prisoner's. Should the two separate by more than 100 yards, the collars explode. When Rogers convinces Hauer that they are on the same frequency, the two escape. Trouble is, they are being pursued not only by the police, but by Hauer's former partners in crime as well. Can the two find the freedom they are looking for - without losing their heads? Originally made for cable television. **103m/C VHS, Beta, LV.** Rutger Hauer, Mimi Rogers, Joan Chen, James Remar, Stephen Tobolowsky, Basil Wallace; ***D:*** Lewis Teague. *VTR, FXV, MED*

Deadlock 2 🦴🦴 *Deadlocked: Escape from Zone 14* **1994 (R)** Same basic plot as in the first TV movie. Tony Archer (Morales) and Allie Thompson (Peeples), two strangers who have been set up by the same corrupt businessman, are being held in a violent correctional facility. Inmates wear electronic collars programmed to explode if they venture too far apart. But Tony figures a way around this trap only to discover he and Allie are caught in another. **120m/C VHS.** Esai Morales, Nia Peeples, Stephen McHattie, Jon Cuthbert; ***D:*** Graeme Campbell. *HMK*

Deadly Advice 🦴🦴 **1993 (R)** Meek bookseller Jodie (Horrocks) and her sister are constantly humiliated by their overbearing mother (Fricker), who also objects to Jodie's romance with the local doctor (Pryce). As life becomes increasingly unbearable, Jodie discovers a book on infamous killers and is visited by their ghosts, including Jack the Ripper, who is happy to suggest ways to get rid of mom. **91m/C VHS.** Jane Horrocks, Imelda Staunton, Brenda Fricker, Jonathan Pryce; ***D:*** Mandie Fletcher. *HMK*

Deadly Alliance 🦴 **1978** Two impecunious filmmakers (who happen to be hunks) and a babe (for good measure) poke their noses in where they're not wanted (in the shady business of an international oil cartel). "Deadly Dull" would be a more appropriate moniker. **90m/C VHS, Beta.** Kathleen Arc, Tony de Fonte, Michele Marsh, Walter Prince; ***D:*** Paul S. Parco. *NO*

The Deadly and the Beautiful 🦴 *Wonder Women* **1973 (PG)** Dr. Tsu sends her "deadly but beautiful" task force to kidnap the world's prime male athletes for use in her private business enterprise. **82m/C VHS, Beta.** *PH* Nancy Kwan, Ross Hagen, Maria de Aragon, Roberta Collins, Tony Lorea, Sid Haig, Vic Diaz, Shirley Washington, Gale Hansen; ***D:*** Robert Vincent O'Neil. *MED*

Deadly Bet 🦴½ **1991 (R)** A made-for-video saga of a kickboxer who loses his money and his girl when he loses the big match. Lots of fight sequences as he works to regain his career. **93m/C VHS, LV.** Jeff Wincott, Charlene Tilton, Steven Leigh; ***D:*** Richard W. Munchkin. *PMH*

Deadly Blessing 🦴🦴 **1981 (R)** A young, recently widowed woman is visited in her rural Pennsylvania home by some friends from the city. Something's not quite right about this country life and they become especially suspicious after meeting their friend's very religious in-laws. **104m/C VHS, Beta.** Maren Jensen, Susan Buckner, Sharon Stone, Ernest Borgnine, Karen Jensen, Jeff East, Lisa Hartman Black, Lois Nettleton; ***D:*** Wes Craven; ***W:*** Wes Craven, Glenn Benest, Matthew F. Barr; ***M:*** James Horner. *SUE*

Deadly Breed 🦴½ **1989** Beware your friendly neighborhood cop. A band of white supremacists has infiltrated the local police force, intent on causing violence, not keeping the peace. **90m/C VHS.** William Smith, Addison Randall, Blake Bahner, Joe Vance; ***D:*** Charles Kanganis. *PMH*

Deadly Business 🦴🦴🦴 **1986** The true story of a man who turned from crime to become a government informant. As a garbage man, he works to stop the illegal dumping of chemicals in New Jersey. An interesting made-for-televison drama. **100m/C VHS.** Alan Arkin, Armand Assante, Michael Learned, Jon Polito, George Morfogen, James Rebhorn; ***D:*** John Korty. *WOV*

Deadly Business 🦴½ **19??** Hard-nosed collection man for a lethal loan shark finds he is the one with the debt to pay as he's stalked through the city street by hit men. **95m/C VHS, Beta.** David Peterson, John Lazarus, Leo Gabrowski. *ACA*

Deadly Companions 🦴🦴½ **1961** Keith is an ex-gunslinger who agrees to escort O'Hara through Apache territory in order to make up for inadvertenly killing her son. Director Peckinpah's first feature film. **90m/C VHS, Beta, LV.** Maureen O'Hara, Brian Keith, Chill Wills, Steve Cochran; ***D:*** Sam Peckinpah; ***C:*** William Clothier. *VTR, NWV*

Deadly Conspiracy 🦴🦴 **1991 (R)** Saxon plays a corrupt businessman who kills an employee about to blow the whistle on his shady dealings. Hauser is the good cop, with the bad personal life, who makes it his mission to bring Saxon to justice. The prolific Hauser brings some fast-paced action to this routine story. **92m/C VHS.** Wings Hauser, John Saxon, Frances Fisher, Patti D'Arbanville, Margaux Hemingway, Greg Mullavey; ***D:*** Paul Leder. *MNC*

Deadly Currents 🦴🦴 **1993 (R)** Scott plays a former sea captain who owns a bar on the island of Curacao and enjoys regaling his patrons with his seagoing tales. Petersen is the exiled CIA agent stuck as the security officer of the American consulate. The dangerous pasts of both men catch them up and find them caught in a web of international intrigue. Based on the novel "The Prince of Malta" by James David Buchanan. **93m/C VHS.** George C. Scott, William L. Petersen, Julie Carmen, Alexei Sayle, Trish Van Devere, Philip Anglim, Maria Ellingsen; ***D:*** Carl Schultz; ***W:*** James David Buchanan. *COL*

Deadly Dancer 🦴½ **1990** It's up to a lone cop to find out who's been offing the hoofers in L.A. **88m/C VHS.** Adolfo "Shabba Doo" Quinones, Smith Wordes, Walter W. Cox, Steve Jonson; ***D:*** Kimberly Casey; ***W:*** David A. Prior. *AIP*

Deadly Daphne's Revenge 🦴½ **1993** Gory story of rape and revenge from the Troma Team. Hitchhiker Cindy is beaten and raped by Charlie Johnson. When she seeks justice via the local police, Johnson makes plans to have her snuffed out. Meantime, another of his victims escapes from the asylum she's been in and comes looking for him with murder on her mind. **98m/C VHS, LV.** *AIP*

Deadly Darling *Woof!* **1985** Muddled, completely awful tale centering on two different rapes with no discernible attempt made to link the two or establish a plot. **91m/C VHS, Beta.** Fonda Lynn, Warren Chan, Bernard Tsui, Cherry Kwok; ***D:*** Karen Young. *UNI*

Deadly Desire 🦴🦴 **1991 (R)** Seduced by the beautiful Harrold, security guard Scalia finds himself putting his life on the line when Harrold asks him to help cheat her husband out of millions in an insurance scam. Trouble ensues when they try to outsmart Harrold's powerful entrepreneurial husband. **93m/C VHS.** Jack Scalia, Kathryn Harrold, Will Patton, Joe Santos; ***D:*** Charles Correll. *PAR, HHE*

Deadly Diamonds 🦴½ **1991** Cop is on the trail of diamond smugglers who leave a trail of death in their wake. **90m/C VHS, Beta.** Dan Haggerty, Troy Donahue, Eli Rich, Kathleen Kane, Kenna Grob, Nicholas Mercer; ***D:*** Thomas Atcheson; ***W:*** Ron Herbst. *DMP, GNS, HHT*

Deadly Dreams 🦴🦴 **1988 (R)** A young boy's parents are killed by a maniac who then commits suicide. Years later, he dreams that he is being stalked anew by the same killer. Nightmares turn into reality in this decent horror/suspense flick. **79m/C VHS, Beta, LV.** Mitchell Anderson, Xander Berkeley, Thom Babbes, Juliette Cummins; ***D:*** Kristine Peterson; ***W:*** Thom Babbes. *NO*

Deadly Embrace *Woof!* **1988** Sordid tale of wealthy man (Vincent) who wants to get rid of his wife—permanantly. He enlists the aid of a beautiful young coed. Soft-core sleaze with nary a redeemable quality. **82m/C VHS, Beta.** Jan-Michael Vincent, Jack Carter, Ty Randolph, Linnea Quigley, Michelle (McClellan) Bauer, Ken Abraham; ***D:*** Ellen Cabot. *PSM*

Deadly Encounter 🦴🦴🦴 **1972** Thrilling actioner in which Hagman portrays a helicopter pilot—a former war ace—who allows an old flame to talk him into helping her escape from the mobsters on her trail. Terrific edge-of-your-seat aerial action. **90m/C VHS, Beta.** Larry Hagman, Susan Anspach, Michael C. Goetz, James Gammon; ***D:*** William A. Graham. *NO*

Deadly Encounter *Woof!* **1978 (R)** Lacking any redeemable qualities, this film shows just how low some people go. Merrill hosts a dinner to garner financial support for a budding playwright, but what we get is a look at the lifestyles of the rich and perverse. **90m/C VHS, Beta.** Dina Merrill, Carl Betz, Leon Ames, Vicki Powers, Mark Rasmussen, Susan Logan; ***D:*** R. John Hugh. *CNG*

Deadly Exposure 🦴🦴 **1993 (R)** Benson stars as a burned-out journalist doing his own investigation of the right-wing extremist group that killed his father. Aspiring reporter Johnson helps out and turns up a conspiracy between the extremists, the government, and a plot to assassinate a U.S. senator. Also available in an unrated version. **100m/C VHS.** Robby Benson, Laura Johnson, Paul Hampton, Andrew Prine, Bentley Mitchum, Isaac Hayes; ***D:*** Lawrence Mortorff; ***W:*** Asher Brauner. *AVE*

Deadly Eyes 🦴½ *The Rats* **1982 (R)** After eating grain laced with steroids a group of rats grows to mammoth proportions (dachshunds in rat drag were used). Their appetites grow accordingly—now they crave humans. Amid the nibbling by the giant ratdogs, romance blooms. Silly adaptation by Charles Eglee of Frank Herbert's "The Rats." **93m/C VHS, Beta.** Sam Groom, Sara Botsford, Scatman Crothers, Lisa Langlois, Cec Linder; ***D:*** Robert Clouse. *WAR*

Deadly Fieldtrip 🦴½ **1974** Four female students and their teacher are abducted by a biker gang and held hostage on a deserted farm. **91m/C VHS, Beta.** Zalman King, Brenda Fogarty, Robert Porter; ***D:*** Earl Barton. *NO*

Deadly Force 🦴½ **1983 (R)** Ex-cop turned private detective stalks a killer in Los Angeles who has left an "X" carved in the forehead of each of his 17 victims. If he had just signed his name, things could have been tidied up much earlier. **95m/C VHS, Beta.** Wings Hauser, Joyce Ingalls, Paul Shenar, Al Ruscio, Arlen Dean Snyder, Lincoln Kilpatrick; ***D:*** Paul Aaron; ***W:*** Robert Vincent O'Neil, Barry Schneider. *SUE, NLC*

Deadly Friend 🦴🦴 **1986 (R)** A well-meaning horror flick? That's what Wes Craven has tried to provide for us. When the girlfriend of a lonely teenage genius is accidentally killed, he decides to insert his robot's "brain" in her body, though the results aren't entirely successful. The same can be said for the film which was based on Diana Henstell's more effective novel "Friend." **91m/C VHS, Beta, LV.** Matthew Laborteaux, Kristy Swanson, Michael Sharrett, Anne Twomey, Richard Marcus, Anne Ramsey; ***D:*** Wes Craven; ***W:*** Bruce Joel Rubin; ***M:*** Charles Bernstein. *WAR*

Deadly Game 🦴🦴 **1982 (R)** A reunion at a remote hotel leads to an ordeal of psychological terror and murderous intrigue. **108m/C VHS, Beta.** George Segal, Robert Morley, Trevor Howard, Emlyn Williams, Alan Webb; ***D:*** George Schaefer. *SUE*

Deadly Game 🦴½ **1983** Much-maligned and preyed-upon witness is protected by a weary cop, who speaks with the use of English subtitles. **90m/C VHS, Beta.** *GE* Mel Ferrer, Helmut Berger, Barbara Sukowa; ***D:*** Karoly Makk, Dieter Geissler. *VCD, GLV*

The Deadly Game 🦴🦴 **198?** East-West intrigue prior to the fall of the Berlin Wall finds a Western operative returning from a dangerous mission, only to walk into a trap set by his own side. **104m/C VHS.** *GB* David Hemmings. *FCT, INJ*

Deadly Game 🦴½ **1991 (R)** Horribly burned, a vengeful millionaire invites seven people he believes have wronged him to spend the weekend on his isolated island. He has promised them each a reward for their good deeds, but instead plans to have a big-game hunt with his "guests" as the prey. **93m/C VHS, Beta.** Roddy McDowall, Jenny Seagrove, Marc Singer, Michael Beck; ***D:*** Tom Wright; ***W:*** Wes Claridge. *PAR*

Deadly Games 🦴½ **1980** Ineffective plot involving a series of murders in a small town is seemingly played out by the principal characters in a horror board game. Film is saved from being a complete waste by Groom's good performance as the local cop. **94m/C VHS, Beta.** Sam Groom, Jo Ann Harris, Steve Railsback, Dick Butkus, June Lockhart, Colleen Camp; ***D:*** Scott Mansfield. *MON*

Deadly Harvest 🦴 **1972 (PG)** Scientists' worst fears have been realized—due to ecological abuse and over-development of the land, food has become extremely scarce. This in turn has caused people to become a bit savage. They are particularly nasty to a farmer and his family. Not a bad plot, but a poorly acted film. **86m/C VHS, Beta.** Clint Walker, Nehemiah Persoff, Kim Cattrall, David G. Brown, Gary Davies; ***D:*** Timothy Bond. *VTR, NWV*

Deadly Hero 🦴🦴🦴 **1975 (R)** Gripping tale of a young woman who becomes the prey of a New York City cop after questioning the brutal methods he employed while saving her from being assaulted, ultimately killing her attacker. Williams makes film debut in this chilling suspenser. **102m/C VHS, Beta.** Don Murray, James Earl Jones, Diahn Williams, Lilia Skala, Conchata Ferrell, George S. Irving, Treat Williams, Josh Mostel; ***D:*** Ivan Nagy; ***M:*** Brad Fiedel. *SUE*

Deadly Illusion 🦴🦴 *Love You to Death* **1987 (R)** Williams is a private detective who manages to get himself tangled in a complex web of intrigue and winds up framed for murder. Decent outing for all. **95m/C VHS, Beta, LV.** Billy Dee Williams, Morgan Fairchild, Vanity, John Beck, Joe Cortese; ***D:*** William Tannen, Larry Cohen; ***W:*** Larry Cohen; ***M:*** Patrick Gleeson. *COL*

Deadly Impact 🦴½ **1984** Las Vegas casinos are targeted for rip-off by means of a computer. Svenson and Williamson give good performances, but that's not enough to save this one. **90m/C VHS, Beta.** *IT* Bo Svenson, Fred Williamson, Marcia Clingan, John Morghen, Vincent Conti; ***D:*** Larry Ludman. *LIV, VES*

Deadly Innocence 🦴½ **1988 (R)** A shy, lonely girl works at an isolated gas station. After her father's death, she takes in a boarder—a mysterious woman being chased by her past. **90m/C VHS.** Mary Crosby, Andrew Stevens, Amanda Wyss; ***D:*** John D. Patterson, Hugh Parks. *NO*

Deadly Intent 🦴🦴 **1988** The widow of a murdered archeologist becomes the target of fortune hunters when they try to get their hands on the priceless jewel her husband brought back from a dig. **83m/C VHS.** Lisa Eilbacher, Steve Railsback, Maud Adams, Lance Henriksen, Fred Williamson, Persis Khambatta; ***D:*** Nigel Dick. *FRH*

Deadly Intruder 🦴½ **1984** Quiet vacation spot is being terrorized by an escapee from a mental institution. So much for a little R and R. **86m/C VHS, Beta.** Chris Holder, Molly Creek. *NO*

Deadly Lessons 🦴🦴 **1994** Misfit Ann gets shunned by the college "in" crowd but then a childhood friend comes to her aid and decides to take revenge on the nasty students. **90m/C VHS.** Andrea Gall, Mat McGinnis, Dana Wise; ***D:*** Leslie Delano. *SWI*

The Deadly Mantis 🦴½ *The Incredible Praying Mantis* **1957** A gigantic praying mantis lies in a million-year-old sleep in the frozen reaches of the Arctic. Then a volcanic eruption releases the critter and the flying beastie does it's destructive best on Washington, DC and New York City until the military can gas it into oblivion. Typically silly fifties sci-fi with decent special effects. **79m/B VHS.** Craig Stevens, William Hopper, Alix Talton, Pat Conway, Donald Randolph; ***D:*** Nathan (Hertz) Juran; ***W:*** Martin Berkeley. *MCA*

Deadly Mission 🦴½ **1978 (R)** Five soldiers in WWII France are convicted of crimes against the Army, only to escape from lock-up and become focal points in a decisive battle. **99m/C VHS, Beta.** Bo Svenson, Peter Hooten, Fred Williamson. *LIV*

Deadly Neighbor 🦴🦴 **1991** New neighbor moves in, dead neighborhood housewives move out. Another neighbor becomes suspicious and investigates. **90m/C VHS.** Don Leifert, George Stover, Lydia Laurans; ***D:*** Donald M. Dohler. *VCI*

Deadly Obsession 🦴½ **1988 (R)** A disfigured lunatic stalks a young co-ed hoping to extort $1 million from the wealthy dean of the school. **93m/C VHS.** Jeffrey R. Iorio; ***D:*** Jeno Hodl; ***W:*** Brian Cox. *REP, FCT*

Deadly Passion 🦴½ **1985 (R)** A James Cain-like thriller about a private eye getting carnally involved with a beautiful and treacherous woman who is manipulating her late husband's estate through murder and double-crossing. **100m/C VHS, Beta.** *SA* Brent Huff, Ingrid Boulting, Harrison Coburn, Lynn Maree; ***D:*** Larry Larson. *LIV*

Deadly Past 🦴½ **1995 (R)** Predictable story finds dumb ex-con bartender (Marquette) making the mistake of getting involved with a femme fatale (Alt) from his past. Also available in an unrated version. **90m/C VHS.** Ron Marquette, Carol Alt, Dedee Pfeiffer, Mark Dacascos. *AVE*

Deadly Possession 🦴🦴 **1988** A college student plays amateur detective when she tries to clear her ex-husband's name after he is accused of the horrible murder of a fellow student. **99m/C VHS, Beta, LV.** *AU* Penny Cook, Anna-Maria Winchester, Liddy Clark, Olivia Hamnett; ***D:*** Craig Lahiff. *LIV, VES*

Deadly Prey *Woof!* **1987 (R)** Prior is up against a fully outfitted army of bloodthirsty mercenaries who are using innocent people as "live targets" at their secret bootcamp. Plot lifted from "The Most Dangerous Game" has more than its share of gruesome violence. **87m/C VHS, Beta.** Cameron Mitchell, Troy Donahue, Ted Prior, Fritz Matthews; ***D:*** David A. Prior; ***W:*** David A. Prior. *NO*

Deadly Reactor 🦴🦴 **1989** In a post-nuclear future a lone preacher turns into an armed vigilante to protect the people of a town being terrorized by a vicious motorcycle gang. **88m/C VHS, Beta.** David Heavener, Stuart Whitman, Darwyn Swalve, Allyson Davis; ***D:*** David Heavener. *AIP*

Deadly Recruits 🦴½ **1986** The Russians did it! The Russians did it! Stamp is convinced that the downfall of several top students at Oxford, amid scandal and rumor, is due to a KGB conspiracy. **92m/C VHS, Beta.** *GB* Terence Stamp, Michael Culver, Carmen Du Sautoy, Robin Sachs; ***D:*** Roger Tucker. *NO*

Deadly Revenge 🦴 **1983 (R)** Action-adventure pic with not much adventure and even less action. Small-town reporter finds himself up against a mob boss when he takes over the nightclub business of a friend killed by the mobsters. Dubbed. **90m/C VHS, Beta.** *IT* Rodolfo Ranni, Julio de Grazia, Silvia Montanari, Fred Commoner; ***D:*** Juan Carlos Sesanzo. *UNI*

Deadly Rivals 🦴🦴 **1992 (R)** Stevens plays a laser specialist in Miami for a top-secret weapons conference. A beauty takes a interest in him but then she's first accused of being a spy and then mistaken for a courier in the pay of a ruthless crime boss. Can Stevens find the truth? **93m/C VHS, LV.** Andrew Stevens, Cela Wise, Joseph Bologna, Margaux Hemingway, Richard Roundtree, Francesco Quinn, Randi Ingerman; ***D:*** James Dodson; ***W:*** Redge Mahaffey; ***M:*** Ashley Irwin. *MCA*

Deadly Sanctuary *Woof!* **1968** Censors stopped production of this film several times. The Marquis de Sade's writings provided the inspiration (though there's nothing inspired about it) for this tale of two recently orphaned young women who get caught up in prostitution, an S&M club, and murder. **92m/C VHS, Beta.** Jack Palance, Mercedes McCambridge, Sylva Koscina, Klaus Kinski, Akim Tamiroff, Romina Power; ***D:*** Jess (Jesus) Franco. *NO*

The Deadly Secret 🦴🦴 **1994** Randall Parks is a successful real estate agent with a past he has managed to hide for twenty years. When he is blackmailed, he decides to take matters into his own hands and track down his accusers. **98m/C VHS.** Joe Estevez, Tracy Spaulding, Reggie Cale, Douglas Stalgren; ***D:*** Jason Hammond; ***W:*** Douglas Stalgren; ***M:*** Erik Hansen. *AIP*

Deadly Sins 🦴🦴½ **1995 (R)** Deputy sheriff Jack Gates (Keith) hooks up with P.I. Christina Herrera (Milano) to investigate a murder in a Catholic girls school. Christina poses as a student and uncovers sinister secrets. **98m/C VHS.** David Keith, Alyssa Milano, Terry David Mulligan, Corrie Clark; ***D:*** Michael Robison; ***W:*** John Langley, Malcolm Barbour. *AVE*

Deadly Spygames **1989** A special agent for the United States Special Operations Bureau finds himself in deep trouble. **?m/C VHS.** Troy Donahue, Tippi Hedren; ***D:*** Jack M. Sell; ***W:*** Jack M. Sell. *UNI*

Deadly Sting 🦴½ **1982** Silva devises an intricate scheme to gain revenge on the men who cheated him out of his share of a gold bullion heist. **90m/C VHS, Beta.** *FR* Henry Silva, Philip Clay, Andre Pousse; ***D:*** Jean-Claude Roy. *NO*

Deadly Stranger 🦴 *Border Heat* **1988** Fluegel's talents could have been put to much better use than as the selfish mistress of a plantation owner who is taking advantage of the migrant workers toiling on his land. Moore is a drifter and hired hand who rallies the workers to stand up to the owner. **93m/C VHS.** Darlanne Fluegel, Michael J. Moore, John Vernon, Ted White; ***D:*** Max Kleven. *MCG*

Deadly Strangers 🦴🦴 **1982** Two people meet up on the road and decide to share a ride. We discover that one of them is an insane killer who's escaped from a mental institution. Suspense builds nicely, but the ending is flawed. **89m/C VHS, Beta.** *GB* Hayley Mills, Simon Ward, Sterling Hayden, Ken Hutchison; ***D:*** Sidney Hayers. *NO*

Deadly Sunday 🦴½ **1982** A family's weekly Sunday drive turns terrifying when desperate jewel thieves detour them and hold them hostage. **85m/C VHS, Beta.** Dennis Ely, Henry Sanders, Gylian Roland, Douglas Alexander; ***D:*** Donald M. Jones. *LIV*

Deadly Surveillance 🦴🦴 **1991 (R)** Two tough policemen investigate a series of drug-related murders and stake out a possible suspect—a beautiful woman who's the lover of one of the lawmen. Tension in this Canadian-made cop opera evaporates in the third act for a standard buddy-buddy action finale. Made for television. **92m/C VHS.** Michael Ironside, Christopher Bondy, Susan Almgren, Vlasta Vrana, David Carradine; ***D:*** Paul Ziller. *REP*

Deadly Target 🦴½ **1994 (R)** Detective Charles Prince (Daniels) is sent to L.A. to return a notorious Chinese gangster to Hong Kong for trial. But Prince finds out his would-be prisoner's escaped and soon he's involved in martial arts mayhem. **90m/C VHS.** Gary Daniels, Kenneth McLeod, Max Gail, Susan Byun. *PMH*

Deadly Thief 🦴🦴 *Shalimar* **1978** A former jewel thief comes out of retirement to challenge those who are now tops in the profession to try and steal the world's most precious ruby from him. Of course all they have to lose is their lives. What could have been an exciting adventure is made curiously boring. **90m/C VHS, Beta.** *IN* Rex Harrison, John Saxon, Sylvia Miles, Dharmendra, Zenat Aman, Shammi Kapoor; ***D:*** Krishna Shah. *PSM*

The Deadly Trackers 🦴 **1973 (PG)** If gorey oaters are your thing, this one's definitely for you; if not, make tracks. Harris plays a spiteful sheriff who heads south of the border to get his pound of flesh from the outlaws who slew his family in a bank robbery. Overlong revenge-o-rama based on Samuel Fuller's short story, "Riata"; might have been bearable if Fuller hadn't been bumped from the director's chair (as it is, he and other contributors refused to be listed in the credits). **104m/C VHS, LV.** Richard Harris, Rod Taylor, Al Lettieri, Neville Brand, William Smith, Paul Benjamin, Pedro Armendariz Jr.; ***D:*** Barry Shear. *WAR, FCT*

The Deadly Trap 🦴 *Death Scream* **1971 (PG)** Confusing thriller that couldn't. Dunaway is the mentally unstable wife of an ex-spy. His former employers have targeted him with plans to use her and her fragile state-of-mind to their advantage. **96m/C VHS.** *FR IT* Faye Dunaway, Frank Langella, Barbara Parkins, Maurice Ronet; ***D:*** Rene Clement. *FCT*

Deadly Twins *Woof!* **1985** After being beaten and gang-raped, twin sister singers are out to get revenge. Nothing new here; don't waste your time. **87m/C VHS, Beta.** Audrey Landers, Judy Landers, Ellie Russell, Wayne Allison; ***D:*** Joe Oaks. *PSM*

Deadly Vengeance 🦴 **1981** It's strictly low budget as the mob kills Jones's boyfriend, forcing her to mount a vengeful but inexpensive offensive against the crime syndicate's bigwigs. **84m/C VHS, Beta.** Grace Jones, Alan Marlowe, Arthur Roberts. *NO*

Deadly Weapon 🦴 **1988 (PG-13)** It's a bit of nerdish wish fulfillment when 15-year-old geek Eastman finds a secret anti-matter weapon conveniently lost by the military in an Arizona stream. You won't like the kid any more than you'll like the story of this low rent boy-gets-back-at-bullies sci fi fiasco. **89m/C VHS.** Rodney Eastman, Gary Frank, Michael Horse, Ed Nelson, Kim Walker; ***D:*** Michael Miner; ***W:*** Michael Miner. *TWE, HHE*

Deadly Weapons 🦴 **1970 (R)** Chesty Morgan, she of the 73-inch bustline, takes on the mob using only her God-given abilities. One of Joe Bob Brigg's "Sleaziest Movies in the History of the World" series, and he is welcome to it. **90m/C VHS.** Chesty Morgan, Harry Reems; ***D:*** Doris Wishman. *NO*

Deadman's Curve 🦴🦴 **1978** Decent bio pic detailing the lives of Jan Berry and Dean Torrence who, as Jan and Dean, started the surf music wave only to wipe out after an almost-fatal car wreck. Shows how they deal with and recover from the tragedy. Made for television. **100m/C VHS.** Richard Hatch, Bruce Davison, Pamela Bellwood, Susan Sullivan, Dick Clark, Wolfman Jack; ***D:*** Richard Compton. *GEM*

Deadtime Stories 🦴½ **1986** Mother Goose it's not. Fairy tales "Little Red Riding Hood" and "Goldilocks and the Three Bears," among others, are presented like you've never before seen them—as low-budget horror tales. **93m/C VHS, Beta, LV.** Michael Mesmer, Brian DePersia, Scott Valentine, Phyllis Craig, Melissa Leo, Nicole Picard; ***D:*** Jeffrey Delman. *NO*

Deadwood 🦴½ **1965** In the untamed West, a young cowboy is mistaken for the notorious Billy the Kid. Cinematography by Vilmos Zsigmond. **100m/C VHS, Beta.** Arch Hall Jr., Jack Lester, Melissa Morgan, Robert Dix; ***D:*** James Landis. *RHI, FCT*

Deadwood Pass 🦴 **1933** Below-standard fare has Tyler rescuing Monti more times than seems reasonable. Monti was once an all-around helper to W.C. Fields. **62m/B VHS.** Tom Tyler, Alice Dahl, Wally Wales, Buffalo Bill Jr., Lafe McKee, Bud Osborne, Charles "Slim" Whitaker, Charlotte (Carlotta) Monti; ***D:*** J.P. McGowan. *DVT, HEG, GPV*

Deal of the Century 🦴🦴 **1983 (PG)** A first-rate hustler and his cohorts sell second-rate weapons to third-world nations; unfortunately, their latest deal threatens to blow up in their faces—literally. **99m/C VHS, Beta, LV.** Chevy Chase, Sigourney Weaver, Gregory Hines, Richard Libertini, Wallace Shawn; ***D:*** William Friedkin; ***W:*** Paul Brickman. *WAR*

Dealers 🦴½ **1989 (R)** Two money-hungry stock traders mix business and pleasure, then set their sights on one final all or nothing score. **92m/C VHS, Beta, LV.** *GB* Rebecca DeMornay, Paul McGann, Derrick O'Connor; ***D:*** Colin Bucksey. *ACA, IME*

Dear America: Letters Home from Vietnam 🦴🦴🦴½ **1988 (PG)** Acclaimed documentary featuring pictures and film of the war with voice-overs by dozens of Hollywood stars reading the words of American GIs. Initially made for cable television. **84m/C VHS, Beta.** ***D:*** Bill Couturie; ***W:*** Bill Couturie; ***M:*** Todd Boekelheide. *HBO, AMB*

Dear Boys 🦴🦴 **1980** A stylized film of sexual fantasies and romance between a moody writer and a carefree young man who relentlessly pursues excitement. Based on the novel by Gerald Reve. **90m/C VHS.** *NL* Hugo Netsers, Hans Dagelet, Bill Van Dijk, Albert Mol; ***D:*** Paul de Lussanet. *FCT*

Dear Brigitte 🦴🦴 **1965** A young American kid ("Lost in Space" tyke Mumy) writes a love letter to Brigitte Bardot and travels to Paris to meet her in person. Based on the novel "Erasmus with Freckles" by John Haase. **100m/C VHS, Beta.** James Stewart, Billy Mumy, Glynis Johns, Fabian, Cindy Carol, John Williams, Jack Kruschen, Brigitte Bardot, Ed Wynn, Alice Pearce; ***D:*** Henry Koster; ***W:*** Hal Kanter. *FOX*

Dear Dead Delilah 🦴½ **1972** Moorehead is Delilah, the matriarch of a southern family, who is on her deathbed. Her heirs are fighting to the bitter—and bloody—end to be the first to find Delilah's money, buried somewhere on her land. **90m/C VHS, Beta.** Agnes Moorehead, Will Geer, Michael Ansara, Patricia Carmichael, Dennis Patrick; ***D:*** John Farris. *SUE*

Dear Detective 🦴🦴 *Dear Inspector; Tendre Poulet* **1977** Comedy/thriller/romance finds female police inspector (Girardot) investigating a murder while romancing a somewhat pompous professor of Greek (Noiret). French with subtitles. **105m/C VHS.** *FR* Annie Girardot, Philippe Noiret, Catherine Alric, Guy Marchand, Simone Renant; ***D:*** Philippe de Broca; ***W:*** Philippe de Broca, Michel Audiard; ***M:*** Georges Delerue. *FRA*

Dear Detective 🦴🦴 **1978** Vaccaro is the head of the police homicide unit who is trying to track down the killer of several politicians. In the midst of her investigation, she falls for an old friend, a professor of Greek language. Made for television and based on a French television series. **90m/C VHS.** Brenda Vaccaro, Arlen Dean Snyder, Michael MacRae, John Dennis Johnston, Jack Ging, Stephen McNally, M. Emmet Walsh, Constance Forslund, R.G. Armstrong; ***D:*** Dean Hargrove; ***M:*** Georges Delerue. *FCT*

Dear Murderer 🦴🦴 **1947** A husband suspects his wife of having an affair, and devises an ingenious, if complicated, trap for her. Inspired performances from the leads, but the plot is grim and confusing. **94m/B VHS, Beta.** *GB* Eric Portman, Greta Gynt, Dennis Price, Jack Warner, Maxwell Reed, Hazel Court, Andrew Crawford, Jane Hylton; ***D:*** Arthur Crabtree. *SNC*

Dear Wife 🦴🦴½ **1949** Comedy about those ties that bind. Even though her father is runnning for reelection to the State Senate, Freeman wants her brother-in-law (Holden) to run against him. Sequel to "Dear Ruth." **88m/B VHS, Beta.** William Holden, Joan Caulfield, Edward Arnold, Billy DeWolfe, Mona Freeman; ***D:*** Richard Haydn. *BAR*

Death and the Maiden 🦴🦴🦴 **1994 (R)** Former political prisoner and torture victim (Weaver) turns the tables on the man she believes was her tormentor 15 years before. Pressing her civil rights lawyer husband (Wilson) into duty as defense attorney, she becomes prosecutor, judge, and jury. The accused (Kingsley) learns the dangers of picking up stranded motorists, as he is bound, gagged, and roughed up by the now empowered and vengeful Paulina. Tense, claustrophobic political thriller features a talented ensemble both on screen and behind the scenes. From the Ariel Dorfman play. **102m/C VHS, LV.** Sigourney Weaver, Ben Kingsley, Stuart Wilson; ***D:*** Roman Polanski; ***W:*** Rafael Yglesias, Ariel Dorfman; ***C:*** Tonino Delli Colli; ***M:*** Wojciech Kilar. Nominations: Independent Spirit Awards '95: Best Director (Polanski). *TTC, NLC, IME*

Death at Love House 🦴½ **1975** A screen writer becomes obsessed when he is hired to write the life story of a long dead silent movie queen. Filmed at the Harold Lloyd estate. Made for television. **74m/C VHS, Beta.** Robert Wagner, Kate Jackson, Sylvia Sidney, Joan Blondell, John Carradine; ***D:*** E.W. Swackhamer. *PSM*

Death Be Not Proud 🦴🦴🦴 **1975** Based on the book by John Gunther detailing the valiant battle fought by his son against the brain tumor that took his life at the age of 17. Wonderfully acted by the three principals, especially Alexander, this film leaves us feeling hopeful despite its subject. Made for television. **74m/C VHS, Beta.** Arthur Hill, Robby Benson, Jane Alexander, Linden Chiles, Wendy Phillips; ***D:*** Donald Wrye. *LCA*

Death Becomes Her 🦴🦴🦴 **1992 (PG-13)** Aging actress Streep will do anything to stay young and beautiful, especially when childhood rival Hawn shows up, 200 pounds lighter and out to revenge the loss of her fiance, Streep's henpecked hubby. Doing anything arrives in the form of a potion that stops the aging process (and keeps her alive forever). Watch for the hilarious party filled with dead celebrities who all look as good as the day they died. Great special effects and fun performances by Streep and Hawn playing their glamour-girl roles to the hilt add merit to this biting commentary on Hollywood's obsession with beauty and youth. **105m/C VHS, Beta, LV.** Meryl Streep, Bruce Willis, Goldie Hawn, Isabella Rossellini, Sydney Pollack, Michael Caine, Ian Ogilvy, Adam Storke, Nancy Fish, Alaina Reed Hall, Michelle Johnson, Mimi Kennedy, Jonathan Silverman; ***Cameos:*** Fabio Lanzoni; ***D:*** Robert Zemeckis; ***W:*** Martin Donovan, David Koepp; ***C:*** Dean Cundey; ***M:*** Alan Silvestri. Academy Awards '92: Best Visual Effects. *MGM, PMS*

Death Before Dishonor 🦴½ **1987 (R)** Formula actioner stars Dryer as a tough Marine sergeant who battles ruthless Middle Eastern terrorists after they slaughter his men and kidnap his commanding officer (Keith). **95m/C VHS, Beta, LV.** Fred Dryer, Brian Keith, Joanna Pacula, Paul Winfield; ***D:*** Terry J. Leonard. *NWV, VTR*

Death Blow 🦴½ **1987 (R)** The victims of a violent rapist team together to stop the criminal after he repeatedly skirts conviction. **90m/C VHS, Beta.** Martin Landau, Frank Stallone, Jerry Van Dyke, Terry Moore, Henry Darrow, Jack Carter, Peter Lapis, Don Swayze, Donna Denton; ***D:*** Raphael Nussbaum. *NO*

Death by Dialogue 🦴 **1988 (R)** Muddled story of some teenagers who discover an old film script from a project never produced because it was haunted by tragic accidents. **90m/C VHS, Beta.** Laura Albert, Ken Sagoes; ***D:*** Tom Dewier. *NO*

Death by Prescription 🦴½ **198?** After adjusting his patients' wills to benefit himself, an evil physician sees to their mysterious deaths. **75m/C VHS, Beta.** Timothy West, Nigel Davenport. *ACA, MOV*

Death Challenge 🦴½ **1980** Gangs battle without weapons, motive or discretion in this kung fu extravaganza. **94m/C VHS, Beta.** Steve Leving, Susan Wong. *UNI*

Death Chase 🦴½ **1987** An average Joe, just jogging down the street, is thrown into a desperate game of cat-and-mouse when a body lands at his feet. **86m/C VHS, Beta.** William Zipp, Paul Smith, Jack Starrett, Bainbridge Scott; ***D:*** David A. Prior. *NO*

Death Collector 🦴½ **1989 (R)** In the future when insurance companies run the world, if you don't pay your premium, you die. **90m/C VHS, Beta.** Daniel Chapman, Ruth Collins; ***D:*** Tom Gniazdowski. *VTR*

Death Cruise 🦴½ **1974** The six winners of a free cruise find that there is a fatal catch to the prize in this made-for-TV movie. **74m/C VHS, Beta.** Kate Jackson, Celeste Holm, Tom Bosley, Edward Albert, Polly Bergen, Michael Constantine, Richard Long; ***D:*** Ralph Senensky. *AHV*

The Death Curse of Tartu *Woof!* **1966** Another aspiring cult classic. (Read: A low-budget flick so bad it's funny). Students accidentally disturb the burial ground of an Indian medicine man who comes to zombie-like life with a deadly prescription. **84m/C VHS, Beta.** Fred Pinero, Doug Hobart, William Grefe. *NO*

Death Dreams 🦴🦴 **1992** Crista thinks she has a perfect life with her wealth, beautiful daughter Jennie, and handsome new husband George. Then Jennie tragically drowns. It appears to be an accident until Jennie contacts her mother from beyond the grave to tell what really happened. Is the tragedy turning Crista's mind or is there truly something sinister going on—something that involves George? Based on the novel by William Katz. Routine suspenser originally appeared on cable television. **94m/C VHS, LV.** Marg Helgenberger, Christopher Reeve, Fionnula Flanagan; ***D:*** Martin Donovan; ***W:*** Robert Glass. *NLC*

Death Driver 🦴½ **1978** In order to make a comeback, a stuntman attempts to do a stunt that was responsible for ending his career ten years earlier. Obviously brave but none too smart. **93m/C VHS, Beta.** Earl Owensby, Mike Allen, Patty Shaw, Mary Ann Hearn; ***D:*** Jimmy Huston. *NO*

Death Drug 🦴½ **1983** Cliched alarmist film about a talented musician ruining his career by becoming addicted to the drug angel dust. **73m/C VHS, Beta.** Philip Michael Thomas, Vernee Watson-Johnson, Rosalind Cash; ***D:*** Oscar Williams. *ACA*

Death Feud **1989** A man tries to save the woman he loves from the man who would destroy her and her former pimp. **98m/C VHS, Beta.** Karen Mayo Chandler, Chris Mitchum, Frank Stallone. *HMD*

Death Force 🦴½ **1978 (R)** When a Vietnam veteran comes to New York City, he becomes a hitman for the Mafia. **90m/C VHS, Beta.** Jayne Kennedy, Leon Isaac Kennedy, James Iglehart, Carmen Argenziano; ***D:*** Cirio H. Santiago. *NO*

Death from a Distance 🦴½ **1936** A reporter and a detective put the moves on a group of astronomers who may be responsible for a murder. **73m/B VHS, Beta.** Russell Hopton, Lola Lane, George F. Marion Sr., John St. Polis, Lee Kohlmar, Lew Kelly, Wheeler Oakman, Robert Frazer, Cornelius Keefe; ***D:*** Frank Strayer. *SNC*

Death Games 🦴½ **1982** Two young men shooting a documentary about an influential music promoter ask too many wrong questions, causing the powers-that-be to want them out of the picture for good. **78m/C VHS, Beta.** Lou Brown, David Clendenning, Jennifer Cluff. *NO*

Death Goes to School 🦴🦴 **1953** A strangler is loose in a girl's school, and the music teacher has a hunch as to who it is. **65m/B VHS, Beta.** *GB* Barbara Murray, Gordon Jackson, Pamela Allan, Jane Aird, Beatrice Varley; ***D:*** Stephen Clarkson. *SNC*

Death House 🦴½ **1988** Derek Keillor is on Death Row at Townsend State Prison when he discovers a plot to use inmates for scientific experiments in biological warfare. He decides the best way to get out is to volunteer, which means convincing the man who put him in prison that they're now on the same side. **92m/C VHS.** Dennis Cole, Anthony (Tony) Franciosa, Michael Pataki, John Saxon; ***D:*** John Saxon. *AIP*

Death Hunt 🦴🦴 **1981 (R)** A man unjustly accused of murder pits his knowledge of the wilderness against the superior numbers of his pursuers. **98m/C VHS, Beta, LV.** Charles Bronson, Lee Marvin, Ed Lauter, Andrew Stevens, Carl Weathers, Angie Dickinson; ***D:*** Peter Hunt; ***W:*** Mark Victor, Michael Grais. *FXV, FOX*

Death in Brunswick 🦴🦴 **1990 (R)** Carl Fitzgerald (Neill) seems to be one of life's born losers— his wife's left him, his mother nags him, his house is falling apart, and he's unemployed. At least until he gets a job as a chef in a sleazy rock 'n' roll club and finds Sophie (Carides), the lovely barmaid, who just happens to be engaged to the club's owner. Of course, with Carl's luck, things go from bad to downright dangerous. Based on the novel by Boyd Oxlade. **106m/C VHS.** *AU* Sam Neill, Zoe Carides, Yvonne Lawley, Boris Brkic, John Clarke; ***D:*** John Ruane; ***W:*** John Ruane, Boyd Oxlade. *COL*

Death in Deep Water 🦴🦴 **1974** A sensuous woman lures a man into a plot to kill her incredibly rich husband. **71m/C VHS, Beta.** Bradford Dillman, Suzan Farmer. *LIV*

Death in the Garden 🦴🦴 *La Mort en Ce Jardin; Evil Eden* **1956** Surreal film, filled with symbolism, about a group of French people, living in a South American settlement, who must flee a riot between soldiers and striking miners. Local adventurer, Chark (Marchal), agrees to lead them to safety but their trek through the jungle is fraught with peril (and not just from the animal life). French with subtitles. **90m/C VHS.** *MX FR* Georges Marchal, Simone Signoret, Charles Vanel, Michele Girardon, Michel Piccoli, Tito Junco; ***D:*** Luis Bunuel; ***W:*** Luis Bunuel, Luis Alcoriza, Raymond Queneau; ***C:*** Jorge Stahl Jr.; ***M:*** Paul Misraki. *INT*

Death in Venice 🦴🦴🦴½ *Morte a Venezia* **1971 (PG)** A lush, decadent adaptation of the Thomas Mann novella about an aging and jaded composer, here suggested to be Gustav Mahler, tragically obsessed with ideal beauty as personified in a young boy. **124m/C VHS, Beta.** *IT* Dirk Bogarde, Mark Burns, Bjorn Andresen, Marisa Berenson, Silvana Mangano; ***D:*** Luchino Visconti; ***C:*** Pasqualino de Santis; ***M:*** Gustav Mahler. Nominations: Academy Awards '71: Best Costume Design; Cannes Film Festival '71: Best Film. *WAR, INJ, PME*

Death is Called Engelchen 🦴🦴🦴½ *For We Too Do Not Forgive* **1963** An influential, important work of the Czech new wave. A survivor of WWII remembers his experiences with the SS leader Engelchen in a series of flashbacks. In Czech with subtitles. **111m/B VHS, Beta.** *CZ* ***D:*** Jan Kadar, Elmar Klos. *FCT*

Death Journey 🦴½ **1976 (R)** Producer and director Williamson portrays private eye Jesse Crowder, hired by the New York D.A. to escort a key witness cross-country. A regular Williamsonfest. **90m/C VHS, Beta.** Fred Williamson, D'Urville Martin, Bernie Kuby, Heidi Dobbs, Stephanie Faulkner; ***D:*** Fred Williamson. *UNI*

The Death Kiss 🦴🦴½ **1933** Creepy thriller about eerie doings at a major Hollywood film studio where a sinister killer does away with his victims while a cast-of-thousands movie spectacular is in production. **72m/B VHS, Beta, 8mm.** Bela Lugosi, David Manners, Adrienne Ames, Edward Van Sloan, Vince Barnett; ***D:*** Edwin L. Marin. *NOS, SNC, CAB*

Death Kiss 🦴½ **1977 (R)** When a man hires a psychopath to murder his wife, his plan doesn't proceed exactly as expected. **90m/C VHS, Beta.** Larry Daniels, Dorothy Moore. *PSM, LSV*

Death Machine 🦴½ **1995 (R)** Exec uncovers questionable scientific project at weapons technology company and the scientist in charge decides to get even by testing his death machine, which works by sensing fear, in corporate headquarters. **99m/C VHS, LV.** Brad Dourif, Ely Pouget, William Hootkins; ***D:*** Stephen Norrington. *VMK*

Death Machines 🦴½ **1976 (R)** Young karate student must face the "Death Machines," a team of deadly assassins who are trained to kill on command. **93m/C VHS, Beta.** Ron Marchini, Michael Chong, Joshua Johnson; ***D:*** Paul Kyriazi. *NO*

Death Magic 🦴½ **1992** A group of five ceremonial magicians performs a spell to bring someone back from the dead, but the man they bring back, a soldier from the Civil War, decides to go on a vicious murdering spree to kill the descendants of the people who convicted him of murder in 1875. A suspenseful first entry from director Clinco. **93m/C VHS.** Anne Coffrey, Keith DeGreen, Jack Dunlap, Danielle Frons, Norman Stone; ***D:*** Paul E. Clinco; ***W:*** Paul E. Clinco. *NO*

Death Mask of the Ninja 🦴½ **198?** Two princes, separated at birth, reunite and kick everyone in the head. Dubbed. **95m/C VHS, Beta.** Joey Lee, Tiger Tung, Jon Chen. *MOV*

Death Match 🦴 **1994 (R)** John Larson gives up kickboxing after a tragedy but when his friend disappears, John is forced into a fighting bout with no rules and only one outcome. **90m/C VHS.** Matthias Hues, Martin Kove, Ian Jacklin, Nick Hill, Renee Ammann; ***D:*** Joe Coppoletta. *MNC*

The Death Merchant 🦴 **1991** Foundering attempt at a nuclear thriller. A modern mad man hopes to sell a computer chip to third world countries but is thwarted by a secret agent. Confusing, illogical plot highlighted by mediocre performances. **90m/C VHS.** Lawrence Tierney, Martina Castle, Melody Munyan, Monika Schnarre; ***D:*** James R. Winburn; ***W:*** Kari Holman. *AIP*

Death Nurse 🦴🦴 **1987** Fresh from "Crazy Fat Ethel II," aspiring Queen of Camp Alden takes takes up residence in a health care establishment, much to the dismay of the patients who give up their lives in exchange for their money. **80m/C VHS.** Priscilla Alden, Michael Flood; ***D:*** Nick Phillips. *VCD*

Death of a Bureaucrat 🦴🦴🦴 **1966** A Cuban hero dies, and in tribute, the Communist government buries him with his union card. His widow, however, needs the card in order to collect a pension, and she enlists her nephew's help to retrieve it. The nephew soon finds himself buried in red tape, and digs himself in ever-deeper as he seeks to disinter his late uncle. A wry satire of the communist bureaucracy in Cuba, brimming with comedic tributes to Harold Lloyd, Buster Keaton and Laurel & Hardy. Alea's film was only briefly released in 1966 and was promptly banned, eventually finding its way to the U.S. in 1979. In Spanish with English subtitles. **87m/B VHS, Beta.** *CU* Salvador Wood, Silvia Planas, Manuel Estanillo, Gaspar de Santelices, Carlos Ruiz de la Tejera, Omar Alfonso, Ricardo Suarez, Luis Romay, Elsa Montero; ***D:*** Thomas Gutierrez Alea. *NYF, FCT, INJ*

Death of a Centerfold 🦴🦴 **1981** Drama based on the life and tragic death of Playboy model and actress Dorothy Stratten. More effectively handled in Bob Fosse's "Star 80." **96m/C VHS, Beta.** Jamie Lee Curtis, Bruce Weitz, Robert Reed, Mitchell Ryan, Bibi Besch; ***D:*** Gabrielle Beaumont. *MGM*

Death of a Gunfighter 🦴🦴 **1969 (PG)** A western town courting eastern investors and bankers seeks a way to kill their ex-gunslinger sheriff. **94m/C VHS, Beta.** Richard Widmark, Lena Horne, Carroll O'Connor, John Saxon, Larry Gates; ***D:*** Donald Siegel; ***W:*** Robert Totten. *MCA*

Death of a Salesman 🦴🦴🦴½ **1986** A powerful made-for-television adaptation of the famous Arthur Miller play. Hoffman won an Emmy (as did Malkovich) for his stirring portrayal of Willy Loman, the aging salesman who realizes he's past his prime and tries to come to grips with the life he's wasted and the family he's neglected. Reid also turns in a fine performance as his long-suffering wife. **135m/C VHS, Beta, LV.** Dustin Hoffman, John Malkovich, Charles Durning, Stephen Lang, Kate Reid, Louis Zorich; ***D:*** Volker Schlondorff; ***C:*** Michael Ballhaus; ***M:*** Alex North. *ORI, FCT, WAR*

Death of a Scoundrel 🦴🦴½ *Loves of a Scoundrel* **1956** A womanizing entrepreneur is murdered and the culprit could be any one of his many jealous romantic conquests. **119m/B VHS, Beta, LV.** George Sanders, Zsa Zsa Gabor, Yvonne De Carlo, Victor Jory; ***D:*** Charles Martin; ***M:*** Max Steiner. *NO*

Death of a Soldier 🦴🦴 **1985 (R)** During WWII, the uneasy U.S.-Australian alliance explodes when a psychotic American soldier murders three Melbourne women. The lawyer hired to defend him has to fight political as well as legal influences. Based on a true story. **93m/C VHS, Beta.** *AU* James Coburn, Reb Brown, Maurie Field, Belinda Darey; ***D:*** Philippe Mora. *FOX*

The Death of Adolf Hitler 🦴🦴½ **1984** British made-for-television film depicting Hitler's last ten days in an underground bunker. Drug-addled, suicidal, and Eva Braun-haunted, he receives the news of the fall of the Third Reich. While the film avoids cliche, it lacks emotional depth. **107m/C VHS, Beta.** *GB* Frank Finlay, Caroline Mortimer; ***D:*** Rex Firlin. *ORI, TLF, WAR*

Death of an Angel 🦴½ **1986** When her crippled daughter runs away to join a cult in Mexico, a recently ordained priest (Bedelia) follows her, only to become caught up herself with the leader of the group. **95m/C VHS, Beta, LV.** Bonnie Bedelia, Nick Mancuso, Pamela Ludwig, Alex Colon; ***D:*** Petru Popescu; ***M:*** Jay Michael Ferguson. *NO*

The Death of Richie 🦴🦴 *Richie* **1976** Gazzara does a fine job as a father driven to kill his drug-addicted teenage son, portrayed by Benson. Occasionally lapses into melodrama, but all-in-all a decent adaptation of Thomas Thompson's book "Richie" which was based on a true story. Made for television. **97m/C VHS, Beta.** Ben Gazzara, Robby Benson, Eileen Brennan, Clint Howard; ***D:*** Paul Wendkos. *PSM, LCA*

Death of the Incredible Hulk 🦴½ **1990** Scientist David Banner's new job just may provide the clues for stopping his transformation into the monstrous Incredible Hulk. But first there are terrorists after the Hulk who need to be defeated and Banner's new romance to contend with. Made for television. **96m/C VHS.** Bill Bixby, Lou Ferrigno, Elizabeth Gracen, Philip Sterling; ***D:*** Bill Bixby. *RHI*

Death of the Rat **1975** A serious/comic meditation on the tragedy of modern technological life. **6m/C VHS, Beta.** ***D:*** Pascal Aubier. *FFM*

Death on the Nile 🦴🦴½ **1978 (PG)** Agatha Christie's fictional detective, Hercule Poirot, is called upon to interrupt his vacation to uncover who killed an heiress aboard a steamer cruising down the Nile. Ustinov's first stint as the Belgian sleuth. Anthony Powell's costume design won an Oscar. **135m/C VHS, Beta, LV.** *GB* Peter Ustinov, Jane Birkin, Lois Chiles, Bette Davis, Mia Farrow, David Niven, Olivia Hussey, Angela Lansbury, Jack Warden, Maggie Smith, George Kennedy, Simon MacCorkindale, Harry Andrews, Jon Finch; ***D:*** John Guillermin; ***W:*** Anthony Shaffer; ***C:*** Jack Cardiff; ***M:*** Nino Rota. Academy Awards '78: Best Costume Design; National Board of Review Awards '78: Best Supporting Actress (Lansbury). *REP*

Death Promise 🦴 **1978 (R)** Ho-hum excuse for a horror flick has murderous landlord trying to evict his tenants using whatever means are necessary. **90m/C VHS, Beta.** Charles Bonet. *NO*

Death Race 2000 🦴🦴½ **1975 (R)** In the 21st century, five racing car contenders challenge the national champion of a cross country race in which drivers score points by killing pedestrians. Gory fun. Based on the 1956 story by Ib Melchior, and followed by "Deathsport." Made for television. **80m/C VHS, Beta.** David Carradine, Simone Griffeth, Sylvester Stallone, Mary Woronov; ***D:*** Paul Bartel; ***W:*** Charles B. Griffith, Robert Thom. *VDM, MRV*

Death Rage 🦴½ **1977 (R)** A hitman comes out of retirement to handle the toughest assignment he has ever faced: search for and kill the man who murdered his brother. He finds out he's the victim of a Mafia doublecross. **92m/C VHS, Beta.** *IT* Yul Brynner, Martin Balsam; ***D:*** Anthony (Antonio Margheriti) Dawson. *NO*

Death Ray *Woof!* **19??** It's a race to the finish as terrorists threaten to unleash the world's most powerful weapon. A very poor James Bond rip-off. **93m/C VHS, Beta.** Gordon Scott; ***D:*** Frank G. Carroll. *BFV, MRV*

Death Ray 2000 🦴½ *T.R. Sloane* **1981** Bondian superspy T.R. Sloane must search out the whereabouts of a stolen military device that could kill all life on Earth. TV pilot for the series "A Man Called Sloane." **100m/C VHS, Beta.** Robert F. Logan, Ann Turkel, Maggie Cooper, Dan O'Herlihy; ***D:*** Lee H. Katzin. *WOV, MOV*

Death Rides the Plains 🦴🦴 **1944** Western with a twist. A man lures prospective buyers to his ranch, kills them, and steals their money. It's up to our heroes to ride to the rescue. **53m/B VHS, Beta.** Bob Livingston, Al "Fuzzy" St. John, Nica Doret, Ray Bennett; ***D:*** Sam Newfield. *VYY, VDM*

Death Rides the Range 🦴½ **1940** Russian spies start a range war as a cover for an operation to pipe helium off a ranch and over the border. Maynard, an undercover FBI agent posing as a cowboy, is out to stop them. **58m/B VHS.** Ken Maynard, Fay McKenzie, Ralph Peters, Julian Rivero, Charles "Blackie" King, John Elliott, Bud Osborne; ***D:*** Sam Newfield. *GPV, NOS, DVT*

Death Ring 🦴 **1993 (R)** Basic action/martial arts tale about three men who must battle the bad guys to ensure their own survival. **91m/C VHS, LV.** Mike Norris, Chad McQueen, Don Swayze, Billy Drago, Isabel Glasser; ***D:*** Robert J. Kizer; ***W:*** George T. LeBrun. *COL, NLC*

Death Row Diner 🦴½ **1988** A movie mogul, executed for a crime he didn't commit, is brought back to life by a freak electrical storm. Nothing will stop him from exacting revenge. **90m/C VHS, Beta.** Jay Richardson, Michelle (McClellan) Bauer, John Content, Tom Schell, Dennis Mooney, Frank Sarcinello Sr., Dana Mason. *NO*

Death Scream 🦴🦴 **1975** Drama based on the New York murder of Kitty Genovese, whose cries for help while being assaulted went ignored by her neighbors. Good casting but the pacing deteriorates. Made for television. **100m/C VHS.** Raul Julia, John P. Ryan, Lucie Arnaz, Ed Asner, Art Carney, Diahann Carroll, Kate Jackson, Cloris Leachman, Tina Louise, Nancy Walker, Eric (Hans Gudegast) Braeden, Allyn Ann McLerie, Tony Dow, Sally Kirkland; ***D:*** Richard T. Heffron; ***W:*** Stirling Silliphant. *ACE*

Death Screams 🦴 **1983 (R)** Attractive college coeds have a party and get hacked to pieces for their troubles by a machete-wielding maniac. **88m/C VHS, Beta.** Susan Kiger, Jennifer Chase, Jody Kay, William T. Hicks, Martin Tucker. *GEM*

Death Sentence 🦴½ *Murder One* **1974** When a woman juror on a murder case finds out that the wrong man is on trial, she is stalked by the real killer. Made for television. **74m/C VHS, Beta.** Cloris Leachman, Laurence Luckinbill, Nick Nolte, William Schallert; ***D:*** E.W. Swackhamer. *PSM*

Death Ship 🦴 **1980 (R)** A luxury liner is destroyed by an ancient, mysterious freighter on open seas, leaving the survivors to confront the ghost ship's inherent evil in this slow-going horror flick. **91m/C VHS, Beta.** *GB CA* George Kennedy, Richard Crenna, Nick Mancuso, Sally Ann Howes, Saul Rubinek, Kate Reid; ***D:*** Alvin Rakoff. *SUE, NLC*

Death Shot 🦴 **1973** Two plainclothes detectives (who seem just as sleazy as the criminals they're trying to bust) try to break up a drug ring and find that, with a little coercion, their best sources of information are the pimps and junkies they want to stop. Senseless attempt to make an action pic. **90m/C VHS.** Richard C. Watt, Frank Himes; ***D:*** Mitch Brown. *NO*

Death Spa *Woof!* **1987 (R)** A health club is possessed by the spirit of a vengeful woman. The fitness craze takes on a campy new twist. **87m/C VHS.** William Bumiller, Brenda Bakke, Merritt Butrick; ***D:*** Michael Fischa. *MPI*

Death Sport 🦴🦴 **1978 (R)** In this sequel to the cult hit "Death Race 2000," a group of humans play a game of death in the year 3000. The object is to race cars and kill as many competitors as possible. Not as good as the original, but still watchable. **83m/C VHS, Beta.** David Carradine, Claudia Jennings, Richard Lynch, William Smithers, Will Walker, David McLean, Jesse Vint; ***D:*** Henry Suso, Allan Arkush. *WAR, OM*

The Death Squad 🦴½ **1973** A police commissioner hires an ex-cop to find a group of vigilante cops who are behind a series of gangland-style executions. Good cast, though that's about all this flick has got going for it. Made for television. **74m/C VHS, Beta.** Robert Forster, Melvyn Douglas, Michelle Phillips, Mark Goddard, Bert Remsen, Claude Akins; ***D:*** Harry Falk. *PSM*

Death Stalk 🦴½ **1974** Dream vacation turns nightmarish for two couples when the wives are taken hostage by several escaped convicts. Made for television. **90m/C VHS, Beta.** Vince Edwards, Vic Morrow, Anjanette Comer, Robert Webber, Carol Lynley, Neville Brand, Norman Fell; ***D:*** Robert Day. *CNG, GEM, HHE*

Death Target 🦴½ **1983** Three former mercenaries team up for one last mission that gets sidetracked when one of the soldiers-of-fortune falls for a worker with a habit. **72m/C VHS, Beta.** Jorge Montesi, Elaine Lakeman; ***D:*** Peter Hyams. *PSM*

Death Tide 🦴🦴 **1958** Hoodlums pirate a ship full of diamonds in this story of death and crime on the high seas. **?m/C VHS.** Frank Silvera. *SNC*

Death Train 🦴½ **1979** Dead man seems to have been struck by a train, but clueless investigator can't figure out where the train came from. **96m/C VHS, Beta.** Hugh Keays-Byrne, Ingrid Mason, Max Meldrum; ***D:*** Igor Auzins. *NO*

Death Valley 🦴½ **1946** Greed turns gold prospectors in Death Valley against each other. **70m/C VHS, Beta.** Robert Lowery, Helen Gilbert, Sterling Holloway; ***D:*** Lew (Louis Friedlander) Landers. *NO*

Death Valley 🦴½ **1981 (R)** Good cast, lousy plot. Youngster (Billingsley) gets caught up with a psycho cowpoke while visiting mom in Arizona. **90m/C VHS, Beta.** Paul LeMat, Catherine Hicks, Peter Billingsley, Wilford Brimley, Edward Herrmann, Stephen McHattie; ***D:*** Dick Richards. *MCA*

Death Valley Days: No Gun Behind His Badge **1965** Western anthology series which ran on television from 1952-1970 and was noted for its longtime sponsor, 20 Mule Team Borax, as well as its hosts, including Stanley Andrews, Ronald Reagan, Robert Taylor, and Dale Robertson. On this tape: the premiere episode plus "Halo for a Bad Man." Each additional tape contains two episodes. **55m/C VHS.** Robert Taylor, Ronald Reagan. *NO*

Death Valley Manhunt 🦴🦴 **1943** A marshal hired to protect a man's oil wells discovers that the company manager is keeping the profits for himself. **55m/B VHS, Beta.** Wild Bill Elliott, George "Gabby" Hayes, Anne Jeffreys; ***D:*** John English. *DVT*

Death Valley Rangers 🦴½ **1944** The hero pretends to be an outlaw to expose a gang robbing gold-laden stagecoaches. **59m/B VHS.** Ken Maynard, Hoot Gibson, Bob Steele, Linda Brent, Kenneth Harlan; ***D:*** Robert Emmett Tansey. *NOS, DVT*

Death Warmed Up 🦴½ **1985** A crazed brain surgeon turns ordinary people into bloodthirsty mutants, and a small group of young people travel to his secluded island to stop him. **83m/C VHS, Beta.** Michael Hurst, Margaret Umbers, David Letch; ***D:*** David Blyth. *LIV, VES*

Death Warrant 🦴🦴 **1990 (R)** Van Damme whams and bams a little less than usual in this cop-undercover-in-prison testosterone fest. As a Royal Canadian Mountie undercover in prison—where inmates are perishing under mysterious circumstances—the pectoral-perfect Muscles from Brussels is on the brink of adding two plus two when an inmate transferee threatens his cover. Contains the requisite gratuitous violence, prison bromide, and miscellaneous other Van Dammages. **111m/C VHS, LV.** Jean-Claude Van Damme, Robert Guillaume, Cynthia Gibb, George Dickerson, Patrick Kilpatrick; ***D:*** Deran Sarafian. *MGM*

Death Watch 🦴🦴🦴 **1980 (R)** In the future, media abuse is taken to an all time high as a terminally ill woman's last days are secretly filmed by a man with a camera in his head. Intelligent, adult science fiction with an excellent cast. **128m/C VHS, LV.** *FR GE* Romy Schneider, Harvey Keitel, Harry Dean Stanton, Max von Sydow; ***D:*** Bertrand Tavernier; ***W:*** Bertrand Tavernier, David Rayfiel. *SUE*

Death Weekend 🦴½ *House by the Lake* **1976** A woman is stalked by a trio of murderous, drunken hoodlums who seek to spoil her weekend. **89m/C VHS, Beta.** *CA* Brenda Vaccaro, Don Stroud, Chuck Shamata, Richard Ayres, Kyle Edwards; ***D:*** William Fruet. *LIV, VES*

Death Wish 🦴🦴½ **1974 (R)** A middle-aged businessman turns vigilante after his wife and daughter are violently attacked and raped by a gang of hoodlums (one is Goldblum in his film debut). He stalks the streets of New York seeking revenge on other muggers, pimps, and crooks, making the neighborhood safer for those less macho. **93m/C VHS, Beta, LV.** Charles Bronson, Vincent Gardenia, William Redfield, Hope Lange, Jeff Goldblum, Stuart Margolin, Olympia Dukakis; ***D:*** Michael Winner; ***W:*** Wendell Mayes; ***M:*** Herbie Hancock. *MGM, PAR*

Death Wish 2 *Woof!* **1982 (R)** Bronson recreates the role of Paul Kersey, an architect who takes the law into his own hands when his family is victimized once again. Extremely violent sequel to the successful 1974 movie. Followed by "Death Wish 3" (1985) and 4 (1987) in which Bronson continues to torture the street scum and the viewers as well. **89m/C VHS, Beta, LV.** J.D. Cannon, Charles Bronson, Jill Ireland, Vincent Gardenia, Anthony (Tony) Franciosa; ***D:*** Michael Winner; ***M:*** Jimmy Page. *WAR, OM*

Death Wish 3 🦴½ **1985 (R)** Once again, Charles Bronson blows away the low lifes who have killed those who were dear to him and were spared in the first two films. **100m/C VHS, Beta, LV.** Charles Bronson, Martin Balsam, Deborah Raffin, Ed Lauter, Alex Winter, Marina Sirtis; ***D:*** Michael Winner; ***M:*** Jimmy Page. *MGM*

Death Wish 4: The Crackdown 🦴 **1987 (R)** The four-times-weary urban vigilante hits crack dealers this time, hard. **100m/C VHS, Beta, LV.** Charles Bronson, John P. Ryan, Kay Lenz; ***D:*** J. Lee Thompson. *MED, VTR*

Death Wish 5: The Face of Death *Woof!* **1994 (R)** Paul Kersey (Bronson) returns to vigilantism when his clothing manufacturer fiancee Olivia (Downs) has her business threatened by mobsters, one of whom turns out to be her sadistic ex (Parks). Bronson looks bored with the rehashed material. Lots of explicit and grisly violence. **95m/C VHS, LV.** Charles Bronson, Lesley-Anne Down, Michael Parks, Kenneth Welsh; ***D:*** Allan Goldstein; ***W:*** Allan Goldstein; ***M:*** Terry Plumer. *VMK*

Death Wish Club 🦴½ *Carnival of Fools* **1983** Young woman gets involved in a club with an unusual mission—suicide. **93m/C VHS, Beta.** Meridith Haze, Rick Barns, J. Martin Sellers, Ann Fairchild; ***D:*** John Carr. *NO*

Deathcheaters 🦴½ **1976 (G)** Australian Secret Service offers two stuntmen a top secret mission in the Philippines. **96m/C VHS, Beta.** John Hargreaves, Grant Page, Noel Ferrer; ***D:*** Brian Trenchard-Smith; ***W:*** Michael Cove. *VES*

Deathdream 🦴🦴½ *Dead of Night; Night Walk; The Veteran* **1972** In this reworking of the "Monkey's Paw" tale, a mother wishes her dead son would return from Vietnam. He does, but he's not quite the person he used to be. Gripping plot gives new meaning to the saying, "Be careful what you wish for—it might come true." **98m/C VHS, Beta.** *CA* John Marley, Richard Backus, Lynn Carlin; ***D:*** Bob (Benjamin) Clark; ***W:*** Alan Ormsby. *MPI*

Deathfight 🦴½ **1993 (R)** Let's face it, no one watches these movies because they have a plot. This is a fast-paced B-grade martial arts flick with numerous butts getting kicked. Oh, all right, if you insist on a plot—Norton's evil half-brother (Guerrero) is trying to turn their legitimate family business into a criminal front by framing Norton for murder. **92m/C VHS.** Richard Norton, Franco Guerrero, Karen Moncrieff, Chuck Jeffreys, Ron Vreeken, Tetchie Agbayani, Jose Mari Avellano; ***D:*** Anthony Maharaj; ***W:*** Tom Huckabee. *ACA*

Deathhead Virgin 🦴½ **1974 (R)** An evil virgin spirit is waiting to possess one of two men eager to find a sunken fortune. The fate of the fortunate one is only death! **94m/C VHS, Beta.** Jock Gaynor, Larry Ward, Diane McBain, Vic Diaz. *NO*

Deathmask 🦴🦴 **1969** A four-year-old boy's corpse is found buried in a cardboard box, and a medical examiner—whose daughter met a similar fate—investigates the murder. Could've been done more tastefully. **102m/C VHS, Beta.** Farley Granger, Ruth Warrick, Danny Aiello; ***D:*** Richard S. Friedman. *PSM, PRD*

Deathmoon 🦴½ **1978** A businessman plagued by recurring werewolf nightmares goes on a Hawaiian vacation to try to forget his troubles. Made for television. **90m/C VHS, Beta.** Robert Foxworth, Joe Penny, Debralee Scott, Dolph Sweet, Charles Haid; ***D:*** Bruce Kessler. *NO*

Deathrow Gameshow 🦴½ **1988** Condemned criminals can either win their freedom or die in front of millions on a new television show that doesn't win the host many friends. **78m/C VHS, Beta, LV.** John McCafferty, Robin Bluthe, Beano, Mark Lasky; ***D:*** Mark Pirro; ***W:*** Mark Pirro. *MED*

Deathstalker *Woof! El Cazador de la Muerte* **1983 (R)** Deathstalker sets his sights on seizing the evil wizard Munkar's magic amulet so he can take over Munkar's castle. The only excuse for making such an idiotic film seems to have been to fill it with half-naked women. Filmed in Argentina and followed by two sequels that were an improvement. **80m/C VHS, Beta, LV.** Richard Hill, Barbi Benton, Richard Brooker, Victor Bo, Lana Clarkson; ***D:*** John Watson; ***W:*** Howard R. Cohen. *LIV, VES*

Deathstalker 2: Duel of the Titans 🦴🦴 **1987 (R)** Campy fantasy comically pits the lead character against an evil wizard. Sword-and-sorcery spoof doesn't take itself too seriously. **85m/C VHS, Beta, LV.** John Terlesky, Monique Gabrielle, John Lazar, Toni Naples, Maria Socas, Queen Kong; ***D:*** Jim Wynorski; ***W:*** Jim Wynorski. *LIV, VES*

Deathstalker 3 🦴½ *Deathstalker 3: The Warriors From Hell* **1989 (R)** Another humorous entry in the Deathstalker saga. This time there's action, romance, magic and the Warriors From Hell. **85m/C VHS, Beta, LV.** John Allen Nelson, Carla Herd, Terri Treas, Thom Christopher; ***D:*** Alfonso Corona; ***W:*** Howard R. Cohen. *LIV, VES, HHE*

Deathstalker 4: Match of Titans 🦴 **1992 (R)** The sword and sorcery epic continues, with our hero revealing yet more musculature in his efforts to defeat an evil queen and her legion of stone warriors. **85m/C VHS.** Richard Hill, Maria Ford, Michelle Moffett, Brent Baxter Clark; ***D:*** Howard R. Cohen. *NHO*

Deathtrap 🦴🦴 **1982 (PG)** A creatively-blocked playwright, his ailing rich wife, and a former student who has written a surefire hit worth killing for, are the principals in this compelling comedy-mystery. Cross and double-cross are explored in this film based on the Broadway hit by Ira Levin. **118m/C VHS, Beta.** Henry Jones, Michael Caine, Christopher Reeve, Dyan Cannon, Irene Worth; ***D:*** Sidney Lumet; ***W:*** Jay Presson Allen. *WAR*

The Decameron 🦴🦴🦴½ **1970 (R)** Pasolini's first epic pageant in his "Trilogy of Life" series. An acclaimed, sexually explicit adaptation of a handful of the Boccaccio tales. In Italian with English subtitles. **111m/C VHS, Beta, LV.** *FR IT GE* Franco Citti, Ninetto Davoli, Angela Luce, Patrizia Capparelli, Jovan Jovanovich, Silvana Mangano, Pier Paolo Pasolini; ***D:*** Pier Paolo Pasolini; ***C:*** Tonino Delli Colli; ***M:*** Ennio Morricone. Berlin International Film Festival '71: Silver Prize. *WBF, INJ, APD*

Decameron Nights 🦴🦴½ **1953** Story of Boccaccio's pursuit of a recently-widowed young women is interwoven amongst the three of the fourteenth-century Italian writer's bawdy tales. **87m/C VHS, Beta.** *GB* Louis Jourdan, Joan Fontaine, Binnie Barnes, Joan Collins, Marjorie Rhodes; ***D:*** Hugo Fregonese. *NOS, MRV, GEM*

Deceit 🦴🦴 **1993 (R)** A sci-fi sex comedy with an environmental premise. Bailey and Brick are two aliens working for their planet's Environmental Protection Agency, whose idea of protection is to vaporize polluter planets. Guess which planet is next on their hit list. But before they get down to business, our two alien studs want to do the horizontal bop with two of the local lovelies, who decide that isn't how they want to spend their last moments on earth. It has a happy ending. **92m/C VHS.** Scott Paulin, Norbert Weisser, Samantha Phillips; ***D:*** Albert Pyun; ***W:*** Kitty Chalmers. *COL*

Deceived 🦴🦴½ **1991 (PG-13)** A successful career woman with a passionate husband and a young daughter feels she has it all until her husband is apparently killed in a bizarre tragedy. But just how well did she know the man she married? Who was he really and what secrets are hidden in his past? As she struggles to solve these mysteries, her own life becomes endangered in this psychological thriller. **115m/C VHS, Beta.** Goldie Hawn, John Heard, Ashley Peldon, Jan Rubes, Amy Wright, Maia Filar, Robin Bartlett, Tom Irwin, Beatrice Straight, Kate Reid; ***D:*** Damian Harris; ***W:*** Mary Agnes Donoghue, Derek Saunders; ***C:*** Jack N. Green; ***M:*** Thomas Newman. *TOU*

The Deceivers 🦴🦴 **1988 (PG-13)** Brosnan stars as a British officer sent on a dangerous undercover mission in 1820s India. He's to infiltrate the notorious Thuggee cult, known for robbing and murdering unwary travelers. Interesting premise falters due to slow pacing and Brosnan's lack of believability. **112m/C VHS, Beta, LV.** *IN GB* Pierce Brosnan, Saeed Jaffrey, Shashi Kapoor, Keith Michell; ***D:*** Nicholas Meyer; ***C:*** Walter Lassally. *WAR*

December 🦴🦴 **1991 (PG)** Four prep-school students in New Hampshire must confront the reality of war when the Japanese bomb Pearl Harbor. A touching story of courage and friendship that takes place in one night during the suprise-attack. **92m/C VHS, LV.** Wil Wheaton, Chris Young, Brian Krause, Balthazar Getty, Jason London; ***D:*** Gabe Torres; ***W:*** Gabe Torres. *NO*

December Bride 🦴🦴½ **1991** Determined young woman (Reeves) becomes the housekeeper to two taciturn Irish farmer/brothers (Hinds and McCann) and proceeds to bully them into prosperity in early 20th century rural Ireland. She also scandalizes the community by sleeping with both men and refusing to marry either—even after she becomes pregnant. Based on the novel by Sam Hanna Bell. **88m/C VHS.** *IR* Saskia Reeves, Ciaran Hinds, Donal McCann, Patrick Malahide, Brenda Bruce; ***D:*** Thaddeus O'Sullivan; ***W:*** David Rudkin; ***C:*** Bruno de Keyzer; ***M:*** Jurgen Knieper. *FXL*

December Flower 🦴🦴½ **19??** A young woman arrives at her aunt's estate so she can nurse her back to health, but she finds her aunt a bit down in the mouth: seems someone is trying to kill her, and she could be next in line. **65m/C VHS.** Jean Simmons, Mona Washbourne, Bryan Forbes. *FCT, MOV*

December 7th: The Movie 🦴🦴½ **1991** Banned for 50 years by the U.S. Government, this planned Hollywood explanation to wartime audiences of the Pearl Harbor debacle offers such "offensive" images as blacks fighting heroically alongside whites, loyal Japanese-Americans, and Uncle Sam asleep on the morning of the attack. The Chief of Naval Operations confiscated the original film, claiming it demeaned the Navy. The battle scenes were so realistic they fooled even documentarians. This isn't the most incisive video on the event—just an unforgettable snapshot. **82m/B VHS.** Walter Huston, Harry Davenport; ***D:*** John Ford. *KIT, CPM, FUS*

Deception 🦴🦴🦴 **1946** Davis is a pianist torn between two loves: her intensely jealous sponsor (Rains) and her cellist boyfriend (Henreid). Plot in danger of going over the melodramatic edge is saved by the very effective performances of the stars. **112m/B VHS, Beta.** Bette Davis, Paul Henreid, Claude Rains, John Abbott, Benson Fong; ***D:*** Irving Rapper. *MGM*

Deception 🦴½ *Ruby Cairo* **1992 (PG-13)** Talented cast is wasted in an old-fashioned mystery that lacks a coherent script. MacDowell is married to Mortensen, the owner of an aircraft salvage company. He's supposedly killed in a plane crash but she thinks he's just pulled a fast one and sets off to find him. Tracking her hubby's secret bank accounts takes her all over the world, and finally to Cairo, Egypt where she meets Neeson. Together they discover Mortensen's scam involves smuggling poison gas and the duo then try to outwit the hoods on their trail. Film was originally released at 110 minutes. **90m/C VHS, LV.** Andie MacDowell, Liam Neeson, Viggo Mortensen, Jack Thompson, Jeff Corey, Miriam Reed, Luis Cortes, Paco Mauri; ***D:*** Graeme Clifford; ***W:*** Robert Dillon, Michael Thomas; ***M:*** John Barry. *LIV*

Deceptions 🦴🦴 **1990 (R)** A risque, semi-erotic thriller about a wealthy society woman (Sheridan) who kills her husband. Sheridan claims that she acted in self-defense, but macho cop Hamlin has a different view. He interrogates her, grows increasingly attracted, and is drawn into her web of seduction. **105m/C VHS, LV.** Harry Hamlin, Nicolette Sheridan. *REP*

The Decline of the American Empire ½ *Le Declin De L'Empire Americain* **1986 (R)** The critically acclaimed French-Canadian film about eight academic intellectuals who spend a weekend shedding their sophistication and engaging in intertwining sexual affairs. Examines the differing attitudes of men and women in regards to sex and sexuality. In French with English subtitles. **102m/C VHS, Beta.** *CA* Dominique Michel, Dorothee Berryman, Louise Portal, Genevieve Rioux; ***D:*** Denys Arcand; ***W:*** Denys Arcand. Genie Awards '87: Best Director (Arcand), Best Film, Best Supporting Actor (Arcand), Best Supporting Actress (Portal); Toronto-City Award '86: Best Canadian Feature Film; Nominations: Academy Awards '86: Best Foreign Language Film. *MCA, INJ*

Decline of Western Civilization 1 **1981** The L.A. hard core punk scene. Music by X, Circle Jerks, Black Flag, Fear and more. **100m/C VHS, Beta, LV.** ***D:*** Penelope Spheeris. *MVD, MED*

Decline of Western Civilization 2: The Metal Years **1988 (R)** Following Spheeris's first documentary about hardcore punk, she in turn delves into the world of heavy metal rock. We are given a look at some of the early rockers, as well as some of the smaller bands still playing L.A. clubs. Features appearances by Alice Cooper, Ozzy Osbourne, Poison, Gene Simmons and Megadeth. **90m/C VHS, Beta.** Alice Cooper, Ozzy Osbourne, Gene Simmons, Lizzie Borden; ***D:*** Penelope Spheeris. *COL, MVD, FCT*

Deconstructing Sarah **1994 (R)** Sarah Vincent (Ticotin) is a high-powered but bored ad exec who assumes an alter-ego, Ruth, when she heads for the wrong side of the tracks in her pursuit of casual sex. Her secret life is discovered when Sarah is murdered and best friend Elizabeth (Kelley) begins to turn up some likely suspects. Fast-paced whodunnit with good cast work. Made for cable TV. **120m/C VHS.** Rachel Ticotin, Sheila Kelley, A. Martinez, David Andrews, John Vickery, Jenifer Lewis, Dwier Brown, Peter Jason; ***D:*** Craig R. Baxley; ***W:*** Lee Rose; ***M:*** Tom Scott. *MCA*

Decoration Day **1990 (PG)** Garner plays a retired Southern judge who aids an angry childhood friend who has refused to accept his long-overdue Medal of Honor. Investigating the past leads to a decades-old mystery and a tragic secret that has repercussions for everyone involved. Based on the novel by John William Corrington. A Hallmark Hall of Fame presentation. **99m/C VHS, LV.** James Garner, Bill Cobbs, Judith Ivey, Ruby Dee, Laurence "Larry" Fishburne, Jo Anderson; ***D:*** Robert Markowitz. *REP*

Decoy ½ **1995 (R)** Two ex-government operatives (Weller and Patrick) are hired by their former commanding officer (Breck) to protect his daughter (Vogel) but they're hunted by a gang of mercenaries in the Canadian wilderness. **98m/C VHS, LV.** Peter Weller, Robert Patrick, Darlene Vogel, Charlotte Lewis, Peter Breck; ***D:*** Victor Rambaldi; ***W:*** Robert Sarno; ***C:*** Jon Kranhouse. *TTC*

Dedee d'Anvers ½ *Dedee; Woman of Antwerp* **1949** A gritty dockside melodrama about a drunken prostitute abused by her pimp. A sailor and a local barkeep don't like it. In French with subtitles. **95m/B VHS, Beta.** Simone Signoret, Marcel Dalio, Bernard Blier, Marcel Pagliero, Jane Marken; ***D:*** Yves Allegret; ***C:*** Jean Bourgoin. *NOS, FCT, INJ*

A Dedicated Man **1986** A lonely woman agrees to act as a wife for a businessman to lend him credibility. A British "Romance Theater" presentation. **60m/C VHS.** *GB* Alec McCowen, Joan Plowright; ***D:*** Robert Knights. *PSM*

The Deep **1977 (PG)** An innocent couple get involved in an underwater search for a shipwreck, and they quickly find themselves in over their heads. Gorgeous photography manages to keep this slow mover afloat. Famous for Bisset's wet T-shirt scene. Based on the novel by Peter Benchley. The laserdisc edition offers widescreen format. **123m/C VHS, Beta, LV.** Nick Nolte, Jacqueline Bisset, Robert Shaw, Louis Gossett Jr., Eli Wallach; ***D:*** Peter Yates; ***W:*** Peter Benchley, Tracy Keenan Wynn; ***M:*** John Barry. Nominations: Academy Awards '77: Best Sound. *GKK*

Deep Cover ½ **1988 (R)** A man dares to go beyond the walls of a mysterious English manor in order to expose the secrets that lie within the manor. **81m/C VHS, Beta.** Tom Conti, Donald Pleasence, Denholm Elliott, Kika Markham, Phoebe Nicholls; ***D:*** Richard Loncraine. *PSM, PAR*

Deep Cover ½ **1992 (R)** Fishburne plays Russell Stevens Jr., a straight-arrow cop who goes undercover to infiltrate a Latin American cocaine cartel. While undercover, he becomes partners with drug dealer David Jason (Goldblum), and undergoes an inner transformation until he realizes he is betraying his cause. Confusing and commercial, yet marked with a moral rage. **107m/C VHS, LV.** Laurence "Larry" Fishburne, Jeff Goldblum, Victoria Dillard, Charles Martin Smith, Sydney Lassick, Clarence Williams III, Gregory Sierra, Robert Guenveur Smith, Cory Curtis, Glynn Turman, Def Jef; ***D:*** Bill Duke; ***W:*** Michael Tolkin, Henry Bean; ***C:*** Bojan Bazelli; ***M:*** Michel Colombier. *NLC*

Deep Down ½ **1994 (R)** When young Andy (Young) moves into a new apartment, he discovers his neighbor (Roberts) is a gorgeous married woman just looking for a little fun on the side. Too bad her husband (Segal) is a violent psychopath, totally suspicious of his wife's fidelity. Just how far will everyone go to get what they want? Also available in an unrated version. **86m/C VHS.** Tanya Roberts, Chris Young, George Segal. *IMP*

Deep End **1970** A 15-year-old boy working as an attendant in a bath house falls in love with a 20-year-old woman in this tragic tale of a young man obsessed. Good British cast and music by Cat Stevens. **88m/C VHS.** *GB GE* Jane Asher, John Moulder-Brown, Diana Dors; ***D:*** Jerzy Skolimowski; ***M:*** Cat Stevens. *NO*

Deep in My Heart ½ **1954** A musical biography of the life and times of composer Sigmund Romberg, with guest appearances by many MGM stars. ♫Leg of Mutton; You Will Remember Vienna; Softly, as in a Morning Sunrise; Mr. & Mrs.; I Love to Go Swimmin' with Wimmin; The Road to Paradise; Will You Remember; It; Serenade. **132m/C VHS, Beta.** Jose Ferrer, Merle Oberon, Paul Henreid, Walter Pidgeon, Helen Traubel, Rosemary Clooney, Jane Powell, Howard Keel, Cyd Charisse, Gene Kelly, Ann Miller; ***D:*** Stanley Donen. *MGM*

Deep in the Heart *Handgun* **1983 (R)** When a young teacher is raped at gunpoint on a second date, she takes the law into her own hands. Just-off-the-target film tries to take a stand against the proliferation of guns in the U.S. Thought-provoking all the same. **99m/C VHS, Beta.** *GB* Karen Young, Clayton Day, Ben Jones, Suzie Humphreys; ***D:*** Tony Garnett; ***W:*** Tony Garnett. *NO*

Deep Red **1994 (R)** When a young girl has an encounter with an extra-terrestrial spacecraft her blood chemistry is mysteriously altered. Now the proteins her body manufactures can lead to immortality and ruthless scientist Newmeyer wants to take advantage of the fact—any way he can. **85m/C VHS, LV.** Michael Biehn, Joanna Pacula, John de Lancie; ***D:*** Craig R. Baxley; ***W:*** D. Brent Mote. *MCA*

Deep Red: Hatchet Murders ½ *The Hatchet Murders; Profundo Rosso; Dripping Deep Red* **1975** A stylish but gruesome rock music-driven tale of a composer who reads a book on the occult which happens to relate to the sadistic, sangfroid murder of his neighbor. When he visits the book's author, he discovers that she has been horribly murdered as well. **100m/C VHS, Beta.** David Hemmings, Daria Nicolodi; ***D:*** Dario Argento. *QVD*

Deep Six ½ **1958** A WWII drama that examines the conflict between pacifism and loyalty. A staunch Quaker is called to active duty as a lieutenant in the U.S. Navy, where his beliefs put him into disfavor with shipmates. **110m/C VHS, Beta.** Alan Ladd, William Bendix, James Whitmore, Keenan Wynn, Efrem Zimbalist Jr., Joey Bishop; ***D:*** Rudolph Mate. *NO*

Deep Space ½ **1987** A flesh-eating alien lands on earth and, after devouring a cop, is stalked by his partner. An "Alien" rip-off. Some humorous moments keep us from thinking too hard about how much the monster resembles our friend from "Alien." **90m/C VHS, Beta.** Charles Napier, Ann Turkel, Ron Glass, Bo Svenson, Julie Newmar; ***D:*** Fred Olen Ray. *TWE*

Deepstar Six ½ **1989 (R)** When futuristic scientists try to set up an undersea research and missile lab, a group of subterranean monsters get in the way. **97m/C VHS, Beta, LV.** Taurean Blacque, Nancy Everhard, Greg Evigan, Miguel Ferrer, Matt McCoy, Nia Peeples, Cindy Pickett, Marius Weyers; ***D:*** Sean S. Cunningham; ***W:*** Lewis Abernathy. *NO*

The Deer Hunter **1978 (R)** A powerful and vivid portrait of Middle America with three steel-working friends who leave home to face the Vietnam War. Controversial, brutal sequences in Vietnam are among the most wrenching ever filmed; the rhythms and rituals of home are just as purely captured. Neither pro- nor anti-war, but rather the perfect evocation of how totally and forever altered these people are by the war. Emotionally shattering; not to be missed. **183m/C VHS, Beta, LV.** Robert De Niro, Christopher Walken, Meryl Streep, John Savage, George Dzundza, John Cazale, Chuck Aspegren, Rutanya Alda, Shirley Stoler, Amy Wright; ***D:*** Michael Cimino; ***W:*** Deric Washburn, Michael Cimino; ***C:*** Vilmos Zsigmond; ***M:*** John Williams. Academy Awards '78: Best Director (Cimino), Best Film Editing, Best Picture, Best Sound, Best Supporting Actor (Walken); Golden Globe Awards '79: Best Director (Cimino); Los Angeles Film Critics Association Awards '78: Best Director (Cimino); New York Film Critics Awards '78: Best Film, Best Supporting Actor (Walken); Nominations: Academy Awards '78: Best Actor (De Niro), Best Cinematography, Best Original Screenplay, Best Supporting Actress (Streep). *MCA, FCT, BTV*

The Deerslayer ½ **1978** Low-budget snoozer based on the classic novel by James Fenimore Cooper. Frontiersman Hawkeye and his Indian companion Chingachgook set out to rescue a beautiful Indian maiden and must fight bands of hostile Indians and Frenchmen along the way. **98m/C VHS, Beta.** Steve Forrest, Ned Romero, John Anderson, Joan Prather; ***D:*** Richard Friedenberg; ***M:*** Andrew Belling. *NO*

Def by Temptation **1990 (R)** A potent horror fantasy about a young black theology student who travels to New York in search of an old friend. There he meets an evil woman who is determined to seduce him and force him to give in to temptation. Great soundtrack. **95m/C VHS, Beta, LV.** James Bond III, Kadeem Hardison, Bill Nunn, Samuel L. Jackson, Minnie Gentry, Rony Clanton; ***D:*** James Bond III; ***W:*** James Bond III. *SGE, IME*

Def-Con 4 ½ **1985 (R)** Three marooned space travelers return to a holocaust-shaken Earth to try to start again, but some heavy-duty slimeballs are in charge and they don't want to give it up. Good special effects bolster a weak script. **85m/C VHS, Beta.** Maury Chaykin, Kate Lynch, Tim Choate; ***D:*** Paul Donovan. *NWV, VTR*

The Defender ½ **1957** CBS "Studio One" presentation of a live courtroom drama. First shown in 1957. Made for television. **112m/B VHS, Beta.** Steve McQueen, William Shatner, Ralph Bellamy, Martin Balsam. *FCT, RHI*

Defenders of the Law **1931** Early action talkie concerned with gang warfare and law enforcement. **64m/B VHS.** John Holland, Mae Busch, Alan Cooke, Joseph Girard, Edmund Breese, Catherine Dale Owen, Robert Gleckler; ***D:*** Joseph Levering. *GPV*

Defending Your Life **1991 (PG)** Brooks' cock-eyed way of looking at the world travels to the afterlife in this uneven comedy/romance. In Judgement City, where everyone goes after death, past lives are examined and judged. If you were a good enough person you get to stay in heaven (where you wear funny robes and eat all you want without getting fat). If not, it's back to earth for another go-round. Brooks plays an L.A. advertising executive who crashes his new BMW and finds himself defending his life. When he meets and falls in love with Streep, his interest in staying in heaven multiplies. Occasionally charming, seldom out-right hilarious. **112m/C VHS, LV, 8mm.** Albert Brooks, Meryl Streep, Rip Torn, Lee Grant, Buck Henry, George Wallace, Lillian Lehman, Peter Schuck; ***D:*** Albert Brooks; ***W:*** Albert Brooks; ***M:*** Michael Gore. *WAR*

The Defense Never Rests 🦴🦴 **1990** Perry Mason, the lawyer who never loses a case, aids his friend and secretary, Della Street, in this made-for-television movie. **95m/C VHS, Beta.** Raymond Burr, Barbara Hale, Al Freeman Jr., William Katt, Patrick O'Neal. *MCG*

Defense of the Realm 🦴🦴🦴½ **1985 (PG)** A British politician is accused of selling secrets to the KGB through his mistress and only a pair of dedicated newspapermen believe he is innocent. In the course of finding the answers they discover a national cover-up conspiracy. An acclaimed, taut thriller. **96m/C VHS, Beta, LV.** *GB* Gabriel Byrne, Greta Scacchi, Denholm Elliott, Ian Bannen, Bill Paterson, Fulton Mackay, Robbie Coltrane; ***D:*** David Drury. British Academy Awards '85: Best Supporting Actor (Elliott). *COL, SUE*

Defense Play 🦴½ **1988 (PG)** Two teenagers are unwittingly stuck in the middle of a Soviet plot to steal the plans that created a technologically advanced helicopter. **95m/C VHS, Beta.** David Oliver, Susan Ursitti, Monte Markham, William Frankfather, Patch MacKenzie; ***D:*** Monte Markham. *TWE*

Defenseless 🦴🦴 **1991 (R)** Hershey tries hard in an unplayable part as a giddy attorney who finds herself trapped in a love-affair/legal case that turns murderous. Good cast and interesting twists contend with a sexist sub-text, which proves a woman can't "have it all." **106m/C VHS, LV.** Barbara Hershey, Sam Shepard, Mary Beth Hurt, J.T. Walsh, Sheree North; ***D:*** Martin Campbell; ***W:*** James Cresson; ***M:*** Trevor Jones. *LIV*

Defiance 🦴🦴 **1979 (PG)** A former merchant seaman moves into a tenement in a run-down area of New York City. When a local street gang begins terrorizing the neighborhood, he decides to take a stand. Familiar plotline handled well in this thoughtful film. **101m/C VHS, Beta.** Jan-Michael Vincent, Art Carney, Theresa Saldana, Danny Aiello; ***D:*** John Flynn; ***W:*** Tom Donnelly; ***M:*** John Beal, Basil Poledouris. *ORI, LIV, VES*

Defiant 🦴½ *The Wild Pack; The Sandpit Generals* **1970** Two rival street gangs clash when one admits a young orphan girl. **93m/C VHS, Beta.** Kent Lane, John Rubinstein, Tisha Sterling; ***D:*** Hall Bartlett. *LIV*

The Defiant Ones 🦴🦴🦴½ **1958** Thought-provoking story about racism revolves around two escaped prisoners (one black, one white) from a chain gang in the rural South. Their societal conditioning to hate each other dissolves as they face constant peril together. Critically acclaimed. **97m/B VHS, Beta.** Tony Curtis, Sidney Poitier, Theodore Bikel, Lon Chaney Jr., Charles McGraw, Cara Williams; ***D:*** Stanley Kramer; ***W:*** Nathan E. Douglas, Harold Jacob Smith; ***C:*** Sam Leavitt; ***M:*** Stephen Dorff. Academy Awards '58: Best Black and White Cinematography, Best Original Screenplay; British Academy Awards '58: Best Actor (Poitier); Edgar Allan Poe Awards '58: Best Screenplay; Golden Globe Awards '59: Best Film—Drama; New York Film Critics Awards '58: Best Director (Kramer), Best Film, Best Screenplay; Nominations: Academy Awards '58: Best Actor (Curtis), Best Actor (Poitier), Best Director (Kramer), Best Film Editing, Best Picture, Best Supporting Actor (Bikel), Best Supporting Actress (Williams). *MGM, FOX*

The Defilers 🦴 **1965 (R)** Disturbing, low-budget J.D. movie in which two thugs imprison a young girl in a basement and force her to be their love slave. **?m/B VHS.** Byron Mabe, Jerome Eden, Mae Johnson; ***D:*** David Friedman. *SNC, TPV*

Deja Vu 🦴 **1984 (R)** A lame romantic thriller about the tragic deaths of two lovers and their supposed reincarnation 50 years later. **95m/C VHS, Beta, LV.** *GB* Jaclyn Smith, Nigel Terry, Claire Bloom, Shelley Winters; ***D:*** Anthony Richmond; ***W:*** Ezra D. Rappaport; ***M:*** Pino Donaggio. *MGM*

Deja Vu 🦴🦴 **1989** Thriller set in 1925 and moving between Chicago and Odessa. A Chicago hitman is hired by the mob to kill a traitor who has fled to Odessa. Niczypur, the traitor, has been using the newly opened Chicago-Constantinople-Odessa shipping line for his own smuggling operation. Filled with shoot-outs, brawls, and chases. In English, Russian, and Polish with English subtitles. **108m/C VHS.** *PL* Jerzy Stuhr, Galina Pietrowa, Nikolai Karaczencow, Wladimir Golowin; ***D:*** Juliusz Machulski. *FCT*

The Deliberate Stranger 🦴🦴🦴 **1986** Harmon is engrossing as charismatic serial killer Ted Bundy, sentenced to death for several Florida murders and suspected in the killings of a least 25 women in several states. After eluding police for five years Bundy was finally arrested in Florida in 1979. His case became a cause celebre on capital punishment as it dragged on for nine years. Bundy was finally executed in 1989. Based on the book "Bundy: The Deliberate Stranger" by Richard W. Larsen. Made for television. **188m/C VHS, Beta.** Mark Harmon, M. Emmet Walsh, Frederic Forrest, John Ashton, George Grizzard, Ben Masters, Glynnis O'Connor, Bonnie Bartlett, Billy Green Bush, Lawrence Pressman; ***D:*** Marvin J. Chomsky. *WAR, PMS*

The Delicate Delinquent 🦴🦴½ **1956** Lewis's first movie without Dean Martin finds him in the role of delinquent who manages to become a policeman with just the right amount of slapstick. **101m/B VHS, Beta, LV.** Jerry Lewis, Darren McGavin, Martha Hyer, Robert Ivers, Horace McMahon; ***D:*** Don McGuire; ***W:*** Don McGuire. *PAR*

Delicatessen 🦴🦴🦴 **1992 (R)** Set in 21st-century Paris, this hilarious debut from directors Jeunot and Caro focuses on the lives of the oddball tenants of an apartment building over a butcher shop. Although there is a famine, the butcher shop is always stocked with fresh meat—made from the building's tenants. Part comedy, part horror, part romance, this film merges a cacophony of sights and sounds with intriguing results. Watch for the scene involving a symphony of creaking bed springs, a squeaky bicycle pump, a cello, and clicking knitting needles. In French with English subtitles. **95m/C VHS, Beta, LV.** *FR* Marie-Laure Dougnac, Dominique Pinon, Karin Viard, Jean Claude Dreyfus, Ticky Holgado, Anne Marie Pisani, Edith Ker, Patrick Paroux, Jean-Luc Caron; ***D:*** Jean-Marie Jeunet, Marc Caro; ***W:*** Gilles Adrien; ***M:*** Carlos D'Alessi. Cesar Awards '92: Best Art Direction/Set Decoration, Best Writing. *PAR, INJ, BTV*

Delightfully Dangerous 🦴🦴 **1945** Often Deadly Dull. A farfetched musical rooted in yesteryear about mismatched sisters, one a 15-year-old farm girl, the other a New York burlesque dancer, in competition on Broadway. ♫I'm Only Teasin'; In a Shower of Stars; Mynah Bird; Through Your Eyes to Your Heart; Delightfully Dangerous; Once Upon a Song. **92m/B VHS.** Jane Powell, Ralph Bellamy, Constance Moore, Arthur Treacher, Louise Beavers; ***D:*** Arthur Lubin. *DVT, NOS, VDM*

Delinquent Daughters 🦴½ **1944** Slow-paced drama about a high school girl who commits suicide and the cop and reporter who try to find out why so darn many kids are getting into trouble. **71m/B VHS, Beta.** June Carlson, Fifi d'Orsay, Teala Loring; ***D:*** Al(bert) Herman. *SNC, VYY, DVT*

Delinquent Parents 🦴½ **1938** A wayward girl gives up her baby for adoption. She turns her life around and becomes a juvenile court judge. Years later, who should come up before her for misdeeds but her long-lost daughter. The Hound cannot improve on a contemporary critic who renamed this "Delinquent Producers." **62m/B VHS.** Doris Weston, Maurice Murphy, Helen MacKellar, Terry Walker, Richard Tucker, Morgan Wallace; ***D:*** Nick Grinde. *NOS, LOO*

Delinquent School Girls *Woof! Bad Girls* **1984 (R)** Three escapees from an asylum get more than they bargained for when they visit a Female Correctional Institute to fulfill their sexual fantasies. Buys into just about every conceivable stereotype. **89m/C VHS, Beta.** Michael Pataki, Bob Minos, Stephen Stucker; ***D:*** Gregory Corarito. *LIV, VES*

Delirious 🦴½ **1991 (PG)** A writer for a television soap opera wakes from a bash on the head to find himself inside the story where murder and mayhem are brewing. Can he write himself back to safety, and find romance along the way? Somehow Candy just isn't believeable as a romantic lead and the film has few laughs. **96m/C VHS, Beta, LV, 8mm.** John Candy, Mariel Hemingway, Emma Samms, Raymond Burr, David Rasche, Dylan Baker, Charles Rocket, Jerry Orbach, Renee Taylor, Robert Wagner; ***D:*** Tom Mankiewicz; ***W:*** Lawrence J. Cohen; ***M:*** Cliff Eidelman. *MGM*

Delirium *Woof! Psycho Puppet* **1977** Homicidal maniac goes on a killing spree and has just one thing in mind—women. Angry group of citizens inadvertently includes the demonic villain in their vigilante club. Nothing redeeming here. **94m/C VHS, Beta.** Turk Cekovsky, Debi Shanley, Terry Ten Broeck; ***D:*** Peter Maris. *NO*

Deliverance 🦴🦴🦴🦴 **1972 (R)** Terrifying exploration of the primal nature of man and his alienation from nature, based on the novel by James Dickey, which he adapted for the film (he also makes an appearance as a sheriff). Four urban professionals, hoping to get away from it all for the weekend, canoe down a southern river, encounter crazed backwoodsmen, and end up battling for survival. Excellent performances all around, especially by Voight. Debuts for Beatty and Cox. Watch for O'Neill as a sheriff, and director Boorman's son Charley as Voight's son. "Dueling Banjos" scene and tune are memorable as is scene where the backwoods boys promise to make the fellows squeal like pigs. **109m/C VHS, Beta, LV.** Jon Voight, Burt Reynolds, Ronny Cox, Ned Beatty, James Dickey, Bill McKinney, Ed O'Neill, Charley Boorman; ***D:*** John Boorman; ***W:*** James Dickey; ***C:*** Vilmos Zsigmond; ***M:*** Eric Weissburg. National Board of Review Awards '72: 10 Best Films of the Year; Nominations: Academy Awards '72: Best Director (Boorman), Best Film Editing, Best Picture. *WAR, FCT*

Delivery Boys 🦴½ **1984 (R)** The "Delivery Boys," three breakdancers aiming to win the $10,000 New York City Break-Off, find unusual perils that may keep them from competing. **94m/C VHS, Beta.** Joss Marcano, Tom Sierchio, Jim Soriero, Mario Van Peebles, Samantha Fox; ***D:*** Ken Handley. *VTR, NWV*

Delos Adventure 🦴 **1986 (R)** A geological expedition in South America stumbles upon covert Russian activities and must battle to survive in this overly-violent actioner. **98m/C VHS, Beta.** Roger Kern, Jenny Neumann, Kevin Brophy; ***D:*** Joseph Purcell. *TWE*

Delta Force 🦴🦴 **1986 (R)** Based on the true hijacking of a TWA plane in June 1985. Arab terrorists take over an airliner; the Delta Force, led by Lee Marvin and featuring Norris as its best fighter, rescue the passengers in ways that cater directly to our nationalistic revenge fantasies. Average thriller, exciting and tense at times, with fine work from Marvin, Norris, and Forster. **125m/C VHS, Beta, LV.** Lee Marvin, Chuck Norris, Shelley Winters, Martin Balsam, George Kennedy, Hanna Schygulla, Susan Strasberg, Bo Svenson, Joey Bishop, Lainie Kazan, Robert Forster, Robert Vaughn, Kim Delaney; ***D:*** Menahem Golan; ***W:*** James Bruner; ***M:*** Alan Silvestri. *MED, VTR*

Delta Force 2: Operation Stranglehold 🦴½ **1990 (R)** Delta Force is back with martial artist and military technician Norris at the helm. Action-packed and tense. **110m/C VHS, Beta, LV.** John P. Ryan, Chuck Norris, Billy Drago, Richard Jaeckel, Paul Perri; ***D:*** Aaron Norris; ***W:*** Lee Reynolds. *MED, BTV, VTR*

Delta Force 3: The Killing Game 🦴½ *Young Commandos* **1991 (R)** A terrorist mastermind plants an atomic bomb in an American city, and the President has only one choice...call in the Delta Force. The leading men in this lackluster thriller are the sons of some of Hollywood's biggest stars. **97m/C VHS, LV.** Nick Cassavetes, Eric Douglas, Mike Norris, Matthew Penn, John P. Ryan, Sandy Ward; ***D:*** Sam Firstenberg; ***W:*** Boaz Davidson. *CAN*

Delta Force Commando 🦴½ **1987 (R)** Two U.S. Fighter pilots fight against terrorism in the deadly Nicaraguan jungle. **90m/C VHS.** Fred Williamson, Bo Svenson. *VES, RHI*

Delta Force Commando 2 🦴 *Priority Red One* **1990 (R)** The celluloid was hardly dry on the first "Delta Force Commando" before the resourceful Italians began grinding out this follow-up, with the lead commando getting the Force entangled in a deadly international conspiracy. **100m/C VHS.** *IT* Richard Hatch, Fred Williamson, Giannina Facio, Van Johnson; ***D:*** Frank Valenti. *LIV*

Delta Fox 🦴🦴 **1977** Delta Fox is carrying a million dollars for the mob, but the mob is carrying a grudge and the chase is on. **90m/C VHS, Beta.** Priscilla Barnes, Richard Lynch, Stuart Whitman, John Ireland; ***D:*** Beverly Sebastian, Ferd Sebastian. *NO*

Delta Heat 🦴🦴 **1992 (R)** A new designer drug hits L.A. and detective Mike Bishop (Edwards) follows his partner to the drug's source in Louisiana. When Bishop arrives he discovers his partner has been tortured and murdered in order to keep the drug lord's foes in line. Bishop must then save himself and find justice in the steamy streets of New Orleans. Routine lone guy vs. bad guys actioner. **91m/C VHS.** Anthony Edwards, Lance Henriksen, Betsy Russell, Linda Dona, Rod Masterson, John McConnell, Clyde Jones; ***D:*** Michael Rischa. *ACA*

Delta of Venus 🦴½ **1995 (R)** Paris, 1940—beautiful young American Elena (England), an aspiring author, falls for handsome Lawrence (Mandylor), a writer of dirty books. But she finds out Lawrence isn't faithful and winds up supporting herself as a nude model and writing her own erotic tales. Lots of sex scenes and an equal amount of pretensions. Based on the erotic novel "Delta of Venus" by Anais Nin. Prague substitutes for Paris as the film location. Also availble unrated; the theatrical version came out as NC-17. **100m/C VHS, LV.** Audie England, Costas Mandylor, Erick Da Silva; ***D:*** Zalman King; ***W:*** Patricia Louisianna Knop, Elisa Rothstein; ***C:*** Eagle Egilsson; ***M:*** George S. Clinton. *NLC*

Deluge 🦴🦴 **1933** Tidal waves caused by earthquakes have destroyed most of New York (though some may think this is no great loss) in this early sci-fi pic. **72m/B VHS, Beta.** Edward Van Sloan, Peggy Shannon, Sidney Blackmer, Fred Kohler Sr., Matt Moore, Samuel S. Hinds, Lane Chandler; ***D:*** Felix Feist. *MWP*

Delusion 🦴½ *The House Where Death Lives* **1984 (R)** Gothic thriller in which invalid Cotten and family are harassed by a possibly supernatural killer as told by Cotten's nurse. Filmed in 1980. Ending is a letdown. **93m/C VHS, Beta.** Patricia Pearcy, David Hayward, John Dukakis, Joseph Cotten, Simone Griffeth; ***D:*** Alan Beattie. *SUE*

Delusion 🦴🦴½ **1991 (R)** A yuppie with an embezzled fortune is held up in the Nevada desert by a psycho hood with a showgirl lover. But who's really in charge here? The snappy, hip, film-noir thriller takes a few unlikely twists and has an open Lady-or-the-Tiger finale that may infuriate. Available in a widescreen edition on laserdisc. **100m/C VHS, LV.** Jim Metzler, Jennifer Rubin, Kyle Secor, Robert Costanzo, Tracey Walter, Jerry Orbach; ***D:*** Carl Colpaert; ***W:*** Carl Colpaert, Kurt Voss; ***M:*** Barry Adamson. *COL*

Delusions of Grandeur 🦴🦴½ *La Folle des Grandeurs* **1976** A French comedy of court intrigue set in 17th-century Spain. In French with English subtitles. Based loosely on Victor Hugo's "Ruy Blas." **85m/C VHS, Beta.** *FR* Yves Montand, Louis de Funes, Alice Sapritch, Karin Schubert, Gabriele Tinti; ***D:*** Gerard Oury. *FCT*

Demented 🦴 **1980 (R)** Beautiful and talented woman is brutally gang-raped by four men, but her revenge is sweet and deadly as she entices each to bed and gives them a big dose of their own medicine. All-too-familiar plot offers nothing new. **92m/C VHS, Beta.** Sallee Elyse, Bruce Gilchrist. *MED*

Dementia 13 🦴🦴½ *The Haunted and the Hunted* **1963** This eerie thriller, set in a creepy castle, is an early Coppola film about the members of an Irish family who are being offed by an axe murderer one-by-one. **75m/B VHS, Beta.** William Campbell, Luana Anders, Bart Patton, Patrick Magee; ***D:*** Francis Ford Coppola; ***W:*** Francis Ford Coppola. *NOS, MRV, SNC*

Demetrius and the Gladiators 🦴🦴½ **1954** A sequel to "The Robe," wherein the holy-robe-carrying slave is enlisted as one of Caligula's gladiators and mixes with the trampy empress Messalina. **101m/C VHS, Beta, LV.** Victor Mature, Susan Hayward, Michael Rennie, Debra Paget, Anne Bancroft, Jay Robinson, Barry Jones, Richard Egan, William Marshall, Ernest Borgnine; ***D:*** Delmer Daves; ***W:*** Philip Dunne; ***C:*** Milton Krasner. *FOX*

The Demi-Paradise 🦴🦴🦴 *Adventure for Two* **1943** Tongue-in-cheek look at people's perceptions of foreigners has Olivier as a Russian inventor (?!) who comes to England with some trepidation. Though the Brits are plenty quirky, he manages to find romance with Ward in this charming look at British life. **110m/B VHS, Beta.** *GB* Laurence Olivier, Penelope Dudley Ward, Margaret Rutherford, Wilfrid Hyde-White; ***D:*** Anthony Asquith. *NOS, VDM, DVT*

Demolition 🦴½ **1977** Ex-international courier finds that the "simple" task he has consented to do for his old employers is deceptively hazardous. **90m/C VHS, Beta.** John Waters, Belinda Giblin, Fred Steele, Vincent Ball; ***D:*** Kevin Dobson. *NO*

Demolition Man 🦴🦴 **1993 (R)** No-brain sci-fier rests on the action skills of Stallone and Snipes. Psychovillain Snipes (a shocking blond!) is pursued by equally violent cop Stallone in the late 1990s. Then they're cryogenically frozen, defrosted in 2032, and back to their old tricks. One problem. This is not a fun future: virtual reality sex is the only kind allowed and puritan ethics and political correctness are enforced to the max. So cop and bad guy get to show this highly orderly society some really violent times. Implausible plot and minimal acting, but lots of action and violence for fans. **115m/C VHS, Beta, LV, 8mm.** Sylvester Stallone, Wesley Snipes, Sandra Bullock, Nigel Hawthorne, Benjamin Bratt, Bob Gunton, Glenn Shadix; ***D:*** Marco Brambilla; ***W:*** Daniel Waters, Robert Reneau, Peter M. Lenkov; ***M:*** Elliot Goldenthal. Nominations: MTV Movie Awards '94: Best Villain (Snipes). *WAR*

The Demolitionist 🦴🦴 **1995 (R)** Tough undercover cop Alyssa Lloyd (Eggert) is killed by a crimelord (Grieco) and then resurrected by a scientist (Abbott) as a hard-hitting futuristic superheroine who's out to save Metro City from evil. **100m/C VHS, LV.** Nicole Eggert, Richard Grieco, Bruce Abbott, Susan Tyrrell; ***D:*** Robert Kurtzman. *APX*

The Demon 🦴½ **1981 (R)** A small town may be doomed to extinction, courtesy of a monster's thirst for the blood of its inhabitants. **94m/C VHS, Beta.** Cameron Mitchell, Jennifer Holmes. *NO*

Demon Barber of Fleet Street 🦴🦴½ *Sweeney Todd: The Demon Barber of Fleet Street* **1936** Loosely based on an actual event, this film inspired the 1978 smash play "Sweeney Todd." Slaughter stars as a mad barber who doesn't just cut his client's hair. He happens to have a deal cooked up with the baker to provide him with some nice 'juicy' filling for his meat pies. Manages to be creepy and funny at the same time. **68m/B VHS, Beta.** *GB* Tod Slaughter, Eve Lister, Bruce Seton; ***D:*** George King. *VYY, MRV, SNC*

Demon City Shinjuku 🦴🦴½ **1993** In the near future the evil Levih Rah has created a Demon City in Shinjuku, located in the heart of Tokyo, where he commands his army of thugs and monsters. Sayama and the streetwise Kyoya venture into Shinjuku in search of Sayama's kidnapped father. They encounter the mystical Mephisto, who may be able to help them, but time is running out—Levih Rah is set to destroy the entire planet in three days! In Japanese with English subtitles. **82m/C VHS, LV.** *JP CPM*

Demon for Trouble 🦴 **1934** Outlaws are murdering land buyers in this routine western. **58m/B VHS, Beta.** Bob Steele. *NOS, RXM*

Demon Hunter 🦴½ **1988** Terror reigns while a deranged killer stalks his next victim. **90m/C VHS, Beta.** George Ellis, Erin Fleming, Marrianne Gordon; ***D:*** Massey Cramer. *NO*

A Demon in My View 🦴🦴½ **1992 (R)** In a role similar to his infamous Norman Bates in "Psycho," Perkins stars as a man who hides a terrible secret—he is a former serial killer. When a fellow tenant in his apartment house accidentally destroys his doll, Perkins' tenuous sanity is shaken and he begins killing again. A smart thriller. Perkins last big-screen role. **98m/C VHS, LV.** Anthony Perkins, Sophie Ward, Stratford Johns; ***D:*** Petra Hafter. *VMK, MOV*

The Demon Lover *Woof!* **1977 (R)** Leader of a satanic cult calls forth the devil when he doesn't get his way. Poorly acted and badly produced. Features comic book artists Val "Howard the Duck" Mayerick and Gunnar "Leatherface" Hansen. Also on video as "Devil Master" and "Master of Evil." **87m/C VHS, Beta.** Christmas Robbins, Val Mayerick, Gunnar Hansen, Tom Hutton, David Howard; ***D:*** Donald G. Jackson, Jerry Younkins; ***W:*** Donald G. Jackson, Jerry Younkins. *UNI, PMR*

Demon Lust 🦴 **19??** A couple's lovely country vacation is turned into a nightmare when two drifters terrorize them. **76m/C VHS, Beta.** ***D:*** Bernard Buys. *GHV*

Demon of Paradise *Woof!* **1987 (R)** Dynamite fishing off the coast of Hawaii unearths an ancient, man-eating lizard-man. Unveven, unexciting horror attempt. **84m/C VHS, Beta.** Kathryn Witt, William Steis, Leslie Huntly, Laura Banks; ***D:*** Cirio H. Santiago. *WAR*

Demon Possessed 🦴½ **1993 (R)** When Tom is critically injured in a snowmobile race in a remote woods, he and his friends find shelter in a deserted children's camp. It turns out the camp was run by a secret religious cult that practiced occult murder and the demon that haunted the place has never left. When Tom dies this satanic spirit finds the perfect host to return to human form and continue its bloody work. **97m/C VHS, LV.** Dawn Laurrie, Aaron Kjenass, David Fields, Eve Montgomery; ***D:*** Christopher Webster; ***W:*** Julian Weaver; ***M:*** John Tatgenhorst. *AIP*

Demon Queen 🦴 **198?** A vampirish woman seduces, then murders, many men. **70m/C VHS, Beta.** Mary Fanaro, Dennis Stewart, Cliff Dance; ***D:*** Donald Farmer. *NO*

Demon Rage 🦴½ *Satan's Mistress; Fury of the Succubus; Dark Eyes* **1982 (R)** Neglected housewife drifts under the spell of a phantom lover. **98m/C VHS, Beta.** Britt Ekland, Lana Wood, Kabir Bedi, Don Galloway, John Carradine, Sherry Scott; ***D:*** James Polakof. *HHE*

Demon Seed 🦴🦴🦴 **1977 (R)** When a scientist and his wife separate so he can work on his computer, the computer takes over the house and impregnates the wife. Bizarre and taut. **97m/C VHS, Beta, LV.** Julie Christie, Fritz Weaver, Gerrit Graham, Berry Kroeger, Ron Hays; ***D:*** Donald Cammell; ***V:*** Robert Vaughn. *MGM*

Demon Wind 🦴½ **1990 (R)** A gateway to Hell opens up on a secluded farm and various heroic types try to close it. Meanwhile, demons attempt to possess those humans in their midst. Zombies abound in this near-woof. **97m/C VHS, Beta, LV.** Eric Larson, Francine Lapensee, Rufus Norris; ***D:*** Charles Philip Moore. *PAR*

Demon Witch Child *Woof!* **1975** A wrongly accused old woman commits suicide and possesses a young girl who takes revenge on everyone. **90m/C VHS, Beta.** *NO*

Demon with a Glass Hand 🦴½ **1964** In the vein of "The Terminator," a man goes back two hundred years in time to escape the evil race that rules the planet. **63m/B VHS, Beta.** Robert Culp, Arlene Martel, Abraham Sofaer. *MGM*

Demonic Toys 🦴½ **1990 (R)** The possessed play-things attack a bunch of unfortunates in a warehouse, and pumped-up lady cop Scoggins deserves an award for keeping a straight face. Skimpily scripted gore from the horror assembly-line at Full Moon Productions. Far more entertaining are the multiple behind-the-scenes featurettes on the tape. **86m/C VHS, Beta, LV.** Tracy Scoggins, Bentley Mitchum, Michael

Russo, Jeff Weston, Daniel Cerney, Pete Schrum; ***D:*** Peter Manoogian. *PAR*

Demonoid, Messenger of Death *Macabra* **1981 (R)** Discovery of an ancient temple of Satan worship drastically changes the lives of a young couple when the husband becomes possessed by the Demonoid, which initially takes on the form of a severed hand. Poor script needs hand, producing a number of unintentionally laughable moments. **85m/C VHS, Beta.** Samantha Eggar, Stuart Whitman, Roy Cameron Jenson; ***D:*** Alfredo Zacharias. *MED*

The Demons **1974 (R)** As she slips into death, a tortured woman curses her torturers. **90m/C VHS, Beta.** Anne Libert, Britt Nichols, Doris Thomas. *UNI*

Demons ½ *Demoni* **1986 (R)** A horror film in a Berlin theater is so involving that its viewers become the demons they are seeing. The new monsters turn on the other audience members. Virtually plotless, very explicit. Rock soundtrack by Accept, Go West, Motley Crue, and others. Revered in some circles, blasted in others. Followed by "Demons 2." **89m/C VHS, Beta, LV.** *IT* Urbano Barberini, Natasha Hovey, Paolo Cozza, Karl Zinny, Fiore Argento, Fabiola Toledo, Nicoletta Elni; ***D:*** Lamberto Bava. *NWV*

Demons 2 ½ **1987** Inferior sequel to "Demons." The son of horror-meister Mario Bava, Lamberto collaborated with Italian auteur Argento (who co-wrote and produced) to create an improbable sequel (storywise) which seems to have been edited by some kind of crazed cutting room slasher with equally hackneyed dubbing. Residents of a chi-chi high rise watching a documentary about the events of "Demons"—a sort of high-tech play-within-a-play ploy—when a demon emerges from the TV, spreads his creepy cooties, and causes the tenants to sprout fangs and claws and nasty tempers. Lots of blood drips from ceilings, plumbing fixtures, and various body parts. **88m/C VHS, LV.** *IT* David Knight, Nancy Brill, Coralina Cataldi Tassoni, Bobby Rhodes, Asia Argento, Virginia Bryant; ***D:*** Lamberto Bava; ***W:*** Dario Argento, Lamberto Bava; ***M:*** Simon Boswell. *IMP*

Demons in the Garden *Demonios En El Jardin* **1982 (R)** Centers on the disintegration of a family after the end of the Spanish Civil War, due to sibling rivalries and a variety of indiscretions. Problems mount as two brothers become involved with their stepsister. Story takes on poignancy in its narration by a young boy. Beautiful cinematography. In Spanish with English subtitles. **100m/C VHS.** *SP* Angela Molina, Ana Belen, Encarna Paso, Imanol Arias; ***D:*** Manuel Gutierrez Aragon. *CVC, TPV, INJ*

Demons of Ludlow **1975** Demons attend a small town's bicentennial celebration intent on raising a little hell of their own. **83m/C VHS, Beta.** Paul von Hauser, Stephanie Cushna, James Robinson, Carol Perry; ***D:*** Steven Kuether. *TWE*

Demons of the Mind **1972 (R)** A sordid psychological horror film about a baron in 19th century Austria who imprisons his children, fearing that mental illness is a family trait. Also on video as "Blood Evil." **85m/C VHS, Beta.** *GB* Michael Hordern, Patrick Magee, Yvonne Mitchell, Robert Hardy, Gillian Hills, Virginia Wetherell, Shane Briant, Paul Jones; ***D:*** Peter Sykes. *REP, MLB*

Demonstone *Heartstone* **1989 (R)** A television reporter becomes possessed by a Filipino demon and carries out an ancient curse against the family of a corrupt government official. **90m/C VHS, Beta, LV.** R. Lee Ermey, Jan-Michael Vincent, Nancy Everhard; ***D:*** Andrew Prowse. *FRH*

Demonstrator ½ **1971** A father and son are at odds when dad heads an Asian military coalition and junior protests. Notable for being one of the first major Australian films to use an entirely native cast. **82m/C VHS.** *AU* Joe James, Irene Inescort, Gerard Maguire, Wendy Lingham, Harold Hopkins; ***D:*** Warwick Freeman. *ACA*

Demonwarp *Woof!* **1987** A vengeance-minded hunter journeys into an evil, primeval forest to kill the monsters that abducted his daughter. **91m/C VHS, Beta.** George Kennedy, Emmett Alston. *VMK*

Dempsey **1983** In this made for television film based on Jack Dempsey's autobiography, Williams plays the role of the famed world heavyweight champ. His rise through the boxing ranks as well as his personal life are chronicled. A bit slow-moving considering the pounding fists and other action. **110m/C VHS, Beta.** Treat Williams, Sam Waterston, Sally Kellerman, Victoria Tennant, Peter Mark Richman, Jesse Vint, Bonnie Bartlett, James Noble; ***D:*** Gus Trikonis; ***M:*** Billy Goldenberg. *MED*

Denial: The Dark Side of Passion **1991 (R)** A strong-willed woman tries to put a destructive love affair behind her—but if she succeeded there'd be no movie. Torrid stuff with a watchable cast. **103m/C VHS, LV.** Robin Wright, Jason Patric, Barry Primus, Christina Harnos, Rae Dawn Chong; ***D:*** Eric Dignam; ***W:*** Eric Dignam. *REP*

Denise Calls Up ½ **1995 (PG-13)** Comedy about futility and complications of urban relationships among overworked professionals. A group of six work-at-home city friends socialize, romance, and date entirely via phone, fax, and computer without ever meeting or leaving their homes, even for a close friend's funeral (who dies, oddly enough, while on the phone). Subplot involves title character, Denise (Ubach) tracking down sperm donor Martin (Gunther) and eventually giving birth, with the help of her cellular coaches. Funny premise is executed well, but doesn't hold up over a (barely) feature length film. **79m/C VHS.** Timothy Daly, Dana Wheeler Nicholson, Caroleen Feeney, Liev Schreiber, Dan Gunther, Aida Turturro, Alanna Ubach, Sylvia Miles; ***D:*** Hal Salwen; ***W:*** Hal Salwen; ***C:*** Mike Mayers; ***M:*** Lynne Geller. *NYR*

Dennis the Menace ½ **1993 (PG)** Straight from the Hughes kiddie farm comes Kevin McAllister—oops!—Dennis Mitchell (newcomer Gamble), curious, crafty, and blond 5-year-old. He dreams and schemes, but everything he does manages to be a threat to the physical and mental well-being of hot-head neighbor Mr. Wilson (Matthau, perfectly cast as the grump). Lloyd is very nasty as protagonist Switchblade Sam; Plowright, Thompson, and Stanton round out the cast as Mrs. Wilson and the Mitchell parents, respectively. Sure to please young kids, but parents may be less enthralled with this adaptation of the popular '50s comic strip and subsequent TV series. **96m/C VHS, Beta, LV, 8mm.** Walter Matthau, Mason Gamble, Joan Plowright, Christopher Lloyd, Lea Thompson, Robert Stanton, Billie Bird, Paul Winfield, Amy Sakasitz, Kellen Hathaway, Arnold Stang; ***D:*** Nick Castle; ***W:*** John Hughes; ***M:*** Jerry Goldsmith. *WAR*

Dennis the Menace: Dinosaur Hunter ½ **1993 (G)** Another version of Hank Ketchum's mischievious cartoon character brought to life to have adventures and disturb his neighbor Mr. Wilson. This time Dennis discovers a huge, primitive bone in his backyard and when an archaeologist declares it's a dinosaur bone, news crews, tourists, and scientists are suddenly everywhere. This badly disturbs Mr. Wilson's retirement and Dennis and his friends must save the day (and their neighborhood). **118m/C VHS, LV.** Victor Dimattia, William Windom, Pat Estrin, Jim Jansen, Patsy Garrett. *VMK*

The Dentist ½ **1932** Fields treats several oddball patients in his office. After watching the infamous tooth-pulling scene, viewers will be sure to brush regularly. **22m/B VHS, Beta.** W.C. Fields, Elise Cavanna, Babe Kane, Bud Jamison, Zedna Farley. *CCB, GVV*

The Denver & Rio Grande ½ **1951** Action-packed western about two rival railroads competing to be the first to complete a line through the Royal Gorge. Plot is predictable, but the scene featuring two trains crashing into each other is worth it (Haskin used actual trains for this stunt). **89m/C VHS.** Edmond O'Brien, Sterling Hayden, Dean Jagger, ZaSu Pitts, J. Carrol Naish; ***D:*** Byron Haskin. *PAR*

Department Store *Bargain Basement* **1935** Confusing crime-drama involving a store manager who mistakes an ex-convict for his employer's heir. Based on a story by H. F. Maltby. **65m/B VHS.** *GB* Garry Marsh, Eve Gray, Sebastian Shaw, Geraldine Fitzgerald, Jack Melford; ***D:*** Leslie Hiscott. *DVT*

The Deputy Drummer ½ **1935** Second-rate early British musical, notable as a later vehicle for silent-era star Lane. He plays a penniless composer who impersonates an aristocrat to attend a party, and catches jewel robbers in the act. **71m/B VHS.** *GB* Lupino Lane, Jean Denis, Kathleen Kelly, Wallace Lupino, Margaret Yarde, Syd Crossley. *NOS*

Deputy Marshall ½ **1950** Hall trails a pair of bankrobbers, fights off landgrabbers, and finds romance as well. **75m/B VHS, Beta.** Jon Hall, Frances Langford, Dick Foran. *RXM*

Der Purimshpiler ½ *The Purim Player; The Jester; The Jewish Jester* **1937** A drifter embarks on a quest for happiness, which takes him to various small towns. In one, he meets and falls in love with a shoemaker's daughter. In Yiddish with English subtitles. **90m/B VHS, Beta.** *PL* Miriam Kressyn, Zygmund Turkow, Hymie Jacobsen; ***D:*** Joseph Green. *ERG*

Deranged **1974 (R)** Of the numerous movies based on the cannibalistic exploits of Ed Gein ("Psycho," "Texas Chainsaw Massacre," etc.), this is the most accurate. A dead-on performance by Blossom and a twisted sense of humor help move things along nicely. The two directors, Gillen and Ormsby, previously worked together on the classic "Children Shouldn't Play with Dead Things." An added attraction is the early special effect work of gore wizard Tom Savini. **82m/C VHS.** *CA* Roberts Blossom, Cosette Lee, Robert Warner, Marcia Diamond, Brian Sneagle; ***D:*** Jeff Gillen, Alan Ormsby. *FRG, MRV*

Deranged ½ **1987 (R)** A mentally unstable, pregnant woman is attacked in her apartment after her husband leaves town. She spends the rest of the movie engaged in psychotic encounters, real and imagined. Technically not bad, but extremely violent and grim. Not to be confused with 1974 movie of the same name. **85m/C VHS.** Jane Hamilton, Paul Siederman, Jennifer Delora, James Gillis, Jill Cumer, Gary Goldman; ***D:*** Chuck Vincent. *REP*

Derby **1971 (R)** The documentary story of the rise to fame of roller-derby stars on the big rink. **91m/C VHS, Beta.** Charlie O'Connell, Lydia Gray, Janet Earp, Ann Colvello, Mike Snell; ***D:*** Robert Kaylor. *PSM, FAF*

Dersu Uzala ½ **1975** An acclaimed, photographically breathtaking film about a Russian surveyor in Siberia who befriends a crusty, resourceful Mongolian. They begin to teach each other about their respective worlds. Produced in Russia; one of Kurosawa's stranger films. **124m/C VHS, Beta.** *JP RU* Yuri Solomin, Maxim Munzuk; ***D:*** Akira Kurosawa. Academy Awards '75: Best Foreign Language Film. *SUE, KIV*

Descending Angel **1990 (R)** The premise is familiar: a swastika-friendly collaborator is forced out of the closet. But the cast and scripting make this made-for-cable there's-a-Nazi-in the-woodwork suspenser better than average, despite its flawed finale. Scott plays a well-respected Romanian refugee—active in the community, in the church, and in Romanian-American activities—whose daughter's fiance (Roberts) suspects him of Nazi collusion. **96m/C VHS, LV.** George C. Scott, Diane Lane, Eric Roberts, Mark Margolis, Vyto Ruginis, Amy Aquino, Richard Jenkins, Jan Rubes; ***D:*** George C. Scott, Jeremy Paul Kagan; ***W:*** George C. Scott. *HBO*

Desert Bloom **1986 (PG)** On the eve of a nearby nuclear bomb test, a beleaguered alcoholic veteran and his family struggle through tensions brought on by a promiscuous visiting aunt and the chaotic, rapidly changing world. Gish shines as the teenage daughter through whose eyes the story unfolds. From a story by Corr and Linda Ramy. **103m/C VHS, Beta, LV.** Jon Voight, JoBeth Williams, Ellen Barkin, Annabeth Gish, Allen (Goorwitz) Garfield, Jay Underwood; ***D:*** Eugene Corr; ***W:*** Eugene Corr; ***C:*** Reynaldo Villalobos; ***M:*** Brad Fiedel. *NO*

Desert Commandos ☠☠ **196?** When the Allies appear to be winning WWII, the Nazis devise a plan to eliminate all of the opposing forces' leaders at once. **?m/C VHS.** Kenneth Clark, Horst Frank, Jeanne Valeri, Carlo Hinterman, Gianni Rizzo. *NO*

The Desert Fox ☠☠☠ *Rommel—Desert Fox* **1951** Big-budgeted portrait of German Army Field Marshal Rommel, played by Mason, focuses on the soldier's defeat in Africa during WWII and his subsequent, disillusioned return to Hitler's Germany. Mason played Rommel again in 1953's "Desert Rats." **87m/B VHS, Beta, LV.** James Mason, Cedric Hardwicke, Jessica Tandy, Luther Adler; ***D:*** Henry Hathaway. *FOX, TLF*

Desert Gold ☠½ **1936** A fierce Indian chief battles a horde of greedy white men over his tribe's gold mine. Based on a novel by Zane Grey. **58m/B VHS, Beta.** Buster Crabbe, Robert Cummings, Marsha Hunt, Tom Keene, Raymond Hatton, Monte Blue, Leif Erickson; ***D:*** Charles T. Barton. *NOS, DVT*

Desert Guns/Six-Shootin' Sheriff ☠☠ **1936** Double feature includes a rare Tearle "B" film and a Maynard oater from 1938. **?m/C VHS.** Conway Tearle, Ken Maynard. *RXM*

Desert Hearts ☠☠☠ **1986 (R)** An upstanding professional woman travels to Reno, Nevada in 1959 to obtain a quick divorce, and slowly becomes involved in a lesbian relationship with a free-spirited casino waitress. **93m/C VHS, Beta, LV.** Helen Shaver, Audra Lindley, Patricia Charbonneau, Andra Akers, Dean Butler, Jeffrey Tambor, Denise Crosby, Gwen Welles; ***D:*** Donna Deitch; ***W:*** Natalie Cooper. *LIV, VES*

Desert Kickboxer ☠☠ **1992 (R)** A border guard takes on a cocaine dealer and his henchmen, fighting for gold and, of course, a beautiful woman. Lots of kickboxing action. **86m/C VHS, LV.** John Haymes Newton, Judie Aronson, Sam DeFrancisco, Paul Smith; ***D:*** Isaac Florentine. *HBO*

Desert of the Lost ☠☠½ **1927** Wales flees to Mexico after shooting a man in self-defense. He's aided by Montgomery and, in turn, helps save her from a forced marriage. **58m/B VHS.** Wally Wales, Peggy Montgomery, William J. Dyer, Edward Cecil, Richard Neill, Kelly Cafford, Ray Murro, George Magrill, Charles "Slim" Whitaker; ***D:*** Richard Thorpe. *GPV*

The Desert of the Tartars ☠ *Le Desert des Tartares* **1976 (PG)** Story of a young soldier who dreams of war and discovers that the real battle for him is with time. **140m/C VHS, Beta.** Jacques Perrin; ***M:*** Ennio Morricone. *SUE*

Desert Phantom ☠½ **1936** Villains threaten to rob a woman of her ranch until a stranger rescues her. **66m/B VHS, Beta, LV.** Johnny Mack Brown, Sheila Mannors, Charles "Blackie" King, Ted Adams, Hal Price, Nelson McDowell; ***D:*** S. Roy Luby. *GPV*

The Desert Rats ☠☠☠ **1953** A crusty British captain (Burton) takes charge of an Australian division during WWII. Thinking they are inferior to his own British troops, he is stiff and uncaring to the Aussies until a kind-hearted drunk and the courage of the division win him over. Crack direction from Wise and Newton's performance (as the wag) simply steal the movie. Mason reprises his role as Germany Army Field Marshal Rommel from "The Desert Fox." **88m/B VHS, Beta.** Richard Burton, Robert Newton, Robert Douglas, Torin Thatcher, Chips Rafferty, Charles Tingwell, James Mason; ***D:*** Robert Wise. Nominations: Academy Awards '53: Best Story & Screenplay. *FXV, FCT*

Desert Snow ☠☠ **1989 (R)** Here's a non-formulaic dope opera oater: cowboys 'n' drug runners battle it out for an out-of-the-way, underpopulated western town. About as clever as the title. **90m/C VHS, Beta.** Frank Capizzi, Flint Carney, Shelley Hinkle, Sam Incorvia, Carolyn Jacobs; ***D:*** Paul de Cruccio. *NO*

The Desert Song ☠☠½ **1953** MacRae secretly leads a band of do-gooders against the evil forces of a dastardly sheik. Grayson is the general's daughter who falls in love with our disguised hero. Third filmed version of the Sigmund Romberg operetta creaks along with the talents of MacRae and Grayson rising about the hackneyed plot. ♫The Desert Song; Gay Parisienne; Long Live the Night; One Alone; One Flower; The Riff Song; Romance. **96m/C VHS.** Gordon MacRae, Kathryn Grayson, Raymond Massey, Steve Cochran, Dick Wesson, Allyn Ann McLerie, Ray Collins, William Conrad; ***D:*** H. Bruce Humberstone; ***W:*** Roland Kibbee; ***C:*** Robert Burks; ***M:*** Max Steiner. *FCT*

Desert Steel ☠½ **1994 (PG)** Rival racers risk their lives in the big off-road race. **89m/C VHS.** David Naughton, Brian Skinner, Amanda Wyss, Russ Tamblyn; ***D:*** Glenn Gebhard. *MNC*

Desert Trail ☠½ **1935** Wayne is a championship rodeo rider accused of bank robbery. **57m/B VHS, Beta.** John Wayne, Paul Fix, Mary Kornman; ***D:*** Robert North Bradbury. *COL, REP, MRV*

Desert Warrior ☠ **1988 (PG-13)** Earth becomes a waste site after a nuclear war. Ferrigno stars as a post-nuke hero in this low-budget action film. Very bad acting. **89m/C VHS, Beta.** Lou Ferrigno, Shari Shattuck, Kenneth Peer, Anthony East; ***D:*** Jim Goldman; ***W:*** Frederick Bailey. *PSM*

The Deserters ☠½ **198?** Sergeant Hawley, a Vietnam-era hawk, hunts deserters and draft-dodgers in Canada. There, he confronts issues of war and peace head-on. **110m/C VHS, Beta.** Alan Scarfe, Dermot Hennelly, Jon Bryden, Barbara March; ***M:*** Michael Conway Baker. *MOV*

Designing Woman ☠☠☠ **1957** Bacall and Peck star in this mismatched tale of romance. She's a chic high-fashion designer, he's a rumpled sports writer. The fun begins when they try to adjust to married life together. Neither likes the other's friends or lifestyle. Things get even crazier when Bacall has to work with her ex-lover Helmore on a fashion show and Peck's former love Gray shows up as well. And as if that weren't enough, Peck is being hunted by the mob because of a boxing story he's written. It's a fun, quick, witty tale that is all entertainment and no message. Bacall's performance is of note because Bogart was dying of cancer at the time. **118m/C VHS, Beta, LV.** Gregory Peck, Lauren Bacall, Dolores Gray, Sam Levene, Tom Helmore, Mickey Shaughnessy, Jesse White, Chuck Connors, Edward Platt, Alvy Moore, Jack Cole; ***D:*** Vincente Minnelli; ***W:*** George Wells; ***C:*** John Alton; ***M:*** Andre Previn. Academy Awards '57: Best Story & Screenplay. *MGM*

Desire ☠☠☠ **1936** Jewel thief Madeleine (Dietrich) manages to involve innocent tourist Tom (Cooper) into carrying her ill-gotten goods across the Spanish border. Then she entices him into joining her at the country estate of her partner-in-crime. By this time Tom is in love—and so is Madeleine but she doesn't think she's good enough for him. Lots of lying until the twosome can figure out what to do. Cooper manages to hold his own with the sophisticated Dietrich in their second film together (after "Morocco"). **96m/B VHS.** Marlene Dietrich, Gary Cooper, John Halliday, William Frawley, Ernest Cossart, Akim Tamiroff, Alan Mowbray; ***D:*** Frank Borzage; ***W:*** Edwin Justus Mayer, Waldemar Young; ***M:*** Friedrich Hollander. *MCA, FCT*

Desire ☠☠ **1993 (R)** A free-spirited woman finds herself attracted to a local fisherman. Hardly her intellectual equal but then what she really wants is his body. **108m/C VHS.** Greta Scacchi, Vincent D'Onofrio; ***D:*** Andrew Birkin. *ACA*

Desire ☠☠ **1995 (R)** Security consultant Lauren Allen (Hodge) is working for a perfume manufacturer whose fragrance, Desire, is the fave of a Beverly Hills serial killer who likes to douse his victims in the scent. The prime suspect is scent expert Gordon Lewis (Kemp) and naturally Lauren falls for him. Standard erotic thriller fare. **90m/C VHS.** Kate Hodge, Martin Kemp, Deborah Shelton, Robert Miranda. *MNC*

Desire and Hell at Sunset Motel ☠½ **1992 (PG-13)** Low-budget thriller takes place at the Sunset Motel in 1950s Anaheim. Fenn is the bombshell wife of a toy salesman who's in town for a sales meeting, while she just wants to visit Disneyland. She's soon fooling around with another guy and her husband hires a psychotic criminal to spy on her as her new lover plots to kill hubby. Very confusing plot isn't worth figuring out. Film's only redeeming quality is the imaginative and creative work used in the visuals. Castle's directorial debut. **90m/C VHS, Beta, LV.** Sherilyn Fenn, Whip Hubley, David Hewlett, David Johansen, Paul Bartel; ***D:*** Alien Castle; ***W:*** Alien Castle. *FXV, VTR*

Desire Under the Elms ☠☠½ **1958** Ives, the patriarch of an 1840s New England farming family, takes a young wife (Loren) who promptly has an affair with her stepson. Loren's American film debut. Based on the play by Eugene O'Neill. **114m/B VHS, Beta, LV.** Sophia Loren, Anthony Perkins, Burl Ives, Frank Overton; ***D:*** Delbert Mann; ***C:*** Daniel F. Fapp; ***M:*** Elmer Bernstein. Nominations: Academy Awards '58: Best Black and White Cinematography. *BAR, FCT, PAR*

Desiree ☠☠½ **1954** A romanticized historical epic about Napoleon and his 17-year-old mistress, Desiree. Based on the novel by Annemarie Selinko. Slightly better than average historical fiction piece. **110m/C Beta, LV.** Marlon Brando, Jean Simmons, Merle Oberon, Michael Rennie, Cameron Mitchell, Elizabeth Sellars, Cathleen Nesbitt; ***D:*** Henry Koster; ***W:*** Daniel Taradash; ***C:*** Milton Krasner; ***M:*** Alex North. Nominations: Academy Awards '54: Best Art Direction/Set Decoration (Color), Best Costume Design (Color). *FOX, IME*

Desk Set ☠☠☠ *His Other Woman* **1957** One of the later and less dynamic Tracy/Hepburn comedies, about an efficiency expert who installs a giant computer in an effort to update a television network's female-run reference department. Still, the duo sparkle as they bicker, battle, and give in to love. Based on William Marchant's play. **103m/C VHS, Beta, LV.** Spencer Tracy, Katharine Hepburn, Joan Blondell, Gig Young, Dina Merrill, Neva Patterson; ***D:*** Walter Lang; ***C:*** Leon Shamroy. *FOX, FCT*

Despair ☠☠☠ **1978** A chilling and comic study of a victimized chocolate factory owner's descent into madness, set against the backdrop of the Nazi rise to power in the 1930s. Adapted from the Nabokov novel by Tom Stoppard. **120m/C VHS, Beta.** *GE* Dirk Bogarde, Andrea Ferreol, Volker Spengler, Klaus Lowitsch; ***D:*** Rainer Werner Fassbinder; ***W:*** Tom Stoppard; ***C:*** Michael Ballhaus; ***M:*** Peer Raben. Nominations: Cannes Film Festival '78: Best Film. *GLV*

Desperado ☠☠☠ *El Mariachi 2* **1995 (R)** Rodriguez's nameless guitar player-turned-gunman returns—this time in the persona of heartthrob Banderas. The director also has a studio budget to play with (a sizable increase over the $7000 for "El Mariachi"), so the action's on a bigger, more violent scale (you'll quickly lose count of flying bodies and bullets) as El Mariachi tracks infamous drug lord Bucho (de Almeida). Gringo Buscemi provides assistance, beautiful bookstore owner Carolina (Hayek) offers solace, and Tarantino meets his well-deserved cameo demise. You'll also find original Mariachi, Gallardo, in a cameo role as a musician/gunslinger amigo of the hero. Filmed in Mexico. **103m/C VHS, LV, 8mm.** Antonio Banderas, Salma Hayek, Joaquim de Almeida, Steve Buscemi, Richard "Cheech" Marin, Carlos Gomez; ***Cameos:*** Quentin Tarantino, Carlos Gallardo; ***D:*** Robert Rodriguez; ***W:*** Robert Rodriguez; ***C:*** Guillermo Navarro. Nominations: MTV Movie Awards '96: Most Desirable Male (Banderas), Best Kiss (Antonio Banderas/Salma Hayek). *COL*

Desperados ☠☠½ **1969 (PG)** After the Civil War, a murderous renegade and two of his sons go on a looting rampage, eventually kidnapping the child of the third son who just wants to live in peace. Made in Spain. **90m/C VHS, Beta.** *SP* Jack Palance, Vince Edwards, Christian Roberts, George Maharis, Neville Brand, Sylvia Syms; ***D:*** Henry Levin; ***W:*** Walter Brough; ***C:*** Sam Leavitt. *COL*

The Desperados ☠½ **198?** When a young woman is raped by outlaws robbing her stagecoach, a bevy of western heroes band together to avenge her. **86m/C VHS.** Keenan Wynn, Henry Silva, Michele Carey, John Anderson, Joe Turkel; ***D:*** Ron Joy. *SIM, COL*

Desperate ☠☠½ **1947** An honest truck driver witnesses a mob crime and must escape with his wife in this minor film noir. Eventually, the law is on his tail, too. **73m/B VHS, Beta.** Steve Brodie, Audrey Long, Raymond Burr, Jason Robards Sr., Douglas Fowley, William Challee, Ilka Gruning, Nan Leslie; ***D:*** Anthony Mann. *TTC*

Desperate Cargo ☠½ **1941** Two showgirls stranded in a Latin American town manage to get aboard a clipper ship with hoodlums who are trying to steal the vessel's cargo. **69m/B VHS, Beta.** Ralph Byrd, Carol Hughes, Jack Mulhall. *NOS, DVT, HEG*

Desperate Characters ☠☠☠ **1971 (R)** A slice-of-city-life story about a middle-class couple living in a once-fashionable section of Brooklyn, New York, who watch their neighborhood disintegrate around them. Their marriage on remote control, the two find their lives a series of small disappointments, routine work, uncertain friendships, and pervasive violence. Excellent performances, especially by MacLaine as the harried wife, but the film's depressing nature made it a complete box office flop. **87m/C VHS.** Shirley MacLaine, Kenneth Mars, Gerald S. O'Loughlin, Sada Thompson, Michael Higgins, Rose Gregorio, Jack Somack, Chris Gampel, Mary Alan Hokanson, Patrick McVey, Carol Kane; ***D:*** Frank D. Gilroy; ***W:*** Frank D. Gilroy. *PAR*

Desperate Crimes ☠☠ **1993** Two rival mobs battle over the prostitution and drug trade. When an innocent woman is murdered her brother looks for revenge with the help of a beautiful prostitute. **92m/C VHS.** Traci Lords, Denise Crosby, Franco Columbu, Van Quattro, Rena Niehaus, Nicoletta Boris, Elizabeth Kaitan, Randi Ingerman; ***D:*** Andreas Marfori. *AIP*

Desperate Hours ☠☠☠ **1955** A tough, gritty thriller about three escaped convicts taking over a suburban home and holding the family hostage. Plenty of suspense and fine acting. Based on the novel and play by Joseph Hayes. **112m/B VHS, Beta.** Humphrey Bogart, Fredric March, Martha Scott, Arthur Kennedy, Gig Young, Dewey Martin, Mary Murphy, Robert Middleton, Richard Eyer; ***D:*** William Wyler; ***C:*** Lee Garmes. Edgar Allan Poe Awards '55: Best Screenplay; National Board of Review Awards '55: Best Director (Wyler). *PAR*

Desperate Hours ☠☠ **1990 (R)** An escaped prisoner holes up in a suburban couple's home, waiting for his lawyer/accomplice to take him to Mexico. Tensions heighten between the separated couple and the increasingly nerve-wracked criminals. Terrific, if not downright horrifying, performance by Rourke in an overall tepid remake of the 1955 thriller. **105m/C VHS, Beta, LV.** Mickey Rourke, Anthony Hopkins, Mimi Rogers, Kelly Lynch, Lindsay Crouse, Elias Koteas, David Morse, Shawnee Smith, Danny Gerard, Matt McGrath; ***D:*** Michael Cimino; ***W:*** Mark Rosenthal. *MGM, FHE*

Desperate Journey ☠☠½ **1942** Flynn and Reagan are two of five Allied fighters shot down over Nazi occupied Poland. They go through various tight squeezes such as stealing Goering's car in Berlin, and eliminating a few Nazis at a chemical factory to get back to the safety of England. All the while they are hunted by Massey as Nazi Major Otto Baumester, who of course bumbles and fumbles the whole affair. Strictly propaganda intended to keep up morale on the homefront. Flynn was not pleased about having Reagan as his co-star, seeing as he was usually paired with female leads. **108m/B VHS, Beta.** Errol Flynn, Ronald Reagan, Raymond Massey, Nancy Coleman, Alan Hale, Arthur Kennedy, Helmut Dantine; ***D:*** Raoul Walsh; ***M:*** Max Steiner. *MGM*

Desperate Lives ☠☠ **1982** High school siblings come into contact with drugs and join their guidance counselor in the war against dope. Average made for TV fare. **100m/C VHS, Beta.** Diana Scarwid, Doug McKeon, Helen Hunt, William Windom, Art Hindle, Tom Atkins, Sam Bottoms, Diane Ladd, Dr. Joyce Brothers; ***D:*** Robert Lewis; ***M:*** Bruce Broughton. *LIV*

Desperate Living ☠☠½ **1977** Typical John Waters trash. A mental patient (Stole) is released and becomes paranoid that her family may be out to kill her. After aiding in the murder of her husband (the hefty maid, Hill, suffocates him by sitting on him), Stole and Hill escape to Mortville, a town populated by outcasts such as transsexuals, murderers, and the woefully disfigured. **90m/C VHS, Beta.** Jean Hill, Mink Stole, Edith Massey, Mary Vivian Pearce, Liz Renay, Susan Lowe; ***D:*** John Waters; ***W:*** John Waters. *NLC*

Desperate Motives ☠☠ *Distant Cousins* **1992 (R)** Keith and his fiancee Helgenberger are a charming couple who arrive to stay with Keith's distant cousin (Katt) and his family. Only what the family doesn't realize is that the duo have escaped from an asylum for the criminally insane and want to take over their lives. **92m/C VHS, LV.** David Keith, Marg Helgenberger, William Katt, Mel Harris, Mary Crosby, Brian Bonsall, Cyndi Pass; ***D:*** Andrew Lane; ***W:*** C. Courtney Joyner. *NLC*

Desperate Moves ☠☠ **1986** An Oregon-transplanted geek in San Francisco sets out to make himself over in order to win his dream girl. Sometimes effective, often sappy treatment of his coming to terms with the big city. **90m/C VHS, Beta.** Isabel Sanford, Steve Tracy, Paul Benedict, Christopher Lee, Eddie Deezen; ***D:*** Oliver Hellman. *TWE*

Desperate Prey ☠½ **1994 (R)** Lucy videotapes herself having sex with a lawyer and then accidentally films his murder. So she's stalked by the killer. **102m/C VHS.** Claudia Karvan. *APX*

Desperate Remedies ☠☠ **1993 (R)** Enjoyment will rest on the viewer's appreciation of campy melodrama. In a Victorian-era New Zealand town, regal shop owner Dorothea Brook (Ward-Lealand) is trying to find a husband for her difficult younger sister Rose (Mills)—who happens to be pregnant and a drug addict. She spots handsome sailor Lawrence (Smith) and decides he'll do but Lawrence is instantly smitten with Dorothea (who's also having heart palpitations over the hunk). Unfortunately, her current lover is Anne (Chappell) and Dorothea has also decided on a marriage of convenience with ambitious politician William (Hurst). It's all very operatic. **92m/C VHS, Beta.** *NZ* Jennifer Ward-Lealand, Kevin Smith, Lisa Chappell, Michael Hurst, Kiri Mills, Clifford Curtis; ***D:*** Stewart Main, Peter Wells; ***W:*** Stewart Main, Peter Wells; ***C:*** Leon Narbey; ***M:*** Peter Scholes. *PAR*

Desperate Scoundrel/The Pride of Pikeville **1922** Two classic comedy films back to back featuring the best of the early silent comics. **44m/B VHS, Beta.** Ford Sterling, Ben Turpin, The Keystone Cops. *CCB*

Desperate Target ☠½ **1980** Courageous people fight against all odds to survive. **90m/C VHS, Beta.** Chris Mitchum. *NO*

Desperate Teenage Lovedolls ☠ **1984** A trashy view of the formation of a tacky all-girl punk group. **60m/C VHS, Beta.** Jennifer Schwartz, Hilary Rubens, Steve McDonald, Tracy Lea; ***D:*** David Markey. *HHT*

The Desperate Trail ☠☠½ **1994 (R)** Prostitute, convicted of killing an abusive client, manages to escape from the marshal who's escorting her to her hanging. She teams up with a con man in a plot to rob a bank while the marshal enlists a posse to track her down. Strong performances augmented by blazing guns, hobbled by weak writing. Made for cable television. **93m/C VHS.** Sam Elliott, Linda Fiorentino, Craig Sheffer, Frank Whaley; ***D:*** P.J. Pesce; ***W:*** P.J. Pesce, Tom Abrams; ***C:*** Michael Bonvillain; ***M:*** Stephen Endelman. *TTC*

Desperate Women ☠½ **1978** Made for television western about three unjustly accused female convicts rescued en route to prison by an ex-hired gun. **98m/C VHS, Beta.** Susan St. James, Dan Haggerty, Ronee Blakley, Ann Dusenberry, Susan Myers; ***D:*** Earl Bellamy. *LIV*

Desperately Seeking Susan ☠☠ **1985 (PG-13)** A bored New Jersey housewife gets her kicks reading the personals. When she becomes obsessed with a relationship between two lovers who arrange their meetings through the columns, she decides to find out for herself who they are. But when she is involved in an accident the housewife loses her memory and thinks she is Susan, the free-spirited woman in the personals. Unfortunately, Susan is in a lot of trouble with all sorts of unsavory folk and our innocent housewife finds herself caught in the middle. Terrific characters, with special appeal generated by Arquette and Madonna. Quinn winningly plays the romantic interest. **104m/C VHS, Beta, LV.** Rosanna Arquette, Madonna, Aidan Quinn, Mark Blum, Robert Joy, Laurie Metcalf, Steven Wright, John Turturro, Richard Hell, Annie Golden, Ann Magnuson; ***D:*** Susan Seidelman; ***W:*** Leora Barish; ***M:*** Thomas Newman. British Academy Awards '85: Best Supporting Actress (Arquette); National Board of Review Awards '85: Best Supporting Actress (Arquette). *FCT*

Destination Moon ☠☠½ **1950** Story of man's first lunar voyage contains Chesley Bonstell's astronomical artwork and a famous Woody Woodpecker cartoon. Includes previews of coming attractions from classic science fiction films. **91m/C VHS, Beta, LV.** Warner Anderson, Tom Powers, Dick Wesson, Erin O'Brien Moore; ***D:*** Irving Pichel; ***C:*** Lionel Lindon. Academy Awards '50: Best Special Effects; Nominations: Academy Awards '50: Best Art Direction/Set Decoration (Color). *SNC, MED*

Destination Moonbase Alpha ☠☠ **1975** In the 21st century, an explosion has destroyed half the moon, causing it to break away from the Earth's orbit. The moon is cast far away, but the 311 people manning Alpha, a research station on the moon, must continue their search for other life forms in outer space. A thankless task. Pilot for the television series "Space: 1999." **93m/C VHS, Beta.** Martin Landau, Barbara Bain, Barry Morse. *FOX*

Destination Saturn ☠☠ *Buck Rogers* **1939** Buck Rogers awakens from suspended animation in the twenty-fifth century. **90m/B VHS, Beta.** Buster Crabbe, Constance Moore; ***D:*** Ford Beebe. *NOS, CAB, VYY*

Destination Tokyo ☠☠ **1943** A weathered WWII submarine actioner, dealing with the search-and-destroy mission of a U.S. sub sent into Tokyo harbor. Available in a colorized version. **135m/B VHS, Beta.** Cary Grant, John Garfield, Alan Hale, Dane Clark, John Ridgely, Warner Anderson, William Prince, Robert Hutton, Tom Tully, Peter Whitney, Faye Emerson, John Forsythe; ***D:*** Delmer Daves. Nominations: Academy Awards '43: Best Story. *MGM*

Destiny Turns on the Radio ☠☠ **1995 (R)** Mystic figure Johnny Destiny (Tarantino) dabbles in the lives of various stock characters in Las Vegas after emerging from a glowing swimming pool. Three years after this grand entrance, he enlists escaped con Julian and partner Thoreau (McDermott and Le Gros, respectively) to help him return to his place of origin. Julian has other plans, which involve getting his ex, Lucille (Travis), back from sleazy casino owner Tuerto (Belushi). Aggressively cheezy, dime novel dialogue and threadbare, convoluted plot wastes talents of interesting cast. Too much time and energy spent trying to be hip. Sadly, Tarantino's only participation was in front of the camera. **101m/C VHS.** Dylan McDermott, Nancy Travis, James LeGros, Quentin Tarantino, Allen (Goorwitz) Garfield, James Belushi, Tracey Walter, Bob(cat) Goldthwait; ***D:*** Jack Baran; ***W:*** Robert Ramsey, Matthew Stone; ***C:*** James L. Carter; ***M:*** Steven Soles. *HBO*

Destroy All Monsters ☠☠½ *Kaiju Soshingeki* **1968 (G)** When alien babes take control of Godzilla and his monstrous colleagues, it looks like all is lost for Earth. Adding insult to injury, Ghidra is sent in to take care of the loose ends. Can the planet possibly survive this madness? Classic Toho monster slugfest also features Mothra, Rodan, Son of Godzilla, Angila, Varan, Baragon, Spigas and others. **88m/C VHS.** *JP* Akira Kubo, Jun Tazaki, Yoshio Tsuchiya, Kyoko Ai, Yukiko Kobayashi, Kenji Sahara, Andrew Hughes; ***D:*** Inoshiro Honda. *FRG*

Destroy All Planets ☠☠ *Gamera Tai Viras; Gamera Tai Uchukaiju Bairasu; Gamera Vs. Viras; Gamera Vs. Outer Space Monster Viras* **1968** Aliens whose spaceships turn into giant flying squids are attacking Earth. It's up to Gammera, the flying, fire-breathing turtle to save the day. **?m/C VHS.** *JP* Peter Williams, Kojiro Hongo, Toru Takatsuka; ***D:*** Noriaki Yuasa. *SNC*

Destroyer ☠☠☠ **1943** Trials and tribulations aboard a WWII destroyer result in tensions, but when the time comes for action, the men get the job done. **99m/B VHS, Beta.** Edward G. Robinson, Glenn Ford, Marguerite Chapman, Edgar Buchanan, Leo Gorcey, Regis Toomey, Edward Brophy, Larry Parks; ***D:*** William A. Seiter. *NO*

Destroyer 🦴 **1988 (R)** Small-budget film crew goes to an empty prison to shoot, and are stalked by the ghost/zombie remains of a huge serial killer given the electric chair 18 months before. **94m/C VHS, Beta, LV.** Anthony Perkins, Deborah Foreman, Lyle Alzado; ***D:*** Robert Kirk. *NO*

The Destructors 🦴🦴 *The Marseille Contract* **1974 (PG)** An American narcotics enforcement officer in Paris seeks the help of a hitman in order to catch a druglord. **89m/C VHS, Beta.** *GB* Anthony Quinn, Michael Caine, James Mason, Maureen Kerwin, Alexandra Stewart; ***D:*** Robert Parrish; ***W:*** Judd Bernard. *LIV, VES, HHE*

Destry Rides Again 🦴🦴🦴🦴 *Justice Rides Again* **1939** An uncontrollably lawless western town is whipped into shape by a peaceful, unarmed sheriff. A vintage Hollywood potpourri with Dietrich's finest post-Sternberg moment; standing on the bar singing "See What the Boys in the Back Room Will Have." The second of three versions of this Max Brand story. First was released in 1932; the third in 1954. **94m/B VHS, Beta, LV.** James Stewart, Marlene Dietrich, Brian Donlevy, Charles Winninger, Mischa Auer, Irene Hervey, Una Merkel, Billy Gilbert, Jack Carson, Samuel S. Hinds, Allen Jenkins; ***D:*** George Marshall; ***W:*** Gertrude Purcell, Felix Jackson, Henry Myers; ***C:*** Hal Mohr; ***M:*** Frank Skinner. *MCA, FCT*

Details of a Duel: A Question of Honor 🦴🦴½ **1989** A butcher and a teacher collide in this comedy, and prodded by the church, militia and town officals, must duel before the entire town. In Spanish with English subtitles. **97m/C VHS.** *SP* ***D:*** Sergio Cabrera. *INJ, FCT*

The Detective 🦴🦴🦴 *Father Brown* **1954** Based on G.K. Chesterton's "Father Brown" detective stories, a slick, funny English mystery in which the famous priest tracks down a notorious, endlessly crafty antique thief. **91m/B VHS, Beta.** *GB* Alec Guinness, Peter Finch, Joan Greenwood, Cecil Parker, Bernard Lee; ***D:*** Robert Hamer; ***M:*** Jerry Goldsmith. *COL*

The Detective 🦴🦴🦴 **1968** A New York detective investigating the mutilation murder of a homosexual finds political and police department corruption. Fine, gritty performances prevail in this suspense thriller. Based on the novel by Roderick Thorpe. **114m/C VHS, Beta, LV.** Frank Sinatra, Lee Remick, Ralph Meeker, Jacqueline Bisset, William Windom, Robert Duvall, Tony Musante, Jack Klugman, Al Freeman Jr.; ***D:*** Gordon Douglas; ***W:*** Abby Mann; ***C:*** Joseph Biroc. *FOX*

Detective Sadie & Son 🦴 **1984** A television movie about an elderly detective and her young son cracking a case. **96m/C VHS, Beta.** Debbie Reynolds, Sam Wanamaker, Brian McNamara. *NO*

Detective School Dropouts 🦴🦴 *Dumb Dicks* **1985 (PG)** Since they couldn't pass detective school, are they smart enough to outwit a kidnapper? Find out and get a few laughs at the same time. **92m/C VHS, Beta.** Lorin Dreyfuss, David Landsberg, Christian de Sica, George Eastman; ***D:*** Filippo Ottoni. *MGM*

Detective Story 🦴🦴🦴½ **1951** Intense drama about a New York City police precinct with a wide array of characters led by a disillusioned and bitter detective (Douglas). Excellent casting is the strong point, as the film can be a bit dated. Based on Sydney Kingsley's Broadway play. **103m/B VHS.** Kirk Douglas, Eleanor Parker, Lee Grant, Horace McMahon, William Bendix, Craig Hill, Cathy O'Donnell, Bert Freed, George Macready, Joseph Wiseman, Gladys George, Frank Faylen, Warner Anderson, Gerald Mohr; ***D:*** William Wyler; ***W:*** Philip Yordan, Robert Wyler; ***C:*** Lee Garmes. Cannes Film Festival '52: Best Actress (Grant); Edgar Allan Poe Awards '51: Best Screenplay; Nominations: Academy Awards '51: Best Actress (Parker), Best Director (Wyler), Best Screenplay, Best Supporting Actress (Grant). *PAR*

Detonator 🦴🦴 *Alistair MacLean's Death Train; Death Train* **1993 (R)** A renegade Russian general has stolen a nuclear bomb and is transporting it from Germany to Iraq via a hijacked train commandeered by his hired band of mercenaries. Stewart is the U.N. troubleshooter delegated to stop the plot, aided by a commando team featuring Brosnan and Paul. Based on the novel "Death Train" by Alistair MacLean. Made for cable television. **98m/C VHS.** Pierce Brosnan, Patrick Stewart, Ted Levine, Alexandra Paul, Christopher Lee; ***D:*** David S. Jackson; ***W:*** David S. Jackson. *NLC*

Detonator 2: Night Watch 🦴🦴½ *Alistair MacLean's Night Watch; Night Watch* **1995 (R)** Made-for-cable movie finds Brosnan and Paul returning as operatives for the secret United Nations Anti-Crime Organization (UNACO). Mike Graham and Sabrina Carver are teamed by their boss Nick Caldwell (Devane) when it's discovered that Rembrandt's "Night Watch" has been replaced by a forgery. This takes our intrepid duo to Hong Kong, a shady computer expert/art collector (Shannon), and a suspicious satellite about to be launched by North Korea. Based on a story by Alistair MacLean. **99m/C VHS, LV.** Pierce Brosnan, Alexandra Paul, William Devane, Michael J. Shannon, Lim Kay Siu, Irene Ng; ***D:*** David S. Jackson; ***W:*** David S. Jackson; ***M:*** John Scott. *NLC*

Detour 🦴🦴🦴 **1946** Considered to be the creme de la creme of "B" movies, a largely unacknowledged but cult-followed noir downer. Well-designed, stylish, and compelling, if a bit contrived and sometimes annoyingly shrill. Shot in only six days with six indoor sets. Down-on-his-luck pianist Neal hitches cross-country to rejoin his fiancee. His first wrong turn involves the accidental death of the man who picked him up, then he's en route to Destiny with a capital "D" when he picks up fatal femme Savage, as vicious a vixen as ever ruined a good man. Told in flashback, it's also been called the most despairing of all "B"-pictures. As noir as they get. **67m/B VHS, Beta, LV.** Tom Neal, Ann Savage, Claudia Drake, Edmund MacDonald; ***D:*** Edgar G. Ulmer. *BAR, MRV, SNC*

Detour to Danger *Woof!* **1945** Two young men set out on a fishing expedition and run into crooks and damsels in distress. Unintentionally hilarious "acting" by the no-name cast make this a grade-Z "B" movie. Of interest only because it was filmed in the three-color Kodachrome process used primarily in documentaries. **56m/C VHS, Beta, 8mm.** Britt Wood, John Day, Nancy Brinckman; ***D:*** Richard Talmadge. *VYY*

Detroit 9000 🦴½ **1973 (R)** A pair of Detroit policemen investigate a robbery that occurred at a black congressman's fundraising banquet. Also on video as "Detroit Heat." **106m/C VHS, Beta.** Alex Rocco, Scatman Crothers, Hari Rhodes, Lonette McKee, Herbert Jefferson Jr.; ***D:*** Arthur Marks. *NO*

Deutschland im Jahre Null 🦴🦴🦴½ **1947** The acclaimed, unsettling vision of post-war Germany as seen through the eyes of a disturbed boy who eventually kills himself. Lyrical and grim, in German with subtitles. **75m/B VHS, Beta.** *GE* Franz Gruber; ***D:*** Roberto Rossellini. *FCT, GLV*

Devastator 🦴 *Kings Ransom; The Destroyers* **1985 (R)** A Vietnam vet exacts violent revenge on the murderer of an old army buddy. **79m/C VHS, Beta.** Richard Hill, Katt Shea Ruben, Crofton Hardester; ***D:*** Cirio H. Santiago. *MGM*

Devi 🦴🦴🦴½ **1960** A minor film in the Ray canon, it is, nonetheless, a strange and compelling tale of religious superstition. An Indian farmer becomes convinced that his beautiful daughter-in-law is the reincarnation of the goddess Kali. The girl is then pressured into accepting a worship that eventually drives her mad. In Bengali with English subtitles. **96m/B VHS, Beta.** *IN* Chhabi Biswas, Sharmila Tagore, Soumitra Chatterjee; ***D:*** Satyajit Ray. *INJ, WFV, DVT*

Devices and Desires 🦴🦴🦴 **1994** Typically complicated mystery adapted from the novel by P.D. James. Scotland Yard Commander Adam Dalgliesh (Marsden) is on holiday on the east coast of England where, of course, there's blackmail, murder, suicide, and trouble at a nearby nuclear power station for him to contend with. Made for TV; on six cassettes. **312m/C VHS.** *GB* Roy Marsden, Susannah York. *TVC, AAE*

The Devil 🦴 **1984** The last remaining humans try to fight off demonic lifeforms that need to feed on their flesh. **90m/C VHS, Beta.** *VCD*

The Devil & Daniel Webster 🦴🦴🦴½ *All That Money Can Buy; Here Is a Man; A Certain Mr. Scratch* **1941** In 1840s New Hampshire, a young farmer, who sells his soul to the devil, is saved from a trip to Hell when Daniel Webster steps in to defend him. This classic fantasy is visually striking and contains wonderful performances. Adapted from the story by Stephen Vincent Benet who based it on Goethe's Faust. **106m/B VHS, Beta, LV.** James Craig, Edward Arnold, Walter Huston, Simone Simon, Gene Lockhart, Jane Darwell, Anne Shirley, John Qualen, H.B. Warner; ***D:*** William Dieterle. Nominations: Academy Awards '41: Best Actor (Huston). *HMV, SUE, CRC*

Devil & Leroy Basset 🦴 **1973 (PG)** Keema Gregwolf kills a deputy, breaks from jail with the Basset brothers, hijacks a church bus, kidnaps a family, and gets into other troublesome situations while on a posse-eluding cross-country adventure. **85m/C VHS, Beta.** Cody Bearpaw, John Goff, George Flower; ***D:*** Robert E. Pearso; ***M:*** Les Baxter. *PSM*

The Devil & Max Devlin 🦴½ **1981 (PG)** Good cast wanders aimlessly in Disney family fantasy. The recently deceased Max Devlin strikes a bargain with the devil. He will be restored to life if he can convince three mortals to sell their souls. **95m/C VHS, Beta.** Elliott Gould, Bill Cosby, Susan Anspach, Adam Rich, Julie Budd; ***D:*** Steven Hilliard Stern; ***W:*** Jimmy Sangster; ***M:*** Marvin Hamlisch, Buddy Baker. *DIS, OM*

The Devil & Miss Jones 🦴🦴🦴½ **1941** Engaging romantic comedy finds a big business boss posing as an ordinary salesclerk to weed out union organizers. He doesn't expect to encounter the wicked management or his beautiful co-worker, however. **90m/B VHS.** Jean Arthur, Robert Cummings, Charles Coburn, Edmund Gwenn, Spring Byington, William Demarest, S.Z. Sakall; ***D:*** Sam Wood; ***C:*** Harry Stradling. Nominations: Academy Awards '41: Best Original Screenplay, Best Supporting Actor (Coburn). *REP*

The Devil at 4 O'Clock 🦴🦴½ **1961** An alcoholic missionary and three convicts work to save a colony of leper children from a South Seas volcano. Quality cast barely compensates for mediocre script. **126m/B VHS, Beta, LV.** Spencer Tracy, Frank Sinatra, Kerwin Mathews, Jean-Pierre Aumont; ***D:*** Mervyn LeRoy; ***C:*** Joseph Biroc; ***M:*** George Duning. *GKK, IME*

The Devil Bat 🦴🦴 *Killer Bats* **1941** Madman Lugosi trains a swarm of monstrous blood-sucking bats to attack whenever they smell perfume. Followed by the sequel "Devil Bat's Daughter." **67m/B VHS, Beta.** Bela Lugosi, Dave O'Brien, Suzanne Kaaren, Yolande Donlan; ***D:*** Jean Yarbrough. *NOS, SNC, PSM*

The Devil Bat's Daughter 🦴½ **1946** A young woman, hoping to avoid becoming insane like her batty father, consults a psychiatrist when she starts to have violent nightmares. Unsuccessful sequel to "Devil Bats." **66m/B VHS, Beta.** Rosemary La Planche, Michael Hale, John James, Molly Lamont; ***D:*** Frank Wisbar. *COL, MRV*

Devil Diamond 🦴🦴 **1937** Mystery-suspense yarn about two amateur detectives who find themselves facing danger after tracking down a gang of evil jewel thieves. **?m/C VHS.** Kane Richmond, Frankie Darro. *SNC, VYY*

Devil Dog: The Hound of Hell 🦴 **1978** A family has trouble with man's best friend when they adopt a dog that is the son of the "Hound of Hell" in this made for television movie. **95m/C VHS, Beta.** Richard Crenna, Yvette Mimieux, Kim Richards, Victor Jory; ***D:*** Curtis Harrington. *NO*

Devil Dogs of the Air 🦴🦴½ **1935** Cagney and O'Brien team up in another air drama with Cagney once again the cocky pilot who, this time, joins the Marine Air Corp. O'Brien plays his flying idol (and later rival). Cagney finds all his wisecracking and luck are no match for knowledge and experience but he learns. Good stunt flying; shot on location at the San Diego naval air base. **85m/B VHS.** James Cagney, Pat O'Brien, Margaret Lindsay, Frank McHugh, Robert Barrat, Russell Hicks, Ward Bond; ***D:*** Lloyd Bacon. *MGM, FCT*

Devil Doll 1936 An escaped convict uses a mad scientist's human-shrinking formula to evil ends—he sends out miniature assassins in the guise of store-bought dolls. Rarely seen horror oldie. **80m/B VHS, Beta.** Lionel Barrymore, Maureen O'Sullivan, Frank Lawton; ***D:*** Tod Browning; ***W:*** Tod Browning, Erich von Stroheim. *MGM, MLB*

Devil Doll 1964 Ventriloquist's dummy, which contains the soul of a former performer, eyes a beautiful victim in the crowd. Newspaper guy senses trouble. Cut above the usual talking, stalking dummy story. **80m/B VHS, Beta.** *GB* Bryant Holiday, William Sylvester; ***D:*** Lindsay Shonteff. *NO*

Devil Girl from Mars ½ 1954 Sexy female from Mars and her very large robot arrive at a small Scottish inn to announce that a Martian feminist revolution has occurred. The distaff aliens then undertake a search of healthy Earth males for breeding purposes. Believe it or not, the humans don't want to go and therein lies the rub. A somewhat enjoyable space farce. **76m/B VHS, Beta.** *GB* Hugh McDermott, Hazel Court, Patricia Laffan, Peter Reynolds, Adrienne Corri, Joseph Tomelty, Sophie Stewart, John Laurie, Anthony Richmond; ***D:*** David MacDonald; ***W:*** John C. Mather, James Eastwood. *NOS, MRV, SNC*

Devil Horse 1932 A boy's devotion to a wild horse marked for destruction as a killer leads him into trouble. A serial in twelve, thirteen-minute chapters. **156m/B VHS, Beta.** Frankie Darro, Harry Carey Sr., Noah Beery Sr.; ***D:*** Otto Brower, Richard Talmadge. *GPV, VCN, DVT*

Devil In a Blue Dress 1995 (R) Down-on-his-luck Easy Rawlins (Washington) is an out of work aircraft worker in 1948 LA. He's hired to find mystery woman Daphne (Beals) by a shady businessman (Sizemore). What he finds are the usual noir staples: government corruption backed by thugs who want him to mind his own business. Easy and Daphne's torrid romance featured in the Walter Mosley novel is missing but the racism and violence are intact. Realism and accuracy in period detail enhance solid performance by Washington, though the deliberate, literary pace is at times lulling. Cheadle takes over whenever he shows up as Mouse, Rawlins' loyal friend and muscle. **102m/C VHS, LV.** Denzel Washington, Jennifer Beals, Don Cheadle, Tom Sizemore, Maury Chaykin, Terry Kinney, Mel Winkler, Albert Hall; ***D:*** Carl Franklin; ***W:*** Carl Franklin; ***C:*** Tak Fujimoto; ***M:*** Elmer Bernstein. Los Angeles Film Critics Association Awards '95: Best Supporting Actor (Cheadle); National Society of Film Critics Awards '95: Best Cinematography, Best Supporting Actor (Cheadle); Nominations: Screen Actors Guild Award '95: Best Supporting Actor (Cheadle). *COL*

The Devil in Silk ½ 1956 A composer marries a woman, not knowing that she is psychotically jealous. After she commits suicide, he must prove to the police that he did not kill her. Original dialogue in German. **102m/B VHS, Beta.** *GE* Lilli Palmer, Curt Jurgens, Winnie Markus; ***D:*** Rolf Hansen. *NOS, SNC*

Devil in the Flesh *Le Diable au Corps* 1946 Acclaimed drama about a French soldier's wife having a passionate affair with a high school student while her husband is away fighting in WWI. From the novel by Raymond Radiguet. Dubbed. Updated and remade in 1987. **112m/B VHS, Beta.** *FR* Gerard Philipe, Micheline Presle, Denise Grey; ***D:*** Claude Autant-Lara. *NOS, FCT, APD*

Devil in the Flesh *Il Diavolo in Corpo* 1987 (R) A angst-ridden, semi-pretentious Italian drama about an obsessive older woman carrying on an affair with a schoolboy, despite her terrorist boyfriend and the objections of the lad's psychiatrist father, who had treated her. In Italian with subtitles. Famous for a graphic sex scene, available in the unrated version. Updated remake of the 1946 French film. **110m/C VHS, Beta, LV.** *IT* Maruschka Detmers, Federico Pitzalis; ***D:*** Marco Bellochio; ***W:*** Marco Bellochio. *ORI, INJ*

Devil Kiss 1977 Gothic horror including zombies, virgins, sorcery, and the inevitable living dead. **93m/C VHS, Beta.** Oliver Mathews, Evelyn Scott. *HMV*

Devil Monster 1946 A world-weary traveler searches for a girl's fiance in the South Pacific, and is attacked by a large manta. **65m/B VHS, Beta, LV.** Barry Norton, Blanche Mehaffey; ***D:*** S. Edwin Graham. *SNC*

Devil of the Desert Against the Son of Hercules ½ 1962 The grandson of Zeus ventures into the wasteland to take on a feisty foe. **?m/C VHS, Beta.** *IT* Kirk Morris, Michele Girardon; ***D:*** Riccardo (Robert Hampton) Freda. *SNC*

Devil on Horseback 1954 A miner's son journeys to London to become a jockey in this comedy/drama. As he tries to bully his way into the racing circuit, he succeeds, but not in the way he anticipated. **88m/B VHS, Beta, 8mm.** *GB* Googie Withers, John McCallum, Jeremy Spenser, Liam Redmond; ***D:*** Cyril Frankel; ***M:*** Malcolm Arnold. *VYY*

The Devil on Wheels 1947 Inspired by his dad's reckless driving, a teenager becomes a hot rodder and causes a family tragedy. A rusty melodrama that can't be described as high-performance. **67m/B VHS.** James B. Cardwell, Noreen Nash, Darryl Hickman, Jan Ford, Damian O'Flynn, Lenita Love. *NOS, LOO*

Devil Rider ½ 1991 A monster from Hell, the Devil Rider, once rode the plains in search of human fodder. In the present day, a pleasure ranch is built on his old territory, and people begin dying in the most horrific manners. Could this mean the return of the Devil Rider? **90m/C VHS.** *NO*

Devil Riders ½ 1944 Unspectacular horse opera has a crooked lawyer trying to get his grubby hands on some choice land. Enter Crabbe to set things straight. **56m/B VHS.** Buster Crabbe, Al "Fuzzy" St. John, Patti McCarty, Charles "Blackie" King, John Merton, Kermit Maynard, Frank LaRue, Jack Ingram, George Chesebro, Edward Cassidy; ***D:*** Sam Newfield. *NOS, MRV*

The Devil Thumbs a Ride 1947 A naive traveller picks up a hitchhiker, not knowing he's wanted for murder. Will history repeat itself in this interesting noir? **63m/B VHS, Beta.** Ted North, Lawrence Tierney, Nan Leslie; ***D:*** Felix Feist. *NO*

The Devil Thumbs a Ride/Having Wonderful Crime 1947 A mystery double feature. In "Devil Thumbs a Ride," a ruthless killer-bank robber hitches a ride from an inebriated travelling salesman. In "Having Wonderful Crime," a criminal lawyer investigates the disappearance of a magician. **132m/B VHS, Beta.** Lawrence Tierney, Pat O'Brien, George Murphy, Carole Landis, Nan Leslie, George Zucco; ***D:*** Felix Feist, Edward Sutherland. *NO*

Devil Times Five ½ *People Toys; The Horrible House on the Hill* 1974 (R) To take revenge for being incarcerated in a mental hospital, five children methodically murder the adults who befriend them. **87m/C VHS, Beta.** Gene Evans, Sorrell Booke, Shelly Morrison; ***D:*** Sean McGregor. *MED*

Devil Wears White 1986 (R) A student's vacation is disrupted when he becomes involved in a war with an insane arms dealer who wants to take over a Latin American Republic. **92m/C VHS, Beta.** Robert Livesy, Jane Higginson, Guy Ecker, Anthony Cordova; ***D:*** Steven A. Hull. *TWE*

Devil Woman *Woof!* 1976 (R) A Filipino Gorgon-woman seeks reptillian revenge on the farmers who killed her family. Bad news. **79m/C VHS.** *PH* Rosemarie Gil; ***D:*** Albert Yu, Felix Vilars. *SNC*

Devilfish 1984 A small seaside community is ravaged by berserk manta rays in this soggy saga. **92m/C VHS, Beta.** *IT* ***D:*** Lamberto Bava. *VMK*

The Devils 1971 (R) In 1631 France, a priest is accused of commerce with the devil and sexual misconduct with nuns. Since he is also a political threat, the accusation is used to denounce and eventually execute him. Based on Aldous Huxley's "The Devils of Loudun," the movie features masturbating nuns and other excesses—shocking scenes typical of film director Russell. Supposedly this was Russell's attempt to wake the public to their desensitization of modern horrors of war. Controversial and flamboyant. **109m/C VHS, Beta.** *GB* Vanessa Redgrave, Oliver Reed, Dudley Sutton, Max Adrian, Gemma Jones, Murray Melvin; ***D:*** Ken Russell; ***W:*** Ken Russell; ***C:*** David Watkin. National Board of Review Awards '71: Best Director (Russell). *WAR, INJ*

Devil's Angels 1967 A motorcycle gang clashes with a small-town sheriff. Cheap 'n' sleazy fare. **84m/C VHS.** John Cassavetes, Beverly Adams, Mimsy Farmer, Salli Sachse, Nai Bonet, Leo Gordon; ***D:*** Daniel Haller; ***W:*** Charles B. Griffith. *NO*

The Devil's Brigade 1968 "Dirty Dozen" style film with Holden as the leader of special commando brigade consisting of the usual misfits and oddballs. The team is trained to take on the Nazis in Scandanavia but has their assignment cancelled. Instead, they take them on in the Italian Alps, making for some perilous adventures. Non-acting notables include former football great Hornung and former boxing champ Gene Fullmer. **130m/C VHS, Beta.** William Holden, Cliff Robertson, Vince Edwards, Michael Rennie, Dana Andrews, Gretchen Wyler, Andrew Prine, Claude Akins, Carroll O'Connor, Richard Jaeckel, Jack Watson, Paul Hornung, Jeremy Slate, Don Megowan, Patric Knowles, James Craig, Richard Dawson, Tom Stern, Luke Askew; ***D:*** Andrew V. McLaglen; ***W:*** William Roberts; ***C:*** William Clothier; ***M:*** Alex North. *MGM*

The Devil's Brother *Fra Diavolo; Bogus Bandits; The Virtuous Tramps* 1933 In one of their lesser efforts, Laurel and Hardy star as bumbling bandits in this comic operetta based on the 1830 opera by Daniel F. Auber. Also available with "Laurel & Hardy's Laughing 20's" on laserdisc. **88m/B VHS.** Stan Laurel, Oliver Hardy, Dennis King, Thelma Todd, James Finlayson, Lucille Browne; ***D:*** Charles R. Rogers, Hal Roach. *MGM, MLB, CCB*

Devil's Canyon 1953 An ex-lawman, serving time in an Arizona prison, is beset by a jailed killer seeking vengeance for his own incarceration. Filmed in 3-D. **92m/B VHS, Beta.** Dale Robertson, Virginia Mayo, Stephen McNally, Arthur Hunnicutt, Robert Keith, Jay C. Flippen, Whit Bissell; ***D:*** Alfred Werker. *TTC*

The Devil's Cargo ½ 1948 When a man is accused of killing a racetrack operator, he calls in the Falcon to clear his name. The master detective finds this to be a most difficult task however, especially when the accused is found poisoned in his cell. One of the final three "Falcon" films, in which Calvert replaced Tom Conway. **61m/B VHS, Beta.** John Calvert, Rochelle Hudson, Roscoe Karns, Lyle Talbot, Tom Kennedy; ***D:*** John F. Link. *SNC*

The Devil's Commandment *I, Vampiri; Lust of the Vampires* 1956 A lurid melodrama about a Parisian newspaperman's journey into a network of crime and perversion. Cinematography by Mario Bava. **90m/B VHS, Beta, LV.** *FR* Gianna Maria Canale, Dario Michaelis, Carlo D'Angelo, Wandisa Guida, Paul Muller, Renato Tontini; ***D:*** Riccardo (Robert Hampton) Freda. *SNC*

Devil's Crude 1971 Adventurous sailor and a young oil heir uncover a conspiracy within a giant corporation. **85m/C VHS, Beta.** *IT* Franco Nero. *TWE*

The Devil's Daughter ½ *Pocomania; Poncomania* 1939 A sister's hatred and voodoo ceremonies play an important part in this all-black drama. **60m/B VHS, Beta.** Nina Mae McKinney, Jack Carter, Ida James, Hamtree Harrington. *SNC, VYY, DVT*

The Devil's Daughter 1991 (R) Satan, in a desperate bid to take over the planet, orders his minions to flood the earth with horrific evil. Only one woman can prevent the HellMaster from succeeding, and she may be too late! **112m/C VHS.** *IT* Kelly Curtis, Herbert Lom, Maria Angela Giordano, Michel Hans Adatte, Carla Cassola, Angelika Maria Boeck, Tomas Arana; ***D:*** Michele (Michael) Soavi; ***W:*** Dario Argento; ***M:*** Pino Donaggio. *REP*

The Devil's Disciple 1959 Entertaining adaptation of George Bernard Shaw play set during the American Revolution. Standout performances by Douglas as a romantic rogue, Lancaster as a New England pastor, and Olivier as British General Burgoyne. Film suffers from choppy direction, but the excellent cast more than makes up for it. **82m/B VHS.** *GB* Burt Lancaster, Kirk Douglas, Laurence Olivier, Janet Scott, Eva LeGallienne, Harry Andrews, Basil Sydney,

George Rose; *D:* Guy Hamilton; *C:* Jack Hildyard; *M:* Richard Rodney Bennett. *MGM*

The Devil's Eye 𝄞𝄞 *Djavulens Oga* **1960** The devil dispatches Don Juan to tempt and seduce a young virgin bride-to-be, a reverend's daughter, no less. Based on the Danish radio play "Don Juan Returns." **90m/B VHS, Beta.** *SW* Bibi Andersson, Jarl Kulle; *D:* Ingmar Bergman; *W:* Ingmar Bergman. *SUE, INJ, NLC*

Devil's Gift *Woof!* **1984** A young boy's toy is possessed by a demon and havoc ensues. **112m/C VHS, Beta.** Bob Mendlesolin, Vicki Saputo, Steven Robertson; *D:* Kenneth Berton. *LIV, VES*

The Devil's Hand 𝄞 *Devil's Doll; The Naked Goddess; Live to Love* **1961** When Alda finds a doll that represents his ideal woman in a curio shop, the shop's owner (Hamilton, aka Commissioner Gordon), tells him the dream girl who modeled for the doll lives nearby. Trouble is, she's part of a voodoo cult, and guess who's head voodoo-man. Big trouble for Alda; big snooze for you. **71m/B VHS.** Linda Christian, Robert Alda, Neil Hamilton, Ariadne Welter; *D:* William Hole Jr. *NOS, SNC, LOO*

The Devil's Harvest *Woof!* **193?** A vintage "Reefer Madness"-style cautionary film about pot, the "smoke of Hell." **52m/B VHS, Beta.** *NO*

The Devil's Mistress 𝄞½ **1968** A gang of criminals on a pillaging spree murder a man and rape his Indian wife, only to find out she's a she-demon who won't let bygones be bygones. Lame. **66m/C VHS.** Joan Stapleton, Robert Gregory, Forrest Westmoreland, Douglas Warren, Oren Williams, Arthur Resley; *D:* Orville Wanzer; *W:* Orville Wanzer. *SNC*

The Devil's Nightmare 𝄞½ *Succubus; The Devil Walks at Midnight* **1971 (R)** A woman leads seven tourists (representing the seven deadly sins) on a tour of a medieval European castle. There they experience demonic tortures. Lots of creepy moments. Euro-horror/sex star Blanc is fantastic in this otherwise mediocre production. **88m/C VHS, Beta.** *BE IT* Erika Blanc, Jean Servais, Daniel Emilfork, Lucien Raimbourg, Jacques Monseau, Colette Emmanuelle, Ivana Novak, Shirley Corrigan, Frederique Hender; *D:* Jean Brismee. *APP*

The Devil's Partner 𝄞½ **1958** Yet another uninspired devil yarn in which an old-timer trades in his senior citizenship by dying and coming back in the form of his younger self. Young again, he takes a new wife and indulges in multiple ritual sacrifices. Noteworthy only by virtue of the cast's later TV notoriety—Buchanan and Foulger would later appear on "Petticoat Junction," Nelson played Dr. Rossi on "Peyton Place," and Crane beached a role on "Hawaiian Eye." **75m/B VHS.** Ed Nelson, Jean Allison, Edgar Buchanan, Richard Crane, Spencer Carlisle, Byron Foulger, Claire Carleton; *D:* Charles R. Rondeau. *SNC, MRV, CNM*

Devil's Party 𝄞𝄞 **1938** A tenement boy's reunion party turns into a night of horror when one of the guests is killed. As a result, the childhood friends band together to uncover the murderer's identity. **65m/B VHS, Beta.** Victor McLaglen, Paul Kelly, William Gargan, Samuel S. Hinds, Scotty Beckett; *D:* Ray McCarey. *NOS, MRV, DVT*

The Devil's Playground 𝄞𝄞𝄞 **1976** Sexual tension rises in a Catholic seminary, distracting the boys from their theological studies. The attentions of the priests only further their sexual confusion. Winner of many Australian film awards. **107m/C Beta.** *AU* Arthur Dignam, Nick Tate, Simon Burke, Charles Frawley, Jonathon Hardy, Gerry Dugan, Thomas Keneally; *D:* Fred Schepisi; *W:* Fred Schepisi; *M:* Bruce Smeaton. Australian Film Institute '76: Best Actor (Tate), Best Actor (Burke), Best Film. *ALL*

The Devil's Possessed 𝄞½ **1974** A Middle Ages despot tortures and maims the peasants in his region until they rise up and enact an unspeakable revenge. **90m/C VHS, Beta.** *AR SP* Paul Naschy; *D:* Leon Klimovsky. *NO*

Devil's Rain 𝄞½ **1975 (PG)** The rituals and practices of devil worship, possession, and satanism are gruesomely related. Interesting cast. **85m/C VHS, Beta, LV.** Ernest Borgnine, Ida Lupino, William Shatner, Eddie Albert, Keenan Wynn, John Travolta, Tom Skerritt; *D:* Robert Fuest. *NO*

The Devil's Sleep 𝄞 **1951** When a crusading woman sets out to break up a teen narcotics ring, the threatened thugs attempt to draw her daughter into their sleazy affairs, thus assuring the mother's silence. **81m/B VHS, Beta.** Lita Grey Chaplin, Timothy Farrell, John Mitchum, William Thomason, Tracy Lynn; *D:* W. Merle Connell. *SNC*

Devil's Son-in-Law *Woof!* **1977 (R)** A black stand-up comic makes a deal with a devil. **95m/C VHS, Beta.** Rudy Ray Moore; *D:* Cliff Roguemore. *NO*

The Devil's Undead 𝄞𝄞½ **1975 (PG)** When a Scottish orphanage is besieged by a rash of cold-blooded murders, the detectives Lee and Cushing are summoned to investigate. Interesting spin on that old possessed by demons theme. **90m/C VHS, Beta.** *GB* Christopher Lee, Peter Cushing; *D:* Peter Sasdy. *MLB*

Devil's Wanton 𝄞𝄞½ *Fangelse; Prison* **1949** A young girl tries to forget an unhappy relationship by beginning a new romance with an equally frustrated beau. Gloomy, but hopeful. **80m/B VHS, Beta.** *SW* Doris Svedlund, Eva Henning, Hasse Ekman; *D:* Ingmar Bergman; *W:* Ingmar Bergman. *VYY, MRV, DVT*

The Devil's Web 𝄞½ **1974 (PG)** A demonic nurse infiltrates, manipulates, and corrupts three beautiful sisters. **73m/C VHS, Beta.** Diana Dors, Andrea Marcovicci, Ed Bishop, Cec Linder, Michael Culver. *LIV*

Devil's Wedding Night *Woof!* **1973 (R)** An archaeologist and his twin brother fight over a ring that lures virgins into Count Dracula's Transylvanian castle. Vampire queen Bay seduces the dimwit twins and strips at every chance she gets. **85m/C VHS, Beta.** Mark Damon, Rosalba (Sara Bay) Neri, Frances Davis; *D:* Paul Solvay. *NO*

Devlin 𝄞𝄞 **1992 (R)** Devlin is a tough cop with an alcohol problem and a bad marriage. His father-in-law, Brennan, is a powerful local political boss. When Brennan's son is murdered, Devlin is the fall guy. Seeking to clear himself, he discovers a conspiracy going back thirty years. Made for cable television. **110m/C VHS, Beta, LV.** Bryan Brown, Roma Downey, Lloyd Bridges; *D:* Rick Rosenthal; *M:* Minette Alton. *FXV, VTR*

The Devlin Connection 𝄞𝄞 **1982** Retired private investigator helps his son learn the ropes as he embarks on a Los Angeles crime fighting career. Hudson's last starring television series, excluding his "Dynasty" role. All thirteen episodes are available separately. **50m/C VHS, Beta.** Rock Hudson, Jack Scalia, Louis Giambalvo, Leigh Taylor-Young, Jack Kruschen; *D:* Christian Nyby. *TWE*

Devonsville Terror 𝄞𝄞 **1983 (R)** Strange things begin to happen when a new school teacher arrives in Devonsville, a town that has a history of torture, murder, and witchcraft. The hysterical townspeople react by beginning a 20th-century witchhunt. **97m/C VHS, Beta.** Suzanna Love, Donald Pleasence, Deanna Haas, Mary Walden, Robert Walker Jr., Paul Wilson; *D:* Ulli Lommel; *W:* Ulli Lommel. *SUE*

Devotion 𝄞𝄞½ **1931** A lovesick British miss disguises herself as a governess so she can be near the object of her affection, a London barrister. **80m/B VHS.** Ann Harding, Leslie Howard, Robert Williams, O.P. Heggie, Louise Closser Hale, Dudley Digges; *D:* Robert Milton. *TTC*

D.I. 𝄞𝄞 **1957** A tough drill sergeant is faced with an unbreakable rebellious recruit, threatening his record and his platoon's status. Webb's film features performances by actual soldiers. **106m/B VHS, Beta.** Jack Webb, Don Dubbins, Jackie Loughery, Lin McCarthy, Virginia Gregg; *D:* Jack Webb. *WAR*

The Diabolical Dr. Z 𝄞𝄞 *Miss Muette; Dans les Griffes du Maniaque* **1965** When dad dies of cardiac arrest after the medical council won't let him make the world a kinder gentler place with his personality-altering technique, his dutiful daughter—convinced the council brought on dad's demise—is out to change some personalities in a big way. **86m/B VHS.** *SP FR* Mabel Karr, Fernando Montes, Estella Blain, Antonio J. Escribano, Howard Vernon; *D:* Jess (Jesus) Franco. *SNC*

Diabolically Yours 𝄞𝄞½ *Diaboliquement Votre* **1967** A French thriller about an amnesiac who struggles to discover his lost identity. Tensions mount when his pretty spouse and friends begin to wonder if it's all a game. Dubbed. **94m/C VHS, Beta.** *FR* Alain Delon, Senta Berger; *D:* Julien Duvivier. *UNI*

Diabolique 𝄞𝄞𝄞½ *Les Diabolique* **1955** The mistress and the wife of a sadistic schoolmaster conspire to murder the man, carry it out, and then begin to wonder if they have covered their tracks effectively. Plot twists and double-crosses abound. In French with English subtitles. Remade for television as "Reflections of Murder." **107m/B VHS, Beta, LV, 8mm.** *FR* Simone Signoret, Vera Clouzot, Paul Meurisse, Charles Vanel, Michel Serrault; *D:* Henri-Georges Clouzot. National Board of Review Awards '55: 5 Best Foreign Films of the Year; New York Film Critics Awards '55: Best Foreign Film. *VYY, NOS, SNC*

Diabolique 𝄞½ **1996 (R)** Remake of the 1955 French noir classic, updated for '90s sensibilities, finds timid teacher Mia (Adjani) married to overbearing school head Guy (Palminteri), who's having an affair with fellow teacher Nicole (Stone). The two women, who loathe Guy equally, plot to kill him. But when a P.I. (Bates) investigates, it seems possible that Guy isn't dead after all. If you're having trouble accessorizing with leopard skin, watch Stone. Otherwise, watch the far superior original. The usually publicity hungry Stone refused to have anything to do with this picture after its release due to a spat with director Chechik. **105m/C VHS, LV.** Sharon Stone, Isabelle Adjani, Chazz Palminteri, Kathy Bates, Spalding Gray, Shirley Knight, Adam Hann-Byrd, Allen (Goorwitz) Garfield; *D:* Jeremiah S. Chechik; *W:* Don Roos; *C:* Peter James; *M:* Randy Edelman. *WAR*

Dial Help 𝄞½ **1988 (R)** A lame Italian-made suspenser about a model plagued by ghostly phone calls. **94m/C VHS, Beta.** *IT* Charlotte Lewis, Marcello Modugno, Mattia Sbragia, Victor Cavallo; *D:* Ruggero Deodato. *PSM*

Dial "M" for Murder 𝄞𝄞𝄞 **1954** An unfaithful husband devises an elaborate plan to murder his wife for her money, but when she accidentally stabs the killer-to-be, with scissors no less, he alters his methods. Part of the "A Night at the Movies" series, this tape simulates a 1954 movie evening with a Daffy Duck cartoon, "My Little Duckaroo," a newsreel, and coming attractions for "Them" and "A Star Is Born." Filmed in 3-D. Based on the play by Frederick Knotts. **123m/C VHS, Beta, LV.** Ray Milland, Grace Kelly, Robert Cummings, John Williams, Anthony Dawson; *D:* Alfred Hitchcock; *C:* Robert Burks; *M:* Dimitri Tiomkin. *WAR, TLF*

Diamond Fleece 𝄞𝄞½ **1992** Rick (Cross) is a convicted diamond thief who's given a parole just so he can guard the world's largest uncut gemstone. But Inspector Outlaw (Dennehy) figures Rick will never be able to resist stealing the gem himself and the law can finally lock Rick away for good. Oh, and Holly, she thinks a maybe-ex-diamond thief will bring a little romance to her life. **93m/C VHS.** Ben Cross, Brian Dennehy, Kate Nelligan; *D:* Al Waxman; *W:* Michael Norell. *PSM*

Diamond Head 𝄞𝄞½ **1962** A Hawaiian landowner brings destruction and misery to his family via his stubbornness. Based on the Peter Gilman novel. **107m/C VHS, Beta, LV.** Charlton Heston, Yvette Mimieux, George Chakiris, France Nuyen, James Darren; *D:* Guy Green; *C:* Sam Leavitt; *M:* John Williams. *COL*

Diamond Ninja Force *Woof!* **198?** Non-adventure minimally hosted by Sho Kosugi pitting reluctant ninjas against indifferent mortal enemies with the usual half-hearted revenge motif. Shabby ninja imitator. **90m/C VHS, Beta.** *TWE*

Diamond Run 𝄞½ **1990 (R)** A streetwise American expatriate frantically searches for his girlfriend after unwittingly involving her in an assassination plot. **89m/C VHS, Beta, LV.** William Bell Sullivan, Ava

Lazar, Ayu Azhari, David Thornton, Peter Fox; ***D:*** Robert Chappell. *NO*

Diamond Trail 🦴½ **1933** East Coast jewel thieves bring their operation to the West, trailed by a New York reporter. **58m/B VHS, Beta.** Rex Bell, Frances Rich, Bud Osborne, Lloyd Whitlock, Norman Feusier; ***D:*** Harry Fraser. *NOS, DVT*

The Diamond Trap 🦴🦴 **1991 (PG)** A Manhatten detective finds himself in the middle of a diamond heist and involved with a con artist. Made for television. **93m/C VHS, LV.** Howard Hesseman, Brooke Shields, Ed Marinaro, Twiggy; ***D:*** Don Taylor; ***W:*** David Peckinpah. *VMK*

Diamonds 🦴🦴 **1972 (PG)** A tense film in which the Israel Diamond Exchange is looted by a motley array of criminal heisters. Shaw plays a dual role as twin brothers. **108m/C VHS, Beta.** *IS* Robert Shaw, Richard Roundtree, Barbara Hershey, Shelley Winters; ***D:*** Menahem Golan. *NLC*

Diamonds Are Forever 🦴🦴🦴½ **1971 (PG)** 007 once again battles his nemesis Blofeld, this time in Las Vegas. Bond must prevent the implementation of a plot to destroy Washington through the use of a space-orbiting laser. Fabulous stunts include Bond's wild drive through the streets of Vegas in a '71 Mach 1. Connery returned to play Bond in this film after being offered the then record-setting salary of one million dollars. **120m/C VHS, Beta, LV.** *GB* Sean Connery, Jill St. John, Charles Gray, Bruce Cabot, Jimmy Dean, Lana Wood, Bruce Glover, Putter Smith, Norman Burton, Joseph Furst, Bernard Lee, Desmond Llewelyn, Laurence Naismith, Leonard Barr, Lois Maxwell, Margaret Lacey, Joe Robinson, Donna Garrat, Trina Parks; ***D:*** Guy Hamilton; ***W:*** Tom Mankiewicz; ***C:*** Ted Moore; ***M:*** John Barry. Nominations: Academy Awards '71: Best Sound. *MGM, TLF*

Diamond's Edge 🦴🦴 *Just Ask for Diamond* **1988 (PG)** An adolescent private eye and his juvenescent brother snoop into the affairs of the Fat Man, and find out that the opera ain't over until they find out what's in the Fat Man's mysterious box of bonbons. A genre-parodying kid mystery, written by Horowitz, based on his novel, "The Falcon's Malteser." **83m/C VHS, Beta.** Susannah York, Peter Eyre, Patricia Hodge, Nickolas Grace; ***D:*** Stephen Bayly; ***W:*** Anthony Horowitz; ***M:*** Trevor Jones. *HBO*

Diamonds of the Night 🦴🦴🦴🦴 *Demanty Noci* **1964** A breakthrough masterpiece of the Czech new wave, about two young men escaping from a transport train to Auschwitz and scrambling for survival in the countryside. Surreal, powerfully expressionistic film, one of the most important of its time. In Czech with English subtitles. Accompanied by Nemec's short "A Loaf of Bread." **71m/B VHS, Beta.** *CZ* Ladislav Jansky, Antonin Kumbera, Ilse Bischofova; ***D:*** Jan Nemec; ***W:*** Arnost Lustig, Jan Nemec. *FCT*

Diamonds on Wheels 🦴🦴 **1973** A Disney film about three British teenagers, amid a big road rally, discovering stolen diamonds and getting pursued by gangsters. **84m/C VHS, Beta.** *DIS*

Diana: Her True Story 🦴🦴½ **1993** Britain's royals are held up to scandalous review in this made for tv adaptaion of Andrew Morton's sympathetic bio of the Princess of Wales. Taking Diana from her lonely childhood to her "fairytale" nuptials and subsequent disillusionment with being a royal, including her bulimia and half-hearted suicide attempts. Charles is portrayed as an arrogant, emotional cold fish, only interested in farming and continuing his liaison with Camilla Parker-Bowles. Handsome production with appropriate inpersonations by the cast. **180m/C VHS.** Serena Scott Thomas, David Threlfall, Elizabeth Garvie, Jemma Redgrave, Tracy Hardwick, Anne Stallybrass, Jeffrey Harmer, Donald Douglas; ***D:*** Kevin Connor; ***W:*** Stephen Zito. *EHV*

Diane 🦴🦴 **1955** Overstuffed medieval drama featuring Turner as Diane de Poitier, the mistress of a sixteenth century French King. Moore plays the king in his Hollywood debut. Gorgeous sets and costumes couldn't boost this film at the box office, which had disappointing figures in spite of the expense bestowed upon it. Based on the novel "Diane de Poitier" by John Erskine. **110m/C VHS, LV.** Lana Turner, Pedro Armendariz Sr., Roger Moore, Marisa Pavan, Cedric Hardwicke, Torin Thatcher, Taina Elg, John Lupton, Henry Daniell, Sean McClory, Michael Ansara; ***D:*** David Miller; ***W:*** Christopher Isherwood; ***M:*** Miklos Rozsa. *MGM*

Diary of a Chambermaid 🦴🦴🦴 **1946** A chambermaid wants to marry a rich man and finds herself the object of desire of a poor servant willing to commit murder for her. Excellent comic drama, but very stylized in direction and set design. Produced during Renoir's years in Hollywood. Adapted from a story by Octave Mirbeau, later turned into a play. Remade in 1964 by Luis Bumel. **86m/B VHS.** Paulette Goddard, Burgess Meredith, Hurd Hatfield, Francis Lederer, Judith Anderson, Florence Bates, Almira Sessions, Reginald Owen; ***D:*** Jean Renoir. *REP, FCT*

Diary of a Chambermaid 🦴🦴🦴½ *Le Journal d'une Femme de Chambre; Il Diario di una Cameriera* **1964** Vintage Bunuelian social satire about a young girl taking a servant's job in a provincial French family, and easing into an atmosphere of sexual hypocrisy and decadence. In French with English subtitles. Remake of the 1946 Jean Renoir film. **97m/C VHS, Beta, LV.** *FR* Jeanne Moreau, Michel Piccoli, Georges Geret, Francoise Lugagne, Daniel Ivernel; ***D:*** Luis Bunuel; ***W:*** Luis Bunuel, Jean-Claude Carriere. *INJ, APD, IME*

Diary of a Country Priest 🦴🦴🦴½ *Le Journal d'un Cure de Campagne* **1950** With "Balthazar" and "Mouchette," this is one of Bresson's greatest, subtlest films, treating the story of an alienated, unrewarded young priest with his characteristic austerity and Catholic humanism. In French and English subtitles. **120m/B VHS, Beta.** *FR* Claude Layou, Jean Riveyre, Nicole Ladmiral; ***D:*** Robert Bresson; ***W:*** Robert Bresson. *DVT, APD, INJ*

Diary of a Hitman 🦴🦴½ **1991 (R)** A hitman is hired to knock off the wife and child of a commodities broker who claims his wife is a drug addict and the infant is a crack baby and not his. The hired killer wants out of the business, but needs to pull off one more job for a down payment on his apartment. Beset by doubts, he breaks conduct by conversing with the victim and discovers the broker lied. Based on the play "Insider's Price" by Pressman. **90m/C VHS, LV.** Forest Whitaker, James Belushi, Sherilyn Fenn, Sharon Stone, Seymour Cassel, Lewis Smith, Lois Chiles, John Bedford-Lloyd; ***D:*** Roy London; ***W:*** Kenneth Pressman; ***M:*** Michel Colombier. *COL*

Diary of a Lost Girl 🦴🦴🦴½ **1929** The second Louise Brooks/G.W. Pabst collaboration (after "Pandora's Box") in which a frail but mesmerizing German girl plummets into a life of hopeless degradation. Dark and gloomy, the film chronicles the difficulties she faces, from rape to an unwanted pregnancy and prostitution. Based on the popular book by Margarete Boehme. Silent. Made after flapper Brooks left Hollywood to pursue greater opportunities and more challenging roles under Pabst's guidance. **99m/B VHS, Beta, LV.** *GE* Louise Brooks, Fritz Rasp, Josef Rovensky, Sybille Schmitz; ***D:*** G.W. Pabst. *GPV, MRV, VDM*

Diary of a Mad Housewife 🦴🦴🦴 **1970 (R)** Despairing of her miserable family life, a housewife has an affair with a writer only to find him to be even more selfish and egotistical than her no-good husband. Snodgress plays her character perfectly, hearing the insensitive absurdity of her husband and her lover over and over again, enjoying her martyrdom even as it drives her crazy. **94m/C VHS, Beta.** Carrie Snodgress, Richard Benjamin, Frank Langella; ***D:*** Frank Perry. Golden Globe Awards '71: Best Actress—Musical/Comedy (Snodgress); National Board of Review Awards '70: 10 Best Films of the Year, Best Supporting Actor (Langella); Nominations: Academy Awards '70: Best Actress (Snodgress). *GKK*

Diary of a Mad Old Man 🦴🦴 *Dagboek Van Een Oude Dwaas* **1988 (PG-13)** A wistful drama about an old man who's lost everything except his desire for his daughter-in-law, which sends him into fits of nostalgia. **93m/C VHS, Beta.** Derek De Lint, Ralph Michael, Beatie Edney. *MED*

Diary of a Madman 🦴🦴 **1963** Price is once again possessed by an evil force in this gothic thriller. Fairly average Price vehicle, based on Guy de Maupassant's story. **96m/C VHS, Beta.** Vincent Price, Nancy Kovack, Chris Warfield, Ian Wolfe, Nelson Olmstead; ***D:*** Reginald LeBorg. *MGM, FCT*

Diary of a Rebel 🦴 **1984** A fictional account of the rise of Cuban rebel leader Che Guevara. **89m/C VHS, Beta.** John Ireland, Francesco Rabal. *NO*

Diary of a Teenage Hitchhiker 🦴 **1982** Teen girl ignores family restrictions and police warnings about a homicidal rapist stalking the area and continues to thumb rides to her job at a beach resort. One night she's picked up for ride she'll never forget. **96m/C VHS, Beta.** Charlene Tilton, Dick Van Patten; ***D:*** Ted Post. *NO*

Diary of a Young Comic 🦴🦴 **1979** New York comedian searches for the meaning of lunacy. He finds it after Improvisation in Los Angeles. **74m/C VHS, Beta.** Stacy Keach, Dom DeLuise, Richard Lewis, Bill Macy, George Jessel, Gary Muledeer, Nina Van Pallandt; ***D:*** Gary Weis. *NO*

The Diary of Anne Frank 🦴🦴🦴½ **1959** In June 1945, a liberated Jewish refugee returns to the hidden third floor of an Amsterdam factory where he finds the diary kept by his youngest daughter, Anne. The document recounts their years in hiding from the Nazis. Based on the actual diary of 13-year-old Anne Frank, killed in a death camp during WWII. **150m/B VHS, Beta, LV.** Millie Perkins, Joseph Schildkraut, Shelley Winters, Richard Beymer, Gusti Huber, Ed Wynn, Lou Jacobi, Diane Baker; ***D:*** George Stevens; ***C:*** William Mellor. Academy Awards '59: Best Art Direction/Set Decoration (B & W), Best Black and White Cinematography, Best Supporting Actress (Winters); Nominations: Academy Awards '59: Best Costume Design (B & W), Best Director (Stevens), Best Picture, Best Supporting Actor (Wynn), Best Original Score. *KUI, FOX, BTV*

Diary of Forbidden Dreams 🦴🦴🦴 *What?; Che?* **1973 (R)** A beautiful young girl finds herself drawn into bizarre incidents at an eccentric millionaire's mansion that cause her to go insane. Set on the Italian Riviera, it's the most offbeat rendition of "Alice in Wonderland" you're apt to find. Unfortunately, the convoluted plot lessens its appeal. Unedited version, under the original title "What!," released at 113 minutes, is also available. **94m/C VHS, Beta.** *IT* Marcello Mastroianni, Hugh Griffith, Sydne Rome, Roman Polanski; ***D:*** Roman Polanski; ***W:*** Roman Polanski, Gerard Brach. *VDM, TWE, FCT*

Diary of the Dead 🦴 **198? (PG)** A newlywed kills his aggravating mother-in-law, only to have her repeatedly return from the grave. **93m/C Beta.** Hector Elizondo, Geraldine Fitzgerald, Salome Jens; ***D:*** Arvin Brown. *NO*

Dick Barton, Special Agent 🦴 **1948** Dick Barton is called in when a mad scientist threatens to attack London with germ-carrying bombs. The first film production for Hammer Studios, later to be known for its horror classics. **70m/B VHS, Beta.** *GB* Don Stannard, Geoffrey Ford, Jack Shaw; ***D:*** Alfred Goulding. *SNC, VYY*

Dick Barton Strikes Back 🦴🦴½ **1948** "Mr. French" Cabot has a nuclear weapon and is willing to use it; that is, until Dick Barton arrives to put the Frenchman out of commission. Generally considered the best of the Dick Barton film series. **73m/B VHS, Beta.** *GB* Don Stannard, Sebastian Cabot, Jean Lodge; ***D:*** Godfrey Grayson. *SNC, VYY*

Dick Tracy **1937** Serial, based on the comic-strip character, in fifteen chapters. Tracy tries to find his kidnapped brother as he faces the fiend "Spider." The first chapter is thirty minutes and each additional chapter is twenty minutes. **310m/B VHS, Beta, LV.** Ralph Byrd, Smiley Burnette, Irving Pichel, Jennifer Jones; ***D:*** John English. *SNC, VYY, VCI*

Dick Tracy 🦴🦴🦴½ **1990 (PG)** Beatty wears the caps of producer, director, and star, performing admirably on all fronts. One minor complaint: his Tracy is somewhat flat in comparison to the outstanding performances and makeup of the unique villains, especially Pacino. Stylistically superior, shot in only 7 colors, the timeless sets capture the essence rather than the reality of the city, successfully bringing the comic strip to life. Madonna is fine as the seductive Breathless Mahoney, belting out Stephen Sondheim like she was born to do it. People expecting the gothic technology of "Batman" may be disappointed, but moviegoers searching for a memory made real will be thrilled. ♫Sooner or Later. **105m/C VHS, Beta, LV.** Warren Beatty, Madonna, Charlie Korsmo, Glenne Headly, Al Pacino, Dustin Hoffman, James Caan, Mandy Patinkin, Paul Sorvino, Charles Durning, Dick Van Dyke, R.G. Armstrong, Catherine O'Hara, Estelle Parsons, Seymour Cassel, Michael J. Pollard, William Forsythe, Kathy Bates, James Tolkan; ***D:*** Warren Beatty; ***W:*** Jim Cash, Jack Epps Jr.; ***M:*** Danny Elfman, Stephen Sondheim. Academy Awards '90: Best Art Direction/Set Decoration, Best Makeup, Best Song ("Sooner or Later"); Nominations: Academy Awards '90: Best Cinematography, Best Costume Design, Best Sound, Best Supporting Actor (Pacino). *TOU, FCT, IME*

Dick Tracy, Detective 🦴🦴 **1945** The first Dick Tracy feature film, in which Splitface is on the loose, a schoolteacher is murdered, the Mayor is threatened, and a nutty professor uses a crystal ball to give Tracy the clues needed to connect the crimes. **62m/B VHS, Beta.** Morgan Conway, Anne Jeffreys, Mike Mazurki, Jane Greer, Lyle Latell; ***D:*** William (Lester Williams) Berke. *SNC, MED, VYY*

Dick Tracy, Detective/The Corpse Vanishes 🦴½ **1942** On one tape, the first Dick Tracy feature film and Lugosi's minor epic about a mad scientist using virgin's blood to restore youth to an aging countess. **126m/B VHS, Beta.** Bela Lugosi, Morgan Conway, Luana Walters, Tristram Coffin, Mike Mazurki, Jane Greer, Lyle Latell; ***D:*** William (Lester Williams) Berke. *AOV*

Dick Tracy Double Feature #1 1945 Mystery-adventure double feature presents Chester Gould's popular comic strip hero in live action. Includes "Dick Tracy, Detective" and "Dick Tracy's Dilemma." **122m/B VHS, Beta.** Ralph Byrd, Lyle Latell, Morgan Conway, Anne Jeffreys. *VCI*

Dick Tracy Double Feature #2 🦴🦴 **1947** Chester Gould's famous comic strip character is personified in "Dick Tracy Meets Gruesome" and "Dick Tracy vs. Cueball," a double-feature videocassette featuring Dick Tracy battling two of his archenemies. **127m/B VHS, Beta.** Boris Karloff, Ralph Byrd, Morgan Conway, Anne Jeffreys. *VCI*

Dick Tracy Meets Gruesome 🦴🦴 *Dick Tracy's Amazing Adventure; Dick Tracy Meets Karloff* **1947** Gruesome and his partner in crime, Melody, stage a bank robbery using the secret formula of Dr. A. Tomic. Tracy has to solve the case before word gets out and people rush to withdraw their savings, destroying civilization as we know it. **66m/B VHS, Beta.** Boris Karloff, Ralph Byrd, Lyle Latell; ***D:*** John Rawlins. *NOS, MRV, SNC*

Dick Tracy Returns 1938 15-chapter serial. Public Enemy Paw Stark and his gang set out on a wave of crime that brings them face to face with dapper Dick. **100m/B VHS, Beta, LV.** Ralph Byrd, Charles Middleton; ***D:*** William Witney. *VCI, IME, MLB*

Dick Tracy: The Original Serial, Vol. 1 🦴🦴🦴 **1937** The first seven parts of the original popular serial. The comic strip character comes to life and tries to stop the spider, a dangerous criminal. **150m/B VHS, Beta.** Ralph Byrd, Smiley Burnette, Kay Hughes, Francis X. Bushman, Lee Van Atta; ***D:*** Ray Taylor; ***W:*** Alan James. *GKK*

Dick Tracy: The Original Serial, Vol. 2 🦴🦴🦴 **1937** The last eight chapters of the highly acclaimed serial. Tracy is still tracking down the Spider in this action-packed adventure. **160m/B VHS, Beta.** Ralph Byrd, Smiley Burnette, Kay Hughes, Francis X. Bushman, Lee Van Atta; ***D:*** Ray Taylor; ***W:*** Alan James. *GKK*

Dick Tracy: The Spider Strikes 1937 Dick Tracy, his bumbling sidekick, and his beautiful, brainy assistant go up against the master criminal, The Spider. **60m/B VHS, Beta.** Ralph Byrd, Francis X. Bushman. *KAR*

Dick Tracy vs. Crime Inc. 1941 Dick Tracy encounters many difficulties when he tries to track down a criminal who can make himself invisible. A serial in 15 chapters. **100m/B VHS, Beta, LV.** Ralph Byrd, Ralph Morgan, Michael Owen; ***D:*** William Witney; ***W:*** John English. *VCI, IME, MLB*

Dick Tracy vs. Cueball 🦴🦴 **1946** Dick Tracy has his work cut out for him when the evil gangster Cueball appears on the scene. Based on Chester Gould's comic strip. **62m/B VHS, Beta.** Morgan Conway, Anne Jeffreys; ***D:*** Gordon Douglas. *NOS, VCI, VYY*

Dick Tracy's Dilemma 🦴🦴 *Mark of the Claw* **1947** The renowned police detective Dick Tracy tries to solve a case involving the Claw. Based on the Chester Gould comic strip. **60m/B VHS, Beta.** Ralph Byrd, Lyle Latell, Kay Christopher, Jack Lambert, Ian Keith, Jimmy Conlin; ***D:*** John Rawlins. *MRV, VCI, VYY*

Dick Turpin 🦴🦴½ **1925** In this rare film, Mix plays the famed English highwayman who seeks adventure in historical Britain. **60m/B VHS, Beta.** Tom Mix, Alan Hale; ***D:*** John Blystone. *GVV*

Didn't You Hear? 🦴 **1983 (PG)** An alienated college student discovers that dreams have a life of their own when he becomes immersed in his own fantasy world. **94m/C VHS, Beta.** Dennis Christopher, Gary Busey, Cheryl Waters, John Kauffman. *PSM*

Die! Die! My Darling! 🦴½ *Fanatic* **1965** A young widow visits her mad ex-mother-in-law in a remote English village, and is imprisoned by the mourning woman as revenge for her son's death. Bankhead's last role. **97m/C Beta.** *GB* Tallulah Bankhead, Stefanie Powers, Peter Vaughan, Maurice Kaufman, Donald Sutherland, Gwendolyn Watts, Yootha Joyce, Winifred Dennis; ***D:*** Silvio Narizzano; ***W:*** Richard Matheson. *COL, MLB*

Die Grosse Freiheit Nr. 7 🦴½ **1945** A man tries to stop his niece's love affair with a sailor. Nazi propaganda minister Goebbels banned this film in Germany, since it showed German soldiers getting drunk and also had Hildebrand cast as a prostitute. After the war, however, it enjoyed great popularity throughout Germany. Albers sings the classic "Auf der Reeperbahn." In German with no English translation. **100m/C VHS, Beta.** *GE* Hans Albers, Hilde Hildebrand. *IHF*

Die Hard 🦴🦴🦴 **1988 (R)** High-voltage action thriller pits a lone New York cop against a band of ruthless high-stakes terrorists who attack and hold hostage the employees of a large corporation as they celebrate Christmas in a new L.A. high rise. It's just as unbelievable as it sounds, but you'll love it anyway. Rickman, who later charmed audiences as the villain in "Robin Hood: Prince of Thieves," turns in a marvelous performance as the chief bad guy. Based on the novel "Nothing Lasts Forever" by Roderick Thorp. **114m/C VHS, Beta, LV.** Bruce Willis, Bonnie Bedelia, Alan Rickman, Alexander Godunov, Paul Gleason, William Atherton, Reginald Vel Johnson, Hart Bochner, James Shigeta, Mary Ellen Trainor, De'voreaux White, Robert Davi, Rick Ducommun; ***D:*** John McTiernan; ***W:*** Jeb Stuart, Steven E. de Souza; ***C:*** Jan De Bont; ***M:*** Michael Kamen. Nominations: Academy Awards '88: Best Film Editing, Best Sound. *FOX*

Die Hard 2: Die Harder 🦴🦴🦴 **1990 (R)** Fast, well-done sequel brings another impossible situation before the wise-cracking, tough-cookie cop. Our hero tangles with a group of terrorists at an airport under siege, while his wife remains in a plane circling above as its fuel dwindles. Obviously a repeat of the plot and action of the first "Die Hard," with references to the former in the script. While the bad guys lack the fiendishness of their predecessors, this installment features energetic and finely acted performances. Fairly gory, especially the icicle-in-the-eyeball scene. Adapted from the novel "58 Minutes" by Walter Wager and characters created by Roderick Thorp. **124m/C VHS, LV.** Bruce Willis, William Atherton, Franco Nero, Bonnie Bedelia, John Amos, Reginald Vel Johnson, Dennis Franz, Art Evans, Fred Dalton Thompson, William Sadler, Sheila McCarthy, Robert Patrick, John Leguizamo, Robert Costanzo, Tom Verica; ***D:*** Renny Harlin; ***W:*** Doug Richardson, Steven E. de Souza; ***M:*** Michael Kamen. *FOX*

Die Hard: With a Vengeance 🦴🦴½ *Die Hard 3* **1995 (R)** Third time is not a charm in the "Die Hard" series. McClane (Willis) is back home in the Big Apple and having another bad day. More Eurotrash terrorists, led by the brilliant and vengeful Simon (Irons), are out to blow things up, snag some gold, and make life miserable for McClane and his reluctant partner, Zeus Carver (Jackson). The claustrophobic settings of the first two outings have been replaced by the exhausting expanse of New York City, to good effect, but frenetic action scenes and good chemistry between Willis and Jackson don't quite compensate for a lackluster script and more cartoony feel. Jackson brings a fresh perspective and vitality to what will probably be the last ride of John McClane. **131m/C VHS, LV.** Bruce Willis, Samuel L. Jackson, Jeremy Irons, Graham Greene, Colleen Camp, Larry Bryggman, Tony Peck, Nick Wyman, Sam Phillips; ***D:*** John McTiernan; ***W:*** Jonathan Hensleigh; ***M:*** Michael Kamen. Nominations: MTV Movie Awards '96: Best Action Sequence. *FXV*

Die Laughing *Woof!* **1980 (PG)** A cab driver unwittingly becomes involved in murder, intrigue, and the kidnapping of a monkey that has memorized a scientific formula that can destroy the world. Writer/actor/composer Benson might consider renaming it "Die from Embarassment." **108m/C VHS, Beta.** Robby Benson, Charles Durning, Bud Cort, Elsa Lanchester, Peter Coyote; ***D:*** Jeff Werner; ***W:*** Robby Benson, Scott Parker; ***M:*** Robby Benson. *WAR*

Die, Monster, Die! 🦴🦴 *Monster of Terror* **1965** A reclusive scientist experiments with a radioactive meteorite and gains bizarre powers. Karloff is great in this adaptation of H.P. Lovecraft's "The Color Out of Space." **80m/C VHS, LV.** *GB* Boris Karloff, Nick Adams, Suzan Farmer, Patrick Magee, Freda Jackson, Terence de Marney; ***D:*** Daniel Haller; ***M:*** Don Banks. *NO*

Die Screaming, Marianne 🦴 *Die, Beautiful Marianne* **1973** A girl is on the run from her father, a crooked judge, who wants to kill her before her 21st birthday, when she will inherit evidence that will put him away for life. **81m/C VHS, Beta.** *GB* Michael Rennie, Susan George, Karin Dor; ***D:*** Pete Walker. *UNI*

Die Sister, Die! 🦴 **1974** Thriller about a gothic mansion with an eerie secret in the basement features a battle between a senile, reclusive sister and her disturbed, tormenting brother. **88m/C VHS, Beta.** Jack Ging, Edith Atwater, Antoinette Bower, Kent Smith, Robert Emhardt; ***D:*** Randall Hood. *NO*

Die Watching 🦴½ **1993 (R)** Sleazy erotic thriller about a video director (Atkins) who not only likes to film some hot Hollywood babes but may also like to kill them as well. His latest discovery just could be the next victim. **92m/C VHS.** Christopher Atkins, Vali Ashton, Tim Thomerson, Carlos Palomino, Mike Jacobs Jr.; ***D:*** Charles Davis; ***W:*** Kenneth J. Hall. *TRI*

A Different Kind of Love 🦴 **1985** A romantic novel on tape, in modern settings. Love, frustration, tragedy. **60m/C Beta.** Joyce Redman. *PSM*

Different Story 🦴🦴½ **1978 (PG)** Romance develops when a lesbian real estate agent offers a homosexual chauffeur a job with her firm. Resorts to stereotypes when the characters decide to marry. **107m/C VHS, Beta.** Perry King, Meg Foster, Valerie Curtin, Peter Donat, Richard Bull; ***D:*** Paul Aaron. *SUE, NLC*

Digby, the Biggest Dog in the World 🦴 **1973 (G)** Poor comedy-fantasy about Digby, a sheepdog, who wanders around a scientific laboratory, drinks an experimental fluid, and grows and grows and grows. **88m/C VHS, Beta.** *GB* Jim Dale, Angela Douglas, Spike Milligan, Dinsdale Landen; ***D:*** Joseph McGrath; ***M:*** Edwin Astley. *PSM*

Digger 🦴🦴½ **1994 (PG)** Digger (Hann-Byrd) arrives at a Pacific Northwest island to stay with relatives, including his Grandma (Dukakis) who's being romanced by the fun-loving Arthur (Nielsen). He makes friends with another youth who turns out to have a terminal heart ailment. **92m/C VHS.** Adam Hann-Byrd, Olympia Dukakis, Leslie Nielsen, Joshua Jackson, Barbara Williams, Timothy Bottoms; ***D:*** Robert Turner; ***W:*** Rodney Gibbons; ***M:*** Todd Boekelheide. *PAR*

Digging Up Business *Woof!* **1991 (PG)** Johnson tries to save the family funeral home business from financial ruin with some unique interment services. This film needs a decent burial. **89m/C VHS.** Lynn-Holly Johnson, Billy Barty, Ruth Buzzi, Murray Langston, Yvonne Craig, Gary Owens; ***D:*** Mark Byers. *NO*

Diggstown ☙☙½ **1992 (R)** Lightweight, good-natured sports comedy about a boxing scam. Con man Gabriel Caine (Woods), fresh out of prison, heads for Diggstown and the unregulated boxing matches arranged by town boss, John Gillon (Dern). The bet is that Caine's one boxer can beat any 10 boxers, chosen by Gillon, in a 24-hour period. So Caine decides to hook up with an old friend, former prizefighter "Honey" Roy Palmer (Gosset Jr.), to run the scam of his life. Dern is sufficiently nasty and Woods his usual nervy self but it's Gossett Jr. who manages to hold everything together as the aging boxer. Based on the novel "The Diggstown Ringers" by Leonard Wise. **97m/C VHS, Beta, LV.** James Woods, Louis Gossett Jr., Bruce Dern, Oliver Platt, Heather Graham, Randall "Tex" Cobb, Thomas Wilson Brown, Duane Davis, Willie Green, George Wallace; ***D:*** Michael Ritchie; ***W:*** Steven McKay; ***M:*** James Newton Howard. *MGM*

Digital Man ☙½ **1994 (R)** High-tech military super-soldier prototype has his programming sabotaged and a team of human and robotic commmandoes must prevent him from starting WWIII. **95m/C VHS.** Ken Olandt, Adam Baldwin, Ed Lauter, Matthias Hues, Kristen Dalton, Paul Gleason; ***D:*** Phillip J. Roth; ***W:*** Phillip J. Roth, Ronald Schmidt. *REP*

Dillinger ☙☙☙ **1945** John Dillinger's notorious career, from street punk to public enemy number one, receives a thrilling fast-paced treatment. Tierney turns in a fine performance in this interesting account of the criminal life. **70m/C VHS, Beta.** Lawrence Tierney, Edmund Lowe, Anne Jeffreys, Elisha Cook Jr.; ***D:*** Max Nosseck; ***W:*** Philip Yordan. Nominations: Academy Awards '45: Best Original Screenplay. *FOX, FCT*

Dillinger ☙☙½ **1973 (R)** The most colorful period of criminality in America is brought to life in this story of bank-robber John Dillinger, "Baby Face" Nelson, and the notorious "Lady in Red." **106m/C VHS, Beta, LV.** Warren Oates, Michelle Phillips, Richard Dreyfuss, Cloris Leachman, Ben Johnson, Harry Dean Stanton; ***D:*** John Milius; ***W:*** John Milius. *LIV, VES*

Dillinger ☙☙½ **1991** Harmon stars as the Depression-era bank robber, who became public enemy number one, in this TV gangster story. Fenn's girlfriend Billy Frenchette, with Patton particularly beady-eyed as G-man Melvin Purvis. **95m/C VHS.** Mark Harmon, Sherilyn Fenn, Will Patton, Patricia Arquette, Vince Edwards, Bruce Abbott; ***D:*** Rupert Wainwright; ***C:*** Donald M. Morgan. *WAR*

Dillinger and Capone ☙☙½ **1995 (R)** Supposedly the FBI has killed the wrong Dillinger and the gangster decides to make a new life. But his old friend Al Capone, newly released from prison, is holding Dillinger's wife and son hostage as insurance that first he'll retrieve $15 million from a mob-owned Chicago bank. **95m/C VHS, LV.** Martin Sheen, F. Murray Abraham, Catherine Hicks, Stephen Davies, Don Stroud, Clint Howard; ***D:*** Jon Purdy; ***W:*** Michael B. Druxman. *NHO*

Dim Sum: A Little Bit of Heart ☙☙☙ **1985 (PG)** The second independent film from the director of "Chan Is Missing." A Chinese-American mother and daughter living in San Francisco's Chinatown confront the conflict between traditional Eastern ways and modern American life. Gentle, fragile picture made with humor and care. In English and Chinese with subtitles. **88m/C VHS, Beta, LV.** Laureen Chew, Kim Chew, Victor Wong, Ida F.O. Chong, Cora Miao, John Nishio, Joan Chen; ***D:*** Wayne Wang; ***W:*** Terrel Seltzer; ***M:*** Todd Boekelheide. *FCT, IME, INJ*

Dimples ☙☙½ **1936 (PG)** When Shirley's pickpocket grandfather is caught red-handed, she steps in, takes the blame, and somehow ends up in show business. Re-issued version is rated. Also available colorized. ♫Hey, What Did the Bluebird Say?; He Was a Dandy; Picture Me Without You; Oh Mister Man Up in the Moon; Dixie-Anna; Get On Board; Swing Low Sweet Chariot. **78m/B VHS, Beta.** Shirley Temple, John Carradine, Frank Morgan, Helen Westley, Berton Churchill, Robert Kent, Delma Byron; ***D:*** William A. Seiter. *FOX*

Diner ☙☙☙½ **1982 (R)** A group of old high school friends meet at "their" Baltimore diner to find that more has changed than the menu. A bittersweet look at the experiences of a group of Baltimore post-teenagers growing up, circa 1959. Particularly notable was Levinson's casting of "unknowns" who have since become household names. Features many humorous moments and fine performances. **110m/C VHS, Beta, LV.** Steve Guttenberg, Daniel Stern, Mickey Rourke, Kevin Bacon, Ellen Barkin, Timothy Daly, Paul Reiser, Michael Tucker; ***D:*** Barry Levinson; ***C:*** Peter Sova. National Society of Film Critics Awards '82: Best Supporting Actor (Rourke); Nominations: Academy Awards '82: Best Original Screenplay. *MGM*

Dingaka ☙☙½ **1965** A controversial drama from the writer and director of "The Gods Must Be Crazy" about a South African tribesman who avenges his daughter's murder by tribal laws, and is then tried by white man's laws. A crusading white attorney struggles to acquit him. **96m/C VHS, Beta.** Stanley Baker, Juliet Prowse, Ken Gampu; ***D:*** Jamie Uys. *COL, NLC, FCT*

The Dining Room ☙☙½ **1986** Six performers play more than 50 roles in this adaptation of A.R. Gurney Jr.'s play set in a dining room, where people live out dramatic and comic moments in their lives. From the "American Playhouse" series. **90m/C VHS, Beta.** Remak Ramsay, Pippa Perthree, John Shea, Frances Sternhagen; ***D:*** Allan Goldstein. *PBS, ACA*

Dinner at Eight ☙☙☙☙ **1933** A social-climbing woman and her husband throw a dinner party for various members of the New York elite. During the course of the evening, all of the guests reveal something about themselves. Special performances all around, especially Barrymore, Dressler, and Harlow. Superb comedic direction by Cukor. Adapted from the play by Edna Ferber and George Kaufman. **110m/C VHS, Beta, LV, 8mm.** John Barrymore, Lionel Barrymore, Wallace Beery, Madge Evans, Jean Harlow, Billie Burke, Marie Dressler, Phillips Holmes, Jean Hersholt, Lee Tracy, Edmund Lowe, Karen Morley, May Robson; ***D:*** George Cukor; ***W:*** Herman J. Mankiewicz, Frances Marion, Donald Ogden Stewart; ***C:*** William H. Daniels. *MGM*

Dinner at Eight ☙☙ **1989** A social-climbing romance novelist throws an elegant dinner party. Made for television remake of the 1933 film does not compare well. **100m/C VHS, Beta.** Lauren Bacall, Charles Durning, Ellen Greene, Harry Hamlin, John Mahoney, Marsha Mason, Tim Kazurinsky; ***D:*** Ron Lagomarsino. *TTC*

Dinner at the Ritz ☙☙½ **1937** Daughter of a murdered Parisian banker vows to find his killer with help from her fiance. **78m/B VHS, Beta.** *GB* David Niven, Annabella, Paul Lukas, Patricia Medina; ***D:*** Harold Schuster. *NOS, MRV, VYY*

Dino ☙½ **1957** Social worker joins a young woman in helping a seventeen-year-old delinquent re-enter society. **96m/B VHS, Beta.** Sal Mineo, Brian Keith, Susan Kohner; ***D:*** Thomas Carr. *REP*

Dinosaur Island ☙ **1993 (R)** Five military men survive a plane crash and discover an island where scantily-clad (leather bikinis being the fashion choice) lascivious ladies live. Will the awesome power of testosterone overcome the fierce dinosaurs which stand between the men and their objects of desire? **85m/C VHS.** Ross Hagen, Richard Gabai, Antonia Dorian, Peter Spellos, Tom Shell, Griffin Drew, Steve Barkett, Toni Naples; ***D:*** Jim Wynorski, Fred Olen Ray; ***W:*** Bob Sheridan, Christopher Wooden. *NHO, HVL*

Dinosaurus! ☙ **1960** Large sadistic dinosaurs appear in the modern world. They eat, burn, and pillage their way through this film. Also includes a romance between a Neanderthal and a modern-age woman. **85m/C VHS, Beta.** Ward Ramsey, Kristina Hanson, Paul Lukather; ***D:*** Irvin S. Yeaworth Jr. *NWV, SNC*

Diplomaniacs ☙☙½ **1933** Wheeler and Woolsey, official barbers on an Indian reservation, are sent to the Geneva peace conference to represent the interests of their tribe. Slim plot nevertheless provides quite a few laughs. Fun musical numbers. **62m/B VHS, Beta, LV.** Bert Wheeler, Robert Woolsey, Marjorie White, Hugh Herbert; ***D:*** William A. Seiter; ***W:*** Joseph L. Mankiewicz, Henry Myers; ***M:*** Max Steiner. *CCB, IME, TTC*

Diplomatic Courier ☙☙☙ **1952** Cold-war espionage saga has secret agent Power attempting to re-steal sensitive documents from the hands of Soviet agents. Involved and exciting thriller. Michael Ansara, Charles Bronson and Lee Marvin made brief appearanes. **97m/B VHS.** Tyrone Power, Patricia Neal, Stephen McNally, Hildegarde Neff, Karl Malden; ***D:*** Henry Hathaway. *TCF*

Diplomatic Immunity ☙½ **1991 (R)** Vicious killer gets off scot-free due to his diplomatic immunity. That is, until the victim's ex-soldier father follows this low-life to the jungles of Paraguay to exact revenge. A heap o' action. **95m/C VHS, Beta, LV.** Bruce Boxleitner, Billy Drago, Meg Foster, Robert Forster; ***D:*** Peter Maris. *FRH, IME*

Direct Hit ☙☙½ **1993 (R)** A CIA assassin discovers retiring is not an option. John Hatch (Forsythe) decides he wants out, particularly when his next kill, Savannah (Champa), turns out to be an innocent pawn. So Hatch turns protector and decides to best the agency at its own deadly game. **91m/C VHS, LV.** William Forsythe, Richard Norton, Jo Champa, John Aprea, Juliet Landau, George Segal; ***D:*** Joseph Merhi; ***W:*** Jacobsen Hart. *REP*

Dirkham Detective Agency ☙½ **1983** Three children team up to form the Dirkham Detective Agency and are hired by a veterinarian to recover two dognapped poodles. **60m/C VHS, Beta.** Sally Kellerman, Stan Shaw, John Quade, Gordon Jump, Randy Morton. *NO*

Dirt Bike Kid ☙½ **1986 (PG)** A precocious brat is stuck with a used motorbike that has a mind of its own. Shenanigans follow in utterly predictable fashion as he battles bankers and bikers with his bad bike. **91m/C VHS, Beta, LV, 8mm.** Peter Billingsley, Anne Bloom, Stuart Pankin, Patrick Collins, Sage Parker, Chad Sheets; ***D:*** Hoite C. Caston; ***W:*** Lewis Colick, David Brandes. *COL, NLC*

Dirt Gang ☙ **1971 (R)** A motorcycle gang terrorizes the members of a film crew on location in the desert. **89m/C VHS, Beta.** Paul Carr, Michael Pataki, Michael Forest; ***D:*** Jerry Jameson. *MPI*

Dirty Dancing ☙☙☙ **1987 (PG-13)** An innocent 17-year-old (Grey) is vacationing with her parents in the Catskills in 1963. Bored with the program at the hotel, she finds the real fun at the staff dances. Falling for the sexy dance instructor (Swayze), she discovers love, sex, and rock and roll dancing. An old story, with little to save it, but Grey and Swayze are appealing, the dance sequences fun, and the music great. Swayze, classically trained in ballet, also performs one of the sound-track songs. ♫(I've Had) the Time of My Life; Be My Baby; Big Girls Don't Cry; Cry to Me; Do You Love Me?; Hey Baby; Hungry Eyes; In the Still of the Nite; Love is Strange. **97m/C VHS, Beta, LV.** Patrick Swayze, Jennifer Grey, Cynthia Rhodes, Jerry Orbach, Jack Weston, Jane Brucker, Kelly Bishop, Lonny Price, Charles "Honi" Coles, Bruce Morrow; ***D:*** Emile Ardolino; ***W:*** Eleanor Bergstein; ***M:*** John Morris. Academy Awards '87: Best Song ("(I've Had) the Time of My Life"); Golden Globe Awards '88: Best Song ("(I've Had) the Time of My Life"); Independent Spirit Awards '88: Best First Feature. *LIV, VES*

Dirty Dishes ☙☙☙ **1982 (R)** A French film sardonically examining the fruitless life of the average housewife as she confronts a series of bizarre but pointless experiences during the day. Dubbed and subtitled versions available. The director is the American daughter-in-law of the late Luis Bunuel. **99m/C VHS, Beta.** *FR* Carol Laurie, Pierre Santini; ***D:*** Joyce Bunuel. *SUE*

The Dirty Dozen 1967 (PG) A tough Army major is assigned to train and command twelve hardened convicts offered absolution if they participate in a suicidal mission into Nazi Germany in 1944. Well-made movie is a standout in its genre. Rough and gruff Marvin is good as the group leader. Three made-for-television sequels followed in the '80s. **149m/C VHS, Beta, LV.** Lee Marvin, Ernest Borgnine, Charles Bronson, Jim Brown, George Kennedy, John Cassavetes, Clint Walker, Donald Sutherland, Telly Savalas, Robert Ryan, Ralph Meeker, Richard Jaeckel, Trini Lopez; ***D:*** Robert Aldrich. Academy Awards '67: Best Sound Effects Editing; Nominations: Academy Awards '67: Best Film Editing, Best Sound, Best Supporting Actor (Cassavetes). *MGM, TLF*

The Dirty Dozen: The Deadly Mission ½ 1987 A second made-for-TV sequel to the '67 movie finds Borgnine ordering another suicide mission. Savalas (killed in the original, he's playing a new character) must pick 12 convicted army prisoners for an assault on a Nazi-held French monastery. Their mission is to rescue six scientists who are working on a deadly new nerve gas. Followed by "The Dirty Dozen: The Fatal Mission." **96m/C VHS.** Ernest Borgnine, Telly Savalas, Vince Edwards, Gary Graham, James Van Patten, Vincent Van Patten, Bo Svenson; ***D:*** Lee H. Katzin. *MGM*

The Dirty Dozen: The Fatal Mission ½ 1988 This third TV sequel has Borgnine learning of a plan to bring a group of high-ranking Nazis to Instanbul via the Orient Express. Naturally, he assigns Savalas the task of getting his motley gang together to thwart the Nazi schemes. To add intrigue, a female has joined the ranks of the Dirty Dozen and a spy may also have infiltrated the group. **91m/C VHS.** Ernest Borgnine, Telly Savalas, Hunt Block, Jeff Conaway, Erik Estrada, Ray "Boom Boom" Mancini, Heather Thomas, Alex Cord; ***D:*** Lee H. Katzin. *MGM*

The Dirty Dozen: The Next Mission ½ 1985 Disappointing made for television sequel to the 1967 hit, with Marvin reprising his role as the leader of the motley pack. In this installment, the rag-tag toughs are sent on yet another suicide mission inside Nazi Germany, this time to thwart an assassination attempt of Hitler. Followed by two more sequels. **97m/C VHS, Beta.** Lee Marvin, Ernest Borgnine, Richard Jaeckel, Ken Wahl, Larry Wilcox, Sonny Landham, Ricco Ross; ***D:*** Andrew V. McLaglen. *MGM*

Dirty Games ½ 1993 Nicola Kendra is part of a team sent to Africa to inspect a nuclear waste site. Once there, the scientists discover terrorists are plotting to blow up the nuclear complex unless Nicola and her new allies can prevent it. **97m/C VHS.** Jan-Michael Vincent, Valentina Vargas, Ronald France, Michael McGovern; ***D:*** Gray Hofmeyr. *AIP*

Dirty Gertie from Harlem U.S.A. 1946 All-black cast performs a variation of W. Somerset Maugham's "Rain." Gertie goes to Trinidad to hide out from her jilted boyfriend. **60m/B VHS, Beta.** Gertie LaRue, Spencer Williams Jr., Francine Everett. *VYY, DVT, VYY*

Dirty Hands *Les Innocents aux Mains Sales* 1976 A woman and her lover conspire to murder her husband. A must for fans of the sexy Schneider. Cinematography provides moments that are both interesting and eerie. **102m/C VHS.** *FR* Rod Steiger, Romy Schneider, Paul Giusti, Jean Rochefort, Hans-Christian Blech; ***D:*** Claude Chabrol. *FCT*

Dirty Harry ½ 1971 (R) Rock-hard cop Harry Callahan attempts to track down a psychopathic rooftop killer before a kidnapped girl dies. Harry abuses the murderer's civil rights, however, forcing the police to return the criminal to the streets, where he hijacks a school bus and Harry is called on once again. The only answer to stop this vicious killer seems to be death in cold blood, and Harry is just the man to do it. Taut, suspenseful direction by Siegel, who thoroughly understands Eastwood's on-screen character. Features Callahan's famous "Do you feel lucky?" line, the precursor to his "Go ahead, make my day." **103m/C VHS, Beta, LV, 8mm.** Clint Eastwood, Harry Guardino, John Larch, Andrew (Andy) Robinson, Reni Santoni, John Vernon; ***D:*** Donald Siegel; ***C:*** Bruce Surtees; ***M:*** Lalo Schifrin. *WAR, TLF*

Dirty Heroes *Dalle Ardenne All'Inferno* 1971 (R) A band of escaped WWII POWs battle the Nazis for a precious treasure in the war's final days. **117m/C VHS, Beta.** John Ireland, Curt Jurgens, Adolfo Celi, Daniela Bianchi, Michael Constantine; ***D:*** Alberto De Martino; ***M:*** Ennio Morricone. *NO*

Dirty Laundry *Woof!* 1987 (PG-13) Insipid wreck of a comedy about a klutz who accidentally gets his laundry mixed up with $1 million dollars in drug money. Features Olympians Lewis and Louganis. Never released theatrically. **81m/C VHS, Beta.** Leigh McCloskey, Jeanne O'Brien, Frankie Valli, Sonny Bono, Carl Lewis, Greg Louganis, Nicholas Worth; ***D:*** William Webb. *NO*

Dirty Mary Crazy Larry 1974 (PG) A racecar driver, his mechanic, and a sexy girl hightail it from the law after pulling off a heist. Great action, great fun, and an infamous surprise ending. **93m/C VHS, Beta, LV.** Peter Fonda, Susan George, Adam Roarke, Vic Morrow, Roddy McDowall; ***D:*** John Hough; ***W:*** Leigh Chapman. *FOX*

Dirty Mind of Young Sally *Woof!* 1972 (R) Sally's erotic radio program broadcasts from a mobile studio, which must stay one step ahead of the police. **84m/C VHS, Beta.** Sharon Kelly. *TPV*

Dirty Rotten Scoundrels 1988 (PG) A remake of the 1964 "Bedtime Story," in which two confidence tricksters on the Riviera endeavor to rip off a suddenly rich American woman, and each other. Caine and Martin are terrific, Martin has some of his best physical comedy ever, and Headly is charming as the prey who's always one step ahead of them. Fine direction from Oz, the man who brought us the voice of Yoda in "The Empire Strikes Back." **112m/C VHS, Beta, LV.** Steve Martin, Michael Caine, Glenne Headly, Anton Rodgers, Barbara Harris, Dana Ivey; ***D:*** Frank Oz; ***W:*** Dale Launer, Stanley Shapiro; ***C:*** Michael Ballhaus; ***M:*** Miles Goodman. *ORI*

Dirty Tricks ½ 1981 (PG) History professor Gould fights with bad guys for a letter written by George Washington. Thoroughly forgettable comedy lacking in laughs. **91m/C VHS, Beta.** *CA* Elliott Gould, Kate Jackson, Arthur Hill, Rich Little; ***D:*** Alvin Rakoff; ***W:*** William W. Norton Sr.; ***M:*** Hagood Hardy. *COL, SUE*

Dirty Work 1992 (R) A drug-dealing bail bondsman (Ashton) steals counterfeit money from the mob and then sets up his partner (Dobson) as the fall guy. Can Dobson survive long enough to set things straight? **88m/C VHS, Beta.** John Ashton, Kevin Dobson, Roxann Biggs, Donnelly Rhodes, Jim Byrnes, Mitchell Ryan; ***D:*** John McPherson; ***W:*** Aaron Julien. *PAR*

Disappearance 1981 (R) A hired assassin discovers an ironic link between his new target and his missing wife. **80m/C VHS, Beta.** *CA* Donald Sutherland, David Hemmings, John Hurt, Christopher Plummer, David Warner, Virginia McKenna; ***D:*** Stuart Cooper. *VES, RHI*

The Disappearance of Aimee 1976 Dramatic recreation of events surrounding the 1926 disappearance of evangelist Aimee Semple McPherson. She claimed she was abducted, but her mother insisted she ran away to have an affair. Excellent made for television movie with an exceptional cast. Originally to star Ann-Margret. **110m/C VHS, Beta.** Faye Dunaway, Bette Davis, James Sloyan, James Woods, John Lehne, Lelia Goldoni, Barry Brown, Severn Darden; ***W:*** Anthony Harvey. *LIV*

The Disappearance of Christina ½ 1993 (PG-13) Successful entrepreneur Joe Seldon (Stamos) is married to heiress Christina (Yarlett) and they seem to be the perfect couple. But when Christina mysteriously vanishes during a sailing trip, was it really an accident? Detective Nora Davis (Pounder) doesn't think so and naturally, Joe is suspect numero uno. **93m/C VHS, LV.** John Stamos, Kim Delaney, Robert Carradine, Claire Yarlett, CCH Pounder; ***D:*** Karen Arthur; ***W:*** Camille Thomasson. *MCA*

Disaster at Silo 7 1988 When the engine of a Titan missile goes on the fritz, the Air Force tries to prevent a nuclear disaster. Based on an actual Titan II missile incident near Little Rock, Arkansas. Made for television. **92m/C VHS.** Peter Boyle, Patricia Charbonneau, Perry King, Michael O'Keefe, Joe Spano, Dennis Weaver; ***D:*** Larry Elikann; ***W:*** Douglas Lloyd McIntosh; ***C:*** Roy Wagner. *TRI*

The Disciple ½ 1915 Vintage silent western wherein Hart's unsmiling good-bad guy tries to clean up a lawless town and win back his wife, who has shamelessly fallen in with a corrupt saloon-keeper. **80m/B VHS, Beta, 8mm.** William S. Hart, Dorothy Dalton, Robert McKim, Jean Hersholt; ***D:*** William S. Hart; ***W:*** Thomas Ince. *VYY, GPV*

Disciple of Death 1972 (R) Raven plays "The Stranger," a ghoul who sacrifices virgins to the Devil. **82m/C VHS, Beta.** *GB* Mike Raven, Ronald Lacey, Stephen Bradley, Virginia Wetherell; ***D:*** Tom Parkinson. *UNI*

Disclosure 1994 (R) Likable, responsible executive and family man (Douglas) finds himself sexually harassed by his ex-lover turned dragon-lady boss (Moore). But when he rejects her lusty come-on, she points the finger at him. One-dimensional characters and hollow material turn sexual harassment into a trivial issue. High-tech saga of corporate politics, while flashy, is nothing we haven't seen before. Douglas just can't pass up these "Regular Joe meets beautiful, horny babe, bad things happen" roles, can he? Based on the Michael Crichton novel. **129m/C VHS, LV.** Michael Douglas, Demi Moore, Donald Sutherland, Caroline Goodall, Dylan Baker, Dennis Miller, Rosemary Forsyth, Roma Maffia; ***D:*** Barry Levinson; ***W:*** Paul Attanasio; ***M:*** Ennio Morricone. Blockbuster Entertainment Awards '95: Drama Actress, Theatrical (Moore); Blockbuster Entertainment Awards '96: Drama Actress, Video (Moore); Nominations: MTV Movie Awards '95: Most Desirable Female (Moore), Best Villain (Moore). *WAR*

Disconnected ½ 1987 "Sorry, Wrong Number" is updated, with more than ample doses of sex and violence. **81m/C VHS, Beta.** Mark Walker. *NO*

Discontent ½ 1916 An early silent film by Lois Weber in which a cantankerous old vet goes to live with his wealthy nephew. The harmonious family life is disrupted by his meddling ways. **30m/B VHS, Beta.** ***D:*** Lois Weber. *GVV*

The Discovery Program ½ 1989 Four award-winning short films on one video: "Ray's Male Heterosexual Dance Hall," "Greasy Lake," "The Open Window," and "Hearts of Stone." The subjects range from humorous and offbeat to tragic and deadly serious. **106m/C VHS, Beta.** Academy Awards '87: Best Live Action Short Film ("Ray's Male Heterosexual Dance Hall"). *FCT*

The Discreet Charm of the Bourgeoisie *Le Charme Discret de la Bourgeoisie* 1972 (R) Bunuel in top form, satirizing modern society. These six characters are forever sitting down to dinner, yet they never eat. Dreams and reality, actual or contrived, prevent their feast. **100m/C VHS, Beta, LV.** *FR* Fernando Rey, Delphine Seyrig, Jean-Pierre Cassel, Bulle Ogier, Michel Piccoli, Stephane Audran, Luis Bunuel; ***D:*** Luis Bunuel; ***W:*** Luis Bunuel, Jean-Claude Carriere. Academy Awards '72: Best Foreign Language Film; British Academy Awards '73: Best Actress (Seyrig), Best Screenplay; National Board of Review Awards '72: 5 Best Foreign Films of the Year; National Society of Film Critics Awards '72: Best Director (Bunuel), Best Film; Nominations: Academy Awards '72: Best Story & Screenplay. *INJ, MED, APD*

Discretion Assured ½ 1993 (R) Successful businessman Trevor McCabe (York) finds himself in a romantic quandry with three women, leading to his involvement in embezzlement and murder. **97m/C VHS.** Michael York, Jennifer O'Neill, Dee Wallace Stone, Elizabeth Gracen; ***D:*** Odorico Mendes. *MNC*

Dishonored ½ 1931 Dated spy drama has Dietrich playing secret agent X-27 in WWI and masquerading on the side as a peasant girl. Although not one of the more famous Dietrich-Sternberg productions, its camp plot and Dietrich's lavish performance make it worth watching. Based on the infamous spy Mata Hari, who was shot by the French in 1917 for espionage. **91m/B VHS.** Marlene Dietrich, Victor McLaglen, Lew Cody, Gustav von Seyffertitz, Warner Oland, Barry Norton, Davison Clark, Wilfrid Lucas; ***D:*** Josef von Sternberg; ***W:*** Josef von Sternberg, Daniel N. Rubin; ***C:*** Lee Garmes. *MCA, FCT*

Dishonored Lady 🦴½ **1947** After her ex-boyfriend is murdered, a female art director finds that she's the number one suspect. When put on trial for the dastardly deed, she takes the fifth in this mediocre melodrama. **85m/B VHS, Beta.** Hedy Lamarr, Dennis O'Keefe, William Lundigan, John Loder; ***D:*** Robert Stevenson. *SNC, NOS, CAB*

Disney's Storybook Classics **1982** A collection of classic children's fables, featuring "Little Toot" (1948, excerpted from "Melody Time"), the story of a little harbor tugboat; "Chicken Little" (1943); "The Grasshopper and the Ant" (1934, a "Silly Symphony"); and "Peter and the Wolf" (1946, excerpted from "Make Mine Music"), a Disneyized version of Prokofiev's famous concert piece. **121m/C VHS, Beta.** Sterling Holloway, The Andrews Sisters. *DIS*

Disorderlies 🦴 **1987 (PG)** Members of the popular rap group cavort as incompetent hospital orderlies assigned to care for a cranky millionaire. Fat jokes abound with performances by the Fat Boys. **86m/C VHS, Beta, LV.** The Fat Boys, Ralph Bellamy; ***D:*** Michael A. Schultz; ***M:*** Anne Dudley. *WAR*

Disorderly Orderly 🦴½ **1964** When Jerry Lewis gets hired as a hospital orderly, nothing stands upright long with him around. Vintage slapstick Lewis running amuck in a nursing home. **90m/C VHS, Beta, LV.** Jerry Lewis, Glenda Farrell, Everett Sloane, Kathleen Freeman, Susan Oliver; ***D:*** Frank Tashlin. *PAR*

Disorganized Crime 🦴🦴 **1989 (R)** On the lam from the law, Bernsen attempts to organize a group of his ex-con buddies to pull off the perfect heist. Before the boys can organize, however, the cops are hot on Bernsen's trail, and he must vacate the meeting place. Good cast attempts to lift this movie beyond script. **101m/C VHS, Beta, LV.** Lou Diamond Phillips, Fred Gwynne, Corbin Bernsen, Ruben Blades, Hoyt Axton, Ed O'Neill, Daniel Roebuck, William Russ; ***D:*** Jim Kouf; ***M:*** David Newman. *TOU*

Disraeli 🦴🦴🦴 **1929** Arliss deservedly won the Best Actor Oscar for his title role as the famed British prime minister to Queen Victoria. This particular slice of the cunning statesman's life depicts his efforts to secure the Suez Canal for England against the Russians. Arliss' wife also played his screen spouse. One of Warner's earliest and best biographical pictures. Based on a play by Louis Napoleon Parker. **87m/B VHS.** George Arliss, Joan Bennett, Florence Arliss, Anthony Bushell, David Torrence, Doris Lloyd, Ivan Simpson, Gwendolyn Logan; ***D:*** Alfred E. Green; ***C:*** Lee Garmes. Academy Awards '30: Best Actor (Arliss); Nominations: Academy Awards '30: Best Picture, Best Writing. *MGM*

Distant Drums 🦴🦴 **1951** A small band of adventurers tries to stop the Seminole War in the Florida Everglades. **101m/C VHS.** Gary Cooper, Mari Aldon, Robert Barrat, Richard Webb, Ray Teal, Arthur Hunnicutt; ***D:*** Raoul Walsh; ***M:*** Max Steiner. *REP, FCT*

Distant Justice 🦴½ **1992 (R)** Tokyo police inspector Rio (Sugawara) is vacationing in Boston with his wife and daughter, where he can also visit old friend, Chief Bradfield (Kennedy). But Rio's wife is murdered and his daughter kidnapped by vicious drug dealer Roy Pennola (Carradine) and Bradfield assigns young officer Charlie Givens (Lutes) to see that Rio doesn't get himself killed as well. **91m/C VHS.** Bunta Sugawara, George Kennedy, David Carradine, Eric Lutes; ***D:*** Toru Murakawa. *COL*

Distant Thunder 🦴🦴🦴½ **1973** A bitter, unrelenting portrait of a small Bengali neighborhood as the severe famines of 1942, brought about by the "distant thunder" of WWII, take their toll. A mature achievement from Ray; in Bengali with English subtitles. **92m/C VHS, Beta.** *IN* Soumitra Chatterjee, Sandhya Roy, Babita, Gobinda Chakravarty, Romesh Mukerji; ***D:*** Satyajit Ray. Berlin International Film Festival '73: Golden Berlin Bear. *FCT*

Distant Thunder 🦴🦴 **1988 (R)** A scarred Vietnam vet, who has become a recluse, and his estranged son reunite in the Washington State wilderness, causing him to reflect on his isolation. Strong premise and cast watered down by weak script. **114m/C VHS, Beta, LV.** *CA* John Lithgow, Ralph Macchio, Kerrie Keane, Janet Margolin, Rick Rosenthal; ***D:*** Rick Rosenberg; ***C:*** Ralf Bode; ***M:*** Maurice Jarre. *PAR*

Distant Voices, Still Lives 🦴🦴🦴 **1988** A profoundly executed, disturbing film chronicling a British middle-class family through the maturation of the three children, under the dark shadow of their abusive, malevolent father. An evocative, heartbreaking portrait of British life from WWII on, and of the rhythms of dysfunctional families. A film festival favorite. **87m/C VHS, Beta, LV.** *GB* Freda Dowie, Pete Postlethwaite, Angela Walsh, Dean Williams, Lorraine Ashbourne; ***D:*** Terence Davies; ***W:*** Terence Davies. Los Angeles Film Critics Association Awards '89: Best Foreign Film. *LIV*

The Distinguished Gentleman 🦴🦴 **1992 (R)** A small-time con man (Murphy) manages to scam his way into a political career and winds up in Congress. The other characters serve mostly as foils for Murphy's comedic talent. Viewers will laugh despite the story's predictablity. **122m/C VHS, LV.** Eddie Murphy, Lane Smith, Sheryl Lee Ralph, Joe Don Baker, Victoria Rowell, Grant Shaud, Kevin McCarthy, Charles S. Dutton, James Garner; ***D:*** Jonathan Lynn; ***W:*** Marty Kaplan; ***M:*** Randy Edelman. *TOU*

Distortions 🦴🦴 **1987 (PG)** Hussey is a widow whose evil aunt (Laurie) is holding her hostage. What the film lacks in suspense throughout most of the movie is made up for in the end. **90m/C VHS, Beta.** Piper Laurie, Steve Railsback, Olivia Hussey, Edward Albert, Rita Gam, Terence Knox; ***D:*** Armand Mastroianni. *ACA*

Disturbance 🦴½ **1989** The two personas of a young schizophrenic get him entangled in a mysterious string of murders. **81m/C VHS, Beta.** Timothy Greeson, Lisa Geoffreion; ***D:*** Cliff Guest. *NO*

Disturbed 🦴 **1990 (R)** Lusty mental hospital director McDowell meets sex starved and suicidal Gidley in this less-than-stellar erotic creeper. Redeemed only by McDowell's performance and more evidence that the droog's career hasn't been just peachy since "Clockwork Orange." **96m/C VHS, LV.** Malcolm McDowell, Geoffrey Lewis, Priscilla Pointer, Pamela Gidley, Clint Howard; ***D:*** Charles Winkler; ***W:*** Emerson Bixby, Charles Winkler. *LIV*

Diva 🦴🦴🦴½ **1982 (R)** While at a concert given by his favorite star, a young French courier secretly tapes a soprano who has refused to record. The film follows the young man through Paris as he flees from two Japanese recording pirates, and a couple of crooked undercover police who are trying to cover-up for the chief who not only has a mistress, but runs a prostitution ring. Brilliant and dazzling photography compliment the eclectic soundtrack. **123m/C VHS, Beta, LV.** *FR* Frederic Andrei, Roland Bertin, Richard Bohringer, Gerard Darmon, Jacques Fabbri, Wilhelmenia Wiggins Fernandez, Dominique Pinon; ***D:*** Jean-Jacques Beineix; ***W:*** Jean-Jacques Beineix; ***C:*** Philippe Rousselot; ***M:*** Vladimir Cosma. Cesar Awards '82: Best Cinematography, Best Sound, Best Score; National Society of Film Critics Awards '82: Best Cinematography. *MGM, APD*

The Dive 🦴🦴 **1989 (PG-13)** Two North Sea oil-rig workers are trapped far below the waves when the lifeline to their diving bell snaps in rough seas. **90m/C VHS, Beta, LV.** Bjorn Sundquist, Frank Grimes, Einride Eidsvold, Michael Kitchen; ***D:*** Tristan De Vere Cole. *NO*

Dive Bomber 🦴🦴🦴 **1941** Exciting aviation film that focuses on medical problems related to flying. Flynn stars as an aviator-doctor who conducts experiments to eliminate pilot-blackout. MacMurray, Toomey, and Heydt perform well as three flyboys stationed in Hawaii. Great flying sequences filmed at San Diego's naval base with extra scenes shot at Pensacola. Warner Bros. released this film just months before the Japanese attacked Pearl Harbor. Based on the story "Beyond the Blue Sky" by Frank Wead. **130m/B VHS.** Errol Flynn, Fred MacMurray, Ralph Bellamy, Alexis Smith, Regis Toomey, Robert Armstrong, Allen Jenkins, Craig Stevens; ***D:*** Michael Curtiz; ***W:*** Frank Wead, Robert Buckner; ***M:*** Max Steiner. Nominations: Academy Awards '41: Best Color Cinematography. *MGM*

Divine 🦴🦴½ **1990** Two Divine flicks from Waters. First, Divine plays a naughty girl who, not surprisingly, since this one is titled "The Diane Linkletter Story," ends up a successful suicide. "The Neon Woman" is a rare live performance, with Divine a woman who owns a strip joint and has a slew of problems you won't read about in Dear Abbey. **110m/C VHS.** Divine; ***D:*** John Waters. *FCT*

The Divine Enforcer 🦴½ **1991** A monsignor in a crime-ridden L.A. neighborhood reaches his wit's end in trying to stave off perpetrators of injustice. Fortunately, help arrives in the form of a mysterious priest who is equally handy with his fists, nunchakus, and guns. From then on it's no more mister nice guy, and the criminals haven't a prayer. **90m/C VHS, Beta.** Jan-Michael Vincent, Erik Estrada, Jim Brown, Judy Landers, Don Stroud, Robert Z'Dar, Michael Foley, Carrie Chambers, Hiroko; ***D:*** Robert Rundle. *PSM*

Divine Madness **1980 (R)** Bette Midler is captured at her best in a live concert at Pasadena Civic Auditorium. **87m/C VHS, Beta, LV.** Bette Midler; ***D:*** Michael Ritchie; ***W:*** Bette Midler, Jerry Blatt. *WAR*

Divine Nymph 🦴½ **1971 (R)** Charts the erotic adventures of the beautiful and young Manuela, who is dangerously pursued by two cousins. **100m/C VHS, Beta.** *IT* Laura Antonelli, Marcello Mastroianni, Terence Stamp; ***D:*** Giuseppe Patroni Griffi; ***M:*** Ennio Morricone. *MPI*

Diving In 🦴🦴 **1990 (PG-13)** Have you heard the one about the acrophobic diver? It seems a paralyzing fear of heights is the only thing between a young diver and Olympic gold. Much splashing about and heartstring-tugging. **92m/C VHS, Beta.** Burt Young, Matt Adler, Kristy Swanson, Matt Lattanzi, Richard Johnson, Carey Scott, Yolanda Jilot; ***D:*** Strathford Hamilton; ***M:*** Guy Moon, Paul Buckmaster. *PAR, FCT*

Divorce American Style 🦴🦴½ **1967** Dated but still amusing look at love, marriage, and the big D. Richard (Van Dyke) and Barbara (Reynolds) Harmon find their longtime marriage in a tailspin as they spend all their time arguing. They split but find single life and the dating game have their own pitfalls. **103m/C VHS.** Dick Van Dyke, Debbie Reynolds, Jason Robards Jr., Jean Simmons, Van Johnson, Lee Grant, Joe Flynn, Shelley Berman, Martin Gabel, Tom Bosley, Dick Gautier, Eileen Brennan; ***D:*** Bud Yorkin; ***W:*** Norman Lear; ***C:*** Conrad Hall; ***M:*** Dave Grusin. Nominations: Academy Awards '67: Best Original Screenplay. *COL*

Divorce His, Divorce Hers 🦴🦴 **1972** The first half of this drama shows the crumbling of a marriage through the husband's eyes. The second half offers the wife's perspective. Made for television. **144m/C VHS, Beta.** Richard Burton, Elizabeth Taylor; ***D:*** Waris Hussein. *NO*

Divorce—Italian Style 🦴🦴🦴½ *Divorzio All'Italiana* **1962** A middle-aged baron bored with his wife begins directing his amorous attentions to a teenage cousin. Since divorce in Italy is impossible, the only way out of his marriage is murder—and the baron finds a little-known law that excuses a man from murdering his wife if she is having an affair (since he would merely be defending his honor). A hilarious comedy with a twist ending. Available in Italian with English subtitles or dubbed in English. **104m/B VHS.** *IT* Marcello Mastroianni, Daniela Rocca, Leopoldo Trieste; ***D:*** Pietro Germi; ***W:*** Pietro Germi, Ennio de Concini, Alfredo Giannetti. Academy Awards '62: Best Screenplay; British Academy Awards '63: Best Actor (Mastroianni); Golden Globe Awards '63: Best Actor—Musical/Comedy (Mastroianni), Best Foreign Film; Nominations: Academy Awards '62: Best Actor (Mastroianni), Best Director (Germi). *HTV, INJ*

The Divorce of Lady X 🦴🦴½ **1938** A spoiled British debutante, in the guise of "Lady X," makes a woman-hating divorce lawyer eat his words through romance and marriage. Based on the play by Gilbert Wakefield. **92m/C VHS, Beta, LV.** *GB* Merle Oberon, Laurence Olivier, Ralph Richardson, Binnie Barnes; ***D:*** Tim Whelan; ***C:*** Harry Stradling; ***M:*** Miklos Rozsa. *NOS, MRV, UNI*

The Divorcee ♂♂½ **1930** Early Leonard film (he'd later direct "The Great Ziegfield" and "Pride and Prejudice") casts Shearer as a woman out to beat her husband at philandering. Married to a journalist, she cavorts with her husband's best friend and a discarded old flame as only a pre-production code gal could. Shearer—who Lillian Hellman described as having "a face unclouded by thought"—grabbed an Oscar. Based on the novel "Ex-Wife" by Ursula Parrott. **83m/B VHS.** Norma Shearer, Chester Morris, Conrad Nagel, Robert Montgomery, Mary Doran, Tyler Brooke, George Irving, Helen Johnson; ***D:*** Robert Z. Leonard. Academy Awards '30: Best Actress (Shearer); Nominations: Academy Awards '30: Best Director (Leonard), Best Picture, Best Writing. *MGM, FCT, BTV*

Dixiana ♂½ **1930** A Southern millionaire falls for a circus performer shortly before the start of the Civil War. Part color. ♫Dixiana; Here's to the Old Days; A Tear, a Kiss, a Smile; My One Ambition is You; A Lady Loved a Soldier; Mr. & Mrs. Sippi; Guiding Star. **99m/B VHS, Beta.** Bebe Daniels, Bert Wheeler, Robert Woolsey, Dorothy Lamour, Bill Robinson; ***D:*** Luther Reed; ***M:*** Max Steiner. *NOS, DVT*

Dixie: Changing Habits ♂♂♂ **1985** A New Orleans madam and a Mother Superior go head to head in this amusing made-for-television movie. In the end all benefit as the nuns discover business sense and pay off a debt, while the former bordello owner cleans up her act. Above-average scripting and directing for the medium. **100m/C VHS.** Suzanne Pleshette, Cloris Leachman, Kenneth McMillan, John Considine, Geraldine Fitzgerald, Judith Ivey; ***D:*** George Englund. *LIV*

Dixie Dynamite ♂ **1976 (PG)** The two daughters of a Georgia moonshiner set out to avenge the murder of their father. The music is performed by Duane Eddy and Dorsey Burnette. **88m/C VHS, Beta.** Warren Oates, Christopher George, Jane Anne Johnstone, Kathy McHaley, R.G. Armstrong, Wes Bishop; ***D:*** Lee Frost. *VCI*

Dixie Jamboree ♂ **1944** Low-budget musical has gangster on the lam using an unusual method to escape from St. Louis—the last Mississippi Showboat. ♫Dixie Showboat; No, No, No; If It's a Dream; You Ain't Right with the Lord; Big Stuff. **69m/B VHS, Beta.** Guy Kibbee, Frances Langford, Louise Beavers, Charles Butterworth; ***D:*** Christy Cabanne. *NOS, VYY, DVT*

Dixie Lanes ♂ **1988** A relentlessly nostalgic comedy set in a small town at the end of WWII. A woman, troubled by her nephew's restless antics, puts him to work. Unfortunately she adds to his plight, as her business involves the Black Market. **92m/C VHS, Beta.** Hoyt Axton, Karen Black, Art Hindle, John Vernon, Ruth Buzzi, Tina Louise, Pamela Springsteen, Nina Foch; ***D:*** Don Cato. *CEL*

Django ♂½ **1968 (PG)** Django is a stranger who arrives in a Mexican-border town to settle a dispute between a small band of Americans and Mexicans. **90m/C VHS, Beta.** Franco Nero, Loredana Nusciak, Angel Alvarez; ***D:*** Sergio Corbucci. *NO*

Django Shoots First ♂½ **1974** Spaghetti western with usual amount of action and plot twists. **96m/C VHS, Beta.** Glen Saxson, Evelyn Stewart, Alberto Lupo. *VYY*

Do or Die ♂½ **1991 (R)** Former "Playboy" centerfolds Speir and Vasquez team up as a couple of federal agent babes who take on international crime boss Morita. But the crimelord is ready for our scantily clad heroines with a sick game of revenge—and the stakes are their very lives! **97m/C VHS, LV.** Erik Estrada, Dona Speir, Roberta Vasquez, Noriyuki "Pat" Morita, Bruce Penhall, Carolyn Liu, Stephanie Schick; ***D:*** Andy Sidaris; ***W:*** Andy Sidaris. *COL*

Do the Right Thing ♂♂♂½ **1989 (R)** An uncompromising, brutal comedy about the racial tensions surrounding a white-owned pizzeria in the Bed-Stuy section of Brooklyn on the hottest day of the summer, and the violence that eventually erupts. Ambivalent and, for the most part, hilarious; Lee's coming-of-age. **120m/C VHS, Beta, LV.** Spike Lee, Danny Aiello, Richard Edson, Ruby Dee, Ossie Davis, Giancarlo Esposito, Bill Nunn, John Turturro, John Savage, Rosie Perez, Frankie Faison; ***D:*** Spike Lee; ***W:*** Spike Lee. Los Angeles Film Critics Association Awards '89: Best Director (Lee), Best Film, Best Supporting Actor (Aiello); Nominations: Academy Awards '89: Best Original Screenplay, Best Supporting Actor (Aiello). *MCA, FCT*

D.O.A. ♂♂♂½ **1949** A man is given a lethal, slow-acting poison. As his time runs out, he frantically seeks to learn who is responsible and why he was targeted for death. Dark film noir remade in 1969 as "Color Me Dead" and in 1988 with Dennis Quaid and Meg Ryan. Also available colorized. **83m/B VHS, Beta.** Edmond O'Brien, Pamela Britton, Luther Adler, Neville Brand, Beverly Garland; ***D:*** Rudolph Mate; ***C:*** Ernest Laszlo; ***M:*** Dimitri Tiomkin. *SNC, NOS, VYY*

D.O.A. ♂♂½ **1988 (R)** Well-done remake of the 1949 thriller with Quaid portraying a college professor who is poisoned and has only 24 hours to identify his killer. His search for the suspect is further complicated by the fact that he is being sought by the police on phony charges of murder. Directed by the same people who brought "Max Headroom" to television screens. **98m/C VHS, Beta, LV.** Dennis Quaid, Meg Ryan, Charlotte Rampling, Daniel Stern, Jane Kaczmarek, Christopher Neame, Jay Patterson; ***D:*** Rocky Morton, Annabel Jankel; ***W:*** Charles Edward Pogue; ***M:*** Chaz Jankel. *TOU*

The Doberman Gang ♂♂ **1972 (PG)** Clever thieves train a gang of Dobermans in the fine art of bank robbery. Sequelled by "The Daring Dobermans." **85m/C VHS, Beta.** Byron Mabe, Hal Reed, Julie Parrish, Simmy Bow, JoJo D'Amore; ***D:*** Byron Ross Chudnow; ***W:*** Frank Ray Perilli. *FOX*

Doc Hollywood ♂♂½ **1991 (PG-13)** A hotshot young physician on his way to a lucrative California practice gets stranded in a small Southern town. Will the wacky woodsy inhabitants persuade the city doctor to stay? There aren't many surprises in this fish-out-of-water comedy, but the cast injects it with considerable charm. Adapted from Neil B. Shulman's book "What?...Dead Again?" **104m/C VHS, Beta, LV, 8mm.** Michael J. Fox, Julie Warner, Woody Harrelson, Barnard Hughes, David Ogden Stiers, Frances Sternhagen, Bridget Fonda, George Hamilton, Roberts Blossom, Helen Martin, Macon McCalman, Barry Sobel; ***D:*** Michael Caton-Jones; ***W:*** Daniel Pyne, Jeffrey Price, Peter S. Seaman; ***M:*** Carter Burwell. *WAR*

Doc Savage ♂♂½ **1975 (PG)** Doc and "The Amazing Five" fight a murderous villain who plans to take over the world. Based on the novels of Kenneth Robeson. **100m/C VHS, Beta.** Ron Ely, Pamela Hensley, Paul Gleason, Paul Wexler, William Lucking; ***D:*** Michael Anderson Sr.; ***W:*** George Pal, Joe Morhaim; ***C:*** Fred W. Koenekamp. *WAR*

Docks of New York ♂♂♂ **1928** Von Sternberg made his mark in Hollywood with this silent drama about two dockside losers finding love amid the squalor. A rarely seen, early masterpiece. **60m/B VHS, Beta.** George Bancroft, Betty Compson, Olga Baclanova; ***D:*** Josef von Sternberg; ***M:*** Gaylord Carter. *PAR*

The Doctor ♂♂½ **1991 (PG-13)** A hotshot doctor develops throat cancer and gets treated at his own hospital, an ordeal that teaches him a respect and compassion for patients that he formerly lacked. Potential melodrama is saved by fine acting and strong direction. Based on the autobiographical book "A Taste of My Own Medicine" by Dr. Edward Rosenbaum. **125m/C VHS, Beta, LV.** William Hurt, Elizabeth Perkins, Christine Lahti, Mandy Patinkin, Wendy Crewson, Charlie Korsmo, Adam Arkin, Bill Macy; ***D:*** Randa Haines; ***W:*** Robert Caswell; ***C:*** John Seale; ***M:*** Michael Convertino. *TOU*

Dr. Alien ♂ **1988 (R)** Alien poses as beautiful scientist and turns a college freshman into a sex-addicted satyr. Likewise, the cast turns this flick into a dog. **90m/C VHS, Beta, LV.** Billy Jacoby, Olivia Barash, Stuart Fratkin, Troy Donahue, Arlene Golonka, Judy Landers; ***D:*** David DeCoteau. *PAR*

The Doctor and the Devils ♂♂½ **1985 (R)** Based on an old screenplay by Dylan Thomas, this is a semi-Gothic tale about two criminals who supply a physician with corpses to study, either digging them up or killing them fresh. **93m/C VHS, Beta.** *GB* Timothy Dalton, Julian Sands, Jonathan Pryce, Twiggy, Stephen Rea, Beryl Reid, Sian Phillips, Patrick Stewart, Phyllis Logan, T.P. McKenna; ***D:*** Freddie Francis; ***W:*** Ronald Harwood; ***M:*** John Morris. *FOX*

Doctor at Large ♂♂½ **1957** A fledgling doctor seeks to become a surgeon at a hospital for the rich. Humorous antics follow. The third of the "Doctor" series. **98m/C VHS, Beta.** *GB* Dirk Bogarde, Muriel Pavlow, James Robertson Justice, Shirley Eaton, Donald Sinden, Anne Heywood; ***D:*** Ralph Thomas. *NO*

Doctor at Sea ♂♂½ **1956** To escape a troublesome romantic entanglement and the stresses of his career, a London physician signs on a cargo boat as a ship's doctor and becomes involved with French bombshell Bardot. The second of the "Doctor" series. **93m/C VHS, Beta.** *GB* James Robertson Justice, Dirk Bogarde, Brigitte Bardot; ***D:*** Ralph Thomas; ***W:*** Jack Davies. *FCT*

Dr. Bethune ♂♂♂ *Bethune, The Making of a Hero* **1990** Canadian surgeon Norman Bethune was a larger-than-life hero with equally great flaws. A crusader for socialized medicine and an outspoken opponent of Fascism (as well as an alcoholic womanizer), he worked for the Loyalist forces in the Spanish Civil War and was instrumental in developing mobile medical units for treating battlefield wounded. He's also credited with bringing modern medical care to China, where he attended to Mao's revolutionary forces. Sutherland's strong performance shows the intensity and vision of a complicated man; he previously played the doctor in 1977's "Bethune." Awkward jumps in time and place rob the story of narrative drive. **115m/C VHS.** *CA FR* Donald Sutherland, Helen Mirren, Helen Shaver, Colm Feore, Anouk Aimee, Ronald Pickup, Harrison Liu; ***D:*** Phillip Borsos; ***W:*** Ted Allan; ***M:*** Alan Reeves. *FXL, ING*

Dr. Black, Mr. Hyde ♂ *Dr. Black and Mr. White; The Watts Monster* **1976 (R)** Not-so-horrifying tale of a black Jekyll who metamorphoses into a white monster with the help of the special potion. Unintended laughs lessen suspense. **88m/C VHS, Beta.** Rosalind Cash, Stu Gilliam, Bernie Casey, Marie O'Henry; ***D:*** William Crain. *VCI*

Doctor Blood's Coffin ♂♂½ **1962** The aptly named doctor performs hideous experiments on the unsuspecting denizens of a lonely village. Good cast in this effective chiller. **92m/C VHS.** *GB* Kieron Moore, Hazel Court, Ian Hunter; ***D:*** Sidney J. Furie. *SNC*

Doctor Butcher M.D. *Woof! Queen of the Cannibals* **1980 (R)** Mad doctor's deranged dream of creating "perfect people" by taking parts of one person and interchanging them with another backfires as his monstrosities develop strange side effects. The M.D., by the way, stands for "Medical Deviate." Dubbed. **81m/C VHS, Beta.** *IT* Ian McCulloch, Alexandra Cole, Peter O'Neal, Donald O'Brien; ***D:*** Frank Martin. *NO*

Dr. Caligari ♂♂ **1989 (R)** The granddaughter of the original Dr. Caligari promotes "better living through chemistry" in her insane asylum while using her patients as guinea pigs in her bizarre sexual experiments. Nothing outstanding here in terms of story or performance, but "Dick Tracy" has nothing on the visually compelling set designs and make-up. **80m/C VHS, LV.** Madeleine Reynal, Fox Harris, Laura Albert, Jennifer Balgobin, John Durbin, Gene Zerna, David Parry, Barry Phillips; ***D:*** Stephen Sayadian. *FCT*

Dr. Christian Meets the Women ♂½ **1940** This entry in the "Dr. Christian" series of films has the small-town physician once again exposing a con man trying to filch the townspeople. **63m/B VHS, Beta, 8mm.** Jean Hersholt, Edgar Kennedy, Rod La Rocque, Dorothy Lovett, Veda Ann Borg; ***D:*** William McGann. *VYY*

Dr. Cyclops ♂♂½ **1940** The famous early Technicolor fantasia about a mad scientist miniaturizing a group of explorers who happen upon his jungle lab. Landmark F/X and a slow-moving story. **76m/C**

VHS, Beta, LV. Albert Dekker, Janice Logan, Victor Kilian, Thomas Coley, Charles Halton, Frank Yaconelli; ***D:*** Ernest B. Schoedsack; ***W:*** Tom Kilpatrick; ***C:*** Winton C. Hoch, Henry Sharp. *MCA, FCT, MLB*

Dr. Death, Seeker of Souls **1973 (R)** Evil doctor discovers a process for transmigrating his soul into the bodies of people he murdered 1000 years ago. Now he seeks to revive his wife. Final role for 77-year-old "Stooge" Moe Howard. **93m/C VHS, Beta.** John Considine, Barry Coe, Cheryl Miller, Stewart Moss, Leon Askin, Jo Morrow, Florence Marly, Sivi Aberg, Athena Lorde, Moe Howard; ***D:*** Eddie Saeta. *PSM*

Doctor Detroit **1983 (R)** Aykroyd is funny in thin film, portraying a meek college professor who gets involved with prostitutes and the mob, under the alias "Dr. Detroit." Aykroyd later married actress Donna Dixon, whom he worked with on this film. Features music by Devo, James Brown, and Pattie Brooks. **91m/C VHS, Beta, LV.** Dan Aykroyd, Howard Hesseman, Donna Dixon, T.K. Carter, Lynn Whitfield, Lydia Lei, Fran Drescher, Kate Murtagh, George Furth, Andrew Duggan, James Brown, Glenne Headly; ***D:*** Michael Pressman; ***W:*** Carl Gottlieb, Robert Boris; ***M:*** Lalo Schifrin. *MCA*

Doctor Dolittle **1967** An adventure about a 19th century English doctor who dreams of teaching animals to speak to him. Realistic premise suffers from poor script. Based on Hugh Lofting's acclaimed stories. ♫Doctor Dolittle; My Friend the Doctor; Talk to the Animals; I've Never Seen Anything Like It; Beautiful Things; When I Look in Your Eyes; After Today; Fabulous Places; Where Are the Words?. **144m/C VHS, Beta, LV.** Rex Harrison, Samantha Eggar, Anthony Newley, Richard Attenborough, Geoffrey Holder, Peter Bull; ***D:*** Richard Fleischer; ***W:*** Leslie Bricusse; ***C:*** Robert L. Surtees; ***M:*** Leslie Bricusse. Academy Awards '67: Best Song ("Talk to the Animals"), Best Visual Effects; Golden Globe Awards '68: Best Supporting Actor (Attenborough); National Board of Review Awards '67: 10 Best Films of the Year; Nominations: Academy Awards '66: Best Cinematography, Best Sound, Best Original Score; Academy Awards '67: Best Film Editing, Best Picture. *FOX, FCT, MLT*

Doctor Duck's Super Secret All-Purpose Sauce **1985** Conglomeration of video, music, and comedy clips directed by the former Monkee done in the style of his popular "Elephant Parts." **90m/C VHS, Beta, LV.** Michael Nesmith, Whoopi Goldberg, Jimmy Buffett, Rosanne Cash, Jay Leno; ***D:*** Michael Nesmith. *MVD*

Doctor Faustus ½ **1968** A stilted, stagy, but well-meaning adaptation of the Christopher Marlowe classic about Faust, who sold his soul to the devil for youth and the love of Helen of Troy. **93m/C VHS, Beta.** Richard Burton, Andreas Teuber, Elizabeth Taylor, Ian Marter; ***D:*** Richard Burton, Nevill Coghill. *COL*

Dr. Frankenstein's Castle of Freaks **1974 (PG)** Dr. Frankenstein and his dwarf assistant reanimate a few Neanderthals that are terrorizing a nearby Rumanian village. **87m/C VHS, Beta.** *IT* Rossano Brazzi, Michael Dunn, Edmund Purdom, Christiane Royce; ***D:*** Robert Oliver. *SNC*

Dr. Giggles **1992 (R)** Drake plays the psycho-genius Dr. Giggles, an escaped mental patient who sets out to avenge the death of his psycho-genius father (dementia runs in the family). He returns to his family home to procure the necessary medical instruments, most notably a hypodermic needle, and starts killing people—on screen with the tools and in the audience with remarkably stupid one-liners. Opening scenes are especially mired in gore. **96m/C VHS, Beta, LV.** Larry Drake, Holly Marie Combs, Glenn Quinn, Keith Diamond, Cliff DeYoung; ***D:*** Manny Coto; ***W:*** Graeme Whifler, Manny Coto. *MCA*

Dr. Goldfoot and the Bikini Machine **1966** A mad scientist employs gorgeous female robots to seduce the wealthy and powerful, thereby allowing him to take over the world. Title song by the Supremes. **90m/C VHS.** Vincent Price, Frankie Avalon, Dwayne Hickman, Annette Funicello, Susan Hart, Kay Elkhardt, Fred Clark, Deanna Lund, Deborah Walley; ***D:*** Norman Taurog; ***M:*** Les Baxter. *AIP*

Dr. Hackenstein ½ **1988 (R)** A doctor tries to revive his wife by "borrowing" parts from unexpected (and unsuspecting) guests. **88m/C VHS, Beta.** David Muir, Stacy Travis, Catherine Davis Cox, Dyanne DiRosario, Anne Ramsey, Logan Ramsey; ***D:*** Richard Clark. *MCG*

Dr. Heckyl and Mr. Hype **1980 (R)** A naughty, comical version of the Jekyll and Hyde story. Exuberantly wicked performances from Reed and Coogan; stellar cast of "B" veterans. **100m/C VHS, Beta.** Oliver Reed, Sunny Johnson, Maia Danzinger, Mel Welles, Virgil Frye, Kedrick Wolfe, Jackie Coogan, Corinne Calvet, Dick Miller, Lucretia Love; ***D:*** Charles B. Griffith; ***W:*** Charles B. Griffith; ***M:*** Richard Band. *NO*

Doctor in Distress ½ **1963** Aging chief surgeon falls in love for the first time. His assistant tries to further the romance as well as his own love life. Comedic fourth in the six-film "Doctor" series. **102m/C VHS, Beta.** *GB* Dirk Bogarde, James Robertson Justice, Leo McKern, Samantha Eggar; ***D:*** Ralph Thomas. *NO*

Doctor in the House ½ **1953** Four medical student/roommates seek only to examine lovely women and make lots of cash. In the process, they are also tempted by the evils of drink, but rally to make their grades. A riotous British comedy with marvelous performances all around. Led to six sequels and a television series. **92m/C VHS.** *GB* Dirk Bogarde, Muriel Pavlow, Kenneth More, Donald Sinden, Kay Kendall, James Robertson Justice, Donald Houston, Geoffrey Keen, George Coulouris, Shirley Eaton, Joan Hickson, Richard Wattis; ***D:*** Ralph Thomas. British Academy Awards '54: Best Actor (More). *PAR, HMV*

Dr. Jack/For Heaven's Sake **1926** In "Dr. Jack" (1922) and "For Heaven's Sake" (1926) Lloyd acts respectively as an unorthodox doctor and as a debonair millionaire who falls in love with a poor girl. Silent comedy shorts from Lloyd. **88m/B VHS, Beta.** Harold Lloyd, Jobyna Ralston; ***D:*** Sam Taylor. *TLF*

Dr. Jekyll and Ms. Hyde ½ **1995 (PG-13)** Chemist Richard Jacks (Daly) stumbles across the secret formula of great-grandad Dr. Jekyll and, after trying to improve the potion, he finds himself transformed into wicked woman Helen Hyde (Young). Cheap cross-gender gags abound. **89m/C VHS.** Timothy Daly, Sean Young, Lysette Anthony, Stephen Tobolowsky, Harvey Fierstein, Polly Bergen, Stephen Shellan; ***D:*** David F. Price; ***W:*** William Davies, William Osborne, Tim John, Oliver Butcher; ***C:*** Tom Priestley; ***M:*** Mark McKenzie. *HBO*

Dr. Jekyll and Mr. Hyde **1920** The first American film version of Robert Louis Stevenson's horror tale about a doctor's experiments that lead to his developing good and evil sides to his personality. Silent. Kino Video's edition also contains the rarely seen 1911 version of the film, as well as scenes from a different 1920 version. **96m/B VHS, LV.** John Barrymore, Martha Mansfield, Brandon Hurst, Charles Lane, J. Malcolm Dunn, Nita Naldi; ***D:*** John S. Robertson. *SNC, REP, MRV*

Dr. Jekyll and Mr. Hyde **1931** The hallucinatory, feverish classic version of the Robert Louis Stevenson story, in which the good doctor becomes addicted to the formula that turns him into a sadistic beast. Possibly Mamoulian's and March's best work, and a masterpiece of subversive, pseudo-Freudian creepiness. Eighteen minutes from the original version, lost until recently, have been restored, including the infamous whipping scene. **96m/B VHS, Beta, LV.** Fredric March, Miriam Hopkins, Halliwell Hobbes, Rose Hobart, Holmes Herbert, Edgar Norton; ***D:*** Rouben Mamoulian; ***C:*** Karl Struss. Academy Awards '32: Best Actor (March); Venice Film Festival '31: Best Actor (March); Nominations: Academy Awards '32: Best Adapted Screenplay, Best Cinematography. *MGM, BTV*

Dr. Jekyll and Mr. Hyde **1941** Strangely cast adaptation of the Robert Louis Stevenson story about a doctor's experiment on himself to separate good and evil. **113m/B VHS, Beta, LV.** Spencer Tracy, Ingrid Bergman, Lana Turner, Donald Crisp; ***D:*** Victor Fleming; ***C:*** Joseph Ruttenberg. Nominations: Academy Awards '41: Best Black and White Cinematography, Best Film Editing, Best Original Score. *MGM*

Dr. Jekyll and Mr. Hyde **1968** Yet another production of Robert Louis Stevenson's classic story of a split-personality. **90m/C VHS, Beta.** Jack Palance. *LIV*

Dr. Jekyll and Mr. Hyde **1973** Dr. Jekyll discovers a potion that turns him into the sinister Mr. Hyde. Based on the classic story by Robert Louis Stevenson. **90m/C VHS, Beta, LV.** Kirk Douglas, Michael Redgrave, Susan George, Donald Pleasence; ***D:*** David Winters. *IME*

Dr. Jekyll and Sister Hyde ½ **1971 (R)** A tongue-in-cheek variation on the split-personality theme, which has the good doctor transforming himself into a sultry, knife-wielding woman who kills prostitutes. **94m/C VHS, Beta.** *GB* Ralph Bates, Martine Beswick, Gerald Sim; ***D:*** Roy Ward Baker; ***W:*** Brian Clemens. *MLB*

Dr. Jekyll and the Wolfman *Dr. Jekyll y el Hombre Lobo* **1971 (R)** Naschy's sixth stint as El Hombre Lobo. This time he visits a mysterious doctor in search of a cure but ends up turning into Mr. Hyde, a man who likes to torture women. **85m/C VHS.** *SP* Paul Naschy, Shirley Corrigan, Jack Taylor; ***D:*** Leon Klimovsky. *SNC*

Dr. Jekyll vs. the Werewolf ½ **1971** A man afflicted with the characteristics of a wolf seeks a cure from Dr. Jekyll's grandson. **?m/C VHS.** Paul Naschy, Jack Taylor. *SNC*

Dr. Jekyll's Dungeon of Death **1982 (R)** Dr. Jekyll and his lobotomized sister, Hilda, scour the streets of San Francisco looking for human blood to recreate his great-grandfather's secret serum. Also on video as "Dr. Jekyll's Dungeon of Darkness." **90m/C VHS, Beta.** James Mathers, Dawn Carver Kelly, John Kearney, Jake Pearson; ***D:*** James Wood. *GHV*

Dr. Kildare's Strange Case **1940** Dr. Kildare administers a daring treatment to a man suffering from a mental disorder of a dangerous nature. One in the film series. **76m/B VHS, Beta.** Lew Ayres, Lionel Barrymore, Laraine Day; ***D:*** Harold Bucquet. *NOS, HHT, DVT*

Dr. Mabuse, Parts 1 & 2 ½ *Doktor Mabuse der Spieler* **1922** The massive, two-part crime melodrama, introducing the raving mastermind/extortionist/villain to the world. The film follows Dr. Mabuse through his life of crime until he finally goes mad. Highly influential and inventive. Lang meant this to be a criticism of morally bankrupt post-WWI Germany. Followed some time later by "Testament of Doctor Mabuse" and "The Thousand Eyes of Dr. Mabuse." Silent. **242m/B VHS, Beta.** *GE* Rudolf Klein-Rogge, Aud Egede Nissen, Alfred Abel, Gertrude Welcker, Lil Dagover, Paul Richter; ***D:*** Fritz Lang. *SNC, MRV, NOS*

Dr. Mabuse vs. Scotland Yard ½ **1964** A sequel to the Fritz Lang classics, this film features the arch-criminal attempting to take over the world with a mind-controlling camera. **90m/B VHS, Beta.** *GE* Sabine Bethmann, Peter Van Eyck; ***D:*** Paul May. *VYY, SNC, GLV*

Doctor Mordrid: Master of the Unknown **1990 (R)** Two immensely powerful sorcerers from the 4th dimension cross over into present time with two very different missions—one wants to destroy the Earth, one wants to save it. **102m/C VHS, Beta.** Jeffrey Combs, Yvette Nipar, Jay Acovone, Brian Thompson; ***D:*** Albert Band, Charles Band; ***M:*** Richard Band. *PAR*

Dr. No **1962 (PG)** The world is introduced to British secret agent 007, James Bond, when it is discovered that a mad scientist is sabotaging rocket launchings from his hideout in Jamaica. The first 007 film is far less glitzy than any of its successors but boasts the sexiest "Bond girl" of them all in Andress, and promptly made stars of her and Connery. On laserdisc, the film is in wide-screen transfer and includes movie bills, publicity photos, location pictures, and the British and American trailers. The sound effects and musical score can be separated from the dialogue. Audio interviews with the director, writer, and editor are included as part of the disc. **111m/C VHS, Beta, LV.** *GB* Sean Connery, Ursula Andress, Joseph Wiseman, Jack Lord, Zena Marshall, Eunice Gayson, Margaret LeWars, John Kitzmiller, Lois Maxwell, Bernard Lee, Anthony Dawson; ***D:*** Terence Young; ***C:*** Ted Moore; ***M:*** John Barry. *MGM, CRC, TLF*

Dr. Orloff's Invisible Horror 🦴½ **1972** In this horror film, Dr. Orloff creates an invisible ape-monster that escapes and goes on a rampage. **?m/C VHS.** Howard Vernon. *SNC*

Dr. Orloff's Monster *Woof!* **1964** As if "The Awful Dr. Orloff" wasn't awful enough, the doctor is back, this time eliminating his enemies with his trusty killer robot. Awful awful. **88m/B VHS.** *SP* Jose Rubio, Agnes Spaak; ***D:*** Jess (Jesus) Franco. *SNC, VYY*

Dr. Otto & the Riddle of the Gloom Beam 🦴½ **1986 (PG)** Ernest is in your face again. Fresh from the TV commercials featuring "Ernest" comes Varney playing a villain out to wreck the global economy. He also plays all the other characters, too. Way bizarre, "Know whut I mean?" **92m/C VHS, Beta.** Jim Varney; ***D:*** John R. Cherry III. *GKK*

Dr. Petiot 🦴🦴 *Le Docteur Petiot* **1990** Based on the true life story of a French WWII doctor who promised to smuggle Jews to freedom but instead killed them for their money and possessions. He was executed in 1946—accused of 60 murders and convicted of 27. The gruesome details are left to the imagination rather than shown. In French with subtitles. **102m/C VHS.** *FR* Michel Serrault, Berangere Bonvoisin; ***W:*** Christian de Chalonge, Dominique Garnier. *WAC, FCT*

Doctor Phibes Rises Again 🦴🦴½ **1972 (PG)** The despicable doctor contines his quest to revive his beloved wife. Fun, superior sequel to "The Abominable Dr. Phibes." **89m/C VHS, Beta.** *GB* Vincent Price, Robert Quarry, Peter Cushing, Beryl Reid, Hugh Griffith, Terry-Thomas; ***D:*** Robert Fuest; ***W:*** Robert Blees. *LIV, VES, ORI*

Doctor Quinn, Medicine Woman 🦴🦴½ **1992** The small western town of Colorado Springs has advertised for a doctor and is pleased to hire Dr. "Mike" Quinn from Boston. Only to the town's surprise, and dismay, who should arrive by Dr. Michaela Quinn. This eastern lady has her work cut out for her just trying to convince the townsfolk that a woman can practice medicine. But she's determined and with the aid of the brooding, handsome Sully she opens her practice. Made for television. **?m/C VHS.** Jane Seymour, Diane Ladd, Joe Lando. *FXV*

Doctor Satan's Robot 🦴🦴½ **1940** Indestructible robot is battled by insane Dr. Satan in reedited serial, "Mysterious Dr. Satan." **100m/B VHS.** Eduardo Ciannelli, Robert Wilcox, William Newell, Ella Neal; ***D:*** William Witney, John English. *VCN*

Dr. Strange 🦴½ **1978** A made-for-television pilot based upon the Marvel Comics character who, with the help of a sorcerer, practices witchcraft in order to fight evil. **94m/C VHS, Beta.** Peter Hooten, Clyde Kusatsu, Jessica Walter, Eddie Benton, John Mills; ***D:*** Philip DeGuere. *MCA*

Dr. Strangelove, or: How I Learned to Stop Worrying and Love the Bomb 🦴🦴🦴🦴 **1964** Sellers plays a tour-de-force triple role in Kubrick's classic black anti-war comedy. While a U.S. President (Sellers) deals with the Russian situation, a crazed general (Hayden) implements a plan to drop the A-bomb on the Soviets. Famous for Pickens' wild ride on the bomb, Hayden's character's "purity of essence" philosophy, Scott's gum-chewing militarist, a soft-drink vending machine dispute, and countless other scenes. Based on the novel "Red Alert" by Peter George. **93m/B VHS, Beta, LV, 8mm.** *GB* Peter Sellers, George C. Scott, Sterling Hayden, Keenan Wynn, Slim Pickens, James Earl Jones, Peter Bull; ***D:*** Stanley Kubrick; ***W:*** Terry Southern, Peter George, Stanley Kubrick; ***M:*** Laurie Johnson. British Academy Awards '64: Best Film; New York Film Critics Awards '64: Best Director (Kubrick); Nominations: Academy Awards '64: Best Actor (Sellers), Best Adapted Screenplay, Best Director (Kubrick), Best Picture. *COL, HMV*

Dr. Syn 🦴🦴 **1937** The story of a seemingly respectable vicar of Dymchurch who is really a former pirate. The last film of George Arliss. **90m/B VHS, Beta.** *GB* George Arliss, Margaret Lockwood, John Loder; ***D:*** Roy William Neill. *NOS, MRV, CAB*

Dr. Syn, Alias the Scarecrow 🦴🦴½ **1964 (G)** A mild-mannered minister is, in reality, a smuggler and pirate avenging King George III's injustices upon the English people. Originally broadcast in three parts on the Disney television show. **129m/C VHS, Beta.** Patrick McGoohan, George Cole, Tony Britton, Michael Hordern, Geoffrey Keen, Kay Cole; ***D:*** James Neilson. *DIS*

Doctor Takes a Wife 🦴🦴🦴 **1940** A fast, fun screwball comedy wherein two ill-matched career people are forced via a publicity mix-up to fake being married. **89m/B VHS, Beta.** Ray Milland, Loretta Young, Reginald Gardiner, Gail Patrick, Edmund Gwenn, George Metaxa, Charles Halton; ***D:*** Alexander Hall; ***W:*** George Seaton. *COL*

Dr. Tarr's Torture Dungeon *Woof!* **1975 (R)** A mysterious man is sent to the forest to investigate the bizarre behavior of Dr. Tarr who runs a torture asylum. **90m/C VHS, Beta.** Claudio Brook, Ellen Sherman, Robert Dumont. *NO*

Dr. Terror's House of Horrors 🦴🦴½ *The Blood Suckers* **1965** On a train, six traveling companions have their fortunes told by a mysterious doctor. Little do they realize that their final destination has changed. Creepy and suspenseful, especially the severed-hand chase sequence. **92m/C VHS.** *GB* Christopher Lee, Peter Cushing, Donald Sutherland; ***D:*** Freddie Francis. *REP, MLB*

Doctor Who 🦴🦴½ **1996** The late British sci-fi series, which ended in 1989, has been resurrected in this TV movie. The TARDIS is forced down in 1999 San Francisco and renegade Time Lord the Master's sluglike remains escape from the Doctor (McCoy) and into a temporary host body (Roberts). Meanwhile, the Doctor's been hospitalized and a botched operation by Dr. Grace Holloway (Ashbrook) leaves him clinically dead—until he manages to regenerate once again (as McGann). With Grace's help, the Doctor tries to stop his enemy from destroying the world on New Year's Eve in a plot that will also give the Master the Doctor's body as his new home. Production design and special effects are lavish (particularly in relation to the cheesiness of the series). **?m/C VHS.** *GB CA* Paul McGann, Eric Roberts, Daphne Ashbrook, Yee Jee Tso, Sylvester McCoy; ***D:*** Geoffrey Sax; ***W:*** Matthew Jacobs; ***C:*** Glen MacPherson; ***M:*** John Debney. *NYR*

Doctor Who: An Unearthly Child **1963** In the long-running British series' first episode, Doctor Who and his granddaughter travel to prehistoric times to witness the discovery of fire. Additional episodes are available. **98m/B VHS.** *GB* William Hartnell; ***D:*** Waris Hussein. *FXV, MOV*

Doctor Who and the Daleks **1965** The Time Lord and his two grandchildren accidentally transport themselves to a futuristic planet inhabited by the Daleks, who capture the travelers and hold them captive. A feature film version of the long-running British television show. **78m/C VHS, Beta.** *GB* Peter Cushing, Roy Castle; ***D:*** Gordon Flemyng. *REP*

Doctor Who: Cybermen—The Early Years **1992** Baker, the 6th Doctor, hosts this look at one of the Time Lord's favorite enemies, the robotic and ruthless Cybermen from their first appearance in "The Tenth Planet" to "Tomb of the Cyberman" and "The Invasion." **120m/C VHS.** *GB FXV, MOV*

Doctor X 🦴🦴½ **1932** An armless mad scientist uses a formula for "synthetic flesh" to grow temporary limbs and commit murder. A classic, rarely seen horror oldie, famous for its very early use of two-color Technicolor. **77m/C VHS, Beta, LV.** Lionel Atwill, Fay Wray, Lee Tracy, Preston Foster; ***D:*** Michael Curtiz. *MGM, MLB*

Doctor Zhivago 🦴🦴🦴 **1965 (PG-13)** Sweeping adaptation of the Nobel Prize-winning Boris Pasternak novel. An innocent Russian poet-intellectual is caught in the furor and chaos of the Bolshevik Revolution. Essentially a poignant love story filmed as a historical epic. Panoramic film popularized the song "Lara's Theme." Overlong, with often disappointing performances, but gorgeous scenery. Lean was more successful in "Lawrence of Arabia," where there was less need for ensemble acting. **197m/C VHS, Beta, LV.** Omar Sharif, Julie Christie, Geraldine Chaplin, Rod Steiger, Alec Guinness, Klaus Kinski, Ralph Richardson, Rita Tushingham, Siobhan McKenna, Tom Courtenay; ***D:*** David Lean; ***W:*** Robert Bolt; ***C:*** Frederick A. (Freddie) Young; ***M:*** Maurice Jarre. Academy Awards '65: Best Adapted Screenplay, Best Art Direction/Set Decoration (Color), Best Color Cinematography, Best Costume Design (Color), Best Original Score; Golden Globe Awards '66: Best Actor—Drama (Sharif), Best Director (Lean), Best Film—Drama, Best Screenplay, Best Score; National Board of Review Awards '65: 10 Best Films of the Year, Best Actress (Christie); Nominations: Academy Awards '65: Best Director (Lean), Best Film Editing, Best Picture, Best Sound, Best Supporting Actor (Courtenay). *MGM, RDG, HMV*

Doctors and Nurses 🦴🦴 **1982** A children's satire of soap operas wherein the adults play the children and vice-versa. **90m/C VHS, Beta.** Rebecca Rigg, Drew Forsythe, Graeme Blundell; ***D:*** Maurice Murphy. *NO*

Doctors' Wives 🦴½ **1970 (R)** An adaptation of the Frank Slaughter potboiler about a large city hospital's doctors, nurses, and their respective spouses, with plenty of affairs, medical traumas, and betrayals. **102m/C VHS, Beta.** Dyan Cannon, Richard Crenna, Gene Hackman, Carroll O'Connor, Rachel Roberts, Janice Rule, Diana Sands, Ralph Bellamy, John Colicos; ***D:*** George Schaefer; ***W:*** Daniel Taradash; ***C:*** Charles B(ryant) Lang; ***M:*** Elmer Bernstein. *COL*

Dodes 'ka-den 🦴🦴🦴½ *Clickety Clack* **1970** In this departure from his samurai-genre films, Kurosawa depicts a throng of fringe-dwelling Tokyo slum inhabitants in a semi-surreal manner. Fascinating presentation and content. **140m/C VHS, Beta.** *JP* Yoshitaka Zushi, Junzaburo Ban, Kiyoko Tange; ***D:*** Akira Kurosawa. Nominations: Academy Awards '71: Best Foreign Language Film. *INJ, SUE*

Dodge City 🦴🦴🦴 **1939** Flynn stars as Wade Hutton, a roving cattleman who becomes the sheriff of Dodge City. His job: to run a ruthless outlaw and his gang out of town. De Havilland serves as Flynn's love interest, as she did in many previous films. A broad and colorful shoot-em-up! **104m/C VHS, Beta, LV.** Errol Flynn, Olivia de Havilland, Bruce Cabot, Ann Sheridan, Alan Hale, Frank McHugh, Victor Jory, Henry Travers, Charles Halton; ***D:*** Michael Curtiz; ***M:*** Max Steiner. *MGM, FOX, FCT*

Dodsworth 🦴🦴🦴½ **1936** The lives of a self-made American tycoon and his wife are drastically changed when they take a tour of Europe. The success of their marriage seems questionable as they re-evaluate their lives. Huston excels as does the rest of the cast in this film, based upon the Sinclair Lewis novel. **101m/B VHS, Beta, LV.** Walter Huston, David Niven, Paul Lukas, John Payne, Mary Astor, Ruth Chatterton, Maria Ouspenskaya, Charles Halton; ***D:*** William Wyler. Academy Awards '36: Best Interior Decoration; New York Film Critics Awards '36: Best Actor (Huston); Nominations: Academy Awards '36: Best Actor (Huston), Best Adapted Screenplay, Best Director (Wyler), Best Picture, Best Sound, Best Supporting Actress (Ouspenskaya). *HBO, SUE*

Does This Mean We're Married? 🦴🦴 **1990 (PG-13)** A stand-up comedian is trying to find success in the comedy clubs of Paris but without her green card she may soon be deported. She finds a sleazy marriage broker who fixes her up with a womanizing songwriter who needs money. As usual, immigration officials suspect that the marriage is a fake and the mismatched couple must live together to prove them wrong. **93m/C VHS, LV.** Patsy Kensit, Stephane Freiss; ***D:*** Carol Wiseman. *COL, NLC*

Dog Day 🦴🦴½ *Canicule* **1983** An American traitor, who is on the lam from the government, and his cronies, takes refuge on a small farm. A surprise awaits him when the farmers come up with an unusual plan to bargain for his life. **101m/C VHS, Beta.** *FR* Lee Marvin, Miou-Miou, Victor Lanoux; ***D:*** Yves Boisset. *LIV*

Dog Day Afternoon 🦴🦴🦴½ **1975 (R)** Based on a true story, this taut, yet fantastic thriller centers on a bi-sexual and his slow-witted buddy who rob a bank to obtain money to fund a sex change operation for the ringleader's lover. Pacino is breathtaking in his role as the frustrated robber, caught in a trap of his own devising. Very controversial for its language and subject matter when released, it nevertheless became a huge success. Director Lumet keeps up the pace, fills the screen with pathos without gross sentiment. **124m/C VHS, Beta, LV.** Al Pacino, John Cazale, Charles Durning, James Broderick, Chris Sarandon, Carol Kane, Lance Henriksen, Dick Williams; ***D:*** Sidney Lumet; ***W:*** Frank Pierson. Academy Awards '75: Best Original Screenplay; British Academy Awards '75: Best Actor (Pacino); National Board of Review Awards '75: 10 Best Films of the Year, Best Supporting Actor (Durning); Nominations: Academy Awards '75: Best Actor (Pacino), Best Director (Lumet), Best Film Editing, Best Picture, Best Supporting Actor (Sarandon). *WAR*

Dog Eat Dog 🦴 *Einer Frisst den Anderen; La Morte Vestita di Dollar* **1964** Centering on a heist scheme by Mitchell, this one has nothing to offer except Mansfield's attributes. **86m/B VHS, Beta, 8mm.** Cameron Mitchell, Jayne Mansfield, Isa Miranda; ***D:*** Ray Nazarro. *VYY, HEG*

A Dog of Flanders 🦴🦴½ **1959** A young Dutch boy and his grandfather find a severely beaten dog and restore it to health. **96m/C VHS, Beta.** David Ladd, Donald Crisp, Theodore Bikel, Max Croiset, Monique Ahrens; ***D:*** James B. Clark. *PAR*

Dog Pound Shuffle 🦴🦴🦴 *Spot* **1975 (PG)** Two drifters form a new song-and-dance act in order to raise the funds necessary to win their dog's freedom from the pound. Charming Canadian production. **98m/C VHS, Beta.** *CA* Ron Moody, David Soul; ***D:*** Jeffrey Bloom; ***W:*** Jeffrey Bloom. *FOX*

The Dog Soldier 🦴½ **1972** This "video novel" dramatically depicts a state of future events whereby a lone human in flight struggles to preserve his right to be free. **40m/B VHS, Beta.** *PCV*

Dog Star Man 🦴🦴🦴 **1964** The silent epic by the dean of experimental American film depicts man's spiritual and physical conflicts through Brakhage's characteristically freeform collage techniques. **78m/C VHS, Beta.** ***D:*** Stan Brakhage. *MFV, FCT, TPV*

The Dog Who Stopped the War 🦴🦴 **1984 (G)** A Canadian children's film about a dog who puts a halt to an escalating snowball fight between rival gangs. **90m/C VHS, Beta.** *CA* ***D:*** Andre Melancon. *NO*

Dogfight 🦴🦴🦴 **1991 (R)** It's 1963 and a baby-faced Marine and his buddies are spending their last night in San Francisco before leaving the U.S. for a tour of duty in Vietnam. They agree to throw a "dogfight," a competition to see who can bring the ugliest date to a party. Birdlace (Phoenix) chooses Taylor, a shy, average-looking waitress who dreams of becoming a folk singer and realizes too late that she doesn't deserve the treatment he's about to subject her to. This quiet film didn't see a wide release, but is worth renting due to an above average script which is held up by the splendid performances of Phoenix and Taylor. **94m/C VHS, Beta, LV, 8mm.** River Phoenix, Lili Taylor, Richard Panebianco, Anthony Clark, Mitchell Whitfield, E.G. Daily, Holly Near, Brendan Fraser, Peg Phillips; ***D:*** Nancy Savoca; ***W:*** Bob Comfort. *WAR*

The Dogfighters 🦴🦴 **1995 (R)** Ex-Air Force pilot Rowdy Wells (Davi) is blackmailed into trying to destroy a plutonium plant in an eastern European country. That is, if Rowdy can survive an air battle with nemisis Lothar Krasna (Godunov). Small budget is reflected in the mediocre aerial sequences. **96m/C VHS, LV.** Robert Davi, Alexander Godunov, Ben Gazzara, Lara Harris; ***D:*** Barry Zetlin; ***W:*** Sean Smith, Anthony Stark; ***C:*** Levie Isaacks; ***M:*** Jimmie Haskell. *LIV*

Dogs in Space 🦴🦴 **1987** A low-budget Australian film about a clique of aimless Melbourne rock kids in 1978, caught somewhere between post-hippiedom and punk, free love and heroin addiction. Acclaimed. Includes music by Hutchence, Brian Eno, Iggy Pop, and others. **109m/C VHS, Beta.** *AU* Michael Hutchence, Saskia Post, Nique Needles, Tony Helou, Deanna Bond; ***D:*** Richard Lowenstein; ***W:*** Richard Lowenstein. *FOX*

Dogs of Hell 🦴½ **1983 (R)** The sheriff of an idyllic resort community must stop a pack of killer dogs from terrorizing the residents. **90m/C VHS, Beta.** Earl Owensby, Bill Gribble, Jerry Rushing; ***D:*** Worth Keeter. *MED*

The Dogs of War 🦴🦴½ **1981 (R)** A graphic depiction of a group of professional mercenaries, driven by nothing but their quest for wealth and power, hired to overthrow the dictator of a new West African nation. Has some weak moments which break up the continuity of the movie. Based on the novel by Frederick Forsyth. **102m/C VHS, Beta, LV.** *GB* Christopher Walken, Tom Berenger, Colin Blakely, Paul Freeman, Hugh Millais, Victoria Tennant, JoBeth Williams; ***D:*** John Irvin; ***W:*** Gary De Vore; ***C:*** Jack Cardiff; ***M:*** Geoffrey Burgon. *MGM*

Doin' Time 🦴 **1985 (R)** At the John Dillinger Memorial Penitentiary, the inmates take over the prison under the supervision of warden "Mongo." Silliness prevails. **80m/C VHS, Beta.** Jeff Altman, Dey Young, Richard Mulligan, John Vernon, Colleen Camp, Melanie Chartoff, Graham Jarvis, Pat McCormick, Eddie Velez, Jimmie Walker, Judy Landers, Nicholas Worth, Mike Mazurki, Muhammad Ali, Melinda Fee, Francesca "Kitten" Natividad, Ron Palillo; ***D:*** George Mendeluk; ***W:*** Dee Caruso; ***M:*** Charles Fox. *WAR*

Doin' Time on Planet Earth 🦴🦴½ **1988 (PG-13)** A young boy feels out of place with his family and is convinced by two strange people (aliens themselves?) that he is really an extraterrestrial. Amusing, aimless fun directed by the son of Walter Matthau. **83m/C VHS, Beta.** Adam West, Candice Azzara, Hugh O'Brian, Matt Adler, Timothy Patrick Murphy, Roddy McDowall, Maureen Stapleton, Andrea Thompson; ***D:*** Charles Matthau. *WAR*

Dolemite 🦴½ **1975 (R)** An ex-con attempts to settle the score with some of his former inmates. He forms a band of kung-fu savvy ladies. Strange combination of action and comedy. **88m/C VHS.** Rudy Ray Moore, Jerry Jones; ***D:*** D'Urville Martin. *XVC*

Dolemite 2: Human Tornado 🦴½ *The Human Tornado* **1976 (R)** Nobody ever said Moore was for everybody's taste. But, hey, when blaxploitation movies were the rage, Rudy the standup comic was out there rapping through a series of trashy movies that, when viewed today, have survived the test of time. This one's just as vile, violent, and sexist as the day it was released. When Rudy is surprised in bed with a white sheriff's wife, he flees and meets up with a madam and a house of kung-fu-skilled girls who are embroiled in a fight with a local mobster. **98m/C VHS.** Rudy Ray Moore, Lady Reed. *XVC*

The Doll 🦴🦴 *La Poupee; He, She or It* **1962** A lonely night watchman happens upon two burglars and, in the chase, the thieves knock over a mannequin. The watchman reports the mannequin stolen, brings it home and begins to have conversations with it. Soon, the doll's needs cause him to steal jewelry and clothes, until his brutish neighbor discovers his secrets. In Swedish with English subtitles. **96m/B VHS.** *SW* Per Oscarsson, Gio Petre, Tor Isedal, Elsa Prawitz; ***D:*** Arne Mattson. *FCT, DVT, AUD*

Doll Face 🦴🦴½ *Come Back to Me* **1946** Story of a stripper who wants to go legit and make it on Broadway. Film was adapted from the play "The Naked Genius" by tease queen Gypsy Rose Lee. ♫Dig You Later; Here Comes Heaven Again; Chico-Chico; Somebody's Walkin' In My Dreams; Red Hot and Beautiful. **80m/B VHS, Beta, LV.** Vivian Blaine, Dennis O'Keefe, Perry Como, Carmen Miranda, Martha Stewart, Reed Hadley; ***D:*** Lewis Seiler. *NOS, HHT, DVT*

The Doll Squad 🦴 *Hustler Squad* **1973 (PG)** Three voluptuous special agents fight an ex-CIA agent out to rule the world. **93m/C VHS, Beta.** Michael Ansara, Francine York, Anthony Eisley, Tura Satana; ***D:*** Ted V. Mikels. *GHV, MRV*

Dollar 🦴🦴 **1938** The actress wife of an industrialist, convinced that he is having an affair, follows him to a ski lodge in attempt to catch him in the act. In Swedish with English subtitles. **74m/B VHS, Beta, LV.** *SW* Georg Rydeberg, Ingrid Bergman, Kotti Chave, Tutta Rolf, Hakan Westergren, Elsa Burnett, Edvin Adolphson, Gosta Cederlund, Eric Rosen; ***D:*** Gustaf Molander. *WAC, INJ*

Dollars 🦴🦴🦴 *The Heist* **1971 (R)** A bank employee and his dizzy call-girl assistant plan to steal the German facility's assets while installing its new security system. Lighthearted fun. **119m/C VHS, Beta, LV.** Warren Beatty, Goldie Hawn, Gert Frobe, Scott Brady, Robert Webber; ***D:*** Richard Brooks; ***W:*** Richard Brooks; ***M:*** Quincy Jones. *GKK*

The Dollmaker 🦴🦴½ **1984** Excellent made for television adaptation of Harriette Arnow's novel. A strong-willed Kentucky mother of five helps move her family to Detroit in the 1940s. Petrie's direction moves the story along and creates a lovely period vision. **140m/C VHS, Beta.** Jane Fonda, Levon Helm, Geraldine Page, Amanda Plummer, Susan Kingsley; ***D:*** Daniel Petrie. *FOX*

Dollman 🦴½ **1990 (R)** An ultra-tough cop from an Earth-like planet (even swear words are the same) crashes in the South Bronx—and on this world he's only 13 inches tall. The filmmakers squander a great premise and cast with bloody shootouts and a sequel-ready non-ending. **86m/C VHS, Beta, LV.** Tim Thomerson, Jackie Earle Haley, Kamala Lopez, Humberto Ortiz, Nicholas Guest, Michael Halsey, Eugene Glazer, Judd Omen, Frank Collison, Vincent Klyn; ***D:*** Albert Pyun. *PAR*

Dollman vs Demonic Toys 🦴🦴 **1993 (R)** Let's combine elements from three separate films and make one disgusting sequel: "Dollman," the 13-inch cop from the planet Arturus; his new girlfriend, Dollchick, who was shrunk to a diminutive 10 inches in "Bad Channels;" and tough cop Judith Grey, who's once again battling those loathsome playthings from "Demonic Toys." If you feel the need for a plot—Dollchick is kidnapped by Baby Doll and needs to be rescued. **84m/C VHS, Beta.** Tim Thomerson, Tracy Scoggins, Melissa Behr, Phil Brock, Phil Fondacaro; ***D:*** Charles Band; ***W:*** Craig Hamann; ***M:*** Richard Band. *PAR*

The Dolls *Woof!* **1983** A tropically located photographer recruits an area beauty into the fashion world with his winning smile and macho charm, only to learn native traditions forbid her to follow him. **96m/C VHS, Beta, LV.** Tetchie Agbayani, Max Thayer, Carina Schally, Richard Seward; ***D:*** Hubert Frank. *LIV, VES*

Dolls 🦴🦴½ **1987 (R)** A group of people is stranded during a storm in an old, creepy mansion. As the night wears on, they are attacked by hundreds of antique dolls. Tongue-in-cheek. **77m/C VHS, Beta.** Ian Patrick Williams, Carolyn Purdy-Gordon, Carrie Lorraine, Stephen Lee, Guy Rolfe, Bunty Bailey, Cassie Stuart, Hilary Mason; ***D:*** Stuart Gordon; ***W:*** Ed Naha; ***M:*** Richard Band. *LIV, VES*

A Doll's House 🦴🦴½ **1959** An all-star cast is featured in this original television production of Henrik Ibsen's classic play about an independent woman's quest for freedom in nineteenth-century Norway. **89m/B VHS, Beta.** Julie Harris, Christopher Plummer, Jason Robards Jr., Hume Cronyn, Eileen Heckart, Richard Thomas. *MGM, FCT*

A Doll's House 🦴🦴½ **1973 (G)** Fonda plays Nora, a subjugated 19th-century housewife who breaks free to establish herself as an individual. Based on Henrik Ibsen's classic play; some controversy regarding Fonda's interpretation of her role. **98m/C Beta.** Jane Fonda, Edward Fox, Trevor Howard, David Warner, Delphine Seyrig; ***D:*** Joseph Losey; ***W:*** Christopher Hampton; ***M:*** John Barry. *PSM*

A Doll's House 🦴🦴🦴 **1989 (G)** A Canadian production of the Henrik Ibsen play about a Norwegian woman's search for independence. **96m/C VHS, Beta, LV.** *CA* Claire Bloom, Anthony Hopkins, Ralph Richardson, Denholm Elliott, Anna Massey, Edith Evans; ***D:*** Patrick Garland. *HMD*

Dolly Dearest 🦴½ **1992 (R)** Strange things start happening after an American family takes over a run-down Mexican doll factory. They create a new doll called "Dolly Dearest" with deadly results. In the same tradition as the "Chucky" series. **94m/C VHS, LV.** Rip Torn, Sam Bottoms, Denise Crosby; ***D:*** Maria Lease. *VMK*

The Dolly Sisters 🦴🦴½ **1945** Competent musical about sisters Jenny (Grable) and Rosie (Haver), who become turn-of-the-century vaudeville stars and also find romance. Good songs, extravagent costuming, fine support work, and the charms of the two leading actresses provide simple enjoyment. ♫I Can't Begin to Tell You; I'm Always Chasing Rainbows; Powder, Lipstick and Rouge; Give Me the Moonlight; On the Mississippi; We Have Been Around; Carolina In the Morning; Arrah Go On, I'm Gonna Go Back to Oregon; The Darktown Strutter's Ball. **114m/C VHS.** Betty Grable, June Haver, John Payne, Frank Latimore, S.Z. Sakall, Reginald Gardiner, Gene Sheldon, Sig Rumann; ***D:*** Irving Cummings; ***W:*** Marian Spitzer, John Larkin; ***C:*** Ernest Palmer. Nominations: Academy Awards '45: Best Song ("I Can't Begin to Tell You"). *FXV*

Dolores Claiborne 🦴🦴🦴 **1994 (R)** Stephen King gets the Hollywood treatment again (the check cleared, King approved), with better results than previous outings (remember "Needful Things"?). Successful but neurotic New York journalist Selena (Leigh) confronts her troubled past when coarse, hard-talking mom Dolores (Bates) is accused of murdering her wealthy employer (Parfitt). Plummer is vengeful detective John Mackey who, like everyone else on the fictitious Maine island, believes Dolores murdered her husband 15 years before. Top-notch performances by Bates and Leigh highlight this sometimes manipulative tale. Straithairn is wonderfully despicable as the stereotypically deadbeat dad. **132m/C VHS, LV.** Kathy Bates, Jennifer Jason Leigh, Christopher Plummer, Judy Parfitt, David Strathairn, John C. Reilly; ***D:*** Taylor Hackford; ***W:*** Tony Gilroy; ***M:*** Danny Elfman. *COL*

The Dolphin 🦴🦴½ **1987** A dolphin visits a Brazilian fishing village each full moon, turns himself into a man, and casts a spell of seduction over the women. Villagers are both enchanted and angered by the dolphin-man, since his presence creates desire in local women but scares fish from the waters. In Portuguese with English subtitles. **95m/C VHS.** *BR* Carlos Alberto Riccelli, Cassia Kiss, Ney Latorraca; ***D:*** Walter Lima Jr.; ***W:*** Walter Lima Jr. *FXL, INJ, FCT*

Dominick & Eugene 🦴🦴🦴 **1988 (PG-13)** Dominick is a little slow, but he makes a fair living as a garbageman—good enough to put his brother through medical school. Both men struggle with the other's faults and weaknesses, as they learn the meaning of family and friendship. Well-acted, especially by Hulce, never melodramatic or weak. **96m/C VHS, Beta, LV.** Ray Liotta, Tom Hulce, Jamie Lee Curtis, Todd Graff, Bill Cobbs, David Strathairn; ***D:*** Robert M. Young; ***W:*** Alvin Sargent, Corey Blechman; ***M:*** Trevor Jones. *ORI, FCT*

Dominion 🦴🦴½ **1994 (R)** Six buddies take off for a weekend hunting trip that turns deadly when a murderous hunter believes they've trespassed on his territory and begins stalking them. **98m/C VHS.** Brad Johnson, Brion James, Tim Thomerson, Woody Brown, Glen Morshower, Richard Riehle, Geoffrey Blake; ***D:*** Michael Kehoe; ***W:*** Woody Brown, Michael Kehoe. *TTC*

Dominique is Dead 🦴🦴 **1979 (PG)** A woman is driven to suicide by her greedy husband; now someone is trying to drive him mad. A.K.A. "Dominique" and "Avenging Spirit." **95m/C VHS, Beta.** Cliff Robertson, Jean Simmons, Jenny Agutter, Simon Ward, Ron Moody; ***D:*** Michael Anderson Sr. *PSM*

Domino 🦴 **1988 (R)** A beautiful woman and a mysterious guy link up for sex, murder and double-crosses. Dubbed. Tries to be arty and avant-garde, but only succeeds in being a piece of soft-core fluff. **95m/C VHS, Beta, LV.** *IT* Brigitte Nielsen, Tomas Arana, Daniela Alzone; ***D:*** Ivana Massetti. *LIV*

The Domino Principle 🦴½ *The Domino Killings* **1977 (R)** It's got nothing to do with pizza. Viet vet Hackman is a doltish convict sprung from the joint by a government organization to do some dirty work: working as a political assassin. Heavy-handed direction and lack of suspense make it less than it should be. **97m/C VHS, Beta.** Gene Hackman, Candice Bergen, Richard Widmark, Mickey Rooney, Edward Albert, Eli Wallach; ***D:*** Stanley Kramer; ***C:*** Fred W. Koenekamp; ***M:*** Billy Goldenberg. *CCB, FOX*

Don Amigo/Stage to Chino **194?** A western double feature: The Cisco Kid and Pancho ride together again in "Don Amigo," and in "Stage to Chino," a postal inspector investigates a gang who robs rival stage lines. **122m/B VHS, Beta.** Duncan Renaldo, Leo Carrillo, George O'Brien, Roy Barcroft; ***D:*** Edward Killy. *TTC*

Don Daredevil Rides Again 🦴 **1951** A greedy political boss tries to take over homesteaders' claims for their mineral rights. One settler adopts the identity of an ancestor (Don Daredevil), and a black mask, and becomes a frontier avenger. A 12-episode serial. **180m/B VHS, Beta.** Ken Curtis, Aline Towne, Roy Barcroft. *REP, MLB, MED*

The Don is Dead 🦴½ *Beautiful But Deadly* **1973 (R)** A violent Mafia saga wherein a love triangle interferes with Family business, resulting in gang wars. **96m/C VHS, Beta.** Anthony Quinn, Frederic Forrest, Robert Forster, Al Lettieri, Ina Balin, Angel Tompkins, Charles Cioffi; ***D:*** Richard Fleischer; ***W:*** Michael Butler; ***M:*** Jerry Goldsmith. *MCA*

Don Juan 🦴🦴🦴½ **1926** Barrymore stars as the swashbuckling Italian duke with Spanish blood who seduces a castleful of women in the 1500s. Many exciting action sequences, including classic sword fights in which Barrymore eschewed a stunt double. Great attention is also paid to the detail of the costumes and settings of the Spanish-Moor period. Noted for employing fledgling movie sound effects and music-dubbing technology, which, ironically, were responsible for eclipsing the movie's reputation. Watch for Loy as an Asian vamp and Oland as a pre-Charlie Chan Cesare Borgia. **90m/B VHS, LV.** John Barrymore, Mary Astor, Willard Louis, Estelle Taylor, Helene Costello, Myrna Loy, June Marlowe, Warner Oland, Montagu Love, Hedda Hopper, Gustav von Seyffertitz; ***D:*** Alan Crosland. *MGM, FCT*

Don Juan DeMarco 🦴🦴½ **1994 (PG-13)** Burned-out clinical psychiatrist Dr. Jack Meckler (Brando) is romantically inspired by a cape-wearing, suicidal man-child from Queens (Depp), who thinks he's legendary lover Don Juan. Delusional Depp recounts, in a convincing Castilian accent, thousands of conquests as the sympathetic shrink decides it's time to bring some spice to his own ho-hum life and marriage (to Dunaway). Depp turns in a sincere, engaging performance that avoids the huge potential for melodrama and compensates for inconsistent pacing. Brando and Dunaway make a charmingly quirky couple. Watch for slain Tejano queen Selena in a musical interlude. **92m/C VHS, LV.** Marlon Brando, Johnny Depp, Faye Dunaway, Geraldine Pailhas, Rachel Ticotin, Bob Dishy, Talisa Soto; ***D:*** Jeremy Leven; ***W:*** Jeremy Leven. Nominations: Academy Awards '95: Best Song ("Have You Ever Really Loved a Woman?"); Golden Globe Awards '96: Best Song ("Have You Ever Really Loved a Woman?"), Best Score. *TTC, NLC*

Don Juan, My Love 🦴🦴🦴 *Don Juan, Mi Querido Fantasma* **1990** Sexy comedy finds the ghost of Don Juan given a chance, after 450 years in Purgatory, to perform a good deed and free his soul. In Spanish with English subtitles. **96m/C VHS, LV.** *SP* Juan Luis Galiardo, Rossy de Palma, Maria Barranco, Loles Leon; ***D:*** Antonio Mercero; ***M:*** Bernardo Bonazzi. *FXL, FCT, INJ*

Don Q., Son of Zorro 🦴🦴 **1925** Zorro's son takes up his father's fight against evil and injustice. Silent sequel to the 1920 classic. **111m/B VHS, Beta, LV.** Douglas Fairbanks Sr., Mary Astor. *NOS, WFV, CCB*

Don Quixote 🦴🦴🦴🦴 **1935** Miguel de Cervantes' tale of the romantic who would rather be a knight in shining armor than shining armor at night. Chaliapin stars as the knight-errant on his nightly errands, tilting at windmills and charging flocks of sheep. Certain scenes were adapted to fit the pre-WWII atmosphere, as it was filmed during the same time that the Nazis were burning books. **73m/B VHS.** Feodor Chaliapin, George Robey, Sidney Fox, Miles Mander, Oscar Asche, Emily Fitzroy, Wally Patch; ***D:*** G.W. Pabst; ***W:*** Paul Morand, Alexandre Arnoux; ***M:*** Jacques Ibert. *NOS, MLB, VEC*

Don Quixote 🦴🦴🦴½ **1957** The lauded, visually ravishing adaptation of the Cervantes classic, with a formal integrity inherited from Eisenstein and Dovshenko. In Russian with English subtitles. **110m/B VHS, Beta.** *SP RU* Nikolai Cherkassov, Yuri Tobubeyev; ***D:*** Grigori Kosintsev. *FCT*

Don Segundo Sombra 🦴🦴½ **1969** An interesting film seen through the eyes of an old gaucho, who is the mentor of a young boy growing to manhood. Based on the novel by Ricardo Guiraldes. In Spanish with English subtitles. **110m/C VHS, Beta.** *SP* Juan Carballido, Juan Carlos Gene, Soledad Silveyra, Alejandra Boero; ***D:*** Manuel Antin. Nominations: Cannes Film Festival '70: Best Film. *MED, INJ*

Don Winslow of the Coast Guard **1943** Serial in 13 episodes features comic-strip character Winslow as he strives to keep the waters of America safe for democracy. **234m/B VHS, Beta.** Don Terry, Elyse Knox; ***D:*** Ford Beebe, Ray Taylor. *NOS, MED, VDM*

Don Winslow of the Navy **1943** Thirteen episodes centered around the evil Scorpion, who plots to attack the Pacific Coast, but is thwarted by comic-strip hero Winslow. **234m/B VHS, Beta.** Don Terry, Walter Sande, Anne Nagel; ***D:*** Ford Beebe, Ray Taylor. *VYY, MED, MLB*

Dona Flor and Her Two Husbands 🦴🦴🦴 *Dona Flor e Seus Dois Maridos* **1978** A woman becomes a widow when her philandering husband finally expires from drink, gambling, and ladies. She remarries, but her new husband is so boring and proper that she begins fantasizing spouse number one's return. But is he only in her imagination? Based on the novel by Jorge Amado. In Portuguese with English subtitles. Remade as "Kiss Me Goodbye." **106m/C VHS, Beta, LV.** *BR* Sonia Braga, Jose Wilker, Mauro Mendonca; ***D:*** Bruno Barreto; ***W:*** Bruno Barreto; ***M:*** Chico Buarque. *FXL, IME, INJ*

Dona Herlinda & Her Son 🦴🦴 *Dona Herlinda y Su Hijo* **1986** A Mexican sex comedy about a mother who manipulates her bisexual son's two lovers (one male, one female), until all four fit together into a seamless unit. In Spanish with English subtitles. Slow, but amusing. **90m/C VHS, Beta, LV.** *MX* Guadalupe Del Toro, Arturo Meza, Marco Antonio Trevino, Leticia Lupersio; ***D:*** Jaime Humberto Hermosillo. *TPV, INJ, CCN*

Donkey Skin 🦴🦴🦴 *Peau d'Ane* **1970** A charming, all-star version of the medieval French fairy tale about a king searching for a suitable wife in a magical realm after his queen dies. In his quest for the most beautiful spouse, he learns that his daughter is that woman. She prefers Prince Charming, however. In French with English subtitles. **89m/C VHS, Beta.** *FR* Catherine Deneuve, Jean Marais, Delphine Seyrig, Jacques Perrin; ***D:*** Jacques Demy; ***C:*** Ghislan Cloquet. *INJ, SUE*

Donner Pass: The Road to Survival 🦴🦴 **1984** Tame retelling of the western wagon-train pioneers who were forced to resort to cannibalism during a brutal snowstorm in the Rockies. The tragedy is lightly implied, keeping the film suitable for family viewing. **98m/C VHS, Beta.** Robert Fuller, Diane McBain, Andrew Prine, John Anderson, Michael Callan; ***D:*** James L. Conway. *VTR, HHE*

The Donor 🦴½ **1994 (R)** Cartel stalks victims and kills them for a human organ black market. **94m/C VHS.** Jeff Wincott, Michelle Johnson, Gordon Thomson; ***D:*** Damian Lee; ***W:*** Neal Dobrofsky, Tippi Dobrofsky. *AVE*

Donor Unknown 🦴🦴 **1995 (R)** Driven businessman Nicholas Stillman (Onorati) has always put work before his family—and both wife Alice (Krige) and teenaged daughter Danielle (Herbst) have suffered from his attitude. When Nick is hit by a massive heart attack and gets a transplant, he insists on knowing everything about the donor. What he uncovers is a black market in organ procurement and Nash Creed (Brown), who'll do anything to stop Nick from exposing his lucrative business. Based on the novel "Corazon" by William H. Mooney. **93m/C VHS.** Peter Onorati, Alice Krige, Clancy Brown, Becky Herbst, Sam Robards, Richard Portnow, T.J. Castranovo, Leo Garcia, John Dorman; ***D:*** John Harrison; ***W:*** John Harrison. *MCA*

Donovan's Brain 🦴🦴🦴 **1953** A scientist maintains the still-living brain of a dead millionaire and begins to be controlled by its powerful force. Based on Curt Siodmak's novel. **85m/B VHS, Beta, LV.** Lew Ayres, Gene Evans, Nancy Davis, Steve Brodie; ***D:*** Felix Feist; ***C:*** Joseph Biroc. *MGM, IME, MLB*

Donovan's Reef 🦴🦴🦴 **1963** Two WWII buddies meet every year on a Pacific atoll to engage in a perpetual bar-brawl, until a stuck-up Bostonian maiden appears to find her dad, a man who has fathered a brood of lovable half-casts. A rollicking, good-natured film from Ford. **109m/C VHS, Beta, LV.** John Wayne, Lee Marvin, Jack Warden, Elizabeth Allen, Dorothy Lamour, Mike Mazurki, Cesar Romero; ***D:*** John Ford; ***C:*** William Clothier. *PAR, TLF*

Don's Party 🦴🦴🦴 **1976** A rather dark comedy focusing on Australian Yuppie-types who decide to watch the election results on television as a group. A lot more goes on at this party, however, than talk of the returns. Sexual themes surface. Cast members turn fine performances, aided by top-notch script and direction. **90m/C VHS, Beta.** *AU* Pat Bishop, Graham Kennedy, Candy Raymond, Veronica Lang, John Hargreaves; ***D:*** Bruce Beresford; ***W:*** David Williamson. Australian Film Institute '77: Best Actress (Bishop). *FCT*

Don't Answer the Phone 🦴 *The Hollywood Strangler* **1980 (R)** Deeply troubled photographer stalks and attacks the patients of a beautiful psychologist talk-show hostess. **94m/C VHS, Beta.** James Westmoreland, Flo Gerrish, Ben Frank; ***D:*** Robert Hammer; ***M:*** Byron Allred. *MED*

Don't Be Afraid of the Dark 🦴🦴½ **1973** A young couple move into their dream house only to find that demonic little critters are residing in their basement and they want more than shelter. Made for TV with creepy scenes and eerie makeup for the monsters. **74m/C VHS, Beta.** Kim Darby, Jim Hutton, Barbara Anderson, William Demarest, Pedro Armendariz Jr.; ***D:*** John Newland. *LIV*

Don't Bother to Knock 🦴🦴½ **1952** As a mentally unstable hotel babysitter, Monroe meets a pilot (Widmark) and has a brief rendezvous with him. When the little girl she is babysitting interrupts, Monroe is furious, and later tries to murder the girl. This is one of Monroe's best dramatic roles. Bancroft's film debut as the Widmark's girlfriend. **76m/B VHS.** Richard Widmark, Marilyn Monroe, Anne Bancroft, Elisha Cook Jr., Jim Backus, Lurene Tuttle, Jeanne Cagney, Donna Corcoran; ***D:*** Roy Ward Baker; ***W:*** Daniel Taradash. *FXV*

Don't Change My World 🦴½ **1983 (G)** To preserve the natural beauty of the north woods, a wildlife photographer must fight a villainous land developer and a reckless poacher. Eco-correct. **89m/C VHS, Beta.** Roy Tatum, Ben Jones, Edie Kramer, George Macrenais, Paul Newmark, David Eidson; ***D:*** Robert Rector. *LIV*

Don't Cry, It's Only Thunder 🦴🦴½ **1982 (PG)** A young army medic who works in a mortuary in Saigon becomes involved with a group of Vietnamese orphans and a dedicated army doctor. Based on a true story. **108m/C VHS, Beta.** Dennis Christopher, Susan St. James, Roger Brown, Li Lu, Thu Thuy, James Whitmore; ***D:*** Peter Werner; ***M:*** Maurice Jarre. *COL*

Don't Do It 🦴🦴½ **1994 (PG-13)** Three twentysomething couples, attempting to find love, all wind up in the same cafe and try to tell the truth about how they feel and whom they desire. **90m/C VHS.** James Marshall, James LeGros, Sheryl Lee, Esai Morales, Alexis Arquette, Balthazar Getty; ***D:*** Eugene Hess; ***W:*** Eugene Hess. *TRI*

Don't Drink the Water 🦴🦴½ **1969 (G)** Based on Woody Allen's hit play, this film places an average Newark, New Jersey, family behind the Iron Curtain, where their vacation photo-taking gets them accused of spying. **100m/C VHS, Beta.** Jackie Gleason, Estelle Parsons, Joan Delaney, Ted Bessell, Michael Constantine; ***D:*** Howard Morris. *COL, SUE*

Don't Go in the House 🦴 **1980 (R)** Long-dormant psychosis is brought to life by the death of a young man's mother. **90m/C VHS, Beta.** Dan Grimaldi, Robert Osth, Ruth Dardick; ***D:*** Joseph Ellison; ***M:*** Richard Einhorn. *MED*

Don't Go in the Woods *Woof!* **1981 (R)** Routine exercise in "don't do that" terror genre (includes warnings about going into houses, answering phones, looking into basements, opening windows, etc.). This time, four young campers are stalked by a crazed killer armed with prerequisite ax. **88m/C VHS, Beta.** *VES*

Don't Go Near the Water 🦴🦴 **1957** Somewhat amusing comedy about the happenings at a Naval installation on a South Pacific tropical paradise. Clark outshines the others in his role as a frustrated officer. Based on the novel by William Brinkley. **107m/C VHS.** Glenn Ford, Gia Scala, Earl Holliman, Anne Francis, Keenan Wynn, Fred Clark, Eva Gabor, Russ Tamblyn; ***D:*** Charles Walters; ***W:*** Dorothy Kingsley, George Wells. *MGM*

Don't Go to Sleep 🦴🦴 **1982** After a fatal car crash, a young girl misses mom and dad so much she returns from the grave to take them where they can be one big happy family again. Better than most made-for-TV junk-food fright-fests, written by Keenan Wynn's son, Ned. **93m/C VHS.** Dennis Weaver, Valerie Harper, Robin Ignico, Kristin Cummings, Ruth Gordon, Robert Webber; ***D:*** Richard Lang; ***W:*** Ned Wynn. *UNI*

Don't Hang Up 🦴🦴½ **1990** Handicapped New York actress Sarah (Arquette) wants to do a production of agoraphobic London writer Joe's (Suchet) play. So she calls him up to get his permission and the two begin a phone relationship that develops from business to romance. **84m/C VHS.** *GB* Rosanna Arquette, David Suchet. *WBF*

Don't Let Your Meat Loaf 🦴½ **1995** Three struggling comedians take their act on the road, including subway stations and street corners, in order to get the money to open their own comedy club. **82m/C VHS.** Leander Sales, Dana S. Hubbard, Brad Albright; ***D:*** Leander Sales. *SDE*

Don't Look Back: The Story of Leroy "Satchel" Paige 🦴🦴½ **1981** Drama of the legendary baseball pitcher who helped break down racial barriers, based on his autobiography. Made-for-TV fare. Gossett hits a home run in the lead, but the overall effort is a ground-rule double. **98m/C VHS.** Louis Gossett Jr., Beverly Todd, Cleavon Little, Clifton Davis, John Beradino, Jim Davis, Ossie Davis, Hal Williams; ***D:*** George C. Scott, Richard A. Colla. *ABC*

Don't Look in the Attic *Woof!* **1981** A couple finds a haunted house with cows in the attic. **90m/C VHS, Beta.** Beba Loncar, Jean-Pierre Aumont; ***D:*** Carl Ausino. *NO*

Don't Look in the Basement 🦴½ **1973 (R)** Things get out of hand at an isolated asylum and a pretty young nurse is caught in the middle. Straight-jacketed by a low budget. **95m/C VHS, Beta.** Rosie Holotik, Anne MacAdams, William Bill McGhee, Rhea MacAdams, Gene Ross, Betty Chandler, Camilla Carr, Robert Dracup, Jessie Kirby, Hugh Feagin, Harryete Warren, Jessie Lee Fulton, Michael Harvey; ***D:*** S.F. Brownrigg. *MPI*

Don't Look Now 🦴🦴🦴 **1973 (R)** A psychological thriller about a couple's trip to Venice after their child drowns. Notable for a steamy love scene and a chilling climax. Based on the novel by Daphne Du Maurier. **110m/C VHS, Beta, LV.** Donald Sutherland, Julie Christie, Hilary Mason; ***D:*** Nicolas Roeg; ***W:*** Chris Bryant, Allan Scott; ***M:*** Pino Donaggio. *PAR*

Don't Mess with My Sister! 🦴🦴½ **1985** A married, New York junkyard worker falls in love with a belly dancer he meets at a party. The affair leads to murder and subsequently, revenge. An interesting, offbeat film from the director of "I Spit on Your Grave." **90m/C VHS, Beta, LV.** Joe Perce, Jeannine Lemay, Jack Gurci, Peter Sapienza, Laura Lanfranchi; ***D:*** Mier Zarchi. *NO*

Don't Open the Door! *Woof!* **1974 (PG)** A young woman is terrorized by a killer located inside her house. **90m/C VHS, Beta.** Susan Bracken, Gene Ross, Jim Harrell; ***D:*** S.F. Brownrigg. *GEM*

Don't Open Till Christmas *Woof!* **1984** A weirdo murders various Santa Clauses in assorted gory ways. Best to take this one back to the department store. **86m/C VHS, Beta.** *GB* Edmund Purdom, Caroline Munro, Alan Lake, Belinda Mayne, Gerry Sundquist, Mark Jones; ***D:*** Edmund Purdom. *LIV, VES*

Don't Raise the Bridge, Lower the River 🦴🦴 **1968 (G)** After his wife leaves him, an American with crazy, get-rich-quick schemes turns his wife's ancestral English home into a Chinese discotheque. Domestic farce that comes and goes; if mad for Lewis, rent "The Nutty Professor." **99m/C VHS, Beta.** Jerry Lewis, Terry-Thomas, Jacqueline Pearce; ***D:*** Jerry Paris. *COL*

Don't Shove/Two Gun Gussie **1919** Two early Harold Lloyd shorts feature the comedian's embryonic comic style as a young fellow impressing his date at a skating rink ("Don't Shove") and a city slicker out West ("Two Gun Gussie"). Silent with piano scores. **27m/B VHS, Beta.** Harold Lloyd, Bebe Daniels, Noah Young, Snub Pollard. *CCB*

Don't Talk to Strangers 🦴🦴½ **1994 (R)** Formula thriller has Brosnan marrying divorcee Reed and becoming instant father to her 9-year-old son. But someone appears to be a whacko—is it the kid's real dad (Quinn) or is Brosnan just too good to be true? **94m/C VHS, LV.** Pierce Brosnan, Shanna Reed, Terry O'Quinn; ***D:*** Robert Lewis; ***W:*** Neill D. Hicks, Jon George, Nevin Schreiner. *MCA*

Don't Tell Her It's Me 🦴 *The Boyfriend School* **1990 (PG-13)** Guttenberg is determined to win the heart of an attractive writer. With the assistance of his sister, he works to become a dream man. Clever premise, promising cast, lame comedy. From the novel by Sarah Bird. **101m/C VHS, Beta, LV.** Steve Guttenberg, Jami Gertz, Shelley Long, Kyle MacLachlan, Madchen Amick; ***D:*** Malcolm Mowbray; ***W:*** Sarah Bird; ***M:*** Michael Gore. *HBO*

Don't Tell Mom the Babysitter's Dead 🦴½ **1991 (PG-13)** Their mother traveling abroad, the title situation leaves a houseful of teenagers with the whole summer to themselves. Eldest daughter Applegate cons her way into the high-powered business world while the metalhead son parties hardy. Many tepid comic situations, not adding up to very much. **105m/C VHS, Beta, LV, 8mm.** Christina Applegate, Keith Coogan, Joanna Cassidy, John Getz, Josh Charles, Concetta Tomei, Eda Reiss Merin; ***D:*** Stephen Herek. *HBO*

The Doolins of Oklahoma 🦴🦴½ *The Great Manhunt* **1949** Scott is the leader of the last of the southwestern outlaw gangs, pursued by lawmen and changing times with the onset of the modern age. Fast-paced and intelligent. **90m/B VHS, Beta.** Randolph Scott, George Macready, Louise Allbritton, John Ireland, Virginia Huston, Charles Kemper, Noah Beery Jr.; ***D:*** Gordon Douglas; ***M:*** George Duning. *GKK*

Doom Asylum *Woof!* **1988 (R)** Several sex kittens wander into a deserted sanatorium and meet up with the grisly beast wielding autopsy instruments. The people involved with this spoof should have been (more) committed. **77m/C VHS, Beta.** Patty Mullen, Ruth Collins, Kristen Davis, William Hay, Kenny L. Price, Harrison White, Dawn Alvan, Michael Rogan; ***D:*** Richard S. Friedman. *ACA*

The Doom Generation 1995 (R) Alienated trio on the road trip to hell (doubling as L.A.). Beautiful 17-year-old druggie Amy Blue (McGowan), her sweetly dim boyfriend Jordan White (Duval), and hot-tempered stud/drifter Xavier Red (Schaech) flee after Red kills a store clerk. They're basically from nowhere, going nowhere, and finding sex and (lots of gruesomely depicted) violence along the way. The subtitle, "A Heterosexual Movie by Gregg Araki," may be technically accurate but the homoerotic subtext is very clear. Terrific performances. Second film in Araki's teen trilogy, following "Totally F***ked Up," and preceding "Nowhere." An unrated version is also available. **84m/C VHS.** Rose McGowan, James Duval, Johnathon Schaech; ***Cameos:*** Parker Posey; ***D:*** Gregg Araki; ***W:*** Gregg Araki; ***C:*** Jim Fealy. Nominations: Independent Spirit Awards '96: Debut Performance (McGowan). *VMK*

Doomed at Sundown ½ 1937 Decent Steele vehicle has the tough cowpoke as a sheriff's son known for playing practical jokes. When his father gets knifed, it's no laughing matter and he takes off after the killers. Based on a story by Fred Myton. **55m/B VHS.** Bob Steele, Laraine Day, Warner Richmond, Harold Daniels, David Sharpe; ***D:*** Sam Newfield; ***W:*** George Plympton. *GPV, DVT*

Doomed Caravan 1941 Hoppy and his pals lend a hand when some villains try to monopolize the wagon train business. Location shooting was done in the valleys of central California. **60m/B VHS.** William Boyd, Russell Hayden, Andy Clyde, Minna Gombell, Morris Ankrum, Georgia Hawkins, Trevor Bardette, Pat O'Brien; ***D:*** Lesley Selander. *NOS*

Doomed Love ½ 1983 Love is hell, especially when the object of your affection happens to be deceased. A professor of literature in the throes of unrequited love decides to reunite himself with his lost love. Won awards when released in Berlin. **75m/C VHS.** Bill Rice; ***D:*** Andrew Horn. *MWF, FCT*

Doomed to Die 1940 Cargo of stolen bonds leads to a tong war and the murder of a shipping millionaire. Part of Mr. Wong series. Worth a look if only for Karloff's performance. **67m/B VHS, Beta.** Boris Karloff, Marjorie Reynolds, Grant Withers; ***D:*** William Nigh. *NOS, MRV, SNC*

Doomsday ½ 1928 Vidor marries for wealth instead of love and, in classic fashion, finds that money doesn't buy happiness. **73m/B VHS.** Florence Vidor, Gary Cooper, Lawrence Grant; ***D:*** Rowland V. Lee. *GPV*

The Doomsday Flight 1966 Uneven made-for-television thriller. O'Brien plants an altitude-triggered bomb on a jet in an effort to blackmail the airline. Search for the bomb provides some suspenseful and well-acted moments. **100m/C VHS, Beta.** Jack Lord, Edmond O'Brien, Van Johnson, John Saxon, Katherine Crawford, Michael Sarrazin, Ed Asner, Greg Morris, Richard Carlson, Don Stewart; ***D:*** William A. Graham; ***W:*** Rod Serling. *MCA*

Doomsday Gun ½ 1994 Fact-based thriller about arms manufacturer Gerald Bull (Langella), who dreams of building the world's biggest gun—a behemoth with a range of 1000 miles. Only problem is Bull's willingness to sell the weapon to the highest bidder, who happens to be Saddam Hussein. This doesn't sit well with Israeli Mossad agent Yossi (Arkin). Made for cable TV. **110m/C VHS.** Frank Langella, Alan Arkin, Kevin Spacey, Tony Goldwyn, James Fox, Michael Kitchen, Francesca Annis, Marianne Denicourt; ***D:*** Robert M. Young; ***W:*** Lionel Chetwynd, Walter Bernstein. *HBO*

Doomwatch ½ 1972 A scientist discovers a chemical company is dumping poison into local waters, deforming the inhabitants of an isolated island when they eat the catch of the day. Unsurprising. **89m/C VHS, Beta.** *GB* Ian Bannen, Judy Geeson, John Paul, Simon Oates, George Sanders; ***D:*** Peter Sasdy. *MON, SUE*

Door to Door 1984 A made-for-cable comedy about two door-to-door salesmen who race to stay one step ahead of the law and their own company. Fairly lightweight, but it has its moments. **93m/C VHS, Beta.** Ron Leibman, Jane Kaczmarek, Arliss Howard, Alan Austin; ***D:*** Patrick Bailey. *MED*

Door to Door Maniac ½ *Five Minutes to Live* 1961 Criminals hold a bank president's wife hostage, unaware that the husband was looking to get rid of her in favor of another woman. Cash's screen debut. Aside from the strange cast ensemble, not particularly worth seeing. **80m/B VHS, Beta.** Johnny Cash, Ron Howard, Vic Tayback, Donald Woods, Cay Forrester, Pamela Mason; ***D:*** Bill Karn. *VDM, AOV*

Door with the Seven Locks ½ 1962 Bizarre Edgar Wallace story of man who leaves seven keys to a treasure vault in his will. Remake of "Chamber of Horrors." **96m/C VHS.** *GE* Eddi Arent, Heinz Drache, Klaus Kinski, Ady Berber; ***D:*** Alfred Vohrer. *SNC*

The Doors ½ 1991 (R) Stone approached Jim Morrison with an early incarnation of this docudrama, but it's hard to believe even the Lizard King could play himself with any more convincing abandon than Kilmer, in a great performance. Trouble is, the story—one of drugs, abuse, and abject self-indulgence—grows tiresome, and the audience, with the exception of die-hard fans, may lose sight of any sympathy they might have had. Ryan is forgettable as Morrison's hippie-chick wife, MacLachlan sports a funny wig and dabbles on the keyboards as Ray Manszarek, and Quinlan is atypically cast as a sado-masochistic journalist paramour. Based on "Riders on the Storm" by John Densmore. **138m/C VHS, LV, 8mm.** Val Kilmer, Meg Ryan, Kevin Dillon, Kyle MacLachlan, Frank Whaley, Michael Madsen, Kathleen Quinlan, Crispin Glover, Josh Evans, John Densmore, William Jordan, Mimi Rogers, Paul Williams, Bill Graham, Billy Vera, William Kunstler, Wes Studi, Costas Mandylor, Billy Idol, Michael Wincott, Dennis Burkley; ***D:*** Oliver Stone; ***W:*** Oliver Stone, Ralph Thomas, Randy Johnson, J. Randall Johnson; ***C:*** Robert Richardson. *COL, FCT, VES*

The Doors: Soft Parade, a Retrospective 1969 The Doors' final TV appearance in 1969 forms the centerpiece of this concert-video tie-in to the Oliver Stone film. Fans should a-Door previously unreleased backstage interviews and a notable version of "The Unknown Soldier." **50m/C VHS, LV.** ***D:*** Ray Manzarek. *MCA*

Dope Mania 1986 A potpourri of anti-drug propaganda spanning from the '30's to the '60's, campily detailing the degradation thought to result instantly from pot and cocaine. **60m/C VHS, Beta.** *RHI*

Doppelganger: The Evil Within 1990 (R) Holly Gooding (Barrymore) seems like such a nice girl—until the police suspect her of the brutal murder of her mother. Her new friend Patrick (Newbern) begins to see another side to the vulnerable Holly—a seductress capable of doing anything to get what she wants. **105m/C VHS, LV.** Drew Barrymore, George Newbern, Dennis Christopher, Sally Kellerman, Leslie Hope; ***D:*** Avi Nesher; ***W:*** Avi Nesher. *FXV*

Dorian Gray ½ *The Secret of Dorian Gray; Il Dio Chiamato a Dorian; Das Bildness des Dorian Gray* 1970 (R) Modern-day version of the famous tale by Oscar Wilde about an ageless young man whose portrait reflects the ravages of time and a life of debauchery. More sex, less acting with Berger in lead. Not nearly as good as the original version, "The Picture of Dorian Gray." **92m/C VHS.** *GE IT* Richard Todd, Helmut Berger, Herbert Lom; ***D:*** Massimo Dallamano. *REP, FCT*

Dorm That Dripped Blood *Woof!* 1982 (R) Five college students volunteer to close the dorm during their Christmas vacation. A series of grisly and barbaric incidents eliminates the youngsters one by one. As the terror mounts, the remaining students slowly realize that they are up against a terrifyingly real psychopathic killer. Merry Christmas. **84m/C VHS, Beta.** Laura Lopinski, Stephen Sachs, Pamela Holland; ***D:*** Stephen Carpenter, Jeffrey Obrow; ***W:*** Stephen Carpenter. *MED*

Dos Cruces en Danger Pass 1971 Charming fairy tale about a widowed king in search of a beautiful wife. Gorgeous color production. Also known as "Peau D'Ane." In French with English subtitles. **0090m/C VHS, Beta.** *FR* Catherine Deneuve, Jacques Perrin, Jean Marais, Delphine Seyrig; ***D:*** Jacques Demy. *SUE*

Double Agents *La Nuit Des Espions; Night Encounter* 1959 Two double agents are sent on a rendezvous to exchange vital government secrets. Dubbed in English. **81m/B VHS, Beta.** *FR* Marina Vlady, Robert Hossein. *VYY*

Double Cross 1992 (R) Tank Polling (Connery), a British journalist, uses the secrets of an ex-hooker (Donohoe) to get back at a corrupt politician who ruined Polling's life five years earlier. Lots of action and a few graphic murders in this thriller. **96m/C VHS.** Amanda Donohoe, Peter Wyngarde, Jason Connery; ***D:*** James Marcus. *VTR*

Double Cross 1994 (R) Man has what seems to be a chance erotic encounter with a beautiful blonde. But this wouldn't be a thriller if it ended there, so there's blackmail and murder to contend with as well. **95m/C VHS.** Patrick Bergin, Jennifer Tilly, Kelly Preston, Matt Craven, Kevin Tighe. *PAR*

Double-Crossed ½ 1991 In 1984 Barry Seal agrees to inform on Colombia's Medellin Cartel and its links to the Sandanista government of Nicaragua in exchange for leniency on drug-smuggling charges. Little does he know that the personal consequences will turn deadly when his cover is blown and the government double-crosses him. Hopper's hyped-up performance as drug smuggler turned DEA informant Seal showcases this true-crime tale. **111m/C VHS, LV.** Dennis Hopper, Robert Carradine, G.W. Bailey, Adrienne Barbeau; ***C:*** Donald M. Morgan; ***M:*** Richard Bellis. *WAR*

Double Deal 1939 An honest man and a gangster are rivals in love. The gangster robs a jewelry store and tries to pin the crime on the good guy. This is a movie with a moral so don't expect him to get away with it. **60m/C VHS.** Monte Hawley, Jeni Le Gon, Edward Thompson, Florence O'Brien; ***D:*** Arthur Dreifuss. *FCT*

Double Deal ½ 1950 Murder, mayhem, and industrial espionage come into play as parties fight over an oil field. **65m/B VHS, Beta.** Marie Windsor, Richard Denning, Taylor Holmes; ***D:*** Abby Berlin. *DVT*

Double Deal ½ 1984 Unfaithful woman and her lover plot to steal priceless opal from hubby. Lifeless and silly. **90m/C VHS, Beta.** Louis Jourdan, Angela Punch McGregor; ***D:*** Brian Kavanagh. *NO*

Double Double Toil and Trouble ½ 1994 The twins come to the financial rescue of their family when Dad's business gets into trouble and their home is threatened. But first they need to get a magic moonstone from their wicked Aunt Agatha (Leachman) and rescue kind Aunt Sophia, all before midnight on Halloween. Made for TV. **93m/C VHS.** Ashley Olsen, Mary-Kate Olsen, Cloris Leachman, Meshach Taylor; ***D:*** Jeff Franklin; ***W:*** Jeff Franklin. *WAR*

Double Dragon ½ 1994 (PG-13) Generally harmless brain candy, based on the videogame, finds orphaned brothers Jimmy (Dacascos) and Billy (Wolf) living in the rubble of post earthquake L.A., circa 2007. They have half of a mystical dragon amulet and obsessed mogul Koga Shuko (Patrick), who possesses the other half, after them. Seems he needs the entire amulet in order to control its vast power. Non-stop action should keep the kiddies amused. **96m/C VHS, LV.** Scott Wolf, Mark Dacascos, Robert Patrick, Alyssa Milano, Kristina Malandro Wagner, Julia Nickson-Soul; ***D:*** Jim Yukich; ***W:*** Michael Paul Davis, Peter Gould; ***M:*** Jay Michael Ferguson. *MCA*

Double Dynamite 🦴½ *It's Only Money* **1951** A bank teller is at a loss when his racetrack winnings are confused with the cash lifted from his bank during a robbery. Forgettable, forgotten shambles. Originally filmed in 1948. **80m/B VHS, Beta.** Frank Sinatra, Jane Russell, Groucho Marx, Don McGuire, Howard Freeman, Harry Hayden, Nestor Paiva, Lou Nova, Joe Devlin; ***D:*** Irving Cummings; ***W:*** Melville Shavelson. *TTC*

Double Edge 🦴🦴 **1992 (PG-13)** The Palestinian-Israeli conflict is the focus of this drama about an ambitious reporter (Dunaway). On her first foreign assignment, New Yorker Faye Milano finds herself way out of her depth when she covers a colleague's beat in Jerusalem. Unable to remain a detached observer, Faye instead becomes an active participant, alternating between her affair with an Israeli reserves officer and her friendship with a family of Palestinian intifada leaders. Dunaway and Kollek are unfortunately stiff in their performances but the location (Israel and the West Bank) is interesting and the story surprisingly balanced. **85m/C VHS, Beta.** *IS* Faye Dunaway, Amos Kollek, Muhamad Bakri, Shmuel Shilo, Makram Khouri, Michael Schneider, Anat Atzman, Ann Belkin; ***D:*** Amos Kollek; ***W:*** Amos Kollek. *WAR*

Double Exposure 🦴🦴 **1982 (R)** A young photographer's violent nightmares become the next day's headlines. Unsurprising vision. **95m/C VHS, Beta.** Michael Callan, James Stacy, Joanna Pettet, Cleavon Little, Pamela Hensley, Seymour Cassel; ***D:*** William B. Hillman. *VES*

Double Exposure 🦴½ **1993 (R)** A possessive husband discovers his wife's infidelity and decides to get revenge, only his plan doesn't work out as he intends. **93m/C VHS, LV.** Ron Perlman, Ian Buchanan, Jennifer Gatti, William R. Moses, James McEachin, Dedee Pfeiffer; ***D:*** Claudia Hoover; ***W:*** Christine Colfer, Bridget Hoffman, Claudia Hoover. *PSM*

Double Exposure: The Story of Margaret Bourke-White 🦴🦴½ *Margaret Bourke-White* **1989** Beautifully shot but slow biography of a woman who became a well-known professional photographer for "Life" magazine during the 1930s and 1940s, as well as the first official female photojournalist of WWII. Made for cable television. **105m/C VHS, LV.** Farrah Fawcett, Frederic Forrest, Mitchell Ryan, David Huddleston, Jay Patterson, Ken Marshall; ***D:*** Lawrence Schiller. *TTC*

Double Face 🦴½ **1970** A wealthy industrialist kills his lesbian wife with a car bomb, but she seems to haunt him through pornographic films. **84m/C VHS, Beta.** Klaus Kinski, Annabella Incontrera. *UNI*

Double Happiness 🦴🦴🦴 **1994 (PG-13)** Slice of life comedy-drama finds twentysomething Chinese-Canadian Jade Li (Oh) struggling to balance her would-be acting career and new world romance with her family's traditional values. Jade wants to please her old world father (Chang) so she endures his arranged dates and puts on a pleasant demeanor for family friends. But Jade must decide who she wants to be when she gets involved with non-Asian college student Mark (Rennie). Fine performances and assured direction from Shum in her feature film debut. **87m/C VHS, LV.** *CA* Sandra Oh, Stephen Chang, Alannah Ong, Frances You, Johnny Mah, Callum Rennie; ***D:*** Mina Shum; ***W:*** Mina Shum; ***C:*** Peter Wunstorf. Genie Awards '94: Best Actress (Oh), Best Film Editing; Nominations: Genie Awards '94: Best Director (Shum), Best Film. *TTC, NLC*

Double Identity 🦴🦴½ **1989 (PG-13)** Former college professor turned criminal Mancuso moves to a corn patch called New Hope in hopes of returning to the straight and narrow. He finds a good woman to stand by him, but, alas, crime, like smoking, is easier to start than to quit. Much intrigue and deceit. **95m/C VHS.** *CA FR* Nick Mancuso, Leah K. Pinsent, Patrick Bauchau, Anne LeTourneau, Jacques Godin; ***D:*** Yves Boisset. *NO*

Double Impact 🦴½ **1991 (R)** Van Damme plays twins re-united in Hong Kong to avenge their parents' murder by local bad guys, but this lunkhead kick-em-up doesn't even take advantage of that gimmick; the basic story would have been exactly the same with just one Jean-Claude. Lots of profane dialogue and some gratuitous nudity for the kiddies. **107m/C VHS, Beta, LV, 8mm.** Jean-Claude Van Damme, Cory Everson, Geoffrey Lewis; ***D:*** Sheldon Lettich; ***W:*** Jean-Claude Van Damme, Sheldon Lettich. *COL, CCB*

Double Indemnity 🦴🦴🦴🦴 **1944** The classic seedy story of an insurance agent seduced by a deadly woman into killing her husband so they can collect together from his company. Terrific, influential film noir, the best of its kind. Based on the James M. Cain novel. **107m/B VHS, Beta, LV.** Fred MacMurray, Barbara Stanwyck, Edward G. Robinson, Tom Powers, Porter Hall, Jean Heather, Byron Barr, Fortunio Bonanova; ***D:*** Billy Wilder; ***W:*** Raymond Chandler, Billy Wilder; ***M:*** Miklos Rozsa. Nominations: Academy Awards '44: Best Actress (Stanwyck), Best Black and White Cinematography, Best Director (Wilder), Best Picture, Best Screenplay, Best Sound, Best Original Score. *MCA, FCT*

Double Jeopardy 🦴🦴 **1992 (R)** Boxleitner stars as a married man who risks his family and life when his sexy ex-lover returns to town. She easily involves him in deception—and murder. A cake-walk for Ward as the femme fatale. Made for cable television. **101m/C VHS, Beta, LV.** Bruce Boxleitner, Rachel Ward, Sela Ward, Sally Kirkland; ***D:*** Lawrence Schiller; ***M:*** Eduard Artemyev. *FXV, PMS*

A Double Life 🦴🦴🦴 **1947** Colman plays a Shakespearean actor in trouble when the characters he plays begin to seep into his personal life and take over. Things begin to look really bad when he is cast in the role of the cursed Othello. Colman won an Oscar for this difficult role, and the moody musical score garnered another for Rosza. **107m/B VHS.** Ronald Colman, Shelley Winters, Signe Hasso, Edmond O'Brien, Ray Collins, Millard Mitchell; ***D:*** George Cukor; ***W:*** Ruth Gordon, Garson Kanin; ***C:*** Milton Krasner; ***M:*** Miklos Rozsa. Academy Awards '47: Best Actor (Colman), Best Score; Golden Globe Awards '48: Best Actor—Drama (Colman); Nominations: Academy Awards '47: Best Director (Cukor), Best Original Screenplay. *REP, FCT, BTV*

The Double Life of Veronique 🦴🦴 *La Double Vie de Veronique* **1991 (R)** They say everyone has a twin, but this is ridiculous. Two women—Polish Veronika and French Veronique—are born on the same day in different countries, share a singing talent, a cardiac ailment, and, although the two never meet, a strange awareness of each other. Jacob is unforgettable as the two women, and director Krzysztof creates some spellbinding scenes but the viewer has to be willing to forgo plot for atmosphere. **96m/C VHS, Beta, LV.** *FR PL* Irene Jacob, Phillipe Volter, Sandrine Dumas, Aleksander Bardini, Louis Ducreux, Claude Duneton, Halina Gryglaszewska, Kalina Jedrusik; ***D:*** Krzysztof Kieslowski; ***W:*** Krzysztof Kieslowski, Krzysztof Piesiewicz; ***C:*** Slawomir Idziak. Cannes Film Festival '91: Best Actress (Jacob); National Society of Film Critics Awards '91: Best Foreign Film. *PAR*

The Double McGuffin 🦴🦴 **1979 (PG)** A plot of international intrigue is uncovered by teenagers—a la the Hardy Boys—when a prime minister and her security guard pay a visit to a small Virginia community. They're not believed, though. Action-packed from the makers of Benji. Dogs do not figure prominently here. **100m/C VHS, Beta.** Ernest Borgnine, George Kennedy, Elke Sommer, Ed "Too Tall" Jones, Lisa Whelchel, Vincent Spano; ***D:*** Joe Camp; ***M:*** Euel Box; ***V:*** Orson Welles. *VES*

The Double Negative 🦴½ *Deadly Companion* **1980** A photojournalist pursues his wife's killer in a confusing story. Based on Ross MacDonald's "The Three Roads." **96m/C VHS, Beta.** *CA* Michael Sarrazin, Susan Clark, Anthony Perkins, Howard Duff, Kate Reid, Al Waxman, Elizabeth Shepherd, John Candy; ***D:*** George Bloomfield; ***W:*** Janis Allen. *BFV*

The Double O Kid 🦴🦴½ **1992 (PG-13)** Lance is a 17-year-old video game master who's interning at the Agency, a covert spy organization. Ordered to rush a package to Los Angeles, Lance discovers that a madman computer virus designer and his henchwoman desperately want what he's carrying. Aided by the prerequisite pretty girl, Lance must avoid all the hazards sent his way. **95m/C VHS, Beta.** Corey Haim, Wallace Shawn, Brigitte Nielsen, Nicole Eggert, John Rhys-Davies, Basil Hoffman, Karen Black; ***Cameos:*** Anne Francis; ***D:*** Duncan McLachlan; ***W:*** Andrea Buck, Duncan McLachlan. *PSM*

Double Obsession 🦴½ **1993 (R)** College roommates Heather (Hemingway) and Claire (d'Abo) are inseparable friends—until Claire falls in love. Heather becomes possessive and, though the years pass, her obsession with Claire only grows. When Heather's affections turn deadly, can Claire stop her? **88m/C VHS.** Margaux Hemingway, Maryam D'Abo, Frederic Forrest, Scott Valentine; ***D:*** Eduardo Montes; ***W:*** Jeffrey Delman, R.J. Marx, Eduardo Montes. *COL*

Double Revenge 🦴½ **1989** Two men feel they have a score to settle after a bank heist gone sour leaves two people dead. **90m/C VHS.** Joe Dallesandro, Nancy Everhard, Leigh McCloskey, Richard Rust, Theresa Saldana; ***D:*** Armand Mastroianni. *REP*

Double Standard 🦴½ **1988** You'll be less concerned with the plot—a community discovers that a prominent judge has maintained two marriages for nearly twenty years—than with the possibility that such dim-witted myopes might actually have existed in the real world. This made-for-TV slice of bigamy is for fans of the oops-I-forgot-I'm-married genre only. **95m/C VHS.** Robert Foxworth, Michelle Greene, Pamela Bellwood, James Kee; ***D:*** Louis Rudolph. *FRH*

Double Suicide 🦴🦴🦴 *Shinju Ten No Amijima* **1969** From a play by Monzarmon Chikamatsu, a tragic drama about a poor salesman in 18th century Japan who falls in love with a geisha and ruins his family and himself trying to requite the hopeless passion. Stylish with Iwashita turning in a wonderful dual performance. In Japanese with subtitles. **105m/B VHS, Beta.** *JP* Kichiemon Nakamura, Shima Iwashita, Yusuke Takita, Hosei Komatsu; ***D:*** Masahiro Shinoda. *INJ*

Double Threat 🦴🦴 **1992 (R)** An aging sex star makes her return to the screen opposite a younger actor with whom she is having an affair. When the director wants to include nude sex scenes in the film she agrees to use a younger body-double. Then the actress discovers her lover is involved in off-screen action with the double as well. This does not please her and she decides to take a deadly revenge. An unrated version is also available. **94m/C VHS.** Sally Kirkland, Andrew Stevens, Lisa Shane, Richard Lynch, Anthony (Tony) Franciosa, Sherrie Rose, Chick Vennera; ***D:*** David A. Prior. *AIP*

Double Trouble 🦴🦴 **1967** When rock star Presley falls in love with an English heiress, he winds up involved in an attempted murder. The king belts out "Long Legged Girl" while evading cops, criminals, and crying women. A B-side. Based on a story by Marc Brandell. **92m/C VHS, Beta.** Elvis Presley, Annette Day, John Williams, Yvonne Romain, Michael Murphy, Chips Rafferty; ***D:*** Norman Taurog; ***W:*** Jo Heims. *MGM*

Double Trouble 🦴 **1991 (R)** Twin brothers—one a cop, one a jewel thief—team up to crack the case of an international jewel smuggling ring headed by a wealthy and politically well-connected businessman and his righthand man. **87m/C VHS, LV.** David Paul, Peter Paul, James Doohan, Roddy McDowall, Steve Kanaly, A.J. Johnson, David Carradine; ***D:*** John Paragon. *COL*

Double Vision 🦴🦴 **1992 (PG-13)** Suspense thriller starring Cattrall as Caroline, a medical student who goes to London to check out the strange disappearance of her twin sister, Lisa. Assuming her identity, Caroline gets deeply involved in a kinky lifestyle that may result in murder. Based on a short story by Mary Higgins Clark. **92m/C VHS.** Kim Cattrall, Gale Hansen, Christopher Lee; ***D:*** Robert Knights. *REP*

Double Wedding 🦴🦴🦴 **1937** Madcap comedy starring Powell as a wacky painter who doesn't believe in working and Loy as a workaholic dress designer. Loy has chosen a fiance for her younger sister, Irene, to marry, but Irene has plans of her own. When Irene and her beau meet bohemian Powell, the fun really begins. Script suffers slightly from too much slapstick and not enough wit, although the stars (in their seventh outing as a duo) play it well.

Based on the play "Great Love" by Ferenc Molnar. **86m/B VHS.** William Powell, Myrna Loy, Florence Rice, John Beal, Jessie Ralph, Edgar Kennedy, Sidney Toler, Mary Gordon; ***D:*** Richard Thorpe; ***W:*** Jo Swerling. *MGM*

Doubting Thomas ½ **1935** Rogers' last film, which was in theatres when he was killed in a plane crash. Silly story of a husband and his doubts about his wife and her amateur-acting career. The show goes on in spite of his doubts, her forgotten lines, and wardrobe goofs. Remake of 1922's silent film "The Torch Bearers." **78m/B VHS.** Will Rogers, Billie Burke, Alison Skipworth, Sterling Holloway; ***D:*** David Butler. *FOX, FCT*

Doughboys ½ *Forward March* **1930** Keaton's second talkie is a so-so comedy about a rich man who mistakenly enlists in the Army during WWI. He manages to bumble his way through basic training and win the heart of a pretty girl. There are a few bright moments, particularly a musical number between Keaton and "Ukulele Ike" Edwards. **80m/B VHS.** Buster Keaton, Cliff Edwards, Edward Brophy, Sally Eilers, Victor Potel, Arnold Korff, Frank Mayo; ***D:*** Edward Sedgwick. *MGM*

Doughnuts & Society ½ **1936** Two elderly ladies who run a coffee shop suddenly strike it rich and find that life among the bluebloods is not all it's cracked up to be. No sprinkles. **70m/B VHS, Beta.** Louise Fazenda, Maude Eburne, Eddie Nugent, Ann Rutherford, Hedda Hopper, Franklin Pangborn. *VYY*

The Dove **1968** A hilarious short spoof of the Ingmar Bergman films "Wild Strawberries," "The Seventh Seal," and "The Silence." English subtitles. **15m/B VHS, Beta.** Madeline Kahn; ***W:*** Sidney Davis; ***M:*** John Barry. *PYR*

The Dove ½ **1974 (PG-13)** The true story of a 16-year-old's adventures as he sails around the world in a 23-foot sloop. The trip took him five years and along the way he falls in love with a girl who follows him to exotic locales. Photography and scenery are magnificent. **105m/C VHS, Beta.** Joseph Bottoms, Deborah Raffin, Dabney Coleman, Peter Gwynne; ***D:*** Charles Jarrott; ***W:*** Peter S. Beagle; ***C:*** Sven Nykvist. *PAR, BMV*

Down Among the Z Men **1952** Enlisted man helps a girl save an atomic formula from spies. Funny in spots but weighed down by musical numbers from a female entourage. From the pre-Monty Python comedy troupe "The Goons." **71m/B VHS, Beta, LV.** *GB* Peter Sellers, Spike Milligan, Harry Secombe, Michael Bentine, Carole Carr; ***D:*** Maclean Rogers. *NO*

Down & Dirty *Brutti, Sporchi, e Cattivi* **1976** A scathing Italian satire about a modern Roman family steeped in petty crime, incest, murder, adultery, drugs, and arson. In Italian with English subtitles. **115m/C VHS, Beta.** *IT* Nino Manfredi, Francesco Anniballi, Maria Bosco; ***D:*** Ettore Scola; ***W:*** Ettore Scola. Cannes Film Festival '76: Best Director (Scola). *MED, INJ*

Down and Out in Beverly Hills ½ **1986 (R)** A modern retelling of Jean Renoir's classic "Boudu Sauve des Eaux" with some nice star turns. A spoiled wealthy couple rescue a suicidal bum from their swimming pool. He, in turn, beds the wife, the maid and the daughter, solves the dog's identity crisis, rescues the man and his son from frustration and finds he doesn't like being a bum. A box-office hit. **103m/C VHS, Beta, LV.** Nick Nolte, Bette Midler, Richard Dreyfuss, Little Richard, Tracy Nelson, Elizabeth Pena, Evan Richards, Valerie Curtin, Barry Primus, Dorothy Tristan, Alexis Arquette; ***D:*** Paul Mazursky; ***W:*** Paul Mazursky, Leon Capetanos; ***M:*** Andy Summers. *TOU*

Down Argentine Way **1940** A lovely young woman falls in love with a suave Argentinian horse breeder. First-rate Fox musical made a star of Grable and was Miranda's first American film. ♫South American Way; Down Argentina Way; Two Dreams Met; Mama Yo Quiero; Sing to Your Senorita. **90m/C VHS, Beta, LV.** Don Ameche, Betty Grable, Carmen Miranda, Charlotte Greenwood, J. Carrol Naish, Henry Stephenson, Leonid Kinskey; ***D:*** Irving Cummings; ***C:*** Leon Shamroy. Nominations: Academy Awards '40: Best Color Cinematography, Best Interior Decoration, Best Song ("Down Argentine Way"). *FOX, MLB*

Down by Law **1986 (R)** In Jarmusch's follow-up to his successful "Stranger than Paradise," he introduces us to three men: a pimp, an out-of-work disc jockey, and an Italian tourist. When the three break out of prison, they wander through the Louisiana swampland with some regrets about their new-found freedom. Slow-moving at times, beautifully shot throughout. Poignant and hilarious, the film is true to Jarmusch form: some will love the film's off-beat flair, and others will find it bothersome. **107m/C VHS, Beta.** John Lurie, Tom Waits, Roberto Benigni, Ellen Barkin, Billie Neal, Rockets Redglare, Vernel Bagneris, Nicoletta Braschi; ***D:*** Jim Jarmusch; ***W:*** Jim Jarmusch; ***M:*** John Lurie, Tom Waits. *FOX*

Down Came a Blackbird ½ **1994 (R)** Anna Lenka (Redgrave), a Holocaust survivor, runs a clinic for healing both the physical and psychological wounds of torture victims. Journalist Helen McNulty (Dern), herself a survivor, decides to write about the clinic but Anna believes Helen's covering up the pain she's never dealt with. Also at the clinic is Tomas Ramirez (Julia), a former college professor with a terrible secret, with whom Helen discovers a special rapport. Conventional script with some fine performances; Julia died shortly after principal photography was completed on the TV film, which is dedicated to his memory. **112m/C VHS, LV.** Vanessa Redgrave, Laura Dern, Raul Julia, Jay O. Sanders, Cliff Gorman, Sarita Choudhury, L. Scott Caldwell, Jeffrey DeMunn; ***D:*** Jonathan Sanger; ***W:*** Kevin Droney; ***C:*** Kees Van Oostrum; ***M:*** Graeme Revell. *REP*

Down Dakota Way ½ **1949** Strange coincidence between a recent murder and a fatal cow epidemic. Rogers helps some locals bring the link to light. **67m/C VHS.** Roy Rogers, Dale Evans, Pat Brady, Monte Montana, Elisabeth Risdon, Byron Barr, James B. Cardwell, Roy Barcroft, Emmett Vogan; ***D:*** William Witney. *REP*

Down Mexico Way **1941** Two cowboys come to the aid of a Mexican town whose residents have been hoodwinked by a phony movie company. Very exciting chase on horseback, motorcycle, and in automobiles. **78m/B VHS, Beta.** Gene Autry, Smiley Burnette, Fay McKenzie, Duncan Renaldo; ***D:*** Joseph Santley. *CCB*

Down, Out and Dangerous **1995 (R)** Expectant couple find out the charming homeless man they've befriended is really a psycho killer. **90m/C VHS, Beta.** Richard Thomas, Bruce Davison; ***D:*** Noel Nosseck; ***W:*** Carey Hayes, Chad Hayes. *PAR*

Down Periscope ½ **1996 (PG-13)** Tom Dodge (Grammer) dreams of commanding a nuclear sub, but gets stuck with an out-of-mothballs, rusting WWII vintage tub with the usual goof-off crew. In order for Dodge to get his dream assignment, he and his losers must beat the nuclear subs of generic mean authority figure Admiral Graham (Dern), in a war game. Predictable comedy is kept afloat by amusing cast, especially Schneider as the weaselly Executive Officer Pascal. Many jokes revolve around Dodge's tattoo, which is on a body part that is normally private first-class. Denied cooperation from the U.S. Navy, the shipyard scenes were filmed on three barges tied together in the San Francisco Bay area, with empty discarded frigates and destroyers belonging to the U.S. Department of Transportation playing the fleet. **92m/C VHS.** Kelsey Grammer, Lauren Holly, Bruce Dern, Fred Schneider, Rip Torn, Harry Dean Stanton, William H. Macy, Ken Campbell, Toby Huss, Duane Martin, Jonathan Penner, Bradford Tatum, Hal Williams; ***D:*** David S. Ward; ***W:*** Hugh Wilson, Andrew Kurtzman, Eliot Wald; ***C:*** Victor Hammer; ***M:*** Randy Edelman. *FXV*

Down Texas Way **1942** One of the "Rough Riders" series. When one of the boys is accused of murdering his best friend, his two companions search for the real killer. **57m/B VHS, Beta.** Buck Jones, Tim McCoy, Raymond Hatton; ***D:*** Howard Bretherton. *NOS, VCN, TIM*

Down the Drain **1989 (R)** A broad-as-a-city-block farce about an unscrupulous criminal lawyer and his assortment of crazy clients. A fine first half but someone pulls the plug in the middle of the bath. **90m/C VHS, Beta, LV.** Andrew Stevens, John Matuszak, Teri Copley, Joseph Campanella, Don Stroud, Stella Stevens, Jerry Mathers, Benny "The Jet" Urquidez; ***D:*** Robert C. Hughes. *COL*

Down the Wyoming Trail **1939** Western hero Ritter battles some rustlers who are terrorizing farmers during the winter, while still managing to find time to warble some tunes. **52m/B VHS.** Tex Ritter, Horace Murphy, Mary Brodel, Bobby Lawson, Charles "Blackie" King, Bob Terry; ***D:*** Al(bert) Herman; ***W:*** Peter Dixon, Roger Merton. *MOV*

Down to Earth **1917** Ever-gallant lover Fairbanks overruns a mental hospital to save his sweetheart. Once inside, he's determined to show the patients that their illness is illusion, and reality's the cure. A quixotic gem from Fairbanks' pre-swashbuckling social comic days. Director Emerson's wife was the scenarist, and Victor Fleming, who went on to direct "The Wizard of Oz" and "Gone with the Wind" (to name a few), was the man behind the camera. **68m/B VHS, Beta.** Douglas Fairbanks Sr., Eileen Percy, Gustav von Seyffertitz, Charles P. McHugh, Charles Gerrard, William H. Keith, Ruth Allen, Fred Goodwine; ***D:*** John Emerson. *GPV, FCT*

Down to Earth **1947** A lackluster musical and box office flop with an impressive cast. Hayworth is the Greek goddess of dance sent to Earth on a mission to straighten out Broadway producer Parks and his play that ridicules the Greek gods. Anita Ellis dubs the singing of Hayworth. A parody of "Here Comes Mr. Jordan," remade in 1980 as "Xanadu." **101m/C VHS, LV.** Rita Hayworth, Larry Parks, Marc Platt, Roland Culver, James Gleason, Edward Everett Horton, Adele Jergens, George Macready, William Frawley, James Burke, Fred F. Sears, Lynn Merrick, Myron Healey; ***D:*** Alexander Hall; ***W:*** Edwin Blum; ***M:*** George Duning. *COL, CCB*

Down to the Sea in Ships ½ *The Last Adventurers* **1922** Bow made her movie debut in this drama about the whalers of 19th-century Massachusetts. Highlighted by exciting action scenes of an actual whale hunt. Silent with music score and original tinted footage. **83m/B VHS, Beta.** Marguerite Courtot, Raymond McKee, Clara Bow; ***D:*** Elmer Clifton. *NOS, CCB, GPV*

Down Twisted **1989 (R)** A young woman gets involved with a thief on the run in Mexico in this "Romancing the Stone" derivative. The muddled plot deserves such a confusing title. **89m/C VHS, Beta.** Carey Lowell, Charles Rocket, Trudi Dochtermann, Thom Mathews, Linda Kerridge, Courteney Cox; ***D:*** Albert Pyun; ***W:*** Albert Pyun; ***C:*** Walt Lloyd; ***M:*** Eric Allaman. *MED*

Down Under **1986** Two gold-hungry beach boys go to Australia looking for riches, and document their adventures on film. Essentially a crudely shot, tongue-in-cheek travelogue narrated by Patrick Macnee. **90m/C VHS, Beta.** Don Atkinson, Donn Dunlop, Patrick Macnee. *NO*

Downhill Racer ½ **1969 (PG)** An undisciplined American skier locks ski-tips with his coach and his new-found love while on his way to becoming an Olympic superstar. Character study on film. Beautiful ski and mountain photography keep it from sliding downhill. **102m/C VHS, Beta, LV.** Robert Redford, Camilla Sparv, Gene Hackman, Dabney Coleman; ***D:*** Michael Ritchie. *PAR*

Downtown ½ **1989 (R)** Urban comedy about a naive white suburban cop who gets demoted to the roughest precinct in Philadelphia, and gains a streetwise black partner. Runs a routine beat. **96m/C VHS, Beta, LV.** Anthony Edwards, Forest Whitaker, Joe Pantoliano, Penelope Ann Miller; ***D:*** Richard Benjamin; ***M:*** Alan Silvestri. *FOX*

D.P. **1985** A black orphan attaches to the only other black in post-WWII Germany. From a story by Kurt Vonnegut, Jr. Made for television. **60m/C VHS.** Stan Shaw, Rosemary Leach, Julius Gordon. *MON, KAR*

Drachenfutter *Dragon's Food; Dragon Chow* **1987** Powerful story dealing with a Pakistani immigrant's attempts to enter the Western world. Themes of alienation and helplessness are emphasized. Dialogues occur in 12 languages, predominantly German and Mandarin Chinese; subtitled in English. **75m/B VHS, Beta.** *GE SI* Bhasker, Ric Young, Buddy Uzzaman; ***D:*** Jan Schutte; ***W:*** Thomas Strittmatter; ***M:*** Claus Bantzer. *NYF, INJ*

Dracula **1931** Lugosi, in his most famous role, plays a vampire who terrorizes the countryside in his search for human blood. From Bram Stoker's novel. Although short of a masterpiece due to slow second half, deservedly rated a film classic. What would Halloween be like without this movie? Sequelled by "Dracula's Daughter." **75m/B VHS, Beta, LV.** Bela Lugosi, David Manners, Dwight Frye, Helen Chandler, Edward Van Sloan; ***D:*** Tod Browning; ***C:*** Karl Freund. *MCA, TLF, HMV*

Dracula ½ **1973** Count on squinty-eyed Palance to shine as the Transylvanian vampire who must quench his thirst for human blood. A made-for-television adaptation of the Bram Stoker novel that really flies. **105m/C VHS, Beta, LV.** Jack Palance, Simon Ward, Fiona Lewis, Nigel Davenport; ***D:*** Dan Curtis. *LIV*

Dracula ½ **1979 (R)** Langella recreates his Broadway role as the count who needs human blood for nourishment. Notable for its portrayal of Dracula as a romantic and tragic figure in history. Overlooked since the vampire spoof "Love at First Bite" came out at the same time. **109m/C VHS, Beta, LV.** Frank Langella, Laurence Olivier, Kate Nelligan, Donald Pleasence; ***D:*** John Badham; ***W:*** W.D. Richter; ***M:*** John Williams. *MCA*

Dracula: A Cinematic Scrapbook **1991** A look at the blood-sucking monster in both film and legend, featuring rare film trailers and interviews with actors such as Bela Lugosi, Christopher Lee, and Lon Chaney, Jr. In color and B&W. **60m/C VHS, Beta.** ***D:*** Ted Newsom; ***W:*** Ted Newsom. *RHI, FCT*

Dracula & Son *Dracula Pere et Fils* **1976 (PG)** Dracula spoof in which the count fathers a son who prefers girls and football to blood. Poor English dubbing and choppy ending drive a stake through the heart. **88m/C VHS, Beta.** *FR* Christopher Lee, Bernard Menez, Marie Breillat; ***D:*** Edouard Molinaro; ***M:*** Vladimir Cosma. *GKK*

Dracula Blows His Cool **1982 (R)** Three voluptuous models and their photographer restore an ancient castle and open a disco in it. The vampire lurking about the castle welcomes the party with his fangs. **91m/C VHS, Beta, LV.** John Garco, Betty Verges; ***D:*** Carlo Ombra; ***W:*** Carlo Ombra. *MED*

Dracula: Dead and Loving It **1995 (PG-13)** King of the spoofs Nielsen takes on the title role as the ever-loving, if clumsy, Count who still enjoys necking—particularly with luscious damsels in distress, Lucy (Anthony) and Mina (Yasbeck). And he's still got his bug-eating minion Renfield (MacNichol) and egomaniacal vampire-hunter Van Helsing (Brooks) around. As usual, Brooks throws everything possible on the screen, hoping some schtick will stick (and some does). **90m/C VHS, LV.** Leslie Nielsen, Mel Brooks, Peter MacNicol, Lysette Anthony, Amy Yasbeck, Steven Weber, Harvey Korman, Anne Bancroft; ***D:*** Mel Brooks; ***W:*** Mel Brooks, Rudy DeLuca, Steve Haberman; ***C:*** Michael D. O'Shea; ***M:*** Hummie Mann. *COL*

Dracula/Garden of Eden **1928** The abridged version of the chilling vampire film "Nosferatu" is coupled with "The Garden of Eden," in which Tini Le Brun meets her Prince Charming while vacationing with her Baroness friend. Silent. **52m/B VHS, Beta.** Max Schreck, Alexander Granach, Corine Griffith, Charles Ray, Louise Dresser. *CCB*

Dracula Has Risen from the Grave ½ **1968 (G)** Lee's Dracula is foiled by the local priest before he can drain the blood from innocent villagers. Effectively gory. One of the Hammer series of Dracula films followed by "Taste the Blood of Dracula." **92m/C VHS.** *GB* Christopher Lee, Rupert Davies, Veronica Carlson, Barbara Ewing, Barry Andrews, Michael Ripper; ***D:*** Freddie Francis; ***M:*** James Bernard. *WAR*

Dracula Rising ½ **1993 (R)** A modern-day art historian (Travis) turns out to have been a witch, burned at the stake, in a past life. She was also the blood-drinking Count's lost love. Now Dracula's a monk and when he sees this reincarnated beauty is he going to be able to keep his hands—er, fangs—off her? **?m/C VHS.** Christopher Atkins, Stacy Travis; ***D:*** Fred Gallo. *NHO*

Dracula (Spanish Version) ½ **1931** Filmed at the same time as the Bela Lugosi version of "Dracula," using the same sets and the same scripts, only in Spanish. Thought to be more visually appealing and more terrifying than the English-language counterpart. The only thing it's missing is a presence like Lugosi. Based on the novel by Bram Stoker. **104m/B VHS.** Carlos Villarias, Lupita Tovar, Eduardo Arozamena, Pablo Alvarez Rubio, Barry Norton, Carmen Guerrero; ***D:*** George Melford; ***W:*** Garrett Fort. *MCA*

Dracula Sucks **1979 (R)** A soft-core edit of a hardcore sex parody about Dracula snacking on the usual bevy of screaming quasi-virgins. **90m/C VHS, Beta.** James Gillis, Reggie Nalder, Annette Haven, Kay Parker, Serena, Seka, John Leslie; ***D:*** Philip Marshak. *UNI, OM*

Dracula: Up in Harlem *Woof!* **1983** When the Prince of Darkness gets together with the people of the night, the Pentagon rolls out the heavy metal. This may suck your brain out. **90m/C VHS, Beta.** *NO*

Dracula vs. Frankenstein **1969** An alien reanimates Earth's most infamous monsters in a bid to take over the planet. Rennie's last role. Also on video as, "Assignment: Terror." **91m/C VHS.** *IT GE SP* Michael Rennie, Paul Naschy, Karin Dor, Patty Shepard; ***D:*** Hugo Fregonese, Tulio Demicheli; ***W:*** Paul Naschy. *UAV*

Dracula vs. Frankenstein *Woof! Blood of Frankenstein; They're Coming to Get You; Dracula Contra Frankenstein; The Revenge of Dracula* **1971 (R)** The Count makes a deal with a shady doctor to keep him in blood. Vampire spoof that's very bad but fun. Last film for both Chaney and Naish. Features a cameo by genre maven Forrest J. Ackerman. **90m/C VHS.** *SP* J. Carrol Naish, Lon Chaney Jr., Regina Carrol, Russ Tamblyn, Jim Davis, Anthony Eisley, Zandor Vorkov, John Bloom, Angelo Rossitto; ***Cameos:*** Forrest J. Ackerman; ***D:*** Al Adamson. *NO*

Dracula's Daughter **1936** Count Dracula's daughter, Countess Marya Zaleska, heads to London supposedly to find the cure to a mysterious illness. Instead she finds she has a taste for human blood, especially female blood. She also finds a man, falls in love, and tries to keep him by casting a spell on him. A good script and cast keep this sequel to Bela Lugosi's "Dracula" entertaining. **71m/B VHS.** Gloria Holden, Otto Kruger, Marguerite Churchill, Irving Pichel, Edward Van Sloan, Nan Grey, Hedda Hopper; ***D:*** Lambert Hillyer. *MCA*

Dracula's Great Love *Woof! Gran Amore del Conde Dracula; Count Dracula's Great Love; Dracula's Virgin Lovers* **1972 (R)** Four travellers end up in Dracula's castle for the night, where the horny Count takes a liking to one of the women. Left out in the sun too long. **96m/C VHS, Beta.** *SP* Paul Naschy, Charo Soriano; ***D:*** Javier Aguirre. *SNC, MPI*

Dracula's Last Rites *Woof! Last Rites* **1979 (R)** Blood-curdling tale of a sheriff and a mortician in a small town who are up to no good. Technically inept: film equipment can be spotted throughout. Don't stick your neck out for this one. **86m/C VHS, Beta.** Patricia Lee Hammond, Gerald Fielding, Victor Jorge; ***D:*** Domonic Paris. *MGM, CAN, FCT*

Dracula's Widow **1988 (R)** Countess Dracula, missing her hubby and desperately in need of a substitute, picks innocent Raymond as her victim. His girlfriend and a cynical cop fight to save his soul from the Countess' damnation. Directed by the nephew of Frances Ford Coppola. **85m/C VHS, Beta.** Sylvia Kristel, Josef Sommer, Lenny Von Dohlen; ***D:*** Christopher Coppola. *HBO*

Dragnet ½ **1954** Sgt. Joe Friday and Officer Frank Smith try to solve a mob slaying but have a rough time. Alexander plays the sidekick in "Dragnet" pre-Morgan days. Just the facts: feature version of the TV show that's suspenseful and well-acted. **88m/C VHS, Beta.** Jack Webb, Ben Alexander, Richard Boone, Ann Robinson; ***D:*** Jack Webb. *MCA*

Dragnet **195?** Detectives Joe Friday and Frank Smith make the streets of Los Angeles safe in this police series which ran from 1951-1959. Two episodes per tape. **55m/C VHS.** Jack Webb, Ben Alexander. *MOV, MRV*

Dragnet **1987 (PG-13)** Semi-parody of the vintage '60s television cop show. Sgt. Joe Friday's straight-laced nephew and his sloppy partner take on the seamy crime life of Los Angeles. Neither Aykroyd nor Hanks can save this big-budget but lackluster spoof that's full of holes. **106m/C VHS, Beta, LV.** Dan Aykroyd, Tom Hanks, Christopher Plummer, Harry (Henry) Morgan, Elizabeth Ashley, Dabney Coleman; ***D:*** Tom Mankiewicz; ***W:*** Dan Aykroyd, Tom Mankiewicz, Alan Zweibel; ***M:*** Ira Newborn. *MCA*

Dragon Force ½ **1982** Korean martial artists fend off Japanese invaders in the 1930s. **101m/C VHS, Beta.** Kangjo Lee; ***D:*** Key-Nam Nam. *CNG*

Dragon Fury ½ **1995** Evil dictator tries to conquer what remains of America in the year 2099—a world peopled by barbarians and victims of a deadly plague. Naturally, there's a martial arts hero around to stop him. **80m/C VHS.** Robert Chapin, Richard Lynch, Chona Jason, Deborah Stamble; ***D:*** David Heavener. *MNC*

Dragon Princess **197?** When the king of karate and his dragon princess confront the blind master of the bloody blades, sparks fly. **90m/C VHS, Beta.** Sonny Chiba, Sue Shiomi. *NO*

Dragon Seed ½ **1944** The lives of the residents of a small Chinese village are turned upside down when the Japanese invade it. Based on the Pearl S. Buck novel. Lengthy and occasionally tedious, though generally well-made with heart-felt attempts to create Oriental characters, without having Asians in the cast. **145m/B VHS, Beta.** Katharine Hepburn, Walter Huston, Agnes Moorehead, Akim Tamiroff, Hurd Hatfield, J. Carrol Naish, Henry Travers, Turhan Bey, Aline MacMahon; ***D:*** Jack Conway. Nominations: Academy Awards '44: Best Black and White Cinematography, Best Supporting Actress (MacMahon). *MGM, FCT*

Dragon: The Bruce Lee Story **1993 (PG-13)** Entertaining, inspiring account of the life of Chinese-American martial-arts legend Bruce Lee. Jason Scott Lee (no relation) is great as the talented artist, exuding his joy of life and gentle spirit, before his mysterious brain disorder death at the age of 32. Ironically, this release coincided with son Brandon's accidental death on a movie set. The martial arts sequences in "Dragon" are extraordinary, but there's also romance as Lee meets and marries his wife (Holly, who acquits herself well). Based on the book "Bruce Lee: The Man Only I Knew" by his widow, Linda Lee Caldwell. **121m/C VHS, LV.** Jason Scott Lee, Lauren Holly, Robert Wagner, Michael Learned, Nancy Kwan, Kay Tong Lim, Sterling Macer, Ric Young, Sven Ole-Thorsen; ***D:*** Rob Cohen; ***W:*** Edward Khmara, John Raffo, Rob Cohen; ***M:*** Randy Edelman. Nominations: MTV Movie Awards '94: Breakthrough Performance (Lee). *MCA, BTV, FCT*

Dragon the Odds **198?** A man named Mo masters Kung Fu "maniac style" in order to repossess the gymnasium that was willed to him. **90m/C VHS, Beta.** *TWE*

Dragon vs. Needles of Death **1982** It's a battle to the finish against the unstoppable deadly needles in this Kung-Fu adventure. **86m/C VHS, Beta.** Don Chien, Wong Ting. *FOX*

Dragonard ½ **1988 (R)** Slaves on a West Indies island rebel against their cruel masters. **93m/C VHS, Beta.** Eartha Kitt, Oliver Reed, Annabel Schofield, Patrick Warburton; ***D:*** Gerard Kikione; ***W:*** R.J. Marx. *WAR*

Dragonfight ½ **1992 (R)** Corporations rule the world and vie for supremacy through gladiator combat in this action-adventure saga set in the near future. Fights are to the death and when the current champ refuses a new challenger the corporate honchos decide to provoke him into battle by having the challenger mow down innocent bystanders. Several execs also decide the slaughter has to stop but they may be the next targets. **84m/C VHS, Beta.** Robert Z'Dar, Michael Pare, Paul Coufos, Charles Napier, James Hong, Alexa Hamilton, Fawna MacLaren. *WAR*

Dragonfly Squadron **1954** Korean war drama about pilots and their romantic problems. Never gets off the ground. **82m/C VHS.** John Hodiak, Barbara Britton, Bruce (Herman Brix) Bennett, Jess Barker; ***D:*** Lesley Selander. *NO*

Dragonheart ½ **1996 (PG-13)** Okay, get past the fact that Connery's Scottish burr is coming out of the teeth-filled mouth of an 18 ft. tall, 43 ft. long dragon and you'll be well on your way to enjoying this 10th-century fantasy. Knightly Bowen (Quaid) is the one-time mentor of evil-hearted King Einon (Thewlis) and it's up to him, Draco the dragon, feisty Kara (Meyer), and some fearful peasants to band together and free themselves from the king's tyranny. There's some slow spots but Bowen and Draco make for an amusing pairing and the dragon does seem, well, real. Work on Draco took more than a year of Industrial Light & Magic's expertise. **103m/C VHS.** Dennis Quaid, David Thewlis, Pete Postlethwaite, Dina Meyer, Julie Christie, Jason Isaacs, Brian Thompson, Wolf Christian, Terry O'Neill; ***D:*** Rob Cohen; ***W:*** Charles Edward Pogue; ***C:*** David Eggby; ***M:*** Randy Edelman; ***V:*** Sean Connery, John Gielgud. *NYR*

Dragon's Claw **198?** A young man's parents are murdered, and he trains in shaolin skills in order to exact revenge. **90m/C VHS, Beta.** Jimmy Liu, Hwang Cheng Li; ***D:*** Joseph Kuo. *GEM*

The Dragon's Showdown **1983** After witnessing the brutal decapitations of his parents, a young man learns Kung-Fu to avenge their deaths. **90m/C VHS, Beta.** Dragon Lee; ***D:*** Godfrey Ho. *GEM*

Dragonslayer **1981 (PG)** A sorcerer's apprentice suddenly finds himself the only person who can save the kingdom from a horrible, firebreathing dragon. Extreme violence but wonderful special effects, smart writing, and a funny performance by Richardson. **110m/C VHS, Beta, LV.** Peter MacNicol, Caitlin Clarke, Ralph Richardson, John Hallam, Albert Salmi, Chloe Salaman; ***D:*** Matthew Robbins; ***W:*** Matthew Robbins, Hal Barwood; ***M:*** Alex North. Nominations: Academy Awards '81: Best Original Score. *PAR, COL*

Dragonworld ½ **1994 (PG)** Five-year-old Johnny McGowan is sent to Scotland to live with his grandfather. A wish for a friend has Johnny mysteriously awakening a baby dragon he names Yowler. Years later, the financially strapped adult Johnny agrees to loan Yowler to an amusement park only to find out the park's owner never intends to give Yowler back. Both baby dragon and young Johnny are unbearably cute. **86m/C VHS, Beta.** Sam Mackenzie, Courtland Mead, Brittney Powell, John Calvin, Andrew Keir, Lila Kaye, John Woodvine; ***D:*** Ted Nicolaou; ***W:*** Ted Nicolaou, Suzanne Glazener Naha; ***M:*** Richard Band. *PAR*

Dragstrip Girl **1957** An 18-year-old girl comes of age while burning rubber at the dragstrip—the world of boys, hot rods, and horsepower. A definite "B" movie that may seem dated. **70m/B VHS.** Fay Spain, Steven Terrell, John Ashley, Frank Gorshin; ***D:*** Edward L. Cahn. *COL*

The Drake Case **1929** A slight courtroom drama made during the waning days of the silent era. You'll probably recognize Brit Lloyd from her later career. **56m/B VHS, Beta.** Robert Frazer, Doris Lloyd, Gladys Brockwell. *GPV, FCT*

The Draughtsman's Contract **1982 (R)** A beguiling mystery begins when a wealthy woman hires an artist to make drawings of her home. Their contract is quite unusual, as is their relationship. Everything is going along at an even pace until murder is suspected, and things spiral down to darker levels. A simple story turned into a bizarre puzzle. Intense enough for any thriller fan. **103m/C VHS.** *GB* Anthony Higgins, Janet Suzman, Anne Louise Lambert, Hugh Fraser; ***D:*** Peter Greenaway; ***W:*** Peter Greenaway; ***M:*** Michael Nyman. *MGM, FCT*

Draw! **1981** Two has-been outlaws warm up their pistols again in this old-fashioned Western. Star power and some smart moments make it worthwhile. Made for TV. **98m/C VHS, Beta.** Kirk Douglas, James Coburn, Alexandra Bastedo, Graham Jarvis; ***D:*** Steven Hilliard Stern. *MED*

Dreadnaught Rivals **198?** A student is taught by his drunken servant how to avenge himself on the culprits who kidnapped his girlfriend. Dubbed. **90m/C VHS, Beta.** Sinon Lin, Kent Ko, Louisa Monk. *MOV*

Dream a Little Dream **1989 (PG-13)** Strange teen transformation drama about an old man and his wife trying mystically to regain their youth. When they collide bikes with the teenagers down the street, their minds are exchanged and the older couple with the now young minds are transported to a permanent dream-like state. Same old switcheroo made bearable by cast. **114m/C VHS, Beta, LV.** Corey Feldman, Corey Haim, Meredith Salenger, Jason Robards Jr., Piper Laurie, Harry Dean Stanton, Victoria Jackson, Alex Rocco, Billy McNamara; ***D:*** Marc Rocco; ***W:*** Marc Rocco. *LIV, VES, HHE*

Dream a Little Dream 2 ½ **1994 (PG-13)** Friends Dinger Holefield (Haim) and Bobby Keller (Feldman) receive a mysterious package containing two pairs of sunglasses, which they discover have magic powers. The wearer of one pair is driven to do the bidding of the wearer of the second pair of specs—whether for good or evil. Naturally, there are evildoers who want the glasses as well. **91m/C VHS.** Corey Haim, Corey Feldman, Stacie Randall, Michael Nicolosi, James Lemmo; ***W:*** David Weissman, Susan Forman. *COL*

Dream Chasers **1984 (PG)** A bankrupt old codger and an 11-year-old boy stricken with cancer run away together during the Great Depression. **97m/C VHS, Beta.** Harold Gould, Justin Dana. *FOX*

Dream Date ½ **1993 (PG-13)** Lovely teenager is wooed by hip, playful suitor until trouble ensues when goofball sidekick enters the picture. Family entertainment. **96m/C VHS.** Tempestt Bledsoe, Clifton Davis, Kadeem Hardison, Anne-Marie Johnson, Pauly Shore, Richard Moll; ***D:*** Anson Williams. *TRI, PMS*

Dream Demon **1988** The appearance of Wilhoite, a visiting American, disrupts the status quo at a spooky British manor where the charming Redgrave debates her impending marriage to wealthy rogue Greenstreet. Aside from a terrific opening dream sequence, most of the scary bits have been done before. **89m/C VHS.** *GB* Jemma Redgrave, Kathleen Wilhoite, Timothy Spall, Jimmy Nail, Mark Greenstreet; ***D:*** Harley Cokliss. *WAR*

A Dream for Christmas **1973** Earl Hamner, Jr. (best known for writing the "The Waltons") wrote this moving story of a black minister whose church in Los Angeles is scheduled to be demolished. Made for television. **100m/C VHS.** Hari Rhodes, Beah Richards, George Spell, Juanita Moore, Joel Fluellen, Robert DoQui, Clarence Muse; ***D:*** Ralph Senensky. *LIV, WAR*

Dream Lover **1985 (R)** Terrifying nightmares after an assault lead McNichol to dream therapy. Treatment causes her tortured unconscious desires to take over her waking behavior, and she becomes a violent schizophrenic. Slow, heavy, and not very thrilling. **105m/C VHS, Beta.** Kristy McNichol, Ben Masters, Paul Shenar, Justin Deas, Joseph Culp, Gayle Hunnicutt, John McMartin; ***D:*** Alan J. Pakula; ***W:*** Jon Boorstin; ***C:*** Sven Nykvist. *MGM*

Dream Lover **1993 (R)** Divorced architect Ray (Spader) meets and marries Lena (Amick), beautiful and seemingly perfect, who nonetheless warns him that she's just your average mixed-up gal. Suspense is supposed to come into play as Ray suspects Lena's been lying to him about her past. Visually appealing (considerably helped by the attractive leads) but good looks don't make up for the lack of substance and the minimal number of surprises expected in a thriller. Directorial debut of Kazan. Also available in an unrated version. **103m/C VHS, LV.** James Spader, Madchen Amick, Frederic Lehne, Bess Armstrong, Larry Miller, Kathleen York, Blair Tefkin, Scott Coffey, William Shockley, Clyde Kusatsu; ***D:*** Nicholas Kazan; ***W:*** Nicholas Kazan; ***M:*** Christopher Young. *PGV*

Dream Machine ½ **1991 (PG)** A childish teen comedy, based on that old urban legend of the lucky kid given a free Porshe by the vengeful wife of a wealthy philanderer. The gimmick is that the husband's body is in the trunk; the murderer is in pursuit. The tape includes an anti-drug commerical—but nothing against reckless driving, which the picture glorifies. **88m/C VHS, LV.** Corey Haim, Evan Richards, Jeremy Slate, Randall England, Tracy Fraim, Brittney Lewis, Susan Seaforth Hayes; ***D:*** Lyman Dayton. *LIV*

Dream Man ½ **1994 (R)** Kris Anderson (Kensit) is a Seattle cop with the clairvoyant ability to see crimes as they're committed. But that doesn't stop her from getting involved with the handsome murder suspect (McCarthy) she's supposed to be investigating. **94m/C VHS, LV.** Patsy Kensit, Andrew McCarthy, Bruce Greenwood; ***D:*** Rene Bonniere; ***W:*** Michael Alexander Miller; ***M:*** Graeme Coleman. *REP*

Dream No Evil ½ **1975** A mentally disturbed woman is forced to commit bizarre murders to protect her warped fantasy world. **93m/C VHS, Beta.** Edmond O'Brien, Brooke Mills, Marc Lawrence, Arthur Franz; ***D:*** John Hayes. *AHV*

A Dream of Kings **1969 (R)** Quinn is exceptional in this Petrakis story of an immigrant working to get his dying son home to Greece. Last film appearance for Stevens before committing suicide at age 36. **107m/C VHS.** Anthony Quinn, Irene Papas, Inger Stevens, Sam Levene, Val Avery; ***D:*** Daniel Mann; ***M:*** Alex North. *WAR*

A Dream of Passion ½ **1978 (R)** A woman imprisoned in Greece for murdering her children becomes the object of a publicity stunt for a production of "Medea," and she and the lead actress begin to exchange personalities. Artificial gobbledygook. **105m/C VHS, Beta.** *GR SI* Ellen Burstyn, Melina Mercouri, Andreas Voutsinas; ***D:*** Jules Dassin; ***W:*** Jules Dassin. *NLC*

Dream Street **1921** A weak morality tale of London's lower classes. Two brothers, both in love with the same dancing girl, woo her in their own way, while a Chinese gambler plans to take her by force. Silent with music score. Based on Thomas Burke's "Limehouse Nights." **138m/B VHS, Beta.** Tyrone Power Sr., Carol Dempster, Ralph Graves, Charles Mack; ***D:*** D.W. Griffith. *VYY*

The Dream Team ½ **1989 (PG-13)** On their way to a ball game, four patients from a mental hospital find themselves lost in New York City after their doctor is knocked out by murderers. Some fine moments from a cast of dependable comics. Watch for numerous nods to "One Flew Over the Cuckoo's Nest," another Lloyd feature. Keaton fans won't want to miss this one. **113m/C VHS, Beta, LV.** Michael Keaton, Christopher Lloyd, Peter Boyle, Stephen Furst, Lorraine Bracco, Milo O'Shea, Dennis Boutsikaris, Philip Bosco, James Remar, Cynthia Belliveau; ***D:*** Howard Zieff; ***W:*** Jon Connolly, David Loucka; ***M:*** David McHugh. *MCA*

Dream to Believe **1985** Slice of the life of your typical high school coed—mom's dying, stepdad's from hell, sports injury hurts, and, oh yeah, championship gymnastic competitions loom. Designed to make you feel oh-so-good in that MTV kind of way. Reeves is most excellent as the girl's blushing beau. **96m/C VHS, Beta.** Rita Tushingham, Keanu Reeves, Olivia D'Abo; ***D:*** Paul Lynch. *HHE*

Dream Trap ½ **1990** A young man is obsessed with a girl in his dreams. When he meets a girl who really exists, fantasy louses up every opportunity for the real thing. **90m/C VHS.** Kristy Swanson, Sasha Jensen, Jeanie Moore; ***D:*** Tom Logan, Hugh Parks; ***W:*** Tom Logan. *NO*

Dreamchild ✗✗✗ **1985 (PG)** A poignant story of the autumn years of Alice Hargreaves, the model for Lewis Carroll's "Alice in Wonderland." Film follows her on a visit to New York in the 1930s, with fantasy sequences including Wonderland characters created by Jim Henson's Creature Shop invoking the obsessive Reverend Dodgson (a.k.a. Carroll). **94m/C VHS, Beta.** *GB* Coral Browne, Ian Holm, Peter Gallagher, Jane Asher, Nicola Cowper, Amelia Shankley, Caris Corfman, Shane Rimmer, James Wilby; ***D:*** Gavin Millar; ***W:*** Dennis Potter; ***C:*** Billy Williams; ***M:*** Max Harris, Stanley Myers. *MGM*

Dreamer ✗✗ **1979 (PG)** The excitement of bowling is exploited for all it's worth in this "strike or die" extravaganza. One of a kind. **86m/C VHS.** Tim Matheson, Susan Blakely, Jack Warden, Richard B. Shull; ***D:*** Noel Nosseck; ***W:*** Larry J. Bischof; ***M:*** Bill Conti. *FOX*

The Dreaming ✗ **1989** A young doctor stumbles upon a dimension where reality and fantasy are blurred, and where the supernatural reigns supreme. **87m/C VHS, Beta.** *AU NO*

Dreaming Lips ✗✗½ **1937** An orchestra conductor's wife falls in love with her husband's violinist friend. Tragedy befalls the couple. Bergner outstanding in a familiar script. **70m/B VHS, Beta.** *GB* Raymond Massey, Elisabeth Bergner, Romney Brent, Joyce Bland, Charles Carson, Felix Aylmer; ***D:*** Paul Czinner, Lee Garmes; ***C:*** Lee Garmes. *VYY, CCB*

Dreaming of Rita ✗✗ **1994** Bob (Oscarsson) named his daughter Rita after long-lost love Sabine's resemblance to Hollywood goddess, Rita Hayworth. Now an elderly widower, Bob suddenly decides to try and find Sabine, taking off across the Swedish countryside. The unhappily married Rita (Lagercrantz), leaving husband and children behind, goes after him—and meets sympathetic hitchhiker Erik (Ersgard), who's happy to offer a little romance. Swedish with subtitles. **108m/C VHS.** *SW* Per Oscarsson, Marika Lagercrantz, Patrick Ersgard, Philip Zanden; ***D:*** Jon Lindstrom; ***W:*** Jon Lindstrom, Rita Holst; ***C:*** Kjell Lagerros. *FCT*

Dreaming Out Loud ✗✗ **1940** Screen debut of popular radio team Lum 'n Abner. The boys get involved in several capers to bring progress to their small Arkansas town. Rural wisecracks make for pleasant outing. First in film series for the duo. **65m/B VHS, Beta.** Frances Langford, Phil Harris, Clara Blandick, Robert Wilcox, Chester Lauck, Norris Goff, Frank Craven, Bobs Watson, Irving Bacon; ***D:*** Harold Young. *NOS, DVT, VYY*

Dreams ✗✗ *Kvinn odrom; Journey into Autumn* **1955** Unfocused film about the lives and loves of two successful women. Subtitled. **86m/B VHS, Beta, LV.** *SW* Harriet Andersson, Gunnar Bjornstrand, Eva Dahlbeck, Ulf Palme; ***D:*** Ingmar Bergman; ***W:*** Ingmar Bergman. *VDM, INJ, SUE*

Dreams Come True ✗ **1984 (R)** Silly young comedy-romance about two young lovers who discover the trick of out-of-body travel, and have various forms of spiritual contact while their bodies are sleeping. **95m/C VHS, Beta.** Michael Sanville, Stephanie Shuford; ***D:*** Max Kalmanowicz. *MED*

Dreams Lost, Dreams Found ✗½ **1987** A young widow journeys from the U.S. to Scotland in search of her heritage. The third "Harlequin Romance Movie," made for cable television. **102m/C VHS.** Kathleen Quinlan, Betsy Brantley, Charles Gray; ***D:*** Willi Patterson. *PAR*

Dreams of Desire ✗ **1982** Engaged couple goes to Hong Kong to enjoy that city's sensual pleasures. **80m/C VHS, Beta.** *NO*

Dreamscape ✗✗½ **1984 (PG-13)** When a doctor teaches a young psychic how to enter into other people's dreams in order to end their nightmares, somebody else wants to use this psychic for evil purposes. The special effects are far more convincing than the one man-saves-the-country-with-his-psychic-powers plot. **99m/C VHS, Beta, LV.** Dennis Quaid, Max von Sydow, Christopher Plummer, Eddie Albert, Kate Capshaw, David Patrick Kelly, George Wendt, Jana Taylor; ***D:*** Joseph Ruben; ***W:*** Chuck Russell; ***M:*** Maurice Jarre. *IME*

Dreamwood ✗✗✗ **1972** A myth-packed experimental film by James Broughton with muse-figures, angels, flower-children, and the like. **45m/C VHS, Beta.** ***D:*** James Broughton. *MFV, TPV*

Dress Gray ✗✗✗ **1986** Fine, exciting adaptation of the Lucian K. Truscott IV novel about a cover-up at an Eastern military academy. Baldwin is cadet Slaight, an upperclassman who finds more secrets than he can handle when a younger cadet (Cassidy), with whom he had an adversarial relationship, is murdered. He's torn between investigating the death or keeping quiet—for the sake of his career if not his life. Originally a television miniseries. **192m/C VHS, Beta.** Alec Baldwin, Hal Holbrook, Eddie Albert, Lloyd Bridges, Susan Hess, Timothy Van Patten, Patrick Cassidy, Alexis Smith, James B. Sikking, Lane Smith; ***D:*** Glenn Jordan; ***W:*** Gore Vidal; ***M:*** Billy Goldenberg. *WAR*

Dressed for Death ✗½ *Straight on Till Morning; Til Dawn Do Us Part* **1974 (R)** A tale of true love gone bad as a woman is chased and murdered in her castle by the psychopath she loves. **121m/C VHS, Beta.** *GB* Rita Tushingham, Shane Briant, Tom Bell, Annie Ross, Katya Wyeth, James Bolam, Claire Kelly; ***D:*** Peter Collinson. *ACA*

Dressed to Kill ✗✗½ **1946** Sherlock Holmes finds that a series of music boxes holds the key to plates stolen from the Bank of England. The plot's a bit thin, but Rathbone/Bruce, in their final Holmes adventure, are always a delight. **72m/B VHS, LV.** Basil Rathbone, Nigel Bruce, Patricia Morison, Edmund Breon, Tom Dillon; ***D:*** Roy William Neill. *CNG, MRV, REP*

Dressed to Kill ✗✗½ **1980 (R)** Contemporary thriller merges bombastic DePalma with a tense Hitchcockian flare. Sexually unsatisfied Dickinson ends up in bed with a man who catches her eye in a museum. Then she's found brutally murdered. Her son teams up with a prostitute to track and lure the killer into their trap. Suspenseful and fast paced. Dickinson's museum scene is wonderfully photographed and edited. DePalma was repeatedly criticized for using a stand-in during the Dickinson shower scene; he titled his next film "Body Double" as a rebuttal. **105m/C VHS, Beta, LV.** Angie Dickinson, Michael Caine, Nancy Allen, Keith Gordon, Dennis Franz, David Margulies, Brandon Maggart; ***D:*** Brian DePalma; ***W:*** Brian DePalma; ***C:*** Ralf Bode; ***M:*** Pino Donaggio. *WAR, OM*

The Dresser ✗✗✗½ **1983 (PG)** Film adaptation of Harwood's play (he also wrote the screen version) about an aging English actor/manager (Finney), his dresser (Courtenay), and their theater company touring England during WWII. Marvelous showbiz tale is lovingly told, superbly acted. **119m/C VHS, Beta, LV.** Albert Finney, Tom Courtenay, Edward Fox, Michael Gough, Zena Walker, Eileen Atkins, Cathryn Harrison; ***D:*** Peter Yates; ***W:*** Ronald Harwood; ***M:*** James Horner. Golden Globe Awards '84: Best Actor—Drama (Courtenay); Nominations: Academy Awards '83: Best Actor (Courtenay), Best Actor (Finney), Best Adapted Screenplay, Best Director (Yates), Best Picture. *COL*

Dressmaker ✗✗½ **1956** French comedian Fernandel stars as a man's tailor who designs dresses in secret so as not to compete with his dressmaker wife. Lightweight but entertaining. English subtitled. **95m/B VHS, Beta, LV.** *FR* Fernandel, Francoise Fabian; ***D:*** Jean Boyer. *NOS, GVV, DVT*

The Dressmaker ✗✗½ **1989** Two sisters in WWII Liverpool must deal with their young niece's romantic involvement with an American soldier. Plowright and Whitelaw turn in fine performances as the two siblings with very different outlooks on life. **90m/C VHS.** *GB* Joan Plowright, Billie Whitelaw, Pete Postlethwaite, Jane Horrocks, Tim Ransom; ***D:*** Jim O'Brien; ***M:*** George Fenton. *CAP, INJ*

Drift Fence ✗✗½ *Texas Desperadoes* **1936** Good early oater about a Texas ranger who goes in search of the man responsible for the murder of his buddy. Routine story saved by high quality production. Based on the story "Nevada" by Zane Grey. **57m/B VHS.** Buster Crabbe, Katherine DeMille, Tom Keene, Benny Baker; ***D:*** Otho Lovering; ***W:*** Stuart Anthony, Robert Yost. *DVT, GPV*

The Drifter ✗✗ **1932** A lumberjack makes sacrifices for the love between his brother and the lumbermill owner's daughter. **56m/B VHS, Beta, LV.** William Farnum, Noah Beery Sr., Phyliss Barrington. *NOS, VYY, HEG*

The Drifter ✗✗½ **1988 (R)** It's psychos, psychos everywhere as a beautiful young woman learns to regret a one-night stand. A good, low-budget version of "Fatal Attraction." Director Brand plays the cop. **90m/C VHS.** Kim Delaney, Timothy Bottoms, Miles O'Keeffe, Al Shannon, Thomas Wagner, Larry Brand; ***D:*** Larry Brand; ***W:*** Larry Brand; ***M:*** Rick Conrad. *MGM*

The Driftin' Kid ✗ **1941** Poorly produced western has Keene posing as a rancher in order to nab a bunch of cattle rusters. So bad that even the sound of the punches are seconds off from the blows. **57m/B VHS.** Tom Keene, Betty Miles, Frank Yaconelli, Slim Andrews, Stanley Price, Glenn Strange; ***D:*** Robert Emmett Tansey; ***W:*** Robert Emmett Tansey, Frances Kavanaugh. *MOV*

Driftin' River ✗✗½ **1946** A shipment of horses bound for the Army is hijacked and the soldiers sent to investigate the theft are murdered. Investigators Deans and Ates are sent to take care of the culprits. Routine oater. **57m/B VHS.** Eddie Dean, Roscoe Ates, Shirley Patterson, William "Bill" Fawcett, Dennis Moore, Bob Callahan, Lottie Harrison, Forrest Taylor; ***D:*** Robert Emmett Tansey; ***W:*** Frances Kavanaugh. *GPV*

Drifting ✗✗½ *Nagooa* **1982** A controversial Israeli film about a homosexual filmmaker surviving in modern-day Jerusalem. First such movie to be made in Israel. In Hebrew with English titles. **103m/C VHS, Beta.** *IS* Jonathan Sagalle, Ami Traub, Ben Levine, Dita Arel; ***D:*** Amos Guttman. *FCT*

Drifting Souls ✗✗ **1932** In order to save her father's life, a beautiful young woman marries for money instead of love. **65m/C VHS, Beta.** Lois Wilson, Theodore von Eltz, Shirley Grey, Raymond Hatton, Gene Gowing, Bryant Washburn; ***D:*** Louis King. *GPV*

Drifting Weeds ✗✗✗½ *Floating Weeds; The Duckweed Story; Ukigusa* **1959** A remake by Ozu of his 1934 silent film about a troupe of traveling actors whose leader visits his illegitimate son and his lover after years of separation. Classic Ozu in his first color film. In Japanese with English subtitles. **128m/B VHS, Beta, LV.** *JP* Ganjiro Nakamura, Machiko Kyo, Haruko Sugimura, Ayako Wakao; ***D:*** Yasujiro Ozu. *HMV, MRV, FCT*

Driller Killer *Woof!* **1974 (R)** Frustrated artist goes insane and begins to kill off Manhattan residents with a carpenter's drill. Likewise, the plot is full of holes. **78m/C VHS, Beta.** Jimmy Laine, Carolyn Marz, Bob DeFrank; ***D:*** Abel Ferrara; ***M:*** Joe Delia. *NO*

Drive-In *Woof!* **1976 (PG)** A low-budget bomb showing a night in the life of teenage yahoos at a Texas drive-in. **96m/C VHS, Beta.** Lisa Lemole, Glen Morshower, Gary Cavagnaro; ***D:*** Rod Amateau. *COL*

Drive-In Massacre *Woof!* **1974 (R)** Two police detectives investigate a bizarre series of slasher murders at the local drive-in. Honk the horn at this one. **78m/C VHS, Beta, LV.** Jake Barnes, Adam Lawrence. *NO*

Driven to Kill ✗✗ **1990** No-name cast assemble in low-rent suspenser portraying the ugly side of love: bent on revenge, a man is out to obliterate the thugs who made his life a horrible experience highlighted by misery and boredom. **?m/C VHS.** Jake Jacobs, Chip Campbell, Michele McNeil. *PMH*

The Driver ✗½ **1978 (PG)** A police detective will stop at nothing to catch "The Driver," a man who has the reputation of driving the fastest getaway car around. Chase scenes win out over plot. **131m/C VHS, Beta.** Ryan O'Neal, Bruce Dern, Isabelle Adjani, Ronee Blakley, Matt Clark; ***D:*** Walter Hill; ***W:*** Walter Hill. *FOX*

Driver's Seat *Woof!* *Psychotic; Identikit* **1973 (R)** Extremely bizarre film with a cult following that was adapted from the novel by Muriel Spark. Liz stars as a deranged woman trying to keep a rendezvous with her strange lover in Rome. In the meantime she wears tacky clothes and delivers stupid lines. **101m/C**

VHS, Beta. *IT* Elizabeth Taylor, Ian Bannen, Mona Washbourne, Andy Warhol; ***D:*** Giuseppe Patroni Griffi. *SUE*

Driving Force **1988 (R)** In an effort to capitalize on the popularity of the "Road Warrior" movies, features a lone trucker battling a gang of roadhogs in another post-holocaust desert. Ultimately, runs off the road. **90m/C VHS, Beta, LV.** Sam Jones, Catherine Bach, Don Swayze; ***D:*** A.J. Prowse; ***W:*** Patrick Edgeworth. *ACA*

Driving Me Crazy ½ **1991 (PG-13)** When an East German car inventor comes to America, it's laughs in the fast lane in this all-star comedy. **88m/C VHS, LV.** Billy Dee Williams, Thomas Gottschalk, Dom DeLuise, Milton Berle, Steve Kanaly, Michelle Johnson, Richard Moll, Morton Downey Jr., George Kennedy; ***D:*** Jon Turteltaub. *NO*

Driving Miss Daisy ½ **1989 (PG)** Tender and sincere portrayal of a 25-year friendship between an aging Jewish woman and the black chauffeur forced upon her by her son. Humorous and thought-provoking, skillfully acted and directed, it subtly explores the effects of prejudice in the South. The development of Aykroyd as a top-notch character actor is further evidenced here. Part of the fun is watching the changes in fashion and auto design. Adapted from the play by Alfred Uhry. **99m/C VHS, Beta, LV, 8mm.** Jessica Tandy, Morgan Freeman, Dan Aykroyd, Esther Rolle, Patti LuPone; ***D:*** Bruce Beresford; ***W:*** Alfred Uhry; ***M:*** Hans Zimmer. Academy Awards '89: Best Actress (Tandy), Best Adapted Screenplay, Best Makeup, Best Picture; British Academy Awards '90: Best Actress (Tandy); Golden Globe Awards '90: Best Actor—Musical/Comedy (Freeman), Best Actress—Musical/Comedy (Tandy), Best Film—Musical/Comedy; National Board of Review Awards '89: 10 Best Films of the Year, Best Actor (Freeman); Writers Guild of America '89: Best Adapted Screenplay; Nominations: Academy Awards '89: Best Actor (Freeman), Best Costume Design, Best Film Editing, Best Supporting Actor (Aykroyd). *WAR, FCT, BTV*

Drop Dead Fred *Woof!* **1991 (PG-13)** As a little girl, Lizzie Cronin had a manic, imaginary friend named Fred, who protected her from her domineering mother. When her husband dumps her twenty years later, Fred returns to "help" as only he can. Although the cast is fine, incompetent writing and direction make this a truly dismal affair. Plus, gutter humor and mean-spirited pranks throw the whole "heart-warming" premise out the window. Filmed in Minneapolis. **103m/C VHS, LV.** Phoebe Cates, Rik Mayall, Tim Matheson, Marsha Mason, Carrie Fisher, Daniel Gerroll, Ron Eldard; ***D:*** Ate De Jong; ***W:*** Carlos Davis, Anthony Fingleton; ***M:*** Randy Edelman. *LIV*

Drop-Out Mother **1988** A woman gives up her executive position to become a housewife and full-time mom; expected domestic turmoil follows. Standard made for television fare and sort of a sequel to "Drop-Out Father," shown in 1982. **100m/C VHS.** Valerie Harper, Wayne Rogers, Carol Kane, Kim Hunter, Danny Gerard; ***D:*** Charles S. Dubin. *FRH*

DROP Squad **1994 (R)** Not quite on target social satire revolving around buppie Burford Jackson, Jr. (La Salle), a token minority ad exec who's job is to push questionable products, using gross stereotypes, to the black community. His family's appalled and Buford becomes a prime target of D.R.O.P. (Deprogramming and Restoration of Pride), a vigilante organization that kidnaps erring black bretheren and leads them back to their cultural heritage. Frequently intense performances but the script raises some serious issues it doesn't deliver on. Based on the short story "The Deprogrammer" by David Taylor. **88m/C VHS, LV.** Eriq La Salle, Vondie Curtis-Hall, Ving Rhames, Kasi Lemmons, Vanessa Williams, Nicole Powell, Afemo Omilami; ***Cameos:*** Spike Lee; ***D:*** David Johnson; ***W:*** David Johnson, Butch Robinson, David Taylor; ***M:*** Michael Bearden. *MCA*

Drop Zone ½ **1994 (R)** Routine action-thriller finds U.S. marshal Pete Nessip (Snipes) and his brother Terry (Warner) assigned to protect drug cartel snitch Earl Leedy (Jeter). The plane they're on is skyjacked by criminal Moncrief (Busey) who parachutes off with Leedy, Terry's killed, and while Pete's on suspension he decides to go undercover into the world of sky-driving with the aid of ex-con cutie Jessie (Butler). Plot holes are big enough to pilot a plane through but the stunts are good and Snipes is never less than professional. **101m/C VHS, Beta.** Wesley Snipes, Gary Busey, Yancy Butler, Michael Jeter, Corin "Corky" Nemec, Kyle Secor, Luca Bercovici, Malcolm Jamal Warner, Rex Linn, Grace Zabriskie, Sam Hennings, Claire Stansfield, Mickey Jones, Andy Romano; ***D:*** John Badham; ***W:*** John Bishop, Peter Barsocchini; ***M:*** Hans Zimmer. *PAR*

The Dropkick **1927** Erstwhile D.W. Griffith leading man Barthelmess stars in this pigskin whodunnit: a coach's suicide looks like murder, and the prime suspect is the team's most valuable player. Cast includes ten bona fide university football players and Hedda "nobody's interested in sweetness and light" Hopper, while The Duke makes cameo. Webb later went on to direct a musical with Eddie Cantor and Rudy Vallee ("Glorifying the American Girl"). Silent. Based on the story "Glitter" by Katherine Brush. **62m/B VHS, Beta.** Richard Barthelmess, Barbara Kent, Dorothy Revier, Eugene Strong, Alberta Vaughn, Brooks Benedict, Hedda Hopper; ***Cameos:*** John Wayne; ***D:*** Millard Webb; ***W:*** Winifred Dunn. *GPV, FCT*

Drowning by Numbers ½ **1987 (R)** Three generations of women, each named Cissie Colpitts, solve their marital problems by drowning their husbands and making deals with a bizarre coroner. Further strange visions from director Greenaway, complemented by stunning cinematography courtesy of Sacha Vierny. A treat for those who appreciate Greenaway's uniquely curious cinematic statements. **121m/C VHS, LV.** *GB* Bernard Hill, Joan Plowright, Juliet Stevenson, Joely Richardson; ***D:*** Peter Greenaway; ***W:*** Peter Greenaway; ***M:*** Michael Nyman. *LIV*

The Drowning Pool **1975 (PG)** Newman returns as detective Lew Harper (of "Harper" by Ross MacDonald) to solve a blackmail case. Uneventful script and stodgy direction, but excellent character work from all the cast members keep this watchable. Title is taken from a trap set for Newman, from which he must escape using most of his female companion's clothing. Adapted from a character created by Ross MacDonald. **109m/C VHS, Beta.** Paul Newman, Joanne Woodward, Anthony (Tony) Franciosa, Murray Hamilton, Melanie Griffith, Richard Jaeckel; ***D:*** Stuart Rosenberg; ***W:*** Tracy Keenan Wynn, Walter Hill; ***C:*** Gordon Willis; ***M:*** Charles Fox. *WAR*

Drug Wars 2: The Cocaine Cartel **1992** Muddled drama featuring crazy unpredictable DEA agents executing the downfall of Colombia's Medellin drug kingpins. Average sequel to the award-winning miniseries "Drug Wars." **200m/C VHS.** Alex McArthur, Dennis Farina, Julie Carmen, John Glover, Karen Young, Michele Placido, Gustav Vintas, Geno Silva; ***D:*** Paul Krasny. *MCA*

Drugstore Cowboy ½ **1989 (R)** A gritty, uncompromising depiction of a pack of early 1970s drugstore-robbing junkies as they travel around looking to score. Brushes with the law and tragedy encourage them to examine other life-styles, but the trap seems impossible to leave. A perfectly crafted piece that reflects the "me generation" era, though it tends to glamorize addiction. Dillon's best work to date. Based on a novel by prison inmate James Fogle. **100m/C VHS, Beta, LV.** Matt Dillon, Kelly Lynch, James Remar, James LeGros, Heather Graham, William S. Burroughs, Beah Richards, Grace Zabriskie, Max Perlich; ***D:*** Gus Van Sant; ***W:*** Gus Van Sant, Daniel Yost; ***M:*** Elliot Goldenthal. Independent Spirit Awards '90: Best Actor (Dillon), Best Cinematography, Best Screenplay, Best Supporting Actor (Perlich); New York Film Critics Awards '89: Best Screenplay; National Society of Film Critics Awards '89: Best Director (Van Sant), Best Film, Best Screenplay. *LIV, FCT*

Drum *Woof!* **1976 (R)** This steamy sequel to "Mandingo" deals with the sordid interracial sexual shenanigans at a Southern plantation. Bad taste at its best. **101m/C VHS, Beta.** Ken Norton, Warren Oates, Pam Grier, Yaphet Kotto, Fiona Lewis, Isela Vega, Cheryl "Rainbeaux" Smith; ***D:*** Steve Carver. *LIV, VES, WAR*

Drum Beat **1954** An unarmed Indian fighter sets out to negotiate a peace treaty with a renegade Indian leader. Bronson is especially believable as chief. Based on historical incident. **111m/C VHS, Beta.** Alan Ladd, Charles Bronson, Marisa Pavan, Robert Keith, Rodolfo Acosta, Warner Anderson, Elisha Cook Jr., Anthony Caruso; ***D:*** Delmer Daves. *NO*

Drum Taps **1933** Maynard saves the day for a young girl who is being pushed off her land by a group of speculators. **55m/B VHS, Beta.** Ken Maynard, Dorothy Dix, Frank "Junior" Coghlan, Kermit Maynard; ***D:*** J.P. McGowan. *NOS, VDM, VYY*

Drums ½ *The Drum* **1938** A native prince helps to save the British army in India from being annihilated by a tyrant. Rich melodrama with interesting characterizations and locale. **96m/B VHS, Beta, LV.** *GB* Sabu, Raymond Massey, Valerie Hobson, Roger Livesey, David Tree; ***D:*** Zoltan Korda. *SUE*

Drums Along the Mohawk ½ **1939** Grand, action-filled saga about pre-Revolutionary America, detailing the trials of a colonial newlywed couple as their village in Mohawk Valley is besieged by Indians. Based on the Walter Edmonds novel, and vintage Ford. **104m/C VHS, Beta, LV.** Henry Fonda, Claudette Colbert, Edna May Oliver, Eddie Collins, John Carradine, Dorris Bowdon, Arthur Shields, Ward Bond, Jessie Ralph, Robert Lowery; ***D:*** John Ford; ***C:*** Ray Rennahan. Nominations: Academy Awards '39: Best Color Cinematography, Best Supporting Actress (Oliver). *FOX*

Drums in the Deep South **1951** A rivalry turns ugly as two former West Point roommates wind up on opposite sides when the Civil War breaks out. Historical drama hampered by familiar premise. **87m/C VHS, Beta.** James Craig, Guy Madison, Craig Stevens, Barbara Payton, Barton MacLane; ***D:*** William Cameron Menzies; ***W:*** Philip Yordan. *NOS, MRV, VGR*

Drums of Fu Manchu **1940** Fu Manchu searches for the scepter of Genghis Khan, an artifact that would give him domination over the East. Brandon smoothly evil as the Devil Doctor. Originally a serial in 15 chapters. **150m/B VHS, Beta.** Henry Brandon, Robert Kellard, George Cleveland, Dwight Frye, Gloria Franklin, Tom Chatterton; ***D:*** William Witney, John English. *VCN, MLB*

Drums of Jeopardy *Mark of Terror* **1931** A father wanders through czarist Russia and the U.S. to seek revenge on his daughter's killer. Cheap copy of "Dr. Fu Manchu." **65m/B VHS.** Warner Oland, June Collyer, Lloyd Hughes, George Fawcett, Mischa Auer; ***D:*** George B. Seitz. *NOS, SNC, DVT*

Drums O'Voodoo *Woof! She Devil* **1934** A voodoo princess fights to eliminate the town bad guy in this all-black feature that is greatly hampered by shoddy production values. **70m/B VHS, Beta.** Laura Bowman, J. Augustus Smith, Edna Barr; ***D:*** Arthur Hoerl. *SNC*

Drunken Angel **1948** Alcoholic doctor gets mixed up with local gangster. Kurosawa's first major film aided by strong performances. With English subtitles. **108m/B VHS, Beta.** *JP* Toshiro Mifune, Takashi Shimura, Choko Iida; ***D:*** Akira Kurosawa. *DVT, MRV, INJ*

A Dry White Season **1989 (R)** A white Afrikaner living resignedly with apartheid confronts the system when his black gardener, an old friend, is persecuted and murdered. A well-meaning expose that, like many others, focuses on white people. **105m/C VHS, Beta, LV.** Donald Sutherland, Marlon Brando, Susan Sarandon, Zakes Mokae, Janet Suzman, Juergen Prochnow, Winston Ntshona, Susannah Harker, Thoko Ntshinga, Rowan Elmes; ***D:*** Euzhan Palcy; ***W:*** Colin Welland, Euzhan Palcy; ***M:*** Dave Grusin. Nominations: Academy Awards '89: Best Supporting Actor (Brando). *FOX, FCT*

Drying Up the Streets **1976** Tepid message tale of a police drug squad out to terminate the pattern that has young women turning to a life of prostitution and drugs. **90m/C VHS, Beta.** *CA* Len Cariou, Don Francks, Sarah Torgov, Calvin Butler; ***D:*** Robin Spry. *LIV, VES*

D2: The Mighty Ducks *The Mighty Ducks 2* **1994 (PG)** When an injury forces Gordon (Estevez) out of the minor leagues, he is tapped by promotor Tibbles (Tucker) to coach Team U.S.A. in the Junior Goodwill Games. Upon arriving in LA, the coach's head is turned by the money to be made in endorsements, and he soon gets a lesson in character-building (hey, it's Disney). The duck redux premise is lame, but kids will want ice time to see more of the hockey action that made the first a hit. **107m/C VHS, LV.** Emilio Estevez, Michael Tucker, Jan Rubes, Kathryn Erbe, Shaun Weiss, Kenan Thompson, Ty O'Neal; ***Cameos:*** Kristi Yamaguchi, Kareem Abdul-Jabbar, Wayne Gretzky; ***D:*** Sam Weisman; ***W:*** Steven Brill; ***M:*** J.A.C. Redford. *DIS*

Dual Alibi 🦴🦴 **1947** Identical twin trapeze artists murder a colleague for a winning lottery ticket. Lom plays the brothers in a dual role. **87m/B VHS, Beta.** *GB* Herbert Lom, Terence de Marney, Phyllis Dixey, Ronald Frankau, Abraham Sofaer, Harold Berens, Sebastian Cabot; ***D:*** Alfred Travers. *NOS, SNC*

Dual Flying Kicks 🦴 **1982** Chinese provincial mayor allies himself to a group of bandits amid much high kicking. **95m/C VHS, Beta.** Chen Hsing, Tan Tao Liang. *WVE*

Dubarry 🦴🦴½ **1930** Early sound version of the romantic experiences of Madame Dubarry, the alluring French heroine of David Belasco's "DuBarry." Talmadge's last film. **81m/B VHS, Beta.** Norma Talmadge, Conrad Nagel, William Farnum, Hobart Bosworth, Alison Skipworth; ***D:*** Sam Taylor. *NOS, DVT, HEG*

DuBarry Was a Lady 🦴🦴½ **1943** Skelton is a washroom attendant who daydreams that he is King Louis XV of France. Dorsey's band gets to dress in period wigs and costumes. ♫DuBarry Was a Lady; Do I Love You, Do I?; Friendship; Well, Did You Evah; Taliostro's Dance; Katie Went to Haiti; Madame, I Love Your Crepes Suzettes; Thinking of You; A Cigarette, Sweet Music and You. **112m/C VHS, Beta.** Lucille Ball, Gene Kelly, Red Skelton, Virginia O'Brien, Zero Mostel, Dick Haymes, Rags Ragland, Donald Meek, George Givot, Louise Beavers; ***D:*** Roy Del Ruth; ***W:*** Irving Brecher; ***C:*** Karl Freund. *MGM, CCB*

Dubeat-E-O 🦴½ **1984** A filmmaker races against time to finish making a documentary about the Los Angeles underground hardcore punk scene, and becomes immersed in the subculture. Somewhat of a haphazard exercise in filmmaking that is best appreciated by rock fans. **84m/C VHS, Beta.** Ray Sharkey, Joan Jett, Derf Scratch, Len Lesser, Nora Gaye; ***D:*** Alan Sacks. *MVD, MED*

The Duchess and the Dirtwater Fox 🦴½ **1976 (PG)** Period western strung together with many failed attempts at humor, all about a music-hall hooker who meets a bumbling card shark on the make. **105m/C VHS, Beta, LV.** George Segal, Goldie Hawn, Conrad Janis, Thayer David; ***D:*** Melvin Frank; ***W:*** Barry Sandler; ***C:*** Joseph Biroc; ***M:*** Charles Fox. *FOX*

The Duchess of Idaho 🦴🦴½ **1950** Williams tries to help her roommate patch up a romance gone bad, but ends up falling in love herself. MGM guest stars liven up an otherwise routine production. ♫Baby Come Out of the Clouds; You Can't Do Wrong Doin' Right; Let's Choo Choo to Idaho; Of All Things; Or Was It Spring; Warm Hands, Cold Heart; Singlefoot Serenade; You Won't Forget Me. **98m/C VHS.** Esther Williams, Van Johnson, John Lund, Paula Raymond, Amanda Blake, Eleanor Powell, Lena Horne; ***D:*** Robert Z. Leonard. *MGM*

Duck Soup 🦴🦴🦴🦴 **1933** The Marx Brothers satiric masterpiece (which failed at the box office). Groucho becomes the dictator of Freedonia, and hires Chico and Harpo as spies. Jam-packed with the classic anarchic and irreverent Marx shtick; watch for the mirror scene. Zeppo plays a love-sick tenor, in this, his last film with the brothers. **70m/B VHS, Beta, LV.** Groucho Marx, Chico Marx, Harpo Marx, Zeppo Marx, Louis Calhern, Margaret Dumont, Edgar Kennedy, Raquel Torres, Leonid Kinskey, Charles Middleton; ***D:*** Leo McCarey; ***W:*** Harry Ruby, Nat Perrin, Bert Kalmar, Arthur Sheekman; ***M:*** Harry Ruby, Bert Kalmar. *MCA, FCT*

DuckTales the Movie: Treasure of the Lost Lamp 🦴🦴½ **1990 (G)** Uncle Scrooge and company embark on a lost-ark quest, ala Harrison Ford, for misplaced treasure (a lamp that can make the sky rain ice cream). Based on the daily Disney cartoon of the same name, it's more like an extended-version Saturday morning sugar smacks'n'milk 'toon. See it with someone young. **74m/C VHS, Beta, LV.** ***D:*** Bob Hathcock; ***W:*** Alan Burnett; ***M:*** David Newman; ***V:*** Alan Young, Christopher Lloyd, Rip Taylor, June Foray, Chuck McCann, Richard Libertini, Russi Taylor, Joan Gerber, Terence McGovern. *DIS, WTA*

Dude Bandit 🦴🦴 **1932** An unscrupulous money-lender tries to gain control of a ranch but Gibson comes to the rescue. Gibson actually plays three roles: the rancher's best friend, an aw-shucks cowpoke disguise in order to find out what's going on, and the title character used to bedevil the crooks. **68m/B VHS, Beta.** Hoot Gibson, Gloria Shea. *VYY, VCI, VCN*

Dude Ranger 🦴🦴½ **1934** Well-acted Zane Grey story about an easterner who gets caught up in a range war and cattle rustling when he takes possession of some property out west. **58m/B VHS, Beta.** Smiley Burnette, George O'Brien, Irene Hervey; ***D:*** Eddie Cline. *VDM*

Dudes 🦴 **1987 (R)** Three city kids head for the desert and run afoul of some rednecks. Tired grade-6 revenge story. **90m/C VHS, Beta, LV.** Jon Cryer, Catherine Mary Stewart, Daniel Roebuck, Flea, Lee Ving, Calvin Bartlett, Pete Willcox, Glenn Withrow; ***D:*** Penelope Spheeris; ***M:*** Charles Bernstein. *NO*

Duel 🦴🦴🦴 **1971 (PG)** Spielberg's first notable film, a made-for-television exercise in paranoia. A docile traveling salesman is repeatedly attacked and threatened by a huge, malevolent tractor-trailer on an open desert highway. Released theatrically in Europe. **90m/C VHS, Beta.** Dennis Weaver, Lucille Benson, Eddie Firestone, Cary Loftin; ***D:*** Steven Spielberg; ***W:*** Richard Matheson; ***M:*** Billy Goldenberg. *MCA*

Duel at Diablo 🦴🦴🦴 **1966** An exceptionally violent film that deals with racism in the Old West. Good casting; western fans will enjoy the action. **103m/C VHS.** James Garner, Sidney Poitier, Bibi Andersson, Dennis Weaver, Bill Travers; ***D:*** Ralph Nelson. *MGM*

Duel in the Sun 🦴🦴🦴 **1946** A lavish, lusty David O. Selznick production of a minor western novel about a vivacious half-breed Indian girl, living on a powerful dynastic ranch, who incites two brothers to conflict. Selznick's last effort at outdoing his epic success with "Gone With the Wind." **130m/C VHS, Beta.** Gregory Peck, Jennifer Jones, Joseph Cotten, Lionel Barrymore, Lillian Gish, Butterfly McQueen, Harry Carey Sr., Walter Huston, Charles Bickford, Herbert Marshall; ***D:*** King Vidor; ***C:*** Ray Rennahan. Nominations: Academy Awards '46: Best Actress (Jones), Best Supporting Actress (Gish). *FOX*

Duel of Champions 🦴 *Orazi e Curiazi* **1961** It's ancient Rome, and the prodigal gladiator has come home. Now the family must have a duel to decide who will rule. **90m/C VHS, Beta.** *IT SP* Alan Ladd, Francesca Bett; ***D:*** Ferdinando Baldi. *NO*

Duel of Fists 🦴 **1989** When the owner of a boxing institute dies, he instructs his son in his will to go searching for his long-lost brother in Thailand. All he can go on is an old photograph and the knowledge that his brother is a Thai boxer. **111m/C VHS, Beta.** David Chiang, Chen Hsing, Ti Lung, Tang Ti. *HMD, MOV*

Duel of Hearts 🦴🦴 **1992 (PG-13)** Beautiful Caroline falls in love with wealthy Lord Vane Brecon, who unfortunately is accused of murder. When Caroline tries to help him clear his name she discovers he's hiding a number of secrets. Based on the romance novel "Duel of Love" by Barbara Cartland. Nothing too inspiring here, although regency romance fans will appreciate the attention to detail. Originally made for cable television. **95m/C VHS, Beta, LV.** *GB* Alison Doody, Michael York, Geraldine Chaplin, Benedict Taylor, Billie Whitelaw, Virginia McKenna, Richard Johnson, Jeremy Kemp, Beryl Reid, Suzanna Hamilton, Jolyon Baker, Julie Kate; ***D:*** John Hough. *TTC*

Duel of the Iron Fist 🦴 **1972 (R)** Master of the martial arts must do battle with a brutal gang to save his own group from extinction. **98m/C VHS, Beta.** David Chiang, Ti Lung, Wang Ping, Yu Hui. *HHT*

Duel of the Seven Tigers 🦴🦴 **1980** Nine of the world's greatest Kung Fu and Karate exponents team up in this martial arts spectacular. **80m/C VHS, Beta.** Cliff Lok, Ka Sa Fa, Chio Chi Ling, Lam Men Wei, Yang Pan Pan, Charlie Chan. *TWE*

The Duellists 🦴🦴🦴 **1977 (PG)** A beautifully photographed picture about the long-running feud between two French officers during the Napoleonic wars. Based on "The Duel" by Joseph Conrad. **101m/C VHS, Beta, LV.** *GB* Keith Carradine, Harvey Keitel, Albert Finney, Edward Fox, Tom Conti, Christina Raines, Diana Quick; ***D:*** Ridley Scott. Nominations: Cannes Film Festival '77: Best Film. *PAR*

Duet for One 🦴🦴 **1986 (R)** A famous concert violinist learns she is suffering from multiple sclerosis and is slowly losing her ability to play. Convinced that her life is meaningless without music, she self-destructively drifts into bitter isolation. From the play by Tom Kempinski. **108m/C VHS, Beta.** Julie Andrews, Max von Sydow, Alan Bates, Liam Neeson; ***D:*** Andrei Konchalovsky. *MGM*

The Duke is Tops 🦴🦴½ **1938** In Horne's earliest existing film appearance, she's off to attempt the "big-time," while her boyfriend joins a traveling medicine show. ♫I Know You Remember. **80m/C VHS, Beta.** Ralph Cooper, Lena Horne, Marie Bryant. *NOS, MRV, VCN*

Duke of the Derby 🦴🦴 *Le Gentleman D'epsom* **1962** A scheming racehorse handicapper bets over his head and ruins his higher-than-means lifestyle. In French with English subtitles. **83m/C VHS, Beta.** *FR* Jean Gabin; ***D:*** Gilles Grangier. *FCT, DVT, HEG*

Duke: The Films of John Wayne **1989** A gift-pack collection of three of Wayne's finest: "Flying Leathernecks," "Fort Apache," and "She Wore a Yellow Ribbon." **332m/C VHS.** John Wayne. *TTC*

Dumb & Dumber 🦴🦴½ **1994 (PG-13)** Moronic limo driver Lloyd Christmas (Carrey) and equally dense dog groomer Harry Dunne (Daniels) travel (in the hilarious "sheep dog" van) from Rhode Island to Colorado—at one point going east!—to return a briefcase full of cash to a beautiful socialite (Holly). Engaging in all sorts of gross-out bathroom, bodily function, and slapstick humor, this one will definitely not appeal to the stuffy critic or arthouse snob. It will provide plenty of laughs, however embarrassingly rendered, for everyone else. Daniels proves a convincing dimwit sidekick, while Carrey mugs shamelessly. Occasional "Seinfeld" writer Farrelly makes his directorial debut. **110m/C VHS, LV.** Jim Carrey, Jeff Daniels, Lauren Holly, Teri Garr, Karen Duffy, Mike Starr, Charles Rocket, Victoria Rowell, Felton Perry; ***D:*** Peter Farrelly; ***W:*** Bennett Yellin, Bobby Farrelly, Peter Farrelly; ***M:*** Todd Rundgren. MTV Movie Awards '95: Best Comedic Performance (Carrey), Best Kiss (Jim Carrey/Lauren Holly); Nominations: MTV Movie Awards '95: Best On-Screen Duo (Jim Carrey/Jeff Daniels). *TTC, NLC*

Dumb Waiter **1987** A mini-play by Harold Pinter about two hitmen awaiting instructions for a job in an empty boardinghouse, and getting comically mixed messages. Made for television. **60m/C VHS, Beta.** John Travolta, Tom Conti; ***D:*** Robert Altman; ***W:*** Harold Pinter. *PSM*

Dumbo 🦴🦴🦴🦴 **1941** Animated Disney classic about a baby elephant growing up in the circus who is ridiculed for his large ears, until he discovers he can fly. The little elephant who could fly then becomes a circus star. Expressively and imaginatively animated, highlighted by the hallucinatory dancing pink elephants sequence. Endearing songs by Frank Churchill, Oliver Wallace, and Ned Washington, including "Baby Mine," "Pink Elephants on Parade," and "I See an Elephant Fly." **63m/C VHS, Beta, LV.** ***D:*** Ben Sharpsteen; ***W:*** Joe Grant, Dick Huemer; ***M:*** Frank Churchill, Oliver Wallace; ***V:*** Sterling Holloway, Edward Brophy, Verna Felton, Herman Bing, Cliff Edwards. Academy Awards '41: Best Score; National Board of Review Awards '41: 10

Best Films of the Year; Nominations: Academy Awards '41: Best Song ("Baby Mine"). *DIS, APD, SCH*

The Dummy Talks **1943** When a ventriloquist is murdered, a midget goes undercover as a dummy to find the killer. Watch closely and you might see his lips move. **85m/B VHS, Beta.** *GB* Jack Warner, Claude Hulbert, Beryl Orde, Derna-Hazell, Ivy Benson, Manning Whiley; ***D:*** Oswald Mitchell. *SNC*

Dune **1984 (PG-13)** Lynch sci-fi opus based on the Frank Herbert novel boasting great set design, muddled scripting, and a good cast. The story: controlling the spice drug of Arrakis permits control of the universe in the year 10991. Paul, the heir of the Atreides family, leads the Freemen in a revolt against the evil Harkhonens who have violently seized control of Arrakis, also known as Dune, the desert planet. That's as clear as it ever gets. **137m/C VHS, Beta, LV.** Kyle MacLachlan, Francesca Annis, Jose Ferrer, Sting, Max von Sydow, Juergen Prochnow, Linda Hunt, Freddie Jones, Dean Stockwell, Virginia Madsen, Brad Dourif, Kenneth McMillan, Silvana Mangano, Jack Nance, Sian Phillips, Paul Smith, Richard Jordan, Everett McGill, Sean Young; ***D:*** David Lynch; ***W:*** David Lynch; ***M:*** Brian Eno. Nominations: Academy Awards '84: Best Sound. *MCA, FCT*

Dune Warriors ½ **1991 (R)** Earth is a parched planet in the year 2040. Renegade bands cruise the desert, making short shrift of civilized people who band together in remote villages. When peaceful farmer Carradine's family falls prey to the pillagers, surely he and the most evil warlord of all must clash. Good action and stunts, if the dummy plot doesn't get you first. **77m/C VHS, LV.** David Carradine, Richard Hill, Luke Askew, Jillian McWhirter, Blake Boyd; ***D:*** Cirio H. Santiago. *COL*

The Dunera Boys **1985 (R)** Hoskins shines in this story about Viennese Jews who, at the onset of WWII, escape to England where they are suspected as German spies. Subsequently, the British shipped them all to an Australian prison camp, where they recreated in peace their Viennese lifestyle. **150m/C VHS, Beta, LV.** *AU* Bob Hoskins, Joe Spano, Warren Mitchell, Joseph Furst, Moshe Kedem, Dita Cobb, John Meillon, Mary-Anne Fahey, Simon Chilvers, Steven Vidler; ***D:*** Sam Lewin. *PSM*

Dungeon of Harrow **1964** Unbelievably cheap tale of shipwrecked comrades who encounter a maniacal family on an otherwise deserted island. Not your stranded-on-a-desert-island fantasy come true. Filmed in San Antonio; a harrowing bore. **74m/B VHS.** Russ Harvey, Helen Hogan, Bill McNulty, Pat Boyette; ***D:*** Pat Boyette. *SNC*

Dungeonmaster ½ *Ragewar* **1983 (PG-13)** A warlord forces a computer wiz to participate in a bizarre "Dungeons and Dragons" styled game in order to save a girl held captive. Consists of seven segments, each by a different director. Save yourself the trouble. **80m/C VHS, Beta, LV.** Jeffrey Byron, Richard Moll, Leslie Wing, Danny Dick; ***D:*** John Carl Buechler, Charles Band, David Allen, Stephen Ford, Peter Manoogian, Ted Nicolaou, Rosemarie Turko; ***W:*** Allen Actor; ***M:*** Richard Band. *LIV*

Dunston Checks In ½ **1995 (PG)** This just in: Hollywood thinks monkeys are funny. But, as far as "stupid people learn important life lessons from a monkey who wears clothes" movies go, this one's not bad. Robert Grant (Alexander) is the manager of a five-star hotel. His Leona Helmsley-esque boss (Dunaway) is convinced that aristocratic guest Lord Rutledge (Everett) is a travel guide critic who is there to bestow an elusive sixth star on the hotel. Actually he's a jewel thief, and Dunston the orangutan is his accomplice. When Dunston flees from his abusive owner, he's adopted by Grant's two children. Together, Dunston and the kids are left to straighten out the whole mess. **88m/C VHS, LV.** Jason Alexander, Faye Dunaway, Eric Lloyd, Rupert Everett, Graham Sack, Paul (Pee Wee Herman) Reubens, Glenn Shadix, Nathan Davis, Jennifer Bassey; ***Cameos:*** Paul (Pee Wee Herman) Reubens; ***D:*** Ken Kwapis; ***W:*** Bruce Graham, John Hopkins; ***C:*** Peter Collister; ***M:*** Miles Goodman. *FXV*

The Dunwich Horror **1970** Young warlock acquires a banned book of evil spells, starts trouble on the astral plane. Stockwell hammy. Loosely based on H. P. Lovecraft story. **90m/C VHS, Beta.** Sandra Dee, Dean Stockwell, Lloyd Bochner, Ed Begley Sr., Sam Jaffe, Joanna Moore; ***D:*** Daniel Haller; ***W:*** Curtis Hanson; ***M:*** Les Baxter. *SUE*

Duplicates **1992 (PG-13)** Harrison and Greist are a married couple whose young son has disappeared. When the boy is found he has no memory of his former life or parents. The couple discover he's the victim of secret experiments which transfer human memories into computer banks. Will they become the next targets? **92m/C VHS, Beta.** Gregory Harrison, Kim Greist, Cicely Tyson, Lane Smith, William Lucking, Kevin McCarthy; ***D:*** Sandor Stern. *PAR, PMS*

Dupont Lajoie *Rape of Innocence* **1974** At a tourist campground Lajoie (Carmet) accidentally kills his son's girlfriend when she resists his sexual advances. To save his life he accuses Arabs of committing the crime and begins a racist campaign of vengeance. French with subtitles. **103m/C VHS.** *FR* Jean Carmet; ***D:*** Yves Boisset. *FCT*

Durango Valley Raiders ½ **1938** Sheriff is the leader of the outlaws, and a young cowboy finds out. **55m/B VHS, Beta.** Bob Steele; ***D:*** Sam Newfield. *VCN, DVT*

Dust **1985** A white woman in South Africa murders her father when he shows affection for a young black servant. Controversial and intense. **87m/C VHS, Beta.** *FR BE* Jane Birkin, Trevor Howard, John Matshikiza, Nadine Uwampa, Lourdes Christina Sayo, Rene Diaz; ***D:*** Marion Hansel; ***W:*** Marion Hansel; ***M:*** Martin St. Pierre. *TPV*

Dust Devil **1993 (R)** Three travelers find themselves in Namibia's vast desert: a policeman, a woman on the run, and her abusive husband. They all have the misfortune of meeting up with a supernatural being known as the "Dust Devil," who kills humans in order to steal their souls and increase his other worldly powers. **87m/C VHS, Beta.** Robert Burke, Chelsea Field, Zakes Mokae, Rufus Swart, John Matshikiza, William Hootkins, Marianne Sagebrecht; ***D:*** Richard Stanley; ***W:*** Richard Stanley; ***M:*** Simon Boswell. *PAR*

Dust to Dust **1985** A short mystery made for British television about an aging gentleman who answers a request for correspondence and discovers ulterior, and evil, motives. **60m/C VHS, Beta.** *GB* Patricia Hodge, Michael Jayston, Judy Campbell. *PSM*

Dusty **1985** Touching story of a wild dingo dog raised by an Australian rancher and trained to herd sheep. Filmed in the Australian bush and based on the children's book by Frank Dalby Davison. **89m/C VHS, Beta.** *AU* Bill Kerr, Noel Trevarthen, Carol Burns, Nicholas Holland, John Stanton; ***D:*** John Richardson. *MED, FCT, FHE*

Dutch ½ **1991 (PG-13)** Working class boob attempts to pick up his girlfriend's son from boarding school. Their trip together gives them an unexpected chance to connect, if they don't kill each other first. Silly premise from the Hughes factory has little innovation and uses type-casting instead of acting. **107m/C VHS.** Ed O'Neill, Ethan Randall, JoBeth Williams; ***D:*** Peter Faiman; ***W:*** John Hughes. *FXV, IME*

Dutch Girls *Woof!* **1987** Muddled mayhem as a horny high school field hockey team travels through Holland, cavorts about, and discovers the meaning of life. **83m/C VHS, Beta.** *GB* Bill Paterson, Colin Firth, Timothy Spall; ***D:*** Giles Foster. *ACA*

Dutch Treat **1986 (R)** Two nerds con a sultry, all-girl rock band into thinking they're powerful record company execs. Nobody's buying. **95m/C VHS, Beta.** Lorin Dreyfuss, David Landsberg; ***D:*** Boaz Davidson. *MGM*

Dutchman **1967** Film presentation of Amiri Baraka's one act play depicting the claustrophobic reality of the black man's situation in America. Black man shares subway conversation with a white woman who questions his race and middle class aspirations. Enraged, one takes the other's life. **55m/C VHS.** *GB* Al Freeman Jr., Shirley Knight; ***D:*** Anthony Harvey; ***M:*** John Barry. Cannes Film Festival '67: Best Film. *CAL*

D.W. Griffith Triple Feature ½ **1913** A collection of three short D.W. Griffith films including "The Battle of Elderbush Gulch," "Iola's Promise," and "The Goddess of Sagebrush Gulch." **50m/B VHS, Beta.** Mae Marsh, Lillian Gish, Mary Pickford, Blanche Sweet, Charles West; ***D:*** D.W. Griffith. *BAR, FCT*

The Dwelling Place ½ **199?** Sixteen-year-old girl struggles to hold her family together after the death of their parents. But her situation turns tragic when she's raped and left pregnant but a drunken young aristocrat. Based on a novel by Catherine Cookson. **145m/C VHS.** *GB GB* Tracy Whitwell, James Fox, Edward Rawle-Hicks. *VCO*

The Dybbuk ½ **1937** A man's bride is possessed by a restless spirit. Set in the Polish-Jewish community before WWI and based on the play by Sholom Anski. Considered a classic for its portrayal of Jewish religious and cultural mores. In Yiddish with English subtitles. **123m/B VHS, Beta.** *PL* Abraham Morewski, Isaac Samberg, Moshe Lipman, Lili Liliana, Dina Halpern; ***D:*** Michal Waszynski. *IHF, FCT, NCJ*

Dying Game **1994** Sorority girls are being stalked and murdered and the detective investigating the crimes falls for the sorority's president. Now, he has to find the killer before his girlfriend becomes the next victim. **85m/C VHS.** Michael Hughes, Mathea Webb, D.J. Boozer; ***D:*** Kris Hughes. *SWI*

Dying Room Only ½ **1973** Travelling through the desert, a woman's husband suddenly disappears after they stop at a secluded roadside diner. Made for television flick is a real spooker. **74m/C VHS.** Cloris Leachman, Ross Martin, Ned Beatty, Louise Latham, Dana Elcar, Dabney Coleman; ***D:*** Philip Leacock; ***W:*** Richard Matheson; ***M:*** Charles Fox. *LIV*

Dying to Remember ½ **1993 (PG-13)** A fashion designer (Gilbert) regresses to a past life during hypnotherapy and discovers she was murdered in 1963. She flies to San Francisco to discover more about her past but finds that someome wants to keep things secret—and is willing to kill again. Tedious and predictable. **87m/C VHS, Beta.** Melissa Gilbert, Ted Shackleford, Scott Plank, Christopher Stone, Jay Robinson; ***D:*** Arthur Seidelman; ***W:*** George Schenck, Frank Cardea, Brian L. Ross. *PAR*

The Dying Truth **1991** A wrongfully accused prisoner lies dying in his cell. Trouble is, he can't die in peace until he solves the murder they say he committed. Interesting mix of the supernatural and mystery, although perhaps not one of Carradine's more memorable roles. **80m/C VHS.** David Carradine, Stephanie Beacham, Stephen Greif, Stephan Chase, Larry Carby, Lesley Dunlop; ***D:*** John Hough. *NO*

Dying Young ½ **1991 (R)** Muted romance has a wealthy leukemia victim hire a spirited, unschooled beauty as his nurse. They fall in love, but the film is either too timid or too unimaginative to mine emotions denoted by the title. Nobody dies, in fact, a grim ending (faithful to the Marti Leimbach novel on which this was based) got scrapped after testing poorly with audiences. The actors try their best, photography is lovely, and Kenny G's mellow music fills the soundtrack, but this is basically overmelodramatic drivel. Scott is the late Dewhurst's son. **111m/C VHS.** Julia Roberts, Campbell Scott, Vincent D'Onofrio, Colleen Dewhurst, Ellen Burstyn, David Selby; ***D:*** Joel Schumacher; ***W:*** Richard Friedenberg; ***C:*** Juan Ruiz-Anchia. *FXV*

Dynamite **1949** Romance explodes as two young demolitions experts vie for the same girl. Stand back. **68m/B VHS, Beta.** William Gargan, Virginia Welles, Richard Crane, Irving Bacon; ***D:*** William H. Pine. *NOS, DVT, HEG*

Dynamite and Gold *Where the Hell's the Gold?* **1988 (PG)** Nelson and crew embark on a search for lost gold, battling hostile Indians, the Mexican army and assorted bandits along the way. A mediocre television movie. **91m/C VHS, LV.** Willie Nelson, Delta Burke, Jack Elam, Alfonso Arau, Gregory Sierra, Michael

Wren, Gerald McRaney; **D:** Burt Kennedy; **W:** Burt Kennedy. *ACA*

The Dynamite Brothers 🦴 **1974 (R)** Two tough guys, one a Hong Kong immigrant with martial arts skills, the other a brother from the streets of the ghetto, team up to rid Los Angeles of a Chinese crimelord. **90m/C VHS.** James Hong, Aldo Ray, Alan Tang, Timothy Brown, Carolyn Ann Speed, Don Oliver; **D:** Al Adamson; **M:** Charles Earland. *RHI*

Dynamite Canyon 🦴🦴 **1941** Average oater has villain Price committing murder in order to keep secret the location of a lode of copper. Standard western fare. **58m/B VHS.** Tom Keene, Evelyn Finley, Sugar Dawn, Stanley Price, Kenne Duncan; **D:** Robert Emmett Tansey; **W:** Robert Emmett Tansey, Frances Kavanaugh. *DVT*

Dynamite Chicken 🦴🦴 **1970 (R)** Melange of skits, songs, and hippie satire is dated. Includes performances by Joan Baez, Lenny Bruce, B.B. King, and others. **75m/C VHS, Beta.** Joan Baez, Richard Pryor, Lenny Bruce, Jimi Hendrix; **D:** Ernie Pintoff. *NO*

Dynamite Dan 🦴½ **1924** A man knocks out the heavyweight boxing champion after he flirts with his girlfriend and decides to give up his day job to become a championship boxer. He is a success, and in the end he has to face the champion again. Will he win? **62m/B VHS, Beta.** Kenneth McDonald, Frank Rice, Boris Karloff, Eddie Harris, Diana Alden, Harry Woods, Jack Richardson; **D:** Bruce Mitchell. *GPV, LSV*

Dynamite Pass 🦴🦴 **1950** Offbeat oater about disgruntled ranchers attempting to stop the construction of a new road. **61m/B VHS, Beta.** Tim Holt, Richard Martin, Regis Toomey, Lynn (Mary Hart) Roberts, Denver Pyle; **D:** Lew (Louis Friedlander) Landers. *MED*

Dynamite Ranch 🦴 **1932** Ranchers fight tooth and nail to keep their rights and property in this Maynard oater. **60m/B VHS, Beta.** Ken Maynard. *NOS, VCI, DVT*

Dynamo 🦴 **1980 (R)** A glamorous advertising executive pursues a kung fu expert to sign a contract with her agency for a kick boxing contest. **81m/C VHS, Beta.** *SUE, ORI*

Dynasty 🦴🦴 **1977** A leader of the Ming Dynasty is killed by evil Imperial Court eunuch and his son the monk sets out to avenge him. In 3-D. Run-of-the-mill kung-fu stunts. **94m/C VHS, Beta.** Bobby Ming, Lin Tashing, Pai Ying, Tang Wei, Jin Gang; **D:** Zhang Meijun. *BFV*

Dynasty 🦴🦴 **1982** Pulitzer Prize-winning author James Michener creates the usual sweeping saga of a family torn by jealousy, deception, and rivalry in love and business as husband, wife, and brother-in-law seek their fortune in the Ohio frontier of the 1820s. **90m/C VHS, Beta.** Sarah Miles, Harris Yulin, Stacy Keach. *TLF*

Dynasty of Fear 🦴½ *Fear in the Night; Honeymoon of Fear* **1972 (PG)** Matters get rather sticky at a British boys' school when the headmaster's wife seduces her husband's assistant. Together they conspire to murder her husband and share his fortune. **93m/C VHS, Beta.** *GB* Peter Cushing, Joan Collins, Ralph Bates, Judy Geeson, James Cossins; **D:** Jimmy Sangster; **W:** Jimmy Sangster. *REP, ACA*

E. Nick: A Legend in His Own Mind **1984** Satire of videos and magazines designed for adults. **75m/C VHS, Beta.** Don Calfa, Cleavon Little, Andra Akers, Pat McCormick; **D:** Robert Hegyes. *LIV*

Each Dawn I Die 🦴🦴½ **1939** Cagney stars as a reporter who is a fervent critic of the political system. Framed for murder and imprisoned, he is subsequently befriended by fellow inmate, Raft, a gangster. Once hardened by prison life, Cagney shuns his friend and becomes wary of the system. Despite its farfetched second half and mediocre script, the film makes interesting viewing thanks to a stellar performance from Cagney. **92m/B VHS, Beta.** James Cagney, George Raft, George Bancroft, Jane Bryan, Maxie "Slapsie" Rosenbloom, Alan Baxter, Thurston Hall, Stanley Ridges, Victor Jory; **D:** William Keighley. *MGM*

The Eagle 🦴🦴🦴 **1925** In this tale of a young Cossack "Robin Hood," Valentino assumes the persona of the Eagle to avenge his father's murder. The romantic rogue encounters trouble when he falls for the beautiful Banky much to the chagrin of the scorned Czarina Dresser. Fine performances from Valentino and Dresser. Silent, based on a Alexander Pushkin story. Released on video with a new score by Davis. **77m/B VHS, Beta, LV.** Rudolph Valentino, Vilma Banky, Louise Dresser, George Nicholls Jr., James Marcus; **D:** Clarence Brown; **C:** George Barnes; **M:** Carl Davis. *NOS, HBO, VYY*

Eagle Claws Champion 🦴 **198?** A ninja master accidentally kills a friend, goes to prison, gets released and returns to fight again. **90m/C VHS, Beta.** Sho Kosugi. *TWE*

The Eagle Has Landed 🦴🦴🦴 **1977 (PG)** Duvall, portraying a Nazi colonel in this WWII spy film, commissions Sutherland's Irish, English-hating character to aid him in his mission to kill Prime Minister Winston Churchill. Adapted from the bestselling novel by Jack Higgins. A restored version is available at 134 minutes. **123m/C VHS, Beta.** Michael Caine, Donald Sutherland, Robert Duvall, Larry Hagman, Jenny Agutter, Donald Pleasence, Treat Williams, Anthony Quayle; **D:** John Sturges; **W:** Tom Mankiewicz; **M:** Lalo Schifrin. *FOX, FCT*

The Eagle Has Two Heads 🦴🦴🦴 *L'Aigle a Deux Tetes; The Eagle with Two Heads* **1948** Set during the 19th century, poet/anarchist Marais sets out to assassinate the queen, but when he sees the beautiful monarch, it's love at first sight. Adapted from Cocteau's hugely successful play. In French with English subtitles. **93m/B VHS.** *FR* Edwige Feuillere, Jean Marais; **D:** Jean Cocteau; **W:** Jean Cocteau. *WBF*

Eagles Attack at Dawn 🦴½ **1974 (PG)** After escaping from an Arab prison, an Israeli soldier vows to return with a small commando force to kill the sadistic warden. **96m/C VHS, Beta.** *IS* Rick Jason, Peter Brown, Joseph Shiloal. *NO*

Eagle's Shadow 🦴 **1984** After a poor orphan boy rescues an aged beggar, the grateful old man tutors the lad in Snake-Fist techniques. **101m/C VHS, Beta.** Jackie Chan, Juan Jan Lee, Simon Yuen, Roy Horan; **D:** Yuen Woo Ping. *WVE*

Eagle's Wing 🦴½ **1979** John Briley, screenwriter of the award-winning epic "Gandhi," attempts to weave the threads of allegory smoothly in this white man vs. red man Western from England. The mediocre story finds Native American Waterston dueling white trapper Sheen in a quest to capture an elusive, exotic white stallion. **111m/C VHS, Beta.** *GB* Martin Sheen, Sam Waterston, Harvey Keitel, Stephane Audran, Caroline Langrishe; **D:** Anthony Harvey; **W:** John Briley; **C:** Billy Williams. *MED*

Early Cinema Vol. 1 **1919** A compendium of early silent shorts, mostly predating 1920, which includes: Melies' "Conquest of the North Pole"; Linder's "Man and the Statue" and "Max's Mother In Law"; Drew's "Auntie's Portrait"; Normand's "Mabel's Dramatic Career"; Mix's "An Angelic Attitude" Sennett and Swain's "Cowboy Ambrose"; Lloyd's "Just Neighbors" and Parrott's "Take the Air." **118m/B VHS, Beta.** Mabel Normand, Harold Lloyd, Sidney Drew, Max Linder, Paul Parrott, Tom Mix, Mack Swain; **D:** Mabel Normand, Harold Lloyd, Max Linder, Georges Melies, Mack Sennett. *FCT*

Early Days 🦴🦴 **1981** A cantankerous, salty, once-powerful politician awaits death. **67m/C VHS, Beta.** Ralph Richardson. *FOX*

Early Frost 🦴½ **1984** Near suspenseful whodunit centering around a simple divorce investigation that leads to the discovery of a corpse. **95m/C VHS, Beta, LV.** Diana McLean, Jon Blake, Janet Kingsbury, David Franklin; **D:** Terry O'Connor. *NO*

An Early Frost 🦴🦴🦴½ **1985** Highly praised, surprisingly intelligent made-for-television drama following the anguish of a successful lawyer who tells his closed-minded family that he is gay and dying of AIDS. Sensitive performance by Quinn in one of the first TV films to focus on the devastating effects of HIV. Rowlands adeptly displays her acting talents as the despairing mother. **97m/C VHS, Beta, LV.** Aidan Quinn, Gena Rowlands, Ben Gazzara, John Glover, D.W. Moffett, Sylvia Sidney; **D:** John Erman. *COL*

Early Russian Cinema, Vol. 1: Beginnings **1911** Four films from 1908-1911, including a documentary and the first film adaptation of a Chekhov play. English subtitles. **45m/B VHS.** *RU MIL*

Early Russian Cinema, Vol. 2: Folklore & Legend **1912** Four films from 1909-1912: two depicting typical Russian folktales and two, directed by Goncharov, featuring national and cultural themes of the day. English subtitles. **55m/B VHS.** *RU* **D:** Vasilii Goncharov. *MIL*

Early Russian Cinema, Vol. 3: Starewicz's Fantasies **1915** Three films by director Starewicz, known for his use of puppet animation. This selection also includes a live-action fantasy from a Gogol story and an anti-German war allegory. English subtitles. **58m/B VHS.** *RU* **D:** Wladislaw Starewicz. *MIL*

Early Russian Cinema, Vol. 4: Provincial Variations **1913** The provincial Latvian film "Wedding Day" highlights Jewish life while the melodrama "Merchant Bashkirov's Daughter" follows a scandal based on an actual murder. English subtitles. **55m/B VHS.** *RU MIL*

Early Russian Cinema, Vol. 5: Chardynin's Pushkin **1913** Actor-director Chardynin's adaptations of two Pushkin stories. English subtitles. **45m/B VHS.** *RU* Ivan Mosjoukine; **D:** Petr Chardynin. *MIL*

Early Russian Cinema, Vol. 6: Class Distinctions **1914** The hardship of rural life and a view of servants and masters are depicted in two films. English subtitles. **94m/B VHS.** *RU* **D:** Vasilii Goncharov, Evgenii Bauer. *MIL*

Early Russian Cinema, Vol. 7: Evgenii Bauer **1915** Three films from the prolific director of some 80 films, covering both melodrama and erotic comedy. English subtitles. **95m/B VHS.** *RU* **D:** Evgenii Bauer. *MIL*

Early Russian Cinema, Vol. 8: Iakov Protazanov **1916** Two films from director Protazanov, including his controversial film on the last days of Tolstoy which provoked legal action from the writer's family due to its scandalous depiction. English subtitles. **104m/B VHS.** *RU* **D:** Yakov Protazanov. *MIL*

Early Russian Cinema, Vol. 9: High Society **1919** Three films covering social and urban topics, including a newsreel on the death of Russia's greatest star of the day. English subtitles. **72m/B VHS.** *RU* **D:** Evgenii Bauer. *MIL*

Early Russian Cinema, Vol. 10: The End of an Era **1917** Three films, including Bauer's last film "For Luck" and a fragment with the husband-wife acting team of Lisenko and Mosjoukine before their departure into exile. English subtitles. **72m/B VHS.** *RU* Ivan Mosjoukine, Natalia Lisenko; **D:** Evgenii Bauer. *MIL*

Early Sound Films **1928** This series of experimental shorts from throughout the silent era depicts the various methods of devising sound film, prior to "The Jazz Singer" in 1927. **90m/B VHS, Beta.** *GVV*

Early Summer 🦴🦴🦴 *Bakushu* **1951** A classic from renowned Japanese director Ozu, this film chronicles family tensions in post-WWII Japan caused by newly-independent women rebelling against the social conventions they are expected to fulfill. Perhaps the best example of this director's work. Winner of Japan's Film of the Year Award. In Japanese with English subtitles. **150m/B VHS, Beta.** *JP* Ichiro Sugai, Chishu Ryu, Setsuko Hara, Chikage Awashima, Chieko Higashiyama, Haruko Sugimura, Kuniko Miyake, Kan Nihon-yanagi, Shuji Sano, Toyoko Takahashi, Seiji Miyaguchi; **D:** Yasujiro Ozu. *FCT, INJ*

The Earrings of Madame De... *Diamond Earrings; Madame De* **1954** A simple story about a society woman who sells a pair of diamond earrings that her husband gave her, then lies about it. Transformed by Ophuls into his most opulent, overwrought masterpiece, the film displays a triumph of form over content. In French with English subtitles. **105m/C VHS, Beta.** *FR* Charles Boyer, Danielle Darrieux, Vittorio De Sica, Lea di Lea, Jean Debucourt; ***D:*** Max Ophuls. Nominations: Academy Awards '54: Best Costume Design (B & W). *FCT, MRV, INJ*

Earth *Zemlya; Soul* **1930** Classic Russian silent film with English subtitles. Problems begin in a Ukrainian village when a collective farm landowner resists handing over his land. Outstanding camera work. Kino release runs 70 minutes. **57m/B VHS, Beta.** *RU* Semyon Svashenko, Mikola Nademsy, Stephan Shkurat, Yelena Maximova; ***D:*** Alexander Dovzhenko. *VYY, CCB, IHF*

Earth Entranced *Terra em Transe* **1966** A complex political lamentation from Rocha, the premiere director of Brazil's own new wave cinema. Here a writer switches his allegiance from one politician to another, only to find that he (and the masses) lose either way. In Portuguese with English subtitles. **105m/C VHS.** *BR* Jose Lewgoy, Paulo Gracindo, Jardel Filho, Glauce Rocha; ***D:*** Glauce Rocha; ***W:*** Glauce Rocha. *FCT*

Earth Girls Are Easy ½ **1989 (PG)** Valley girl Valerie is having a bad week: first she catches her fiancee with another woman, then she breaks a nail, then furry aliens land in her swimming pool. What more could go wrong? When the aliens are temporarily stranded, she decides to make amends by giving them a head-to-toe makeover. Devoid of their excessive hairiness, the handsome trio of fun-loving extraterrestrials set out to experience the Southern California lifestyle. Sometimes hilarious sci-fi/musical, featuring bouncy shtick and a gleeful dismantling of modern culture. **100m/C VHS, Beta, LV.** Geena Davis, Jeff Goldblum, Charles Rocket, Julie Brown, Jim Carrey, Damon Wayans, Michael McKean, Angelyne, Larry Linville, Rick Overton; ***D:*** Julien Temple; ***W:*** Julie Brown, Charlie Coffey, Terrance McNally; ***M:*** Nile Rodgers. *LIV, VES*

Earth vs. the Flying Saucers ½ *Invasion of the Flying Saucers* **1956** Extraterrestrials land on Earth and issue an ultimatum to humans concerning their constant use of bombs and missiles. Peace is threatened when the military disregards the extraterrestrials' simple warning. Superb special effects by Ray Harryhausen. **83m/B VHS, Beta, LV.** Hugh Marlowe, Joan Taylor, Donald Curtis, Morris Ankrum; ***D:*** Fred F. Sears; ***W:*** Curt Siodmak. *COL, MLB*

Earth vs. the Spider *The Spider* **1958** Man-eating giant mutant (teenage ninja?) tarantula makes life miserable for a small town in general and high school partyers in particular. Silly old drive-in fare is agony for many, camp treasure for a precious few. **72m/B VHS.** Edward Kemmer, June Kennedy, Gene Persson, Gene Roth, Hal Torey, Mickey Finn; ***D:*** Bert I. Gordon; ***W:*** Laszlo Gorog, George Worthing Yates; ***C:*** Jack Marta. *COL, MLB*

Earthling ½ **1980 (PG)** A terminally ill Holden helps a young Schroder survive in the Australian wilderness after the boy's parents are killed in a tragic accident. Lessons of life and the power of the human heart are passed on in this panoramic, yet mildly sentimental film. **102m/C VHS, Beta.** *AU* William Holden, Rick Schroder, Jack Thompson, Olivia Hamnett, Alwyn Kurts; ***D:*** Peter Collinson; ***W:*** Lanny Cotler. *LIV, VES*

Earthquake **1974 (PG)** Less-than mediocre drama centers on a major earthquake in Los Angeles and its effect on the lives of an engineer, his spoiled wife, his mistress, his father-in-law, and a suspended policeman. Filmed in much-hyped Sensurround—a technique intended to shake up the theater a bit, but which will have no effect on your television set. Good special effects, but not enough to compensate for lackluster script. **123m/C VHS, Beta, LV.** Charlton Heston, Ava Gardner, George Kennedy, Lorne Greene, Genevieve Bujold, Richard Roundtree, Marjoe Gortner, Barry Sullivan, Victoria Principal, Lloyd Nolan, Walter Matthau, Scott Hylands; ***D:*** Mark Robson; ***W:*** Mario Puzo; ***M:*** John Williams. Academy Awards '74: Best Sound, Best Visual Effects; Nominations: Academy Awards '74: Best Art Direction/Set Decoration, Best Cinematography, Best Film Editing. *MCA*

Earthworm Tractors ½ **1936** Ambitious tractor salesman Alexander Botts will do anything to make a sale. Brown excels as the fast-talking lead. Comedy is strengthened by its supporting cast. Based on characters first appearing in the "Saturday Evening Post." **63m/B VHS.** Joe E. Brown, June Travis, Guy Kibbee, Dick Foran, Carol Hughes, Gene Lockhart, Olin Howlin; ***D:*** Ray Enright. *NOS, RXM, HEG*

East and West **1923** Morris Brown, a worldly New York Jew, returns home to Galicia with his daughter Mollie for a traditional family wedding. She teaches the young villagers to dance and box but meets her romantic match in a young yeshiva scholar who forsakes tradition to win her heart. Picon shines as the exuberant flapper. With English and Yiddish intertitles. **85m/B VHS.** Molly Picon, Jacob Kalish, Sidney Goldin; ***D:*** Sidney Goldin. *NCJ*

East End Hustle **1976 (R)** High-priced call girl rebels against her pimp and sets out to free other prostitutes as well. Also available in an 88-minute unrated version. **86m/C VHS, Beta.** *LIV, VES*

East L.A. Warriors ½ **1989** A mobster, Hilton-Jacobs, manipulates Los Angeles gangs in this non-stop action adventure. **90m/C VHS, Beta.** Tony Bravo, Lawrence-Hilton Jacobs, Kamar Reyes, William Smith; ***D:*** Addison Randall. *PAR*

East of Borneo ½ **1931** Tropical adventure involving a "lost" physician whose worried wife sets out to find him in the jungle. She locates her love only to discover he has a prestigious new job tending to royalty and didn't want to be found. **76m/B VHS, Beta.** Charles Bickford, Rose Hobart, Georges Renavent; ***D:*** George Melford. *SNC, DVT, CAB*

East of Eden **1954** Steinbeck's contemporary retelling of the biblical Cain and Abel story receives superior treatment from Kazan and his excellent cast. Dean, in his first starring role, gives a reading of a young man's search for love and acceptance that defines adolescent pain. Though filmed in the 1950s, this story still rivets today's viewers with its emotional message. **115m/C VHS, Beta, LV.** James Dean, Julie Harris, Richard Davalos, Raymond Massey, Jo Van Fleet, Burl Ives, Albert Dekker; ***D:*** Elia Kazan; ***W:*** Paul Osborn; ***M:*** Leonard Rosenman. Academy Awards '55: Best Supporting Actress (Van Fleet); Golden Globe Awards '56: Best Film—Drama; National Board of Review Awards '55: 10 Best Films of the Year; Nominations: Academy Awards '55: Best Actor (Dean), Best Director (Kazan), Best Screenplay. *WAR, BTV, HMV*

East of Eden ½ **1980** Remade into a television mini series, this Steinbeck classic tells the tale of two brothers who vie for their father's affection and the woman who comes between them. Seymour is notable as the self-serving mother who abandons her babies to lead a disreputable life. Rife with biblical symbolism and allusions. **375m/C VHS, Beta, LV.** Jane Seymour, Bruce Boxleitner, Warren Oates, Lloyd Bridges, Anne Baxter, Timothy Bottoms, Soon-Teck Oh, Karen Allen, Hart Bochner, Sam Bottoms, Howard Duff, Richard Masur, Wendell Burton, Nicholas Pryor, Grace Zabriskie, M. Emmet Walsh, Matthew "Stymie" Beard; ***D:*** Harvey Hart. *VTR, LIV*

East of Elephant Rock ½ **1976** In 1948, a young first secretary of the British Embassy returns from leave in England to a tense atmosphere in a colony in southeast Asia. Beautiful scenery can't make up for weak plot. **93m/C VHS, Beta.** *GB* John Hurt, Jeremy Kemp, Judi Bowker, Christopher Cazenove; ***D:*** Don Boyd; ***W:*** Don Boyd. *SUE*

East of Kilimanjaro **1957** A freelance photographer and a doctor search frantically to find the carrier of a fatal disease near the slopes of the majestic Mt. Kilimanjaro. Routine killer virus flick filmed in Africa. Also know as "The Big Search." **75m/C VHS.** Marshall Thompson, Gaby Andre, Fausto Tozzi; ***D:*** Arnold Belgard. *SUE*

East Side Kids **1940** Early East Side kids. A hoodlum wants to prevent his brother from beginning a similar life of crime. **60m/B VHS, Beta.** Leon Ames, Harris Berger, Dennis Moore, Joyce Bryant; ***D:*** Robert F. "Bob" Hill. *NOS, MRV, DVT*

East Side Kids/The Lost City **1935** The first East Side Kids film introduces some soon-familiar faces. "The Lost City" is a composite of all twelve episodes of the serial; edited for brevity. **135m/B VHS, Beta.** Dennis Moore, Vince Barnett, William "Stage" Boyd, Kane Richmond. *AOV*

East Side, West Side **1949** Stanwyck and Mason try hard to make this simple-minded soaper work, with mixed results. A wealthy couple experiences marital woes, aggravated by a ambitious young woman and a soft-hearted man suffering from unrequited love. Based on the popular novel by Marcia Davenport. **110m/B VHS.** Barbara Stanwyck, James Mason, Ava Gardner, Van Heflin, Gale Sondergaard, William Frawley, Nancy Davis; ***D:*** Mervyn LeRoy; ***C:*** Charles Rosher; ***M:*** Miklos Rozsa. *MGM*

Easter Parade ½ **1948** A big musical star (Astaire) splits with his partner (Miller) claiming that he could mold any girl to replace her in the act. He tries and finally succeeds after much difficulty. Astaire and Garland in peak form, aided by a classic Irving Berlin score. ♫Happy Easter; Drum Crazy; It Only Happens When I Dance With You; Everybody's Doin' It; I Want to Go Back to Michigan; Beautiful Faces Need Beautiful Clothes; A Fella With an Umbrella; I Love a Piano; Snookey Ookums. **103m/C VHS, Beta, LV.** Fred Astaire, Judy Garland, Peter Lawford, Ann Miller, Jules Munshin, Joi Lansing; ***D:*** Charles Walters; ***W:*** Sidney Sheldon; ***C:*** Harry Stradling; ***M:*** Irving Berlin. Academy Awards '48: Best Score. *MGM, HMV*

Easy Come, Easy Go **1967** Elvis, as a Navy frogman, gets excited when he accidentally discovers what he believes is a vast sunken treasure. Music is his only solace when he finds his treasure to be worthless copper coins. ♫Easy Come, Easy Go; The Love Machine; Yoga is as Yoga Goes; Sing, You Children; You Gotta Stop; I'll Take Love. **96m/C VHS, Beta.** Elvis Presley, Dodie Marshall, Pat Priest, Elsa Lanchester, Frank McHugh, Pat Harrington; ***D:*** John Rich. *PAR*

Easy Kill ½ **1989** A man takes the law into his own hands to exact revenge on drug lords. **100m/C VHS, Beta.** Jane Badler, Cameron Mitchell, Frank Stallone; ***D:*** Josh Spencer. *NO*

The Easy Life **1963** Haunting film about a hedonistic man from a small Italian village who takes a mild-mannered student pleasure-seeking. The ride turns sour and the playboy is ultimately destroyed by his own brutality. **105m/B VHS.** *IT* Vittorio Gassman, Catherine Spaak, Jean-Louis Trintignant, Luciana Angiolillo; ***D:*** Dino Risi. *FST*

Easy Living ½ **1949** Compromised melodrama about an over-the-hill football player who must cope with his failing marriage and looming retirement. Based on an Irwin Shaw story. **77m/B VHS, Beta, LV.** Victor Mature, Lucille Ball, Jack Paar, Lizabeth Scott, Sonny Tufts, Lloyd Nolan, Paul Stewart; ***D:*** Jacques Tourneur. *MED, TTC*

Easy Money **1983 (R)** A basic slob has the chance to inherit $10 million if he can give up his loves: smoking, drinking, and gambling among others. Dangerfield is surprisingly restrained in this harmless, though not altogether unpleasing comedy. **95m/C VHS, Beta, LV.** Rodney Dangerfield, Joe Pesci, Geraldine Fitzgerald, Jennifer Jason Leigh, Tom Ewell, Candice Azzara, Taylor Negron; ***D:*** James Signorelli; ***W:*** Rodney Dangerfield, Dennis Blair. *VES*

Easy Rider ½ **1969 (R)** Slim-budget, generation-defining movie. Two young men in late 1960s undertake a motorcycle trek throughout the Southwest in search of the real essence of America. Along the way they encounter hippies, rednecks, prostitutes, drugs, Nicholson, and tragedy. One of the highest-grossing pictures of the decade, undoubtedly an influence on two generations of "youth-oriented dramas," which all tried unsuccessfully to duplicate the original accomplishment. Psychedelic scenes and a great role for Nicholson are added bonuses. Look for the graveyard dancing scene in New Orleans. Features one of the best '60s rock scores around, including "Mean Streets" and "The Wanderers." **94m/C VHS, Beta, LV, 8mm.** Peter Fonda, Dennis Hopper, Jack Nicholson, Karen Black, Toni Basil, Robert Walker Jr.; ***D:*** Dennis Hopper; ***W:*** Terry Southern. New York Film Critics Awards '69: Best Supporting Actor (Nicholson); National Society of Film Critics Awards '69: Best Supporting Actor (Nicholson); Nominations: Academy Awards '69: Best Story & Screenplay, Best Supporting Actor (Nicholson). *COL, CCB*

Easy Street ᘛᘛᘛ **1916** Chaplin portrays a derelict who, using some hilarious methods, reforms the residents of Easy Street. Chaplin's row with the town bully is particularly amusing. Silent with musical soundtrack added. **20m/B VHS, Beta.** Charlie Chaplin; ***D:*** Charlie Chaplin. *CAB*

Easy to Love ᘛᘛ½ **1953** Williams is in love with her boss, but he pays her no attention until a handsome singer vies for her affections. Set at Florida's Cypress Gardens, this aquatic musical features spectacular water ballet productions choreographed by Busby Berkeley, and the title song penned by Cole Porter. ♫Easy to Love; Coquette; Beautiful Spring; That's What Rainy Day is For; Look Out! I'm Romantic; Didja Ever. **96m/C VHS.** Esther Williams, Van Johnson, Tony Martin, John Bromfield, King Donovan, Carroll Baker; ***D:*** Charles Walters; ***W:*** William Roberts. *MGM*

Easy Virtue ᘛᘛ½ **1927** Hitchcock directs this adaptation of a Noel Coward play as a social melodrama. Larita is an unhappily married socialite with a lover. When her husband discovers her infidelity they divorce and she is marked as a woman of loose morals. Her reputation is not enhanced by her marriage to a younger man whose family diapproves. **79m/B VHS, Beta.** *GB* Isabel Jeans, Ian Hunter, Frank Dyall, Eric Bransby Williams, Robin Irvine, Violet Farebrother; ***D:*** Alfred Hitchcock. *GPV, MRV, NOS*

Easy Wheels ᘛᘛ½ **1989** Like most decent biker movies, "Wheels" is propelled by bad taste and a healthy dose of existentialist nihilism. But there's an unusual plot twist in this parody. A biker named She-Wolf and her gang kidnap female babies and let wolves rear the children. Their elaborate plan is to create a race of super women who will subdue the troublesome male population. But can this "noble" plan succeed? **94m/C VHS, Beta, LV.** Paul LeMat, Eileen Davidson, Marjorie Bransfield, Jon Menick, Mark Holton, Karen Russell, Jami Richards, Roberta Vasquez, Barry Livingston, George Plimpton; ***D:*** David O'Malley; ***W:*** Ivan Raimi, Celia Abrams, David O'Malley; ***M:*** John Ross. *FRH*

Eat a Bowl of Tea ᘛᘛᘛ **1989 (PG-13)** Endearing light drama-comedy concerning a multi-generational Chinese family. They must learn to deal with the problems of life in America and in particular, marriage, when Chinese women are finally allowed to immigrate with their husbands to the United States following WWII. Adaptation of Louis Chu's story, directed by the man who brought us "Dim Sum." A PBS "American Playhouse" presentation. **102m/C VHS, Beta, LV.** Cora Miao, Russell Wong, Lau Siu Ming, Eric Tsiang Chi Wai, Victor Wong, Jessica Harper, Lee Sau Kee; ***D:*** Wayne Wang; ***W:*** Judith Rascoe; ***M:*** Mark Adler. *COL*

Eat and Run ᘛ **1986 (R)** A bloody comedy about a 400-pound alien with a taste for Italian (people, that is). **85m/C VHS, Beta.** Ron Silver, R.L. Ryan, Sharon Schlarth; ***D:*** Christopher Hart. *VTR, NWV*

Eat Drink Man Woman ᘛᘛᘛ½ **1994 (R)** In Taipei, widowed master chef serves weekly feast of elaborate food and familial guilt to his three grown daughters, all of whom still live at home. They spend their time sorting out professional and romantic difficulties, searching for independence, and fulfilling traditional family obligations. Each character has a lot going on, but no one's story gets lost in the mix. Lee uses irony to great effect, introducing us to the culinary artist who has lost his sense of taste and has a daughter who works at a Wendy's. Food preparation scenes (more than 100 recipes are served up) illustrate a careful attention to detail (and are guaranteed to make you hungry). Lee's follow-up to "The Wedding Banquet" is a finely observed, comic tale of generational drift, the richness of tradition, and the power of love to redeem or improve. In Chinese with subtitles or dubbed. **123m/C VHS, LV.** *TW* Sihung Lung, Kuei-Mei Yang, Yu-Wen Wang, Chien-Lien Wu, Sylvia Chang, Winston Chao; ***D:*** Ang Lee; ***W:*** Hui-Ling Wang, James Schamus, Ang Lee; ***C:*** Jong Lin. National Board of Review Awards '94: Best Foreign Film; Nominations: Academy Awards '94: Best Foreign Language Film; Golden Globe Awards '95: Best Foreign Language Film; Independent Spirit Awards '95: Best Actor (Lung), Best Actress (Wu), Best Cinematography, Best Director (Lee), Best Film, Best Screenplay. *HMK*

Eat My Dust ᘛᘛ **1976 (PG)** Teenage son of a California sheriff steals the best stock cars from a race track to take the town's heartthrob for a joy ride. Subsequently he leads the town on a wild car chase. Brainless but fast-paced. **89m/C VHS, Beta.** Ron Howard, Christopher Norris, Warren Kemmerling, Rance Howard, Clint Howard, Corbin Bernsen; ***D:*** Charles B. Griffith. *SUE*

Eat the Peach ᘛᘛ½ **1986** An idiosyncratic Irish comedy about two young unemployed rebels who attempt to break free from their tiny coast town by becoming motorcycle champs after seeing the Elvis Presley film "Roustabout." Together they create the "wall of death,"—a large wooden barrel in which they can perform various biker feats. **90m/C VHS, Beta.** *IR* Stephen Brennan, Eamon Morrissey, Catherine Byrne, Niall Toibin, Tony Doyle, Joe Lynch; ***D:*** Peter Ormrod; ***W:*** Peter Ormrod, John Kelleher; ***M:*** Donal Lunny. *FOX*

Eat the Rich ᘛ **1987 (R)** A British farce about a group of terrorists who take over the popular London restaurant, Bastard's. Led by a former, disgruntled transvestite employee, they turn diners into menu offerings. Music by Motorhead. **89m/C VHS, Beta.** *GB* Nosher Powell, Lanah Pellay, Fiona Richmond, Ronald Allen, Sandra Dorne; ***Cameos:*** Paul McCartney, Bill Wyman, Koo Stark, Miranda Richardson; ***D:*** Peter Richardson. *COL*

Eaten Alive ᘛᘛ *Death Trap; Starlight Slaughter; Legend of the Bayou; Horror Hotel Massacre* **1976 (R)** A Southerner takes an unsuspecting group of tourists into a crocodile death trap. Director Tobe Hooper's follow-up to "The Texas Chainsaw Massacre." Englund is more recognizable with razor fingernails as Freddy Krueger of the "Nightmare on Elm Street" films. **96m/C VHS, Beta.** Neville Brand, Mel Ferrer, Carolyn Jones, Marilyn Burns, Stuart Whitman, Robert Englund; ***D:*** Tobe Hooper; ***M:*** Wayne Bell. *PSM*

Eating ᘛᘛ½ **1990 (R)** Set in Southern California, women gather to celebrate birthdays for three of their friends who are turning 30, 40 and 50. As the party commences, women from two generations discuss their attitudes towards food and men...and discover hilarious parallels. **110m/C VHS, Beta, LV.** Nelly Alard, Frances Bergen, Mary Crosby, Lisa Richards, Gwen Welles, Daphna Kastner, Elizabeth Kemp, Marlena Giovi, Marina Gregory, Toni Basil; ***D:*** Henry Jaglom; ***W:*** Henry Jaglom. *PAR*

Eating Raoul ᘛᘛᘛ½ **1982 (R)** The Blands are a happily married couple who share many interests: good food and wine, entrepreneurial dreams, and an aversion to sex. The problem is, they're flat broke. So, when the tasty swinger from upstairs makes a pass at Mary and Paul accidentally kills him, they discover he's got loads of money; Raoul takes a cut in the deal by disposing of—or rather recycling—the body. This may just be the way to finance that restaurant they've been wanting to open. Wonderful, offbeat, hilariously dark comedy. **83m/C VHS, Beta.** Mary Woronov, Paul Bartel, Buck Henry, Ed Begley Jr., Edie McClurg, Robert Beltran, John Paragon; ***D:*** Mary Woronov, Paul Bartel; ***W:*** Paul Bartel, Richard Blackburn. *FOX*

Ebbtide ᘛᘛ½ **1994 (R)** Lawyer Jeff Warren (Hamlin) takes on the case of a mother who says her son's died from chemicals dumped by the Poseidon Pacific Co. Jeff got the case when the previous lawyer died mysteriously but this doesn't stop him checking out the chemical company or its beautiful president. **90m/C VHS.** Harry Hamlin, Judy McIntosh, Susan Lyons, John Gregg, Frankie J. Holden; ***D:*** Craig Lahiff; ***W:*** Robert Ellis, Peter Goldsworthy. *PAR*

Ebony Dreams **1980** WWII documentary focuses on the experience of female factory workers during and after the war. Five contemporary women relate their personal endeavors and struggles to retain their jobs once the war ended. Excellent use of newsreel footage and interesting interviews with the women. **85m/C VHS.** Philomena Nowlin; ***D:*** Bill Brame. *NO*

Ebony Tower ᘛᘛ½ **1986** Based on the John Fowles novel about a crusty old artist who lives in a French chateau with two young female companions. They are visited by a handsome young man, thereby initiating sexual tension and recognizably Fowlesian plot puzzles. Made for British television. Features some partial nudity. **80m/C Beta.** *GB* Laurence Olivier, Roger Rees, Greta Scacchi, Toyah Wilcox; ***D:*** Robert Knights; ***M:*** Richard Rodney Bennett. *NO*

Echo Murders ᘛ½ **1945** A Sexton Blake mystery wherein he investigates a mine owner's mysterious death, opening up a veritable can of murdering, power-hungry worms. **75m/B VHS, Beta.** David Farrar, Dennis Price. *NOS, VYY*

Echo Park ᘛᘛ½ **1986 (R)** An unsung sleeper comedy about three roommates living in Los Angeles' Echo Park: a body builder, a single-mother waitress, and an itinerant songwriter. Charts their struggles as they aim for careers in showbiz. Offbeat ensemble effort. **93m/C VHS, Beta, LV.** *AU* Tom Hulce, Susan Dey, Michael Bowen, Richard "Cheech" Marin, Christopher Walker, Shirley Jo Finney, Cassandra Peterson, Yana Nirvana, Timothy Carey; ***D:*** Robert Dornhelm; ***W:*** Michael Ventura; ***M:*** David Rickets. *BAR*

Echoes ᘛᘛ **1983 (R)** A young painter's life slowly comes apart as he is tormented by nightmares that his stillborn twin brother is attempting to murder him. **90m/C VHS, Beta.** Gale Sondergaard, Mercedes McCambridge, Richard Alfieri, Ruth Roman, John Spencer, Nathalie Nell; ***D:*** Arthur Seidelman; ***W:*** Richard Alfieri, Richard J. Anthony. *NO*

Echoes in the Darkness ᘛᘛ½ **1987** Television mini series based on the true-life Joseph Wambaugh bestseller about the "Main Line" murder investigation in Pennsylvania in 1979. Police are baffled when a teacher is murdered and her children vanish. Suspicion falls on a charismatic coworker and the school's principal. On two tapes. **234m/C VHS.** Peter Coyote, Robert Loggia, Stockard Channing, Peter Boyle, Cindy Pickett, Gary Cole, Zeljko Ivanek, Alex Hyde-White, Treat Williams; ***D:*** Glenn Jordan. *NWV*

Echoes of Conflict ᘛᘛ **1989** The turbulent Middle East and Arab-Israeli tensions are spotlighted in three new wave films from Israel. Includes "The Cage," "The Movie," and "Don't Get Involved." In Hebrew with English subtitles. In color and black and white. **91m/C VHS.** *IS* *FCT, INJ, KIV*

Echoes of Paradise ᘛ½ *Shadows of the Peacock* **1986 (R)** After a series of earth-shattering events, a depressed woman journeys to an island where she falls for a Balinese dancer. Soon she must choose between returning home or beginning life anew in paradise. **90m/C VHS, Beta, LV.** *AU* Wendy Hughes, John Lone, Rod Mullinar, Peta Toppano, Steve Jacobs, Gillian Jones; ***D:*** Phillip Noyce. *ACA*

The Eclipse ᘛᘛᘛ½ *L'eclisse* **1966** The last of Antonioni's trilogy (after "L'Avventura" and "La Notte"), wherein another fashionable and alienated Italian woman passes from one lover to another searching unsuccessfully for truth and love. Highly acclaimed. In Italian with subtitles. **123m/B VHS, Beta.** *IT* Monica Vitti, Alain Delon, Francesco Rabal, Louis Seigner; ***D:*** Michelangelo Antonioni; ***W:*** Michelangelo Antonioni; ***C:*** Carlo DiPalma. *TPV, MRV, FCT*

Ecstasy ᘛᘛ½ *Extase; Ekstase; Symphony of Love* **1933** A romantic, erotic story about a young woman married to an older man, who takes a lover. Features Lamarr, then Hedy Kiesler, before her discovery in Hollywood. Film subsequently gained notoriety for Lamarr's nude scenes. In Czech with English subtitles. **90m/B VHS, Beta, 8mm.** *CZ* Hedy Lamarr, Jaromir Rogoz; ***D:*** Gustav Machaty. *VYY, NOS, MRV*

Ecstasy *Woof!* **1984 (R)** Soft core fluff about a film director's wife's erotic adventures. **82m/C VHS, Beta.** Tiffany Bolling, Franc Luz, Jack Carter, Britt Ekland, Julie Newmar. *MGM*

Ed *Woof!* **1996 (PG)** A must see for all fans of flatulent animatronic chimpanzees who play third base. Everyone else should stay away. LeBlanc (who should've been tipped off when they couldn't even get a real chimp to appear) plays Coop, a phenom pitcher stuck on a losing team in the minor leagues. After Ed the chimpanzee is bequeathed to the team by the late Mickey Mantle, (forgive them Mick, they know not what they do) he starts playing the hot corner like Brooks Robinson. Surprise! Ed becomes a national sensation, the team goes on a winning streak and sets up the showdown game climax. Most of the humor is derived from Ed tearing things up and passing gas, while LeBlanc yells in pop-eyed exasperation. Cameo from Tommy Lasorda playing a fat major league manager. **94m/C VHS, LV.** Matthew LeBlanc, Jayne Brook, Bill Cobbs, Jack Warden, Doren Fein, Patrick Kerr, Charlie Schlatter, Carl Anthony Payne II, Curt Kaplan, Zack Ward, Mike McGlone, James Caviezel, Valente Rodriguez; ***D:*** Bill Couturie; ***W:*** David Mickey Evans; ***C:*** Alan Caso; ***M:*** Stephen Endelman. *MCA*

Ed and His Dead Mother 🦴🦴 **1993 (PG-13)** Ed's just an average guy who happens to really love his mother. So much so that when she dies Ed tries to bring her back from the dead—and succeeds. Only death has made a few changes in Mom's personality. Now she's a bug-eating, chainsaw-wielding fiend. Just what's a good son supposed to do? **93m/C VHS, LV.** Ned Beatty, Steve Buscemi, John Glover, Miriam Margolyes; ***D:*** Jonathan Wacks; ***W:*** Chuck Hughes. *FXV*

Ed Wood 🦴🦴🦴½ **1994 (R)** Leave it to Burton to bring to the screen the story of a director many consider to be the worst of all time (he's at least in the top three) and who now occupies a lofty position as a cult icon. In this hilarious and touching tribute to a Hollywood maverick with grade-Z vision, detailed homage is paid to Wood's single-mindedness and optimism in the face of repeated failure and lack of financing, even down to the black and white photography. Depp is convincing (and engaging) as Ed Wood, Jr., the cross-dressing, angora-sweater-wearing, low-budget auteur of such notoriously "bad" cult films as "Glen or Glenda" and "Plan 9 From Outer Space." Depp is supported by terrific portrayals of the motley Wood crew, led by Landau's morphine-addicted, down-on-his-luck Bela Lugosi. Burton focuses on Wood's relationship with Lugosi, whose career is over by the time Wood befriends him. Based on Rudolph Grey's book, "Nightmare of Ecstasy: The Life and Art of Edward D. Wood, Jr." **127m/B VHS, LV.** Johnny Depp, Sarah Jessica Parker, Martin Landau, Bill Murray, Jim Myers, Patricia Arquette, Jeffrey Jones, Lisa Marie, Vincent D'Onofrio; ***D:*** Tim Burton; ***W:*** Scott Alexander, Larry Karaszewski. Academy Awards '94: Best Makeup, Best Supporting Actor (Landau); Golden Globe Awards '95: Best Supporting Actor (Landau); Los Angeles Film Critics Association Awards '94: Best Cinematography, Best Supporting Actor (Landau), Best Original Score; New York Film Critics Awards '94: Best Cinematography, Best Supporting Actor (Landau); Screen Actors Guild Award '94: Best Supporting Actor (Landau); Nominations: British Academy Awards '95: Best Supporting Actor (Landau); Golden Globe Awards '95: Best Actor—Musical/Comedy (Depp), Best Film—Musical/Comedy. *TOU*

Ed Wood: Look Back in Angora **1994** Biography of the eccentric low-budget filmmaker frequently considered the worst director in Hollywood and now a cult fave. Wood was responsible for "Plan 9 from Outer Space," among other movie disasters but his private peculiarities (including an angora fetish) rivaled his professional ones. Director Tim Burton brings Wood's life to the big screen with the theatrical release of "Ed Wood." **51m/C VHS.** *AVE*

The Ed Wood Story: The Plan 9 Companion **1995** Explores Ed Wood's life and work using interviews, film clips, and commentary. Features interviews with "Plan 9 from Outer Space" cast members. Includes a tour of Quality Studios, where Wood filmed "Plan 9." **111m/C VHS.** *MPI*

Eddie 🦴🦴 **1996 (PG-13)** Basketball nut Edwina (Goldberg) wins a chance to be honorary coach of her beloved Knicks in a free throw contest. When some of her courtside advice works, and the other fans seem to respond to her, the publicity-seeking maverick owner (Langella) gives her the job full-time. Predictable comedy with the usual "new team member leads underdogs to contention" characters won't suprise, or particularly thrill, anyone. Goldberg's lively performance somewhat redeems standard script but reduces everyone around her, including an All-Star roster of NBA players, to window dressing. Basically the hoops version of "Little Big League." **100m/C VHS.** Whoopi Goldberg, Frank Langella, Dennis Farina, Richard Jenkins, Lisa Ann Walter, John Benjamin Hickey, John Salley; ***D:*** Steve Rash; ***W:*** Jon Connolly, David Loucka, Eric Champnella, Keith Mitchell, Steve Zacharias, Jeff Buhai; ***C:*** Victor Kemper; ***M:*** Stanley Clarke. *NYR*

Eddie and the Cruisers 🦴🦴 **1983 (PG)** In the early 1960s, rockers Eddie and the Cruisers score with one hit album. Amid their success, lead singer Pare dies mysteriously in a car accident. Years later, a reporter decides to write a feature on the defunct group, prompting a former band member to begin a search for missing tapes of the Cruisers' unreleased second album. Questions posed at the end of the movie are answered in the sequel. Enjoyable soundtrack by John Cafferty and the Beaver Brown Band. **90m/C VHS, Beta, LV, 8mm.** Tom Berenger, Michael Pare, Ellen Barkin, Joe Pantoliano, Matthew Laurance; ***D:*** Martin Davidson; ***W:*** Martin Davidson, Arlene Davidson; ***C:*** Fred Murphy. *MVD, SUE, NLC*

Eddie and the Cruisers 2: Eddie Lives! 🦴½ **1989 (PG-13)** A sequel to the minor cult favorite, in which a rock star believed to be dead emerges under a new name in Montreal to lead a new band. The Beaver Brown Band again provides the music. **106m/C VHS, Beta, LV.** *CA* Michael Pare, Marina Orsini, Matthew Laurance, Bernie Coulson; ***D:*** Jean-Claude Lord; ***W:*** Charles Zev Cohen; ***M:*** Leon Aronson. *CCB, IME*

Eddie Macon's Run 🦴🦴 **1983 (PG)** Based on a true story; Eddie Macon has been unjustly jailed in Texas and plans an escape to run to Mexico. He is followed by a tough cop who is determined to catch the fugitive. Film debut of Goodman. **95m/C VHS, Beta, LV.** Kirk Douglas, John Schneider, Lee Purcell, John Goodman, Leah Ayres; ***D:*** Jeff Kanew; ***M:*** Wendy Blackstone. *MCA*

Eddie Murphy: Raw 🦴🦴 **1987 (R)** Murphy's second stand-up performance film, featuring many of his woman-bashing observations on life. **90m/C VHS, Beta, LV, 8mm.** Eddie Murphy; ***D:*** Robert Townsend. *PAR*

The Eddy Duchin Story 🦴🦴 **1956** Glossy tearjerker that profiles the tragic life of Eddy Duchin, the famous pianist/bandleader of the 30s and 40s. Features almost 30 songs, including classics by Cole Porter, George and Ira Gershwin, Hammerstein, Chopin, and several others. **123m/C VHS, LV.** Tyrone Power, Kim Novak, Victoria Shaw, James Whitmore, Rex Thompson; ***D:*** George Sidney; ***C:*** Harry Stradling; ***M:*** George Duning. Nominations: Academy Awards '56: Best Color Cinematography, Best Sound, Best Story, Best Original Score. *COL, MVD, TVC*

Eden 🦴🦴 **1992** Eden is a luxury resort designed to cater to personal fantasies and filled with numerous intrigues. Part-owner Eve Sinclair faces a number of professional and personal complications, including the tragic death of her husband, a brother-in-law who's interested in more than business, and an old friend with uncertain motives. Lots of sex in beautiful settings. Made for cable television. **?m/C VHS.** Barbara Alyn Woods, Jack Armstrong, Steve Chase, Darcy Demoss, Jeff Griggs; ***D:*** Victor Lobl; ***W:*** Stephen Black, Henry Stern. *UND*

Eden 2 🦴🦴 **1993 (R)** The continuing saga of the luxury resort Eden. Owner Eve is still having erotic dreams of late husband Grant while fending off the very real advances of his brother Josh and becoming attracted to Paul, her late husband's best friend. The guests are equally caught up in erotic dilemmas involving sexual blackmail. Made for cable television. **102m/C VHS.** Barbara Alyn Woods, Jack Armstrong, Steve Chase, Darcy Demoss, Jeff Griggs; ***D:*** Kristine Peterson; ***W:*** Stephen Black, Henry Stern. *UND*

Eden 3 🦴🦴 **1993 (R)** Yet another chapter in this sexy made for cable saga. Eve Sinclair risks losing her share of the tropical resort unless she remarries, which she doesn't want to do, although fitness trainer Randi would be delighted to pick up the option. Meanwhile, an heiress discovers her new bridegroom has murderous intentions. **?m/C VHS.** Barbara Alyn Woods, Jack Armstrong, Steve Chase, Darcy Demoss, Jeff Griggs, Dean Scofield; ***D:*** Victor Lobl. *UND*

Eden 4 🦴🦴 **1993 (R)** Further adventures in the cable series. Eve, Eden's co-owner, must cope with both Josh's jealous rage and Randi's continuing scheming as she tries to keep her guests happy at the posh resort. One of the guests, a beautiful author, gets too caught up in her sexual fantasies and may find herself in danger. **?m/C VHS.** Barbara Alyn Woods, Jack Armstrong, Steve Chase, Darcy Demoss, Jeff Griggs, Dean Scofield; ***D:*** Kristine Peterson. *UND*

Edge of Darkness 🦴🦴🦴½ **1943** Compelling war-drama about the underground movement in Norway during Nazi takeover of WWII. Flynn plays a Norwegian fisherman who leads the local underground movement and Sheridan is his loyal fiancee. Although several problems occurred throughout filming, this picture earned high marks for its superb performances and excellent camerawork. Based on the novel by William Woods. **120m/B VHS.** Errol Flynn, Ann Sheridan, Walter Huston, Nancy Coleman, Helmut Dantine, Judith Anderson, Ruth Gordon, John Beal; ***D:*** Lewis Milestone; ***W:*** Robert Rossen. *MGM*

Edge of Darkness 🦴🦴 **1986** Originally produced as a mini series for British television, this mystery involves a police detective who investigates his daughter's murder and uncovers a web of espionage and intrigue. **307m/C VHS, Beta.** *GB* Bob Peck, Joe Don Baker, Jack Woodson, John Woodvine, Joanne Whalley; ***D:*** Martin Campbell; ***M:*** Eric Clapton, Michael Kamen. *FOX, TVC, VCO*

Edge of Honor 🦴½ **1991 (R)** Young Eagle Scouts camping in the Pacific Northwest discover a woodland weapons cache and wage guerilla war against killer lumberjacks out to silence them. A boneheaded, politically correct action bloodbath; you don't have to like the logging industry to disapprove of the broad slurs against its men shown here. **92m/C VHS.** Corey Feldman, Meredith Salenger, Scott Reeves, Ken Jenkins, Christopher Neame, Don Swayze; ***D:*** Michael Spence; ***W:*** David O'Malley. *ACA*

Edge of Sanity 🦴½ **1989 (R)** An overdone Jekyll-Hyde reprise, with cocaine serving as the villainous substance. The coke-created Hyde is posited as a prototype for Jack the Ripper. Not for the easily queazy. Available in a 90 minute, unrated version. **85m/C VHS, Beta, LV.** *GB* Anthony Perkins, Glynis Barber, David Lodge, Sarah Maur-Thorp; ***D:*** Gerard Kikione. *NO*

Edge of the Axe **1989** A small town is held in the grip of terror by a demented slasher. **91m/C VHS, Beta.** Barton Faulks, Christina Marie Lane, Page Moseley, Fred Hollyday; ***D:*** Joseph Braunstein. *MCG*

Edge of the World 🦴🦴🦴 **1937** Moody, stark British drama of a mini-society in its death throes, expertly photographed on a six-square-mile island in the Shetlands. A dwindling fishing community of fewer than 100 souls agonize over whether to migrate to the mainland; meanwhile the romance of a local girl with an off-islander takes a tragic course. Choral effects were provided by the Glasgow Orpheus Choir. **80m/B VHS.** *GB* Finlay Currie, Niall MacGinnis, Grant Sutherland, John Laurie, Michael Powell; ***D:*** Michael Powell; ***W:*** Michael Powell. *NOS*

Edie in Ciao! Manhattan ✭✭ *Ciao! Manhattan* **1972 (R)** Real-life story of Edie Sedgwick, Warhol superstar and international fashion model, whose life in the fast lane led to ruin. **84m/C VHS, Beta.** Edie Sedgwick, Baby Jane Holzer, Roger Vadim, Paul America, Viva. *FCT, PBS*

Edison the Man ✭✭½ **1940** Story of Tommy Edison's early years of experimentation in the basement. The young genious eventually invents light bulbs, motion pictures, and a sound recording device. Well played by Tracy. **108m/C VHS, Beta.** Spencer Tracy, Rita Johnson, Lynne Overman, Charles Coburn, Gene Lockhart, Henry Travers, Felix Bressart; ***D:*** Clarence Brown. Nominations: Academy Awards '40: Best Story. *MGM*

Edith & Marcel ✭½ **1983** A fictionalization of the love affair between chanteuse Edith Piaf and boxer Marcel Cerdan (played by his son, Marcel Cerdan, Jr.). In French, with English subtitles. **104m/C VHS, Beta.** *FR* Evelyne Bouix, Marcel Cerdan Jr., Charles Aznavour, Jacques Villeret; ***D:*** Claude Lelouch. *MED*

Educating Rita ✭✭✭½ **1983 (PG)** Walters and Caine team beautifully in this adaptation of the successful Willy Russell play which finds an uneducated hairdresser determined to improve her knowledge of literature. In so doing, she enlists the aid of a tutor: a disillusioned alcoholic, adeptly played by Caine. Together, the two find inspiration in one another's differences and experiences. Ultimately, the teacher receives a lesson in how to again appreciate his work and the classics as he observes his pupil's unique approach to her studies. Some deem this a "Pygmalion" for the '80s. **110m/C VHS, Beta, LV, 8mm.** *GB* Michael Caine, Julie Walters, Michael Williams, Maureen Lipman; ***D:*** Lewis Gilbert; ***W:*** Willy Russell. British Academy Awards '83: Best Actor (Caine), Best Actress (Walters), Best Film; Golden Globe Awards '84: Best Actor—Musical/Comedy (Caine), Best Actress—Musical/Comedy (Walters); Nominations: Academy Awards '83: Best Actor (Caine), Best Actress (Walters), Best Adapted Screenplay. *COL*

The Education of Sonny Carson ✭✭½ **1974 (R)** Chilling look at the tribulations of a black youth living in a Brooklyn ghetto amid drugs, prostitution, crime, and other forms of vice. Based on Sonny Carson's autobiography. Still pertinent some twenty years after its theatrical release. **104m/C VHS, Beta.** Rony Clanton, Don Gordon, Paul Benjamin; ***D:*** Michael Campus. *MED*

Edvard Munch ✭✭ **1974** Biographical portrait of the Norwegian Expressionist painter and his tormented life in the stuffy society of 19th-century Oslo. Concentrates mainly on his early years, including the deaths of his mother and younger sister, his brother's suicide, Munch's affair with a married woman, and his struggle to maintain his sanity. Based on Munch's memoirs. In German and Norwegian with English subtitles. **167m/C VHS.** *NO* Geir Westby, Gro Fraas, Eli Ryg; ***D:*** Peter Watkins; ***W:*** Peter Watkins. *FCT, NYF*

Edward and Mrs. Simpson ✭✭ **1980** Made-for-television dramatic reconstruction of the years leading to the abdication of King Edward VIII, who forfeited the British throne in 1936 so that he could marry American divorcee Wallis Simpson. Originally aired on PBS. **270m/C VHS, Beta.** Edward Fox, Cynthia Harris; ***D:*** Waris Hussein. *HBO, TVC*

Edward Scissorhands ✭✭✭ **1990 (PG-13)** Depp's a young man created by loony scientist Price, who dies before he can attach hands to his boy-creature. Then the boy is rescued from his lonely existence outside of suburbia by an ingratiating Avon lady. With scissors in place of hands, he has more trouble fitting into suburbia than would most new kids on the block, and he struggles with being different and lonely in a cardboard-cutout world. Visually captivating fairy tale full of splash and color, however predictable the Hollywood-prefab denouement. **100m/C VHS, Beta, LV.** Johnny Depp, Winona Ryder, Dianne Wiest, Vincent Price, Anthony Michael Hall, Alan Arkin, Kathy Baker, Conchata Ferrell, Caroline Aaron, Dick Anthony Williams, Robert Oliveri, John Davidson; ***D:*** Tim Burton; ***W:*** Caroline Thompson, Tim Burton; ***M:*** Danny Elfman. Nominations: Academy Awards '90: Best Makeup. *FOX, FCT*

Edward II ✭✭½ **1992 (R)** Jarman's controversial adaptation of Christopher Marlowe's play "The Troublesome Reign of Edward II" portrays the weak-willed monarch as neglecting his kingdom for love. Unfortunately, it's not for his queen but for his commoner male lover. His neglect of both queen and country lead to a swift and brutal downfall. Jarman's use of contemporary anachronisms, stream of conscienceness approach, and heavy symbolism may leave more than one viewer wondering what's going on. **91m/C VHS, LV.** *GB* Steven Waddington, Kevin Collins, Andrew Tiernan, John Lynch, Dudley Sutton, Tilda Swinton, Jerome Flynn, Jody Graber, Nigel Terry, Annie Lennox; ***D:*** Derek Jarman; ***W:*** Derek Jarman; ***M:*** Simon Fisher Turner. Venice Film Festival '92: Best Actress (Swinton). *COL, INJ*

Eegah! *Woof!* **1962** Another Arch Hall (Merriwether) epic in which an anachronistic Neanderthal falls in love in '60s California. Reputed to be one of the worst films of all time. **93m/C VHS, Beta.** Marilyn Manning, Richard Kiel, Arch Hall Jr., William Waters; ***D:*** Ray Dennis Steckler. *RHI, FCT*

The Effect of Gamma Rays on Man-in-the-Moon Marigolds ✭✭✭ **1973 (PG)** A wonderful drama based on the Pulitzer Prize winning play by Paul Zindel. The story centers around eccentric young Matilda and her depressed family. Matilda is preparing her experiment for the school science fair, determined to beat her competition. Her exhibit shows how radiation sometimes kills the helpless marigolds, but sometimes causes them to grow into even more beautiful mutations. This mirrors Matilda, who flowers even amidst the drunkenness of her mother and the dullness of her sister. **100m/C VHS.** Joanne Woodward, Nell Potts, Roberta Wallach, Judith Lowry, Richard Venture; ***D:*** Paul Newman. Cannes Film Festival '73: Best Actress (Woodward); Nominations: Cannes Film Festival '73: Best Film. *NO*

Effi Briest ✭✭✭½ *Fontane Effi Briest* **1974** A 19th-century tragedy well-played by Schygulla and empowered with Fassbinder's directorial skills. Effi (Schygulla) is a 17 year-old beauty, unhappily married to a much older man. She drifts into a brief affair, which is not discovered for several years. When her husband does discover her past infidelity, the Prussian legal code permits him a chilling revenge. Based on a popular 19th-century novel by Theodor Fontane. In German with English subtitles. **135m/B VHS.** *GE* Hanna Schygulla, Wolfgang Schenck, Lilo Pempeit, Ulli Lommel; ***D:*** Rainer Werner Fassbinder; ***W:*** Rainer Werner Fassbinder. *NYF, INJ, PMS*

The Efficiency Expert ✭✭½ *Spotswood* **1992 (PG)** Lighthearted Australian comedy about a dingy moccasin factory where a rigid efficiency consultant is invited to save the eccentric family-run company from bankruptcy. Predictable ending contains a nevertheless timely message about the importance of the bottom line. **97m/C VHS, Beta.** *AU* Anthony Hopkins, Ben Mendelsohn, Alwyn Kurts, Bruno Lawrence, Angela Punch McGregor, Russell Crowe, Rebecca Rigg, Toni Collette; ***D:*** Mark Joffe; ***W:*** Andrew Knight, Max Dann; ***M:*** Ricky Fataar. *PAR, BTV*

Egg ✭✭½ **1988** Striking film from Holland chronicles the life of a quiet, middle-aged baker who answers a personal ad from a schoolteacher. After much correspondence, the teacher visits the baker in his village, and the townspeople take great interest in what happens next. In Dutch with English subtitles. **58m/C VHS, LV.** *NL* Johan Leysen, Marijke Vengelers; ***D:*** Danniel Danniel. *KIV, LUM, INJ*

Egg and I ✭✭✭ **1947** Based on the true-life adventures of best-selling humorist Betty MacDonald. A young urban bride agrees to help her new husband realize his life-long dream of owning a chicken farm. A dilapidated house, temperamental stove, and suicidal chickens test the bride's perseverance, as do the zany antics of her country-bumpkin neighbors, Ma and Pa Kettle, who make their screen debut. Plenty of old-fashioned laughs. **104m/B VHS, Beta, LV.** Claudette Colbert, Fred MacMurray, Marjorie Main, Percy Kilbride, Louise Allbritton, Richard Long, Billy House, Donald MacBride; ***D:*** Chester Erskine; ***C:*** Milton Krasner. Nominations: Academy Awards '47: Best Supporting Actress (Main). *MCA*

The Egyptian ✭✭½ **1954** Based on the sword-and-sandal novel by Mika Waltari, this is a ponderous big-budget epic about a young Egyptian in Akhnaton's epoch who becomes physician to the Pharaoh. **140m/C VHS, Beta, LV.** Edmund Purdom, Victor Mature, Peter Ustinov, Bella Darvi, Gene Tierney, Henry Daniell, Jean Simmons, Michael Wilding, Judith Evelyn, John Carradine, Carl Benton Reid; ***D:*** Michael Curtiz; ***W:*** Philip Dunne, Casey Robinson; ***C:*** Leon Shamroy. Nominations: Academy Awards '54: Best Color Cinematography. *FOX, IME*

The Eiger Sanction ✭✭ **1975 (R)** An art teacher returns to the CII (a fictionalized version of the CIA) as an exterminator hired to assassinate the killers of an American agent. In the process, he finds himself climbing the Eiger. Beautiful Swiss Alps scenery fails to totally compensate for several dreary lapses. Based on the novel by Trevanian. **125m/C VHS, Beta, LV.** Clint Eastwood, George Kennedy, Vonetta McGee, Jack Cassidy, Thayer David; ***D:*** Clint Eastwood; ***M:*** John Williams. *MCA, TLF*

8 1/2 ✭✭✭✭ *Otto E Mezzo; Federico Fellini's 8 1/2* **1963** The acclaimed Fellini self-portrait of a revered Italian film director struggling with a fated film project wanders through his intermixed life, childhood memories, and hallucinatory fantasies. Subtitled in English. **135m/B VHS, Beta, LV.** *IT* Marcello Mastroianni, Claudia Cardinale, Anouk Aimee, Sandra Milo, Barbara Steele, Rossella Falk, Eddra Gale, Mark Herron, Madeleine LeBeau, Caterina Boratto; ***D:*** Federico Fellini; ***W:*** Tullio Pinelli, Ennio Flaiano, Brunello Rondi, Federico Fellini; ***M:*** Nino Rota. Academy Awards '63: Best Costume Design (B & W), Best Foreign Language Film; National Board of Review Awards '63: 5 Best Foreign Films of the Year; New York Film Critics Awards '63: Best Foreign Film; Nominations: Academy Awards '63: Best Art Direction/Set Decoration (B & W), Best Director (Fellini), Best Story & Screenplay. *VES, MRV, MPI*

800 Leagues Down the Amazon ✭½ **1993 (PG-13)** A 19th-century journey down the Amazon on a raft with a planter, his daughter, and various complications. Based on a novel by Jules Verne. **100m/C VHS.** Daphne Zuniga, Barry Bostwick, Adam Baldwin, Tom Verica, E.E. Bell; ***D:*** Luis Llosa; ***W:*** Laura Schiff, Jackson Barr. *NHO*

Eight Men Out ✭✭✭½ **1988 (PG)** Taken from Eliot Asinof's book, a moving, full-blooded account of the infamous 1919 "Black Sox" scandal, in which members of the Chicago White Sox teamed to throw the World Series for $80,000. A dirge of lost innocence, this is among Sayles' best films. Provides an interesting look at the "conspiracy" that ended "shoeless" Joe Jackson's major-league career. The actual baseball scenes are first-rate, and Straithairn, Sweeney, and Cusack give exceptional performances. Sayles makes an appearance as Ring Lardner. Enjoyable viewing for even the non-sports fan. **121m/C VHS, Beta, LV.** John Cusack, D.B. Sweeney, Perry Lang, Jace Alexander, Bill Irwin, Clifton James, Michael Rooker, Michael Lerner, Christopher Lloyd, Studs Terkel, David Strathairn, Charlie Sheen, Kevin Tighe, John Mahoney, John Sayles, Gordon Clapp, Richard Edson, James Reed, Don Harvey, John Anderson, Maggie Renzi; ***D:*** John Sayles; ***W:*** John Sayles; ***C:*** Robert Richardson; ***M:*** Mason Daring. *ORI, FCT*

8 Million Ways to Die ✭✭ **1985 (R)** An ex-cop hires himself out to rescue a pimp-bound hooker, and gets knee-deep in a mess of million-dollar drug deals, murder, and prostitution. Slow-moving but satisfying. Based on the book by Lawrence Block. **115m/C VHS, Beta, LV.** Jeff Bridges, Rosanna Arquette, Andy Garcia, Alexandra Paul; ***D:*** Hal Ashby; ***W:*** Oliver Stone; ***M:*** James Newton Howard. *FOX*

8 Seconds ✭✭½ *The Lane Frost Story* **1994 (PG-13)** Love, not sports, dominates the true-life story of rodeo star Lane Frost (Perry), a world champion bull rider killed in the ring at the age of 25 in 1990. A decent guy, he finds quick success on the rodeo circuit, marries (to Geary), and finds his career getting in the way of their happiness. Bull-riding sequences are genuinely stomach churning, the performances low-key. Title refers to the amount of time a rider must stay aboard his animal. **104m/C VHS, LV.** Luke Perry, Cynthia Geary, Stephen Baldwin, James Rebhorn, Carrie Snodgress, Red Mitchell, Ronnie Clair Edwards; ***D:*** John G. Avildsen; ***W:*** Monte Merrick; ***M:*** Bill Conti. *NLC*

Eight Witnesses **1954** Suspense thriller about a man being murdered in front of eight blind witnesses. **?m/C VHS.** Peggy Ann Garner. *LOO*

18 Again! ½ **1988 (PG)** After a bump on the head, an 81-year-old man and his 18-year-old grandson mentally switch places, giving each a new look at his life. Lightweight romp with Burns in especially good form, but not good enough to justify redoing this tired theme. **100m/C VHS, Beta, LV.** George Burns, Charlie Schlatter, Anita Morris, Jennifer Runyon, Tony Roberts, Red Buttons, Miriam Flynn, George DiCenzo; ***D:*** Paul Flaherty; ***W:*** Jonathan Prince, Josh Goldstein; ***M:*** Billy Goldenberg. *VTR, NWV*

Eighteen Jade Arhats **1984** A kung fu epic with a blind heroine who nevertheless kicks other people in the eyes. **95m/C VHS, Beta.** Chia Ling, Ou-Yang Ksiek, Sun Chia-Lin, Otae Mofo. *UNI*

1860 **1933** During the Battle of Calatafimi in May of 1860, Sicilian peasants revolted against the King of Naples' army. The story focuses on four people caught up in the fighting: the spouse of a revolutionary, a foppish intellectual, a rebel priest, and the young shepherd who is sent with a message to Genoa asking for assistance. Blasetti made great use of location filming and natural light. In Italian with English subtitles. **72m/C VHS.** *IT* ***D:*** Alessandro Blasetti. *FCT, INJ, WBF*

The Eighth Day ½ *Le Huitieme Jour* **1995** Sugary story about workaholic businessman Harry (Auteuil), whose wife Julie (Miou-Miou) has just left him, taking their daughters. Driving home, Harry finds Georges (Duquenne) by the side of the road. Georges, who has Downs syndrome, has left the institution he's been living in and, though Harry tries to take him to the nearest police station, Georges refuses to leave him. Naturally, the emotionally deprived Harry begins to loosen up and, when Georges is finally returned to his group home, all his friends decide to help with Harry's attempts to win back his family. Thick with whimsy but the lead performances are excellent. French with subtitles. **114m/C VHS.** *FR BE* Daniel Auteuil, Pascal Duquenne, Miou-Miou, Henri Garcin, Fabienne Loriaux, Isabelle Sadoyan, Helene Roussel, Michele Maes; ***D:*** Jaco Van Dormael; ***W:*** Jaco Van Dormael; ***C:*** Walther Van Ende; ***M:*** Pierre Van Dormael. Cannes Film Festival '96: Best Actor (Auteuil), Best Actor (Duquenne). *NYR*

The Eighties ½ **1983** A comic, pseudo-documentary romp through the making of a musical. Not just another dime-a-dozen song-and-dance flick, but plays with the genre with humor and intelligence, treating us to an insider's view of a performance arranged at a shopping plaza, from the rigorous auditions to the tedium of the production of songs and routines. Treated in a light-hearted, sensitive, just on the verge of laughable manner, it concludes with 30 minutes of song and dance. In French with English subtitles. **86m/C VHS.** *FR* Aurore Clement, Lio, Magali Noel, Pascale Salkin; ***D:*** Chantal Akerman; ***W:*** Chantal Akerman, Jean Gruault. *WAC, FCT, INJ*

84 Charing Cross Road **1986 (PG)** A lonely woman in New York and a book-seller in London begin corresponding for business reasons. Over a twenty-year period, their relationship grows into a friendship, and then a romance, though they communicate only by mail. Based on a true story. **100m/C VHS, Beta, LV.** Anne Bancroft, Anthony Hopkins, Judi Dench, Jean De Baer, Maurice Denham, Eleanor David, Mercedes Ruehl, Daniel Gerroll, Hugh Whitemore; ***D:*** David Jones; ***M:*** George Fenton. British Academy Awards '87: Best Actress (Bancroft). *COL, TVC, HMV*

84 Charlie Mopic **1989 (R)** A widely acclaimed drama about the horrors of Vietnam seen through the eyes of a cameraman assigned to a special front-line unit. Filled with a cast of unknowns, this is an unsettling film that sheds new light on the subject of the Vietnam war. Powerful and energetic; music by Donovan. **89m/C VHS, Beta, LV.** Richard Brooks, Christopher Burgard, Nicholas Cascone, Jonathon Emerson, Glen Morshower, Jason Tomlins, Byron Thames; ***D:*** Patrick Duncan; ***W:*** Patrick Duncan; ***M:*** Donovan. *COL*

Eijanaika ½ *Why Not?* **1981** A gripping story of a poor Japanese man who returns to his country after a visit to America in the 1860s. Memorable performances make this an above-average film. In Japanese with English subtitles. **151m/C VHS, LV.** *JP* Ken Ogata, Shigeru Izumiya; ***D:*** Shohei Imamura. *KIV, FCT, INJ*

El Amor Brujo *Love, the Magician* **1986** An adaptation of the work of Miguel de Falla, in which flamenco dancers enact the story of a tragic romance. **100m/C VHS, Beta, LV.** Antonio Gades, Christina Hoyos, Laura Del Sol; ***D:*** Carlos Saura. *CTH, FCT, APD*

El Barbaro **1984** In the beginning of civilization, when evil powers rule, a barbarian has two ambitions in life: to seek revenge for his friend's death and to rescue the world from a sorcerer's power. **88m/C VHS, Beta.** *SP* Andrea Occhipinti, Maria Scola, Violeta Cela, Sabrina Sellers. *MED*

El Bruto ½ *The Brute* **1952** A mid-Mexican-period Bunuel drama, about a brainless thug who is used as a bullying pawn in a struggle between a brutal landlord and discontented tenants. In Spanish with English titles. **83m/B VHS, Beta.** *MX* Pedro Armendariz Sr., Katy Jurado, Andres Soler, Rosita Arenas; ***D:*** Luis Bunuel. *INJ, FCT, APD*

El Cid **1961** Charts the life of Rodrigo Diaz de Bivar, known as El Cid, who was the legendary eleventh-century Christian hero who freed Spain from Moorish invaders. Noted for its insanely lavish budget, this epic tale is true to its setting and features elaborate battle scenes. **184m/C VHS, Beta, LV.** Charlton Heston, Sophia Loren, Raf Vallone, Hurd Hatfield, Genevieve Page; ***D:*** Anthony Mann; ***W:*** Philip Yordan; ***C:*** Robert Krasker; ***M:*** Miklos Rozsa. Nominations: Academy Awards '61: Best Art Direction/Set Decoration (Color), Best Song ("Love Theme (The Falcon and the Dove)"), Best Original Score. *BFV, FCT, KAR*

El Cochecito *The Wheelchair* **1960** Great Spanish actor Isbert stars as the head of a large family whose closest friends are all joined together in a kind of fraternity defined by the fact that they each use a wheelchair. He feels excluded because he does not have or need one, so he goes to great lengths to gain acceptance in this "brotherhood." In Spanish with English subtitles. **90m/B VHS, Beta.** *SP* Jose Isbert; ***D:*** Marco Ferreri. *FCT*

El Condor ½ **1970 (R)** Two drifters search for gold buried in a Mexican fort. **102m/C VHS.** *SP* Jim Brown, Lee Van Cleef, Patrick O'Neal, Marianna Hill, Iron Eyes Cody, Elisha Cook Jr.; ***D:*** John Guillermin; ***W:*** Larry Cohen, Steven W. Carabatsos; ***M:*** Maurice Jarre. *WAR*

El Diablo ½ **1990 (PG-13)** A young man finds the West more wild than he expected. He finds "help" in the shape of Gossett as he tries to free a young girl who's being held by the notorious El Diablo. Made for television. Better than average. **107m/C VHS.** Louis Gossett Jr., Anthony Edwards, John Glover, Robert Beltran, M.C. Gainey, Miguel Sandoval, Sarah Trigger, Joe Pantoliano; ***D:*** Peter Markle; ***W:*** John Carpenter, Bill Phillips. *WAR, HBO*

El Diablo Rides ½ **1939** A fierce feud between cattlemen and sheepmen develops, with touches of comedy in between. **57m/B VHS, Beta.** Bob Steele, Carleton Young, Kit Guard. *VDM, VCN, VYY*

El Diputado *The Deputy* **1978** A famous politician jeopardizes his career when he has an affair with a young man. In Spanish with English subtitles. **111m/C VHS.** *SP* Jose Sacristan, Maria Luisa San Jose, Jose Alonso; ***D:*** Eloy De La Iglesia. *FCT*

El Dorado **1967** A gunfighter rides into the frontier town of El Dorado to aid a reckless cattle baron in his war with farmers over land rights. Once in town, the hired gun meets up with an old friend—the sheriff—who also happens to be the town drunkard. Switching allegiances, the gunslinger helps the lawman sober up and defend the farmers. This Hawks western displays a number of similarities to the director's earlier "Rio Bravo" (1959), staring Wayne, Dean Martin, and Ricky Nelson—who charms viewers as the young sidekick "Colorado" much like Caan does as "Mississippi" in El Dorado. **126m/C VHS, Beta, LV.** John Wayne, Robert Mitchum, James Caan, Charlene Holt, Ed Asner, Arthur Hunnicutt, Christopher George, R.G. Armstrong, Jim Davis, Paul Fix, Johnny Crawford, Michele Carey; ***D:*** Howard Hawks. *PAR, TLF*

El Mariachi **1993 (R)** Extremely low-budget but clever mixture of humor and violence in a tale of mistaken identity set in a small Mexican border town. 24-year-old director Rodriguez makes his feature film debut with this $7000 feature, originally intended only for the Spanish-language market. Film festival awards and critical attention brought the work to wider release. In Spanish with English subtitles or dubbed. The laserdisc version includes director's commentary and Rodriguez's 8 minute film "Bedhead." **81m/C VHS, Beta, LV, 8mm.** *MX* Carlos Gallardo, Consuelo Gomez, Peter Marquardt, Jaime de Hoyos, Reinol Martinez, Ramiro Gomez; ***D:*** Robert Rodriguez; ***W:*** Carlos Gallardo, Robert Rodriguez. Independent Spirit Awards '94: Best First Feature; Sundance Film Festival '93: Audience Award; Nominations: Independent Spirit Awards '94: Best Director (Rodriguez). *COL, FCT, BTV*

El Muerto ½ **1975** In 19th-century Buenos Aires, a young man flees his home after killing an enemy. Arriving in Montevideo, he becomes a member of a smuggling ring. In Spanish with English subtitles. **103m/C VHS, Beta.** *SP* Thelma Biral, Juan Jose Camero, Francesco Rabal; ***D:*** Hector Olivera. *INJ, MED*

El Norte **1983 (R)** Gripping account of a Guatemalan brother and sister, persecuted in their homeland, who make an arduous journey north ("El Norte") to America. Their difficult saga continues as they struggle against overwhelming odds in an attempt to realize their dreams. Passionate, sobering, and powerful. In English and Spanish with English subtitles. Produced in association with the "American Playhouse" series for PBS. Produced by Anna Thomas who also co-wrote the story with Nava. **139m/C VHS, Beta.** *SP* David Villalpando, Zaide Silvia Gutierrez, Ernesto Cruz, Eracio Zepeda, Stella Quan, Alicia del Lugo, Lupe Ontiveros; ***D:*** Gregory Nava; ***W:*** Anna Thomas, Gregory Nava. Nominations: Academy Awards '84: Best Original Screenplay. *FOX, APD*

El Paso Stampede ½ **1953** Cowboy investigates raids on cattle herds used to feed Americans fighting in the Spanish-American War. **50m/B VHS, Beta.** Allan "Rocky" Lane, Eddy Waller, Phyllis Coates; ***D:*** Harry Keller. *VCN*

El Super **1979** A Cuban refugee, still homesick after many years, struggles to make a life for himself in Manhattan as an apartment superintendent. In Spanish with English subtitles; an American production shot on location in New York City. **90m/C VHS.** *SP* Raymundo Hidalgo-Gato, Orlando Jiminez-Leal, Zully Montero, Raynaldo Medina, Juan Granda, Hilda Lee, Elizabeth Pena; ***D:*** Leon Ichaso; ***W:*** Leon Ichaso, Manuel Arce. *APD, INJ, NYF*

El: This Strange Passion **1952** Disturbing drama in which a man, convinced he is cuckolded, slowly descends into madness. Bunuel's surreal, almost Freudian look at the Spanish male's obsession with female fidelity. In Spanish with English subtitles. **82m/B VHS.** *SP* Arturo de Cordova, Delia Garces, Luis Beristain, Aurora Walker; ***D:*** Luis Bunuel. *HTV, FCT*

Ele, My Friend ½ **1993** The British Raj still rules India in the 1920s, when 10-year-old Charles comes across a herd of wild elephants living in the jungle. Charles befriends a baby elephant he names Ele but what can he do when hunters also discover the animals? Filmed on location in south India. **104m/C VHS.** Jacob Paul Guzman, Gazan Khan, R.S. Shivaji, Amjad Khan, Prabhu; ***D:*** Dharan Mandrayar; ***W:*** Dharan Mandrayar; ***M:*** Barry Phillips. *VCI, BTV*

Eleanor & Franklin ½ **1976** An exceptional television dramatization of the personal lives of President Franklin D. Roosevelt and his wife Eleanor. Based on Joseph Lash's book, this Emmy award-winning film features stunning performances by Alexander and Herrmann in the title roles. **208m/C VHS, Beta.** Jane Alexander, Edward Herrmann, Ed Flanders, Rosemary Murphy, MacKenzie Phillips, Pamela Franklin, Anna Lee, Linda Purl, Linda Kelsey, Lindsay Crouse; ***D:*** Daniel Petrie; ***M:*** John Barry. *SIG, TLF*

Eleanor: First Lady of the World ½ **1982 (G)** Stapleton plays the former first lady after her husband's death as she goes on to work at the United Nations and emerges as even more of an influential public figure. Made for television. **96m/C VHS.** Jean Stapleton, E.G. Marshall, Coral Browne, Joyce Van Patten, Gail Strickland, Kenneth Kimmins; ***D:*** John Erman; ***M:*** John Addison. *COL*

Electra Glide in Blue **1973 (R)** An Arizona motorcycle cop uses his head in a world that's coming apart at the seams. Good action scenes; lots of violence. **113m/C VHS, LV.** Robert (Bobby) Blake, Billy Green Bush, Mitchell Ryan, Jeannine Riley, Elisha Cook Jr., Royal Dano; ***D:*** James W. Guercio; ***W:*** Robert Boris; ***C:*** Conrad Hall. Nominations: Cannes Film Festival '73: Best Film. *MGM*

Electric Dreams ½ **1984 (PG)** A young man buys a computer that yearns to do more than sit on a desk. First it takes over his apartment, then it sets its sights on the man's cello-playing neighbor—the same woman his owner is courting. To win her affections, the over-eager computer tries to dazzle her with a variety of musical compositions from his unique keyboard. Cort supplies the voice of Edgar the computer in this film that integrates a rock-music video format. **95m/C VHS, Beta, LV.** Lenny Von Dohlen, Virginia Madsen, Maxwell Caulfield, Bud Cort, Koo Stark; ***D:*** Steven Barron. *MGM*

The Electric Horseman ½ **1979 (PG)** Journalist Fonda sets out to discover the reason behind the kidnapping of a prized horse by an ex-rodeo star. The alcoholic cowboy has taken the horse to return it to its native environment, away from the clutches of corporate greed. As Fonda investigates the story she falls in love with rebel Redford. Excellent Las Vegas and remote western settings. **120m/C VHS, Beta, LV.** Robert Redford, Jane Fonda, John Saxon, Willie Nelson, Valerie Perrine, Wilford Brimley, Nicolas Coster, James B. Sikking; ***D:*** Sydney Pollack; ***M:*** Dave Grusin. Nominations: Academy Awards '79: Best Sound. *MCA*

The Electronic Monster *Escapement; The Electric Monster* **1957** Insurance claims investigator Cameron looks into the death of a Hollywood starlet and discovers an exclusive therapy center dedicated to hypnotism. At the facility, people vacation for weeks in morgue-like body drawers, while evil Dr. Illing uses an electronic device to control the sleeper's dreams and actions. Eerie. Intriguingly, it is one of the first films to explore the possibilities of brainwashing and mind control. **72m/B VHS.** *GB* Rod Cameron, Mary Murphy, Meredith Edwards, Peter Illing; ***D:*** Montgomery Tully. *SNC*

The Elegant Criminal ½ **1992** Based on the true story of France's most infamous killer, Pierre Lacenaire. The film begins with Lacenaire in prison, writing his memoirs, receiving his admirers, and awaiting his execution (in 1836). A series of flashbacks detail his life and the supposed social clime which hindered his better instincts and turned him to the criminal life. However, Auteuil has such a wonderful time playing the charming bad guy that any blame to society fails to convince. In French with English subtitles. **120m/C VHS.** *FR* Daniel Auteuil, Jean Poiret, Jacques Weber, Marie-Armelle DeGuy, Maiwenn Le Besco, Patrick Pineau; ***D:*** Francois Girod; ***W:*** George Conchon, Francois Girod. *ORI, BTV, FCT*

The Element of Crime ½ *Forbrydelsens Element* **1984** In a monochromatic, post-holocaust future, a detective tracks down a serial killer of young girls. Made in Denmark, this minor festival favorite features an impressive directional debut and awaits cult status. Filmed in Sepiatone. **104m/C VHS, Beta.** *DK* Michael Elphick, Esmond Knight, Jerold Wells, Meme Lei, Astrid Henning-Jensen, Preben Leerdorff-Rye, Gotha Andersen; ***D:*** Lars von Trier. Nominations: Cannes Film Festival '84: Best Film. *UNI, INJ, TPV*

Elena and Her Men *Paris Does Strange Things; Elena et les Hommes* **1956** The romantic entanglements and intrigues of a poor Polish princess are explored in this enjoyable French film. Beautiful cinematography by Claude Renoir. In French with subtitles. **98m/C VHS, Beta, LV.** *FR* Ingrid Bergman, Jean Marais, Mel Ferrer, Jean Richard, Magali Noel, Pierre Bertin, Juliette Greco; ***D:*** Jean Renoir. *INT, FCT, INJ*

Eleni **1985 (PG)** The true story of "New York Times" reporter Nicholas Gage and his journey to Athens to discover the truth about his mother's execution by Communists during the Greek rebellion after WWII. Adapted by Steve Tesich from Gage's bestselling book. **117m/C VHS, Beta, LV, 8mm.** John Malkovich, Kate Nelligan, Linda Hunt, Oliver Cotton, Ronald Pickup, Dimitra Arliss, Rosalie Crutchley; ***D:*** Peter Yates; ***W:*** Steve Tesich; ***C:*** Billy Williams; ***M:*** Bruce Smeaton. *COL, IGP, INJ*

Elephant Boy **1937** An Indian boy helps government conservationists locate a herd of elephants in the jungle. Sabu's first film. Available in digitally remastered stereo. **80m/B VHS, Beta, LV.** *GB* Sabu, Walter Hudd, W.E. Holloway; ***D:*** Robert Flaherty, Zoltan Korda. Venice Film Festival '37: Best Director (Flaherty). *HBO, SUE, WAR*

The Elephant Man **1980 (PG)** A biography of John Merrick, a severely deformed man who, with the help of a sympathetic doctor, moved from freak shows into posh London society. Lynch's first mainstream film, shot in black and white, it presents a startlingly vivid picture of the hypocrisies evident in the social moves of the Victorian era. Moving performance from Hurt in title role. **125m/B VHS, Beta, LV.** Anthony Hopkins, John Hurt, Anne Bancroft, John Gielgud, Wendy Hiller, Freddie Jones, Kenny Baker; ***D:*** David Lynch; ***W:*** Eric Bergren, Christopher DeVore, David Lynch; ***M:*** John Morris, Samuel Barber. British Academy Awards '80: Best Actor (Hurt), Best Film; Cesar Awards '82: Best Foreign Film; National Board of Review Awards '80: 10 Best Films of the Year; Nominations: Academy Awards '80: Best Actor (Hurt), Best Art Direction/Set Decoration, Best Costume Design, Best Director (Lynch), Best Film Editing, Best Picture, Best Original Score. *PAR*

Elephant Walk ½ **1954** Sri Lanka's balmy jungles provide the backdrop for a torrid love triangle in this post-prime Dieterle effort. Taylor, ignored by her wealthy drunkard hubby, finds solace in the arms of her spouse's sexy right-hand man. As if keeping the affair secret weren't a big enough task, she also braves a cholera epidemic and a pack of vengeful elephants who take an unscheduled tour of her humble home. Lethargic lead performances make this more of a sleep walk, but Sofaer and Biberman's supporting roles are worth the price of rental. Taylor replaced Vivian Leigh early in the filming after she fell ill, but footage of Leigh in faraway shots is included. **103m/C VHS.** Elizabeth Taylor, Dana Andrews, Peter Finch, Abraham Sofaer, Abner Biberman; ***D:*** William Dieterle; ***C:*** Loyal Griggs. *PAR, FCT*

11 Harrowhouse *Anything for Love; Fast Fortune* **1974 (PG)** The Consolidated Selling System at 11 Harrowhouse, London, controls much of the world's diamond trade. Four adventurous thieves plot a daring heist relying on a very clever cockroach. A rather successful stab at spoofing detailed "heist" films. **95m/C VHS, Beta.** *GB* Charles Grodin, Candice Bergen, James Mason, Trevor Howard, John Gielgud; ***D:*** Aram Avakian; ***W:*** Jeffrey Bloom. *FOX*

Eli Eli ½ **1940** An American Yiddish film about a family forced to live apart because of their farm's failure. Lighthearted and fun. In Yiddish with English titles. **85m/B VHS, Beta.** Esther Feild, Lazar Fried, Muni Serebroff; ***D:*** Joseph Seiden; ***M:*** Sholom Secunda. *VYY, AUD, FCT*

The Eliminators **1986 (PG)** A cyborgian creature endeavors to avenge himself on his evil scientist creator with help from a kung fu expert and a Mexican. The group uses time travel and other devices to achieve their mission. **95m/C VHS, Beta.** Roy Dotrice, Patrick Reynolds, Denise Crosby, Andrew Prine, Conan Lee; ***D:*** Peter Manoogian; ***W:*** Danny Bilson, Paul DeMeo; ***M:*** Richard Band. *FOX*

Elisa, Vida Mia *Elisa, My Love; Elisa, My Life* **1977** A long-estranged father and daughter are reunited when he falls ill. She stays to help him write his biography and gradually begins to see things through his perspective. The shifting narrative can confuse but worth seeing are Rey and Chaplin's subtle performances. Spanish with subtitles. **125m/C VHS.** *SP* Fernando Rey, Geraldine Chaplin, Norman Brisky, Isabel Mestres, Joaquin Hinojosa; ***D:*** Carlos Saura; ***W:*** Carlos Saura; ***M:*** Erik Satie. Cannes Film Festival '77: Best Actor (Rey). *FCT*

Elizabeth of Ladymead **1948** Four generations of a British family live through their experiences in the Crimean War, Boer War, WWI, and WWII. Neagle, playing the wives in all four generations, aptly explores the woman's side of war. Enjoyable performances from husband and wife team Neagle and Wilcox. **97m/C VHS, Beta.** Anna Neagle, Hugh Williams, Bernard Lee, Michael Lawrence, Nicholas Phipps, Isabel Jeans; ***D:*** Herbert Wilcox. *DVT, VEC*

Elizabeth R **1972** Jackson is outstanding in the title role of this TV drama focusing on the life of Elizabeth I, from 17 to 70. Constantly besieged by court intrigue and political machinations, the Virgin Queen managed to restore England to glory and power amidst private and public turmoil. Six 90-minute cassettes. **540m/C VHS.** *GB* Glenda Jackson, Rosalie Crutchley, Robin Ellis, Robert Hardy, Peter Jeffrey, Stephen Murray, Vivian Pickles, Sarah Frampton, Ronald Hines; ***D:*** Claude Whatham, Herbert Wise, Roderick Graham, Richard Martin, Donald Whatham; ***W:*** Hugh Whitemore, John Hale, Julian Mitchell, John Prebble, Ian Rodger, Rosemary Anne Sisson. *FOX*

Elizabeth, the Queen *The Private Lives of Elizabeth and Essex* **1968** Historical drama recreates the struggle for power by Robert Devereaux, Earl of Essex, whom the aging Queen Elizabeth I both loved and feared, and whose downfall she finally invoked. Part of "George Schaefer's Showcase Theatre." **76m/C VHS, Beta.** Judith Anderson, Charlton Heston; ***D:*** George Schaefer. *FHS*

Eliza's Horoscope ½ **1970** A frail Canadian woman uses astrology in her search for love in Montreal, and experiences bizarre and surreal events. An acclaimed Canadian film. **120m/C VHS, Beta.** *CA* Tommy Lee Jones, Elizabeth Moorman; ***D:*** Gordon Sheppard. *AHV*

Elke ½ *Friend of the Family* **1995** While backpacking across the U.S., Elke (O'Brien) is invited to stay in Malibu with the Stillman family— husband Jeff, wife Linda, and their twenty-something children, Josh and Montana. Naturally, the sexy Elke becomes very involved with the family. **98m/C VHS.** Shauna O'Brien, C.T. Miller, Griffin Drew, Lisa Boyle. *TRI*

Ella Cinders **1926** The American mania for breaking into the movies is satirized in this look at a girl who wins a trip to Hollywood in a small-town beauty contest. Silent with original organ score. **60m/B VHS, Beta.** Colleen Moore, Harry Langdon, Lloyd Hughes, Jed Prouty, Vera Lewis; ***D:*** Alfred E. Green. *NOS, GPV, VYY*

Ellie ½ **1984 (R)** A murderous widow's stepdaughter tries to save her father from being added to the woman's extensive list of dearly departed husbands. **90m/C VHS, Beta.** Shelley Winters, Sheila Kennedy, Pat Paulsen, George Gobel, Edward Albert; ***D:*** Peter Wittman. *LIV, VES*

Elmer ½ **1976 (G)** Follows the adventures of a temporarily blinded youth and a lovable hound dog who meet in the wilderness and together set off in search of civilization. **82m/C VHS, Beta.** Elmer Swanson, Phillip Swanson; ***D:*** Christopher Cain. *LIV, WTA*

Elmer Gantry ½ **1960** The classic multi-Oscar-winning adaptation of the Sinclair Lewis novel written to expose and denounce the flamboyant, small-town evangelists spreading through America at the time. In the film, Lancaster is the amoral Southern preacher who exacts wealth and power from his congregation, and takes a nun as a mistress. Jones stars as his ex-girlfriend who resorts to a life of prostitution. **146m/C VHS, Beta, LV.** Burt Lancaster, Shirley Jones, Jean Simmons, Dean Jagger, Arthur Kennedy, Patti Page, Edward Andrews, John McIntire, Hugh Marlowe, Rex Ingram; ***D:*** Richard Brooks; ***W:*** Richard Brooks; ***C:*** John Alton; ***M:*** Andre Previn. Academy Awards '60: Best Actor (Lancaster), Best Adapted Screenplay, Best Supporting Actress (Jones); National Board of Review Awards '60: 10 Best Films of the Year, Best Supporting Actress (Jones); Nominations: Academy Awards '60: Best Picture, Best Original Score. *FOX, MGM, FCT*

Elsa, Elsa **1985** Satire of moviemaking life finds a scriptwriter-director distracted by the loss of his girlfriend and unable to concentrate on writing a memoir of his career as a child actor. He creates a subplot dealing with his romantic problems, and puts the film in jeopardy. Fine acting and witty dialogue. In French with English subtitles. **85m/C VHS.** *FR* ***D:*** Didier Haudepin. *FCT*

The Elusive Corporal 🦴🦴🦴½ *Le Caporal Epingle* **1962** Set in a P.O.W. camp on the day France surrendered to Germany, this is the story of the French and Germans, complete with memories of a France that is no more. **108m/B VHS, Beta, LV.** Jean-Pierre Cassel, Claude Brasseur, O.E. Hasse, Claude Rich; ***D:*** Jean Renoir. *VYY, INT, APD*

The Elusive Pimpernel 🦴🦴½ *The Fighting Pimpernel* **1950** Niven sparkles in this otherwise undistinguished adaptation of Baroness Orczy's "The Scarlet Pimpernel." **109m/C VHS, Beta.** *GB* David Niven, Margaret Leighton, Jack Hawkins, Cyril Cusack, Robert Coote, Edmund Audran, Danielle Godet, Patrick Macnee; ***D:*** Michael Powell; ***W:*** Michael Powell, Emeric Pressburger. *HMV, FCT*

Elves 🦴 **1989 (PG-13)** A group of possessed, neo-Nazi elves performs serious human harm at Christmas time in this tongue-in-check thriller. **95m/C VHS, Beta.** Dan Haggerty, Deanna Lund, Julie Austin, Borah Silver; ***D:*** Jeffrey Mandel. *AIP*

Elvira Madigan 🦴🦴🦴 **1967 (PG)** Chronicles the 19th-century Swedish romance between a young officer and a beautiful circus tight-rope walker. Based on a true incident. Exceptional direction and photography. In Swedish with English subtitles. **90m/C VHS, Beta, LV.** *SW* Pia Degermark, Thommy Berggren, Lennart Malmer, Nina Widerberg, Cleo Jensen; ***D:*** Bo Widerberg; ***W:*** Bo Widerberg. Cannes Film Festival '67: Best Actress (Degermark); National Board of Review Awards '67: 5 Best Foreign Films of the Year. *WAC, FCT, TPV*

Elvira, Mistress of the Dark 🦴🦴 **1988 (PG-13)** A manic comedy based on Peterson's infamous B-movie horror-hostess character. The mega-busted terror-queen inherits a house in a conservative Massachusetts town and causes double-entendre chaos when she attempts to sell it. **96m/C VHS, Beta, LV.** Cassandra Peterson, Jeff Conaway, Susan Kellerman, Edie McClurg, Daniel Greene, W. Morgan Shepherd; ***D:*** James Signorelli. *VTR, NWV*

Elvis and Me 🦴½ **1988** A TV mini series based on Priscilla Beaulieu Presley's autobiography about her life with the Pelvis. Features many of Presley's biggest hits, sung by country star Ronnie McDowell. Film may aggravate Elvis fans, however, as the King is often depicted negatively from his ex-wife's point of view. **187m/C VHS, Beta.** Dale Midkiff, Susan Walters, Billy Green Bush, Linda Miller, Jon Cypher; ***D:*** Larry Peerce. *VTR, NWV*

Elvis in Hollywood 🦴🦴🦴 **1993** A tribute highlighting Presley's first four films, "Love Me Tender," "Loving You," "Jailhouse Rock," and "King Creole," completed prior to his reporting for active duty in the army. Features his 1956 screen test at Paramount Studios; photos from the movie sets; interviews with co-stars, directors, writers, business associates, songwriters, and friends; and home movies as well as out-take footage from "Jailhouse Rock." **65m/C VHS, LV.** ***D:*** Frank Martin. *BMG, BTV*

Elvis Stories **1989** Collection of humorous shorts dealing with the King, from Mojo Nixon's song "Elvis Is Everywhere" to Cusack as a burger maker who claims to receive messages from Elvis through his patties. **30m/C VHS, Beta.** John Cusack, Ben Stiller, Joel Murray, Mojo Nixon, Rick Saucedo. *MVD, RHI*

Elvis: The Movie 🦴🦴½ **1979** A made-for-television biography of the legendary singer, from his high school days to his Las Vegas comeback. Russell gives a convincing performance and lip syncs effectively to the voice of the King (provided by country singer Ronnie McDowell). Also available in 150-minute version. **117m/C VHS, Beta.** Kurt Russell, Season Hubley, Shelley Winters, Ed Begley Jr., Dennis Christopher, Pat Hingle, Bing Russell, Joe Mantegna; ***D:*** John Carpenter. *LIV, VES*

Emanon 🦴½ **1986 (PG-13)** A coming-of-age tale about a young kid and the Christ-like vagabond, named Emanon (or "no name" if spelled in reverse), he befriends. **101m/C VHS, Beta.** Stuart Paul, Cheryl Lynn, Jeremy Miller; ***D:*** Stuart Paul. *NLC*

Embassy 🦴🦴 *Target: Embassy* **1972** In this mediocre espionage thriller, von Sydow is a Soviet defector under asylum at the U.S. embassy in Beirut. Colonel Connors, a Russian spy, penetrates embassy security and wounds von Sydow. He is caught, escapes, is captured, escapes, and is caught again. Great cast, but script is often too wordy and contrived. **90m/C VHS.** *GB* Richard Roundtree, Chuck Connors, Max von Sydow, Ray Milland, Broderick Crawford, Marie-Jose Nat; ***D:*** Gordon Hessler. *WVE*

Embassy 🦴🦴 **1985** A made-for-television movie about an American family in Rome that unknowingly possesses a secret computer chip, and thus is pursued by ruthless agents. **104m/C VHS, Beta.** Nick Mancuso, Blanche Baker, Eli Wallach, Sam Wanamaker, Richard Gilliland, Mimi Rogers, George Grizzard, Richard Masur, Kim Darby; ***D:*** Robert Lewis. *NO*

Embrace of the Vampire 🦴🦴 **1995 (R)** Innocent young Charlotte (Milano) must make a choice between her college boyfriend and a new nighttime lover (Kemp) with some decidedly different habits. Seems Charlotte looks exactly like a love lost hundreds of years ago and he's not going to take no for an answer. Also available in an unrated version. **92m/C VHS, LV.** Alyssa Milano, Martin Kemp, Harrison Pruett, Charlotte Lewis; ***Cameos:*** Jennifer Tilly; ***D:*** Anne Goursaud; ***W:*** Halle Eaton, Nicole Coady, Rick Bitzelberger; ***M:*** Joseph Williams. *TTC, IME*

Embryo 🦴🦴 *Created to Kill* **1976 (PG)** An average sci-fi drama about a scientist who uses raw genetic material to artificially produce a beautiful woman, with ghastly results. **108m/C VHS, Beta.** Rock Hudson, Barbara Carrera, Diane Ladd, Roddy McDowall, Ann Schedeen, John Elerick, Dr. Joyce Brothers; ***D:*** Ralph Nelson; ***C:*** Fred W. Koenekamp. *LIV*

The Emerald Forest 🦴🦴🦴 **1985 (R)** Captivating adventure about a young boy who is kidnapped by a primitive tribe of Amazons while his family is traveling through the Brazilian jungle. Boothe is the father who searches 10 years for him. An engrossing look at tribal life in the vanishing jungle. Beautifully photographed and based upon a true story. Features the director's son as the kidnapped youth. **113m/C VHS, Beta, LV, 8mm.** Powers Boothe, Meg Foster, Charley Boorman, Dira Pass, Rui Polonah; ***D:*** John Boorman; ***W:*** Rospo Pallenberg; ***C:*** Philippe Rousselot. *SUE, NLC*

Emerald Jungle 🦴½ *Eaten Alive by Cannibals* **1980** While searching for her missing sister in the jungle, Agren encounters cannibal tribes and a colony of brainwashed cult followers. Originally titled "Eaten Alive by Cannibals," this Italian feature was cut for its U.S. release. **92m/C VHS, Beta.** *IT* Robert Kerman, Janet Agren, Mel Ferrer, Luciano Martino, Mino Loy; ***D:*** Umberto Lenzi. *NO*

Emerald of Artama 🦴 **1967** Anyone viewing the most precious and sought after stone in the history of man does not live to tell about it. **93m/C VHS.** Rory Calhoun. *NO*

Emergency 🦴🦴🦴 **1968** Scenes from the Living Theatre's works after their return to America from four years of self-imposed exile, including "Frankenstein," "Mysteries," and "Paradise Now." **29m/C VHS, Beta.** Julian Beck, Judith Malina; ***D:*** Gwen Brown. *MFV*

The Emigrants 🦴🦴🦴 *Utvandrarna* **1972 (PG)** Farmer von Sydow decides to gather his wife (Ullmann) and family together and leave 19th-century Sweden for the promise of a new life in America. Film is divided into their leaving, the voyage over, and the journey to a settlement in Minnesota. Pacing is somewhat slow; notable cinematography (by director Troell). Adapted from the novels by Vilhelm Moberg. Dubbed into English. Followed by "The New Land." Also edited with the sequel for TV as "The Emigrant Saga." **151m/C VHS.** *SW* Max von Sydow, Liv Ullmann, Allan Edwall, Eddie Axberg, Svenolof Bern, Aina Alfredsson, Monica Zetterlund, Pierre Lindstedt; ***D:*** Jan Troell; ***W:*** Jan Troell, Bengt Forslund; ***M:*** Erik Nordgren. New York Film Critics Awards '72: Best Actress (Ullmann); Nominations: Academy Awards '72: Best Actress (Ullmann), Best Adapted Screenplay, Best Director (Troell), Best Picture. *WAR, MOV*

Emil and the Detectives 🦴🦴½ *Emil Und Die Detektive* **1964** A German ten-year-old is robbed of his grandmother's money by gangsters, and subsequently enlists the help of pre-adolescent detectives to retrieve it. Good Disney dramatization of the Erich Kastner children's novel. Remake of the 1931 German film starring Rolf Wenkhaus. **99m/C VHS, Beta.** Bryan Russell, Walter Slezak, Roger Mobley; ***D:*** Peter Tewkesbury; ***W:*** A.J. Carothers. *DIS*

Emily *Woof!* **1977** Returning from her exclusive Swiss finishing school, licentious young Emily discovers mama is a prostitute and deals with the scalding news by delving into a series of erotic encounters at the hands of her willing "instructors." Stark's first venture into the realm of soft porn. **87m/C VHS, Beta.** Koo Stark; ***D:*** Henry Herbert; ***C:*** Jack Hildyard. *MGM*

Eminent Domain 🦴🦴½ **1991 (PG-13)** A communist party member wakes up to find himself stripped of power in a Kafkaesque purge, not knowing what he is accused of—or why. A potent premise, indifferently handled despite filming on location in Poland. Based on actual events that befell the family of scriptwriter Androej Krakowski. **102m/C VHS.** Donald Sutherland, Anne Archer, Paul Freeman, Bernard Hepton, Francoise Michaud, Jodhi May; ***D:*** John Irvin; ***W:*** Andrzej Krakowski, Richard Greggson; ***M:*** Zbigniew Preisner. *IME*

Emissary 🦴🦴 **1989 (R)** An American politician and his wife are blackmailed in Africa by the Russians into revealing state secrets that could spark WWIII. **98m/C VHS, Beta, LV.** *SA* Robert Vaughn, Ted Leplat, Terry Norton, Andre Jacobs; ***D:*** Jan Scholtz. *NO*

Emma 🦴🦴🦴 **1996** Jane Austen's 1816 novel about a young woman (Paltrow) who makes it her goal to "fix" the lives of all her friends, while ignoring her own problems (the modern adaptation was "Clueless"). Emma Woodhouse focuses much of her attention on Harriet Smith (Collete), a simple young woman who Emma believes is in need of the perfect mate. After the success of "Sense and Sensibility," Austen's name is making it in the movies in the footsteps of the likes of John Grisham. **111m/C VHS.** Gwyneth Paltrow, Jeremy Northam, Greta Scacchi, Toni Collette, Alan Cummings, Juliet Stevenson, Polly Walker, Ewan McGregor, James Cosmo, Sophie Thompson, Phyllida Law; ***D:*** Douglas McGrath; ***W:*** Douglas McGrath; ***C:*** Ian Wilson; ***M:*** Rachel Portman. *NYR*

Emmanuelle 🦴🦴½ **1974** Filmed in Bangkok, a young, beautiful woman is introduced by her husband to an uninhibited world of sensuality. Above-average soft-core skin film, made with sophistication and style. Kristel maintains a vulnerability and awareness, never becoming a mannequin. **92m/C VHS, Beta.** *FR* Sylvia Kristel, Alain Cuny, Marika Green; ***D:*** Just Jaeckin; ***M:*** Pierre Bachelet. *COL*

Emmanuelle 4 🦴 **1984 (R)** Emmanuelle flees a bad relationship and undergoes plastic surgery to mask her identity. Ultimately, she becomes a beautiful young model in the form of a different actress, of course. **95m/C VHS, Beta.** *FR* Sylvia Kristel, Mia Nygren, Patrick Bauchau; ***D:*** Francis Giacobetti. *MGM*

Emmanuelle 5 🦴½ **1987 (R)** This time around sexy Emmanuelle flees aboard a convenient yacht when she's chased by adoring fans at the Cannes Film Festival. But she winds up being forced to join an Arab sheik's harem of slaves. A good example of a series that should have quit while it was ahead. **78m/C VHS.** *FR* Monique Gabrielle, Charles Foster; ***D:*** Steve Barnett, Walerian Borowczyk; ***M:*** Pierre Bachelet. *NHO*

Emmanuelle 6 🦴 **1992 (R)** The saga of the sexy beauty continues. This time Emmanuelle and a group of models head for the paradise of an Amazon jungle where they promptly become the prized captives of a drug lord. **80m/C VHS.** *NHO*

Emmanuelle & Joanna 🦴 **1986** A mistreated newlywed bride goes to her sister's whorehouse and stumbles across lots of soft-core antics. **90m/C VHS, Beta.** *FR* Sherry Buchanan, Danielle Dublino. *MED*

Emmanuelle in Bangkok 🦴 **1978 (R)** Emanuelle's exotic, erotic experiences in the Far East include a royal masseuse, suspense, and the Asian art of love. **94m/C VHS, Beta.** *FR NO*

Emmanuelle in Soho 🦴 **198? (R)** Yet another episode of the sleaze-queen's sexual exploits, this time in London's porn-saturated Soho district. **90m/C VHS, Beta.** *FR PSM*

Emmanuelle in the Country 🦴 **1978** Emmanuelle becomes a nurse in an attempt to bring comfort and other pleasures to those in need. **90m/C VHS, Beta, LV.** *FR* Laura Gemser. *IME*

Emmanuelle on Taboo Island 🦴½ **1976 (R)** Marooned young man discovers a beautiful woman on his island. This delights him. **95m/C VHS, Beta.** *FR* Laura Gemser, Paul Giusti, Arthur Kennedy. *NO*

Emmanuelle, the Joys of a Woman 🦴 **1976** The amorous exploits of a sensuous, liberated couple take them and their erotic companions to exotic Hong Kong, Bangkok, and Bali. **92m/C VHS, Beta, LV, 8mm.** *FR* Sylvia Kristel, Umberto Orsini, Catherine Rivet, Frederic Lagache; ***D:*** Francis Giacobetti. *PAR*

Emmanuelle, the Queen 🦴 **1975** Seeking revenge, Emmanuelle plots the murder of her sadistic husband. The lecherous assassin she hires tries to blackmail her, and she challenges him at his own game of deadly seduction. **90m/C VHS, Beta.** Laura Gemser. *NO*

Emmanuelle's Daughter 🦴 **1979** A Greek-made thriller in which a vapidly sensuous heroine cavorts amid episodes of murder, blackmail, and rape. **91m/C Beta.** *GR* Laura Gemser, Gabriele Tinti, Livia Russa, Vagelis Varton, Nadia Neri. *NO*

Emma's Shadow 🦴🦴🦴 *Skyggen Af Emma* **1988** In the 1930s, a young girl fakes her own kidnapping to get away from her inattentive family and comes to befriend an ex-convict sewer worker. In Danish with English subtitles. Winner of the Prix de la Jeunesse at Cannes, it was voted 1988's Best Danish Film. **93m/C VHS.** *DK* Bjorje Ahistedt, Line Kruse; ***D:*** Soeren Kragh-Jacobsen. *ORI, FCT, INJ*

Emperor Jones 🦴🦴½ **1933** Loosely based on Eugene O'Neill's play, film portrays the rise and fall of a railroad porter whose exploits take him from a life sentence on a chain gang to emperor of Haiti. Robeson recreates his stage role in his first screen appearance. **72m/B VHS, Beta, LV.** Paul Robeson, Dudley Digges, Frank Wilson, Fredi Washington, Ruby Elzy; ***D:*** Dudley Murphy. *SNC, NOS, HHT*

Emperor Jones/Paul Robeson: Tribute to an Artist **1933** A classic, rarely viewed version of the Eugene O'Neill play about a criminal who schemes his way into becoming the king of a Caribbean island. Robeson's only true dramatic film appearance. The film is accompanied by a documentary profile of Robeson, made in 1979. **102m/B VHS, Beta.** Paul Robeson, Dudley Digges, Frank Wilson; ***D:*** Dudley Murphy. *COL, SUE, HMV*

Emperor of the Bronx 🦴 **1989** A look at crime, sleaze, violence, and the actions of bad guys in the inner-city. **90m/C VHS, Beta.** William Smith. *HHE*

Emperor Waltz 🦴🦴½ **1948** Typical Hollywood musical finds phonograph salesman Crosby travelling to Vienna, hoping to sell his goods to the Austrian royal family of Emperor Franz Joseph. He meets up with the Emperor's snobby niece (Fontaine) and attempts to charm her into an audience with her royal uncle. Naturally the two fall in love and everything ends in a happy fade-out. ♫The Emperor's Waltz; Friendly Mountains; Get Yourself a Phonograph; The Kiss in Your Eyes; I Kiss Your Hand, Madame; The Whistler and His Dog. **106m/C VHS.** Bing Crosby, Joan Fontaine, Roland Culver, Richard Haydn, Lucile Watson, Sig Rumann, Harold Vermilyea; ***D:*** Billy Wilder; ***W:*** Billy Wilder, Charles Brackett; ***C:*** George Barnes; ***M:*** Victor Young. *MCA*

The Emperor's New Clothes **1984** The story of an emperor and the unusual outfit he gets from his tailor. A "Faerie Tale Theatre" presentation. **60m/C VHS, Beta.** Art Carney, Alan Arkin, Dick Shawn; ***D:*** Peter Medak. *KUI, FOX, FCT*

The Empire of Passion 🦴🦴🦴 **1976** A peasant woman and her low-life lover kill the woman's husband, but find the future they planned with each other is not to be. The husband's ghost returns to haunt them, and destroy the passionate bond which led to the murder. Oshima's follow-up to "In the Realm of the Senses." In Japanese with English subtitles. **110m/C VHS.** *JP* Nagisa Oshima, Kazuko Yoshiyuki, Tatsuya Fuji, Takahiro Tamura, Takuzo Kawatani; ***D:*** Nagisa Oshima. Cannes Film Festival '78: Best Director (Oshima); Nominations: Cannes Film Festival '78: Best Film. *FCT*

Empire of the Ants 🦴½ **1977 (PG)** A group of enormous, nuclear, unfriendly ants stalk a real estate dealer and prospective buyers of undeveloped oceanfront property. Story originated by master science-fiction storyteller H. G. Wells. **90m/C VHS, Beta.** Joan Collins, Robert Lansing, John David Carson, Albert Salmi, Jacqueline Scott, Robert Pine; ***D:*** Bert I. Gordon; ***W:*** Bert I. Gordon; ***C:*** Reginald Morris. *SUE*

Empire of the Dragon 🦴 **198?** Rip-roaring martial arts adventure featuring standard number of wide-ranging kicks. **90m/C VHS, Beta.** Chen Tien Tse, Chia Kai, Chang Shan. *NO*

Empire of the Sun 🦴🦴🦴 **1987 (PG)** Spielberg's mature, extraordinarily vivid return to real storytelling, from the best-selling J.G. Ballard novel. Yearns to be a great film, but occasional flat spots keep it slightly out of contention. Young, wealthy British Bale lives in Shanghai, but is thrust into a life of poverty and discomfort when China is invaded by Japan at the onset of WWII and he's separated from his family and interred in a prison camp. A mysterious, breathtaking work, in which Spielberg's heightened juvenile romanticism has a real, heartbreaking context. Two other 1987 releases explore the WWII memories of young boys: "Au Revoir Les Enfants" and "Hope and Glory." **153m/C VHS, Beta, LV, 8mm.** Christian Bale, John Malkovich, Miranda Richardson, Nigel Havers, Joe Pantoliano, Leslie Phillips, Robert Frazer, Ben Stiller, Robert Stephens, Burt Kwouk, Masato Ibu, Emily Richard; ***Cameos:*** J.G. Ballard; ***D:*** Steven Spielberg; ***W:*** Tom Stoppard; ***C:*** Allen Daviau; ***M:*** John Williams. National Board of Review Awards '87: 10 Best Films of the Year, Best Director (Spielberg); Nominations: Academy Awards '87: Best Art Direction/Set Decoration, Best Cinematography, Best Costume Design, Best Film Editing, Best Sound, Best Original Score. *WAR, INJ*

Empire Records 🦴🦴 **1995 (PG-13)** Well, the soundtrack's good and that's about all this frantic movie has going for it (besides a photogenic cast). Joe's (LaPaglia) the manager of an independent record store about to be taken over by a faceless conglomerate unless he and his young-and-crisis-prone staff can come up with the cash to buy the place within 24 hours. **91m/C VHS.** Anthony LaPaglia, Rory Cochrane, Liv Tyler, Renee Zellweger, Johnny Whitworth, Robin Tunney, Ethan Randall, Maxwell Caulfield, Debi Mazar; ***D:*** Allan Moyle; ***W:*** Carol Heikkinen; ***C:*** Walt Lloyd. *WAR*

Empire State 🦴 **1987 (R)** When his friend disappears from a posh London nightclub, a young man searches for him and finds more action and intrigue than he can handle. Even so, this movie's still pretty bland. **102m/C VHS, Beta.** *GB* Cathryn Harrison, Martin Landau, Ray McAnally; ***D:*** Ron Peck. *VMK*

The Empire Strikes Back 🦴🦴🦴🦴 **1980 (PG)** Second film in the epic "Star Wars" trilogy finds young Luke Skywalker and the Rebel Alliance plotting new strategies as they prepare to battle the evil Darth Vader and the forces of the Dark Side. Luke learns the ways of a Jedi knight from master Yoda, while Han and Leia find time for romance and a few adventures of their own. Introduces the charismatic Lando Calrissian, vulgar and drooling Jabba the Hut, and a mind-numbing secret from Vadar. Offers the same superb special effects and hearty plot as set by 1977's excellent "Star Wars." Followed by "Return of the Jedi" in 1983. Also available on Laserdisc with "The Making of 'Star Wars'." **124m/C VHS, Beta, LV.** Mark Hamill, Carrie Fisher, Harrison Ford, Billy Dee Williams, Alec Guinness, David Prowse, Kenny Baker, Frank Oz, Anthony Daniels, Peter Mayhew, Clive Revill, Julian Glover, John Ratzenberger; ***D:*** Irvin Kershner; ***W:*** Leigh Brackett, Lawrence Kasdan; ***C:*** Peter Suschitzsky; ***M:*** John Williams; ***V:*** James Earl Jones. Academy Awards '80: Best Sound, Best Visual Effects; People's Choice Awards '81: Best Film; Nominations: Academy Awards '80: Best Art Direction/Set Decoration, Best Original Score. *FOX, FCT, RDG*

Employees' Entrance 🦴🦴🦴 **1933** William stars as a ruthless department store manager in this story about commerce and compromise during the Depression. Young gives an excellent performance as the wife of one of his employees. Outrageous, and racy, this pre-Code film was expertly-directed by veteran craftsman Del Ruth. Based on a play by David Boehm. **74m/B VHS.** Warren William, Loretta Young, Wallace Ford, Alice White, Allen Jenkins; ***D:*** Roy Del Ruth; ***W:*** Robert Presnell. *MGM*

The Empty Beach 🦴½ **1985** A tough private detective investigates the disappearance of a wealthy business tycoon. **87m/C VHS, Beta.** *AU* Bryan Brown, Anna Maria Monticelli; ***D:*** Chris Thomson. *LIV*

An Empty Bed 🦴🦴🦴 **1990** Award-winning independent production depicting Bill Frayne, an older homosexual, and the challenges of his everyday life. Told mostly in flashbacks as Bill encounters people and places during the course of one day, this is a delicate drama with important statements about homosexuality, aging and honesty. **60m/C VHS.** John Wylie, Mark Clifford Smith, Conan McCarty, Dorothy Stinnette, Kevin Kelly, Thomas Hill, Harriet Bass; ***D:*** Mark Gasper; ***W:*** Mark Gasper. *YOC, FCT, INJ*

Empty Canvas 🦴½ *La Noia: L'Ennui Et Sa Diversion, L'Erotisme* **1964** A spiritually-bankrupt artist becomes obsessively jealous of his mistress who refuses to marry him in the hope that someone better will come along. Based on the Alberto Moravia novel. **118m/B VHS, Beta.** *FR IT* Horst Buchholz, Catherine Spaak, Bette Davis; ***D:*** Damiano Damiani; ***M:*** Luis Bacalov. *SUE, MLB*

Enchanted April 🦴🦴½ **1992 (PG)** Two women, tired of their overbearing husbands, rent a villa in Portofino, Italy for a month with two other very different women—a beautiful but bored socialite, and a crusty old woman with an impeccable literary pedigree. The effects of the charming villa, with plenty of wisteria and sunshine, do wonders for the women. A charming and romantic period piece. Based on the 1922 novel by Elizabeth von Arnim. **93m/C VHS, Beta, LV.** *GB* Miranda Richardson, Joan Plowright, Josie Lawrence, Polly Walker, Alfred Molina, Jim Broadbent, Michael Kitchen, Adriana Fachetti; ***D:*** Mike Newell; ***W:*** Peter Barnes; ***M:*** Richard Rodney Bennett. Golden Globe Awards '93: Best Actress—Musical/Comedy (Richardson), Best Supporting Actress (Plowright); Nominations: Academy Awards '92: Best Adapted Screenplay, Best Costume Design, Best Supporting Actress (Plowright). *PAR, MOV, WAR*

The Enchanted Cottage 🦴🦴½ **1945** Represents Hollywood's "love conquers all" fantasy hokum, as a disfigured war vet and a homely girl retreat from the horrors of the world into a secluded cottage, where they both regain youth and beauty. A four-tissue heart-tugger. Adopted from the Arthur Pinero play. **91m/B VHS, Beta, LV.** Dorothy McGuire, Robert Young, Herbert Marshall, Mildred Natwick, Spring Byington, Hillary Brooke, Richard Gaines, Robert Clarke; ***D:*** John Cromwell. Nominations: Academy Awards '45: Best Original Score. *NOS, TTC*

The Enchanted Forest ½ **1945** An elderly man teaches a boy about life and the beauty of nature when the boy gets lost in a forest. **78m/C VHS, Beta, LV.** *AR* Harry Davenport, Edmund Lowe, Brenda Joyce; ***D:*** Lew (Louis Friedlander) Landers. *NOS, NWV, HEG*

Enchanted Island ½ **1958** Sailor stops on an island to find provisions and ends up falling in love with a cannibal princess. Thinly based upon Herman Melville's "Typee." **94m/C VHS, Beta.** Jane Powell, Dana Andrews, Arthur Shields; ***D:*** Allan Dwan. *NO*

The Enchantress ½ *I Skiachtra* **1985** A daring boy experiences his first true loves and passions when he journeys through a mystical land in order to find a beautiful fairy. In Greek with subtitles. **93m/C VHS, Beta.** *GR* Alkis Kourkoulos, Sofia Aliberti, Lily Kokodi, Antogone Amanitou, Vicky Koulianou, Nicols Papaconstantinou, Stratos Pachis; ***D:*** Manoussos Manoussakis. *FCT*

Encino Man *California Man* **1992 (PG)** Two, like, totally uncool Valley dudes dig up a 10,000-year old caveman in the backyard. After giving him a makeover and teaching him the necessities like the four basic food groups (Milk Duds in the dairy group, Sweet Tarts in the fruit group), they use the gnarly caveman as their ticket to popularity and dates to the prom. Juvenile humor appealing to teens; strictly brain candy. **88m/C VHS, Beta.** Sean Astin, Brendan Fraser, Pauly Shore, Megan Ward, Robin Tunney, Rick Ducommun, Mariette Hartley, Richard Masur, Michael DeLuise; ***D:*** Les Mayfield; ***W:*** Shawn Schepps. Golden Raspberry Awards '92: Worst New Star (Shore). *HPH*

Encore **1952** The third W. Somerset Maugham omnibus (following "Quartet" and "Trio") which includes: "Winter Cruise," "The Ant and the Grasshopper," and "Gigolo and Gigolette." **85m/B VHS, Beta.** *GB* Nigel Patrick, Kay Walsh, Roland Culver, John Laurie, Glynis Johns, Ronald Squire, Noel Purcell, Peter Graves; ***D:*** Pat Jackson, Anthony Pelissier, Harold French. *NO*

Encounter at Raven's Gate ½ **1988 (R)** Punk rockers and extraterrestrials meet amid hard rock and gallons of gore. **85m/C VHS, Beta, LV.** Eddie Cleary, Steven Vidler; ***D:*** Rolf de Heer. *IME*

Encounter with the Unknown ½ **1975** Relates three fully documented supernatural events including a death prophesy and a ghost. **90m/C VHS, Beta.** Rosie Holotik, Gene Ross; ***D:*** Harry Z. Thomason. *VCI*

The End **1978 (R)** Reynolds plays a young man who discovers he is terminally ill. He decides not to prolonging his suffering and attempts various tried-and-true methods for committing suicide, receiving riotous help from the crazed DeLuise. **100m/C VHS, Beta, LV.** Burt Reynolds, Sally Field, Dom DeLuise, Carl Reiner, Joanne Woodward, Robby Benson, Kristy McNichol, Norman Fell, Pat O'Brien, Myrna Loy, David Steinberg; ***D:*** Burt Reynolds; ***W:*** Jerry Belson; ***M:*** Paul Williams. *MGM, FOX*

End of August **1982 (PG)** A spinster of New Orleans Creole aristocracy, circa 1900, breaks out of her sheltered life and experiences new sexual and romantic awareness. Adapted from "The Awakening" by Kate Chopin. **104m/C VHS, Beta.** Sally Sharp, David Marshall Grant, Paul Roebling; ***D:*** Bob Graham; ***W:*** Anna Thomas, Gregory Nava; ***C:*** John Bailey. *NLC*

End of Desire **1962** Schell discovers that her husband, Marquand, has married her for her money and is having an affair with the maid in this melodrama based on De Maupassant's story, "Une Vie." A period piece that is a little on the slow side. In French with English subtitles. **86m/C VHS.** *FR* Maria Schell, Christian Marquand, Pascale Petit, Ivan Desny; ***D:*** Alexandre Astruc. *NO*

The End of Innocence **1990 (R)** In her attempts to please everyone in her life, a woman experiences a nervous breakdown. Released two years after Schaeffer's murder. **102m/C VHS, Beta.** Dyan Cannon, John Heard, George Coe, Lola Mason, Rebecca Schaeffer, Stephen Meadows, Billie Bird, Michael Madsen, Madge Sinclair, Renee Taylor, Viveka Davis; ***D:*** Dyan Cannon; ***W:*** Dyan Cannon; ***M:*** Michael Convertino. *PAR, FCT*

The End of St. Petersburg ½ **1927** A Russian peasant becomes a scab during a workers' strike in 1914. He is then forced to enlist in the army prior to the 1917 October Revolution. Fascinating, although propagandistic film commissioned by the then-new Soviet government. Silent. **75m/B VHS, Beta.** Ivan Chuvelov; ***D:*** Vsevolod Pudovkin. *NOS, MRV, WFV*

End of the Line ½ **1988 (PG)** Two old-time railroad workers steal a locomotive for a cross-country jaunt to protest the closing of the local railroad company. Produced by Steenburgen. **103m/C VHS, Beta, LV.** Wilford Brimley, Levon Helm, Mary Steenburgen, Kevin Bacon, Holly Hunter, Barbara Barrie, Bob Balaban, Howard Morris, Bruce McGill, Clint Howard, Trey Wilson, Rita Jenrette; ***D:*** Jay Russell; ***W:*** John Wohlbruck; ***M:*** Andy Summers. *BAR, WAR*

End of the Road ½ **1970 (X)** Keach is a troubled college professor whose bizarre treatment by his psychologist (Jones) produces tragic results. He eventually enters into an affair with the wife of a co-worker. Fascinating, if uneven script adapted from John Barth's story. Rated X upon release for adult story and nudity. **110m/C VHS, Beta.** Stacy Keach, James Earl Jones, James Coco, Harris Yulin, Dorothy Tristan; ***D:*** Aram Avakian; ***W:*** Terry Southern; ***C:*** Gordon Willis. *FOX*

End of the World *Woof!* **1976 (PG)** A coffee machine explodes, sending a man through a window and into a neon sign, where he is electrocuted. A priest witnesses this and retreats to a convent where he meets his alien double and heads for more trouble with outer space invaders. Interesting premise. **88m/C VHS, Beta.** Christopher Lee, Sue Lyon, Lew Ayres, MacDonald Carey, Dean Jagger, Kirk Scott; ***D:*** John Hayes; ***M:*** Andrew Belling. *MED*

Endangered ½ **1994** Environmentalists battle bad guys for survival in the wilderness. **91m/C VHS.** Rick Aiello, Martin Kove, Sandra Hess, Tim Quill, Richard Hench, Dale Dye, Craig Alan, Kent MacLachlan, Renee Estevez; ***D:*** Nick Kellis; ***W:*** Nick Kellis. *ACA*

Endangered Species ½ **1982 (R)** Offbeat thriller with sci-fi leanings about a retired New York cop on vacation in America's West who is drawn into a female sheriff's investigation of a mysterious series of cattle killings. Could it be UFOs? Based on a true story. **97m/C VHS, Beta.** Robert Urich, JoBeth Williams, Paul Dooley, Hoyt Axton, Peter Coyote, Harry Carey Jr., Dan Hedaya, John Considine; ***D:*** Alan Rudolph; ***W:*** Alan Rudolph, John Binder. *MGM*

Endgame **1985** Grotesquely deformed survivors of WWIII fight their way out of radioactive New York City to seek a better life. **98m/C VHS, Beta.** Al Oliver, Moira Chen, Jack Davis, Bobby Rhodes, Jill Elliot; ***D:*** Steve Benson. *MED*

Endless Descent *Woof! La Grieta* **1990 (R)** At least it seems endless. A group of scientist-types set out in search of a sunken sub, but somehow take a wrong turn into the rift, the deepest chasm at the bottom of the sea. There, they discover unimaginable horrors—that is, if you've never seen "Alien," or just about any other icky-monster flick. A Spanish film, shot in English, by director Simon, whose other works of art include "Pieces" and "Slugs." **79m/C VHS, Beta, LV.** *SP* Jack Scalia, R. Lee Ermey, Ray Wise, Deborah Adair, Ely Pouget; ***D:*** J. Piquer Simon; ***W:*** David Coleman. *LIV*

The Endless Game **1989 (PG-13)** Cold War suspenser has British secret-agent-man Finney attempting to solve the murder of his erstwhile fellow agent-lover, much to the dismay of the government. Written by director Forbes, this made-for-cable would-be thriller is a decidedly mediocre waste of a talented cast. Also of note, it was actor-director Sir Anthony Quayle's final appearance. **123m/C VHS.** *GB* Albert Finney, George Segal, Derek De Lint, Monica Guerritore, Ian Holm, John Standing, Anthony Quayle, Kristin Scott Thomas; ***M:*** Ennio Morricone. *PSM, FCT*

Endless Love **1981 (R)** Although only 17, David and Jade are in love. Her parents think they are too serious and demand that the two spend time apart. David attempts to win her parents' affection and approval, goes mad in the process, and commits a foolish act (he burns the house down) that threatens their love forever. Based on the novel by Scott Spencer. Of interest only to those with time on their hands or smitten by a love so bad that this movie will seem grand in comparison. Features Cruise's first film appearance. **115m/C VHS, Beta, LV.** Brooke Shields, Martin Hewitt, Don Murray, Shirley Knight, Beatrice Straight, Richard Kiley, Tom Cruise, James Spader, Robert Moore, Jami Gertz; ***D:*** Franco Zeffirelli; ***W:*** Judith Rascoe; ***C:*** David Watkin. Nominations: Academy Awards '81: Best Song ("Endless Love"). *LIV, VES*

Endless Night *Agatha Christie's Endless Night* **1971** An adaptation of an Agatha Christie tale. Focuses on a young chauffeur who wants to build a dream house, and his chance meeting with an American heiress. **95m/C VHS, Beta, LV.** *GB* Hayley Mills, Hywel Bennett, Britt Ekland, George Sanders, Per Oscarsson, Peter Bowles; ***D:*** Sidney Gilliat. *REP*

The Endless Summer **1966** Classic surfing documentary about the freedom and sense of adventure that surfing symbolizes. Director Brown follows two young surfers around the world in search of the perfect wave. (They finally find it at a then-unknown break off Cape Saint Francis in South America.) Besides the excellent surfing photography, Big Kahuna Brown provides the amusing tongue-in-cheek narrative. Considered by many to be the best surf movie ever. **90m/C VHS, Beta, LV.** Mike Hynson, Robert August; ***D:*** Bruce Brown; ***W:*** Bruce Brown. *FCT, HMV, PBS*

The Endless Summer 2 *Bruce Brown's The Endless Summer 2* **1994 (PG)** You don't have to personally hang ten to get stoked about this long-awaited sequel that once again follows two surfer dudes in their quest for the perfect wave. This time out pro surfers O'Connell and Weaver circle the globe seeking adventure and the world's best waves. Traces the evolution of surfing from the lazy, golden days of the '60s to the worldwide phenomenon it is today, complete with its own pro tour circuit. Breathtaking scenery and spectacular surfing sequences highlight this look at a unique subculture. Thirty years later and it's still a great ride, though the travelogue wears thin and the sub-culture's now fairly well exploited. **107m/C VHS, LV.** Robert "Wingnut" Weaver, Pat O'Connell, Robert August; ***D:*** Bruce Brown; ***W:*** Bruce Brown, Dana Brown. *NLC*

Endplay ½ **1975** An Australian-made crime/horror drama in which two brothers cover for each other in a series of murders involving blonde hitchhikers. Based on a novel by Russell Braddon. **110m/C VHS.** *AU* George Mallaby, John Waters, Ken Goodiet, Delvene Delaney, Charles Tingwell, Robert Hewett, Kevin Miles; ***D:*** Tim Burstall. *ACA*

Enemies, a Love Story ½ **1989 (R)** A wonderfully resonant, subtle tragedy based on the novel by Isaac Bashevis Singer. A post-Holocaust Jew, living in Coney Island, can't choose between three women—his current wife (who hid him during the war), his tempestuous lover, and his reappearing pre-war wife he presumed dead. A hilarious, confident tale told with grace and patience. **119m/C VHS, Beta, LV.** Ron Silver, Lena Olin, Anjelica Huston, Margaret Sophie Stein, Paul Mazursky, Alan King, Judith Malina, Rita Karin, Phil Leeds, Elya Baskin, Marie-Adele Lemieux; ***D:*** Paul Mazursky; ***W:*** Paul Mazursky; ***C:*** Fred Murphy; ***M:*** Maurice Jarre. New York Film Critics Awards '89: Best Director (Mazursky), Best Supporting Actress (Olin); Nominations: Academy Awards '89: Best Adapted Screenplay, Best Supporting Actress (Huston, Olin). *MED, VTR*

Enemy Below 1957 Suspenseful WWII sea epic, in which an American destroyer and a German U-Boat chase one another and square off in the South Atlantic. **98m/C VHS, Beta.** Robert Mitchum, Curt Jurgens, David Hedison, Theodore Bikel, Doug McClure, Russell Collins; ***D:*** Dick Powell. Academy Awards '57: Best Special Effects; National Board of Review Awards '57: 10 Best Films of the Year. *FOX, FCT*

Enemy Gold ½ **1993 (R)** A crime czar and a beautiful killer without a conscience go after federal agents who have stumbled across a cache of Confederate gold. Basically, a babes-with-guns blowout. **92m/C VHS, Beta, LV.** Bruce Penhall, Rodrigo Obregon, Mark Barriere, Suzi Simpson, Tai Collins, Julie Strain; ***D:*** Drew Sidaris; ***W:*** Wess Rahn, Christian Sidaris. *PSM*

Enemy Mine **1985 (PG-13)** A space fantasy in which two pilots from warring planets, one an Earthling, the other an asexual reptilian Drac, crash land on a barren planet and are forced to work together to survive. **108m/C VHS, Beta, LV.** Dennis Quaid, Louis Gossett Jr., Brion James, Richard Marcus, Lance Kerwin, Carolyn McCormick; ***D:*** Wolfgang Petersen; ***W:*** Edward Khmara; ***M:*** Maurice Jarre. *FOX*

Enemy of the Law ½ **1945** Texas rangers battle evil in an old frontier town. **59m/B VHS, Beta.** Tex Ritter, Dave O'Brien; ***D:*** Harry Fraser. *NOS, VCN, DVT*

Enemy of Women ½ *The Private Life of Paul Joseph Goebbels* **1944** Chronicles the life and loves of Nazi propagandist Dr. Joseph Goebbels. **90m/B VHS, Beta.** Claudia Drake, Paul Andor, Donald Woods, H.B. Warner, Sigrid Gurie, Ralph Morgan, Gloria Stuart, Charles Halton; ***D:*** Alfred Zeisler; ***W:*** Alfred Zeisler. *NOS, DVT, GLV*

Enemy Territory **1987 (R)** A handful of citizens trapped in a New York City housing project after dark are stalked by a violent, murderous street gang. **89m/C VHS, Beta.** Ray Parker Jr., Jan-Michael Vincent, Gary Frank, Frances Foster; ***D:*** Peter Manoogian. *FOX*

Enemy Unseen **1991 (R)** A bickering squad of merceneries slog through the African jungle to find a girl abducted by crocodile-worshipping natives. Dull Jungle-Jim-style adventure, notable for the hilariously phony crocs that occasionally clamp onto the characters. **90m/C VHS.** Vernon Wells, Stack Pierce, Ken Gampu, Michael McCabe, Angela O'Neill; ***D:*** Elmo De Witt. *AIP*

The Enemy Within ½ **1994** Cable TV remake of the 1964 political thriller "Seven Days in May." Set in the late 1990's, President William Foster's (Waterston) approval rating is at an all-time low and his heavy defense cuts have certain government officials plotting a coup. Hero of the tale is Joint Chief of Staffs officer, Col. Mac Casey (Whitaker), whose military career is warring with his sense of ethics. The updating is fairly clunky; for true suspense stick with the original. **86m/C VHS.** Forest Whitaker, Sam Waterston, Josef Sommer, Jason Robards Jr., Dana Delany, George Dzundza; ***D:*** Jonathan Darby; ***W:*** Darryl Ponicsan, Ronald Bass. *HBO*

The Enforcer ½ *Murder, Inc* **1951** A district attorney goes after an organized gang of killers in this film noir treatment of the real-life "Murder, Inc." case. **87m/B VHS, LV.** Humphrey Bogart, Zero Mostel, Ted de Corsia, Everett Sloane, Roy Roberts, Lawrence Tolan, King Donovan, Bob Steele, Adelaide Klein, Don Beddoe, Tito Vuolo, John Kellogg; ***D:*** Bretaigne Windust, Raoul Walsh; ***W:*** Martin Rackin; ***C:*** Robert Burks. *REP*

The Enforcer ½ **1976 (R)** Dirty Harry takes on a female partner and a vicious terrorist group that is threatening the city of San Francisco. See how many "punks" feel lucky enough to test the hand of the tough cop. **96m/C VHS, Beta, LV.** Clint Eastwood, Tyne Daly, Harry Guardino, Bradford Dillman, John Mitchum; ***D:*** James Fargo; ***W:*** Stirling Silliphant. *WAR*

Enforcer from Death Row **1978** An ex-con is recruited by a secret international peace-keeping organization to track down and eliminate a band of murderous spies. **87m/C VHS, Beta.** Cameron Mitchell, Leo Fong, Darnell Garcia, Booker T. Anderson, John Hammond, Mariwin Roberts. *LIV, GHV*

An Englishman Abroad **1983** During the Cold War, a British actress visits Moscow and chances to meet a notorious English defector. Behind their gossip and small talk is a tragicomic portrait of the exiled traitor/spy. He was the infamous Guy Burgess; the actress was Coral Browne, here playing herself in a pointed recreation. Made for British TV; nuances may be lost on yank viewers. Winner of several British awards. **63m/C VHS.** *GB* Alan Bates, Coral Browne, Charles Gray; ***D:*** John Schlesinger; ***W:*** Alan Bennett; ***M:*** George Fenton. *FOX, FCT, PRV*

The Englishman Who Went Up a Hill But Came Down a Mountain **1995 (PG)** Charming if slight tale of town pride based on writer/director Monger's family stories. In 1917 two English cartographers—pompous George (McNeice) and naive Reginald (Grant)—travel into Wales to measure the height of Ffynnon Garw (a running gag has the surveyors struggling with the Welsh language). To the proud locals it is the first mountain in Wales, and without that designation they might as well redraw the maps and be part of England—God forbid. But in order to be designated a mountain Ffynnon Garw must be 1000 feet high, and she measures only 984. Grant stammers boyishly as the Englishman who is not only captivated by the village, but by spirited local lass Betty (Fitzgerald), with whom he starred in "Sirens." Meaney slyly shines as innkeeper Morgan the Goat, leading the townful of color characters. Wales is shown to great advantage by cinematographer Layton. **96m/C VHS, LV.** *GB* Hugh Grant, Tara Fitzgerald, Colm Meaney, Ian McNeice, Ian Hart, Kenneth Griffith; ***D:*** Christopher Monger; ***W:*** Christopher Monger; ***C:*** Vernon Layton; ***M:*** Stephen Endelman. *TOU*

Enid Is Sleeping *Over Her Dead Body* **1990 (R)** Well-done comedy noir in the now-popular there's-a-corpse-in-the-closet subgenre. A woman in a mythical New Mexican town tries to hide the body of her sister Enid, who she's accidentally killed. Enid, it turns out, wasn't thrilled to discover her sister sleeping with her police-officer husband. Phillips and Perkins restored the film to its original state after it was ruthlessly gutted by the studio. **105m/C VHS.** Elizabeth Perkins, Judge Reinhold, Rhea Perlman; ***D:*** Maurice Phillips; ***W:*** Maurice Phillips. *VES, LIV*

Enigma **1982 (PG)** Trapped behind the Iron Curtain, a double agent tries to find the key to five pending murders by locating a Russian coded microprocessor holding information that would unravel the assassination scheme. **101m/C VHS, Beta, LV.** *FR GB* Martin Sheen, Brigitte Fossey, Sam Neill, Derek Jacobi, Frank Finlay, Michael Lonsdale, Warren Clarke; ***D:*** Jeannot Szwarc; ***W:*** John Briley. *SUE*

Enigma Secret **1979** Three Polish mathematicians use their noggins to break the Nazi secret code machine during WWII. Based on a true story; in Polish with English subtitles. **158m/C VHS.** *PL* Tadeusz Borowski, Piotr Fronczewski, Piotr Garlicki. *FCT*

Enjo *Conflagration; The Flame of Torment* **1958** True story of a tormented young monk, studying at the Golden Pavilion in Kyoto, who becomes disillusioned by the pervasive corruption of the temple. In desperation, he sets fire to the national shrine in an attempt to preserve the monument from further contamination. Very disturbing yet beautiful to watch. Adapted from Mishima's novel "Temple of the Golden Pavilion." Japanese with subtitles. **98m/B VHS.** *JP* Raizo Ichikawa, Ganjiro Nakamura, Tatsuya Nakadai; ***D:*** Kon Ichikawa; ***W:*** Natto Wada, Keiji Hasebe, Toshiro Mayazumi. *NYF*

Enola Gay: The Men, the Mission, the Atomic Bomb **1980** Based on the bestselling book by Gordon Thomas and Max Gordon Witts, this made for television drama tells the story of the airmen aboard the B-29 that dropped the first atomic bomb. Details the events during WWII leading up to the decision to bomb Hiroshima and the concerns of the crew assigned the task. **150m/C VHS, Beta.** Patrick Duffy, Billy Crystal, Kim Darby, Gary Frank, Gregory Harrison, Ed Nelson, Robert Walden, Stephen Macht, Robert Pine, James Shigeta, Henry Wilcoxon; ***D:*** David Lowell Rich; ***M:*** Maurice Jarre. *PSM*

Enormous Changes *Enormous Changes at the Last Minute* **1983** Three stories about New York City women and their personal relationships. Based on the stories of Grace Paley. **115m/C VHS, Beta, LV.** Ellen Barkin, David Strathairn, Ron McLarty, Maria Tucci, Lynn Milgrim, Kevin Bacon; ***D:*** Mirra Bank; ***W:*** John Sayles. *VMK*

Enrapture ½ **1990 (R)** A chauffeur is the prime suspect when a promiscuous passenger is murdered in his limousine. The driver did it? **87m/C VHS, LV.** Ona Simms, Harvey Siegel, Richard Parnes; ***D:*** Chuck Vincent. *ATL*

Ensign Pulver **1964** A continuation of the further adventures of the crew of the U.S.S. Reluctant from "Mister Roberts," which was adapted from the Broadway play. **104m/C VHS, Beta.** Walter Matthau, Robert Walker Jr., Larry Hagman, Jack Nicholson, Millie Perkins, James Coco, James Farentino, Burl Ives, Gerald S. O'Loughlin, Al Freeman Jr.; ***D:*** Joshua Logan. *WAR*

Entangled **1993 (R)** David Mirkin (Nelson) is a struggling writer living in Paris with his beautiful girlfriend Annabelle (Treil). As she becomes ever more successful as a fashion model, David becomes ever more jealous and mistrustful. So he hires a detective (Brosnan) to spy on her. And then there's the small matter of a murder. Adapted from the novel "Les Veufs" by Boileau Narcejac. **98m/C VHS, LV.** Judd Nelson, Pierce Brosnan, Laurence Treil, Roy Dupuis; ***D:*** Max Fischer. *COL*

Enter Laughing **1967** Based on Reiner's semi-autobiographical novel and play, depicts the botched efforts of a Bronx-born schlump to become an actor. Worthwhile, but doesn't live up to the original. **112m/C VHS, Beta.** Reni Santoni, Jose Ferrer, Elaine May, Shelley Winters, Jack Gilford, Don Rickles, Michael J. Pollard, Janet Margolin, Rob Reiner; ***D:*** Carl Reiner; ***W:*** Carl Reiner; ***C:*** Joseph Biroc; ***M:*** Quincy Jones. *NO*

Enter the Dragon *The Deadly Three* **1973 (R)** The American film that broke Bruce Lee worldwide combines Oriental conventions with 007 thrills. Spectacular fighting sequences including Karate, Judo, Tae Kwon Do, and Tai Chi Chuan are featured as Lee is recruited by the British to search for opium smugglers in Hong Kong. **98m/C VHS, Beta, LV.** Bruce Lee, John Saxon, Jim Kelly; ***D:*** Robert Clouse; ***M:*** Lalo Schifrin. *WAR*

Enter the Ninja **1981 (R)** First and most serious of the Cannon canon of relatively well-done ninja epics (faint praise) that created original box-office stir for genre (mostly among adolescents needing outlet). Ninja Nero visits old friend in Philippines who's being pressured by ruthless evil guy George to give up the farm. Nero dispatches numerous thugs before indulging in ninja slugfest with Kosugi. **99m/C VHS, Beta.** Franco Nero, Susan George, Sho Kosugi, Christopher George, Alex Courtney; ***D:*** Menahem Golan; ***W:*** Judd Bernard. *MGM*

Enter the Panther **1979** Amidst, and regardless of, a double-crossing plot featuring a treacherous family and a sought-after gold mine, a young man kicks heads and punches his way to fame. **91m/C VHS, Beta.** Bruce Li, Tsai Chin, Tse Lan. *GEM*

Enter Three Dragons **1981 (R)** Kung Fu artistry abounds in this head-kicking action-adventure film. **90m/C VHS.** Dragon Lee, Bruce Lea, Yang Tsze, Samuel Walls, Chang Li, Bruce Li, Jackie Chin. *SUN*

The Entertainer ½ **1960** Splendid drama of a down and out vaudevillian who tries vainly to gain the fame his dying father once possessed. His blatant disregard for his alcoholic wife and his superficial sons brings his world crashing down around him, and he discovers how self-destructive his life has been. Remade in 1975 for television. Adapted from the play by John Osborne. **97m/B VHS.** *GB* Laurence Olivier, Brenda de Banzie, Roger Livesey, Joan Plowright, Daniel Massey, Alan Bates, Shirley Anne Field, Albert Finney, Thora Hird; ***D:*** Tony Richardson; ***W:*** John Osborne; ***C:*** Oswald Morris; ***M:*** John Addison. Nominations: Academy Awards '60: Best Actor (Olivier). *FCT, TPV*

Entertaining Mr. Sloane ☠☠½ **1970** Playwright Joe Orton's masterpiece of black comedy concerning a handsome criminal who becomes the guest and love interest of a widow and her brother. **90m/C VHS, Beta.** Beryl Reid, Harry Andrews, Peter McEnery, Alan Webb; ***D:*** Douglas Hickox. *NO*

The Entity ☠☠ **1983 (R)** Supposedly based on a true story about an unseen entity that repeatedly rapes a woman. Hershey's the victim whom nobody believes. She eventually ends up at a university for talks with parapsychologist Silver. Pseudo-science to the rescue as the over-sexed creature is frozen dead in its tracks. Exploitative violence, gore, and nudity aplenty, balanced to a degree by Hershey's strong performance. **115m/C VHS, Beta.** Barbara Hershey, Ron Silver, Alex Rocco; ***D:*** Sidney J. Furie; ***W:*** Frank de Felitta; ***C:*** Stephen Burum; ***M:*** Charles Bernstein. *FOX*

Entr'acte **1924** Clair's famous dada-surrealist classic short, reflecting his sense of humor, as various eccentric characters become involved in a crazy chase. Silent. **21m/B VHS, Beta.** *FR* ***D:*** Rene Clair. *MRV, INJ, GVV*

Entre-Nous ☠☠☠½ *Between Us; Coup de Foudre* **1983 (PG)** Two attractive, young French mothers find in each other the fulfillment their husbands cannot provide. One of the women was confined in a concentration camp during WWII; the other is a disaffected artist. In French with English subtitles. **112m/C VHS, Beta.** *FR* Isabelle Huppert, Miou-Miou, Guy Marchand; ***D:*** Diane Kurys; ***W:*** Diane Kurys; ***M:*** Luis Bacalov. Nominations: Academy Awards '83: Best Foreign Language Film. *MGM, INJ*

Epitaph ☠ **1987** An average American family's life is disrupted by the mother's habitual axe-murdering. **90m/C VHS, Beta.** ***D:*** Joseph Merhi. *NO*

The Equalizer: Memories of Manon ☠☠½ **1988** Feature-length episode of the popular television crime thriller about an ex-agent who uses guns and espionage tactics to help people who are being persecuted by ruthless villians on the streets of New York City. In this installment, McCall, the Equalizer, learns that he has a daughter and that her life is in peril. **96m/C VHS, Beta.** Edward Woodward, Melissa Sue Anderson, Anthony Zerbe, George DiCenzo, Jon Polito, Robert Lansing, Keith Szarabajka; ***D:*** Tony Wharmby. *MCA*

Equalizer 2000 ☠ **1986 (R)** A warrior in a post-holocaust future plots to overthrow a dictatorship by using a high-powered gun. **85m/C VHS, Beta.** Richard Norton, Corinne Wahl, William Steis; ***D:*** Cirio H. Santiago. *MGM*

Equinox ☠☠☠ **1971 (PG)** Young archaeologists uncover horror in a state forest. The ranger, questing for a book of spells that the scientists have found, threatens them with wonderful special effects, including winged beasts, huge apes, and Satan. Though originally an amateur film, it is deemed a minor classic in its genre. **80m/C VHS.** Edward Connell, Barbara Hewitt, Frank Bonner, Robin Christopher, Jack Woods; ***D:*** Jack Woods. *NO*

Equinox ☠☠ **1993 (R)** Modine gets to try his hand (and does well) at a dual role, with his portrayal of identical twins, separated at birth and raised in completely different environs. Garage worker Henry lives in a tenement while slick brother Freddie is a gangster's chauffeur married to the materialistic Sharon (Singer). Fate brings the brothers together when a janitor discovers a letter that reveals their parentage and the fact that a fortune has been left to them. Set in the near future, in the surreal and decaying city of Empire, this is typical Rudolph with its moody stylized appearance and convoluted plot. **110m/C VHS, LV.** Matthew Modine, Lara Flynn Boyle, Lori Singer, Marisa Tomei, Fred Ward, M. Emmet Walsh, Tyra Ferrell, Tate Donovan, Kevin J. O'Connor, Gailard Sartain; ***D:*** Alan Rudolph; ***W:*** Alan Rudolph; ***C:*** Elliot Davis. Nominations: Independent Spirit Awards '94: Best Actor (Modine), Best Cinematography, Best Film, Best Supporting Actress (Boyle). *COL, FCT*

Equinox Flower ☠☠ **1958** Ozu's first color film tells the sensitive story of two teenage girls who make a pact to protect each other from the traditional prearranged marriages their parents have set up. Lovely film that focuses on the generation gap between young and old in the Japanese family. In Japanese with English subtitles. **118m/C VHS.** *JP* Shin Saburi, Kinuyo Tanaka, Ineko Arima, Miyuki Kuwano, Chishu Ryu; ***D:*** Yasujiro Ozu. *NYF, FCT, ING*

Equus ☠☠½ **1977 (R)** A psychiatrist undertakes the most challenging case of his career when he tries to figure out why a stable-boy blinded horses. Based upon the successful play by Peter Shaffer, but not well transferred to film. **138m/C VHS, Beta, LV.** Richard Burton, Peter Firth, Jenny Agutter, Joan Plowright, Colin Blakely, Harry Andrews; ***D:*** Sidney Lumet; ***W:*** Peter Shaffer; ***C:*** Oswald Morris; ***M:*** Richard Rodney Bennett. British Academy Awards '77: Best Supporting Actress (Agutter); Golden Globe Awards '78: Best Actor—Drama (Burton), Best Supporting Actor (Firth); Nominations: Academy Awards '77: Best Actor (Burton), Best Adapted Screenplay, Best Supporting Actor (Firth). *MGM*

ER **1994** TV pilot for the hit medical series about the trials and traumas of the Chicago emergency room of an urban teaching hospital. Edwards is Dr. Mark Greene, the standards-setting team leader trying to juggle professional and personal resonsibilities, Douglas Ross (Clooney) is a womanizing pediatric resident, Susan Lewis (Stringfield) a workaholic second-year resident, Peter Benton (La Salle) is the perfectionist surgical resident with no people skills, which disconcerts third year medical student John Carter (Wyle) who falls under Benton's stern gaze. Fast-paced action is enough to make you dizzy. **88m/C VHS.** Anthony Edwards, George Clooney, Eriq La Salle, Noah Wyle, Sherry Stringfield, Julianna Margulies, Christina Harnos, William H. Macy. *WAR*

Era Notte a Roma ☠☠☠ **1960** An American, Russian, and British soldier each escape from a concentration camp in the waning days of WWII and find refuge in the home of a young woman. **145m/C VHS.** *IT* ***D:*** Roberto Rossellini; ***W:*** Roberto Rossellini. *NO*

Eraser ☠☠½ **1996 (R)** Arnold returns to familiar big-budget action territory and looks right at home. He plays elite U.S. Marshal John Kruger, who protects federal witnesses by "erasing" their previous identities. When a beautiful witness uncovers a high-level conspiracy, the two go on the run to stay alive long enough to expose the truth. Fans of the big bang Schwarzenegger of yore will not be disappointed. Rumors of production delays and budget overruns, not to mention difficulties between director Russell and producer Kopelson, brought up the spectre of "Waterworld," but the final result is more reminiscent of the success of "True Lies." **115m/C VHS.** Arnold Schwarzenegger, Vanessa Williams, James Caan, James Coburn, Robert Pastorelli, Andy Romano, James Cromwell, Danny Nucci, Nicholas Chinlund, Mark Rolston, Gerry Becker; ***D:*** Chuck Russell; ***W:*** Walon Green, Tony Puryear; ***C:*** Adam Greenberg; ***M:*** Alan Silvestri. *NYR*

Eraserhead ☠☠☠ **1978** The infamous cult classic about a numb-brained everyman wandering through what amounts to a sick, ironic parody of the modern urban landscape, innocently impregnating his girlfriend and fathering a pestilent embryonic mutant. Surreal and bizarre, the film has an inner, completely unpredictable logic all its own. Lynch's first feature-length film stars Nance, who later achieved fame in Lynch's "Twin Peaks" as Pete the Logger. **90m/B VHS, Beta, LV.** Jack Nance, Charlotte Stewart, Jack Fisk, Jeanne Bates; ***D:*** David Lynch; ***W:*** David Lynch. *COL, OM*

Erendira ☠☠½ **1983** Based on Gabriel Garcia-Marquez's story about a teenage girl prostituting herself to support her witch-like grandmother after accidentally torching the elder's house. The film follows the two as they travel across the desert trying out new and inventive ways to survive. Unusual ending tops off a creative, if not eclectic, movie. In Spanish with English subtitles. **103m/C VHS, Beta.** *FR MX GE* Irene Papas, Claudia Ohana, Michael Lonsdale, Rufus, Jorge Fegan; ***D:*** Ruy Guerra. Nominations: Cannes Film Festival '83: Best Film. *XVC, MED, APD*

Eric ☠☠☠ **1975** Made-for-television tear-jerker about a young athlete who fights for his life after he's diagnosed with leukemia. Based on the true-life account written by Eric's mother Doris Lund. **100m/C VHS, Beta.** Patricia Neal, John Savage, Claude Akins, Sian Barbara Allen, Mark Hamill, Nehemiah Persoff, Tom Clancy; ***D:*** James Goldstone; ***M:*** Dave Grusin. *LIV*

Erik ☠☠ **1990** An ex-government agent working in Central America finds his loyalties divided when he is approached by a female activist and his old CIA friends. They want him to help expose his current boss as a drug smuggler. **90m/C VHS, Beta.** Stephen McHattie, Deborah Van Valkenburgh. *NO*

Erik, the Viking ☠ **1972** The Norse Warrior discovers not only the New World but traitorous subordinates among his crew, calling for drastic measures. **95m/C VHS, Beta.** Giuliano Gemma, Gordon Mitchell. *UNI*

Erik the Viking ☠½ **1989 (PG-13)** A mediocre Monty Pythonesque farce about a Viking who grows dissatisfied with his barbaric way of life and decides to set out to find the mythical Asgaard, where Norse gods dwell. Great cast of character actors is wasted. **104m/C VHS, Beta, LV.** *GB* Tim Robbins, Terry Jones, Mickey Rooney, John Cleese, Imogen Stubbs, Anthony Sher, Gordon John Sinclair, Freddie Jones, Eartha Kitt; ***D:*** Terry Jones; ***W:*** Terry Jones. *ORI*

Ernest Goes to Camp ☠½ **1987 (PG)** A screwball, slapstick summer camp farce starring the character Ernest P. Worrell as an inept camp counselor. When progress threatens the camp, Ernest leads the boys on a turtle-bombing, slop-shooting attack on the construction company. Followed by "Ernest Saves Christmas" and "Ernest Goes to Jail." **92m/C VHS, Beta.** Jim Varney, Victoria Racimo, John Vernon, Iron Eyes Cody, Lyle Alzado, Gailard Sartain, Daniel Butler, Hakeem Abdul-Samad; ***D:*** John R. Cherry III; ***W:*** John R. Cherry III. *TOU*

Ernest Goes to Jail ☠☠ **1990 (PG)** The infamous loon Ernest P. Worrell winds up in the jury box and the courtroom will never be the same again. Jury duty suddenly becomes hard-time in the slammer for poor Ernest when he is mistaken for a big-wig organized crime boss. Sequel to "Ernest Goes to Camp" and "Ernest Saves Christmas." **81m/C VHS, LV.** Jim Varney, Gailard Sartain, Randall "Tex" Cobb, Bill Byrge, Barry Scott, Charles Napier; ***D:*** John R. Cherry III; ***W:*** Charlie Cohen; ***M:*** Bruce Arntson. *TOU*

Ernest Goes to School ☠☠½ **1994 (PG)** Ernest must finish high school if he wants to keep his job as school janitor. He's "aided" by two crazy science teachers who give him an experimental IQ booster. **89m/C VHS.** Jim Varney, Linda Kash, Bill Byrge; ***D:*** Coke Sams. *MNC*

The Ernest Green Story ☠☠½ **1993** Made-for-cable drama based on the integration of Central High in Little Rock, Arkansas by nine black students in 1957. Green was the only senior in the group and the movie follows a year of verbal and physical abuse, vandalism, and unfair academic treatment, as he struggles to withstand every difficulty in order to graduate. **92m/C VHS.** Morris Chestnut, CCH Pounder, Gary Grubbs, Tina Lifford, Avery Brooks, Ruby Dee, Ossie Davis; ***D:*** Eric Laneuville. *DIS*

Ernest Rides Again ☠☠½ **1993 (PG)** Ernest P. "KnowwhutImean?" Worrell (Varney) is back, aiding a college professor friend who has a cockamamie theory that the British crown jewels were hidden in a Revolutionary War cannon. Naturally he's right and Ernest must battle British spies and a greedy antiquities collector to get the gems back. Goofy slapstick sticks to the formula of the other films. **93m/C VHS.** Jim Varney, Ron James, Duke Ernsberger, Jeffrey Pillars, Linda Kash, Tom Butler; ***D:*** John R. Cherry III; ***W:*** John R. Cherry III, William M. Akers; ***M:*** Bruce Arntson, Kirby Shelstad. *MNC*

Ernest Saves Christmas ½ **1988 (PG)** Ernest P. Worrell is back. When Santa decides that it's time to retire, Ernest must help him recruit a has-been children's show host who is a bit reluctant. For Ernest fans only, and only the most dedicated of those. Second in the series featuring the nimble-faced Varney, the first of which was "Ernest Goes to Camp," followed by "Ernest Goes to Jail." **91m/C VHS, Beta, LV.** Jim Varney, Douglas Seale, Oliver Clark, Noelle Parker, Billie Bird; ***D:*** John R. Cherry III. *TOU*

Ernest Scared Stupid ½ **1991 (PG)** Pea-brained Ernest P. Worrell returns yet again in this silly comedy. When he accidentally releases a demon from a sacred tomb a 200-year-old curse threatens to destroy his hometown, unless Ernest can come to the rescue. Would you want your town depending on Ernest's heroics? Who would have thought that the annoying Ernest P. Worrell could appear in one movie, let alone four? **93m/C VHS, Beta.** Jim Varney, Eartha Kitt, Austin Nagler, Jonas Moscartolo, Shay Astar; ***D:*** John R. Cherry III; ***W:*** John R. Cherry III; ***M:*** Bruce Arntson. *TOU*

Ernesto ½ **1979** A lushly erotic Italian film depicting the troubled relationship between a young, devil-may-care gay youth and his older, coolly seducing lover. In Italian with subtitles. **98m/C VHS, Beta.** *IT* Martin Halm, Michele Placido; ***D:*** Salvatore Samperi. *FCT*

Ernie Kovacs: Between the Laughter **1984** A made for television version of the television comic's life and career, ending with his tragic death in a car accident in 1962. Shows the brand of humor that made Kovacs famous as well as the devastation that he suffered after the tragic kidnapping of his children by his first wife during divorce proceedings. Kovac's second wife, Edie Adams, makes a brief appearance. **95m/C VHS, Beta.** Jeff Goldblum, Cloris Leachman, Melody Anderson, Madolyn Smith, John Glover; ***Cameos:*** Edie Adams; ***D:*** Lamont Johnson; ***M:*** Ralph Burns. *NO*

Erotic Dreams *Woof!* **1987** The Devil tries to persuade a young guy to come to Hell by showing him a tableau of lusty soft-core vignettes. **70m/C VHS, Beta.** *CEL*

Erotic Escape **1986** Soft-core fun about party girls taking over a small French town. Originally in French, but dubbed in English. Check your brain at the door. **86m/C VHS, Beta.** *FR* Marie-Claire Davy, Pauline Larrieu. *MED*

Erotic Images *Woof!* **1985 (R)** A beautiful psychology teacher publishes her doctoral thesis on sex and becomes a best-selling author, which threatens her marriage. **93m/C VHS, Beta.** Britt Ekland, Edd Byrnes, John McCann; ***D:*** Declan Langan. *LIV, VES*

Erotic Touch of Hot Skin **1965** Sex, murder, false identities, car crashes, and striptease in the Riviera. **78m/B VHS, Beta.** Fabienne Dali, Sophie Hardy, Jean Valmont, Francois Dryek; ***D:*** Max Pecas. *VDM*

The Errand Boy ½ **1961** Jerry Lewis' patented babbling schnook hits Hollywood in search of a job. When he lands a position as an errand boy, Hollywood may never be the same again in this prototypical comedy; a must for Lewis fans only. **92m/B VHS, Beta, LV.** Jerry Lewis, Brian Donlevy, Dick Wesson, Howard McNear, Felicia Atkins, Fritz Feld, Sig Rumann, Renee Taylor, Doodles Weaver, Mike Mazurki, Lorne Greene, Michael Landon, Dan Blocker, Pernell Roberts, Snub Pollard, Kathleen Freeman; ***D:*** Jerry Lewis; ***W:*** Jerry Lewis. *LIV*

The Errors of Youth *Wild Oats* **1978** Dimitri (Zhdanko), a construction worker in Siberia, is disillusioned over a failed love affair and moves to Leningrad where he falls in with black marketeers and a marriage of convenience. Because of political problems, director Frumin left the film unfinished when he emigrated to the U.S. and it wasn't until 1989 that he returned to Leningrad to complete the project. Russian with subtitles. **87m/C VHS.** *RU* Stanislav Zhdanko, Marina Neyelova, Natalia Varley, Mikhail Vaskov; ***D:*** Boris Frumin. *FCT*

Escapade **1955** Sons thinking their parents are en route to divorce court create a scheme to achieve peace worldwide. The pacifist father's reaction juxtaposes idealistic youth with the cynicism of adulthood. Adapted from a play by Roger MacDougall. **87m/B VHS.** *GB* John Mills, Yvonne Mitchell, Alastair Sim, Jeremy Spenser, Andrew Ray, Marie Lohr, Peter Asher; ***D:*** Philip Leacock. *VYY, MOV*

Escapade in Florence **1962** As two students in Florence paint their way to immortality, an elaborate art-forging ring preys upon their talents. **81m/C VHS, Beta.** Tommy Kirk, Ivan Desny; ***D:*** Steve Previn. *DIS*

Escapade in Japan **1957** A Japanese youth helps an American boy frantically search the city of Tokyo for his parents. Shot in Japan. **93m/C VHS, Beta.** Cameron Mitchell, Teresa Wright, Jon Provost, Roger Nakagawa, Philip Ober, Clint Eastwood; ***D:*** Arthur Lubin; ***M:*** Max Steiner. *NO*

Escape ½ **1990 (R)** A woman attempts to track down her brother's killer and finds an entire town mysteriously controlled by a sadistic and powerful man. Features General Hospital's bad-boy Shriner. **100m/C VHS.** Elizabeth Jeager, Kim Richards, Kin Shriner; ***D:*** Richard Styles. *HHE*

Escape **1990 (PG)** A fun-loving, care-free Irish officer is sent to oversee the toughest POW prison in Scotland. There, he becomes consumed with keeping the facility secure despite the intricate escape plans laid out by a group of rioters. **90m/C VHS.** Brian Keith, Helmut Griem; ***D:*** Lamont Johnson. *NO*

The Escape Artist **1982 (PG)** Award-winning cinematographer Deschanel's first directorial effort is this quirky film about a teenage escape artist who sets out to uncover the identity of his father's killers. **96m/C VHS, Beta, LV.** Griffin O'Neal, Raul Julia, Teri Garr, Joan Hackett, Desi Arnaz Sr., Gabriel Dell, Huntz Hall, Jackie Coogan; ***D:*** Caleb Deschanel; ***W:*** Melissa Mathison; ***C:*** Stephen Burum; ***M:*** Georges Delerue. *LIV, VES*

Escape from Alcatraz **1979 (PG)** A fascinating account of the one and only successful escape from the maximum security prison at Alcatraz in 1962. The three men were never heard from again. **112m/C VHS, Beta, LV.** Clint Eastwood, Patrick McGoohan, Roberts Blossom, Fred Ward, Danny Glover; ***D:*** Donald Siegel; ***C:*** Bruce Surtees. *PAR*

Escape from Cell Block 3 **1978** Five escaped female convicts take it on the lam for Mexico and freedom. **82m/C VHS, Beta.** Carolyn Judd, Teri Guzman, Bonita Kalem. *PSM*

Escape from Death Row **1976 (R)** Convicted criminal mastermind, sentenced to die, devises a brilliant and daring plan of escape on the eve of his execution. **85m/C VHS, Beta.** Lee Van Cleef, James Lane, Barbara Moore, Alice Belios. *NO*

Escape from DS-3 **198?** Bostwick and "Police Academy" alumnus Smith team up in a familiar story: framed for a serious crime, a man attempts to escape from a maximum security satellite prison. About as good as you'd expect. **88m/C VHS.** Jackson Bostwick, Bubba Smith. *MOV*

Escape from El Diablo **1983 (PG)** Two juvenile delinquents harass guards at a Mexican prison. Being from California, they use frisbees and skateboards to help their escape. **92m/C VHS, Beta.** *SP GB* Jimmy McNichol, Timothy Van Patten, John Ethan Wayne; ***D:*** Gordon Hessler. *MED*

Escape from Fort Bravo ½ **1953** A Civil War era western set in an Arizona stockade. Holden is the hard-bitten Union cavalry officer who ruthlessly guards his Confederate prisoners, who are led by Forsythe. Parker is a southern spy whose job is to break the rebels out of jail by seducing Holden from his duty, which she does. When Holden discovers what's happened, he recaptures his prisoners only to be beset by hostile Mescalero Indians while trying to get everyone back to the fort. It's an old story but well-executed with lots of action. **98m/C VHS, Beta.** William Holden, Eleanor Parker, John Forsythe, William Demarest, William Campbell, Polly Bergen, Richard Anderson, Carl Benton Reid, John Lupton, Howard McNear, Alex Montoya, Forrest Lewis, Fred Graham, William Newell; ***D:*** John Sturges; ***W:*** Frank Fenton; ***C:*** Robert L. Surtees. *MGM, FCT*

Escape from Galaxy Three **1976 (G)** A pair of space travelers fight off a bevy of evil aliens. **90m/C VHS, Beta.** James Milton, Cheryl Buchanan. *PSM*

Escape from Hell *Woof! Hellfire on Ice, Part 2: Escape from Hell* **1989** Two scantily clad women escape from a jungle prison and are pursued by their sadistic warden. **?m/C VHS.** Anthony Steffen, Ajita Wilson; ***D:*** Edward Muller. *HHE*

Escape from L.A. ½ *John Carpenter's Escape from L.A* **1996 (R)** Well, Snake Plissken is back (Russell once again) and so's Carpenter, who did the original "Escape from New York" saga, and technology's advanced a lot in 15 years, so sit back and enjoy the action. In 2013, L.A.'s been turned into a gang-infested island, thanks to a 9.6 earthquake, where Snake is forced to find a doomsday weapon in just 10 hours. Seems he's been injected with a virus that will kill him unless he can complete his job and escape to get the antidote. Naturally, there's lots of bad guys who'll try to stop him. Russell not only reprises his old role but found Snake's original leathers, which still fit, and wore the outfit in some scenes of the sequel. **?m/C VHS.** Kurt Russell, Georges Corraface, Stacy Keach, Peter Fonda, Steve Buscemi, Pam Grier, Valeria Golino, Cliff Robertson; ***D:*** John Carpenter; ***W:*** Kurt Russell, John Carpenter, Debra Hill. *NYR*

Escape from New York ½ **1981 (R)** The ultimate urban nightmare: a ruined, future Manhattan is an anarchic prison for America's worst felons. When convicts hold the President hostage, a disgraced war hero unwillingly attempts an impossible rescue mission. Cynical but largely unexceptional sci-fi action, putting a good cast through tight-lipped peril. **99m/C VHS, Beta, LV.** Kurt Russell, Lee Van Cleef, Ernest Borgnine, Donald Pleasence, Isaac Hayes, Adrienne Barbeau, Harry Dean Stanton, Season Hubley; ***D:*** John Carpenter; ***W:*** John Carpenter, Nick Castle; ***C:*** Dean Cundey; ***M:*** John Carpenter. *SUE, NLC, FUS*

Escape from Planet Earth *The Doomsday Machine* **1967** A spaceship is damaged deep in space and only a few of the crew can make it back to Earth. But who will decide who lives or dies? (Unfortunately, the Earth has been totally destroyed so who cares anyway.) Lousy special effects. **91m/B VHS.** Grant Williams, Bobby Van, Ruta Lee, Henry Wilcoxon, Mala Powers, Casey Kasem, Mike Farrell, Harry Hope; ***D:*** Lee Sholem. *ACA*

Escape from Safehaven *Woof!* **1988 (R)** Brutal slimeballs rule a mad, sadistic world in the post-apocalyptic future, and a family tries to escape them. In very poor taste. **87m/C VHS, Beta.** Rick Gianasi, Mollie O'Mara, John Wittenbauer, Roy MacArthur, William Beckwith; ***D:*** Brian Thomas Jones, James McCalmont. *NO*

Escape from Sobibor **1987 (PG-13)** Nail-biting, true account of the largest successful escape from a Nazi prison camp, adapted from Richard Rashke's book. Made for TV. **120m/C VHS.** Alan Arkin, Joanna Pacula, Rutger Hauer, Hartmut Becker, Jack Shepherd; ***D:*** Jack Gold; ***M:*** Georges Delerue. *LIV*

Escape from the Bronx **1985 (R)** Invading death squads seek to level the Bronx. Local street gangs cry foul and ally to defeat the uncultured barbarians. Sequel to "1990: The Bronx Warriors." **82m/C VHS, Beta.** Mark Gregory, Henry Silva, Valeria D'Obici, Timothy Brent, Andrea Coppola; ***D:*** Enzo G. Castellari. *MED*

Escape from the KGB *Woof!* **1987** A CIA agent escapes from a Soviet prison, taking plans for a new space installation with him. **99m/C VHS, Beta.** Thomas Hunter, Ivan Desny, Marie Versini, Walter Barns; ***D:*** Harald Phillipe. *NO*

Escape from the Planet of the Apes **1971 (G)** Reprising their roles as intelligent, English-speaking apes, McDowall and Hunter flee their world before it's destroyed, and travel back in time to present-day America. In L.A. they become the subjects of a relentless search by the fearful population, much like humans Charlton Heston and James Franciscus were targeted for experimentation and destruction in simian society in the earlier "Planet of the Apes" and "Beneath the Planet of the Apes." Sequelled by "Conquest of the Planet of the Apes" and a television series. **98m/C VHS, Beta, LV.** Roddy McDowall, Kim Hunter, Sal Mineo, Ricardo Montalban, William Windom, Bradford Dillman, Natalie Trundy, Eric (Hans Gudegast) Braeden; ***D:*** Don Taylor; ***C:*** Joseph Biroc; ***M:*** Jerry Goldsmith. *FOX, FUS*

Escape Me Never ☆½ **1947** Flynn plays a struggling composer in this sappy period piece about poverty-stricken artists in Italy at the turn of the century. Flynn falls for his brother's wealthy fiancee (Parker), although he is married to the faithful Lupino. Atypical role for Flynn and definitely not one of his best. Based on the novel "The Fool of the Family," by Margaret Kennedy and the play "Escape Me Never" by Kennedy. **101m/B VHS.** Errol Flynn, Ida Lupino, Eleanor Parker, Gig Young, Reginald Denny, Isobel Elsom; ***D:*** Peter Godfrey; ***W:*** Thomas Williamson. *MGM*

Escape to Athena ☆☆½ **1979 (PG)** A motley group is stuck in a German P.O.W. camp on a Greek island during WWII. **102m/C VHS, Beta.** *GB* Roger Moore, Telly Savalas, David Niven, Claudia Cardinale, Richard Roundtree, Stefanie Powers, Sonny Bono, Elliott Gould, William Holden; ***D:*** George P. Cosmatos; ***W:*** Edward Anhalt; ***M:*** Lalo Schifrin. *FOX*

Escape to Burma ☆½ **1955** A man on the run for a murder he did not commit finds refuge and romance in an isolated jungle home. **86m/C VHS, Beta.** Barbara Stanwyck, Robert Ryan, Reginald Denny; ***D:*** Allan Dwan. *DIS, TOU*

Escape to Love ☆½ **1982** Beautiful student helps a famous dissident escape from Poland, only to lose him to another heroic venture. **105m/C Beta.** Clara Perryman, Louis Jourdan; ***D:*** Herbert Stein. *PSM*

Escape to Paradise ☆½ **1939** The last of Breen's films for RKO has him as a South American motorcycle-taxi driver acting as a guide for tourist Taylor. When Breen sets Taylor up with Shelton, trouble ensues. ♫Tra-La-La; Rhythm of the Rio; Ay, Ay, Ay. **60m/B VHS.** Bobby Breen, Kent Taylor, Marla Shelton, Joyce Compton, Rosina Galli, Frank Yaconelli; ***D:*** Erle C. Kenton. *NOS, RXM*

Escape to the Sun ☆½ *Habricha el Hashemesh* **1972 (PG)** Pair of Russian university students plan to flee their homeland so they can be allowed to live and love free from oppression. **94m/C VHS, Beta.** *IS* Laurence Harvey, Josephine Chaplin, John Ireland, Jack Hawkins, Lila Kedrova, Clive Revill; ***D:*** Menahem Golan. *NO*

Escape to Witch Mountain ☆☆☆ **1975 (G)** Two young orphans with supernatural powers find themselves on the run from a greedy millionaire who wants to exploit their amazing gift. Adapted from a novel by Alexander Key. **97m/C VHS, Beta, LV.** Kim Richards, Ike Eisenmann, Eddie Albert, Ray Milland, Donald Pleasence; ***D:*** John Hough. *DIS, BTV*

Escape 2000 *Woof! Turkey Shoot* **1981 (R)** In a future society where individuality is considered a crime, those who refuse to conform are punished by being hunted down in a jungle. Gross, twisted takeoff of Richard Connell's "The Most Dangerous Game." **80m/C VHS, Beta.** *AU* Steve Railsback, Olivia Hussey, Michael Craig; ***D:*** Brian Trenchard-Smith; ***W:*** George Schenck. *SUE, VTR*

Escapes ☆☆ **1986** In the tradition of "The Twilight Zone," Vincent Price introduces five short thrillers featuring time travel, aliens, and telepathy. Produced with computer assistance for sharper, more contrasted images. **72m/C VHS, Beta.** Vincent Price, Jerry Grisham, Lee Canfield, John Mitchum, Gil Reade; ***D:*** David Steensland. *PSM*

Escapist *Woof!* **1983** A professional escape artist becomes involved in a perverted corporate plot and must escape to save his life and livelihood. **87m/C VHS, Beta.** Bill Shirk, Peter Lupus; ***D:*** Eddie Beverly Jr. *LIV, VES*

E.S.P. **1983** A young man is given the amazing power of extra-sensory perception. **96m/C VHS, Beta.** Jim Stafford, George Deaton. *BFV*

Estate of Insanity ☆ **1970** An English lord and his second wife become involved in a web of death when a maniac stalks their ancient estate. **90m/C VHS, Beta.** John Turner, Heather Sears, Ann Lynn; ***D:*** Robert Hartford-Davis. *NO*

Esther and the King ☆½ **1960** Biblical costumer with Egan as Persian king and Collins as the Judean maiden he wants in place of the murdered queen. Long, rambling, and torturous. **109m/C VHS.** *IT* Joan Collins, Richard Egan, Denis O'Dea, Sergio Fantoni; ***D:*** Raoul Walsh; ***W:*** Raoul Walsh, Michael Elkins; ***M:*** Angelo Francesco Lavagnino. *FXV*

Et La Tenoresse?...Bordel! ☆☆ **1984** A French comedy about a color-blind painter and his kinky fashion photographer roommate living in Paris. In French with subtitles. **100m/C VHS, Beta.** *FR* ***D:*** Patrick Schulmann. *FCT*

E.T.: The Extra-Terrestrial ☆☆☆☆ **1982 (PG)** Spielberg's famous fantasy, one of the most popular films in history, portrays a limpid-eyed alien stranded on earth and his special bonding relationship with a young boy. A modern fairy tale providing warmth, humor and sheer wonder. Held the first place spot as the highest grossing movie of all time for years until a new Spielberg hit replaced it—"Jurassic Park." Debra Winger contributed to the voice of E.T. **115m/C VHS, Beta, LV.** Henry Thomas, Dee Wallace Stone, Drew Barrymore, Robert MacNaughton, Peter Coyote, C. Thomas Howell, Sean Frye, K.C. Martel; ***D:*** Steven Spielberg; ***W:*** Melissa Mathison; ***C:*** Allen Daviau; ***M:*** John Williams. Academy Awards '82: Best Sound, Best Visual Effects, Best Original Score; Golden Globe Awards '83: Best Film—Drama, Best Score; Los Angeles Film Critics Association Awards '82: Best Director (Spielberg), Best Film; National Society of Film Critics Awards '82: Best Director (Spielberg); People's Choice Awards '83: Best Film; Writers Guild of America '82: Best Original Screenplay; Nominations: Academy Awards '81: Best Film Editing; Academy Awards '82: Best Cinematography, Best Director (Spielberg), Best Picture, Best Sound. *MCA, APD, RDG*

Eternal Evil ☆ **1987 (R)** A bored television director is taught how to have out-of-body experiences by his devil-worshipping girlfriend. He eventually realizes that when he leaves his body, it runs around killing people. **85m/C VHS, Beta, LV.** Karen Black, Winston Rekert, Lois Maxwell; ***D:*** George Mihalka. *LIV*

Eternal Return ☆☆½ *L'Eternel Retour; Love Eternal* **1943** A lush modern retelling of the Tristan/Isolde legend. Patrice (Marais) brings the beautiful Nathalie (Sologne) to his family's castle, as his uncle's (Murat) intended bride. But thanks to a love potion, it's Nathalie and Patrice who fall in love—with tragic results. In French with English subtitles. **111m/B VHS, Beta.** *FR* Jean Marais, Madeleine Sologne, Jean Murat; ***D:*** Jean Delannoy; ***W:*** Jean Cocteau. *WBF, INJ, NLC*

The Eternal Waltz ☆☆ *Ewiger Walzer* **1954** Overly sentimental chronicle of the life of composer Johann Strauss. Only director Verhoeven's touch holds the viewer's interest, though the production values are excellent. **97m/C VHS.** Bernhard Wicki, Hilde Krahl, Annemarie Duerringer, Friedl Loor, Eduard Strauss Jr., Gert Frobe, Arnulf Schroeder; ***D:*** Paul Verhoeven. *NOS*

Eternally Yours ☆☆½ **1939** A witty magician's career threatens to break up his marriage. **95m/B VHS, Beta.** David Niven, Loretta Young, Hugh Herbert, Broderick Crawford, Sir C. Aubrey Smith, Billie Burke, Eve Arden, ZaSu Pitts; ***D:*** Tay Garnett. Nominations: Academy Awards '39: Best Original Score. *NOS, MRV, HHT*

Eternity ☆ **1990 (R)** While trying to uncover corrupt corporate America a television reporter falls in love with a model who works for a media king and puts his credibility on the line. He believes he and the woman shared romance in a past life. **122m/C VHS.** Jon Voight, Armand Assante, Wilford Brimley, Eileen Davidson, Kaye Ballard, Lainie Kazan, Joey Villa, Steven Keats, Eugene Roche, Frankie Valli, John P. Ryan; ***D:*** Steven Paul. *ACA*

Ethan ☆½ **1971** A missionary in the Philippines falls in love with a woman and exiles himself for his fall from grace. **91m/C VHS, Beta.** Robert Sampson, Rosa Rosal, Eddie Infante; ***D:*** Michael DuPont. *GHV*

Ethan Frome ☆☆½ **1992 (PG)** Neeson stars as the lonely, poverty-stricken 19th-century New England farmer who has long and faithfully cared for his bitter, invalid wife. When his wife's distant young cousin comes to take over as housekeeper they both succumb to their forbidden passion with tragic results. The performers carry the burden of the film's sluggish pacing, where the bleak setting of Massachusetts in winter tends to overwhelm the events. Based on the novel by Edith Wharton. **107m/C VHS, Beta, LV.** Liam Neeson, Patricia Arquette, Joan Allen, Tate Donovan, Katharine Houghton, Stephen Mendillo; ***D:*** John Madden; ***W:*** Richard Nelson. *TOU, FCT*

Eubie! **1982** The popular Broadway musical revue based on the life and songs of Eubie Blake is presented in a video transfer. Some of Eubie's best known songs, performed here by members of the original cast, include "I'm Just Wild About Harry," "Memories of You," "In Honeysuckle Time" and "The Charleston Rag." **100m/C VHS, Beta.** Gregory Hines, Maurice Hines, Leslie Dockery, Alaina Reed, Lynnie Godfrey, Mel Johnson Jr., Jeffrey V. Thompson; ***D:*** Julianne Boyd. *WAR, OM*

Eureka! ☆☆½ **1981 (R)** A bizarre, wildly symbolic slab of Roegian artifice that deals with the dream-spliced life of a rich, bored gold tycoon who becomes tortured over his daughter's marriage and his own useless wealth. Eventually he is bothered by the Mafia and led to the courtroom by business competitors. From the book by Paul Mayersberg. **130m/C VHS, Beta.** *GB* Gene Hackman, Theresa Russell, Joe Pesci, Rutger Hauer, Mickey Rourke, Ed Lauter, Jane Lapotaire; ***D:*** Nicolas Roeg. *MGM*

Eureka Stockade ☆☆ *Massacre Hill* **1949** Four early Australian gold prospectors join forces to fight their governor and the police for the rights to dig on the continent. **103m/B VHS, Beta.** *AU* Chips Rafferty, Peter Finch, Jane Barrett, Peter Illing; ***D:*** Harry Watt. *NOS, DVT, HEG*

Europa, Europa ☆☆☆½ **1991 (R)** The incredible, harrowing and borderline-absurdist true story of Solomon Perel, a young Jew who escaped the Holocaust by passing for German at an elite, Nazi-run academy. Such a sharp evocation of the era that the modern German establishment wouldn't submit it for the Academy Awards. In German and Russian with English subtitles. **115m/C VHS.** *GE* Marco Hofschneider, Klaus Abramowsky, Michele Gleizer, Rene Hofschneider, Nathalie Schmidt, Delphine Forest, Julie Delpy; ***D:*** Agnieszka Holland; ***W:*** Agnieszka Holland. Golden Globe Awards '92: Best Foreign Film; National Board of Review Awards '91: Best Foreign Film; New York Film Critics Awards '91: Best Foreign Film; Nominations: Academy Awards '91: Best Adapted Screenplay. *ORI, INJ, BTV*

Europa '51 ☆☆½ *The Greatest Love* **1952** The despairing portrait of post-war malaise, as an American woman, whose son committed suicide, lives in Rome searching for some semblance of meaning, and ends up in an asylum. One of Bergman & Rossellini's least-loved films. In Italian with subtitles. **110m/B VHS, Beta.** Ingrid Bergman, Alexander Knox, Ettore Giannini, Giulietta Masina; ***D:*** Roberto Rossellini. *FCT*

The Europeans ☆☆☆ **1979** Fine adaptation of Henry James's satiric novel. British brother and sister visit their staid American cousins in 19th-century New England in an effort to improve their prospects through fortuitous marriages. **90m/C VHS, Beta.** Lee Remick, Lisa Eichhorn, Robin Ellis, Wesley Addy, Tim Woodward; ***D:*** James Ivory; ***W:*** Ruth Prawer Jhabvala. National Board of Review Awards '79: 10 Best Films of the Year; Nominations: Academy Awards '79: Best Costume Design; Cannes Film Festival '79: Best Film. *CVC, INJ, LUM*

Evangeline ☆☆½ **1929** Based on the Henry Wadsworth Longfellow poem about the struggles of Evangeline and the tragedy of lost love. **79m/B VHS.** Dolores Del Rio, Roland Drew, Alec B. Francis, George F. Marion Sr.; ***D:*** Edwin Carewe. *FCT*

Eve of Destruction *Woof!* **1990 (R)** Hell knows no fury like a cutting-edge android-girl on the warpath. Modeled after her creator, Dr. Eve Simmons, Eve VII has android-babe good looks and a raging nuclear capability. Wouldn't you know, something goes haywire during her trial run, and debutante Eve turns into a PMS nightmare machine, blasting all the good Doctor's previous beaux. That's where military agent Hines comes in, though you wonder why. Dutch actress Soutendijk plays dual Eves in her first American film. **101m/C VHS, Beta, LV.** Gregory Hines, Renee Soutendijk, Kevin McCarthy, Ross Malinger; ***D:*** Duncan Gibbins; ***W:*** Duncan Gibbins. *COL, NLC, SUE*

Evel Knievel 🦴🦴 **1972 (PG)** The life of motorcycle stuntman Evel Knievel is depicted in this movie, as portrayed by George Hamilton. Stunts will be appreciated by Evel Knievel fans. **90m/C VHS, Beta.** George Hamilton, Bert Freed, Rod Cameron, Sue Lyon; ***D:*** Marvin J. Chomsky; ***W:*** John Milius. *NO*

Evelyn Prentice 🦴🦴½ **1934** Powell and Loy again team up as a married couple (after their "The Thin Man" success) but this time things aren't so rosy. He is an attorney with a wandering eye who has an affair with Russell (in her film debut). Loy finds out and turns for sympathy to Stephens but then she decides to stay with her husband after all. Only she's written some steamy letters to Stephens and he tries blackmailing her—and winds up dead. Dramatic courtroom scene straightens things out. Adapted from the novel by W.E. Woodward. Film was remade as "Stronger Than Desire" in 1939. **78m/B VHS.** Myrna Loy, William Powell, Harvey Stephens, Isabel Jewell, Una Merkel, Rosalind Russell, Henry Wadsworth, Edward Brophy, Cora Sue Collins, Jessie Ralph, Sam Flint, Pat O'Malley; ***D:*** William K. Howard; ***W:*** Lenore Coffee. *MGM*

Even Angels Fall 🦴🦴 **1990** One of heartthrob singer Humperdinck's scattered dramatic projects, a mystery thriller about a romance novelist moving into a New York brownstone whose previous inhabitant committed suicide—or was it murder? **?m/C VHS.** Morgan Fairchild, Engelbert Humperdinck; ***D:*** Thomas Calabrese. *NO*

Even Cowgirls Get the Blues 🦴½ **1994 (R)** '70s counterculture loses its ill-defined charm in a meandering adaptation of cult author Tom Robbins' 1976 novel. An interesting failure, but likely to alienate both Van Sant and Robbins fans. Sissy Hackshaw (Thurman) possesses enormous thumbs which she hopes will make her the greatest hitchhiker in the world. But first they take her to a NYC modeling career for The Countess (Hurt in a high camp performance), who sends her to the Rubber Rose ranch, recently liberated by female cowhands, who are happy to welcome her. Theatrical release was delayed numerous times as Van Sant recut but it doesn't matter—the only successful feature is the soundtrack. **106m/C VHS, LV.** Uma Thurman, John Hurt, Rain Phoenix, Lorraine Bracco, Noriyuki "Pat" Morita, Angie Dickinson, Keanu Reeves; ***Cameos:*** Sean Young, Crispin Glover, Roseanne, Ed Begley Jr.; ***D:*** Gus Van Sant; ***W:*** Gus Van Sant; ***C:*** Eric Alan Edwards, John Campbell; ***M:*** k.d. lang, Ben Mink. Nominations: Golden Raspberry Awards '94: Worst Actress (Thurman). *COL*

An Evening with Robin Williams **1983** Robin Williams explodes all over the screen in this live nightclub performance taped at the Great American Music Hall in San Francisco. **92m/C VHS, Beta, LV.** Robin Williams. *PAR*

Evergreen 🦴🦴½ **1934** The daughter of a retired British music hall star is mistaken for her mother and it is thought that she has discovered the secret of eternal youth. ♫Daddy Wouldn't Buy Me a Bow-Wow; When You've Got a Little Springtime in Your Heart; If I Give in to You; Tinkle, Tinkle, Tinkle; Dear, Dear; Dancing on the Ceiling; Just by Your Example; Over My Shoulder. **91m/B VHS, Beta, LV.** *GB* Jessie Matthews, Sonnie Hale, Betty Balfour, Barry Mackay; ***D:*** Victor Saville; ***M:*** Richard Rodgers, Harry Woods, Lorenz Hart, Harry Woods. *VYY, HMV, VMK*

The Everlasting Secret Family 🦴🦴 **1988** Politics and family life make strange bedfellows. A top political figure joins a secret homosexual organization in his search for power. **93m/C VHS.** *AU* Arthur Dignam, Mark Lee, Dennis Miller, Heather Mitchell; ***D:*** Michael Thornhill. *FCT, CCN, TPV*

Eversmile New Jersey 🦴½ **1989 (PG)** A dentist travels through Patagonia, offering dental care and advice to anyone in need, and a young woman, taken with the dental knight, dumps her boyfriend and stows away with him. When he discovers his admirer, he is less than ecstatic, but a chance tooth extraction on the road reveals the young woman's natural dental talents, and the two bond. From the director of "The Official Story." **88m/C VHS, Beta, LV.** *AR* Daniel Day-Lewis, Mirjana Jokovic; ***D:*** Carlos Sorin; ***W:*** Jorge Goldenberg, Roberto Scheuer, Carlos Sorin. *FXV, MED*

Every Breath 🦴🦴 **1993 (R)** A kinky couple's games can be deadly and now they have someone new to play with. Jimmy couldn't resist the wife's seductive allure and if he wants to survive, he'll have to beat them at their own game. **88m/C VHS.** Judd Nelson, Joanna Pacula, Patrick Bauchau; ***D:*** Steve Bing; ***W:*** Judd Nelson, Andrew Fleming, Steve Bing; ***M:*** Nils Lofgren. *COL*

Every Day's a Holiday 🦴🦴½ **1938** In the 1890s, West stars as confidence woman Peaches O'Day, who sells the Brooklyn Bridge and is run out of New York City. But she comes back, in disguise as a French singer, to expose some crooked cops. The Hays office again came down heavily on Mae's suggestive behavior, which left her with little to rely on. West's last film for Paramount. **79m/B VHS.** Mae West, Edmund Lowe, Charles Butterworth, Charles Winninger, Walter Catlett, Lloyd Nolan, Herman Bing; ***D:*** Edward Sutherland; ***W:*** Mae West. *MCA, BTV*

Every Girl Should Be Married 🦴🦴½ **1948** A shopgirl sets her sights on an eligible bachelor doctor. **84m/B VHS, Beta, LV.** Cary Grant, Betsy Drake, Diana Lynn, Franchot Tone; ***D:*** Don Hartman. *TTC*

Every Girl Should Have One 🦴½ **1978** A rambunctious comedy about a chase following a million-dollar diamond theft. **90m/C VHS, Beta.** Zsa Zsa Gabor, Robert Alda, Alice Faye, Sandra Vacey, John Lazar. *GEM*

Every Man for Himself & God Against All 🦴🦴🦴🦴 *The Mystery of Kaspar Hauser; Jeder Fur Sich Und Gott Gegen Alle; The Enigma of Kaspar Hauser* **1975** Kaspar Hauser is a young man who mysteriously appears in the town square of Nuremberg, early in the 19th century. He cannot speak or stand upright and is found to have been kept in a dungeon for the first 18 years of his life. He becomes an attraction in society with his alternate vision of the world and attempts to reconcile with reality. A lovely, though demanding film which is based on a true story. In German with English subtitles. **110m/C VHS, Beta.** *GE* Bruno S, Brigitte Mira, Walter Ladengast, Hans Musaus, Willy Semmelrogge, Michael Kroecher, Henry van Lyck; ***D:*** Werner Herzog; ***W:*** Werner Herzog; ***M:*** Albinoni Pachelbel, Orlando Di Lasso. Nominations: Cannes Film Festival '75: Best Film. *NYF, APD, GLV*

Every Man's Law 🦴½ **1935** A cowboy who poses as a hired gunman is almost lynched by ranchers who think he is a murderer. **60m/B VHS, Beta.** Johnny Mack Brown. *VCN*

Every Time We Say Goodbye 🦴🦴½ **1986 (PG-13)** In 1942, Jerusalem, an American flyboy falls in love with a young Sephardic Jewish girl, whose family resists the match. **97m/C VHS, Beta, LV.** Tom Hanks, Christina Marsillach, Benedict Taylor, Anat Atzman, Gila Almagor; ***D:*** Moshe Mizrahi; ***W:*** Moshe Mizrahi, Leah Appet; ***M:*** Philippe Sarde. *LIV*

Every Which Way But Loose 🦴🦴 **1978 (R)** Fairly pointless Eastwood foray featuring Clint as a beer-guzzling, country-music loving truck driver earning a living as a barroom brawler. He and his orangutan travel to Colorado in pursuit of the woman he loves. Behind him are a motorcycle gang and an L.A. cop. All have been victims of his fists. Sequel is "Any Which Way You Can." **119m/C VHS, Beta, LV.** Clint Eastwood, Sondra Locke, Geoffrey Lewis, Beverly D'Angelo, Ruth Gordon; ***D:*** James Fargo; ***M:*** Stephen Dorff. *WAR*

Everybody Sing 🦴🦴 **1938** A down-on-their-luck theatrical family, including Garland (who is kicked out of boarding school for singing Mendelssohn with a swing beat) decides to put on a show in hopes of making a comeback. Dumb plot and boring songs make this one for die-hard Garland fans only. ♫Swing, Mr. Mendelssohn, Swing; The One I Love; Down on Melody Farms; The Show Must Go On; I Wanna Swing; Never Was There Such a Perfect Day; Quainty Dainty Me; Why? Because; Snooks. **80m/B VHS.** Allan Jones, Fanny Brice, Judy Garland, Reginald Owen, Billie Burke, Reginald Gardiner, Lynne Carver, Monty Woolley; ***D:*** Edwin L. Marin; ***M:*** George Bassman. *MGM, MVD*

Everybody Wins 🦴 **1990 (R)** A mystery-romance about a befuddled private eye trying to solve a murder and getting caught up with the bizarre prostitute who hired him. Arthur Miller based this screenplay on his stage drama "Some Kind of Love Story." Confused and, given its pedigree, disappointing mystery. **110m/C VHS, Beta, LV.** Nick Nolte, Debra Winger, Will Patton, Jack Warden, Kathleen Wilhoite, Frank Converse, Frank Military, Judith Ivey; ***D:*** Karel Reisz; ***W:*** Arthur Miller. *ORI*

Everybody's All American 🦴🦴 **1988 (R)** Shallow, sentimental melodrama about a college football star and his cheerleader wife whose lives, subsequent to their youthful glories, is a string of disappointments and tragedies. Decently acted and based on Frank Deford's novel. **127m/C VHS, Beta, LV, 8mm.** Jessica Lange, Dennis Quaid, Timothy Hutton, John Goodman, Carl Lumbly, Ray Baker, Savannah Smith; ***D:*** Taylor Hackford; ***M:*** James Newton Howard. *WAR*

Everybody's Dancin' 🦴½ **1950** A ballroom proprietor's business is marred by random killings in her establishment as the bands play on. ♫Foolish Tears; Oblivious; Deep Freeze Dinah; I Shook; Rhumba Boogie. **66m/B VHS, Beta, LV.** Spade Cooley, Dick Lane, Hal Derwin, The Pioneers, Roddy McDowall; ***D:*** Will Jason. *NO*

Everybody's Fine 🦴🦴½ *Stanno Tutti Bene* **1990 (PG-13)** Mastroianni stars in this bittersweet story of a father on a mission to reunite his five grown children. His journey takes him all over Italy as he tries to bring them together in this touching film about enduring family love. In Italian with English subtitles. **115m/C VHS, LV.** *IT* Marcello Mastroianni, Salvatore Cascio, Valeria Cavalli, Norma Martelli, Marino Cenna, Roberto Nobile, Michele Morgan, Fabio Iellini; ***D:*** Giuseppe Tornatore; ***W:*** Giuseppe Tornatore, Tonino Guerra; ***M:*** Ennio Morricone. *COL, INJ*

Everything Happens at Night 🦴🦴🦴 **1939** Rival reporters Milland and Cummings are torn between the woman they love and the story of a lifetime. One of Henie's best romantic skating vehicles due to the strong performances by the leading men. Henie does take to the ice for a couple of numbers, but this film was largely designed to expand her image as a serious actress. Although it failed to do that, it's good entertainment nonetheless. **76m/B VHS.** Sonja Henie, Ray Milland, Robert Cummings, Maurice Moscovich, Leonid Kinskey, Alan Dinehart, Fritz Feld; ***D:*** Irving Cummings; ***W:*** Art Arthur, Robert Harari. *FXV*

Everything You Always Wanted to Know about Sex (But Were Afraid to Ask) 🦴🦴🦴 **1972 (R)** Satiric comical sketches about sex includes a timid sperm cell, an oversexed court jester, a sheep folly, and a giant disembodied breast. Quite entertaining in its own jolly way. Based on the book by Dr. David Reuben. **88m/C VHS, Beta, LV.** Woody Allen, John Carradine, Lou Jacobi, Louise Lasser, Anthony Quayle, Geoffrey Holder, Lynn Redgrave, Tony Randall, Burt Reynolds, Gene Wilder, Robert Walden, Jay Robinson; ***D:*** Woody Allen; ***W:*** Woody Allen. *MGM, FOX, FCT*

The Evictors *Woof!* **1979 (PG)** Young couple moves into an abandoned, haunted farmhouse in a small Louisiana town. Unfortunately, they don't know anything about its horrible bloody history. And the real estate agent acts kinda funny. AIP Amityville scare-a-thon. **92m/C VHS, Beta.** Vic Morrow, Michael Parks, Jessica Harper, Sue Ane Langdon, Dennis Fimple; ***D:*** Charles B. Pierce; ***W:*** Charles B. Pierce. *LIV, VES*

The Evil 🦴🦴 **1978 (R)** A psychologist must destroy an evil force that is killing off the members of his research team residing at an old mansion. **80m/C VHS, Beta.** Richard Crenna, Joanna Pettet, Andrew Prine, Victor Buono, Cassie Yates; ***D:*** Gus Trikonis. *SUE*

Evil Altar 🦴 **1989 (R)** A man controls a small town, but only so long as he offers sacrifices to the devil! **90m/C VHS.** William Smith, Robert Z'Dar, Pepper Martin, Theresa Cooney, Ryan Rao; ***D:*** James R. Winburn. *HMD*

The Evil Below 🦴 **1987** A couple hits the high seas in search of the lost treasure ship "El Diablo," resting on the ocean floor. In the process they trigger an evil curse and then must attempt to thwart it. **90m/C VHS, Beta.** *SA* June Chadwick, Wayne Crawford; ***D:*** Jean-Claude Dubois. *NO*

Evil Clutch 🦴½ **1989 (R)** A young couple vacationing in the Alps encounter several creepy locals when they find themselves in the midst of a haunted forest. The cinematography is extremely amateurish in this Italian gorefest and the English dubbing is atrocious. However, the special makeup effects are outstanding and the musical score adds a touch of class to this otherwise inept horror film. **88m/C VHS, LV.** *IT* Coralina Cataldi Tassoni, Diego Riba, Elena Cantarone, Luciano Crovato, Stefano Molinari; ***D:*** Andreas Marfori; ***W:*** Andreas Marfori. *UND, RHI*

Evil Dead 🦴🦴½ **1983 (NC-17)** Five vacationing college students unwittingly resurrect demons which transform the students into evil monsters. Exuberantly gory low-budgeter followed by two sequels. **126m/C VHS, Beta, LV.** Bruce Campbell, Ellen Sandweiss, Betsy Baker, Hal Delrich; ***D:*** Sam Raimi; ***W:*** Sam Raimi. *IME*

Evil Dead 2: Dead by Dawn 🦴🦴½ **1987 (R)** A gory, tongue-in-cheek sequel/remake of the original festival of gag and gore, in which an ancient book of magic invokes a crowd of flesh-snacking, joke-tossing ghouls. Followed by yet a third bloodfest. **84m/C VHS, Beta, LV.** Bruce Campbell, Sarah Berry, Dan Hicks, Kassie Wesley, Theodore (Ted) Raimi, Denise Bixler, Richard Domeier; ***D:*** Sam Raimi; ***W:*** Sam Raimi, Scott Spiegel; ***M:*** Joseph Lo Duca. *LIV, VES*

Evil Judgement 🦴½ **1985** A young girl investigates a series of murders and finds the culprit is a psychopathic judge. **93m/C VHS, Beta.** Pamela Collyer, Jack Langedijk, Nanette Workman; ***D:*** Claude Castravelli. *MED*

Evil Laugh *Woof!* **1986 (R)** Medical students and their girlfriends party at an abandoned orphanage, until a serial killer decides to join them. **90m/C VHS.** Tony Griffin, Kim McKamy, Jody Gibson, Dominick Brascia; ***D:*** Dominick Brascia. *CEL*

The Evil Mind 🦴🦴½ *The Clairvoyant* **1934** A fraudulent mind reader predicts many disasters that start coming true. **80m/B VHS, Beta.** *GB* Claude Rains, Fay Wray, Jane Baxter, Felix Aylmer; ***D:*** Maurice Elvey; ***W:*** Charles Bennett. *SNC, NOS, BAR*

The Evil of Frankenstein 🦴🦴 **1964** The third of the Hammer Frankenstein films, with the mad doctor once again finding his creature preserved in ice and thawing him out. Preceded by "The Revenge of Frankenstein" and followed by "Frankenstein Created Woman." **84m/C VHS, Beta.** *GB* Peter Cushing, Duncan Lamont, Peter Woodthorpe, Sandor Eles, Kiwi Kingston, Katy Wild; ***D:*** Freddie Francis; ***M:*** Don Banks. *MCA, MLB*

Evil Spawn 🦴 *Deadly Sting; Alive by Night; Alien Within* **1987** A fading movie queen takes an experimental drug to restore her youthful beauty, but it only turns her into a giant silverfish. Releases under several alternate titles, and with varying running times. **70m/C VHS, Beta.** Bobbie Bresee, John Carradine, Drew Godderis, John Terrance, Dawn Wildsmith; ***D:*** Kenneth J. Hall. *NO*

Evil Spirits 🦴½ **1991 (R)** Boardinghouse tenants are murdered while the crazy landlady cashes their social security checks. This seedy horror cheapie doesn't take itself seriously, and like-minded genre buffs may enjoy the cult-film cast. **95m/C VHS, Beta, LV.** Karen Black, Arte Johnson, Virginia Mayo, Michael Berryman, Martine Beswick, Bert Remsen, Yvette Vickers, Robert Quarry, Mikel Angel, Debra Lamb; ***D:*** Gary Graver; ***W:*** Mikel Angel. *PSM*

The Evil That Men Do 🦴🦴 **1984 (R)** A hitman comes out of retirement to break up a Central American government's political torture ring and, in the process, brings a friend's killer to justice. Based on the novel by R. Lance Hill. **90m/C VHS, Beta, LV, 8mm.** Charles Bronson, Theresa Saldana, Joseph Maher, Jose Ferrer, Rene Enriquez, John Glover, Raymond St. Jacques, Antoinette Bower, Enrique Lucero, Jorge Luke; ***D:*** J. Lee Thompson; ***W:*** John Crowther. *COL*

Evil Toons 🦴½ **1990 (R)** A quartet of lovely coeds on a cleaning job venture into a deserted mansion. There they accidentally release a vulgar, lustful, animated demon who proceeds to cause their clothes to fall off. Can the girls escape the haunted mansion with their sanity, virtue and wardrobes intact? **86m/C VHS, Beta.** David Carradine, Dick Miller, Monique Gabrielle, Suzanne Ager, Stacy Nix, Madison Stone, Don Dowe, Arte Johnson, Michelle (McClellan) Bauer; ***D:*** Fred Olen Ray. *PSM*

Evil Town 🦴 **1987 (R)** In this poorly made film, a wandering guy discovers a town overrun with zombies created by a mad doctor. **88m/C VHS, Beta.** Dean Jagger, James Keach, Robert Walker Jr., Doria Cook, Michele Marsh; ***D:*** Edward Collins. *TWE, HHE*

Evil under the Sun 🦴🦴 **1982 (PG)** An opulent beach resort is the setting as Hercule Poirot attempts to unravel a murder mystery. Based on the Agatha Christie novel. **112m/C VHS, Beta, LV.** *GB* Peter Ustinov, Jane Birkin, Maggie Smith, Colin Blakely, Roddy McDowall, Diana Rigg, Sylvia Miles, James Mason, Nicholas Clay; ***D:*** Guy Hamilton; ***W:*** Anthony Shaffer. *REP*

The Evil Within *Woof! Baby Blood* **1994 (R)** Parasitic beast, with an unquenchable thirst for blood, slithers from the center of the earth into the convenient womb of a young woman. She takes to murdering everyone within reach while preparing to give birth. As disgusting as it sounds. **88m/C VHS.** Emmanuelle Escourrou, Jean-Francois Guillotte; ***D:*** Alain Robak; ***W:*** Alain Robak, Serge Cukier. *APX*

Evil's Commandment 🦴🦴½ **1956** Original vampire film which started the classic Italian horror cycle. A gorgeous Countess needs blood to stay young, otherwise she reverts to a 200-year-old vampire. **?m/B VHS.** *IT* Gianna Maria Canale; ***D:*** Riccardo (Robert Hampton) Freda. *SMW*

Evils of the Night 🦴 **1985** Teenage campers are abducted by sex-crazed alien vampires. Bloody naked mayhem follows. **85m/C VHS, Beta.** John Carradine, Julie Newmar, Tina Louise, Neville Brand, Aldo Ray, Karrie Emerson, Bridget Hollman; ***D:*** Mardi Rustam; ***W:*** Phillip D. Connors. *LIV*

Evilspeak *Woof!* **1982 (R)** Bumbling misfit enrolled at a military school is mistreated by the other cadets. With the help of his computer, he retaliates with satanic power. Bits, bytes, and gore. **89m/C VHS, Beta.** Clint Howard, Don Stark, Lou Gravance, Lauren Lester, R.G. Armstrong, Joe Cortese, Claude Earl Jones, Haywood Nelson; ***D:*** Eric Weston. *FOX*

Evolver 🦴½ **1994 (R)** Teenager wins a robot patterned after a video arcade game but the robot has a secret military weapon's program built into its brain, causing it to evolve into a killing machine. **90m/C VHS, LV.** Ethan Randall, John de Lancie, Cassidy Rae, Cindy Pickett, Paul Dooley; ***D:*** Mark Rosman; ***V:*** William H. Macy. *VMK*

The Ewok Adventure 🦴🦴½ **1984 (G)** Those adorable, friendly and funny characters from "Return of the Jedi" make the jump from film to television in a new adventure from George Lucas. In this installment, the Ewoks save a miraculous child from harm with the help of a young human. This fun-filled adventure has Lucas's thumbprint all over it and great special effects. Followed by "Ewoks: The Battle for Endor." **96m/C VHS, Beta, LV.** Warwick Davis, Eric Walker, Aubree Miller, Fionnula Flanagan; ***D:*** John Korty; ***M:*** Elmer Bernstein, Peter Bernstein. *MGM, FCT*

The Ewoks: Battle for Endor 🦴🦴½ **1985** A television movie based on the furry creatures from "Return of the Jedi," detailing their battle against an evil queen to retain their forest home. Preceded by "The Ewok Adventure." **98m/C VHS, Beta, LV.** Wilford Brimley, Warwick Davis, Aubree Miller, Sian Phillips, Paul Gleason, Eric Walker, Carel Struycken, Niki Bothelo; ***D:*** Jim Wheat, Ken Wheat; ***M:*** Peter Bernstein. *MGM, FCT*

Ex-Cop 🦴🦴 **1993** Pete Danberg is a cop with a drinking problem. He's fired from the force but not before he puts away the "Las Vegas Slasher." Unfortunately for Pete the Slasher makes parole and is out for revenge—using Pete's kidnapped daughter as bait. **97m/C VHS.** Rick Savage, Sandy Hackett, Joan Chamberlain, Douglas Terry, Angi Davidson, Richard Cornell, Jim Williams; ***D:*** Patrick Kerby; ***W:*** Daniel S. Sample. *AIP*

Ex-Lady 🦴🦴 **1933** Davis stars as a liberated woman who loves advertising writer Raymond, but doesn't want to marry him. However, she believes living together is the most suitable arrangement. The two open up an ad agency and complications ensue. Remake of "Illicit," which was filmed only two years earlier with Barbara Stanwyck in the lead role. **65m/B VHS.** Bette Davis, Gene Raymond, Frank McHugh, Claire Dodd, Monroe Owsley, Ferdinand Gottschalk; ***D:*** Robert Florey. *MGM*

Ex-Mrs. Bradford 🦴🦴🦴 **1936** Amateur sleuth Dr. Bradford teams up with his ex-wife to solve a series of murders at the race track. Sophisticated comedy-mystery; witty dialogue. **80m/B VHS, Beta, LV.** William Powell, Jean Arthur, James Gleason, Eric Blore, Robert Armstrong; ***D:*** Stephen Roberts. *NOS, MED*

Excalibur 🦴🦴🦴½ **1981 (R)** A sweeping, visionary retelling of the life of King Arthur, from his conception, to the sword in the stone, to the search for the Holy Grail and the final battle with Mordred. An imperfect, sensationalized version, but still the best yet filmed. **140m/C VHS, Beta, LV.** Nigel Terry, Nicol Williamson, Nicholas Clay, Helen Mirren, Cherie Lunghi, Paul Geoffrey, Gabriel Byrne, Liam Neeson, Patrick Stewart, Charley Boorman, Corin Redgrave; ***D:*** John Boorman; ***W:*** John Boorman, Rospo Pallenberg; ***M:*** Trevor Jones. Nominations: Academy Awards '81: Best Cinematography; Cannes Film Festival '81: Best Film. *WAR, TVC*

Excessive Force 🦴½ **1993 (R)** Routine actioner lives up to its title by offering lots of violence, but little else. Gang leader Young seeks revenge on the cops who he believes ruined a $3 million drug deal. Loner cop Griffith is the only one to survive the grudge killings and goes after Young himself. Talented cast underachieves. Limited theatrical release sent this one almost straight to video. **87m/C VHS, LV.** Thomas Ian Griffith, Lance Henriksen, James Earl Jones, Charlotte Lewis, Tony Todd, Burt Young, W. Earl Brown; ***D:*** Jon Hess; ***W:*** Thomas Ian Griffith; ***C:*** Donald M. Morgan; ***M:*** Charles Bernstein. *NLC, IME*

Excessive Force 2: Force on Force 🦴½ **1995 (R)** Special agent Harly Cordell (Randall) volunteers to hunt down an assassination squad that is turning L.A. into murder central. Seems her former lover Francis Lydell (Gauthier) is head killer and Harly's got a score to settle. Lots of action and nifty weapons. **88m/C VHS, LV.** Stacie Randall, Dan Gauthier, Jay Patterson, John Mese; ***D:*** Jonathan Winfrey; ***W:*** Mark Sevi; ***C:*** Russ Brandt; ***M:*** Kevin Kiner. *NLC, IME*

The Execution 🦴½ **1985** A made-for-television film about five female friends who discover that the Nazi doctor who brutalized them in a concentration camp during WWII is now living a normal life in California. Together they plot his undoing. **92m/C VHS, Beta.** Loretta Swit, Valerie Harper, Sandy Dennis, Jessica Walter, Rip Torn, Barbara Barrie, Robert Hooks, Michael Lerner; ***D:*** Paul Wendkos; ***M:*** Georges Delerue. *PSM*

The Execution of Private Slovik 🦴🦴🦴½ **1974** This quiet powerhouse of a TV movie recounts in straightforward terms the case of Eddie Slovik, a WWII misfit who became the only American soldier executed for desertion since the Civil War. The Levinson/Link screenplay (based on the book by William Bradford Huie) ends up deifying Slovik, which some might find hard to take. But there's no arguing the impact of the drama, or of Sheen's unaffected lead performance. **122m/C VHS.** Martin Sheen, Mariclare Costello, Ned Beatty, Gary Busey, Matt Clark, Ben Hammer, Warren Kemmerling; ***D:*** Lamont Johnson; ***W:*** Richard Levinson, William Link. *MCA*

Execution of Raymond Graham ♂♂½ **1985** The lawyers and family of Raymond Graham struggle to keep him from being executed for murder. Based on a true story; made for television. **104m/C VHS, Beta.** Morgan Freeman, Jeff Fahey, Kate Reid, Laurie Metcalf, Josef Sommer; ***D:*** Daniel Petrie. *NO*

The Executioner ♂♂ **1970 (PG)** A thriller wherein a British spy must prove that his former colleague is a double agent. Elements of backstabbing, betrayal, and espionage abound. **107m/C VHS, Beta.** *GB* Judy Geeson, Oscar Homolka, Charles Gray, Nigel Patrick, George Peppard, Joan Collins, Keith Michell; ***D:*** Sam Wanamaker. *COL, GKK*

The Executioner ♂ *Like Father, Like Son; Massacre Mafia Style* **1978 (R)** A very cheap, very "Godfather"-like story of a mafia family gone awry. Also known as "Like Father, Like Son" and "Massacre Mafia Style." **84m/C VHS, Beta.** Duke Mitchell, Vic Caesar, Dominic Micelli, John Strong, Jim Williams, Lorenzo Dodo; ***D:*** Duke Mitchell; ***W:*** Duke Mitchell. *GEM, MRV*

Executioner of Venice ♂ **1963** Marauding pirates with time on hands swarm in from the Adriatic Sea and attempt to rob the Venetians blind. The Doge and his godson come to the rescue. **90m/C VHS, Beta.** Guy Madison, Lex Barker, Alessandra Panaro; ***D:*** Louis Capauno. *NO*

The Executioner, Part 2: Frozen Scream ♂ **1984 (R)** Brutal feud rocks the Mafia, and a crime kingpin's passionate son seeks revenge on his father's slayers. Not a sequel to any other films bearing similar titles. Strange thing is, no "Executioner, Part I" was ever made. Pretty laughable. **150m/C VHS, Beta.** Chris Mitchum, Aldo Ray, Antoine John Mottet, Renee Harmon; ***D:*** James Bryant. *GEM*

The Executioner's Song ♂♂½ **1982** European version of the television movie based on Norman Mailer's Pulitzer Prize-winner, recounting the life and death of convicted murderer Gary Gilmore. Features adult-minded footage not seen in the U.S. version. **157m/C VHS, Beta.** Tommy Lee Jones, Rosanna Arquette, Eli Wallach, Christine Lahti, Jenny Wright, Jordan Clark, Steven Keats; ***D:*** Lawrence Schiller. *LIV*

Executive Action ♂♂½ **1973 (PG)** Political thriller providing a different look at the events leading to the assassination of JFK. In this speculation, a millionaire pays a professional spy to organize a secret conspiracy to kill President Kennedy. Ryan's final film. Adapted by Dalton Trumbo from Mark Lane's "Rush to Judgement." **91m/C VHS, Beta, LV.** Burt Lancaster, Robert Ryan, Will Geer, Gilbert Green, John Anderson; ***D:*** David Miller; ***C:*** Robert Steadman; ***M:*** Randy Edelman. *WAR*

Executive Decision ♂♂ **1996 (R)** Those wacky terrorists are at it again. You would think that after getting their butts kicked in almost every action picture since 1980 that they would learn. But here they are again, hijacking a 747, cutting off communications, and affixing a nerve gas bomb to the plane. This time a group of high tech commandos, led by Russell and (briefly) Seagal, must sneak onto the plane and generally mess up the bad guys plans. Brave stewardess Berry helps tango with the central casting mad dog terrorists. The title refers to the President's decision on whether or not to blow the plane up in order to avert disaster. Or maybe "Die Hard: Ad Nauseum" wasn't available. **132m/C VHS, LV.** Kurt Russell, Halle Berry, Oliver Platt, John Leguizamo, Steven Seagal, Joe Morton, David Suchet, B.D. Wong, Len Cariou, Whip Hubley, J.T. Walsh; ***D:*** Stuart Baird; ***W:*** Jim Thomas, John Thomas; ***C:*** Alex Thomson; ***M:*** Jerry Goldsmith. *WAR*

Executive Suite ♂♂♂ **1954** One of the first dog-eat-dog dramas about high finance and big business. The plot centers on the question of a replacement for the freshly buried owner of a gigantic furniture company. **104m/B VHS, Beta.** William Holden, June Allyson, Barbara Stanwyck, Fredric March, Walter Pidgeon, Louis Calhern, Shelley Winters, Paul Douglas, Nina Foch, Dean Jagger; ***D:*** Robert Wise; ***W:*** Ernest Lehman. Nominations: Academy Awards '54: Best Art Direction/Set Decoration (B & W), Best Black and White Cinematography, Best Costume Design (B & W), Best Supporting Actress (Foch). *MGM*

Exiled in America ♂♂ **1990** A Central American freedom fighter (Albert) flees his country for the United States, settling in a small town with his wife. She gets a waitressing job at a local diner, telling the owner her husband died in an accident, and the owner's son winds up falling in love with her. Things get complicated when the death squad, led by a corrupt CIA agent, follows Albert to his hiding place, and the local sheriff threatens to blow his cover. **84m/C VHS.** Maxwell Caulfield, Edward Albert, Viveca Lindfors, Kamala Lopez, Stella Stevens, Wings Hauser; ***D:*** Paul Leder; ***W:*** Paul Leder. *PSM*

Exiled to Shanghai ♂♂½ **1937** A couple of newsreel men invent a television device that revolutionizes the business. **65m/B VHS.** Wallace Ford, June Travis, Dean Jagger, William "Billy" Bakewell, Arthur Lake, Jonathan Hale, William Harrigan, Sarah Padden; ***D:*** Nick Grinde. *NOS, DVT, HEG*

Exit ♂½ **1995 (R)** Pair of criminals take a strip club's dancers as hostages when their robbery attempt goes bad. Exotic dancer Whirry manages to escape and hook up with bodyguard Bradley to stop the creeps. Lame action, silly dialogue, very attractive Whirry. **90m/C VHS.** Shannon Whirry, David Bradley, Larry Manetti; ***D:*** Ric Roman Waugh. *REP*

Exit the Dragon, Enter the Tiger ♂½ **1976** Story about the death of karate master Bruce Lee. **84m/C VHS, Beta.** *TWE*

Exit to Eden ♂½ **1994 (R)** Anne Rampling's (aka Anne Rice) novel focused on fulfilling S&M sexual fantasies, but director Marshall goes for laughs with a buddy cops-out-of-water sitcom subplot, as undercover cops Aykroyd and O'Donnell track a suspected jewel thief to the fantasy resort of Eden, run by dominatrix Delany. (What was the pitch for this one? Think "Another Stakeout" meets "Tie Me Up, Tie Me Down." It'll be great. Really.) Neither plot works, resulting in a kinky movie with no kink, and a comedy with few laughs. O'Donnell holds up her end, providing what few yuks there are. Everyone else, especially Aykroyd and Delany, seem to be sleepwalking. Lucky for them. **113m/C VHS.** Dan Aykroyd, Rosie O'Donnell, Dana Delany, Paul Mercurio, Hector Elizondo, Stuart Wilson, Iman, Sandi Korn; ***D:*** Garry Marshall; ***W:*** Deborah Amelon, Bob Brunner; ***M:*** Patrick Doyle. Golden Raspberry Awards '94: Worst Supporting Actress (O'Donnell). *HBO*

Exodus ♂♂♂ **1960** Chronicles the post-WWII partition of Palestine into a homeland for Jews; the anguish of refugees from Nazi concentration camps held on ships in the Mediterranean; the struggle of the tiny nation with forces dividing it from within and destroying it from the outside; and the heroic men and women who saw a job to be done and did it. Based on the novel by Leon Uris; filmed in Cyprus and Israel. Preminger battled the Israeli government, the studio, and the novel's author to complete this epic. Cost more than $4 million, a phenomenal amount at the time. **208m/C VHS, Beta, LV.** Paul Newman, Eva Marie Saint, Lee J. Cobb, Sal Mineo, Ralph Richardson, Hugh Griffith, Gregory Ratoff, Felix Aylmer, Peter Lawford, Jill Haworth, John Derek, David Opatoshu, Marius Goring, Alexandra Stewart, Michael Wager, Martin Benson, Paul Stevens, George Maharis; ***D:*** Otto Preminger; ***W:*** Dalton Trumbo; ***M:*** Ernest Gold. Academy Awards '60: Best Original Score; Golden Globe Awards '61: Best Supporting Actor (Mineo); Nominations: Academy Awards '60: Best Color Cinematography, Best Supporting Actor (Mineo). *FOX, SWC*

Exorcism ♂½ **1974** A satanic cult in a small English village commits a series of gruesome crimes that have the authorities baffled. **90m/C VHS, Beta.** Paul Naschy, Maria Perschy; ***D:*** Juan Bosch. *HHE*

Exorcism's Daughter ♂ *House of Insane Women* **1974 (R)** While running an insane asylum, a man discovers that a woman has lost her mind because as a child, she witnessed her mother's death during an exorcism. Pretty grim but interesting for genre fans. A natural double feature with "House of Psychotic Women." **93m/C VHS.** *SP* Amelia Gade, Francesco Rabal, Espartaco Santoni; ***D:*** Rafael Morena Alba. *SNC*

The Exorcist ♂♂♂½ **1973 (R)** Truly terrifying story of a young girl who is possessed by a malevolent spirit. Brilliantly directed by Friedkin, with underlying themes of the workings and nature of fate. Impeccable casting and unforgettable, thought-provoking performances. A rare film that remains startling and engrossing with every viewing, it spawned countless imitations and changed the way horror films were made. Based on the bestseller by Blatty, who also wrote the screenplay. Not for the squeamish. When first released, the film created mass hysteria in theaters, with people fainting and paramedics on the scene. **120m/C VHS, Beta, LV.** Ellen Burstyn, Linda Blair, Jason Miller, Max von Sydow, Jack MacGowran, Lee J. Cobb, Kitty Winn; ***D:*** William Friedkin; ***W:*** William Peter Blatty; ***C:*** Owen Roizman; ***M:*** Jack Nitzsche. Academy Awards '73: Best Adapted Screenplay, Best Sound; Golden Globe Awards '74: Best Director (Friedkin), Best Film—Drama, Best Screenplay, Best Supporting Actress (Blair); Nominations: Academy Awards '73: Best Actress (Burstyn), Best Art Direction/Set Decoration, Best Cinematography, Best Director (Friedkin), Best Film Editing, Best Picture, Best Supporting Actor (Miller), Best Supporting Actress (Blair). *WAR*

The Exorcist 2: The Heretic ♂♂ **1977 (R)** Unnecessary sequel to the 1973 hit "The Exorcist" which featured extensive recutting by Boorman. After four years, Blair is still under psychiatric care, suffering from the effects of being possessed by the devil. Meanwhile, a priest investigates the first exorcist's work as he tries to help the head-spinning lass. Decent special effects. **118m/C VHS, Beta.** Richard Burton, Linda Blair, Louise Fletcher, Kitty Winn, James Earl Jones, Ned Beatty, Max von Sydow; ***D:*** John Boorman; ***M:*** Ennio Morricone. *WAR*

Exorcist 3: Legion ♂♂ **1990 (R)** Apparently subscribing to the two wrongs make a right school of sequels, this time novelist Blatty is the director. The result is slightly better than the first sequel, but still a far cry from the original. Fifteen years after later, Detective Kinderman (Scott) is faced with a series of really gross murders bearing the mark of a serial killer who was flambeed in the electric chair on the same night as the exorcism of the pea-soup expectorating devil of the original. With the aid of priests Flanders and Douriff the detective stalks the transmigratory terror—without the help of Linda Blair, who was at the time spoofing "The Exorcist" in "Repossessed." **105m/C VHS, Beta, LV.** George C. Scott, Ed Flanders, Jason Miller, Nicol Williamson, Scott Wilson, Brad Dourif, Nancy Fish, George DiCenzo, Viveca Lindfors; ***D:*** William Peter Blatty; ***W:*** William Peter Blatty. *FOX, CCB*

Exotica ♂♂♂ **1994 (R)** Daunting look at eroticism, secrecy, and despair. Christina (Kirshner) is at the center of some complicated relationships. She dresses as a schoolgirl while working at the Exotica strip club in Toronto, where her former lover Eric (Koteas) is the creepily suggestive DJ. Christina's also the obsession of seemingly mild-mannered tax man Francis (Greenwood), who has turned her table dancing into a strange private ritual. Lest this seem to make sense be assured that director Egoyan has much, much more going on—not all of it clear and most of it disturbing. **104m/C VHS, LV.** *CA* Mia Kirshner, Elias Koteas, Bruce Greenwood, Don McKellar, Victor Garber, Arsinee Khanjian, Sarah Polley; ***D:*** Atom Egoyan; ***W:*** Atom Egoyan; ***M:*** Mychael Danna. Genie Awards '94: Best Art Direction/Set Decoration, Best Cinematography, Best Costume Design, Best Director (Egoyan), Best Film, Best Screenplay, Best Supporting Actor (McKellar), Best Original Score; Toronto-City Award '94: Best Canadian Feature Film; Nominations: Genie Awards '94: Best Actor (Greenwood), Best Actor (Koteas). *MAX*

Expect No Mercy 🦴 **1995 (R)** Government agent must rescue a fellow agent being held in a virtual reality center that trains assassins to commit murder. **91m/C VHS.** Billy Blanks, Jalal Merhi. *AVE*

The Expendables 🦴½ **1989 (R)** A rugged captain turns a platoon of criminals and misfits into a tough fighting unit for a particularly dangerous mission from which they might not return. See the "Dirty Dozen" instead. **89m/C VHS, Beta, LV.** Anthony Finetti, Peter Nelson, Loren Haynes, Kevin Duffis; ***D:*** Cirio H. Santiago; ***W:*** Phillip Alderton. *MED*

Experience Preferred... But Not Essential 🦴🦴½ **1983 (PG)** An English schoolgirl gets her first job at a resort where she learns about life. Made for British television. **77m/C VHS, Beta.** *GB* Elizabeth Edmonds, Sue Wallace, Geraldine Griffith, Karen Meagher, Ron Bain, Alun Lewis, Robert Blythe; ***D:*** Peter Duffell; ***W:*** June Roberts; ***C:*** Phil Meheux. *MGM*

Experiment in Terror 🦴🦴🦴 **1962** A psychopath kidnaps a girl in order to blackmail her sister, a bank teller, into embezzling $100,000. **123m/B VHS, Beta, LV.** Lee Remick, Glenn Ford, Stefanie Powers, Ross Martin; ***D:*** Blake Edwards; ***M:*** Henry Mancini. *COL, IME*

Experiment Perilous 🦴🦴🦴 **1945** A psychologist and a recently widowed woman band together to find her husband's murderer. An atmospheric vintage mystery. **91m/B VHS, Beta.** Hedy Lamarr, Paul Lukas, George Brent, Albert Dekker; ***D:*** Jacques Tourneur. Nominations: Academy Awards '45: Best Interior Decoration. *MED*

The Expert 🦴🦴 **1995 (R)** Special operations expert John Lomax (Speakman) helps catch the creep who murdered his sister. But the killer gets a slap-on-the-wrist sentence, ticking Lomax off mightily. Now, the duo prepare for a deadly last confrontation. **92m/C VHS.** Jeff Speakman, James Brolin, Michael Shaner, Alex Datcher, Wolfgang Bodison, Elizabeth Gracen, Red West, Jim Varney; ***D:*** Rick Avery; ***W:*** Max Allan Collins; ***C:*** Levie Isaacks; ***M:*** Ashley Irwin. *ORI*

The Experts 🦴🦴 **1989 (PG-13)** When the KGB needs real Americans for their spies to study, they kidnap two out-of-work New Yorkers who mistakenly believe that they have been hired to open a nightclub in Nebraska. Shot on location in Canada. Sometimes funny and directed by former Second City TV MacKenzie Brother, Dave Thomas. **94m/C VHS, Beta, LV, 8mm.** John Travolta, Arye Gross, Charles Martin Smith, Kelly Preston, James Keach, Deborah Foreman, Brian Doyle-Murray; ***D:*** Dave Thomas; ***W:*** Nick Thiel, Eric Alter; ***M:*** Marvin Hamlisch. *PAR*

Explorers 🦴🦴½ **1985 (PG)** Intelligent family fare involving three young boys who use a contraption from their makeshift laboratory to travel to outer space. From the director of "Gremlins," displaying Dante's characteristic surreal wit and sense of irony. **107m/C VHS, Beta, LV.** Ethan Hawke, River Phoenix, Jason Presson, Amanda Peterson, Mary Kay Place, Dick Miller, Robert Picardo, Dana Ivey, Meshach Taylor, Brooke Bundy; ***D:*** Joe Dante; ***W:*** Eric Luke; ***M:*** Jerry Goldsmith. *PAR*

Explosion 🦴½ **1969 (R)** Distraught and disturbed young man evades the draft after losing a brother in Vietnam. Arriving in Canada, he meets another draft-dodger with whom he embarks on a murderous rampage. **96m/C VHS, Beta.** Don Stroud, Gordon Thomson, Michele Chicione, Richard Conte; ***D:*** Jules Bricken. *TWE*

Exposed 🦴🦴 **1983 (R)** High fashion model Kinski falls in with a terrorist gang through a connection with violinist Nureyev. Weak plotting undermines the end of this political thriller. However, Kinski is brilliant, stripping the barrier between performance and audience. **100m/C VHS, Beta.** Nastassia Kinski, Rudolf Nureyev, Harvey Keitel, Ian McShane, Bibi Andersson; ***D:*** James Toback; ***W:*** James Toback; ***M:*** Georges Delerue. *MGM*

Exposure 🦴 **1991 (R)** A rugged American photographer (Coyote) on assignment in Rio turns vigilante to locate the vicious killer of a young prostitute. Coyote and his girlfriend (Pays) get caught up in the deadly underworld of international arms trading and drug running as they search for the murderer. **99m/C VHS.** Peter Coyote, Amanda Pays, Tcheky Karyo; ***M:*** Todd Boekelheide. *HBO*

Express to Terror 🦴½ **1979** Passengers aboard an atomic-powered train en route to Los Angeles attempt to kill a sleazy theatrical agent. Pilot for the "Supertrain" series. **120m/C VHS, Beta.** Steve Lawrence, George Hamilton, Vic Morrow, Broderick Crawford, Robert Alda, Don Stroud, Fred Williamson, Stella Stevens, Don Meredith; ***D:*** Dan Curtis. *PSM*

Exquisite Corpses 🦴½ **1988** An Oklahoma hayseed charges to New York with a new, slick image. He meets the wife of a wealthy man, and together they organize a murderous operation. **95m/C VHS, LV.** Zoe Tamerlaine Lund, Gary Knox, Daniel Chapman, Ruth Collins; ***D:*** Temistocles Lopez. *NO*

The Exterminating Angel 🦴🦴🦴½ **1962** A fierce, funny surreal nightmare, wherein dinner guests find they cannot, for any definable reason, leave the dining room; full of dream imagery and characteristically scatological satire. One of Bunuel's best, in Spanish with English subtitles. **95m/B VHS, Beta.** *MX SP* Silvia Pinal, Enrique Rambal, Jacqueline Andere, Jose Baviera, Augusto Benedico, Luis Beristain; ***D:*** Luis Bunuel. *INJ, HTV, FCT*

Exterminator 🦴 **1980 (R)** Vietnam veteran hunts down the gang that assaulted his friend and becomes the target of the police, the CIA and the underworld in this bloody banal tale of murder and intrigue. Followed by creatively titled "Exterminator II." **101m/C VHS, Beta, LV.** Christopher George, Samantha Eggar, Robert Ginty; ***D:*** James Glickenhaus. *SUE, NLC*

Exterminator 2 🦴 **1984 (R)** The Exterminator battles the denizens of New York's underworld after his girlfriend is crippled, then murdered by the ruthless Mr. X. Violence galore. **88m/C VHS, Beta.** Robert Ginty, Mario Van Peebles, Deborah Geffner, Frankie Faison; ***D:*** Mark Buntzman; ***W:*** Mark Buntzman. *MGM*

Exterminators of the Year 3000 *Woof!* **1983 (R)** The Exterminator and his mercenary girlfriend battle with nuclear mutants over the last remaining tanks of purified water on Earth. Low-budget Road Warrior rip-off. **101m/C VHS, Beta.** *IT SP* Robert Jannucci, Alicia Moro, Alan Collins, Fred Harris; ***D:*** Jules Harrison. *NO*

Extra Girl 🦴🦴 **1923** A silent melodrama/farce about a farm girl, brilliantly played by Normand, who travels to Hollywood to be a star. Once in the glamour capital, she gets used and abused for her trouble. **87m/B VHS, Beta, LV, 8mm.** Mabel Normand, Ralph Graves, Vernon Dent; ***D:*** F. Richard Jones; ***W:*** Mack Sennett. *VYY, GPV*

Extramuros 🦴🦴 **1985** A nun (Maura), living in a convent during the Spanish Inquisition, tries to repress her lesbian desires while the convent vies for fame and money through faked visions. Spanish with subtitles. **120m/C VHS.** *SP* Carmen Maura; ***D:*** Miguel Picazo. *FCT*

The Extraordinary Adventures of Mr. West in the Land of the Bolsheviks 🦴🦴 **1924** The first achievement from the Kuleshov workshop, a wacky satire on American insularity depicting a naive and prejudiced American visiting Russia and being taken advantage of. Silent. **55m/B VHS, Beta.** Vsevolod Pudovkin, Boris Barnet; ***D:*** Lev Kuleshov. *FCT, INJ*

Extreme Justice 🦴🦴½ **1993 (R)** A violent expose of the Special Investigations Section of the Los Angeles Police Department, an elite, undercover squad which specialized in catching violent repeat offenders. But their tactics left something to be desired. They were accused of stalking their prey until they committed a crime and then dealing with the criminal by shooting them in the act. Lots of gunplay. Originally a theatrical film that was pulled for release in the wake of the Rodney King verdict. **96m/C VHS, LV.** Lou Diamond Phillips, Scott Glenn, Yaphet Kotto, Ed Lauter, Chelsea Field; ***W:*** Robert Boris. *VMK*

Extreme Prejudice 🦴🦴 **1987 (R)** A redneck Texas Ranger fights a powerful drug kingpin along the U.S.-Mexican border. Once best friends, they now fight for justice and the heart of the woman they both love. **104m/C VHS, Beta, LV.** Nick Nolte, Powers Boothe, Maria Conchita Alonso, Michael Ironside, Rip Torn; ***D:*** Walter Hill; ***W:*** Deric Washburn; ***M:*** Jerry Goldsmith. *LIV*

Extreme Vengeance 🦴🦴 **1993** Police officer David puts mafia crime boss Mario Blanco away for ten years, then exposes police corruption and goes into hiding. When Blanco gets out, he seeks revenge on David's family, forcing David out of hiding to protect what is his. Available in Spanish subtitles. **97m/C VHS, LV.** *NHO*

Extremities 🦴🦴 **1986 (R)** An adaptation of the topical William Mastrosimone play about an intended rape victim who turns on her attacker, captures him, and plots to kill him. Violent and exploitive. **83m/C VHS, Beta, LV, 8mm.** Farrah Fawcett, Diana Scarwid, James Russo, Alfre Woodard; ***D:*** Robert M. Young; ***W:*** William Mastrosimone. *PAR*

The Eye Creatures 🦴 **1965** Alien creatures in the form of eyeballs are fought off by a teenager and his girlfriend. A low-budget, gory, science fiction feature. **80m/B VHS.** John Ashley, Cynthia Hull, Warren Hammack, Chet Davis, Bill Peck; ***D:*** Larry Buchanan. *NOS, SNC*

An Eye for an Eye 🦴🦴 **1981 (R)** A story of pursuit and revenge with Norris as an undercover cop pitted against San Francisco's underworld and high society. **106m/C VHS, Beta.** Chuck Norris, Christopher Lee, Richard Roundtree, Matt Clark, Mako, Maggie Cooper; ***D:*** Steve Carver; ***W:*** James Bruner; ***M:*** William Goldstein. *SUE, NLC*

An Eye for an Eye 🦴 **1995 (R)** A made-for-TV script that ended up on the feature film pile (and we do mean pile). Manipulative story has Karen McCann (Field) listening on the phone as her daughter is raped and killed by a scuzzball drifter (Sutherland). He's caught, but released on a technicality, driving Mom to join a vigilante group and plot revenge. Not a great career move for the director or surprisingly distinguished cast, who are given nothing but cardboard characters and push-button emotional cliches to work with. Shamelessly plays on middle class fears of crime and doubts about the judicial system. Based on the novel by Erika Holzer. **102m/C VHS, Beta.** Sally Field, Ed Harris, Kiefer Sutherland, Beverly D'Angelo, Joe Mantegna, Keith David; ***D:*** John Schlesinger; ***W:*** Amanda Silver, Rick Jaffa; ***C:*** Amir M. Mokri; ***M:*** James Newton Howard. *PAR*

Eye of the Demon 🦴 **1987** A couple moves to a small town in Massachusetts and discovers that the area had once been a haven for witchcraft. To their horror, they soon find that old habits die hard, and the spellcasting continues in a nearby graveyard. Made for cable television. **92m/C VHS.** Tim Matheson, Pamela Sue Martin, Woody Harrelson, Barbara Billingsley, Susan Ruttan; ***D:*** Carl Schenkel. *VMK*

Eye of the Eagle 🦴½ **1987 (R)** A special task force is given a dangerous assignment during the Vietnam war. **84m/C VHS, Beta.** Brett Clark, Ed Crick, Robert Patrick, William Steis, Cec Verrell; ***D:*** Cirio H. Santiago. *MGM*

Eye of the Eagle 2 🦴 **1989 (R)** When his platoon is betrayed and killed in Vietnam, a surviving soldier joins with a beautiful girl and seeks revenge. **79m/C VHS, Beta.** Todd Field, Andy Wood, Ken Jacobson, Ronald Lawrence; ***D:*** Carl Franklin. *MGM*

Eye of the Eagle 3 🦴½ **1991 (R)** Filipino-made Vietnam-War shoot-em-up, rack-em-up, shoot-em-up again, with U.S. forces pinned down against seemingly overwhelming odds. Violent. **90m/C VHS.** Steve Kanaly, Ken Wright, Peter Nelson, Carl Franklin; ***D:*** Cirio H. Santiago; ***W:*** Carl Franklin. *NHO*

Eye of the Needle 🦴🦴½ **1981 (R)** Based on Ken Follett's novel about a German spy posing as a shipwrecked sailor on a deserted English island during WWII. Lonely, sad, yet capable of terrible violence, he is stranded on an isolated island while en route to report to his Nazi commander. He becomes involved with an English woman living on the island, and begins to contemplate his role in the war. **112m/C VHS, Beta.** Donald Sutherland, Kate Nelligan, Ian Bannen, Christopher Cazenove, Philip Brown; ***D:*** Richard Marquand; ***M:*** Miklos Rozsa. *MGM, FOX*

Eye of the Octopus ♪ **1982** Based on a true story of a boy who traveled to a Pacific Island to learn the ways of the people there. **23m/C VHS, Beta.** *JOU*

Eye of the Storm ♪♪½ **1991 (R)** At the highway gas station/motel/diner where they live, two young brothers witness their parent's murder. Their younger brother is blinded in the same incident. Ten years later both brothers are still there and the tragedy may have turned one of them psychotic. When the abusive Gladstone and his young and sexy wife are stranded at the gas station it brings out the worst in everyone, with a violent climax during an equally violent thunderstorm. **98m/C VHS.** Craig Sheffer, Bradley Gregg, Lara Flynn Boyle, Dennis Hopper, Leon Rippy; ***D:*** Yuri Zeltser. *NLC*

Eye of the Stranger ♪½ **1993 (R)** Suspenser about a nameless stranger who sets out to solve the mystery of a small western town and its corrupt mayor. **96m/C VHS.** David Heavener, Sally Kirkland, Martin Landau, Don Swayze, Stella Stevens, John Pleshette, Joe Estevez, Thomas F. Duffy; ***D:*** David Heavener; ***W:*** David Heavener; ***M:*** Robert Garrett. *MNC*

Eye of the Tiger ♪♪ **1986 (R)** A righteous ex-con battles a crazed, crack-dealing motorcycle gang that terrorized and murdered his wife, and is moving on to infest his town. **90m/C VHS, Beta.** Gary Busey, Yaphet Kotto, Seymour Cassel, Bert Remsen, William Smith; ***D:*** Richard Sarafian. *LIV*

Eye of the Wolf ♪♪½ **1995 (PG-13)** Zoologist (Fahey) brings a wild wolf into civilization and then must fight to save the animal from execution. Kazan (a wolf-dog mix) is the true star—and rightly so. **96m/C VHS.** Jeff Fahey, Sophie Duez. *VMK*

Eye on the Sparrow ♪♪½ **1991 (PG)** A couple (Winningham and Carradine) desperately want to raise a child of their own, but the system classifies them as unfit parents since they are both blind. Together they successfully fight the system in this inspiring made for television movie that was based on a true story. **94m/C VHS.** Mare Winningham, Keith Carradine, Conchata Ferrell, Sandy McPeak, Karen Lee, Bianca Rose; ***D:*** John Korty. *REP*

Eye Witness ♪♪½ *Your Witness* **1949** An American attorney goes abroad to free a friend from the British legal system. A book of poems becomes the necessary device in deducing the whereabouts of the witness testifying to his friend's alibi. **104m/B VHS.** *GB* Robert Montgomery, Felix Aylmer, Leslie Banks, Michael Ripper, Patricia Wayne; ***D:*** Robert Montgomery; ***M:*** Malcolm Arnold. *NOS, SNC, RXM*

Eyeball *Woof! Gatto Rossi In Un Labirinto Do Vetro* **1978 (R)** An intrepid policeman is stumped by a madman who is removing eyeballs from his victims. At least they won't have to watch this movie. **87m/C VHS, Beta.** *IT* John Richardson, Martine Brochard; ***D:*** Umberto Lenzi. *PSM*

Eyes Behind the Stars ♪ **1972** A news photographer accidentally gets a few pictures of invading aliens, but nobody takes him seriously, particularly the government. **95m/C VHS, Beta.** *IT* Martin Balsam, Robert Hoffman, Nathalie Delon, Sherry Buchanan; ***D:*** Roy Garrett. *NO*

Eyes of a Stranger *Woof!* **1981 (R)** Terrifying maniac stalks his female prey by watching their every move. Tewes is cast as a journalist, the stronger of the two sisters in this exploitative slasher. **85m/C VHS, Beta.** Lauren Tewes, John Disanti, Jennifer Jason Leigh; ***D:*** Ken Wiederhorn; ***W:*** Eric L. Bloom; ***M:*** Richard Einhorn. *WAR*

Eyes of a Witness ♪♪½ **1994** American businessman Roy Baxter (Travanti) travels to Kenya to rescue his daughter (Grey) from danger in the African bush. But Roy is falsely charged with murdering a government official and must take on the police to prove his innocence. **90m/C VHS, LV.** Daniel J. Travanti, Jennifer Grey, Carl Lumbly. *NLC, IME*

Eyes of an Angel ♪♪½ **1991 (PG-13)** A widower (Travolta), who's heavily involved in gambling, is forced to go on the run with his young daughter (Raab) when a deal goes sour. She must abandon the family dog, who manages to follow them from Chicago to California anyway. Talk about loyalty! **91m/C VHS, LV.** John Travolta, Elie Raab, Jeffrey DeMunn; ***D:*** Robert Harmon. *LIV*

Eyes of Fire ♪♪ **1984 (R)** In early rural America, a group of pioneers set up camp in the wilderness and are besieged during the night by Indian witchcraft. **86m/C VHS, Beta, LV.** Dennis Lipscomb, Rebecca Stanley, Fran Ryan, Rob Paulsen, Guy Boyd, Karlene Crockett; ***D:*** Avery Crounse; ***W:*** Avery Crounse; ***M:*** Brad Fiedel. *VES*

Eyes of Julia Deep ♪♪ **1918** Rare silent film featuring the ill-fated Minter as Julia, a woman who prevents Terry (Forrest) from killing himself. Piano scored. **54m/B VHS.** Mary Miles Minter, Alan Forrest, Alice Wilson, George Periolat; ***D:*** Lloyd Ingraham. *GPV*

Eyes of Laura Mars ♪♪½ **1978 (R)** A photographer exhibits strange powers—she can foresee a murder before it happens through her snapshots. In time she realizes that the person responsible for a series of killings is tracking her. Title song performed by Barbra Streisand. **104m/C VHS, Beta, LV.** Faye Dunaway, Tommy Lee Jones, Brad Dourif, Rene Auberjonois, Raul Julia, Darlanne Fluegel, Michael Tucker; ***D:*** Irvin Kershner; ***W:*** John Carpenter, David Zelag Goodman. *GKK*

Eyes of Texas ♪½ **1948** Bryant, a lawyer who uses a pack of killer dogs to get the land she wants, is pursued by a U.S Marshal played decently by Rogers. **54m/B VHS, Beta.** Roy Rogers, Lynn (Mary Hart) Roberts, Andy Devine, Nana Bryant, Roy Barcroft; ***D:*** William Witney. *NOS, VCN, TIM*

The Eyes of the Amaryllis ♪½ **1982 (R)** A young girl becomes involved in a mysterious game when she arrives in Nantucket to care for her insane, invalid grandmother. Based on the story by Natalie Babbitt and filmed on location on Nantucket Island. **94m/C VHS, Beta.** Martha Byrne, Ruth Ford, Guy Boyd, Jonathan Bolt, Katharine Houghton; ***D:*** Frederick King Keller. *LIV, VES*

Eyes of the Beholder ♪♪ **1992 (R)** Janice is a psychopathic serial killer who suffered brain damage from a botched surgical attempt to reverse his insanity. Now he's escaped from the state mental institution, heading straight for the secluded home of the doctor who made him crazier than ever. During a raging storm, Janice stalks the doctor, his wife, and their two hapless dinner guests in a sadistic game of cat-and-mouse. **89m/C VHS, LV.** Lenny Von Dohlen, Joanna Pacula, Matt McCoy, George Lazenby, Kylie Travis, Charles Napier; ***D:*** Lawrence L. Simeone; ***W:*** Lawrence L. Simeone; ***M:*** Greg Turner. *COL*

Eyes of the Panther **1990** One of Shelley Duvall's "Nightmare Classics" series, this adaptation of an Ambrose Bierce story concerns a pioneer girl haunted for years by the animal urges of a wild cat. **60m/C VHS, Beta, LV.** Daphne Zuniga, C. Thomas Howell, John Stockwell; ***D:*** Noel Black. *NO*

Eyes of Turpin Are Upon You! ♪♪ **1921** Two early Turpin silent comedies: "Idle Eyes" and "A Small Town Idol." **56m/B VHS, Beta.** Ben Turpin, Ramon Novarro, Marie Prevost, James Finlayson. *VYY*

The Eyes of Youth ♪♪ **1919** A young woman searches her soul for answers: to marry or not to marry is the question. A little foresight, in the form of a glimpse into the hypothetical future, helps her make the right choice. Very early Valentino fare in which the sheik plays a cad. **78m/B VHS, Beta.** Clara Kimball Young, Edmund Lowe, Rudolph Valentino. *VYY, FCT, VYY*

Eyes Right! ♪♪ **1926** Based on a story by Ernest Grayman, this portrayal of life in a military prep school has its main character experience struggle, recognition, love, jealousy, and triumph. Silent. **46m/B VHS, Beta.** Francis X. Bushman. *VYY, GPV*

The Eyes, the Mouth ♪♪ **1983 (R)** A young man has an affair with his dead twin brother's fiancee. Happiness eludes them as they are haunted by the deceased's memory and the family's grief. In Italian with English subtitles. **100m/C VHS, Beta.** *FR IT* Lou Castel, Angela Molina; ***D:*** Marco Bellochio; ***W:*** Marco Bellochio. *COL, INJ*

Eyewitness ♪♪½ *The Janitor* **1981 (R)** When a murder occurs in the office building of a star-struck janitor, he fabricates a tale in order to initiate a relationship with the television reporter covering the story. Unfortunately the killers think he's telling the truth, which plunges the janitor and reporter into a dangerous and complicated position, pursued by both police and foreign agents. Somewhat contrived, but Hurt and Weaver are always interesting. Woods turns in a wonderful performance as Hurt's somewhat-psychotic best friend. **102m/C VHS, Beta, LV.** William Hurt, Sigourney Weaver, Christopher Plummer, James Woods, Kenneth McMillan, Pamela Reed, Irene Worth, Steven Hill, Morgan Freeman; ***D:*** Peter Yates; ***W:*** Steve Tesich. *FXV, FOX*

Eyewitness to Murder ♪½ **1993** Stevens plays a cop who is assigned to protect beautiful artist Wolter. They both have their tragic flaws: he is a grieving widower, she has been blinded by an unknown attacker. Their flaws may draw them together. Somewhat more engaging than a television police action drama. **75m/C VHS.** Andrew Stevens, Adrian Zmed, Sherilyn Wolter, Carl Strano, Robin Drue; ***D:*** Jag Mundhra. *NHO*

F. Scott Fitzgerald in Hollywood ♪♪ **1976** Dramatization begins in the late 1930s when Fitzgerald was lured to Hollywood to work in the burgeoning film industry. It covers the period when, with his wife in a mental institution, he lived with Sheila Graham and struggled against alcoholism. Interesting story made dull and depressing by Miller's uninspired performance, but it's almost saved by Weld's portrayal of Zelda. Made for television. **98m/C VHS, Beta.** Jason Miller, Tuesday Weld, Julia Foster, Dolores Sutton, Michael Lerner, James Woods; ***D:*** Anthony Page. *NO*

F/X ♪♪♪ **1986 (R)** A Hollywood special effects expert is contracted by the government to fake an assassination to protect a mob informer. After completing the assignment, he learns that he's become involved in a real crime and is forced to reach into his bag of F/X tricks to survive. Twists and turns abound in this fast-paced story that was the sleeper hit of the year. Followed by a sequel. **109m/C VHS, Beta, LV.** Bryan Brown, Cliff DeYoung, Diane Venora, Brian Dennehy, Jerry Orbach, Mason Adams, Joe Grifasi, Martha Gehman; ***D:*** Robert Mandel; ***W:*** Robert T. Megginson, Gregory Fleeman; ***M:*** Bill Conti. *FCT*

F/X 2: The Deadly Art of Illusion ♪♪ **1991 (PG-13)** Weak follow-up finds the special-effects specialist set to pull off just one more illusion for the police. Once again, corrupt cops use him as a chump for their scheme, an over-complicated business involving a stolen Vatican treasure. **107m/C VHS, LV.** Bryan Brown, Brian Dennehy, Rachel Ticotin, Philip Bosco, Joanna Gleason; ***D:*** Richard Franklin; ***W:*** Bill Condon; ***M:*** Michael Boddicker, Lalo Schifrin. *ORI, IME*

Fabiola ♪♪♪ **1948** The first of the big Italian spectacle movies, this one opened the door for a flood of low-budget imitators. Fabiola, the daughter of a Roman senator, becomes a Christian when her father's Christian servants are accused of murdering him. In the meantime, the Emperor Constantine speeds toward Rome to convert it to Christian status. You can bet plenty of Christians will lose their heads, be thrown to the lions and generally burn at the stake before he does. **96m/C VHS.** *IT* Michel Simon, Henri Vidal, Gino Cervi; ***D:*** Alessandro Blasetti. *SNC, FCT*

The Fable of the Beautiful Pigeon Fancier 🦴🦴½ *Fabula de la Bella Palomera* **1988** A powerful man who has always gotten what he wanted spies a beautiful young married woman and sets out to make her his own. Based on the Gabriel Gracia Marquez novel "Love in the Time of Cholera." In Spanish with English subtitles. **73m/C VHS, LV.** *SP* Ney Latorraca, Claudia Ohana, Tonia Carrero, Dina Stat, Chico Diaz; ***D:*** Ruy Guerra. *FXL, FCT, INJ*

Fabulous Adventures of Baron Munchausen 🦴🦴 **1961** The legendary Baron Munchausen, known for his tall tales, relates the story of his trek to the strange and beautiful land of Trukesban in a mixture of live action and animation. Wonderful special effects but a boring storyline. In German with English subtitles. **84m/C VHS, Beta.** *GE* Milos Kopecky, Jana Brejchova, Rudolph Jelinek, Jan Werich; ***D:*** Karel Zeman. *LIV, VES, TPV*

The Fabulous Baker Boys 🦴🦴🦴 **1989 (R)** Two brothers have been performing a tired act as nightclub pianists for fifteen years. When they hire a sultry vocalist to revitalize the routine, she inadvertently triggers long-suppressed hostility between the "boys." The story may be a bit uneven, but fine performances by the three leading actors, the steamy 1940s atmosphere, and Pfeiffer's classic rendition of "Makin' Whoopee," are worth the price of the rental. **116m/C VHS, Beta, LV, 8mm.** Michelle Pfeiffer, Jeff Bridges, Beau Bridges, Elie Raab, Jennifer Tilly; ***D:*** Steven Kloves; ***W:*** Steven Kloves; ***C:*** Michael Ballhaus; ***M:*** Dave Grusin. Golden Globe Awards '90: Best Actress—Drama (Pfeiffer); Los Angeles Film Critics Association Awards '89: Best Actress (Pfeiffer), Best Cinematography; National Board of Review Awards '89: Best Actress (Pfeiffer); New York Film Critics Awards '89: Best Actress (Pfeiffer); National Society of Film Critics Awards '89: Best Actress (Pfeiffer), Best Cinematography, Best Supporting Actor (Bridges); Nominations: Academy Awards '89: Best Actress (Pfeiffer), Best Cinematography, Best Film Editing, Best Original Score. *LIV, FCT*

The Fabulous Dorseys 🦴🦴 **1947** The musical lives of big band leaders Tommy and Jimmy Dorsey are portrayed in this less than fabulous biography that's strong on song but weak on plot. Guest stars include Art Tatum, Charlie Barnet, Ziggy Elman, Bob Eberly and Helen O'Connell. Highlights are the tunes. ♫At Sundown; I'll Never Say Never Again; To Me; Green Eyes; Dorsey Concerto; Art's Blues; Everybody's Doin' It; The Object of My Affection; Runnin' Wild. **91m/B VHS, LV.** Tommy Dorsey, Jimmy Dorsey, Janet Blair, Paul Whiteman, Sara Allgood, Arthur Shields; ***D:*** Alfred E. Green. *NOS, MRV, HHT*

Fabulous Joe 🦴🦴 **1947** A talking dog named Joe gets involved in the life of a hen-pecked husband. **54m/C VHS, Beta.** Walter Abel, Donald Meek, Margot Grahame, Marie Wilson; ***D:*** Harve Foster. *NOS*

The Face at the Window 🦴🦴 **1939** Melodramatic crime story of a pair of ne'er-do-well brothers who terrorize Paris to conceal their bank robberies. **65m/B VHS.** Tod Slaughter, Marjorie Taylor, John Warwick, Robert Adair, Harry Terry; ***D:*** George King. *NOS, MRV, HEG*

A Face in the Crowd 🦴🦴🦴½ **1957** Journalist (Neal) discovers a down-home philosopher (Griffith) and puts him on her television show. His aw-shucks personality soon wins him a large following and increasing influence—even political clout. Off the air he reveals his true nature to be insulting, vengeful, and power-hungry—all of which Neal decides to expose. Marks Griffith's spectacular film debut as a thoroughly despicable character and debut of Remick as the pretty cheerleader in whom he takes an interest. Schulburg wrote the screenplay from his short story "The Arkansas Traveler." He and director Kazan collaborated equally well in "On the Waterfront." **126m/B VHS, Beta.** Andy Griffith, Patricia Neal, Lee Remick, Walter Matthau, Anthony (Tony) Franciosa; ***D:*** Elia Kazan; ***W:*** Budd Schulberg; ***C:*** Harry Stradling. *WAR, FCT*

A Face in the Fog 🦴🦴 **1936** Two newspaper reporters set out to solve a number of murders that have plagued the cast of a play. Also interested is the playwright. Good low-budget thriller. **66m/B VHS, Beta.** June Collyer, Lloyd Hughes, Lawrence Gray, Al "Fuzzy" St. John, Jack Mulhall, Jack Cowell, John Elliott, Sam Flint, Forrest Taylor, Edward Cassidy; ***D:*** Robert F. "Bob" Hill. *NOS, SNC*

Face of Another 🦴🦴 **1966** A severely burned man gets a second chance when a plastic surgeon makes a mask to hide the disfigurement. Unfortunately this face leads him to alienation, rape, infidelity, and murder. In Japanese with English subtitles. **124m/B VHS, Beta.** *JP* Tatsuya Nakadai, Machiko Kyo; ***D:*** Hiroshi Teshigahara. *INJ*

Face of the Screaming Werewolf 🦴½ *La Casa Del Terror; House of Terror* **1959** Originally a Mexican horror/comedy that was bought for U.S. distribution by Jerry Warren, who earned his spot in the horror hall of fame with "The Incredible Petrified World" and "Teenage Zombies." A scientist brings a mummy back to life, but when he removes the bandages (gasp), the subject turns out to be of the canine persuasion. Suffers from comic evisceration; not much to scream about. **60m/B VHS.** *MX* Lon Chaney Jr., Landa Varle, Raymond Gaylord; ***D:*** Gilberto Martinez Solares, Jerry Warren. *SNC, MRV*

Face the Music 🦴½ **1992 (PG-13)** Ringwald and Dempsey were once stormily married and pursuing successful, collaborative careers as singer/songwriters for the movies. But they've abandoned the work, along with the marriage, until a movie producer makes them a very lucrative offer for a new song. Only Dempsey's new girlfriend has some voracious objections. **93m/C VHS.** Patrick Dempsey, Molly Ringwald, Lysette Anthony. *LIV*

Face to Face 🦴🦴½ **1952** Dramatic adaptation of two short stories, "The Secret Sharer," by Joseph Conrad, and Stephen Crane's "The Bride Comes to Yellow Sky." The Conrad story features Mason as a sea captain who discovers a fugitive stowaway aboard his ships. The Crane story features Preston as a sheriff threatened by an old-time gunfighter. **92m/B VHS.** Bretaigne Windust, James Mason, Michael Pate, Robert Preston, Marjorie Steele, Gene Lockhart, Minor Watson; ***D:*** John Brahm. *NO*

Face to Face 🦴🦴🦴 **1976** Bergman's harrowing tale of a mental breakdown. Ullmann has a bravura role as a psychiatrist deciding to vacation at her grandparent's house in the country. Once there she begins to experience depression and hallucinations tied to her past with both her mother and grandmother. Her deeply repressed feelings eventually lead to a suicide attempt, which brings some much needed help. Originally a four-hour series made for Swedish television. In Swedish with English subtitles. **136m/C VHS.** *SW* Liv Ullmann, Erland Josephson, Gunnar Bjornstrand, Aino Taube-Henrikson, Sven Lindberg; ***D:*** Ingmar Bergman; ***W:*** Ingmar Bergman; ***C:*** Sven Nykvist. Golden Globe Awards '77: Best Foreign Film; Los Angeles Film Critics Association Awards '76: Best Actress (Ullmann), Best Foreign Film; National Board of Review Awards '76: Best Actress (Ullmann); New York Film Critics Awards '76: Best Actress (Ullmann); Nominations: Academy Awards '76: Best Actress (Ullmann), Best Director (Bergman). *PAR*

Faces 🦴🦴🦴½ **1968 (R)** Cassavettes' first independent film to find mainstream success portrays the breakup of the 14-year marriage of middle-aged Richard (Marley) and Maria (Carlin) Forst. Both seek at least momentary comfort with others—Richard with prostitute Jeannie (Rowlands) and Maria with aging hippie Chet (Cassel). The director's usual improvisational and documentary style can either be viewed as compelling or tedious but the performances are first-rate. **129m/B VHS.** John Marley, Lynn Carlin, Gena Rowlands, Seymour Cassel, Val Avery, Dorothy Gulliver, Joanne Moore Jordan, Fred Draper, Darlene Conley; ***D:*** John Cassavetes; ***W:*** John Cassavetes; ***C:*** Al Ruban; ***M:*** Jack Ackerman. National Society of Film Critics Awards '68: Best Screenplay, Best Supporting Actor (Cassel); Nominations: Academy Awards '68: Best Screenplay, Best Supporting Actor (Carlin), Best Supporting Actress (Cassel). *FXL*

Faces of Women 🦴🦴 **1985** Two stories about women in contemporary Africa. In the first, an unhappy young woman is married to a very jealous man. When her brother-in-law visits, she decides to give her husband something to worry about. The second story finds a businesswoman running into problems when she tries to open a restaurant—problems that her daughter helps to solve. French and indigenous languages with English subtitles. **103m/C VHS.** Eugenie Cisse Roland, Sidiki Bakaba, Albertine N'Guessan; ***D:*** Desire Ecare. *NYF*

Fade to Black *Woof!* **1980 (R)** Young man obsessed with movies loses his grip on reality and adopts the personalities of cinematic characters (Hopalong Cassidy and Dracula among them) to seek revenge on people who have wronged him. Thoroughly unpleasant, highlighted by clips from old flicks. **100m/C VHS, Beta.** Dennis Christopher, Tim Thomerson, Linda Kerridge, Mickey Rourke, Melinda Fee; ***D:*** Vernon Zimmerman. *MED, MLB*

Fade to Black 🦴🦴 **1993 (R)** Busfield stars as a college professor with voyeuristic tendencies and a handy camcorder. After viewing his latest tape, he realizes he's filmed his neighbor's murder and that he can recognize the killer. Before he can warn the killer's girlfriend, she disappears and our nosy prof is framed for the death. **84m/C VHS, Beta.** Timothy Busfield, Heather Locklear, Michael Beck, Louis Giambalvo, Cloris Leachman, David Byron; ***D:*** John McPherson; ***W:*** Douglas Barr. *PAR*

Fahrenheit 451 🦴🦴🦴 **1966** Chilling adaptation of the Ray Bradbury novel about a futuristic society that has banned all reading material and the firemen whose job it is to keep the fires at 451 degrees: the temperature at which paper burns. Werner is a fireman who begins to question the rightness of his actions when he meets the book-loving Christie—who also plays the dual role of Werner's TV-absorbed wife. Truffaut's first color and English-language film. **112m/C VHS, Beta, LV.** *FR* Oskar Werner, Julie Christie, Cyril Cusack, Anton Diffring; ***D:*** Francois Truffaut. *MCA, MLB, INJ*

Fail-Safe 🦴🦴🦴½ **1964** A nail-biting nuclear age nightmare, in which American planes have been erroneously sent to bomb the USSR, with no way to recall them. An all-star cast impels this bitterly serious thriller, the straight-faced flipside of "Dr. Strangelove." **111m/B VHS, Beta, LV.** Henry Fonda, Dan O'Herlihy, Walter Matthau, Larry Hagman, Fritz Weaver, Dom DeLuise; ***D:*** Sidney Lumet; ***W:*** Walter Bernstein. *COL*

Fair Game *Woof!* **1982 (R)** Three young women decide to ditch their private school for a weekend of fun but find out the resort town they've chosen is run by sociopaths who get their kicks by stalking our chicks. **90m/C VHS, Beta.** *AU* Kim Trengove, Kerry Mack, Marie O'Loughlina, Karen West; ***D:*** Christopher Fitchett. *IMP*

Fair Game *Woof!* **1985** In the Australian outback, three loathesome excuses for human beings come across a beautiful woman alone on a remote farm. Naturally, they try to do despicable things but she fights back. **83m/C VHS.** *AU* Cassandra Delaney, Peter Ford, David Sandford, Gary Who; ***D:*** Mario Andreacchio. *ORI*

Fair Game *Woof!* **1989 (R)** A psychotic but imaginative ex-boyfriend locks his former girlfriend in her apartment with a lethal giant Mamba snake. Understandably uninterested in its serpentine attention, the young woman must trespass against the Hollywood code and keep her wits in the face of danger. Guaranteed not to charm you. **81m/C VHS, LV.** Greg Henry, Trudie Styler, Bill Moseley; ***D:*** Mario Orfini. *VMK*

Fair Game 🦴🦴½ **1995 (R)** Miami police detective Max (Baldwin) defies orders so he can protect family attorney Kate (Crawford, in her big-screen debut) from high-tech assassins. Nice work if you can get it. Generic action plot provides Crawford and first-time director Sipes with relatively safe proving ground. Cindy wears the "Die Hard" dirty white tank top look fetchingly enough (and showers when the action slackens), while Baldwin is no slouch in the babe department (male division) either. Based on Paula Gosling's 1978 novel "Fair Game," which was previously filmed as 1986's "Cobra." **91m/C VHS, LV.** William Baldwin, Cindy Crawford, Miguel Sandoval, Christopher McDonald, Johann Carlo, Salma Hayek, John Bedford

Lloyd, Jenette Goldstein; ***D:*** Andrew Sipes; ***W:*** Charlie Fletcher; ***C:*** Richard Bowen; ***M:*** Mark Mancina. Nominations: Golden Raspberry Awards '95: Worst New Star (Crawford). *WAR*

Fairy Tales 🦴🦴 *Fairytales* **1976 (R)** A ribald musical fantasy follows the equally risque "Cinderella." In order to save the kingdom, the prince must produce an heir. The problem is that only the girl in the painting of "Princess Beauty" can "interest" the prince and she must be found. Good-natured smut. **83m/C VHS, Beta.** Don Sparks, Prof. Irwin Corey, Brenda Fogarty, Sy Richardson, Nai Bonet, Martha Reeves; ***D:*** Harry Tampa. *MED*

Faith 🦴 **1992 (R)** When young dancer Faith's parents are killed in an accident she winds up in a frightening foster home. Running away, she meets a gentlemanly mobster who helps her attain her dance dreams. Laughably implausible. **104m/C VHS, LV.** Sylvia Seidel, Ami Dolenz, Richard Maldone. *VMK*

Faithful 🦴🦴½ **1995 (R)** Black comedy about depressed, rich housewife Margaret (Cher) who is rudely interrupted by Tony the hitman (Palminteri) while trying to commit suicide on her 20th wedding anniversary. Unfaithful hubby Jack (O'Neal), who has put the contract out on Margaret, is conveniently away on business. As Margaret sits tied to a chair and Tony waits for a call to confirm the hit, the two connect and decide to turn the tables. Director Mazursky succeeds in bringing Palminteri's three-character play to the screen, even if it does suffer at times from too much stage talk and not enough action. First film for Cher since 1990's "Mermaids" and the first for O'Neal since 1989's "Chances Are." Big rift between Mazursky and the film's producers over final cut led him to threaten to pull his name from the credits. Mazursky cameos as the hitman's therapist. **91m/C VHS, LV.** Cher, Ryan O'Neal, Chazz Palminteri; ***Cameos:*** Paul Mazursky; ***D:*** Paul Mazursky; ***W:*** Chazz Palminteri; ***C:*** Fred Murphy. *NLC*

Fake Out 🦴 *Nevada Heat* **1982** Nightclub singer is caught between the mob and the police who want her to testify against her gangland lover. Typical vanity outing for Zadora. **89m/C VHS, Beta.** Pia Zadora, Telly Savalas, Desi Arnaz Jr.; ***D:*** Matt Cimber. *CNG*

Falcon 🦴 **1974** Brave knight battles for the honor of a beautiful maiden; with or without the Falcon's help. **105m/C VHS, Beta.** Franco Nero. *TWE*

The Falcon and the Snowman 🦴🦴🦴 **1985 (R)** True story of Daulton Lee and Christopher Boyce, two childhood friends who, almost accidentally, sell American intelligence secrets to the KGB in 1977. Hutton and Penn are excellent, creating a relationship we care about and strong characterizations. **110m/C VHS, Beta, LV.** Sean Penn, Timothy Hutton, Lori Singer, Pat Hingle, Dorian Harewood, Richard Dysart, David Suchet, Jennifer Runyon, Priscilla Pointer, Nicholas Pryor, Joyce Van Patten, Mady Kaplan, Michael Ironside; ***D:*** John Schlesinger; ***W:*** Steven Zaillian; ***M:*** Lyle Mays, Pat Metheny. *LIV, VES*

The Falcon in Hollywood 🦴🦴½ **1944** The falcon gets caught up with the murder of an actor who was part of a Tinseltown love triangle. The film takes place on RKO's back lot for a behind-the-scenes view of Hollywood. Part of the popular "Falcon" series from the 1940s. **67m/B VHS.** Tom Conway, Barbara Hale, Veda Ann Borg, Sheldon Leonard, Frank Jenks, Rita (Paula) Corday, John Abbott; ***D:*** Gordon Douglas. *MED*

The Falcon in Mexico 🦴½ **1944** When paintings from a supposedly dead artist turn up for sale in New York City, the Falcon and the artist's daughter wind up journeying to Mexico to solve the mystery. Part of "The Falcon" series. **70m/B VHS, Beta.** Tom Conway, Mona Maris, Nestor Paiva; ***D:*** William (Lester Williams) Berke. *MED*

The Falcon Takes Over/Strange Bargain 🦴🦴 **1949** A mystery double feature. In "The Falcon Takes Over," The Falcon becomes involved in a series of murder and an ex-con's last love, and in "Strange Bargain," an underpaid bookkeeper gets in on an insurance swindle. **131m/B VHS, Beta.** George Sanders, Ward Bond, Allen Jenkins, Martha Scott, Harry (Henry) Morgan, James Gleason, Anne Revere, Hans Conried, Turhan Bey; ***D:*** Irving Reis. *TTC*

The Falcon's Adventure/Armored Car Robbery 🦴½ **1950** A mystery double feature: The Falcon uncovers a vicious plot to steal a formula for synthetic diamonds in "The Falcon's Adventure," and four participants in an armored car robbery flee after slaying a policeman in "Armored Car Robbery." **122m/B VHS, Beta.** Tom Conway, Madge Meredith, William Talman, Charles McGraw, Adele Jergens; ***D:*** William (Lester Williams) Berke. *TTC*

The Falcon's Brother 🦴🦴 **1942** Enemy agents intent on killing a South American diplomat are foiled by the Falcon's brothers at a steep personal cost. The plot enabled Sanders' real-life brother Conway to take over the title role in "The Falcon" mystery series, a role which he played nine more times. **64m/B VHS, Beta.** Tom Conway, George Sanders, Keye Luke, Jane Randolph; ***D:*** Stanley Logan. *MED*

Fall and Rise of Reginald Perrin 1 🦴🦴🦴 **1978** Starring Leonard Rossiter, this BBC show has Reginald getting out of the rat race. **107m/C VHS.** *GB* Leonard Rossiter. *VCO, HMV, FUS*

Fall and Rise of Reginald Perrin 2 🦴🦴🦴 **1978** After part one's escape from the rat race, this time Reginald is back in suburbia. **120m/C VHS.** *GB* Leonard Rossiter. *VCO, HMV, FUS*

Fall from Grace 🦴🦴½ **1994** American and British intelligence officers take deadly risks in 1943 Europe in an effort to convince Hitler to end the war. **180m/C VHS.** *GB* James Fox, Michael York, Patsy Kensit, Gary Cole; ***D:*** Waris Hussein. *AVE, FCT*

Fall from Innocence 🦴½ **1988** A girl is driven to a life of prostitution and drugs by the sexual abuse inflicted upon her by her father. **81m/C VHS.** Isabelle Mejias, Thom Haverstock, Amanda Smith, Rob McEwan; ***D:*** Carey Connor. *NO*

The Fall of the House of Usher 🦴 **1949** Lord Roderick Usher is haunted by his sister's ghost in this poor adaptation of the Poe classic. **70m/B VHS.** *GB* Kay Tendeter, Gwen Watford, Irving Steen, Lucy Pavey; ***D:*** Ivan Barnett. *SNC, FCT*

The Fall of the House of Usher 🦴🦴🦴 *House of Usher* **1960** The moody Roger Corman/Vincent Price interpretation, the first of their eight Poe adaptations, depicting the collapse of the famous estate due to madness and revenge. Terrific sets and solid direction as well as Price's inimitable presence. **85m/C VHS, Beta.** Vincent Price, Myrna Fahey, Mark Damon; ***D:*** Roger Corman; ***W:*** Richard Matheson; ***C:*** Floyd Crosby; ***M:*** Les Baxter. *NO*

The Fall of the House of Usher 🦴½ **1980 (PG)** Another version of Edgar Allan Poe's classic tale of a family doomed to destruction. Stray to the Roger Corman/Vincent Price version to see how it should have been done. **101m/C VHS, Beta.** Martin Landau, Robert Hays, Charlene Tilton, Ray Walston; ***D:*** James L. Conway. *NO*

The Fall of the Roman Empire 🦴🦴🦴 **1964** An all-star, big budget extravaganza set in ancient Rome praised for its action sequences. The licentious son of Marcus Aurelius arranges for his father's murder and takes over as emperor while Barbarians gather at the gate. Great sets, fine acting, and thundering battle scenes. **187m/C VHS, Beta, LV.** Sophia Loren, Alec Guinness, James Mason, Stephen Boyd, Christopher Plummer, John Ireland, Anthony Quayle, Eric Porter, Mel Ferrer, Omar Sharif; ***D:*** Anthony Mann; ***W:*** Philip Yordan; ***C:*** Robert Krasker. Golden Globe Awards '65: Best Score; Nominations: Academy Awards '64: Best Original Score. *BFV, KAR, FCT*

Fall Time 🦴🦴 *Falltime* **1994 (R)** Crime drama set in small-town Minnesota, circa 1957. Three high schoolers set in motion a prank that turns bad when they pull up in front of the local bank. David (Arquette), Joe (Blechman), and Tim (London) intend to stage a mock robbery—too bad a real robbery is going down and the teens wind up the terrified hostages of creepy criminals Forence (Rourke) and Leon (Baldwin). Promising premise derailed by narrative inadequacies. **88m/C VHS, LV.** Mickey Rourke, Stephen Baldwin, Jason London, David Arquette, Jonah Blechman, Sheryl Lee; ***D:*** Paul Warner; ***W:*** Steve Alden, Paul Skemp; ***C:*** Mark J. Gordon. *LIV*

Fallen Angel 🦴🦴½ **1981** Television movie about a child pornographer and a particular young girl he finds easily exploitable because of her unbalanced home situation. Fine cast, solid direction. **100m/C Beta.** Dana Hill, Richard Masur, Melinda Dillon, Ronny Cox; ***D:*** Robert Lewis; ***M:*** Richard Bellis. *COL*

Fallen Angels 1 🦴🦴🦴 **1993** Trilogy of hard-boiled, film noirish tales set in Los Angeles. "The Frightening Frammis" concerns a grifter (Gallagher) who meets his match in a mystery woman (Rossellini) in this adaptation of a Jim Thompson story. Cruise's directorial debut. "Murder, Obliquely" finds a plain Jane (Dern) falling for a heel (Rickman) who may have murdered his previous girl in a Cornell Woolrich tale. "Since I Don't Have You" has Buzz Meeks (Busey) hired to find a dame sought by both Howard Hughes (Matheson) and gangster Mickey Cohen (Woods). From a story by James Elroy. Made for cable television. **90m/C VHS.** Peter Gallagher, Isabella Rossellini, Nancy Travis, John C. Reilly, Bill Erwin, Laura Dern, Alan Rickman, Diane Lane, Robin Bartlett, Gary Busey, Tim Matheson, James Woods, Aimee Graham, Dick Miller, Ken Lerner; ***D:*** Tom Cruise, Alfonso Cuaron, Jonathan Kaplan; ***W:*** Jon Robin Baitz, Howard A. Rodman, Amanda Silver, Steven Katz; ***M:*** Elmer Bernstein. *PGV*

Fallen Angels 2 🦴🦴🦴 **1993** Three more film noir stories set in L.A. "Dead End for Delia" finds a police detective (Oldman) arriving at a murder scene to find his estranged wife (Anwar) the victim. Based on a short story by William Campbell Gault. "I'll Be Waiting" has Kirby as a hapless hotel detective who falls for a beautiful guest (Helgenberger) and winds up a mob pawn. Adaptation of a Raymond Chandler tale. "The Quiet Room" has Bedelia and Mantegna as a pair of corrupt cops who find their shakedown schemes going very wrong. From a story by Jonathan Craig. Made for cable television. **90m/C VHS.** Gary Oldman, Gabrielle Anwar, Meg Tilly, Patrick Masset, Vondie Curtis-Hall, Paul Guilfoyle, Dan Hedaya, John Putch, Wayne Knight, Bruno Kirby, Marg Helgenberger, Jon Polito, Peter Scolari, Dick Miller, Joe Mantegna, Bonnie Bedelia, Vinessa Shaw, J.E. Freeman, Peter Gallagher, Patrick Breen, Genia Michaela, Wayne Grace; ***Cameos:*** Tom Hanks; ***D:*** Phil Joanou, Tom Hanks, Steven Soderbergh; ***W:*** Scott Frank, C. Gaby Mitchell, Howard A. Rodman. *PGV*

Fallen Champ: The Untold Story of Mike Tyson 🦴🦴🦴 **1993** Director Kopple's provocative documentary on the boxing champ, from his roots in a Brooklyn ghetto to his conviction for rape in 1991. Tyson is shown as pathetic, vulnerable, and violent—psychologically unprepared for both acclaim and responsibility, as well as easily manipulated by promoters and opportunists. A mixture of ring footage and interviews with sportswriters, promoters, trainers, and others as well as media coverage of Tyson. Made for television. **93m/C VHS.** ***D:*** Barbara Kopple. *COL, BTV*

The Fallen Idol 🦴🦴🦴 *The Lost Illusion* **1949** A young boy wrongly believes that a servant he admires is guilty of murdering his wife. Unwittingly, the child influences the police investigation of the crime so that the servant becomes the prime suspect. Richardson as the accused and Henrey as the boy are notable. Screenplay adapted by Greene from his short story, "The Basement Room." **92m/B VHS, Beta, LV.** *GB* Ralph Richardson, Bobby Henrey, Michele Morgan, Sonia Dresdel, Jack Hawkins, Bernard Lee; ***D:*** Carol Reed; ***W:*** Graham Greene; ***C:*** Georges Perinal. British Academy Awards '48: Best Film; National Board of Review Awards '49: 10 Best Films of the Year, Best Actor (Richardson); Nominations: Academy Awards '49: Best Director (Reed), Best Screenplay. *NOS, MRV, PSM*

The Fallen Sparrow 🦴🦴🦴 **1943** Garfield is superb as a half-mad veteran of the Spanish Civil War. Captured and brutalized, he never revealed the whereabouts of a valuable possession. His return to the U.S. continues his torture as Nazi agent Slezak uses the woman Garfield loves to set a trap and finish the job. Solid performances and good plot are highlights. **94m/B VHS, Beta.** John Garfield, Maureen O'Hara, Walter Slezak, Patricia Morison, Martha O'Driscoll, Bruce Edwards, John Miljan, John Banner, Hugh Beaumont; ***D:*** Richard Wallace. Nominations: Academy Awards '43: Best Original Score. *MED, IME*

Falling Down **1993 (R)** Douglas is "D-FENS" (taken from his license plate), a normally law-abiding white-collar geek who snaps while stuck in a traffic jam on a hot day in LA. Like Charles Bronson in "Death Wish," he decides to take matters into his own hands. Unlike Bronson, he is not avenging an attack by a specific criminal, but raging against whomever gets in his way. Duvall is a detective on his last day before retirement, Hershey has the thankless role of Douglas' ex. Essentially a revenge fantasy that was vilified by some for catering to the baser emotions. **112m/C VHS, LV.** Michael Douglas, Robert Duvall, Barbara Hershey, Rachel Ticotin, Tuesday Weld, Frederic Forrest, Lois Smith, D.W. Moffett, Dedee Pfeiffer, Vondie Curtis-Hall, Michael Paul Chan, Raymond J. Barry, Jack Kehoe, John Diehl; ***D:*** Joel Schumacher; ***W:*** Ebbe Roe Smith; ***M:*** James Newton Howard. Nominations: Cannes Film Festival '93: Best Film. *WAR, FCT*

Falling from Grace ½ **1992 (PG-13)** Bud Parks (Mellencamp) is a successful country singer who, accompanied by his wife and daughter, returns to his small Indiana hometown to celebrate his grandfather's 80th birthday. He's tired of both his career and his marriage and finds himself taking up once again with an old girlfriend (Lenz), who is not only married to Bud's brother but is also having an affair with his father. Bud believes he's better off staying in his old hometown but the problems caused by his return may change his mind. Surprisingly sedate, although literate, family drama with good ensemble performances. Actor-director debut for Mellencamp. **100m/C VHS, LV.** John Cougar Mellencamp, Mariel Hemingway, Kay Lenz, Claude Akins, Dub Taylor, Brent Huff, Deidre O'Connell, Larry Crane; ***D:*** John Cougar Mellencamp; ***W:*** Larry McMurtry. *COL, FCT*

Falling in Love ½ **1984 (PG-13)** Two married New Yorkers unexpectedly fall in love after a coincidental meeting at the Rizzoli Book Store. Weak but gracefully performed reworking of "Brief Encounter," where no one seems to ever complete a sentence. An unfortunate re-teaming for Streep and De Niro after their wonderful work in "The Deer Hunter." **106m/C VHS, Beta, LV.** Robert De Niro, Meryl Streep, Harvey Keitel, Dianne Wiest, George Martin, Jane Kaczmarek, David Clennon; ***D:*** Ulu Grosbard; ***W:*** Michael Cristofer; ***M:*** Dave Grusin. *PAR*

Falling in Love Again ½ *In Love* **1980 (PG)** Romantic comedy about middle-aged dreamer Gould and realistic wife York. They travel from Los Angeles to their hometown of New York for his high school reunion, where Gould is suddenly attacked by nostalgia vibes for his youth, seen in countless flashbacks, and prominently featuring Pfeiffer, notable in her film debut. Like watching a home movie about people you don't care about. **103m/C VHS, Beta.** Elliott Gould, Susannah York, Michelle Pfeiffer; ***D:*** Steven Paul; ***W:*** Ted Allan. *SUE*

False Arrest ½ **1992** A woman is falsely accused of killing her husband's business partner and winds up in prison where she continues to fight to prove her innocence. Mills does well in this less-than-glamorous role. Based on a true story. Made for television. **102m/C VHS, Beta.** Donna Mills, Steven Bauer, James Handy, Lane Smith, Lewis Van Bergen, Dennis Christopher, Robert Wagner; ***D:*** Bill W.L. Norton. *TTC, PMS*

False Colors **1943** Hopalong Cassidy unmasks a crook posing as a ranch heir. This was the 49th Hopalong Cassidy feature. **54m/B VHS, Beta.** William Boyd, Robert Mitchum, Andy Clyde, Jimmy Rogers; ***D:*** George Archainbaud. *NOS, MRV, VYY*

False Faces ½ **1918** Secret agent known as The Lone Wolf is working in France for the Allies when he learns a German master spy is headed for the U.S. to cause trouble. So he heads for New York to stop him. Lots of thrills. **65m/B VHS.** Henry B. Walthall, Lon Chaney Sr., Mary Anderson, Milton Ross; ***D:*** Irvin Willat. *FCT*

False Faces ½ **1932** A ruthless, money-hungry quack is hounded by the law and the victims of his unscrupulous plastic surgery. **80m/B VHS, Beta.** Lowell Sherman, Peggy Shannon, Lila Lee, Joyce Compton, Berton Churchill, David Landau, Eddie Anderson, Ken Maynard, Veda Ann Borg; ***D:*** Lowell Sherman. *VYY*

False Identity ½ **1990 (PG-13)** A radio psychologist buys a Purple Heart medal at a garage sale and then tries to find out about the original recipient. But her questions are making a number of folks uneasy, including a potentially dangerous stranger. **97m/C VHS, Beta, LV.** Genevieve Bujold, Stacy Keach, Veronica Cartwright, Tobin Bell, Mimi Maynard; ***D:*** James Keach; ***W:*** Sandra K. Bailey. *PAR*

False Note ½ **1972** Against a background of vibrant colors and collages, a little, crippled beggar-musician roams through a modern city, playing his small barrel organ which inevitably emits a sour note. He discovers a kindred spirit in an abandoned carousel horse. **10m/C VHS, Beta.** *IFB*

False Witness ½ **1989** A New Orleans district attorney and her lover, a private investigator, find themselves working the same rape-murder case. When their methods disagree both find themselves in danger. Adapted from a novel by Dorothy Uhnak. Made for television. **96m/C VHS.** Phylicia Rashad, Philip Michael Thomas, Terri Austin, George Grizzard; ***D:*** Arthur Seidelman; ***M:*** Charles Fox. *VTR*

Fame **1980 (R)** Follows eight talented teenagers from their freshmen year through graduation from New York's High School of Performing Arts. Insightful and absorbing, director Parker allows the kids to mature on screen, revealing the pressures of constantly trying to prove themselves. A faultless parallel is drawn between these "special" kids and the pressures felt by high schoolers everywhere. Great dance and music sequences. The basis for the television series. ♫Fame; Red Light; I Sing the Body Electric; Dogs in the Yard; Hot Lunch Jam; Out Here On My Own; Is It OK If I Call You Mine?. **133m/C VHS, Beta, LV.** Irene Cara, Barry Miller, Paul McCrane, Anne Meara, Joanna Merlin, Richard Belzer, Maureen Teefy; ***D:*** Alan Parker; ***M:*** Michael Gore. Academy Awards '80: Best Song ("Fame"), Best Original Score; Golden Globe Awards '81: Best Song ("Fame"); Nominations: Academy Awards '80: Best Film Editing, Best Film Editing, Best Original Screenplay, Best Song ("Out Here on My Own"), Best Sound. *MGM, FCT*

Fame Is the Spur ½ **1947** A lengthy but interesting look at the way power corrupts, plus an insight into the Conservative versus Labor dynamics of British government. Redgrave is a poor, idealistic worker who decides to help his fellow workers by running for Parliament. There, he falls prey to the trappings of office with surprising consequences. Look hard for Tomlinson, who went on to star in "Mary Poppins" and "Bedknobs and Broomsticks" for Disney. **116m/B VHS.** *GB* Michael Redgrave, Rosamund John, Bernard Miles, Hugh Burden, Guy Verney, Carla Lehmann, Seymour Hicks, David Tomlinson; ***D:*** Roy Boulting. *NOS, VEC*

The Family ½ **1973** As a New Orleans hitman who resists joining the mob, Bronson initiates an all-out war on the syndicate and its boss, played by Savalas. A poorly dubbed Italian action film. **94m/C VHS, Beta.** *IT* Charles Bronson, Jill Ireland, Telly Savalas; ***D:*** Sergio Sollima. *MPI*

The Family *La Famiglia* **1987** An 80-year-old patriarch prepares for his birthday celebration reminiscing about his family's past triumphs, tragedies and enduring love. The charming flashbacks, convincingly played, all take place in the family's grand old Roman apartment. In Italian with English subtitles or dubbed. **128m/C VHS, Beta, LV.** *IT* Vittorio Gassman, Fanny Ardant, Philippe Noiret, Stefania Sandrelli, Andrea Occhipinti, Jo Ciampa; ***D:*** Ettore Scola; ***W:*** Ettore Scola, Ruggero Maccari, Furio Scarpelli; ***M:*** Armando Trovajoli. Nominations: Academy Awards '87: Best Foreign Language Film. *LIV, VES, INJ*

Family Business ½ **1989 (R)** A bright Ivy Leaguer, impressed by the exploits and vitality of his criminal grandfather, recruits him and his ex-con dad to pull off a high-tech robbery, which goes awry. Caper film, with its interest in family relationships and being true to one's nature. Casting Connery, Hoffman, and Broderick as the three leaves a big believability problem in the family department. **114m/C VHS, Beta, LV, 8mm.** Sean Connery, Dustin Hoffman, Matthew Broderick, Rosana De Soto, Janet Carroll, Victoria Jackson, Bill McCutcheon, Deborah Rush, Marilyn Cooper, Salem Ludwig, Rex Everhart, James Tolkan; ***D:*** Sidney Lumet; ***W:*** Vincent Patrick; ***M:*** Cy Coleman. *COL, FCT*

Family Dog: Complete Series **1992** Ten episodes from the animated television series executive produced by Tim Burton and Steven Spielberg. This put-upon pup is property of the Binfords family and succeeds in getting himself involved in all sorts of unhappy situations. **235m/C VHS, LV.** ***D:*** Chris Buck; ***W:*** Dennis Klein; ***V:*** Daniel Mann, Martin Mull, Molly Cheek, Zak Huxtable Epstein, Cassie Cole. *MCA*

Family Enforcer *Death Collector* **1976 (R)** A small-time hoodlum is bent on becoming the best enforcer in an underworld society. **82m/C VHS, Beta.** Joe Cortese, Lou Criscuola, Joe Pesci, Anne Johns, Keith Davis; ***D:*** Ralph De Vito. *VCI, VTR*

The Family Game **1983** An obsessive satire about a poor, belligerent college student hired by a wealthy contemporary Japanese family to tutor their spoiled teenage son. Provides an all-out cultural assault on the Japanese bourgeoisie. From an original story by Yohei Honma. In Japanese with English subtitles. **107m/C VHS, Beta.** *JP* Junichi Tsujita, Yusaku Matsuda, Juzo Itami, Saori Yuki, Ichirota Miyagawa; ***D:*** Yoshimitsu Morita; ***W:*** Yoshimitsu Morita. *FCT, INJ*

Family Jewels **1965** A spoiled child-heiress has to choose among her six uncles to decide which should be her new father. If you like Jerry Lewis, you can't miss this! In addition to playing all six uncles, Lewis plays the chauffeur, as well as serving as producer, director, and coauthor of the script. **100m/C VHS.** Jerry Lewis, Donna Butterworth, Sebastian Cabot, Robert Strauss; ***D:*** Jerry Lewis; ***W:*** Jerry Lewis. *PAR*

Family Life *Zycie Rodzinne* **1971** Melancholy mood piece finds an engineer reluctantly returning to his family's delapidated country mansion after six years in Warsaw. He must confront his own life as well as his alcoholic father and slightly mad sister. Polish with subtitles. **93m/C VHS.** *PL* Daniel Olbrychski, Jan Nowicki, Jan Kreczmar, Maja Komorowska, Halina Mikolajska; ***D:*** Krzysztof Zanussi; ***W:*** Krzysztof Zanussi; ***M:*** Wojciech Kilar. *FCT*

Family Life ½ *Wednesday's Child* **1971** A portrait of a 19-year-old girl battling her parents to establish her own identity. She is subjected to increasingly vigorous psychological interventions in this documentary-style effort originally made for British television. **108m/C VHS, Beta.** *GB* Sandy Ratcliff, Bill Dean, Grace Cave; ***D:*** Ken Loach. *COL*

The Family Man **1979** A brief encounter between a married Manhattanite (Asner) and a much younger single woman (Baxter Birney) is sensitively handled in this film which explores their passionate affair. Made-for-television. **98m/C VHS, Beta.** Ed Asner, Meredith Baxter, Paul Clemens, Mary Joan Negro, Anne Jackson, Martin Short, Michael Ironside; ***D:*** Glenn Jordan; ***M:*** Billy Goldenberg. *TLF*

A Family Matter *Vendetta: Secrets of a Mafia Bride* **1991 (R)** A Mafia chieftain adopts a child whose father was killed by hit men. She grows into a beautiful woman bent on revenge. Melodramatic Italian-American co-production, made for TV. **100m/C VHS, LV.** Eric Roberts, Carol Alt, Eli Wallach, Burt Young. *VMK*

Family Pictures **1993** A photographer remembers growing up in the 50's with her autistic brother, the mother who lavished her attention on him almost to the exclusion of her five other children, and the father who blamed his wife for their son's deficiencies. Interesting portrait of a typical American family, which eventually cracks under pressure and splits up. Adapted from the novel by Sue Miller (no relation to screenwriter Jennifer). **240m/C VHS.** Anjelica Huston, Sam Neill, Kyra Sedgwick, Dermot Mulroney, Gemma Barry, Tara Charendoff, Torri Higginson, Jamie Harold; ***D:*** Philip Saville; ***W:*** Jennifer Miller. *NYR*

Family Plot 🦴🦴½ **1976 (PG)** Alfred Hitchcock's last film focuses on the search for a missing heir which is undertaken by a phony psychic and her private-eye boyfriend, with all becoming involved in a diamond theft. Campy, lightweight mystery that stales with time and doesn't fit well into Hitchcock's genre. **120m/C VHS, Beta, LV.** Karen Black, Bruce Dern, Barbara Harris, William Devane, Ed Lauter, Katherine Helmond; ***D:*** Alfred Hitchcock; ***W:*** Ernest Lehman; ***M:*** John Williams. Edgar Allan Poe Awards '76: Best Screenplay; National Board of Review Awards '76: 10 Best Films of the Year. *MCA*

Family Prayers 🦴🦴½ **1991 (PG)** Coming-of-age drama, set in 1969 Los Angeles, about 13-year-old Andrew and his family troubles. His father Martin (Mantegna) is a compulsive gambler which causes wife Rita (Archer) untold anxiety and constant friction between the two. Tension is heightened by Nan (LuPone), Rita's opinionated older sister who has bailed the family out of their money problems more than once. Meanwhile, Andrew tries to look out for his younger sister and prepare for his bar-mitzvah. A little too much of a nostalgic golden glow surrounds what is essentially a family tragedy. **109m/C VHS.** Tzvi Ratner-Stauber, Joe Mantegna, Anne Archer, Patti LuPone, Paul Reiser, Allen (Goorwitz) Garfield, Conchata Ferrell, David Margulies; ***D:*** Scott Rosenfelt; ***W:*** Steven Ginsburg. *COL*

Family Reunion 🦴½ **1988** A young man brings a pretty hitchhiker to his family reunion where they mistake her for his fiancee (who recently dumped him). **97m/C VHS, Beta.** David Eisner, Rebecca Jenkins, Henry Beckman, Linda Sorensen; ***D:*** Dick Sarin. *NO*

Family Secrets 🦴🦴½ **1984** A made-for-television drama about a daughter, mother, and grandmother overprotecting and manipulating each other during a weekend together. **96m/C Beta.** Maureen Stapleton, Stefanie Powers, Melissa Gilbert, James Spader; ***D:*** Jack Hofsiss. *NO*

Family Sins 🦴🦴 **1987** A television movie about a domineering father who dotes on his sports-oriented son while willfully neglecting the other. Eventually this leads to calamity. **93m/C VHS.** James Farentino, Jill Eikenberry, Andrew Bendarski, Mimi Kuzyk, Brent Spiner, Michael Durrell, Tom Bower; ***D:*** Jerrold Freedman. *REP*

A Family Thing 🦴🦴🦴 **1996 (PG-13)** Racial issues are addressed in this character-driven story of two brothers. Southerner Earl Pilcher (Duvall) learns his biological mother was black and that she died during his birth. In a letter written by the recently deceased woman who raised him, Earl discovers he also has a half brother, Ray (Jones), who is black and living in Chicago. He drives to Chicago, and seeks out Ray, who to Earl's surprise knows about him already, and is not exactly thrilled about the family ties, either. As the two brothers, expertly played by Duvall and Jones, slowly find common ground, Hall steals the show as the irascible Aunt T. **109m/C VHS.** Robert Duvall, James Earl Jones, Irma P. Hall, Michael Beach, Grace Zabriskie, Regina Taylor, Mary Jackson, Paula Marshall, Jim Harrell; ***D:*** Richard Pearce; ***W:*** Billy Bob Thornton, Tom Epperson; ***C:*** Fred Murphy. *NYR*

Family Upside Down 🦴🦴🦴 **1978** An aging couple fight their separation after the husband has a heart attack and is put into a nursing home. The fine cast received several Emmy nominations, with Astaire the winner. Made-for-television. **100m/C VHS, Beta.** Helen Hayes, Fred Astaire, Efrem Zimbalist Jr., Patty Duke; ***D:*** David Lowell Rich; ***M:*** Henry Mancini. *COL*

Family Viewing 🦴🦴🦴 **1987** Surrealistic depiction of a family—obsessed with television and video—whose existence is a textbook model of home sweet dysfunctional home. An early, experimental film from Canada's Egoyan, it won considerable praise for its social commentary. **92m/C VHS, LV.** *CA* David Hemblen, Adian Tierney, Gabrielle Rose, Arsinee Khanjian; ***D:*** Atom Egoyan; ***W:*** Atom Egoyan; ***M:*** Mychael Danna. Toronto-City Award '87: Best Canadian Feature Film. *FXL, FCT, INJ*

Famous Five Get into Trouble 🦴🦴 **1987** Four precocious youngsters and a dog get involved with a criminal plot and cutely wile their way out of it. Scandinavian; dubbed in English. **90m/C VHS, Beta.** Astrid Villaume, Ove Sprogoe, Lily Broberg; ***D:*** Trine Hedman. *TWE*

The Fan 🦴🦴 **1981 (R)** A Broadway star is threatened and her immediate circle cut down when a lovestruck fan feels he has been rejected by his idol. The stellar cast makes this bloody and familiar tale seem better than it is. **95m/C VHS, Beta, LV.** Lauren Bacall, Maureen Stapleton, James Garner, Hector Elizondo, Michael Biehn, Griffin Dunne; ***D:*** Edward Bianchi; ***W:*** Priscilla Chapman; ***M:*** Pino Donaggio. *PAR*

The Fan 🦴🦴½ **1996 (R)** Obsessed baseball fan Gil Renard (De Niro, who owns the copyright on playing deranged) stalks favorite player Bobby Rayburn (Snipes) who just signed a big contract with the hometown team. When Rayburn goes into a slump, Renard figures he can help his idol—by any means necessary. As an added bonus, Gil's a knife salesman. De Niro does the psycho thing with his usual aplomb, while Snipes successfully returns to the diamond. Scott keeps the familiar storyline from becoming tedious. Based on the book by Peter Abrahams. **?m/C VHS.** Robert De Niro, Wesley Snipes, Ellen Barkin, John Leguizamo, Benicio Del Toro, Patti D'Arbanville; ***D:*** Tony Scott; ***W:*** Phoef Sutton. *NYR*

Fancy Pants 🦴🦴½ **1950** Remake of "Ruggles of Red Gap" features Hope, a British actor posing as a butler. Also featuring Ball, an amusing contrast. Fine performances all around. ♫Fancy Pants; Home Cookin'. **92m/C VHS, Beta, LV.** Bob Hope, Lucille Ball, Bruce Cabot, Jack Kirkwood, Lea Penman, Eric Blore, John Alexander, Norma Varden; ***D:*** George Marshall; ***C:*** Charles B(ryant) Lang. *PAR*

Fandango 🦴🦴½ **1985 (PG)** Five college friends take a wild weekend drive across the Texas Badlands for one last fling before graduation and the prospect of military service. Expanded by Reynolds with assistance from Steven Spielberg, from his student film. Provides a look at college and life during the '60s Vietnam crisis. **91m/C VHS, Beta.** Judd Nelson, Kevin Costner, Sam Robards, Chuck Bush, Brian Cesak, Elizabeth Daily, Suzy Amis, Glenne Headly, Pepe Serna, Marvin J. McIntyre; ***D:*** Kevin Reynolds; ***W:*** Kevin Reynolds; ***M:*** Alan Silvestri. *WAR*

Fangoria's Weekend of Horrors **1986** A documentary about the making of horror films, featuring interviews with the industry's most scream-invoking artists. Copious film clips. **60m/C VHS, Beta.** Rick Baker, Wes Craven, Tobe Hooper, Robert Englund. *MED*

Fangs 🦴½ **1975 (R)** Unfriendly reptile-stomping villagers take the life of Mr. Snakey's favorite serpent. He sends his slithering pets on a vengeful and poisonous spree. **90m/C VHS, Beta.** Les Tremayne, Janet Wood, Bebe Kelly, Marvin Kaplan, Alice Nunn; ***D:*** Vittorio Schiraldi. *GEM, MRV*

Fangs of Fate 🦴½ **1925** A gang of bad guys battles the town's new marshal. **67m/B VHS, Beta, 8mm.** Bill Patton, Dorothy Donald. *GPV, VYY*

Fangs of the Living Dead 🦴½ *Malenka, the Vampire; La Nipote del Vampiro; The Niece of the Vampire; The Vampire's Niece* **1968** When a young woman inherits a castle, her uncle, who happens to be a vampire, tries to persuade her to remain among the undead. **80m/C VHS.** *SP IT* Anita Ekberg, Rossana Yanni, Diana Lorys, Fernando Bilbao, Paul Muller, Julian Ugarte, Andriana Ambesi; ***D:*** Armando de Ossorio; ***W:*** Armando de Ossorio. *SNC*

Fangs of the Wild 🦴🦴 *Follow the Hunter* **1954** When a young boy witnesses a murder at his father's hunting lodge, no one but the killer believes him. When the killer decides to get rid of the boy, Buck the Wonder Dog gets involved. **72m/B VHS.** Charles Chaplin Jr., Onslow Stevens, Margia Dean, Freddy Ridgeway, Phil Tead, Robert Stevenson; ***D:*** William Claxton. *NOS, DVT, HEG*

Fanny 🦴🦴🦴🦴 **1932** Second part of Marcel Pagnol's trilogy depicting the lives of the people of Provence, France. The poignant tale of Fanny, a young woman who marries an older man when Marius, her young lover, leaves her pregnant when he goes to sea. Remade several times but the original holds its own very well. "Marius" was first in the trilogy; "Cesar" was third. **128m/B VHS, Beta, LV.** *FR* Raimu, Charpin, Orane Demazis, Pierre Fresnay, Alida Rauffe; ***D:*** Marc Allegret; ***W:*** Marcel Pagnol; ***M:*** Vincent Scotto. *INT, MRV, HHT*

Fanny 🦴🦴🦴 **1961** Young girl falls in love with an adventurous sailor, and finds herself pregnant after he returns to the sea. With the help of the sailor's parents, she finds, marries, and eventually grows to love a much older man, who in turn cares for her and adores her son as if he were his own. When the sailor returns, all involved must confront their pasts and define their futures. Beautifully made, with fine performances and a plot which defies age or nationality. Part of the "A Night at the Movies" series, this tape simulates a 1961 movie evening, with a Tweety Pie cartoon, a newsreel and coming attractions for "Splendor in the Grass" and "The Roman Spring of Mrs. Stone." **148m/C VHS, Beta.** *FR* Leslie Caron, Maurice Chevalier, Charles Boyer, Horst Buchholz, Lionel Jeffries; ***D:*** Joshua Logan; ***W:*** Julius J. Epstein, Philip C. Epstein; ***C:*** Jack Cardiff. National Board of Review Awards '61: 10 Best Films of the Year; Nominations: Academy Awards '60: Best Color Cinematography; Academy Awards '61: Best Actor (Boyer), Best Film Editing, Best Picture, Best Original Score. *NOS, WAR*

Fanny and Alexander 🦴🦴🦴🦴 *Fanny Och Alexander* **1983 (R)** The culmination of Bergman's career, this autobiographical film is set in a rural Swedish town in 1907. It tells the story of one year in the lives of the Ekdahl family, as seen by the young children, Fanny and Alexander. Magic and religion, love and death, reconciliation and estrangement are skillfully captured in this carefully detailed, lovingly photographed film. In Swedish with English subtitles or dubbed. **197m/C VHS, Beta, LV.** *SW* Pernilla Allwin, Bertil Guve, Gunn Walgren, Allan Edwall, Ewa Froling, Erland Josephson, Harriet Andersson, Jarl Kulle, Jan Malmsjo; ***D:*** Ingmar Bergman; ***W:*** Ingmar Bergman; ***C:*** Sven Nykvist; ***M:*** Daniel Bell. Academy Awards '83: Best Art Direction/Set Decoration, Best Cinematography, Best Costume Design, Best Foreign Language Film; Cesar Awards '84: Best Foreign Film; Golden Globe Awards '84: Best Foreign Film; Los Angeles Film Critics Association Awards '83: Best Cinematography, Best Foreign Film; New York Film Critics Awards '83: Best Director (Bergman), Best Foreign Film; Nominations: Academy Awards '83: Best Director (Bergman), Best Original Screenplay. *COL, INJ, NLC*

Fanny Hill 🦴🦴 **1983 (R)** A softcore adaptation of the racy Victorian classic. **80m/C VHS, Beta.** *GB* Lisa Raines, Shelley Winters, Wilfrid Hyde-White, Oliver Reed. *MGM*

Fanny Hill: Memoirs of a Woman of Pleasure *Woof!* **1964** Sexual exploits of an innocent in bawdy 18th-century London, as directed by notorious "Super Vixen" Meyer (though by Meyer standards, proceedings are fairly innocuous, if inept). Based on the novel. **105m/B VHS, Beta.** Miriam Hopkins, Walter Giller, Alexander D'Arcy, Leticia Roman; ***D:*** Russ Meyer. *NO*

Fantasia 🦴🦴🦴🦴 **1940** Disney's most personal animation feature first bombed at the box office and irked purists who couldn't take the plotless, experimental mix of classical music and cartoons. It became a cult movie, embraced by more liberal generations of moviegoers. Reissue of the original version, painstakingly restored, ceased because of a planned remake. ♫Toccata & Fugue in D; The Nutcracker Suite; The Sorcerer's Apprentice; The Rite of Spring; Pastoral Symphony; Dance of the Hours; Night on Bald Mountain; Ave Maria; The Cossack Dance. **116m/C VHS, LV.** *DIS, FCT, RDG*

Fantasies *Woof! And Once Upon a Love* **1973 (R)** Teenage lovers Derek and Hooten return to their Greek island home and decide to improve their village by turning it into a tourist haven. First collaboration of the Dereks is a loser, lacking plot, direction, and decent acting. Bo shows no talent but the obvious one and is actually credited as Kathleen Collins. **81m/C VHS, Beta.** Bo Derek, Peter Hooten, Anna Alexiades; ***D:*** John Derek. *FOX*

The Fantasist ✂ **1989 (R)** Sex crime thriller features a deranged killer who makes obscene, yet seductive phone calls to young ladies before murdering them. **98m/C VHS.** Timothy Bottoms, Christopher Cazenove; ***D:*** Robin Hardy. *REP*

Fantastic Balloon Voyage ✂ **197? (G)** Three men embark on a journey across the equator in a balloon, experiencing myriad adventures along the way. Much hot air. **100m/C VHS, Beta.** Hugo Stiglitz, Jeff Cooper. *GEM*

Fantastic Planet ✂✂✂ *La Planete Sauvage* **1973 (PG)** A critically acclaimed French, animated, sci-fi epic based on the drawings of Roland Topor. A race of small humanoids are enslaved and exploited by a race of giants on a savage planet, until one of the small creatures manages to unite his people and fight for equality. **68m/C VHS, Beta.** *FR* ***D:*** Rene Laloux; ***W:*** Rene Laloux; ***V:*** Barry Bostwick. Nominations: Cannes Film Festival '73: Best Film. *VYY, MRV, SNC*

Fantastic Seven ✂½ **1982** The Fantastic Seven is a daredevil team sent to rescue a Hollywood sex symbol who has been kidnapped and held for ransom while shooting on location off the coast of Miami. **96m/C VHS, Beta.** Elke Sommer, Christopher Connelly. *TLF*

Fantastic Voyage ✂✂✂ *Microscopia; Strange Journey* **1966** An important scientist, rescued from behind the Iron Curtain, is so severely wounded by enemy agents that traditional surgery is impossible. After being shrunk to microscopic size, a medical team journeys inside his body where they find themselves threatened by the patient's natural defenses. Great action, award-winning special effects. **100m/C VHS, Beta, LV.** Stephen Boyd, Edmond O'Brien, Raquel Welch, Arthur Kennedy, Donald Pleasence, Arthur O'Connell, William Redfield, James Brolin; ***D:*** Richard Fleischer; ***C:*** Ernest Laszlo. Academy Awards '66: Best Art Direction/Set Decoration (Color), Best Visual Effects; Nominations: Academy Awards '66: Best Color Cinematography, Best Film Editing. *FOX, CCB*

The Fantastic World of D.C. Collins ✂✂ **1984** Gary Coleman plays a daydreaming teenager who thinks he is being pursued by mysterious strangers seeking a videotape that was unknowingly slipped to him. Made for television. **100m/C VHS.** Gary Coleman, Bernie Casey, Shelley Smith, Fred Dryer, Marilyn McCoo, Philip Abbott, George Gobel, Michael Ansara; ***D:*** Leslie Martinson. *VTR, NWV*

Fantasy Island ✂ **1976** Three people fly ("De plane, boss!") to an island paradise and get to live out their fantasies for a price. Made for television; the basis for the TV series. **100m/C VHS, Beta.** Ricardo Montalban, Bill Bixby, Sandra Dee, Peter Lawford, Carol Lynley, Hugh O'Brian, Eleanor Parker, Dick Sargent, Victoria Principal; ***D:*** Richard Lang. *PSM*

Fantasy Man ✂½ **1984** A restless middle-aged man tries to relieve his mid-life crisis with the help of three women. **100m/C VHS, Beta.** *AU* Harold Hopkins, Jeanie Drynan, Kerry Mack, Kate Fitzpatrick; ***D:*** John Meagher; ***W:*** John Meagher. *VCD*

Far and Away ✂✂½ **1992 (PG-13)** Meandering old-fashioned epic about immigrants, romance, and settling the American West. In the 1890s, Joseph Donelly (Cruise) is forced to flee his Irish homeland after threatening the life of his landlord, and emigrates to America in the company of the landlord's daughter, feisty Shannon Christie (Kidman). Particularly brutal scenes of Cruise earning his living as a bare-knuckled boxer contrast with the expansiveness of the land rush ending. Slow, spotty, and a little too slick for its own good, though real-life couple Cruise and Kidman are an attractive pair. Filmed in 70-mm Panavision on location in Ireland and Montana. Also available in a letter boxed version. **140m/C VHS, Beta, LV.** Tom Cruise, Nicole Kidman, Thomas Gibson, Robert Prosky, Barbara Babcock, Colm Meaney, Eileen Pollock, Michelle Johnson, Cyril Cusack, Clint Howard, Rance Howard; ***D:*** Ron Howard; ***W:*** Bob Dolman; ***C:*** Mikael Salomon; ***M:*** John Williams. *MCA*

Far Away and Long Ago ✂✂½ **1974** Based on the autobiographical novel by Guillermo Hudson which details the memories which haunted his childhood—the Argentinian pampas, its gauchos, witchcraft, and women. In Spanish with English subtitles. **91m/C VHS.** *AR* Juan Jose Camero, Leonor Manso; ***D:*** Manuel Antin. *INJ*

Far Country ✂✂✂ **1955** Cattlemen must battle the elements and frontier lawlessness in this classic. Stewart leads his herd to the Yukon in hopes of large profits, but ends up having to kidnap it back from the crooked sheriff and avenging the deaths of his friends. Entertaining and the Yukon setting takes it out of the usual Western arena. **97m/C VHS, Beta.** James Stewart, Ruth Roman, Walter Brennan, Harry (Henry) Morgan, Corinne Calvet, Jay C. Flippen, John McIntire; ***D:*** Anthony Mann; ***C:*** William H. Daniels; ***M:*** Henry Mancini. *BAR*

Far Cry from Home ✂ **197?** A battered wife attempts to escape from her domineering husband before it's too late. **87m/C VHS, Beta.** Mary Ann McDonald, Richard Monette. *TWE*

Far East ✂½ **1985** Two ex-lovers meet in Southeast Asia and join forces to find the woman's missing husband, a reporter. **105m/C VHS, Beta.** Bryan Brown, Helen Morse; ***D:*** John Duigan. *ORI, VTR*

Far from Home ✂✂ **1989 (R)** Drew Barrymore is the seductive teen being scoped by a psychotic killer while on vacation with her father. Lots of over-the-top performances by the familiar cast. **86m/C VHS, LV.** Matt Frewer, Drew Barrymore, Richard Masur, Karen Austin, Susan Tyrrell, Anthony Rapp, Jennifer Tilly, Andras Jones, Dick Miller; ***D:*** Meiert Avis; ***M:*** Jonathan Elias. *LIV, VES*

Far from Home: The Adventures of Yellow Dog ✂✂ **1994 (PG)** Stalwart lad Angus (Bradford) and his faithful pooch Yellow (Dakotah) battle the elements, wild animals and fatigue as they try to get back home after being shipwrecked on a remote island in British Columbia. Good thing Dad (Davidson) gave them all those cool survival tips before they left, or else they never would've known that you can eat bugs. (Okay, the dog probably knew that already.) Mom (Rogers) does her bit by making sure the search mission stays focused. You usually can't go wrong with a kid and his dog lost in the wilderness, but this one is really short—on time and drama. Nice scenery, though. **81m/C VHS, LV.** Jesse Bradford, Bruce Davison, Mimi Rogers, Tom Bower; ***D:*** Phillip Borsos; ***W:*** Phillip Borsos. *FXV*

Far from the Madding Crowd ✂✂✂ **1967 (PG)** A lavish, long adaptation of Thomas Hardy's nineteenth century classic about the beautiful Bathsheba and the three very different men who love her. Her first love is a handsome and wayward soldier (Stamp), her second the local noble lord (Finch) and her third the ever-loving and long-patient farmer (Bates). Christie is well cast as the much-desired beauty. Gorgeous cinematography by Nicolas Roeg. **165m/C VHS, Beta, LV.** *GB* Julie Christie, Terence Stamp, Peter Finch, Alan Bates, Prunella Ransome; ***D:*** John Schlesinger; ***W:*** Frederic Raphael; ***M:*** Richard Rodney Bennett. National Board of Review Awards '67: 10 Best Films of the Year, Best Actor (Finch); Nominations: Academy Awards '67: Best Original Score. *MGM*

Far Frontier ✂✂ **1948** Roy Rogers saves the day by thwarting a band of outlaws who are being smuggled across the border in soybean oil cans. Includes musical numbers and horse tricks. **60m/B VHS.** Roy Rogers, Andy Devine, Clayton Moore. *NOS, TIM, REP*

Far North ✂✂½ **1988 (PG-13)** Quirky comedy about a woman who returns to her rural family homestead after her father is seriously injured by a horse, and tries to deal with her eccentric family's travails. Fine cast never reaches its potential. Shepard's directing debut. **96m/C VHS, Beta, LV, 8mm.** Jessica Lange, Charles Durning, Tess Harper, Donald Moffat, Ann Wedgeworth, Patricia Arquette, Nina Draxton; ***D:*** Sam Shepard; ***W:*** Sam Shepard; ***C:*** Robbie Greenberg. *NLC*

A Far Off Place ✂✂ **1993 (PG-13)** Adolescent boy, adolescent girl, adolescent bushperson, and mature dog set out across the African desert to escape elephant poachers who want to kill them. The boy and girl find romance in the sand, bushperson finds water by listening, and dog gets very nice walk. Strong performances by the youthful leads lend charm to this Disney/Amblin flick, particularly Bok as the bushperson. Unusually violent film for studios involved (animals and people bite sand), though care is taken to edit actual blood shed on screen. Filmed in Zimbabwe and Namibia and based on the books "A Story Like the Wind" and "A Far Off Place" by Laurens van der Post. **107m/C VHS, Beta, LV.** Reese Witherspoon, Ethan Randall, Sarel Bok, Jack Thompson, Maximilian Schell, Robert Burke, Patricia Kalember, Daniel Gerroll, Miles Anderson; ***D:*** Mikael Salomon; ***W:*** Robert Caswell, Jonathan Hensleigh, Sally Robinson; ***C:*** Juan Ruiz-Anchia; ***M:*** James Horner. *DIS*

Far Out Man *Woof!* **1989 (R)** An unalterable middle-aged hippie is sent by his worried family and his psychiatrist on a cross-country journey to rediscover himself. The script makes no sense and has very few laughs. **105m/C VHS, Beta, LV.** Thomas Chong, Rae Dawn Chong, C. Thomas Howell, Shelby Chong, Martin Mull, Paris Chong, Paul Bartel, Judd Nelson, Michael Winslow, Richard "Cheech" Marin; ***D:*** Thomas Chong; ***W:*** Thomas Chong. *COL*

The Far Pavilions ✂✂½ *Blade of Steel* **1984** A British officer falls in love with an Indian princess during the second Afghan War. Cross is appropriately noble and stiff-upper-lipped but Irving is miscast as his ethnic love. Based on the romantic bestseller by M.M. Kaye, this lavish production was made for cable television. **108m/C VHS, Beta.** Ben Cross, Amy Irving, Omar Sharif, Benedict Taylor, Rossano Brazzi, Christopher Lee; ***D:*** Peter Duffell; ***M:*** Carl Davis. *KAR*

Faraway, So Close! ✂✂ *In Weiter Ferne, So Nah!* **1993 (PG-13)** Wenders' erratic follow-up to his magnificent "Wings of Desire." Cassiel (Sander), the angel left behind when Damiel (Ganz) chose to become human, once again surveys Berlin, noticing the changes (not necessarily for the better). Angelic companion Raphaela (Kinski) watches events passively, including an old man's (Ruhamnn) reflections on life and the philosophical musings of Emit Flesti (Dafoe, Time Itself, get it?), even as Cassiel impulsively chooses humanity over his heavenly world. Falk makes a return appearance to little effect. Overlong and under-developed. **146m/C VHS, LV.** *GE* Otto Sander, Peter Falk, Horst Buchholz, Nastassia Kinski, Heinz Ruhmann, Bruno Ganz, Solveig Dommartin, Ruediger Vogler, Willem Dafoe, Lou Reed; ***D:*** Wim Wenders; ***W:*** Ulrich Zieger, Richard Reitinger, Wim Wenders; ***M:*** Laurent Petitgrand. Cannes Film Festival '93: Grand Jury Prize; Nominations: Cannes Film Festival '93: Best Film; Golden Globe Awards '94: Best Song ("Stay"). *COL*

Farewell My Concubine ✂✂ *Bawang Bie Ji* **1993 (R)** Exotic film covers 50 years of sexual, social, and political Chinese history wrapped around the story of two male Peking Opera stars. Deposited as boys at the Opera's training school Douzi and Shitou become fast friends in their hermetically sealed world, but their friendship is tested during the chaos of Communism and the cultural revolution. Sumptuous and well-acted, but the sheer length and emotional detachment prove to be drawbacks. Adapted from a novel by Lee, who based the work on a 2000-year-old Chinese opera about an imperial concubine. Filmed on location in Beijing. In Mandarin Chinese with subtitles. **157m/C VHS, LV.** *HK* Leslie Cheung, Zhang Fengyi, Gong Li, Lu Qi, Ying Da, Ge You; ***D:*** Chen Kaige; ***W:*** Lilian Lee, Lu Wei; ***C:*** Gu Changwei; ***M:*** Zhao Jiping. British Academy Awards '93: Best Foreign Film; Cannes Film Festival '93: Best Film; Los Angeles Film Critics Association Awards '93: Best Foreign Film; National Board of Review Awards '93: Best Foreign Film; New York Film Critics Awards '93: Best Foreign Film, Best Supporting Actress (Li); Nominations: Academy Awards '93: Best Cinematography, Best Foreign Language Film; British Academy Awards '93: Best Foreign Language Film; Golden Globe Awards '94: Best Foreign Language Film. *TOU*

Farewell, My Lovely 1975 (R) A remake of the 1944 Raymond Chandler mystery, "Murder, My Sweet," featuring private eye Phillip Marlowe hunting for an ex-convict's lost sweetheart in 1941 Los Angeles. Perhaps the most accurate of Chandler adaptations, but far from the best, this film offers a nicely detailed production. Mitchum is a bit too world-weary as the seen-it-all detective. **95m/C VHS, Beta.** *GB* Robert Mitchum, Charlotte Rampling, Sylvia Miles, John Ireland, Anthony Zerbe, Jack O'Halloran, Harry Dean Stanton, Sylvester Stallone, Cheryl "Rainbeaux" Smith; ***D:*** Dick Richards; ***W:*** David Zelag Goodman; ***C:*** John A. Alonzo; ***M:*** David Shire. National Board of Review Awards '75: 10 Best Films of the Year; Nominations: Academy Awards '75: Best Supporting Actress (Miles). *SUE*

A Farewell to Arms 1932 The original film version of Ernest Hemingway's novel about the tragic love affair between an American ambulance driver and an English nurse during the Italian campaign of WWI. The novelist disavowed the ambiguous ending, but the public loved the film. Fine performances and cinematography. **85m/B VHS, Beta, LV.** Helen Hayes, Gary Cooper, Adolphe Menjou, Mary Philips, Jack LaRue, Blanche Frederici; ***D:*** Frank Borzage; ***C:*** Charles B(ryant) Lang. Academy Awards '33: Best Cinematography, Best Sound; National Board of Review Awards '32: 10 Best Films of the Year; Nominations: Academy Awards '33: Best Interior Decoration, Best Picture. *CNG, MRV, NOS*

Farewell to the King ½ 1989 (PG-13) During WWII, a ship-wrecked American deserter becomes the chief of a tribe of Borneo headhunters until his jungle kingdom is caught between the forces of the U.S. and Japanese. With the help of a British officer he helps them defend themselves when the Japanese invade. An old-fashioned war epic with a beautiful location and solid if uninspired-performances by the leads. Based on Pierre Schoendoerffer's novel "L'Adieu Au Roi." **114m/C VHS, Beta, LV.** Nick Nolte, Nigel Havers, Marius Weyers, Frank McRae, Marilyn Tokuda, Elan Oberon, William Wise, James Fox, Aki Aleong; ***D:*** John Milius; ***W:*** John Milius; ***C:*** Dean Semler; ***M:*** Basil Poledouris. *ORI*

Fargo 1996 (R) Another malicious comedy from the Coen brothers. Car salesman Jerry Lundegaard (Macy) hires a couple of losers to kidnap his wife so he can swindle the ransom money out of his father-in-law. Naturally, the scheme begins to unravel and the very pregnant police chief Marge Gunderson (McDormand) treks through the frozen tundra of Minnesota to put the pieces of the puzzle together. McDormand's performance as the chatty competent chief is first rate. Needling the flat-accented Midwestern neighbors of their youth, the Coens have also returned to their filmmaking roots after the disappointing big-budget "Hudsucker Proxy." **97m/C VHS.** William H. Macy, Frances McDormand, Steve Buscemi, Peter Stormare, Harve Presnell, Steve Reevis, John Carroll Lynch, Kristin Rudrud, Steve Park; ***Cameos:*** Jose Feliciano; ***D:*** Ethan Coen; ***W:*** Ethan Coen, Joel Coen; ***C:*** Roger Deakins; ***M:*** Carter Burwell. Cannes Film Festival '96: Best Director (Coen). *PGV*

Fargo Express ½ 1932 When the kid brother of Maynard's true love is falsely accused of robbing a stagecoach, Maynard works to clear his name. Routine stuff. **60m/B VHS, Beta.** Ken Maynard, Helen Mack, Paul Fix; ***D:*** Alan James. *NOS, VCN, DVT*

Farinelli *Farinelli the Castrato; Farinelli Il Castrato* 1994 (R) A movie to make men cringe. Floridly depicts the complex professional and personal ties of 18th-century opera composer Riccardo Broschi (Lo Verso) and his younger brother Carlo (Dionisi), a celebrated castrato singer under the stage name "Farinelli." In part, because of an early church prohibition against women singing in public, boys were castrated before puberty to preserve their pure soprano voices while vocal power and agility grew as they became men. Castrati were the rock stars of their day and Farinelli lived a flamboyant life before retiring to the Spanish court of Philip V. The castrato voice heard in the movie is an electronic mixture of countertenor Derek Lee Ragin and soprano Ewa Mallas Godlewska. French and Italian with subtitles. **110m/C VHS, LV.** *FR IT BE* Stefano Dionisi, Enrico Lo Verso, Jeroen Krabbe, Elsa Zylberstein, Caroline Cellier, Omero Antonutti, Jacques Boudet; ***D:*** Gerard Corbiau; ***W:*** Gerard Corbiau, Andree Corbiau, Marcel Beaulieu; ***C:*** Walther Vanden Ende; ***M:*** Christopher Rousset. Cesar Awards '95: Best Art Direction/Set Decoration, Best Sound; Golden Globe Awards '95: Best Foreign Film; Nominations: Academy Awards '94: Best Foreign Language Film. *COL*

The Farmer Takes a Wife ½ 1935 Henry Fonda's first film, recreating his stage role, as a mid-nineteenth century farmer at odds with the Erie canal builders and struggling to court the woman he loves. Remade as a musical in 1953. **91m/B VHS.** Janet Gaynor, Henry Fonda, Charles Bickford, Slim Summerville, Jane Withers; ***D:*** Victor Fleming. *TCF*

The Farmer Takes a Wife 1953 Poor musical remake of the 1935 drama, about the trials of a struggling 1850s farmer and the Erie canal boat cook he loves. Contains no memorable music and Robertson can't compete with Henry Fonda's original role as the farmer. ♫We're in Business; On the Erie Canal; We're Doing it for the Natives in Jamaica; When I Close My Door; Today I Love Everybody; Somethin' Real Special; With The Sun Warm Upon Me; Can You Spell Schenectady?. **81m/C VHS, Beta, LV.** Betty Grable, Dale Robertson, Thelma Ritter, John Carroll, Eddie Foy Jr.; ***D:*** Henry Levin. *FOX*

The Farmer's Daughter 1947 Young portrays Katrin Holmstrom, a Swedish farm girl who becomes a maid to Congressman Cotten and winds up running for office herself (not neglecting to find romance as well). The outspoken and multi-talented character charmed audiences and was the basis of a television series in the 1960s. **97m/B VHS, Beta.** Loretta Young, Joseph Cotten, Ethel Barrymore, Charles Bickford, Harry Davenport, Lex Barker, James Arness, Rose Hobart; ***D:*** H.C. Potter; ***C:*** Milton Krasner. Academy Awards '47: Best Actress (Young); Nominations: Academy Awards '47: Best Supporting Actor (Bickford). *FOX, BTV*

The Farmer's Other Daughter *Farm Girl* 1965 A rural comedy about Farmer Brown whose lovely daughter is eyed by all the farmhands. He also has to contend with dastardly Mr. Barksnapper who wants to take his farm away from him until one of his daughter's beaus comes to the rescue. **84m/C VHS.** Ernest Ashworth, Judy Pennebaker, Bill Michael; ***D:*** John Patrick Hayes. *COL*

The Farmer's Wife ½ 1928 Silent British comedy about a recently widowed farmer searching for a new wife. Meanwhile, his lovely housekeeper would be the perfect candidate. Based on Eden Philpott's play. **97m/B VHS.** *GB* Jameson Thomas, Lillian Hall-Davis, Gordon Harker; ***D:*** Alfred Hitchcock; ***W:*** Alfred Hitchcock. *REP, SNC, MLB*

Fashions of 1934 *Fashions* 1934 A typical, lightweight thirties musical with impressive choreography by Busby Berkeley. Powell plays a disreputable clothing designer who goes to Paris to steal the latest fashion designs and winds up costuming a musical and falls in love. ♫Spin a Little Web of Dreams; Broken Melody. **78m/B VHS, Beta.** Bette Davis, William Powell, Frank McHugh, Hugh Herbert, Reginald Owen, Busby Berkeley; ***D:*** William Dieterle. *VDM*

Fass Black 1977 (R) Yet another man against the mob flick straight out of Bartlett's familiar plot lines. Amidst gratuitous music and violence, a disco owner locks horns with the syndicate after they try to take over his place. There's a good reason disco is dead. **105m/C VHS.** John Poole, Jeanne Bell, Cal Wilson, Harold Nicholas, Nicholas Lewis; ***D:*** D'Urville Martin. *XVC*

The Fast and the Furious 1954 On the lam after being falsely charged with murder, Ireland picks up a fast car and a loose woman (or is it a loose car and a fast woman?) and makes a run for the border by entering the Pebble Beach race. **73m/B VHS.** John Ireland, Dorothy Malone, Bruce Carlisle, Iris Adrian; ***D:*** John Ireland, Edwards Sampson. *NOS*

Fast Break ½ 1979 (PG) New York deli clerk who is a compulsive basketball fan talks his way into a college coaching job. He takes a team of street players with him, with predictable results on and off the court. Kaplan's screen debut. **107m/C VHS, Beta.** Gabe Kaplan, Harold Sylvester, Randee Heller; ***D:*** Jack Smight; ***M:*** David Shire. *GKK*

Fast Bullets ½ 1944 Texas Rangers fight a gang of smugglers and rescue a kidnap victim in this typical western. **52m/B VHS, Beta.** Tom Tyler, Rex Lease. *NOS, VCN, DVT*

Fast Company 1978 The life story of champion race car driver Lonnie Johnson including women, money, and the drag racing sponsors. **90m/C VHS, Beta.** William Smith, John Saxon, Claudia Jennings, Nicholas Campbell, Don Francks; ***D:*** David Cronenberg; ***W:*** David Cronenberg. *AOV*

Fast Food 1989 A super-cheap, strangulated attempt at low comedy, wherein an entrepreneurial hamburger peddler invents a secret aphrodisiac sauce. Look for former porn-star Traci Lords. **90m/C VHS, Beta, LV.** Clark Brandon, Tracy Griffith, Randal Patrick, Traci Lords, Kevin McCarthy, Michael J. Pollard, Jim Varney; ***D:*** Michael A. Simpson; ***W:*** Clark Brandon. *FRH*

Fast Forward ½ 1984 (PG) A group of eight teenagers from Ohio learn how to deal with success and failure when they enter a national dance contest in New York City. A break-dancing variation on the old show business chestnut. ♫Fast Forward; How Do You Do; As Long As We Believe; Pretty Girl; Mystery; Curves; Showdown; Do You Want It Right Now?; Hardrock. **110m/C VHS, Beta, LV.** John Scott Clough, Don Franklin, Tracy Silver, Cindy McGee; ***D:*** Sidney Poitier; ***W:*** Richard Wesley; ***M:*** Tom Bahler. *COL*

Fast Getaway 1991 (PG) Chases scenes proliferate when a teen criminal mastermind plots bank heists for his outlaw father. Relatively painless adolescent action-comedy, cleverly acted, quickly forgotten. **91m/C VHS, LV, 8mm.** Corey Haim, Cynthia Rothrock, Leo Rossi, Ken Lerner, Marcia Strassman; ***D:*** Spiro Razatos. *COL*

Fast Getaway 2 ½ 1994 (PG-13) Ex-bank robber Nelson (Haim) has given up a life of crime to open a business with gal pal Patrice (Buxton) while waiting for his partner/dad Sam (Rossi) to get out of jail. Then Nelson gets set up by Lily (Rothrock) and finds himself trying to convince an FBI agent of his innocence. Innocuous. **90m/C VHS.** Corey Haim, Sarah Buxton, Leo Rossi, Cynthia Rothrock, Peter Paul Liapis; ***D:*** Oley Sassone; ***W:*** Mark Sevi; ***M:*** David Robbins. *LIV*

Fast Gun ½ 1993 (R) Weapons-loving ex-CIA spook decides to take over a town—with your basic one lone hero to stop him. **90m/C VHS.** Richard Hill, Kaz Garas, Robert Dryer, Brenda Bakke, Cirio H. Santiago. *NHO*

Fast Kill 1973 A terrorist plot begins to fall apart when the conspirators fight among themselves. **94m/C VHS, Beta.** Tom Adams, Susie Hampton, Michael Culver, Peter Halliday; ***D:*** Lindsay Shonteff. *GEM*

Fast Lane Fever 1982 (R) A drag racer challenges a factory worker to a no-holds-barred race. **94m/C VHS, Beta.** *MGM*

Fast Money ½ 1983 Three pals can't resist the temptation of big bucks from flying drugs in from Mexico, but they find danger along the way. **92m/C VHS, Beta.** Sammy Allred, Sonny Carl Davis; ***D:*** Doug Holloway. *LIV*

Fast Talking 1986 The story of a quick-talking, incorrigible, fifteen-year-old Australian boy's humorous though tragic criminal schemes. The young protagonist slides his way through a life marked by a degenerate home life, a brother who forces him to sell drugs, and a future that holds no promise. **93m/C VHS, Beta.** *AU* Steve Bisley, Tracey Mann, Peter Hehir, Dennis Moore, Rod Zuanic, Toni Allaylis, Chris Truswell; ***D:*** Ken Cameron; ***W:*** Ken Cameron. *SUE, NLC*

Fast Times at Ridgemont High **1982 (R)** Teens at a Southern California high school revel in sex, drugs, and rock 'n' roll. A full complement of student types meet at the Mall—that great suburban microcosm percolating with angst-ridden teen trials—to contemplate losing their virginity, plot skipping homeroom, and move inexorably closer to the end of their adolescence. The talented young cast became household names: Sean Penn is most excellent as the California surfer dude who antagonizes teacher, Walston, aka "Aloha Mr. Hand." Based on the best-selling book by Cameron Crowe, it's one of the best of this genre. **91m/C VHS, Beta, LV.** Sean Penn, Jennifer Jason Leigh, Judge Reinhold, Robert Romanus, Brian Backer, Phoebe Cates, Ray Walston, Scott Thomson, Vincent Schiavelli, Amanda Wyss, Forest Whitaker, Kelli Maroney, Eric Stoltz, Pamela Springsteen, James Russo, Martin Brest, Anthony Edwards; ***D:*** Amy Heckerling; ***W:*** Cameron Crowe. *MCA*

Fast Walking **1982 (R)** A prison guard is offered fifty-thousand dollars to help a militant black leader escape from jail, the same man his cousin has contracted to kill. **116m/C VHS, Beta.** James Woods, Kay Lenz, M. Emmet Walsh, Robert Hooks, Tim McIntire, Timothy Carey, Susan Tyrrell; ***D:*** James B. Harris. *FOX, HHE*

Faster Pussycat! Kill! Kill! **1966** It doesn't get any better than this! Three sexy go-go dancers get their after-work kicks by hot-rodding in the California desert. They soon find themselves enveloped in murder, kidnapping, lust and robbery after a particular race gets out of hand. Easily the most watchable, fun and funny production to spring from the mind of Russ Meyer. Those who haven't seen this cannot truly be called "cool." **83m/B VHS.** Tura Satana, Haji, Lori Williams, Susan Bernard, Stuart Lancaster, Paul Trinka, Dennis Busch, Ray Barlow, Mickey Foxx; ***D:*** Russ Meyer; ***W:*** Jack Moran, Russ Meyer. *RMF, FCT, TPV*

Fastest Guitar Alive ½ **1968** Debut of the legendary Orbison is strictly for inveterate fans only. Rebel operative/crooner during the Civil War, whose rhythm is good but timing is bad, steals a Union gold supply, but the war ends before he makes it back to the land of Dixie. Seems that makes him a common thief. **88m/C VHS, Beta.** Roy Orbison, Sammy Jackson, Margaret Pierce, Joan Freeman; ***D:*** Michael Moore; ***M:*** Fred Karger. *MGM, MVD*

Fastest Gun Alive **1956** Suspenseful western with ex-gunfighter Ford challenged to a showdown by Crawford. **89m/C VHS.** Glenn Ford, Jeanne Crain, Broderick Crawford, Russ Tamblyn, Allyn Joslyn, Leif Erickson, John Dehner, Noah Beery Jr., J.M. Kerrigan, Rhys Williams; ***D:*** Russel Rouse; ***W:*** Russel Rouse, Frank D. Gilroy; ***M:*** Andre Previn. *MGM*

Fat and the Lean **1961** An early short film from Roman Polanski that satirizes government tyranny and absurdity. **16m/C VHS, Beta.** ***D:*** Roman Polanski. *IHF, FLI, GVV*

Fat City ½ **1972 (PG)** One of Huston's later triumphs, a seedy, street-level drama based on the Leonard Gardner novel about an aging alcoholic boxer trying to make a comeback and his young worshipful protege. Highly acclaimed. Tyrrell earned an Oscar nomination as the boxer's world-weary lover. **93m/C VHS, Beta.** Stacy Keach, Jeff Bridges, Susan Tyrrell, Candy Clark, Nicholas Colasanto; ***D:*** John Huston; ***C:*** Conrad Hall; ***M:*** Marvin Hamlisch. Nominations: Academy Awards '72: Best Supporting Actress (Tyrrell). *COL*

Fat Guy Goes Nutzoid *Woof! Zeisters* **1986** A crude farce about an obese mental patient who escapes from the mental hospital and joins two teenagers on a wild trip to New York City. **85m/C VHS, Beta.** Tibor Feldman, Peter Linari, John MacKay, Joan Allen; ***D:*** John Golden. *PSM*

Fat Man and Little Boy ½ **1989 (PG-13)** A lavish, semi-fictional account of the creation of the first atomic bomb, and the tensions between J. Robert Oppenheimer and his military employer, Gen. Leslie Groves. Overlong but interesting. Cusack, whose character never existed, is especially worthwhile as an idealistic scientist. **127m/C VHS, Beta, LV, 8mm.** Paul Newman, Dwight Schultz, Bonnie Bedelia, John Cusack, Laura Dern, John C. McGinley, Natasha Richardson, Ron Frazier; ***D:*** Roland Joffe; ***W:*** Bruce Robinson, Tony Garnett, Roland Joffe; ***M:*** Ennio Morricone. *PAR, FCT, HMV*

Fatal Attraction *Head On* **1980 (R)** Couple meet after an auto accident. They begin an affair which turns dark and bizarre. Fine cast doesn't get far with this peculiar premise, although every one tries hard. **90m/C VHS, Beta.** *CA* Sally Kellerman, Stephen Lack, John Huston, Lawrence Dane; ***D:*** Michael Grant. *VES*

Fatal Attraction **1987 (R)** When a very married New York lawyer is seduced by a beautiful blonde associate, the one-night stand leads to terror as she continues to pursue the relationship. She begins to threaten his family and home with possessive, violent acts. An expertly made, manipulative thriller; one of the most hotly discussed films of the 1980s. A successful change of role for Close as the sexy, scorned, and deadly other woman. Also available in a special "director's series" edition, featuring Lyne's original, controversial ending. **120m/C VHS, Beta, LV, 8mm, CD-I.** Michael Douglas, Glenn Close, Anne Archer, Stuart Pankin, Ellen Hamilton-Latzen, Ellen Foley, Fred Gwynne, Meg Mundy, J.J. Johnston; ***D:*** Adrian Lyne; ***W:*** James Dearden; ***M:*** Maurice Jarre. People's Choice Awards '88: Best Film—Drama; Nominations: Academy Awards '87: Best Actress (Close), Best Adapted Screenplay, Best Director (Lyne), Best Film Editing, Best Picture, Best Supporting Actress (Archer). *PAR, FCT, CCB*

Fatal Beauty ½ **1987 (R)** A female undercover cop in Los Angeles tracks down a drug dealer selling cocaine (from which the title is taken). Elliott is the mob bodyguard who helps her out. Violent and sensational, the film tries to capitalize on the success of "Beverly Hills Cop" and fails miserably. Goldberg is wasted in this effort and the picture tiptoes around the interracial romance aspects that are implied. **104m/C VHS, Beta, LV.** Whoopi Goldberg, Sam Elliott, Ruben Blades, Harris Yulin, Richard "Cheech" Marin, Brad Dourif; ***D:*** Tom Holland; ***M:*** Harold Faltermeyer. *MGM*

Fatal Bond ½ **1991 (R)** Blair plays a small-town hairdresser caught in an obsessive love affair with a drifter. When she suspects her boyfriend is committing a string of rape-murders, will she turn him in or protect him? Or is she next? **89m/C VHS.** Linda Blair, Jerome Elhers, Stephen Leeder, Donal Gibson, Caz Lederman, Tao Gerbert, Penny Pederson, Joe Bugner; ***D:*** Vincent Monton; ***W:*** Phillip Avalon. *COL*

Fatal Charm **1992 (R)** There's a serial killer at work in a small town. So far six women have been raped and murdered. But cute-teen Valerie can't believe it when the townspeople accuse that sweet guy Adam, especially since he's the one boy Valerie is so very attracted to. **90m/C VHS.** Christopher Atkins, Amanda Peterson, Mary Frann, James Remar, Andrew (Andy) Robinson, Peggy Lipton; ***D:*** Alan Smithee; ***W:*** Nicholas Niciphor. *ACA*

Fatal Chase *Nowhere to Hide* **1977** Van Cleef is a U.S. Marshal assigned to protect ex-hitman Musante from his vengeful former employers. And you thought you didn't get along with your boss. Typical made-for-TV fodder written by Anhalt, who usually manages to be a trifle more entertaining. **78m/C VHS.** Lee Van Cleef, Tony Musante, Charles Robinson, Lelia Goldoni, Noel Fournier, Russell Johnson, Edward Anhalt; ***D:*** Jack Starrett; ***W:*** Edward Anhalt. *SIM*

Fatal Confinement ½ **1964** Wrenching drama finds Crawford, having lived 15 years in seclusion with her young daughter, forced to sell her land to a giant corporation bent on expansion. Interesting also for the similarities to Crawford's real-life "Mommie Dearest" lifestyle. **70m/C VHS.** *GB* Joan Crawford, Paul Burke, Charles Bickford; ***D:*** Robert Guest. *FCT, MOV, TPV*

Fatal Error ½ *Outsider in Amsterdam; The Outsider; Grijpstra and de Gier* **1983** Dutch police thriller about the investigation of a cop killing. Based on the mystery series by Janwillem van de Wetering. Dubbed. **85m/C VHS, Beta.** *NL* Rutger Hauer, Rijk de Gooyer, Willeke Van Ammelrooy, Donald M. Jones; ***D:*** Wim Verstappen; ***M:*** Ennio Morricone. *NO*

Fatal Exposure **1990** The insatiably sanguinary Jack the Ripper lives on in the form of his great grandson, who avails himself of modern technology to capture those magic moments on videotape. Just goes to show home movies don't have to be bland. **?m/C VHS.** Blake Bahner, Ena Henderson, Julie Austin, Dan Schmale, Renee Cline, Gary Wise, Joy Ovington. *HHE*

Fatal Exposure **1991 (PG-13)** A divorcee on vacation with her young sons accidentally picks up the wrong snapshots at the developers'. It turns out she has her hands on some incriminating photos, and the subject will resort to anything, even murder, to keep her quiet. Originally made for television. **89m/C VHS, Beta, LV.** Mare Winningham, Nick Mancuso, Christopher McDonald, Geoffrey Blake, Christopher Pettiet; ***D:*** Alan Metzger. *PAR*

Fatal Fix ½ **198?** A French film expose of urban heroin addiction. Music by the Pretenders. **90m/C VHS, Beta.** *FR* Helmut Berger, Corinne Clery; ***D:*** Massimo Pirri. *NO*

Fatal Games ½ **1984** Young female athletes are mysteriously disappearing at the Falcon Academy of Athletics and a crazed killer is responsible. **88m/C VHS, Beta.** Sally Kirkland, Lynn Banashek, Sean Masterson. *MED*

The Fatal Glass of Beer **1933** Fields' son returns to his home in the north woods after serving a jail term in this slapstick comedy short. **18m/B VHS, Beta.** W.C. Fields, Rosemary Theby, George Chandler, Richard Cramer. *CCB, GVV*

The Fatal Hour ½ **1940** Karloff is enlisted to aid police in solving the murder of a detective. As Karloff is rounding up suspects, three more murders take place. Feeble. **68m/B VHS, Beta, 8mm.** Boris Karloff, Marjorie Reynolds, Grant Withers, Charles Trowbridge, John Hamilton, Frank Puglia, Jason Robards Sr.; ***D:*** William Nigh. *VYY, SNC*

The Fatal Image ½ **1990** A mother and daughter on vacation in Paris inadvertantly videotape an international mob hit, making them the target of ruthless assassins. Filmed on location in Paris. Made for television. **96m/C VHS.** Michele Lee, Justine Bateman, Francois Dunoyer, Jean-Pierre Cassel, Sonia Petrovna; ***D:*** Thomas J. Wright. *WOV*

Fatal Images **1982** A camera mysteriously causes all the models who pose for it to die, prompting the photographer to investigate. **90m/C VHS, Beta.** Lane Coyle; ***D:*** Dennis Devine. *AHV*

Fatal Instinct ½ **1992 (R)** A tough-guy cop trying to solve a murder instead finds himself a victim of sexual obsession in this erotic thriller. Also available in an unrated version. Not to be confused with (but doesn't everything sound familiar) "Basic Instinct." **93m/C VHS.** Michael Madsen, Laura Johnson, Tony Hamilton; ***D:*** John Dirlam. *NLC, COL*

Fatal Instinct **1993 (PG-13)** Spoof on erotic thrillers such as "Fatal Attraction" and "Basic Instinct." Suave Assante plays a guy with dual careers—he's both cop and attorney, defending the criminals he's arrested. Young plays a lovelorn psycho who's lost her panties. Plot is worth mentioning only in passing, since the point is to mercilessly skewer the entire film noir tradition. The gags occasionally hit deep-chuckle level, though for every good joke there's at least three that misfire. Clemmons of "E Street Band" fame wanders around with sax for background music purposes, typical of the acute self-consciousness of the film. **90m/C VHS, LV.** Armand Assante, Sean Young, Sherilyn Fenn, Kate Nelligan, Christopher McDonald, James Remar, Tony Randall; ***Cameos:*** Clarence Clemmons, Doc Severinsen; ***D:*** Carl Reiner; ***W:*** David O'Malley; ***M:*** Richard Gibbs. *MGM*

Fatal Justice **199?** Mars is a topnotch assassin who's been in the business too long and knows too much so the agency he works for decides to kill him off. They send young and beautiful professional Diana to do the job but will she be able to when she discovers Mars is actually her father? **90m/C VHS.** Joe Estevez. *AIP*

Fatal Mission ☙ **1989 (R)** A Vietnam soldier captures a female Chinese guerilla and uses her as his hostage and guide through the jungle. **84m/C VHS, Beta, LV.** Peter Fonda, Mako, Tia Carrere, Ted Markland, Jim Mitchum; ***D:*** George Rowe; ***C:*** Phil Parmet. *MED, VTR*

Fatal Passion ☙☙ **1994** Two sisters escape from the city after an accidental murder but run straight into the middle of a sacrifical backwoods cult. **90m/C VHS.** Lisa Hayland, Joseph Pilato. *SWI*

Fatal Past ☙☙ **1994 (R)** Bodyguard gets up close and personal with his client—who happens to be a mobster's mistress. As if this weren't trouble enough their pasts provide doom and gloom as well. **85m/C VHS, Beta.** Costas Mandylor, Kaisa Figura; ***D:*** Clive Fleury; ***W:*** Richard Ryan. *PAR*

Fatal Pulse *Woof!* **1988** Sorority girls are being killed off in grisly ways. Basic slasher/gore. **90m/C VHS, Beta.** Michelle McCormick, Ken Roberts, Joe Phelan, Alex Courtney. *CEL*

Fatal Skies ☙ **1990** An evil schemer plots to dump toxic waste in a small town's water supply until a group of teens comes to the rescue. **88m/C VHS, Beta.** Timothy Leary. *AIP*

Fatal Vision ☙☙½ **1984** The television film version of Joe McGinniss' controversial book about the murder trial of Dr. Jeffrey MacDonald, the former Green Berets physician accused of murdering his whole family and blaming the killings on crazed hippies. McGinniss first believed MacDonald may have been innocent but his subsequent investigation, and his book, proved otherwise. The starring debut for Cole. MacDonald still protests his innocence. **192m/C VHS, Beta, LV.** Gary Cole, Karl Malden, Eva Marie Saint, Andy Griffith, Barry Newman; ***D:*** David Greene. *COL*

Fatally Yours ☙☙ **1995** Real-estate agent Danny (Rossovich) decides to restore a long-vacant house where a mob massacre occurred in 1928. While in the house, he's "contacted" by the ghostly Sara (MacDonnell), whose husband and gangster father were among the dead. Sara tells him about a hidden treasure of jewels, which leads some present-day gangsters to take an interest in Danny's new property. **90m/C VHS.** Rick Rossovich, George Lazenby, Roddy McDowall, Sage Stallone, Sarah MacDonnell; ***D:*** Tim Everitt. *MNC*

Fate ☙☙½ **1990 (PG-13)** Sweet comedy. A young man plans his love-affair carefully, but his biggest problem is meeting the girl of his dreams. Cheerful acting from Lynn and Paul. Stylish and charming. **115m/C VHS.** Cheryl Lynn, Stuart Paul, Kaye Ballard, Susannah York; ***D:*** Stuart Paul. *ACA*

Father ☙☙☙ **1967** After WWII, a Hungarian youth makes up stories about his dead father's heroism that enhance his own position. Eventually he becomes obsessed with the facts surrounding his father's death at the hands of the enemy and, learning the truth, lays the past to rest. In Hungarian with English subtitles. **89m/B VHS, Beta, LV.** *HU* Andras Balint, Miklos Gabor; ***D:*** Istvan Szabo; ***W:*** Istvan Szabo. *VYY, DVT, INJ*

Father ☙☙ **1990 (PG-13)** A woman receives an anonymous telephone call telling her to watch a television news program and learn the truth about her beloved father. What she sees is her father's face superimposed over that of a young Nazi soldier and an aging, unstable woman accusing her father of war crimes. The daughter fiercely believes her father to be a victim of mistaken identity but questions keep nagging at her. Very similiar in plot to "Music Box" and just as pedestrian in spite of some good performances. **106m/C VHS.** *AU* Max von Sydow, Carol Drinkwater, Julia Blake, Steve Jacobs; ***D:*** John Power. Australian Film Institute '90: Best Actor (von Sydow), Best Actress (Blake). *MNC*

Father and Scout ☙☙½ **1995 (PG)** Would-be Eagle Scout has a problem when he takes his city-bred, whiny, basically incompetent, dad on a camping trip. Made for TV. **92m/C VHS, LV.** Bob Saget, Brian Bonsall, Heidi Swedberg, Stuart Pankin, David Graf, Troy Evans; ***D:*** Richard Michaels; ***M:*** David Kitay. *TTC*

The Father Clements Story ☙☙½ **1987** The true story of a black priest in Chicago who battled the Roman Catholic hierarchy in order to adopt a troubled teenager. Made for television. **100m/C VHS.** Louis Gossett Jr., Malcolm Jamal Warner, Carroll O'Connor, Leon Robinson, Rosetta LeNoire, Ron McClarty; ***D:*** Edwin Sherin. *LIV*

Father Figure ☙½ **1980** When a divorced man attends his ex-wife's funeral, he discovers that he must take care of his estranged sons. Based on young adult writer Richard Peck's novel; a well-done made-for-television movie. **94m/C VHS, Beta.** Hal Linden, Timothy Hutton, Cassie Yates, Martha Scott, Jeremy Licht; ***D:*** Jerry London; ***M:*** Billy Goldenberg. *NO*

Father Goose ☙☙½ **1964** During WWII, a liquor-loving plane-spotter stationed on a remote Pacific isle finds himself stuck with a group of French refugee schoolgirls and their teacher. Some predictable gags, romance, and heroism fill out the running time pleasantly. Scriptwriters Stone and Tarloff, who were competitors, not collaborators on the project, shared an Oscar. **116m/C VHS.** Cary Grant, Leslie Caron, Trevor Howard; ***D:*** Ralph Nelson; ***W:*** Peter Stone, Frank Tarloff; ***C:*** Charles B(ryant) Lang; ***M:*** Cy Coleman. Academy Awards '64: Best Story & Screenplay; Nominations: Academy Awards '64: Best Film Editing, Best Sound. *REP*

Father Hood ☙ **1993 (PG-13)** Family drama has Swayze playing a small-time criminal whose daughter tracks him down after leaving the foster-care shelter where she and her brother are being abused. The family takes to the road, running from both the police and a journalist (Berry) who wants to expose the corrupt foster-care system. The children are obnoxious, Swayze is miscast, and the entire film is a misfire. **94m/C VHS, LV.** Patrick Swayze, Halle Berry, Sabrina Lloyd, Brian Bonsall, Diane Ladd, Michael Ironside, Bob Gunton; ***D:*** Darrell Roodt; ***W:*** Scott Spencer. *TOU*

Father of the Bride ☙☙☙½ **1950** A classic, quietly hilarious comedy about the tribulations of a father preparing for his only daughter's wedding. Tracy is suitably overwhelmed as the loving father and Taylor radiant as the bride. A warm vision of American family life, accompanied by the 1940 MGM short "Wedding Bills." Also available in a colorized version. Followed by "Father's Little Dividend" and later a television series. Remade in 1991. **106m/C VHS, Beta, LV.** Spencer Tracy, Elizabeth Taylor, Joan Bennett, Billie Burke, Leo G. Carroll, Russ Tamblyn, Don Taylor, Moroni Olsen; ***D:*** Vincente Minnelli; ***W:*** Frances Goodrich, Albert Hackett; ***C:*** John Alton. Nominations: Academy Awards '50: Best Actor (Tracy), Best Picture, Best Screenplay. *MGM*

Father of the Bride ☙☙½ **1991 (PG)** Remake of the 1950 comedy classic portrays one of the most overextravagant weddings in recent film history, but falls short of the original. Predictable plot and characters don't hide any surprises, but nothing detracts from the purpose of the film: to be a nice, charming movie. Martin is fine as the reluctant dad but Keaton is little more than window dressing as the bride's mom; Short is annoying as a pretentious wedding coordinator. Williams pulls off a nice film debut—and was almost immediately cast in a TV ad as a young-bride-to-be calling her dad long distance to tell him she's engaged. Adapted from a novel by Edward Streeter. **105m/C VHS, Beta, LV.** Steve Martin, Diane Keaton, Kimberly Williams, Kieran Culkin, George Newbern, Martin Short, B.D. Wong, Peter Michael Goetz, Kate McGregor Stewart, Martha Gehman; ***Cameos:*** Eugene Levy; ***D:*** Charles Shyer; ***W:*** Charles Shyer, Nancy Meyers; ***C:*** John Lindley; ***M:*** Alan Silvestri. *TOU*

Father of the Bride Part II ☙☙½ **1995 (PG)** Sweetly sentimental update of the 1951 film "Father's Little Dividend" finds George Banks (Martin) once again thrown for a loop—first by his beloved daughter Annie's (Williams) pregnancy and then by wife Nina's (the radiant Keaton) announcement that they are about to become parents themselves. George doesn't deal very well with either situation but, aided by fey party planner Franck (Short), he manages to get through the predictable chaos. Martin's physical expressiveness and sly charm are a big plus. **106m/C VHS, LV.** Steve Martin, Diane Keaton, Kimberly Williams, Martin Short, George Newbern, Kieran Culkin, Peter Michael Goetz, Kate McGregor Stewart, Eugene Levy, B.D. Wong, Jane Adams; ***D:*** Charles Shyer; ***W:*** Nancy Myers, Charles Shyer; ***C:*** William A. Fraker; ***M:*** Alan Silvestri. Nominations: Golden Globe Awards '96: Best Actor—Musical/Comedy (Martin). *TOU*

Father Was a Fullback ☙☙½ **1949** College football coach (MacMurray) has a losing team, problems with the administration and alumni, and two daughters with growing pains at home. Wife O'Hara supplies the sympathetic shoulder. **99m/B VHS.** Fred MacMurray, Maureen O'Hara, Betty Lynn, Rudy Vallee, Thelma Ritter, Natalie Wood, Jim Backus; ***D:*** John M. Stahl. *FCT*

Fatherland ☙☙½ **1994** It's 1964 and 20 years earlier Hitler has won WWII in this what-if TV movie. The Nazi leader is about to sign a historic alliance with the U.S. President in Berlin when a series of murders of high-ranking Third Reich officers begins. SS detective Xavier March (Hauer) investigates, along with visiting American journalist Charlie Maguire (Richardson), leading the two to the Gestapo coverup of the Holocaust. If the secret gets out it could ruin the summit, so guess who's in big danger? Intriguing premise but the thriller fails to sustain tension. Based on the novel by Robert Harris. Filmed in Prague, Czech Republic. **106m/C VHS.** Rutger Hauer, Miranda Richardson, Peter Vaughan, Jean Marsh, Michael Kitchen, John Woodvine, John Shrapnel, Clare Higgins; ***D:*** Christopher Menaul; ***W:*** Stanley Weiser, Ron Hutchinson; ***C:*** Peter Sova; ***M:*** Gary Chang. *WAR*

Fathers and Sons ☙½ **1992 (R)** Max is a brooding, former bad-boy movie director living on the Jersey Shore. His wife's death causes him to rethink his life and deal with his drinking problem. He also tries to get to know his equally brooding teenage son, Ed. Turns out addiction may run in the family as Ed experiments with drugs. Ill-fitting subplot deals a serial killer stalking the community. Goldblum brings an uneasy gentleness to the father's role in an otherwise slow, talky, and obviously symbolic flick. **100m/C VHS, LV.** Jeff Goldblum, Rory Cochrane, Mitchell Marchand, Famke Janssen, Natasha Gregson Wagner, Ellen Greene, Samuel L. Jackson, Joie Lee, Rosanna Arquette, Michael Disend; ***D:*** Paul Mones; ***W:*** Paul Mones; ***M:*** Mason Daring. *COL*

Father's Little Dividend ☙☙☙ **1951** Tracy expects a little peace and quiet now that he's successfully married off Taylor in this charming sequel to "Father of the Bride." However, he's quickly disillusioned by the news he'll soon be a grandfather - a prospect that causes nothing but dismay. Reunited the stars, director, writers, and producer from the successfull first film. **82m/B VHS, Beta, LV.** Spencer Tracy, Joan Bennett, Elizabeth Taylor, Don Taylor, Billie Burke, Russ Tamblyn, Moroni Olsen; ***D:*** Vincente Minnelli; ***W:*** Frances Goodrich, Albert Hackett. *CNG, MRV, NOS*

A Father's Revenge ☙☙½ **1988 (R)** Dennehy is the only reason to bother with this average hostage drama. He's the father of a stewardess who's one of a group being held by terrorists. They're scheduled to die in 72 hours unless Dennehy can find a way to rescue them. Made for television. **93m/C VHS, LV.** Brian Dennehy, Joanna Cassidy, Ron Silver; ***D:*** John Herzfeld; ***M:*** Klaus Doldinger. *VMK*

Fatso ☙½ **1980 (PG)** After the shocking death of his obese cousin, an obsessive overeater struggles to overcome his neurosis with the aid of his sister and a self-help group called "Chubby Checkers." Bancroft's first work as both writer and director. **93m/C VHS, Beta.** Dom DeLuise, Anne Bancroft, Ron Carey, Candice Azzara; ***D:*** Anne Bancroft; ***W:*** Anne Bancroft. *FOX*

Fatty and Mabel Adrift/Mabel, Fatty and the Law **1916** Fatty and Mabel have problems enjoying their wedded bliss in these two silent shorts, which have a newly recorded orchestral score on the soundtrack. **40m/B VHS, Beta.** Fatty Arbuckle, Mabel Normand, Al "Fuzzy" St. John, Minta Durfee. *CCB, GVV*

Fatty Finn 🦴½ **1984** A children's gagfest about young kids and bullies during the Depression, based on Syd Nicholls' comic strip. **91m/C VHS, Beta.** *AU* Ben Oxenbould, Bart Newton; ***D:*** Maurice Murphy. *NO*

Faust 🦴🦴🦴½ **1926** The classic German silent based upon the legend of Faust, who sells his soul to the devil in exchange for youth. Based on Goethe's poem, and directed by Murnau as a classic example of Germanic expressionism. Remade as "All That Money Can Buy" in 1941. **117m/B VHS, Beta.** *GE* Emil Jannings, Warner Fuetterer, Gosta Ekman, Camilla Horn; ***D:*** F.W. Murnau. *GPV, MRV, NOS*

Faust **1973** Joan Sutherland introduces the opera based on Goethe's dramatic poem telling of a man who makes a pact with the devil. Some of the most beautiful moments in French opera are presented. Puppet characters help explain the story and make it accessible to youngsters. **30m/C VHS, Beta.** Joan Sutherland. *BFA*

The Favor 🦴🦴½ **1992 (R)** Lighthearted romance rife with comic confusion, vivid fantasies, secrets, and the all-important favor. Kathy (Kozak) seeks to relieve the boredom of her marriage through best friend Emily's (McGovern) tryst with Kathy's old beau, Tom. Or so she thinks, until Em spills all the juicy details. In a change of pace, the males take a back seat to the women. Good comic performances from Kozak and McGovern and witty dialogue help overcome the plot's sheer silliness. Damian Elwes (actor Cary's brother) provided Pitt's paintings. Theatrical release was delayed three years due to financial crisis at Orion Pictures. **97m/C VHS, LV.** Harley Jane Kozak, Elizabeth McGovern, Bill Pullman, Brad Pitt, Ken Wahl, Larry Miller, Holland Taylor; ***D:*** Donald Petrie; ***W:*** Josann McGibbon, Sara Parriott; ***M:*** Thomas Newman. *ORI*

The Favor, the Watch, & the Very Big Fish 🦴🦴 **1992 (R)** Set in a fairytale version of Paris. Hoskins is a photographer of religious subjects searching for a man to pose as Jesus. He discovers his subject in the hirsute Goldblum, a mad bar pianist who actually thinks he's the savior. Richardson plays the object of Hoskin's shy affections, an actress who does dubbing work by providing the moaning and groaning for porno flicks. Messy attempt at screwball-comedy with some brief humorous moments. **89m/C VHS, LV.** *GB FR* Bob Hoskins, Jeff Goldblum, Natasha Richardson, Michel Blanc, Jacques Villeret, Angela Pleasence, Jean-Pierre Cassel, Bruce Altman; ***D:*** Ben Lewin; ***W:*** Ben Lewin; ***M:*** Vladimir Cosma. *VMK, FCT*

The Favorite Son 🦴🦴🦴 *Le Fils Prefere* **1994** Troubled family history is examined between three adult French brothers and their Italian immigrant father. A dutiful son, hotel manager Jean-Paul (Lanvin) regularly visits elderly father Raphael (Herlitzka). But Jean-Paul has problems. Desperate for cash to pay his loan shark, he approaches estranged younger brother Philippe (Barr), a wealthy lawyer, who is loath to help, while older schoolteacher brother Francis (Giraudeau) has little spare cash. Jean-Paul decides to take out a life insurance policy on dad—who promptly disappears—leaving the brothers to reluctantly come to terms in order to find him. French with subtitles. **100m/C VHS.** *FR* Gerard Lanvin, Jean-Marc Barr, Bernard Giraudeau, Roberto Herlitzka, Margherita Buy; ***D:*** Nicole Garcia; ***W:*** Nicole Garcia; ***C:*** Eric Gautier; ***M:*** Philippe Sarde. Cesar Awards '95: Best Actor (Lanvin); Nominations: Cesar Awards '95: Best Director (Garcia), Best Film. *NYR*

Fawlty Towers **1977** Cleese stars as the most obnoxious and inept hotel proprietor on earth in these three comedy episodes from the BBC series: "A Touch of Class," "Hotel Inspectors," and "The Germans," (which features Cleese's extraordinary goose-stepping). Additional episodes available. **90m/C VHS.** *GB* John Cleese, Prunella Scales, Connie Booth, Andrew Sachs; ***W:*** John Cleese, Connie Booth. *FOX, MOV, SIG*

FBI Girl 🦴🦴 **1952** An FBI clerk is used as bait to trap a murderer and break up a gang. Burr, pre-Perry Mason, plays a bad guy. **74m/B VHS, Beta, LV.** Cesar Romero, George Brent, Audrey Totter, Raymond Burr, Tom Drake; ***D:*** William (Lester Williams) Berke. *RXM*

The FBI Murders 🦴🦴🦴 **1988** A fact-based chiller about the bloody 1986 shootout between Miami FBI agents and a pair of violent killers (Soul and Gross playing against type). This made for television drama was shown on TV as "In the Line of Duty: The FBI Murders." **95m/C VHS.** David Soul, Michael Gross, Ronny Cox, Bruce Greenwood, Doug Sheehan, Teri Copley; ***D:*** Dick Lowry; ***W:*** Tracy Keenan Wynn. *CAF*

The FBI Story 🦴🦴🦴 **1959** Mr. Stewart goes to Washington in this anatomy of the Federal Bureau of Investigation. If you're a fan of the gangster genre (LeRoy earlier directed "Little Caesar"), and not especially persnickety about fidelity to the facts, this actioner offers a pseudo-factual (read fictional) glimpse—based on actual cases from the 1920s through the 1950s—into the life of a fictitious agent-family man. **149m/C VHS, LV.** James Stewart, Vera Miles, Nick Adams, Murray Hamilton, Larry Pennell; ***D:*** Mervyn LeRoy; ***C:*** Joseph Biroc; ***M:*** Max Steiner. *WAR, FCT, CCB*

Fear 🦴🦴 **1946** An impoverished medical student murders the professor he believes is tormenting him and his life suddenly gets better. He falls in love and gets a scholarship but the police are closing in on his crime. Except...did any of it really happen? Or is he suffering from hallucinations. Low-budget psychodrama with some good paranoid moments. **68m/B VHS.** Peter Cookson, Warren William, Anne Gwynne, James B. Cardwell, Nestor Paiva; ***D:*** Alfred Zeisler. *VES*

Fear 🦴 **1988 (R)** A vacationing family is plagued by a murderous Vietnam vet and other psychotic cons. **96m/C VHS, Beta, LV.** Frank Stallone, Cliff DeYoung, Kay Lenz, Robert Factor; ***D:*** Robert A. Ferretti. *NO*

Fear 🦴🦴½ **1990 (R)** A young psychic (Sheedy) delves into the minds of serial killers and writes novels about her experiences. But what happens when the next killer is also a psychic and decides to play mind-games with her? Above average suspense sustains this made-for-cable thriller. **98m/C VHS.** Ally Sheedy, Lauren Hutton, Michael O'Keefe, Stan Shaw, Dina Merrill, John Agar, Marta DuBois; ***D:*** Rockne S. O'Bannon; ***M:*** Henry Mancini. *VES*

The Fear 🦴½ **1994 (R)** Student psychologist (Bowz) takes a group to a remote cabin to explore their fears as part of his research project. Then, they begin to die horribly and gradually figure out that the cabin's wooden mascot, Morty (Weiss), is coming to life and doing them in. **98m/C VHS.** Eddie Bowz, Darin Heames, Anna Karin, Leland Hayward, Monique Mannen, Heather Medway, Antonio Todd, Erick Weiss, Vince Edwards, Ann Turkel; ***Cameos:*** Wes Craven; ***D:*** Vincent Robert; ***W:*** Ron Ford. *APX*

Fear 🦴½ *No Fear* **1996 (R)** Wahlberg (the former Marky Mark) is a parents' worse nightmare: the violent, obsessed boyfriend of a sixteen-year old girl (Witherspoon) as "Fatal Attraction" goes to the prom. Some cleverness, but ultimately follows a familiar, cliched path littered with one-dimensional characters and predictable plot twists. Gory, unconvincing climax kills any credibility that was left. The one standout is Petersen as the girl's protective father. **96m/C VHS.** Reese Witherspoon, Mark Wahlberg, William L. Petersen, Amy Brenneman, Alyssa Milano, Tracy Fraim, Christopher Gray, Todd Caldecott; ***D:*** James Foley; ***W:*** Christopher Crowe; ***C:*** Thomas Kloss; ***M:*** Carter Burwell. *NYR*

Fear, Anxiety and Depression 🦴½ **1989 (R)** A neurotic aspiring playwright in New York has various problems with his love life. Sub-Woody Allen comedy attempt, with a few bright spots. The dregs of New York, with all the violence and degradation, are brought to the screen here. **84m/C VHS, Beta.** Todd Solondz, Stanley Tucci; ***D:*** Todd Solondz; ***W:*** Todd Solondz. *NO*

The Fear Chamber *Woof! Torture Zone; Chamber of Fear; La Camara Del Terror* **1968** Hardly a Karloff vehicle. Boris shot the footage for this and three other Mexican "horror" films in LA, an unfortunate swan song to his career, though he was fortunate to be quickly written out of this story. The near plot concerns a mutant rock that thrives on human fear. Doctor Karloff and his assistants make sure the rock is rolling in sacrificial victims (women, of course). A prodigious devaluation of the "B"-grade horror flick, it's so bad it's just bad. **88m/C VHS.** *MX* Boris Karloff, Yerye Beirut, Julissa, Carlos East; ***D:*** Juan Ibanez, Jack Hill. *SNC, MPI*

Fear City 🦴½ **1985 (R)** Two partners who own a talent agency are after the psychopath who is killing off their prized strippers with the aid of a local cop. Sleazy look at Manhattan low life. **93m/C VHS, Beta, LV.** Billy Dee Williams, Tom Berenger, Jack Scalia, Melanie Griffith, Rae Dawn Chong, Joe Santos, Maria Conchita Alonso, Rossano Brazzi; ***D:*** Abel Ferrara; ***W:*** Nicholas St. John. *NO*

Fear in the City 🦴 **1981** The Sicilian Mafia and a black crime gang battle for control of the streets. **90m/C VHS, Beta.** *IT* Michael Constantine, Fred Williamson, Gianni Manera; ***D:*** Gianni Manera. *NO*

Fear in the Night 🦴🦴🦴 **1947** Suspenseful tale of a murder committed by a man under hypnosis. Fearing his nightmares are real Kelley talks his detective friend into investigating his "crime", which leads them to a mansion, a mirrored room, and a plot that takes some clever and unexpected twists. Remade in 1956 as "Nightmare." **72m/B VHS.** Paul Kelly, DeForest Kelley, Ann Doran, Kay Scott, Robert Emmett Keane; ***D:*** Maxwell Shane. *SNC*

The Fear Inside 🦴🦴½ **1992 (R)** Lahti plays a woman suffering from agoraphobia who, because of her fear, has not left her home in more than a year. To help out, Lahti invites a seemingly charming college student to live with her. When the young woman's equally charming "brother" comes to visit, Lahti discovers the two aren't so charming after all. A standard woman-in-terror film with a better-than-average cast. Made for cable television. **100m/C VHS, Beta, LV.** Christine Lahti, Jennifer Rubin, Dylan McDermott, David Ackroyd, Thomas Ian Nicholas, Paul Linke, Leon Ichaso; ***W:*** David Birke. *FXV, VTR*

Fear No Evil 🦴🦴 **1980 (R)** A teenager who is the human embodiment of the demon Lucifer commits acts of demonic murder and destruction. His powers are challenged by an 18-year-old girl, who is the embodiment of the archangel Gabriel. First feature from La Loggia is better than it sounds. **90m/C VHS, Beta.** Stefan Arngrim, Kathleen Rowe McAllen, Elizabeth Hoffman; ***D:*** Frank Laloggia; ***W:*** Frank Laloggia. *COL, SUE*

Fear of a Black Hat 🦴🦴 **1994 (R)** Think "Spinal Tap" as gangsta rap and you've the plot of this good-natured imitator. The dim-witted Ice Cold (Cundileff), Tone-Def (Lawrence), and Tasty-Taste (Scott), the trio known as NWH (Niggaz With Hats), are touring in support of their album and trying to convince filmmaker Nina Blackburn (Lemmons) of their street credibility. Like Taps metalheads, the more they explain themselves, the less sense they make. **87m/C VHS.** Larry B. Scott, Mark Christopher Lawrence, Kasi Lemmons, Rusty Cundieff; ***D:*** Rusty Cundieff; ***W:*** Rusty Cundieff. *FXV*

Fear Strikes Out 🦴🦴🦴 **1957** Perkins plays Jimmy Piersall, star outfielder for the Boston Red Sox, and Malden, his demanding father, in the true story of the baseball star's battle for sanity. One of Perkins' best screen performances. **100m/B VHS, Beta, LV.** Anthony Perkins, Karl Malden, Norma Moore, Adam Williams, Perry Wilson; ***D:*** Robert Mulligan; ***W:*** Raphael David Blau; ***M:*** Elmer Bernstein. *PAR*

Fearless 🦴 **1978** An Italian detective has found a Viennese banker's daughter, but continues to pursue the unanswered questions of the case, embroiling himself in a web of intrigue and plotting. **89m/C VHS, Beta.** Joan Collins, Maurizio Merli, Franz Antel. *NWV*

Fearless 🦴🦴🦴 **1993 (R)** Two plane crash survivors reach out to each other as they try and cope with everday life. Bridges is riveting as the transformed Max, and Perez compelling as the sorrowful Carla. Hulce provides dead-on amusement as a casualty lawyer who knows he's slime but can't help himself. Opening sequences of smoke in the corn fields are haunting as are flashbacks of the crash itself. Weir provides an engrossing look at facing death, both psychological and spiritual, but the ending is something of a letdown in its sappiness. Based on the novel by Yglesias. **122m/C VHS, Beta, LV.** Jeff Bridges, Isabella Rossellini, Rosie Perez, Tom Hulce, John Turturro, Benicio Del Toro, Deidre O'Connell, John de Lancie; ***D:*** Peter Weir; ***W:*** Rafael Yglesias; ***C:*** Allen Daviau; ***M:*** Maurice Jarre. Los Angeles Film Critics Association Awards '93: Best Supporting Actress (Perez); Nominations: Academy Awards '94: Best Supporting Actress (Perez); Golden Globe Awards '94: Best Supporting Actress (Perez). *WAR*

Fearless Tiger ꝭ½ **1994 (R)** Martial arts action flick includes the usual combination of fierce swordplay, hand-to-hand showdowns, and the intrigue of exotic locations. **?m/C VHS, LV.** Bolo Yeung, Monika Schnarre, Jamie Farr, Jalal Merhi; ***D:*** Ron Hulme; ***W:*** Ron Hulme; ***M:*** Varouje. *IMP*

The Fearless Vampire Killers ꝭꝭꝭ *Pardon Me, Your Teeth are in My Neck; Dance of the Vampires* **1967** Underrated, off-off-beat, and deliberately campy spoof of vampire films in which Tate is kidnapped by some fangy villains. Vampire trackers MacGowran and Polanski pursue the villains to the haunted castle and attempt the rescue. Only vampire movie with a Jewish bloodsucker ("Boy, have you got the wrong vampire," he proclaims to a maiden thrusting a crucifix at him). Inside the castle, Polanski is chased by the count's gay vampire son. Highlight is the vampire ball with a wonderful mirror scene. Many other amusing moments. **98m/C VHS, Beta, LV.** *GB* Jack MacGowran, Roman Polanski, Alfie Bass, Jessie Robbins, Sharon Tate, Ferdinand "Ferdy" Mayne, Iain Quarrier; ***D:*** Roman Polanski; ***W:*** Roman Polanski, Gerard Brach. *MGM*

Fearmaker *House of Fear; Violent Rage* **1989 (PG)** After the mysterious death of her father, the heiress to his fortune is tangled in a web of treachery created by other potential inheritors. **90m/C VHS, Beta.** *MX* Katy Jurado, Paul Picerni, Sonia Amelio, Carlos East; ***D:*** Anthony Carras. *PSM*

Feast for the Devil ꝭ½ **197?** A woman searches for her missing sister in a mysterious coastal village, only to fall under the occult spell of a mad doctor. **90m/C VHS, Beta.** Krista Nell, Teresa Gimpera. *NO*

Feast of July ꝭꝭ **1995 (R)** Victorian-era drama, adapted from an H. E. Bates novel, has young Bella (Davidtz) pregnant and abandoned by supercad Arch (Wise) whom she sets out to find. After a miscarriage, she is taken in by the Wainwright family where she becomes the object of the affections of the three grown sons. Predictably, she falls for and weds the troubled loafer, Con (Chaplin). Naturally (this being Victorian England) tragedy results. Well-crafted, a given considering the producers, but ultimately a familiar telling of an average story. Feature film debut for director Menaul, after an award-winning career in British television. **116m/C VHS, LV.** Embeth Davidtz, Ben Chaplin, Tom Bell, Gemma Jones, James Purefoy, Kenneth Anderson, Greg Wise; ***D:*** Christopher Menaul; ***W:*** Christopher Neame; ***C:*** Peter Sova; ***M:*** Zbigniew Preisner. *TOU*

Federal Agent ꝭꝭ **1936** Lots of cliches fill this crime film about a federal agent chasing foreign spys who are looking for a new explosive. **53m/B VHS, Beta.** William Boyd, Charles A. Browne, Irene Ware, George Cooper, Lentia Lace, Dan Alvarado; ***D:*** Sam Newfield. *GPV*

Federal Agents vs. Underworld, Inc. *Golden Hands of Kurigal* **1949** Super G-Man Dave Worth goes up against Nila, a greedy villainess bent on finding the golden hands of Kurigal so she may rule the world. A 12-episode serial edited onto two cassettes. **167m/B VHS.** Kirk Alyn, Rosemary La Planche, Roy Barcroft, Carol Forman, James Dale, Bruce Edwards; ***D:*** Fred Brannon. *REP, MLB*

Federal Hill ꝭꝭ **1994 (R)** Familiar plot and characters are still well-handled by cast and first time writer/director Corrente. Federal Hill is a working-class, Little Italy section of Providence, Rhode Island. Five buddies, mostly losers, hang out together at a weekly card game. Nicky's (De Sando) a small-time dealer who meets his uptown Brown University sweetie, Wendy (Langdon), when he sells her cocaine. His friends try to warn him, especially short-fused burglar Ralphie (Turturro). And, of course, things go very wrong for practically everyone. The video is available colorized or in the director's version in B&W. **100m/B VHS, LV.** Anthony De Sando, Nicholas Turturro, Libby Langdon, Michael Raynor, Jason Andrews, Frank Vincent, Robert Turano; ***D:*** Michael Corrente; ***W:*** Michael Corrente; ***C:*** Richard Crudo; ***M:*** Bob Held, David Bravo. Nominations: Independent Spirit Awards '95: Best Supporting Actor (Turturro). *VMK*

Federal Operator 99 ꝭꝭ½ **1945** A fortune in stolen jewels, a chemical plant, and a priceless violin all figure in this 12 chapter serial. And it's up to Jerry Blake, Federal Operator 99, to save the day. Part of "The Cliffhanger Serials" series. **169m/B VHS.** Marten Lamont, Helen Talbot, George Lewis. *REP, MOV*

Feds ꝭ½ **1988 (PG-13)** Two women enter the FBI Academy and take on the system's inherent sexism with feebly comic results. **82m/C VHS, Beta, LV.** Rebecca DeMornay, Mary Gross, Ken Marshall, Fred Dalton Thompson, Larry Cedar, James Luisi, Raymond Singer; ***D:*** Dan Goldberg; ***W:*** Dan Goldberg, Len Blum; ***M:*** Randy Edelman. *WAR*

Feel My Pulse ꝭꝭ **1928** Silent comedy about a rich fanatic who leaves everything in his will to his young niece on the stipulation that she lead a germ-free life; when she reaches 21, she moves into the sanitarium she's inherited, not knowing it has become a base for prohibition-era rum runners. **86m/B VHS, Beta.** Bebe Daniels, Richard Arlen, William Powell; ***D:*** Gregory La Cava. *VYY*

Feel the Motion ꝭ **1986** A female auto-mechanic wants to make it big in the music biz. She sees her chance when she slips her demo tape onto a hit TV-music show. **98m/C VHS, Beta.** Sissy Kelling, Frank Meyer-Brockman, Ingold Locke, Falco, Meat Loaf. *VMK*

Feelin' Screwy ꝭ **1990** A couple of misfit dweebs attempt to rid their town of the local drug dealer in order to impress a couple of babes in this limp coming-of-ager. **90m/C VHS.** Quincy Reynolds, Larry Gamal, Darin McBride, Hassan Jamal, Marsha Carter, Brooks Morales, Anna Fuentes; ***D:*** Riffat A. Khan; ***W:*** Riffat A. Khan. *NO*

Feelin' Up *Woof!* **1976 (R)** A young man sells all his possessions to come to New York in search of erotic adventures. **84m/C VHS, Beta.** Malcolm Groome, Kathleen Seward, Rhonda Hansome, Tony Collado, Charles Douglass; ***D:*** David Secter. *LIV, VES*

Feet First ꝭꝭ½ **1930** A shoe salesman puts on "upper crust" airs as he begins a shipboard romance with a girl who thinks he's wealthy. Lloyd's second sound film shows him grappling with technique and has scenes that recall highlights of his silent hits. **85m/B VHS, Beta.** Harold Lloyd, Barbara Kent, Robert McWade; ***D:*** Clyde Bruckman. *TLF*

Feet Foremost ꝭ½ **1985** A made-for-British-television horror story about an industrialist haunted by the spirit of a teenage girl. **60m/C VHS, Beta.** *GB* Jeremy Kemp. *PSM*

Felix the Cat: The Movie ꝭ½ **1991** Classic cartoon creation Felix returns in a trite feature. The feline and his bag of tricks enter a dimension filled with He-Man/Mutant Ninja Turtles leftovers; new-age princess, comic reptiles, robots and a Darth Vader clone who's defeated with ridiculous ease. Strictly for undemanding kids. **83m/C VHS, Beta.** ***D:*** Tibor Hernadi; ***V:*** Chris Phillips, Alice Playten, Maureen O'Connell. *TOU, FCT, WTA*

Fellini Satyricon ꝭꝭꝭ *Satyricon* **1969 (R)** Fellini's famous, garish, indulgent pastiche vision of ancient Rome, based on the novel "Satyricon" by Petronius, follows the adventures of two young men through the decadences of Nero's reign. Actually an exposition on the excesses of the 1960s, with the actors having little to do other than look good and react to any number of sexual situations. Crammed with excesses of every variety. In Italian with English subtitles. Also available on laserdisc with additional footage and letterboxing. **129m/C VHS, Beta, LV.** *IT* Martin Potter, Capucine, Hiram Keller, Salvo Randone, Max Born; ***D:*** Federico Fellini; ***W:*** Federico Fellini; ***C:*** Giuseppe Rotunno; ***M:*** Nino Rota. Nominations: Academy Awards '70: Best Director (Fellini). *MGM, FCT, INJ*

Fellini's Roma ꝭꝭ½ *Roma* **1972 (R)** Fellini reviews his youth in this stream-of-consciousness homage to Rome and Italy. Best left for fervent Fellini fans. **128m/C VHS, Beta, LV.** *FR IT* Peter Gonzales, Britta Barnes, Pia de Doses, Fiona Florence, Marne Maitland, Renato Giovannoli; ***D:*** Federico Fellini; ***W:*** Federico Fellini; ***M:*** Nino Rota; ***V:*** Federico Fellini. *MGM, FCT, APD*

Fellow Traveler ꝭꝭꝭ **1989** Two old friends, an actor and a screenwriter, both successful, get blacklisted for reputed Communist leanings in 1950s Hollywood. Good performances and a literate script. Made for cable television. **97m/C VHS, Beta.** Ron Silver, Hart Bochner, Daniel J. Travanti, Imogen Stubbs, Katherine Borowitz, Jonathan Hyde; ***D:*** Philip Saville; ***M:*** Colin Towns. *PAR*

Felony ꝭ½ **1995 (R)** Police seek revenge when 12 cops are murdered. Turns out the culprit is a rogue CIA agent, whose spree was captured on video by a tabloid-show cameraman. **90m/C VHS.** Lance Henriksen, Leo Rossi, Joe Don Baker, Charles Napier, Ashley Laurence, Cory Everson; ***D:*** David A. Prior; ***W:*** David A. Prior. *NLC*

Female ꝭꝭ½ **1933** Feminist look at life in the 30's stars Chatterton as the wealthy president of an auto factory who wines and dines the office men and then gives them the strictly business line the next day. However, she finally meets her match when Brent walks through the door. (The two stars were a real-life married couple at the time.) Funny, role-reversal story directed by Curtiz of "Casablanca" fame. Based on a story by Donald Henderson Clark. **60m/B VHS.** Ruth Chatterton, George Brent, Philip Reed, Ruth Donnelly, Johnny Mack Brown, Lois Wilson, Gavin Gordon, Ferdinand Gottschalk; ***D:*** Michael Curtiz, William Dieterle; ***W:*** Gene Markey, Kathryn Scola. *MGM*

The Female Bunch *Woof!* **1969 (R)** The man-free world of an all-woman settlement is shattered by the arrival of a handsome stranger. Some of this garbage was filmed on location at the notorious Charles Manson ranch, and that's the least of its flaws. **86m/C VHS.** Jennifer Bishop, Russ Tamblyn, Lon Chaney Jr., Nesa Renet, Geoffrey Land, Regina Carrol; ***D:*** Al Adamson, John Cardos. *SNC*

The Female Jungle ꝭ *The Hangover* **1956** Below-average whocares whodunnit directed by Roger Corman stock-company actor Ve Sota. Police sergeant Tierney is caught between a rock and a hard place. The prime suspect in a murder case, Tierney discovers a series of clues that implicate his friend Carradine. Interesting only for the screen debut of the nympho-typecast Miss Jayne—of whom Bette Davis said "Dramatic art in her opinion is knowing how to fill a sweater." **56m/B VHS.** Lawrence Tierney, John Carradine, Jayne Mansfield, Burt Kaiser, Kathleen Crowley, James Kodl, Rex Thorson, Jack Hill; ***D:*** Bruno Ve Sota. *COL, FCT*

Female Trouble ꝭꝭ½ **1974 (R)** Divine leads a troublesome existence in this $25,000 picture. She turns to a life of crime and decadence, seeking to live out her philosophy: "Crime is beauty." Look closely at the Divine rape scene where she plays both rapist and victim. Climax of her deviant ways comes with her unusual night club act, for which the law shows no mercy. Trashy, campy; for die-hard Waters fans. **95m/C VHS, Beta.** Divine, David Lochary, Mary Vivian Pearce, Mink Stole, Edith Massey, Danny Mills, Cookie Mueller, Susan Walsh; ***D:*** John Waters; ***W:*** John Waters. *NO*

Femme Fatale ꝭꝭ½ *Fatal Woman* **1990 (R)** When a man's new bride disappears he teams up with an artist pal to track her down. Their search reveals her secret double life and takes them to L.A.'s avant-garde art scene—and deeper into deception and mystery. Billy Zane (Elijah) and Lisa Zane are brother and sister. **96m/C VHS, LV.** Colin Firth, Lisa Zane, Billy Zane, Scott Wilson, Lisa Blount; ***D:*** Andre Guttfreund; ***W:*** John Brancato. *REP*

Femme Fontaine: Killer Babe for the C.I.A. *Woof!* **1995 (R)** Beautiful assassin Drew "Killer Babe" Fontaine (Hope) gets help from CIA-agent-turned-monk Master Sun (Hong) in order to avenge her father's death. Fishnet-clad women with big guns are always a Troma treat. **93m/C VHS.** Margot Hope, James Hong, Arthur Roberts, Catherine Dao, David Shark, Kevin Fry, Harry Mok; ***D:*** Margot Hope; ***W:*** Margot Hope; ***C:*** Gary Graver; ***M:*** Gardner Cole. *TTV*

Femmes de Paris 🦴🦴 **1953** A funny and risque French musical comedy about the comings and goings of the cast of a naughty nightclub shows. In French with English subtitles. **79m/C VHS, Beta.** *FR* Robert Dhery, Collette Brosset, Louis de Funes. *VDM, TPV*

The Fence 🦴🦴½ **1994** Interesting presentation of standard bad boy grows up, attempts to go straight. Terry Griff (Wirth) has been bounced from juvenile detention to prison since he was 15. On the streets for the first time in 14 years, Terry wants to lead a clean life with potential girlfriend Jackie (Gimp). But when Terry gets on the wrong side of his dishonest parole officer, the harsh world of the streets pulls him back. Bleak urban drama with sincere performances. **90m/C VHS.** Billy Wirth, Erica Gimpel, Marc Alaimo, Paul Benjamin, Lorenzo Clemons; ***D:*** Peter Pistor; ***W:*** Peter Fedorenko; ***M:*** Jeff Beal. *TRI*

Fer-De-Lance 🦴½ *Operation Serpent* **1974** A stricken submarine is trapped at the bottom of the sea, with a nest of deadly snakes crawling through the ship. Made for television. **120m/C VHS, Beta.** David Janssen, Hope Lange, Ivan Dixon, Jason Evers; ***D:*** Russ Mayberry. *WOV*

Fergie & Andrew: Behind Palace Doors 🦴🦴 **1993** More soap-opera from the British royals in this tale of feisty redhead, Sarah Ferguson, and the neglectful Prince Andrew. He's away a lot, she's bored by all the palace propriety and causes too many scandals, and their marriage falls apart. Made for television. **92m/C VHS, Beta.** Pippa Hinchley, Sam Miller, Peter Cellier, Harold Innocent, Edita Brychta; ***D:*** Michael Switzer. *TTC*

Fernandel the Dressmaker 🦴🦴½ **1957** Fernandel dreams of designing exquisite dresses, but when the opportunity arises, he finds his cheating partners get in the way. In French with English subtitles. **95m/B VHS, Beta, 8mm.** *FR* Fernandel, Suzy Delair, Francoise Fabian, Georges Chamarat; ***D:*** Jean Boyer. *VYY, FCT*

Ferngully: The Last Rain Forest 🦴🦴½ **1992 (G)** Animated eco-musical follows the adventures of independent-minded flying sprite Crysta, who lives in a rain forest beset by pollution. She discovers the outside world and becomes smitten with the human Zak, who is helping to cut down the forest. Crysta decides to reduce him to her size and show him the error of his ways. She's aided by fellow sprite, Pips, and a crazy bat (Batty Koda with a voice provided by the lively Williams). So-so script with politically pristine environmental message may grow tiresome for both adults and children, though decent animation and brilliant coloring enlivens the tale. **72m/C VHS.** ***D:*** Bill Kroyer; ***W:*** Jim Cox; ***M:*** Alan Silvestri; ***V:*** Samantha Mathis, Christian Slater, Robin Williams, Tim Curry, Jonathan Ward, Grace Zabriskie, Richard "Cheech" Marin, Thomas Chong, Tone Loc, Jim Cox. *FXV, MLT*

Ferocious Female Freedom Fighters 🦴 **1988** A typical foreign-made action flick with female wrestlers is spoofed by the L.A. Connection comedy troupe which did the totally ridiculous dubbed dialog. **90m/C VHS, Beta, LV.** Eva Arnaz, Barry Prima. *MED, IME*

Ferris Bueller's Day Off 🦴🦴🦴 **1986 (PG-13)** It's almost graduation and if Ferris can get away with just one more sick day—it had better be a good one. He sweet talks his best friend into borrowing his dad's antique Ferrari and sneaks his girlfriend out of school to spend a day in Chicago. Their escapades lead to fun, adventure, and almost getting caught. Broderick is charismatic as the notorious Bueller with Grey amusing as his tattle-tale sister doing everything she can to see him get caught. Early Sheen appearance as a juvenile delinquent who pesters Grey. Led to TV series. One of Hughes' more solid efforts. **103m/C VHS, Beta, LV, 8mm.** Matthew Broderick, Mia Sara, Alan Ruck, Jeffrey Jones, Jennifer Grey, Cindy Pickett, Edie McClurg, Charlie Sheen, Del Close, Virginia Capers, Max Perlich, Louis Anderson; ***D:*** John Hughes; ***W:*** John Hughes; ***C:*** Tak Fujimoto; ***M:*** Ira Newborn. *PAR, TLF*

Ferry to Hong Kong 🦴½ **1959** World-weary, heavy drinking traveler comes aboard the "Fat Annie," a ship skippered by the pompous Captain Hart. The two men clash, until an act of heroism brings them together. Embarrassingly hammy performance by Welles as the ferry skipper. **103m/C VHS, Beta.** Curt Jurgens, Orson Welles, Sylvia Syms; ***D:*** Lewis Gilbert. *SUE*

The Feud 🦴🦴 **1990 (R)** A wacky comedy about the ultimate "family feud." The Bullards of Millville and the Bealers of Hornbeck engage in a battle of the witless, and no one in either town is safe. A silly, irreverent comedy of the slapstick variety. Based on a novel by Thomas Berger. **87m/C VHS.** Rene Auberjonois, Ron McLarty, Joe Grifasi, David Strathairn, Gale Mayron; ***D:*** Bill D'Elia; ***W:*** Bill D'Elia. *VMK*

Feud Maker 🦴½ **1938** Steele rides to the rescue in this range war between the bad guys and the cowmen. Hackett plays a schemer who falsely befriends both sides, plotting to buy up cheap land when the participants have killed each other off. Based on a story by Harry F. Olmsted. **55m/B VHS.** Bob Steele, Marion Weldon, Karl Hackett, Frank Ball, Budd Buster, Lew Meehan, Roger Williams; ***D:*** Sam Newfield; ***W:*** George Plympton. *MOV*

Feud of the Trail 🦴 **1937** A cowboy saves a range family's gold and falls in love with their daughter in the process. Tyler plays both the hero and the villain here. **56m/B VHS, Beta.** Tom Tyler, Harlin Wood, Guinn "Big Boy" Williams; ***D:*** Robert F. "Bob" Hill. *NOS, DVT*

Feud of the West 🦴½ **1935** Old West disagreements settled with guns in this outing for cowboy star Gibson, here portraying a rodeo performer. **60m/B VHS, Beta.** Hoot Gibson, Buzz Barton, Robert F. (Bob) Kortman, Edward Cassidy, Joan Barclay, Nelson McDowell, Reed Howes, Lew Meehan; ***D:*** Harry Fraser. *NOS, VCI, VCN*

Fever 🦴🦴🦴 **1981** Controversial Polish film based on Andrzej Strug's novel "The Story of One Bomb." Focusing on a period in Polish history marked by anarchy, violence, resistance, and revolution, it was banned before it won eventual acclaim at the Gdansk Film Festival. In Polish with English subtitles. **115m/C VHS.** *PL* ***D:*** Agnieszka Holland. *FCT*

Fever 🦴 **1988 (R)** A once-honest cop trades his good life in for a shot at dealing drugs. Meanwhile, his wife's lover wants to murder him. **83m/C VHS, Beta, LV.** Bill Hunter, Gary Sweet, Mary Regan, Jim Holt; ***D:*** Craig Lahiff. *ACA*

Fever 🦴🦴 **1991 (R)** An ex-con and a high-powered lawyer join forces to rescue the woman both of them love from a vicious killer. Made for cable television. Available in Spanish. **99m/C VHS.** Armand Assante, Sam Neill, Marcia Gay Harden, Joe Spano; ***D:*** Larry Elikann; ***W:*** Larry Brothers. *HBO*

Fever Mounts at El Pao 🦴🦴½ *Los Ambiciosos* **1959** A minor effort from director Bunuel about the regime of a dictator in an imaginary South American country. In Spanish with English subtitles. **97m/B VHS, Beta.** *MX* Gerard Philipe, Jean Servais; ***D:*** Luis Bunuel. *NOS, FCT, FST*

Fever Pitch *Woof!* **1985 (R)** Sordid story of a sports writer (O'Neal) who becomes addicted to gambling. Very poor script. **95m/C VHS, Beta.** Ryan O'Neal, Catherine Hicks, Giancarlo Giannini, Bridgette Anderson, Chad Everett, John Saxon, William Smith, Patrick Cassidy, Chad McQueen; ***D:*** Richard Brooks; ***W:*** Richard Brooks; ***M:*** Thomas Dolby. *FOX*

A Few Good Men 🦴🦴🦴½ **1992 (R)** Strong performances by Cruise and Nicholson carry this story of a peacetime military coverup. Cruise is a smart aleck Navy lawyer sleepwalking through his comfortable career in DC. He's ready to write off two soldiers pinned for the murder of their cohort until he interviews their commanding officer, Nicholson. Cruise smells a rat, but Nicholson practically dares him to prove it. Moore is another military lawyer assigned to the case, though her function seems to be holding Kaffee's hand (there's no actual romance between the two). Incredible fireworks between Cruise and Nicholson in the courtroom. Based on the play by Sorkin, who also wrote the screenplay. **138m/C VHS, Beta, LV, 8mm.** Tom Cruise, Jack Nicholson, Demi Moore, Kevin Bacon, Kevin Pollak, Kiefer Sutherland, James Marshall, J.T. Walsh, Christopher Guest, J.A. Preston, Matt Craven, Wolfgang Bodison, Xander Berkeley, Cuba Gooding Jr.; ***D:*** Rob Reiner; ***W:*** Aaron Sorkin; ***C:*** Robert Richardson; ***M:*** Marc Shaiman. Chicago Film Critics Awards '93: Best Supporting Actor (Nicholson); MTV Movie Awards '93: Best Film; National Board of Review Awards '92: Best Supporting Actor (Nicholson); People's Choice Awards '93: Best Film, Best Film—Drama; Nominations: Academy Awards '92: Best Film Editing, Best Picture, Best Sound, Best Supporting Actor (Nicholson). *COL, CRC, MOV*

A Few Moments with Buster Keaton and Laurel and Hardy 🦴🦴🦴 **1963** Three short appearances: "The Tree in a Test Tube," a government film with Stan & Ollie about wood's role in the war effort; an episode of "The Ed Sullivan Show," with the duo, and a commercial for Simon Pure Beer featuring Keaton. **17m/B VHS, Beta, 8mm.** Stan Laurel, Oliver Hardy, Buster Keaton, Ed Sullivan, Pete Smith. *VYY*

ffolkes 🦴🦴 *Assault Force; North Sea Hijack* **1980 (PG)** Rufus Excalibur Ffolkes is an eccentric underwater expert who is called upon to stop a madman (Perkins, indulging himself) from blowing up an oil rig in the North Sea. Entertaining farce with Moore playing the opposite of his usual suave James Bond character. **99m/C VHS, Beta.** Roger Moore, James Mason, Anthony Perkins, David Hedison, Michael Parks; ***D:*** Andrew V. McLaglen. *MCA*

Fiances 🦴🦴 *The Engagement; I Fidanzati* **1963** Young man from Milan takes a welding job in Sicily that will separate him from his fiancee for 18 months. He thinks the separation will be good for them but loneliness and the strange environment makes him long for her. Non-professional leads provide strength. Italian with subtitles. **84m/B VHS.** *IT* Carlo Carbrini, Anna Canzi; ***D:*** Ermanno Olmi; ***W:*** Ermanno Olmi; ***C:*** Lamberto Caimi; ***M:*** Gianni Ferrio. *FCT*

Fiction Makers 🦴🦴 **1967** Roger Moore stars as Simon Templar, also known as "The Saint," a sophisticated detective who is hired to help Amos Klein. Klein turns out to be an alias for a beautiful novelist who is being threatened by the underworld crime ring. Based on the Leslie Chateris' character. **102m/C VHS, Beta.** Roger Moore, Sylvia Syms. *FOX*

Fictitious Marriage **1988** Eldad Ilan, a high school teacher experiencing a mid-life crisis, travels to Israel to get away from his family in order to consider his life's direction. In Hebrew with English subtitles. **90m/C VHS.** Shlomo Bar-Aba, Irit Sheleg, Ofra Veingarten; ***D:*** Haim Bouzaglo. *ERG*

Fiddler on the Roof 🦴🦴🦴½ **1971 (G)** Based on the long-running Broadway musical. The poignant story of Tevye, a poor Jewish milkman at the turn of the century in a small Ukrainian village, and his five dowry-less daughters, his lame horse, his wife, and his companionable relationship with God. Topol, an Israeli who played the role in London, is charming, if not quite as wonderful as Zero Mostel, the Broadway star. Finely detailed set decoration and choreography, strong performances from the entire cast create a sense of intimacy in spite of near epic proportions of the production. Play was based on the Yiddish stories of Tevye the Dairyman, written by Sholem Aleichem. ♫Tradition; Matchmaker, Matchmaker; If I Were a Rich Man; Sabbath Prayer; To Life; Miracle of Miracles; Tevye's Dream; Sunrise, Sunset; Wedding Celebration. **184m/C VHS, Beta, LV.** Chaim Topol, Norma Crane, Leonard Frey, Molly Picon; ***D:*** Norman Jewison; ***C:*** Oswald Morris; ***M:*** John Williams. Academy Awards '71: Best Cinematography, Best Sound, Best Score;

Golden Globe Awards '72: Best Actor—Musical/Comedy (Topol), Best Film—Musical/Comedy; Nominations: Academy Awards '71: Best Actor (Topol), Best Art Direction/Set Decoration, Best Director (Jewison), Best Picture, Best Supporting Actor (Frey). *FOX, MGM, TLF*

The Fiddlin' Buckaroo 🦴½ **1933** Maynard plays a government agent who disguises himself as a musical ventriloquist to capture Kohler and his band of outlaws. Everybody sings a lot. **63m/B VHS.** Ken Maynard, Gloria Shea, Fred Kohler Sr., Frank Rice, Jack Mower, Charles "Slim" Whitaker, Robert F. (Bob) Kortman, Hank Bell, Jack Rockwell; ***D:*** Ken Maynard; ***W:*** Nate Gatzert. *GPV*

The Field 🦴🦴🦴½ **1990 (PG-13)** After an absence from the big screen, intense and nearly over the top Harris won acclaim as an iron-willed peasant fighting to retain a patch of Irish land he's tended all his life, now offered for sale to a wealthy American. His uncompromising stand divides the community in this glowing adaptation of John B. Keane's classic play, an allegory of Ireland's internal conflicts. **113m/C VHS, LV.** *GB* Richard Harris, Tom Berenger, John Hurt, Sean Bean, Brenda Fricker, Frances Tomelty, Sean McGinley, Jenny Conroy; ***D:*** Jim Sheridan; ***W:*** Jim Sheridan. Nominations: Academy Awards '90: Best Actor (Harris). *LIV, TVC*

Field of Dreams 🦴🦴🦴½ **1989 (PG)** Uplifting mythic fantasy based on W.P. Kinsella's novel "Shoeless Joe." Iowa corn farmer heeds a mysterious voice that instructs "If you build it, he will come" and cuts a baseball diamond in his corn field. Soon the ball field is inhabited by the spirit of Joe Jackson and others who were disgraced in the notorious 1919 "Black Sox" baseball scandal. Jones, as a character based on reclusive author J.D. Salinger, is reluctantly pulled into the mystery. It's all about chasing a dream, maintaining innocence, finding redemption, reconciling the child with the adult, and celebrating the mythic lure of baseball. Costner and Madigan are strong, believable characters. **106m/C VHS, Beta, LV.** Kevin Costner, Amy Madigan, James Earl Jones, Burt Lancaster, Ray Liotta, Timothy Busfield, Frank Whaley, Gaby Hoffman; ***D:*** Phil Alden Robinson; ***W:*** Phil Alden Robinson; ***M:*** James Horner. Nominations: Academy Awards '89: Best Adapted Screenplay, Best Picture, Best Original Score. *MCA, FCT, HMV*

Field of Fire 🦴🦴 **1992 (R)** One of America's top military experts has been taken hostage and it's up to a top general to rescue him. But the rescue doesn't come off as planned and all must fight their way through the Cambodian jungle to safety. **96m/C VHS, LV.** David Carradine; ***D:*** Cirio H. Santiago; ***W:*** Thomas McKelvey Cleaver. *HBO*

Field of Honor 🦴🦴½ **1986 (R)** A look at the harrowing experience of jungle combat through the eyes of a Dutch infantryman in Korea. **93m/C VHS, Beta, LV.** Everett McGill, Ron Bradsteder, Hey Young Lee; ***D:*** Hans Scheepmaker. *MGM*

Field of Honor 🦴🦴½ *Champ d'Honneur* **1987 (PG)** A quiet French anti-war drama set during the Franco-Prussian war in 1869 in which a peasant boy volunteers to fight in place of a rich man's son. He is befriended behind enemy lines by a young boy and both try to avoid capture. In French with English subtitles. **87m/C VHS, Beta.** *FR* Cris Campion, Eric Wapler, Pascale Rocard, Frederic Mayer; ***D:*** Jean-Pierre Denis. Cesar Awards '88: Best Score. *ORI, INJ*

The Fiend 🦴 **1971 (R)** A religious cultist, already unbalanced, grabs a knife and starts hacking away Jack-the-Ripper style. **87m/C VHS, Beta.** *GB* Ann Todd, Patrick Magee, Tony Beckley, Madeline Hinde, Suzanna Leigh, Percy Herbert; ***D:*** Robert Hartford-Davis. *NO*

Fiend *Woof!* **1983** Glowing supernatural thing flits around graveyard before animating dead guy who needs to kill in order to go on living. Murderous dead guy becomes a small-town music teacher feeding parasitically on his students to satisfy his supernatural hunger. His neighbor suspects some discord. Low-budget time waster. **93m/C VHS, Beta.** Don Leifert, Richard Nelson, Elaine White, George Stover; ***D:*** Donald M. Dohler. *PSM*

Fiend Without a Face 🦴🦴 **1958** An isolated air base in Canada is the site for a scientist using atomic power in an experiment to make a person's thoughts materialize. Only his thoughts are evil and reveal themselves as flying brains with spinal cords that suck human brains right out of the skull. Tons of fun for fifties SF fans and anyone who appreciates the sheer silliness of it all. **77m/B VHS, LV.** Marshall Thompson, Kim Parker, Terence Kilburn, Michael Balfour, Gil Winfield, Shane Cordell; ***D:*** Arthur Crabtree. *CCB, REP, MLB*

The Fiendish Plot of Dr. Fu Manchu *Woof!* **1980 (PG)** A sad farewell from Sellers, who in his last film portrays Dr. Fu in his desperate quest for the necessary ingredients for his secret life-preserving formula. Sellers portrays both Dr. Fu and the Scotland Yard detective on his trail, but it's not enough to save this picture, flawed by poor script and lack of direction. **100m/C VHS, Beta, LV.** *GB* Peter Sellers, David Tomlinson, Sid Caesar, Helen Mirren; ***D:*** Piers Haggard. *WAR, FCT*

Fiesta 🦴🦴 **1947** A girl comes from Mexico City to her father's hacienda where her old boyfriend awaits her return with a proposal of marriage. Full of authentic Mexican dances and music. ♫Fantasia Mexican; La Bamba; La Luna Enamorada; Miriano; Romeria Vasca. **44m/C VHS, Beta.** Ann Ayars, George Negrete, Armida; ***D:*** Richard Thorpe; ***C:*** Charles Rosher. Nominations: Academy Awards '47: Best Original Score. *VYY, DVT*

The Fifteen Streets 🦴🦴½ **1990** Kind-hearted dock worker John O'Brien (Teale) is the quiet one in a boozing, brawling Irish family living in near poverty in late-Victorian England. He meets well-bred schoolteacher Mary Llewellyn (Holman) and the two fall in love but bigotry, scandal, and tragedy challenge their chances at happiness. Based on a novel by Catherine Cookson. **108m/C VHS.** *GB* Owen Teale, Clare Holman, Sean Bean, Billie Whitelaw, Ian Bannen, Jane Horrocks, Anny Tobin, Leslie Schofield; ***D:*** David Wheatley; ***W:*** Rob Bettinson. *VCO*

Fifth Avenue Girl 🦴½ **1939** An unhappy millionaire brings home a poor young woman to pose as his mistress to make his family realize how they've neglected him. As this below-par social comedy drones toward its romantic conclusion, the rich folks see the error of their ways and love conquers all. **83m/B VHS, Beta, LV.** Ginger Rogers, Walter Connolly, Tim Holt, James Ellison, Franklin Pangborn; ***D:*** Gregory La Cava. *IME, TTC*

Fifth Day of Peace 🦴🦴 **1972 (PG)** In the aftermath of the WWI armistice, two German soldiers are tried and executed for desertion by their commander, even though the Allies forbade German military trials. An interesting plot that is marred by too obvious plot twists. Based on a true story. **95m/C VHS, Beta.** *IT* Richard Johnson, Franco Nero, Larry Aubrey, Helmut Schneider; ***D:*** Guiliano Montaldo. *PSM*

The Fifth Floor *Woof!* **1980 (R)** College disco dancer overdoses on drugs and winds up in an insane asylum, complete with menacing attendant Hopkins and apathetic doctor Ferrer. Pathetic, exploitative trash. **90m/C VHS, Beta.** Bo Hopkins, Dianne Hull, Patti D'Arbanville, Mel Ferrer; ***D:*** Howard (Hikmet) Avedis; ***W:*** Howard (Hikmet) Avedis. *MED*

The Fifth Monkey 🦴½ **1990 (PG-13)** A man embarks on a journey to sell four monkeys in order to fill a dowry for his bride, but along the way he encounters all sorts of obstacles and adventures. Filmed on location in Brazil **93m/C VHS, LV.** Ben Kingsley; ***D:*** Eric Rochant; ***W:*** Eric Rochant. *COL, FCT*

The Fifth Musketeer 🦴🦴 *Behind the Iron Mask* **1979 (PG)** A campy adaptation of Dumas's "The Man in the Iron Mask," wherein a monarch's evil twin impersonates him while imprisoning the true king. A good cast and rich production shot in Austria make for a fairly entertaining swashbuckler. **90m/C Beta.** *GB* Beau Bridges, Sylvia Kristel, Ursula Andress, Cornel Wilde, Ian McShane, Alan Hale Jr., Helmut Dantine, Olivia de Havilland, Jose Ferrer, Rex Harrison, Helmut Dantine; ***D:*** Ken Annakin; ***W:*** David Ambrose; ***C:*** Jack Cardiff. *COL*

The Fifth Seal 🦴🦴 **1976** A group of friends are arrested when one makes a casual remark that offends a commandant. This leads to a series of tasks that test their commitment to their moral ideals. Set at the close of WWII in Hungary. In Hungarian with English subtitles. **116m/C VHS.** *HU* ***D:*** Zoltan Fabri. *FCT*

Fifty/Fifty 🦴🦴 **1993 (R)** Jake and Frenchie are a couple of mercenaries forced by the CIA not only to work together but with a bunch of incompetent guerillas to overthrow a Southeast Asian dictator. Weller handles the violence, Hays handles the comedy, and both get chased a lot. **101m/C VHS, LV.** Robert Hays, Peter Weller, Ramona Rahman, Charles Martin Smith; ***D:*** Charles Martin Smith; ***W:*** Dennis Shryack, Michael Butler; ***M:*** Peter Bernstein. *WAR, CAN*

$50,000 Reward 🦴½ **1925** Maynard's first western finds him being victimized by an unscrupulous banker who wants Maynard's land deeds for property on which a new dam is being built. **49m/B VHS, Beta.** Ken Maynard, Esther Ralston. *GPV, CCB, HEG*

52 Pick-Up 🦴🦴½ **1986 (R)** After a fling, a wealthy industrialist is blackmailed by a trio of repulsive criminals and determines to save himself. First he becomes deeply caught in their web of murder. Based on an Elmore Leonard novel with lots of gruesome violence and good performances. **111m/C VHS, Beta, LV.** Roy Scheider, Ann-Margret, Vanity, John Glover, Doug McClure, Clarence Williams III, Kelly Preston, Robert Trebor, Lonny Chapman; ***D:*** John Frankenheimer; ***W:*** John Steppling, Elmore Leonard; ***M:*** Gary Chang. *MED, VTR*

55 Days at Peking 🦴🦴🦴 **1963** A costume epic depicting the Chinese Boxer Rebellion and the fate of military Britishers caught in the midst of the chaos. Standard fare superbly handled by director Ray and an all-star cast. **150m/C VHS, Beta, LV.** Charlton Heston, Ava Gardner, David Niven, John Ireland, Flora Robson, Paul Lukas, Jacques Sernas; ***D:*** Nicholas Ray; ***W:*** Philip Yordan; ***C:*** Jack Hildyard. Nominations: Academy Awards '63: Best Song ("So Little Time"), Best Original Score. *BFV, KAR*

The Fig Tree **1987** After her mother passes away, Miranda becomes tormented by the fear of death. Now her aunt must help her cope with this difficult part of life. Adapted from the short story by Katherine Anne Porter. Aired on PBS as part of the "Wonderworks" family movie series. **58m/C VHS.** Olivia Cole, William Converse-Roberts, Doris Roberts, Teresa Wright, Karron Graves; ***D:*** Calvin Skaggs. *PME, FCT, BTV*

Fight for Gold 🦴 **1986** In the frozen wastes of the North, a man becomes embroiled in a violent quest for gold. **107m/C VHS.** *GE* Doug McClure, Harald Leipnitz, Heinz Reinl, Roberto Bianco, Angelica Ott, Kristina Nel; ***D:*** Harald Reinl. *ACA*

A Fight for Jenny 🦴🦴 **1990 (PG)** Miami Viceroy Thomas and Warren play an interracial couple who fight for custody of the wife's child from a previous marriage. Standard made-for-TV meaningful drama (bite-sized issues served with a modicum of melodrama). **95m/C VHS.** Philip Michael Thomas, Lesley Ann Warren, Jean Smart, Lynne Moody, William Atherton; ***D:*** Gilbert Moses. *PSM*

Fight for Survival 🦴½ **1977 (R)** Young female aspirant of kung fu must recover sacred books that were stolen by disguised kung fu masters. **101m/C VHS, Beta.** Shangkuan Ling-Feng. *FOX*

Fight for the Title 🦴🦴 **1957** Benny Leonard's reign as the lightweight boxing champ has just begun when WWII is declared. Against his manager's wishes, Benny decides to enlist. **30m/C VHS.** Michael Landon, George Brenlin; ***D:*** Eric Kenton. *FCT, RHI*

Fight for Us 🦴½ *L'Insoumis* **1989 (R)** A social activist, recently released from prison, takes on the death squads terrorizing the countryside in post-Marcos Philippines. In Spanish with English subtitles. **92m/C VHS, Beta, LV.** Phillip Salvador, Dina Bonnevie, Gina Alajar, Benbol Roco. *NO*

Fight for Your Life 🦴 **1979** Three escaped convicts—a white bigot, an Asian, and a Chicano—take a black minister's family hostage. After suffering all manner of vicious torture, the family exacts an equally brutal revenge. Shades of "The Desperate Hours" and "Extremities," but with much more graphic violence and a racial twist. **89m/C VHS, Beta.** *CA* William Sanderson, Robert Judd, Lela Small. *NO*

Fight to the Death **1983** An evil businessman hires a group of deadly assassins to assist with the Japanese invasion of China at the start of WWII. Includes self-defense tips segment. **100m/C VHS.** Chang Li, Ron Van Cliff. *NO*

The Fighter *The First Time* **1952** A Mexican patriot, involved in a struggle to overthrow a dictator, falls for a co-revolutionist. Flashbacks show the destruction of his family and village, and his pugilistic expertise, which he uses to fight for a huge purse to help the cause. Adapted from Jack London's "The Mexican." **78m/B VHS.** Richard Conte, Vanessa Brown, Lee J. Cobb, Frank Silvera, Roberta Haynes, Hugh Sanders, Claire Carleton, Martin Garralaga; ***D:*** Herbert Kline. *DVT, HEG*

The Fighter ½ **1995 (R)** French soldier Charlemont (Gruner) gets involved with desperate farmers opposing a greedy landlord (Ermey) and is forced to compete against former rival Ziegfield (Singer). Strange western/kickboxing hybrid that does have lots of action. **91m/C VHS.** Olivier Gruner, Marc Singer, R. Lee Ermey, Ian Ziering, James Brolin, Ashley Laurence; ***D:*** Isaac Florentine. *APX*

Fighter Attack **1953** Story of a WWII pilot, based in Corsica, who is shot down during a mission to destroy a Nazi supply station. He meets with a woman of the Italian underground, and succeeds in destroying his target with her help. **80m/C VHS.** Sterling Hayden, J. Carrol Naish, Joy Page; ***D:*** Lesley Selander. *REP*

Fightin' Ranch **1930** A famous lawman saves his reputation, previously tainted. A Maynard classic. **60m/B VHS, Beta.** Ken Maynard. *NO*

The Fighting American **1924** A frat boy proposes to a girl on a brotherly dare, and, unflattered by the fraternal proposal, the girl flees to the Far East to return to the bosom of her family. But it turns out the boy really does love the girl, by golly, and he's got just enough of that fighting American spirit to prove it. Predates Oland's Charlie Chan career by seven years. **65m/B VHS, Beta.** Pat O'Malley, Mary Astor, Raymond Hatton, Warner Oland; ***D:*** Tom Forman. *GPV, FCT*

Fighting Back *Death Vengeance* **1982 (R)** Reactionary tale of an angry resident in a crime-ridden Philadelphia neighborhood who organizes a patrol of armed civilian vigilantes. The police attempt to head off a racial confrontation in this effective drama graced with some fine performances. **96m/C VHS, Beta.** Tom Skerritt, Patti LuPone, Michael Sarrazin, Yaphet Kotto; ***D:*** Lewis Teague; ***W:*** David Zelag Goodman. *PAR*

Fighting Black Kings **1976 (PG)** Martial arts and karate masters appear in this tale of action. **90m/C VHS, Beta.** William Oliver, Charles Martin, Willie Williams, Mas Oyama. *WAR, OM*

Fighting Caballero **1935** Lease and his pals effectively handle a gang of mine-harassing outlaws. **60m/B VHS, Beta.** Rex Lease; ***D:*** Elmer Clifton. *NO*

Fighting Caravans *Blazing Arrows* **1931** In this early big-budget western, based on a story by Zane Grey, a wagon train sets out west from Missouri. Cooper emerges as the hero after warding off an Indian attack that takes the lives of the original leaders. **80m/B VHS, Beta.** Gary Cooper, Ernest Torrence, Tully Marshall, Fred Kohler Sr., Lili Damita; ***D:*** Otto Brower, David Burton. *NOS, MRV, VYY*

Fighting Champ **1933** Cowpunching gives way to boxing as Steele steps into the ring and takes on all comers. Poor combination of riding and boxing makes for a disappointing Western. **57m/B VHS.** Bob Steele, Arletta Duncan, George "Gabby" Hayes, Charles "Blackie" King, Lafe McKee, Kit Guard, George Chesebro; ***D:*** John P. McCarthy; ***W:*** Wellyn Totman. *MOV*

Fighting Cowboy **1933** Bill settles a tungsten mine dispute with a greedy miner and some outlaws. **50m/B VHS, Beta, LV.** Buffalo Bill Jr.; ***D:*** Victor Adamson. *NO*

Fighting Devil Dogs **1938** Two Marine lieutenants are assigned the task of obtaining a deadly secret weapon controlled by crooks. A serial in twelve chapters. **195m/B VHS.** Lee Powell, Bruce (Herman Brix) Bennett; ***D:*** John English, William Witney. *REP, VCN, MLB*

Fighting Father Dunne **1948** Mega-hokey Hollywood steamroller about a tough priest caring for St. Louis newsboys in the early 1900s. Based on a true story. **92m/B VHS, Beta.** Pat O'Brien, Darryl Hickman, Charles Kemper, Una O'Connor, Arthur Shields, Harry Shannon, Joseph Sawyer, Anna Q. Nilsson, Donn Gift, Myrna Dell; ***D:*** Ted Tetzlaff. *TTC*

Fighting Fists of Shanghai Joe **1965** Fearsome fighting man from the Far East engages a vile American land baron in a battle of honor. **94m/C VHS, Beta.** Klaus Kinski, Gordon Mitchell, Carla Romanelli, Robert Hundar, Chen Lee; ***D:*** Mario Ciano. *TWE*

Fighting Fool **1932** Average oater has McCoy as a sheriff constantly in pursuit of an outlaw named "The Shadow." Of course, romance blossoms between McCoy and Day, too. The real identity of "The Shadow" turns out to be quite a surprise for McCoy. **57m/B VHS.** Tim McCoy, Marceline Day, Robert Ellis, Arthur Rankin, Dorothy Granger; ***D:*** Lambert Hillyer. *MOV*

Fighting Jack **1926** After he saves a girl from a watery death, a man is accused of horse stealing and trespassing. **52m/B VHS, Beta.** Bill Bailey, Hazel Deane, Frona Hale, John Byron, Sailor Sharkey, Herma Cordova; ***D:*** Louis Chaudet. *GPV*

The Fighting Kentuckian ½ **1949** Homeward bound from the Battle of New Orleans in 1814, a Kentucky rifleman lingers in a French settlement in Alabama. His romance with the daughter of a French general is blocked by the father until the American saves the community from an assault by land grabbers. Hardy as a frontiersman is well worth the view. An action-packed, well-photographed hit. **100m/B VHS.** John Wayne, Oliver Hardy, Vera Ralston, Marie Windsor, Philip Dorn, John Howard, Hugo Haas, Grant Withers; ***D:*** George Waggner. *REP*

The Fighting Legion **1930** Maynard shows his foresight here, making this one of the first westerns to fully exploit sound by adding music and singing. Standard plot has Maynard going after the villain who murdered his brother. **69m/B VHS.** Ken Maynard, Dorothy Dwan, Ernie Adams, Stanley Blystone, Frank Rice; ***D:*** Harry Joe Brown. *GPV, DVT, HEG*

Fighting Life **1980** The tale of two brothers who overcome immense physical and emotional handicaps and become vital members of society. The two stars of the film are both physically handicapped. **90m/C VHS, Beta.** *NO*

Fighting Mad ½ **1939** A singing Mountie tangles with border-crossing robbers and saves the reputation of a woman they exploit. One of the "Renfrew of the Mounties" series. **57m/B VHS, Beta.** James Newill, Milburn Stone, Sally Blane; ***D:*** Sam Newfield. *VDM*

Fighting Mad ½ **1976 (R)** A peaceful land owner is driven to violence when he discovers that the business men who want his property are planning to murder two of his family members in order to get it. The local sheriff's apathy forces the man to take the law into his own hands. Unlike other Fonda films of the time which consist of chaotic violence and car crashes, this story is a well performed character study. **90m/C VHS.** Peter Fonda, Lynn Lowry, John Doucette, Phil Carey, Scott Glenn, Kathleen Miller; ***D:*** Jonathan Demme; ***W:*** Jonathan Demme. *NO*

Fighting Mad ½ *Fierce* **1977 (R)** Soldiers leave their buddy for dead in wartime Vietnam. He is alive, but captured by Japanese soldiers who believe they are still fighting in WWII. **96m/C VHS.** James Iglehart, Jayne Kennedy, Leon Isaac Kennedy; ***D:*** Cirio H. Santiago. *NO*

Fighting Marines ½ **1936** U.S. Marines are trying to establish an air base on Halfway Island in the Pacific, but are thwarted by the "Tiger Shark," a modern-day pirate. First appeared as a serial. **69m/B VHS, Beta.** Jason Robards Sr., Grant Withers, Ann Rutherford, Pat O'Malley; ***D:*** Joseph Kane, B. Reeves Eason. *VYY, VCN, VDM*

The Fighting Marshal **1932** After serving time for a crime he didn't commit, McCoy assumes the identity of a dead sheriff and tries to find the felons who done him wrong. **58m/B VHS.** Tim McCoy, Dorothy Gulliver, Mary Carr, Matthew Betz, Pat O'Malley; ***D:*** David Ross Lederman. *MOV*

Fighting Parson **1935** In order to infiltrate a lawless town Gibson, a gunsliging cowboy, dresses as a revivalist preacher. **65m/B VHS, Beta.** Hoot Gibson, Marceline Day, Robert Frazer, Stanley Blystone, Skeeter Bill Robbins, Charles "Blackie" King; ***D:*** Harry Fraser. *VCI, GPV*

Fighting Pilot **1935** Talmadge is a real fighter in this classic talkie. His assignment is to rescue the plans for a secret aircraft from ill fate. **62m/B VHS, Beta.** Richard Talmadge, Victor Mace, Gertrude Messinger, Eddie Davis, Robert Frazer; ***D:*** Noel Mason Smith. *NOS, DVT, GPV*

The Fighting Prince of Donegal ½ **1966** An Irish prince battles the invading British in 16th Century Ireland. Escaping their clutches, he leads his clan in rescuing his mother and his beloved in this Disney swashbuckler. Based on the novel "Red Hugh, Prince of Donegal" by Robert T. Reilly. **110m/C VHS, Beta.** Peter McEnery, Susan Hampshire, Tom Adams, Gordon Jackson, Andrew Keir; ***D:*** Michael O'Herlihy; ***M:*** George Bruns. *DIS*

The Fighting Redhead **1950** Final entry in the "Red Ryder" series has Hart as a cattle rustling murderer and Bannon as the hero, Red Ryder. Based on the comic strip, "Red Ryder." **55m/C VHS.** Jim Bannon, Don Reynolds, Emmett Lynn, Marin Sais, Peggy Stewart, John Hart, Lane Bradford; ***D:*** Lewis D. Collins; ***W:*** Paul Franklin, Jerry Thomas. *MOV*

Fighting Renegade ½ **1939** The search for an Indian burial ground in Mexico prompts two murders and McCoy, disguised as a notorious bandit part of the time, is wrongly accused. Justice triumphs in the end. **60m/B VHS, Beta.** Tim McCoy; ***D:*** Sam Newfield. *NOS, VCN, DVT*

The Fighting Rookie ½ **1934** LaRue, better known for playing hoods, is a rookie cop set up and disgraced by the mob. But he fights back to regain his honor and bring the gang to justice. **65m/B VHS, Beta, 8mm.** Jack LaRue; ***D:*** Spencer Gordon Bennet. *VYY*

Fighting Seabees ½ **1944** As a hot-tempered construction foreman who battles Navy regulations as well as the Japanese, Wayne emerges as a larger-than-life hero in this action-packed saga of the Pacific theater of WWII. Extremely popular patriotic drama depicts the founding of the Seabees, the naval construction corps, amidst the action and the would-be romance with a woman reporter. Also available colorized. **100m/B VHS.** John Wayne, Susan Hayward, Dennis O'Keefe, William Frawley; ***D:*** Edward Ludwig. Nominations: Academy Awards '44: Best Original Score. *REP*

Fighting Shadows ½ **1935** McCoy plays a tough lawman who rids his town of an unscrupulous bandit gang guilty of harassing the locals. Highlighted by some excellent trick riding—for which Western star McCoy was known. **58m/B VHS.** Tim McCoy, Robert Allen, Geneva Mitchell, Ward Bond, Si Jenks; ***D:*** David Selman; ***W:*** Ford Beebe. *MOV*

The Fighting Sheriff **1931** Routine oater mixes action and romance when a sheriff is thrown together with a society debutante. **65m/B VHS.** Buck Jones, Loretta Sayers, Robert Ellis, Harlan E. Knight, Paul Fix, Lilian Worth; ***D:*** Louis King; ***W:*** Stuart Anthony. *MOV*

The Fighting 69th **1940** Cornball but entertaining WWI drama with lots of action. Cagney is a Brooklyn street tough who joins the all-Irish 69th New York regiment but could care less about its famed military history. He promptly defies his superiors and barely scrapes through his training. Sent to France the swaggering Cagney turns coward when confronted by the horrors of war but eventually redeems himself. O'Brien is the famed regimental chaplain Father Duffy, while Brent is commander "Wild Bill" Donovan, who would later found the OSS in WWII. Lots of heart-tugging emotion backed with a fine supporting cast. **90m/B VHS.** James Cagney, Pat O'Brien, George Brent, Jeffrey Lynn, Alan Hale, Frank McHugh, Dennis (Stanley Morner) Morgan, William Lundigan, Dick Foran, Guinn "Big Boy" Williams, Henry O'Neill, John Litel, George Reeves; ***D:*** William Keighley; ***W:*** Fred Niblo, Norman Reilly Raine, Dean Franklin; ***C:*** Gaetano Antonio "Tony" Gaudio. *MGM, FCT*

The Fighting Stallion 🦴🦴🦴 **1926** Canutt stars as a drifter hired by a rancher who's determined to capture a beautiful wild stallion (played by Boy the Wonder Horse). Silent with original organ score. **76m/B VHS, Beta, 8mm.** Yakima Canutt, Neva Gerber, Bud Osborne. *GPV, VYY*

The Fighting Sullivans 🦴🦴🦴½ *The Sullivans* **1942** The true story of five brothers killed on the Battleship Juneau at Guadalcanal during WWII. The tale tells of the fury felt by the siblings after Pearl Harbor, their enlistment to fight for their country, and their tragic fate in the heat of battle. Truly a stirring tribute to all lives lost in combat. **110m/B VHS.** Anne Baxter, Thomas Mitchell, Selena Royle, Eddie Ryan, Trudy Marshall, James B. Cardwell, Roy Roberts, Ward Bond, Mary McCarty, Bobby Driscoll, Addison Richards, Selmer Jackson, Mae Marsh, Harry Strang, Barbara Brown; ***D:*** Lloyd Bacon. *IVY*

Fighting Texans 🦴 **1933** An entire town invests in an oil well, on the advice of young salesman Bell, that the bankers are sure is a dud. Imagine their surprise when it turns out to be a gusler. **60m/B VHS.** Rex Bell, Luana Walters, Betty Mack, Gordon DeMain; ***D:*** Armand Schaefer. *NOS, DVT*

Fighting Thru 🦴 *California in 1878* **1930** Maynard fights off the bad guys and wins the girl after some nifty riding in his first all-talkie western. **60m/B VHS, Beta.** Ken Maynard, Jeanette Loff; ***D:*** William Nigh. *NOS, DVT*

The Fighting Trooper 🦴½ **1934** Based on the James Oliver Curwood story, "Footprints," this frontier tale presents a Mountie who goes undercover as a trapper in the Northwest. He is out to catch a murderer. **57m/B VHS, Beta.** Kermit Maynard. *NOS, VDM, DVT*

Fighting Valley 🦴🦴 **1943** Texas Rangers O'Brien, Newill, and Wilkerson ride off to break up an outlaw gang that is trying to monopolize the ore smelting business. O'Brien later went on to directing for TV and also wrote for Red Skelton. **60m/B VHS.** Dave O'Brien, James Newill, Guy Wilkerson, Patti McCarty, John Merton, Curly Dresden; ***D:*** Oliver Drake; ***W:*** Oliver Drake. *DVT, HEG*

Fighting Vigilantes 🦴🦴 **1947** A villainous food distributor is terrorizing his rivals until LaRue whips him. Holt and her father put together a committee called "The Vigilantes" to help out. Holt is the daughter of movie good guy Jack Holt. **61m/B VHS.** Lash LaRue, Al "Fuzzy" St. John, Jennifer Holt, George Chesebro, Lee Morgan, Russell Arms, Steve Clark; ***D:*** Ray Taylor. *NOS*

The Fighting Westerner 🦴½ *Rocky Mountain Mystery* **1935** Scott stars as a mining engineer who becomes entangled in mysterious murders. Mrs. Leslie Carter stars in a rare screen role. **54m/B VHS, Beta, 8mm.** Randolph Scott, Chic Sale, Ann Sheridan, Charles T. Barton. *VYY, MRV*

Fighting with Kit Carson **1933** Famous guide and Indian fighter lead bands of settlers westward. Action-packed. Twelve chapters. **230m/B VHS, Beta.** Johnny Mack Brown, Noah Beery Sr., Noah Beery Jr., Betsy King Ross; ***D:*** Armand Schaefer, Colbert Clark. *VYY, VCN, VDM*

Film House Fever 🦴 **1986** A compilation of clips from sleazy, cult-type movies, including "Blood Feast" and "Hot Night at the Go Go Lounge." **58m/C VHS, Beta.** Jamie Lee Curtis, James Keach, Lon Chaney Jr., Harvey Korman. *LIV, VES*

Films by Peter Thompson **1987** Three semi-experimental documentary shorts by Thompson, each using film form to comment on matters of both personal and public history: "Two Portraits," a memoir about Thompson's parents; "Universal Hotel," a meditation on photographs of a Polish POW forced into deep-cold medical experiments in Dachau, and "Universal Citizen," about a Guatemalan smuggler who was once an inmate at Dachau. **74m/C VHS, Beta.** ***D:*** Peter Thompson. *FCT*

The Final Alliance 🦴 **1989 (R)** A tough loner takes on a vicious motorcycle gang that's terrorizing a small town, and realizes that they're also responsible for his family's death. **90m/C VHS, Beta, LV.** David Hasselhoff, John Saxon, Bo Hopkins, Jeanie Moore; ***D:*** Mario Di Leo. *COL*

Final Analysis 🦴🦴½ **1992 (R)** Glossy thriller starring Gere as a San Francisco psychiatrist who falls for the glamorous sister of one of his patients. Basinger plays the femme fatale and Thurman is Gere's sexually neurotic patient. Although heavily influenced by "Vertigo," this film never comes close to attaining the depth of Hitchcock's cinematic masterpiece. Roberts gives the most gripping performance in this slick suspense movie as Basinger's sleazy gangster husband. **125m/C VHS, LV.** Richard Gere, Kim Basinger, Uma Thurman, Eric Roberts, Paul Guilfoyle, Keith David, Robert Harper, Jolyon Baker, Harris Yulin, Agustin Rodriguez; ***D:*** Phil Joanou; ***W:*** Wesley Strick, Robert Berger; ***M:*** George Fenton. *WAR*

Final Appeal 🦴🦴½ **1993 (PG-13)** Christine Biondi (Williams) is an abused wife, living in terror of her drug-addicted doctor husband, Ed. When Christine walks in on Ed and his mistress, she's forced to kill him in self-defense. But Ed's mistress swears it was murder and Christine's on trial. Now her only chance is her hard-drinking lawyer brother Perry (Dennehy)—who doesn't believe her story. Fact-based made for TV fare. **94m/C VHS.** JoBeth Williams, Brian Dennehy, Lindsay Crouse, Tom Mason, Eddie Jones, Ashley Crow, Betsy Brantley, Michael Beach; ***M:*** Charles Bernstein. *REP*

Final Approach 🦴🦴 **1991 (R)** Test pilot Jason Halsey (Sikking) crashes in the desert and awakens in the office of psychiatrist Dio Gottlieb (Elizondo). Halsey can't remember anything about his past, or his own name for that matter, but through word association games and psychological tests, he begins to remember as Gottlieb tries to pry information from his brain. Showy computer effects are excellent, but they only serve to fill holes in a story that has an unsatisfying ending. Notable as first film mde with digital sound. Also available in a letterboxed version. **100m/C VHS, LV.** James B. Sikking, Hector Elizondo, Madolyn Smith, Kevin McCarthy, Cameo Kneuer, Wayne Duvall; ***D:*** Eric Steven Stahl. *VMK*

Final Assignment 🦴 **1980** A Canadian television reporter agrees to smuggle a dissident Soviet scientist's ill granddaughter out of Russia for treatment along with a videotape documenting tragic experiments on children with steroids. She manages to evade the KGB while carrying on with a Russian press officer, and enlists the support of a Jewish fur trader. Location shooting in Canada instead of Russia is just one pitfall of this production. Also on video as, "The Moscow Chronicle." **101m/C VHS, Beta.** *CA* Genevieve Bujold, Michael York, Burgess Meredith, Colleen Dewhurst; ***D:*** Paul Almond. *LIV, VES*

Final Comedown 🦴 **1972 (R)** A black revolutionary attempts to get white radicals behind his war against racism. He fails and starts a racial bloodbath. **84m/C VHS, Beta.** Billy Dee Williams, D'Urville Martin, Celia Kaye, Raymond St. Jacques, Pamela Jones, R.G. Armstrong; ***D:*** Oscar Williams. *NLC, SIM*

The Final Conflict 🦴½ *The Omen 3* **1981 (R)** Unwelcomed third installment in the "Omen" series, concerning Satan's son Damien. Now 32, and the head of an international conglomerate, he is poised for world domination but fears another savior is born. Several monks and many babies meet gruesome deaths before he gets his comeuppance. The last theatrical release was then followed by a made-for-television movie called "Omen 4: The Awakening" (1991). **108m/C VHS, Beta, LV.** Sam Neill, Lisa Harrow, Barnaby Holm, Rossano Brazzi; ***D:*** Graham Baker; ***W:*** Andrew Birkin; ***C:*** Phil Meheux; ***M:*** Jerry Goldsmith. *FOX*

The Final Countdown 🦴🦴🦴 **1980 (PG)** A U.S. nuclear-powered aircraft carrier, caught in a time warp, is transported back to 1941, just hours before the bombing of Pearl Harbor. The commanders face the ultimate decision—leave history intact or stop the incident and thus avoid WWII. Excellent photography and a surprise ending. **92m/C VHS, Beta, LV.** Kirk Douglas, Martin Sheen, Katharine Ross, James Farentino, Charles Durning; ***D:*** Don Taylor; ***W:*** Thomas Hunter, David Ambrose. *VES*

Final Cut 🦴½ **1988** While filming in a secluded swampland, a crew stumbles on a local sheriff's crooked scheme and one by one, the crew members disappear. **92m/C VHS, Beta.** Carla De Lane, T.J. Kennedy, Joe Rainer, Brett Rice, Jordan Williams; ***D:*** Larry G. Brown. *VMK*

The Final Cut 🦴🦴🦴 **1995** Follows "House of Cards" and "To Play the King" in portraying the political adventures of Francis Urquardt (Richardson), Prime Minister. At 65, Urquardt has two goals: he wants to beat Margaret Thatcher's 11-year reign and he wants to establish a secret retirement fund (the plot involves Cyprus and could—finally—leads to Urquardt's downfall). Author Michael Dobbs objected to the adaptation and insisted his name be removed from the script. On 2 cassettes. **200m/C VHS.** *GB* Ian Richardson, Diane Fletcher, Paul Freeman, Isla Blair, Nick Brimble, Erika Hoffman, Nickolas Grace, Julian Fellowes; ***D:*** Mike Vardy; ***W:*** Andrew Davies; ***C:*** Ian Punter; ***M:*** Jim Parker. *FOX, FCT*

The Final Days 🦴🦴½ **1989 (PG)** TV drama follows the presidency of Richard Nixon (Smith) from Watergate through his resignation. Based on the Pulitzer Prize-winning book by Bob Woodward and Carl Bernstein. **150m/C VHS.** Lane Smith, Richard Kiley, David Ogden Stiers, Ed Flanders, Theodore Bikel; ***D:*** Richard Pearce. *REP*

Final Embrace 🦴½ **1992 (R)** When Laurel's famous sister is murdered she decides to do a little investigating on her own. She's aided by a young cop who just happened to be obsessed with the murdered woman. **?m/C VHS, LV.** Robert Rusler, Nancy Valen, Dick Van Patten, Linda Dona; ***D:*** Oley Sassone; ***W:*** R.J. Robertson, Jim Wynorski; ***M:*** Daniel Licht. *NHO*

Final Equinox 🦴½ **1995** Mysterious alien artifact, which has the power to spontaneously create new life, is stolen and both the government and the mob try to be the first to find—and control—it. Cop Kove opposes them both. **90m/C VHS.** Martin Kove, Joe Lara, David Warner. *MNC*

Final Exam *Woof!* **1981 (R)** Psychotic killer stalks college students during exam week. This one's too boring to be scary. You root for the psycho to off everyone just to have the movie over. **90m/C VHS, Beta.** Cecile Bagdadi, Joel Rice; ***D:*** Jimmy Huston. *COL, SUE*

The Final Executioner 🦴 *The Last Warrior* **1983** A valiant man finds a way to stop the slaughter of innocent people in a post-nuclear world. **95m/C VHS, Beta.** William Mang, Marina Costa, Harrison Muller, Woody Strode; ***D:*** Romolo Guerrieri. *MGM*

Final Extra 🦴🦴 **1927** Ambitious reporter's career gets a boost when he's assigned to investigate the murder of a rival. Silent with music score. **60m/B VHS, Beta, 8mm.** Grant Withers, Marguerite de la Motte. *NOS, VYY, DVT*

Final Impact 🦴½ **1991 (R)** Nick Taylor seeks vengeance on reigning kickboxing champ Jake Gerard through his prodigy, Danny Davis. Will sweet revenge for the wicked beating, suffered at the hands of Gerard years earlier, be his? **99m/C VHS.** Lorenzo Lamas, Kathleen Kinmont, Mimi Lesseos, Kathrin Lautner, Jeff Langton, Mike Worth; ***D:*** Joseph Merhi, Stephen Smoke; ***M:*** John Gonzalez. *PMH*

Final Judgement 🦴🦴 **1992 (R)** Daniel Tyrone (Dourif) is a former gang member, now a troubled priest, who's the prime suspect in the Los Angeles murder of a beautiful stripper. Determined to find the killer Father Tyrone heads into L.A.'s underground sex industry to search for clues, which brings him face to face with evil and his own desires. **90m/C VHS.** Brad Dourif, Isaac Hayes, Maria Ford, Karen Black, Orson Bean, David Ledingham; ***D:*** Louis Morneau; ***W:*** Kirk Honeycutt, Louis Morneau. *COL*

Final Justice 🦴 **1984 (R)** A small-town Texan sheriff wages a war against crime and corruption that carries him to Italy and the haunts of Mafia hitmen. **90m/C VHS, Beta.** Joe Don Baker, Rossano Brazzi, Patrizia Pellegrino; ***D:*** Greydon Clark; ***M:*** David Bell. *VES*

Final Mission 🦴 **1984** Vengeful one-man army follows the professional hit man who slaughtered his family from L.A. to Laos. His pursuit leads to a jungle showdown. Gee, sounds like "Rambo, First Blood," though obviously less grand and glorious. **97m/C VHS, Beta.** Richard Young, John Dresden, Kaz Garas, Christine Tudor; ***D:*** Cirio H. Santiago. *REP*

Final Mission 🦴🦴 **1993 (R)** Virtual reality becomes a weapon in a military conspiracy when pilots start dying. Air Force jets are supposed to be unstoppable thanks to the new technology and a general is only too willing to blame the deaths on pilot error but one fly boy is out to find the truth. **91m/C VHS, LV.** Billy Wirth, Corbin Bernsen, Elizabeth Gracen, Steve Railsback. *VMK*

Final Notice 🦴 **1989** A detective tracking a serial killer has as his only evidence a trail of shredded photos of nude women. Not released theatrically. **91m/C VHS, Beta, LV.** Gil Gerard, Steve Landesburg, Jackie Burroughs, Melody Anderson, Louise Fletcher, David Ogden Stiers, Kevin Hicks; ***D:*** Steven Hilliard Stern; ***W:*** John Gay; ***M:*** Tom Scott. *PAR*

The Final Option 🦴 *Who Dares Wins* **1982 (R)** An agent of England's Special Air Services team goes undercover as one of a band of anti-nuclear terrorists that take over the U.S. Embassy in London. Violent, but unconvincing. **125m/C VHS, Beta.** *GB* Lewis Collins, Judy Davis, Richard Widmark, Robert Webber, Edward Woodward, Ingrid Pitt, Kenneth Griffith, Tony Doyle, John Duttine; ***D:*** Ian Sharp; ***W:*** Reginald Rose; ***C:*** Phil Meheux. *MGM*

The Final Programme 🦴🦴½ *The Last Days of Man on Earth* **1973** In this futuristic story, a man must rescue his sister—and the world—from their brother, who holds a microfilmed plan for global domination. Meanwhile, he must shield himself from the advances of a bisexual computer programmer who wants to make him father to a new, all-purpose human being. Based on the Michael Moorcock "Jerry Cornelius" stories, the film has gained a cult following. **85m/C VHS, Beta.** *GB* Hugh Griffith, Harry Andrews, Jon Finch, Jenny Runacre, Sterling Hayden, Patrick Magee, Sarah Douglas; ***D:*** Robert Fuest. *SUE*

Final Round 🦴½ **1993 (R)** A kickboxer and his girlfriend are kidnapped by a millionaire who stages hunt the humans games for the pleasure of his gambling syndicate. Stiff but with a few good action sequences. **90m/C VHS.** Lorenzo Lamas, Anthony de Longis, Kathleen Kinmont, Clark Johnson, Isabelle Jamieson; ***D:*** George Erschbamer; ***W:*** Arne Olsen; ***M:*** Graeme Coleman. *WOV*

Final Sanction 🦴🦴½ **1989** After a nuclear holocaust exhausts their military resources, the U.S. and the Soviets each send one-man armies to battle each other for final control of the world. **90m/C VHS, Beta.** Robert Z'Dar, Ted Prior; ***D:*** David A. Prior; ***W:*** David A. Prior. *AIP, HHE*

Final Shot: The Hank Gathers Story 🦴🦴½ **1992** Inspirational story of Gathers, who rose from the ghetto to become one of America's top college basketball stars at Loyola Marymount, until tragedy strikes during a game. **92m/C VHS, Beta.** Victor Love, Duane Davis, Nell Carter, George Kennedy. *PSM*

The Final Terror 🦴🦴 *Campsite Massacre; Bump in the Night; The Forest Primeval* **1983 (R)** Group of young campers is stalked by a mad killer in a desolate, backwoods area. Better-than-average stalked-teens entry is notable for the presence of some soon-to-be stars. **90m/C VHS, Beta, LV.** John Friedrich, Rachel Ward, Adrian Zmed, Daryl Hannah, Joe Pantoliano, Ernest Harden, Mark Metcalf, Lewis Smith, Cindy Harrel, Akosua Busia; ***D:*** Andrew Davis. *LIV, VES*

Final Verdict 🦴🦴½ **1991** A trial lawyer defends a man he knows is guilty, throwing his life and his family into turmoil. Made for cable television. **93m/C VHS, Beta.** Treat Williams, Glenn Ford, Amy Wright, Olivia Burnette; ***D:*** Jack Fisk. *TTC*

Final Warning 🦴🦴½ *Chernobyl: The Final Warning* **1990** A dramatization of actual events surrounding the 1986 melt-down of the nuclear power plant at Chernobyl. Made for television. **94m/C VHS.** Jon Voight, Jason Robards Jr., Sammi Davis; ***D:*** Anthony Page. *TTC*

Find the Lady 🦴½ *Call the Cops: Kopek and Broom* **1975 (R)** Candy assumes a supporting role as a bumbling cop who is part of an incompetent police team trying to rescue a kidnapped socialite. **100m/C VHS, Beta.** *CA* John Candy, Peter Cook, Mickey Rooney, Lawrence Dane, Alexandra Bastedo; ***D:*** John Trent. *NO*

Finders Keepers 🦴🦴 **1984 (R)** A wild assortment of characters on board a train en route from California to Nebraska search for five million dollars hidden in the baggage car. **96m/C VHS, Beta.** Michael O'Keefe, Beverly D'Angelo, Ed Lauter, Louis Gossett Jr., Pamela Stephenson, Jim Carrey, David Wayne, Brian Dennehy, John Schuck; ***D:*** Richard Lester; ***W:*** Ronny Graham. *FOX*

Fine Gold 🦴🦴 **1988** A false charge of embezzlement leaves a man without home and family, so he decides to turn the tables on those who betrayed him. **91m/C VHS, Beta.** Andrew Stevens, Ray Walston, Ted Wass, Stewart Granger, Lloyd Bochner, Jane Badler; ***D:*** J. Anthony Loma. *MCG*

A Fine Madness 🦴🦴🦴 **1966** A near-classic comedy about a lusty, rebellious poet thrashing against the pressures of the modern world, and fending off a bevy of lobotomy-happy psychiatrists. Shot on location in New York City, based on Elliot Baker's novel. **104m/C VHS, Beta.** Sean Connery, Joanne Woodward, Jean Seberg, Patrick O'Neal, Colleen Dewhurst, Clive Revill, John Fiedler; ***D:*** Irvin Kershner; ***M:*** John Addison. *WAR*

A Fine Mess 🦴½ **1986 (PG)** Two buffoons cash in when one overhears a plan to dope a racehorse, but they are soon fleeing the plotters' slapstick pursuit. The plot is further complicated by the romantic interest of a gangster's wife. The television popularity of the two stars did not translate to the big screen; perhaps it's Edwards' fault. **100m/C VHS, Beta, LV.** Ted Danson, Howie Mandel, Richard Mulligan, Stuart Margolin, Maria Conchita Alonso, Paul Sorvino; ***D:*** Blake Edwards; ***W:*** Blake Edwards; ***C:*** Harry Stradling Jr.; ***M:*** Henry Mancini. *COL*

A Fine Romance 🦴🦴 **1992 (PG-13)** An improbable romance set in Paris features Andrews and Mastroianni as abandoned spouses falling in love. Andrews is the prim English Pamela who has been abandoned by her docter husband. Mastroianni is the irrepresible Cesareo, whose wife has just happened to run off with the aforementioned doctor. They meet to plan how to get their spouses back and wind up with opposites attracting. Not much story and the charm is spread thin. Based on the play "Tchin, Tchin" by Francois Billetdoux. **83m/C VHS.** Julie Andrews, Marcello Mastroianni, Ian Fitzgibbon, Jean-Pierre Castaldi, Jean-Jacques Dulon, Maria Machado, Jean-Michel Cannone, Catherine Jarrett, Gene Saks; ***W:*** Ronald Harwood; ***M:*** Pino Donaggio. *ACA*

Fine Things 🦴🦴½ *Danielle Steel's Fine Things* **1990** Bernie Fine thinks everything will be dandy now that he has a beautiful new bride and a cute stepdaughter. Then his wife dies and his stepdaughter's unreliable father wants sole custody. What's a nice guy to do? Based on the novel by Danielle Steel. Made for television. **145m/C VHS.** D.W. Moffett, Tracy Pollan, Judith Hoag, Cloris Leachman, Noley Thornton; ***D:*** Tom Moore; ***W:*** Peter Lefcourt. *CMB, WOV*

Finessing the King 🦴🦴½ **1984** Private eyes Tommy and Tuppence follow a mysterious newspaper notice to a masked ball where a murder is about to occur. Based on the Agatha Christie story. Made for British television. **60m/C VHS, Beta.** *GB* James Warwick, Francesca Annis. *TPV*

The Finest Hour 🦴½ **1991 (R)** Two Navy buddies have a falling out when they both fall for the same woman. But they must put aside their differences when their next mission sends them to Iraq to deal with the deadly threat of biological warfare. **105m/C VHS, LV.** Rob Lowe, Gale Hansen, Tracy Griffith, Eb Lottimer; ***D:*** Shimon Dotan; ***W:*** Shimon Dotan. *COL*

The Finger Man 🦴🦴½ **1955** An ex-con cooperates with the feds rather than return to jail. The deal is that he gets the dirt on an underworld crime boss. Solid performances. **82m/B VHS.** Frank Lovejoy, Forrest Tucker, Peggy Castle, Timothy Carey, Glenn Gordon; ***D:*** Harold Schuster. *REP*

Finger on the Trigger 🦴🦴 *El Dedo En El Gatillo* **1965** Veterans from both sides of the Civil War are after a hidden supply of gold, but find that they must band together to fend off an Indian attack. Routine. **89m/C VHS, Beta.** Rory Calhoun, James Philbrook, Todd Martin, Silvia Solar, Brad Talbot; ***D:*** Sidney Pink. *NO*

Fingerprints Don't Lie 🦴 **1951** A fingerprint expert pins the murder of the town mayor on an innocent guy, then suspects a frame-up. **56m/B VHS, Beta, LV.** Richard Travis, Sheila Ryan, Tom Neal; ***D:*** Sam Newfield. *NO*

Fingers 🦴🦴🦴 **1978 (R)** Keitel is Johnny Fingers, a mobster's son, reluctantly working as a mob debt-collector, all the while dreaming of his ambitions to be a concert pianist. The divisions between his dreams and reality cause him to crack. Toback's first film generates psychological tension and excellent performances. **89m/C VHS, Beta.** Harvey Keitel, Tisa Farrow, Jim Brown, Danny Aiello, Tanya Roberts, Marian Seldes, Michael V. Gazzo, James Toback; ***D:*** James Toback; ***W:*** James Toback; ***C:*** Michael Chapman; ***M:*** George Barrie. *TTC*

Finian's Rainbow 🦴🦴🦴 **1968 (G)** A leprechaun comes to America to steal back a pot of gold taken by an Irishman and his daughter in this fanciful musical comedy based on a 1947 Broadway hit. Both the sprite and the girl find romance; the sharecropping locals are saved by the cash; a bigot learns the error of his ways; and Finian (Astaire) dances off to new adventures. The fine production and talented cast are not used to their best advantage by the director who proved much better suited for "The Godfather." Entertaining, nonetheless. ♫How Are Things in Glocca Morra?; Look To the Rainbow; That Old Devil Moon; If This Isn't Love; Something Sort of Grandish; The Be-Gat; This Time of Year; The Great Come and Get It Day; When I'm Not Near the Girl I Love. **141m/C VHS, Beta, LV.** Fred Astaire, Petula Clark, Tommy Steele, Keenan Wynn, Al Freeman Jr., Don Francks, Susan Hancock, Dolph Sweet; ***D:*** Francis Ford Coppola. Nominations: Academy Awards '68: Best Sound, Best Original Score. *WAR, MVD*

Finish Line 🦴🦴½ **1989** A high school track star turns to steroids to enhance his performance after being pushed by an overzealous father. The father-and-son Brolins play the pair. Made for cable. **100m/C VHS.** James Brolin, Josh Brolin, Mariska Hargitay, Kristoff St. John, John Finnegan, Billy Vera, Stephen Lang; ***D:*** John Nicolella. *TTC*

Finishing School 🦴½ **1933** Girls' school roommates Rogers and Dee experience heartaches and loves lost while enduring disinterested parents and snobbish peers. Box office bomb when released, despite a strong cast. **73m/B VHS, Beta.** Ginger

Rogers, Frances Dee, George Nicholls Jr., Beulah Bondi, Bruce Cabot, Billie Burke, John Halliday, Sara Haden, Jack Norton, Joan Barclay, Jane Darwell; ***D:*** George Nicholls Jr.; ***M:*** Max Steiner. *TTC*

The Finishing Touch 𝄞𝄞 **1992 (R)** Someone is stalking L.A.'s most gorgeous women and Detective Sam Stone (Nader) is assigned to the case. Stone discovers his prime suspect is a video artist with a taste for pornography. When Stone's investigation is cut short, his ex-wife, Detective Hannah Stone (Hack) is brought in to take over the case. Unfortunately, she finds herself falling for the suspect in this erotic thriller. **82m/C VHS.** Michael Nader, Shelley Hack, Arnold Vosloo, Art Evans, Clark Johnson, Theodore (Ted) Raimi; ***D:*** Fred Gallo. *COL*

Finnegan Begin Again 𝄞𝄞 **1984** A middle-aged schoolteacher and a grouchy, 65-year-old newspaper editor find romance despite their other obligations. Winning performances add charm to this cable TV movie. **112m/C VHS, Beta.** Mary Tyler Moore, Robert Preston, Sam Waterston, Sylvia Sidney, David Huddleston; ***D:*** Joan Micklin Silver. *CNG, KAR*

Finnegan's Wake *Passages from "Finnegans Wake"; Passages from James Joyce's "Finnegans Wake"* **1963** Portions of the filmed adaptation of James Joyce's novel are shown in this program along with an interview with producer/director Mary Ellen Bute. **92m/B VHS, Beta.** *CMR, NYS*

Fiorile 𝄞𝄞𝄞 *Wild Flower* **1993 (PG-13)** Covers several generations of a Tuscan clan living under a family curse which dates back to Napoleon's invasion of Italy. At that time Jean, a handsome French lieutenant, falls in love with Tuscan peasant girl Elisabetta, nicknamed Fiorile. When Jean is executed for a theft committed by her brother, the pregnant Fiorile vows revenge. Throughout sucessive generations, haunted by the past, the family's personal bad luck persists. Several of the actors play their character's ancestors, lending continuity. Attractive cast does well with the Taviani brothers' visual style and romantic narrative. In Italian with English subtitles. **118m/C VHS, LV.** *IT* Michael Vartan, Galatea Ranzi, Claudio Bigagli, Lino Capolicchio, Constanze Engelbrecht, Athina Cenci, Giovanni Guidelli, Chiara Caselli; ***D:*** Paolo Taviani, Vittorio Taviani; ***W:*** Paolo Taviani, Vittorio Taviani, Sandro Petraglia; ***M:*** Nicola Piovani. *NLC*

Fire 𝄞½ **1977** A fire started by an escaped convict rages through Oregon timberland in this suspenseful made-for-television Irwin Allen disaster drama. **98m/C VHS, Beta.** Ernest Borgnine, Vera Miles, Patty Duke, Alex Cord, Donna Mills; ***D:*** Earl Bellamy. *WAR*

Fire Alarm 𝄞 **1938** A change of scene for Western star Brown as he portrays a fireman who, in-between his work, romances a career girl. **67m/B VHS, Beta, LV.** Johnny Mack Brown, Noel Francis; ***D:*** Karl Brown. *NOS, VYY, HEG*

Fire and Ice 𝄞𝄞½ **1983 (PG)** An animated adventure film that culminates in a tense battle between good and evil, surrounded by the mystical elements of the ancient past. Designed by Frank Frazetta. **81m/C VHS, Beta, LV.** Randy Norton, Cynthia Leake; ***D:*** Ralph Bakshi; ***W:*** Ralph Bakshi, Willy Bogner, Gerry Conway; ***V:*** Susan Tyrrell, William Ostrander. *COL, WTA*

Fire and Ice 𝄞 **1987 (PG)** A tale of love on the slopes. Two skiers realize that their feelings for each other are perhaps even stronger than their feelings about skiing. You won't care though, except for some fine ski footage. **83m/C VHS, Beta, LV.** Suzy Chaffee, John Eaves; ***D:*** Willy Bogner; ***W:*** George Schlatter; ***M:*** Harold Faltermeyer. *SUE*

Fire and Rain 𝄞𝄞 **1989** Based on the real-life crash of a Delta Airlines plane in Dallas and the rescue efforts made following the disaster. Familiar cast-members turn in decent performance. Made for television. **89m/C VHS, Beta, LV.** Angie Dickinson, Charles Haid, Tom Bosley, David Hasselhoff, Robert Guillaume, Susan Ruttan, John Beck, Patti LaBelle, Dean Jones, Lawrence Pressman, Penny Fuller; ***D:*** Jerry Jameson; ***W:*** Gary Sherman. *PAR*

Fire and Sword 𝄞 **1982** A Cornish knight must choose between loyalty for king and country and the love of an Irish woman in this medieval drama. A not very inspired retelling of the Tristan and Isolde legend. **84m/C VHS, Beta.** *GB* Peter Firth, Leigh Lawson, Antonia Preser, Christopher Waitz; ***D:*** Veith von Furstenberg. *LIV*

Fire Birds 𝄞 *Wings of the Apache* **1990 (PG-13)** Army attack helicopters and the people who fly them are used in the war on drugs in South America. Failed to match either the exciting flight sequences, the romantic interest or the box office of "Top Gun." **85m/C VHS, Beta, LV.** Nicolas Cage, Tommy Lee Jones, Sean Young, Bryan Kestner, Dale Dye, Mary Ellen Trainor, J.A. Preston, Peter Onorati; ***D:*** David Green; ***W:*** Nick Thiel, Paul F. Edwards; ***M:*** David Newman. *TOU*

Fire Down Below 𝄞½ **1957** Hayworth is the been-around-the-block beauty who persuades Mitchum and Lemmon, two small-time smugglers, to take her to a safe haven, no questions asked. Both men fall for her obvious charms, causing them to have a falling out until a life or death situation puts their friendship to the test. An unoriginal melodrama indifferently acted by everyone but Lemmon. Good location work in Trinidad and Tobago. **116m/C VHS, Beta, LV.** *GB* Robert Mitchum, Jack Lemmon, Rita Hayworth, Herbert Lom, Anthony Newley; ***D:*** Robert Parrish. *COL, COL, CCB*

Fire, Ice and Dynamite 𝄞½ **1991 (PG)** Moore is onscreen only briefly as an eccentric tycoon who fakes suicide to watch several teams of challengers scramble in a madcap winter-sports contest for his millions. A German-made avalanche of crazy stunts, bad jokes, and product plugs for countless European companies, commencing with a literal parade of guests, from astronaut Buzz Aldrin to soul man Isaac Hayes. Numbing; must be seen to be believed. **105m/C VHS.** Roger Moore, Shari Belafonte, Simon Shepherd, Uwe Ochsenknecht, Marjoe Gortner; ***D:*** Willy Bogner. *VES, LIV*

Fire in the Night 𝄞½ **1985** In a small Southern town, a beautiful and sure-footed woman battles the limitless resources of the town's predominant dynastic family. **89m/C VHS, Beta.** Graciela Casillas, John Martin. *VTR, NWV*

Fire in the Sky 𝄞𝄞 **1993 (PG-13)** Mysterious disappearance of Sweeney sparks a criminal investigation, until he returns, claiming he was abducted by aliens. Though everybody doubts his story, viewers won't, since the alleged aliens have already made an appearance, shifting the focus to Sweeney as he tries to convince skeptics that his trauma is genuine. Perhaps this mirrors what director Lieberman went through while trying to convince backers the film should be made. He could have benefitted by understanding the difference between what he was telling viewers and what he was showing them. Captivating special effects are one of the few bright spots. Based on a story that might be true. **98m/C VHS, Beta, LV.** D.B. Sweeney, Robert Patrick, Craig Sheffer, Peter Berg, James Garner, Henry Thomas; ***D:*** Robert Liebmann; ***W:*** Tracy Torme; ***M:*** Mark Isham. *PAR*

The Fire in the Stone 𝄞𝄞 **1985** A young boy discovers an opal mine and dreams of using the treasure to reunite his family. However, when the jewels are stolen from him, he enlists his friends to help get them back. Based on the novel by Colin Thiele. **97m/C VHS, Beta.** *AU* Paul Smith, Linda Hartley, Theo Pertsindis. *WAR*

Fire Maidens from Outer Space 𝄞 **1956** Fire maidens prove to be true to the space opera code that dictates that all alien women be in desperate need of male company. Astronauts on an expedition to Jupiter's thirteenth moon discover the lost civilization of Atlantis, which, as luck would have it, is inhabited by women only. Possibly an idea before its time, it might've been better had it been made in the sixties, when space-exploitation came into its own. **80m/B VHS.** *GB* Anthony Dexter, Susan Shaw, Paul Carpenter, Harry Fowler, Jacqueline Curtiss, Sydney Tafler, Maya Koumani, Jan Holden, Kim Parker; ***D:*** Cy Roth; ***W:*** Cy Roth. *CNM, MLB*

Fire Monsters Against the Son of Hercules 𝄞𝄞 **1962** The son of the muscular one does battle with a hydra-headed monster in this average sword and sandal adventure. **?m/C VHS.** Reg Lewis. *SNC*

The Fire Next Time 𝄞𝄞½ **1993** In the year 2017, the United States is being ravaged by an ecological holocaust caused by a deadly combination of pollution and global warming. Nelson, Bedelia and their children are forced from their Louisiana home by a natural disaster and decide to head for better times in Canada. Their travels aren't easy. Made for television. **195m/C VHS.** Craig T. Nelson, Bonnie Bedelia, Juergen Prochnow, Richard Farnsworth, Justin Whalin, Charles Haid, Sal Lopez, Shawn Toovey, Ashley Jones; ***Cameos:*** Odetta; ***D:*** Tom McLoughlin; ***W:*** James Henerson. *CAF*

Fire Over England 𝄞𝄞𝄞 **1937** Young naval officer volunteers to spy at the Spanish court to learn the plans for the invasion of his native England and to identify the traitors among the English nobility. He arouses the romantic interest of his queen, Elizabeth I, one of her ladies, and a Spanish noblewoman who helps with his missions, and later leads the fleet to victory over the huge Spanish Armada. The first on-screen pairing of Olivier and Leigh is just one of the many virtues of this entertaining drama. **81m/B VHS, Beta.** *GB* Flora Robson, Raymond Massey, Laurence Olivier, Vivien Leigh, Leslie Banks, James Mason; ***D:*** William K. Howard; ***C:*** James Wong Howe. *NOS, MRV, VYY*

Fire with Fire 𝄞𝄞 **1986 (PG-13)** A boy at a juvenile detention center and a Catholic school girl fall in love. However, they find themselves on the run from the law when he escapes to be with her. Sheffer and Madsen are appealing in this otherwise unspectacular film. **103m/C VHS.** Craig Sheffer, Virginia Madsen, Jon Polito, Kate Reid, Jean Smart, D.B. Sweeney; ***D:*** Duncan Gibbins; ***W:*** Bill Phillips, Paul Boorstin, Sharon Boorstin; ***M:*** Howard Shore. *PAR*

The Fire Within 𝄞𝄞𝄞 *Le Feu Follet; Fuoco Fatuo* **1964** Ronet plays an alcoholic writer recently released from a sanitorium after a breakdown. Believing his life will only continue its downward spiral, he pays a final visit to friends and calmly plots his suicide. Malle clearly and pitilessly describes a man beyond despair. Based on a novel by Pierre Drieu La Rochelle, which itself fictionalized the suicide of writer Jacques Rigaut. In French with English subtitles. **104m/B VHS.** *FR* Maurice Ronet, Lena Skerla, Yvonne Clech, Hubert Deschamps, Jean-Paul Moulinot; ***D:*** Louis Malle; ***W:*** Louis Malle; ***C:*** Ghislan Cloquet. *NYF, INJ, PMS*

Fireback 𝄞½ **1978.** A Vietnam vet's wife is kidnapped by the mob, causing him to take up arms and spill blood yet again. **90m/C VHS, Beta.** Bruce Baron, Richard Harrison. *LIV*

Fireball Forward 𝄞𝄞½ **1972 (PG)** A battalion fighting in France during WWII is having a bad time until Gazzara takes over and turns them into a crack fighting team. Uses some battle footage from the movie "Patton." Made for television. **100m/C VHS.** Ben Gazzara, Eddie Albert, Ricardo Montalban, Dana Elcar, L.Q. Jones, Anne Francis; ***D:*** Marvin J. Chomsky. *QVD*

Fireballs 𝄞½ **1990** Sexploitaton pic set at a firehouse, where a batch of female recruits turn up the heat for three stud hose-bearers. The title should give you some idea of the intellectual level. **89m/C VHS.** Mike Shapiro, Goren Kalezik; ***D:*** Mike Shapiro. *ATL*

Firebird 2015 A.D. 𝄞 **1981 (PG)** Dreary action adventure set in a 21st century society where automobile use is banned because of an extreme oil shortage. Private cars are hunted down for destruction by the Department of Vehicular Control. One over-zealous enforcer decides to make it a package deal and throws in the owners as well. Everyone connected with effort should have been cited for running stop sign. **97m/C VHS, Beta.** Darren McGavin, George Touliatos, Doug McClure; ***D:*** David Robertson. *SUE*

Firecracker **1971** Female martial arts expert retaliates against the crooks who murdered her sister. **83m/C VHS, Beta.** Jillian Kesner, Darby Hinton; ***D:*** Cirio H. Santiago. *NO*

Firecreek ½ **1968** Fonda and his thugs terrorize a small town protected by part-time sheriff Stewart. Beautiful photography and competent cast, but meandering and long. **104m/C VHS.** Henry Fonda, James Stewart, Inger Stevens, Gary Lockwood, Dean Jagger, Ed Begley Sr., Jay C. Flippen, Jack Elam, Barbara Luna; ***D:*** Vincent McEveety; ***C:*** William Clothier. *WAR, VTR, MTX*

Firefall *Freefall* **1994** Wildlife photog Katy Mazur (Gidley) has a brief affair with sportsman Grant Orion (Roberts) while on assignment in Africa. When they meet again, Orion tells Katy he's actually an Interpol agent who's assigned to protect her—although she has no idea why. Katy's fiance (Fahey) thinks this is strange. **95m/C VHS, LV.** Pamela Gidley, Eric Roberts, Jeff Fahey; ***D:*** John Irvin. *VMK*

Firefight **1987** After a nuclear holocaust, convicted criminals endeavor to rule the wasteland. **100m/C VHS, Beta.** James Pfeiffer, Janice Carraher, Jack Tucker; ***D:*** Scott Pfeiffer. *TWE*

The Firefly ½ **1937** Although slow-paced and long, this adaptation of the 1912 Rudolf Friml operetta was one of MacDonald's most popular films. Co-star Jones gets to sing the best song in the film, "Donkey Serenade," while MacDonald sings most of the others. ♫Love Is Like a Firefly; English March; A Woman's Kiss; He Who Loves and Runs Away; When a Maid Comes Knocking at Your Heart; When the Wine Is Full of Fire; The Donkey Serenade; Giannina Mia; Sympathy. **140m/B VHS.** Jeanette MacDonald, Allan Jones, Warren William, Billy Gilbert, Henry Daniell, Douglass Dumbrille, George Zucco; ***D:*** Robert Z. Leonard. *MGM*

Firefox ½ **1982 (PG)** A retired pilot sneaks into the Soviet Union for the Pentagon to steal a top-secret, ultra-sophisticated warplane and fly it out of the country. Best for the low-altitude flight and aerial battle sequences, but too slow on character and much too slow getting started. **136m/C VHS, Beta, LV.** Clint Eastwood, Freddie Jones, David Huffman, Warren Clarke, Ronald Lacey, Kenneth Colley, Nigel Hawthorne, Kai Wulff; ***D:*** Clint Eastwood; ***C:*** Bruce Surtees; ***M:*** Maurice Jarre. *WAR*

Firehawk **1992 (R)** Several American soldiers survive the crash of their helicopter into the jungles of Vietnam. They think their only enemy is the Vietcong but when they discover the copter has been sabotaged the hunt is on for the traitor among them. **92m/C VHS, LV.** Martin Kove, Matt Salinger, Vic Trevino; ***D:*** Cirio H. Santiago; ***W:*** Jeff Yonis. *LIV*

Firehead ½ **1990 (R)** A pyrokinetic Soviet defector begins using his powers to destroy American munitions in the name of peace. When a clandestine pro-war organization hears of this, they attempt to capture the man and use him for their own evil purposes. **88m/C VHS, Beta, LV.** Christopher Plummer, Chris Lemmon, Martin Landau, Gretchen Becker, Brett Porter; ***D:*** Peter Yuval. *AIP*

Firehouse **1972** Tempers ignite in a lily-white firehouse when a black rookie replaces an expired veteran. March—of "Paper Lion" renown—directed this made-for-TV emergency clone, which ran ever-so-briefly as an adventure series on TV in 1974 (with a largely different cast). **73m/C VHS.** Richard Roundtree, Vince Edwards, Andrew Duggan, Richard Jaeckel, Sheila Frazier, Val Avery, Paul LeMat, Michael Lerner; ***D:*** Alex March. *XVC*

Firehouse **1987 (R)** In the style of "Police Academy," three beautiful and sex-starved fire-fighting recruits klutz up an urban firehouse. A softcore frolic. **91m/C VHS, Beta.** Barrett Hopkins, Shannon Murphy, Violet Brown, John Anderson; ***D:*** J. Christian Ingvordsen. *ACA*

The Fireman ½ **1916** Chaplin portrays a fireman who becomes a hero. Silent with musical soundtrack added. **20m/B VHS, Beta.** Eric Campbell, Edna Purviance, Charlie Chaplin; ***D:*** Charlie Chaplin. *CAB, GVV, VYY*

The Firemen's Ball **1968** A critically acclaimed comedy about a small-town ball held for a retiring fire chief. Plans go amusingly awry as beauty contestants refuse to show themselves, raffle prizes and other items—including the gift for the guest of honor—are stolen, and the firemen are unable to prevent an old man's house from burning down. Forman's second film is sometimes interpreted as political allegory; Czech with subtitles. **73m/C VHS, Beta.** *CZ* Vaclav Stockel, Josef Svet; ***D:*** Milos Forman. Nominations: Academy Awards '68: Best Foreign Language Film. *HMV, INJ, COL*

Firepower ½ **1979 (R)** Loren blames her chemist husband's death on a rich industrialist and hires hitman Coburn to take care of the matter. Less than compelling. **104m/C VHS, Beta.** Sophia Loren, James Coburn, O.J. Simpson, Christopher F. Bean; ***D:*** Michael Winner; ***W:*** Michael Winner; ***M:*** Gato Barbieri. *FOX*

Firepower ½ **1993 (R)** Two cops chase "The Swordsman" into a federally sanctioned area of legalized gambling, prostitution and crime (Las Vegas?), risking life and limb in the treacherous "Caged Ring of Death." **?m/C VHS, LV.** Chad McQueen, Gary Daniels, Jim Hellwig, Joseph Ruskin, George Murdock. *PMH*

Fires on the Plain *Nobi* **1959** A grueling Japanese antiwar film about an unhinged private in the Philippines during WWII who roams the wartorn countryside encountering all manner of horror and devastation. In Japanese with English subtitles. **105m/B VHS, Beta.** *JP* Eiji Funakoshi, Osamu Takizawa, Mickey Custis, Asao Suno; ***D:*** Kon Ichikawa. *SUE, MRV, HHT*

Fires Within **1991 (R)** A curiously flat romance with political overtones. After eight years as a political prisoner in Cuba, Nestor (Smits) is released and goes to Miami to be reunited with his wife and daughter. Once there he finds his wife has fallen in love with another man. Now Nestor must choose between his politics and the chance to win back his family. Secondary plot lines fizzle out and a talented cast is largely wasted. Scacchi is beautiful but hardly believable as the Cuban wife. **90m/C VHS, Beta.** Jimmy Smits, Greta Scacchi, Vincent D'Onofrio; ***D:*** Gillian Armstrong; ***W:*** Cynthia Cidre. *MGM*

Firesign Theatre Presents Nick Danger in the Case of the Missing Yolks ½ **1983** Firesign characters Nick Danger and Rocky Rococo are featured in this story of a truly interactive family who live through their television set. **60m/C VHS, Beta.** Phil Proctor, Phil Austin, Peter Bergman. *NO*

Firestarter **1984 (R)** A C.I.A.-like organization is after a little girl who has the ability to set anything on fire in this filmed adaptation of Stephen King's bestseller. Good special effects help a silly plot. **115m/C VHS, Beta, LV.** David Keith, Drew Barrymore, Freddie Jones, Martin Sheen, George C. Scott, Heather Locklear, Louise Fletcher, Moses Gunn, Art Carney, Antonio Fargas, Drew Snyder; ***D:*** Mark L. Lester; ***M:*** Tangerine Dream. *MCA*

Firestorm: 72 Hours in Oakland ½ **1993** Residents of an Oakland community face the threat of a big brush fire. **94m/C VHS.** LeVar Burton, Jill Clayburgh, Michael Gross; ***D:*** Michael Tuchner. *ABC*

Firewalker **1986 (PG)** An "Indiana Jones" clone about three mercenaries endeavoring to capture a fortune in hidden gold. Paper-mache sets and a villain with an eye patch that consistently changes eyes are just some of the gaffes that make this one of the worst edited movies in history. **106m/C VHS, Beta, LV.** Chuck Norris, Louis Gossett Jr., Melody Anderson; ***D:*** J. Lee Thompson; ***W:*** Norman Aladjem; ***M:*** Gary Chang. *MED, VTR*

The Firing Line **1991** The Central American government hires a mercenary rebel-buster to squash insurgents. Everything's great until he finds out he agrees with the rebel cause, and he trains them to fight the government. Below average renegade-with-a-hidden-heart warpic. **93m/C VHS, LV.** Reb Brown, Shannon Tweed; ***D:*** John Gale. *AIP*

The Firm **1993 (R)** Top-flight cast promises a good time—the script based on the top-selling 1991 novel by John Grisham nearly guarantees it. Ambitious, idealistic Ivy League law school grad Cruise accepts a great offer from a small but wealthy Memphis law firm. As with anything that seems too good to be true, he discovers too late that nothing in life is free. Good performances by nearly everyone involved makes up for predictability. Sorvino has an uncredited cameo as a mob boss. Book fans beware: the script is fairly faithful until the end. The movie rights were snapped up before the book was published. Placed third in the 1993 race for top box office gross. **154m/C VHS, Beta, LV, CD-I.** Tom Cruise, Jeanne Tripplehorn, Gene Hackman, Hal Holbrook, Terry Kinney, Wilford Brimley, Ed Harris, Holly Hunter, David Strathairn, Gary Busey, Steven Hill, Tobin Bell, Barbara Garrick, Jerry Hardin, Karina Lombard, John Beal; ***Cameos:*** Paul Sorvino; ***D:*** Sydney Pollack; ***W:*** Robert Towne, David Rayfiel; ***C:*** John Seale; ***M:*** Dave Grusin. Nominations: Academy Awards '93: Best Original Screenplay, Best Supporting Actress (Hunter); MTV Movie Awards '94: Best Actor (Cruise), Most Desirable Male (Cruise). *PAR, BTV, FCT*

First Affair **1983** A made-for-television film about a young innocent girl undergoing the pressures of freshman life at college, including her first love affair, which is with the husband of a female professor. **95m/C VHS, Beta.** Loretta Swit, Melissa Sue Anderson, Joel Higgins; ***D:*** Gus Trikonis. *FOX*

First & Ten **1985** A failing football team emphasizes sexual, rather than athletic conquests, under the guidance of their female owner. Made for cable TV and followed by "First & Ten: The Team Scores Again." **88m/C VHS, Beta.** Delta Burke, Geoffrey Scott, Reid Shelton, Ruta Lee, Fran Tarkenton; ***D:*** Donald Kushner. *LIV, VES*

First & Ten: The Team Scores Again **1985** A sequel to the made-for-cable-television comedy "First and Ten" about a football team's relationship with their female owner. **101m/C VHS, Beta.** Delta Burke, Geoffrey Scott, Ruta Lee, Reid Shelton, Clayton Landey, Fran Tarkenton. *LIV, VES*

First Blood **1982 (R)** Stallone is a former Green Beret survivor of Vietnam whose nightmares of wartime horrors are triggered by a wrongful arrest in a small town. He escapes into the mountains of the Northwest and leads his pursuers to all manner of bloody ends. Finally, the Army is summoned to crush him. Extremely violent and frequently confused, fueled on the revenge fantasy and not much concerned with the rules of plot realism. Screen debut of Caruso. Based on David Morrell's novel. A box-office hit that launched the "Rambo" series. Followed by "Rambo: First Blood, Part 2." **96m/C VHS, Beta, LV.** Sylvester Stallone, Richard Crenna, Brian Dennehy, Jack Starrett, David Caruso; ***D:*** Ted Kotcheff; ***W:*** Sylvester Stallone; ***M:*** Jerry Goldsmith. *LIV, TLF*

First Born ½ **1984 (PG-13)** In search of romance, divorced mother Garr finds an intriguing man, Weller. Trouble erupts when her son learns Weller is a cocaine dealer. Talented cast makes most of story. **100m/C VHS, Beta, LV.** Teri Garr, Peter Weller, Christopher Collet, Corey Haim, Sarah Jessica Parker, Robert Downey Jr.; ***D:*** Michael Apted. *PAR*

The First Deadly Sin ½ **1980 (R)** Police lieutenant Sinatra tracks down a homicidal killer in spite of wife Dunaway's illness and his impending retirement. Read Lawrence Sanders' bestselling novel; it's a lot more exciting than this. **112m/C VHS, Beta, LV.** Frank Sinatra, Faye Dunaway, David Dukes, Brenda Vaccaro, James Whitmore; ***D:*** Brian G. Hutton; ***C:*** Jack Priestley. *WAR*

First Degree ½ **1995 (R)** New York City homicide detective goes up against the mob while investigating the murder of a rich man and falling for the widow. Made for cable. **98m/C VHS.** Rob Lowe, Leslie Hope. *PGV*

First Family ½ **1980 (R)** Flat satire of life in the White House. The humor is weak and silly at best, despite the excellent comedy cast. Henry's first directorial effort. **100m/C VHS, Beta.** Bob Newhart, Madeline Kahn, Gilda Radner, Richard Benjamin; **D:** Buck Henry; **W:** Buck Henry; **M:** Ralph Burns. *WAR*

First Knight ✂½ **1995 (PG-13)** King Arthur/Camelot legend comes to life again, but isn't worth the time it takes to watch. Wandering swordsman Lancelot (Gere) saves beautiful Guinevere (Ormond), soon to be Arthur's (Connery) queen, from evil renegade knight Malagant. They yearn, they gaze, they kiss—you gag. Written like a Harlequin romance, the dialogue (especially when uttered by Gere) is unintentionally funny, and the plot will cause much eye-rolling. Connery's regal (he knows his costume epics) and Ormond's lovely, but Gere is badly miscast. He offers a contemporary take on the flawed hero complete with American accent, an amazing feat in the 13th century. Big-scale battles, betrayals, passion, even Disneyland-like Camelot sets—the pieces for a tremendous epic are all here, it just doesn't work. **134m/C VHS, LV, 8mm.** Sean Connery, Richard Gere, Julia Ormond, Ben Cross, John Gielgud, Liam Cunningham, Christopher Villiers, Valentine Pelka; **D:** Jerry Zucker; **W:** William Nicholson; **C:** Adam Greenberg; **M:** Jerry Goldsmith. *COL*

First Legion ✂✂½ **1951** Boyer and Addy are seminarians struggling with their faith when they are confronted with a supposed miracle. Low-key examination of religion and conflict within a religious community. **77m/B VHS, Beta.** Charles Boyer, Barbara Rush, William Demarest, Leo G. Carroll; **D:** Douglas Sirk. *LIV*

First Love ✂✂½ **1939** Best known for Durbin's first screen kiss, this lightweight romance finds orphaned Connie Harding moving to New York to live with her wealthy Uncle James Clinton (Pallette) and his family. Connie meets handsome rich boy Ted Drake (Stack's screen debut) but her snobby debutante cousin Barbara (Parrish) already has Ted in her sights. Barbara tries to prevent Connie from going to the Drakes fancy dance but, in Cinderella fashion, the Clinton family servants help her become the belle of the ball. Durbin also does some singing. ♫One Fine Day; Amapola; Sympathy; A Change of Heart; Deserted; Spring In My Heart; Home Sweet Home. **85m/B VHS.** Deanna Durbin, Robert Stack, Eugene Pallette, Helen Parrish, Leatrice Joy, June Storey, Frank Jenks, Kathleen Howard, Charles Coleman, Mary Treen; **D:** Henry Koster; **W:** Bruce Manning, Lionel Houser; **C:** Joseph Valentine; **M:** Frank Skinner. *MCA*

First Love ✂✂½ **1970 (R)** A sixteen year old lad falls in love with a slightly older woman only to have his feelings rejected and to discover that she's his father's mistress. Actor Schell's directorial debut. **90m/C VHS, Beta.** *GE SI* John Moulder-Brown, Dominique Sanda, Maximilian Schell, Valentina Cortese; **D:** Maximilian Schell; **C:** Sven Nykvist. *CNG*

First Love ✂✂½ **1977 (R)** A story of an idealistic college student who takes love (and especially making love) more seriously than the rest of his peers, including his girlfriend. Based on Harold Brodkey's story "Sentimental Education." Darling's directorial debut. **92m/C VHS, Beta.** William Katt, Susan Dey, John Heard, Beverly D'Angelo, Robert Loggia; **D:** Joan Darling; **M:** John Barry. *PAR*

First Man into Space ✂✂ *Satellite of Blood* **1959** An astronaut returns to Earth covered with strange space dust and with an organism feeding inside him (shades of "Alien"). The alien needs human blood to survive and starts killing in order to get it. **78m/B VHS, Beta.** Marshall Thompson, Marla Landi, Bill Edwards; **D:** Robert Day. *DVT, RHI, HEG*

First Men in the Moon ✂✂ **1964** A fun, special effects-laden adaptation of the H. G. Wells novel about an Edwardian civilian spacecraft visiting the moon and the creature found there. Visual effects by Ray Harryhausen. Finch makes a brief appearance. **103m/C VHS, Beta, LV.** *GB* Martha Hyer, Edward Judd, Lionel Jeffries, Erik Chitty, Peter Finch; **D:** Nathan (Hertz) Juran; **W:** Nigel Kneale, Jan Read. *COL, MLB*

First Monday in October ✂✂½ **1981 (R)** A comedy concerning the first woman appointed to the Supreme Court, a conservative, and her colleague, a crusty but benign liberal judge. Though based on a Broadway hit, it ended up seeming to foreshadow the real-life appointment of Sandra Day O'Connor, which occurred at about the time the film was released. The title refers to the date the court begins its sessions. **99m/C VHS, Beta, LV.** Walter Matthau, Jill Clayburgh, Barnard Hughes, James Stephens, Jan Sterling; **D:** Ronald Neame; **C:** Fred W. Koenekamp. *PAR*

The First Movie Cowboy **1913** Three shorts featuring the very first movie cowboy, Bronco Billy. **47m/B VHS, Beta, 8mm.** "Broncho" Billy Anderson; **D:** "Broncho" Billy Anderson. *VYY*

First Name: Carmen ✂✂✂ *Prenom: Carmen* **1983** Carmen, although posing as an aspiring filmmaker, really is a bank robber and terrorist. She is also such a femme fatale that during a bank robbery one of the guards decides to run away with her. Godard cast himself as Carmen's uncle. Amusing late Godard. **95m/C VHS, Beta, LV.** *FR* Maruschka Detmers, Jacques Bonaffe, Jean-Luc Godard, Myriem Roussel, Christophe Odent; **D:** Jean-Luc Godard; **W:** Anne-Marie Mieville. *CVC, INJ, TPV*

The First Nudie Musical ✂✂ **1975 (R)** A producer tries to save his studio by staging a 1930s style musical, but with a naked cast and risque lyrics. Has attained semi-cult/trash status. ♫The First Nudie Musical; The Lights and the Smiles; Orgasm; Lesbian Butch Dyke; Dancing Dildos; Perversion; Honey, What Ya Doin' Tonight; Let 'Em Eat Cake; I Don't Have to Hide Anymore. **93m/C VHS, Beta.** Cindy Williams, Stephen Nathan, Diana Canova, Bruce Kimmel; **D:** Mark Haggard. *MED, HHT*

The First Olympics: Athens 1896 ✂✂½ **1984** Recounts the organization and drama surrounding the first modern-day Olympic games when the inexperienced American team shocked the games with their success. Made for television. **260m/C VHS, Beta.** Louis Jourdan, Angela Lansbury, David Ogden Stiers, Virginia McKenna, Jason Connery, Alex Hyde-White, Honor Blackman, Bill Travers; **D:** Alvin Rakoff; **M:** Bruce Broughton. *COL*

The First Power ✂½ **1989** A detective and psychic join forces to track down a serial killer who, after being executed, uses his satanic powers to kill again. **90m/C VHS, Beta, LV, 8mm.** Lou Diamond Phillips, Tracy Griffith, Jeff Kober, Mykelti Williamson, Elizabeth Arlen; **D:** Robert Resnikoff; **W:** Robert Resnikoff; **M:** Stewart Copeland. *COL, SUE, NLC*

First Spaceship on Venus ✂✂✂ *Der Schweigende Stern; Milczaca Gwiazda* **1960** Eight scientists from various countries set out for Venus and find the remains of a civilization far in advance of Earth's that perished because of nuclear weapons. A sometimes compelling anti-nuclear sci-fi effort made with German and Polish backing. Originally released at 130 minutes. **78m/C VHS, Beta.** *GE PL* Yoko Tani, Oldrich Lukes, Ignacy Machowski, Julius Ongewe, Michal Postnikow, Kurt Rackelmann, Gunther Simon, Tang-Hua-Ta, Lucyna Winnicka; **D:** Kurt Maetzig. *NOS, MRV, SNC*

First Strike ✂ **1985** The United States and the USSR engage in nuclear submarine warfare when the Soviets hijack a U.S. sub and aims its weapons at Arab oil fields. **90m/C VHS, Beta.** Stuart Whitman, Persis Khambatta. *VCD*

The First Time ✂½ *You Don't Need Pajamas at Rosie's; The Beginners Three; The Beginners; They Don't Wear Pajamas at Rosie's; Doin' It* **1969 (R)** It's pre-Porky's zaniness as a vacationing youth understandably wants to spend his "first time" with Bisset. Other than her presence, this film has little to offer. **90m/C VHS.** Jacqueline Bisset, Wes Stern, Rick Kelman, Wink Roberts; **D:** James Neilson. *NO*

First Time ✂✂½ *Doin' It* **1982 (R)** A comedy about a college student who can't quite succeed with women, despite coaching from his roommate and counseling from a psychology professor whose assistance is part of a research project. **96m/C VHS, Beta.** Tim Choate, Krista Errickson, Marshall Efron, Wallace Shawn, Wendie Jo Sperber, Cathryn Damon; **D:** Charles Loventhal. *NO*

First Turn On ✂ **1983 (R)** Not to be confused with "The Thomas Edison Story," this sex-comedy follows the adventures of several young campers who decide to die happy when an avalanche leaves them trapped in a cave. A longer unrated version is available. **84m/C VHS, Beta.** Georgia Harrell, Michael Sanville, Googy Gress, Jenny Johnson, Heide Basset, Vincent D'Onofrio, Sheila Kennedy; **D:** Michael Herz, Lloyd (Samuel Weil) Kaufman. *LIV*

First Yank into Tokyo ✂✂ *Mask of Fury* **1945** An American army pilot who grew up in Japan undergoes plastic surgery in order to infiltrate Japanese lines and get information from an American scientist. Some last minute editing to capitalize on current events made this the first American film to deal with the atomic bomb. **83m/B VHS, Beta.** Tom Neal, Richard Loo, Barbara Hale, Marc Cramer; **D:** Gordon Douglas. *TTC*

A Fish Called Wanda ✂✂✂ **1988 (R)** Absurd, high-speed farce about four criminals trying to retrieve $20 million they've stolen from a safety deposit box—and each other. Meanwhile, barrister Cleese falls in love with the female thief (Curtis). Some sick, but tastelessly funny, humor involves Palin's problem with stuttering and some very dead doggies. Written by Monty Python alum Cleese and director Crichton, who understand that silence is sometimes funnier than speech, and that timing is everything. Wickedly funny. **98m/C VHS, Beta, LV.** John Cleese, Kevin Kline, Jamie Lee Curtis, Michael Palin, Tom Georgeson, Maria Aitken, Patricia Hayes, Geoffrey Palmer; **D:** Charles Crichton; **W:** John Cleese, Charles Crichton; **M:** John Du Prez. Academy Awards '88: Best Supporting Actor (Kline); British Academy Awards '88: Best Actor (Cleese), Best Supporting Actor (Palin); Nominations: Academy Awards '88: Best Director (Crichton), Best Original Screenplay. *MGM, BTV, FOX*

Fish Hawk ✂½ **1979 (G)** When an alcoholic Indian, Fish Hawk, meets a young boy in the forest, they strike up a friendship and he attempts to clean up his act. Attempts to be heartwarming. **95m/C VHS, Beta.** *CA* Will Sampson, Charlie Fields; **D:** Donald Shebib. *MED, VTR*

The Fish that Saved Pittsburgh ✂✂ **1979 (PG)** A floundering basketball team hires an astrologer to try and change their luck. She makes sure all the team members' signs are compatible with their star's Pisces sign (the fish). Produced a disco soundtrack with several Motown groups who also performed in the movie. **104m/C VHS, Beta.** Jonathan Winters, Stockard Channing, Flip Wilson, Julius Erving, Margaret Avery, Meadowlark Lemon, Nicholas Pryor, James Bond III, Kareem Abdul-Jabbar, Jack Kehoe, Debbie Allen; **D:** Gilbert Moses; **M:** Thom Bell. *ORI, WAR*

The Fisher King ✂✂✂ **1991 (R)** In derelict-infested Manhattan a down-and-out radio deejay meets a crazed vagabond (Williams) obsessed with medieval history and in search of the Holy Grail. At first the whimsical mix of Arthurian myth and modern urban hell seems amazingly wrongheaded. In retrospect it still does. But while this picture runs it weaves a spell that pulls you in, especially in its quiet moments. Your reaction to the silly ending depends entirely on how well you're bamboozled by a script that equates madness with enlightment and the homeless with holy fools. Filmed on the streets of New York, with many street people playing themselves. **138m/C VHS, Beta, LV, 8mm.** Robin Williams, Jeff Bridges, Amanda Plummer, Mercedes Ruehl, Michael Jeter, Harry Shearer, John de Lancie, Kathy Najimy, David Hyde Pierce; **D:** Terry Gilliam; **W:** Richard LaGravenese. Academy Awards '91: Best Supporting Actress (Ruehl); Chicago Film Critics Awards '91: Best Supporting Actress (Ruehl); Golden Globe Awards '92: Best Actor—Musical/Comedy (Williams), Best Supporting Actress (Ruehl); Nominations: Academy Awards '91: Best Actor (Williams), Best Art Direction/Set Decoration, Best Original Screenplay, Best Original Score. *COL, CCB*

Fisherman's Wharf ✂½ **1939** Breen stars as an orphan adopted by a San Francisco fisherman who runs away when his aunt and bratty cousin come to live with them. **72m/B VHS.** Bobby Breen, Leo

Carrillo, Henry Armetta, Lee Patrick, Rosina Galli, Leon Belasco; *D:* Bernard Vorhaus. *NOS*

F.I.S.T. ½ **1978 (R)** A young truck driver turns union organizer for idealistic reasons, but finds himself teaming with gangsters to boost his cause. His rise to the top of the union comes at the cost of his integrity, as Stallone does a character resembling Jimmy Hoffa. **145m/C VHS, Beta, LV.** Sylvester Stallone, Rod Steiger, Peter Boyle, David Huffman, Melinda Dillon, Tony LoBianco, Kevin Conway, Peter Donat, Cassie Yates, Brian Dennehy; *D:* Norman Jewison; *W:* Sylvester Stallone; *M:* Bill Conti. *MGM, FOX*

Fist **1979 (R)** Street fighter battles his way through the urban jungle seeking personal freedom and revenge. **84m/C VHS, Beta.** Richard Lawson, Annazette Chase, Dabney Coleman. *NO*

Fist Fighter ½ **1988 (R)** The ups and downs of a professional bare-knuckle fighter as he avenges a friend's murder. **99m/C VHS, Beta, LV.** George Rivero, Edward Albert, Brenda Bakke, Mike Connors, Simon Andrew, Matthias Hues; *D:* Frank Zuniga; *W:* Max Bloom. *NO*

Fist of Fear, Touch of Death **1977 (R)** Madison Square Garden is the scene for a high stakes martial arts face-off. Standard kung-fu film highlighted by short clips of the late Bruce Lee. **90m/C VHS, Beta.** Fred Williamson, Ron Van Cliff, Adolph Caesar, Aaron Banks, Bill Louie; *D:* Matthew Mallinson. *LIV*

Fist of Glory ½ **1995 (R)** In the waning days of the Vietnam War, a commando searches for the comrade who saved his life. He discovers his pal is a drug-addicted POW who's forced to fight in order to survive. **93m/C VHS.** Dale "Apollo" Cook, Maurice Smith, Robert Marius, Eric Hahn; *D:* Jose Mari Avellano. *VMK*

Fist of Honor **1992 (R)** A young boxer seeks to avenge his fiance's death, a beautiful girl squares off against a bad-cop, and two mobster leaders try to take control of the same city. When a member of one family breaks a truce and begins killing rival family members, the violence escalates and old scores will be settled. **90m/C VHS.** Sam Jones, Joey House, Harry Guardino, Nicholas Worth, Frank Sivero, Abe Vigoda, Bubba Smith; *D:* Richard Pepin; *W:* Charles Kanganis. *PMH*

Fist of Steel ½ **1993** In this futuristic martial arts film, modern day gladiators fight to the death in tournaments run by a vicious syndicate. When top gladiator Amp makes an escape bid he's hunted by henchman Mainframe, who plans to meet Amp in a fixed fight in order to become the new champion. **97m/C VHS, LV.** Dale "Apollo" Cook, Greg Douglass, Cynthia Khan, Don Nakaya Nielsen, Jim Gaines, Ned Hourani, Nick Nicholson, Kris Aguilar; *D:* Irvin Johnson; *W:* Anthony Jesu. *AIP*

The Fist, the Kicks, and the Evils **1980** A young man who's father is murdered learns kung fu and sets out for revenge. **90m/C VHS, Beta.** Kao Fei, Bruce Liang. *MGI*

Fistful of Death **1967** Kinski portrays a vengefully violent and desperate cowpoke in the days of the old West. **84m/C VHS, Beta.** Klaus Kinski. *TWE*

A Fistful of Dollars **1964 (R)** The epitome of the "spaghetti western" pits Eastwood as "the man with no name" against two families who are feuding over land. A remake of Kurosawa's "Yojimbo," and followed by Leone's "For a Few Dollars More", and "The Good, The Bad, and The Ugly." **101m/C VHS, Beta, LV.** *IT* Clint Eastwood, Gian Marie Volonte, Marianne Koch; *D:* Sergio Leone; *M:* Ennio Morricone. *MGM, FCT, TLF*

A Fistful of Dynamite *Duck, You Sucker; Giu la Testa* **1972 (PG)** A spaghetti western, with Leone's trademark humor and a striking score by Morricone. An Irish demolitions expert and a Mexican peasant team up to rob a bank during a revolution in Mexico. **138m/C VHS, Beta, LV.** *IT* James Coburn, Rod Steiger, Romolo Valli; *D:* Sergio Leone; *M:* Ennio Morricone. *MGM*

Fists of Blood ½ **1987** A martial arts expert seeks revenge on the drug baron who murdered his friend and kidnapped his girl. **90m/C VHS, Beta.** *AU* Eddie Stazak; *D:* Brian Trenchard-Smith. *CEL*

Fists of Dragons **1969** Vengeful, sacrificial bloodshed abounds in this Chinese boxing extravaganza. **92m/C VHS, Beta.** Huang I Lung, Ou Ti; *D:* Yeh Yung Chu. *TWE*

Fists of Fury *The Big Boss* **1973 (R)** Bruce Lee stars in this violent but charming Kung Fu action adventure in which he must break a solemn vow to avoid fighting in order to avenge the murder of his teacher by drug smugglers. **102m/C VHS, Beta.** Bruce Lee, Maria Yi; *D:* Lo Wei. *FOX*

Fists of Fury 2 ½ **1980 (R)** Chen Shan must survive the Organizations' onslaughts to kill him. He escapes their perilous plots only to return to battle against them after they kill his mother for her inability to disclose Chen's hiding place. Finally Chen defeats the Evil Organization himself. **90m/C VHS, Beta.** Bruce Li, Ho Chung Do, Shum Shim Po. *GEM*

Fists of Iron ½ **1994 (R)** Tough guy, skilled in martial arts, seeks revenge on the fighter and promoter who caused the death of his best friend. **94m/C VHS, LV.** Mike Worth, Matthias Hues, Sam Jones, Marshall Teague, Jenilee Harrison. *WEA*

Fit for a King **1937** A reporter becomes a princess' knight in shining armor when he foils an assassination plot in this screwball romance. **73m/B VHS, Beta.** Joe E. Brown, Leo Carrillo, Helen Mack, Paul Kelly, Harry Davenport; *D:* Edward Sedgwick; *C:* Paul Vogel. *NOS, DVT*

Fit to Kill ½ **1993 (R)** Once again special agents Donna Hamilton and Nicole Justine (former Playboy centerfolds Speir and Vasquez) reteam for an adventure that matches them with an old enemy, double agents, diamonds, and revenge. Filmed on location in Hawaii. **94m/C VHS.** Dona Speir, Roberta Vasquez, R.J. Moore, Bruce Penhall, Julie Strain, Rodrigo Obregon, Cynthia Brimhall, Tony Peck; *D:* Andy Sidaris; *W:* Andy Sidaris. *COL*

Fitzcarraldo **1982 (PG)** Although he failed to build a railroad across South America, Fitzcarraldo is determined to build an opera house in the middle of the Amazon jungles and have Enrico Caruso sing there. Based on a true story of a charismatic Irishman's impossible quest at the turn of the century. Of note: No special effects were used in this movie—everything you see actually occurred during filming, including hauling a large boat over a mountain. **157m/C VHS, Beta.** *GE* Klaus Kinski, Claudia Cardinale, Jose Lewgoy, Miguel Angel Fuentes, Paul Hittscher; *D:* Werner Herzog; *W:* Werner Herzog; *M:* Popul Vuh. Cannes Film Festival '82: Best Director (Herzog); Nominations: Cannes Film Festival '82: Best Film. *WAR, APD, INJ*

Five Came Back **1939** When a plane with twelve passengers crashes in the South American jungle, only five can ride in the patched-up wreck. Since the remainder will be left to face head hunters, intense arguments ensue. Same director remade this as "Back from Eternity" in 1956. **93m/B VHS, Beta, LV.** Lucille Ball, Chester Morris, John Carradine, Wendy Barrie, Kent Taylor, Joseph Calleia, Sir C. Aubrey Smith, Patric Knowles; *D:* John Farrow. *TTC*

Five Card Stud ½ **1968 (PG)** Five members of a lynching party are being killed one by one, and a professional gambler, who tried to prevent the lynching, attempts to ensnare the killer with the aid of a preacher with a gun. The poor script was based on a novel by Ray Gaulden. **103m/C VHS, Beta.** Robert Mitchum, Dean Martin, Inger Stevens, Roddy McDowall, Yaphet Kotto, John Anderson, Katherine Justice; *D:* Henry Hathaway; *M:* Maurice Jarre. *PAR*

Five Corners **1988 (R)** A quixotic, dramatic comedy about the inhabitants of the 5 Corners section of the Bronx in 1964, centering around a girl being wooed by a psychotic rapist, her crippled boyfriend, and the hero-turned-racial-pacifist who cannot rescue her out of principle. **92m/C VHS, Beta.** Jodie Foster, John Turturro, Todd Graff, Tim Robbins, Elizabeth Berridge, Rose Gregorio, Gregory Rozakis, Rodney Harvey, John Seitz; *D:* Tony Bill; *W:* John Patrick Shanley; *C:* Fred Murphy; *M:* James Newton Howard. Independent Spirit Awards '89: Best Actress (Foster). *MGM*

Five Days One Summer **1982 (PG)** Set in 1932, the story of a haunting and obsessive love affair between a married Scottish doctor and a young woman who happens to be his niece. While on vacation in the Swiss Alps, the doctor must vie for her love with their handsome young mountain climbing guide. Based on a story by Kay Boyle. **108m/C VHS, Beta.** Sean Connery, Betsy Brantley, Lambert Wilson; *D:* Fred Zinnemann; *W:* Michael Austin; *M:* Elmer Bernstein. *WAR*

Five Easy Pieces **1970 (R)** Nicholson's superb acting brings to life this character study of a talented musician who has given up a promising career and now works on the oil rigs. After twenty years he returns home to attempt one last communication with his dying father and perhaps, reconcile himself with his fear of failure and desire for greatness. Black, Anspach, and Bush create especially memorable characters. Nicholson ordering toast via a chicken salad sandwich is a classic. **98m/C VHS, Beta, LV, 8mm.** Jack Nicholson, Karen Black, Susan Anspach, Lois Smith, Billy Green Bush, Fannie Flagg, Ralph Waite, Sally Struthers, Helena Kallianiotes; *D:* Bob Rafelson; *W:* Adrien (Carole Eastman) Joyce, Bob Rafelson. Golden Globe Awards '71: Best Supporting Actress (Black); National Board of Review Awards '70: Best Supporting Actress (Black); New York Film Critics Awards '70: Best Director (Rafelson), Best Film, Best Supporting Actress (Black); Nominations: Academy Awards '70: Best Actor (Nicholson), Best Picture, Best Story & Screenplay, Best Supporting Actress (Black). *COL, WME*

Five Fighters from Shaolin **197?** Five high-kicking fighters endeavor to recapture their temple from an evil duke. **88m/C VHS, Beta.** Chang Shen, Lung Kwan, Dhiu Min Shien; *D:* Ko Shu-How. *MPI, MOV*

Five Fingers ½ *Operation Cicero* **1952** Under the alias "Cicero," Albanian valet Mason joins the espionage ring, selling highly confidential British war papers to the Germans during WWII. True story with odd real-life ending—unconvinced of document authenticity, the Nazis never acted on the information, even when they had the time and date of the European invasion! Fast-paced and absorbing. Adapted from the book "Operation Cicero" by L.C. Moyzisch. **108m/B VHS.** James Mason, Danielle Darrieux, Michael Rennie, Walter Hampden, Oscar Karlweis, Herbert Berghof, John Wengraf, Michael Pate, Ivan Triesault, Hanne Axman, David Wolfe, Nestor Paiva, Richard Loo, Keith McConnell; *D:* Joseph L. Mankiewicz; *W:* Michael Wilson; *M:* Bernard Herrmann. Golden Globe Awards '53: Best Screenplay. *FXV*

Five for Hell **1967** The army picks five of its meanest men for a suicide mission during WWII. They must go behind German lines and find the plans for the enemy offensive. **88m/C VHS, Beta.** *IT* Klaus Kinski, Gianni "John" Garko, Nick Jordan, Margaret Lee; *D:* Frank Kramer. *TWE*

Five Giants from Texas *I Cinque Della Vendetta* **1966** El cheapo spaghetti western features Madison, television's former Wild Bill Hickock, as a rancher fighting off displaced Mexican peasants and outlaws. **103m/C VHS, Beta.** Guy Madison, Monica Randall; *D:* Aldo Florio. *TWE*

Five Golden Dragons **1967** A typical action film about an American running afoul of ruthless gold trafficking in Hong Kong. Even this stellar cast can't help the script. **92m/C VHS, Beta.** *GB* Robert Cummings, Christopher Lee, Brian Donlevy, Klaus Kinski, George Raft, Dan Duryea, Margaret Lee; *D:* Jeremy Summers. *NO*

The Five Heartbeats **1991 (R)** Well told story of five black singers in the 1960s, their successes and failures as a group and as individuals. Although every horror story of the music business is included, the story remains fresh and the acting excellent. Music is fine, but secondary to the people. Well written characters with few cliches. Skillfully directed by Townsend (of "Hollywood Shuffle") who did research by talking to the Dells. Less than memorable showing at the box office but fun and entertaining. **122m/C VHS, Beta, LV.** Robert Townsend, Tressa Thomas, Michael Wright, Harry J. Lennix, Diahann Carroll, Leon, Hawthorne James, Chuck Patterson, Roy Fegan, Tico Wells, John Canada Terrell, Harold Nicholas, Paul Benjamin, Norma Donaldson; ***D:*** Robert Townsend; ***W:*** Robert Townsend, Keenen Ivory Wayans; ***M:*** Stanley Clarke. *FXV*

Five Miles to Midnight **1980** Brett and Danny have to depend on a photographer (Collins) for help to smuggle a gangster out of Italy. From the British "Persuaders" adventure series. Made for television. **52m/C VHS.** *GB* Roger Moore, Tony Curtis, Joan Collins. *NO*

Five Minutes to Love 🦴 *The Rotten Apple; It Only Take Five Minutes* **1963** McClanahan (one of TV's "Golden Girls") plays a young, sleazy hussy named "Poochie, the girl from the shack." This exploitation schlocker appears to be McClanahan's first film. **85m/B VHS.** Rue McClanahan, Paul Leder, King Moody; ***D:*** John Hayes. *SNC, TPV*

The Five of Me 🦴🦴½ **1981** A man with five personalities finds that livin' ain't easy and seeks professional help. Made for television, based on the autobiography of Henry Hawksworth. **100m/C VHS.** David Birney, Dee Wallace Stone, Mitchell Ryan, John McLiam, James Whitmore Jr., Ben Piazza; ***D:*** Paul Wendkos. *LIV*

The Five Pennies 🦴🦴½ **1959** Sentimental biography starring Kaye as famed jazzman Red Nichols features performances by legendary musicians Bob Crosby, Bobby Troup, Ray Anthony and Louis Armstrong. This movie marked Weld's film debut. ♫Good Night Sleep Tight; The Five Pennies; Battle Hymn of the Republic; When the Saints Go Marching In; The Music Goes 'Round and Around; Jingle Bells; Carnival of Venice; Paradise. **117m/C VHS, Beta.** Danny Kaye, Louis Armstrong, Barbara Bel Geddes, Tuesday Weld, Harry Guardino; ***D:*** Melville Shavelson; ***W:*** Melville Shavelson, Jack Rose; ***C:*** Daniel F. Fapp. Nominations: Academy Awards '59: Best Color Cinematography, Best Costume Design (Color), Best Song ("The Five Pennies"), Best Original Score. *PAR*

The 5000 Fingers of Dr. T 🦴🦴🦴 **1953 (G)** In Dr. Seuss' only non-animated movie, a boy tries to evade piano lessons and runs right into the castle of the evil Dr. Terwilliger, where hundreds of boys are held captive for piano lessons. Worse yet, they're forced to wear silly beanies with "happy fingers" waving on top. Luckily, the trusted family plumber is on hand to save the day through means of an atomic bomb. Wonderful satire, horrible music, mesmerizing Seussian sets. The skating brothers (who are joined at their beards) are a treat. **88m/C VHS, Beta, LV.** Peter Lind Hayes, Mary Healy, Tommy Rettig, Hans Conried; ***D:*** Roy Rowland; ***W:*** Theodore "Dr. Seuss" Geisel, Allan Scott. Nominations: Academy Awards '53: Best Original Score. *COL, XVC, FCT*

Five Weeks in a Balloon 🦴🦴 **1962 (PG)** This adaptation of the Jules Verne novel follows the often-comic exploits of a 19th-century British expedition that encounters many adventures on a balloon trek across Africa. Pleasant fluff with a good cast. **101m/C VHS, Beta, LV.** Fabian, Peter Lorre, Red Buttons, Cedric Hardwicke, Barbara Eden; ***D:*** Irwin Allen; ***W:*** Charles Bennett, Irwin Allen; ***C:*** Winton C. Hoch. *FXV, FCT*

The $5.20 an Hour Dream 🦴🦴 **1980** Lavin is a divorced mother and factory worker burdened with debt and determined to get and keep a job on the higher-paying, traditionally all-male assembly line. Lesser feminist drama on the heels of "Norma Rae." Made for television. **96m/C VHS, Beta.** Linda Lavin, Richard Jaeckel, Nicholas Pryor, Pamela McMyler, Mayf Nutter, Taurean Blacque, Robert Davi, Dennis Fimple, Dana Hill, Ernie Hudson; ***D:*** Russ Mayberry. *TLF*

The Fix 🦴 *The Agitators* **1984** A group of cocaine smugglers get their just desserts as the federal government catches them in a sting operation. **95m/C VHS, Beta.** Vince Edwards, Richard Jaeckel, Julie Hill, Charles Dierkop, Byron Cherry, Robert Tessier; ***D:*** Will Zens. *NO*

The Fixer 🦴🦴🦴 **1968 (PG-13)** Based on the true story of a Jewish handyman (Bates) in 1911 Tsarist Russia who's accused of murdering a gentile boy. Wrongly imprisoned he's tortured to confess to the crime, which he refuses to do. Bogarde is the lawyer who tries to help him. Strong direction and acting in an unrelenting drama. Adapted from Bernard Malamud's Pulitzer Prize-winning novel. **132m/C VHS.** Alan Bates, Dirk Bogarde, Georgia Brown, Hugh Griffith, Elizabeth Hartman, Ian Holm, David Opatoshu, David Warner, Carol White, Murray Melvin, Peter Jeffrey, William Hutt; ***D:*** John Frankenheimer; ***W:*** Dalton Trumbo; ***M:*** Maurice Jarre. Nominations: Academy Awards '68: Best Actor (Bates). *MGM*

Flambards 🦴🦴½ **19??** In the early 1900's teenaged orphan Christine is sent to live with her tyrannical Uncle Russell and his two sons on their crumbling English estate, Flambards. Bitter rivalries and jealousies abound between arrogant, tradition bound Mark and younger brother William, who's obsessed with the new-fangled airplane. Quarrels intensify as both young men fall in love with Christine and WWI begins, leading to sacrifice and tragedy. Based on the trilogy by K.M. Peyton. Made for British television; 12 episodes on 6 cassettes. **676m/C VHS.** *GB* Christine McKenna, Stephen Grives, Alan Parnaby, Edward Judd, Sebastian Abineri, Peter Settelen, Carol Leader, Frank Mills. *TVC, VCO*

The Flame & the Arrow 🦴🦴🦴 **1950** Dardo the Arrow, a Robin Hood-like outlaw in medieval Italy, leads his band of mountain fighters against a mercenary warlord who has seduced his wife and kidnapped his son. Spectacular acrobatics, with Lancaster performing his own stunts, add interest to the usual swashbuckling. **88m/C VHS, Beta, LV.** Burt Lancaster, Virginia Mayo, Aline MacMahon, Nick Cravat, Robert Douglas, Frank Allenby; ***D:*** Jacques Tourneur; ***M:*** Max Steiner. Nominations: Academy Awards '50: Best Color Cinematography, Best Original Score. *WAR*

The Flame Is Love 🦴½ **1979** A made-for-television adaptation of one of Barbara Cartland's romantic novels. An American heiress falls tragically in love with a Parisian journalist despite her engagement to an Englishman. Takes place at the turn of the century. **98m/C VHS, Beta.** Linda Purl, Timothy Dalton, Shane Briant; ***D:*** Michael O'Herlihy. *LIV*

Flame of the Barbary Coast 🦴🦴½ **1945** A rancher from Montana vies with a gambling czar for a beautiful dance hall queen and control of the Barbary Coast district of San Francisco. The great earthquake of 1906 provides the plot with a climax. Also available colorized. **91m/B VHS.** John Wayne, Ann Dvorak, Joseph Schildkraut, William Frawley; ***D:*** Joseph Kane. Nominations: Academy Awards '45: Best Sound, Best Original Score. *MED, REP*

Flame of the Islands 🦴🦴 **1955** De Carlo plays a smoldering, passionate chanteuse who struggles with love and gangsters for possession of a Bahamian casino in this tropical heat wave. **92m/C VHS, Beta.** Yvonne De Carlo, Howard Duff, Zachary Scott, James Arness, Kurt Kasznar, Barbara O'Neil; ***D:*** Edward Ludwig. *NO*

Flame Over India 🦴🦴🦴 *Northwest Frontier* **1960** When Moslems lay siege to a British fortress in India, Governess Wyatt (Bacall) and Captain Scott (More) save the Maharaja's son and escape by commandeering a train. Along the way they find treason, adventure and love. **130m/C VHS.** *GB* Kenneth More, Lauren Bacall, Herbert Lom, Wilfrid Hyde-White, I.S. Johar, Ursula Jeans, Ian Hunter, Eugene Deckers, Jack Gwillim, Govind Raja Ross, Frank Olegario; ***D:*** J. Lee Thompson; ***C:*** Geoffrey Unsworth. *HEG, SUE, DVT*

Flame to the Phoenix 🦴½ **1985** A WWII drama about the Polish cavalry forces' decimation to German Panzer tanks. **80m/C VHS, Beta.** *GB* Paul Geoffrey, Ann Firbank, Frederick Treves; ***D:*** William Brayne. *NO*

The Flame Trees of Thika 🦴🦴🦴 **1981** In 1913, a British family travels to East Africa to start a coffee plantation. Seen through the eyes of the young daughter, her childhood consists of the local Masai and Kikuyu tribes, the eccentric and sometimes unhappy English neighbors, and the wild animals that roam the plains. Based on the memoirs of writer Elspeth Huxley. 4 cassettes; shown on PBS "Masterpiece Theatre." **366m/C VHS.** *GB* Hayley Mills, Holly Aird, David Robb, Ben Cross. *SIG, TVC*

Flaming Bullets 🦴🦴 **1945** Last of the Texas Rangers series has solid action scenes, but little else. Ritter leads the Texas Rangers in breaking up a gang with a devious scheme: breaking men out of jail, then killing them for the cash reward. **55m/B VHS.** *MOV*

Flaming Frontiers **1938** A frontier scout matches wits against gold mine thieves. In fifteen episodes. **300m/B VHS, Beta.** Johnny Mack Brown, Eleanor Hanson, Ralph Bowman; ***D:*** Ray Taylor. *VYY, VCN, NOS*

Flaming Lead 🦴½ **1939** A hard-drinkin' ranch owner hires a nightclub cowboy to help him get an Army horse contract. **57m/B VHS.** Ken Maynard, Eleanor Stewart, Walter Long, Tom London; ***D:*** Sam Newfield. *NOS, DVT, HEG*

Flaming Signal 🦴½ **1933** Featuring Flash the Wonder Labrador, this action-packed film deals with a pilot who crash-lands near a Pacific island, just as the natives, provoked by an exploitative German trader, are rising up against the whites. Both Flash and his master manage to rescue the missionary's pretty daughter. **64m/B VHS, Beta, LV.** Noah Beery Sr., Marceline Day, Carmelita Geraghty, Mischa Auer, Henry B. Walthall. *SNC, LSV, RXM*

Flaming Star 🦴🦴🦴 **1960** In 1870s Texas, a family with a white father and an Indian mother is caught in the midst of an Indian uprising. The mixed-blood youth, excellently played by Presley, must choose a side with tragic results for all. A stirring, well-written drama of frontier prejudice and one of Presley's best films. **101m/C VHS, Beta.** Elvis Presley, Dolores Del Rio, Barbara Eden, Steve Forrest, John McIntire, Richard Jaeckel, L.Q. Jones; ***D:*** Donald Siegel. *FOX, MVD*

The Flaming Teen-Age 🦴 **1956** Schlocky pseudo-documentary demonstrating the evils of drugs and alcohol. Exploitative, and the teenagers look really old. Cheaply made, and it shows. **67m/B VHS.** Noel Reyburn, Ethel Barrett, Jerry Frank, Shirley Holmes; ***D:*** Irvin S. Yeaworth Jr., Charles Edwards. *SNC*

The Flaming Urge **1953** A small town is plagued by mysterious fires. Could a pyromaniac be on the loose? **67m/B VHS, Beta.** Harold Lloyd Jr., Cathy Downs. *SNC*

The Flamingo Kid 🦴🦴🦴 **1984 (PG-13)** Brooklyn teen Dillon gets a summer job at a fancy beach club on Long Island. His father, a plumber, remembers how to dream but is also aware of how rough the world is on dreamers. Suddenly making lots of money at a mostly easy job, the kid's attracted to the high style of the local sports car dealer, and finds his father's solid life a bore. By the end of the summer, he's learned the true value of both men, and the kind of man he wants to be. Excellent performances all around, nice ensemble acting among the young men who play Dillon's buddies. Great sound track. Film debut of Jones, who seems a little old for her part as a California college sophomore. **100m/C VHS, Beta, LV.** Matt Dillon, Hector Elizondo, Molly McCarthy, Martha Gehman, Richard Crenna, Jessica Walter, Carole Davis, Janet Jones, Fisher Stevens, Bronson Pinchot; ***D:*** Garry Marshall. *PAR, VES, LIV*

Flamingo Road 🦴🦴🦴 **1949** A scandalously entertaining melodrama in which Crawford portrays a carnival dancer who intrigues Scott and Brian in a small Southern town where the carnival stops. Crawford shines in a role that demands her to be both tough and sensitive in a corrupt world full of political backstabbing and sleazy characters. Remade as a TV movie and television soap-opera series in 1980. **94m/B VHS, LV.** Joan Crawford, Zachary Scott, David Brian, Sydney Greenstreet, Gertrude Michael, Gladys George, Virginia Huston, Fred Clark, Alice White; ***D:*** Michael Curtiz; ***W:*** Edmund H. North, Robert Wilder; ***M:*** Max Steiner. *MGM*

The Flash **1990** When police scientist Barry Allen is accidentally doused by chemicals and then struck by lightening the combination makes him into a new superhero. His super quickness help his quest in fighting crime in Central City where he's aided by fellow scientist Tina McGee (the only other person to know his secret). In this adventure, the Flash seeks out the violent and mesmerizing leader of a biker gang who caused the death of Barry's brother. Based on the DC comic book character, this is the pilot episode for the short-lived television series. The look is dark and stylized and not played for camp. **94m/C VHS, Beta, LV.** John Wesley Shipp, Amanda Pays, Michael Nader; ***M:*** Danny Elfman. *WAR*

The Flash 2: Revenge of the Trickster ½ **1991** Every good superhero needs his nemesis—and this time around the Flash (Shipp) has that murderous mischiefmaker the Trickster (Hamill) who, along with his femme fatale sidekick Prank, is determined to outwit our hero. Can super speed and strength be enough to keep Central City safe? Based on the DC comic book character and taken from two episodes of the television series. **92m/C VHS, Beta.** John Wesley Shipp, Amanda Pays, Mark Hamill, Richard Belzer. *WAR*

Flash & Firecat **1975 (PG)** A beautiful blonde and a crazy thief steal and race their way across the country in a dune buggy with the police hot on their trail. **90m/C VHS, Beta.** Roger Davis, Tricia Sembera, Dub Taylor, Richard Kiel; ***D:*** Ferd Sebastian. *NO*

Flash Gordon **1980 (PG)** Camp version of the adventures of Flash Gordon in outer space. This time, Flash and Dale Arden are forced by Dr. Zarkov to accompany him on a mission to far-off Mongo, where Ming the Merciless is threatening the destruction of Earth. Music by Queen. **111m/C VHS, Beta, LV.** Sam Jones, Melody Anderson, Chaim Topol, Max von Sydow, Ornella Muti, Timothy Dalton, Brian Blessed; ***D:*** Mike Hodges; ***M:*** Howard Blake. *MCA*

Flash Gordon Conquers the Universe *Purple Death from Outer Space* **1940** Ravaging plague strikes the earth and Flash Gordon undertakes to stop it. A serial in twelve chapters. **240m/B VHS, Beta.** Buster Crabbe, Carol Hughes, Charles Middleton, Frank Shannon. *VYY, MRV, SNC*

Flash Gordon: Mars Attacks the World *The Deadly Rays From Mars; Flash Gordon's Trip to Mars* **1938** The earth is plagued by the evil Ming, but Flash Gordon steps in. From the serial. **87m/B VHS, Beta.** Buster Crabbe, Jean Rogers, Charles Middleton; ***D:*** Robert F. "Bob" Hill, Ford Beebe. *CAB*

Flash Gordon: Rocketship ½ *Spaceship to the Unknown; Perils from Planet Mongo; Space Soldiers; Atomic Rocketship* **1936** Re-edited from the original Flash Gordon serial in which Flash and company must prevent the planet Mongo from colliding with Earth. Good character acting and good clean fun. **97m/B VHS, Beta.** Buster Crabbe, Jean Rogers, Frank Shannon, Charles Middleton, Priscilla Lawson, Jack Lipson; ***D:*** Frederick Stephani. *VYY, PSM, CAB*

Flash Gordon: Vol. 1 **1953** Join Flash Gordon and Dale Arden as they struggle to maintain peace in the galaxy in this pair of episodes from the series. **60m/B VHS, Beta.** Steve Holland, Irene Champlin. *DVT*

Flash Gordon: Vol. 2 **1953** Flash and Dale continue their quest for intergalactic tranquility in this pair of episodes from the series. **60m/B VHS, Beta.** Steve Holland, Irene Champlin. *DVT*

Flash Gordon: Vol. 3 **1953** The struggle for intergalactic peace continues as Flash Gordon battles Ming the Merciless in this pair of episodes from the series. **60m/B VHS, Beta.** *DVT*

A Flash of Green **1985** A crooked politician is helping a construction firm exploit valuable waterfront property. He enlists the influence of a hesitant local journalist, who then falls for the woman leading the homeowner's conservation drive against the development plan. Made for American Playhouse and produced by costar Jordon. Based on the work of John D. MacDonald. **122m/C VHS, Beta.** Ed Harris, Blair Brown, Richard Jordan, George Coe; ***D:*** Victor Nunez; ***W:*** Victor Nunez; ***M:*** Charles Engstrom. *MED*

Flashback **1989 (R)** FBI agent Sutherland's assignment sounds easy: escort aging 1960s radical Hopper to prison. But Hopper is cunning and decides not to go without a fight. He uses his brain to outwit the young Sutherland and to turn him against himself. Good moments between the two leads and with Kane, as a woman who never left the sixties behind. **108m/C VHS, Beta, LV.** Dennis Hopper, Kiefer Sutherland, Carol Kane, Cliff DeYoung, Paul Dooley, Michael McKean, Richard Masur; ***D:*** Franco Amurri; ***M:*** Barry Goldberg. *PAR*

Flashdance **1983 (R)** 18-year-old Alex wants to dance. She works all day as a welder (and has a hot affair going with her boss), dances at a local bar at night, and hopes someday to get enough courage to audition for a spot at the School of Ballet. Glossy music video redeemed somewhat by exciting choreography with Marine Jahan doing the dancing for Beals. Oscar-winning title song sung by Irene Cara. Inspired the torn-sweatshirt trend in fashion of the period. ♫Flashdance...What a Feeling; I Love Rock 'n Roll; Manhunt; Gloria; Lady, Lady, Lady; Seduce Me Tonight. **95m/C VHS, Beta, LV, 8mm.** Jennifer Beals, Michael Nouri, Belinda Bauer, Lilia Skala, Cynthia Rhodes, Sunny Johnson, Lee Ving, Kyle T. Heffner, Ron Karabatsos, Robert Wuhl, Elizabeth Sagal; ***D:*** Franca Pasut. Academy Awards '83: Best Song ("Flashdance...What a Feeling"); Golden Globe Awards '84: Best Song ("Flashdance...What a Feeling"), Best Score; Nominations: Academy Awards '83: Best Cinematography, Best Film Editing, Best Song ("Maniac"). *PAR*

Flashfire ½ **1994 (R)** The torching of an apartment building and the murder of a cop seem unrelated until troubled detective Jack Flinder (Zane) becomes involved. Soon, he and murder witness Lisa (Minter) are on the run from the arsonists and crooked police. **88m/C VHS.** Billy Zane, Kristin Minter, Louis Gossett Jr.; ***D:*** Elliot Silverstein; ***W:*** John Warren, Dan York; ***M:*** Sylvester Levay. *VMK*

Flashpoint **1984 (R)** A pair of Texas border patrolmen discover an abandoned jeep that contains a fortune in cash, apparently from the 1960s. As they try to figure out how it got there, they become prey to those who want to keep the secret. With this cast, flick ought to be better. **95m/C VHS, Beta, LV.** Treat Williams, Kris Kristofferson, Tess Harper, Rip Torn, Miguel Ferrer, Roberts Blossom; ***D:*** William Tannen; ***W:*** Michael Butler. *NO*

Flashpoint Africa ½ **1984** When a news team follows a terrorist group's activities it winds up in a power struggle with terrifying consequences. **99m/C VHS, Beta.** Trevor Howard, Gayle Hunnicutt, James Faulkner. *NO*

Flat Top ½ **1952** The training of Navy fighter pilots aboard "flat top" aircraft carriers during WWII provides the drama here. A strict commander is appreciated only after the war when the pilots realize his role in their survival. The film makes good use of actual combat footage; fast-paced and effective. **85m/C VHS, Beta, LV.** Sterling Hayden, Richard Carlson, Keith Larsen, John Bromfield; ***D:*** Lesley Selander. Nominations: Academy Awards '52: Best Film Editing. *REP, FCT*

Flatbed Annie and Sweetiepie: Lady Truckers ½ *Flatbed Annie* **1979** A couple of good ol' gals hit the road and encounter a variety of bad guys out to steal their truck. Made for television. **100m/C VHS, Beta.** Annie Potts, Kim Darby, Harry Dean Stanton, Arthur Godfrey, Rory Calhoun, Bill Carter; ***D:*** Robert Greenwald. *HBO, CNG*

Flatfoot *The Knock-Out Cop* **1978 (PG)** Tough police officer will let nothing stop him from finding and arresting drug smugglers. Good for laughs as well as lots of action. **113m/C VHS, Beta.** *IT GE* Bodo, Werner Pochat, Bud Spencer, Enzo Cannavale, Dagmar Lassander, Joe Stewardson; ***D:*** Steno. *NO*

Flatliners **1990 (R)** A group of medical students begin after-hours experimentation with death and out-of-body experiences. Some standard horror film images but Roberts and Sutherland create an energy that makes it worth watching. **111m/C VHS, Beta, LV, 8mm.** Kiefer Sutherland, Julia Roberts, William Baldwin, Oliver Platt, Kevin Bacon, Kimberly Scott, Joshua Rudoy; ***D:*** Joel Schumacher; ***M:*** James Newton Howard. *COL*

Fled **1996 (R)** Charles Piper (Fishburne) and Luke Dodge (Baldwin) are two combative prison escapees who need to find a stash of cash and a computer disk that could save them from both the Cuban mob and the cops. Hayek is the bombshell who helps the pair and tries to get steamy with Piper. The climatic battle (the film was shot around Atlanta) takes place in a sightseeing gondola at Georgia's Stone Mountain. **?m/C VHS.** Laurence "Larry" Fishburne, Stephen Baldwin, Salma Hayek, Will Patton, Robert John Burke; ***D:*** Kevin Hooks; ***W:*** Preston A. Whitmore II; ***C:*** Matthew F. Leonetti; ***M:*** Graeme Revell. *NYR*

Flesh **1968** An Andy Warhol-produced seedy urban farce about a bisexual street hustler who meets a variety of drug-addicted, deformed, and sexually deviant people. Dallesandro fans will enjoy his extensive exposure (literally). **90m/C VHS, Beta.** Joe Dallesandro, Geraldine Smith, Patti D'Arbanville; ***D:*** Paul Morrissey. *TPV, PAR, FCT*

Flesh and Blood **1922** An unjustly convicted lawyer is released from prison to find out his wife has died. He vows revenge on those who falsely imprisoned him and assumes the disguise of a crippled beggar to begin his plot. Silent with musical score. **75m/B VHS, Beta, 8mm.** Lon Chaney Sr.; ***D:*** Irving Cummings. *SNC, VYY, GVV*

Flesh and Blood ½ *The Rose and the Sword* **1985 (R)** A rowdy group of 16th Century hellions makes off with a princess who is already spoken for and pillage and plunder their way to revenge. Hauer leads the motley group through sword fights, raids, and the like. Dutch director Verhoeven's first English language film. Not for children; with rape scenes, nudity, and graphic sex. **126m/C VHS, Beta, LV.** Rutger Hauer, Jennifer Jason Leigh, Tom Burlinson, Susan Tyrrell, Jack Thompson, Ronald Lacey, Brion James, Bruno Kirby; ***D:*** Paul Verhoeven; ***W:*** Paul Verhoeven, Gerard Soeteman; ***C:*** Jan De Bont; ***M:*** Basil Poledouris. *LIV, VES*

Flesh and Blood Show *Asylum of the Insane* **1973 (R)** Rehearsal turns into an execution ritual for a group of actors at a mysterious seaside theatre. Truth in titling: features blood, gore, and some sex. Shot in part in 3-D. **93m/C VHS, Beta.** *GB* Robin Askwith, Candace Glendenning, Tristan Rogers, Ray Brooks, Jenny Hanley, Luan Peters, Patrick Barr; ***D:*** Pete Walker. *NO*

Flesh and Bone **1993 (R)** Quaid is exact as a vending machine distributor with a desolate rural Texas circuit, haunted by the memory of a decades-old murder committed by his father (Caan) during a botched farm-house robbery. Alcoholic Ryan (Quaid's real-life wife) emerges from a bad marriage and helps Quaid rebuild his life, never suspecting that they may have met before. Challenging but successful role for Ryan, better known for her girlish, romantic-comedy appeal. Paltrow's unforgettable as a heartless casket robber and Caan's partner/girlfriend. Director Kloves extracts moments of earthy beauty from the bleak, humble West Texas setting. **127m/C VHS, Beta, LV.** Dennis Quaid, Meg Ryan, James Caan, Gwyneth Paltrow, Scott Wilson, Christopher Rydell; ***D:*** Steven Kloves; ***W:*** Steven Kloves; ***M:*** Thomas Newman. *PAR*

The Flesh and the Devil ½ **1927** Classic Garbo at her seductive best as a woman who causes a feud between two friends. Gilbert is an Austrian officer, falls for the married Garbo and winds up killing her husband in a duel. Banished to the African Corps he asks his best friend (Hanson) to look after his lady love. But Hanson takes his job too seriously, falling for the lady himself. Great silent movie with surprise ending to match. The first Gilbert and Garbo pairing. **112m/B VHS.** John Gilbert, Greta Garbo, Lars Hanson, Barbara Kent, George Fawcett, Eugenie Besserer; ***D:*** Clarence Brown; ***C:*** William H. Daniels. *MGM*

Flesh and the Spur 🦴½ **1957** A cowboy tracks the killer of his brother. Future Mannix Mike Connors (nicknamed 'Touch' at the time) joins the search. Unedifying western with oddball touches, notably a theme song by Chipmunks creator Ross Bagdasarian. **78m/C VHS.** John Agar, Marla English, Mike Connors, Raymond Hatton, Maria Monay, Joyce Meadows, Kenne Duncan; ***D:*** Edward L. Cahn. *NOS, LOO*

The Flesh Eaters 🦴½ **1964** A claustrophobic low-budget thriller about a film queen and her secretary who crash-land on an island inhabited by your basic mad scientist. His latest experiment is with tiny flesh-eating sea creatures. Shock ending. **87m/C VHS, Beta.** Martin Kosleck, Rita Morley, Byron Sanders, Barbara Wilkin, Ray Tudor; ***D:*** Jack Curtis. *SNC*

Flesh Eating Mothers 🦴 **1989** Housewives are transformed into cannibals after a mystery virus hits their town. Their kids must stop the moms from eating any more people. **90m/C VHS, Beta.** Robert Lee Oliver, Donatella Hecht, Valorie Hubbard, Neal Rosen, Terry Hayes; ***D:*** James Aviles Martin. *ACA*

Flesh Feast *Woof!* **1969 (R)** Classically horrendous anti-Nazi bosh, in which a mad female plastic surgeon (Lake) rejuvenates Hitler and then tortures him to death with maggots to avenge her mother's suffering. Lake's last film, and the sorriest sign-off any actress ever had. **72m/C VHS, Beta.** Veronica Lake, Phil Philbin, Heather Hughes, Martha Mischon, Yanka Mann, Dian Wilhite, Chris Martell; ***D:*** Brad F. Ginter. *NO*

Flesh Gordon 🦴 **1972** Soft-core spoof of the "Flash Gordon" series. Flesh takes it upon himself to save Earth from the evil Wang's sex ray; Wang, of course, being the leader of the planet Porno. Lackluster special effects and below par story dull an already ridiculous movie. Look for cameo by real-life porn starlet Candy Samples. The restored (90-minute) version also includes the theatrical trailer; a 72-minute R-rated version is also available. **90m/C VHS, LV.** Jason Williams, Suzanne Fields, Joseph Hudgins, John Hoyt, Howard Zieff, Michael Benveniste; ***Cameos:*** Candy Samples; ***D:*** Mike Light; ***V:*** Craig T. Nelson. *HTV, IME, MED*

Flesh Gordon 2: Flesh Gordon Meets the Cosmic Cheerleaders 🦴 **1990** Emperor Wang (Hunt) threatens the Universe with his powerful Impotence ray. Flesh (Murdocco), along with Dale (Kelly) and Dr. Flexi Jerkoff (Travis), do battle with a belt of farting asteroids and other weirdos. Director Ziehm delivers this one on a shoestring of under $1 million, even improving technically on the original. The sex scenes are, however, more watered down in an apparent attempt to gain a wider audience. Scatological jokes are the basis for much of the humor. **98m/C VHS.** *CA* Vince Murdocco, Tony Travis, William Dennis Hunt, Robyn Kelly; ***D:*** Howard Ziehm. *NHO*

Fleshburn 🦴🦴 **1984 (R)** An Indian Vietnam War veteran escapes from a mental institution to get revenge on the four psychiatrists who committed him. **91m/C VHS, Beta.** Steve Kanaly, Karen Carlson, Sonny Landham, Macon McCalman; ***D:*** George Gage. *MED*

Fleshpot on 42nd Street 🦴 **1971** Stark, realistic look at the streetwalking profession. Dusty leaves her blue collar boyfriend to move in with a transvestite and then she meets a dashing young Staten Island native (like the director). Their romance blooms until he is run over by a car, sending Dusty into a tailspin which lands her back on 42nd Street. Along the way, various rustic hookers and venerable old floozies liven up director Mulligan's version of New York. Less emphasis on the sleaze than the grittiness. **78m/C VHS.** Diana Lewis, Lynn Flanagan, Bob Walters; ***D:*** Andy Milligan. *SMW, TPV*

Fleshtone 🦴🦴 **1994 (R)** Artist Matthew Greco's (Kemp) work is not for the faint-hearted since he paints grisly suicides and murders. No wonder he's lonely—so lonely that he answers a phone-sex ad and is hooked up with Edna (Cutter), who becomes an obsession. Matthew even depicts her murder in one of his paintings and then she's found dead—only it turns out not to be Edna, who doesn't exist. Just what has Matthew gotten himself into? Provocative but ending is a letdown. An unrated version is also available. **89m/C VHS, LV.** Martin Kemp, Lise Cutter, Tim Thomerson; ***D:*** Harry Hurwitz; ***W:*** Harry Hurwitz. *PSM*

Fletch 🦴🦴 **1985 (PG)** Somewhat charming comedy. When newspaper journalist Fletch goes undercover to get the scoop on the local drug scene, a wealthy young businessman enlists his help in dying. Something's rotten in Denmark when the man's doctor knows nothing of the illness and Fletch comes closer to the drug scene than he realizes. Throughout the entire film, Chevy Chase assumes a multitude of flippant comic characters to discover the truth. Based on Gregory McDonald's novel. **98m/C VHS, Beta, LV.** Chevy Chase, Tim Matheson, Joe Don Baker, Dana Wheeler-Nicholson, M. Emmet Walsh, Kenneth Mars, Geena Davis, Richard Libertini, George Wendt, Kareem Abdul-Jabbar, Alison La Placa; ***D:*** Michael Ritchie; ***W:*** Andrew Bergman; ***M:*** Harold Faltermeyer. *MCA*

Fletch Lives 🦴🦴 **1989 (PG)** In this sequel to "Fletch," Chase is back again as the super-reporter. When Fletch learns of his inheritance of a Southern estate he is eager to claim it. During his down-home trip he becomes involved in a murder and must use his disguise skills to solve it before he becomes the next victim. Based on the novels of Gregory MacDonald. **95m/C VHS, Beta, LV.** Chevy Chase, Hal Holbrook, Julianne Phillips, Richard Libertini, R. Lee Ermey, Cleavon Little; ***D:*** Michael Ritchie; ***W:*** Leon Capetanos; ***M:*** Harold Faltermeyer. *MCA*

Flicks *Hollyweird; Loose Joints* **1985 (R)** A compilation of skits parodying the tradition of Saturday afternoon matinees, including coming attractions and a cartoon. Never released theatrically. **79m/C VHS, Beta.** Martin Mull, Joan Hackett, Pamela Sue Martin, Betty Kennedy, Richard Belzer; ***D:*** Peter Winograd. *MED*

The Flight 🦴🦴 **1989** A non-narrative view of glider planes as they soar over the countryside and rivers of the Laurentians and Canadian Rockies. Useful in language arts classes. **96m/C VHS, Beta, LV.** Eli Danker, Sandy McPeak, Lindsay Wagner; ***D:*** Paul Wendkos. *VES, IME*

Flight from Glory 🦴🦴½ **1937** A group of pilots fly supplies over the Andes from their isolated base camp to even more isolated mines. Morris is their leader who watches as, one by one, the men are killed on their dangerous flights. To make a bad situtation worse, Heflin arrives as a new recruit—along with his pretty wife. **66m/B VHS, Beta.** Chester Morris, Onslow Stevens, Whitney Bourne, Van Heflin; ***D:*** Lew (Louis Friedlander) Landers. *NO*

Flight from Singapore 🦴½ **1962** Transporting desperately needed blood to Malaysia, a flight crew is forced to crash land in the jungle. Nicely done if trite. **74m/B VHS, Beta.** *GB* Patrick Allen, Patrick Holt, William Abney, Harry Fowler; ***D:*** Dudley Birch; ***W:*** Dudley Birch. *SNC*

Flight from Vienna 🦴🦴 **1958** A high-ranking Hungarian security officer, disenchanted with communism, stages a daring escape from his country. In Vienna, he asks the British for political asylum, but is sent back to Hungary to help a scientist escape in order to prove his loyalty. Cold war drama hangs together on strength of Bikel's performance. **54m/B VHS, Beta.** Theodore Bikel, John Bentley, Donald Gray. *VYY*

Flight of Black Angel 🦴🦴½ **1991 (R)** Wacked-out F-16 pilot fancies himself an angel of death, and, after annihilating a number of trainees, sets out to make Las Vegas a nuked-out ghost town. Squadron commander Strauss, however, is not pleased with his pilot's initiative. Made for cable TV script runs out of gas and heads into a nosedive. **102m/C VHS.** Peter Strauss, William O'Leary, James O'Sullivan, Michael Keys Hall; ***D:*** Jon Mostow; ***W:*** Henry Dominick. *VMK*

Flight of Dragons 🦴🦴½ **1982** Animated tale takes place between the Age of Magic and the Age of Science, in a century when dragons ruled the skies. **98m/C VHS, Beta.** ***D:*** Arthur Rankin Jr., Jules Bass; ***V:*** John Ritter, Victor Buono, James Earl Jones, Don Messick, Larry Storch. *WAR, WTA*

A Flight of Rainbirds 🦴🦴 **1981** In a dual role, Krabbe plays a biologist who dreams he must lose his virginity within a week or die and his alter ego who joins him in the search for the perfect woman. In Dutch with English subtitles. **94m/C VHS, LV.** *NL* Jeroen Krabbe; ***D:*** Ate De Jong. *INJ*

Flight of the Eagle 🦴🦴½ **1982** Based on the actual ill-fated expedition of Salomon Andree who, with two friends, attempted to fly from Sweden to the North Pole in a hydrogen balloon in 1897. The last half of the film drags somewhat as the three struggle to survive in the frozen north after their balloon crashes. Beautifully photographed adventure. In Swedish with English subtitles. **115m/C VHS, Beta, LV.** *SW* Max von Sydow, Goran Stangertz, Clement Harari, Sverre Anker; ***D:*** Jan Troell. Nominations: Academy Awards '82: Best Foreign Language Film. *AHV*

Flight of the Grey Wolf 🦴½ **1976** A tame, innocent wolf is mistaken for a killer and must run for his life with the help of his boy-owner. **82m/C VHS, Beta.** Bill Williams, Barbara Hale, Jeff East. *DIS*

Flight of the Innocent 🦴🦴½ **1993 (R)** The innocent 10-year-old Vito comes from a family who make their living as kidnappers. He is the only witness (and the only survivor) when his family is massacred by a rival gang. Vito flees the carnage and sets off to find his cousin who lives in Rome. But his journey truly ends when he is taken in by a wealthy industrialist family whose own son has been kidnapped. Directorial debut of Carlei who tends to rely on striking visuals rather than his characters. In Italian with English subtitles. **105m/C VHS, LV.** *IT* Manuel Colao, Francesca Neri, Jacques Perrin, Frederico Pacifici, Sal Borgese; ***D:*** Carlo Carlei; ***W:*** Carlo Carlei, Gualtiero Rosella. Nominations: Golden Globe Awards '94: Best Foreign Language Film. *MGM*

Flight of the Intruder 🦴½ **1990 (PG-13)** Vietnam naval pilots aboard an aircraft carrier don't like the way the war is being handled, so they go rogue and decide to go on a mission to bomb an enemy air base in Hanoi. Loads of male bonding. **115m/C VHS, Beta, LV.** Danny Glover, Willem Dafoe, Brad Johnson, Rosanna Arquette, Tom Sizemore; ***D:*** John Milius; ***W:*** Robert Dillon; ***C:*** Fred W. Koenekamp; ***M:*** Basil Poledouris. *PAR*

Flight of the Navigator 🦴🦴½ **1986 (PG)** A boy boards an alien spacecraft and embarks on a series of time-travel adventures with a crew of wise-cracking extraterrestrial creatures. When he returns home eight years later, a NASA investigation ensues. Paul Reubens, better known as Pee Wee Herman, provides the voice of the robot. **90m/C VHS, Beta, LV.** Joey Cramer, Veronica Cartwright, Cliff DeYoung, Sarah Jessica Parker, Matt Adler, Howard Hesseman; ***D:*** Randal Kleiser; ***W:*** Michael Burton, Matt MacManus; ***M:*** Alan Silvestri; ***V:*** Paul (Pee Wee Herman) Reubens. *DIS*

The Flight of the Phoenix 🦴🦴🦴 **1965** A group of men stranded in the Arabian desert after a plane crash attempt to rebuild their plane in order to escape before succumbing to the elements. Big budget, all-star survival drama based on the novel by Elleston Trevor. **147m/C VHS, Beta, LV.** James Stewart, Richard Attenborough, Peter Finch, Hardy Kruger, Dan Duryea, George Kennedy, Ernest Borgnine, Ian Bannen; ***D:*** Robert Aldrich; ***C:*** Joseph Biroc. Nominations: Academy Awards '65: Best Film Editing, Best Supporting Actor (Bannen). *FOX*

Flight to Fury 🦴½ **1966** A cheap independent adventure film, featuring the novice Hellman-Nicholson team, about a few assorted mercenaries searching for a horde of diamonds when their plane crashes in the wilderness of the Philippines. Based on a story by director/producer Hellman. **73m/B VHS, Beta.** Jack Nicholson, Dewey Martin, Fay Spain, Vic Diaz, Jacqueline Hellman; ***D:*** Monte Hellman; ***W:*** Jack Nicholson. *WAR*

Flight to Mars 🦴🦴 **1952** An expedition crash lands on the red planet and discovers an advanced underground society that wants to invade earth using the U.S. spacecraft. Includes previews of coming attractions from classic science fiction films. First movie of this genre to be shot in color. **72m/C**

VHS, Beta, LV. Cameron Mitchell, Marguerite Chapman, Arthur Franz; ***D:*** Lesley Selander. *MED, IME*

Flight to Nowhere *Woof!* **1946** An FBI agent tracks down a stolen map of atomic bomb source material with the help of a charter pilot and a dizzy blonde. Muddled plot and no discernable acting. **74m/B VHS, Beta, LV.** Alan Curtis, Evelyn Ankers, Jack Holt; ***D:*** William Rowland. *SNC, VYY*

Flim-Flam Man *One Born Every Minute* **1967** A con man teams up with an army deserter to teach him the fine art of flim-flamming as they travel through small southern towns. Love may lead the young man back to the straight and narrow, but not his reprobate mentor. Scott is wonderful; and the slapstick episodes move at a good pace. **104m/C VHS, Beta.** George C. Scott, Michael Sarrazin, Slim Pickens, Sue Lyon, Jack Albertson, Harry (Henry) Morgan; ***D:*** Irvin Kershner; ***C:*** Charles B(ryant) Lang; ***M:*** Jerry Goldsmith. *FOX*

Flinch **1994 (R)** Two models, who work as live mannequins, witness a murder and wonder if they'll be the next victims. **90m/C VHS.** Judd Nelson, Nick Mancuso, Gina Gershon; ***D:*** George Erschbamer. *PAR*

The Flintstones **1960** The foibles of the two Stone Age families, the Flintstones and the Rubbles, are chronicled in these two animated episodes of the classic series. **50m/C VHS, Beta.** ***V:*** Alan Reed, Mel Blanc, Jean Vander Pyl, Bea Benadaret. *TTC*

The Flintstones ½ **1994 (PG)** Preceded by massive hype, popular '60s cartoon comes to life thanks to a huge budget and creative sets and props. Seems that Fred's being set up by evil corporate types MacLachlan and Barry to take the fall for their embezzling scheme. Soon he gives up dining at RocDonald's for Cavern on the Green and cans best buddy Barney (Moranis). Forget the lame plot (32 writers took a shot at it) and sit back and enjoy the spectacle. Goodman's an amazingly true-to-type Fred, O'Donnell has Betty's giggle down pat, and Perkins looks a lot like Wilma. Wilma's original voice, VanderPyl, has a cameo; listen for Korman's voice as the Dictabird. Add half a bone if you're under 12. **92m/C VHS, LV.** John Goodman, Rick Moranis, Elizabeth Perkins, Rosie O'Donnell, Elizabeth Taylor, Kyle MacLachlan, Halle Berry, Jonathan Winters, Richard Moll, Irwin Keyes, Dann Florek; ***Cameos:*** Laraine Newman, Jean VanDerPyl, Jay Leno; ***D:*** Brian Levant; ***W:*** Tom S. Parker, Jim Jennewein, Steven E. de Souza; ***M:*** David Newman; ***V:*** Harvey Korman. Golden Raspberry Awards '94: Worst Supporting Actress (O'Donnell), Worst Screenplay; Nominations: MTV Movie Awards '95: Most Desirable Female (Berry); Golden Raspberry Awards '94: Worst Remake/Sequel, Worst Supporting Actress (Taylor). *MCA*

Flipper **1963** A fisherman's son befriends an injured dolphin, is persuaded to return him to the wild, and earns the animal's gratitude. Prime kids' fare, as its sequels and television series attest. **87m/C VHS, Beta.** Chuck Connors, Luke Halpin, Kathleen Maguire, Connie Scott; ***D:*** James B. Clark. *MVD, MGM*

Flipper **1964** Widower Porter Ricks (Kelly) is the chief ranger at Coral Key Park, Florida, who lives with sons, 15-year-old Sandy (Halpin) and 10-year-old Bud (Norden), and their pet dolphin Flipper. Adventures usually involved Flipper rescuing his trouble-prone charges from assorted acquatic dangers. The series ran from 1964-1968; two episodes are included per tape. Oh yes, Flipper was played by a girl dolphin named Suzy. **60m/C VHS.** Brian Kelly, Luke Halpin, Tommy Norden. *HMK*

Flipper **1996 (PG)** They still call him Flipper! Flipper, who in some scenes is played by a robot dolphin, reappears in a feature film for the first time since 1966. Sullen 14-year-old city boy Sandy Ricks (Wood) must spend the summer with crusty bachelor uncle Porter (Hogan), who would rather fish than look after his troublesome nephew. The duo witness the heartless killing of Flipper's family and are adopted by him. In addition to causing their seafood bill to skyrocket, the dolphin helps them uncover an illegal toxic waste dumper, who happens to be the same guy who made Flipper's mama sleep with the fishes. Updated along with the story is the soundtrack, which features a version of the famous theme song by Matthew Sweet. **94m/C VHS.** Elijah Wood, Paul Hogan, Chelsea Field, Isaac Hayes, Jonathan Banks, Luke Halpin; ***D:*** Alan Shapiro; ***W:*** Alan Shapiro; ***C:*** Bill Butler; ***M:*** Joel McNeely. *NYR*

Flipper's New Adventure *Flipper and the Pirates* **1964** Believing they are to be separated, Flipper and Sandy travel to a remote island. Little do they know, a British family is being held for ransom on the island they have chosen. It's up to the duo to save the day. An enjoyable, nicely done family adventure. **103m/C VHS, Beta.** Luke Halpin, Pamela Franklin, Tom Helmore, Francesca Annis, Brian Kelly, Joe Higgins, Ricou Browning; ***D:*** Leon Benson. *MGM, FCT*

Flipper's Odyssey **1966** Flipper has disappeared and his adopted family goes looking for him, but when one of the boys gets trapped in a cave, Flipper is his only hope. **77m/C VHS, Beta.** Luke Halpin, Brian Kelly, Tommy Norden; ***D:*** Paul Landres. *CNG, PSM*

Flirt ½ **1995** Three variations on the same theme: love, jealousy, and the problems of committing are what comprise this interesting portrait of modern romance in three countries. One character in each of the three stories is faced with an ultimatum to commit and is given a 90-minute deadline. Each are already involved in various other romantic entanglements. The best scenes show the confused flirts receiving very amusing advice from strangers. First episode is the best, as the pace subsequently slows. **84m/C VHS.** *GE JP* William Sage, Parker Posey, Martin Donovan, Dwight Ewell, Dominik Bender, Geno Lechner, Miho Nikaidoh, Toshizo Fujisawa; ***D:*** Hal Hartley; ***W:*** Hal Hartley; ***C:*** Michael Spiller; ***M:*** Ned Rifle. *NYR*

Flirtation Walk ½ **1934** West point musical that has cadet Powell falling in love with the general's daughter (Keeler), who is already engaged to lieutenant Eldredge. Some fairly good numbers, including "Mr. and Mrs. Is The Name," and "Flirtation Walk." In an attempt to change her image, Keeler hardly dances at all, which is too bad for the viewer. Based on a story by Lou Edelman and Delmer Daves. **98m/B VHS.** Dick Powell, Ruby Keeler, Pat O'Brien, Ross Alexander; ***D:*** Frank Borzage; ***W:*** Delmer Daves. *MGM*

Flirting **1989 (R)** Set in an Australian boarding school in 1965, a charming story following the misadventures of the adolescent Danny Embling, who has the misfortune to be both bright and sensitive, putting him seriously at odds with his masculine peers. He finds love with an outcast at the neighboring girls boarding school, the daughter of a diplomat from Uganda. Kidman has a supporting role as a snobbish older boarding school girl, not quite as bad as she seems. Tender and amusing. The second of director Duigan's coming-of-age trilogy, preceded by "The Year My Voice Broke" (the third film isn't yet completed). **100m/C VHS, LV.** *AU* Noah Taylor, Thandie Newton, Nicole Kidman, Bartholomew Rose, Felix Nobis, Josh Picker, Kiri Paramore, Marc Gray, Joshua Marshall, David Wieland, Craig Black, Leslie Hill; ***D:*** John Duigan; ***W:*** John Duigan. Australian Film Institute '90: Best Film. *VMK, BTV*

Flirting with Disaster **1995 (R)** Mel Coplin (Stiller) is your average neurotic New York entomologist searching for his birth parents so he can finally name his 4-month-old child and make love to his wife. Tagging along on his bumpy ride are his wife Nancy (Arquette), a beautiful quirky adoption agency shrink (Leoni), and a pair of bisexual FBI agents. The excellent cast also features Moore as Mel's bra baring adoptive mother, Segal as his weirdly paranoid adoptive father, and Alda and Tomlin as hilarious send-ups of ex-hippie mentality. As events spin madly out of control, every type of relationship is satired, and every character is left in their underwear. This is director Russell's first big budget movie, and is as close to a vintage screwball comedy as you'll see in the 90s. **92m/C VHS.** Ben Stiller, Patricia Arquette, Tea Leoni, Alan Alda, Mary Tyler Moore, George Segal, Lily Tomlin, Josh Brolin, Richard Jenkins, Celia Weston, Glenn Fitzgerald, Beth Ostrosky, Cynthia Lamontagne, David Patrick Kelly, John Ford Noonan, Charlet Oberly; ***D:*** David O. Russell; ***W:*** David O. Russell; ***C:*** Eric Alan Edwards; ***M:*** Stephen Endelman. *NYR*

Flirting with Fate **1916** Early Fairbanks-cum-acrobat vehicle. Having hired a hitman to rub himself out, a young man decides he doesn't want to die, after all. Seems there's a girl involved... **51m/B VHS, Beta.** Douglas Fairbanks Sr., Jewel Carmen, Howard Gaye, William E. Lawrence, George Beranger, Dorothy Hadel, Lillian Langdon; ***D:*** Christy Cabanne. *NOS, GPV, FCT*

Flood! **1976** Irwin Allen's first made-for-television disaster film. A dam bursts and devastates a small town, so a helicopter pilot must save the day. Good cast is swept along in a current of disaster-genre cliches. **98m/C VHS, Beta.** Robert Culp, Martin Milner, Barbara Hershey, Richard Basehart, Carol Lynley, Roddy McDowall, Cameron Mitchell, Teresa Wright, Francine York; ***D:*** Earl Bellamy. *WAR*

The Floorwalker **1917** Chaplin becomes involved with a dishonest floorwalker in a department store. Silent. **20m/B VHS, Beta.** Charlie Chaplin; ***D:*** Charlie Chaplin. *CAB, GVV*

The Floorwalker/By the Sea **1915** Two early Chaplin short comedies, featuring a hilarious scene on an escalator in the first film. Silent. **51m/B VHS, Beta, 8mm.** Charlie Chaplin, Edna Purviance, Eric Campbell; ***D:*** Charlie Chaplin. *VYY*

Flor Silvestre *Wild Flower* **1958** The son of a rich rancher romances a young woman against the background of the Mexican Revolution. **90m/B VHS, Beta.** *MX* Dolores Del Rio, Pedro Armendariz Sr.; ***D:*** Emilio Fernandez. *MAD*

The Florida Connection **1974** An action thriller set in the Florida Swamps with a collection of villains and a vague plot about smuggling. **90m/C VHS, Beta.** Dan Pastorini, June Wilkinson. *UNI*

Florida Straits **1987 (PG-13)** A recently released Cuban prisoner hires a few losers and their boat to return to the island, supposedly to find the girl he loves. The real quest is for gold buried during the Bay-of-Pigs invasion in this none-too-original made-for-cable movie that at least offers a good cast. **98m/C VHS, Beta, LV.** Raul Julia, Fred Ward, Daniel H. Jenkins, Antonio Fargas; ***D:*** Mike Hodges; ***W:*** Stephen Metcalfe; ***M:*** Michel Colombier. *ORI*

Floundering ½ **1994 (R)** Misguided satire uses the 1992 L.A. riots as a backdrop to tell the saga of unemployed James Boyz (LeGros), whose life is a walking disaster. He owes the IRS, his unemployment compensation has run out, his brother (Hawke) has fled from a drug rehab clinic, and he finds his girlfriend (Zane) in bed with another man. John drags himself among the city's downtrodden as he fantasizes about life. Drag pretty much sums up the film despite good performances by LeGros and Hawke. **97m/C VHS.** James LeGros, Ethan Hawke, Steve Buscemi, John Cusack, Lisa Zane, Sy Richardson; ***D:*** Peter McCarthy; ***W:*** Peter McCarthy. *APX*

Flower Drum Song **1961** The Rodgers and Hammerstein musical played better on Broadway than in this overblown adaptation of life in San Francisco's Chinatown. Umeki plays the young girl who arrives from Hong Kong for an arranged marriage. Her intended (Soo) is a fast-living nightclub owner already enjoying the love of singer Kwan. Meanwhile Umeki falls for the handsome Shigeta. Naturally, everything comes together in a happy ending. ♫I Enjoy Being A Girl; Don't Marry Me; Grant Avenue; You Are Beautiful; A Hundred Million Miracles; Fan Tan Fanny; Chop Suey; The Other Generation; I Am Going to Like It Here. **133m/C VHS, Beta, LV.** Nancy Kwan, Jack Soo, James Shigeta, Miyoshi Umeki, Juanita Hall; ***D:*** Henry Koster; ***C:*** Russell Metty; ***M:*** Richard Rodgers, Oscar Hammerstein. Nominations: Academy Awards '61: Best Art Direction/Set Decoration (Color), Best Color Cinematography, Best Costume Design (Color), Best Sound, Best Original Score. *MCA, FCT*

The Flower of My Secret *La Flor de My Secreto* **1995 (R)** Emotional yet restrained story about middle-aged Leo (Paredes), whose longtime marriage is fast ending (and it's not her idea). Leo writes hugely popular romance novels under a pseudonym but her current work is so bleak it's unpublishable. So, Leo gets a job at a newspaper where editor Angel (Echanove) immediately falls for her, and indeed, lives up to his name as her guardian. Willfully myopic about her own life, Leo undergoes further trials until she slowly realizes the mess she's in and becomes willing to change. Surprisingly subdued given Almodovar's usual flamboyance but it's a welcome change of pace. Spanish with subtitles. **105m/C VHS.** *SP FR* Marisa Paredes, Juan Echanove, Imanol Arias, Carmen Elias, Rossy de Palma, Chus Lampreave, Joaquin Cortes, Manuela Vargas; ***D:*** Pedro Almodovar; ***W:*** Pedro Almodovar; ***C:*** Alfonso Beato; ***M:*** Alberto Iglesias. *NYR*

Flowers in the Attic 🦴½ **1987 (PG-13)** Based on the V.C. Andrews bestseller, a would-be thriller about four young siblings locked for years in their family's old mansion by their grandmother with their mother's selfish acquiescence. A chicken-hearted, clumsy flop that skimps on the novel's trashier themes. **93m/C VHS, Beta, LV.** Victoria Tennant, Kristy Swanson, Louise Fletcher, Jeb Stuart Adams; ***D:*** Jeffrey Bloom; ***W:*** Jeffrey Bloom. *NWV, VTR*

Flowers of Reverie 🦴🦴 **1984** A former soldier is imprisoned for his work in the resistance during the Hungarian Revolution (1848-9), leading to tragedy. In Hungarian with English subtitles. **106m/C VHS.** *HU* ***D:*** Laszlo Lugossy. *FCT*

The Flowers of St. Francis 🦴🦴🦴 **1950** Rossellini's presentation of St. Francis and his friars' attainment of spiritual harmony. In Italian with English subtitles. This is the British release version, 10-15 minutes longer than the U.S. version. **75m/B VHS, Beta.** *IT* Federico Fellini; ***D:*** Roberto Rossellini. *FCT*

Fluke 🦴🦴 **1995 (PG)** "Ghost" meets "Oh, Heavenly Dog" as Tom (Modine) dies in a suspicious car accident and is reincarnated as a dog who remembers his past life. He returns to his former family (Travis and Pomeranc) to protect them from his former business partner (Stoltz), battling such puppy perils as cosmetic testing labs and dogcatchers along the way. While there's plenty of squishy sentimentality to go around, some of the scenes involving animal abuse may be a little much for the target audience of pre-teen kids. Jackson and Stoltz trade "Pulp Fiction" for pup fiction, but this dog won't hunt. Based on the novel by James Herbert. **96m/C VHS, LV.** Matthew Modine, Nancy Travis, Eric Stoltz, Max Pomeranc, Ron Perlman, Jon Polito, Bill Cobbs, Frederico Pacifici, Collin Wilcox Paxton; ***D:*** Carlo Carlei; ***W:*** James Carrington, Carlo Carlei; ***C:*** Raffaele Mertes; ***M:*** Carlo Siliotto; ***V:*** Samuel L. Jackson. *MGM*

Flush 🦴🦴 **1981** Unorthodox comedy involving funny noises. **90m/C VHS.** William Calloway, William Bronder, Jeannie Linero; ***D:*** Andrew J. Kuehn. *NO*

Flush It **1976 (R)** While working in the honey factory, Harvey finds a clue that leads him on a wild escapade in search of a buried treasure. Surprises abound along the way. **90m/C VHS, Beta.** *NO*

The Flustered Comedy of Leon Errol 🦴🦴 **1939** The popular Depression-era comedian Errol is showcased in three shorts: "Crime Rave," "Man-I-Cured," and "A Panic in the Parlor." **56m/B VHS, Beta, 8mm.** Leon Errol, Vivian Tobin, Dorothy Granger, Frank Faylen, Virginia Vale. *VYY*

The Fly 🦴🦴🦴 **1958** The historic, chillingly original '50s sci-fi tale about a hapless scientist experimenting with teleportation who accidentally gets anatomically confused with a housefly. Campy required viewing; two sequels followed, and a 1986 remake which itself has spawned one sequel. **94m/C VHS, Beta, LV.** Vincent Price, David Hedison, Herbert Marshall, Patricia Owens; ***D:*** Kurt Neumann; ***W:*** James Clavell; ***C:*** Karl Struss. *FOX*

The Fly 🦴🦴🦴 **1986 (R)** A sensitive, humanistic remake of the 1958 horror film about a scientist whose flesh is genetically intermixed with a housefly via his experimental transportation device. A thoughtful, shocking horror film, with fine performances from Goldblum and Davis and a brutally emotional conclusion. Followed by "The Fly II" in 1989. **96m/C VHS, Beta, LV.** Jeff Goldblum, Geena Davis, John Getz, Joy Boushel; ***D:*** David Cronenberg; ***W:*** David Cronenberg, Charles Edward Pogue; ***M:*** Howard Shore. Academy Awards '86: Best Makeup. *FOX*

The Fly 2 🦴½ **1989 (R)** Inferior sequel to Cronenberg's opus, in which the offspring of Seth Brundle achieves full genius maturity in three years, falls in love, and discovers the evil truth behind his father's teleportation device and the corporate auspices that backed it. **105m/C VHS, Beta, LV.** Eric Stoltz, Daphne Zuniga, Lee Richardson, John Getz, Harley Cross; ***D:*** Chris Walas; ***W:*** Mick Garris, Jim Wheat, Ken Wheat, Frank Darabont. *FOX, CCB*

Fly by Night 🦴🦴 **1993 (PG-13)** Mismatched New York rappers Rich and I join forces to make it big as hard-core gangstas. When they're propelled to the top of the charts, forces both personal and professional work to tear them apart. **93m/C VHS.** Jeffrey D. Sams, Ron Brice; ***D:*** Steve Gomer; ***W:*** Todd Graff. Sundance Film Festival '93: Filmmakers Trophy. *COL*

Fly with the Hawk 🦴🦴 **19??** A troubled teenager gets lost in the wilderness for a year, and learns some important things from nature to take back to civilization. **90m/C VHS.** Peter Ferri, Peter Snook, Shelley Lynne Speigel; ***D:*** Robert Tanos. *NO*

Flying Blind 🦴½ **1941** Foreign agents are thwarted in their attempt to steal a vital air defense secret. Unconvincing espionage plot cobbled into a story about a Los Angeles-Las Vegas puddle jumper. **69m/B VHS, Beta.** Richard Arlen, Jean Parker, Marie Wilson. *NOS, DVT*

The Flying Deuces 🦴🦴🦴 *Flying Aces* **1939** Ollie's broken heart lands Laurel and Hardy in the Foreign Legion. The comic pair escape a firing squad only to suffer a plane crash that results in Hardy's reincarnation as a horse. A musical interlude with a Laurel soft shoe while Hardy sings "Shine On, Harvest Moon" is one of the film's highlights. **65m/B VHS, Beta, LV.** Stan Laurel, Oliver Hardy, Jean Parker, Reginald Gardiner, James Finlayson; ***D:*** Edward Sutherland. *CNG, MRV, NOS*

Flying Discman from Mars **1951** A Martian warlord battles a brave pilot and his secretary in this exciting serial not seen in 30 years. The original 12 episodes are edited together on two cassettes. **167m/B VHS.** *REP, MLB*

Flying Down to Rio 🦴🦴½ **1933** The first Astaire-Rogers musical, although they are relegated to supporting status behind Del Rio and Raymond. Still, it was enough to make them stars and a team that epitomizes the height of American musical films. The slim story revolves around singer Del Rio's two suitors and receives a splendid, art deco production. Showgirls dancing on plane wings in flight provide another memorable moment. ♫Music Makes Me; The Carioca; Orchids in the Moonlight; Flying Down to Rio. **89m/B VHS, Beta.** Fred Astaire, Ginger Rogers, Dolores Del Rio, Eric Blore, Gene Raymond, Franklin Pangborn; ***D:*** Thornton Freeland; ***M:*** Vincent Youmans, Max Steiner. Nominations: Academy Awards '34: Best Song ("Carioca"). *TTC, MED*

The Flying Fool 🦴🦴 **1929** Ace pilot Bill returns from the war to find his younger brother has fallen for a singer. When Bill meets the lady, he also notices her charms and the two brothers have a duel in the skies to see who'll get the girl. **75m/B VHS, Beta.** William Boyd, Marie Prevost, Russell Gleason; ***D:*** Tay Garnett; ***W:*** James Gleason. *VYY, RXM, GPV*

Flying from the Hawk 🦴½ **1986** A 12-year-old boy sees something he shouldn't and soon finds that his friends and relatives are mysteriously vanishing. **110m/C VHS, Beta.** John Ireland, Diane McBain. *NO*

Flying Karamazov Brothers Comedy Hour 🦴½ **1983** The wild and crazy Karamazov brothers show what they can do in this fun-filled video of comedy, acrobatics, and juggling. **59m/C VHS, Beta.** The Flying Karamazov Brothers. *MCG*

Flying Leathernecks 🦴🦴🦴 **1951** Tough squadron leader Wayne fights with his fellow officer Ryan in Guadalcanal when their leadership styles clash. But when the real fighting begins all is forgotten as Wayne leads his men into victorious battle, winning the admiration and devotion of his fliers. Memorable WWII film deals with war in human terms. **102m/C VHS, Beta, LV.** John Wayne, Robert Ryan, Janis Carter; ***D:*** Nicholas Ray. *TLF, TTC*

The Flying Saucer 🦴½ **1950** U.S. and Russian scientists clash over their search for a huge flying saucer that is hidden under a glacier. The first movie to deal with flying saucers. The cassette includes animated opening and closing sequences plus previews of coming attractions. **120m/B VHS, Beta.** Mikel Conrad, Pat Garrison, Hanz von Teuffen; ***D:*** Mikel Conrad. *MWP, SNC*

Flying Saucers Over Hollywood: The Plan 9 Companion **1993** This documentary looks at what many consider to be the worst film of all time, "Plan 9 from Outer Space," released in 1959. The cult classic, directed by the equally bizarre Edward D. Wood, Jr., is revealed in all its absurdity, including interviews with cast, crew, and fans. **111m/C VHS.** ***W:*** Mark Patrick Carducci. *ATM*

The Flying Scotsman 🦴½ **1929** A fired railroad worker tries to wreck an express train on the engineer's last journey. The daughter of the intended victim saves the day. Silent, with sound added. **60m/B VHS, Beta.** Ray Milland, Pauline Johnson, Moore Marriott; ***D:*** Castleton Knight. *NOS, DVT, HEG*

Flying Tigers 🦴🦴½ **1942** Salutes the All-American Volunteer Group which flew for China under General Claire Chennault against the Japanese before the U.S. entered WWII. A squadron leader and a brash new recruit both vie for the affections of a pretty nurse in-between their flying missions. Romance and a few comic touches take a back seat to graphic scenes of aerial battles and dramatization of heroic sacrifice in this rousing war film. **101m/B VHS, LV.** John Wayne, Paul Kelly, John Carroll, Anna Lee, Mae Clarke, Gordon Jones; ***D:*** David Miller. Nominations: Academy Awards '42: Best Sound, Best Original Score. *REP*

Flying Wild 🦴½ **1941** A gang of saboteurs is out to steal top-secret airplane blueprints. Who else but the Bowery Boys could conceivably stop them? **62m/B VHS.** Leo Gorcey, Bobby Jordan, Donald Haines, Joan Barclay, David Gorcey, Bobby Stone, Sammy Morrison; ***D:*** William West. *NOS, LOO*

FM 🦴🦴 *Citizen's Band* **1978 (PG-13)** The disc jockeys at an L.A. radio station rebel in the name of rock'n'roll. Despite the promising cast and setting (Mull makes his movie debut as a memorable space case), this is just disjointed and surprisingly unhip; one producer took his name off it due to creative difficulties. The decent soundtrack includes concert footage of Jimmy Buffet and Linda Ronstadt. ♫FM; Do It Again; FM Reprise; Livingston Saturday Night; The Key To My Kingdom; Green Grass and High Tides; Life In The Fast Lane; Bad Man; Poor, Poor, Pitiful Me. **104m/C VHS, LV.** Eileen Brennan, Alex Karras, Cleavon Little, Martin Mull, Cassie Yates, Linda Ronstadt, Jimmy Buffett; ***D:*** Lamont Johnson. *MCA*

The Fog 🦴🦴 **1978 (R)** John Carpenter's blustery follow-up to his success with "Halloween." An evil fog containing murderous, vengeful ghosts envelops a sleepy seaside town and subjects the residents to terror and mayhem. **91m/C VHS, Beta, LV, 8mm.** Hal Holbrook, Adrienne Barbeau, Jamie Lee Curtis, Janet Leigh, John Houseman; ***D:*** John Carpenter; ***W:*** John Carpenter; ***C:*** Dean Cundey; ***M:*** John Carpenter. *COL, SUE*

Fog Island 🦴½ **1945** Murder and terror lurk after a greedy inventor, who was framed for fraud by his business partner, is released from prison. He plots revenge by inviting his foes to his island home. **72m/B VHS, Beta.** George Zucco, Lionel Atwill, Terry Morse, Jerome Cowan, Veda Ann Borg; ***D:*** Terry Morse. *NOS, SNC, VCN*

Folks! ☠ **1992 (PG-13)** Selleck is a Chicago stockbroker whose wife and kids have left him, the FBI is after him, and, worst of all, his parents have moved in with him. His parents don't want to be a burden, so Selleck decides that the best way to solve his financial woes is to help his parents commit suicide so he can collect on their insurance policies. Tasteless comedy that makes fun of aging and Alzheimer's Disease. Selleck is too sweet and cuddly for his role, but Ameche is good as the senile father, and Ebersole is great as Selleck's unpleasant sister. **109m/C VHS.** Tom Selleck, Don Ameche, Anne Jackson, Christine Ebersole, Wendy Crewson, Robert Pastorelli, Michael Murphy, Kevin Timothy Chevalia, Margaret Murphy; ***D:*** Ted Kotcheff; ***M:*** Michel Colombier. *FXV*

Follies Girl ☠☠ **1943** There's folly in expecting that this wartime tuner would hold up today. An army private romances a dress designer and a musical show somehow results. ♫Keep the Flag A-Flying; No Man In The House; Someone to Love; I Told A Lie; Shall We Gather at the Rhythm?; Fascination; I Knew Your Father's Son; Thoity Poiple Boids. **74m/B VHS.** Wendy Barrie, Doris Nolan, Gordon Oliver, Anne Barrett, Arthur Pierson; ***D:*** William Rowland. *NOS, LOO*

Follies in Concert **1985** A filmed record of the famed Stephen Sondheim musical play, performed at Lincoln Center in New York with an all-star cast. Songs include "I'm Still Here," "Losing My Mind," "Broadway Baby" and "The Ladies Who Lunch." **90m/C VHS, Beta, LV.** Carol Burnett, Lee Remick, Betty Comden, Andre Gregory, Adolph Green, Mandy Patinkin, Phyllis Newman, Elaine Stritch, Jim Walton, Licia Albanese. *MVD, FRH*

Follow Me ☠☠ **1969 (G)** Round-the-world odyssey of three moon doggies searching for adventure—and the perfect wave. Spectacular surfing scenes are complemented by songs performed by Dino, Desi, and Billy. **90m/C VHS.** Claude Codgen, Mary Lou McGinnis, Bob Purvey; ***D:*** Gene McCabe. *NO*

Follow Me, Boys! ☠☠☠ **1966** A Disney film about a simple man who decides to put down roots and enjoy the quiet life, after one year too many on the road with a ramshackle jazz band. That life is soon interrupted when he volunteers to lead a high-spirited boy scout troop. **120m/C VHS, Beta.** Fred MacMurray, Vera Miles, Lillian Gish, Charlie Ruggles, Elliott Reid, Kurt Russell, Luana Patten, Ken Murray; ***D:*** Norman Tokar; ***M:*** George Bruns. *DIS*

Follow Me Quietly ☠☠☠ **1949** Serial strangler who only kills in the rain is stalked by Lundigan. Very good little thriller which packs a punch in less than an hour. **59m/B VHS, Beta.** William Lundigan, Dorothy Patrick, Jeff Corey, Nestor Paiva, Charles D. Brown, Paul Guilfoyle; ***D:*** Richard Fleischer. *TTC, MLB, RXM*

Follow That Camel ☠½ *Carry On Follow That Camel* **1967** Foreign Legion sergeant who invents acts of heroism finally gets a chance to really help out a friend in need. Part of the "Carry On" series. **95m/C VHS, Beta.** *GB* Phil Silvers, Kenneth Williams, Anita Harris, Jim Dale; ***D:*** Gerald Thomas. *NO*

Follow That Car ☠ **1980 (PG)** Three southern kids become FBI agents and begin a thigh-slappin', rip-snortin' down-home escapade. **96m/C VHS, Beta.** Dirk Benedict, Tanya Tucker, Teri Nunn; ***D:*** Daniel Haller. *NLC*

Follow That Dream ☠☠ **1961 (G)** Elvis plays a musical hillbilly whose family is trying to homestead on government land along the sunny Florida coast. Based on Richard C. Powell's novel "Pioneer Go Home." The songs-the only reason to see this movie—include "Angel", and "What a Wonderful Life", and the title track. **111m/C VHS, Beta, LV.** Elvis Presley, Arthur O'Connell, Anne Helm, Simon Oakland, Jack Kruschen, Joanna Moore, Howard McNear; ***D:*** Gordon Douglas. *MGM*

Follow That Rainbow ☠ **1966** Believing that her long-lost father is a popular touring singer, a young lass pursues him from Switzerland to South Africa. **90m/C VHS, Beta.** Joe Stewardson, Memory Jane, Joan Bickhill. *NO*

Follow the Boys ☠☠☠ **1944** Vaudeville performer Tony West (Raft) heads out to California to try his luck and gets a double break when he's noticed by leading lady Gloria Vance (Zorina). Not only does he become a star but he marries Gloria as well. When WWII breaks out Tony's turned down for military service, so he organizes camp shows for the soldiers. They're a big success but misunderstandings have put his marriage in jeopardy. Plot's merely an excuse to have haute Hollywood (including Marlene Dietrich, Orson Welles, Jeanette MacDonald, and W.C. Fields) sing, dance, and tell jokes. ♫Beyond the Blue Horizon; I'll See You In My Dreams; The Bigger the Army and the Navy; Some of These Days; I'll Get By; I'll Walk Alone; Mad About Him Blues; The House I Live In. **111m/B VHS.** George Raft, Vera Zorina, Grace McDonald, Charles Butterworth, Martha O'Driscoll, Charley Grapewin, Elizabeth Patterson; ***D:*** Edward Sutherland; ***W:*** Lou Breslow, Gertrude Purcell. *MCA*

Follow the Fleet ☠☠☠ **1936** A song-and-dance man joins the Navy and meets two sisters in need of help in this Rogers/Astaire bon-bon featuring a classic Berlin score. Look for Betty Grable, Lucille Ball, and Tony Martin in minor roles. Hilliard went on to be best known as the wife of Ozzie Nelson in TV's "The Adventures of Ozzie and Harriet." ♫Let's Face the Music and Dance; We Saw the Sea; I'm Putting All My Eggs In One Basket; Get Thee Behind Me, Satan; But Where Are You?; I'd Rather Lead a Band; Let Yourself Go. **110m/B VHS, Beta, LV.** Fred Astaire, Ginger Rogers, Randolph Scott, Harriet Hilliard Nelson, Betty Grable, Lucille Ball; ***D:*** Mark Sandrich; ***M:*** Irving Berlin, Max Steiner. *MED, TTC, IME*

Follow the Leader ☠☠ *East of the Bowery* **1944** On leave from the Army, Hall and Gorcey discover that one of the gang has been jailed on a trumped-up charge and set about finding the real culprit. ♫Now and Then; All I Want to Do Play the Drums. **65m/B VHS.** Leo Gorcey, Huntz Hall, Gabriel Dell, Jack LaRue, Joan Marsh, Billy Benedict, Mary Gordon, Sammy Morrison; ***D:*** William Beaudine; ***M:*** Gene Austin. *NOS*

Follow the River ☠☠½ **1995 (PG)** It's 1775 and Mary Ingles (Lee) is living with her husband and family on a frontier farm in the Blue Ridge Mountains. The community is raided by the Shawnee, lead by Wildcat (Schweig), who take Mary and several other settlers miles away to their home camp. Once there, Mary befriends another captive, the older Gretl (Burstyn), proves her courage to the smitten Wildcat, and plots to escape and find her way home. Based on the 1981 novel by James Alexander Thom; filmed in North Carolina. **93m/C VHS.** Sheryl Lee, Eric Schweig, Ellen Burstyn, Tim Guinee, Renee O'Connor; ***D:*** Martin Davidson. *HMK*

Food of the Gods *Woof!* **1976 (PG)** On a secluded island giant rats, chickens, and other creatures crave human flesh, blood, bones, etc. This cheap, updated version of the H. G. Wells novel suffers from lousy performances and a lack of imagination. **88m/C VHS, Beta.** Marjoe Gortner, Pamela Franklin, Ralph Meeker, Ida Lupino, Jon Cypher; ***D:*** Bert I. Gordon. *LIV, VES*

Food of the Gods: Part 2 *Woof! Gnaw: Food of the Gods 2* **1988 (R)** The killer beasts and animals of the first film (and of H.G. Wells' classic novel) strike again; gigantic rats maim young girls. Easily as bad as the original. **93m/C VHS, Beta, LV.** Paul Coufos, Lisa Schrage; ***D:*** Damian Lee; ***W:*** E. Kim Brewster. *NO*

A Fool and His Money ☠☠½ **1988 (R)** An adman (Penner) decides to market a shady new religion based on greed but, naturally, finds the true road. Bullock is the skeptical girlfriend. **84m/C VHS.** Jonathan Penner, Sandra Bullock, Gerald Orange, George Plimpton; ***D:*** Daniel Adams. *VMK*

Fool for Love ☠☠ **1986 (R)** Explores the mysterious relationship between a modern-day drifter and his long-time lover, who may or may not be his half-sister, as they confront each other in a seedy New Mexico motel. Adapted by Shepard from his play. **108m/C VHS, Beta.** Sam Shepard, Kim Basinger, Randy Quaid, Harry Dean Stanton; ***D:*** Robert Altman; ***W:*** Sam Shepard; ***M:*** George Burt. *MGM*

The Fool Killer ☠☠½ *Violent Journey* **1965** In the post-Civil War south, a 12 year-old boy learns that a terrifying legend about an axe-murderer may be all too real. Offbeat film with striking visuals and photography. Debut film for Albert and another choice psycho role for Perkins. **100m/B VHS.** Anthony Perkins, Edward Albert, Dana Elcar, Henry Hull, Salome Jens, Arnold Moss; ***D:*** Servando Gonzalez. *REP*

A Fool There Was ☠☠½ **1914** The rocket that blasted Theda Bara to stardom and launched the vamp film genre. One of the few extant Bara films, it tells the now familiar story of a good man whom crumbles from the heights of moral rectitude thanks to the inescapable influence of an unredeemable vamp. Bette Davis described Bara as "divinely, hysterically, insanely malevolent." Much heavy emoting; subtitled (notoriously) "Kiss Me, My Fool!" Based on Rudyard Kipling's "The Vampire." **70m/B VHS, Beta.** Theda Bara, Edward Jose, Runa Hodges, Clifford Bruce; ***D:*** Frank Powell. *VYY, FCT, GVV*

Foolin' Around ☠☠½ **1980 (PG)** An innocent Oklahoma farm boy arrives at college and falls in love with a beautiful heiress. He will stop at nothing to win her over, including crashing her lavish wedding ceremony. **101m/C VHS, Beta.** Gary Busey, Annette O'Toole, Eddie Albert, Tony Randall, Cloris Leachman; ***D:*** Richard T. Heffron; ***W:*** Michael Kane; ***M:*** Charles Bernstein. *SUE*

Foolish Wives ☠☠☠½ **1922** A remake of Von Stroheim's classic depicting the confused milieu of post-war Europe as reflected through the actions of a bogus count and his seductive, corrupt ways. Comes as close as possible to the original film. **107m/B VHS, Beta, LV.** Erich von Stroheim, Mae Busch, Maude George, Cesare Gravina, Harrison Ford; ***D:*** Erich von Stroheim. *KIV, CCB, HHT*

Fools ☠ **1970 (PG)** Two lonely people—he an aging horror film actor and she a young woman estranged from her husband—start a warm romance when they meet in San Francisco. The husband reacts violently. Good cast seems lost. **93m/C VHS, Beta.** Jason Robards Jr., Katharine Ross, Scott Hylands; ***D:*** Tom Gries. *PSM*

Fools of Fortune ☠☠½ **1990 (PG-13)** Adaptation of William Trevor's novel depicting Willie Clinton's childhood and adult experiences of family dramatics played against the backdrop of post-WWI Ireland. During the Irish war for independence, a family is attacked by British soldiers, creating emotional havoc for the survivors. Though well-acted and poignant, it's a rather disjointed and straying shamrock opera. **104m/C VHS, LV.** *GB* Mary Elizabeth Mastrantonio, Iain Glen, Julie Christie, Michael Kitchen, Sean McClory, Frankie McCafferty; ***D:*** Pat O'Connor; ***W:*** Michael Hirst; ***M:*** Hans Zimmer. *COL, FCT*

Footlight Frenzy ☠☠ **1984** The Law Moan Spectacular comedy troupe are at it again as they perform a benefit play where everything goes wrong. **110m/C VHS, Beta.** *GB* Alan Shearman, Diz White, Ron House, Frances Tomelty, Michael Aldridge, Ron Pember. *NO*

Footlight Parade ☠☠☠ **1933** Broadway producer Cagney is out of work. Sound films have scared off his backers until his idea for staging live musical numbers before the cinema features lures them back. Lots of authentic backstage action precedes three spectacular Busby Berkeley-choreographed numbers that climax the film, including the giant water ballet featuring more than 100 performers. ♫Ah, the Moon is Here; Sittin' on a Backyard Fence; Honeymoon Hotel; By A Waterfall; Shanghai Lil. **104m/B Beta, LV.** James Cagney, Joan Blondell, Dick Powell, Ruby Keeler, Guy Kibbee, Ruth Donnelly; ***D:*** Lloyd Bacon; ***C:*** George Barnes. *MGM, FOX*

Footlight Serenade ☠☠½ **1942** A boxer falls for a beautiful dancer with whom he's costarring in a Broadway play. Unfortunately, she's secretly married to another of the actors and her husband is becoming jealous of the boxer's intentions. Light, fun musical. One of a series of Grable movies made to boost morale during WWII. ♫Are You Kidding?; I'm Still Crazy About You; I Hear the Birdies Sing; Living High; I'll Be Marching to a Love Song; Land On Your Feet; I'm Stepping Out With a Memory Tonight. **80m/B VHS, Beta.** Betty Grable, Victor Mature, John Payne, Jane Wyman, Phil Silvers, James Gleason, Mantan Moreland; ***D:*** Gregory Ratoff; ***C:*** Lee Garmes. *FOX*

Footloose ♪♪½ **1984 (PG)** When a city boy moves to a small Midwestern town, he discovers some disappointing news: rock music and dancing have been forbidden by the local government. Determined to bring some '80s-style life into the town, he sets about changing the rules and eventually enlists the help of the daughter of the man responsible for the law. Rousing music, talented young cast, and plenty of trouble make this an entertaining musical-drama. ♫Footloose; Let's Hear it for the Boy; The Girl Gets Around; Dancing in the Sheets; Somebody's Eyes; Almost Paradise; I'm Free; Never; Holding Out for a Hero. **107m/C VHS, Beta, LV, 8mm.** Kevin Bacon, Lori Singer, Christopher Penn, John Lithgow, Dianne Wiest, John Laughlin, Sarah Jessica Parker; ***D:*** Herbert Ross; ***M:*** Miles Goodman. Nominations: Academy Awards '84: Best Song ("Footloose"), Best Song ("Let's Hear It for the Boy"). *PAR*

Footsteps in the Dark ♪♪½ **1941** Fairly amusing comedy-mystery with investment counselor Flynn doubling as detective. Based on the play "Blondie White" by Ladislaus Fodor, Bernard Merivale, and Jeffrey Dell. **96m/B VHS.** Errol Flynn, Brenda Marshall, Ralph Bellamy, Alan Hale, Lee Patrick, Allen Jenkins, Lucile Watson, William Frawley, Roscoe Karns, Grant Mitchell, Maris Wrixon, Noel Madison, Jack LaRue, Turhan Bey; ***D:*** Lloyd Bacon, Hugh MacMullen; ***W:*** Lester Cole, John Wexley. *MGM*

For a Few Dollars More ♪♪½ **1965 (PG)** The Man With No Name returns as a bounty hunter who teams up with a gunslinger/rival to track down the sadistic leader of a gang of bandits. Violent. Sequel to "A Fistful of Dollars" (1964) and followed by "The Good, The Bad, and The Ugly". Letterboxed laserdisc edition features the original movie trailer. **127m/C VHS, Beta, LV.** *IT* Clint Eastwood, Lee Van Cleef, Klaus Kinski, Gian Marie Volonte; ***D:*** Sergio Leone; ***M:*** Ennio Morricone. *FOX, MGM, FCT*

For a Lost Soldier ♪♪ **1993** Middle-aged Dutch choreorapher Jeroen (Krabbe), working on a piece about the Allied liberation, recalls his relationship with a Canadian soldier more than 40 years before. During WWII, the 13-year-old Jeroen (Smit) is sent from Amsterdam to live in the country with a foster family. With the first twinges of puberty and sexuality he longs for a special friend, whom he finds in Walt (Kelley), a young gay Canadian soldier who is part of the Allied liberation forces. Very provocative subject, delicately handled, without any implication of child abuse. In English and Dutch with subtitles. **92m/C VHS.** *NL* Marten Smit, Andrew Kelley, Jeroen Krabbe, Feark Smink, Elsje de Wijn, Derk-Jan Kroon; ***D:*** Roeland Kerbosch; ***W:*** Roeland Kerbosch; ***M:*** Joop Stokkermans. *FXL, ORI*

For Auld Lang Syne: The Marx Brothers **1932** Four classic comedy shorts: "Monkey Business Special," "Gai Dimanche," "Hooks and Jabs," and "For Auld Lang Syne." **46m/B VHS, Beta.** Chico Marx, Groucho Marx, Alan Marx, Harpo Marx. *VYY*

For Better and For Worse ♪♪½ **1992 (PG)** A nice young couple is planning to have your average nice wedding when one of their friends gets hold of an invitation and decides to jokingly invite the Pope to attend. But the joke is on them when the Pope accepts. Talk about upstaging the bride! **94m/C VHS, LV.** Patrick Dempsey, Kelly Lynch. *LIV*

For Better or Worse ♪♪ **1995 (PG-13)** Pathetic loser Michael Makeshift (Alexander, also making his directorial debut) falls in love with his new sister-in-law Valerie (Davidovich) even as he gets entangled in his brother Reggie's (Woods) business scams. Made for cable TV. **95m/C VHS.** Jason Alexander, Lolita Davidovich, James Woods, Joe Mantegna, Jay Mohr, Beatrice Arthur, Robert Costanzo, John Amos, Eda Reiss Merin; ***Cameos:*** Rob Reiner, Rip Torn; ***D:*** Jason Alexander; ***W:*** Jeff Nathanson; ***C:*** Wayne Keenan; ***M:*** Miles Goodman. *TTC*

For Heaven's Sake ♪♪♪ **1926** Lloyd's first film for Paramount has him making an accidental donation to a skid row mission, then marrying the preacher's daughter and converting all the neighborhood tough guys. **60m/B VHS.** Harold Lloyd, Jobyna Ralston, Noah Young, James Mason, Paul Weigel; ***D:*** Sam Taylor. *NO*

For Heaven's Sake ♪½ **1979** A bumbling basketball team is lent some heavenly assistance in the form of a meddling angel. But can he hit the jumper? Made for television. **90m/C VHS.** Ray Bolger, Kent McCord. *LIV*

For Keeps ♪½ **1988 (PG-13)** Two high school sweethearts on the verge of graduating get married after the girl becomes pregnant, and suffer all the trials of teenage parenthood. Tends toward the unrealistic and trite. **98m/C VHS, Beta, LV.** Molly Ringwald, Randall Batinkoff, Kenneth Mars; ***D:*** John G. Avildsen; ***W:*** Tim Kazurinsky, Denise DeClue; ***M:*** Bill Conti. *COL*

For Ladies Only ♪♪ **1981** A struggling actor takes a job as a male stripper to pay the rent. Among the leering ladies is Davis, daughter of former President Reagan. Made for television. **100m/C VHS, Beta.** Gregory Harrison, Patricia Davis, Dinah Manoff, Louise Lasser, Lee Grant, Marc Singer, Viveca Lindfors, Steven Keats; ***D:*** Mel Damski. *NO*

For Love Alone ♪♪ **1986** A young Australian college co-ed in the 1930s falls in love with a handsome, controversial teacher and follows him to London, only to discover he's not her Mr. Right after all. **102m/C VHS, Beta.** *AU* Helen Buday, Sam Neill, Hugo Weaving; ***D:*** Stephen Wallace. *LIV*

For Love of Ivy ♪♪ **1968 (PG)** Poitier is a trucking executive who has a gambling operation on the side. Ivy is the Black maid of a rich white family who is about to leave her job to look for romance. The two are brought together but the road to true love doesn't run smooth. Based on a story by Poitier. **102m/C VHS, Beta.** Sidney Poitier, Abbey Lincoln, Beau Bridges, Carroll O'Connor, Nan Martin; ***D:*** Daniel Mann; ***M:*** Quincy Jones. Nominations: Academy Awards '68: Best Song ("For Love of Ivy"). *FOX*

For Love or Money ♪♪ **1963** A super-rich hotel owner wants her lawyer to find her three beautiful daughters. However, she doesn't trust him enough not to meddle in the search. Lavish production and a good cast can't overcome the mediocrity of the script and direction. **108m/C VHS.** Kirk Douglas, Mitzi Gaynor, Thelma Ritter, William Bendix, Julie Newmar, Gig Young, Leslie Parrish, William Windom, Dick Sargent; ***D:*** Michael Gordon. *NO*

For Love or Money ♪½ **1984** Made-for-television fare about game-show contestants finding money and romance. **91m/C VHS, Beta.** Jamie Farr, Suzanne Pleshette, Gil Gerard, Ray Walston, Lawrence Pressman, Mary Kay Place; ***D:*** Terry Hughes; ***M:*** Billy Goldenberg. *IME*

For Love or Money ♪♪ **1988 (PG)** A real estate man with Career on the mind has to choose between the woman in his life and the condo development that stands firmly between them and happily-ever-afterdom. **?m/C VHS.** Timothy Daly, Haviland Morris, Kevin McCarthy. *NO*

For Love or Money ♪♪½ **1993 (PG)** Struggling hotel concierge with a heart of gold finds himself doing little "favors" for a slimy entrepreneur who holds the key to his dreams—the cash to open an elegant hotel of his own. Romantic comedy is reminiscent of the classic screwball comedies of the '30s and '40s, but lacks the trademark tight writing and impeccable timing. Fox is appealing and likable as the wheeling and dealing concierge, a role undermined by a mediocre script offering too few laughs. **89m/C VHS, LV.** Michael J. Fox, Gabrielle Anwar, Isaac Mizrahi, Anthony Higgins, Michael Tucker, Bobby Short, Dan Hedaya, Bob Balaban, Udo Kier, Patrick Breen, Paula Laurence; ***D:*** Barry Sonnenfeld; ***W:*** Mark Rosenthal, Larry Konner; ***M:*** Bruce Broughton. *MCA*

For Me and My Gal ♪♪½ **1942** In his film debut, Kelly plays an opportunistic song-and-dance man who lures a young vaudevillian (Garland) away from her current partners. WWI interrupts both their career and romance, but you can count on them being reunited. Loaded with vintage tunes. ♫For Me and My Gal; They Go Wild, Simply Wild Over Me; The Doll Shop; Oh, Johnny, Oh; Oh, You Beautiful Doll; When You Wore A Tulip; Don't Leave Me Daddy; Do I Love You; By The Beautiful Sea. **104m/B VHS, Beta, LV.** Gene Kelly, Judy Garland, George Murphy, Martha Eggerth, Ben Blue, Richard Quine, Keenan Wynn, Stephen McNally; ***D:*** Busby Berkeley; ***M:*** George Bassman. Nominations: Academy Awards '42: Best Original Score. *MGM*

For Pete's Sake ♪♪ *July Pork Bellies* **1974 (PG)** Topsy-turvy comedy about a woman whose efforts to get together enough money to put her husband through school involve her with loan sharks, a madame, and even cattle rustling in New York City. Not one of Streisand's best. **90m/C VHS, Beta.** Barbra Streisand, Michael Sarrazin, Estelle Parsons, William Redfield, Molly Picon; ***D:*** Peter Yates; ***M:*** Artie Butler. *COL*

For Richer, For Poorer ♪½ *Father, Son and the Mistress* **1992 (PG)** A very rich, successful businessman notices his son is happy just to sit back and let dad earn all the dough while he waits for his share. In order to teach his son a lesson, Dad decides to give all his money away. But the plan backfires when both realize that earning a second fortune may not be as easy as they assumed. Below average made for cable fare. **90m/C VHS.** Jack Lemmon, Talia Shire, Joanna Gleason, Jonathan Silverman, Madeline Kahn, George Wyner; ***D:*** Jay Sandrich; ***W:*** Stan Daniels. *HBO*

For the Boys ♪♪ **1991 (R)** Midler stars as Dixie Leonard, a gutsy singer-comedian who hooks up with Eddie Sparks (Caan) to become one of America's favorite USO singing, dancing, and comedy teams. The movie spans 50 years and three wars—including Korea and Vietnam—and raises such issues as the blacklist and the role of politics in showbiz. Glitzy Hollywood entertainment falters despite Midler's strong performance. ♫Billy-A-Dick; Come Rain or Come Shine; In My Life; Stuff Like That There. **120m/C VHS.** Bette Midler, James Caan, George Segal, Patrick O'Neal, Christopher Rydell, Arye Gross, Norman Fell, Rosemary Murphy, Dori Brenner, Bud Yorkin, Jack Sheldon, Melissa Manchester, Brandon Call; ***Cameos:*** Arliss Howard; ***D:*** Mark Rydell; ***W:*** Marshall Brickman, Neal Jimenez, Lindy Laub; ***M:*** Dave Grusin. Golden Globe Awards '92: Best Actress—Musical/Comedy (Midler); Nominations: Academy Awards '91: Best Actress (Midler). *FXV*

For the First Time ♪♪½ **1959** In his last film, Lanza plays an opera singer who tours European cities to raise money for his deaf girlfriend's medical treatment. ♫Oh Mon Amour; Bavarian Drinking Song; Ave Maria; Vesti La Giubba; La Donna e Mobile; Niun Mi Tema; Grand March; O Solo Mio; Ich Liebe Dich. **97m/C VHS.** Mario Lanza, Zsa Zsa Gabor, Johanna von Koczian, Kurt Kasznar, Hans Sohnker, Peter Capell, Renzo Cesana, Sandro Giglio; ***D:*** Rudolph Mate; ***W:*** Andrew Solt. *MGM*

For the Love of Angela ♪½ **1986** Pretty and young shop clerk involves herself with both the shopkeeper and his son. **90m/C Beta.** Louis Jourdan. *PSM*

For the Love of Benji ♪♪ **1977 (G)** In this second "Benji" film, the adorable little dog accompanies his human family on a Greek vacation. He is kidnapped to be used as a messenger for a secret code, but escapes, to have a series of comic adventures in this entertaining family fare. **85m/C VHS, Beta.** Benji, Patsy Garrett, Cynthia Smith, Allen Finzat, Ed Nelson; ***D:*** Joe Camp; ***W:*** Joe Camp; ***M:*** Euel Box. *FCT, APD, BFV*

For the Love of It ♪½ **1980** Television stars galore try to hold together this farce about car chases in California, stolen secret documents, and (of course) true love. Outstandingly mediocre. Made for television. **100m/C VHS, Beta.** Deborah Raffin, Jeff Conaway, Tom Bosley, Norman Fell, Don Rickles, Henry Gibson, Noriyuki "Pat" Morita, William Christopher, Lawrence-Hilton Jacobs, Adrian Zmed, Barbi Benton, Adam West; **D:** Hal Kanter. *FRH*

For the Moment 🦴🦴½ **1994 (PG-13)** Aussie aviator Lachlan (Crowe) has joined the British Commonwealth Training Plan in 1942, a crash course for fighter pilots that drew men from several countries to bases across Canada. Stationed with best buddy Johnny (Outerbridge) in Manitoba, Lachlan falls for the married Lill (Hirt), sister of Johnny's honey Kate (McMillan), whose husband is away fighting. The emotional stakes are high for all concerned since they know the fliers will soon be sent off to combat. Old-fashioned (and sometimes slow-moving) romance with excellent performances and some gorgeous scenery. **120m/C VHS.** *CA* Russell Crowe, Christianne Hirt, Peter Outerbridge, Sara McMillan, Wanda Cannon, Scott Kraft; **D:** Aaron Kim Johnston; **W:** Aaron Kim Johnston; **C:** Ian Elkin; **M:** Victor Davies. *NYR*

For Those About to Rock: Monsters in Moscow 🦴🦴½ **1991 (R)** A tribute to the young people who defended Russia's new freedom during 1991's attempted coup. The first open-air festival-style concert ever to take place in Russia features the music of AC/DC, Metallica, The Black Crowes, Pantera, and Russia's Electro Shock Therapy. **84m/C VHS, Beta, LV. D:** Wayne Isham. *WAR, MVD, PMS*

For Us, the Living 🦴🦴🦴 **1988** The life and assassination of civil rights activist Medgar Evers are dramatically presented in this production of "American Playhouse" for PBS. Provides insight into Evers' character, not just a recording of the events surrounding his life. Adapted from the biography written by Evers' widow. **84m/C VHS, Beta.** Howard E. Rollins Jr., Rocky Aoki, Paul Winfield, Irene Cara, Margaret Avery, Roscoe Lee Browne, Laurence "Larry" Fishburne, Janet MacLachlan, Dick Anthony Williams; **D:** Michael A. Schultz. *MED, FCT*

For Whom the Bell Tolls 🦴🦴🦴½ **1943** Hemingway novel, gorgeously translated to the big screen, features a star-crossed romantic tale of derring-do. American schoolteacher Robert Jordan (Cooper) decides to join the Spanish Civil War and fight the fascists. He's ordered to rendezvous with peasant guerillas, to aid in blowing up a bridge, and in the rebel camp Jordan meets the beautiful Maria (Bergman). Lots of heroics (and some romance under the stars). Both leads were personally selected by the author. Originally released at 170 minutes. **130m/C VHS.** Gary Cooper, Ingrid Bergman, Akim Tamiroff, Katina Paxinou, Arturo de Cordova, Vladimir Sokoloff, Mikhail Rasumny, Fortunio Bonanova, Victor Varconi; **D:** Sam Wood; **W:** Dudley Nichols; **C:** Ray Rennahan; **M:** Victor Young. Academy Awards '43: Best Supporting Actress (Paxinou); Nominations: Academy Awards '43: Best Actor (Cooper), Best Actress (Bergman), Best Art Direction/Set Decoration (Color), Best Color Cinematography, Best Film Editing, Best Picture, Best Supporting Actor (Tamiroff), Best Score. *MCA*

For Your Eyes Only 🦴🦴🦴 **1981 (PG)** In this James Bond adventure, 007 must keep the Soviets from getting hold of a valuable instrument aboard a sunken British spy ship. Sheds the gadgetry of its more recent predecessors in the series in favor of some spectacular stunt work and the usual beautiful girl and exotic locale. Glen's first outing as director, though he handled second units on previous Bond films. Sheena Easton sang the hit title tune. **136m/C VHS, Beta, LV.** *GB* Roger Moore, Carole Bouquet, Chaim Topol, Lynn-Holly Johnson, Julian Glover, Cassandra Harris, Jill Bennett, Michael Gothard, John Wyman, Jack Hedley, Lois Maxwell, Desmond Llewelyn, Geoffrey Keen, Walter Gotell, Charles Dance; **D:** John Glen; **W:** Michael G. Wilson; **M:** Bill Conti. Nominations: Academy Awards '81: Best Song ("For Your Eyes Only"). *MGM, FOX, TLF*

For Your Love Only 🦴🦴 **1979** A beautiful young student falls in love with her teacher and is blackmailed, leading her to murder her tormentor. Soap opera made for German television. Dubbed in English. **90m/C VHS, Beta.** *GE* Nastassia Kinski, Christian Quadflieg, Judy Winter, Klaus Schwarzkopf; **D:** Wolfgang Petersen. *GLV*

Forbidden 🦴🦴½ **1985** In Nazi Germany, a German countess has an affair with a Jewish intellectual, and she winds up hiding him from the S.S. Based on the novel "The Last Jews of Berlin" by Leonard Gross. Slow made-for-cable movie. **116m/C VHS, Beta.** Jacqueline Bisset, Juergen Prochnow, Irene Worth, Peter Vaughan, Amanda Cannings, Avis Bunnage; **D:** Anthony Page; **W:** Leonard Gross. *SWC*

Forbidden Choices 🦴🦴 *The Beans of Egypt, Maine* **1994 (R)** Problems and attractions of the white trash Bean family as observed by enthralled neighbor girl Earlene (Plimpton). Hot-tempered Reuben Bean (Hauer) has just landed a long prison term, leaving his brood of nine in the care of lover Roberta (Lynch), who's also involved with Bean nephew Beal (McGaw). Downtrodden Earlene is only too eager to give in to handsome Beal's charms, leading to more heartbreak. Based on Carolyn Chute's novel "The Beans of Egypt, Maine." Directorial debut of Warren. **109m/C VHS, LV.** Martha Plimpton, Kelly Lynch, Rutger Hauer, Patrick McGaw, Richard Sanders; **D:** Jennifer Warren; **W:** Bill Phillips. Nominations: Independent Spirit Awards '95: Best Cinematography, Best Supporting Actress (Lynch). *WEA*

The Forbidden City 🦴🦴 **1918** San San is a young Chinese maiden who has the misfortune to fall in love with a Western diplomat. After he is sent away on business San San keeps secret the fact she has born her lover a child but her actions are unforgiven by her father, a deposed mandarin. **72m/B VHS, Beta.** Norma Talmadge, Thomas Meighan; **D:** Sidney Franklin. *VYY, GVV, GPV*

The Forbidden Dance *Woof!* **1990 (PG-13)** The first of several quickies released in 1990 applying hackneyed plots to the short-lived Lambada dance craze. The nonsensible plot has a Brazilian princess coming to the U.S. in order to stop further destruction of the rain forest. Instead, she winds up falling for a guy, teaching him to Lambada, and going on TV for a dance contest. Features an appearance by Kid Creole and the Coconuts. **90m/C VHS, Beta, LV.** Laura Herring, Jeff James, Sid Haig, Richard Lynch; **D:** Greydon Clark. *COL*

Forbidden Fruit 🦴🦴🦴 *Le Fruit Defendu* **1952** Widowed country doctor (Fernandel), who lives with his domineering mother (Sylvie), marries an equally demanding woman (Nollier) and then finds himself involved with a compliant young prostitute (Arnoul). Comic Fernandel does very well with his change of pace role as a man whose illusions of middle-class respectibility are destroyed. Based on "Letter a Mon Juge" by Georges Simenon. French with subtitles. **103m/B VHS.** *FR* Fernandel, Francoise Arnoul, Claude Nollier, Sylvie, Jacques Castelot; **D:** Henri Verneuil; **W:** Jacques Companeez, Jean Manse, Henri Verneuil; **C:** Henri Alekan; **M:** Paul Durand. *FCT*

Forbidden Games 🦴🦴🦴🦴 *Les Jeux Interdits* **1952** Famous anti-war drama about two French children play-acting the dramas of war amid the carnage of WWII. Young refugee Fossey sees her parents and dog killed. She meets a slightly older boy whose family takes the girl in. The children decide to bury the animals they have seen killed in the same way that people are buried—even stealing crosses from the cemetery to use over the animal graves. Eventually they are discovered and Fossey is again separated from her newfound home. Acclaimed; available in both dubbed and English-subtitled versions. **90m/B VHS, Beta, LV.** *FR* Brigitte Fossey, Georges Poujouly, Amedee, Louis Herbert; **D:** Rene Clement. Academy Awards '52: Best Foreign Language Film; British Academy Awards '53: Best Film; National Board of Review Awards '52: 5 Best Foreign Films of the Year; New York Film Critics Awards '52: Best Foreign Film; Venice Film Festival '52: Best Film; Nominations: Academy Awards '54: Best Story. *NOS, SUE, APD*

Forbidden Love 🦴 **1982** A man in his early 20's falls in love with a woman twice his age, much to the chagrin of her daughters. Made for television. **96m/C VHS, Beta.** Andrew Stevens, Yvette Mimieux, Dana Elcar, Lisa Lucas, Jerry Hauser, Randi Brooks, Lynn Carlin, Hildy Brooks, John Considine; **D:** Steven Hilliard Stern; **M:** Hagood Hardy. *CNG*

Forbidden Passion: The Oscar Wilde Movie 🦴🦴½ **1987** A British-made look at Wilde's later years, emphasizing his homosexuality and the Victorian repression that accompanied it. **120m/C VHS, Beta.** *GB* Michael Gambon, Robin Lermitte. *VMK*

Forbidden Planet 🦴🦴🦴½ **1956** In 2200 A.D., a space cruiser visits the planet Altair-4 to uncover the fate of a previous mission of space colonists. They are greeted by Robby the Robot and discover the only survivors of the Earth colony which has been preyed upon by a terrible space monster. A classic science fiction version of the Shakespearean classic "The Tempest." Laserdisc features formerly "cut" scenes, production and publicity photos, the original screen treatment, and special effects outtakes. **98m/C VHS, Beta, LV.** Walter Pidgeon, Anne Francis, Leslie Nielsen, Warren Stevens, Jack Kelly, Richard Anderson, Earl Holliman, George Wallace; **D:** Fred M. Wilcox; **M:** Bebe Barron, Louis Barron. *MGM, CRC*

Forbidden Sun 🦴 **1989 (R)** An Olympic gymnastics coach and her dozen beautiful students go to Crete to train. When one of them is brutally raped, vengeance is meted out by the girls. **88m/C VHS, Beta, LV.** Lauren Hutton, Cliff DeYoung, Renee Estevez; **D:** Zelda Barron. *ACA*

Forbidden Trails 🦴½ **1941** Rough Riders adventure has Silver the horse saving his owner from the vengeance of two outlaws. Two more heroes go under cover to bring the bad guys to justice. **60m/B VHS, Beta.** Buck Jones, Tim McCoy, Raymond Hatton; **D:** Robert North Bradbury. *NOS, VCN, DVT*

Forbidden World *Woof! Mutant* **1982 (R)** Lives of a genetic research team become threatened by the very life form they helped to create: a man-eating organism capable of changing its genetic structure as it grows and matures. Corman-produced quickie follow-up to "Galaxy of Terror" is a graphically violent rip-off of "Alien." **82m/C VHS, Beta, LV.** Jesse Vint, Dawn Dunlap, June Chadwick, Linden Chiles; **D:** Allan Holzman; **W:** Jim Wynorski, R.J. Robertson, Tim Curnen. *SUE*

Forbidden Zone 🦴½ **1980 (R)** A sixth dimension kingdom is ruled by the midget, King Fausto, and inhabited by dancing frogs, bikini-clad tootsies, robot boxers, and degraded beings of all kinds. Original music by Oingo Boingo, and directed by founding member Elfman. **75m/B VHS, Beta.** Herve Villechaize, Susan Tyrrell, Viva; **D:** Richard Elfman; **W:** Matthew Bright, Richard Elfman; **M:** Danny Elfman. *MED*

Forbidden Zone: Alien Abduction 🦴 **1996 (R)** Three babes sharing a sauna also share sexual confidences and discover they've each had an encounter with the same unusual man. Then one of the girls figures out they've had an alien encounter of the very close kind. **90m/C VHS.** Darcy Demoss, Pia Reyes, Dumitri Bogmaz, Carmen Lacatus, Alina Chivulescu, Florin Chiriac, Meredyth Holmes; **D:** Lucian S. Diamonde; **W:** Vernon Lumley; **C:** Adolfo Bartoli; **M:** Reg Powell. *AFE*

The Force 🦴🦴 **1994 (R)** Rookie LAPD cop Cal Warner (Gedrick) crosses paths with maverick homicide detective Des Flynn (Hudson), who's on the trail of a brutal killer. But when Flynn dies mysteriously, it's Cal who's haunted by bizarre dreams—and finding the truth could be equally deadly. **94m/C VHS, LV.** Jason Gedrick, Gary Hudson, Cyndi Pass, Kim Delaney. *REP*

Force Five 🦴🦴 **1975** A group of ex-cons form an anti-crime undercover force turning their skills toward justice. Nothing new in this made for television pilot. **78m/C VHS, Beta.** Gerald Gordon, Nicholas Pryor, James Hampton, David Spielberg, Leif Erickson, Bradford Dillman; **D:** Walter Grauman. *MED*

Force: Five 🦴 **1981 (R)** Mercenary gathers a group of like-minded action groupies together to rescue the daughter of a powerful man from a religious cult. All action and no brains. **95m/C VHS, Beta.** Joe Lewis, Pam Huntington, Master Bong Soo Han; **D:** Robert Clouse; **W:** Robert Clouse; **M:** William Goldstein. *MED*

Force of Evil 🦴🦴🦴 **1949** A cynical attorney who works for a mob boss and for Wall Street tries to save his brother from the gangster's takeover of the numbers operation. The honorable, though criminal, brother refuses the help of the amoral lawyer, and he is finally forced to confront his conscience. Garfield's sizzling performance and the atmospheric photography have made this a film noir classic. **82m/B VHS, LV.** John Garfield, Thomas Gomez, Marie Windsor, Sheldon Leonard, Roy Roberts; ***D:*** Abraham Polonsky; ***W:*** Abraham Polonsky; ***C:*** George Barnes. *REP*

Force of Evil 🦴 **1977** A paroled murderer returns to his hometown to brutalize the family that refused to fabricate an alibi for him. Made for television. **100m/C VHS, Beta, LV.** Lloyd Bridges, Eve Plumb, William Watson, Pat Crowley; ***D:*** Richard Lang. *WOV, GKK*

Force of Impulse 🦴🦴 **1960** J.D. schlocker featuring an impressive cast involved with everything from hot rods to robbery to parental problems. **?m/C VHS.** J. Carrol Naish, Robert Alda, Tony Anthony, Christina Crawford, Jody McCrea, Lionel Hampton. *SNC*

Force of One 🦴🦴 **1979 (PG)** A team of undercover narcotics agents is being eliminated mysteriously, and karate expert Norris saves the day in this sequel to "Good Guys Wear Black." **91m/C VHS, Beta.** Chuck Norris, Bill Wallace, Jennifer O'Neill, Clu Gulager; ***D:*** Paul Aaron. *MED*

Force on Thunder Mountain 🦴 **1977** A father and son go camping and encounter ancient Indian lore and flying saucers. **93m/C VHS, Beta.** Christopher Cain, Todd Dutson. *VCI*

Force 10 from Navarone 🦴🦴 **1978 (PG)** So-so sequel to Alistair MacLean's "The Guns of Navarone," follows a group of saboteurs whose aim is to blow up a bridge vital to the Nazi's in Yugoslavia. Keep an eye out for Ford, Nero, and Bach. Lots of double-crosses and action sequences, but doesn't quite hang together. **118m/C VHS, Beta, LV.** Robert Shaw, Harrison Ford, Barbara Bach, Edward Fox, Carl Weathers, Richard Kiel, Franco Nero; ***D:*** Guy Hamilton; ***W:*** Robin Chapman. *WAR, OM*

Forced Entry 🦴 *The Last Victim* **1975 (R)** Psychopathic killer-rapist hesitates over one of his victims, and she murders him instead. **92m/C VHS, Beta.** Tanya Roberts, Ron Max, Nancy Allen; ***D:*** Jim Sotos. *NO*

Forced March 🦴🦴½ **1990** On location in Hungary, an actor portrays a poet who fought in WWII and became a victim of the Holocaust. However, the deeper he gets into his role, the thinner the line between illusion and reality becomes. Flat drama. **104m/C VHS, Beta, LV.** Chris Sarandon, Renee Soutendijk, Josef Sommer, John Seitz; ***D:*** Rick King. *SGE, MOV, IME*

Forced to Kill 🦴½ **1993 (R)** A repo man is on his way to deliver a Jaguar when he's captured by a bizarre family and forced to fight in an illegal barefist tournament run by the local lunatic sheriff. Professional stuntman Eubanks has his work cut out for him in this actioner. **91m/C VHS, LV.** Corey Michael Eubanks, Michael Ironside, Rance Howard, Don Swayze, Clint Howard, Brian Avery, Kari Whitman, Mickey Jones, Carl Ciarfalio, Cynthia J. Blessington, Alan Gelfant; ***D:*** Russell Solberg; ***W:*** Corey Michael Eubanks; ***M:*** Martin D. Bolin. *PMH*

Forced Vengeance 🦴🦴 **1982 (R)** Vietnam vet pits himself against the underworld in Hong Kong. With Norris in the lead, you can take it for granted there will be plenty of martial arts action. **103m/C VHS, Beta.** Chuck Norris, Mary Louise Weller; ***D:*** James Fargo; ***M:*** William Goldstein. *MGM*

Ford: The Man & the Machine 🦴½ **1987** Episodic biography of ruthless auto magnate Henry Ford I from the building of his empire to his personal tragedies. The cast lacks spark and Robertson (Ford) is positively gloomy. The only one appearing to have any fun is Thomas (Ford's mistress). Based on the biography by Robert Lacey. **200m/C VHS.** Cliff Robertson, Hope Lange, Heather Thomas, Michael Ironside, Chris Wiggins, R.H. Thomson; ***D:*** Allan Eastman. *CAF*

Foreign Affairs 🦴🦴🦴 **1993** Vinnie Miller (Woodward) is a prim New England college teacher off to London on a research sabbatical. On the flight Vinnie's seatmate is boisterous good-ole-boy Chuck Mumpson (Dennehy), with whom she appears to have nothing in common. Naturally the two middle-aged romantics find a funny, though bittersweet, love together. A rather distracting subplot find's Vinnie's young colleague Fred (Stolz) involved in an affair with an older, eccentric British actress (Beacham). Based on the novel by Alison Lurie. Made for cable television. **100m/C VHS, LV.** Joanne Woodward, Brian Dennehy, Eric Stoltz, Stephanie Beacham, Ian Richardson, Robert Hands; ***D:*** Jim O'Brien; ***W:*** Chris Bryant. National Academy of Cable Programming ACE Awards '93: Best Actor (Dennehy). *TTC*

Foreign Body 🦴🦴½ **1986 (PG-13)** An Indian (played by "Passage to India" star, Banerjee) visiting London pretends to be a doctor and finds women flocking to him. Excellent overlooked British comedy. Based on the novel by Roderick Mann. **108m/C VHS.** *GB* Victor Banerjee, Warren Mitchell, Trevor Howard, Geraldine McEwan, Amanda Donohoe, Denis Quilley, Eve Ferret, Anna Massey; ***D:*** Ronald Neame; ***W:*** Celine La Freniere; ***M:*** Ken Howard. *HBO*

Foreign Correspondent 🦴🦴🦴🦴 **1940** A classic Hitchcock tale of espionage and derring-do. A reporter is sent to Europe during WWII to cover a pacifist conference in London, where he becomes romantically involved with the daughter of the group's founder and befriends an elderly diplomat. When the diplomat is kidnapped, the reporter uncovers a Nazi spy-ring headed by his future father-in-law. **120m/B VHS, Beta, LV.** Joel McCrea, Laraine Day, Herbert Marshall, George Sanders, Robert Benchley, Albert Basserman, Edmund Gwenn, Eduardo Ciannelli, Harry Davenport, Martin Kosleck, Charles Halton; ***D:*** Alfred Hitchcock; ***W:*** Robert Benchley, Charles Bennett, Joan Harrison, James Hilton; ***M:*** Alfred Newman. National Board of Review Awards '40: 10 Best Films of the Year; Nominations: Academy Awards '40: Best Black and White Cinematography, Best Interior Decoration, Best Original Screenplay, Best Picture, Best Supporting Actor (Basserman). *WAR*

A Foreign Field 🦴🦴½ **1993** Comedy/drama focuses on several WW2 veterans returning to the Normandy beaches in honor of the 50th anniversary of the invasion. Blustery British Cyril (McKern) and equally demanding Yank Waldo (Randolph) also must deal with their 50-year rivalry over their wartime love, the cheerfully vulgar Angelique (Moreau). Veteran performers get the chance to show their stuff but film descends into pathos. **90m/C VHS.** *GB* Leo McKern, John Randolph, Jeanne Moreau, Lauren Bacall, Alec Guinness, Edward Herrmann, Geraldine Chaplin; ***D:*** Charles Sturridge; ***W:*** Roy Clarke; ***M:*** Geoffrey Burgon. *FOX*

Foreign Student 🦴🦴½ **1994 (R)** In 1956 Philippe (Hofschneider) is a French exchange student at a tradition-bound Virginia college. At a professor's home he meets part-time housekeeper April (Givens), who wants to practice her schoolbook French (amongst other things). They begin a romance but, since April is black, there's trouble. Hofschneider is charming though Givens appears too glamorous and self-aware. Dutton and Battle are notable in their small roles as blues musicians Howlin' Wolf and Sonny Boy Williamson. Directorial debut for Sereny. Based on the novel "The Foreign Student" by Philippe Labro. **96m/C VHS.** Marco Hofschneider, Robin Givens, Jack Coleman, Edward Herrmann, Rick Johnson, Charlotte Ross, Charles S. Dutton, Hinton Battle; ***D:*** Eva Sereny; ***W:*** Menno Meyjes; ***M:*** Jean-Claude Petit. *MCA*

The Foreigner 🦴 **1978** Secret agent who comes to New York City to meet his contact becomes entrapped in a series of mysterious events revolving around the underground club scene. **90m/B VHS, Beta.** Eric Mitchell, Patti Astor, Deborah Harry; ***D:*** Amos Poe; ***W:*** Amos Poe. *FCT*

The Foreman Went to France 🦴½ *Somewhere in France* **1942** Industrial engineer travels to France during WWII to help prevent secret machinery from falling into the hands of the Nazis and their allies. **88m/B VHS, Beta.** *GB* Clifford Evans, Constance Cummings, Robert Morley; ***D:*** Charles Frend. *NOS, MRV, DVT*

Foreplay *Woof! The President's Women* **1975** Inane trilogy of comedy segments involving characters with White House connections. Stories are introduced by former President Mostel discussing his downfall in a television interview. Lame rather than risque, wasting talents of all involved. Each segment was scripted and directed by a different team. **100m/C VHS, Beta.** Pat Paulsen, Jerry Orbach, Estelle Parsons, Zero Mostel; ***D:*** Bruce Malmuth, John G. Avildsen; ***C:*** Ralf Bode. *LIV, VES*

The Forest 🦴 **1983** Spooks and a cannibalistic killer terrorize a group of campers. Nothing that hasn't been done countless times before. **90m/C VHS, Beta.** ***D:*** Donald M. Jones. *PSM*

Forest of Little Bear 🦴🦴 **1979** A man returns to his impoverished family in 1928 and decides to seek the reward put on the head of a one-eared man-eating bear. He kills the bear but faces a dilemma when he sees the bear left a helpless cub behind. In Japanese with English subtitles. **124m/C VHS.** *JP* ***D:*** Toshio Goto. *FCT*

Forever 🦴🦴½ **1978** A teenage girl experiences true love for the first time and struggles with its meaning. Made for television adaptation of Judy Blume's novel. **100m/C VHS.** Stephanie Zimbalist, Dean Butler, John Friedrich, Beth Raines, Diana Scarwid; ***D:*** John Korty. *GEM*

Forever: A Ghost of a Love Story 🦴🦴½ **1992 (R)** Coogan is a hot-shot music video director who moves into a haunted house and soon meets the resident ghost, who just happens to be a beautiful woman. He falls for the ghostly presence but his all-too-real female agent is also making her moves. **93m/C VHS, Beta.** Keith Coogan, Sean Young, Diane Ladd, Sally Kirkland, Terence Knox, Nicholas Guest, Renee Taylor, Steve Railsback; ***D:*** Thomas Palmer Jr.; ***W:*** Thomas Palmer Jr. *PSM*

Forever Amber 🦴🦴½ **1947** Seventeenth century rags to riches story features Darnell as the poverty stricken girl who uses sex to gain wealth and status. She makes it to the bed of King Charles II, only to lose the one man she ever really loved (Wilde). The censorship of the 1940s hindered the film's erotic potential. Adapted from the best-selling novel by Kathleen Winsor. **140m/C VHS.** Linda Darnell, Cornel Wilde, Richard Greene, George Sanders, Richard Haydn, Jessica Tandy, Anne Revere, John Russell, Leo G. Carroll, Robert Coote, Margaret Wycherly, Alma Kruger, Edmund Breon, Alan Napier, Bill Ward, Richard Bailey, Skelton Knaggs, Norma Varden, Edith Evanson, Ellen Corby; ***D:*** Otto Preminger; ***W:*** Philip Dunne, Ring Lardner Jr.; ***C:*** Leon Shamroy; ***M:*** David Raksin. *FXV*

Forever and a Day 🦴🦴🦴🦴 **1943** Tremendous salute to British history centers around a London manor originally built by an English admiral during the Napoleonic era and the exploits of succeeding generations. The house even manages to survive the blitz of WWII showing English courage during wartime. Once-in-a-lifetime casting and directing. **104m/B VHS.** Brian Aherne, Robert Cummings, Ida Lupino, Charles Laughton, Herbert Marshall, Ray Milland, Anna Neagle, Merle Oberon, Claude Rains, Victor McLaglen, Buster Keaton, Jessie Matthews, Roland Young, Sir C. Aubrey Smith, Edward Everett Horton, Elsa Lanchester, Edmund Gwenn; ***D:*** Rene Clair, Edmund Goulding, Cedric Hardwicke, Frank Lloyd, Victor Saville, Robert Stevenson, Herbert Wilcox, Kent Smith; ***W:*** Charles Bennett, Michael Hogan, Peter Godfrey, Christopher Isherwood, Gene Lockhart, Donald Ogden Stewart. *HTV, MLB, TPV*

Forever Darling 🦴🦴 **1956** Mixed effort from the reliable comedy duo sees Desi playing a dedicated chemist who neglects his wife while pursuing the next great pesticide. Lucy calls on her guardian angel (Mason) to help her rekindle her marriage. He advises her to go with Desi when he tests his new bug killer, and a series of hilarious, woodsy calamities occur. Lucy and Desi are always fun to watch, but '60s TV sitcom fans will enjoy the fact that Mrs. Howell (Schaefer) and Jane Hathaway (Kulp) appear in the same picture. **91m/C VHS, Beta.** Lucille Ball, Desi Arnaz

Sr., James Mason, Louis Calhern, John Emery, John Hoyt, Natalie Schafer, Nancy Kulp; **D:** Alexander Hall. *MGM, CCB*

Forever Emmanuelle 🦴 **1982 (R)** Sensual young woman finds love and the ultimate erotic experience in the wilds of the South Pacific in this sequel to the porn-with-production-values "Emmanuelle." **89m/C VHS, Beta, LV.** Annie Belle, Emmanuelle Arsan, Al Cliver. *LIV, VES*

Forever Evil 🦴 **1987** The vacationing denizens of a secluded cabin are almost killed off by the cult followers of a mythic god. **107m/C VHS, Beta.** Red Mitchell, Tracey Huffman, Charles Trotter, Howard Jacobsen, Kent Johnson. *VCI*

Forever Female 🦴🦴🦴 **1953** Bright comedy about show business, egos, and love. Holden is a young playwright whose first play is accepted by stage producer Douglas on the condition that the lead role, featuring a 19-year-old heroine, be rewritten for his ex-wife Rogers. She's an aging leading lady smitten by Holden's charms—as is the ingenue Crowley, who would be perfect for the role as written. Complications and manipulations abound as the play makes its way to production. Adaptation of the Sir James Barrie play "Rosalind." **93m/B VHS.** Ginger Rogers, William Holden, Paul Douglas, Pat Crowley, James Gleason, Jesse White, George Reeves, Marjorie Rambeau, King Donovan, Vic Perrin, Marion Ross; **D:** Irving Rapper; **W:** Julius J. Epstein, Philip C. Epstein. *PAR*

Forever James Dean **1988** A profile of the legendary actor/cult hero, examining his life, short career and remaining legacy. Also includes the original previews of his three feature films. A must for serious Dean fans. **69m/C VHS, Beta.** James Dean, Julie Harris, William Bast, Kenneth Kendall; **D:** Ara Chekmayan. *WAR, FCT*

Forever, Lulu 🦴 *Crazy Streets* **1987 (R)** A down-on-her-luck novelist winds up involved with the mob and a gangster's girlfriend. Completely laughless comedy with amateurish direction. **86m/C VHS, Beta, LV.** Hanna Schygulla, Deborah Harry, Alec Baldwin, Annie Golden, Paul Gleason, Dr. Ruth Westheimer; **D:** Amos Kollek. *COL*

Forever Mary 🦴🦴🦴 *Mery per Sempre* **1989** A teacher tries to better the lives of the boys sentenced to a reformatory in Palermo, Sicily, when a teenage transvestite prostitute (the title character) is admitted to the school. In Italian with English subtitles. **100m/C VHS.** *IT* Michele Placido, Alesandro DiSanzo, Francesco Benigno; **D:** Marco Risi; **W:** Sandro Petraglia. *CCN, INJ*

Forever Young 🦴🦴 **1985** A young boy immerses himself in Catholicism. Admiring a priest, he is unaware that the priest's friend is involved with his mother. Tangled, but delicate handling of the coming-of-age story. Made originally for British television. **85m/C VHS, Beta.** *GB* James Aubrey, Nicholas Gecks, Alec McCowen; **D:** David Drury; **W:** Ray Connelly. *MGM*

Forever Young 🦴🦴½ **1992 (PG)** When test pilot Gibson's girlfriend is hit by a car and goes into a coma, he volunteers to be cryogenically frozen for one year. Oops!—he's left frozen for fifty years, until he is accidentally thawed out by a couple of kids. Predictable, designed to be a tear jerker, though it serves mostly as a star vehicle for Gibson who bumbles with 90s technology, finds his true love, and escapes from government heavies, adorable as ever. Through all the schmaltz, the relationship Gibson develops with the young Wood turns out to be the most authentic and endearing love in the film. **102m/C VHS, LV, 8mm.** Mel Gibson, Jamie Lee Curtis, Elijah Wood, Isabel Glasser, George Wendt, Joe Morton, Nicolas Surovy, David Marshall Grant, Art LaFleur; **D:** Steve Miner; **W:** Jeffrey Abrams; **M:** Jerry Goldsmith. *WAR, BTV*

Forger of London 🦴🦴 **1961** Edgar Wallace tale in which Scotland Yard investigates a counterfeit ring connected to a prime suspect, an amnesiac playboy. **91m/C VHS.** *GE* Eddi Arent, Karin Dor, Viktor de Kowa, Hellmut Lange, Robert Graf; **D:** Harald Reinl. *SNC*

Forget Mozart 🦴🦴 *Zabudnite na Mozarta* **1985** On the day of Mozart's death, the head of the secret police gathers a group together for questioning. They include the composer's wife, his lyricist, the head of a Masonic lodge, and Salieri, Mozart's rival. Each has a different story to tell to the investigator about the composer's life and death. The film makes use of a number of sets and costumes from "Amadeus" and was also filmed on location in Prague. In German with English subtitles. **93m/C VHS.** *GE* Armin Mueller-Stahl, Catarina Raacke; **D:** Salvo Luther. *WBF*

Forget Paris 🦴🦴½ **1995 (PG-13)** Pro basketball referee Mickey (Crystal) and airline executive Ellen (Winger) meet in Paris, fall in love and get married. But once the honeymoon is over, the marital bliss unravels due to conflicting work schedules and the lack of romantic scenery. This look at yuppie love and courtship finds Crystal in pre-"City Slickers 2" form, launching three-point one-liners and "When Harry Met Sally" sentiment. Bland direction and an obligation to be cute intensify the "been-there-seen-that" feeling. Winger's presence may hint of miscasting, but she has one of the films funniest scenes involving a stray pet and a pigeon. **101m/C VHS, LV.** Billy Crystal, Debra Winger, Joe Mantegna, Cynthia Stevenson, Richard Masur, Julie Kavner, William Hickey, Cathy Moriarty, John Spencer; **D:** Billy Crystal; **W:** Billy Crystal, Lowell Ganz, Babaloo Mandel; **C:** Kent Beyda; **M:** Marc Shaiman. *COL*

The Forgotten 🦴🦴 **1989** After 17 years as POWs, six Green Berets are freed, only to face a treacherous government conspiracy aimed at eliminating them. Made for television. **96m/C VHS, Beta, LV.** Keith Carradine, Steve Railsback, Stacy Keach, Pepe Serna, Don Opper, Richard Lawson; **D:** James Keach; **W:** Keith Carradine, Steve Railsback, James Keach. *PAR*

The Forgotten One 🦴½ **1989 (R)** An uninspired author and a female reporter become mixed up in a century-old murder and the restless ghost it spawned. **89m/C VHS, Beta, LV.** Kristy McNichol, Terry O'Quinn, Blair Parker, Elisabeth Brooks; **D:** Phillip Badger. *ACA*

Forgotten Prisoners 🦴🦴 *Forgotten Prisoners: The Amnesty Files* **1990 (R)** Celluloid proof that conviction and true grit do not always entertainment make. Greenwald—whose credits range from "Xanadu" to "The Burning Bed"—directed this righteous but stationary drama about an Amnesty International official (Silver) who's assigned to look into the incarceration and egregious mistreatment of Turkish citizens. Made for cable TV. **92m/C VHS, Beta.** Ron Silver, Roger Daltrey, Hector Elizondo; **D:** Robert Greenwald; **M:** Brad Fiedel. *TTC, FCT*

A Forgotten Tune for the Flute 🦴🦴🦴 **1988** A delightful, Glasnost-era romantic comedy. A bureaucrat caught up in a dull, stuffy existence has a heart attack and winds up falling in love with his nurse. He then must decide between his comfortable, cared-for life or the love which beckons him. In Russian with English subtitles. **131m/C VHS, Beta, LV.** *RU* Leonid Filatov, Tatiana Dogileva, Irina Kupchenko; **D:** Edgar Ryazanov. *FRH, INJ*

Forgotten Warrior 🦴½ **1986 (R)** Vengeance is the name of the game as a Vietnam vet tracks down the fellow officer who tried to kill him and shot his commander. **76m/C VHS, Beta.** Quincy Frazer, Sam T. Lapuzz, Ron Marchini, Joe Meyer; **D:** Nick Cacas, Charlie Ordonez. *NO*

Forlorn River 🦴½ **1937** Nevada and Weary, two law-abiding men, seek to return their hometown to peace by eliminating a gang of outlaws. Based on a novel by Zane Grey. **62m/B VHS.** Buster Crabbe, June Martel, John D. Patterson, Harvey Stephens, Chester Conklin, Lew Kelly, Syd Saylor; **D:** Charles T. Barton. *NOS, DVT, RXM*

The Formula 🦴½ **1980 (R)** Convoluted story about a secret formula for synthetic fuel that meanders it's way from the end of WWII to the present. A U.S. soldier waylays, and then joins forces with, a German general entrusted with the formula. Years later, after the American is murdered, his friend, a hard-nosed L.A. cop, starts investigating, meeting up with spies and a reclusive oil billionaire. Scott and Brando have one good confrontation scene but the rest of the movie is just hot air. From the novel by Steve Shagan. **117m/C VHS, Beta.** Marlon Brando, George C. Scott, Marthe Keller, G.D. Spradlin, Beatrice Straight, John Gielgud, Richard Lynch; **D:** John G. Avildsen; **M:** Bill Conti. Nominations: Academy Awards '80: Best Cinematography. *MGM*

Formula for a Murder 🦴 **1985** A very rich but paralyzed woman marries a scheming con artist who plots to kill her and inherit everything. **89m/C VHS, Beta.** Christina Nagy, David Warbeck, Rossano Brazzi. *LIV*

Forrest Gump 🦴🦴🦴🦴 **1994 (PG-13)** Grandly ambitious and slightly flawed, amounting to a wonderful bit of movie magic. As the intelligence-impaired Gump with a heart of gold and more than enough character and dignity, Hanks supplies another career highlight. Field contributes a nice turn as his dedicated mama (they were last together in "Punchline"), while Sinise is particularly effective as a handicapped Vietnam veteran with a bad attitude. Incredible special effects put Gump in the middle of historic events over a four decade period, but the real story is the life-affirming, non-judgmental power of Gump to transform the lives of those around him. From the novel by Winston Groom. **142m/C VHS, Beta.** Tom Hanks, Robin Wright, Sally Field, Gary Sinise, Mykelti Williamson; **D:** Robert Zemeckis; **W:** Eric Roth; **C:** Don Burgess. Academy Awards '94: Best Actor (Hanks), Best Adapted Screenplay, Best Director (Zemeckis), Best Film Editing, Best Picture, Best Visual Effects; Chicago Film Critics Awards '94: Best Actor (Hanks); Directors Guild of America Awards '94: Best Director (Zemeckis); Golden Globe Awards '95: Best Actor—Drama (Hanks), Best Director (Zemeckis), Best Film—Drama; National Board of Review Awards '94: Best Actor (Hanks), Best Film, Best Supporting Actor (Sinise); Writers Guild of America '94: Best Adapted Screenplay; Blockbuster Entertainment Awards '95: Movie, Theatrical, Drama Actor, Theatrical (Hanks); Nominations: Academy Awards '94: Best Art Direction/Set Decoration, Best Cinematography, Best Makeup, Best Sound, Best Supporting Actor (Sinise), Best Original Score; Golden Globe Awards '95: Best Screenplay, Best Supporting Actor (Sinise), Best Supporting Actress (Wright), Best Original Score; MTV Movie Awards '95: Best Film, Best Male Performance (Hanks), Breakthrough Performance (Williamson). *PAR*

Forsaking All Others 🦴🦴½ **1935** Screwball comedy featuring several MGM superstars. Friends since childhood, Gable has been in love with Crawford for 20 years, but she never realizes it and plans to marry Montgomery. Crawford is very funny in this delightful story of a wacky romantic triangle. **84m/B VHS.** Joan Crawford, Clark Gable, Robert Montgomery, Charles Butterworth, Billie Burke, Rosalind Russell, Frances Drake; **D:** Woodbridge S. Van Dyke; **W:** Joseph L. Mankiewicz. *MGM*

Fort Apache 🦴🦴🦴½ **1948** The first of director Ford's celebrated cavalry trilogy, in which a fanatical colonel (Fonda) leads his reluctant men to an eventual slaughter, recalling George Custer at Little Big Horn. In residence: Ford hallmarks of spectacular landscapes and stirring action, as well as many vignettes of life at a remote outpost. Don't forget to catch "She Wore a Yellow Ribbon" and "Rio Grande," the next films in the series. Also available in a colorized version. **125m/B VHS, Beta, LV.** John Wayne, Henry Fonda, Shirley Temple, John Agar, Pedro Armendariz Sr., Victor McLaglen, Ward Bond, Anna Lee; **D:** John Ford; **C:** Archie Stout. *TTC, TLF*

Fort Apache, the Bronx 🦴🦴🦴 **1981 (R)** A police drama set in the beleaguered South Bronx of New York City, based on the real-life experiences of two former New York cops who served there. Newman is a decent cop who goes against every kind of criminal and crazy and against his superiors in trying to bring law and justice to a downtrodden community. **123m/C VHS, Beta, LV.** Paul Newman, Ed Asner, Ken Wahl, Danny Aiello, Rachel Ticotin, Pam Grier, Kathleen Beller; **D:** Daniel Petrie; **W:** Heywood Gould. *WAR, VES, CCB*

Fort Saganne 🦴🦴 **1984** Charles Saganne (Depardieu), a soldier from a peasant background, is posted to the French Sahara, where he becomes a natural leader. He gains fame and fortune, marries, and then WWI begins. Good, if cliched, adventure saga. Based on the novel by Louis Gardel. French with subtitles. **180m/C VHS.** *FR* Gerard Depardieu, Catherine Deneuve, Philippe Noiret, Sophie Marceau, Michael Duchaussoy; ***D:*** Alain Corneau; ***W:*** Alain Corneau, Louis Gardel; ***M:*** Philippe Sarde. *CVC*

Fortress ♂ **1985 (R)** A teacher and her class are kidnapped from their one-room schoolhouse in the Australian outback. They must use their ingenuity and wits to save their lives in this violent made-for-cable-television suspense drama. **90m/C VHS, Beta.** *AU* Rachel Ward, Sean Garlick, Rebecca Rigg; ***D:*** Arch Nicholson; ***M:*** Danny Beckerman. *CNG, HBO*

Fortress ♂♂ **1993 (R)** How come the future is never a place you'd want to be? Thanks to overpopulation a woman is only allowed one pregnancy. When John and Karen Brennick are caught trying to have a second child they are shipped to the Fortress, an underground prison in the middle of the desert. Discipline is enforced with numerous sadistic toys, including the intestinator, so-called because it's implanted in the stomach of each prisoner and infractions result in excruciating laser-activated pain. Lambert does well with his action hero but it's character actor Smith as the warden, a techno-human with some sick fantasies, who has the real fun in this horrific depiction of the future. **91m/C VHS, LV.** Christopher Lambert, Kurtwood Smith, Loryn Locklin, Lincoln Kilpatrick; ***D:*** Stuart Gordon; ***W:*** Steve Feinberg, Troy Neighbors, Terry Curtis Fox. *LIV*

Fortress of Amerikka ♂½ **1989** In the not-too-distant future, mercenaries get their hands on a secret weapon that could allow them to take over the USA. **?m/C VHS.** Gene Le Brock, Kellee Bradley. *IMP*

Fortune and Men's Eyes ♂♂ **1971 (R)** Exploitative and depressing film about life in a Canadian prison. A naive young man is sent to prison for marijuana possession and has to make a difficult choice—be regularly sodomized by a man who will protect him or be raped by everyone else. Based on the play by John Herbert. **102m/C VHS.** Wendell Burton, Michael Greer, Zooey Hall, Danny Freedman; ***D:*** Harvey Hart; ***W:*** John Herbert. *MGM*

The Fortune Cookie ♂♂♂ *Meet Whiplash Willie* **1966** After receiving a minor injury during a football game, a TV cameraman is convinced by his seedy lawyer brother-in-law to exaggerate his injury and start an expensive lawsuit. A classic, biting comedy by Wilder. First of several Lemmon-Matthau comedies. The letterbox laserdisc version contains the original theatrical trailer. **125m/B VHS, Beta, LV.** Jack Lemmon, Walter Matthau, Ron Rich, Cliff Osmond, Judi West, Lurene Tuttle; ***D:*** Billy Wilder; ***W:*** Billy Wilder, I.A.L. Diamond; ***C:*** Joseph LaShelle; ***M:*** Andre Previn. Academy Awards '66: Best Supporting Actor (Matthau); Nominations: Academy Awards '66: Best Art Direction/Set Decoration (B & W), Best Black and White Cinematography, Best Story & Screenplay. *FOX, MGM, FCT*

Fortune Dane ♂½ **1986 (PG)** Police detective Fortune Dane goes undercover to clear his name after he is framed for murder. **83m/C VHS, Beta.** Carl Weathers, Adolph Caesar; ***D:*** Nicholas Sgarro; ***W:*** Charles Correll. *VMK*

Fortune's Fool ♂♂ **1921** A beef king and profiteer marries a younger woman and soon discovers the problems that ambition can cause. Silent. **60m/B VHS, Beta.** *GE* Emil Jannings, Daguey Servaes, Reinhold Schunzel; ***D:*** Reinhold Schunzel. *NOS, MRV, VYY*

Fortunes of War ♂♂♂ **1987** British professor Guy Pringle arrives with his bride, Harriet, to take up a teaching post in the Balkans in 1939. The idealistic Guy soon becomes enmeshed in anti-fascist politics and involved with the local members of the British embassy. When threatened by war they travel to Athens and then Cairo, where Guy's increasing involvement in the political situation, and his neglect of Harriet, causes a crisis in their marriage. Slow-moving drama with some self-centered characters is redeemed by the acting skills of those involved. Based on the autobiographial novels of Olivia Manning. Originally shown on "Masterpiece Theater" on PBS. **160m/C VHS.** *GB* Kenneth Branagh, Emma Thompson, Rupert Graves, Ronald Pickup, Robert Stephens, Charles Kay, James Villiers, Harry Burton, Ciaran Madden, Diana Hardcastle, Greg Hicks, Alan Bennett, Jeremy Brundell, Jeremy Sinden; ***D:*** James Cellan Jones; ***W:*** Alan Plater. *FOX, FCT, TVC*

Fortunes of War ♂♂ **1994 (R)** Peter Kernan (Salinger) is a burned-out relief worker in Thailand. Desperate for money, he agrees to smuggle a rare medicine across the Cambodian border to a rural war lord. Travelling with refugee Khoy Thoun (Ngor) and French Red Cross worker, Johanna (Jenkins), Peter begins to realize his need to do the right thing, even if the cost is high. Filmed on location in Manila. **107m/C VHS, LV.** Matt Salinger, Michael Ironside, Haing S. Ngor, Sam Jenkins, Martin Sheen, Michael Nouri; ***D:*** Thierry Notz; ***W:*** Mark Lee. *COL*

Forty Carats ♂♂½ **1973 (PG)** Ullmann plays the just-turned forty divorcee who has a brief fling with the half-her-age Albert while on vacation in Greece. She figures she'll never see him again but, back in New York, he turns up on the arm of her beautiful daughter (Raffin). Except he's still interested in mom. The rest of the movie is spent trying to convince Ullmann that love can conquer all. Ullmann's very attractive but not well-suited for the part; Raffins's screen debut. Based on the Broadway hit. **110m/C VHS, Beta.** Liv Ullmann, Edward Albert, Gene Kelly, Binnie Barnes, Deborah Raffin, Nancy Walker; ***D:*** Milton Katselas; ***W:*** Jay Presson Allen; ***C:*** Charles B(ryant) Lang. *COL*

Forty Days of Musa Dagh ♂♂ **1985** Based on the true story of Armenia's fight for freedom against Turkey in the 1914 uprising and the dreadful cost. From the novel by Franz Werfel. **120m/C VHS, Beta.** Michael Constantine, David Opatoshu. *VCD*

The Forty-Niners ♂ **1932** A forgettable oater about the hysteria surrounding the finding of gold in California. **59m/B VHS.** Tom Tyler, Betty Mack, Alan Bridge, Fern Emmett, Gordon Wood, Frank Ball; ***D:*** John P. McCarthy. *DVT, HEG, GPV*

The Forty-Ninth Parallel ♂♂♂ *The Invaders* **1941** Six Nazi servicemen, seeking to reach neutral American land, are trapped and their U-boat sunk by Royal Canadian Air Force bombers, forcing them into Canada on foot, where they run into an array of stalwart patriots. Dated wartime propaganda made prior to the U.S. entering the war; riddled with entertaining star turns. **90m/B VHS, Beta, LV.** *GB* Laurence Olivier, Leslie Howard, Eric Portman, Raymond Massey, Glynis Johns, Finlay Currie, Anton Walbrook; ***D:*** Michael Powell; ***W:*** Emeric Pressburger, Rodney Ackland. *NO*

40 Pounds of Trouble ♂♂½ **1962** Lake Tahoe casino/hotel manager Steve McCluskey (Curtis) likes to avoid complications in his life. But first he's charmed by his boss' niece Chris (Pleshette), the hotel's new headliner, and then he becomes a surrogate father to five-year-old Penny (Wilcox), abandoned by her debt-ridden dad. So what does Steve decide to do? Why take them to Disneyland, of course! Director Jewison's feature film debut. **106m/C VHS.** Tony Curtis, Suzanne Pleshette, Claire Wilcox, Phil Silvers, Larry Storch, Howard Morris, Stubby Kaye, Edward Andrews, Mary Murphy, Kevin McCarthy, Sharon Farrell; ***D:*** Norman Jewison; ***W:*** Marion Hargrove; ***M:*** Mort Lindsay. *MCA*

Forty Thousand Horsemen ♂♂½ **1941** The story of the ANZACS of Australia, created to fight Germany in the Middle East during WWII. This Australian war drama is full of cavalry charges, brave young lads, and "Waltzing Matilda." **86m/B VHS, Beta.** *AU* Chips Rafferty, Grant Taylor, Betty Bryant, Pat Twohill. *VYY, FCT*

42nd Street ♂♂♂♂ **1933** A Broadway musical producer faces numerous problems in his efforts to reach a successful opening night. Choreography by Busby Berkeley. A colorized version of the film is also available. ♫You're Getting to Be a Habit With Me; Shuffle Off to Buffalo; Young and Healthy; Forty-Second Street; It Must Be June. **89m/B VHS, Beta, LV.** Warner Baxter, Ruby Keeler, Bebe Daniels, George Brent, Dick Powell, Guy Kibbee, Ginger Rogers, Una Merkel, Busby Berkeley, Ned Sparks, George E. Stone; ***D:*** Lloyd Bacon; ***W:*** Rian James, James Seymour; ***M:*** Harry Warren, Al Dubin. Nominations: Academy Awards '33: Best Picture, Best Sound. *MGM, FOX, HMV*

47 Ronin, Part 1 ♂♂♂ *The Loyal 47 Ronin; 47 Samurai* **1942** Turn of the 18th-century epic chronicling the samurai legend. The warriors of Lord Asano set out to avenge their leader, tricked into committing a forced seppuku, or hara-kiri. The photography is generously laden with views of 18th century gardens as well as panoramic vistas. This is the largest and most popular film of the Kabuki version of the story by Seika Mayama. In Japanese with English subtitles. **111m/C VHS.** *JP* ***D:*** Kenji Mizoguchi. *INJ*

47 Ronin, Part 2 ♂♂♂ **1942** Second half of the film in which the famous Japanese folklore tale of Lord Asano and his warriors is told. The film follows Asano's samurai as they commit themselves to avenging their leader in 1703. In Japanese with English subtitles. **108m/C VHS.** *JP* ***D:*** Kenji Mizoguchi. *INJ*

48 Hrs. ♂♂♂ **1982 (R)** An experienced San Francisco cop (Nolte) springs a convict (Murphy) from jail for 48 hours to find a vicious murdering drug lord. Murphy's film debut is great and Nolte is perfect as his gruff foil. **97m/C VHS, Beta, LV.** Nick Nolte, Eddie Murphy, James Remar, Annette O'Toole, David Patrick Kelly, Sonny Landham, Brion James, Denise Crosby; ***D:*** Walter Hill; ***W:*** Walter Hill, Larry Gross, Steven E. de Souza, Roger Spottiswoode; ***M:*** James Horner. *PAR*

48 Hours to Live ♂ *Man in the Middle* **1960** A reporter travels to a nuclear scientist's secluded island only to find the scientist held hostage by nuclear weapon-seeking terrorists. **86m/B VHS, Beta.** Anthony Steel, Ingemar Johannson, Marlies Behrens. *NO*

Foul Play ♂♂ **1976** Bearing no similarity to the Goldie Hawn vehicle of the same name, this Polish crimer is based on a true story, and stars two of Poland's Olympic boxers. A young man, accused of theft, is coerced by the Warsaw police to go undercover in return for having the charges against him dropped. With English subtitles. **98m/C VHS.** *PL* Marek Powowski, Jan Szcepanski, Jerzy Kulej. *FCT*

Foul Play ♂♂♂ **1978 (PG)** Hawn is a librarian who picks up a hitchhiker which leads to nothing but trouble. She becomes involved with San Francisco detective Chase in an effort to expose a plot to kill the Pope during his visit to the city. Also involved is Moore as an English orchestra conductor with some kinky sexual leanings. Chase is charming (no mugging here) and Hawn both bubbly and brave. A big winner at the box office; features Barry Manilow's hit tune "Ready to Take a Chance Again." **116m/C VHS, Beta, LV, 8mm.** Goldie Hawn, Chevy Chase, Dudley Moore, Burgess Meredith, Billy Barty, Rachel Roberts, Eugene Roche, Brian Dennehy, Chuck McCann, Bruce Solomon; ***D:*** Colin Higgins; ***M:*** Charles Fox. Nominations: Academy Awards '78: Best Song ("Ready to Take a Chance Again"). *PAR*

Found Alive ♂ **1934** After a painful divorce, a woman kidnaps her son and steals away into the Mexican jungle, with only the help of her faithful butler. **65m/B VHS, Beta.** Barbara Bedford, Maurice Murphy, Robert Frazer, Edwin Cross; ***D:*** Charles Hutchinson. *SNC*

The Fountainhead ♂♂♂ **1949** Cooper is an idealistic, uncompromising architect who refuses to change his designs. When he finds out his plans for a public housing project have been radically altered he blows up the building and winds up in court defending his actions. Neal is the sub-plot love interest. Based on the novel by Ayn Rand. **113m/C VHS, Beta.** Gary Cooper, Patricia Neal, Raymond Massey, Ray Collins, Henry Hull; ***D:*** King Vidor; ***C:*** Robert Burks; ***M:*** Max Steiner. *MGM, FOX*

Four Adventures of Reinette and Mirabelle ♂♂♂ **1989** Small but touching Rohmer tale of the friendship between two women—one a naive country girl (Miquel, as Reinette), the other a sophisticated Parisian (Forde, as Mirabelle)—who share an apartment and a number of experiences, but who have a very different manner of inhabiting those experiences. A thoroughly French human comedy, one of Rohmer's better studies. In French with English subtitles. **95m/C VHS.** *FR* Joelle Miquel, Jessica

Forde, Philippe Laudenbach, Marie Riviere, Beatrice Romand, Yasmine Haury; ***D:*** Eric Rohmer; ***W:*** Eric Rohmer. *NYF, FCT, INJ*

Four Bags Full ½ **1956** A bitter comedy about two smugglers during WWII who try to get a slaughtered pig to the black market under the Nazis' noses. In French with English subtitles. **82m/C VHS, Beta.** *FR* Jean Gabin, Louis de Funes, Bourvil, Jeanette Batti; ***D:*** Claude Autant-Lara. *VDM, FCT*

Four Daughters **1938** Classic, three-hankie outing in which four talented daughters of music professor Rains fall in love and marry. Garfield shines, in a role tailor-made for him, as the world-weary suitor driven to extremes in the name of love. Great performances from all. Based on the novel "Sister Act" by Fannie Hurst. **90m/B VHS.** Claude Rains, John Garfield, May Robson, Priscilla Lane, Lola Lane, Rosemary Lane, Gale Page, Dick Foran, Jeffrey Lynn; ***D:*** Michael Curtiz; ***M:*** Max Steiner. Nominations: Academy Awards '38: Best Director (Curtiz), Best Picture, Best Screenplay, Best Sound, Best Supporting Actor (Garfield). *MGM, CCB*

Four Days in July **1985** Two couples from Belfast, one Catholic and one Protestant, find they have something in common when they meet in the maternity ward as both couples become first-time parents. Script and dialog were mainly improvised, which provides both dull stretches and the film's charm. Made for British television. **99m/C VHS.** *GB* Des McAleer, Brid Brennan, Charles Lawson, Paula Hamilton, Shane Connaughton, Eileen Pollock, Stephen Rea; ***D:*** Mike Leigh. *WBF, BTV*

Four Deuces ½ **1975** Gang war is underway between the Chico Hamilton mob and Vic Morano and the Four Deuces during the Depression. Comedy and action combine with elements of strong language, strong sex, and strong violence. **87m/C VHS, Beta.** Jack Palance, Carol Lynley, Warren Berlinger, Adam Roarke; ***D:*** William H. Bushnell Jr. *VTR*

Four Eyes and Six Guns ½ **1993** In 1882 a New York optometrist, who's a fan of the popular dime-store western novels, moves to Tombstone, Arizona in search of adventure. He's just in time too because Sheriff Wyatt Earp is trying to rid the town of those pesky Doom Brothers but is having a problem with his eyesight (causing his gunshots to go astray). Now if the greenhorn can just get Earp to wear his new glasses. Silly but harmless fluff. Made for cable television. **92m/C VHS, Beta.** Judge Reinhold, Patricia Clarkson, Dan Hedaya, M. Emmet Walsh, Austin Pendleton, Fred Ward; ***D:*** Piers Haggard; ***W:*** Leon Prochnik. *TTC*

Four Faces West ½ *They Passed This Way* **1948** McCrea is an honest rancher who nevertheless robs the local bank in order to save his father's ranch from foreclosure. His humanity in helping a diphtheria-ridden family leads to his capture, but the sheriff promises a light sentence, since he is not a typical bad guy. Fine performances strengthen this low-key western. **90m/B VHS.** Joel McCrea, Frances Dee, Charles Bickford; ***D:*** Alfred E. Green. *REP*

The Four Feathers **1939** A grand adventure from a story by A.E.W. Mason. After resigning from the British Army a young man is branded a coward and given four white feathers as symbols by three of his friends and his lady love. Determined to prove them wrong he joins the Sudan campaign of 1898 and rescues each of the men from certain death. They then take back their feathers as does his girl upon learning of his true courage. Excellent performances by Smith and Richardson. **99m/C VHS, Beta, LV.** *GB* John Clements, Ralph Richardson, Sir C. Aubrey Smith, June Duprez, Donald Gray, Jack Allen, Clive Barker, Allan Jeayes; ***D:*** Zoltan Korda; ***W:*** R.C. Sherriff; ***C:*** Georges Perinal; ***M:*** Miklos Rozsa. Nominations: Academy Awards '39: Best Color Cinematography. *SUE, FCT, HMV*

The Four Feathers **1978** Determined to return the symbols of cowardice, four feathers, to his friends and fiancee, a man courageously saves his friends' lives during the British Sudan campaign and regains the love of his lady. Made-for-television movie is the fifth remake. **95m/C VHS, Beta.** Beau Bridges, Jane Seymour, Simon Ward, Harry Andrews, Richard Johnson, Robert Powell; ***D:*** Don Sharp. *REP*

Four for Texas **1963** Perhaps Aldrich's later success with "The Dirty Dozen" can be attributed, in part, to this exercise in how not to make a comic western; poorly made, over long, and far too dependant on the feminine charisma of Ekberg and Andress. Slow-moving Sinatra-Martin vehicle tells the tale of con men in the Old West who battle bandits and bad bankers for a stash of loot. **124m/C VHS, Beta, LV.** Frank Sinatra, Dean Martin, Anita Ekberg, Ursula Andress, Charles Bronson, Victor Buono, Jack Elam; ***D:*** Robert Aldrich; ***C:*** Ernest Laszlo. *WAR, FCT*

Four Friends *Georgia's Friends* **1981 (R)** The magical good and bad dream of the 1960s is remembered in this story of four friends. A young woman and the three men in love with her first come together in high school and then separate, learning from college, war and drug abuse, and each other in this ambitious movie from Steve Tesich, the writer of "Breaking Away." Good performances by all. **114m/C VHS, Beta.** James Leo Herlihy, Craig Wasson, Jodi Thelen, Michael Huddleston, Jim Metzler, Reed Birney; ***D:*** Arthur Penn; ***W:*** Steve Tesich; ***C:*** Ghislan Cloquet. *WAR, OM*

The Four Horsemen of the Apocalypse ½ **1921** Silent classic and star maker for Valentino concerning an Argentine family torn apart by the outbreak of WWI. Valentino is a painter who moves from his native Argentina to France and is persuaded to enlist by a recruiter who invokes the image of the Biblical riders. His excellence as a soldier, however, proves to be his undoing. The 1962 remake can't hold a candle to original, adapted from a novel by Vicente Blasco-Ibanez. **110m/B VHS.** Rudolph Valentino, Alice Terry, Pomeroy Cannon, Josef Swickard, Alan Hale, Mabel van Buren, Nigel de Brulier, Bowditch Turner, Wallace Beery; ***D:*** Rex Ingram. *NO*

The Four Horsemen of the Apocalypse ½ **1962** The members of a German family find themselves fighting on opposite sides during WWII. This remake of the vintage Valentino silent failed at the box office, with complaints about its length, disjointed script, and uninspired performances. The title refers to the horrors of conquest, pestilence, war, and death. Adapted from the book by Vincente Blasco-Ibanez. **153m/C VHS, Beta.** Glenn Ford, Charles Boyer, Lee J. Cobb, Paul Henreid, Yvette Mimieux; ***D:*** Vincente Minnelli; ***W:*** John Gay; ***C:*** Milton Krasner; ***M:*** Andre Previn. *MGM*

The 400 Blows *Les Quartre Cents Coups* **1959** The classic, ground-breaking semi-autobiography that initiated Truffaut's career and catapulted him to international acclaim, about the trials and rebellions of a 12-year-old French schoolboy. One of the greatest and most influential of films, and the first of Truffaut's career-long Antoine Doinel series. With English subtitles. **97m/B VHS, Beta, LV.** *FR* Jean-Pierre Leaud, Claire Maurier, Albert Remy, Guy Decomble, Georges Flament, Patrick Auffay, Jeanne Moreau, Jean-Claude Brialy, Jacques Demy, Francois Truffaut; ***D:*** Francois Truffaut; ***W:*** Marcel Moussey, Francois Truffaut; ***M:*** Jean Constantin. Cannes Film Festival '59: Best Director (Truffaut); New York Film Critics Awards '59: Best Foreign Film; Nominations: Academy Awards '59: Best Story & Screenplay. *HMV, MRV, APD*

Four in a Jeep ½ **1951** In Vienna in 1945, soldiers from different countries are serving as an international military police force. They clash as a result of political demands and their love for the same woman. Shot on location in Austria. **83m/B VHS, Beta.** Ralph Meeker, Viveca Lindfors, Joseph Yadin, Michael Medwin; ***D:*** Leopold Lindtberg. *NOS*

Four Jacks and a Jill **1941** Four musicians are left in the lurch when their band singer leaves them for her gangster boyfriend and they must frantically search for a replacement. Not completely uninteresting, but rather bland and old now. Earlier versions of the story were released as "Street Girl" and "That Girl from Paris." ♫I'm in Good Shape For the Shape I'm In; You Go Your Way and I'll Go Crazy; I Haven't A Thing to Wear; Wherever You Are; Boogie Woogie Conga. **68m/B VHS, Beta.** Anne Shirley, Ray Bolger, Desi Arnaz Sr., Jack Durant, June Havoc, Eddie Foy Jr., Fritz Feld; ***D:*** Jack Hively. *TTC*

The Four Musketeers *The Revenge of Milady* **1975 (PG)** A fun-loving continuation of "The Three Musketeers," reportedly filmed simultaneously. Lavish swashbuckler jaunts between France, England, and Italy, in following the adventures of D'Artagnan and his cohorts. Pictures give an amusing depiction of Lester-interpreted seventeenth-century Europe, with fine performances especially by Dunaway as an evil countess seeking revenge on our heroes and Welch as the scatterbrained object of York's affections. Followed, in 1989, by "The Return of the Musketeers." **108m/C VHS, Beta.** Michael York, Oliver Reed, Richard Chamberlain, Frank Finlay, Raquel Welch, Christopher Lee, Faye Dunaway, Jean-Pierre Cassel, Geraldine Chaplin, Simon Ward, Charlton Heston, Roy Kinnear, Nicole Calfan; ***D:*** Richard Lester; ***M:*** Lalo Schifrin. Nominations: Academy Awards '75: Best Costume Design. *LIV, OM*

Four Robbers **197?** The ruthless Ma initiates his series of crimes throughout the Far East, somehow staying ahead of the cops. When the final showdown occurs, it's an all out kung fu massacre. **90m/C VHS, Beta.** Lau Chun, Shek Hon, Kong Seng, Lee Wing Shan. *MGI*

Four Rode Out **1969** A Mexican outlaw is pursued by his girlfriend, one-time partner, and the law. Brutal, inferior western. **99m/C VHS.** Pernell Roberts, Sue Lyon, Leslie Nielsen, Julian Mateos; ***D:*** John Peyser. *NO*

Four Rooms **1995 (R)** Four stories by four hot indie filmers set in the same L.A. hotel on New Year's Eve are tied together by bellboy Roth, stumbling around in a Jerry/Carrey-like stupor. Leading off is Anders's roomful of witches trying to resurrect spirit of '50s stripper DeCadenet. After this disappointing start is Rockwell's bland look at infidelity, with wife Beals tied and gagged by her husband (Proval) over an alleged fling with Roth. Bandaras heads the best seg as a mobster who leaves his demonic children in Roth's hands. Tarantino is the anchor man with his take on Hitchcock, dealing with a macabre bet involving the removal of body parts. Altogether disjointed and uninspired. **109m/C VHS.** Tim Roth, Antonio Banderas, Jennifer Beals, Paul Calderone, Sammi Davis, Valeria Golino, Madonna, Ione Skye, Marisa Tomei, Tamlyn Tomita, Bruce Willis, David Proval, Lili Taylor, Alicia Witt, Amanda DeCadenet, Danny Verduzco, Lana McKissack, Quentin Tarantino; ***Cameos:*** Salma Hayek; ***D:*** Quentin Tarantino, Alexandre Rockwell, Robert Rodriguez, Allison Anders; ***W:*** Quentin Tarantino, Alexandre Rockwell, Robert Rodriguez, Allison Anders; ***C:*** Phil Parmet, Guillermo Navarro, Andrzej Sekula, Rodrigo Garcia; ***M:*** Combustible Edison, Esquivel. Golden Raspberry Awards '95: Worst Supporting Actress (Madonna). *TOU*

The Four Seasons ½ **1981 (PG)** Three upper-middle-class New York couples share their vacations together, as well as their friendship, their frustrations and their jealousies. Alda's first outing as a film director is pleasant and easy on the eyes. **108m/C VHS, Beta, LV.** Alan Alda, Carol Burnett, Sandy Dennis, Len Cariou, Jack Weston, Rita Moreno, Bess Armstrong; ***D:*** Alan Alda; ***W:*** Alan Alda. *MCA*

Four Sided Triangle **1953** Two mad scientists find their friendship threatened when they discover that they are both in love with the same woman. So they do what anyone would do in this situation—they invent a machine and duplicate her. **81m/B VHS.** *GB* James Hayter, Barbara Payton, Stephen Murray, John Van Eyssen, Percy Marmont; ***D:*** Terence Fisher; ***M:*** Malcolm Arnold. *NOS, SNC, MLB*

Four Ways Out ½ **1957** Four average guys are fed up by their lot in life and stage a box-office robbery of their local soccer stadium. They don't get to enjoy their ill-gotten gains. In Italian with subtitles or dubbed. **77m/B VHS.** *IT* Gina Lollobrigida, Renalto Baldini, Paul Muller; ***D:*** Pietro Germi. *SNC, VYY*

Four Weddings and a Funeral 🦴🦴🦴 **1994 (R)** Refreshing, intelligent adult comedy brimming with stiff upper-lip wit and sophistication. Thirty-ish Brit bachelor Charles (Grant) spends his time attending the weddings of his friends, but manages to avoid taking the plunge himself. Then he falls for Carrie (MacDowell), who's about to wed another. Great beginning offers loads of laughs as the first two weddings unfold, then becomes decidedly bittersweet. While Grant makes this a star turn as the romantic bumbler, MacDowell charms without seeming particularly needed. Supporting characters are superb, especially Coleman as the "flirty" Scarlett and Atkinson as a new minister. Surprising box office hit found a broad audience. **118m/C VHS, LV.** *GB* Hugh Grant, Andie MacDowell, Simon Callow, Kristin Scott Thomas, James Fleet, John Hannah, Charlotte Coleman, David Bower, Corin Redgrave, Rowan Atkinson; ***D:*** Mike Newell; ***W:*** Richard Curtis; ***M:*** Richard Rodney Bennett. Australian Film Institute '94: Best Foreign Film; British Academy Awards '94: Best Actor (Grant), Best Director (Newell), Best Film, Best Supporting Actress (Scott Thomas); Golden Globe Awards '95: Best Actor—Musical/Comedy (Grant); Writers Guild of America '94: Best Original Screenplay; Nominations: Academy Awards '94: Best Original Screenplay, Best Picture; Directors Guild of America Awards '94: Best Director (Newell); Golden Globe Awards '95: Best Actress—Musical/Comedy (MacDowell), Best Film—Musical/Comedy, Best Screenplay; MTV Movie Awards '95: Breakthrough Performance (Grant). *PGV*

The 4D Man 🦴🦴½ **1959** A physicist makes two fateful discoveries while working on a special project that gets out of control, leaving him able to pass through matter and see around corners. He also finds that his touch brings instant death. Cheap but effective sci-fier. Young Duke has a small part. **85m/C VHS, Beta, LV.** Robert Lansing, Lee Meriwether, James Congdon, Guy Raymond, Robert Strauss, Patty Duke; ***D:*** Irvin S. Yeaworth Jr. *NWV, MLB*

1492: Conquest of Paradise 🦴🦴½ **1992 (PG-13)** Large-scale Hollywood production striving for political correctness is a drawn-out account of Columbus's (Depardieu) discovery and subsequent exploitation of the "New World." Skillful directing by Ridley Scott and impressive scenery add interest, yet don't make up for a script which chronicles events but tends towards trite dialogue and characterization. Available in both pan-and-scan and letterbox formats. **142m/C VHS, Beta, LV.** Gerard Depardieu, Sigourney Weaver, Armand Assante, Frank Langella, Loren Dean, Angela Molina, Fernando Rey, Michael Wincott, Steven Waddington, Tcheky Karyo, Kario Salem; ***D:*** Ridley Scott; ***W:*** Roselyne Bosch; ***M:*** Vangelis. *PAR, BTV*

The 4th Man 🦴🦴🦴½ *Blunt* **1979** Steeped in saturated colors and jet black comedy, with an atmospheric score, Verhoeven's nouveau noir mystery enjoyed considerable art-house success but was not released in the US until 1984. The story is decidedly non-linear, the look stylish and symbolic. Krabbe is an alcoholic bisexual Catholic writer who inadvertently becomes the hypotenuse of a love triangle involving Herman, a young man he encounters at a railway station, and his lover Christine, who owns the Sphinx beauty parlor and whose three husbands died, shall we say, mysteriously. In Dutch with English subtitles. **104m/C VHS, Beta, LV.** *NL* Jeroen Krabbe, Renee Soutendijk, Thom Hoffman, Jon DeVries, Geert De Jong; ***D:*** Paul Verhoeven; ***C:*** Jan De Bont; ***M:*** Loek Dikker. Los Angeles Film Critics Association Awards '84: Best Foreign Film. *XVC, MED, INJ*

The Fourth Protocol 🦴🦴🦴 **1987 (R)** Well-made thriller based on the Frederick Forsyth bestseller about a British secret agent trying to stop a young KGB agent from destroying NATO and putting the world in nuclear jeopardy. Brosnan, as the totally dedicated Russkie, gives his best performance to date while Caine, as usual, is totally believable as he goes about the business of tracking down the bad guys. **119m/C VHS, Beta, LV.** *GB* Michael Caine, Pierce Brosnan, Ned Beatty, Joanna Cassidy, Julian Glover, Ray McAnally, Michael Gough, Ian Richardson, Betsy Brantley, Matt Frewer, Peter Cartwright, David Conville; ***D:*** John MacKenzie; ***W:*** Frederick Forsyth, Richard Burridge, George Axelrod; ***C:*** Phil Meheux; ***M:*** Lalo Schifrin, Francis Shaw. *ORI, WAR*

Fourth Story 🦴🦴🦴 **1990 (PG-13)** A misfit detective is hired by a beautiful woman to find her missing husband. The investigation reveals some unseemly facts about the gentleman. Characterizations and plot twists keep this made-for-cable mystery interesting. **91m/C VHS, Beta, LV.** Mark Harmon, Mimi Rogers, Cliff DeYoung, Paul Gleason, M. Emmet Walsh; ***D:*** Ivan Passer; ***W:*** Andrew Guerdat. *MED, IME, VTR*

The Fourth War 🦴🦴 **1990 (R)** Scheider and Prochnow are American and Russian colonels, respectively, assigned to guard the West German-Czechoslovakian border against each other. With the end of the cold war looming, these two frustrated warriors begin to taunt each other with sallies into the other's territory, threatening to touch off a major superpower conflict. **109m/C VHS, Beta, LV.** Roy Scheider, Juergen Prochnow, Tim Reid, Lara Harris, Harry Dean Stanton; ***D:*** John Frankenheimer; ***M:*** Bill Conti. *HBO*

Fourth Wise Man 🦴🦴 **1985** A Biblical Easter story about a rich physician searching for Christ in Persia. **72m/C VHS, Beta.** Martin Sheen, Lance Kerwin, Alan Arkin, Harold Gould, Eileen Brennan, Ralph Bellamy, Adam Arkin, Richard Libertini. *LIV, VES, IGP*

Fourth Wish 🦴🦴 **1975** When a single father learns that his son is dying, he vows to make his son's last months as fulfilling as possible. Bring lots of hankies. **107m/C VHS, Beta.** John Meillon, Robert Bettles, Robyn Nevin; ***D:*** Don Chaffey. Australian Film Institute '75: Best Actor (Meillon). *SUE*

Fowl Play *Woof!* **1983** An unlikely threesome encounter various hardships and mishaps on their way to the first cock-fighting Olympics. Let's hope it's the last cock-fighting Olympics. **90m/C VHS, Beta.** Nancy Kwan. *NO*

Fox and His Friends 🦴🦴🦴½ *Faustrecht der Freiheit; Fist Right of Freedom* **1975** Fassbinder's breakthrough tragi-drama, about a lowly gay carnival barker who wins the lottery, thus attracting a devious, exploiting lover, who takes him for everything he has. In German with English subtitles. **123m/C VHS, Beta.** *GE* Rainer Werner Fassbinder, Peter Chatel, Karl-Heinz Boehm, Adrian Hoven, Harry Baer, Ulla Jacobsson, Kurt Raab; ***D:*** Rainer Werner Fassbinder; ***C:*** Michael Ballhaus. *FCT, NYF, INJ*

The Fox and the Hound 🦴🦴🦴 **1981 (G)** Sweet story of the friendship shared by a fox and hound. Young and naive, the animals become friends and swear their allegiance to one another when they are separated for a season. Upon return, the hound has become his master's best hunting dog and warns his friend the fox to stay clear of their hunting grounds, for the master is determined to catch the docile fox. Saddened, the fox retreats but soon finds himself boldly standing his ground against a bear that attacks the hound, and the hound inevitably protects the fox from the mean-spirited hunter. Very good animation, but not in the same class as other Disney favorites like "Beauty and the Beast." **83m/C VHS, Beta.** ***D:*** Art Stevens, Ted Berman, Richard Rich; ***W:*** Art Stevens, Peter Young, Steve Hulett, Earl Kress, Vance Gerry, Laury Clemmons, Dave Michener, Burny Mattinson; ***M:*** Buddy Baker; ***V:*** Mickey Rooney, Kurt Russell, Pearl Bailey, Jack Albertson, Sandy Duncan, Jeanette Nolan, Pat Buttram, John Fiedler, John McIntire, Richard Bakalayan, Paul Winchell, Keith Mitchell, Corey Feldman. *DIS, OM*

Foxes 🦴🦴 **1980 (R)** Four young California girls grow up with little supervision from parents still trying to grow up themselves. They rely on each other in a world where they have to make adult choices, yet are not considered grown-up. They look for no more than a good time and no tragic mistakes. **106m/C VHS, Beta.** Jodie Foster, Cherie Currie, Marilyn Kagan, Scott Baio, Sally Kellerman, Randy Quaid, Laura Dern; ***D:*** Adrian Lyne; ***W:*** Gerald Ayres. *MGM, FOX*

Foxfire 🦴🦴🦴 **1987 (PG)** In the role that won her Tony and Emmy awards, Tandy stars as Annie Nations, a woman who has lived her entire life in the Blue Ridge Mountains. Widowed, all she has left are the memories of her beloved husband, with whom she regularly communes. Her son tries to convince her to move, and it becomes a clash of the wills as Annie tries to decide to stay in her past or change her future. Made for television. **118m/C VHS.** Jessica Tandy, Hume Cronyn, John Denver, Gary Grubbs, Harriet Hall; ***D:*** Jud Taylor. National Media Owl Awards '88: Second Prize. *REP*

Foxfire Light 🦴 **1984 (PG)** A young woman vacationing in the Ozarks is drawn into a romance with a cowboy. But her mother's social ambitions and her own indecesion may tear them apart. **102m/C VHS, Beta.** Tippi Hedren, Lara Parker, Leslie Nielsen, Barry Van Dyke; ***D:*** Allen Baron. *PSM*

Foxstyle 🦴½ **1973** A wealthy nightclub owner struggles with his country roots and his city sophistication. **84m/C VHS, Beta.** Juanita Moore, Richard Lawson, John Taylor, Jovita Bush; ***D:*** Clyde Houston. *MOV*

Foxtrap 🦴 **1985** An L.A. courier is hired to find a runaway girl and, upon finding her in Europe, discovers he's been led into a trap. A low budget Italian co-production. **89m/C VHS, Beta.** *IT* Fred Williamson, Christopher Connelly, Arlene Golonka; ***D:*** Fred Williamson. *FCT, VES*

Foxtrot 🦴🦴 *The Other Side of Paradise* **1976 (R)** A wealthy count isolates himself, his wife, and their two servants, on an island but cannot escape his past or the horrors of WWII. Even the good cast can't save the pretentious script and inadequate production. **91m/C VHS, Beta.** *Sl MX* Peter O'Toole, Charlotte Rampling, Max von Sydow, Jorge Luke; ***D:*** Arturo Ripstein. *NLC*

Foxy Brown 🦴 **1974 (R)** A bitter woman poses as a prostitute to avenge the mob-backed deaths of her drug dealer brother and undercover cop boyfriend. Extremely violent black exploitation flick. **92m/C VHS, Beta.** Pam Grier, Terry Carter, Antonio Fargas, Kathryn Loder; ***D:*** Jack Hill. *ORI, FCT*

F.P. 1 🦴🦴 **1933** An artifical island (Floating Platform 1) in the Atlantic is threatened by treason. This slow-moving 1930s technothriller is the English-language version of the German "F.P. 1 Antwortet Nicht" ("F.P. 1 Doesn't Answer"). Both were directed at the same time by Hartl, using different casts. **74m/B VHS.** *GE* Leslie Fenton, Conrad Veidt, Jill Esmond. *NOS*

F.P. 1 Doesn't Answer 🦴🦴 *F.P. 1 Antwortet Nicht* **1933** A mid-Atlantic refueling station (Floating Platform 1) is threatened by treason and a pilot sets out to put things right. Features pre-Hollywood vintage Lorre; Albers was Germany's number one box office draw at the time. In German. **74m/B VHS.** *GE* Hans Albers, Sybille Schmitz, Paul Hartmann, Peter Lorre, Hermann Speelmanns; ***D:*** Karl Hartl. *SNC, LSV*

Frame by Frame 🦴🦴½ **1995 (R)** Cops who share a passion on and off the job become implicated in murder. Cable thriller. **97m/C VHS.** Michael Biehn, Marg Helgenberger; ***D:*** Douglas Barr. *REP*

Frame Up 🦴🦴 **1991 (R)** A small town sheriff is trying to investigate a murder tied to a fraternity's initiation. However, he runs into opposition from the most powerful man in town. **90m/C VHS, LV.** Wings Hauser, Bobby DiCicco, Frances Fisher, Dick Sargent, Robert Picardo; ***D:*** Paul Leder. *REP*

Framed 🦴🦴 **1975 (R)** A nightclub owner is framed for murder, which understandably irks him. He's determined to get paroled and then seek revenge on the crooked cops responsible for his incarceration. This action melodrama features the writer, director and star of "Walking Tall." **106m/C VHS, Beta.** Joe Don Baker, Gabriel Dell, Brock Peters, Conny Van Dyke, John Marley; ***D:*** Phil Karlson; ***W:*** Mort Briskin. *PAR*

Framed 🦴🦴 **1990** An art forger gets tripped up by a beautiful con artist. However, when they meet again he is willingly drawn into her latest swindle. **87m/C VHS.** Jeff Goldblum, Kristin Scott Thomas, Todd Graff; ***D:*** Dean Parisot. *HBO*

Fran 🦴🦴 **1985** A young woman is torn between her desperate need for a male companion and the care of her children. Well made, albeit depressing, Australian production. **92m/C VHS, Beta.** *AU* Noni Hazlehurst, Annie Byron, Alan Fletcher; ***D:*** Glenda Hambly. Australian Film Institute '85: Best Actress (Hazlehurst). *NO*

France/Tour/Detour/Deux/ Enfants 🦴🦴🦴 **1978** A twelve-part television series made for French television in which Godard and Mieville chronicle, in their characteristically reflexive fashion, the lives of two French schoolchildren and how their everyday growth is informed by television and the media. In French with English subtitles. **26m/C VHS, Beta.** *FR* ***D:*** Jean-Luc Godard, Anne-Marie Mieville. *EAI*

Frances 🦴🦴🦴 **1982** The tragic story of Frances Farmer, the beautiful and talented screen actress of the 30's and early 40's, who was driven to a mental breakdown by bad luck, drug and alcohol abuse, a neurotic, domineering mother, despicable mental health care, and her own stubbornness. After being in and out of mental hospitals, she is finally reduced to a shadow by a lobotomy. Not nearly as bleak as it sounds, this film works because Lange understands this character from the inside out, and never lets her become melodramatic or weak. **134m/C VHS, Beta, LV.** Jessica Lange, Kim Stanley, Sam Shepard; ***D:*** Graeme Clifford; ***W:*** Christopher DeVore, Nicholas Kazan, Eric Bergren; ***M:*** John Barry. Nominations: Academy Awards '82: Best Actress (Lange), Best Supporting Actress (Stanley). *REP*

Francesco 🦴🦴 **1993 (PG-13)** Set in 13th-century Italy and depicting the life of St. Francis of Assisi. Follows the pleasure-loving son of a wealthy merchant through his religious awakening, and the founding of the Franciscan order of monks. Rourke, in a definite change-of-pace role, is actually believable, while Bonham Carter offers fine support as a devoted disciple. **119m/C VHS, LV.** Mickey Rourke, Helena Bonham Carter, Paolo Bonacelli, Andrea Ferreol, Hanns Zischler, Peter Berling; ***D:*** Liliana Cavani; ***W:*** Liliana Cavani. *HMD*

The Franchise Affair 🦴🦴 **1952** A teenage girl in need of an alibi accuses two reclusive women of kidnapping and abusing her. It's up to a lawyer to sort out the truth. Based on the novel by Josephine Tey. **149m/C VHS.** *GB* Michael Denison, Dulcie Gray, Anthony Nicholls, Marjorie Fielding, Athene Seyler, Ann Stephens, Patrick Troughton; ***D:*** Lawrence Huntington. *FCT*

The Franchise Affair 🦴🦴½ **19??** A scandal is about to overtake the sleepy village of Milford in 1947. An elderly lady and her daughter, the owners of a forbidding country house, are accused of kidnapping and beating a teenaged girl until she agreed to work as their servant. A British TV production based on the novel by Josephine Tey and previously filmed for the big screen in 1952. **155m/C VHS.** *GB* Patrick Malahide, Rosalie Crutchley, Joanna McCallum. *VCO*

Francis Covers the Big Town 🦴🦴½ **1953** The fourth in the series finds Peter Stirling (O'Connor) trying to become an ace reporter with a New York newspaper. Thanks to Francis he gets some big scoops but then runs afoul of the mob and is accused of murder. And it's up to his smarter pal to come to the rescue. **86m/B VHS.** Donald O'Connor, Yvette Dugay, Gene Lockhart, Nancy Guild, Larry Gates, Gale Gordon; ***D:*** Arthur Lubin; ***W:*** Oscar Brodney; ***C:*** Carl Guthrie; ***M:*** Joseph Gershenson; ***V:*** Chill Wills. *MCA*

Francis Gary Powers: The True Story of the U-2 Spy 🦴🦴½ **1976** A television dramatization of the true experiences of Gary Powers, a CIA spy pilot whose plane was shot down over the Soviet Union in 1960. His capture, trial, and conviction are all portrayed in detail, taken from Power's own reminiscences. **120m/C VHS, Beta.** Lee Majors, Noah Beery Jr., Nehemiah Persoff, Lew Ayres, Brooke Bundy; ***D:*** Delbert Mann. *WOV*

Francis Goes to the Races 🦴🦴½ **1951** The second in the talking-mule series finds O'Connor and Francis taking up residence on Kellaway's failing horse ranch. When mobsters seize control of the property to pay off a debt, Francis decides to check with the horses at the Santa Anita race track and find a sure winner to bet on. **88m/B VHS.** Donald O'Connor, Piper Laurie, Cecil Kellaway, Jesse White, Barry Kelley, Hayden Rorke, Vaughn Taylor, Larry Keating; ***D:*** Arthur Lubin; ***W:*** Oscar Brodney; ***M:*** Frank Skinner; ***V:*** Chill Wills. *MCA*

Francis Goes to West Point 🦴🦴½ **1952** Peter (O'Connor) and Francis get into West Point where the unfortunate freshman winds up last in his class. But thanks to Francis, Peter makes it past school hazing, grades, and other campus hijicks. Look for Leonard Nimoy in the bit role of a football player. Third in the series. **81m/B VHS.** Donald O'Connor, Lori Nelson, William Reynolds, Gregg Palmer, Alice Kelley, Les Tremayne, David Janssen, Paul Burke; ***D:*** Arthur Lubin; ***W:*** Oscar Brodney; ***C:*** Carl Guthrie; ***M:*** Joseph Gershenson; ***V:*** Chill Wills. *MCA*

Francis in the Haunted House 🦴½ **1956** The sixth and last entry in the series finds star Donald O'Connor, director Arthur Lubin, and even Chill Wills (the voice of Francis) all abandoning the sinking series. So, its left to Rooney (as hapless David Prescott) to get himself into trouble (trapped in a haunted house with thieves) and for Francis to get him out. Ho-hum. **80m/B VHS.** Mickey Rooney, Virginia Welles, James Flavin, Paul Cavanagh, David Janssen, Richard Deacon; ***D:*** Charles Lamont; ***W:*** Herbert Margolis, William Raynor; ***C:*** George Robinson; ***M:*** Joseph Gershenson; ***V:*** Paul Frees. *MCA*

Francis in the Navy 🦴🦴 **1955** The precocious talking mule, Francis, is drafted, and his buddy, played by O'Connor, comes to the rescue. The loquacious beast proves he has the superior grey matter however, and ends up doing all the thinking. Look for Clint Eastwood in his second minor role. **80m/B VHS.** Donald O'Connor, Martha Hyer, Jim Backus, Paul Burke, David Janssen, Clint Eastwood, Martin Milner; ***D:*** Arthur Lubin. *MCA*

Francis Joins the WACs 🦴🦴½ **1954** The fifth entry in the series finds O'Connor working as a bank clerk when he is mistakenly drafted back into the military—and sent to a WAC base. Francis tries to keep him out of trouble with the ladies. Wills, the voice of Francis, also turns up as a general. **94m/B VHS.** Donald O'Connor, Julie Adams, Chill Wills, Mamie Van Doren, Lynn Bari, ZaSu Pitts, Joan Shawlee, Mara Corday, Allison Hayes; ***D:*** Arthur Lubin; ***V:*** Chill Wills. *MCA*

Francis the Talking Mule 🦴🦴🦴 *Francis* **1949** The first of the silly but funny series about, what else, a talking mule. Peter Stirling (O'Connor) is the dim-bulb G.I. who hooks up with Francis while fighting in Burma. Francis helps Peter become a war hero but of course everyone thinks he's crazy when Peter insists the mule can talk. The joke is that Francis is smarter than any of the humans. O'Connor starred in six of the films, with Mickey Rooney taking over the final adventure. Director Lubin went on to create the television series "Mr. Ed," about a talking horse. **91m/B VHS, LV.** Donald O'Connor, Patricia Medina, ZaSu Pitts, Ray Collins, John McIntire, Eduard Franz, Howland Chamberlin, Frank Faylen, Tony Curtis; ***D:*** Arthur Lubin; ***M:*** Frank Skinner; ***V:*** Chill Wills. *MCA*

Frank and Jesse 🦴🦴½ **1994 (R)** Another revisionist western finds outlaw Jesse James (Lowe) brooding about his violent existence while brother Frank (Paxton) keeps the gang together and they all try to avoid capture by a vengeful Alan Pinkerton (Atherton) and his detective agency. **106m/C VHS, LV.** Rob Lowe, Bill Paxton, Randy Travis, William Atherton, Alexis Arquette; ***D:*** Robert Boris; ***W:*** Robert Boris. *VMK*

Frank and Ollie 🦴🦴🦴 **1995 (PG)** If you have children, chances are you have a collection of Disney classics, including "Cinderella," "Snow White and the Seven Dwarfs," or "Bambi." Look closely at any of the opening credits and you'll see that two of those names, part of Disney's famed "Nine Old Men," are 80-something animators Frank Thomas and Ollie Johnston. Documentary, from Thomas's son Theodore, highlights the 60-plus year friendship and storied careers of these two pioneers, who are still well-known thanks to the recent animation craze. Seven years from conception to release, the film has many great pencil drawings and scenes from the movies, but focuses as much on the men's longtime friendship. **89m/C VHS.** ***D:*** Theodore Thomas; ***W:*** Theodore Thomas; ***C:*** Erik Daarstad; ***M:*** James Stemple. *NYR*

Frankenhooker 🦴½ **1990 (R)** Jeffrey Franken is a nice guy; he didn't mean to mow his fiancee down in the front lawn. But sometimes bad things just happen to good people. Luckily Jeff thought to save her head and decides to pair it up with the body of some sexy streetwalkers. Voila! You have Frankenhooker: the girlfriend with more than a heart. The posters say it best, "A Terrifying Tale of Sluts and Bolts." Also available in an "R" rated version. **90m/C VHS, LV.** James Lorinz, Patty Mullen, Charlotte J. Helmkamp, Louise Lasser; ***D:*** Frank Henenlotter. *SGE, FCT*

Frankenstein 🦴🦴🦴🦴 **1931** The definitive expressionistic Gothic horror classic that set the mold. Adapted from the Mary Shelley novel about Dr. Henry Frankenstein, the scientist who creates a terrifying, yet strangely sympathetic monster. Great performance by Karloff as the creation, which made him a monster star. Several powerful scenes, excised from the original version, have been restored. Side two of the laser disc version contains the original theatrical trailer, plus a collection of photos and scenes replayed for study purposes. **71m/B VHS, Beta, LV.** Boris Karloff, Colin Clive, Mae Clarke, John Boles, Dwight Frye, Edward Van Sloan, Frederick Kerr, Lionel Belman; ***D:*** James Whale; ***W:*** Francis Edwards Faragoh, Garrett Fort, John Balderston, Robert Florey; ***M:*** David Broeckman. *MCA, TLF, HMV*

Frankenstein 🦴🦴½ **1973** A brilliant scientist plays God, unleashing a living monster from the remains of the dead. A TV movie version of the legendary horror story. Good atmosphere provided by producer Dan "Dark Shadows" Curtis. **130m/C VHS, Beta.** Robert Foxworth, Bo Svenson, Willie Aames, Susan Strasberg; ***D:*** Glenn Jordan. *MPI*

Frankenstein 🦴🦴½ **1982** A remake of the horror classic, closely following the original story, wherein the creature speaks (and waxes philosophical), the doctor sees him as his dark subconscious, and the two die in an arctic confrontation. **81m/C VHS, Beta.** Robert Powell, Carrie Fisher, David Warner, John Gielgud; ***D:*** James Ormerod. *LIV*

Frankenstein 🦴🦴½ **1993** Yet another remake of Mary Shelley's 1818 novel. Bergin stars as Dr. Victor Frankenstein, fanatically believing in the power of science to solve all mankind's ills. This leads him to prove his theories on the "secret of life" with his creation of the monster (Quaid), which Frankenstein finds he cannot ultimately control. Slow-moving story but while the monster isn't really terrifying, he's vengeful and intelligent enough to be a good enemy. Made for cable television. **117m/C VHS.** Patrick Bergin, Randy Quaid, John Mills, Lambert Wilson, Fiona Gilles, Jacinta Mulcahy, Timothy Stark; ***D:*** David Wickes; ***W:*** David Wickes. *TTC, BTV*

Frankenstein: A Cinematic Scrapbook **1991** A behind the scenes look at the world's most infamous monster, featuring interviews with Boris Karloff, Bela Lugosi and Lon Chaney, Jr. Also included are original movie trailers. In color and B&W. **60m/C VHS, Beta.** ***D:*** Ted Newsom; ***W:*** Ted Newsom. *RHI, FCT*

Frankenstein and the Monster from Hell 🦴🦴 **1974 (R)** A young doctor is discovered conducting experiments with human bodies and thrown into a mental asylum run by none other than Dr. Frankenstein himself. They continue their gruesome work together, creating a monster who develops a taste for human flesh. This really lame film was the last of the Hammer Frankenstein series. **93m/C VHS.** Peter Cushing, Shane Briant, Madeleine Smith, David Prowse, John Stratton; ***D:*** Terence Fisher; ***M:*** James Bernard. *PAR*

Frankenstein '80 *Woof!* **1979** Guy named Frankenstein pieces together a monster who goes on a killing spree. Bottom of the barrel Italian production with funky music and lots of gore. **88m/C VHS, Beta.** *IT GE* John Richardson, Gordon Mitchell, Leila Parker, Dada Galloti, Marisa Travers; ***D:*** Mario Mancini. *NO*

Frankenstein General Hospital *Woof!* **1988** A completely laughless horror spoof wherein the twelfth grandson of the infamous scientist duplicates his experiments in the basement of a modern hospital. A must see for Frankenstein fans; considered by some the worst Frankenstein movie ever made. **90m/C VHS, Beta, LV.** Mark Blankfield, Kathy Shower, Leslie Jordan, Irwin Keyes; ***D:*** Deborah Roberts. *NO*

Frankenstein Island *Woof!* **1981 (PG)** Four balloonists get pulled down in a storm and end up on a mysterious island. They are greeted by one Sheila Frankenstein and encounter monsters, amazons, and other obstacles. Completely inept; Carradine "appears" in a visionary sequence wearing his pajamas. **97m/C VHS, Beta.** Cameron Mitchell, Andrew Duggan, John Carradine; ***D:*** Jerry Warren. *NO*

Frankenstein Meets the Space Monster *Woof! Mars Invades Puerto Rico; Frankenstein Meets the Spacemen; Duel of the Space Monsters* **1965** A classic grade-Z epic about a space robot gone berserk among Puerto Rican disco dancers. **80m/B VHS, Beta.** James Karen, Nancy Marshall, Marilyn Hanold, David Kerman, Robert Reilly, Lou Cutell; ***D:*** Robert Gaffney; ***W:*** George Garret; ***C:*** Saul Midwall. *PSM*

Frankenstein Meets the Wolfman 🦴🦴🦴 **1942** The two famous Universal monsters meet and battle it out in this typical grade-B entry, the fifth from the series. The Werewolf wants Dr. Frankenstein to cure him, but only his monster (played by Lugosi) remains. **73m/C VHS, Beta, LV.** Lon Chaney Jr., Bela Lugosi, Patric Knowles, Lionel Atwill, Maria Ouspenskaya; ***D:*** Roy William Neill. *MCA, MLB*

Frankenstein Sings...The Movie 🦴½ **1995 (PG)** Musical horror spoof finds young couple seeking shelter in a creepy mansion that happens to belong to Dr. Frankenstein. Also visiting (it just happens to be Halloween) are Mr. and Mrs. Dracula, the Wolfman and his mother, and the mummified remains of Elvis and his agent. Some amusing one-liners and mediocre music; adapted from a stage musical. **83m/C VHS, LV.** Candace Cameron, Ian Bohen, Jimmie Walker, Anthony Crivello; ***D:*** Joel Cohen, Alec Sokolow. *TTC*

Frankenstein Unbound 🦴🦴🦴 *Roger Corman's Frankenstein Unbound* **1990 (R)** Corman returns after nearly 20 years with a better than ever B movie. Hurt plays a nuclear physicist time traveler who goes back to the 1800s and runs into Lord Byron, Percy and Mary Shelley and their neighbor Dr. Frankenstein and his monster. Great acting, fun special effects, intelligent and subtle message, with a little sex to keep things going. **86m/C VHS, Beta, LV.** John Hurt, Raul Julia, Bridget Fonda, Jason Patric, Michael Hutchence, Catherine Rabett, Nick Brimble, Catherine Corman, Mickey Knox; ***D:*** Roger Corman; ***W:*** Roger Corman, F.X. Feeney; ***M:*** Carl Davis; ***V:*** Terri Treas. *FOX*

Frankenstein's Daughter 🦴 *She Monster of the Night* **1958** Demented descendant of Dr. Frankenstein sets a den of gruesome monsters loose, including the corpse of a teenaged girl he revitalizes, as he continues the mad experiments of his forefathers. **85m/B VHS, Beta.** John Ashley, Sandra Knight; ***D:*** Richard Cunha. *NOS, MRV, RHI*

Frankenstein's Great Aunt Tillie *Woof!* **1983** An excrutiatingly bad send up of the Frankenstein saga with the good doctor about to be evicted from his estate because of back taxes. Gabor appears for a few seconds in a flashback. **99m/C VHS, Beta.** Donald Pleasence, Yvonne Furneaux, Aldo Ray, June Wilkinson, Zsa Zsa Gabor; ***D:*** Myron G. Gold; ***W:*** Myron G. Gold. *VCD*

Frankenweenie 🦴🦴½ **1984 (PG)** "Frankenweenie" is the tale of a lovable spunky dog named Sparky and his owner, Victor Frankenstein. When Sparky is hit by a car, Victor brings him back to life through the use of electric shock. This affectionate parody of "Frankenstein" launched renowned director Burton's career. **27m/B VHS, Beta.** Shelley Duvall, Daniel Stern, Barret Oliver, Paul Bartel; ***D:*** Tim Burton; ***W:*** Tim Burton. *TOU*

Frankie and Johnny 🦴 **1936** Based on the song of the same name, famed torch singer Morgan portrays a singer in a bordello who shoots her unfaithful lover. Release was delayed two years by the Hays Office's intervention in how a house of prostitution could be portrayed on screen. Too bad they reached an agreement. Not even Morgan's rendition of the title song redeems this. **68m/B VHS, Beta.** Helen Morgan, Chester Morris; ***D:*** Chester Erskine. *CCB*

Frankie and Johnny 🦴🦴½ **1965** Elvis is a riverboat gambler/singer with lousy luck until Kovack changes the odds. This upsets his girlfriend Douglas who shoots him (but not fatally). Elvis wears period costumes, but this is otherwise similar to his contemporary films. ♫When the Saints Go Marching In; Look Out Broadway; Shout It Out; Frankie and Johnny; Chesay; Come Along; Petunia; The Gardner's Daughter; Beginner's Luck. **88m/C VHS, Beta.** Elvis Presley, Donna Douglas, Harry (Henry) Morgan, Audrey Christie, Anthony Eisley, Sue Ane Langdon, Robert Strauss, Nancy Kovack; ***D:*** Fred de Cordova. *MGM*

Frankie and Johnny 🦴🦴🦴 **1991 (R)** Ex-con gets a job as a short-order cook and falls for a world-weary waitress. She doesn't believe in romance, but finally gives into his pleas for a chance and finds out he may not be such a bad guy after all. Nothing can make Pfeiffer dowdy enough for this role, but she and Pacino are charming together. In a change of pace role, Nelligan has fun as a fellow waitress who loves men. Based on the play "Frankie and Johnny in the Clair de Lune" by McNally who also wrote the screenplay. **117m/C VHS, LV.** Al Pacino, Michelle Pfeiffer, Hector Elizondo, Nathan Lane, Kate Nelligan, Jane Morris, Greg Lewis, Al Fann, K. Callan, Phil Leeds, Tracy Reiner, Dey Young; ***D:*** Garry Marshall; ***W:*** Terrance McNally; ***C:*** Dante Spinotti; ***M:*** Marvin Hamlisch. British Academy Awards '91: Best Supporting Actress (Nelligan); National Board of Review Awards '91: 10 Best Films of the Year, Best Supporting Actress (Nelligan). *PAR, CCB*

Frankie Starlight 🦴🦴½ **1995 (R)** Bernadette (Parillaud) leaves France after WWII, smuggled aboard an American troop ship. By the time the ship reaches Ireland, she's pregnant and gives birth to her dwarf son, Frankie, in Dublin. She's taken in by the family of customs officer Jack Kelly (Byrne), who instills in the boy a lifelong love of the stars. The adult Frankie (Walker) becomes a celebrity when he writes a novel combining his obsession with the cosmos and his mother's erotic history. Raymo adapts from his 1993 novel "The Dork of Cork." Great performances by both Pentony and Walker as the child and adult Frankies. **100m/C VHS, LV.** *IR* Corban Walker, Alan Pentony, Gabriel Byrne, Anne Parillaud, Matt Dillon, Georgina Cates, Darbnia Molloy, Niall Toibin, Rudi Davies; ***D:*** Michael Lindsay-Hogg; ***W:*** Chet Raymo, Ronan O'Leary; ***C:*** Paul Laufer; ***M:*** Elmer Bernstein. *NLC*

Frantic 🦴🦴🦴 *Elevator to the Gallows; Ascenseur Pour L'Echafaud* **1958** From Louis Malle comes one of the first French New Wave film noir dramas. A man kills his boss with the connivance of the employer's wife, his lover, and makes it look like suicide. Meanwhile, teenagers have used his car and gun in the murder of a tourist couple and he is indicted for that crime. Their perfectly planned murder begins to unravel into a panic-stricken nightmare. A suspenseful and captivating drama. Director Malle's first feature film. Musical score by jazz legend Miles Davis. **92m/B VHS, Beta, 8mm.** *FR* Maurice Ronet, Jeanne Moreau, Georges Poujouly; ***D:*** Louis Malle; ***M:*** Miles Davis. *SNC, NOS, VYY*

Frantic 🦴🦴🦴 **1988 (R)** While in Paris, an American surgeon's wife is kidnapped when she inadvertantly picks up the wrong suitcase. Her kidnappers want their hidden tresure returned, which forces the husband into the criminal underground and into unexpected heroism when he seeks to rescue her. Contrived ending weakens on the whole, but Polanski is still master of the dark film thriller. **120m/C VHS, Beta, LV.** Harrison Ford, Betty Buckley, John Mahoney, Emmanuelle Seigner, Jimmie Ray Weeks, Yorgo Voyagis, David Huddleston, Gerard Klein; ***D:*** Roman Polanski; ***W:*** Gerard Brach, Roman Polanski; ***M:*** Ennio Morricone. *WAR, FCT*

Franz 🦴 **1972** A French mercenary and an insecure woman struggle with a doomed love affair. In French with English subtitles. **90m/C VHS, Beta.** *FR* Jacques Brel; ***D:*** Jacques Brel. *BAR, INJ*

Frasier the Sensuous Lion 🦴🦴 *Frasier the Lovable Lion* **1973 (PG)** A zoology professor is able to converse with Frasier, a lion known for his sexual stamina and whose potency is coveted by a billionaire (shadow of monkey glands rejuvenation therapy). A fairly typical, if slightly risque, talking critter film. **97m/C VHS, Beta.** Michael Callan, Katherine Justice, Frank De Kova, Malachi Throne, Victor Jory, Peter Lorre Jr., Marc Lawrence; ***D:*** Pat Shields. *PSM*

Fraternity Vacation 🦴 **1985 (R)** Two college fraternity men show a nerd the greatest time of his life while he's on vacation in Palm Springs. **95m/C VHS, Beta, LV.** Stephen Geoffreys, Sheree J. Wilson, Cameron Dye, Leigh McCloskey, Tim Robbins, Matt McCoy, Amanda Bearse, John Vernon, Nita Talbot, Barbara Crampton, Kathleen Kinmont, Max Wright, Julie Payne, Franklin Ajaye, Charles Rocket, Britt Ekland; ***D:*** James Frawley; ***M:*** Brad Fiedel. *NWV, VTR*

Frauds 🦴½ **1993 (R)** Collins is an immoral insurance investigator who takes his victims for everything he can. Then he meets a couple who are out to beat him at his own game. **94m/C VHS, LV.** Phil Collins, Hugo Weaving, Josephine Byrnes. *LIV*

Freaked 🦴🦴 **1993 (PG-13)** Bizarre little black comedy throws everything at the screen, hoping some of the gross-out humor will prove amusing (and some does). Greedy TV star Ricky Coogin (Winter) agrees to be the spokesman for E.E.S. Corporation, which markets a toxic green slime fertilizer to the third world. He's sent to South America to promote the product and is captured by the mad scientist proprietor (Quaid) of a mysterious sideshow, who douses him with the fertilizer. Before you know it he's an oozing half-man, half-beast, perfect to join other freaks as the latest attraction. Lots of yucky makeup. Reeves has an uncredited cameo as the Dog Boy. **80m/C VHS, LV.** Alex Winter, Randy Quaid, Megan Ward, Michael Stoyanov, Brooke Shields, William Sadler, Derek McGrath, Alex Zuckerman, Karyn Malchus, Mr. T, Morgan Fairchild; ***Cameos:*** Keanu Reeves, Tom Stern; ***D:*** Alex Winter, Tom Stern; ***W:*** Alex Winter, Tom Stern, Tim Burns; ***M:*** Kevin Kiner; ***V:*** Bob(cat) Goldthwait. *FXV*

The Freakmaker 🦴🦴 *Mutations; The Mutation* **1973 (R)** Mad professor attempts to breed plants with humans in his lab and has the usual bizarre results. Experiments that fail go to Dunn, a dwarf who runs a freak show. Shamelessly includes real freaks as if plot was not strange enough. **90m/C VHS, Beta.** *GB* Donald Pleasence, Tom Baker, Brad Harris, Julie Ege, Michael Dunn, Jill Haworth; ***D:*** Jack Cardiff. *VDC*

Freaks 🦴🦴🦴½ *Nature's Mistakes; Forbidden Love; The Monster Show* **1932** The infamous, controversial, cult-horror classic about a band of circus freaks that exact revenge upon a beautiful aerialist and her strongman lover after enduring humiliation and exploitation. Based on Ted Robbins story "Spurs." It was meant to out-horror "Frankenstein" but was so successful that it was repeatedly banned. Browning's film may be a shocker but it is never intended to be exploitative since the "Freaks" are the only compassionate, loyal, and loving people around. **66m/B VHS, Beta, LV.** Wallace Ford, Olga Baclanova, Leila Hyams, Roscoe Ates, Harry Earles; ***D:*** Tod Browning. *MGM*

Freakshow 🦴🦴 **1995 (R)** Two teens wander into the sideshow at a local carnival and meet the Freakmaster (Hansen), whose grisly exhibits have equally grisly stories to tell. Campy horror with routine special effects. **102m/C VHS.** Gunnar Hansen, Veronica Carlson, Brian D. Kelly, Shannon Michelle Parsons; ***D:*** William Cooke, Paul Talbot. *AVI*

Freaky Friday 🦴🦴½ **1976 (G)** A housewife and her teenage daughter inadvertently switch bodies and each then tries to carry on the other's normal routine. Mary Rodgers' popular book is brought to the screen with great charm in this above average Disney film. **95m/C VHS, Beta.** Barbara Harris, Jodie Foster, Patsy Kelly, Dick Van Patten, Ruth Buzzi; ***D:*** Gary Nelson. *DIS*

Freddie the Frog ½ *Freddie as F.R.O.7* **1992 (G)** Prince Frederick's life is shattered when his father is killed by his evil Aunt Messina, who wants to rule the kingdom. She even changes Frederick into a frog—but he manages to escape her with the help of friendly sea monster Nessie. But Freddie discovers that he has also been given super-frog powers, just in time to save Britain's landmarks, which are disappearing thanks to Aunt Messina's spells. **72m/C VHS.** *GB* ***D:*** Jon Acevski; ***W:*** Jon Acevski, David Ashton; ***V:*** Ben Kingsley, Nigel Hawthorne, Jenny Agutter, John Sessions, Brian Blessed, Billie Whitelaw, Jonathan Pryce, Phyllis Logan, Michael Hordern. *MCA*

Freddy's Dead: The Final Nightmare *Nightmare on Elm Street 6: Freddy's Dead* **1991 (R)** Freddy's daughter journeys to Springwood, Ohio to put a stop to her father's evil ways. Will she be able to destroy this maniac, or is a new reign of terror just beginning? The sixth, and supposedly last, film in the "Nightmare" series. **96m/C VHS, LV.** Robert Englund, Lisa Zane, Shon Greenblatt, Leslie Deane, Ricky Dean Logan, Breckin Majer, Yaphet Kotto, Elinor Donahue, Roseanne, Johnny Depp, Alice Cooper; ***D:*** Rachel Talalay; ***W:*** Michael De Luca. *COL, NLC*

Free Amerika Broadcasting **1989** A drama about an alternate reality in which Richard Nixon was assassinated, leaving Spiro Agnew president. As a result, the country turns to violent revolution. **80m/C VHS.** Brian Kincaid; ***D:*** Dean Wilson. *NO*

Free and Easy ½ *Easy Go* **1930** Keaton plays the incompetent manager of a beauty contest winner (Page) from Gopher City, Kansas. Page and her overbearing mother, accompanied by Keaton, go to Hollywood to make the girl a star. They gate-crash the MGM studio where all cause havoc and it turns out Keaton is the one who lands in front of the cameras (Page has to settle for romancing Montgomery). Provides a behind-the-scenes look at the MGM studio, with a number of MGM stars making cameo appearances. **92m/B VHS.** Buster Keaton, Anita Page, Robert Montgomery, Trixie Friganza, Fred Niblo; ***Cameos:*** Cecil B. DeMille, Jackie Coogan, Lionel Barrymore, William Haines; ***D:*** Edward Sedgwick. *MGM*

Free Grass *Scream Free!* **1969** A gang of thoughtless hippie drug smugglers and abusers escape from the police, drink acid-spiked wine, shoot each other, and have love-ins. **82m/C VHS, Beta, LV.** Russ Tamblyn, Richard Beymer, Casey Kasem, Lana Wood, Warren Finnerty. *NO*

Free Ride **1986 (R)** A kooky kid steals a sportscar to impress a girl, and gets involved with local hoods. They chase each other around. **92m/C VHS, Beta, LV.** Gary Hershberger, Reed Rudy, Dawn Schneider, Peter DeLuise, Brian MacGregor; ***W:*** Robert Bell. *LIV*

A Free Soul ½ **1931** Tippling litigator Barrymore helps low-life mobster Gable beat a murder rap, only to discover the hood has stolen his daughter's heart. Bargaining with his ditzy daughter, he vows to eschew the bottle if she'll stay away from good-for-nothing Gable. Directed by Brown, best known for his work with Garbo, and based on the memoirs of Adela Rogers St. John. The final courtroom scene—a cloak-and-gavel classic—cinched Barrymore's Oscar. Remade with Liz Taylor as "The Girl Who Had Everything" (although, ironically, the earlier version is the racier of the two). **94m/B VHS.** Norma Shearer, Leslie Howard, Lionel Barrymore, Clark Gable, James Gleason, Lucy Beaumont; ***D:*** Clarence Brown; ***C:*** William H. Daniels. Academy Awards '31: Best Actor (Barrymore); Nominations: Academy Awards '31: Best Actress (Shearer), Best Director (Brown). *MGM, FCT, BTV*

Free to Love **1925** Screen idol Bow plays a young woman, fresh out of prison, who is taken in by a kindly, affluent patron. But, as the silent drama axiom would have it, there's no escaping the past, and she's forced to defend her former life when her guardian is murdered. **61m/B VHS, Beta.** Clara Bow, Donald Keith, Raymond McKee; ***D:*** Frank O'Connor. *GPV, FCT*

Free, White, and 21 **1962** A black motel owner is accused of raping a white civil rights worker. Produced in a "pseudo-documentary" form which sometimes drags. **104m/B VHS.** Frederick O'Neal, Annalena Lund, George Edgely, John Hicks, Hugh Crenshaw, George Russell; ***D:*** Larry Buchanan. *NO*

Free Willy ½ **1993 (PG)** Sentimental story about a 12-year-old runaway (Richter) who befriends a whale. Should appeal to children for its heartwarming story and delightful sea acrobatics. An electronically operated stand-in whale was used for far-off shots; a domesticated performing whale named Keiko for the close-ups. Director Wincer was known to grumble about the temperamental Keiko during shooting. Suggested viewing for students of animal behavior. Proof that family films can make money, "Free Willy" placed tenth for total box office receipts in 1993. **112m/C VHS, LV, 8mm.** Jason James Richter, Lori Petty, Jayne Atkinson, August Schellenberg, Michael Madsen; ***D:*** Simon Wincer; ***W:*** Keith A. Walker, Corey Blechman; ***C:*** Robbie Greenberg; ***M:*** Basil Poledouris. MTV Movie Awards '94: Best Song ("Will You Be There"); Nominations: MTV Movie Awards '94: Breakthrough Performance (Richter), Best Kiss (Jason James Richter/Willy). *WAR, BTV*

Free Willy 2: The Adventure Home ½ **1995 (PG)** While camping in the Pacific Northwest, Jesse is reunited with his orca-pal Willy, who has found a new home along with his whale siblings. But an offshore oil spill separates Willy from his family and threatens their lives, so his human friends must once again come to the rescue. All the principal characters are back, except for Willy (real name Keiko), who is recuperating from a skin virus in Mexico. Animatronics and Gump-like digital effects were used to replicate the real Willy. **98m/C VHS, LV.** Jason James Richter, Michael Madsen, Jayne Atkinson, August Schellenberg, Jon Tenney, Elizabeth Pena; ***D:*** Dwight Little; ***W:*** Corey Blechman, John Mattson; ***C:*** Laszlo Kovacs; ***M:*** Basil Poledouris. *WAR*

Freebie & the Bean ½ **1974 (R)** Two San Francisco cops nearly ruin the city in their pursuit of a numbers-running mobster. Top-flight car chases and low-level, bigoted humor combine. Watch for Valerie Harper's appearance as Arkin's wife. Followed by a flash-in-the-pan television series. **113m/C VHS, Beta, LV.** Alan Arkin, James Caan, Loretta Swit, Valerie Harper, Jack Kruschen, Mike Kellin; ***D:*** Richard Rush. *WAR*

Freedom ½ **1981** A young man finds the price of freedom to be very high when he tries to escape from Australian society in a silver Porsche. **102m/C VHS, Beta.** Jon Blake, Candy Raymond, Jad Capelja, Reg Lye, John Clayton. *NO*

Freedom Is Paradise **1989** With his mother dead and his father missing, thirteen-year-old Sasha is growing up in a bleak reform school. Every time he runs away he is caught and severely beaten upon his return. When Sasha learns of his father's whereabouts he sets out on a 1,000 mile journey to the gulag-style prison where is father is being held. Bodrov's directorial debut. In Russian with English subtitles. **75m/C VHS.** *RU* ***D:*** Sergei Bodrov. Montreal World Film Festival '89: Best Film. *FCT*

Freedom Road **1979** A made for television drama about a Reconstruction Era ex-slave, portrayed by heavyweight champion Ali, who is elected to the U.S. Senate and subsequently killed while trying to obtain total freedom for his race. Based on a novel by Howard Fast. **186m/C VHS, Beta.** Ron O'Neal, Edward Herrmann, John McLiam, Ernest Dixon, Alfre Woodard, Kris Kristofferson, Muhammad Ali; ***D:*** Jan Kadar. *WOV, FCT*

Freejack ½ **1992 (R)** Futuristic thriller set in the year 2009, where pollution, the hole in the ozone layer, and the financial gap between the social classes have grown to such horrific proportions that the rich must pillage the past to find young bodies to replace their own. Estevez is a young race car driver whose sudden death makes him an ideal candidate for this bizarre type of surgery. Once transported to the future, he becomes a "Freejack" who must run for his life. Good cast including Jagger and Hopkins brings this one up slightly. Adapted from the novel "Immortality Inc." by Robert Sheckley. **110m/C VHS, Beta, LV.** Emilio Estevez, Mick Jagger, Rene Russo, Anthony Hopkins, Jonathan Banks, David Johansen, Amanda Plummer, Grand Bush, Frankie Faison, Esai Morales, John Shea; ***D:*** Geoff Murphy; ***W:*** Dan Gilroy, Ronald Shusett, Steven Pressfield; ***M:*** Trevor Jones, Michael Boddicker. *WAR*

Freeway ½ **1988 (R)** A nurse attempts to find the obsessive killer who shot her husband. The murderer phones a radio psychiatrist from his car, using Biblical quotes, while cruising for new victims. Okay thriller, based on the L.A. freeway shootings. **91m/C VHS, Beta, LV.** Darlanne Fluegel, James Russo, Billy Drago, Richard Belzer, Michael Callan, Steve Franken, Kenneth Tobey, Clint Howard; ***D:*** Francis Delia; ***W:*** Larry Ketron, Darrell Fetty, Francis Delia; ***M:*** Joe Delia. *NWV, VTR*

The Freeway Maniac **1988 (R)** A low budget thriller about an escaped convict who ends up on a movie set where he continues his former career: murder. Music by former "Doors" guitarist Robby Krieger. **94m/C VHS, Beta.** Loren Winters, James Courtney, Shepard Sanders, Donald Hotton; ***D:*** Paul Winters; ***M:*** Robby Krieger. *MED*

Freeze-Die-Come to Life ½ *Zamri Oumi Voskresni* **1990** First feature film from Kanevski, who spent 8 years in a labor camp before glasnost. The story of two children who overcome the crushing poverty and bleakness of life in a remote mining community with friendship and humor. Beautifully filmed images, fine acting, touching but never overly sentimental story. The title comes from a children's game of tag. In Russian with English subtitles. **105m/B VHS.** *RU* Pavel Nazarov, Dinara Drukarova; ***D:*** Vitaly Kanevski. *FXL, BST, ING*

Freeze Frame ½ **1992** Doherty is a high school TV reporter who's determined to capture a biotech conspiracy on video in this funny, fast-paced action flick. Nothing objectionable here. **78m/C VHS, LV.** Shannen Doherty, Charles Haid, Robyn Douglass, Seth Michaels; ***D:*** William Bindley; ***W:*** William Bindley. *COL, NLC*

French Can-Can *Only the French Can!* **1955** Dramatically sparse but visually stunning depiction of the can-can's revival in Parisian nightclubs. Gabin plays the theater impressario who discovers laundress Arnoul and decides to turn her into the dancing star of his new revue at the Moulin Rouge. In French with English subtitles. **93m/C VHS, Beta, LV.** *FR* Jean Gabin, Francoise Arnoul, Maria Felix, Jean-Roger Caussimon, Edith Piaf, Patachou; ***D:*** Jean Renoir. *INT, APD, INJ*

The French Connection ½ **1971 (R)** Two NY hard-nosed narcotics detectives stumble onto what turns out to be one of the biggest narcotics rings of all time. Cat-and-mouse thriller will keep you on the edge of your seat; contains one of the most exciting chase scenes ever filmed. Hackman's portrayal of Popeye Doyle is exact and the teamwork with Scheider special. Won multiple awards. Based on a true story from the book by Robin Moore. Followed in 1975 by "French Connection 2." **102m/C VHS, Beta, LV.** Gene Hackman, Roy Scheider, Fernando Rey, Tony LoBianco, Eddie Egan, Sonny Grosso, Marcel Bozzuffi; ***D:*** William Friedkin; ***C:*** Owen Roizman. Academy Awards '71: Best Actor (Hackman), Best Adapted Screenplay, Best Director (Friedkin), Best Film Editing, Best Picture; British Academy Awards '72: Best Actor (Hackman); Directors Guild of America Awards '71: Best Director (Friedkin); Edgar Allan Poe Awards '71: Best Screenplay; Golden Globe Awards '72: Best Actor—Drama (Hackman), Best Director (Friedkin), Best Film—Drama; National Board of Review Awards '71: 10 Best Films of the Year, Best Actor (Hackman); Writers Guild of America '71: Best Adapted Screenplay; Nominations: Academy Awards '71: Best Cinematography, Best Sound, Best Supporting Actor (Scheider). *FOX*

French Connection 2 **1975 (R)** New York policeman "Popeye" Doyle goes to Marseilles to crack a heroin ring headed by his arch nemesis, Frog One, who he failed to stop in the United States. Dour, super-gritty sequel to the 1971 blockbuster, and featuring one of Hackman's most uncompromising performances. **118m/C VHS, Beta,**

LV. Gene Hackman, Fernando Rey, Bernard Fresson; ***D:*** John Frankenheimer; ***W:*** Robert Dillon. *FOX*

The French Detective 🦴🦴🦴 **1975** Two detectives, one an old-time tough guy and the other a young cynic, are after a ruthless politician and his pet hood. Grim but entertaining. **90m/C VHS, Beta.** *FR* Lino Ventura, Patrick Dewaere, Victor Lanoux; ***D:*** Pierre Granier-Deferre. *COL*

French Fried Vacation **1979** Zany antics erupt when a group of unattached and consenting adults vacation in Africa. French with English subtitles. **90m/C VHS.** Josiane Balasko, Michel Blanc, Mariann Chazel; ***D:*** Patrice Leconte. *FRA*

French Intrigue 🦴🦴 **19?? (R)** International agents track drug lords from the U.S. to France in a so-so spy thriller. **90m/C VHS, Beta.** Jane Birkin, Curt Jurgens. *BFV*

French Kiss 🦴🦴½ **1995 (PG-13)** Ultra cute Kate (Ryan) has a fear of flying but she's more afraid of losing her fiance (Hutton) to a newly met French babe. She jets off to Paris and on the way meets a dashing, but disheveled, French rogue (Kline). What happens next is predictable, but amusing just the same. Plot drags a bit in the middle, but the scenery and banter between Ryan and Kline are a pleasant enough diversion. Kline is at his charming best, while Ryan is typically perky. Watch for Spielvogel's stereotypically rude French hotel concierge. He's a hoot. **111m/C VHS, LV.** Meg Ryan, Kevin Kline, Timothy Hutton, Jean Reno, Francois Cluzet, Renee Humphrey, Michael Riley, Susan Anbeh, Laurent Spielvogel; ***D:*** Lawrence Kasdan; ***W:*** Adam Brooks; ***C:*** Owen Roizman; ***M:*** James Newton Howard. *FXV*

The French Lesson 🦴🦴½ *The Frog Prince* **1986 (PG)** A romantic British farce from a screenplay by cartoonist Simmonds, dealing with an English girl who goes to school in Paris and finds love. **90m/C VHS, Beta.** *GB* Alexandre Sterling, Jane Snowdon; ***D:*** Brian Gilbert; ***W:*** Posy S. Simmonds. *WAR*

The French Lieutenant's Woman 🦴🦴🦴½ **1981 (R)** Romantic love and tragedy in the form of two parallel stories, that of an 19th-century woman who keeps her mysterious past from the scientist who loves her, and the lead actor and actress in the film of the same story managing an illicit affair on the set. Extraordinary performances and beautifully shot. Based on the John Fowles novel. **124m/C VHS, Beta, LV.** Meryl Streep, Jeremy Irons, Leo McKern, Lynsey Baxter; ***D:*** Karel Reisz; ***W:*** Harold Pinter; ***M:*** Carl Davis. British Academy Awards '81: Best Actress (Streep); Golden Globe Awards '82: Best Actress—Drama (Streep); Los Angeles Film Critics Association Awards '81: Best Actress (Streep); Nominations: Academy Awards '81: Best Actress (Streep), Best Adapted Screenplay, Best Art Direction/Set Decoration, Best Costume Design, Best Film Editing. *MGM, FOX*

The French Line 🦴🦴 **1954** A millionairess beauty travels incognito while trying to sort out which men are after her money, and which ones aren't. The 3-D presentation of Russell's physique in skimpy costumes earned this the condemnation of the Catholic Legion of Decency, which pumped the box office even higher. Lacks the charm of "Gentlemen Prefer Blonds," which it imitates. ♫Comment Allez-Vous; Well, I'll Be Switched; Any Gal From Texas; What Is This That I Feel?; With A Kiss; By Madame Fuelle; Wait Till You See Paris; Poor Andre; The French Line. **102m/C VHS, Beta.** Jane Russell, Gilbert Roland, Craig Stevens, Kim Novak, Arthur Hunnicutt, Joi Lansing; ***D:*** Lloyd Bacon. *CCB, TTC*

French Postcards 🦴🦴 **1979 (PG)** Three American students study all aspects of French culture when they spend their junior year of college at the Institute of French Studies in Paris. By the same writers who penned "American Graffiti" a few years earlier. **95m/C VHS, Beta.** Miles Chapin, Blanche Baker, Valerie Quennessen, Debra Winger, Mandy Patinkin, Marie-France Pisier; ***D:*** Willard Huyck; ***W:*** Gloria Katz, Willard Huyck. *PAR*

French Quarter 🦴🦴½ **1978 (R)** A dual story about a young girl in the modern-day French Quarter of New Orleans who is also the reincarnation of a turn-of-the-century prostitute. Everyone gets to play two roles but this film is more curiosity than anything else. **101m/C VHS, Beta.** Bruce Davison, Virginia Mayo, Lindsay Bloom, Alisha Fontaine, Lance LeGault, Anne Michelle; ***D:*** Dennis Kane. *NO*

French Quarter Undercover 🦴 **1985 (R)** Two undercover cops in New Orleans thwart a terrorist plot aimed at the World's Fair. **84m/C VHS, Beta.** Michael Parks, Bill Holiday; ***D:*** Joe Catalanotto. *LIV*

French Silk 🦴🦴½ **1994 (PG-13)** Homicide detective (Horsley) falls for a lingerie designer (Lucci) who's a murder suspect. Filmed on location in New Orleans. Made for TV production with additional footage. "R" rating is for nudity (not Lucci's). Based on the novel by Sandra Brown. **90m/C VHS, LV.** Susan Lucci, Lee Horsley, Shari Belafonte, R. Lee Ermey, Sarah Marshall, Bobby Hosea, Jim Metzler, Joe Warfield, Paul Rosenberg; ***D:*** Noel Nosseck. *APX*

The French Touch 🦴🦴½ **1954** Fernandel stars in this French farce about a shepherd who decides to open his own clip joint as a hairdresser and finds himself a hit among the Parisiennes. Fair to middling comedy. **84m/B VHS.** *FR* Fernandel, Renee Devillers, Georges Chamarat; ***D:*** Jean Boyer. *NOS*

French Twist 🦴🦴½ *Bushwhacked; Gazon Maudit* **1995 (R)** Romantic comedy about housewife Loli (Abril), tiredly coping with her realtor/husband Laurent (Chabat) and their two sons. Then Loli meets appealing stranger Marijo (Balasko), a very matter-of-fact lesbian, and when she discovers her hubby is a chronic philanderer, Loli gets revenge by inviting Marijo to move in with them. Laurent realizes he loves his wife but she's having too much fun and there's finally an interesting showdown between Laurent and Marijo over Loli. The French title, which translates literally to "Cursed Lawn," is an old slang term for lesbian. French with subtitles. **105m/C VHS.** *FR* Victoria Abril, Alain Chabat, Josiane Balasko, Ticky Holgado; ***D:*** Josiane Balasko; ***W:*** Josiane Balasko, Telsche Boorman; ***C:*** Gerard de Battista; ***M:*** Manuel Malou. Nominations: Cesar Awards '96: Best Actor (Chabat), Best Director (Balasko), Best Film, Best Screenplay, Best Supporting Actor (Holgado). *NYR*

The French Way 🦴🦴½ **1940** One of the legendary Baker's few films, in which she portrays a Parisian nightclub owner playing matchmaker for a young couple. In French with English subtitles. **72m/B VHS, Beta.** *FR* Josephine Baker, Micheline Presle, Georges Marchal; ***D:*** Jacques de Baroncelli. *VDM, FCT*

The French Woman 🦴 **1979 (R)** Soft-core story of blackmail, murder, and sex involving French cabinet ministers mixing passion and politics. From the director of "Emmanuelle." **97m/C VHS, Beta.** Francoise Fabian, Klaus Kinski; ***D:*** Just Jaeckin; ***M:*** Serge Gainsbourg. *NO*

Frenchman's Farm 🦴½ **1987 (R)** A young woman witnesses a killing at a deserted farmhouse. When she tells the police, they tell her that the murder happened forty years before. Average thriller that probably won't keep you on the edge of your seat. **90m/C VHS, Beta.** *AU* Tracey Tanish, David Reyne, John Meillon, Norman Kaye, Tui Bow; ***D:*** Ron Way. *NO*

Frenzy 🦴🦴½ *Latin Quarter* **1946** A sculptor, pushed over the brink of sanity when he discovers that his wife is having an affair, turns to his art for solace...and seals his wife's corpse in a statue. Creepy. **75m/B VHS.** *GB* Derrick DeMarney, Frederick Valk, Joan Greenwood, Joan Seton, Valentine Dyall, Martin Miller; ***D:*** Vernon Sewell; ***W:*** Vernon Sewell. *SNC*

Frenzy 🦴🦴🦴 **1972 (R)** The only film in which Hitchcock was allowed to totally vent the violence and perverse sexuality of his distinctive vision, in a story about a strangler stalking London women in the late '60s. Finch plays the convicted killer-only he's innocent and must escape prison to find the real killer. McGowen is wonderful as the put-upon police inspector. A bit dated, but still ferociously hostile and cunningly executed. **116m/C VHS, Beta, LV.** *GB* Jon Finch, Barry Foster, Barbara Leigh-Hunt, Anna Massey, Alec McCowen, Vivien Merchant, Billie Whitelaw, Jean Marsh; ***D:*** Alfred Hitchcock; ***W:*** Anthony Shaffer. National Board of Review Awards '72: 10 Best Films of the Year. *MCA*

Fresh 🦴🦴½ **1994 (R)** Intelligent 12-year-old boy runs heroin in the morning and sells crack after school in a tough Brooklyn neighborhood. Enterprising young man draws life lessons from chess-hustler father Jackson and heroin-dealing mentor Esposito, so he looks for a way out of the dead-end business. First time director Yakin plays it straight, foregoing the usual Hollywood-style rap and automatic weapons approach to convey the message that circumstances can kill innocence just as effectively as a bullet. Startling but subdued atmosphere allows the plot and characters to become more complicated than first suspected. Excellent performance by newcomer Nelson as the kid. **114m/C VHS, Beta, LV.** Samuel L. Jackson, Giancarlo Esposito, Sean Nelson, N'Bushe Wright; ***D:*** Boaz Yakin; ***W:*** Boaz Yakin; ***C:*** Adam Holender. Independent Spirit Awards '95: Debut Performance (Nelson); Sundance Film Festival '94: Special Jury Prize, Filmmakers Trophy; Nominations: Independent Spirit Awards '95: Best Supporting Actor (Esposito). *MAX*

Fresh Horses 🦴🦴 **1988 (PG-13)** A wrong-side-of-the-tracks Depression-era romance. McCarthy is the engaged college boy who falls for backwoods girl Ringwald, who turns out to have a destructive secret. **92m/C VHS, Beta, LV.** Molly Ringwald, Andrew McCarthy, Patti D'Arbanville, Ben Stiller; ***D:*** David Anspaugh; ***M:*** David Foster. *COL*

Fresh Kill 🦴 **1987** A young guy from Chicago goes to Hollywood, and gets mixed up in drugs and murder. Made for video. **90m/C VHS, Beta.** Flint Keller, Patricia Parks; ***D:*** Joseph Merhi. *NO*

The Freshman 🦴🦴🦴🦴 **1925** Country boy Lloyd goes to college and, after many comic tribulations, saves the day with the winning touchdown at the big game and wins the girl of his dreams. This was one of the comedian's most popular films. **75m/B VHS, Beta.** Harold Lloyd, Jobyna Ralston, Brooks Benedict, James Anderson, Hazel Keener; ***D:*** Fred Newmeyer, Sam Taylor; ***W:*** Sam Taylor. *TLF*

The Freshman 🦴🦴½ **1990 (PG)** Brando, in an incredible parody of his Don Corleone character, makes this work. Broderick is a college student in need of fast cash, and innocent enough to believe that any work is honest. A good supporting cast and a twisty plot keep things interesting. Sometimes heavy handed with its sight gags, but Broderick and Brando push the movie to hilarious conclusion. Don't miss Burt Parks' musical extravaganza. **102m/C VHS, Beta, LV, 8mm.** Marlon Brando, Matthew Broderick, Penelope Ann Miller, Maximilian Schell, Bruno Kirby, Frank Whaley, Jon Polito, Paul Benedict, Richard Gant, B.D. Wong, Bert Parks; ***D:*** Andrew Bergman; ***W:*** Andrew Bergman; ***M:*** David Newman. *COL, FCT*

Frida 🦴🦴½ **1984** The life of controversial Mexican painter Frido Kahlo is told via deathbed flashbacks using the artist's paintings to set the scenes. In Spanish with English subtitles. **108m/C VHS, Beta, LV.** *SP* Ofelia Medina, Juan Jose Gurrola, Max Kerlow; ***D:*** Paul Leduc. *CVC, IME, APD*

Friday 🦴🦴½ **1995 (R)** It's "Boyz N' the Hood" meets "Good Times". Ice Cube wrote and stars as Craig in this humorous look into life in the 'hood. Craig's just lost his job and spends his time sitting on the porch with his pot smoking sidekick Smokey (Tucker), with the two getting mixed up in a variety of crazy antics involving their kooky neighbors. The laughs come at the expense of overworn cliches and sterotypical characters, but there's originality in the movie's energy and boldness (i.e. the local dope dealer is also the neighborhood ice cream man). To some, this "Friday" could be something to look forward to. **91m/C VHS, LV.** Ice Cube, Chris Tucker, Bernie Mac, John Witherspoon, Regina King, Nia Long, Tiny Lister; ***D:*** F. Gary Gray; ***W:*** Ice Cube, DJ Pooh; ***C:*** Gerry Lively; ***M:*** Frank Fitzpatrick. Nominations: MTV Movie Awards '96: Breakthrough Performance (Tucker), Best On-Screen Duo (Chris Tucker/Ice Cube), Best Comedic Performance (Tucker). *NLC, TTC*

Friday Foster ⚲½ **1975 (R)** A beautiful, young photographer investigates an assassination attempt and uncovers a conspiracy against black politicians. Based on the Chicago Tribune comic strip. **90m/C VHS, Beta.** Pam Grier, Yaphet Kotto, Thalmus Rasulala, Carl Weathers, Godfrey Cambridge; ***D:*** Arthur Marks. *ORI, FCT*

Friday the 13th ⚲⚲ **1980 (R)** Notable as among the first in a very long series of slasher flicks, with effects by Tom Savini. A New Jersey camp reopens after it's been closed for 20 years after a history of "accidental" deaths. And the horror begins again. Six would-be counselors arrive to get the place ready. Each is progressively murdered: knifed, speared, and axed. Followed by numerous, equally gory sequels. **95m/C VHS, Beta, LV.** Betsy Palmer, Adrienne King, Harry Crosby, Laurie Bartrarr, Mark Nelsor, Kevin Bacon; ***D:*** Sean S. Cunningham. *PAR*

Friday the 13th, Part 2 *Woof!* **1981 (R)** New group of teen camp counselors are gruesomely executed by the still undead Jason. Equally as graphic as the first installment; followed by several more gorefests. **87m/C VHS, Beta, LV.** Amy Steel, John Furey, Adrienne King, Betsy Palmer; ***D:*** Steve Miner. *PAR*

Friday the 13th, Part 3 *Woof!* **1982 (R)** Yet another group of naive counselors at Camp Crystal Lake fall victim to the maniacal Jason. The 3-D effects actually helped lessen the gory effects, but this is still awful. Followed by more disgusting sequels. **96m/C VHS, Beta, LV.** Dana Kimmell, Paul Krata, Richard Brooker; ***D:*** Steve Miner. *PAR*

Friday the 13th, Part 4: The Final Chapter *Woof!* **1984 (R)** Jason escapes from the morgue to once again slaughter and annihilate teenagers at a lakeside cottage. Preceded by three earlier "Friday the 13th" films, equally as graphic. The title's also a lie since there's several more sequels to look forward to. **90m/C VHS, Beta, LV.** Erich Anderson, Judie Aronson, Kimberly Beck, Peter Barton, Tom Everett, Corey Feldman, Crispin Glover; ***D:*** Joseph Zito; ***W:*** Barney Cohen. *PAR*

Friday the 13th, Part 5: A New Beginning *Woof!* **1985 (R)** Jason rises from the dead to slice up the residents of a secluded halfway house. The sequels, and the sameness, never stop. See Part 6... **92m/C VHS, Beta, LV.** John Shepherd, Melanie Kinnaman, Shavar Ross, Richard Young, Juliette Cummins, Corey Feldman; ***D:*** Danny Steinmann; ***W:*** David M. Cohen. *PAR*

Friday the 13th, Part 6: Jason Lives *Woof!* **1986 (R)** One of the few youths not butchered by Jason digs him up and discovers he's not (and never will be) dead. Carnage ensues...and the sequels continue. **87m/C VHS, Beta, LV.** Thom Mathews, Jennifer Cooke, David Kagen; ***D:*** Tom McLoughlin. *PAR*

Friday the 13th, Part 7: The New Blood *Woof!* **1988 (R)** A young camper with telekinetic powers accidentally unchains Jason from his underwater lair with the now-familiar results. There's still another bloody sequel to go. **90m/C VHS, Beta, LV.** Lar Park Lincoln, Kevin Blair, Susan Blu; ***D:*** John Carl Buechler; ***W:*** Daryl Haney. *PAR*

Friday the 13th, Part 8: Jason Takes Manhattan ⚲ **1989 (R)** Yet another sequel, with the ski-masked walking slaughterhouse transported to New York. Most of the previous action in the movie takes place on a cruise ship. This one is less gruesome than others in the series. Followed by "Jason Goes to Hell: The Final Friday." **96m/C VHS, Beta, LV.** Jensen Daggett, Scott Reeves, Peter Mark Richman, Barbara Bingham; ***D:*** Rob Hedden; ***W:*** Rob Hedden. *PAR*

Fridays of Eternity ⚲⚲ **1981** A romantic comedy about loyalty, fidelity, love, and lovers all with a tinge of the supernatural. In Spanish with English subtitles. **89m/C VHS.** *AR* Thelma Biral, Hector Alterio; ***D:*** Hector Olivera. *INJ*

Fried Green Tomatoes ⚲⚲⚲ **1991 (PG-13)** Two stories about four women, love, friendship, Southern charm, and eccentricity are untidily held together by wonderful performances. Unhappy, middle-aged Evelyn (Bates), meets the talkative 83-year-old Ninny Threadgoode (Tandy). Ninny reminisces about her Depression-era life in the town of Whistle Stop, Alabama and the two women, Idgie (Masterson) and Ruth (Parker), who ran the local cafe. Back-and-forth narrative as it tracks multiple storylines is occasionally confusing, though strong character development holds interest. Surprising box office hit adapted by Fannie Flagg from her novel "Fried Green Tomatoes at the Whistle Stop Cafe." **130m/C VHS, Beta, LV.** Kathy Bates, Jessica Tandy, Mary Stuart Masterson, Mary-Louise Parker, Cicely Tyson, Chris O'Donnell, Stan Shaw, Gailard Sartain, Timothy Scott, Gary Basaraba, Lois Smith, Grace Zabriskie; ***D:*** Jon Avnet; ***W:*** Fannie Flagg, Carol Sobieski; ***M:*** Thomas Newman. National Media Owl Awards '92: First Prize; Nominations: Academy Awards '91: Best Adapted Screenplay, Best Supporting Actress (Tandy). *MCA*

Frieda ⚲⚲½ **1947** An RAF officer brings his German wife home after the war and she is naturally distrusted by his family and neighbors. An interesting look at post-war bigotry. **97m/B VHS.** *GB* David Farrar, Glynis Johns, Mai Zetterling, Flora Robson, Albert Lieven; ***D:*** Basil Dearden. *NOS, VYY, VEC*

Friendly Fire ⚲⚲⚲ **1979** Based on a true story of an American family in 1970 whose soldier son is killed by "friendly fire" in Vietnam, and their efforts to uncover the circumstances of the tragedy. Touching and powerful, with an excellent dramatic performance by Burnett. Made for television. **146m/C VHS, Beta.** Carol Burnett, Ned Beatty, Sam Waterston, Timothy Hutton; ***D:*** David Greene. *FOX*

Friendly Persuasion ⚲⚲⚲ *Except For Me and Thee* **1956** Earnest, solidly acted tale about a peaceful Quaker family struggling to remain true to its ideals in spite of the Civil War which touches their farm life in southern Indiana. Cooper and McGuire are excellent as the parents with Perkins fine as the son worried he's using his religion to hide his cowardice. Based on a novel by Jessamyn West. **140m/C VHS, Beta, LV.** Gary Cooper, Dorothy McGuire, Anthony Perkins, Marjorie Main, Charles Halton; ***D:*** William Wyler; ***C:*** Ellsworth Fredericks; ***M:*** Dimitri Tiomkin. Cannes Film Festival '57: Best Film; Nominations: Academy Awards '56: Best Adapted Screenplay, Best Director (Wyler), Best Picture, Best Song ("Friendly Persuasion (Thee I Love)"), Best Sound, Best Supporting Actor (Perkins). *FOX*

Friends ⚲ **1971 (R)** Ho-hum drama about an orphaned French girl and an unloved English boy who meet, become friends, and decide to run away together, setting up house in a deserted beach cottage. They even have a baby before they're discovered. Provides no insight into the teenagers dilemmas. Followed by "Paul and Michelle." **101m/C VHS.** *GB* Sean Bury, Anicee Alvina, Pascale Roberts, Sady Rebbot, Ronald Lewis; ***D:*** Lewis Gilbert; ***M:*** Elton John. *PAR*

Friends ⚲⚲ **1995** Story of three South African women sharing an apartment in Johannesburg. Fox is a white political activist, Burgers, an Afrikaner archaeologist, and Kente, a black teacher. When Fox plants a bomb that takes two innocent lives, their loyalties are tested. Debut for director Proctor. **109m/C VHS.** Kerry Fox, Michele Burgers, Dambisa Kente; ***D:*** Elaine Proctor; ***W:*** Elaine Proctor. *ICA*

Friends Forever ⚲⚲⚲ **1986** Conformity, sexuality, and friendship are explored in this coming-of-age drama. Kristian is a shy, conformist sixteen-year-old, starting off at a new school. He finds himself drawn to two different young men who equally dominate his class. Henrik's androgynous sexual charm is equaled by his independence while the moody Patrick is the leader of a band of troublemakers. Kristian gains in self-confidence by their friendship but is tested when he learns Patrick is gay. **95m/C VHS.** *DK* ***D:*** Stefan Christian Henszelman. *FCT*

Friends, Lovers & Lunatics ⚲½ *Crazy Horse; She Drives Me Crazy* **1989** A weekend turns into a romantic nightmare/laugh-fest when a man visits his ex-girlfriend and her new "friend", and winds up in a new romance himself. **87m/C VHS, Beta, LV.** *CA* Daniel Stern, Deborah Foreman, Sheila McCarthy, Page Fletcher, Elias Koteas; ***D:*** Stephen Withrow. *FRH, IME*

A Friendship in Vienna ⚲⚲½ **1988** The friendship of two young teenage girls, one Jewish, and the other the daughter of a Nazi collaborator, is tested as WWII looms over Europe and the Nazis begin their persecution of Austrian Jews. Adapted from the book "Devil in Vienna" by Doris Orgel. Made for cable television. **100m/C VHS.** Jenny Lewis, Ed Asner, Jane Alexander, Stephen Macht, Rosemary Forsyth, Ferdinand "Ferdy" Mayne, Kamie Harper; ***D:*** Arthur Seidelman; ***W:*** Richard Alfieri. *DIS*

Fright ⚲ *Spell of the Hypnotist* **1956** A woman—convinced that she died in 1889 as part of a suicide pact with Prince Rudolph of Austria—seeks help from a psychiatrist who promptly falls in love with her (didn't Freud say it was supposed to be the other way around?). **?m/B VHS.** Nancy Malone, Eric Fleming, Frank Marth, Humphrey Davis, Ned Glass, Norman Burton; ***D:*** W. Lee Wilder. *SNC*

Fright ⚲⚲ *Night Legs* **1971 (PG)** A baby-sitter is menaced by a mental hospital escapee. He turns out to be the father of the boy she is watching. Tense but violent thriller. **84m/C VHS.** *GB* Susan George, Honor Blackman, Ian Bannen, John Gregson, George Cole, Dennis Waterman; ***D:*** Peter Collinson. *REP, MOV*

Fright House ⚲ **1989 (R)** Two stories of terror. "Fright House" features witches preparing an old mansion for a visit from the Devil. "Abandon" explains the prolonged youth of a teacher to her young student. **110m/C VHS, Beta.** Al Lewis, Duane Jones; ***D:*** Len Anthony. *NO*

Fright Night ⚲⚲½ **1985 (R)** It's Dracula-versus-the-teens time when Charley suspects that his new neighbor descends from Count Vlad's line. He calls in the host of "Fright Night," the local, late-night, horror-flick series, to help de-ghoul the neighborhood. But they have a problem when the vampire discovers their plans (and nobody belives them anyway). Sarandon is properly seductive as the bloodsucker. Followed by sequel. **106m/C VHS, Beta, LV.** William Ragsdale, Chris Sarandon, Amanda Bearse, Roddy McDowall, Stephen Geoffreys, Jonathan Stark, Dorothy Fielding; ***D:*** Tom Holland; ***W:*** Tom Holland; ***M:*** Brad Fiedel. *COL*

Fright Night 2 ⚲⚲ **1988 (R)** The sequel to the 1985 release "Fright Night," in which the harassed guy from the original film learns slowly that the vampire's sister and her entourage have come to roost around his college. Not quite as good as the original but the special effects are worth a look. **108m/C VHS, Beta, LV.** Roddy McDowall, William Ragsdale, Traci Lind, Julie Carmen; ***D:*** Tommy Lee Wallace; ***W:*** Tommy Lee Wallace, Tim Metcalfe; ***M:*** Brad Fiedel. *LIV*

The Frighteners ⚲⚲½ **1996 (R)** Con man Frank Bannister (Fox) has a unique scam—he works with a group of ghosts who haunt a home until Frank comes along to drive them out, for the right price. But the small town of Fairwater is plagued by a serial killer's evil spirit and Frank and his spiritual cronies face the challenge of getting rid of the ghost before the police decide to get rid of Frank. Interesting horror-comedy takes a lot of twists and turns to get where its going, but the payoff in gore and humor is worth it for fans of the genre. New Zealand helmer Jacobson makes his American directorial debut. **?m/C VHS.** Michael J. Fox, Trini Alvarado, Peter Dobson, Dee Wallace Stone, John Astin, Jeffrey Combs, Troy Evans, Chi McBride, Jake Busey, R. Lee Ermey; ***D:*** Peter Jackson; ***W:*** Peter Jackson, Frances Walsh; ***C:*** Alun Bollinger, John Buck; ***M:*** Danny Elfman. *NYR*

Frightmare ⚲⚲½ *Frightmare 2* **1974 (R)** A seemingly quiet British couple do indulge in one strange habit—they're cannibals. Released on video as "Frightmare 2" to avoid confusion with the 1981 film. **86m/C VHS, Beta.** *GB* Deborah Fairfax, Kim Butcher, Rupert Davies, Sheila Keith; ***D:*** Pete Walker. *PSM*

Frightmare ☠ **1981 (R)** Great horror star dies, but he refuses to give up his need for adoration and revenge. **84m/C VHS, Beta.** Ferdinand "Ferdy" Mayne, Luca Bercovici, Nita Talbot, Peter Kastner; ***D:*** Norman Thaddeus Vane. *VES*

Frightshow **1984** Four independent short horror films; "Nightfright," "Thing in the Basement," "Dr. Dobermind," and "Illegal Alien." **60m/C VHS.** *MPI*

The Fringe Dwellers ☠☠½ **1986 (PG)** An Aborigine family leave their shantytown and move to the white, middle-class suburbs of Australia, encountering prejudice and other difficulties. Well acted and interesting but the ending's a letdown. **98m/C VHS, Beta, LV.** *AU* Kristina Nehm, Justine Saunders, Bob Maza, Kylie Belling, Denis Walker, Ernie Dingo; ***D:*** Bruce Beresford; ***W:*** Bruce Beresford, Rhoisin Beresford; ***M:*** George Dreyfus. *NO*

The Frisco Kid ☠☠ *No Knife* **1979 (R)** An innocent orthodox rabbi (Wilder) from Poland is sent to the wilds of San Francisco during the 1850s gold rush to lead a new congregation. He lands in Philadelphia, joins a wagon train and is promptly robbed and abandoned. He eventually meets up with a not-too-bright robber (Ford) who finds himself unexpectly befriending the man and undergoing numerous tribulations in order to get them both safely to their destination. This isn't a laugh riot and some scenes fall distinctly flat but Wilder is sweetness personified and lends the movie its charm. **119m/C VHS, Beta.** Gene Wilder, Harrison Ford, Ramon Bieri, Val Bisoglio, George DiCenzo, Penny Peyser, William Smith; ***D:*** Robert Aldrich; ***W:*** Michael Elias; ***C:*** Robert B. Hauser. *WAR*

Fritz the Cat ☠☠☠ **1972** Ralph Bakshi's animated tale for adults about a cat's adventures as he gets into group sex, college radicalism, and other hazards of life in the '60s. Loosely based on the underground comics character by Robert Crumb. Originally X-rated. **77m/C VHS, Beta.** ***D:*** Ralph Bakshi; ***W:*** Ralph Bakshi; ***M:*** Ed Bogas. *WAR, OM*

Frog **1989** A boy adds a frog to his reptile collection but gets the surprise of his life when he finds it's really an enchanted Prince! Followed by "Frogs!" Part of the "Wonderworks" series. **55m/C VHS, Beta, LV.** Paul Williams, Scott Grimes, Shelley Duvall, Elliott Gould, David Grossman. *ORI, IME*

Frogs ☠☠½ **1972 (PG)** An environmental photographer working on a small island in Florida interrupts the birthday celebration of a patriarch. He and the folks at the party soon realize that various amphibians in the surrounding area are going berserk and attacking humans. One of the first environmentally-motivated animal-vengeance films, and one of the best to come out of the '70s. **91m/C VHS, Beta.** Ray Milland, Sam Elliott, Joan Van Ark, Adam Roarke, Judy Pace, Lynn Borden, Mae Mercer, David Gilliam, George Skaff; ***D:*** George McCowan; ***W:*** Robert Blees; ***M:*** Les Baxter. *WAR, OM*

Frogs! **199?** Arlo is almost the most popular boy in school and is hoping to be crowned the king of his school's Spring Fling dance—until he and his friend Gus are turned into frogs by a witch. When Arlo and Gus discover their frog pond is being poisoned, they turn to the geeky Hannah for help. A sequel to "Frog." A viewers' guide is included. Part of the "Wonderworks" series. **55m/C VHS.** Shelley Duvall, Elliott Gould, Paul Williams, Scott Grimes, Judith Ivey. *PME, HMV, BTV*

Frolics on Ice ☠☠ **1940** Pleasant comedy-musical about a family man saving to buy the barber shop he works at. Irene Dare is featured in several ice skating production numbers. **65m/B VHS, Beta.** Roscoe Karns, Lynn (Mary Hart) Roberts, Irene Dare, Edgar Kennedy. *VYY*

From Beyond ☠☠☠ **1986 (R)** A gruesome, tongue-in-cheek adaptation of the ghoulish H.P. Lovecraft story. Scientists discover another dimension through experiments with the pineal gland. From the makers of "Re-Animator," and just as funny. **90m/C VHS, Beta, LV.** Jeffrey Combs, Barbara Crampton, Ted Sorel, Ken Foree, Carolyn Purdy-Gordon, Bunny Summers, Bruce McGuire; ***D:*** Stuart Gordon; ***W:*** Dennis Paoli, Brian Yuzna; ***M:*** Richard Band. *LIV, VES*

From Beyond the Grave ☠☠ *Creatures* **1973 (PG)** This horror compendium revolves around a mysterious antique shop whose customers experience various supernatural phenomena, especially when they try to cheat the shop's equally mysterious owner. **98m/C VHS, Beta.** *GB* Peter Cushing, David Warner, Ian Bannen, Donald Pleasence, Margaret Leighton, Lesley-Anne Down, Diana Dors, Ian Ogilvy; ***D:*** Kevin Connor. *WAR*

From Dusk Till Dawn ☠☠½ **1995 (R)** Escaped cons Seth and Richie Gecko (Clooney and Tarantino) pick up an ex-preacher (Keitel) and his two kids (Lewis and Liu) as hostages en route to their Mexican rendezvous spot, a raunchy biker joint run (unbenownst to them) by vampires. Feels like two movies in one, as Rodriguez's and Tarantino's styles don't necessarily mesh as much as they coexist. The first half features Tarantino's gift for snappy dialogue and somewhat sympathetic scumbags while the barroom finale shows off Rodriguez's mastery of the go-for-broke action set piece. Clooney proves the jump from TV to movies can be made successfully. Penned by Tarantino in 1990 during his video store days, he used the fee to get "Reservoir Dogs" off the ground. **100m/C VHS.** George Clooney, Quentin Tarantino, Harvey Keitel, Juliette Lewis, Fred Williamson, Richard "Cheech" Marin, Salma Hayek, Michael Parks, Tom Savini, Ernest Liu, Kelly Preston, John Saxon, Danny Trejo; ***D:*** Robert Rodriguez; ***W:*** Quentin Tarantino; ***C:*** Guillermo Navarro; ***M:*** Graeme Revell. MTV Movie Awards '96: Breakthrough Performance (Clooney). *TOU*

From Hell to Borneo ☠½ **1964 (PG)** A mercenary must defend his secluded island from pirates and gangsters. **90m/C VHS, Beta.** George Montgomery, Torin Thatcher, Julie Gregg, Lisa Moreno; ***D:*** George Montgomery. *NO*

From Hell to Victory ☠☠ **1979 (PG)** Group of friends of different nationalities vow to meet each year in Paris on the same date but WWII interrupts their lives and friendships. Director Lenzi used the alias Hank Milestone. Good battle scenes but nothing special. **100m/C VHS, Beta.** *SP FR* George Peppard, George Hamilton, Horst Buchholz, Jean-Pierre Cassel, Capucine, Sam Wanamaker, Anny Duperey, Ray Lovelock; ***D:*** Umberto Lenzi. *MED, HHE, VTR*

From Here to Eternity ☠☠☠☠ **1953** Complex, hard-hitting look at the on and off-duty life of soldiers at the Army base in Honolulu in the days before the Pearl Harbor attack. There's sensitive Pvt. Pruitt (Clift), his always in trouble best friend Maggio (Sinatra), and their good-guy top sergeant (Lancaster) who just happens to be having a torrid affair with the commander's wife (Kerr). Pruitt, meanwhile, is introduced to a club "hostess" (Reed) who is a lot more vulnerable than she's willing to admit. A movie filled with great performances. Still has the best waves-on-the-beach love scene in filmdom. Based on the novel by James Jones, which was toned down by the censors. **118m/B VHS, Beta, LV, 8mm.** Burt Lancaster, Montgomery Clift, Frank Sinatra, Deborah Kerr, Donna Reed, Ernest Borgnine, Philip Ober, Jack Warden, Mickey Shaughnessy, George Reeves, Claude Akins; ***D:*** Fred Zinnemann; ***W:*** Daniel Taradash; ***C:*** Burnett Guffey; ***M:*** George Duning. Academy Awards '53: Best Black and White Cinematography, Best Director (Zinnemann), Best Film Editing, Best Picture, Best Screenplay, Best Sound, Best Supporting Actor (Sinatra), Best Supporting Actress (Reed); Golden Globe Awards '54: Best Supporting Actor (Sinatra); National Board of Review Awards '53: 10 Best Films of the Year; New York Film Critics Awards '53: Best Actor (Lancaster), Best Director (Zinnemann), Best Film; Nominations: Academy Awards '53: Best Actor (Clift), Best Actor (Lancaster), Best Actress (Kerr), Best Costume Design (B & W); Golden Globe Awards '54: Best Director (Zinnemann). *COL, BTV*

From Here to Eternity ☠☠½ **1979 (PG-13)** From here to eternity...and back on the silver screen. Remake of the 1953 classic is based on James Jones' novel about life on a Hawaiian military base just before WWII. Decent actioner, but no Oscar-winner this time around. Made for television. **110m/C VHS, Beta, LV.** Natalie Wood, Kim Basinger, William Devane, Steve Railsback, Peter Boyle, Will Sampson, Andy Griffith, Roy Thinnes, Barbara Hershey; ***D:*** Buzz Kulik. *VMK, FCT*

From Here to Maternity ☠☠½ **1985** A made-for-television soap opera-based spoof about modern maternity. Three women want to be pregnant but their significant others aren't interested in paternity. **40m/C VHS, Beta.** Carrie Fisher, Arleen Sorkin, Lauren Hutton, Griffin Dunne, Paul Reiser. *LIV, VES*

From Hollywood to Deadwood ☠☠ **1989 (R)** A beautiful starlet is kidnapped and the private eye searching for her discovers blackmail and danger. **90m/C VHS, Beta, LV.** Scott Paulin, Jim Haynie, Barbara Schock; ***D:*** Rex Pickett. *MED, FCT, IME*

From Noon Till Three ☠☠½ **1976 (PG)** A change of pace role for Bronson as a two-bit gunfighter in a spoof of western legends. Bronson has a brief romance with Ireland who, believing him dead, fictionalizes their relationship in a series of books and builds the mediocre Dorsey into a western hero. When he turns up alive no one, including Ireland, believes that he is the real Dorsey and he's gradually driven crazy. Good script, weak direction but Bronson is likeable. **99m/C VHS.** Charles Bronson, Jill Ireland, Douglas Fowley, Stan Haze, Damon Douglas; ***D:*** Frank D. Gilroy; ***W:*** Frank D. Gilroy; ***M:*** Elmer Bernstein. *MGM*

From Russia with Love ☠☠☠½ **1963 (PG)** Bond is back and on the loose in exotic Istanbul looking for a super-secret coding machine. He's involved with a beautiful Russian spy and has the SPECTRE organization after him, including villainess Rosa Klebb (she of the killer shoe). Lots of exciting escapes but not an over-reliance on the gadgetry of the later films. The second Bond feature, thought by many to be the best. The laserdisc edition includes interviews with director Terence Young and others on the creative staff. The musical score and special effects can be separated from the actors' dialogue. Also features publicity shots, American and British trailers, on-location photos, and movie posters. **125m/C VHS, Beta, LV.** *GB* Sean Connery, Daniela Bianchi, Pedro Armendariz Sr., Lotte Lenya, Robert Shaw, Eunice Gayson, Walter Gotell, Lois Maxwell, Bernard Lee, Desmond Llewelyn, Nadja Regin, Alizia Gur, Martine Beswick, Leila; ***D:*** Terence Young; ***C:*** Ted Moore; ***M:*** John Barry. *MGM, CRC, TLF*

From "Star Wars" to "Jedi": The Making of a Saga **1983** Using copious amounts of actual footage from the films, this movie follows the production of all three "Star Wars" sagas, concentrating on the special effects involved. **65m/C VHS, Beta.** David Prowse, Harrison Ford, Carrie Fisher, Billy Dee Williams, Alec Guinness; ***D:*** George Lucas. *FOX, FLI*

From the Dead of Night ☠☠☠ **1989** A spooky chiller about a near-death experience. Fashion designer Wagner narrowly escapes death but gets close enough to the other side that six of the dead feel cheated that she didn't join them. They decide to rectify the mistake and Wagner is pursued by the shadowy figures. Based on the novel "Walkers" by Gary Bradner. Made for television. **192m/C VHS.** Lindsay Wagner, Bruce Boxleitner, Diahann Carroll, Robert Prosky, Robin Thomas, Merritt Butrick, Joanne Linville; ***D:*** Paul Wendkos. *AIP*

From the Earth to the Moon ☠☠ **1958** A mad scientist invents a new energy source and builds a rocket which takes him, his daughter, and two other men for some adventures on the moon. Based on the novel by Jules Verne. **100m/C VHS, Beta, LV.** George Sanders, Joseph Cotten, Debra Paget, Don Dubbins; ***D:*** Byron Haskin; ***W:*** Robert Blees. *NO*

From the Hip ☠☠ **1986 (PG)** A young lawyer (Nelson) gets the chance of a lifetime when his office assigns a murder case to him. The only problem is that he suspects his client is very guilty indeed and must discover the truth without breaking his code of ethics. Nelson's courtroom theatrics are a bit out of hand, as he flares his nostrils at every opportunity. The movie is encumbered by a weak script and plot as well as a mid-story switch from comedy to drama.

112m/C VHS, Beta, LV. Judd Nelson, Elizabeth Perkins, John Hurt, Ray Walston; ***D:*** Bob (Benjamin) Clark; ***W:*** Bob (Benjamin) Clark, David Kelly. *ORI, WAR*

From the Life of the Marionettes **1980 (R)** A repressed man in a crumbling marriage rapes and kills a young prostitute. Another look at the powers behind individual motivations from Bergman, who uses black and white and color to relate details of the incident. **104m/C VHS, Beta, LV.** *SW* Robert Atzorn, Christine Buchegger, Martin Benrath, Rita Russek, Lola Muethel, Walter Schmidinger, Heinz Bennent; ***D:*** Ingmar Bergman; ***W:*** Ingmar Bergman; ***C:*** Sven Nykvist. *LIV*

From the Manger to the Cross **1915** This version of the Passion play was the first film to be done on location in Palestine. Re-enacts the Nativity, the flight into Egypt, and the crucifixion. Color-tinted. **71m/C VHS.** R. Henderson-Bland, Alice Hollister, Gene Gauthier; ***D:*** Sidney Olcott; ***W:*** Gene Gauthier, Sidney Olcott. *KIV*

From the Mixed-Up Files of Mrs. Basil E. Frankweiler ½ **1995 (PG)** Runaway siblings (Barnwell and Lee) secretly hide out in a New York art museum. They get caught up in trying to determine the authenticity of a sculpture (could it be the work of Michelangelo?) and turn to the statue's last owner, elusive art patron Mrs. Basil E. Frankweiler (Bacall). Based on the Newbery Award-winning novel by E.L. Konigsburg. Made for TV. **92m/C VHS.** Lauren Bacall, Jean Marie Barnwell, Jesse Lee; ***D:*** Marcus Cole. *HMK*

From the Terrace ½ **1960** Newman is a wealthy Pennsylvania boy who goes to New York and marries into even more money and social position when he weds Woodward. He gets a job with her family's investment company and neglects his wife for business. She turns to another man and when he goes home for a visit he also finds a new romance which leads to some emotional soul searching. The explicitness of O'Hara's very long novel was diluted by the censors and Newman's performance is a stilted disappointment. Loy, as Newman's alcoholic mother, earned the best reviews. **144m/C VHS, Beta, LV.** Paul Newman, Joanne Woodward, Myrna Loy, Ina Balin, Felix Aylmer, Leon Ames, George Grizzard, Patrick O'Neal, Barbara Eden, Mae Marsh; ***D:*** Mark Robson; ***W:*** Ernest Lehman; ***M:*** Elmer Bernstein. *FOX*

The Front **1976 (PG)** Woody is the bookmaker who becomes a "front" for blacklisted writers during the communist witch hunts of the 1950s in this satire comedy. The scriptwriter and several of the performers suffered blacklisting themselves during the Cold War. Based more or less on a true story. **95m/C VHS, Beta, LV.** Woody Allen, Zero Mostel, Herschel Bernardi, Michael Murphy, Danny Aiello, Andrea Marcovicci; ***D:*** Martin Ritt; ***W:*** Walter Bernstein; ***C:*** Michael Chapman; ***M:*** Dave Grusin. National Board of Review Awards '76: 10 Best Films of the Year; Nominations: Academy Awards '76: Best Original Screenplay. *COL*

The Front Page ½ **1931** The original screen version of the Hecht-MacArthur play about the shenanigans of a battling newspaper reporter and his editor in Chicago. O'Brien's film debut here is one of several hilarious performances in this breathless pursuit of an exclusive with an escaped death row inmate. **101m/B VHS, Beta.** Adolphe Menjou, Pat O'Brien, Edward Everett Horton, Mae Clarke, Walter Catlett; ***D:*** Lewis Milestone; ***C:*** Hal Mohr. National Board of Review Awards '31: 10 Best Films of the Year; Nominations: Academy Awards '31: Best Actor (Menjou), Best Director (Milestone), Best Picture. *NOS, MRV, HHT*

The Front Page ½ **1974 (PG)** A remake of the Hecht-MacArthur play about the managing editor of a 1920s Chicago newspaper who finds out his ace reporter wants to quit the business and get married. But first an escaped convicted killer offers the reporter an exclusive interview. **105m/C VHS, LV.** Jack Lemmon, Walter Matthau, Carol Burnett, Austin Pendleton, Vincent Gardenia, Charles Durning, Susan Sarandon; ***D:*** Billy Wilder; ***W:*** Billy Wilder, I.A.L. Diamond. *MCA*

Frontier Days ½ **1934** Cody goes undercover to capture the leader of a gang of stagecoach robbers. He also manages to capture a killer along the way. **60m/B VHS, Beta.** Bill Cody, Ada Ince, Wheeler Oakman; ***D:*** Sam Newfield. *NOS, DVT*

Frontier Fugitives ½ **1945** When a trapper is murdered—allegedly by Indians—the Texas Rangers ride in to investigate. **58m/B VHS.** Tex Ritter, Dave O'Brien, Guy Wilkerson, Lorraine Miller, I. Stanford Jolley, Jack Ingram; ***D:*** Harry Fraser. *NOS*

Frontier Horizon **1939** Wayne and the Three Mesquiteers help out ranchers whose land is being bought up by crooked speculators. **55m/B VHS, Beta.** John Wayne, Jennifer Jones, Ray Corrigan, Raymond Hatton; ***D:*** George Sherman. *REP, CAB*

Frontier Justice **1935** Gibson is the foolish son of a cattle owner who has been forced into an insane asylum because of a battle over water rights. Naturally, he must take on responsibility and rescue his father. **56m/B VHS, Beta.** Hoot Gibson, Richard Cramer; ***D:*** Robert McGowan. *NOS, VCN, DVT*

Frontier Law ½ **1943** Hayden and the boys ride into town to clean out the bad guys and clear a friend wrongly accused of murder. **55m/B VHS.** Russell Hayden, Jennifer Holt, Dennis Moore, Fuzzy Knight, Jack Ingram, Hal Taliaferro; ***D:*** Elmer Clifton; ***W:*** Elmer Clifton. *MOV*

Frontier Outlaws **1944** A gang of villains is selling stolen cattle, and Crabbe poses as an interested buyer to catch them in the act. Laughs are provided by Lynn as a judge, and "Fuzzy" St. John as Crabbe's sidekick. **58m/B VHS.** Buster Crabbe, Al "Fuzzy" St. John, Frances Gladwin, Marin Sais, Charles "Blackie" King, Jack Ingram, Kermit Maynard, Edward Cassidy, Emmett Lynn, Budd Buster; ***D:*** Sam Newfield. *GPV, MRV, NOS*

Frontier Pony Express **1939** Roy and Trigger do their best to help the Pony Express riders who are being attacked by marauding gangs in California during the time of the Civil War. Plenty of action here. **54m/B VHS, Beta.** Roy Rogers; ***D:*** Joseph Kane. *NOS, MED, DVT*

Frontier Scout **1938** Action-packed western has Wild Bill Hickock, portrayed by former opera singer Houston, forcing Lee's surrender in the Civil War before pursuing cattle rustlers out West. **60m/B VHS, Beta.** George Houston, Mantan Moreland; ***D:*** Sam Newfield. *NOS, DVT, RXM*

Frontier Uprising ½ **1961** Stunning cinematography makes up for weak narrative in this otherwise routine oater. Davis stars as a frontier scout battling hordes of Mexicans and Indians while trying to gain control of California for the U.S. Based on the short story "Kit Carson" by George Bruce. **68m/B VHS.** Jim Davis, Nancy Hadley, Ken Mayer, Nestor Paiva, Don O'Kelly; ***D:*** Edward L. Cahn; ***W:*** Owen Harris. *DVT*

Frontier Vengeance ½ **1940** Barry is falsely accused of murder and works to clear his name while at the same time romancing a stagecoach driver who's trying to win a race with a rival stagecoach line. **54m/B VHS, Beta.** Donald (Don "Red") Barry, Nate Watt. *MED, RXM*

The Frontiersmen **1938** Things plod along at the little red schoolhouse until Hoppy and the guys have to take off after some rustlers. Features the members of the St. Brendan Boys Choir as the schoolboys. Unusual for its lack of gunplay until near the end. **71m/B VHS.** William Boyd, George "Gabby" Hayes, Russell Hayden, Evelyn Venable, Clara Kimball Young, Charles Hughes, Dick Jones, Roy Barcroft, Emily Fitzroy; ***D:*** Lesley Selander. *NOS*

Frostbiter: Wrath of the Wendigo *Woof!* **1994 (R)** Woe to the hunters who disturb the final resting place of the dreaded demon "Wendigo." Try to maintain a high level of suspended belief. Based on the comic book character of the same name. **90m/C VHS.** Ron Asheton, Lori Baker, Patrick Butler, Devlin Burton; ***D:*** Tom Chaney; ***W:*** Tom Chaney. *TTV*

Frozen Alive **1964** A scientist experiments with suspended animation but, wouldn't you know, someone murders his wife while he's on ice. Apparently being frozen stiff does not an alibi make, and he becomes the prime suspect. Much unanimated suspense. **80m/B VHS.** *GB GE* Mark Stevens, Marianne Koch, Delphi Lawrence, Joachim Hansen, Walter Rilla, Wolfgang Lukschy; ***D:*** Bernard Knowles. *MOV*

Frozen Assets **1992 (PG-13)** Pathetic attempt at comedy from Long and Bernsen. He's an ambitious executive who finds the "bank" of his corporation's latest acquisition deals in sperm and not cash. Still, he expects this acquisition to be a success and comes up with a number of tacky ways, much to the horror of the facility's administrator, to make that profit margin grow. **93m/C VHS.** Corbin Bernsen, Shelley Long, Larry Miller, Dody Goodman, Gerrit Graham, Paul Sand, Teri Copley, Matt Clark; ***D:*** George Miller; ***W:*** Don Klein, Tom Kartozian. *FXV*

Frozen Terror **1980 (R)** A madman resembling both Jack Frost and Jack the Ripper claims victims at random. **93m/C VHS, Beta.** Bernice Stegers; ***D:*** Lamberto Bava. *LIV, VES*

Fu Manchu **1956** Villainous arch-criminal Fu Manchu plots to enslave the world in "The Golden God" and "The Master Plan," two episodes from the television series. **60m/B VHS, Beta.** Glenn Gordon, Laurette Luez, Clark Howat, Lee Matthews. *DVT*

The Fugitive **1948** Fonda is a priest devoted to God and the peasants under his care when he finds himself on the run after religion is outlawed in this nameless South-of-the-border dictatorship. Despite the danger of capture, he continues to minister to his flock. His eventual martyrdom unites the villagers in prayer. Considered Fonda's best performance; Ford's favorite film. Shot on location in Mexico. Excellent supporting performances. Based on the Graham Greene novel "The Power and the Glory" although considerably cleaned up for the big screen—Greene's priest had lost virtually all of his faith and moral code. Here the priest is a genuine Ford hero. A gem. **99m/B VHS, Beta, LV.** Henry Fonda, Dolores Del Rio, Pedro Armendariz Sr., J. Carrol Naish, Leo Carrillo, Ward Bond, Robert Armstrong, John Qualen; ***D:*** John Ford; ***W:*** Dudley Nichols. *TTC*

The Fugitive ½ **1993 (PG-13)** Exciting big-screen version of the '60s TV series with the same basic storyline: Dr. Richard Kimble's wife is murdered and he's implicated, so he goes on the lam to find the real killer, the mysterious one-armed man. Lots of mystery and action, particularly a spectacular train/bus crash sequence, keeps the tension high. Due to illness, Richard Jordan was replaced by Krabbe after production had begun. Alec Baldwin was originally slated to star as Kimble, but backed out and Ford was cast. Sound familiar? Ford also replaced Baldwin as Jack Ryan in "Patriot Games." The second highest grossing movie of 1993. **127m/C VHS, LV.** Harrison Ford, Tommy Lee Jones, Jeroen Krabbe, Julianne Moore, Sela Ward, Joe Pantoliano, Andreas Katsulas, Daniel Roebuck; ***D:*** Andrew Davis; ***W:*** David N. Twohy, Jeb Stuart; ***C:*** Michael Chapman; ***M:*** James Newton Howard. Academy Awards '93: Best Supporting Actor (Jones); Golden Globe Awards '94: Best Supporting Actor (Jones); Los Angeles Film Critics Association Awards '93: Best Supporting Actor (Jones); MTV Movie Awards '94: Best On-Screen Duo (Harrison Ford/Tommy Lee Jones), Best Action Sequence; Blockbuster Entertainment Awards '95: Action Actor, Video (Ford); Nominations: Academy Awards '93: Best Cinematography, Best Film Editing, Best Original Screenplay, Best Picture, Best Sound, Best Sound Effects Editing; British Academy Awards '93: Best Supporting Actor (Jones); Directors Guild of America Awards '93: Best Director (Davis); Golden Globe Awards '94: Best Actor—Drama (Ford), Best Director (Davis). *WAR*

Fugitive Alien *Woof!* **1986** Alien and Earth forces battle it out. Dubbed for Japanese. **103m/C VHS, Beta.** *JP CEL*

Fugitive Among Us **1992** Dedicated cop is determined to return an escaped rapist to a life behind bars and he's aided by a victim who would really rather forget the whole thing. Made for TV. **97m/**

C VHS. Peter Strauss, Eric Roberts, Elizabeth Pena, Lauren Holly. *ABC, PAR*

The Fugitive Kind 🦴🦴½ **1960** A young drifter walks into a sleepy Mississippi town and attracts the attention of three of its women with tragic results. Based upon the Tennessee Williams' play "Orpheus Descending." good performances but the writing never hangs well-enough together for coherence. **122m/B VHS, Beta.** Marlon Brando, Anna Magnani, Joanne Woodward, Victor Jory, R.G. Armstrong, Maureen Stapleton; ***D:*** Sidney Lumet; ***C:*** Boris Kaufman. *MGM, FOX*

The Fugitive: Premiere Episode 1963 In this introductory episode to the television series, Janssen plays Dr. Richard Kimble, who's wrongly convicted of murdering his wife. After a train taking him to prison derails, he makes his escape and begins his search for the real culprit, the mysterious one-armed man. But Kimble's pursued by the relentless Lt. Gerard. Additional episodes available. **45m/B VHS.** David Janssen, Barry Morse, Vera Miles, Brian Keith. *MOV, GKK*

Fugitive Road 🦴🦴 **1934** The great von Stroheim stars as a crusty but soft-hearted border guard who arbitrarily detains people at the crossing. **69m/B VHS.** Erich von Stroheim, Wera Engels, Leslie Fenton, Harry Holman; ***D:*** Frank Strayer. *NOS*

The Fugitive: Taking of Luke McVane 🦴🦴 **1915** An early silent western in which Hart upholds the cowboy code of honor. **28m/B VHS, Beta.** William S. Hart, Enid Markey. *VYY*

The Fugitive: The Final Episode 1967 The final episode of the acclaimed series, aired on August 29, 1967, in which Dr. Richard Kimble meets up with the one-armed man who murdered his wife and tries to bring him to justice before Lt. Gerard can bring Kimble in. Episode was the most watched television program up to that time. **78m/C VHS.** David Janssen, Barry Morse, Bill Raisch, Diane Baker, Joseph Campanella, Michael Constantine. *MOV*

Fugitive Valley 🦴½ **1941** Muddled plot has villains-turned-heroes on the trail of some outlaws and stolen money. Terhune shows off some of his vaudeville skills, and King sings some songs. **61m/B VHS.** Ray Corrigan, John "Dusty" King, Max Terhune, Julie Duncan, Glenn Strange, Robert F. (Bob) Kortman, Tom London, Reed Howes; ***D:*** S. Roy Luby. *NOS, HEG*

Fulfillment 🦴🦴½ *The Fulfillment of Mary Gray* **1989 (PG-13)** Ladd stars as Mary Gray, a turn-of-the-century woman comfortably married to good but unexciting farmer, Jonathan (Levine). He's unable to give his wife the child they both desperately want and when his younger brother, Aaron (Smith), visits, the hope is Aaron can be persuaded to help out. The naturally volatile situation is heightened by the fact Mary is very drawn to the handsome Aaron anyway, and the feeling is mutual. Based on the novel "The Fulfillment" by LaVyrle Spencer. Made for television. **96m/C VHS.** Cheryl Ladd, Ted Levine, Lewis Smith; ***D:*** Piers Haggard. *REP*

Full Body Massage 🦴🦴 **1995 (R)** Wealthy art gallery owner Nina (Rogers) spends much of her time alone at her California dream home—except for a weekly appointment with young masseur Douglas (Burgard). But one week, the older Fitch (Brown) comes instead and begins discussing life and personal spirituality while he massages away the self-indulgent cares of the world-weary Nina. Good work by the leads in a chatty cable movie. **93m/C VHS.** Mimi Rogers, Bryan Brown, Christopher Burgard, Elizabeth Barondes; ***D:*** Nicolas Roeg; ***W:*** Dan Gurskis; ***C:*** Anthony B. Richmond; ***M:*** Harry Griegson-Williams. *PAR*

Full Circle 🦴🦴 *The Haunting of Julia* **1977 (R)** Peter Straub wrote this eerie tale about a grief-stricken young woman whose child has recently died. To overcome her loss, she moves into a new house—which is haunted by the ghost of a long-dead child. **96m/C VHS, Beta.** *CA GB* Mia Farrow, Keir Dullea, Tom Conti, Jill Bennett, Robin Gammell; ***D:*** Richard Loncraine; ***M:*** Colin Towns. *MED*

Full Contact 🦴🦴 **1993 (R)** Farmhand Luke Powers heads for the decadence of Los Angeles to find his older brother. When three thugs make the mistake of trying to rob him, Luke shows off his martial arts skills. When Luke finds out his brother has been murdered by gamblers involved in an illegal back alley kickboxing circuit, he vows to get revenge. **97m/C VHS.** Jerry Trimble, Howard Jackson, Alvin Prouder, Gerry Blanck, Denise Buick; ***D:*** Rick Jacobson; ***W:*** Beverly Gray. *COL*

Full Eclipse 🦴🦴 **1993 (R)** Max Dire (Van Peebles) is seduced by the fetching Casey (Kensit) into joining a fierce elite group of underground cops whose mission is to wipe out crime. However, Max soon learns that the secret of their power is a serum which turns them into werewolves. Max is now faced with a decision: join forces with them, or expose them. Either way, blood will flow. Interesting special effects. Unrated version also available. **97m/C VHS, LV.** Mario Van Peebles, Patsy Kensit, Bruce Payne, Anthony John Denison; ***D:*** Anthony Hickox. *HBO*

Full Exposure: The Sex Tape Scandals 🦴½ **1989 (R)** Sleazy drama about a murdered call girl who was blackmailing her clients with sex videos. A cop and his inexperienced female partner are assigned to catch the killer. Made for television. **95m/C VHS.** Jennifer O'Neill, Lisa Hartman Black, Vanessa Williams, Anthony John Denison, Peter Jurasik; ***D:*** Noel Nosseck; ***W:*** Stephen Zito; ***M:*** Dana Kaproff. *WOV*

Full Fathom Five 🦴½ **1990 (PG)** Central American militants, angered by America's invasion of Panama, hijack a submarine and threaten a nuclear assault on Houston. Boring and dumb. **81m/C VHS, Beta.** Michael Moriarty, Maria Rangel, Michael Cavanaugh, John Lafayette, Todd Field, Daniel Faraldo; ***D:*** Carl Franklin; ***W:*** Bart Davis. *MGM*

Full Hearts & Empty Pockets 🦴½ **1963** Follows the happy-go-lucky adventures of a young, handsome, impoverished gentleman on the loose in Rome. Dubbed in English. **88m/B VHS, Beta.** *IT GE* Linda Christian, Gino Cervi, Senta Berger; ***D:*** Camillo Mastrocinque. *VYY*

Full Metal Jacket 🦴🦴🦴½ **1987 (R)** A three-act Vietnam War epic, about a single Everyman impetuously passing through basic training then working in the field as an Army photojournalist and fighting at the onset of the Tet offensive. First half of the film is the most realistic bootcamp sequence ever done. Unfocused but powerful. Based on the novel by Hasford, who also co-scripted. **116m/C VHS, Beta, LV, 8mm.** Matthew Modine, R. Lee Ermey, Vincent D'Onofrio, Adam Baldwin, Dorian Harewood, Arliss Howard, Kevyn Major Howard, Ed O'Ross; ***D:*** Stanley Kubrick; ***W:*** Gustav Hasford, Stanley Kubrick, Michael Herr. Nominations: Academy Awards '87: Best Adapted Screenplay. *WAR, FCT*

Full Metal Ninja 🦴 **1989** When his family is kidnapped, a trained martial artist trails their abductors and swears revenge. **90m/C VHS, Beta.** Patrick Allen, Pierre Kirby, Sean Odell, Jean Paul, Renato Sala; ***D:*** Charles Lee. *IMP*

Full Moon in Blue Water 🦴🦴½ **1988 (R)** His wife's been dead a year, he owes back taxes on his bar, his father has Alzheimer's, and his only form of entertainment is watching old home movies of his wife. Floyd has problems. Enter Louise, a lonely spinster who feels that it is her personal duty to change his life. If she doesn't do it, the bizarre things that happen after her arrival will. **96m/C VHS, Beta, LV.** Gene Hackman, Teri Garr, Burgess Meredith, Elias Koteas, Kevin Cooney, David Doty; ***D:*** Peter Masterson; ***W:*** Bill Bozzone; ***M:*** Phil Marshall. *MED, VTR*

Full Moon in Paris 🦴🦴½ *Les Nuits De La Pleine* **1984 (R)** A young woman in Paris moves out on her architect lover in order to experience freedom. Through a couple of random relationships, she soon finds that what she hoped for is not what she really wanted. **101m/C VHS, Beta.** *FR* Pascale Ogier, Tcheky Karyo, Fabrice Luchini; ***D:*** Eric Rohmer; ***W:*** Eric Rohmer. Venice Film Festival '84: Best Actress (Ogier). *XVC, MED, INJ*

Full of Life 🦴🦴½ **1956** Holliday stars in this domestic comedy about a non-religious young woman who had married, in a civil ceremony, into a strict, Italian-Catholic family. Although she is now eight months pregnant the family still wants the couple to have a church wedding. Holliday is a winning personality and the humor is lightly handled. **91m/C VHS.** Judy Holliday, Richard Conte, Salvatore Baccaloni, Esther Minciotti; ***D:*** Richard Quine. *FCT*

The Fuller Brush Girl 🦴🦴½ **1950** Lots of slapstick with Ball as a door-to-door saleswoman unexpectedly involved in a murder. She and dim-bulb boyfriend Albert are chased by cops, murderers, and smugglers in this frantic farce. Sequel to Red Skelton's (who has a cameo) 1948 film "The Fuller Brush Man." **84m/B VHS.** Lucille Ball, Eddie Albert, Carl Benton Reid, Gale Robbins, Jeff Donnell, John Litel, Fred Graham, Lee Patrick; ***Cameos:*** Red Skelton; ***D:*** Lloyd Bacon; ***W:*** Frank Tashlin. *COL*

The Fuller Brush Man 🦴🦴½ *That Man Mr. Jones* **1948** A newly hired Fuller Brush man becomes involved in murder and romance as he tries to win the heart of his girlfriend. A slapstick delight for Skelton fans. **93m/B VHS, Beta, LV.** Red Skelton, Janet Blair, Don McGuire, Adele Jergens; ***D:*** Frank Tashlin. *COL*

Fun Down There *Woof!* **1988** This smalltown boy-comes-to-the-big city is so bad, it's...bad. A naive—and unsympathetic—gay man from upstate New York moves to Greenwich Village and has fun down there (and they don't mean Australia). **110m/C VHS.** Michael Waite, Nickolas Nagurney, Gretschen Somerville, Martin Goldin, Kevin Och; ***D:*** Roger Stigliano; ***W:*** Michael Waite, Roger Stigliano. *WBF, FCT, INJ*

Fun in Acapulco 🦴🦴 **1963** Former trapeze artist Elvis romances two beauties and acts as a part-time lifeguard and night club entertainer. He must conquer his fear of heights for a climactic dive from the Acapulco cliffs. Features ten musical numbers. ♫Fun in Acapulco; Vino, Dinero y Amor; Mexico; The Bullfighter Was A Lady; El Toro; Marguerita; (There's) No Room To Rhumba (In A Sports Car); I Think I'm Going To Like It Here; You Can't Say No In Acapulco. **97m/C VHS, Beta.** Elvis Presley, Ursula Andress, Elsa Cardenas, Paul Lukas, Alejandro Rey, Larry Domasin, Howard McNear; ***D:*** Richard Thorpe; ***C:*** Daniel F. Fapp. *FOX, MVD*

Fun with Dick and Jane 🦴🦴 **1977 (PG)** An upper-middle class couple turn to armed robbery to support themselves when the husband is fired from his job. Though it has good performances, the film never develops its intended bite. **104m/C VHS, Beta.** George Segal, Jane Fonda, Ed McMahon; ***D:*** Ted Kotcheff; ***W:*** Jerry Belson, David Giler, Mordecai Richler; ***C:*** Fred W. Koenekamp; ***M:*** Ernest Gold. *COL*

The Funeral 🦴🦴🦴½ **1984** A sharp satire of the clash of modern Japanese culture with the old. The hypocrisies, rivalries and corruption in an average family are displayed at the funeral of its patriarch who also happened to own a house of ill repute. Itami's breakthrough film; Japanese with subtitles. **112m/C VHS.** *JP* Tsutomu Yamazaki, Nobuko Miyamoto, Kin Sugai, Ichiro Zaitsu, Nekohachi Edoya, Shoji Otake; ***D:*** Juzo Itami. *REP, FCT, INJ*

Funeral for an Assassin 🦴½ **1977 (PG)** A professional assassin seeks revenge for his imprisonment by the government of South Africa, a former client. Planning to kill all of the country's leading politicians, he masquerades as a black man, a cover which is designed to fool the apartheid establishment. **92m/C VHS, Beta.** Vic Morrow, Peter Van Dissel; ***D:*** Ivan Hall. *GEM, MRV, VTR*

Funeral Home 🦴½ *2 Cries in the Night* **1982** Terrified teen spends her summer vacation at her grandmother's tourist home, a former funeral parlor. Rip-off of "Psycho." **90m/C VHS, Beta.** *CA* Lesleh Donaldson, Kay Hawtry; ***D:*** William Fruet. *NO*

Funeral in Berlin 🦴🦴🦴 **1966** Second of the Caine/Harry Palmer espionage films (following up "Ipcress File"), in which the deadpan British secret serviceman arranges the questionable defection of a Russian colonel. Good look at the spy biz and postwar Berlin. "Billion Dollar Brain" continues the series. **102m/C VHS, Beta, LV.** Michael Caine, Eva Renzi, Oscar Homolka; ***D:*** Guy Hamilton; ***W:*** Evan Jones. *PAR*

The Funhouse 𝅘½ **1981 (R)** Four teenagers spend the night at a carnival funhouse, witness a murder, and become next on the list of victims. From the director of cult favorite "Texas Chainsaw Massacre," but nothing that hasn't been seen before. **96m/C VHS, Beta, LV.** Elizabeth Berridge, Shawn Carson, Cooper Huckabee, Largo Woodruff, Sylvia Miles; ***D:*** Tobe Hooper; ***W:*** Larry Block; ***M:*** John Beal. *MCA*

Funland 𝅘 **1989 (PG-13)** In the world's weirdest amusement park a clown goes nuts over the new corporate owners' plans for the place and decides to seek revenge. **86m/C VHS, LV.** David Lander, William Windom, Bruce Mahler, Michael McManus; ***D:*** Michael A. Simpson. *LIV, IME, VES*

Funny About Love 𝅘½ **1990 (PG-13)** Fairly absurd tale with dashes of inappropriate black humor about a fellow with a ticking biological clock. Nimoy sheds his Spock ears to direct a star-studded cast in this lame tale of middle-aged cartoonist Wilder who strays from wife Lahti after having problems on the conception end into the welcoming arms of fertile college co-ed Masterson in his quest to contribute to the population count. **107m/C VHS, Beta, LV, 8mm.** Gene Wilder, Christine Lahti, Mary Stuart Masterson, Robert Prosky, Stephen Tobolowsky, Anne Jackson, Susan Ruttan, David Margulies; ***D:*** Leonard Nimoy; ***W:*** Norman Steinberg, David Frankel. *PAR*

Funny Bones 𝅘𝅘𝅘 **1994 (R)** Struggling comedian Tommy Fawkes (Platt) bombs in Vegas bigtime while his Mr. Showbiz father George (Lewis) easily overshadows him at every turn. So Tommy decides to head back to his childhood home in Blackpool, England and figure out his life. What he discovers are the Parkers, a family of British vaudevillians, and the fact that his father stole their routines and, briefly, Mrs. Parker (Caron), resulting in half-brother Jack (Evans) who has all the natural talent Tommy can only dream about. Serious, funny, and hostile with notable performances from Platt and Evans. **128m/C VHS, LV.** Oliver Platt, Lee Evans, Leslie Caron, Jerry Lewis, Oliver Reed, Ian McNeice, Ruta Lee, Richard Griffith, George Carl, Freddie Davies; ***D:*** Peter Chelsom; ***W:*** Peter Chelsom, Peter Flannery; ***C:*** Eduardo Berra; ***M:*** John Altman. *TOU*

Funny, Dirty Little War 𝅘𝅘½ **1983** An Argentinian farce about the petty rivalries in a small village erupting into a violent, mini-civil war. In Spanish with English subtitles. **80m/C VHS, Beta.** *AR* Federico Luppi, Julio de Grazia, Miguel Angel Sola; ***D:*** Hector Olivera. *XVC, MED, INJ*

Funny Face 𝅘𝅘𝅘 **1957** A musical satire on beatniks and the fashion scene also features the May-December romance between Astaire and the ever-lovely Hepburn. He is a high-fashion photographer (based on Richard Avedon); she is a Greenwich Village bookseller fond of shapeless, drab clothing. He decides to take her to Paris and show her what modeling's all about. The elegant musical score features classic Gershwin. The laserdisc includes the original theatrical trailer and is available in widescreen. ♫Let's Kiss and Make Up; He Loves and She Loves; Funny Face; How Long Has This Been Going On?; Clap Yo' Hands; S'Wonderful; Bonjour Paris; On How To Be Lovely; Marche Funebre. **103m/C VHS, Beta, LV, 8mm.** Fred Astaire, Audrey Hepburn, Kay Thompson, Suzy Parker; ***D:*** Stanley Donen; ***M:*** George Gershwin, Ira Gershwin. Nominations: Academy Awards '57: Best Art Direction/Set Decoration, Best Cinematography, Best Costume Design, Best Story & Screenplay. *PAR, FCT*

The Funny Farm 𝅘½ **1982** Comedy about a group of ambitious young comics striving to make it in the crazy world of comedy at Los Angeles' famous comedy club, The Funny Farm. **90m/C VHS, Beta.** *CA* Miles Chapin, Eileen Brennan, Peter Aykroyd; ***D:*** Ron Clark; ***W:*** Ron Clark. *VTR*

Funny Farm 𝅘𝅘 **1988 (PG)** Chevy Chase as a New York sportswriter finds that life in the country is not quite what he envisioned. The comedy is uneven throughout, with the best scenes coming at the end. **101m/C VHS, LV.** Chevy Chase, Madolyn Smith, Joseph Maher, Jack Gilpin, Brad Sullivan, MacIntyre Dixon; ***D:*** George Roy Hill; ***W:*** Jeffrey Boam; ***M:*** Elmer Bernstein. *WAR*

Funny Girl 𝅘𝅘𝅘 **1968 (G)** Follows the early career of comedian Fanny Brice, her rise to stardom with the Ziegfeld Follies and her stormy romance with gambler Nick Arnstein in a fun and funny look at back stage music hall life in the early 1900s. Streisand's film debut followed her auspicious performance of the role on Broadway. Score was augmented by several tunes sung by Brice during her performances. Excellent performances from everyone, captured beautifully by Wyler in his musical film debut. Followed by "Funny Lady." ♫My Man; Second Hand Rose; I'd Rather Be Blue Over You; People; Don't Rain On My Parade; I'm The Greatest Star; Sadie, Sadie; His Love Makes Me Beautiful; You Are Woman, I Am Man. **151m/C VHS, Beta, LV.** Barbra Streisand, Omar Sharif, Walter Pidgeon, Kay Medford, Anne Francis; ***D:*** William Wyler; ***C:*** Harry Stradling. Academy Awards '68: Best Actress (Streisand); Golden Globe Awards '69: Best Actress—Musical/Comedy (Streisand); Nominations: Academy Awards '68: Best Cinematography, Best Film Editing, Best Picture, Best Song ("Funny Girl"), Best Sound, Best Supporting Actress (Medford), Best Original Score. *COL, BTV*

Funny Lady 𝅘𝅘½ **1975 (PG)** A continuation of "Funny Girl," recounting Fanny Brice's tumultuous marriage to showman Billy Rose in the 1930s and her lingering affection for first husband Nick Arnstein. One of the rare sequels which are just as good, or at least almost, as the original. ♫How Lucky Can You Get?; Great Day; More Than You Know; Blind Date; So Long, Honey Lamb; Isn't This Better; Let's Hear It For Me; I Like Him/I Like Her; It's Only a Paper Moon. **137m/C VHS, Beta, LV.** Barbra Streisand, Omar Sharif, James Caan, Roddy McDowall, Ben Vereen, Carole Wells, Larry Gates, Heidi O'Rourke; ***D:*** Herbert Ross; ***W:*** Jay Presson Allen, Arnold Schulman; ***C:*** James Wong Howe. Nominations: Academy Awards '75: Best Cinematography, Best Costume Design, Best Song ("How Lucky Can You Get"), Best Sound, Best Original Score. *COL, FCT*

Funny Money 𝅘 **1982** Pointed, satirical look at the British habit of financing life with the almighty credit card. Sometimes uneven comedy. **92m/C VHS, Beta.** *GB* Greg Henry, Elizabeth Daily, Gareth Hunt, Derren Nesbitt, Annie Ross; ***D:*** James Kenelm Clarke. *LIV*

A Funny Thing Happened on the Way to the Forum 𝅘𝅘𝅘 **1966** A bawdy Broadway farce set in ancient Rome where a conniving, slave plots his way to freedom by aiding in the romantic escapades of his master's inept son. Terrific performances by Mostel and Gilford. Keaton's second-to-last film role. The Oscar-winning score includes such highlights as "Comedy Tonight," "Lovely," and "Everybody Ought to Have a Maid." **100m/C VHS, Beta, LV.** Zero Mostel, Phil Silvers, Jack Gilford, Buster Keaton, Michael Hordern, Michael Crawford, Annette Andre; ***D:*** Richard Lester; ***M:*** Ken Thorne. Academy Awards '66: Best Score. *FOX, FCT*

Furious 𝅘 **1983 (PG)** The sister of a young martial arts apprentice is killed by the master, with a great deal of action and special effects. **85m/C VHS, Beta.** Simon Rhee, Howard Jackson, Arlene Montano. *VHE*

The Furious Avenger 𝅘 **1976** A released convict, on his way to avenging his family's murder, stops a rape and takes on one opponent after another in this rousing kickfest. Dubbed. **84m/C VHS, Beta.** Hsiung Fei, Fan Ling, Chen Pei Ling, Tien Yeh, Wang Mo Chou. *UNI*

The Further Adventures of Tennessee Buck 𝅘 **1988 (R)** Mercenary adventurer travels through tropical jungles acting as a guide to a dizzy couple. Along the way, they encounter cannibals, headhunters, and other bizarre jungle things in this lame take on "Indiana Jones." Shot on location in Sri Lanka. **90m/C VHS, Beta, LV.** David Keith, Kathy Shower, Brant Van Hoffman; ***D:*** David Keith; ***M:*** John Debney. *MED, VTR*

Further Adventures of the Wilderness Family, Part 2 𝅘𝅘½ *Wilderness Family, Part 2* **1977 (G)** Also known as the "Further Adventures of the Wilderness Family." Depicts the Robinson family who left civilization for the freedom of the Colorado wild. Predictable retread, but more good family adventure drama from the makers of "Adventures of the Wilderness Family." **104m/C VHS, Beta.** Heather Rattray, Ham Larsen, George Flower, Robert F. Logan, Susan Damante Shaw; ***D:*** Frank Zuniga. *MED, VTR*

Fury 𝅘𝅘𝅘½ **1936** Tracy gives an excellent performance as an innocent young man framed for kidnapping and then nearly murdered by a lynch mob. His plans for revenge are thwarted by his girlfriend, who fears that he will turn into the murderer he has been accused of being. Powerful anti-violence message is well-made, with strong ensemble acting. Lang's favorite of his American-made films. **96m/B VHS, Beta.** Spencer Tracy, Sylvia Sidney, Walter Abel, Bruce Cabot, Edward Ellis, Walter Brennan, Frank Albertson; ***D:*** Fritz Lang; ***C:*** Joseph Ruttenberg. Nominations: Academy Awards '36: Best Story. *MGM*

The Fury 𝅘𝅘 **1978 (R)** The head of a government institute for psychic research finds that his own son is snatched by supposed terrorists who wish to use his lethal powers. The father tries to use another a young woman with psychic power to locate him, with bloody results. A real chiller. **117m/C VHS, Beta.** Kirk Douglas, John Cassavetes, Carrie Snodgress, Andrew Stevens, Amy Irving, Charles Durning, Daryl Hannah; ***D:*** Brian DePalma; ***M:*** John Williams. *FOX*

Fury 𝅘 **198?** A man and woman meet in the Amazonian jungle and the sparks begin to fly. **75m/C VHS, Beta.** Stuart Whitman, Laura Gemser. *NO*

Fury is a Woman 𝅘𝅘𝅘½ **1961** A Polish version of Shakespeare's Macbeth which ranks with the greatest film translations of his work. In Czarist Russia the passionate wife of a plantation owner begins an affair with a farm hand, and poisons her father-in-law when he finds them out. As her madness grows, she plots the murder of the husband. Letterbox format. In Serbian with English subtitles. **93m/B VHS.** *RU* Olivera Markovic, Ljuba Tadic, Kapitalina Eric; ***D:*** Andrzej Wajda. *HTV, INJ*

The Fury of Hercules 𝅘½ *La Furia Di Ercole; Fury of Samson* **1961** It's up to the mighty son of Zeus to free an enslaved group of people from an oppressive, evil ruler. Surely all who stand in his way will be destroyed. Another Italian muscleman film. **95m/C VHS.** *IT* Brad Harris, Brigitte Corey, Mara Berni, Carlo Tamberlani, Serge Gainsbourg, Elke Arendt, Alan Steel; ***D:*** Gianfranco Parolini. *GKK, SNC*

The Fury of the Wolfman 𝅘 **1970** A murdering werewolf is captured by a female scientist who tries to cure his lycanthropy with drugs and brain implants. Pretty slow going, but hang in there for the wolfman versus werewoman climax. **80m/C VHS, Beta.** *SP* Paul Naschy, Perla Cristal; ***D:*** Jose Maria Zabalza; ***W:*** Paul Naschy. *UNI, NLC, LOO*

Fury on Wheels 𝅘 **1971 (PG)** Tale of men who race cars and wreak havoc and vice versa. **89m/C VHS, Beta.** Judd Hirsch, Tom Ligon, Paul Sorvino, Logan Ramsey, Collin Wilcox-Horne. *NO*

Fury to Freedom: The Life Story of Raul Ries 𝅘𝅘 **1985** A young man raised in the volatile world of abusive and alcoholic parents grows into an abusive and violent adult. One night, however, he meets something he can't beat up, and it changes his life. **78m/C VHS.** Gil Gerard, John Quade, Tom Silardi. *VCI*

Future Cop 𝅘𝅘 *Trancers* **1976** A hard-nosed, old-fashioned cop is forced to team with the ultimate partner—a robot. Silly made-for-TV movie, but likable leads. **78m/C VHS.** Ernest Borgnine, Michael J. Shannon, John Amos, John Larch, Herbert Nelson, Ronnie Clair Edwards; ***D:*** Jud Taylor; ***W:*** Danny Bilson, Paul DeMeo. *PAR*

Future Force 🦴 **1989 (R)** In the crime-filled future cops can't maintain order. They rely on a group of civilian mercenaries to clean up the streets. **90m/C VHS, Beta.** David Carradine, Robert Tessier, Anna Rapagna, William Zipp. *AIP*

Future Hunters 🦴 **1988** In the holocaust-blitzed future, a young couple searches for a religious artifact that may decide the future of the planet. **96m/C VHS, Beta, LV.** Robert Patrick, Linda Carol, Ed Crick, Bob Schott; ***D:*** Cirio H. Santiago. *LIV, VES*

Future Kill 🦴 **1985 (R)** Anti-nuclear activists battle fraternity brothers in this grim futuristic world. Shaky political alliances form between revenge-seeking factions on both sides. **83m/C VHS, Beta, LV.** Edwin Neal, Marilyn Burns, Doug Davis; ***D:*** Ronald W. Moore; ***W:*** Ronald W. Moore. *LIV, VES*

Future Shock 🦴🦴 **1993 (PG-13)** Dr. Russell Langdon is a psychiatrist who has been experimenting with virtual reality technology. Unbeknownst to three of his patients he decides to use them as guinea pigs in his work. But confronting their deepest fears only leads to new terrors. Also available in an unrated version. **93m/C VHS.** Bill Paxton, Vivian Schilling, Brion James, Martin Kove; ***D:*** Eric Parkinson, Matt Reeves, Oley Sassone. *HMD*

Future Zone 🦴🦴 **1990 (R)** In an attempt to save his father from being murdered, a young man travels backwards in time. **88m/C VHS, LV.** David Carradine, Charles Napier, Ted Prior; ***D:*** David A. Prior. *AIP*

Futurekick 🦴½ **1991 (R)** In the not so distant future, a kickboxer with an attitude and cyborg capabilities must use every ounce of strength in a battle against evil. **80m/C VHS.** Don "The Dragon" Wilson, Meg Foster, Christopher Penn, Eb Lottimer; ***D:*** Damian Klaus; ***W:*** Damian Klaus. *NHO*

Futureworld 🦴🦴 **1976 (PG)** In the sequel to "Westworld," two reporters junket to the new "Futureworld" theme park, where they first support a scheme to clone and control world leaders. Includes footage shot at NASA locations. **107m/C VHS, Beta, LV.** Peter Fonda, Blythe Danner, Arthur Hill, Yul Brynner, Stuart Margolin; ***D:*** Richard T. Heffron; ***W:*** George Schenck. *WAR, OM*

Futz 🦴½ **1969** Story from off-Broadway is of a man who loves his pig and the world that can't understand the attraction. Better in original stage production. **90m/C VHS, Beta.** John Pakos, Victor Lipari, Sally Kirkland; ***D:*** Tom O'Horgan. *NO*

Fuzz 🦴🦴½ **1972 (PG)** Reynolds in the Boston cop on the track of a bomber killing policemen, punks setting winos on fire, and some amorous fellow officers. Combines fast action and some sharp-edged humor. **92m/C VHS, Beta.** Burt Reynolds, Tom Skerritt, Yul Brynner, Raquel Welch, Jack Weston, Charles Martin Smith; ***D:*** Richard A. Colla; ***M:*** Dave Grusin. *MGM, FOX*

Fyre 🦴½ **1978 (R)** Young beautiful girl moves from the Midwest to Los Angeles and becomes a prostitute. **90m/C VHS, Beta.** Allen (Goorwitz) Garfield, Lynn Theel, Tom Baker, Cal Haynes, Donna Wilkes, Bruce Kirby; ***D:*** Richard Grand. *MED*

"G" Men 🦴🦴🦴½ **1935** Powerful story based loosely on actual events that occurred during FBI operations in the early 1930s, with Cagney on the right side of the law, though still given to unreasonable fits of anger. Raised and educated by a well-known crime kingpin, a young man becomes an attorney. When his friend the FBI agent is killed in the line of duty, he joins the FBI to seek vengeance on the mob. But his mob history haunts him, forcing him to constantly prove to his superiors that he is not under its influence. Tense and thrilling classic. **86m/B VHS, Beta.** James Cagney, Barton MacLane, Ann Dvorak, Margaret Lindsay, Robert Armstrong, Lloyd Nolan, William Harrigan, Regis Toomey; ***D:*** William Keighley. *MGM, CCB*

G-Men Never Forget *Code 645* **1948** Moore, former stunt-man and future Lone Ranger, stars in this 12-part serial about FBI agents battling the bad guys. Lots of action. On two cassettes. **167m/B VHS.** Clayton Moore, Roy Barcroft, Ramsay Ames, Drew Allen, Tommy Steele, Eddie Acuff; ***D:*** Fred Brannon, Yakima Canutt. *REP, MLB*

G-Men vs. the Black Dragon **1943** Reedited serial of "Black Dragon of Manzanar" stars Cameron as Fed who battles Asian Axis agents during WWII. Action-packed. **244m/B VHS, LV.** Rod Cameron, Roland Got, Constance Worth, Nino Pipitone, Noel Cravat; ***D:*** William Witney. *REP, MED, MLB*

Gabriel Over the White House 🦴🦴🦴 **1933** Part political satire, part fantasy, and completely fascinating. Huston is a venal politician, completely in thrall to his crooked cohorts, who manages to get elected President. While recuperating from an auto accident Huston thinks he's sees a vision of the Archangel Gabriel, who essentially tells him to change his crooked ways. From bought man Huston changes to righteous do-gooder, much to the dismay of his criminal companions, who'll stop at nothing to get rid of the man they think has simply gone insane. Huston gives a powerful performance in this decidedly oddball film. **86m/B VHS.** Walter Huston, Karen Morley, Arthur Byron, Franchot Tone, Dickie Moore, C. Henry Gordon, David Landau, Samuel S. Hinds, Jean Parker; ***D:*** Gregory La Cava. *MGM, MOV, BTV*

Gabriela 🦴🦴 **1984 (R)** A sultry romance develops between a Brazilian tavern keeper and the new cook he's just hired. Derived from Jorge Amado's novel. In Portuguese with English subtitles. **102m/C VHS, Beta.** *BR* Sonia Braga, Marcello Mastroianni, Nelson Xavier, Antonio Cantafora; ***D:*** Bruno Barreto; ***W:*** Bruno Barreto; ***M:*** Antonio Carlos. *MGM, INJ*

Gaby: A True Story 🦴🦴🦴 **1987 (R)** The story of a woman with congenital cerebral palsy who triumphs over her condition with the help of family and loved ones, and ends up a college graduate and acclaimed author. Based on a true story. **115m/C VHS, Beta, LV.** Rachel Levin, Liv Ullmann, Norma Aleandro, Robert Loggia, Lawrence Monoson, Robert Beltran, Tony Goldwyn; ***D:*** Luis Mandoki; ***W:*** Martin Salinas, Michael James Love; ***C:*** Lajos Koltai; ***M:*** Maurice Jarre. Nominations: Academy Awards '87: Best Supporting Actress (Aleandro). *COL*

Gaiety 🦴½ **1943** Explores the lighter side of lion hunting. **40m/B VHS, Beta.** Antonio Moreno, Armida, Ann Ayars. *NO*

Gal Young 'Un 🦴🦴🦴 **1979** Set during the Prohibition era, a rich, middle-aged woman living on her property in the Florida backwoods finds herself courted by a much younger man. She discovers she is being used to help him set up a moonshining business. Unsentimental story of a strong woman. Based on a Marjorie Kinnan Rawlings story. **105m/C VHS, Beta.** Dana Preu, David Peck, J. Smith; ***D:*** Victor Nunez. Sundance Film Festival '81: Grand Jury Prize. *ACA, ICA*

Galactic Gigolo *Woof!* **1987 (R)** An alien broccoli (yes, the vegetable) descends to earth on vacation, and discovers he's irresistible to Connecticut women. Must be something in the water. Amateurish effort intended as science-fiction satire, but there's more sleaze than humor. **80m/C Beta.** Carmine Capobianco, Debi Thibeault, Ruth Collins, Angela Nicholas, Frank Stewart; ***D:*** Gorman Bechard. *AFE*

Galaxies are Colliding 🦴🦴½ **1992 (R)** Adam (Brown) is so afraid of tying the knot that he abandons his bride at the altar and takes off on a journey of enlightenment, accompanied by best friend Peter (Grammer). They naturally meet any number of eccentrics along the way. **97m/C VHS.** Dwier Brown, Kelsey Grammer, Susan Walters, Karen Medak; ***D:*** John Ryman; ***W:*** John Ryman; ***C:*** Philip Lee; ***M:*** Stephen Barber. *PAR*

Galaxina 🦴½ **1980 (R)** In the 31st century, a beautiful robot woman capable of human feelings is created. Stumbling parody of superspace fantasies features murdered Playmate Stratten in one of few film appearances. **95m/C VHS, Beta, LV.** Dorothy Stratten, Avery Schreiber, Stephen Macht; ***D:*** William Sachs. *MCA*

Galaxis 🦴½ **1995 (R)** The physically impressive Nielsen stars as space- and time-traveling freedom fighter Landera, who beams down to Earth to battle your basic evil, intergalatic villain Kyla (Moll) who has the power source that could save her civilization. **91m/C VHS.** Brigitte Nielsen, Richard Moll, Craig Fairbrass; ***D:*** William Mesa. *TTC*

Galaxy Invader 🦴 **1985 (PG)** Chaos erupts when an alien explorer crash lands his spacecraft in a backwoods area of the United States. **90m/C VHS, Beta.** Richard Ruxton, Faye Tilles, Don Leifert. *NO*

Galaxy of Terror 🦴½ *Mindwarp: An Infinity of Terror; Planet of Horrors* **1981 (R)** Astronauts sent to rescue a stranded spaceship get killed by vicious aliens. Big first: Moran (Joanie on "Happy Days") explodes. Inferior Corman-produced "Alien" imitation still manages to shock and displays generous gore. Followed by "Forbidden World." **85m/C VHS, Beta, LV.** Erin Moran, Edward Albert, Ray Walston, Grace Zabriskie, Zalman King; ***D:*** B.D. Clark; ***W:*** Mark Siegler, B.D. Clark. *SUE*

Gallagher's Travels 🦴 **1987** A screwball male/female reporting team chase an animal smuggling ring through the wilds of Australia. **94m/C VHS, Beta.** *AU* Ivar Kants, Joanne Samuel, Stuart Campbell, Jennifer Hagan; ***D:*** Michael Caulfield. *TWE*

The Gallant Fool 🦴½ **1933** A man is wrongly accused of murder and tries to clear his name while eluding the law. **57m/B VHS.** Bob Steele, Arletta Duncan, George "Gabby" Hayes, John Elliott; ***D:*** Robert North Bradbury; ***W:*** Robert North Bradbury. *GPV*

The Gallant Hours 🦴🦴🦴 **1960** Biography of Admiral "Bull" Halsey (Cagney) covers five weeks, October 18 through December 1, 1942, in the WWII battle of Guadalcanal in the South Pacific. Director Montgomery forgoes battle scenes to focus on the human elements in a war and what makes a great leader. Fine performance by Cagney. **115m/B VHS.** James Cagney, Dennis Weaver, Ward Costello, Richard Jaeckel, Les Tremayne, Robert Burton, Raymond Bailey, Karl Swenson, Harry Landers, James T. Goto; ***D:*** Robert Montgomery; ***W:*** Frank D. Gilroy. *MGM*

Gallipoli 🦴🦴🦴🦴 **1981 (PG)** History blends with the destiny of two friends as they become part of the legendary WWI confrontation between Australia and the German-allied Turks. A superbly filmed, gripping commentary on the wastes of war. Haunting score; excellent performances by Lee and a then-unknown Gibson. Remake of a lesser 1931 effort "Battle of Gallipoli." **111m/C VHS, Beta, LV.** *AU* Mel Gibson, Mark Lee, Bill Kerr, David Argue, Tim McKenzie, Robert Grubb; ***D:*** Peter Weir; ***W:*** David Williamson, Peter Weir; ***C:*** John Seale. Australian Film Institute '81: Best Actor (Gibson), Best Film. *PAR*

Galloping Dynamite 🦴½ **1937** Early western based on a James Oliver Curwood story. A ranger avenges the death of his brother killed for gold. **58m/B VHS, Beta.** Kermit Maynard; ***D:*** Harry Fraser. *VDM*

The Galloping Ghost 🦴🦴½ **1931** A 12-chapter serial starring football great "Red" Grange about big games, gambling, and underworld gangs. Grange is ousted from football when he's accused of throwing a game and he sets out to prove his innocence. **226m/B VHS, Beta.** Harold "Red" Grange, Dorothy Gulliver, Walter Miller, Tom Dugan; ***D:*** B. Reeves Eason. *VYY, VDM, NOS*

Galloping Romeo 🦴½ **1933** Steele stars as a heartthrob on horseback in this romantic Western. Steele had a hard time pulling off the light comedy he was asked to do, so clips from his previous films were used to pad the movie. **59m/B VHS.** Bob Steele, Doris Hill, George "Gabby" Hayes, Frank Ball, Ernie Adams; ***D:*** Robert North Bradbury; ***W:*** Harry Fraser. *GPV, MOV*

Gallowglass 🦴🦴🦴 **1995** A "gallowglass" is an ancient Gaelic term for a servant willing to sacrifice his life for his master. In this moody TV mystery that is dim Joe (Sheen), whose life was saved by manipulative, handsome Sandor (Rhys), who now demands his absolute loyalty. Sandor needs his help in kidnapping Nina (Whitely), an unhappy ex-model who was the victim of a kidnapping years before in Italy and now lives with her husband in wealthy seclusion in the country. There, Nina is under the protection of bodyguard/chauffeur Paul (McArdle), and their mutual attraction leads to unexpected complications. Based on the thriller by Ruth Rendell (writing as Barbara Vine). **150m/C VHS.** *GB* Paul Rhys, Michael Sheen, Arkie Whiteley, John McArdle, Claire Hackett, Gary Waldhorn; ***D:*** Tim Fywell. *FOX*

Galyon **1977 (PG)** Soldier of fortune is recruited by an oil tycoon to find his daughter and son-in-law who have been kidnapped by terrorists in South America. **92m/C VHS, Beta.** Stan Brock, Lloyd Nolan, Ina Balin. *NO*

Gambit ½ **1966** Caine's first Hollywood film casts him as a burglar who develops a "Topkapi"-style scheme to steal a valuable statue with MacLaine as the lure and Lom as the equally devious owner. Once Caine's careful plan is put into operation, however, everything begins to unravel. **109m/C VHS, Beta.** Shirley MacLaine, Michael Caine, Herbert Lom, Roger C. Carmel; ***D:*** Ronald Neame; ***W:*** Alvin Sargent, Jack Davies; ***M:*** Maurice Jarre. Nominations: Academy Awards '66: Best Art Direction/Set Decoration (Color), Best Costume Design (Color), Best Sound. *MCA*

The Gamble **1988 (R)** A young man (Modine) seeks to rescue his father from gambling debts by wagering himself against a lustful countess (Dunaway). When he loses the bet, however, he flees and joins up with a runaway (Beals) with the countess and her henchmen in close pursuit. **108m/C VHS, Beta, LV.** Matthew Modine, Jennifer Beals, Faye Dunaway; ***D:*** Carlo Vanzina. *PSM*

Gamble on Love **1986** Woman returns to her father's Las Vegas casino and falls for the man who manages the gaming room. **90m/C Beta.** Beverly Garland; ***D:*** Jim Balden. *PSM*

The Gambler **1974 (R)** College professor Axel Freed has a gambling problem so vast that it nearly gets him killed by his bookies. He goes to Las Vegas to recoup his losses and wins big, only to blow the money on stupid sports bets that get him deeper into trouble. Excellent character study of a compulsive loser on a downward spiral. **111m/C VHS, Beta, LV.** James Caan, Lauren Hutton, Paul Sorvino, Burt Young, James Woods; ***D:*** Karel Reisz; ***W:*** James Toback. *PAR*

The Gambler & the Lady ½ **1952** A successful London-based gambler and casino owner endeavors to climb the social ladder by having an affair with a member of the British aristocracy. He not only has to contend with his jilted nightclub singer girlfriend but also with the gangsters who would like to take over his clubs. Dull direction and a mediocre script. **72m/B VHS, Beta, LV.** *GB* Dane Clark, Naomi Chance, Kathleen Byron; ***D:*** Patrick Jenkins. *NO*

The Gambler Returns: The Luck of the Draw ½ **1993** You'll see lots of familiar western television stars as Rogers returns yet again as debonair gambler Brady Hawkes. This time he's on a cross country trip to San Francisco and the biggest card game around—only some varmints are out to stop him playing that first hand. **180m/C VHS.** Kenny Rogers, Reba McEntire, Rick Rossovich, Chuck Connors, Patrick Macnee, Linda Evans, James Drury, Mickey Rooney, Jere Burns, Clint Walker, Claude Akins, Gene Barry, Doug McClure, Hugh O'Brian, Brian Keith, Park Overall, Jack Kelly, David Carradine, Johnny Crawford, Marianne Rogers; ***D:*** Dick Lowry. *CAF*

Gambler's Choice **1944** A police lieutenant and his boyhood friend find themselves on opposite sides of the law in this crime drama. Even though both men are romantically involved with the same woman, their friendship remains intact. **66m/B VHS.** Chester Morris, Nancy Kelly, Russell Hayden, Sheldon Leonard, Lee Patrick, Lloyd Corrigan, Tom Dugan, Lyle Talbot, Charles Arnt; ***D:*** Frank McDonald. *NOS*

The Gambling Samurai *Kunisada Chuji* **1960** A samurai returns to his village to find it besieged by a ruthless government. Instead of attacking, he bides his time and works to undermine the government—finally achieving his revenge. In Japanese with English subtitles. **101m/C VHS, Beta.** *JP* Toshiro Mifune, Michiyo Aratama; ***D:*** Senkichi Taniguhi. *VDA*

The Gambling Terror **1937** A cowboy goes after a mobster selling protection to hapless ranchers. **53m/B VHS, Beta.** Johnny Mack Brown, Charles "Blackie" King; ***D:*** Sam Newfield. *NOS, VCN, HEG*

The Game **1989** Three friends arrange a puzzle-murder-mystery for a selected group of guilty people, with $1 million as the prize—and death for the losers. **91m/C VHS, Beta, LV.** Tom Blair, Debbie Martin; ***D:*** Curtis Brown; ***W:*** Curtis Brown. *TWE*

Game for Vultures ½ **1986 (R)** Racial unrest in Rhodesia is the backdrop for this tale of a black revolutionary who fights racist sanctions. The noble topic suffers from stereotypes and oversimplification. **113m/C VHS, Beta.** *GB* Richard Harris, Richard Roundtree, Joan Collins, Ray Milland; ***D:*** James Fargo. *TWE*

The Game is Over ½ **1966 (R)** A wealthy neglected wife falls in love with her grown stepson, causing her to divorce her husband and shatter her life. A good performance by Fonda, then Vadim's wife. Modern version of Zola's "La Curee." **96m/C VHS, Beta.** *FR* Jane Fonda, Peter McEnery, Michel Piccoli; ***D:*** Roger Vadim; ***M:*** Jean Bouchety. *MED*

A Game of Crime **1960** Intriguing murder story with strong horror overtones. **?m/C VHS.** John Blythe Barrymore Jr., Luisa Rivelli. *LOO*

Game of Death *Goodbye Bruce Lee: His Last Game of Death; Bruce Lee's Game of Death* **1979 (R)** Bruce Lee's final kung fu thriller about a young martial arts movie star who gets involved with the syndicate. Lee died halfway through the filming of this movie and it was finished with out-takes and a double. **100m/C VHS, Beta, LV.** Bruce Lee, Dean Jagger, Kareem Abdul-Jabbar, Colleen Camp, Chuck Norris; ***D:*** Robert Clouse; ***M:*** John Barry. *FOX*

The Game of Love **1990 (PG)** Olin presides over Henry's bar, the lost and found of lonely hearts and lust, where people go to quench that deep thirst for love. **94m/C VHS, LV.** Ed Marinaro, Belinda Bauer, Ken Olin, Robert Rusler, Tracy Nelson, Max Gail, Janet Margolin, Brynn Thayer; ***D:*** Bobby Roth. *ACA*

Game of Seduction **1986** A murdering, womanizing playboy pursues a married woman and gets caught up in a treacherous cat-and-mouse game. Dubbed. **81m/C VHS, Beta.** Sylvia Kristel, Jon Finch, Nathalie Delon; ***D:*** Roger Vadim. *NO*

Game of Survival **1989** A young rebel warrior from another planet is sent to earth to battle six of the galaxy's most brutal warriors. **85m/C VHS, Beta.** Nikki Hill, Cindy Coatman, Roosevelt Miller Jr.; ***D:*** Armand Gazarian. *NO*

Gamera, the Invincible ½ *Gamera; Gammera; Daikaiju Gamera* **1966** This Japanese monster flick features the ultimate nuclear super-turtle who flies around destroying cities and causing panic. First in the series of notoriously bad films, this one is cool in black and white and has some impressive special effects. Dubbed in English. **86m/B VHS, LV.** *JP* Brian Donlevy, Albert Dekker, Diane Findlay, John Baragrey, Dick O'Neill, Eiji Funakoshi; ***D:*** Noriaki Yuasa. *JFK, SNC*

Gamera vs. Barugon ½ *Gamera Tai Barugon; Gambara vs. Barugon; The War of the Monsters* **1966** The monstrous turtle returns to Earth from his outer space prison, now equipped with his famous leg-jets. He soon wishes he had stayed airborne, however, when he is forced to do battle with 130-foot lizard Barugon and his rainbow-melting ray. Tokyo and Osaka get melted in the process. **101m/C VHS, Beta.** *JP* Kojiro Hongo, Kyoko Enami; ***D:*** Shigeo Tanaka. *JFK*

Gamera vs. Gaos ½ *The Return of the Giant Monsters; Gamera vs. Gyaos; Boyichi and the Supermonster; Gamera Tai Gaos* **1967** Now fully the good guy, Gamera slugs it out with a bat-like critter named Gaos. Suspense rules the day when Gaos tries to put out the super turtle's jets with his built-in fire extinguisher but luckily for Earth, Gamera has a few tricks of his own up his shell. **87m/C VHS, Beta, LV.** *JP* Kojiro Hongo, Kichijiro Ueda, Naoyuki Abe; ***D:*** Noriaki Yuasa. *JFK*

Gamera vs. Guiron *Attack of the Monsters; Gamera Tai Guiron* **1969** Gamera risks it all to take on an evil, spear-headed monster on a distant planet. Highlight is the sexy, leotard clad aliens who want to eat the little Earth kids' brains. **88m/C VHS, Beta.** *JP* Nobuhiro Kashima, Christopher Murphy, Miyuki Akiyama, Yuko Hamada, Eiji Funakoshi; ***D:*** Noriaki Yuasa. *JFK*

Gamera vs. Zigra *Gamera Tai Shinkai Kaiju Jigara; Gamera vs. the Deep Sea Monster Zigra* **1971** Gamera the flying turtle chose an ecological theme for this, his final movie. It seems that the alien Zigrans have come to Earth to wrest the planet from the hands of the pollutive humans who have nearly destroyed it. The aliens kill the staunch turtle, but the love and prayers of children revive him that he may defend Earth once more. **91m/C VHS, Beta, LV.** *JP* Reiko Kasahara, Mikiko Tsubouchi, Koji Fujiyama, Arlene Zoellner, Gloria Zoellner; ***D:*** Noriaki Yuasa. *JFK*

Games Girls Play ½ *The Bunny Caper; Sex Play* **1975** The daughter of an American diplomat organizes a contest at a British boarding school to see which of her classmates can seduce important dignitaries. **90m/C VHS, Beta.** Christina Hart, Jane Anthony, Jill Damas, Drina Pavlovic; ***D:*** Jack Arnold. *NO*

The Gamma People *Woof!* **1956** A journalist discovers a Balkan doctor shooting children with gamma rays, creating an army of brainless zombies. Cult-renowned grade-Z tripe. **83m/B VHS, Beta.** *GB* Walter Rilla, Paul Douglas, Eva Bartok; ***D:*** John Gilling; ***C:*** Ted Moore. *NO*

Gandhi ½ **1982 (PG)** The biography of Mahatma Gandhi from the prejudice he encounters as a young attorney in South Africa, to his role as spiritual leader to the people of India and his use of passive resistance against the country's British rulers, and his eventual assassination. Kingsley is a marvel in his Academy Award-winning role and the picture is a generally riveting epic worthy of its eight Oscars. **188m/C VHS, Beta, LV.** *GB* Ben Kingsley, Candice Bergen, Edward Fox, John Gielgud, John Mills, Saeed Jaffrey, Trevor Howard, Ian Charleson, Roshan Seth, Athol Fugard, Martin Sheen, Daniel Day-Lewis, Rohini Hattangady; ***D:*** Richard Attenborough; ***W:*** John Briley; ***C:*** Billy Williams; ***M:*** George Fenton. Academy Awards '82: Best Actor (Kingsley), Best Art Direction/Set Decoration, Best Cinematography, Best Costume Design, Best Director (Attenborough), Best Film Editing, Best Original Screenplay, Best Picture; British Academy Awards '82: Best Actor (Kingsley), Best Director (Attenborough), Best Film, Best Supporting Actress (Hattangady); Golden Globe Awards '83: Best Actor—Drama (Kingsley), Best Director (Attenborough), Best Foreign Film, Best Screenplay; Los Angeles Film Critics Association Awards '82: Best Actor (Kingsley); National Board of Review Awards '82: Best Actor (Kingsley); New York Film Critics Awards '82: Best Actor (Kingsley), Best Film; Nominations: Academy Awards '82: Best Makeup, Best Original Score. *COL, BTV, HMV*

Gang Bullets **1938** Mobster tries to continue his dirty systems in a new town, but finds the legal force incorruptible. **62m/B VHS, Beta.** Anne Nagel, Robert Kent, Charles Trowbridge, Morgan Wallace, J. Farrell MacDonald, Arthur Loft, John Merton; ***D:*** Lambert Hillyer. *SNC*

Gang Busters ½ **1955** Prisoners plan a breakout. Slow and uninteresting adaptation of the successful radio series. Filmed in Oregon. **78m/B VHS.** Myron Healey, Sam Edwards, Frank Gerstle; ***D:*** Bill Karn. *NOS, SNC*

Gang Justice **1994** Low-budget melodrama finds sensitive Asian student Paul (Kim) battling racists at school and his crippled alcoholic father at home. Some martial arts fight scenes but this is amateur time. **92m/C VHS, LV.** Joon Kim, Jonathan Gorman, Erik Estrada, Angel Dashek; ***D:*** Richard W. Park. *AIP*

Gang War **1940** Low-budget gangster film with an all-back cast about two gangs fighting for control of the city's jukebox business. **60m/B VHS.** Ralph Cooper, Gladys Snyder, Reggie Fenderson, Lawrence Criner, Monte Hawley, Jesse C. Brooks, Maceo B. Sheffield; ***D:*** Leo Popkin. *NOS, RXM*

Gang Wars *Devil's Express* **1975 (R)** There's a riot going on as Puerto Rican, Black, and Chinese gangs fight it out for control of the city. **82m/C VHS.** Warhawk Tanzania, Larry Fleishman, Sam DeFazio, Wilfred Roldan, Elsie Roman, Sarah Nyrick; ***D:*** Barry Rosen. *SUN*

Gangbusters **1938** Men battle crime in the city in this serial in thirteen episodes based on the popular radio series of the same name. **253m/B VHS, Beta.** Kent Taylor, Irene Hervey, Robert Armstrong. *NOS, CAB, VCN*

The Gang's All Here ½ **1940** Darro joins a trucking firm whose rigs are being run off the road and hijacked by a competitor. Features "Charlie Chan" regulars Luke and Moreland. **63m/B VHS.** Frankie Darro, Marcia Mae Jones, Jackie Moran, Mantan Moreland, Keye Luke; ***D:*** Jean Yarbrough. *NOS, RXM, MOV*

Gangs, Inc. *Crimes, Inc.; Paper Bullets* **1941** A woman is sent to prison for a hit-and-run accident, actually the fault of a wealthy playboy. When she learns his identity she vows revenge and turns to crime to achieve her evil ends. Okay thriller suffers from plot problems. Ladd has a minor role filmed before he became a star. **72m/B VHS, Beta.** Joan Woodbury, Lash LaRue, Linda Ware, John Archer, Vince Barnett, Alan Ladd; ***D:*** Phil Rosen. *NOS, MRV, DVT*

The Gangster ½ **1947** Sullivan plays a small-time slum-bred hood who climbs to the top of the underworld, only to lose his gang because he allows his fears to get the better of him. (There's nothing to fear except when someone knows you're afeared.) Noir crimer with an interesting psychological perspective, though a bit sluggish at times. **84m/B VHS.** Barry Sullivan, Joan Lorring, Akim Tamiroff, Harry (Henry) Morgan, John Ireland, Fifi d'Orsay, Shelley Winters; ***D:*** Gordon Wiles. *FOX, FCT*

Gangster Wars **1981** A specially edited-for-video version of the television mini-series "The Gangster Chronicles." Based on fact, it deals with the growth of organized crime in America from the early days of this century, through the eyes of three ghetto kids who grow up to become powerful mobsters. **121m/C VHS, Beta.** Michael Nouri, Joe Penny, Brian Benben, Kathleen Lloyd, Madeleine Stowe, Robert Davi; ***D:*** Richard Sarafian. *MCA*

Gangsters **1979** City is ruled by the mob and nothing can stop their bloody grip except "The Special Squad." **90m/C VHS, Beta.** *IT* Michael V. Gazzo, Tony Page, Vicki Sue Robinson, Nai Bonet; ***D:*** Mac Ahlberg. *VCD, HHE, MTX*

Gangster's Den **1945** A gang of renegades scare a woman out of buying a gold-laden piece of land and Billy the Kid comes to her rescue. **56m/B VHS, Beta.** Buster Crabbe, Kermit Maynard, Al "Fuzzy" St. John, Charles "Blackie" King; ***D:*** Sam Newfield. *VDM*

Gangster's Law *Woof!* **1986** A look at a seedy gangster's downfall. Filmed on location in Italy. Dubbed. **89m/C VHS, Beta.** Klaus Kinski, Maurice Poli, Susy Anderson, Max Delys; ***D:*** Siro Marcellini. *TWE*

Gangsters of the Frontier **1944** The people of Red Rock are forced to work in the town mines by two prison escapees until Ritter and his friends ride to the rescue. Part of the "Texas Ranger" series. **56m/B VHS, Beta.** Tex Ritter, Dave O'Brien; ***D:*** Elmer Clifton; ***W:*** Elmer Clifton. *NOS, DVT, RXM*

Gangway ½ **1937** Pat Wayne (Matthews), a London newspaper reporter, is mistaken for a jewel thief and kidnapped by gangsters aboard a New York-bound ocean liner. In the meantime, the real thief is aboard posing as a Hollywood actress (Blakeney), and it's up to Scotland Yard inspector Bob Deering (Mackay) to solve the crime. Matthews was considered by many to be the English equivalent of America's Eleanor Powell. Based on an original story by Dwight Taylor. **90m/B VHS.** *GB* Jessie Matthews, Barry Mackay, Olive Blakeney, Liane Ordeyne, Patrick Ludlow, Nat Pendleton, Noel Madison, Alastair Sim, Doris Rogers, Laurence Anderson, Bennie Dorn; ***D:*** Sonnie Hale; ***W:*** Sonnie Hale, Lesser Samuels. *HEG*

Ganjasaurus Rex **1987 (R)** Monster spoof about a giant green dinosaur emerging from the pot-laden hills of California. Maybe it's all in your head, man. **100m/C VHS, Beta.** Paul Bassis, Dave Fresh, Rosie Jones; ***D:*** Ursi Reynolds. *RHI*

Gappa the Trifibian Monster ½ *Daikyoju Gappa; Monster from a Prehistoric Planet* **1967 (PG)** Researchers visiting a tropical island find a giant egg and take it back to Tokyo with them, dismaying the egg's giant monster parents. Dubbed. **90m/C VHS, Beta.** *JP ORI*

The Garbage Pail Kids Movie *Woof!* **1987 (PG)** The disgusting youngsters, stars of bubblegum cards, make their first and last film appearance in this live action dud. The garbage is where it should be thrown. **100m/C VHS, Beta, LV.** Anthony Newley, MacKenzie Astin, Katie Barberi; ***D:*** Rod Amateau; ***W:*** Rod Amateau. *PAR, BAR, IME*

Garbo Talks **1984 (PG-13)** A dying eccentric's last request is to meet the reclusive screen legend Greta Garbo. Bancroft amusingly plays the dying woman whose son goes to extreme lengths in order to fulfill his mother's last wish. **104m/C VHS, Beta.** Anne Bancroft, Ron Silver, Carrie Fisher, Catherine Hicks, Steven Hill, Howard da Silva, Dorothy Loudon, Harvey Fierstein, Hermione Gingold; ***D:*** Sidney Lumet; ***M:*** Cy Coleman. *MGM, FOX*

The Garden **1990** Eternally provocative director Jarman does another take on sex and religion. He examines the role of the Church in the persecution of homosexuality by recreating the story of the Passion and replacing the figure of Christ in some sequences with two male lovers, who are arrested, humiliated, and tortured. **90m/C VHS.** *GB* Tilda Swinton, Johnny Mills, Philip MacDonald, Roger Cook, Kevin Collins, Pete Lee-Wilson, Spencer Lee, Jody Graber; ***D:*** Derek Jarman; ***W:*** Derek Jarman; ***M:*** Simon Fisher Turner. *FXL, FCT*

The Garden of Allah **1936** Dietrich finds hyper-romantic encounters in the Algerian desert with Boyer, but his terrible secret may doom them both. This early Technicolor production, though flawed, is an absolute must for Dietrich fans. Yuma, Arizona substituted for the exotic locale. **85m/C VHS, LV.** Marlene Dietrich, Charles Boyer, Basil Rathbone, Sir C. Aubrey Smith, Tilly Losch, Joseph Schildkraut, Henry Kleinbach (Brandon), John Carradine; ***D:*** Richard Boleslawski; ***C:*** William Howard Greene; ***M:*** Max Steiner. Nominations: Academy Awards '36: Best Original Score. *FOX*

The Garden of Delights **1970** A wicked black comedy about a millionaire, paralyzed and suffering from amnesia after a car accident. His horrendously greedy family tries to get him to remember and reveal his Swiss bank account number. Acclaimed; in Spanish with English subtitles. **95m/C VHS, Beta.** *SP* Jose Luis Lopez Vasquez, Lina Canelajas, Luchy Soto, Francisco Pierra, Charo Soriano; ***D:*** Carlos Saura. *HMV, CVC, FCT*

The Garden of Eden **1928** Milestone—whose "Two Arabian Nights" had won an Academy Award the previous year, and who went on to direct "All Quiet on the Western Front" and "Of Mice and Men"—directed this sophisticated ersatz Lubitsch sex comedy. Griffith, the so-called "Orchid Lady," is a young girl who dreams of diva-dom but falls deep into the underbelly of the seedy side of Budapest. With the aid of a fallen baroness, however, she finds her way to Monte Carlo and has her turn in the limelight. A handsome production designed by William Cameron Menzies, art director for "Gone With the Wind." **115m/B VHS, Beta, 8mm.** Corine Griffith, Louise Dresser, Charles Ray, Lowell Sherman; ***D:*** Lewis Milestone. *NOS, VYY*

The Garden of the Finzi-Continis *Il Giardino Del Finzi-Contini* **1971 (R)** Acclaimed film by De Sica about an aristocratic Jewish family living in Italy under increasing Fascist oppression on the eve of WWII. The garden wall symbolizes the distance between the Finzi-Continis and the Nazi reality about to engulf them. Flawless acting and well-defined direction. Based on the novel by Giorgio Bassani, who collaborated on the script but later repudiated the film. Music by De Sica's son, Manuel. In Italian with English subtitles or dubbed. **90m/C VHS, Beta, LV.** *IT* Dominique Sanda, Helmut Berger, Lino Capolicchio, Fabio Testi, Romolo Valli; ***D:*** Vittorio De Sica; ***W:*** Cesare Zavattini; ***M:*** Manuel De Sica. Academy Awards '71: Best Foreign Language Film; Berlin International Film Festival '71: Golden Berlin Bear; National Board of Review Awards '71: 5 Best Foreign Films of the Year; Nominations: Academy Awards '71: Best Adapted Screenplay. *VLL, IME, APD*

Gardens of Stone **1987 (R)** A zealous young cadet during the Vietnam War is assigned to the Old Guard patrol at Arlington Cemetery, and clashes with the patrol's older officers and various pacifist civilians. Falls short of the mark, although Jones turns in an excellent performance. **112m/C VHS, Beta, LV.** James Caan, James Earl Jones, D.B. Sweeney, Anjelica Huston, Dean Stockwell, Lonette McKee, Mary Stuart Masterson, Bill Graham, Sam Bottoms, Casey Siemaszko, Laurence "Larry" Fishburne; ***D:*** Francis Ford Coppola; ***W:*** Ronald Bass; ***M:*** Carmine Coppola. *FOX*

Gargoyles, The Movie: The Heroes Awaken ½ **1994 (G)** Mythical crimefighting creatures, trapped in stone by day thanks to a sorcerer's spell but released to live at night, are displaced in time from their medieval Scottish home, winding up in modern-day New York City. But they discover they still have old enemies to fight. First aired as a five-episode part of the animated TV series. **80m/C VHS.** ***V:*** Ed Asner, Keith David, Jonathon Frakes, Marina Sirtis, Bill Fagerbakke, Salli Richardson, Frank Welker, Thom Adcox, Jeff Bennett. *TOU*

Garringo **1969** Lawmen attempt to bring to justice a man who is intent on killing the soldiers responsible for his father's death. **95m/C VHS, Beta.** *IT SP* Anthony Steffen, Peter Lee Lawrence, Jose Bodalo; ***D:*** Rafael Romero Marchent. *MAD*

Gas *Woof!* **1981 (R)** This dog has tycoon Hayden buying up all the gas stations in town to create a crisis that will make him richer. Everyone in the cast wastes their time, especially Sutherland as a hip DJ reporting on the gas shortage. **94m/C VHS, Beta.** *CA* Donald Sutherland, Susan Anspach, Sterling Hayden, Peter Aykroyd, Howie Mandel, Helen Shaver; ***D:*** Les Rose; ***W:*** Dick Wolf. *PAR*

Gas Food Lodging **1992 (R)** Saga casts Adams as Nora, a weary waitress in Laramie, New Mexico, trying her best to raise two teenaged daughters on her own. The daughters, Skye and Balk, are disillusioned about love and family. Balk's special friend is Darius, an eccentric window dresser, played by Leitch, Skye's brother. Nothing works out quite as intended but multi-dimensional characters, poignant situtations, and enormous emotional appeal highlight the directorial debut of Anders. Based on the Richard Peck novel "Don't Look and It Won't Hurt." **100m/C VHS, LV.** Brooke Adams, Ione Skye, Fairuza Balk, James Brolin, Rob Knepper, Donovan Leitch, David Lansbury, Jacob Vargas, Chris Mulkey, Tiffany Anders; ***D:*** Allison Anders; ***W:*** Allison Anders; ***M:*** J. Mascis, Barry Adamson. Independent Spirit Awards '93: Best Actress (Balk). *COL*

Gas Pump Girls ½ **1979 (R)** Comedy about five lovely ladies who manage a gas station and use their feminine wiles to win the battle against a shady oil sheik. **102m/C VHS, Beta, LV.** Kirsten Baker, Dennis Bowen, Huntz Hall, Steve Bond, Leslie King, Linda Lawrence; ***D:*** Joel Bender. *VES*

Gas-s-s-s! ½ *Gas-s-s-s... or, It May Become Necessary to Destroy the World in Order to Save It* **1970 (PG)** A gas main leak in an Alaskan defense plant kills everyone beyond thirtysomething and the post-apocalyptic pre-boomer survivors are left to muddle their way through the brume. Trouble is, AIP edited the heck out of the movie, much to Corman's chagrin, and the result is a truncated comedy; Corman was so displeased, in fact, he left to create New World studios. **79m/C VHS, Beta.** Robert Corff, Elaine Giftos, Pat Patterson, George Armitage, Alex Wilson, Ben Vereen, Cindy Williams, Bud Cort, Talia Shire; ***D:*** Roger Corman; ***W:*** George Armitage. *NO*

Gaslight ½ *Angel Street* **1939** A forgotten British classic that fell victim to the American production of the same title and theme that was filmed only five years later. Set in late Victorian London, Wynyard is the rich innocent married to the calculating Walbrook, who slowly tries driving his bride insane in order to discover some hidden family jewels. She comes under the protection of a Scotland Yard detective (Pettingell) who suspects Walbrook has already murdered once. An outstandingly eerie psychological thriller. Based on the play "Angel Street" by Patrick Hamilton. **84m/C VHS.** *GB* Anton Walbrook, Diana Wynyard, Frank Pettingell, Cathleen Cordell; ***D:*** Thorold Dickinson. *FCT*

Gaslight ½ *The Murder in Thorton Square* **1944** Lavish remake of the 1939 film, based on the Patrick Hamilton play "Angel Street." A man tries to drive his beautiful wife insane while searching for priceless jewels. Her only clue to his evil acts is the frequent dimming of their gaslights. A suspenseful Victorian era mystery. Lansbury's film debut, as the tarty maid. **114m/B VHS, Beta, LV.** Charles Boyer, Ingrid Bergman, Joseph Cotten, Angela Lansbury, Terry Moore, May Whitty, Barbara Everest, Emil Rameau, Edmund Breon, Halliwell Hobbes, Tom Stevenson; ***D:*** George Cukor; ***C:*** Joseph Ruttenberg. Academy Awards '44: Best Actress (Bergman), Best Interior Decoration; Golden Globe Awards '45: Best Actress—Drama (Bergman); Nominations: Academy Awards '44: Best Actor (Boyer), Best Black and White Cinematography, Best Picture, Best Screenplay, Best Supporting Actress (Lansbury). *MGM, BTV, VEC*

The Gate **1987 (PG-13)** Kids generally like to explore and Dorff and Tripp are no exception. When a large hole is exposed in their backyard, it would be a childhood sin not to see what's in it, right? What they don't know is that this hole is actually a gateway to and from Hell. The terror they unleash includes more than just run-of-the-mill demons. Good special effects. Followed by "Gate 2." **85m/C VHS, Beta, LV.** Christa Denton, Stephen Dorff, Louis Tripp; ***D:*** Tibor Takacs. *LIV, VES*

Gate 2 ½ **1992 (R)** Tripp returns in his role as Terry, a young student of demonology in this lame sequel to "The Gate." Terry and a few of his teen buddies call up a group of demons that have been confined behind a gate for billions of years. The demons are used to grant modest wishes, but the wishes end up having very evil effects. Incredibly weak plot saved only by the special monster effects, which include live action and puppetry. **90m/C VHS, LV.** Louis Tripp, Simon Reynolds, Pamela Segall, James Villemaire, Neil Munro, James Kidnie, Andrea Ladanyi; ***D:*** Tibor Takacs; ***W:*** Michael Nankin; ***M:*** George Blondheim. *COL*

Gate of Hell ½ *Jigokumen* **1954** Set in 12th-century Japan. A warlord desires a beautiful married woman and seeks to kill her husband to have her. However, he accidentally kills her instead. Filled with shame and remorse, the warlord abandons his life to seek solace as a monk. Heavily awarded and critically acclaimed; the first Japanese film to use color photography. In Japanese with English subtitles. **89m/C VHS, Beta, 8mm.** *JP* Kazuo Hasegawa, Machiko Kyo; ***D:*** Teinosuke Kinugasa. Academy Awards '54: Best Costume Design (Color), Best Foreign Language Film; Cannes Film Festival '54: Best Film; National Board of Review Awards '54: 10 Best Films of the Year. *VYY, SUE, DVT*

Gates of Hell *Woof! Paura Nella Citta Dei Morti Viventi; City of the Living Dead; The Fear; Twilight of the Dead; Fear in the City of the Living Dead* **1983** Salem, Massachusetts, must battle the risen dead in this gorefest that tried to disguise itself under many other titles. **90m/C VHS, Beta.** Christopher George, Janet Agren, Katherine MacColl, Robert Sampson; ***D:*** Lucio Fulci. *IGP*

The Gathering ½ **1977** A dying man seeks out the wife and family he has alienated for a final Christmas gathering. James Poe authored this well-acted holiday tearjerker that won the 1977-78 Emmy for outstanding TV drama special. **94m/C VHS, Beta.** Ed Asner, Maureen Stapleton, Lawrence Pressman, Stephanie Zimbalist, Bruce Davison, Gregory Harrison, Veronica Hamel, Gail Strickland; ***D:*** Randal Kleiser; ***M:*** John Barry. *WOV*

A Gathering of Eagles ½ **1963** Hudson portrays a hard-nosed Air Force colonel during peacetime whose British wife must adjust to being a military spouse. **115m/C VHS.** Rock Hudson, Rod Taylor, Mary Peach, Barry Sullivan, Kevin McCarthy, Henry Silva, Leif Erickson; ***D:*** Delbert Mann; ***M:*** Jerry Goldsmith. *MGM*

The Gathering: Part 2 **1979** Sequel in which a widow has a Christmas reunion with her family, but conflict arises when she introduces a new man in her life. Not as effective as the original, also made for TV. **98m/C VHS.** Maureen Stapleton, Efrem Zimbalist Jr., Jameson Parker, Bruce Davison, Lawrence Pressman, Gail Strickland, Veronica Hamel; ***D:*** Charles S. Dubin. *TTC*

The Gathering Storm **1974** Based on the first book of memoirs from Sir Winston Churchill, this drama examines the pre-WWII years. **72m/C Beta.** Richard Burton, Virginia McKenna, Ian Bannen; ***D:*** Herbert Wise. *PSM*

The Gatling Gun ½ *King Gun* **1972 (PG)** Poor tale of the Cavalry, Apache Indians, and renegades all after the title weapon. **93m/C VHS.** Guy Stockwell, Woody Strode, Patrick Wayne, Robert Fuller, Barbara Luna, John Carradine, Pat Buttram, Phil Harris; ***D:*** Robert Gordon. *HHE*

Gator **1976 (PG)** Sequel to "White Lightning" (1973) follows the adventures of Gator (Reynolds), who is recruited to gather evidence to convict a corrupt political boss who also happens to be his friend. Reynolds in his good ole' boy role with lots of chase scenes. Talk show host Michael Douglas made his film debut in the role of the governor. First film Reynolds directed. **116m/C VHS, Beta.** Burt Reynolds, Jerry Reed, Lauren Hutton, Jack Weston, Alice Ghostley, Dub Taylor; ***D:*** Burt Reynolds; ***W:*** William W. Norton Sr.; ***M:*** Charles Bernstein. *MGM, FOX*

Gator Bait ½ **1973 (R)** The Louisiana swamp is home to the beautiful Desiree, and woe be unto any man who threatens her family. Aims to please fans of the raunchy and violent. Followed by an equally vile sequel. **91m/C VHS, Beta, LV.** Claudia Jennings, Clyde Ventura, Bill Thurman, Janet Baldwin; ***D:*** Ferd Sebastian, Beverly Sebastian; ***W:*** Ferd Sebastian, Beverly Sebastian. *PAR*

Gator Bait 2: Cajun Justice **1988 (R)** A city girl comes to the Louisiana swamp and turns violent in an effort to exact revenge on the men who have been tormenting her. **94m/C VHS, Beta, LV.** Jan MacKenzie, Tray Loren, Paul Muzzcat, Brad Kepnick, Jerry Armstrong, Ben Sebastian; ***D:*** Ferd Sebastian, Beverly Sebastian; ***W:*** Ferd Sebastian, Beverly Sebastian. *PAR*

The Gauntlet **1977 (R)** A cop is ordered to Las Vegas to bring back a key witness for an important trial—but the witness turns out to be a beautiful prostitute being hunted by killers. Violence-packed action. **111m/C VHS, Beta, LV.** Clint Eastwood, Sondra Locke, Pat Hingle, Bill McKinney; ***D:*** Clint Eastwood; ***W:*** Michael Butler. *WAR, TLF*

The Gay Divorcee *The Gay Divorce* **1934** Astaire pursues Rogers to an English seaside resort, where she mistakes him for the hired correspondent in her divorce case. Based on the musical play "The Gay Divorce" by Dwight Taylor and Cole Porter. The title was slightly changed for the movie because of protests from the Hays Office. ♫Don't Let It Bother You; A Needle in a Haystack; Let's K-nock K-nees; Night and Day; The Continental. **107m/B VHS, Beta, LV.** Fred Astaire, Ginger Rogers, Edward Everett Horton, Eric Blore, Alice Brady, Erik Rhodes, Betty Grable; ***D:*** Mark Sandrich; ***M:*** Max Steiner. Academy Awards '34: Best Song ("The Continental"); Nominations: Academy Awards '34: Best Interior Decoration, Best Picture, Best Sound, Best Score. *MED, TTC*

The Gay Lady ½ *Trottie True* **1949** Light romantic comedy set in the 1890s about an actress who climbs to stardom in London theater and winds up marrying into the aristocracy. Look for Christopher Lee and Roger Moore in early bit parts. **95m/C VHS.** *GB* Jean Kent, James Donald, Hugh Sinclair, Lana Morris, Bill Owen, Michael Medwin, Andrew Crawford; ***D:*** Brian Desmond Hurst. *MOV, UNI*

Gay Purr-ee **1962** Delightful tale of feline romance in the City of Lights. For all ages. **85m/C VHS, LV.** ***D:*** Abe Levitow; ***W:*** Chuck Jones; ***M:*** Harold Arlen; ***V:*** Judy Garland, Robert Goulet, Red Buttons, Hermione Gingold, Mel Blanc. *WAR, FCT, WTA*

The Gay Ranchero **1942** Rogers, without Dale Evans, in an average tale of old west meets new crooks. Rogers is the sheriff who foils gangsters trying to take over an airport. The action doesn't stop him from singing a duet with leading lady Frazee on "Wait'll I Get My Sunshine in the Moonlight." **55m/B VHS, Beta.** Roy Rogers, Andy Devine, Tito Guizar, Jane Frazee, Estelita Rodriguez; ***D:*** William Witney. *NOS, VCN, CAB*

The Gazebo **1959** Wacky comedy about a TV writer who is being blackmailed by someone who has nude photos of his Broadway star wife. He decides murder is the only solution to this problem. Reynolds sings "Something Called Love." Based on a play by Alec Coppel from a story by Myra and Alec Coppel. **102m/B VHS.** Glenn Ford, Debbie Reynolds, Carl Reiner, John McGiver, Doro Merande, Bert Freed, Martin Landau; ***D:*** George Marshall; ***W:*** George Wells. *MGM*

Geek Maggot Bingo *The Freak From Suckweasel Mountain* **1983** It's too bad director Zed waited until mid-"Bingo" to post a sign warning "Leave Now, It Isn't Going Get Any Better!" Conceived by the New York underground's don of the "Cinema of Transgression" to be an off-the-rack cult classic, this horror spoof is too long on in-jokes and short on substance to earn its number in the cult hall of fame. It does, however, boast Death as Scumbalina the vampire queen and Hell as a punk cowboy crooner (before alternative country hit the airwaves). TV horror-meister Zacherle narrates. **70m/C VHS.** Richard Hell, Donna Death, John Zacherle; ***D:*** Nick Zedd. *MWF, MOV*

Geheimakte WB1 *Secret Paper WB1* **1942** Historical drama centering on the invention of the U-boat by Sergeant Wilhelm Bauer during Denmark's WWII blockade of the ports of Schleswig-Holstein. In German with no subtitles. **91m/B VHS, Beta.** *GE* Alexander Golling; ***D:*** Herbert Selpin. *IHF*

A Geisha *Gion Bayashi; Gion Festival Music* **1953** Miyoharu (Kogure) is a passive elderly geisha who agrees to train the naive young Eiko (Wakao) in her new role. But Eiko discovers her romantic notions of the geisha life are far from it's modern reality. Poignant look at the changing status of the geisha in Japan after WWII and the country's social upheavals. In Japanese with English subtitles. **86m/B VHS.** *JP* Michiyo Kogure, Ayako Wakao, Seizaburo Kawazu, Chieko Naniwa, Eitaro Shindo; ***D:*** Kenji Mizoguchi; ***W:*** Yoshikata Yoda; ***M:*** Ichiro Saito. *NYF, FCT, BTV*

The Geisha Boy **1958** Jerry is a floundering magician who joins the USO and tours the Far East. His slapstick confrontations with the troupe leader and an officer who dreams of attending his own funeral provide hearty laughs, plus Lewis finds romance with a Japanese widow after her son claims him as a father. Pleshette's film debut, with an appearance by the Los Angeles Dodgers. **98m/C VHS.** Jerry Lewis, Marie McDonald, Sessue Hayakawa, Barton MacLane, Suzanne Pleshette, Nobu McCarthy; ***D:*** Frank Tashlin. *PAR*

Geisha Girl ½ **1952** Forgotten sci-fi film about a mad scientist and his Japanese cohorts who develop small explosive pills that are more powerful than nuclear bombs. Their plans of world conquest are thwarted when the pills inadvertently fall into the hands of two American G.I.s. **67m/B VHS.** Martha Hyer, William Andrews, Archer MacDonald, Kekao Yokoo, Teddy Nakamura; ***D:*** George Breakston, C. Ray Stahl; ***W:*** C. Ray Stahl. *SNC*

Gemini Affair **198?** Two women go to Hollywood to become rich and famous but end up being very disappointed. **88m/C VHS, Beta.** Marta Kristen, Kathy Kersh, Anne Seymour. *UNI*

Gene Autry Matinee Double Feature #1 **1953** Includes "Blue Canadian Rockies" (1952), where Autry must investigate a series of murders, and "Last of the Pony Riders" (1953), in which the final days of the pony express yield a sinister conspiracy. **117m/C VHS.** Gene Autry; ***D:*** George Archainbaud. *NO*

Gene Autry Matinee Double Feature #2 **1953** An exciting western double feature: A cowboy goes after the man who stole his rodeo winnings in "Melody Trail" and a territorial ranger investigates a series of Indian raids in "Winning of the West." **117m/B VHS, Beta.** Gene Autry, Smiley Burnette, Alan Bridge; ***D:*** George Archainbaud, Joseph Kane. *NO*

Gene Autry Matinee Double Feature #3 **1953** Gene stars in "Prairie Moon," in which he teaches some tough kids a lesson about life, and "On Top of Old Smokey," which sees a young woman trying to save her small town. **113m/B VHS, Beta.** Gene Autry, Smiley Burnette; ***D:*** George Archainbaud, Ralph Staub. *NO*

The Gene Krupa Story 🦴🦴½ **1959** The story of the famous jazz drummer and his career plunge after a drug conviction. Krupa recorded the soundtrack, mimed by Mineo, who was too young for a convincing portrayal. Gavin McLeod (of "Love Boat" fame) has a small part as Mineo's dad. **101m/B VHS, Beta.** Sal Mineo, James Darren, Susan Kohner, Susan Oliver, Anita O'Day, Red Nichols; ***D:*** Don Weis. *COL, FCT*

The General 🦴🦴🦴🦴 **1927** Keaton's masterpiece and arguably the most formally perfect and funniest of silent comedies. Concerns a plucky Confederate soldier who single-handedly retrieves a pivotal train from Northern territory. Full of eloquent man-vs-machinery images and outrageous sight gags. Remade as "The Great Locomotive Chase" in 1956 with Fess Parker. **78m/B VHS, Beta, LV, 8mm.** Buster Keaton, Marion Mack, Glen Cavender, Jim Farley, Joe Keaton; ***D:*** Buster Keaton, Clyde Bruckman. *VYY, HHT, NOS*

The General Died at Dawn 🦴🦴🦴 **1936** A clever, atmospheric suspense film about an American mercenary in Shanghai falling in love with a beautiful spy as he battles a fierce Chinese warlord who wants to take over the country. Playwright-to-be Odets' first screenplay; he, O'Hara and '30s gossip hound Skolsky have cameos as reporters. **93m/B VHS, Beta.** Gary Cooper, Madeleine Carroll, Akim Tamiroff, Dudley Digges, Porter Hall, William Frawley, Philip Ahn; ***Cameos:*** John O'Hara, Clifford Odets, Sidney Skolsky; ***D:*** Lewis Milestone; ***W:*** Clifford Odets; ***C:*** Victor Milner. Nominations: Academy Awards '36: Best Cinematography, Best Supporting Actor (Tamiroff), Best Original Score. *MCA*

The General Line 🦴🦴🦴🦴 *The Old and the New* **1929** Eisenstein's classic pro-Soviet semi-documentary about a poor farm woman who persuades her village to form a cooperative. Transgresses its party-line instructional purpose by vivid filmmaking. The director's last silent film. **90m/B VHS, Beta.** *RU* Marfa Lapkina; ***D:*** Sergei Eisenstein. National Board of Review Awards '30: 5 Best Foreign Films of the Year. *NOS, MRV, DVT*

General Spanky 🦴🦴 **1936** The only feature "Our Gang" comedy goofed by transplanting them to a Civil War milieu popular at the time. Confederate kids Spanky and Alfalfa play soldier, ultimately outsmarting Union troops. The rascals are still funny sometimes, but Buckwheat's role as an eager slave is disturbing today. **73m/B VHS, LV.** George "Spanky" McFarland, Phillips Holmes, Ralph Morgan, Irving Pichel, Rosina Lawrence, Billie "Buckwheat" Thomas, Carl "Alfalfa" Switzer, Louise Beavers; ***D:*** Fred Newmeyer. Nominations: Academy Awards '36: Best Sound. *MGM, FCT*

Generale Della Rovere 🦴🦴🦴½ *Il Generale Della-Rovere* **1960** A WWII black marketeer is forced by the Nazis to go undercover in a local prison. To find out who the resistance leaders are, he poses as a general. But when prisoners begin to look to him for guidance, he finds the line between his assumed role and real identity diminished, leading to a tragic conclusion. Acclaimed film featuring a bravura lead performance by veteran director De Sica. In Italian with English subtitles. **139m/B VHS, Beta.** *IT* Vittorio De Sica, Otto Messmer, Sandra Milo; ***D:*** Roberto Rossellini. *NOS, CVC, HHT*

A Generation 🦴🦴🦴 **1954** During WWII, a young man escapes from the Warsaw Ghetto and finds his way to the Polish Resistance. He falls in love with the leader of the local group and finds the courage to fight for his freedom. Strong directorial debut from Wajda. Part 1 of his "War Trilogy," followed by "Kanal" and "Ashes and Diamonds." Scripted by Czeszko from his novel "Pokolenie." Polish with subtitles. **90m/B VHS.** *PL* Tadeusz Lomnicki, Ursula Modrzynska, Zbigniew Cybulski, Roman Polanski; ***D:*** Andrzej Wajda; ***W:*** Bohdan Czeszko. *FCT, HMV, PME*

Generation 🦴🦴 *A Time For Caring* **1969** A very pregnant bride informs everyone she'll give birth at home without doctors, and creates a panic. Based on the Broadway play by William Goodhart. **109m/C VHS, Beta.** David Janssen, Kim Darby, Carl Reiner, Peter Duel, Andrew Prine, James Coco, Sam Waterston; ***D:*** George Schaefer; ***W:*** William Goodhart; ***C:*** Lionel Lindon; ***M:*** Dave Grusin. *SUE*

Generations: Mind Control-From the Future 🦴 **1980** Max Lang has lost all self-control and is being driven by evil forces beyond time, forced to kill while fleeing total extinction. **54m/C VHS, Beta.** *NO*

Genevieve 🦴🦴🦴 **1953** A 1904 Darracq roadster is the title star of this picture which spoofs "classic car" owners and their annual rally from London to Brighton. Two married couples challenge each other to a friendly race which becomes increasingly intense as they near the finish line. **86m/C VHS, Beta.** *GB* John Gregson, Dinah Sheridan, Kenneth More, Kay Kendall; ***D:*** Henry Cornelius; ***M:*** Larry Adler. British Academy Awards '53: Best Film; Golden Globe Awards '55: Best Foreign Film; Nominations: Academy Awards '54: Best Story & Screenplay, Best Original Score. *LCA*

Genghis Cohn 🦴🦴½ **1993** Black comedy follows the misadventures of a former Nazi concentration camp commander (Lindsay) who has settled in a small Bavarian town and taken on the position of police chief. But his quiet life is rocked by a series of murders, an affair with a kinky Baroness (Rigg), and by the ghost of Jewish comedian Genghis Cohn (Sher), a victim of the camps whose haunting presence exacts a particularly appropriate revenge. Adapted from Romain Gary's novel "The Dance of Genghis Cohn." Made for British TV. **100m/C VHS.** *GB* Robert Lindsay, Diana Rigg, Anthony Sher; ***D:*** Elijah Moshinsky; ***W:*** Stanley Price. *AAE*

Genie of Darkness 🦴 **1960** The ashes of Nostradamus himself are retrieved in a bid to destroy his vampiric descendent. Edited from a Mexican serial; if you were able to sit through this one, look for "Curse of Nostradamus" and "The Monster Demolisher." **?m/B VHS.** *MX* German Robles; ***D:*** Frederick Curiel. *SNC, NOS, LOO*

Gentle Giant 🦴🦴 **1967** An orphaned bear is taken in by a boy and his family and grows to be a 750 pound giant who must be returned to the wild. "Gentle Ben" TV series was derived from this feature. **93m/C VHS.** Dennis Weaver, Vera Miles, Ralph Meeker, Clint Howard, Huntz Hall; ***D:*** James Neilson. *REP*

Gentle Savage 🦴🦴½ *Camper John* **1973 (R)** When an Indian is wrongly accused of raping and beating a white woman, the white community seeks revenge. The vengeful mob, led by the victim's stepfather, is unaware that it's really their ringleader who is responsible for the crime. When the accused's brother is slain, the Indian community retaliates. Violent but well-crafted. **85m/C VHS.** William Smith, Gene Evans, Barbara Luna, Joe Flynn; ***D:*** Sean McGregor. *LIV*

A Gentle Woman 🦴🦴 *A Gentle Creature; Une Femme Douce* **1969** Adaptation of Dostoevsky's short story about a young married woman who kills herself. Sanda marries pawnbroker Frangin, is miserable in her marriage, toys with killing her husband, and commits suicide instead, leaving the bewildered Frangin to try to figure out why. Several theories are offered but nothing is ever made clear. Debut of Sanda; Bressons' first film in color. French with subtitles. **89m/C VHS.** *FR* Dominique Sanda, Guy Frangin, Jane Lobre; ***D:*** Robert Bresson; ***W:*** Robert Bresson; ***C:*** Ghislan Cloquet; ***M:*** Jean Wiener. *NYF, FCT*

Gentleman Bandit 🦴🦴 **1981** So-so drama about Father Bernard Pagano, a Boston priest mistakenly arrested as a stickup artist. Based on a true story. Made for television. **96m/C VHS, Beta.** Ralph Waite, Julie Bovasso, Jerry Zaks, Joe Grifasi, Estelle Parsons, Tom Aldredge; ***D:*** Jonathan Kaplan. *MTI*

The Gentleman from California 🦴 *The Californian* **1937** The dashing son of a Mexican landowner returns home and finds his people's land stolen from them by greedy tax collectors. **56m/B VHS, Beta, 8mm.** Ricardo Cortez, Marjorie Weaver, Katherine DeMille; ***D:*** Gus Meins. *VYY*

Gentleman from Dixie 🦴🦴 **1941** After LaRue is released from prison, he looks to change his life by joining his brother on a farm and seeking revenge on the man who put him in the pokey. **61m/B VHS.** Jack LaRue, Marian Marsh, Clarence Muse, Mary Ruth, Robert Kellard, John Holland, Herbert Rawlinson; ***D:*** Al(bert) Herman. *MOV*

Gentleman from Texas 🦴 **1946** Ropin', ridin', and romance figure in this less than dramatic oater. **55m/B VHS.** Johnny Mack Brown, Raymond Hatton, Claudia Drake, Reno Blair, Christine McIntyre; ***D:*** Lambert Hillyer. *NOS, DVT*

Gentleman Jim 🦴🦴🦴½ **1942** A colorful version of the life of old-time heavyweight boxing great Jim Corbett, transformed from a typical Warner Bros. bio-pic by director Walsh into a fun-loving, anything-for-laughs donnybrook. Climaxes with Corbett's fight for the championship against the great John L. Sullivan. One of Flynn's most riotous performances. **104m/B VHS, Beta, LV.** Errol Flynn, Alan Hale, Alexis Smith, Jack Carson, Ward Bond, Arthur Shields, William Frawley; ***D:*** Raoul Walsh. *MGM, FOX*

The Gentleman Killer 🦴 **1978** A man-with-no-name clears a ravaged border town of murdering bandits. **95m/C VHS, Beta.** Anthony Steffen, Silvia Solar. *UNI*

Gentleman's Agreement 🦴🦴🦴 **1947** A magazine writer (Peck) looks for a new angle for an article on anti-Semitism by pretending to be Jewish. His new identity pervades his life in unexpected ways, almost destroys his relationships, but contributes to the success of his magazine series. This movie was Hollywood's first major attack on anti-Semitism. Controversial in its day, yet still timely. **118m/B VHS, LV.** Gregory Peck, Dorothy McGuire, John Garfield, Celeste Holm, Anne Revere, June Havoc, Albert Dekker, Jane Wyatt, Dean Stockwell, Nicholas Joy; ***D:*** Elia Kazan; ***W:*** Moss Hart; ***C:*** Arthur C. Miller. Academy Awards '47: Best Director (Kazan), Best Picture, Best Supporting Actress (Holm); New York Film Critics Awards '47: Best Director (Kazan), Best Film; Nominations: Academy Awards '46: Best Actress (McGuire); Academy Awards '47: Best Actor (Peck), Best Film Editing, Best Screenplay, Best Supporting Actress (Revere). *FXV, BTV, JCF*

Gentlemen Prefer Blondes 🦴🦴🦴 **1953** Amusing satire involving two show-business girls from Little Rock trying to make it big in Paris. Seeking rich husbands or diamonds, their capers land them in police court. Monroe plays Lorelei Lee, Russell is her sidekick. Despite an occasionally slow plot, the music, comedy, and performances are great fun. Film version of a Broadway adaption of a story by Anita Loos. Followed by (but without Monroe) "Gentlemen Marry Brunettes." ♫ A (Two) Little Girl(s) From Little Rock; Bye, Bye Baby; Ain't There Anyone Here For Love?; When Love Goes Wrong; Diamonds Are A Girl's Best Friend. **91m/C VHS, Beta, LV.** Marilyn Monroe, Jane Russell, Charles Coburn, Elliott Reid, Tommy Noonan, George Winslow; ***D:*** Howard Hawks. *FOX*

Genuine Risk 🦴½ **1989 (R)** Gorgeous young woman turns off her crime boss boyfriend bigtime when she seduces his bodyguard. Genuine tripe. **89m/C VHS, LV.** Terence Stamp, Michelle Johnson, Peter Berg, M.K. Harris; ***D:*** Kurt Voss; ***W:*** Kurt Voss. *COL*

George! 🦴½ **1970 (G)** A carefree bachelor takes his girlfriend and his 250-pound St. Bernard on a trip to the Swiss Alps where he proves that a dog is not always man's best friend. **87m/C VHS, Beta.** Marshall Thompson, Jack Mullaney, Inge Schoner; ***D:*** Wallace C. Bennett; ***W:*** Wallace C. Bennett. *VCI*

George Balanchine's The Nutcracker 🦴🦴½ *The Nutcracker* **1993 (G)** Pas de deux redeux. Tchaikovsky's classic ballet about the magic of Christmas and a little girl (Cohen) who dreams on Christmas Eve that she is in an enchanted kingdom. Culkin lamely grins through his wooden performance as the Nutcracker Prince, but the talent of the Sugarplum Fairy (Kistler) and the other dancers is such that conventional camera techniques sometimes fail to keep up with their exacting moves. Adapted from the 1816 book by E.T.A. Hoffmann. **93m/C VHS, LV, 8mm.** Macaulay Culkin, Jessica Lynn Cohen, Bart Robinson Cook, Darci Kistler, Damian Woetzel, Kyra Nichols, Wendy Whelan, Gen Horiuchi, Margaret Tracey; ***D:*** Emile Ardolino; ***W:*** Susan Cooper. *WAR*

The George McKenna Story 🦴🦴½ **1986** Washington stars as the newly appointed principal of George Washington High in Los Angeles. The school is located in South Central, a gang and drug-infested war zone where the students are armed for their own protection. The situation appears hopeless but McKenna refuses to give up. Based on a true story. Made for television. **95m/C VHS.** Denzel Washington, Lynn Whitfield, Akosua Busia, Richard Masur; ***D:*** Eric Laneuville; ***W:*** Charles Eric Johnson; ***M:*** Herbie Hancock. *PSM*

George Washington 🦴🦴½ **1984** Bostwick stars as the father of our country in this made for television adaptation of James Thomas Flexner's biography. The destitute young Washington develops a close friendship with the wealthy Will Fairfax (Dukes), who provides him with the support to pursue his dreams, even though Washington has secretly fallen in love with Sally (Smith), Will's flirtatious wife. George himself has married the widowed Martha (Duke) and begins his military career, leading the American colonies against the Brits in the Revolutionary War. On three cassettes. **398m/C VHS, Beta.** Barry Bostwick, David Dukes, Jaclyn Smith, Patty Duke, Hal Holbrook, Lloyd Bridges, Jose Ferrer, Trevor Howard, Richard Kiley, James Mason, Clive Revill, Robert Stack; ***W:*** Richard Fielder. *WAR*

George Washington Slept Here 🦴🦴🦴 **1942** Hilarious side-splitter about a couple who moves from their Manhattan apartment to an old, broken-down country home in Connecticut. It's one catastrophe after another as the couple tries to renovate their home and deal with a greedy neighbor. Based on the play by George S. Kaufman and Moss Hart. **93m/B VHS.** Jack Benny, Ann Sheridan, Charles Coburn, Percy Kilbride, Hattie McDaniel, William Tracy; ***D:*** William Keighley. Nominations: Academy Awards '42: Best Interior Decoration. *MGM*

George Washington: The Forging of a Nation 🦴🦴½ **1986** Sequel to the "George Washington" miniseries finds Bostwick and Duke reprising their roles as George and Martha. Unfortunately, the later part of Washington's life isn't nearly as exciting. **208m/C VHS.** Barry Bostwick, Patty Duke, Penny Fuller, Jeffrey Jones, Richard Bekins; ***D:*** William A. Graham; ***M:*** Bruce Broughton. *MGM*

George White's Scandals 🦴🦴 **1945** A lightweight musical comedy look at the show biz world and why the show must go on. Based on White's Broadway extravaganzas. Jazz numbers by Gene Krupa and his band. Preceded by "George White's Scandals" of 1934 and 1935. ♫Bolero in the Jungle; E.H.S.; Leave Us Leap; I Want to be a Drummer in the Band; How Did You Get Out of My Dreams?; I Wake Up in the Morning; Who Killed Vaudeville?; Scandals; Liza. **95m/B VHS, Beta.** Joan Davis, Jack Haley, Jane Greer, Phillip Terry, Margaret Hamilton, Martha Holliday; ***D:*** Felix Feist. *CCB*

George's Island 🦴🦴🦴 **1991 (PG)** When young George is placed with the worst foster parents in the world, his eccentric grandfather helps him escape. They wind up on Oak's Island, where, legend has it, Captain Kidd's ghost and buried treasure reside. They soon find out the legends are true! **89m/C VHS, LV.** Ian Bannen, Sheila McCarthy, Maury Chaykin, Nathaniel Moreau, Vicki Ridler, Brian Downey, Gary Reineke; ***D:*** Paul Donovan; ***W:*** J. William Ritchie; ***M:*** Marty Simon. *COL, NLC*

Georgia 🦴🦴 **1987** Tough lawyer Nina Bailey (Davis) explores her past when she begins a search for information on her biological mother, Georgia White, a photographer who drowned herself years before. Only Nina has no idea about the Pandora's box of secrets she's about to unleash. Frequent flashbacks to Georgia's mysterious life and death (Davis well plays both roles). **90m/C VHS.** *AU* Judy Davis, Julia Blake, John Bach; ***D:*** Ben Lewin. *ORI, FXL*

Georgia 🦴🦴🦴 **1995 (R)** Character study about sibling rivalry, self-destruction, and the Seattle music scene. Struggling rock singer Sadie (Leigh), who relies on booze, drugs, and men to help her make it through the night, returns to Seattle to crash with big-sister Georgia (Winningham). Settled, with loving husband and kids, the much more talented Georgia is also a popular folk icon and has the type of personal/career success angry and ambitious Sadie can only dream about. Fine performances—particularly from the chameonlike Leigh; both leads do their own singing. Screenwriter Turner is Leigh's mother. **117m/C VHS.** Jennifer Jason Leigh, Mare Winningham, Ted Levine, Max Perlich, John Doe, John C. Reilly, Jimmy Witherspoon; ***D:*** Ulu Grosbard; ***W:*** Barbara Turner; ***C:*** Jan Kiesser. Independent Spirit Awards '96: Best Supporting Actress (Winningham); Montreal World Film Festival '95: Best Actress (Leigh), Best Film; New York Film Critics Awards '95: Best Actress (Leigh); Nominations: Academy Awards '95: Best Supporting Actress (Winningham); Independent Spirit Awards '96: Best Actress (Leigh), Best Director (Grosbard), Best Supporting Actor (Perlich). *TOU*

Georgia, Georgia 🦴½ **1972 (R)** Sands is a black entertainer on tour in Sweden who falls for a white photographer. Her traveling companion, who hates whites, takes drastic action to separate the lovers. Poor acting, script, and direction. Based on a book by Maya Angelou. **91m/C VHS, Beta.** Diana Sands, Dirk Benedict, Minnie Gentry; ***D:*** Stig Bjorkman; ***W:*** Maya Angelou. *PSM*

Georgy Girl 🦴🦴🦴 **1966** Redgrave finely plays the overweight ugly-duckling Georgy who shares a flat with the beautiful and promiscuous Meredith (Rampling). Georgy is, however, desired by the wealthy and aging Mason and soon by Meredith's lover (Bates) who recognizes her good heart. When Meredith becomes pregnant, Georgy persuades her to let her raise the baby, leaving Georgy with the dilemma of marrying the irresponsible Bates (the baby's father) or the settled Mason. The film and title song (sung by the Seekers) were both huge hits. Based on the novel by Margaret Foster who also co-wrote the screenplay. **100m/B VHS, Beta, LV.** *GB* Lynn Redgrave, James Mason, Charlotte Rampling, Alan Bates, Bill Owen, Claire Kelly, Rachel Kempson; ***D:*** Silvio Narizzano. Golden Globe Awards '67: Best Actress—Musical/Comedy (Redgrave); National Board of Review Awards '66: 10 Best Films of the Year; New York Film Critics Awards '66: Best Actress (Redgrave); Nominations: Academy Awards '66: Best Actress (Redgrave), Best Black and White Cinematography, Best Song ("Georgy Girl"), Best Supporting Actor (Mason). *FCT, COL*

Germany in Autumn 🦴🦴 *Deutschland im Herbst* **1978** Twelve West German filmmakers offer political statements and artistic commentary on the political situation in their country after the kidnapping and murder of industrialist Hans Martin Schleyer. In German with English subtitles. **124m/C VHS.** *GE* ***D:*** Volker Schlondorff, Rainer Werner Fassbinder, Alf Brustellin, Alexander Kluge, Maximiliane Mainka, Edgar Reitz, Katja Rupe, Hans Peter Cloos, Bernhard Sinkel, Beate Mainka-Jellinghaus, Peter Schubert, Heinrich Boll; ***W:*** Heinrich Boll. *WAC, FCT*

Germicide 🦴 **1974** Scientist tries to warn the world of the threat posed by a horrifying bacterial weapon. Terrorists and his mistress hatch plots against him. **90m/C Beta.** Rod Taylor, Bibi Andersson. *PSM*

Germinal 🦴🦴🦴 **1993 (R)** Recounts the struggle of working-class coal miners in France, led by Depardieu and wife Miou-Miou, to stave off poverty. While greedy investors debate how far they should lower miners' wages, the Maheu family, spurred on by newly arrived Marxist and off-camera French pop star Renaud, lead a strike. Minor themes revolving around management's adulterous adventures provide some momentary relief to relieve short attention spans. Seems so self-consciously an epic drama, however, that the overall effect is ponderous. Adaptation of the 19th century novel by Zola. In French with English subtitles. **158m/C VHS, LV.** *FR* Gerard Depardieu, Miou-Miou, Bernard Fresson, Jean Carmet, Laurent Terzieff, Anny Duperey, Renaud, Jacques Dacqmine; ***D:*** Claude Berri; ***W:*** Claude Berri, Arlette Langmann; ***C:*** Yves Angelo; ***M:*** Jean-Louis Roques. Cesar Awards '94: Best Cinematography, Best Costume Design. *COL*

Geronimo 🦴🦴½ **1962** In typical Hollywood casting Connors stars as the Indian leader on the warpath against the cavalry over broken treaties. Lots of action and the Indians are actually the good guys. **101m/C VHS, LV.** Chuck Connors, Ross Martin, Pat Conway, Kamala Devi, Adam West, Lawrence Dobkin, Denver Pyle, Enid Jaynes, Armando Silvestre, John Anderson; ***D:*** Arnold Laven. *MGM*

Geronimo 🦴🦴🦴 **1993** Not to be confused with the big screen version, this made for cable television drama uses three actors to portray the legendary Apache warrior (1829-1909) at various stages of his life. The intrepid teenager who leads attacks on Mexican troops, the adult fighting the duplicitous bluecoats, and the aged man witnessing the destruction of his way of life. The true story is told from the point of view of Native American culture and historical records. Somewhat overly earnest. **120m/C VHS.** Joseph Runningfox, Jimmy Herman, Ryan Black, Nick Ramus, Michelle St. John, Michael Greyeyes, Tailinh Forest Flower, Kimberly Norris, August Schellenberg, Geno Silva, Harrison Lowe; ***D:*** Roger Young; ***W:*** J.T. Allen; ***M:*** Patrick Williams. *TTC*

Geronimo: An American Legend 🦴🦴½ **1993 (PG-13)** Well-intentioned bio-actioner about the legendary Apache leader who fought the U.S. Army over forcing Native Americans onto reservations. Narrator is young Army officer Gatewood (Patric), whose division is to round up the renegades led by Geronimo (Studi), whom he naturally comes to admire. Hackman and Duvall (as a General and a scout respectively) steal any scene they're in although the leads manage to hold their own. Too noble for its own good and somewhat plodding. Great location filming around Moab, Utah. **115m/C VHS, LV, 8mm.** Wes Studi, Jason Patric, Robert Duvall, Gene Hackman, Matt Damon, Rodney Grant, Kevin Tighe, Carlos Palomino, Stephen McHattie; ***D:*** Walter Hill; ***W:*** John Milius, Larry Gross; ***C:*** Lloyd Ahern; ***M:*** Ry Cooder. Nominations: Academy Awards '93: Best Sound. *COL*

Geronimo's Revenge 🦴½ **1960** When Geronimo starts a battle with the settlers, a rancher he has befriended finds himself caught in the middle. The fourth soggy Disney TV oater from the "Tales of Texas John Slaughter" series. **77m/C VHS, Beta.** Tom Tryon, Darryl Hickman; ***D:*** Harry Keller. *NO*

Gertrud 🦴🦴🦴½ **1964** The simple story of an independent Danish woman rejecting her husband and lovers in favor of isolation. Cold, dry, minimalistic techniques make up Dreyer's final film. In Danish with subtitles. **116m/B VHS, Beta.** *DK* Nina Pens Rode, Bendt Rothe, Ebbe Rode; ***D:*** Carl Theodor Dreyer; ***W:*** Carl Theodor Dreyer. National Board of Review Awards '65: 5 Best Foreign Films of the Year. *FCT, DVT, HEG*

Gervaise 🦴🦴🦴 **1956** The best of several films of Emile Zola's "L'Assommoir." A 19th-century middle-class family is destroyed by the father's plunge into alcoholism despite a mother's attempts to save them. Well acted but overwhelmingly depressing. In

French with English subtitles. **89m/B VHS, Beta.** *FR* Maria Schell, Francois Perier, Suzy Delair, Armand Mestral; ***D:*** Rene Clement; ***M:*** Georges Auric. British Academy Awards '56: Best Actor (Perier), Best Film; National Board of Review Awards '57: 5 Best Foreign Films of the Year; New York Film Critics Awards '57: Best Foreign Film; Venice Film Festival '56: Best Actress (Schell); Nominations: Academy Awards '56: Best Foreign Language Film. *DVT, FST, WFV*

Get Christie Love! 🦴🦴 **1974** Vintage blaxploitation from the genre's halcyon days, when going undercover meant a carte blanche for skimpy outfits. Based on Dorothy Uhnak's detective novel, the eponymous policewoman goes undercover to bring a thriving drug empire to it knees. The outcome: a TV series. Graves previously appeared on television as one of the "Laugh-In" party girls. **95m/C VHS.** Teresa Graves, Harry Guardino, Louise Sorel, Paul Stevens, Andy Romano, Debbie Dozier; ***D:*** William A. Graham. *XVC*

Get Crazy 🦴🦴½ **1983** The owner of the Saturn Theatre is attempting to stage the biggest rock-and-roll concert of all time on New Year's Eve 1983, and everything is going wrong in this hilarious, offbeat film. **90m/C VHS, Beta, LV.** Malcolm McDowell, Allen (Goorwitz) Garfield, Daniel Stern, Gail Edwards, Ed Begley Jr., Lou Reed, Bill Henderson; ***D:*** Allan Arkush; ***M:*** Michael Boddicker. *SUE, NLC*

Get Out Your Handkerchiefs 🦴🦴🦴½ *Preparez Vous Mouchoirs* **1978 (R)** Unconventional comedy about a husband desperately attempting to make his sexually frustrated wife happy. Determined to go to any lengths, he asks a Mozart-loving teacher to become her lover. She is now, however, bored by both men. Only when she meets a 13-year-old genius at the summer camp where the three adults are counselors does she come out of her funk and find her sexual happiness. Laure is a beautiful character, but Depardieu and Dewaere are wonderful as the bewildered would-be lovers. Academy Award winner for best foreign film. In French with English subtitles. **109m/C VHS, Beta, LV.** *FR* Gerard Depardieu, Patrick Dewaere, Carole Laure; ***D:*** Bertrand Blier; ***W:*** Bertrand Blier; ***M:*** Georges Delerue. Academy Awards '78: Best Foreign Language Film; Cesar Awards '79: Best Score; National Society of Film Critics Awards '78: Best Film. *WAR, INT, INJ*

Get Rita 🦴🦴 *Gun Moll; Poopsie; Oopsie Poopsie; La Puppa del Gangster* **1975** Italian prostitute sets up her gangster boyfriend for a murder she committed and she winds up as mob boss. **90m/C VHS, Beta.** Sophia Loren, Marcello Mastroianni; ***D:*** Tom Rowe. *CTC*

Get Shorty 🦴🦴🦴 **1995 (R)** Low-level Miami loan shark and film buff Chili Palmer (Travolta) heads to Hollywood via Las Vegas, looking for a deadbeat drycleaner (Paymer) and a grade-Z movie producer (Hackman) who owes Vegas $150,000. Aided by B-movie scream-queen (Russo), Palmer is pitted against a variety of shady Hollywood-types, including egomaniacal star (DeVito) while trying to get into showbiz himself. Snappy scripting and performances finally do screen justice to an Elmore Leonard novel. DeVito, with the smaller title role, was originally cast as Chili Palmer, a role Travolta twice turned down until the ubiquitous Quentin Tarantino advised him to take it. **105m/C VHS, LV.** John Travolta, Gene Hackman, Danny DeVito, Rene Russo, Dennis Farina, Delroy Lindo, David Paymer, James Gandolfini; ***Cameos:*** Bette Midler, Harvey Keitel, Penny Marshall; ***D:*** Barry Sonnenfeld; ***W:*** Scott Frank; ***C:*** Don Peterman; ***M:*** John Lurie. Golden Globe Awards '96: Best Actor—Musical/Comedy (Travolta); Nominations: Golden Globe Awards '96: Best Film—Musical/Comedy, Best Screenplay; Screen Actors Guild Award '95: Cast; Writers Guild of America '95: Best Adapted Screenplay. *MGM*

Get Smart, Again! 🦴🦴½ **1989** Would you believe Maxwell Smart is back again as CONTROL's most incompetent agent? How about Agent 99 as his sidekick? Hymie the robot and those no-good-niks at KAOS? Well, it's all true. This second reunion movie (following "The Nude Bomb") from the '60s TV show highlights all the wacky gadgetry, including the shoe phone, but fails to find the show's original outlandishness. Made for television. **93m/C VHS.** Don Adams, Barbara Feldon, Dick Gautier, Bernie Kopell, Kenneth Mars, Harold Gould, Roger Price, Fritz Feld, Robert Karvelas, King Moody; ***D:*** Gary Nelson. *WOV*

Get That Girl 🦴 **1932** Minor western action pic marred by former silent-screen player Talmadge's heavy German accent which soon lead to him giving up acting for a directing career. **54m/B VHS.** Richard Talmadge, Shirley Grey, Carl Stockdale; ***D:*** George Crone. *GPV*

Get That Man 🦴🦴 **1935** When a cabby is mistaken for the murdered heir to a vast fortune, his life suddenly becomes complex. **57m/B VHS, Beta, LV.** Wallace Ford, Leon Ames, Lillian Miles, E. Alyn Warren; ***D:*** Spencer Gordon Bennet. *NOS*

The Getaway 🦴🦴 **1972 (PG)** McQueen plays a thief released on a parole arranged by his wife (McGraw) only to find out a corrupt politician wants him to rob a bank. After the successful holdup, McQueen finds out his cohorts are in the politician's pocket and trying to doublecross him. McQueen and McGraw are forced into a feverish chase across Texas to the Mexican border, pursued by the politician's henchmen and the state police. Completely amoral depiction of crime and violence with McQueen taciturn as always and McGraw again showing a complete lack of acting skills. Based on a novel by Jim Thompson. McQueen and McGraw had a romance during filming and later married. Remade in 1993. **123m/C VHS, Beta.** Steve McQueen, Ali MacGraw, Ben Johnson, Sally Struthers, Al Lettieri, Slim Pickens, Jack Dodson, Dub Taylor, Bo Hopkins; ***D:*** Sam Peckinpah; ***W:*** Walter Hill; ***C:*** Lucien Ballard; ***M:*** Quincy Jones. *FCT*

The Getaway 🦴½ **1993 (R)** It was a bad movie in 1972 and the remake hasn't improved the situation. Doc and Carol are husband and wife crooks (played by marrieds Basinger and Baldwin). Doc gets double-crossed and winds up in a Mexican jail; Carol gets a well-connected crook (Woods) to spring her hubby—by sleeping with him and promising Doc will pull off another heist. The robbery's botched, there are double-crosses galore, and the couple go on the run. The stars are pretty but everything's predictable. An unrated version is also available. **110m/C VHS, LV.** Alec Baldwin, Kim Basinger, James Woods, Michael Madsen, Jennifer Tilly, David Morse; ***D:*** Roger Donaldson; ***W:*** Walter Hill, Amy Holden Jones; ***M:*** Mark Isham. Nominations: MTV Movie Awards '94: Most Desirable Female (Basinger). *MCA*

Getting Away With Murder *Woof!* **1996 (R)** An utterly distasteful bomb that proves the Holocaust just isn't as funny as it used to be. College professor Aykroyd takes matters into his own hands when he learns that his kindly neighbor (Lemmon) is a Nazi war criminal. After finding out he may have been a wee bit hasty, he marries the coot's daughter as penance. Writer-director Miller tries to squeeze gags out of such topics as Nazi death camps and Holocaust denial. Definitely career lows for everyone involved. One of the last films released (with no advance warning and no advance screenings) by Savoy pictures. **92m/C VHS.** Dan Aykroyd, Lily Tomlin, Jack Lemmon, Bonnie Hunt, Brian Kerwin; ***D:*** Harvey Miller; ***W:*** Harvey Miller; ***C:*** Frank Tidy; ***M:*** John Debney. *HBO*

Getting Even 🦴½ *Hostage: Dallas* **1986 (R)** A maniac threatens to poison the entire population of Texas with a deadly gas unless he gets $50 million. An adventurous businessman sets out to stop him. **90m/C VHS, Beta.** Edward Albert, Joe Don Baker, Audrey Landers; ***D:*** Dwight Little. *LIV, VES*

Getting Even 🦴🦴 **1992 (R)** Dundee and Evans served together in Vietnam. Fifteen years later they're reunited by the FBI to track a former Marine, who once betrayed Evans to the enemy. Seems he's now a drug traffiker and arms dealer who also gets his sadistic pleasures by killing women. The two ex-Marines find they have one last battle to fight. **93m/C VHS.** Richard Roundtree, Michael J. Aronin; ***D:*** Leandro Lucchetti. *COL*

Getting Even with Dad 🦴½ **1994 (PG)** Crook Danson can't find the money he stole in his last heist. Why? because his precocious son has hidden it with the intention of blackmailing dear old dad into going straight and acting like a real father. Title is unintentionally funny in light of Mac's domineering dad Kit, who makes everybody in Hollywood want to go hide when he appears. Fairly bland family film squanders charm of Danson and Culkin, running formulaic plot into ground. Headly is likewise wasted as district attorney who prosecutes and then falls for Pops. And hey, Macaulay's precocious days are down to a precious few. **108m/C VHS, LV.** Macaulay Culkin, Ted Danson, Glenne Headly, Hector Elizondo, Saul Rubinek, Gailard Sartain, Kathleen Wilhoite, Sam McMurray; ***D:*** Howard Deutch; ***W:*** Tom S. Parker, Jim Jennewein. Nominations: Golden Raspberry Awards '94: Worst Actor (Culkin). *MGM*

Getting Gotti 🦴🦴½ **1994 (R)** Story of the seven year investigation and six-month trial by U.S. Attorney's Office prosecutor Diane Giacalone (Bracco) against reputed mobster "Teflon Don" John Gotti. (She lost.) Made for television. **93m/C VHS.** Lorraine Bracco, Anthony John Denison, Kathleen Lasky, August Schellenberg, Kenneth Welsh, Ellen Burstyn, Lawrence Bayne; ***D:*** Roger Young; ***W:*** James Henerson; ***M:*** Patrick Williams. *ACA*

Getting In 🦴½ *Student Body* **1994 (R)** Pressured by the family tradition of attending Johns Hopkins Medical School, Gabriel Higgs (Mailer) decides to bribe the rivals ahead of him on the waiting list. But one of them (McCarthy) decides the easiest thing to do is murder the other candidates and frame Gabe. **94m/C VHS, LV.** Steven Mailer, Kristy Swanson, Andrew McCarthy, Dave Chappelle; ***D:*** Doug Liman; ***W:*** P.J. Posner, Joel Posner, Jonathan Lewin. *VMK*

Getting It On 🦴 **1983 (R)** High school student uses his new-found video equipment for voyeuristic activity. **100m/C VHS, Beta.** Martin Yost, Heather Kennedy, Jeff Edmond, Kathy Rockmeier, Mark Alan Ferri; ***D:*** William Olsen. *LIV, VES*

Getting It Right 🦴🦴½ **1989 (R)** A sweet-natured British comedy about an inexperienced, shy adult male who is quite suddenly pursued by a middle-aged socialite, a pregnant, unstable rich girl, and a modest single mother. Novel and screenplay by Elizabeth Jane Howard. **101m/C VHS, Beta, LV.** *GB* Jesse Birdsall, Helena Bonham Carter, Lynn Redgrave, Peter Cook, John Gielgud, Jane Horrocks, Richard Huw, Shirley Anne Field, Pat Haywood, Judy Parfitt, Bryan Pringle; ***D:*** Randal Kleiser; ***W:*** Elizabeth Jane Howard; ***M:*** Colin Towns, Steve Tyrell. *VTR*

The Getting of Wisdom 🦴🦴½ **1977** A 13-year-old girl from the Australian outback tries to establish her identity, and her individuality, within the restricting confines of a Victorian girl's boarding school. Based on the novel by Henry Handel Richardson. **100m/C VHS, Beta.** *AU* Susannah Fowle, Hilary Ryan, Alix Longman, Sheila Helpmann, Patricia Kennedy, Barry Humphries, John Waters; ***D:*** Bruce Beresford. *FOX*

Getting Out 🦴🦴½ **1994** Arlie (DeMornay) is an ex-con on her way home to Georgia after an eight year prison stint and what she hopes will be a reunion with the son she bore in jail. She thinks he's in a foster home but instead her mother (Burstyn) had the child adopted and if she interferes, Arlie's parole will be revoked. Arlie's trying desperately to rehabilitate herself but the system and old contacts are close to dragging her back down. TV movie adapted from Marsha Norman's 1977 play. **92m/C VHS, LV.** Rebecca DeMornay, Ellen Burstyn, Rob Knepper, Richard Jenkins, Carol Mitchell-Leon, Tandy Cronyn, Norman Skaggs; ***D:*** John Korty; ***W:*** Eugene Corr, Ruth Shapiro; ***M:*** Mason Daring. *HMK*

Getting Over 🦴 **1981** A black promoter is hired as a figurehead by a bigoted record company president and proceeds to try to run the company his own way. He develops an all-girl group called "The Love Machine" and gets involved in a singer's kidnapping and a record company run by gangsters. Filled with cliches and stereotypes. **108m/C VHS, Beta.** John Daniels, Gwen Brisco, Mary Hopkins, John Goff, Andrew "Buzz" Cooper; ***D:*** Bernie Rollins; ***W:*** Bernie Rollins. *UNI*

Getting Physical ½ **1984** After being mugged, a secretary decides to get in shape and enters the world of female body building. Crammed with workout scenes and disco music. Made for television. **95m/C VHS, Beta.** Alexandra Paul, Sandahl Bergman, David Naughton; ***D:*** Steven Hilliard Stern; ***M:*** William Goldstein. *FOX*

Getting Straight **1970 (R)** A returning Vietnam soldier (Gould) goes back to his alma mater to secure a teaching degree and gets involved in the lives of his fellow students and the turbulence of the end of the '60s, including campus riots. A now-dated "youth" picture somewhat watchable for Gould's performance. **124m/C VHS, Beta.** Elliott Gould, Candice Bergen, Jeff Corey, Cecil Kellaway, Jeannie Berlin, Harrison Ford, John Rubinstein, Robert F. Lyons, Max Julien; ***D:*** Richard Rush. *COL*

Getting Up and Going Home ½ **1992** Jack (Skerritt) is a married man with a midlife crisis. So what does he do? Get involved with not one, but two, other women. Is he asking for trouble or what? Adapted from the book by Robert Anderson. **93m/C VHS, Beta.** Tom Skerritt, Blythe Danner, Roma Downey, Julianne Phillips, Bruce Kirby, Gary Frank, Dorian Harewood, Paul Sand; ***D:*** Steven Schachter; ***W:*** Peter Nelson. *PSM*

Getting Wasted ½ **1980 (PG)** Set in 1969 at a military academy for troublesome young men, chaos ensues when the cadets meet hippies. **98m/C VHS, Beta.** Brian Kerwin, Stephen Furst, Cooper Huckabee. *NO*

Gettysburg ½ **1993 (PG)** Civil War buff Ted Turner (who has a cameo as a Confederate soldier) originally intended Michael Shaara's Pulitzer Prize-winning novel "The Killer Angels" to be adapted as a three-part miniseries for his "TNT" network, but the lure of the big screen prevailed, marking the first time the battle has been committed to film and the first time a film crew has been allowed to film battle scenes on the Gettysburg National Military Park battlefield. The greatest battle of the war and the bloodiest in U.S. history is realistically staged by more than 5,000 Civil War re-enactors. The all-male cast concentrates on presenting the human cost of the war, with Daniels particularly noteworthy as the scholarly Colonel Chamberlain, determined to hold Little Big Top for the Union. Last film role for Jordan, to whom the movie is co-dedicated. The full scale recreation of Pickett's Charge is believed to be the largest period scale motion-picture sequence filmed in North America since D.W. Griffith's "Birth of a Nation." **254m/C VHS.** Jeff Daniels, Martin Sheen, Tom Berenger, Sam Elliott, Richard Jordan, Stephen Lang, Kevin Conway, C. Thomas Howell, Maxwell Caulfield, Andrew Prine, James Lancaster, Royce D. Applegate, Brian Mallon; ***Cameos:*** Ken Burns, Ted Turner; ***D:*** Ronald F. Maxwell; ***W:*** Ronald F. Maxwell; ***M:*** Randy Edelman. *TTC*

The Ghastly Ones *Woof!* **1968** Three couples must stay in a haunted mansion to inherit an estate, but they're soon being violently killed off. No budget and no talent. Remade as "Legacy of Blood." **81m/C VHS, Beta.** Don Williams, Maggie Rogers, Hal Belsoe, Veronica Redburn; ***D:*** Andy Milligan. *NO*

Ghetto Blaster **1989 (R)** A Vietnam vet takes on out-of-control street gangs to make his neighborhood safe. **86m/C VHS, Beta.** R.G. Armstrong, Richard Hatch, Richard Jaeckel, Harry Caesar, Rose Marie; ***D:*** Alan L. Stewart. *PSM*

Ghetto Revenge **19??** An embittered Vietnam vet gets caught between white supremacists and black radical activists in this coming home story. He returns and tries to build a life but succumbs to the desire for vengeance and things are never the same. **?m/C VHS.** Mike Sims. *NO*

Ghidrah the Three Headed Monster ½ *Ghidorah Sandai Kaiju Chikyu Saidai No Kessan; Ghidora, The Three-Headed Monster; Ghidrah; The Greatest Battle on Earth; The Biggest Right on Earth; Monster of Monsters* **1965** When a three-headed monster from outer-space threatens the world, humans, having nowhere else to turn, appeal to the friendly Mothra, Rodan, and Godzilla. Rock'em, sock 'em giant thrashing about as Tokyo once again gets trampled. Dependable afternoon monster fare complete with usual dubious dubbing. **85m/C VHS, Beta.** *JP* Yosuke Natsuki, Yuriko Hoshi; ***D:*** Inoshiro Honda. *HHT, VCN, VHE*

The Ghost ½ *Lo Spettro* **1963** A woman is driven mad by her supposedly dead husband and their evil housekeeper. Sequel to "The Horrible Dr. Hichcock." **96m/C VHS, Beta.** *IT* Barbara Steele, Peter Baldwin, Leonard Eliott, Harriet White; ***D:*** Riccardo (Robert Hampton) Freda. *SNC*

Ghost **1990 (PG-13)** Zucker, known for overboard comedies like "Airplane!" and "Ruthless People," changed tack and directed this undemanding romantic thriller, which was the surprising top grosser of 1990. Swayze is a murdered investment consultant attempting (from somewhere near the hereafter) to protect his lover, Moore, from imminent danger when he learns he was the victim of a hit gone afoul. Goldberg is the medium who suddenly discovers that the powers she's been faking are real. A winning blend of action, special effects (from Industrial Light and Magic) and romance. **127m/C VHS, Beta, LV, 8mm.** Patrick Swayze, Demi Moore, Whoopi Goldberg, Tony Goldwyn, Rick Aviles, Vincent Schiavelli, Gail Boggs, Armelia McQueen, Phil Leeds; ***D:*** Jerry Zucker; ***W:*** Bruce Joel Rubin; ***M:*** Maurice Jarre. Academy Awards '90: Best Original Screenplay, Best Supporting Actress (Goldberg); Golden Globe Awards '91: Best Supporting Actress (Goldberg); People's Choice Awards '91: Best Film—Drama; Nominations: Academy Awards '90: Best Film Editing, Best Picture, Best Original Score. *PAR, FCT, BTV*

The Ghost and Mrs. Muir **1947** A charming, beautifully orchestrated fantasy about a feisty widow who, with her young daughter, buys a seaside house and refuses to be intimidated by the crabby ghost of its former sea captain owner. When the widow falls into debt, the captain dictates his sea adventures, which she adapts into a successful novel. The ghost also falls in love with the beautiful lady. Tierney is exquisite and Harrison is sharp-tongued and manly. Based on R. A. Dick's novel. **104m/B VHS, Beta, LV.** Gene Tierney, Rex Harrison, George Sanders, Edna Best, Anna Lee, Vanessa Brown, Robert Coote, Natalie Wood, Isobel Elsom; ***D:*** Joseph L. Mankiewicz; ***W:*** Philip Dunne; ***C:*** Charles B(ryant) Lang; ***M:*** Bernard Herrmann. Nominations: Academy Awards '47: Best Black and White Cinematography. *FOX, HMV*

The Ghost and Mr. Chicken ½ **1966** Fraidy cat Luther Heggs (Knotts) works for a small town newspaper and longs to be a hot-shot reporter. One night he thinks he sees a woman's corpse at the vacant Simmons mansion but of course there's no body when the cops come. The house is considered haunted and there is a 20-year-old murder scandal, so Luther is very reluctantly persuaded to spend the night and solve the sinister goings-on. **90m/C VHS.** Don Knotts, Joan Staley, Dick Sargent, Liam Redmond, Skip Homeier, Reta Shaw, Lurene Tuttle, Philip Ober; ***D:*** Alan Rafkin; ***W:*** James Fritzell; ***C:*** William Margulies; ***M:*** Vic Mizzy. *MCA*

The Ghost and the Guest ½ **1943** Newlyweds spend their honeymoon in a house in the country only to find that gangsters are using the place as a hideout. Chases involving secret passages ensue. **59m/B VHS, Beta.** James Dunn, Florence Rice, Mabel Todd; ***D:*** William Nigh; ***W:*** Morey Amsterdam. *SNC, VYY*

The Ghost Breakers **1940** As a follow-up to the Hope/Goddard 1939 comedy thriller "The Cat and the Canary," this spooky comedy was even better. Lots of laughs and real chills as Hope and Goddard investigate a haunted mansion that she's inherited in Cuba. Effective horror scenes are expertly handled by director Marshall. Remade in 1953 as "Scared Stiff" with Dean Martin and Jerry Lewis. Based on the play by Paul Dickey and Charles Goddard. **83m/B VHS, LV.** Bob Hope, Paulette Goddard, Richard Carlson, Paul Lukas, Willie Best, Pedro de Cordoba, Noble Johnson, Anthony Quinn; ***D:*** George Marshall; ***C:*** Charles B(ryant) Lang. *MCA, BTV*

The Ghost Brigade ½ *The Killing Box* **1993 (R)** Civil War ghost story finds a Union general (Sheen) trying to discover who's slaughtering both Confederate and Union soldiers on the battlefield. So he sends Captain Harling (Pasdar) to investigate, with the help of rebel prisoner Strayn (Bernsen) and a slave (Williams). What they find is an evil brigade of soldiers—who already happen to be dead—and are eager for new recruits. **80m/C VHS.** Adrian Pasdar, Corbin Bernsen, Martin Sheen, Cynda Williams, Ray Wise, Roger Wilson; ***D:*** George Hickenlooper; ***W:*** Matt Greenberg. *TTC*

The Ghost Camera ½ **1933** Slight story of a man falsely accused of murder. A photograph taken at the murder scene can prove his innocence if only the missing camera can be discovered. **68m/B VHS.** *GB* Henry Kendall, Ida Lupino, John Mills; ***D:*** Bernard Vorhaus. *HCV*

Ghost Chase ½ **1988 (PG-13)** A young filmmaker desperate for funds inherits his dead relative's clock, from which issues the ghost of the deceased's butler. The ghostly retainer aids in a search for the departed's secret fortune. Neither scary nor funny. **89m/C VHS, Beta, LV.** Jason Lively, Jill Whitlow, Tim McDaniel, Paul Gleason, Chuck "Porky" Mitchell; ***D:*** Roland Emmerich. *NO*

Ghost Chasers ½ **1951** The Bowery Boys become mixed up in supernatural hijinks when a seance leads to the appearance of a ghost that only Sach can see. **70m/B VHS.** Leo Gorcey, Huntz Hall, Billy Benedict, David Gorcey, Buddy Gorman, Bernard Gorcey, Jan Kayne, Philip Van Zandt, Lloyd Corrigan; ***D:*** William Beaudine. *WAR*

Ghost City **1932** Our hero must deal with a masked gang that is "haunting" a town. **60m/B VHS.** Bill Cody, Helen Foster, Ann Rutherford, John Shelton, Reginald Owen; ***D:*** Harry Fraser. *NOS, DVT, HEG*

Ghost Crazy **1944** Three wild comedians and a gorilla create mayhem in a haunted house. **?m/C VHS.** Shemp Howard, Billy Gilbert, Maxie "Slapsie" Rosenbloom. *LOO*

Ghost Dad **1990 (PG)** A widowed workaholic dad is prematurely killed and returns from the dead to help his children prepare for the future. Cosby walks through doors, walls, and other solid objects for the sake of comedy—only none of it is funny. **84m/C VHS, Beta, LV.** Bill Cosby, Denise Nicholas, Ian Bannen, Christine Ebersole, Dana Ashbrook, Arnold Stang; ***D:*** Sidney Poitier; ***W:*** S.S. Wilson, Brent Maddock; ***M:*** Henry Mancini. *MCA*

Ghost Dance **1983** Sacred Indian burial ground is violated, with grim results. **93m/C VHS, Beta.** Sherman Hemsley, Henry Ball, Julie Amato; ***D:*** Peter Bufa. *TWE*

Ghost Fever *Woof!* **1987 (PG)** Two bumbling cops try to evict the inhabitants of a haunted house and get nowhere. A bad rip-off of "Ghostbusters." Alan Smithee is a pseudonym used when a director does not want his or her name on a film—no wonder. **86m/C VHS, Beta, LV.** Sherman Hemsley, Luis Avalos; ***D:*** Alan Smithee; ***W:*** Oscar Brodney. *NLC*

The Ghost Goes West **1936** A brash American family buys a Scottish castle and transports the pieces to the United States along with the Scottish family ghost (Donat). Also along is the ghost's modern-day descendant (also played by Donat) who is the new castle caretaker and in love with the new owner's daughter. It turns out to be up to the ghost to get the two lovers together and find his own eternal rest. A rather lovable fantasy. Rene Clair's first English film. Available in digitally remastered stereo with original movie trailer. **85m/B VHS, Beta.** *GB* Robert Donat, Jean Parker, Eugene Pallette, Elsa Lanchester; ***D:*** Rene Clair; ***W:*** Robert Sherwood. *HBO, SUE*

Ghost in the Machine ½ **1993 (R)** Serial killer dies while undergoing an X-ray scan and somehow, because of a lightning storm and a power outage, his soul manages to infiltrate the hospital's computer and go on to terrorize more victims via their home computers and appliances. (You expect this to make sense?) Outlandish, predictable flick hovers between high-tech horror and satiric comedy and wastes some pretty decent talent. Horror buffs may get a kick out of it but be forewarned: You may never view your microwave, dishwasher, or electrical outlets in quite the same way again. **104m/C VHS, LV.** Karen Allen, Chris Mulkey, Ted Marcoux, Jessica Walter, Rick Ducommun, Wil Horneff, Nancy Fish, Brandon Adams; ***D:*** Rachel Talalay; ***W:*** William Davies, William Osborne; ***M:*** Graeme Revell. *FXV*

Ghost in the Noonday Sun *Woof!* **1974** Crew of a treasure-seeking pirate ship sets sail for high sea silliness in this slapstick adventure film. Not a theatrical release for one obvious reason—it's terrible. **90m/C VHS, Beta.** *GB* Peter Sellers, Spike Milligan, Anthony (Tony) Franciosa, Clive Revill, Rosemary Leach, Peter Boyle; ***D:*** Peter Medak. *NO*

Ghost Keeper 🦴 **1980** Three girls are trapped in a mansion with an old hag and various supernatural apparitions. **87m/C VHS, Beta.** Riva Spier, Murray Ord, Georgie Collins; ***D:*** Vernon Sewell. *NWV*

The Ghost of Fletcher Ridge 198? Two friends on a hunting trip run into some backwoodsmen and uncover their moonshining operation. When one of the men is killed, the other flees to the forest in a desperate bid for survival. **90m/C VHS.** Campbell Scott, Bernie White, Virginia Lantry, Len Lesser; ***D:*** Michael Bordon. *NO*

The Ghost of Frankenstein 🦴🦴½ **1942** Fourth Frankenstein film in the Universal Studios series with Chaney filling in for Karloff as the monster. Not as good as its predecessors, but the cast is enjoyable, especially Lugosi as the monster's deformed sidekick, Ygor. Based on a story by Eric Taylor. **68m/B VHS.** Cedric Hardwicke, Lon Chaney Jr., Lionel Atwill, Ralph Bellamy, Bela Lugosi, Evelyn Ankers, Dwight Frye; ***D:*** Erle C. Kenton; ***W:*** W. Scott Darling; ***C:*** Milton Krasner. *MCA, FCT*

Ghost of Hanley House 🦴🦴 **1968** Obscure, low-budget ghost story, shot in Texas. **?m/B VHS.** *SMW*

The Ghost of Rashmon Hall 🦴 *Night Comes Too Soon* **1947** Doctor tries to rid his home of the ghosts of a sailor, his wife and her lover. **52m/B VHS, Beta.** Valentine Dyall, Anne Howard, Alex Flavorsham, Howard Douglas, Beatrice Marsden, Arthur Brander. *SNC, MWP*

The Ghost of Yatsuya 🦴½ **1958** Based on the Japanese legend of a man who must betray his wife to get the power he seeks. When he does, however, what follows is a horrifying revenge. In Japanese with English subtitles. **100m/C VHS, Beta.** *JP* Shigeru Amachi. *VDA, TPV*

Ghost on the Loose 1943 The Bowery Boys take on Nazi spies. **65m/C VHS.** Leo Gorcey, Huntz Hall, Bela Lugosi; ***D:*** William Beaudine. *GPV*

Ghost Patrol 🦴½ **1936** A cowboy duo kidnaps the inventor of a ray gun in order to hijack mail planes, but they're stopped by G-Man McCoy and friends. An odd hybrid of science fiction and western, to say the least. **57m/B VHS, Beta.** Tim McCoy, Walter Miller, Wheeler Oakman; ***D:*** Sam Newfield. *GPV, VCI, VCN*

Ghost Rider 🦴 **1935** A lawman is aided in his outlaw-nabbing efforts by the ghost of a gunfighter. **56m/B VHS, Beta.** Rex Lease, Bobby Nelson, Franklyn Farnum, Lloyd Ingraham, Ed Parker, Lafe McKee; ***D:*** Jack Levine. *NOS, GPV*

Ghost Rider 🦴🦴 **1943** Former footballer Brown rides the range once again, this time with an element of the supernatural nipping at his heels. **58m/B VHS.** Johnny Mack Brown, Raymond Hatton, Tim Seidel, Beverly Boyd, Milburn Morante; ***D:*** Wallace Fox. *GPV*

Ghost Ship 🦴½ **1953** Young couple is tortured by ghostly apparitions when they move into an old yacht with a dubious past. Grade "b" haunting featuring the murdered wife of the ship's former owner as the poltergeist. **69m/B VHS, Beta.** *GB* Dermot Walsh, Hazel Court, Hugh Burden, John Robinson; ***D:*** Vernon Sewell. *NOS, SNC*

Ghost Stories: Graveyard Thriller **1986** A compilation of stories with ghosts, vampires and other creatures of the night. **56m/C VHS, Beta.** ***D:*** Lynn Silver. *LIV, VES*

Ghost Story 🦴🦴 **1981 (R)** Four elderly men, members of an informal social club called the Chowder Society, share a terrible secret buried deep in their pasts—a secret that comes back to haunt them to death. Has moments where it's chilling, but unfortunately they're few. Based on the best-selling novel by Peter Straub. **110m/C VHS, Beta, LV.** Fred Astaire, Melvyn Douglas, Douglas Fairbanks Jr., John Houseman, Craig Wasson, Alice Krige, Patricia Neal; ***D:*** John Irvin; ***W:*** Lawrence D. Cohen; ***C:*** Jack Cardiff. *MCA*

Ghost Town 🦴 **1937** Good guy Carey saves a mine from claim jumpers, but not before he is mistakenly incarcerated as his friend's murderer, and then proved innocent. **65m/B VHS, Beta, LV.** Harry Carey Sr.; ***D:*** Harry Fraser. *VDM*

Ghost Town 🦴🦴½ **1988 (R)** Fine sleeper about a modern sheriff who follows a gal through a supernatural sandstorm and discovers a literal ghost town of bad guys. **85m/C VHS, LV.** Franc Luz, Catherine Hickland, Jimmie F. Skaggs, Penelope Windust, Bruce Glover, Blake Conway, Laura Schaefer; ***D:*** Richard Governor; ***W:*** Duke Sandefur; ***M:*** Harvey R. Cohen. *NWV*

Ghost Town Gold 🦴 **1936** The Three Mesquiteers series continues as the trio outwits bank robbers who have hidden their loot in a ghost town. **53m/B VHS, Beta.** Bob Livingston, Ray Corrigan, Max Terhune; ***D:*** Joseph Kane. *NOS, DVT*

Ghost Town Law 🦴½ **1942** The Rough Riders step in to save the day when a group of outlaws defend their hideout by murdering anyone who approaches. **62m/B VHS, Beta.** Buck Jones, Tim McCoy, Raymond Hatton; ***D:*** Howard Bretherton. *NOS, VCN, CAB*

Ghost Town Renegades 🦴 **1947** A pair of government agents prevent a crook from gaining control of a mining town. **57m/B VHS, Beta.** Lash LaRue, Al "Fuzzy" St. John, Jennifer Holt; ***D:*** Ray Taylor. *COL*

Ghost Town Riders 🦴½ **1938** An outlaw gang is holed up in an abandoned town, threatening to steal Shannon's gold mine, until Baker comes to the rescue. **55m/B VHS.** Bob Baker, Fay Shannon, George Cleveland, Glenn Strange, Forrest Taylor, Hank Worden, Murdock McQuarrie; ***D:*** George Waggner. *GPV*

The Ghost Train 🦴🦴 **1941** Passengers stranded at a train station are told tales of a haunted train. Forced to stay at the station overnight, they encounter a number of comically spooky situations. **85m/B VHS, Beta.** *GB* Arthur Askey, Richard Murdock, Kathleen Harrison; ***D:*** Walter Forde. *NOS, SNC*

Ghost Valley 🦴🦴½ **1932** When Keene and Kennedy inherit land rich in unmined ore, the administrator (Harris) attempts to scare them off. To foil his plan, Keene conceals his identity and takes a job as the administrator's assistant. Based on a story by Adele Buffington. **54m/B VHS.** Tom Keene, Merna Kennedy, Mitchell Harris, Billy Franey, Harry Bowen, Kate Campbell, Ted Adams, Buck Moulton, Harry Semels, Al Taylor, Charles "Slim" Whitaker; ***D:*** Fred Allen. *HEG*

The Ghost Walks 🦴🦴 **1934** A playwright has his new masterpiece acted out in front of an unsuspecting producer, who thinks that a real murder has taken place. But when the cast really does start disappearing, who's to blame? **69m/B VHS.** John Miljan, June Collyer, Richard Carle, Spencer Charters, Johnny Arthur, Henry Kolker; ***D:*** Frank Strayer. *SNC, NOS, DVT*

Ghost Writer 🦴 **1989 (PG)** A writer discovers the ghost of a movie star haunting her beach house, and together they solve the dead vamp's murder. **94m/C VHS, Beta.** Audrey Landers, Judy Landers, Jeff Conaway, David Doyle, Anthony (Tony) Franciosa, Joey Travolta, John Matuszak, David Paul, Peter Paul; ***D:*** Kenneth J. Hall. *PSM*

Ghostbusters 🦴🦴🦴 **1984 (PG)** After losing their scholastic funding, a group of "para-normal" investigators decide to go into business for themselves, aiding New York citizens in the removal of ghosts, goblins and other annoying spirits. This comedy-thriller about Manhattan being overrun by ghosts, contains great special effects, zany characters, and some of the best laughs of the decade. Also available in a laserdisc version with letterboxing, analysis of all special effects, complete screenplay, and original trailer. Followed by a sequel. **103m/C VHS, Beta, LV, 8mm.** Bill Murray, Dan Aykroyd, Harold Ramis, Rick Moranis, Sigourney Weaver, Annie Potts, Ernie Hudson, William Atherton; ***D:*** Ivan Reitman; ***W:*** Dan Aykroyd, Harold Ramis; ***M:*** Elmer Bernstein. Nominations: Academy Awards '84: Best Song ("Ghostbusters"). *COL, APD, CRC*

Ghostbusters 2 🦴🦴½ **1989 (PG)** After being sued by the city for the damages they did in the original "Ghostbusters," the boys in khaki are doing kiddie shows at birthday parties. When a river of slime that is actually the physical version of evil is discovered running beneath the city, the Ghostbusters are back in action. They must do battle with a wicked spirit in a painting or the entire world will fall pray to its ravaging whims. **102m/C VHS, Beta, LV, 8mm.** Bill Murray, Dan Aykroyd, Sigourney Weaver, Harold Ramis, Rick Moranis, Ernie Hudson, Peter MacNicol, David Margulies, Wilhelm von Homburg, Harris Yulin, Annie Potts; ***D:*** Ivan Reitman; ***W:*** Dan Aykroyd, Harold Ramis; ***C:*** Michael Chapman; ***M:*** Randy Edelman. *COL*

Ghosthouse 🦴 **1988** It looks like an average suburban house, but it's haunted by the ghost of a little girl—and when she comes, evil is sure to follow. **91m/C VHS, Beta.** Lara Wendell, Gregg Scott; ***D:*** Humphrey Humbert. *IMP*

Ghostriders 🦴 **1987** One hundred years after their hanging, a band of ghostly outlaws take revenge on the townfolk's descendents. **85m/C VHS, Beta.** Bill Shaw, Jim Peters, Ricky Long, Cari Powell, Mike Ammons, Arland Bishop; ***D:*** Alan L. Stewart. *PSM*

Ghosts Can Do It 🦴½ **1990** The Hound doesn't like jumping to conclusions, but is it possible this obscurity was titled to be reminiscent of the more publicized Bo Derek vehicle "Ghosts Can't Do It" comedy about a man who returns to his sexy wife despite her efforts at killing him. **88m/C VHS.** Garry McDonald, Pamela Stephenson. *ATL, HHE*

Ghosts Can't Do It 🦴 **1990 (R)** Another wet-shirted, Bo-dacious softcore epic, involving a young woman who would like to have the spirit of her virile, but unfortunately dead, husband return to inhabit a living body. **91m/C VHS, Beta, LV.** Bo Derek, Anthony Quinn, Don Murray, Leo Damian; ***D:*** John Derek. Golden Raspberry Awards '90: Worst Picture, Worst Actress (Derek), Worst Director (Derek). *COL, TTC*

Ghosts of Berkeley Square 🦴🦴½ **1947** The ghosts of two retired soldiers of the early 18th century are doomed to haunt their former home, and only a visit from a reigning monarch can free them. **85m/B VHS, Beta.** Wilfrid Hyde-White, Robert Morley, Felix Aylmer; ***D:*** Vernon Sewell. *VYY*

The Ghosts of Hanley House 🦴½ **1968** No-budget spooker with no-brain plot. Several unlucky guests spend an evening in a creepy mansion...sound familiar? Shot in Texas. **80m/C VHS, Beta.** Barbara Chase, Wilkie De Martel, Elsie Baker, Cliff Scott. *SNC*

Ghosts That Still Walk 🦴 **1977** Spooky phenomena occur. The demons possessing a young lad's soul may be responsible. **92m/C VHS, Beta.** Ann Nelson, Matt Boston, Jerry Jenson, Caroline Howe, Rita Crafts; ***D:*** James T. Flocker. *VCI, MRV*

Ghostwarrior 🦴 *Swordkill* **1986 (R)** A 16th century samurai warrior's ice-packed body is revived and runs amuck in the streets of modern-day Los Angeles. **86m/C VHS, Beta.** Hiroshi Fujioka, Janet Julian, Andy Wood, John Calvin; ***D:*** Larry Carroll; ***W:*** Tim Curnen. *VES*

Ghostwriter 🦴🦴 **1984** Based on Philip Roth's best-selling novel, the story is of a writer coming to terms with his past. Roth co-wrote the screenplay. First seen on PBS. **90m/C VHS, Beta.** Sam Wanamaker, Claire Bloom, Rose Arrick, MacIntyre Dixon, Cecile Mann, Joseph Wiseman, Mark Linn-Baker, Paulette Smit; ***D:*** Tristam Powell; ***W:*** Phillip J. Roth. *PBS*

The Ghoul ½ **1934** An eccentric English Egyptologist desires a sacred jewel to be buried with him and vows to come back from the grave if the gem is stolen. When that happens, he makes good on his ghostly promise. A minor horror piece with Karloff only appearing at the beginning and end of the film. This leaves the middle very dull. **73m/B VHS.** *GB* Boris Karloff, Cedric Hardwicke, Ernest Thesiger, Dorothy Hyson, Ralph Richardson, Anthony Bushell; ***D:*** T. Hayes Hunter. *VYY, SNC, DVT*

The Ghoul **1975 (R)** A defrocked clergyman has a cannibal son to contend with—especially after the drivers in a local auto race begin to disappear. Hurt is the lunatic family gardener. **88m/C VHS, Beta.** *GB* Peter Cushing, John Hurt, Alexandra Bastedo, Don Henderson, Stewart Bevan; ***D:*** Freddie Francis. *MED*

Ghoul School **1990 (R)** A spoof of horror films and college flicks, with lots of scantily clad women and bloody creatures in dark hallways. **90m/C VHS.** Joe Franklin, Nancy Siriani, William Friedman. *HHE*

Ghoulies **1984 (PG-13)** A young man gets more than he bargained for when he conjures up a batch of evil creatures when dabbling in the occult. Ridiculous but successful. Followed by two sequels. **81m/C VHS, Beta.** Lisa Pelikan, Jack Nance, Scott Thomson, Tamara DeTreaux, Mariska Hargitay, Bobbie Bresee; ***D:*** Luca Bercovici; ***W:*** Luca Bercovici; ***M:*** Richard Band. *LIV, VES, HHE*

Ghoulies 2 **1987 (R)** Inept sequel to "Ghoulies" (1985), wherein the little demons haunt a failing carnival horror house, whose revenues begin to soar. Followed by a second sequel. **89m/C VHS, Beta, LV.** Damon Martin, Royal Dano, Phil Fondacaro, J. Downing, Kerry Remsen; ***D:*** Albert Band. *LIV, VES*

Ghoulies 3: Ghoulies Go to College *Woof!* **1991 (R)** Third in the series has the best special effects and the worst storyline. Not satisfied with ripping off "Gremlins," this one imposes Three Stooges personae upon a trio of demons at large on a beer- and babe-soaked campus. **94m/C VHS.** Kevin McCarthy, Griffin O'Neal, Evan Mackenzie; ***D:*** John Carl Buechler. *VES, LIV*

Ghoulies 4 ½ **1993 (R)** Dopey series continues with the satanic creatures roaming the streets of Los Angeles, searching for a way to return to their netherworld home. They get their chance when they meet a Satan-worshipping dominatrix out on a killing spree. **84m/C VHS.** Barbara Alyn Woods, Peter Paul Liapis; ***D:*** Jim Wynorski; ***W:*** Mark Sevi. *COL*

G.I. Blues **1960** Three G.I.'s form a musical combo while stationed in Germany. Prowse is the nightclub singer Presley falls for. Presley's first film after his military service. ♫Shopping Around; Tonight Is So Right For Love; What's She Really Like?; Frankfurt Special; Didya Ever; Big Boots; Pocketful of Rainbows; Doin' the Best I Can; Blue Suede Shoes. **104m/C VHS, Beta, LV.** Elvis Presley, Juliet Prowse, Robert Ivers, Leticia Roman, Ludwig Stossel, James Douglas, Jeremy Slate; ***D:*** Norman Taurog; ***C:*** Loyal Griggs. *FOX, MVD*

G.I. Executioner *Wit's End; Dragon Lady* **1971 (R)** An adventure set in Singapore featuring a Vietnam veteran turned executioner. **86m/C VHS, Beta.** Tom Kenna, Victoria Racimo, Angelique Pettyjohn, Janet Wood, Walter Hill; ***D:*** Joel M. Reed. *VES*

G.I. Jane **1951** A television producer faints when he gets his draft notice and dreams his company is stranded at a desert post with a company of WACs. **62m/B VHS, Beta, LV.** Jean Porter, Tom Neal, Iris Adrian, Jimmy Lloyd, Mara Lynn, Michael Whalen; ***D:*** Reginald LeBorg. *NO*

Giant ½ **1956** Based on the Edna Ferber novel, this epic saga covers two generations of a wealthy Texas cattle baron (Hudson) who marries a strong-willed Virginia woman (Taylor) and takes her to live on his vast ranch. It explores the problems they have adjusting to life together, as well as the politics and prejudice of the time. Dean plays the resentful ranch hand (who secretly loves Taylor) who winds up striking oil and beginning a fortune to rival that of his former boss. Dean's last movie—he died in a car crash shortly before filming was completed. **201m/C VHS, Beta, LV.** Elizabeth Taylor, Rock Hudson, James Dean, Carroll Baker, Chill Wills, Dennis Hopper, Rod Taylor, Earl Holliman, Jane Withers, Sal Mineo, Mercedes McCambridge; ***D:*** George Stevens; ***C:*** William Mellor. Academy Awards '56: Best Director (Stevens); Directors Guild of America Awards '56: Best Director (Stevens); Nominations: Academy Awards '56: Best Actor (Dean), Best Actor (Hudson), Best Adapted Screenplay, Best Art Direction/Set Decoration (Color), Best Costume Design (Color), Best Film Editing, Best Picture, Best Supporting Actress (McCambridge), Best Original Score. *WAR, BTV*

The Giant Claw ½ **1957** Giant, winged (and stringed) bird attacks from outer space and scientists Morrow, Corday and Ankrum attempt to pluck it. Good bad movie; Corday was Playboy's Miss October, 1958. **76m/B VHS.** Jeff Morrow, Mara Corday, Morris Ankrum, Louis D. Merrill, Edgar Barrier, Robert Shayne, Morgan Jones, Clark Howat; ***D:*** Fred F. Sears. *MOV*

Giant from the Unknown *Woof!* **1958** Giant conquistador is revived after being struck by lightning and goes on a murderous rampage. Unbelievably bad. **80m/B VHS, Beta.** Edward Kemmer, Buddy Baer, Bob Steele, Sally Fraser; ***D:*** Richard Cunha. *NOS, SNC, MWP*

The Giant Gila Monster ½ **1959** A giant lizard has the nerve to disrupt a local record hop, foolishly bringing upon it the wrath of the local teens. Rear-projection monster isn't particularly effective, but the film provides many unintentional laughs. **74m/B VHS.** Don Sullivan, Lisa Simone, Shug Fisher, Jerry Cortwright, Beverly Thurman, Don Flourney, Pat Simmons; ***D:*** Ray Kellogg. *NOS, RHI, SNC*

The Giant of Marathon **1960** Reeves shrugs off the role of Hercules to play Philippides, a marathoner (who uses a horse) trying to save Greece from invading Persian hordes. Lots of muscle on display, but not much talent. Cinematography by Mario Bava. **90m/C VHS.** *IT* Steve Reeves, Mylene Demongeot, Daniela Rocca, Ivo Garrani, Alberto Lupo, Sergio Fantoni; ***D:*** Jacques Tourneur. *SNC, MLB*

The Giant of Metropolis *Il Gigante Di Metropolis* **1961** Muscle-bound hero goes shirtless to take on the evil, sadistic ruler of Atlantis (still above water) in 10,000 B.C. Ordinary Italian adventure, but includes interesting sets and bizarre torture scenes. **92m/C VHS.** *IT* Gordon Mitchell, Roldano Lupi, Bella Cortez, Liana Orfei; ***D:*** Umberto Scarpelli. *SNC*

The Giant Spider Invasion **1975 (PG)** A meteorite carrying spider eggs crashes to Earth and soon the alien arachnids are growing to humongous proportions. Notoriously bad special effects, but the veteran "B" cast has a good time. **76m/C VHS.** Steve Brodie, Barbara Hale, Leslie Parrish, Robert Easton, Alan Hale Jr., Dianne Lee Hart, Bill Williams, Christianne Schmidtmer; ***D:*** Bill Rebane. *MOV*

Giant Steps **19??** Williams plays Slate Hopson, a moody jazz legend idolized by a talented young trumpet player. When the two meet Hopson clues the boy into some of life's lessons and rediscovers his own joy at making music. **94m/C VHS.** Billy Dee Williams, Michael Mahonen; ***M:*** Eric Leeds. *MNC*

Giants of Rome *Woof!* **1963** Rome is in peril at the hands of a mysterious secret weapon that turns out to be a giant catapult. Ludicrous all around. **87m/C VHS, Beta.** *IT* Richard Harrison, Ettore Manni. *SNC*

The Giants of Thessaly **1960** Jason and Orpheus search for the Golden Fleece, encountering and defeating monsters, wizards, and a scheming witch. **86m/C VHS.** *IT* Roland Carey, Ziva Rodann, Massimo Girotti, Alberto Farnese; ***D:*** Riccardo (Robert Hampton) Freda. *SNC*

Gideon's Trumpet ½ **1980** True story of Clarence Earl Gideon, a Florida convict whose case was decided by the Supreme Court and set the precedent that everyone is entitled to defense by a lawyer, whether or not they can pay for it. Based on the book by Anthony Lewis. Made for television. **104m/C VHS, Beta.** Henry Fonda, Jose Ferrer, John Houseman, Dean Jagger, Sam Jaffe, Fay Wray; ***D:*** Robert Collins. *WOV*

Gidget **1959** A plucky, boy-crazy teenage girl (whose nickname means girl midget) discovers romance and wisdom on the beaches of Malibu when she becomes involved with a group of college-aged surfers. First in a series of Gidget/surfer films. Based on a novel by Frederick Kohner about his daughter. **95m/C VHS, Beta, LV.** Sandra Dee, James Darren, Cliff Robertson, Mary Laroche, Arthur O'Connell, Joby Baker; ***D:*** Paul Wendkos; ***C:*** Burnett Guffey. *COL*

Gidget Goes Hawaiian **1961** Gidget is off to Hawaii with her parents and is enjoying the beach (and the boys) when she is surprised by a visit from boyfriend "Moondoggie." Sequel to "Gidget" and followed by "Gidget Goes to Rome." **102m/C VHS, Beta.** Deborah Walley, James Darren, Carl Reiner, Peggy Cass, Michael Callan, Eddie Foy Jr.; ***D:*** Paul Wendkos. *COL*

Gidget Goes to Rome ½ **1963** Darren returns in his third outing as boyfriend "Moondoggie" to yet another actress playing "Gidget" as the two vacation in Rome and find themselves tempted by other romances. Second sequel to "Gidget." **104m/C VHS, Beta.** Cindy Carol, James Darren, Jeff Donnell, Cesare Danova, Peter Brooks, Jessie Royce Landis; ***D:*** Paul Wendkos; ***M:*** John Williams. *COL*

The Gift ½ **1982 (R)** Story of a 55-year-old man who chooses early retirement in the hopes of changing his dull and boring life. Unbeknownst to him, his co-workers arrange the ultimate retirement gift - a woman. Silly French sexual farce. Dubbed. **105m/C VHS, Beta.** *FR* Pierre Mondy, Claudia Cardinale, Clio Goldsmith, Jacques Francois, Cecile Magnet, Remy Laurent; ***D:*** Michael Lang. *FCT*

The Gift **19??** Real life husband and wife Farrell and Niccoli play fictitious characters of the same names in this darkly comic look into the world of the junkie. They revolve between the streets, drug treatment centers, and the shooting gallery they call home as the film moves toward its inevitable conclusion. Farrell is a former member of the band "Jane's Addiction." **83m/C VHS.** *WEA*

The Gift Horse *Glory at Sea* **1952** A WWII British naval officer dispatches his duties with an iron hand in an attempt to overturn the legacy of a court-martial eight years earlier. Angry rumblings from his crew threaten to upset the ship's stability. Against this foreboding backdrop, the Nazis give battle. Not historically accurate, but exciting. Based on a story by Ivan Goff and Ben Roberts. **99m/B VHS, Beta.** *GB* Trevor Howard, Richard Attenborough, Sonny Tufts, Bernard Lee; ***D:*** Compton Bennett. *DVT*

The Gift of Love ½ **1990** Saccharine, made-for-television adaption of O. Henry's Christmas romance "The Gift of the Magi." **96m/C VHS.** James Woods, Marie Osmond, Timothy Bottoms, June Lockhart, David Wayne; ***D:*** Don Chaffey. *MON, KAR*

The Gig ½ **1985** In this small, independently-made film, a band of middle-aged amateur jazz musicians give up their stable occupations for a once-in-a-lifetime shot at a two-week gig in the Catskills. Film succeeds on the strength of it's well fleshed-out characters. **95m/C VHS, Beta, LV.** Wayne Rogers, Cleavon Little, Warren Vache, Joe Silver, Daniel Nalbach, Andrew Duncan, Jay Thomas, Jerry Matz; ***D:*** Frank D. Gilroy; ***W:*** Frank D. Gilroy. *ORI, WAR*

Gigi **1958** Based on Colette's story of a young Parisian girl (Caron) trained to become a courtesan to the wealthy Gaston (Jourdan). But he finds out he prefers her to be his wife rather than his mistress. Chevalier is Gaston's roguish uncle, who casts an always admiring eye on the ladies. Gingold is Gigi's grandmother and former Chevalier flame, and Gabor amuses as Gaston's current, and vapid, mistress. One of the first MGM movies to be shot on location, this extravaganza features some of the best tributes to the French lifestyle ever filmed. Score includes memorable classics. ♫Gigi; Ah Yes, I Remember It Well; Thank Heaven For Little Girls; The Night They Invented Champagne; She's Not Thinking of Me; It's a Bore; Gossip; I'm Glad I'm Not Young Anymore; The Parisians. **119m/C VHS, Beta, LV, 8mm.**

Leslie Caron, Louis Jourdan, Maurice Chevalier, Hermione Gingold, Eva Gabor, Isabel Jeans, Jacques Bergerac; ***D:*** Vincente Minnelli; ***W:*** Alan Jay Lerner; ***C:*** Joseph Ruttenberg; ***M:*** Frederick Loewe. Academy Awards '58: Best Adapted Screenplay, Best Art Direction/Set Decoration, Best Color Cinematography, Best Costume Design, Best Director (Minnelli), Best Film Editing, Best Picture, Best Song ("Gigi"), Best Score; Directors Guild of America Awards '58: Best Director (Minnelli); Golden Globe Awards '59: Best Director (Minnelli), Best Film—Musical/Comedy, Best Supporting Actress (Gingold). *MGM, BTV*

Gilda 🦴🦴🦴½ **1946** An evil South American gambling casino owner hires young American Ford as his trusted aide, unaware that Ford and his sultry wife Hayworth have engaged in a steamy affair. Hayworth does a striptease to "Put the Blame on Mame" in this prominently sexual film. This is the film that made Hayworth into a Hollywood sex goddess. **110m/B VHS, Beta, LV.** Rita Hayworth, Glenn Ford, George Macready, Joseph Calleia, Steve Geray; ***D:*** Charles Vidor. *COL*

The Gilded Cage 🦴🦴 **1954** Two brothers are falsely accused of art theft and must find the real crooks in order to clear their names. **77m/B VHS, Beta.** *GB* Alex Nicol, Veronica Hurst, Clifford Evans, Ursula Howells, Elwyn Brook-Jones, John Stuart; ***D:*** John Gilling. *SNC*

Gilligan's Island: Meet the Crew **1964** Join Gilligan and the Skipper of the S.S. Minnow and their unfortunate passengers—Ginger, Mary Ann, the Professor, and Mr. and Mrs. Thurston Howell III—as they try to survive life (and each other) on an uncharted desert isle. Three episodes per cassette from the slapstick television series. Additional episodes available. **?m/B VHS.** Bob Denver, Alan Hale Jr., Jim Backus, Natalie Schafer, Tina Louise, Russell Johnson, Dawn Wells. *CMB*

Gimme an F *Woof! T & A Academy 2* **1985 (R)** The handsome cheerleading instructor at Camp Beaver View ruffles a few pom-poms when he discovers that the camp's owner is about to enter into a shady deal with some foreigners. The film certainly deserves an "F" for foolishness if nothing else. **100m/C VHS, Beta.** Stephen Shellan, Mark Keyloun, John Karlen, Jennifer Cooke; ***D:*** Paul Justman. *FOX*

Gimme Shelter **1970** The sixties ended as violence occurred at a December 1969 free Rolling Stones concert attended by 300,000 people in Altamont, California. This "Woodstock West" became a bitter remembrance in rock history, as Hell's Angels (hired for security) do some ultimate damage to the spectators. A provocative look at an out-of-control situation. **91m/C VHS, Beta, LV.** Mick Jagger, Keith Richards, Charlie Watts, Bill Wyman, Mick Taylor; ***D:*** David Maysles; ***C:*** Haskell Wexler. *COL, MVD*

Gin Game 🦴🦴🦴 **1984** Taped London performance of the Broadway play about an aging couple who find romance in an old age home. Two-character performance won awards; touching and insightful. **82m/C VHS, Beta.** Jessica Tandy, Hume Cronyn; ***D:*** Mike Nichols. *TTC*

Ginger 🦴 **1972** Fabulous super-sleuth Ginger faces the sordid world of prostitution, blackmail and drugs. Prequel to "The Abductors" and followed eventually by "Girls Are for Loving." **90m/C VHS, Beta.** Cheri Caffaro, William Grannell; ***D:*** Don Schain. *MON*

Ginger Ale Afternoon 🦴 **1989** A smutty comedy revolving around a triangle formed by a married couple and their sexy next-door neighbor. The film tries for fizz but only comes up flat. **88m/C VHS, Beta, LV.** Dana Anderson, John M. Jackson, Yeardley Smith; ***D:*** Rafal Zeilinski; ***W:*** Gina Wendkos; ***M:*** Willie Dixon. *ACA, IME*

Ginger & Fred 🦴🦴🦴 **1986 (PG-13)** An acclaimed story of Fellini-esque poignancy about an aging dance team. Years before they had gained success by reverently impersonating the famous dancing duo of Astaire and Rogers. Now, after thirty years, they reunite under the gaudy lights of a high-tech television special. Wonderful performances by the aging Mastroianni and the still sweet Masina. In Italian with English subtitles. **126m/C VHS, Beta.** *IT* Marcello Mastroianni, Giulietta Masina, Franco Fabrizi, Frederick Von Ledenberg, Martin Blau, Toto Mignone; ***D:*** Federico Fellini; ***W:*** Federico Fellini, Tonino Guerra, Tullio Pinelli; ***C:*** Tonino Delli Colli; ***M:*** Nicola Piovani. *MGM, FCT, APD*

Ginger in the Morning 🦴🦴 **1973** A salesman is enamored of a young hitchhiker whom he picks up on the road. This is the same year Spacek played the innocent-gone-twisted in "Badlands." **90m/C VHS, Beta.** Sissy Spacek, Slim Pickens, Monte Markham, Susan Oliver, Mark Miller; ***D:*** Gordon Wiles. *NO*

The Girl 🦴🦴🦴 **1968** The first of Meszaros' trilogy, dealing with a young girl who leaves an orphanage to be reunited with her mother, a traditional country peasant. In Hungarian with English subtitles. Meszaros' first film. Followed by "Riddance" (1973) and "Adoption" (1975). **86m/B VHS, Beta.** *HU* ***D:*** Marta Meszaros. *KIV, INJ*

The Girl 🦴½ **1986 (R)** Nero is a wealthy attorney who agrees to pay Powney 300 crowns to have his way with her. Although somewhat ambivalent because of her scandalous age, he takes her anyway. Soon he informs his wife he needs to go on a long business trip, which fits in with her own adulterous plans. A snooping reporter (Brennan) out for some dirt upsets the apple cart, eventually leading to murder. **104m/C VHS, Beta.** Franco Nero, Christopher Lee, Bernice Stegers, Clare Powney, Frank Brennan; ***D:*** Arne Mattson. *VTR, NWV*

Girl 6 🦴🦴½ **1996 (R)** Aspiring actress (Randle) takes job as a phone sex operator in order to make ends meet. After finally finding stardom in the world of titillating telecommunications, she starts to take her work home. Bound to be compared, unfairly and probably unfavorably, to Lee's debut "She's Gotta Have It." Terrific performance by Randle is hampered by the lack of a strong story and too many unresolved subplots. Features the obligatory Lee cameo, while Tarantino shows up as a young hotshot director. Prince provides old and new tunes (as well as his previous moniker, apparently) to the proceedings. **107m/C VHS.** Theresa Randle, Isaiah Washington, Ron Silver, John Turturro, Naomi Campbell, Halle Berry, Madonna, Quentin Tarantino, Debi Mazar, Peter Berg, Richard Belzer, Spike Lee, Jenifer Lewis, Michael Imperioli, Kristen Wilson, Dina Pearlman, Maggie Rush, Desi Moreno, Susan Batson; ***D:*** Spike Lee; ***W:*** Suzan-Lori Parks; ***C:*** Malik Hassan Sayeed; ***M:*** Prince. *FXV*

A Girl, a Guy and a Gob 🦴🦴 *The Navy Steps Out* **1941** A shy rich boy falls in love with a girl who has her sights on another. Silly but enjoyable cast. **91m/B VHS, Beta.** Lucille Ball, Edmond O'Brien, George Murphy, Franklin Pangborn, Henry Travers, Lloyd Corrigan; ***D:*** Richard Wallace. *TTC*

The Girl Can't Help It 🦴🦴½ **1956** Satiric rock and roll musical comedy about a retired mobster who hires a hungry talent agent to promote his girlfriend, a wannabe no-talent singer. Mansfield's first starring role. Classic performances by some of the early greats including Eddie Cochran, Gene Vincent, The Platters, Little Richard and Fats Domino. **99m/B VHS, Beta, LV.** Jayne Mansfield, Tom Ewell, Edmond O'Brien, Julie London, Ray Anthony; ***D:*** Frank Tashlin. *FOX*

Girl Crazy 🦴🦴🦴 *When the Girls Meet the Boys* **1943** A wealthy young playboy is sent to an all-boy school in Arizona to get his mind off girls. Once there, he still manages to fall for a local girl who can't stand the sight of him. The eighth film pairing for Rooney and Garland. ♫Sam and Delilah; Embraceable You; I Got Rhythm; Fascinating Rhythm; Treat Me Rough; Bronco Busters; Bidin' My Time; But Not For Me; Do. **99m/B VHS, Beta, LV.** Mickey Rooney, Judy Garland, Nancy Walker, June Allyson; ***D:*** Norman Taurog; ***C:*** William H. Daniels; ***M:*** George Gershwin, Ira Gershwin. *MGM, TTC, FCT*

Girl from Calgary 🦴 **1932** A female rodeo champ ropes her boyfriends much like she ropes her cows, but not without a knock-down, drag-out fight between the two which forces our cowgirl to make the choice she seems to know is fated. Stock rodeo footage is intercut with the heroine riding an obviously mechanical bucking bronc. **66m/B VHS, Beta, LV.** Fifi d'Orsay, Paul Kelly; ***D:*** Philip H. Whitman. *VYY*

Girl from Chicago 🦴🦴 **1932** In this crime melodrama a secret service agent falls in love while on assignment in Mississippi. When he's back in New York he finds a good friend of his girl's in serious trouble with the numbers racket. **69m/C VHS.** Starr Calloway, Grace Smith, Eugene Brooks, Frank Wilson; ***D:*** Oscar Micheaux. *FCT, BTV*

Girl from Hunan 🦴🦴🦴 **1986** Turn-of-the-century China, a 12-year-old girl is married to a 2-year-old boy in a typical arranged marriage. She grows into womanhood treating her toddler husband with sibling affection, but conducts a secret love affair with a farmer. Intolerant village laws against adultry place her life in jeopardy. In Mandarin with English subtitles. **99m/C VHS.** Na Renhua, Deng Xiaotuang, Yu Zhang; ***D:*** Xie Fei. *NYF, INJ*

The Girl from Missouri 🦴🦴🦴 *One Hundred Percent Pure* **1934** Cute comedy in which Harlow tries to snag a millionaire without sacrificing her virtues. Lots of laughs and hilarious action, especially the scene where Harlow arrives at the yacht in Florida. Kelly is great as Harlow's wise-cracking girlfriend. Witty dialogue by Emerson and Loos, who also wrote "Gentleman Prefer Blondes." **75m/B VHS.** Jean Harlow, Lionel Barrymore, Franchot Tone, Lewis Stone, Patsy Kelly, Alan Mowbray, Clara Blandick, Russell Hopton; ***D:*** Jack Conway; ***W:*** Anita Loos, John Emerson. *MGM*

The Girl from Petrovka 🦴½ **1974 (PG)** A high-spirited Russian ballerina falls in love with an American newspaper correspondent. Their romance is complicated by the suspicious KGB. Bittersweet with a bleak ending. **103m/C VHS, Beta.** Goldie Hawn, Hal Holbrook, Anthony Hopkins; ***D:*** Robert Ellis Miller; ***W:*** Chris Bryant, Allan Scott; ***M:*** Henry Mancini. *MCA*

The Girl from Tobacco Row 🦴 **1966** A Southern slut involved with a cache of stolen cash fools with both a convict and the sheriff. **90m/C VHS, Beta.** Tex Ritter, Rachel Romen, Earl Richards, Tim Ormond, Rita Faye, Ralph Emery; ***D:*** Ron Ormond. *NO*

Girl Happy 🦴🦴 **1965** The King's fans will find him in Fort Lauderdale, Florida this time as the leader of a rock 'n' roll group. His mission: to chaperone the daughter of a Chicago mobster who naturally falls for him. Why not? ♫Girl Happy; Cross My Heart and Hope to Die; Do Not Disturb; Spring Fever; Wolf Call; Do the Clam; Fort Lauderdale Chamber of Commerce; Puppet On a String; I've Got to Find About My Baby. **96m/C VHS, Beta.** Elvis Presley, Harold J. Stone, Shelley Fabares, Gary Crosby, Nita Talbot, Mary Ann Mobley, Jackie Coogan; ***D:*** Boris Sagal; ***W:*** Harvey Bulloch. *MGM*

Girl Hunters 🦴🦴½ **1963** That intrepid private eye, Mike Hammer (played by his creator, Spillane), is caught up with communist spies, wicked women, and a missing secretary. Hammer is his usual judge-and-jury character but the action is fast-paced. **103m/B VHS, Beta.** Mickey Spillane, Lloyd Nolan, Shirley Eaton, Hy Gardner, Scott Peters; ***D:*** Roy Rowland. *SNC, NOS, DVT*

A Girl in a Million 🦴🦴 **1946** Williams dumps his verbose wife and seeks peace and quiet in a men-only War Department office. All is well until the arrival of a colonel and his daughter, mute from trauma. Finding her silence appealing, he marries her, but another trauma restores her speech. Sexist comedy may have played better in its day. **90m/B VHS.** *GB* Hugh Williams, Joan Greenwood, Naunton Wayne, Wylie Watson, Garry Marsh; ***D:*** Francis Searle. *NOS*

The Girl in a Swing 🦴½ **1989 (R)** An Englishman impulsively marries a beautiful German girl and both are subsequently haunted by phantoms from her past - are they caused by her psychic powers? Cliche-ridden silliness. Based on the Richard Adams novel. **119m/C VHS, Beta, LV.** Meg Tilly, Rupert Frazer, Elspet Gray, Lynsey Baxter, Nicholas Le Prevost, Jean Both; ***D:*** Gordon Hessler. *HBO*

Girl in Black ☆☆ **1956** The shy daughter of a once wealthy household gets the chance to escape her genteel poverty when she falls in love with the young man boarding with her family. He is attracted to her but a shocking tragedy changes everything. In Greek with English subtitles. **100m/C VHS, Beta.** *GR* Ellie Lambetti; ***D:*** Michael Cacoyannis. *FCT*

Girl in Black Stockings ☆☆ **1957** Beautiful women are mysteriously murdered at a remote, Utah hotel. Interesting, little known thriller similar to Hitchcock's "Psycho," but pre-dating it by three years. **75m/B VHS.** Lex Barker, Anne Bancroft, Mamie Van Doren, Ron Randell, Marie Windsor, John Dehner, John Holland, Diana Van Der Vlis; ***D:*** Howard W. Koch; ***M:*** Les Baxter. *FRG*

The Girl in Blue ☆☆ **1974 (R)** A lawyer, ill at ease with his current romance, suddenly decides to search for a beautiful woman he saw once, and instantly fell in love with, years before. **103m/C VHS, Beta.** *CA* Maud Adams, David Selby, Gay Rowan, William Osler, Diane Dewey, Michael Kirby; ***D:*** George Kaczender. *PSM*

A Girl in Every Port ☆☆½ **1952** Navy buddies acquire an ailing racehorse and try to conceal it aboard ship along with a healthy horse they plan to switch it with in an upcoming race. Groucho flies without his brothers in this zany film. **86m/B VHS, Beta, LV.** Groucho Marx, William Bendix, Marie Wilson, Don DeFore, Gene Lockhart; ***D:*** Chester Erskine. *CCB*

Girl in Gold Boots ☆ **1969** Aspiring starlet meets up with a draft evader and a biker on her way to Hollywood where she gets a job as a go-go dancer in a sleazy club. But things don't go smoothly when a murder and a drug theft are revealed. ♫Do You Want to Laugh or Cry?; For You; Hello, Michelle; One Good Time, One Good Place; Lonesome Man; You Gotta Come Down; Everything I Touch Turns to Gold; Cowboy Santa; Wheels of Love. **94m/C VHS, Beta.** Jody Daniels, Leslie McRae, Tom Pace, Mark Herron; ***D:*** Ted V. Mikels. *NO*

Girl in His Pocket ☆☆ *Amour de Poche; Nude in His Pocket* **1957** Mad scientist creates a potion that turns things into three-inch statues. He uses it mostly to have trystes with his lab assistant so his fiancee won't find out. Based on "The Diminishing Draft" by Waldemar Kaempfert. **82m/C VHS.** *FR* Jean Marais, Genevieve Page, Agnes Laurent; ***D:*** Pierre Kast; ***C:*** Ghislan Cloquet. *SNC*

The Girl in Lover's Lane ☆☆ **1960** A drifter falls in love with a small town girl but becomes a murder suspect when she turns up dead. Interesting mainly for Elam's uncharacteristic portrayal of a village idiot. **78m/B VHS, Beta.** Brett Halsey, Joyce Meadows, Lowell Brown, Jack Elam; ***D:*** Charles R. Rondeau. *SNC*

The Girl in Room 2A *Woof!* **1976 (R)** A young woman is trapped in a mansion with the elderly owner and her demented son. Routine horrorfest. **90m/C VHS, Beta.** Raf Vallone, Daniela Giordano. *PSM*

Girl in the Cadillac ☆☆½ **1994 (R)** Modern-day B-movie wannabe loosely adapted from the James M. Cain novella "The Enchanted Isle." 17-year-old freespirited Amanda (Eleniak) wants to get out of stifling small town Texas. She buys a bus ticket to find her long-gone daddy and winds up with not-too-smart cowpoke Rick (McNamara) instead. A bank robbery gone bad finds the twosome on the loose with $75 thou, a cherry red El Dorado convertible, and Rick's partners after them. Appealing lead performers can't overcome the cliches. **89m/C VHS.** Erika Eleniak, William McNamara, Michael Lerner, Bud Cort, Valerie Perrine, Ed Lauter, William Shockley; ***D:*** Lucas Platt; ***W:*** John Warren; ***C:*** Nancy Schreiber; ***M:*** Anton Sanko. *TTC*

The Girl in the Picture ☆☆½ **1986 (PG-13)** Sinclair stars in this light comedy as an unlucky photo clerk who discovers only too late that his ex-girlfriend may be the woman of his dreams. Typical understated but entertaining effort. **89m/C VHS, Beta.** *GB* John Gordon-Sinclair, Irina Brook, David McKay, Catherine Guthrie, Paul Young, Gregory Fisher; ***D:*** Cary Parker. *VES*

The Girl Most Likely ☆☆½ **1957** Light musical comedy about a romance-minded girl who dreams of marrying a wealthy, handsome man. She runs into a problem when she finds three prospects. Remake of 1941's "Tom, Dick and Harry" with Ginger Rogers. Choreography by great Gower Champion. ♫The Girl Most Likely; All the Colors of the Rainbow; I Don't Know What I Want; Balboa; We Gotta Keep Up With the Joneses; Crazy Horse. **98m/C VHS, Beta, LV.** Jane Powell, Cliff Robertson, Tommy Noonan, Kaye Ballard, Una Merkel; ***D:*** Mitchell Leisen. *NO*

Girl of the Golden West ☆☆ **1938** A musical version of the David Belasco chestnut about a Canadian frontier girl loving a rogue. One of Eddy and MacDonald's lesser efforts but features Ebsen's song and dance talents. ♫Camptown Races; Shadows on the Moon; Soldiers of Fortune; Soldiers of Fortune Reprise; Shadows on the Moon Reprise; The Wind in the Trees; Liebestraum; Ave Maria; Senorita. **120m/B VHS, Beta.** Jeanette MacDonald, Nelson Eddy, Walter Pidgeon, Leo Carrillo, Buddy Ebsen, Leonard Penn, Priscilla Lawson, Bob Murphy, Olin Howlin, Cliff Edwards, Billy Bevan; ***D:*** Robert Z. Leonard. *MGM*

A Girl of the Limberlost **1990** A young Indiana farmgirl fights to bring her estranged parents back together, in spite of a meddling aunt and the unexplained phenomena that haunt her. Fine acting and beautiful scenery. Originally broadcast on public television as part of the "Wonderworks" family movie series, it's best appreciated by young teens. Adapted from Gene Stratton Porter's much-filmed novel. **120m/C VHS.** Annette O'Toole, Joanna Cassidy, Heather Fairfield. *PME, HMV, FCT*

Girl on a Chain Gang *Woof!* **1965** A girl on the run gets caught by police and does her time on a chain gang—an otherwise all-male chain gang. Predictable. **96m/B VHS, Beta.** William Watson, Julie Ange, R.K. Charles; ***D:*** Jerry Gross; ***W:*** Jerry Gross. *SNC*

The Girl on a Motorcycle ☆☆ *Naked Under Leather; La Motocyclette* **1968 (R)** Singer Faithfull is a bored housewife who dons black leather and hops on her motorcycle to meet up with her lover (Delon), all the while remembering their other erotic encounters. **92m/C VHS, Beta.** *GB* Alain Delon, Marianne Faithfull, Roger Mutton; ***D:*** Jack Cardiff. *MLB*

A Girl on Her Own ☆☆ **1976** A young actress embarking on her first big role in Paris must also deal with family and political considerations in this drama set during the political upheaval of 1935. **112m/C VHS.** *FR* Sophie Chemineau, Bruno La Brasca; ***D:*** Philippe Nahoun. *FCT*

Girl Rush ☆ **1944** Two bad vaudeville comics are stuck in California during the gold rush and are promised sacks of gold if they can persuade some women to come to a rowdy mining town. ♫Annabella's Bustle; Rainbow Valley; If Mother Could Only See Us Now; Walking Arm in Arm With Jim. **65m/B VHS, Beta.** Wally Brown, Alan Carney, Frances Langford, Vera Vague, Robert Mitchum, Paul Hurst, Patti Brill, Sarah Padden, Cy Kendall; ***D:*** Gordon Douglas. *TTC*

The Girl Said No ☆½ *With Words and Music* **1937** A sleazy bookie poses as a theatrical producer in order to get even with a dance hall floozy who once stiffed him. **72m/B VHS, Beta.** Robert Armstrong, Irene Hervey, William Haines; ***D:*** Andrew L. Stone; ***W:*** Andrew L. Stone. Nominations: Academy Awards '37: Best Sound. *NOS, DVT, VYY*

Girl Shy ☆☆☆ **1924** Harold is a shy tailor's apprentice who is trying to get a collection of his romantic fantasies published. Finale features Lloyd chasing wildly after girl of his dreams. **65m/B VHS, Beta.** Harold Lloyd, Jobyna Ralston, Richard Daniels; ***D:*** Fred Newmeyer; ***W:*** Sam Taylor. *TLF*

The Girl, the Body and the Pill ☆ **1967** Sexploitation pic from director Lewis has a high school instructor getting fired for her sex education lectures—so she continues them in the privacy of her own home. Meanwhile, her students take up playing musical beds and learn about "the pill." **?m/C VHS.** Bill Rogers, Nancy Lee Noble; ***D:*** Herschell Gordon Lewis. *MOV*

A Girl to Kill For ☆½ **1990 (R)** A temptress lures a randy college guy into a plot of murder and betrayal. **85m/C VHS, Beta, LV.** Sasha Jensen, Karen Austin, Alex Cord, Rod McCary, Karen Medak; ***D:*** Richard Oliver. *COL*

Girl Under the Sheet ☆ **196?** A con-man/archaeologist moves into an ancient castle and begins romancing a beautiful resident ghost. **89m/C VHS, Beta.** Chelo Alonso, Walter Chiari. *NO*

The Girl Who Had Everything ☆☆½ **1953** Good melodrama with top cast, intelligent script and smooth direction. Taylor plays the spoiled daughter of a criminal lawyer (Powell) who falls for her father's client (Lamas), a suave, underground syndicate boss. Remake of the 1931 film "A Free Soul," which starred Norma Shearer, Clark Gable, and Lionel Barrymore. Based on the novel of the same name by Adela Rogers St. John. **69m/B VHS.** Elizabeth Taylor, Fernando Lamas, William Powell, Gig Young, James Whitmore, Robert Burton; ***D:*** Richard Thorpe; ***M:*** Andre Previn. *MGM*

The Girl Who Spelled Freedom ☆☆☆ **1986** A young Cambodian girl, speaking little English, strives to adjust to life in Chattanooga, Tennessee. She faces her challenges by becoming a champion at the national spelling bee. Based on a true story. Made-for-television. **90m/C VHS, Beta.** Wayne Rogers, Mary Kay Place, Jade Chinn, Kieu Chinh, Kathleen Sisk; ***D:*** Simon Wincer. *DIS*

The Girl with the Hat Box ☆☆ **1927** Early Russian production about a poor working girl who's paid with a lottery ticket rather than rubles (an ironic pre-communist theme?). When she strikes it rich in the lottery, her boss gives chase and silent antics ensue. Silent with orchestral score. **67m/B VHS.** *RU* Anna Sten, Vladimar Fogel, Serafina Birman, Ivan Koval-Samborsky; ***D:*** Boris Barnet. *KIV, FCT, INJ*

The Girl with the Hungry Eyes ☆☆ **1994 (R)** In 1937, top fashion model and hotel owner Louise (Fulton) kills herself over a cheating fiancee. Except Louise doesn't die, instead she becomes a vampire and, in the present-day, decides to return to her now-derelict haunts. Louise is determined to restore her hotel to its former glory and get her revenge on men in general. Filmed in Miami's South Beach. Adapted from a short story by Fritz Leiber. **84m/C VHS.** Christina Fulton, Isaac Turner, Leon Herbert, Bret Carr, Susan Rhodes; ***D:*** Jon Jacobs; ***W:*** Jon Jacobs; ***M:*** Paul Inder. *COL*

Girlfriend from Hell ☆ **1989 (R)** The Devil inhabits the body of a teenage wallflower and turns her into an uncontrollable vamp. **95m/C VHS, Beta, LV.** Liane Curtis, Dana Ashbrook, Leslie Deane, James Daughton, Anthony Barrie, James Karen; ***D:*** Daniel M. Peterson; ***W:*** Daniel M. Peterson. *LIV*

Girlfriends ☆☆☆ **1978 (PG)** Bittersweet story of a young Jewish photographer learning to make it on her own. Directorial debut of Weill reflects her background in documentaries as the true-to-life episodes unfold. **87m/C VHS, Beta.** Melanie Mayron, Anita Skinner, Eli Wallach, Christopher Guest, Amy Wright, Viveca Lindfors, Bob Balaban; ***D:*** Claudia Weill; ***W:*** Vicki Polon. Sundance Film Festival '78: Grand Jury Prize. *WAR*

Girls Are for Loving ☆ **1973** Undercover agent Ginger faces real adventure when she battles it out with her counterpart, a seductive enemy agent. Her third adventure following "Ginger" (1970) and "The Abductors" (1971). **90m/C VHS, Beta.** Cheri Caffaro, Timothy Brown; ***D:*** Don Schain. *MON*

A Girl's Folly ☆☆½ **1917** A country girl falls in love with the leading man of a film shooting on location. She wants to become a rich actress, but fails miserably. The actor offers her all the luxuries she wants if she'll become his mistress. When she finally agrees, her mother shows up. What will our country maid do now? **66m/B VHS, Beta, 8mm.** Robert Warwick, Doris Kenyon, June Elvidge, Johnny Hines; ***D:*** Maurice Tourneur. *VYY, GPV*

Girls! Girls! Girls! 🦴🦴 **1962** Poor tuna boat fisherman Elvis moonlights as a nightclub singer to get his father's boat out of hock. He falls for a rich girl pretending to be poor; and after some romantic trials, there's the usual happy ending. ♫The Nearness of You; Never Let Me Go; Girls, Girls, Girls; Return to Sender; We're Coming in Loaded; A Boy Like Me, A Girl Like You; Song of the Shrimp; Earth Boy; The Walls Have Ears. **106m/C VHS, Beta.** Elvis Presley, Stella Stevens, Laurel Goodwin, Jeremy Slate, Benson Fong, Robert Strauss, Ginny Tiu, Guy Lee, Beulah Quo; ***D:*** Norman Taurog; ***W:*** Edward Anhalt; ***C:*** Loyal Griggs. *FOX, MVD*

Girls in Chains 🦴½ **1943** Girls in a reformatory, a teacher, a corrupt school official, and the detective trying to nail him. There's also a murder with the killer revealed at the beginning of the film. **72m/B VHS, Beta.** Arline Judge, Roger Clark, Robin Raymond, Barbara Pepper, Dorothy Burgess, Clancy Cooper; ***D:*** Edgar G. Ulmer. *NOS, SNC, DVT*

Girls in Prison 🦴½ **1956** Anne Carson is sent to prison for a bank robbery she didn't commit, and although the prison chaplain believes her story, the other prisoners think she knows where the money is hidden. They plan a prison break, forcing Carson to go with them and get the money, but they soon run across the real robber, also searching for the loot. A below-average "B" prison movie, lacking the camp aspects of so many of these films. **87m/B VHS.** Richard Denning, Joan Taylor, Adele Jergens, Helen Gilbert, Lance Fuller, Jane Darwell, Raymond Hatton; ***D:*** Edward L. Cahn. *COL*

Girls Just Want to Have Fun 🦴½ **1985 (PG)** An army brat and her friends pull out all the stops and defy their parents for a chance to dance on a national television program. Based loosely upon Cyndi Lauper's song of the same name. **90m/C VHS, Beta, LV.** Sarah Jessica Parker, Helen Hunt, Ed Lauter, Holly Gagnier, Morgan Woodward, Lee Montgomery, Shannen Doherty, Biff Yeager; ***D:*** Alan Metter; ***M:*** Thomas Newman. *NWV, VTR*

Girls Next Door 🦴 **1979 (R)** A bevy of boisterous beauties cavort and cause havoc in buffoon-cluttered suburbia. **85m/C VHS, Beta, LV.** Kirsten Baker, Perry Lang, Leslie Cederquist, Richard Singer; ***D:*** James Hong. *NO*

Girls Night Out 🦴 *The Scaremaker* **1983 (R)** Ex-cop must stop a killer who is murdering participants in a sorority house scavenger hunt and leaving cryptic clues on the local radio station. **96m/C VHS, Beta.** Hal Holbrook, Rutanya Alda, Julia Montgomery, James Carroll; ***D:*** Robert Deubel. *NO*

The Girls of Huntington House 🦴🦴 **1973** A teacher in a school for unwed mothers finds herself becoming increasingly absorbed in her students' lives. Made for television. **73m/C VHS.** Shirley Jones, Mercedes McCambridge, Sissy Spacek, William Windom, Pamela Sue Martin, Darrell Larson; ***D:*** Alf Kjellin. *LIV*

Girls of the White Orchid 🦴 *Death Ride to Osaka* **1985** A naive American girl thinks she's getting a job singing in a Japanese nightclub, but it turns out to be a front for a prostitution ring run by the Japanese Yakuza. A made-for-television movie based on real stories, though the producers concentrate on the seamy side. **96m/C VHS, Beta.** Ann Jillian, Jennifer Jason Leigh; ***D:*** Jonathan Kaplan; ***M:*** Brad Fiedel. *ORI*

Girls on the Road 🦴½ **1973 (PG)** Two girls are just out for fun cruising the California coast. But that handsome hitchhiker turns out to be a deadly mistake. **91m/C VHS, Beta.** *CA* Kathleen Cody, Michael Ontkean, Dianne Hull, Ralph Waite; ***D:*** Thomas J. Schmidt. *UNI*

Girls Riot 🦴 **1988** Young, female juvenile delinquents have had enough! They decide to give their warden-like headmistress a taste of her own violence. **100m/C VHS, Beta.** Jocelyne Boisseau, Cornelia Calwer, Angelica Domrose, Ute Freight; ***D:*** Manfred Purzer. *ACN*

Girls School Screamers 🦴 **1986 (R)** Six young women and a nun are assigned to spend the weekend checking the contents for sale in a scary mansion bequeathed to their school. Unfortunately, the psychotic killer inhabiting the place doesn't think that's a good idea. **85m/C VHS, Beta.** Mollie O'Mara, Sharon Christopher, Vera Gallagher; ***D:*** John P. Finegan. *LIV*

Girls' Town 🦴 *The Innocent and the Damned* **1959** Typical bad girls and drag racing fifties flick has Van Doren sent to a correctional institute, run by nuns. This tough girl sees the error of her wicked ways and turns into a goody-two-shoes. **90m/B VHS.** Mamie Van Doren, Mel Torme, Paul Anka, Ray Anthony, Maggie Hayes, Cathy Crosby, Elinor Donahue, Gigi Perreau, Jim Mitchum, Gloria Talbott, Harold Lloyd Jr., Charles Chaplin Jr.; ***D:*** Charles Haas; ***W:*** Robert Smith; ***M:*** Van Alexander. *REP*

Girls Town 🦴🦴 **1995** Tough look at the lives of three working-class high school seniors who are shattered by the suicide of Nikki (Ellis), the fourth member of their group, who killed herself from guilt over an undisclosed rape. Single mom Patti (Taylor), ambitious Emma (Grace), and strong-willed Angela (Harris) argue, commiserate, battle their foes (Patti's abusive boyfriend, Nikki's rapist), and lean on each other as they struggle to figure out themselves and their ambiguous futures. Lots of time's spent in the girls' bathroom at school (how realistic can you get?) **88m/C VHS.** Lili Taylor, Anna Grace, Bruklin Harris, Aunjanue Ellis; ***D:*** Jim McKay; ***W:*** Lili Taylor, Anna Grace, Bruklin Harris, Aunjanue Ellis, Jim McKay, Denise Hernandez; ***C:*** Russell Fine. Sundance Film Festival '96: Filmmakers Trophy. *NYR*

Girly 🦴 *Mumsy, Nanny, Sonny, and Girly* **1970 (R)** An English gothic about an excessively weird family that lives in a crumbling mansion and indulges in murder, mental aberration, and sexual compulsion. **101m/C VHS, Beta.** *GB* Michael Bryant, Ursula Howells, Pat Heywood, Howard Trevor, Vanessa Howard, Michael Ripper; ***D:*** Freddie Francis. *PSM*

Git! 🦴½ **1965** A young runaway and his faithful dog are taken in by a wealthy dog-breeder and trained by him into a crack hunting team. **90m/C VHS, Beta.** Jack Chaplain, Richard Webb, Heather North; ***D:*** Ellis Kadisan. *COL, NLC*

Git Along Little Dogies 🦴½ **1937** It's cattle ranchers versus oil men with Autry caught in the middle of the petro/cow war. But Gene still finds a little time to romance the town banker's pretty daughter. **60m/B VHS, Beta.** Gene Autry, Judith Allen, Smiley Burnette, William Farnum; ***D:*** Joseph Kane. *NOS, VYY, DVT*

Give a Girl a Break 🦴🦴½ **1953** Three talented but unknown babes vie for the lead in a stage production headed for Broadway after the incumbent prima donna quits. After befriending one of the various men associated with the production, each starlet thinks she's a shoe-in for the part. Entertaining but undistinguished musical with appealing dance routines of Fosse and the Champions. Ira Gershwin, collaborating for the first and only time with Burton Lane, wrote the lyrics to two of the songs. ♫Give the Girl a Break; In Our United State; It Happens Every Time; Nothing is Impossible; Applause, Applause; Challenge Dance. **84m/C VHS.** Marge Champion, Gower Champion, Debbie Reynolds, Helen Wood, Bob Fosse, Kurt Kasznar, Richard Anderson, William Ching, Larry Keating, Donna Martell; ***D:*** Stanley Donen; ***M:*** Andre Previn. *MGM, TTC, FCT*

Give 'Em Hell, Harry! **1975** James Whitmore's one-man show as Harry S. Truman filmed in performance on stage; Whitmore was nominated for a Tony. **103m/C VHS, Beta.** James Whitmore; ***D:*** Steve Binder. Nominations: Academy Awards '75: Best Actor (Whitmore). *WOV*

Give Me a Sailor 🦴🦴½ **1938** Hope and Whiting play brothers, and fellow Naval officers, who meet sisters Grable and Raye on shore leave. Naturally, there's comic romantic complications until a double wedding ends the farce. Not much of a musical score from Ralph Rainger and Leo Robin but the movie's fun. Based on a play by Anne Nichols. ♫What Goes Here in My Heart?; A Little Kiss at Twilight; Give Me a Sailor; The US and You; It Don't Make Sense. **71m/B VHS.** Bob Hope, Martha Raye, Betty Grable, Jack Whiting, Clarence Kolb, Nana Bryant, Emerson Treacy; ***D:*** Elliott Nugent; ***W:*** Frank Butler, Doris Anderson. *MCA*

Give My Regards to Broad Street 🦴🦴 **1984 (PG)** McCartney film made for McCartney fans. Film features many fine versions of the ex-Beatle's songs that accompany his otherwise lackluster portrayal of a rock star in search of his stolen master recordings. ♫Eleanor Rigby; Ballroom Dancing; Good Day, Sunshine; Silly Love Songs; No Values; No More Lonely Nights; Yesterday; Not Such a Bad Boy; The Long and Winding Road. **109m/C VHS, Beta, LV.** *GB* Paul McCartney, Bryan Brown, Ringo Starr, Barbara Bach, Tracey Ullman, Ralph Richardson, Linda McCartney; ***D:*** Peter Webb. *MVD, FOX*

The Gladiator 🦴🦴🦴½ **1938** Brown stars as a mild-mannered collegiate who accidently ingests a serum which turns him into a real he-man. Things take a turn for the funniest when the effects wear off, just as he is to wrestle Man Mountain Dean. Chock-full of Brown's trademark physical humor. **70m/B VHS.** Joe E. Brown, Man Mountain Dean, June Travis, Dickie Moore, Lucien Littlefield, Robert Kent, Ethel Wales; ***D:*** Edward Sedgwick. *NOS*

The Gladiator 🦴½ **1986** An angry Los Angeles citizen turns vigilante against drunk drivers after his brother is one of their victims. Made for television. **94m/C VHS, Beta, LV.** Ken Wahl, Nancy Allen, Robert Culp, Stan Shaw, Rosemary Forsyth; ***D:*** Abel Ferrara. *VTR, NWV, HHE*

Gladiator 🦴½ **1992 (R)** When suburban Golden Gloves boxing champion Tommy Riley (Marshall) is forced to move to the inner city because of his father's gambling debts, he becomes involved with an evil boxing promotor who thrives on pitting different ethnic races against each other in illegal boxing matches. Eventually Riley is forced to fight his black friend Lincoln (Gooding), even though Lincoln has been warned that another blow to the head could mean his life. Although this film tries to serve some moral purpose, it falls flat on the mat. **98m/C VHS, LV.** Cuba Gooding Jr., James Marshall, Robert Loggia, Ossie Davis, Brian Dennehy, Cara Buono, John Heard, John Seda, Lance Slaughter; ***D:*** Rowdy Herrington. *COL*

Gladiator Cop: The Swordsman 2 🦴½ **1995 (R)** A legendary sword, believed to have magic powers, is stolen and an ex-detective winds up fighting modern-day gladiators and a man who believes himself to be a reincarnation of Alexander the Great. **92m/C VHS.** Lorenzo Lamas. *MNC*

Gladiator of Rome 🦴 *Il Gladiatore Di Roma* **1963** A gladiator flexes his pecs to save a young girl from death at the hands of evil rulers. **105m/C VHS.** *IT* Gordon Scott, Wandisa Guida, Roberto Risso, Ombretta Colli, Alberto Farnese; ***D:*** Mario Costa. *SNC*

The Gladiators 🦴 *The Peace Game; Gladiatorerna* **1970** Televised gladiatorial bouts are designed to subdue man's violent tendencies in a futuristic society until a computer makes a fatal error. **90m/C VHS, Beta.** Arthur Pentelow, Frederick Danner; ***D:*** Peter Watkins. *NO*

Gladiators 7 🦴½ **1962** Sparta must be freed from the tyrannical rule of the Romans. In lieu of samurai or cowboys, who better than the Gladiators 7 to do the deed? Plenty of sword-to-sword action and scantily clad Italian babes. **92m/C VHS, Beta.** *SP IT* Richard Harrison, Loredana Nusciak, Livio Lorenzon, Gerard Tichy, Edoardo Toniolo, Joseph Marco, Barta Barry; ***D:*** Pedro Lazaga. *SNC*

Glass 🦴½ **1990** A normally complacent man is driven to the brink of savagery when a killer begins stalking his employees. **92m/C VHS.** Alan Lovell, Lisa Peers, Adam Stone, Natalie McCurry. *ATL*

The Glass Bottom Boat 🦴🦴½ **1966** A bubbly but transparent Doris Day comedy, in which she falls in love with her boss at an aerospace lab. Their scheme to spend time together get her mistaken for a spy. Made about the time they stopped making them like this anymore, it's innocuous slapstick romance with a remarkable 1960's cast, including a Robert Vaughn cameo as the Man From U.N.C.L.E. Doris sings "Que Sera, Sera" and a few other numbers. **110m/C VHS, Beta, LV.** Doris Day, Rod Taylor, Arthur Godfrey, Paul Lynde, Eric Fleming, Alice Pearce, Ellen Corby, John McGiver, Dom DeLuise, Dick Martin, Edward Andrews; ***Cameos:*** Robert Vaughn; ***D:*** Frank Tashlin; ***W:*** Everett Freeman; ***C:*** Leon Shamroy. *MGM*

The Glass House ✂✂✂ *Truman Capote's The Glass House* **1972** Alda stars as a middle-aged college professor, convicted on a manslaugter charge, who is sent to a maximum security prison and must learn to deal with life inside. Filmed at Utah State Prison, real-life prisoners as supporting cast add to the drama. Still has the power to chill, with Morrow particularly effective as one of the inmate leaders. Adapted from a Truman Capote story. Made for television. **92m/C VHS, Beta.** Alan Alda, Vic Morrow, Clu Gulager, Billy Dee Williams, Dean Jagger, Kristopher Tabori; ***D:*** Tom Gries; ***M:*** Billy Goldenberg. *MOV, HHT*

The Glass Jungle **1988** Will a cab driver save Los Angeles? When armed terrorists and the FBI battle it out in the sunny California city an innocent cabby seems to hold the solution to survival. **94m/C VHS, Beta.** Lee Canalito, Joe Filbeck, Diana Frank, Mark High, Frank Scala; ***D:*** Joseph Merhi. *HHE*

The Glass Key ✂✂✂ **1942** The second version of Dashiell Hammet's novel, a vintage mystery movie concerning a nominally corrupt politician (Donlevy) being framed for murder, and his assistant sleuthing out the real culprit. One of Ladd's first starring vehicles; Lake is the mystery woman who loves him, and Bendix a particularly vicious thug. **85m/B VHS, Beta, LV.** Alan Ladd, Veronica Lake, Brian Donlevy, William Bendix, Bonita Granville, Richard Denning, Joseph Calleia, Moroni Olsen, Dane Clark; ***D:*** Stuart Heisler. *MCA*

The Glass Menagerie ✂✂✂ **1987 (PG)** An aging Southern belle deals with her crippled daughter Laura, whose one great love is her collection of glass animals. The third film adaptation of the Tennessee Williams classic, which preserves the performances of the Broadway revival cast, is a solid-but-not-stellar adaptation of the play. All-star acting ensemble. **134m/C VHS, Beta, LV.** Joanne Woodward, Karen Allen, John Malkovich, James Naughton; ***D:*** Paul Newman; ***W:*** Tennessee Williams; ***C:*** Robert Burks; ***M:*** Henry Mancini, Max Steiner. *MCA*

The Glass Shield ✂✂½ **1995 (PG-13)** Timely look at racism and corruption in the Los Angeles sheriff's department as seen through the eyes of African American rookie J.J. Johnson (Boatman). His dream of being a police officer turns to disillusionment when he slowly realizes his own department is framing a black man (Ice Cube) for a murder he did not commit. First half grabs your attention, but the momentum is lost in murky plot twists and a rushed ending. Made on a shoestring, but has an interesting cast, including the reliably slimy Ironside as (what else) one of the bad cops and an almost unrecognizable Petty, who becomes Johnson's only ally on the force. **109m/C VHS, LV.** Michael Boatman, Lori Petty, Michael Ironside, M. Emmet Walsh, Ice Cube, Richard Anderson, Elliott Gould; ***D:*** Charles Burnett; ***W:*** Charles Burnett; ***C:*** Elliot Davis; ***M:*** Stephen James Taylor. *TOU*

The Glass Slipper ✂✂ **1955** In this version of the "Cinderella" saga, Caron plays an unglamourous girl gradually transformed into the expected beauty. Winwood is the fairy godmother who inspires the girl to find happiness, rather then simply providing it for her magically. The film is highlighted by the stunning dance numbers, choreographed by Roland Petit and featuring the Paris ballet. **93m/C VHS, Beta.** Leslie Caron, Michael Wilding, Keenan Wynn, Estelle Winwood, Elsa Lanchester, Barry Jones, Amanda Blake, Lurene Tuttle; ***D:*** Charles Walters. *MGM, FCT*

Glass Tomb ✂✂ *The Glass Cage* **1955** At a circus, a man performs the world's longest fast inside a glass cage, and becomes the raison d'etre for murder. **59m/B VHS, Beta, LV.** John Ireland, Honor Blackman, Eric Pohlmann, Tonia Bern, Sidney James; ***D:*** Montgomery Tully. *NO*

Gleaming the Cube ✂½ **1989 (PG-13)** A skateboarding teen investigates his brother's murder. Film impresses with its stunt footage only. For those with adolescent interests. **102m/C VHS, Beta, LV.** Christian Slater, Steven Bauer, Min Luong, Art Chudabala, Le Tuan; ***D:*** Graeme Clifford; ***W:*** Michael Tolkin; ***M:*** Jay Michael Ferguson. *LIV, VES*

Glen and Randa ✂✂½ **1971 (R)** Two young people experience the world after it has been destroyed by nuclear war. Early McBride, before the hired-gun success of "The Big Easy." **94m/C VHS, Beta, LV.** Steven Curry, Shelley Plimpton; ***D:*** Jim McBride; ***W:*** Rudy Wurlitzer, Jim McBride. *VCI, IME*

Glen or Glenda: Confessions of Ed Wood *Woof! He or She; I Changed My Sex; I Led Two Lives; The Transvestite* **1953** An appalling, quasi-docudrama about transvestism, interspersed with meaningless stock footage, inept dream sequences and Lugosi sitting in a chair spouting incoherent prattle at the camera. Directorial debut of Wood, who, using a pseudonym, played the lead; one of the phenomenally bad films of this century. An integral part of the famous anti-auteur's canon. **70m/B VHS, Beta.** Bela Lugosi, Edward D. Wood Jr., Lyle Talbot, Donald Woods; ***D:*** Edward D. Wood Jr. *NOS, MRV, SNC*

Glengarry Glen Ross ✂✂✂ **1992 (R)** A seven-character study chronicling 48-hours in the lives of some sleazy real estate men in danger of getting the ax from their hard-driving bosses. A standout cast includes Pacino as the glad-handing sales leader, Lemmon as the hustler fallen on dim prospects, and Baldwin, briefly venomous, as the company hatchet-man. Brutal and hard-edged with very strong language. Mamet scripted from his Tony-award winning Broadway play. **100m/C VHS, LV.** Al Pacino, Jack Lemmon, Ed Harris, Alec Baldwin, Alan Arkin, Kevin Spacey, Jonathan Pryce, Bruce Altman, Jude Ciccolella; ***D:*** James Foley; ***W:*** David Mamet; ***C:*** Juan Ruiz-Anchia; ***M:*** James Newton Howard. National Board of Review Awards '92: Best Actor (Lemmon); Venice Film Festival '93: Best Actor (Lemmon); Nominations: Academy Awards '92: Best Supporting Actor (Pacino). *LIV, MOV, BTV*

The Glenn Miller Story ✂✂✂ **1954 (G)** The music of the Big Band Era lives again in this warm biography of the legendary Glenn Miller, following his life from the late '20s to his untimely death in a WWII plane crash. Stewart's likably convincing and even fakes the trombone playing well. ♫Moonlight Serenade; In the Mood; Tuxedo Junction; Little Brown Jug; Adios; String of Pearls; Pennsylvania 6-5000; Stairway to the Stars; American Patrol. **113m/C VHS, Beta, LV.** James Stewart, June Allyson, Harry (Henry) Morgan, Gene Krupa, Louis Armstrong, Ben Pollack; ***D:*** Anthony Mann; ***W:*** Oscar Brodney; ***C:*** William H. Daniels; ***M:*** Henry Mancini. Academy Awards '54: Best Sound; Nominations: Academy Awards '54: Best Story & Screenplay, Best Original Score. *MCA, RDG*

Glitch! ✂½ **1988 (R)** A throng of beautiful Hollywood hopefuls draw two youngsters unconnected with the film into posing as the film's director and producer in the hopes of conducting personal interviews on the casting couch. Straight to video. **88m/C VHS, Beta, LV.** Julia Nickson-Soul, Will Egan, Steve Donmyer, Dan Speaker, Dallas Cole, Ji Tu Cumbuka, Dick Gautier, Ted Lange, Teri Weigel, Fernando Carzon, John Kreng, Lindsay Carr; ***D:*** Nico Mastorakis; ***W:*** Nico Mastorakis. *ACA*

The Glitter Dome ✂½ **1984** Two policemen discover the sleazier side of Hollywood when they investigate the murder of a pornographer. Based upon the novel by Joseph Wambaugh. Made for television. **90m/C VHS, Beta.** Stuart Margolin, John Marley, James Garner, John Lithgow, Margot Kidder, Colleen Dewhurst; ***D:*** Stuart Margolin. *NO*

Glitz ✂✂½ **1988** A Miami cop and an Atlantic City lounge singer team up to investigate a call-girl's death and wind up too close to a drug ring. Based on the novel by Elmore Leonard. Made for television. **96m/C VHS, Beta.** Jimmy Smits, John Diehl, Markie Post, Ken Foree, Madison Mason, Robin Strasser; ***D:*** Sandor Stern. *WAR*

A Global Affair ✂½ **1963** Hope is a department head in the United Nations who finds an abandoned baby in the building. The inept bachelor is wooed by a number of international beauties seeking to adopt the child for their various countries but he becomes increasingly attached to the little tyke. **84m/B VHS, Beta.** Bob Hope, Lilo (Liselotte) Pulver, Michele Mercier, Yvonne De Carlo, Miiko Taka, Robert Sterling, Nehemiah Persoff, John McGiver, Mickey Shaughnessy; ***D:*** Jack Arnold; ***W:*** Charles Lederer, Arthur Marx, Bob Fisher; ***C:*** Joseph Ruttenberg. *MGM, FCT*

Gloria ✂✂½ **1980 (PG)** She used to be a Mafia moll, now she's outrunning the Mob after taking in the son of a slain neighbor. He's got a book that they want, and they're willing to kill to get it. Trademark Cassavetes effort in which he has actors plumb their souls to discomfiting levels. **123m/C VHS, Beta, LV.** Gena Rowlands, John Adams, Buck Henry, Julie Carmen; ***D:*** John Cassavetes; ***M:*** Bill Conti. Venice Film Festival '80: Best Film; Golden Raspberry Awards '80: Worst Supporting Actor (Adams); Nominations: Academy Awards '80: Best Actress (Rowlands). *COL*

Glorifying the American Girl ✂✂ **1930** Eaton's a chorus girl performing in the Ziegfeld Follies, which lends itself to numerous production numbers. The only film Ziegfeld ever produced. ♫What I Wouldn't Do For That Man; Blue Skies; I'm Just a Vagabond Lover; Baby Face; At Sundown; Beautiful Changes; Sam the Old Accordian Man; There Must Be Someone Waiting For Me. **96m/B VHS, Beta.** Mary Eaton, Dan Healey, Eddie Cantor, Rudy Vallee; ***D:*** Millard Webb. *NOS, HHT, DVT*

Glory ✂✂ **1956** O'Brien is a racehorse owner who tussles with her grandmother over how to keep the family farm open on a shoestring budget. Brennan enters the picture as the financial guru who lands them back on track, with enough left over to enter their prize filly in the Kentucky Derby. Lupton plays O'Brien's love interest. No surprises here. **100m/C VHS, Beta.** Margaret O'Brien, Walter Brennan, Charlotte Greenwood; ***D:*** David Butler. *NO*

Glory ✂✂✂½ **1989 (R)** A rich, historical spectacle chronicling the 54th Massachusetts, the first black volunteer infantry unit in the Civil War. The film manages to artfully focus on both the 54th and their white commander, Robert Gould Shaw. Based on Shaw's letters, the film uses thousands of accurately costumed "living historians" (re-enactors) as extras in this panoramic production. A haunting, bittersweet musical score pervades what finally becomes an anti-war statement. Stunning performances throughout, with exceptional work from Freeman and Washington. **122m/C VHS, Beta, LV, 8mm.** Matthew Broderick, Morgan Freeman, Denzel Washington, Cary Elwes, Jihmi Kennedy, Andre Braugher, John Finn, Donovan Leitch, John Cullum, Bob Gunton, Jane Alexander, Raymond St. Jacques, Cliff DeYoung; ***D:*** Edward Zwick; ***W:*** Kevin Jarre; ***C:*** Freddie Francis; ***M:*** James Horner. Academy Awards '89: Best Cinematography, Best Sound, Best Supporting Actor (Washington); Nominations: Academy Awards '89: Best Film Editing. *COL, FCT, BTV*

The Glory Boys ✂½ **1984** A secret agent is hired to protect an Israeli scientist who is marked for assassination by the PLO and IRA. **78m/C VHS, Beta.** Rod Steiger, Anthony Perkins, Gary Brown, Aaron Harris; ***D:*** Michael Ferguson. *VCO, VTR, PSM*

Glory Enough for All: The Discovery of Insulin ✂✂½ **1992** The drama behind the discovery of insulin in the 1920s focuses on the research of four men, sometimes not-so-friendly rivals, searching for a treatment for diabetes mellitus. Dr. Frederick Banting and science student Charles Best are granted permission by James Macleod, a Professor of Physiology at the University of Toronto, to conduct experiments on the pancreas. Macleod then assigns biochemist James Collip to assist them on developing a viable serum, an extract named insulin. Banting and Macleod were awarded the Nobel prize in 1923 for their discovery (though Banting felt Macleod was undeserving). Adapted from "The Discovery of Insulin" by Michael Bliss. Made for Canadian television. **196m/C VHS.** *CA* R.H.

Thomson, Robert Wisden, John Woodvine, Michael Zelniker, Martha Henry, Heather Hess; *D:* Eric Till; *W:* Grahame Woods. *CCC*

Glory! Glory! **1990 (R)** Slashing satire about TV evangelism. Thomas as the meek son of founder of Church of the Champions of Christ brings in lewd female rock singer to save the money-machine ministry from financial ruin. Rock music, sex, and MTV-like camera work make it worth seeing. Whitmore is a treat. **152m/C VHS, Beta, LV.** Ellen Greene, Richard Thomas, Barry Morse, James Whitmore, Winston Reckert; *D:* Lindsay Anderson; *W:* Stan Daniels. *ORI, IME*

The Glory Stompers *Woof!* **1967** Hopper prepares for his Easy Rider role as the leader of a motorcycle gang who battles with a rival leader over a woman. Very bad, atrocious dialogue, and a "love-in" scene that will be best appreciated by insomniacs. **85m/C VHS.** Dennis Hopper, Jody McCrea, Chris Noel, Jock Mahoney, Lindsay Crosby, Robert Tessier, Casey Kasem; *D:* Anthony M. Lanza. *NO*

The Glory Trail ½ *Glorious Sacrifice* **1936** A group of railroad workers and soldiers are constantly harassed by Indian attacks. **63m/B VHS.** Tom Keene, Joan Barclay, James Bush, Frank Melton, Walter Long; *D:* Lynn Shores. *GPV*

Glory Years **1987** Three old friends find themselves in charge of the scholarship fund at their 20th high school reunion. Unfortunately, they decide to increase the fund by gambling in Las Vegas and lose it all on a fixed fight! **150m/C VHS, Beta.** George Dzundza, Archie Hahn, Tim Thomerson, Tawny Kitaen, Donna Pescow, Donna Denton; *D:* Arthur Seidelman. *HBO*

The Glove ½ *The Glove: Lethal Terminator; Blood Mad* **1978 (R)** Ex-cop turned bounty hunter has his toughest assignment ever. It's his job to bring in a six-and-a-half foot, 250-pound ex-con who's been wreaking havoc with an unusual glove—it's made of leather and steel. **93m/C VHS, Beta.** John Saxon, Roosevelt Grier, Joanna Cassidy, Joan Blondell, Jack Carter, Aldo Ray; *D:* Ross Hagen. *MED*

The Gnome-Mobile **1967** A lumber baron and his two grandchildren attempt to reunite a pair of forest gnomes with a lost gnome colony. Brennan has a dual role as both a human and a gnome grandfather. Wynn's last film. Based on a children's novel by Upton Sinclair. **84m/C VHS, Beta.** Walter Brennan, Richard Deacon, Ed Wynn, Karen Dotrice, Matthew Garber; *D:* Robert Stevenson; *C:* Edward Colman; *M:* Buddy Baker. *DIS, OM*

The Go-Between ½ **1971 (PG)** Wonderful tale of hidden love. Young boy Guard acts as a messenger between the aristocratic Christie and her former lover Bates. But tragedy befalls them all when the lovers are discovered. The story is told as the elderly messenger (now played by Redgrave) recalls his younger days as the go-between and builds to a climax when he is once again asked to be a messenger for the lady he loved long ago. Based on a story by L.P. Hartley. **116m/C VHS.** *GB* Julie Christie, Alan Bates, Dominic Guard, Margaret Leighton, Michael Redgrave, Michael Gough, Edward Fox; *D:* Joseph Losey; *W:* Harold Pinter. British Academy Awards '71: Best Screenplay, Best Supporting Actor (Fox), Best Supporting Actress (Leighton); Nominations: Academy Awards '71: Best Supporting Actress (Leighton). *COL*

Go Down Death ½ **1941** In this early all-black film, a minister is caught in a moral dilemma literally between Heaven and Hell. Scenes of the afterlife are taken from early silent films. **63m/B VHS, Beta.** Myra D. Hemmings, Samuel H. James, Eddy L. Houston, Spencer Williams Jr., Amos Droughan; *D:* Spencer Williams Jr. *VYY, DVT, TIM*

Go Fish **1994 (R)** Low-budget girl-meets-girl romantic comedy finds Kia (McMillan) playing matchmaker for her roommate, energetic Max (Turner), by setting her up with shy Ely (Brodie). The opposites do, eventually, attract, with their friends eager for every detail. Good-natured and candid, with a welcome lack of melodrama. **87m/B VHS.** Guinevere Turner, V.S. Brodie, T. Wendy McMillan, Anastasia Sharp, Migdalia Melendez; *D:* Rose Troche; *W:* Guinevere Turner, Rose Troche; *C:* Ann T. Rossetti; *M:* Brendan Dolan, Jennifer Sharpe. Nominations: Independent Spirit Awards '95: Best Supporting Actress (Brodie). *HMK, FCT*

Go for Broke! ½ **1951** Inexperienced officer Johnson heads a special WWII attack force which is made up of Japanese Americans. Sent to fight in Europe, they prove their bravery and loyalty to all. Good, offbeat story. **92m/B VHS, Beta.** Van Johnson, Gianna Maria Canale, Warner Anderson, Lane Nakano, George Miki; *D:* Robert Pirosh; *C:* Paul Vogel. Nominations: Academy Awards '51: Best Story & Screenplay. *NOS, MRV, VYY*

Go for Broke **1990** Motorcycle stunts, fights, and car chases highlight this action film. **?m/C VHS.** *VYY*

Go for It **1983 (PG)** Oddball supercops go after a mad scientist—who has created a deadly "K"-bomb—and they encounter killer whales, karate busboys and malevolent Shirley Temple clones along the way. **109m/C VHS, Beta.** *IT* Bud Spencer, Terence Hill, David Huddleston; *D:* E.B. Clucher. *WAR*

Go for the Gold **1984** A young marathon runner risks his girlfriend's love when he decides to pursue fame and fortune. **98m/C VHS, Beta.** James Ryan, Cameron Mitchell, Sandra Horne. *LIV*

Go-Get-'Em-Haines **1935** Newsman Boyd follows a fleeing bankrupt utilities tycoon onto an ocean liner for an interview only to end up trying to solve the tycoon's murder. **61m/C VHS.** William Boyd, Sheila Terry, Eleanor Hunt, Leroy Mason, Lloyd Ingraham, Jimmy Aubrey, Clarence Geldert, Louis Natheaux, Lee Shumway; *D:* Sam Newfield. *GPV*

The Go-Getter **1954** Wild slapstick fun in the world of business. **?m/C VHS.** Hank McCune, Beverly Garland. *LOO*

Go, Johnny Go! **1959** Rock promoter Alan Freed molds a young orphan into rock sensation "Johnny Melody." Musical performances include Ritchie Valens (his only film appearance), Eddie Cochran, Jackie Wilson. **75m/B VHS, Beta, LV.** Alan Freed, Sandy Stewart, Chuck Berry, Jimmy Clanton, Eddie Cochran, Jackie Wilson, Ritchie Valens; *D:* Paul Landres. *MED, AOV, VTR*

Go Kill and Come Back **1968 (PG)** A bounty hunter tracks down a notoriously dangerous train robber. **95m/C VHS, Beta.** Gilbert Roland, George Helton, Edd Byrnes; *D:* Enzo G. Castellari. *MON*

The Go-Masters *Mikan No Taikyoku* **1982** Historic co-production between Japan and China, centering on the ancient strategy board game "Go." A young competitor becomes obsessed with winning at any price. Episodic tale of the relationships between a Japanese and Chinese family spans 30 years and was critically acclaimed in both China and Japan. In Japanese and Chinese with English subtitles. **134m/C VHS, Beta.** *JP CH* Huang Zong-Ying, Du Peng, Yu Shao-Kang, Lui Xin, Yoshiko Mita, Keiko Matsuzaka, Mayumi Ogawa, Rentaro Mikuni, Sun Dao-Lin, Shen Guan-Chu, Misako Honno; *D:* Junya Sato, Duan Jishun. Montreal World Film Festival '83: Best Film. *INJ, FCT*

Go Tell It On the Mountain ½ **1984** Young black boy tries to gain the approval of his stern stepfather in this fine adaptation of James Baldwin's semiautobiographical novel. Set in the 1930s; originally a PBS "American Playhouse" presentation. **100m/C VHS.** Paul Winfield, Olivia Cole, Ruby Dee, Alfre Woodard, James Bond III, Rosalind Cash, Linda Hopkins; *D:* Stan Lathan. *MON*

Go Tell the Spartans **1978 (R)** In Vietnam, 1964, a hard-boiled major is ordered to establish a garrison at Muc Wa with a platoon of burned out Americans and Vietnamese mercenaries. Blundering but politically interesting war epic pre-dating the flood of 1980s American-Vietnam apologetics. Based on Daniel Ford's novel. **114m/C VHS, Beta, LV.** Burt Lancaster, Craig Wasson, David Clennon, Marc Singer; *D:* Ted Post; *W:* Wendell Mayes; *C:* Harry Stradling Jr. *VES*

Go West ½ **1940** The brothers Marx help in the making and un-making of the Old West. Weak, late Marx Bros., but always good for a few yucks. **80m/B VHS, Beta, LV.** Groucho Marx, Chico Marx, Harpo Marx, John Carroll, Diana Lewis; *D:* Edward Buzzell; *M:* George Bassman. *MGM, CCB*

Go West, Young Man ½ **1936** West is a movie star whose latest film is premiering in a small town, where she's naturally a sensation. Scott is the muscular farm boy who catches her eye and she decides to hang around in order to catch the rest of him as well. The censors again cut West's most overt sexual and satiric barbs. **80m/B VHS.** Mae West, Randolph Scott, Warren William, Alice Brady, Elizabeth Patterson, Lyle Talbot, Isabel Jewell; *D:* Henry Hathaway; *W:* Mae West; *C:* Karl Struss. *MCA, BTV*

The Goalie's Anxiety at the Penalty Kick ½ **1971** A chilling landmark film that established Wenders as one of the chief film voices to emerge from post-war Germany. The story deals with a soccer player who wanders around Vienna after being suspended, commits a random murder, and slowly passes over the brink of sanity and morality. A suspenseful, existential adaptation of the Peter Handke novel. In German with English subtitles. **101m/C VHS, Beta.** *GE* Arthur Brauss, Erika Pluhar, Kai Fischer; *D:* Wim Wenders. *FCT, GLV, INJ*

Goblin *Woof!* **1993** Newlywed couple regret the purchase of their new home when the devilish creature once brought to life by the previous homeowner, a witchcraft performing farmer, is raised from the depths of hell to rip to pieces anyone in its view. Any movie whose promo says "You won't believe your eyes...until he rips them from their sockets" is sure to be a crowd pleaser. Enjoy. **75m/C VHS.** Bobby Westrick, Jenny Admire. *TEM*

God Bless the Child **1988** A young single mother loses her home and she and her seven-year-old daughter are forced to live on the streets. Harrowing made for television drama providing no easy answers to the plight of the homeless. **93m/C VHS.** Mare Winningham, Dorian Harewood, Grace Johnston, Charlaine Woodard, Obba Babatunde, L. Scott Caldwell; *D:* Larry Elikann; *W:* Dennis Nemec; *M:* David Shire. *WOV*

God, Man and Devil ½ **1949** A wager between God and Satan begins this allegory of money versus the spirit. A poor Torah scribe, Hershele Dubrovner, has a life that glorifies God until Satan, disguised as a business partner, turns him greedy and dishonest. Dubrovner's success destroys both his religion and his community leaving only betrayal and abandonment. In Yiddish with English subtitles. **100m/B VHS.** Mikhal Mikhalesko, Gustav Berger; *D:* Joseph Seiden. *NCJ*

God Told Me To ½ *Demon* **1976 (R)** A religious New York cop is embroiled in occult mysteries while investigating a series of grisly murders. He investigates a religious cult that turns out to be composed of half-human, half-alien beings. A cult-fave Larry Cohen epic. **89m/C VHS, Beta, LV.** Tony LoBianco, Deborah Raffin, Sylvia Sidney, Sandy Dennis, Richard Lynch; *D:* Larry Cohen; *W:* Larry Cohen. *NLC*

Godard/Truffaut Shorts **1958** A pair of early shorts directed by two French "new wave" masters: Jean-Luc Godard's "All the Boys Are Called Patrick" from 1957 and Francois Truffaut's "Les Mistons" from 1958. **39m/B VHS, Beta.** *FR* *D:* Francois Truffaut, Jean-Luc Godard. *DVT, MRV, INJ*

The Goddess **1958** Sordid story of a girl who rises to fame as a celluloid star by making her body available to anyone who can help her career. When the spotlight dims, she keeps going with drugs and alcohol to a bitter end. **105m/B VHS, Beta, LV.** Kim Stanley, Lloyd Bridges, Patty Duke; *D:* John Cromwell; *W:* Paddy Chayefsky. Nominations: Academy Awards '58: Best Story & Screenplay. *NO*

The Godfather **1972 (R)** Coppola's award-winning adaptation of Mario Puzo's novel about a fictional Mafia family in the late 1940s. Revenge, envy, and parent-child conflict mix with the rituals of Italian mob life in America. Minutely detailed, with excellent performances by Pacino, Brando, and Caan as the violence-prone Sonny. Film debut of Coppola's daughter Sophia, the infant in the baptism scene, who returns in "Godfather III." The horrific horse scene is an instant chiller. Indisputably an instant piece of American culture. Followed by two sequels. **171m/C VHS, Beta, LV, 8mm.** Marlon Brando, Al Pacino, Robert Duvall, James Caan, Diane Keaton, John Cazale, Talia Shire, Richard Conte, Richard Castellano, Abe Vigoda, Alex Rocco, Sterling Hayden, John Marley, Al Lettieri, Sofia Coppola, Al Martino, Morgana King; ***D:*** Francis Ford Coppola; ***W:*** Mario Puzo, Francis Ford Coppola; ***C:*** Gordon Willis; ***M:*** Nino Rota. Academy Awards '72: Best Actor (Brando), Best Adapted Screenplay, Best Picture; Directors Guild of America Awards '72: Best Director (Coppola); Golden Globe Awards '73: Best Actor—Drama (Brando), Best Director (Coppola), Best Film—Drama, Best Screenplay, Best Score; National Board of Review Awards '72: 10 Best Films of the Year, Best Supporting Actor (Pacino); National Society of Film Critics Awards '72: Best Actor (Pacino); Writers Guild of America '72: Best Adapted Screenplay; Nominations: Academy Awards '72: Best Costume Design, Best Director (Coppola), Best Film Editing, Best Sound, Best Supporting Actor (Caan, Duvall, Pacino). *PAR, BTV*

The Godfather 1902-1959: The Complete Epic 🦴🦴🦴🦴 **1981** Coppola's epic work concerning the lives of a New York crime family. Comprises the first two "Godfather" films, reedited into a chronological framework of the Corleone family history, with much previously discarded footage restored. **386m/C VHS, Beta.** Marlon Brando, Al Pacino, Robert Duvall, James Caan, Richard Castellano, Diane Keaton, Robert De Niro, John Cazale, Lee Strasberg, Talia Shire, Michael V. Gazzo, Troy Donahue, Joe Spinell, Abe Vigoda, Alex Rocco, Sterling Hayden, John Marley, Richard Conte, G.D. Spradlin, Bruno Kirby, Harry Dean Stanton, Roger Corman, Al Lettieri; ***D:*** Francis Ford Coppola; ***W:*** Mario Puzo, Francis Ford Coppola; ***M:*** Nino Rota. *PAR, FCT*

The Godfather, Part 2 🦴🦴🦴🦴 **1974 (R)** A continuation and retracing of the first film, interpolating the maintenance of the Corleone family by the aging Michael, and its founding by the young Vito (De Niro, in a terrific performance) 60 years before in New York City's Little Italy. Often considered the second half of one film, the two films stand as one of American film's greatest efforts, and as a 1970s high-water mark. Combined into one work for television presentation. Followed by a sequel. **200m/C VHS, Beta, LV, 8mm.** Al Pacino, Robert De Niro, Diane Keaton, Robert Duvall, James Caan, Danny Aiello, John Cazale, Lee Strasberg, Talia Shire, Michael V. Gazzo, Troy Donahue, Joe Spinell, Abe Vigoda, Marianna Hill, Fay Spain, G.D. Spradlin, Bruno Kirby, Harry Dean Stanton, Roger Corman, Kathleen Beller, John Aprea, Morgana King; ***D:*** Francis Ford Coppola; ***W:*** Mario Puzo, Francis Ford Coppola; ***C:*** Gordon Willis; ***M:*** Nino Rota, Carmine Coppola. Academy Awards '74: Best Adapted Screenplay, Best Art Direction/Set Decoration, Best Director (Coppola), Best Picture, Best Supporting Actor (De Niro), Best Original Score; Directors Guild of America Awards '74: Best Director (Coppola); National Society of Film Critics Awards '74: Best Director (Coppola); Writers Guild of America '74: Best Adapted Screenplay; Nominations: Academy Awards '74: Best Actor (Pacino), Best Costume Design, Best Supporting Actor (Gazzo, Strasberg), Best Supporting Actress (Shire). *PAR, BTV*

The Godfather, Part 3 🦴🦴🦴 **1990 (R)** Don Corleone (Pacino), now aging and guilt-ridden, determines to buy his salvation by investing in the Catholic Church, which he finds to be a more corrupt brotherhood than his own. Meanwhile, back on the homefront, his young daughter discovers her sexuality as she falls in love with her first cousin. Weakest entry of the trilogy is still a stunning and inevitable conclusion to the story; Pacino adds exquisite finishing touches to his time-worn character. Beautifully photographed in Italy by Gordon Willis. Video release contains the final director's cut featuring nine minutes of footage not included in the theatrical release. **170m/C VHS, Beta, LV, 8mm.** Al Pacino, Diane Keaton, Andy Garcia, Joe Mantegna, George Hamilton, Talia Shire, Sofia Coppola, Eli Wallach, Don Novello, Bridget Fonda, John Savage, Al Martino, Raf Vallone, Franc D'Ambrosio, Donal Donnelly, Richard Bright, Helmut Berger; ***D:*** Francis Ford Coppola; ***W:*** Mario Puzo, Francis Ford Coppola; ***C:*** Gordon Willis; ***M:*** Nino Rota, Carmine Coppola. Golden Raspberry Awards '90: Worst Supporting Actress (Coppola), Worst New Star (Coppola); Nominations: Academy Awards '90: Best Art Direction/Set Decoration, Best Cinematography, Best Director (Coppola), Best Film Editing, Best Picture, Best Song ("Promise Me You'll Remember"), Best Supporting Actor (Garcia). *PAR, FCT*

God's Bloody Acre *Woof!* **1975 (R)** Three backwoods mountain-dwelling brothers kill construction workers in order to defend their land, and then begin preying on vacationers. **90m/C VHS, Beta.** Scott Lawrence, Jennifer Gregory, Sam Moree, Shiang Hwa Chyang; ***D:*** Harry Kerwin. *TWE*

God's Country 🦴🦴 **1946** A loner kills a man in self-defense and escapes the pursuing law by disappearing into California Redwood country with his dog. **62m/C VHS, Beta, LV.** Robert Lowery, Helen Gilbert, William Farnum, Buster Keaton; ***D:*** Robert Emmett Tansey. *NO*

God's Country and the Man 🦴🦴 **1937** Typical western adventurer about a cowboy out to nab a gunman who's been threatening the life of a dance hall girl. Plenty of two-fisted action when law-abiding Keene shows up. **56m/B VHS.** Tom Keene, Betty Compson, Charlotte Henry, Charles "Blackie" King, Billy Bletcher, Ed Parker; ***D:*** Robert North Bradbury; ***W:*** Robert Emmett. *MOV*

God's Gun 🦴 *A Bullet from God* **1975 (R)** Preacher who was once a gunfighter seeks revenge on the men who tried to kill him. **93m/C VHS, Beta.** Richard Boone, Lee Van Cleef, Jack Palance, Sybil Danning; ***D:*** Frank Kramer. *CCB*

God's Little Acre 🦴🦴🦴 **1958** Delves into the unexpectedly passionate lives of Georgia farmers. One man, convinced there's buried teasure on his land, nearly brings himself and his family to ruin trying to find it. Based on the novel by Erskine Caldwell. **110m/B VHS, Beta.** Robert Ryan, Tina Louise, Michael Landon, Buddy Hackett, Vic Morrow, Jack Lord, Aldo Ray, Fay Spain; ***D:*** Anthony Mann; ***W:*** Philip Yordan; ***M:*** Elmer Bernstein. *PSM, VEC*

The Gods Must Be Crazy 🦴🦴🦴½ **1984 (PG)** An innocent and charming film. A peaceful Bushman travels into the civilized world to return a Coke bottle "to the gods." Along the way he meets a transplanted schoolteacher, an oafishly clumsy microbiologist and a gang of fanatical terrorists. A very popular film, disarmingly crammed with slapstick and broad humor of every sort. Followed by a weak sequel. **109m/C VHS, Beta, LV.** N!xau, Marius Weyers, Sandra Prinsloo, Louw Verwey, Jamie Uys, Michael Thys, Nic de Jager; ***D:*** Jamie Uys; ***M:*** Johnny Bishop, John Boshoff. *FOX, FCT, TVC*

The Gods Must Be Crazy 2 🦴🦴½ **1989 (PG)** A slapdash sequel to the original 1981 African chortler, featuring more ridiculous shenanigans in the bush. This time the bushman's children find themselves in civilization and N!xau must use his unique ingenuity to secure their safe return. **90m/C VHS, Beta, LV.** N!xau, Lena Farugia, Hans Strydom, Eiros Nadies, Eric Bowen; ***D:*** Jamie Uys; ***M:*** Charles Fox. *COL, TTC, FCT*

Gods of the Plague 🦴🦴🦴 *Gotter der Pest* **1969** Fassbinder goes noir—or grey with lots of sharp lighting—in this gangster-auteur tale of robbery gone awry. The requisite trappings of the crime genre (guys and dolls and cops and robbers) provide a vague backdrop (and a vague plot) for a moody story full of teutonic angst and alienation, and that certain Fassbinder feeling (which, need we say, isn't to everyone's taste). An early effort by the director, who remade the story later the same year as "The American Soldier" (Fassbinder acts in both). In German with (difficult-to-read) English subtitles. **92m/C VHS.** *GE* Hanna Schygulla, Harry Bear; ***D:*** Rainer Werner Fassbinder. *TPV, INJ*

The Godsend 🦴 **1979 (R)** "Omen" rip-off about a little girl who is thrust upon a couple. After adopting her, they lose their natural family to her evil ways. **93m/C VHS, Beta.** *CA* Cyd Hayman, Malcolm Stoddard, Angela Pleasence, Patrick Barr; ***D:*** Gabrielle Beaumont. *VES*

Godson 🦴🦴🦴 **1972** Emotionless assassin lives a barren life under the surveillance of Paris police who suspect him in a recent killing. He suddenly discovers that his boss has a contract out on his life. Delon's performance raises this to an above-average crime drama. **103m/C VHS.** *FR* Alain Delon, Nathalie Delon, Francois Perier; ***D:*** Jean-Pierre Melville. *PSV*

Godzilla, King of the Monsters 🦴🦴½ *Gojira* **1956** An underwater prehistoric reptile emerges from the depths to terrorize Tokyo after he has been awakened by atomic testing. Burr's scenes are intercut in the American version, where he serves as a narrator telling the monster's tale in flashbacks. Ridiculously primitive special effects even in its own day. One of the first post-WWII Japanese films to break through commercially in the U.S. **80m/B VHS, Beta, LV.** *JP* Raymond Burr, Takashi Shimura; ***D:*** Terry Morse. *PAR, VES*

Godzilla 1985 🦴½ **1985 (PG)** Godzilla is awakened from underwater slumber by trolling nuclear submarines belonging to the superpowers near Japan. The giant monster's newly acquired appetite for nuclear energy inadvertently precipitates an international incident. Burr is called in (as the only living American witness to Godzilla's destructive 1955 outburst) to help mediate the conflict. Film released to coincide with the 30th anniversary of the original. **91m/C VHS, Beta, LV.** *JP* Raymond Burr, Keiju Kobayashi, Ken Tanaka, Yasuka Sawaguchi; ***D:*** Kohji Hashimoto, Robert J. Kizer. *NWV, VTR*

Godzilla on Monster Island 🦴🦴 *Godzilla vs. Gigan* **1972** Even Godzilla himself cannot hope to take on both Ghidra and Gigan alone and hope to succeed. Therefore he summons his pal Angillus for help. Together, they offer Earth its only hope of survival. Though the terror may repel you, the movie is a must for Godzilla fans; it's his first speaking part. **89m/C VHS.** *JP* Hiroshi Ichikawa, Tomoko Umeda, Yuriko Hishimi, Minoru Takashima, Zan Fujita; ***D:*** Jun Fukuda. *SNC, MRV, NWV*

Godzilla Raids Again 🦴🦴 *Gigantis, the Fire Monster; Godzilla's Counter Attack* **1959** Warner Bros. had a problem securing rights to Godzilla's name. Yearning for a change of pace, the King of Monsters opts to destroy Osaka instead of Tokyo, but the spiny Angorous is out to dethrone our hero. Citizens flee in terror when the battle royale begins. The first Godzilla sequel. **78m/B VHS.** *JP* Hugo Grimaldi, Makayama, Minoru Chiaki. *VTR*

Godzilla vs. Biollante 🦴🦴 **1989 (PG)** Doctor Surigama's secret plant formula could free the industrialized world from oil dependency. He also runs his pet Godzilla experiment from the same laboratory. When terrorist thieves attempt to steal the plant formula, a petri dish mixup unleashes the abominable fury of Biollante. The return of the real Godzilla is the world's only hope, but not before another Japanese city is crushed in the reptilian rumble. **104m/C VHS.** *JP* ***D:*** Kazuki Ohmori; ***W:*** Kazuki Ohmori. *NO*

Godzilla vs. Megalon 🦴½ *Gojira Tai Megaro* **1976 (G)** Godzilla's creators show their gratitude to misguided but faithful American audiences by transforming the giant monster into a good guy. This time, the world is threatened by Megalon, the giant cockroach, and Gigan, a flying metal creature, simultaneously. Fortuneately, the slippery hero's robot pal Jet Jaguar is on hand to slug it out side by side with Tokyo's ultimate defender. **80m/C VHS.** *JP* Katsuhiko Sasakai, Hiroyuki Kawase, Yutaka Hayashi, Robert Dunham; ***D:*** Jun Fukuda. *NOS, MRV, NWV*

Godzilla vs. Monster Zero 🦴🦴 *Monster Zero; Battle of the Astros; Invasion of the Astro-Monsters; Invasion of the Astros; Invasion of Planet X; Kaiju Daisenso* **1968 (G)** Novel Godzilla adventure with the big guy and Rodan in outer space. Suspicious denizens of Planet X require the help of Godzilla and Rodan to rid themselves of the menacing Ghidra, whom they refer to as Monster Zero. Will they, in return, help Earth as promised, or is this just one big, fat double cross? **93m/C VHS, Beta.** *JP* Nick Adams; ***D:*** Inoshiro Honda. *PAR, FUS*

Godzilla vs. Mothra ☙☙ *Godzilla vs. the Thing; Godzilla vs. the Giant Moth; Godzilla Fights the Giant Moth; Mothra vs. Godzilla; Mosura Tai Goira* **1964** Mighty Mothra is called in to save the populace from Godzilla, who is on a rampage; and he's aided by two junior Mothras who hatch in the nick of time. The hesitant moth avoids the fire-breathing behemoth until succumbing to the pleadings of the Peanut Sisters to save humanity. Hilarious special effects inspire more laughter from derision than anything else. **88m/C VHS, Beta.** *JP* Akira Takarada, Yuriko Hoshi, Hiroshi Koizumi; ***D:*** Inoshiro Honda. *PAR, FUS*

Godzilla vs. the Cosmic Monster ☙☙ *Godzilla Versus the Bionic Monster; Godzilla vs. Mechagodzilla; Gojira Tai Meka-Gojira* **1974 (G)** Godzilla's worst nightmares become a reality as he is forced to take on the one foe he cannot defeat - a metal clone of himself! To make matters worse, Earth is in dire peril at the hands of cosmic apes. We all need friends, and Godzilla is never more happy to see his buddy King Seeser, who gladly lends a claw. **80m/C VHS.** *JP* Masaki Daimon, Kazuya Aoyama, Reiko Tajima, Barbara Lynn, Akihiko Hirata; ***D:*** Jun Fukuda. *NWV, MRV, VYY*

Godzilla vs. the Sea Monster *Woof! Nankai No Kai Ketto; Ebirah, Terror of the Deep; Big Duel in the North* **1966** Godzilla makes friends with former rival Mothra (a giant moth) and together they bash on Ebirah, an enormous lobster backed by an evil cadre of (human) totalitarians. The unrepentant crusteacean turns the tables on our heroes, however, by growing a new tentacle everytime one is ripped off. Meanwhile, a frenzied batch of helpless humans are trapped on an island about to explode, if they aren't drowned first in a shower of reptilian backwash. **80m/C VHS, Beta.** *JP* ***D:*** Jun Fukuda. *DVT, MRV, HHT*

Godzilla vs. the Smog Monster ☙ *Gojira Tai Hedora; Godzilla vs. Hedora* **1972 (G)** Godzilla battles a creature borne of pollution, a 400-pound sludge blob named Hedora. Early 1970's period piece conveys interesting attitude towards pollution; it's treated as a sinister force that people are powerless to stop. Japanese teenagers marshal their dancing talents to combat the threat amid the hypnotic swirl of disco lighting. Great opening song: "Save the Earth." Dubbed in English. **87m/C VHS, Beta.** *JP* Akira Yamauchi, Hiroyuki Kawase, Toshio Shibaki; ***D:*** Yoshimitu Banno. *ORI*

Godzilla's Revenge ☙ *Oru Kaiju Daishingeki* **1969** A young boy who is having problems dreams of going to Monster Island to learn from Minya, Godzilla's son. Using the lessons in real life, the boy captures some bandits and outwits a bully. Uses footage from "Godzilla vs. the Sea Monster" and "Son of Godzilla" for battle scenes. One of the silliest Godzilla movies around. **70m/C VHS.** *JP* Kenji Sahara, Tomonori Yazaki, Machiko Naka, Sachio Sakai, Chotaro Togin, Yoshibumi Tajima; ***D:*** Inoshiro Honda. *NO*

Goetz von Berlichingen ☙☙ *Iron Hand* **1980** During the reign of Emperor Maximilian, a brave knight fights injustice in the service of the Emperor and becomes a hunted man. In German with English subtitles. **100m/C VHS, Beta.** *GE VCD, GLV*

Goin' Coconuts ☙ **1978 (PG)** Donny and Marie are miscast as Donny and Marie in this smarmy story of crooks and jewels. Seems someone covets the chanteuse's necklace, and only gratuitous crooning can spare the twosome from certain swindling. Big bore on the big island. **93m/C VHS.** Donny Osmond, Marie Osmond, Herb Edelman, Kenneth Mars, Ted Cassidy, Marc Lawrence, Harold Sakata; ***D:*** Howard Morris. *NO*

Goin' South ☙☙☙ **1978 (PG)** An outlaw is saved from being hanged by a young woman who agrees to marry him in exchange for his help working a secret gold mine. They try to get the loot before his old gang gets wind of it. A tongue-in-cheek western that served as Nicholson's second directorial effort. Movie debuts of Steenburgen and Belushi. **109m/C VHS, Beta, LV.** Jack Nicholson, Mary Steenburgen, John Belushi, Christopher Lloyd, Veronica Cartwright, Richard Bradford, Danny DeVito, Luana Anders, Ed Begley Jr., Anne Ramsey; ***D:*** Jack Nicholson; ***W:*** Charles Shyer; ***M:*** Perry Botkin. *PAR*

Goin' to Town ☙☙½ **1935** Complicated yarn with West as a woman who inherits an oil field and becomes the wealthiest woman in the state. She falls for British engineer Cavanagh and decides to become a "lady" in order to get his attention. There's a subplot about Buenos Aires and a crooked horse race, an in-name-only marriage to a high society type, and a murder before Mae finally gets her man. **71m/B VHS.** Mae West, Paul Cavanagh, Gilbert Emery, Ivan Lebedeff, Marjorie Gateson, Tito Coral, Monroe Owsley; ***D:*** Alexander Hall; ***W:*** Mae West; ***C:*** Karl Struss. *MCA, BTV*

Going Ape! ☙☙ **1981 (PG)** Danza inherits a bunch of orangutans. If the apes are treated well, a legacy of $5 million will follow. This is all you need to know. **87m/C VHS, Beta.** Tony Danza, Jessica Walter, Danny DeVito, Art Metrano, Rick Hurst; ***D:*** Jeremy Joe Kronsberg; ***M:*** Elmer Bernstein. *PAR*

Going Back ☙½ **1983** Four friends reunite after college to relive a memorable summer they spent together after graduating from high school. **85m/C VHS, Beta.** Bruce Campbell, Christopher Howe, Perry Mallette, Susan W. Yamasaki; ***D:*** Ron Teachworth. *LIV, VES*

Going Bananas ☙☙ **1988 (PG)** Wacky adventure about a chimp who is being chased by a sinister circus owner. The monkey runs through Africa dragging along a boy, his caretaker, and a guide. The cast says it all. **95m/C VHS, Beta.** Dom DeLuise, Jimmie Walker, David Mendenhall, Herbert Lom; ***D:*** Boaz Davidson. *MED, VTR*

Going Berserk ☙½ **1983 (R)** The members of SCTV's television comedy troupe are featured in this comedy which lampoons everything from religious cults to kung fu movies to "Father Knows Best." Should have been more fun. **85m/C VHS, Beta, LV.** *CA* John Candy, Joe Flaherty, Eugene Levy, Paul Dooley, Pat Hingle, Richard Libertini, Ernie Hudson; ***D:*** David Steinberg. *MCA*

Going for the Gold: The Bill Johnson Story ☙☙ **1985** Biographical tale of the American downhill skier who went from hard-luck punk to Olympic champion in the 1984 games at Sarajevo, Yugoslavia. **100m/C VHS.** Anthony Edwards, Dennis Weaver, Sarah Jessica Parker, Deborah Van Valkenburgh, Wayne Northrop; ***D:*** Don Taylor. *COL*

Going Hollywood ☙☙☙ **1933** Amusing musical/romantic fluff about a French teacher (Davies) who falls in love with a radio crooner (Crosby in his first MGM film). He's got the movie bug and heads for Hollywood, where he becomes an overnight sensation with a sultry costar (D'Orsay). Davies follows and proceeds to get Crosby out of D'Orsay's clutches and winds up replacing her rival in the film, promptly becoming a star herself. The underrated Davies was a fine light comedienne and supplied glamour to the production as well. Kelly, in her film debut, supplied the slapstick. The last Hearst-Cosmopolitan production made with MGM. ♫Temptation; We'll Make Hay While the Sun Shines; Going Hollywood; Our Big Love Scene; After Sundown; Cinderella's Fella; Beautiful Girl; Just an Echo in the Valley. **78m/B VHS.** Marion Davies, Bing Crosby, Fifi d'Orsay, Stuart Erwin, Patsy Kelly, Ned Sparks; ***D:*** Raoul Walsh; ***W:*** Donald Ogden Stewart. *MGM*

Going Home ☙☙½ **1986** During WWI, Canadian soldiers held in British camps awaiting transport back home stage a riot over the endless delays and intolerable conditions. A fact-based story of the events leading up to this tragedy. **100m/C VHS.** Nicholas Campbell, Paul Maxwell, Eugene Lipinski. *NO*

Going in Style ☙☙☙½ **1979 (PG)** Three elderly gentlemen, tired of doing nothing, decide to liven up their lives by pulling a daylight bank stick-up. They don't care about the consequences because anything is better than sitting on a park bench all day long. The real fun begins when they get away with the robbery. Great cast makes this a winner. **91m/C VHS, Beta.** George Burns, Art Carney, Lee Strasberg; ***D:*** Martin Brest; ***W:*** Martin Brest. *WAR*

Going My Way ☙☙☙½ **1944** A musical-comedy about a progressive young priest assigned to a downtrodden parish who works to get the parish out of debt, but clashes with his elderly curate, who's set in his ways. Followed by "The Bells of St. Mary's." Fitzgerald's Oscar-winning Supporting Actor performance was also nominated in the Best Actor category. ♫The Day After Forever; Swinging on a Star; Too-ra-loo-ra-loo-ra; Going My Way; Silent Night; Habanera; Ave Maria. **126m/B VHS, Beta, LV.** Bing Crosby, Barry Fitzgerald, Rise Stevens, Frank McHugh, Gene Lockhart, Porter Hall; ***D:*** Leo McCarey; ***W:*** Frank Butler, Frank Cavett, Leo McCarey; ***C:*** Lionel Lindon. Academy Awards '44: Best Actor (Crosby), Best Director (McCarey), Best Picture, Best Song ("Swinging on a Star"), Best Story & Screenplay, Best Supporting Actor (Fitzgerald); National Board of Review Awards '44: 10 Best Films of the Year; New York Film Critics Awards '44: Best Actor (Fitzgerald), Best Director (McCarey), Best Film; Nominations: Academy Awards '44: Best Actor (Fitzgerald), Best Black and White Cinematography, Best Film Editing. *MCA, IGP, BTV*

Going Overboard ☙ *Babes Ahoy* **1989 (R)** Cruise ship waiter dreams of becoming a comedian and gets his big break when the ship's comic disappears. **99m/C VHS.** Adam Sandler, Burt Young, Billy Zane, Peter Berg; ***D:*** Valerie Breiman. *VMK*

Going Places ☙☙☙ *Les Valseuses; Making It* **1974 (R)** A cynical, brutal satire about two young thugs traversing the French countryside raping, looting and cavorting as they please. Moreau has a brief role as an ex-con trying to go straight. An amoral, controversial comedy that established both its director and two stars. In French with English subtitles or dubbed. **122m/C VHS, Beta, LV.** *FR* Gerard Depardieu, Patrick Dewaere, Miou-Miou, Isabelle Huppert, Jeanne Moreau, Brigitte Fossey; ***D:*** Bertrand Blier; ***W:*** Bertrand Blier. *COL, INT, INJ*

Going to Congress/Don't Park There **1924** Two typical silent Rogers shorts. With original organ score. **57m/B VHS, Beta, 8mm.** Will Rogers. *VYY*

Going to Town ☙ **1944** Radio team Lum and Abner in one of their last films, as two conmen who scheme to make money from a phony oil well. **77m/B VHS, Beta.** Barbara Hale, Grady Sutton, Florence Lake. *GVV*

Going Under **1991 (PG)** Subsurface military satire about the U.S.S. Sub Standard, the worst nuclear vessel in the Navy. It's so poorly constructed that the brass would rather sink than inspect it - if only they could. Interesting cast sinks with script headed for dry dock. **81m/C VHS, Beta.** Bill Pullman, Wendy Schaal, Ned Beatty, Robert Vaughn, Bud Cort, Michael Winslow. *WAR*

Going Undercover ☙ **1988 (PG-13)** A bumbling private investigator is hired to protect a rich, beautiful, and spoiled young woman on her European vacation. Poor excuse for a comedy. **90m/C VHS, Beta, LV.** Lea Thompson, Jean Simmons, Chris Lemmon; ***D:*** James Kenelm Clarke. *VMK*

The Gold & Glory ☙ **1988 (PG-13)** Two brothers, one a musician, the other an athlete, vie for the affections of the same girl by competing in a footrace for a golden purse. **102m/C VHS, Beta, LV.** Colin Friels, Josephine Smulders, Grant Kenny. *LIV*

Gold Diggers of 1933 ☙☙☙½ **1933** In this famous period musical, showgirls help a songwriter save his Busby Berkeley-choreographed show. Followed by two sequels. ♫We're in the Money; Shadow Waltz; I've Got to Sing a Torch Song; Pettin' in the Park; Remember My Forgotten Man. **96m/B VHS, Beta, LV.** Joan Blondell, Ruby Keeler, Aline MacMahon, Dick Powell, Guy Kibbee, Warren William, Ned Sparks, Ginger Rogers; ***D:*** Mervyn LeRoy. Nominations: Academy Awards '33: Best Sound. *MGM, FOX*

Gold Diggers of 1935 🦴🦴🦴 **1935** The second Gold Diggers film, having something to do with a New England resort, romance, and a charity show put on at the hotel. Plenty of Berkeleian large-scale drama, especially the bizarre, mock-tragic "Lullaby on Broadway" number, which details the last days of a Broadway baby. ♫I'm Going Shopping With You; The Words Are in My Heart; Lullaby of Broadway. **95m/B VHS, Beta, LV.** Dick Powell, Adolphe Menjou, Gloria Stuart, Alice Brady, Frank McHugh, Glenda Farrell, Grant Mitchell, Hugh Herbert, Wini Shaw; ***D:*** Busby Berkeley; ***C:*** George Barnes. *MGM, MLB*

Gold Diggers: The Secret of Bear Mountain 🦴🦴½ **1995 (PG)** Thirteen-year-old Beth (Ricci) moves to the small town of Wheaton, Washington and forms an unlikely friendship with rebellious tomboy Jody (Chlumsky). Together, the girls set out on a treasure hunt that takes them into a dangerous trek through sea-coast mountain terrain. The grownups are dumb (and the story's fairly boring) but the two heroines have real appeal. **94m/C VHS, LV.** Christina Ricci, Anna Chlumsky, Polly Draper, Brian Kerwin, Diana Scarwid, David Keith; ***D:*** Kevin J. Dobson; ***W:*** Barry Glasser; ***C:*** Ross Berryman; ***M:*** Joel McNeely. *MCA*

The Gold of Naples 🦴🦴🦴 *L'Oro Di Napoli* **1954** A four-part omnibus film about life in Naples, filled with romance and family tragedies, by turns poignant, funny and pensive. Originally six tales; two were trimmed for U.S. release. In Italian with subtitles. **107m/B VHS, Beta.** *IT* Vittorio De Sica, Eduardo de Filippo, Paolo Stoppa, Sophia Loren, Silvana Mangano; ***D:*** Vittorio De Sica. *NOS, FCT, APD*

Gold of the Amazon Women 🦴 *Amazon Women* **1979** When two explorers set out to find gold, they stumble onto a society of man-hungry women who follow them into the urban jungle of Manhattan. Made for television. There is also a European "R" rated version. **94m/C VHS, Beta.** Bo Svenson, Anita Ekberg, Bond Gideon, Donald Pleasence; ***D:*** Mark L. Lester. *SUE*

Gold Raiders 🦴 **1951** Larry, Moe, and Shemp team up with an insurance agent to take on the bad guys in the wild west. The Stooges are long past their prime. **56m/B VHS.** George O'Brien, Moe Howard, Moe Howard, Shemp Howard, Larry Fine, Sheila Ryan, Clem Bevans, Lyle Talbot; ***D:*** Edward L. Bernds. *MED*

Gold Raiders 🦴½ **1984** Team of secret agents are sent to the Jungles of Laos to find a plane carrying $200 million worth of gold, and nothing will get in their way. **106m/C VHS, Beta.** Robert Ginty, Sarah Langenfeld, William Steven. *MED*

The Gold Rush 🦴🦴🦴🦴 **1925** Chaplin's most critically acclaimed film. The best definition of his simple approach to film form; adept maneuvering of visual pathos. The "Little Tramp" searches for gold and romance in the Klondike in the mid-1800s. Includes the dance of the rolls, pantomime sequence of eating the shoe, and Chaplin's lovely music. **85m/B VHS, Beta, LV, 8mm.** Charlie Chaplin, Mack Swain, Tom Murray, Georgia Hale; ***D:*** Charlie Chaplin. *CNG, NOS, CAB*

Gold Rush/Payday **1925** Chaplin drifts along the Arctic tundra, searching for gold and love in "The Gold Rush." In "Payday," he goes out drinking with his buddies. **92m/B VHS, Beta.** Charlie Chaplin, Georgia Hale, Mack Swain; ***D:*** Charlie Chaplin. *FOX*

Golden Age of Comedy **1958** The great comedians of silent cinema are seen in clips from some of their funniest films. **78m/B VHS, Beta, LV.** Ben Turpin, Harry Langdon, Will Rogers, Jean Harlow, Carole Lombard, Stan Laurel, Oliver Hardy, The Keystone Cops. *MLB*

Golden Age of Hollywood **1977** This episode of "Life Goes to the Movies" examines Hollywood as it quickly became the ultimate dream factory, providing escape from the grimness of the depression. **34m/C VHS, Beta.** Henry Fonda, Shirley MacLaine. *TLF*

Golden Boy 🦴🦴🦴 **1939** Holden plays a young and gifted violinist who earns money for his musical education by working as a part-time prizefighter. Fight promoter Menjou has Stanwyck cozy up to the impressionable young man to convince him to make the fight game his prime concern. She's successful but it leads to tragedy. Holden's screen debut, with Cobb as his immigrant father and Stanwyck successfully slinky as the corrupting love interest. Classic pugilistic drama with well-staged fight scenes. Based on Clifford Odets' play with toned down finale. **99m/B VHS, Beta, LV.** William Holden, Adolphe Menjou, Barbara Stanwyck, Lee J. Cobb, Joseph Calleia, Sam Levene, Don Beddoe, Charles Halton; ***D:*** Rouben Mamoulian; ***W:*** Daniel Taradash, Victor Heerman, Sarah Y. Mason. Nominations: Academy Awards '39: Best Original Score. *GKK*

The Golden Child 🦴🦴 **1986 (PG-13)** When a Tibetan child with magic powers is kidnapped and transported to Los Angeles, Chandler, a professional "finder of lost children" must come to the rescue. The search takes him through Chinatown in a hunt that cliches every Oriental swashbuckler ever made. Good fun. **94m/C VHS, Beta, LV, 8mm.** Eddie Murphy, Charlotte Lewis, Charles Dance, Victor Wong, Randall "Tex" Cobb, James Hong; ***D:*** Michael Ritchie; ***M:*** Michel Colombier. *PAR*

The Golden Coach 🦴🦴🦴 *Le Carrosse D'Or* **1952** Based on a play by Prosper Merimee, the tale of an 18th-century actress in Spanish South America who takes on all comers, including the local viceroy who creates a scandal by presenting her with his official coach. Rare cinematography by Claude Renoir. **101m/C VHS, Beta, LV.** *FR* Anna Magnani, Odoardo Spadaro, Nada Fiorelli, Dante Rino, Duncan Lamont; ***D:*** Jean Renoir. *FCT, CRC, INT*

Golden Demon 🦴🦴½ *Konjiki Yasha* **1953** An acclaimed Japanese epic, from the novel by Koyo Ozaki, about the destructive powers of wealth on the lives of two star-crossed lovers in medieval Japan. In Japanese with English subtitles. **95m/C VHS, Beta.** *JP* Jun Negami, Fujiko Yamamoto; ***D:*** Koji Shima. *SUE, NLC, INJ*

Golden Earrings 🦴🦴½ **1947** Enjoyable, yet incredulous story about British agent Milland joining up with gypsy Dietrich for espionage work. Absurd film was so bad it became a camp classic overnight. Although Dietrich and Milland couldn't stand each other and battled constantly during production, the movie did quite well at the box office. Based on a novel by Yolanda Foldes. **95m/B VHS.** Ray Milland, Marlene Dietrich, Bruce Lester, Dennis Hoey, Quentin Reynolds, Reinhold Schunzel, Ivan Triesault, Mitchell Leisen; ***W:*** Abraham Polonsky, Frank Butler, Helen Deutsch; ***C:*** Daniel F. Fapp. *MCA, FCT*

Golden Exterminators 🦴 **197?** Two brothers battle the forces of evil who have killed their martial arts master with the heels of their formidable feet. **86m/C VHS, Beta.** Raymond Chan. *UNI*

Golden Gate 🦴🦴 **1993 (R)** Young Fed Dillon is thrown into the hysteria of the communist witch hunt in 1952 San Francisco. He snares Song, a Chinese labor activist, on some very dubious charges. Ten years later he finds himself getting involved with Song's daughter Marilyn (Chen), who knows nothing about her lover's involvement with her family. Then she finds out. Everchanging moods, sometimes film noir, sometimes a love story, sometimes a nostalgic look back, are confusing. Promising storyline meanders and fades as Director Madden tries to do too much in a short time. Beware of broad stereotypes in every character. **95m/C VHS, LV.** Matt Dillon, Joan Chen, Bruno Kirby, Teri Polo, Tzi Ma, Stan Egi, Peter Murnik; ***D:*** John Madden; ***W:*** David Henry Hwang; ***M:*** Elliot Goldenthal. *TOU*

Golden Lady 🦴½ **1979** Beautiful woman leads her female gang in a deadly game of international intrigue. **90m/C VHS, Beta.** Christina World, Suzanne Danielle, June Chadwick; ***D:*** Joseph Larraz. *NO*

Golden Ninja Warrior 🦴 **198?** Lady ninjas endeavor to capture a golden statue and gain superiority over chauvinists everywhere. **92m/C VHS, Beta.** *TWE*

Golden Rendezvous 🦴🦴 *Nuclear Terror* **1977** A tale of treachery aboard a "gambler's paradise" luxury liner which is hijacked and held for ransom. Based on Alistair MacLean's novel. **103m/C VHS, Beta.** Richard Harris, David Janssen, John Carradine, Burgess Meredith, Ann Turkel, John Vernon; ***D:*** Ashley Lazarus. *VES*

The Golden Salamander 🦴🦴 **1951** Howard shines in otherwise lackluster adventure about archaeologist searching for ancient ruins in Tunisia who must deal with gun runners and their evil leader, while torridly romancing a beautiful Tunisian girl. Filmed on location in Tunis. Based on the novel by Victor Canning. **96m/B VHS.** *GB* Trevor Howard, Anouk Aimee, Herbert Lom, Miles Malleson, Walter Rilla, Jacques Sernas, Wilfrid Hyde-White, Peter Copely, Eugene Deckers, Henry Edwards, Marcel Poncin, Percy Walsh, Sybilla Binder, Kathleen Boutall, Valentine Dyall; ***D:*** Ronald Neame; ***C:*** Oswald Morris. *FCT*

The Golden Seal 🦴🦴½ **1983 (PG)** Tale of a small boy's innocence put in direct conflict, because of his love of a rare wild golden seal and her pup, with the failed dreams, pride and ordinary greed of adults. **94m/C VHS, Beta, LV, 8mm.** Steve Railsback, Michael Beck, Penelope Milford, Torquil Campbell; ***D:*** Frank Zuniga; ***M:*** John Barry. *SUE*

The Golden Stallion 🦴½ **1949** Trigger falls in love with a stunning mare. He sees her villainous owners abusing her and kills them. Roy takes the blame for his equine pal, but true love triumphs to save the day. **67m/B VHS.** Roy Rogers, Dale Evans, Estelita Rodriguez, Pat Brady, Douglas Evans, Frank Fenton; ***D:*** William Witney. *REP*

Golden Sun 🦴 **198?** Young Kung Fu student decides to investigate the death of his hero, Bruce Lee, and comes up against a sinister conspiracy. **90m/C VHS, Beta.** Lei Hsiao Lung, Chen Pei Ling, Ou-Yang Chung. *UNI*

The Golden Triangle 🦴½ **1980 (PG)** Big battle of the drug pushers set in the mountainous region surrounded by Laos, Thailand, and Burma. Rival gangs fight for control of the world's opium crop. **90m/C VHS, Beta.** Lo Lieh, Sambat Metanen, Tien Ner. *MGI*

Golden Voyage of Sinbad 🦴🦴½ **1973 (G)** In the mysterious ancient land of Lemuria, Sinbad and his crew encounter magical and mystical creatures. A statue of Nirvana comes to life and engages in a sword fight with Sinbad. He later meets up with a one-eyed centaur and a griffin. Ray Harryhausen can once again claim credit for the unusual and wonderful mythical creatures springing to life. **105m/C VHS, Beta, LV.** John Phillip Law, Caroline Munro, Tom Baker, Douglas Wilmer, Martin Shaw, John David Garfield, Gregoire Aslan; ***D:*** Gordon Hessler; ***W:*** Brian Clemens; ***C:*** Ted Moore; ***M:*** Miklos Rozsa. *COL, MLB*

Goldeneye 🦴🦴🦴 **1995 (PG-13)** Bond is back, in the long-awaited (eight years) debut of Brosnan as legendary Brit agent 007. Since we're through the Cold War, Bond has to make do with the villainy of the Russian Mafia, who are planning to sabotage global financial markets utilizing the "Goldeneye" satellite weapon. There's a spectacularly impossible stunt to start things out in familiar territory and lots more noisy (if prolonged) action pieces. Brosnan (who looks great in a tux) is slyly self-aware that his character is more myth than man and Janssen does a suitably over-the-top job as bad Bond girl Xenia Onatopp. Tina Turner sings the dreary title track. **130m/C VHS, LV.** Pierce Brosnan, Famke Janssen, Sean Bean, Izabela Scorupco, Joe Don Baker, Robbie Coltrane, Judi Dench, Tcheky Karyo, Gottfried John, Alan Cumming, Desmond Llewelyn, Michael Kitchen, Serena Gordon, Samantha Bond; ***Cameos:*** Minnie Driver; ***D:*** Martin Campbell; ***W:*** Michael France, Jeffrey Caine; ***C:*** Phil Meheux; ***M:*** Eric Serra. Blockbuster Entertainment Awards '96: Action Actor, Theatrical (Brosnan). *MGM*

Goldengirl **1979 (PG)** A neo-Nazi doctor tries to make a superwoman of his daughter who has been specially fed, exercised, and emotionally conditioned since childhood to run in the Olympics. Anton's starring debut. **107m/C VHS, Beta.** Susan Anton, James Coburn, Curt Jurgens, Robert Culp, Leslie Caron, Harry Guardino, Jessica Walter; ***D:*** Joseph Sargent; ***M:*** Bill Conti. *COL, SUE*

Goldenrod ½ **1977** A successful rodeo champion is forced to reevaluate his life when he sustains a crippling accident in the ring. Made for television. **100m/C VHS, Beta.** *CA* Tony LoBianco, Gloria Carlin, Donald Pleasence, Donnelly Rhodes; ***D:*** Harvey Hart. *PSM*

Goldfinger **1964 (PG)** Ian Fleming's James Bond, Agent 007, attempts to prevent international gold smuggler Goldfinger and his pilot Pussy Galore from robbing Fort Knox. Features villainous assistant Oddjob and his deadly bowler hat. The third in the series is perhaps the most popular. Shirley Bassey sings the theme song. The laserdisc edition includes audio interviews with the director, the writer, the editor, and the production designer; music and sound effects/ dialogue separation; publicity stills, movie posters, trailers, and on-location photos. A treat for Bond fans. **117m/C VHS, Beta, LV.** *GB* Sean Connery, Honor Blackman, Gert Frobe, Shirley Eaton, Tania Mallet, Harold Sakata, Cec Linder, Bernard Lee, Lois Maxwell, Desmond Llewelyn, Nadja Regin; ***D:*** Guy Hamilton; ***C:*** Ted Moore; ***M:*** John Barry. Academy Awards '64: Best Sound Effects Editing. *MGM, CRC, TLF*

Goldilocks & the Three Bears **1983** Entry from "Faerie Tale Theatre" tells the story of Goldilocks, who wanders through the woods and finds the home of three bears—only in this version Goldilocks is a nasty child, and it's the bears who'll get your sympathy. **60m/C VHS, Beta, LV.** Tatum O'Neal, Alex Karras, Brandis Kemp, Donovan Scott, Hoyt Axton, John Lithgow, Carole King; ***D:*** Gilbert Cates. *KUI, FOX, FCT*

The Goldwyn Follies **1938** Lavish disjointed musical comedy about Hollywood. A movie producer chooses a naive girl to give him advice on his movies. George Gershwin died during the filming. ♫Romeo and Juliet; Water Nymph; Here, Pussy, Pussy; Serenade To a Fish; Love Walked In; Love is Here to Stay; Spring Again; I Was Doing Alright; La Serenata. **115m/C VHS, Beta, LV.** Adolphe Menjou, Vera Zorina, The Ritz Brothers, Helen Jepson, Phil Baker, Bobby Clark, Ella Logan, Andrea Leeds, Edgar Bergen; ***D:*** George Marshall; ***C:*** Gregg Toland; ***M:*** George Gershwin, Ira Gershwin. Nominations: Academy Awards '38: Best Interior Decoration, Best Score. *SUE, HBO*

Goldy: The Last of the Golden Bears ½ **1984** Orphaned child and a lonely prospector risk their lives to save a Golden Bear from a circus owner. Followed by "Goldy 2: The Saga of the Golden Bear." **91m/C VHS, Beta.** *LIV, VES*

Goldy 2: The Saga of the Golden Bear **1985** Continues the adventures in the High Sierras of an orphan girl and her friend, the Golden Bear. **96m/C VHS, Beta.** *LIV, VES*

The Golem ½ **1920** A huge clay figure is given life by a rabbi in hopes of saving the Jews in the ghetto of medieval Prague. Rarely seen Wegener expressionist myth-opus that heavily influenced the "Frankenstein" films of the sound era. **80m/B VHS, Beta.** *GE* Paul Wegener, Albert Steinruck, Ernst Deutsch, Syda Salmonava; ***D:*** Paul Wegener. *SNC, NOS, MRV*

Goliath Against the Giants ½ *Goliath Contro I Giganti; Goliat Contra Los Gigantes; Goliath and the Giants* **1963** Goliath takes on Bokan, who has stolen his throne. Goliath must fight Amazons, storms, and sea monsters to save the lovely Elea. Goliath conquers all. **95m/C VHS, Beta.** *IT SP* Brad Harris, Gloria Milland, Fernando Rey, Barbara Carroll; ***D:*** Guido Malatesta. *SNC*

Goliath and the Barbarians *Il Terror Dei Baraberi* **1960** Goliath and his men go after the barbarians who are terrorizing and ravaging the Northern Italian countryside during the fall of the Roman Empire. A basic Reeves muscleman epic. **86m/C VHS, Beta.** *IT* Steve Reeves, Bruce Cabot; ***D:*** Carlo Campogalliani; ***M:*** Les Baxter. *MGM*

Goliath and the Dragon *Woof! La Vendetta De Ercole* **1961** Even Goliath must have doubts as he is challenged by the evil and powerful King Eurystheus. A must for fans of ridiculous movies with ridiculous monsters. **90m/C VHS, Beta.** *IT FR* Bruce Cabot, Mark Forest, Broderick Crawford, Gaby Andre, Leonora Ruffo; ***D:*** Vittorio Cottafavi; ***M:*** Les Baxter. *SNC*

Goliath and the Sins of Babylon *Maciste, L'Eroe Piu Grande Del Mondo* **1964** Well-sculpted Forest plays yet another mesomorph to the rescue in this poorly dubbed spaghetti legend. Goliath must spare twenty-four virgins whom the evil Crisa would submit as human sacrifice. Forest—who played the mythic Maciste in a number of films—was randomly assigned the identity of Goliath, Hercules or Samson for US viewing; go figure. **80m/C VHS.** *IT* Mark Forest, Eleanora Bianchi, Jose Greco, Giuliano Gemma, Paul Muller; ***D:*** Michele Lupo. *SNC*

Goliath Awaits **1981** Harmon plays an oceanographer who discovers a ship that was sunk by German U-boats during WWI. Nothing much new there, except that the survivors still reside on board the vessel, some 40 years after the oceanliner was torpedoed. And get this: they're living a quasi-Utopian existence. Kind of hard to swallow. Made for TV, it originally aired in two parts. **110m/C VHS, LV.** Mark Harmon, Robert Forster, Christopher Lee, Eddie Albert, John Carradine, Alex Cord, Emma Samms, Jean Marsh; ***D:*** Kevin Connor; ***M:*** George Duning. *VMK*

Goliathon *Woof! The Mighty Peking Man* **1979** A ten-story-tall gorilla resides in the jungle and is sought by a group of Hong Kong businessman who want to display the creature. Johnny, the hunter hired to find the beast, discovers both the gorilla and a beautiful jungle goddess. Incredibly campy, with badly dubbed and hilariously awful dialogue. **81m/C VHS.** *HK* Lee Hassen, Evelyn Kraft. *VYY*

Gone are the Days ½ *The Man From C.O.T.T.O.N., Purlie Victorious* **1963** Shaky adaptation of the play, "Purlie Victorious." A black preacher wants to cause the ruin of a white plantation owner. Alda's screen debut. **97m/B VHS, Beta.** Ossie Davis, Ruby Dee, Sorrell Booke, Godfrey Cambridge, Alan Alda, Beah Richards; ***D:*** Nicholas Webster; ***W:*** Ossie Davis; ***C:*** Boris Kaufman. *DIS*

Gone are the Days **1984** Government agent (Korman) is assigned to protect a family who witnessed an underworld shooting, but the family would like to get away from both the mob and the police. Made-for-cable Disney comedy is well-acted but done in by cliches. **90m/C VHS, Beta.** Harvey Korman, Susan Anspach, Robert Hogan; ***D:*** Gabrielle Beaumont. *DIS*

Gone in 60 Seconds ½ **1974** Car thief working for an insurance adjustment firm gets double-crossed by his boss and chased by the police. Forty minutes are consumed by a chase scene which destroyed more than 90 vehicles. **105m/C VHS, Beta.** H.B. Halicki, Marion Busia, George Cole, James McIntyre, Jerry Daugirda; ***D:*** H.B. Halicki. *MED*

Gone to Ground **1976** Mad killer terrorizes a group of vacationers who are trapped in an isolated beach house. **74m/C VHS, Beta.** Charles Tingwell, Elaine Lee, Eric Oldfield, Marion Johns, Robyn Gibbes, Judy Lynne, Dennis Grosvenor, Alan Penney, Marcus Hale. *NO*

Gone with the West ½ **1972** Little Moon and Jud McGraw seek revenge upon the man who stole their cattle. **92m/C VHS, Beta.** James Caan, Stefanie Powers, Sammy Davis Jr., Aldo Ray, Michael Conrad, Michael Walker Jr.; ***D:*** Bernard Giraudeau. *UNI*

Gone with the Wind **1939** Epic Civil War drama focuses on the life of petulant southern belle Scarlett O'Hara. Starting with her idyllic lifestyle on a sprawling plantation, the film traces her survival through the tragic history of the South during the Civil War and Reconstruction, and her tangled love affairs with Ashley Wilkes and Rhett Butler. Classic Hollywood doesn't get any better than this; one great scene after another, equally effective in intimate drama and sweeping spectacle. The train depot scene, one of the more technically adroit shots in movie history, involved hundreds of extras and dummies, and much of the MGM lot was razed to simulate the burning of Atlanta. Based on Margaret Mitchell's novel, screenwriter Howard was assisted by producer Selznick and novelist F. Scott Fitzgerald. For its 50th anniversary, a 231-minute restored version was released that included the trailer for "The Making of a Legend: GWTW." The laserdisc is available in a limited, numbered edition, fully restored to Technicolor from the original negative, with an enhanced soundtrack and seven minutes of rare footage, including the original trailer. **231m/C VHS, Beta, LV.** Clark Gable, Vivien Leigh, Olivia de Havilland, Leslie Howard, Thomas Mitchell, Hattie McDaniel, Butterfly McQueen, Evelyn Keyes, Harry Davenport, Jane Darwell, Ona Munson, Barbara O'Neil, William "Billy" Bakewell, Rand Brooks, Ward Bond, Laura Hope Crews, Yakima Canutt, George Reeves, Marjorie Reynolds, Ann Rutherford, Victor Jory, Carroll Nye, Paul Hurst, Isabel Jewell, Cliff Edwards, Eddie Anderson, Oscar Polk, Eric Linden, Violet Kemble-Cooper; ***D:*** Victor Fleming; ***W:*** Sidney Howard; ***C:*** Ray Rennahan; ***M:*** Max Steiner. Academy Awards '39: Best Actress (Leigh), Best Color Cinematography, Best Director (Fleming), Best Film Editing, Best Interior Decoration, Best Picture, Best Screenplay, Best Supporting Actress (McDaniel); New York Film Critics Awards '39: Best Actress (Leigh); Nominations: Academy Awards '39: Best Actor (Gable), Best Sound, Best Special Effects, Best Supporting Actress (de Havilland), Best Original Score. *MGM, FUS, BTV*

Gonza the Spearman ½ **1986** A gifted samurai lancer is accused of having an affair with the wife of the lord of his province. The lancer must leave to save the woman's honor, because to stay would mean death to them both. In Japanese with English subtitles. **126m/C VHS, LV.** *JP* Hiromi Goh, Shima Iwashita; ***D:*** Masahiro Shinoda. *KIV, INJ*

A Good Day to Die ½ *Children of the Dust* **1995 (R)** Western made-for-TV saga, set during the 1880s land rush of the Oklahoma Territory, and adapted from the novel by Clancy Carlile. Half-black, half-Cherokee gunslinger Gypsy Smith (Poitier) reluctantly agrees to lead a wagontrain of freed slaves west to found their own community. Naturally, there's trouble with the Klan and Gypsy isn't the only one involved—young Cherokee brave White Wolf (Wirth), who has been raised among whites, has a forbidden romance with his foster sister, Rachel (Going), leading to lots of heartbreak. Fawcett has a brief role as the young Rachel's high-strung mother. Filmed in Alberta, Canada. **120m/C VHS.** Sidney Poitier, Michael Moriarty, Joanna Going, Billy Wirth, Regina Taylor, Hart Bochner, Shirley Knight, Robert Guillaume, Farrah Fawcett; ***D:*** David Greene; ***W:*** Joyce Eliason; ***M:*** Mark Snow. *VMK*

The Good Earth ½ **1937** Pearl S. Buck's classic recreation of the story of a simple Chinese farm couple beset by greed and poverty. Outstanding special effects. MGM's last film produced by master Irving Thalberg and dedicated to his memory. Rainer won the second of her back-to-back Best Actress Oscars for her portrayal of the self-sacrificing O-Lan. **138m/B VHS, Beta.** Paul Muni, Luise Rainer, Charley Grapewin, Keye Luke, Walter Connolly; ***D:*** Sidney Franklin; ***C:*** Karl Freund. Academy Awards '37: Best Actress (Rainer), Best Cinematography; Nominations: Academy Awards '37: Best Director (Franklin), Best Film Editing, Best Picture. *MGM, BTV, CCB*

Good Evening, Mr. Wallenberg ½ **1993** Raoul Wallenberg was an upper-class Swede who imported luxury goods from Hungary. He was also responsible for saving thousands of Hungarian Jews from extermination by the Nazis. Using phony documents he first had small groups of Jews smuggled to safety but when he learns that the 65,0000 Jews of the Budapest ghetto are to be killed he uses a bluff to prevent the deaths. Later taken prisoner by the Soviet Army, Wallenberg's fate has never been determined. Characters are dwarfed by the immensity of the events and Wallenberg remains an enigma. In Swedish, German, and Hungarian with English subtitles. **115m/C VHS.** *SW* Stellan Skarsgard, Erland Josephson, Katharina Thalbach; ***D:*** Kjell Grede; ***W:*** Kjell Grede. *ORI, FCT*

The Good Father 🦴🦴🦴 **1987 (R)** An acclaimed British TV movie about a bitter divorced man trying to come to terms with his son, his ex-wife, and his own fury by supporting the courtroom divorce battle of a friend. **90m/C VHS, Beta.** *GB* Anthony Hopkins, Jim Broadbent, Harriet Walter, Frances Viner, Joanne Whalley, Simon Callow, Michael Byrne; ***D:*** Mike Newell; ***W:*** Christopher Hampton; ***M:*** Richard Hartley. *MED, FOX*

The Good Fight 🦴🦴½ **1992** Grace Cragin (Lahti) is a lawyer at a small firm who's asked by her son's best friend to represent him in a tough case against a powerful corporation. The young man is dying of mouth cancer and he wants to sue the tobacco company that makes the chewing tobacco he blames for his illness. Grace is wary of the high-powered litigation necessary but with the increasingly personal aid of her prominent lawyer ex-husband (O'Quinn), she is ready to battle the odds. Another fine performance by Lahti in this made for cable television drama. **91m/C VHS, Beta.** Christine Lahti, Terry O'Quinn, Kenneth Welsh, Lawrence Dane, Adam Trese, Tony Rosato, Andrea Roth, Jonathan Crombie; ***D:*** John David Coles; ***W:*** Beth Gutcheon; ***M:*** W.G. Snuffy Walden. *PSM*

Good Girls Don't 🦴½ **1995** Two women are framed for murder and take it on the lam in a red convertible with a half million in cash. It's a comedy. **?m/C VHS.** Christopher Knight, Renee Estevez, Julia Parton, Mary Woronov. *LEO*

Good Grief, Charlie Brown **1983** That lovably misunderstood Charlie Brown is featured again in this Peanuts production. **30m/C VHS.** ***D:*** Bill Melendez, Sam Jaimes, Phil Roman. *BAR*

The Good Guys and the Bad Guys 🦴🦴½ **1969 (PG)** When Kennedy is abandoned by his gang of outlaws for being too old to keep up, he finds himself being hunted by lifelong marshall nemesis Mitchum. **91m/C VHS.** Robert Mitchum, George Kennedy, David Carradine, Tina Louise, Douglas Fowley, Lois Nettleton, Martin Balsam, John Carradine; ***D:*** Burt Kennedy; ***W:*** Ronald M. Cohen; ***C:*** Harry Stradling Jr. *WAR*

Good Guys Wear Black 🦴🦴 **1978 (PG)** A mild-mannered professor keeps his former life as leader of a Vietnam commando unit under wraps until he discovers that he's number one on the CIA hit list. Sequel is "A Force of One." **96m/C VHS, Beta, LV.** Chuck Norris, Anne Archer, James Franciscus; ***D:*** Ted Post; ***W:*** Mark Medoff. *WAR, HBO, VES*

A Good Man in Africa 🦴🦴 **1994 (R)** Bumbling low-level British diplomat gets caught up in the high-level political turmoil of a newly independent African state. Confusing plot has borderline incompetent blackmailed by corrupt politician into bribing respected doctor for local land rights. Wow, corrupt officials, ineffectual bureaucrats—go figure! Does to the British diplomatic corps what "A Fish Called Wanda" did to England's legal community, without the humor. Performances by Connery, Gossett and Lithgow almost make up for shortcomings in key areas such as writing and direction. Adapted from the novel by William Boyd. **95m/C VHS.** Colin Friels, Sean Connery, Louis Gossett Jr., John Lithgow, Joanne Whalley, Diana Rigg; ***D:*** Bruce Beresford; ***W:*** William Boyd. *MCA*

Good Men and Bad 🦴🦴½ **1994** Rampant violence in Texas, following President Lincoln's assassination, finds an innocent woman killed in the crossfire. Now her husband seeks revenge on the killers. **90m/C VHS.** Christopher Reeve, Raoul Trujillo, Tony Todd, Kim Coates; ***D:*** Steven Hilliard Stern. *CAF*

Good Morning, Babylon 🦴🦴🦴 *Good Morning Babilonia* **1987 (PG-13)** The Taviani brothers' first American film. Two young Italian brothers skilled in cathedral restoration come to America and find success building the sets to D.W. Griffith's "Intolerance." Eventually, their fortune is shattered by the onslaught of WWI. **113m/C VHS, Beta, LV.** Vincent Spano, Joaquim de Almeida, Greta Scacchi, Charles Dance, Desiree Becker, Omero Antonutti, David Brandon; ***D:*** Paolo Taviani, Vittorio Taviani; ***W:*** Paolo Taviani, Vittorio Taviani, Tonino Guerra; ***M:*** Nicola Piovani. *LIV, VES*

Good Morning, Vietnam 🦴🦴🦴 **1987 (R)** Based on the story of Saigon DJ Adrian Cronauer, although Williams' portrayal is reportedly a bit more extroverted than the personality of Cronauer. Williams spins great comic moments that may have been scripted but likely were not as a man with no history and for whom everything is manic radio material. The character ad-libs, swoops, and swerves, finally accepting adult responsibility. Engaging all the way with an outstanding period soundtrack. **121m/C VHS, Beta, LV, 8mm.** Robin Williams, Forest Whitaker, Bruno Kirby, Richard Edson, Robert Wuhl, J.T. Walsh, Noble Willingham, Floyd Vivino, Tung Thanh Tran, Chintara Sukapatana; ***D:*** Barry Levinson; ***W:*** Mitch Markowitz; ***C:*** Peter Sova; ***M:*** Alex North. Golden Globe Awards '88: Best Actor—Musical/Comedy (Williams); Nominations: Academy Awards '87: Best Actor (Williams). *TOU*

The Good Mother 🦴🦴½ **1988 (R)** A divorced mother works at creating a fulfilling life for herself and her daughter, with an honest education for her daughter about every subject, including sex. But her ex-husband, unsure of how far this education is being taken, fights her for custody of their 8-year old daughter after allegations of sexual misconduct against the mother's new lover. Based on Sue Miller's bestselling novel. Well acted, weakly edited and scripted. **104m/C VHS, Beta, LV.** Diane Keaton, Liam Neeson, Jason Robards Jr., Ralph Bellamy, James Naughton, Teresa Wright, Asia Vieira, Joe Morton, Katey Sagal, Tracy Griffith, Charles Kimbrough; ***D:*** Leonard Nimoy; ***W:*** Michael Bortman; ***C:*** David Watkin; ***M:*** Elmer Bernstein. *TOU*

Good Neighbor Sam 🦴🦴🦴 **1964** A married advertising executive (Lemmon) agrees to pose as a friend's husband in order for her to collect a multimillion-dollar inheritance. Complications ensue when his biggest client mistakes the friend for his actual wife and decides they're the perfect couple to promote his wholesome product—milk. **130m/C VHS, Beta.** Jack Lemmon, Romy Schneider, Dorothy Provine, Mike Connors, Edward G. Robinson, Joyce Jameson; ***D:*** David Swift. *GKK*

Good News 🦴🦴½ **1947** A vintage Comden-Green musical about the love problems of a college football star, who will flunk out if he doesn't pass his French exams. Revamping of the 1927 Broadway smash features the unlikely sight of Lawford in a song-and-dance role. ♫Varsity Drag; He's a Lady's Man; Good News; Tait Song; Students Are We; Just Imagine; If You're Not Kissing Me; Football; I Feel Pessimistic. **92m/C VHS, Beta, LV.** June Allyson, Peter Lawford, Joan McCracken, Mel Torme; ***D:*** Charles Walters; ***W:*** Betty Comden. Nominations: Academy Awards '47: Best Song ("Pass That Peace Pipe"). *MGM, FCT*

The Good Old Boys 🦴🦴½ **1995** Debuting as both director and co-writer, Jones also stars as aging cowpoke Hewey Calloway. The n'er-do-well Hewey makes a surprise visit to the hardscrabble 1906 Texas farm of brother Walter (Kinney), whose wife Eve (McDormand) is none too happy to see the wanderer. But Walter needs help, the local banker (Brimley) is about to foreclose, and Hewey is also taken with spirited schoolmarm Spring Renfro (Spacek, who also starred with Jones in "Coal-Miner's Daughter"). And even Hewey realizes that the twentieth century is going to change his way of life forever. Easy-going drama with a fine cast. **118m/C VHS.** Tommy Lee Jones, Sissy Spacek, Terry Kinney, Frances McDormand, Wilford Brimley, Sam Shepard, Walter Olkewicz, Matt Damon, Bruce McGill, Park Overall; ***D:*** Tommy Lee Jones; ***W:*** Tommy Lee Jones, J.T. Allen; ***M:*** John McEuen. *TTC*

Good Sam 🦴🦴 **1948** An incurable "Good Samaritan" finds himself in one jam after another as he tries too hard to help people. Lots of missed opportunities for laughs with McCrarey's mediocre direction. **116m/B VHS.** Gary Cooper, Ann Sheridan, Ray Collins, Edmund Lowe, Joan Lorring, Ruth Roman; ***D:*** Leo McCarey. *REP*

The Good Son 🦴🦴 **1993 (R)** In a grand departure from cute, Culkin tackles evil as a 13-year-old obsessed with death and other unseemly hobbies. During a stay with his uncle, Mark (Wood) watches as his cousin (Culkin) gets creepier and creepier, and tries to alert the family. But will they listen? Nooo—they choose to ignore the little warning signs like the doll hanging by a noose in Culkin's room. And then there's the untimely death of a sibling. Hmmm. Culkin isn't as bad as expected, but doesn't quite get all the way down to bone-chilling terror either. Original star Jesse Bradford was dropped when Papa Culkin threatened to pull Mac off "Home Alone 2" if he wasn't cast in the lead. **87m/C VHS, LV.** Macaulay Culkin, Elijah Wood, Wendy Crewson, David Morse, Daniel Hugh-Kelly, Quinn Culkin; ***D:*** Joseph Ruben; ***W:*** Ian McEwan; ***C:*** John Lindley; ***M:*** Elmer Bernstein. Nominations: MTV Movie Awards '94: Best Villain (Culkin). *FXV*

The Good, the Bad, and Huckleberry Hound **1988** Journeying out West to begin a ranch, Huckleberry Hound winds up becoming a sheriff in the small town of Two-Bit. Huckleberry stands up against a group of bully brothers who have been terrorizing the town. **94m/C VHS, Beta.** ***D:*** Ray Patterson; ***V:*** Daws Butler. *TTC, IME, WTA*

The Good, the Bad and the Ugly 🦴🦴🦴½ **1967** Léone's grandiloquent, shambling tribute to the American Western. Set during the Civil War, it follows the seemingly endless adventures of three dirtbags in search of a cache of Confederate gold buried in a nameless grave. Violent, exaggerated, beautifully crafted, it is the final and finest installment of the "Dollars" trilogy: a spaghetti Western chef d'oeuvre. **161m/C VHS, Beta, LV.** *IT* Clint Eastwood, Eli Wallach, Lee Van Cleef, Chelo Alonso, Luigi Pistilli; ***D:*** Sergio Leone; ***W:*** Sergio Leone; ***C:*** Tonino Delli Colli; ***M:*** Ennio Morricone. *FOX, MGM, FCT*

Good Time with a Bad Girl 🦴 *A Good Time, A Bad Girl* **1967** A married millionaire visiting Las Vegas experiments with exotic sexual pleasures when he meets up with Sue, a teenage nymphomaniac. **61m/B VHS, Beta.** *VDM, TPV*

The Good Wife 🦴🦴½ *The Umbrella Woman* **1986 (R)** A bored and sexually frustrated wife scandalizes her small Australian town by taking up with the new hotel barman. There's no denying Ward's sexuality, but overall the movie is too predictable. **97m/C VHS, Beta, LV.** *AU* Rachel Ward, Bryan Brown, Sam Neill, Steven Vidler, Bruce Barry, Jennifer Claire; ***D:*** Ken Cameron; ***M:*** Cameron Allan. *BAR, IME*

Goodbye Again 🦴🦴½ *Aimez-Vous Brahms* **1961** A romantic drama based on the novel by Francoise Sagan. Bergman is a middle-aged interior decorator whose lover, Montand, has a roaming eye. She finds herself drawn to the son (Perkins) of a client and begins an affair—flattered by the young man's attentions. Montand is outraged and vows to change his ways and marry Bergman if she will give up the young man. A bit soapy, but a must for Bergman fans. **120m/B VHS.** Jessie Royce Landis, Ingrid Bergman, Anthony Perkins, Yves Montand, Diahann Carroll; ***D:*** Anatole Litvak. Cannes Film Festival '61: Best Actor (Perkins). *MGM, FCT*

The Goodbye Bird 🦴🦴½ **1993 (G)** Frank is accused by his school principal of stealing her prized talking parrot. With the aid of a kindly veterinarian Frank tries to discover who the thief really is. **91m/C VHS.** Cindy Pickett, Concetta Tomei, Wayne Rogers, Christopher Pettiet; ***D:*** William Clark. *WOV*

Goodbye Columbus 🦴🦴🦴 **1969 (PG)** Philip Roth's novel about a young Jewish librarian who has an affair with the spoiled daughter of a nouveau riche family is brought to late-'60s life, and vindicated by superb performances all around. Benjamin and McGraw's first starring roles. **105m/C VHS, Beta, LV.** Richard Benjamin, Ali MacGraw, Jack Klugman, Nan Martin, Jaclyn Smith; ***D:*** Larry Peerce; ***M:*** Charles Fox. Writers Guild of America '68: Best Adapted Screenplay; Nominations: Academy Awards '69: Best Adapted Screenplay. *PAR*

Goodbye Cruel World ☆½ **1982 (R)** Black comedy about a suicidal television anchorman who decides to spend his last day filming the relatives who drove him to the brink. **90m/C VHS, Beta.** Dick Shawn, Cynthia Sikes, Chuck "Porky" Mitchell; ***D:*** David Irving. *LIV*

Goodbye Emmanuelle ☆½ **1979 (R)** Follows the further adventures of Emmanuelle in her quest for sexual freedom and the excitement of forbidden pleasures. The second sequel to "Emmanuelle." **92m/C VHS, Beta.** Sylvia Kristel. *NO*

The Goodbye Girl ☆☆☆ **1977 (PG)** Neil Simon's story of a former actress, her precocious nine-year-old daughter and the aspiring actor who moves in with them. The daughter serves as catalyst for the other two to fall in love. While Mason's character is fairly unsympathetic, Dreyfuss is great and Simon's dialogue witty. **110m/C VHS, Beta, LV.** Richard Dreyfuss, Marsha Mason, Quinn Cummings, Barbara Rhoades, Marilyn Sokol; ***D:*** Herbert Ross; ***W:*** Neil Simon; ***M:*** Dave Grusin. Academy Awards '77: Best Actor (Dreyfuss); British Academy Awards '78: Best Actor (Dreyfuss); Golden Globe Awards '78: Best Actor—Musical/Comedy (Dreyfuss), Best Actress—Musical/Comedy (Mason), Best Film—Musical/Comedy, Best Screenplay; Los Angeles Film Critics Association Awards '77: Best Actor (Dreyfuss); Nominations: Academy Awards '76: Best Picture; Academy Awards '77: Best Actress (Mason), Best Original Screenplay, Best Supporting Actress (Cummings). *MGM, BTV*

Goodbye Love ☆½ **1934** Dull comedy about a group of ex-husbands who refuse to pay alimony and end up in jail. **65m/B VHS.** Charlie Ruggles, Verree Teasdale, Sidney Blackmer, Mayo Methot, Phyllis Barry, Ray Walker, John Kelly, Hale Grace, Luis Alberni; ***D:*** Herbert Ross. *FCT*

Goodbye, Miss 4th of July ☆☆½ **1988** Inspired by the true story of the teenage daughter of Greek immigrants living in pre-WWI West Virginia, the prejudice they encounter, the relationship that begins between the family and an aging African-American ex-boxer, and the girl's efforts in the influenza epidemic. Based on the 1985 book by her brother. **89m/C VHS.** Roxana Zal, Louis Gossett Jr., Chris Sarandon, Chantal Contouri, Chynna Phillips, Mitchell Anderson, Conchata Ferrell, Ed Lauter; ***D:*** George Miller. *DIS*

Goodbye, Mr. Chips ☆☆☆½ **1939** An MGM classic, the sentimental rendering of the James Hilton novel about a shy Latin professor in an English school who marries the vivacious Garson only to tragically lose her. He spends the rest of his life devoting himself to his students and becoming a school legend. Multi award-winning soaper featuring Garson's first screen appearance, which was Oscar nominated. Special two-tape letterboxed laserdisc edition includes the original trailer and an extra-special production featurette. Remade in 1969 as a fairly awful musical starring Peter O'Toole. **115m/B VHS, Beta, LV.** Robert Donat, Greer Garson, Paul Henreid, John Mills; ***D:*** Sam Wood; ***C:*** Frederick A. (Freddie) Young. Academy Awards '39: Best Actor (Donat); National Board of Review Awards '39: 10 Best Films of the Year; Nominations: Academy Awards '39: Best Actress (Garson), Best Director (Wood), Best Film Editing, Best Picture, Best Screenplay, Best Sound. *MGM, BTV, HMV*

Goodbye, Mr. Chips ☆☆ **1969** Ross debuted as director with this big-budget (but inferior musical re-make) of the classic James Hilton novel about a gentle teacher at an English all-boys private school and the woman who helps him demonstrate his compassion and overcome his shyness. O'Toole, although excellent, is categorically a non-singer, while Clark, a popular singer at the time ("Downtown"), musters very little talent in front of the camera. The plot is altered unnecessarily and updated to the WWII era for little reason; the music is thoroughly forgettable. ♫Fill The World With Love; Where Did My Childhood Go; London is London; And the Sky Smiled; When I Am Older; Walk Through the World; What Shall I Do with Today?; What a Lot of Flowers; Schooldays. **151m/C VHS, Beta, LV.** Peter O'Toole, Petula Clark, Michael Redgrave, George Baker, Sian Phillips, Michael Bryant, Jack Hedley, Herbert Ross; ***D:*** Herbert Ross; ***C:*** Oswald Morris; ***M:*** Leslie Bricusse, John Williams. Golden Globe Awards '70: Best Actor—Musical/Comedy (O'Toole); National Board of Review Awards '69: Best Actor (O'Toole); National Society of Film Critics Awards '69: Best Supporting Actress (Phillips); Nominations: Academy Awards '69: Best Actor (O'Toole), Best Original Score. *MGM*

Goodbye, My Lady ☆☆ **1956** Based on the novel by James Street, this is a tear-jerking film about a young Mississippi farmboy who finds and cares for a special dog that he comes to love but eventually must give up. **95m/B VHS, Beta, LV.** Brandon de Wilde, Walter Brennan, Sidney Poitier, Phil Harris, Louise Beavers; ***D:*** William A. Wellman. *WAR, FCT*

Goodbye, New York ☆☆ **1985 (R)** A New York yuppie on a vacation finds herself penniless and stranded in Israel. She makes the best of the situation by joining a kibbutz and falling for a part-time soldier. Well, of course. **90m/C VHS, Beta, LV.** *IS* Julie Hagerty, Amos Kollek, Shmuel Shilo; ***D:*** Amos Kollek; ***M:*** Michael Abene. *VES*

Goodbye, Norma Jean ☆ **1975 (R)** Detailed and sleazy recreation of Marilyn Monroe's early years in Hollywood. Followed by "Goodnight, Sweet Marilyn." **95m/C VHS, Beta.** Misty Rowe, Terrence Locke, Patch MacKenzie; ***D:*** Larry Buchanan; ***M:*** Joe Beck. *NO*

The Goodbye People ☆☆½ **1983** Balsam is an elderly man who decides to reopen his Coney Island hot dog stand that folded 22 years earlier. Hirsch and Reed help him realize his impossible dream in this sweetly sentimental film. **104m/C VHS, Beta, LV.** Judd Hirsch, Martin Balsam, Pamela Reed, Ron Silver; ***D:*** Herb Gardner; ***W:*** Herb Gardner. *COL, SUE*

Goodbye Pork Pie ☆½ **1981 (R)** With the police on their trail, two young men speed on a 1000-mile journey in a small, brand-new, yellow stolen car. Remember: journey of thousand miles always begin in stolen car. **105m/C VHS, Beta.** *NZ* Tony Barry, Kelly Johnson; ***D:*** Geoff Murphy. *SUE*

Goodfellas ☆☆☆☆ **1990 (R)** Quintessential picture about "wiseguys," at turns both violent and funny. A young man grows up in the mob, works hard to advance himself through the ranks, and enjoys the life of the rich and violent, oblivious to the horror of which he is a part. Cocaine addiction and many wiseguy missteps ultimately unravel his climb to the top. Excellent performances (particularly Liotta and Pesci, with De Niro pitching in around the corners), with visionary cinematography and careful pacing. Watch for Scorsese's mom as Pesci's mom. Based on the life of Henry Hill, ex-mobster now in the Witness Protection Program. Adapted from the book by Nicholas Pileggi. **146m/C VHS, Beta, LV, 8mm.** Robert De Niro, Ray Liotta, Joe Pesci, Paul Sorvino, Lorraine Bracco, Frank Sivero, Mike Starr, Frank Vincent, Samuel L. Jackson, Henny Youngman, Tony Darrow, Chuck Low, Frank DiLeo, Christopher Serrone, Jerry Vale; ***D:*** Martin Scorsese; ***W:*** Nicholas Pileggi, Martin Scorsese; ***C:*** Michael Ballhaus. Academy Awards '90: Best Supporting Actor (Pesci); British Academy Awards '90: Best Adapted Screenplay, Best Director (Scorsese), Best Film; Los Angeles Film Critics Association Awards '90: Best Cinematography, Best Director (Scorsese), Best Film, Best Supporting Actor (Pesci), Best Supporting Actress (Bracco); New York Film Critics Awards '90: Best Actor (De Niro), Best Director (Scorsese), Best Film; National Society of Film Critics Awards '90: Best Director (Scorsese), Best Film; Nominations: Academy Awards '90: Best Adapted Screenplay, Best Director (Scorsese), Best Film Editing, Best Picture, Best Supporting Actress (Bracco). *WAR, FCT, BTV*

Goodnight God Bless ☆ **1987 (R)** A depressing movie about a mentally disturbed priest who wanders into an elementary school with murder on his mind. He kills the teacher and all the children—except one. Will he find that one too? It's not worth it to find out. **90m/C VHS, Beta.** *NO*

Goodnight, Michelangelo ☆☆½ **1989 (R)** Funny, engaging and somewhat confusing story of the life of an Italian immigrant family as seen through the eyes of its youngest member, eight-year-old Michelangelo. Winner of the 1990 Best Comedy Award at the Greater Fort Lauderdale Film Festival. **91m/C VHS.** *IT* Lina Sastri, Kim Cattrall, Giancarlo Giannini, Daniel Desanto; ***D:*** Carlo Liconti; ***W:*** Carlo Liconti. *NO*

Goodnight, Sweet Marilyn ☆ **1989 (R)** Supposed "never-before-told" story of Marilyn Monroe's tragic death. According to this, her death was the result of pre-arranged "mercy-killing." Follow-up to director Buchanan's "Goodbye, Norma Jean" (1977) with Lane as the 1960s Marilyn intercut with scenes of Rowe from the first film as young Marilyn. You'd be better off leaving "Sweet Marilyn" to rest in peace. **100m/C VHS, Beta.** Paula Lane, Jeremy Slate, Misty Rowe; ***D:*** Larry Buchanan. *NO*

Goof Balls *Woof!* **1987 (R)** The tourist denizens of a island golf resort putt and cavort about, and golf isn't all that's on their minds. **87m/C VHS, Beta.** Ben Gordon, Laura Robinson. *ACA*

A Goofy Movie ☆☆½ **1994 (G)** The dog finally gets his day. After 63 years of supporting roles, Disney's Goofy stars in his own movie along with his teenage son Max. When it comes to Goofy's attention that his rock music obsessed son is goofing off in school, Goofy decides to spend some quality time with Max via a road trip through the country. Their journey is plagued with mishaps, but through the obstacles, father and son bridge their generational gap and bond in the true Disney sense. A modest animated treat with six new songs that may induce some finger snapping and toe tapping. **78m/C VHS.** ***D:*** Kevin Lima; ***W:*** Jymn Magon, Brian Pimental, Chris Matheson; ***V:*** Bill Farmer, Jason Marsden, Jim Cummings, Kellie Martin, Rob Paulsen, Wallace Shawn, Florence Stanley, Jo Anne Worley. *DIS*

Goon Movie ☆☆ *Stand Easy* **1953** The cast of "The Goon Show," Britain's popular radio comedy series, perform some of their best routines in this, their only film appearance. **75m/B VHS, Beta.** Peter Sellers, Spike Milligan, Harry Secombe. *VDM*

The Goonies ☆☆½ **1985 (PG)** Two brothers who are about to lose their house conveniently find a treasure map. They pick up a couple of friends and head for the "X." If they can recover the treasure without getting caught by the bad guys, then all will be saved. Steven Spielberg produced this high-energy action fantasy for kids of all ages. The laserdisc edition comes in a widescreen format. **114m/C VHS, Beta, LV.** Sean Astin, Josh Brolin, Jeff B. Cohen, Corey Feldman, Martha Plimpton, John Matuszak, Robert Davi, Anne Ramsey, Mary Ellen Trainor, Jonathan Ke Quan, Kerri Green, Joe Pantoliano; ***D:*** Richard Donner; ***W:*** Chris Columbus, Steven Spielberg; ***M:*** Dave Grusin. *WAR*

Gor ☆½ **1988 (PG)** Sword and sorcery: a magic ring sends a meek college professor to "Gor," a faraway world in which survival goes to the fittest and the most brutal. Followed by "Outlaw of Gor." **95m/C VHS, Beta.** Urbano Barberini, Rebecca Ferratti, Jack Palance, Paul Smith, Oliver Reed; ***D:*** Fritz Kiersch; ***W:*** R.J. Marx. *WAR*

Gorath ☆☆ *Yosei Gorasu* **1964** The world's top scientists are racing to stop a giant meteor from destroying the Earth. **77m/C VHS, Beta.** *JP* ***D:*** Inoshiro Honda. *GEM, PSM*

Gordon's War ☆☆ **1973 (R)** When a Vietnam vet returns to his Harlem home, he finds his wife overdosing on the drugs that have infiltrated his neighborhood. He leads a vigilante group in an attempt to clean up the area, which makes for a lot of action; however, there's also an excessive amount of violence. **89m/C VHS, Beta.** Paul Winfield, Carl Lee, David Downing, Tony King, Grace Jones; ***D:*** Ossie Davis; ***M:*** Angelo Badalamenti. *FOX*

Gordy ☆½ **1995 (G)** Perky talking porker Gordy manages to escape his fate as future bacon and find a couple of equally perky kids—motherless country-song-singing Jinnie Sue (Young) and lonely rich boy Hanky (Roescher), whom the pig manages to save from drowning. Plot scarcely matters and all the 25 piggies who performed as Gordy generally manage to outshine the humans, though country singer Stone (in his film debut) displays an easy charm. **90m/C VHS.** Doug Stone, Michael Roescher, Kristy Young, James Donadio, Deborah Hobart, Tom Lester, Ted Manson; ***D:*** Mark Lewis; ***W:*** Leslie Stevens; ***C:*** Richard Michalak; ***M:*** Tom Bahler; ***V:*** Justin Garms. *TOU*

The Gore-Gore Girls ✗ **1972** Splatter horror director Lewis' final film follows a detective's search for a madman who's been mutilating and killing beautiful young bar dancers. **84m/C VHS.** ***D:*** Herschell Gordon Lewis. *MOV*

Gore-Met Zombie Chef From Hell *Woof!* **1987** A demon/vampire opens up a seafood restaurant and slaughters his customers. Deliberately campy and extremely graphic. **90m/C VHS, Beta.** Theo Depuay, Kelley Kunicki, C.W. Casey, Alan Marx, Michael O'Neill; ***D:*** Don Swan. *NO*

Gore Vidal's Billy the Kid ✗✗½ **1989** An unusual treatment of the William Bonney legend in which the Kid is merely a misunderstood teenager caught up in the midst of the brutal range wars. Made for cable television. **100m/C VHS.** Val Kilmer, Duncan Regehr, Wilford Brimley, Julie Carmen, Michael Parks, Rene Auberjonois, Albert Salmi; ***D:*** William A. Graham. *TTC*

Gore Vidal's Lincoln ✗✗½ *Lincoln* **1988** Waterston is a low-key but sympathetic Lincoln, with Moore as his high-strung wife Mary, in this made for television adaptation of the Vidal best-seller. Follows the couple from their first day in Washington, through the Civil War, family tragedies, up to the day of the President's burial. **190m/C VHS.** Sam Waterston, Mary Tyler Moore, John Houseman, Richard Mulligan, John McMartin, Ruby Dee, Cleavon Little, Jeffrey DeMunn, James Gammon, Deborah Adair, Robin Gammell; ***D:*** Lamont Johnson; ***W:*** Ernest Kinoy; ***M:*** Ernest Gold. *PAP, AVE*

The Gorgeous Hussy ✗ **1936** Crawford stars in this fictionalized biography of Peggy Eaton, Andrew Jackson's notorious belle, who disgraces herself and those around her. A star-studded cast complete with beautiful costumes isn't enough to save this overly long and dull picture. **102m/B VHS.** Joan Crawford, Robert Taylor, Lionel Barrymore, Melvyn Douglas, James Stewart, Franchot Tone, Louis Calhern; ***D:*** Clarence Brown. Nominations: Academy Awards '36: Best Cinematography, Best Supporting Actress (Bondi). *MGM*

Gorgo ✗✗½ **1961** An undersea explosion off the coast of Ireland brings to the surface a prehistoric sea monster, which is captured and brought to a London circus. Its irate mother appears looking for her baby, creating havoc in her wake. **76m/C VHS, Beta, LV.** *GB* Bill Travers, William Sylvester, Vincent Winter, Bruce Seton, Christopher Rhodes; ***D:*** Eugene Lourie; ***C:*** Frederick A. (Freddie) Young. *NOS, MRV, VCI*

The Gorgon ✗✗ **1964** In pre-WWI Germany, the lovely assistant to a mad brain surgeon moonlights as a snake-haired gorgon, turning men to stone. A professor arrives in the village to investigate, only to become another victim. **83m/C VHS, Beta, LV.** *GB* Peter Cushing, Christopher Lee, Richard Pasco, Barbara Shelley, Michael Goodliffe, Patrick Troughton; ***D:*** Terence Fisher; ***M:*** James Bernard. *GKK, MLB*

The Gorilla ✗✗ **1939** Bumbling Ritzes are hired to protect a country gentleman receiving threats from a killer. Lugosi portrays the menacing butler. Derived from the play by Ralph Spence. **67m/B VHS, Beta, LV.** The Ritz Brothers, Anita Louise, Patsy Kelly, Lionel Atwill, Bela Lugosi; ***D:*** Allan Dwan. *NOS, SNC, MRV*

Gorilla ✗✗ **1956** A rampaging gorilla is sought by the local game warden and a journalist researching the natives. Filmed on location in the Belgian Congo. **79m/B VHS, Beta.** *SW* Gio Petre, Georges Galley; ***D:*** Sven Nykvist, Lar Henrik Ottoson. *FCT, VYY*

Gorillas in the Mist ✗✗✗ **1988 (PG-13)** The life of Dian Fossey, animal rights activist and world-renowned expert on the African gorilla, from her pioneering contact with mountain gorillas to her murder at the hands of poachers. Weaver is totally appropriate as the increasingly obsessed Fossey, but the character moves away from us, just as we need to see and understand more about her. Excellent special effects. **117m/C VHS, Beta, LV.** Sigourney Weaver, Bryan Brown, Julie Harris, Iain Cuthbertson, John Omirah Miluwi, Constantin Alexandrov, Waigwa Wachira; ***D:*** Michael Apted; ***W:*** Anna Hamilton Phelan; ***C:*** John Seale; ***M:*** Maurice Jarre. Golden Globe Awards '88: Best Actress—Drama (Weaver); Golden Globe Awards '89: Best Score; Nominations: Academy Awards '88: Best Actress (Weaver), Best Adapted Screenplay, Best Film Editing, Best Sound, Best Original Score. *MCA, HMV*

Gorky Park ✗✗✗ **1983 (R)** Adaptation of Martin Cruz Smith's bestseller. Three strange, faceless corpses are found in Moscow's Gorky Park. There are no clues for the Russian police captain investigating the incident. He makes the solution to this crime his personal crusade, and finds himself caught in a web of political intrigue. Excellent police procedure yarn. **127m/C VHS, Beta, LV.** William Hurt, Lee Marvin, Brian Dennehy, Joanna Pacula; ***D:*** Michael Apted; ***W:*** Dennis Potter; ***C:*** Ralf Bode; ***M:*** James Horner. Edgar Allan Poe Awards '83: Best Screenplay. *VES*

Gorp *Woof!* **1980 (R)** Sex, fun, and lewd, sophomoric humor reign at a summer camp. For the bored and witless or those who aspire. **90m/C VHS, Beta.** Dennis Quaid, Rosanna Arquette, Michael Lembeck, Philip Casnoff, Frank Drescher; ***D:*** Joseph Ruben. *HBO*

Gospa ✗✗½ **1994 (PG)** Based on the true story of Father Jozo Zovko (Sheen), who was put on trial for treason by the communist government in Yugoslavia in 1981 when he protected six Coatian children who repeatedly claimed that they saw visions of the Virgin Mary. Somewhat ponderous but well-meaning story that also suffers from a plethora of accents. "Gospa" means "Our Lady" in Croatian. **121m/C VHS.** Martin Sheen, Michael York, Morgan Fairchild, Frank Finlay; ***D:*** Jakov Sedlar; ***W:*** Ivan Aralica, Paul Gronseth; ***C:*** Vjekoslav Vrdoljak; ***M:*** Nona Hendryx. *NYR*

The Gospel According to St. Matthew ✗✗✗✗ *Il Vangelo Secondo Matteo; L'Evangile Selon Saint-Matthieu* **1964** Perhaps Pasolini's greatest film, retelling the story of Christ in gritty, neo-realistic tones and portraying the man less as a divine presence than as a political revolutionary. The yard-stick by which all Jesus-films are to be measured. In Italian with English subtitles or dubbed. **142m/B VHS, Beta, LV, 8mm.** *IT* Enrique Irazoqui, Susanna Pasolini, Margherita Caruso, Marcello Morante, Mario Socrate; ***D:*** Pier Paolo Pasolini; ***W:*** Pier Paolo Pasolini; ***C:*** Tonino Delli Colli; ***M:*** Luis Bacalov. National Board of Review Awards '66: 5 Best Foreign Films of the Year; Nominations: Academy Awards '66: Best Art Direction/Set Decoration (B & W), Best Costume Design (B & W), Best Original Score. *NOS, MRV, WBF*

The Gospel According to Vic ✗✗ *Heavenly Pursuits* **1987 (PG-13)** A Scottish comedy about a skeptical teacher at a remedial school, who, having survived miraculously from a fall, is taken for proof of the sainthood of the school's patron namesake. **92m/C VHS, Beta.** *GB* Tom Conti, Helen Mirren; ***D:*** Charles Gormley. *FOX*

Gotcha! ✗✗½ **1985 (PG-13)** The mock assassination game "Gotcha!" abounds on the college campus and sophomore Edwards is one of the best. What he doesn't know is that his "assassination" skills are about to take on new meaning when he meets up with a female Czech graduate student who is really an international spy. **97m/C VHS, Beta, LV.** Anthony Edwards, Linda Fiorentino, Alex Rocco, Nick Corri, Marla Adams, Klaus Loewitsch, Christopher Rydell; ***D:*** Jeff Kanew; ***W:*** Dan Gordon; ***M:*** Bill Conti. *MCA*

Gotham ✗✗✗ **1988** A wealthy financier hires private-eye Jones to track down beautiful wife Madsen. It seems that she keeps dunning her husband for money. Sounds easy enough to Jones until he learns that she has been dead for some time. Mystery ventures into the afterlife and back as it twists its way to its surprise ending. Intriguing throwback to '40s detective flicks. Made for television. **100m/C VHS, LV.** Tommy Lee Jones, Virginia Madsen, Colin Bruce, Kevin Jarre, Denise Stephenson, Frederic Forrest; ***D:*** Lloyd Fonvielle; ***M:*** George S. Clinton. *CAN*

Gothic ✗✗✗ **1987 (R)** Mary Shelley, Lord Byron, Percy Bysshe Shelley, and John Polidori spend the night in a Swiss villa telling each other ghost stories and experimenting with laudanum and sexual partner combinations. The dreams and realizations of the night will color their lives ever after. Interesting premise, well-carried out, although burdened by director Russell's typical excesses. Soundtrack by Thomas Dolby. **87m/C VHS, Beta, LV.** Julian Sands, Gabriel Byrne, Timothy Spall, Natasha Richardson, Miriam Cyr; ***D:*** Ken Russell; ***W:*** Stephen Volk; ***M:*** Thomas Dolby. *LIV, VES*

Gotta Dance, Gotta Sing **1984** Compilation of memorable dance routines from great Hollywood films. **53m/C VHS, Beta.** Fred Astaire, Ginger Rogers, Shirley Temple, Carmen Miranda, Betty Grable. *NO*

Government Agents vs. Phantom Legion **1951** Agent Hal Duncan must stop an evil group who is stealing uranium shipments from under the government's nose. Edited from 12 episodes of the original serial on two cassettes. **167m/B VHS, Beta.** Walter Reed, Mary Ellen Kay, Dick Curtis, John Pickard. *REP, MLB*

The Grace Kelly Story ✗✗½ **1983** Ladd stars as the beautiful Philadelphia society girl who became an Oscar-winning actress and a seemingly fairy tale princess when she leaves Hollywood behind to marry Prince Rainier of Monaco. Standard TV bio but Ladd does look the part. **104m/C VHS.** Cheryl Ladd, Diane Ladd, Lloyd Bridges, Ian McShane, Alejandro Rey, William Schallert, Marta DuBois, Salome Jens, Edith Fellows; ***D:*** Anthony Page; ***W:*** Cynthia Mandelberg. *COL*

Grace Quigley ✗½ *The Ultimate Solution of Grace Quigley* **1984 (PG)** An elderly woman, tired of life, hires a hitman to kill her. Instead they go into business together, bumping off other elderly folk who decide they'd rather be dead. Notoriously inept black comedy noted for being the career embarrassment for both of its stars. **87m/C VHS, Beta.** Katharine Hepburn, Nick Nolte, Walter Abel, Chip Zien, Elizabeth Wilson, Kit Le Fever, William Duell, Jill Eikenberry; ***D:*** Anthony Harvey; ***M:*** John Addison. *MGM*

Grad Night ✗ **1981 (R)** The anticipation for graduation in a small town high school brings surprises no one could have predicted, unless they've seen all the other typical adolescent films. **85m/C VHS, Beta.** Joey Johnson, Suzanna Fagan, Barry Stolze, Sam Whipple, Caroline Bates; ***D:*** John Tenorio. *NO*

The Graduate ✗✗✗✗ **1967 (PG)** Famous, influential slice of comic Americana stars Hoffman as Benjamin Braddock, a shy, aimless college graduate who, without any idea of responsibility or ambition, wanders from a sexual liaison with a married woman (the infamous Mrs. Robinson) to pursuit of her engaged daughter. His pursuit of Elaine right to her wedding has become a film classic. Extremely popular and almost solely responsible for establishing both Hoffman and director Nichols. The career advice given to Benjamin, "plastics," became a catchword for the era. Watch for Dreyfuss in the Berkeley rooming house, Farrell in the hotel lobby, and screenwriter Henry as the desk clerk. Based on the novel by Charles Webb. Laserdisc edition includes screen tests, promotional stills, and a look at the creative process involved in making a novel into a movie. A 25th Anniversary Limited Edition is also available, presented in a wide-screen format and including the original movie trailer and interviews with the cast and crew. **106m/C VHS, Beta, LV, 8mm.** Dustin Hoffman, Anne Bancroft, Katharine Ross, Murray Hamilton, Brian Avery, Marion Lorne, Alice Ghostley, William Daniels, Elizabeth Wilson, Norman Fell, Buck Henry, Richard Dreyfuss, Mike Farrell; ***D:*** Mike Nichols; ***W:*** Buck Henry, Calder Willingham; ***C:*** Robert L. Surtees; ***M:*** Paul Simon, Art Garfunkel, Dave Grusin. Academy Awards '67: Best Director (Nichols); British Academy Awards '68: Best Director (Nichols), Best Film, Best Screenplay; Directors Guild of America Awards '67: Best Director (Nichols); Golden Globe Awards '68: Best Actress—Musical/Comedy (Bancroft), Best Director (Nichols), Best Film—Musical/Comedy; National Board of Review Awards '67: 10 Best Films of the Year; New York Film Critics Awards '67: Best Director (Nichols); Nominations: Academy Awards '66: Best Adapted Screenplay, Best Cinematography, Best Supporting Actress (Ross). *NLC, CRC, BTV*

Graduation Day ✗ **1981 (R)** Another teen slasher about the systematic murder of members of a high school track team. Notable mainly for brief appearance by Vanna White. **85m/C VHS, Beta.** Christopher George, Patch MacKenzie, E. Danny Murphy, Vanna White; ***D:*** Herb Freed. *COL*

Graffiti Bridge 🦴½ **1990 (PG-13)** Prince preaches love instead of sex and the result is boring. The Lavender One is a Minneapolis nightclub owner who battles with Day over the love of a beautiful woman. Chauvinistic attitudes toward women abound, but the females in the film don't seem to mind. Which must mean they were "acting." Visually interesting, although not as experimental as "Purple Rain." Music made Top Ten. **90m/C VHS, Beta, LV.** Prince, Morris Day, Jerome Benton, Jill Jones, Mavis Staples, George Clinton, Ingrid Chavez; ***D:*** Prince; ***W:*** Prince. *MVD, WAR*

Grain of Sand 🦴🦴🦴 **1984** Based on a true story, an understated French drama about a troubled woman searching her past, and her home town in Corsica, for the man of her dreams. Directorial debut of Meffre. In French with English subtitles. **90m/C VHS, Beta.** *FR* Delphine Seyrig, Genevieve Fontanel, Coralie Seyrig, Michel Aumont; ***D:*** Pomme Meffre. *FCT*

Grambling's White Tiger 🦴🦴½ **1981** The true story of Jim Gregory, the first white man to play on Grambling College's all-black football team. Jenner's a little too old, but Belafonte, in his TV acting debut, is fine as legendary coach Eddie Robinson. Based on book by Bruce Behrenberg. Made for television. **98m/C VHS, Beta.** Bruce Jenner, Harry Belafonte, LeVar Burton, Ray Vitte, Byron Stewart; ***D:*** Georg Stanford Brown; ***M:*** John D'Andrea. *MCA*

Grampa's Monster Movies **1990** Grampa (star of "The Munsters" TV show) hosts a tribute to Frankenstein, Dracula, Wolfman and the Mummy, with legends Bela Lugosi, Boris Karloff, Lon Chaney Jr. and Vincent Price. **65m/C VHS, Beta.** *NO*

Grampa's Sci-Fi Hits **1990** Sequel to Grampa's "Monster Movies," this one carries some of the more fantastic of sci-fi creatures from beyond. **65m/C VHS, Beta.** *NO*

Grand Canyon 🦴🦴🦴 **1991 (R)** Diverse group of characters is thrown together through chance encounters while coping with urban chaos in L.A. The main focus is the growing friendship between an immigration lawyer (Kline) and a tow-truck driver (Glover) who meet when Kline's car breaks down in a crime-ridden neighborhood. First-rate performances by the cast make up for numerous moral messages thrown at viewers with the subtlety of a brick. Sometimes funny, sometimes preachy became more relevant in light of the violence that exploded in L.A. during the summer of '92. **134m/C VHS.** Danny Glover, Kevin Kline, Steve Martin, Mary McDonnell, Mary-Louise Parker, Alfre Woodard, Jeremy Sisto, Tina Lifford, Patrick Malone, Mary Ellen Trainor; ***D:*** Lawrence Kasdan; ***W:*** Lawrence Kasdan, Meg Kasdan; ***C:*** Owen Roizman; ***M:*** James Newton Howard. National Board of Review Awards '91: 10 Best Films of the Year; Nominations: Academy Awards '91: Best Original Screenplay. *FXV*

Grand Canyon Trail 🦴½ **1948** Our hero is the owner of a played-out silver mine who is the target of an unscrupulous engineer who thinks there's silver to be found if you know where to look. The first appearance of the Riders of the Purple Sage, who replaced the Sons of the Pioneers. **68m/B VHS, Beta.** Roy Rogers, Andy Devine, Charles Coleman, Jane Frazee, Robert Livingston; ***D:*** William Witney. *NOS, MED, DVT*

The Grand Duchess and the Waiter 🦴🦴🦴 **1926** Menjou is a French millionaire who disguises himself as a waiter in order to enter the service of a grand duchess with whom he has fallen in love. **70m/B VHS, Beta.** Adolphe Menjou, Florence Vidor, Lawrence Grant; ***D:*** Malcolm St. Clair. *GVV*

The Grand Duel 🦴🦴 **1973** More spaghetti thrills as Lee plays a mysterious gunman who also acts as protector of a young ruffian falsely accused of murder. **?m/C VHS.** *IT* Lee Van Cleef, Peter O'Brien, Jess Hahn, Horst Frank. *SNC, VTR*

Grand Hotel 🦴🦴🦴½ **1932** A star-filled cast is brought together by unusual circumstances at Berlin's Grand Hotel and their lives become hopelessly intertwined over a 24 hour period. Adapted (and given the red-carpet treatment) from a Vicki Baum novel; notable mostly for Garbo's world-weary ballerina. Time has taken its toll on the concept and treatment, but still an interesting star vehicle. **112m/B VHS, Beta, LV.** Greta Garbo, John Barrymore, Joan Crawford, Lewis Stone, Wallace Beery, Jean Hersholt, Lionel Barrymore; ***D:*** Edmund Goulding; ***C:*** William H. Daniels. Academy Awards '32: Best Picture. *MGM, FCT, BTV*

Grand Illusion 🦴🦴🦴🦴 **1937** Unshakably classic anti-war film by Renoir, in which French prisoners of war attempt to escape from their German captors during WWI. An indictment of the way Old World, aristocratic nobility was brought to modern bloodshed in the Great War. Renoir's optimism remains relentless, but was easier to believe in before WWII. In French, with English subtitles. The laserdisc version includes an audio essay by Peter Crowe. **111m/B VHS, Beta, LV, 8mm.** *FR* Jean Gabin, Erich von Stroheim, Pierre Fresnay, Marcel Dalio, Julien Carette, Gaston Modot, Jean Daste, Dita Parlo; ***D:*** Jean Renoir. National Board of Review Awards '38: 5 Best Foreign Films of the Year; New York Film Critics Awards '38: Best Foreign Film; Nominations: Academy Awards '38: Best Picture. *VYY, MRV, FOX*

Grand Isle 🦴🦴½ **1992** At the turn of the century Grand Isle is the place Louisiana gentry leisurely spend their summers. This is where Edna Pontellier (McGillis), the wife of a rich stockbroker, meets sensitive Creole artist Robert LeBrun (Pasdar). Robert gives Edna all the attention sorely lacking in her marriage and they fall in love. However, Edna's attempts to liberate herself from the strictures of society lead her to tragedy. Based on "The Awakening" by Kate Chopin. Made for cable television. **94m/C VHS, LV.** Kelly McGillis, Adrian Pasdar, Julian Sands, Jon DeVries, Glenne Headly, Anthony De Sando, Ellen Burstyn; ***D:*** Mary Lambert; ***W:*** Hesper Anderson. *TTC*

Grand Larceny 🦴🦴 **1992** The daughter of a millionaire/thief has to prove that she can take over the family "business." Lots of action and stunts. **95m/C VHS.** Marilu Henner, Omar Sharif, Ian McShane, Louis Jourdan; ***D:*** Jeannot Szwarc. *CAF*

Grand Prix 🦴🦴 **1966** A big-budget look at the world of Grand Prix auto racing, as four top competitors circle the world's most famous racing circuits. Strictly for those who like cars racing round and round; nothing much happens off the track. Letterboxed screen is featured in the laserdisc format. **161m/C VHS, Beta, LV.** James Garner, Eva Marie Saint, Yves Montand, Toshiro Mifune, Brian Bedford; ***D:*** John Frankenheimer; ***C:*** Lionel Lindon; ***M:*** Maurice Jarre. Academy Awards '66: Best Film Editing, Best Sound, Best Sound Effects Editing. *MGM, FCT*

Grand Theft Auto 🦴🦴 **1977 (PG)** In Howard's initial directorial effort, a young couple elopes to Las Vegas in a Rolls Royce owned by the bride's father. The father, totally against the marriage and angered by the stolen Rolls, offers a reward for their safe return and a cross-country race ensues. **84m/C VHS, Beta.** Ron Howard, Nancy Morgan, Marion Ross, Barry Cahill, Clint Howard; ***D:*** Ron Howard; ***W:*** Ron Howard. *WAR*

Grand Tour: Disaster in Time 🦴🦴 **1992 (PG-13)** Greenglen is a quiet, small Midwestern town, until it is visited by a sinister group of time traveling aliens. Daniels plays a widowed innkeeper who must save the town from destruction and save his daughter from being kidnapped by the fiends. Made for cable television. **98m/C VHS, LV.** Jeff Daniels, Ariana Richards, Emilia Crow, Jim Haynie, Nicholas Guest, Marilyn Lightstone, George Murdock; ***D:*** David N. Twohy; ***W:*** David N. Twohy. *ACA*

Grandes Amigos 🦴 *Great Friends* **197?** A young boy finds out the meaning of having a true friend in this comedy-drama in Spanish. **105m/C VHS, Beta.** *SP* Nino Del Arco. *MAD*

Grandma's House 🦴 **1988 (R)** A brother and sister discover that the house in which they live with their grandmother is chock-full of secrets and strange happenings, including madness, incest, and murder. **90m/C VHS, Beta, LV.** Eric Foster, Kim Valentine, Brinke Stevens, Ida Lee; ***D:*** Peter Rader. *ACA*

Grandview U.S.A. 🦴🦴½ **1984 (R)** A low-key look at low-rent middle America, centering on a foxy local speedway owner and the derby-obsessed boys she attracts. Pre-"Dirty Dancing" choreography from Patrick Swayze and wife Lisa Niemi. **97m/C VHS, Beta.** Jamie Lee Curtis, Patrick Swayze, C. Thomas Howell, M. Emmet Walsh, Troy Donahue, William Windom, Jennifer Jason Leigh, Ramon Bieri, John Cusack, Joan Cusack, Jason Court; ***D:*** Randal Kleiser; ***M:*** Thomas Newman. *FOX*

The Granny 🦴½ **1994 (R)** Evil Granny Gargoli (Stevens) is so mean that just before she dies she swallows an ancient potion, enabling her to haunt her survivors. When Kelly (Whirry), the only one to really care for Granny, is cheated out of her inheritance, the rest of the family is in for some nasty shocks from the zombiefied oldster. Can't decide whether to be camp or horrific. **85m/C VHS.** Shannon Whirry, Stella Stevens; ***D:*** Luca Bercovici; ***W:*** Luca Bercovici. *AVE*

The Grapes of Wrath 🦴🦴🦴½ **1940** John Steinbeck's classic American novel about the Great Depression. We follow the impoverished Joad family as they migrate from the dust bowl of Oklahoma to find work in the orchards of California and as they struggle to maintain at least a little of their dignity and pride. A sentimental but dignified, uncharacteristic Hollywood epic. **129m/B VHS, Beta, LV.** Henry Fonda, Jane Darwell, John Carradine, Charley Grapewin, Zeffie Tilbury, Dorris Bowdon, Russell Simpson, John Qualen, Eddie Quillan, O.Z. Whitehead, Grant Mitchell; ***D:*** John Ford; ***W:*** Nunnally Johnson; ***C:*** Gregg Toland. Academy Awards '40: Best Director (Ford), Best Supporting Actress (Darwell); New York Film Critics Awards '40: Best Director (Ford), Best Film; Nominations: Academy Awards '40: Best Actor (Fonda), Best Adapted Screenplay, Best Picture, Best Sound, Best Original Score. *FXV, BTV, HMV*

The Grass is Always Greener Over the Septic Tank 🦴🦴 **1978** Based on Erma Bombeck's best-seller. A city family's flight to the supposed peace of the suburbs turns out to be a comic compilation of complications. Made for television. **98m/C VHS, Beta.** Carol Burnett, Charles Grodin, Linda Gray, Alex Rocco, Robert Sampson, Vicki Belmonte, Craig Richard Nelson, Anrae Walterhouse, Eric Stoltz; ***D:*** Robert Day. *NO*

The Grass is Greener 🦴🦴½ **1961** An American millionaire invades part of an impoverished Earl's mansion and falls in love with the lady of the house. The Earl, who wants to keep his wife, enlists the aid of an old girlfriend in a feeble attempt to make her jealous. The two couples pair off properly in the end. **105m/C VHS, LV.** Cary Grant, Deborah Kerr, Jean Simmons, Robert Mitchum; ***D:*** Stanley Donen. *REP*

Grave of the Fireflies 🦴🦴🦴 **1988** In post-war Japan, in the city of Kobe's train station, a young boy lies dying. A janitor finds a metal canister lying next to the boy and when he opens it ashes fall out. As fireflies gather around, ghostly figures of the boy and his little sister appear, as the story flashes back to the orphaned, homeless Seita and his sister. The two youngsters struggle in the Japanese countryside but find they cannot escape the hardships of war and have no chance for survival. Stunning animated testimony to the human spirit. Based on the novel by Akiyuki Nosaka. In Japanese with English subtitles. **88m/C VHS, LV.** *JP* ***D:*** Isao Takahata; ***W:*** Isao Takahata. *CPM, WTA*

Grave of the Vampire 🦴 *Seed of Terror* **1972 (R)** A vampire rapes and impregnates a modern-day girl. Twenty years later, their son, who grows up to be a bitter bloodsucker, sets out to find his father and kill him. **95m/C VHS, Beta.** William Smith, Michael Pataki, Lyn Peters, Diane Holden, Jay Adler, Kitty Vallacher, Jay Scott, Lieux Dressler; ***D:*** John Hayes. *UNI*

Grave Secrets 🦴½ **1989 (R)** A professor of psychic phenomena teams up with a medium to find out who—or what—is controlling the life of a young woman. **90m/C VHS, LV.** Paul LeMat, Renee Soutendijk, David Warner, Olivia Barash, Lee Ving; ***D:*** Donald P. Borchers. *SGE*

Grave Secrets: The Legacy of Hilltop Drive 1992 The Williams family finds out their dream house is built on the site of an old graveyard. The spirits are not only restless, they're deadly. Based on a true story. **94m/C VHS.** Jonelle Allen, Patty Duke, David Selby, David Soul, Blake Clark; **D:** John D. Patterson. *WOV, PMS*

The Graveyard *Persecution; Terror of Sheba; Sheba* **1974** A mommy spends many years torturing her little boy, David. In one blood-filled day, the fellow seeks his revenge. **90m/C VHS, Beta.** Lana Turner, Trevor Howard, Ralph Bates, Olga Georges-Picot, Suzan Farmer; **D:** Don Chaffey. *ELV*

Graveyard of Horror 1971 His wife and baby dead, a man seeking revenge discovers a horrible secret: his brother, a doctor, is stealing the heads from corpses. Dubbed. **105m/C VHS, Beta.** *SP* Bill Curran, Francisco (Frank) Brana, Beatriz Lacy; **D:** Miguel Madrid. *NO*

Graveyard Shift ½ **1987 (R)** A New York cabby on the night shift is actually a powerful vampire who uses his fares to build an army of vampires. Not to be confused with the 1990 Stephen King scripted film. Followed by "Understudy: Graveyard Shift II." **89m/C VHS, Beta.** *IT* Silvio Oliviero, Helen Papas, Cliff Stoker; **D:** Gerard Ciccoritti. *VTR*

Graveyard Shift *Stephen King's Graveyard Shift* **1990 (R)** Just because Stephen King wrote the original story doesn't mean its celluloid incarnation is guaranteed to stand your hair on end; unless that's your response to abject boredom. When a man takes over the night shift at a recently reopened textile mill, he starts to find remnants...and they aren't fabric. Seems there's a graveyard in the neighborhood. **89m/C VHS, Beta, LV.** David Andrews, Kelly Wolf, Stephen Macht, Brad Dourif; **D:** Ralph S. Singleton; **W:** Stephen King, John Esposito; **M:** Brian Banks. *PAR, FCT*

Gray Lady Down **1977 (PG)** A nuclear submarine sinks off the coast of Cape Cod and with their oxygen running out, a risky escape in an experimental diving craft seems to be their only hope. Dull, all-semi-star suspenser. **111m/C VHS, Beta.** Charlton Heston, David Carradine, Stacy Keach, Ned Beatty, Ronny Cox, Christopher Reeve, Michael O'Keefe, Rosemary Forsyth; **D:** David Greene. *MCA*

Grayeagle **1977 (PG)** When a frontier trapper's daughter is kidnapped by Cheyenne Indians, he launches a search for her recovery. More style than pace in this Western, but worth a look for fans of Johnson. **104m/C VHS, Beta.** Ben Johnson, Iron Eyes Cody, Lana Wood, Alex Cord, Jack Elam, Paul Fix, Cindy Butler, Charles B. Pierce; **D:** Charles B. Pierce; **W:** Charles B. Pierce. *WAR, OM*

Grazuole 1969 A nine-year-old girl is mockingly made "Beauty Queen" by her malicious playmates. **71m/B VHS, Beta. D:** Arunas Zhebrunas. *IHF*

Grease **1978 (PG)** Film version of the hit Broadway musical about summer love. Set in the 1950s, this spirited musical follows a group of highschoolers throughout their senior year. The story offers a responsible moral: act like a tart and you'll get your guy; but, hey, it's all in fun anyway. Followed by a weak sequel. ♫Grease; Summer Nights; Hopelessly Devoted To You; You're the One That I Want; Sandy; Beauty School Dropout; Look at Me, I'm Sandra Dee; Greased Lightnin'; It's Raining on Prom Night. **110m/C VHS, Beta, LV.** John Travolta, Olivia Newton-John, Jeff Conaway, Stockard Channing, Eve Arden, Frankie Avalon, Sid Caesar; **D:** Randal Kleiser. People's Choice Awards '79: Best Film; Nominations: Academy Awards '78: Best Song ("Hopelessly Devoted to You"). *PAR, FCT*

Grease 2 **1982 (PG)** Continuing saga of the T-Birds, the Pink Ladies, and young love at Rydell High. Newton-John and Travolta have graduated, leaving Pfeiffer to lead on love-struck book-neb Caulfield. Some okay tunes, though lame story lacks good-humor flair of the original. **115m/C VHS, Beta, LV.** Maxwell Caulfield, Michelle Pfeiffer, Adrian Zmed, Lorna Luft, Didi Conn, Eve Arden, Sid Caesar, Tab Hunter; **D:** Patricia Birch; **M:** Artie Butler. *PAR*

Greased Lightning ½ **1977 (PG)** The story of the first black auto racing champion, Wendell Scott, who had to overcome racial prejudice to achieve his success. Slightly-better-than-average Pryor comedy vehicle. **95m/C VHS, Beta.** Richard Pryor, Pam Grier, Beau Bridges, Cleavon Little, Vincent Gardenia; **D:** Michael A. Schultz; **W:** Leon Capetanos, Melvin Van Peebles. *WAR*

Greaser's Palace ½ **1972** Seaweed-head Greaser, owner of the town's saloon, faces his arch-nemesis in this wide-ranging satiric Christ allegory from the director of "Putney Swope." **91m/C VHS, Beta.** Albert Henderson, Allan Arbus; **D:** Robert Downey; **M:** Jack Nitzsche. *COL, OM*

The Great Adventure ½ *Det Stora Aventyret* **1953** Two farm boys capture and attempt to train a wild otter. Unfortunately, the otter longs to once again join his kind despite the boys' efforts. Arne Sucksdorff won an Oscar for his arresting view of animal life. **73m/B VHS, Beta.** *SW* Anders Norberg, Kjell Sucksdorff, Arne Sucksdorff; **D:** Arne Sucksdorff; **W:** Arne Sucksdorff. *MED*

Great Adventure **1975 (PG)** In the severe environment of the gold rush days on the rugged Yukon territory, a touching tale unfolds of a young orphan boy and his eternal bond of friendship with a great northern dog. Based on a Jack London story. Paul Elliots is a pseudonym for Gianfranco Baldanello and Fred Romer is actually Fernando Romero. **90m/C VHS, Beta.** *IT SP* Jack Palance, Joan Collins, Fred Romer, Elisabetta Virgili, Remo de Angelis, Manuel de Blas; **D:** Paul Elliotts. *MED, VTR*

The Great Alligator *Il Fiume Del Grande Caimano* **1981** As if you couldn't guess, this one's about a huge alligator who does what other huge alligators do...terrorizes the people at a resort. **89m/C VHS, Beta.** Barbara Bach, Mel Ferrer, Richard Johnson; **D:** Sergio Martino. *MPI*

The Great American Broadcast 1941 Two WWI vets want more than anything to strike it rich. After many failed endeavors, the two try that new-fangled thing called radio. The station takes off, as does the plot. The girlfriend of one vet falls for his partner and numerous other misunderstandings and complications ensue. Charming and crazy musical with an energetic cast. ♫I've Got a Bone To Pick With You; It's All In a Lifetime; I Take to You; Long Ago Last Night; Where You Are; The Great American Broadcast; Albany Bound; Give My Regards to Broadway; If I Didn't Care. **92m/B VHS.** Alice Faye, John Payne, Jack Oakie, Cesar Romero, James Newill, Mary Beth Hughes; **D:** Archie Mayo; **C:** Leon Shamroy. *MLB*

The Great American Sex Scandal ½ *Jury Duty* **1994 (PG-13)** Sanford Lagelfust (Pinchot) is an meek accountant on trial for embezzlement, but when the prosecution's main witness turns out to be his sexy girlfriend Hope (Scoggins) the case turns into a courtroom sex scandal. Silly Canadian TV production. **94m/C VHS.** *CA* Bronson Pinchot, Tracy Scoggins, Heather Locklear, Stephen Baldwin, Lynn Redgrave, Alan Thicke, Madchen Amick, Barbara Bosson, Ilene Graff, Mark Blankfield, Danny Pintauro, Reginald Veljohnson, Jacklyn Zeman; **D:** Michael A. Schultz. *APX*

Great American Traffic Jam ½ *Gridlock* **1980 (PG)** A made-for-television farce about the humorous variety of characters interacting on the interstate during a massive California traffic jam. **97m/C VHS, Beta.** Ed McMahon, Vic Tayback, Howard Hesseman, Abe Vigoda, Noah Beery Jr., Desi Arnaz Jr., John Beck, Shelley Fabares, James Gregory; **D:** James Frawley. *FOX*

The Great American Western Collection: Roy Rogers 194? Series of three Roy Rogers classics. "West of the Badlands" is an adaptation of Zane Grey's novel "Border Legion." Rogers plays an outlaw who sacrifices himself to save a pair of lovers. In "Jesse James at Bay," Rogers plays a romanticized version of James, stealing from the rich and powerful railroad to help the poor settlers keep their land. Rogers and Dale Evans star together in the singing western classic, Yellow Rose of Texas. **180m/B VHS.** Roy Rogers, George "Gabby" Hayes, Dale Evans. *BPG*

The Great Armored Car Swindle **1964** An anonymous English businessman becomes involved in international intrigue when he becomes a pawn in a plan to transfer money to a Middle Eastern government under communist rule. But thanks to his wife things don't go off as planned. **58m/B VHS, Beta.** Peter Reynolds, Dermot Walsh, Joanna Dunham, Lisa Gastoni, Brian Cobby; **D:** Lance Comfort. *SNC*

Great Balls of Fire ½ **1989 (PG-13)** A florid, comic-book film of the glory days of Jerry Lee Lewis, from his first band to stardom. Most of the drama is derived from his marriage to his 13-year-old cousin. Somewhat overacted but full of energy. The soundtrack features many of the "Killer's" greatest hits re-recorded by Jerry Lee Lewis for the film. **108m/C VHS, Beta, LV.** Dennis Quaid, Winona Ryder, Alec Baldwin, Trey Wilson, John Doe, Lisa Blount, Steve Allen, Stephen Tobolowsky, Lisa Jane Persky, Michael St. Gerard, Peter Cook; **D:** Jim McBride; **W:** Jack Baran, Jim McBride; **M:** Jack Baran, Jim McBride. *ORI*

Great Bank Hoax ½ *The Great Georgia Bank Hoax; Shenanigans* **1978 (PG)** Three bank managers decide to rob their own bank to cover up the fact that all the assets have been embezzled. **89m/C VHS, Beta.** Richard Basehart, Ned Beatty, Burgess Meredith, Michael Murphy, Paul Sand, Arthur Godfrey; **D:** Joseph Jacoby; **C:** Walter Lassally. *WAR*

Great Bikini Off-Road Adventure ½ **1994 (R)** Duke Abbey is about to lose his jeep tour company because business is so slow that he can't pay the rent. Then Duke's niece Lori decides to get her bikini-clad friends to hire on as drivers, showing lots of sights on their desert tours. **90m/C VHS, LV.** Avalon Anders, Lauren Hays, Floyd Irons, Laura Hudspeth, Dan Frank; **D:** Gary Orona. *IMP, IME*

The Great Caruso ½ **1951** The story of opera legend Enrico Caruso's rise to fame, from his childhood in Naples, Italy, to his collapse on the stage of the Metropolitan Opera House. Lanza is superb as the singer, and there are 27 musical numbers to satisfy the opera lover. ♫The Loveliest Night of the Year; Over the Waves; Vesti la Giubba; M'Appari; Celeste Aida; Numi, Pieta; La Fatal Pietra; Sextet from Lucia di Lammermoor; La Donne a Mobile. **113m/C VHS, Beta, LV.** Mario Lanza, Ann Blyth, Dorothy Kirsten; **D:** Richard Thorpe; **C:** Joseph Ruttenberg. Academy Awards '51: Best Sound; Nominations: Academy Awards '51: Best Costume Design (Color), Best Original Score. *MGM*

Great Chase ½ **1963** A historical anthology of the funniest and most suspenseful classic movie chases, especially "The General." **79m/B VHS, Beta.** Buster Keaton, Lillian Gish, Pearl White, Noah Beery Jr.; **M:** Larry Adler. *SUE, NLC*

The Great Commandment 1941 Young man throws himself into a revolution against the overbearing Roman Empire in 30 A.D. His brother joins him but is killed. The man, who has become influenced by the teachings of Christ, decides to give up his revolution and go off with his brother's widow. (He always loved her anyway.) **78m/B VHS.** John Beal, Maurice Moscovich, Albert Dekker, Marjorie Cooley, Warren McCollum; **D:** Irving Pichel. *REP*

Great Dan Patch ½ **1949** The story of the great Dan Patch, the horse that went on to become the highest-earning harness racer in history. **92m/B VHS, Beta.** Dennis O'Keefe, Gail Russell, Ruth Warrick; **D:** Joseph M. Newman. *VEC*

Great Day ½ **1946** A soap opera set around the wartime visit of first lady Eleanor Roosevelt to a small British town. It focuses mainly on the wife and daughter of a bitter, alcoholic WWI vet. **62m/B VHS, Beta.** Eric Portman, Flora Robson, Sheila Sim, Isabel Jeans, Walter Fitzgerald, Philip Friend, Marjorie Rhodes, Maire O'Neill, Beatrice Varley; **D:** Lance Comfort. *TTC*

Great Day in the Morning ½ **1956** A rebel sympathizer and a Northern spy are both after Colorado gold to help finance the Civil War. But our Southern gentlemen soon find themselves equally interested in the local ladies. **92m/C VHS, Beta.** Robert Stack, Ruth Roman, Raymond Burr, Virginia Mayo, Alex Nicol, Regis Toomey; ***D:*** Jacques Tourneur. *NO*

The Great Dictator 🦴🦴🦴🦴 **1940** Chaplin's first all-dialogue film, a searing satire on Nazism in which he has dual roles as a Jewish barber with amnesia who is mistaken for a Hitlerian dictator, Adenoid Hynkel. A classic scene involves Hynkel playing with a gigantic balloon of the world. Hitler banned the film's release to the German public due to its highly offensive portrait of him. The film also marked Chaplin's last wearing of the Little Tramp's (and Hitler's equally little) mustache. **126m/B VHS, Beta, LV.** Charlie Chaplin, Paulette Goddard, Jack Oakie, Billy Gilbert, Reginald Gardiner, Henry Daniell, Maurice Moscovich; ***D:*** Charlie Chaplin; ***W:*** Charlie Chaplin; ***C:*** Karl Struss. National Board of Review Awards '40: 10 Best Films of the Year; New York Film Critics Awards '40: Best Actor (Chaplin); Nominations: Academy Awards '40: Best Actor (Chaplin), Best Original Screenplay, Best Picture, Best Supporting Actor (Oakie), Best Original Score. *FOX, HMV, GLV*

The Great Elephant Escape 🦴🦴½ **1995** Vacationing American teen Gordon-Levitt teams up with Kenyan M'Cormac, who works at an animal orphanage, to save a baby elephant from an unscrupulous businessman and his poacher friends. Made for TV. **90m/C VHS.** Joseph Gordon-Levitt, Frederick M'Cormac, Stephanie Zimbalist, Leo Burmester, Julian Sands; ***D:*** George Miller; ***W:*** John Sweet, Christopher Canaan. *CAF*

The Great Escape 🦴🦴🦴½ **1963** During WWII, troublesome allied POW's are thrown by the Nazis into an escape-proof camp, where they join forces in a single mass break for freedom. One of the great war movies, with a superb ensemble cast and lots of excitement. The story was true, based on the novel by Paul Brickhill. McQueen performed most of the stunts himself, against the wishes of director Sturges. Laserdisc features an analysis of the true story that inspired the movie, actual photos of the camp, prisoners, and guards, commentary by director Sturges, composer Bernstein, and stuntman Bud Ekins, excerpts from the script by novelist/screenwriter Clavell, over 250 production photos, and the original movie trailer. Followed by a made for TV movie 25 years later. **170m/C VHS, Beta, LV.** Steve McQueen, James Garner, Richard Attenborough, Charles Bronson, James Coburn, Donald Pleasence, David McCallum, James Donald, Gordon Jackson; ***D:*** John Sturges; ***W:*** James Clavell, W.R. Burnett; ***C:*** Daniel F. Fapp; ***M:*** Elmer Bernstein. National Board of Review Awards '63: 10 Best Films of the Year. *MGM, FOX, CRC*

The Great Escape 2: The Untold Story 🦴🦴 **1988** Bland actioner can't decide whether it's a remake of the original or a sequel; it pretends to be a sequel yet spends a lot of time retelling—poorly—the first great escape. Once it gets around to the sequel part, it dispenses with protocol: Pleasance, an escapee in the original, is a Nazi bad guy in this go-round. Poor casting, especially Reeves, unconvincing as a German-speaking British officer who rallies the surviving escapees in revenge against their WWII captors. Made for television and originally shown in two parts, but mercifully shortened for video. **93m/C VHS.** Christopher Reeve, Judd Hirsch, Ian McShane, Donald Pleasence, Anthony John Denison, Jud Taylor, Charles Haid; ***D:*** Michael Nader, Paul Wendkos. *VMK, TLF*

Great Expectations 🦴🦴🦴🦴 **1946** Lean's magisterial adaptation of the Dickens tome, in which a young English orphan is graced by a mysterious benefactor and becomes a well-heeled gentleman. Hailed and revered over the years; possibly the best Dickens on film. Well-acted by all, but especially notable is Hunt's slightly mad and pathetic Miss Havisham. Remake of the 1934 film. **118m/B VHS, Beta, LV.** *GB* John Mills, Valerie Hobson, Anthony Wager, Alec Guinness, Finlay Currie, Jean Simmons, Bernard Miles, Francis L. Sullivan, Martita Hunt, Ivan Barnard, Freda Jackson, Torin Thatcher, Eileen Erskine, Hay Petrie; ***D:*** David Lean; ***W:*** David Lean; ***C:*** Guy Green. Academy Awards '47: Best Art Direction/Set Decoration (B & W), Best Black and White Cinematography; National Board of Review Awards '47: 10 Best Films of the Year; Nominations: Academy Awards '47: Best Director (Lean), Best Picture, Best Screenplay. *PAR, LCA, HMV*

Great Expectations 🦴🦴 **1981** A British television mini-series adaptation of the Dickens epic about Pip and his mysterious benefactor in Victorian London. On two tapes. **300m/C VHS, Beta.** *GB* Gerry Sundquist, Stratford Johns, Joan Hickson. *NO*

Great Expectations 🦴🦴🦴 **1989** Dickens classic retold on 3 cassettes. A mysterious benefactor turns a poor orphan boy into a gentleman of means. **325m/C VHS, Beta.** *GB* Jean Simmons, Anthony Hopkins, John Rhys-Davies; ***D:*** Kevin Connor. *DIS*

Great Expectations: The Untold Story 🦴🦴½ **1987** Magwitch is an escaped convict, hiding out in the Victorian English countryside, who is aided by the young orphan, Pip. Captured and sent to the penal colonies in Australia, Magwitch serves his time and then discovers a fortune in gold, which he decides to use to make Pip into a gentleman. But Magwitch's enemies would like to get Pip's inheritance for themselves. Based on the Dickens classic, this three-tape miniseries is also available in a 102-minute feature length version. **287m/C VHS.** John Stanton, Sigrid Thornton, Robert Coleby, Todd Boyce, Anne Louise Lambert, Ron Haddrick, Noel Ferrier; ***D:*** Tim Burstall. *FCT*

Great Flamarion 🦴🦴½ **1945** A woman-hating trick-shot artist is nevertheless duped into murdering the husband of his femme fatale assistant after he comes to believe she loves him. He's wrong. **78m/B VHS, Beta.** Dan Duryea, Erich von Stroheim, Mary Beth Hughes; ***D:*** Anthony Mann. *SNC, NOS, DVT*

The Great Gabbo 🦴🦴 **1929** A ventriloquist can express himself only through his dummy, losing his own identity and going mad at the end. Von Stroheim's first talkie. May quite possibly be the first mentally-twisted-ventriloquist story ever put on film. Von Stroheim hated the movie, believing it to be analogous to his own life. When he tried to buy the rights to the film, presumably to destroy the prints, he found that the property had been already purchased by real-life ventriloquist, Edgar Bergen. Based on a story by Ben Hecht. ♫The New Step; I'm Laughing Ickey; I'm in Love With You; The Ga-Ga Bird; The Web of Love; Every Now and Then. **82m/B VHS, Beta.** Erich von Stroheim, Betty Compson, Don Douglas, Marjorie Kane; ***D:*** James Cruze. *SNC, NOS, DVT*

The Great Gatsby 🦴🦴½ **1974 (PG)** Adaptation of F. Scott Fitzgerald's novel of the idle rich in the 1920s. A mysterious millionaire crashes Long Island society, and finds his heart captured by an impetuous and emotionally impoverished girl. Skillful acting and directing captures the look and feel of this era, but the movie doesn't have the power of the book. **144m/C VHS, Beta, LV.** Robert Redford, Mia Farrow, Bruce Dern, Karen Black, Patsy Kensit, Sam Waterston, Howard da Silva, Edward Herrmann; ***D:*** Jack Clayton; ***W:*** Francis Ford Coppola; ***M:*** Nelson Riddle. Academy Awards '74: Best Adapted Score, Best Costume Design; Golden Globe Awards '75: Best Supporting Actress (Black). *PAR, FCT*

The Great Gildersleeve 🦴🦴 **1943** Throckmorton P. Gildersleeve adds another problem to his list; the sister of a local judge wants to marry him. His niece and nephew won't allow it and his attempts to juggle everyone's desires make for fine fun. Peary was also the voice for the popular radio series of the same name. **62m/B VHS.** Harold Peary, Jane Darwell, Nancy Gates, Charles Arnt, Thurston Hall; ***D:*** Gordon Douglas. *MED*

Great Gold Swindle 🦴🦴 **1984** A dramatization of the 1982 swindling of the Perth Mint in Australia of over $650,000 worth of gold. **101m/C VHS, Beta.** John Hargreaves, Robert C. Hughes, Tony Rickards, Barbara Llewellyn. *LIV*

The Great Gundown 🦴½ **1975** A violent tale set in the Old West. The peace of frontier New Mexico erupts when a half-breed Indian leads a brutal assault on an outlaw stronghold. **98m/C VHS, Beta.** Robert Padilla, Richard Rust, Milila St. Duval; ***D:*** Paul Hunt. *HHT*

Great Guns 🦴🦴 **1941** Stan and Ollie enlist in the army to protect a spoiled millionaire's son but wind up being targets at target practice instead. Not one of their better efforts. **74m/B VHS, Beta.** Stan Laurel, Oliver Hardy, Sheila Ryan, Dick Nelson; ***D:*** Montague Banks. *FOX, MLB*

Great Guy 🦴½ *Pluck of the Irish* **1936** One of Cagney's lesser roles as an ex-boxer turned food inspector who wipes out graft in his town. **50m/B VHS, Beta.** James Cagney, Mae Clarke, Edward Brophy; ***D:*** John Blystone. *NOS, MRV, PSM*

The Great Hunter 🦴 **1975** A village militia captain and his girlfriend seek to destroy the men who killed the girl's father. **91m/C VHS, Beta.** Chia Ling, Wang Yu, Hsu Feng. *UNI*

The Great Impostor 🦴🦴½ **1961** The true story of Ferdinand Waldo Demara, Jr., who during the 1950s, hoodwinked people by impersonating a surgeon, a college professor, a monk, a prison warden and a schoolteacher, with the FBI always one step behind him. **112m/C VHS, Beta.** Tony Curtis, Edmond O'Brien, Arthur O'Connell, Gary Merrill, Raymond Massey, Karl Malden, Mike Kellin, Frank Gorshin; ***D:*** Robert Mulligan; ***C:*** Robert Burks; ***M:*** Henry Mancini. *MCA*

Great Jesse James Raid 🦴½ **1949** Jesse James comes out of retirement to carry out a mine theft. Routine. **73m/C VHS, Beta.** Willard Parker, Barbara Payton, Tom Neal, Wallace Ford; ***D:*** Reginald Le-Borg. *RXM, MRV*

Great K & A Train Robbery 🦴🦴½ **1926** A railroad detective is hired to find and stop the bandits who have been preying on the K & A Railroad. Silent. **55m/B VHS, Beta.** Tom Mix, Dorothy Dwan, William Walling, Harry Grippe, Carl Miller; ***D:*** Lewis Seiler. *GPV, GVV*

The Great Land of Small 🦴🦴 **1986 (G)** Two children enter a fantasy world and try to save it from Evil. For kids. **94m/C VHS, Beta.** Karen Elkin, Michael Blouin, Michael Anderson Jr., Ken Roberts; ***D:*** Vojtech Jasny. *VTR, NWV, HHE*

Great Leaders of the Bibles **197?** The inspiring stories of two Old Testament heroes, Gideon and Samson, are dramatized in this beautifully constructed film. **105m/C VHS, Beta.** Ivo Garrani, Fernando Rey, Giorgio Ceridni. *VCI*

The Great Lie 🦴🦴🦴 **1941** A great soaper with Davis and Astor as rivals for the affections of Brent, an irresponsible flyer. Astor is the concert pianist who marries Brent and then finds out she's pregnant after he's presumed dead in a crash. The wealthy Davis offers to raise the baby so Astor can continue her career. But when Brent does return, who will it be to? Sparkling, catty fun. Astor's very short, mannish haircut became a popular trend. **107m/B VHS, Beta, LV.** Bette Davis, Mary Astor, George Brent, Lucile Watson, Hattie McDaniel, Grant Mitchell, Jerome Cowan; ***D:*** Edmund Goulding; ***C:*** Gaetano Antonio "Tony" Gaudio; ***M:*** Max Steiner. Academy Awards '41: Best Supporting Actress (Astor). *MGM, BTV*

The Great Locomotive Chase 🦴🦴½ *Andrews' Raiders* **1956** During the Civil War, Parker and his fellow soldiers head into Confederate territory to disrupt railroad supply lines. They take over a locomotive, but are pursued by Confederate Hunter, the conductor of another train; and soon a pursuit is underway. Based on the true story of Andrew's Raiders. **85m/C VHS, Beta.** Fess Parker, Jeffrey Hunter, Kenneth Tobey; ***D:*** Francis D. Lyon. *DIS*

The Great Los Angeles Earthquake 🦴½ **1991** Made-for-TV disaster movie is the same old story; multiple soap-opera plotlines are spun around terrifying special effects, as L.A. is devastated by three major earth tremors and attendant disasters. Condensed from a two-part miniseries, also known as "The Big One: The Great Los Angeles Earthquake." **106m/C VHS.** Ed Begley Jr., Joanna Kerns; ***D:*** Larry Elikann. *VMK*

Great Love Experiment ☆ **1984** Everyone in a high school learns a valuable lesson about beauty and friendship when four popular students try to change the personality of an awkward classmate. **52m/C VHS, Beta.** Tracy Pollan, Esai Morales, Kelly Wolf, Scott Benderer. *NO*

The Great Lover ☆☆½ **1949** Aboard an ocean liner, a bumbler chaperoning school kids gets involved with a gambler, a duchess and a murder. Vintage Bob Hope. **80m/B VHS, Beta.** Bob Hope, Rhonda Fleming, Roland Young, Roland Culver, George Reeves, Jim Backus; ***D:*** Alexander Hall. *COL, FCT*

The Great Madcap ☆☆ **1949** A wealthy man believes in lavishly indulging himself which drives his excessively conservative family crazy. Bunuel satirizes behavioral extremes, Christianity, advertising, sex, and a number of other popular absurdities. In Spanish with English subtitles. **90m/B VHS.** *MX* Fernando Soler, Rosario Granados, Ruben Rogo; ***D:*** Luis Bunuel. *WBF, INJ*

The Great Man Votes ☆☆☆ **1938** Alcoholic college professor Barrymore falls into a deep depression after his wife's death. His children then plan to create a situation wherein his vote will decide the fate of the new town mayor, thus instilling in him a newly found sense of importance for himself and his children. Satiric and funny. **72m/B VHS, Beta.** John Barrymore, Peter Holden, Virginia Weidler, Katherine Alexander, Donald MacBride, Elisabeth Risdon, Granville Bates, Luis Alberni, J.M. Kerrigan, William Demarest, Roy Gordon; ***D:*** Garson Kanin; ***C:*** Russell Metty. *TTC*

The Great Man's Lady ☆☆½ **1942** Stanwyck stars in a "stand by your man" story in which she supported and was responsible for the good deeds of a now past town hero. Told in flashback sequence, Stanwyck's character, 109-year-old Hanna Sampler, reveals to a young biographer the trials and tribulations of her life with Ethan Hoyt, founder of Hoyt City, who is being honored with the dedication of a statue in the opening of the film. The picture reveals their secrets and the truth about the woman behind the man. Based on the story "The Human Side" by Vina Delmar. **91m/B VHS.** Barbara Stanwyck, Joel McCrea, Brian Donlevy; ***D:*** William A. Wellman; ***W:*** Seena Owen, W.L. Rivers, Adela Rogers St. John; ***C:*** William Mellor; ***M:*** Victor Young. *MCA*

The Great McGinty ☆☆☆½ *Down Went McGinty* **1940** Sturges' directorial debut, about the rise and fall of a small-time, bribe-happy politician is an acerbic, ultra-cynical indictment of modern politics that stands, like much of his other work, as bracingly courageous as anything that's ever snuck past the Hollywood censors. Political party boss Tamiroff chews the scenery with gusto while Donlevy, in his first starring role, is more than his equal as the not-so-dumb political hack. **82m/B VHS, Beta, LV.** Brian Donlevy, Muriel Angelus, Akim Tamiroff, Louis Jean Heydt, Arthur Hoyt, William Demarest; ***D:*** Preston Sturges; ***W:*** Preston Sturges; ***C:*** William Mellor. Academy Awards '40: Best Original Screenplay. *MCA*

Great McGonagall ☆½ **1975** Tale of an unemployed Scot trying to become Britain's poet laureate. Sellers adds a semi-bright spot with his portrayal of Queen Victoria! **95m/C VHS.** *GB* Peter Sellers, Spike Milligan, Julia Foster; ***D:*** Joseph McGrath. *MOV, VTR*

The Great Mike ☆☆½ **1944** Unlikely but moving story of a young boy who convinces track management that his work horse has a chance against the touted thoroughbred. Sentimental, with little innovation, but generally well-acted. **72m/B VHS.** Stuart Erwin, Robert "Buzzy" Henry, Pierre Watkin, Gwen Kenyon, Carl "Alfalfa" Switzer, Edythe Elliott, Marion Martin; ***D:*** Wallace Fox. *NOS*

Great Missouri Raid ☆☆ **1951** Follows the famous adventures of the James/Younger gang and their eventual demise. **81m/C VHS, Beta.** Wendell Corey, MacDonald Carey, Ellen Drew, Ward Bond; ***D:*** Gordon Douglas; ***C:*** Ray Rennahan. *BAR*

The Great Moment ☆☆ **1944** Story of the Boston dentist who discovered ether's use as an anesthetic in 1845. Confusing at times, changing from comedy to drama and containing flashbacks that add little to the story. Surprisingly bland result from ordinarily solid cast and director. **87m/B VHS, Beta.** Joel McCrea, Betty Field, Harry Carey Sr., William Demarest, Franklin Pangborn, Porter Hall; ***D:*** Preston Sturges; ***C:*** Victor Milner. *MCA*

The Great Mouse Detective ☆☆☆ *The Adventures of the Great Mouse Detective* **1986 (G)** Animated version of the book "Basil of Baker Street" by Eve Titus. Fun adventure about Sherlock-of-the-mouse-world. Not as good as some of the other Disney animated features, but kids will enjoy it nonetheless. In 1992 it was rereleased. **74m/C VHS, Beta, LV.** ***D:*** John Musker, Ron Clements, Dave Michener, Burny Mattinson; ***W:*** Ron Clements, Dave Michener; ***M:*** Henry Mancini; ***V:*** Vincent Price, Barrie Ingham, Val Bettin, Susanne Pollatschek, Candy Candido, Eve Brenner, Alan Young, Melissa Manchester. *DIS, OM*

Great Movie Stunts & the Making of Raiders of the Lost Ark **1981** Two television specials: "Movie Stunts" demonstrates how major action sequences were designed and executed, and "Making of Raiders" captures the cast and crew as they tackle the many problems created in filming the spectacular scenes. **107m/C VHS, Beta, LV.** Harrison Ford. *PAR*

The Great Muppet Caper ☆☆☆ **1981 (G)** A group of hapless reporters (Kermit, Fozzie Bear, and Gonzo) travel to London to follow up on a major jewel robbery. **95m/C VHS, Beta, LV.** Jim Henson's Muppets, Charles Grodin, Diana Rigg; ***Cameos:*** John Cleese, Robert Morley, Peter Ustinov, Peter Falk, Jack Warden; ***D:*** Jim Henson; ***W:*** Jack Rose; ***C:*** Oswald Morris; ***V:*** Frank Oz. Nominations: Academy Awards '81: Best Song ("The First Time It Happens"). *JHV, FOX*

The Great Northfield Minnesota Raid ☆☆½ **1972 (PG)** The Younger/James gang decides to rob the biggest bank west of the Mississippi, but everything goes wrong. Uneven, offbeat western, but Duvall's portrayal of the psychotic Jesse James and Robertson's cunning Cole Younger are notable. **91m/C VHS, Beta.** Cliff Robertson, Robert Duvall, Elisha Cook Jr., Luke Askew, R.G. Armstrong, Donald Moffat, Matt Clark; ***D:*** Philip Kaufman; ***W:*** Philip Kaufman; ***C:*** Bruce Surtees; ***M:*** Dave Grusin. *MCA*

The Great Outdoors ☆☆ **1988 (PG)** Good cast is mostly wasted in another John Hughes' tale of vacation gone bad. A family's peaceful summer by the lake is disturbed by their uninvited, trouble-making relatives. Aykroyd and Candy are two funny guys done in by a lame script that awkwardly examines friendship and coming of age and throws in a giant bear when things get unbearably slow. May be fun for small fry. **91m/C VHS, Beta, LV.** Dan Aykroyd, John Candy, Stephanie Faracy, Annette Bening, Chris Young, Lucy Deakins; ***D:*** Howard Deutch; ***W:*** John Hughes; ***M:*** Thomas Newman. *MCA*

Great Race ☆☆½ **1965** A dastardly villain, a noble hero and a spirited suffragette are among the competitors in an uproarious New York-to-Paris auto race circa 1908, complete with pie fights, saloon brawls, and a confrontation with a feisty polar bear. Overly long and only sporadically funny. **160m/C VHS, Beta, LV.** Jack Lemmon, Tony Curtis, Natalie Wood, Peter Falk, Keenan Wynn, George Macready; ***D:*** Blake Edwards; ***M:*** Henry Mancini. Academy Awards '65: Best Sound Effects Editing; Nominations: Academy Awards '65: Best Color Cinematography, Best Film Editing, Best Song ("The Sweetheart Tree"), Best Sound. *WAR, FCT*

Great Ride ☆ **1978** State police are after two dirt bikers who are riding through areas where bike riding is illegal. **90m/C VHS, Beta.** Perry Lang, Michael MacRae, Michael Sullivan; ***D:*** Don Hulette. *NO*

The Great Riviera Bank Robbery ☆☆½ **1979** A genius executes a bank robbery on the French Riviera netting fifteen million dollars. Based on a true story, the film chronicles the unfolding of the heist. **98m/C VHS, Beta.** Ian McShane, Warren Clarke, Stephen Greif, Christopher Malcolm; ***D:*** Francis Megahy. *MPI*

The Great Rupert ☆☆☆ **1950** Durante and family are befriended by a helpful squirrel (a puppet) in obtaining a huge fortune. Good fun; Durante shines. **86m/B VHS, Beta.** Jimmy Durante, Terry Moore, Tom Drake, Frank Orth, Sara Haden, Queenie Smith; ***D:*** Irving Pichel. *DVT, HEG, VYY*

The Great St. Louis Bank Robbery ☆☆½ **1959** Three career criminals (Denton, Clarke, Dukas) and young turk McQueen are brought together for a bank heist. They don't trust each other, which proves fatal when the heist goes bad. Based on a true story and filmed in semi-documentary style. Nineteen-year-old McQueen's follow-up to "The Blob." **86m/B VHS.** Graham Denton, David Clarke, James Dukas, Steve McQueen, Molly McCarthy; ***D:*** Charles Guggenheim. *IVY*

The Great St. Trinian's Train Robbery ☆☆ **1966** Train robbers hide their considerable loot in an empty country mansion only to discover, upon returning years later, it has been converted into a girls' boarding school. When they try to recover the money, the thieves run up against a band of pestiferous adolescent girls, with hilarious results. Based on the cartoon by Ronald Searle. Sequel to "The Pure Hell of St. Trinian's." **90m/C VHS, Beta.** *GB* Dora Bryan, Frankie Howerd, Reg Varney, Desmond Walter Ellis; ***D:*** Sidney Gilliat, Frank Launder; ***M:*** Malcolm Arnold. *NO*

The Great Santini ☆☆☆ *Ace* **1980 (PG)** Lt. Col. Bull Meechum, the "Great Santini," a Marine pilot stationed stateside, fights a war involving his frustrated career goals, repressed emotions, and family. His family becomes his company of marines, as he abuses them in the name of discipline, because he doesn't allow himself any other way to show his affection. With a standout performance by Duvall, the film successfully blends warm humor and tenderness with the harsh cruelties inherent with dysfunctional families and racism. Based on Pat Conroy's autobiographical novel, the movie was virtually undistributed when first released, but re-released due to critical acclaim. **118m/C VHS, Beta, 8mm.** Robert Duvall, Blythe Danner, Michael O'Keefe, Julie Ann Haddock, Lisa Jane Persky, David Keith; ***D:*** Lewis John Carlino; ***W:*** Lewis John Carlino; ***M:*** Elmer Bernstein. Montreal World Film Festival '80: Best Actor (Duvall); National Board of Review Awards '80: 10 Best Films of the Year; Nominations: Academy Awards '80: Best Actor (Duvall), Best Supporting Actor (O'Keefe). *WAR*

Great Scout & Cathouse Thursday ☆½ *Wildcat* **1976 (PG)** Marvin and Reed vow to take revenge on their third partner, Culp, who made off with all their profits from a gold mine. The title refers to Marvin's May-December romance with prostitute Lenz. Already forgotten, unfunny, all-star comedy with cutesy title. **96m/C VHS, Beta.** Lee Marvin, Oliver Reed, Robert Culp, Elizabeth Ashley, Kay Lenz; ***D:*** Don Taylor. *LIV, VES*

The Great Skycopter Rescue ☆ **1982** Ruthless businessmen hire a motorcycle gang to terrorize and scare away the inhabitants of an oil-rich town. A local teenage flying enthusiast organizes his friends into an attack force to fight back. **96m/C VHS, Beta.** William Marshall, Aldo Ray, Russell Johnson, Terry Michos, Terry Taylor; ***D:*** Lawrence Foldes. *MGM*

Great Smokey Roadblock ☆☆ *Last of the Cowboys* **1976 (PG)** While in the hospital, a sixty-year-old truck driver's rig is repossessed by the finance company. Deciding that it's time to make one last perfect cross country run, he escapes from the hospital, steals his truck, picks up six prostitutes, heads off into the night with the police on his tail, and becomes a folk hero. **84m/C VHS, Beta.** Henry Fonda, Eileen Brennan, Susan Sarandon, John Byner; ***D:*** John Leone. *MED*

The Great Texas Dynamite Chase ☆½ *Dynamite Women* **1976 (R)** Two sexy young women drive across Texas with a carload of dynamite. They leave a trail of empty banks with the cops constantly on their trail. **90m/C VHS, Beta.** Claudia

Jennings, Jocelyn Jones, Johnny Crawford, Chris Pennock, Tara Strohmeier, Miles Watkins, Bart Braverman; ***D:*** Michael Pressman. *WAR, OM*

The Great Train Robbery *The First Great Train Robbery* **1979 (PG)** A dapper thief arranges to heist the Folkstone bullion express in 1855, the first moving train robbery. Well-designed, fast-moving costume piece based on Crichton's best-selling novel. **111m/C VHS, Beta, LV.** *GB* Sean Connery, Donald Sutherland, Lesley-Anne Down, Alan Webb; ***D:*** Michael Crichton; ***W:*** Michael Crichton; ***C:*** Geoffrey Unsworth; ***M:*** Jerry Goldsmith. *MGM, FCT, HMV*

The Great Train Robbery: Cinema Begins **1903** Three pioneering film shorts: "Billy Whiskers," a collection of Lumiere footage from their most famous films, and the title short. **42m/B VHS, Beta, 8mm.** "Broncho" Billy Anderson; ***D:*** Edwin S. Porter, Auguste Lumiere, Hans A. Spanuth. *VYY*

Great Treasure Hunt **197?** Four Western rogues help a blind man steal a wealthy crook's gold. **90m/C VHS, Beta.** Mark Damon, Stan Cooper, Luis Marin; ***D:*** Tonino Ricci. *TWE*

The Great Waldo Pepper **1975 (PG)** Low key and (for Hill) less commercial film about a WWI pilot-turned-barnstormer who gets hired as a stuntman for the movies. Features spectacular vintage aircraft flying sequences. **107m/C VHS, Beta, LV.** Robert Redford, Susan Sarandon, Margot Kidder, Bo Svenson, Scott Newman, Geoffrey Lewis, Edward Herrmann; ***D:*** George Roy Hill; ***W:*** William Goldman; ***C:*** Robert L. Surtees; ***M:*** Henry Mancini. *MCA*

A Great Wall *The Great Wall is a Great Wall* **1986 (PG)** A Chinese-American family travels to mainland China to discover the country of their ancestry and to visit relatives. They experience radical culture shock. Wang's first independent feature. In English and Chinese with subtitles. **103m/C VHS, Beta, LV.** Peter Wang, Sharon Iwai, Kelvin Han Yee, Lin Qinqin, Hy Xiaoguang; ***D:*** Peter Wang; ***W:*** Peter Wang, Shirley Sun; ***M:*** David Liang, Ge Ganru. *FCT, IME, APD*

The Great Wallendas **1978** The true story of the tragedies and triumphs of the Wallendas, a seven-person acrobatic family, who were noted for creating a pyramid on the high wire without nets below them. Made for television. **96m/C VHS, Beta.** Lloyd Bridges, Britt Ekland, Cathy Rigby; ***D:*** Larry Elikann. *NO*

The Great Waltz **1938** The first of two musical biographies on the life of Johann Strauss sees the musician quit his banking job to pursue his dream of becoming a successful composer. A fine, overlooked production rich with wonderful music and romantic comedy. ♫Tales of Vienna Woods; There'll Come A Time; One Day When We Were Young; Voices of Spring; Du und Du; The Bat; I'm In Love With Vienna; Revolutionary March. **102m/B VHS, LV.** Luise Rainer, Fernand Gravet, Milza Korjus, Hugh Herbert, Lionel Atwill, Curt Bois, Leonid Kinskey, Al Shear, Minna Gombell, George Houston, Bert Roach, Herman Bing, Alma Kruger, Sig Rumann; ***D:*** Julien Duvivier; ***C:*** Joseph Ruttenberg. Nominations: Academy Awards '38: Best Film Editing, Best Supporting Actress (Korjus). *MGM, FOX, FCT*

The Great War *La Grande Guerre* **1959** Two Italian soldiers find themselves in the midst of WWI, much against their will. They try a number of schemes to get out of fighting and working, but their circumstance dictates otherwise. Slightly muddled, but generally good acting. **118m/B VHS.** *FR IT* Vittorio Gassman, Alberto Sordi, Silvana Mangano, Folco Lulli; ***D:*** Mario Monicelli; ***M:*** Nino Rota. Nominations: Academy Awards '59: Best Foreign Language Film. *FCT*

The Great White Hope ½ **1970 (PG)** A semi-fictionalized biography of boxer Jack Johnson, played by Jones, who became the first black heavyweight world champion in 1910. Alexander makes her film debut as the boxer's white lover, as both battle the racism of the times. Two Oscar-nominated performances in what is essentially an "opened-out" version of the Broadway play. **103m/C VHS, Beta.** James Earl Jones, Jane Alexander, Lou Gilbert, Joel Fluellen, Chester Morris, Robert Webber, Hal Holbrook, R.G. Armstrong, Moses Gunn, Scatman Crothers; ***D:*** Martin Ritt; ***C:*** Burnett Guffey. Nominations: Academy Awards '70: Best Actor (Jones), Best Actress (Alexander). *FOX, FCT*

The Great White Hype ½ **1996 (R)** Screenwriter Shelton, who penned "Bull Durham" and "White Men Can't Jump," returns to the sports arena with this satire of the sleazy world of boxing. Jackson's the Don King-esque promoter and manager of heavyweight champ Wayans. Noticing that pay-per-view revenues are slipping, he searches for a white boxer to generate interest and dollars and finds boxer-turned-musician Berg, who beat the champ in their Golden Glove days, and the publicity machine is cranked up for a veritable Lollapalooka. Jackson's performance as the flamboyant Rev. Fred Sultan fuels the entire movie. Concentrating on the shady wheeling and dealing, the boxing action is kept to a minimum however. **90m/C VHS.** Samuel L. Jackson, Damon Wayans, Peter Berg, Jeff Goldblum, Jon Lovitz, Corbin Bernsen, Richard "Cheech" Marin, John Rhys-Davies, Salli Richardson, Rocky Carroll, Jamie Foxx, Michael Jace; ***D:*** Reginald Hudlin; ***W:*** Ron Shelton, Tony Hendra; ***C:*** Ron Garcia; ***M:*** Marcus Miller. *NYR*

The Great Ziegfeld ½ **1936** Big bio-pic of the famous showman; acclaimed in its time as the best musical biography ever done, still considered the textbook for how to make a musical. Look for cameo roles by many famous stars, as well as a walk-on role by future First Lady Pat Nixon. The movie would have stood up as a first-rate biography of Ziegfeld, even without the drop-dead wonderful songs. ♫Won't You Come Play With Me?; It's Delightful to be Married; If You Knew Susie; Shine On Harvest Moon; A Pretty Girl is Like a Melody; You Gotta Pull Strings; She's a Follies Girl; You; You Never Looked So Beautiful. **179m/B VHS, Beta, LV.** William Powell, Luise Rainer, Myrna Loy, Frank Morgan, Reginald Owen, Nat Pendleton, Ray Bolger, Virginia Bruce, Harriet Hocter, Ernest Cossart, Robert Greig, Gilda Gray, Leon Errol, Dennis (Stanley Morner) Morgan, Mickey Daniels, William Demarest; ***Cameos:*** Fanny Brice; ***D:*** Robert Z. Leonard; ***W:*** William Anthony McGuire. Academy Awards '36: Best Actress (Rainer), Best Picture; New York Film Critics Awards '36: Best Actress (Rainer), Best Actress (Rainer); Nominations: Academy Awards '36: Best Director (Leonard), Best Film Editing, Best Interior Decoration, Best Story. *MGM, BTV*

The Greatest ½ **1977 (PG)** Autobiography of Cassius Clay, the fighter who could float like a butterfly and sting like a bee. Ali plays himself, and George Benson's hit "The Greatest Love of All" is introduced. **100m/C VHS, Beta.** Muhammad Ali, Robert Duvall, Ernest Borgnine, James Earl Jones, John Marley, Roger E. Mosley, Dina Merrill, Paul Winfield; ***D:*** Tom Gries; ***W:*** Ring Lardner Jr.; ***C:*** Harry Stradling Jr. *COL*

The Greatest Question ½ **1919** Gish is a girl menaced by a married couple whom she saw commit a murder years before. A rush job by Griffith to fulfill his studio obligations but Gish's performance is fine. **80m/B VHS.** Lillian Gish, Robert "Bobbie" Harron, Ralph Graves, Eugenie Besserer, George Fawcett, George Nicholls Jr., Josephine Crowell, Carl Stockdale; ***D:*** D.W. Griffith. *GPV*

The Greatest Show on Earth **1952** DeMille is in all his epic glory here in a tale of a traveling circus wrought with glamour, romance, mysterious clowns, a tough ringmaster, and a train wreck. **149m/C VHS, Beta, LV.** Betty Hutton, Cornel Wilde, James Stewart, Charlton Heston, Dorothy Lamour, Lawrence Tierney; ***D:*** Cecil B. DeMille. Academy Awards '52: Best Picture, Best Story; Golden Globe Awards '53: Best Director (DeMille), Best Film—Drama; Nominations: Academy Awards '52: Best Costume Design (Color), Best Director (DeMille), Best Film Editing. *PAR, BTV*

The Greatest Story Ever Told **1965** Christ's journey from Galilee to Golgotha is portrayed here in true international-all-star-epic treatment by director Stevens. A lackluster version of Christ's life, remarkable only for Heston's out-of-control John the Baptist. **196m/C VHS, Beta, LV.** Max von Sydow, Charlton Heston, Sidney Poitier, Claude Rains, Jose Ferrer, Telly Savalas, Angela Lansbury, Dorothy McGuire, John Wayne, Donald Pleasence, Carroll Baker, Van Heflin, Robert Loggia, Shelley Winters, Ed Wynn, Roddy McDowall; ***D:*** George Stevens; ***C:*** William Mellor, Loyal Griggs. National Board of Review Awards '65: 10 Best Films of the Year; Nominations: Academy Awards '65: Best Art Direction/Set Decoration (Color), Best Color Cinematography, Best Costume Design (Color). *MGM, RDG, TVC*

Greed **1924** A wife's obsession with money drives her husband to murder. Although the original version's length (eight hours) was trimmed to 140 minutes, it remains one of the greatest and most highly acclaimed silent films ever made. Effective use of Death Valley locations. Adapted from the Frank Norris novel, "McTeague." **140m/B VHS, LV.** Dale Fuller, Gibson Gowland, ZaSu Pitts, Jean Hersholt, Chester Conklin; ***D:*** Erich von Stroheim. *MGM*

The Greed of William Hart *Horror Maniacs* **1948** Reworking of the Burke and Hare legend has grave robbers providing Edinburgh medical students with the requisite cadavers. **78m/B VHS.** *GB* Tod Slaughter, Henry Oscar, Jenny Lynn, Winifred Melville; ***D:*** Oswald Mitchell. *SNC*

Greedy ½ **1994 (PG-13)** Money-grubbing family suck up to elderly millionaire uncle (Douglas) when they fear he'll leave his money to the sexy, young former pizza delivery girl (d'Abo) he's hired as his nurse. Fox is the long-lost nephew who comes to the rescue. Wicked comedy from veterans Ganz and Mandel should zing, but instead falls flat thanks to a descent into the maudlin. Fox bares his backside and Douglas has fun as the mean old miser, but check out Hartman, a riot as a snarky relative. **109m/C VHS, LV.** Kirk Douglas, Michael J. Fox, Olivia D'Abo, Phil Hartman, Nancy Travis, Ed Begley Jr., Bob Balaban, Colleen Camp, Jere Burns, Khandi Alexander; ***Cameos:*** Jonathan Lynn; ***D:*** Jonathan Lynn; ***W:*** Lowell Ganz, Babaloo Mandel; ***M:*** Randy Edelman. *MCA*

Greedy Terror **1978** A cross-country motorcycle trip becomes a real nightmare when two young men realize they're being stalked by a maniac with a thirst for blood. **90m/C VHS, Beta.** Michael MacRae, Perry Lang. *NO*

Greek Street *Latin Love* **1930** The owner of small cafe in London discovers a poor girl singing in the street for food. He takes her in and spotlights her songs in his cafe. **51m/B VHS, Beta.** *GB* Sari Maritza, Arthur Ahmbling, Martin Lewis; ***D:*** Sinclair Hill. *VYY, DVT, HEG*

The Greek Tycoon ½ **1978 (R)** Old familiar story about widow of an American president who marries a billionaire shipping magnate and finds that money cannot buy happiness. A transparent depiction of the Onassis/Kennedy marriage, done to a turn. **106m/C VHS, Beta.** Anthony Quinn, Jacqueline Bisset, James Franciscus, Raf Vallone, Edward Albert; ***D:*** J. Lee Thompson. *MCA*

Green Archer **1940** Fifteen episodes of the famed serial, featuring a spooked castle complete with secret passages and tunnels, trapdoors, and the mysterious masked figure, the Green Archer. **283m/B VHS, Beta.** Victor Jory, Iris Meredith, James Craven, Robert Fiske; ***D:*** James W. Horne. *VYY, NOS, VCN*

The Green Berets *Woof!* **1968 (G)** Cliched wartime heroics co-directed by Wayne and based on Robin Moore's novel. The Duke stars as a Special Forces colonel, leading his troops against the Viet Cong. Painfully insipid pro-war propaganda, notable as the only American film to come out in support of U.S. involvement in Vietnam. Truly embarrassing but did spawn the hit single "Ballad of the Green Beret" by Barry Sadler. **135m/C VHS, Beta, LV.** John Wayne, David Janssen, Jim Hutton, Aldo Ray, George Takei, Raymond St. Jacques; ***D:*** John Wayne; ***C:*** Winton C. Hoch; ***M:*** Miklos Rozsa. *WAR, TLF*

Green Card ½ **1990 (PG-13)** Some marry for love, some for money, others for an apartment in the Big Apple. Refined, single MacDowell covets a rent-controlled apartment in Manhattan, but the lease stipulates that the apartment be let to a married couple. Enter brusque and burly Depardieu, who covets the elusive green card. The counterpoint between MacDowell, as a stuffy horticulturist, and Depardieu, as a French composer works well, and the two adroitly play a couple whose relationship covers the romantic continuum. Director Weir wrote the screenplay with Depardieu in mind. Depardieu's English-language debut. **108m/C VHS, Beta, LV.** Gerard Depardieu, Andie MacDowell, Bebe Neuwirth, Gregg Edelman, Robert Prosky, Jessie Keosian, Ann Wedgeworth, Ethan Phillips, Mary Louise Wilson, Lois Smith, Simon Jones; ***D:*** Peter Weir; ***W:*** Peter Weir; ***M:*** Hans Zimmer. Golden Globe Awards '91: Best Actor—Musical/Comedy (Depardieu), Best Film—Musical/Comedy; Nominations: Academy Awards '90: Best Original Screenplay; Golden Globe Awards '91: Best Actress—Musical/Comedy (MacDowell). *TOU*

Green Dolphin Street 🦴🦴½ **1947** Flimsy romantic epic set in 19th century New Zealand. A young girl marries the beau she and her sister are battling over in this Oscar-winning special effects show which features one big earthquake. Based on the Elizabeth Goudge novel, this was one of MGM's biggest hits in 1947. **161m/B VHS, Beta.** Lana Turner, Van Heflin, Donna Reed, Edmund Gwenn; ***D:*** Victor Saville. Academy Awards '47: Best Special Effects; Nominations: Academy Awards '47: Best Black and White Cinematography, Best Film Editing, Best Sound. *MGM*

Green Dragon Inn 🦴 **1982** When trying to escort an accused murderer to trial, a Ming court emissary finds himself battling against Kung Fu masters. **94m/C VHS, Beta.** Yue Hwa, Lo Lei, Shangkuan Ling-Feng. *WVE*

Green Eyes 🦴½ **1934** A costume party in a country mansion sets the scene for a routine murder mystery when the guests find their host stabbed to death in a closet. Based on the novel "The Murder of Stephen Kester" by H. Ashbrook. **68m/B VHS.** Shirley Grey, Charles Starrett, Claude Gillingwater, John Wray, Dorothy Revier; ***D:*** Richard Thorpe; ***W:*** Melville Shyer. *SNC*

Green Eyes 🦴🦴🦴½ **1976** Winfield, an ex-GI, returns to postwar Vietnam to search for his illegitimate son who he believes will have green eyes. A highly acclaimed, made-for-television drama featuring moving performances from Winfield and Jonathan Lippe. **100m/C VHS.** Paul Winfield, Rita Tushingham, Jonathon Lippe, Victoria Racimo, Royce Wallace, Claudia Bryar; ***D:*** John Erman. *LIV*

Green Fields 🦴🦴½ *Grine Felder; Gruner Felder* **1937** A quiet romance based on Peretz Hirschbein's legendary tale of a young scholar of the Talmud who leaves the shelter of the synagogue in order to learn about people in the real world. The search takes him to the countryside where he finds himself in the middle of a battle between two families who both want him as a tutor and a suitor for their daughters. In Yiddish with English subtitles. **95m/B VHS, Beta.** Michael Goldstein, Herschel Bernardi, Helen Beverly; ***D:*** Jacob Ben-Ami. *ERG, NCJ*

Green Fire 🦴🦴½ **1955** The screen sizzles when emerald miner Granger meets plantation-owner Kelly in the exotic jungles of South America. Usual plot complications muddle the story, but who cares when the stars are this attractive? **100m/C VHS.** Stewart Granger, Grace Kelly, Paul Douglas, John Ericson, Murvyn Vye, Jose Torvay, Robert Tafur, Nacho Galindo; ***D:*** Andrew Marton; ***W:*** Ivan Goff, Ben Roberts; ***M:*** Miklos Rozsa. *MGM*

Green for Danger 🦴🦴 **1947** A detective stages a chilling mock operation to find a mad killer stalking the corridors of a British hospital during WWII. Sim's first great claim to fame (pre-"A Christmas Carol"). **91m/B VHS, Beta, LV.** *GB* Trevor Howard, Alastair Sim, Leo Genn; ***D:*** Sidney Gilliat. *HMV, RXM*

The Green Glove 🦴🦴½ **1952** A jewel thief steals a beautiful relic from a tiny church. WWII makes it impossible for him to fence it and the church finds a relentless ally to track the thief. Excellent action sequences lift this standard plot slightly above the ordinary. **88m/B VHS.** Glenn Ford, Geraldine Brooks, Cedric Hardwicke, George Macready, Gaby Andre, Roger Treville, Juliette Greco, Jean Bretonniere; ***D:*** Rudolph Mate; ***W:*** Charles Bennett. *NOS, FCT, HEG*

Green Grow the Rushes 🦴🦴 *Brandy Ashore* **1951** The English government tries to put a stop to brandy smuggling on the coast, but the townspeople drink up the evidence. A young Burton highlights this watered-down comedy. Based on a novel by co-scripter Harold Clewes. **77m/B VHS.** *GB* Roger Livesey, Honor Blackman, Richard Burton, Frederick Leister; ***D:*** Derek Twist. *HMV, NOS, VYY*

Green Horizon 🦴½ *Afurika Monogatari; A Tale of Africa* **1983** A bucolic old codger faces a dilemma when he must choose between his granddaughter's future and his disaster-prone natural environment. **80m/C VHS, Beta.** James Stewart, Philip Sayer, Elenora Vallone. *FHE*

The Green Hornet **1939** The feature version of the original serial, in which the Green Hornet and Kato have a series of crime-fighting adventures. **100m/B VHS, Beta.** Gordon Jones, Keye Luke, Anne Nagel, Wade Boteler, Walter McGrail, Douglas Evans, Cy Kendall. *NOS, GKK, MLB*

Green Ice 🦴½ **1981** An American electronics expert gets involved with a brutal South American government dealing with emeralds and plans a heist with his girlfriend and other cohorts. A little bit of romance, a little bit of action, a lot of nothing much. **109m/C VHS, Beta, LV.** *GB* Ryan O'Neal, Anne Archer, Omar Sharif, John Larroquette; ***D:*** Ernest Day; ***W:*** Edward Anhalt, Robert De Laurentis. *NO*

Green Inferno 🦴 **198?** A wealthy eccentric who lives deep in the South American jungle incites the natives to rebel. Mercenary agents are then hired to kill him. **90m/C VHS, Beta.** Richard Yesteran, Didi Sherman, Caesar Burner. *NO*

The Green Man 🦴🦴🦴 **1991** Maurice Allington (Finney), the alcoholic and randy owner of the Green Man Inn in rural England, jokes about the spirits that supposedly haunt the inn. It's not too funny, however, when he discovers the spirits are real and he has to figure out who the spirit of a 17th-century murderer is inhabiting before he kills again. A classy ghost story based on the novel by Kingsley Amis. **150m/C VHS.** *GB* Albert Finney, Sarah Berger, Linda Marlowe, Michael Hordern, Nickolas Grace, Michael Culver; ***D:*** Elijah Moshinsky; ***W:*** Malcolm Bradbury. *AAE, INJ, BTV*

Green Mansions 🦴🦴 **1959** Screen adaptation of W. H. Hudson's novel suffers due to miscasting of Hepburn as Rima the Bird Girl, who is not permitted to leave her sanctuary. Perkins is good as the male lead who fled to the jungle in search of wealth and instead finds a powerful love. Hepburn was married to director Ferrer at the time. **104m/C VHS.** Audrey Hepburn, Anthony Perkins, Lee J. Cobb, Sessue Hayakawa, Henry Silva, Nehemiah Persoff, Michael Pate; ***D:*** Mel Ferrer; ***W:*** Dorothy Kingsley; ***C:*** Joseph Ruttenberg. *MGM*

Green Pastures 🦴🦴🦴 **1936** An adaptation of Marc Connelly's 1930 Pulitzer Prize-winning play which attempts to retell Biblical stories in Black English Vernacular of the '30s. Southern theater owners boycotted the controversial film which had an all-Black cast. **93m/C VHS, Beta.** Rex Ingram, Oscar Polk, Eddie Anderson, George Reed, Abraham Graves, Myrtle Anderson, Frank Wilson; ***D:*** William Keighley, Marc Connelly; ***C:*** Hal Mohr. National Board of Review Awards '36: 10 Best Films of the Year. *MGM, MOV, FOX*

The Green Promise 🦴🦴 *Raging Waters* **1949** A well-meaning but domineering farmer and his four motherless children face disaster as a result of the father's obstinacy. But when he is laid up, the eldest daughter takes over, tries modern methods and equipment, and makes the farm a success. **90m/B VHS, Beta.** Walter Brennan, Marguerite Chapman, Robert Paige, Natalie Wood; ***D:*** William D. Russell. *NOS, DVT, HEG*

The Green Room 🦴🦴 *La Chambre Verte* **1978 (PG)** Truffaut's haunting tale of a man who, valuing death over life, erects a shrine to all the dead he has known. Offered a chance at love, he cannot overcome his obsessions to take the risk. Based on the Henry James story "Altar of the Dead." In French with subtitles. **95m/C VHS, Beta.** *FR* Francois Truffaut, Nathalie Baye, Jean Daste; ***D:*** Francois Truffaut; ***C:*** Nestor Almendros. *MGM*

The Green Slime *Woof! Gamma Sango Uchu Daisakusen; Battle Beyond the Stars; Death and the Green Slime* **1968 (G)** Danger and romance highlight the journey of a space ship assigned to intercept an oncoming asteroid. Little do the astronauts realize, but they have brought aboard the ship the malevolent alien creatures known as green slime (and we ain't talking jello here). Cheap, U.S./Japanese co-production will leave you feeling lousy in the morning. The title song is legendary among genre aficionados. **90m/C VHS, Beta.** *JP* Robert Horton, Richard Jaeckel, Luciana Paluzzi, Bud Widom, Ted Gunther, Robert Dunham; ***D:*** Kinji Fukasaku. *MGM*

The Green Wall 🦴🦴🦴 **1970** A city-dwelling young man attempts to homestead with his family in the Amazon. A lovely and tragic film with stunning photography of the Peruvian forests. First Peruvian feature to be shown in the U.S. In Spanish with English subtitles. **110m/C VHS.** *SP* Julio Aleman, Sandra Riva; ***D:*** Armando Robles Godoy; ***W:*** Armando Robles Godoy. *FCT, DVT, HEG*

Greenstone 🦴🦴 **1985 (G)** The green stone is a glowing rock in the forbidden forest that conveys a young boy into an exciting new world. **48m/C VHS, Beta.** Joseph Corey, John Riley, Kathleen Irvine, Jack Mauck; ***D:*** Kevin Irvine. *AHV*

Greetings 🦴🦴🦴 **1968 (R)** De Niro stars in this wild and crazy comedy about a man who tries to help his friend flunk his draft physical. One of DePalma's first films, and a pleasantly anarchic view of the late '60s, wrought with a light, intelligent tone. Followed by the sequel "Hi, Mom." **88m/C VHS, Beta, LV.** Robert De Niro, Gerrit Graham, Allen (Goorwitz) Garfield; ***D:*** Brian DePalma; ***W:*** Brian DePalma. *VMK*

Gregory's Girl 🦴🦴🦴½ **1980** Sweet, disarming comedy established Forsyth. An awkward young Scottish schoolboy falls in love with the female goalie of his soccer team. He turns to his 10-year-old sister for advice, but she's more interested in ice cream than love. His best friend is no help, either, since he has yet to fall in love. Perfect mirror of teenagers and their instantaneous, raw, and all-consuming loves. Very sweet scene with Gregory and his girl lying on their backs in an open space illustrates the simultaneous simplicity and complexity of young love. **91m/C VHS, Beta.** *GB* Gordon John Sinclair, Dee Hepburn, Jake D'Arcy, Chic Murray, Alex Norton, John Bett, Clare Grogan; ***D:*** Bill Forsyth; ***W:*** Bill Forsyth. British Academy Awards '81: Best Screenplay. *SUE, TVC*

Gremlins 🦴🦴🦴 **1984 (PG)** Comedy horror with deft satiric edge. Produced by Spielberg. Fumbling gadget salesman Rand Peltzer is looking for something really special to get his son Billy. He finds it in a small store in Chinatown. The wise shopkeeper is reluctant to sell him the adorable "mogwai" but relents after fully warning him "Don't expose him to bright light, don't ever get him wet, and don't ever, ever feed him after midnight." Naturally, this all happens and the result is a gang of nasty gremlins who decide to tear up the town on Christmas Eve. Followed by "Gremlins 2, the New Batch" which is less black comedy, more parody, and perhaps more inventive. **106m/C VHS, Beta, LV, 8mm.** Zach Galligan, Phoebe Cates, Hoyt Axton, Polly Holliday, Frances Lee McCain, Keye Luke, Dick Miller, Corey Feldman, Judge Reinhold; ***D:*** Joe Dante; ***W:*** Chris Columbus; ***M:*** Jerry Goldsmith. *WAR, TLF*

Gremlins 2: The New Batch 🦴🦴🦴½ **1990 (PG-13)** The sequel to "Gremlins" is superior to the original, which was quite good. Set in a futuristic skyscraper in the Big Apple, director Dante presents a less violent but far more campy vision, paying myriad surreal tributes to scores of movies, including "The Wizard of Oz" and musical extravaganzas of the past. Also incorporates a Donald Trump parody, takes on television news, and body slams modern urban living. Great fun. **107m/C VHS, Beta, LV, 8mm.** Phoebe Cates, Christopher Lee, John Glover, Zach Galligan; ***Cameos:*** Jerry Goldsmith; ***D:*** Joe Dante; ***M:*** Jerry Goldsmith. *WAR, HHE*

Grendel, Grendel, Grendel ☙☙ **1982** An utterly urbane dragon wants to be friends, but for some reason people are just terrified of Grendel. It's true, he bites a head off once in a while, but nobody's perfect! An ingenious, animated retelling of Beowulf. **90m/C VHS, Beta.** *AU* ***D:*** Alexander Stitt; ***M:*** Bruce Smeaton; ***V:*** Peter Ustinov, Arthur Dignam, Julie McKenna, Keith Michell. *FHE*

Greta ☙☙☙ **1986** During WWII, a young Polish boy escapes from a detention camp. Now on the run, several bizarre twists of fate place him in the care of Greta, a young girl whose father is an officer in the S.S. In Polish with English subtitles. **60m/C VHS, Beta.** *PL* Janusz Grabowski, Agnieszka Kruszewska, Eva Borowik, Tomasz Grochoczki, Andrzej Precig; ***D:*** Krzysztof Gruber. *EVD, INJ*

The Grey Fox ☙☙☙½ **1983 (PG)** A gentlemanly old stagecoach robber tries to pick up his life after thirty years in prison. Unable to resist another heist, he tries train robbery, and winds up hiding out in British Columbia where he meets an attractive photographer, come to document the changing West. Farnsworth is perfect as the man who suddenly finds himself in the 20th century trying to work at the only craft he knows. Based on the true story of Canada's most colorful and celebrated outlaw, Bill Miner. **92m/C VHS, Beta, LV.** *CA* Richard Farnsworth, Jackie Burroughs, Wayne Robson, Timothy Webber, Ken Pogue; ***D:*** Phillip Borsos; ***M:*** Michael Conway Baker. Genie Awards '83: Best Director (Borsos), Best Film, Best Supporting Actress (Burroughs). *MED*

Greyfriars Bobby ☙☙½ **1961** A true story of a Skye terrier named Bobby who, after his master dies, refuses to leave the grave. Even after being coaxed by the local children into town, he still returns to the cemetery each evening. Word of his loyalty spreads, and Bobby becomes the pet of 19th century Edinburgh. Nicely told, with fine location photography and good acting. Great for children and animal lovers. **91m/C VHS.** Donald Crisp, Laurence Naismith, Kay Walsh; ***D:*** Don Chaffey. *DIS*

Greystoke: The Legend of Tarzan, Lord of the Apes ☙☙ **1984 (PG)** The seventh Earl of Greystoke becomes a shipwrecked orphan and is raised by apes. Ruling the ape-clan in the vine-swinging persona of Tarzan, he is discovered by an anthropologist and returned to his ancestral home in Scotland, where he is immediately recognized by his grandfather. The contrast between the behavior of man and ape is interesting, and Tarzan's introduction to society is fun, but there's no melodrama or cliff-hanging action, as we've come to expect of the Tarzan genre. Due to her heavy southern accent, Andie MacDowell (as Jane) had her voice dubbed by Glenn Close. **130m/C VHS, Beta, LV.** Christopher Lambert, Ralph Richardson, Ian Holm, James Fox, Andie MacDowell, Ian Charleson, Cheryl Campbell, Nigel Davenport; ***D:*** Hugh Hudson; ***W:*** Michael Austin. New York Film Critics Awards '84: Best Supporting Actor (Richardson); Nominations: Academy Awards '84: Best Adapted Screenplay, Best Makeup, Best Supporting Actor (Richardson). *WAR*

Grief ☙☙ **1994** Mark (Chester) is a writer on the syndicated daytime TV show "The Love Judge." Still numb from his lover's death from AIDS the previous year, Mark begins to take an interest in fellow writer Bill (Arquette), while writer Paula (Gutteridge) desires to become the show's new producer and secretary Leslie (Douglas) wants to take her place as the new writer. Present producer Jo (Beat) tries to keep her office family in line while sorting out her personal life. Writer-director Glatzer knows his territory since he spent five years writing for "Divorce Court." **86m/C VHS.** Craig Chester, Alexis Arquette, Lucy Gutteridge, Illeana Douglas, Jackie Beat, Carlton Wilborn; ***D:*** Richard Glatzer; ***W:*** Richard Glatzer. *ACA, SHV*

Grievous Bodily Harm ☙☙ **1989 (R)** Morris Martin's wife Claudine is missing. When he finds a videotape of Claudine in very compromising positions, he becomes murderously determined to find out where she has gone. **136m/C VHS, Beta.** John Waters, Colin Friels, Bruno Lawrence; ***D:*** Mark Joffe. *FRH*

Griffin and Phoenix: A Love Story ☙☙½ **1976** A sentimental film about the mortality of two vital people. Falk deserts his family when he learns he has terminal cancer. Clayburgh, also terminally ill, meets him for a short but meaningful affair. Good performances help overcome the tear-jerker aspects of the story. Made for television. **110m/C VHS.** Peter Falk, Jill Clayburgh, Dorothy Tristan, John Lehne; ***D:*** Daryl Duke. *FOX*

Griffith Biograph Program **1909** Some of the best Biograph shorts are featured: "The Lonely Villa," "The Lonedale Operator," "The New York Hat," "Friends," and "The Unseen Enemy," all produced between 1909 and 1912. **50m/B VHS, Beta, LV.** Mary Pickford, Blanche Sweet, Lillian Gish, Dorothy Gish; ***D:*** D.W. Griffith. *GVV*

The Grifters ☙☙☙½ **1990 (R)** Evocative rendering of a terrifying sub-culture. Huston, Cusak, and Bening are con artists, struggling to stay on top in a world where violence, money, and lust are the prizes. Bening and Huston fight for Cusak's soul, while he's determined to decide for himself. Seamless performances and dazzling atmosphere, along with superb pacing, make for a provocative film. Based on a novel by Jim Thompson. **114m/C VHS, Beta, LV.** Anjelica Huston, John Cusack, Annette Bening, Pat Hingle, J.T. Walsh, Charles Napier, Henry Jones, Gailard Sartain; ***D:*** Stephen Frears; ***W:*** Donald E. Westlake; ***M:*** Elmer Bernstein. Independent Spirit Awards '91: Best Actress (Huston), Best Film; Los Angeles Film Critics Association Awards '90: Best Actress (Huston); National Society of Film Critics Awards '90: Best Actress (Huston), Best Supporting Actress (Bening); Nominations: Academy Awards '90: Best Actress (Huston), Best Adapted Screenplay, Best Director (Frears), Best Supporting Actress (Bening). *MCA, HBO, FCT*

Grim ☙ **1995 (R)** Lives up to its title as an extremely icky and evil subterranean creature is awakened from a long sleep by miners. Apparently not long enough, since he proceeds to rip apart anyone he comes in contact with. **86m/C VHS, LV.** Emmanuel Xuereb, Tres Handley, Peter Tregloan; ***D:*** Paul Matthews. *APX*

Grim Prairie Tales ☙☙ **1989 (R)** A city slicker and a crazed mountain man meet by a campfire in the high plains one night and pass the time sharing four tales of Western horror. Dourif and Jones are fun, the stories scary, making for an interesting twist on both the horror and the Western genres. **90m/C VHS, LV.** Brad Dourif, James Earl Jones, Marc McClure, William Atherton, Scott Paulin; ***D:*** Wayne Coe; ***W:*** Wayne Coe; ***C:*** Janusz Kaminski. *ACA, FCT*

The Grim Reaper ☙☙☙ *La Commare Secca* **1962** 22-year-old Bertolucci directed his first feature with this grim and brutal treatment of the investigation of the murder of a prostitute, told via flashbacks and from the disparate perspectives of three people who knew the woman. A commercial bust, the critics were no kinder than the public at the time; not until two years later, with "Before the Revolution," did Bertolucci earn his directorial spurs. The script was written by Pasolini, with whom the erstwhile poet had collaborated on "Accattone" the previous year (as assistant). In Italian with English subtitles. **100m/B VHS, LV.** *IT* Francesco Rulu, Giancarlo de Rosa; ***D:*** Bernardo Bertolucci; ***W:*** Pier Paolo Pasolini. *CVC, FCT, INJ*

Grim Reaper ☙½ **1981 (R)** Mia Farrow's sister is one of a group of American students vacationing on a Greek island. Farrow learns of the twisted cannibalistic murderer who methodically tries to avenge the tragic deaths of his family. **81m/C VHS, Beta.** *IT* Tisa Farrow, George Eastman; ***D:*** Joe D'Amato. *NO*

Grisbi ☙☙ *Hands Off the Loot; Honour Among Thieves; Touchez Pas Au Grisbi* **1953** King of the French underworld, Gabin finds there's no honor among thieves when a gold heist goes wrong and the loot comes up missing. Moreau is the quintessential moll. Dubbed. **94m/C VHS.** *FR* Jean Gabin, Jeanne Moreau, Lino Ventura, Daniel Cauchy, Gaby Basset; ***D:*** Jacques Becker; ***W:*** Jacques Becker, Maurice Griffe; ***M:*** Jean Wiener. Venice Film Festival '54: Best Actor (Gabin). *FCT*

The Grissom Gang ☙☙☙ **1971 (R)** Remake of the 1948 British film "No Orchids for Miss Blandish." Darby is a wealthy heiress kidnapped by a family of grotesques, led by a sadistic mother. The ransom gets lost in a series of bizarre events, and the heiress appears to be falling for one of her moronic captors. Director Robert Aldrich skillfully blends extreme violence with dark humor. Superb camera work, editing, and 1920s period sets. **127m/C VHS.** Kim Darby, Scott Wilson, Tony Musante, Ralph Waite, Connie Stevens, Robert Lansing, Wesley Addy; ***D:*** Robert Aldrich; ***C:*** Joseph Biroc. *FOX*

Grit of the Girl Telegrapher/In the Switch Tower **1915** A pair of silent railroad dramas, which feature thrilling chase sequences, nefarious schemers and virginal heroines. Silent with piano scores. **47m/B VHS, Beta.** Anna Q. Nilsson, Hal Clements, Walter Edwards, Frank Borzage; ***M:*** Jon Mirsalis. *CCB, PEN, GVV*

Grizzly ☙ *Killer Grizzly* **1976 (PG)** Giant, killer grizzly terrorizes a state park in this blatant "Jaws" rip-off. From the same folks who produced "Abby," a blatant "Exorcist" rip-off. Filmed in Georgia. **92m/C VHS, Beta.** Christopher George, Richard Jaeckel, Andrew Prine, Victoria (Vicki) Johnson, Charles Kissinger; ***D:*** William Girdler. *MED*

Grizzly Adams: The Legend Continues ☙½ **1990** A small town is saved from three desperados by Grizzly and his huge grizzly bear pet, Martha. **90m/C VHS.** Gene Edwards, Link Wyler, Red West, Tony Caruso, Acquanetta, L.Q. Jones; ***D:*** Ken Kennedy. *NO*

The Groove Tube ☙☙½ **1972 (R)** A television series called "The Groove Tube" is the context for these skits that spoof everything on television from commercials to newscasts. Chevy Chase's movie debut. **75m/C VHS, Beta.** Lane Sarasohn, Chevy Chase, Richard Belzer, Marcy Mendham, Bill Kemmill; ***D:*** Ken Shapiro. *MED*

Gross Anatomy ☙☙½ **1989 (PG-13)** Lightweight comedy/drama centers on the trials and tribulations of medical students. Modine is the very bright, but somewhat lazy, future doctor determined not to buy into the bitter competition among his fellow students. His lack of desire inflames Lahti, a professor dying of a fatal disease who nevertheless believes in modern medicine. She pushes and inspires him to focus on his potential, and his desire to help people. Worth watching, in spite of cheap laughs. Interesting cast of up-and-comers. **107m/C VHS, Beta, LV.** Matthew Modine, Daphne Zuniga, Christine Lahti, John Scott Clough, Alice Carter, Robert Desiderio, Zakes Mokae, Todd Field; ***D:*** Thom Eberhardt; ***W:*** Ron Nyswaner; ***M:*** David Newman. *TOU*

Gross Misconduct ☙☙ **1993 (R)** Charismatic university professor Justin Thorne (Smits) makes the nearly fatal mistake of getting involved with his student, Jennifer (Watts). Seems she's one of those obsessive types and when Thorne wants to break off the affair for the sake of his marriage, Jennifer goes over the edge. Thorne's charged with rape and unless Jennifer changes her story his life is over. Based on a true story that happened in the '50s but this version is set in the '90s. **97m/C VHS.** *AU* Jimmy Smits, Naomi Watts, Sarah Chadwick, Adrian Wright, Alan Fletcher; ***D:*** George Miller; ***W:*** Lance Peters, Gerard Maguire. *AEE*

Grosse Fatigue ☙☙☙ *Dead Tired* **1994 (R)** Diminutive comic everyman Blanc successfully takes up the challenge of a dual role of mistaken identity (as well as directing and writing chores). He first plays himself, bewildered by accusations of lechery and other escapades, who learns he has a psychopath double who's stolen his celebrity. So it's up to Michel and pal Carole (the gorgeous Bouquet) to track down the mischief-maker before Blanc's reputation is in complete tatters. French with subtitles. **85m/C VHS, LV.** *FR* Michel Blanc, Carole Bouquet, Philippe Noiret, Josiane Balasko; ***Cameos:*** Charlotte Gainsbourg, Mathilda May, Thierry Lhermitte, Roman Polanski; ***D:*** Michel Blanc; ***W:*** Michel Blanc; ***C:*** Eduardo Serra; ***M:*** Rene Marc Bini. *TOU*

Grotesque *Woof!* **1987 (R)** After slaughtering a young woman's family as they vacationed in a remote mountain cabin, a gang of bloodthirsty punks are attacked by the family secret, the deformed son. The title says it all. **79m/C VHS, Beta, LV.** Linda Blair, Tab Hunter, Guy Stockwell, Donna Wilkes, Nels Van Patten; ***D:*** Joe Tornatore. *MED*

Ground Zero 🦴🦴🦴 **1988 (R)** Political thriller, set in the Australian outback in the fifties, in which a man searches for the reasons for his father's murder in the films of the British nuclear tests. **109m/C VHS, Beta, LV.** *AU* Colin Friels, Jack Thompson, Donald Pleasence, Natalie Bate, Simon Chilvers, Neil Fitzpatrick, Bob Maza, Peter Cummins; ***D:*** Bruce Myles, Michael Pattinson. *LIV*

Ground Zero 🦴½ **1988 (R)** Ground Zero is the term used to describe the site of a nuclear explosion. San Francisco is threatened with just such a new name in this story of nuclear blackmail. Someone plants an atomic bomb on the Golden Gate Bridge. It must be defused and the culprit caught. **90m/C VHS, Beta.** Ron Casteel, Melvin Belli, Yvonne D'Angiers; ***D:*** James T. Flocker. *GHV, VTR*

Groundhog Day 🦴🦴🦴 **1993 (PG)** Phil (Murray), an obnoxious weatherman, is in Punxatawney, Pennsylvania to cover the annual emergence of the famous rodent from its hole. After he's caught in a blizzard that he didn't predict, he finds himself trapped in a time warp, doomed to relive the same day over and over again until he gets it right. Lighthearted romantic comedy takes a funny premise and manages to carry it through to the end. Murray has fun with the role, although he did get bitten by the groundhog during the scene when they're driving. Elliott, who has been missed since his days as the man under the seats on "Late Night with David Letterman" is perfectly cast as a smart-mouthed cameraman. **103m/C VHS, LV.** Bill Murray, Andie MacDowell, Chris Elliott, Stephen Tobolowsky, Brian Doyle-Murray, Marita Geraghty, Angela Paton; ***D:*** Harold Ramis; ***W:*** Harold Ramis, Daniel F. Rubin; ***M:*** George Fenton. British Academy Awards '93: Best Original Screenplay. *COL, FCT, BTV*

The Groundstar Conspiracy 🦴🦴🦴 **1972 (PG)** Spy thriller brings to life L.P. Davies' novel, "The Alien." After an explosion kills all but one space project scientist, Peppard is sent to investigate suspicions of a cover-up. Meanwhile, the surviving scientist (Sarrazin) suffers from disfigurement and amnesia. He pursues his identity while Peppard accuses him of being a spy. Splendid direction by Lamont Johnson. Sarrazin's best role. **96m/C VHS.** *CA* George Peppard, Michael Sarrazin, Christine Belford, Cliff Potts, James Olson, Tim O'Connor, James McEachin, Alan Oppenheimer; ***D:*** Lamont Johnson. *MCA*

The Group 🦴🦴½ **1966** Based upon the novel by Mary McCarthy, the well-acted story deals with a group of graduates from a Vassar-like college as they try to adapt to life during the Great Depression. Has some provocative subject matter, including lesbianism, adultery, and mental breakdowns. Soapy, but a good cast with film debuts of Bergen, Hackett, Pettet, Widdoes, and Holbrook. **150m/C VHS, Beta.** Candice Bergen, Joanna Pettet, Shirley Knight, Joan Hackett, Elizabeth Hartman, Jessica Walter, Larry Hagman, James Broderick, Kathleen Widdoes, Hal Holbrook, Mary-Robin Redd, Richard Mulligan, Carrie Nye; ***D:*** Sidney Lumet; ***C:*** Boris Kaufman. *FOX*

Group Marriage 🦴🦴½ **1972 (R)** Six young professionals fall into a marriage of communal convenience and rapidly discover the many advantages and drawbacks of their thoroughly modern arrangement. **90m/C VHS, Beta.** Victoria Vetri, Aimee Eccles, Zack Taylor, Jeff Pomerantz, Claudia Jennings, Jayne Kennedy, Milt Kamen; ***D:*** Stephanie Rothman. *NO*

Growing Pains 🦴½ **1982** A young couple discover that their newly adopted son possesses extraordinary powers. **60m/C VHS, Beta.** Gary Bond, Barbara Keilermann, Norman Beaton. *LIV*

Grown Ups 🦴🦴 **1980** A newly married couple move into their first home only to discover that the wife's ditzy sister expects to live with them and that their next door neighbor was their former high school teacher. Made for British television. **95m/C VHS.** *GB* Philip Davis, Leslie Manville, Sam Kelly, Lindsay Duncan, Brenda Blethyn, Janine Duvitsky; ***D:*** Mike Leigh; ***W:*** Mike Leigh. *WBF, BTV, FCT*

Grown Ups 🦴🦴 **1986** A journalist watches his family slowly disintegrating around him in this adaptation of Jules Feiffer's play. **106m/C VHS, Beta.** Jean Stapleton, Martin Balsam, Charles Grodin, Marilu Henner, Kerry Segal; ***D:*** John Madden. *ORI, WAR*

Gruesome Twosome 🦴 **1967** Another guts/cannibalism/mutilation fun-fest by Lewis, about someone who's marketing the hair of some very recently deceased college coeds. **75m/C VHS, Beta.** Elizabeth Davis, Chris Martell; ***D:*** Herschell Gordon Lewis. *NO*

Grumpier Old Men 🦴🦴 **1995 (PG-13)** Max (Matthau) and John (Lemmon) are back at each other's throats, but with John happily married to Ariel (Ann-Margaret), he's not much of an adversary. Enter Maria (Loren), who wants to turn the boys' favorite bait shop into an Italian restaurant. In a twist that should surprise no one, Max soon falls for the beautiful Maria, and she with him. Jokes are similar but more adolescent than in the first, and subplots involving John and Max's kids' wedding and Grandpa's (Meredith) romantic interests are forced. Suffers the standard sequel fate of not measuring up to the original. **101m/C VHS, LV.** Jack Lemmon, Walter Matthau, Ann-Margret, Sophia Loren, Kevin Pollak, Burgess Meredith, Daryl Hannah, Ann Guilbert; ***D:*** Howard Deutch; ***W:*** Mark Steven Johnson; ***C:*** Tak Fujimoto; ***M:*** Alan Silvestri. *WAR*

Grumpy Old Men 🦴🦴🦴 **1993 (PG-13)** Lemmon and Matthau team for their seventh movie, in parts that seem written just for them. Boyhood friends and retired neighbors, they have been feuding for so long that neither of them can remember why. Doesn't matter much, when it provides a reason for them to spout off at each other every morning and play nasty practical jokes every night. This, and ice-fishing, is life as they know it, until feisty younger woman Ann-Margret moves into the neighborhood and lights some long-dormant fires. 83-year-old Meredith is a special treat playing Lemmon's 90-something father. Filmed in Wabasha, Minnesota, and grumpy, in the most pleasant way. **104m/C VHS, LV, 8mm.** Jack Lemmon, Walter Matthau, Ann-Margret, Burgess Meredith, Daryl Hannah, Kevin Pollak, Ossie Davis, Buck Henry, Christopher McDonald; ***D:*** Donald Petrie; ***W:*** Mark Steven Johnson; ***M:*** Alan Silvestri. *WAR*

Grunt! The Wrestling Movie *Woof!* **1985 (R)** A spoof of documentaries about the behind-the-scenes world of wrestling. For fans only. **91m/C VHS, Beta.** Wally Greene, Steven Cepello, Dick Murdoch, John Tolos; ***D:*** Allan Holzman. *VTR, NWV*

Gryphon **1988** Ricky's new teacher can do all sorts of magical things. Hidden among her tricks are lessons about creativity, beauty, and imagination. Adapted from the short story by Charles Baxter. Aired on PBS as part of the "Wonderworks" family movie series. **58m/C VHS.** Amanda Plummer, Sully Diaz, Alexis Cruz; ***D:*** Mark Cullingham. *PME, FCT, BTV*

Guadalcanal Diary 🦴🦴½ **1943** A vintage wartime flag-waver, with a typical crew of Marines battling the "Yellow Menace" over an important base on the famous Pacific atoll. Based on Richard Tregaskis' first-hand account. **93m/B VHS, Beta, LV.** Preston Foster, Lloyd Nolan, William Bendix, Richard Conte, Anthony Quinn, Richard Jaeckel, Roy Roberts, Minor Watson, Miles Mander, Ralph Byrd, Lionel Stander, Reed Hadley; ***D:*** Lewis Seiler. *FOX, IME*

The Guardian 🦴½ **1984 (R)** Residents of a chic New York apartment building hire a security expert/ex-military man to aid them in combatting their crime problem. But one of the liberal tenants thinks their guard's methods may come at too high a cost. Made for cable television. **102m/C VHS, Beta, LV.** Martin Sheen, Louis Gossett Jr., Arthur Hill; ***D:*** David Greene. *LIV, VES*

The Guardian 🦴 **1990 (R)** A young couple unwittingly hires a human sacrificing druid witch as a babysitter for their child. Based on the book "The Nanny" by Dan Greenburg. **92m/C VHS, Beta, LV.** Jenny Seagrove, Dwier Brown, Carey Lowell; ***D:*** William Friedkin; ***W:*** William Friedkin. *MCA*

Guardian Angel 🦴🦴½ *Beyond Justice* **1994 (R)** Detective Christy McKay (Rothrock) quits the force after her partner/lover is killed by icy seductress Nina (Denier), who manages to escape from jail. When McKay is hired to protect playboy Lawton Hobbs (McVicar), she finds that the threat comes from a psycho ex-girlfriend. Guess who. **97m/C VHS.** Cynthia Rothrock, Lydie Denier, Daniel McVicar, Kenneth McLeod, Marshall Teague, John O'Leary, Dale Jacoby; ***D:*** Richard W. Munchkin. *PMH*

Guardian of the Abyss 🦴 **1982** A young couple who buy an antique mirror get more than they bargained for when they discover that it is the threshold to Hell and the devil wants to come through. **60m/C VHS, Beta.** Ray Lonnen, Rosalyn Landor, Paul Darrow, Barbara Ewing; ***D:*** Don Sharp. *LIV*

Guarding Tess 🦴🦴 **1994 (PG-13)** Long-suffering Secret Service agent Cage is nearing the end of his three year assignment to crotchety widowed First Lady MacLaine when the Prez extends his tour of duty. Feels like a TV movie, not surprising since writers Torokvei and Wilson have several sitcoms to their credit, including "WKRP in Cinncinnati." Nice chemistry between Cage and MacLaine results in a few funny moments, but there are too many formulaic plot twists. End result: a pleasant, if somewhat slow buddy comedy. **98m/C VHS, LV, 8mm.** Shirley MacLaine, Nicolas Cage, Austin Pendleton, Edward Albert, Richard Griffiths; ***D:*** Hugh Wilson; ***W:*** Peter Torokvei, Hugh Wilson; ***C:*** Brian Reynolds; ***M:*** Michael Convertino. Nominations: Golden Globe Awards '95: Best Actress—Musical/Comedy (MacLaine). *COL*

The Guardsman 🦴🦴🦴 **1931** Broadway's illustrious couple Lunt and Fontanne shine in this adaptation of the clever marital comedy by French playwright Molnar in which they also starred. This sophisticated comedy was their only starring film, although they were offered large sums of money to appear in other movies—they just couldn't tear themselves away from the stage. Remade as "The Chocolate Soldier" and "Lily in Love." **89m/B VHS.** Alfred Lunt, Lynn Fontanne, Roland Young, ZaSu Pitts, Maude Eburne, Herman Bing, Ann Dvorak; ***D:*** Sidney Franklin. Nominations: Academy Awards '32: Best Actor (Lunt), Best Actress (Fontanne). *MGM*

Guerilla Brigade 🦴🦴½ *Riders* **1939** A rarely seen Ukrainian epic about Russian/Ukrainian solidarity during the Civil War. In Russian with English subtitles. **90m/B VHS, Beta.** *RU* ***D:*** Igor Savchenko. *FCT*

Guess What We Learned in School Today? *Woof!* **1970 (R)** Parents in a conservative suburban community protest sex education in the schools. Intended as a satire, but it only reinforces stereotypes. **85m/C VHS, Beta.** Richard Carballo, Devin Goldenberg; ***D:*** John G. Avildsen. *NO*

Guess Who's Coming to Dinner 🦴🦴🦴 **1967** Controversial in its time. A young white woman brings her black fiance home to meet her parents. The situation truly tests their open-mindedness and understanding. Hepburn and Tracy (in his last film appearance) are wonderful and serve as the anchors in what would otherwise have been a rather sugary film. Houghton, who portrays the independent daughter, is the real-life niece of Hepburn. **108m/C VHS, Beta, LV.** Katharine Hepburn, Spencer Tracy, Sidney Poitier, Katharine Houghton, Cecil Kellaway; ***D:*** Stanley Kramer; ***W:*** William Rose; ***C:*** Sam Leavitt. Academy Awards '67: Best Actress (Hepburn), Best Original Screenplay; British Academy Awards '68: Best Actor (Tracy), Best Actress (Hepburn); Nominations: Academy Awards '66: Best Actor (Tracy), Best Picture, Best Supporting Actor (Kellaway). *COL, FCT, COL*

Guest in the House 🦴🦴½ **1945** A seemingly friendly young female patient is invited to stay in the family home of her doctor. She skillfully attempts to dissect the family's harmony in the process. **121m/B VHS, Beta.** Anne Baxter, Ralph Bellamy, Ruth Warrick, Marie McDonald, Margaret Hamilton; ***D:*** John Brahm; ***C:*** Lee Garmes. Nominations: Academy Awards '45: Best Original Score. *NOS, CAB, VYY*

Guest Wife 🦴🦴½ **1945** Determined to impress his sentimental boss, a quick-thinking bachelor talks his best friend's wife into posing as his own wife, but the hoax gets a bit out of hand and nearly ruins the real couple's marriage. **90m/B VHS.** Claudette Colbert, Don Ameche, Dick Foran, Charles Dingle, Wilma Francis; ***D:*** Sam Wood; ***C:*** Joseph Valentine. Nominations: Academy Awards '45: Best Original Score. *REP*

A Guide for the Married Man 🦴🦴🦴 **1967** One suburban husband instructs another in adultery, with a cast of dozens enacting various slapstick cameos. Based on Frank Tarloff's novel of the same name. Followed by "A Guide for the Married Woman." **91m/C VHS, Beta.** Walter Matthau, Robert Morse, Inger Stevens, Sue Ane Langdon, Claire Kelly, Elaine Devry; ***Cameos:*** Lucille Ball, Sid Caesar, Jack Benny, Wally Cox, Jayne Mansfield, Louis Nye, Carl Reiner, Phil Silvers, Terry-Thomas, Sam Jaffe, Jeffrey Hunter, Polly Bergen; ***D:*** Gene Kelly; ***W:*** Frank Tarloff; ***M:*** John Williams. *FOX*

A Guide for the Married Woman 🦴½ **1978** A bored housewife tries to take the romantic advice of a girlfriend to add a little spice to her life. A poor made-for-television follow-up to "A Guide for the Married Man." **96m/C VHS, Beta.** Cybill Shepherd, Barbara Feldon, Eve Arden, Chuck Woolery, Peter Marshall, Charles Frank; ***D:*** Hy Averback. *FOX*

Guilty as Charged 🦴½ **1992 (R)** A butcher rigs his own private electric chair and captures and executes paroled killers in his personal quest for justice. But when a politician frames an innocent man for murder how far will this vigilante go? **95m/C VHS, LV.** Rod Steiger, Lauren Hutton, Heather Graham, Isaac Hayes; ***D:*** Sam Irvin; ***M:*** Steve Bartek. *COL*

Guilty as Sin 🦴🦴 **1993 (R)** Johnson is a ruthless Casanova accused of murdering his very wealthy wife and decides lawyer DeMornay is just the woman to defend him. Question is, who'll defend DeMornay from him? Johnson has fun as the menacing smoothie but DeMornay's supposedly hotshot criminal attorney is just plain dumb. It sounds like "Jagged Edge" but there's no sexual involvement between client and lawyer and no thrill in this thriller. **120m/C VHS, Beta, LV.** Don Johnson, Rebecca DeMornay, Jack Warden, Stephen Lang, Dana Ivey, Ron White, Sean McCann, Luis Guzman; ***D:*** Sidney Lumet; ***W:*** Larry Cohen. *HPH, BTV, TOU*

Guilty by Suspicion 🦴🦴½ **1991 (PG-13)** Examination of the 1950's McCarthy investigations by the House Un-American Activities Committee comes off like a bland history lesson. De Niro plays a director who attended a Communist party meeting in the '30s but who otherwise doesn't have any red connections. He takes the moral high ground and refuses to incriminate his buddy (Wendt) to get off the hook and finds himself blacklisted. Characterized by average performances (excepting Wettig who goes overboard) and a lightweight script. "The Front" (1976) does a better job on this topic. Directorial debut for producer Winkler. Available in widescreen on laserdisc. **105m/C VHS, LV, 8mm.** Robert De Niro, Annette Bening, George Wendt, Patricia Wettig, Sam Wanamaker, Chris Cooper, Ben Piazza, Martin Scorsese, Barry Primus, Gailard Sartain, Stuart Margolin, Barry Tubb, Roxann Biggs, Robin Gammell, Brad Sullivan, Luke Edwards, Adam Baldwin; ***D:*** Irwin Winkler; ***W:*** Irwin Winkler; ***C:*** Michael Ballhaus; ***M:*** James Newton Howard. *WAR*

Guilty of Innocence 🦴🦴 **1987 (PG)** A young African-American man finds he's guilty until proven innocent when he runs into the law in Texas. A bold lawyer joins his fight for justice. Based on a true story and made for television. **95m/C VHS.** Dorian Harewood, Dabney Coleman, Hoyt Axton, Paul Winfield, Dennis Lipscomb, Debbi Morgan, Marshall Colt, Victor Love; ***D:*** Richard T. Heffron. *VMK*

Guilty of Treason 🦴🦴½ **1950** A documentary on the life and times of Joszef Cardinal Mindszenty of Hungary, who was imprisoned by the communists as an enemy of the state for speaking out against the totalitarian regime. At the trial, it was revealed that the Cardinal's confession was obtained only by the use of drugs, hypnosis, and torture. A realistic look at the dark side of Communism. **86m/B VHS.** Charles Bickford, Paul Kelly, Bonita Granville, Richard Derr, Berry Kroeger, Elisabeth Risdon, Roland Winters, John Banner; ***D:*** Felix Feist. *NOS, MRV*

The Guinea Pig 🦴🦴½ *The Outsider* **1948** Jack Read (Attenborough), the son of a tobacconist, is sent to a posh public school as an experiment but finds problems between his simple upbringing and the reactions of teachers and other students. **97m/B VHS.** *GB* Richard Attenborough, Joan Hickson, Bernard Miles, Sheila Sim, Robert Flemyng, Timothy Bateson; ***D:*** Roy Boulting; ***W:*** Bernard Miles, Roy Boulting. *FCT*

Guitarman 🦴 **1995** Modern version of "The Pied Piper of Hamlin" finds a mysterious musician saving a farming community's crops from a plague of locusts. But when the mayor reneges on paying the piper (so to speak), he takes the town's children instead. **92m/C VHS.** Nicholas Campbell, Donnelly Rhodes, Andrea Martin, Shawn Ashmore, Jack Semple; ***D:*** Will Dixon. *SDE*

Gulag 🦴🦴½ **1985** An American sportscaster is wrongly sentenced to ten years of hard labor in a Soviet prison, and plans his escape from the cruel guards. Good suspense. Made for television. **130m/C VHS, Beta.** *GB* David Keith, Malcolm McDowell, David Suchet, Warren Clarke, John McEnery; ***D:*** Roger Young; ***M:*** Elmer Bernstein. *PSM*

Gulliver's Travels 🦴🦴½ **1939** The Fleischer Studio's animated version of Jonathan Swift's classic about the adventures of Gulliver, an English sailor who is washed ashore in the land of Lilliput, where everyone is about two inches tall. **74m/C VHS, LV.** ***D:*** Dave Fleischer; ***V:*** Lanny Ross, Jessica Dragonette. Nominations: Academy Awards '39: Best Song ("Faithful Forever"), Best Original Score. *CNG, MRV, NOS*

Gulliver's Travels 🦴🦴 **1977 (G)** In this partially animated adventure the entire land of Lilliput has been constructed in miniature. Cartoon and real life mix in a 3-dimensional story of Dr. Lemuel Gulliver and his discovery of the small people in the East Indies. From the classic by Jonathan Swift. **80m/C VHS, Beta.** *GB* Richard Harris, Catherine Schell; ***D:*** Peter Hunt. *VTR, HHE, RDG*

Gulliver's Travels 🦴🦴½ **1995 (PG)** Faithful TV version of Jonathan Swift's 1726 satiric novel. Lemuel Gulliver (Danson) is confined to Bedlam, an English insane asylum, after having been lost at sea for eight years. While in the asylum he relates his very odd adventures—in the tiny land of Lilliput, among the giants of Brobdingnag, with the silly and impractical intellectuals of Laputa, and finally amidst the brutish human Yahoos, who are ruled by rational talking horses, the Houyhnhnms. Meanwhile, Gulliver's wife Mary (Steenburgen) and son Tom (Sturridge) struggle to prove his sanity and win his release. On two cassettes. **187m/C VHS, LV.** Ted Danson, Mary Steenburgen, Edward Fox, Thomas Sturridge, Edward Woodward, Nicholas Lyndhurst, Peter O'Toole, Phoebe Nicholls, Ned Beatty, Kate Maberly, Alfre Woodard, Geraldine Chaplin, John Gielgud, Kristin Scott Thomas, Omar Sharif, John Standing, Warwick Davis, Robert Hardy, Shashi Kapoor, Karyn Parsons, Edward Petherbridge; ***D:*** Charles Sturridge; ***W:*** Simon Moore; ***C:*** Howard Atherton; ***M:*** Trevor Jones. *HMK*

Gumball Rally 🦴🦴 **1976 (PG)** An unusual assortment of people converge upon New York for a cross country car race to Long Beach, California where breaking the rules is part of the game. **107m/C VHS, Beta.** Michael Sarrazin, Gary Busey, Raul Julia, Nicholas Pryor, Tim McIntire, Susan Flannery; ***D:*** Chuck Bail; ***W:*** Leon Capetanos. *WAR*

Gumby: The Movie 🦴🦴½ **1995 (G)** Gumby and his musical group, the Clayboys, seek to save their neighbors' farms from foreclosure by putting on a benefit concert. And yes, pal Pokey is along to help out. But 90 minutes of our gentle clay hero stretches the patience of even the most enthusiastic fan. **90m/C VHS.** ***D:*** Art Clokey; ***W:*** Art Clokey. *KID*

Gumshoe 🦴🦴½ **1972 (G)** An homage to American hard-boiled detectives. Finney plays a small-time worker in a Liverpool nightclub who decides to become a detective like his movie heroes. He bumbles through a number of interconnecting cases, but finds his way in the end. Good satire of film noir detectives. **85m/C VHS, Beta.** *GB* Albert Finney, Billie Whitelaw, Frank Finlay, Janice Rule, Carolyn Seymour; ***D:*** Stephen Frears; ***C:*** Chris Menges; ***M:*** Andrew Lloyd Webber. *NO*

The Gumshoe Kid 🦴 *The Detective Kid* **1989 (R)** A college-bound kid enters the family detective business to prevent his mother from being evicted. He gets in over his head though, trying to track the fiancee of a wealthy mobster. **98m/C VHS, Beta, LV.** Jay Underwood, Tracy Scoggins, Vince Edwards, Arlene Golonka, Pamela Springsteen; ***D:*** Joseph Manduke. *ACA*

Gun Cargo 🦴 **1949** Muddled story about a conniving shipowner who fires his crew for demanding shore leave. He replaces them with assorted lowlifes, resulting in the usual hijinks. A terrible performance by an otherwise great cast. **49m/C VHS, Beta, 8mm.** Rex Lease, Smith Ballew, William Farnum, Gibson Gowland. *VYY*

Gun Code 🦴½ **1940** The white-hatted cowboy-hero puts a stop to small-town racketeering. **52m/B VHS, Beta.** Tim McCoy, Ina Guest; ***D:*** Sam Newfield. *VDM*

Gun Crazy 🦴🦴🦴 *Deadly is the Female* **1949** Annie Laurie Starr—Annie Oakley in a Wild West show—meets gun-lovin' Bart Tare, who says a gun makes him feel good inside, "like I'm somebody." Sparks fly, and the two get married and live happily ever after—until the money runs out and fatal femme Laurie's craving for excitement and violence starts to flare up. The two become lovebirds-on-the-lam. Now a cult fave, it's based on a MacKinlay Kantor story. Ex-stuntman Russell Harlan's photography is daring; the realism of the impressive robbery scenes is owed in part to the technical consultation of former train robber Al Jennings. And watch for a young Tamblyn as the 14-year-old Bart. **87m/B VHS.** Peggy Cummins, John Dall, Berry Kroeger, Morris Carnovsky, Anabel Shaw, Nedrick Young, Trevor Bardette, Russ Tamblyn; ***D:*** Joseph H. Lewis; ***W:*** Dalton Trumbo. *FOX, FCT*

Gun Crazy 🦴🦴½ *A Talent for Loving* **1969** A gambler becomes enmeshed in an arranged marriage with a cursed Mexican family. Lightweight comedy, good cast. **110m/C VHS.** Richard Widmark, Chaim Topol, Cesar Romero, Genevieve Page, Judd Hamilton, Caroline Munro; ***D:*** Richard Quine. *SIM*

Gun Fight at Red Sands 🦴🦴 *Gringo; Duello Nel Texas* **1963** Landmark western in the history of Italian cinema. Long before Leone's Eastwood trilogy, this film introduced the theme of an avenging stranger to the genre. Harrison stars as the dark, brooding hero who is out for revenge after learning that his family has been attacked by a gang of bandits. **?m/C VHS.** *IT* Richard Harrison, Giacomo "Jack" Rossi-Stuart, Sara Lezana; ***M:*** Ennio Morricone. *SNC*

Gun Fury 🦴🦴½ **1953** A panoramic western about a Civil War veteran pursuing the bandits who kidnapped his beautiful bride-to-be. First screened as a 3-D movie. **83m/C VHS, Beta, LV.** Rock Hudson, Donna Reed, Phil Carey, Lee Marvin; ***D:*** Raoul Walsh. *COL*

Gun Girls 🦴 **1956** Campy exploitation flick about a gun-toting gang of girls who rob anything or anyone. The guy who fences their goods ends up getting one of them pregnant. **?m/C VHS.** Timothy Farrell, Jean Ferguson, Jacquelyn Park, Jean Ann Lewis; ***D:*** Robert Deltano. *SNC*

Gun Glory 🦴🦴½ **1957** Granger plays Tom Early, a gunslinger who returns home after three years to find the town would rather not have him. He regains the town's respect when he stops a murderer from invading the town with his cattle herd. Based on the novel "Man of the West" by Philip Yordan. **88m/C**

VHS. Stewart Granger, Rhonda Fleming, Chill Wills, Steve Rowland, James Gregory, Jacques Aubuchon, Arch Johnson, William "Bill" Fawcett, Lane Bradford, Michael Dugan, Bud Osborne, May McAvoy, Charles Herbert, Carl Pitti; ***D:*** Roy Rowland; ***W:*** William Ludwig; ***M:*** Jeff Alexander. *MGM*

Gun Grit 🦴½ **1936** An FBI agent is sent west to break up a protection racket. **51m/B VHS.** Jack Perrin, Ethel Beck, David Sharpe, Roger Williams, Budd Buster; ***D:*** William (Lester Williams) Berke. *GPV*

The Gun in Betty Lou's Handbag 🦴🦴 **1992 (PG-13)** Shy, small town librarian with a dull marriage is looking for excitement when she stumbles across a gun used in a murder. She decides excitement will follow her (false) confession to the crime leaving her husband thunderstruck, the police confused, and the gossip line humming. She also intrigues the real bad guy, who comes looking for her. Lame silliness is redeemed somewhat by Miller, but there's some surprisingly nasty violence given the comedy label. **99m/C VHS, Beta, LV.** Penelope Ann Miller, Eric Thal, Alfre Woodard, Cathy Moriarty, William Forsythe, Julianne Moore, Xander Berkeley, Michael O'Neill, Christopher John Fields; ***D:*** Allan Moyle; ***W:*** Grace Cary Bickley; ***M:*** Richard Gibbs. *TOU*

A Gun in the House 🦴 **1981** While being attacked in her own home, a woman shoots one of her assailants. The police find no conclusive evidence of attack and arrest the woman for murder. Exploitive drama on gun control. Made-for-television. **100m/C VHS, Beta.** Sally Struthers, David Ackroyd, Joel Bailey, Jeffrey Tambor; ***D:*** Ivan Nagy. *VHE, HHE*

Gun Law 🦴½ **1933** The hero tackles the Sonora Kid, an outlaw terrorizing Arizona folk. One of the few sound westerns with Hoxie, a silent-era star who hung up his spurs when his voice proved nonphotogenic. **59m/B VHS, Beta.** Jack Hoxie, Paul Fix, Mary Carr, Edmund Cobb, Robert Burns; ***D:*** Lewis D. Collins *GPV*

Gun Lords of Stirrup Basin 🦴🦴 **1937** A cattleman and the daughter of a homesteader are in love in the Old West, but a seedy lawyer wants to douse their flame. Bullets and fists fly as a result. **55m/B VHS.** Bob Steele, Louise Stanley, Karl Hackett, Ernie Adams, Frank LaRue, Frank Ball, Steve Clark; ***D:*** Sam Newfield. *NOS, DVT*

Gun Packer 🦴🦴 **1938** When an outlaw gang robs stagecoaches of their gold and uses the booty to salt barren mine shafts so the unsuspecting can be swindled out of their money on worthless gold mine certificates, hard-riding Randall is called in to save the day. **51m/B VHS.** Jack Randall, Louise Stanley, Charles "Blackie" King, Glenn Strange; ***D:*** Wallace Fox; ***W:*** Robert Emmett. *MOV*

Gun Play 🦴🦴 *Lucky Boots* **1936** Brother and sister venture west to run their father's ranch. Mexican bandits believe the ranch's property houses a revolutionary fortune, and set about recovering it. The brother defends his father's ranch along with a sidekick, who sweeps the sister off her feet. **59m/B VHS.** Guinn "Big Boy" Williams, Frank Yaconelli, Marion Shilling, Wally Wales, Charles French; ***D:*** Al(bert) Herman. *NOS, DVT, GPV*

The Gun Ranger 🦴½ **1934** Our hero plays a Texas Ranger who becomes fed up with soft judges and shady prosecutors and decides to take the law into his own hands. **56m/B VHS, Beta.** Bob Steele, Eleanor Stewart, John Merton, Ernie Adams, Budd Buster; ***D:*** Robert North Bradbury. *NOS, DVT, GPV*

Gun Riders 🦴½ *Five Bloody Graves; Five Bloody Days to Tombstone; Lonely Man* **1969** Gunman must seek out and stop a murderer of innocent people. **98m/C VHS, Beta.** Scott Brady, Jim Davis, John Carradine; ***D:*** Al Adamson. *CCB*

Gun Smugglers/Hot Lead 🦴 **1951** A western double feature: Tim Holt and his sidekick Chito must recover a shipment of stolen guns in "Gun Smugglers," and the duo gallop into action against a gang of train robbers in "Hot Lead." **120m/B VHS, Beta.** Tim Holt, Richard Martin, Martha Hyer. *TTC*

Gunblast 🦴 **197?** A convict is released from San Quentin and wastes no time in getting involved with mob-powered drug smuggling. **70m/C VHS, Beta.** Lloyd Allan, Christine Cardan, James Cunningham. *NO*

Guncrazy 🦴🦴 **1992 (R)** Girl from the wrong side of the tracks, abused her entire life, finds her freedom in a gun. She winds up killing the man who raped her, takes up with an equally lost ex-con, and the two armed misfits go on the run from the law. Barrymore's convincing and the movie is another well-made variation on the lovers-on-the-run theme. Film was inspired by, but is not a remake of, the 1949 movie "Gun Crazy." **97m/C VHS, Beta, LV.** Drew Barrymore, James LeGros, Billy Drago, Rodney Harvey, Ione Skye, Joe Dallesandro, Michael Ironside; ***D:*** Tamra Davis; ***W:*** Matthew Bright. *ACA, PMS*

A Gunfight 🦴🦴 **1971 (PG)** When Cash is stranded in a small Western town, he meets up with fellow old-time gunfighter Douglas. The two strike up a friendship, but discover the town folk expect a gun battle. Needing money, the two arrange a gunfight for paid admission — winner take all. Cash makes his screen debut. **90m/C Beta.** Kirk Douglas, Johnny Cash, Jane Alexander, Karen Black, Dana Elcar, Keith Carradine, Raf Vallone; ***D:*** Lamont Johnson; ***W:*** Harold Jack Bloom. *ALL, MTX*

Gunfight at Sandoval 🦴½ **1959** A Texas Ranger investigates the headquarters of a criminal gang while hunting for the bandits who killed his partner. Adapted from the "Texas John Slaughter" episodes of the Disney television series. **72m/C VHS, Beta.** Tom Tryon, Beverly Garland, Dan Duryea. *DIS*

Gunfight at the O.K. Corral 🦴🦴🦴 **1957** The story of Wyatt Earp and Doc Holliday joining forces in Dodge City to rid the town of the criminal Clanton gang. Filmed in typical Hollywood style, but redeemed by its great stars. **122m/C VHS, Beta, LV.** Burt Lancaster, Kirk Douglas, Rhonda Fleming, Jo Van Fleet, John Ireland, Kenneth Tobey, Lee Van Cleef, Frank Faylen, DeForest Kelley, Earl Holliman; ***D:*** John Sturges; ***W:*** Leon Uris; ***C:*** Charles B(ryant) Lang. Nominations: Academy Awards '57: Best Sound. *PAR, FCT*

The Gunfighter 🦴🦴🦴½ **1950** A mature, serious, Hollywood-western character study about an aging gunfighter searching for peace and quiet but unable to avoid his reputation and the duel-challenges it invites. One of King's best films. **85m/B VHS, Beta, LV.** Gregory Peck, Helen Westcott, Millard Mitchell, Jean Parker, Karl Malden, Skip Homeier, Mae Marsh; ***D:*** Henry King; ***C:*** Arthur C. Miller. Nominations: Academy Awards '50: Best Story. *FOX*

The Gunfighters 🦴½ **1987** Lackluster pilot of a proposed Canadian series pits three individualistic relatives against a powerful empire-builder. **100m/C VHS, LV.** *CA* Art Hindle, Reiner Schoene, Tony Addabbo, George Kennedy, Michael Kane, Lori Hallier; ***D:*** Clay Borris. *VMK*

Gunfire 🦴½ **1950** A Frank James look-alike cavorts, robs and loots the countryside until the real James decides to set things straight. **59m/B VHS, Beta, LV.** Donald (Don "Red") Barry, Robert Lowery, Pamela Blake, Wally Vernon; ***D:*** William (Lester Williams) Berke. *HHE*

Gunfire 🦴🦴 *China 9, Liberty 37* **1978** A gunfighter is rescued from the hangman's noose by railroad tycoons who want him to kill a farmer. He doesn't kill the man, but runs off with his wife instead, and the incensed railway honchos send assassins after the double-crossing gunman. Peckinpah's part is pretty puny in this leisurely horse opera. **94m/C VHS.** *IT* Fabio Testi, Warren Oates, Jenny Agutter, Sam Peckinpah; ***D:*** Monte Hellman; ***M:*** Pino Donaggio. *SIM*

Gung Ho! 🦴🦴 **1943** Carlson's Raiders are a specially trained group of Marine jungle fighters determined to retake the Pacific island of Makin during WWII. **88m/B VHS, Beta.** Robert Mitchum, Randolph Scott, Noah Beery Jr., Alan Curtis, Grace McDonald; ***D:*** Ray Enright; ***C:*** Milton Krasner. *REP, MRV, CNG*

Gung Ho 🦴🦴½ **1985 (PG-13)** A Japanese firm takes over a small-town U.S. auto factory and causes major cultural collisions. Keaton plays the go-between for employees and management while trying to keep both groups from killing each other. From the director of "Splash" and "Night Shift." Made into a short-lived television series. **111m/C VHS, Beta, LV, 8mm.** Michael Keaton, Gedde Watanabe, George Wendt, Mimi Rogers, John Turturro, Clint Howard, Michelle Johnson, So Yamamura, Sab Shimono; ***D:*** Ron Howard; ***W:*** Babaloo Mandel, Lowell Ganz; ***M:*** Thomas Newman. *PAR*

Gunga Din 🦴🦴🦴🦴 **1939** The prototypical "buddy" film. Three veteran British sergeants in India try to suppress a native uprising, but it's their water boy, the intrepid Gunga Din, who saves the day. Friendship, loyalty, and some of the best action scenes ever filmed. Based loosely on Rudyard Kipling's famous poem, the story is credited to Ben Hecht, Charles MacArthur and William Faulkner (who is uncredited). Also available colorized. **117m/B VHS, Beta, LV.** Cary Grant, Victor McLaglen, Douglas Fairbanks Jr., Sam Jaffe, Eduardo Ciannelli, Montagu Love, Joan Fontaine, Abner Biberman, Robert Coote, Lumsden Hare, Cecil Kellaway; ***D:*** George Stevens; ***W:*** Fred Guiol, Joel Sayre; ***M:*** Alfred Newman. Nominations: Academy Awards '39: Best Black and White Cinematography. *TTC, MLB*

Gunman from Bodie 🦴½ *Gun Man from Bodie* **1941** Second of the Rough Rider series. Jones, McCoy, and Hatton rescue a baby orphaned by rustlers and then go after the bad guys. **62m/B VHS, Beta.** Tim McCoy, Buck Jones, Raymond Hatton; ***D:*** Spencer Gordon Bennet. *NOS, MRV, VCN*

Gunmen 🦴🦴 **1993 (R)** A reluctant buddy team face down some bad guys. DEA agent Cole (Van Peebles) teams up with smuggler Dani (Lambert) to find stolen drug money also wanted by wheelchair-bound villain Loomis (Stewart) and his violence-loving henchman (Leary). Adds comedy to the mix as well as shameless action rip-offs from spaghetti westerns. **90m/C VHS, LV.** Christopher Lambert, Mario Van Peebles, Denis Leary, Patrick Stewart, Kadeem Hardison, Sally Kirkland; ***Cameos:*** Big Daddy Kane, Ed Lover, Eric B. Rakim, Dr. Dre; ***D:*** Deran Sarafian; ***W:*** Stephen Sommers; ***M:*** John Debney. *LIV*

Gunners & Guns 🦴 **1934** Vintage western starring King. **51m/B VHS, Beta.** Black King, Edmund Cobb, Edna Asetin, Eddie Davis; ***D:*** Robert Hoyt. *VCN*

Gunplay 🦴½ **1951** Two cowboys befriend a boy whose father has been killed and search for the murderer. **61m/B VHS, Beta.** Tim Holt, Joan Dixon, Richard Martin. *MED*

Gunpowder 🦴 **1984** Two Interpol agents endeavor to stop a crime lord from causing the collapse of the world economy. **85m/C VHS, Beta.** David Gilliam, Martin Potter, Gordon Jackson, Anthony Schaeffer. *LIV, VES*

The Gunrunner 🦴½ **1984 (R)** Costner plays a Canadian mobster, involved in liquor smuggling, who aids a Chinese rebellion in this 1920s drama. Interesting concept. Received more attention after Costner gained notoriety in later films. **92m/C VHS, LV.** *CA* Kevin Costner, Sara Botsford, Paul Soles; ***D:*** Nardo Castillo. *VTR, HHE*

Guns 🦴🦴 **1990 (R)** An international gunrunner puts the moves on buxom women between hair-raising adventures. **95m/C VHS, LV.** Erik Estrada, Dona Speir; ***D:*** Andy Sidaris; ***W:*** Andy Sidaris. *COL*

The Guns and the Fury 🦴½ **1983** Two American oil riggers in the Middle East, circa 1908, are forced to fight off an attack by a vicious Arab sheik and his tribe. **90m/C VHS, Beta.** Peter Graves, Cameron Mitchell, Michael Ansara, Albert Salmi; ***D:*** Tony Zarindast. *NO*

Guns at Batasi 🦴🦴½ **1964** Attenborough plays a tough British Sergeant Major stationed in Africa during the anti-colonial 1960s. Ultimately the regiment is threatened by rebel Africans. Fine performances make this rather predictable film watchable. **103m/B VHS.** *GB* Richard Attenborough, Jack Hawkins, Mia Farrow, Flora Robson, John Leyton; ***D:*** John Guillermin; ***M:*** John Addison. *TCF, RXM*

Guns Don't Argue 🦴🦴 **1957** Entertaining schlocker about the rise and fall of famous criminal Dillinger. Non-stop action also features Bonnie and Clyde, Pretty Boy Floyd and Baby Face Nelson. **?m/C VHS.** Myron Healey, Jim Davis, Richard Crane. *SNC*

Guns for Dollars 🦴🦴 *They Call Me Hallelujah* **1973** Mex-Western has four men, including a secret agent and a cossack, tangled up in the Mexican Revolution as they search for a fortune in smuggled jewels. **94m/C VHS.** *MX* George Hilton, Charles Southwood, Agata Flory, Roberto Camardiel, Paolo Gozlino, Rick Boyd; ***D:*** Anthony Ascot. *ACA*

Guns in the Dark 🦴 **1937** A cowboy vows never to use a gun again when he believes that he accidentally shot his best friend. **60m/C VHS, Beta.** Johnny Mack Brown, Claire Rochelle; ***D:*** Sam Newfield. *NOS, DVT, RXM*

Guns of Diablo 🦴🦴 **1964** Wagon train master Bronson has to fight a gang that controls the supply depot, all the while showing his young helper (beardless boy Russell) the fascinating tricks of the trade. **91m/C VHS.** Charles Bronson, Kurt Russell, Susan Oliver; ***D:*** Boris Sagal. *ACE, MTX, VTR*

Guns of Fury 🦴½ **1945** Cisco and Pancho solve the troubles of a small boy in this standard oater. **60m/B VHS, Beta.** Duncan Renaldo. *NOS, VCI, VCN*

Guns of Justice 🦴 *Colorado Ranger* **1950** Undercover Colorado rangers stop a swindler from forcing homesteaders off their land. **60m/B VHS, Beta, LV.** James Ellison, Russell Hayden, Tom Tyler, Raymond Hatton; ***D:*** Thomas Carr. *NO*

The Guns of Navarone 🦴🦴🦴½ **1961** During WWII, British Intelligence in the Middle East sends six men to the Aegean island of Navarone to destroy guns manned by the Germans. Consistently interesting war epic based on the Alistair MacLean novel, with a vivid cast. **159m/C VHS, Beta, LV.** Gregory Peck, David Niven, Anthony Quinn, Richard Harris, Stanley Baker, Anthony Quayle, James Darren, Irene Papas; ***D:*** J. Lee Thompson; ***C:*** Oswald Morris. Academy Awards '61: Best Special Effects; Golden Globe Awards '62: Best Film—Drama, Best Score; Nominations: Academy Awards '60: Best Adapted Screenplay, Best Director (Thompson). *COL*

Guns of the Law 🦴½ **1944** The Texas Rangers try to stop a shifty lawyer who attempts to swindle a family out of a potential fortune in property. **56m/B VHS.** Dave O'Brien, James Newill, Guy Wilkerson, Jack Ingram, Robert F. (Bob) Kortman, Bob Barron; ***D:*** Elmer Clifton; ***W:*** Elmer Clifton. *MOV*

Guns of the Magnificent Seven 🦴🦴½ **1969 (G)** The third remake of "The Seven Samurai." Action-packed western in which the seven free political prisoners and train them to kill. The war party then heads out to rescue a Mexican revolutionary being held in an impregnable fortress. **106m/C VHS.** George Kennedy, Monte Markham, James Whitmore, Reni Santoni, Bernie Casey, Joe Don Baker, Scott Thomas, Michael Ansara, Fernando Rey; ***D:*** Paul Wendkos; ***M:*** Elmer Bernstein. *MGM*

Guns of War **1975** This is the true story of how a group of Yugoslavians formed a partisan army to stop the reign of Nazi terror in their native land. **114m/C VHS, Beta.** *YU NO*

The Gunslinger 🦴½ **1956** A woman marshall struggles to keep law and order in a town overrun by outlaws. Unique western with a surprise ending. **83m/C VHS.** John Ireland, Beverly Garland, Allison Hayes, Jonathan Haze, Dick Miller, Bruno Ve Sota; ***D:*** Roger Corman; ***W:*** Charles B. Griffith. *MLB, TIM, SNC*

Gunslinger 🦴½ **197?** Armed to the teeth with weaponry, Sartana shows a mining town's heavies how to sling a gun or two. **90m/C VHS, Beta.** Gianni "John" Garko, Antonio Vilar; ***D:*** Anthony Ascot. *VDC*

Gunsmoke: Return to Dodge 🦴🦴½ **1987** The first of the made-for-television movies which reunited most of the cast of the classic television western. Matt Dillon returns to Dodge and Miss Kitty after 12 years only to be trailed by a ruthless adversary. **100m/C VHS.** James Arness, Amanda Blake, Buck Taylor, Fran Ryan, Earl Holliman, Steve Forrest; ***D:*** Vincent McEveety. *FXV*

Gunsmoke Trail 🦴½ **1938** Cowpoke Randall saves an heiress from losing her estate to a phony uncle in low-budget Western. Also features the prolific "Fuzzy" St. John in his cowboy's sidekick stage (interestingly, St. John, a nephew of Fatty Arbuckle, later co-starred in the "Lone Rider" series with Randall's brother, Robert Livingston). **59m/C VHS.** Jack Randall, Al "Fuzzy" St. John. *NOS, MRV, MOV*

Gus 🦴🦴½ **1976 (G)** A Disney film about the California Atoms, a football team that has the worst record in the league until they begin winning games with the help of their field goal kicking mule of a mascot, Gus. The competition then plots a donkey-napping. Enjoyable comedy for the whole family. **96m/C VHS, Beta, LV.** Ed Asner, Tim Conway, Dick Van Patten, Ronnie Schell, Bob Crane, Tom Bosley; ***D:*** Vincent McEveety; ***W:*** Arthur Alsberg; ***M:*** Robert F. Brunner. *COL, DIS*

GUY: Awakening of the Devil 🦴🦴 **1993** Guy and Raina, two despicable intergalactic soldiers of fortune, embark on a continuous sky-raid adventure. Available in general release and uncut versions. Japanese with English subtitles. **?m/C VHS.** *JP CPM, WTA*

The Guy from Harlem 🦴🦴 **1977** He's mad, he's from Harlem, and he's not going to take it any more. **86m/C VHS.** Loye Hawkins, Cathy Davis, Patricia Fulton, Wanda Starr; ***D:*** Rene Martinez Jr. *XVC*

A Guy Named Joe 🦴🦴½ **1944** A sentimental, patriotic Hollywood fantasy about the angel of a dead WWII pilot guiding another young pilot through battle and also helping him to romance his girl, who's still too devoted to his memory. Remade in 1989 as "Always." **121m/B VHS, Beta.** Spencer Tracy, Irene Dunne, Van Johnson, Ward Bond, James Gleason, Lionel Barrymore, Esther Williams; ***D:*** Victor Fleming; ***W:*** Dalton Trumbo; ***C:*** Karl Freund. Nominations: Academy Awards '44: Best Story. *MGM*

The Guyana Tragedy: The Story of Jim Jones 🦴🦴 **1980** Dramatization traces the story of the Reverend Jim Jones and the People's Temple from its beginnings in 1953 to the November 1978 mass suicide of more than 900 people. Boothe is appropriately hypnotic as the Reverend. Made for television. **240m/C VHS, Beta.** Powers Boothe, Ned Beatty, Randy Quaid, Brad Dourif, Brenda Vaccaro, LeVar Burton, Colleen Dewhurst, James Earl Jones; ***D:*** William A. Graham; ***M:*** Elmer Bernstein. *VHE, HHE*

Guys and Dolls 🦴🦴🦴 **1955** New York gambler Sky Masterson takes a bet that he can romance a Salvation Army lady. Based on the stories of Damon Runyon with Blaine, Kaye, Pully, and Silver re-creating their roles from the Broadway hit. Brando's not-always-convincing musical debut. ♫More I Cannot Wish You; My Time of Day; Guys and Dolls; Fugue for Tinhorns; Follow the Fold; Sue Me; Take Back Your Mink; If I Were a Bell; Luck Be a Lady. **150m/C VHS, Beta, LV.** Marlon Brando, Jean Simmons, Frank Sinatra, Vivian Blaine, Stubby Kaye, Sheldon Leonard, Veda Ann Borg; ***D:*** Joseph L. Mankiewicz; ***W:*** Joseph L. Mankiewicz; ***C:*** Harry Stradling; ***M:*** Frank Loesser. Golden Globe Awards '56: Best Actress—Musical/Comedy (Simmons), Best Film—Musical/Comedy; Nominations: Academy Awards '55: Best Art Direction/Set Decoration (Color), Best Color Cinematography, Best Costume Design (Color), Best Original Score. *FOX, FCT*

The Guyver 🦴½ **1991** A young college student is transformed into a super-human fighting machine thanks to his discovery of an alien device, "The Guyver." A CIA agent (Hamill) must keep the secret device from falling into the hands of human mutants, the Zoanoids. Based on a Japanese comic book. **92m/C VHS.** Mark Hamill, Vivian Wu, David Gale, Jeffrey Combs, Michael Berryman; ***D:*** Steve Wang. *COL, NLC*

Guyver 2: Dark Hero 🦴½ **1994 (R)** The Guyver discovers an alien ship filled with weapons capable of destroying the planet. Naturally, he must battle the evil mutant Zoanoids in order to save the world. Adapted from a Japanese comic book. **127m/C VHS, LV.** David Hayter, Kathy Christopherson, Christopher Michael; ***D:*** Steve Wang; ***W:*** Nathan Long. *COL*

Gymkata 🦴 **1985 (R)** A gymnast (Olympian Thomas) must use his martial arts skills to conquer and secure a military state in a hostile European country. **89m/C VHS, Beta.** Kurt Thomas, Tetchie Agbayani, Richard Norton, Conan Lee; ***D:*** Robert Clouse; ***W:*** Charles Robert Carner. *MGM*

Gypsy 🦴🦴🦴 **1962** The life story of America's most famous striptease queen, Gypsy Rose Lee. Russell gives a memorable performance as the infamous Mama Rose, Gypsy's stage mother. Based on both Gypsy Rose Lee's memoirs and the hit Broadway play by Arthur Laurents. ♫Small World; All I Need is the Girl; You'll Never Get Away From Me; Let Me Entertain You; Some People; Everything's Coming Up Roses; You Gotta Have a Gimmick; Baby Jane and the Newsboys; Mr. Goldstone, I Love You. **144m/C VHS, Beta, LV.** Rosalind Russell, Natalie Wood, Karl Malden, Ann Jillian, Parley Baer, Paul Wallace, Betty Bruce; ***D:*** Mervyn LeRoy; ***C:*** Harry Stradling. Golden Globe Awards '63: Best Actress—Musical/Comedy (Russell); Nominations: Academy Awards '62: Best Color Cinematography, Best Costume Design (Color), Best Original Score. *WAR*

Gypsy 🦴🦴 **1975** A modern day gypsy-blooded Robin Hood cavorts between heists and romantic trysts. Dubbed. **90m/C VHS, Beta.** Alain Delon, Annie Girardot, Paul Meurisse; ***D:*** Jose Giovanni. *FCT*

Gypsy 🦴🦴½ **1993** If you like Bette brassy and larger than life, as only she can be, than this is the production for you. This television recreation of the 1959 Broadway musical stars Midler as notorious stage mother Mama Rose, who tries to realize all her frustrated ambitions by pushing her two young daughters, June and Louise, into vaudeville show biz. Her wish eventually comes true, in an unexpected fashion, when an adult Louise (Gibb) transforms herself into stripper Gypsy Rose Lee. ♫Everything's Coming Up Roses; You've Gotta Have a Gimmick; All I Need Is the Girl; Rose's Turn; Some People; Mr. Goldstone, I Love You; You'll Never Get Away From Me; Together, Wherever We Go. **150m/C VHS, LV.** Bette Midler, Peter Riegert, Cynthia Gibb, Ed Asner, Christine Ebersole, Michael Jeter, Andrea Martin, Jennifer Beck, Linda Hart, Rachel Sweet; ***D:*** Emile Ardolino; ***W:*** Arthur Laurents; ***C:*** Ralf Bode; ***M:*** Jule Styne, Stephen Sondheim. *CAF*

Gypsy Angels 🦴 **1994 (R)** A daredevil stunt pilot has a terrifying accident and develops amnesia. With the help of a stripper (who is in love with him), he tries to rebuild his life, this time with her in it. White's no actress and unless you like stunt flying (and there's a lot of it), fly by this one. (You'll note the director won't admit to this, since Smithee is a pseudonym.) **92m/C VHS.** Vanna White, Richard Roundtree, Gene Bicknell; ***D:*** Alan Smithee. *VMK*

Gypsy Blood 🦴🦴 **1918** One of the first screen versions of "Carmen," closer to Prosper Merrimee's story than to the opera, depicting the fated love between a dancing girl and a matador. Lubitsch's first notable film. Silent. **104m/B VHS, Beta.** Pola Negri; ***D:*** Ernst Lubitsch. *FCT, GPV*

Gypsy Colt 🦴🦴½ **1954 (G)** Gypsy is the horse beloved by the young Corcoran. But a drought forces her family to sell the animal to a racing stable 500 miles from their home. Gypsy is having none of this, escapes the stables, and returns home to be with Corcoran. Both horse and child actress are naturally appealing. **72m/C VHS.** Donna Corcoran, Ward Bond, Frances Dee, Lee Van Cleef, Larry Keating; ***D:*** Andrew Marton. *MGM, FCT*

The Gypsy Warriors 🦴½ **1978** Two Army captains during WWII infiltrate Nazi-occupied France in order to prevent the distribution of a deadly toxin and are aided by a band of Gypsies. Made for television. **77m/C VHS, Beta.** Tom Selleck, James Whitmore Jr., Joseph Ruskin, Lina Raymond; ***D:*** Lou Antonio. *MCA*

H 🦴🦴 **1990** Two junkies try to kick their heroin addiction and face the difficult withdrawal period. Includes glimpses into their past that shed light on the reasons they turned to drugs. Contains explicit footage. **93m/C VHS.** *CA* Martin Neufeld, Pascale Montpetit; ***D:*** Darrell Wasyk. Toronto-City Award '90: Best Canadian Feature Film. *NYR*

H-Bomb *Woof!* **1971** Mitchum stars as a CIA agent who is sent to Bangkok to retrieve two stolen nuclear warheads from a terrorist. It just so happens that his ex-girlfriend's father is the terrorist he must contend with in this stupid movie. **98m/C VHS, Beta.** Olivia Hussey, Chris Mitchum, Krung Savilai; ***D:*** P. Chalong. *NO*

H-Man *Woof! Bijo to Ekitainigen* **1959** A Japanese sci-fi woofer about a radioactive mass of slime festering under Tokyo. Extremely lame special effects get quite a few unintentional laughs. Dubbed. **79m/C VHS, Beta.** *JP* Koreya Senda, Kenji Sahara, Yumi Shirakawa, Akihiko Hirata; ***D:*** Inoshiro Honda. *COL*

The Habitation of Dragons 🦴½ **1991** Family fueds and melodrama in 1930s West Texas. Wandering lawyer George Tolliver (Davis) argues with successful businessman brother Leonard (Forrest) while matriarch Leonora (Stapleton) presides and family skeletons rattle. Confusing hodgepodge. **94m/C VHS.** Jean Stapleton, Frederic Forrest, Brad Davis, Pat Hingle, Hallie Foote, Maureen O'Sullivan; ***D:*** Michael Lindsay-Hogg; ***W:*** Horton Foote; ***M:*** David Shire. *TTC*

Hack O'Lantern 🦴 **1987** Granddad worships Satan, and gets his grandson involved: the result is much bloodshed, violence and evil. **90m/C VHS, Beta.** ***D:*** Jag Mundhra. *NO*

Hackers 🦴🦴 **1995 (PG-13)** Group of teenaged computer cyber-geeks surf the 'net and become the prime suspects in an industrial conspiracy when hacker Dade (Miller) breaks into the computer at Ellingson Oil Company. It's really an inside job but just try getting anyone (read "adult") to believe him. So the techno whiz kids band together, with cops and security all wanting to shut them down. Jolie (hacker Acid Burn) is the daughter of actor Jon Voight. **105m/C VHS, LV.** Jonny Lee Miller, Angelina Jolie, Fisher Stevens, Lorraine Bracco, Jesse Bradford, Wendell Pierce, Alberta Watson, Laurence Mason, Renoly Santiago, Matthew Lillard, Penn Jillette; ***D:*** Iain Softley; ***W:*** Rafael Moreu; ***C:*** Andrzej Sekula; ***M:*** Simon Boswell. *MGM*

Hadley's Rebellion 🦴½ **1984 (PG)** A Georgia farm boy adjusts to relocation at an elitist California boarding school by flaunting his wrestling abilities. **96m/C VHS, Beta.** Griffin O'Neal, Charles Durning, William Devane, Adam Baldwin, Dennis Hage, Lisa Lucas; ***D:*** Fred Walton; ***W:*** Fred Walton. *FOX*

Hail 🦴🦴 *Hail to the Chief; Washington, B.C* **1973 (PG)** A biting satire of what-might-have-been if certain key cabinet members had their way. **85m/C VHS, Beta.** Richard B. Shull, Dick O'Neill, Phil Foster, Joseph Sirola, Dan Resin, Willard Waterman, Gary Sandy; ***D:*** Fred Levinson. *NO*

Hail Caesar 🦴🦴½ **1994 (PG)** His job at an eraser factory is the only thing standing between Julius Caesar MacGruder (Hall) and fame and fortune as a rock 'n roll singer. **93m/C VHS, Beta, LV.** Anthony Michael Hall, Robert Downey Jr., Frank Gorshin, Samuel L. Jackson, Judd Nelson, Nicholas Pryor, Leslie Danon, Bobbie Philips; ***D:*** Anthony Michael Hall; ***W:*** Robert Mittenthal; ***M:*** Roger Tallman. *PSM*

Hail, Hero! 🦴½ **1969 (PG)** A dated Vietnam War era drama about a confused hippie rebelling against his parents and the draft. First film for both Douglas and Strauss. Adapted from the novel by John Weston. Includes music by Gordon Lightfoot. **97m/C VHS, Beta.** Michael Douglas, Arthur Kennedy, Teresa Wright, John Larch, Charles Drake, Deborah Winters, Peter Strauss; ***D:*** David Miller; ***C:*** Robert B. Hauser. *FOX*

Hail Mary 🦴🦴½ *Je Vous Salue Marie* **1985 (R)** A modern-day virgin named Mary inexplicably becomes pregnant in this controversial film that discards notions of divinity in favor of the celebration of a lively, intellectual humanism. Godard rejects orthodox narrative structure and bourgeois prejudices. Very controversial, but not up to his breathless beginning work. In French with English subtitles. **107m/C VHS, Beta, LV.** *FR SI GB* Myriem Roussel, Thierry Rode, Philippe Lacoste, Manon Anderson, Juliette Binoche, Johan Leysen; ***D:*** Jean-Luc Godard; ***W:*** Jean-Luc Godard. *LIV, VES, INJ*

Hail the Conquering Hero 🦴🦴🦴½ **1944** A slight young man is rejected by the Army. Upon returning home, he is surprised to find out they think he's a hero. Biting satire with Demarest's performance stealing the show. **101m/B VHS.** Eddie Bracken, Ella Raines, William Demarest, Franklin Pangborn, Raymond Walburn; ***D:*** Preston Sturges. Nominations: Academy Awards '44: Best Original Screenplay. *MCA*

Hair 🦴🦴🦴½ **1979 (PG)** Film version of the explosive 1960s Broadway musical about the carefree life of the flower children and the shadow of the Vietnam War that hangs over them. Great music, as well as wonderful choreography by Twyla Tharp help portray the surprisingly sensitive evocation of the period so long after the fact. Forman has an uncanny knack for understanding the textures of American life. Watch for a thinner Nell Carter. **122m/C VHS, Beta, LV.** Treat Williams, John Savage, Beverly D'Angelo, Annie Golden, Nicholas Ray; ***D:*** Milos Forman; ***W:*** Michael Weller. *MGM*

The Hairdresser's Husband 🦴🦴 **1992 (R)** Antoine (Rochefort) has had an odd obsession since boyhood—hairdressers—and in middle age he finds love with Mathilde (Galiena), a hairdresser he meets and proposes to as she cuts his hair. She accepts, and the two live their quiet lives in her barber shop as she cuts hair and he watches, occasionally breaking out in Arabian dances. A dark and odd yet refreshing film with fine performances by Rochefort and Galiena in this story about fetishism, obsession, and hair. In French with English subtitles. **84m/C VHS, LV.** *FR* Jean Rochefort, Anna Galiena, Roland Bertin, Maurice Chevit, Philippe Clevenot, Jacques Mathou, Claude Aufaure; ***D:*** Patrice Leconte; ***W:*** Patrice Leconte; ***M:*** Michael Nyman. *PAR, BTV*

Hairspray 🦴🦴🦴 **1988 (PG)** Waters' first truly mainstream film, if that's even possible, and his funniest. Details the struggle among teenagers in 1962 Baltimore for the top spot in a local TV dance show. Deals with racism and stereotypes, as well as typical "teen" problems (hair-do's and don'ts). Filled with refreshingly tasteful, subtle social satire (although not without typical Waters touches that will please die-hard fans). Lake is lovable and appealing as Divine's daughter; Divine, in his last film, is likeable as an iron-toting mom. Look for Waters in a cameo and Divine as a man. Great '60s music, which Waters refers to as "the only known remedy to today's Hit Parade of Hell." **94m/C VHS, Beta, LV.** Ricki Lake, Divine, Jerry Stiller, Colleen Fitzpatrick, Sonny Bono, Deborah Harry, Ruth Brown, Pia Zadora, Ric Ocasek, Michael St. Gerard, Leslie Ann Powers, Shawn Thompson; ***Cameos:*** John Waters; ***D:*** John Waters; ***W:*** John Waters. *NLC, FCT*

The Hairy Ape 🦴🦴 **1944** Screen adaptation of the Eugene O'Neill play. A beast-like coal stoker becomes obsessed with a cool and distant passenger aboard an ocean liner. **90m/B VHS.** William Bendix, Susan Hayward, John Loder, Dorothy Comingore, Roman Bohnen, Alan Napier; ***D:*** Alfred Santell. Nominations: Academy Awards '44: Best Original Score. *NOS, MRV, FCT*

Half a Lifetime **1986** The stakes are too high for four friends playing a game of poker. **85m/C VHS, Beta.** Keith Carradine, Gary Busey, Nick Mancuso, Saul Rubinek. *HBO*

Half a Loaf of Kung Fu 🦴 **1985** The worthy bodyguards of Sern Chuan are called upon to deliver a valuable jade statue. Thwarted again and again by ruthless robbers, they falter. Only Chan carries on, meeting the enemy alone. Fast action, good story. **98m/C VHS, Beta.** Jackie Chan. *NO*

Half a Sixpence 🦴🦴 **1967** Former musician Sidney, who earlier directed "Showboat" and "Kiss Me Kate," shows a bit less verve in this production. Based on H.G. Wells' 1905 novel, "Kipps," it sports much of the original cast from its Broadway incarnation. Edwardian orphan Steele, a cloth-dealer-in-training, comes into a large sum of money and proceeds to lose it with great dispatch. Somewhere along the way he loses his girlfriend, too, but she takes him back because musicals end happily. ♫Half a Sixpence; Flash, Bang, Wallop!; All In The Cause Of Economy; I'm Not Talking To You; Money To Burn; The Race Is On; I Don't Believe A Word Of It; A Proper Gentleman; She's Too Far Above Me. **148m/B VHS.** Tommy Steele, Julia Foster, Penelope Horner, Cyril Ritchard, Grover Dale; ***D:*** George Sidney; ***W:*** Beverley Cross; ***C:*** Geoffrey Unsworth. *PAR, FCT*

Half a Soldier 🦴🦴 **1940** A spoiled girl gets a big surprise when she steals a car and discovers the body of a gangster in the trunk. **59m/B VHS, Beta.** Heather Angel, John "Dusty" King. *NOS, DVT, HEG*

The Half-Breed 🦴🦴 **1951** Routine oater with settlers and Apaches fighting, and the obligatory half-breed stuck in the middle. **81m/B VHS, Beta.** Robert Young, Jack Buetel, Janis Carter, Barton MacLane, Reed Hadley, Porter Hall, Connie Gilchrist; ***D:*** Stuart Gilmore. *TTC*

Half Human 🦴½ **1958** Dull Japanese monster movie about an ape-human who terrorizes Northern Japan. When released in the U.S., Carradine and Morris were added. Without subtitles, just Carradine's narration. Director Honda made better movies before and after, with Godzilla and Rodan. **78m/B VHS.** *JP* John Carradine, Akira Takarada, Morris Ankrum; ***D:*** Inoshiro Honda. *SNC, MLB*

Half Moon Street 🦴🦴 *Escort Girl* **1986 (R)** A brilliant woman scientist supplements her paltry fellowship salary by becoming a hired escort and prostitute, which leads her into various incidents of international intrigue. Adapted from a story by Paul Theroux, "Dr. Slaughter." **90m/C VHS, Beta, LV, 8mm.** Sigourney Weaver, Michael Caine, Keith Buckley, Ian MacInnes; ***D:*** Bob Swaim. *SUE, NLC*

Half of Heaven 🦴🦴🦴 *La Mitad del Cielo* **1986** A critically popular film about a young Spanish woman who begins to share certain telepathic powers with her wizened grandmother. In Spanish with English subtitles. **95m/C VHS, Beta.** *SP* Angela Molina, Margarita Lozano; ***D:*** Manuel Gutierrez Aragon. *PBS, FCT, APD*

Half-Shot at Sunrise 🦴🦴 **1930** Madcap vaudeville comedians play AWOL soldiers loose in 1918 Paris. Continuous one-liners, sight gags, and slapstick nonsense. First film appearance of comedy team Wheeler and Woolsey. **78m/B VHS, Beta.** Bert Wheeler, Robert Woolsey, Dorothy Lee, Robert Rutherford, Edna May Oliver; ***D:*** Paul Sloane; ***M:*** Max Steiner. *VYY, CAB, DVT*

Half Slave, Half Free 🦴🦴½ *Solomon Northrup's Odyssey* **1985** The true story of a free black man in the 1840s who is kidnapped and forced into slavery for 12 years. Made for television as part of the "American Playhouse" series on PBS. Followed by "Charlotte Forten's Mission: Experiment in Freedom." **113m/C VHS, Beta.** Avery Brooks, Mason Adams, Petronia Paley, John Saxon, Joe Seneca, Michael Tolan, Lee Bryant, Rhetta Greene, Janet League; ***D:*** Gordon Parks. *XVC, KAR, KUI*

The Halfback of Notre Dame 🦴🦴½ **1996 (G)** Star football player (and coach's son) Craig Modeau (Hogan) is a lumbering misfit, ripe for high school teasing, anywhere but on the gridiron. But French exchange student Esmeralda (Vaugier) thinks he's sweet—much to the dismay of current boyfriend, obnoxious quarterback Archie (Cutler). Then Craig decides to quit the team right before the big game when dad says no fraternizing and it's up to his French flame to get the jock to change his mind. Made for TV reworking of Victor Hugo's "The Hunchback of Notre Dame." **97m/C VHS, LV.** Gabriel Hogan, Emmanuelle Vaugier, Scott Hylands, Sandra Nelson, Allen Cutler; ***D:*** Rene Bonniere; ***W:*** Richard Clark, Mark Trafficante; ***C:*** Maris Jansons; ***M:*** George Blondheim. *HMK*

Hallelujah! 🦴🦴🦴½ **1929** Haynes plays an innocent young man who turns to religion and becomes a charasmatic preacher after a family tragedy. He retains all his human weaknesses, however, including falling for the lovely but deceitful McKinney. Great music included traditional spirituals and songs by Berlin, such as "At the End of the Road" and "Swanee Shuffle." Shot on location in Tennessee. The first all-black feature film and the first talkie for director Vidor was given the go-ahead by MGM production chief Irving Thalberg, though he knew the film would be both controversial and get minimal release in the deep South. **90m/B VHS.** Daniel L. Haynes, Nina Mae McKinney, William Fontaine, Harry Gray, Fannie Belle DeKnight, Everett McGarrity; ***D:*** King Vidor; ***M:*** Irving Berlin. Nominations: Academy Awards '30: Best Director (Vidor). *MGM, MOV, BTV*

Hallelujah, I'm a Bum 🦴🦴½ *Hallelujah, I'm a Tramp; The Heart of New York; Happy Go Lucky; Lazy Bones* **1933** A happy-go-lucky hobo reforms and begins a new life for the sake of a woman. Bizarre Depression-era musical with a Rodgers and Hart score and continuously rhyming dialogue. The British version, due to the slang meaning of "bum," was retitled, substituting "tramp." ♫You Are Too Beautiful; I'll Do It Again; I've Got To Get Back To New York; What Do You Want With Money?; Hallelujah, I'm A Bum; My Pal Bumper; Dear June; Bumper Found a Grand. **83m/B VHS, Beta.** Al Jolson, Madge Evans, Frank Morgan, Chester Conklin; ***D:*** Lewis Milestone; ***W:*** Ben Hecht, S.N. Behrman; ***M:*** Richard Rodgers, Lorenz Hart. *LCA, MLB*

The Hallelujah Trail 🦴🦴 **1965** Denver mining town in the late 1800s is about to batten down the hatches for a long winter, and there's not a drop of whiskey to be had. The U.S. Cavalry sends a shipment to the miners, but temperance leader Cora Templeton Massingale (Remick) and her bevy of ladies against liquor stand between the shipment and the would-be whistle whetters. Limp Western satire directed by Preston Sturges' brother, who fared much better when he kept a straight face (he also directed "The Great Escape"). Based on Bill Gulick's novel, "The Hallelujah Train." Two-laserdisc set includes additional footage (though it's already overlong), the original trailer, and a letterboxing. **166m/C VHS, LV.** Burt Lancaster, Lee Remick, Jim Hutton, Pamela Tiffin, Donald Pleasence, Brian Keith, Martin Landau; ***D:*** John Sturges; ***W:*** John Gay; ***C:*** Robert L. Surtees; ***M:*** Elmer Bernstein. *MGM, FCT*

Halloween 🦴🦴🦴½ **1978 (R)** John Carpenter's horror classic has been acclaimed "the most successful independent motion picture of all time." A deranged youth returns to his hometown with murderous intent after fifteen years in an asylum. Very, very scary—you feel this movie more than see it. **90m/C VHS, Beta, LV.** Jamie Lee Curtis, Donald Pleasence, Nancy Loomis, P.J. Soles; ***D:*** John Carpenter; ***W:*** John Carpenter, Debra Hill; ***C:*** Dean Cundey; ***M:*** John Carpenter. *MED, VTR*

Halloween 2: The Nightmare Isn't Over! 🦴½ **1981 (R)** Trying to pick up where "Halloween" left off, the sequel begins with the escape of vicious killer Michael, who continues to murder and terrorize the community of Haddonfield, Illinois. Lacking the innovative intentions of its predecessor, it relies on old-fashioned buckets of blood. No chills, just trauma. Co-scripted by Carpenter, director of the original. **92m/C VHS, Beta, LV.** Jamie Lee Curtis, Donald Pleasence, Jeffrey Kramer, Charles Cyphers, Lance Guest; ***D:*** Rick Rosenthal; ***W:*** John Carpenter, Debra Hill; ***M:*** John Carpenter. *MCA*

Halloween 3: Season of the Witch 🦴🦴 **1982 (R)** Modern druid plans to kill 50 million children with his specially made Halloween masks. Produced by John Carpenter, this second sequel to the 1978 horror classic is not based on the events or characters of its predecessors or successors. Followed by "Halloween 4," and "Halloween 5: The Revenge of Michael Myers" (1989). **98m/C VHS, Beta, LV.** Tom Atkins, Stacey Nelkin, Dan O'Herlihy, Ralph Strait; ***D:*** Tommy Lee Wallace; ***M:*** John Carpenter. *MCA*

Halloween 4: The Return of Michael Myers 🦴 **1988 (R)** The third sequel, wherein the lunatic that won't die returns home to kill his niece. **88m/C VHS, Beta, LV.** Donald Pleasence, Ellie Cornell, Danielle Harris, Michael Pataki; ***D:*** Dwight Little. *FOX*

Halloween 5: The Revenge of Michael Myers 🦴½ **1989 (R)** Fifth in the series, this Halloween is an improvement over 2, 3, and 4, thanks to a few well-directed scare scenes. Unfortunately, the plot remains the same: a psycho behemoth chases down and kills more teens. An open ending promises yet another installment. **96m/C VHS, Beta, LV.** Donald Pleasence, Ellie Cornell, Danielle Harris, Don Shanks, Betty Carvalho; ***D:*** Dominique Othenin-Girard; ***W:*** Shem Bitterman. *FOX*

Halloween 6: The Curse of Michael Myers 🦴 **1995 (R)** First the return. Then his revenge. And now, his curse, aimed square at the viewer. Lame series entry connects Michael Meyers to an ancient Celtic ritual that drives him to murder whole families in his old stompin' grounds of Haddonfield. Before he finishes his reign of terror, Meyers has to contend with Dr. Loomis (Pleasence), the man who knows his true evil. Though still a profit-making monster (the entire franchise had a combined budget of $20 million and grossed over $200 million), Michael should probably join Freddy and Jason at the old slashers' retirement home. Film marks the final screen appearance of Pleasance, who died shortly after its completion. **88m/C VHS.** Donald Pleasence, Mitchell Ryan, Marianne Hagan, Leo Geter, George P. Wilbur; ***D:*** Joe Chappelle; ***W:*** Daniel Farrands; ***C:*** Billy Dickson; ***M:*** Alan Howarth. *TOU*

Halloween Night 🦴🦴 **1990 (R)** Ancient evil rises up to destroy the perfect small town. **90m/C VHS.** Hy Pyke, Katrina Garner; ***D:*** Emilio P. Miraglio. *ATL*

Halloween with the Addams Family *Woof!* **1979** A really pathetic production spawned during the "reunion" craze of the late '70s, sparked only by the lively performance of Coogan's Uncle Fester and the always lovable Lurch. Made for television. **87m/C VHS, Beta.** John Astin, Carolyn Jones, Jackie Coogan, Ted Cassidy. *GKK*

The Halls of Montezuma 🦴🦴½ **1950** Large, bombastic WWII combat epic. Depicts the Marines fighting the Japanese in the Pacific. **113m/C VHS, Beta.** Richard Widmark, Jack Palance, Reginald Gardiner, Robert Wagner, Karl Malden, Richard Boone, Richard Hylton, Skip Homeier, Jack Webb, Neville Brand, Martin Milner, Bert Freed; ***D:*** Lewis Milestone. *FOX*

Hallucination *Woof! Hallucination Generation* **1967** Early flower-power exploiter about expatriate acid heads who murder an antique dealer under the influence of LSD and then attempt to hide at a monastery. Depicts LSD as the catalyst in bringing out the group's criminal behavior. In sepia while everyone's cool, breaking into color during the head trips. **90m/C VHS, Beta.** George Montgomery, Danny Stone; ***D:*** Edward Mann. *VDC*

Hallucinations of a Deranged Mind 🦴 **1970** A compilation of all the magic moments ever censored by the Brazilian military dictatorship. Includes scenes banned from over 10 different Marins films, including his "Coffin Joe" character. In Spanish with English subtitles. **?m/C VHS.** *BR* Jose Mojica Marins; ***D:*** Jose Mojica Marins. *SMW, FCT*

Hambone & Hillie 🦴🦴 **1984 (PG)** An elderly woman makes a 3000-mile trek across the United States to search for the dog she lost in an airport. **97m/C VHS, Beta.** Lillian Gish, Timothy Bottoms, Candy Clark, O.J. Simpson, Robert Walker Jr., Jack Carter, Alan Hale Jr., Anne Lockhart; ***D:*** Roy Watts; ***W:*** Sandra K. Bailey. *VTR*

Hamburger Hill 🦴🦴½ **1987 (R)** Popular war epic depicting the famous battle between Americans and Viet Cong over a useless hill in Vietnam. Made in the heyday of 1980s Vietnam backlash, and possibly the most realistic and bloodiest of the lot. **104m/C VHS, Beta, LV.** Michael Dolan, Daniel O'Shea, Dylan McDermott, Tommy Swerdlow, Courtney B. Vance, Anthony Barille, Michael Boatman, Don Cheadle, Tim Quill, Don James, Michael A. Nickles; ***D:*** John Irvin; ***W:*** Jim Carabatsos; ***M:*** Philip Glass. *LIV, VES, FCT*

Hamburger...The Motion Picture 🦴 **1986 (R)** The life and times of students at Busterburger U., the only college devoted to hamburger franchise management. **90m/C VHS, Beta, LV.** Leigh McCloskey, Dick Butkus, Randi Brooks, Sandy Hackett; ***D:*** Mike Marvin; ***M:*** Elmer Bernstein. *MED*

Hamlet 🦴🦴🦴🦴 **1948** Splendid adaptation of Shakespeare's dramatic play. Hamlet vows vengeance on the murderer of his father in this tight version of the four hour stage play. Some scenes were cut out, including all of Rosencrantz and Guildenstern. Beautifully photographed in Denmark. An Olivier triumph. Remade several times. **153m/B VHS.** *GB* Laurence Olivier, Basil Sydney, Felix Aylmer, Jean Simmons, Stanley Holloway, Peter Cushing, Christopher Lee, Eileen Herlie, John Laurie, Esmond Knight, Anthony Quayle; ***D:*** Laurence Olivier; ***W:*** Alan Dent; ***M:*** William Walton; ***V:*** John Gielgud. Academy Awards '48: Best Actor (Olivier), Best Art Direction/Set Decoration (B & W), Best Costume Design (B & W), Best Picture; British Academy Awards '48: Best Film; Golden Globe Awards '49: Best Actor—Drama (Olivier); New York Film Critics Awards '48: Best Actor (Olivier); Nominations: Academy Awards '48: Best Director (Olivier), Best Supporting Actress (Simmons), Best Original Score. *PAR, BTV, HMV*

Hamlet 🦴🦴½ **1969 (G)** Williamson brings to the screen his stage performance as the classic Shakespeare character. Something is lost in the process, although there are some redeeming moments including those with Faithfull as Ophelia. **114m/C VHS, Beta.** *GB* Nicol Williamson, Anthony Hopkins, Marianne Faithfull, Gordon Jackson, Judy Parfitt, Mark Dingham, Anjelica Huston; ***D:*** Tony Richardson. *COL*

Hamlet 🦴🦴🦴½ **1990 (PG)** Zeffirelli—in his fourth attempt at Shakespeare—creates a surprisingly energetic and accessible interpretation of the Bard's moody play. Gibson brings charm, humor and a carefully calculated sense of violence, not to mention a good deal of solid flesh, to the eponymous role, and handles the language skillfully (although if you seek a poetic Dane, stick with Olivier). Exceptional work from Scofield and Bates; Close seems a tad hysterical (not to mention too young to play Gibson's mother), but brings insight and nuance to her role. Purists beware: this isn't a completely faithful adaptation. Beautifully costumed; shot on location in Northern Scotland. **135m/C VHS, Beta, LV, 8mm.** Mel Gibson, Glenn Close, Alan Bates, Paul Scofield, Ian Holm, Helena Bonham Carter, Nathaniel Parker, Pete Postlethwaite; ***D:*** Franco Zeffirelli; ***W:*** Franco Zeffirelli, Christopher DeVore; ***C:*** David Watkin. Nominations: Academy Awards '90: Best Art Direction/Set Decoration, Best Costume Design. *WAR, BTV, FCT*

Hammersmith is Out 🦴½ **1972 (R)** A violent lunatic cons an orderly into letting him escape. Chases, romance and craziness follow. **108m/C VHS, Beta.** Richard Burton, Elizabeth Taylor, Peter Ustinov, Beau Bridges, John Schuck; ***D:*** Peter Ustinov. *PSM*

Hammett 🦴🦴 **1982 (PG)** After many directors and script rewrites, Wenders was assigned to this arch neo-noir what-if scenario. Depicts Dashiell Hammett solving a complex crime himself, an experience he uses in his novels. Interesting, but ultimately botched studio exercise, like many from executive producer Francis Coppola, who is said to have reshot much of the film. **98m/C VHS, Beta.** Frederic Forrest, Peter Boyle, Sylvia Sidney, Elisha Cook Jr., Marilu Henner; ***D:*** Wim Wenders; ***C:*** Joseph Biroc; ***M:*** John Barry. Nominations: Cannes Film Festival '82: Best Film. *WAR, INJ*

Hamsin 🦴🦴🦴 **1983** A Jewish landowner and an Arab worker encounter difficulties in their relationship when the government announces plans to confiscate Arab land. In Hebrew with English subtitles. **90m/C VHS, Beta.** Shlomo Tarshish, Yasin Shawap, Hemda Levy, Ruth Geler; ***D:*** Daniel Wachsmann. *ERG*

The Hand 🦴½ **1960** During WWII, three British POWs are tortured by the Japanese. Refusing to give information, two of them have their right hands cut off. The third opts to talk, thereby keeping his hand. After the war, a series of murders occur in London where the victims have their hands amputated. Could there be a connection? **61m/B VHS, Beta.** *GB* Derek Bond, Ronald Lee Hunt, Reed de Rouen, Ray Cooney, Brian Coleman; ***D:*** Henry Cass. *SNC*

The Hand 🦴🦴🦴 **1981 (R)** A gifted cartoonist's hand is severed in a car accident. Soon, the hand is on the loose with a mind of its own, seeking out victims with an obsessive vengeance. Stone's sophomore directorial outing is a unique, surreal psycho-horror pastiche consistently underrated by most critics. **105m/C VHS, Beta.** *GB* Michael Caine, Andrea Marcovicci, Annie McEnroe, Bruce McGill, Viveca Lindfors; ***D:*** Oliver Stone; ***W:*** Oliver Stone; ***M:*** James Horner. *WAR*

Hand Gun ♪♪½ **1993 (R)** Jack McCallister (Cassel) is wounded in a shoot-out with police but still manages to get away with half-a-million from a robbery. When word gets out, everybody begins looking for Jack, including his two sons—gun happy George (Williams) and small time con artist Michael (Schulze). **90m/C VHS, LV.** Seymour Cassel, Treat Williams, Paul Schulzie, Michael Rapaport; ***D:*** Whitney Ransick; ***W:*** Whitney Ransick. *TRI*

The Hand that Rocks the Cradle ♪♪½ **1992 (R)** DeMornay is Peyton Flanders, the nanny from hell, in an otherwise predictable thriller. Sciorra's role is a thankless one as pregnant and unbelievably naive Claire Bartel, who unwittingly starts a horrific chain of events when she levels charges of molestation against her obstetrician. Transparent plot preys on the worst fears of viewers, and doesn't offer anything innovative or new. See this one for DeMornay's Jekyll and Hyde performance. **110m/C VHS, Beta.** Annabella Sciorra, Rebecca DeMornay, Matt McCoy, Ernie Hudson, Julianne Moore, Madeline Zima, John de Lancie, Mitchell Laurance; ***D:*** Curtis Hanson; ***W:*** Amanda Silver; ***M:*** Graeme Revell. MTV Movie Awards '92: Best Villain (DeMornay). *HPH*

A Handful of Dust ♪♪♪ **1988 (PG)** A dry, stately adaptation of the bitter Evelyn Waugh novel about a stuffy young aristocrat's wife's careless infidelity and how it sends her innocent husband to a tragic downfall. A well-meaning version that captures Waugh's cynical satire almost in spite of itself. Set in post-WWI England. **114m/C VHS, Beta.** *GB* James Wilby, Kristin Scott Thomas, Rupert Graves, Alec Guinness, Anjelica Huston, Judi Dench, Cathryn Harrison, Pip Torrens; ***D:*** Charles Sturridge; ***W:*** Tim Sullivan, Derek Granger, Charles Sturridge; ***M:*** George Fenton. British Academy Awards '88: Best Supporting Actress (Dench); Nominations: Academy Awards '88: Best Costume Design. *COL, TVC*

The Handmaid's Tale ♪♪½ **1990 (R)** A cool, shallow but nonetheless chilling nightmare based on Margaret Atwood's bestselling novel, about a woman caught in the machinations of a near-future society so sterile it enslaves the few fertile women and forces them into being child-bearing "handmaids." **109m/C VHS, Beta, LV.** Natasha Richardson, Robert Duvall, Faye Dunaway, Aidan Quinn, Elizabeth McGovern, Victoria Tennant, Blanche Baker, Traci Lind; ***D:*** Volker Schlondorff; ***W:*** Harold Pinter. *HBO, FCT, IME*

Hands Across the Border ♪½ **1943** A musical western in which Roy helps a woman find the men who killed her father. **72m/B VHS.** Roy Rogers, Ruth Terry, Guinn "Big Boy" Williams, Onslow Stevens, Mary Treen, Joseph Crehan; ***D:*** Joseph Kane. *NOS, DVT, TIM*

Hands Across the Table ♪♪♪ **1935** Regi Allen (Lombard) is a fortune-hunting manicurist in a swanky hotel barber shop. Has-been millionaire playboy Theodore Drew, III (MacMurray) falls for her but he's about to marry money (Allwyn) and Regi's got a wheelchair-bound rich man (Bellamy) just waiting for her to say "I do." Snappy dialogue and light-hearted performances. Based on the story "Bracelets" by Vina Delmar. **80m/B VHS.** Carole Lombard, Fred MacMurray, Ralph Bellamy, Astrid Allwyn, Ruth Donnelly, Marie Prevost, William Demarest, Edward Gargan; ***D:*** Mitchell Leisen; ***W:*** Norman Krasna, Vincent Lawrence, Herbert Fields; ***C:*** Ted Tetzlaff. *MCA*

Hands of a Murderer ♪♪½ *Sherlock Holmes and the Prince of Crime* **1990** Sherlock Holmes (Woodward) and the faithful Dr. Watson (Hillerman) are in pursuit of the great detective's most evil nemesis—the nefarious Moriarty (Andrews). This time, the fiend has escaped the gallows and stolen government secrets from the safe of Holmes' brother Mycroft. TV movie. **100m/C VHS.** Edward Woodward, John Hillerman, Anthony Andrews, Kim Thomson, Peter Jeffrey, Warren Clarke; ***D:*** Stuart Orme; ***W:*** Charles Edward Pogue. *TVC*

Hands of a Stranger ♪♪ **1962** Another undistinguished entry in the long line of remakes of "The Hands of Orlac." A pianist who loses his hands in an accident is given the hands of a murderer, and his new hands want to do more than tickle the ivories. Kellerman has a very small role as does former "Sheena" McCalla. **95m/B VHS.** Paul Lukather, Joan Harvey, James Stapleton, Sally Kellerman, Irish McCalla; ***D:*** Newton Arnold. *SNC*

Hands of a Stranger ♪♪½ **1987** Policeman's wife is raped during an adulterous tryst. As the painful truth dawns on the cop, he himself dallies with a compassionate lady D.A. while hunting the attacker. About as sordid as a network TV-movie gets without toppling into sleaze; strong acting and a sober script pull it through. But the plot, from Robert Daly's novel, doesn't justify miniseries treatment; the two-cassette package is excessively long. **179m/C VHS.** Armand Assante, Beverly D'Angelo, Blair Brown, Michael Lerner, Philip Casnoff, Arliss Howard; ***D:*** Larry Elikann; ***W:*** Arthur Kopit. *WOV*

Hands of Death ♪ **1988** Thieves use their Ninja skills to stop any one in their path to evil. Action-packed, somewhat contrived. **90m/C VHS, Beta.** Richard Harrison, Mike Abbott; ***D:*** Godfrey Ho. *IMP*

The Hands of Orlac ♪♪ **1925** Classic silent film about a pianist whose hands are mutilated in an accident. His hands are replaced by those of a murderer, and his urge to kill becomes overwhelming. Contains restored footage. **?m/B VHS.** *AT* Conrad Veidt, Fritz Kortner, Carmen Cartellieri, Paul Adkonas; ***D:*** Robert Wiene. *LSV*

The Hands of Orlac ♪♪ *Hands of the Strangler* **1960** Third remake of Maurice Renard's classic tale. When a concert pianist's hands are mutilated in an accident, he receives a graft of a murderer's hands. Obsession sweeps the musician, as he believes his new hands are incapable of music, only violence. Bland adaptation of the original story. **95m/B VHS.** *GB FR* Mel Ferrer, Christopher Lee, Felix Aylmer, Basil Sydney, Donald Wolfit, Donald Pleasence; ***D:*** Edmond T. Greville; ***M:*** Claude Bolling. *SNC*

Hands of Steel *Woof!* **1986 (R)** A ruthless cyborg carries out a mission to find and kill an important scientist. Terrible acting, and lousy writing: an all-around woofer! **94m/C VHS, Beta.** Daniel Greene, John Saxon, Janet Agren, Claudio Cassinelli, George Eastman; ***D:*** Martin Dolman. *LIV*

Hands of the Ripper ♪♪½ **1971 (R)** Jack the Ripper's daughter returns to London where she works as a medium by day and stalks the streets at night. Classy Hammer horror variation on the perennial theme. **85m/C VHS, Beta.** *GB* Eric Porter, Angharad Rees, Jane Merrow, Keith Bell; ***D:*** Peter Sasdy; ***M:*** Christopher Gunning. *MLB*

Hands Up ♪♪½ **1926** Jaunty Confederate spy (played by much-overlooked American comedian Griffith) attempts, amidst much comic nonsense, to thwart Yankee gold mining during the Civil War. Silent. **50m/B VHS, Beta.** Raymond Griffith, Mack Swain, Marion Nixon, Montagu Love; ***D:*** Clarence Badger. *GPV*

Hands Up ♪♪♪ *Rece do Gory* **1981** Famed Polish film finished in 1967 but not released until 1981 for political reasons (prologue shot in '81 included). Doctors at a medical school reunion reflect upon the effect of Stalinist rule on their education and lives. In Polish with English subtitles. **78m/C VHS, Beta.** *PL* ***D:*** Jerzy Skolimowski. *FCT*

Hang 'Em High ♪♪½ **1967** A cowboy is saved from a lynching and vows to hunt down the gang that nearly killed him in this American-made spaghetti western. Eastwood's first major vehicle made outside of Europe. **114m/C VHS, Beta, LV.** Clint Eastwood, Inger Stevens, Ed Begley Sr., Pat Hingle, James MacArthur; ***D:*** Ted Post. *MGM, TLF*

Hangar 18 ♪½ *Invasion Force* **1980 (PG)** Silly sci-fi drama about two astronauts who collide with a UFO during a shuttle flight. Later they learn that the government is hiding it in a hangar and they try to prove its existence. Shown on TV as "Invasion Force" with an entirely new ending. **97m/C VHS, Beta.** Darren McGavin, Robert Vaughn, Gary Collins, James Hampton, Philip Abbott, Pamela Bellwood, Tom Hallick, Cliff Osmond, Joseph Campanella; ***D:*** James L. Conway; ***W:*** David O'Malley. *WOV*

The Hanged Man ♪♪ **1974** Tale of a gunslinger in the Old West who mystically escapes death by hanging. Reborn, he re-evaluates the meaning of justice. Made for television. **78m/C VHS.** Steve Forrest, Cameron Mitchell, Sharon Acker, Dean Jagger, Will Geer, Barbara Luna, Rafael Campos; ***D:*** Michael Caffey. *NO*

Hangfire ♪♪ **1991 (R)** When a New Mexican prison is evacuated thanks to a nasty chemical explosion, several prisoners decide it's time for a furlough, and they elect the local sheriff's wife as a traveling companion. Another mediocre actioner from director Maris, it gets an extra bone for stunts kids shouldn't try at home. **91m/C VHS, LV.** Brad Davis, Yaphet Kotto, Lee DeBroux, Jan-Michael Vincent, George Kennedy, Kim Delaney; ***D:*** Peter Maris; ***W:*** Brian D. Jeffries. *COL*

Hangin' with the Homeboys ♪♪♪ **1991 (R)** One night in the lives of four young men. Although the Bronx doesn't offer much for any of them, they have little interest in escaping its confines, and they are more than willing to complain. Characters are insightfully written and well portrayed, with strongest work from Serrano as a Puerto Rican who is trying to pass himself off as Italian. Lack of plot may frustrate some viewers. **89m/C VHS, LV.** Mario Joyner, Doug E. Doug, John Leguizamo, Nestor Serrano, Kimberly Russell, Mary B. Ward; ***D:*** Joseph B. Vasquez; ***W:*** Joseph B. Vasquez. Sundance Film Festival '91: Best Screenplay. *NLC, FCT*

Hanging on a Star ♪ **1978 (PG)** A small rock band encounters many comic adventures as it climbs its way up the charts. Raffin stars as the band's persistent and competent road agent. **92m/C VHS, Beta.** Deborah Raffin, Lane Caudell, Wolfman Jack, Jason Parker, Danil Torppe; ***D:*** Mike MacFarland. *MGM*

The Hanging Tree ♪♪♪ **1959** Cooper plays a frontier doctor who rescues a thief (Piazza) from a lynch mob and nurses a temporarily blind girl (Schell). Malden is the bad guy who tries to attack Schell and Cooper shoots him. The townspeople take Cooper out to "The Hanging Tree" but this time it's Schell and Piazza who come to his rescue. Slow-paced western with good performances. Scott's screen debut. **108m/B VHS.** Gary Cooper, Maria Schell, Ben Piazza, Karl Malden, George C. Scott, Karl Swenson, Virginia Gregg, King Donovan; ***D:*** Delmer Daves; ***W:*** Wendell Mayes, Halsted Welles; ***M:*** Max Steiner. Nominations: Academy Awards '59: Best Song ("The Hanging Tree"). *WAR*

The Hanging Woman ♪♪½ *Return of the Zombies; Beyond the Living Dead* **1972 (R)** A man is summoned to the reading of a relative's will, and discovers the corpse of a young woman hanging in a cemetery. As he investigates the mystery, he uncovers a local doctor's plans to zombify the entire world. Not bad at all and quite creepy once the zombies are out in force. Euro-horror star Naschy plays the necrophiliac grave digger, Igor. **91m/C VHS, Beta.** *SP IT* Stan Cooper, Vickie Nesbitt, Marcella Wright, Catherine Gilbert, Gerard Tichy, Paul Naschy; ***D:*** John Davidson. *NO*

Hangman's Knot ♪♪½ **1952** Members of the Confederate Cavalry rob a Union train, not knowing that the war is over. Now facing criminal charges, they are forced to take refuge in a stagecoach stop. Well-done horse opera with a wry sense of humor. **80m/C VHS, Beta.** Randolph Scott, Donna Reed, Claude Jarman Jr., Frank Faylen, Glenn Langan, Richard Denning, Lee Marvin, Jeanette Nolan; ***D:*** Roy Huggins. *GKK*

Hangmen *Woof!* **1987 (R)** Ex-CIA agents battle it out on the East side of New York. If you're into very violent, very badly-acted films, then this one's for you. **88m/C VHS, Beta.** Jake La Motta, Rick Washburne, Doug Thomas; ***D:*** J. Christian Ingvordsen. *ACA*

Hank Aaron: Chasing the Dream ♪♪♪ **1995** Docudrama combines archival footage, interviews, and reenactments to tell the story of the life and career of Henry Aaron. Follows Aaron's development as a Hall of Fame outfielder for the Milwaukee and Atlanta Braves and as a leader in the civil rights movement. Emphasis on personal and societal issues, as well as on-the-field accomplishments, raises this one above most sports biography documentaries. **120m/C VHS.** *TTC*

Hanky Panky ♪½ **1982 (PG)** Insipid comic thriller in which Wilder and Radner become involved in a search for top-secret plans. **107m/C VHS, Beta, LV.** Gene Wilder, Gilda Radner, Richard Widmark, Kathleen Quinlan; ***D:*** Sidney Poitier. *COL*

Hanna K. ♪♪ **1983 (R)** Story of divided passions set in the tumultuous state of Israel. American lawyer Clayburgh tries to settle her personal and political affairs with various Middle-Eastern men. Mediocre Disappointing. Release generated controversy over pro-Palestine stance. **111m/C VHS, Beta.** *FR* Jill Clayburgh, Gabriel Byrne, Jean Yanne, Muhamad Bakri, David Clennon, Oded Kotler; ***D:*** Constantin Costa-Gavras. *MCA*

Hannah and Her Sisters ♪♪♪½ **1986 (PG)** Allen's grand epic about a New York showbiz family, its three adult sisters and their various complex romantic entanglements. Excellent performances by the entire cast, especially Caine and Hershey. Classic Allen themes of life, love, death, and desire are explored in an assured and sensitive manner. Witty, ironic, and heartwarming. **103m/C VHS, Beta, LV.** Mia Farrow, Barbara Hershey, Dianne Wiest, Michael Caine, Woody Allen, Maureen O'Sullivan, Lloyd Nolan, Sam Waterston, Carrie Fisher, Max von Sydow, Julie Kavner, Daniel Stern, Tony Roberts, John Turturro; ***D:*** Woody Allen; ***W:*** Woody Allen; ***C:*** Carlo DiPalma. Academy Awards '86: Best Original Screenplay, Best Supporting Actor (Caine), Best Supporting Actress (Wiest); Golden Globe Awards '87: Best Film—Musical/Comedy; Los Angeles Film Critics Association Awards '86: Best Film, Best Screenplay, Best Supporting Actress (Wiest); New York Film Critics Awards '86: Best Director (Allen), Best Film, Best Supporting Actress (Wiest); Writers Guild of America '86: Best Original Screenplay; Nominations: Academy Awards '85: Best Art Direction/Set Decoration; Academy Awards '86: Best Director (Allen), Best Film Editing, Best Picture. *BTV*

Hanna's War ♪♪½ **1988 (PG-13)** A moving film about Hanna Senesh, a young Hungarian Jew living in Palestine, who volunteered for a suicide mission behind Nazi lines during WWII. After her capture by the Germans, she was killed, and is now considered by many to have been a martyr. Detmers is very believable as Hanna and Burstyn puts in a good performance as her mother. **148m/C VHS, Beta, LV.** Ellen Burstyn, Maruschka Detmers, Anthony Andrews, Donald Pleasence, David Warner, Denholm Elliott, Vincenzo Ricotta, Ingrid Pitt; ***D:*** Menahem Golan; ***W:*** Menahem Golan; ***M:*** Dov Seltzer. *CCB, MED, SWC*

Hannie Caulder ♪♪ **1972 (R)** A woman hires a bounty hunter to avenge her husband's murder and her own rape at the hands of three bandits. Excellent casting but uneven direction. Boyd is uncredited as the preacher. **87m/C VHS.** Raquel Welch, Robert Culp, Ernest Borgnine, Strother Martin, Jack Elam, Christopher Lee, Diana Dors, Stephen Boyd; ***D:*** Burt Kennedy; ***W:*** Burt Kennedy. *PAR, FCT, VTR*

Hanoi Hilton ♪½ **1987 (R)** A brutal drama about the sufferings of American POWs in Vietnamese prison camps. Non-stop torture, filth, and degradation. **126m/C VHS, Beta, LV.** Michael Moriarty, Paul LeMat, Jeffrey Jones, Lawrence Pressman, Stephen Davies, David Soul, Rick Fitts, Aki Aleong, Gloria Carlin; ***D:*** Lionel Chetwynd; ***W:*** Lionel Chetwynd. *WAR*

Hanover Street ♪♪ **1979 (PG)** An American bomber pilot and a married British nurse fall in love in war-torn Europe. Eventually the pilot must work with the husband of the woman he loves on a secret mission. A sappy, romantic tearjerker. **109m/C VHS, Beta, LV.** Harrison Ford, Lesley-Anne Down, Christopher Plummer, Alec McCowen; ***D:*** Peter Hyams; ***W:*** Peter Hyams; ***C:*** David Watkin; ***M:*** John Barry. *COL*

Hans Brinker ♪♪½ **1969** Young Hans Brinker and his sister participate in an ice skating race, hoping to win a pair of silver skates. A musical version of the classic tale. **103m/C VHS, Beta.** Robin Askwith, Eleanor Parker, Richard Basehart, Cyril Ritchard, John Gregson; ***D:*** Robert Scheerer. *WAR, OM*

Hans Christian Andersen ♪♪ **1952** Sentimental musical story of Hans Christian Andersen, a young cobbler who has a great gift for storytelling. Digitally remastered editions available with stereo sound and original trailer. ♫The King's New Clothes; I'm Hans Christian Andersen; Wonderful Copenhagen; Thumbelina; The Ugly Duckling; Anywhere I Wander; The Inch Worm; No Two People. **112m/C VHS, Beta, LV.** Danny Kaye, Farley Granger, Zizi Jeanmarie, Joey Walsh; ***D:*** Charles Vidor; ***W:*** Moss Hart; ***M:*** Frank Loesser. Nominations: Academy Awards '52: Best Art Direction/Set Decoration (Color), Best Color Cinematography, Best Costume Design (Color), Best Song ("Thumbelina"), Best Sound, Best Original Score. *HBO, SUE, FCT*

Hansel and Gretel **1982** From Shelly Duvall's "Faerie Tale Theatre" comes the story of two young children who get more than they bargained for when they eat a gingerbread house. **51m/C VHS, Beta, LV.** Rick Schroder, Joan Collins, Paul Dooley, Bridgette Anderson; ***D:*** James Frawley. *KUI, FOX, FCT*

Hanussen ♪♪♪½ **1988 (R)** The third of Szabo and Brandauer's price-of-power trilogy (after "Mephisto" and "Colonel Redl"), in which a talented German magician and clairvoyant (based on a true life figure) collaborates with the Nazis during their rise to power in the 1930s, although he can foresee the outcome of their reign. In German with English subtitles. **110m/C VHS, Beta, LV.** *GE HU* Klaus Maria Brandauer, Erland Josephson, Walter Schmidinger; ***D:*** Istvan Szabo; ***C:*** Lajos Koltai. Nominations: Academy Awards '88: Best Foreign Language Film. *COL, INJ*

The Happiest Days of Your Life ♪♪♪ **1950** During the London Blitz, a girls academy is evacuated to the country and mistakeningly billeted with a boys school. The headmaster and headmistress clash and the bewildered students all try to get along. Good cast, lots of laughs. Adapted from a play by John Dighton. **81m/B VHS.** *GB* Alastair Sim, Margaret Rutherford, Joyce Grenfell, Edward Rigby, Guy Middleton, John Bentley, Bernadette O'Farrell, Richard Wattis, Muriel Aked, Patricia Owens, John Turnbull, Arthur Howard; ***D:*** Frank Launder; ***W:*** Frank Launder, John Dighton; ***M:*** Mischa Spoliansky. *HMV, ING*

The Happiest Millionaire ♪♪ **1967** A Disney film about a newly immigrated lad who finds a job as butler in the home of an eccentric millionaire. Based on the book "My Philadelphia Father," by Kyle Chrichton. ♫What's Wrong With That?; Watch Your Footwork; Valentine Candy; Strengthen the Dwelling; I'll Always Be Irish; Bye-Yum Pum Pum; I Believe in This Country; Detroit; There Are Those. **118m/C VHS, Beta.** Fred MacMurray, Tommy Steele, Greer Garson, Geraldine Page, Lesley Ann Warren, John Davidson; ***D:*** Norman Tokar; ***W:*** A.J. Carothers; ***C:*** Edward Colman. Nominations: Academy Awards '67: Best Costume Design. *DIS, OM*

Happily Ever After ♪♪ **1982** Las Vegas star-maker recruits and manipulates two green performers. Show business life in Vegas is given a truthful treatment in made-for-television drama. **95m/C VHS, Beta.** Suzanne Somers, John Rubinstein, Eric (Hans Gudegast) Braeden; ***D:*** Robert Scheerer. *TLF*

Happily Ever After ♪♪ *Alem Da Paixao* **1986** A Brazilian housewife meets a bisexual transvestite and has a passionate affair, bringing her into the depths of the criminal underworld. In Portuguese with English subtitles. Contains nudity. **106m/C VHS.** *BR* Regina Duarte, Paul Castelli; ***D:*** Bruno Barreto. *FCT, INJ, TPV*

Happily Ever After ♪½ **1993 (G)** Sequel to "Snow White" begins where the original ends, but isn't connected to the Walt Disney classic. Snow White and her Prince prepare for their wedding when the Wicked Queen is found dead by her brother, who vows revenge. So it's up to Snow and the Dwarfelles (Disney said no to using the Dwarfs), female cousins of the original Dwarfs, to rescue him. Interesting choices from the casting department: Diller is Mother Nature and Asner provides the voice of a rapping owl. Poorly animated drivel designed to ride in on Disney's coattails. While the kids might enjoy it, save your money for the original, finally slated for a video release. **74m/C VHS.** ***D:*** John Howley; ***W:*** Martha Moran, Robby London; ***V:*** Dom DeLuise, Phyllis Diller, Zsa Zsa Gabor, Ed Asner, Sally Kellerman, Irene Cara, Carol Channing, Tracey Ullman. *REP, WTA, WOV*

Happiness ♪♪ **1934** Another zany comedy from the land of the hammer and sickle. Banned in Russia for 40 years, it was deemed to be risque and a bit too biting with the social satire. Silent with orchestral score. **69m/B VHS.** *RU* ***D:*** Alexander Medvedkin. *KIV, FCT, INJ*

Happy Anniversary 007: 25 Years of James Bond **1987** Film clip retrospective of the dashing British spy created by Ian Fleming. Hosted by Roger Moore. **59m/C VHS, Beta.** Sean Connery, Roger Moore, George Lazenby, Timothy Dalton; ***D:*** Mel Stuart. *FOX*

Happy Birthday, Gemini ♪½ **1980 (R)** A coming-of-age comedy about a young man on his 21st birthday worrying about his sexual identity. Based on the play "Gemini" by Albert Innaurato. The closeness of the characters on stage did not translate to the screen. **107m/C VHS.** Robert Viharo, Madeline Kahn, Rita Moreno, Alan Rosenberg, Sarah Holcomb, David Marshall Grant, David McIlwraith; ***D:*** Richard Benner; ***W:*** Richard Benner. *MGM*

Happy Birthday to Me ♪½ **1981 (R)** Several elite seniors at an exclusive private school are mysteriously killed by a deranged killer who has a fetish for cutlery. **108m/C VHS, Beta, LV.** *CA* Melissa Sue Anderson, Glenn Ford, Tracy Bregman, Jack Blum, Matt Craven; ***D:*** J. Lee Thompson; ***W:*** Timothy Bond. *COL*

The Happy Ending ♪♪½ **1969 (PG)** Woman struggles with a modern definition of herself and her marriage, causing pain and confusion for her family. Simmons is solid as the wife and mother seeking herself. Michel LeGrand's theme song "What Are You Doing With the Rest of Your Life?" was a big hit. **112m/C VHS.** Jean Simmons, John Forsythe, Lloyd Bridges, Shirley Jones, Teresa Wright, Dick Shawn, Nanette Fabray, Bobby Darin, Tina Louise; ***D:*** Richard Brooks; ***W:*** Richard Brooks; ***C:*** Conrad Hall. Nominations: Academy Awards '69: Best Actress (Simmons), Best Song ("What Are You Doing the Rest of Your Life?"). *NO*

Happy Gilmore ♪♪ **1996 (PG-13)** Skating-impaired hockey player Gilmore (Sandler) translates his slap shot into a 400-foot tee shot and joins the pro golf tour. His unique style brings a new, less refined breed of fan to the game and upsets the reigning tour hotshot (McDonald). Sandler improves on "Billy Madison," but there's still plenty of ammo for his many detractors. Replacing bathroom humor with abusive behavior, he swears at or beats up about 90% of the supporting cast, including Bob Barker in a charity pro-am. Unfortunately, it won't make anyone forget "Caddyshack II." **92m/C VHS.** Adam Sandler, Christopher McDonald, Carl Weathers, Julie Bowen, Francis Bay, Ben Stiller, Richard Kiel, Joe Flaherty, Kevin Nealon, Alan Covert, Robert Smigel, Bob Barker, Dennis Dugan; ***D:*** Dennis Dugan; ***W:*** Adam Sandler, Tim Herlihy; ***C:*** Arthur Albert; ***M:*** Mark Mothersbaugh. MTV Movie Awards '96: Best Fight (Adam Sandler/Bob Barker); Nominations: MTV Movie Awards '96: Best Comedic Performance (Sandler). *MCA*

Happy Go Lovely ♪♪ **1951** An unscrupulous theatrical producer casts a chorus girl in a leading role in order to get closer to her boyfriend's fortune. Tired plot, but good performances in this lightweight musical. ♫One-Two-Three; Would You, Could You; London Town. **95m/C VHS, Beta.** Vera-Ellen, David Niven, Cesar Romero, Bobby Howes; ***D:*** H. Bruce Humberstone. *NOS, MRV, DVT*

The Happy Hooker ♪♪½ **1975 (R)** Xaviera Hollander's cheeky (and bestselling) memoir of her transition from office girl to "working girl" has been brought to the screen with a sprightly (though sanitary) air of naughtiness, with Redgrave enjoyable in title role. Followed by "The Happy Hooker Goes to Washington" and "The Happy Hooker Goes Hollywood." **96m/C VHS, Beta, LV.** Lynn Redgrave, Jean-Pierre Aumont, Nicholas Pryor; ***D:*** Nicholas Sgarro. *CAN, VES*

The Happy Hooker Goes Hollywood ♪ **1980 (R)** Third film inspired by the title of Xaviera Hollander's memoirs, in which the fun-loving Xaviera comes to Hollywood with the intention of making a movie based on her book, but soon meets up with a series of scheming, would-be producers. **86m/C VHS, Beta, LV.** Martine Beswick, Chris Lemmon, Adam West, Phil Silvers; ***D:*** Alan Roberts. *CAN, MCA*

The Happy Hooker Goes to Washington 🦴½ **1977 (R)** Further adventures of the world's most famous madam. Heatherton (not Redgrave) is Xaviera Hollander this time, testifying before the U.S. Senate in defense of sex. Fairly stupid attempt to milk box office of original. Second in the holy trilogy of Happy Hooker pictures, which also include "The Happy Hooker" and "The Happy Hooker Goes Hollywood." **89m/C VHS, Beta.** Joey Heatherton, George Hamilton, Ray Walston, Jack Carter; ***D:*** William A. Levey. *CAN, VES*

Happy Hour 🦴½ **1987 (R)** A young brewing scientist discovers a secret formula for beer, and everyone tries to take it from him. Little turns in a good performance as a superspy. **88m/C VHS, Beta, LV.** Richard Gilliland, Jamie Farr, Tawny Kitaen, Ty Henderson, Rich Little; ***D:*** John DeBello; ***W:*** John DeBello. *LIV*

Happy Landing 🦴🦴½ **1938** Predictable, yet entertaining Henie vehicle about a plane that makes a forced landing in Norway near Henie's home. Romance follows with bandleader Romero and manager Ameche. ♫Hot and Happy; Yonny and his Oompah; You Are The Music to the Words in my Heart; A Gypsy Told Me; You Appeal to Me. **102m/B VHS.** Sonja Henie, Don Ameche, Jean Hersholt, Ethel Merman, Cesar Romero, Billy Gilbert, Wally Vernon, El Brendel; ***D:*** Roy Del Ruth; ***W:*** Milton Sperling, Boris Ingster. *FXV*

Happy New Year 🦴🦴🦴 *The Happy New Year Caper* **1974** Charming romantic comedy in which two thieves plan a robbery but get sidetracked by the distracting woman who works next door to the jewelry store. Available in both subtitled and dubbed versions. Remade in 1987. **114m/C VHS, Beta.** *FR IT* Francoise Fabian, Lino Ventura, Andre Falcon; ***D:*** Claude Lelouch; ***W:*** Claude Lelouch. *SUE*

A Happy New Year! 🦴🦴 **1979** Two men and a woman, all engineers in a chemical plant, try to fight off a hangover as they deal with the comings and goings of friends throughout the day and night. In Hungarian with English subtitles. **84m/C VHS.** *HU* Istvan Bujtor, Erika Bodnar, Cecilia Esztergalyos, Andras Balint; ***D:*** Reszo Szoreny; ***W:*** Peter Modos, Reszo Szoreny. *FCT*

Happy New Year 🦴🦴½ **1987 (PG)** Two sophisticated thieves plan and execute an elaborate jewel heist that goes completely awry. Remake of the 1974 French film of the same name. **86m/C VHS, Beta.** Peter Falk, Wendy Hughes, Tom Courtenay, Charles Durning, Joan Copeland; ***D:*** John G. Avildsen; ***W:*** Warren Lane; ***M:*** Bill Conti. Nominations: Academy Awards '87: Best Makeup. *COL*

Happy New Year, Charlie Brown **1982** Strife upsets the Peanuts gang as the New Year's Eve gala becomes a source of tension. **25m/C VHS, Beta.** ***D:*** Bill Melendez, Sam Jaimes. *BAR, KAR, WTA*

Happy Since I Met You 🦴🦴🦴 **1989** Comedy-drama about a scatterbrained drama teacher and a struggling young actor who become romantically involved. **55m/C VHS, Beta.** *GB* Julie Walters, Duncan Preston; ***Cameos:*** Tracey Ullman, Jim Bowen; ***D:*** Baz Taylor; ***W:*** Victoria Wood. *BIJ, WOM*

Happy Together 🦴 **1989 (PG-13)** An eager freshman accidentally gets a beautiful, impulsive girl as his roommate. Together they meet the challenges of secondary education. **102m/C VHS, Beta, LV.** Helen Slater, Patrick Dempsey, Dan Schneider, Marius Weyers, Barbara Babcock; ***D:*** Mel Damski; ***M:*** Robert Folk. *LIV*

Hard-Boiled 🦴🦴½ *Lashou Shentan* **1992** Police Inspector Yuen (Woo regular Yun-fat) is investigating, with his usual excessive force, the Triads organized crime syndicate and a group of gun smugglers who killed his partner. He joins forces with Tony, an undercover cop who's working as a gangster hitman. There's lots of gunplay and betrayals among all the participants. Usual Woo way with violence and action sequences although the plot is more contrived. In Mandarin and Chinese with English subtitles. **126m/C VHS.** *HK* Chow Yun-fat, Tony Leung, Philip Chan, Anthony Wong, Teresa Mo; ***D:*** John Woo; ***W:*** Barry Wong; ***M:*** Michael Gibbs. *ORI, FCT*

Hard-Boiled Mahoney 🦴🦴½ **1947** Slip, Sach, and the rest of the Bowery Boys try to solve a mystery involving mysterious women and missing men. The last film in the series for Bobby Jordan, whose career was ended when he was injured in an accident involving a falling elevator. **64m/B VHS.** Leo Gorcey, Huntz Hall, Bobby Jordan, Billy Benedict, David Gorcey, Gabriel Dell, Teala Loring, Dan Seymour, Bernard Gorcey, Patti Brill, Betty Compson; ***D:*** William Beaudine. *WAR*

Hard Bounty 🦴🦴½ **1994 (R)** After five years of chasing desperadoes, bounty hunter Martin B. Kanning hangs up his guns to open a saloon—complete with frontier prostitutes. When one of his ladies is murdered, the other gals decide to chase after the killer. Naturally, Kanning can't let them go alone. **90m/C VHS.** Matt McCoy, Kelly Le Brock, Rochelle Swanson, Felicity Waterman, Kimberly Kelly; ***D:*** Jim Wynorski. *TRI*

Hard Choices 🦴🦴🦴 **1984** A 15-year-old Tennessee boy is unjustly charged as an accessory to murder, until a female social worker decides to help him. From then on, nothing is predictable. Excellent work by Klenck, McCleery, and Seitz. Don't miss Sayles as an unusual drug dealer. Intelligent, surprising, and powerful. Based on a true story, this is a low profile film that deserves to be discovered. **90m/C VHS, Beta.** Margaret Klenek, Gary McCleery, John Seitz, John Sayles, Liane Curtis, J.T. Walsh, Spalding Gray; ***D:*** Rick King; ***W:*** Rick King. *BAR, ORI, WAR*

Hard Country 🦴🦴½ **1981 (PG)** Caught between her best friend's success as a country singer and the old values of a woman's place, a small town girl questions her love and her life style. A warm and intelligent rural drama. Basinger's debut. **104m/C VHS, LV.** Jan-Michael Vincent, Kim Basinger, Michael Parks, Gailard Sartain, Tanya Tucker, Ted Neeley, Daryl Hannah, Richard Moll; ***D:*** David Greene; ***W:*** Michael Kane; ***M:*** Michael Martin Murphy. *NO*

A Hard Day's Night 🦴🦴🦴½ **1964** The Beatles' first film is a joyous romp through an average "day in the life" of the Fab Four, shot in a pseudo-documentary style with great flair by Lester and noted as the first music video. Laser version includes original trailer and an interview with Lester. ♫A Hard Day's Night; Tell Me Why; I Should Have Known Better; She Loves You; I'm Happy Just To Dance With You; If I Fell; And I Love Her; This Boy; Can't Buy Me Love. **90m/B VHS, Beta, LV, CD-I.** *GB* John Lennon, Paul McCartney, George Harrison, Ringo Starr; ***D:*** Richard Lester. Nominations: Academy Awards '64: Best Story & Screenplay, Best Original Score. *MVD, MPI, CRC*

Hard Drive 🦴½ **1994** A high tech, interactive network offers shared fantasies to Will and Delilah. Then they become obsessed with making their dreams a reality. **92m/C VHS, LV.** Matt McCoy, Christina Fulton, Edward Albert, Leo Damian, Stella Stevens; ***D:*** James Merendino; ***W:*** James Merendino. *TRI*

Hard Drivin' 🦴 **1960** Rowdy action featuring Southern stock car drivers with well shot race scenes from the Southern 500. **92m/C VHS, Beta.** Rory Calhoun, John Gentry, Alan Hale Jr.; ***D:*** Paul Helmick. *NO*

Hard Evidence 🦴🦴½ **1994 (R)** Trent Turner (Harrison) winds up with major regrets when he joins his mistress (Timmins) on a business trip. Seems her "business" involves drug smuggling and he's forced to shoot a DEA agent to protect them. Some protection—now Turner and his wife (Severance) are caught up in murder, drugs, and blackmail. **100m/C VHS.** Gregory Harrison, Joan Severance, Cali Timmins, Andrew Airlie, Nathaniel Deveaux; ***D:*** Michael Kennedy; ***W:*** William Martel; ***C:*** Bruce Worrall; ***M:*** Barron Abramovitch. *AVE*

Hard Frame 🦴½ *Hunters Are For Killing* **1970** An ex-con returns home hoping all will turn to sweetness and light when he attempts to make nice-nice with his stepdad, who wouldn't stick by him during his trial. Reynolds' debut into TV moviedom; could be the hirsute actor was thinking of this one when he said his movies were the kind they show in prisons and airplanes because nobody can leave. **100m/C VHS.** Burt Reynolds, Melvyn Douglas, Suzanne Pleshette, Larry Storch, Martin Balsam, Peter Brown, Jill Banner, Donald (Don "Red") Barry, Angus Duncan, Ivor Francis; ***D:*** Bernard Girard. *SIM*

Hard Hombre 🦴🦴 **1931** Gibson rides and shoots across the screen in one of his best western adventures. **60m/B VHS, Beta.** Hoot Gibson, Lena Basquette, Skeeter Bill Robbins, Jack Byron, Glenn Strange; ***D:*** Otto Brower. *GPV, VCN, VCI*

Hard Hunted 🦴½ **1992 (R)** Three macho undercover agents try to avoid death at the hands of high-tech guerillas trying to steal nuclear weapons. No-brain actioner, heavy on the display of feminine charms. **97m/C VHS.** Dona Speir, Roberta Vasquez, Cynthia Brimhall, Bruce Penhall, R.J. Moore, Tony Peck, Rodrigo Obregon, Al Leong, Michael J. Shane; ***D:*** Andy Sidaris; ***W:*** Andy Sidaris. *COL*

Hard Justice 🦴🦴 **1995 (R)** Bureau of Alcohol, Tobacco & Firearms agent Nick Adams (Bradley) goes undercover in prison to find his partner's killer and discovers that Warden Pike (Napier) is running an illegal gun operation. Now, who's he gonna trust? Lots of action thrills in a routine story. **95m/C VHS, LV.** David Bradley, Charles Napier, Yuji Okumoto, Vernon Wells; ***D:*** Greg Yaitanes; ***W:*** Nicholas Amendolare, Chris Bold; ***C:*** Moshe Levin; ***M:*** Don Peake. *TTC*

Hard Knocks 🦴🦴½ **1980** An ex-con goes from one tragic situation to another, and is eventually stalked by shotgun-wielding rednecks in this grim, powerful drama. Excellent performance by Mann holds this picture together. **85m/C Beta.** *AU* Tracey Mann, John Arnold, Bill Hunter, Max Cullen, Tony Barry; ***D:*** Don McLennan. Australian Film Institute '80: Best Actress (Mann). *NO*

Hard Knocks 🦴 **19??** A young man on the run is tormented by an aging actress and her husband. His attempt to leave a past of violence and pain creates even more havoc. **90m/C VHS, Beta.** Michael Christian, John Crawford, Donna Wilkes, Keenan Wynn. *NO*

Hard Knox 🦴 **1983** A hard-nosed Marine pilot is dumped from the service and takes up command at a military school filled with undisciplined punks. A made-for-television movie. **96m/C VHS, Beta.** Robert Conrad, Frank Howard, Alan Ruck, Red West, Bill Erwin, Dean Hill, Joan Sweeney; ***D:*** Peter Werner. *BAR, ORI*

Hard Labour 🦴🦴 **1973** Middle-aged housekeeper is humiliated at home by her children and tyrannical daughter-in-law. Made for British television. **70m/C VHS.** *GB* Alison Steadman, Ben Kingsley, Clifford Kershaw; ***D:*** Mike Leigh. *WBF, FCT*

Hard Part Begins 🦴 **198?** A naive country singer gets sucked into the pratfalls of show business. **87m/C VHS, Beta.** Donnelly Rhodes, Nancy Belle Fuller, Paul Bradley. *TWE*

Hard Promises 🦴🦴 **1992 (PG)** Absence doesn't necessarily make the heart fonder, as Joey finds out when he's accidentally invited to his wife's wedding. He's been away from home for so long he doesn't even realize he's been divorced and hightails it home to win his sweetheart back. Average performances and script round out this innocuous domestic comedy-drama. Originally made for cable television. **95m/C VHS, LV, 8mm.** Sissy Spacek, William L. Petersen, Brian Kerwin, Mare Winningham, Peter MacNicol, Ann Wedgeworth, Amy Wright, Lois Smith, Rip Torn; ***D:*** Martin Davidson; ***M:*** George S. Clinton. *COL*

Hard Rain-The Tet 1968 **1989** An American platoon stationed in Saigon must mobilize in the wake of the North Vietnamese Army's Tet offensive. An episode of television's "Tour of Duty." Other episodes are also available on tape. **89m/C VHS.** Terence Knox, Stephen Caffrey; ***D:*** Bill W.L. Norton. *NWV*

The Hard Ride 🦴🦴½ **1971 (PG)** Above average biker movie about a Vietnam vet who brings the body of a black buddy back home, then tries to persuade the dead man's white girlfriend and the leader of his motorcycle gang to attend the funeral. **93m/C VHS.** Robert Fuller, Sherry Bain, Tony Russell, Marshall Reed, Biff Elliot, William Bonner, R.L. Armstrong; *D:* Burt Topper; *W:* Burt Topper. *ORI*

Hard Rock Zombies ½ **1985 (R)** Four heavy metal band members die horribly on the road and are brought back from the dead as zombies. This horror/heavy metal spoof is somewhat amusing in a goofy way. **90m/C VHS, Beta.** E.J. Curcio, Sam Mann; *D:* Krishna Shah; *W:* David Ball. *LIV, VES*

Hard Target ½ **1993 (R)** Van Damme continues his action-hero ways as Chance Boudreaux, a Cajun (which explains the accent) merchant seaman, who comes to the rescue of Natasha (Butler), albeit with lots of violence. Brimley provides the humor as Chance's bayou uncle. It's another variation of "The Most Dangerous Game" story but it moves. American directorial debut of over-the-top Hong Kong action director Woo who had to tone down his usual stylistic effects and repeatedly cut some of the more violent scenes to earn an "R" rating. **97m/C VHS, LV.** Jean-Claude Van Damme, Lance Henriksen, Yancy Butler, Arnold Vosloo, Wilford Brimley, Kasi Lemmons; *D:* John Woo; *W:* Chuck Pfarrer; *C:* Russell Carpenter; *M:* Graeme Revell. Nominations: MTV Movie Awards '94: Most Desirable Male (Van Damme), Best Action Sequence. *MCA, BTV*

Hard Ticket to Hawaii **1987 (R)** A shot-on-video spy thriller about an agent trying to rescue a comrade in Hawaii from a smuggling syndicate. Supporting cast includes many Playboy Playmates. **96m/C VHS, Beta.** Ron Moss, Dona Speir, Hope Marie Carlton, Cynthia Brimhall; *D:* Andy Sidaris. *BAR, ORI, WAR*

Hard Times **1975 (PG)** A Depression-era drifter becomes a bare knuckle street fighter, and a gambler decides to promote him for big stakes. One of grade-B meister Hill's first genre films. A quiet, evocative drama. **92m/C VHS, Beta, LV.** Charles Bronson, James Coburn, Jill Ireland, Strother Martin; *D:* Walter Hill; *W:* Walter Hill. *GKK*

Hard to Die *Tower of Terror* **1990** Director Wynorski's comic homage to Carol Frank's "Sorority House Massacre." Five beauties (former Playboy Playmates Harris, Taylor, Dare, Moore, and Carney) find employment moving boxes in a deserted lingerie factory. The film takes off from there as they uncover a mysterious spirit called the Sorority House Killer in an ancient "Soul Box." Desperate to extinguish the evil threat, they focus their efforts in an armed struggle involving high-powered weaponry against the building maintenance man, whom they fear is possessed by the spirit. Accompanied by a lovely, touching group shower scene. **77m/C VHS.** Robin Harris, Melissa Moore, Debra Dare, Lindsay Taylor, Bridget Carney, Forrest J. Ackerman; *D:* Jim Wynorski. *NHO*

Hard to Hold ½ **1984 (PG)** Rockin' Rick's lukewarm film debut where he falls in love with a children's counselor after an automobile accident. Springfield sings "Love Somebody" with music by Peter Gabriel. **93m/C VHS, Beta, LV.** Rick Springfield, Janet Eilber, Patti Hansen, Albert Salmi, Monique Gabrielle; *D:* Larry Peerce. *MCA*

Hard to Kill **1989 (R)** Policeman Seagal is shot and left for dead in his bedroom, but survives against the odds, though his wife does not. After seven years, he is well enough to consider evening the score with his assailants. He hides while training in martial arts for the final battle. Strong outing from Seagal, with good supporting cast. **96m/C VHS, Beta, LV, 8mm.** Steven Seagal, Kelly Le Brock, William Sadler, Frederick Coffin, Bonnie Burroughs, Zachary Rosencrantz, Dean Norris; *D:* Bruce Malmuth; *M:* Charles Fox. *WAR*

Hard Traveling **1985 (PG)** An unemployed Depression-era farmworker is accused of murder. He must fight a hostile court system to maintain his dignity and salvage the love and respect of his wife. Based on a novel by Alvah Bessie. **99m/C VHS, Beta.** J.E. Freeman, Ellen Geer, Barry Corbin, James Gammon, Jim Haynie; *D:* Dan Bessie; *W:* Dan Bessie. *VTR, NWV*

The Hard Truth ½ **1994 (R)** By-the-book actioner finds cop Jonah (Rooker) suspended for having an itchy trigger finger. His gal Lisa (Anthony) knows her sleazy boss has lots of mob money handy and proposes they grab it. But then Lisa gets a look at Chandler (Roberts), the electronic whiz blackmailed to assist in the heist, and the triangle leads to trouble. **100m/C VHS.** Michael Rooker, Eric Roberts, Lysette Anthony, Ray Baker, Don Yesso; *D:* Kristine Peterson; *W:* Jonathan Tydor; *C:* Ross Berryman. *LIV*

Hard Vice ½ **1994 (R)** Vice cops Joe Owens (Jones) and Andrea Thompson (Tweed) have their work cut out for them on their Las Vegas beat. When the bodies start piling up, the prime suspects turn out to be a group of high-priced hookers. **86m/C VHS, LV.** Shannon Tweed, Sam Jones, James Gammon, Rebecca Ferratti; *D:* Joey Travolta; *W:* Joey Travolta. *APX*

Hard Way **1980** A world-weary assassin is pressured by his boss to perform one last assignment. A surprise awaits him if he accepts. **88m/C VHS, Beta.** Patrick McGoohan, Lee Van Cleef, Donal McCann, Edna O'Brien; *D:* Mihael Dryhurst. *TWE*

The Hard Way **1991 (R)** Hollywood superstar Fox is assigned to hardened NYC cop Woods to learn the ropes as he trains for a role. Nothing special in the way of script or direction, but Woods and Fox bring such intensity and good humor to their roles that the package works. Fox pokes fun at the LA lifestyle as the annoying, self-absorbed actor, and Marshall has an entertaining appearance as his agent. Woods is on familiar over-the-edge turf as the brittle but dedicated detective. Silly finale almost destroys the film, but other small vignettes are terrific. **91m/C VHS, Beta, LV.** James Woods, Michael J. Fox, Annabella Sciorra, Stephen Lang, L.L. Cool J., John Capodice, Christina Ricci, Karen Gorney, Luis Guzman; *Cameos:* Penny Marshall; *D:* John Badham; *W:* Daniel Pyne, Lem Dobbs; *C:* Robert Primes; *M:* Arthur B. Rubinstein. *MCA*

Hardbodies **1984 (R)** Three middle-aged men hit the beaches of Southern California in search of luscious young girls. They find them. Mid-life crisis done stupidly. Followed by a sequel. **88m/C VHS, Beta, LV.** Grant Cramer, Teal Roberts, Gary Wood, Michael Rapport, Sorrels Pickard, Roberta Collins, Cindy Silver, Courtney Gains, Kristi Somers, Crystal Shaw, Kathleen Kinmont, Joyce Jameson; *D:* Mark Griffiths; *W:* Eric Alter. *COL*

Hardbodies 2 *Woof!* **1986 (R)** A sequel to the original comedy hit, dealing with film crew in Greece that is distracted by hordes of nude natives. Sophomoric humor dependent on nudity and profanity for laughs. **89m/C VHS, Beta, LV.** Brad Zutaut, Brenda Bakke, Fabiana Udenio, James Karen; *D:* Mark Griffiths; *W:* Eric Alter; *M:* Eddie Arkin. *COL*

Hardcase and Fist **1989 (R)** A framed cop leaves prison with his mind on revenge. The godfather who used him is just his first target. **92m/C VHS, Beta.** Maureen Lavette, Ted Prior; *D:* Tony Zarindast. *MCG*

Hardcore ½ *The Hardcore Life* **1979 (R)** A Midwestern businessman who is raising a strict Christian family learns of his daughter's disappearance while she is on a church trip. After hiring a streetwise investigator, he learns that his daughter has become an actress in pornographic films out in California. Strong performance by Scott and glimpse into the hardcore pornography industry prove to be convincing points of this film, though it exploits what it condemns. **106m/C VHS, Beta, LV.** George C. Scott, Season Hubley, Peter Boyle, Dick Sargent; *D:* Paul Schrader; *W:* Paul Schrader; *C:* Michael Chapman; *M:* Jack Nitzsche. *COL*

The Harder They Come ½ **1972 (R)** A poor Jamaican youth becomes a success with a hit reggae record after he has turned to a life of crime out of desperation. Songs, which are blended nicely into the framework of the film, include "You Can Get It If You Really Want it" and "Sitting In Limbo." **93m/C VHS, Beta, LV.** Jimmy Cliff, Janet Barkley, Carl Bradshaw; *D:* Perry Henzell. *CRC, FCT*

The Harder They Fall **1956** A cold-eyed appraisal of the scum-infested boxing world. An unemployed reporter (Bogart in his last role) promotes a fighter for the syndicate, while doing an expose on the fight racket. Bogart became increasingly debilitated during filming and died soon afterward. Based on Budd Schulberg's novel. **109m/B VHS, Beta.** Humphrey Bogart, Rod Steiger, Jan Sterling, Mike Lane, Max Baer Sr.; *D:* Mark Robson; *W:* Philip Yordan; *C:* Burnett Guffey. Nominations: Academy Awards '56: Best Black and White Cinematography. *CCB, COL*

Hardhat & Legs **1980** Comic complications arise when a New York construction worker falls in love with the woman who's teaching the modern sexuality course in which he's enrolled. Made for television. **96m/C VHS, Beta.** Sharon Gless, Kevin Dobson, Raymond Serra, Elva Josephson, Bobby Short, Jacqueline Brookes, W.T. Martin; *D:* Lee Philips; *W:* Ruth Gordon; *M:* Brad Fiedel. *NO*

Hardly Working **1981 (PG)** A circus clown finds it difficult to adjust to real life as he fumbles about from one job to another. Lewis's last attempt at resuscitating his directorial career. His fans will love it, but others need not bother. **90m/C VHS, Beta.** Jerry Lewis, Susan Oliver, Roger C. Carmel, Gary Lewis, Deanna Lund; *D:* Jerry Lewis; *W:* Jerry Lewis. *FOX*

Hardware ½ **1990 (R)** Rag-tag ripoff in which McDermott is a post-apocalyptic garbage picker who gives girlfriend Travis some robot remains he collected (ours is not to ask why), oblivious to the fact that the tidy android was a government-spawned population controller programmed to destroy warm bodies. Seems old habits die hard, and that spells danger, danger, Will Robinson. Much violence excised to avoid x-rating. **94m/C VHS, Beta, LV.** Dylan McDermott, Stacy Travis, John Lynch, Iggy Pop; *D:* Richard Stanley; *M:* Simon Boswell. *HBO, WAR*

Hardware Wars & Other Film Farces **1981 (G)** A collection of four award-winning spoofs of big-budget film epics, featuring "Hardware Wars," "Porklips Now," "Bambi Meets Godzilla," and "Closet Cases of the Nerd Kind." Some black-and-white segments. **48m/C VHS, Beta.** *WAR, OM*

Harem **1985** A beautiful stockbroker gets kidnapped by a wealthy OPEC oil minister and becomes part of his harem. Kingsley stars as the lonely sheik who longs for the love of a modern woman. **107m/C VHS, Beta, LV.** *FR* Ben Kingsley, Nastassia Kinski; *D:* Arthur Joffe. *LIV, VES*

Harem **1986** In the early 1900s, a dastardly Turkish sultan kidnaps an American beauty to add to his harem—mightily displeasing his jealous first wife. Lots of overwrought romance and drama until she is finally rescued. Made for television. **200m/C VHS.** Omar Sharif, Nancy Travis, Ava Gardner, Julian Sands, Art Malik, Sarah Miles, Yaphet Kotto, Cherie Lunghi; *D:* Billy Hale. *VTR*

Harlan County, U.S.A. **1976 (PG)** The emotions of 180 coal mining families are seen up close in this classic documentary about their struggle to win a United Mine Workers contract in Kentucky. Award-winning documentary. **103m/C VHS, Beta.** *D:* Barbara Kopple; *C:* Phil Parmet. Academy Awards '76: Best Feature Documentary; National Board of Review Awards '77: 10 Best Films of the Year. *COL, ICA*

Harlem Nights **1989 (R)** Two Harlem nightclub owners in the 1930s battle comically against efforts by the Mob and crooked cops to take over their territory. High-grossing, although somewhat disappointing effort from Murphy, who directed, wrote, produced, and starred in this film. **118m/C VHS, Beta, LV.** Eddie Murphy, Richard Pryor, Redd Foxx, Danny Aiello, Jasmine Guy, Michael Lerner, Arsenio Hall, Della Reese; *D:* Eddie Murphy; *M:* Herbie Hancock. Golden Raspberry Awards '89: Worst Screenplay; Nominations: Academy Awards '89: Best Costume Design. *PAR*

Harlem on the Prairie *Bad Man of Harlem* **1938** This first-ever western with an all-black cast has Jeffries helping a young lady find hidden gold and foiling a villain. Even though the technical standards and acting are below par, this is worth watching for the singing and a comedy routine done by a well-known contemporary black team. ♫Harlem On The Prairie; Romance In The Rain. **54m/B VHS.** Herbert Jeffries, Mantan Moreland, F.E. Miller, Connie Harris, Maceo B. Sheffield, William Spencer Jr.; ***D:*** Sam Newfield. *NOS*

Harlem Rides the Range 🦴½ **1939** Jeffries must outsmart villainous Brooks, who means to swindle a radium mine away from its rightful owner. Early oater of interest only because of its atypical all-black cast and crew. **58m/B VHS.** Herbert Jeffries, Lucius Brooks, Artie Young, F.E. Miller, Spencer Williams Jr., Clarence Brooks, Tom Southern, Wade Dumas, Leonard Christmas; ***D:*** Richard C. Kahn; ***W:*** F.E. Miller, Spencer Williams Jr. *NOS, MRV, TPV*

Harley 🦴🦴 **1990 (PG)** Diamond is Harley, an L.A. thug-on-a-hog, who's on his way to an extended stay at one of the state's luxury institutions when he's sent to a Texas rehabilitation community. There, he bonds with an ex-biker, and may just find his way back down the straight and narrow. And the local longhorn rednecks applaud his efforts...not. **80m/C VHS.** Lou Diamond Phillips, Eli Cummins, DeWitt Jan, Valentine Kim; ***D:*** Fred Holmes; ***W:*** Frank Kuntz, Sandy Kuntz. *VMK*

Harley Davidson and the Marlboro Man 🦴 **1991 (R)** An awful rehash of "Butch Cassidy and the Sundance Kid" with blatant vulgarity and pointless sci-fi touches. The title duo are near-future outlaws who rob a bank to save their favorite bar, then find they've stolen mob money. Some action, but it's mostly talk: lewd, meant-to-be-whimsical soul-probing chats between H.D. and M.M. that would bore even the biker crowd—and did. **98m/C VHS, Beta, LV, 8mm.** Mickey Rourke, Don Johnson, Chelsea Field, Tom Sizemore, Vanessa Williams, Robert Ginty, Daniel Baldwin; ***D:*** Simon Wincer. *MGM*

Harlow 🦴🦴½ **1965** The more lavish of the two Harlow biographies made in 1965, both with the same title. A sensationalized "scandal sheet" version of Jean Harlow's rise to fame that bears little resemblance to the facts of her life. **125m/C VHS, Beta.** Carroll Baker, Martin Balsam, Red Buttons, Mike Connors, Angela Lansbury, Peter Lawford, Raf Vallone, Leslie Nielsen; ***D:*** Gordon Douglas; ***W:*** John Michael Hayes; ***C:*** Joseph Ruttenberg. *PAR*

Harmagedon 🦴🦴 **1983** When Princess Luna's jetliner explodes she is thrown into a psychic plane where she must battle Genma, an eternal being who has destroyed half the universe. Luna gathers together the heroic Psyonic Warriors and the cyborg Vega to aid in her battle. Animated; in Japanese with English subtitles. **131m/C VHS, LV.** *JP CPM, WTA*

Harmon of Michigan 🦴🦴½ **1941** College football hero Harmon starred in this loosely adapted story of his life in and out of the pros and his career at Michigan. **65m/B VHS.** Tom Harmon, Anita Louise, Forest Evashevski, Oscar O'Shea, Warren Ashe, Stanley Crown, Ken Christy, Tim Ryan, Lloyd Bridges, William Hall, Chester Conklin, Larry Parks; ***D:*** Charles T. Barton; ***W:*** Howard J. Green. *GPV*

Harmony Lane 🦴🦴 **1935** Highly romanticised rendition of the life of American composer, Stephen Collins Foster (1826-1864). Montgomery, as Foster, manages to lend a hint of credibility to the syrupy, melodramatic script. Very little attention is given to historical fact and almost every scene is orchestrated to showcase the composer's songs. The music steals the show. ♫Beautiful Dreamer; Old Folks at Home; Swanee River; Oh! Susanna; De Camptown Races. **84m/B VHS.** Douglass Montgomery, Evelyn Venable, Adrienne Ames, Joseph Cawthorn, William Frawley, Florence Roberts, Smiley Burnette, Hattie McDaniel; ***D:*** Joseph Santley. *DVT, NOS, VYY*

Harmony Trail 🦴½ **1944** Maynard stars in another rip-roaring western adventure. **60m/B VHS, Beta.** Ken Maynard. *NOS, VCN, DVT*

Harold and Maude 🦴🦴🦴🦴 **1971 (PG)** Cult classic pairs Cort as a dead-pan disillusioned 20-year-old obsessed with suicide (his staged attempts are a highlight) and a loveable Gordon as a fun-loving 80-year-old eccentric. They meet at a funeral (a mutual hobby), and develop a taboo romantic relationship, in which they explore the tired theme of the meaning of life with a fresh perspective. The script was originally the 20-minute long graduate thesis of UCLA student Higgins, who showed it to his landlady, wife of film producer Lewis. Features music by the pre-Islamic Cat Stevens. **92m/C VHS, Beta, LV, 8mm.** Ruth Gordon, Bud Cort, Cyril Cusack, Vivian Pickles, Charles Tyner, Ellen Geer; ***D:*** Hal Ashby; ***W:*** Colin Higgins; ***C:*** John A. Alonzo; ***M:*** Cat Stevens. *PAR*

Harper 🦴🦴🦴 *The Moving Target* **1966** A tight, fast-moving genre piece about cynical LA private eye Newman investigating the disappearence of Bacall's wealthy husband. From a Ross McDonald novel, adapted by William Golding. Later sequelled in "The Drowning Pool." **121m/C VHS, Beta, LV.** Paul Newman, Shelley Winters, Lauren Bacall, Julie Harris, Robert Wagner, Janet Leigh, Arthur Hill; ***D:*** Jack Smight; ***C:*** Conrad Hall. Edgar Allan Poe Awards '66: Best Screenplay. *WAR*

Harper Valley P.T.A. 🦴🦴 **1978 (PG)** Eden raises hell in Harper Valley after the PTA questions her parental capabilities. Brain candy was adapted from a hit song; TV series followed. **93m/C VHS, Beta.** Barbara Eden, Nanette Fabray, Louis Nye, Pat Paulsen, Ronny Cox, Ron Masak, Audrey Christie, John Fiedler, Bob Hastings; ***D:*** Richard Bennett; ***W:*** Barry Schneider. *VES*

Harrad Experiment 🦴½ **1973 (R)** Adaptation of Robert Rimmer's love-power bestseller in which an experiment-minded college establishes a campus policy of sexual freedom. Famous for the Hedren/Johnson relationship, shortly before Johnson married Hedren's real-life daughter Melanie Griffith. Followed by "The Harrad Summer." **98m/C VHS, Beta.** James Whitmore, Tippi Hedren, Don Johnson, Bruno Kirby, Laurie Walters, Victoria Thompson, Elliot Street, Sharon Taggart, Robert Middleton, Billy Sands, Melanie Griffith; ***D:*** Ted Post; ***M:*** Artie Butler. *VES*

Harrad Summer 🦴🦴 **1974 (R)** Sequel to "The Harrad Experiment." College coeds take their sex-education to the bedroom where they can apply their knowledge by more intensive means. **103m/C VHS.** Richard Doran, Victoria Thompson, Laurie Walters, Robert Reiser, Bill Dana, Marty Allen; ***D:*** Steven Hilliard Stern. *NO*

Harriet Craig 🦴🦴🦴 **1950** Tailor-made Crawford role finds her as seemingly perfect wife Harriet Craig. In reality, she's a domineering shrew, who's also a bully and a clean freak. Harriet squelches husband Walter's (Corey) promotion because it means he'll be travelling abroad, ruins his relationship with best friend Billy (Joslyn), and manages to sabotage her young cousin Clare's (Stevens) romance before anybody stands up to her. Third film adaptation of George Kelly's 1925 play "Craig's Wife." **94m/B VHS.** Joan Crawford, Wendell Corey, Allyn Joslyn, William Bishop, K.T. Stevens, Lucile Watson, Raymond Greenleaf, Ellen Corby; ***D:*** Vincent Sherman; ***W:*** James Gunn; ***C:*** Joseph Walker; ***M:*** George Duning. *COL*

Harriet the Spy 🦴🦴½ **1996 (PG)** Sixth-grader Harriet M. Welsch spies on everyone around her and, encouraged by her nanny Golly, writes down everything going on in her secret notebook, because she's determined to become a great writer. Unfortunately, Harriet's imagination sometimes gets the best of her and when her notebook is found, her friends and family are not too happy about its contents. Based on the award-winning novel by Louise Fitzhugh. **?m/C VHS.** Michelle Trachtenberg, Rosie O'Donnell, Vanessa Lee Chester, Gregory Edward Smith, Robert Joy, Eartha Kitt, J. Smith-Cameron; ***D:*** Bronwen Hughes; ***W:*** Douglas Petrie, Theresa Rebeck. *NYR*

Harry & Son 🦴🦴 **1984 (PG)** A widowed construction worker faces the problems of raising his son. Newman is miscast as the old man and we've all seen Benson play the young role too many times. **117m/C VHS, Beta, LV.** Paul Newman, Robby Benson, Ellen Barkin, Wilford Brimley, Judith Ivey, Ossie Davis, Morgan Freeman, Joanne Woodward; ***D:*** Paul Newman; ***M:*** Henry Mancini. *VES*

Harry and the Hendersons 🦴🦴½ **1987 (PG)** Ordinary American family vacationing in the Northwest has a collision with Bigfoot. Thinking that the big guy is dead, they throw him on top of the car and head home. Lo and behold, he revives and starts wrecking the furniture and in the process, endears himself to the at-first frightened family. Nice little tale efficiently told, with Lithgow fine as the frustrated dad trying to hold his Bigfoot-invaded home together. Basis for the television series. **111m/C VHS, Beta, LV.** John Lithgow, Melinda Dillon, Don Ameche, David Suchet, Margaret Langrick, Joshua Rudoy, Kevin Peter Hall, Lainie Kazan, M. Emmet Walsh; ***D:*** William Dear; ***W:*** William Dear, William E. Martin, Ezra D. Rappaport; ***M:*** Bruce Broughton. Academy Awards '87: Best Makeup. *MCA, APD*

Harry and Tonto 🦴🦴🦴 **1974** A gentle comedy about an energetic septuagenarian who takes a cross-country trip with his cat, Tonto. Never in a hurry, still capable of feeling surprise and joy, he makes new friends and visits old lovers. Carney deserved his Oscar. Mazursky has seldom been better. **115m/C VHS, Beta.** Art Carney, Ellen Burstyn, Larry Hagman, Geraldine Fitzgerald, Chief Dan George, Arthur Hunnicutt, Josh Mostel; ***D:*** Paul Mazursky; ***W:*** Paul Mazursky; ***M:*** Bill Conti. Academy Awards '74: Best Actor (Carney); Golden Globe Awards '75: Best Actor—Musical/Comedy (Carney); National Board of Review Awards '74: 10 Best Films of the Year; Nominations: Academy Awards '74: Best Original Screenplay. *FOX, FCT, BTV*

Harry & Walter Go to New York 🦴🦴 **1976 (PG)** At the turn of the century, two vaudeville performers are hired by a crooked British entrepreneur for a wild crime scheme. The cast and crew try their hardest, but it's not enough to save this boring comedy. The vaudeville team of Caan and Gould perhaps served as a model for Beatty and Hoffman in "Ishtar." **111m/C VHS, Beta, LV.** James Caan, Elliott Gould, Michael Caine, Diane Keaton, Burt Young, Jack Gilford, Charles Durning, Lesley Ann Warren, Carol Kane; ***D:*** Mark Rydell; ***W:*** John Byrum; ***M:*** David Shire. *COL*

Harry Black and the Tiger 🦴🦴 *Harry Black* **1958** Jungle adventure involving a one-legged hunter and a man-eating tiger. The hunter initally teams up with the old war buddy who cost him his leg. The motivation grows with each failure to catch the beast and to make matters worse, the friend's wife and son are lost somewhere in the perilous jungle. Filmed in India. **107m/C VHS.** *GB* Stewart Granger, Barbara Rush, Anthony Steel; ***D:*** Hugo Fregonese. *TCF*

Harry Tracy 🦴🦴½ *Harry Tracy—Desperado* **1983 (PG)** Whimsical tale of the legendary outlaw whose escapades made him both a wanted criminal and an exalted folk hero. **111m/C VHS, Beta.** *CA* Bruce Dern, Gordon Lightfoot, Helen Shaver, Michael C. Gwynne; ***D:*** William A. Graham. *VES*

Harry's War 🦴🦴 **1984 (PG)** A middle-class, middle-aged American declares military war on the IRS in this overdone comedy. **98m/C VHS, Beta.** Edward Herrmann, Geraldine Page, Karen Grassle, David Ogden Stiers; ***D:*** Keith Merrill. *TPI*

Harum Scarum 🦴🦴 *Harem Holiday* **1965** Elvis tune-fest time! When a movie star (Presley) travels through the Middle East, he becomes involved in an attempted assassination of the king and falls in love with his daughter. He also sings at the drop of a veil: "Shake That Tambourine," "Harem Holiday," and seven others. **95m/C VHS, Beta.** Elvis Presley, Mary Ann Mobley, Fran Jeffries, Michael Ansara, Billy Barty, Theo Marcuse, Jay Novello; ***D:*** Gene Nelson. *MGM*

Harvest 🦴🦴🦴🦴 **1937** A classically Pagnolian rural pageant-of-life melodrama, wherein a pair of loners link up together in an abandoned French town and completely revitalize it and the land around it. From the novel by Jean Giono. In French with English subtitles. **128m/B VHS, Beta.** *FR* Fernandel, Gabriel Gabrio, Orane Demazis, Edouard Delmont, Henri Poupon; ***D:*** Marcel Pagnol; ***W:*** Marcel Pagnol; ***M:*** Arthur Honegger. National Board of Review Awards '39: 5 Best Foreign Films of the Year; New York Film Critics Awards '39: Best Foreign Film. *INT, MRV, FCT*

The Harvest 🦴🦴½ **1992 (R)** Sultry temptress Leilani sends Miguel's internal thermometer into convulsions with her preference for ice during lovemaking. However, their tryst turns sour (for him) when she takes Miguel to the beach where mystery thugs beat him unconscious and swipe his kidney. Bizarre story sure to ignite a small cult following. **97m/C VHS, LV.** Miguel Ferrer, Leilani Sarelle Ferrer, Harvey Fierstein, Anthony John Denison, Tim Thomerson, Matt Clark, Henry Silva; ***D:*** David Marconi; ***W:*** David Marconi; ***M:*** Dave Allen, Rick Boston. *COL*

Harvest Melody 🦴🦴 **1943** Singing star Gilda Parker travels to farm country for a mere publicity stunt but decides to stay. Corny in more ways than one. ♫You Could Have Knocked Me Over With A Feather; Put It In Reverse; Let's Drive Out To The Drive-In; Tenderly. **70m/B VHS.** Rosemary Lane, Johnny Downs, Sheldon Leonard, Charlotte Wynters, Luis Alberni, Claire Rochelle, Syd Saylor; ***D:*** Sam Newfield. *NOS, LOO*

Harvey 🦴🦴🦴½ **1950** Straightforward version of the Mary Chase play about a friendly drunk with an imaginary 6-foot rabbit friend named Harvey, and a sister who tries to have him committed. A fondly remembered, charming comedy. Hull is a standout, well deserving her Oscar. **104m/B VHS, Beta, LV.** James Stewart, Josephine Hull, Victoria Horne, Peggy Dow, Cecil Kellaway, Charles Drake, Jesse White, Wallace Ford, Nana Bryant; ***D:*** Henry Koster; ***W:*** Oscar Brodney; ***C:*** William H. Daniels. Academy Awards '50: Best Supporting Actress (Hull); Golden Globe Awards '51: Best Supporting Actress (Hull); Nominations: Academy Awards '50: Best Actor (Stewart). *MCA, BTV, RDG*

The Harvey Girls 🦴🦴🦴 **1946** Lightweight musical about a restaurant chain that sends its waitresses to work in the Old West. ♫In the Valley Where the Evening Sun Goes Down; Wait and See; On the Atchison, Topeka and Santa Fe; It's a Great Big World; The Wild Wild West. **102m/C VHS, Beta, LV.** Judy Garland, Ray Bolger, John Hodiak, Preston Foster, Angela Lansbury, Virginia O'Brien, Marjorie Main, Chill Wills, Kenny L. Baker, Selena Royle, Cyd Charisse; ***D:*** George Sidney; ***M:*** Harry Warren, Johnny Mercer. Academy Awards '46: Best Song ("On the Atchison, Topeka and Santa Fe"); Nominations: Academy Awards '46: Best Song ("On the Atchison, Topeka and Santa Fe"), Best Original Score. *MGM, FCT*

A Hash House Fraud/The Sultan's Wife **1915** "A Hash House Fraud" (1915) features a frenetic Keystone chase. "The Sultan's Wife" (1917) concerns a woman who attracts the unwanted attention of a sultan. **33m/B VHS, Beta.** Louise Fazenda, Hugh Fay, Chester Conklin, Gloria Swanson, Bobby Vernon. *CCB*

The Hasty Heart 🦴🦴 **1986** A rowdy, terminally ill Scotsman brings problems and friendships to a makeshift war-time hospital built in the jungles of Burma. Remake of 1949 flick with Richard Todd and Ronald Reagan in leading roles. **100m/C VHS, Beta.** Gregory Harrison, Cheryl Ladd, Perry King; ***D:*** Martin Speer. *BAR, ORI, WAR*

Hat Box Mystery 🦴🦴 **1947** A detective's secretary is tricked into shooting a woman and private eye Neal is determined to save her from prison. Although not outstanding, it's worth seeing as perhaps the shortest detective film (a mere 44 min.) to ever make it as a feature. **44m/B VHS, Beta, LV.** Tom Neal, Pamela Blake, Allen Jenkins; ***D:*** Lambert Hillyer. *SNC, VYY*

Hatari! 🦴🦴🦴 **1962** An adventure-loving team of professional big game hunters ventures to East Africa to round up animals for zoos around the world. Led by Wayne, they get into a couple of scuffs along the way, including one with lady photographer Martinelli who is doing a story on the expedition. Extraordinary footage of Africa and the animals brought to life by a fantastic musical score. **158m/C VHS, Beta, LV.** John Wayne, Elsa Martinelli, Red Buttons, Hardy Kruger, Gerard Blain, Bruce Cabot; ***D:*** Howard Hawks; ***M:*** Henry Mancini. Nominations: Academy Awards '62: Best Color Cinematography. *PAR*

Hatchet for the Honeymoon 🦴 *Blood Brides; Una Hacka Para la Luna de Miel; Il Roso Segmo Della Pollias* **1970** A rather disturbed young man goes around hacking young brides to death as he tries to find out who murdered his wife. Typical sick Bava horror flick; confusing plot, but strong on vivid imagery. **90m/C VHS, Beta.** *SP IT* Stephen Forsythe, Dagmar Lassander, Laura Betti, Gerard Tichy; ***D:*** Mario Bava. *MED, HEG, FCT*

Hate 🦴🦴🦴 *La Haine; Hatred* **1995** Twenty-hours in the lives of young, disenfranchised Said (Taghmaoui), Vinz (Cassel), and Hubert (Kounde), who are living in a housing project outside Paris. A riot breaks out, thanks to police brutality of an Arab resident, and Vinz finds a gun the cops lost. A Paris sojourn leads to a police interrogation of Hubert and Said, a fight with some skinheads, a return to their home turf, and an unexpected conclusion. Intelligent look at the idiocy engendered by societal oppression and a buildup of hatred. French with subtitles. **95m/B VHS.** *FR* Vincent Cassel, Hubert Kounde, Said Taghmaoui, Francois Levantal; ***D:*** Mathieu Kassovitz; ***W:*** Mathieu Kassovitz; ***C:*** Pierre Aim, Georges Diane. Cannes Film Festival '95: Best Director (Kassovitz); Cesar Awards '96: Best Film, Best Film Editing; Nominations: Cesar Awards '96: Best Actor (Cassel), Best Cinematography, Best Director (Kassovitz), Best Screenplay, Best Sound. *PGV*

The Hatfields & the McCoys 🦴🦴 **1975** A made-for-television re-telling of the most famous feud in American history—the legendary mountain war between the Hatfields and the McCoys. **90m/C VHS, Beta.** Jack Palance, Steve Forrest, Richard Hatch, Karen Lamm; ***D:*** Clyde Ware. *WOV*

Hats Off 🦴 **1937** Clarke and Payne star as opposing press agents in this tedious musical. The only bright spot is the finale, which features white-robed girls on a cloud-covered carousel. ♫Where Have You Been All My Life?; Little Old Rhythm; Twinkle, Twinkle, Little Star; Let's Have Another; Zilch's Hats; Hats Off. **65m/B VHS.** Mae Clarke, John Payne, Helen Lynd, Luis Alberni, Richard "Skeets" Gallagher, Franklin Pangborn; ***D:*** Boris L. Petroff. *NOS, MLB*

The Haunted 🦴 **1979** The ancient curse of an Indian woman haunts a present day family by possessing the body of a beautiful girl. Through the girl, a horrible vengeance is carried out. **81m/C VHS, Beta.** Aldo Ray, Virginia Mayo, Anne Michelle, Jim Negele; ***D:*** Michael de Gaetano. *VHE, HHE*

Haunted 🦴🦴½ **1995 (R)** At their Sussex home, David Ash watches helplessly as his younger sister Juliet drowns. Flash-forward to 1925 and the grown-up David (Quinn) returns to teach a university course debunking the supernatural. Still, he's drawn to a supposedly haunted mansion, inhabited by artist Robert Mariell (Andrews), his sister Christina (Beckinsale), brother Simon (Lowe), and their elderly nanny (Massey). David starts experiencing visions of his dead sister, while mysterious fires and other unexplained manifestations occur—all of which seem tied to the unholy Mariell trio. Based on a novel by James Herbert. **108m/C VHS.** *GB* Aidan Quinn, Kate Beckinsale, Anthony Andrews, Alex Lowe, Anna Massey, Geraldine Somerville, Victoria Shalet; ***Cameos:*** John Gielgud; ***D:*** Lewis Gilbert; ***W:*** Lewis Gilbert, Bob Kellett, Tim Prager; ***C:*** Tony Pierce-Roberts; ***M:*** Debbie Wiseman. *HMK*

The Haunted Castle 🦴🦴🦴 *Schloss Vogelod* **1921** One of Murnau's first films, and a vintage, if crusty, example of German expressionism. A nobleman entertains guests at his country mansion when strange things start to occur. Silent, with English titles. **56m/B VHS, Beta.** Arnold Korff, Lulu Keyser-Korff; ***D:*** F.W. Murnau. *SNC, NOS, VYY*

Haunted Gold 🦴🦴 **1932** A young Wayne, in his first Western for Warners, battles gold-hungry desperadoes and a mysterious cloaked phantom. Remake of "The Phantom City." **57m/B VHS.** John Wayne, Sheila Terry, Harry Woods; ***D:*** Mack V. Wright; ***W:*** Adele Buffington. *MGM, GPV*

Haunted Harbor 🦴🦴½ *Pirate's Harbor* **1944** A high-seas financier has been murderd by a crooked crony and Captain Jim Marsden's alibi is all wet. He's got to find the gold, the girl, and avoid the goons. Part of "The Cliffhanger Serials" series. **243m/B VHS.** Kane Richmond, Kay Aldridge, Roy Barcroft. *REP, MOV*

Haunted Honeymoon 🦴 **1986 (PG)** Arthritic comedy about a haunted house and a couple trapped there. Sad times for the Mel Brooks alumni participating in this lame horror spoof. **82m/C VHS, Beta, LV.** Gene Wilder, Gilda Radner, Dom DeLuise, Jonathan Pryce, Paul Smith, Peter Vaughan, Bryan Pringle, Roger Ashton-Griffiths, Jim Carter; ***D:*** Gene Wilder; ***W:*** Gene Wilder. *NO*

The Haunted Palace 🦴🦴½ **1963** Price plays both a 17th-century warlock burned at the stake and a descendant who returns to the family dungeon and gets possessed by the mutant-breeding forebearer. The movie has its own identity crisis, with title and ambience from Poe but story from H.P. Lovecraft's "The Case of Charles Dexter Ward." Respectable but rootless chills, also available with the quasi-Lovecraft "Curse of the Crimson Altar" on laser disc. **87m/C VHS, Beta, LV.** Vincent Price, Debra Paget, Lon Chaney Jr., Frank Maxwell, Leo Gordon, Elisha Cook Jr., John Dierkes; ***D:*** Roger Corman. *HBO, MLB*

Haunted Ranch 🦴½ **1943** Reno Red has been murdered and a shipment of gold bullion is missing. A gang on the lookout for the gold tries to convince people that Red's ranch is haunted by his ghost. **56m/B VHS, Beta.** John "Dusty" King, David Sharpe, Max Terhune, Rex Lease, Julie Duncan; ***D:*** Robert Emmett Tansey. *NOS, DVT, VYY*

The Haunted Strangler 🦴🦴½ *The Grip of the Strangler* **1958** Boris Karloff is a writer investigating a 20-year old murder who begins copying some of the killer's acts. **78m/B VHS, Beta.** *GB* Boris Karloff, Anthony Dawson, Elizabeth Allan; ***D:*** Robert Day. *MED, MPI*

Haunted Summer 🦴🦴 **1988 (R)** Soft-focus, sex-and-drugs period piece of the bacchanalian summer of 1816 spent by free spirits Lord Byron, Percy Shelley, Mary Shelley, and John Polidori and others that led Mary Shelley to write "Frankenstein." Based on the novel of the same name by Anne Edwards. **106m/C VHS, Beta, LV.** Alice Krige, Eric Stoltz, Philip Anglim, Laura Dern, Alex Winter; ***D:*** Ivan Passer; ***W:*** Lewis John Carlino. *MED*

Haunted Symphony 🦴🦴 **1994 (R)** In the 18th century, a deranged composer (Wert) is discovered creating a symphony for the devil and killed by a mob. Years later, his niece Gabrielle (Burns) discovers the unfinished symphony hidden in an old piano and hires choir master Marius (Cross) to complete the score. But when he tries, demonic things begin to occur. **85m/C VHS.** Jennifer Burns, Ben Cross, Doug Wert, Beverly Garland; ***D:*** David Tausik. *NHO*

Haunted: The Ferryman 🦴🦴 **1974** Adapted by Julian Bond from a Kingsley Amis story, the film deals with a novelist who is mysteriously confronted with various events and macabre set-pieces from his own novel, including a dead ferryman rising from the grave. **50m/C VHS, Beta.** *GB* Jeremy Brett, Natasha Parry, Lesley Dunlop; ***D:*** John Irvin. *PSM*

HauntedWeen 🦴½ **1991** All trick, no treat, as a guy nailed by a frat house prank twenty years ago comes-back-for-revenge. **?m/C VHS.** Brien Blakely, Blake Pickett, Brad Hanks, Bart White, Leslee Lacey, Ethan Adler; ***D:*** Doug Robertson. *CVD*

The Haunting 🦴🦴🦴½ **1963** A subtle, bloodless horror film about a weekend spent in a monstrously haunted mansion by a parapsychologist, the mansion's skeptic heir, and two mediums. A chilling adaptation of Shirley Jackson's "The Haunting of Hill House," in which the psychology of the heroine is forever in question. **113m/B VHS, Beta, LV.** Julie Harris, Claire Bloom, Russ Tamblyn, Richard Johnson; ***D:*** Robert Wise. *MGM, FCT*

Haunting Fear 🦴 **1991** Poe's "The Premature Burial" inspired this pale cheapie about a wife with a fear of early interment. After lengthy nightmares and graphic sex, her greedy husband uses her phobia in a murder plot. **88m/C VHS.** Jan-Michael Vincent, Karen Black, Brinke Stevens, Michael Berryman; ***D:*** Fred Olen Ray; ***W:*** Sherman Scott. *RHI*

The Haunting of Barney Palmer **199?** Barney Palmer is sure he has inherited the family magic powers because he is haunted by the ghost of his great uncle. To destroy the curse, he must conquer his fears. Based on the book "The Haunting" by Margaret Mahy. Includes a viewers' guide. Part of the

"Wonderworks" series. **58m/C VHS.** Ned Beatty, Alexis Banas, Eleanor Gibson. *PME, FCT, BTV*

Haunting of Harrington House 🦴 **1982** A tame teenage haunted house film originally produced for television. **50m/C VHS, Beta.** Dominique Dunne, Roscoe Lee Browne, Edie Adams, Phil Leeds; ***D:*** Murray Golden. *GEM*

The Haunting of Morella 🦴 **1991 (R)** Poe-inspired cheapjack exploitation about a an executed witch living again in the nubile body of her teen daughter. Ritual murders result, in between lesbian baths and nude swims. Producer Roger Corman did the same story with more class and less skin in his earlier anthology "Tales of Terror." **82m/C VHS, LV.** David McCallum, Nicole Eggert, Maria Ford, Lana Clarkson; ***D:*** Jim Wynorski; ***W:*** Jim Wynorski, R.J. Robertson. *NHO*

Haunting of Sarah Hardy 🦴🦴 **1989** Ward, as a recently wed heiress, returns to the scene of her unhappy childhood home. In a standard plot, Ward is torn between an apparent haunting and the question of her own sanity. Made for TV film is redeemed by the creditable acting. **92m/C VHS, Beta, LV.** Sela Ward, Michael Woods, Roscoe Born, Polly Bergen, Morgan Fairchild; ***D:*** Jerry London. *PAR*

The Haunting of Seacliff Inn 🦴🦴½ **1994 (PG-13)** Susan and Mark Enright struggle to start a bed-and-breakfast in their newly acquired Mendocino Victorian manse. But psychic Susie senses something—seems the former owner died violently, and, a hundred years ago, an owner was accused of murdering his wife in the house. Not-too-frightening ghost story but good cast work. Made for cable TV. **94m/C VHS, LV.** Ally Sheedy, William R. Moses, Louise Fletcher, Lucinda Weist, Maxine Stuart, Tom McCleister, James Horan; ***D:*** Walter Klenhard; ***W:*** Walter Klenhard, Tom Walla. *MCA*

The Haunting Passion 🦴🦴½ **1983** Newlywed Seymour moves into a haunted house only to be seduced by the ghost of the former occupant's dead lover. Effective and erotic presentation. Made for Television. **100m/C VHS, Beta.** Jane Seymour, Gerald McRaney, Millie Perkins, Ruth Nelson, Paul Rossilli, Ivan Bonar; ***D:*** John Korty. *LIV*

Haunts 🦴½ *The Veil* **1977 (PG)** Tormented woman has difficulty distinguishing between fantasy and reality after a series of brutal slayings lead police to the stunning conclusion that dead people have been committing the crimes. **97m/C VHS, Beta.** Cameron Mitchell, Aldo Ray, May Britt, William Gray Espy, Susan Nohr; ***D:*** Herb Freed; ***M:*** Pino Donaggio. *MED*

Haunts of the Very Rich 🦴🦴½ **1972** A loose remake of "Outward Bound" in which a group of spoiled people on a vacation find themselves spiritually dead. Made for TV. **72m/C VHS, Beta.** Lloyd Bridges, Anne Francis, Donna Mills, Tony Bill, Robert Reed, Moses Gunn, Cloris Leachman, Ed Asner; ***D:*** Paul Wendkos. *VMK*

Havana 🦴🦴½ **1990 (R)** During the waning days of the Batista regime, a gambler travels to Havana in search of big winnings. Instead, he meets the beautiful wife of a communist revolutionary. Unable to resist their mutual physical attraction, the lovers become drawn into a destiny which is far greater than themselves. Reminiscent of "Casablanca." **145m/C VHS, Beta, LV.** Robert Redford, Lena Olin, Alan Arkin, Raul Julia, Tomas Milian, Tony Plana, Betsy Brantley, Lise Cutter, Richard Farnsworth, Mark Rydell, Daniel Davis; ***D:*** Sydney Pollack; ***W:*** Judith Rascoe, David Rayfiel; ***C:*** Owen Roizman; ***M:*** Dave Grusin. Nominations: Academy Awards '90: Best Original Score. *MCA, FCT, MOV*

Have Rocket Will Travel 🦴🦴½ **1959** Three janitors (guess who) help a scientist who is about to lose her job if she can't send a rocket to Venus. They accidently initiate the launch while still on board and introduce their brand of slapstick to a whole new planet. First of the late 50's-early 60's feature films to capitalize on the renewed popularity of the Three Stooges. **76m/B VHS.** Moe Howard, Larry Fine, Joe DeRita, Anna-Lisa, Jerome Cowan, Bob Colbert; ***D:*** David Lowell Rich; ***W:*** Raphael Hayes. *COL*

Having It All 🦴🦴 **1982** A wry television comedy about a love triangle. Dyan Cannon stars as a successful business woman with a husband on each coast, who finds dividing her time is more than she bargained for. **100m/C VHS, Beta, LV.** Dyan Cannon, Barry Newman, Hart Bochner, Melanie Chartoff, Sylvia Sidney; ***D:*** Edward Zwick; ***M:*** Miles Goodman. *LIV*

Having Wonderful Crime 🦴🦴½ **1945** Madcap comedy-thriller about a newly married couple who combine sleuthing with a honeymoon. With their criminal lawyer friend along, the trio winds up searching for a magician who has vanished. Fast-paced action and quick dialogue. **70m/B VHS, LV.** Pat O'Brien, George Murphy, Carole Landis, Lenore Aubert, George Zucco; ***D:*** Edward Sutherland. *TTC, FCT, IME*

Having Wonderful Time 🦴½ **1938** A young girl tries to find culture and romance on her summer vacation at a resort in the Catskills. Film debut of comic Red Skelton, who wasn't always as old as the hills. Based on a Broadway hit by Arthur Kober. **71m/B VHS, Beta.** Ginger Rogers, Lucille Ball, Eve Arden, Red Skelton, Douglas Fairbanks Jr.; ***D:*** Alfred Santell. *NO*

Having Wonderful Time/Carnival Boat 🦴🦴½ **1938** A Ginger Rogers double feature: "Having Wonderful Time" (1938)-fun and frolic at an adult summer camp in the Catskills; and "Carnival Boat" (1932)-the lives and loves of rugged loggers in the Pacific Northwest. **134m/B VHS, Beta.** Ginger Rogers, Douglas Fairbanks Jr., Lucille Ball, Ann Miller, Red Skelton, William Boyd. *TTC*

Hawaii 🦴🦴🦴 **1966** James Michener's novel about a New England farm boy who decides in 1820 that the Lord has commanded him to the island of Hawaii for the purpose of "Christianizing" the natives. Filmed on location. Also available in a 181 minute version with restored footage. Available in director's cut version with an additional 20 minutes. **161m/C VHS, Beta, LV.** Max von Sydow, Julie Andrews, Richard Harris, Carroll O'Connor, Bette Midler, Gene Hackman, Jocelyn Lagarde; ***D:*** George Roy Hill; ***W:*** Daniel Taradash, Dalton Trumbo; ***M:*** Elmer Bernstein. Golden Globe Awards '67: Best Supporting Actress (Lagarde), Best Score; Nominations: Academy Awards '66: Best Color Cinematography, Best Costume Design (Color), Best Song ("My Wishing Doll"), Best Sound, Best Supporting Actress (Lagarde), Best Original Score. *FOX*

Hawaii Calls 🦴🦴 **1938** Two young stowaways on a cruise ship are allowed to stay on after one of them (Breen) struts his stuff as a singer. The two then turn sleuth to catch a gang of spies. More ham than a can of Spam, but still enjoyable. ♫That's The Hawaiian In Me; Hawaii Calls; Down Where The Trade Winds Blow; Macushia; Aloha Oe. **72m/B VHS.** Bobby Breen, Ned Sparks, Irvin S. Cobb, Warren Hull, Gloria Holden, Pua Lani, Raymond Paige, Philip Ahn, Ward Bond; ***D:*** Eddie Cline. *DVT, NOS, HEG*

Hawaiian Buckaroo 🦴 **1938** A couple of cowboys fight to save their pineapple plantation from a sneaky foreman. **62m/B VHS.** Smith Ballew, Evalyn Knapp, Benny Burt, Harry Woods, Pat O'Brien; ***D:*** Ray Taylor. *NOS, DVT, GPV*

The Hawk 🦴🦴½ **1993 (R)** Okay thriller about suburban housewife Annie (Mirren) who suspects that her husband Stephen (Costigan) is a serial killer known as the Hawk. Since Annie has a history of depression and her husband is a known louse, her suspicions are dismissed as delusional. Some surprise twists help the weak story along. Contains some graphic views of corpses. Based on the novel by Ransley. **84m/C VHS.** *GB* Helen Mirren, George Costigan, Owen Teale, Rosemary Leach; ***D:*** David Hayman; ***W:*** Peter Ransley; ***M:*** Nick Bicat. *ACA*

Hawk and Castile **19??** Bandits murder, pillage, and terrorize the nobility in Medieval Europe until the Hawk comes onto the scene. **95m/C VHS, Beta.** Tom Griffith, Jerry Cobb, Nurla Forway, Mari Real. *NO*

The Hawk of Powder River 🦴 **1948** Cheapie western has Dean getting involved with a beautiful outlaw gang leader with a murderous streak. A large part of this film was lifted from earlier Dean oaters, as are all the tunes. **54m/B VHS.** Eddie Dean, Roscoe Ates, Jennifer Holt, June Carlson, Terry Frost, Lane Bradford; ***D:*** Ray Taylor. *MOV*

Hawk of the Wilderness *Lost Island of Kioga* **1938** A man, shipwrecked as an infant and reared on a remote island by native Indians, battles modern day pirates after an explorer finds a cache of treasure. Serial in 12 episodes. **213m/B VHS.** Bruce (Herman Brix) Bennett, Mala, William Boyle; ***D:*** William Witney. *REP, MLB, VCN*

Hawk the Slayer 🦴½ **1981** A comic book fantasy. A good warrior struggles against his villainous brother to possess a magical sword that bestows upon its holder great powers of destruction. Violent battle scenes; Palance makes a great villain. **93m/C VHS, Beta, LV.** Jack Palance, John Terry, Harry Andrews, Roy Kinnear, Ferdinand "Ferdy" Mayne; ***D:*** Terry Marcel. *LIV*

Hawken's Breed 🦴🦴 **1987 (R)** Drifter meets American Indian beauty and hears her tale of woe; the two fall for each other and set out together to avenge the murder of the woman's husband and son. Nothing much to crow about. **93m/C VHS, Beta, LV.** Peter Fonda, Serene Hedin, Jack Elam; ***D:*** Charles B. Pierce. *VMK, IME*

Hawkeye 🦴½ **1988** After his best friend is murdered by gangsters in a seedy drug deal, Hawkeye, a rough and tumble Texas cop, and his slick new partner hit the streets of Las Vegas with a vengeance. **90m/C VHS, Beta.** Troy Donahue, Chuck Jeffreys, George Chung, Stan Wertlieb; ***D:*** Leo Fong. *NO*

Hawkeye: Premiere Episode **1995** Frontier scout Hawkeye (Horsley) and best friend Chingachgook (Grant) come to the aid of Elizabeth Shields (Carter), whose trading post owner husband has been captured during the French and Indian war. **82m/C VHS.** Lee Horsley, Rodney Grant, Lynda Carter. *MOV*

Hawks 🦴½ **1989 (R)** Somewhere on the road to black-comedy this film gets waylaid by triviality. Two terminally ill men break out of the hospital, determined to make their way to Amsterdam for some last-minute fun. Mediocre at best. **105m/C VHS, Beta, LV, 8mm.** *GB* Anthony Edwards, Timothy Dalton, Janet McTeer, Jill Bennett, Sheila Hancock, Connie Booth, Camille Coduri; ***D:*** Robert Ellis Miller; ***W:*** Roy Clarke. *PAR*

The Hawks & the Sparrows 🦴🦴 *Uccellacci e Uccellini* **1967** Shortly after "Mr. Ed" came Pasolini's garrulous crow, which follows a father and son's travels through Italy spouting pithy bits of politics. A comic Pasolinian allegory-fest full of then-topical political allusions, the story comes off a bit wooden. Worth watching to see Toto, the Italian comic, in his element. **91m/B VHS, LV.** *IT* Toto, Ninetto Davoli, Femi Benussi; ***D:*** Pier Paolo Pasolini; ***W:*** Pier Paolo Pasolini; ***M:*** Ennio Morricone. *WBF, INJ*

Hawmps! *Woof!* **1976 (G)** Idiotic comedy about a Civil War lieutenant who trains his men to use camels. When the soldiers and animals begin to grow fond of each other, Congress orders the camels to be set free. Hard to believe this was based on a real life incident. **98m/C VHS, Beta.** James Hampton, Christopher Connelly, Slim Pickens, Denver Pyle; ***D:*** Joe Camp; ***W:*** William Bickley; ***M:*** Euel Box. *VES*

Hawthorne of the USA 🦴🦴½ **1919** Reid stars as Anthony Hamilton Hawthorne, American extraordinaire. After gambling a fortune away in Monte Carlo, Hawthorne heads to mainland Europe for rest and revelry. Instead, he finds the love of a princess and a Communist coup in the making. Silent with orchestral score. **55m/B VHS, Beta.** Wallace Reid, Harrison Ford, Lila Lee, Tully Marshall; ***D:*** James Cruze. *GPV*

Hazel's People 🦴½ **1975 (G)** Bitter and hostile college student attends his friend's funeral in Mennonite country. He discovers not only a way of life he never knew existed, but a personal faith in a living Christ. From the Merle Good novel, "Happy as the Grass Was Green." **105m/C VHS, Beta.** Geraldine Page, Pat Hingle, Graham Beckel, Charles Davis. *VCI*

He is My Brother ⅅ½ **1975 (G)** Two boys survive a shipwreck, landing on an island that houses a leper colony. **90m/C VHS, Beta.** Keenan Wynn, Bobby Sherman, Robbie Rist; ***D:*** Edward Dmytryk. *NO*

He Kills Night After Night After Night ⅅ½ **1970** British police are baffled as they seek the man who has been killing women in the style of Jack the Ripper. And he keeps doing it. **88m/C VHS, Beta.** Jack May, Linda Marlowe, Justine Lord. *NO*

He Knows You're Alone ⅅ **1980 (R)** Lame horror flick that focuses on a psychotic killer terrorizing a bride-to-be and her bridal party in his search for a suitable bride of his own. **94m/C VHS, Beta.** Don Scardino, Elizabeth Kemp, Tom Rolfing, Paul Gleason, Caitlin O'Heaney, Tom Hanks, Patsy Pease; ***D:*** Armand Mastroianni; ***W:*** Scott Parker. *MGM*

He Lives: The Search for the Evil One ⅅ **1988** A man who was imprisoned by Nazis as a child attempts to keep Hitler, now living in Buenos Aires, from starting a 4th Reich. **90m/C VHS, Beta.** Lee Patterson. *NO*

He Said, She Said ⅅⅅ½ **1991 (R)** Romance is the topic, but this isn't a typical dating film, instead a couple's relationship unfolds from differing points of view: first, the guy's (by Kwapis) and then the girl's (by Silver). Bacon and Perkins, Baltimore journalists and professional rivals, tell how their romance wound up on the rocks, and why (or so they say). The end result is overlong and lacks the zing of other war between the sexes movies, but real-life couple Silver and Kwapis do humorously highlight the fact that men and women often view the same incidents very differently. Bacon overacts, Perkins overreacts, and Stone shines as Bacon's ex-girl. **115m/C VHS, LV.** Elizabeth Perkins, Kevin Bacon, Sharon Stone, Nathan Lane, Anthony LaPaglia, Stanley Anderson, Charlaine Woodard, Danton Stone, Phil Leeds, Rita Karin; ***D:*** Marisa Silver, Ken Kwapis; ***W:*** Brian Hohlfield; ***M:*** Miles Goodman. *PAR, CCB*

He Walked by Night ⅅⅅⅅ½ **1948** Los Angeles homicide investigators track down a cop killer in this excellent drama. Based on a true story from the files of the Los Angeles police, this first rate production reportedly inspired Webb to create "Dragnet." **80m/B VHS, Beta.** Richard Basehart, Scott Brady, Roy Roberts, Jack Webb, Whit Bissell; ***D:*** Alfred Werker, Anthony Mann; ***C:*** John Alton. *SNC, NOS, BAR*

He Who Gets Slapped ⅅⅅⅅ **1924** Chaney portrays a brilliant scientist whose personal and professional humiliations cause him to join a travelling French circus as a masochistic clown (hence the title). There he falls in love with a beautiful circus performer and plans a spectacular revenge. Brilliant use of lighting and Expressionist devices by director Sjostrom (who used the Americanized version of his name-Seastrom-in the credits). Adapted from the Russian play "He, The One Who Gets Slapped" by Leonid Andreyev. **85m/B VHS.** Lon Chaney Sr., Norma Shearer, John Gilbert, Tully Marshall, Ford Sterling, Marc McDermott; ***D:*** Victor Sjostrom; ***W:*** Carey Wilson, Victor Sjostrom. *FCT*

He Who Walks Alone **1978** Made-for-television film documents the life of Thomas E. Gilmore, who became the South's first elected black sheriff in the 1960s. **74m/C VHS, Beta.** Louis Gossett Jr., Clu Gulager, Mary Alice, James McEachin, Barton Heyman, Barry Brown, Lonny Chapman; ***D:*** Jerrold Freedman. *NO*

The Head ⅅⅅ **1959** A scientist comes up with a serum that can keep the severed head of a dog alive. Before too long, he tries the stuff out on a woman, transferring the head from her own hunch-backed body to that of a beautiful stripper. Weird German epic sports poor special effects and unintentional laughs, but is interesting nonetheless. **92m/B VHS.** *GE* Horst Frank, Michel Simon, Paul Dahlke, Karin Kernke, Helmut Schmidt; ***D:*** Victor Trivas; ***W:*** Victor Trivas. *SNC*

Head ⅅⅅⅅ **1968 (G)** Infamously plotless musical comedy starring the television fab four of the '60s, the Monkees, in their only film appearance. A number of guest stars appear and a collection of old movie clips are also included. ♫Circle Sky; Can You Dig It; Long Title: Do I Have To Do This All Over Again; Daddy's Song; As We Go Along; The Porpoise Song. **86m/C VHS, Beta, LV.** Peter Tork, Mickey Dolenz, Davy Jones, Michael Nesmith, Frank Zappa, Annette Funicello, Teri Garr; ***D:*** Bob Rafelson; ***W:*** Jack Nicholson, Bob Rafelson. *RHI, COL, MVD*

Head of the Family ⅅⅅ½ **1971 (PG)** After a woman sacrifices her political ideals and career goals for her role as a family matriarch, she eventually falls apart. **105m/C VHS, Beta.** *IT FR* Nino Manfredi, Leslie Caron, Ugo Tognazzi, Claudine Auger; ***D:*** Nanni Loy; ***W:*** Nanni Loy. *GEM*

Head Office ⅅⅅ **1986 (PG-13)** A light comedy revolving around the competition between corporate management and the lower echelon for the available position of chairman. **90m/C VHS, Beta.** Danny DeVito, Eddie Albert, Judge Reinhold, Rick Moranis, Jane Seymour; ***D:*** Ken Finkleman; ***M:*** James Newton Howard. *NO*

Head Over Heels ⅅⅅⅅ **1967** A model married to an older man has an affair with a younger one and cannot decide between them. In French with subtitles. **89m/C VHS, Beta.** *FR* Brigitte Bardot, Laurent Terzieff, Michael Sarne; ***D:*** Serge Bourguignon. *FCT*

Head Winds ⅅⅅ **1925** Silent romance in which Mr. Right spares helpless girl against her will from marrying Mr. Wrong. **52m/B VHS, Beta.** House Peters Sr., Patsy Ruth Miller. *GPV*

Headhunter ⅅ½ **1989** Voodoo-esque killers are leaving headless bodies all around Miami. Plenty of prosthetic make-up. **92m/C VHS, Beta, LV.** Kay Lenz, Wayne Crawford, John Fatooh, Steve Kanaly, June Chadwick, Sam Williams; ***D:*** Francis Schaeffer. *ACA, IME*

Headin' for the Rio Grande ⅅ **1936** A cowboy and his sheriff brother drive off cattle-rustlers in this Western saga. Ritter's film debut. Songs include "Campfire Love Song," "Jailhouse Lament," and "Night Herding Song." **60m/B VHS, Beta.** Tex Ritter, Eleanor Stewart, Syd Saylor, Warner Richmond, Charles "Blackie" King; ***D:*** Robert North Bradbury. *NOS, DVT*

Heading for Heaven ⅅⅅ **1947** A mistaken medical report leaves a frazzled realtor believing he has only three months to live, and when he disappears the family suspects the worst. A minor comedy based on a play by Charles Webb. **65m/B VHS.** Stuart Erwin, Glenda Farrell, Russ Vincent, Irene Ryan, Milburn Stone, George O'Hanlon; ***D:*** Lewis D. Collins. *NOS*

Heading Home ⅅⅅ½ **1924** A very early version of the Babe Ruth story—starring none other than the Babe himself. A fair print, this film is orchestra scored. **56m/B VHS, Beta.** Babe Ruth. *GPV*

Headless Body in Topless Bar ⅅⅅ½ **1996** Based on a famous New York Post headline and the crime that inspired it, this black comedy contains more than its lurid title lets on. Except for street footage at the opening and closing, the entire movie is set in a seedy strip club. After shooting the bartender in a robbery attempt, a crazed ex-con holds the patrons and employees hostage. He forces them to play a mind game called "Nazi truth," revealing the distasteful truth about the captives. Director Bruce and screenwriter Koper first worked together filming re-creations for "America's Most Wanted." The cast worked for "hostage scale," meaning if those playing captives stole the gun from the robber (a plot point), they got his pay for the day. If not, then he got their wages. **105m/C VHS.** Raymond J. Barry, Jennifer MacDonald, David Selby, Taylor Nichols, Paul Williams, Biff Yeager, Rustam Branaman, April Grace; ***D:*** James Bruce; ***W:*** Peter Koper; ***C:*** Kevin Morrisey; ***M:*** Charles P. Barnett. *NYR*

Headless Eyes ⅅ½ **1983** Gory entry into the psycho-artist category. An artist is miffed when mistaken by a woman as a burglar he loses an eye. Not one to forgive and forget, he becomes quite the eyeball fetishist, culling donations from unsuspecting women. An eye for an eye ad finitum. **78m/C VHS.** Bo Brundin, Gordon Raman, Mary Jane Early; ***D:*** Kent Bateman; ***W:*** Kent Bateman. *NO*

Headline Woman ⅅⅅ **1935** An ongoing feud between a police commissioner and a newspaper's city editor causes a reporter to make a deal with a policeman in exchange for news. A good cast makes this otherwise tired story tolerable. **75m/B VHS, Beta.** Heather Angel, Roger Pryor, Jack LaRue, Ford Sterling, Conway Tearle; ***D:*** William Nigh. *NOS, DVT, HEG*

Heads ⅅⅅ½ **1993 (R)** Unassuming copyreader Guy Franklin (Cryer) gets promoted to reporter and his first assignment is a doozy. He's to cover a series of decapitation murders in a small town. Can he do the job without become the next victim—or being accused of the crimes? Made for cable TV; filmed in Manitoba, Canada. **102m/C VHS.** *CA* Jon Cryer, Jennifer Tilly, Ed Asner, Roddy McDowall; ***D:*** Paul Shapiro; ***W:*** Adam Brooks. *REP*

Healer ⅅ½ *Little Pal* **1936** A doctor forgets his pledge to help the lame and becomes a fashionable physician. A young crippled lad helps him eventually remember his original purpose was to serve others. **80m/B VHS, Beta.** Mickey Rooney, Ralph Bellamy, Karen Morley, Judith Allen, Robert McWade; ***D:*** Reginald Barker. *DVT*

Hear My Song ⅅⅅⅅ½ **1991 (R)** Mickey O'Neill (Dunbar) is an unscrupulous club promoter, who books singers with names like Franc Cinatra, while trying to revive his failing nightclub in this charming, hilarious comedy. He hires the mysterious Mr. X, who claims he is really the legendary exiled singer Josef Locke, only to find out he is an imposter. To redeem himself with his fiancee and her mother, he goes to Ireland to find the real Locke (Beatty) and bring him to Liverpool to sing. Dunbar is appealing in his role, and Beatty is magnificent as the legendary Locke—so much so that he was nominated for a Golden Globe for Best Supporting Actor. **104m/C VHS, Beta.** *GB* Ned Beatty, Adrian Dunbar, Shirley Anne Field, Tara Fitzgerald, William Hootkins, David McCallum; ***D:*** Peter Chelsom; ***W:*** Peter Chelsom; ***M:*** John Altman. *PAR*

Hear No Evil ⅅ½ **1993 (R)** Below average thriller with a deaf victim (Matlin) involved in a game of cat-and-mouse with a corrupt cop (Sheen) who's looking for a valuable coin. Weak script plays up the woman in jeopardy theme but lacks the crucial element of suspense. A waste of an otherwise talented cast. **98m/C VHS, LV.** Marlee Matlin, D.B. Sweeney, Martin Sheen, John C. McGinley, Christina Carlisi, Greg Elam, Charley Lang; ***D:*** Robert Greenwald; ***W:*** Randall Badat, Kathleen Rowell; ***M:*** Graeme Revell. *FXV*

Hearing Voices ⅅ½ **1990** Joyless Erica is a commercial model who suffers from a form of scoliosis. If she capitalized on her infirmity by advertising medical aids, she could make a lot of money but she firmly refuses her lover's pleas to do this. When her doctor suggests reconstructive surgery, she storms out of his office but not before attracting the attention of Lee, his gay lover. Erica and Lee begin a complex emotional relationship, upsetting to everyone around them. Uninvolving characters, inert direction, and amateurish acting work against Greytak's feature film debut. **87m/C VHS.** Erika Nagy, Stephen Gatta, Tim Ahearn, Michael Davenport; ***D:*** Sharon Greytak; ***W:*** Sharon Greytak. *WAC, FCT*

The Hearse *Woof!* **1980 (PG)** Incredibly boring horror film in which a young school teacher moves into a mansion left to her by her late aunt and finds her life threatened by a sinister black hearse. **97m/C VHS, Beta.** Trish Van Devere, Joseph Cotten; ***D:*** George Bowers; ***W:*** William Bleich. *MED*

The Hearst and Davies Affair ⅅⅅ½ **1985** Married, middle-aged newspaper tycoon William Randolph Hearst falls for teenage Ziegfeld girl Marion Davies and tries to turn her into a Hollywood star. Davies was generally thought to be talented as a comedienne but Hearst insisted on choosing ill-suited dramatic roles for the blonde and her career was problematic. Their lavish lifestyle was enhanced when Hearst built San Simeon for Davies and their scandalous affair lasted 35 years. Made for television. **97m/C VHS.** Robert Mitchum, Virginia Madsen, Fritz Weaver; ***D:*** David Lowell Rich. *ABC, PSM*

Heart 🦴½ **1987 (R)** A down-and-out small-time boxer is given a chance to make a comeback, and makes the Rocky-like most of it. **93m/C VHS, Beta.** Brad Davis, Jesse Doran, Sam Gray, Steve Buscemi, Frances Fisher; ***D:*** James Lemmo. *VTR, NWV*

Heart and Souls 🦴🦴½ **1993 (PG-13)** Reincarnation comedy casts Downey, Jr. as a mortal whose body is inhabited by four lost souls who died on the night he was born. Now an adult, he must finish what they could not, no matter how outrageous it may be. Talented cast wears plot that's old hat. Downey Jr. must be looking to do a trilogy of tired reincarnated soul roles—this is his second, "Chances Are" was his first. **104m/C VHS, LV.** Robert Downey Jr., Charles Grodin, Tom Sizemore, Alfre Woodard, Kyra Sedgwick, Elisabeth Shue, David Paymer; ***D:*** Ron Underwood; ***W:*** Brent Maddock, S.S. Wilson, Gregory Hansen, Erik Hansen; ***M:*** Marc Shaiman. *MCA, BTV*

Heart Beat 🦴🦴½ **1980 (R)** The fictionalized story of Jack Kerouac (author of "On the Road"), his friend and inspiration Neal Cassady, and the woman they shared, Carolyn Cassady. Based on Carolyn Cassady's memoirs. Strong performances, with Nolte as Cassady and Spacek as his wife, overcome the sometimes shaky narrative. **105m/C VHS, Beta.** Nick Nolte, John Heard, Sissy Spacek, Ann Dusenberry, Ray Sharkey, Tony Bill, Steve Allen, John Larroquette; ***D:*** John Byrum; ***W:*** John Byrum; ***M:*** Jack Nitzsche. *WAR*

Heart Condition 🦴🦴½ **1990 (R)** A deceased black lawyer's heart is donated to a bigoted Los Angeles cop who was stalking the lawyer when he was alive. Soon afterwards the lawyer's ghost returns to haunt the police officer, hoping the officer will help to avenge his murder. Both Hoskins and Washington display fine performances given the unlikely script. **95m/C VHS, Beta, LV.** Bob Hoskins, Denzel Washington, Chloe Webb, Ray Baker, Ja'net DuBois, Alan Rachins, Roger E. Mosley, Jeffrey Meek; ***D:*** James D. Parriott. *NLC*

The Heart is a Lonely Hunter 🦴🦴🦴 **1968 (G)** Set in the South, Carson McCuller's tale of angst and ignorance, loneliness and beauty comes to the screen with the film debuts of Keach and Locke. Arkin gives an instinctive, gentle performance as the deaf mute; Locke's screen debut. **124m/C VHS, Beta.** Alan Arkin, Cicely Tyson, Sondra Locke, Stacy Keach, Chuck McCann, Laurinda Barrett; ***D:*** Robert Ellis Miller; ***C:*** James Wong Howe; ***M:*** Dave Grusin. New York Film Critics Awards '68: Best Actor (Arkin); Nominations: Academy Awards '68: Best Actor (Arkin), Best Supporting Actress (Locke). *WAR*

Heart Like a Wheel 🦴🦴½ **1983 (PG)** The story of Shirley Muldowney, who rose from the daughter of a country-western singer to the leading lady in drag racing. The film follows her battles of sexism and choosing whether to have a career or a family. Bedelia's perfomance is outstanding. Fine showings from Bridges and Axton in supporting roles. **113m/C VHS, Beta, LV.** Bonnie Bedelia, Beau Bridges, Bill McKinney, Leo Rossi, Hoyt Axton, Dick Miller, Anthony Edwards; ***D:*** Jonathan Kaplan; ***W:*** Ken Friedman. Nominations: Academy Awards '83: Best Costume Design. *FOX*

Heart of a Champion: The Ray Mancini Story 🦴🦴 **1985** Made-for-TV movie based on the life of Ray "Boom Boom" Mancini, former lightweight boxing champion. Inspired by the career his father never had due to WWII, Mancini fought his way to the top. Sylvester Stallone staged the fight sequences. **94m/C VHS, Beta.** Robert (Bobby) Blake, Doug McKeon, Mariclare Costello; ***D:*** Richard Michaels. *FOX*

Heart of a Nation 🦴🦴🦴 *Untel Pere et Fils* **1943** Saga of the Montmarte family and their life during three wars, beginning with the Franco-Prussian War and ending with the Nazi occupation in France. Although ordered to be destroyed by the Nazis, this film was saved, along with many others, by the French "Cinema Resistance." In French with English subtitles. **111m/B VHS.** *FR* Louis Jouvet, Raimu, Suzy Prim, Michele Morgan, Renee Devillers; ***D:*** Julien Duvivier. *NOS, DVT, HEG*

Heart of Darkness 🦴🦴 **1993** Joseph Conrad's 1902 menacing novella set in the Belgian Congo is told through flashbacks by Marlow (Roth), whose employers, a Belgian trading company, hire him to find Kurtz (Malkovich), head of a remote trading station, who is rumored to be hoarding a huge cache of ivory. Marlow's journey up the river is beset by obstacles and Kurtz is rumored to be either insane or a prophet in his jungle kingdom. Filmed in Belize; made for television. Francis Ford Coppola's updated adaptation became "Apocalyse Now." **120m/C VHS, LV.** Tim Roth, John Malkovich, James Fox, Isaach de Bankole, Patrick Ryecart, Geoffrey Hutchings, Peter Vaughan, Phoebe Nicholls, Allan Corduner, Alan Scarfe, Iman, Timothy Bateson; ***D:*** Nicolas Roeg; ***W:*** Benedict Fitzgerald; ***M:*** Stanley Myers. *TTC*

The Heart of Dixie 🦴🦴 **1989 (PG)** Three college co-eds at a southern university in the 1950s see their lives and values change with the influence of the civil rights movement. College newspaper reporter Sheedy takes up the cause of a black man victimized by racial violence. Lightweight social-conscience fare. **96m/C VHS, Beta, LV.** Virginia Madsen, Ally Sheedy, Phoebe Cates, Treat Williams, Kyle Secor, Francesca Roberts, Barbara Babcock, Don Michael Paul, Kurtwood Smith, Richard Bradford; ***D:*** Martin Davidson. *ORI*

Heart of Glass 🦴🦴🦴 **1974** A pre-industrial Bavarian village becomes deeply troubled when their glassblower dies without imparting the secret of making his unique Ruby glass. The townspeople go to extremes, from madness to murder to magic, to discover the ingredients. From German director Herzog (who hypnotized his cast daily), this somewhat apocalyptic tale is based on legend. The colors are incredible in their intensity. In German with English subtitles. **93m/C VHS.** *GE* Josef Bierbichler, Stefan Autter, Scheitz Clemens, Volker Prechtel, Sonia Skiba; ***D:*** Werner Herzog. *NYF, INJ, FCT*

Heart of Humanity **1918** An intense drama of love, patriotism, and sacrifice just before the war in a small Canadian village. A traveler who is really a Prussian army lieutenant finds his way to the house of a young man who is about to wed. He ends up falling in love with his fiancee and war is declared just before the wedding. A silent film with music score. **133m/B VHS, Beta, 8mm.** Dorothy Phillips, Erich von Stroheim; ***D:*** Allen Holubar. *GPV, VYY, GVV*

Heart of Midnight 🦴🦴½ **1989 (R)** An emotionally unstable young woman inherits a seedy massage parlor. She works hard to turn it, and herself, into something better. Nice performance by Leigh. **93m/C VHS, Beta, LV.** Jennifer Jason Leigh, Brenda Vaccaro, Frank Stallone, Peter Coyote, Gale Mayron, Sam Schacht, Denise Dumont; ***D:*** Matthew Chapman; ***W:*** Matthew Chapman; ***M:*** Yanni. *NO*

Heart of Texas Ryan 🦴½ **1916** Flamboyant cowboy star fights with kidnappers and wins in this silent film. **50m/B VHS, Beta.** Tom Mix. *GPV, NOS, DVT*

Heart of the Golden West 🦴🦴 **1942** Roy protects ranchers of Cherokee City from unjust shipping charges. **65m/B VHS, Beta.** Roy Rogers, Smiley Burnette, George "Gabby" Hayes, Bob Nolan, Ruth Terry; ***D:*** Joseph Kane. *NOS, VYY, VCN*

Heart of the Rio Grande 🦴½ **1942** Spoiled young rich girl tries to trick her father into coming to her "rescue" at a western dude ranch. **70m/B VHS, Beta.** Gene Autry, Smiley Burnette, Fay McKenzie, Edith Fellows, Joseph Stauch Jr.; ***D:*** William M. Morgan. *CCB, VCN*

Heart of the Rockies 🦴½ **1937** The Three Mesquiteers stop a mountain family's rustling and illegal game trappers. **54m/B VHS, Beta.** Bob Livingston, Ray Corrigan, Max Terhune, Lynn (Mary Hart) Roberts, Yakima Canutt, J.P. McGowan; ***D:*** Joseph Kane. *NOS, VCN, MED*

Heart of the Rockies 🦴½ **1951** Roy, along with his trusty horse and dog, takes care of a highway construction project. **67m/B VHS.** Roy Rogers, Penny Edwards, Gordon Jones, Ralph Morgan, Fred Graham, Mira McKinney; ***D:*** William Witney. *NOS, DVT, TIM*

Heart of the Stag 🦴🦴½ **1984 (R)** On an isolated sheep ranch in the New Zealand outback, a father and daughter suffer the repercussions of an incestuous relationship when she becomes enamored with a hired hand. **94m/C VHS, Beta, LV.** *NZ* Bruno Lawrence, Mary Regan, Terence Cooper; ***D:*** Michael Firth. *VTR, NWV*

Heartaches 🦴🦴 **1947** A reporter tries to track down a murderer who has killed twice. **71m/B VHS, Beta.** Chill Wills, Sheila Ryan, Edward Norris, James Seay. *NOS, DVT, HEG*

Heartaches 🦴🦴🦴 **1982** A young pregnant woman (Potts) meets up with a crazy girlfriend (Kidder) in this touching film about love and friendship. Although a study in contrasts, the two end up sharing an apartment together in Toronto. Fine performances from Potts and Kidder give life to this romantic comedy. **90m/C VHS, Beta, LV.** *CA* Margot Kidder, Annie Potts, Robert Carradine, Winston Rekert; ***D:*** Donald Shebib. Genie Awards '82: Best Actress (Kidder). *LIV, VES*

Heartbeat 🦴🦴½ **1946** If you thought pointless Hollywood remakes of French films were a new phenomenon (see "Pure Luck," for example), then note this lighthearted remake of a 1940 Gallic farce. Rogers becomes the best student in a Parisian school for pickpockets, but when she tries out her skills on a dashing diplomat they fall in love instead. **100m/B VHS.** Ginger Rogers, Jean-Pierre Aumont, Adolphe Menjou, Basil Rathbone, Melville Cooper, Mona Maris, Henry Stephenson, Eduardo Ciannelli; ***D:*** Sam Wood; ***C:*** Joseph Valentine. *NOS, HEG*

Heartbeeps 🦴🦴 **1981 (PG)** In 1995, two domestic robot servants fall in love and run off together. On a beach they encounter the Energizer Bunny. No, that's not right. Young kids may enjoy the romantic robotic duo of Kaufman and Peters. **79m/C VHS, Beta.** Andy Kaufman, Bernadette Peters, Randy Quaid, Kenneth McMillan, Christopher Guest, Melanie Mayron, Jack Carter; ***D:*** Allan Arkush; ***M:*** John Williams. Nominations: Academy Awards '81: Best Makeup. *MCA*

Heartbreak Hotel 🦴🦴½ **1988 (PG-13)** Johnny Wolfe kidnaps Elvis Presley from his show in Cleveland and drives him home to his mother, a die-hard Elvis fan. Completely unbelievable, utterly ridiculous, and still a lot of fun. **101m/C VHS, Beta, LV.** David Keith, Tuesday Weld, Charlie Schlatter, Angela Goethals, Jacque Lynn Colton, Chris Mulkey, Karen Landry, Tudor Sherrard, Paul Harkins; ***D:*** Chris Columbus; ***W:*** Chris Columbus; ***M:*** Georges Delerue. *TOU*

Heartbreak House 🦴🦴½ **1986** A production of George Bernard Shaw's classic play about a captain and his daughter who invite an odd assortment of people into their home for a few days. In the course of their visit, each person shares his ambitions, hopes, and fears. From the "American Playhouse" television series. **118m/C VHS, Beta.** Rex Harrison, Rosemary Harris, Amy Irving; ***D:*** Anthony Page. *ACA, PBS*

The Heartbreak Kid 🦴🦴🦴 **1972 (PG)** Director May's comic examination of love and hypocrisy. Grodin embroils himself in a triangle with his new bride and a woman he can't have, an absolutely gorgeous and totally unloving woman he shouldn't want. Walks the fence between tragedy and comedy, with an exceptional performance from Berlin. Based on Bruce Jay Friedman's story. **106m/C VHS, Beta, LV.** Charles Grodin, Cybill Shepherd, Eddie Albert, Jeannie Berlin, Audra Lindley, Art Metrano; ***D:*** Elaine May; ***W:*** Neil Simon; ***C:*** Owen Roizman. New York Film Critics Awards '72: Best Supporting Actress (Berlin); National Society of Film Critics Awards '72: Best Supporting Actor (Albert), Best Supporting Actress (Berlin); Nominations: Academy Awards '72: Best Supporting Actor (Albert), Best Supporting Actress (Berlin). *MED, VTR*

Heartbreak Ridge 🦴🦴🦴 **1986 (R)** An aging Marine recon sergeant is put in command of a young platoon to whip them into shape to prepare for combat in the invasion of Grenada. Eastwood whips this old story into shape too, with a fine performance of a man who's given everything to the Marines. The invasion of Grenada, though, is not epic material. (Also available in English with Spanish subtitles.) **130m/C**

VHS, Beta, LV, 8mm. Clint Eastwood, Marsha Mason, Everett McGill, Arlen Dean Snyder, Bo Svenson, Moses Gunn, Eileen Heckart, Boyd Gaines, Mario Van Peebles; ***D:*** Clint Eastwood; ***W:*** Jim Carabatsos; ***C:*** Jack N. Green; ***M:*** Lennie Niehaus. Nominations: Academy Awards '86: Best Sound. *WAR, TLF*

Heartbreaker 🦴½ **1983 (R)** Eastern Los Angeles explodes with vicious turf wars when Beto and Hector battle for the affection of Kim, the neighborhood's newest heartbreaker. **90m/C VHS, Beta, LV.** Fernando Allende, Dawn Dunlap, Michael D. Roberts, Robert Dryer, Apollonia; ***D:*** Frank Zuniga. *MED*

Heartbreakers 🦴🦴🦴 **1984 (R)** Two male best friends find themselves in the throes of drastic changes in their careers and romantic encounters. On target acting makes this old story new, with a fine performance by Wayne, in her last film before her death. **98m/C VHS, Beta.** Peter Coyote, Nick Mancuso, Carole Laure, Max Gail, James Laurenson, Carol Wayne, Jamie Rose, Kathryn Harrold; ***D:*** Bobby Roth; ***W:*** Bobby Roth; ***C:*** Michael Ballhaus; ***M:*** Tangerine Dream. *VES*

Heartburn 🦴🦴🦴 **1986 (R)** Based on Nora Ephron's own semi-autobiographical novel about her marital travails with writer Carl Bernstein, this is a tepid, bitter modern romance between writers already shell-shocked from previous marriages. **109m/C VHS, Beta, LV, 8mm.** Meryl Streep, Jack Nicholson, Steven Hill, Richard Masur, Stockard Channing, Jeff Daniels, Milos Forman, Catherine O'Hara, Maureen Stapleton, Karen Akers, Joanna Gleason, Mercedes Ruehl, Caroline Aaron, Yakov Smirnoff, Anna Maria Horsford, Wilfrid Hyde-White; ***D:*** Mike Nichols; ***W:*** Nora Ephron; ***C:*** Nestor Almendros; ***M:*** Carly Simon. *PAR*

Heartland 🦴🦴🦴½ **1981 (PG)** Set in 1910, this film chronicles the story of one woman's life on the Wyoming Frontier, the hazards she faces, and her courage and spirit. Stunningly realistic and without cliche. Based on the diaries of Elinore Randall Stewart. **95m/C VHS, Beta.** Conchata Ferrell, Rip Torn, Barry Primus, Lilia Skala, Megan Folson; ***D:*** Richard Pearce. Sundance Film Festival '81: Grand Jury Prize. *NO*

Hearts & Armour 🦴🦴 **1983** A holy war between Christians and Moors erupts when a Moorish princess is kidnapped. Based on Ludovico Ariosto's "Orlando Furioso." **101m/C VHS, Beta.** *IT* Tanya Roberts, Leigh McCloskey, Ron Moss, Rick Edwards, Giovanni Visentin; ***D:*** Giacomo Battiato. *WAR*

Heart's Desire 🦴½ **1937** Opera great Tauber stars in this musical of an unknown Viennese singer who falls in love with an English girl. **79m/B VHS, Beta.** *GB* Richard Tauber, Lenora Corbett, Kathleen Kelly, Paul Graetz; ***D:*** Paul Stein. *NO*

Heart's Haven 🦴🦴½ **1922** An insensitive wife (Adams), who doesn't appreciate how wonderful her husband is, winds up running away with another man. **61m/B VHS, Beta.** Claire Adams, Robert McKim, Carl Gantvoort, Jean Hersholt; ***D:*** Benjamin B. Hampton. *GPV, FCT*

Hearts of Darkness: A Filmmaker's Apocalypse 🦴🦴🦴🦴 **1991 (R)** This riveting, critically acclaimed documentary about the making of Francis Ford Coppola's masterpiece "Apocalypse Now" is based largely on original footage shot and directed by his wife Eleanor. Also included are recent interviews with cast and crew members including Coppola, Martin Sheen, Robert Duvall, Frederic Forrest and Dennis Hopper. **96m/C VHS, Beta.** Sam Bottoms, Eleanor Coppola, Francis Ford Coppola, Robert Duvall, Laurence "Larry" Fishburne, Frederic Forrest, Albert Hall, Dennis Hopper, George Lucas, John Milius, Martin Sheen; ***D:*** Fax Bahr, George Hickenlooper; ***W:*** Fax Bahr, George Hickenlooper; ***M:*** Todd Boekelheide. National Board of Review Awards '91: Best Feature Documentary. *PAR*

Hearts of Fire 🦴 **1987** A trio of successful rock 'n roll stars work out their confused romantic entanglements. Barely released and then, not even in the U.S. Sad outing for the cast, especially legendary Dylan. **90m/C VHS, Beta, LV.** Bob Dylan, Fionna, Rupert Everett, Julian Glover; ***D:*** Richard Marquand; ***W:*** Joe Eszterhas; ***M:*** John Barry. *ORI, WAR*

Hearts of Humanity 🦴🦴 **1932** Mawkish melodrama concerning a Jewish antique dealer and his relationship with the son of an Irish cop. An early "Chico and the Man" variant. **56m/B VHS.** Jean Hersholt, Jackie Searl, J. Farrell MacDonald, Claudia Dell, Charles Delaney, Lucille LaVerne, George Humbert; ***D:*** Christy Cabanne. *NOS, HEG*

Hearts of the West 🦴🦴🦴½ *Hollywood Cowboy* **1975 (PG)** A fantasy-filled farm boy travels to Hollywood in the 1930s and seeks a writing career. Instead, he finds himself an ill-suited western movie star in this small offbeat comedy-drama that's sure to charm. **103m/C VHS, Beta.** Jeff Bridges, Andy Griffith, Donald Pleasence, Alan Arkin, Blythe Danner; ***D:*** Howard Zieff; ***W:*** Rob Thompson. National Board of Review Awards '75: 10 Best Films of the Year; New York Film Critics Awards '75: Best Supporting Actor (Arkin). *MGM*

Hearts of the World 🦴🦴🦴 **1918** A vintage Griffith epic about a young boy who goes off to WWI and the tribulations endured by both him and his family on the homefront. Overly sentimental but powerfully made melodrama, from Griffith's waning years. Silent with music score. **152m/B VHS, Beta, LV, 8mm.** Lillian Gish, Robert "Bobbie" Harron, Dorothy Gish, Erich von Stroheim, Ben Alexander, Josephine Crowell, Noel Coward, Mary Gish; ***D:*** D.W. Griffith. *GPV, REP, GVV*

Heartstopper 🦴 **1992** Benjamin Latham, an innocent physician in Pittsburgh, was accused of being a vampire in colonial times and hung. 200 years later, he emerges from the grave, unscathed. While trying to figure out what has happened, he falls in love with a photojournalist, who helps him find his own descendent, Matthew Latham. Unfortunately, his deep freeze has left him with the compulsion to kill, but only evil members of society. **96m/B VHS.** Moon Zappa, Tom Savini, Kevin Kindlan. *TEM, MOV*

Heartstrings 🦴🦴 **1995** Melissa wants everything in her life to be perfect, including having the perfect man, which she thinks is New York gallery owner Peter. But will Melissa's heart compromise her ambitions? **94m/C VHS.** Michelle Little, Phyllis Diller. *SWI*

Heat 🦴🦴🦴 **1972** Another Andy Warhol-produced journey into drug-addled urban seediness. Features a former child actor/junkie and a has-been movie star barely surviving in a run-down motel. This is one of Warhol's better film productions; even nonfans may enjoy it. **102m/C VHS, Beta.** Joe Dallesandro, Sylvia Miles, Pat Ast; ***D:*** Paul Morrissey. *TPV, PAR, FCT*

Heat 🦴½ **1987 (R)** A Las Vegas bodyguard avenges the beating of an old flame by a mobster's son, and incites mob retaliation. Based on the William Goldman novel. **103m/C VHS, Beta, LV.** Burt Reynolds, Karen Young, Peter MacNicol, Howard Hesseman; ***D:*** R.M. Richards; ***W:*** William Goldman; ***M:*** Michael Gibbs. *PAR*

Heat 🦴🦴🦴½ **1995 (R)** Pacino and De Niro in the same scene. Together. Finally. Obsessive master thief McCauley (De Niro) leads a crack crew on various military-style heists across L.A. while equally obsessive detective Hanna (Pacino) tracks him. Each man recognizes and respects the other's ability and dedication, even as they express the willingness to kill each other, if necessary. Excellent script with all the fireworks you'd expect, as well as a surprising look into emotional and personal sacrifice. Beautiful cinematography shows industrial landscape to great effect. Writer-director Mann held onto the screenplay for twelve years. **171m/C VHS, LV.** Robert De Niro, Al Pacino, Val Kilmer, Jon Voight, Diane Venora, Ashley Judd, Wes Studi, Tom Sizemore, Mykelti Williamson, Amy Brenneman, Ted Levine, Dennis Haysbert, William Fichtner, Natalie Portman, Hank Azaria, Henry Rollins, Kevin Gage; ***Cameos:*** Tone Loc, Bud Cort, Jeremy Piven; ***D:*** Michael Mann; ***W:*** Michael Mann; ***C:*** Dante Spinotti; ***M:*** Elliot Goldenthal. *WAR*

Heat and Dust 🦴🦴🦴 **1982 (R)** A young bride joins her husband at his post in India and is inexorably drawn to the country and its prince of state. Years later her great niece journeys to modern day India in search of the truth about her scandalous and mysterious relative. More than the story of two romances, this is the tale of women rebelling against an unseen caste system which keeps them second-class citizens. Ruth Jhabvala wrote the novel and screenplay. **130m/C VHS, Beta.** *GB* Julie Christie, Greta Scacchi, Shashi Kapoor, Christopher Cazenove, Nickolas Grace; ***D:*** James Ivory; ***W:*** Ruth Prawer Jhabvala; ***C:*** Walter Lassally. British Academy Awards '83: Best Adapted Screenplay; Nominations: Cannes Film Festival '83: Best Film. *MCA*

Heat and Sunlight 🦴½ **1987** A photographer becomes obsessively jealous of his lover as their relationship comes to an end. Director Nilsson again used a unique improvisational, video-to-film technique, as he did with his previous film, "Signal 7." **98m/B VHS, Beta, LV.** Rob Nilsson, Consuelo Faust, Bill Bailey, Don Bajema, Ernie Fosselius; ***D:*** Rob Nilsson; ***W:*** Rob Nilsson. Sundance Film Festival '88: Grand Jury Prize. *CVC*

Heat of Desire 🦴🦴 *Plein Sud* **1984 (R)** A philosophy professor abandons everything (including his wife) for a woman he barely knows and is conned by her "relatives." With English subtitles. **90m/C VHS, Beta, LV.** *FR* Clio Goldsmith, Patrick Dewaere, Jeanne Moreau, Guy Marchand; ***D:*** Luc Beraud. *COL*

The Heat of the Day **1991** A British officer is accused of treason. As he attempts to find those who framed him, he meets a lovely woman all too willing to help. But whose side is she really on? Set in WWII. Tense and well-acted. Originally made for Masterpiece Theatre. **120m/C VHS.** Michael York, Patricia Hodge, Peggy Ashcroft, Anna Carteret, Michael Gambon; ***W:*** Harold Pinter. *PBS*

Heat of the Flame 🦴 **1982** A vicious woodsman captures and rapes a beautiful girl. Psychological games, eroticism and exploitive nudity ensue. **88m/C VHS, Beta.** Tony Ferrandis, Ellie MacLure, Raymond Young, Anthony Mayans. *VCD*

Heat Street 🦴 **1987** Two thugs exact revenge on street gangs for the murders of loved ones. Made for video. **90m/C VHS, Beta.** Quincy Adams, Deborah Gibson, Wendy MacDonald, Del Zamora; ***D:*** Joseph Merhi. *HHE*

Heat Wave 🦴½ **1954** A writer gets involved with a "femme fatale" who kills her wealthy husband for the love of a young pianist. **60m/B VHS, Beta, LV.** *GB* Alex Nicol, Hillary Brooke, Sidney James, Susan Stephen, Paul Carpenter; ***D:*** Ken Hughes; ***W:*** Ken Hughes. *NO*

Heat Wave 🦴🦴🦴 **1990 (R)** The Watts ghetto uprising of 1965 is a proving ground for a young black journalist. Excellent cast and fine script portrays the anger and frustration of blacks in Los Angeles and the U.S. in the 1960s and the fear of change felt by blacks and whites when civil rights reform began. Strong drama with minimal emotionalism. Made for cable TV. **92m/C VHS, Beta.** Blair Underwood, Cicely Tyson, James Earl Jones, Sally Kirkland, Margaret Avery, David Strathairn, Robert Hooks, Adam Arkin, Paris Vaughan, Charlie Korsmo. *TTC*

Heated Vengeance 🦴 **1987 (R)** A Vietnam vet returns to the jungle to find the woman he left behind, and runs into some old enemies. **91m/C VHS, Beta.** Richard Hatch, Michael J. Pollard, Mills Watson, Cameron Dye; ***D:*** Edward Murphy. *MED*

Heathers 🦴🦴🦴½ **1989 (R)** Clique of stuck-up girls named Heather rule the high school social scene until the newest member (not a Heather) decides that enough is enough. She and her outlaw boyfriend embark (accidentally on her part, intentionally on his) on a murder spree disguised as a rash of teen suicides. Dense, take-no-prisoners black comedy with buckets of potent slang, satire and unforgiving hostility. Humor this dark is rare; sharply observed and acted, though the end is out of place. Slater does his best Nicholson impression. **102m/C VHS, Beta, LV.** Winona Ryder, Christian Slater, Kim Walker, Shannen Doherty, Lisanne Falk, Penelope Milford, Glenn Shadix, Lance Fenton, Patrick Laborteaux; ***D:*** Michael Lehmann; ***M:*** David Newman. Edgar Allan Poe Awards '89: Best Screenplay; Independent Spirit Awards '90: Best First Feature. *VTR, NWV, FCT*

The Heat's On 🦴 *Tropicana* **1943** Gaxton is a broadway producer with a failing musical and an unhappy star in West. He cranks up the publicity machine and gets the show declared immoral by the Legion of Purity which results in its closing (not what he expected). Gaxton then runs a scam to become the producer of West's new show, which just happens to be financed by some Legion members. Very uneven plot and performances with thrown-in musical numbers. West wrote her own dialogue but unlike her early films she had little control over the production and it showed. West didn't make another movie for 27 years (the appalling "Myra Breckenridge"). ♫Just a Stranger in Town; Hello, Mi Amigo; The White Keys and the Black Keys; There Goes That Guitar; Antonio; The Caissons Go Rolling Along; There Goes My Heart. **79m/B VHS.** Mae West, William Gaxton, Victor Moore, Almira Sessions, Lester Allen, Mary Roche, Alan Dinehart, Lloyd Bridges; ***D:*** Gregory Ratoff; ***W:*** Fitzroy Davis, George S. George, Fred Schiller. *FCT*

Heatseeker 🦴🦴 **1995 (R)** Corporations use mechanical fighters to participate in brutal kickboxing contests in 2019 New America. Human Chance (Cooke) must battle cyborg opponent Xao if he wants to save his kidnapped trainer. Lots of action and even some intentional humor. **91m/C VHS.** Keith Cooke, Gary Daniels, Norbert Weisser, Thom Mathews; ***D:*** Albert Pyun. *VMK*

Heatwave 🦴🦴🦴 **1983 (R)** Local residents oppose a multi-million dollar residential complex in Australia. Davis portrays a liberal activist, who wages war with the developers, and, in return, becomes involved with a possible murder case. **92m/C VHS, Beta.** *AU* Judy Davis, Richard Moir, Chris Haywood, Bill Hunter, John Gregg, Anna Jemison; ***D:*** Phillip Noyce. *NO*

Heaven 🦴🦴 **1987 (PG-13)** An exploration of "heaven" including the idea, the place, and people's views about it. Questions such as "How do you get there?" and "What goes on up there?" are discussed. Offbeat interviews mixed with a collage of celestial images. **80m/C VHS, Beta, LV.** ***D:*** Diane Keaton; ***M:*** Howard Shore. *LTY, FCT*

Heaven & Earth 🦴🦴🦴 **1990 (PG-13)** A samurai epic covering the battle for the future of Japan between two feuding warlords. The overwhelming battle scenes were actually filmed on location in Canada. In Japanese with English subtitles. **104m/C VHS, LV.** *JP* Masahiko Tsugawa, Takaai Enoki, Atsuko Asano, Tsunehiko Watase, Naomi Zaizen, Binpachi Ito. *LIV, INJ*

Heaven and Earth 🦴🦴 **1993 (R)** Conclusion of Stone's Vietnam trilogy (after "Platoon" and "Born on the Fourth of July") focuses on Vietnamese woman (film debut of Le) and her life under the French and American occupations. Jones is the American soldier who marries her and eventually brings her to the U.S. Not one for subtleties, Stone chases melodramatic excess with finesse of lumberjack, sawing away at guilt and remorse from a "woman's point of view." Cranky Tommy Lee shows up too late to save flick and is saddled with a perplexing I.D. to boot. Flawed, ambitious, and interesting if a student of Stone. Based on the two autobiographies of Le Ly Haslip, "When Heaven and Earth Changed Places" and "Child of War, Woman of Peace." Filmed on location in Thailand. **142m/C VHS, LV.** Hiep Thi Le, Tommy Lee Jones, Joan Chen, Haing S. Ngor, Debbie Reynolds, Conchata Ferrell, Dustin Nguyen, Liem Whatley, Dale Dye; ***D:*** Oliver Stone; ***W:*** Oliver Stone; ***C:*** Robert Richardson; ***M:*** Kitaro. Golden Globe Awards '94: Best Original Score. *WAR*

Heaven Can Wait 🦴🦴🦴 **1943** Social satire in which a rogue tries to convince the Devil to admit him into Hell by relating the story of his philandering life and discovers that he was a more valuable human being than he thought. A witty Lubitsch treat based on the play "Birthdays." **112m/C VHS, Beta, LV.** Don Ameche, Gene Tierney, Laird Cregar, Charles Coburn, Marjorie Main, Eugene Pallette, Allyn Joslyn, Spring Byington, Signe Hasso, Louis Calhern, Dickie Moore, Florence Bates, Scotty Beckett, Charles Halton; ***D:*** Ernst Lubitsch. Nominations: Academy Awards '43: Best Color Cinematography, Best Director (Lubitsch), Best Picture. *FOX, FCT*

Heaven Can Wait 🦴🦴🦴 **1978 (PG)** A remake of 1941's "Here Comes Mr. Jordan," about a football player who is mistakenly summoned to heaven before his time. When the mistake is realized, he is returned to Earth in the body of a corrupt executive about to be murdered by his wife. Not to be confused with the 1943 film of the same name. **101m/C VHS, Beta, LV.** Warren Beatty, Julie Christie, Charles Grodin, Dyan Cannon, James Mason, Jack Warden; ***D:*** Buck Henry; ***W:*** Warren Beatty, Elaine May; ***C:*** William A. Fraker; ***M:*** Dave Grusin. Academy Awards '78: Best Art Direction/Set Decoration; Golden Globe Awards '79: Best Actor—Musical/Comedy (Beatty), Best Film—Musical/Comedy, Best Supporting Actress (Cannon); Nominations: Academy Awards '78: Best Actor (Beatty), Best Adapted Screenplay, Best Director (Beatty, Henry), Best Picture, Best Supporting Actor (Warden), Best Supporting Actress (Cannon), Best Original Score. *PAR, FOX, HMV*

Heaven Help Us 🦴🦴½ *Catholic Boys* **1985 (R)** Three mischievous boys find themselves continually in trouble with the priests running their Brooklyn Catholic high school during the mid-1960s. Realistic and humorous look at adolescent life. **102m/C VHS, Beta, LV.** Andrew McCarthy, Mary Stuart Masterson, Kevin Dillon, Malcolm Danare, Jennie Dundas, Kate Reid, Wallace Shawn, Jay Patterson, John Heard, Donald Sutherland, Yeardley Smith, Sherry Steiner, Calvert Deforest, Philip Bosco, Patrick Dempsey, Christopher Durang; ***D:*** Michael Dinner; ***W:*** Charles Purpura; ***M:*** James Horner. *NO*

Heaven is a Playground 🦴🦴½ **1991 (R)** On Chicago's South Side an inner city basketball coach and an idealistic young lawyer are determined to change the fate of a group of high school boys. The men use the incentive of athletic scholarships to keep their team in school and away from drugs and gangs. **104m/C VHS, LV.** D.B. Sweeney, Michael Warren, Richard Jordan, Victor Love; ***D:*** Randall Fried; ***W:*** Randall Fried. *COL*

Heaven on Earth 🦴🦴½ **1989** The story of two orphaned British children who, along with thousands of orphans shipped from England to Canada between 1867 and 1914, try to make new lives in the Canadian wilderness. **101m/C VHS, Beta.** *CA* R.H. Thomson, Sian Leisa Davies, Torquil Campbell, Fiona Reid; ***D:*** Allen Kroeker; ***W:*** Margaret Atwood. *NO*

Heaven Tonight 🦴🦴½ **1993 (R)** Ex-rock star dad copes with midlife crisis by trying for his big comeback, this time with his son. **97m/C VHS.** *AU* John Waters, Rebecca Gilling, Guy Pearce, Kim Gyngell; ***D:*** Pino Amenta. *ACA*

Heavenly Bodies *Woof!* **1984 (R)** A young woman who dreams of owning a health club will stop at nothing to accomplish her goals. When a rival tries to put her out of business, a "dance-down" takes place in this lame low-budget aerobics musical. **99m/C VHS, Beta.** *CA* Cynthia Dale, Richard Rebrere, Laura Henry, Stuart Stone, Walter George Alton, Cec Linder; ***D:*** Lawrence Dane; ***W:*** Lawrence Dane, Ron Base. *FOX*

Heavenly Creatures 🦴🦴🦴½ **1994 (R)** Haunting and surreal drama chronicles the true-life case of two young schoolgirls, Pauline and Juliet, who were charged with clubbing to death Pauline's mother in Christchurch, New Zealand in 1954. Opens two years before the murder, and follows the friendship as the two teens become obsessed with each other, retreating into a rich fantasy life. They create an elaborate, medieval kingdom where they escape to their dream lovers and romantic alter egos. Elaborate morphing and animation effects vividly express the shared inner fantasy world, while innovative camerawork creates the sensations of hysteria and excitement that the girls experience as their infatuation becomes uncontrollable. Leads Lynsky and Winslet are convincing as the awkward, quiet Pauline and the pretty, intelligent, upper class Juliet. Bizarre crime story is stylish and eerily compelling, and made more so by real life events: after the film was released, mystery writer Anne Perry was revealed as Juliet Hulme. **110m/C VHS, LV.** *NZ* Melanie Lynskey, Kate Winslet, Sarah Pierse, Diana Kent, Clive Merrison, Simon O'Connor; ***D:*** Peter Jackson; ***W:*** Peter Jackson, Frances Walsh. Nominations: Academy Awards '94: Best Original Screenplay; Australian Film Institute '95: Best Foreign Film. *TOU*

The Heavenly Kid 🦴🦴 **1985 (PG-13)** Leather-jacketed "cool" guy who died in a sixties hot rod crash finally receives an offer to exit limbo and enter heaven. The deal requires that he educate his dull earthly son on more hip and worldly ways. A big problem is that the soundtrack and wardrobe are 1955, whereas the cocky cool greaser supposedly died seventeen years ago in 1968. Mildly entertaining. **92m/C VHS, Beta.** Lewis Smith, Jane Kaczmarek, Jason Gedrick, Richard Mulligan; ***D:*** Cary Medoway; ***W:*** Cary Medoway, Martin Copeland. *NO*

Heaven's a Drag 🦴🦴½ *To Die For* **1994** Low-budget British cross between a tearjerker and a supernatural comedy. HIV-positive London drag performer Mark (Williams) lives with Simon (Arklie), a TV repairman who keeps his sexuality a secret from his co-workers and his emotional distance from his stricken lover. When Mark dies, Simon is quick to get on with his life—too quick for Mark, who's ghostly presence puts a damper on Simon's dating possibilities and brings up some old resentments. **96m/C VHS.** *GB* Thomas Arklie, Ian Williams, Dilly Keane, Tony Slattery, Jean Boht, John Altman; ***D:*** Peter MacKenzie Litten; ***W:*** Johnny Byrne; ***C:*** John Ward. *ICA*

Heavens Above 🦴🦴🦴 **1963** A sharp, biting satire on cleric life in England. Sellers stars as the quiet, down-to-earth reverend who is appointed to a new post in space. **113m/B VHS, Beta.** *GB* Peter Sellers, Cecil Parker, Isabel Jeans, Eric Sykes, Ian Carmichael; ***D:*** John Boulting, Roy Boulting; ***M:*** Richard Rodney Bennett. *FCT*

Heaven's Gate 🦴🦴 **1981 (R)** The uncut version of Cimino's notorious folly. A fascinating, plotless, and exaggerated account of the Johnson County cattle war of the 1880s. Ravishingly photographed, the film's production almost single-handedly put United Artists out of business. **220m/C VHS, Beta, LV.** Kris Kristofferson, Christopher Walken, Isabelle Huppert, John Hurt, Richard Masur, Mickey Rourke, Brad Dourif, Joseph Cotten, Jeff Bridges, Sam Waterston, Terry O'Quinn, Geoffrey Lewis; ***D:*** Michael Cimino; ***W:*** Michael Cimino; ***C:*** Vilmos Zsigmond. Golden Raspberry Awards '81: Worst Director (Cimino); Nominations: Academy Awards '81: Best Art Direction/Set Decoration; Cannes Film Festival '81: Best Film. *MGM, FCT*

Heaven's Heroes **1987** Dennis Hill, a dedicated policeman, was killed in the line of duty on August 27, 1977. This film recalls his life and deep faith in Jesus. **72m/C VHS, Beta.** David Ralphe, Heidi Vaughn, James O'Hagen; ***D:*** Donald W. Thompson.

Heaven's Prisoners 🦴🦴½ **1995 (R)** Dave Robicheaux (Baldwin) is an ex-New Orleans homicide detective and recovering alcoholic, living a quiet life on a bayou with patient wife Annie (Lynch). They witness a plane crash and Dave rescues the only survivor, a young Salvadoran girl, whom they adopt. But the crash wasn't an accident and Dave's snooping around involves him with drug runners and local crime bosses, including old high school buddy, Bubba Rocque (Roberts), and his sirenish wife, Claudette (Hatcher). Convoluted plot with some moody touches but Baldwin scores as the flawed hero. Based on the mystery series by James Lee Burke. **126m/C VHS.** Alec Baldwin, Kelly Lynch, Mary Stuart Masterson, Eric Roberts, Teri Hatcher, Vondie Curtis-Hall, Badja Djola, Joe Viterelli, Hawthorne James; ***D:*** Phil Joanou; ***W:*** Scott Frank, Harley Peyton; ***C:*** Harris Savides; ***M:*** George Fenton. *NYR*

Heavy 🦴🦴 **1994** Leisurely-paced character study with good performances. Victor (Vince) is an obese, socially withdrawn, 30-ish cook, living with his domineering mother (a subdued Winters) and helping her run their roadside diner, along with veteran waitress Delores (Harry). Then beautiful teenager Callie (Tyler) is hired and Victor begins to dream of a new life. Mom lands in the hospital, Delores puts the moves on him, Callie's life takes some unexpected turns, and Victor manages a few small steps into society. **119m/C VHS.** Pruitt Taylor Vince, Shelley Winters, Liv Tyler, Deborah Harry, Evan Dando, Joe Grifasi; ***D:*** James Mangold; ***W:*** James Mangold; ***M:*** Thurston Moore. Sundance Film Festival '95: Special Jury Prize. *NYR*

Heavy Metal 🦴🦴🦴 **1981 (R)** Yes, the animated cult flick is now legally available on video, its copyright disputes finally resolved. A collection of science fiction and fantasy stories, inspired by the same-titled magazine and offered in a variety of graphic styles, that all encompass the theme of good versus evil. And don't always bet on the good. Features a soundtrack complied from the work of many top metal artists of the time as well as Bernstein's score with the London Philharmonic Orchestra. A three-minute transitional segment, called "Neverwhere Land," that was cut from the original version has been restored as an epilogue. **90m/C VHS, LV.** *CA* ***D:*** Gerald Potterton; ***W:*** Dan Goldberg, Len Blum; ***M:*** Elmer Bernstein; ***V:*** John Candy, Joe Flaherty, Don Francks, Eugene Levy. *COL*

Heavy Petting 🦴🦴½ **1989** A hilarious compilation of "love scene" footage from feature films of the silent era to the sixties, newsreels, news reports, educational films, old TV shows, and home movies. **75m/C VHS, Beta, LV.** David Byrne, Josh Mostel, Sandra Bernhard, Allen Ginsberg, Ann Magnuson, Spalding Gray, Laurie Anderson, John Oates, Abbie Hoffman, Jacki Ochs; ***D:*** Obie Benz. *SUE, ACA*

Heavy Traffic 🦴🦴🦴 **1973** Ralph Bakshi's animated fantasy portrait of the hard-edged underside of city life. A young cartoonist draws the people, places, and paranoia of his environment. **76m/C VHS, Beta.** ***D:*** Ralph Bakshi; ***W:*** Ralph Bakshi; ***M:*** Ed Bogas. *WAR, OM*

Heavyweights 🦴 **1994 (PG)** A product of Disney's sometimes assembly line approach to family entertainment (think "Mighty Ducks"). Nothing new saga of overweight youngsters sent to a fat camp run by tyrannical fitness guru Tony Perkis (Stiller). His methods cause the kids to band together and overthrow him and his "evil" tactics. Oh, by the way, there's a baseball competition with the more athletic camp kids on the other side of the lake. Guess who wins. Stiller as the fame obsessed fitness fanatic, sporting a David Copperfield make-over, is the only highlight in this exercise of excess fluff. Directorial debut of Brill. **98m/C VHS, LV.** Jeffrey Tambor, Ben Stiller, Jerry Stiller, Anne Meara, Shaun Weiss, Kenan Thompson; ***D:*** Steven Brill; ***W:*** Judd Apatow, Steven Brill; ***C:*** Victor Hammer; ***M:*** J.A.C. Redford. *DIS*

Heck's Way Home 🦴🦴½ **1995** Heck is the Neufeld family dog and best friend of 11-year-old Luke (Krowchuk). The family is moving from Winnipeg to Australia and have a three-day layover in Vancouver. Heck is supposed to come along but instead, unbeknownst to the family, he gets captured by the local dogcatcher (Arkin) and the family are forced to leave without him. Naturally, Heck escapes and starts off on a 2000-mile journey to find his family before they fly away forever. Made for cable. **92m/C VHS.** Chad Krowchuk, Alan Arkin, Michael Riley, Shannon Lawson; ***D:*** Michael Scott. *HMK*

Hector's Bunyip **1986** What's a bunyip? People think it's just Hector's scaly imaginary friend. It therefore comes as quite a surprise when Hector gets kidnapped—by his supposed imaginary friend! Aired on PBS as part of the "Wonderworks" series. **58m/C VHS.** Scott Bartle, Robert Coleby, Barbara Stephens, Tushka Hose; ***D:*** Mark Callan. *PME, FCT, BTV*

Hedd Wyn 🦴🦴 **1992** True story of talented young poet Ellis Evans (Garmon), writing under the pseudonym Hedd Wyn, who dreams of winning a coveted literary prize. His hopes are put on hold when he's forced to fight in WWI, although he submits his antiwar poem "The Hero" to the competition. Welsh with subtitles. **123m/C VHS.** *GB* Huw Garmon, Catrin Fychan, Ceri Cunnington, Llio Silyn; ***D:*** Paul Turner; ***W:*** Alan Llwyd; ***C:*** Ray Orton; ***M:*** John E.R. Hardy. Nominations: Academy Awards '93: Best Foreign Language Film. *FXL*

Hedda 🦴🦴½ **1975** A dramatization of the Henrik Ibsen play, "Hedda Gabler," about a middle-class pregnant woman. The story finds her frustrated with her life and manipulating those around her with tragic results. **102m/C VHS, Beta.** *GB* Glenda Jackson, Peter Eyre, Timothy West, Jennie Linden, Patrick Stewart; ***D:*** Trevor Nunn. Nominations: Academy Awards '75: Best Actress (Jackson). *MED*

Hedda Hopper's Hollywood **1942** Newsreel version of the gossip-hound's column, featuring scoops on Ball, Cooper, Minelli and many more. **58m/B VHS.** Hedda Hopper, Gary Cooper, Lucille Ball, Gloria Swanson, Liza Minnelli. *REP*

Heidi 🦴🦴½ **1937** Johanna Spyri's classic tale puts Shirley Temple in the hands of a mean governess and the loving arms of her Swiss grandfather. Also available colorized. Remade in 1967. Also available with "Poor Little Rich Girl" on Laser Disc. **88m/B VHS, Beta.** Shirley Temple, Jean Hersholt, Helen Westley, Arthur Treacher; ***D:*** Allan Dwan; ***C:*** Arthur C. Miller. *FXV, HMV, MLT*

Heidi 🦴🦴½ **1952** The Swiss do their own version of the children's classic by Johanna Spyri. A precocious little girl enjoys life in the Swiss Alps with her grandfather, until her stern aunt takes her away to live in the village in the valley. **98m/B VHS.** *SI* Elsbeth Sigmund, Heinrich Gretler, Thomas Klameth, Elsie Attenoff; ***D:*** Luigi Comencini. *CNG, MRV, KAR*

Heidi 🦴🦴🦴 **1965** The classic story from Johanna Spyri's novel is filmed beautifully in the Swiss Alps in Eastmancolor. Heidi is kidnapped by her mean aunt and forced to work as a slave for a rich family. Her kindly old grandfather comes to her rescue. Family entertainment for all, dubbed in English. **95m/C VHS.** *AT GE* Eva Maria Singhammer, Gustav Knuth, Lotte Ledl; ***D:*** Werner Jacobs. *NO*

Heidi 🦴🦴 **1967** The second American adaptation of the classic Johanna Spyri novel tells the story of an orphaned girl who goes to the Swiss Alps to live with her grandfather. Made for television. **100m/C VHS, Beta.** Maximilian Schell, Jennifer Edwards, Michael Redgrave, Jean Simmons; ***D:*** Delbert Mann; ***M:*** John Williams. *LIV, VES, GLV*

Heidi 🦴🦴🦴 **1993 (G)** Yet another version of the children's classic, from German writer Johanna Spyri's 1881 novel. Thornton is charming as the orphan shuttled from relative to relative until she happily ends up with her crotchety grandfather (Robards) in his mountain cabin. Then her cousin comes along and whisks her off to the city to be a companion to the invalid Klara (Randall). Seymour is the snobbish, scowling governess. This "Heidi" is spunky enough to keep the sugar level tolerable. Filmed on location in Austria. Made for television. **167m/C VHS, LV.** Noley Thornton, Jason Robards Jr., Jane Seymour, Lexi Randall, Sian Phillips, Patricia Neal, Benjamin Brazier, Michael Simkins, Andrew Bicknell, Jane Hazlegrove; ***D:*** Michael Rhodes; ***W:*** Jeanne Rosenberg; ***M:*** Lee Holdridge. *DIS*

The Heidi Chronicles 🦴🦴½ **1995** Some 25 years of boomer angst and friendship are covered in this cable adaptation of Wasserstein's 1988 Pulitzer Prize-winning play. Heidi Holland (Curtis) goes from prep school to Vassar to an art history career while searching for self-fulfillment, feminist ideals, and some romance along the way. The romance is on-and-off, thanks to caddish journalist Scoop (Friedman), but Heidi can always depend on soul mate, gay pediatrician Peter (Hulce), and Susan (Cattrall), her follow-the-fads confidante. Heidi's sometimes too morose for her own good but you won't mind spending a couple of hours in her company. **94m/C VHS.** Jamie Lee Curtis, Tom Hulce, Kim Cattrall, Peter Friedman, Eve Gordon, Shari Belafonte, Sharon Lawrence, Julie White, Debra Eisenstadt, Roma Maffia; ***D:*** Paul Bogart; ***W:*** Wendy Wasserstein; ***C:*** Isidore Mankofsky; ***M:*** David Shire. *TTC*

The Heiress 🦴🦴🦴½ **1949** Based on the Henry James novel "Washington Square," about a wealthy plain Jane, her tyrannical father, and the handsome fortune-seeking scoundrel who seeks to marry her. **115m/B VHS, Beta, LV.** Olivia de Havilland, Montgomery Clift, Ralph Richardson, Miriam Hopkins; ***D:*** William Wyler; ***M:*** Aaron Copland. Academy Awards '49: Best Actress (de Havilland), Best Art Direction/Set Decoration (B & W), Best Costume Design (B & W), Best Original Score; Golden Globe Awards '50: Best Actress—Drama (de Havilland); National Board of Review Awards '49: 10 Best Films of the Year, Best Actor (Richardson); Nominations: Academy Awards '49: Best Black and White Cinematography, Best Director (Wyler), Best Picture, Best Supporting Actor (Richardson). *MCA, MLB, BTV*

The Heist 🦴🦴 **1988 (R)** An explosive crime thriller... **93m/C VHS.** Lee Van Cleef, Karen Black, Edward Albert, Lionel Stander, Robert Alda. *NO*

The Heist 🦴🦴 **1989** A made-for-cable-television film about an ex-con who, upon regaining his freedom, sets out to rip off the crook who framed him. Entertaining enough story with a first-rate cast. **97m/C VHS, Beta.** Pierce Brosnan, Tom Skerritt, Wendy Hughes; ***D:*** Stuart Orme. *HBO, HHE*

Helas Pour Moi 🦴🦴 *Oh Woe is Me* **1994** Perplexing, contemplative film on faith and love—and maybe a miracle. Told in flashback, publisher Alexander Klimt (Verley) travels to a Swiss lakeside town where it's rumored that the beautiful Rachel Donnadieu (Masliah) has been "visited" by God, who wishes to experience the pleasures of love, in the form of her own husband, simple fisherman Simon (Depardieu). Story is derived from the Greek myth concerning Zeus, who seduced Alcmene in the shape of her husband Amphitryon. French with subtitles. **84m/C VHS.** *FR SI* Gerard Depardieu, Laurence Masliah, Bernard Verley; ***D:*** Jean-Luc Godard; ***W:*** Jean-Luc Godard; ***C:*** Caroline Champtier. *FCT*

Held for Murder 🦴 *Her Mad Night* **1932** When a vacationing daughter is accused of murder, her mom lovingly takes the blame. Will the daughter come back to clear her mom, or will she let her fry in the electric chair? **67m/B VHS, Beta.** Irene Rich, Conway Tearle, Mary Carlisle, Kenneth Thomson, William B. Davidson; ***D:*** E. Mason Hopper. *SNC*

Held Hostage 🦴🦴 **1991** The true story of Jerry Levin, a reporter kidnapped by terrorists while on assignment in Beirut, and his wife, Sis, who struggled with the State Department for his release. Made for television. **95m/C VHS.** Marlo Thomas, David Dukes, G.W. Bailey, Ed Winter, Robert Harper, William Schallert; ***D:*** Roger Young. *SDE*

Helen of Troy 🦴½ **1956** Mythological fantasy finds Helen (Podesta), the beautiful daughter of Zeus, falling in love with Trojan prince Paris (Sernas)—an event that leads to the siege of Troy. Ignores script for lavish effects. Video includes behind-the-scenes footage. **135m/C VHS, LV.** Rossana Podesta, Jacques Sernas, Cedric Hardwicke, Stanley Baker, Niall MacGinnis, Nora Swinburne, Robert Douglas, Torin Thatcher, Harry Andrews, Janette Scott, Ronald Lewis, Brigitte Bardot; ***D:*** Robert Wise; ***W:*** John Twist, N. Richard Nash; ***C:*** Harry Stradling; ***M:*** Max Steiner. *WAR, MOV*

Hell Comes to Frogtown 🦴 **1988 (R)** In a post-nuclear holocaust land run by giant frogs, a renegade who is one of the few non-sterile men left on earth must rescue some fertile women and impregnate them. Sci-fi spoof is extremely low-budget, but fun. Stars "Rowdy" Roddy Piper of wrestling fame. **88m/C VHS, Beta, LV.** Roddy Piper, Sandahl Bergman, Rory Calhoun, Donald G. Jackson; ***D:*** Robert J. Kizer. *VTR, NWV*

Hell Commandos 🦴½ **1969** Soldiers in WWII struggle to prevent the Nazis from releasing a deadly bacteria that will kill millions. Dubbed. **92m/C VHS, Beta.** *IT* Guy Madison, Stan Cooper; ***D:*** J.L. Merino. *NO*

Hell Fire Austin 🦴½ **1932** Maynard finds himself mixed up with outlaws in the Old West. **60m/B VHS, Beta.** Ken Maynard, Nat Pendleton, Jack Perrin; ***D:*** Forrest Sheldon. *NOS, VCN, DVT*

Hell Harbor 🦴🦴 **1930** Caribbean love, murder and greed combine to make this early talkie. Exterior shots were filmed on the west coast of Florida and the beauty of the Tampa area in the 1930s is definitely something to see. **65m/B VHS, Beta.** Lupe Velez, Gibson Gowland, Jean Hersholt, John Holland; ***D:*** Henry King. *GVV*

Hell High 🦴 **1986 (R)** Four high schoolers plan a night of torture and humiliation for an annoying teacher, only to find she has some deadly secrets of her own. Dumber than it sounds. **84m/C VHS, Beta.** Christopher Stryker, Christopher Cousins, Millie Prezioso, Jason Brill; ***D:*** Douglas Grossman. *PSM*

Hell Hounds of Alaska 🦴 **1973 (G)** The Yukon, Yugoslav-style. European co-production goes back to the Gold Rush days for an adventure about a frontiersman tracking down a stolen shipment of the precious ore while trying to save the life of an injured boy. **90m/C VHS, Beta.** Doug McClure, Harald Leipnitz, Angelica Ott; ***D:*** Harald Reinl. *NO*

Hell Hunters 🦴 **1987** Nazi-hunters foil the plot of an old German doctor to poison the population of L.A. Meanwhile, a daughter avenges the death of her mother by blowing up the doctor's jungle compound. **98m/C VHS, Beta.** Stewart Granger, Maud Adams, George Lazenby, Candice Daly, Romulo Arantes, William Berger. *NO*

Hell in the Pacific 🦴🦴🦴 **1969 (PG)** A marvelously photographed (by Conrad Hall) psycho/macho allegory, about an American and a Japanese soldier stranded together on a tiny island and the mini-war they fight all by themselves. Overly obvious anti-war statement done with style. **101m/C VHS, Beta, LV.** Lee Marvin, Toshiro Mifune; ***D:*** John Boorman; ***C:*** Conrad Hall; ***M:*** Lalo Schifrin. *FOX*

Hell is for Heroes 🦴🦴🦴½ **1962** McQueen stars as the bitter leader of a small infantry squad outmanned by the Germans in this tight WWII drama. A strong cast and riveting climax make this a must for action fans. **90m/B VHS, Beta, LV.** Steve McQueen, Bobby Darin, Fess Parker, Harry Guardino, James Coburn, Mike Kellin, Nick Adams, Bob Newhart; ***D:*** Donald Siegel; ***W:*** Robert Pirosh, Richard Carr. *PAR*

Hell Night *Woof!* **1981 (R)** Several young people must spend the night in a mysterious mansion as part of their initiation into Alpha Sigma Rho fraternity in this extremely dull low-budget horror flick. **100m/C VHS, Beta.** Linda Blair, Vincent Van Patten, Kevin Brophy, Peter Barton, Jenny Neumann; ***D:*** Tom De Simone; ***W:*** Randy Feldman. *MED*

Hell on Frisco Bay 🦴🦴½ **1955** An ex-waterfront cop, falsely imprisoned for manslaughter, sets out to clear his name. His quest finds him taking on the Mob, in this thirties-style gangster film. Good performances all around, especially Robinson, who steals every scene he's in. **93m/C VHS, Beta.** Alan Ladd, Edward G. Robinson, Joanne Dru, Fay Wray, William Demarest, Jayne Mansfield; ***D:*** Frank Tuttle; ***M:*** Max Steiner. *NO*

Hell on the Battleground 🦴½ **1988 (R)** Group of inexperienced recruits are led into combat by two battle-hardened veterans. Their only hope for survival is a counterattack by U.S. tanks. **91m/C VHS, Beta.** William Smith, Ted Prior, Fritz Matthews; ***D:*** David A. Prior; ***W:*** David A. Prior. *AIP*

Hell on Wheels 🦴🦴 **1967** Two successful brothers in the racing industry are torn apart by the same girl. Brotherly love diminishes into a hatred so deep that murder becomes the sole purpose of both. **96m/C VHS, Beta.** Marty Robbins, Jennifer Ashley, John Ashley, Gigi Perreau, Robert Dornan, Connie Smith, Frank Gerstle; ***D:*** Will Zens. *ACA*

Hell Raiders 🦴½ **1968** A force invades a supposedly defenseless Pacific island, and finds itself fiercely attacked. **90m/C VHS, Beta.** John Agar, Richard Webb, Joan Huntington; ***D:*** Larry Buchanan. *JEF*

Hell River 🦴🦴 **1975 (PG)** In 1941 Yugoslavia, Yugoslav partisans and Nazis battle it out at a place called Hell River. **100m/C VHS, Beta.** Rod Taylor, Adam West; ***D:*** Stole Jankovic. *VCD*

Hell-Ship Morgan 🦴🦴½ **1936** Bancroft is a womanizing tuna boat captain who falls for and marries Sothern. When they set up married life on the boat, she starts eyeing first mate Jory. And Bancroft finds out. **65m/B VHS.** George Bancroft, Ann Sothern, Victor Jory, George Regas, Howard Hickman, Ralph Byrd; ***D:*** David Ross Lederman. *GPV*

Hell Ship Mutiny 🦴½ **1957** Man comes to the aid of a lovely island princess, whose people have been forced to hand over their pearls to a pair of ruthless smugglers. Excellent cast in an unfortunately tepid production. **66m/B VHS, Beta.** Jon Hall, John Carradine, Peter Lorre, Roberta Haynes, Mike Mazurki, Stanley Adams; ***D:*** Lee Sholem, Elmo Williams. *SNC, HEG*

Hell Squad 🦴½ **1958** Lost in North Africa during WWII, five American GIs wander through the desert. They find numerous pitfalls and unexpected help. Overall, dismal and disappointing. **64m/B VHS.** Wally Campo, Brandon Carroll; ***D:*** Burt Topper. *NOS*

Hell Squad 🦴 **1985 (R)** Unable to release his son from the Middle Eastern terrorists who kidnapped him, a U.S. ambassador turns to the services of nine Las Vegas showgirls. These gals moonlight as vicious commandos in this low-budget action film with skin. **88m/C VHS, Beta.** Bainbridge Scott, Glen Hartford, Tina Lederman; ***D:*** Kenneth Hartford; ***W:*** Kenneth Hartford; ***M:*** Charles P. Barnett. *MGM, GHV*

Hell to Eternity 🦴🦴½ **1960** The true story of how WWII hero Guy Gabaldon persuaded 2,000 Japanese soldiers to surrender. Features several spectacular scenes. **132m/B VHS, Beta.** Jeffrey Hunter, Sessue Hayakawa, David Janssen, Vic Damone, Patricia Owens; ***D:*** Phil Karlson. *FOX*

Hell Up in Harlem *Woof!* **1973 (R)** A black crime lord recuperates from an assassination attempt and tries to regain his power. Poor sequel to the decent film "Black Caesar." **98m/C VHS, Beta.** Fred Williamson, Julius W. Harris, Margaret Avery, Gerald Gordon, Gloria Hendry; ***D:*** Larry Cohen; ***W:*** Larry Cohen. *ORI*

Hellbenders 🦴½ *Il Crudeli; Los Despiadados* **1967 (PG)** A confederate veteran robs a Union train and must fight through acres of Civil War adversity. Dubbed. Poorly directed and acted. **92m/C VHS, Beta.** *IT SP* Joseph Cotten, Norman Bengell, Julian Mateos; ***D:*** Sergio Corbucci; ***M:*** Ennio Morricone. *COL, SUE*

Hellbent **1990** A crazed musician and a revenge-obsessed housewife embark on an unusual adventure that challenges their very sanity. **90m/C VHS, Beta.** Phil Ward, Lynn Levand, Cheryl Slean, David Marciano; ***D:*** Richard Casey; ***W:*** Richard Casey. *NO*

Hellbound 🦴🦴½ **1994 (R)** Prosatanos (Neame), a powerful 12th-century wizard, is imprisoned and the source of his power (a scepter) is supposedly destroyed. Fast-forward several hundred years when Prosatanos manages to free himself and seek out the pieces of his scepter. Which happens to lead him to Chicago and a couple of unsuspecting cops (Norris, Levels). **95m/C VHS.** Chuck Norris, Christopher Neame, Calvin Levels, Sheree J. Wilson; ***D:*** Aaron Norris. *WAR*

Hellbound: Hellraiser 2 🦴🦴 *Hellraiser 2* **1988 (R)** In this, the first sequel to Clive Barker's interdimensional nightmare, the traumatized daughter from the first film is pulled into the Cenobites' universe. Gore and weird imagery abound. An uncut, unrated version is also available. **96m/C VHS, Beta, LV.** *GB* Ashley Laurence, Clare Higgins, Kenneth Cranham, Imogen Boorman, William Hope, Oliver Smith, Sean Chapman, Doug Bradley; ***D:*** Tony Randel; ***W:*** Peter Atkins. *VTR, NWV*

Hellcats *Woof!* **1968 (R)** A mob of sleazy, leather-clad female bikers terrorize small Midwestern towns in this violent girl-gang thriller. Even biker movie fans might find this one unworthy. **90m/C VHS, Beta.** Ross Hagen, Dee Duffy, Sharyn Kinzie, Sonny West, Bob Slatzer; ***D:*** Bob Slatzer. *ACA*

Hellcats of the Navy 🦴½ **1957** Soggy true saga of the WWII mission to sever the vital link between mainland Asia and Japan. The only film that Ronald and Nancy Davis Reagan starred in together and the beginning of their grand romance. **82m/B VHS, Beta.** Ronald Reagan, Nancy Davis, Arthur Franz, Robert Arthur; ***D:*** Nathan (Hertz) Juran. *GKK*

Helldorado 🦴🦴 *Heldorado* **1946** A lively western starring the singing cowboy, Roy Rogers. **54m/B VHS, Beta.** Roy Rogers, George "Gabby" Hayes, Dale Evans, Paul Harvey; ***D:*** William Witney. *NOS, VCN, CAB*

Heller in Pink Tights 🦴🦴 **1960** The Louis L'Amour story follows the adventures of a colorful theatrical troupe that visits the 1880s West. Performing amid Indians, bill collectors, and thieves, they are often just one step ahead of the law themselves in this offbeat western. **100m/C VHS, Beta.** Sophia Loren, Anthony Quinn, Margaret O'Brien, Steve Forrest, Edmund Lowe, Ramon Novarro; ***D:*** George Cukor; ***W:*** Walter Bernstein. *BAR, PAR, FCT*

Hellfighters 🦴🦴 **1968 (G)** Texas oil well fire fighters experience trouble between themselves and the women they love. **121m/C VHS, Beta, LV.** John Wayne, Katharine Ross, Jim Hutton, Vera Miles, Bruce Cabot, Jay C. Flippen; ***D:*** Andrew V. McLaglen; ***C:*** William Clothier. *MCA*

Hellfire 🦴🦴 **1948** A gambler promises to build a church and follow the precepts of the Bible after a minister sacrifices his life for him. **90m/B VHS.** William Elliott, Marie Windsor, Forrest Tucker, Jim Davis; ***D:*** R.G. Springsteen. *REP*

The Hellfire Club 🦴🦴 **1961** In 18th century Britain, a young man reaches adulthood and attempts to claim the estate of his father. No ordinary dad, his led the infamous Hellfire Club, an organization specializing in debauchery and depravity. His cousin challenges his claim and kidnaps his fiancee. Historical hokum, complete with swordplay. **88m/C VHS, Beta.** *GB* Keith Michell, Kai Fischer, Adrienne Corri, Peter Arne, David Lodge, Bill Owen, Peter Cushing, Francis Matthews, Desmond Walter Ellis; ***D:*** Robert S. Baker, Monty Berman; ***W:*** Jimmy Sangster. *SNC*

Hellgate *Woof!* **1989 (R)** A woman hitchhiking turns out to be one of the living dead. Her benefactor lives to regret picking her up. **96m/C VHS, LV.** Abigail Wolcott, Ron Palillo; ***D:*** William A. Levey. *VMK*

Hellhole 🦴 **1985 (R)** A young woman who witnesses her mother's murder is sent to a sanitarium where the doctors are perfecting chemical lobotomies. Extremely weak script and poor acting make this a suspenseless thriller. **93m/C VHS, Beta, LV.** Judy Landers, Ray Sharkey, Mary Woronov, Marjoe Gortner, Edy Williams, Terry Moore, Dyanne Thorne; ***D:*** Pierre De Moro. *COL*

Hellmaster 🦴 **1992** Your basic sicko mad scientist experiments on some unsuspecting college students by injecting them with an addictive drug. The drug also causes some horrifying mutations and makes its victims superhuman (but also super-ugly). Lots of gore. Creative special effects and make-up will appeal to fans of horror. **92m/C VHS.** John Saxon, David Emge, Amy Raasch; ***D:*** Douglas Schulze; ***W:*** Douglas Schulze. *AIP*

Hello Again 🦴🦴 **1987 (PG)** The wife of a successful plastic surgeon chokes to death on a piece of chicken. A year later she returns to life, with comical consequences, but soon discovers that life won't be the same. **96m/C VHS, Beta, LV.** Shelley Long, Corbin Bernsen, Judith Ivey, Gabriel Byrne, Sela Ward, Austin Pendleton, Carrie Nye, Robert Lewis, Madeleine Potter; ***D:*** Frank Perry; ***M:*** William Goldstein. *TOU*

Hello, Dolly! 🦴🦴 **1969 (G)** Widow Dolly Levi, while matchmaking for her friends, finds a match for herself. Based on the hugely successful Broadway musical adapted from Thornton Wilder's play "Matchmaker." Lightweight story needs better actors with stronger characterizations. Original Broadway score helps. ♫Hello Dolly; Just Leave Everything to Me; Love is Only Love; Dancing; Walter's Gavotte; It Only Takes a Moment; Ribbons Down My Back; Elegance; It Takes a Woman. **146m/C VHS, Beta, LV.** Barbra Streisand, Walter Matthau, Michael Crawford, Louis Armstrong, E.J. Peaker, Marianne McAndrew, Tommy Tune; ***D:*** Gene Kelly; ***W:*** Ernest Lehman; ***C:*** Harry Stradling; ***M:*** Jerry Herman. Academy Awards '69: Best Art Direction/Set Decoration, Best Sound, Best Score; Nominations: Academy Awards '69: Best Cinematography, Best Costume Design, Best Film Editing, Best Picture. *FOX, FCT*

Hello, Frisco, Hello 🦴🦴½ **1943** San Francisco's wild Barbary Coast is the setting for this romantic musical. Smoothie Payne opens up a saloon that features Faye, who's in love with him, as the star singing attraction. Unfortunately, Payne is involved with a society snob and Faye heads off to European success. When she returns, it's to a sadder and wiser man. ♫Hello, Frisco, Hello; You'll Never Know; San Francisco; Ragtime Cowboy Joe; Sweet Cider Time; Has Anybody Here Seen Kelly; King Chanticleer; When You Wore a Tulip; Strike Up the Band, Here Comes a Sailor. **98m/C VHS.** Alice Faye, John Payne, Jack Oakie, Lynn Bari, Laird Cregar, June Havoc, Ward Bond, Aubrey Mather, John Archer; **D:** H. Bruce Humberstone; **W:** Robert Ellis, Helen Logan. Academy Awards '43: Best Song ("You'll Never Know"); Nominations: Academy Awards '43: Best Color Cinematography. *FXV*

Hello Mary Lou: Prom Night 2 ♪½ *The Haunting of Hamilton High; Prom Night 2* **1987 (R)** A sequel to the successful slasher flick, wherein a dead-for-30-years prom queen relegates the current queen to purgatory and comes back to life in order to avenge herself. Wild special effects. **97m/C VHS, Beta, LV.** Michael Ironside, Wendy Lyon, Justin Louis, Lisa Schrage, Richard Monette; **D:** Bruce Pittman; **W:** Ron Oliver. *NO*

Hello Trouble **1932** A Texas Ranger accidentally kills his friend, who was a former Ranger turned bandit, causing him to hang up his guns. **63m/C VHS.** Buck Jones, Lena Basquette, Wallace MacDonald, "Spec" O'Donnell, Ward Bond, Frank Rice, Ruth Warren; **D:** Lambert Hillyer. *GPV*

Hellraiser ♪♪½ **1987 (R)** A graphic, horror fantasy about a woman who is manipulated by the monstrous spirit of her husband's dead brother. In order for the man who was also her lover to be brought back to life, she must lure and kill human prey for his sustenance. Grisly and inventive scenes keep the action fast-paced; not for the faint-hearted. **94m/C Beta, LV.** *GB* Andrew (Andy) Robinson, Clare Higgins, Ashley Laurence, Sean Chapman, Oliver Smith, Robert Hines; **D:** Clive Barker; **W:** Clive Barker; **M:** Christopher Young. *VTR, NWV*

Hellraiser 3: Hell on Earth ♪♪ **1992 (R)** Pinhead is back in this film based on characters created by horrormeister Clive Barker. A strange black box holds the key to sending Pinhead back to Hell and is sought by the heroine, a TV newswoman (Farrell). But Pinhead's human henchman, a nasty nightclub owner, isn't going to make things easy. Imaginative special effects and Bradley's commanding presence as Pinhead aid this shocker, which becomes unfortunately mired in excessive gore. An unrated version at 97 minutes is also available. **91m/C VHS, LV.** Doug Bradley, Terry Farrell, Kevin Bernhardt, Paula Marshall, Ken Carpenter, Peter Boynton, Ashley Laurence; **D:** Anthony Hickox; **W:** Peter Atkins. *PAR*

Hellraiser 4: Bloodline ♪ **1995 (R)** You can't keep a bad Pinhead in Hell, as this unfortunate sequel demonstrates. Bradley reprises his role as the big bad S&M pincushion in the latest and supposedly last installment of Clive Barker's blood drenched series. Tracing the origin of the infernal Rubik's Cube that releases Pinhead, the plot jumps between 18th century France, present day New York and a 22nd century space station. Along the way, the Pointy One gets to flay, skewer, and impale to his evil heart's content. Special f/x guru Kevin Yeagher was so embarrassed by this outing that he took his director's credit off of the picture. Bad acting, bad plot, bad complexion. **101m/C VHS.** Bruce Ramsey, Valentina Vargas, Doug Bradley, Kim Myers, Christina Harnos, Charlotte Chatton, Paul Perri, Mickey Cotrell; **D:** Alan Smithee; **W:** Peter Atkins; **C:** Gerry Lively; **M:** Daniel Licht. *NYR*

Hellriders *Woof!* **1984 (R)** A motorcycle gang rides into a small town and subjects its residents to a reign of terror. **90m/C VHS, Beta.** Adam West, Tina Louise. *TWE*

Hell's Angels ♪♪♪ **1930** Classic WWI aviation movie is sappy and a bit lumbering, but still an extravagant spectacle with awesome air scenes. Studio owner Hughes fired directors Howard Hawks and Luther Reed, spent an unprecedented $3.8 million, and was ultimately credited as director (although Whale also spent some time in the director's chair). Three years in the making, the venture cost three pilots their lives and lost a bundle. Harlow replaced Swedish Greta Nissen when sound was added and was catapulted into blond bombshelldom as a two-timing dame. And the tinted and two-color scenes—restored in 1989—came well before Ted Turner ever wielded a crayola. **135m/B VHS.** Jean Harlow, Ben Lyon, James Hall, John Darrow, Lucien Prival; **D:** Howard Hughes; **W:** Harry Behn, Howard Estabrook, Joseph Moncure March. Nominations: Academy Awards '30: Best Cinematography. *MCA, MRV*

Hell's Angels Forever **1983 (R)** A revealing ride into the world of honor, violence, and undying passion for motorcycles on the road. Documentary was filmed with cooperation of the Angels. Features appearances by Willie Nelson, Jerry Garcia, Bo Diddley, Kevin Keating and Johnny Paycheck. **93m/C VHS, Beta.** Willie Nelson, Jerry Garcia, Johnny Paycheck, Bo Diddley; **D:** Richard Chase. *MED*

Hell's Angels on Wheels ♪♪½ **1967** Low-budget, two-wheeled Nicholson vehicle that casts him as a gas station attendant who joins up with the Angels for a cross country trip. Laszlo Kovacs is responsible for the photography. One of the better 1960s biker films. **95m/C VHS, Beta.** Jack Nicholson, Adam Roarke, Sabrina Scharf, Jana Taylor, John Garwood; **D:** Richard Rush. *VMK*

Hell's Angels '69 ♪♪ **1969 (PG)** Figuring on robbing Caesar's Palace for the thrill, two wealthy brothers plot a deadly game by infiltrating the ranks of the Hell's Angels. Upon figuring out that they've been duped, the Angels seek revenge. Average biker epic filmed in Nevada features Hell's Angels Oakland chapter. **97m/C VHS, Beta.** Tom Stern, Jeremy Slate, Conny Van Dyke; **D:** Lee Madden; **W:** Tom Stern, Jeremy Slate. *MED*

Hell's Belles ♪½ *Girl in the Leather Suit* **1969** Biker has his ride stolen by a rival, who leaves a chick as payment. The two team up to get revenge, chasing the gang across the Arizona desert and picking them off one by one. **95m/C VHS.** Jeremy Slate, Adam Roarke, Jocelyn Lane, Angelique Pettyjohn, Michael Walker, William Lucking; **D:** Maury Dexter; **W:** James Gordon White, Robert McMullen; **M:** Les Baxter. *ORI*

Hell's Brigade: The Final Assault *Woof!* **1980 (PG)** Low-budget, poorly acted film in which a small band of American commandos is ordered on the most dangerous and important mission of WWII. **99m/C VHS, Beta.** Jack Palance, John Douglas, Carlos Estrada; **D:** Henry Mankiewirk. *MPI*

Hell's Headquarters ♪ **1932** A startling tale of murder and greed involving a hunt for a fortune in African ivory. **59m/B VHS.** Jack Mulhall, Barbara Weeks, Frank Mayo; **D:** Andrew L. Stone. *SNC, NOS, DVT*

Hell's Hinges ♪½ **1916** The next to last Hart western, typifying his good/bad cowboy character. Perhaps Hart's best film. **65m/B VHS, Beta.** William S. Hart, Clara Williams, Jack Standing, Robert McKim; **D:** William S. Hart. *GPV, VYY, GVV*

Hell's House ♪♪ **1932** After his mother dies, young lad Durkin goes to the city to live with relatives, gets mixed up with moll Davis and her bootlegger boyfriend O'Brien, and is sent to a brutal reform school. Interesting primarily for early appearances by Davis and O'Brien (before he was typecast as the indefatigable good-guy). **80m/B VHS, Beta.** Junior Durkin, Pat O'Brien, Bette Davis, Frank "Junior" Coghlan, Charley Grapewin, Emma Dunn; **D:** Howard Higgin. *NOS, MRV, CNG*

Hell's Wind Staff ♪ **1982** Two boys uncover a plot to sell their townsmen as slaves to other South East Asian countries. **95m/C VHS, Beta.** Hwang Jang Lee, Mang Yuen Man, Mang Hai. *WVE*

The Hellstrom Chronicle ♪♪♪ **1971 (G)** A powerful quasi-documentary about insects, their formidable capacity for survival, and the conjectured battle man will have with them in the future. **90m/C VHS, Beta.** Lawrence Pressman; **D:** Walon Green; **W:** David Seltzer. Academy Awards '71: Best Feature Documentary. *COL, OM*

Helltown ♪½ **1938** A western programmer based on Zane Grey's novel in which Wayne tracks down a cattle rustler. **60m/B VHS, Beta.** John Wayne; **D:** Charles T. Barton. *NOS, DVT, VCN*

Help! ♪♪♪ **1965 (G)** Ringo's ruby ring is the object of a search by an Arab cult who chase the Fab Four all over the globe in order to acquire the bauble. The laserdisc version includes a wealth of Beatles memorabilia, rare footage behind the scenes and at the film's premiere, and extensive publicity material. ♫Help!; You're Gonna Lose That Girl; You've Got To Hide Your Love Away; The Night Before; Another Girl; Ticket To Ride; I Need You. **90m/C VHS, Beta, LV.** John Lennon, Paul McCartney, Ringo Starr, George Harrison, Leo McKern, Eleanor Bron; **D:** Richard Lester; **W:** Charles Wood, Marc Behm; **C:** David Watkin. *MPI, MVD, CRC*

Help Wanted Female ♪ **1968** Jo Jo, a prostitute with kung fu skills who likes to rob traveling salesmen, is in a quandary over her lesbian roommate's acid dropping friends, including Mr. Gregory, who has a penchant for murder. After recounting a previous trip in which he murdered an acquaintance, he succeeds in alienating his current companions, who must fight for their life to escape him. **71m/B VHS.** Sebastian Gregory, Inga Olsen; **D:** Harold Perkins. *SMW, TPV*

Help Wanted: Male ♪½ **1982** When a magazine publisher discovers that her fiance cannot have children, she looks for someone else who can do the job right. Made for television. **97m/C VHS, Beta.** Suzanne Pleshette, Gil Gerard, Bert Convy, Dana Elcar, Harold Gould, Caren Kaye; **D:** William Wiard. *WOV*

Helter Skelter ♪♪½ **1976** The harrowing story of the murder of actress Sharon Tate and four others at the hands of Charles Manson and his psychotic "family." Based on the book by prosecutor Vincent Bugliosi, adapted by J.P. Miller. Features an outstanding performance by Railsback as Manson. A TV mini-series. **194m/C VHS, Beta.** Steve Railsback, Nancy Wolfe, George DiCenzo, Marilyn Burns; **D:** Tom Gries; **M:** Billy Goldenberg. *FOX*

The Henderson Monster ♪♪½ **1980** Experiments of a genetic scientist are questioned by a community and its mayor. A potentially controversial television drama turns into typical romantic fluff. **105m/C VHS, Beta.** Jason Miller, Christine Lahti, Stephen Collins, David Spielberg, Nehemiah Persoff, Larry Gates; **D:** Waris Hussein. *LIV*

Hennessy ♪♪½ **1975 (PG)** An IRA man plots revenge on the Royal family and Parliament after his family is violently killed. Tense political drama, but slightly far-fetched. **103m/C VHS.** *GB* Rod Steiger, Lee Remick, Richard Johnson, Trevor Howard, Peter Egan, Eric Porter; **D:** Don Sharp; **W:** John Gay. *NO*

Henry IV ♪♪½ **1985** The adaptation of the Luigi Pirandello farce about a modern-day recluse who shields himself from the horrors of the real world by pretending to be mad and acting out the fantasy of being the medieval German emperor Henry IV. In Italian with English subtitles. **94m/C VHS, Beta.** *IT* Marcello Mastroianni, Claudia Cardinale, Leopoldo Trieste, Paolo Bonacelli, Luciano Bartoli, Latou Chardons; **D:** Marco Bellochio; **W:** Tonino Guerra, Marco Bellochio, Astor Piazzolla. *MED, APD, INJ*

Henry V ♪♪♪♪ **1944** Classic, epic adaptation of the Shakespeare play, and Olivier's first and most successful directorial effort, dealing with the medieval British monarch that defeated the French at Agincourt. Distinguished by Olivier's brilliant formal experiment of beginning the drama as a 16th Century performance of the play in the Globe Theatre, and having the stage eventually transform into realistic historical settings of storybook color. Filmed at the height of WWII suffering in Britain (and meant as a parallel to the British fighting the Nazis), the film was not released in the U.S. until 1946. **136m/C VHS, Beta.** *GB* Laurence Olivier, Robert Newton, Leslie Banks, Esmond Knight, Renee Asherson, Leo Genn, George Robey, Ernest Thesiger, Felix Aylmer, Ralph Truman; **D:** Laurence Olivier; **W:** Laurence Olivier, Alan Dent; **C:** Robert Krasker; **M:** William Walton. National Board of Review Awards '46: 10 Best Films of the Year, Best Actor (Olivier); Nominations: Academy Awards '46: Best Actor (Olivier), Best Interior Decoration, Best Picture, Best Original Score. *PAR, HMV*

Henry V ♪♪♪♪ **1989** Stirring, expansive retelling of Shakespeare's drama about the warrior-king of England. Branagh stars as Henry, leading his troops and uniting his kingdom against France. Very impressive production rivals Olivier's 1945 rendering but differs by stressing the high cost of war—showing the ego-mania, doubts, and subterfuge that underlie conflicts. Marvelous film-directorial debut for Branagh (who also adapted the screenplay). Wonderful supporting cast includes some of Britain's finest actors. **138m/C VHS, LV.** *GB* Kenneth Branagh, Derek Jacobi, Brian Blessed, Alec McCowen, Ian Holm, Richard Briers, Robert Stephens, Robbie Coltrane, Christian Bale, Judi Dench, Paul Scofield, Michael Maloney, Emma Thompson; ***D:*** Kenneth Branagh; ***W:*** Kenneth Branagh; ***M:*** Patrick Doyle. Academy Awards '89: Best Costume Design; British Academy Awards '89: Best Director (Branagh); National Board of Review Awards '89: Best Director (Branagh); Nominations: Academy Awards '89: Best Actor (Branagh), Best Director (Branagh). *FOX, SIG, TVC*

Henry & June 🦴🦴🦴½ **1990 (NC-17)** Based on the diaries of writer Anais Nin which chronicled her triangular relationship with author Henry Miller and his wife June, a relationship that provided the erotic backdrop to Miller's "Tropic of Capricorn." Set in Paris in the early '30s, the setting moves between the impecunious expatriate's cheap room on the Left bank—filled with artists, circus performers, prostitutes, and gypsies—to the conservative, well-appointed home of Nin and her husband. Captures the heady atmosphere of Miller's gay Paris; no one plays an American better than Ward (who replaced Alec Baldwin). Notable for having prompted the creation of an NC-17 rating because of its adult theme. **136m/C VHS, LV.** Fred Ward, Uma Thurman, Maria De Medeiros, Richard E. Grant, Kevin Spacey; ***D:*** Philip Kaufman; ***W:*** Philip Kaufman; ***C:*** Philippe Rousselot. Nominations: Academy Awards '90: Best Cinematography. *MCA, FCT*

Henry: Portrait of a Serial Killer 🦴🦴🦴🦴 **1990 (X)** Based on the horrific life and times of serial killer Henry Lee Lucas, this film has received wide praise for its straight-forward and uncompromising look into the minds of madmen. The film follows Henry and his roommate Otis as they set out on mindless murder sprees (one of which they videotape). Extremely disturbing and graphic film. Unwary viewers should be aware of the grisly scenes and use their own discretion when viewing this otherwise genuinely moving film. **90m/C VHS, Beta, LV.** Michael Rooker, Tom Towles, Tracy Arnold; ***D:*** John McNaughton; ***W:*** Richard Fire, John McNaughton. *MPI*

Hepburn & Tracy **1984** The finest moments from the legendary film careers of Hepburn and Tracy, as a team and on their own. Some sequences in black and white. A must for fans. **45m/C VHS, Beta.** Katharine Hepburn, Spencer Tracy. *NO*

Her Alibi 🦴🦴 **1988 (PG)** When successful murder-mystery novelist Phil Blackwood runs out of ideas for good books, he seeks inspiration in the criminal courtroom. There he discovers a beautiful Romanian immigrant named Nina who is accused of murder. He goes to see her in jail and offers to provide her with an alibi. Narrated by Blackwood in the tone of one of his thriller novels. Uneven comedy, with appealing cast and arbitrary plot. **95m/C VHS, Beta, LV, 8mm.** Tom Selleck, Paulina Porizkova, William Daniels, James Farentino, Hurd Hatfield, Patrick Wayne, Tess Harper, Joan Copeland; ***D:*** Bruce Beresford; ***W:*** Charlie Peters; ***M:*** Georges Delerue. *WAR*

Her First Romance 🦴🦴½ *The Right Man* **1940** Mixed-up romance with Fellows and Wells as sisters, Linden their cousin, and Ladd her fiance. The sisters fall for Evans and use Ladd in their schemes, causing him to believe Evans is actually after Linden. Eventually, everyone pairs up properly. **77m/B VHS.** Edith Fellows, Jacqueline Wells, Alan Ladd, Judith Linden, Wilbur Evans, Roger Daniel; ***D:*** Edward Dmytryk; ***W:*** Adele Comandini. *FCT*

Her Husband's Affairs 🦴 **1947** Tone is an advertising wonder and Ball is his loving wife who always gets credit for his work. Tone does the advertising for an inventor who is searching for the perfect embalming fluid in this rather lifeless comedy. **83m/B VHS.** Lucille Ball, Franchot Tone, Edward Everett Horton, Gene Lockhart, Larry Parks; ***D:*** Sylvan Simon; ***M:*** George Duning. *GKK*

Her Life as a Man 🦴½ **1983** A female reporter is refused a job as a sportswriter because of her gender. She makes herself up as a man, gets the job, and creates havoc when she has to deal with lustful women on the job. A made-for-television movie. **93m/C VHS, Beta.** Robyn Douglass, Joan Collins, Robert Culp, Marc Singer, Laraine Newman; ***D:*** Robert Ellis Miller. *ORI*

Her Silent Sacrifice 🦴½ **1918** A silent melodrama about a French girl torn between material wealth and true love. **42m/B VHS, Beta.** Alice Brady, Henry Clive. *VYY*

Herbie Goes Bananas 🦴½ **1980 (G)** While Herbie the VW is racing in Rio de Janeiro, he is bothered by the syndicate, a pickpocket, and a raging bull. The fourth and final entry in the Disney "Love Bug" movies, but Herbie later made his way to a television series. **93m/C VHS, Beta.** Cloris Leachman, Charles Martin Smith, Harvey Korman, John Vernon, Alex Rocco, Richard Jaeckel, Fritz Feld; ***D:*** Vincent McEveety. *DIS*

Herbie Goes to Monte Carlo 🦴🦴 **1977 (G)** While participating in a Paris-to-Monte-Carlo race, Herbie the VW takes a detour and falls in love with a Lancia. Third in the Disney "Love Bug" series. **104m/C VHS, Beta.** Dean Jones, Don Knotts, Julie Sommars, Roy Kinnear; ***D:*** Vincent McEveety; ***W:*** Arthur Alsberg. *DIS*

Herbie Rides Again 🦴🦴½ **1974 (G)** In this "Love Bug" sequel, Herbie comes to the aid of an elderly woman who is trying to stop a ruthless tycoon from raising a skyscraper on her property. Humorous Disney fare. Two other sequels followed. **88m/C VHS, Beta, LV.** Helen Hayes, Ken Berry, Stefanie Powers, John McIntire, Keenan Wynn; ***D:*** Robert Stevenson; ***M:*** George Bruns. *DIS*

Hercules 🦴🦴½ *La Tatiche de Ercole* **1958** The one that started it all. Reeves is perfect as the mythical hero Hercules who encounters many dangerous situations while trying to win over his true love. Dubbed in English. Cinematography by Mario Bava. **107m/C VHS, Beta, LV.** *IT* Steve Reeves, Sylva Koscina, Fabrizio Mioni, Gianna Maria Canale, Arturo Dominici; ***D:*** Pietro Francisci. *MRV, IME, VDM*

Hercules 🦴 **1983 (PG)** Lackluster remake of 1957 original finds legendary muscle guy Hercules in the person of Ferrigno's Hulkster fighting against the evil King Minos for his own survival and the love of Cassiopeia, a rival king's daughter. **100m/C VHS, Beta, LV.** *IT* Lou Ferrigno, Sybil Danning, William Berger, Brad Harris, Ingrid Anderson; ***D:*** Lewis (Luigi Cozzi) Coates; ***W:*** Lewis (Luigi Cozzi) Coates; ***M:*** Pino Donaggio. Golden Raspberry Awards '83: Worst Supporting Actress (Danning), Worst New Star (Ferrigno). *MGM, IME*

Hercules 2 🦴 *The Adventures of Hercules* **1985 (PG)** The muscle-bound demi-god returns to do battle with more evil foes amidst the same stunningly cheap special effects. **90m/C VHS.** *IT* Lou Ferrigno, Claudio Cassinelli, Milly Carlucci, Sonia Viviani, William Berger, Carlotta Green; ***D:*** Lewis (Luigi Cozzi) Coates; ***M:*** Pino Donaggio. *MGM*

Hercules Against the Moon Men 🦴 *Maciste la Regina di Samar* **1964** It's no holds barred for the mighty son of Zeus when evil moon men start killing off humans in a desperate bid to revive their dead queen. **88m/C VHS, Beta.** *IT FR* Alan Steel, Jany Clair, Anna Maria Polani; ***D:*** Giacomo Gentilomo. *SNC, MRV*

Hercules and the Captive Women 🦴🦴 *Hercules and the Haunted Women; Hercules and the Conquest of Atlantis; Ercole Alla Conquista di Atlantide* **1963** Hercules' son is kidnapped by the Queen of Atlantis, and the bare-chested warrior goes on an all-out rampage to save the boy. Directed by sometimes-lauded Cottafavi. **93m/C VHS, Beta.** *IT* Reg Park, Fay Spain, Ettore Manni; ***D:*** Vittorio Cottafavi. *RHI, MRV, CCB*

Hercules and the Princess of Troy 🦴🦴½ **1965** Hercules is up to his pecs in trouble as he battles a hungry sea monster in order to save a beautiful maiden. Originally a pilot for a prospective television series, and shot in English, not Italian, with Hercules played by erstwhile Tarzan Scott. Highlights are special effects and color cinematography. **?m/C VHS, Beta.** *IT* Gordon Scott, Diana Hyland, Paul Stevens, Everett Sloane. *SNC, MLB*

Hercules in New York 🦴½ *Hercules: The Movie; Hercules Goes Bananas* **1970 (G)** Motion picture debut of Schwarzenegger (his voice is dubbed) as a Herculean mass of muscle sent by dad Zeus to Manhattan, where he behaves likes a geek out of water and eventually becomes a professional wrestling superstar. 250 pounds of stupid, lighthearted fun. **93m/C VHS, Beta.** Arnold Schwarzenegger, Arnold Stang, Deborah Loomis, James Karen, Ernest Graves; ***D:*** Arthur Seidelman. *MPI*

Hercules in the Haunted World 🦴🦴½ *Ercole al Centro Della Terra* **1964** Long before the days of 24-hour pharmacies, Hercules—played yet again by Reeves-clone Park—must journey to the depths of Hell in order to find a plant that will cure a poisoned princess. Better than most muscle operas, thanks to Bava. **91m/C VHS, Beta.** *IT* Reg Park, Leonora Ruffo, Christopher Lee, George Ardisson; ***D:*** Mario Bava. *CCB, RHI, MRV*

Hercules, Prisoner of Evil 🦴 **1964** Spaghetti myth-opera in which Hercules battles a witch who is turning men into werewolves. Made for Italian television by director Dawson (the nom-de-cinema of Antonio Margheriti). **?m/C VHS.** *IT* Reg Park; ***D:*** Anthony (Antonio Margheriti) Dawson. *SNC*

Hercules Unchained 🦴🦴 *Ercole e la Regina de Lidia* **1959** Sequel to "Hercules" finds superhero Reeves must use all his strength to save the city of Thebes and the woman he loves from the giant Antaeus. **101m/C VHS, Beta, LV.** *IT* Steve Reeves, Sylva Koscina, Silvia Lopel, Primo Carnera; ***D:*** Pietro Francisci. *VDM, SUE, MRV*

Here and Elsewhere *Ici et Ailleurs* **197?** Godard, Gorin, and Mieville contrast the story of a French family with a look at the Palestine revolution as seen through the media of television, books, and pictures. The film was originally titled "Until Victory" and commissioned by the Palestinians to examine life in the Palestinian camps. After the defeat of the Palestinian army in the Six Day War, Godard and his cohorts transformed the film with their French family ("Here") and their impressions of Palestine ("Elsewhere"). In French with English subtitles. **?m/C VHS.** *FR* Anne-Marie Mieville; ***D:*** Jean-Pierre Gorin, Jean-Luc Godard. *FCT*

Here Come the Co-Eds 🦴🦴½ **1945** Bud & Lou are the caretakers of an all-girl college which is about to go bankrupt unless the boys can find a way to pay off the mortgage. And come to the rescue they do, including Bud getting into the wrestling ring with the "Masked Marvel" (Chaney, Jr. as the villain). There's also a classic silent scene with Lou served a bowl of oyster stew containing a live oyster, which promptly grabs his tie, bites his fingers, and squirts in his face. **90m/B VHS.** Bud Abbott, Lou Costello, Lon Chaney Jr., Peggy Ryan, Martha O'Driscoll, June Vincent, Donald Cook, Charles Dingle; ***D:*** Jean Yarbrough; ***W:*** Arthur T. Horman, John Grant. *MCA, FCT*

Here Come the Girls 🦴½ **1953** An unfunny musical-comedy about a chorus boy (Hope) fired for incompetence and then rehired to set a trap when the new singer (Martin) is stalked by a killer. Weak script, weak songs. ♫Girls Are Here To Stay; Never So Beautiful; You Got Class; Desire; When You Love Someone; Ali Baba Be My Baby; Heavenly Days; See the Circus; Peace. **100m/C VHS.** Bob Hope, Tony Martin, Arlene Dahl, Rosemary Clooney, Millard Mitchell, William Demarest, Fred Clark, Robert Strauss; ***D:*** Claude Binyon; ***W:*** Hal Kanter. *PAR*

Here Come the Littles: The Movie 🦴½ **1985** A twelve-year-old boy finds many new adventures when he meets The Littles—tiny folks who reside within the walls of people's houses. Adapted from the books and TV series. **76m/C VHS, Beta.** ***D:*** Bernard Deyries. *WTA, FOX*

Here Come the Marines ☠☠ *Tell It To the Marines* **1952** The Bowery Boys accidentally join the marines and wind up breaking up a gambling ring. **66m/B VHS.** Leo Gorcey, Huntz Hall, Tim Ryan; ***D:*** William Beaudine. *NOS*

Here Come the Waves ☠☠☠ **1944** Easy-going wartime musical finds Der Bingle as a singing idol drafted into the Navy, assigned to direct WAVE shows. The crooner meets identical twins (both played by Hutton) and falls hard. Only problem is he can't tell the gals apart—and one twin can't stand him. Amusing romantic complications mix well with some spoofing of a star's life. ♫Ac-cent-tchu-ate the Positive; I Promise You; Let's Take the Long Way Home; That Old Black Magic; There's a Fellow Waiting in Poughkeepsie; Here Come the Waves; My Mama Thinks I'm a Star; Join the Navy. **99m/B VHS.** Bing Crosby, Betty Hutton, Sonny Tufts, Ann Doran, Noel Neill, Mae Clarke, Gwen Crawford, Catherine Craig; ***D:*** Mark Sandrich; ***W:*** Zion Myers. *MCA*

Here Comes Kelly ☠½ **1943** Controlling his temper and hanging on to his job is more than our hero can handle. **63m/C VHS, Beta.** Eddie Quillan, Joan Woodbury, Maxie "Slapsie" Rosenbloom; ***D:*** William Beaudine. *GPV*

Here Comes Mr. Jordan ☠☠☠☠ **1941** Montgomery is the young prizefighter killed in a plane crash because of a mix-up in heaven. He returns to life in the body of a soon-to-be murdered millionaire. Rains is the indulgent and advising guardian angel. A lovely fantasy/romance remade in 1978 as "Heaven Can Wait." Laserdisc edition includes actress Elizabeth Montgomery talking about her father Robert Montgomery as well as her television show "Bewitched." **94m/B VHS, Beta, LV.** Robert Montgomery, Claude Rains, James Gleason, Evelyn Keyes, Edward Everett Horton, Rita Johnson, John Emery; ***D:*** Alexander Hall; ***W:*** Sidney Buchman, Seton I. Miller; ***M:*** Friedrich Hollander. Academy Awards '41: Best Story & Screenplay; National Board of Review Awards '41: 10 Best Films of the Year. *COL, CRC, FCT*

Here Comes Santa Claus ☠½ **1984** A young boy and girl travel to the North Pole to deliver a very special wish to Santa Claus. **78m/C VHS, Beta.** Karen Cheryl, Armand Meffre; ***D:*** Christian Gion. *NWV, VTR*

Here Comes the Groom ☠☠ **1951** Late, stale Capra-corn, involving a rogue journalist who tries to keep his girlfriend from marrying a millionaire by becoming a charity worker. Includes a number of cameos. ♫In the Cool, Cool, Cool of the Evening; Bonne Nuit, Good Night; Misto Cristofo Columbo; Your Own Little House. **114m/B VHS, Beta, LV.** Bing Crosby, Jane Wyman, Franchot Tone, Alexis Smith, James Barton, Connie Gilchrist, Robert Keith, Anna Maria Alberghetti, Charles Halton; ***Cameos:*** Dorothy Lamour, Phil Harris, Louis Armstrong; ***D:*** Frank Capra. Academy Awards '51: Best Song ("In the Cool, Cool, Cool of the Evening"); Nominations: Academy Awards '51: Best Story. *PAR*

Here We Go Again! ☠☠ **1942** Fibber McGee and Molly are planning a cross-country trip for their 20th anniversary celebration, but complications abound. Based on the popular NBC radio series. **76m/B VHS, Beta.** Marian Jordan, Jim Jordan, Harold Peary, Gale Gordon, Edgar Bergen, Ray Noble; ***D:*** Allan Dwan. *CCB*

The Hereafter ☠ **1987** An old church is suddenly overrun by zombies. **92m/C VHS, Beta.** *NO*

Here's Looking at You, Warner Bros. ☠☠☠ **1993** The 90-year history of Warner Bros. studios is profiled from the silent-era to its current success. Highlights cover the creation of Warners' gangster films, Busby Berkeley musicals, and "Looney Tunes" as well as bloopers and early screen tests by Marlo Brando, Paul Newman, Lana Turner, and Orson Welles. Includes interviews with stars, directors, and producers and numerous film clips. **108m/C VHS, LV.** ***D:*** Robert Guenette; ***W:*** Robert Guenette. *WAR*

Heritage of the Desert ☠½ **1933** One of the earlier westerns made by the rugged Scott. **62m/B VHS, Beta.** Randolph Scott, Sally Blane, Guinn "Big Boy" Williams; ***D:*** Henry Hathaway. *DVT, TIM*

The Hero ☠½ *Bloomfield* **1971 (PG)** A popular soccer player agrees to throw a game for big cash, and then worries about losing the respect of a young boy who idolizes him. Nothing new in this overly sentimental sports drama. **97m/C VHS, Beta.** Richard Harris, Romy Schneider, Kim Burfield, Maurice Kaufman; ***D:*** Richard Harris. *SUE*

Hero ☠☠☠ **1992 (PG-13)** Interesting twist on Cinderella fable and modern media satire has television reporter Davis looking for the man who saved her life, expecting a genuine hero, and accepting without question the one who fits her vision. Critically considered disappointing, but wait—Garcia and Hoffman make a great team, and Davis is fetching as the vulnerable media person. Strong language and dark edges may keep away some of the kids, but otherwise this is a fine fable. **116m/C VHS, LV, 8mm.** Geena Davis, Dustin Hoffman, Andy Garcia, Joan Cusack, Kevin J. O'Connor, Chevy Chase, Maury Chaykin, Stephen Tobolowsky, Christian Clemenson, Tom Arnold, Warren Berlinger, Susie Cusack, James Madio, Richard Riehle, Don Yesso, Darrell Larson; ***D:*** Stephen Frears; ***W:*** David Peoples; ***M:*** George Fenton. *COL*

A Hero Ain't Nothin' But a Sandwich ☠☠½ **1978 (PG)** A young urban black teenager gets involved in drugs and is eventually saved from ruin. Slow-moving, over-directed and talky. However, Scott turns in a fine performance. Based on Alice Childress' novel. **107m/C VHS, Beta.** Cicely Tyson, Paul Winfield, Larry B. Scott, Helen Martin, Glynn Turman, David Groh; ***D:*** Ralph Nelson. *PAR, FCT*

Hero and the Terror ☠½ **1988 (R)** Perennial karate guy Norris plays a sensitive policeman who conquers his fear of a not-so-sensitive maniac who's trying to kill him. Plenty of action and a cheesy subplot to boot. **96m/C VHS, Beta, LV.** Chuck Norris, Brynn Thayer, Steve James, Jack O'Halloran, Ron O'Neal, Billy Drago; ***D:*** William Tannen; ***W:*** Michael Blodgett. *MED, VTR*

Hero at Large ☠☠½ **1980 (PG)** An unemployed actor foils a robbery while dressed in a promotional "Captain Avenger" suit, and instant celebrity follows. Lightweight, yet enjoyable. **98m/C VHS, Beta.** John Ritter, Anne Archer, Bert Convy, Kevin McCarthy, Kevin Bacon; ***D:*** Martin Davidson; ***W:*** A.J. Carothers. *MGM*

Hero Bunker ☠☠ **1971** Hero bunk about a platoon of heroic Greek soldiers who attempt, at the expense of their personal longevity, to defend an important bunker from enemy invasion. **93m/C VHS, Beta.** John Miller, Maria Xenia; ***D:*** George Andrews. *LIV*

Hero of Rome **1963** Rome has many who could be called "hero," but one stands biceps and pecs above the rest. **?m/C VHS, Beta.** *IT* Gordon Scott, Gabriella Pallotti. *SNC*

Hero of the Year ☠☠ **1985** The characters from Falk's "Top Dog" return in this story of a Polish television personality who loses his job and is forced to face unemployment and job-seeking. **115m/C VHS.** *PL* ***D:*** Feliks Falk. *FCT*

Herod the Great ☠ **1960** Biblical epic of the downfall of Herod, the ruler of ancient Judea. Scantily clad women abound. Dubbed. **93m/C VHS.** *IT* Edmund Purdom, Sandra Milo, Alberto Lupo; ***D:*** Arnaldo Genoino. *SNC*

Heroes ☠☠ **1977 (PG)** An institutionalized Vietnam vet (Winkler) escapes, hoping to establish a worm farm which will support all his crazy buddies. On the way to the home of a friend he hopes will help him, he encounters Field. Funny situations don't always mix with serious underlying themes of mental illness and post-war adjustment. **97m/C VHS, Beta.** Henry Winkler, Sally Field, Harrison Ford; ***D:*** Jeremy Paul Kagan; ***W:*** Jim Carabatsos; ***M:*** Jack Nitzsche. *MCA*

Heroes Die Young ☠½ **1960** A cheap independent feature depicting an American command mission with orders to sabotage German oil fields during WWII. **76m/B VHS, Beta.** Krika Peters, Scott Borland, Robert Getz, James Strother. *FOX, FCT*

Heroes for Sale ☠☠☠ **1933** Fascinating melodrama about a WWI veteran who returns home and manages to survive one disaster after another. Barthelmess is great in his performance as an American Everyman who must deal with everything from morphine addiction to finding work during the Depression. Fast-paced, patriotic film is helped by ambitious script and the expert direction of Wellman. **72m/B VHS.** Richard Barthelmess, Loretta Young, Aline MacMahon, Robert Barrat, Grant Mitchell, Douglass Dumbrille, Charley Grapewin, Ward Bond; ***D:*** William A. Wellman; ***W:*** Robert Lord, Wilson Mizner. *MGM*

Heroes in Blue ☠☠ **1939** Two brothers join the police force, but one goes astray and hooks up with gangsters. Plenty of action distracts from the cliched story. **60m/B VHS, Beta.** Dick Purcell, Charles Quigley, Bernadene Hayes, Edward Keane; ***D:*** William Watson. *SNC*

Heroes in Hell ☠½ **1967** Two escaped WWII POWs join the Allied underground in an espionage conspiracy against the Third Reich. **90m/C VHS, Beta.** Klaus Kinski, Ettore Manni. *NO*

The Heroes of Desert Storm ☠☠ **1991** The human spirit of the people who fought in the high-tech Persian Gulf War is captured in this film that also features real war footage from ABC News. **93m/C VHS, Beta.** Daniel Baldwin, Angela Bassett, Marshall Bell, Michael Alan Brooks, William Bumiller, Michael Champion, Maria Diaz; ***D:*** Don Ohlmeyer; ***W:*** Lionel Chetwynd. *PSM*

Heroes of the Alamo ☠½ **1937** Remember the Alamo...but forget this movie. Dull, threadbare dramatization of the battle that was scorned even back in '37. **75m/B VHS, Beta.** Rex Lease, Lane Chandler, Roger Williams, Earle Hodgins, Julian Rivero; ***D:*** Harry Fraser. *GPV*

Heroes of the Hills ☠½ **1938** The Three Mesquiteers back up a plan that would allow trusted prisoners to work for neighboring ranchers. Part of "The Three Mesquiteers" series. **54m/B VHS, Beta.** Bob Livingston, Ray Corrigan, Max Terhune. *MED*

Heroes of the West ☠½ **1932** Early sound action western serial. **70m/B VHS, Beta.** Noah Beery Jr. *VCN, MLB*

Heroes Stand Alone ☠ **1989 (R)** When a U.S. spy plane is downed in Central America, a special force is sent in to rescue the crew. Another "Rambo" rip-off. **84m/C VHS, Beta.** Bradford Dillman, Chad Everett, Wayne Grace, Rick Dean; ***D:*** Mark Griffiths; ***W:*** Thomas McKelvey Cleaver. *MGM*

Heroes Three ☠☠ **1984** When his crewmate is murdered while on leave in in the Far East, a Navy officer enlists the aid of a Chinese detective to track down the killer. **90m/C VHS, Beta.** Rowena Cortes, Mike Kelly, Laurens C. Postma, Lawrence Tan; ***D:*** S.H. Lau. *IMP*

The Heroic Trio ☠☠½ **1993** Three superheroines battle the Lord of the Underground to prevent him from stealing any more human babies. Lots of martial arts and supernatural action. Chinese with subtitles or dubbed. **104m/C VHS, LV.** *HK* Michelle Yeoh, Maggie Cheung, Anita Mui, Anthony Wong; ***D:*** Ching Siu Tung, Johnny To. *TAI*

He's My Girl ☠½ **1987 (PG-13)** When a rock singer wins a trip for two to Hollywood, he convinces his agent to dress up as a woman so they can use the free tickets. **104m/C VHS, Beta.** David Hallyday, T.K. Carter, Misha McK, Jennifer Tilly; ***D:*** Gabrielle Beaumont; ***W:*** Terence H. Winkless, Taylor Ames, Charles F. Bohl. *LIV*

He's Your Dog, Charlie Brown! **1968** An animated Peanuts adventure wherein Charlie Brown decides to send Snoopy back to the Daisy Hill Puppy Farm for obedience lessons. **30m/C VHS, Beta.** *MED, WTA*

Hester Street 🦴🦴🦴½ **1975** Set at the turn of the century, the film tells the story of a young Jewish immigrant who ventures to New York City to be with her husband. As she re-acquaints herself with her husband, she finds that he has abandoned his Old World ideals. The film speaks not only to preserving the heritage of the Jews, but to cherishing all heritages and cultures. Highly regarded upon release, unfortunately forgotten today. **89m/C VHS, Beta.** Carol Kane, Doris Roberts, Steven Keats, Mel Howard; ***D:*** Joan Micklin Silver; ***M:*** William Bolcom. Nominations: Academy Awards '75: Best Actress (Kane). *VES, FRV, INJ*

Hexed 🦴½ **1993 (R)** Walter Mitty lives in the person of bellboy Matthew Welsh, who enjoys masquerading as a debonair bon vivant. He finagles his way into the life of Hexina, a beautiful psychotic model who has checked into the hotel where Matthew works in order to murder her blackmailer. She tries to kill Matthew, apparently getting in a little practice, but he'll still follow her anywhere. Inane, charmless comedy that intends to satirize "Fatal Attraction" and similar films. **93m/C VHS, LV.** Arye Gross, Claudia Christian, Adrienne Shelly, R. Lee Ermey, Norman Fell, Michael E. Knight; ***D:*** Alan Spencer; ***W:*** Alan Spencer. *COL*

Hey, Babu Riba 🦴🦴½ **1988 (R)** A popular Yugoslavian fit of nostalgia about four men convening at the funeral of a young girl they all loved years before, and their happy, Americana-bathed memories therein. In Serbo-Croatian with English subtitles. **109m/C VHS, Beta, LV.** *YU* Gala Videnovic, Nebojsa Bakocevic, Dragan Bjelogrlic, Marko Todorovic, Goran Radakovic, Relja Basic, Milos Zutic; ***D:*** Jovan Acin; ***W:*** Jovan Acin. *ORI, INJ*

Hey Good Lookin' **1982** Ralph Bakshi's irreverent look at growing up in the 1950s bears the trademark qualities that distinguish his other adult animated features, "Fritz the Cat" and "Heavy Traffic." **87m/C VHS, Beta.** ***D:*** Ralph Bakshi; ***W:*** Ralph Bakshi. *WAR, WTA*

Hey There, It's Yogi Bear 🦴🦴 **1964** When Yogi Bear comes out of winter hibernation to search for food, he travels to the Chizzling Brothers Circus. The first feature-length cartoon to come from the H-B Studios. **98m/C VHS, Beta, LV.** ***D:*** William Hanna; ***V:*** Daws Butler, James Darren, Mel Blanc, J. Pat O'Malley, Julie Bennett. *WOV, IME, WTA*

Hi-De-Ho 🦴🦴½ **1935** The great Cab Calloway and his red hot jazz are featured in this film, which has the band caught between rival gangsters. The plot is incidental to the music, anyway. ♫Hi-De-Ho; I Got A Gal Named Nettie; Little Old Lady From Baltimore; A Rainy Sunday. **60m/B VHS, Beta.** Cab Calloway, Ida James; ***D:*** Josh Binney. *MVD, NOS, DVT*

Hi-Di-Hi **1988** A British television comedy about the shenanigans that inevitably follow when a stuffy Cambridge professor becomes the entertainment manager for a holiday camp. **91m/C VHS, Beta.** *GB* Simon Cadell, Ruth Madoc, Paul Shane, Jeffrey Holland, Leslie Dwyer. *FOX*

Hi Diddle Diddle 🦴🦴½ *Diamonds and Crime; Try and Find It* **1943** Topsy-turvy comedy features young lovers who long for conventional happiness. Instead they are cursed with con-artist parents who delight in crossing that law-abiding line. **72m/B VHS, Beta.** Adolphe Menjou, Martha Scott, Dennis O'Keefe, Pola Negri; ***D:*** Andrew L. Stone. Nominations: Academy Awards '43: Best Original Score. *NOS, DVT, HEG*

Hi-Jacked 🦴 **1950** When a parolee trucker's cargo is stolen, he inevitably becomes a suspect and must set out to find the true culprits. **66m/B VHS, Beta, LV.** Jim Davis, Paul Cavanagh, Marsha Jones. *RXM*

Hi, Mom! 🦴🦴🦴 *Confessions of A Peeping John; Blue Manhattan* **1970 (R)** DePalma's follow-up to "Greetings" finds amateur pornographer/movie maker De Niro being advised by a professional in the field (Garfield) of sleazy filmmaking. De Niro films the residents of his apartment building and eventually marries one of his starlets. One of De Palma's earlier and better efforts with De Niro playing a crazy as only he can. **87m/C VHS.** Robert De Niro, Charles Durnham, Allen (Goorwitz) Garfield, Lara Parker, Jennifer Salt, Gerrit Graham; ***D:*** Brian DePalma; ***W:*** Brian DePalma. *FCT, HHE*

Hi-Riders 🦴 **1977 (R)** A revenge-based tale about large, mag-wheeled trucks and their drivers. **90m/C VHS, Beta.** Mel Ferrer, Stephen McNally, Neville Brand, Ralph Meeker; ***D:*** Greydon Clark. *VCI*

The Hidden 🦴🦴🦴 **1987 (R)** A seasoned cop (Nouri) and a benign alien posing as an FBI agent (MacLachlan) team up to track down and destroy a hyper-violent alien who survives by invading the bodies of humans, causing them to go on murderous rampages. Much acclaimed, high velocity action film with state-of-the-art special effects. **98m/C VHS, Beta, LV.** Kyle MacLachlan, Michael Nouri, Clu Gulager, Ed O'Ross, Claudia Christian, Clarence Felder, Richard Brooks, William Boyett; ***D:*** Jack Sholder; ***W:*** Bob Hunt; ***M:*** Michael Convertino. *MED, CDV, VTR*

The Hidden 2 🦴🦴½ **1994 (R)** The hyper-violent alien of the 1987 movie returns. With its love of fast cars, high-caliber weapons, and heavy metal music, this body-possessing creature appears to be unstoppable. **91m/C VHS, LV.** Raphael Sbarge, Kate Hodge, Michael Nouri; ***D:*** Seth Pinsker; ***W:*** Seth Pinsker; ***M:*** David McHugh. *NLC, IME*

Hidden Agenda 🦴🦴½ **1990 (R)** A human rights activist and an American lawyer uncover brutality and corruption among the British forces in Northern Ireland. Slow-paced but strong performances. The Northern Irish dialect is sometimes difficult to understand as are the machinations on the British police system. Generally worthwhile. **108m/C VHS, LV.** Frances McDormand, Brian Cox, Brad Dourif, Mai Zetterling, John Benfield, Des McAleer, Jim Norton, Maurice Roeves; ***D:*** Ken Loach; ***W:*** Jim Allen; ***M:*** Stewart Copeland. Cannes Film Festival '90: Special Jury Prize. *HBO, FCT*

Hidden City 🦴🦴 **1987** A film archivist and a statistician become drawn into a conspiracy when a piece of revealing film is spliced onto the end of an innocuous government tape. **112m/C VHS, Beta.** Charles Dance, Cassie Stuart, Alex Norton, Tusse Silberg, Bill Paterson; ***D:*** Stephen Poliakoff. *NO*

Hidden Enemy 🦴½ **1940** During WWII, a scientist develops a new metal alloy that is stronger than steel yet lighter than aluminum. His nephew must protect his scientist/uncle from spies who would steal the formula to use against the Allies. **63m/B VHS, Beta.** Warren Hull, Kay Linaker, William von Brinken, George Cleveland; ***D:*** Howard Bretherton. *SNC, RXM*

Hidden Fears 🦴🦴½ **1993** Maureen Dietz (Foster) carries the gruesome memories of her husband's murder with her. Years later she goes to the police with new evidence to reopen her husband's case. Only the killers find out and return to finish off the eyewitnesses, and she's next! Based on the novel "Exercise in Terror" by Kaminsky, who also wrote the screenplay. **90m/C VHS, Beta.** Meg Foster, Frederic Forrest, Wally Taylor, Bever-Leigh Banfield, Marc Macaulay, Patrick Cherry, Scott Hayes; ***D:*** Jean Bodon; ***W:*** Stuart Kaminsky. *PSM*

The Hidden Fortress 🦴🦴🦴½ *Kakushi Toride No San Akunin; Three Rascals in the Hidden Fortress; Three Bad Men in the Hidden Fortress* **1958** Kurosawa's tale of a warrior who protects a princess from warring feudal lords. An inspiration for George Lucas' "Star Wars" series and deserving of its excellent reputation. In Japanese with English subtitles. The laserdisc edition is letterboxed to retain the film's original integrity. **139m/B VHS, Beta, LV.** *JP* Toshiro Mifune, Misa Vehara, Minoru Chiaki; ***D:*** Akira Kurosawa. Berlin International Film Festival '59: Best Director (Kurosawa). *HMV, FCT, CRC*

Hidden Gold 🦴½ **1933** Routine western for Mix, which has him going undercover to win the confidence of three outlaws and discover where they have hidden their loot. **57m/B VHS, Beta.** Tom Mix, Judith Barrie, Raymond Hatton; ***D:*** Arthur Rosson. *GPV, VCN, DVT*

Hidden Guns 🦴🦴🦴 **1956** Above-average tale of father-and-son lawmen out to reform a town and put the bad guys away. When dad is killed, son goes up against the villain alone. A Greek chorus adds an interesting twist to the action. Erich von Stroheim, Jr. is listed as assistant director. **66m/B VHS.** Bruce (Herman Brix) Bennett, Richard Arlen, John Carradine, Faron Young, Angie Dickinson, Guinn "Big Boy" Williams; ***D:*** Albert C. Gannaway. *NOS*

Hidden Obsession 🦴½ **1992 (R)** Newscaster Ellen is taking a much needed vacation at an isolated cabin when she learns that a serial killer has escaped from a nearby prison. Luckily, she has a hunky police officer neighbor for protection. But though the escaped killer is captured, the killings go on—with Ellen as the next target. **92m/C VHS, LV.** Heather Thomas, Jan-Michael Vincent, Nicholas Celozzi; ***D:*** John Stewart; ***W:*** David Reskin. *MCA*

The Hidden Room 🦴🦴🦴 *Obsession* **1949** A doctor finds out about his wife's affair and decides to get revenge on her lover. He kidnaps him, imprisons him in a cellar, and decides to kill him—slowly. Tense melodrama. **98m/B VHS, Beta.** *GB* Robert Newton, Sally Gray, Naunton Wayne, Phil Brown, Olga Lindo; ***D:*** Edward Dmytryk; ***M:*** Nino Rota. *NOS, SNC, RXM*

Hidden Valley 🦴🦴 **1932** Early Steele western in which everyone is fighting over a map that leads to hidden treasure in the valley. **60m/B VHS.** Bob Steele, Gertrude Messinger, Francis McDonald; ***D:*** Robert North Bradbury. *GPV*

Hide and Go Shriek 🦴 **1987 (R)** Several high school seniors are murdered one by one during a graduation party. Also available in an unrated, gorier version. **90m/C VHS, Beta, LV.** Annette Sinclair, Brittain Frye, Rebunkah Jones; ***D:*** Skip Schoolnik. *NO*

Hide and Seek 🦴 **1977** When a high school hacker converts his computer into a nuclear weapon, he finds that it has developed a mind of its own. **60m/C VHS, Beta.** Bob Martin, Ingrid Veninger, David Patrick. *ORI*

Hide and Seek 🦴 **1980** A study of children living in the land that would soon become Israel. Although they play as normal children, life is particularly difficult. This adversity will lay the foundation for their Israeli citizenry. In Hebrew with English subtitles. **90m/C VHS, Beta.** Gila Almagor, Doron Tavori, Chaim Hadaya; ***D:*** Dan Wolman. *ERG, INJ, TPV*

Hide in Plain Sight 🦴🦴🦴 **1980 (PG)** A distraught blue-collar worker searches for his children who disappeared when his ex-wife and her mobster husband are given new identities by federal agents. Caan's fine directorial debut is based on a true story. **96m/C VHS, Beta.** James Caan, Jill Eikenberry, Robert Viharo, Kenneth McMillan, Josef Sommer, Danny Aiello; ***D:*** James Caan. *MGM*

Hide-Out 🦴🦴½ **1934** A man running from the law winds up at a small farm, falls in love, and becomes reformed by the good family that takes him in. Good supporting cast includes a very young Rooney. **83m/B VHS.** Robert Montgomery, Maureen O'Sullivan, Edward Arnold, Elizabeth Patterson, Mickey Rooney, Edward Brophy; ***D:*** Woodbridge S. Van Dyke. Nominations: Academy Awards '34: Best Original Screenplay. *MGM*

Hideaway 🦴🦴 **1994 (R)** Hodge podge movie finds Hatch Harrison (Goldblum) brought back from the other side after suffering injuries from a near-fatal car accident. He returns with the ability to psychically connect with Vassago (Sisto), a sadistic serial killer of young girls. Coincidentally, Harrison has a teenage daughter, Regina (Silverstone), and Vassago has her lined up as his next victim. The visual effects of spirits floating down a cosmic vortex are entertaining, but plot originality must have been hidden away to make room for the nifty special effects. Based on a novel by Dean R. Koontz. **103m/C VHS, LV.** Jeff Goldblum, Christine Lahti, Alicia Silverstone, Jeremy Sisto, Rae Dawn Chong; ***D:*** Brett Leonard; ***W:*** Andrew Kevin Walker, Neal Jimenez; ***C:*** Gale Tattersall; ***M:*** Trevor Jones. *COL*

The Hideaways 🦴🦴½ *From the Mixed-Up Files of Mrs. Basil E. Frankweiler* **1973 (G)** A 12-year-old girl and her younger brother run away and hide in the Metropolitan Museum of Art. The girl becomes enamored of a piece of sculpture and sets out to discover its creator. Based on the children's novel by E.L. Konigsburg. **105m/C VHS, Beta.** Richard Mulligan, George Rose, Ingrid Bergman, Sally Prager, Johnny Doran, Madeline Kahn; ***D:*** Fielder Cook. *WAR, VHE, FCT*

Hideous Sun Demon 🦴½ *Blood On His Lips; Terror From the Sun; The Sun Demon* **1959** A physicist exposed to radiation must stay out of sunlight or he will turn into a scaly, lizard-like creature. Includes previews of coming attractions from classic sci-fi films. **75m/B VHS, Beta.** Robert Clarke, Patricia Manning, Nan Peterson; ***D:*** Robert Clarke. *NOS, MRV, RHI*

Hider in the House 🦴🦴½ **1990 (R)** In a peaceful neighborhood a family is about to spend an evening of terror when they discover a psychopath is hiding in the attic of their home. **109m/C VHS, Beta, LV.** Michael McKean, Gary Busey, Mimi Rogers, Kurt Christopher Kinder, Candy Hutson, Elizabeth Ruscio, Bruce Glover; ***D:*** Michael Patrick. *VES, LIV*

Hiding Out 🦴🦴 **1987 (PG-13)** A young stockbroker testifies against the Mafia and must find a place to hide in order to avoid being killed. He winds up at his cousin's high school in Delaware, but can he really go through all these teenage troubles once again? **99m/C VHS, Beta.** Jon Cryer, Keith Coogan, Gretchen Cryer, Annabeth Gish, Tim Quill; ***D:*** Bob Giraldi; ***M:*** Anne Dudley. *HBO*

The Hiding Place 🦴🦴 **1975** True story of two Dutch Christian sisters sent to a concentration camp for hiding Jews during WWII. Film is uneven but good cast pulls it through. Based on the Corrie Ten Boom book and produced by Billy Graham's Evangelistic Association. **145m/C VHS.** Julie Harris, Eileen Heckart, Arthur O'Connell, Jeanette Clift; ***D:*** James F. Collier. *VBL, REP, COV*

High & Low 🦴🦴🦴½ *Tengoku To Jigoku* **1962 (R)** Fine Japanese film noir about a wealthy businessman who is being blackmailed by kidnappers who claim to have his son. When he discovers that they have mistakenly taken his chauffeur's son he must decide whether to face financial ruin or risk the life of a young boy. Based on an Ed McBain novel. In Japanese with English subtitles. **143m/B VHS, Beta, LV.** *JP* Toshiro Mifune, Tatsuya Mihashi, Tatsuya Nakadai; ***D:*** Akira Kurosawa. *IME, INJ, TPV*

High Anxiety 🦴🦴 **1977 (PG)** Brooks tries hard to please in this low-brow parody of Hitchcock films employing dozens of references to films like "Psycho," "Spellbound," "The Birds," and "Vertigo." Tells the tale of a height-fearing psychiatrist caught up in a murder mystery. The title song performed a la Sinatra by Brooks is one of the film's high moments. Brooks also has a lot of fun with Hitchcockian camera movements. Uneven (What? Brooks?) but amusing tribute. **92m/C VHS, Beta, LV.** Mel Brooks, Madeline Kahn, Cloris Leachman, Harvey Korman, Ron Carey, Howard Morris, Dick Van Patten; ***D:*** Mel Brooks; ***W:*** Mel Brooks, Ron Clark, Barry Levinson, Rudy DeLuca. *FOX*

High Ballin' 🦴🦴 **1978 (PG)** Truckers Fonda and Reed team up with lady trucker Shaver to take on the gang trying to crush the independent drivers. **100m/C VHS, Beta.** *CA* Peter Fonda, Jerry Reed, Helen Shaver; ***D:*** Peter Carter; ***W:*** Paul F. Edwards. *LIV, VES*

High Command 🦴🦴½ **1937** To save his daughter from an ugly scandal, the British general of an isolated Colonial African outpost traps a blackmailer's killer. **84m/B VHS, Beta.** *GB* Lionel Atwill, Lucie Mannheim, James Mason; ***D:*** Thorold Dickinson. *NOS, MRV, VYY*

High Country 🦴🦴½ *The First Hello* **1981 (PG)** Two misfits, one handicapped, the other an ex-con, on the run from society learn mutual trust as they travel through the Canadian Rockies. **101m/C VHS, Beta.** *CA* Timothy Bottoms, Linda Purl, George Sims, Jim Lawrence, Bill Berry; ***D:*** Harvey Hart. *VES*

High Country Calling 🦴½ **1975 (G)** Wolf pups escape their man-made home and set off a cross-country chase. **84m/C VHS, Beta.** *GEM, CNG*

High Crime 🦴🦴 **1973** A "French Connection"-style suspense story about the heroin trade. Features high-speed chases and a police commissioner obsessed with capturing the criminals. **91m/C VHS, Beta.** James Whitmore, Franco Nero, Fernando Rey; ***D:*** Enzo G. Castellari. *MED*

High Desert Kill 🦴🦴 **1990 (PG)** A science-fiction tale will keep you guessing. Aliens landing in the New Mexican desert want something totally unexpected, and a trio of friends will be the first to find out what it is. Written for cable by Cook ("The China Syndrome"). **93m/C VHS, Beta.** Chuck Connors, Marc Singer, Anthony Geary, Micah Grant; ***D:*** Harry Falk; ***W:*** T.S. Cook. *MCA*

High Frequency 🦴🦴 **1988** Two young men monitoring a satellite relay station witness the murder of a woman. Believing they know who the killer's next victim will be, they set out to warn her. Lack of development mars what could have been a tidy little thriller. **105m/C VHS, LV.** *IT* Oliver Benny, Vincent Spano, Isabelle Pasco, Anne Canovos; ***D:*** Faliero Rosati. *MCG*

High Gear 🦴 **1933** Heartstring-tugger about a race car driver, his girlfriend and the orphan son of a driver killed in a crash. Try to guess the outcome. **65m/B VHS.** James Murray, Joan Marsh, Jackie Searl, Theodore von Eltz, Lee Moran, Gordon DeMain; ***D:*** Leigh Jason. *NOS, RXM*

High Heels 🦴🦴 *Docteur Popaul; Scoundrel in White* **1972** A black comedy about a doctor who believes beauty is only skin deep and marries a plain woman. However, when he meets her beautiful sister, he begins to wonder. In French with English subtitles. **100m/C VHS, Beta.** *FR* Laura Antonelli, Jean-Paul Belmondo, Mia Farrow, Daniel Ivernel; ***D:*** Claude Chabrol. *NO*

High Heels 🦴🦴🦴 *Tacones Lejanos* **1991 (R)** An outrageous combination murder-melodrama-comedy from Almodovar. Rebecca is a TV anchorwoman in Madrid whose flamboyant singer/actress mother has returned to the city for a concert. Rebecca happens to be married to one of her mother's not-so-ex-flames. When her husband winds up dead, Rebecca confesses to his murder during her newscast—but is she telling the truth or just covering up for mom? Mix in a drag queen/judge, a dancing chorus of women prison inmates, and a peculiar police detective, and see if the plot convolutions make sense. In Spanish with English subtitles. **113m/C VHS, Beta.** *SP* Victoria Abril, Marisa Paredes, Miguel Bose, Feodor Atkine, Bibi Andersen, Rocio Munoz; ***D:*** Pedro Almodovar; ***W:*** Pedro Almodovar; ***M:*** Ryuichi Sakamoto. Cesar Awards '93: Best Foreign Film. *PAR*

High Hopes 🦴🦴🦴 **1988** A moving yet nasty satiric comedy about a pair of ex-hippies maintaining their counterculture lifestyle in Margaret Thatcher's England, as they watch the signs of conservative "progress" overtake them and their geriatric, embittered Mum. Hilarious and mature. **110m/C VHS, Beta.** *GB* Philip Davis, Ruth Sheen, Edna Dore, Philip Jackson, Heather Tobias, Leslie Manville, David Bamber; ***D:*** Mike Leigh; ***W:*** Mike Leigh; ***M:*** Andrew Dixon. *ACA*

High Ice 🦴½ **1980** Forest ranger and a lieutenant colonel are involved in a clash of wills over a rescue mission high in the snow-capped Washington state peaks. **97m/C VHS, Beta.** David Janssen, Tony Musante; ***D:*** Eugene S. Jones. *VES*

High Lonesome 🦴🦴½ **1950** Barrymore is a drifter in Big Bend country, suspected in a series of mysterious murders. While he is being held captive, the real killers - thought dead - return to exact revenge on those they hold responsible for the range war in which they were wounded. This was LeMay's only stint as a director. **80m/C VHS.** John Blythe Barrymore Jr., Chill Wills, John Archer, Lois Butler, Kristine Miller, Basil Ruysdael, Jack Elam; ***D:*** Alan LeMay; ***W:*** Alan LeMay. *NOS*

High Noon 🦴🦴🦴🦴 **1952** Landmark Western about Hadeyville town marshal Will Kane (Cooper) who faces four professional killers alone, after being abandoned to his fate by the gutless townspeople who profess to admire him. Cooper is the ultimate hero figure, his sheer presence overwhelming. Note the continuing use of the ballad written by Dimitri Tiomkin, "Do Not Forsake Me, Oh My Darlin'" (sung by Tex Ritter) to heighten the tension and action. Laserdisc includes the original trailer, an essay by Howard Suber on audio 2, a photo essay of production stills, Carl Foreman's original notes of the film and the complete text of "The Tin Star," the story on which the film is based. ♫High Noon (Do Not Forsake Me, Oh My Darlin'). **85m/B VHS, LV.** Gary Cooper, Grace Kelly, Lloyd Bridges, Lon Chaney Jr., Thomas Mitchell, Otto Kruger, Katy Jurado, Lee Van Cleef, Harry (Henry) Morgan, Robert J. Wilke, Sheb Wooley; ***D:*** Fred Zinnemann; ***W:*** Carl Foreman; ***C:*** Floyd Crosby; ***M:*** Dimitri Tiomkin. Academy Awards '52: Best Actor (Cooper), Best Film Editing, Best Song ("High Noon (Do Not Forsake Me, Oh My Darlin')"), Best Score; Golden Globe Awards '53: Best Actor—Drama (Cooper), Best Supporting Actress (Jurado), Best Score; National Board of Review Awards '52: 10 Best Films of the Year; New York Film Critics Awards '52: Best Director (Zinnemann), Best Film; Nominations: Academy Awards '52: Best Director (Zinnemann), Best Picture, Best Screenplay. *REP, TLF, BTV*

High Noon: Part 2 🦴 **1980** Majors attempts to fill Gary Cooper's shoes, as Marshal Kane returns a year after the events of the original "High Noon" to remove the corrupt marshal who replaced him. Subtitled "The Return of Will Kane." Made for television. **96m/C VHS, Beta.** Lee Majors, David Carradine, Pernell Roberts, Kathy Cannon; ***D:*** Jerry Jameson. *FRH, VTR*

High Plains Drifter 🦴🦴½ **1973 (R)** A surreal, violent western focusing on a drifter who defends a town from gunmen intent on meting out death. One of Eastwood's most stylistic directorial efforts, indebted to his "Man with No Name" days with Sergio Leone. Laser format is letterboxed and includes chapter stops and the original theatrical trailer. **105m/C VHS, Beta, LV.** Verna Bloom, Mitchell Ryan, Marianna Hill, Clint Eastwood; ***D:*** Clint Eastwood; ***M:*** Dee Barton. *MCA, TLF*

High Risk 🦴½ **1976 (R)** Improbable action-adventure of four unemployed Americans who battle foreign armies, unscrupulous gunrunners, and jungle bandits in a harrowing attempt to steal five million dollars from an expatriate American drug dealer living in the peaceful splendor of his Columbian villa. Interesting in its own run-on way. **94m/C VHS, Beta.** James Brolin, Anthony Quinn, Lindsay Wagner, James Coburn, Ernest Borgnine, Bruce Davison, Cleavon Little; ***D:*** Stewart Raffill. *SUE, VTR*

High Road to China 🦴🦴 **1983 (PG)** A hard-drinking former WWI air ace is recruited by a young heiress who must find her father before his ex-partner takes over his business. Post-"Raiders of the Lost Ark" thrills and romance, but without that tale's panache. **105m/C VHS, Beta, LV.** Bess Armstrong, Tom Selleck, Jack Weston, Robert Morley, Wilford Brimley, Brian Blessed; ***D:*** Brian G. Hutton; ***M:*** John Barry. *WAR*

High Rolling in a Hot Corvette 🦴 *High Rolling* **1977 (PG)** Two carnival workers leave their jobs and hit the road in search of adventure and excitement, eventually turning to crime. **82m/C VHS, Beta.** *AU* Joseph Bottoms, Greg Taylor, Judy Davis, Wendy Hughes; ***D:*** Igor Auzins. *VES*

High School Caesar 🦴 **1956** A seedy teenage exploitation flick about a rich teenager, with no parental supervision, who starts his own gang to run his high school. **75m/B VHS, Beta.** John Ashley; ***D:*** O'Dale Ireland. *RHI, SNC*

High School Confidential 🦴🦴 *Young Hellions* **1958** Teen punk Tamblyn transfers to Santo Bello high school from Chicago and causes havoc among the locals. He soon involves himself in the school drug scene and looks to be the top dog in dealing, but what no one knows is that he's really a narc! A must for midnight movie fans thanks to high camp values, "hep cat" dialogue and the gorgeous Van Doren as Tamblyn's sex-crazed "aunt." **85m/B VHS, Beta.** Russ Tamblyn, Jan Sterling, John Blythe Barrymore Jr., Mamie Van Doren, Diane Jergens, Jerry Lee Lewis, Ray Anthony, Jackie Coogan, Charles Chaplin Jr., Burt Douglas, Michael Landon, Jody Fair, Phillipa Fallon, Robin Raymond, James Todd, Lyle Talbot, William Wellman Jr.; ***D:*** Jack Arnold. *REP*

High School High 🦴🦴½ **1996** Idealistic teacher Richard Clark (Lovitz) leaves the private school world for notorious inner city Marion Barry High. This school is so bad it has its own cemetery (it's a parody, folks), but Clark is determined to get through to the kids. "Clockers" star Phifer shows up as a helpful student. Penned by David Zucker of "Airplane!" fame, so don't expect a "Mr. Holland's Opus." **?m/C VHS.** Jon Lovitz, Tia Carrere, Mekhi Phifer, Louise Fletcher; ***D:*** Hart Bochner; ***W:*** David Zucker, Robert Locash. *NYR*

High School USA 🦴½ **1984** A high school class clown confronts the king of the prep-jock-bullies. Antics ensue in this made-for-television flick which features many stars from fifties and sixties sitcoms. **96m/C VHS, Beta.** Michael J. Fox, Nancy McKeon, Bob Denver, Angela Cartwright, Elinor Donahue, Dwayne Hickman, Lauri Hendler, Dana Plato, Tony Dow, David Nelson; ***D:*** Rod Amateau; ***M:*** Miles Goodman. *ORI, WAR*

High Season 🦴🦴½ **1988 (R)** A satire about a beautiful English photographer (Bisset) stranded on an idyllic Greek island with neither money nor inspiration, and the motley assembly of characters who surround her during the tourist season. **95m/C VHS, Beta, LV, 8mm.** *GB* Jacqueline Bisset, James Fox, Irene Papas, Sebastian Shaw, Kenneth Branagh, Robert Stephens, Leslie Manville; ***D:*** Clare Peploe; ***W:*** Mark Peploe, Clare Peploe; ***C:*** Chris Menges; ***M:*** Jason Osborn. *SUE, FCT, NLC*

High Sierra 🦴🦴🦴 **1941** Bogart is Roy "Mad Dog" Earle, an aging gangster whose last job backfires, so he's hiding out from the police in the High Sierras. Bogart's first starring role. Based on the novel by W.R. Burnett. Remade in 1955 as "I Died A Thousand Times." Also available colorized. **96m/B VHS, Beta, LV.** Humphrey Bogart, Ida Lupino, Arthur Kennedy, Joan Leslie, Cornel Wilde, Henry Travers, Henry Hull; ***D:*** Raoul Walsh; ***W:*** John Huston, W.R. Burnett; ***C:*** Gaetano Antonio "Tony" Gaudio. National Board of Review Awards '41: 10 Best Films of the Year. *FOX*

High Society 🦴🦴🦴 **1956** A wealthy man attempts to win back his ex-wife who's about to be remarried in this enjoyable remake of "The Philadelphia Story." Letterboxed laserdisc format also includes the original movie trailer. ♫High Society Calypso; Little One; Who Wants to Be a Millionaire?; True Love; You're Sensational; I Love You, Samantha; Now You Has Jazz; Well, Did You Evah?; Mind if I Make Love to You?. **107m/C VHS, Beta, LV, 8mm.** Frank Sinatra, Bing Crosby, Grace Kelly, Louis Armstrong, Celeste Holm, Sidney Blackmer, Louis Calhern; ***D:*** Charles Walters; ***C:*** Paul Vogel; ***M:*** Cole Porter. Nominations: Academy Awards '56: Best Song ("True Love"), Best Story, Best Original Score. *MGM*

High Spirits 🦴🦴 **1988 (PG-13)** An American inherits an Irish castle and a sexy 200-year-old ghost. A painful, clumsy comedy by the fine British director that was apparently butchered by the studio before its release. **99m/C VHS, Beta, LV.** Daryl Hannah, Peter O'Toole, Steve Guttenberg, Beverly D'Angelo, Liam Neeson, Martin Ferrero, Peter Gallagher, Jennifer Tilly; ***D:*** Neil Jordan; ***W:*** Neil Jordan; ***M:*** George Fenton. *MED, VTR*

High Stakes 🦴🦴 **1989 (R)** Kirkland stars as a prostitute who's battling the Mob and falling in love. Limited release in theaters but another fine performance from Kirkland. Also released as "Melanie Rose." **102m/C VHS, LV.** Sally Kirkland, Robert LuPone, Richard Lynch, Sarah Gellar, Kathy Bates, W.T. Martin; ***D:*** Amos Kollek. *VMK*

High Strung 🦴½ **1991 (PG)** Writer Thane Furrows (Oedekerk) thinks his life can't get any worse since he's plagued by a nagging mom, pressuring boss, and an insurance salesman. Then mysterious voices and images (played by Carrey) tell him he'll die that night. Naturally, Thane tries to think of a way out of his predicament. You'll hope he dies sooner since the movie is so lame. Beware, Carrey has very little screen time in spite of the advertising. **96m/C VHS.** Steve Oedekerk, Thomas F. Wilson, Fred Willard, Jim Carrey. *PAR*

High Tide 🦴🦴🦴 **1987 (PG-13)** A strong and strange drama once again coupling the star and director of "My Brilliant Career." A small-time rock 'n' roll singer who is stranded in a small, beach town fortuitously meets up with her previously-abandoned teenage daughter. Acclaimed. **120m/C VHS, Beta, LV, 8mm.** *AU* Judy Davis, Jan Adele, Claudia Karvan, Colin Friels, John Clayton, Mark Hembrow, Frankie J. Holden, Monica Trapaga; ***D:*** Gillian Armstrong; ***W:*** Laura Jones; ***M:*** Peter Best, Ricky Fataar, Mark Moffiatt. Australian Film Institute '87: Best Actress (Davis); National Society of Film Critics Awards '88: Best Actress (Davis). *SUE, FCT, NLC*

High Velocity 🦴½ **1976 (PG)** Lame adventure about two mercenaries involved in the challenge of a lifetime—rescuing a kidnapped executive from Asian terrorists. Filmed in Manila. **105m/C VHS, Beta.** Ben Gazzara, Paul Winfield, Britt Ekland, Keenan Wynn; ***D:*** Remi Kramer; ***M:*** Jerry Goldsmith. *MED*

High Voltage 🦴🦴 **1929** A fast-moving comedy adventure set in the High Sierras. **62m/B VHS, Beta.** Carole Lombard, William Boyd, Gwen Moore, Billy Bevan; ***D:*** Howard Higgin. *NOS, MRV, BAR*

Higher and Higher 🦴🦴 **1944** Bankrupt aristocrat conspires with servants to regain his fortune, and tries to marry his daughter into money. Sinatra's first big-screen role. ♫You Belong in a Love Song; A Most Important Affair; The Music Stopped; Today I'm A Debutante; A Lovely Way To Spend An Evening; I Couldn't Sleep a Wink Last Night; You're On Your Own; I Saw You First; Disgustingly Rich. **90m/B VHS, Beta, LV.** Frank Sinatra, Leon Errol, Michele Morgan, Jack Haley, Mary McGuire; ***D:*** Tim Whelan. Nominations: Academy Awards '44: Best Song ("I Couldn't Sleep A Wink Last Night"), Best Original Score. *CCB, IME, TTC*

Higher Education 🦴🦴 **1988 (R)** Andy leaves his small town for a big city college and falls head over heels for a student and a teacher. He didn't know college could be so much fun. **83m/C VHS.** Kevin Hicks, Isabelle Mejias, Lori Hallier, Maury Chaykin, Richard Monette; ***D:*** John Sheppard. *VTR*

Higher Learning 🦴🦴 **1994 (R)** Racism, idealism, and the struggle for identity converge in this stylistically shot but rarely enlightening commentary on campus life and strife, focusing on three very different freshmen at fictional Columbus University—a bright track star (Ebbs) who questions the exploitation of black student athletes; a sheltered, sexually confused beauty from the 'burbs (Swanson); and a goony, paranoid loner who falls in with a group of skinheads (Rapaport). Singleton's honorable intention—to make a movie that makes a difference—is marred by cardboard supporting characters, a penchant for in-your-face irony, and a predictable, simplistic conclusion. **127m/C VHS, LV.** Omar Epps, Kristy Swanson, Michael Rapaport, Laurence "Larry" Fishburne, Jennifer Connelly, Ice Cube, Tyra Banks, Jason Wiles, Cole Hauser, Regina King; ***D:*** John Singleton; ***W:*** John Singleton. *COL*

The Highest Honor 🦴🦴½ **1984 (R)** True story set during WWII of a friendship between an Australian army officer, captured while attempting to infiltrate Singapore, and a Japanese security officer. Too long, but gripping. **99m/C VHS, Beta, LV.** *AU* John Howard, Atsuo Nakamura, Stuart Wilson, Michael Aitkens, Steve Bisley; ***D:*** Peter Maxwell. *SUE, VTR*

Highlander 🦴🦴🦴 **1986 (R)** A strange tale about an immortal 16th-century Scottish warrior who has had to battle his evil immortal enemy through the centuries. The feud comes to blows in modern-day Manhattan. Connery makes a memorable appearance as the good warrior's mentor. Spectacular battle and death scenes. A cult favorite which spawned a weak sequel and a television series. Based on a story by Gregory Widen. **110m/C VHS, Beta, LV.** Christopher Lambert, Sean Connery, Clancy Brown, Roxanne Hart, Beatie Edney, Alan North, Sheila Gish, Jon Polito; ***D:*** Russell Mulcahy; ***W:*** Gregory Widen, Peter Bellwood, Larry Ferguson; ***M:*** Michael Kamen. *REP*

Highlander 2: The Quickening 🦴½ **1991 (R)** The saga of Connor MacLeod and Juan Villa-Lobos continues in this sequel set in the year 2024. An energy shield designed to block out the sun's harmful ultraviolet rays has left planet Earth in perpetual darkness, but there is evidence that the ozone layer has repaired itself. An environmental terrorist and her group begin a sabotage effort and are joined by MacLeod and Villa-Lobos in their quest to save Earth. Stunning visual effects don't make up for the lack of substance. A director's cut is available at 108 minutes. **90m/C VHS, LV, 8mm.** Christopher Lambert, Sean Connery, Virginia Madsen, Michael Ironside, John C. McGinley; ***D:*** Russell Mulcahy; ***W:*** Peter Bellwood; ***C:*** Phil Meheux; ***M:*** Stewart Copeland. *COL*

Highlander: The Final Dimension 🦴½ *Highlander 3: The Magician; Highlander 3: The Sorcerer* **1994 (R)** Immortal Conner MacLeod (Lambert) battles master illusionist Kane (Van Peebles), who seeks to rule the world. Aiding MacLeod is Alex Smith (Unger), a research scientist who discovers Kane was once buried beneath a mystical mountain along with three other immortal warriors some 300 years before. MacLeod returns to his old Scottish stomping grounds to prepare for battle. Lots of action and special effects, really dumb storyline and overacting—even for a fantasy film. Original theatrical release was PG-13 and 94 minutes; the director's cut has been re-edited and footage added. **99m/C VHS, LV.** Christopher Lambert, Mario Van Peebles, Deborah Unger, Mako; ***D:*** Andrew Morahan; ***W:*** Paul Ohl; ***M:*** J. Peter Robinson. *TOU*

Highlander: The Gathering 🦴🦴½ **1993 (PG-13)** Re-edited episodes from the syndicated TV series finds good immortals Connor MacLeod (Lambert) and distant relative Duncan (Paul) battling against an evil immortal (Moll as a particularly nasty villain) and a misguided human (Vanity). Lots of sword-play and a little bit of romance (courtesy of Vandernoot). **98m/C VHS.** Christopher Lambert, Adrian Paul, Richard Moll, Vanity, Alexandra Vandernoot, Stan Kirsh; ***D:*** Thomas J. Wright, Ray Austin; ***W:*** Lorain Despres, Dan Gordon. *HMD*

Highpoint 🦴 **1980 (PG)** When an unemployed man becomes the chauffeur of a wealthy family, he finds himself in the middle of a mysterious murder and part of an international CIA plot. Hard to figure what's happening in this one. **91m/C VHS, Beta, LV.** *CA* Richard Harris, Christopher Plummer, Beverly D'Angelo, Kate Reid, Saul Rubinek; ***D:*** Peter Carter. *VTR, SUE*

Highway 61 🦴🦴 **1991 (R)** Shy barber Pokey Jones lives in the small Canadian town of Pickerel Falls and becomes a celebrity when he discovers the frozen corpse of an unknown young man in his backyard. Jackie Bangs, a rock roadie who's stolen her band's stash of drugs, finds herself stranded in the same small town. So begins a wild road trip. Lackluster direction undercuts much of the first-rate acting and amusing story quirks. **110m/C VHS.** Valerie Buhagiar, Don McKellar, Earl Pastko, Peter Breck, Art Bergmann; ***D:*** Bruce McDonald; ***W:*** Don McKellar. *PAR, FCT*

Highway 13 🦴½ **1948** When a trucker witnesses an "accidental" death at the loading warehouse, he falls under suspicion. He then sets out to clear his name. **60m/B VHS, Beta, LV.** Robert Lowery, Pamela Blake, Lyle Talbot, Michael Whalen, Maris Wrixon, Clem Bevans; ***D:*** William (Lester Williams) Berke. *NO*

Highway to Hell 🦴🦴 **1992 (R)** Bergen plays the devil in a horror-comedy about going to hell—even if you're not dead yet. Lowe and Swanson are newlyweds on their way to Las Vegas when they're stopped by a "hellcop," who kidnaps the bride and takes her to the netherworld to be the devil's new plaything. Her human hubby doesn't take kindly to this and goes to hell to rescue his bride. Campy flick is played for laughs and has some good special effects. **93m/C VHS.** Patrick Bergin, Adam Storke, Chad Lowe, Kristy Swanson, Richard Farnsworth, C.J. Graham, Lita Ford, Kevin Peter Hall, Pamela Gidley, Brian Helgeland; ***Cameos:*** Gilbert Gottfried; ***D:*** Ate De Jong. *HBO*

Hijazo de Mi Vidaza 🦴 *Son of My Life* **197?** The history of a family as told by a mother to her son. In Spanish. **90m/C VHS, Beta.** Enrique Cuenca, Eduardo Manzano, Maria Fernanda, Fernando Casanova. *MAD*

Hill Number One **1951** A dramatization of the story of Easter, featuring Dean in one of his first major roles as John the Baptist. Made for television. **57m/B VHS, Beta.** James Dean, Michael Ansara, Leif Erickson, Ruth Hussey, Roddy McDowall. *RHI, FCT, HEG*

Hill Street Blues, Vol. 1: Hill Street Station **1981** Landmark police drama which effectively combined a large cast of characters with plots filled with humor and tragedy. Set in an urban ghetto of a large (unnamed) American city, the precinct was run by Capt. Frank Furillo (Travanti) and staffed with "let's be careful out there!" Sgt. Phil Esterhaus (Conrad), as well as a host of offbeat detectives and beat cops. The pilot epsiode introduced the characters and the characteristic mayhem. Additional episodes available. **50m/C VHS.** Daniel J. Travanti, Veronica Hamel, Michael Conrad, Bruce Weitz, James B. Sikking, Joe Spano, Taurean Blacque, Kiel Martin, Rene Enriquez, Michael Warren, Charles Haid, Betty Thomas, Ed Marinaro, Barbara Babcock. *MOV, MTM*

Hill 24 Doesn't Answer 🦴🦴🦴 **1955** Four Zionist soldiers defend a strategic entrance to Jerusalem. While at their posts, they reflect on their lives and devotion to the cause. Made in Israel, in English. The first Israeli feature film. **101m/B VHS, Beta.** *IS* Edward Mulhare, Haya Harareet, Michael Wager; ***D:*** Thorold Dickinson. *ERG, INJ*

Hillbillies in a Haunted House *Woof!* **1967** Two country and western singers en route to the Nashville jamboree encounter a group of foreign spies "haunting" a house. Features Rathbone's last film performance. Sequel to "Las Vegas Hillbillies" (1966). Giant step down for everyone involved. **88m/C VHS, Beta.** Ferlin Husky, Joi Lansing, Don Bowman, John Carradine, Lon Chaney Jr., Basil Rathbone; ***D:*** Jean Yarbrough. *VCI, AOV*

Hillbilly Blitzkrieg 🦴 *Enemy Round-Up* **1942** Two soldiers are sent to the boonies to guard a top-secret missile site from enemy agents. Come-to-life comic strip characters Snuffy Smith, Barney Google and Spark Plug join in the antics. **63m/B VHS.** Bud Duncan, Cliff Nazarro, Edgar Kennedy, Doris Linden, Lucien Littlefield, Alan Baldwin; ***D:*** Roy Mack. *NOS, RXM*

The Hills Have Eyes *Woof!* **1977 (R)** Desperate family battles for survival and vengeance against a brutal band of inbred hillbilly cannibals. Craven gore-fest followed by Hills II. **83m/C VHS, Beta, LV.** Susan Lanier, Robert Houston, Martin Speer, Dee Wallace Stone, Russ Grieve, John Steadman, James Whitworth, Michael Berryman; ***D:*** Wes Craven; ***W:*** Wes Craven. *NO*

The Hills Have Eyes, Part 2 🦴 **1984** Craven reprises Hills with Eyes number one to ill effect. Ignorant teens disregard warnings of a "Hills Have Eyes" refugee, and go stomping into the grim reaper's proving grounds. Predictably bad things happen. **86m/C VHS, Beta.** Michael Berryman, Kevin Blair, John Bloom, Janus Blythe, John Laughlin, Tamara Stafford; ***D:*** Wes Craven; ***W:*** Wes Craven. *REP*

The Hills of Home 🦴🦴🦴 *Master of Lassie* **1948 (G)** Warm sentimental tale about a Scottish doctor and his beloved pet collie. One of the better films in the "Lassie" series. **97m/C VHS.** Edmund Gwenn, Donald Crisp, Tom Drake, Janet Leigh; ***D:*** Fred M. Wilcox; ***W:*** William Ludwig. *MGM, FCT*

Hills of Oklahoma 🦴🦴 **1950** Allen stars as the leader of a cattlemen's association who decides not to deal with dishonest meatpacker Keane, so he drives his herd across the desert to a slaughterhouse run by an honest businesswoman. Based on an original story by Cooper. **67m/B VHS.** Rex Allen, Elisabeth Fraser, Elisabeth Risdon, Fuzzy Knight, Roscoe Ates, Robert Emmett Keane, Trevor Bardette; ***D:*** R.G. Springsteen; ***W:*** Olive Cooper, Victor Arthur. *MOV*

Hills of Utah 🦴½ **1951** Autry finds himself in the middle of a feud between the local mine operator and a group of cattlemen, while searching for his father's murderer. **70m/B VHS, Beta.** Gene Autry, Pat Buttram, Denver Pyle; ***D:*** John English. *CCB*

The Hillside Strangler 🦴½ *The Case of the Hillside Stranglers* **1989** Made-for-television, crime-of-the-week drama about the investigation to apprehend the serial killer responsible for 10 deaths in 1977-78. **91m/C VHS, Beta.** Richard Crenna, Dennis Farina, Billy Zane, Tony Plana, James Tolkan, Tasia Valenza; ***D:*** Steven Gethers. *FRH*

Himatsuri 🦴🦴🦴 *Fire Festival* **1985** An acclaimed film detailing the conflicts between man and nature, as a lumberjack in a Japanese forest believes he's the protector of the mountains through his divine relationship with the ancient gods. Outraged by the destruction, pollution, and commercial exploitation of the land he turns to violence. In Japanese with English subtitles. **120m/C VHS, Beta.** *JP* Kinya Kitaoji, Kwako Taichi, Ryota Nakamoto, Norihei Miki; ***D:*** Mitsuo Yanagimachi; ***W:*** Kenji Nakagami; ***M:*** Toru Takemitsu. *ORI, WAR, AUD*

The Hindenburg 🦴🦴 **1975 (PG)** A dramatization of what might have happened on the fateful night the Hindenburg exploded. Scott plays an investigator who is aware that something is up, and has numerous suspects to interrogate. The laser edition features wide-screen format, digital Stereo Surround, the original trailer and chapter stops. **126m/C VHS, Beta, LV.** George C. Scott, Anne Bancroft, William Atherton, Roy Thinnes, Gig Young, Burgess Meredith, Charles Durning, Richard Dysart; ***D:*** Robert Wise; ***C:*** Robert L. Surtees; ***M:*** David Shire. Academy Awards '75: Best Sound Effects Editing, Best Visual Effects; Nominations: Academy Awards '75: Best Art Direction/Set Decoration, Best Cinematography, Best Sound. *MCA*

Hips, Hips, Hooray 🦴🦴½ **1934** Two supposed "hot shot" salesmen are hired by a cosmetic company to sell flavored lipstick. This lavish musical comedy is one of Wheeler and Woolsey's best vehicles. ♫Tired of It All; Keep Romance Alive; Keep On Doin' What You're Doin'. **68m/B VHS, Beta, LV.** Robert Woolsey, Bert Wheeler, Ruth Etting, Thelma Todd, Dorothy Lee; ***D:*** Mark Sandrich. *CCB*

Hired Hand 🦴🦴½ **1971** Two drifters settle on a farm belonging to one of their wives, only to leave again seeking to avenge the murder of a friend. TV prints include Larry Hagman in a cameo role. **93m/C VHS, Beta.** Peter Fonda, Warren Oates, Verna Bloom, Severn Darden, Robert Pratt; ***Cameos:*** Larry Hagman; ***D:*** Peter Fonda. *BAR*

Hired to Kill 🦴½ *The Italian Connection* **1973 (R)** A pair of Mafia hoods plot against each other over a $6 million drug shipment. **90m/C Beta.** Henry Silva, Woody Strode, Adolfo Celi, Mario Adorf. *NO*

Hired to Kill 🦴½ **1991 (R)** The granite-hewn Thompson plays a male-chauvinist commando grudgingly leading a squad of beautiful mercenaryettes on an international rescue mission. Not as bad as it sounds (mainly because the ladies aren't complete bimbos), but between senseless plotting, gratuitous catfights, and a love scene indistinguishable from rape, the Hound found plenty to dislike. **91m/C VHS, Beta.** Brian Thompson, George Kennedy, Jose Ferrer, Oliver Reed, Penelope Reed, Michelle Moffett, Barbara Lee Alexander, Jordanna Capra; ***D:*** Nico Mastorakis, Peter Rader; ***W:*** Nico Mastorakis. *PAR*

Hiroshima 🦴🦴🦴 **1995 (PG)** Haunting depiction recreates the circumstances surrounding the dropping of the first atomic bomb in 1945. Juxtaposes scenes between the U.S., Japan, and their leaders—President Truman (Welsh) and Emperor Hirohito (Umewaka)—with the development of the Manhattan Project, the bombing itself, and its consequences. Filmed primarily in B&W, with newsreel and contemporary witness interviews in color; Japanese sequences are subtitled in English. Filmed on location in Montreal, PQ, and Tokyo, Japan; made for cable TV. **180m/C VHS.** *JP CA* Kenneth Welsh, Naohiko Umewaka, Wesley Addy, Richard Masur, Hisashi Igawa, Ken Jenkins, Jeffrey DeMunn, Leon Pownall, Saul Rubinek, Timothy West, Koji Takahashi, Kazuo Kato; ***D:*** Roger Spottiswoode, Koreyoshi Kurahara; ***W:*** John Hopkins, Toshiro Ishido; ***C:*** Pierre Mignot, Shohei Ando. *HMK*

Hiroshima Maiden **1988** An American family gains new perspective when they meet a young survivor of the atomic bomb. Based on true stories of Japanese women who stayed with Americans while undergoing surgery to minimize their scars. Originally aired on PBS as part of the "Wonderworks" family movie series. **58m/C VHS.** Susan Blakely, Richard Masur, Tamlyn Tomita; ***D:*** Joan Darling. *PME, WNE, HMV*

Hiroshima, Mon Amour 🦴🦴🦴🦴 **1959** A profoundly moving drama exploring the shadow of history over the personal lives of a lonely French actress living in Tokyo and a Japanese architect with whom she's having an affair. Presented in a complex network of flashbacks. Highly influential; adapted by Marguerite Duras from her book. In Japanese with English subtitles. **88m/B VHS, Beta, 8mm.** *JP FR* Emmanuelle Riva, Eiji Okada, Bernard Fresson, Stella Dassas, Pierre Barbaud; ***D:*** Alain Resnais; ***W:*** Marguerite Duras; ***M:*** Georges Delerue, Giovanni Fusco. National Board of Review Awards '60: 5 Best Foreign Films of the Year; New York Film Critics Awards '60: Best Foreign Film; Nominations: Academy Awards '60: Best Story & Screenplay. *VYY, MRV, SUE*

Hiroshima: Out of the Ashes 🦴🦴🦴 **1990 (PG)** The terrible aftermath of the bombing of Hiroshima, August, 1945, as seen through the eyes of American and Japanese soldiers, the Japanese people, and a priest. Carefully detailed and realistic, creates an amazing emotional response. Don't miss the scene in which Nelson and his buddy find themselves surrounded by Japanese—the enemy—only to realize that their "captors" have been blinded by the blast. Created as an homage for the 45th anniversary of the bombing. **98m/C VHS.** Max von Sydow, Judd Nelson, Mako, Tamlyn Tomita, Stan Egi, Sab Shimono, Noriyuki "Pat" Morita, Kim Miyori; ***D:*** Peter Werner. *VMK*

His Brother's Ghost 🦴🦴 **1945** When Fuzzy is rubbed out by bandits, Billy Carson (no longer called Billy the Kid thanks to mothers' protestations) convinces his twin brother to impersonate him in order to make the bandits believe they are the victims of hocus pocus from the otherworld. Crabbe—who dressed noir before it was chic—made this during his post sci-fi western period, when he slugged it through some fifty low-rent oaters (usually under the direction of Newfield at PRC studios). **54m/C VHS.** Buster Crabbe, Al "Fuzzy" St. John, Charles "Blackie" King, Bud Osborne, Karl Hackett, Archie Hall; ***D:*** Sam Newfield. *NOS, MRV, HEG*

His Butler's Sister 🦴🦴 **1943** Bachelor composer Charles Gerard (Tone) lives a sybarite's life in his Manhattan penthouse, which is run by his butler Martin Murphy (O'Brien). When Murphy's stepsister Ann Carter (Durbin) arrives unexpectedly, she's delighted to hear who Murphy works for because she's a singer and wants an audition—an absolute taboo in Gerard's household. So she fools him into thinking she's the new maid until she can get her big break. Nothing new but Durbin does get to work her pretty pipes. ♫Nessun Dorma; In the Spirit of the Moment; When You're Away; Is It True What They Say About Dixie?. **87m/B VHS.** Deanna Durbin, Franchot Tone, Pat O'Brien, Evelyn Ankers, Akim Tamiroff, Alan Mowbray, Frank Jenks, Walter Catlett, Hans Conried, Florence Bates, Roscoe Karns, Franklin Pangborn; ***D:*** Frank Borzage; ***W:*** Samuel Hoffenstein, Bety Reinhardt; ***C:*** Woody Bredell; ***M:*** Hans J. Salter. *MCA*

His Double Life 🦴🦴½ **1933** When a shy gentleman's valet dies, his master assumes the dead man's identity and has a grand time. From the play "Buried Alive" by Arnold Bennett. Remade in 1943 as "Holy Matrimony." **67m/B VHS, Beta.** Roland Young, Lillian Gish, Montagu Love; ***D:*** Arthur Hopkins. *NOS, MRV, BAR*

His Fighting Blood 🦴½ **1935** Northwest Mounties in action. Based on a James Oliver Curwood story. **63m/B VHS, Beta.** Kermit Maynard. *VDM*

His First Command 🦴½ **1929** An early talkie wherein a playboy falls in love with the daughter of a cavalry officer, and enlists in order to win her affections. **60m/B VHS, Beta, 8mm.** William Boyd, Dorothy Sebastian, Gavin Gordon; ***D:*** Gregory La Cava. *VYY*

His First Flame 🦴🦴🦴 **1926** A classic Langdon silent romantic comedy. **62m/B VHS, Beta.** Harry Langdon, Vernon Dent, Natalie Kingston; ***W:*** Frank Capra. *NOS, VYY, GPV*

His Girl Friday 🦴🦴🦴🦴 **1940** Classic, unrelentingly hilarious war-between-the-sexes comedy in which a reporter and her ex-husband editor help a condemned man escape the law—while at the same time furthering their own ends as they try to get the big scoop on political corruption in the town. One of Hawks' most furious and inventive screen combats in which women are given uniquely equal (for Hollywood) footing, with staccato dialogue and wonderful performances. Based on the Hecht-MacArthur play

"The Front Page," which was originally filmed in 1931. Remade again in 1974 as "The Front Page," and in 1988 as "Switching Channels." Also available colorized. **92m/B VHS, Beta.** Cary Grant, Rosalind Russell, Ralph Bellamy, Gene Lockhart, John Qualen, Porter Hall, Roscoe Karns, Abner Biberman, Cliff Edwards, Billy Gilbert, Helen Mack, Ernest Truex, Clarence Kolb, Frank Jenks; ***D:*** Howard Hawks; ***W:*** Charles Lederer; ***M:*** Morris Stoloff. *CNG, MRV, NOS*

His Kind of Woman 𝄞𝄞𝄞 **1951** A fall guy, being used to bring a racketeer back to the U.S. from Mexico, discovers the plan and tries to halt it. **120m/B VHS, Beta.** Robert Mitchum, Jane Russell, Vincent Price, Tim Holt, Charles McGraw, Raymond Burr, Jim Backus; ***D:*** John Farrow. *NO*

His Majesty O'Keefe 𝄞𝄞½ **1953** Lancaster stars as a South Seas swashbuckler dealing in the lucrative coconut-oil trade of the mid-1800s. The natives see him as a god and allow him to marry a beautiful maiden. When his reign is threatened by unscrupulous traders, Lancaster springs into action to safeguard his kingdom. Based on a real-life American adventurer, this was the first movie ever filmed in the Fiji Islands. **92m/C VHS, Beta, LV.** Burt Lancaster, Joan Rice, Benson Fong, Philip Ahn, Grant Taylor; ***D:*** Byron Haskin. *WAR*

His Majesty, the American 𝄞𝄞½ **1919** William Brooks (Fairbanks) is a young man whose heritage is unknown to him. It turns out he's an heir to a small European kingdom. When Brooks arrives in Alaine he discovers the war minister is trying to overthrow the present king. With his usual dash, our hero saves the day and also wins the hand of a beautiful princess. First picture released by United Artists studios, formed by Fairbanks, Mary Pickford, Charles Chaplin, and D.W. Griffith. **100m/B VHS.** Douglas Fairbanks Sr., Marjorie Daw, Lillian Langdon, Frank Campeau; ***D:*** Joseph Henabery. *GPV, GVV*

His Majesty, the Scarecrow of Oz/ The Magic Cloak of Oz 𝄞𝄞½ **1914** The creator of the Oz stories, L. Frank Baum, wrote, produced and directed these two stories himself, with all the characters from his best-selling children's books. **80m/B VHS, Beta.** ***D:*** L. Frank Baum. *GVV*

His Name was King *Woof!* **1985** A man goes after the gang who murdered his brother and raped his young wife in the old West. **90m/C VHS, Beta.** *IT* Richard Harrison, Klaus Kinski, Anne Puskin; ***D:*** Don Reynolds. *NO*

His Picture in the Papers 𝄞𝄞 **1916** An early silent comedy wherein the robust, red-meat-eating son of a health food tycoon must get his father's permission to marry by getting his picture favorably in the paper for advertising's sake. **68m/B VHS, Beta, 8mm.** Douglas Fairbanks Sr.; ***D:*** John Emerson; ***W:*** Anita Loos, John Emerson. *NOS, VYY, GPV*

His Prehistoric Past/The Bank **1915** Two of Chaplin's classic early shorts. **54m/B VHS, Beta.** Charlie Chaplin, Mack Swain, Edna Purviance; ***D:*** Charlie Chaplin. *VYY, GVV*

His Private Secretary 𝄞½ **1933** Wayne plays the jet-setting son of a wealthy businessman who wants his boy to settle down. And he does - after he meets the minister's beautiful daughter. **68m/B VHS, Beta.** John Wayne, Evalyn Knapp, Alec B. Francis, Reginald Barlow, Natalie Kingston, Arthur Hoyt, Al "Fuzzy" St. John; ***D:*** Philip H. Whitman. *DVT, HEG*

His Royal Slyness/Haunted Spooks **1920** Two Harold Lloyd shorts. "His Royal Slyness" (1919) offers Harold impersonating the king of a small kingdom, while in "Haunted Spooks" (1920), Harold gets suckered into living in a haunted mansion. Both films include music score. **52m/B VHS, Beta.** Harold Lloyd; ***D:*** Harold Lloyd. *VYY, CCB, GVV*

His Wife's Lover 𝄞𝄞𝄞 *Zayn Vaybs Lubovnik* **1931** An actor disguised as an old man wins the heart of a lovely young woman. He decides to test her fidelity by reverting to his handsome young self and attempting to seduce her. An enchanting comedy in Yiddish with English subtitles. **77m/B VHS, Beta.** Ludwig Satz, Michael Rosenberg, Isadore Cashier, Lucy Levine; ***D:*** Sidney Goldin. *ERG, FCT, INJ*

History is Made at Night 𝄞𝄞𝄞 **1937** A wife seeks a divorce from a jealous husband while on an Atlantic cruise; she ends up finding both true love and heartbreak in this story of a love triangle at sea. **98m/B VHS, Beta, LV.** Charles Boyer, Jean Arthur, Leo Carrillo, Colin Clive; ***D:*** Frank Borzage; ***C:*** Gregg Toland. *WAR, FCT*

History of the World: Part 1 𝄞𝄞 **1981 (R)** More misses than hits in this Brooks' parody of historic epics. A bluntly satiric vision of human evolution, from the Dawn of Man to the French Revolution told in an episodic fashion. Good for a few laughs. **90m/C VHS, Beta, LV.** Mel Brooks, Dom DeLuise, Madeline Kahn, Harvey Korman, Cloris Leachman, Gregory Hines, Pamela Stephenson, Paul Mazursky, Beatrice Arthur, Fritz Feld, John Hurt, Jack Carter, John Hillerman, John Gavin, Barry Levinson, Ron Carey, Howard Morris, Sid Caesar, Jackie Mason; ***D:*** Mel Brooks; ***W:*** Mel Brooks. *FOX*

The History of White People in America **1985** A pseudo-documentary look at the complicated life of a white midwestern family. Succeeds in making hilarious fun of many traditional prejudices. Originally made for cable television. **48m/C VHS, Beta.** Martin Mull, Fred Willard, Mary Kay Place, Teri Garr, Bob Eubanks; ***D:*** Harry Shearer. *MCA*

The History of White People in America: Vol. 2 **1985** Mull's television-special comedy satirizing WASP society in America. **40m/C VHS, Beta.** Martin Mull; ***D:*** Harry Shearer. *MCA*

Hit! 𝄞𝄞 **1973 (R)** When the 15-year-old daughter of a government agent dies of a drug overdose, he deals his revenge to top French heroin traffickers. **135m/C VHS.** Billy Dee Williams, Richard Pryor, Gwen Welles, Paul Hampton, Warren Kemmerling, Sid Melton; ***D:*** Sidney J. Furie; ***W:*** Alan R. Trustman, David M. Wolf; ***M:*** Lalo Schifrin. *PAR*

The Hit 𝄞𝄞½ **1985 (R)** A feisty young hooker gets mixed-up with two strong-armed hired killers as they escort an unusual stool-pigeon from his exile in Spain to their angry mob bosses. Minor cult-noir from the director of "My Beautiful Launderette" and "Dangerous Liaisons." **105m/C VHS, Beta, LV.** *GB* Terence Stamp, John Hurt, Laura Del Sol, Tim Roth, Fernando Rey, Bill Hunter; ***D:*** Stephen Frears; ***W:*** Peter Prince; ***M:*** Eric Clapton. *SUE, NLC*

Hit & Run 𝄞 *Revenge Squad* **1982** David Marks, a Manhattan cab driver, is haunted by recurring flashbacks of a freak hit-and-run accident in which his wife was struck down on a city street. **96m/C VHS, Beta.** Paul Perri, Claudia Cron; ***D:*** Charles Braverman; ***M:*** Brad Fiedel. *NO*

Hit Lady 𝄞𝄞 **1974** An elegant cultured woman becomes a hit lady for the syndicate in this predictable, yet slick gangster movie. Made for television. **74m/C VHS, Beta.** Yvette Mimieux, Dack Rambo, Clu Gulager, Keenan Wynn; ***D:*** Tracy Keenan Wynn. *PSM*

The Hit List 𝄞𝄞 **1988 (R)** A regular guy fights back brutally when his wife and child are mistakenly kidnapped by the Mafia. Fast-paced action makes up for thin plot. **87m/C VHS, Beta, LV.** Jan-Michael Vincent, Leo Rossi, Lance Henriksen, Charles Napier, Rip Torn; ***D:*** William Lustig; ***W:*** Peter Brosnan. *COL*

The Hit List 𝄞𝄞½ **1993 (R)** Charles Pike (Fahey) is a professional hitman working for attorney Peter Mayhew (Coburn) to wipe out drug lords. Then Mayhew gives Pike a new assignment. He introduces him to sexy widow Jordan Henning (Butler), who wants Pike to kill the man who murdered her husband. Pike finds himself mixing business with pleasure in a deadly combination that sees him dodging crooked cops and trained assassins. **97m/C VHS, LV.** Jeff Fahey, Yancy Butler, James Coburn; ***D:*** William Webb; ***W:*** Reed Steiner. *COL*

The Hit Man 𝄞𝄞 *Il Sicario* **1961** A crime drama that profiles the crisis of a man unfit to commit murder but who does for a price. **100m/B VHS, Beta.** *CIG*

Hit Men 𝄞½ **1973** Double crosses and gun battles highlight this tale of inner-city crime. **90m/C VHS, Beta.** Henry Silva, Mario Adorf, Woody Strode, Adolfo Celi. *VDC*

Hit the Deck 𝄞½ **1955** Second-rate studio musical about sailors on leave and looking for romance. Based on the 1927 Broadway musical. ♫Sometimes I'm Happy; Hallelujah; Why, Oh Why; Keeping Myself For You; More Than You Know; I Know That You Know; Lucky Bird. **112m/C VHS, Beta, LV.** Jane Powell, Tony Martin, Debbie Reynolds, Walter Pidgeon, Vic Damone, Gene Raymond, Ann Miller, Russ Tamblyn, J. Carrol Naish, Kay Armen, Richard Anderson; ***D:*** Roy Rowland; ***M:*** Vincent Youmans. *MGM*

Hit the Dutchman 𝄞𝄞 **1992 (R)** Routine gangster flick about Dutch Schultz trying to rise to the top of the New York crime community—with or without the help of underworld pals Legs Diamond and Lucky Luciano. An unrated version is also available. **116m/C VHS.** Bruce Nozick, Sally Kirkland, Will Kempe; ***D:*** Menahem Golan. *VMK*

Hit the Ice 𝄞𝄞 **1943** Newspaper photographers Bud and Lou are mistaken as gangsters in Chicago and the usual complications ensue. Includes an appearance by Johnny Long & His Orchestra. ♫I'm Like A Fish Out Of Water; Happiness Bound; I'd Like to Set You to Music; Slap Polka. **89m/C VHS, Beta.** Bud Abbott, Lou Costello, Patric Knowles, Elyse Knox, Ginny Simms; ***D:*** Charles Lamont. *MCA*

Hit the Saddle 𝄞𝄞 **1937** The Three Mesquiteers track down a gang involved in capturing wild horses in protected areas although one of three is more interested in the charms of a dance hall girl (played by starlet Rita Cansino who would soon become Rita Hayworth). **54m/B VHS, Beta.** Bob Livingston, Ray Corrigan, Max Terhune, J.P. McGowan, Yakima Canutt, Rita Hayworth; ***D:*** Mack V. Wright. *NOS, VCN, REP*

Hit Woman: The Double Edge 𝄞𝄞½ **1993 (R)** Lucci plays a dual role as an FBI agent and the look-alike killer-for-hire that she's tracking. Originally made for television, the video version contains additional footage that earned the "R" rating. **92m/C VHS.** Susan Lucci, Robert Urich, Michael Woods, Robert Prosky. *APX*

The Hitch-Hiker 𝄞𝄞𝄞 **1953** Two young men off on the vacation of their dreams pick up a psychopathic hitchhiker with a right eye that never closes, even when he sleeps. Taut suspense makes this flick worth seeing. **71m/B VHS.** Edmond O'Brien, Frank Lovejoy, William Talman, Jose Torvay; ***D:*** Ida Lupino. *SNC*

Hitchcock Classics Collection: Trailers on Tape **1985** Collection of 20 previews for such Hitchcock favorites as "Shadow of a Doubt," "Rear Window," "Vertigo," "North by Northwest" and "Psycho." Some trailers are in black and white. **55m/C VHS, Beta.** ***D:*** Alfred Hitchcock. *SFR*

Hitchcock Collection **1987** A collector's set containing three films from the master of suspense. Includes: "The Lady Vanishes," "The 39 Steps," "Vintage Hitchcock"—see him from a set designer to a director. In B/W and color. **200m/C VHS, Beta.** Alfred Hitchcock, Michael Redgrave, Paul Lukas, Robert Donat, Madeleine Carroll; ***D:*** Alfred Hitchcock. *MPI*

The Hitcher 𝄞𝄞½ **1986 (R)** A young man picks up a hitchhiker on a deserted stretch of California highway only to be tormented by the man's repeated appearances: is he real or a figment of his imagination? Ferociously funny, sadomasochistic comedy with graphic violence. **98m/C VHS, Beta, LV.** Rutger Hauer, C. Thomas Howell, Jennifer Jason Leigh, Jeffrey DeMunn, John M. Jackson; ***D:*** Robert Harmon; ***W:*** Eric Red; ***M:*** Mark Isham. *NO*

The Hitchhiker **1985** HBO's chilling horror anthology series contains a trio of terrifying tales. Additional episodes are available. In this first collection, Hamlin stars in "The Curse," about Yuppie occult vengeance; "W.G.O.D.," finds Busey and Page caught up in radio religion; and "Hired Help," finds Black with a less than human handyman. **90m/C VHS,**

Beta, LV. Harry Hamlin, Gary Busey, Geraldine Page, Karen Black. *WAR, MOV*

Hitchhiker 2 **1985** Three more episodes from HBO's horror series: "Dead Man's Curve," "Nightshift," and "Last Scene." **90m/C VHS, Beta, LV.** Peter Coyote, Margot Kidder, Darren McGavin, Susan Anspach. *WAR*

Hitchhiker 3 **1987** Three episodes from the anthology mystery series: "Ghost Writer," "And If We Dream," and "True Believer." Made-for-cable television. **90m/C VHS, Beta, LV.** Ornella Muti, Willem Dafoe, Barry Bostwick, Dayle Haddon, Stephen Collins, Robert Weiss, Tom Skerritt. *ORI, WAR*

Hitchhiker 4 **1987** Three episodes of the cable-television suspense series: "Man's Best Friend," about a lonely man whose pet dog tears his enemies to bits. "Face to Face," about the revenge exacted upon a drug-abusing cosmetic surgeon after he mucks up an operation; and "Videodate," about a guy being lured into a sinister video performance piece via his use of video dating services. **90m/C VHS, Beta, LV.** Michael O'Keefe, Sybil Danning, Sonja Smits, Robert Vaughn, Shannon Tweed, Greg Henry. *ORI, WAR*

Hitchhikers *Woof!* **1972 (R)** Trash film about a bunch of scantily clad female hitchhikers who rob the motorists who stop to pick them up. Keep right on going when you spot this roadkill. **90m/C VHS, Beta.** Misty Rowe, Norman Klar, Linda Avery; ***D:*** Ferd Sebastian. *NO*

The Hitchhiker's Guide to the Galaxy **1981** The six episode BBC television adaptation of Douglas Adams' hilarious science-fiction books. Features the intergalatic Ford Prefect, sent to Earth to update its planetary listing in the Hitchhiker's Guide; hapless hero Arthur Dent, a typical Englishman caught up in space mayhem; and an odd assortment of aliens, including Marvin the Paranoid Android. The show's sheer cheesiness is part of the charm. Available in both single-cassette and double-cassette versions, the latter includes a copy of the book and a dedication from Adams. **194m/C VHS, LV.** *GB* Simon Jones, David Dixon, Sandra Dickinson, Mark Wing-Davey; ***D:*** Alan Bell. *FOX, MOV, FUS*

Hitler 𝔅𝔅½ *Women of Nazi Germany* **1962** The true story of the infamous Nazi dictator's rise to power and his historic downfall. **103m/B VHS, Beta.** Richard Basehart, Maria Emo, Cordula Trantow; ***D:*** Stuart Heisler. *FOX*

Hitler: Dead or Alive 𝔅𝔅 **1943** Three ex-cons devise a scheme to gain a million-dollar reward for capturing Adolf Hitler in this low-budget production. **64m/B VHS, Beta.** Ward Bond, Dorothy Tree, Bruce Edwards, Warren Hymer, Paul Fix, Russell Hicks, Bobby Watson; ***D:*** Nick Grinde. *NOS, MRV, DVT*

Hitler: The Last Ten Days 𝔅𝔅 **1973 (PG)** Based on an eyewitness account, the story of Hitler's last days in an underground bunker gives insight to his madness. **106m/C VHS, Beta.** Alec Guinness, Simon Ward, Adolfo Celi; ***D:*** Ennio de Concini. *PAR, GLV*

Hitler's Children 𝔅𝔅𝔅 **1943** Two young people, a German boy and an American girl, are caught in the horror of Nazi Germany. He's attracted to Hitler's rant, she's repelled. Exploitative yet engrossing. **83m/B VHS, Beta.** Tim Holt, Bonita Granville, Otto Kruger, H.B. Warner, Irving Reis, Hans Conried, Lloyd Corrigan; ***D:*** Edward Dmytryk. *MED, IHF*

Hitler's Daughter 𝔅 **1990 (R)** Made for TV movie following the trials and tribulations of the illegitimate daughter of Adolf Hitler. She's all grown up now...and wants to rule the United States. She secures a position of power during an election and now Nazi-hunters must figure out her identity before she takes over the world! **88m/C VHS, Beta.** Kay Lenz, Veronica Cartwright, Melody Anderson, Patrick Cassidy, Carolyn Dunn, Lindsay Merrithew, George R. Robertson; ***D:*** James A. Contner. *PAR*

The Hitman 𝔅𝔅 **1991 (R)** Norris plays a cop undercover as a syndicate hit man in Seattle, where he cleans up crime by triggering a three-way mob bloodbath between beastly Italian mafiosi, snooty French-Canadian hoods, and fanatical Iranian scum. But he teaches a black kid martial arts, so you know he's politically correct. Action addicts will give this a passing grade; all others need not apply. **95m/C VHS, LV, 8mm.** Chuck Norris, Michael Parks, Al Waxman, Alberta Watson, Salim Grant, Ken Pogue, Marcel Sabourin, Bruno Gerussi, Frank Ferrucci; ***D:*** Aaron Norris. *CAN, WAR*

The Hitter 𝔅𝔅 **1979 (R)** A former prizefighter, his girlfriend, and a washed-up promoter are all on the run in this adventure tale. **94m/C VHS.** Ron O'Neal, Adolph Caesar, Sheila Frazier; ***D:*** Christopher Leitch. *NO*

Hittin' the Trail 𝔅 **1937** The Good Cowboy is mistaken for a murdering varmint, and must prove his innocence. **57m/B VHS, Beta.** Tex Ritter, Charles "Blackie" King, Ray Whitley, The Range Ramblers; ***D:*** Robert North Bradbury. *NOS, VDM*

Hitz 𝔅½ **1992 (R)** In a Los Angeles barrio, Musico, a Loco gang member, kills two rival gang members. Arrested and convicted when a young boy named Pepe is coerced into testifying against him, Musico is killed in the courtroom. But the violence doesn't stop. The judge, who wants to reform the juvenile court system, tries to protect Pepe, and both are targeted for death by the Loco gang. **90m/C VHS.** Elliott Gould, Emilia Crow, Karen Black, Cuba Gooding Jr. *VMK*

The Hobbit 𝔅𝔅𝔅 **1978** An animated interpretation of J.R.R. Tolkien's novel of the same name. The story follows Bilbo Baggins and his journeys in Middle Earth and encounters with the creatures who inhabit it. He joins comrades to battle against evil beings and creatures. Made for television. **76m/C VHS, Beta, 8mm.** ***D:*** Arthur Rankin Jr., Jules Bass; ***V:*** Orson Bean, John Huston, Otto Preminger, Richard Boone. *WAR, CHI, FCT*

Hobgoblins 𝔅 **198?** Little creatures escape from a studio vault and wreak havoc. **92m/C VHS, Beta.** Jeffrey Culver, Tom Bartlett; ***D:*** Rick Sloane. *TWE*

The Hoboken Chicken Emergency **1984** Arthur's supposed to pick up a turkey for the family Thanksgiving dinner. Instead he returns with a 266-pound live chicken named Henrietta. Originally aired on PBS as part of the "Wonderworks" series. **55m/C VHS.** Dick Van Patten, Peter Billingsley, Gabe Kaplan, Arlene Golonka; ***D:*** Peter Baldwin. *PME, FCT, BTV*

Hobo's Christmas 𝔅𝔅 **1987** A man who left his family to become a hobo comes home for Christmas 25 years later. Hughes turns in a delightful performance as the hobo in this made for television special. **94m/C VHS, Beta.** Barnard Hughes, William Hickey, Gerald McRaney, Wendy Crewson; ***D:*** Will MacKenzie. *NO*

Hobson's Choice 𝔅𝔅𝔅 **1953** A prosperous businessman in the 1890s tries to keep his daughter from marrying, but the strong-willed daughter has other ideas. Remade for television in 1983. **107m/B VHS, Beta, LV.** *GB* Charles Laughton, John Mills, Brenda de Banzie; ***D:*** David Lean; ***C:*** Jack Hildyard; ***M:*** Malcolm Arnold. British Academy Awards '54: Best Film. *ING, NLC, HMV*

Hobson's Choice 𝔅𝔅 **1983** Made-for-television remake of the old family comedy about a crusty, penny-pinching businessman whose headstrong daughter proves to him she'll not become an old maid. Instead she marries one of his employees. Not bad, but not as good as the original. **95m/C VHS, Beta.** Jack Warden, Sharon Gless, Richard Thomas, Lillian Gish; ***D:*** Gilbert Cates. *FOX*

Hockey Night 𝔅𝔅½ **1984** A movie for pre- and early teens in which a girl goalie makes the boys' hockey team. **77m/C VHS, Beta.** *CA* Megan Follows, Rick Moranis, Gail Youngs, Martin Harburg, Henry Ramer; ***D:*** Paul Shapiro. *FHE*

Hocus Pocus 𝔅𝔅½ **1993 (PG)** The divine Miss M is back, but this time she's not so sweet. Midler, Najimy, and Parker are 17th century witches accidentally conjured up in the 20th century, appropriately enough on Halloween in Salem, Massachusetts. Seems they were hung 300 years back and they take their revenge in some surprisingly gruesome ways, given the Disney label. They rant, they rave, they sing (only once), they fly. See this one for the three stars who make up for the lack of substance with their comedic talents. **95m/C VHS, Beta, LV.** Bette Midler, Kathy Najimy, Sarah Jessica Parker, Thora Birch, Doug Jones, Omri Katz, Vinessa Shaw, Stephanie Faracy, Charles Rocket; ***Cameos:*** Penny Marshall, Garry Marshall; ***D:*** Kenny Ortega; ***W:*** Neil Cuthbert, Mick Garris; ***M:*** John Debney. *DIS, BTV*

Hoffa 𝔅𝔅𝔅 **1992 (R)** The story of union organizer James R. Hoffa who oversaw the rise of the Teamsters, a labor union composed mostly of truck drivers, from its fledgling infancy during the Great Depression to a membership of 2 million by the 1970's. Powerful performances by Nicholson in the title role and DeVito, who plays a union aide, a fictitious composite of several men who actually served Hoffa. This almost affectionate biographical treatment stands out in contrast from a career bristling with tension and violence. Proceeds through a series of flashbacks from the day Hoffa disappeared, July 30, 1975. **140m/C VHS, LV.** Jack Nicholson, Danny DeVito, Armand Assante, J.T. Walsh, Frank Whaley, Kevin Anderson, John P. Ryan, Robert Prosky, Natalija Nogulich, Nicholas Pryor, John C. Reilly, Karen Young, Cliff Gorman; ***D:*** Danny DeVito; ***W:*** David Mamet; ***C:*** Stephen Burum; ***M:*** David Newman. Nominations: Academy Awards '92: Best Cinematography, Best Makeup. *FXV*

Hog Wild 𝔅½ **1980 (PG)** A clique of high school nerds exact revenge on bullies from the local mean motorcycle gang, and a girl is torn between the two factions. **97m/C VHS, Beta.** *CA* Patti D'Arbanville, Tony Rosato, Michael Biehn; ***D:*** Les Rose. *NLC*

The Holcroft Covenant 𝔅𝔅 **1985 (R)** Based upon the complex Robert Ludlum novel. Details the efforts of a man trying to release a secret fund that his Nazi father humanistically set up to relieve the future sufferings of Holocaust survivors. Confusing, and slow, but interesting, nonetheless. **112m/C VHS, Beta, LV.** *GB* Michael Caine, Victoria Tennant, Anthony Andrews, Lilli Palmer, Mario Adorf, Michael Lonsdale; ***D:*** John Frankenheimer; ***W:*** Edward Anhalt, John Hopkins, George Axelrod. *MGM*

Hold 'Em Jail 𝔅𝔅½ **1932** Some good laughs with Wheeler and Woolsey starting a competitive football team at Kennedy's Bidemore Prison. **65m/B VHS, Beta.** Bert Wheeler, Robert Woolsey, Edgar Kennedy, Betty Grable, Edna May Oliver; ***D:*** Norman Taurog. *CCB*

Hold Me, Thrill Me, Kiss Me 𝔅𝔅½ **1993 (R)** "Offbeat" barely begins to describe this comedy about a hapless loser who finds true love. Eli (Parrish) has escaped marriage to a rich girl named Twinkle (Young), unfortunately it took a little shooting to do it and now Eli's hiding out in a tacky pink trailer park where Sabra (Naschak), an insatiable stripper with a fondness for sex toys, immediately goes after Eli's bod. But he falls for her naive (and virginal) sister, Dannie (Shelly). Hershman manages to keep all the free-wheeling goings on under control. Film debut of former model Parrish; directorial debut feature of Hershman. **92m/C VHS.** Max Parrish, Adrienne Shelly, Andrea Naschak, Sean Young, Diane Ladd, Bela Lehoczky, Ania Suli; ***Cameos:*** Timothy Leary; ***D:*** Joel Hershman; ***W:*** Joel Hershman. *LIV*

Hold That Ghost 𝔅𝔅𝔅 *Oh, Charlie* **1941** Abbott and Costello inherit an abandoned roadhouse where the illicit loot of its former owner, a "rubbed out" mobster, is supposedly hidden. **86m/B VHS, Beta.** Bud Abbott, Lou Costello, Joan Davis, Richard Carlson, Mischa Auer, The Andrews Sisters; ***D:*** Arthur Lubin. *MCA*

Hold the Dream 𝔅 **1985** A made-for-television mini-series sequel to Barbara Taylor Bradford's "A Woman of Substance." **195m/C VHS, Beta.** Jenny Seagrove, Stephen Collins, Deborah Kerr, James Brolin; ***D:*** Don Sharp. *NO*

Hold Your Man 🦴🦴🦴 **1933** Great star vehicle that turns from comedy to drama with Harlow falling for hustler Gable. Harlow and Gable are at their best in this unlikely story of a crooked couple. Direction drags at times, but snappy dialogue and the stars' personalities more than make up for it. **86m/B VHS.** Jean Harlow, Clark Gable, Stuart Erwin, Dorothy Burgess, Garry Owen, Paul Hurst, Elizabeth Patterson, Laura La Plante; ***D:*** Sam Wood; ***W:*** Anita Loos, Howard Emmett Rogers. *MGM*

A Hole in the Head 🦴🦴½ **1959** A comedy-drama about a shiftless but charming lout who tries to raise money to save his hotel from foreclosure and learn to be responsible for his young son. Notable for the introduction of the song "High Hopes." ♫High Hopes; All My Tomorrows. **120m/C VHS, Beta, LV.** Frank Sinatra, Edward G. Robinson, Thelma Ritter, Carolyn Jones, Eleanor Parker, Eddie Hodges, Keenan Wynn, Joi Lansing; ***D:*** Frank Capra; ***W:*** Arnold Schulman; ***C:*** William H. Daniels. Academy Awards '59: Best Song ("High Hopes"). *MGM*

Hole in the Sky 🦴🦴½ *The Ranger, the Cook and a Hole in the Sky* **1995 (PG)** Teenaged Mac (O'Connell) is working for the Montana forestry service in the summer of 1919 under the tutelage of taciturn legend Bill Bell (a mustache-less Elliott). Mac learns some lessons about growing up, first love, card-playing—and never to rile the camp cook. Based on an autobiographical story by Norman MacLean. Made for TV; filmed on location in British Columbia. **94m/C VHS.** Sam Elliott, Jerry O'Connell, Ricky Jay, Molly Parker; ***D:*** John Kent Harrison; ***W:*** Robert W. Lenski. *HMK*

The Holes 🦴🦴½ *Les Gaspards* **1972 (PG)** A Parisian book shop owner's daughter vanishes along with other local citizens and American tourists, and he decides to investigate when the police won't. In French with subtitles. **92m/C VHS, Beta.** *FR* Philippe Noiret, Charles Denner, Michael Serrault, Gerard Depardieu. *FHE, FCT*

Holiday 🦴🦴🦴½ *Free to Live; Unconventional Linda* **1938** The classically genteel screwball comedy about a rich girl who steals her sister's fiance. A yardstick in years to come for sophisticated, urbane Hollywood romanticism. Based on the play by Philip Barry who later wrote "The Philadelphia Story." **93m/B VHS, Beta, LV.** Cary Grant, Katharine Hepburn, Doris Nolan, Edward Everett Horton, Ruth Donnelly, Lew Ayres, Binnie Barnes; ***D:*** George Cukor; ***W:*** Donald Ogden Stewart, Sidney Buchman. Nominations: Academy Awards '36: Best Interior Decoration. *COL*

Holiday Affair 🦴🦴½ **1949** Hollywood yuletide charmer about a pretty widow being courted by two very different men. **86m/B VHS, Beta, LV.** Robert Mitchum, Janet Leigh, Griff Barnett, Wendell Corey, Esther Dale, Henry O'Neill, Harry (Henry) Morgan, Larry J. Blake; ***D:*** Don Hartman. *TTC*

Holiday Hotel 🦴🦴 **1977 (R)** A group of wild French vacationers let loose at their favorite little resort hotel along the Brittany coast. Available in French with English subtitles or dubbed into English. **109m/C VHS, Beta.** *FR* Sophie Barjae, Daniel Ceccaldi; ***D:*** Michael Lang. *SUE*

Holiday in Havana 🦴🦴 **1949** Desi Arnaz is back in Cuba winning hearts and dance contests. Watch only for Desi's presence. ♫Holiday in Havana; The Arnaz Jam; Straw Hat Song; Rhumba Rumbero; Copacobana; Made For Each Other; I'll Take Romance. **73m/B VHS.** Desi Arnaz Sr., Lolita Valdez, Mary Hatcher, Ann Doran; ***D:*** Jean Yarbrough. *GKK*

Holiday in Mexico 🦴🦴½ **1946** Pidgeon plays the U.S. ambassador to Mexico whose teenage daughter (Powell) tries to run his life along with his household. He falls for a singer while she develops a crush on an older, respected pianist (Iturbi playing himself). Lots of lively production numbers featuring Xavier Cugat and his orchestra. ♫I Think Of You; Walter Winchell Rhumba; Yo Te Amo Mucho—And That's That; And Dreams Remain; Holiday in Mexico; Ave Maria; Les Filles de Cadiz; Italian Street Song; Polonaise in A Flat Major. **127m/C VHS.** Walter Pidgeon, Jane Powell, Ilona Massey, Jose Iturbi, Roddy McDowall, Xavier Cugat, Hugo Haas; ***D:*** George Sidney; ***W:*** Isobel Lennart; ***C:*** Harry Stradling; ***M:*** Georgie Stoll. *MGM*

Holiday Inn 🦴🦴🦴 **1942** Fred Astaire and Bing Crosby are rival song-and-dance men who decide to work together to turn a Connecticut farm into an inn, open only on holidays. Remade in 1954 as "White Christmas." ♫White Christmas; Be Careful, It's My Heart; Plenty to Be Thankful For; Abraham, Abraham; Let's Say It With Firecrackers; I Gotta Say I Love You Cause I Can't Tell A Lie; Let's Start the New Year Right; Happy Holidays; Song of Freedom. **101m/B VHS, Beta, LV.** Bing Crosby, Fred Astaire, Marjorie Reynolds, Walter Abel, Virginia Dale; ***D:*** Mark Sandrich. Academy Awards '42: Best Song ("White Christmas"); Nominations: Academy Awards '42: Best Story, Best Original Score. *MCA*

Holiday Rhythm 🦴½ **1950** A television promoter is knocked out and dreams of a world-wide trip full of entertainment, comedy, and insanity. **61m/B VHS, Beta, LV.** Mary Beth Hughes, Tex Ritter, David Street, Donald MacBride. *NO*

Hollow Gate **1988** Trick or Treat?? Four kids find out when they run into a guy with hungry dogs. **90m/C VHS, Beta.** Addison Randall. *NO*

Hollywood After Dark 🦴 **1965** McClanahan plays a young starlet trying to make it big in Hollywood. Pure exploitation schlock. Not released theatrically until 1968. **?m/C VHS.** Rue McClanahan. *SNC, TPV*

Hollywood Bloopers 🦴🦴½ **195?** Hilarious outtakes from some of Hollywood's finest movies, featuring stars such as Bette Davis, James Cagney, Humphrey Bogart, Rosalind Russell, Errol Flynn, Kirk Douglas, and many more. **85m/B VHS, Beta.** Lauren Bacall, Ronald Reagan, James Stewart, Joan Blondell, Rosalind Russell, Errol Flynn, Kirk Douglas, Barbara Stanwyck. *VDM*

Hollywood Boulevard 🦴🦴½ **1976 (R)** Behind-the-scenes glimpse of shoestring-budget movie making offers comical sex, violence, sight gags, one-liners, comedy bits, and mock-documentary footage. Commander Cody and His Lost Planet Airmen are featured. **93m/C VHS, Beta.** Candice Rialson, Mary Woronov, Rita George, Jonathan Kaplan, Jeffrey Kramer, Dick Miller, Paul Bartel; ***D:*** Joe Dante, Allan Arkush. *WAR, OM*

Hollywood Boulevard 2 🦴 **1989 (R)** A "B" movie studio finds its top actresses being killed off and terror reigns supreme as the mystery grows more intense. Could that psycho-bimbo from outer space have something to do with it? **82m/C VHS, Beta.** Ginger Lynn Allen, Kelly Monteith, Eddie Deezen, Ken Wright, Steve Vinovich; ***D:*** Steve Barnett. *MGM*

Hollywood Canteen 🦴🦴🦴🦴 **1944** Star-studded extravaganza with just about every Warner Bros. lot actor in this tribute to love and nationalism. Lovesick G.I. Hutton falls for Leslie, wins a date with her in a phony raffle set up at the Hollywood Canteen, and the sparks fly right away. But he thinks she tricked him as he boards his train and she's not there to see him off. Lame story is redeemed by the talented cast and wonderful musical numbers which make this picture fly with charm and style. Before production began there were arguments over "unpatriotic" actors—labeled as such due to their lack of participation in this, and other similar movies produced at the time. ♫Don't Fence Me In; Sweet Dreams, Sweetheart; You Can Always Tell A Yank; We're Having a Baby; What Are You Doin' the Rest of Your Life; The General Jumped At Dawn; Gettin' Corns For My Country; Voodoo Moon; Tumblin' Tumbleweeds. **124m/B VHS.** Robert Hutton, Dane Clark, Janis Paige, Jonathan Hale, Barbara Brown, James Flavin, Eddie Marr, Ray Teal, Bette Davis, Joan Leslie, Jack Benny, Jimmy Dorsey, Joan Crawford, John Garfield, Barbara Stanwyck, Ida Lupino, Eddie Cantor, Jack Carson, Eleanor Parker, Alexis Smith, S.Z. Sakall, Peter Lorre, Sydney Greenstreet, Helmut Dantine; ***D:*** Delmer Daves; ***W:*** Delmer Daves. Nominations: Academy Awards '44: Best Song ("Sweet Dreams Sweetheart"), Best Sound, Best Original Score. *FOX, FCT*

Hollywood Chainsaw Hookers 🦴🦴 **1988 (R)** A campy, sexy, very bloody parody about attractive prostitutes who dismember their unsuspecting customers. **90m/C VHS, Beta.** Linnea Quigley, Gunnar Hansen, Jay Richardson, Michelle (McClellan) Bauer; ***D:*** Fred Olen Ray. *NO*

Hollywood Chaos 🦴½ **1989** Director Ballantine's stars quit his production before it even starts, so he gets the next best thing - star look-alikes. However, his problems are just beginning. One of his new "stars" is kidnapped, and his reclusive stage manager is hunted as the object of desire for a female motorcycle gang. **90m/C VHS.** Carl Ballantine, Tricia Leigh Fisher, Kathleen Freeman; ***D:*** Sean McNamara. *WLA*

Hollywood Clowns **1985** Glenn Ford narrates this tribute to the screen's greatest comedians, with clips from many classic scenes. **60m/C VHS, Beta.** Buster Keaton, W.C. Fields, Charlie Chaplin, Harold Lloyd, Bud Abbott, Lou Costello, Stan Laurel, Oliver Hardy, Groucho Marx, Harpo Marx, Chico Marx, Jerry Lewis, Dean Martin, Red Skelton, Danny Kaye, Betty Hutton, Bob Hope. *MGM*

Hollywood Come Home **1962** Ray Milland hosts this look at the history of the movie industry from WWII to the early 60's. Also on this tape is "Hollywood Historama," a collection of video biographies of such luminaries as Mae West and John Barrymore. **54m/B VHS, Beta, 8mm.** Ray Milland. *VYY*

Hollywood Confidential 🦴 **193?** A beautiful Eastern girl goes to Hollywood and suffers irrevocable corruption. **55m/B VHS, Beta.** *NO*

Hollywood Cop 🦴½ **1987 (R)** A tough cop in Hollywood goes up against the mob for the sake of a kidnapped boy. **101m/C VHS, Beta.** Jim Mitchum, David Goss, Cameron Mitchell, Troy Donahue, Aldo Ray; ***D:*** Amir Shervan. *CEL*

Hollywood Crime Wave **196?** An examination of crime and criminals as seen in vintage Hollywood gangster films. Features scenes with Humphrey Bogart, James Cagney and Edward G. Robinson. **60m/B VHS, Beta.** *MPI*

The Hollywood Detective 🦴🦴 **1989 (PG)** An average TV movie that spoofs "Kojak." A TV detective tries it out for real, and gets into troubles for which he can't pause "for a message from our sponsor." **88m/C VHS, Beta.** Telly Savalas, Helene Udy, George Coe, Joe Dallesandro, Tom Reese; ***D:*** Kevin Connor. *MCA*

Hollywood Dreams 🦴½ **1994 (R)** Starlet on the Hollywood casting couch saga of a midwestern gal that comes to California with dreams of making it big. **90m/C VHS.** Kelly Cook, Danny Smith, Debra Beatty; ***D:*** Ralph Portillo. *CEL*

Hollywood Erotic Film Festival 🦴 **1987** A package of soft-core shorts, animated as well as live action, from around the world. **75m/C VHS, Beta.** *PAR*

Hollywood Ghost Stories **1986** A view of supernatural activity in Hollywood, on the screen and behind the scenes. Includes interviews with William Peter Blatty, Sir Arthur Conan Doyle, Elke Sommer and others. **75m/C VHS, Beta.** *WAR*

Hollywood Goes to War **1954** Five shorts produced for the entertainment of G.I.'s overseas or for home front bond drives: "The All-Star Bond Rally" features Hope, Crosby, Harry James and His Orchestra, Sinatra, Grable, Marx, and the Talking Pin-Ups; "Hollywood Canteen Overseas Special" features Shore, Cantor, Durante, and Skelton; "Mail Call (Strictly G.I.)" is a filmed "Mail Call" radio program; "G.I. Movie Weekly-Sing with the Stars" features Miranda and her fruit-basket hat and a Portuguese follow-the-bouncing-ball sing-along; and "Invaders in Greasepaint," the story of the North African USO tour of the "Four Jills in a Jeep." Also includes the Jill's memorable rendition of the wartime classic "Snafu," banned from the airwaves for its racy lyrics. **41m/B VHS, Beta.** Bob Hope, Bing Crosby, Frank Sinatra, Betty Grable, Harpo Marx, Jimmy Durante, Eddie Cantor, Red Skelton, Bud Abbott, Lou Costello, Dinah Shore, Dorothy Lamour, Carmen Miranda. *NO*

Hollywood Harry 🦴 *Harry's Machine* **1986 (PG-13)** A private-eye mystery/parody, about an inept detective who searches for a missing porn actress. **99m/C VHS, Beta.** Robert Forster, Kathrine Forster, Joe Spinell, Shannon Wilcox; ***D:*** Robert Forster; ***W:*** Curt Allen. *MED*

Hollywood Heartbreak 🦴🦴 **1989** It's heartbreak in tinseltown for a young writer who's trying to pitch his movie script but winds up defending himself from slimy agents and persistent starlets. Another entry for Bartlett's familiar plotlines. **90m/C VHS.** Mark Moses, Carol Mayo Jenkins, Ron Karabatsos, Richard Romanus, James LeGros; ***D:*** Lance Dickson. *VTR*

Hollywood High 🦴 **1977 (R)** Four attractive teen couples converge on the mansion of an eccentric silent-film star for an unusual vacation experience in this teenage skin flick. Followed by a sequel. **81m/C VHS, Beta.** Marcy Albrecht, Sherry Hardin, Rae Sperling, Susanne Kevin Mead; ***D:*** Patrick Wright. *LIV, VES*

Hollywood High, Part 2 🦴 **1981 (R)** Ignored by their boyfriends for the lure of sun and surf, three comely high school students try their best to regain their interest. **86m/C VHS, Beta.** April May, Donna Lynn, Camille Warner, Lee Thornburg; ***D:*** Caruth C. Byrd. *LIV, VES*

Hollywood Home Movies **1987 (PG)** The home movies of more than 60 celebrities are compiled in this program. Offers a nostalgic look at how the demi-gods of yesteryear lived, worked, played, and relaxed. **58m/B VHS, Beta.** Marilyn Monroe, John Wayne, Gregory Peck, Robert Mitchum, Ann-Margret. *IHF, MPI*

Hollywood Hot Tubs 🦴 **1984 (R)** Teen sex romp has adolescent picking up some extra cash and a lot of fun repairing the hot tubs of the rich and famous. **103m/C VHS, Beta.** Donna McDaniel, Michael Andrew, Katt Shea Ruben, Paul Gunning, Edy Williams, Jewel Shepard; ***D:*** Chuck Vincent. *LIV, VES, VTR*

Hollywood Hot Tubs 2: Educating Crystal 🦴 **1989 (R)** A softcore comedy about a well-tanned ingenue learning about business in Hollywood during numerous hot tub trysts. **103m/C VHS, Beta, LV.** Jewel Shepard, Patrick Day, Remy O'Neill, David Tiefen, Bart Braverman; ***D:*** Ken Raich. *CCB*

Hollywood in Trouble 🦴 **1987** A bumbling middle-aged fool decides to break into the wacky movie-making business. **90m/C VHS, Beta.** Vic Vallard, Jean Levine, Jerry Tiffe, Pamela Dixon, Jerry Cleary. *NO*

Hollywood Man 🦴🦴 **1976 (R)** A Hollywood actor wants to make his own film but when his financial support comes from the mob there's trouble ahead. **90m/C VHS, Beta.** William Smith, Don Stroud, Jennifer Billingsley, Mary Woronov; ***D:*** Jack Starrett. *NO*

Hollywood Mystery 🦴½ *Hollywood Hoodlum* **1934** A publicity agent stops at nothing to promote his would-be starlet girlfriend. **53m/B VHS.** June Clyde, Frank Albertson, Joe Crespo; ***D:*** B. Reeves Eason. *NOS, LOO*

Hollywood or Bust 🦴🦴½ **1956** The zany duo take their act on the road as they head for Tinsel Town in order to meet Lewis' dream girl Ekberg. This was the last film for the Martin & Lewis team and it's not the swan song their fans would have hoped for. **95m/C VHS.** Dean Martin, Jerry Lewis, Anita Ekberg, Pat Crowley, Maxie "Slapsie" Rosenbloom, Willard Waterman; ***D:*** Frank Tashlin. *PAR, CCB*

Hollywood Outtakes & Rare Footage **1983** A collection of rare and unusual film clips and excerpts that feature dozens of Hollywood stars in screen tests, promotional shorts, home movies, outtakes, television appearances and WWII propaganda shorts. Some segments in black and white. **85m/C VHS, Beta, LV.** Marilyn Monroe, James Dean, Joan Crawford, Judy Garland, Humphrey Bogart, Ronald Reagan, Bette Davis, Vivien Leigh, Carole Lombard. *COL, RXM*

Hollywood Party 🦴🦴½ **1934** Durante plays a film star who decides to throw a Hollywood bash. Any plot is incidental as it is mainly an excuse to have numerous stars of the day appear in brief comic bits or musical numbers. Mickey Mouse and the Big Bad Wolf of Disney fame also appear in color animated footage combined with live action. Numerous MGM directors worked on parts of the film but Dwan was given the task of trying to pull the various scenes together (he is uncredited onscreen). ♫Hollywood Party; Hello; Reincarnation; I've Had My Moments; Feeling High; Hot Chocolate Soldiers. **72m/B VHS.** Jimmy Durante, Stan Laurel, Oliver Hardy, Lupe Velez, Ted Healy, Moe Howard, Curly Howard, Larry Fine, Robert Young, Charles Butterworth, Polly Moran, George Givot, Tom Kennedy; ***D:*** Allan Dwan; ***V:*** Walt Disney, Billy Bletcher. *MGM*

Hollywood Scandals and Tragedies **1988** A look at the skeletons-in-the-closet surrounding the deaths and private turmoils of James Dean, Rock Hudson, Vivien Leigh, Frances Farmer, Sal Mineo, Sharon Tate, Jayne Mansfield, and others. **90m/C VHS, Beta.** *MPI*

Hollywood Shuffle 🦴🦴½ **1987 (R)** Townsend's autobiographical comedy about a struggling black actor in Hollywood trying to find work and getting nothing but stereotypical roles. Written, directed, financed by Townsend, who created this often clever and appealing film on a $100,000 budget. **81m/C VHS, Beta, LV.** Robert Townsend, Anne-Marie Johnson, Starletta DuPois, Helen Martin, Keenen Ivory Wayans, Damon Wayans, Craigus R. Johnson; ***D:*** Robert Townsend; ***W:*** Robert Townsend, Keenen Ivory Wayans; ***M:*** Patrice Rushen, Udi Harpaz. *NO*

Hollywood Stadium Mystery 🦴🦴 **1938** A boxer turns up dead before a big match and a D.A. investigates. Performances hold this one up, especially by Hamilton who later played Commissioner Gordon on TV's "Batman." **66m/B VHS, Beta.** Neil Hamilton, Evelyn Venable, Jimmy Wallington, Barbara Pepper, Lucien Littlefield, Lynn (Mary Hart) Roberts, Charles Williams, James Spottswood, Reed Hadley, Smiley Burnette; ***D:*** David Howard. *SNC*

The Hollywood Strangler Meets the Skid Row Slasher *Woof! The Model Killer* **1979 (R)** Voiced-over narration, canned music and an unfathomable plot are but a few of this would-be fright fest's finer points. Uninhibited by any narrative connection, two terrors strike fear in the heart of Tinseltown. While a psycho photographer cruises L.A. taking pictures of models he subsequently strangles, a woman working in a bare-bums magazine store takes a stab (with a knife) at lowering the city's derelict population. There's a word for this sort of dribble, and it isn't versimilitude. Steckler used an alias (not surprisingly) for this one—Wolfgang Schmidt. **72m/C VHS.** Pierre Agostino, Carolyn Brandt, Forrest Duke, Chuck Alford; ***D:*** Ray Dennis Steckler. *NO*

Hollywood Uncensored **1987** A history of Hollywood censorship, including long-suppressed scenes from "King Kong," "The Outlaw," "Carnal Knowledge," "Baby Doll," "Easy Rider," "Woodstock," and more. **75m/C VHS, Beta.** *LIV, FCT*

Hollywood Varieties **1950** A virtually plotless no-star conglomeration of comedy, music, and burlesque. **60m/B VHS, Beta, LV.** The 3 Rio Brothers, Robert Alda, Glenn Vernon, Eddie Ryan. *NO*

Hollywood Vice Sqaud 🦴 **1986 (R)** Explores the lives of Hollywood police officers and the crimes they investigate. Contains three different story lines involving prostitution, child pornography, and organized crime. The film can't decide to be a comedy send-up of crime stories or a drama and is also crippled by a poor script. Written by the real-life chief of the Hollywood Vice Squad. **100m/C VHS, LV.** Trish Van Devere, Ronny Cox, Frank Gorshin, Leon Isaac Kennedy, Carrie Fisher, Ben Frank, Robin Wright; ***D:*** Penelope Spheeris; ***M:*** Michael Convertino. *VTR, HHE, MTX*

Hollywood without Makeup **1965** Home movie footage taken over the years by Ken Murray includes candid shots of over 100 stars of the film world. **51m/C VHS, Beta, 8mm.** *HHT, MRV, VYY*

Hollywood Zap *Woof!* **1986 (R)** Two losers, one a Southern orphan, the other a video game nut, hit Hollywood and engage in antics that are meant to be funny, but are actually tasteless. **85m/C VHS, Beta.** Ben Frank, Ivan E. Roth, De Waldron, Annie Gaybis, Chuck "Porky" Mitchell; ***D:*** David M. Cohen; ***W:*** David M. Cohen. *PSM*

Hollywood's New Blood 🦴 **1988** Young actors making a movie are haunted by a film crew from hell. **90m/C VHS, Beta.** Bobby Johnson, Francine Lapensee; ***D:*** James Shyman. *VTR*

Holocaust 🦴🦴🦴½ **1978** The war years of 1935 to 1945 are relived in this account of the Nazi atrocities, focusing on the Jewish Weiss family, destroyed by the monstrous crimes, and the Dorf family, Germans who thrived under the Nazi regime. Highly acclaimed riveting made-for-television mini-series with an exceptional cast. Won eight Emmys. **475m/C VHS, Beta.** Michael Moriarty, Fritz Weaver, Meryl Streep, James Woods, Joseph Bottoms, Tovah Feldshuh, David Warner, Ian Holm, Michael Beck, Marius Goring; ***D:*** Marvin J. Chomsky. *REP, SWC, WOV*

Holocaust Survivors...Remembrance of Love 🦴🦴 *Remembrance of Love* **1983** A concentration camp survivor and his daughter attend the 1981 World Gathering of Holocaust Survivors in Tel-Aviv and both find romance. Made for television. **100m/C VHS, Beta.** Kirk Douglas, Pam Dawber, Chana Eden, Yoram Gal, Robert Clary; ***D:*** Jack Smight; ***M:*** William Goldstein. *VMK*

Hologram Man 🦴🦴 **1995 (R)** Futuristic thriller finds psycho/terrorist Slash Gallagher (Lurie) captured by rookie cop Kurt Decoda (Lara). His prison term is to be served in Holographic Stasis, which means his mind is stored on a computer. Slash's gang manges to break his mind out of the computer but since his body is destroyed, Slash roams as a powerful electro-magnetic hologram. And it's up to cop Decoda to get Slash back. **96m/C VHS, LV.** Joe Lara, Evan Lurie, William Sanderson, Tiny Lister, Michael Nouri, John Amos; ***D:*** Richard Pepin; ***W:*** Evan Lurie; ***M:*** John Gonzalez. *PMH*

Holt of the Secret Service **1942** Secret service agent runs afoul of saboteurs and fifth-columnists in this 15-episode serial. **290m/B VHS.** Jack Holt, Evelyn Brent, Montague Shaw, Tristram Coffin, John Ward, George Chesebro; ***D:*** James W. Horne. *VYY, MED, DVT*

The Holy Innocents 🦴🦴🦴 *Los Santos Inocentes* **1984 (PG)** A peasant family is torn asunder by their feudal obligations to their patrons. Set in the 1960s in Franco's Spain. In Spanish with English subtitles. **108m/C VHS, Beta.** *SP* Alfredo Landa, Francesco Rabal; ***D:*** Mario Camus. Cannes Film Festival '84: Best Actor (Landa), Best Actor (Rabal); Nominations: Cannes Film Festival '84: Best Film. *ORI, APD, INJ*

Holy Matrimony 🦴🦴½ **1994 (PG-13)** Mild-mannered and pleasant comedy in spite of its potentially salacious plot. Thieves Peter (Donovan) and Havana (Arquette) take off to Canada to hide out in the Hutterite religious community where Peter grew up and where he's welcomed as the prodigal son. Peter hides their stolen loot but neglects to pass the word on before he's killed in an accident. Wanting to stay and search for the money, Havana uses the colony's reliance on biblical law to marry Peter's brother, Zeke (Gordon-Levitt). Only problem is Zeke is 12 and doesn't even like girls. Strictly brother-sister affection develops between the two. Amusing performances by both. **93m/C VHS, LV.** Patricia Arquette, Joseph Gordon-Levitt, Armin Mueller-Stahl, Tate Donovan, John Schuck, Lois Smith, Courtney B. Vance, Jeffrey Nordling, Richard Riehle; ***D:*** Leonard Nimoy; ***W:*** David Weisberg, Douglas S. Cook; ***M:*** Bruce Broughton. *TOU*

Holy Terror 🦴🦴 **1965** The story of Florence Nightingale, who shocked Victorian society by organizing a nursing staff to aid British soldiers in the Crimean War, is told in this presentation from "George Schaefer's Showcase Theatre." **76m/C VHS, Beta.** Julie Harris, Denholm Elliott, Torin Thatcher, Kate Reid; ***D:*** George Schaefer. *FHS*

Hombre 🦴🦴🦴 **1967** A white man in the 1880s, raised by a band of Arizona Apaches, is forced into a showdown. In helping a stagecoach full of settlers across treacherous country, he not only faces traditional bad guys, but prejudice as well. Based on a story by Elmore Leonard. **111m/C VHS, Beta, LV.** Paul Newman, Fredric March, Richard Boone, Diane Cilento, Cameron Mitchell, Barbara Rush, Martin Balsam; ***D:*** Martin Ritt; ***W:*** Harriet Frank Jr., Irving Ravetch; ***C:*** James Wong Howe. *FOX*

Home Alone 🦴🦴🦴 **1990 (PG)** 8-year-old Kevin is accidentally left behind when his entire (and large) family makes a frantic rush for the airport. That's the plausible part. Alone and besieged by burglars, Culkin turns into a pint-sized Rambo defending his suburban castle with the wile and resources of a boy genius with perfect timing and unlimited wherewithal. That's the implausible part. Pesci and Stern, the targets of Macauley's wrath, enact painful slapstick with considerable vigor, while Candy has a small but funny part as the leader of a polka band traveling cross-country with mom O'Hara. The highest-grossing picture of 1990, surpassing "Ghost" and "Jaws." **105m/C VHS, Beta, LV.** Macaulay Culkin, Catherine O'Hara, Joe Pesci, Daniel Stern, John Heard, Roberts Blossom, John Candy, Catherine O'Hara, Billie Bird, Angela Goethals, Devin Ratray, Kieran Culkin; ***D:*** Chris Columbus; ***W:*** John Hughes; ***M:*** John Williams. Nominations: Academy Awards '90: Best Song ("Somewhere in My Memory"), Best Original Score. *FXV, IME, RDG*

Home Alone 2: Lost in New York 🦴🦴½ **1992 (PG)** In an almost exact duplication of the original blockbuster, the harebrained McCallister family leaves Kevin behind in the shuffle to start their Florida vacation. Boarding the wrong plane, Kevin lands in NYC, where wonder of wonders, he meets crooks Pesci and Stern, prison escapees who somehow survived the torture meted out in the first film. And they want revenge. Loaded with cartoon violence and shameless gag replicas from HA1, mega-hit still produces genuine laughs and manages to incorporate fresh material. Culkin is as adorable as ever, with supporting cast all delivering fine performances. Filmed in New York City. **120m/C VHS, LV.** Macaulay Culkin, Joe Pesci, Daniel Stern, Catherine O'Hara, John Heard, Tim Curry, Brenda Fricker, Devin Ratray, Hillary Wolf, Eddie Bracken, Dana Ivey, Rob Schneider, Kieran Culkin, Gerry Bamman; ***Cameos:*** Donald Trump; ***D:*** Chris Columbus; ***W:*** John Hughes; ***M:*** John Williams. People's Choice Awards '93: Best Film—Musical/Comedy. *FXV, BTV*

The Home and the World 🦴🦴🦴½ *Ghare Baire* **1984** Another masterpiece from India's Ray, this film deals with a sheltered Indian woman who falls in love with her husband's friend and becomes politically committed in the turmoil of 1907-1908. Based on Rabindranath Tagore's novel. In Bengali with English subtitles. **130m/C VHS, Beta.** *IN* Victor Banerjee, Soumitra Chatterjee; ***D:*** Satyajit Ray. *COL, INJ, SUE*

Home at Last **1988** An orphan in turn of the century New York finds himself shipped to Nebraska on an orphan train. There he works on the farm of his adopted family, whose own son has died. The boy finds that he must adjust to a new lifestyle as well as strive to be accepted as someone other than a replacement for the couple's son. From the "Wonderworks" series. **58m/C VHS.** Adrien Brody, Frank Converse, Caroline Lagerfelt, Sascha Radetsky. *PME, HMV, FCT*

Home Before Midnight 🦴½ **1984** A young songwriter falls in love with a 14-year-old, is discovered, and is subsequently charged with statutory rape. **115m/C VHS, Beta.** James Aubrey, Alison Elliott; ***D:*** Pete Walker. *ORI, WAR*

Home for Christmas 🦴🦴½ **1990** An elderly homeless man, with the love of a young girl, teaches a wealthy family the spirit of Christmas. **96m/C VHS.** Mickey Rooney, Joel Kaiser; ***D:*** Peter McCubbin. *RHI*

Home for the Holidays 🦴🦴 *Deadly Desires* **1972** Four daughters are called home on Christmas by their father who is convinced that his second wife is trying to poison him. Made for television. **74m/C VHS, Beta.** Eleanor Parker, Walter Brennan, Sally Field, Jessica Walter, Julie Harris; ***D:*** John Llewellyn Moxey. *VMK*

Home for the Holidays 🦴🦴½ **1995 (PG-13)** Frantic dysfunctional family saga finds eldest daughter Claudia Larson (Hunter) on her way to Baltimore to spend Thanksgiving with her family. Frazzled Claudia must deal with badly bewigged mom Adele (Bancroft), genial dad Henry (Durning), and her siblings—frenzied gay brother Tommy (Downey, Jr.) and self-righteous sister Joanne (Stevenson), as well as screwy Aunt Glady (Chaplin) and Tommy's handsome friend Leo Fish (McDermott). Yes, there are moments of deja vu about your very own family holidays but the film seems badly paced and ultimately irritating. Adapted from a short story by Chris Radant. **103m/C VHS, LV.** Holly Hunter, Anne Bancroft, Charles Durning, Robert Downey Jr., Dylan McDermott, Cynthia Stevenson, Geraldine Chaplin, Steve Guttenberg, Claire Danes; ***Cameos:*** David Strathairn, Austin Pendleton; ***D:*** Jodie Foster; ***W:*** W.D. Richter; ***C:*** Lajos Koltai; ***M:*** Mark Isham. *PGV*

Home Free All 🦴🦴½ **1984** A Vietnam vet turned revolutionary, turned writer, tries to reacquaint himself with childhood friends only to find one has joined the mob and another is settled in suburbia and none of them are dealing well with adulthood. **92m/C VHS, Beta.** Allan Nicholls, Roland Caccavo, Maura Ellyn, Shelley Wyant, Lucille Rivim; ***D:*** Stuart Bird. *LIV, VES*

Home from the Hill 🦴🦴🦴 **1960** A solemn, brooding drama about a southern landowner and his troubled sons, one of whom is illegitimate. This one triumphs because of casting. Cinematography by Milton Krasner. **150m/C VHS, Beta, LV.** Robert Mitchum, George Peppard, George Hamilton, Eleanor Parker, Everett Sloane, Luana Parker, Constance Ford; ***D:*** Vincente Minnelli; ***W:*** Harriet Frank Jr., Irving Ravetch; ***C:*** Milton Krasner. National Board of Review Awards '60: Best Actor (Mitchum). *MGM*

Home in Oklahoma 🦴🦴 **1947** A boy will be swindled out of his inheritance and a killer will escape justice until Roy comes to the rescue. Standard series fare. **72m/B VHS, Beta.** Roy Rogers, Dale Evans, George "Gabby" Hayes, Carol Hughes; ***D:*** William Witney. *NOS, TIM, CAB*

Home Is Where the Hart Is 🦴🦴 **1988 (PG-13)** A rich 103-year-old is kidnapped by a nurse wanting to marry him and become heir to his estate. It's up to his sons, all in their 70s, to rescue him. **94m/C VHS, Beta, LV.** Martin Mull, Leslie Nielsen, Valri Bromfield, Stephen E. Miller, Eric Christmas, Ted Stidder; ***D:*** Rex Bromfield; ***W:*** Rex Bromfield. *PAR, IME*

Home Movies 🦴½ **1979 (PG)** Brian DePalma and his film students at Sarah Lawrence College devised this loose, sloppy comedy which hearkens back to DePalma's early films. Tells the story of a nebbish who seeks therapy to gain control of his absurdly chaotic life. **89m/C VHS, Beta, LV.** Kirk Douglas, Nancy Allen, Keith Gordon, Gerrit Graham, Vincent Gardenia, Mary Davenport; ***D:*** Brian DePalma; ***W:*** Brian DePalma; ***M:*** Pino Donaggio. *LIV, VES, IME*

Home of Angels 🦴🦴½ **1994** Billy sneaks his granddad out of his nursing home in Philadelphia and together the twosome begin a perilous journey back to Billy's home in Long Island, New York so they can have a family Christmas. They're aided by a homeless man when they run into trouble with a street gang. **90m/C VHS.** Lance Robinson, Abe Vigoda, Sherman Hemsley, Joe Frazier; ***D:*** Nick Stagliano. *SDE*

A Home of Our Own **1975** An American priest sets up a home in Mexico for orphan boys and changes their lives for the better. A true story of Father William Wasson. **100m/C VHS, Beta.** Jason Miller. *WOV*

A Home of Our Own 🦴🦴½ **1993 (PG-13)** Semi-autobiographical tearjerker based on screenwriter Duncan's childhood. Widowed and poor mother of six (Bates) is fired from her job at a Los Angeles potato chip factory, packs up the tribe and heads for a better life and a home to call their own. They end up in Idaho, in a ramshackle house owned by lonely Mr. Moon (Oh) and what follows is a winter of discontent. Bates provides an intense performance as a poor but proud woman with a tough exterior. Furlong provides the story's narration as the eldest son. A story of spiritual triumph, this one is sure to make your heart weep. **104m/C VHS, LV.** Kathy Bates, Edward Furlong, Soon-Teck Oh, Amy Sakasitz, Tony Campisi; ***D:*** Tony Bill; ***W:*** Patrick Duncan. *PGV*

Home of the Brave 🦴🦴🦴 **1949** A black soldier is sent on a top secret mission in the South Pacific, but finds that he must battle with his white comrades as he is subjected to subordinate treatment and constant racial slurs. Hollywood's first outstanding statement against racial prejudice. **86m/B VHS, Beta, LV.** Lloyd Bridges, James Edwards, Frank Lovejoy, Jeff Corey; ***D:*** Mark Robson. National Board of Review Awards '49: 10 Best Films of the Year. *REP, FCT*

Home Remedy 🦴🦴 **1988** An introverted New Jersey bachelor's isolated lifestyle is invaded by a flirtatious housewife and her jealous husband. **92m/C VHS, Beta.** Seth Barrish, Maxine Albert; ***D:*** Maggie Greenwald. *INJ*

Home Sweet Home 🦴🦴½ **1914** Suggested by the life of John Howard Payne (actor, poet, dramatist, critic, and world-wanderer) who wrote the title song amid the bitterness of his sad life. Silent with musical score. **62m/B VHS, Beta.** Lillian Gish, Dorothy Gish, Henry B. Walthall, Mae Marsh, Blanche Sweet, Donald Crisp, Robert "Bobbie" Harron; ***D:*** D.W. Griffith. *VYY, KIV, GPV*

Home Sweet Home 🦴½ *Slasher in the House* **1980** A murdering psychopath escapes from the local asylum, and rampages through a family's Thanksgiving dinner. **84m/C VHS, Beta.** Jake Steinfeld, Sallee Elyse, Peter de Paula; ***D:*** Nettie Pena. *MED*

Home Sweet Home 🦴🦴 **1982** Postman Stan fancies himself a ladies man, but his wife has left him. So Stan decides to assauge his loneliness by seducing his co-workers wives. Black comedy look at British social classism. Made for British television. **90m/C VHS.** *GB* Eric Richard, Timothy Spall, Tim Barker, Su Elliot, Frances Barber, Kay Stonham; ***D:*** Mike Leigh; ***W:*** Mike Leigh. *WBF, FCT*

Home to Stay 🦴🦴 **1979** A farmer who has suffered a stroke is fighting off repeated lapses into senility. His son and daughter have conflicting interests as to whether he should be committed to a nursing home. Made for television. **74m/C VHS, Beta.** Henry Fonda, Frances Hyland, Michael McGuire; ***D:*** Delbert Mann; ***M:*** Hagood Hardy. *TLF*

Home Town Story 🦴🦴 **1951** A politician is convinced big business is behind his election loss. Fair drama. Watch for Monroe in a bit part. **61m/B VHS.** Jeffrey Lynn, Donald Crisp, Marjorie Reynolds, Alan Hale Jr., Marilyn Monroe, Barbara Brown, Melinda Plowman; ***D:*** Arthur Pierson. *NOS, TPV*

Homebodies 🦴🦴 **1974 (PG)** Six senior citizens, disgusted when they learn that they will be callously tossed out of their home, become violent murderers in their shocking attempt to solve their problem. An odd little film made in Cincinnati. **96m/C VHS, Beta.** Ruth McDevitt, Linda Marsh, William Hansen, Peter Brocco, Frances Fuller; ***D:*** Larry Yust. *SUE*

Homeboy 🦴🦴 **1988 (R)** A small-time club boxer who dreams of becoming middleweight champ is offered his big break, but the opportunity is jeopardized by his dishonest manager's dealings. Never released theatrically. **118m/C VHS, Beta, LV.** Mickey Rourke, Christopher Walken, Debra Feuer, Kevin Conway, Antony Alda, Ruben Blades; ***D:*** Michael Seresin; ***M:*** Eric Clapton, Michael Kamen. *NO*

Homeboy 🦴½ **198?** A Black boxer owes his career to the mob. When he tries to break free his wife is murdered - and he seeks revenge. **93m/C VHS.** Dabney Coleman, Philip Michael Thomas. *NO*

Homeboys 🦴 **1992** Two East L.A. brothers find themselves on opposite sides of the law in this quickie designed to cash in on gang violence and ghetto dramas. **91m/C VHS, LV.** Todd Bridges, David Garrison, Ron Odriozola, Ken Michaels; ***D:*** Lindsay Norgard. *AIP*

Homecoming ♂♂♂ **1928** Two German prisoners of war escape from a Siberian lead mine. One reaches home first and has an affair with his comrade's wife. Silent. **74m/B VHS, Beta.** *GE* Dita Parlo, Lars Hanson, Gustav Froehlich; ***D:*** Joe May. *GLV*

Homecoming ♂♂ **1948** Average soap opera starring Gable and Turner set amidst the trenches of WW II. Gable plays a selfish doctor who leaves behind his wife and colleague to enlist in the Medical Corps as a major. Turner is the battlefield nurse who forever changes his life. Film is hindered by a story which is far below the talents of the excellent cast. Although voted by the New York Critics as one of the ten worst movies of 1948, the public loved it. Based on the story "The Homecoming of Ulysses" by Sidney Kingsley. **113m/B VHS.** Clark Gable, Lana Turner, Anne Baxter, John Hodiak, Ray Collins, Gladys Cooper, Cameron Mitchell, Art Baker, Lurene Tuttle; ***D:*** Mervyn LeRoy; ***W:*** Paul Osborn, Jan Lustig. *MGM*

Homecoming ♂♂½ **1996 (PG)** Disturbed mother abandons her four children at a Connecticut shopping mall in the care of 13-year-old eldest daughter Dicey (Peterson). The children slowly make their way to a relative's (Bedelia) home in Bridgeport, but when she proves equally uncaring Dicey decides to continue the family trek to their maternal grandmother Ab's (Bancroft) house in Chrisfield, Maryland. No surprise when crazy grandma doesn't want them either but this time Dicey is determined to make them all a home. Based on the Newbery Medal-winning children's novel by Cynthia Voight. Made for cable TV. **?m/C VHS.** Anne Bancroft, Kimberlee Peterson, Bonnie Bedelia, Trever O'Brien, Hanna Hall, William Greenblatt. *HMK*

Homecoming: A Christmas Story ♂♂½ **1971** Made-for-television heart-tugger that inspired the television series "The Waltons." A depression-era Virginia mountain family struggles to celebrate Christmas although the whereabouts and safety of their father are unknown. Adapted from the autobiographical novel by Earl Hamner, Jr. **98m/C VHS, Beta.** Richard Thomas, Patricia Neal, Edgar Bergen, Cleavon Little, Ellen Corby; ***D:*** Fielder Cook. *FOX*

Homer and Eddie ♂ **1989 (R)** A witless road comedy with Goldberg as a dying sociopath and a mentally retarded Belushi. They take off cross-country to make a little trouble, learn a little about life, and create a less than entertaining movie. **100m/C VHS, Beta, LV.** Whoopi Goldberg, James Belushi, Karen Black; ***D:*** Andrei Konchalovsky; ***W:*** Patrick Cirillo; ***C:*** Lajos Koltai; ***M:*** Eduard Artemyev. *HBO*

Homer Comes Home ♂♂ **1920** A homely and diligent inventor finds nothing but failure, but sticks it out in hopes of turning his luck around. Silent comedy starring down-home Ray. **55m/B VHS, Beta.** Charles Ray. *GPV*

Homesteaders of Paradise Valley ♂½ **1947** The Hume brothers oppose Red Ryder and a group of settlers building a dam in Paradise Valley. **54m/B VHS, Beta.** Allan "Rocky" Lane, Robert (Bobby) Blake. *NOS, VCN, CAB*

Hometown Boy Makes Good ♂♂½ **1993 (R)** Smalltown boy Boyd Geary moved to the big city to go to medical school. But what he never told his proud mom was that he dropped out and doesn't have the successful psychiatry practice she thinks he has, instead he's a barely surviving waiter. But when Boyd travels back home to confess to mom, the local mayor makes him an offer to set up his own practice and won't take no for an answer. **88m/C VHS, LV.** Anthony Edwards, Grace Zabriskie, Cynthia Bain; ***D:*** David Burton Morris; ***W:*** Allen Rucker; ***M:*** Barry Goldberg. *IMP, IME*

Hometown U.S.A. *Woof!* **1979 (R)** Set in Los Angeles in the late 50s' this teenage cruising movie is the brainchild of director Baer who is better known as Jethro from that madcap television series "The Beverly Hillbillies." **97m/C VHS, Beta.** Brian Kerwin, Gary Springer, David Wilson, Cindy Fisher, Sally Kirkland; ***D:*** Max Baer Jr. *LIV, VES*

Homeward Bound ♂ **1980 (G)** A dying teenager tries to reunite his long-estranged father and grandfather. Made for television. **96m/C VHS, Beta.** David Soul, Moosie Drier, Barnard Hughes; ***D:*** Richard Michaels. *HMV*

Homeward Bound 2: Lost in San Francisco ♂♂½ **1996 (G)** House pets Chance, the feisty bulldog (Fox), Sassy the sophisticated feline (Field), and Shadow the sage golden retriever (Waite) find themselves on the loose again, this time in the tough streets of San Francisco. The animals escape from the airport as the family departs for a Canadian holiday, and on their way back home, encounter some tough mutts—a gang of streetwise dogs, (most notably comedian Sinbad as Riley) and, of course, some dog nappers. Chance even finds romance along the way with Delilah (Gugino). Not too scary for the little ones, flick carries the same charm of the first adventure. **88m/C VHS.** Robert Hays, Kim Greist, Veronica Lauren, Kevin Timothy Chevalia, Michael Rispoli, Max Perlich; ***D:*** David R. Ellis; ***W:*** Julie Hickson, Chris Hauty; ***C:*** Jack Conroy; ***V:*** Michael J. Fox, Sally Field, Ralph Waite, Al Michaels, Tommy Lasorda, Bob Uecker, Jon Polito, Adam Goldberg, Sinbad, Carla Gugino. *TOU*

Homeward Bound: The Incredible Journey ♂♂♂ **1993 (G)** Successful remake of the 1963 Disney release "The Incredible Journey." Two dogs and a cat once again try to find their way home after their family relocates, armed with greater depth of character than the original. Hard not to shed a tear for the brave animal trio who develop a trusting bond through assorted misadventures. Based on the novel by Sheila Burnford. Superior family fare. **85m/C VHS, LV.** Robert Hays, Kim Greist, Jean Smart, Benj Thall, Veronica Lauren, Kevin Timothy Chevalia; ***D:*** Duwayne Dunham; ***W:*** Linda Woolverton, Carolyn Thompson; ***M:*** Bruce Broughton; ***V:*** Don Ameche, Michael J. Fox, Sally Field. *DIS, BTV*

Homework ♂ **1982 (R)** Young man's after-school lessons with a teacher are definitely not part of the curriculum. Yawning sexploitation. **90m/C VHS, Beta, LV.** Joan Collins, Michael Morgan, Betty Thomas, Shell Kepler, Wings Hauser, Lee Purcell; ***D:*** James Beshears. *MCA*

Homewrecker ♂♂ **1992 (PG-13)** Benson stars as a scientist who invents a computer, with a female voice, as the ultimate domestic worker. Only the computer turns possessive and against Benson's estranged wife. **88m/C VHS, Beta.** Robby Benson, Sydney Walsh, Sarah Rose Karr; ***D:*** Fred Walton; ***W:*** Eric Harlacher; ***V:*** Kate Jackson. *PAR*

Homicidal Impulse ♂½ **1992 (R)** When Assistant D.A. Tim Casey has an affair with his boss' ambitious niece he doesn't realize the danger he's in. His lover decides to kill her uncle so boyfriend Tim will get his job. Some women will do anything for love. Also available in an unrated version. **84m/C VHS.** Scott Valentine, Vanessa Angel. *LIV*

Homicide ♂♂♂½ **1991 (R)** Terrific police thriller with as much thought as action; a driven detective faces his submerged Jewish identity while probing an anti-Semitic murder and a secret society. Playwright/filmmaker Mamet creates nail-biting suspense and shattering epiphanies without resorting to Hollywood glitz. Rich (often profane) dialogue includes a classic soliloquy mystically comparing a lawman's badge with a Star of David. **100m/C VHS, LV, 8mm.** Joe Mantegna, William H. Macy, Natalija Nogulich, Ving Rhames, Rebecca Pidgeon; ***D:*** David Mamet; ***W:*** David Mamet; ***C:*** Roger Deakins. National Board of Review Awards '91: 10 Best Films of the Year. *COL, BTV*

Homo Eroticus/Man of the Year ♂ **1971** Handsome servant finds it difficult to satisfy the desires of Bergamo, Italy's socialite. **93m/C VHS, Beta.** *IT* Lando Buzzanca, Rossana Podesta. *NO*

Hondo ♂♂♂ **1953** In 1874, whites have broken their treaty with the Apache nation who are now preparing for war. Calvary dispatch rider Hondo Lane (Wayne) encounters Angie (Page) and her young son at an isolated ranch and warns her of the danger but she refuses to leave. After various Indian attacks, Hondo persuades Angie (they've fallen in love) to leave for California with him. Based on the story "The Gift of Cochise" by Louis L'Amour. **84m/C VHS.** John Wayne, Geraldine Page, Ward Bond, Michael Pate, James Arness, Rodolfo Acosta, Leo Gordon, Lee Aaker, Paul Fix; ***D:*** John Farrow; ***W:*** James Edward Grant; ***C:*** Robert Burks, Archie Stout. *MPI*

Honey ♂½ **1981** Attractive writer pays an unusual visit to the home of a distinguished publisher. Brandishing a pistol, she demands that he read aloud from her manuscript. As he reads, a unique fantasy unfolds, a dreamlike erotic tale that may be the writer's own sexual awakening. Or maybe not. **89m/C VHS, Beta.** *IT SP* Clio Goldsmith, Fernando Rey, Catherine Spaak; ***D:*** Gianfranco Angelucci. *VES*

Honey, I Blew Up the Kid ♂♂½ **1992 (PG)** Screwball suburban inventor Moranis reverses his shrinking process and this time manages to enlarge his two-year-old into a 112-foot giant who gets bigger every time he comes in contact with electricity. Yikes! Loaded with great special effects, this is a charming and funny film that's fit for the whole family. Sequel to "Honey I Shrunk the Kids." **89m/C VHS, Beta, LV.** Rick Moranis, Marcia Strassman, Robert Oliveri, Daniel Shalikar, Joshua Shalikar, Lloyd Bridges, John Shea, Keri Russell, Gregory Sierra, Julia Sweeney, Kenneth Tobey, Peter Elbling; ***D:*** Randal Kleiser; ***W:*** Thom Eberhardt, Garry Goodrow; ***M:*** Bruce Broughton. *DIS*

Honey, I Shrunk the Kids ♂♂½ **1989 (G)** The popular Disney fantasy about a suburban inventor. His shrinking device accidentally reduces his kids to 1/4 inch tall, and he subsequently throws them out with the garbage. Now they must journey back to the house through the jungle that was once the back lawn. Accompanied by "Tummy Trouble," the first of a projected series of Roger Rabbit Maroon Cartoons. Followed by "Honey, I Blew Up the Kids." **101m/C VHS, Beta, LV.** Rick Moranis, Matt Frewer, Marcia Strassman, Kristine Sutherland, Thomas Wilson Brown, Jared Rushton, Amy O'Neill, Robert Oliveri; ***D:*** Joe Johnston, Rob Minkoff; ***W:*** Ed Naha, Tom Schulman, Stuart Gordon; ***M:*** James Horner; ***V:*** Charles Fleischer, Kathleen Turner, Lou Hirsch, April Winchell. *DIS, MOV, RDG*

The Honey Pot ♂♂½ *It Comes Up Murder; Anyone for Venice?; Mr. Fox of Venice* **1967** A millionaire feigns death to see the reaction of three of his former lovers. Amusing black comedy with fine performances from all. Based on Moliere's "Volpone." **131m/C VHS.** Rex Harrison, Susan Hayward, Cliff Robertson, Capucine, Edie Adams, Maggie Smith, Adolfo Celi; ***D:*** Joseph L. Mankiewicz; ***W:*** Joseph L. Mankiewicz; ***M:*** John Addison. *MGM*

Honeybaby ♂♂ **1974 (PG)** A smooth international soldier of fortune and a bright, sexy American interpreter are entangled in Middle-Eastern turbulence when they must rescue a politician kidnapped by terrorists. **94m/C VHS.** Calvin Lockhart, Diana Sands; ***D:*** Michael A. Schultz. *GEM, MRV, CNG*

Honeyboy ♂½ **1982** Estrada tries to win fame, fortune, and a ticket out of the barrio as an up-and-coming boxer. Outstanding fight scenes, but little else in this made for television drama of the boxing scene. **100m/C VHS, Beta.** Erik Estrada, Morgan Fairchild, James McEachin, Robert Costanzo, Yvonne Wilder; ***D:*** John Berry. *LIV*

Honeymoon ♂♂ **1987** A young French woman visiting New York learns she will be deported when her boyfriend is arrested for drug-smuggling. To stay, she is set up in a marriage of convenience and told her new husband will never see or bother her. But hubby has other plans! **96m/C VHS, Beta.** John Shea, Nathalie Baye, Richard Berry, Peter Donat; ***D:*** Patrick Jamain; ***W:*** Phillip Setbon. *ORI, WAR*

Honeymoon Academy ♂♂ *For Better or For Worse* **1990 (PG-13)** Newly married man has lots to learn in this comic outing. His new wife never told him about her unusual line of business—as an undercover agent! **94m/C VHS, LV.** Robert Hays, Kim Cattrall, Leigh Taylor-Young; ***D:*** Gene Quintano; ***W:*** Gene Quintano; ***M:*** Robert Folk. *HBO, IME*

Honeymoon Horror 197? Stranded on an island, three honeymooning couples soon realize their romantic retreat is a nightmare. A crazy man with an axe is tracking them down. Minimally effective. **90m/C VHS, Beta.** Cheryl Black, William F. Pecchi, Bob Wagner. *NO*

Honeymoon in Vegas ½ **1992 (PG-13)** Romantic comedy turns frantic after Cage loses his fiancee to Caan in a high stakes Vegas poker game. Cage displays lots of talent for manic comedy as the distraught young groom-to-be who encounters numerous obstacles on his way to the altar. Lightweight and funny, featuring a bevy of Elvis impersonators in every size, shape, and color and new versions of favorite Elvis tunes. Look for former Las Vegas U basketball coach Jerry Tarkanian as one of Caan's gambling buddies. **95m/C VHS, LV.** James Caan, Nicolas Cage, Sarah Jessica Parker, Noriyuki "Pat" Morita, John Capodice, Robert Costanzo, Anne Bancroft, Peter Boyle, Seymour Cassel, Tony Shalhoub; ***D:*** Andrew Bergman; ***W:*** Andrew Bergman; ***M:*** David Newman. *COL, NLC, IME*

Honeymoon Killers *The Lonely Hearts Killers* **1970 (R)** A grim, creepy filmization of a true multiple-murder case wherein an overweight woman and slimy gigolo living on Long Island seduce and murder one lonely woman after another. Independently made and frankly despairing. **103m/C VHS, Beta, LV.** Tony LoBianco, Shirley Stoler, Mary Jane Higby, Dortha Duckworth, Doris Roberts, Marilyn Chris, Kip McArdle, Mary Breen, Barbara Cason, Ann Harris, Guy Sorel; ***D:*** Leonard Kastle. *LIV, VES*

The Honeymoon Machine ½ **1961** A lightweight comedy about two American sailors and a computer scam. McQueen and Mullaney hook up with computer expert Hutton to use their ship's computer to beat the gambling odds at an Italian casino. Their commander misinterprets the signals and thinks the ship is being attacked. Fast paced and the computer angle was new territory in '61. **87m/C VHS.** Steve McQueen, Jack Mullaney, Jim Hutton, Dean Jagger, Paula Prentiss, Brigid Bazlen, Jack Weston; ***D:*** Richard Thorpe. *MGM, MOV*

The Honeymooners "Classic 39": TV or Not TV/Honeymooners Highlights **1955** Captain Video and his video rangers are a Kramden household name after Ralph and Ed pool their resources to buy a television. Also includes clips from each of the remaining 38 episodes in "The Honeymooners" series. Video cover illustration by C.F. Payne. This 20 volumes series contains two episodes per tape. **60m/C VHS.** *FXV*

Honeymooners Hidden Episodes, Vol. 1 *The Honeymooners: The Lost Episodes* **1953** Three recently-retrieved episodes of the Honeymooners sketches, which were initially aired live as part of the "Jackie Gleason Show." In "Letter to the Boss," Jackie sends some nasty correspondence to his employer when he mistakenly believes that he has been canned. In "Suspense," Ralph fears that Alice is planning his murder when he eavesdrops on her acting practice. In "Dinner Guest," Ralph's plans to suck up to his supervisor meet with hilarious disaster. This "Honeymooners" series contains 28 volumes, which are available separately for purchase. **53m/B VHS, Beta.** Jackie Gleason, Audrey Meadows, Art Carney, Joyce Randolph. *MPI, FOX, MOV*

Honeysuckle Rose ½ *On the Road Again* **1980 (PG)** A road-touring country-Western singer whose life is a series of one night stands, falls in love with an adoring young guitar player who has just joined his band. This nearly costs him his marriage when his wife, who while waiting patiently for him at home, decides she's had enough. Easygoing performance by Nelson, essentially playing himself. **120m/C VHS, Beta, LV.** Willie Nelson, Dyan Cannon, Amy Irving, Slim Pickens, Joey Floyd, Charles Levin, Priscilla Pointer; ***D:*** Jerry Schatzberg; ***W:*** William D. Wittliff, John Binder, Carol Sobieski; ***M:*** Willie Nelson, Richard Baskin. Golden Raspberry Awards '80: Worst Supporting Actress (Irving); Nominations: Academy Awards '80: Best Song ("On the Road Again"). *WAR, MVD*

Hong Kong Nights ½ **1935** Two agents attempt to break up a Chinese smuggling ring run by an unscrupulous madman. Good, action-packed low-budget film. **59m/B VHS, Beta.** Tom Keene, Wera Engels, Warren Hymer, Tetsu Komai, Cornelius Keefe; ***D:*** E. Mason Hopper. *SNC*

Hong Kong '97 **1994 (R)** On the eve of China's takeover of Hong Kong from Great Britain, special agent Reg Cameron (Patrick) murders a Chinese general. With a $10 million bounty on his head, Cameron tries to escape with his partners and girlfriend in tow. Lots of action, good use of Hong Kong setting. **91m/C VHS, LV.** Robert Patrick, Ming-Na Wen, Brion James, Tim Thomerson; ***D:*** Albert Pyun. *VMK*

Honky ½ **1971 (R)** An innocent friendship between a black woman and a white man develops into a passionate romance that has the whole town talking. **92m/C VHS, Beta.** Brenda Sykes, John Nielson, Maria Donzinger; ***D:*** William A. Graham; ***M:*** Quincy Jones. *UNI*

Honky Tonk **1941** A western soap opera in which ne'er do well Clark marries Lana and tries to live a respectable life. In this, the first of several MGM teamings between Gable and Turner, the chemistry between the two is evident. So much so in fact that Gable's then wife Carole Lombard let studio head Louis B. Mayer know that she was not at all thrilled. The public was pleased however, and made the film a hit. **106m/B VHS, Beta.** Clark Gable, Lana Turner, Frank Morgan, Claire Trevor, Marjorie Main, Albert Dekker, Chill Wills, Henry O'Neill, John Maxwell, Morgan Wallace, Betty Blythe, Francis X. Bushman, Veda Ann Borg; ***D:*** Jack Conway. *MGM, CCB*

Honky Tonk Freeway **1981 (PG)** An odd assortment of people become involved in a small town Mayor's scheme to turn a dying hamlet into a tourist wonderland. You can find better things to do with your evening than watch this accident. **107m/C VHS, Beta.** Teri Garr, Howard Hesseman, Beau Bridges, Hume Cronyn, William Devane, Beverly D'Angelo, Geraldine Page; ***D:*** John Schlesinger; ***W:*** Edward Clinton; ***C:*** John Bailey; ***M:*** Elmer Bernstein, Stephen Dorff. *NO*

Honky Tonk Girl **1937** Hilarious exploitation film about a hitch-hiking prostitution ring. Also known as "Highway Hell." **?m/C VHS.** Mary Chauning. *SNC*

Honkytonk Man **1982 (PG)** Unsuccessful change-of-pace Eastwood vehicle set during the Depression. Aging alcoholic country singer tries one last time to make it to Nashville, hoping to perform at the Grand Ole Opry. This time he takes his nephew (played by Eastwoood's real-life son) with him. **123m/C VHS, Beta, LV.** Clint Eastwood, Kyle Eastwood, John McIntire, Alexa Kenin, Verna Bloom; ***D:*** Clint Eastwood; ***W:*** Clancy Carlile; ***C:*** Bruce Surtees; ***M:*** Stephen Dorff. *WAR*

Honkytonk Nights **197? (R)** A honky-tonkin' romp through an evening in a country/western bar, featuring legendary topless dancer Carol Doda, Georgina ("Devil in Mrs. Jones") Spelvin, and the music of The Hot Licks (minus front man Dan Hicks). **90m/C VHS, Beta.** Carol Doda, Georgina Spelvin, Ramblin' Jack Elliot. *TPV*

Honolulu ½ **1939** A screwball comedy with Powell providing the musical numbers. Young takes on the dual role of a Hollywood star who meets his exact double, a Hawaii plantation owner. They decide to switch identities to give their lives a little oomph. The star sails to Hawaii, falling for fellow passenger Powell, only to discover he's expected to get married upon his arrival in Honolulu. Anderson and Burns and Allen provide the comic relief. ♫The Leader Doesn't Like Music; This Night Was Made For Dreaming; Honolulu; Hymn To The Sun. **83m/B VHS.** Robert Young, Eleanor Powell, George Burns, Gracie Allen, Rita Johnson, Eddie Anderson, Clarence Kolb; ***D:*** Edward Buzzell; ***W:*** Frank Partos, Herbert Fields; ***M:*** Franz Waxman. *MGM*

Honor Among Thieves ½ *Farewell, Friend* **1968 (R)** Two former mercenaries reteam for a robbery that doesn't come off as planned. Not as fast paced as others in Bronson canon. **115m/C VHS, Beta.** *FR IT* Charles Bronson, Alain Delon, Brigitte Fossey, Olga Georges-Picot, Bernard Fresson; ***D:*** Jean Herman. *CCB, MPI, VTR*

Honor and Glory **1992 (R)** Tracy Pride, an FBI agent and martial arts expert, teams up with an Interpol agent, who doubles as a TV anchorwoman, to stop an international banker from getting his greedy hands on the key to a nuclear arsenal. These fighting gals are up against a team of assassins but they can more than handle themselves. **90m/C VHS, LV.** Cynthia Rothrock, Donna Jason, Chuck Jeffreys, Gerald Klein, Robin Shou, Richard Yuen; ***D:*** Godfrey Hall; ***W:*** Herb Borkland. *IMP*

Honor of the Range **1934** The good sheriff's lady is whisked away by his evil twin brother and the sheriff must go undercover to get her back. Odd plot twists for a seemingly normal western. **60m/B VHS.** Ken Maynard, Cecilia Parker, Fred Kohler Sr.; ***D:*** Ken Maynard. *NOS, DVT, HEG*

Honor Thy Father **1973** The everyday life of a real-life Mafia family as seen through the eyes of Bill Bonanno, the son of mob chieftain Joe Bonanno. Adapted from the book by Gay Talese. Made for television. **97m/C Beta.** Raf Vallone, Richard Castellano, Brenda Vaccaro, Joseph Bologna; ***D:*** Paul Wendkos; ***M:*** George Duning. *PSM*

Honor Thy Father and Mother: The True Story of the Menendez Brothers ½ **1994** First Amy Fisher won the true-sleaze-on-TV award and now its the turn of Lyle and Erik Menendez. Accused of the gruesome 1989 shotgun murders of their wealthy parents, the trial provided numerous sordid details, including alledged sexual abuse of the brothers by both parents. (Both Menendez trials ended in hung juries and will be retried). Composite characters and compressed time sequences play fast and loose with the facts of the case. Based on public records and on the book "Blood Brothers," by reporters John Johnson and Ronald L. Soble. Made for television. **90m/C VHS.** Billy Warlock, David Beron, Jill Clayburgh, James Farentino, Susan Blakely, Erin Gray, Elaine Joyce, John Beck, John David Conti, Stanley Kamel; ***D:*** Paul Schneider; ***W:*** Michael J. Murray. *AVE*

Hooch ½ **1976 (PG)** Comedy about three members of the New York Mafia who get some unexpected southern hospitality when they try to muscle in on a southern family's moonshine operation. **96m/C VHS, Beta.** Gil Gerard, Erika Fox, Melody Rogers, Danny Aiello, Mike Allen, Raymond Serra; ***D:*** Edward Mann. *PSM*

The Hooded Terror **1938** A merciless group of murderers take on a G-man. **70m/B VHS.** Tod Slaughter, Greta Gynt. *NOS, HEG*

The Hoodlum **1951** A criminal does his best to rehabilitate and, with a little help from his brother, is able to hold a steady job. However the crime bug dies hard and when he spots an armored car, he just can't resist the temptation. Tierney's real brother, Edward, plays his screen brother. **61m/B VHS, Beta.** Lawrence Tierney, Allene Roberts, Marjorie Riordan, Lisa Golm, Edward Tierney; ***D:*** Max Nosseck. *SNC*

Hoodlum Empire **1952** A senator enlists the aid of a former gangster, now a war hero, in his battle against the syndicate. Loosely based on the Kefauver investigations of 1950-51. **98m/B VHS.** Brian Donlevy, Claire Trevor, Forrest Tucker, Vera Ralston, Luther Adler, John Russell, Gene Lockhart, Grant Withers, Taylor Holmes, Roy Barcroft, Richard Jaeckel; ***D:*** Joseph Kane. *REP*

The Hoodlum Priest **1961** Biography of the Rev. Charles Dismas Clark (Murray), a Jesuit priest who dedicated his life to working with juvenile delinquents and ex-cons in St. Louis. Dullea made his screen debut as Billy Lee Jackson, a thief who finds the straight and narrow is a hard road with more detours than he can handle. Fine performances with Murray co-scripting under the pseudonym Don

Deer. **101m/B VHS, Beta.** Don Murray, Keir Dullea, Larry Gates, Logan Ramsey, Cindi Wood; ***D:*** Irvin Kershner; ***W:*** Don Murray, Joseph Landon; ***C:*** Haskell Wexler. *MGM, FCT*

Hoodoo Ann 🦴🦴 **1916** The story of Hoodoo Ann, from her days in the orphanage to her happy marriage. Silent. **27m/B VHS, Beta.** Mae Marsh, Robert "Bobbie" Harron. *CCB*

Hook 🦴🦴 **1991 (PG)** Although he said he was never gonna to do it, Peter Pan has grown up. Uptight Peter Banning places work before family and has forgotten all about Neverland and the evil Captain Hook, until Hook kidnaps the Banning kids and takes them to Neverland. With the help of Tinkerbell, her magic pixie dust, and happy thoughts, Peter rescues his kids and rediscovers his youth while visiting with the Lost Boys. The sets and special effects are spectacular; the direction less so. Big-budget fantasy lacks the charm it needs to really fly. Still, kids seem to love it. You'll have to look hard to spot pirates Crosby and Close. Futurizes the J.M. Barrie classic. **142m/C VHS, Beta, LV, 8mm.** Dustin Hoffman, Robin Williams, Julia Roberts, Bob Hoskins, Maggie Smith, Charlie Korsmo, Caroline Goodall, Amber Scott, Phil Collins, Arthur Malet, Dante Basco, Gwyneth Paltrow; ***Cameos:*** Glenn Close, David Crosby; ***D:*** Steven Spielberg; ***W:*** Nick Castle; ***C:*** Dean Cundey; ***M:*** John Williams. Nominations: Academy Awards '91: Best Art Direction/Set Decoration, Best Costume Design, Best Makeup, Best Song ("When You're Alone"), Best Visual Effects. *COL*

Hook, Line and Sinker 🦴🦴 **1930** A couple of insurance investigators try to help a young woman restore a hotel, and they find romance and run-ins with crooks. Directed by Cline, who later directed W.C. Fields in "The Bank Dick," "My Little Chickadee," and "Never Give a Sucker an Even Break." **75m/B VHS, LV.** Bert Wheeler, Robert Woolsey, Dorothy Lee, Jobyna Howland, Ralf Harolde, Natalie Moorhead, George F. Marion Sr., Hugh Herbert; ***D:*** Eddie Cline; ***W:*** Rod Amateau. *NOS, TTC, FCT*

The Hooked Generation 🦴 **1969 (R)** A group of drug pushers kidnap defenseless victims, rape innocent girls, and even murder their own Cuban drug contacts (and all without the aid of a cohesive plot). Many gory events precede their untimely deaths; few will be entertained. **92m/C VHS.** Jeremy Slate, Steve Alaimo. *NO*

Hoop Dreams 🦴🦴🦴🦴 **1994 (PG-13)** Exceptional documentary follows two inner-city basketball phenoms' lives through high school as they chase their dreams of playing in the NBA. We meet Arthur Agee and William Gates as they prepare to enter St. Joseph, a predominantly white Catholic school that has offered them partial athletic scholarships. The coach tabs Gates as the "next Isiah Thomas," alluding to the school's most famous alum. There's plenty of game footage, but the more telling and fascinating parts of the film deal with the kids' families and home life. Both players encounter dramatic reversals of fortune on and off the court, demonstrating the incredibly long odds they face. **169m/C VHS, LV.** Arthur Agee, William Gates; ***D:*** Steve James. Chicago Film Critics Awards '94: Best Film; Los Angeles Film Critics Association Awards '94: Best Feature Documentary; MTV Movie Awards '95: Best New Filmmaker Award (James); National Board of Review Awards '94: Best Feature Documentary; New York Film Critics Awards '94: Best Feature Documentary; National Society of Film Critics Awards '94: Best Feature Documentary; Sundance Film Festival '94: Audience Award; Nominations: Academy Awards '94: Best Film Editing. *NLC*

Hooper 🦴🦴½ **1978 (PG)** Lightweight behind-the-scenes satire about the world of movie stuntmen. Reynolds is a top stuntman who becomes involved in a rivalry with an up-and-coming young man out to surpass him. Dated good-ole-boy shenanigans. **94m/C VHS, Beta, LV.** Burt Reynolds, Jan-Michael Vincent, Robert Klein, Sally Field, Brian Keith, John Marley, Adam West; ***D:*** Hal Needham. Nominations: Academy Awards '78: Best Sound. *WAR*

Hoosiers 🦴🦴🦴 **1986 (PG)** In Indiana, where basketball is the sport of the gods, a small town high school basketball team gets a new, but surprisingly experienced coach. He makes the team, and each person in it, better than they thought possible. Classic plot rings true because of Hackman's complex and sensitive performance coupled with Hopper's touching portrait of an alcoholic basketball fanatic. **115m/C VHS, Beta, LV.** Gene Hackman, Barbara Hershey, Dennis Hopper, David Neidorf, Sheb Wooley, Fern Parsons, Brad Boyle, Steve Hollar, Brad Long; ***D:*** David Anspaugh; ***W:*** Angelo Pizzo; ***C:*** Fred Murphy; ***M:*** Jerry Goldsmith. Los Angeles Film Critics Association Awards '86: Best Supporting Actor (Hopper); Nominations: Academy Awards '86: Best Supporting Actor (Hopper), Best Original Score. *LIV*

Hootch Country Boys 🦴 *Redneck County; The Great Lester Boggs* **1975 (PG)** A film packed with moonshine, sheriffs, busty country girls, and chases. **90m/C VHS, Beta.** Alex Karras, Scott MacKenzsie, Dean Jagger, Willie Jones, Bob Ridgely, Susan Denbo, Bob Ginnaven, David Haney; ***D:*** Harry Z. Thomason. *ACA*

Hopalong Cassidy 🦴🦴🦴 *Hopalong Cassidy Enters* **1935** In this first of a long series of "Hopalong Cassidy" films, Hoppy and his pals intervene in a brewing range war. A gang of rustlers is helped by a two-timing foreman who's playing both sides off each other. After a career in silent films, Boyd was pretty much washed up before taking on the role of Cassidy. He was originally asked to play the villain and declined, but agreed to be the good guy if the character was cleaned up. "Gabby" Hayes' stock character was killed off in this episode, but was brought back for later installments. **60m/B VHS.** William Boyd, James Ellison, Paula Stone, Robert Warwick, Charles Middleton, Frank McGlynn, Kenneth Thomson, George "Gabby" Hayes, James Mason, Franklyn Farnum; ***D:*** Howard Bretherton. *NOS, MRV*

Hopalong Cassidy: Borrowed Trouble 🦴½ **1948** Hoppy must save a righteous teacher from the clutches of kidnappers who plan to place a saloon right next to the school. **61m/B VHS.** William Boyd, Andy Clyde, Rand Brooks, Elaine Riley, John Kellogg, Helen Chapman; ***D:*** George Archainbaud. *NO*

Hopalong Cassidy: Dangerous Venture 🦴🦴 **1948** "Dangerous Venture" was one of Hoppy's last ventures, produced the final year of the series' 13-year tenure. Hoppy and the gang hunt for Aztec ruins in the great Southwest, and have to deal with renegade Indians and a band of treacherous looters along the way. **55m/B VHS, Beta.** William Boyd, Andy Clyde, Rand Brooks. *NO*

Hopalong Cassidy: False Paradise 🦴🦴 **1948** Another late Hopalong has the noir-clad cowboy rushing to the aid of a girl and her dad when control of their ranch is threatened by swindlers with false mining claims. **59m/B VHS, Beta.** William Boyd, Andy Clyde, Rand Brooks; ***D:*** George Archainbaud. *NO*

Hopalong Cassidy: Hoppy's Holiday 🦴🦴 **1947** Boyd—the only celluloid incarnation of Clarence Mulford's pulp hero—plays the Hopster yet again. This time, the non-drinking, non-smoking (what does he do for kicks?) hero and a passel of Bar-20 cowboys visit Mesa City for some well-earned R and R, but find themselves caught in a web of corruption. **60m/B VHS, Beta.** William Boyd, Andy Clyde, Rand Brooks, Jeff Corey; ***D:*** George Archainbaud. *NO*

Hopalong Cassidy: Renegade Trail 🦴🦴 **1939** Hoppy comes to the aid of both a small town sheriff and a widow. **61m/B VHS, Beta.** William Boyd, George "Gabby" Hayes, Russell Hayden, Charlotte Wynters, Russell Hopton, Sonny Bupp, Jack Rockwell, Roy Barcroft, John Merton, Robert F. (Bob) Kortman; ***D:*** Lesley Selander. *HEG*

Hopalong Cassidy: Riders of the Deadline 🦴🦴 **1943** Hoppy turns into a baddie in this episode in order to infiltrate a treacherous gang and apprehend their leader. **70m/B VHS, Beta.** William Boyd, Andy Clyde, Jimmy Rogers, Robert Mitchum; ***D:*** Lesley Selander. *NO*

Hopalong Cassidy: Silent Conflict 🦴🦴 **1948** Lucky is tricked and hypnotized by a traveling medicine man who commands him to rob and kill Hoppy. **61m/B VHS, Beta.** William Boyd, Andy Clyde, Rand Brooks; ***D:*** George Archainbaud. *NO*

Hopalong Cassidy: Sinister Journey 🦴🦴 **1948** Mysterious accidents are plaguing a railroad where an old friend of Hoppy's works, so Hoppy, California, and Lucky take railroad jobs to find out what gives. **58m/B VHS, Beta.** William Boyd, Andy Clyde, Rand Brooks; ***D:*** George Archainbaud. *NO*

Hopalong Cassidy: The Dead Don't Dream 🦴🦴 **1948** Hoppy's sidekick Lucky decides to get married, but happily-ever-afterdom is threatened when the father of Mrs. Lucky-to-be is murdered. When Hoppy sets out to find the killer, he finds himself suspected of the dastardly deed. **55m/B VHS, Beta.** William Boyd, Andy Clyde, Rand Brooks, John Parrish; ***D:*** George Archainbaud. *NO*

Hopalong Cassidy: The Devil's Playground 🦴🦴 **1946** Strange things are afoot in a peaceful valley adjacent to a desolate, forbidding wasteland. When Hoppy and a young woman set out across the wasteland to make a gold delivery, they encounter a band of desperados and begin to unravel the secrets of a dishonest political ring. **65m/B VHS, Beta.** William Boyd, Andy Clyde, Rand Brooks, Elaine Riley; ***D:*** George Archainbaud. *NO*

Hopalong Cassidy: The Marauders 🦴🦴 **1947** After seeking shelter in an abandoned church one rainy night, Hoppy and the boys must defend the kirk when it is threatened by a marauder and his gang. **64m/B VHS, Beta.** William Boyd, Andy Clyde, Rand Brooks; ***D:*** George Archainbaud. *NO*

Hopalong Cassidy: Unexpected Guest 🦴🦴½ **1947** When a small fortune is left to a California family, the head count starts to dwindle, and Hoppy aims to find out why. **59m/B VHS, Beta.** William Boyd, Andy Clyde, Rand Brooks, Una O'Connor; ***D:*** George Archainbaud. *NO*

Hope and Glory 🦴🦴🦴½ **1987 (PG-13)** Boorman turns his memories of WWII London into a complex and sensitive film. Father volunteers, and mother must deal with the awakening sexuality of her teen-age daughter, keep her son in line, balance the ration books, and try to make it to the bomb shelter in the middle of the night. Seen through the boy's eyes, war creates a playground of shrapnel to collect and wild imaginings come true. Nice companion film to "Empire of the Sun" and "Au Revoir Les Enfants," two more 1987 releases that explore WWII from the recollections of young boys. **97m/C VHS, Beta, LV, 8mm.** *GB* Sebastian Rice Edwards, Geraldine Muir, Sarah Miles, Sammi Davis, David Hayman, Derrick O'Connor, Susan Wooldridge, Jean-Marc Barr, Ian Bannen, Jill Baker, Charley Boorman, Annie Leon, Katrine Boorman, Gerald James; ***D:*** John Boorman; ***W:*** John Boorman; ***C:*** Philippe Rousselot. British Academy Awards '87: Best Film, Best Supporting Actress (Wooldridge); Los Angeles Film Critics Association Awards '87: Best Director (Boorman), Best Film, Best Screenplay; National Board of Review Awards '87: 10 Best Films of the Year; National Society of Film Critics Awards '87: Best Cinematography, Best Director (Boorman), Best Film, Best Screenplay; Nominations: Academy Awards '87: Best Art Direction/Set Decoration, Best Cinematography, Best Director (Boorman), Best Original Screenplay, Best Picture. *SUE, FCT, HMV*

Hoppity Goes to Town *Mr. Bug Goes to Town* **1941** Full-length animated feature from the Max Fleischer studios tells the story of the inhabitants of Bugville, who live in a weed patch in New York City. **77m/C VHS, LV.** ***D:*** Dave Fleischer; ***M:*** Frank Loesser, Hoagy Carmichael. *REP, MRV, FCT*

Hoppy Serves a Writ 🦴🦴 **1943** In this last of the series to be based on the writings of the original author, Texas sheriff Cassidy tries to bring a gang of outlaws to justice. Look for a young Robert Mitchum as one of the villains. **67m/B VHS.** William Boyd, Andy Clyde, Jay Kirby, Victor Jory, George Reeves, Hal Taliaferro, Robert Mitchum, Byron Foulger, Earle Hodgins, Roy Barcroft; ***D:*** George Archainbaud. *NOS, MRV*

Hopscotch ☠☠☠ **1980 (R)** A C.I.A. agent drops out when his overly zealous chief demotes him to a desk job. When he writes a book designed to expose the dirty deeds of the CIA, he leads his boss and KGB pal on a merry chase. Amiable comedy well-suited for Matthau's rumpled talents. **107m/C VHS, Beta, LV.** Walter Matthau, Glenda Jackson, Ned Beatty, Sam Waterston, Herbert Lom; ***D:*** Ronald Neame. *COL, SUE*

Horizons West ☠☠½ **1952** Two brothers go their separate ways after the Civil War. One leads a peaceful life as a rancher but the other, corrupted by the war, engages in a violent campaign to build his own empire. Ryan's outstanding performance eclipses that of the young Hudson. **81m/C VHS.** Robert Ryan, Julie Adams, Rock Hudson, Raymond Burr, James Arness, John McIntire, Dennis Weaver, Frances Bavier; ***D:*** Budd Boetticher; ***M:*** Henry Mancini. *MCA*

The Horizontal Lieutenant ☠☠½ **1962** Hutton and Prentiss team up again in this moderately funny romantic-comedy about an officer's escapades during WWII. Based on the novel "The Bottletop Affair" by Gordon Cotler. **90m/C VHS.** Jim Hutton, Paula Prentiss, Jack Carter, Jim Backus, Charles McGraw, Miyoshi Umeki; ***D:*** Richard Thorpe; ***W:*** George Wells. *MGM*

The Horn Blows at Midnight ☠☠☠ **1945** A band trumpeter falls asleep and dreams he's a bumbling archangel, on Earth to blow the note bringing the end of the world. But a pretty girl distracts him, and...A wild, high-gloss, well-cast fantasy farce, uniquely subversive in its lighthearted approach to biblical Doomsday. Benny made the film notorious by acting ashamed of it in his later broadcast routines. **78m/B VHS.** Jack Benny, Alexis Smith, Dolores Moran, Allyn Joslyn, Reginald Gardiner, Guy Kibbee, John Alexander, Margaret Dumont; ***D:*** Raoul Walsh. *MGM, FCT*

Hornet's Nest ☠☠½ **1970** Captain Turner (Hudson) is the lone survivor of an Army commando unit which parachuted into the Italian countryside in an effort to blow up a dam being held by the Nazis. He's rescued by a group of boys, the survivors of a German massacre of their nearby town. Turner wants the boys to help him blow up the dam—and they want his help in getting revenge on the Nazis who have occupied their homes. **110m/C VHS.** Rock Hudson, Sylva Koscina, Sergio Fantoni, Jacques Sernas, Giacomo "Jack" Rossi-Stuart, Andrea Bosic, Gerard Herter, Tom Felleghi; ***D:*** Phil Karlson; ***W:*** S.S. Schweitzer. *MGM*

The Horrible Dr. Hichcock ☠☠½ *L'Orribile Segreto Del Dr. Hichcock* **1962** A sicko doctor, who accidentally killed his first wife while engaged in sexual antics, remarries to bring the first missus back from the dead using his new wife's blood. Genuinely creepy. Sequelled by "The Ghost." **76m/C VHS.** *IT* Robert Flemyng, Barbara Steele; ***D:*** Riccardo (Robert Hampton) Freda. *SNC*

The Horror Chamber of Dr. Faustus ☠☠☠½ *Eyes Without a Face; Les Yeux Sans Visage; Occhi Senza Volto* **1959** A wickedly intelligent, inventive piece of Grand Guignol about a mad doctor who kills young girls so he may graft their skin onto the face of his accidentally mutilated daughter. In French with English subtitles. **84m/B VHS, Beta, LV.** *FR* Alida Valli, Pierre Brasseur, Edith Scob, Francois Guerin; ***D:*** Georges Franju; ***C:*** Eugene Eugen Shufftan Shuftan; ***M:*** Maurice Jarre. *SNC, TPV, INT*

Horror Express ☠☠½ *Panic on the Trans-Siberian Express; Panico en el Transiberiano* **1972 (R)** A creature from prehistoric times, that was removed from its tomb, is transported on the Trans-Siberian railroad. Passengers suddenly discover strange things happening—such as having their souls sucked out of them. **88m/C VHS, Beta.** *SP* Christopher Lee, Peter Cushing, Telly Savalas; ***D:*** Gene Martin. *SNC, MRV, PSM*

Horror Hospital ☠ *Computer Killers* **1973 (R)** Patients are turned into zombies by a mad doctor in this hospital where no anesthesia is used. Those who try to escape are taken care of by the doctor's guards. **91m/C VHS, Beta.** *GB* Michael Gough, Robin Askwith, Vanessa Shaw, Ellen Pollock, Skip Martin, Dennis Price; ***D:*** Antony Balch. *GRG*

Horror Hotel ☠☠½ *The City of the Dead* **1960** A young witchcraft student visits a small Massachusetts town which has historic ties to witch burnings and discovers a new, and deadly, coven is now active. Well done and atmospheric. **76m/B VHS, LV.** *GB* Christopher Lee, Patricia Jessel, Betta St. John, Dennis Lotis, Venetia Stevenson, Valentine Dyall; ***D:*** John Llewellyn Moxey; ***W:*** George L. Baxt. *NOS, MRV, SNC*

Horror House on Highway 5 *Woof!* **1986** Someone in a Nixon mask kills people in this extremely cheap dud. **90m/C VHS, Beta.** ***D:*** Richard Casey; ***W:*** Richard Casey. *NO*

The Horror of Dracula ☠☠☠½ *Dracula* **1958** The first Hammer Dracula film, in which the infamous vampire is given a new, elegant and ruthless persona, as he battles Prof. Van Helsing after coming to England. Possibly the finest, most inspired version of Bram Stoker's macabre chestnut, and one that single-handedly revived the horror genre. **82m/C VHS, Beta, LV.** *GB* Peter Cushing, Christopher Lee, Michael Gough, Melissa Stribling, Carol Marsh, John Van Eyssen, Valerie Gaunt; ***D:*** Terence Fisher; ***W:*** Jimmy Sangster; ***M:*** James Bernard. *WAR, FCT, MLB*

The Horror of Frankenstein ☠☠ **1970** Spoof of the standard Frankenstein story features philandering ex-med student Baron Frankenstein, whose interest in a weird and esoteric branch of science provides a shocking and up-to-date rendition of the age-old plot. Preceded by "Frankenstein Must Be Destroyed" and followed by "Frankenstein and the Monster from Hell." **93m/C VHS, Beta.** *GB* Ralph Bates, Kate O'Mara, Dennis Price, David Prowse; ***D:*** Jimmy Sangster; ***W:*** Jimmy Sangster. *MLB*

The Horror of It All **1991** A multi-faceted look at popular horror stars, including Karloff, Chaney, Lugosi, Price, and others, plus an examination of the dark side of the imaginative minds that produce horror. Also includes a behind-the-scenes peek at the creation of great horror scenes. **58m/C VHS.** Boris Karloff, Lon Chaney Sr., Bela Lugosi, John Barrymore, Lionel Atwill, John Carradine, Vincent Price. *MPI, FCT*

Horror of Party Beach *Woof! Invasion of the Zombies* **1964** Considered to be one of the all-time worst films. Features a mob of radioactive seaweed creatures who eat a slew of nubile, surf-minded teenagers. ♫Zombie Stomp. **71m/C VHS, Beta.** John Scott, Alice Lyon, Allen Laurel; ***D:*** Del Tenney. *PSM*

Horror of the Blood Monsters *Woof! Vampire Men of the Lost Planet; Horror Creatures of the Prehistoric Planet; Creatures of the Prehistoric Planet; Creatures of the Red Planet; Flesh Creatures of the Red Planet; The Flesh Creatures; Space Mission of the Lost Planet* **1970 (PG)** John Carradine made a career out of being in bad movies, and this one competes as one of the worst. This is an editor's nightmare, made up of black & white film spliced together and colorized. Vampires from outer space threaten to suck all the blood from the people of Earth. **85m/C VHS, Beta.** *PH* John Carradine, Robert Dix, Vicki Volante, Jennifer Bishop; ***D:*** Al Adamson, George Joseph. *REP*

Horror of the Zombies ☠ *El Buque Maldito* **1974 (R)** Bikinied models are pursued by hooded zombies on board a pleasure yacht...the horror. Effete final installment in the "blind dead" trilogy; see also "Tombs of the Blind Dead" and "Return of the Evil Dead." **90m/C VHS.** *SP* Maria Perschy, Jack Taylor; ***D:*** Armando de Ossorio; ***W:*** Armando de Ossorio. *NO*

Horror Planet *Woof! Inseminoid* **1980 (R)** Alien creature needs a chance to breed before moving on to spread its horror. When a group of explorers disturbs it, the years of waiting are over, and the unlucky mother-to-be will never be the same. Graphic and sensationalistic, capitalizing on the popularity of "Aliens." **93m/C VHS, Beta, LV.** *GB* Robin Clarke, Jennifer Ashley, Stephanie Beacham, Judy Geeson, Stephen Grives, Victoria Tennant; ***D:*** Norman J. Warren. *SUE*

Horror Rises from the Tomb ☠☠ **1972** A 15th century knight and his assistant are beheaded for practicing witchcraft. Five hundred years later, they return to possess a group of vacationers and generally cause havoc. **89m/C VHS, Beta.** *SP* Paul Naschy, Vic Winner, Emma Cohen, Helga Line; ***D:*** Carlos Aured. *FCT, NLC, LOO*

The Horror Show ☠ *House 3* **1989 (R)** Serial killer fries in electric chair, an event that really steams him. So he goes after the cop who brought him in. Standard dead guy who won't die and wants revenge flick. **95m/C VHS, Beta.** Brion James, Lance Henriksen, Rita Taggart, Dedee Pfeiffer, Aron Eisenberg, Matt Clark; ***D:*** James Isaac; ***W:*** Alan Smithee, Leslie Bohem. *MGM*

Horrors of Burke & Hare ☠ **1971** A gory tale about the exploits of a bunch of 19th-century grave robbers. **94m/C VHS, Beta, LV.** Derren Nesbitt, Harry Andrews, Yootha Joyce; ***D:*** Vernon Sewell. *NWV*

Horrors of Spider Island ☠ *It's Hot in Paradise; Ein Toter Hing im Netz; A Corpse Hangs in the Web* **1959** D'Arcy is a Hollywood talent scout who sniffs a goldmine in a team of young female dancers whom he schedules to perform for him in Singapore. Their transport plane crashes in the Pacific Ocean and he and the girls are forced to take refuge on an uncharted isle. Upon landing there they discover it is infested with giant crab-sized spiders. Lots of potential for both shock and arousal, which was probably why it was originally released in both "horror" and "girlie" versions. D'Arcy later admitted to taking over for director Bottger and adding all the horror sequences himself. Dubbed from the German. **77m/C VHS.** *GE* Alexander D'Arcy, Ursula Lederstger; ***D:*** Fritz Bottger. *SMW, TPV*

Horrors of the Red Planet ☠ *The Wizard of Mars* **1964** Cheapo epic sees astronauts crash on Mars, meet its Wizard, and stumble into a few Oz-like creatures. Technically advised by Forrest J. Ackerman. **81m/C VHS, Beta.** John Carradine, Roger Gentry, Vic McGee; ***D:*** David L. Hewitt. *GHV, MRV, REP*

The Horse ☠☠☠½ *Horse, My Horse* **1982** A moving, mature Turkish film about a father and son trying to overcome socioeconomic obstacles and their own frailties in order to make enough money to send the boy to school. In Turkish with English subtitles. **116m/C VHS, Beta.** *TU* ***D:*** Ali Ozgenturk. *KIV, INJ*

Horse Feathers ☠☠☠½ **1932** Huxley College has to beef up its football team to win the championship game, and the corrupt new college president knows just how to do it. Features some of the brothers' classic routines, and the songs "Whatever It Is, I'm Against It" and "Everyone Says I Love You." **67m/B VHS, Beta, LV.** Groucho Marx, Chico Marx, Harpo Marx, Zeppo Marx, Thelma Todd, David Landau, Nat Pendleton; ***D:*** Norman Z. McLeod. *MCA*

A Horse for Danny ☠☠½ **1995 (G)** Horse trainer Eddie (Urich), dogged by bad luck, and his 11-year-old niece Danny (Sobieski), come across a thoroughbred named Tom Thumb, who may be their chance at racing's winners circle. TV movie. **92m/C VHS.** Robert Urich, Leelee Sobieski, Ron Brice, Karen Carlson, Gary Basaraba; ***D:*** Dick Lowry. *HMK*

The Horse in the Gray Flannel Suit ☠☠½ **1968 (G)** Disney comedy portrays an advertising executive who links his daughter's devotion to horses with a client's new ad campaign. **114m/C VHS, Beta.** Dean Jones, Ellen Janov, Fred Clark, Diane Baker, Lloyd Bochner, Kurt Russell; ***D:*** Norman Tokar; ***M:*** George Bruns. *DIS, OM*

The Horse of Pride ☠☠½ *Le Cheval D'Orgeuil* **1980** Chabrol takes a telling look at the everyday life of the peasants of Breton—both their pleasures and their sorrows. In French with English subtitles. French script booklet available. **118m/C VHS, Beta.** *FR* Jacques Dufilho, Francois Cluzet; ***D:*** Claude Chabrol. *INT, APD, AUD*

The Horse Soldiers ☠☠½ **1959** An 1863 Union cavalry officer is sent 300 miles into Confederate territory to destroy a railroad junction and is accompanied by a fellow officer who is also a pacifist doctor. Based on a true Civil War incident. **114m/C VHS, Beta.** John Wayne, William Holden, Hoot Gibson, Anna Lee, Russell Simpson, Strother Martin; ***D:*** John Ford; ***C:*** William Clothier. *MGM, FOX*

The Horse Thief ♪♪♪ *Daoma Zei* **1987** Noted as the first movie from the People's Republic of China to be released on video, this epic tells the tale of Norbu, a man who, exiled from his people for horse thievery, is forced to wander the Tibetan countryside with his family in search of work. His son dies while he is in exile, and he, a devout Buddhist, is ultimately forced to accept tribal work in a ritual exorcism, after which he pleads to be accepted back into his clan. Beautiful and image-driven, offering a rare glimpse into the Tibet you won't see in travel brochures. Filmed on location with locals as actors. In Mandarin with English subtitles. **88m/C VHS.** *CH* ***D:*** Tian Zhuangzhuang. *KIV, FCT, INJ*

The Horse Without a Head ♪♪½ **1963** Stolen loot has been hidden in a discarded toy horse which is now the property of a group of poor children. The thieves, however, have different plans. Good family fare originally shown on the Disney television show. **89m/C VHS, Beta.** Jean-Pierre Aumont, Herbert Lom, Leo McKern, Pamela Franklin, Vincent Winter; ***D:*** Don Chaffey. *DIS*

The Horseman on the Roof ♪♪½ *Le Hussard sur le Toit* **1995 (R)** Lavish costume drama set in Provence in the 1830s, during a cholera epidemic. Italian officer/revolutionary Angelo (Martinez) is on the run and eventually meets up with beautiful Pauline de Theus (Binoche), who hides him in a quarantined French village. Pauline's in search of her husband and Angelo reluctantly agrees to help her. Together they manage to escape a military cordon and travel to another plague town. There's lots of riding through the countryside and hiding out and not much actually happens. Nice scenery, attractive stars. Based on the 1951 novel by Jean Giono. French with subtitles. **135m/C VHS.** *FR* Olivier Martinez, Juliette Binoche, Francois Cluzet, Isabelle Carre, Jean Yanne, Claudio Amendola, Pierre Arditti; ***Cameos:*** Gerard Depardieu; ***D:*** Jean-Paul Rappeneau; ***W:*** Jean-Paul Rappeneau, Jean-Claude Carriere, Nina Companeez; ***C:*** Thierry Arbogast; ***M:*** Jean-Claude Petit. Nominations: Cesar Awards '96: Best Actress (Binoche), Best Art Direction/Set Decoration, Best Cinematography, Best Costume Design, Best Director (Rappeneau), Best Film, Best Film Editing, Best Sound, Best Score. *NYR*

Horsemasters ♪♪ **1961** A group of young riders enter a special training program in England to achieve the ultimate equestrian title of horsemaster, with Annette having to overcome her fear of jumping. Originally a two-part Disney television show, and released as a feature film in Europe. **85m/C VHS, Beta.** Tommy Kirk, Annette Funicello, Janet Munro, Tony Britton, Donald Pleasence, Jean Marsh, John Fraser, Millicent Martin; ***D:*** William Fairchild. *DIS*

The Horsemen ♪½ **1970 (PG)** An Afghani youth enters the brutal buzkashi horse tournament to please his macho-minded father. Beautifully shot in Afghanistan and Spain by Claude Renoir. **109m/C VHS, Beta.** Omar Sharif, Leigh Taylor-Young, Jack Palance, David De, Peter Jeffrey; ***D:*** John Frankenheimer; ***W:*** Dalton Trumbo; ***M:*** Georges Delerue. *COL*

The Horseplayer ♪½ **1991 (R)** A loner is drawn into a mysterious triangle of decadence and desire in this riveting psychothriller. **?m/C VHS, LV.** Brad Dourif, Sammi Davis, M.K. Harris, Vic Tayback; ***D:*** Kurt Voss. *REP*

The Horse's Mouth ♪♪♪ *The Oracle* **1958** An obsessive painter discovers that he must rely upon his wits to survive in London. A hilarious adaptation of the Joyce Cary novel. The laserdisc version is accompanied by an episode of the British documentary series "The Art of Film" profiling Guinness and his screen career. **93m/C VHS, Beta, LV.** *GB* Alec Guinness, Kay Walsh, Robert Coote, Renee Houston, Michael Gough; ***D:*** Ronald Neame. National Board of Review Awards '58: 5 Best Foreign Films of the Year, Best Supporting Actress (Walsh); Nominations: Academy Awards '58: Best Adapted Screenplay. *HMV, ING, NLC*

The Hospital ♪♪♪½ **1971 (PG)** Cult favorite providing savage, unrelentingly sarcastic look at the workings of a chaotic metropolitan hospital beset by murders, witchdoctors, madness, and plain ineptitude. **101m/C VHS, Beta.** George C. Scott, Diana Rigg, Barnard Hughes, Stockard Channing, Nancy Marchand, Richard Dysart; ***D:*** Arthur Hiller; ***W:*** Paddy Chayefsky. Academy Awards '71: Best Story & Screenplay; Berlin International Film Festival '72: Silver Prize; British Academy Awards '72: Best Screenplay; Golden Globe Awards '72: Best Screenplay; Writers Guild of America '71: Best Original Screenplay; Nominations: Academy Awards '71: Best Actor (Scott). *MGM, FOX*

Hospital Massacre *Woof! X-Ray; Ward 13; Be My Valentine, Or Else* **1981 (R)** Psychopathic killer is loose in a hospital. Seems he holds a grudge against the woman who laughed at his valentine when they were children twenty years earlier, and too bad for her that she just checked in as a patient. Former "Playboy" and Hefner playmate Benton frolics in dangerous health care situation presented by the Cannon organization. **89m/C VHS, Beta.** Barbi Benton, Jon Van Ness, Chip Lucio; ***D:*** Boaz Davidson; ***W:*** Marc Behm. *MGM*

Hospital of Terror ♪♪ *Nurse Sherri; Terror Hospital; Beyond the Living* **1978 (R)** A transmigratory religious fanatic who died on the operating table manages to possess a nurse (Jacobson) before he kicks the bucket, and once in his candystripe incarnation, vents his spleen on the doctors who botched his operation. It's got a little more plasma than Adamson's "AstroZombies," considered by many to be a world-class boner. **88m/C VHS.** Jill Jacobson, Geoffrey Land, Marilyn Joi, Mary Kay Pass, Prentiss Moulden, Clayton Foster; ***D:*** Al Adamson. *NO*

The Hostage ♪♪½ **1967 (PG)** A young teenager is witness to a gruesome and clandestine burial. The two murderers responsible take it upon themselves to see that their secret is never told. **84m/C VHS.** Don O'Kelly, Harry Dean Stanton, John Carradine, Danny Martins; ***D:*** Russell S. Doughten Jr. *NO*

Hostage ♪½ **1987 (R)** Arab terrorists hijack a plane and the passengers start to fight back. Filmed in South Africa. **94m/C VHS, Beta.** Karen Black, Kevin McCarthy, Wings Hauser; ***D:*** Hanro Mohr; ***M:*** Brad Fiedel. *COL*

Hostage ♪♪ **1992 (R)** British Secret Service agent John Rennie is fed up after a difficult mission in Argentina. He thinks he can walk away clean but his superiors beg to differ. He's marked for murder but Rennie has a dangerous plan that could guarantee his safety—only if he returns to Argentina to set things in motion. Based on the novel "No Place to Hide" by Ted Allbeury. **100m/C VHS, Beta.** Sam Neill, Talisa Soto, James Fox; ***D:*** Robert W. Young. *PAR, PMS*

Hostage for a Day ♪♪½ **1994** Married to a shrew, toiling for an overbearing father-in-law, and suffering a midlife crisis, Wendt decides to fake his own kidnapping, take the ransom money, and head off for a better life. A series of comedic complications abound. Candy's directorial debut. Made for TV. **92m/C VHS, LV.** George Wendt, John Vernon, Robin Duke, Peter Torokvei, Don Lake, Frank Moore, John Hemphill, Christopher Templeton; ***Cameos:*** John Candy; ***D:*** John Candy; ***W:*** Peter Torokvei, Robert Crane, Kari Hildebrand; ***M:*** Ian Thomas. *VMK*

The Hostage Tower ♪♪ **1980 (PG)** In France, a group of international crime figures capture the visiting U.S. president's mother, hold her hostage in the Eiffel Tower and demand $30 million in ransom. Made for television. **97m/C VHS, Beta, LV.** Peter Fonda, Maud Adams, Britt Ekland, Billy Dee Williams, Keir Dullea, Douglas Fairbanks Jr., Rachel Roberts, Celia Johnson; ***D:*** Claudio Guzman. *SUE*

Hostages ♪ **1979** A gang of criminals kidnap a family on vacation at a Caribbean island. **93m/C VHS, Beta.** Stuart Whitman, Marisa Mell. *NO*

Hostages ♪♪♪ **1993 (R)** Harrowing docudrama about the Beirut hostage crisis combines acutal news footage with scenes of the prisoners and their families. Under desperate conditions hostages John McCarthy, Brian Keenan, Terry Anderson, Thomas Sutherland, Frank Reed, and Terry Waite try to hold on to their sanity and humanity as their families struggle for their release. Filmed on location in England, Israel, and Lebanon. Made for cable TV. **90m/C VHS.** Colin Firth, Ciaran Hinds, Jay O. Sanders, Josef Sommer, Harry Dean Stanton, Kathy Bates, Natasha Richardson, Conrad Asquith; ***D:*** David Wheatley; ***W:*** Bernard MacLaverty. *IMP*

Hostile Guns ♪♪½ **1967** A law man discovers a woman he once loved is now an inmate he is transporting across the Texas badlands. Routine with the exception of cameos by veteran actors. Based on a story by Sloan Nibley and James Edward Grant. **91m/C VHS, LV.** George Montgomery, Yvonne De Carlo, Tab Hunter, John Russell; ***Cameos:*** Brian Donlevy, Richard Arlen, Fuzzy Knight, Donald (Don "Red") Barry; ***D:*** R.G. Springsteen; ***W:*** Steve Fisher, Sloan Nibley. *PAR*

Hostile Intentions ♪♪ **1995 (R)** Three girlfriends head for a weekend of fun in the sun in Tijuana and find themselves turned into fugitives through a series of misunderstandings. In order to get home, they must risk a night border crossing with a group of illegal immigrants. **90m/C VHS.** Tia Carrere, Lisa Dean Ryan, Tricia Leigh Fisher, Carlos Gomez; ***D:*** Catherine Cyran; ***W:*** Catherine Cyran. *AVE*

Hostile Takeover ♪½ *Office Party* **1988 (R)** A mild-mannered accountant finally cracks and takes his co-workers hostage. He faces the police in a tense showdown. **93m/C VHS, Beta, LV.** David Warner, Michael Ironside, Kate Vernon, Jayne Eastwood; ***D:*** George Mihalka. *LIV*

Hot Blood **1989** Two bank robbers take an innocent woman hostage and thrust her in the midst of a huge family battle. Another lukewarm entry from the director of "The Arrogant." **89m/C VHS, Beta.** Sylvia Kristel, Alicia Moro, Aldo Sambrel, Gaspar Cano; ***D:*** Philippe Blot. *CAN*

Hot Box *Woof!* **1972 (R)** A Filipino-shot, low budget woofer. Prison flick about women who break out and foment a revolution. **85m/C VHS, Beta.** Andrea Cagan, Margaret Markov, Rickey Richardson, Laurie Rose; ***D:*** Joe Viola; ***W:*** Joe Viola, Jonathan Demme. *SUE*

Hot Bubblegum ♪ **1981 (R)** Three teenagers discover sex, the beach, rock 'n' roll, sex, drag racing, and sex. **94m/C VHS, Beta.** Jonathan Segall, Zachi Noy, Yftach Katzur. *NO*

Hot Child in the City ♪ **1987** A country girl goes to Los Angeles and searches through the city's fleshpots for her sister's killer. Music by Nick Glider, Lou Reed, Billy Idol, and Fun Boy Three. **85m/C VHS, Beta.** Leah Ayres Hendrix, Shari Shattuck, Geof Pryssir; ***D:*** John Florea. *PSM, PAR*

Hot Chocolate ♪♪ **1992 (PG-13)** Derek is a sultry Texas tycoon who wants to buy out the French chocolate factory run by Hays. After getting a look at her, work isn't all that's on his mind. **93m/C VHS, LV.** Bo Derek, Robert Hays. *LIV*

Hot Dog...The Movie! ♪½ **1983 (R)** There's an intense rivalry going on between an Austrian ski champ and his California challenger during the World Cup Freestyle competition in Squaw Valley. Snow movie strictly for teens or their equivalent. **96m/C VHS, Beta.** David Naughton, Patrick Houser, Shannon Tweed, Tracy N. Smith; ***D:*** Peter Markle; ***M:*** Peter Bernstein. *MGM, FOX*

Hot Foot/A Happy Married Couple **1920** Two silent comedies: "Hot Foot" (1920), is about Dunn's hobo character in the Chaplin mold; "A Happy Married Couple" (1916), is about a young married couple whose puppy, as described in a letter, is mistaken for a baby by their parents. **51m/B VHS, Beta, 8mm.** Bobbie Dunn, Neal Burns, Betty Compson. *VYY*

Hot Lead ♪♪ **1951** Typical Holt oater which has the cowpoke and his sidekick Martin trying to avenge the death of a close friend who was killed by a gang of train robbers. **60m/B VHS.** Tim Holt, Joan Dixon, Ross Elliott, John Dehner; ***D:*** Stuart Gilmore. *MOV*

Hot Lead & Cold Feet 1978 (G) Twin brothers (one a gunfighter, the other meek and mild) compete in a train race where the winner will take ownership of a small western town. Dale not only plays both brothers, but also their tough father. Standard Disney fare. **89m/C VHS, Beta.** Jim Dale, Don Knotts, Karen Valentine; ***D:*** Robert Butler; ***W:*** Arthur Alsberg; ***M:*** Buddy Baker. *DIS*

The Hot Line ½ *The Day the Hot Line Got Hot; Le Rouble a Deux Faces; El Rublo de las dos Caras* **1969** The world's two superpowers become befuddled when the hot line connecting Washington and Moscow breaks down. Taylor's final film. **87m/C VHS.** Robert Taylor, Charles Boyer, George Chakiris, Dominique Fabre, Gerard Tichy; ***D:*** Etienne Perier. *REP*

Hot Millions 1968 Hysterical comedy about high-class swindling operation with Ustinov as a refined embezzler. Excellent cast and sharp script. Although it didn't do well at the box office, this amusing romp became one of the biggest sleepers of the year. **106m/C VHS.** *GB* Peter Ustinov, Maggie Smith, Karl Malden, Bob Newhart, Robert Morley, Cesar Romero; ***D:*** Eric Till; ***W:*** Peter Ustinov, Ira Wallach. *MGM*

Hot Money 1979 A small-town drama about an ex-con who poses as an assistant sheriff and plots a million-dollar robbery during the town's 4th of July parade. Made shortly before Welles' death, and kept on the shelf for more than five years. **78m/C VHS, Beta.** Orson Welles, Michael Murphy, Bobby Pickett, Michelle Finney. *VMK*

Hot Moves 1984 (R) Four high school boys make a pact to lose their virginity before the end of the summer. **89m/C VHS, Beta.** Michael Zorek, Adam Silbar, Jill Schoelen, Deborah Richter, Monique Gabrielle, Tami Holbrook, Virgil Frye; ***D:*** Jim Sotos. *VES*

Hot Potato 1976 (PG) Black Belt Jones rescues a senator's daughter from a megalomaniacal general by using skull-thwacking footwork. **87m/C VHS, Beta.** Jim Kelly, George Memmoli, Geoffrey Binney; ***D:*** Oscar Williams. *WAR*

Hot Pursuit ½ 1984 (PG) A woman who has been framed for murder runs from the law and a relentless hitman. **94m/C VHS, Beta.** Mike Preston, Dina Merrill, Kerrie Keane. *VMK*

Hot Pursuit ½ 1987 (PG-13) A prep-school bookworm resorts to Rambo-like tactics in tracking down his girlfriend and her family after being left behind for a trip to the tropics. **93m/C VHS, Beta, LV.** John Cusack, Robert Loggia, Jerry Stiller, Wendy Gazelle; ***D:*** Steven Lisberger; ***W:*** Steven W. Carabatsos. *PAR*

Hot Resort ½ 1985 (R) Young American lads mix work and play when they sign on as summer help at an island resort. Typical teen sex fantasy. **92m/C VHS, Beta.** Bronson Pinchot, Tom Parsekian, Michael Berz, Linda Kenton, Frank Gorshin; ***D:*** John Robins; ***W:*** Boaz Davidson, John Robins. *MGM*

The Hot Rock *How To Steal a Diamond in Four Easy Lessons* **1970 (PG)** A motley crew of bumbling thieves conspire to steal a huge, priceless diamond; a witty, gritty comedy that makes no moral excuses for its characters and plays like an early-'70s crime thriller gone awry. Adapted from the novel by Donald E. Westlake. The sequel, 1974's "Bank Shot," stars George C. Scott in the role created by Redford. **97m/C VHS, Beta, LV.** Robert Redford, George Segal, Ron Leibman, Zero Mostel, Moses Gunn, William Redfield, Charlotte Rae, Topo Swope; ***M:*** Quincy Jones. Nominations: Academy Awards '72: Best Film Editing. *FOX*

Hot Rod *Rebel of the Road* **1979** A young California hotrodder battles the evil sponsor of a drag race championship. **97m/C VHS, Beta.** Greg Henry, Robert Culp, Pernell Roberts, Robin Mattson, Grant Goodeve; ***D:*** George Armitage. *NLC*

Hot Rod Girl *Hot Car Girl* **1956** A concerned police officer (Conners) organizes supervised drag racing after illegal drag racing gets out of hand in his community. **75m/B VHS.** Lori Nelson, Chuck Connors, John W. Smith; ***D:*** Leslie Martinson; ***W:*** John McGreevey. *SNC, NOS, MRV*

Hot Shot ½ 1986 (PG) An inspirational tale involving a young soccer player who goes to great lengths to take training from a soccer star, played - of course - by Pele. **90m/C VHS, Beta.** Pele, Jim Youngs, Billy Warlock, Weyman Thompson, Mario Van Peebles, David Groh; ***D:*** Rick King. *WAR, MVD*

Hot Shots! 1991 (PG-13) Another entry from "The Naked Gun" team of master movie parodists, this has lots of clever sight gags but the verbal humor often plummets to the ground. Spoofs "Top Gun" and similar gung-ho air corps adventures but doesn't forget other popular films including "Dances with Wolves" and "The Fabulous Baker Boys." Sheen is very funny as ace fighter pilot Sean "Topper" Harley who's to avenge the family honor. Great when you're in the mood for laughs that don't require thought. **83m/C VHS.** Charlie Sheen, Cary Elwes, Valeria Golino, Lloyd Bridges, Kevin Dunn, Jon Cryer, William O'Leary, Kristy Swanson, Efrem Zimbalist Jr., Bill Irwin, Heidi Swedberg, Judith Kahan, Pat Proft; ***Cameos:*** Charles Barkley, Bill Laimbeer; ***D:*** Jim Abrahams; ***W:*** Pat Proft, Jim Abrahams; ***M:*** Sylvester Levay. *FXV*

Hot Shots! Part Deux ½ 1993 (PG-13) Second "Hot Shots" outing doesn't live up to the first, but it's not bad either. Admiral Tug Benson (Bridges) is elected President (yes, of the U.S.) and calls on Sheen's newly pumped-up Topper to take on Saddam Hussein Rambo-style. Love interest Ramada (Golino), returns but this time she's competing with Michelle (Bakke), a sexy CIA agent. Crenna spoofs his role in the "Rambo" films as Sheen's mentor; look for real-life dad Martin in a take-off of "Apocalypse Now." Shtick flies as fast and furious as the bodies, with Bridges getting a chance to reprise his glory days of "Sea Hunt." Don't miss the credits. **89m/C VHS, LV.** Charlie Sheen, Lloyd Bridges, Valeria Golino, Brenda Bakke, Richard Crenna, Miguel Ferrer, Rowan Atkinson, Jerry Haleva, Mitchell Ryan, Gregory Sierra, Ryan Stiles, Michael Colyar; ***Cameos:*** Martin Sheen, Bob Vila; ***D:*** Jim Abrahams; ***W:*** Pat Proft, Jim Abrahams; ***M:*** Basil Poledouris. *FXV, BTV*

Hot Spell ½ 1958 In an attempt to repair her marriage and unify her family, a mother plans a reunion-birthday party for her husband. Despair reigns in this sultry, Southern melodrama. **86m/B VHS, Beta.** Shirley Booth, Anthony Quinn, Shirley MacLaine, Earl Holliman, Eileen Heckart; ***D:*** Daniel Mann; ***C:*** Loyal Griggs; ***M:*** Alex North. *BAR*

The Hot Spot ½ 1990 (R) An amoral drifter arrives in a small Texas town and engages in affairs with two women, including his boss's oversexed wife and a young woman with her own secrets. Things begin to heat up when he decides to plot a bank robbery. Based on Charles Williams' 1952 novel "Hell Hath No Fury." **120m/C VHS, LV.** Don Johnson, Virginia Madsen, Jennifer Connelly, Charles Martin Smith, William Sadler, Jerry Hardin, Barry Corbin, Leon Rippy, Jack Nance; ***D:*** Dennis Hopper; ***W:*** Charles Williams, Nona Tyson; ***M:*** Jack Nitzsche. *ORI, FCT*

Hot Stuff 1980 (PG) Officers on a burglary task force decide the best way to obtain convictions is to go into the fencing business themselves. **91m/C VHS, Beta, LV.** Dom DeLuise, Jerry Reed, Suzanne Pleshette, Ossie Davis; ***D:*** Dom DeLuise; ***W:*** Donald E. Westlake, Michael Kane. *COL*

Hot Summer in Barefoot County 1974 (R) A state law enforcement officer on the search for illegal moonshiners finds more than he bargained for. **90m/C VHS, Beta.** Sherry Robinson, Tonia Bryan, Dick Smith; ***D:*** Will Zens. *NO*

Hot T-Shirts *Woof!* 1979 (R) A small town bar owner needs a boost for business, finding the answer in wet T-shirt contests. Softcore trash. **86m/C VHS, Beta.** Ray Holland, Stephanie Lawlor, Pauline Rose, Corinne Alphen; ***D:*** Chuck Vincent. *MCA*

Hot Target 1985 (R) An ideal mother becomes obsessed with the stranger who seduced her, even after she finds out he's a thief planning to rob her home. **93m/C VHS, Beta, LV.** *NZ* Simone Griffeth, Steve Marachuk; ***D:*** Denis Lewiston. *LIV, VES*

The Hot, the Cool, and the Vicious 198? A quiet town turns into a bloody, martial arts playground when three hombres trade blows in a tavern. **?m/C VHS.** Wang Tao, Tommy Lee, Sun Chia-Lin. *MGI*

Hot Times 1974 (R) Low-budget comedy about a high school boy who, after striking out with the high school girls, decides to go to New York and have the time of his life. **80m/C VHS, Beta.** Gail Lorber, Amy Farber, Henry Cory; ***D:*** Jim McBride; ***W:*** Jim McBride. *MON*

Hot to Trot! 1988 (PG) A babbling idiot links up with a talking horse in an updated version of the "Francis, the Talking Mule" comedies, by way of Mr. Ed. The equine voice is provided by Candy. Some real funny guys are wasted here. **90m/C VHS, Beta, LV.** Bob(cat) Goldthwait, Dabney Coleman, Virginia Madsen, Jim Metzler, Cindy Pickett, Tim Kazurinsky, Santos Morales, Barbara Whinnery, Garry Kluger; ***D:*** Michael Dinner; ***W:*** Charlie Peters; ***M:*** Danny Elfman; ***V:*** John Candy. *WAR*

Hot Touch *Woof!* 198? An art forger with a large heist is besieged by a slashing maniac, and must discover the culprit. **92m/C VHS, Beta.** Wayne Rogers, Samantha Eggar, Marie-France Pisier, Melvyn Douglas. *TWE, HHE*

Hot Under the Collar ½ 1991 (R) Jerry is a weasel who tries to seduce the luscious Monica by using hypnosis. But his plans backfire and instead Monica enters a convent and takes a vow of chastity. This isn't going to stop Jerry, he tries posing as a priest and even dressing as a nun in order to get her out. Things get even more complicated when a mobster, looking for a fortune in stolen diamonds, sneaks into the convent. **87m/C VHS.** Richard Gabai, Angela Visser, Daniel Friedman, Mindy Clarke, Tane McClure; ***D:*** Richard Gabai. *HBO*

Hot Water/Safety Last 1924 Two classic Harold Lloyd silent comedies, "Hot Water" (1924) and "Safety Last" (1923). "Safety Last" features one of Lloyd's most famous stunt scenes, where he is hanging from the hands of a giant clock on the side of a building, high above the city. **81m/B VHS, Beta.** Harold Lloyd. *TLF*

Hot Wire ½ 197? Tired comedy about the unscrupulous side of the car repossession racket. **92m/C VHS, Beta.** George Kennedy, Strother Martin. *NO*

Hotel ½ 1967 (PG) A pale rehash of the "Grand Hotel" formula about an array of rich characters interacting in a New Orleans hotel. From the Arthur Hailey potboiler; the basis for the television series. **125m/C VHS, Beta.** Rod Taylor, Catherine Spaak, Karl Malden, Melvyn Douglas, Merle Oberon, Michael Rennie, Richard Conte, Kevin McCarthy; ***D:*** Richard Quine; ***W:*** Wendell Mayes; ***C:*** Charles B(ryant) Lang. *WAR*

Hotel Colonial ½ 1988 (R) A young Italian idealist ventures to Columbia to retrieve the body of his brother, who reportedly killed himself. Once there, he finds the dead man is not his brother, and decides to investigate. **103m/C VHS, Beta, LV, 8mm.** *IT* Robert Duvall, John Savage, Rachel Ward, Massimo Troisi; ***D:*** Cinzia Torrini; ***W:*** Ira Barmak, Enzo Monteleone; ***M:*** Pino Donaggio. *SUE, NLC*

Hotel du Lac 1986 A made-for-British-television adaptation of the Anita Brookner novel about a woman writer languishing at a Swiss lakefront hotel. **75m/C VHS, Beta.** *GB* Anna Massey, Denholm Elliott, Googie Withers; ***D:*** Giles Foster; ***M:*** Carl Davis. *FOX, TVC, VCO*

Hotel Imperial 1927 Set in 1917 Budapest, six Hungarian soldiers ride into a frontier town and find it occupied by Russians. Hall plays Lieutenant Almasy, who takes refuge in the Hotel Imperial. Orchestra scored. **84m/B VHS.** Pola Negri, James Hall, George Siegmann, Max Davidson; ***D:*** Mauritz Stiller. *GPV*

The Hotel New Hampshire 1984 (R) The witless, amoral adaptation of John Irving's novel about a very strange family's adventures in New Hampshire, Vienna and New York City, which include gang rape, incest, and Kinski in a bear suit. **110m/C VHS, Beta, LV.** Jodie Foster, Rob Lowe, Beau

Bridges, Nastassia Kinski, Wallace Shawn, Wilford Brimley, Amanda Plummer, Anita Morris, Matthew Modine, Lisa Banes, Seth Green; ***D:*** Tony Richardson; ***W:*** Tony Richardson; ***C:*** David Watkin. *VES*

Hotel Paradiso 𝔏𝔏½ **1966** Slightly amusing bedroom farce has timid Guinness trying to carry on affair with Italian sexpot Lollibrigida. Guinness fans won't be disappointed, although it's not a top-rate production. Based on the play "L'Hotel du Libre Echange" by Georges Feydeau and Maurice Desvalliers. **100m/C VHS.** *GB* Alec Guinness, Gina Lollobrigida, Akim Tamiroff, Marie Bell, Derek Fowlds; ***D:*** Peter Glenville; ***W:*** Peter Glenville, Jean-Claude Carriere. *MGM*

Hotel Reserve 𝔏𝔏𝔏 **1944** A Nazi spy is reportedly afoot in a French resort during WWII, and tension mounts as the guests attempt to flush him out. Critical response to this film is wildly split; some find it obvious, while others call it well-done and suspenseful. Based on the novel "Epitaph for a Spy" by Eric Ambler. **79m/B VHS, Beta.** *GB* James Mason, Lucie Mannheim, Raymond Lovell, Julien Mitchell, Martin Miller, Herbert Lom, Frederick Valk, Valentine Dyall, Patricia Medina; ***D:*** Victor Hanbury, Lance Comfort, Max Greene. *TTC, RXM*

Hotel Room 𝔏𝔏½ *David Lynch's Hotel Room* **1993** A trilogy of stories set in the same drab New York hotel room in three different time periods. "Getting Rid of Robert," set in 1992, has three girlfriends swilling champagne and discussing Sasha's slick, movie exec boyfriend whom she wants to dump. "Tricks," set in 1969, features Darlene, a bored, druggy prostitute; her client, Moe; and the sudden appearance of Moe's talkative friend, Lou. "Blackout" is set in 1936 and features a young husband trying to cope with the madness of his beautiful wife. Unfortunately, all three stories are rambling and lacking in energy. Made for cable television. **100m/C VHS.** Deborah Unger, Mariska Hargitay, Chelsea Field, Griffin Dunne, Glenne Headly, Harry Dean Stanton, Freddie Jones, Crispin Glover, Alicia Witt, Clark Heathcliffe Brolly, Camilla Overbye Roos; ***D:*** James Signorelli, David Lynch; ***W:*** Barry Gifford, Jay McInerney; ***M:*** Angelo Badalamenti. *WOV, FCT*

Hothead 𝔏𝔏 *Coup de Tete* **1978** A heedless, impulsive soccer player's behavior gets him cut from the team, fired from his mill job, and booted out of his favorite bar. In French with English subtitles or dubbed. **98m/C VHS, Beta.** *FR* Patrick Dewaere, Jean Bouise, Michel Aumont, France Dougnac; ***D:*** Jean-Jacques Annaud; ***W:*** Francis Veber. Cesar Awards '80: Best Supporting Actor (Bouise). *COL*

Hotline 𝔏𝔏 **1982** After taking a job answering phones at a crisis center, a woman becomes the next target of a psychotic killer. Made for television. **96m/C VHS.** Lynda Carter, Steve Forrest, Granville Van Dusen, Monte Markham, James Booth; ***D:*** Jerry Jameson. *NO*

H.O.T.S. 𝔏 *T & A Academy* **1979 (R)** A sex-filled sorority rivalry film, starring a slew of ex-Playboy Playmates in wet shirts. Screenplay co-written by exploitation star Caffaro. **95m/C VHS, Beta.** Susan Kiger, Lisa London, Kimberly Cameron, Danny Bonaduce, Steve Bond; ***D:*** Gerald Seth Sindell; ***W:*** Cheri Caffaro. *LIV, VES*

Houdini 𝔏𝔏½ **1953** Historically inaccurate but entertaining biopic of the infamous magician and escapologist. Chronicles his rise to stardom, his efforts to contact his dearly departed mother through mediums (a prequel to "Ghost"?), and his heart-stopping logic-defying escapes. First screen teaming of Leigh and Curtis, who had already been married for two years. **107m/C VHS.** Tony Curtis, Janet Leigh, Torin Thatcher, Angela Clark, Stefan Schnabel, Ian Wolfe, Sig Rumann, Michael Pate, Connie Gilchrist, Mary Murphy, Tor Johnson; ***D:*** George Marshall; ***W:*** Philip Yordan. *PAR, FCT*

The Hound of London 𝔏𝔏½ *Sherlock Holmes in The Hound of London* **1993** Inspector Lestrade brings Sherlock Holmes (Macnee) his latest case, a double murder that has taken place at the Strand Theatre. And among the suspects is the only woman Holmes has ever admired, the lovely Irene Adler. Eccentric characters, a sword duel, backstage mischief, and Holmes and Watson together once more. Based on the play by Craig Bowlsby. **72m/C VHS.** *CA* Patrick Macnee, John Scott-Paget, Colin Skinner, Jack McCreath, Carolyn Wilkinson, Sophia Thornley, Drew Kemp, Ned Lemley, Craig Bowlsby; ***D:*** Gil Letourneau, Peter Reynolds-Long; ***W:*** Craig Bowlsby. *IPI*

The Hound of the Baskervilles 𝔏𝔏𝔏 **1939** The curse of a demonic hound threatens descendants of an English noble family until Holmes and Watson solve the mystery. Also available with "Sherlock Holmes Faces Death" on Laser Disc. **80m/B VHS, Beta.** *GB* Basil Rathbone, Nigel Bruce, Richard Greene, John Carradine, Wendy Barrie, Lionel Atwill, E.E. Clive; ***D:*** Sidney Lanfield. *FOX*

The Hound of the Baskervilles 𝔏𝔏½ **1959** Cushing's not half bad as Sherlock Holmes as he investigates the mystery of a supernatural hound threatening the life of a Dartmoor baronet. Dark and moody. **86m/C VHS, Beta, LV.** *GB* Peter Cushing, Christopher Lee, Andre Morell; ***D:*** Terence Fisher; ***M:*** James Bernard. *MGM, MLB, FOX*

The Hound of the Baskervilles *Woof!* **1977** Awful spoof of the Sherlock Holmes classic with Cook as Holmes and Moore as Watson (and Holmes' mother). Even the cast can't save it. **84m/C VHS.** Dudley Moore, Peter Cook, Denholm Elliott, Joan Greenwood, Spike Milligan, Jessie Matthews, Roy Kinnear; ***D:*** Paul Morrissey; ***W:*** Dudley Moore, Peter Cook, Paul Morrissey; ***M:*** Dudley Moore. *ATU*

The Hound of the Baskervilles 𝔏𝔏 **1983** Another remake of the Sherlock Holmes story which finds the great detective investigating the murder of Sir Charles Baskerville and a mysterious haunted moor. **100m/C VHS, Beta.** *GB* Ian Richardson, Donald Churchill, Martin Shaw, Nicholas Clay, Denholm Elliott, Brian Blessed, Ronald Lacey; ***D:*** Douglas Hickox. *PAR*

Hour of Decision 𝔏½ **1957** When a newspaper columnist turns up dead, a reporter investigates the murder. Things get hairy when he finds the prime suspect is his own wife. **81m/B VHS, Beta.** *GB* Jeff Morrow, Hazel Court, Lionel Jeffries, Anthony Dawson, Mary Laura Wood; ***D:*** C.M. Pennington-Richards. *SNC*

Hour of the Assassin 𝔏½ **1986 (R)** A mercenary is hired to assassinate a South American ruler, and a CIA operative is sent to stop him. Shot in Peru. **96m/C VHS, Beta.** Erik Estrada, Robert Vaughn; ***D:*** Luis Llosa. *MGM*

Hour of the Gun 𝔏𝔏 **1967** Western saga chronicles what happens after the gunfight at the OK Corral. Garner plays the grim Wyatt Earp on the trail of vengeance after his brothers are killed. Robards is excellent as the crusty Doc Holliday. **100m/C VHS.** James Garner, Jason Robards Jr., Robert Ryan, Albert Salmi, Charles Aidman, Steve Ihnat, Jon Voight; ***D:*** John Sturges; ***W:*** Edward Anhalt; ***M:*** Jerry Goldsmith. *MGM*

The Hour of the Star 𝔏𝔏𝔏½ *A Hora Da Estrela* **1985** The poignant, highly acclaimed feature debut by Amaral, about an innocent young woman moving to the city of Sao Paulo from the impoverished countryside of Brazil, and finding happiness despite her socioeconomic failures. Based on Clarice Lispector's novel. In Portuguese with English subtitles. **96m/C VHS, Beta.** *BR* Marcelia Cartaxo; ***D:*** Suzana Amaral. Berlin International Film Festival '85: Best Actress (Cartaxo). *KIV, INJ, FCT*

Hour of the Wolf 𝔏𝔏𝔏½ **1968** An acclaimed, surreal view into the tormented inner life of a painter as he and his wife are isolated on a small northern island. Cinematography by Sven Nykvist. In Swedish with English subtitles. **89m/B VHS, Beta.** *SW* Max von Sydow, Liv Ullmann, Ingrid Thulin, Erland Josephson, Gertrud Fridh, Gudrun Brost; ***D:*** Ingmar Bergman; ***W:*** Ingmar Bergman; ***C:*** Sven Nykvist. National Board of Review Awards '68: Best Actress (Ullmann); National Society of Film Critics Awards '68: Best Director (Bergman). *MGM, MRV, FCT*

Hourglass 𝔏𝔏 **1995 (R)** Fashion industry honcho risks his reputation and his life when he becomes involved with a potentially deadly seductress. **91m/C VHS, LV.** C. Thomas Howell, Sofia Shinas, Ed Begley Jr., Timothy Bottoms, Anthony Clark; ***D:*** C. Thomas Howell; ***W:*** C. Thomas Howell, Darren Dalton; ***C:*** John Lambert; ***M:*** Chris Saranec. *LIV*

The Hours and Times 𝔏𝔏𝔏 **1992** A concise drama based on one point of fact used to quietly evoke differences in class, talent, sexual orientation, and unrequited love. The fact is that in the spring of 1963 Brian Epstein, the Beatles brilliant homosexual manager, shared a four-day Barcelona vacation with John Lennon. Director Munch speculates that the sophisticated Epstein was hopelessly in love with the younger, working-class Lennon who is friendly but unresponsive to the courtship. A tender and rueful depiction of friendship longing to be something more. **60m/B VHS.** David Angus, Ian Hart, Stephanie Pack, Robin McDonald, Sergio Moreno, Unity Grimwood; ***D:*** Christopher Munch; ***W:*** Christopher Munch. Sundance Film Festival '92: Special Jury Prize. *FXL, BTV*

House 𝔏𝔏𝔏 **1986 (R)** A horror novelist moves into his dead aunt's supposedly haunted house only to find that the monsters don't necessarily stay in the closets. His worst nightmares come to life as he writes about his Vietnam experiences and is forced to relive the tragic events, but these aren't the only visions that start springing to life. It sounds depressing, but is actually a funny, intelligent "horror" flick. Followed by several lesser sequels. **93m/C VHS, Beta, LV.** William Katt, George Wendt, Richard Moll, Kay Lenz, Michael Ensign, Mary Stavin, Susan French; ***D:*** Steve Miner; ***W:*** Ethan Wiley; ***M:*** Harry Manfredini. *NWV, VTR*

House 2: The Second Story 𝔏 **1987 (PG-13)** The flaccid sequel to the haunted-house horror flick concerns two innocent guys who move into the family mansion and discover Aztec ghosts. Has none of the humor which helped the first movie along. **88m/C VHS, Beta, LV.** John Ratzenberger, Arye Gross, Royal Dano, Bill Maher, Jonathan Stark; ***D:*** Ethan Wiley; ***W:*** Ethan Wiley. *NWV, VTR*

House 4: Home Deadly Home 𝔏½ **1991 (R)** Another bad real estate epic on a par with the other unusually inept "House" efforts. When her husband (Katt) is killed in an auto accident, a young woman and her daughter move into a mysterious old house. Terror begins to confront them at every turn, threatening to destroy them both. We can only hope. **93m/C VHS, LV.** Terri Treas, Scott Burkholder, Melissa Clayton, William Katt, Ned Romero; ***D:*** Lewis Abernathy. *COL, NLC*

House Across the Bay 𝔏𝔏½ **1940** Raft, an imprisoned nightclub owner, finds that he is being duped by his attorney who's eager to get his hooks into the lingerie-clad prisoner's wife. But prison isn't going to stop the bitter husband from getting his revenge. **88m/B VHS, Beta.** George Raft, Walter Pidgeon, Joan Bennett, Lloyd Nolan, Gladys George; ***D:*** Archie Mayo. *NO*

House Arrest 𝔏½ **1996 (PG)** Another tired kids-think-they-know-best formula film. When Grover Beindorf (Howard) and his younger sister learn that their constantly fighting parents (Curtis and Pollak) are separating, they lock them in the basement so they'll be forced to sort things out. Word gets around and some school pals kidnap their problem parents and stash them in the basement with the Beindorfs. Most of the movie was actually shot in a basement; watch for Curtis hanging upside down in a laundry chute "True Lies" style. **107m/C VHS.** Jamie Lee Curtis, Kevin Pollak, Kyle Howard, Jennifer Tilly, Ray Walston, Wallace Shawn, Russell Harper; ***D:*** Harry Winer; ***W:*** Michael Hitchcock. *NYR*

The House by the Cemetery 𝔏 *Quella Villa Accanto Al Cimitero* **1983 (R)** When a family moves into a house close to a cemetery, strange things start to happen to them. **84m/C VHS, Beta.** *IT* Katherine MacColl, Paolo Malco; ***D:*** Lucio Fulci. *LIV, VES*

House Calls 𝔏𝔏𝔏 **1978 (PG)** A widowed surgeon turns into a swinging bachelor until he meets a witty but staid English divorcee. Wonderful dialogue. Jackson is exceptional. Made into a short-lived TV series. **98m/C VHS, Beta, LV.** Walter Matthau, Glenda Jackson, Art Carney, Richard Benjamin, Candice Azzara; ***D:*** Howard Zieff; ***W:*** Charles Shyer; ***M:*** Henry Mancini. *MCA*

The House in Marsh Road **1960** A faithless husband decides to rid himself of She Who Must Be Obeyed, but his wife's ghost-friend intervenes. **70m/B VHS.** *GB* Tony Wright, Patricia Dainton, Sandra Dorne, Derek Aylward, Sam Kydd; ***D:*** Montgomery Tully. *SNC*

A House In The Hills **1993 (R)** A struggling actress is housesitting at a luxurious estate and innocently lets in the exterminator. Except he's an ex-con looking for revenge on the home's current occupant (whom the actress is pretending to be) and may just exterminate her instead. **89m/C VHS, LV.** Helen Slater, Michael Madsen. *LIV*

House of Angels *Anglagard; Colin Nutley's House of Angels* **1992 (R)** Charming comedy, with some serious overtones, about what happens to the gossipy inhabitants of a small Swedish village when two free-spirited newcomers come to stay. Fanny and her friend Zac, who are cabaret performers, show up at the funeral of eccentric Erik, who turns out to be the grandfather Fanny never knew. With her outrageous clothes and attitude, Fanny has most of the neighbors scandalized but what the generous Fanny wants is some information about her past, including who her father might be. What the neighbors want is for Fanny and Zac to leave as quickly as possible. In Swedish with English subtitles. **119m/C VHS.** *SW* Helena Bergstrom, Rikard Wolff, Sven Wollter, Jakob Eklund, Viveka Seldahl, Ernst Gunter, Reine Brynolfsson, Per Oscarsson; ***D:*** Colin Nutley; ***W:*** Susanne Falck. *COL, FCT*

House of Cards **1990** Depicts the political machinations of Machiavellian Tory whip Francis Urquhart (Richardson), who schemes to bring down the present government so that he can become the next Prime Minister. And there's absolutely nothing "F.U." (as he's appropriately known) won't do to achieve power. Followed by "To Play the King" and "The Final Cut;" based on the novel Michael Dobbs. On 2 cassettes. **200m/C VHS.** *GB* Ian Richardson, Susannah Harker. *FOX, TVC*

House of Cards ½ **1992 (PG-13)** Precocious 6-year-old Sally (Menina) suddenly stops talking after her father is killed in an accident at an archeological site in Mexico. Mom Ruth (Turner) fights to bring her daughter out of her fantasy world and seeks medical advice from a psychiatrist (a sympathetic Jones) but ignores it when it clashes with her own theories. The ethereal Menina, in her acting debut, gives the best performance in this weakly plotted and confusing family saga. **109m/C VHS, LV.** Kathleen Turner, Asha Menina, Tommy Lee Jones, Shiloh Strong, Esther Rolle, Park Overall, Michael Horse, Anne Pitoniak; ***D:*** Michael Lessac; ***W:*** Michael Lessac. *LIV, BTV, FCT*

House of Dark Shadows **1970 (PG)** A 150-year-old vampire, accidentally released by a handyman, wreaks havoc on the inhabitants of the Collinswood mansion. Based on the TV daytime soap. **97m/C VHS, Beta.** Jonathan Frid, Joan Bennett, Grayson Hall, Kathryn Leigh Scott, Roger Davis, Nancy Barrett, John Karlen, Thayer David; ***D:*** Dan Curtis. *MGM, FUS*

House of Death **1982 (R)** The ex-Playmate of the Year runs in hysterical fear from a knife-wielding lunatic. **88m/C VHS, Beta.** Susan Kiger, William T. Hicks, Jody Kay, Martin Tucker, Jennifer Chase. *GEM*

The House of Dies Drear **1988** A modern-day African American family moves into an old house that turns out to be haunted by the ghost of a long dead abolitionist. The family is transported back to the days of slavery as they interact with the ghost. Based on the story by Virginia Hamilton. Aired on PBS as part of the "Wonderworks" family movie series. **107m/C VHS.** Howard E. Rollins Jr., Moses Gunn, Shavar Ross, Gloria Foster, Clarence Williams III; ***D:*** Allan Goldstein. *HMV, PME, FCT*

House of Dracula **1945** Sequel to "House of Frankenstein" features several of the Universal monsters. Overly ambitious story gets a bit hokey, but it's entertaining, nonetheless. **67m/B VHS, LV.** Lon Chaney Jr., Martha O'Driscoll, John Carradine, Lionel Atwill, Onslow Stevens, Glenn Strange, Jane Adams, Ludwig Stossel; ***D:*** Erle C. Kenton; ***W:*** Edward T. Lowe. *MCA, FCT*

House of Dreams **1964** Berry is a blocked writer coping with domestic difficulties whose dreams reveal a disturbing future. Contains a bit part for Goodnow, now a CNN talking head. **80m/B VHS.** Robert Berry, Pauline Elliott, Charlene Bradley, Lance Bird, David Goodnow; ***D:*** Robert Berry. *LSV*

The House of Eliott **1992** BBC miniseries set in 1920s London finds the orphaned Beatrice and Evangeline Eliott struggling to begin their fashion business as couturiers to the rich and influential, which eventually leads to their founding of the House of Eliott. Lots of romance and intrigue along the way. Boxed set of six cassettes. **600m/C VHS.** *GB* Stella Gonet, Louise Lombard, Aden Gillett, Richard Lintern. *SIG, AAE, PAP*

House of Errors ½ **1942** Two deliverymen pose as reporters to safeguard a prototype machine gun from the bad guys. Contrived plot consisting of outdated comic routines. This was Marsh's last film. **63m/B VHS.** Harry Langdon, Marian Marsh, Ray Walker, Betty Blythe, John Holland; ***D:*** Bernard B. Ray. *NOS*

House of Fear ½ **1945** Holmes and Watson investigate the murders of several members of the Good Comrades Club, men who were neither good nor comradely. **69m/B VHS, Beta.** Basil Rathbone, Nigel Bruce, Dennis Hoey, Aubrey Mather, Paul Cavanagh, Gavin Muir; ***D:*** Roy William Neill. *FOX*

House of Frankenstein ½ **1944** An evil scientist (Karloff) escapes from prison, and, along with his hunchback manservant, revives Dracula, Frankenstein's monster, and the Wolfman to carry out his dastardly deeds. An all-star cast helps this horror fest along. **71m/B VHS, LV.** Boris Karloff, J. Carrol Naish, Lon Chaney Jr., John Carradine, Elena Verdugo, Anne Gwynne, Lionel Atwill, Peter Coe, George Zucco, Glenn Strange, Sig Rumann; ***D:*** Erle C. Kenton. *MCA*

House of Games **1987 (R)** The directorial debut of playwright Mamet is a tale about an uptight female psychiatrist who investigates the secret underworld of con-artistry and becomes increasingly involved in an elaborate con game. She's led along her crooked path by smooth-talking con-master Mantegna. A taut, well plotted psychological suspense film with many twists and turns. Stylishly shot, with dialogue which has that marked Mamet cadence. Most of the leads are from Mamet's theater throng (including his wife, Crouse). **102m/C VHS, Beta, LV.** Joe Mantegna, Lindsay Crouse, Lilia Skala, J.T. Walsh, Meshach Taylor, Ricky Jay, Mike Nussbaum, Willo Hausman; ***D:*** David Mamet; ***W:*** David Mamet; ***C:*** Juan Ruiz-Anchia; ***M:*** Alaric Jans. *HBO, FCT*

House of Horrors ½ **1946** Deformed murderer "The Creeper" (Hatton) is used by a mad sculptor in a twisted revenge plot. Marcel De Lange (Kosleck) believes his work has been vilely abused by art critics so he uses his friend's homicidal urges to get rid of anyone who stands in his way. **76m/B VHS.** Martin Kosleck, Rondo Hatton, Robert Lowery, Virginia Grey, Bill Goodwin, Alan Napier, Joan Shawlee, Howard Freeman; ***D:*** Jean Yarbrough; ***W:*** George Bricker. *MCA*

The House of Lurking Death ½ **1984** Detectives Tommy and Tuppence find a box of chocolates laced with arsenic at the home of Lois Hargreaves, and the maid old maid is the prime suspect. Based on the Agatha Christie story. Made for British television. **60m/C VHS, Beta.** *GB* James Warwick, Francesca Annis. *TPV*

House of Mystery **1934** For a shot at some priceless jewels stolen by the host from a Hindu princess, several guests gather for a weekend in a spine-tingling mansion. A creepy curse keeps them looking over their shoulders. **62m/C VHS.** Ed Lowry, Verna Hillie, Brandon Hurst, George "Gabby" Hayes; ***D:*** William Nigh. *SNC, DVT, MLB*

House of Mystery ½ *At the Villa Rose* **1941** Splendid British remake of 1934 film in which the detective does some true sleuthing to catch the culprits. An old widow is killed for her jewels, but the murderers can't locate the goods. After they try a series of fiendish plans to retrieve them, the detective must work to stop the crooks. **61m/B VHS.** *GB* Keneth Kent, Judy Kelly, Peter Murray Hill, Walter Rilla, Ruth Maitland; ***D:*** Walter Summers. *NOS, DVT*

The House of 1000 Dolls *Haus Der Tausend Freuden* **1967** Doleful, not dollful, exploitation thriller as magician Price drugs young girls and sells them to slavery rings. An international production set in Tangiers; dialogue is dubbed. **79m/C VHS, Beta.** *GE SP GB* Vincent Price, Martha Hyer, George Nader, Ann Smyrner, Maria Rohm; ***D:*** Jeremy Summers. *HBO*

House of Psychotic Women *Woof! Los Ojos Azules de la Muneca Rota* **1973 (R)** Naschy, Spain's premier horror movie star, plays a studly drifter who winds up in the home of three sisters, one with an artifical arm, one confined to a wheelchair and the other a nymphomaniac. No problemo thinks the hirsute Spaniard, until a series of bizarre murders—in which the victims eyes are ripped out—spoils his fun. Naschy, who usually sprouts fur and fangs, actually doesn't turn into a werewolf. Catchy but inappropriate score. A must for Naschy/bad movie fans. **87m/C VHS, Beta.** *SP* Paul Naschy, Maria Perschy, Diana Lorys, Eva Leon, Ines Morales, Tony Pica; ***D:*** Carlos Aured; ***W:*** Paul Naschy. *NO*

The House of Secrets **1937** A Yank travels to Britain to collect an inheritance and stays in a dusty old mansion filled with an odd assortment of characters. **70m/B VHS, Beta.** Leslie Fenton, Muriel Evans, Noel Madison, Sidney Blackmer, Morgan Wallace, Holmes Herbert; ***D:*** Roland D. Reed. *SNC*

The House of Seven Corpses **1973 (PG)** A crew attempts to film a horror movie in a Victorian manor where seven people died in a variety of gruesome manners. Things take a turn for the ghoulish when a crew member becomes possesed by the house's evil spirits. Good, low budget fun with a competent "B" cast. Filmed in what was the Utah governor's mansion. **90m/C VHS.** John Ireland, Faith Domergue, John Carradine, Carole Wells; ***D:*** Paul Harrison. *GEM, MRV, CNG*

House of Shadows ½ **1983** A 20-year-old murder comes back to haunt the victim's friends in this tale of mystery and terror. **90m/C VHS, Beta.** John Gavin, Yvonne De Carlo, Leonor Manso; ***D:*** Richard Wulicher. *MED*

House of Strangers ½ **1949** Conte, in a superb performance, swears vengeance on his brothers, whom he blames for his father's death. Robinson, in a smaller part than you'd expect from his billing, is nevertheless excellent as the ruthless banker father who sadly reaps a reward he didn't count on. Based on Philip Yordan's "I'll Never Go There Again." **101m/B VHS.** Edward G. Robinson, Susan Hayward, Richard Conte, Luther Adler, Efrem Zimbalist Jr., Debra Paget; ***D:*** Joseph L. Mankiewicz; ***W:*** Philip Yordan; ***C:*** Milton Krasner. Cannes Film Festival '49: Best Actor (Robinson). *FOX, FCT*

House of Terror **1987** A woman and her boyfriend plot to kill her rich boss, while they too are being stalked by some undefined horror. **91m/C VHS, Beta.** Jennifer Bishop, Arell Blanton, Jacquelyn Hyde. *TWE*

The House of the Arrow **1953** Investigating the murder of a French widow, who was killed by a poisoned arrow, a detective must sort through a grab bag of potential suspects. Superior adaptation of the A.E.W. Mason thriller. **73m/B VHS, Beta.** *GB* Oscar Homolka, Yvonne Furneaux, Robert Urquhart; ***D:*** Michael Anderson Sr. *NOS, SNC*

House of the Black Death ½ *Blood of the Man Devil; Night of the Beast* **1965** Horror titans Chaney and Carradine manage to co-star in this as warring warlocks, yet they share no scenes together! Chaney is the evil warlock (the horns are a giveaway) holding people hostage in the title edifice. **89m/B VHS.** Lon Chaney Jr., John Carradine, Katherine Victor, Tom Drake, Andrea King; ***D:*** Harold Daniels, Reginald LeBorg. *NOS, LOO*

House of the Damned ½ **1971** A young woman, a mental hospital, a murdered father, a priceless gold statue—mix together and you get a mystery horror movie. A woman tries to solve her father's murder. **89m/C VHS, Beta.** Donald Pleasence, Michael Dunn; ***D:*** Gonzolo Suarez. *NO*

House of the Dead 🦴 **1980** Man is trapped inside a haunted house. Scary. **100m/C VHS.** John Ericson, Charles Aidman, Bernard Fox, Ivor Francis. *NO*

House of the Living Dead 🦴 *Doctor Maniac* **1973 (PG)** Brattling Manor harbors a murderous and flesh-eating secret ready to lure the unsuspecting. Don't you be one. **87m/C VHS, Beta.** *SA* Mark Burns, Shirley Anne Field, David Oxley; ***D:*** Ray Austin. *VCI, HHE*

House of the Long Shadows 🦴½ **1982 (PG)** Comedy mixes with gore, as four of the horror screen's best leading men team up for the first time, although they have only minor roles. Might have been a contender, but Arnaz is miscast as author who stays in spooky house on a bet with Todd. Some wit but not enough. Based on the play "Seven Keys to Baldpate" by George M. Cohan (and novel by Earl Derr Biggers). **96m/C VHS, Beta.** Vincent Price, Christopher Lee, Peter Cushing, John Carradine, Desi Arnaz Jr., Sheila Keith, Richard Todd; ***D:*** Pete Walker; ***W:*** Michael Armstrong. *MGM*

House of the Rising Sun 🦴½ **1987** A Los Angeles reporter goes under cover for a story on an exclusive brothel only to discover the owner is a psychopath who has very permanent ways of dealing with troublesome employees. **86m/C VHS, Beta.** John York, Bud Davis, Deborah Wakeham, Frank Annese; ***D:*** Greg Gold; ***M:*** Tina Turner, Bryan Ferry. *PSM, PAR*

The House of the Spirits 🦴🦴 **1993 (R)** Star-studded adaptation of the novel by Isabel Allende is a multi-generational saga following the fortunes of the powerful Trueba family. The ambitious Esteban (Irons) marries the clairvoyant Clara (Streep), exploits the peasants on his property, and becomes a conservative senator. Their rebellious daughter Blanca (Ryder) falls for rabble-rousing peasant Pedro (Banderas), and the country undergoes a bloody revolution. Magical realism of the novel is lost in screen melodrama, with the international cast ill-served by tepid direction. The child Clara is played by Streep's daughter, Mary Willa (listed in the credits as Jane Gray). **109m/C VHS, LV.** Meryl Streep, Jeremy Irons, Glenn Close, Winona Ryder, Antonio Banderas, Armin Mueller-Stahl, Vanessa Redgrave, Sarita Choudhury, Maria Conchita Alonso, Vincent Gallo; ***D:*** Bille August; ***W:*** Bille August; ***M:*** Hans Zimmer. *LIV*

House of the Yellow Carpet 🦴½ **1984** A couple try to sell an ancient Persian carpet heirloom, and in doing so transgress some unwritten mystical law. Havoc ensues. **90m/C VHS, Beta.** Roland Josephson, Beatrice Romand; ***D:*** Carlo Lizzani. *LIV*

The House of Usher 🦴 **1988 (R)** Some serious overacting by Reed (as Roderick) and Pleasance (as his balmy brother) almost elevate this Poe retread to "so bad it's good" status, and there are a few admirably grisly moments. But, without other camp virtues, it's merely dreary. Adapted by Michael J. Murray and filmed in South Africa. **92m/C VHS, LV.** Oliver Reed, Donald Pleasence, Romy Windsor; ***D:*** Alan Birkinshaw; ***W:*** Michael J. Murray; ***M:*** Gary Chang. *COL*

House of Wax 🦴🦴🦴 **1953 (PG)** A deranged sculptor (Price, who else?) builds a sinister wax museum which showcases creations that were once alive. A remake of the early horror flick "Mystery of the Wax Museum," and one of the 50s' most popular 3-D films. This one still has the power to give the viewer the creeps, thanks to another chilling performance by Price. Look for a very young Charles Bronson, as well as Carolyn "Morticia Addams" Jones as a victim. **88m/C VHS, Beta, LV.** Vincent Price, Frank Lovejoy, Carolyn Jones, Phyllis Kirk, Paul Cavanagh, Charles Bronson; ***D:*** Andre de Toth. *WAR, MLB*

House of Whipcord *Woof!* **1975** Beautiful young women are kidnapped and tortured in this British gore-o-rama. Awful and degrading. **102m/C VHS, Beta.** *GB* Barbara Markham, Patrick Barr, Ray Brooks, Penny Irving, Anne Michelle; ***D:*** Pete Walker. *MON, LIV*

The House on Carroll Street 🦴½ **1988 (PG)** New York 1951, the middle of the McCarthy era. A young woman overhears a plot to smuggle Nazi war criminals into the U.S. She's already lost her job because of accusations of subversion, and it's not easy persuading FBI agent Daniels that she knows what she's talking about. Contrived plot and melodramatic finale help sink this period piece. **111m/C VHS, Beta, LV.** Kelly McGillis, Jeff Daniels, Mandy Patinkin, Jessica Tandy; ***D:*** Peter Yates; ***W:*** Walter Bernstein; ***M:*** Georges Delerue. *HBO*

The House on Chelouche Street 🦴🦴½ **1973** In Tel-Aviv, during the summer of 1946, 15-year-old Sami, an Egyptian immigrant, tries to help support his mother and family during the upheavals of Palestine under the British mandate. A well thought-out story detailing the struggles of a North African Jewish family before the creation of the country of Israel. In Hebrew with English subtitles. **111m/C VHS, Beta.** *IS* Gila Almagor, Michal Bat-Adam, Shai K. Ophir; ***D:*** Moshe Mizrahi. *VYY, NCJ, AUD*

The House on Garibaldi Street 🦴🦴½ **1979** Spy drama about the capture of Nazi war criminal Adolph Eichmann in Argentina and his extradition to Israel for trial. Based on the book by Isser Harel. Made for television. **96m/C VHS, Beta.** Chaim Topol, Nick Mancuso, Martin Balsam, Janet Suzman, Leo McKern, Charles Gray, Alfred Burke; ***D:*** Peter Collinson; ***M:*** Charles Bernstein. *FRH, SWC*

House on Haunted Hill 🦴🦴½ **1958** A wealthy man throws a haunted house party and offers ten thousand dollars to anyone who can survive the night there. Vintage cheap horror from the master of the macabre Castle. Remembered for Castle's in-theater gimmick of dangling a skeleton over the audiences' heads in the film's initial release. Also available with "Attack of the 50-Foot Woman" on laserdisc. **75m/B VHS, Beta, LV.** Vincent Price, Carol Ohmart, Richard Long, Alan Marshal; ***D:*** William Castle. *FOX, SNC, FCT*

House on 92nd Street 🦴🦴🦴 **1945** Documentary-style thriller finds federal investigator George Briggs (Nolan) contacted by German-American student Bill Dietrich (Eythe), who's been sought out by Nazi spies. Briggs encourages Dietrich to play along and report their nefarious activities to the feds. What Dietrich discovers is that a scientist, working on the atomic bomb project, is actually a Nazi agent. Lots of atmosphere and action, with director Hathaway incorporating newsreel footage to highlight the true-to-life feel. Title refers the the house where the head of the Nazi spies resides. **89m/B VHS.** William Eythe, Lloyd Nolan, Signe Hasso, Gene Lockhart, Leo G. Carroll, William Post Jr., Harry Bellaver; ***D:*** Henry Hathaway; ***W:*** Barre Lyndon, John Monks Jr., Charles G. Booth; ***C:*** Norbert Brodine; ***M:*** David Buttolph. Academy Awards '45: Best Story. *FXV*

The House on Skull Mountain 🦴½ **1974 (PG)** The four surviving relatives of a deceased voodoo priestess are in for a bumpy night as they gather at the House on Skull Mountain for the reading of her will. **85m/C VHS, Beta.** Victor French, Janee Michelle, Mike Evans, Jean Durand; ***D:*** Ron Honthaner. *FOX*

The House on Sorority Row 🦴½ *House of Evil; Seven Sisters* **1983** Less-than-harrowing story of what happens when seven sorority sisters have a last fling and get back at their housemother at the same time. **90m/C VHS, Beta, LV.** Eileen Davidson, Kathy McNeil, Robin Meloy; ***D:*** Mark Rosman; ***M:*** Richard Band. *VES*

The House on Straw Hill 🦴½ *Expose* **1976 (R)** A successful novelist is intrigued by an attractive woman who lives in an isolated farmhouse. Her presence inspires gory hallucinations, lust and violence. **84m/C VHS, Beta.** Udo Kier, Linda Hayden, Fiona Richmond; ***D:*** James Kenelm Clarke. *NWV, MED*

House on the Edge of the Park *Woof! La Casa Nel Parco* **1984** A frustrated would-be womanizer takes revenge on a parade of women during an all-night party. **91m/C VHS, Beta.** *IT* David Hess, Annie Belle, Lorraine De Selle; ***D:*** Ruggero Deodato. *LIV, VES*

The House on Todville Road 🦴 **1995 (R)** Fact-based story about a dangerous cult and its followers. **94m/C VHS.** David Harrod, Terri Harrel, Lisa Marie Newmeyer. *TCE*

The House on Tombstone Hill 🦴½ **1992** An old, abandoned mansion seems like a good investment to a group of friends. Wrong! The original owner is still around and doesn't like strangers coming to visit. **95m/C VHS.** Doug Gibson, John Cerna, Sarah Newhouse; ***D:*** J. Riffel; ***W:*** J. Riffel. *AIP*

House Party 🦴🦴🦴 **1990 (R)** Light-hearted, black hip-hop version of a '50s teen comedy with rap duo Kid 'n' Play. After his father grounds him for fighting, a high-schooler attempts all sorts of wacky schemes to get to his friend's party. Sleeper hit features real-life music rappers and some dynamite dance numbers. **100m/C VHS, Beta, LV.** Christopher Reid, Christopher Martin, Martin Lawrence, Tisha Campbell, Paul Anthony, A.J. Johnson, Robin Harris; ***D:*** Reginald Hudlin; ***W:*** Reginald Hudlin; ***M:*** Marcus Miller. Sundance Film Festival '90: Best Cinematography. *NLC, FCT*

House Party 2: The Pajama Jam 🦴🦴½ **1991 (R)** Rap stars Kid 'N' Play are back in this hip-hop sequel to the original hit. At Harris University Kid 'N' Play hustle up overdue tuition by holding a campus "jammie jam jam." A stellar cast shines in this rap-powered pajama bash. **94m/C VHS, LV.** Christopher Reid, Christopher Martin, Tisha Campbell, Iman, Queen Latifah, Georg Stanford Brown, Martin Lawrence, Eugene Allen, George Anthony Bell, Kamron, Tony Burton, Helen Martin, William Schallert; ***D:*** Doug McHenry, George Jackson; ***W:*** Rusty Cundieff, Daryl G. Nickens; ***M:*** Vassal Benford. *NLC*

House Party 3 🦴 **1994 (R)** Kid is engaged to be married and Play tries to set up a blowout bachelor party. The duo are also working on their record producer careers by trying to sign a feisty female rap group (real life TLC). Strikes out early for easy profanity while never coming within spitting distance of first two flicks. **93m/C VHS, LV.** Christopher Reid, Christopher Martin, Angela Means, Tisha Campbell, Bernie Mac, Barbara Edwards, Michael Colyar, David Edwards, Betty Lester, Christopher Tucker; ***D:*** Eric Meza; ***W:*** Takashi Bufford; ***M:*** David Allen Jones. *COL, IME*

The House that Bled to Death 🦴 **1981** Strange things happen to a family when they move into a run-down house where a murder occurred years before. **60m/C VHS, Beta.** Nicholas Ball, Rachel Davies, Brian Croucher, Pat Maynard, Emma Ridley. *LIV*

The House that Dripped Blood 🦴🦴½ **1971 (PG)** A Scotland Yard inspector discovers the history of an English country house while investigating an actor's disappearance. Four horror tales comprise the body of this omnibus creeper, following the successful "Tales from the Crypt" mold. Duffell's debut as director. **101m/C VHS, Beta.** *GB* Christopher Lee, Peter Cushing, Jon Pertwee, Denholm Elliott, Ingrid Pitt, John Bennett, Tom Adams, Joss Ackland, Chloe Franks; ***D:*** Peter Duffell; ***W:*** Robert Bloch. *PSM*

The House that Vanished 🦴 *Scream and Die* **1973 (R)** Semi-exploitative fare about a beautiful young model who witnesses a murder in a house but later can't find the place. Her boyfriend is skeptical. **84m/C VHS, Beta.** *GB* Andrea Allan, Karl Lanchbury, Judy Matheson, Maggie Walker; ***D:*** Joseph Larraz. *MED, LIV*

House Where Evil Dwells 🦴½ **1982 (R)** An American family is subjected to a reign of terror when they move into an old Japanese house possessed by three deadly samurai ghosts. The setting doesn't upgrade the creepiness of the plot. **88m/C VHS, Beta.** Edward Albert, Susan George, Doug McClure, Amy Barett; ***D:*** Kevin Connor. *MGM*

A House Without a Christmas Tree 🦴🦴½ **1972** A frustrated middle-aged man denies his young daughter her one desire—a Christmas tree. Charming made for cable television holiday fare. **90m/C VHS, Beta.** Jason Robards Jr., Lisa Lucas, Mildred Natwick; ***D:*** Paul Bogart. *FXV, FCT*

Houseboat 🦴🦴½ **1958** Widower Grant with three precocious kids takes up residence on a houseboat with Italian maid Loren who is actually a socialite, incognito. Naturally, they fall in love. Light, fun Hollywood froth. **110m/C Beta, LV.** Cary Grant, Sophia Loren, Martha Hyer, Eduardo Ciannelli, Murray Hamilton, Harry Guardino; ***D:*** Melville Shavelson; ***W:*** Melville Shavelson, Jack Rose; ***M:*** George Duning. Nominations: Academy Awards '58: Best Song ("Almost in Your Arms (Love Song from Houseboat)"), Best Story & Screenplay. *PAR*

Houseguest 🦴🦴½ **1994 (PG)** Dumb comedy about mistaken identity finds hard luck dreamer Kevin Franklin (Sinbad) on the run from loan sharks. Fortunately, while trying to make a getaway at the airport, he's mistaken for the childhood buddy (who's also an eminent dentist prompting some hygiene humor) of family guy/lawyer Gary Young (Hartman), who opens his suburban home to his long lost pal. Street smart Kevin naturally manages to solve every dysfunctional family problem that arises while avoiding some inept Mafia thugs. Everyone is oh-so-good-natured but there's nothing new to hold much interest. **109m/C VHS, LV.** Sinbad, Phil Hartman, Jeffrey Jones, Kim Greist, Stan Shaw, Tony Longo, Mason Adams, Paul Ben-Victor, Chauncey Leopardi, Ron Glass, Talia Seider, Kim Murphy; ***D:*** Randall Miller; ***W:*** Michael J. Di Gaetano, Laurence Gay; ***C:*** Jerzy Zielinski; ***M:*** John Debney. *TOU*

Household Saints 🦴🦴🦴 **1993 (R)** Chronicling one family from post-WWII Little Italy through the 1970's, this is a quirky little story about sausage, religion, women, and families (not necessarily in that order). Joseph (D'Onofrio) wins his bride (Ullman) in a pinochle game, much to his superstitious Catholic mother's (Malina) chagrin. The product of that union is a slightly obsessive girl (Taylor), who sees visions and wants to be a saint. Interesting study of Italian-American families, and the roles religion and food play in the culture of Little Italy. **124m/C VHS.** Tracey Ullman, Vincent D'Onofrio, Lili Taylor, Judith Malina, Michael Rispoli, Victor Argo, Michael Imperioli, Rachael Bella, Illeana Douglas, Joe Grifasi; ***D:*** Nancy Savoca; ***W:*** Richard Guay, Nancy Savoca. Independent Spirit Awards '94: Best Supporting Actress (Taylor); Nominations: Independent Spirit Awards '94: Best Actor (D'Onofrio), Best Screenplay. *COL*

The Householder 🦴🦴 *Gharbar* **1963** An early Merchant-Ivory collaboration featuring a young Indian schoolteacher whose widowed mother arranges his marriage to a woman he doesn't know. The immature couple find their adjustment to marriage fraught with, sometimes amusing, complications. **101m/B VHS, LV.** *IN* Shashi Kapoor, Leela Naidu, Durga Khote; ***D:*** James Ivory; ***W:*** Ruth Prawer Jhabvala. *CVC, INJ*

The Housekeeper 🦴🦴 *A Judgement in Stone* **1986 (R)** Tushingham's portrayal of a deranged housekeeper brings this movie to life even as she kills off her employers. **97m/C VHS, Beta, LV.** *CA* Rita Tushingham, Ross Petty, Jackie Burroughs, Tom Kneebone, Shelly Peterson, Jessica Stern, Jonathan Crombie; ***D:*** Ousama Rawi. *WAR*

Housekeeping 🦴🦴🦴 **1987 (PG)** A quiet but bizarre comedy by Forsyth (his first American film). A pair of orphaned sisters are cared for by their newly arrived eccentric, free-spirited aunt in a small and small-minded community in Oregon in the 1950s. Conventional townspeople attempt to intervene, but the sisters' relationship with their offbeat aunt has become strong enough to withstand the coercion of the townspeople. May move too slowly for some viewers. Based on novel by Marilynne Robinson. **117m/C VHS, Beta.** Christine Lahti, Sarah Walker, Andrea Burchill; ***D:*** Bill Forsyth; ***W:*** Bill Forsyth; ***M:*** Michael Gibbs. *COL*

Housemaster 🦴🦴½ **1938** In a British boys' school the housemaster is kind and understanding of his sometimes-unruly charges. The stern new headmaster is not, and the students conspire against him. An okay but dated comedy, featuring characters with names like Bimbo and Button. Based on "Bachelor Born" by Ian Hay, a London stage hit at the time. **95m/B VHS.** Otto Kruger, Diana Churchill, Phillips Holmes, Rene Ray, Walter Hudd, George L. Baxt, Cecil Parker, Michael Shepley, Jimmy Hanley, Rosamund Barnes; ***D:*** Herbert Brenon. *NOS, MLB*

Housesitter 🦴🦴½ **1992 (PG)** Newton Davis (Martin), an architect/dreamer, builds his high school sweetheart (Delany) a beautiful house and surprises her with a marriage proposal. Delany says no, he has a one-night stand with Gwen (Hawn), and Hawn moves into his empty house and assumes the position of Davis's wife, unbeknownst to him. Gwen spins whoppers of lies and soon has the entire town, including Davis's parents and ex-girlfriend, believing her wacky stories. This romantic screwball comedy is a delight, not only because of Martin and Hawn, but also because of the array of other characters who complicate the stories they spin. **102m/C VHS, Beta, LV.** Steve Martin, Goldie Hawn, Dana Delany, Julie Harris, Donald Moffat, Peter MacNicol, Richard B. Shull, Laurel Cronin, Christopher Durang; ***D:*** Frank Oz; ***W:*** Mark Stein, Brian Grazer; ***C:*** John A. Alonzo; ***M:*** Miles Goodman. *MCA, PMS, BTV*

Housewife 🦴🦴 **1972 (R)** A vengeful black man holds an unhappily married Beverly Hills couple hostage in their home. **96m/C VHS, Beta.** Yaphet Kotto, Andrew Duggan, Joyce Van Patten, Jeannie Berlin; ***D:*** Larry Cohen. *NWV*

How Come Nobody's On Our Side? 🦴 **1973 (PG)** Two out-of-work stuntmen try astrology to find the best time to make some easy money smuggling marijuana out of Mexico. **84m/C VHS, Beta.** Adam Roarke, Larry Bishop, Alexandra Hay, Rob Reiner, Penny Marshall; ***W:*** Leigh Chapman. *NO*

How Funny Can Sex Be? 🦴🦴 **1976 (R)** Eight risque sketches about love and marriage Italian style. **97m/C VHS, Beta.** *IT* Giancarlo Giannini, Laura Antonelli, Dulio Del Prete; ***D:*** Dino Risi. *FOX*

How Green Was My Valley 🦴🦴🦴🦴 **1941** Compelling story of the trials and tribulations of a Welsh mining family, from the youthful perspective of the youngest child (played by a 13-year-old McDowall). Spans 50 years, from the turn of the century, when coal mining was a difficult but fair-paying way of life, and ends, after unionization, strikes, deaths, and child abuse, with the demise of a town and its culture. Considered by many to be director Ford's finest work. When WWII prevented shooting on location, producer Zanuck built a facsimile Welsh valley in California (although Ford, born Sean Aloysius O'Fearna, was said to have been thinking of his story as taking place in Ireland rather than Wales). Based on the novel by Richard Llewellyn. **118m/C VHS, Beta.** Walter Pidgeon, Maureen O'Hara, Donald Crisp, Anna Lee, Roddy McDowall, John Loder, Sara Allgood, Barry Fitzgerald, Patric Knowles, Rhys Williams, Arthur Shields, Ann Todd, Mae Marsh; ***D:*** John Ford; ***W:*** Philip Dunne; ***C:*** Arthur C. Miller; ***M:*** Alfred Newman. Academy Awards '41: Best Black and White Cinematography, Best Director (Ford), Best Interior Decoration, Best Picture, Best Supporting Actor (Crisp); Nominations: Academy Awards '41: Best Film Editing, Best Screenplay, Best Sound, Best Supporting Actress (Allgood), Best Original Score. *FOX, FUS, BTV*

How I Got into College 🦴🦴 **1989 (PG-13)** A slack, uninspired satire about a high school senior who barely manages to get into a local college so he may pursue the girl of his dreams. **87m/C VHS, Beta, LV.** Corey Parker, Lara Flynn Boyle, Christopher Rydell, Anthony Edwards, Phil Hartman, Brian Doyle-Murray, Nora Dunn, Finn Carter, Charles Rocket; ***D:*** Steve Holland; ***W:*** Terrel Seltzer. *FOX*

How I Learned to Love Women 🦴 **196?** A British comedy of errors involving a car-loving youth who learns about women and love. **95m/C VHS, Beta.** *GB* Anita Ekberg. *NO*

How I Won the War 🦴🦴 **1967 (PG)** An inept officer must lead his battalion out of England into the Egyptian desert to conquer a cricket field. Indulgent, scarcely amusing Richard Lester comedy; Lennon, in a bit part, provides the brightest moments. **111m/C VHS, Beta, LV.** *GB* John Lennon, Michael Crawford, Michael Hordern; ***D:*** Richard Lester; ***W:*** Charles Wood; ***C:*** David Watkin. *MGM*

How Many Miles to Babylon? 🦴🦴 **1982** During WWI, two young men become friends despite their different backgrounds. But one is court-martialed for desertion, and the other is supposed to oversee his execution. Made for British television. **106m/C VHS, Beta.** *GB* Daniel Day-Lewis, Christopher Fairbank; ***D:*** Moira Armstrong. *FOX, TVC, FUS*

How Sweet It Is! 🦴 **1968** Typical American family takes a zany European vacation. Looks like a TV sitcom and is about as entertaining. National Lampoon's version is a lot more fun. **99m/C VHS.** James Garner, Debbie Reynolds, Maurice Ronet, Paul Lynde, Erin Moran, Marcel Dalio, Terry-Thomas; ***D:*** Jerry Paris; ***W:*** Jerry Belson. *WAR*

How Tasty Was My Little Frenchman 🦴🦴 *Como Era Gostoso O Meu Frances* **1971** French explorer is captured by a cannibal tribe in the jungles of Brazil. He's treated very well and attempts to learn tribal customs to avoid his fate—he's going to be the main course in a ceremonial dinner. French and Tupi with subtitles. **80m/C VHS.** *BR* Arduino Colasanti, Ana Maria Magalhaes, Ital Natur, Eduardo Embassahy; ***D:*** Nelson Pereira dos Santos. *NYF*

How the Grinch Stole Christmas 🦴🦴🦴 **1965** Classic television Christmas special from the Dr. Seuss book about a Christmas-hating grinch who steals Christmas from the town of Whoville. Fun for the whole family. **26m/C VHS, Beta.** ***V:*** Boris Karloff. *MGM, KUI, WTA*

How the West was Fun 🦴🦴½ **1995** The Olsen gals are visiting great godmother Natty's dude ranch, which is in financial difficulty, and must outsmart her greedy son Bart (Mull), a land grabber who wants to turn the ranch into an environmentally unfriendly western theme park. Made for TV. **93m/C VHS.** Mary-Kate Olsen, Ashley Olsen, Martin Mull, Michelle Greene, Patrick Cassidy, Leon Pownall, Peg Phillips; ***D:*** Stuart Margolin; ***M:*** Richard Bellis. *WAR*

How the West Was Won 🦴🦴🦴 **1963 (G)** A panoramic view of the American West, focusing on the trials, tribulations and travels of three generations of one family, set against the background of wars and historical events. Particularly notable for its impressive cast list and expansive western settings. **165m/C VHS, Beta, LV.** John Wayne, Carroll Baker, Lee J. Cobb, Spencer Tracy, Gregory Peck, Karl Malden, Robert Preston, Eli Wallach, Henry Fonda, George Peppard, Debbie Reynolds, Carolyn Jones, Richard Widmark, James Stewart, Walter Brennan, Andy Devine, Raymond Massey, Agnes Moorehead, Harry (Henry) Morgan, Thelma Ritter, Russ Tamblyn; ***D:*** John Ford, Henry Hathaway, George Marshall; ***W:*** James R. Webb; ***C:*** Milton Krasner, Charles B(ryant) Lang. Academy Awards '63: Best Film Editing, Best Sound, Best Story & Screenplay; National Board of Review Awards '63: 10 Best Films of the Year; Nominations: Academy Awards '63: Best Art Direction/Set Decoration (Color), Best Color Cinematography, Best Costume Design (Color), Best Picture, Best Original Score. *MGM*

How to Be a Perfect Person in Just Three Days **1984** Fun comedy for the whole family shows the efforts of a kid striving for perfection before realizing that individuality is more fun. Based on the book by Stephen Mane. Aired on PBS as part of the "Wonderworks" series. **58m/C VHS.** Wallace Shawn, Ilan Mitchell-Smith, Hermione Gingold, Joan Micklin Silver. *PME, FCT, HMV*

How to Beat the High Cost of Living 🦴½ **1980 (PG)** Three suburban housewives decide to beat inflation by taking up robbery, and they start by planning a heist at the local shopping mall. Comedic talent can't salvage whipped script and direction. **105m/C VHS, Beta.** Jessica Lange, Susan St. James, Jane Curtin, Richard Benjamin, Eddie Albert, Dabney Coleman, Fred Willard, Cathryn Damon, Art Metrano; ***D:*** Robert Scheerer. *LIV, VES*

How to Break Up a Happy Divorce 🦴🦴 **1976** A divorced woman starts a vigorous campaign to win her ex-husband back by dating another man to make him jealous. Lightweight made-for-television comedy. **74m/C VHS, Beta.** Barbara Eden, Hal Linden, Peter Bonerz, Marcia Rodd, Harold Gould; ***D:*** Jerry Paris. *WOV*

How to Commit Marriage ♂½ **1969** **(PG)** Hope and Wyman have been married for 20 years when they decide to divorce—just when their daughter (Cameron) decides to marry her college boyfriend (Matheson). His father (Gleason) tries to stop the wedding, fails, but sticks around to cause more trouble. Subplots involve the divorced duo's new loves and the fact that they're about to become grandparents but the comedy is completely uninspired. **96m/C VHS.** Bob Hope, Jane Wyman, Jackie Gleason, Joanna Cameron, Tim Matheson, Beatrice Arthur, Leslie Nielsen, Tina Louise, Paul Stewart, Prof. Irwin Corey; ***D:*** Norman Panama; ***W:*** Ben Starr, Michael Kanin; ***M:*** Joseph J. Lilley. *COL*

How to Get Ahead in Advertising ♂♂♂ **1989 (R)** A cynical, energetic satire about a manic advertising idea man who becomes so disgusted with trying to sell a pimple cream that he quits the business. Ultimately he grows a pimple of his own that talks and begins to take over his life. Acerbic and hilarious. **95m/C VHS, Beta, LV.** *GB* Richard E. Grant, Rachel Ward, Susan Wooldridge, Mick Ford, Richard Wilson, John Shrapnel, Jacqueline Tong; ***D:*** Bruce Robinson; ***W:*** Bruce Robinson; ***M:*** David Dundas, Rick Wentworth. *NO*

How to Kill 400 Duponts ♂ **1965** Bumbling Scotland Yard detective is off to France to stop a master criminal from trying to kill off the rich Dupont family. Why? So he'll be the only one left with any claim to the remaining family fortune. **98m/C VHS, Beta.** Terry-Thomas, Johnny Dorelli, Margaret Lee. *VCD*

How to Make a Doll ♂ **1968** Lewis' sex farce about an extremely shy professor whose ineptness with women inspires him to invent android females to satisfy his sexual needs. **?m/C VHS.** Robert Wood, Jim Vance, Pamela Rhea; ***D:*** Herschell Gordon Lewis. *MOV, TPV*

How to Make a Monster ♂♂ **1958** In-joke from the creators of youth-oriented '50s AIP monster flicks; a mad makeup man's homebrew greasepaint brainwashes the actors. Disguised as famous monsters, they kill horror-hating movie execs. Mild fun if—and only if—you treasure the genre. Conway repeats his role as Teenage Frankenstein, but the studio couldn't get Michael Landon for the Teenage Werewolf. **73m/B VHS.** Robert Harris, Paul Brinegar, Gary Conway, Gary Clarke, Malcolm Atterbury, Dennis Cross, John Ashley, Morris Ankrum, Walter Reed, Heather Ames; ***D:*** Herbert L. Strock. *COL, MLB*

How to Make an American Quilt ♂♂½ **1995 (PG-13)** Slow-moving take on female friendship and marriage revolves around perennial grad student Finn (the mopey Ryder), who is frantic to both finish her third attempted thesis and to answer a marriage proposal from practically perfect beau Sam (Mulroney). She takes a summer refuge with her grandmother (Burstyn), where a variety of family friends work on her wedding quilt as they tell stories of loves lost and won. Lots of (somewhat overextended) flashbacks and with so many characters, naturally some get the short end of the script. Based on the novel by Whitney Otto. **109m/C VHS, LV.** Winona Ryder, Ellen Burstyn, Anne Bancroft, Lois Smith, Jean Simmons, Kate Nelligan, Maya Angelou, Alfre Woodard, Dermot Mulroney, Kate Capshaw, Rip Torn, Derrick O'Connor, Loren Dean, Samantha Mathis, Joanna Going, Tim Guinee, Johnathon Schaech, Claire Danes, Jared Leto, Esther Rolle, Melinda Dillon, Alicia (Lecy) Goranson, Maria Celedonio, Mykelti Williamson; ***D:*** Jocelyn Moorhouse; ***W:*** Jane Anderson; ***C:*** Janusz Kaminski; ***M:*** Thomas Newman. Nominations: MTV Movie Awards '96: Best Kiss (Winona Ryder/Dermot Mulroney); Screen Actors Guild Award '95: Cast. *MCA*

How to Marry a Millionaire ♂♂½ **1953** Three models pool their money and rent a lavish apartment in a campaign to trap millionaire husbands. Clever performances by three lead women salvage a vehicle intended primarily to bolster Monroe's career. The opening street scene, with the accompanying theme music, was a state-of-the-art achievement of screen and sound in the first movie to be filmed in CinemaScope. Remake of "The Greeks Had a Word for Them." **96m/C VHS, Beta, LV.** Lauren Bacall, Marilyn Monroe, Betty Grable, William Powell, David Wayne, Cameron Mitchell; ***D:*** Jean Negulesco; ***W:*** Nunnally Johnson; ***M:*** Alfred Newman. Nominations: Academy Awards '53: Best Costume Design (Color). *FOX*

How to Murder Your Wife ♂♂♂ **1964** While drunk, a cartoonist marries an unknown woman and then frantically tries to think of ways to get rid of her — even contemplating murder. Frantic comedy is tailored for Lemmon. **118m/C VHS, Beta, LV.** Jack Lemmon, Terry-Thomas, Virna Lisi, Eddie Mayehoff, Sidney Blackmer, Claire Trevor, Mary Wickes, Jack Albertson; ***D:*** Richard Quine; ***W:*** George Axelrod; ***C:*** Harry Stradling. *MGM*

How to Pick Up Girls ♂♂ **1978** Comic tale based on Eric Weber's bestseller follows the exploits of a small-town boy who moves to New York City and finds the secret to picking up women. Made for television. **93m/C VHS, Beta.** Desi Arnaz Jr., Bess Armstrong, Fred McCarren, Polly Bergen, Richard Dawson, Alan King, Abe Vigoda, Deborah Raffin; ***D:*** Bill Persky. *TWE*

How to Seduce a Woman *Woof!* **1974** A playboy attempts to bed five supposedly unattainable women. **108m/C VHS, Beta.** Angus Duncan, Marty Ingels, Lillian Randolph. *PSM*

How to Steal a Million ♂♂♂ **1966** Sophisticated comedy-crime caper involving a million-dollar heist of a sculpture in a Paris art museum. Hepburn and O'Toole are perfectly cast as partners in crime and Griffith gives a good performance as Hepburn's art-forging father. A charming, lightweight script and various Parisian locales combine for fun, above-average fluff. Original title was "How to Steal a Million Dollars and Live Happily Ever After." Based on the story "Venus Rising" by George Bradshaw. **127m/C VHS.** Audrey Hepburn, Peter O'Toole, Eli Wallach, Hugh Griffith, Charles Boyer, Fernand Gravet, Marcel Dalio, Jacques Marin; ***D:*** William Wyler; ***W:*** Harry Kurnitz; ***C:*** Charles B(ryant) Lang; ***M:*** John Williams. *FXV, TVC*

How to Stuff a Wild Bikini ♂♂ **1965** Tired next to last feature in the overlong tradition of Frankie and Annette doing the beach thing, featuring a pregnant Funicello (though this is hidden and not part of the plot). Avalon actually has only a small role as the jealous boyfriend trying to see if Annette will remain faithful while he's away on military duty. Keaton is the witch doctor who helps Frankie keep Annette true. "Playboy" playmates wander about in small swimsuits, garage band extraordinaire "The Kingsmen" play themselves, and Brian Wilson of the "Beach Boys" drops by. Followed by "Ghost in the Invisible Bikini," the only movie in the series that isn't on video. ♫After the Party; Better Be Ready; Follow Your Leader; Give Her Lovin'; How About Us?; How to Stuff a Wild Bikini; I'm the Boy Next Door; Madison Avenue; The Perfect Boy. **90m/C VHS, Beta.** Annette Funicello, Dwayne Hickman, Frankie Avalon, Beverly Adams, Buster Keaton, Harvey Lembeck, Mickey Rooney, Brian Donlevy, Jody McCrea, John Ashley, Marianne Gaba, Len Lesser, Irene Tsu, Bobbi Shaw, Luree Holmes; ***D:*** William Asher; ***W:*** William Asher, Leo Townsend; ***C:*** Floyd Crosby; ***M:*** Les Baxter. *NO*

How to Succeed in Business without Really Trying ♂♂♂½ **1967** Classic musical comedy about a window-washer who charms his way to the top of a major company. Robert Morse repeats his Tony winning Broadway role. Loosely based on a non-fiction book of the same title by Shepherd Mead, whose book Morse purchases on his first day of work. Excellent transfer of stage to film, with choreography by Moreda expanding Bob Fosse's original plan. Dynamite from start to finish. ♫I Believe In You; The Company Way; Coffee Break; The Brotherhood of Man; A Secretary Is Not A Toy; Grand Old Ivy; Been A Long Day; Rosemary; Finch's Frolic. **121m/C VHS, LV.** Robert Morse, Michele Lee, Rudy Vallee, Anthony Teague, George Fenneman, Maureen Arthur; ***D:*** David Swift; ***W:*** David Swift, Abe Burrows; ***C:*** Burnett Guffey; ***M:*** Frank Loesser. *MGM*

How to Succeed with Girls ♂ **1964** Marginally funny comedy about pious wax salesman (Leder) with a secret fantasy life who unwittingly enlists the aid of his wife's lover (Schrier) to help him overcome his shyness. Several fantasy sequences (in color; the rest of the film is black and white) include an Arabian harem, an old West saloon, and a science laboratory. Brubaker's secretary (Mathes) was Playboy's Miss June 1962. Pete's girlfriend (McClanahan of television's Golden Girls) is credited as either Patty Leigh or Helen Goodman. **83m/C VHS.** Marissa Mathes, Rue McClanahan, Paul Leder, Leon Schrier; ***D:*** Edward A. Biery. *SMW, TPV*

How U Like Me Now? ♂♂♂ **1992 (R)** Comedy set on Chicago's south side focuses on Thomas, an attractive but unmotivated guy with low earning potential, and his girl Valerie, a pretentious overachiever who wants much more than he's able to offer. Robert's second directorial effort offers a fresh look at African Americans on film with plenty of lively supporting characters and witty dialogue. Filmed on a $600,000 budget. **109m/C VHS, LV.** Darnell Williams, Salli Richardson, Daniel Gardner, Raymond Whitefield, Debra Crable, Jonelle Kennedy, Byron Stewart, Charnele Brown, Daryll Roberts; ***D:*** Daryll Roberts; ***W:*** Daryll Roberts; ***M:*** Kahil El Zabar, Chuck Webb. *MCA*

Howard the Duck ♂ **1986 (PG)** A big-budget Lucasfilm adaptation of the short-lived Marvel comic book about an alien, resembling a cigar-chomping duck, who gets sucked into a vortex, lands on Earth and saves it from the Dark Overlords. While he's at it, he befriends a nice young lady in a punk rock band and starts to fall in love. A notorious box-office bomb and one of the '80s' worst major films, although it seems to work well with children, given the simple story line and good special effects. **111m/C VHS, Beta, LV.** Lea Thompson, Jeffrey Jones, Tim Robbins; ***D:*** Willard Huyck; ***W:*** Willard Huyck, Gloria Katz; ***M:*** Sylvester Levay, John Barry. Golden Raspberry Awards '86: Worst Picture, Worst Screenplay. *MCA*

Howard's End ♂♂♂♂ **1992 (PG)** E.M. Forster's 1910 novel about property, privilege, class differences, and Edwardian society is brought to enchanting life by the Merchant Ivory team. A tragic series of events occurs after two impulsive sisters become involved with a working class couple and a wealthy family. Tragedy aside, this is a visually beautiful effort with subtle performances where a glance or a gesture says as much as any dialog. The winner of numerous awards and wide critical acclaim. Thompson is especially notable as the compassionate Margaret, while Hopkins plays the repressed English gentleman brilliantly. **143m/C VHS, LV, 8mm.** *GB* Anthony Hopkins, Emma Thompson, Helena Bonham Carter, Vanessa Redgrave, James Wilby, Sam West, Jemma Redgrave, Nicola Duffett, Prunella Scales, Joseph Bennett; ***Cameos:*** Simon Callow; ***D:*** James Ivory; ***W:*** Ruth Prawer Jhabvala; ***C:*** Tony Pierce-Roberts. Academy Awards '92: Best Actress (Thompson), Best Adapted Screenplay, Best Art Direction/Set Decoration; British Academy Awards '92: Best Actress (Thompson); Chicago Film Critics Awards '92: Best Actress (Thompson); Golden Globe Awards '93: Best Actress—Drama (Thompson); Los Angeles Film Critics Association Awards '92: Best Actress (Thompson); National Board of Review Awards '92: Best Actress (Thompson), Best Director (Ivory), Best Film; New York Film Critics Awards '92: Best Actress (Thompson); National Society of Film Critics Awards '92: Best Actress (Thompson); Nominations: Academy Awards '92: Best Cinematography, Best Costume Design, Best Director (Ivory), Best Picture, Best Supporting Actress (Redgrave), Best Original Score; Cannes Film Festival '92: Best Film. *COL, CRC, MOV*

The Howards of Virginia ♂♂½ *Tree of Liberty* **1940** A lavish Hollywood historical epic, detailing the adventures of a backwoodsman and the rich Virginia girl he marries as their families become involved in the Revolutionary War. **117m/B VHS, Beta.** Cary Grant, Martha Scott, Cedric Hardwicke, Alan Marshal, Richard Carlson, Paul Kelly, Irving Bacon, Tom Drake, Anne Revere, Ralph Byrd, Alan Ladd; ***D:*** Frank Lloyd. Nominations: Academy Awards '40: Best Sound, Best Original Score. *COL*

The Howling **1981 (R)** A pretty television reporter takes a rest at a clinic and discovers slowly that its denizens are actually werewolves. Crammed with inside jokes, this horror comedy pioneered the use of the body-altering prosthetic make-up (by Rob Bottin) now essential for on-screen man-to-wolf transformations. At last count, followed by five sequels. **91m/C VHS, Beta, LV.** Dee Wallace Stone, Patrick Macnee, Dennis Dugan, Christopher Stone, Belinda Balaski, Kevin McCarthy, John Carradine, Slim Pickens, Elisabeth Brooks, Robert Picardo, Dick Miller; ***D:*** Joe Dante; ***W:*** John Sayles, Terence H. Winkless; ***M:*** Pino Donaggio. *COL, SUE*

Howling 2: Your Sister is a Werewolf **1985 (R)** A policeman (the brother of one of the first film's victims) investigates a Transylvanian werewolf-ridden castle and gets mangled for his trouble. Followed by four more sequels. **91m/C VHS, Beta, LV.** *FR IT* Sybil Danning, Christopher Lee, Annie McEnroe, Marsha Hunt, Reb Brown, Ferdinand "Ferdy" Mayne; ***D:*** Philippe Mora; ***W:*** Gary Brandner. *REP*

Howling 3: The Marsupials **1987 (PG-13)** Australians discover a pouch-laden form of lycanthrope. Third "Howling" (surprise), second from Mora and better than his first. **94m/C VHS, Beta, LV.** *AU* Barry Otto, Imogen Annesley, Dasha Blahova, Max Fairchild, Ralph Cotterill, Leigh Biolos, Frank Thring Jr., Michael Pate; ***D:*** Philippe Mora. *LIV*

Howling 4: The Original Nightmare **1988 (R)** A woman novelist hears the call of the wild while taking a rest cure in the country. This werewolf tale has nothing to do with the other sequels. **94m/C VHS, Beta, LV.** Romy Windsor, Michael T. Weiss, Antony Hamilton, Susanne Severeid, Lamya Derval; ***D:*** John Hough. *LIV*

Howling 5: The Rebirth **1989 (R)** The fifth in the disconnected horror series, in which a varied group of people stranded in a European castle are individually hunted down by evil. **99m/C VHS, Beta, LV.** Philip Davis, Victoria Catlin, Elizabeth She, Ben Cole, William Shockley; ***D:*** Neal Sundstrom. *LIV*

Howling 6: The Freaks ½ **1990 (R)** Hideous werewolf suffers from multiple sequels, battles with vampire at freak show, and discovers that series won't die. Next up: "Howling 7: The Nightmare that Won't Go Away." **102m/C VHS, LV.** Brendan Hughes, Michelle Matheson, Sean Gregory Sullivan, Antonio Fargas, Carol Lynley, Jered Barclay, Bruce Martyn Payne; ***D:*** Hope Perello. *LIV, IME*

The Howling: New Moon Rising ½ **1995 (R)** Small desert town is plagued by a series of terrifying murders believed to be the work of a werewolf, whose victims then join his vicious pack. **92m/C VHS, LV.** ***D:*** Clive Turner; ***W:*** Clive Turner. *NLC*

Huck and the King of Hearts ½ **1993 (PG)** When a cardshark and his young friend Huck travel the country searching for Huck's long-lost grandfather, they find adventure everywhere from Hannibal, Missouri to L.A. to Vegas. Loose, contemporary adaptation of Mark Twain's "The Adventures of Huckleberry Finn." **103m/C VHS, Beta, LV.** Chauncey Leopardi, Graham Greene, Dee Wallace Stone, Joe Piscopo, John Astin, Gretchen Becker; ***D:*** Michael Keusch; ***W:*** Christopher Sturgeon; ***M:*** Chris Saranec. *PSM*

Huckleberry Finn **1974 (G)** The musical version of the Mark Twain story about the adventures a young boy and a runaway slave encounter along the Mississippi River. **114m/C VHS, Beta, LV.** Jeff East, Paul Winfield, Harvey Korman, David Wayne, Arthur O'Connell, Gary Merrill, Natalie Trundy, Lucille Benson; ***D:*** J. Lee Thompson. *MGM, FOX, FCT*

Huckleberry Finn ½ **1975 (G)** Whitewashed version of the Twain classic features post Opie Howard as the incredible Huck and Dano as the sharp witted short storyist. Stars four members of the Howard clan. Made for TV. **74m/C VHS, Beta.** Ron Howard, Donny Most, Royal Dano, Antonio Fargas, Jack Elam, Merle Haggard, Rance Howard, Jean Howard, Clint Howard, Shug Fisher, Sarah Selby, Bill Erwin; ***D:*** Robert Totten. *KUI, FXV, FCT*

Huckleberry Finn ½ **1981** A version of the classic Mark Twain novel about the adventures a young boy and a runaway slave encounter as they travel down the Mississippi River. **72m/C VHS, Beta.** *LIV, WTA*

The Hucksters **1947** Account of a man looking for honesty and integrity in the radio advertising world and finding little to work with. All performances are excellent; but Greenstreet, as the tyrannical head of a soap company, is a stand out. Deborah Kerr's American debut. **115m/B VHS, Beta.** Clark Gable, Deborah Kerr, Sydney Greenstreet, Adolphe Menjou, Ava Gardner, Keenan Wynn, Edward Arnold; ***D:*** Jack Conway. *MGM, FCT*

Hud **1963** Newman is a hard-driving, hard-drinking, woman-chasing young man whose life is a revolt against the principles of stern father Douglas. Neal is outstanding as the family housekeeper. Excellent photography. **112m/B VHS, Beta, LV.** Paul Newman, Melvyn Douglas, Patricia Neal, Brandon de Wilde, John Ashley; ***D:*** Martin Ritt; ***W:*** Irving Ravetch, Harriet Frank Jr.; ***C:*** James Wong Howe; ***M:*** Elmer Bernstein. Academy Awards '63: Best Actress (Neal), Best Black and White Cinematography, Best Supporting Actor (Douglas); National Board of Review Awards '63: 10 Best Films of the Year, Best Actress (Neal), Best Supporting Actor (Douglas); Nominations: Academy Awards '63: Best Actor (Newman), Best Adapted Screenplay, Best Art Direction/Set Decoration (B & W), Best Director (Ritt). *PAR, BTV*

Hudson Hawk **1991 (R)** A big-budget star vehicle with little else going for it. Willis plays a master burglar released from prison, only to find himself trapped by the CIA into one last theft. Everyone in the cast tries to be extra funny, resulting in a disjointed situation where no one is. Weakly plotted, poorly paced. **95m/C VHS, Beta, LV, 8mm.** Bruce Willis, Danny Aiello, Andie MacDowell, James Coburn, Sandra Bernhard, Richard E. Grant, Frank Stallone; ***D:*** Michael Lehmann; ***W:*** Steven E. de Souza, Daniel Waters. Golden Raspberry Awards '91: Worst Picture, Worst Director (Lehmann), Worst Screenplay. *COL*

The Hudsucker Proxy **1993 (PG)** In an effort to scare off would-be investors in a public stock offering dim bulb mailboy Robbins is installed as the Prez of Hudsucker Industries (in 1958) by Board Director Newman after corporate magnate Hudsucker (Durning) takes a swan dive from the 44th floor. First truly mainstream effort from the maverick Coen brothers is peppered with obscure references to numerous points on the historical map of cinematic style, and trots out an equally old but instantly recognizable story. Will delight Coen fans, but may be too dark for others. Destined to keep art history profs busy for decades. **115m/C VHS, LV.** Tim Robbins, Paul Newman, Jennifer Jason Leigh, Charles Durning, John Mahoney, Jim True, Bill Cobbs, Bruce Campbell; ***Cameos:*** Peter Gallagher; ***D:*** Joel Coen; ***W:*** Ethan Coen, Joel Coen, Sam Raimi; ***C:*** Roger Deakins; ***M:*** Carter Burwell. *WAR*

Hue and Cry **1947** Nobody believes a young boy when he discovers crooks are sending coded messages in a weekly children's magazine. A detective writer finally believes his story and they set off to capture the crooks. **82m/B VHS.** *GB* Alastair Sim, Jack Warner, Frederick Piper, Jack Lambert, Joan Dowling; ***D:*** Charles Crichton. *SNC, NOS, FCT*

Hugh Hefner: Once Upon a Time **1992 (R)** Fascinating look at the "Bunny" king and Playboy Enterprises. His celebrated life of isolation and excess at the Playboy mansions is portrayed as is the founding of "Playboy" magazine in 1953 and the Playboy clubs (with their notorious Bunnies). Includes interviews, home movies, and photographs. Admiring yet not without a few sharp edges. **91m/C VHS, LV.** Hugh Hefner; ***D:*** Robert Heath. *UND, BTV*

Hughes & Harlow: Angels in Hell **1977 (R)** The story of the romance that occurred between Howard Hughes and Jean Harlow during the filming of "Hell's Angels" in 1930. **94m/C VHS, Beta.** Lindsay Bloom, Victor Holchak, David McLean, Royal Dano, Adam Roarke, Linda Cristal; ***D:*** Larry Buchanan. *NO*

Hugo the Hippo **1976 (G)** Animated musical about a forlorn baby hippo who struggles to survive in the human jungle of old Zanzibar. **90m/C VHS, Beta.** ***W:*** Thomas Baum; ***V:*** Paul Lynde, Burl Ives, Robert Morley, Marie Osmond. *FOX*

Hula ½ **1928** Unflappable flapper Bow and her gang frolic on a Pacific island. **64m/B VHS, Beta.** Clara Bow, Clive Brook, Patricia Dupont, Arnold Kent, Agaslino Borgato; ***D:*** Victor Fleming. *GPV, FCT, DVT*

Hullabaloo Over Georgie & Bonnie's Pictures ½ **1978** A young maharajah has inherited a priceless collection of Indian miniature paintings he doesn't appreciate and which his greedy sister is anxious for him to sell. They're beseiged by art dealers and collectors who learn about the treasure trove and will do anything to possess it. Among them are the British Ashcroft, who wants the art for the British Museum, and competing American collector Pine. Made for British television. **85m/C VHS, Beta.** *GB* Victor Banerjee, Aparna Sen, Larry Pine, Saeed Jaffrey, Peggy Ashcroft; ***D:*** James Ivory; ***W:*** Ruth Prawer Jhabvala; ***C:*** Walter Lassally. *SUE, INJ, NLC*

Human Beasts **1980** Jewel robbers face a tribe of hungry cannibals. **90m/C VHS, Beta.** *SP JP* Paul Naschy, Eiko Nagashima; ***D:*** Paul Naschy; ***W:*** Paul Naschy. *NO*

The Human Comedy ½ **1943** A small-town boy experiences love and loss and learns the meaning of true faith during WWII. Straight, unapologetically sentimental version of the William Saroyan novel. **117m/B VHS, Beta, LV.** Mickey Rooney, Frank Morgan, James Craig, Fay Bainter, Ray Collins, Donna Reed, Van Johnson, Barry Nelson, Robert Mitchum, Jackie "Butch" Jenkins; ***D:*** Clarence Brown; ***W:*** William Saroyan; ***C:*** Harry Stradling. Academy Awards '43: Best Story; Nominations: Academy Awards '43: Best Actor (Rooney), Best Black and White Cinematography, Best Director (Brown), Best Picture. *MGM*

The Human Condition: A Soldier's Prayer **1961** A Japanese pacifist escapes from his commanders and allows himself to be captured by Russian troops, hoping for better treatment as a P.O.W. The final part of the trilogy preceded by "The Human Condition: No Greater Love" and "The Human Condition: Road to Eternity." In Japanese with English subtitles. **190m/B VHS, Beta.** *JP* Tatsuya Nakadai, Michiyo Aratama, Yusuke Kawazu, Tamao Nakamura, Chishu Ryu, Taketoshi Naito, Reiko Hitomi, Kyoko Kishida, Keijiro Morozumi, Koji Kiyomura, Nobuo Kaneko, Fujio Suga; ***D:*** Masaki Kobayashi. *INJ*

The Human Condition: No Greater Love **1958** First of a three-part series of films. A pacifist is called into military service and subsequently sent to a run a military mining camp. A gripping look at one man's attempt to retain his humanity in the face of war. Followed by "The Human Condition: Road to Eternity" and "The Human Condition: A Soldier's Prayer." In Japanese with English subtitles. **200m/B VHS, Beta.** *JP* Tatsuya Nakadai, Michiyo Aratama, So Yamamura, Eitaro Ozawa, Akira Ishihama, Chikage Awashima, Ineko Arima, Keiji Sada, Shinji Nambara, Seiji Miyaguchi, Toru Abe, Masao Mishima, Eijiro Tono, Yasushi Nagata, Yoshio Kosugi; ***D:*** Masaki Kobayashi. *INJ*

The Human Condition: Road to Eternity *No Greater Love; Ningen No Joken* **1959** A Japanese pacifist is on punishment duty in Manchuria where he is beaten by sadistic officers who try to destroy his humanity. The second part of the trilogy, preceded by "The Human Condition: No Greater Love" and followed by "The Human Condition: A Soldier's Prayer." In Japanese with English subtitles. **180m/B VHS, Beta.** *JP* Tatsuya Nakadai, Michiyo Aratama, Kokinji Katsura, Jun Tatara, Michio Minami, Keiji Sada, Minoru Chiaki, Ryohei Uchida, Kan Yanagidani, Kenjiro Uemura, Yusuke Kawazu, Susumu Fujita; ***D:*** Masaki Kobayashi. *INJ*

Human Desire ½ **1954** Femme fatale Grahame and jealous husband Crawford turn out the lights on Crawford's boss (seems there's some confusion about how Miss Gloria managed to convince the guy to let her hubby have his job back). Ford's wise to them but plays see no evil because he's gone crackers for Grahame, who by now has decided she'd like a little help to rid herself of an unwanted husband. Bleak, melodramatic, full of big heat, its Lang through and through. Based on the Emile Zola novel "La Bete Humaine," which inspired Renoir's 1938 telling as well. **90m/B VHS.** Glenn Ford, Gloria Grahame, Broderick Crawford, Edgar Buchanan, Kathleen Case; ***D:*** Fritz Lang; ***C:*** Burnett Guffey. *GKK*

The Human Duplicators ☙½ **1964** Kiel is an alien who has come to Earth to make androids out of important folk, thus allowing the "galaxy beings" to take over. Cheap stuff, but earnest performances make this more fun than it should be. **82m/C VHS, Beta.** George Nader, Barbara Nichols, George Macready, Dolores Faith, Hugh Beaumont, Richard Kiel, Richard Arlen; ***D:*** Hugo Grimaldi. *LIV*

Human Experiments ☙ **1979 (R)** Psychiatrist in a women's prison conducts a group of experiments in which he destroys the "criminal instinct" in the inmates through brute fear. **82m/C VHS, Beta.** Linda Haynes, Jackie Coogan, Aldo Ray; ***D:*** Gregory Goodell. *NO*

The Human Factor ☙½ **1975 (R)** Kennedy stars as a computer expert who tracks down his family's murderers using technology. Bloody and violent. **96m/C VHS, Beta.** *GB IT* George Kennedy, John Mills, Raf Vallone, Rita Tushingham, Barry Sullivan, Arthur Franz; ***D:*** Edward Dmytryk; ***M:*** Ennio Morricone. *LIV*

The Human Factor ☙☙½ **1979 (R)** Unexciting spy caper has a British Secret Service agent (Williamson) betraying his country in order to aid a friend. As a result of his actions an innocent man is killed and Williamson is forced to defect to the Soviet Union. Based on a novel by Graham Greene. **115m/C VHS.** *GB* Nicol Williamson, Richard Attenborough, John Gielgud, Derek Jacobi, Robert Morley, Ann Todd, Richard Vernon, Iman; ***D:*** Otto Preminger; ***W:*** Tom Stoppard. *MGM*

Human Gorilla ☙ *Behind Locked Doors* **1948** A thriller involving a mad scientist, an insane asylum, a reporter, and various other mysterious trappings. **58m/B VHS, Beta.** Richard Carlson, Lucille Bremer, Tor Johnson. *NO*

Human Hearts ☙☙ **1922** A creaky old silent starring "Phantom of the Opera" leading lady Philbin. A family is torn apart by a con man and his femme fatale. **99m/B VHS, Beta, 8mm.** House Peters Sr., Russell Simpson, Mary Philbin. *VYY*

The Human Monster ☙☙½ *Dark Eyes of London* **1939** Scotland Yard inspector investigates five drownings of the blind patients a phony Dr. Orloff (Lugosi) is exploiting for insurance money. Superior Lugosi effort that's modestly violent and tasteless. Based on the Edgar Wallace novel. **73m/B VHS, Beta.** *GB* Bela Lugosi, Hugh Williams, Greta Gynt; ***D:*** Walter Summers; ***W:*** Walter Summers. *NOS, MRV, SNC*

The Human Shield ☙☙ **1992 (R)** A man risks his life on a mission to save his brother during the Persian Gulf War. **88m/C VHS, LV.** Michael Dudikoff, Tommy Hinkley, Steve Inwood; ***D:*** Ted Post. *WAR, CAN*

The Human Vapor ☙ *Gasu Ningen Daiichigo* **1968** A normal human being has the ability to vaporize himself at will and use it to terrorize Tokyo. **81m/C VHS, Beta.** *JP GEM, PSM, CNG*

Humanoid Defender ☙☙ **1985** A made-for-television film about a scientist and an android rebelling against the government that wants to use the android as a warfare prototype. **94m/C VHS, Beta.** Terence Knox, Gary Kasper, Aimee Eccles, William Lucking; ***D:*** William Lucking. *MCA*

Humanoids from the Deep *Woof! Monster* **1980 (R)** Mutated salmon-like monsters rise from the depths of the ocean and decide to chop on some bikinied babes. Violent and bloody. **81m/C VHS, Beta.** Doug McClure, Ann Turkel, Vic Morrow, Cindy Weintraub, Anthony Penya, Denise Balik; ***D:*** Barbara Peeters; ***W:*** Frank Arnold; ***M:*** James Horner. *WAR, OM*

Humongous *Woof!* **1982 (R)** Brain-dead bevy of teens shipwreck on an island where they encounter a deranged mutant giant who must kill to survive. You'll be rooting for the monster. **93m/C VHS, Beta.** *CA* Janet Julian, David Wallace, Janet Baldwin; ***D:*** Paul Lynch. *SUE, NLC*

Humoresque ☙☙☙½ **1946** A talented but struggling young musician finds a patron in the married, wealthy, and older Crawford. His appreciation is not as romantic as she hoped. Stunning performance from Crawford, with excellent supporting cast, including a young Robert Blake. Fine music sequences (Isaac Stern dubbed the violin), and lush production values. Laserdisc version features the original movie trailer. **123m/B VHS, LV.** Joan Crawford, John Garfield, Oscar Levant, J. Carrol Naish, Joan Chandler, Tom D'Andrea, Peggy Knudsen, Ruth Nelson, Craig Stevens, Paul Cavanagh, Richard Gaines, John Abbott, Robert (Bobby) Blake; ***D:*** Jean Negulesco. Nominations: Academy Awards '46: Best Original Score. *MGM, BTV, FCT*

The Hunchback of Notre Dame ☙☙☙ **1923** The first film version of Victor Hugo's novel about the tortured hunchback bellringer of Notre Dame Cathedral, famous for the contortions of Lon Chaney's self-transformations via improvised makeup. Also available at 68 minutes. **100m/B VHS, LV.** Lon Chaney Sr., Patsy Ruth Miller, Norman Kerry, Ernest Torrence; ***D:*** Wallace Worsley. *KIV, MRV, NOS*

The Hunchback of Notre Dame ☙☙☙☙ **1939** Best Hollywood version of the Victor Hugo classic, infused with sweep, sadness and an attempt at capturing a degree of spirited, Hugoesque detail. Laughton is Quasimodo, a deformed Parisian bellringer, who provides sanctuary to a young gypsy woman accused by church officials of being a witch. The final scene of the townspeople storming the cathedral remains a Hollywood classic. Great performances all around; the huge facade of the Notre Dame cathedral was constructed on a Hollywood set for this film. Remake of several earlier films, including 1923's Lon Chaney silent. Remade in 1957 and later for television. **117m/B VHS, Beta, LV.** Charles Laughton, Maureen O'Hara, Edmond O'Brien, Cedric Hardwicke, Thomas Mitchell, George Zucco, Alan Marshal, Walter Hampden, Harry Davenport, Curt Bois, George Tobias, Rod La Rocque; ***D:*** William Dieterle; ***W:*** Sonya Levien, Bruno Frank; ***M:*** Alfred Newman. Nominations: Academy Awards '39: Best Sound, Best Score. *TTC, MED, CCB*

The Hunchback of Notre Dame ☙☙☙ *Hunchback* **1982 (PG)** It's not often that a classic novel is remade into a classic movie that's remade into a made-for-TV reprise, and survives its multiple renderings. But it's not often a cast so rich in stage trained actors is assembled on the small screen. Hopkins gives a textured, pre-Hannibal Lecter interpretation of Quasimodo, the Hunchback in Hugo's eponymous novel. Impressive model of the cathedral by production designer John Stoll. **102m/C VHS.** Anthony Hopkins, Derek Jacobi, Lesley-Anne Down, John Gielgud, Tim Pigott-Smith, Rosalie Crutchley, Robert Powell; ***D:*** Michael Tuchner. *VMK*

The Hunchback of Notre Dame ☙☙☙ **1996 (G)** Animated/musical version of Victor Hugo's story about deformed bellringer Quasimodo (Hulce) and his love for the beautiful gypsy Esmerelda (Moore). The original isn't exactly fun fare but you can expect Disney to find a way to leave everybody humming (and happy). The sweeping music was provided by "Pocahontas" tunesmiths Alan Menken and Stephen Schwartz. Comic relief is supplied by three gargoyles, companions to Quasimodo, who are voiced wonderfully by Alexander, Kimbrough and Wickes. Wickes, 85, died six weeks after voicing her role. Looks like another boatload of box office, merchandising, and video sale cash is making its way into old Walt's vaults. **86m/C VHS.** ***D:*** Kirk Wise, Gary Trousdale; ***M:*** Stephen Schwartz, Alan Menken; ***V:*** Tom Hulce, Demi Moore, Kevin Kline, Tony Jay, Charles Kimbrough, Jason Alexander, Mary Wickes, David Ogden Stiers. *NYR*

Hundra ☙ **1985** A warrior queen vows revenge when her all-female tribe is slain by men. Nothing can stop her fierce vendetta—except love. **96m/C VHS, Beta.** *IT* Laurene Landon, John Gaffari, Ramiro Oliveros, Marissa Casel; ***D:*** Matt Cimber; ***M:*** Ennio Morricone. *MED*

A Hungarian Fairy Tale ☙☙☙ *Hol Volt, Hol Nem Volt* **1987** Political satire meets fantasy in a magical tale of a fatherless young boy searching for a surrogate dad. Unusual characters as well as an homage to Mozart's "The Magic Flute." In Hungarian with English subtitles. **97m/B VHS.** *HU* Arpad Vermes, Maria Varga, Frantisek Husak, Eszter Csakanyi, Szilvia Toth, Judith Pogany, Geza Balkay; ***D:*** Gyula Gazdag. *FXL, INJ, EVD*

Hungarian Rhapsody ☙☙☙ **1978** In 1911, a Hungarian nobleman joins the ranks of the rebelling peasants in order to oppose his brother, who represents aristocratic repression. One of Jancso's clearest political films, and one that continues the filmmaker's experiments with long, uncut sequences and dynamic mise-en-scene. In Hungarian with English subtitles. **101m/C VHS, Beta.** *HU* Gyorgy Cserhalmi, Lajos Balaszovits, Gabor Koncz, Bertalan Solti; ***D:*** Miklos Jancso. Nominations: Cannes Film Festival '79: Best Film. *FCT, AUD*

Hunger ☙☙ *Sult* **1966** In the late 1800's a starving Norwegian writer, unable to sell his work, rejects charity out of pride, and retains his faith in his talent. Based on a novel "Sult" by Knut Hamsun. In Danish with English subtitles. **100m/B VHS.** *DK* Per Oscarsson, Gunnel Lindblom; ***D:*** Henning Carlsen; ***W:*** Henning Carlsen. Cannes Film Festival '66: Best Actor (Oscarsson); National Society of Film Critics Awards '68: Best Actor (Oscarsson). *FCT, INJ, CVC*

The Hunger ☙☙ **1983 (R)** A beautiful 2000-year-old vampire needs new blood when she realizes that her current lover, Bowie, is aging fast. Visually sumptuous but sleepwalking modern vampire tale, complete with soft-focus lesbian love scenes between Deneuve and Sarandon. Features a letterboxed screen and original movie trailer on the laserdisc format. **100m/C VHS, Beta, LV.** Catherine Deneuve, David Bowie, Susan Sarandon, Cliff DeYoung, Ann Magnuson, Dan Hedaya, Willem Dafoe; ***D:*** Tony Scott; ***W:*** Michael Thomas, Ian Davis. *MGM*

Hunk ☙☙ **1987 (PG)** A computer nerd sells his soul to the devil for a muscular, beach-blonde physique. Answers the question, "Was it worth it?" **102m/C VHS, Beta, LV.** John Allen Nelson, Steve Levitt, Deborah Shelton, Rebecca Bush, James Coco, Avery Schreiber; ***D:*** Lawrence Bassoff; ***W:*** Lawrence Bassoff. *COL*

The Hunt ☙☙☙ *La Caza* **1967** A teenage boy accompanies three Spanish Civil War veterans on what is supposed to be a friendly rabbit hunt. Things turn violent, however, when old rivalries and tensions begin to surface. In Spanish with English subtitles. **93m/B VHS.** *SP* Alfredo Mayo, Ismael Merlo, Jose Maria Prada, Emilio Gutierrez-Caba, Fernando Sanchez Polack; ***D:*** Carlos Saura. *INJ, TPV, CVC*

The Hunt for Red October ☙☙☙ **1990 (PG)** Based on Tom Clancy's blockbuster novel, a high-tech Cold War yarn about a Soviet nuclear sub turning rogue and heading straight for U.S. waters, as both the U.S. and the U.S.S.R. try to stop it. Complicated, ill-plotted potboiler that succeeds breathlessly due to the cast and McTiernan's tommy-gun direction. Introduces the character of CIA analyst Jack Ryan who returns in "Patriot Games," though in the guise of Harrison Ford. **137m/C VHS, Beta, LV, 8mm, CD-I.** Sean Connery, Alec Baldwin, Richard Jordan, Scott Glenn, Joss Ackland, Sam Neill, James Earl Jones, Peter Firth, Tim Curry, Courtney B. Vance, Jeffrey Jones, Fred Dalton Thompson; ***D:*** John McTiernan; ***W:*** Larry Ferguson, Donald Stewart; ***C:*** Jan De Bont; ***M:*** Basil Poledouris. Academy Awards '90: Best Sound Effects Editing; Nominations: Academy Awards '90: Best Film Editing, Best Sound. *PAR*

The Hunt for the Night Stalker ☙☙ **1991 (PG-13)** Another one of those True-Detective quickies so beloved by network TV, following two hardworking L.A. cops who tracked down satanic serial killer Richard Ramirez in the mid-1980s. It originally aired (under the title "Manhunt: The Search for the Night Stalker") on the date of the killer's death-sentence verdict; the videotape lacks that particular timely sparkle. **95m/C VHS, LV.** Richard Jordan, A. Martinez, Lisa Eilbacher, Julie Carmen, Alan Feinstein; ***D:*** Bruce Seth Green. *ACA*

Hunt the Man Down 🦴🦴½ **1950** An innocent man is charged with murder, and a public defender must find the real killer before time runs out. **68m/B VHS, Beta.** Gig Young, Lynn (Mary Hart) Roberts, Gerald Mohr; ***D:*** George Archainbaud. *NO*

Hunt the Man Down/Smashing the Rackets 🦴🦴½ **1950** A double feature: In "Hunt the Man Down" (1950) a public defender tries to clear a captured fugitive's name, and in "Smashing the Rackets" (1938) a special prosecutor takes on the gangsters who have corrupted a big city. **137m/B VHS, Beta.** Gig Young, Lynn (Mary Hart) Roberts, Chester Morris, Frances Mercer, Willard Parker, Gerald Mohr, Paul Frees; ***D:*** George Archainbaud. *NO*

Hunted! 🦴🦴 **1979** A young Jewish boy teams up with a resistance fighter to find his mother in Nazi Germany during WWII. **90m/C VHS, Beta.** *GE GEM*

Hunted 🦴🦴 **1988 (PG)** WWII prisoner attempts to escape from demented officer who seems to enjoy bugging him. Hunted by the MPs, he relies on unorthodox guide to sustain feature length footage. **75m/C VHS.** Andrew Buckland, Richard Carlson, Ron Smerczak, Mercia Van Wyk; ***D:*** David Lister. *ACA*

The Hunted 🦴½ **1994 (R)** American businessman in Japan meets, beds, and witnesses the assassination of a mysterious woman and is forced on the run by the modern-day ninja clan that committed the crime. Only a notch above the low-budget, badly dubbed martial arts flicks of the 70's, this shameless bloodfest features unintentionally campy performances by Lambert and Lone and lots of silly dialogue. Beware, the cliches pile up as quickly as the bodies. **110m/C VHS.** Christopher Lambert, John Lone, Joan Chen, Yoshio Harada, Yoko Shimada, Maria Natsuki, Tak Kubota; ***D:*** Jonathan Lawton; ***W:*** Jonathan Lawton; ***C:*** Jack Conroy; ***M:*** Motofumi Yamaguchi. *MCA*

The Hunted Lady 🦴½ **1977** In this television pilot, Mills is an undercover policewoman who is framed by the mob. Tired and predictable. **100m/C VHS.** Donna Mills, Robert Reed, Lawrence Casey, Andrew Duggan, Will Sampson, Alan Feinstein; ***D:*** Richard Lang. *WOV*

Hunter 🦴½ **1973** Pilot for a television series that never emerged. A government agent uncovers an enemy brainwashing scam. **90m/C VHS.** John Vernon, Steve Ihnat, Fritz Weaver, Edward Binns, Sabrina Scharf, Barbara Rhoades; ***D:*** Leonard Horn. *ORI*

Hunter 🦴 **1977** An attorney is falsely accused of a crime and imprisoned. Released after eight years, he sets out to even the score with the mysterious millionaire who set him up. Made for television. **120m/C VHS, Beta.** James Franciscus, Linda Evans, Broderick Crawford. *ORI, WAR*

The Hunter 🦴🦴½ **1980 (PG)** Action drama based on the real life adventures of Ralph (Papa) Thorson, a modern day bounty hunter who makes his living by finding fugitives who have jumped bail. McQueen's last. **97m/C VHS, Beta, LV.** Steve McQueen, Eli Wallach, Kathryn Harrold, LeVar Burton; ***D:*** Buzz Kulik; ***W:*** Peter Hyams; ***C:*** Fred W. Koenekamp; ***M:*** Charles Bernstein. *PAR*

Hunter in the Dark 🦴🦴 **1980** Set in 18th-century Japan, where power, betrayal, and corruption are the dark side of the samurai world. Tanuma is a powerful shogunate minister who becomes involved with Gomyo, the leader of a secret underworld organization of thieves and murderers with a violent honor code. In Japanese with English subtitles. **138m/C VHS, LV.** *JP* Tatsuya Nakadai, Tetsuro Tamba, Sonny Chiba; ***D:*** Hideo Gosha. *INJ*

The Hunters 🦴🦴½ **1958** A motley crew of pilots learn about each other and themselves in this melodrama set during Korean war. Incredible aerial photography sets this apart from other films of the genre. **108m/C VHS.** Robert Mitchum, Robert Wagner, Richard Egan, May Britt, Lee Philips; ***D:*** Dick Powell; ***W:*** Wendell Mayes. *NO*

Hunter's Blood 🦴½ **1987 (R)** Five urbanites plunge into the Southern wilderness to hunt deer, and are stalked by maniacal hillbillies. **102m/C VHS, Beta, LV.** Sam Bottoms, Kim Delaney, Clu Gulager, Mayf Nutter; ***D:*** Robert C. Hughes; ***W:*** Emmett Alston. *SUE, NLC*

Hunters of the Golden Cobra 🦴 **1982 (R)** Two American soldiers plot to recover the priceless golden cobra from the Japanese general who stole the prized relic during the last days of WWII. **95m/C VHS, Beta.** David Warbeck, Almanta Suska, Alan Collins, John Steiner; ***D:*** Anthony (Antonio Margheriti) Dawson. *LIV, VES*

The Hunting 🦴🦴 **1992 (R)** A married woman falls for a ruthless businessman and is drawn into a web of blackmail and murder in this low-budget erotic thriller. **97m/C VHS, Beta.** John Savage, Kerry Armstrong, Guy Pearce, Rebecca Rigg; ***D:*** Frank Howson; ***W:*** Frank Howson. *PAR*

The Hurricane 🦴🦴🦴 **1937** A couple on the run from the law are aided by a hurricane and are able to build a new life for themselves on an idyllic island. Filmed two years before the Academy's "special effects" award came into being, but displaying some of the best effects of the decade. Boringly remade in 1979. **102m/B VHS, Beta, LV.** Jon Hall, Dorothy Lamour, Mary Astor, Sir C. Aubrey Smith, Raymond Massey, Thomas Mitchell, John Carradine; ***D:*** John Ford. Academy Awards '37: Best Sound; Nominations: Academy Awards '37: Best Supporting Actor (Mitchell), Best Original Score. *SUE*

Hurricane 🦴 **1974** Television's answer to the disaster movie craze of the early 1970s. Realistic hurricane footage and an adequate cast cannot save this catastrophe. **78m/C VHS.** Larry Hagman, Martin Milner, Jessica Walter, Barry Sullivan, Will Geer, Frank Sutton; ***D:*** Jerry Jameson. *NO*

Hurricane *Woof! Forbidden Paradise* **1979 (PG)** And the wind cried, "turkey." Robards is the governor of a tropical island beset with environmental and personal concerns. Virginal daughter Farrow falls for hunky native, standard colonial power/indigenous people complications ensue, vital explanatory footage is cut, and overacting reaches epidemic heights. Then too late the big wind blows in, leveling the place. Expensive (most of the $22 million must have gone to catering) and essentially misdirected remake of the 1937 semi-classic. **120m/C VHS, Beta.** Mia Farrow, Jason Robards Jr., Trevor Howard, Max von Sydow, Timothy Bottoms, James Keach; ***D:*** Jan Troell; ***C:*** Sven Nykvist; ***M:*** Nino Rota. *PAR*

Hurricane Express **1932** Twelve episodes of the vintage serial, in which the Duke pits his courage against an unknown, powerful individual out to sabotage a railroad. **223m/B VHS, Beta.** John Wayne, Joseph Girard, Conway Tearle, Shirley Grey; ***D:*** J.P. McGowan, Armand Schaefer. *SNC, NOS, RHI*

Hurricane Smith 🦴🦴 **1992 (R)** Weathers stars as a roughneck Texan who travels to Australia's Gold Coast in search of his missing sister. While in the land of Oz, he gets entangled in a Mafia-style drug and prostitution ring around the "Surfer's Paradise" section of the Gold Coast. Packed with mind-blowing stunts and a good performance from Weathers, this fast-paced action thriller won't disappoint fans of this genre. **86m/C VHS.** Carl Weathers, Juergen Prochnow, Tony Bonner, Cassandra Delaney; ***D:*** Colin Budds. *WAR*

Hurricane Sword 🦴½ **197?** Thriller sets savage sword play against a background of murder, betrayal, prostitution, and reunion. **86m/C VHS, Beta.** Chen Sau Kei, Li Tai Shing. *NO*

Hurry, Charlie, Hurry 🦴 **1941** Husband gets in trouble when he bows out of a trip with his social-climber wife when he tells her he must travel to Washington to see the Vice President. **65m/B VHS, Beta.** Leon Errol. *MLB*

Hurry Up or I'll Be Thirty 🦴🦴 **1973** A Brooklyn bachelor celebrates his thirtieth birthday by becoming morose, depressed, and enraged. His friends try to help; they fail, but he finds love anyway. For those seeking a better life through celluloid. **87m/C VHS, Beta.** Danny DeVito, John Lefkowitz, Steve Inwood, Linda DeCoff, Ronald Anton, Maureen Byrnes, Francis Gallagher; ***D:*** Joseph Jacoby. *LIV, VES*

Husband Hunting 🦴 **196?** Working girls hit the beach in search of husbands, and find that love isn't easy to find or hold on to. **90m/C VHS, Beta.** *IT* Walter Chiari. *NO*

Husbands and Lovers 🦴🦴 **1991 (R)** Controversial and confusing film focuses on a couple's untraditional marriage. Stephen (Sands) and Alina (Pacula) have agreed to be totally honest with each other and when Alina decides to take a lover, Stephen agrees on the condition that she report back to him every intimate detail of her affair. In the confusion and excitement of this kinky love triangle, everyone starts losing control as sexual boundaries are pushed to the limit. Also available in an unrated version. **91m/C VHS.** Julian Sands, Joanna Pacula, Tcheky Karyo; ***D:*** Mauro Bolognini; ***W:*** Sergio Bazzini; ***M:*** Ennio Morricone. *COL*

Husbands and Wives 🦴🦴🦴½ **1992 (R)** Art imitates life as Allen/Farrow relationship dissolves onscreen (and off) and Woody becomes involved with young student. Mature, penetrating look at modern pair bonding and loneliness offers more painful honesty and sadness than outright laughs, though still retains essential Allen charm. Stylistically burdened by experiment with pseudo-documentary telling of tale and spasmodic hand-held cameras that annoy more than entertain. Excellent, intriguing cast, notably Davis as the overwhelming, overbearing wife/friend. Trailers became unintentionally funny in light of the highly publicized personal problems of Allen and Farrow. **107m/C VHS, LV.** Woody Allen, Mia Farrow, Judy Davis, Sydney Pollack, Liam Neeson, Juliette Lewis, Lysette Anthony, Blythe Danner; ***D:*** Woody Allen; ***W:*** Woody Allen; ***C:*** Carlo DiPalma. British Academy Awards '92: Best Original Screenplay; Chicago Film Critics Awards '93: Best Supporting Actress (Davis); Los Angeles Film Critics Association Awards '92: Best Supporting Actress (Davis); National Board of Review Awards '92: Best Supporting Actress (Davis); National Society of Film Critics Awards '92: Best Supporting Actress (Davis); Nominations: Academy Awards '92: Best Original Screenplay, Best Supporting Actress (Davis). *COL, MOV*

Husbands, Wives, Money, and Murder 🦴 **1986** A couple is pushed over the edge by a nosey census taker and then must dispose of the consequences. **92m/C VHS, Beta.** Garrett Morris, Greg Mullavey, Meredith MacRae, Timothy Bottoms; ***D:*** Bruce Cook Jr. *TWE, HHE*

Hush, Hush, Sweet Charlotte 🦴🦴🦴 **1965** A fading southern belle finds out the truth about her fiance's murder when the case is reopened thirty-seven years later by her cousin in an elaborate plot to drive her crazy. Grisly, superbly entertaining Southern Gothic horror tale, with vivid performances from the aging leads. **134m/B VHS, Beta, LV.** Bette Davis, Olivia de Havilland, Joseph Cotten, Agnes Moorehead, Mary Astor, Bruce Dern; ***D:*** Robert Aldrich; ***C:*** Joseph Biroc. Edgar Allan Poe Awards '64: Best Screenplay; Golden Globe Awards '65: Best Supporting Actress (Moorehead); Nominations: Academy Awards '64: Best Art Direction/Set Decoration (B & W), Best Black and White Cinematography, Best Costume Design (B & W), Best Film Editing, Best Song ("Hush, Hush, Sweet Charlotte"), Best Supporting Actress (Moorehead), Best Original Score. *FOX*

Hush Little Baby, Don't You Cry 🦴 **1986** A made-for-television drama about a seemingly normal middle-aged family man who is in actuality a child abuser/murderer. **110m/C VHS, Beta.** Emery L. Kedocia, Gary Giem, Tony Grant, Burt Douglas; ***D:*** Don Hawks. *PSM*

Hussy 🦴 **1980 (R)** Hooker and her boyfriend find themselves trapped in a web of gangsters and drugs. **95m/C VHS, Beta, LV.** *GB* Helen Mirren, John Shea, Jenny Runacre; ***D:*** Matthew Chapman; ***W:*** Matthew Chapman; ***M:*** George Fenton. *VES*

The Hustle 🦴🦴 **1975 (R)** Gritty urban adventure with Reynolds as an L.A. detective investigating a young call girl's death. He becomes romantically entangled with high-priced call girl Deneuve. **120m/C**

VHS, Beta. Burt Reynolds, Catherine Deneuve; ***D:*** Robert Aldrich; ***C:*** Joseph Biroc. *PAR*

The Hustler **1961** The original story of Fast Eddie Felsen and his adventures in the seedy world of professional pool. Newman plays the naive, talented and self-destructive Felsen perfectly, Laurie is oustanding as his lover, and Gleason epitomizes the pool great Minnesota Fats. Rivetingly atmospheric, and exquisitely photographed. Parent to the reprise "The Color of Money," made 25 years later. **134m/B VHS, Beta, LV.** Paul Newman, Jackie Gleason, Piper Laurie, George C. Scott, Myron McCormick, Murray Hamilton, Michael Constantine, Jake La Motta, Vincent Gardenia; ***D:*** Robert Rossen; ***W:*** Robert Rossen; ***C:*** Eugene Eugen Shufftan Shuftan. Academy Awards '61: Best Art Direction/Set Decoration (B & W), Best Black and White Cinematography; British Academy Awards '61: Best Actor (Newman), Best Film; National Board of Review Awards '61: 10 Best Films of the Year, Best Supporting Actor (Gleason); Nominations: Academy Awards '61: Best Actor (Newman), Best Actress (Laurie), Best Adapted Screenplay, Best Director (Rossen), Best Picture, Best Supporting Actor (Gleason, Scott). *FOX, FCT*

Hustler Squad **1976 (R)** U.S. Army major and Philippine guerrilla leader stage a major operation to help rid the Philippines of Japanese Occupation forces: they have four combat-trained prostitutes infiltrate a brothel patronized by top Japanese officers. Verrrrry clever. **98m/C VHS, Beta.** John Ericson, Karen Ericson, Lynda Sinclaire, Nory Wright; ***D:*** Ted V. Mikels. *VCI, MRV*

Hustling **1975** A reporter writing a series of articles on prostitution in New York City takes an incisive look at their unusual and sometimes brutal world. Notable performance by Remick as the reporter and Clayburgh as a victimized hooker. Made for TV and based on a novel by Gail Sheehy. **96m/C VHS, Beta.** Jill Clayburgh, Lee Remick, Alex Rocco, Monte Markham; ***D:*** Joseph Sargent. *WOV*

Hyena of London **1962** A doctor steals the hyena of London's corpse and injects the rabid protoplasm into his own brain with deadly results. **?m/C VHS.** Diana Martin, Bernard Price. *LOO*

Hyper-Sapien: People from Another Star ½ **1986 (PG)** Two cuddly aliens run away from home, are befriended by a lonely farmboy, and are chased all over the wilds of Wyoming. **93m/C VHS, Beta, LV.** Sydney Penny, Keenan Wynn, Gail Strickland, Ricky Paull Goldin, Peter Jason, Talia Shire; ***D:*** Peter Hunt; ***W:*** Richard Adcock, Christopher Blue. *WAR*

The Hypothesis of the Stolen Painting *L'Hypothese du Tableau Vole* **1978** An art collector guides an interviewer around six paintings by Frederic Tonnerre, an academic 19th century painter, in an attempt to solve the mysterious disappearance of a seventh painting. The film presents the paintings as tableaux vivants in which the actors hold poses as they are examined. Based on the novel "Baphomet" by Pierre Klossowski. In French with English subtitles. **87m/B VHS.** ***D:*** Raul Ruiz; ***W:*** Raul Ruiz. *WAC, INJ*

Hysteria ½ **1964 (PG)** When an American becomes involved in an accident and has amnesia, a mysterious benefactor pays all his bills and gives the man a house to live in. But a series of murders could mean he's the murderer—or the next victim. **85m/B VHS, Beta.** *GB* Robert Webber, Sue Lloyd, Maurice Denham; ***D:*** Freddie Francis; ***W:*** Jimmy Sangster; ***M:*** Don Banks. *MGM, MLB*

Hysterical **1983 (PG)** Odd little attempt at a horror flick parody features the Hudson Brothers and involves a haunted lighthouse occupied by the vengeful spirit of a spurned woman. Late-night fun. **86m/C VHS, Beta, LV.** Brett Hudson, William Hudson, Mark Hudson, Cindy Pickett, Richard Kiel, Julie Newmar, Bud Cort; ***D:*** Chris Bearde; ***M:*** Robert Alcivar. *SUE*

I Accuse My Parents ½ **1945** Juvenile delinquent tries to blame a murder and his involvement in a gang of thieves on his mom and dad's failure to raise him properly. **70m/B VHS, Beta.** Mary Beth Hughes, Robert Lowell, John Miljan. *SNC, NOS, DVT*

I Am a Camera **1955** A young English writer develops a relationship with a reckless young English girl in Berlin during the 1930s. Based on the Berlin stories by Christopher Isherwood, later musicalized as "Cabaret." **99m/B VHS, Beta.** *GB* Julie Harris, Shelley Winters, Laurence Harvey, Patrick McGoohan; ***D:*** Henry Cornelius; ***C:*** Guy Green; ***M:*** Malcolm Arnold. *MON*

I Am a Fugitive from a Chain Gang *I Am a Fugitive From the Chain Gang* **1932** WWI veteran Muni returns home with dreams of traveling across America. After a brief stint as a clerk, he strikes out on his own. Near penniless, Muni meets up with a tramp who takes him to get a hamburger. He becomes an unwilling accomplice when the bum suddenly robs the place. Convicted and sentenced to a Georgia chain gang, he's brutalized and degraded, though he eventually escapes and lives the life of a criminal on the run. Based on the autobiography by Robert E. Burns. Brutal docu-details combine with powerhouse performances to create a classic. Timeless and thought-provoking. **93m/B VHS, Beta.** Paul Muni, Glenda Farrell, Helen Vinson, Preston Foster, Edward Ellis, Allen Jenkins; ***D:*** Mervyn LeRoy; ***W:*** Howard J. Green. National Board of Review Awards '32: 10 Best Films of the Year; Nominations: Academy Awards '33: Best Actor (Muni), Best Picture, Best Sound. *MGM, FOX, CCB*

I Am Cuba **1964** Agitprop Russian-Cuban co-production illustrates different aspects of the Cuban revolution from the toppling of Batista's decadent Havana to idealistic soldiers and student revolutionaries. Lots of oratory and deliberate artificiality combined with cinematographer Urusevky's stunning high-contrast photography. Spanish and Russian with subtitles. **141m/B VHS.** *CU RU* Luz Maria Collazo, Jose Gallardo, Sergio Corrieri, Jean Bouise, Raul Garcia, Celia Rodriguez; ***D:*** Mikhail Kalatozov; ***W:*** Yevgeny Yevtushenko, Enrique Pineda Barnet; ***C:*** Sergei Urusevsky; ***M:*** Carlos Farinas. Nominations: Independent Spirit Awards '96: Best Foreign Language Film. *MIL*

I Am Curious (Yellow) ½ **1967** A woman sociologist is conducting a sexual survey on Swedish society, which leads her to have numerous sexual encounters in all sorts of places. Very controversial upon its U.S. release because of the nudity and sexual content but tame by today's standards. Followed by "I Am Curious (Blue)" which was filmed at the same time. In Swedish with English subtitles. **95m/B VHS.** *SW* Lena Nyman, Peter Lindgren; ***D:*** Vilgot Sjoman. *HTV*

I Am the Cheese **1983** An institutionalized boy undergoes psychiatric treatment; with the aid of his therapist (Wagner) he relives his traumatic childhood and finds out the truth about the death of his parents. A bit muddled, but with its moments. Adapted from a Robert Cormier teen novel. **95m/C VHS, Beta.** Robert MacNaughton, Hope Lange, Don Murray, Robert Wagner, Sudie Bond; ***D:*** Robert Jiras. *LIV, VES*

I Am the Law **1938** Robinson is given the task of stopping gangster activity in the city. Although regularly a law professor, he is made special prosecutor and starts canvassing for people to testify. His witnesses become murder victims as an enemy on the inside attempts to thwart the game plan. Robinson is dismissed from the case but continues to pursue justice in streetclothes. Fine performances but somewhat predictable. **83m/B VHS, Beta, LV.** Edward G. Robinson, Otto Kruger, John Beal, Barbara O'Neil, Wendy Barrie, Arthur Loft, Marc Lawrence, Charles Halton; ***D:*** Alexander Hall; ***W:*** Jo Swerling. *COL*

I Beheld His Glory **1953** Story based on the experience of Cornelius, the Roman centurion who guarded Christ's tomb. **53m/C VHS.** George Macready, Robert Wilson, Virginia Wave. *REP, MVC*

I Bury the Living **1958** A cemetery manager sticks pins in his map of a graveyard and people mysteriously start to die. Well-done suspense film. **76m/B VHS.** Richard Boone, Theodore Bikel, Peggy Maurer; ***D:*** Albert Band. *SNC, MRV*

I Can't Escape **1934** A man attempts to piece his life back together after serving time for a crime he didn't commit. To prove himself to his girlfriend, he tries to break up an illegal stock scam. **60m/B VHS, Beta.** Onslow Stevens, Lila Lee, Russell Gleason, Otis Harlan, Hooper Atchley, Clara Kimball Young; ***D:*** Otto Brower. *SNC*

I Can't Sleep *J'ai Pas Sommeil* **1993** Serial killers, French style. Gay, black Camille (Courcet), an immigrant from Martinique, and his white lover Raphael (Dupont) live in a Paris hotel and murder elderly women. Though they also rob them, the motive for their horrific crimes is vague (seemingly even to themselves). Not much actually happens—Camille visits his brother, who longs to return home, and their status as outsiders is juxtaposed against another immigrant, Daiga (Golubeva) from Lithuania, who takes little interest in the crimes but unwittingly crosses paths with Camille. Atmospheric if nothing else. Based on the 1987 "Granny Killer" slayings of 20 women. French with subtitles. **110m/C VHS.** *FR* Richard Courcet, Vincent Dupont, Katerina Golubeva, Alex Descas, Beatrice Dalle, Laurent Grevill; ***D:*** Claire Denis; ***W:*** Claire Denis, Jean-Pol Fargeau; ***C:*** Agnes Godard. *NYR*

I, Claudius, Vol. 1: A Touch of Murder/Family Affairs **1991** Award-winning Masterpiece Theatre series tells the true story of the Roman Empire and the people determined to rule it. In these first two episodes, Augustus tries to control his conniving second wife, the beautiful Livia, who is determined that her son Tiberius will be the next Roman ruler. Her manipulations lead to bloody mayhem. Brilliant acting. Based on the books by Robert Graves. Also available as a seven-volume set. Made for television. **120m/C VHS.** *GB* Sian Phillips, Brian Blessed, Derek Jacobi; ***D:*** Herbert Wise. *PBS, FCT, SIG*

I, Claudius, Vol. 2: Waiting in the Wings/What Shall We Do With Claudius? **1980** Continuation of the Masterpiece Theatre series portraying the true story of the Roman Empire and its rulers. In the third and fourth episodes, Tiberius and his mother Livia attempt to capture the throne with a series of brutal manipulations. Young cousin Claudius, considered an ugly dimwit, watches from afar. Based on the books of Robert Graves. Also available as a seven-volume set. Made for television. **120m/C VHS.** Derek Jacobi, Sian Phillips, Brian Blessed; ***D:*** Herbert Wise. *PBS, FCT, SIG*

I, Claudius, Vol. 3: Poison is Queen/Some Justice **1980** Episodes 5 and 6 see Emperor Augustus murdered and Tiberius on the throne he's coveted for so long. But how long can he stay, hiding the treachery that brought him there? Good question. Agrippina, wife of his latest victim, is determined to see him punished, and the Roman masses, not so stupid after all, have begun to see a pattern in the deaths of their best and brightest. Based on the books of Robert Graves. Also available as a seven-volume set. Made for television. **120m/C VHS.** Derek Jacobi, Sian Phillips, Brian Blessed; ***D:*** Herbert Wise. *PBS, FCT, SIG*

I, Claudius, Vol. 4: Queen of Heaven/Reign of Terror **1980** In episodes 7 and 8, Caligula begins his evil manipulation of Tiberius, involving him in a wide variety of amoral activities and creating a trail of blood. Based on the books of Robert Graves. Also available as a seven-volume set. Made for television. **120m/C VHS.** Derek Jacobi, Sian Phillips. *PBS, FCT, SIG*

I, Claudius, Vol. 5: Zeus, By Jove!/Hail Who? **1980** Caligula's schemes result in his rise to the throne after Tiberius. Debauchery rules and murder is a standard procedure that returns to remove the emperor. At last, patient Claudius, the only remaining heir, thought too foolish to be dangerous, ascends the throne. Award-winning Masterpiece Theatre production created by the BBC. Based on the books of Robert Graves. The first episode on this cassette contains the graphic scene of Caligula's evisceration of his sister, as he enacts the life of Zeus in demented belief that he is the god—be forewarned. Also available as a seven-volume set. Made for television. **120m/C VHS.** Derek Jacobi, John Hurt; ***D:*** Herbert Wise. *PBS, FCT, SIG*

I, Claudius, Vol. 6: Fool's Luck/A God in Colchester **1980** Episodes 11 and 12 see Emperor Claudius wise in the ways of statesmanship, but foolish in the ways of love. His young wife Messalina creates a furor when her sexual practices become known. In spite of his love, the emperor must punish her. Award-winning BBC production, shown in U.S. on Masterpiece Theatre. Based on the books of Robert Graves. Also available as a seven-volume set. **120m/C VHS.** Derek Jacobi; ***D:*** Herbert Wise. *PBS, FCT, SIG*

I, Claudius, Vol. 7: Old King Log **1980** Claudius, aging and sad, resigns himself to his destiny, as his wife makes plans for his death. Claudius wants only the time to complete the journal of his life. Brilliant acting from Jacobi in this BBC production shown in the U.S. on Masterpiece Theatre. Based on the books of Robert Graves. Also available as a seven-volume set. **60m/C VHS.** Derek Jacobi; ***D:*** Herbert Wise. *PBS, FCT, SIG*

I Come in Peace 🦴🦴 *Dark Angel* **1990 (R)** A tough, maverick Texas cop embarks on a one-way ride to Nosebleed City when he attempts to track down a malevolent alien drug czar who kills his victims by sucking their brains. Mindless thrills. **92m/C VHS, Beta, LV.** Dolph Lundgren, Brian Benben, Betsy Brantley, Jesse Vint, Michael J. Pollard; ***D:*** Craig R. Baxley; ***M:*** Jan Hammer. *MED, VTR*

I Confess 🦴🦴½ **1953** When a priest (Clift) hears a murderer's confession, the circumstances seem to point to him as the prime suspect. Tepid, overly serious and occasionally interesting mid-career Hitchcock. Adapted from Paul Anthelme's 1902 play. **95m/B VHS, Beta, LV.** Montgomery Clift, Anne Baxter, Karl Malden, Brian Aherne; ***D:*** Alfred Hitchcock; ***C:*** Robert Burks. *WAR, FCT, MLB*

I Conquer the Sea 🦴½ **1936** Two brothers, who works as whalers, cast their affection on the same woman. Drowns in its own melodrama. **68m/B VHS, Beta, 8mm.** Steffi Duna, Dennis (Stanley Morner) Morgan, Douglas Walton, George Cleveland, Johnny Pirrone; ***D:*** Victor Halperin. *VYY*

I Could Go on Singing 🦴🦴½ **1963** An aging American songstress, on a tour in Britain, becomes reacquainted with her illegitimate son and his British father, but eventually goes back to the footlights. Garland's last film. Songs include "By Myself" and "It Never Was You." A must for Garland fans. Letterboxed. **99m/C VHS, Beta, LV.** Judy Garland, Dirk Bogarde, Jack Klugman, Aline MacMahon; ***D:*** Ronald Neame. *MGM*

I Cover the Waterfront 🦴🦴½ **1933** A reporter is assigned to write about a boatman involved in a fishy scheme to smuggle Chinese immigrants into the country wrapped in shark skins. While trying to get the story, the journalist falls in love with the fisherman's daughter. Torrance passed away before its release. **70m/B VHS, Beta.** Claudette Colbert, Ben Lyon, Ernest Torrence, Hobart Cavanaugh; ***D:*** James Cruze. *NOS, MRV, VYY*

I Died a Thousand Times 🦴🦴 **1955** Aging gangster Mad Dog Earle (pushup prince Palance) plans one last death-defying heist while hiding from police in the mountains. Meanwhile, the hard boiled gangster softens a bit thanks to surgery-needing girlfriend, but moll Winters doesn't seem to think that three's company. A low rent "High Sierra." From the novel by W.R. Burnett. **109m/C VHS, LV.** Jack Palance, Shelley Winters, Lori Nelson, Lee Marvin, Earl Holliman, Lon Chaney Jr., Howard St. John; ***D:*** Stuart Heisler; ***W:*** W.R. Burnett. *WAR, FCT*

I Dismember Mama *Woof! Poor Albert and Little Annie* **1974 (R)** Classless story of an asylum inmate who escapes to kill his mother. Although he hates women, he likes little girls as evidenced by his nine-year-old love interest. Notably lacking in bloody scenes. **81m/C VHS, Beta.** Zooey Hall, Joanne Moore Jordan, Greg Mullavey, Marlene Tracy; ***D:*** Paul Leder. *GEM*

I Do! I Do! **1984** This Los Angeles production of the Broadway musical covers 50 years of a marriage, beginning just before the turn of the century. **116m/C VHS, Beta.** Lee Remick, Hal Linden. *TTC*

I Don't Buy Kisses Anymore 🦴🦴½ **1992 (PG)** Heartwarming story starring Alexander and Peeples as two mismatched lovers who end up realizing that they're made for each other. Alexander plays Bernie Fishbine, an overweight Jewish shoe store owner who falls for a psychology graduate student (Peeples). Little does he know, but Peeples is studying him for her term paper, appropriately titled "The Psychological Study of an Obese Male." Alexander gives a great performance, as do Kazan and Jacobi who play Bernie's parents. **112m/C VHS, Beta.** Jason Alexander, Nia Peeples, Lainie Kazan, Lou Jacobi, Eileen Brennan, Larry Storch, Arleen Sorkin; ***D:*** Robert Marcarelli; ***W:*** Jonnie Lindsell; ***M:*** Cobb Bussinger. *PAR*

I Don't Give a Damn 🦴🦴 **1988 (R)** An embittered wounded soldier returns home to his loved ones, rejects them, and becomes more and more uninterested in life itself. Subtitled. **94m/C VHS, Beta.** *IS* Ika Sohar, Anat Waxman; ***D:*** Shmuel Imberman. *TWE*

I Don't Want to Be Born 🦴 *The Devil Within Her* **1975 (R)** It's got all the right ingredients for overnight camp: a spurned dwarf, a large, howling baby-thing, slice and dice murder and mayhem, and Collins. It could've been so bad. Instead, this "Rosemary's Baby" rehash is just stupid bad. **90m/C VHS.** *GB* Joan Collins, Eileen Atkins, Donald Pleasence, Ralph Bates, Caroline Munro; ***D:*** Peter Sasdy. *NO*

I Don't Want to Talk About It 🦴🦴½ *De Eso No Se Habla* **1994** Fable set in a small South American town in the '30s. The widowed Leonor (Brando) is the community leader, a woman determined to see that her daughter Charlotte (Podesta) be as happy and accomplished as possible. Leonor refuses to acknowledge Charlotte is a dwarf and size is never permitted to be mentioned in her presence. Her zealous protectiveness is challenged by worldly and charming newcomer Ludovico (Mastroianni) who becomes entranced by Charlotte. Mastroianni is masterly as always but the moody film proves slight. Based on story by Julio Llinas. Spanish with subtitles. **102m/C VHS, LV.** *AR* Marcello Mastroianni, Luisina Brando, Alejandra Podesta; ***D:*** Maria-Luisa Bemberg; ***W:*** Maria-Luisa Bemberg, Jorge Goldenberg. *COL*

I Dood It 🦴🦴 *By Hook or By Crook* **1943** Young tailor's assistant Skelton falls hard for young actress Powell working near his shop. She agrees to date, and eventually marry him, but only to spite her boyfriend who has just run off with another woman. All's well however, when Skelton stumbles across a spy ring, is hailed a hero and helps Powell realize she really loves him. ♫Star Eyes; Taking a Chance on Love; Jericho; One O'Clock Jump; So Long Sarah Jane; Hola E Pae; Swing the Jinx Away. **102m/B VHS.** Red Skelton, Eleanor Powell, Richard Ainley, Patricia Dane, Sam Levene, Thurston Hall, Lena Horne, Butterfly McQueen; ***D:*** Vincente Minnelli. *MGM, CCB*

I Dream of Jeannie 🦴 **1952** The third and worst bio of Stephen Foster has Foster as a bookkeeper-cum-songwriter alternating between writing tunes and chasing Lawrence. When she dumps him, he goes into a funk. Will he be able to complete the title song? The suspense will kill you. Lots of singing, but not much else. **90m/C VHS.** Ray Middleton, Bill Shirley, Muriel Lawrence, Lynn Bari, Rex Allen; ***D:*** Allan Dwan. *NOS, VEC*

I Dream Too Much 🦴🦴 **1935** A musical vehicle for opera star Pons, as a French singer who marries an American composer played by Fonda. Songwriter falls into wife's shadow after pushing her into a singing career; she then raises his spirits a couple of octaves by helping him sell a musical comedy. Went into production after a rival company, Columbia, launched opera singer Grace Moore's acting career. Ball later bought this studio, where she was given her second starring role. ♫The Jockey on the Carousel; I'm the Echo; I Got Love; I Dream Too Much; Bell Song; Caro Nome. **90m/B VHS, Beta.** Lily Pons, Henry Fonda, Eric Blore, Lucille Ball, Mischa Auer, Scotty Beckett; ***D:*** John Cromwell; ***M:*** Max Steiner. Nominations: Academy Awards '35: Best Sound. *HHT, TTC*

I Drink Your Blood 🦴½ **1971 (R)** Hippie satanists looking for kicks spike an old man's drink with LSD. To get revenge, the old codger's grandson sells the nasty flower children meat pies injected with the blood of a rabid dog. The hippies then turn into cannibalistic maniacs, infecting anyone they bite. From the man responsible for "I Spit on Your Grave;" originally played on a double bill with "I Eat Your Skin." **83m/C VHS.** Bhasker, Jadine Wong, Ronda Fultz, Elizabeth Marner-Brooks, George Patterson, Riley Mills, Iris Brooks, John Damon; ***D:*** David E. Durston. *FRG, TPV*

I Eat Your Skin *Woof! Zombies; Voodoo Blood Bath; Zombie* **1964** Cannibalistic zombies terrorize a novelist and his girlfriend on a Caribbean island. Blood and guts, usually shown on a gourmet double bill with "I Drink Your Blood." **82m/B VHS.** William Joyce, Heather Hewitt, Betty H. Lindon; ***D:*** Del Tenney. *RHI, SNC, FCT*

I Hate Blondes 🦴🦴½ *Odio le Bionde* **1983** A group of criminals use a ghostwriter's burglaring stories as instructional manuals. The writer becomes involved with the gang. Relies heavily on visual humor. Notably among the comedy scenes is the author's search for jewels at a get-together. **90m/C VHS, Beta.** *IT* ***D:*** Giorgio Capitani, Giorgio Capitani. *NO*

I Heard the Owl Call My Name 🦴🦴½ **1973** Poignant story of an Anglican priest who is relocated to an Indian fishing village on the ouskirts of Vancouver, British Columbia. Made for television and based on a Margaret Craven book. **74m/C Beta.** Tom Courtenay, Dean Jagger, Paul Stanley; ***D:*** Daryl Duke. *PSM*

I Killed Rasputin 🦴½ **1967** The "Mad Monk" who rose to power before the Russian Revolution lost his life in a bizarre assassination by Felix Youssoupoff. Film deals with the friendship between the men that ended in betrayal. Well-intentioned, but overwrought. Dubbed. **95m/C VHS, Beta.** *FR IT* Geraldine Chaplin, Gert Frobe, Peter McEnery; ***D:*** Robert Hossein; ***M:*** Don Banks. *NO*

I Killed That Man 🦴🦴½ **1942** A prisoner scheduled to die in the electric chair is given an early ticket out when he is found poisoned. Evidence points to an unusual group of suspects. Effective low-budget thriller offers a few unexpected surprises. **72m/B VHS, Beta.** Ricardo Cortez, Joan Woodbury, Iris Adrian, George Pembroke, Herbert Rawlinson, Pat Gleason, Ralf Harolde, Jack Mulhall, Vince Barnett, Gavin Gordon, John Hamilton; ***D:*** Phil Rosen. *SNC*

I Know Where I'm Going 🦴🦴🦴 **1945** A young woman (Hiller), who believes that money brings happiness, is on the verge of marrying a rich old man, until she meets a handsome naval officer (Livesey) and finds a happy, simple life. Early on the female lead appears in a dream sequence filmed in the mode of surrealist painter Salvador Dali and avant garde director Luis Bunuel. Scottish setting and folk songs give a unique flavor. Brown provides a fine performance as a native Scot. **91m/B VHS, Beta, LV.** *GB* Roger Livesey, Wendy Hiller, Finlay Currie, Pamela Brown; ***D:*** Michael Powell. *HMV, LCA*

I Know Why the Caged Bird Sings 🦴🦴🦴 **1979** A black writer's memories of growing up in the rural South during the 1930s. Strong performances from Rolle and Good. Made-for-television film is based on the book by Maya Angelou. **100m/C VHS, Beta.** Diahann Carroll, Ruby Dee, Esther Rolle, Roger E. Mosley, Paul Benjamin, Constance Good; ***D:*** Fielder Cook. *KUI, LIV*

I Like Bats **1985** Can a psychiatrist help a vampire become a human? Polish dialogue with English subtitles. **90m/C VHS.** ***D:*** Grzegorz Warchol. *FCT*

I Like It Like That 🦴🦴🦴 **1994 (R)** Chaotic family life and loves in the Bronx are the setting for this tale of a Cinderella in the record industry. Strong-willed black-Latina Lisette (Velez) has been married for 10 years to macho Latin, Chino (Seda), who has a wandering eye. When Chino is jailed for looting during a blackout, Lisette, needing to support their three kids, talks her way into a job with WASP record promoter Stephen Price (Dunne). When local gossips make it seem Lisette is having an affair, the newly sprung Chino retaliates by turning to lusty Magdalena (Vidal). Lisette, meanwhile, gathers support from her transvestite brother and proves to have inner resources previously unnoticed. Great Latino soundtrack illuminates the complications. Modest-budget sleeper quickly exited the theater but proves to be a strong debut for director/writer Martin, reputed to be the first African American woman to be given the reins by a major studio. **106m/C VHS, LV.** Lauren Velez, John Seda, Lisa Vidal, Jesse Borrego, Griffin Dunne, Rita Moreno, Tomas Melly, Desiree Casado, Isaiah Garcia; ***D:*** Darnell Martin; ***W:*** Darnell Martin; ***M:*** Sergio George. Nominations: Independent Spirit Awards '95: Best Actor (Seda), Best Actress (Velez), Best Cinematography, Best First Feature. *COL*

I Like to Play Games ½ **1995 (R)** Michael is looking for a woman who enjoys playing sexual games—and he seems to have the perfect partner in Suzanne. But just how far will their kinks take them? Also available unrated. **95m/C VHS, LV.** Lisa Boyle, Ken Steadman. *APX*

I Live in Fear *Record of a Living Being; Kimono No Kiroku* **1955** Nakajima, an elderly, wealthy owner of a foundry, becomes increasingly fearful of atomic war and the threats to his family's safety. He tries to persuade them to leave Japan and move with him to Brazil but they fear the family will be ruined financially. Nakajima then burns down his foundry to force his children to move but instead they go to court and have him declared mentally incompetent. He is placed in an institution where he finds peace in the delusion that he has escaped to another planet and that the Earth has indeed suffered a nuclear holocaust. Provocative look at the fear of atomic warfare and radiation. In Japanese with English subtitles. **105m/C VHS.** *JP* Toshiro Mifune, Takashi Shimura, Eiko Miyoshi, Haruko Togo; ***D:*** Akira Kurosawa. *FCT*

I Live in Grosvenor Square *A Yank In London* **1946** An American soldier in Great Britain falls in love with a major's fiancee. Entertaining if a bit drawn out. **106m/B VHS.** *GB* Anna Neagle, Rex Harrison, Dean Jagger, Robert Morley, Jane Darwell; ***D:*** Herbert Wilcox. *NOS, DVT*

I Live My Life ½ **1935** Stylish glossy flick with Crawford playing a bored New York debutante who travels to Greece and meets a dedicated archaelogist (Aherne). A love/hate relationship ensues in this typical Crawford vehicle where she is witty and parades around in sophisticated fashions, but there is little substance here. **92m/B VHS.** Joan Crawford, Brian Aherne, Frank Morgan, Aline MacMahon, Eric Blore, Fred Keating, Jessie Ralph, Arthur Treacher, Frank Conroy, Sterling Holloway, Vince Barnett, Hedda Hopper, Lionel Stander; ***D:*** Woodbridge S. Van Dyke; ***W:*** Joseph L. Mankiewicz, Gottfried Reinhardt, Ethel B. Borden. *MGM*

I Live with Me Dad ½ **1986** A vagrant drunk and his son fight the authorities for the right to be together. **86m/C VHS, Beta.** *AU* Peter Hehir, Haydon Samuels; ***D:*** Paul Maloney. *FOX*

I Love All of You ½ **1983** Deneuve relives experiences with three former lovers - a composer, a well-intentioned nobody, and a rock star - as she enters into a relationship with a widower. **103m/C VHS, Beta.** *FR* Catherine Deneuve, Jean-Louis Trintignant, Gerard Depardieu, Serge Gainsbourg; ***D:*** Claude Berri. *NO*

I Love Lucy **1952** Everyone's favorite redhead in scrape after scrape, along with her Cuban bandleader husband, Ricky Ricardo, and their neighbors Fred and Ethel Mertz. Episodes on this tape are "Lucy Does a TV Commercial" and "Lucy's Italian Movie." Other episodes available. **51m/B VHS, LV.** Lucille Ball, Desi Arnaz Sr., Vivian Vance, William Frawley. *FOX, MOV*

I Love Melvin ½ **1953** Reynolds wants to be a Tinseltown goddess, and O'Connor just wants Reynolds; so he passes himself off as chief lenseman for a famous magazine and promises her a shot at the cover of "Look." Seems he has a little trouble on the follow through. Choreographed by Robert Alton, it's got a best ever football ballet (with Reynolds as pigskin). ♫A Lady Loves; Saturday Afternoon Before The Game; I Wanna Wander; We Have Never Met As Of Yet; Life Has Its Funny Little Ups And Downs; Where Did You Learn To Dance?; And There You Are. **77m/C VHS.** Donald O'Connor, Debbie Reynolds, Una Merkel, Richard Anderson, Jim Backus, Allyn Joslyn, Les Tremayne, Noreen Corcoran, Robert Taylor, Howard Keel; ***D:*** Don Weis. *MGM, TTC, FCT*

I Love My...Wife **1970 (R)** A medical student plays doctor with hospital nurses when he and his wife stop having sex during her pregnancy. The marriage becomes more strained when their son is born and his mother-in-law moves in. A comedy without the proper dosage of laughs. **98m/C VHS, Beta.** Elliott Gould, Brenda Vaccaro, Angel Tompkins; ***D:*** Mel Stuart. *MCA*

I Love N.Y. **1987** A young metropolitan couple struggles to find true love amidst disapproving parents and doubting friends. Choppy direction and poor writing contribute to its failure. **100m/C VHS, Beta, LV.** Scott Baio, Kelley Van Der Velden, Christopher Plummer, Jennifer O'Neill, Jerry Orbach, Virna Lisi; ***D:*** Alan Smithee; ***M:*** Bill Conti. *NO*

I Love Trouble ½ **1994 (PG)** Veteran reporter Peter Brackett (sexy veteran Nolte) and ambitious cub reporter Sabrina Petersen (young and sexy Roberts) are competitors working for rival Chicago newspapers. When they begin to secretly exchange information on a big story, they find their lives threatened and their rivalry turning to romance. Some action, simplistic retro script, one big star, one sorta big star, and you've got the perfect movie package for the Prozac decade. Written, produced and directed by husband/wife team Meyers and Shyer. **123m/C VHS, LV.** Julia Roberts, Nick Nolte, Saul Rubinek, Robert Loggia, James Rebhorn; ***D:*** Charles Shyer; ***W:*** Nancy Myers, Charles Shyer; ***C:*** John Lindley. *TOU*

I Love You ½ **1981 (R)** Man down on his luck mistakenly assumes that a woman he meets is a hooker. She plays along, only to find that they are becoming emotionally involved. Pretentious cat-and-mouse game. **104m/C VHS, Beta.** *BR* Sonia Braga, Paulo Cesar Pereio, Vera Fischer, Tarcisio Meria; ***D:*** Arnaldo Jabor. *MGM*

I Love You Again ½ **1940** A classic screwball comedy with Powell and Loy working together (wonderfully) in something other than their "Thin Man" series. Powell is a gloomy businessman who's about to be divorced by Loy. But after an accident it turns out Powell had been suffering from amnesia and has now regained his memory (which he keeps a secret). It seems Mr. Respectable used to be a con man and he decides to revert to his criminal ways. He also doesn't remember Loy but falls instantly in love with her and must decide what kind of life he wants. Witty dialog, amusing situations, fine direction. **97m/B VHS, LV.** William Powell, Myrna Loy, Frank McHugh, Edmund Lowe; ***D:*** Woodbridge S. Van Dyke. *MGM*

I Love You, Alice B. Toklas! ½ *Kiss My Butterfly* **1968** A straight uptight lawyer decides to join the peace and love generation in this somewhat maniacal satire of the hippie culture. Authored by Paul Mazursky and Larry Tucker. Incidentally, the title's Alice B. Toklas was actually the lifemate of "Lost Generation" author Gertrude Stein. **94m/C VHS, Beta, LV.** Peter Sellers, Jo Van Fleet, Leigh Taylor-Young, Joyce Van Patten; ***D:*** Hy Averback; ***W:*** Paul Mazursky; ***M:*** Elmer Bernstein. *WAR, FCT*

I Love You ... Goodbye **1973** A frustrated housewife, fed up with the constant role of wife and mother, leaves her family in an effort to find a more challenging and fulfilling life. A good performance by Lange compensates for some of its muddledness. **74m/C VHS, Beta.** Hope Lange, Earl Holliman. *LCA*

I Love You Rosa ½ **1972** Rosa, a young Jewish widow, wrestles big time with old world values. Required by custom to marry her dearly departed's eldest brother, she's not enamored with her newly betrothed. Not that he's not a nice guy; he seems to plan to take his marital duties very seriously. It's just that he's a tad youthful (eleven years old, to be exact). Much rabbi consulting and soul searching. **90m/C VHS.** Michal Bat-Adam, Gabi Oterman, Yoseph Shiloah; ***D:*** Moshe Mizrahi; ***W:*** Moshe Mizrahi. Nominations: Academy Awards '72: Best Foreign Language Film; Cannes Film Festival '72: Best Film. *FCT, NCJ*

I Love You to Death ½ **1990 (R)** Dry comedy based on a true story, concerns a woman who tries to kill off her cheating husband. Lots of stars, but they never shine. Hurt and Reeves are somewhat amusing as drugged up hit men who struggle with the lyrics to the National Anthem. Watch for director Kasdan as Devo's lawyer. Cates, Kline's real-life wife, has an unbilled part as one of his one-night stands. **110m/C VHS, Beta, LV.** Kevin Kline, Tracey Ullman, Joan Plowright, River Phoenix, William Hurt, Keanu Reeves, James Gammon, Victoria Jackson, Miriam Margolyes, Heather Graham; ***Cameos:*** Phoebe Cates; ***D:*** Lawrence Kasdan; ***W:*** John Kostmayer; ***C:*** Owen Roizman; ***M:*** James Horner. *COL*

I, Madman **1989 (R)** A novel-loving horror actress is stalked by the same mutilating madman that appears in the book she's presently reading. We call that bad luck. **90m/C VHS, Beta, LV.** Jenny Wright, Clayton Rohner, William Cook; ***D:*** Tibor Takacs; ***W:*** David Chaskin. *MED*

I Married a Centerfold **1984** Television movie fluff about a young man's amorous pursuit of a model. **100m/C VHS, Beta, LV.** Teri Copley, Timothy Daly, Diane Ladd, Bert Remsen, Anson Williams; ***D:*** Peter Werner. *NO*

I Married a Monster from Outer Space ½ **1958** The vintage thriller about a race of monster-like aliens from another planet who try to conquer earth. Despite its head-shaking title, an effective '50s sci-fi creeper. **78m/B VHS, Beta.** Tom Tryon, Gloria Talbott, Maxie "Slapsie" Rosenbloom, Mary Treen, Ty Hardin, Ken Lynch, John Eldridge; ***D:*** Gene Fowler Jr. *PAR, MLB*

I Married a Vampire **1987** A country girl in the city is romanced and wed by a dashing vampire. Troma-produced hyper-camp. **85m/C VHS, Beta.** Rachel Gordon, Brendan Hickey; ***D:*** Jay Raskin. *PSM*

I Married a Witch **1942** A witch burned at the stake during the Salem witch trials comes back to haunt the descendants of her accusers and gets romantic with one of them. Wonderfully played fantasy/comedy. **77m/B VHS, Beta, LV.** Veronica Lake, Fredric March, Susan Hayward, Broderick Crawford; ***D:*** Rene Clair. Nominations: Academy Awards '42: Best Original Score. *MLB, WAR*

I Married a Woman **1956** Advertising executive marries beautiful blonde woman, but finds it very difficult to balance his career and marriage. Low on laughs. Shot in black and white, but includes a fantasy scene in color that features John Wayne. Pay attention to see young Angie Dickinson. **84m/B VHS, Beta, LV.** George Gobel, Diana Dors, Adolphe Menjou, Nita Talbot; ***D:*** Hal Kanter. *NO*

I Married an Angel ½ **1942** The last MacDonald/Eddy film. A playboy is lured away from his usual interests by a beautiful angel. Adapted from Rodgers and Hart Broadway play. Strange and less than compelling. ♫I Married An Angel; I'll Tell the Man in the Street; Spring is Here; Tira Lira La; A Twinkle in Your Eye; Aloha Oe; Caprice Viennoise; Chanson Boheme; Anges Purs. **84m/C VHS, Beta.** Jeanette MacDonald, Nelson Eddy, Binnie Barnes, Edward Everett Horton, Reginald Owen, Mona Maris, Janis Carter, Inez Cooper, Douglass Dumbrille, Leonid Kinskey, Marion Rosamond, Anne Jeffreys, Marek Windheim, Veda Ann Borg; ***D:*** Woodbridge S. Van Dyke; ***W:*** Anita Loos; ***M:*** Richard Rodgers, Lorenz Hart. *MGM, MVD*

I Met a Murderer ½ **1939** A man kills his nagging wife after a bitter argument and flees from her vengeful brother. Fine fugitive drama with a number of interesting twists. **79m/B VHS.** James Mason, Pamela Kellino, Sylvia Coleridge; ***D:*** Roy Kellino. *SNC, NOS, DVT*

I, Mobster ½ **1958** Cochran tells a Senate Sub-Committee of his rise in the ranks of the Underworld—from his humble beginning as a bet collector for a bookie to his position as kingpin of the crime syndicate. **80m/B VHS.** Steve Cochran, Lita Milan, Robert Strauss, Celia Lovsky; ***D:*** Roger Corman; ***C:*** Floyd Crosby. *NO*

I Never Promised You a Rose Garden **1977 (R)** A disturbed 16-year-old girl spirals down into madness and despair while a hospital psychiatrist struggles to bring her back to life. Based on the Joanne Greenberg bestseller. Compelling and unyielding exploration of the clinical treatment of schizophrenia. **90m/C VHS, Beta.** Kathleen Quinlan, Bibi Andersson, Sylvia Sidney, Diane Varsi; ***D:*** Anthony Page; ***W:*** Gavin Lambert, Lewis John Carlino. Nominations: Academy Awards '77: Best Adapted Screenplay. *WAR, OM*

I Never Sang For My Father ½ **1970 (PG)** A devoted son must choose between caring for his cantankerous but well-meaning father, and moving out West to marry the divorced doctor whom he loves. While his mother wants him to stay near home, his sister, who fell out of her father's favor by marrying out of the family faith, argues that he should do what he wants. An introspective, stirring story based on the Robert Anderson play. **90m/C VHS, Beta, LV.** Gene Hackman, Melvyn Douglas, Estelle Parsons, Dorothy Stickney; ***D:*** Gilbert Cates; ***W:*** Robert Anderson. National Board of Review Awards '70: 10 Best Films of the Year; Writers Guild of America '70: Best Adapted Screenplay; Nominations: Academy Awards '70: Best Actor (Douglas), Best Adapted Screenplay, Best Supporting Actor (Hackman). *COL*

I Only Want You to Love Me **1976** Peter's been denigrated by his family his entire life, so he decides to move with his wife to the city and show them he can make something of himself. But his desires become compulsions and he cracks under the strain of work and marriage, leading to a terrifying crackup. German with subtitles. **104m/C VHS.** *GE* ***D:*** Rainer Werner Fassbinder; ***W:*** Rainer Werner Fassbinder. *WBF*

I Ought to Be in Pictures **1982 (PG)** After hitch-hiking from New York to Hollywood to break into the movies, a teen-aged actress finds her father, a screenwriter turned alcoholic-gambler. Late, desperately unfunny Neil Simon outing, adapted from a Simon play. **107m/C VHS, Beta.** Walter Matthau, Ann-Margret, Dinah Manoff, Lance Guest, Michael Dudikoff; ***D:*** Herbert Ross; ***W:*** Neil Simon; ***M:*** Marvin Hamlisch. *FOX*

I Posed for Playboy **1991 (R)** Three women—one a college co-ed, one a stockbroker, and one a 37-year-old mother—quench their private passions by posing for Playboy Magazine. Made for television with additional footage added to give it an "R" rating. **98m/C VHS, LV.** Lynda Carter, Michelle Greene, Amanda Peterson, Brittany York; ***D:*** Stephen Stafford. *REP*

I Remember Mama ½ **1948** A true Hollywood heart tugger chronicling the life of a Norwegian immigrant family living in San Francisco during the early 1900s. Dunne triumphs as the mother, with a perfect Norwegian accent, and provides her family with wisdom and inspiration. A kindly father and four children round out the nuclear family. A host of oddball characters regularly pop in on the household—three high-strung aunts and an eccentric doctor who treats a live-in uncle. Adapted from John Van Druten's stage play, based on Kathryn Forbes memoirs, "Mama's Bank Account;" a TV series came later. **95m/B VHS, Beta, LV.** Irene Dunne, Barbara Bel Geddes, Oscar Homolka, Ellen Corby, Cedric Hardwicke, Edgar Bergen, Rudy Vallee, Barbara O'Neil, Florence Bates; ***D:*** George Stevens. Golden Globe Awards '49: Best Supporting Actress (Corby); Nominations: Academy Awards '48: Best Actress (Dunne), Best Black and White Cinematography, Best Supporting Actor (Homolka), Best Supporting Actress (Corby, Bel Geddes). *CCB, TTC*

I See a Dark Stranger *The Adventuress* **1946** Cynical yet whimsical postwar British spy thriller about an angry Irish lass who agrees to steal war plans for the Nazis in order to battle her native enemies, the British—then she falls in love with a British officer. A sharply performed, decidedly jaded view of nationalism and wartime "heroism." **112m/B VHS, Beta.** *GB* Deborah Kerr, Trevor Howard, Raymond Huntley; ***D:*** Frank Launder. *NO*

I Sent a Letter to My Love **1981** An aging spinster, faced with the lonely prospect of the death of her paralyzed brother, places a personal ad for a companion in a local newspaper, using a different name. Unknown to her, the brother is the one who answers it, and they begin a romantic correspondence. Well-acted, touching account of relationships that change lives, but it takes its time in telling the story. **102m/C VHS, Beta.** *FR* Simone Signoret, Jean Rochefort, Delphine Seyrig; ***D:*** Moshe Mizrahi; ***W:*** Moshe Mizrahi, Gerard Brach; ***C:*** Ghislan Cloquet. *NO*

I Shot Billy the Kid ½ **1950** Billy the Kid decides to turn over a new leaf and live a decent life. The cards are stacked against him though: He's killed a man for nearly every year of his life, and old habits are hard to break. **58m/B VHS, Beta, LV.** Donald (Don "Red") Barry, Robert Lowery, Tom Neal, Jack Perrin; ***D:*** William (Lester Williams) Berke. *NO*

I Shot Jesse James **1949** In his first film, director Fuller breathes characteristically feverish, maddened fire into the story of Bob Ford (Ireland) after he killed the notorious outlaw. An essential moment in Fuller's unique, America-as-tabloid-nightmare canon, and one of the best anti-westerns ever made. **83m/B VHS, Beta.** John Ireland, Barbara Britton, Preston Foster, Reed Hadley; ***D:*** Samuel Fuller; ***W:*** Samuel Fuller. *RXM*

I Spit on Your Corpse *Woof! Girls For Rent* **1974 (R)** A vicious female hired killer engages in a series of terrorist activities. Stars Spelvin in a non-pornographic role. **90m/C VHS, Beta.** Georgina Spelvin, Susan McIver, Kent Taylor; ***D:*** Al Adamson. *REP*

I Spit on Your Grave *Woof! Day of the Woman* **1977 (R)** Woman vacationing at an upstate New York lake house is brutally attacked and raped by four men. Left for dead, she recovers and seeks revenge. Not to be confused with the 1962 film of the same title, this one is worth zero as a film; lots of violent terror and gory death, totally irresponsibly portrayed. Also available in a 102-minute version. **98m/C VHS, Beta, LV.** Camille Keaton, Eron Tabor, Richard Pace, Gunter Kleeman; ***D:*** Mier Zarchi; ***W:*** Mier Zarchi. *VES*

I Stand Condemned ½ *Moscow Nights* **1936** A Russian officer is tricked into borrowing money from a spy and is condemned for treason. He's saved when a girl who loves him gives herself to a profiteer. Worth seeing only for young Olivier's performance. **90m/B VHS, Beta, 8mm.** *GB* Laurence Olivier, Penelope Dudley Ward, Robert Cochran; ***D:*** Anthony Asquith. *NOS, MRV, VYY*

I Take This Oath **1940** A cop is shocked to discover that his uncle is a wanted mobster, responsible for the death of a man. Hackneyed plot. **64m/B VHS, Beta.** Gordon Jones, Joyce Compton, Craig Reynolds, J. Farrell MacDonald, Robert E. Homans, Veda Ann Borg; ***D:*** Sam Newfield. *SNC*

I, the Jury **1982 (R)** A remake of the 1953 Mike Hammer mystery in which the famed PI investigates the murder of his best friend. Assante mopes around as Hammer and looks out of place in this slowed-down version. **111m/C VHS, Beta.** Armand Assante, Barbara Carrera, Laurene Landon, Alan King, Geoffrey Lewis, Paul Sorvino, Jessica James, Leigh Anne Harris, Lynette Harris; ***D:*** Richard T. Heffron; ***W:*** Larry Cohen; ***M:*** Bill Conti. *FOX*

I, the Worst of All *Yo, la Peor de Todas* **1990** Portrayal of 17-century Mexican poet, Sister Juana Ines del la Cruz (Serna). She develops a passionate but chaste friendship with Maria Luisa (Sanda), the wife of the Spanish viceroy in Mexico, and writes love poems to her. However, the newly-appointed archbishop (Murua) is a religious fanatic who condemns Juana's work, burns her books, and proceeds to persecute her. Adapted from the novel, "The Traps of Faith," by Octavio Paz. Spanish with subtitles. **105m/C VHS.** *SP* Assumpta Serna, Dominique Sanda, Lautaro Murua, Hector Alterio; ***D:*** Maria-Luisa Bemberg; ***W:*** Maria-Luisa Bemberg, Antonio Larreta; ***C:*** Felix Monti; ***M:*** Luis Maria Serra. *ICA*

I Vitelloni ½ *The Young and the Passionate; Vitelloni; Spivs* **1953** Fellini's semi-autobiographical drama, argued by some to be his finest work. Five young men grow up in a small Italian town. As they mature, four of them remain in Romini and limit their opportunities by roping themselves off from the rest of the world. The characters are multi-dimensional, including a loafer who is supported by his sister and a young stud who impregnates a local woman. The script has some brilliant insights into youth, adulthood and what's in between. **104m/B VHS, LV.** *IT* Alberto Sordi, Franco Interlenghi, Franco Fabrizi, Leopoldo Trieste; ***D:*** Federico Fellini; ***W:*** Federico Fellini, Ennio Flaiano; ***M:*** Nino Rota. Nominations: Academy Awards '57: Best Story & Screenplay. *MOV, APD, INJ*

I Wake Up Screaming *Hot Spot* **1941** An actress' promoter is accused of her murder. Entertaining mystery with a surprise ending. Remade as "Vicki." **82m/B VHS, Beta.** Betty Grable, Victor Mature, Carole Landis, Laird Cregar, William Gargan, Alan Mowbray, Allyn Joslyn; ***D:*** H. Bruce Humberstone. *FOX*

I Walked with a Zombie ½ **1943** The definitive and eeriest of the famous Val Lewton/Jacques Tourneur horror films. Dee, a young American nurse, comes to Haiti to care for the catatonic matriarch of a troubled family. Local legends bring themselves to bear when the nurse takes the ill woman to a local voodoo ceremony for "healing." Superb, startling images and atmosphere create a unique context for this serious "Jane Eyre"-like story; its reputation has grown through the years. **69m/B VHS, Beta, LV.** Frances Dee, Tom Conway, James Ellison, Christine Gordon, Edith Barrett, Darby Jones, Sir Lancelot; ***D:*** Jacques Tourneur. *MED, FCT, MLB*

I Wanna Be a Beauty Queen **1985** Divine hosts the "Alternative Miss World" pageant featuring all sorts of bizarre contestants. **81m/C VHS, Beta.** Divine, Little Nell, Andrew Logan. *AHV, FCT, HHE*

I Wanna Hold Your Hand ½ **1978 (PG)** Teenagers try to crash the Beatles' appearance on the Ed Sullivan show. **104m/C VHS, Beta, LV.** Nancy Allen, Bobby DiCicco, Wendie Jo Sperber, Marc McClure, Susan Kendall Newman, Theresa Saldana, Eddie Deezen, William Jordan; ***D:*** Robert Zemeckis; ***W:*** Robert Zemeckis. *WAR, FCT*

I Want to Live! **1958** Based on a scandalous true story, Hayward gives a riveting, Oscar-winning performance as a prostitute framed for the murder of an elderly woman and sentenced to death in the gas chamber. Producer Walter Wanger's seething indictment of capital punishment. **120m/B VHS, Beta, LV.** Susan Hayward, Simon Oakland, Theodore Bikel; ***D:*** Robert Wise; ***C:*** Lionel Lindon; ***M:*** Johnny Mandel. Academy Awards '58: Best Actress (Hayward); Golden Globe Awards '59: Best Actress—Drama (Hayward); New York Film Critics Awards '58: Best Actress (Hayward); Nominations: Academy Awards '58: Best Adapted Screenplay, Best Black and White Cinematography, Best Director (Wise), Best Sound. *MGM, BTV, CCB*

I Want What I Want **1972 (R)** A young Englishman wants a sex-change, lives as a woman, falls in love, complications ensue. Not as shocking to watch as it might seem, but more a melodramatic gender-bender. **91m/C VHS, Beta.** *GB* Anne Heywood, Harry Andrews, Jill Bennett; ***D:*** John Dexter. *PSM*

I Was a Male War Bride ☠☠☠ **1949** Hilarious WWII comedy. French officer Grant falls in love with and marries WAC lieutenant Sheridan in occupied Europe. Planning to leave the continent and settle down in the U.S., the couple hits a road-block of red tape and Grant must cross-dress in order to accompany his bride on the troop ship taking her home. Worth watching for Grant's performance alone. Based on the novel by Henri Rochard. **105m/B VHS.** Cary Grant, Ann Sheridan, Randy Stuart, Kenneth Tobey, William Neff, Marion Marshall; ***D:*** Howard Hawks; ***W:*** Charles Lederer, Leonard Spigelgass, William Neff; ***M:*** Cyril Mockridge. *FXV*

I Was a Teenage TV Terrorist *Woof! Amateur Hour* **1987** Two teenagers pull on-the-air pranks at the local cable television, blaming it all on an imaginary terrorist group. Poorly acted, cheaply made, and pointless. **85m/C VHS, Beta.** Adam Nathan, Julie Hanlon; ***D:*** Stanford Singer; ***W:*** Kevin McDonough. *LIV*

I Was a Teenage Werewolf ☠☠½ **1957** "Rebel Without a Cause" meets "The Curse of the Werewolf" in this drive-in rock'n'roll horror. A troubled young man (pre-Bonanza Landon, in his first feature film appearance) suffers from teen angst and low production values, and falls victim to shrink Bissel. The good doctor turns out to be a bad hypnotist, and Landon's regression therapy takes him beyond childhood into his, gasp, primal past, where he sprouts a premature beard and knuckle hair. Misconstrued and full of terrible longings, the hairy high-schooler is understood only by girlfriend Lime and misunderstood hair-sprouting teen viewers. Directorial debut of Fowler. **70m/B VHS.** Michael Landon, Yvonne Lime, Whit Bissell, Tony Marshall, Dawn Richard, Barney Phillips, Ken Miller, Cindy Robbins, Michael Rougas, Robert Griffin, Joseph Mell, Malcolm Atterbury, Eddie Marr, Vladimir Sokoloff, Louise Lewis, S. John Launer, Guy Williams, Dorothy Crehan; ***D:*** Gene Fowler Jr.; ***W:*** Ralph Thornton. *COL, FCT, MLB*

I Was a Teenage Zombie ☠ **1987** Spoof of high school horror films features a good zombie against a drug-pushing zombie. Forget the story and listen to the music by Los Lobos, the Fleshtones, the Waitresses, Dream Syndicate and Violent Femmes. **92m/C VHS, Beta, LV.** Michael Rubin, Steve McCoy, Cassie Madden, Allen Rickman; ***D:*** John E. Michalakis. *NLC*

I Was a Zombie for the FBI ☠½ **1982** Intelligence agency toughens its hiring criteria. Much McCarthyian mirth. **105m/B VHS, Beta.** James Raspberry, Larry Raspberry, John Gillick, Christina Wellford, Anthony Isbell, Laurence Hall, Rick Crowe; ***D:*** Maurice Penczner; ***C:*** Rick Dupree. *NO*

I Will Fight No More Forever ☠☠☠ **1975** A vivid recounting of the epic true story of the legendary Chief Joseph who led the Nez Perce tribe on a 1,600-mile trek to Canada in 1877. Disturbing and powerful. Made for television. **100m/C VHS, Beta.** James Whitmore, Ned Romero, Sam Elliott; ***D:*** Richard T. Heffron. *CNG, MRV, GEM*

I Will, I Will for Now ☠☠ **1976 (R)** Tacky sex clinic comedy with Keaton and Gould trying to save their marriage through kinky therapy. **109m/C VHS, Beta.** Diane Keaton, Elliott Gould, Paul Sorvino, Victoria Principal, Robert Alda, Warren Bellinger; ***D:*** Norman Panama; ***W:*** Norman Panama; ***C:*** John A. Alonzo. *MED*

I Wonder Who's Killing Her Now? ☠☠ **1976** Husband pays to have his wife murdered, then changes his mind. On-again, off-again comedy. **87m/C VHS.** Bob Dishy, Joanna Barnes, Bill Dana, Vito Scotti; ***D:*** Steven Hilliard Stern. *LIV*

Ice ☠☠½ **1993 (R)** Charley and Ellen Reed are thieves whose latest heist is $60 million in diamonds from mob boss Vito Malta. There's trouble when they try to fence the goods and Ellen is left with the merchandise and on the run from Malta's henchmen. **91m/C VHS, LV.** Traci Lords, Phillip Troy, Zach Galligan, Jorge Rivero, Michael Bailey Smith, Jamie Alba, Jean Pflieger, Floyd Levine; ***D:*** Brook Yeaton; ***W:*** Sean Dash. *PMH*

Ice Castles ☠☠ **1979 (PG)** A young figure skater's Olympic dreams are dimmed when she is blinded in an accident, but her boyfriend gives her the strength, encouragement, and love necessary to perform a small miracle. Way too schmaltzy. **110m/C VHS, Beta.** Robby Benson, Lynn-Holly Johnson, Tom Skerritt, Colleen Dewhurst, Jennifer Warren, David Huffman; ***D:*** Donald Wrye; ***W:*** Donald Wrye, Gary L. Bain; ***M:*** Marvin Hamlisch. Nominations: Academy Awards '79: Best Song ("Theme from Ice Castles-Through the Eyes of Love"). *COL*

Ice Cream Man ☠ **1995 (R)** Quite disgusting horror tale of a dweeby, demented ice cream man who delivers gore and death along with his frozen treats. **96m/C VHS.** Clint Howard, Sandahl Bergman, Olivia Hussey, Lee Majors II, David Naughton, Jan-Michael Vincent, David Warner, Steve Garvey; ***D:*** Norman Apstein. *APX*

The Ice Flood ☠☠ **1926** Silent family type comedy of a son who proves to the old man that he wrote the book on life, wagering the successful supervision of dad's lumberjacks. **63m/B VHS, Beta.** Kenneth Harlan, Viola Dana; ***D:*** George B. Seitz. *GPV*

Ice House ☠☠ **1989** A sophisticated young lady flees Texas for Hollywood, searching for a better life. When her ex-lover shows up and wants her to go back, the lackless turmoil begins. Pairs real-life couple Gilbert and Brinkman. **81m/C VHS, Beta.** Melissa Gilbert, Bo Brinkman, Andreas Manolikakis, Buddy Quaid; ***D:*** Bo Brinkman, Eagle Pennell; ***W:*** Bo Brinkman. *NO*

Ice Palace ☠☠ **1960** Two rugged adventurers maintain a lifelong rivalry in the primitive Alaskan wilderness, their relationship dramatizing the development of the 49th state. Silly but entertaining. Based on Edna Ferber's novel. **143m/C VHS, Beta.** Richard Burton, Robert Ryan, Carolyn Jones, Shirley Knight, Martha Hyer, Jim Backus, George Takei; ***D:*** Vincent Sherman; ***C:*** Joseph Biroc; ***M:*** Max Steiner. *WAR*

Ice Pawn ☠☠ **1992** Alex Dalton may finally get to realize his dream of becoming a gold medal ice skater if he can beat Misha, his Russian rival. He soon finds out that Misha isn't his only problem, as he unknowingly becomes a pawn in a game of corruption and greed that could totally ruin his career. **102m/C VHS.** Paul Cross, Dan Haggerty, Robert Budaska, Chris Thomas; ***D:*** Barry Samson; ***W:*** Paul Cross. *NO*

Ice Pirates ☠½ **1984 (PG)** Space pirates in the far future steal blocks of ice to fill the needs of a thirsty galaxy. Cool plot has its moments. **91m/C VHS, Beta, LV.** Robert Urich, Mary Crosby, Michael D. Roberts, John Matuszak, Anjelica Huston, Ron Perlman, John Carradine, Robert Symonds; ***D:*** Stewart Raffill; ***W:*** Stewart Raffill; ***M:*** Bruce Broughton. *MGM*

The Ice Runner ☠☠½ **1993 (R)** Low-key Cold War thriller, filmed in 1991, about a U.S. spy who escapes from the Soviet gulag. Jeffrey West (Albert) gets caught in a botched payoff to a Soviet minister and when the diplomats wash their hands of him a rigged trial has West sentenced to 12 years hard labor. A convenient train wreck lets him assume a different prisoner's name which gets him to a minimum security camp under the eyes of a suspicious commander. Now West needs to escape and cross 39 miles of icy tundra separating his Russian prison from American freedom. **116m/C VHS.** Edward Albert, Eugene Lazarev, Olga Kabo, Victor Wong, Alexander Kuznitsov, Basil Hoffman, Bill Bordy, Sergei Ruban; ***D:*** Barry Samson; ***W:*** Joyce Warren, Clifford Coleman, Joshua Stallings. *MNC*

Ice Station Zebra ☠☠½ **1968 (G)** A nuclear submarine races Soviet seamen to find a downed Russian satellite under a polar ice cap. Suspenseful Cold War adventure based on the novel by Alistair MacLean. **148m/C VHS, Beta, LV.** Rock Hudson, Ernest Borgnine, Patrick McGoohan, Jim Brown, Lloyd Nolan, Tony Bill; ***D:*** John Sturges; ***C:*** Daniel F. Fapp; ***M:*** Michel Legrand. Nominations: Academy Awards '68: Best Cinematography. *MGM*

Icebox Murders *Woof!* **198?** A crazed, motiveless, faceless killer hangs his victims in a walk-in freezer. Store this one. **90m/C VHS, Beta.** Jack Taylor, Mirta Miller. *NO*

Iced ☠ **1988** Wild fun turns to horror on a ski trip as a group of college friends are hunted by a maniac on the loose. It's all downhill. **86m/C VHS, Beta.** Debra Deliso, Doug Stevenson, Ron Kologie, Elizabeth Gorcey, Alan Johnson; ***D:*** Jeff Kwitny. *PSM*

Iceland ☠☠ **1942** Labored romance of an Iceland girl and a Marine with plenty of skating thrown in for good measure. Skating and singing interludes are the best part of an otherwise average film. ♫You Can't Say No to a Soldier; There Will Never Be Another You; Lover's Knot; Let's Bring New Glory to Old Glory; I Like a Military Tune. **79m/B VHS.** Sonja Henie, John Payne, Jack Oakie, Felix Bressart, Osa Massen, Fritz Feld; ***D:*** H. Bruce Humberstone; ***W:*** Robert Ellis, Helen Logan. *FXV*

Iceman ☠☠☠ **1984 (PG)** A frozen prehistoric man is brought back to life, after which severe culture shock takes hold. Underwritten but nicely acted, especially by Lone as the primal man. **101m/C VHS, Beta, LV.** *CA* Timothy Hutton, Lindsay Crouse, John Lone, David Strathairn, Josef Sommer, Danny Glover; ***D:*** Fred Schepisi; ***W:*** Chip Proser; ***M:*** Bruce Smeaton. *MCA*

The Icicle Thief ☠☠☠ *Ladri di Saponette* **1989** "The Naked Gun" for the art-house crowd. As a stark, black-and-white neo-realist tragedy airs on TV, bright color commercials disrupt the narrative. Soon ads invade the the movie itself, and the film's director jumps into his picture to fix the damage. Study up on your postwar Italian cinema and this'll seem hilarious; otherwise the real fun doesn't kick in until the halfway point. In Italian with English subtitles. **93m/C VHS.** *IT* Maurizio Nichetti, Cateria Sylos Labini, Claudio G. Fava, Renato Scarpa, Heidi Komarek; ***D:*** Maurizio Nichetti. *FXL, FCT, APD*

Icy Breasts ☠☠☠ **1975** A French psychiatrist tries to prevent his beautiful but psychotic patient from continuing her murdering spree. Dubbed. **105m/C VHS, Beta.** *FR* Alain Delon, Mireille Darc; ***D:*** Georges Lautner. *FCT*

I'd Climb the Highest Mountain ☠☠☠ **1951** Sincere, sentimental piece of Americana about a country preacher (Lundigan) and his city wife (Hayward) as they adjust to life in a small town in Southern hill country. Filmed on location in Georgia. Film was a big hit, especially in the South. Based on the novel by Corra Harris. **88m/C VHS.** Susan Hayward, William Lundigan, Rory Calhoun, Gene Lockhart, Ruth Donnelly, Barbara Bates, Lynn Bari, Alexander Knox; ***D:*** Henry King; ***W:*** Lamar Trotti. *FXV*

I'd Give My Life ☠½ **1936** A gangster's ex-wife is presently married to the governor. He tries to use their honest but framed son to blackmail her. **73m/B VHS, Beta.** Guy Standing, Frances Drake, Tom Brown, Janet Beecher; ***D:*** Edwin L. Marin. *VYY*

Idaho ☠½ **1943** On a mission to close down houses of ill repute, Rodgers teams up with Autry's old sidekick Burnette. **70m/B VHS, Beta.** Roy Rogers, Harry Shannon, Virginia Grey, Smiley Burnette, Ona Munson; ***D:*** Joseph Kane. *NOS, VDM, VCN*

Idaho Transfer *Woof! Deranged* **1973 (PG)** Fonda's second directorial effort; Carradine's first screen appearance. An obnoxious group of teens travel through time to Idaho in the year 2044. Environmental wasteland story is dull and confused. **90m/C VHS, Beta.** Keith Carradine, Kelley Bohanan; ***D:*** Peter Fonda. *MPI, FCT*

Identity Crisis ☠ **1990 (R)** Campy fashion maven and flamboyant rapper switch identities causing much tedious overacting. Lifeless murder comedy from father and son Van Peebles. **98m/C VHS, LV.** Mario Van Peebles, Ilan Mitchell-Smith, Nicholas Kepros, Shelly Burch, Richard Clarke; ***D:*** Melvin Van Peebles. *ACA*

Identity Unknown ☠☠½ **1945** Shell-shocked veteran goes AWOL to discover who he is, meeting grieving relatives along the way. Interesting premise is sometimes moving. **70m/B VHS, Beta, 8mm.** Richard Arlen, Cheryl Walker, Roger Pryor, Bobby Driscoll; ***D:*** Walter Colmes. *VYY*

The Idiot ♪♪♪♪ **1951** Dostoevski's Russian novel is transported by Kurosawa across two centuries to post-war Japan, where the madness and jealousy continue to rage. In Japanese with English subtitles. **166m/B VHS.** Toshiro Mifune, Masayuki Mori, Setsuko Hara, Yoshiko Kuga, Takashi Shimura; ***D:*** Akira Kurosawa. *NYF, INJ*

Idiot's Delight ♪♪♪ **1939** At an Alpine hotel, a song and dance man meets a gorgeous Russian countess who reminds him of a former lover. Incredibly, Gable sings and dances through "Puttin' on the Ritz," the film's big highlight. Based on the Pulitzer Prize-winning play by Robert Sherwood. **107m/B VHS, Beta, LV.** Clark Gable, Norma Shearer, Burgess Meredith, Edward Arnold, Charles Coburn, Joseph Schildkraut; ***D:*** Clarence Brown; ***C:*** William H. Daniels. *CCB, MGM*

The Idol Dancer ♪♪½ **1920** Romance and adventure in the South Seas with a drunken American beachcomber inspired by love to change his ways. There's also a native uprising for added excitement. Minor Griffith but nice Nassau scenery. **93m/B VHS.** Richard Barthelmess, Clarine Seymour, Creighton Hale, George MacQuarrie, Kate Bruce, Anders Randolf, Walter James, Thomas Carr; ***D:*** D.W. Griffith. *GPV, GVV*

Idolmaker ♪♪½ **1980 (PG)** A conniving agent can make a rock star out of anyone. Well-acted fluff with Sharkey taking a strong lead. The first film by hack-meister Hackford and somewhat based on true-life teen fab Fabian. **119m/C VHS, Beta, LV.** Ray Sharkey, Tovah Feldshuh, Peter Gallagher, Paul Land, Joe Pantoliano, Maureen McCormick, John Aprea, Richard Bright, Olympia Dukakis, Steven Apostlee Peck; ***D:*** Taylor Hackford; ***C:*** Adam Holender; ***M:*** Jeff Barry. Golden Globe Awards '81: Best Actor—Musical/Comedy (Sharkey). *MGM*

If... ♪♪♪♪ **1969 (R)** Three unruly seniors at a British boarding school refuse to conform. A popular, anarchic indictment of staid British society, using the same milieu as Vigo's "Zero de Conduite," with considerably more violence. The first of Anderson and McDowell's trilogy, culminating with "O Lucky Man!" and "Britannia Hospital." In color and black and white. **111m/C VHS, Beta, LV.** *GB* Malcolm McDowell, David Wood, Christine Noonan, Richard Warwick, Robert Swann, Arthur Lowe, Mona Washbourne, Graham Crowden, Simon Ward; ***D:*** Lindsay Anderson. Cannes Film Festival '69: Best Film. *PAR*

If Ever I See You Again ♪ **1978 (PG)** The creator of "You Light Up My Life" stars in the sentimental melodrama. Two adolescent lovers meet again years later and try to rekindle old passions. Done with as much skill as "Light" minus a hit song. **105m/C VHS, Beta.** Joseph Brooks, Shelley Hack, Jerry Keller, Jimmy Breslin; ***D:*** Joseph Brooks; ***W:*** Joseph Brooks; ***M:*** Joseph Brooks. *COL*

If I Were Rich ♪♪ *Cash; For Love or Money* **1933** Gwenn is arranging a meeting at his home for a group of financiers he hopes will back a scheme to save his ailing business. Meanwhile he has to dodge bill collectors and others determined to ruin his plans. **63m/B VHS, Beta.** *GB* Edmund Gwenn, Wendy Barrie, Robert Donat, Clifford Heatherly; ***D:*** Zoltan Korda. *VYY, FCT, NOS*

If It's a Man, Hang Up ♪½ **1975** A model is terrified by harrowing telephone calls from a stranger. **71m/C VHS, Beta.** Carol Lynley, Gerald Harper. *LIV*

If It's Tuesday, This Must Be Belgium ♪♪♪ **1969 (G)** A fast-paced, frantic, and funny look at a group of Americans on a whirlwind European tour. The group does a nine-country, 18-day bus tour with clashing, comic personalities and lots of romantic possibilities. Remade as a 1987 television movie. **99m/C VHS, LV.** Suzanne Pleshette, Ian McShane, Mildred Natwick, Norman Fell, Michael Constantine, Peggy Cass, Murray Hamilton, Marty Ingels, Sandy Baron, Pamela Britton, Luke Halpin; ***D:*** Mel Stuart. *MGM, MOV*

If Looks Could Kill ♪♪ **1986 (R)** Would-be film noir about a man spying on a female embezzler and falling in love. **90m/C VHS.** Alan Fisler, Tim Gail, Kim Lambert, Jeanne Marie; ***D:*** Chuck Vincent. *REP*

If Looks Could Kill ♪♪½ **1991 (PG-13)** TV stud Grieco makes film debut as a high school class cutup who travels to France with his class to parlez vous for extra credit. Mistaken for a CIA agent, he stumbles into a plot to take over all the money in the whole wide world, and much implausible action and eyelash batting follows. Extra kibbles for supporting characterizations. Oh, and don't be put off by the fact that the Parisian scenes were shot in Montreal. **89m/C VHS, Beta, LV, 8mm.** Richard Grieco, Linda Hunt, Roger Rees, Robin Bartlett, Gabrielle Anwar, Roger Daltrey, Geraldine James, Carole Davis; ***D:*** William Dear; ***W:*** Fred Dekker; ***M:*** David Foster. *WAR*

If Lucy Fell ♪♪ **1995 (R)** Schaeffer serves as writer/director/star of this predictable 90s-style romantic comedy. Ludicrous premise has psychotherapist Lucy (Parker) bent on realizing a 10-year-old pact with longtime friend Joe (Schaeffer) that stipulates they both jump off the Brooklyn Bridge if neither one has found true love by age 30. With the big birthday approaching, Lucy takes a desperate shot with eccentric painter Bwick (Stiller), while Joe finally goes for the object of his desire, asking beautiful neighbor Jane (MacPherson) to a showing of his paintings. Highlights come in the casting, with Parker a solid and energetic neurotic and MacPherson showing that there's something beyond her more obvious talents. **94m/C VHS.** Sarah Jessica Parker, Eric Schaeffer, Ben Stiller, Elle Macpherson, James Rebhorn, Dominic Luchese; ***D:*** Eric Schaeffer; ***W:*** Eric Schaeffer, Tony Spiridakis; ***C:*** Ron Fortunato; ***M:*** Amanda Kravat, Charles Pettis. *NYR*

If Things Were Different ♪½ **1979** Feisty woman struggles to hold her family together after her husband is hospitalized with a nervous breakdown. **96m/C VHS, Beta.** Suzanne Pleshette, Tony Roberts, Arte Johnson, Chuck McCann, Don Murray; ***D:*** Robert Lewis. *WOV*

If You Could See What I Hear ♪½ **1982 (PG)** Irritatingly upbeat true-life story of blind singer-musician, Tom Sullivan. Covers his life from college days to marriage. Sophomoric comedy centers around the hero's irresponsible, and often life-endangering, behavior. **103m/C VHS, Beta, LV.** *CA* Marc Singer, R.H. Thomson, Sarah Torgov, Shari Belafonte; ***D:*** Eric Till. Genie Awards '83: Best Supporting Actor (Thomson). *VES*

If You Don't Stop It...You'll Go Blind ♪½ **1977 (R)** A series of gauche and tasteless vignettes from various little-known comedians. **80m/C VHS, Beta.** Pat McCormick, George Spencer, Patrick Wright; ***D:*** I. Robert Levy, Keefe Brasselle. *MED*

If You Knew Susie ♪♪ **1948** Two retired vaudeville actors find a letter from George Washington which establishes them as descendants of a colonial patriot and the heirs to a seven billion dollar fortune. ♫If You Knew Susie; My Brooklyn Love Song; What Do I Want With Money?; We're Living the Life We Love; My, How the Time Goes By. **90m/B VHS, Beta.** Eddie Cantor, Joan Davis, Allyn Joslyn, Charles Dingle, Charles Halton; ***D:*** Gordon Douglas. *CCB*

Igor & the Lunatics ♪ **1985 (R)** Tasteless tale of a cannibal cult leader released from prison who picks up where he left off. **79m/C VHS, Beta.** Joseph Eero, Joe Niola, T.J. Michaels; ***D:*** Billy Parolini. *LIV*

Iguana ♪♪ **1989** The videocassette box art makes this look like a horror movie, but it's really a stiff, solemn period drama about a deformed sailor with lizardlike features. After a life of mistreatment he reigns mercilessly over a handful of island castaways. An international coproduction with mostly English dialogue, some Spanish and Portuguese with subtitles. **?m/C VHS.** Everett McGill; ***D:*** Monte Hellman. *IMP*

Ike ♪♪½ *Ike: The War Years* **1979** Duvall is top brass in this made-for television epic biography tracing Eisenhower's career during WWII. Previously a six-hour mini-series; also titled "Ike: The War Years." **291m/C VHS, Beta, LV.** Robert Duvall, Lee Remick, Darren McGavin, Dana Andrews, Laurence Luckinbill; ***D:*** Melville Shavelson. *VMK*

Ikiru ♪♪♪♪ *To Live* **1952** When a clerk finds out he is dying of cancer, he decides to build a children's playground and give something of himself back to the world. Highly acclaimed, heartbreaking drama from the unusually restrained Kurosawa; possibly his most "eastern" film. In Japanese with English subtitles. **134m/B VHS, Beta, LV.** *JP* Takashi Shimura, Nobuo Kaneko, Kyoko Seki, Miki Odagari, Yunosuke Ito; ***D:*** Akira Kurosawa. *HMV, CRC, FCT*

Il Bell'Antonio ♪♪½ **1960** The boastful Antonio has a reputation as a womanizer but when he finally marries, to a lovely young woman, he faces the loss of his libido. Satire of machismo, marriage, and Catholicism. In Italian with English subtitles. **115m/C VHS.** *IT* Marcello Mastroianni, Claudia Cardinale, Pierre Brasseur; ***D:*** Mauro Bolognini; ***W:*** Pier Paolo Pasolini, Gino Vissentini. *KIV, FCT*

Il Grido ♪♪ *The Cry; The Outcry* **1957** A jilted husband takes his young daughter from village to village in search of the woman who deserted them for another man. Set in the desolate Po Valley of director Antonioni's childhood. In Italian with English subtitles. **116m/B VHS.** *IT* Steve Cochran, Alida Valli, Dorian Gray, Betsy Blair, Gabriella Pallotti; ***D:*** Michelangelo Antonioni; ***W:*** Michelangelo Antonioni, Ennio de Concini; ***M:*** Giovanni Fusco. *KIV, FCT*

Il Sorpasso ♪♪½ **1963** A braggart, who has failed at everything, spends all his time traveling around Italy in his sportscar. He takes a repressed law student under his wing and decides to teach him how to have fun. In Italian with English subtitles. **116m/B VHS.** *IT* Vittorio Gassman, Jean-Louis Trintignant; ***D:*** Dino Risi. *INJ*

I'll Cry Tomorrow ♪♪♪ **1955** Hayward brilliantly portrays actress Lillian Roth as she descends into alcoholism and then tries to overcome her addiction. Based on Roth's memoirs. ♫Sing You Sinners; When The Red Red Robin Comes Bob Bob Bobbin' Along; Happiness Is Just a Thing Called Joe; Vagabond King Waltz. **119m/B VHS, Beta, LV.** Susan Hayward, Richard Conte, Eddie Albert, Jo Van Fleet, Margo, Don Taylor, Ray Danton, Veda Ann Borg; ***D:*** Daniel Mann; ***M:*** Alex North. Academy Awards '55: Best Costume Design (B & W); Cannes Film Festival '56: Best Actress (Hayward); Nominations: Academy Awards '55: Best Actress (Hayward), Best Art Direction/Set Decoration (B & W), Best Black and White Cinematography. *MGM*

I'll Do Anything ♪♪½ **1993 (PG-13)** Hollywood satire finds unemployed actor Matt (Nolte) suddenly forced to care for his six-year-old daughter Jeannie (Wright), whom he hasn't seen in three years. Matt also finally gets a job—as a chauffeur to an obnoxious producer (well-played by Brooks) whose company winds up making the manipulative demon Jeannie into a hot child star. Great work by Kavner as the owner of a test-screening service who romances Brooks. Originally intended as a musical, the test screenings were so disastrous that the numbers were axed. What's left is less jerky than expected; Brooks reportedly based his character in part on mega-mogul Joel Silver. **115m/C VHS, LV, 8mm.** Nick Nolte, Albert Brooks, Julie Kavner, Whittni Wright, Joely Richardson, Tracey Ullman; ***D:*** James L. Brooks; ***W:*** James L. Brooks; ***M:*** Hans Zimmer. *COL*

I'll Get You ♪♪ *Escape Route* **1953** An FBI agent goes to England on the trail of a kidnapping ring. **79m/B VHS, Beta, LV.** George Raft, Sally Gray, Clifford Evans; ***D:*** Seymour Friedman. *RXM*

I'll Name the Murderer ♪♪ **1936** Suspense film in which a gossip columnist starts his own investigation into the murder of a club singer. **?m/C VHS.** Ralph Forbes, Marion Shilling; ***D:*** Raymond K. Johnson. *SNC*

I'll See You in My Dreams ♪♪½ **1951** Hokey but fun musical biography of songwriter Gus Kahn (Thomas) and his wife Grace LeBoy (Day). Kahn gets his start in Ziegfeld shows but loses both his career and wife after the 1929 crash. However, she soon returns and everything ends happily ever after. ♫Ain't We Got Fun; Ukelele Lady; The One I Love Belongs To Somebody Else; I'll See You In My

Dreams; It Had To Be You; Swingin' Down the Lane; My Buddy; Makin' Whoopee!; Yes Sir, That's My Baby. **109m/B VHS.** Danny Thomas, Doris Day, Frank Lovejoy, Patrice Wymore, James Gleason, Mary Wickes, Jim Backus, Minna Gombell, William Forrest; ***D:*** Michael Curtiz; ***W:*** Melville Shavelson, Jack Rose. *WAR, MVD*

I'll Take Sweden 𝓏𝓏½ **1965** Overprotective father Hope disapproves of teenaged daughter Weld's guitar-playing boyfriend (Avalon). So to keep her out of harm's way he finagles a company transfer to Sweden. Dad falls for an interior decorator (Merrill) while Weld gets involved with a Swedish playboy (Slate). Deciding Avalon is the lesser of two evils, Hope schemes to get the two back together. **96m/C VHS, Beta.** Bob Hope, Tuesday Weld, Frankie Avalon, Dina Merrill, Jeremy Slate, Walter Sande, John Qualen, Roy Roberts, Maudie Prickett; ***D:*** Fred de Cordova; ***W:*** Arthur Marx, Bob Fisher, Nat Perrin; ***C:*** Daniel F. Fapp. *MGM, FCT*

Illegal 𝓏𝓏½ **1955** Crime melodrama stars Robinson as an attorney who risks all to acquit his assistant of murder. Early Mansfield appearance. Remake of "The Mouthpiece." **88m/B VHS.** Edward G. Robinson, Nina Foch, Hugh Marlowe, Jayne Mansfield, Albert Dekker, Ellen Corby, DeForest Kelley, Howard St. John; ***D:*** Lewis Allen. *NO*

Illegal Entry: Formula for Fear 𝓏½ **1993** Tracie's scientist father has invented a formula that could change the world. When he's murdered the formula falls into her unsuspecting hands. Tracie might not know what she has but that doesn't stop some very ruthless efforts to get the information others want. **88m/C VHS.** Sabryn Gene't, Barbara Lee Alexander, Gregory Vignolle, Arthur Roberts, Carol Hoyt; ***D:*** Henri Charr; ***W:*** John B. Pfeifer. *PMH*

Illegal in Blue 𝓏𝓏 **1995 (R)** Chris (Gauthier) the cop falls for sultry blues singer Kari (Dash) and then realizes she could be a suspect in the murder he's investigating. Will libido win out over loyalty to the job? Also available unrated. **94m/C VHS, LV.** Dan Gauthier, Stacey Dash, Louis Giambalvo, Michael Durrell, David Groh; ***D:*** Stu Segall; ***W:*** Noel Hynd; ***M:*** Steve Edwards. *ORI*

Illegally Yours 𝓏 **1987 (PG)** Miscast comedy about a college student serving on the jury in trial of old girlfriend. Bring down the gavel on this one. **94m/C VHS, Beta.** Rob Lowe, Colleen Camp, Kenneth Mars; ***D:*** Peter Bogdanovich. *MGM*

Illicit 𝓏𝓏 **1931** In love, Stanwyck fears that marrying Rennie will only ruin their wonderful relationship. Two years after their marriage her fears are realized when each searches for happiness with a past lover. A melodramatic performance that doesn't quite hit its mark. Remade two years later as "Ex-Lady" with Bette Davis in the lead. Based on the play by Edith Fitzgerald and Robert Riskin. **76m/B VHS.** Barbara Stanwyck, Ricardo Cortez, Natalie Moorhead, Charles Butterworth, Joan Blondell, Claude Gillingwater; ***D:*** Archie Mayo; ***W:*** Harvey Thew. *MGM*

Illicit Behavior 𝓏𝓏½ **1991 (R)** A dangerous manipulative woman (Severance) is out to claim a $2 million inheritance in this intricate and seductive police thriller. Included among her victims are her husband; a Hollywood vice cop suspended for use of excessive force; his partner; her husband's internal affairs adversary; and her own psychiatrist. Also available in an uncut, unrated version. **101m/C VHS.** Joan Severance, Robert Davi, James Russo, Jack Scalia, Kent McCord; ***D:*** Worth Keeter. *PSM*

Illicit Dreams 𝓏½ **1994** A lonely housewife fantasizes about a dream lover who then becomes real. Too bad her possessive and vicious tycoon hubby would rather kill than lose her. **93m/C VHS.** Shannon Tweed, Andrew Stevens. *REP*

Illumination 𝓏𝓏 *Illuminacja* **1973** Cryptic drama about a young scientist who believes that rational analysis can solve every crisis. Until he must confront the accidental death of a close friend and his problematic affair with an older woman. Intercutting of documentary material can prove disconcerting. Polish with subtitles. **91m/C VHS.** *PL* Stanislaw Latallo, Monika Denisiewicz-Olbrzychska, Malgorzata Pritulak, Edward Zebrowski; ***D:*** Krzysztof Zanussi; ***W:*** Krzysztof Zanussi; ***C:*** Edward Klosinski; ***M:*** Wojciech Kilar. *FCT*

The Illusion Travels by Streetcar 𝓏𝓏𝓏 *La Ilusion en Travnia* **1953** Odd but enchanting story of two men who restore a streetcar, only to find that it will not be used by the city. In a gesture of defiance, they steal the streetcar and take it for one last ride, picking up an interesting assortment of characters along the way. In Spanish with English subtitles. Not released in the U.S. until 1977. **90m/B VHS.** *MX* Lilia Prado, Carlos Navarro, Domingo Soler, Fernando Soto, Agustin Isunza, Miguel Manzano; ***D:*** Luis Bunuel. *CVC, FCT*

Illusions 𝓏𝓏 **1991 (R)** Jan (Locklear) is trying to recover from a nervous breakdown and improve her crumbling marriage when her husband's sexy sister arrives and things start to heat up. Jan thinks her husband and sister-in-law are just a little too close, but when she lets her landlord in on her suspicions, he reacts quite strangely. Will Jan have another nervous breakdown? Mysterious with lots of plot twists. Based on Colley's play "I'll Be Back Before Midnight." **95m/C VHS, Beta.** Robert Carradine, Heather Locklear, Emma Samms, Ned Beatty; ***D:*** Victor Kulle; ***W:*** Peter Colley. *PSM*

The Illustrated Man 𝓏𝓏𝓏 **1969 (PG)** A young drifter meets a tattooed man. Each tattoo causes a fantastic story to unfold. A strange, interesting, but finally limited attempt at literary sci-fi. Based on the story collection by Ray Bradbury. **103m/C VHS, Beta.** Rod Steiger, Claire Bloom, Robert Drivas, Don Dubbins; ***D:*** Jack Smight; ***M:*** Jerry Goldsmith. *WAR, FCT, MLB*

Ilsa, Harem Keeper of the Oil Sheiks *Woof!* **1976 (R)** The naughty Ilsa works for an Arab sheik in the slave trade. More graphic violence and nudity. Plot makes an appearance. **45m/C VHS, LV.** Dyanne Thorne, Michael Thayer. *CIC*

Ilsa, She-Wolf of the SS *Woof!* **1974 (R)** The torture-loving Ilsa runs a medical camp for the Nazis. Plot is incidental to nudity and violence. **45m/C VHS, LV.** Dyanne Thorne, Greg Knoph; ***D:*** Don Edmunds. *CIC*

Ilsa, the Tigress of Siberia *Woof!* **1979** Everyone's favorite torturer has been working her wiles on political prisoners in Russia. After escaping to Canada, her past threatens to catch up with her. As usual, no plot, violence. **85m/C VHS.** Dyanne Thorne, Michel Morin, Tony Angelo, Terry Coady, Howard Mauer; ***D:*** Jean LaFleur. *NO*

Ilsa, the Wicked Warden *Woof! Ilsa, the Absolute Power; Greta the Mad Butcher* **1978 (R)** Ilsa is now a warden of a woman's prison in South America, behaving just as badly as she always has, until the prisoners stage an uprising. Lots of skin, no violence, no acting. Also: no plot. **90m/C VHS, LV.** Dyanne Thorne, Lina Romay, Jess (Jesus) Franco; ***D:*** Jess (Jesus) Franco. *CIC*

I'm All Right Jack 𝓏𝓏𝓏 **1959** Sellers plays a pompous communist union leader in this hilarious satire of worker-management relations. Based on Alan Hackney's novel "Private Life." **101m/B VHS, Beta.** Peter Sellers, Ian Carmichael, Terry-Thomas, Victor Maddern; ***D:*** John Boulting. British Academy Awards '59: Best Actor (Sellers), Best Screenplay; National Board of Review Awards '60: 5 Best Foreign Films of the Year. *FCT*

I'm Dancing as Fast as I Can 𝓏𝓏 **1982 (R)** A successful television producer hopelessly dependent on tranquilizers tries to stop cold turkey. Good story could be better; based on Barbara Gordon's memoirs. **107m/C VHS, Beta, LV.** Jill Clayburgh, Nicol Williamson, Dianne West, Joe Pesci, Geraldine Page, John Lithgow, Daniel Stern; ***D:*** Jack Hofsiss; ***W:*** David Rabe; ***C:*** Jan De Bont. *PAR*

I'm Dangerous Tonight 𝓏½ **1990 (R)** Wallflower Amick (Shelley the Waitress in Twin Peaks) turns into party monster when she dons red dress made from evil ancient Aztec cloak. Many dead soldiers when this girl parties. Based on a Cornell Woolrich short story, it's another in a series of ever more disappointing entries from Hooper, whose cult fave "Texas Chainsaw Massacre" had low as they come production values, but far better scares. Originally cable fare. **92m/C VHS.** Madchen Amick, Corey Parker, R. Lee Ermey, Mary Frann, Dee Wallace Stone, Anthony Perkins; ***D:*** Tobe Hooper; ***W:*** Alice Wilson. *MCA*

I'm from Arkansas 𝓏 **1944** The little town of Pitchfork, Arkansas, goes nuts when a pig gives birth to ten piglets. **68m/B VHS, Beta.** El Brendel, Slim Summerville, Iris Adrian, Harry Harvey, Bruce (Herman Brix) Bennett; ***D:*** Lew (Louis Friedlander) Landers. *NOS, MRV, DVT*

I'm Gonna Git You Sucka 𝓏𝓏𝓏 **1988 (R)** Parody of "blaxploitation" films popular during the '60s and '70s. Funny and laced with out-right bellylaughs. A number of stars who made "blaxploitation" films, including Jim Brown, take part in the gags. **89m/C VHS, Beta, LV.** Keenen Ivory Wayans, Bernie Casey, Steve James, Isaac Hayes, Jim Brown, Ja'net DuBois, Anne-Marie Johnson, Antonio Fargas, Eve Plumb, John Vernon, Clu Gulager, Kadeem Hardison, Damon Wayans, Gary Owens, Clarence Williams III, David Alan Grier, Kim Wayans, Robin Harris, Chris Rock, Dawnn Lewis, Jester Hairston; ***Cameos:*** Robert Townsend; ***D:*** Keenen Ivory Wayans; ***W:*** Keenen Ivory Wayans; ***M:*** David Michael Frank. *MGM*

I'm No Angel 𝓏𝓏𝓏 **1933** "Beulah, peel me a grape." Well, you'd be hungry too if you spent your time eyeing playboy Grant as West does. She's a circus floozy who's prone to extorting money from her men (after hashing over their shortcomings with her seen-it-all-maid, the aforementioned Beulah). However, after wooing Grant, she sues for breach of promise. This leads to a comic courtroom scene with Grant bringing in all West's ex-lovers as witnesses. Grant's second film with West, following "She Done Him Wrong." **88m/B VHS.** Mae West, Cary Grant, Gregory Ratoff, Edward Arnold, Ralf Harolde, Kent Taylor, Gertrude Michael, Russell Hopton, Dorothy Peterson, William B. Davidson, Gertrude Howard; ***D:*** Wesley Ruggles; ***W:*** Mae West. *MCA, BTV*

I'm on My Way/The Non-Stop Kid **1918** Two classic shorts: "I'm on My Way" (1919), in which Lloyd's dreams of an idyllic marriage are shattered; and "The Non-Stop Kid" (1918), in which Lloyd must contend with a rival for the affection of his beloved. **30m/B VHS, Beta.** Harold Lloyd, Snub Pollard, Bebe Daniels; ***D:*** Harold Lloyd. *CCB, GVV*

I'm the Girl He Wants to Kill 𝓏½ **1974** A woman sees a murder committed, and the murderer sees her. Now he's after her. **71m/C VHS, Beta.** Julie Sommars, Anthony Steel. *NO*

I'm the One You're Looking For 𝓏𝓏½ **1988** A famous model obsessively combs Barcelona for the man who raped her. Suspenseful thriller based on a short story by Gabriel Garcia Marquez. In Spanish with English subtitles. **85m/C VHS, LV.** *SP* Patricia Adriani, Chus Lampreave, Ricard Borras, Toni Canto, Angel Alcazar, Marta Fedz, Frank Muro, Miriam DeMaeztu; ***D:*** Jaime Chavarri. *FXL, FCT, IME*

The Image 𝓏𝓏½ **1989** Anchorman Finney, the unscrupulous czar of infotainment, does a little soul delving when a man he wrongly implicated in a savings and loan debacle decides to check into the hereafter ahead of schedule. Seems the newsmonger's cut a few corners en route to the bigtime, and his public is mad as hell and...oops, wrong movie (need we say there are not a few echoes of "Network"?). Finney's great. Made for cable. **91m/C VHS.** Albert Finney, John Mahoney, Kathy Baker, Swoosie Kurtz, Marsha Mason, Spalding Gray; ***D:*** Peter Werner; ***M:*** James Newton Howard. *HBO*

Image of Bruce Lee 𝓏 **197? (G)** Martial arts fight scenes prevail in this story about a jeweler who is swindled out of $1 million worth of diamonds. **88m/C VHS, Beta.** Bruce Li, Chang Wu Lang, Chang Lei, Dana. *MED*

Image of Death 𝓏 **1977** Woman plots to take the life of an old school chum, assume her identity, and then blow up the Capitol. **83m/C VHS, Beta.** Cathy Paine, Cheryl Waters, Tony Banner, Barry Pierce, Sheila Helpmann, Pennie Hackforth-Jones; ***D:*** Kevin Dobson. *NO*

Image of Passion 1986 Weak account of male stripper/lovely advertising executive romance. **90m/C Beta.** James Horan, Susan Damante Shaw, Edward Bell; ***D:*** Susan Orlikoff-Simon. *PSM*

Imagemaker ½ 1986 (R) Uneven story of a presidential media consultant who bucks the system and exposes corruption. **93m/C VHS, Beta, LV.** Michael Nouri, Jerry Orbach, Jessica Harper, Farley Granger; ***D:*** Hal Wiener. *LIV, VES*

Imaginary Crimes 1994 (PG) Ray Weiler (Keitel) is a well-meaning salesman with dreams much bigger than his reach. After the death of his wife (Lynch), Ray tries to raise his two daughters, Sonya (Balk) and Greta (Moss). But gifted high school senior (in 1962) Sonya is resentful of being her sister's maternal anchor and having her father's schemes come to nothing even as she acknowledges how much Ray cares and how he wants to improve their lives. Remarkable performances by Keitel and Balk. From the novel by Sheila Ballantyne. **106m/C VHS, LV.** Harvey Keitel, Fairuza Balk, Kelly Lynch, Vincent D'Onofrio, Elissabeth Moss, Diane Baker, Christopher Penn, Seymour Cassel, Annette O'Toole; ***D:*** Tony Drazan; ***W:*** Kristine Johnson, Davia Nelson; ***M:*** Stephen Endelman. *WAR*

Imitation of Life 1959 Remake of the successful 1939 Claudette Colbert outing of the same title, and based on Fanny Hurst's novel, with a few plot changes. Turner is a single mother, more determined to achieve acting fame and fortune than function as a parent. Her black maid, Moore, is devoted to her own daughter (Kohner), but loses her when the girl discovers she can pass for white. When Turner discovers that she and her daughter are in love with the same man, she realizes how little she knows her daughter, and how much the two of them have missed by not having a stronger relationship. Highly successful at the box office. **124m/C VHS, Beta.** Lana Turner, John Gavin, Troy Donahue, Sandra Dee, Juanita Moore, Susan Kohner; ***D:*** Douglas Sirk; ***C:*** Russell Metty. Golden Globe Awards '60: Best Supporting Actress (Kohner); Nominations: Academy Awards '59: Best Supporting Actress (Kohner), Best Supporting Actress (Moore). *MCA, FCT*

Immediate Family ½ 1989 (PG-13) Childless couple contact a pregnant, unmarried girl and her boyfriend in hopes of adoption. As the pregnancy advances, the mother has doubts about giving up her baby. A bit sugar-coated in an effort to woo family trade. **112m/C VHS, Beta, LV.** Glenn Close, James Woods, Kevin Dillon, Mary Stuart Masterson, Kevin Dillon, Linda Darlow, Jane Greer, Jessica James, Mimi Kennedy; ***D:*** Jonathan Kaplan; ***W:*** Barbara Benedek; ***M:*** Brad Fiedel. National Board of Review Awards '89: Best Supporting Actress (Masterson). *COL*

The Immigrant ½ 1917 Chaplin portrays a newly arrived immigrant who falls in love with the first girl he meets. Silent with musical soundtrack added. **20m/B VHS, Beta.** Charlie Chaplin; ***D:*** Charlie Chaplin. *CAB, GVV*

Immortal Bachelor ½ 1980 (PG) Good cast can't overcome the silliness of this one. A juror daydreams about the dead husband of a cleaning woman on trial for killing her adulterous spouse. She decides the dead man seems a lot more exciting than her own dull and tiresome husband. **94m/C VHS, Beta.** *IT* Giancarlo Giannini, Monica Vitti, Claudia Cardinale, Vittorio Gassman; ***D:*** Marcello Fondato. *NO*

Immortal Battalion *The Way Ahead* 1944 Entertaining wartime psuedo-documentary follows newly recruited soldiers as they are molded from an ordinary group of carping civilians into a hardened battalion of fighting men by Niven. Some prints run to 116 minutes. **89m/B VHS, Beta.** David Niven, Stanley Holloway, Reginald Tate, Raymond Huntley, William Hartnell, James Donald, Peter Ustinov; ***D:*** Carol Reed; ***W:*** Peter Ustinov, Eric Ambler; ***C:*** Guy Green. *NOS, MRV, VYY*

Immortal Beloved 1994 (R) The death of Ludwig van Beethoven prompts his loyal secretary to seek the identity of a mystery love to whom the composer has bequeathed his estate. While Beethoven's genius is awesome and his music breathtaking, his lovelife is neither, and the ensuing confessions of the maestro's former loves only get in the way of flashbacks that hint at his torment and triumph. Oldman is darkly intense, and a scene in which the aged Beethoven remembers his terrifying childhood amid the strains of "Ode to Joy" is simply stunning, but an unfocused script undoes what might have been a fine tribute to the master. The London Symphony Orchestra and soloists Murray Perahia, Emanuel Ax, and Yo Yo Ma contributed to the splendid soundtrack. **121m/C VHS, LV.** Gary Oldman, Jeroen Krabbe, Isabella Rossellini, Johanna Ter Steege, Marco Hofschneider, Miriam Margolyes, Barry Humphries, Valeria Golino, Christopher Fulford; ***D:*** Bernard Rose; ***W:*** Bernard Rose. *COL*

Immortal Combat ½ 1994 (R) An army of men trained in ninja and guerilla warfare have seemingly immortal powers. Can our two violent heroes find an equally destructive way to stop the killing? **109m/C VHS, LV.** Roddy Piper, Sonny Chiba, Tiny Lister, Meg Foster; ***D:*** Daniel Neira. *APX*

Immortal Sergeant ½ 1943 After the battle death of the squad leader, an inexperienced corporal takes command of North African troops during WWII. Fonda gives a strong performance. Based on a novel by John Brody. **91m/B VHS, Beta.** Henry Fonda, Thomas Mitchell, Maureen O'Hara, Allyn Joslyn, Reginald Gardiner, Melville Cooper, Morton Lowry; ***D:*** John M. Stahl; ***W:*** Lamar Trotti; ***C:*** Clyde De Vinna. *FOX*

Immortal Sins 1991 (R) Michael and Susan inherited an old Spanish Castle, complete with its own curse, which comes in the form of a seductive women that has haunted families for centuries. **80m/C VHS.** Cliff DeYoung, Maryam D'Abo; ***W:*** Thomas McKelvey Cleaver. *NO*

The Immortalizer 1989 (R) A mad doctor transfers people's brains into young bodies for a price, although it's not as simple as it sounds. **85m/C VHS, Beta, LV.** Ron Kay, Chris Crone, Melody Patterson, Clarke Lindsley, Bekki Armstrong; ***D:*** Joel Bender. *COL*

The Immortals 1995 (R) Nightclub owner recruits eight terminally ill criminals in an elaborate heist that calls for simultaneously hitting targets citywide. But when they compare notes, the team fear a doublecross. **92m/C VHS.** Eric Roberts, Tia Carrere, William Forsythe, Joe Pantoliano, Clarence Williams III, Tony Curtis, Chris Rock, Kieran Mulroney, Kevin Bernhardt; ***D:*** Brian Grant; ***W:*** Kevin Bernhardt. *HMK*

Impact 1949 A woman and her lover plan the murder of her rich industrialist husband, but the plan backfires. More twists and turns than a carnival ride. **83m/B VHS, Beta.** Brian Donlevy, Ella Raines; ***D:*** Arthur Lubin. *NOS, MRV, DVT*

The Imperial Japanese Empire 1985 Epic of the WWII Pacific seen through Japanese eyes. **130m/C VHS, Beta.** *JP* Tetsuro Tamba, Tomokazu Miura, Teruhiko Saigo, Teruhiko Aoi, Saburo Shinoda, Keiko Sekine, Masako Natsume, Akiko Kana. *VCD*

Imperial Navy 198? A WWII epic as seen from the Japanese perspective, concentrating on their great navy and its suicide squadrons. Dubbed. **145m/C VHS, Beta.** *JP* ***D:*** Paul Aaron. *MOV*

Imperial Venus 1971 (PG) Biography of Napoleon's sister, Paolina Boneparte—with particular focus on her many loves, lusts and tribulations. **121m/C VHS, Beta.** Gina Lollobrigida, Stephen Boyd, Raymond Pellegrin; ***D:*** Jean Delannoy. *NO*

Importance of Being Earnest 1952 Fine production of classic Oscar Wilde comedy-of-manners. Cast couldn't be better or the story funnier. **95m/C VHS, Beta.** Michael Redgrave, Edith Evans, Margaret Rutherford, Michael Denison, Joan Greenwood; ***D:*** Anthony Asquith. *PAR, HMV*

The Imported Bridegroom 1989 A comedy set at the turn of the century about a man who returns to Poland in order to find his daughter a proper husband. **93m/C VHS.** Eugene Troobarck, Avi Hoffman, Greta Cowan, Annette Miller; ***D:*** Pamela Berger; ***W:*** Pamela Berger. *ERG, INJ*

The Impossible Spy 1987 True story of Elie Cohen, an unassuming Israeli who doubled as a top level spy in Syria during the 1960s. Cohen became so close to Syria's president that he was nominated to become the Deputy Minister of Defense before his double life was exposed. Well-acted spy thriller made for cable and is worth a look for espionage fans. **96m/C VHS.** *GB* John Shea, Eli Wallach, Michal Bat-Adam, Rami Danon, Sasson Gabray, Chaim Girafi; ***D:*** Jim Goddard. *NCJ, FCT*

The Impossible Years 1968 Unattractive, leering sex farce about psychiatrist Nivens who has problems with his own young daughter. Dismal adaptation of the hit Broadway play by Bob Fisher and Arthur Marx. **97m/C VHS.** David Niven, Lola Albright, Chad Everett, Ozzie Nelson, Christina Ferrare, Jeff Cooper, John Harding; ***D:*** Michael Gordon; ***W:*** George Wells. *MGM*

The Imposter ½ 1984 Improbable tale of a con artist/ex-con who impersonates a high school principal in order to regain his estranged girlfriend, who works as a teacher. Complications ensue when he tackles the school's drug problems. Made for television. **95m/C VHS, Beta.** Anthony Geary, Billy Dee Williams, Lorna Patterson; ***D:*** Michael Pressman. *PSM*

Imposters 1984 A comedy centering on the romantic problems between a self-indulgent young man and the woman who cheats on him. **110m/C VHS, Beta.** Ellen McElduff, Charles Ludlam, Lisa Todd, Peter Evans. *NO*

Impromptu 1990 (PG-13) A smart, sassy, romantic comedy set in 1880s Europe among the era's artistic greats—here depicted as scalawags, parasites and early beatniks. The film's ace is Davis in a lusty, dynamic role as mannish authoress George Sand, obsessively in love with the dismayed composer Chopin. Though he's too pallid a character for her attraction to be credible, a great cast and abundant wit make this a treat. Beautiful score featuring Chopin and Liszt. Film debut of stage director Lapine; screenplay written by his wife, Sarah Kernochan. **108m/C VHS, LV.** Judy Davis, Hugh Grant, Mandy Patinkin, Bernadette Peters, Julian Sands, Ralph Brown, Georges Corraface, Anton Rodgers, Emma Thompson, Anna Massey; ***D:*** James Lapine; ***W:*** Sarah Kernochan. Independent Spirit Awards '92: Best Actress (Davis). *TVC, MOV*

Improper Channels 1982 (PG) Mediocre comedy about a couple trying to recover their daughter after being accused of child abuse. **91m/C VHS, Beta, LV.** Monica Parker, Alan Arkin, Mariette Hartley; ***D:*** Eric Till; ***W:*** Adam Arkin. *VES*

Improper Conduct 1994 (R) Ad agency employee is sexually harassed by her boss but loses her court case. Her sister decides to get revenge by getting hired and setting the slimeball up for a fall. **95m/C VHS.** Steven Bauer, Lee Ann Beaman, John Laughlin, Kathy Shower, Tahnee Welch, Nia Peeples, Stuart Whitman, Adrian Zmed, Patsy Pease; ***D:*** Jag Mundhra; ***W:*** Carl Austin. *MNC*

Impulse ½ 1955 When his wife leaves for a visit with her mother, a young man is thrust into cahoots with gangsters, and wrapped up in an affair with another woman. **81m/B VHS.** *GB* Arthur Kennedy, Constance Smith, Joy Shelton; ***D:*** Charles De Latour. *FCT*

Impulse *Woof! Want a Ride, Little Girl?; I Love to Kill* 1974 (PG) Shatner, a crazed killer, is released from prison and starts to kill again in this low-budget, predictable, critically debased film about child-molesting. **85m/C VHS, Beta.** William Shatner, Ruth Roman, Harold Sakata, Kim Nicholas, Jennifer Bishop, James Dobbs; ***D:*** William Grefe. *LIV, VES*

Impulse 1984 (R) Small town residents can't control their impulses, all because of government toxic waste in their milk. A woman worried about her mother's mental health returns to town with her doctor boyfriend to discover most of the inhabitants are quite mad. Starts strong but... **95m/C VHS, Beta, LV.** Tim Matheson, Meg Tilly, Hume Cronyn, John Karlen, Bill Paxton, Amy Stryker, Claude Earl Jones, Sherri Stoner; ***D:*** Graham Baker; ***W:*** Bart Davis. *PAR*

Impulse 🦴🦴½ **1990 (R)** A beautiful undercover vice cop poses as a prostitute, and gives in to base desires. Russell gives a fine performance in this underrated sleeper. **109m/C VHS, Beta, LV.** Theresa Russell, Nicholas Mele, Eli Danker, Charles McCaughan, Jeff Fahey, George Dzundza, Alan Rosenberg, Lynne Thigpen, Shawn Elliott; ***D:*** Sondra Locke; ***W:*** John DeMarco, Leigh Chapman; ***M:*** Michel Colombier. *WAR*

Impure Thoughts 🦴🦴 **1986 (PG)** Four friends meet in the afterlife and discuss their Catholic school days. Odd premise never catches fire. **87m/C VHS, Beta.** Brad Dourif, Lane Davies, John Putch, Terry Beaver; ***D:*** Michael A. Simpson. *NLC*

In a Glass Cage 🦴🦴½ *Tras el Cristal* **1986** A young boy who was tortured and sexually molested by a Nazi official seeks revenge. Years after the war, he shows up at the Nazi's residence in Spain and is immediately befriended by his tormentor's family. Confined to an iron lung, the official is at the mercy of the young man who tortuously acts out the incidents detailed in the Nazi's journal. Suspenseful and extremely graphic, it's well crafted and meaningful but may be just too horrible to watch. Sexual and violent acts place it in the same league as Pasolini's infamous "Salo, or The 120 Days in Sodom." Definitely not for the faint of heart. In Spanish with English subtitles. **110m/C VHS.** *SP* Gunter Meisner, David Sust, Marisa Paredes, Gisela Echevarria; ***D:*** Agustin Villaronga; ***W:*** Agustin Villaronga. *CCN, FCT, INJ*

In a Lonely Place 🦴🦴🦴½ **1950** Bogart is outstanding as a volatile Hollywood screenwriter who has an affair with starlet Grahame while under suspicion of murder. Offbeat, yet superb film noir entry became one of the most memorable of the genre. Expertly directed by Ray. Based on the novel by Dorothy B. Hughes and an adaptation by Edmund H. North. **93m/B VHS, Beta.** Humphrey Bogart, Gloria Grahame, Frank Lovejoy, Carl Benton Reid, Art Smith, Jeff Donnell; ***D:*** Nicholas Ray; ***W:*** Andrew Solt; ***C:*** Burnett Guffey. *COL*

In a Moment of Passion 🦴½ **1993 (R)** A two-bit actor wants to be a star—in the worst way possible. So he kills off the lead actor of a new film, takes his place, and proceeds to eliminate any obstacle that gets in his way. The problem comes in when an aspiring actress falls for the actor and then figures out what's going on. **100m/C VHS.** Maxwell Caulfield, Chase Masterson, Vivian Schilling, Julie Araskog, Joe Estevez, Robert Z'Dar, Zbigniew Kaminski; ***Cameos:*** Jeff Conaway; ***W:*** Charles Haigh. *HMD*

In a Shallow Grave 🦴🦴 **1988 (R)** Shallow treatment of James Purdy's novel about a WWII veteran, badly disfigured in combat at Guadalcanal, who returns to Virginia in an attempt to return to the life he once had with the woman he still loves. Handsome Biehn plays the disfigured vet, Mueller's his ex-fiancee, and Dempsey's the drifter who adds a bisexual hypotenuse to the love triangle. Pokey American Playhouse coproduction. **92m/C VHS.** Michael Biehn, Maureen Mueller, Patrick Dempsey, Michael Beach, Thomas Boyd Mason; ***D:*** Kenneth Bowser; ***W:*** Kenneth Bowser. *WAR*

In a Stranger's Hand 🦴🦴½ **1992** Urich stars a respected businessman who happens to find a doll which belongs to a kidnapped young girl. The police have their suspicions but Urich teams up with the child's mother to find the girl and winds up uncovering a child-selling ring. Made for television. **93m/C VHS.** Robert Urich, Megan Gallagher, Brett Cullen, Vondie Curtis-Hall, Dakin Matthews, Alan Rosenberg, Maria O'Brien; ***D:*** David Greene. *TTC*

In a Year of 13 Moons 🦴🦴 *In a Year with 13 Moons; In Einem Jahr Mit 13 Monden* **1978** Notorious Fassbinder tale of Erwin who becomes Elvira and is subjected to a series of humiliating relationships with men. Finally, with the aid of his/her ex-wife and a prostitute, Elvira looks into the past in an effort to resolve the present. Alternatingly depressing and pretentious. German with subtitles. **119m/C VHS.** *GE* Volker Spengler, Ingrid Caven, Gottfried John, Elisabeth Trissenaar, Eva Mattes; ***D:*** Rainer Werner Fassbinder; ***W:*** Rainer Werner Fassbinder; ***M:*** Peer Raben. *NYF*

In an Old Manor House 🦴🦴½ **1984** Residents of an old house are tormented by the vindictive ghost of a murdered adultress whose husband didn't approve of the, uh, affection she showed his son from a previous marriage. Based on the play by Stanislaw Witkiewicz. In Polish with English subtitles. **90m/C VHS.** *PL* ***D:*** Jerzy Kotkowski. *FCT*

In Between 🦴🦴½ **1992 (PG-13)** When Margo, Jack, and Amy wake up they expect it to be another average day. Instead, these three strangers find themselves together in a peculiar house. An angel informs them that the house is a way station between life and the hereafter. The three must look at their pasts, imagine their futures, and decide whether to return to their old lives or accept death and go on to an afterlife. **92m/C VHS.** Wings Hauser, Robin Mattson, Alexandra Paul, Robert Forster. *NO*

In Celebration 🦴🦴🦴 **1975 (PG)** Three successful brothers return to the old homestead for their parents' 40th wedding celebration. Intense drama but somewhat claustrophobic. Based on a play by David Storey. **110m/C VHS.** *GB CA* Alan Bates, James Bolam, Brian Cox; ***D:*** Lindsay Anderson. *NO*

In Cold Blood 🦴🦴🦴½ **1967** Truman Capote's supposedly factual novel provided the basis for this hard-hitting docu-drama about two ex-cons who ruthlessly murder a Kansas family in 1959 in order to steal their non-existent stash of money. Blake is riveting as one of the killers. **133m/B VHS, Beta, LV.** Robert (Bobby) Blake, Scott Wilson, John Forsythe; ***D:*** Richard Brooks; ***W:*** Richard Brooks; ***C:*** Conrad Hall; ***M:*** Quincy Jones. National Board of Review Awards '67: 10 Best Films of the Year, Best Director (Brooks); Nominations: Academy Awards '67: Best Adapted Screenplay, Best Cinematography, Best Director (Brooks), Best Original Score. *COL*

In Country 🦴🦴½ **1989 (R)** Based on Bobbie Ann Mason's celebrated novel, the story of a young Kentuckian high schooler (perfectly played by Lloyd) and her search for her father, killed in Vietnam. Willis plays her uncle, a veteran still struggling to accept his own survival, and crippled with memories. Moving scene at the Vietnam Veterans Memorial. **116m/C VHS, Beta, LV, 8mm.** Bruce Willis, Emily Lloyd, Joan Allen, Kevin Anderson, Richard Hamilton, Judith Ivey, Peggy Rea, John Terry, Patricia Richardson, Jim Beaver; ***D:*** Norman Jewison; ***W:*** Frank Pierson, Cynthia Cidre; ***M:*** James Horner. *WAR, MVD*

The In Crowd 🦴🦴 **1988 (PG)** A bright high school student gets involved with a local television dance show circa 1965, and must choose between uncertain fame and an Ivy League college. A fair nostalgic look at the period. Leitch is the son of psychedelic folk singer Donovan. **96m/C VHS, Beta, LV.** Donovan Leitch, Jennifer Runyon, Scott Plank, Joe Pantoliano; ***D:*** Mark Rosenthal; ***W:*** Mark Rosenthal. *ORI*

In Custody 🦴🦴 *Hifazaat* **1994 (PG)** Producer Merchant makes his feature directorial debut with this dreamy tale of small-town teacher Deven (Puri) who's urged by a publishing friend to interview Nur (Kapoor), the greatest living poet in the disappearing Urdu language. The worshipful Deven is dismayed to find his idol a wreck, surrounded by sycophants and a shrewish second wife who's plagiarizing her husband's work, and soon finds himself hopelessly entangled in the writer's life. Unabashedly literary (the poetry recited is by Faiz Ahmed Faiz) with a star cast. Based on the 1987 novel by Anita Desai. Urdu with subtitles. **123m/C VHS.** *IN* Shashi Kapoor, Om Puri, Shabana Azmi, Sushma Seth, Neena Gupta, Ajay Sahni, Tinnu Anand; ***D:*** Ismail Merchant; ***W:*** Anita Desai, Shahrukh Husain; ***C:*** Larry Pizer; ***M:*** Zakir Hussain, Ustad Sultan Khan. *COL*

In Dangerous Company 🦴 **1988 (R)** Beautiful babe balances beaux and battles abound. A brow lowering experience. **92m/C VHS.** Tracy Scoggins, Cliff DeYoung, Chris Mulkey, Henry Darrow, Steven Keats, Richard Portnow; ***D:*** Ruben Preuss; ***W:*** Mitch Brown. *NO*

In Deadly Heat 🦴 **1987** Crime, revenge, murder, and urban warfare are done once again. **98m/C VHS, Beta.** William Dame, Catherine Dee, M.R. Murphy; ***D:*** Don Nardo. *JEF*

In Desert and Wilderness 🦴🦴½ **1973** Two kidnapped children escape and are thrust into the wilds of Africa, where they must survive with wits and courage. Based on a novel by Nobel prize-winning author Henyk Sienkiewicz. In Polish with English subtitles. **144m/C VHS.** *PL* ***D:*** Wladyslaw Slesicki. *FCT*

In for Treatment 🦴🦴🦴 **1982** A terminally ill cancer patient, lost in the bureaucracy of the hospital, fights to rediscover the joy of life. Strong and disturbing story. In Dutch with English subtitles. **92m/C VHS, Beta.** *NL* Helmut Woudenberg, Frank Groothof, Hans Man Int Veld; ***D:*** Eric Van Zuylen, Marja Kok. *NO*

In Gold We Trust 🦴½ **1991** Vincent leads an elite battalion of fighters against a group of rogue American MIAs (!) laying waste to the Vietnemese countryside. **89m/C VHS.** Jan-Michael Vincent, Sam Jones; ***D:*** P. Chalong; ***M:*** Hummie Mann. *AIP*

In Harm's Way 🦴🦴 **1965** Overdone story about two naval officers and their response to the Japanese attack at Pearl Harbor. Even the superb cast members (and there are plenty of them) can't overcome the incredible length and overly intricate plot. **165m/B VHS, Beta, LV.** John Wayne, Kirk Douglas, Tom Tryon, Patricia Neal, Paula Prentiss, Brandon de Wilde, Burgess Meredith, Stanley Holloway, Henry Fonda, Dana Andrews, Franchot Tone, Jill Haworth, George Kennedy, Carroll O'Connor, Patrick O'Neal, Slim Pickens, Bruce Cabot, Larry Hagman, Hugh O'Brian, Jim Mitchum, Barbara Bouchet; ***D:*** Otto Preminger; ***W:*** Wendell Mayes; ***C:*** Loyal Griggs; ***M:*** Jerry Goldsmith. British Academy Awards '65: Best Actress (Neal); Nominations: Academy Awards '65: Best Black and White Cinematography. *PAR*

In Hot Pursuit 🦴½ **1982** Convicted for drug smuggling, two young men stage a daring but not too exciting escape from a southern prison. **90m/C VHS, Beta.** Bob Watson, Don Watson, Debbie Washington. *NO*

The In-Laws 🦴🦴🦴 **1979 (PG)** A wild comedy with Falk, who claims to be a CIA agent, and Arkin, a dentist whose daughter is marrying Falk's son. The fathers foil a South American dictator's counterfeiting scheme in a delightfully convoluted plot. **103m/C VHS, Beta, LV.** Peter Falk, Alan Arkin, Richard Libertini, Nancy Dussault, Penny Peyser, Arlene Golonka, Michael Lembeck, Ed Begley Jr., Rosana De Soto, Art Evans; ***D:*** Arthur Hiller; ***W:*** Andrew Bergman; ***M:*** John Morris. *WAR*

In Like Flint 🦴🦴½ **1967** Sequel to "Our Man Flint" sees our dapper spy confronting an organization of women endeavoring to take over the world. Spy spoofery at its low-level best. **107m/C VHS, Beta, LV.** James Coburn, Lee J. Cobb, Anna Lee, Andrew Duggan, Jean Hale; ***D:*** Gordon Douglas; ***C:*** William H. Daniels; ***M:*** Jerry Goldsmith. *FOX*

In Love and War 🦴🦴½ **1991 (R)** Woods plays Navy pilot Jim Stockdale, whose plane was grounded over hostile territory and who endured nearly eight years of torture as a POW. Meanwhile, wife Sybil is an organizer of POW wives back in the States. Low octane rendering of the US Navy Commander's true story. Aaron earlier directed "The Miracle Worker," and you may recognize Ngor from "The Killing Fields." **96m/C VHS, LV.** James Woods, Jane Alexander, Haing S. Ngor, Concetta Tomei, Richard McKenzie, James Pax; ***D:*** Paul Aaron; ***W:*** Carol Schreder. *VMK*

In Love with an Older Woman 🦴🦴 **1982** Ritter takes fewer pratfalls than usual in this film; after all, it's a romantic comedy. Adapted from "Six Months with an Older Woman," the novel by David Kaufelt. Made for television. **100m/C VHS, Beta.** John Ritter, Karen Carlson, Jamie Rose, Robert Mandan, Jeff Altman, George Murdock; ***D:*** Jack Bender. *FRH*

In Memoriam 🦴🦴½ **1976** Tragic and gripping drama about one man's ability, albeit too late, to cope with his unforgettable past. Based on a story by Adolfo Bioy Casares. In Spanish with English subtitles. **96m/C VHS.** *SP* Geraldine Chaplin, Jose Luis Gomez; ***D:*** Enrique Braso. *FCT, INJ*

In 'n Out 🦴½ **1986** An American loser ventures to Mexico to recover a long-lost inheritance, meeting with mildly comic obstacles along the way. **85m/C VHS, Beta.** Sam Bottoms, Pat Hingle. *VTR, NWV*

In Name Only 🦴🦴½ **1939** Somber drama about a heartless woman who marries for wealth and prestige and holds her husband to a loveless marriage. Based on "Memory of Love" by Bessie Brewer. **102m/B VHS, Beta, LV.** Carole Lombard, Cary Grant, Kay Francis; ***D:*** John Cromwell. *CCB, MLB, TTC*

In Old Caliente 🦴½ **1939** Rogers battles the bad guys in the frontier town of Caliente. **60m/B VHS, Beta.** Roy Rogers, Lynn (Mary Hart) Roberts, George "Gabby" Hayes. *NOS, VCN, DVT*

In Old California 🦴🦴½ **1942** Plucky story of a young Boston pharmacist who searches for success in the California gold rush and runs into the local crime boss. Also available colorized. **88m/B VHS.** John Wayne, Patsy Kelly, Binnie Barnes, Albert Dekker, Charles Halton; ***D:*** William McGann. *REP*

In Old Cheyenne 🦴½ **1941** Bank holdups, cattle rustling, fist fights, and even car crashes mix with some good ol' guitar plunking in this western. **60m/B VHS, Beta.** Roy Rogers, George "Gabby" Hayes. *NOS, CAB, TIM*

In Old Chicago 🦴🦴🦴 **1938** The O'Leary family travels to Chicago to seek their fortune, with mom working as a washerwoman to support her sons. Brothers Power and Ameche become powerbroking rivals and when mom comes to break up a brawl between the two, she neglects to properly restrain the family cow. This leads to the great Chicago fire of 1871, supposedly started when the cow kicks over a latern and sets the barn ablaze. The city burns down in a spectacular 20-minute sequence. Based on the story "We the O'Learys" by Niven Busch. **115m/B VHS.** Tyrone Power, Alice Faye, Don Ameche, Alice Brady, Andy Devine, Brian Donlevy, Phyllis Brooks, Tom Brown, Sidney Blackmer, Gene Reynolds, Berton Churchill, Bobs Watson; ***D:*** Henry King; ***W:*** Lamar Trotti, Sonya Levien. Nominations: Academy Awards '38: Best Picture. *FXV*

In Old Colorado 🦴🦴½ **1941** Ankrum and his cronies try to stir up trouble over water rights, but Boyd and his pals ride to the rescue. **67m/B VHS.** William Boyd, Russell Hayden, Andy Clyde, Margaret Hayes, Morris Ankrum, Sarah Padden, Cliff Nazarro, Stanley Andrews, James Seay, Morgan Wallace; ***D:*** Howard Bretherton. *NOS*

In Old Montana 🦴 **1939** A Cavalry lieutenant tries to settle a cattleman vs. sheep-herding war. **60m/B VHS, Beta.** Fred Scott, Jeanne Carmen, Harry Harvey, John Merton; ***D:*** Raymond K. Johnson. *VDM, GPV*

In Old New Mexico 🦴 **1945** The Cisco Kid and Pancho reveal the murderer of an old woman—a mysterious doctor who was after an inheritance. **60m/B VHS, Beta.** Duncan Renaldo, Martin Garralaga, Gwen Kenyon, Pedro de Cordoba. *NOS, VCI, VYY*

In Old Santa Fe 🦴🦴½ **1934** Cowboy star Maynard's best western, and the first film ever with Autry and Burnette. Maynard is framed for murder and his pals save him. **60m/B VHS, Beta.** Ken Maynard, Gene Autry, Smiley Burnette, Evalyn Knapp, George "Gabby" Hayes, Kenneth Thomson, Wheeler Oakman, George Chesebro; ***D:*** David Howard, Joseph Kane. *NOS, VCN, DVT*

In Person 🦴🦴½ **1935** Spry comedy about a movie star who disguises herself to take a vacation incognito and falls in love with a country doctor who is unaware of her identity. ♫Don't Mention Love To Me; Out of Sight, Out of Mind; Got a New Lease on Life. **87m/B VHS, Beta, LV.** Ginger Rogers, George Brent, Alan Mowbray, Grant Mitchell; ***D:*** William A. Seiter; ***M:*** Oscar Levant. *TTC*

In Praise of Older Women 🦴🦴 **1978** Berenger is just right as a young Hungarian who is corrupted by WWII and a large number of older women. Based on a novel by Stephen Vizinczey. **110m/C VHS, Beta, LV.** *CA* Karen Black, Tom Berenger, Susan Strasberg, Helen Shaver, Alexandra Stewart; ***D:*** George Kaczender. *FOX, SUE*

In Pursuit of Honor 🦴🦴½ **1995 (PG-13)** Based on the true story of five American cavalry soldiers who find themselves being phased out in the 1935 Army. Ordered by General Douglas MacArthur to destroy their horses, they instead try to outrun an elite tank division to get some 400 horses to safety in Canada. Rugged performances and the violence towards the horses is aptly disturbing. Filmed on location in Australia and New Zealand; made for cable TV. **?m/C VHS.** Don Johnson, Craig Sheffer, Gabrielle Anwar, Bob Gunton, Rod Steiger, James B. Sikking, John Dennis Johnston, Robert Coleby; ***D:*** Ken Olin; ***W:*** Dennis Lynton Clark; ***C:*** Stephen Windon; ***M:*** John Debney. *HBO*

In Search of a Golden Sky 🦴🦴 **1984 (PG)** Following their mother's death, a motley group of children move in with their secluded cabin-dwelling uncle, much to the righteous chagrin of the welfare department. **94m/C VHS, Beta.** Charles Napier, George Flower, Cliff Osmond; ***D:*** Jefferson Richard. *FOX*

In Search of Anna *Woof!* **1979** When a convict is released from jail, he hits the road with a flighty model in search of the girlfriend who corresponded with him in prison. There auto be a law. **90m/C VHS, Beta.** *AU* Judy Morris, Richard Moir, Chris Hayward, Bill Hunter; ***D:*** Esben Storm. *AHV*

In Search of the Castaways 🦴🦴🦴 **1962** Stirring adventure tale of a teenage girl and her younger brother searching for their father, a ship's captain lost at sea years earlier. Powerful special effects and strong cast make this a winning Disney effort. Based on a story by Jules Verne. **98m/C VHS, Beta.** *GB* Hayley Mills, Maurice Chevalier, George Sanders, Wilfrid Hyde-White, Michael Anderson Jr.; ***D:*** Robert Stevenson. *DIS*

In Self Defense 🦴½ **1993 (PG)** Purl is supposed to be protected from the killer she testified against but it doesn't quite work out that way. **94m/C VHS.** Linda Purl, Yaphet Kotto, Billy Drago; ***D:*** Bruce Seth Green; ***M:*** Patrick Gleeson. *TTC*

In Society 🦴🦴½ **1944** The duo play dimwitted plumbers who are mistakenly invited to a high society party, where they promptly create catastrophe. **84m/B VHS.** Bud Abbott, Lou Costello, Marion Hutton, Kirby Grant, Ann Gillis, Arthur Treacher, Thomas Gomez, Steve Geray, Margaret Irving, Thurston Hall; ***Cameos:*** Sid Fields; ***D:*** Jean Yarbrough; ***W:*** Sid Fields, Hal Fimberg, Edmund Hartmann, John Grant. *MCA, FCT*

In the Aftermath: Angels Never Sleep 🦴½ **1987** Mix of animation and live-action in this post-nuclear wasteland tale never quite works. **85m/C VHS, Beta.** Tony Markes, Rainbow Dolan; ***D:*** Carl Colpaert. *VTR, NWV*

In the Army Now 🦴 **1994 (PG)** Pauly dude gets his head shaved, man. Service comedy about a slacker who joins the Army hoping to cash in on military benefits but who winds up in combat instead. Shore drops the Valley Guy shtick and ventures into the land of action when he gets sent on a mission to the Sahara. Strictly for Shore's fans. **92m/C VHS, LV.** Pauly Shore, Esai Morales, Lori Petty, David Alan Grier, Ernie Hudson, Andy Dick; ***D:*** Dan Petrie Jr.; ***W:*** Dan Petrie Jr., Ken Kaufman, Fax Bahr, Stu Krieger, Adam Small; ***M:*** Robert Folk. *HPH*

In the Cold of the Night 🦴 **1989 (R)** Another drowsy entry into the "to sleep perchance to have a nightmare genre." A photographer with a vivid imagination dreams he murders a woman he doesn't know, and when said dream girl rides into his life on the back of a Harley, Mr. Foto's faced with an etiquette quandary: haven't they met before? Cast includes Hedren (Hitchcock's Marnie and Melanie Griffith's mother). **112m/C VHS, LV.** Jeff Lester, Adrienne Sachs, Shannon Tweed, David Soul, John Beck, Tippi Hedren, Marc Singer; ***D:*** Nico Mastorakis. *REP*

In the Custody of Strangers 🦴🦴🦴 **1982** A teenager's parents refuse to help when he is arrested for being drunk and he ends up spending the night in jail. Realistic handling of a serious subject. Sheen and Estevez play the father and son, mimicking their real-life relationship. Made for television. **100m/C VHS.** Martin Sheen, Jane Alexander, Emilio Estevez, Kenneth McMillan, Ed Lauter, Matt Clark, John Hancock; ***D:*** Robert Greenwald. *MOV*

In the Days of the Thundering Herd & the Law & the Outlaw **1914** In the first feature, a pony express rider sacrifices his job to accompany his sweetheart on a westward trek to meet her father. In the second show, a fugitive falls in love with a rancher's daughter and risks recognition. **76m/B VHS, Beta.** Tom Mix, Myrtle Stedman; ***D:*** Colin Campbell. *CCB, GPV*

In the Deep Woods 🦴🦴 **1991** Children's author Joanna Warren (Arquette) gets too close to mayhem when a childhood friend is murdered by the Deep Woods Killer. A mysterious private detective (Perkins) is on the killer's trail but when Joanna comes into the picture will she be a suspect or a victim? Based on the book by Nicholas Conde. **?m/C VHS.** Rosanna Arquette, Anthony Perkins, Will Patton, D.W. Moffett, Christopher Rydell, Harold Sylvester, Kimberly Beck; ***D:*** Charles Correll; ***W:*** Robert Nathan, Robert Rosenbaum; ***C:*** James Glennon. *AEL*

In the Good Old Summertime 🦴🦴🦴 **1949** This pleasant musical version of "The Shop Around the Corner" tells the story of two bickering co-workers who are also anonymous lovelorn pen pals. Minnelli made her second screen appearance at 18 months in the final scene. ♫I Don't Care; Meet Me Tonight In Dreamland; Play That Barbershop Chord; In the Good Old Summertime; Put Your Arms Around Me Honey; Wait Till the Sun Shines Nellie; Chicago; Merry Christmas. **104m/C VHS, Beta, LV.** Judy Garland, Van Johnson, S.Z. Sakall, Buster Keaton, Spring Byington, Liza Minnelli, Clinton Sundberg; ***D:*** Robert Z. Leonard; ***C:*** Harry Stradling. *MGM*

In the Heat of Passion 🦴½ **1991 (R)** A low-budget ripoff of "Body Heat" and "Fatal Attraction" starring Kirkland as a married woman who involves a much younger man in a very steamy affair that leads to murder. This movie wants to be a thriller, but is little more than a soft-core sex flick. Also available in an unrated version that contains explicit footage. **84m/C VHS, LV.** Sally Kirkland, Nick Corri, Jack Carter, Michael Greene; ***D:*** Rodman Flender; ***W:*** Rodman Flender. *COL*

In the Heat of Passion 2: Unfaithful 🦴½ **1994 (R)** Philip Donovan (Bostwick) is having an affair with his stepdaughter Casey (Hill) and the duo murder hapless wife/mother (Down) to get her money. But it seems someone else knows about their crime. **88m/C VHS, LV.** Barry Bostwick, Teresa Hill, Lesley-Anne Down, Michael Gross; ***D:*** Catherine Cyran. *NHO*

In the Heat of the Night 🦴🦴🦴½ **1967** A wealthy industrialist in a small Mississippi town is murdered. A black homicide expert is asked to help solve the murder, despite resentment on the part of the town's chief of police. Powerful script with underlying theme of racial prejudice is served well by taut direction and powerhouse performances. Poitier's memorable character Virgil Tibbs appeared in two more pictures, "They Call Me Mister Tibbs" and "The Organization." **109m/C VHS, Beta, LV.** Sidney Poitier, Rod Steiger, Warren Oates, Lee Grant; ***D:*** Norman Jewison; ***W:*** Stirling Silliphant; ***C:*** Haskell Wexler; ***M:*** Quincy Jones. Academy Awards '67: Best Actor (Steiger), Best Film Editing, Best Picture, Best Sound; British Academy Awards '67: Best Actor (Steiger); Edgar Allan Poe Awards '67: Best Screenplay; Golden Globe Awards '68: Best Actor—Drama (Steiger), Best Film—Drama, Best Screenplay; New York Film Critics Awards '67: Best Actor (Steiger), Best Director (Nichols), Best Film; National Society of Film Critics Awards '67: Best Actor (Steiger), Best Cinematography; Nominations: Academy Awards '67: Best Director (Jewison). *MGM, FOX, BTV*

In the King of Prussia 🦴½ **1983** Recreation of the trial of the "Plowshares Eight" radicals who were jailed for sabotaging two nuclear missiles at an electric plant in Pennsylvania. **92m/C VHS, Beta.** Martin Sheen, Rev. Daniel Berrigan. *MPI, BUL*

In the Kingdom of the Blind the Man with One Eye is King ☌☌ **1994 (R)** The title doesn't seem to mean anything and you may feel the same way about this standard crime drama, despite a strong cast. Mobster Tony (Petersen) gets police assistance from detective Al (Vallelonga) in discovering who murdered a mob boss' brother. **99m/C VHS.** Nick Vallelonga, William L. Petersen, Michael Biehn, Paul Winfield, James Quarter; ***D:*** Nick Vallelonga; ***W:*** Nick Vallelonga. *AVI*

In the Land of the Owl Turds **1987** The story of a decidely eccentric young man who drives a dada art gallery on wheels while searching for love. Blank's senior thesis film. **30m/C VHS, Beta.** ***D:*** Harrod Blank. *FFM*

In the Line of Duty: Ambush in Waco ☌☌½ **1993 (R)** Insta-television movie made by NBC even before the fire which engulfed the Texas compound and ended the standoff between self-proclaimed "prophet" David Koresh and the federal government. Daly does well as the manipulative, charasmatic Branch Davidian cult leader whose stockpiling of illegal weapons lead to an investigation by the Bureau of Alcohohol, Tobacco and Firearms and a botched raid which caused the ultimately fatal siege. Filmed on location outside Tulsa, Oklahoma. **93m/C VHS.** Timothy Daly, Dan Lauria, William O'Leary; ***D:*** Dick Lowry; ***W:*** Phil Penningroth. *REP*

In the Line of Fire ☌☌☌½ **1993 (R)** Aging Secret Service agent meets his match in a spooky caller who threatens his honor and the president in an exciting, fast paced cat and mouse game. Terrific performance by Eastwood includes lots of dry humor and an unscripted emotional moment, but is nearly overshadowed by Malkovich's menacing bad guy. Eerie special effects add to the mood. The Secret Service cooperated and most scenes are believable, with a few Hollywood exceptions; the end result clearly pays homage to the agents who protect our presidents. Intriguing trailer showed the number "6" in "1963" slowly turning to "9" to become "1993." The seventh highest grossing movie of 1993. **128m/C VHS, LV, 8mm.** Clint Eastwood, John Malkovich, Rene Russo, Dylan McDermott, Gary Cole, Fred Dalton Thompson, John Mahoney, Gregory Alan Williams; ***D:*** Wolfgang Petersen; ***W:*** Jeff Maguire; ***C:*** John Bailey; ***M:*** Ennio Morricone. Nominations: Academy Awards '93: Best Film Editing, Best Original Screenplay, Best Supporting Actor (Malkovich); Golden Globe Awards '94: Best Supporting Actor (Malkovich); MTV Movie Awards '94: Best Villain (Malkovich). *COL, BTV*

In the Money ☌ **1934** Veteran vaudevillian "Skeets" Gallagher introduces a muddled mass of acts, including a poor imitator of boxing great Gene Tunney, a mad scientist who talks to rabbits and writes rubber checks, and a limp-wristed lisper. **66m/B VHS.** Lois Wilson, Warren Hymer, Arthur Hoyt, Frank "Junior" Coghlan, Louise Beavers; ***D:*** Frank Strayer. *NOS*

In the Mood ☌☌½ **1987 (PG-13)** Based on fact, this is the story of teenager Sonny Wisecarver, nicknamed "The Woo Woo Kid," who in 1944, seduced two older women and eventually landed in jail after marrying one of them. Look for Wisecarver in a cameo role as a mailman in the film. **98m/C VHS, Beta, LV.** Patrick Dempsey, Beverly D'Angelo, Talia Balsam, Michael Constantine, Betty Jinnette, Kathleen Freeman, Peter Hobbs, Edith Fellows; ***Cameos:*** Ellsworth Wisecarver; ***D:*** Phil Alden Robinson; ***W:*** Phil Alden Robinson; ***M:*** Ralph Burns. *WAR, ORI, BAR*

In the Mouth of Madness ☌☌ **1995 (R)** Standard horror flick pays homage to or pokes fun at Stephen King (you decide) with story of successful horror novelist whose fans become a bit too engrossed in his stories—seems his readers tend to slip into dementia and carry out the grisly acts depicted within the pages. Neill plays an insurance investigator who must track down the missing author while combating the psychotic, axe-wielding residents of the seemingly quiet east coast hamlet where the author resides. Worth a look for the above average special effects and makeup provided by Industrial Light and Magic (ILM). **95m/C VHS, LV.** Sam Neill, Juergen Prochnow, Julie Carmen, Charlton Heston, David Warner, John Glover, Bernie Casey, Peter Jason, Francis Bay; ***D:*** John Carpenter; ***W:*** Michael De Luca; ***M:*** John Carpenter, Jim Lang. *TTC, NLC*

In the Name of the Father ☌☌☌½ **1993 (R)** Compelling true story of Gerry Conlon and the Guildford Four, illegally imprisoned in 1974 by British officials after a tragic IRA bombing near London. The British judicial system receives a black eye, but so does the horror and cruelty of IRA terrorism. Politics and family life in a prison cell share the focus, as Sheridan captures superior performances from Day-Lewis and Postlethwaite (beware the thick Belfast brogue). Thompson was accused of pro-IRA sympathies in the British press for her role as the lawyer who believed in Conlon's innocence. Adapted from "Proved Innocent," Conlon's prison memoirs; reunites Sheridan and Day-Lewis after "My Left Foot." Includes original songs by U2's Bono, with a haunting theme sung by Sinead O'Connor. **133m/C VHS, LV.** *GB IR* Daniel Day-Lewis, Pete Postlethwaite, Emma Thompson, John Lynch, Corin Redgrave, Beatie Edney, John Benfield, Paterson Joseph, Marie Jones, Gerard McSorley, Frank Harper, Mark Sheppard, Don Baker, Britta Smith, Aidan Grennell, Daniel Massey, Bosco Hogan; ***D:*** Jim Sheridan; ***W:*** Jim Sheridan, Terry George; ***M:*** Trevor Jones, Bono, Sinead O'Connor. Berlin International Film Festival '94: Golden Berlin Bear; Nominations: Academy Awards '93: Best Actor (Day-Lewis), Best Adapted Screenplay, Best Director (Sheridan), Best Film Editing, Best Picture, Best Supporting Actor (Postlethwaite), Best Supporting Actress (Thompson); Golden Globe Awards '94: Best Actor—Drama (Day-Lewis), Best Film—Drama, Best Song ("(You Made Me the) Thief of Your Heart"), Best Supporting Actress (Thompson). *MCA*

In the Name of the Pope-King ☌☌☌ **1985** An acclaimed historical epic about the politics and warfare raging around the 1867 Italian wars that made the Pope the sole ruler in Rome. In Italian with English subtitles. **115m/C VHS, Beta.** Nino Manfredi, Danilo Mattei, Carmen Scarpitta, Giovannella Grifea, Carlo Bagno; ***D:*** Luigi Magni. *WBF, TPV, FCT*

In the Navy ☌☌½ *Abbott and Costello in the Navy* **1941** Abbott and Costello join the Navy in one of four military-service comedies they cranked out in 1941 alone. The token narrative involves about a singing star (Powell) in uniform to escape his female fans, but that's just an excuse for classic A & C routines. With the Andrews Sisters. ♫Starlight, Starbright; You're Off To See The World; Hula Ba Lua; Gimme Some Skin; A Sailor's Life For Me; We're In The Navy; Anchors Aweigh (instrumental); You're A Lucky Fellow, Mr. Smith (instrumental). **85m/B VHS, LV.** Lou Costello, Bud Abbott, Dick Powell, The Andrews Sisters; ***D:*** Arthur Lubin; ***C:*** Joseph Valentine. *MCA*

In the Realm of Passion ☌☌ *Empire of Passion* **1980 (R)** A wife and her lover murder her husband and dump the body in an abandoned well. Guilt over their actions drive the lovers to return to the scene where they are greeted by the vengeful ghost of the betrayed husband—or is it only their consciences torturing them? In Japanese with English subtitles. **108m/C VHS.** Kazuko Yoshiyuki, Takahiro Tamura, Tatsuya Fuji; ***D:*** Nagisa Oshima. *FXL, INJ*

In the Realm of the Senses ☌☌☌ **1976 (NC-17)** Taboo-breaking story of a woman and man who turn their backs on the militaristic rule of Japan in the mid-1930s by plunging into an erotic and sensual world all their own. Striking, graphic work that was seized by U.S. customs when it first entered the country. Violent with explicit sex, and considered by some critics as pretentious, while others call it Oshima's masterpiece. In Japanese with English subtitles. **105m/C VHS.** *JP FR* Tatsuya Fuji, Eiko Matsuda, Aio Nakajima, Meika Seri; ***D:*** Nagisa Oshima. *FXL, CVC*

In the Region of Ice ☌☌☌ **1976** Award-winning short reveals the complexities of the relationship between a nun and a disturbed student. **38m/B VHS, Beta.** Fionnula Flanagan, Peter Lempert; ***D:*** Peter Werner. *BFA*

In the Secret State ☌☌ **19??** Inspector Strange finds himself faced with the apparent suicide of a colleague on the day of his own retirement from the force. His private investigation into the case finds him mired in murder and espionage. **107m/C VHS.** Frank Finlay, Matthew Marsh, Thorley Walters. *MOV*

In the Shadow of Kilimanjaro *Woof!* **1986 (R)** A pack of hungry baboons attacks innocent people in the wilderness of Kenya. Based on a true story but the characters are contrived and just plain stupid at times. Quite gory as well. Filmed on location in Kenya. **105m/C VHS, Beta.** *GB* John Rhys-Davies, Timothy Bottoms, Michele Carey, Irene Miracle, Calvin Jung, Donald Blakely; ***D:*** Raju Patel. *LIV*

In the Soup ☌☌½ **1992 (R)** Adolpho is a naive New York filmmaker barely scraping by. He decides to sell his script in a classified ad which is answered by the fast-talking Joe, a would-be film producer who's true profession is as a con artist. The two then try numerous (and humorous) ways to raise the money to begin filming. Also available colorized. **93m/B VHS, LV.** Steve Buscemi, Seymour Cassel, Jennifer Beals, Will Patton, Pat Moya, Sully Boyar, Stanley Tucci, Rockets Redglare, Elizabeth Bracco, Ruth Maleczech; ***Cameos:*** Jim Jarmusch, Carol Kane; ***D:*** Alexandre Rockwell; ***W:*** Tim Kissell, Alexandre Rockwell; ***C:*** Phil Parmet; ***M:*** Mader. Sundance Film Festival '92: Grand Jury Prize. *ACA*

In the Spirit ☌☌½ **1990 (R)** New Age couple move from Beverly Hills to New York, where they meet an air-headed mystic and are forced to hide from a murderer. Falk gives solid performance in sometimes rocky production. Berlin is the real-life daughter of May. **94m/C VHS, Beta.** Elaine May, Marlo Thomas, Jeannie Berlin, Peter Falk, Melanie Griffith, Olympia Dukakis, Chad Burton, Thurn Hoffman, Michael Emil, Christopher Durang, Laurie Jones; ***D:*** Sandra Seacat; ***W:*** Jeannie Berlin, Laurie Jones; ***M:*** Patrick Williams. *ACA*

In the Steps of a Dead Man ☌½ **1974** A family grieving for a fallen soldier is earmarked for evil by a young man who bears an uncanny resemblance to the dead man. A friend of the family has her suspicions and must find out the truth before something terrible happens. **71m/C VHS, Beta.** Skye Aubrey, John Nolan. *NO*

In the White City ☌☌☌ *Dans la Ville Blanche* **1983** A sailor jumps ship in Lisbon and uses a movie camera to record himself and his search through the twisted streets and alleys of the city for something or someone to connect to. In French, Portuguese, and German with English subtitles. **108m/C VHS.** *PT SI* Bruno Ganz, Teresa Madruga; ***D:*** Alain Tanner. *NYF, INJ*

In This House of Brede ☌☌☌ **1975** A sophisticated London widow turns her back on her worldly life to become a cloistered Benedictine nun. Rigg is outstanding as the woman struggling to deal with the discipline of faith. Made for television and based on the novel by Rumer Godden. **105m/C VHS, Beta.** Diana Rigg; ***D:*** George Schaefer. *LCA, OM*

In This Our Life ☌☌½ **1942** Histrionic melodrama handled effectively by Huston about a nutsy woman who steals her sister's husband, rejects him, manipulates her whole family and eventually leads herself to ruin. Vintage star vehicle for Davis, who chews scenery and fellow actors alike. Adapted by Howard Koch from the Ellen Glasgon novel. **101m/B VHS, Beta.** Bette Davis, Olivia de Havilland, Charles Coburn, Frank Craven, George Brent, Dennis (Stanley Morner) Morgan, Billie Burke, Hattie McDaniel, Lee Patrick, Walter Huston, Ernest Anderson; ***D:*** John Huston; ***M:*** Max Steiner. *MGM*

In Too Deep ☌½ **1990 (R)** A rock star and a beautiful woman are physically drawn to one another in spite of the fact that any contact between them could have disasterous results. **106m/C VHS, Beta.** Hugo Race, Santha Press, Rebekah Elmaloglou, John Flaus, Dominic Sweeney; ***D:*** Colin South. *PAR*

In Trouble *Woof!* **1967** Hard-to-follow and frequently aimless story of a pregnant girl who invents a fake rape story that her dull-witted brothers take seriously, embarking on a cross-country search for the culprit. **82m/C VHS, Beta.** *CA* Julie LaChapelle, Katherine Mousseau, Daniel Pilon; ***D:*** Gilles Carle. *NWV*

In Which We Serve 🦴🦴🦴½ **1943** Much stiff upper-lipping in this classic that captures the spirit of the British Navy during WWII. The sinking of the destroyer HMS Torrin during the Battle of Crete is told via flashbacks, with an emphasis on realism that was unusual in wartime flag-wavers. Features the film debuts of Johnson and Attenborough, and the first Lean directorial effort. Coward received a special Oscar for his "outstanding production achievement," having scripted, scored, codirected and costarred. **114m/B VHS, Beta.** *GB* Noel Coward, John Mills, Bernard Miles, Celia Johnson, Kay Walsh, James Donald, Richard Attenborough; ***D:*** Noel Coward, David Lean; ***W:*** Noel Coward; ***M:*** Noel Coward. National Board of Review Awards '42: 10 Best Films of the Year; New York Film Critics Awards '42: Best Film; Nominations: Academy Awards '43: Best Original Screenplay, Best Picture. *NOS, SUE*

In Your Face 🦴½ *Abar, the First Black Superman* **1977 (R)** Little known blaxploitation film about a black family harrassed in a white suburb. A black motorcycle gang comes to their rescue. **90m/C VHS.** J. Walter Smith, Tobar Mayo, Roxie Young, Tina James; ***D:*** Frank Packard. *XVC, HHE*

The Incident 🦴🦴½ **1967** A gritty, controversial (at-the-time) drama about two abusive thugs who take over a New York subway car late at night, humiliating and terrorizing each passenger in turn. Film debut for Sheen and Musante as the thugs. **99m/B VHS, Beta, LV.** Martin Sheen, Tony Musante, Beau Bridges, Ruby Dee, Jack Gilford, Thelma Ritter, Brock Peters, Ed McMahon, Gary Merrill, Donna Mills, Jan Sterling, Mike Kellin; ***D:*** Larry Peerce; ***M:*** Charles Fox. *FOX*

The Incident 🦴🦴🦴 **1989** Political thriller set during WWII in Lincoln Bluff, Colorado. Matthau is excellent in his TV debut as a small-town lawyer who must defend a German prisoner of war accused of murder at nearby Camp Bremen. An all-star cast lends powerful performances to this riveting made for TV drama. **95m/C VHS.** Walter Matthau, Susan Blakely, Harry (Henry) Morgan, Robert Carradine, Barnard Hughes, Peter Firth, William Schallert; ***D:*** Joseph Sargent. *CAF*

Incident at Channel Q 🦴½ **1986** A heavy-metal rock musical about a suburban neighborhood declaring war on a chain-and-leather deejay. **85m/C VHS, Beta, LV.** Al Corley. *MVD, BMG*

Incident at Deception Ridge 🦴🦴½ **1994 (R)** After five years in prison, Jack Bolder (O'Keefe) is finally a free man, and headed for Seattle by bus. Unfortunately, also aboard is weasely bank manager Jack Davis (Begley, Jr.) who's bolted with the ransom money for his kidnapped wife, Helen (Purl). Now Helen is left at the mercy of her kidnappers, who've discovered where their money is and decide to go after it—no matter who gets in their way. Filmed in Vancouver, British Columbia. Made for cable. **94m/C VHS, LV.** Michael O'Keefe, Ed Begley Jr., Linda Purl, Miguel Ferrer, Colleen Flynn, Michelle Johnson, Ian Tracey; ***D:*** John McPherson, John McPherson; ***W:*** Ken Hixon, Randy Kornfield; ***C:*** David Geddes. *MCA*

Incident at Map-Grid 36-80 🦴🦴 **1983** A Soviet-made combination of espionage and sea-battle. Gripping and fascinating look at the U.S. from the pre-Glasnost era. **85m/C VHS.** *RU KIV, TPV*

Incident at Oglala: The Leonard Peltier Story 🦴🦴🦴 **1992 (PG)** Offers a detailed account of the violent events leading to the murder of two FBI agents in Oglala, South Dakota in 1975. American Indian activist Leonard Peltier was convicted of the murders and is presently serving two consecutive life sentences, but he's cited as a political prisoner by Amnesty International. The documentary examines the highly controversial trial and the tensions between the government and the Oglala Nation stemming back to the Indian occupation of Wounded Knee in 1973. Director Apted is sympathetic to Peltier and offers reasons why he should be allowed a retrial; he examined similar incidents in his film "Thunderheart." **90m/C VHS.** ***D:*** Michael Apted; ***M:*** John Trudell, Jackson Browne. *LIV, FCT*

An Inconvenient Woman 🦴🦴 **1991** When an older married man has an affair with a young seductress, there's suicide, murder, a nasty gossip columnist, a reporter, a knowing society wife, and a lot of cover-ups among the rich and famous. From the novel by Dominick Dunne and based on the Alfred Bloomingdale scandal. Originally a made for television mini-series. **126m/C VHS, Beta.** Rebecca DeMornay, Jason Robards Jr., Jill Eikenberry, Peter Gallagher, Roddy McDowall, Chad Lowe. *ABC, PSM*

The Incredible Hulk 🦴🦴½ **1977** Bixby is a scientist who achieves superhuman strength after he is exposed to a massive dose of gamma rays. But his personal life suffers, as does his wardrobe. Ferrigno is the Hulkster. The pilot for the television series is based on the Marvel Comics character. **94m/C VHS, Beta, LV.** Bill Bixby, Susan Sullivan, Lou Ferrigno, Jack Colvin; ***D:*** Kenneth Johnson. *MCA*

The Incredible Hulk Returns 🦴½ **1988** The beefy green mutant is back and this time he wages war against a Viking named Thor. Very little substance in this made for television flick, so be prepared to park your brain at the door. Followed by "The Trial of the Incredible Hulk." **100m/C VHS, LV.** Bill Bixby, Lou Ferrigno, Jack Colvin, Lee Purcell, Charles Napier, Steve Levitt; ***D:*** Nick Corea. *VTR, NWV*

The Incredible Journey 🦴🦴½ **1963** A labrador retriever, bull terrier and Siamese cat mistake their caretaker's intentions when he leaves for a hunting trip, believing he will never return. The three set out on a 250 mile adventure-filled trek across Canada's rugged terrain. Entertaining family adventure from Disney taken from Sheila Burnford's book. **80m/C VHS, Beta, LV.** ***D:*** Fletcher Markle. *DIS*

The Incredible Journey of Dr. Meg Laurel 🦴🦴🦴 **1979** A young doctor returns to her roots to bring modern medicine to the Appalachian mountain people during the 1930's. Made for television featuring Wagner in a strong performance. **143m/C VHS, Beta.** Lindsay Wagner, Jane Wyman, Dorothy McGuire, James Woods, Gary Lockwood; ***D:*** Guy Green. *COL*

Incredible Master Beggars 🦴 **1982 (R)** Against all odds, the Beggars challenge the Great Iron Master, using "Tam Leg" tactics versus the "Iron Cloth" fighting style. **88m/C VHS, Beta.** Tan Tao Liang, Ku Feng, Han Kuo Tsai, Li Tang Ming, Li Hai Sheng, Lui I. Fan, Pan Yao Kun. *GEM*

Incredible Melting Man *Woof!* **1977 (R)** Two transformations change an astronaut's life after his return to earth. First, his skin starts to melt, then he displays cannibalistic tendencies. Hard to swallow. Special effects by Rick Baker. Look for director Jonathan Demme in a bit part. **85m/C VHS, Beta.** Alex Rebar, Burr de Benning, Cheryl "Rainbeaux" Smith; ***D:*** William Sachs. *LIV, VES*

The Incredible Mr. Limpet 🦴🦴 **1964** Limp comedy about a nebbish bookkeeper who's transformed into a fish, fulfilling his aquatic dreams. Eventually he falls in love with another fish, and helps the U.S. Navy find Nazi subs during WWII. Partially animated, beloved by some, particularly those under the age of seven. Based on Theodore Pratt's novel. **99m/C VHS, Beta, LV.** Don Knotts, Jack Weston, Carole Cook, Andrew Duggan, Larry Keating, Elizabeth McRae; ***D:*** Arthur Lubin; ***W:*** Jameson Brewer. *WAR, WTA*

The Incredible Petrified World *Woof!* **1958** Divers are trapped in an underwater cave when volcanic eruptions begin. Suffocating nonsense. **78m/B VHS.** John Carradine, Allen Windsor, Phyllis Coates, Lloyd Nelson, George Skaff; ***D:*** Jerry Warren. *NOS, SNC*

The Incredible Rocky Mountain Race 🦴🦴 **1977** The townspeople of St. Joseph, fed up with Mark Twain's destructive feud with a neighbor, devise a shrewd scheme to rid the town of the troublemakers by sending them on a road race through the West. Made for television comedy starring the F-Troop. **97m/C VHS, Beta.** Christopher Connelly, Forrest Tucker, Larry Storch, Mike Mazurki; ***D:*** James L. Conway. *VTR*

The Incredible Sarah 🦴🦴 **1976 (PG)** A limp adapted stage biography from "Reader's Digest" of the great actress Sarah Bernhardt. Jackson chews scenery to no avail. **105m/C VHS, Beta, LV.** Glenda Jackson, Daniel Massey, Yvonne Mitchell, Douglas Wilmer; ***D:*** Richard Fleischer; ***M:*** Elmer Bernstein. Nominations: Academy Awards '76: Best Art Direction/Set Decoration, Best Costume Design. *IME*

The Incredible Shrinking Man 🦴🦴🦴½ **1957** Adapted by Richard Matheson from his own novel, the sci-fi classic is a philosophical thriller about a man who is doused with radioactive mist and begins to slowly shrink. His new size means that everyday objects take on sinister meaning and he must fight for his life in an increasingly hostile, absurd environment. A surreal, suspenseful allegory with impressive special effects. Endowed with the tension usually reserved for Hitchcock films. **81m/B VHS, Beta, LV.** Grant Williams, Randy Stuart, April Kent, Paul Langton, Raymond Bailey; ***D:*** Jack Arnold; ***W:*** Richard Matheson. *MCA, MLB*

The Incredible Shrinking Woman 🦴🦴½ **1981 (PG)** "...Shrinking Man" spoof and inoffensive social satire finds household cleaners producing some strange side effects on model homemaker Tomlin, slowly shrinking her to doll-house size. She then encounters everyday happenings as big tasks and not so menial. Her advertising exec husband has a hand in the down-sizing. Sight gags abound but the cuteness wears thin by the end. **89m/C VHS, Beta, LV.** Lily Tomlin, Charles Grodin, Ned Beatty, Henry Gibson; ***D:*** Joel Schumacher; ***W:*** Jane Wagner. *MCA*

The Incredible Two-Headed Transplant *Woof!* **1971 (PG)** Mad scientist Dern has a criminal head transplanted on to the shoulder of big John Bloom and the critter runs amuck. Low-budget special effects guaranteed to give you a headache or two. Watch for onetime Pat "Marilyn Munster" Priest in a bikini. **88m/C VHS.** Bruce Dern, Pat Priest, Casey Kasem, Albert Cole, John Bloom, Berry Kroeger; ***D:*** Anthony M. Lanza; ***M:*** John Barber. *NO*

Incredibly Strange Creatures Who Stopped Living and Became Mixed-Up Zombies *Woof! The Teenage Psycho Meets Bloody Mary; The Incredibly Strange Creatures* **1963** The infamous, super-cheap horror spoof that established Steckler (for whom Cash Flagg is a pseudonym), about a carny side show riddled with ghouls and bad rock bands. Assistant cinematographers include the young Laszlo Kovacs and Vilmos Zsigmond. A must-see for connoisseurs of cult and camp. **90m/C VHS, Beta.** Cash Flagg, Carolyn Brandt, Brett O'Hara, Atlas King, Sharon Walsh; ***D:*** Ray Dennis Steckler. *NO*

The Incredibly True Adventure of Two Girls in Love 🦴🦴½ **1995 (R)** Gentle low-budget romantic comedy about first love between two high school girls. Tomboyish working-class Randy (Holloman) lives with her lesbian aunt and works part-time at the local gas station where she spots the rich and beautiful Evie (Parker), one of the popular girls in school. Some sparks fly but Evie's confused, though she's willing to be wooed and, later, defend her new relationship. The issue of race (Randy's white, Evie's black) is only briefly alluded to—more is made of the differences between the girls' social classes and their vulnerability. Directorial debut for Maggenti. **95m/C VHS.** Laurel Holloman, Nicole Parker, Kate Stafford, Stephanie Berry; ***D:*** Maria Maggenti; ***W:*** Maria Maggenti. *NLC*

Incubus *Woof!* **1982 (R)** A doctor and his teenaged daughter settle in a quiet New England community, only to encounter the incubus, a terrifying, supernatural demon who enjoys sex murders. Offensive trash. **90m/C VHS, Beta, LV.** *CA* John Cassavetes, Kerrie Keane, Helen Hughes, Erin Flannery, John Ireland; ***D:*** John Hough; ***C:*** Conrad Hall. *VES*

Indecency 🦴🦴 **1992 (PG-13)** Ellie (Beals) is still recovering from a mental breakdown when she goes to work for Marie (Clarkson) at her ad agency. There Ellie must deal with manipulative associate Nia

(Davis) and Marie's charming, estranged husband Mick (Remar), who draws the fragile Ellie into an affair. Then Marie commits suicide—or maybe it was murder. **88m/C VHS, LV.** Jennifer Beals, James Remar, Sammi Davis, Barbara Williams, Christopher John Fields, Ray McKinnon; ***D:*** Marisa Silver; ***W:*** Amy Holden Jones, Holly Goldberg Sloan, Alan Ormsby. *MCA*

Indecent Behavior ﾜﾜ **1993 (R)** Tweed is a sex therapist who's accused of murder when one of her clients overdose's on the latest designer drug. Hudson, who plays the genre's hard-boiled cop figure, gets very personally involved investigating the allegations, which really upsets Tweed's hubby, Vincent. Also available in an unrated version. **93m/C VHS.** Shannon Tweed, Gary Hudson, Jan-Michael Vincent, Michelle Moffett, Lawrence-Hilton Jacobs, Penny Peyser; ***D:*** Lawrence Lanoff. *AVE*

Indecent Behavior 2 ﾜ½ **1994 (R)** Sex therapist Rebecca is targeted for blackmail as she finds out all sorts of unhealthy things about her patients. Meanwhile, she's practicing her technique with a fellow therapist. Also available unrated. **96m/C VHS.** Shannon Tweed, James Brolin, Chad McQueen, Elizabeth Sandifer, Craig Stepp, Rochelle Swanson; ***D:*** Carlo Gustaff. *AVE*

Indecent Behavior 3 ﾜ **1995 (R)** Sex therapist becomes the obsessed object of desire for a decidedly deadly client. Also available unrated. **90m/C VHS.** Shannon Tweed, Sam Hennings, Colleen Coffey, Doug Jeffrey, Beau Billingslea, Laura Rogers; ***D:*** Kelley Cauthen; ***W:*** Hel Styverson. *AVE*

An Indecent Obsession ﾜﾜ½ **1985** Colleen McCullough's bestseller about WWII Australian soldiers recuperating in a field hospital mental ward. Hughes plays the nurse everyone's in love with. **100m/C VHS, Beta.** *AU* Wendy Hughes, Gary Sweet, Richard Moir, Jonathan Hyde, Bill Hunter, Bruno Lawrence; ***D:*** Lex Marinos; ***W:*** Denise Morgan. *NO*

Indecent Proposal ﾜﾜ½ **1993 (R)** High-gloss movie that had couples everywhere discussing the big question: Would you let your wife sleep with a billionaire in exchange for a million bucks? Probably, if all were as goodlooking as the weathered, yet ever gorgeous Redford. Moore and Harrelson are the financially down on their luck, but happy, couple who venture to Vegas on a last-ditch gambling effort. Surreally slick direction from Lyne, but an ultimately empty film that explores the values of marriage in a terribly angst-ridden fashion. Based on the novel by Jack Engelhard. Proof that average movies can make a killing at the box office, landing in sixth place for 1993. **119m/C VHS, Beta, CD-I.** Robert Redford, Demi Moore, Woody Harrelson, Seymour Cassel, Oliver Platt, Billy Bob Thornton, Rip Taylor, Billy Connolly, Joel Brooks; ***Cameos:*** Sheena Easton, Herbie Hancock; ***D:*** Adrian Lyne; ***W:*** Amy Holden Jones; ***M:*** John Barry. MTV Movie Awards '94: Best Kiss (Demi Moore/Woody Harrelson); Golden Raspberry Awards '93: Worst Picture, Worst Supporting Actor (Harrelson), Worst Screenplay; Nominations: MTV Movie Awards '94: Best Actress (Moore), Most Desirable Female (Moore). *PAR*

Independence **1976** Dramatically recreates the debates, concerns, and events that led up to the U.S. Declaration of Independence in 1776. **30m/C VHS, Beta.** Eli Wallach, Anne Jackson, Pat Hingle, Patrick O'Neal; ***D:*** John Huston. *MPI, KAR, VEC*

Independence Day ﾜﾜ *Follow Your Dreams* **1983 (R)** Uneven romantic drama about a small-town photographer, yearning for the big city, who falls in love with a racing car enthusiast, whose sister is a battered wife. Strong cast, particularly Wiest as the abused wife, is left occasionally stranded by a script reaching too hard for social significance. **110m/C VHS, Beta.** Kathleen Quinlan, David Keith, Frances Sternhagen, Dianne Wiest, Cliff DeYoung, Richard Farnsworth, Josef Sommer, Cheryl "Rainbeaux" Smith; ***D:*** Robert Mandel; ***M:*** Charles Bernstein. *WAR, CCB*

Independence Day ﾜﾜﾜ **1996 (PG-13)** The biggest of the new wave of disaster flicks paying tribute to the Irwin Allen celebrity-fests of the '70s finds an alien armada descending on Earth to create some fireworks on the July 4th weekend. The fate of the world rests in the hands of an unlikely band of Earthlings led by President Whitmore (Pullman), a computer expert (Goldblum), and a Marine fighter pilot (Smith). Special effects, despite forgoing some of the more expensive newer technology, don't disappoint. Strong (if not A-list) cast and plenty of action. Devlin and Emmerich wrote the script while promoting "Stargate," after a reporter asked Emmerich if he believed in aliens. **?m/C VHS.** Bill Pullman, Will Smith, Jeff Goldblum, Brent Spiner, Judd Hirsch, Randy Quaid, Mary McDonnell, Harry Connick Jr., Robert Loggia, Harvey Fierstein; ***D:*** Roland Emmerich; ***W:*** Roland Emmerich, Dean Devlin; ***C:*** Karl Walter Lindenlaub; ***M:*** David Arnold. *NYR*

The Indestructible Man ﾜ **1956** Chaney, electrocuted for murder and bank robbery, is brought back to life by a scientist. Naturally, he seeks revenge on those who sentenced him to death. Chaney does the best he can with the material. **70m/B VHS.** Lon Chaney Jr., Marian Carr, Max Casey Adams Showalter; ***D:*** Jack Pollexfen. *NOS, MRV, SNC*

The Indian Fighter ﾜﾜﾜ **1955** Exciting actioner has Douglas as a scout hired to lead a wagon train to Oregon in 1870. The train must past through dangerous Sioux territory and Douglas tries to make peace with the Sioux leader but a secret Indian gold mine and romance cause friction and keep things lively. **88m/C VHS.** Kirk Douglas, Elsa Martinelli, Walter Abel, Walter Matthau, Diana Douglas, Lon Chaney Jr., Eduard Franz, Alan Hale Jr., Elisha Cook Jr., Harry Landers; ***D:*** Andre de Toth; ***W:*** Ben Hecht. *MGM*

The Indian in the Cupboard ﾜﾜ½ **1995 (PG)** On his ninth birthday, Omri receives a three-inch plastic indian named Little Bear and an old wooden medicine cabinet. (Guess they were out of Power Rangers.) When placed in the cabinet, Little Bear magically comes to life, taking Omri on adventures and teaching him important lessons. Blue screen techniques allow them appear together onscreen although they were actually shot together only once. Based on the best-selling children's book by Lynne Reid Banks. **97m/C VHS, LV, 8mm.** Hal Scardino, Litefoot, Lindsay Crouse, Richard Jenkins, Rishi Bhat; ***D:*** Frank Oz; ***W:*** Melissa Mathison; ***C:*** Russell Carpenter; ***M:*** Miles Goodman. *COL*

Indian Paint ﾜﾜ **1964** A pleasant children's film about an Indian boy's love for his horse and his rite of passage. Silverheels was Tonto on television's "The Lone Ranger," while Crawford was the "Rifleman's" son. **90m/C VHS, Beta.** Jay Silverheels, Johnny Crawford, Pat Hogan, Robert Crawford Jr., George Lewis; ***D:*** Norman Foster. *NO*

The Indian Runner ﾜﾜ **1991 (R)** In Penn's debut as a writer-director, he brings us the story of two brothers in Nebraska during the late '60s, who are forced to change their lives with the loss of their family farm. Joe is a good cop and family man who can't deal with the rage of his brother Frank, who has just returned from Vietnam and is turning to a life of crime. Penn does a decent job of representing the struggle between the responsible versus the rebellious side of human nature. Based on the song "Highway Patrolman" by Bruce Springsteen. **127m/C VHS, LV.** David Morse, Viggo Mortensen, Sandy Dennis, Charles Bronson, Valeria Golino, Patricia Arquette, Dennis Hopper; ***D:*** Sean Penn; ***W:*** Sean Penn. *MGM*

The Indian Scarf ﾜﾜ **1963** Heirs to a dead man's fortune are being strangled one by one at the benefactor's country estate. An Edgar Wallace suspense tale. **85m/C VHS.** *GE* Heinz Drache, Gisela Uhlen, Klaus Kinski; ***D:*** Alfred Vohrer. *SNC*

Indian Summer ﾜﾜ **1993 (PG-13)** Yet another addition to the growing 30-something nostalgia genre. Delete the big house, add a crusty camp director (Arkin), change the characters' names (but not necessarily their lives) and you feel like you're experiencing deja vu. This time seven friends and the requisite outsider reconvene at Camp Tamakwa, the real-life summer camp to writer/director Binder. The former campers talk. They yearn. They save Camp Tamakwa and experience personal growth. A must see for those who appreciate listening to situational jokes that are followed by "I guess you had to be there." **108m/C VHS, Beta, LV.** Alan Arkin, Matt Craven, Diane Lane, Bill Paxton, Elizabeth Perkins, Kevin Pollak, Sam Raimi, Vincent Spano, Julie Warner, Kimberly Williams, Richard Chevolleau; ***D:*** Mike Binder; ***W:*** Mike Binder; ***M:*** Miles Goodman. *TOU, FCT*

Indian Uprising ﾜﾜ **1951** An army captain tries to keep local settlers from causing trouble with Geronimo and his people when gold is discovered on their territory. **75m/C VHS, Beta.** George Montgomery, Audrey Long, Carl Benton Reid, John Baer, Joseph Sawyer; ***D:*** Ray Nazarro. *GKK*

Indiana Jones and the Last Crusade ﾜﾜﾜ **1989 (PG)** In this, the third and last (?) Indiana Jones adventure, the fearless archaeologist is once again up against the Nazis in a race to find the Holy Grail. Connery is perfectly cast as Indy's father; opening sequence features Phoenix as a teenage Indy and explains his fear of snakes and the origins of the infamous fedora. Returns to the look and feel of the original with more adventures, exotic places, dastardly villains, and daring escapes than ever before; a must for Indy fans. **126m/C VHS, Beta, LV, 8mm.** Harrison Ford, Sean Connery, Denholm Elliott, Alison Doody, Julian Glover, John Rhys-Davies, River Phoenix, Michael Byrne, Alex Hyde-White; ***D:*** Steven Spielberg; ***W:*** Jeffrey Boam; ***M:*** John Williams. Nominations: Academy Awards '89: Best Sound, Best Original Score. *PAR, TLF*

Indiana Jones and the Temple of Doom ﾜﾜﾜ **1984 (PG)** Daredevil archaeologist Indiana Jones is back. This time he's on the trail of the legendary Ankara Stone and a ruthless cult that has enslaved hundreds of children. More gore and violence than the original; Capshaw's whining character is an irritant, lacking the fresh quality that Karen Allen added to the original. Enough action for ten movies, special effects galore, and the usual booming Williams score make it a cinematic roller coaster ride, but with less regard for plot and pacing than the original. Though second in the series, it's actually a prequel to "Raiders of the Lost Ark." Followed by "Indiana Jones and the Last Crusade." **118m/C VHS, Beta, LV, 8mm.** Harrison Ford, Kate Capshaw, Ke Huy Quan, Amrish Puri; ***D:*** Steven Spielberg; ***W:*** Willard Huyck, Gloria Katz; ***M:*** John Williams. Academy Awards '84: Best Visual Effects; Nominations: Academy Awards '84: Best Original Score. *PAR, APD*

Indictment: The McMartin Trial ﾜﾜﾜ **1995 (R)** Woods stars as attorney Danny Davis, who has the unenviable task of providing a defense in the notorious McMartin child molestation trial. In 1983, Manhattan Beach, California was rocked by reports that some 60 preschoolers had been abused at a day-care center. Seven defendants were accused thanks to lurid videotaped interviews with the children. The trial lasted six years (the longest and most expensive on record) and all charges were eventually dismissed. It's clear from this telepic that public hysteria and media hype lead to a grave miscarriage of justice that put the legal system on trial as well. **132m/C VHS, LV.** James Woods, Henry Thomas, Mercedes Ruehl, Shirley Knight, Sada Thompson, Mark Blum, Alison Elliott, Chelsea Field, Richard Bradford, Lolita Davidovich; ***D:*** Mick Jackson; ***W:*** Abby Mann, Myra Mann; ***C:*** Rodrigo Garcia; ***M:*** Peter Melnick. *HBO*

Indio ﾜ **1990 (R)** A Marine-trained half-breed takes it on himself to save the Amazon rain forest. Not a peaceful demonstrator, his tactics are violent ones. **94m/C VHS, Beta, LV.** Marvin Hagler, Francesco Quinn, Brian Dennehy; ***D:*** Anthony (Antonio Margheriti) Dawson. *MED, VTR*

Indio 2: The Revolt ﾜ **1992 (R)** Greedy developers are cutting a highway into the Amazon jungle, destroying everything in their path. All is not lost though, because U.S. Marine Sgt. Iron is on top of things, continuing his struggle to unite the Amazon tribes and save the rainforest, no matter what it takes. **104m/C VHS.** Marvin Hagler, Charles Napier; ***M:*** Pino Donaggio. *LIV*

Indiscreet ♪½ **1931** Empty-headed romantic comedy about a fashion designer whose past catches up with her when her ex-lover starts romancing her sister. No relation to the classic 1958 film with Cary Grant and Ingrid Bergman. ♫Come To Me; If You Haven't Got Love. **81m/B VHS, Beta.** Gloria Swanson, Ben Lyon, Barbara Kent; ***D:*** Leo McCarey. *NOS, MRV, REP*

Indiscreet ♪♪♪ **1958** A charming American diplomat in London falls in love with a stunning actress, but protects himself by saying he is married. Needless to say, she finds out. Stylish romp with Grant and Bergman at their sophisticated best. Adapted by Norman Krasna from his stage play "Kind Sir." **100m/C VHS.** Cary Grant, Ingrid Bergman, Phyllis Calvert; ***D:*** Stanley Donen; ***C:*** Frederick A. (Freddie) Young; ***M:*** Richard Rodney Bennett. *REP, MLB*

Indiscreet ♪½ **1988 (PG)** Indistinctive made for TV rehash of the charming 1958 Grant/Bergman romantic comedy in which a suave American falls for an English actress. Both versions derive from the play "Kind Sir" by Norman Krasna, but this one suffers by comparison. **94m/C VHS.** Robert Wagner, Lesley-Anne Down, Maggie Henderson, Robert McBain, Jeni Barnett; ***D:*** Richard Michaels. *REP*

Indiscretion of an American Wife ♪♪ *Indiscretion; Terminus Station; Terminal Station Indiscretion* **1954** Set almost entirely in Rome's famous Terminal Station, where an ill-fated couple say goodbye endlessly while the woman tries to decide whether to join her husband in the States. Trimmed down from 87 minutes upon U.S. release. **63m/C VHS, Beta.** *IT* Jennifer Jones, Montgomery Clift, Richard Beymer; ***D:*** Vittorio De Sica; ***W:*** Truman Capote; ***C:*** Oswald Morris. Nominations: Academy Awards '54: Best Costume Design (B & W). *NOS, FOX, HEG*

Indochine ♪♪♪ **1992 (PG-13)** Soapy melodrama follows the fortunes of Eliane (Deneuve), a Frenchwoman born and reared in Indochina, from 1930 to the communist revolution 25 years later. She contends with the changes to her country as well as her adopted daughter as she grows up and becomes independent. Deneuve's controlled performance (and unchanging beauty) is eminently watchable. Filmed on location in Vietnam with breathtaking cinematography by Francois Catonne. In French with English subtitles. **155m/C VHS, LV, 8mm.** *FR* Catherine Deneuve, Linh Dan Pham, Vincent Perez, Jean Yanne, Dominique Blanc, Henri Marteau, Carlo Brandt, Gerard Lartigau; ***D:*** Regis Wargnier; ***W:*** Erik Orsenna, Louis Gardel, Catherine Cohen, Regis Wargnier; ***M:*** Patrick Doyle. Academy Awards '92: Best Foreign Language Film; Cesar Awards '93: Best Actress (Deneuve), Best Art Direction/Set Decoration, Best Cinematography, Best Sound, Best Supporting Actress (Blanc); National Board of Review Awards '92: Best Foreign Film; Nominations: Academy Awards '92: Best Actress (Deneuve); British Academy Awards '93: Best Foreign Language Film. *COL, FCT, BTV*

Indomitable Teddy Roosevelt ♪♪½ **1983** Entertaining mix of newsreel footage and staged scenes traces the career of the feisty president. **93m/C VHS, Beta.** ***D:*** Harrison Engle. *PSM, CHF*

Infamous Crimes ♪♪ *Philo Vance Returns* **1947** Philo investigates the murders of a playboy and his girlfriends. One of the last of the series whose character was based on the S.S. Van Dine stories. **64m/B VHS, Beta, 8mm.** William Wright, Terry Austin, Leon Belasco, Clara Blandick, Iris Adrian, Frank Wilcox; ***D:*** William Beaudine. *VYY*

Infernal Trio ♪♪½ **1974** An attorney comes up with a plan involving two sisters (who are his lovers) which will make them both wealthy; but it will also make them both murderers. Sophisticated black comedy based on a true story. In French with English subtitles or dubbed. **100m/C VHS.** *FR IT* Romy Schneider, Michel Piccoli, Mascha Gonska; ***D:*** Francois Girod. *CVC, INJ*

Inferno ♪♪ **1978 (R)** Uneven occult horror tale about a young man who arrives in New York to investigate the mysterious circumstances surrounding his sister's death. Dubbed. **83m/C VHS, Beta.** *IT* Leigh McCloskey, Elenora Giorgi, Irene Miracle, Sacha Pitoeff; ***D:*** Dario Argento; ***W:*** Dario Argento; ***M:*** Keith Emerson. *FOX*

Inferno in Paradise ♪ **1988** Mucho macho firefighter and bimbous gal pal photographer get hot while trailing a murderous pyromaniac. More like purgatory in the living room (that is, unless you thought Forsyth's earlier "Chesty Anderson, US Navy" was divine comedy). **115m/C VHS.** Richard Young, Betty Ann Carr, Jim Davis, Andy Jarrell, Dennis Chun; ***D:*** Ed Forsyth. *ACA*

The Infiltrator ♪♪½ **1995 (R)** Based on the true story of Yaron Svoray (Platt), an Israeli journalist and the son of Holocaust survivors, whose latest assignment is to go to Berlin and investigate the rising Neo-Nazi movement. Eventually, Svoray manages to meet leaders of the Nationalist Front and then finds himself enmeshed in a worldwide political network. Based on the book "In Hitler's Shadow" by Yaron Svoray and Nick Taylor. Made for cable TV. **102m/C VHS.** Oliver Platt, Arliss Howard, Peter Riegert, Alan King, Tony Haygarth, Michael Byrne, Julian Glover, Alex Kingston; ***D:*** John MacKenzie; ***W:*** Guy Andrews; ***M:*** Hal Lindes. *HBO*

The Informer ♪½ **1929** Hanson wants to flee Ireland's poverty for America, using the reward money he gets for turning in an IRA comrade. But things don't turn out as planned and instead he's haunted by the guilt of his betrayal. Based on the novel by Liam O'Flaherty and filmed to much greater effect by John Ford in 1935. **83m/B VHS.** *GB* Lars Hanson, Lya de Putti, Warwick Ward, Dennis Wynham; ***D:*** Arthur Robison; ***W:*** Benn W. Levy, Rolfe E. Vanlo. *GPV*

The Informer ♪♪♪♪ **1935** Based on Liam O'Flaherty's novel about the Irish Sinn Fein Rebellion of 1922, it tells the story of a hard-drinking Dublin man (McLaglen) who informs on a friend (a member of the Irish Republican Army) in order to collect a 20-pound reward. When his "friend" is killed during capture, he goes on a drinking spree instead of using the money, as planned, for passage to America. Director Ford allowed McLaglen to improvise his lines during the trial scene in order to enhance the realism, leading to excruciating suspense. Wonderful score. **91m/B VHS, Beta, LV.** Victor McLaglen, Heather Angel, Wallace Ford, Margot Grahame, Joseph Sawyer, Preston Foster, Una O'Connor, J.M. Kerrigan, Donald Meek; ***D:*** John Ford; ***W:*** Dudley Nichols; ***M:*** Max Steiner. Academy Awards '35: Best Actor (McLaglen), Best Director (Ford), Best Screenplay, Best Original Score; National Board of Review Awards '35: 10 Best Films of the Year; New York Film Critics Awards '35: Best Director (Ford), Best Film; Nominations: Academy Awards '35: Best Film Editing, Best Picture. *MED, BTV, TTC*

Infra-Man *Woof! The Super Inframan; The Infra Superman* **1976 (PG)** If you're looking for a truly bad, hokey flick, this could be it. Infra-man is a superhero who must rescue the galaxy from the clutches of the evil Princess Dragon Mom and her army of prehistoric monsters. Outlandish dialogue (delivered straight) combines with horrible special effects and costumes to create what may well be one of the best camp classics to date. Poorly dubbed in English. **92m/C VHS, Beta.** *HK* Li Hsiu-hsien, Wang Hsieh, Yuan Man-tzu, Terry Liu, Tsen Shu-yi, Huang Chien-lung, Lu Sheng; ***D:*** Hua-Shan; ***W:*** Peter Fernandez. *PSM*

Inga **1967** Story of a teenage girl becoming a woman. Sensitive and well-acted. **86m/B VHS, Beta.** *SW VPL*

Inherit the Wind ♪♪♪½ **1960** Powerful courtroom drama, based on the Broadway play, is actually a fictionalized version of the infamous Scopes "Monkey Trial" of 1925. Tracy is the defense attorney for the schoolteacher on trial for teaching Darwin's Theory of Evolution to a group of students in a small town ruled by religion. March is the prosecutor seeking to put the teacher behind bars and restore religion to the schools. **128m/B VHS, Beta, LV.** Spencer Tracy, Fredric March, Florence Eldridge, Gene Kelly, Dick York; ***D:*** Stanley Kramer; ***C:*** Ernest Laszlo; ***M:*** Ernest Gold. Berlin International Film Festival '60: Best Actor (March); National Board of Review Awards '60: 10 Best Films of the Year; Nominations: Academy Awards '60: Best Actor (Tracy), Best Adapted Screenplay, Best Black and White Cinematography, Best Film Editing. *FOX, FCT*

Inheritance ♪♪♪ *Uncle Silas* **1947** Victorian-era melodrama of a young heiress endangered by her guradian, who plots to murder his charge for her inheritance. Chilling and moody story based on a novel by Sheridan Le Fanu. **103m/B VHS, Beta.** *GB* Jean Simmons, Katina Paxinou, Derrick DeMarney, Derek Bond; ***D:*** Charles Frank. *DVT*

The Inheritance ♪♪½ *L'Eredita Ferramonti* **1976 (R)** Wealthy partiarch becomes sexually involved with scheming daughter-in-law. Tawdry tale is nonetheless engaging. **121m/C VHS, Beta.** *IT* Anthony Quinn, Fabio Testi, Dominique Sanda; ***D:*** Mauro Bolognini; ***M:*** Ennio Morricone. Cannes Film Festival '76: Best Actress (Sanda); Nominations: Cannes Film Festival '76: Best Film. *NO*

The Inheritor ♪♪ **1990 (R)** Set in a small New England town, this mystery centers on the death of a young woman and her sister's attempts to uncover the murderer. The local celebrity, a writer, seems to be at the heart of the mystery and the sister finds herself growing interested. Keeps you guessing. **83m/C VHS.** Dan Haggerty; ***D:*** Brian Savegar. *NO*

The Inheritors ♪½ **1985** Not-too-subtle tale of a young German boy who becomes involved with a Nazi youth group as his home life deteriorates. Heavy-going anti-fascism creates more message than entertainment. In German with English subtitles or dubbed. **89m/C VHS, Beta.** *GE* Nikolas Vogel, Roger Schauer, Klaus Novak, Johanna Tomek; ***D:*** Walter Bannert; ***W:*** Walter Bannert. *SUE, APD, GLV*

Inhibition ♪ **1986** A beautiful heiress has lots of sex with different people in exotic locales. Softcore soap. **90m/C VHS, Beta.** Claudine Beccaire, Ilona Staller. *MED*

The Initiation ♪ **1984 (R)** Trying to rid herself of a troublesome nightmare, a coed finds herself face-to-face with a psycho. Gory campus slaughterfest. **97m/C VHS, Beta.** Vera Miles, Clu Gulager, James Read, Daphne Zuniga; ***D:*** Larry Stewart. *VTR*

Initiation of Sarah ♪ **1978** College freshman joins a sorority, undergoes abusive initiation, and gains a supernatural revenge. Made-for-television "Carrie" rip-off. **100m/C VHS, Beta.** Kay Lenz, Shelley Winters, Kathryn Crosby, Morgan Brittany, Tony Bill, Tisa Farrow, Robert Hays, Morgan Fairchild; ***D:*** Robert Day. *WOV*

The Inkwell ♪♪½ **1994 (R)** Quiet teenager Drew Tate finds first love when his family spends their vacation with relatives on Martha's Vineyard. Drew is drawn into the party atmosphere of the Inkwell, the area where affluent black professionals have summered for decades. Meanwhile, political differences between Drew's former Black Panther father and his conservative uncle threaten family harmony. Everything about the film has a sugary aura, with conflicts handled tastefully. Rich directs broadly, leading to some overacting. Film is set in 1976. **112m/C VHS, LV.** Larenz Tate, Joe Morton, Phyllis Stickney, Jada Pinkett; ***D:*** Matty Rich; ***W:*** Tom Ricostronza, Paris Qualles; ***M:*** Terence Blanchard. *TOU*

Inn of Temptation ♪ **1986** A bunch of bowling buddies take off for Bangkok on an impulsive weekend, and meet lots of Oriental women. **72m/C VHS, Beta.** Michael Jacot, Claude Martin. *MED*

Inn of the Damned ♪½ **1974** Detective looks into an inn where no one ever gets charged for an extra day; they simply die. Anderson is watchable. **92m/C VHS, Beta.** *AU* Alex Cord, Judith Anderson, Tony Bonner, Michael Craig, John Meillon; ***D:*** Terry Burke. *NO*

The Inn of the Sixth Happiness ♪♪♪ **1958** Inspiring story of Gladys Aylward, an English missionary in 1930s' China, who leads a group of children through war-torn countryside. Donat's last film. **158m/C VHS, Beta.** Ingrid Bergman, Robert Donat, Curt Jurgens; ***D:*** Mark Robson; ***C:*** Frederick A. (Freddie) Young; ***M:*** Malcolm Arnold. National Board of Review Awards '58: Best Actress (Bergman); Nominations: Academy Awards '58: Best Director (Robson). *FXV*

Inn on the River ♪♪½ **1962** Scotland Yard investigates a series of murders taking place on the waterfront by the "Shark's" gang. Remake of "The Return of the Frog." **95m/C VHS.** *GE* Klaus Kinski,

Joachim Fuchsberger, Brigitte Grothum, Richard Much; *D:* Alfred Vohrer. *SNC*

The Inner Circle ♂½ **1946** A private detective, framed for murder by his secretary, has a limited amount of time to find the real murderer. Confusing. **57m/B VHS, Beta.** Adele Mara, Warren Douglas, William Frawley, Ricardo Cortez, Virginia Christine; *D:* Philip Ford. *SNC*

The Inner Circle ♂♂♂ **1991 (PG-13)** Ivan Sanshin is a meek, married man working as a movie projectionist for the KGB in 1935 Russia. Sanshin is taken by the KGB to the Kremlin to show movies, primarily Hollywood features, to leader Joseph Stalin, a job he cannot discuss with anyone, even his wife. Under the spell of Stalin's personality, Sanshin sees only what he's told and overlooks the oppression and persecution of the times. Based on the life of the projectionist who served from 1935 until Stalin's death in 1953. Filmed on location at the Kremlin. **122m/C VHS, LV, 8mm.** Tom Hulce, Lolita Davidovich, Bob Hoskins, Alexandre Zbruev, Maria Baranova, Feodor Chaliapin Jr, Bess Meyer; *D:* Andrei Konchalovsky; *W:* Andrei Konchalovsky, Anatoli Usov; *M:* Eduard Artemyev. *COL*

Inner Sanctum ♂♂ **1948** Adequate tale of a young girl accosted by a gypsy who claims that tragedy awaits her. Based on a radio show of the same name. **62m/B VHS.** Chuck Russell, Mary Beth Hughes, Lee Patrick, Nana Bryant; *D:* Lew (Louis Friedlander) Landers. *SNC*

Inner Sanctum *Woof!* **1991 (R)** Cheating husband hires sensuous nurse to tend invalid wife. You can guess the rest; in fact, you have to because the plot ultimately makes no sense. Available in R-rated and sex-drenched unrated editions. **87m/C VHS, LV.** Tanya Roberts, Margaux Hemingway, Joseph Bottoms, Valerie Wildman, William Butler, Brett Clark; *D:* Fred Olen Ray. *COL*

Inner Sanctum 2 ♂½ **1994 (R)** Jennifer Reed (Swope) had a breakdown and killed her husband in the first film. Now under a doctor's (Warner) care, Jennifer is under siege from her brother-in-law's (Nouri) evil plot to send her over the edge again and claim her fortune. As if that's not enough, Jennifer's also being stalked by a murderer. Also available in an unrated version. **90m/C VHS, LV.** Michael Nouri, Tracy Brooks Swope, Sandahl Bergman, David Warner, Jennifer Ciesar, Margaux Hemingway; *D:* Fred Olen Ray; *W:* Sherman Scott; *M:* Chuck Cirino. *COL*

Innerspace ♂♂½ **1987 (PG)** A space pilot, miniaturized for a journey through a lab rat a la "Fantastic Voyage," is accidentally injected into a nebbish supermarket clerk, and together they nab some bad guys and get the girl. Award-winning special effects support some funny moments between micro Quaid and nerdy Short, with Ryan producing the confused romantic interest. **120m/C VHS, Beta, LV, 8mm.** Dennis Quaid, Martin Short, Meg Ryan, Kevin McCarthy, Fiona Lewis, Henry Gibson, Robert Picardo, John Hora, Wendy Schaal, Orson Bean, Chuck Jones, William Schallert, Dick Miller, Vernon Wells, Harold Sylvester, Kevin Hooks, Kathleen Freeman, Kenneth Tobey; *D:* Joe Dante; *W:* Jeffrey Boam, Chip Proser; *M:* Jerry Goldsmith. Academy Awards '87: Best Visual Effects. *WAR*

Innocence Unprotected ♂♂½ **1968** A film collage that contains footage from the 1942 film "Innocence Unprotected," the story of an acrobat trying to save an orphan from her wicked stepmother, newsreels from Nazi-occupied Yugoslavia, and interviews from 1968 with people who were in the film. Confiscated by the Nazis during final production, "Innocence Unprotected" was discovered by director Makavejev, who worked it into the collage. Filmed in color and black and white; in Serbian with English subtitles. **78m/C VHS.** *YU* Dragoljub Aleksic, Ana Milosavljevic, Vera Jovanovic; *D:* Dusan Makavejev; *W:* Dusan Makavejev. *FCT*

The Innocent ♂♂♂½ *L'Innocente* **1976 (R)** The setting: turn of the century Rome, ablaze with atheism and free love. The story: Giannini's a Sicilian aristocrat who ignores wife Antonelli and dallies with scheming mistress O'Neill. Discovering his wife's infidelity, he's profoundly disillusioned, and his manly notion of self disintegrates. Visconti's last film, it was an art house fave and is considered by many to be his best. Lavishly photographed, well set and costumed, and true to the Gabrielle D'Annunzio's novel. In Italian with English subtitles. **125m/C VHS, Beta.** *IT* Laura Antonelli, Jennifer O'Neill, Giancarlo Giannini; *D:* Luchino Visconti; *C:* Pasqualino de Santis. *VES, FCT, INJ*

The Innocent ♂♂½ **1993 (R)** Cold War thriller has naive British engineer Leonard Markham (Scott) sent to Berlin in 1955 by Brits who are warily cooperating with the U.S. forces. He's turned over to CIA operator Bob Glass (Hopkins) and asked to intercept communications between East Germany and the Soviet Union. Glass continually warns Markham not to trust anyone, including Maria (Rossellini), the married German woman with whom he begins an affair. Failure to build necessary suspense and performances leads to disappointing one-note display. Based on the novel by McEwan. **97m/C VHS, LV.** *GE GB* Anthony Hopkins, Campbell Scott, Isabella Rossellini, Hart Bochner, James Grant, Jeremy Sinden, Ronald Nitschke; *D:* John Schlesinger; *W:* Ian McEwan; *M:* Gerald Gouriet. *MAX*

Innocent Blood ♂♂ **1992 (R)** A mediocre modern-day vampire/gangster combo with the beautiful (though red-eyed) Parillaud as the woman with a taste for someone "Italian." Unfortunately, she doesn't finish off her latest meal—mobster Loggia—who finds being undead very useful to his vicious work. LaPaglia plays the bewildered, love-struck cop involved with the vamp. Parillaud appears nude in several scenes and the gore and violence are stomach-turning. **112m/C VHS, Beta, LV.** Anne Parillaud, Anthony LaPaglia, Robert Loggia, David Proval, Don Rickles, Rocco Sisto, Kim Coates; *D:* John Landis; *M:* Ira Newborn. *WAR, PMS*

Innocent Lies ♂♂½ **1995 (R)** In 1938, British policeman Alan Cross (Dunbar) heads for an island off the French coast to look into the suicide of a colleague who was investigating the expatriate Graves family. There are family tensions, skeletons in the closet, and some Nazi-sympathizers all mixed together in an old-fashioned but satisfying stew. **88m/C VHS.** *FR GB* Adrian Dunbar, Stephen Dorff, Gabrielle Anwar, Joanna Lumley; *D:* Patrick Dewolf; *W:* Kerry Crabbe, Patrick Dewolf; *C:* Patrick Blossier; *M:* Alexandre Desplat. *PGV*

An Innocent Man ♂♂½ **1989 (R)** Uneven story of Selleck, an ordinary family man and airline mechanic, framed as a drug dealer and sent to prison. **113m/C VHS, Beta, LV.** Tom Selleck, F. Murray Abraham, Laila Robins, David Rasche, Richard Young, Badja Djola; *D:* Peter Yates; *W:* Larry Brothers; *M:* Howard Shore. *TOU*

Innocent Prey ♂♂ **1988 (R)** When a woman finally summons the courage to bid hasta la vista to her abusive husband, it turns out he's not so quick to say ciao. Definitely not a highlight in Balsam's career. **88m/C VHS.** *AU* P.J. Soles, Martin Balsam, Kit Taylor, Grigor Taylor, John Warnock, Susan Stenmark, Richard Morgan; *D:* Colin Eggleston. *NO*

Innocent Sorcerers ♂♂ *Niewinni Czarodzieje* **1960** Ironic comedy about aimless sixties Polish youth that finds a young doctor having trouble committing himself to his superficial girlfriend and coping with the problems of his cynical friends. Polish with subtitles. **86m/B VHS.** *PL* Tadeusz Lomnicki, Zbigniew Cybulski, Roman Polanski, Krystyna Stypulkowska, Jerzy Skolimowski; *D:* Andrzej Wajda; *W:* Jerzy Skolimowski, Andrzej Wajda; *M:* Krzysztof Komeda. *FCT*

Innocent Victim ♂ *The Tree of Hands* **1990 (R)** Convoluted tale of revenge and madness. Bacall plays a mad grandmother who kidnaps a boy to take the place of her dead grandson. The kidnapped boy's stepfather then is accused of murdering him, and starts murdering others to get the boy back. **100m/C VHS.** Lauren Bacall, Helen Shaver, Paul McGann, Peter Firth; *D:* Giles Foster. *ACA*

The Innocents ♂♂♂½ **1961** Incredibly creepy version of Henry James' "The Turn of the Screw." Minister's daughter, Miss Giddens (Kerr), is hired by Redgrave (known only as "The Uncle") as governess to young Flora (Franklin) and her brother Miles (Stephens) at his country estate. Miss Giddens begins to see the specters of a man and a woman and is told her descriptions match that of former estate manager Peter Quint and the last governess, his mistress, whose influence on the children was thought to be malevolent. Indeed, Miss Giddens believes the children are possessed by evil—but is it true or a product of her own hysteria? **99m/B VHS.** *GB* Deborah Kerr, Michael Redgrave, Pamela Franklin, Martin Stephens, Peter Wyngarde, Megs Jenkins, Clytie Jessop, Isla Cameron; *D:* Jack Clayton; *W:* Truman Capote, William Archibald; *C:* Freddie Francis; *M:* Georges Auric. *FXV*

The Innocents Abroad ♂♂½ **1984** Entertaining adaptation of Mark Twain's novel about a group of naive Americans cruising the Mediterranean. Ensemble cast offers some surprising performances. Originally produced for PBS. **116m/C VHS.** Craig Wasson, Brooke Adams, David Ogden Stiers. *MCA*

Innocents in Paris ♂♂½ **1953** A group of seven Britons visit Paris for the first time. A bit long but enough ooo-la-la to satisfy. **89m/B VHS, Beta.** *GB* Alastair Sim, Laurence Harvey, Jimmy Edwards, Claire Bloom, Margaret Rutherford; *D:* Gordon Parry. *NO*

The Inquiry ♂♂½ **1987** A new twist on the resurrection of Christ. Carradine senses a cover-up when he's sent from Rome to investigate the problem of Christ's missing corpse. He retraces Christ's final days to solve the case in this interesting, offbeat film. Dubbed. **107m/C VHS.** *IT* Keith Carradine, Harvey Keitel, Phyllis Logan, Angelo Infanti, Lina Sastri; *D:* Damiano Damiani. *NO*

Inquisition ♂½ **1976** Naschy is a 16th century witch hunting judge who finds himself accused of witchcraft. **85m/C VHS, Beta.** *SP* Paul Naschy, Daniela Giordano, Juan Gallardo; *D:* Paul Naschy; *W:* Paul Naschy. *VCD*

Insanity ♂ **1982** A film director becomes violently obsessed with a beautiful actress. **101m/C VHS, Beta.** Terence Stamp, Fernando Rey, Corinne Clery. *NO*

The Insect Woman ♂♂♂ *The Insect; Nippon Konchuki* **1963** Chronicles 45 years in the life of a woman who must work with the diligence of an ant in order to survive. Thoughtfully reflects the exploitation of women and the cruelty of human nature in Japanese society. Beautiful performance from Hidari, who ages from girlhood to middle age. In Japanese with English subtitles. **123m/B VHS.** *JP* Sachiko Hidari, Yitsuko Yoshimura, Hiroyuki Nagaes, Sumie Sasaki; *D:* Shohei Imamura. *CVC*

Inserts ♂ **1976 (R)** A formerly successful director has been reduced to making porno films in this pretentious, long-winded effort set in a crumbling Hollywood mansion in the 1930s. Affected, windbaggish performances kill it. **99m/C VHS.** *GB* Richard Dreyfuss, Jessica Harper, Veronica Cartwright, Bob Hoskins; *D:* John Byrum; *W:* John Byrum. *FOX*

Inside Daisy Clover ♂♂½ **1965** Wood is the self-sufficient, junior delinquent waif who becomes a teenage musical star and pays the price for fame in this Hollywood saga set in the 1930s. Discovered by tyrannical studio head Plummer, Daisy is given her big break and taken under his wing for grooming as Swan Studio's newest sensation. She falls for fellow performer, matinee idol Redford, who has some secrets of his own, and eventually has a breakdown from the career pressure. Glossy melodrama is filled with over-the-top performances but its sheer silliness makes it amusing. **128m/C VHS, LV.** Natalie Wood, Christopher Plummer, Robert Redford, Ruth Gordon, Roddy McDowall, Katharine Bard; *D:* Robert Mulligan; *W:* Gavin Lambert; *C:* Charles B(ryant) Lang; *M:* Andre Previn. Golden Globe Awards '66: Best Supporting Actress (Gordon); Nominations: Academy Awards '65: Best Art Direction/Set Decoration (Color), Best Costume Design (Color), Best Supporting Actress (Gordon). *WAR*

Inside Edge 🦴🦴 **1992 (R)** Urban crime thriller is a complex yet surprisingly uninteresting story of a police officer who falls for the girlfriend of the drug lord he is chasing. Filled with the standard genre violence. **84m/C VHS.** Michael Madsen, Richard Lynch, Rosie Vela, Tony Peck, George Jenesky, Branscombe Richmond; ***D:*** Warren Clark; ***W:*** William Tannen. *ATV*

Inside Information 🦴 **1934** With Tarzan's help, a cop searches out the leader of a ring of jewel thieves. **51m/B VHS, Beta, LV.** Rex Lease, Marion Shilling, Philo McCullough. *NO*

The Inside Man 🦴🦴½ **1984** Double agents struggle to find a submarine-detecting laser device. Based on true incidents in which a soviet sub ran aground in Sweden. Made in Sweden; dubbed. **90m/C VHS, Beta.** *SW* Dennis Hopper, Hardy Kruger, Gosta Ekman, David Wilson; ***D:*** Tom Clegg. *CEL, VTR*

Inside Monkey Zetterland 🦴🦴 **1993 (R)** Monkey Zetterland (Antin) is a screenwriter and former actor with an eccentric family. His actress mother is neurotically insecure and a nag; his father is an aging hippie who only shows up at Thanksgiving; his lesbian sister Grace is trying to get over a failed relationship; and his brother Brent is totally self-absorbed. Add to this menage his equally lunatic friends: Imogene, the compulsive talker and exhibitionist; his vicious girlfriend Daphne; and frightening married couple Sophie and Sasha. Meanwhile, Monkey tries to survive amidst the chaos. Interesting cast but lots of camera tricks do not a successful film make and the effort to be hip is all too apparent. **92m/C VHS, LV.** Steve Antin, Patricia Arquette, Sandra Bernhard, Sofia Coppola, Tate Donovan, Katherine Helmond, Bo Hopkins, Debi Mazar, Martha Plimpton, Rupert Everett, Ricki Lake; ***D:*** Jefery Levy; ***W:*** Steve Antin. Nominations: Independent Spirit Awards '94: Best Supporting Actor (Donovan). *PSM*

Inside Moves 🦴🦴½ **1980 (PG)** A look at handicapped citizens trying to make it in everyday life, focusing on the relationship between an insecure, failed suicide and a volatile man who is only a knee operation away from a dreamed-about basketball career. **113m/C VHS, Beta, LV.** John Savage, Diana Scarwid, David Morse, Amy Wright; ***D:*** Richard Donner; ***W:*** Valerie Curtin, Barry Levinson; ***M:*** John Barry. Nominations: Academy Awards '80: Best Supporting Actress (Scarwid). *FOX*

Inside Out 🦴🦴½ *The Golden Heist; Hitler's Gold* **1975 (PG)** An ex-GI, a jewel thief and a German POW camp commandant band together to find a stolen shipment of Nazi gold behind the Iron Curtain. To find the gold, they help a Nazi prisoner who knows the secret to break out of prison. Good action caper. **97m/C VHS, Beta.** *GB* Telly Savalas, Robert Culp, James Mason, Aldo Ray, Doris Kunstmann; ***D:*** Peter Duffell. *WAR*

Inside Out 🦴🦴½ **1991 (R)** Hiding in his apartment from a world which terrifies him, Jimmy doesn't feel he's missing much—since he has the necessary women and bookies come to him. He soon finds he's not quite as safe as he thought, and the only way out is "out there." Fine performance from Gould, suspenseful pacing. **87m/C VHS.** Elliott Gould, Jennifer Tilly, Howard Hesseman, Beah Richards, Timothy Scott, Sandy McPeak, Dana Elcar, Meshach Taylor, Nicole Norman; ***D:*** Robert Taicher; ***W:*** Robert Taicher. *NO*

Inside the Law 🦴🦴 **1942** A gang of crooks takes over a bank and must stay "inside the law" and resist their natural inclinations. Lots of comic situations. **65m/B VHS.** Wallace Ford, Frank Sully, Harry Holman, Luana Walters, Lafayette McKee, Danny Duncan, Earle Hodgins; ***D:*** Hamilton MacFadden. *NOS*

Inside the Lines 🦴🦴 **1930** A WWI tale of espionage and counter-espionage. **73m/B VHS, Beta.** Betty Compson, Montagu Love, Mischa Auer, Ralph Forbes. *VYY*

Inside the Third Reich 🦴🦴½ **1982** A made-for-television mini-series detailing the rise to power within the Third Reich of Albert Speer, top advisor to Hitler. Based on Speer's rather self-serving memoires. **250m/C VHS, Beta, LV.** Derek Jacobi, Rutger Hauer, John Gielgud, Blythe Danner, Maria Schell, Ian Holm, Trevor Howard, Randy Quaid, Viveca Lindfors, Robert Vaughn, Stephen Collins, Elke Sommer, Renee Soutendijk; ***D:*** Marvin J. Chomsky. *SUE, GLV*

Insignificance 🦴🦴🦴 **1985** A film about an imaginary night spent in a New York hotel by characters who resemble Marilyn Monroe, Albert Einstein, Joe McCarthy, and Joe DiMaggio. Entertaining and often amusing as it follows the characters as they discuss theory and relativity, the Russians, and baseball among other things. **110m/C VHS, Beta, LV.** *GB* Gary Busey, Tony Curtis, Theresa Russell, Michael Emil, Will Sampson; ***D:*** Nicolas Roeg; ***W:*** Terry Johnson; ***M:*** Hans Zimmer. *ORI, WAR*

The Inspector General 🦴🦴🦴 *Happy Times* **1949** Classic Kaye craziness of mistaken identities with the master comic portraying a carnival medicine man who is mistaken by the villagers for their feared Inspector General. If you like Kaye's manic performance, you'll enjoy this one. ♫The Gypsy Drinking Song; Onward Onward; The Medicine Show; The Inspector General; Lonely Heart; Soliloquy For Three Heads; Happy Times; Brodny. **103m/C VHS, Beta.** Danny Kaye, Walter Slezak, Barbara Bates, Elsa Lanchester, Gene Lockhart, Walter Catlett, Alan Hale; ***D:*** Henry Koster. Golden Globe Awards '50: Best Score. *MGM, MRV, NOS*

The Inspector General 🦴🦴½ **1954** The filmed performance of Gogol's great play by the Moscow Art Theatre, wherein a provincial town panics when they mistake a wandering moron for the Inspector come to check up on them. In Russian with English subtitles. **128m/B VHS, Beta.** *RU* ***D:*** Vladimir Petrov. *FCT, AUD, INJ*

Inspector Hornleigh 🦴🦴½ **1939** A pair of bumbling detectives arrive on the scene when a Chancellor's fortune is stolen. Fine comedy, although the Scottish and British accents can be rather thick now and again. **76m/B VHS, Beta.** *GB* Gordon Harker, Alastair Sim, Miki Hood, Wally Patch, Steve Geray, Edward Underdown, Hugh Williams, Gibb McLaughlin; ***D:*** Eugene Forde. *NOS, SNC*

Inspiration of Mr. Budd **1975** A clever barber helps police trap a murderer. Based on a short story by Dorothy L. Sayers. Part of EBE's "Orson Welles' Great Mysteries" series. **25m/C VHS, Beta.** Orson Welles. *BRT*

Instant Justice 🦴½ *Marine Issue* **1986 (R)** A professional Marine jeopardizes his military career by avenging his sister's murder, vigilante style. Exclusive action. **101m/C VHS, Beta.** *GB* Michael Pare, Tawny Kitaen, Charles Napier; ***D:*** Craig T. Rumar. *WAR*

Instant Karma 🦴½ **1990** Would be comedy depicts young man's far fetched attempts to score babewise. Ask no more what happened to erstwhile teen heart throb Cassidy: he suffers from a major bout of bad karma. **94m/C VHS, Beta.** Craig Sheffer, Chelsea Noble, David Cassidy, Alan Blumenfeld, Glen Hirsch, Marty Ingels, Orson Bean; ***D:*** Roderick Taylor. *MGM*

Instant Kung-Fu Man 🦴 **1984** Twin brothers get involved in a case of mistaken identity in this martial arts effort. **104m/C VHS, Beta.** John Liu, Hwang Jang Lee, Yeh Fei Yang. *WVE*

The Instructor 🦴 **1983** The head of a karate school proves the value of his skill when threatened by the owner of a rival school. **91m/C VHS, Beta.** Don Bendell, Bob Chaney, Bob Saal, Lynday Scharnott; ***D:*** Don Bendell. *LIV, VES*

Interceptor 🦴🦴 **1992 (R)** Hijackers attempt to steal a Stealth Bomber in this action-adventure saga which features virtual reality computer-generated imagery in its combat sequences. **92m/C VHS, LV.** Juergen Prochnow, Andrew Divoff, Elizabeth Morehead; ***D:*** Michael Cohn; ***W:*** John Brancato. *VMK*

Interface 🦴½ **1984** A computer game gets out of hand at a university, turning the tunnels beneath the campus into a battleground of good and evil. **88m/C VHS, Beta.** John Davies, Laura Lane, Matthew Sacks. *LIV, VES*

Interiors 🦴🦴🦴½ **1978 (R)** Ultra serious, Bergmanesque drama about three neurotic adult sisters, coping with the dissolution of their family. When Father decides to leave mentally unbalanced mother for a divorcee, the daughters are shocked and bewildered. Depressing and humorless, but fine performances all the way around, supported by the elegant camera work of Gordon Willis. Original theatrical trailer available on the laserdisc format. **95m/C VHS, Beta, LV.** Diane Keaton, Mary Beth Hurt, E.G. Marshall, Geraldine Page, Richard Jordan, Sam Waterston, Kristin Griffith, Maureen Stapleton; ***D:*** Woody Allen; ***W:*** Woody Allen; ***C:*** Gordon Willis. British Academy Awards '78: Best Supporting Actress (Page); Los Angeles Film Critics Association Awards '78: Best Supporting Actress (Stapleton); Nominations: Academy Awards '78: Best Actress (Page), Best Director (Allen), Best Original Screenplay, Best Supporting Actress (Stapleton). *MGM*

Intermezzo 🦴🦴🦴 *Interlude* **1936** Married violinist Ekman meets pianist Bergman and they fall in love. He deserts his family to tour with Bergman, but the feelings for his wife and children become too much. When Bergman sees their love won't last, she leaves him. Shakily, he returns home and as his daughter runs to greet him, she is hit by a truck and he realizes that his family is his true love. One of the great grab-your-hanky melodramas. In Swedish with English subtitles. 1939 English re-make features Bergman's American film debut. **88m/B VHS, LV.** *SW* Gosta Ekman, Inga Tidblad, Ingrid Bergman, Bullen Berglund; ***D:*** Gustaf Molander. *WAC, TPV, LUM*

Intermezzo 🦴🦴🦴 *Intermezzo: A Love Story* **1939** Fine, though weepy, love story of a renowned, married violinist who has an affair with his stunningly beautiful protege (Bergman), but while on concert tour realizes that his wife and children hold his heart, and he returns to them. A re-make of the 1936 Swedish film, it's best known as Bergman's American debut. Howard's violin playing was dubbed by Jascha Heifetz. **70m/B VHS, Beta, LV.** *IT* Ingrid Bergman, Leslie Howard, Edna Best, Ann Todd; ***D:*** Gregory Ratoff; ***C:*** Gregg Toland; ***M:*** Max Steiner. Nominations: Academy Awards '39: Best Black and White Cinematography, Best Score. *FOX, FCT*

Internal Affairs 🦴🦴½ **1990 (R)** Wild, sexually charged action piece about an Internal Affairs officer for the L.A.P.D. (Garcia) who becomes obsessed with exposing a sleazy, corrupt street cop (Gere). Drama becomes illogical, but boasts excellent, strung out performances, especially Gere as the creepy degenerate you'd love to bust. **114m/C VHS, Beta, LV, 8mm.** Richard Gere, Andy Garcia, Laurie Metcalf, Ron Vawter, Marco Rodriguez, Nancy Travis, William Baldwin, Richard Bradford, Annabella Sciorra, Michael Beach; ***D:*** Mike Figgis; ***W:*** Henry Bean; ***C:*** John A. Alonzo; ***M:*** Brian Banks, Mike Figgis. *PAR*

International Crime 🦴🦴 **1937** Radio hero The Shadow solves a tough crime in this adventure film. **62m/B VHS, Beta.** Rod La Rocque, Astrid Allwyn, William von Brinken; ***D:*** Charles Lamont. *SNC, NOS, AOV*

International House 🦴🦴½ **1933** A wacky Dada-esque Hollywood farce about an incredible array of travelers quarantined in a Shanghai hotel where a mad doctor has perfected television. Essentially a burlesque compilation of skits, gags, and routines. Guest stars Rudy Vallee, Baby Rose Marie and Cab Calloway appear on the quaint "television" device, in musical sequences. ♫Tea Cup; Thank Heaven For You; My Bluebirds are Singing the Blues; Reefer Man. **72m/B VHS, Beta, LV.** W.C. Fields, Peggy Hopkins Joyce, Rudy Vallee, George Burns, Cab Calloway, Sari Maritza, Gracie Allen, Bela Lugosi, Sterling Holloway, Baby Rose Marie; ***D:*** Edward Sutherland. *MCA, MLB*

International Velvet 🦴🦴½ **1978 (PG)** In this long overdue sequel to "National Velvet," adult Velvet, with live-in companion (Plummer), grooms her orphaned niece (O'Neal) to become an Olympic champanion horsewoman. Good photography and performances by Plummer and Hopkins manage to keep the sentiment at a trot. **126m/C VHS, Beta.** *GB* Tatum O'Neal, Anthony Hopkins, Christopher Plummer; ***D:*** Bryan Forbes. *MGM*

Internecine Project ✂✂½ **1973 (PG)** Stylistic espionage tale with Coburn's English professor acting as the mastermind behind an unusual series of murders where industrial spies kill each other, so Coburn can garner a top government job in D.C. Unexpected ending is worth the viewing. Based on Mort Elkind's novel. **89m/C VHS, Beta.** *GB* James Coburn, Lee Grant, Harry Andrews, Keenan Wynn; ***D:*** Ken Hughes; ***W:*** Barry Levinson; ***C:*** Geoffrey Unsworth. *FOX*

Internes Can't Take Money ✂✂½ **1937** With the help of McCrea and gangster Nolan, widow Stanwyck is desperately trying to find the daughter her bank robber husband hid before he died. Young doctor McCrea must save the life of another gangster who knows the whereabouts of the toddler. The first film featuring writer Max Brand's Dr. Kildare characters, which later became part of a series starring Lew Ayres and Laraine Day. **79m/B VHS.** Barbara Stanwyck, Joel McCrea, Lloyd Nolan, Stanley Ridges, Lee Bowman, Irving Bacon; ***D:*** Alfred Santell; ***W:*** Rian James, Theodore Reeves; ***C:*** Theodor Sparkuhl; ***M:*** Gregory Stone. *MCA*

The Interns ✂✂½ **1962** Finessed hospital soaper about interns on the staff of a large city hospital, whose personal lives are fraught with trauma, drugs, birth, death, and abortion. Good performances and direction keep this medical melodrama moving in a gurney-like manner. Followed by the "The New Interns" and the basis for a television series. Adapted from a novel by Richard Frede. **120m/C VHS, Beta, LV.** Cliff Robertson, James MacArthur, Michael Callan, Nick Adams, Stefanie Powers, Suzy Parker, Buddy Ebsen, Telly Savalas, Haya Harareet; ***D:*** David Swift. *COL*

The Interrogation ✂✂✂ *Przesluchanie* **1982** Grueling depiction of Stalin-era Poland proves that nobody makes anticommunist movies better than those who knew tyranny firsthand. A 1950s cabaret starlet is arrested on false charges and endures years of torment in custody. Banned under Polish martial law in 1982, it circulated illegally in the country until 1989. Janda won an award at Cannes for her transformation from showgirl floozy to defiant heroine. In Polish with English subtitles. **118m/C VHS.** *PL* Krystyna Janda, Janusz Gajos, Adam Ferency, Agnieszka Holland, Anna Romantowska; ***D:*** Richard Bugajski. *KIV, FCT, INJ*

Interrupted Journey ✂✂½ **1949** A married man runs away to start a new life with another woman. When she is killed in a train accident, he becomes the prime suspect in her murder. Lots of action and speed, but a disappointing ending. **80m/B VHS.** *GB* Richard Todd, Valerie Hobson; ***D:*** Daniel Birt. *NOS, SNC*

Interrupted Melody ✂✂✂ **1955** True story of opera diva Marjorie Lawrence's courageous battle with polio and her fight to appear once more at the Metropolitan Opera. Parker was nominated for an Oscar in her excellent portrayal of the Australian singer who continues her career despite her handicap. Vocals dubbed by opera star Eileen Farrell. Based on the book by Marjorie Lawrence. **106m/C VHS.** Glenn Ford, Eleanor Parker, Roger Moore, Cecil Kellaway, Evelyn Ellis, Walter Baldwin; ***D:*** Curtis Bernhardt; ***W:*** William Ludwig, Sonya Levien; ***C:*** Paul Vogel. Nominations: Academy Awards '55: Best Screenplay (Ludwig), Best Screenplay (Levien). *MGM*

Intersection ✂½ **1993 (R)** Successful architect Vincent (Gere) is torn between his aloof wife/partner, Sally (Stone), and a sexy journalist mistress, Olivia (Davidovitch). Who to choose? Since he's a completely self-involved boor, you won't care either way. Another retooling of a French film ("Les Choses de la Vie") as a Hollywood star vehicle that doesn't work. Lousy dialogue doesn't help. Does boast some nice location shots of Vancouver, BC. **98m/C VHS, Beta, LV.** Richard Gere, Sharon Stone, Lolita Davidovich, Martin Landau, David Selby, Jenny Morrison; ***D:*** Mark Rydell; ***W:*** Marshall Brickman, David Rayfiel; ***C:*** Vilmos Zsigmond; ***M:*** James Newton Howard. Golden Raspberry Awards '94: Worst Actress (Stone). *PAR*

Interval ✂✂ **1973 (PG)** A middle-aged, globe-trotting woman becomes involved with a young American painter while running from her past. Oberon, 62 at the time, produced and played in this, her last film. Filmed in Mexico. **84m/C VHS, Beta.** Merle Oberon, Robert Wolders; ***D:*** Daniel Mann. *NLC*

Interview with the Vampire ✂✂ **1994 (R)** Portrayal of the elegantly decadent world of vampires and their prey, which features the perverse Lestat (Cruise) who decides to make 18th-century New Orleans aristocrat Louis (Pitt) his latest recruit. Only problem is Louis is horrified by his blood-sucking nature and whines about it for 200 years (it does get tedious). Lestat even makes a child-vampire, Claudia (Dunst), for their own very dysfunctional family but this doesn't turn out well. Director Jordan brings some much needed humor to the dark mix along with some overdone gore. The first book in Anne Rice's "The Vampire Chronicles" was a 17-year film project beset by controversy, including the casting of Cruise (who looks nothing like Rice's description of the character, although Pitt does), leading to an outcry among the cult book's fans though Rice finally came around. Slater replaced the late River Phoenix as the interviewer. **123m/C VHS, LV.** Tom Cruise, Brad Pitt, Kirsten Dunst, Christian Slater, Antonio Banderas, Stephen Rea, Domiziana Giordano; ***D:*** Neil Jordan; ***W:*** Anne Rice; ***C:*** Philippe Rousselot; ***M:*** Elliot Goldenthal. Chicago Film Critics Awards '94: Most Promising Actress (Dunst); MTV Movie Awards '95: Best Male Performance (Pitt), Breakthrough Performance (Dunst), Most Desirable Male (Pitt); Nominations: Academy Awards '94: Best Art Direction/Set Decoration, Best Original Score; Golden Globe Awards '95: Best Supporting Actress (Dunst), Best Original Score; MTV Movie Awards '95: Best Film, Most Desirable Male (Slater, Cruise), Best On-Screen Duo (Tom Cruise/Brad Pitt), Best Villain (Cruise). *WAR*

Intervista ✂✂✂ *Federico Fellini's Intervista* **1987** A pseudo-documentary look at director Fellini's love of the movies, "Intervista" is a mixture of recollection, parody, memoir, satire, self-examination and fantasy. Fellini himself is the master of ceremonies in this joyous celebration of the studio community that features actors, actresses, bit players, make-up artists, scene painters, publicity agents, technicians, and gate-crashers. The high point of the film arrives with the stars of "La Dolce Vita" re-screening the Fellini masterpiece at Ekberg's country villa. It's a special moment of fantasy vs. reality in this glorious tribute to cinema history. In Italian with English subtitles. **108m/C VHS.** *IT* Marcello Mastroianni, Anita Ekberg, Federico Fellini, Sergio Rubini, Lara Wendell, Antonio Cantafora, Antonella Ponziani, Maurizio Mein, Paola Liguori, Nadia Ottaviani; ***D:*** Federico Fellini; ***W:*** Federico Fellini, Gianfranco Angelucci; ***C:*** Tonino Delli Colli; ***M:*** Nicola Piovani. *TRI*

Interzone ✂½ **1988** Humans battle mutants in a post-holocaust world. **97m/C VHS, Beta.** Bruce Abbott; ***D:*** Deran Sarafian. *MED*

Intimate Contact ✂✂✂ **1987 (PG)** Top executive discovers he has AIDS after a business trip fling. Powerful drama as he and his wife try to cope. Excellent, understated performances from Massey and Bloom. Originally made for cable television. **140m/C VHS, Beta.** *GB* Claire Bloom, Daniel Massey, Abigail Cruttenden, Mark Kingston, Sylvia Syms, Sally Jane Jackson; ***D:*** Waris Hussein; ***W:*** Alma Cullen. *HBO*

Intimate Power ✂✂½ **1989 (R)** True story of French schoolgirl sold into slavery to an Ottoman sultan who becomes the harem queen. She bears an heir and begins to teach her son about his people's rights, in the hope that he will bring about reform in Turkey where he grows up to be a sultan. Good cast supports the exotic storytelling in this made for cable drama. **104m/C VHS, Beta, LV.** F. Murray Abraham, Maud Adams, Amber O'Shea; ***D:*** Jack Smight. *HBO*

Intimate Story ✂✂½ **1981** Intimate story of a husband and wife trying unsuccessfully to have a baby, amid the lack of privacy in a Kibbutz. Each blames the other for the problem and tries to escape the problems by focusing on personal fantasies. In Hebrew with English subtitles. **95m/C VHS, Beta.** *IS* Chava Alberstein, Alex Peleg; ***D:*** Israeli Nadav Levitan. *ERG, INJ, TPV*

Intimate Stranger ✂½ **1991 (R)** Sexy, would-be rock star by day, Harry sets out in search of a steadier source of income. Rather than wait on tables all day, she chooses instead to become a phone-sex girl. This turns out to be an unwise career move, as she promptly finds herself the target of a phone-psycho who just can't take "no" for an answer. Will Debbie be able to shake this loser, or will he put a permanent end to her life-long dreams? Made for television. **96m/C VHS, Beta, LV.** Deborah Harry, James Russo, Tim Thomerson, Paige French, Grace Zabriskie; ***D:*** Allan Holzman. *PAR*

Intimate Strangers ✂✂½ **1977** Taut made-for-television expose on battering and its effects on the family. Weaver and Struthers outshine the material, but the finest performance is a cameo by Douglas as Weaver's irascible aged father. **96m/C VHS, Beta.** Dennis Weaver, Sally Struthers, Quinn Cummings, Tyne Daly, Larry Hagman, Rhea Perlman; ***Cameos:*** Melvyn Douglas; ***D:*** John Llewellyn Moxey. *WOV*

Into the Badlands ✂✂ **1992 (R)** Mild made for cable TV thriller presents three suspense tales in "Twilight Zone" fashion, linked by the appearance of a mysterious Man in Black. No, it's not Johnny Cash, but Dern as a sinister bounty hunter in the old west, who inspires strange events on the trail. **89m/C VHS.** Bruce Dern, Mariel Hemingway, Helen Hunt, Dylan McDermott, Lisa Pelikan, Andrew (Andy) Robinson; ***D:*** Sam Pillsbury; ***W:*** Dick Beebe, Marjorie David, Gordon Dawson. *MCA*

Into the Darkness ✂½ **1986** In the world of fashion models, a maniacal, demented killer stalks his prey. **90m/C VHS, Beta.** Donald Pleasence, Ronald Lacey. *NO*

Into the Fire ✂ **1988 (R)** Thriller about a young drifter who, against the backdrop of a Canadian winter, happens upon a roadside lodge and diner, where he gets involved in sex and murder. Title gives a good idea of what to do with this one. **88m/C VHS, Beta, LV.** *CA* Susan Anspach, Art Hindle, Olivia D'Abo, Lee Montgomery; ***D:*** Graeme Campbell. *LIV, VES*

Into the Homeland ✂✂ **1987** Seasoned ex-cop (Boothe) infiltrates a white supremacist group which had kidnapped his teenage daughter. Failed "message" about neo-nazi ethics, but good confrontation between Boothe and his son (Howell) make this so-so viewing. Made for cable television. **95m/C VHS, Beta, LV.** Powers Boothe, C. Thomas Howell, Paul LeMat; ***D:*** Lesli Linka Glatter. *BAR, ORI, WAR*

Into the Night ✂✂ **1985 (R)** Campy, off-beat thriller about a middle-aged, jilted deadbeat (Goldblum), who meets a beautiful woman (Pfeiffer) when she suddenly drops onto the hood of his car, with a relentless gang of Iranians pursuing. During their search through L.A. and other parts of California for the one person who can help her out of this mess, a whole crew of Hollywood directors make cameo appearances, making this a delight for film buffs, but occasionally tedious for general audiences. B.B. King sings the title song. **115m/C VHS, Beta, LV.** Jeff Goldblum, Michelle Pfeiffer, David Bowie, Carl Perkins, Richard Farnsworth, Dan Aykroyd, Paul Mazursky, Roger Vadim, Irene Papas, Bruce McGill, Vera Miles, Clu Gulager, Don Steel, Kathryn Harrold; ***Cameos:*** Jim Henson, Paul Bartel, David Cronenberg, Jack Arnold, Jonathan Demme, Lawrence Kasdan, Amy Heckerling, Donald Siegel, Richard Franklin, Colin Higgins, Andrew Marton; ***D:*** John Landis; ***W:*** Ron Koslow; ***M:*** Ira Newborn. *MCA*

Into the Sun ✂½ **1992 (R)** Hall plays a Hollywood star who encounters real-life danger while hanging out with an Air Force pilot (Pare) to prepare for an upcoming role. Spectacular aerial scenes steal the show, which isn't hard to do in this lackluster movie. **101m/C VHS, LV.** Anthony Michael Hall, Michael Pare, Terry Kiser, Deborah Maria Moore; ***D:*** Fritz Kiersch; ***W:*** John Brancato. *VMK*

Into the West ✂✂✂ **1992 (PG)** Enchanting horse tale set amid the mystic isle of Eire. Brooding, drunken Riley (Byrne), once the leader of a band of travelers (the Irish version of gypsies), leaves the road after his wife's death and settles in a Dublin slum with his two boys. The boys are enraptured when their grandfather turns up with a beautiful white horse, but their happiness is shattered when the police take it away. Boys and horse eventually escape in a wild ride across Ireland and into the west. Spiritual and mythic, with an awe-inspiring performance by the horse. Fitzgerald and Conroy make a run at best performances by kids, while Byrne is convincingly sodden and sulky. Meany and Barkin shine in small parts as sibling travellers. **97m/C VHS, LV.** *IR* Gabriel Byrne, Ellen Barkin, Ciaran Fitzgerald, Ruaidhri Conroy, David Kelly, Colm Meaney; ***D:*** Mike Newell; ***W:*** Jim Sheridan; ***M:*** Patrick Doyle. *TOU*

Into Thin Air 🦴🦴🦴 **1985** A mother searches tirelessly for her college bound son who disappeared on a cross-country drive. Well-done television drama with a good performance from Burstyn. **100m/C VHS, Beta, LV.** Ellen Burstyn, Robert Prosky, Sam Robards, Tate Donovan, Caroline McWilliams, Nicholas Pryor, John Dennis Johnston; ***D:*** Roger Young; ***W:*** George Rubio, Larry Cohen; ***M:*** Brad Fiedel. *VTR*

Intolerance 🦴🦴🦴🦴 **1916** Griffith's largest film in every aspect. An interwoven, four-story epic about human intolerance, with segments set in Babylon, ancient Judea, and Paris. One of the cinema's grandest follies, and greatest achievements. Silent with music score. Laserdisc version contains supplemental material including cuts from other Griffith works. Black and white with some restored color footage. **175m/B VHS, LV.** Lillian Gish, Mae Marsh, Constance Talmadge, Bessie Love, Elmer Clifton, Erich von Stroheim, Eugene Pallette, Seena Owen, Alfred Paget; ***D:*** D.W. Griffith. *GPV, MRV, KIV*

Intrigue 🦴🦴½ **1990 (PG)** Former CIA agent (Loggia) defects to the KGB, but wants to return to the US when he realizes he has a progressive illness. Underground agent and old buddy (Glenn) is recruited with orders to smuggle his former colleague out. Tension continues throughout as murder comes along with the orders. Loads of suspense and twist ending in this made for television nail-biter. **96m/C VHS, LV.** Scott Glenn, Robert Loggia, William Atherton, Martin Shaw, Cherie Lunghi, Eleanor Bron; ***D:*** David Drury. *VMK*

Intruder 🦴🦴 **1977** A man and his stepson are terrorized by a stranger in a panel truck as they travel from Rome to Paris. **98m/C VHS, Beta.** Jean-Louis Trintignant, Mireille Darc, Adolfo Celi. *NO*

Intruder 🦴🦴 **1988 (R)** A psychotic killer stalks an all-night convenience store shopping for fresh meat (customers beware). Slasher movie fans should get a kick out of the plot twist at the end. **90m/C VHS, Beta, LV.** Elizabeth Cox, Renee Estevez, Alvy Moore; ***D:*** Scott Spiegel; ***W:*** Lawrence Bender. *PAR*

Intruder in the Dust 🦴🦴🦴½ **1949** A small southern community develops a lynch mob mentality when a black man is accused of killing a white man. Powerful, but largely ignored portrait of race relations in the South. Solid performances from the whole cast; filmed in Mississippi. Adapted from a novel by William Faulkner. **87m/B VHS.** David Brian, Claude Jarman Jr., Juano Hernandez, Porter Hall, Elizabeth Patterson; ***D:*** Clarence Brown; ***C:*** Robert L. Surtees. *MGM, MOV, BTV*

Intruder Within 🦴 **1981** Half-baked thriller about crew on an isolated oil rig in Antarctica who, while drilling, unearth a nasty creature that goes around terrorizing the frost-bitten men and occasional stray woman. Made for television. **91m/C VHS, Beta.** Chad Everett, Joseph Bottoms, Jennifer Warren; ***D:*** Peter Carter. *TWE*

Intruders 🦴🦴 **1992** Follows the story of three people who have unexplained lapses of time in their lives which they eventually believe are connected to visits by aliens. The three are brought together by a skeptical psychiatrist. The aliens are your typical bugged-eyed, white-faced spooks but part of the film is genuinely unsettling. **162m/C VHS.** Richard Crenna, Mare Winningham, Susan Blakely, Ben Vereen, Steven Berkoff, Daphne Ashbrook; ***D:*** Dan Curtis. *FXV*

Invader 🦴🦴 **1991 (R)** When a news reporter is sent to cover a mysterious massacre, he begins to realize that the culprits are vicious aliens thirsty for blood...and now they're after him! **95m/C VHS, LV.** Hans Bachman, A. Thomas Smith, Rich Foucheux, John Cooke, Robert Diedermann, Allison Sheehy, Ralph Bluemke; ***D:*** Phillip Cook. *VMK*

The Invaders 🦴🦴 *Erik the Conqueror; Gli Invasori; La Ruee Des Vikings; Fury of the Vikings* **1963** Two Viking brothers battle each other and the Britons. **88m/C VHS, Beta.** *FR IT* Cameron Mitchell, George Ardisson, Andrea Checchi, Francoise Christophe, Joe Robinson; ***D:*** Mario Bava; ***M:*** Les Baxter. *NO*

The Invaders **1967** The popular science fiction series created by Larry Cohen stars Thinnes, as David Vincent, who attempts to convince people he has witnessed an alien landing and that they want to take over Earth. "Beach Head" is the pilot episode. Additional episodes available. **53m/C VHS.** Roy Thinnes, Kent Smith, Diane Baker, J.D. Cannon, James Daly, John Milford, Ellen Corby, Vaughn Taylor; ***D:*** Joseph Sargent. *GKK, MOV*

The Invaders 🦴🦴½ **1995** TV mini is an updated continuation of the 1967 sci-fi series that finds the pollution-loving aliens gradually conquering Earth by allowing humans to destroy their own ecosystem (which we're so good at anyway). Bewildered hero Nolan Wood (Bakula) is trying to get everyone to believe in the alien invasion but since he's just gotten out of prison, it's an uphill climb. Still, the aliens (lead by effectively evil Thomas) would like to permanently shut Nolan up. Thinnes, who starred in the original series, briefly reprises his role as David Vincent. **180m/C VHS, LV.** Scott Bakula, Richard Thomas, DeLane Matthews, Terence Knox, Elizabeth Pena, Raoul Trujillo, Richard Belzer, Jon Polito, Roy Thinnes, Jon Cypher, Todd Susman, Jack Kehler, Elinor Donahue; ***D:*** Paul Shapiro; ***W:*** James Dott; ***C:*** Alan Kivilo; ***M:*** Joseph Vitarelli. *REP*

Invaders from Mars 🦴🦴½ **1953** Young boy cries "martian" in this sci-fi cheapy classic. He can't convince the townspeople of this invasion because they've already been possessed by the alien beings. His parents are zapped by the little green things first, making this perhaps an allegory for the missing Eisenhower/Stepford years. Includes previews of coming attractions from classic science fiction films. Remade in 1986 by Tobe Hooper. **78m/C VHS, Beta.** Helena Carter, Arthur Franz, Jimmy Hunt, Leif Erickson; ***D:*** William Cameron Menzies. *MED, MLB*

Invaders from Mars 🦴½ **1986 (PG)** A high-tech remake of Menzies' 1953 semi-classic about a Martian invasion perceived only by one young boy and a sympathetic (though hysterical) school nurse, played by mother and son Black and Carson. Instant camp. **102m/C VHS, Beta, LV.** Hunter Carson, Karen Black, Louise Fletcher, Laraine Newman, Timothy Bottoms, Bud Cort; ***D:*** Tobe Hooper; ***W:*** Dan O'Bannon, Don Jakoby. *MED, IME*

Invasion 🦴🦴½ **1965** A hospital opens its doors to an accident victim, and his attractive female visitors don't seem sympathetic to the idea of a long hospital stay. Turns out he's an escaped alien prisoner, and the alien babes, intent on intergalactic extradition, place a force field around the hospital and demand his return. Early effort of director Bridges, who later did "The Shooting Party." Interesting, creepy, atmospheric, with very cool camera moves. **82m/B VHS.** *GB* Edward Judd, Yoko Tani, Valerie Gearon, Lyndon Brook, Tsai Chin, Barrie Ingham; ***D:*** Alan Bridges. *MOV*

Invasion Earth: The Aliens Are Here! 🦴 **1987** A cheap spoof of monster movies, as an insectoid projectionist takes over the minds of a movie audience. Clips of Godzilla, Mothra and other beasts are interpolated. **84m/C VHS, Beta, LV.** Janice Fabian, Christian Lee; ***D:*** George Maitland. *VTR, NWV*

Invasion Force 🦴 **1990** A terrorist army parachutes into a remote region where a film crew is preparing to set up for an action movie. The moviemakers must scare away the terrorists with their smokepots and blanks. Sounds promising, but proves to be as empty as the movie props used to scare the terrorists. **93m/C VHS.** Richard Lynch, David Shark, Renee Cline, Douglas Hartier, Graham Times, Angie Synodis; ***D:*** David A. Prior. *AIP*

The Invasion of Carol Enders 🦴½ **1974** A woman, almost killed by a prowler, awakens with an expanded consciousness, and tries to convince her near husband that her death wasn't an accident. **72m/C VHS, Beta.** Meredith Baxter, Christopher Connelly, Charles Aidman. *LIV*

Invasion of Privacy 🦴🦴 **1992 (R)** Alex is a psycho prison inmate obsessed with high profile journalist, Hilary. When Hilary interviews Alex for a magazine cover story, his obsession only grows stronger. Then Alex gets paroled and goes to work for Hilary. When he discovers Hilary isn't interested in him, Alex turns his fantasies to her daughter, who has no notion what she's getting into. An unrated version is also available. Made for cable television. **95m/C VHS.** Robby Benson, Jennifer O'Neill, Lydie Denier, Ian Ogilvy; ***D:*** Kevin Meyer; ***W:*** Kevin Meyer. *PSM*

Invasion of the Animal People *Woof!* *Terror in the Midnight Sun; Space Invasion of Lapland; Horror in the Midnight Sun; Space Invasion from Lapland* **1962** Hairy monster from outer space attacks Lapland. Narrated by Carradine, the only American in the cast. Pretty silly. **73m/C VHS.** *SW* Robert Burton, Barbara Wilson, John Carradine; ***D:*** Virgil W. Vogel, Jerry Warren. *VMK, SNC, NOS*

Invasion of the Bee Girls 🦴🦴🦴 *Graveyard Tramps* **1973** California girls are mysteriously transformed into deadly nymphomaniacs in this delightful campy science fiction romp. Written by Meyer who later directed "Star Trek II: The Wrath of Khan." **85m/C VHS.** Victoria Vetri, William Smith, Anitra Ford, Cliff Osmond, Wright King, Ben Hammer; ***D:*** Denis Sanders; ***W:*** Nicholas Meyer; ***M:*** Charles Bernstein. *SUE*

Invasion of the Blood Farmers *Woof!* **1972 (PG)** In a small New York town, members of an ancient Druidic cult murder young women, taking their blood in the hope of finding the precise, rare blood type to keep their queen alive. A real woofer. **86m/C VHS, Beta.** Norman Kelley, Tanna Hunter, Bruce Detrick, Jack Neubeck, Cythia Fleming, Paul Craig Jennings; ***D:*** Ed Adlum. *NO*

Invasion of the Body Snatchers 🦴🦴🦴 **1956** The one and only post-McCarthy paranoid sci-fi epic, where a small California town is infiltrated by pods from outer space that replicate and replace humans. A chilling, genuinely frightening exercise in nightmare dislocation. Based upon a novel by Jack Finney. Remade in 1978. The laserdisc version contains commentary by Maurice Yacowar, the text of an interview with Siegel, and the original theatrical trailer. The film itself is presented in its original wide-screen format. **80m/B VHS, LV.** Kevin McCarthy, Dana Wynter, Carolyn Jones, King Donovan, Donald Siegel; ***D:*** Donald Siegel; ***W:*** Sam Peckinpah; ***C:*** Ellsworth Fredericks. *REP, CRC, MLB*

Invasion of the Body Snatchers 🦴🦴🦴½ **1978 (PG)** One of the few instances where a remake is an improvement on the original, which was itself a classic. This time, the "pod people" are infesting San Francisco, with only a small group of people aware of the invasion. A ceaselessly inventive, creepy version of the alien-takeover paradigm, with an intense and winning performance by Sutherland. **115m/C VHS, Beta, LV.** Donald Sutherland, Brooke Adams, Veronica Cartwright, Leonard Nimoy, Jeff Goldblum, Kevin McCarthy, Donald Siegel, Art Hindle; ***D:*** Philip Kaufman; ***W:*** W.D. Richter; ***C:*** Michael Chapman. *MGM*

Invasion of the Body Stealers *Woof!* *Thin Air; The Body Stealers* **1969 (PG)** Aliens are thought to be the captors when sky-divers begin vanishing in mid-air. Uneven sci-fi with nothing going for it. **115m/C VHS, Beta.** *GB* George Sanders, Maurice Evans, Patrick Allen; ***D:*** Gerry Levy. *LIV*

Invasion of the Flesh Hunters *Woof!* *Cannibals in the Streets; Savage Apocalypse; The Slaughterers; Cannibals in the City; Virus* **1982** Group of tortured Vietnam veterans returns home carrying a cannibalistic curse with them. Smorgasbord of gore and sensationalism is not for discriminating tastes. **90m/C VHS, Beta.** *IT* John Saxon, Elizabeth Turner; ***D:*** Anthony (Antonio Margheriti) Dawson; ***W:*** Anthony (Antonio Margheriti) Dawson. *LIV, VES*

Invasion of the Girl Snatchers *Woof!* **1973** Aliens from another planet, in cahoots with a cult kingpin, subdue young earth girls and force them to undergo bizarre acts that may just rob them of their dignity. Save a bit of your own dignity by staying away. Cheap look, cheap feel, cheap thrills. **90m/C VHS, Beta.** Elizabeth Rush, Ele Grigsby, David Roster; ***D:*** Lee Jones. *NO*

Invasion of the Saucer Men 🦴 **1957** Suburban teenagers (Terrell, Castillo) are detained by a little green man at lovers lane. When they return with police to the scene, only the corpse of the town drunk (Gorshin) remains. Fortunately, the dead man's roommate (Osborn) believes them but the trio must convince authorities before the alien creatures multiply and take over the world. **69m/B VHS.** Steven Terrell, Gloria Castillo, Frank Gorshin, Lyn Osborn, Ed Nelson, Angelo Rossitto; ***D:*** Edward L. Cahn; ***M:*** Ronald Stein. *COL*

Invasion of the Space Preachers **1990** Hideous creatures from outer space arrive on Earth with plans for conquest. Led by the seemingly human Reverend Lash, they prey on the innocent and trusting, fleecing God-fearing folk out of their hard earned cash! **100m/C VHS, Beta.** Jim Wolfe, Guy Nelson, Eliska Hahn, Gary Brown, Jesse Johnson, John Riggs; ***D:*** Daniel Boyd; ***W:*** Daniel Boyd. *RHI*

Invasion of the Vampires 🦴 *La Invasion de Los Vampiros* **1961** Burrito bat fest has Count Frankenhausen doing his vampire thing in a small, 16th century village. Atmospheric sets are highlight. Not a good substitute for No Doze. **78m/B VHS.** *MX* Carlos Agosti, Rafael Etienne, Bertha Moss, Tito Junco, Erna Martha Bauman, Fernando Soto, Enrique Garcia Alvarez, David Reynoso; ***D:*** Miguel Morayta; ***W:*** Miguel Morayta. *SNC*

Invasion of the Zombies 🦴 **1961** Barefisted wrestler Santo faces of brace of zombies in order to prove that men with short necks can hug other men and still be mucho macho. **85m/B VHS.** *MX* Santo; ***D:*** Benito Alazraki. *SNC, HHT*

Invasion U.S.A. 🦴½ **1952** Cheap Red Scare movie using tons of stock footage showing actual bombings and air battles. O'Herlihy is a stranger who visits a New York bar and convinces the patrons that the H-bomb has been unleashed on America, while Mohr romances Castle. Full of propaganda and overacting. Based on a story by Robert Smith and Franz Spencer. **73m/B VHS.** Gerald Mohr, Peggy Castle, Dan O'Herlihy, Robert Bice, Tom Kennedy, Phyllis Coates; ***D:*** Alfred E. Green; ***W:*** Robert Smith. *SNC*

Invasion U.S.A. 🦴 **1985 (R)** A mercenary defends nothing less than the entire country against Russian terrorists landing in Florida and looking for condos. A record-setting amount of people killed. Count them—it's not like you'll miss anything important. Norris is a bit less animated than a wooden Indian, and the acting is more painful to endure than the violence. Glasnost saved the movie industry from additional paranoia movies of this kind. **108m/C VHS, Beta, LV.** Chuck Norris, Richard Lynch, Melissa Prophet, Alex Colon, Billy Drago; ***D:*** Joseph Zito; ***W:*** James Bruner. *MGM*

Investigation 🦴🦴½ **1979** A Frenchman plans to murder his wife so he can marry his pregnant mistress, guaranteeing an heir. Subtle study of small town people so concerned with their own welfare that the dirty deeds of the lead character might be overlooked. Fine performances and story development make this worth investigating. In French with English subtitles. **116m/C VHS, Beta.** *FR* Victor Lanoux, Valerie Mairesse; ***D:*** Etienne Perier. *SUE*

Invincible 🦴½ **1980 (R)** Martial arts student must find and correct another student who has turned evil. For Bruce Lee fans, as if they haven't already memorized all the memorable lines-"hiyaah," "ugh," "oof," etc. **93m/C VHS, Beta.** Chen Sing, Ho Chung Dao. *GEM*

Invincible Armor 🦴 **197?** Wrong man is accused of murder when an ambitious minister of justice unleashes a sinister plot. **92m/C VHS, Beta.** *TWE*

Invincible Barbarian *Woof!* **1983** A young man leads a tribe of amazing Amazon warriors in a sneak attack against the tribe that annihilated his native village. One of those movies that presumes "primitivism" can be recreated through bad acting. **92m/C VHS, Beta.** Diana Roy, David Jenkins. *PSM*

The Invincible Gladiator 🦴½ *Il Gladiatore Invincibile* **1963** A gladiator who saves the evil man ruling a land for a boy-king is given command of an army. He eventually leads the army in revolt when the evil man tries to take over the throne. Plodding with stock characters. **96m/C VHS.** *IT SP* Richard Harrison, Isabel Corey, Livio Lorenzon; ***D:*** Frank Gregory. *SNC*

Invincible Gladiators *Woof!* **1964** The sons of Hercules labor to aid a prince whose bride had been kidnapped by an evil queen. Laborious to watch. **87m/C VHS, Beta.** Richard Lloyd, Claudia Lange, Tony Freeman; ***D:*** Robert Mauri. *NO*

Invincible Mr. Disraeli 🦴🦴½ **1963** Presentation from "George Schaefer's Showcase Theatre" deals with the life and career of Benjamin Disraeli, novelist, philosopher, first Earl of Beaconsfield, statesman, and Prime Minister. Basically a tribute. Made for television. **76m/C VHS, Beta.** Trevor Howard, Greer Garson, Hurd Hatfield, Kate Reid; ***D:*** George Schaefer. *FHS*

The Invincible Six 🦴🦴 **1968** An unlikely band of thieves running from the law winds up protecting a small village from marauding bandits. Plenty of action, as you would expect when thieves take on bandits, but with no scene-stealers or sympathetic characters the story lacks interest. Unremarkable choreography by ballet great Rudolf Nureyev. Filmed in Iran. **96m/C VHS, Beta.** Stuart Whitman, Elke Sommer, Curt Jurgens, Jim Mitchum, Ian Ogilvy; ***D:*** Jean Negulesco. *NO*

Invisible Adversaries 🦴🦴 **1977** A photographer uncovers an extra-terrestrial plot to cause excessive aggression in humans. She and her lover attempt to hold on to their crumbling humanity. Movies like this make you mad enough to tear something up. Enjoyed a meek cult following. In German with English subtitles. **112m/C VHS, Beta.** *GE* Susanne Widl, Peter Weibel; ***D:*** Valie Export. *FCT*

Invisible Agent 🦴🦴 **1942** Hall plays an agent using the secret formula to outwit the Nazis in this third sequel to "The Invisible Man." Especially enjoyable for the kids. Based on characters suggested in H.G. Well's "The Invisible Man." **83m/B VHS.** Ilona Massey, Jon Hall, Peter Lorre, Cedric Hardwicke, J. Edward Bromberg, Albert Basserman, John Litel, Holmes Herbert; ***D:*** Edwin L. Marin; ***W:*** Curt Siodmak. *MCA, FCT*

The Invisible Avenger 🦴🦴 *Bourbon St. Shadows* **1958** Based on the vintage radio character "The Shadow." A detective who can make himself invisible investigates the murder of a New Orleans jazz musician. The mysterious element successful on radio is lost on film, and only the Shadow knows why. **60m/B VHS, Beta.** Richard Derr, Marc Daniels, Helen Westcott, Jeanne Neher; ***D:*** John Sledge, Ben Parker. *SNC, SMW, RXM*

The Invisible Boy 🦴🦴½ **1957 (G)** Science fiction story about a young boy and his robot (Robby the Robot from "Forbidden Planet"). Kids will enjoy this adventure as told through the viewpoint of the child. Based on a story by Edmund Cooper. **89m/C VHS.** Richard Eyer, Diane Brewster, Philip Abbott, Harold J. Stone; ***D:*** Herman Hoffman; ***W:*** Cyril Hume; ***M:*** Les Baxter. *MGM, FCT*

The Invisible Dead 🦴 *Orloff Against the Invisible Man* **1970** So many invisible man movies, so little time. A scientist creates an invisible man, imprisons and tortures him. A bit miffed with his host, he who can't be seen escapes, and vents his invisible spleen. **90m/C VHS.** *IT* Howard Vernon, Britt Carva; ***D:*** Jess (Jesus) Franco. *NO*

The Invisible Dr. Mabuse 🦴🦴🦴 *The Invisible Horror; Die Unsichtbaren Krallen des Dr. Mabuse* **1962** Possibly the best of the Dr. Mabuse series sees the mad scientist using an invisibility agent in an attempt to take over the world. Preiss also played the title villian in Fritz Lang's "The Thousand Eyes of Dr. Mabuse." **89m/B VHS, Beta.** *GE* Lex Barker, Karin Dor, Siegfried Lowitz, Wolfgang Preiss, Rudolf Fernau; ***D:*** Harald Reinl. *SNC*

The Invisible Ghost 🦴½ **1941** A man carries out a series of grisly stranglings while under hypnosis by his insane wife. Typically bad low-budget exploiter about a fun-lovin' crazy couple bringing down property values in the neighborhood. **70m/B VHS, Beta.** Bela Lugosi, Polly Ann Young; ***D:*** Joseph H. Lewis. *VYY, MRV, SNC*

Invisible Invaders 🦴 **1959** Short, cheap, and silly aliens-try-to-take-over-the-earth flick. This time they're moonmen who use the bodies of dead earthlings (ugh) to attack the living until Agar can save the day. Carradine has a brief role as a formerly-dead scientist. **67m/B VHS.** John Agar, Robert Hutton, Hal Torey, Jean Byron, Philip Tonge, John Carradine; ***D:*** Edward L. Cahn; ***W:*** Samuel Newman; ***C:*** Maury Gertsman. *MGM*

The Invisible Kid 🦴 **1988** A shy teen manages to make himself invisible, a feat which ironically permits him to get people to notice him. Now he can visit places he's only dreamed of, including the girls' locker room. For those who have dreamed about girls' locker rooms. **95m/C VHS, Beta, LV.** Karen Black, Jay Underwood, Chynna Phillips, Wally Ward, Brother Theodore; ***D:*** Avery Crounse; ***W:*** Avery Crounse. *MED, VTR*

The Invisible Killer 🦴½ **1940** Someone is killing folks by sending poison through telephone lines. A detective and a reporter team up to find the scoundrel by setting up an answering machine that automatically plays back messages to the caller. Bad connection of events leads to a static resolution. **61m/B VHS, Beta.** Grace Bradley, Roland Drew, William Newell; ***D:*** Sam Newfield. *SNC, MLB*

The Invisible Man 🦴🦴🦴🦴 **1933** The vintage horror-fest based on H. G. Wells' novella about a scientist whose formula for invisibility slowly drives him insane. His mind definitely wandering, he plans plans to use his recipe to rule the world. Rains' first role; though his body doesn't appear until the final scene, his voice characterization is magnificent. The visual detail is excellent, setting standards that are imitated because they are difficult to surpass; with special effects by John P. Fulton. **71m/B VHS, Beta, LV.** Claude Rains, Gloria Stuart, Dudley Digges, William Harrigan, Una O'Connor, E.E. Clive, Dwight Frye; ***D:*** James Whale; ***W:*** R.C. Sherriff. *MCA, MLB*

The Invisible Man Returns 🦴🦴🦴 **1940** Price stars as the original invisible man's brother. Using the same invisibility formula, Price tries to clear himself after being charged with murder. He reappears at the worst times, and you gotta love that floating gun. Fun sequel to 1933's classic "The Invisible Man." **81m/B VHS.** Cedric Hardwicke, Vincent Price, John Sutton, Nan Grey; ***D:*** Joe May; ***C:*** Milton Krasner. *MCA, MLB*

The Invisible Maniac *Woof!* **1990 (R)** A crazy voyeur perfects a serum for invisibility and promptly gets a job as a physics teacher in a high school. There he leers at girls taking showers and slaughters students when he is caught. For voyeurs. Get outta here, you maniac. **87m/C VHS.** Noel Peters, Shannon Wilsey, Melissa Moore, Robert Ross, Rod Sweitzer, Eric Champnella, Kalei Shellabarger, Gail Lyon, Debra Lamb; ***D:*** Rif Coogan; ***W:*** Rif Coogan. *REP*

The Invisible Man's Revenge 🦴🦴½ **1944** Left for dead on a safari five years before, Hall seeks revenge against Sondergaard and Matthews, aided by scientist Carradine who renders Hall invisible. Only problem is Hall doesn't stay that way. Fifth in Universal's "Invisible Man" film series. **78m/B VHS.** Jon Hall, John Carradine, Gale Sondergaard, Lester Matthews, Evelyn Ankers, Alan Curtis, Leon Errol, Doris Lloyd; ***D:*** Ford Beebe; ***W:*** Bertram Millhauser; ***C:*** Milton Krasner. *MCA*

The Invisible Monster *Slaves of the Invisible Monster* **1950** Special investigators Lane Carlson and Carol Richards battle a mad scientist ready to take over the world with his invisible army. 12 episodes of the original serial edited onto two cassettes. **167m/B VHS.** Richard Webb, Aline Towne, Lane Bradford, Stanley Price, John Crawford, George Meeker; ***D:*** Fred Brannon. *REP*

The Invisible Ray 🦴🦴½ **1936** For a change, this horror film features Lugosi as the hero, fighting Karloff, a scientist who locates a meteor that contains a powerful substance. Karloff is poisoned and becomes a murdering megalomaniac. Watching Karloff and Lugosi interact, and the great special effects—including a hot scene where a scientist bursts into flames—helps you ignore a generally hokey script. **82m/B VHS, Beta, LV.** Boris Karloff, Bela Lugosi, Frances Drake, Frank Lawton, Beulah Bondi, Walter Kingsford; ***D:*** Lambert Hillyer. *MCA, MLB*

The Invisible Strangler 🦴½ **1976 (PG)** A death-row murderer can make himself invisible and rubs out witnesses who helped put him away; woman risks her life to expose him when the police fail to see the problem. Very violent collection of brutal scenes. Not released theatrically until 1984. **85m/C VHS, Beta.** Robert Foxworth, Stefanie Powers, Elke Sommer, Sue Lyon, Leslie Parrish, Marianna Hill; ***D:*** John Florea. *TWE*

The Invisible Terror 🦴🦴 **1963** A maniac steals a mad scientist's invisibility formula and uses it on a number of innocent victims. **?m/C VHS.** Herbert Stass, Ellen Scheirs. *SNC*

Invisible: The Chronicles of Benjamin Knight 🦴🦴½ **1993 (R)** Scientist Benjamin Knight is rendered invisible during a terrible laboratory accident. His only hope of regaining his visible form is a desperate search by Knight and his fellow scientists for just the right chemical antidote. **80m/C VHS, Beta.** Brian Cousins, Jennifer Nash, Michael DellaFemina, Curt Lowens, David Kaufman, Alan Oppenheimer, Aharon Ipale; ***D:*** Jack Ersgard; ***W:*** Earl Kenton. *PAR*

The Invisible Woman 🦴🦴🦴 **1940** Above average comedy about zany professor Barrymore discovering the secret of invisibility and making luscious model Bruce transparent. Great cast makes this a very likeable movie. Based on a story by Curt Siodmak and Joe May, the same team that wrote "The Invisible Man Returns." **73m/B VHS.** John Barrymore, Virginia Bruce, John Howard, Charlie Ruggles, Oscar Homolka, Margaret Hamilton, Donald MacBride, Edward Brophy, Shemp Howard, Charles Lane, Thurston Hall; ***D:*** Edward Sutherland; ***W:*** Robert Lees, Fred Rinaldo, Gertrude Purcell. *MCA, FCT*

Invitation au Voyage 🦴🦴½ **1982 (R)** Follows the journey of a twin who refuses to accept the death of his sister, a rock singer. The obsession is played fairly well, but it's a no-twin situation, even though the guy can't admit it. Perversity is played to the point of overkill. From the novel "Moi, Ma Soeur Images," by Jean Bany. In French with English subtitles. **90m/C VHS, Beta.** *FR* Laurent Malet, Nina Scott, Aurore Clement, Mario Adorf; ***D:*** Peter Del Monte. Nominations: Cannes Film Festival '82: Best Film. *COL, INJ*

Invitation to a Gunfighter 🦴🦴 **1964** Small town politics change when a paid assassin ambles into town and creates a lot of talk among the neighbors. Like a long joke in which the teller keeps forgetting the important details, the plot grows confusing though it's not complicated. Brynner is interesting as an educated, half-black/half-creole, hired gun. **92m/C VHS, Beta.** Yul Brynner, George Segal, Strother Martin, William Hickey, Janice Rule, Mike Kellin, Pat Hingle; ***D:*** Richard Wilson. *MGM, HHE*

Invitation to Hell *Woof!* **1984** Tormented maiden has a devil of a time discovering a secret power that can enable her to gracefully decline a satanic summoning. The cliched evil is tormenting. **100m/C VHS, Beta.** Becky Simpson, Joseph Sheahan, Colin Efford, Stephen Longhurst. *NO*

Invitation to Hell 🦴½ **1984** "Faust" meets "All My Children" in celluloid suburbia. Never Emmied Lucci is the devil's dirty worker, persuading upwardly mobile suburbanites to join a really exclusive country club in exchange for a little downward mobility. Urich, a space scientist, and family are new in town, and soul searching Lucci's got her devil vixen sights set on space jock and brood. Bound to disappoint both fans of Craven's early independent work ("Last House on the Left") and his later high gloss ("Nightmare on Elm Street") formulas. Made for the small screen. **100m/C VHS, Beta.** Susan Lucci, Robert Urich, Joanna Cassidy, Kevin McCarthy, Patty McCormack, Joe Regalbuto, Soleil Moon Frye; ***D:*** Wes Craven. *NO*

Invitation to the Dance 🦴🦴½ **1956** Three classic dance sequences, "Circus," "Ring Around the Rosy," and "Sinbad the Sailor." For dance lovers, featuring excellent performances by Kelly. **93m/C VHS, Beta.** Gene Kelly, Igor Youskevitch, Tamara Toumanova; ***D:*** Gene Kelly. Berlin International Film Festival '56: Golden Berlin Bear. *MGM, CCB*

Invitation to the Wedding 🦴🦴 **1973 (PG)** When the best friend of a bridegroom falls in love with the bride, he stops at nothing to halt the wedding. Not exactly the Gielgud movie of the year, but there are some excellent scenes between him and Richardson. **89m/C VHS, Beta.** John Gielgud, Ralph Richardson, Paul Nicholas, Elizabeth Shepherd; ***D:*** Joseph Brooks; ***M:*** Joseph Brooks. *VES*

The Ipcress File 🦴🦴🦴 **1965** The first of the Harry Palmer spy mysteries that made Caine a star. Based upon the bestseller by Len Deighton, it features the flabby, nearsighted spy investigating the kidnapping of notable British scientists. Solid scenes, including a scary brainwashing session, and tongue-firmly-in-British-cheek humor. Lots of camera play to emphasize Caine's myopia. Two sequels: "Funeral in Berlin" and "Billion Dollar Brain." **108m/C VHS, Beta.** *GB* Michael Caine, Nigel Green, Guy Doleman, Sue Lloyd; ***D:*** Sidney J. Furie; ***M:*** John Barry. British Academy Awards '65: Best Film. *MCA*

Iphigenia 🦴🦴🦴 **1977** Based on the classic Greek tragedy by Euripides, this story concerns the Greek leader Agamemnon, who plans to sacrifice his lovely daughter, Iphigenia, to please the gods. Mere mortals protest and start a save-the-babe movement, but Euripides' moral—you can't please 'em all—is devastatingly realized. Fine adaptation that becomes visually extravagant at times, with an equally fine musical score. In Greek with English subtitles. **130m/C VHS, Beta.** *GR* Irene Papas, Costa Kazakos, Tatiana Papamoskou; ***D:*** Michael Cacoyannis; ***M:*** Mikis Theodorakis. Nominations: Academy Awards '77: Best Foreign Language Film; Cannes Film Festival '77: Best Film. *COL, FHS, INJ*

I.Q. 🦴🦴½ **1994 (PG)** Albert Einstein (the irascible Matthau) thinks his co-ed niece (Ryan) is in need of a little romance, so he engineers a plan to get her into the arms of Robbins, a local auto mechanic. Robbins and Ryan are comfortable in their comic roles, although they're both above the material. Matthau shines as the famous physicist. Plot gets a little farfetched with its central contrivance of making Robbins look like a brilliant scientist, which leaves second half of story flat. However, chemistry between leads is undeniable and you can't help but cheer on the inevitable. Visually pleasing with Ryan costumed in cool, elegant '50s fashions. Filmed in Princeton, New Jersey. **95m/C VHS, Beta.** Tim Robbins, Meg Ryan, Walter Matthau, Lou Jacobi, Gene Saks, Joseph Maher, Stephen Fry, Tony Shalhoub, Frank Whaley; ***D:*** Fred Schepisi; ***W:*** Michael Leeson, Andy Breckman; ***M:*** Jerry Goldsmith. *PAR*

Iran: Days of Crisis 🦴🦴½ **1991** An insightful made-for-cable-TV miniseries recounts America's humiliation at the hands of Iranian radicals in 1979, told from the vantage of a U.S. embassy official married to a Tehran woman. Former Carter administration aides Hamilton Jordan and Gerald Rafshoon devised the docudrama, which spares neither them nor their president in showing how bungled and shortsighted policies led to 52 Americans held hostage for over a year. **185m/C VHS.** Arliss Howard, Alice Krige, George Grizzard, Jeff Fahey, Tony Goldwyn, Ronald Guttman, Valerie Kaprisky, Daniel Gelin; ***D:*** Kevin Connor. *TTC*

Irezumi 🦴🦴🦴 *Spirit of Tattoo* **1983** A Japanese woman has her body elaborately tattooed to please her lover. Things start off well enough. He's an inept lover, so she has directions tattooed, but then he discovers a "Dear John" letter on her foot just as she gives him the boot. Actually proves an interesting study in obsession and eroticism, with the tattoos drawing the lovers deeper and deeper until they get under each other's skin. In Japanese with English subtitles. **88m/C VHS, Beta, LV.** *JP INJ*

Iris 🦴🦴 **1989** Drama follows the passionate and tragic life of New Zealand writer Iris Wilkinson, an international novelist, poet, and journalist. Wilkinson achieved a great deal of acclaim as a writer, but suffered many personal tragedies, and eventually took her own life at age 33. Well intentioned but clunky treatment of powerful subject matter. **90m/C VHS, Beta.** *NZ* Helen Morse. *WOM*

Irish Cinderella 🦴🦴 **1922** A silent version of the Cinderella legend set in Ireland, with thematic stress on Irish politics and patriotism. **72m/B VHS, Beta, 8mm.** Pattie MacNamara. *VYY*

Irish Luck 🦴🦴 **1939** A bellhop turns detective to figure out the mysterious happenings in his hotel. Becomes terminally cute by playing on a luck o' the Irish theme. **58m/B VHS.** Frankie Darro, Dick Purcell, Sheila Darcy, Grant Withers; ***D:*** Howard Bretherton. *NOS, DVT, HEG*

The Irishman 🦴🦴½ **1978** Set in 1920s Australia, the tale of a proud North Queensland family and their struggles to stay together. The Irish immigrant father is a teamster whose horse-drawn wagons are threatened by progress. His fight to preserve old ways is impressive, but gives way to sentimentality. **108m/C VHS, Beta.** *AU* Lou Brown, Michael Craig, Simon Burke, Robyn Nevin, Bryan Brown; ***D:*** Donald Crombie. *VES*

Irma La Douce 🦴🦴½ **1963** A gendarme pulls a one-man raid on a back-street Parisian joint and falls in love with one of the hookers he arrests. Lemmon is great as a well-meaning, incompetent boob, and MacLaine gives her all as the hapless hooker. A plodding pace, however, robs it of the original's zip, though it was a box office smash. Broadway musical is lost without the music. **144m/C VHS, Beta, LV.** Jack Lemmon, Shirley MacLaine, Herschel Bernardi; ***D:*** Billy Wilder; ***W:*** Billy Wilder, I.A.L. Diamond; ***M:*** Andre Previn. Academy Awards '63: Best Original Score; Golden Globe Awards '64: Best Actress—Musical/Comedy (MacLaine); Nominations: Academy Awards '63: Best Actress (MacLaine), Best Color Cinematography. *MGM, IME, FOX*

Iron & Silk 🦴🦴½ **1991 (PG)** A young American searches for himself while he teaches English and learns martial arts in mainland China. Based on the true story of Salzman's travels. His studies of martial arts and Chinese culture provide a model for his students in their studies of American language and culture. Beautiful photography. Fine performances. **94m/C VHS, LV.** Mark Saltzman, Pan Qingfu, Jeanette Lin Tsui, Vivian Wu; ***D:*** Shirley Sun; ***W:*** Mark Saltzman, Shirley Sun; ***M:*** Michael Gibbs. *LIV*

Iron Angel 🦴½ **1964** During the Korean War a squadron sets out to silence North Korean guns. They do. Judging by their eternal bickering they must have put the enemy to sleep. **84m/B VHS.** Jim Davis, Margo Woode, Donald (Don "Red") Barry, L.Q. Jones; ***D:*** Ken Kennedy; ***W:*** Ken Kennedy. *NOS, LOO*

Iron Cowboy 🦴🦴 **1968** Actor finds romance with film editor while audience stifles yawns. Filmed on the set of "Blue," this pre-"Deliverance" Reynolds comedy never made it to the theaters. (Smithee is actually director Jud Taylor.) **86m/C VHS.** Burt Reynolds, Barbara Loden, Terence Stamp, Noam Pitlik, Ricardo Montalban, Patricia Casey, Jane Hampton, Joseph Perry; ***D:*** Alan Smithee. *ACE*

The Iron Crown 🦴🦴 **1941** A 13th-century legend inspired this sometime violent spectacle involving the title totem, a symbol of justice ignored by a powerful king at his peril. There's wonderful pagentry and a notable Tarzan imitator, but the pace is terribly slow. Italian dialogue with English subtitles. **100m/C VHS.** ***D:*** Alessandro Blasetti. *FST*

Iron Dragon Strikes Back **1984** Man seeks out the men who murdered his martial arts instructor. **90m/C VHS, Beta.** Bruce Li. *TWE*

The Iron Duke ½ **1934** Fair to middlin' historical account of the life of the Duke of Wellington, victor over Napoleon at Waterloo. **88m/B VHS, Beta.** *GB* George Arliss, Gladys Cooper, A.E. Matthews, Emlyn Williams, Felix Aylmer; ***D:*** Victor Saville. *NOS, WFV, BAR*

Iron Eagle ½ **1986 (PG-13)** A teenager teams with a renegade fighter pilot to rescue the youth's father from captivity in the Middle East. Predictable but often exciting. Followed by two sequels. **117m/C VHS, Beta, LV.** Louis Gossett Jr., Jason Gedrick, Tim Thomerson, David Suchet, Larry B. Scott, Caroline Lagerfelt, Jerry Levine, Michael Bowen, Robbie Rist, Bobby Jacoby, Melora Hardin; ***D:*** Sidney J. Furie; ***W:*** Kevin Elders, Sidney J. Furie; ***M:*** Basil Poledouris. *FOX*

Iron Eagle 2 **1988 (PG)** Lower-budget extended adventures of a maverick fighter pilot after he is reinstated in the Air Force. This time he links with an equally rebellious commie fighter and blasts away at nuke-happy Ivan. Yahoo fun for all overt Yankees! Followed by "Aces: Iron Eagle 3." Available in Spanish. **102m/C VHS, Beta, LV.** *CA IS* Louis Gossett Jr., Mark Humphrey, Stuart Margolin, Alan Scarfe, Maury Chaykin, Sharon H. Brandon; ***D:*** Sidney J. Furie; ***W:*** Sidney J. Furie, Kevin Elders; ***M:*** Amin Bhatia. *LIV*

Iron Eagle 4 ½ **1995 (PG-13)** Series has gotten old and tired though Gossett, Jr. shows professionalism in his father figure role of retired Air Force General "Chappy" Sinclair. He's running the Iron Eagle Flight School—a training center/holding cell for troubled teens—along with pilot Doug Masters (Cadieux). Masters and his would-be pilots discover suspicious activities at a local air base, leading to biological weapons and an Air Force conspiracy. **95m/C VHS, LV.** *CA* Louis Gossett Jr., Jason Cadieux, Al Waxman, Joanne Vannicola, Rachel Blanchard, Sean McCann, Ross Hill, Karen Gayle; ***D:*** Sidney J. Furie; ***W:*** Michael Stokes; ***C:*** Curtis Petersen; ***M:*** Paul Zaza. *VMK*

Iron Horsemen *J.C* **1971 (R)** A motorcycle gang leader has a prophetic vision while tripping on LSD, and returns to his former town to challenge its religious establishment. Also available on video under its original title "J.C." **97m/C VHS, Beta.** William F. McGaha, Hannibal Penny, Joanna Moore, Burr de Benning, Slim Pickens, Pati Delaney; ***D:*** William F. McGaha. *NLC*

The Iron Major ½ **1943** Frank Cavanaugh, a famous football coach, becomes a hero in WWI. Standard flag-waving biography to increase morale back home, but fairly well-made. **85m/B VHS, Beta.** Pat O'Brien, Ruth Warrick, Robert Ryan, Leon Ames, Russell Wade, Bruce Edwards; ***D:*** Ray Enright. *TTC*

The Iron Mask ½ **1929** Early swashbuckling extravaganza with a master swordsman defending the French king from a scheme involving substitution by a lookalike. Still fairly exciting, thanks largely to director Dwan's flair. Based on Alexandre Dumas' "Three Musketeers" and "The Man in the Iron Mask" with talking sequences. **87m/B VHS, Beta, LV.** Douglas Fairbanks Sr., Nigel de Brulier, Marguerite de la Motte; ***D:*** Allan Dwan. Nominations: Academy Awards '29: Best Interior Decoration. *NOS, CCB, DVT*

Iron Maze ½ **1991 (R)** A fascinating notion forms the center of this dramatic scrapheap; the classic Japanese "Rashomon" plot shifted to a rusting Pennsylvania steel town. When a Tokyo businessman is found bludgeoned, witnesses and suspects (including his American-born wife) tell contradictory stories. It's too convoluted and contrived to work, with a hollow happy ending tacked on. Oliver Stone helped produce. **102m/C VHS, LV.** Jeff Fahey, Bridget Fonda, Hiroaki Murakami, J.T. Walsh, Gabriel Damon, John Randolph, Peter Allas; ***D:*** Hiroaki Yoshida; ***W:*** Tim Metcalfe. *ACA*

Iron Thunder ½ **1989** Liberty is in peril and only much kicking and pec flexing will make the world a kinder gentler place. A thundering bore. **85m/C VHS.** Iron "Amp" Elmore, George M. Young, Julius Dorsey. *XVC, HHE*

The Iron Triangle **1989 (R)** A U.S. officer taken prisoner by the Viet Cong forms a bond with one of his captors. Film lends the viewer an opportunity to see things from the other sides perspective. **94m/C VHS, Beta, LV.** Beau Bridges, Haing S. Ngor, Liem Whatley; ***D:*** Eric Weston; ***W:*** John Bushelman. *LIV*

Iron Warrior **1987 (R)** A barbarian hacks his way through a fantastical world to get to a beautiful princess. **82m/C VHS, Beta.** Miles O'Keeffe, Savina Gersak, Tim Lane; ***D:*** Al Bradley; ***W:*** Al Bradley. *MED, VTR*

Iron Will ½ **1993 (PG)** Okay Disney family movie based on a true story. Will Stoneman is a 17-year-old farm kid from South Dakota. It's 1917 and because of his father's death there's no money to send Will to college. So he decides to enter the 500 mile winner-take-all dog sled race, with its $10,000 prize. Lots of obstacles, several villains, but Will perseveres. **109m/C VHS, LV.** MacKenzie Astin, Kevin Spacey, David Ogden Stiers, August Schellenberg, George Gerdes, John Terry; ***D:*** Charles Haid; ***W:*** John Michael Hayes, Jeffrey Arch, Djordje Milicevic; ***M:*** Joel McNeely. *DIS*

Ironclads ½ **1990** Memorable dramatization of the five-hour naval battle between the Confederate's Merrimac and the Union's Monitor during the Civil War. The special effects are the only thing worth watching in this overlong tale that includes standard subplots of loyalty, lost loves, and death from war. **94m/C VHS.** Virginia Madsen, Alex Hyde-White, Reed Edward Diamond, E.G. Marshall, Fritz Weaver, Philip Casnoff; ***D:*** Delbert Mann. *TTC*

Ironheart ½ **1992** Slimy Milverstead and his henchman meet lovely young women at dance clubs, drug them, and sell them into slavery. But the trouble really starts when they kill a cop and his former partner, John Keem (Lee), lashes out with his blazing martial arts skill to still the perpetrators. **?m/C VHS, LV.** Britton Lee, Bolo Yeung, Richard Norton, Karman Kruschke; ***D:*** Robert Clouse; ***W:*** Lawrence Riggins. *IMP*

Ironmaster **1983** When a primitive tribesman is exiled from his tribe, he discovers a mysteriously power-filled iron staff on a mountainside. **98m/C VHS, Beta.** George Eastman, Pamela Field. *PSM*

Ironweed **1987 (R)** Grim and gritty drama about bums living the hard life in Depression-era Albany. Nicholson excels as a former ballplayer turned drunk bothered by visions of the past, and Streep is his equal in the lesser role of a tubercular boozer. Waits also shines. Another grim view from "Pixote" director Babenco. Kennedy scripted based on his Pulitzer Prize-winning tragedy. **135m/C VHS, Beta, LV.** Jack Nicholson, Meryl Streep, Tom Waits, Carroll Baker, Michael O'Keefe, Fred Gwynne, Diane Venora, Margaret Whitton, Jake Dengel, Nathan Lane, James Gammon, Joe Grifasi, Bethel Leslie, Ted Levine, Frank Whaley; ***D:*** Hector Babenco; ***W:*** William Kennedy; ***M:*** John Morris. Los Angeles Film Critics Association Awards '87: Best Actor (Nicholson); New York Film Critics Awards '87: Best Actor (Nicholson); Nominations: Academy Awards '87: Best Actor (Nicholson), Best Actress (Streep). *LIV*

Irreconcilable Differences ½ **1984 (PG)** When her Beverly Hills parents spend more time working and fretting than giving hugs and love, a ten-year-old girl sues them for divorce on the grounds of "irreconcilable differences." The media has a field day when they hear that she would rather go live with the maid. Well cast, with well-developed characterizations. The script, by the creators of "Private Benjamin," is humanely comic rather than uproariously funny. **112m/C VHS, Beta, LV.** Ryan O'Neal, Shelley Long, Drew Barrymore, Sam Wanamaker, Allen (Goorwitz) Garfield, Sharon Stone, Luana Anders; ***D:*** Charles Shyer; ***W:*** Charles Shyer, Nancy Meyers. *LIV, VES*

Irving Berlin's America **1986** A documentary depicting Berlin's legacy of patriotic pop tunes, shown in a variety of film and performance clips, plus interviews with the stars who sang them. **83m/C Beta.** Ginger Rogers, Mary Martin, Howard Keel, Kate Smith, Fred Astaire. *CMR*

Is Paris Burning? *Paris Brule-t-il?* **1968** A spectacularly star-studded but far too sprawling account of the liberation of Paris from Nazi occupation. The script, in which seven writers had a hand, is based on Larry Collins and Dominique Lapierre's best-seller. **173m/C VHS.** *FR* Jean-Paul Belmondo, Charles Boyer, Leslie Caron, Jean-Pierre Cassel, George Chakiris, Claude Dauphin, Alain Delon, Kirk Douglas, Glenn Ford, Gert Frobe, Daniel Gelin, E.G. Marshall, Yves Montand, Anthony Perkins, Claude Rich, Simone Signoret, Robert Stack, Jean-Louis Trintignant, Pierre Vaneck, Orson Welles, Bruno Cremer, Suzy Delair, Michael Lonsdale; ***D:*** Rene Clement; ***W:*** Gore Vidal, Francis Ford Coppola; ***M:*** Maurice Jarre. *PAR, FCT*

Is There Life Out There? ½ **1994** Wife, mother, and waitress Lily Marshall (McEntire) decides it's time to do something for herself—so she goes to work on her college degree. But there's unexpected family resentments, a breast cancer scare, and the interest of a young teaching assistant to turn her head away from her studies. Filmed in Nashville, Tennessee. Based on a song by McEntire; made for TV. **92m/C VHS.** Reba McEntire, Keith Carradine, Mitchell Anderson, Donald Moffat, Genia Michaela; ***D:*** David Jones; ***W:*** Dalene Young. *CAF*

Is There Sex After Death? **1971 (R)** Often funny satire on the sexual revolution is constructed as a behind-the-scenes view of the porn film world. Odd cast includes Henry and Warhol superstar Woodlawn. Originally rated "X." **97m/C VHS, Beta.** Buck Henry, Alan Abel, Marshall Efron, Holly Woodlawn, Earl Doud; ***D:*** Alan Abel, Jeanne Abel. *NO*

Is This Goodbye, Charlie Brown? **1983** Charlie Brown and the gang struggle to understand their loss when a friend moves away. **25m/C VHS.** *MED, VTR, WTA*

Isadora *The Loves of Isadora* **1968** A loose, imaginative biography of Isadora Duncan, the cause celebre dancer in the 1920s who became famous for her scandalous performances, outrageous behavior, public love affairs, and bizarre, early death. Redgrave is exceptional in the lead, and Fox provides fine support. Restored from its original 131-minute print length by the director. **153m/C VHS, Beta.** Vanessa Redgrave, Jason Robards Jr., James Fox, Ivan Tchenko, John Fraser, Bessie Love; ***D:*** Karel Reisz; ***W:*** Melvin Bragg; ***M:*** Maurice Jarre. Cannes Film Festival '69: Best Actress (Redgrave); National Board of Review Awards '69: 10 Best Films of the Year; National Society of Film Critics Awards '69: Best Actress (Redgrave); Nominations: Academy Awards '68: Best Actress (Redgrave); Cannes Film Festival '69: Best Film. *MCA, HEG*

Ishtar **1987 (PG-13)** Two astoundingly untalented performers have a gig in a fictional Middle Eastern country and become involved in foreign intrigue. A big-budget box-office bomb produced by Beatty offering few laughs, though it's not as bad as its reputation. Considering the talent involved, though, it's a disappointment, with Beatty and Hoffman laboring to create Hope and Crosby chemistry. Anyone for a slow night? **107m/C VHS, Beta, LV.** Dustin Hoffman, Warren Beatty, Isabelle Adjani, Charles Grodin; ***D:*** Elaine May; ***W:*** Elaine May; ***M:*** Dave Grusin. Golden Raspberry Awards '87: Worst Director (May). *COL*

The Island ½ *Hadaka No Shima; Naked Island* **1961** Poetic examination of a peasant family's daily struggle for existence on a small island. No dialogue in this slow but absorbing work by one of Japan's master directors. **96m/B VHS, Beta, LV, 8mm.** *JP* Nobuko Otowa, Taiji Tonoyama, Shinji Tanaka, Masanori Horimoto; ***D:*** Kaneto Shindo. National Board of Review Awards '62: 5 Best Foreign Films of the Year. *IHF, VYY, HHT*

The Island *Woof!* **1980 (R)** New York reporter embarks on a Bermuda triangle investigation, only to meet with the murderous but sterile descendants of seventeenth century pirates on a deserted island. Caine is designated as stud service for the last remaining fertile woman. Almost surreal in its badness. Adapted by Benchley from his novel. **113m/C VHS, Beta, LV.** Michael Caine, David Warner, Angela Punch McGregor, Frank Middlemass, Don Henderson; ***D:*** Michael Ritchie; ***W:*** Peter Benchley; ***M:*** Ennio Morricone. *MCA*

The Island at the Top of the World ½ **1974 (G)** A rich Englishman, in search of his missing son, travels to the Arctic Circle in 1908. The rescue party includes an American archeologist, a French astronaut, and an Eskimo guide. Astonishingly, they discover an unknown, "lost" Viking kingdom. This Jules Verne-style adventure doesn't quite measure up, but kids will like it. **93m/C VHS, Beta, LV.** David Hartman, Donald Sinden, Jacques Marin, Mako, David Gwillim; ***D:*** Robert Stevenson; ***M:*** Maurice Jarre. Nominations: Academy Awards '74: Best Art Direction/Set Decoration. *DIS*

Island Claw *Woof! Night of the Claw* **1980** A group of marine biologists experimenting on a tropical island discover the "Island Claw," who evolved as the result of toxic waste seeping into the ocean. A festering, oozing woofer. **91m/C VHS, Beta.** Barry Nelson, Robert Lansing; ***D:*** Hernan Cardenas. *LIV, VES*

Island in the Sun **1957** Racial tension pulls apart the lives of the residents of a Caribbean island. Good cast, but a very poor adaptation of Alec Waugh's novel. Marvelous location shots. **119m/C VHS.** James Mason, Joan Fontaine, Dorothy Dandridge, John Williams, Harry Belafonte; ***D:*** Robert Rossen; ***C:*** Frederick A. (Freddie) Young; ***M:*** Malcolm Arnold. *TCF*

Island Monster ½ **1953** Also called "Monster of the Island," this film deals with ruthless, kidnapping drug-smugglers led by "monster" Karloff, and the efforts to bring them to justice. **87m/B VHS, Beta.** *IT* Boris Karloff, Renata Vicario, Franco Marzi; ***D:*** Robert Montero. *SNC, HHT, LSV*

Island of Adventure ½ **1981** Four children explore an island and find a gang of criminals inhabiting it. **85m/C VHS, Beta.** *SUE*

Island of Blood ½ **1986** Buckets of blood abound on a remote island when a film crew's beset by berserk butcher. **84m/C VHS.** Jim Williams, Dean Richards. *AIP, MOV*

Island of Desire *Saturday Island* **1952** An Army nurse, a doctor, and a young Navy Adonis are trapped on a deserted island. Not surprisingly, a love triangle develops. **93m/C VHS, Beta.** *GB* Tab Hunter, Linda Darnell, Donald Gray; ***D:*** Stuart Heisler. *MLB*

Island of Dr. Moreau ½ **1977 (PG)** This remake of the "Island of the Lost Souls" (1933) is a bit disappointing but worth watching for Lancaster's solid performance as the scientist who has isolated himself on a Pacific island in order to continue his chromosome research—he can transform animals into near-humans and humans into animals. Neat-looking critters. Adaptation of the H.G. Wells novel of the same title. **99m/C VHS, Beta.** Burt Lancaster, Michael York, Nigel Davenport, Barbara Carrera, Richard Basehart; ***D:*** Don Taylor. *WAR, OM*

The Island of Dr. Moreau **1996** Success depends on the frightening "manimals" rather than on Brando's mad scientist in this updated version of the grisly 1896 H.G. Wells novel, which finds Moreau doing DNA experiments on a remote Pacific Isle in an effort to literally make animals into men. Kilmer is the doctors's right-hand hybrid with Thewlis a U.N. lawyer investigating the bizarre goings-on. Filming hit some big rocks when "creative differences" caused original director Richard Stanley to be replaced and Rob Morrow (originally the lawyer) to ask for his release. Previously filmed under the same title in 1977 and (terrifically) as "Island of Lost Souls" in 1933. **?m/C VHS.** Marlon Brando, Val Kilmer, David Thewlis, Fairuza Balk, Marco Hofschneider, Temuera Morrison; ***D:*** John Frankenheimer. *NYR*

Island of Lost Girls *Woof!* **1973 (R)** Young women are taken to an unknown location in the Far East to be sold as part of a white slave ring. **85m/C VHS, Beta.** Brad Harris, Tony Kendall, Monica Pardo. *SNC*

Island of Lost Souls ½ **1932** Horrifying adaptation of H.G. Wells "The Island of Dr. Moreau" was initially banned in parts of the U.S. because of its disturbing contents. Laughton is a mad scientist on a remote island obsessed with making men out of jungle animals. When a shipwreck survivor gets stranded on the island, little does he know that Laughton wants to mate him with Lota, the Panther Woman, to produce the first human-animal child. As unsettling today as it was in the '30s. Burke beat out more than 60,000 young women in a nationwide search to play the Panther Woman, winning the role because of her "feline" look. Remade as "The Island of Dr. Moreau." **71m/B VHS.** Charles Laughton, Bela Lugosi, Richard Arlen, Leila Hyams, Kathleen Burke, Stanley Fields, Robert F. (Bob) Kortman; ***Cameos:*** Alan Ladd, Randolph Scott, Buster Crabbe; ***D:*** Erle C. Kenton; ***W:*** Philip Wylie, Waldemar Young; ***C:*** Karl Struss. *MCA, FCT, BTV*

The Island of Nevawuz **1980** A beautiful island is in trouble when J.B. Trumphorn decides to make lots of money by building factories and refineries on it. Will the Island of Nevawuz end up a polluted mess? **50m/C VHS, Beta.** *SUE*

Island of Terror *Night of the Silicates; The Creepers* **1966** First-rate science fiction chiller about an island overrun by shell-like creatures that suck the bones out of their living prey. Good performances and interesting twists make for prickles up the spine. **90m/C VHS.** *GB* Peter Cushing, Edward Judd, Carole Gray, Sam Kydd, Niall MacGinnis; ***D:*** Terence Fisher. *MCA, SNC, MLB*

Island of the Blue Dolphins ½ **1964** Based on a popular children's book by Scott O'Dell, this is a true story of a young Native American girl who, with her brother, are stranded on a deserted island when their people accidentally leave them. When the boy is killed, the girl learns to survive by her skills and by befriending the leader of a pack of wild dogs. Good family fare. **99m/C VHS, Beta.** Celia Kaye, Larry Domasin, Ann Daniel, George Kennedy; ***D:*** James B. Clark. *MCA*

Island of the Burning Doomed ½ *Island of the Burning Damned; Night of the Big Heat* **1967** A brutal heat wave accompanies invading aliens in this British-made outing. Lee and Cushing carry the picture. **94m/C VHS.** *GB* Christopher Lee, Peter Cushing, Patrick Allen, Sarah Lawson, Jane Merrow; ***D:*** Terence Fisher. *NO*

Island of the Lost ½ **1968** An anthropologist's family must fight for survival when they become shipwrecked on a mysterious island. **92m/C VHS.** Richard Greene, Luke Halpin; ***D:*** John Florea; ***M:*** George Bruns. *REP, GHV*

Island Trader **1971** Young lad battles pirates and a crooked tug captain who seek hidden gold that he knows about. **95m/C VHS, Beta.** John Ewart, Ruth Cracknell, Eric Oldfield; ***D:*** Harold Rubie. *NO*

The Islander **1988** Sixteen-year-old Inga comes of age among the commercial fishermen of Lake Michigan. **99m/C VHS, Beta.** Kit Wholihan, Jeff Weborg, Celia Klehr, Jacob Mills, Julie Johnson, Mary Ann McHugh, Michael Rock, Sheri Parish; ***D:*** Phyllis Berg-Pigorsch. *NO*

Islands **1987** A made-for-television drama about a middle-aged ex-hippie and a young rebellious punk who clash during a summer together on a secluded island. **55m/C VHS, Beta.** Louise Fletcher. *NWV*

Islands in the Stream ½ **1977 (PG)** Based on Ernest Hemingway's novel, this film is actually two movies in one. An American painter/sculptor, Thomas Hudson, lives a reclusive life on the island of Bimini shortly before the outbreak of WWII. The first part is a sensitive story of a broken family and the coming of the artist's three sons to live with their father after a four year separation. The second part is a second rate action-adventure. **105m/C VHS, Beta, LV.** George C. Scott, David Hemmings, Claire Bloom, Susan Tyrrell, Gilbert Roland; ***D:*** Franklin J. Schaffner; ***C:*** Fred W. Koenekamp; ***M:*** Jerry Goldsmith. Nominations: Academy Awards '77: Best Cinematography. *PAR*

Isle of Forgotten Sins **1943** Deep sea divers and an evil ship's captain vie for treasure. Good cast and direction but unremarkable material. Also released under the title "Monsoon." **82m/B VHS, Beta, 8mm.** John Carradine, Gale Sondergaard, Sidney Toler, Frank Fenton, Veda Ann Borg; ***D:*** Edgar G. Ulmer. *SNC, VYY*

Isle of Secret Passion **1985** A romance novel comes to video life as two lovers thrash out their problems on a Greek island. **90m/C VHS, Beta.** Patch MacKenzie, Michael MacRae, Zohra Lampert. *PSM*

Isle of the Dead ½ **1945** A Greek general is quarantined with seemingly all manner of social vermin on a plague-infested island in the early 1900s. The fear is that vampires walk among them. Characteristically spooky Val Lewton production with some original twists. **72m/B VHS, Beta, LV.** Boris Karloff, Ellen Drew, Marc Cramer; ***D:*** Mark Robson. *TTC, MED, FCT*

Isn't Life Wonderful **1924** Outstanding Griffith film depicts the unbearable conditions in post-WWI Germany. Filmed on location. **90m/B VHS, Beta.** Carol Dempster, Neil Hamilton, Lupino Lane, Hans von Schlettow; ***D:*** D.W. Griffith; ***W:*** D.W. Griffith. *GPV, GVV*

Istanbul ½ **1957** Adventurer Jim Brennan (Flynn) finds a fortune in smuggled diamonds, which he hides in a hotel room. Unfortunately, he's deported before he can retrieve the gems and it takes him five years to make it back to Istanbul. Then he's hounded by the original smugglers who want their gems back and discovers his lost love Stephanie (Borchers). Cole croons a couple of songs in his role as a lounge singer. Remake of 1947's "Singapore." ♫When I Fall In Love; I Was a Little Too Lonely. **85m/C VHS.** Errol Flynn, Cornell Borchers, John Bentley, Torin Thatcher, Leif Erickson, Peggy Knudsen, Martin Benson, Nat King Cole, Werner Klemperer; ***D:*** Joseph Pevney; ***W:*** Seton I. Miller, Barbara Gray; ***C:*** William H. Daniels. *MCA*

Istanbul **1985 (R)** An American charms a Belgian student into taking part in a kidnap scheme. **90m/C VHS, Beta.** *FR* Brad Dourif, Dominique Deruddere, Ingrid De Vos, Francois Beukelaers; ***D:*** Marc Didden. *NO*

Istanbul *Istanbul, Keep Your Eyes Open* **1990 (PG-13)** Believing he has stumbled upon the best story of his career, a journalist soon discovers that he has been pulled into a world of guns and violence. **88m/C VHS, Beta, LV.** *TU SW* Robert Morley, Timothy Bottoms, Twiggy; ***D:*** Mats Arehn. *IME*

It ½ **1927** A department store clerk with plenty of sex appeal desires her rich boss. Established Bow as a prominent screen siren. Otherwise, it's not particularly interesting. Silent. Adapted by Elinor Glyn from her own story; Glyn also makes an appearance. **71m/B VHS, Beta, LV.** Clara Bow, Gary Cooper, Antonio Moreno; ***D:*** Clarence Badger. *GPV, CRC, CCB*

It Came from Beneath the Sea **1955** A giant octopus arises from the depths of the sea to scour San Francisco for human food. Ray Harryhausen effects are special. **80m/B VHS, Beta, LV.** Kenneth Tobey, Faith Domergue, Ian Keith, Donald Curtis; ***D:*** Robert Gordon. *GKK, MLB*

It Came from Hollywood **1982 (PG)** A compilation of scenes from "B" horror and science fiction films of the 1950s, highlighting the funny side of these classic schlock movies. Some sequences in black and white. **87m/C VHS, Beta, LV.** ***D:*** Malcolm Leo. *PAR*

It Came From Outer Space **1953** Aliens take on the form of local humans to repair their spacecraft in a small Arizona town. Good performances and outstanding direction add up to a fine science fiction film. Based on the story "The Meteor" by Ray Bradbury, who also wrote the script. Originally filmed in 3-D. **81m/B VHS.** Richard Carlson, Barbara Rush, Charles Drake, Russell Johnson; ***D:*** Jack Arnold; ***W:*** Ray Bradbury, Harry Essex; ***M:*** Herman Stein. *MCA, MLB, GKK*

It Came Upon a Midnight Clear ½ **1984** A heavenly miracle enables a retired (and dead) New York policeman to keep a Christmas promise to his grandson. Made for television. **96m/C VHS, Beta.** Mickey Rooney, Scott Grimes, George Gaynes, Annie Potts, Lloyd Nolan, Barrie Youngfellow; ***D:*** Peter H. Hunt. *GKK*

It Conquered the World 𝄞𝄞½ **1956** Vegetable critters from Venus follow a probe satellite back to Earth and drop in on scientist Van Cleef, who'd been their intergalactic pen pal (seems he thought a Venusian invasion would improve the neighborhood). Their travelling companions, little bat creatures, turn earth dwellers into murderous zombies, and it starts to look like the Venusians are trying to make earth their planetary exurbia. Early- vintage zero-budget Corman, for schlock connoisseurs. Remade for television as "Zontar, the Thing from Venus." **68m/B VHS.** Peter Graves, Beverly Garland, Lee Van Cleef, Sally Fraser, Charles B. Griffith, Russ Bender, Jonathan Haze, Dick Miller, Karen Kadler, Paul Blaisdell; ***D:*** Roger Corman. *COL, FCT, MLB*

It Could Happen to You 𝄞½ **1937** Stepbrothers raised by a gentle immigrant take different paths in life. When one ends up killing someone during a botched robbery, the other—a lawyer—defends him. Standard '30s morality play. **64m/B VHS.** Alan Baxter, Andrea Leeds, Owen Davis Jr., Astrid Allwyn, Walter Kingsford, Al Shear; ***D:*** Phil Rosen. *NOS, BAR*

It Could Happen to You 𝄞𝄞 **1939** A drunken advertising executive is charged with murder after a dead nightclub singer is found in his car. His wife sets out to clear him. **64m/C VHS, Beta.** Stuart Erwin, Gloria Stuart, Raymond Walburn, Douglas Fowley, June Gale, Paul Hurst, Richard Lane; ***D:*** Alfred Werker. *NO*

It Could Happen to You 𝄞𝄞½ *Cop Tips Waitress $2 Million* **1994 (PG)** NYC cop Charlie Lang (Cage) doesn't have any change to leave coffee shop waitress Yvonne (Fonda) a tip, so he promises to split his lottery ticket with her. When he nets four million dollars, he makes good on the promise, much to the chargrin of his upwardly mobile wife (Perez). Capra-corn for the X-crowd is pleasant dinnertime diversion as Cage and Perez shine as henpecked nice guy and the wife committed to making him miserable. Don't look for the diner on your next trip to NYC; it was specially built in TriBeCa and dismantled after the shoot. **101m/C VHS, LV, 8mm.** Bridget Fonda, Nicolas Cage, Rosie Perez, Red Buttons, Isaac Hayes, Seymour Cassel, Stanley Tucci, J.E. Freeman, Richard Jenkins, Ann Dowd, Wendell Pierce; ***D:*** Andrew Bergman; ***W:*** Jane Anderson, Andrew Bergman; ***C:*** Caleb Deschanel. *COL*

It Couldn't Happen Here 𝄞 **1988 (PG-13)** Fans of the techno-pop duo The Pet Shop Boys can test their loyalty by enduring this feature music-video that actually played a few theaters. The dour pair journey across a surreal England, encountering a sinister blind priest, a philisophical ventriloquist's dummy, and more. Songs, sometimes presented only as muted incidental music, include the title track, "West End Girls," "It's a Sin" and "Always on My Mind." **87m/C VHS, LV.** *GB* Neil Tennant, Chris Lowe, Joss Ackland, Neil Dickson, Carmen Du Sautoy, Gareth Hunt; ***D:*** Jack Bond. *COL, MVD*

It Happened at Nightmare Inn 𝄞𝄞 **1970** Average thriller in which Geeson travels to Spanish inn and confronts two mad sisters who run the hotel. Also known as "Nightmare Hotel." **95m/C VHS.** *SP* Judy Geeson, Aurora Bautista, Esperanza Roy, Victor Alcocer, Lone Fleming; ***D:*** Eugenio Martin. *SNC*

It Happened at the World's Fair 𝄞𝄞½ **1963** Fun and light romance comedy has Elvis and a companion (O'Brien) being escorted through the Seattle World's Fair by a fetching Chinese girl. ♫I'm Falling In Love Tonight; They Remind Me Too Much Of You; Take Me To The Fair; Relax; How Would You Like To Be; Beyond the Bend; One Broken Heart For Sale; Cotton Candy Land; A World Of Our Own. **105m/C VHS, Beta.** Elvis Presley, Joan O'Brien, Gary Lockwood, Kurt Russell, Edith Atwater, Yvonne Craig; ***D:*** Norman Taurog. *MGM*

It Happened in Brooklyn 𝄞𝄞 **1947** Former sailor with blue eyes bunks with janitor with big nose in Brooklyn. Sailor and cronies encounter many musical opportunities. Lots of songs and falling in love, little entertainment. **104m/B VHS.** Frank Sinatra, Kathryn Grayson, Jimmy Durante, Peter Lawford, Gloria Grahame; ***D:*** Richard Whorf. *MGM, FCT*

It Happened in New Orleans 𝄞½ *Rainbow on the River* **1936** A young boy is cared for by a former slave in post-Civil War New Orleans until his Yankee grandmother claims him and tåkes him to New York. The boy is resented by his family but manages to overcome their hostilities. **86m/B VHS, Beta.** Bobby Breen, May Robson, Alan Mowbray, Benita Hume. *VYY*

It Happened in the Park 𝄞𝄞½ **1956** A rare film exercise for De Sica, wherein the patrons of the Villa Borghese parks are surveyed for a 24-hour period. In French with English dialogue. **72m/B VHS, Beta.** *FR* ***D:*** Vittorio De Sica. *NOS, FCT, INJ*

It Happened One Night 𝄞𝄞𝄞𝄞 **1934** Classic Capra comedy about an antagonistic couple determined to teach each other about life. Colbert is an unhappy heiress who runs away from her affluent home in search of contentment. On a bus she meets newspaper reporter Gable, who teaches her how "real" people live. She returns the favor in this first of the 1930s screwball comedies. The plot is a framework for an amusing examination of war between the sexes. Colbert and Gable are superb as affectionate foes. Remade as the musicals "Eve Knew Her Apples" and "You Can't Run Away From It." **105m/B VHS, Beta, LV.** Clark Gable, Claudette Colbert, Roscoe Karns, Walter Connolly, Alan Hale, Ward Bond; ***D:*** Frank Capra; ***W:*** Robert Riskin. Academy Awards '34: Best Actor (Gable), Best Actress (Colbert), Best Adapted Screenplay, Best Director (Capra), Best Picture; National Board of Review Awards '34: 10 Best Films of the Year. *COL, BTV, HMV*

It Happens Every Spring 𝄞𝄞𝄞½ **1949** A chemistry professor, working on a bug repellant for trees, accidentally invents a potion that repels any kind of wood that it comes in contact with. Since he needs some big bucks to pop the question to his sweetie, the prof, who also loves baseball, gets a tryout as a pitcher with a major league team and uses the solution on the baseballs he pitches. Naturally, it's strikeout time and the prof becomes a pitching phenom. Now, if he can only keep his little secret. Wacky baseball footage is a highlight. **87m/B VHS.** Ray Milland, Jean Peters, Paul Douglas, Ed Begley Sr., Ted de Corsia, Ray Collins, Jessie Royce Landis, Alan Hale Jr., Gene Evans; ***D:*** Lloyd Bacon; ***W:*** Valentine Davies; ***M:*** Leigh Harline. *FXV*

It Means That to Me 𝄞𝄞 **1963** Espionage thriller in which Constantine plays a reporter who's hired by the government to transport top secret micro-film. **?m/C VHS.** *FR* Eddie Constantine, Jean-Louis Richard. *SNC*

It Rained All Night the Day I Left 𝄞𝄞 **1978 (R)** Two drifters find their fortunes change when they are hired by a wealthy widow. Interesting romance adventure. **100m/C VHS, Beta.** Louis Gossett Jr., Sally Kellerman, Tony Curtis; ***D:*** Nicolas Gessner. *NO*

It Should Happen to You 𝄞𝄞𝄞 **1954** An aspiring model attempts to boost her career by promoting herself on a New York City billboard. The results, however, are continually surprising. Fine comedy teamwork from master thespians Holliday and Lemmon in this, the latter's first film. **87m/B VHS, Beta, LV.** Judy Holliday, Jack Lemmon, Peter Lawford; ***D:*** George Cukor; ***W:*** Ruth Gordon, Garson Kanin; ***C:*** Charles B(ryant) Lang. Nominations: Academy Awards '54: Best Costume Design (B & W). *GKK*

It Started in Naples 𝄞𝄞𝄞 **1960** Good performances by both Gable and Loren in this comedy-drama about an American lawyer in Italy who, upon preparing his late brother's estate, finds that his brother's nephew is living with a stripper. A custody battle ensues, but love wins out in the end. Loren is incredible in nightclub scenes. **100m/C VHS.** Clark Gable, Sophia Loren, Marietto, Vittorio De Sica, Paolo Carlini, Claudio Ermelli, Giovanni Filidoro; ***D:*** Melville Shavelson; ***W:*** Melville Shavelson, Jack Rose. Nominations: Academy Awards '60: Best Art Direction/Set Decoration (Color). *PAR*

It Started with a Kiss 𝄞𝄞½ **1959** Reynolds plays a showgirl who impulsively marries an Air Force sargeant (Ford). When he's transfered to Spain they try to make a go of their hasty marriage among numerous comic complications. Flimsy farce with likeable leads. **104m/C VHS.** Debbie Reynolds, Glenn Ford, Eva Gabor, Gustavo Rojo, Fred Clark, Edgar Buchanan, Robert Warwick, Harry (Henry) Morgan, Frances Bavier; ***D:*** George Marshall. *MGM, MOV*

It Started with Eve 𝄞𝄞𝄞 **1941** Funny comedy about a grumpy old millionaire (Laughton) whose dying wish is to meet the young lady his son Johnny is to wed. Unfortunately, the bride-to-be is unavailable, so Johnny (Cummings) finds a replacement in hatcheck girl Durbin. Of course, Durbin steals the old man's heart and he miraculously makes a full-blown recovery, which means big trouble for Cummings. Remade in 1964 as "I'd Rather Be Rich." Based on the story "Almost An Angel" by Hans Kraly. ♫Clavelitos; Going Home. **92m/B VHS.** Deanna Durbin, Charles Laughton, Robert Cummings, Guy Kibbee, Margaret Tallichet, Catherine Doucet, Walter Catlett, Charles Coleman, Clara Blandick; ***D:*** Henry Koster; ***W:*** Norman Krasna, Leo Townsend. *MCA*

It Takes a Thief 𝄞𝄞 *The Challenge* **1959** Tough cookie Jayne's a buxom gangstress who does the hokey pokey with her criminal minions. A former lover who's been released from the big house seems to think she's been minding the mint for him. Au contraire. **93m/B VHS.** *GB* Jayne Mansfield, Anthony Quayle, Carl Mohner, Peter Reynolds, John Bennett; ***D:*** John Gilling. *BBF*

It Takes Two 𝄞𝄞 **1988 (PG-13)** A young man spends his last ten days of bachelorhood cruising down Texas highways with a beautiful car saleswoman. Meanwhile, back at the altar, his bride waits patiently. Upbeat with some genuinely funny moments. From the director of "Pass the Ammo." **79m/C VHS, Beta.** George Newbern, Leslie Hope, Kimberly Foster, Barry Corbin; ***D:*** David Beaird; ***M:*** Carter Burwell. *MGM*

It Takes Two 𝄞 **1995 (PG)** Vapid sugary comedy finds the nine-year-old Olsen twins playing a duo from opposite sides of the tracks who change identities in an effort to get their respective adults (Guttenberg and Alley) together. See "The Parent Trap" instead. **100m/C VHS, LV.** Ashley Olsen, Mary-Kate Olsen, Kirstie Alley, Steve Guttenberg, Philip Bosco, Jane Sibbett, Lawrence Dane, Gerard Parkes; ***D:*** Andy Tennant; ***W:*** Deborah Dean Davis; ***C:*** Kenneth Zunder; ***M:*** Sherman Foote, Ray Foote. *WAR*

It! The Terror from Beyond Space 𝄞𝄞½ *It! The Vampire From Beyond Space* **1958** The sole survivor of a Martian expedition is believed to have murdered his colleagues. He's arrested and brought back to Earth via space ship. En route, a vicious alien, the actual culprit, is discovered on board and begins killing the crew members. A fun science fiction thriller which, 20 years later, would provide Ridley Scott with the plot for "Alien." **68m/B VHS, Beta.** Marshall Thompson, Shawn Smith, Kim Spalding, Ann Doran, Dabbs Greer, Paul Langton, Ray Corrigan; ***D:*** Edward L. Cahn. *MGM, MLB*

It Was a Short Summer, Charlie Brown **1969** The Peanuts gang enjoys the summer until it's time to go back to school. **26m/C VHS.** ***D:*** Bill Melendez. *WTA*

Italian **1915** The story of an Italian immigrant family living in the slums of New York during the turn of the century. **78m/B VHS, Beta.** George Beban, Clara Williams, Leo Wills, J. Frank Burke, Fanny Midgley. *GPV, GVV*

The Italian Job 𝄞𝄞½ **1969 (G)** Caine and Coward pair up to steal $4 million in gold by causing a major traffic jam in Turin, Italy. During the jam, the pair steals the gold from an armored car. Silliness and chases through the Swiss mountains ensue, culminating in a hilarious ending. **99m/C VHS, LV.** *GB* Michael Caine, Noel Coward, Benny Hill, Raf Vallone, Tony Beckley, Rossano Brazzi, Margaret Blye; ***D:*** Peter Collinson; ***M:*** Quincy Jones. *PAR*

The Italian Stallion 🦴 **1973** Stallone plays a man with only one thing on his mind...sex! **90m/C VHS, Beta.** Sylvester Stallone, Henrietta Holm. *JEF*

Italian Straw Hat 🦴🦴🦴 *Un Chapeau de Paille d'Italie* **1927** Classic silent about the chain of errors that ensues when a man's horse eats a woman's hat. His vast, unending struggle to replace the hat is the source of continual comedy. From Eugene Labiche's play. **72m/B VHS, Beta.** *FR* Albert Prejean; ***D:*** Rene Clair. *VYY, MRV, INT*

Italianamerican/The Big Shave 197? Two shorts by Scorsese. "Italianamerican" (1974) features dinner and conversation with his parents in their Little Italy (New York) apartment. In "The Big Shave," (1967) a young man nicks himself shaving and suddenly has a frightening religious experience. **54m/C VHS.** ***D:*** Martin Scorsese. *HMV*

It's a Bundyful Life 1992 The outrageous family from television's "Married with Children" does Christmas in their own inimitable fashion. This parody of "It's a Wonderful Life" features Kinison earning his wings as father Al's guardian angel. See what the family would have been like if Al had never been born...and what Al decides to do about it. Those seeking traditional family fare should look elsewhere. **47m/C VHS.** Ed O'Neill, Katey Sagal, Christina Applegate, David Faustino, Sam Kinison, Amanda Bearse, Ted McGinley; ***D:*** Gerry Cohen. *COL*

It's a Date 🦴🦴 **1940** A mother and daughter, both actresses, continually get their professional and romantic lives intertwined. It begins when Durbin (the daughter) is offered Kay's (the mother) Broadway role. It continues in Hawaii where the man that Kay is in love with tries to court Durbin. As it's a comedy, of course, all is put right in the end. ♫Musetta's Waltz; Ave Maria; Loch Lomond; Love Is All; It Happened in Kaloha; Rhythm of the Islands; Hawaiian War Chant. **103m/B VHS.** Deanna Durbin, Kay Francis, Walter Pidgeon, Samuel S. Hinds, S.Z. Sakall, Henry Stephenson, Charles Lane, Leon Belasco; ***D:*** William A. Seiter; ***W:*** Norman Krasna; ***C:*** Joseph Valentine. *FOX, FCT, MLB*

It's a Dog's Life 🦴🦴½ *The Bar Sinister* **1955** The hero and narrator of this story is a wily bull terrier called Wildfire. Wildfire is a tough dog on the mean streets of the Bowery in turn-of-the-century New York. His master has him in dog fights in the local saloon but eventually abandons him. Wildfire is then taken in by the kindly employee of the rich and dog-hating Jagger but naturally manages to win the codger over. Based on the short story "The Bar Sinister" by Richard Harding Davis. **87m/C VHS.** Jeff Richards, Edmund Gwenn, Dean Jagger; ***D:*** Herman Hoffman; ***W:*** John Michael Hayes; ***M:*** Elmer Bernstein. *FCT*

It's A Gift 🦴🦴🦴½ **1934** A grocery clerk moves his family west to manage orange groves in this classic Fields comedy. Several inspired sequences. The supporting cast shines too. A real find for the discriminating comedy buff. Remake of the silent "It's the Old Army Game." **71m/B VHS, Beta, LV.** W.C. Fields, Baby LeRoy, Kathleen Howard; ***D:*** Norman Z. McLeod. *MCA, BAR*

It's a Great Feeling 🦴🦴½ **1949** Another Carson and Day team-up where Carson plays a camera-hogging show-off whom no one wants to direct. He's such an industry piranha that he ends up directing himself! He cons Day, a waitress and would-be actress, by promising her a part in his new film. Some executives hear her sing before she heads back home to Wisconsin, fed up with Hollywood. They make Carson track her down to star in the new picture, but when he arrives she is at the altar with her high school sweetheart. **85m/C VHS, LV.** Dennis (Stanley Morner) Morgan, Doris Day, Jack Carson, Bill Goodwin, Errol Flynn, Gary Cooper, Joan Crawford, Ronald Reagan, Sydney Greenstreet, Danny Kaye, Eleanor Parker, Edward G. Robinson, Jane Wyman; ***D:*** David Butler. Nominations: Academy Awards '49: Best Song ("It's a Great Feeling"). *FOX, FCT, MLB*

It's a Great Life 🦴🦴½ **1943** Blondie wants Dagwood to buy a house but instead he buys a horse. He's scheming to impress a client of Mr. Dither's by participating in a fox hunt. Blondie comes to the rescue. 13th entry in series. **75m/B VHS.** Penny Singleton, Arthur Lake, Larry Simms, Hugh Herbert, Jonathan Hale, Danny Mummert, Alan Dinehart, Irving Bacon, Douglas Leavitt, Marjorie Ann Mutchie; ***D:*** Frank Strayer; ***W:*** Karen De Wolf, Connie Lee. *MOV*

It's a Joke, Son! 🦴🦴 **1947** Follows the fictional politician, Senator Claghorn from the Fred Allen radio show, during his first run for the U.S. Senate. **67m/B VHS.** Kenny Delmar, Una Merkel; ***D:*** Ben Stoloff. *NOS, MRV, DVT*

It's a Mad, Mad, Mad, Mad World 🦴🦴 **1963** Overblown epic comedy with a cast of notables desperately seeking the whereabouts of stolen money. Ultimately exhausting film undone by its length and overbearing performances. Laserdisc contains 20 minutes of supplemental footage, including interviews with some of the surviving cast members. **155m/C VHS, Beta, LV.** Spencer Tracy, Sid Caesar, Milton Berle, Ethel Merman, Jonathan Winters, Jimmy Durante, Buddy Hackett, Mickey Rooney, Phil Silvers, Dick Shawn, Edie Adams, Dorothy Provine, Buster Keaton, Terry-Thomas, Moe Howard, Larry Fine, Joe DeRita, Jim Backus, William Demarest, Peter Falk, Leo Gorcey, Edward Everett Horton, Joe E. Brown, Carl Reiner, ZaSu Pitts, Eddie Anderson, Jack Benny, Jerry Lewis; ***D:*** Stanley Kramer; ***C:*** Ernest Laszlo; ***M:*** Ernest Gold. Academy Awards '63: Best Sound Effects Editing; Nominations: Academy Awards '63: Best Color Cinematography, Best Song ("It's a Mad, Mad, Mad, Mad World"), Best Sound, Best Original Score. *MGM, FOX, FCT*

It's a Mystery, Charlie Brown 1987 Peanuts adventure in which Snoopy interrogates everyone on the disappearance of Woodstock's birdhouse. **30m/C VHS, Beta.** ***D:*** Phil Roman. *BAR, WTA*

It's a Wonderful Life 🦴🦴🦴🦴 **1946** American classic about a man saved from suicide by a considerate angel, who then shows the hero how important he's been to the lives of loved ones. Corny but inspirational and heartwarming, with an endearing performance by Travers as angel Clarence. Stewart and Reed are typically wholesome. Perfect film for people who want to feel good, joyfully teetering on the border between Hollywood schmaltz and genuine heartbreak. Also available colorized. The laserdisc version includes production and publicity stills, the theatrical trailer, and commentary by film professor Jeanine Basinger. Also available in a 160-minute Collector's Edition with original preview trailer, "The Making of 'It's a Wonderful Life,'" and a new digital transfer from the original negative. **125m/B VHS, LV.** James Stewart, Donna Reed, Henry Travers, Thomas Mitchell, Lionel Barrymore, Samuel S. Hinds, Frank Faylen, Gloria Grahame, H.B. Warner, Ellen Corby, Sheldon Leonard, Beulah Bondi, Ward Bond, Frank Albertson, Todd Karns, Mary Treen, Charles Halton; ***D:*** Frank Capra; ***W:*** Frances Goodrich, Albert Hackett, Jo Swerling; ***M:*** Dimitri Tiomkin. Golden Globe Awards '47: Best Director (Capra); Nominations: Academy Awards '46: Best Actor (Stewart), Best Director (Capra), Best Film Editing, Best Picture, Best Sound. *IGP, MRV, CNG*

It's Alive! 🦴 **1968** Slow-moving dud about a farmer feeding passersby to the area's cave-dwelling lizard man. The ping pong ball-eyed monster puts in a belated appearance that's not worth the wait. **80m/C VHS.** Tommy Kirk, Shirley Bonne, Bill Thurman; ***D:*** Larry Buchanan; ***W:*** Larry Buchanan. *NOS, LOO*

It's Alive 🦴🦴🦴 **1974 (PG)** Cult film about a mutated baby that is born to a normal Los Angeles couple, who escapes and goes on a bloodthirsty, murderous rampage, is a sight to behold. Fantastic score by Bernard Herrmann makes this chilling film a memorable one. **91m/C VHS, Beta.** John P. Ryan, Sharon Farrell, Andrew Duggan, Guy Stockwell, James Dixon, Michael Ansara; ***D:*** Larry Cohen; ***W:*** Larry Cohen. *WAR, FCT*

It's Alive 2: It Lives Again *Woof!* **1978 (R)** In this sequel to "It's Alive," the original hellspun baby meets up with two more of the same and all three terrorize the city, murdering everyone they can find. Truly horrendous. **91m/C VHS, Beta.** Frederic Forrest, Kathleen Lloyd, John P. Ryan, Andrew Duggan, John Marley, Eddie Constantine; ***D:*** Larry Cohen. *WAR, FCT*

It's Alive 3: Island of the Alive 🦴 **1987 (R)** The second sequel to the tongue-in-cheek horror film, in which the infant mutant of the previous films has been left with other mutations to spawn on a desert island. **94m/C VHS, Beta.** Michael Moriarty, Karen Black, Laurene Landon, Gerrit Graham, James Dixon, Neal Israel, MacDonald Carey; ***D:*** Larry Cohen; ***W:*** Larry Cohen. *WAR*

It's All True 🦴🦴 **1993 (G)** A look at auteur Welles' ill-fated WWII filmmaking project. Welles served as a special cultural ambassador to South America and, in 1942, began a documentary covering the area's complex political and social issues. Includes footage from "Four Men on a Raft," Welles' recreation about the peasant fishermen of Brazil; surviving excerpts from "The Story of Samba," a Technicolor musical about Carnaval in Rio de Janeiro; and footage from "My Friend Bonito," set against a backdrop of bullfighting in Mexico. **85m/C VHS, LV.** ***D:*** Richard Wilson, Bill Krohn, Myron Meise, Orson Welles; ***W:*** Richard Wilson, Bill Krohn, Myron Meise; ***M:*** Jorge Arriagada. *PAR*

It's Always Fair Weather 🦴🦴 **1955** Three WWII buddies meet again at a 10-year reunion and find that they don't like each other very much. A surprisingly cynical film. Director Donen produced "Seven Brides for Seven Brothers" the previous year. ♫Stillman's Gym; March, March; Why Are We Here? (Blue Danube); Music Is Better Than Words; Once Upon A Time; The Time For Parting; I Like Myself; Baby You Knock Me Out; Thanks A Lot But No Thanks. **102m/C VHS, Beta, LV.** Gene Kelly, Cyd Charisse, Dan Dailey, Michael Kidd; ***D:*** Stanley Donen; ***W:*** Betty Comden, Adolph Green; ***M:*** Betty Comden, Adolph Green, Andre Previn. Nominations: Academy Awards '55: Best Story & Screenplay, Best Original Score. *MGM, FHE*

It's an Adventure, Charlie Brown! 1983 A collection of six vignettes featuring Charlie Brown and the whole Peanuts gang. **50m/C VHS, Beta.** ***D:*** Bill Melendez. *WTA, SHV, VTR*

It's Arbor Day, Charlie Brown 1983 Tribulations aplenty for Charlie Brown as his baseball team turns his field into an Arbor Day garden. **26m/C VHS, Beta.** *BAR, WTA*

It's Called Murder, Baby 🦴 **1982 (R)** The famed porn star gives the viewer a lesson in English vocabulary in this tale of a blackmailed movie queen. **94m/C VHS, Beta.** John Leslie, Cameron Mitchell, Lisa Trego; ***D:*** Sam Weston. *LIV*

It's Flashbeagle, Charlie Brown/She's a Good Skate, Charlie Brown 1984 A Peanuts double header: In "It's Flashbeagle Charlie Brown," Snoopy infects the Peanuts gang with dance fever, and in "She's a Good Skate Charlie Brown," Snoopy trains Peppermint Patty to become a figure skating champion. **55m/C VHS, Beta.** ***D:*** Bill Melendez. *SHV*

It's Good to Be Alive 🦴🦴½ **1974** The true story of how Brooklyn Dodgers' catcher Roy Campanella learned to face life after an automobile accident left him a quadriplegic. Good performances in this television drama. **100m/C VHS, Beta.** Paul Winfield, Ruby Dee, Louis Gossett Jr.; ***D:*** Michael Landon. *PSM*

It's in the Bag 🦴🦴½ *The Fifth Chair* **1945** A shiftless flea circus owner sells chairs he has inherited, not knowing that a fortune is hidden in one of them. **87m/B VHS, LV.** Fred Allen, Don Ameche, Jack Benny, William Bendix, Binnie Barnes, Robert Benchley; ***D:*** Richard Wallace. *REP, MED*

It's Love Again 🦴🦴½ **1936** A streetwise chorus girl poses as a fictional socialite in a light music-hall comedy. ♫It's Love Again; Heaven In Your Arms. **83m/B VHS, Beta.** *GB* Jessie Matthews, Robert Young, Sonnie Hale; ***D:*** Victor Saville. *NOS, DVT, HEG*

It's Magic, Charlie Brown/Charlie Brown's All Star 1981 In the first of these two stories, Snoopy, "The Great Houndini," makes Charlie Brown disappear. Problems begin when Snoopy finds it difficult conjuring his master back to reality. In the second story, Charlie Brown's baseball team has lost 999 games in a row, and prospects are bleak. New hope arrives when he gets an offer to have the team sponsored in a real league. **55m/C VHS, Beta.** ***D:*** Phil Roman. *SHV, VTR, WTA*

It's My Party ☠☠½ **1995 (R)** When L.A. architect Nick Stark (Roberts) learns that he's developed untreatable brain lesions from AIDS that will essentially leave him helpless, he decides to throw himself a monumental farewell bash before taking a drug overdose. Friends and family all turn up as does, awkwardly enough, Brandon Theis (Harrison), Nick's former live-in who couldn't handle his HIV-positive diagnosis but would like a last reapproachment. Fine, sympathetic performances, espcially by the two leads, and yes, it's a weepie. Based on a true story. **120m/C VHS, LV.** Eric Roberts, Gregory Harrison, Marlee Matlin, Lee Grant, George Segal, Bronson Pinchot, Bruce Davison, Devon Gummersall, Roddy McDowall, Margaret Cho, Paul Regina, Olivia Newton-John, Christopher Atkins, Dennis Christopher, Ron Glass; ***D:*** Randal Kleiser; ***W:*** Randal Kleiser; ***C:*** Bernd Heinl; ***M:*** Basil Poledouris. *MGM*

It's My Turn ☠☠ **1980 (R)** A mathematics professor (Clayburgh) struggles in her relationship with live-in lover (Grodin) who sells real-estate in Chicago. She meets retired baseball player (Douglas) and falls in love. "Ho-hum" just about describes the rest. **91m/C VHS, Beta, LV.** Jill Clayburgh, Michael Douglas, Charles Grodin, Beverly Garland, Steven Hill, Dianne Wiest, Daniel Stern; ***D:*** Claudia Weill; ***W:*** Eleanor Bergstein. *COL*

It's Not the Size That Counts *Woof! Percy's Progress* **1974** After the Earth's drinking water is contaminated, Lawson is the only man on Earth not to be struck by impotency. Limp sequel to "Percy," the British comedy about the first man to receive a penis transplant. Promising comedy doesn't deliver. **90m/C VHS.** Leigh Lawson, Elke Sommer, Denholm Elliott, Vincent Price; ***D:*** Ralph Thomas. *SUE*

It's Pat: The Movie *Woof!* **1994 (PG-13)** This movie is so bad, let's pray it sounds the death knell to big-screen versions of "Saturday Night Live" sketch characters— who possessed little humor to begin with. For what it's worth, the androgynous Pat (Sweeney) falls for the equally gender-suspect Chris (Foley, from Canada's version of SNL, "Kids in the Hall") and all sorts of embarrassing situations arise. Pat's quest to find Pat's self is sketch material stretched see-through thin. **78m/C VHS.** Julia Sweeney, Dave Foley, Charles Rocket, Kathy Griffin, Julie Haydon, Tim Meadows, Arleen Sorkin; ***Cameos:*** Sally Jesse Raphael, Kathy Najimy; ***D:*** Adam Bernstein; ***W:*** Julia Sweeney, Jim Emerson, Stephen Hibbert. Nominations: Golden Raspberry Awards '95: Worst Picture, Worst New Star (Sweeney). *TOU*

It's the Great Pumpkin, Charlie Brown **1988** It's Halloween, and Charlie Brown and his friends are going trick-or-treating, but Linus faithfully awaits the arrival of the Great Pumpkin. **25m/C VHS, Beta.** *PAR, MED, VTR*

It's the Old Army Game **1926** Classic Fields gags in three of his best Ziegfeld Follies sketches: "The Drug Store," "A Peaceful Morning," and "The Family Flivver." The beautiful Brooks serves as his comic foil. **75m/B VHS, Beta.** W.C. Fields, Louise Brooks, Blanche Ring, William Gaxton; ***D:*** Edward Sutherland. *GPV*

It's Three Strikes, Charlie Brown **1986** Misfortunes abound in the baseball diamond for the Peanuts gang. **41m/C VHS, Beta.** ***D:*** Bill Melendez, Phil Roman, Robert E. Balzer, Sam Nicholson. *BAR, WTA*

It's Your First Kiss, Charlie Brown/ Someday You'll Find Her, Charlie Brown **1977** In "It's Your First Kiss, Charlie Brown," our hero has to escort the school's homecoming queen to the ball. What's worse, he actually has to kiss her in front of everyone! In "Someday You'll Find Her, Charlie Brown," Charlie Brown sees "the most beautiful girl in the world" on television and, after recruiting Linus, embarks upon a door-to-door search to find her. **55m/C VHS, Beta.** ***D:*** Phil Roman. *SHV, VTR*

Ivan the Terrible, Part 1 ☠☠☠☠ **1944** Contemplative epic of Russia's first czar is a classic, innovative film from cinema genius Eisenstein. Visually stunning, with a fine performance by Cherkassov. Ivan's struggles to preserve his country is the main concern of the first half of Eisenstein's masterwork (which he originally planned as a trilogy). In Russian with English subtitles. **96m/B VHS, Beta, LV, 8mm.** *RU* Nikolai Cherkassov, Ludmila Tselikovskaya, Serafina Birman, Piotr Kadochnikev; ***D:*** Sergei Eisenstein; ***W:*** Sergei Eisenstein; ***M:*** Sergei Prokofiev. *NOS, MRV, WST*

Ivan the Terrible, Part 2 ☠☠☠½ **1946** Landed gentry conspire to dethrone the czar in this continuation of the innovative epic. More stunning imagery from master Eisenstein, who makes no false moves in this one. Slow going, but immensely rewarding. Russian dialogue with English subtitles; contains color sequences. **84m/B VHS, Beta, LV, 8mm.** *RU* Nikolai Cherkassov, Ludmila Tselikovskaya, Serafina Birman, Piotr Kadochnikev; ***D:*** Sergei Eisenstein. *NOS, MRV, WST*

Ivanhoe ☠☠☠ **1952** Knights fight each other and woo maidens in this chivalrous romance derived from the Sir Walter Scott classic. Taylor is suitably noble, while Sanders is familiarly serpentine. Remade in 1982. **107m/C VHS, Beta.** Robert Taylor, Elizabeth Taylor, Joan Fontaine, George Sanders, Finlay Currie, Felix Aylmer; ***D:*** Richard Thorpe; ***C:*** Frederick A. (Freddie) Young; ***M:*** Miklos Rozsa. Nominations: Academy Awards '52: Best Color Cinematography, Best Picture, Best Original Score. *MGM*

Ivanhoe ☠☠½ **1982** A version of Sir Walter Scott's classic novel of chivalry and knighthood in 12th century England. Made for television. Remake of the 1953 film classic. **142m/C VHS, Beta.** Anthony Andrews, James Mason, Lysette Anthony, Sam Neill, Olivia Hussey, Michael Hordern, Julian Glover, George Innes, Ronald Pickup, John Rhys-Davies, Chloe Franks; ***D:*** Douglas Camfield. *TVC, COL*

I've Always Loved You ☠☠½ *Concerto* **1946** The drama of love and jealousy explored in an extravagant production filled with classical music. **117m/C VHS, LV.** Philip Dorn, Catherine McLeod; ***D:*** Frank Borzage; ***C:*** Gaetano Antonio "Tony" Gaudio. *REP, FCT*

I've Heard the Mermaids Singing ☠☠☠ **1987** Independent Canadian semi-satiric romantic comedy details the misadventures of a klutzy woman who suddenly obtains a desirable job in an art gallery run by a lesbian on whom she develops a crush. Good-natured tone helped considerably by McCarthy's winning performance. **81m/C VHS, Beta, LV.** *CA* Sheila McCarthy, Paule Baillargeon, Ann-Marie MacDonald, John Evans; ***D:*** Patricia Rozema; ***M:*** Mark Korven. Genie Awards '88: Best Actress (McCarthy), Best Supporting Actress (Baillargeon). *NLC, FCT*

Ivory Hunters ☠☠½ *The Last Elephant* **1990** Conservationists team up to thwart a massacre of elephants by poachers. Predictable made-for-cable entertainment co-produced by the National Audubon Society. **94m/C VHS, Beta.** John Lithgow, Isabella Rossellini, James Earl Jones, Tony Todd, Olek Krupa; ***D:*** Joseph Sargent; ***W:*** Richard Guttman, Bill Bozzone; ***M:*** Charles Bernstein. *TTC*

Izzy & Moe ☠☠½ **1985** Carney and The Great One are reunited for the last time on screen as former vaudevillians who become federal agents and create havoc amid speak-easies and bathtub gin during Prohibition. A made-for-television movie based on true stories. **92m/C VHS, Beta, LV.** Jackie Gleason, Art Carney, Cynthia Harris, Zohra Lampert, Drew Snyder, Dick Latessa; ***D:*** Jackie Cooper. *VMK*

J. Edgar Hoover ☠☠ **1987** Made for cable adaptation from "My 30 years in Hoover's FBI" by William G. Sullivan and William S. Brown. Biographical drama deals with Hoover's fifty-five year career with the government. Included are his FBI days. **110m/C VHS, Beta, LV.** Treat Williams, Rip Torn, David Ogden Stiers, Andrew Duggan, Art Hindle, Louise Fletcher; ***D:*** Robert Collins. *MCG*

J-Men Forever! ☠☠☠ **1979 (PG)** A spoof on early sci-fi/spy serials in which an alien takeover is attempted via rock-n-roll (your parents warned you). Employs an amusing technique of dubbing footage from dozens of Republic dramas intercut with new film featuring the "Firesign Theater" crew. **73m/B VHS, Beta.** Peter Bergman, Phil Proctor; ***D:*** Richard Patterson. *VES*

Jabberwalk ☠☠ **1979 (R)** A "Mondo Cane," American-style. A reckless and funny view of the bizarre in U.S. life. **110m/C VHS, Beta.** *VCD*

Jabberwocky ☠☠½ **1977 (PG)** Pythonesque chaos prevails in the medieval cartoon kingdom of King Bruno the Questionable, who rules with cruelty, stupidity, lust and dust. Jabberwocky is the big dragon mowing everything down in its path until hero Palin decides to take it on. Uneven, but real funny at times. **104m/C VHS, Beta, LV.** *GB* Michael Palin, Eric Idle, Max Wall, Deborah Fallender, Terry Jones, John Le Mesurier; ***D:*** Terry Gilliam; ***W:*** Terry Gilliam. *COL*

Jacare ☠☠ **1942** First adventure thriller filmed in the Amazon jungle. **?m/C VHS.** Frank Buck; ***M:*** Miklos Rozsa. *SNC, VYY*

J'Accuse ☠☠☠ *I Accuse; That They May Live* **1937** A Frenchman creates a device he believes will stop the war but it is confiscated by the government and used as part of the national defense. Subsequently, he goes mad. Gance (known for his 1927 "Napoleon"), remade his 1919 silent film, retelling the powerful anti-war message with great sensitivity. Banned in Nazi Germany. **125m/B VHS.** *FR* Victor Francen, Jean Max, Deltaire, Renee Devillers; ***D:*** Abel Gance. *CVC, SNC, FCT*

Jack ☠☠½ **1996 (PG-13)** Ten-year-old Jack Powell (Williams) suffers from a rare genetic disorder that causes him to age at four times the normal rate so he looks like a 40-year-old. His family, fearing ridicule, has kept him isolated but since Jack's so lonely, they finally agree to let him attend school. This new fourth grader isn't the only one with a lot to learn. **?m/C VHS.** Robin Williams, Bill Cosby, Diane Lane, Brian Kerwin, Fran Drescher, Prof. Irwin Corey; ***D:*** Francis Ford Coppola. *NYR*

Jack and His Friends ☠☠ **1992 (R)** Comic satire of the tribulations of Jack the shoe salesman (Garfield), who is shown the front door by his unfaithful wife. Beset by grief, he drives the streets aimlessly until he is kidnapped by a young couple (Rockwell and Reyes) on the run from the law, who force Jack to take them to his summer house where they all try to decide what to do with their lives. **93m/C VHS.** Allen (Goorwitz) Garfield, Sam Rockwell, Judy Reyes; ***D:*** Bruce Ornstein. *FCT*

Jack and Sarah ☠☠½ **1996 (R)** Widowed London lawyer (Grant) hires American waitress (Mathis), to help raise his infant daughter Sarah. Complications arise because Amy has no child rearing skills and Jack's parents and in-laws disapprove of the whole situation. Performances are nice (especially the scene-stealing infants), and there's some fine moments combining tragedy with romance, but the plot is a little thin and the whole film is slow moving (it takes more than half the movie to get the three protagonists in place). An edited version is rated PG. **110m/C VHS.** *GB* Richard E. Grant, Samantha Mathis, Ian McKellen, Judi Dench, Cherie Lunghi, Eileen Atkins, Imogen Stubbs; ***D:*** Tim Sullivan; ***W:*** Tim Sullivan; ***C:*** Jean-Yves Escoffier; ***M:*** Simon Boswell. *PGV*

Jack & the Beanstalk ☠☠ **1952** While baby-sitting, Lou falls asleep and dreams he's Jack in this spoof of the classic fairy tale. **78m/C VHS, Beta, LV.** Bud Abbott, Lou Costello, Buddy Baer; ***D:*** Jean Yarbrough. *NOS, VTR*

Jack & the Beanstalk ☠☠ **1976** An animated musical version of the familiar story of Jack, the young boy who climbs a magic beanstalk up into the clouds, where he meets a fearsome giant. **80m/C VHS, Beta.** ***D:*** Peter J. Solmo; ***W:*** Peter J. Solmo. *COL*

Jack & the Beanstalk **1983** From the "Faerie Tale Theatre" comes this classic tale of Jack, who sells his family's cow for 5 magic beans, climbs the huge beanstalk that sprouts from them, and encounters an unfriendly giant. **60m/C VHS, Beta, LV.** Dennis Christopher, Katherine Helmond, Elliott Gould, Jean

Stapleton, Mark Blankfield; *D:* Lamont Johnson. *KUI, FOX, FCT*

Jack Be Nimble ✂✂ **1994 (R)** Siblings Jack (Arquette) and Dora (Kennedy) were separated as children and adopted by different families. Jack's family turns out to be sadistic and he suffers much abuse, until he enacts a violent revenge; Dora begins to hear voices and soon realizes it's Jack crying out to her. The duo finally reunite but between Jack's rage and Dora's telepathic abilities, life takes on further bizarre twists. Much psychological terror rather than gore. **93m/C VHS.** *NZ* Alexis Arquette, Sarah Kennedy, Bruno Lawrence; *D:* Garth Maxwell; *W:* Garth Maxwell; *M:* Chris Neal. *TRI*

Jack Frost ✂✂½ **1943** Moving biographical drama that follows a man from the sweat factories of London to his eventual rise to success. **89m/B VHS, Beta, 8mm.** Michael O'Shea, Susan Hayward. *VYY*

The Jack Knife Man ✂✂✂ **1920** Sentimental silent treatment of the relationship between a boy and a man. A new mother close to death hands over her bundle of joy to a kindly old river man, and the two bond in a familial way despite incessant adversity. Made the year following Vidor's debut as a feature film director. **70m/B VHS, Beta.** Fred Turner, Harry Todd, Bobby Kelso, Willis Marks, Lillian Leighton, James Corrigan; *D:* King Vidor; *W:* William Parker. *VYY, GPV, FCT*

Jack London ✂½ *The Adventures of Jack London; The Life of Jack London* **1944** Dramatizes London's most creative years during his careers as oyster pirate, prospector, war correspondent and author. Based on "The Book of Jack London" by Charmian London. **94m/B VHS, Beta.** Michael O'Shea, Susan Hayward, Harry Davenport, Virginia Mayo, Frank Craven; *D:* Alfred Santell. Nominations: Academy Awards '44: Best Original Score. *NOS, MRV, DVT*

Jack-O ✂½ **1995 (R)** Halloween nightmares in the small town of Oakmoor Crossing. When warlock Walter Machen (Carradine) was hung 100 years before, he invoked a demon creature to take his revenge. Now partyers, fooling around in the local cemetery, have stumbled onto horrific Jack-O's remains and manage to once again unleash the evil within. Cheesy grade-Z horror features old footage of deceased actors Carradine and Mitchell incorporated into what little plot there is. **90m/C VHS, LV.** Linnea Quigley, Ryan Latshaw, Cameron Mitchell, John Carradine; *D:* Steve Latshaw. *TRI, IME*

Jack the Bear ✂½ **1993 (PG-13)** Exercise in misery centers on a father and his two sons, trying to pick up the pieces after the death of wife and mother Marcovicci. Dad DeVito is the host of a late-night horror show who's cuddly as a bear—when he's not drinking. While the talent and circumstances might have been enough to create a sensitive study, the emotion is completely overwrought by contrived plot twists, including a kidnapping by the local Nazi. TV's "thirtysomething" director Herskovitz creates an effect not unlike a cement block being dropped on a card house. Point made, but so much for subtlety. Based on a novel by Dan McCall. **98m/C VHS, LV.** Danny DeVito, Robert J. Steinmiller Jr., Miko Hughes, Gary Sinise, Art LaFleur, Andrea Marcovicci, Julia Louis-Dreyfus, Reese Witherspoon; *D:* Marshall Herskovitz; *W:* Steven Zaillian; *C:* Fred Murphy; *M:* James Horner. *FXV*

Jack the Giant Killer ✂✂✂ **1962 (G)** A young farmer joins a medieval princess on a journey to a distant convent. Along the way, they combat an evil wizard, dragons, sea monsters and other mystical creatures, and are assisted by leprechauns, a dog and a chimp. Generally considered a blatant ripoff of "The Seventh Voyage of Sinbad," the film nonetheless delivers plenty of fun and excitement. Jim Danforth of "Gumby" fame provided the stop-motion animation. **95m/C VHS, Beta, LV.** Kerwin Mathews, Judi Meredith, Torin Thatcher, Walter Burke, Roger Mobley, Barry Kelley, Don Beddoe, Anna Lee, Robert Gist; *D:* Nathan (Hertz) Juran. *MGM, FCT*

Jack the Ripper ✂✂ **1960** An American detective joins Scotland Yard in tracking down the legendary and elusive Jack the Ripper. More gory than most. The last scene is in color. **88m/B VHS.** *GB* Lee Patterson, Betty McDowall, Barbara Burke, John Le Mesurier, George Rose; *D:* Monty Berman, Robert S. Baker; *M:* Stanley Black. *SNC, PAR*

Jack the Ripper ✂✂ **1980 (R)** The inimitable Kinski assumes the role of the most heinous criminal of modern history—Jack the Ripper. **82m/C VHS, Beta.** Klaus Kinski, Josephine Chaplin; *D:* Jess (Jesus) Franco. *VES*

Jack the Ripper ✂✂✂ **1988** Another retelling of the life of the legendary serial killer. Caine is the Scotland Yard inspector who tracks down the murderer. Ending is based on recent evidence found by director/co-writer Wickes. Extremely well done made-for-television film. **200m/C VHS.** Michael Caine, Armand Assante, Ray McNally, Susan George, Jane Seymour, Lewis Collins, Ken Bones; *D:* David Wickes; *W:* David Wickes. *VES, LIV*

Jackie Chan's Police Force ✂✂½ *The Police Story; Police Force; Jackie Chan's Police Story* **1985 (PG-13)** Chopsocker Chan's assigned to protect a witness in a drug case. Faced by unsavory thugs, he flies through the air with the greatest of ease. Very cool stunts. **89m/C VHS.** *CH* Jackie Chan, Bridget Lin, Maggie Cheung, Cho Yuen, Bill Tung, Kenneth Tong; *D:* Jackie Chan. *NO*

The Jackie Robinson Story ✂✂✂ **1950** Chronicles Robinson's rise from UCLA to his breakthrough as the first black man to play baseball in the major league. Robinson plays himself; the film deals honestly with the racial issues of the time. **76m/B VHS, Beta.** Jackie Robinson, Ruby Dee, Minor Watson, Louise Beavers, Richard Lane, Harry Shannon, Joel Fluellen, Ben Lessy; *D:* Alfred E. Green. *MGM, MRV, MOV*

Jacknife ✂✂✂ **1989 (R)** The well-crafted story of a Vietnam veteran who visits his old war buddy and tries to piece together what's happened to their lives since their homecoming. During his visit he encounters anger and hostility from the other veteran, and tenderness from his friend's sister. A masterfully acted, small-scale drama, adapted by Stephen Metcalfe from his play. **102m/C VHS, Beta, LV.** Robert De Niro, Kathy Baker, Ed Harris, Loudon Wainwright III, Charles S. Dutton; *D:* David Jones; *W:* Stephen Metcalfe; *M:* Bruce Broughton. *HBO, IME*

Jacko & Lise ✂✂ **1982 (R)** A French lad falls in love with a young girl, and abandons his previously decadent lifestyle to win her. Available with English subtitles or dubbed. **92m/C VHS, Beta.** *FR* Laurent Malet, Annie Girardot; *D:* Walter Bal. *SUE*

The Jackpot ✂✂ **1950** An average Joe wins a bushel of money from a radio quiz show but can't pay the taxes. Maybe that was funny before the age of read-my-lips economics, but the all-star cast doesn't deliver on its promise. Lang, noted for mostly mediocre pictures, went on to direct "The King and I." **87m/C VHS.** James Stewart, Natalie Wood, Barbara Hale, James Gleason, Fred Clark, Patricia Medina; *D:* Walter Lang; *C:* Joseph LaShelle. *FXV*

Jack's Back ✂✂✂ **1987 (R)** When a lunatic is killing Los Angeles prostitutes Jack-the-Ripper style, twin brothers get mistakenly involved (Spader in both roles). One of the brothers is accused of the murders and it is up to the other either to clear his name or to provide the final evidence of guilt. A well thought out story with enough twists and turns for any suspense buff. **97m/C VHS, Beta, LV.** James Spader, Cynthia Gibb, Rod Loomis, Rex Ryon, Robert Picardo, Jim Haynie, Chris Mulkey, Danitza Kingsley; *D:* Rowdy Herrington. *PAR*

Jackson County Jail ✂✂½ **1976 (R)** While driving cross-country, a young woman is robbed, imprisoned, and raped by a deputy, whom she kills. Faced with a murder charge, she flees, with the law in hot pursuit. Also known by its later remade-for-television name, "Outside Chance," this is a minor cult film. **84m/C VHS, Beta.** Yvette Mimieux, Tommy Lee Jones, Robert Carradine, Severn Darden, Howard Hesseman, Mary Woronov; *D:* Michael Miller; *W:* Donald Stewart. *WAR*

The Jacksons: An American Dream ✂✂½ **1992** Made for television miniseries covering the career of the Jackson 5, the working-class family from Gary, Indiana which became a celebrated show business success. The series begins with the courtship of Joseph and Katherine Jackson and ends with the group's farewell tour in 1984, covering both family and career turmoils. Simplistic, glossy biography. **225m/C VHS.** Lawrence-Hilton Jacobs, Angela Bassett, Wylie Draper, Angel Vargas, Jacen Wilkerson, Terrence DaShon Howard, Jason Weaver, Jermaine Jackson II, Billy Dee Williams, Vanessa Williams, Holly Robinson, Margaret Avery; *D:* Karen Arthur. *PGV*

Jacob ✂✂½ **1994** Jacob (Modine), second son of Isaac (Ackland), tricks his father into giving him the blessing meant for eldest son Esau (Bean). Jacob is forced to run away to his Uncle Laban (Giannini), where he promptly falls in love with his cousin Rachel (Boyle). But Laban tricks Jacob into marrying eldest daughter Leah (Aubrey), before allowing his marriage to Rachel. Finally, Jacob settles on his own land with his wives and children (who will become the tribes of Israel). Diginified retelling of the Biblical story; filmed on location in Morocco. Made for cable TV. **120m/C VHS.** Matthew Modine, Lara Flynn Boyle, Sean Bean, Juliet Aubrey, Giancarlo Giannini, Joss Ackland, Irene Papas, Christoph Waltz; *D:* Peter Hall; *W:* Lionel Chetwynd; *M:* Marco Frisina. *TTC*

Jacob Have I Loved **1988** A teenage girl struggles to overcome her jealousy of her twin sister and find her own place in life as she comes of age on a Chesapeake island. Based on the book by Katherine Paterson. Part of the "Wonderworks" family movie series from PBS. **57m/C VHS.** Bridget Fonda, Jenny Robertson, John Kellogg; *D:* Victoria Hochberg. *PME, WNE, RHU*

Jacob's Ladder ✂✂½ **1990 (R)** A man struggles with events he experienced while serving in Vietnam. Gradually, he becomes unable to separate reality from the strange, psychotic world into which he increasingly lapses. His friends and family try to help him before he's lost forever. Great story potential is flawed by too many flashbacks, leaving the viewer more confused than the characters. **116m/C VHS, Beta, LV.** Tim Robbins, Elizabeth Pena, Danny Aiello, Matt Craven, Pruitt Taylor Vince, Jason Alexander, Patricia Kalember, Eriq La Salle, Ving Rhames, Macaulay Culkin; *D:* Adrian Lyne; *W:* Bruce Joel Rubin; *M:* Maurice Jarre. *LIV, FCT*

Jacqueline Bouvier Kennedy ✂½ **1981** A made-for-television biography of the former First Lady, from her childhood to "Camelot," the glorious years with JFK in the White House. Smith bears a physical resemblance to Jackie, but this drama is far too glossy. **150m/C VHS, Beta.** Jaclyn Smith, James Franciscus, Rod Taylor, Donald Moffat, Dolph Sweet, Stephen Elliott; *D:* Steven Gethers; *M:* Billy Goldenberg. *VMK*

Jacquot ✂✂ *Jacquot de Nantes* **1991 (PG)** Director Varda offers a loving tribute to her husband, filmmaker Jacques Demy. Based on the memoirs of her husband's childhood as a boy obsessed with movies, Varda re-stages scenes and also uses clips from various Demy films to illustrate her points. In French with English subtitles. **118m/C VHS.** *FR* Philippe Maron, Edouard Joubeaud, Laurent Monnier, Brigitte de Villepoix, Daniel Dublet; *D:* Agnes Varda; *W:* Agnes Varda; *M:* Joanne Bruzdowicz. *COL*

Jade ✂½ **1995 (R)** Sleazy whodunnit scraped from the bottom of the Eszterhas barrel (and it's a deep one) has hot-shot San Francisco Assistant D.A. David Corelli (Caruso) tracking a trail of pubic hairs across San Francisco. Seems he's caught up in the murder of a millionaire that points to his ex-lover, psychologist Katrina Gavin (Fiorentino), as the killer. Oh yeah, she's also a kinky call girl of choice to California's rich and famous, and happens to be married to Corelli's best friend (Palminteri). Psycho-thriller with little of either injects lots of lurid details (and a car chase scene that Friedkin has done much better elsewhere) in an attempt to curtail boredom; it doesn't work. Combine it with "Showgirls" for the No Self-Respect Film Festival, then go to confession. **94m/C VHS.** David Caruso, Linda Fiorentino, Chazz Palminteri, Michael Biehn, Richard Crenna, Kenneth King; ***D:*** William Friedkin; ***W:*** Joe Eszterhas; ***C:*** Andrzej Bartkowiak; ***M:*** James Horner. *PAR*

The Jade Mask ½ **1945** Chan discovers a murderer and his wife use puppets and masks to make it appear their victims are still alive. Another in the detective series with nothing noteworthy about it. Luke, the brother of actor Keye Luke, takes on the role of Chan's Number Four son. **66m/B VHS.** Sidney Toler, Mantan Moreland, Edwin Luke, Janet Warren, Hardie Albright, Edith Evanson; ***D:*** Phil Rosen. *MGM*

JAG ½ **1995** TV pilot episode features Navy pilot-turned-lawyer Lt. Harmon Rabb, Jr. (Elliott) assigned to investigate the case of a young female pilot who disappears from an aircraft carrier. Seems some of her fellow sailors resented having women on board so was it an accident or murder? JAG stands for the office of the Judge Advocate General, whose Navy lawyers serve as investigators, prosecutors, and defense attorneys. **94m/C VHS.** David James Elliott, Andrea Parker, Terry O'Quinn; ***D:*** Donald P. Bellisario; ***W:*** Donald P. Bellisario; ***M:*** Bruce Broughton. *PAR*

The Jagged Edge ½ **1985 (R)** The beautiful wife of successful newspaper editor, Jack Forester, is killed and the police want to point the guilty finger at Jack. Attorney Teddy Barnes is brought in to defend him and accidentally falls in love. Taut murder mystery will keep you guessing "whodunit" until the very end. **108m/C VHS, Beta, LV, 8mm.** Jeff Bridges, Glenn Close, Robert Loggia, Peter Coyote, John Dehner, Leigh Taylor-Young, Lance Henriksen, James Karen, Karen Austin, Michael Dorn, Guy Boyd, Marshall Colt, Louis Giambalvo; ***D:*** Richard Marquand; ***W:*** Joe Eszterhas; ***M:*** John Barry. Nominations: Academy Awards '85: Best Supporting Actor (Loggia). *COL*

Jaguar **1956** Three men leave their homes in Niger in order to find jobs in the cities. When they return to their village, they bring back with them their experiences. **93m/C VHS.** ***D:*** Jean Rouch; ***M:*** Van Alexander. *INT*

Jaguar Lives **1979 (PG)** A high-kicking secret agent tracks down bad boy drug kings around the world. **91m/C VHS, Beta.** Joe Lewis, Barbara Bach, Christopher Lee, Woody Strode, Donald Pleasence, Joseph Wiseman, John Huston, Capucine; ***D:*** Ernie Pintoff. *TWE*

Jail Bait ½ *Hidden Face* **1954** Early Wood film about a group of small-time crooks who are always in trouble with the law; they blackmail a plastic surgeon into using his talents to help them ditch the cops. Not as "bad" as Wood's "Plan 9 From Outer Space," but still bad enough for camp fans to love (check the cheesy score leftover from an equally cheesy Mexican mad-scientist flick). **80m/B VHS, Beta.** Timothy Farrell, Clancy Malone, Lyle Talbot, Steve Reeves, Herbert Rawlinson; ***D:*** Edward D. Wood Jr. *SNC, AOV, LSV*

Jailbait **1993 (R)** A cop gets involved with an alleged murder witness, a teenaged runaway named Kyle. What they discover is an international crime syndicate that kidnaps runaways to exploit as sex slaves. Now they know too much. An unrated version is also available. **100m/C VHS.** C. Thomas Howell, Renee Humphrey; ***D:*** Rafal Zielinksi; ***W:*** Robert Vincent O'Neil, Alien Castle. *PAR*

Jailbait: Betrayed By Innocence ½ **1986 (R)** A man is on trial for statutory rape. Made-for-television. **90m/C VHS, Beta.** Barry Bostwick, Lee Purcell, Paul Sorvino, Cristen Kauffman, Isaac Hayes; ***D:*** Elliot Silverstein. *HHE*

Jailbird Rock ½ **1988** We'd like to tell you that this isn't really a sweet-young-thing-in-prison musical, but it is. When Antin shoots her stepfather (he told her to turn that damn noise down?) she tries to bring down the Big House with song and dance. No kidding. **90m/C VHS, Beta.** Ronald Lacey, Rhonda Aldrich, Robin Antin; ***D:*** Phillip Schuman. *TWE*

Jailbird's Vacation *Les Grandes Gueules* **1965** Two ex-cons pose as lumberjacks in order to exact revenge on the bum that put them away. In French with English subtitles. **125m/C VHS, Beta.** *FR* Lino Ventura, Bourvil, Marie DuBois; ***D:*** Robert Enrico. *FCT, BAR, INJ*

Jailbreakin' **1972** A faded country singer and a rebellious youth team up to break out of jail. **90m/C VHS, Beta.** Erik Estrada. *GEM*

Jailhouse Rock **1957 (G)** While in jail for manslaughter, a teenager learns to play the guitar. After his release, he slowly develops into a top recording star. Probably the only film that captured the magnetic power of the young Elvis Presley; an absolute must for fans. Also available in a colorized version. ♫Jailhouse Rock; Treat Me Nice; Baby, I Don't Care; Young and Beautiful; Don't Leave Me Now; I Wanna Be Free; One More Day. **96m/B VHS, Beta, LV.** Elvis Presley, Judy Tyler, Vaughn Taylor, Dean Jones, Mickey Shaughnessy, William Forrest, Glenn Strange; ***D:*** Richard Thorpe. *MGM*

Jakarta ½ **1988 (R)** A love-hardened CIA operative is whisked away to Jakarta for reasons unknown, only to find his thought-to-be-dead lover still alive and caught in a deadly game of espionage. **94m/C VHS, Beta, LV.** Christopher Noth, Sue Francis Pai, Ronald Hunter; ***D:*** Charles Kaufman. *NO*

Jake Speed ½ **1986 (PG)** Comic-book mercenary Jake and his loyal associate Remo rescue a beautiful girl from white slave traders. Supposedly a parody of the action adventure genre. **93m/C VHS, Beta, LV.** Wayne Crawford, John Hurt, Karen Kopins, Dennis Christopher; ***D:*** Andrew Lane; ***W:*** Wayne Crawford. *NWV, VTR*

Jamaica Inn **1939** In old Cornwall, an orphan girl becomes involved with smugglers. Remade in 1982; based on the story by Daphne Du Maurier. **98m/B VHS, Beta.** *GB* Charles Laughton, Maureen O'Hara, Leslie Banks, Robert Newton; ***D:*** Alfred Hitchcock; ***C:*** Harry Stradling. *SNC, NOS, CAB*

Jamaica Inn ½ **1982** A made-for-television mini-series based on the old Daphne Du Maurier adventure about highwaymen and moor-lurking thieves in Cornwall. Remake of the 1939 Hitchcock film. **192m/C VHS, Beta.** Patrick McGoohan, Jane Seymour; ***D:*** Lawrence Gordon Clark. *VTR, NWV*

James and the Giant Peach **1996 (PG)** Combo of live action and stop-motion animation in this adaptation of Roald Dahl's 1961 children's book. Orphaned James is sent to live with his wicked aunts. When magic "crocodile tongues," given to James by a hobo, spill at the base of a peach tree, one fruit grows to such a tremendous size that James crawls inside, meets six insect friends, and goes on numerous adventures, all the while trying to face his fears. Dahl's books are creepy and since the people who brought you "Nightmare Before Christmas" are also doing "James," expect the visuals to be astonishing but too scary for the little ones. **80m/C VHS.** Paul Terry, Pete Postlethwaite, Joanna Lumley, Miriam Margolyes; ***D:*** Henry Selick; ***C:*** Pete Kozachik, Hiro Narita; ***M:*** Randy Newman; ***V:*** Richard Dreyfuss, Susan Sarandon, David Thewlis, Simon Callow, Jane Leeves. *TOU*

James Dean *The Legend* **1976** Dean's friend Bast wrote this behind-the-scenes look at the short life of the enigmatic movie star. Made for television. **99m/C VHS, Beta.** Stephen McHattie, Michael Brandon, Candy Clark, Amy Irving, Brooke Adams, Dane Clark, Jayne Meadows, Meg Foster; ***D:*** William Bast, Robert Butler; ***W:*** William Bast; ***M:*** Billy Goldenberg. *NWV*

James Dean **1985** Production reflects an exhaustive search through archival film, videotape and photographs, and includes many exclusive interviews with friends of the late actor. **120m/C VHS, Beta.** James Dean; ***D:*** Claudio Masenza. *BAR*

James Dean Story **1957** An intimate portrait of James Dean presented by Robert Altman. The program includes never-before-seen out-takes from "East of Eden" and rare footage from the Hollywood premiere of "Giant" and the infamous Highway Public Safety message Dean made for television. **80m/B VHS, Beta, LV.** James Dean; ***D:*** George W. George. *FCT, PMS, VEC*

James Dean: The First American Teenager **1976 (PG)** A look at the life and legend of the charismatic filmstar, with scenes from his films and comments from those who knew him best. **83m/C VHS, Beta.** James Dean, Elizabeth Taylor, Sammy Davis Jr., Rock Hudson, Sal Mineo, Natalie Wood, Julie Harris, Jack Larson, Nicholas Ray. *NO*

James Joyce: A Portrait of the Artist as a Young Man **1977** A moving, lyrical adaptation of the author's autobiography, told through the character of Stephen Dedalus. Joyce's characterizations, words, and scenes are beautifully translated to the medium of film. Excellent casting. **93m/C VHS.** John Gielgud, T.P. McKenna, Bosco Hogan. *MFV*

James Joyce's Women **1985 (R)** Adapted from her one-woman stage show as well as produced by Flanagan, this acclaimed film features enacted portraits of three real-life Joyce associates, including his wife (Nora Barnacle) and three of his famous characters. **91m/C VHS, Beta.** Fionnula Flanagan, Timothy E. O'Grady, Chris O'Neill; ***D:*** Michael Pearce; ***W:*** Fionnula Flanagan. *MCA*

James Stewart: A Wonderful Life **1987** Tribute to the popular, slow-talking actor is highlighted by interviews and visits to the sets of some of Stewart's most popular films. **88m/C VHS, Beta.** *MGM, FCT, BTV*

Jamon, Jamon *Ham Ham* **1993** Comedic melodrama satirizing various aspects of the Spanish character, including machismo, sex, and food. A small Spanish town is dominated by two businesses—an underwear factory and a brothel—both run by strong-minded women. The brothel's Carmen and the factory's Conchita clash when Carmen's daughter, Silvia, becomes pregnant by Conchita's son, Manuel. Conchita's appalled and hires stud Raul to seduce Silvia—only to fall for him herself. Oh yes, Raul attributes his sexual prowess to a steady diet of ham and garlic. In Spanish with English subtitles. **95m/C VHS, LV.** *SP* Penelope Cruz, Anna Galiena, Javier Bardem, Stefania Sandrelli, Juan Diego, Jordi Molla; ***D:*** Bigas Luna; ***W:*** Bigas Luna, Cuca Canals; ***M:*** Nicola Piovani. *ACA*

Jane & the Lost City ½ **1987 (PG)** A British farce based on the age-old, barely dressed comic-strip character, Jane, as she stumbles on ancient cities, treasures, villains, and blond/blue-eyed heroes. Low-budget camp fun. **94m/C VHS, Beta.** *GB* Kristen Hughes, Maud Adams, Sam Jones; ***D:*** Terry Marcel; ***W:*** Mervyn Haisman; ***M:*** Harry Robertson. *NWV, VTR*

Jane Austen in Manhattan ½ **1980** Two acting-teachers vie to stage a long-lost play written by a youthful Jane Austen. Dreary, despite the cast. Hodiak is the real-life daughter of Baxter. **108m/C VHS, Beta.** Anne Baxter, Robert Powell, Michael Wager, Sean Young, Kurt Johnson, Katrina Hodiak; ***D:*** James Ivory; ***W:*** Ruth Prawer Jhabvala. *NLC*

Jane Doe ½ **1983** Valentine plays a young amnesia victim who is linked to a series of brutal slayings. Quite suspenseful for a television movie. **100m/C VHS, Beta.** Karen Valentine, William Devane, Eva Marie Saint, Stephen E. Miller, Jackson Davies; ***D:*** Ivan Nagy. *LIV*

Jane Eyre **1934** Stiff, early version of Charlotte Bronte's classic gothic romance. English orphan grows up to become the governess of a mysterious manor. Notable as the first talkie version. Remade several times. **67m/B VHS.** Virginia Bruce, Colin Clive, Beryl Mercer, Jameson Thomas, Aileen Pringle, David Torrence; ***D:*** Christy Cabanne. *SNC*

Jane Eyre **1944** Excellent adaptation of the Charlotte Bronte novel about the plain governess with the noble heart and her love for the mysterious and tragic Mr. Rochester. Fontaine has the proper backbone and yearning in the title role but to accommodate Welles' emerging popularity the role of Rochester was enlarged. Excellent bleak romantic-Gothic look. Taylor, in her third film role, is seen briefly in the early orphanage scenes. **97m/B VHS.** Joan Fontaine, Orson Welles, Margaret O'Brien, Peggy Ann Garner, John Sutton, Sara Allgood, Henry Daniell, Agnes Moorehead, Aubrey

Mather, Edith Barrett, Barbara Everest, Hillary Brooke, Elizabeth Taylor; **D:** Robert Stevenson; **W:** John Houseman, Aldous Huxley, Robert Stevenson; **C:** George Barnes; **M:** Bernard Herrmann. *FXV, FCT, BTV*

Jane Eyre ☙☙☙ **1983** A made-for-British-television mini-series based on the famed Charlotte Bronte novel about the maturation of a homeless English waif, her love for the tormented Rochester, and her quest for permanent peace. **239m/C VHS, Beta, LV.** *GB* Timothy Dalton, Zelah Clarke; **D:** Julian Aymes. *PBS, FOX, SIG*

Jane Eyre ☙☙☙ **1996 (PG)** Zeffirelli creates an eloquent yet spare interpretation of Charlotte Bronte's 1847 masterpiece, about a meek governess and her mysterious employer, in its fourth film incarnation. Everything about it, from the lighting to the score, is muted and somber. Still a beautiful film, it seems to lack a certain passion that earlier versions (especially the 1944 version) brought to the screen. Strong performances all around, including Oscar-winner Paquin and French star Gainsbourg as the younger and older Jane, and Hurt as the tormented Rochester. **112m/C VHS.** William Hurt, Anna Paquin, Charlotte Gainsbourg, Joan Plowright, Elle Macpherson, Geraldine Chaplin, Fiona Shaw, John Wood, Amanda Root, Marc Schneider, Josephine Serre; **D:** Franco Zeffirelli; **W:** Franco Zeffirelli, Hugh Whitemore; **C:** David Watkin; **M:** Alessio Vlad, Claudio Capponi. *NYR*

Janis: A Film ☙☙½ **1974 (R)** The famous biographical film about Janis Joplin, from her Texas origins to Woodstock and superstardom, featuring performances with Big Brother and the Holding Company and rare interviews. **79m/C VHS, Beta. D:** Howard Alk. *MVD, MCA, FCT*

The January Man ☙☙ **1989 (R)** An unorthodox cop, previously exiled by a corrupt local government to the fire department, is brought back to the force in New York City to track down a serial killer. Written by the "Moonstruck" guy, Shanley, who apparently peaked with the earlier movie. **97m/C VHS, Beta, LV.** Kevin Kline, Susan Sarandon, Mary Elizabeth Mastrantonio, Harvey Keitel, Rod Steiger, Alan Rickman, Danny Aiello; **D:** Pat O'Connor; **W:** John Patrick Shanley, Pat O'Connor; **M:** Marvin Hamlisch. *MGM, FXV*

Japanese Connection ☙ **1982** Warring crime chiefs fight furiously with deadly kung-fu action until end of movie. **96m/C VHS, Beta.** Li Chao, Yang Wei, Wu Ming-Tsai. *GEM*

The Jar **1984** A recluse discovers a disgusting creature in a jar. He keeps it, only to discover that it is out to kill him. **90m/C VHS, Beta.** Gary Wallace, Karen Sjoberg; **D:** Bruce Toscano. *NO*

Jason and the Argonauts ☙☙☙ **1963 (G)** Jason, son of the King of Thessaly, sails on the Argo to the land of Colchis, where the Golden Fleece is guarded by a seven-headed hydra. Superb special effects and multitudes of mythological creatures; fun for the whole family. **104m/C VHS, Beta, LV, 8mm.** *GB* Todd Armstrong, Nancy Kovack, Gary Raymond, Laurence Naismith, Nigel Green, Michael Gwynn, Honor Blackman; **D:** Don Chaffey; **W:** Jan Read, Beverley Cross. *COL, MLB, FUS*

Jason Goes to Hell: The Final Friday *Woof!* **1993 (R)** The supposed last, at least so far, in the "Friday the 13th" gore series. Only through the bodies—dead or alive—of his Vorhees kin can supernatural killer Jason be reborn, and only at their hands can he truly die. One can only hope that this is finally true. An unrated, even gorier, version is also available. **89m/C VHS, LV.** Kane Hodder, John D. LeMay, Kari Keegan, Steven Williams, Steven Culp, Erin Gray, Richard Gant, Leslie Jordan, Billy Green Bush, Rusty Schwimmer; **D:** Adam Marcus; **W:** Dean Lorey, Jay Huguely-Cass; **M:** Harry Manfredini. *NLC, IME*

Jason's Lyric ☙☙ **1994 (R)** A romantic triangle, sibling rivalry, family bonds, and neighborhood violence all set on the wrong side of the Houston tracks. Jason (Payne) is the responsible young man who works hard and helps out his mom; younger brother Joshua (Woodbine) has just gotten out of jail and is headed straight for more trouble. Between the two is Lyric (Pinkett), a soul-food waitress whose bad news half-brother Alonzo (Treach) is naturally one of Joshua's homies. Good-looking but ultimately empty storytelling. **119m/C VHS.** Allen Payne, Bokeem Woodbine, Jada Pinkett, Suzanne Douglas, Forest Whitaker, Treach; **D:** Doug McHenry; **W:** Bobby Smith Jr.; **M:** Matt Noble. *PGV*

Java Head ☙☙☙ **1935** Young Chinese wife commits suicide so her husband can marry an English girl. Set in mid-1800s England. Based on the novel by Joseph Hergesheimer. **70m/B VHS, Beta, 8mm.** *GB* Anna May Wong, Elizabeth Allan, John Loder, Edmund Gwenn, Ralph Richardson, George Curzan; **D:** J. Walter Ruben. *VYY*

Jaws ☙☙☙½ **1975 (PG)** Early directorial effort by Spielberg from the Peter Benchley potboiler. A tight, very scary, and sometimes hilarious film about the struggle to kill a giant great white shark that is terrorizing an eastern beach community's waters. The characterizations by Dreyfuss, Scheider, and Shaw are much more endurable than the shock effects. Memorable score. Sequeled by "Jaws 2" in 1978, "Jaws 3" 1983, and "Jaws the Revenge" in 1987. Look for Benchley as a TV reporter. **124m/C VHS, Beta, LV.** Roy Scheider, Robert Shaw, Richard Dreyfuss, Lorraine Gary, Murray Hamilton, Carl Gottlieb; ***Cameos:*** Peter Benchley; **D:** Steven Spielberg; **W:** Carl Gottlieb, Peter Benchley; **M:** John Williams. Academy Awards '75: Best Film Editing, Best Sound, Best Original Score; Golden Globe Awards '76: Best Score; People's Choice Awards '76: Best Film; Nominations: Academy Awards '75: Best Picture. *MCA*

Jaws 2 ☙☙½ **1978 (PG)** Unsatisfactory sequel to "Jaws." It's been four years since the man-eating shark feasted on the resort town of Amity; suddenly a second shark stalks the waters and the terror returns. Scheider—who must by now wonder at his tendancy to attract large aquatic carnivores with lunch on their minds— battles without his compatriots from the original. And we haven't seen the last of the mechanical dorsal fin yet; two more sequels follow. **116m/C VHS, Beta, LV.** Roy Scheider, Lorraine Gary, Murray Hamilton; **D:** Jeannot Szwarc; **W:** Carl Gottlieb; **M:** John Williams. *MCA*

Jaws 3 ☙☙ *Jaws 3-D* **1983 (PG)** Same monster, new setting: in a Sea World-type amusement park, a great white shark escapes from its tank and proceeds to cause terror and chaos. Little connection to the previous "Jaws" sagas. Followed by one more sequel, "Jaws: The Revenge." **98m/C VHS, Beta, LV.** Dennis Quaid, Bess Armstrong, Louis Gossett Jr., Simon MacCorkindale, Lea Thompson; **D:** Joe Alves; **W:** Richard Matheson, Carl Gottlieb; **M:** John Williams. *MCA*

Jaws of Death ☙☙ *Mako: The Jaws of Death* **1976** "Jaws"-like saga of shark terror. Jaeckel illogically strikes out to protect his "friends," the sharks. **91m/C VHS, Beta.** Richard Jaeckel, Harold Sakata, Jennifer Bishop, John Chandler, Buffy Dee; **D:** William Grefe. *NO*

Jaws of Justice ☙½ **1933** A Canadian Mountie and his trusty German shepherd track down outlaws in the Canadian Northwest. **55m/B VHS, Beta, 8mm.** Richard Terry, Lafe McKee. *VYY*

Jaws of Satan *Woof! King Cobra* **1981 (R)** Weaver is terrorized by a slimy snake who is, in actuality, the Devil. Not released for 2 years after it was filmed, and generally considered a bomb of the first caliber. Unfortunate work for usually worthwhile Weaver. **92m/C VHS.** Fritz Weaver, Gretchen Corbett, Jon Korkes, Norman Lloyd, Christina Applegate; **D:** Bob Claver. *NO*

Jaws: The Revenge ☙ **1987 (PG-13)** The third sequel, in which Mrs. Brody is pursued the world over by a seemingly personally motivated Great White Shark. Includes footage not seen in the theatrical release. Each sequel in this series is progressively inferior to the original. **87m/C VHS, Beta, LV.** Lorraine Gary, Lance Guest, Karen Young, Mario Van Peebles, Michael Caine, Judith Barsi, Lynn Whitfield; **D:** Joseph Sargent; **W:** Michael deGuzman. *MCA*

The Jayhawkers ☙☙ **1959** Chandler and Parker battle for power and women in pre-Civil War Kansas. **100m/C VHS.** Jeff Chandler, Fess Parker, Nicole Maurey, Henry Silva, Herbert Rudley, Frank De Kova, Don Megowan, Leo Gordon; **D:** Melvin Frank. *PAR, FCT*

The Jayne Mansfield Story ☙ *Jayne Mansfield: A Symbol of the '50s* **1980** Television movie recounting the blond bombshell's career from her first career exposure, through her marriage to a body-builder, to the famous car crash that beheaded her. **97m/C VHS, Beta.** Loni Anderson, Arnold Schwarzenegger, Raymond Buktenica, Kathleen Lloyd, G.D. Spradlin, Dave Shelley; **D:** Dick Lowry. *LIV*

The Jazz Singer ☙☙½ **1927** A Jewish cantor's son breaks with his family to become a singer of popular music. Of historical importance as the first successful part-talkie; a very early Loy performance. With the classic line "You ain't heard nothing yet!" Remade several times. ♫Toot, Toot, Tootsie Goodbye; Blue Skies; My Gal Sal; Waiting for the Robert E. Lee; Dirty Hands, Dirty Face; Mother, I Still Have You; Kol Nidre; Yahrzeit; My Mammy. **89m/B VHS, Beta, LV.** Al Jolson, May McAvoy, Warner Oland, William Demarest, Eugenie Besserer, Myrna Loy; **D:** Alan Crosland; **C:** Hal Mohr. Nominations: Academy Awards '28: Best Adapted Screenplay. *FOX, FCT, MLB*

The Jazz Singer *Woof!* **1980 (PG)** Flat and uninteresting (if not unintentionally funny) remake of the 1927 classic about a Jewish boy who rebels against his father and family tradition to become a popular entertainer. Stick with the original, this is little more than a vehicle for Diamond to sing. ♫America; You Baby Baby; Jerusalem; Love on the Rocks; Summer Love; On the Robert E. Lee; Louise; Songs of Life; Hello Again. **115m/C VHS, Beta, LV, 8mm.** Neil Diamond, Laurence Olivier, Lucie Arnaz, Catlin Adams, Franklin Ajaye; **D:** Richard Fleischer. Golden Raspberry Awards '80: Worst Actor (Diamond), Worst Supporting Actor (Olivier). *REP, PAR*

Jazzman ☙☙☙ **1984** A comedy set in the late 1920s with a young musician forming a jazz band with two street musicians and a saxophonist who played in the czar's marching band. Their music is condemned as a product of bourgeois society but that doesn't stop them. In Russian with English subtitles. **80m/C VHS.** *RU* Igor Sklyar, Alexander Chorny; **D:** Karen Chakhnazarov. *KIV, FCT*

J.D.'s Revenge ☙☙½ **1976 (R)** Attorney in training Glynn Turman is possessed by the spirit of a gangster who was murdered on Bourbon Street in the early 1940s and grisly blaxploitation results. Ever so slightly better than others of the genre. Shot in New Orleans, with a soundtrack by a then-unknown Prince. **95m/C VHS.** Louis Gossett Jr., Glynn Turman; **D:** Arthur Marks; **M:** Prince. *ORI, FCT*

Je Tu Il Elle ☙☙½ *I You She He* **1974** A hyperactive young woman desperately seeking the answers to life gradually gains experience and maturity as she travels around France. The directorial debut of Ackerman. In French with English subtitles. **90m/B VHS.** *FR* Niels Arestrup, Claire Wauthion, Chantal Akerman; **D:** Chantal Akerman. *WAC, FCT, INJ*

Jealousy **1984** Three dramatic episodes dealing with jealousy. Made for TV. **95m/C VHS, Beta.** Angie Dickinson, Paul Michael Glaser, David Carradine, Bo Svenson; **D:** Jeffrey Bloom. *IMP*

Jean de Florette ☙☙☙½ **1987 (PG)** The first of two films (with "Manon of the Spring") based on Marcel Pagnol's novel. A single spring in drought-ridden Provence, France is blocked by two scheming countrymen (Montand and Auteuil). They await the imminent failure of the farm nearby, inherited by a city-born hunchback, whose chances for survival fade without water for his crops. A devastating story with a heartrending performance by Depardieu as the hunchback. Lauded and awarded; in French with English subtitles. **122m/C VHS, Beta, LV.** *FR* Gerard Depardieu, Yves Montand, Daniel Auteuil, Elisabeth Depardieu, Ernestine Mazurowna; **D:** Claude Berri; **W:** Gerard Brach, Claude Berri. British Academy Awards '87: Best Adapted Screenplay, Best Film, Best Supporting Actor (Auteuil); National Board of Review Awards '87: 5 Best Foreign Films of the Year. *ORI, IME, FCT*

Jeeves & Wooster: Jeeves' Arrival **1991** Based on P.G. Wodehouse's spoofs of upper-crust British life in the 1920s. The bungling Bertie Wooster, a young man who just can't stay out of trouble, is taken in hand by the unflappable "gentleman's gentleman," Jeeves. Wonderful period detail and fine acting add up to a charming and funny hour. Additional episodes available. **60m/C VHS.** *GB* Hugh Laurie, Stephen Fry. *MOV, TVC, PBS*

Jefferson in Paris ½ **1994 (PG-13)** Costume drama explores the impact Thomas Jefferson's (Nolte) five years in pre-revolutionary Paris (as American ambassador to Versailles) had on his private life. Jefferson confronts the personal and political issues of slavery in America, as well as his feelings for Sally Hemings (Newton), a Monticello slave brought to Paris by Jefferson's daughter. The Jefferson-Hemings legend may or may not be true (more likely not, according to many historians), but it seems to be the central theme here. Merchant Ivory's trademark tasteful production values and earnest characters can't camouflage the fact that they're playing fast and loose with the historical facts. **139m/C VHS, LV.** Nick Nolte, Greta Scacchi, Gwyneth Paltrow, Thandie Newton, Jean-Pierre Aumont, Seth Gilliam, Todd Boyce, James Earl Jones; ***D:*** James Ivory; ***W:*** Ruth Prawer Jhabvala; ***M:*** Richard Robbins. *TOU*

Jeffrey ½ **1995 (R)** AIDS-fearing Jeffrey (Weber) decides to give celibacy a try until a trip to the gym brings Mr. Right into the picture. Steve (Weiss) is a hunk, but he happens to be HIV-positive, which prompts Jeffrey to do some serious soul-searching. Hence the message: AIDS sucks, but don't let it destroy life's joys. Musical fantasy numbers, phallic fireworks, and a game show are a bit crass and the high theatrics can get annoying, but wicked barbs and one-liners score lots of laughs. Scene-stealer Stewart is caustically funny as Jeffrey's flamboyantly effeminate best friend Sterling, who works as an interior decorator and dates a "Cats" chorus boy. Adapted from the Paul Rudnick play. **92m/C VHS, LV.** Steven Weber, Patrick Stewart, Michael T. Weiss, Bryan Batt, Sigourney Weaver, Olympia Dukakis, Kathy Najimy, Nathan Lane; ***D:*** Christopher Ashley; ***W:*** Paul Rudnick; ***C:*** Jeffery Tufano; ***M:*** Stephen Endelman. *ORI*

Jekyll and Hyde ½ **1990** Unmemorable remake of the Robert Louis Stevenson tale of a doctor whose scientific experiments lead to a horrifyingly violent split personality. Caine does have a good time with his dual role. Made for TV. **100m/C VHS.** Michael Caine, Cheryl Ladd, Joss Ackland, Ronald Pickup, Kim Thomson, Lionel Jeffries, Kevin McNally, Lee Montague; ***D:*** David Wickes; ***W:*** David Wickes. *VMK*

Jekyll & Hyde...Together Again **1982 (R)** New Wave comic version of the classic story. This time, a serious young surgeon turns into a drug-crazed punk rocker after sniffing a mysterious powder. Mad scientist Blankfield fires and misfires, occasionally eliciting a snort. **87m/C VHS, Beta.** Mark Blankfield, Bess Armstrong, Krista Errickson, Tim Thomerson; ***D:*** Jerry Belson; ***W:*** Monica Johnson, Michael Leeson, Harvey Miller, Jerry Belson. *PAR*

Jennifer ½ *Jennifer (The Snake Goddess)* **1978 (PG)** Elaboration of that old "Carrie" theme: a teenage girl outcast who likes snakes wreaks havoc on her catty classmates in this supernatural thriller. **90m/C VHS, Beta.** Lisa Pelikan, Bert Convy, Nina Foch, John Gavin, Wesley Eure; ***D:*** Brice Mack. *LIV, VES*

Jennifer 8 **1992 (R)** Mix of familiar genres results in a film about a burned-out cop moving to the suburbs where he finds the eighth victim of a serial killer and falls in love with the chief witness. Garcia is John Berlin, the cop who discovers the hand of the blind female victim, which leads him to her school and Helena Robertson (Thurman), another blind woman who may have the information he needs. Dark and mysterious atmosphere is dramatic, but plot lacks logic and sense of thrill. **127m/C VHS, Beta, LV.** Andy Garcia, Uma Thurman, Lance Henriksen, Kathy Baker, Graham Beckel, Kevin Conway, John Malkovich; ***D:*** Bruce Robinson; ***W:*** Bruce Robinson. *PAR, BTV*

Jenny **1970 (PG)** A loveless marriage of convenience between a draft-dodger and a film buff gets turned around as they fall in love despite themselves. **90m/C VHS, Beta.** Marlo Thomas, Alan Alda, Marian Hailey, Elizabeth Wilson, Vincent Gardenia, Charlotte Rae; ***D:*** George Bloomfield. *FOX*

Jenny Lamour *Quai des Orfevres* **1947** A dark mystery thriller about a singer accused of murdering a man he thought was stealing his woman. Acclaimed genre piece, dubbed into English. **95m/B VHS, Beta.** *FR* Louis Jouvet, Suzy Delair, Bernard Blier, Simone Renant; ***D:*** Henri-Georges Clouzot. *NOS, FCT*

Jenny's War ½ **1985 (PG)** An unbelievable WWII adventure story of an American teacher (Cannon) who outwits the Gestapo and infiltrates a Nazi POW camp in search of her missing soldier son. Actually based on a true story. From the book by Jack Stoneley. Made for television. **192m/C VHS.** Dyan Cannon, Elke Sommer, Robert Hardy, Nigel Hawthorne, Christopher Cazenove, Patrick Ryecart, Hartmut Becker; ***D:*** Steven Gethers; ***W:*** Steven Gethers. *COL*

Jeremiah Johnson **1972 (PG)** The story of a man who turns his back on civilization, circa 1850, and learns a new code of survival in a brutal land of isolated mountains and hostile Indians. In the process, he becomes part of the mountains and their wildlife. A notable and picturesque film. **107m/C VHS, Beta, LV.** Robert Redford, Will Geer; ***D:*** Sydney Pollack; ***W:*** Edward Anhalt, John Milius. Nominations: Cannes Film Festival '72: Best Film. *WAR, FCT*

Jericho *Dark Sands* **1938** Adventures in Africa occur as a court-martialed captain pursues a murderous deserter. **77m/B VHS, Beta.** *GB* Paul Robeson, Henry Wilcoxon, Wallace Ford; ***D:*** Thornton Freeland. *NOS, HHT, DVT*

Jericho Fever ½ **1993 (PG-13)** A group of terrorists assassinate Palestinian and Israeli negotiators engaged in peace talks in Mexico. Infected with a deadly disease they escape to the U.S., tracked by Israeli Mossad agents, a border patrolman, and two investigators from the Centers for Disease Control who want to stop the spread of the plague. **88m/C VHS, Beta.** Stephanie Zimbalist, Perry King, Branscombe Richmond, Alan Scarfe, Elyssa Davalos, Ari Barak; ***D:*** Sandor Stern; ***W:*** I.C. Rapoport; ***M:*** Cameron Allan. *PAR*

The Jericho Mile **1979** A made-for-television drama about a track-obsessed convicted murderer who is given a chance at the Olympics. **97m/C VHS, Beta.** Peter Strauss, Roger E. Mosley, Brian Dennehy; ***D:*** Michael Mann. *NLC, SUE*

The Jerk ½ **1979 (R)** A jerk tells his rags-to-riches-to-rags story in comedic flashbacks, from "I was born a poor Black child," through his entrepreneurial success in his invention of the "Optigrab," to his inevitable decline. Only film in history with a dog named "Shithead." Martin's first starring role, back in his wild and crazy days; his ridiculous misadventures pay tribute to Jerry Lewis movies of the late sixties. Followed by a TV version released in 1984 as "The Jerk Too," with Mark Blankfield as the Jerk. **94m/C VHS, Beta, LV.** Steve Martin, Bernadette Peters, Catlin Adams, Bill Macy, Jackie Mason; ***D:*** Carl Reiner; ***W:*** Steve Martin, Carl Gottlieb, Michael Elias. *MCA*

The Jerky Boys *Woof!* **1995 (R)** Quick! Let's make a Jerky Boys movie and exploit their popularity before everyone realizes what a lame, one-joke act it is! Too late, guys. In what passes for a plot, Johnny and Kamal prank call an irritable mob boss (Arkin), pretending to be Chicago hitmen in need of a hide-out. The wiseguys soon figure out the truth, but the requisite dumb cop (Sullivan) pads the film by not catching on. All these "twists" serve only one purpose—to get our heroes to the next phone. Don't accept the charges for this one. **82m/C VHS, LV.** Johnny Brennan, Kamal Ahmed, Alan Arkin, William Hickey, Alan North, James Lorinz, Brad Sullivan, Vinny Pastore, Ozzy Osbourne, Paul Bartel, Suzanne Shepherd; ***Cameos:*** Tom Jones; ***D:*** James Melkonian; ***W:*** Johnny Brennan, Kamal Ahmed, Rich Wilkes, James Melkonian. *TOU*

Jersey Girl ½ **1992 (PG-13)** Toby Mastellone (Gertz) is a bright single gal from the Jersey shore who wants something better in her life. Her hard-working dad (Bologna) has fixed her up with an apprentice plumber but she wants a Manhattan guy. And then Toby meets cute with Sal (McDemott), who seems just the ticket, but can you really take the Jersey out of the girl? **95m/C VHS.** Jami Gertz, Dylan McDermott, Joseph Bologna, Aida Turturro, Star Jasper, Sheryl Lee, Joseph Mazzello, Molly Price; ***D:*** David Burton Morris; ***W:*** Gina Wendkos; ***M:*** Stephen Bedell. *COL*

Jesse **1988 (PG)** A heroic nurse ministers to remote Death Valley residents, and state bureaucats hound her for practicing medicine without a license. Although based on a true case and well-acted, this made-for-TV drama just lacks import and impact. **94m/C VHS.** Lee Remick, Scott Wilson, Leon Rippy, Priscilla Lopez, Albert Salmi; ***D:*** Glenn Jordan; ***M:*** David Shire. *REP*

Jesse James **1939** A Hollywood biography of the famed outlaw. One of director King's best efforts. **105m/C VHS, Beta, LV.** Henry Fonda, Tyrone Power, Randolph Scott, Henry Hull, Jane Darwell, Brian Donlevy, Charles Halton; ***D:*** Henry King. *FOX*

Jesse James at Bay **1941** Rogers is the do-good Jesse who's warring against some crooked railroad execs. Interesting perspective. **54m/B VHS, Beta.** Roy Rogers, George "Gabby" Hayes, Sally Payne; ***D:*** Joseph Kane. *NOS, MRV, VCN*

Jesse James Meets Frankenstein's Daughter ½ **1965** The gunslinger and Frankenstein's granddaughter, Maria, meet up in the Old West in this wacky combination of western and horror genres. **95m/C VHS, Beta.** John Lupton, Cal Bolder, Narda Onyx, Steve Geray, Estelita, Jim Davis, William "Bill" Fawcett, Nestor Paiva; ***D:*** William Beaudine. *NOS, SUE*

Jesse James Rides Again **1947** Originally a serial, this feature depicts the further adventures of the West's most notorious outlaw. **181m/B VHS.** Clayton Moore, Linda Stirling, Roy Barcroft, Tristram Coffin; ***D:*** Fred Brannon, Thomas Carr. *REP, MLB*

Jesse James Under the Black Flag ½ **1921** An interesting western/pseudo biography/flashback in which Coates and James Jr. (the outlaw's son) play themselves. As Coates attempts to gather information from Jesse's decendants, a stranger appears and falls for Jesse's granddaughter, who shuns him. He proceeds to read the Coates biography and the flashback begins, in the Jesse was really a good guy forced off the straight and narrow vein. **59m/B VHS, Beta.** Jesse James Jr., Franklin Coates, Diana Reed, Marguerite Hungerford; ***D:*** Franklin Coates. *GPV, FCT*

The Jesse Owens Story **1984** The moving story of the four-time Olympic Gold medal winner's triumphs and misfortunes. A made-for-television movie. **174m/C VHS, Beta.** Dorian Harewood, Debbi Morgan, Georg Stanford Brown, LeVar Burton, George Kennedy, Tom Bosley, Ben Vereen; ***D:*** Richard Irving. *PAR, FCT*

Jessie's Girls ½ *Wanted Women* **1975 (R)** In retaliation for the murder of her husband, an angry young woman frees three female prisoners, and they embark on a bloody course of revenge. Together, they track down the killers, and one by one, they fight to even the score. **86m/C VHS, Beta.** Sondra Currie, Regina Carrol, Jennifer Bishop; ***D:*** Al Adamson. *MON*

Jesus **1979 (G)** A supposedly authenticated life of Christ, using real artifacts. **118m/C VHS, Beta.** Brian Deacon; ***D:*** Peter Sykes, John Kirsh. *VBL*

Jesus Christ, Superstar **1973 (G)** A rock opera that portrays, in music, the last seven days in the earthly life of Christ, as reenacted by young tourists in Israel. Outstanding musical score was the key to the success of the film. Based on the stage play by Tim Rice and Andrew Lloyd Webber, film is sometimes stirring while exhibiting the usual heavy-handed Jewison approach. ♫Jesus Christ, Superstar; I Don't Know How To Love Him; What's The Buzz?; Herod's Song; Heaven On Their Minds; Strange Thing, Mystifying; Then We Are Decided; Everything's Alright; This Jesus Must Die. **108m/C**

VHS, Beta, LV. Ted Neeley, Carl Anderson, Yvonne Elliman, Josh Mostel; ***D:*** Norman Jewison; ***W:*** Melvin Bragg. Nominations: Academy Awards '73: Best Original Score. *MCA*

Jesus of Montreal 🦴🦴🦴½ *Jesus de Montreal* **1989 (R)** A vagrant young actor (stage-trained Canadian star Bluteau) is hired by a Montreal priest to produce a fresh interpretation of an Easter passion play. Taking the good book at its word, he produces a contemporized literal telling that captivates audiences, inflames the men of the cloth, and eventually wins the players' faith. Quebecois director Arcand (keep an eye out for him as the judge) tells a compelling, acerbically satirical and haunting story that never forces its Biblical parallels. In French with English subtitles. **119m/C VHS, LV.** *FR CA* Gilles Pelletier, Lothaire Bluteau, Catherine Wilkening, Robert Lepage, Johanne-Marie Tremblay, Remy Girard, Marie-Christine Barrault; ***D:*** Denys Arcand; ***W:*** Denys Arcand. Cannes Film Festival '89: Special Jury Prize; Genie Awards '90: Best Actor (Girard), Best Director (Arcand), Best Film, Best Supporting Actor (Girard); Nominations: Academy Awards '89: Best Foreign Language Film. *ORI, FCT, INJ*

Jesus of Nazareth 🦴🦴½ **1928** A dramatic recreation of the life of Christ from the Annunciation through the Ascension. The film titles are taken from descriptive biblical passages. **85m/B VHS, Beta, 8mm.** Philip Van Loan, Anna Lehr, Charles McCaffrey. *VYY, FCT*

Jesus of Nazareth 🦴🦴🦴 **1977** An all-star cast vividly portrays the life of Christ in this made-for-television mini-series. Wonderfully directed and sensitively acted. On three cassettes. **371m/C VHS, Beta.** Robert Powell, Anne Bancroft, Ernest Borgnine, Claudia Cardinale, James Mason, Laurence Olivier, Anthony Quinn; ***D:*** Franco Zeffirelli; ***M:*** Maurice Jarre. *LIV, FOX, IGP*

The Jesus Trip 🦴½ **1971** Hunted motorcyclists take a young nun hostage in the desert. **86m/C VHS, Beta.** Robert Porter, Tippy Walker; ***D:*** Russ Mayberry. *UNI*

Jet Attack/Paratroop Command 🦴🦴 **1958** A double feature of "B" war movies. "Jet Attack" is a bad movie about a scientist whose plane gets shot down over Korea. He amazingly survives, only to be taken to a hospital and brainwashed. Enter a squad of soldiers leading a rescue mission who meet up with a beautiful Russian aide and some life-saving guerillas. This movie is so bad it's funny. In "Paratroop Command," a paratrooper accidentally kills a member of his squadron. In order to regain his dignity, the paratrooper sets off land mines in North Africa to prove himself. **139m/B VHS.** John Agar, Audrey Totter, Gregory Walcott, James Dobson, Richard Bakalayan, Jack Hogan, Jimmy Murphy, Ken Lynch; ***D:*** Edward L. Cahn, William Witney. *COL*

Jet Benny Show **1986** A Buck Rogers/Star Wars-style spoof of Jack Benny's classic TV show. **76m/C VHS, Beta.** Steve Norman, Kevin Dees, Polly MacIntyre, Ted Luedemann; ***D:*** Roger Evans. *NLC*

Jet Over the Atlantic 🦴½ **1959** Dangerous situation arises as a bomb is discovered aboard a plane en route from Spain to New York. **92m/B VHS, Beta.** Guy Madison, George Raft, Virginia Mayo, Brett Halsey; ***D:*** Byron Haskin. *NO*

Jet Pilot 🦴🦴 **1957** An American Air Force colonel (Wayne) in charge of an Alaskan Air Force base falls in love with a defecting Russian jet pilot (Leigh). They marry, but Wayne suspects Leigh is a spy planted to find out top U.S. secrets. He pretends to defect with her back to Russia to see what he can find out, but they again flee. Ludicrous plot is saved only by spectacular flying scenes, some performed by Chuck Yeager. Although this was filmed in 1950, it took seven more years to be released because producer Hughes couldn't keep his hands off it. **112m/B VHS, LV.** John Wayne, Janet Leigh, Jay C. Flippen, Paul Fix, Richard Rober, Roland Winters, Hans Conried, Ivan Triesault; ***D:*** Josef von Sternberg; ***C:*** Winton C. Hoch. *MCA*

The Jetsons Meet the Flintstones **1988** Trouble arises when young Elroy Jetson's time machine takes him and his family back to the 25th century B.C. There they meet the Flintstones and the Rubbles, who accidentally get transported into the future. Will either family ever get back home? **100m/C VHS, Beta, LV.** ***V:*** Mel Blanc, Daws Butler, Jean VanDerPyl, George O'Hanlon, Penny Singleton. *TTC, IME, WTA*

Jetsons: The Movie 🦴🦴 **1990 (G)** The famous outer space family of '60s TV is given a new silver-screened life. George gets a promotion that puts him in charge of an asteroid populated by furry creatures. Ecological concerns are expressed; while this is rare for a cartoon, the story is overall typical. **82m/C VHS, Beta, LV.** ***D:*** William Hanna, Joseph Barbera; ***M:*** John Debney; ***V:*** George O'Hanlon, Mel Blanc, Penny Singleton, Tiffany, Patric Zimmerman, Don Messick, Jean VanDerPyl, Ronnie Schell, Patti Deutsch, Dana Hill, Russi Taylor, Paul Kreppel, Rick Dees. *MCA, APD, WTA*

The Jewel in the Crown **1984** Epic saga of the last years of British rule in India from 1942-1947 concentrating on a controversial love affair between the Indian Hari Kumar and the English Daphne Manners, which profoundly affects the lives of many. Based on "The Raj Quartet" by Paul Scott. Originally shown on British television, it aired in the United States on the PBS series "Masterpiece Theatre." An excellent mini-series that was shown in fourteen segments. Available on eight cassettes. **750m/C VHS, Beta.** *GB* Charles Dance, Susan Wooldridge, Art Malik, Tim Pigott-Smith, Geraldine James, Peggy Ashcroft, Judy Parfitt; ***D:*** Christopher Morahan, Jim O'Brien; ***M:*** George Fenton. *AAE, PAP, VCO*

The Jewel of the Nile 🦴🦴½ **1985 (PG)** Sequel to "Romancing the Stone" with the same cast but new director. Romance novelist Joan thought she found her true love in Jack but finds that life doesn't always end happily ever. After they part ways, Jack realizes that she may be in trouble and endeavors to rescue her from the criminal hands of a charming North African president. Of course, he can always check out this "jewel" at the same time. Chemistry is still there, but the rest of the film isn't quite up to the "Stone's" charm. **106m/C VHS, Beta, LV.** Michael Douglas, Kathleen Turner, Danny DeVito, Avner Eisenberg, The Flying Karamazov Brothers, Spiros Focas, Holland Taylor; ***D:*** Lewis Teague; ***W:*** Mark Rosenthal, Larry Konner; ***C:*** Jan De Bont; ***M:*** Jack Nitzsche. *FOX*

The Jeweller's Shop 🦴🦴 **1990** A highly spiritual tale of two married couples in Poland whose children meet and fall in love much later in Canada. Based on a play by Karol Wojtyla—who later became Pope Jean-Paul II. Adapted under strict Vatican supervision. **90m/C VHS.** Burt Lancaster, Ben Cross, Olivia Hussey. *IGP*

Jezebel 🦴🦴🦴½ **1938** Davis is a willful Southern belle who loses fiance Fonda through her selfish and spiteful ways in this pre-Civil War drama. When he becomes ill, she realizes her cruelty and rushes to nurse him back to health. Davis' role won her an Oscar for Best Actress, and certainly provided Scarlett O'Hara with a rival for most memorable female character of all time. **105m/B VHS, Beta, LV.** Bette Davis, George Brent, Henry Fonda, Margaret Lindsay, Fay Bainter, Donald Crisp, Spring Byington, Eddie Anderson; ***D:*** William Wyler; ***M:*** Max Steiner. Academy Awards '38: Best Actress (Davis), Best Supporting Actress (Bainter); Nominations: Academy Awards '38: Best Cinematography, Best Picture, Best Score. *MGM, FCT, BTV*

Jezebel's Kiss 🦴🦴 **1990 (R)** A sizzling young beauty returns to the town where she grew up and proceeds to destroy any man she pleases. **96m/C VHS, LV.** Meg Foster, Malcolm McDowell, Meredith Baxter, Everett McGill, Katherine Barrese; ***D:*** Harvey Keith; ***W:*** Harvey Keith. *COL*

JFK 🦴🦴🦴½ **1991 (R)** Highly controversial examination of President John F. Kennedy's 1963 assassination, from the viewpoint of New Orleans district attorney Jim Garrison. Hotly debated because of Stone's conspiracy theory, it sparked new calls to open the sealed government records from the 1977 House Select Committee on Assassinations investigation. Outstanding performances from all-star principal and supporting casts, stunning cinematography, and excellent editing. Even Garrison himself shows up as Chief Justice Earl Warren. Considered by some to be a cinematic masterpiece, others see it as revisionist history that should be taken with a grain of salt. Extended version adds 17 minutes. **189m/C VHS, Beta, LV.** Kevin Costner, Sissy Spacek, Kevin Bacon, Tommy Lee Jones, Laurie Metcalf, Gary Oldman, Michael Rooker, Jay O. Sanders, Beata Pozniak, Joe Pesci, Donald Sutherland, John Candy, Jack Lemmon, Walter Matthau, Ed Asner, Vincent D'Onofrio, Sally Kirkland, Brian Doyle-Murray, Wayne Knight, Tony Plana, Tomas Milian, Sean Stone; ***Cameos:*** Lolita Davidovich, Frank Whaley, Jim Garrison; ***D:*** Oliver Stone; ***W:*** Oliver Stone, Zachary Sklar; ***C:*** Robert Richardson; ***M:*** John Williams. Academy Awards '91: Best Cinematography, Best Film Editing; Golden Globe Awards '92: Best Director (Stone); Nominations: Academy Awards '91: Best Adapted Screenplay, Best Director (Stone), Best Picture, Best Sound, Best Supporting Actor (Jones), Best Original Score. *WAR*

The JFK Conspiracy **1991** Did Lee Harvey Oswald act alone? Opinions of government officials, eyewitnesses, and director Oliver Stone, in addition to testimony, photographs, documents, and other evidence, address the perennial American question. Includes footage from the House Select Committee on Assassination. Made for television. **98m/C VHS, LV.** *BMG, VTR*

JFK: Reckless Youth 🦴🦴½ **1993** Glossy made for TV docudrama detailas the youthful exploits of Kennedy as both ladies man and emerging leader and comes perilously close to being a tacky soap. Follows the president-to-be from his party-hearty years at prep school, through his naval career (and PT-109 heroics), and his first forays into politics. Excellent portrayal by Dempsey details JFK's chronic ill health, his ambitions, and the family ties that provided both friction and support. Based on the controversial biography by Nigel Hamilton. **182m/C VHS.** Patrick Dempsey, Terry Kinney, Loren Dean, Diana Scarwid, Yolanda Jilot, Robin Tunney, Andrew Lowery, Stan Cahill, James Rebhorn, Malachy McCourt; ***D:*** Harry Winer; ***W:*** William Broyles Jr.; ***M:*** Cameron Allan. *CAF*

JFK Remembered **1988** A look at John F. Kennedy's 1000-day Presidential term, released on the 25th anniversary of his assassination, features interviews, rare film clips, and famous news footage. **54m/C VHS, Beta.** *LIV, VES*

Jigsaw 🦴🦴🦴 *Gun Moll* **1949** Crime drama with a smattering of cameos by Hollywood favorites. A newspaper reporter is murdered. The dead man's friend, an assistant district attorney, seeks the punks responsible. They send in a seductress to keep the D.A. busy, but she too is murdered. Action and tension in a well-made flick. Based on a story by John Roeburt. **70m/B VHS.** Franchot Tone, Jean Wallace, Myron McCormick, Marc Lawrence, Winifred Lenihan, Betty Harper, Robert Gist; ***Cameos:*** Marlene Dietrich, Henry Fonda, Burgess Meredith, John Garfield; ***D:*** Fletcher Markle. *SNC, DVT*

Jigsaw 🦴🦴 *Man on the Move* **1971** Missing persons lawman is lured into a cover-up more complex than he had bargained for. A tense drama originated as the pilot for a series. **100m/C VHS.** James Wainwright, Vera Miles, Richard Kiley, Andrew Duggan, Edmond O'Brien; ***D:*** William A. Graham. *LIV*

Jigsaw 🦴🦴 **1990** A developer is found dead the day after his wedding. His widow and a cop team up to find out who, what, where, and why. Lukewarm Australian mystery export. **85m/C VHS.** Rebecca Gibney, Dominic Sweeney, Michael Coard. *ATL*

The Jigsaw Man 🦴🦴 **1984 (PG)** A British-Russian double agent is sent back to England to retrieve a list of Soviet agents which he hid there many years before. **90m/C VHS, Beta, LV.** *GB* Michael Caine, Laurence Olivier, Susan George, Robert Powell, Charles Gray, David Patrick Kelly, Michael Medwin; ***D:*** Terence Young. *REP*

Jigsaw Murders **1989** A macho detective is out to solve a grisly murder, but the only available leads are a jigsaw puzzle and the victim's severed, tattooed lower limb. **98m/C VHS, Beta.** Chad Everett, Michelle Johnson, Yaphet Kotto; ***D:*** Jag Mundhra. *MGM*

Jim Thorpe: All American 𝓑𝓑½ *Man of Bronze* **1951** The life story of Thorpe, a Native American athlete who gained international recognition for his excellence in many different sports. A must for sports fans. **105m/B VHS, Beta.** Burt Lancaster, Phyllis Thaxter, Charles Bickford, Steve Cochran, Dick Wesson; ***D:*** Michael Curtiz; ***W:*** Douglas S. Morrow; ***M:*** Max Steiner. *WAR*

Jimmy Hollywood 𝓑½ **1994 (R)** Wanna-be Hollywood actor Pesci has never acted in his life but longs for stardom—which he gets after he accidentally becomes a community vigilante. Burned-out sidekick Slater helps create the videotapes that will bring Jimmy his 15 minutes of fame. Although appropriately desperate, Pesci's role comes off as mostly shtick; two dogs in a row for the usually talented Levinson (after "Toys"). **118m/C VHS, Beta, LV.** Joe Pesci, Christian Slater, Victoria Abril; ***Cameos:*** Barry Levinson, Rob Weiss; ***D:*** Barry Levinson; ***W:*** Barry Levinson; ***C:*** Peter Sova; ***M:*** Robbie Robertson. *PAR*

Jimmy, the Boy Wonder 𝓑½ **1966** Goremeister Lewis' attempt at a "family" film turns out just as weird as expected. A young boy goes on a magical trip to find out who stopped time and meets an absent-minded astronomer, the evil Mr. Fig, and then discovers what happens at world's end. **?m/C VHS.** ***D:*** Herschell Gordon Lewis. *MOV, TPV*

Jimmy the Kid 𝓑𝓑 **1982 (PG)** A young boy becomes the unlikely target for an improbable gang of would-be crooks on a crazy, "fool-proof" crime caper. Kiddie comic caper. **95m/C VHS, Beta.** Gary Coleman, Cleavon Little, Fay Hauser, Ruth Gordon, Dee Wallace Stone, Paul LeMat, Don Adams; ***D:*** Gary Nelson; ***W:*** Sam Bobrick. *NO*

Jinxed 𝓑𝓑 **1982 (R)** Las Vegas nightclub singer tries to convince a gullible blackjack dealer to murder her crooked boyfriend, but the plan backfires when the gangster electrocutes himself while taking a shower. Offscreen cast disputes were probably much more interesting than onscreen comedy. **104m/C VHS, Beta.** Bette Midler, Ken Wahl, Rip Torn; ***D:*** Donald Siegel; ***W:*** David Newman, Frank D. Gilroy; ***M:*** Miles Goodman. *MGM*

Jit 𝓑𝓑 **1994** Unpretentious romantic comedy finds the easy-going U.K., who runs errands for his uncle in a Zimbabwe town, falling in love with the beautiful Sofi, who already has a boyfriend. But U.K. won't be stopped by this or Sofi's greedy father. "Jit" refers to the infectious local music, a fusion of traditional African rhythms and reggae-pop. **98m/C VHS.** Dominic Makuvachuma, Sibongile Nene, Faria Sevenzo, Winnie Ndemera; ***D:*** Michael Raeburn. *HMV*

The Jitters 𝓑 **1988 (R)** The murdered dead turn into zombies and seek revenge on their killers. **80m/C VHS, Beta.** Sal Viviano, Marilyn Tokuda, James Hong, Frank Dietz; ***D:*** John Fasano. *PSM*

Jive Junction 𝓑𝓑 **1943** A group of patriotic teenagers convert a barn into a canteen for servicemen and name it "Jive Junction." **62m/B VHS, Beta.** Dickie Moore, Tina Thayer, Gerra Young, Johnny Michaels, Jan Wiley, Beverly Boyd, William Halligan; ***D:*** Edgar G. Ulmer. *NOS, GVV*

Jive Turkey 𝓑½ **1976** Cool dude busts heads. **?m/C VHS.** Paul Harris, Frank De Kova, Serena; ***D:*** Bill Brame. *MOV*

Jo Jo Dancer, Your Life is Calling 𝓑𝓑½ **1986 (R)** Pryor directed and starred in this semi-autobiographical price-of-fame story of a comic, hospitalized for a drug-related accident, who must re-evaluate his life. A serious departure from Pryor's slapstick comedies that doesn't quite make it as a drama; Pryor nevertheless deserves credit for the honesty he demonstrates in dealing with his real-life problems. **97m/C VHS, Beta, LV.** Richard Pryor, Debbie Allen, Art Evans, Fay Hauser, Barbara Williams, Paula Kelly, Wings Hauser, Carmen McRae, Diahnne Abbott, Scoey Mitchell, Billy Eckstine, Virginia Capers, Dennis Farina; ***D:*** Richard Pryor; ***W:*** Richard Pryor, Rocco Urbisci; ***M:*** Herbie Hancock. *COL*

Joan of Arc 𝓑𝓑½ **1948** A touching and devout look at the life of Joan of Arc. Perhaps unfortunately, the film is accurately based on the play by Maxwell Anderson, and adds up to too much talk and too little action. **100m/C VHS, Beta, LV.** Ingrid Bergman, Jose Ferrer, John Ireland, Leif Erickson; ***D:*** Victor Fleming; ***C:*** Joseph Valentine. Academy Awards '48: Best Color Cinematography, Best Costume Design; National Board of Review Awards '48: 10 Best Films of the Year; Nominations: Academy Awards '48: Best Actress (Bergman), Best Art Direction/Set Decoration (Color), Best Film Editing, Best Supporting Actor (Ferrer), Best Original Score. *IGP, HMV*

Joan of Paris 𝓑𝓑𝓑½ **1942** A French resistance leader dies so that Allied pilots can escape from the Nazis. A well done, but obviously dated propaganda feature. **91m/B VHS, Beta.** Michele Morgan, Paul Henreid, Thomas Mitchell, Laird Cregar, May Robson, Alexander Granach, Alan Ladd; ***D:*** Robert Stevenson; ***W:*** Charles Bennett. Nominations: Academy Awards '42: Best Original Score. *TTC*

Jock Petersen 𝓑 *Petersen* **1974 (R)** A lighthearted story about a blonde hunk who enrolls in college, cavorting and seducing his way to questionable fame and fortune. **97m/C VHS, Beta.** Jack Thompson, Wendy Hughes; ***D:*** Tim Burstall. *NLC*

Jocks 𝓑½ **1987 (R)** A whiz-kid tennis team competes in a pro meet in Las Vegas, and paints the town red. **90m/C VHS, Beta.** Christopher Lee, Perry Lang, Richard Roundtree, Scott Strader; ***D:*** Steve Carver; ***W:*** Jeff Bukai. *COL*

Joe 𝓑𝓑½ **1970 (R)** An odd friendship grows between a businessman and a blue-collar worker as they search together for the executive's runaway daughter. Thrust into the midst of the counter-culture, they react with an orgy of violence. **107m/C VHS, Beta, LV.** Peter Boyle, Susan Sarandon, Dennis Patrick; ***D:*** John G. Avildsen. Nominations: Academy Awards '70: Best Story & Screenplay. *MGM, VES*

Joe Kidd 𝓑𝓑½ **1972 (PG)** A land war breaks out in New Mexico between Mexican natives and American land barons. Eastwood, once again portraying the "mysterious stranger," must decide with whom he should side, all the while falling in love with Garcia. Lackluster direction results in a surprisingly tedious western, in spite of the cast. One of Eastwood's lowest money grossers. The laserdisc edition is letterboxed and features chapter stops, the original trailer and digital sound. **88m/C VHS, Beta, LV.** Clint Eastwood, Robert Duvall, John Saxon, Don Stroud, Stella Garcia, James Wainwright, Paul Koslo, Gregory Walcott, Dick Van Patten, Lynn Marta; ***D:*** John Sturges; ***W:*** Elmore Leonard; ***C:*** Bruce Surtees; ***M:*** Lalo Schifrin. *MCA*

The Joe Louis Story 𝓑𝓑 **1953** The story of Joe Louis' rise to fame as boxing's Heavyweight Champion of the world. **88m/B VHS, Beta.** Coley Wallace, Paul Stewart, Hilda Simms; ***M:*** George Bassman. *NOS, DVT, FCT*

Joe Panther 𝓑𝓑𝓑 **1976 (G)** Family drama about a young Seminole Indian who stakes his claim in the Anglo world by wrestling alligators. Montalban plays a wise old chieftain who helps the youth handle the conflict between Indian and white societies. **110m/C VHS.** Brian Keith, Ricardo Montalban, Alan Feinstein, Cliff Osmond, A. Martinez, Robert Hoffman; ***D:*** Paul Krasny. *WAR*

Joe Versus the Volcano 𝓑𝓑 **1990 (PG)** Expressionistic goofball comedy about a dopey guy who, after finding out he has only months to live, contracts with a millionaire to leap into a volcano alive. Imaginative farce with great "Metropolis"-pastiche visuals that eventually fizzle out. Watch for Ryan in not one, but three roles, and mysterious symbolism throughout. Special effects courtesy of Industrial Light and Magic. **106m/C VHS, Beta, LV, 8mm.** Tom Hanks, Meg Ryan, Lloyd Bridges, Robert Stack, Amanda Plummer, Abe Vigoda, Dan Hedaya, Barry McGovern, Ossie Davis; ***D:*** John Patrick Shanley; ***W:*** John Patrick Shanley; ***M:*** Georges Delerue. *WAR*

Joe's Apartment 𝓑𝓑 **1996** Fresh-from-Iowa Joe (O'Connell) comes to New York, finds a squalid apartment, and then discovers its other occupants are hordes of singing, joking cockroaches. Lucky for Joe, his unwelcome roommates are on his side, even helping out with his love life, when necessary. Gross but interesting, throw in Robert Vaughn as a panty-wearing politician and you've got yourself a potential cult-movie favorite. Neat freaks probably won't enjoy it much. Flick took three years to finish as computer-animated roaches had to do all the dancing and singing. Feature directorial debut for writer Payson, who created the original 1992 live-action/animation MTV short. **?m/C VHS.** Jerry O'Connell, Megan Ward, Robert Vaughn, Jim Turner, Don Ho, Don Ho; ***D:*** John Payson; ***W:*** John Payson; ***V:*** Billy West, Reginald Hudlin. *NYR*

Joe's Bed-Stuy Barbershop: We Cut Heads 𝓑𝓑½ **1983** Lee's first film takes place inside a neighborhood landmark, the corner barbershop. Lee displays the social awareness and urban humor that he honed in his later, bigger films. **60m/C VHS, Beta.** Leon Errol, Morris Carnovsky, Elyse Knox, Billy House, Trudy Marshall; ***D:*** Spike Lee; ***W:*** Spike Lee. *ICA*

Joey 𝓑½ **1985 (PG)** Daddy, a former doo-wop-per, looks back on his years of musical success as a waste of time. His son takes to the world of rock guitar with blind fervor. Their argument plays against the backdrop of the "Royal Doo-Wopp Show" at New York City's Radio Music Hall. Features multi-generational rock songs. **90m/C VHS, Beta.** Neill Barry, James Quinn. *NO*

Joey Breaker 𝓑𝓑𝓑 **1993 (R)** Joey (cult-fave Edson) is a hot-shot Manhattan talent agent who's consumed by his job. A series of encounters (romantic and otherwise) expands his outlook, first among them with Cyan (Marley), a young Jamaican waitress. On his journey to possible enlightenment Joey also meets AIDS-stricken Fondren, who helps Joey see another side of life. Quirky with a reggae beat, small pic works large message with sense of humor and sincere performances. Dedicated to Fondren, who died of AIDS in 1992. Marley, daughter of late reggae superstar Bob, shares a tune on the soundtrack with brother Ziggy. Filmed in da Big Apple and St. Lucia, West Indies. **92m/C VHS, Beta.** Richard Edson, Cedella Marley, Erik King, Gina Gershon, Philip S. Hoffman, Fred Fondren; ***D:*** Steven Starr; ***W:*** Steven Starr; ***M:*** Paul Aston. *PAR, FCT*

John and the Missus 𝓑½ **1987 (PG)** After the discovery of a copper mine threatens to destroy a nearby town, the Canadian government begins a relocation process. However, one man refuses to give up his generations-old home. Canadian Pinsent's directorial debut, adapting his own 1973 novel. **98m/C VHS, Beta.** *CA* Gordon Pinsent, Jackie Burroughs, Randy Follet, Jessica Steen; ***D:*** Gordon Pinsent. Genie Awards '87: Best Actor (Pinsent). *NO*

John & Yoko: A Love Story 𝓑 **1985** Appalling television movie version of the rock legend's life and marriage. With original Beatles tunes. **146m/C VHS, Beta, LV.** Mark McGann, Kim Miyori, Kenneth Price, Peter Capaldi, Richard Morant, Philip Walsh; ***D:*** Sandor Stern. *IME*

John Cleese on How to Irritate People *How to Irritate People* **1968** Cleese, a master at causing irritation, demonstrates how to take care of all those annoying people who irritate you, including job interviewers, bank clerks, waiters, and salesmen. Monty Python alumni Palin and Chapman also join Cleese in the "Airline Pilots" sketch about bored pilots deliberately trying to terrify their passengers. **65m/C VHS.** John Cleese, Michael Palin, Graham Chapman, Connie Booth. *WST, FUS*

John Paul Jones 𝓑𝓑½ **1959** Big bio of the Revolutionary War naval hero ("I have not yet begun to fight!") who wins a lot of battles but can't convince Congress to maintain a strong navy at war's end. He's sent to win sea battles for the Empress Catherine the Great of Russia and then spends his last years in France. Great action scenes, otherwise tedious. **126m/C VHS.** Robert Stack, Charles

Coburn, MacDonald Carey, Marisa Pavan, Jean-Pierre Aumont, Peter Cushing, Erin O'Brien, Bruce Cabot, David Farrar, Basil Sydney, John Crawford; ***Cameos:*** Bette Davis; ***D:*** John Farrow; ***W:*** John Farrow, Jesse Lasky Jr.; ***M:*** Max Steiner. *WAR*

John Wayne Anthology: Star Packer/Lawless Range **1934** In addition to two of Wayne's films, this program captures 40 years of the actor's career. **156m/B VHS.** John Wayne; ***D:*** Robert North Bradbury. *SIM*

Johnnie Gibson F.B.I. 🦴 *Johnnie Mae Gibson: FBI* **1987** Supposedly based on a true story, the adventures of a beautiful, black FBI agent who falls in love with a man she's investigating. **96m/C VHS, Beta.** Howard E. Rollins Jr., Lynn Whitfield, William Allen Young, Richard Lawson; ***D:*** Bill Duke; ***M:*** Billy Goldenberg. *ACA, PTB*

Johnny Angel 🦴🦴🦴 **1945** Merchant Marine captain unravels mystery of his father's murder aboard a ship. Tense film noir. **79m/B VHS, Beta, LV.** George Raft, Claire Trevor, Signe Hasso, Lowell Gilmore, Hoagy Carmichael; ***D:*** Edwin L. Marin. *CCB, TTC*

Johnny Apollo 🦴🦴½ **1940** Upright college student Power keeps his nose clean until Dad's sent to jail for playing with numbers. Scheming to free his old man (Arnold) from the big house, he decides crime will pay for the stiff price tag of freedom. Predictable and melodramatic, but well directed. **93m/B VHS, Beta.** Tyrone Power, Dorothy Lamour, Lloyd Nolan, Edward Arnold, Charley Grapewin, Lionel Atwill; ***D:*** Yves Allegret; ***C:*** Arthur C. Miller. *FOX, FCT*

Johnny Appleseed **1986** True story of the legendary American who spent his life planting apple trees across the country. Comedy the entire family will enjoy from Shelly Duvall's "Tall Tales and Legends" series. Originally broadcast on cable television. **60m/C VHS.** Martin Short, Rob Reiner, Molly Ringwald. *FOX*

Johnny Be Good 🦴 **1988 (R)** A too-talented high school quarterback is torn between loyalty to his best friend and to his girlfriend amid bribery and schemings by colleges eager to sign him up. **91m/C VHS, Beta, LV.** Anthony Michael Hall, Robert Downey Jr., Paul Gleason, Uma Thurman, John Pankow, Steve James, Seymour Cassel, Michael Greene, Marshall Bell, Deborah May; ***D:*** Bud Smith; ***W:*** Jeff Bukai; ***M:*** Jay Michael Ferguson. *ORI*

Johnny Belinda 🦴🦴🦴 **1948** A compassionate physician cares for a young deaf mute woman and her illegitimate child. Tension builds as the baby's father returns to claim the boy. **103m/B VHS, Beta.** Jane Wyman, Lew Ayres, Charles Bickford, Agnes Moorehead; ***D:*** Jean Negulesco; ***M:*** Max Steiner. Academy Awards '48: Best Actress (Wyman); Golden Globe Awards '49: Best Actress—Drama (Wyman), Best Film—Drama; Nominations: Academy Awards '48: Best Actor (Ayres), Best Art Direction/Set Decoration (B & W), Best Black and White Cinematography, Best Director (Negulesco), Best Film Editing, Best Picture, Best Screenplay, Best Sound, Best Supporting Actor (Bickford), Best Supporting Actress (Moorehead), Best Original Score. *MGM, BTV, CCB*

Johnny Belinda 🦴🦴 **1982** A television movie adaptation of the Elmer Harris weepie about a small town doctor who befriends an abused deaf girl. Remake of the 1948 film. **95m/C VHS, Beta.** Richard Thomas, Rosanna Arquette, Dennis Quaid, Candy Clark, Roberts Blossom, Fran Ryan; ***D:*** Anthony Page. *LIV*

Johnny Come Lately 🦴🦴½ *Johnny Vagabond* **1943** An elderly editor helps out an ex-newspaperman with a police charge. The two then team up to expose political corruption despite threats from a rival newspaperman. **97m/B VHS, LV.** James Cagney, Grace George, Marjorie Main, Marjorie Lord, Hattie McDaniel, Ed McNamara; ***D:*** William K. Howard. Nominations: Academy Awards '43: Best Original Score. *REP*

Johnny Dangerously 🦴🦴 **1984 (PG-13)** A gangster spoof about Johnny Dangerously, who turned to crime in order to pay his mother's medical bills. Now, Dangerously wants to go straight, but competitive crooks would rather see him dead than law-abiding and his mother requires more and more expensive operations. Crime pays in comic ways. **90m/C VHS, Beta.** Michael Keaton, Joe Piscopo, Danny DeVito, Maureen Stapleton, Marilu Henner, Peter Boyle, Griffin Dunne, Glynnis O'Connor, Dom DeLuise, Richard Dimitri, Ray Walston, Dick Butkus, Alan Hale Jr., Bob Eubanks; ***D:*** Amy Heckerling; ***W:*** Norman Steinberg, Harry Colomby. *FOX*

Johnny Eager 🦴🦴🦴 **1942** Glossy crime melodrama starring Taylor as an unscrupulous racketeer and Turner as the daughter of D.A. Arnold who falls for him and ends up becoming a pawn in his schemes. Heflin won an Oscar for his outstanding performance as Taylor's alcoholic confidant. Excellent direction by LeRoy makes this a top-rate gangster film. Based on a story by James Edward Grant. **107m/B VHS.** Robert Taylor, Lana Turner, Edward Arnold, Van Heflin, Robert Sterling, Patricia Dane, Glenda Farrell, Barry Nelson, Henry O'Neill, Charles Dingle, Cy Kendall; ***D:*** Mervyn LeRoy; ***W:*** James Edward Grant, John Lee Mahin. Academy Awards '42: Best Supporting Actor (Heflin). *MGM*

Johnny Firecloud 🦴 **1975** A modern Indian goes on the warpath when the persecution of his people reawakens his sense of identity. **94m/C VHS, Beta.** Victor Mohica, Ralph Meeker, Frank De Kova, Sacheen Little Feather, David Canary, Christina Hart; ***D:*** William Allen Castleman. *PSM*

Johnny Frenchman 🦴🦴 **1946** Rival fishing groups battle it out, complicated by a romance across the water. Featured in the cast are real fishermen and villagers from Cornwall, as well as authentic Free French Resistance fighters from WWII. **104m/B VHS.** *GB* Francoise Rosay, Tom Walls, Patricia Roc, Ralph Michael, Frederick Piper, Pierre Richard, Carroll O'Connor; ***D:*** Charles Frend. *NOS*

Johnny Got His Gun 🦴🦴 **1971 (R)** Dalton Trumbo's story of a young war veteran who realizes that his arms and legs have been amputated. **111m/C VHS, Beta, LV.** Timothy Bottoms, Jason Robards Jr., Donald Sutherland, Diane Varsi, Kathy Field; ***D:*** Dalton Trumbo. Cannes Film Festival '71: Grand Jury Prize; Nominations: Cannes Film Festival '71: Best Film. *MED*

Johnny Guitar 🦴🦴🦴½ **1953** Women strap on six-guns in Nicholas Ray's unintentionally hilarious, gender-bending western. A guitar-playing loner wanders into a small town feud between lovelorn saloon owner Crawford and McCambridge, the town's resident lynch mob-leading harpy. This fascinating cult favorite has had film theorists arguing for decades: is it a parody, a political McCarthy-era allegory, or Freudian exercise? The off-screen battles of the two female stars are equally legendary. Stick around for the end credits to hear Peggy Lee sing the title song. **116m/C VHS, LV.** Joan Crawford, Ernest Borgnine, Sterling Hayden, Mercedes McCambridge, Scott Brady, Ward Bond, Royal Dano, John Carradine; ***D:*** Nicholas Ray; ***W:*** Philip Yordan; ***C:*** Harry Stradling. *REP*

Johnny Handsome 🦴🦴🦴 **1989 (R)** An ugly, deformed hood, after he's been double-crossed and sent to prison, volunteers for a reconstructive surgery experiment and is released with a new face, determined to hunt down the scum that set him up. A terrific modern B-picture based on John Godey's "The Three Worlds of Johnny Handsome." **96m/C VHS, Beta, LV.** Mickey Rourke, Ellen Barkin, Lance Henriksen, Elizabeth McGovern, Morgan Freeman, Forest Whitaker, Scott Wilson, Blake Clark; ***D:*** Walter Hill; ***W:*** Ken Friedman; ***M:*** Ry Cooder. *LIV*

Johnny Mnemonic 🦴🦴 **1995 (R)** Robo-yuppie data courier Johnny (Reeves), has over extended the storage capacity in his head and must download his latest job before his brain turns to applesauce. Aided by an implant-enhanced bodyguard (Meyer), underground hacker rebels called LoTeks, and a former doctor (Rollins) battling a technology-induced epidemic, Johnny is on the run from the corporation that wants his head (literally). Freshman director Longo can't seem to get a handle on the plot and doesn't get much help from Gibson, who combined characters and scenarios from his other books. Action sequences and computer effects are appropriately spiffy, preventing a total system crash. **98m/C VHS, LV, 8mm.** Keanu Reeves, Dina Meyer, Ice-T, Takeshi, Dolph Lundgren, Henry Rollins, Udo Kier, Barbara Sukowa, Denis Akiyama; ***D:*** Robert Longo; ***W:*** William Gibson; ***C:*** Francois Protat; ***M:*** Brad Fiedel. *COL*

Johnny Nobody 🦴🦴½ **1961** A mysterious stranger murders a writer who has been taunting the residents of a quaint Irish town. A sleeper of a thriller, especially in the treatment of the town's reaction to this murder. **88m/B VHS, Beta.** *GB* William Bendix, Aldo Ray, Nigel Patrick, Yvonne Mitchell, Cyril Cusack; ***D:*** Nigel Patrick. *NO*

Johnny Reno 🦴½ **1966** Laughable western that has U.S. Marshal Andrews trying to save an accused killer from lynching. Of interest for star-watching only. Based on a story by Steve Fisher, A.C. Lyles, and Andrew Craddock. **83m/C VHS.** Dana Andrews, Jane Russell, Lon Chaney Jr., John Agar, Lyle Bettger, Tom Drake, Richard Arlen, Robert Lowery; ***D:*** R.G. Springsteen; ***W:*** Steve Fisher. *PAR*

Johnny Shiloh 🦴🦴 **1963** An underage youth becomes a heroic drummer during the Civil War. Originally a two-part Disney television show. **90m/C VHS, Beta.** Kevin Corcoran, Brian Keith, Darryl Hickman, Skip Homeier; ***D:*** James Neilson. *DIS*

Johnny Stecchino 🦴🦴🦴 **1992 (R)** A breathless, charming comedy about mistaken identity, with Benigni starring as both Dante, a mild-mannered Roman bus driver, and his double, a notorious Mafioso known as "Johnny Toothpick." Dante happens to meet a lovely woman who takes exceptional interest in him, even inviting him to visit her home in Palermo. The reason she's interested is that Dante is the exact double of her husband, who has ratted on his fellow mobsters and needs a patsy to take the fall. Benigni's expressive body language and sweetness of character is well-showcased. In Italian with English subtitles. **100m/C VHS, LV.** *IT* Roberto Benigni, Nicoletta Braschi, Paolo Bonacelli, Ignazio Pappalardo, Franco Volpi; ***D:*** Roberto Benigni; ***W:*** Roberto Benigni, Vincenzo Cerami; ***M:*** Evan Lurie. *NLC, IME, FCT*

Johnny Suede 🦴🦴½ **1992 (R)** Hip kid with big hair wanders the city seeking an identity via retro black suede elevator shoes. Sleepy surreal comedy walks Pitt through two romantic entanglements and a rendezvous with his own rock idol in his quest for musical talent and pop singer nirvana (not necessarily in that order). Candidate for induction into the David Lynch Movie Musuem of the Weird. **97m/C VHS, LV.** Brad Pitt, Calvin Levels, Nick Cave, Wilfredo Giovanni Clark, Alison Moir, Peter McRobbie, Tina Louise, Michael Mulheren, Catherine Keener, Samuel L. Jackson; ***D:*** Tom DiCillo; ***W:*** Tom DiCillo; ***M:*** Jim Farmer. *PAR*

Johnny Tiger 🦴🦴½ **1966** A teacher has his hands full when he arrives at the Seminole Reservation in Florida to instruct the Indian children. **100m/C VHS, Beta.** Robert Taylor, Geraldine Brooks, Chad Everett, Brenda Scott; ***D:*** Paul Wendkos. *REP*

Johnny Tremain & the Sons of Liberty 🦴🦴 **1958** The story of the gallant American patriots who participated in the Boston Tea Party. **85m/C VHS, Beta.** Sebastian Cabot, Hal Stalmaster, Luana Patten, Richard Beymer; ***D:*** Robert Stevenson. *DIS*

Johnny We Hardly Knew Ye 🦴🦴½ **1977** Well-made biographical drama recounts John F. Kennedy's first political campaign for local office in Boston in 1946. Made for television. **90m/C VHS, Beta.** Paul Rudd, Kevin Conway, William Prince, Burgess Meredith, Tom Berenger, Brian Dennehy, Kenneth McMillan; ***D:*** Gilbert Cates. *TLF*

Johnny's Girl 🦴🦴½ **1995** After her mom's death, a 16-year-old (Kirshner) moves to Anchorage, Alaska to live with her wayward dad (Williams). He's a kinda con man involved in shady deals, who tries to go legit in order to give his daughter a proper home. TV movie based on the novel by Kim Rich. **92m/C VHS.** Mia Kirshner, Treat Williams, Ron White, Gloria Reuben, Shirley Douglas, Janne Mortil; ***D:*** John Kent Harrison. *HMK*

A Joke of Destiny, Lying in Wait Around the Corner Like a Bandit 🦴🦴 *A Joke of Destiny* **1984 (PG)** A irreverent satire about a Minister of the Interior (Tognazzi, of "La Cage aux Folles" fame) who becomes trapped in his high-tech limousine before a vital press conference. An exaggerated vision of Italian bureaucracy. With English subtitles. **105m/C VHS, Beta.** *IT* Ugo Tognazzi, Piera Degli Esposti, Gastone Moschin, Renzo Montagnani, Valeria Golino; ***D:*** Lina Wertmuller; ***W:*** Lina Wertmuller. *ORI, APD*

Jokes My Folks Never Told Me ☆ **1977** Series of blackouts and sketches featuring a bevy of beautiful women. **82m/C VHS, Beta.** Sandy Johnson, Mariwin Roberts; ***D:*** Gerry Woolery. *SUE*

The Jolly Paupers ☆☆½ *Freylekhe Kabtsonim* **1938** A pre-war comedy made in Warsaw about two small-town Jews who try to achieve fame and fortune in the face of setbacks, community quarrels, and insanity. In Yiddish with English subtitles. **62m/B VHS.** Shimon Dzigan, Yisroel Shumacher, Max Bozyk, Menasha Oppenheim; ***D:*** Zygmund Turkow. *ALD*

Jolson Sings Again ☆☆ **1949** This sequel to "The Jolson Story" brings back Larry Parks as the ebullient entertainer, with Jolson himself dubbing Parks's voice for the songs. Picking up where the other film ended, the movie chronicles Jolson's comeback in the 1940s and his tireless work with the USO overseas during WWII and the Korean War. ♫After You've Gone; Chinatown, My Chinatown; Give My Regards to Broadway; I Only Have Eyes For You; I'm Just Wild About Harry; You Made Me Love You; I'm Looking Over a Four-Leaf Clover; Is It True What They Say About Dixie?; Ma Blushin' Rose. **96m/C VHS, Beta, LV.** Larry Parks, William Demarest, Barbara Hale, Bill Goodwin; ***D:*** Henry Levin; ***M:*** George Duning. Nominations: Academy Awards '49: Best Color Cinematography, Best Story & Screenplay, Best Original Score. *COL*

The Jolson Story ☆☆☆ **1946** A smash Hollywood bio of Jolson, from his childhood to superstardom. Features dozens of vintage songs from Jolson's parade of hits. Jolson himself dubbed the vocals for Parks, rejuvenating his own career in the process. ♫Swanee; You Made Me Love You; By the Light of the Silvery Moon; I'm Sitting On Top of the World; There's a Rainbow Round My Shoulder; My Mammy; Rock-A-Bye Your Baby With a Dixie Melody; Liza; Waiting for the Robert E. Lee. **128m/C VHS, Beta, LV.** Larry Parks, Evelyn Keyes, William Demarest, Bill Goodwin, Tamara Shayne, John Alexander, Jimmy Lloyd, Ludwig Donath, Scotty Beckett; ***D:*** Alfred E. Green; ***M:*** Morris Stoloff. Academy Awards '46: Best Sound, Best Score; Nominations: Academy Awards '46: Best Actor (Parks), Best Color Cinematography, Best Film Editing, Best Supporting Actor (Demarest). *COL*

Jon Jost's Frameup ☆☆ *Frameup* **1993** Cocky ex-con Ricky Lee hooks up with dizzy waitress Beth Ann and they head out on a 3000-mile nightmare road trip to California. Free-form story shot in 10 days. **91m/C VHS.** Howard Swain, Nancy Carlin; ***D:*** Jon Jost; ***W:*** Jon Jost. *WAC*

Jonah Who Will Be 25 in the Year 2000 ☆☆☆½ *Jonas—Qui Aura 25 Ans en l'an 2000* **1976** A group of eight friends, former 60s radicals, try to adjust to growing older and coping with life in the 70s. The eccentric octet include a disillusioned journalist turned gambler, an unorthodox teacher, and a grocery store cashier who gives away food to the elderly. Wonderful performances highlight this social comedy. In French with English subtitles. **110m/C VHS.** *SI* Jean-Luc Bideau, Myriam Meziere, Miou-Miou, Jacques Denis, Rufus, Dominique Labourier, Roger Jendly, Miriam Boyer, Raymond Bussieres, Jonah; ***D:*** Alain Tanner; ***W:*** Alain Tanner. National Society of Film Critics Awards '76: Best Screenplay. *NYF*

Jonathan Livingston Seagull ☆☆½ **1973 (G)** Based on the best-selling novella by Richard Bach, this film quietly envisions a world of love, understanding, achievement hope and individuality. **99m/C VHS, Beta.** James Franciscus, Juliet Mills; ***D:*** Hall Bartlett; ***M:*** Neil Diamond. Golden Globe Awards '74: Best Score; Nominations: Academy Awards '73: Best Cinematography, Best Film Editing. *PAR, WSH*

Joni ☆☆ **1979 (G)** An inspirational story based on the real life of Tada (playing herself) who was seriously injured in a diving accident, and her conquering of the odds. A born-again feature film based on the book by Tada. **75m/C VHS, Beta.** Joni Eareckson Tada, Bert Remsen, Katherine De Hetre, Cooper Huckabee; ***D:*** James F. Collier. *LIV*

Jornada de Muerte ☆ **198?** An ex-cop is hired to bring an important anti-Mob witness to trial via transcontinental train, and must fend off Mob attack squads in the process. In Spanish. **90m/C VHS, Beta.** *SP* Fred Williamson, Bernie Kuby, Heidi Dobbs. *UNI*

Jory ☆☆ **1972 (PG)** A young man's father is killed in a saloon fight, and he must grow up quickly to survive. **96m/C VHS, Beta.** Robby Benson, B.J. Thomas, John Marley; ***D:*** Jorge Fons. *COL, SUE*

Joseph ☆☆½ **1995** Following "Abraham" and "Jacob" comes the Old Testament story of young Joseph (Mercurio), beloved son of Jacob, who's sold into slavery by his envious older brothers. Joseph is bought by the Pharoah's chief steward, Potiphar (Kingsley), and, after a long series of tribulations, rises to become a power in Egypt, which unexpectedly leads Joseph to hold the fate of his long-lost family in his hands. Filmed in Morocco. **240m/C VHS.** Paul Mercurio, Ben Kingsley, Martin Landau, Lesley Ann Warren, Warren Clarke, Alice Krige, Dominique Sanda, Stefano Dionisi, Valeria Cavalli, Peter Eyre, Timothy Bateson, Jamie Glover, Mike Attwell; ***D:*** Roger Young; ***W:*** Lionel Chetwynd, James Carrington; ***C:*** Raffaele Mertes; ***M:*** Marco Frisina. *TTC*

Joseph & His Brethren ☆ *The Story of Joseph and His Brethren; Joseph Sold by His Brothers* **1960** A full-length dramatization of the Old Testament story. **103m/C VHS, Beta.** Geoffrey Horne, Robert Morley; ***D:*** Irving Rapper. *VCI, KEP*

Joseph Andrews ☆☆ **1977 (R)** This adaptation of a 1742 Henry Fielding novel chronicles the rise of Joseph Andrews from servant to personal footman (and fancy) of Lady Booby. **99m/C VHS, Beta.** *GB* Ann-Margret, Peter Firth, Jim Dale, Michael Hordern, Beryl Reid; ***D:*** Tony Richardson; ***W:*** Chris Bryant, Allan Scott; ***C:*** David Watkin; ***M:*** John Addison. *PAR*

Josepha ☆☆☆ **1982 (R)** A husband and wife, both actors, are forced to re-examine their relationship when the wife finds a new love while on a film location. In French with English subtitles. **114m/C VHS, Beta.** *FR* Miou-Miou, Claude Brasseur, Bruno Cremer; ***D:*** Christopher Frank. *COL, INJ*

The Josephine Baker Story ☆☆☆ **1990 (R)** Made-for-cable bio of exotic entertainer/activist Josephine Baker, an Afro-American woman from St. Louis who found superstardom in pre-WWII Europe, but repeated racism and rejection in the U.S. At times trite treatment turns her eventful life into a standard rise-and-fall showbiz tale, but a great cast and lavish scope pull it through. Whitfield recreates Baker's (sometimes topless) dance routines; Carol Dennis dubs her singing. Filmed on location in Budapest. **129m/C VHS.** Lynn Whitfield, Ruben Blades, David Dukes, Craig T. Nelson, Louis Gossett Jr., Kene Holliday, Vivian Bonnell; ***D:*** Brian Gibson; ***M:*** Ralph Burns. Emmy Awards '91: Best Actress (Whitfield), Best Director (Gibson). *HBO, FCT*

Josh and S.A.M. ☆☆ **1993 (PG-13)** Road movie for youngsters with a twist: the driver can barely see over the dashboard. Josh and Sam are brothers whose parents are splitting. They cope by taking off on their own. Sam, meanwhile has been convinced by Josh that he's not a real boy at all, but rather a S.A.M.: Strategically Altered Mutant. Weber's directorial debut will appeal to young kids, but adults will see over the dashboard and through the transparent plot. **97m/C VHS, LV.** Jacob Tierney, Noah Fleiss, Martha Plimpton, Joan Allen, Christopher Penn, Stephen Tobolowsky, Ronald Guttman; ***D:*** Billy Weber; ***W:*** Frank Deese; ***C:*** Don Burgess; ***M:*** Thomas Newman. *NLC*

Josh Kirby...Time Warrior: Chapter 1, Planet of the Dino-Knights ☆☆½ **1995 (PG)** Time-traveling 14-year-old Josh Kirby is accidently zapped to the 25th-century where fierce warriors ride dinosaurs and a madman is out to destroy the universe. The first tale in a fantasy series designed as an old-fashioned movie serial, complete with cliff-hanger ending. **88m/C VHS, Beta.** Corbin Allred, Jennifer Burns, Derek Webster, John De Mita; ***D:*** Ernest Farino; ***W:*** Ethan Reiff, Cyrus Voris, Paul Callisi. *PAR*

Josh Kirby...Time Warrior: Chapter 2, The Human Pets ☆☆½ **1995 (PG)** Josh and his friends now find themselves in the year 70,370—held hostage by the enormous Fatlings, who regard their human finds as pet-like action toys. **90m/C VHS, Beta.** Corbin Allred, Jennifer Burns; ***D:*** Frank Arnold; ***W:*** Ethan Reiff, Cyrus Voris, Paul Callisi. *PAR*

Josh Kirby...Time Warrior: Chapter 3, Trapped on Toyworld ☆☆½ **1995 (PG)** Josh is stranded away from his friends on the strange planet of Toyworld and must rely on the life-like creations of a toy magnate to defend himself from the villainous Dr. Zoetrope. **90m/C VHS, Beta.** Corbin Allred, Jennifer Burns, Derek Webster, Sharon Lee Jones, Buck Kartalian, Barrie Ingham; ***D:*** Frank Arnold; ***W:*** Nick Paine. *PAR*

Josh Kirby...Time Warrior: Chapter 4, Eggs from 70 Million B.C. ☆☆½ **1995 (PG)** Josh and his pals finds themselves in a military compound that is under attack and encounter some very hungry alien worms. **93m/C VHS, Beta.** Corbin Allred, Jennifer Burns, Derek Webster, Gary Kasper, Barrie Ingham; ***D:*** Mark Manos. *PAR*

Josh Kirby...Time Warrior: Chapter 5, Journey to the Magic Cavern ☆☆½ **1996 (PG)** Josh and pals find themselves in the center of a planet where they are befriended by the weird Mushroom People who are under siege by a monster known as "the Muncher." **93m/C VHS, Beta.** Corbin Allred, Jennifer Burns, Derek Webster, Michael Hagiwara, Barrie Ingham; ***D:*** Ernest Farino; ***W:*** Ethan Reiff, Cyrus Voris. *PAR*

Josh Kirby...Time Warrior: Chapter 6, Last Battle for the Universe ☆☆½ **1996 (PG)** Josh is ready to get back to his own time but first he must survive a battle between long-feuding rivals of the timebelt. **90m/C VHS, Beta.** Corbin Allred, Jennifer Burns, Derek Webster, Barrie Ingham; ***D:*** Frank Arnold; ***W:*** Ethan Reiff, Cyrus Voris. *PAR*

Joshua ☆ *Black Rider* **1976 (R)** Western drama about a vigilante who tracks down the group of outlaws that killed his mother. **75m/C VHS.** Fred Williamson, Isela Vega; ***D:*** Larry Spangler. *NO*

Joshua Then and Now ☆☆☆ **1985 (R)** When a Jewish-Canadian novelist (Woods) is threatened by the breakup of his marriage to his WASPy wife, compounded by a gay scandal, he re-examines his picaresque history, including his life with his gangster father (Arkin). A stirring story that is enhanced by a strong performance by Woods, as well as a picturesque Canadian backdrop. Adapted by Mordecai Richler from his own novel. **102m/C VHS, Beta.** *CA* James Woods, Gabrielle Lazure, Alan Arkin, Michael Sarrazin, Chuck Shamata, Linda Sorensen, Alan Scarfe, Alexander Knox, Robert Joy, Ken Campbell; ***D:*** Ted Kotcheff; ***W:*** Mordecai Richler; ***M:*** Philippe Sarde. Genie Awards '86: Best Supporting Actor (Arkin), Best Supporting Actress (Sorensen). *FOX*

Jour de Fete ☆☆☆½ *The Big Day; Holiday* **1948** Tati's first film, dealing with a French postman's accelerated efforts at efficiency after viewing a motivational film of the American post service. Wonderful slapstick moments. In French with English subtitles. **79m/B VHS, Beta, LV.** *FR* Jacques Tati, Guy Decomble, Paul Fankeur; ***D:*** Jacques Tati. *VDM, SUE, CRC*

Journey ☆ **1977 (PG)** Violent story of a girl who is rescued from the Sagueney River and falls in love with her rescuer. Choosing to remain in the remote pioneer community of this "hero," she brings everyone bad luck and misery. **87m/C VHS, Beta.** *CA* Genevieve Bujold, John Vernon; ***D:*** Paul Almond. *NO*

Journey ☆☆½ **1995 (PG)** Eleven-year-old Journey (Pomeranc) and his teenaged sister Cat (Dushku) are abandoned by their unhappy, restless mother Min (Tilly) at the home of her parents, Marcus (Robards) and Lottie (Fricker). Marcus is an amatuer photographer and Journey searches through the family photo albums to find reasons for his mother's leaving as he and his grandfather slowly build their relationship. Based on the book by Patricia MacLachlan. **98m/C VHS.** Max Pomeranc, Jason Robards Jr., Brenda Fricker, Eliza Dushku, Meg Tilly; ***D:*** Tom McLoughlin; ***W:*** Patricia MacLachlan; ***C:*** Kees Van Oostrum. *HMK*

Journey Back to Oz **1971** Animated special features Dorothy and Toto returning to visit their friends in the magical land of Oz. **90m/C VHS, Beta.** ***V:*** Liza Minnelli, Ethel Merman, Paul Lynde, Milton Berle, Mickey Rooney, Danny Thomas. *FHE, KAR, HHE*

Journey Beneath the Desert 🦴🦴 *Antinea, l'Amante Della Citta Sepolta* **1961** Three engineers discover the lost-but-always-found-in-the-movies kingdom of Atlantis when their helicopter's forced down in the sunny Sahara. A poor hostess with a rotten disposition, the mean sub-saharan queen doesn't roll out the welcome mat for her grounded guests, so a beautiful slave babe helps them make a hasty exit. Dawdling Euro production with adequate visuals. **105m/C VHS, Beta.** *FR IT* Haya Harareet, Jean-Louis Trintignant, Brad Fulton, Amedeo Nazzari, George Riviere, Giulia Rubini, Gabriele Tinti, Gian Marie Volonte; ***D:*** Edgar G. Ulmer, Giuseppe Masini, Frank Borzage. *SNC*

Journey for Margaret 🦴🦴🦴 **1942** Young and Day star as an expectant American couple living in London during WWII so Young can cover the war for a newspaper back home. After she loses her baby during an air raid, Day heads back to the States. Young stays in London where he meets two young orphans and takes them under his wing. He decides to take them back to the United States and adopt them, but problems arise. A real tearjerker and a good story that shows the war through the eyes of children. O'Brien's first film. Based on the book by William L. White. **81m/B VHS.** Robert Young, Laraine Day, Fay Bainter, Signe Hasso, Margaret O'Brien, Nigel Bruce, G.P. Huntley Jr., William Severn, Doris Lloyd, Halliwell Hobbes, Jill Esmond; ***D:*** Woodbridge S. Van Dyke. *MGM, FCT*

Journey into Fear 🦴🦴🦴 **1942** During WWII, an American armaments expert is smuggled out of Istanbul, but Axis agents are close behind. From the novel by Eric Ambler; remade for television in 1974. **71m/B VHS, Beta, LV.** Joseph Cotten, Dolores Del Rio, Orson Welles, Agnes Moorehead, Norman Foster; ***D:*** Norman Foster; ***C:*** Karl Struss. *MED, RXM, TTC*

Journey into Fear 🦴½ *Burn Out* **1974** A remake of the 1942 Orson Welles classic about a geologist ensnared in Turkish intrigue and murder. **96m/C VHS, Beta.** *CA* Sam Waterston, Vincent Price, Shelley Winters, Donald Pleasence, Zero Mostel, Yvette Mimieux, Ian McShane; ***D:*** Daniel Mann; ***M:*** Alex North. *LIV*

Journey into the Beyond **1976 (R)** A brain-incinerating look at the inexplicable world of the supernatural. Includes examinations of voodoo, barehanded surgery and psychic sex that are guaranteed to fry your soul. **83m/C VHS, Beta.** *FHE*

The Journey of August King 🦴🦴½ **1995 (PG-13)** Adapted by Ehle from his own 1971 novel, set in 1815, about a runaway slave (Newton) protected by a lonely farmer against the landowner and posse tracking her down. August King (Patric), a widower on his way home from town, comes upon Annalees (Newton), prize possession of powerful slaveowner Olaf Singletary (Drake). August, a highly principled man, resists helping her at first, for fear of breaking the law and losing his farm and only remaining possessions. But he rises to higher moral ground, deciding to help her find freedom, whatever the consequences. Director Duigan ("Sirens") crafts a thoughtful, but not particularly suspenseful, period piece of early American history. Patric/Newton relationship reflects the gradual feel of the film. Drake booms as slaveowner. Includes brief brutal scene of slave torture. **91m/C VHS, LV.** Jason Patric, Thandie Newton, Larry Drake, Sam Waterston; ***D:*** John Duigan; ***W:*** John Ehle; ***C:*** Slawomir Idziak; ***M:*** Stephen Endelman. *TOU*

Journey of Honor 🦴🦴½ **1991 (PG-13)** During a civil war in 17th century Japan, a nearly defeated Shogun sends his son, Lord Mayeda, to Spain to buy guns from King Phillip III. Along the way he must fight shipboard spies and fierce storms, and once Mayeda arrives in Spain, he is confronted by the evil Duke Don Pedro. In defeating Don Pedro, Mayeda saves King Phillip, gets his guns, and wins the love of Lady Cecilia. To get revenge, Don Pedro plots to capture the Japanese ship and enslave everyone on board. Lots of action and fine acting. Based on a story by martial artist Sho Kosugi. **107m/C VHS, Beta, LV.** Sho Kosugi, David Essex, Kane Kosugi, Christopher Lee, Norman Lloyd, Ronald Pickup, John Rhys-Davies, Dylan Kussman, Toshiro Mifune; ***D:*** Gordon Hessler. *MCA*

Journey of Hope 🦴🦴🦴½ **1990 (PG)** Powerful drama about Kurdish family that sells its material possessions in hopes of emigrating legally to Switzerland, where life will surely be better. During the perilous journey, smugglers take their money and the family must attempt crossing the formidable slopes of the Swiss Mountains on foot. Based on a true story. In Turkish with English subtitles. **111m/C VHS, LV.** *SI* Necmettin Cobanoglu, Nur Surer, Emin Sivas, Yaman Okay, Mathias Gnaedinger, Dietmar Schoenherr; ***D:*** Xavier Koller; ***W:*** Xavier Koller. Academy Awards '90: Best Foreign Language Film. *WAR, HBO, INJ*

The Journey of Natty Gann 🦴🦴🦴½ **1985 (PG)** With the help of a wolf (brilliantly portrayed by a dog) and a drifter, a 14-year-old girl travels across the country in search of her father in this warm and touching film. Excellent Disney representation of life during the Great Depression. **101m/C VHS, Beta, LV.** Meredith Salenger, John Cusack, Ray Wise, Scatman Crothers, Lainie Kazan, Verna Bloom; ***D:*** Jeremy Paul Kagan; ***W:*** Jeanne Rosenberg; ***M:*** James Horner. Nominations: Academy Awards '85: Best Costume Design. *DIS*

Journey Through Rosebud **1972** A re-enactment of the 1970s protest at Wounded Knee by Native Americans. **93m/C VHS, Beta.** Robert Forster, Eddie Little Sky; ***D:*** Tom Giles. *NLC*

Journey to Spirit Island 🦴🦴½ **1992 (PG)** A young Native American girl dreams of her ancestors who are buried on Spirit Island, an ancient burial ground. However, the island is now scheduled to be developed into a resort. With the help of three friends the girl tries to protect the land. Filmed in the Pacific Northwest. **93m/C VHS.** Brandon Douglas, Gabriel Damon, Tony Acierto, Nick Ramus, Marie Antoinette Rodgers, Tarek McCarthy; ***D:*** Laszlo Pal. *ACA*

Journey to the Center of the Earth 🦴🦴🦴 **1959** A scientist and student undergo a hazardous journey to find the center of the earth and along the way they find the lost city of Atlantis. Based upon the Jules Verne novel. **132m/C VHS, Beta, LV.** James Mason, Pat Boone, Arlene Dahl, Diane Baker, Thayer David, Alan Napier, Peter Ronson; ***D:*** Henry Levin. Nominations: Academy Awards '59: Best Art Direction/Set Decoration (Color), Best Sound. *FXV, FCT, FUS*

Journey to the Center of the Earth **1976** An animated version of the Jules Verne classic adventure about a scientist's quest to reach the earth's core. **50m/C VHS, Beta.** *MGM, WTA*

Journey to the Center of the Earth **1988 (PG)** A young nanny and two teenage boys discover Atlantis while exploring a volcano. **83m/C VHS, Beta, LV.** Nicola Cowper, Paul Carafotes, Ilan Mitchell-Smith; ***D:*** Rusty Lemorande; ***W:*** Rusty Lemorande, Kitty Chalmers. *CAN*

Journey to the Center of Time 🦴½ **1967** A scientist and his crew are hurled into a time trap when a giant reactor explodes. **83m/C VHS, Beta.** Lyle Waggoner, Scott Brady, Gigi Perreau, Anthony Eisley; ***D:*** David L. Hewitt. *ACA, GHV*

Journey to the Far Side of the Sun 🦴🦴🦴 *Doppelganger* **1969 (G)** Chaos erupts in the Earth's scientific community when it is discovered that a second, identical Earth is on the other side of the Sun. Both planets end up sending out identical exploratory missions. The denouement is worth the journey. **92m/C VHS, Beta, LV.** *GB* Roy Thinnes, Ian Hendry, Lynn Loring, Patrick Wymark, Loni von Friedl, Herbert Lom, Ed Bishop; ***D:*** Robert Parrish; ***W:*** Gerry Anderson. *MCA*

Journey to the Lost City 🦴½ *Tiger of Bengal* **1958** Architect living in India happens upon a lost city, the rulership of which is being contested by two brothers. In the midst of fighting snakes and tigers, he falls in love with Paget, a beautiful dancer. This feature is actually a poorly edited hybrid of two Lang German adventures, "Der Tiger von Eschnapur" and "Das Indische Grabmal" merged for U.S. release. **95m/C VHS, Beta.** *FR IT GE* Debra Paget, Paul Christian, Walter Reyer, Claus Holm, Sabine Bethmann, Valeri Inkizhinov, Rene Deltgen, Luciana Paluzzi; ***D:*** Fritz Lang. *SNC*

Journeys from Berlin/1971 🦴🦴½ **1984** This is the true story about a woman who tries to find a solution to her own problems in life. **125m/C VHS, Beta.** *NO*

Joy House 🦴🦴 *The Love Cage; Les Felins* **1964** An American woman befriends a handsome French playboy when her husband sends gangsters to kill him. **98m/B VHS, Beta.** Jane Fonda, Alain Delon, Lola Albright; ***D:*** Rene Clement; ***W:*** Rene Clement. *NO*

The Joy Luck Club 🦴🦴🦴 **1993 (R)** Universal themes in mother/daughter relationships are explored in a context Hollywood first rejected as too narrow, but which proved to be a modest sleeper hit. Tan skillfully weaves the plot of her 1989 best-seller into a screenplay which centers around young June's going-away party. Slowly the stories of four Chinese women, who meet weekly to play mah-jongg, are unraveled. Each vignette reveals life in China for the four women and the tragedies they survived, before reaching into the present to capture the relationships between the mothers and their daughters. Powerful, relevant, and moving. **136m/C VHS, LV.** Tsai Chin, Kieu Chinh, France Nuyen, Rosalind Chao, Tamlyn Tomita, Lisa Lu, Lauren Tom, Ming-Na Wen, Michael Paul Chan, Andrew McCarthy, Christopher Rich, Russell Wong, Victor Wong, Vivian Wu, Jack Ford, Diane Baker; ***D:*** Wayne Wang; ***W:*** Amy Tan, Ronald Bass. *TOU, HPH*

The Joy of Knowledge 🦴½ **1965** Godard's experimental use of language and image in a plotless narrative. Berto and Leaud sit together on a bare sound stage and are exposed to popular culture through images, word association, and conversation. In French with English subtitles. Also known as "Le Gai Savoir." **96m/C VHS.** *FR* Juliet Berto, Jean-Pierre Leaud; ***D:*** Jean-Luc Godard; ***W:*** Jean-Luc Godard. *FCT*

Joy of Living 🦴🦴🦴 **1938** Vintage screwball farce about a randy playboy trying to win over a pragmatic songstress. ♫You Couldn't Be Cuter; A Heavenly Party; What's Good About Goodnight; Just Let Me Look At You. **90m/B VHS, Beta, LV.** Irene Dunne, Douglas Fairbanks Jr., Alice Brady, Guy Kibbee, Jean Dixon, Eric Blore, Lucille Ball, Warren Hymer, Billy Gilbert, Frank Milan; ***D:*** Tay Garnett; ***M:*** Jerome Kern, Dorothy Fields. *TTC*

Joy of Sex 🦴 **1984 (R)** An undercover narcotics agent is sent to Southern California's Richard M. Nixon High School to investigate the school's extracurricular activities. Typical teen sex flick; no relation to the book. **93m/C VHS, Beta.** Cameron Dye, Michelle Meyrink, Colleen Camp, Christopher Lloyd, Ernie Hudson, Lisa Langlois; ***D:*** Martha Coolidge; ***W:*** Kathleen Rowell. *PAR*

Joy Ride to Nowhere 🦴 **1978 (PG)** Two young women steal a Cadillac with two million dollars in the trunk and ride away with the owner hot on their tail. **86m/C VHS, Beta.** Leslie Ackerman, Sandy Serrano, Len Lesser, Mel Welles, Ron Ross, Speed Stearns. *NO*

Joy Sticks *Woof!* **1983 (R)** Joy sticks in question are down at the arcade. Businessman wants to shut down local video game palace. Inhabitants just say no. **88m/C VHS, Beta, LV.** Joe Don Baker, Leif Green, Jim Greenleaf, Scott McGinnis, Jonathan Gries; ***D:*** Greydon Clark. *VES*

Joyful Laughter 🦴🦴 **1954** The dreary life of an Italian movie bit player draws strength from Magnani's powerful emotions as she repeatedly comes near to success only to find disappointment. Set in Rome. With English subtitles. **106m/C VHS.** *IT* ***D:*** Mario Monicelli. *FST*

Joyless Street ☆☆☆½ **1925** Silent film focuses on the dismal life of the middle class in Austria during an economic crisis. Lovely piano score accompanies the film. **96m/B VHS, Beta, LV.** *GE* Greta Garbo, Werner Krauss, Asta Nielson; ***D:*** G.W. Pabst. *VYY, MRV, FST*

Joyride ☆½ **1977 (R)** Mistreated by a union official, three friends steal a car for a joy ride and plummet into a life of crime. **91m/C VHS, Beta.** Desi Arnaz Jr., Robert Carradine, Melanie Griffith, Anne Lockhart; ***D:*** Joseph Ruben. *LIV, VES*

Ju Dou ☆☆☆☆ **1990 (PG-13)** Breath-taking story of an aging factory owner in search of an heir. He takes a third wife, but she finds caring in the arms of another man, when her husband's brutality proves too much. Beautiful color cinematography, excellent acting and epic story. Oscar nominee for Best Foreign Film. In Chinese with English subtitles. **98m/C VHS, LV.** *CH* Gong Li, Li Bao-Tian, Li Wei, Zhang Yi, Zheng Jian; ***D:*** Zhang Yimou; ***C:*** Gu Changwei. Nominations: Academy Awards '90: Best Foreign Language Film. *LIV, BTV, INJ*

Juarez ☆☆ **1939** A revolutionary leader overthrows the Mexican government and then becomes President of the country. Based on the true story of Benito Pablo Juarez. **132m/B VHS, Beta.** Paul Muni, John Garfield, Bette Davis, Claude Rains, Gale Sondergaard, Charles Halton; ***D:*** William Dieterle; ***C:*** Gaetano Antonio "Tony" Gaudio. Nominations: Academy Awards '39: Best Black and White Cinematography, Best Supporting Actor (Aherne). *MGM, FCT*

Jubal ☆☆ **1956** A rancher (Borgnine) seeks advice from a cowhand (Ford) about pleasing his wife, but another cowhand (Steiger) implies that Ford is "advising" Borgnine's wife, as well. A western take on "Othello." **101m/C VHS, Beta, LV.** Glenn Ford, Rod Steiger, Ernest Borgnine, Felicia Farr, Charles Bronson, Valerie French, Noah Beery Jr.; ***D:*** Delmer Daves. *IME*

Jubilee Trail ☆☆½ **1954** Wagon trail western follows the lives of a group of pioneers from New Orleans to California. A woman goes through a marriage, a baby, and her husband's death. Ralston has some good tunes in this lush picture. **103m/C VHS.** Vera Ralston, Joan Leslie, Forrest Tucker, John Russell, Ray Middleton, Pat O'Brien; ***D:*** Joseph Kane. *REP*

Jud ☆½ **1971 (PG)** Society's refusal to understand a young soldier returning from the Vietnam conflict leads him to violence and tragedy. Jennings' first film; music by Phillips of Creedence Clearwater Revival. **80m/C VHS, Beta.** Joseph Kaufmann, Robert Deman, Alix Wyeth, Norman Burton, Claudia Jennings, Maurice Sherbanee, Vic Dunlop, Bonnie Bittner; ***D:*** Gunther Collins; ***M:*** Stu Phillips. *PSM*

Jud Suess ☆☆☆ **1940** Classic, scandalous Nazi anti-Semitic tract about a Jew who rises to power under the duchy of Wuerttemberg by stepping on, abusing, and raping Aryans. A film that caused riots at its screenings and tragedy for its cast and crew, and the Third Reich's most notorious fictional expression of policy. In German with English subtitles. **100m/B VHS, Beta.** *GE* Ferdinand Marian, Werner Krauss, Heinrich George, Kristina Soderbaum, Eugene Klopfer; ***D:*** Veit Harlan. *NOS, VCD, IHF*

The Judas Project: The Ultimate Encounter ☆½ **1994 (PG-13)** Religious fantasy finds Jesse battling corruption and pseudo-religious figures in a fight to save a violent and decaying world. But Jesse's destroyed by his own disciple, Jude. Sound familiar? (There's even a cruxifixion scene.) **98m/C VHS.** John O'Bannion, Ramy Zada, Richard Herd. *HMD*

Jude the Obscure ☆☆½ **1971** Thomas Hardy's last novel is a tragic, bleak story of mismatched lovers and blighted ambitions. Jude is a poor stonemason whose dream is to get a proper education and marry his beloved cousin. Failing to get into Oxford he is seduced by a farm girl, whom he marries and fathers a child by (a gnome-like creature named "Father Time"). Meanwhile, his cousin marries a schoolteacher who disgusts her. Finally, the two thwarted lovers marry, only to find themselves living in poverty and hopelessness. After this novel (said to be Hardy's favorite), he devoted the rest of his long life to poetry. On three cassettes. **262m/C VHS.** *GB* Robert Powell, Daphne Heard, Alex Marshall, John Franklyn-Robbins, Fiona Walker; ***D:*** Hugh David; ***W:*** Harry Green. *FOX, FCT, VCO*

Judex ☆☆½ **1964** Judex, a sensitive cloaked hero-avenger, fights master criminal gangs. In French with English subtitles. Remake of the silent French serial. **103m/B VHS, Beta.** *FR IT* Channing Pollock, Francine Berge, Jacques Jouanneau; ***D:*** Georges Franju; ***M:*** Maurice Jarre. *NOS, SNC, HHT*

The Judge ☆½ **1949** A courtroom crime-drama about the consequences of infidelity. A lawyer sends an acquitted hit man to kill his wife and her lover. Things go amiss and the lawyer winds up dead. **69m/B VHS.** Milburn Stone, Katherine DeMille, Paul Guilfoyle, Jonathan Hale; ***D:*** Elmer Clifton. *SNC*

The Judge and the Assassin ☆☆☆½ *Le Juge et L'assassin* **1975** Intriguing courtroom drama. A prejudiced judge has his values challenged when he must decide if a child-killer is insane or not. The relationship that develops between the judge and the killer is the film's focus. Excellent direction by Tavernier. In French with English subtitles. **130m/C VHS, Beta, LV.** *FR* Philippe Noiret, Michel Galabru, Isabelle Huppert, Jean-Claude Brialy; ***D:*** Bertrand Tavernier; ***W:*** Bertrand Tavernier. Cesar Awards '77: Best Writing, Best Score. *CVC, IME, INJ*

Judge Dredd ☆½ **1995 (R)** Futuristic lawman Dredd (Stallone), who acts as cop, judge, jury, and executioner, is framed for murder by his "brother" Rico (Assante), a renegade misfit. With the help of a female Judge (Lane) and an ex-con (Schneider), Dredd fights to clear his name and save the people of Mega City One. Big names, big bangs, big budget—big disappointment. Dialogue makes "Rambo" sound like Shakespeare, and the choppy, convoluted plot doesn't help. Schneider provides a rare bright spot while acting circles around Sly, who hoped (in vain) that the project would provide him with another profitable action franchise. The source comic book has been a cult favorite in England for 20 years. **96m/C VHS, LV.** Sylvester Stallone, Armand Assante, Diane Lane, Rob Schneider, Joan Chen, Juergen Prochnow, Max von Sydow; ***D:*** Danny Cannon; ***W:*** Steven E. de Souza, Michael De Luca, William Wisher; ***M:*** Alan Silvestri. Nominations: Golden Raspberry Awards '95: Worst Actor (Stallone). *TOU*

Judge Horton and the Scottsboro Boys ☆☆½ **1976** A courtroom drama focusing on a famous 1931 trial. A courageous judge must battle the South in the case of nine black men charged with gang-raping two white women. Made for television. **100m/C VHS.** Arthur Hill, Vera Miles, Ken Kercheval, Suzanne Lederer, Tom Ligon; ***D:*** Fielder Cook. *LIV*

Judge Priest ☆☆☆ **1934** Small-town judge in the old South stirs up the place with stinging humor and common-sense observances as he tangles with prejudices and civil injustices. Funny, warm slice-of-life is occasionally defeated by racist characterizations. Ford remade it later as "The Sun Shines Bright." Taken from the Irvin S. Cobb stories. **80m/B VHS, Beta.** Will Rogers, Stepin Fetchit, Anita Louise, Henry B. Walthall; ***D:*** John Ford. *NOS, MRV, PSM*

Judge Roy Bean **1955** This western series set in Langtry, Texas in 1870 starred Buchanan as the self-appointed "Law West of the Pecos," trying to maintain order in a lawless territory. Two episodes per tape. **55m/B VHS, Beta.** Edgar Buchanan, Jack Beutel, Jackie Loughery. *MOV, MVC*

The Judge Steps Out ☆☆½ **1949** Pleasant, light comedy about a hen-pecked, Bostonian judge who decides he's had enough and heads for balmy California. There he finds a job in a restaurant and, more importantly, a sympathetic friend in its female owner. He soon finds himself falling for the woman, and realizes he faces an important decision. **91m/B VHS.** Alexander Knox, Ann Sothern, George Tobias, Sharyn Moffett, Florence Bates, Frieda Inescort, Myrna Dell, Ian Wolfe, H.B. Warner; ***D:*** Boris Ingster. *TTC*

Judgment ☆☆☆ **1990 (PG-13)** A devout Catholic couple are shocked to learn that their young son has been molested by the popular priest of their small Louisiana parish. When they find out their son is not the first victim, and other families have been coerced into silence, they vow to fight back. Tasteful treatment of a real court case. Made for cable. **89m/C VHS.** Keith Carradine, Blythe Danner, Jack Warden, David Strathairn, Bob Gunton, Mitchell Ryan, Michael Faustino; ***D:*** Tom Topor; ***W:*** Tom Topor. *HBO*

Judgment at Nuremberg ☆☆☆☆ **1961** It's 1948 and a group of high-level Nazis are on trial for war crimes. Chief Justice Tracy must resist political pressures as he presides over the trials. Excellent performances throughout, especially by Dietrich and Garland. Considers to what extent an individual may be held accountable for actions committed under orders of a superior officer. Consuming account of the Holocaust and WWII; deeply moving and powerful. Based on a "Playhouse 90" television program. **178m/B VHS, Beta, LV.** Spencer Tracy, Burt Lancaster, Richard Widmark, Montgomery Clift, Maximilian Schell, Judy Garland, Marlene Dietrich, William Shatner; ***D:*** Stanley Kramer; ***W:*** Abby Mann; ***C:*** Ernest Laszlo; ***M:*** Ernest Gold. Academy Awards '61: Best Actor (Schell), Best Adapted Screenplay; Golden Globe Awards '62: Best Actor—Drama (Schell), Best Director (Kramer); New York Film Critics Awards '61: Best Actor (Schell), Best Screenplay; Nominations: Academy Awards '61: Best Actor (Tracy), Best Art Direction/Set Decoration (B & W), Best Black and White Cinematography, Best Costume Design (B & W), Best Director (Kramer), Best Film Editing, Best Picture, Best Supporting Actor (Clift), Best Supporting Actress (Garland). *MGM, FOX, BTV*

Judgment Day ☆ **1988 (PG-13)** Four college buddies pick the wrong New England town for their vacation. It seems that the town made a deal with the Devil in 1689 to save themselves from the plague, and now the Dark Master is here to collect. **93m/C VHS, Beta.** Kenneth McLeod, David Anthony Smith, Monte Markham, Gloria Hayes, Peter Mark Richman, Cesar Romero; ***D:*** Ferde Grofe Jr. *NO*

Judgment in Berlin ☆☆½ *Escape to Freedom* **1988 (PG)** East German family hijacks a U.S. airliner into West Germany, and then must stand trial in Berlin before a troubled American judge. Based on a true 1978 incident and the book by Herbert J. Stern. **92m/C VHS, Beta, LV.** Martin Sheen, Sam Wanamaker, Max Gail, Sean Penn, Heinz Hoenig, Carl Lumbly, Max Volkert Martens, Harris Yulin, Jutta Speidel, Juerger Hemrich; ***D:*** Leonard Penn; ***W:*** Joshua Sinclair; ***M:*** Peter Goldfoot. *COL*

Judgment Night ☆☆ **1993 (R)** Four macho buddies on their way to a boxing match detour a highway traffic jam via surface streets and find themselves witnesses to a murder. The rest of their guys-night-out is spent trying to escape a gloomy ghetto and determined killer (played convincingly by Leary). All of the action takes place after dark on the streets and in the sewers and, subsequently, the scenes are extremely dark with only a burnt orange lighting. Lots of action and a little oomph. Based on a story by Lewis Colick and Jere Cunningham. **109m/C VHS, LV.** Emilio Estevez, Cuba Gooding Jr., Stephen Dorff, Denis Leary, Jeremy Piven, Peter Greene; ***D:*** Stephen Hopkins; ***W:*** Lewis Colick; ***M:*** Alan Silvestri. *MCA*

Judicial Consent ☆☆½ **1994** Gwen Warwick (Bedelia) is an accomplished criminal court judge with a bland husband (Patton) and a lot of unfulfilled desires. At least one desire is taken care of when Gwen succumbs to the charms of handsome law clerk Martin (Wirth). Then her colleague Charles (Coleman) is murdered and all the evidence points to Gwen. She knows she's been set up but can Gwen prove her innocence? Familiar plot, good performances although Patton gets stuck in an underwritten role. **101m/C VHS.** Bonnie Bedelia, Dabney Coleman, Billy Wirth, Will Patton, Lisa Blount; ***D:*** William Bindley; ***W:*** William Bindley; ***M:*** Christopher Young. *AVE*

Judith of Bethulia ☆☆☆ **1914** A young widow uses her charm and wits to save her city from attack by the Assyrians. Based on the Apocrypha, this is the last film Griffith directed for Biograph. It was re-released as "Her Condoned Sin" in 1971, including two reels of Griffith's outtakes. **65m/B VHS, LV.** Blanche Sweet, Henry B. Walthall, Mae Marsh, Robert "Bobbie" Harron, Lillian Gish, Dorothy Gish, Kate Bruce, Harry Carey Sr.; ***D:*** D.W. Griffith; ***W:*** D.W. Griffith. *GPV, NOS, VYY*

Juggernaut 🦴½ **1937** Not the classic disaster film of the '70s. A young woman hires a sinister doctor (Karloff) to murder her wealthy husband. The doctor, who happens to be insane, does away with the husband and then goes on a poisoning spree. Seems to drag on forever. **64m/B VHS, Beta.** Boris Karloff, Mona Goya, Arthur Margetson. *NOS, SNC, VYY*

Juggernaut 🦴🦴🦴 **1974 (PG-13)** Well-done drama about a doomed luxury liner. A madman plants bombs aboard a cruise ship and mocks the crew about his plan over the wireless. The countdown ensues, while the bomb experts struggle to find the explosives. Suspenseful with good direction. **109m/C VHS.** *GB* Richard Harris, Omar Sharif, David Hemmings, Anthony Hopkins, Shirley Knight, Ian Holm, Roy Kinnear, Freddie Jones; ***D:*** Richard Lester. *MGM, FOX*

The Juggler of Notre Dame 🦴🦴½ **1984** A hobo and a street juggler embark on an unusual journey that will change the lives of the people they meet. Based on a medieval folktale about the special gift given to the Virgin Mary on Christmas morning. **110m/C VHS, Beta.** Carl Carlson, Patrick Collins, Melinda Dillon, Merlin Olsen, Gene Roche. *PAU*

Juice 🦴🦴½ **1992 (R)** Day-to-day street life of four Harlem youths as they try to earn respect ("juice") in their neighborhood. Q, an aspiring deejay, is talked into a robbery by his friends but everything takes a turn for the worse when one of the others, Bishop, gets hold of a gun. The gritty look and feel of the drama comes naturally to Dickerson in his directorial debut. Prior to his first film, Dickerson served as cinematographer for Spike Lee's "Do the Right Thing" and "Jungle Fever." **95m/C VHS.** Omar Epps, Jermaine Hopkins, Tupac Shakur, Khalil Kain, Cindy Herron, Vincent Laresca, Samuel L. Jackson; ***D:*** Ernest R. Dickerson; ***W:*** Gerard Brown, Ernest R. Dickerson. *PAR*

Juke Joint 🦴½ **1947** "Amos 'n Andy" star Spencer Williams acted in and directed this tale of two men who arrive in Hollywood with only 25 cents between them. Features an all-black cast and musical numbers. **60m/B VHS, Beta.** Spencer Williams Jr., Judy Jones, Mantan Moreland; ***D:*** Spencer Williams Jr. *NOS, VCN, DVT*

Jules and Jim 🦴🦴🦴🦴 *Jules et Jim* **1962** Beautiful film with perfect casting, particularly Moreau. Spanning from 1912 to 1932, it is the story of a friendship between two men and their twenty-year love for the same woman. Werner is the shy German Jew and Serre the fun-loving Frenchman, who meet as students. The two men discover and woo the bohemian, destructive Moreau, although it is Werner she marries. After WWI, the friends are reunited but the marriage of Moreau and Werner is in trouble and she has an affair with Serre, which leads to tragedy for all three. Adapted from the novel by Henri-Pierre Roche. In French with English subtitles. **104m/B VHS, Beta, LV.** *FR* Jeanne Moreau, Oskar Werner, Henri Serre, Marie DuBois, Vanna Urbino; ***D:*** Francois Truffaut; ***W:*** Jean Gruault; ***M:*** Georges Delerue. *HMV, APD, FOX*

Julia 🦴🦴🦴½ **1977 (PG)** The story recounted in Lillian Hellman's fictional memoir "Pentimento." Fonda plays Hellman as she risks her life smuggling money into Germany during WWII for the sake of Julia, her beloved childhood friend (Redgrave), who is working in the Resistance. All cast members shine in their performances; watch for Streep in her screen debut. **118m/C VHS, Beta, LV.** Jane Fonda, Jason Robards Jr., Vanessa Redgrave, Maximilian Schell, Hal Holbrook, Rosemary Murphy, Meryl Streep, Lisa Pelikan; ***D:*** Fred Zinnemann; ***W:*** Alvin Sargent; ***M:*** Georges Delerue. Academy Awards '77: Best Adapted Screenplay, Best Supporting Actor (Robards), Best Supporting Actress (Redgrave); Golden Globe Awards '78: Best Actress—Drama (Fonda), Best Supporting Actress (Redgrave); National Board of Review Awards '77: 10 Best Films of the Year; New York Film Critics Awards '77: Best Supporting Actor (Schell); Writers Guild of America '77: Best Adapted Screenplay; Nominations: Academy Awards '77: Best Actress (Fonda), Best Cinematography, Best Costume Design, Best Director (Zinnemann), Best Film Editing, Best Picture, Best Supporting Actor (Schell), Best Original Score. *FOX, BTV*

Julia and Julia 🦴🦴½ **1987 (R)** A beautiful American woman in Trieste is tossed between two seemingly parallel dimensions, one in which her husband died six years earlier in a car crash, and the other in which he didn't. A purposefully obscure Italian-made psychological thriller, filmed in high-definition video and then transferred to film stock, it has a very different look and feel from other films of the genre. Intriguing and engaging most of the time, slow moving and confusing some of the time, it ultimately challenges but fails adequately to reward the viewer. **98m/C VHS, Beta, LV.** Kathleen Turner, Sting, Gabriel Byrne, Gabriele Ferzetti, Angela Goodwin; ***D:*** Peter Del Monte; ***W:*** Peter Del Monte; ***M:*** Maurice Jarre. *FOX*

Julia Has Two Lovers 🦴🦴 **1991 (R)** Minimalist comedy-drama about a woman torn between two men—her dull fiance and a mysterious phone caller. Mostly a long phone conversation; don't expect blistering action. **87m/C VHS.** Daphna Kastner, David Duchovny, David Charles; ***D:*** Bashar Shbib. *HMD*

Julia Misbehaves 🦴🦴🦴 **1948** Charming comedy that has Garson returning to ex-husband Pidgeon and daughter Taylor after an 18-year absence. Taylor is about to be married at a chateau in France and wants Garson to be there. While traveling to France from England, Garson encounters a bunch of colorful circus characters who are taking their act to Paris. Wonderful slapstick scenes give the stars a chance to have some real fun. Based on the novel "The Nutmeg Tree" by Margery Sharp. **99m/B VHS.** Greer Garson, Walter Pidgeon, Peter Lawford, Cesar Romero, Elizabeth Taylor, Lucile Watson, Nigel Bruce, Mary Boland, Reginald Owen, Veda Ann Borg, Joi Lansing; ***D:*** Jack Conway. *MGM*

Juliet of the Spirits 🦴🦴🦴 *Giulietta Degli Spiriti* **1965** Fellini uses the sparse story of a woman (Fellini's real-life wife) deliberating over her husband's possible infidelity to create a wild, often senseless surrealistic film. With a highly symbolic internal logic and complex imagery, Fellini's fantasy ostensibly elucidates the inner life of a modern woman. In Italian with English subtitles. **142m/C VHS, Beta, LV.** *IT* Giulietta Masina, Valentina Cortese, Sylva Koscina, Mario Pisu; ***D:*** Federico Fellini; ***W:*** Federico Fellini, Tullio Pinelli, Ennio Flaiano, Brunello Rondi; ***M:*** Nino Rota. National Board of Review Awards '65: 5 Best Foreign Films of the Year; New York Film Critics Awards '65: Best Foreign Film; Nominations: Academy Awards '66: Best Art Direction/Set Decoration (Color), Best Costume Design (Color). *VYY, MRV, VDM*

Julius Caesar 🦴🦴🦴½ **1953** All-star version of the Shakespearean tragedy, heavily acclaimed and deservedly so. Working directly from the original Shakespeare, director Mankiewicz produced a lifelike, yet poetic production. **121m/B VHS, Beta, LV.** James Mason, Marlon Brando, John Gielgud, Greer Garson, Deborah Kerr, Louis Calhern, Edmond O'Brien, George Macready, John Hoyt, Michael Pate; ***D:*** Joseph L. Mankiewicz; ***W:*** Joseph L. Mankiewicz; ***C:*** Joseph Ruttenberg; ***M:*** Miklos Rozsa. Academy Awards '53: Best Art Direction/Set Decoration (B & W); British Academy Awards '53: Best Actor (Brando), Best Actor (Gielgud); Nominations: Academy Awards '53: Best Actor (Brando), Best Black and White Cinematography, Best Picture, Best Original Score. *MGM*

Julius Caesar 🦴🦴 **1970** Subpar adaptation of the Shakespeare play about political greed and corruption within the Roman Empire. **116m/C VHS, Beta.** *GB* Charlton Heston, John Gielgud, Jason Robards Jr., Richard Chamberlain, Robert Vaughn, Diana Rigg; ***D:*** Stuart Burge. *NOS, REP, APD*

July Group 🦴½ **197?** A Quaker family's peaceful existence is threatened when kidnappers invade their home and hold them for ransom. **75m/C VHS, Beta.** Nicholas Campbell, Calvin Butler, Maury Chaykin. *TWE*

Jumanji 🦴🦴½ **1995 (PG)** For the past 26 years Alan Parish (Williams) has been stuck in the netherworld of Jumanji, a jungle-themed board game that sucks players into its alternate universe. When unsuspecting youngsters Judy (Dunst) and Peter (Pierce) happen upon the game and begin to play, they release Williams and a jungle full of rampaging beasts from the game and into the present. Loosely based on Chris Van Allsburg's children's book, the film version relies too heavily on cutting-edge special effects to make up for a thin story. Many of the creatures and effects are utterly too bizarre and unsettling for younger audiences. With a $65 million pricetag, Jumanji is definitely a roll of the dice. **104m/C VHS, LV.** Robin Williams, Kirsten Dunst, Bonnie Hunt, Bradley Michael Pierce, Bebe Neuwirth, Jonathan Hyde, David Alan Grier; ***D:*** Joe Johnston; ***W:*** Jonathan Hensleigh; ***C:*** Thomas Ackerman; ***M:*** James Horner. *COL*

The Jumper 🦴🦴½ *Der Todesspringer* **1985** An abstract, theatrical narrative about a cast of tragicomic characters floundering through their meaningless lives. In German with English subtitles. **90m/C VHS, Beta.** *GE* ***D:*** Benno Trachtmann. *FCT, VCD, GLV*

Jumpin' at the Boneyard 🦴🦴 **1992 (R)** Gritty family drama about the trials of two dispossessed brothers, set on the streets of New York. Deeply depressed, out-of-work, divorced Manny hates his recently deceased father, adores his mother, and is estranged from his younger brother, Danny. Danny is a scared crack addict who's supported by a hooker/girlfriend. The two brothers reunite for a trip into their scarred past when Danny tries to rob his brother's apartment to get dope money. Manny starts to believe that the only way to redeem his own life is to get his brother into a rehab program. Good acting helps to overcome some script weaknesses but this is one depressing movie. **107m/C VHS, LV.** Tim Roth, Alexis Arquette, Danitra Vance, Samuel L. Jackson, Kathleen Chalfant, Luis Guzman; ***D:*** Jeff Stanzler; ***W:*** Jeff Stanzler. *FXV*

Jumpin' Jack Flash 🦴🦴½ **1986 (R)** A bank worker is humorously embroiled in international espionage when her computer terminal picks up distress signals from a British agent in Russia. Marshall's directing debut. Good performances from a fun cast and a particularly energetic effort by Goldberg are held back by an average and predictable script. **98m/C VHS, Beta, LV.** Whoopi Goldberg, Stephen Collins, Carol Kane, Annie Potts, Jonathan Pryce, James Belushi, Jon Lovitz, John Wood; ***Cameos:*** Michael McKean, Tracey Ullman, Roscoe Lee Browne, Sara Botsford, Jeroen Krabbe, Phil Hartman, Tracy Reiner, Paxton Whitehead, Jamey Sheridan, Garry Marshall, Peter Michael Goetz; ***D:*** Penny Marshall; ***W:*** David Franzoni; ***M:*** Thomas Newman. *FOX, OM*

Jumping Jacks 🦴🦴 **1952** Martin and Lewis are a couple of nightclub performers who wind up in the paratroop corps instead of performing their act for the soldiers. Martin gets to sing and Lewis gets to parachute into enemy territory and capture a general. **96m/B VHS, LV.** Dean Martin, Jerry Lewis, Mona Freeman, Don DeFore, Robert Strauss, Ray Teal; ***D:*** Norman Taurog; ***C:*** Daniel F. Fapp. *PAR*

Junction 88 🦴 **1940** Early all-black musical chock full of great dancing and hot music. **60m/B VHS, Beta.** Noble Sissle, Bob Howard. *NOS, DVT*

June Bride 🦴🦴🦴 **1948** Fast-paced and entertaining comedy in which Davis and Montgomery are teamed up as magazine writers. A hilarious battle of the sexes erupts as they're sent to Indiana to do a feature story on June brides. Look for Debbie Reynolds in her film debut. **97m/B VHS.** Bette Davis, Robert Montgomery, Fay Bainter, Betty Lynn, Tom Tully, Barbara Bates, Jerome Cowan, Mary Wickes; ***D:*** Bretaigne Windust; ***W:*** Ranald MacDougall. *MGM*

June Night 🦴🦴 *Juninatten* **1940** A woman who was victimized by a shooting incident cannot escape the public eye due to her former promiscuous behavior. In Swedish with English subtitles. **90m/C VHS, Beta, LV.** *SW* Ingrid Bergman, Marianne Lofgren, Gunnar Sjoberg, Olaf Widgren; ***D:*** Per Lindberg. *WAC, TPV, LUM*

Jungle 🦴 **1952** A princess and an American adventurer lead an expedition into the Indian wilds to discover the source of recent elephant attacks. **74m/B VHS, Beta, LV.** Rod Cameron, Cesar Romero, Marie Windsor; ***D:*** William (Lester Williams) Berke; ***C:*** Clyde De Vinna. *NO*

Jungle Assault 1989 Two Vietnam vets with nothing left to lose are called back into the bloodiest action of their lives. Their assignment is to locate and destroy a terrorist base and bring back an American general's brainwashed daughter. **86m/C VHS, Beta.** William Smith, Ted Prior, William Zipp; ***D:*** David A. Prior. *AIP*

The Jungle Book *Rudyard Kipling's Jungle Book* **1942** A lavish version of Rudyard Kipling's stories about Mowgli, the boy raised by wolves in the jungles of India. **109m/C VHS, LV.** Sabu, Joseph Calleia, Rosemary DeCamp, Ralph Byrd, John Qualen; ***D:*** Zoltan Korda; ***C:*** Lee Garmes; ***M:*** Miklos Rozsa. *CNG, MRV, REP*

The Jungle Book 1967 Based on Kipling's classic, a young boy raised by wolves must choose between his jungle friends and human "civilization." Along the way he meets a variety of jungle characters including zany King Louie, kind-hearted Baloo, wise Bagherra and the evil Shere Khan. Great, classic songs including "Trust in Me," "I Wanna Be Like You," and Oscar-nominated "Bare Necessities." Last Disney feature overseen by Uncle Walt himself and a must for kids of all ages. **78m/C VHS, Beta, LV.** ***D:*** Wolfgang Reitherman; ***M:*** George Bruns; ***V:*** Phil Harris, Sebastian Cabot, Louis Prima, George Sanders, Sterling Holloway, J. Pat O'Malley, Verna Felton, Darlene Carr. Nominations: Academy Awards '67: Best Song ("The Bare Necessities"). *DIS, TOU, FCT*

Jungle Bride ½ **1933** Three people are shipwrecked and one of them is a suspected murderer. **66m/B VHS, Beta, LV.** Anita Page, Charles Starrett. *SNC, NOS, VYY*

Jungle Drums of Africa *U-238 and the Witch Doctor* **1953** Jungle adventures abound as Moore and Coates encounter lions, wind tunnels, voodoo and enemy agents in deepest Africa. A 12-episode serial re-edited onto two cassettes. **167m/B VHS.** Clayton Moore, Phyllis Coates, Roy Glenn, John Cason; ***D:*** Fred Brannon. *REP, MLB*

Jungle Fever **1991 (R)** Married black architect's affair with his white secretary provides the backdrop for a cold look at interracial love. Focuses more on the discomfort of friends and families than with the intense world created by the lovers for themselves. Provides the quota of humor and fresh insight we expect from Lee, but none of the joyous sexuality experienced by the lovers in "She's Gotta Have It." In fact, Lee tells viewers that interracial love is unnatural, never more than skin deep, never more than a blind obsession with the allure of the opposite race. Very fine cast but if you don't agree with Lee, a real disappointment as well. **131m/C VHS, Beta, LV.** Wesley Snipes, Annabella Sciorra, John Turturro, Samuel L. Jackson, Ossie Davis, Ruby Dee, Lonette McKee, Anthony Quinn, Spike Lee, Halle Berry, Tyra Ferrell, Veronica Webb, Frank Vincent, Tim Robbins, Brad Dourif; ***D:*** Spike Lee; ***W:*** Spike Lee; ***M:*** Terence Blanchard. National Board of Review Awards '91: 10 Best Films of the Year; New York Film Critics Awards '91: Best Supporting Actor (Jackson). *MCA, CCB, FCT*

Jungle Goddess ½ **1949** Two mercenaries set out for the reward offered for finding a wealthy heiress last seen in the jungles of Africa. **61m/B VHS, Beta, LV.** George Reeves, Wanda McKay, Ralph Byrd, Armida; ***D:*** Lewis D. Collins. *NO*

Jungle Heat ½ *Dance of the Dwarfs* **1984 (PG)** While searching for a pygmy tribe, an anthropologist and her pilot run into a pack of anthropoid mutants. **93m/C VHS, Beta.** Peter Fonda, Deborah Raffin; ***D:*** Gus Trikonis. *TWE*

Jungle Hell 1955 Sabu comes to the rescue of an Indian tribe being harassed by flying saucers, death rays and radioactive debris. **?m/B VHS, Beta.** Sabu, David Bruce, George E. Stone, K.T. Stevens; ***D:*** Norman A. Cerf. *SNC*

Jungle Holocaust 1985 One member of a scientific team survives an attack by a cannibal tribe and in an effort of self-preservation becomes one of them. **90m/C VHS, Beta.** *VCD*

Jungle Inferno 197? Nature boy, a fugitive from the government, fights lions, tigers and pursuing feds in this story of escape and survival. **90m/C VHS, Beta.** Brad Harris. *NO*

Jungle Master 1956 Noble British types hunt for Karzan, the jungle's number one guy, with the aid of a tribal priestess and a lovely photo-journalist. Must see for trash movie fans. **90m/C VHS, Beta.** John Kitzmiller, Simone Blondell, Edward Mann; ***D:*** Miles Deem. *NO*

Jungle Patrol ½ **1948** In 1943 New Guinea, a squadron of entrapped fliers are confronted with a beautiful USO entertainer. Romance and show tunes follow. **72m/B VHS, Beta.** Kristine Miller, Arthur Franz, Richard Jaeckel, Ross Ford, Tommy Noonan, Gene Reynolds; ***D:*** Joseph M. Newman. *NO*

Jungle Raiders ½ *Legenda Del Rudio Malese; Captain Yankee* **1985 (PG-13)** An Indiana Jones-esque mercenary searches the steamy jungles of Malaysia for a valuable jewel, the Ruby of Gloom. **102m/C VHS, Beta.** Lee Van Cleef, Christopher Connelly, Marina Costa; ***D:*** Anthony (Antonio Margheriti) Dawson. *MGM*

Jungle Siren 1942 Nazis in Africa try to foment rebellion amongst the black natives against the white residents. Crabbe and a white woman raised in the jungle set things right. **68m/B VHS, Beta.** Ann Corio, Buster Crabbe, Evelyn Wahl, Milton Kibbee; ***D:*** Sam Newfield. *SNC, MLB*

The Jungle Trap 1954 Steve Davis thought he could escape his past living in Africa. However, when the judge who wrongly sentenced his brother to death arrives, he plots revenge. **30m/B VHS.** Ronald Reagan. *RHI*

Jungle Warriors ½ **1984 (R)** Seven fashion models are abducted by a Peruvian cocaine dealer. To escape him, they must become Jungle Warriors. **96m/C VHS, Beta.** *GE MX* Sybil Danning, Marjoe Gortner, Nina Van Pallandt, Paul Smith, John Vernon, Alex Cord, Woody Strode, Kai Wulff; ***D:*** Ernst R. von Theumer. *MED*

Jungleground ½ **1995 (R)** Jungleground is a urban wasteland controlled by rival gangs. Lt. Jake Cornel (Piper) gets caught in a shoot-out when a sting operation goes bad and winds up before psychotic gang leader Odin. Odin offers him one chance—Cornel's going to be hunted in Jungleground's abandoned streets and if he can escape before dawn, he gets to live. **90m/C VHS, LV.** Roddy Piper, Torri Higginson, Peter Williams; ***D:*** Don Allan; ***W:*** Michael Stokes. *TRI*

Junior *Woof!* **1986** A raving, drooling lunatic cuts up girls with a chainsaw. **80m/C VHS, Beta.** Suzanne DeLaurentis, Linda Singer, Jeremy Ruthford, Michael McKeever. *PSM*

Junior **1994 (PG-13)** Out of the way women! Schwarzenegger trades the war room for the delivery room to experience the miracle of birth. As scientists, he and DeVito take a dip in the gene pool once again to test an anti-miscarriage drug. Thompson provides the egg and some surprisingly good physical comedy as the klutzy cryogenics expert who moves into their university digs. Every pregnancy cliche is explored as Schwarzenegger and DeVito bring the concept to term. Sorry, action fans...nothing blows up except Arnold. **109m/C VHS, LV.** Arnold Schwarzenegger, Danny DeVito, Emma Thompson, Frank Langella, Pamela Reed, Judy Collins, James Eckhouse, Aida Turturro; ***D:*** Ivan Reitman; ***W:*** Kevin Wade, Chris Conrad; ***M:*** James Newton Howard. Nominations: Academy Awards '94: Best Song ("Look What Love Has Done"); Golden Globe Awards '95: Best Actor—Musical/Comedy (Schwarzenegger), Best Actress—Musical/Comedy (Thompson), Best Song ("Look What Love Has Done"). *MCA*

Junior Bonner **1972 (PG)** A rowdy modern-day western about a young drifting rodeo star who decides to raise money for his father's new ranch by challenging a formidable bull. **100m/C VHS, Beta.** Steve McQueen, Robert Preston, Ida Lupino, Ben Johnson, Joe Don Baker, Barbara Leigh; ***D:*** Sam Peckinpah; ***C:*** Lucien Ballard. *FOX*

Junior G-Men **1940** The Dead End Kids fight Fifth Columnists who are trying to sabotage America's war effort. Twelve episodes. **237m/B VHS, Beta.** Billy Halop, Huntz Hall. *VYY, VCN, NOS*

Junior G-Men of the Air ½ **1942** The Dead End Kids become teen-age flyboys in this twelve-episode serial adventure. **215m/B VHS, Beta.** Billy Halop, Huntz Hall. *SNC, NOS, MED*

Junior High School ½ **1978** A comically, on target film detailing the romantic yearnings, petty cruelties, and claustrophobia of 8th grade existence. **60m/C VHS, Beta.** Paula Abdul. *PIC*

The Juniper Tree ½ **1987** Based on a tale by the Brothers Grimm, this Icelandic curio finds sisters Margit (Bjork) and Katla (Bragadottir) fleeing across the medieval countryside after their mother is burned at the stake for witchcraft. The sisters have their own special powers, which they turn on each other when they become romantic rivals over a young widower (Flygenring). **78m/B VHS.** *IC* Bjork, Bryndis Petra Bragadottir, Vladimar Orn Flygenring; ***D:*** Nietzchka Keene. *RHI*

The Junkman ½ **1982 (R)** Movie maker whose new film is about to be premiered is being chased by a mysterious killer. Promoted as "the ultimate car chase film" since the production used and destroyed over 150 automobiles. From the makers of "Gone in 60 Seconds." **97m/C VHS, Beta.** H.B. Halicki, Christopher Stone, Susan Shaw, Hoyt Axton, Lynda Day George; ***D:*** H.B. Halicki. *TWE*

Juno and the Paycock ½ **1930** Perhaps if Hitchcock hadn't been so faithful to O'Casey this early effort would have been less stagey and more entertaining. In Dublin during the civil uprising, a poor family is torn apart when they receive news of an imminent fortune. Hitchcock's reported to have said that "drama is life with the dull bits left out," though here too many dull bits remain. **96m/B VHS.** Sara Allgood, Edward Chapman, John Longden, John Laurie, Maire O'Neill; ***D:*** Alfred Hitchcock; ***W:*** Alfred Hitchcock. *NOS, VEC, HHT*

Jupiter's Darling **1955** This spoof of Hannibal (Keel) and Amytis (Williams) gravely misses the mark in making funny the world of the Roman Empire. Amytis has the job of distracting Hannibal from attacking the Eternal City, and does so through musical interludes and unfunny jokes. ♫I Have A Dream; If This Be Slav'ry; I Never Trust A Woman; Hannibal's Victory March; Don't Let This Night Get Away; The Life Of An Elephant; Horatio's Narration. **96m/C LV.** Esther Williams, Howard Keel, George Sanders, Gower Champion, Marge Champion, Norma Varden, Richard Haydn, William Demarest, Douglass Dumbrille, Michael Ansara, Martha Wentworth, Chris Alcaide, William Tannen; ***D:*** George Sidney; ***C:*** Charles Rosher. *MGM*

Jupiter's Thigh ½ **1981** A madcap married pair of treasure-hunters honeymoon in Greece in search of an ancient statue's lost thigh. Available in French with English subtitles, or dubbed into English. **96m/C VHS, Beta.** *FR* Annie Girardot, Philippe Noiret; ***D:*** Philippe de Broca. *SUE, FCT*

Jurassic Park ½ **1993 (PG-13)** Crichton's spine-tingling thriller translates well (but not faithfully) due to its main attraction: realistic, rampaging dinosaurs. Genetically cloned from prehistoric DNA, all is well until they escape from their pens—smarter and less predictable than expected. Contrived plot and thin characters (except Goldblum), but who cares? The true stars are the dinos, an incredible combination of models and computer animation. Violent, suspenseful, and realistic with gory attack scenes. Not for small kids, though much of the marketing is aimed at them. Spielberg knocked his own "E.T." out of first place as "JP" became the highest grossing movie of all time. Also available in a letterbox version. **127m/C VHS, LV.** Sam Neill, Laura Dern, Jeff Goldblum, Richard Attenborough, Bob Peck, Martin Ferrero, B.D. Wong, Joseph Mazzello, Ariana Richards, Samuel L. Jackson, Wayne Knight; ***D:*** Steven Spielberg; ***W:*** David Koepp, Michael Crichton; ***C:*** Dean Cundey; ***M:*** John Williams; ***V:*** Richard Kiley. Academy Awards '93: Best Sound, Best

Sound Effects Editing, Best Visual Effects; Nominations: MTV Movie Awards '94: Best Film, Best Villain (T-Rex), Best Action Sequence. *MCA*

The Juror 🦴½ **1996 (R)** Plucky single mom (Moore) ends up on the jury in the trial of a powerful mobster and draws the attention of the smooth enforcer (Baldwin) who muscles her into providing a certain verdict. The usual good-vs.-evil, family-in-danger action ensues. Despite boasting a fine cast and impressive attention to detail, flick is guilty of ludicrous situations, a mechanical plot and a dopey ending. Based on the novel by George Dawes Green. **107m/C VHS, LV, 8mm.** Demi Moore, Alec Baldwin, Joseph Gordon-Levitt, Anne Heche, James Gandolfini, Lindsay Crouse, Tony LoBianco, Michael Constantine, Matt Craven; ***D:*** Brian Gibson; ***W:*** Ted Tally; ***C:*** Jamie Anderson; ***M:*** James Newton Howard. *COL*

Jury Duty 🦴 **1995 (PG-13)** Mama's boy loser Tommy Collins (Shore) gets jury duty on a serial-killer case and tries to keep what seems to be an open-and-shut case going so he can continue to get free room and board. He falls for babe juror Monica (Carrere) and really drags the trial (and the film) out in a pathetic attempt to woo her. Shore is even more annoying and unfunny than ever. Low-rent bastardization of "Twelve Angry Men" tries to pass off lame O.J references and Shore falling out of chairs as humor. Creates reasonable doubt as to Shore's talent and movie execs' judgement. **88m/C VHS, LV.** Pauly Shore, Tia Carrere, Shelley Winters, Brian Doyle-Murray, Abe Vigoda, Stanley Tucci, Charles Napier; ***Cameos:*** Andrew Dice Clay; ***D:*** John Fortenberry; ***W:*** Barbara Williams, Fax Bahr. Golden Raspberry Awards '95: Worst Actor (Shore). *COL*

Just a Gigolo 🦴🦴½ **1979 (R)** Bowie stars in this unusual melodrama about a Prussian war vet turned male prostitute. He spends most of his time working for the sexiest of women. Splendid cast, but a bit incoherent. **105m/C VHS, LV.** *GE* David Bowie, Sydne Rome, Kim Novak, David Hemmings, Maria Schell, Curt Jurgens, Marlene Dietrich; ***D:*** David Hemmings. *INJ, MOV, LUM*

Just Another Girl on the I.R.T. 🦴🦴½ **1993 (R)** Double debut from two African American women, writer/director Harris, and actress Johnson, captures the sass and wit of a girl from the projects. Seventeen-year-old Chantal has a plan for her life and challenges authority with assurance, even after an unexpected pregnancy puts a twist into her plan. Strong initial statement tends to become weak and cloudy as Chantal loses her focus. This doesn't dismiss the remarkable realism and raw talent portrayed in a picture filmed in just seventeen days for $130,000. Winner of a special jury prize at the Sundance Film Festival. **96m/C VHS, LV.** Ariyan Johnson, Kevin Thigpen, Ebony Jerido, Jerard Washington, Chequita Jackson, William Badget; ***D:*** Leslie Harris; ***W:*** Leslie Harris. Sundance Film Festival '93: Special Jury Prize; Nominations: Independent Spirit Awards '94: Best Actress (Johnson). *LIV, FCT*

Just Another Pretty Face 🦴🦴½ *Be Beautiful but Shut Up* **1958** An aging detective catches a gang of jewel smugglers, and gets involved with their young moll. In French with English subtitles. **110m/B VHS, Beta.** *FR* Henri Vidal, Mylene Demongeot, Isa Miranda; ***D:*** Henri Verneuil. *FCT, INJ*

Just Around the Corner 🦴½ **1938 (G)** Temple helps her Depression-poor father get a job after she befriends a cantankerous millionaire. Temple duets with Bill "Bojangles" Robinson with the fourth time. Also available colorized. ♫This Is A Happy Little Ditty; I'm Not Myself Today; I'll Be Lucky With You; Just Around the Corner; I Love To Walk in the Rain; Brass Buttons and Epaulets. **71m/B VHS.** Shirley Temple, Charles Farrell, Bert Lahr, Joan Davis, Bill Robinson, Cora Witherspoon, Franklin Pangborn; ***D:*** Irving Cummings. *FXV*

Just Before Dawn 🦴🦴 **1980 (R)** Another murderers stalk campers story; humans resort to their animal instincts in their struggle for survival. Not to be confused with the William Castle film (1946) from the "Crime Doctor" series. **90m/C VHS, Beta.** Chris Lemmon, Deborah Benson, Greg Henry, George Kennedy; ***D:*** Jeff Lieberman; ***M:*** Brad Fiedel. *NO*

Just Between Friends 🦴🦴 **1986 (PG-13)** Two women become friends, not knowing that one is having an affair with the husband of the other. Allan Burns directorial debut. **110m/C VHS, Beta.** Mary Tyler Moore, Christine Lahti, Sam Waterston, Ted Danson, Jim MacKrell, Jane Greer; ***D:*** Allan Burns; ***W:*** Allan Burns. *NO*

Just Cause 🦴🦴 **1994 (R)** Incoherent mystery/thriller set in the Florida Everglades. Retired attorney, Paul Armstrong, now a Harvard law professor, decides to defend Bobby Earl (Underwood), on death row for the murder of a white girl. As Armstrong investigates the case, he discovers that the arresting officer Tanny Brown, (Fishburne) is corrupt and tortured the confession out of Bobby. Starts off promising with the electricity of Connery's and Fishburne's presence and a frigthening cameo by Ed Harris as an incarcerated serial killer, but once the barrage of plot twists start, creating gator size holes in the plot, the movie drifts into a murkey swamp of absurdity. Adapted from the legal thriller by John Katzenbach. **102m/C VHS, LV.** Sean Connery, Laurence "Larry" Fishburne, Kate Capshaw, Blair Underwood, Ruby Dee, Daniel J. Travanti, Ned Beatty, Lynne Thigpen, George Plimpton, Chris Sarandon, Kevin McCarthy, Ed Harris; ***D:*** Arne Glimcher; ***W:*** Jeb Stuart, Robert Stone; ***C:*** Lajos Koltai; ***M:*** James Newton Howard. *WAR*

Just for the Hell of It *Woof! Destruction, Inc* **1968** A quartet of teenage punks ruthlessly terrorize their suburban Miami 'hood while an innocent kid gets blamed. More exploitation from schlock king Lewis, who also wrote the theme song, "Destruction Inc" (pic's alternate title). Essentially the same cast as the director's "She Devils on Wheels," filmed simultaneously. **85m/C VHS.** Rodney Bedell, Ray Sager, Nancy Lee Noble, Agi Gyenes, Steve White; ***D:*** Herschell Gordon Lewis. *NO*

Just for You 🦴🦴½ **1952** Entertaining musical about producer Crosby who doesn't have time for his kids until Wyman steps in and shows him the way. Based on Stephen Vincent Benet's novel "Famous." ♫Zing A Little Zong; He's Just Crazy For Me; The Live Oak Tree; A Flight of Fancy; I'll Si-Si Ya In Bahia; On the 10:10; Just for You. **95m/C VHS.** Bing Crosby, Jane Wyman, Ethel Barrymore, Robert Arthur, Natalie Wood, Cora Witherspoon; ***D:*** Elliott Nugent; ***W:*** Robert Carson. *PAR*

Just Like a Woman 🦴🦴 **1995 (R)** Sweet-natured film about an unlikely romance with some decided quirks. Young American Gerald (Pasdar) is working for a London bank and renting a flat from lonely older divorcee Monica (Walters). Ideal tenant Gerald is also recently divorced and a mutual attraction develops, in fact Gerald trusts Monica enough to confess his darkest secret—seems his marriage broke up over women's lingerie—the ones Gerald likes to wear when he cross-dresses in his female persona of Geraldine. Does this put Monica off? Well, she turns out to be very understanding indeed. Based on the memoir "Geraldine" by Monica Jay. **102m/C VHS.** *GB* Adrian Pasdar, Julie Walters, Paul Freeman, Susan Wooldridge, Gordon Kennedy; ***D:*** Christopher Monger; ***W:*** Nick Evans; ***C:*** Alan Hume; ***M:*** Michael Storey. *HMK*

Just Like Weather 🦴🦴🦴 **1986** Contemporary Hong Kong and the city's looming return to control by mainland China provide the backdrop for the troubled marriage of a young couple. Couple endure abortion, arrest, and veterinarian episodes before departing for on U.S. trip with high hopes. **98m/C VHS.** *HK* Christine Lee, Lee Chi-Keung, Allen Fong; ***D:*** Allen Fong. *FCT*

Just Me & You 🦴½ **1978** An "It Happened One Night" made-for-television tale of an unlikely couple who fall in love with each other when chance brings them together on a cross-country drive. **100m/C VHS, Beta.** Louise Lasser, Charles Grodin; ***D:*** Charles Erman; ***W:*** Louise Lasser. *NO*

Just One of the Girls 🦴½ **1993 (R)** Teen star Haim transfers to a new high school where he dresses in drag in order to avoid the itinerant leader of the school's toughest gang whom he has unwittingly enraged. Palling around with Eggert becomes one of his costume's unexpected perks. Sort of a cross between "Some Like it Hot" and "90210." **94m/C VHS, LV.** Corey Haim, Nicole Eggert, Cameron Bancroft; ***D:*** Michael Keusch; ***M:*** Amin Bhatia. *VMK*

Just One of the Guys 🦴🦴 **1985 (PG-13)** When the school newspaper refuses to accept the work of an attractive young girl, she goes undercover as a boy to prove that her work is good. She goes on to befriend the school's nerd, and even helps him grow out of his awkward stage, falling for him in the process. Very cute, but predictable. **100m/C VHS, Beta, LV.** Joyce Hyser, Clayton Rohner, Billy Jacoby, Toni Hudson, Leigh McCloskey, Sherilyn Fenn; ***D:*** Lisa Gottlieb. *COL*

Just Suppose 🦴🦴½ **1926** Prince in waiting decides he'd prefer the simple life, travels to the land of the free in search of honest work and is felled by cupid's arrow. All's well 'til duty calls, and his princely presence is expected back in the royal fold. Features beautiful boy Barthelmess, whom Lillian Gish described as having "the most beautiful face of any man who ever went before a camera." Silent. **90m/B VHS, Beta.** Richard Barthelmess, Lois Moran, Geoffrey Kerr, Henry Vibart, George Spelvin; ***D:*** Kenneth Webb. *GPV*

Just Tell Me What You Want 🦴🦴½ **1980 (R)** A wealthy, self-made married man finally drives his longtime mistress away when he refuses to let her take over the operation of a failing movie studio he has acquired. After she falls for another man, the tycoon does everything he can to win her back. The department store battle between MacGraw and King is priceless. **112m/C VHS, Beta.** Alan King, Ali MacGraw, Myrna Loy, Keenan Wynn, Tony Roberts; ***D:*** Sidney Lumet; ***W:*** Jay Presson Allen; ***C:*** Oswald Morris. *WAR*

Just Tell Me You Love Me 🦴 **1980 (PG)** Three budding con artists plot to make easy money in this Hawaiian romp. **90m/C VHS, Beta.** Robert Hegyes, Debralee Scott, Lisa Hartman Black, Ricci Martin, June Lockhart; ***D:*** Tony Mordente. *LIV, VES*

Just the Way You Are 🦴 **1984 (PG)** An attractive musician struggles to overcome a physical handicap and winds up falling in love while on vacation in the French Alps. **96m/C VHS, Beta.** Kristy McNichol, Robert Carradine, Kaki Hunter, Michael Ontkean, Alexandra Paul, Lance Guest, Timothy Daly, Patrick Cassidy; ***D:*** Edouard Molinaro; ***W:*** Allan Burns; ***M:*** Vladimir Cosma. *MGM*

Just William's Luck 🦴🦴 **1947** A precocious English brat sneaks into an old mansion, which just happens to be the headquarters for a gang of thieves. Based on British series of children's books. **87m/B VHS, Beta.** *GB* William A. Graham, Garry Marsh; ***D:*** Val Guest. *VYY*

Justice 🦴🦴 **1955** A crusading attorney tries to keep a waterfront kangaroo court from applying its harsh justice to an admitted killer. A television crime-drama also titled "Flight from Fear." **26m/B VHS, Beta.** William Prince, Jack Klugman, Biff McGuire, Jack Warden. *VYY*

Justice of the West 🦴 **1961** The Lone Ranger and his sidekick, Tonto, perform good deeds in the Old West, including helping to retrieve stolen gold, helping to build an Indian school, and giving a blind man a fresh perspective on life. **71m/C VHS, Beta.** Clayton Moore, Jay Silverheels; ***D:*** Earl Bellamy. *MGM*

Justice Rides Again 🦴½ **193?** Mix tries to uphold law and order, but he's up against some very tough outlaws. **55m/B VHS, Beta.** Tom Mix. *VCN*

Justin Morgan Had a Horse 🦴🦴 **1981** The true story of a colonial school teacher in post-Revolutionary War Vermont who first bred the Morgan horse, the first and most versatile American breed. **91m/C VHS, Beta.** Don Murray, Lana Wood, Gary Crosby; ***D:*** Hollingsworth Morse. *DIS*

Justine 1969 In the 1930s, a prostitute who marries an Egyptian banker becomes involved with a variety of men and a plot to arm Palestinian Jews in their revolt against English rule. A condensed film version of Lawrence Durrell's "The Alexandria Quartet." **115m/C VHS, Beta.** *IS* Anouk Aimee, Michael York, Dirk Bogarde, Philippe Noiret, Michael Constantine, John Vernon, Jack Albertson; ***D:*** George Cukor; ***W:*** Lawrence B. Marcus; ***C:*** Leon Shamroy; ***M:*** Jerry Goldsmith. *FOX, HHE*

K-9 ½ **1989 (PG-13)** After having his car destroyed by a drug dealer, "I work alone" Belushi is forced to take on a partner—a German Shepherd. Together they work to round up the bad guys and maybe chew on their shoes a little. Sometimes amusing one-joke comedy done in by a paper-thin script. Both the dog and Belushi are good, however. **111m/C VHS, Beta, LV.** James Belushi, Mel Harris, Kevin Tighe, Ed O'Neill, Cotter Smith, James Handy, Jerry Lee; ***D:*** Rod Daniel; ***W:*** Steven Siegel, Scott Myers; ***M:*** Miles Goodman. *MCA*

K-9000 **1989** The Hound salutes the idea behind this standard sci-fi crime-fighter; a cyberdog fights the forces of evil with the aid of a cop, a lady reporter, and the usual cliches. Made For television. **96m/C VHS.** Chris Mulkey, Catherine Oxenberg; ***D:*** Kim Manners; ***M:*** Jan Hammer. *FRH*

Kafka ½ **1991 (PG-13)** Disappointing and gloomy Soderbergh film that serves no purpose whatsoever. Irons plays Kafka, an insurance workers by day and a writer by night. The movie exists largely without interest until Kafka uncovers an office conspiracy and makes his way to the enemy's castle headquarters. From then on, "Kafka" is nothing but a conventional horror film. Irons is wasted in a role that requires nothing but an impeccable British accent. On the plus side, the film is exquisitely shot in black and white until the castle scenes, when the cinematography is switched to color. **100m/C VHS, Beta, LV.** Jeremy Irons, Theresa Russell, Joel Grey, Ian Holm, Jeroen Krabbe, Armin Mueller-Stahl, Alec Guinness, Brian Glover, Robert Flemyng; ***D:*** Steven Soderbergh; ***W:*** Lem Dobbs; ***C:*** Walt Lloyd. Independent Spirit Awards '92: Best Cinematography. *PAR, INJ, PMS*

Kagemusha ½ *The Shadow Warrior; The Double* **1980 (PG)** A thief is rescued from the gallows because of his striking resemblance to a warlord in 16th Century Japan. When the ambitious warlord is fatally wounded, the thief is required to pose as the warlord. In Japanese with English subtitles. **160m/C VHS, Beta, LV.** *JP* Tatsuya Nakadai, Tsutomu Yamazaki, Kenichi Hagiwara; ***D:*** Akira Kurosawa. British Academy Awards '80: Best Director (Kurosawa); Cannes Film Festival '80: Best Film; Cesar Awards '81: Best Foreign Film; National Board of Review Awards '80: 5 Best Foreign Films of the Year; Nominations: Academy Awards '80: Best Art Direction/Set Decoration, Best Foreign Language Film. *FOX, APD, INJ*

Kalifornia ½ **1993 (R)** "Badlands" meets the '90s in a road trip with the hitchhikers from hell. Early Grayce (Pitt) is your average slimeball who murders his landlord and hops a ride with his waifish girlfriend Adele (Lewis) from Kentucky to California with Brian (Duchovny), a yuppie writer interested in mass murderers, and his sultry photographer girlfriend Carrie (Forbes). Pitt and Lewis were still an item when they made this. Pitt reportedly wanted to play against type, and as pretty boy gone homicidal, he succeeds. Extremely violent and disturbing. Also available in an unrated version. **117m/C VHS, LV.** Brad Pitt, Juliette Lewis, David Duchovny, Michele Forbes, Sierra Pecheur, Lois Hall, Gregory Mars Martin; ***D:*** Dominic Sena; ***W:*** Tim Metcalfe; ***C:*** Bojan Bazelli; ***M:*** Carter Burwell. *PGV, BTV*

Kameradschaft ½ **1931** A great, early German sound film about Germans struggling to free themselves and French miners trapped underground on the countries' border. In German and French with English subtitles. **80m/B VHS, Beta.** *GE* Ernst Busch, Alexander Granach, Fritz Kampers; ***D:*** G.W. Pabst. National Board of Review Awards '32: 10 Best Films of the Year. *SUE, MRV, IHF*

Kamikaze **1945** A Japanese WWII action drama about suicide pilots. **100m/B VHS, Beta.** *JP VCD, RXM*

Kamikaze '89 **1983** German director Fassbinder has the lead acting role (his last) in this offbeat story of a police lieutenant in Berlin, circa 1989, who investigates a puzzling series of bombings. In German with English subtitles. **90m/C VHS, Beta.** *GE* Rainer Werner Fassbinder, Gunther Kaufman, Boy Gobert; ***D:*** Wolf Gremm; ***M:*** Tangerine Dream. *MGM, FCT, GLV*

Kamikaze Hearts **1991** A quasi-documentary set in the world of two lesbian-junkies (Sharon the actress and Tina the director/producer) making underground X-rated movies. **80m/C VHS.** Sharon Mitchell, Tina "Tigr" Mennett; ***D:*** Juliet Bashore; ***W:*** Tina "Tigr" Mennett. *FCT*

Kanal ½ *They Loved Life* **1956** Wajda's first major success, a grueling account of Warsaw patriots, upon the onset of the Nazis toward the end of the war, fleeing through the ruined city's sewers. Highly acclaimed. Part 2 of Wajda's "War Trilogy," preceded by "A Generation" and followed by "Ashes and Diamonds." In Polish with English subtitles or dubbed. **96m/B VHS, Beta.** *PL* Teresa Izewska, Tadeusz Janczar; ***D:*** Andrzej Wajda. Cannes Film Festival '57: Grand Jury Prize. *ING, NLC, HMV*

Kandyland **1987 (R)** An over-the-hill stripper takes a young innocent stripper under her wing. **94m/C VHS, Beta, LV.** Sandahl Bergman, Kimberly Evenson, Charles Laulette, Bruce Baum; ***D:*** Robert Allen Schnitzer. *VTR, NWV*

Kangaroo **1986 (R)** An Australian adaptation of the semi-autobiographical D.H. Lawrence novel. A controversial English novelist and his wife move to the Outback in 1922, and are confronted with all manner of prejudice and temptation. **115m/C VHS, Beta.** *AU* Judy Davis, Colin Friels, John Walton, Hugh Keays-Byrne, Julie Nihill; ***D:*** Tim Burstall; ***W:*** Evan Jones; ***M:*** Nathan Waks. Australian Film Institute '86: Best Actress (Davis). *MCA*

The Kansan **1943** The marshall in a Kansas town won't rest until he's stamped out all traces of corruption. **79m/B VHS, Beta.** Richard Dix, Victor Jory, Albert Dekker; ***D:*** George Archainbaud. Nominations: Academy Awards '43: Best Original Score. *NOS, MRV, HEG*

Kansas **1988 (R)** Two young men, one a lawless rebel, the other a rational loner, stage a bank heist, and then go on the lam. Lame plot and very weak acting combine to make this film a dud. **111m/C VHS, Beta, LV.** Matt Dillon, Andrew McCarthy, Leslie Hope, Kyra Sedgwick; ***D:*** David Stevens; ***M:*** Pino Donaggio. *MED*

Kansas City Confidential **1952** An ex-cop on the wrong side of the law launches a sophisticated armored car heist. A disgruntled ex-con gets arrested for the crime on circumstantial evidence. When released, he scours the underworld for the real thieves. **98m/B VHS.** John Payne, Coleen Gray, Preston Foster, Neville Brand, Lee Van Cleef, Jack Elam; ***D:*** Phil Karlson. *NOS, MGM, RXM*

Kansas City Massacre ½ **1975** A made-for-television film chronicling the efforts of Melvin Purvis, as he tracked down Depression-era hoods. First called "Melvin Purvis, G-Man." **99m/C VHS, Beta.** Dale Robertson, Sally Kirkland, Bo Hopkins, Scott Brady, Lynn Loring, Matt Clark, Mills Watson, Robert Walden; ***D:*** Dan Curtis. *VMK*

Kansas Pacific **1953** A group of Confederate sympathizers try to stop the Kansas Pacific Railroad from reaching the West Coast in the 1860s. **73m/C VHS, Beta.** Sterling Hayden, Eve Miller, Barton MacLane, Reed Hadley, Douglas Hadley; ***D:*** Ray Nazarro. *NOS, MRV, DVT*

The Kansas Terrors **1939** The "Three Mesquiteers" head for the Caribbean to deliver a herd of horses and wind up in a battle against local despot. **57m/B VHS.** Bob Livingston, Raymond Hatton, Duncan Renaldo, Jacqueline Wells, Yakima Canutt, Richard Alexander, Maureen McCormack; ***D:*** George Sherman. *NOS*

Kaos *Chaos-Kaos* **1985 (R)** The Taviani brothers adaptation of four stories by Luigi Pirandello ("The Other Son," "Moonstruck," "The Jar," and "Requiem"), which look at peasant life in Sicily, ranging from the comic to the tragic. A fictional epilog, "Conversing with Mother," has Pirandello talking with the spirit of his dead mother. As with any anthology some stories are stronger than others but all possess the Taviani's great visual style and some fine acting. In Italian with English subtitles. **188m/C VHS.** *IT* Margarita Lozano, Claudio Bigagli, Massimo Bonetti, Omero Antonutti, Enrica Maria Modugno, Ciccio Ingrassia, Franco Franchi, Biagio Barone, Salvatore Rossi, Franco Scaldati, Pasquale Spadola, Regina Bianchi; ***D:*** Paolo Taviani, Vittorio Taviani; ***W:*** Paolo Taviani, Vittorio Taviani, Tonino Guerra. *MGM, BTV*

Kapo **1959** A 14-year-old Jewish girl and her family are imprisoned by the Nazis in a concentration camp. There, the girl changes identities with the help of the camp doctor, and rises to the position of camp guard. She proceeds to become taken with her power until a friend commits suicide and jolts the girl back into harsh reality. An Academy Award nominee for Best Foreign Film (lost to "The Virgin Spring"). Primarily English dialogue, with subtitles for foreign language. **116m/B VHS.** *IT FR YU* Susan Strasberg, Laurent Terzieff, Emmanuelle Riva, Gianni "John" Garko; ***D:*** Gillo Pontecorvo; ***W:*** Gillo Pontecorvo. Nominations: Academy Awards '60: Best Foreign Language Film. *DVT, HEG*

Karate Cop ½ **1993 (R)** In a future without law or order John Travis (Marchini) is the last cop on earth. He saves Rachel, a beautiful scientist, from a band of scavengers and together they hunt for a hidden crystal with mysterious powers. Only first John has to defeat a gladiator in a martial arts fight to the death. **?m/C VHS, LV.** Ron Marchini, Carrie Chambers, David Carradine, Michael Bristow, D.W. Landingham, Michael Foley, Dana Bentley; ***D:*** Alan Roberts. *IMP, IME, VTR*

The Karate Kid ½ **1984 (PG)** A teenage boy finds out that Karate involves using more than your fists when a handyman agrees to teach him martial arts. The friendship that they develop is deep and sincere; the Karate is only an afterthought. From the director of the original "Rocky," this movie is easy to like. **126m/C VHS, Beta, LV, 8mm.** Ralph Macchio, Noriyuki "Pat" Morita, Elisabeth Shue, Randee Heller, Martin Kove, Chad McQueen; ***D:*** John G. Avildsen; ***W:*** Robert Mark Kamen; ***M:*** Bill Conti. Nominations: Academy Awards '84: Best Supporting Actor (Morita). *COL*

The Karate Kid: Part 2 ½ **1986 (PG)** Sequel to the first film wherein our high-kicking hero tests his mettle in real-life karate exchanges in Okinawa, and settles a long-standing score. Followed by a second sequel. **95m/C VHS, Beta, LV, 8mm.** Ralph Macchio, Noriyuki "Pat" Morita, Danny Kamekona, Martin Kove, Tamlyn Tomita, Nobu McCarthy, Yuji Okumoto; ***D:*** John G. Avildsen; ***W:*** Robert Mark Kamen; ***M:*** Bill Conti. Nominations: Academy Awards '86: Best Song ("Glory of Love"). *COL*

The Karate Kid: Part 3 ½ **1989 (PG)** Second sequel takes a tired plot and doesn't do much to perk it up. Macchio again battles an evil nemesis and learns about himself, but this time Morita refuses to be a part of his training until, of course, Macchio desperately needs his help. Followed by "The Next Karate Kid" which introduces a new kid—a girl. **105m/C VHS, Beta, LV, 8mm.** Ralph Macchio, Noriyuki "Pat" Morita, John G. Avildsen, Thomas Ian Griffith, Martin Kove, Sean Kanan, Robyn Elaine; ***D:*** John G. Avildsen; ***W:*** Robert Mark Kamen; ***M:*** Bill Conti. *COL*

Karate Polish Style **1982** Polish painter duo paint, plaster and draw blood. A sort of "Dances with Poles" in Warsaw's Mazurian Lake District. In Polish with English subtitles. Not a Polish joke. **91m/C VHS.** *PL* ***D:*** Jerzy Wojcik. *FCT*

Karate Warrior ½ **1988** Young martial artist is beaten and left for dead by Filipino crime syndicate. Bones mended, he prescribes a dose of their medicine. Plenty of rest and retaliation. **90m/C VHS, Beta.** Jared Martin, Ken Watanabe. *IMP*

Karate Warriors **197?** Chiba takes his battle against crime to the streets. **90m/C VHS, Beta.** Sonny Chiba. *NO*

Kashmiri Run 🦴🦴 **1969 (R)** Action adventure about trio on the lam from Chinese communists chasing them through Tibet. **101m/C VHS.** *SP* Pernell Roberts, Alexandra Bastedo, Julian Mateos, Gloria Gamata; ***D:*** John Peyser. *LIV*

Katherine 🦴 *The Radical* **1975** A young heiress rejects her pampered lifestyle and becomes a violent revolutionary, rebelling against social injustices and the system that spawned them. Made for television. **98m/C VHS, Beta, LV.** Sissy Spacek, Art Carney, Jane Wyatt, Henry Winkler, Julie Kavner, Hector Elias, Jenny Sullivan; ***D:*** Jeremy Paul Kagan. *VTR, NWV, IME*

Kavik the Wolf Dog 🦴½ *The Courage of Kavik, the Wolf Dog* **1984** Heartwarming story of a courageous dog's love and suffering for the boy he loves. Made for television. **99m/C VHS, Beta.** Ronny Cox, Linda Sorensen, Andrew Ian McMillian, Chris Wiggins, John Ireland; ***D:*** Peter Carter. *MED*

Kazaam 🦴🦴½ **1996 (PG)** Twelve-year-old Max (Capra) is having problems—bullies are chasing him and his single mom's just found a new boyfriend. But his luck seems ready to change when a battered boombox reveals a seven-foot rappin' genie named Kazaam (O'Neal). While Shaq isn't your typical leading man, the audience for this light-hearted film probably won't care. Director Glaser thought up the part for the tall guy just before he met him at an NBA All-Star Game. **?m/C VHS.** Francis Capra, Shaquille O'Neal, Ally Walker, John Costelloe; ***D:*** Paul Michael Glaser; ***W:*** Christian Ford, Roger Soffer. *NYR*

Keaton's Cop 🦴 **1990 (R)** Another cheap cop comedy involving the mistaken identity of an important mob witness. **95m/C VHS, Beta, LV.** Lee Majors, Abe Vigoda, Don Rickles; ***D:*** Robert Burge. *MGM, OM*

The Keep 🦴🦴 **1983 (R)** At the height of the Nazi onslaught, several German soldiers unleash an unknown power from a medieval stone fortress. Technically impressive but lacking in all other aspects. **96m/C VHS, Beta, LV.** Scott Glenn, Alberta Watson, Juergen Prochnow, Robert Prosky, Gabriel Byrne; ***D:*** Michael Mann; ***W:*** Michael Mann, Dennis Lynton Clark. *PAR*

Keep 'Em Flying 🦴🦴 **1941** Bud and Lou star in the this wartime morale-booster that hasn't aged well. The duo follow their barnstorming friend into flight academy; a not-too-taxing plot includes five musical numbers and two Martha Rayes (she plays twins). ♫Pig Foot Pete; Together; I'm Looking for the Boy with the Wistful Eyes; Let's Keep 'Em Flying; I'm Getting Sentimental Over You. **86m/B VHS, LV.** Bud Abbott, Lou Costello, Martha Raye; ***D:*** Arthur Lubin. *MCA*

Keep My Grave Open 🦴🦴 *The House Where Hell Froze Over* **1980 (R)** A woman lives in an isolated house where a series of strange murders take place. She attributes them to her brother, but does he really exist? Made cheaply, but not without style; filmed in Harrison County, Texas. **85m/C VHS, Beta.** Camilla Carr, Gene Ross, Stephen Tobolowsky, Ann Stafford, Sharon Bunn, Chelcie Ross; ***D:*** S.F. Brownrigg. *UNI*

Keep Punching 🦴🦴 **1939** A gambler/boxer is almost destroyed by life in the fast lane, as well as by a seductive woman. **80m/C VHS.** Henry Armstrong, Mae Johnson; ***Cameos:*** Canada Lee; ***D:*** John Clein. *FCT*

Keep Talking Baby 🦴🦴 **1961** Action-packed thriller that finds Eddie in prison after being framed for murder. He escapes and is out for revenge on the organization that put him there. **?m/C VHS.** Eddie Constantine. *SNC*

Keep the Change 🦴🦴 **1992 (PG-13)** Joe Starling is an artist with painter's block, living in California with his girlfriend Astrid. He decides to revisit the family ranch in Deadrock, Montana, and his crackpot Uncle Smitty and saintly Aunt Lureen. The family ranch is coveted by the evil Overstreet (typecasting for Palance), whose daughter was once loved by Joe but is now married to his ex-best friend. Character more than plot rules this moody, low-key story based on a novel by Thomas McGuane. Made for cable television. **95m/C VHS, LV.** William L. Petersen, Lolita Davidovich, Rachel Ticotin, Buck Henry, Jack Palance, Fred Dalton Thompson, Jeff Kober, Lois Smith; ***D:*** Andy Tennant. *TTC*

Keeper 🦴🦴 **1984** Wealthy patients at Underwood Asylum suffer unspeakable horrors while under the care of Lee. Detective Dick Driver investigates. Obscure horror spoof. **96m/C VHS, Beta.** *CA* Christopher Lee, Tell Schreiber, Sally Gray; ***D:*** Tom Drake; ***W:*** Tom Drake. *TWE, HHE*

Keeper of the City 🦴🦴½ **1992 (R)** Gossett stars as a tough detective out to get a vigilante (LaPaglia) who is roaming the streets of Chicago. LaPaglia turns in a good performance as the son of a Mafia operative who wants to rid himself of the Mafia ties that have controlled him. As he pursues his deadly course of action, a newspaper journalist tags him "The Gangster Killer." Coyote plays the crusading journalist who is always interfering in Gossett's business. Good performances and an intriguing story line combine to make this action-packed thriller worthwhile, although the script isn't as good as Di Pega's novel, which he adapted himself. **95m/C VHS, Beta, LV.** Louis Gossett Jr., Peter Coyote, Anthony LaPaglia, Renee Soutendijk, Aeryk Egan, Tony Todd; ***D:*** Bobby Roth; ***W:*** Gerald Di Pega. *FXV, VTR*

Keeper of the Flame 🦴🦴½ **1942** Tracy and Hepburn manage to keep the murk of this story at bay as war correspondent Steven O'Malley (Tracy) is assigned to write about super patriot Robert V. Forrest, who's just died in an accident. Reclusive widow Christine Forrest (Hepburn) finally agrees to help O'Malley out but what our intrepid reporter discovers is that the hero was really a heel—something Christine still doesn't want known. Based on the novel by I.A.R. Wylie. **100m/B VHS.** Spencer Tracy, Katharine Hepburn, Richard Whorf, Margaret Wycherly, Donald Meek, Stephen McNally, Audrey Christie, Frank Craven, Forrest Tucker, Percy Kilbride, Howard da Silva, Darryl Hickman; ***D:*** George Cukor; ***W:*** Donald Ogden Stewart; ***C:*** William H. Daniels; ***M:*** Bronislau Kaper. *TTC*

Keeping On 🦴🦴½ **1981** Television movie with a pro-union stance. A preacher, who is also a millworker, teams up with an organizer to try to unionize the mill. Originally produced for the PBS "American Playhouse" series. **75m/C VHS.** Dick Anthony Williams, Carol Kane, James Broderick, Marcia Rodd, Rosalind Cash, Carl Lee, Danny Glover, Guy Boyd; ***D:*** Barbara Kopple. *TWE*

Keeping Track 🦴 **1986 (R)** Two tourists witness a murder and robbery and find the stolen $5 million on a New York-bound train. The two are relentlessly pursued by everyone, including the CIA and Russian spies. **102m/C VHS, Beta, LV.** Michael Sarrazin, Margot Kidder, Alan Scarfe, Ken Pogue, Vlasta Vrana, Donald Pilon; ***D:*** Robin Spry. *NLC*

Keetje Tippel 🦴🦴 *Katie's Passion; Cathy Tippel; Hot Sweat* **1975 (R)** In 1881 Amsterdam, a young Dutch prostitute works her way out of poverty and enters a world of education and wealth. A Victorian tale of exploitation with a tough and intelligent Cinderella heroine. In Dutch with English subtitles. **104m/C VHS, Beta, LV.** *NL* Monique Van De Ven, Rutger Hauer, Eddie Brugman, Hannah De Leeuwe, Andrea Domburg; ***D:*** Paul Verhoeven; ***C:*** Jan De Bont. *TPV, CVC, IME*

Kelly of the Secret Service 🦴🦴 **1936** Agent tries to find out who stole the plans for a guided missile system. Fast-pace rides over the silliness of the plot. **69m/B VHS.** Lloyd Hughes, Sheila Mannors, Fuzzy Knight, Syd Saylor, Jack Mulhall, Forrest Taylor; ***D:*** Robert F. "Bob" Hill; ***W:*** Al Martin. *SNC*

Kelly the Second 🦴½ **1936** Slow-moving boxing comedy about a punch-drunk fighter trying to win again with the encouragement of his trainer and manager. **70m/B VHS.** Guinn "Big Boy" Williams, Patsy Kelly, Charley Chase, Pert Kelton, Edward Brophy, Maxie "Slapsie" Rosenbloom, Harold Huber, DeWitt Jennings, Billy Gilbert, Syd Saylor; ***D:*** Gus Meins. *RXM*

Kelly's Heroes 🦴🦴½ **1970 (PG)** A misfit band of crooks are led by Eastwood on a daring mission: to steal a fortune in gold from behind enemy lines. In the process, they almost win WWII. Sutherland is superb, as is McLeod, in his pre-Love Boat days. **145m/C VHS, Beta, LV.** Clint Eastwood, Donald Sutherland, Telly Savalas, Gavin MacLeod, Don Rickles, Carroll O'Connor, Stuart Margolin, Harry Dean Stanton; ***D:*** Brian G. Hutton; ***M:*** Lalo Schifrin. *MGM, TLF*

Kemek 🦴 **1988 (R)** An eccentric chemical company owner has his mistress push a new mind-control drug on an American writer, and has them killed after discovering their subsequent affair. Unfortunately, he didn't count on the woman's ex-husband seeking revenge. **82m/C VHS, Beta.** David Hedison, Helmut Snider, Mary Woronov, Alexandra Stewart, Cal Haynes. *GHV*

Kennedy 🦴🦴 **1983** The long television mini-series biography of JFK from his inauguration to assassination. **278m/C VHS, Beta.** Martin Sheen, Blair Brown, Vincent Gardenia, Geraldine Fitzgerald, E.G. Marshall, John Shea; ***D:*** Richard Hartley. *PSM*

The Kennedys Don't Cry **1983** A sensitive and detailed look at the triumphs and tragedies of the Kennedy clan. Rare footage and interviews trace the growth of Joseph P. Kennedy's children and their influence on American history. Some segments are in black and white. **100m/C VHS, Beta.** *MPI*

The Kennel Murder Case 🦴🦴 **1933** Debonair detective Philo Vance suspects that a clear-cut case of suicide is actually murder. Fourth Vance mystery starring Powell. Remade as "Calling Philo Vance" in 1940. **73m/B VHS, Beta.** William Powell, Mary Astor, Jack LaRue, Ralph Morgan, Eugene Pallette; ***D:*** Michael Curtiz. *SNC, NOS, HHT*

Kenny Rogers as the Gambler 🦴🦴½ **1980** Rogers stars as Brady Hawkes, debonair gambler searching for a son he never knew he had. Based on the Rogers song of the same name. One of the highest rated TV movies ever. Followed by several sequels. **94m/C VHS.** Kenny Rogers, Christine Belford, Bruce Boxleitner, Harold Gould, Clu Gulager, Lance LeGault, Lee Purcell, Noble Willingham; ***D:*** Dick Lowry. *WKV*

Kenny Rogers as the Gambler, Part 2: The Adventure Continues 🦴½ **1983** The surprise success of the made-for-TV western based on the popular Kenny Rogers' song spawned this equally popular sequel. Rogers returns as Brady Hawkes, this time searching for his kidnapped son. Followed by two more sequels. **195m/C VHS, Beta, 8mm.** Kenny Rogers, Bruce Boxleitner, Linda Evans, Harold Gould, David Hedison, Clu Gulager, Johnny Crawford; ***D:*** Dick Lowry. *WKV*

Kenny Rogers as the Gambler, Part 3: The Legend Continues 🦴🦴 **1987** Roger's third attempt at humanizing the gambler from his hit '70s song. This time, the Gambler gives a hand with the mediating between the warring U.S. government and the Sioux nation. Sitting Bull and Buffalo Bill add credibility to this average undertaking. Made for TV. **190m/C VHS, Beta.** Kenny Rogers, Bruce Boxleitner, Linda Gray, Melanie Chartoff, Matt Clark, George Kennedy, Dean Stockwell, Charles Durning, Jeffrey Jones, George American Horse; ***D:*** Dick Lowry. *WKV*

Kent State 🦴🦴 **1981** Made-for-television drama recounts the tragic events that took place at Kent State University in 1970, when student demonstrators faced National Guardsmen. Goldstone won an Emmy for Outstanding Direction. **120m/C VHS, Beta.** Talia Balsam, Ellen Barkin, Jane Fleiss, John Getz, Keith Gordon; ***D:*** James Goldstone. *MCA*

The Kentuckian 🦴🦴½ **1955** Burt Lancaster stars as a rugged frontiersman who leaves with his son to go to Texas. On their journey the two are harassed by fighting mountaineers. **104m/C VHS, Beta.** Burt Lancaster, Walter Matthau, Diana Lynn, John McIntire, Dianne Foster, Una Merkel, John Carradine; ***D:*** Burt Lancaster; ***C:*** Ernest Laszlo. *MGM*

Kentucky Blue Streak 🦴½ **1935** Young jockey is framed for murder while riding at an "illegal" racetrack. Later, almost eligible for parole, he escapes from jail to ride "Blue Streak" in the Kentucky Derby. **61m/B VHS, Beta.** Eddie Nugent, Frank "Junior" Coghlan, Patricia Scott, Ben Carter. *VYY*

Kentucky Fried Movie 🦴🦴🦴 **1977 (R)** A zany potpourri of satire about movies, television, commercials, and contemporary society. Written by Abrahams and the Zuckers, who were later known for "Airplane!" **85m/C VHS, Beta, LV.** Bill Bixby, Jerry Zucker, Jim Abrahams, David Zucker, Donald Sutherland, Henry Gibson, George Lazenby; ***D:*** John Landis; ***W:*** Jerry Zucker, Jim Abrahams, David Zucker. *MED*

Kentucky Jubilee 🦴½ **1951** At the jubilee, a movie director is kidnapped and the master of ceremonies, among others, decides to find him. **67m/B VHS, Beta, LV.** Jerry Colonna, Jean Porter, James Ellison, Raymond Hatton, Fritz Feld. *RXM*

Kentucky Kernels 🦴🦴 *Triple Trouble* **1934** A pair of down and out magicians (thirties comic duo Wheeler and Woolsey) happen upon a young boy (Little Rascal Spanky) who happens to be heir to a fortune. The three head for the rascal's Kentucky home, where they're welcomed with southern inhospitality. Much feuding and slapsticking. **75m/B VHS, LV.** Bert Wheeler, Robert Woolsey, Mary Carlisle, George "Spanky" McFarland, Noah Beery Sr., Lucille LaVerne, Willie Best; ***D:*** George Stevens; ***M:*** Max Steiner. *TTC, FCT, GVV*

Kentucky Rifle 🦴½ **1955** A Comanche Indian tribe will let a group of stranded pioneers through their territory only if they agree to sell the Kentucky rifles aboard their wagon. **80m/C VHS, Beta.** Chill Wills, Lance Fuller, Cathy Downs, Jess Barker, Sterling Holloway, Jeanne Cagney; ***D:*** Carl K. Hittleman. *MON, HHE*

Kept Husbands 🦴🦴 **1931** A factory worker saves two lives in an industrial accident, and the boss invites him home to dinner. When he meets the boss' daughter, romance blooms. But their different backgrounds cause difficulties. A bit dull, and dated by its chauvinism. **76m/B VHS.** Dorothy Mackaill, Joel McCrea, Robert McWade, Florence Roberts, Clara Kimball Young, Mary Carr, Ned Sparks, Bryant Washburn; ***D:*** Lloyd Bacon; ***M:*** Max Steiner. *NOS, HEG*

The Kettles in the Ozarks 🦴🦴½ **1956** Since Kilbride retired after the seventh comedy, Hunnicutt played a new male character, Uncle Sledge, in the eighth film. Ma (Main) takes the young'uns to visit their uncle in the Ozarks and finds she must help him and fiancee Bedelia (Merkel) save the failing farm from bootleggers. **81m/B VHS.** Marjorie Main, Arthur Hunnicutt, Una Merkel, Ted de Corsia, Richard Eyer, Joseph Sawyer, Richard Deacon; ***D:*** Charles Lamont; ***W:*** Kay Lenard. *MCA*

The Kettles on Old MacDonald's Farm 🦴🦴½ **1957** The ninth and last in the series finds Ma (Main in her final film) and Pa (Kennelly replacing the retired Kilbride) playing matchmakers for humble lumberman Brad (Smith). Seems he wants to marry the boss' spoiled daughter, Sally (Talbott), whom Ma decides needs a little backwoods seasoning before she'll make the proper wife. **82m/B VHS.** Marjorie Main, Parker Fennelly, John Smith, Gloria Talbott, Claude Akins, Roy Barcroft, Patricia Morrow, George Dunn; ***D:*** Virgil W. Vogel; ***W:*** Herbert Margolis, William Raynor. *MCA*

The Key 🦴🦴½ **1958** A long, slow WWII drama about the key to an Italian girl's apartment that gets passed from tugboat skipper to tugboat skipper before dangerous missions. Ultimately she finds true love, or does she? Based on the novel "Stella" by Jan de Hartog. **134m/B VHS, Beta, LV.** *GB* William Holden, Sophia Loren, Trevor Howard, Oscar Homolka, Kieron Moore; ***D:*** Carol Reed; ***W:*** Carl Foreman; ***C:*** Oswald Morris; ***M:*** Malcolm Arnold. British Academy Awards '58: Best Actor (Howard). *COL*

Key Exchange 🦴🦴½ **1985 (R)** Kevin Scott and Paul Kurta based this contemporary look at love and commitments on Kevin Wade's popular play. Two New York City "yuppies" have reached a point in their relationship where an exchange of apartment keys commonly occurs—but they are hesitant. **96m/C VHS, Beta.** Brooke Adams, Ben Masters, Daniel Stern, Tony Roberts, Danny Aiello, Annie Golden, Nancy Mette; ***D:*** Barnet Kellman; ***W:*** Kevin Scott, Paul Kurta; ***M:*** Jonathan Elias. *FOX*

Key Largo 🦴🦴🦴½ **1948** A gangster melodrama set in Key West, Florida, where hoods take over a hotel in the midst of a hurricane. Based on a play by Maxwell Anderson. **101m/B VHS, Beta, LV.** Humphrey Bogart, Lauren Bacall, Claire Trevor, Edward G. Robinson, Lionel Barrymore; ***D:*** John Huston; ***W:*** Richard Brooks, John Huston; ***C:*** Karl Freund; ***M:*** Max Steiner. Academy Awards '48: Best Supporting Actress (Trevor). *MGM, FOX, TLF*

The Key Man 🦴½ *Life at Stake* **1957** A radio show host manages to get mixed up with gangsters after recreating a crime on the air. He uses his knowledge of crime to thwart the crooks. **63m/B VHS, Beta.** *GB* Lee Patterson, Hy Hazell, Colin Gordon, Philip Leaver, Paula Byrne; ***D:*** Montgomery Tully; ***M:*** Les Baxter. *NOS, SNC*

The Key to Rebecca 🦴🦴½ **1985** The Nazis and the British go head-to-head in war torn North Africa. As the Germans push their way across Egypt, they find an unexpected ally in a half-German/half-Arab killer behind the British lines. Tense, well made thriller, originally a mini-series. On two cassettes. Made for television. **190m/C VHS.** David Soul, Cliff Robertson, Robert Culp, Season Hubley, Lina Raymond, Anthony Quayle, David Hemmings; ***D:*** David Hemmings. *WOV*

Key to the City 🦴🦴½ **1950** Light comedy featuring Gable and Young as two small town mayors who meet and fall in love at a convention in San Francisco. Throw in some sharp lines, a little slapstick, and a bit of satire for an amusing picture. Based on the story by Albert Beich. **99m/B VHS.** Clark Gable, Loretta Young, Frank Morgan, Marilyn Maxwell, Raymond Burr, James Gleason, Lewis Stone, Raymond Walburn; ***D:*** George Sidney; ***W:*** Robert Riley Crutcher. *MGM*

The Keys of the Kingdom 🦴🦴🦴 **1944** An earnest adaptation of A.J. Cronin's novel about a young Scottish missionary spreading God's word in 19th Century China. **137m/B VHS, Beta, LV.** Gregory Peck, Thomas Mitchell, Edmund Gwenn, Vincent Price, Roddy McDowall, Cedric Hardwicke, Peggy Ann Garner, James Gleason, Anne Revere, Rose Stradner, Sara Allgood, Abner Biberman, Arthur Shields; ***D:*** John M. Stahl; ***W:*** Joseph L. Mankiewicz, Nunnally Johnson; ***C:*** Arthur C. Miller. Nominations: Academy Awards '45: Best Actor (Peck), Best Black and White Cinematography, Best Interior Decoration, Best Original Score. *FOX, IGP*

The KGB: The Secret War 🦴½ *Lethal* **1986 (PG-13)** Reheated Cold War fare. **90m/C VHS, LV.** Sally Kellerman, Michael Ansara, Michael Billington; ***W:*** Sandra K. Bailey. *HHE*

Khartoum 🦴🦴½ **1966** A sweeping but talky adventure epic detailing the last days of General "Chinese" Gordon as the title city is besieged by Arab tribes in 1884. **134m/C VHS, Beta, LV.** Charlton Heston, Laurence Olivier, Ralph Richardson, Richard Johnson, Alexander Knox, Hugh Williams, Nigel Green, Michael Hordern, Johnny Sekka; ***D:*** Basil Dearden. Nominations: Academy Awards '66: Best Story & Screenplay. *MGM, CCB*

The Kick Fighter 🦴 **1991** Would you believe the hero has to kickbox to finance his kid sister's operation? Grungy, Bangkok-set chopsocky cheapie leaves no cliche untouched, but fights are well-staged. A strange end credit lauds real-life champ Urquidez, here a bad guy. **92m/C VHS.** Richard Norton, Benny "The Jet" Urquidez, Glen Ruehland, Franco Guerrero, Erica Van Wagener, Steve Rackman; ***D:*** Anthony Maharaj. *AIP*

Kick of Death: The Prodigal Boxer 🦴 **198? (R)** A young boxer is accused of a murder he didn't commit, and fights a battle to the death to prove it. **90m/C VHS, Beta.** Mang Sei, Suma Wah Lung, Pa Hung; ***D:*** Chai Yang Min. *GEM*

Kickboxer 🦴½ **1989 (R)** The brother of a permanently crippled kickboxing champ trains for a revenge match. **97m/C VHS, Beta, LV.** Jean-Claude Van Damme, Rochelle Ashana, Dennis Chan, Dennis Alexio; ***D:*** Mark DiSalle; ***W:*** Jean-Claude Van Damme, Mark DiSalle, Glenn A. Bruce. *HBO, WAR*

Kickboxer 2: The Road Back 🦴½ **1990 (R)** Mitchell takes over for Van Damme in this action sequel which finds our athletic hero seeking revenge on the kickboxer who murdered his brother. **90m/C VHS, LV.** Sasha Mitchell, Peter Boyle, John Diehl; ***D:*** Albert Pyun. *WAR, MOV, HBO*

Kickboxer 3: The Art of War 🦴½ **1992 (R)** Mitchell returns in this second sequel. This time the American kickboxing champ flies to Rio for a big match which turns out to be fixed by a local mobster. For a little more fun our hero saves a kidnapped girl and fights a hired killer. **92m/C VHS, LV.** Sasha Mitchell, Dennis Chan, Richard Comar, Noah Verduzco, Althea Miranda, Ian Jacklin; ***D:*** Rick King. *LIV*

Kickboxer 4: The Aggressor 🦴🦴½ **1994 (R)** Martial arts expert David Sloan (Mitchell) was framed by sworn enemy Tong Po but now he's back and looking for revenge. **90m/C VHS, LV.** Sasha Mitchell, Kamal Krifia, Nicholas Guest, Deborah Mansy, Brad Thornton; ***D:*** Albert Pyun. *LIV*

Kickboxer the Champion 🦴 **1991** The opium trade is in for a kick to the stomach when Archer challenges the big man in charge to a deathly duel. **?m/C VHS.** Don Murray, Wayne Archer; ***D:*** Alton Cheung. *WLA*

Kicking and Screaming 🦴🦴🦴 **1995 (R)** Baumbach's deft, though slightly self-conscious directorial debut examines the post-college grad angst of Grover (Hamilton) and his three other slacker roomies. In denial of their recently achieved non-student status, the four bond together in pursuit of the inane and trivial, while their various girlfriends slip more easily into adulthood. Funny and tender flashback scenes of Grover and girlfriend Jane (D'Abo) add depth without all the dialogue, well-written though it is. Hilarious highlight occurs as roommate Otis interviews for that most popular of low-budget, Gen-X movie jobs—video store clerk. **96m/C VHS.** Josh Hamilton, Olivia D'Abo, Carlos Jacott, Christopher Eigeman, Eric Stoltz, Jason Wiles, Parker Posey, Cara Buono, Elliott Gould; ***D:*** Noah Baumbach; ***W:*** Oliver Berkman, Noah Baumbach; ***C:*** Steven Bernsein; ***M:*** Phil Marshall. *VMK*

Kicks 🦴½ **1985** Two well-off San Francisco professionals play high-risk games with each other, culminating in a life-or-death hunt. Made for television. **97m/C VHS, Beta.** Anthony Geary, Shelley Hack, Tom Mason, Ian Abercrombie, James Avery; ***D:*** William Wiard; ***M:*** Peter Bernstein. *NO*

The Kid 🦴🦴🦴 **1921** Sensitive and sassy film about a tramp who takes home an orphan. Chaplin's first feature. Also launched Coogan as the first child superstar. **60m/B VHS.** Charlie Chaplin, Jackie Coogan, Edna Purviance; ***D:*** Charlie Chaplin. *FCT, MLB*

Kid 🦴🦴½ **1990 (R)** Young guy carries grudge for the murder of his parents and seeks pound of flesh. Enter mysterious beautiful woman and copious complications. Good sound FX. **94m/C VHS, Beta, LV.** C. Thomas Howell, R. Lee Ermey, Brian Austin Green, Sarah Trigger; ***D:*** John Mark Robinson. *LIV, IME*

Kid and the Killers 🦴 **198? (PG)** Young orphan and a hardened criminal band together to pursue a villain. **90m/C VHS, Beta.** Jon Cypher. *NO*

The Kid Brother 🦴🦴🦴½ **1927** The shy, weak son of a tough sheriff, Harold fantasizes about being a hero like his father and big brothers, falls in love with a carnival lady, and somehow saves the day. Classic silent comedy. **84m/B VHS, Beta.** Harold Lloyd, Walter James, Jobyna Ralston; ***D:*** Ted Wilde. *TLF*

Kid Colter 🦴🦴½ **1985** Enjoyable family film about a city kid who goes to visit his dad in a remote wilderness area of the Pacific Northwest. While there he is abducted by two grizzly mountain men and left for dead, but survives and pursues his abductors relentlessly. Received the Film Advisory Board Award of Excellence and the Award of Merit from the Academy of Family Films. **101m/C VHS, Beta.** Jim Stafford, Jeremy Shamos, Hal Terrance, Greg Ward, Jim Turner; ***D:*** David O'Malley; ***W:*** David O'Malley. *FOX*

Kid Courageous ☠ **1935** An athlete goes west, tracks ore mine thieves and prevents a hot-blooded spitfire from marrying the wrong man. **53m/B VHS, Beta.** Bob Steele. *NOS*

Kid Dynamite *Queen of Broadway* **1943** A Bowery Boys series episode. Gorcey is a boxer who is kidnapped to prevent his participation in a major fight. The real fighting occurs when his brother is substituted, and Gorcey is smitten. **73m/B VHS.** Leo Gorcey, Huntz Hall, Bobby Jordan, Gabriel Dell, Pamela Blake; ***D:*** Wallace Fox. *NOS, HEG*

A Kid for Two Farthings ☠☠½ **1955** An episodic, sentimental portrait of the Jewish quarter in London's East End, centered on a boy with a malformed goat he thinks is a magic unicorn capable of granting wishes and bringing happiness to his impoverished 'hood. Acclaimed adaptation of a novel by screenwriter Wolf Mankowitz, also on tape in a shorter rehash as "The Unicorn." **96m/C VHS.** Jonathan Ashmore. *HMV, FCT*

Kid from Brooklyn ☠☠ **1946** A shy, musically inclined milkman becomes a middleweight boxer by knocking out the champ in a street brawl. Remake of "The Milky Way" by Harold Lloyd. Available with digitally remastered stereo and original movie trailer. ♫Sunflower Song; Hey, What's Your Name; You're the Cause Of It All; Welcome, Burleigh; I Love An Old-Fashioned Song; Josie. **113m/C VHS, Beta, LV.** Danny Kaye, Virginia Mayo, Eve Arden, Fay Bainter, Walter Abel; ***D:*** Norman Z. McLeod; ***C:*** Gregg Toland. *HBO, SUE*

Kid from Gower Gulch ☠ **1947** A singing, non-horse-riding cowboy enters a rodeo through a clever ruse. **56m/B VHS, Beta, LV.** Spade Cooley. *NOS*

The Kid from Left Field ☠☠ **1979** Bat boy for the San Diego Padres transforms the team from losers to champions when he passes on the advice of his father, a "has-been" ballplayer, to the team members. A made-for-television remake of the 1953 classic. **80m/C VHS, Beta.** Gary Coleman, Robert Guillaume, Ed McMahon, Tab Hunter; ***D:*** Adell Aldrich. *VES*

Kid from Not-So-Big ☠☠ **1978 (G)** A family film that tells the story of Jenny, a young girl left to carry on her grandfather's frontier-town newspaper. When two con-men come to town, Jenny sets out to expose them. **87m/C VHS, Beta.** Jennifer McAllister, Veronica Cartwright, Robert Viharo, Paul Tulley; ***D:*** William Crain. *WAR, OM*

Kid Galahad ☠☠☠ *The Battling Bellhop* **1937** Well acted boxing drama with Robinson playing an honest promoter who wants to make Morris into a prize fighter. Davis plays the girl they both want. Remade as "The Wagons Roll at Night" and then made again as an Elvis Presley vehicle. Shown on television. **101m/B VHS.** Edward G. Robinson, Bette Davis, Humphrey Bogart, Wayne Morris, Jane Bryan, Harry Carey Sr., Veda Ann Borg; ***D:*** Michael Curtiz; ***W:*** Seton I. Miller; ***C:*** Gaetano Antonio "Tony" Gaudio; ***M:*** Max Steiner. *MGM*

Kid Galahad ☠☠ **1962** The King plays a young boxer who weathers the fight game, singing seven songs along the way. ♫King of the Whole Wide World; This Is Living; I Got Lucky; A Whistling Tune; Home Is Where The Heart Is; Riding the Rainbow; Love Is For Loves. **95m/C VHS, Beta, LV.** Elvis Presley, Lola Albright, Charles Bronson, Ned Glass, Joan Blackman, Ed Asner, Gig Young; ***D:*** Phil Karlson; ***C:*** Burnett Guffey. *MGM*

The Kid/Idle Class ☠☠☠ **1921** The Little Tramp adopts a homeless orphan in "The Kid," Chaplin's first feature-length film. This tape also includes "The Idle Class," a rare Chaplin short. **85m/B VHS, Beta.** Charlie Chaplin, Jackie Coogan, Edna Purviance, Chuck Reisner, Lita Grey Chaplin; ***D:*** Charlie Chaplin. *FOX*

A Kid in King Arthur's Court ☠½ **1995 (PG)** Lame adaptation of Mark Twain's "A Connecticut Yankee in King Arthur's Court" finds insecure California teen Calvin Fuller (Nicholas), falling down a hole created by an earthquake and landing in Camelot. Arthur's (Ackland) a doddering old man with a cute teen daughter, Princess Katey (Baeza), who needs some help in defeating the evil Lord Belasco (Malik). Naturally, Calvin helps out and gains confidence in himself. Okay time-waster for the kids. **91m/C VHS.** Thomas Ian Nicholas, Joss Ackland, Art Malik, Paloma Baeza, Kate Winslet, Ron Moody, Daniel Craig; ***D:*** Michael Gottlieb; ***W:*** Michael Part, Robert L. Levy; ***C:*** Elemer Ragaly; ***M:*** J.A.C. Redford. *TOU*

Kid Millions ☠☠½ **1934** Vintage musical comedy in which a dull-witted Brooklyn boy must travel to exotic Egypt to collect an inherited fortune. The finale is filmed in early three-strip Technicolor. Lucille Ball appears as a Goldwyn Girl. ♫Your Head on My Shoulder; Ice Cream Fantasy; An Earful of Music; When My Ship Comes In; Okay Toots; I Want to be a Minstrel Man; Mandy. **90m/B VHS, Beta.** Eddie Cantor, Ethel Merman, Ann Sothern, George Murphy; ***D:*** Roy Del Ruth. *SUE*

Kid 'n' Hollywood and Polly Tix in Washington **1933** These two "Baby Burlesks" shorts star a cast of toddlers, featuring the most famous moppet of all time, Shirley Temple, in her earliest screen appearances. **20m/B VHS, Beta.** Shirley Temple. *CCB*

Kid Ranger ☠ **1936** A ranger shoots an innocent man, but later sets things straight by bringing the real culprit to justice. **57m/B VHS, Beta.** Bob Steele, William Farnum; ***D:*** Robert North Bradbury. *VYY*

Kid Sister ☠½ **1945** A young girl is determined to grab her sister's boyfriend for herself, and enlists the aid of a burglar to do it. **56m/B VHS, Beta.** Roger Pryor, Judy Clark, Frank Jenks, Constance Worth. *VYY*

Kid Vengeance ☠½ **1975 (R)** After witnessing the brutal slaying of his family, a boy carries out a personal vendetta against the outlaws. **90m/C VHS, Beta.** Leif Garrett, Jim Brown, Lee Van Cleef, John Marley, Glynnis O'Connor; ***D:*** Joseph Manduke. *NO*

The Kid Who Loved Christmas ☠☠ **1990** After his adoptive mother is killed in a car accident, a young boy is taken from his adoptive father. The boy, upset about being removed from his new family, writes to Santa Claus for help. A touching yuletide drama. This was Sammy Davis, Jr.'s last film. Made for television. **118m/C VHS.** Cicely Tyson, Michael Warren, Sammy Davis Jr., Gilbert Lewis, Ken Page, Della Reese, Esther Rolle, Ben Vereen, Vanessa Williams, John Beal, Trent Cameron, Arthur Seidelman. *PAR*

The Kid with the Broken Halo ☠☠ **1982** Coleman and Guillaume are paired again in this unsuccessful pilot for a TV series. A young angel, out to earn his wings, must try to help three desperate families, with the help of an experienced angel. **100m/C VHS.** Gary Coleman, Robert Guillaume, June Allyson, Mason Adams, Ray Walston, John Pleshette, Kim Fields, Georg Stanford Brown, Telma Hopkins; ***D:*** Leslie Martinson. *NO*

The Kid with the 200 I.Q. ☠☠ **1983** When an earnest boy genius enters college at age 13, predictable comic situations arise that involve his attempts at impressing his idolized astronomy professor (Guillaume), as well as an equally unrequited bout of first love. Harmless comedy, one of a series of squeaky-clean made-for-TV family fare starring Coleman. **96m/C VHS, Beta.** Gary Coleman, Robert Guillaume, Harriet Hilliard Nelson, Dean Butler, Karli Michaelson, Christina Murrull, Mel Stewart; ***D:*** Leslie Martinson. *LIV*

Kidco ☠☠ **1983 (PG)** The true story of a money-making corporation headed and run by a group of children ranging in age from nine to sixteen. **104m/C VHS, Beta.** Scott Schwartz, Elizabeth Gorcey, Cinnamon Idles, Tristine Skyler; ***D:*** Ronald F. Maxwell. *FOX*

Kidnap Syndicate ☠½ **1976 (R)** Kidnappers swipe two boys, releasing one—the son of a wealthy industrialist who meets their ransom demands. When they kill the other boy, a mechanic's son, the father goes on a revengeful killing spree. **105m/C VHS, Beta.** *IT* James Mason, Valentina Cortese; ***D:*** Fernando Di Leo. *NO*

Kidnapped ☠☠½ **1960** A young boy is sold by his wicked uncle as a slave, and is helped by an outlaw. A Disney film based on the Robert Louis Stevenson classic. **94m/C VHS, Beta.** Peter Finch, James MacArthur, Peter O'Toole; ***D:*** Robert Stevenson. *DIS*

Kidnapped *Woof!* **1987 (R)** When a teenage girl is kidnapped by pornographers, her sister seeks help from a tough cop and together they go undercover to find her. Plot is flimsy cover for what is actually an exploitative piece. **100m/C VHS, Beta, LV.** David Naughton, Barbara Crampton, Lance LeGault, Chick Vennera, Charles Napier; ***D:*** Howard (Hikmet) Avedis; ***W:*** Howard (Hikmet) Avedis. *NO*

Kidnapping of Baby John Doe **1988** Tragedy strikes a family's newborn, and they must make the terrifying decision between life and death. A doctor and nurse, however, take matters into their own hands to save the baby. **90m/C VHS, Beta.** Helen Hughes, Jayne Eastwood, Janet-Laine Green, Geoffery Boues, Peter Gerretsen. *NO*

The Kidnapping of the President ☠☠½ **1980 (R)** The U.S. president is taken hostage by Third World terrorists. The Secret Service is on the ball trying to recover the nation's leader. Well-integrated subplot involves the vice president in a scandal. Engrossing political thriller. Based on novel by Charles Templeton. **113m/C VHS, Beta.** *CA* William Shatner, Hal Holbrook, Van Johnson, Ava Gardner, Miguel Fernandez; ***D:*** George Mendeluk. *NO*

Kids ☠☠ **1995** Very controversial docudrama about 24 hours in the lives of some aimless New York teenagers. The sullen Telly (Fitzpatrick) enjoys bragging about his skill in deflowering virgins but his promiscuity has lead Jennie (Sevigny) to test H.I.V. positive—something Telly is as yet unaware of. Telly'd rather hang around with best friend Casper (Pierce) anyway, out on the streets, being generally profane and obnoxious. Can either be regarded as a brutally realistic look at teen life today or a lot of fuss about nothing. Korine was 19 when he wrote the screenplay. The MPAA rated the film NC-17, after a protest the distributors chose to release it unrated. **90m/C VHS, LV.** Leo Fitzpatrick, Justin Pierce, Chloe Sevigny, Rosario Dawson; ***D:*** Larry Clark; ***W:*** Harmony Korine; ***C:*** Eric Alan Edwards; ***M:*** Louis Barlow. Independent Spirit Awards '96: Debut Performance (Pierce); Nominations: Independent Spirit Awards '96: Best First Feature, Best Supporting Actress (Sevigny). *VMK*

Kid's Auto Race/Mabel's Married Life ☠☠ *Kid Auto Races at Venice* **1915** "Kid's Auto Race" (1914) concerns a kiddie-car contest; "Mabel's Married Life" (1915) is about flirtations in the park between married individuals. Piano and organ scores. **21m/B VHS, Beta.** Charlie Chaplin, Mabel Normand, Mack Swain; ***D:*** Mack Sennett. *CCB, GVV*

Kids In the Hall Brain Candy ☠☠ **1996 (R)** The Kids bring their Monty Python-meets-SCTV humor to the big screen with moderate success. Dr. Cooper (McDonald), facing corporate downsizing, allows his new, untested anti-depressant to be released to the public after it shows promise. The drug, Gleemonex, sweeps the country by forcing the user's mind to focus on a favorite memory. As befits the troupe's twisted vision, these happy memories aren't always pleasant to the "Family Values" crowd. The easily offended should be warned—there's a character named "Cancer Boy." The story wanders a bit, giving everyone a chance to show their versatility (these Kids collectively play 32 different roles). Sophomore director Makin served the same duty on many of the TV episodes. **88m/C VHS.** Dave Foley, Bruce McCulloch, Kevin McDonald, Scott Thompson, Mark McKinney, Janeane Garofalo; ***D:*** Kelly Makin; ***W:*** Bruce McCulloch, Kevin McDonald, Scott Thompson, Mark McKinney, Norm Hiscock; ***C:*** David Makin; ***M:*** Craig Northey. *NYR*

Kid's Last Ride ☠ **1941** Three tough guys come into town to settle a feud. **55m/B VHS.** Ray Corrigan, John "Dusty" King, Max Terhune, Luana Walters, Edwin Brian; ***D:*** S. Roy Luby. *NOS, DVT*

Kika ☠☠ **1994** Another flamboyant comedy from Almodovar finds irrepressible beautician Kika (Forque) involved with kinky photographer Ramon (Casanovas) and his stepfather Nicholas (Coyote), a sinister American pulp novelist. There's also Andrea Scarface (Jean-Paul Gaultier-costumed Abril), the host of a vile tabloid TV show called "Today's Worst," and Kika's lesbian maid Juana (de Palma) whose brother happens to be an escaped con/porn star, leading to an outlandish rape and...well, it's all pretty nonsensical, anyway. Spanish with subtitles. **115m/C VHS.** *SP* Veronica Forque, Peter Coyote, Victoria Abril, Alex Casanovas, Rossy de Palma; ***D:*** Pedro Almodovar; ***W:*** Pedro Almodovar. *VMK*

The Kill ½ **1973** A rough, cynical, hard-boiled, womanizing detective tracks down stolen cash in downtown Macao. **81m/C VHS, Beta.** Richard Jaeckel, Henry Duval, Judy Washington. *NWV*

Kill Alex Kill *Woof!* **1983** A Vietnam POW returns to find his family murdered, and uses the crime underworld to take revenge. **88m/C VHS, Beta.** Tony Zarindast, Tina Bowmann, Chris Ponti. *GEM*

Kill and Go Hide *The Child* **1976** A young girl visits her mother's grave nightly to communicate with and command the ghoul-like creatures that haunt the surrounding woods. **95m/C VHS, Beta.** *NO*

Kill and Kill Again ½ **1981 (PG)** A martial arts champion attempts to rescue a kidnapped Nobel Prize-winning chemist who has developed a high-yield synthetic fuel. Colorful, tongue-in-cheek, and fun even for those unfamiliar with the genre. **100m/C VHS, Beta.** James Ryan, Anneline Kriel, Stan Schmidt, Bill Flynn, Norman Robinson, Ken Gampu, John Ramsbottom; ***D:*** Ivan Hall; ***W:*** John Crowther. *MED*

Kill, Baby, Kill *Curse of the Living Dead; Operacione Paura* **1966** A small Transylvania town is haunted by the ghost of a seven-year-old witchcraft victim, and the town's suicide victims all seem to have hearts of gold (coins, that is). Lots of style and atmosphere in this Transylvanian tale from horror tongue in cheekster Bava. Considered by many genre connoisseurs to be the B man's finest, except that it bears early symptoms of the director's late onset infatuation with the zoom shot. **83m/C VHS.** *IT* Erika Blanc, Giacomo "Jack" Rossi-Stuart, Fabienne Dali, Giana Vivaldi; ***D:*** Mario Bava. *SNC, FRG*

Kill Castro **1980 (R)** Ever hear the one about the exploding cigar? Key West boat skipper is forced to carry a CIA agent to Cuba on a mission to assassinate Castro. Low-budget adventure that's deadly dull. **90m/C VHS, Beta.** Sybil Danning, Albert Salmi, Michael V. Gazzo, Raymond St. Jacques, Woody Strode, Stuart Whitman, Robert Vaughn, Caren Kaye; ***D:*** Chuck Workman. *NO*

Kill Cruise **1990 (R)** The depressed and alcoholic skipper of the yacht Bella Donna gives up sailing until he meets two beautiful young women who want to sail to Bermuda for a taste of the good life. The calm of the Atlantic is disturbed when they are plagued by bad weather and fierce storms, and tensions rise as the two women's jealousies erupt. Will it set the climate for murder? **99m/C VHS, Beta, LV.** Juergen Prochnow, Patsy Kensit, Elizabeth Hurley; ***D:*** Peter Keglevic; ***W:*** Peter Keglevic. *MCA*

Kill Factor *Woof! Death Dimension; Black Eliminator; The Freeze Bomb* **1978 (R)** Something stupid about a killer bomb tht could freeze the planet. So inept your brain cells will also be frozen if you watch it. **91m/C VHS, Beta.** Jim Kelly, George Lazenby, Aldo Ray, Harold Sakata, Terry Moore; ***D:*** Al Adamson. *ACA*

Kill Line **1991 (R)** Kim stars as Joe, a street fighter who seeks to clear his name after serving a 10-year prison sentence for a crime he didn't commit. When he finds his brother's family has been murdered by criminals looking for the millions he supposedly stole, Joe wages a one-man martial arts war against a corrupt police force and the gang of thugs who are looking for the money. **93m/C VHS.** Bobby Kim, Michael Parker, Marlene Zimmerman, H. Wayne Lowery, C.R. Valdez, Mark Williams, Ben Pfeifer; ***D:*** Richard H. Kim; ***W:*** Richard H. Kim. *HMD*

Kill Me Again ½ **1989 (R)** Director Dahl does the contemporary noir thing through the Nevada desert with Whalley-Kilmer as a beautiful femme fatale. She asks a detective (real-life husband Kilmer) to fake her death, which gets him targeted not only by the police, but also the mob and her psycho-boyfriend (Madsen). Fun and full of plot twists that will satisfy fans of the noir persuasion. **93m/C VHS, Beta.** Val Kilmer, Joanne Whalley, Michael Madsen, Jonathan Gries, Bibi Besch; ***D:*** John Dahl; ***W:*** John Dahl, David Warfield. *MGM*

Kill My Wife...Please! **19??** Comic adventure of a despicable husband trying to bump off his wife in order to cash in on her insurance policy. **90m/C VHS.** Bob Dishy, Joanna Barnes, Bill Dana; ***D:*** Steven Hilliard Stern. *HHE*

Kill or Be Killed **1980 (PG)** Martial arts champion is lured to a phony martial arts contest by a madman bent on revenge. **90m/C VHS, Beta.** James Ryan, Charlotte Michelle, Norman Combes; ***D:*** Ivan Hall. *MED*

Kill or Be Killed ½ **1993** Michael Julian just spent eight years in jail for saving his brother Charlie's life. He must wonder why he bothered since Charlie has stolen his girl Beth and set up a drug empire. Michael ambushes Charlie's men and steals a million dollars to use as leverage but Charlie thinks rival drug lords are out to get him and starts a street war. **97m/C VHS.** David Heavener, Joseph Nuzzolo, Paulo Tocha, Lynn Levand; ***D:*** Joe Straw; ***W:*** Joseph Nuzzolo. *AIP*

The Kill Reflex **1989 (R)** A tough black cop and his beautiful rookie partner battle the mob and corruption. **90m/C VHS, Beta, LV.** Maud Adams, Fred Williamson, Bo Svenson, Phyllis Hyman; ***D:*** Fred Williamson. *COL*

Kill Slade **1989 (PG-13)** When a United Nations food-aid diversion conspiracy is uncovered by a beautiful journalist, a plan to kidnap her is put into action. Romance follows. **90m/C VHS, Beta, LV.** *SA* Patrick Dollaghan, Lisa Brady, Anthony Fridjhon, Danny Keogh, Alfred Nowke; ***D:*** Bruce McFarlane. *SUE, NLC*

Kill Squad **1981 (R)** Squad of martial arts masters follow a trail of violence and bloodshed to a vengeful, deadly battle of skills. **85m/C VHS, Beta.** Jean Claude, Jeff Risk, Jerry Johnson, Bill Cambra, Cameron Mitchell. *VTR*

Kill the Golden Goose **1979 (R)** Two martial arts masters work on opposite sides of a government corruption and corporate influence peddling case. **91m/C VHS, Beta.** Brad von Beltz, Ed Parker, Master Bong Soo Han; ***D:*** Elliot Hong. *GEM*

Killcrazy **1989 (R)** On the way to a weekend camping trip, five Vietnam vets released from a mental hospital are slowly massacred by a group of dangerous killers until one of the vets decides to fight back. **94m/C VHS, LV.** David Heavener, Danielle Brisebois, Burt Ward, Lawrence-Hilton Jacobs, Bruce Glover, Gary Owens, Rachelle Carson; ***D:*** David Heavener; ***W:*** David Heavener. *MED, IME*

Killer **197?** An ex-convict sets up an ingenious bank robbery, and gets double-crossed himself. **87m/C VHS, Beta.** Henry Silva. *NO*

The Killer ½ *Die Xue Shuang Xiong* **1990 (R)** Jeffrey Chow is a gangster gunman who wants out. He's hired by his best friend to perform one last killing, but it doesn't go as smoothly as he wanted. He's almost caught by "Eagle" Lee, a detective who vows to hunt him down using Jennie, a singer blinded by Chow in crossfire. Lots of action and gunfights, but also pretty corny and sentimental. Very similar to American action movies, but using Chinese and Asian cultural conventions. A good introduction to the Chinese gangster-flick genre. Available with subtitles or dubbed in English. **110m/C VHS.** *HK* Chow Yun-fat, Sally Yeh, Danny Lee, Kenneth Tsang, Chu Kong; ***D:*** John Woo; ***W:*** John Woo. *FXL, BTV, FCT*

Killer Bait ½ **1949** Muddled drama about an innocent couple who find a large sum of money accidentally dropped into their car by mobsters. Possession of the money leads the greedy wife to ruin when she gets involved with gangsters, blackmail, and murder. Also known as "Killer Bait." **99m/C VHS.** Lizabeth Scott, Don DeFore, Dan Duryea, Arthur Kennedy, Kristine Miller, Barry Kelley; ***D:*** Byron Haskin. *SNC*

Killer Commandos **19??** Mercenaries go to the rescue of an oppressed African nation to overthrow the sinister white supremacy dictator. **87m/C VHS.** Cameron Mitchell, Anthony Eisley. *NO*

Killer Dill ½ **1947** Also killer dull. A meek salesman is misidentified as a death-dealing gangster, and the comic mixups begin. **71m/B VHS.** Stuart Erwin, Anne Gwynne, Frank Albertson, Mike Mazurki, Milburn Stone, Dorothy Granger; ***D:*** Lewis D. Collins. *NOS, VYY*

Killer Diller ½ **1948** All-black musical revue featuring Nat King Cole and his Trio. **70m/B VHS, Beta.** Dusty Fletcher, Nat King Cole, Butterfly McQueen, Moms Mabley, George Wiltshire; ***D:*** Josh Binney. *MVD, NOS, DVT*

Killer Elephants **1976** A Thai man struggles to save his plantation, his wife, and his baby from the terrorists hired by a land baron to drive him away from his property. **83m/C VHS, Beta.** Sung Pa, Alan Yen, Nai Yen Ne, Yu Chien. *UNI*

The Killer Elite ½ **1975 (PG)** Straight-ahead Peckinpah fare examining friendship and betrayal. Two professional assassins begin as friends but end up stalking each other when they are double-crossed. This minor Peckinpah effort is murky and doesn't have a clear resolution, but is plenty bloody. Lots of Dobermans roam through this picture too. **120m/C VHS, Beta, LV.** James Caan, Robert Duvall, Arthur Hill, Gig Young, Burt Young, Mako, Bo Hopkins, Helmut Dantine; ***D:*** Sam Peckinpah; ***W:*** Marc Norman, Stirling Silliphant. *MGM*

Killer Fish *Deadly Treasure of the Piranha* **1979 (PG)** A scheme to steal and then hide a fortune in emeralds at the bottom of a tank full of piranhas backfires as the criminals find it impossible to retrieve them...as if that took a lot of foresight. Director Dawson is AKA Antonio Margheriti. Filmed in Brazil. **101m/C VHS, Beta.** *BR GB* Lee Majors, James Franciscus, Margaux Hemingway, Karen Black, Roy Brocksmith, Marisa Berenson; ***D:*** Anthony (Antonio Margheriti) Dawson. *FOX*

Killer Force ½ **1975 (R)** Predictable adventure involving international diamond smuggling. **100m/C VHS, Beta.** Telly Savalas, Peter Fonda, Maud Adams, Hugh O'Brian; ***D:*** Val Guest. *LIV, VES*

Killer Image **1992 (R)** A photographer unwittingly sees more than he should and becomes involved in a lethal political coverup. At the same time a wealthy senator targets him and he must fight for his life. Viewers might feel they have to fight their boredom. **97m/C VHS, Beta, LV.** John Pyper-Ferguson, Michael Ironside, M. Emmet Walsh, Krista Errickson; ***D:*** David Winning. *PAR*

A Killer in Every Corner **1974** Three psychology students visit a loony professor and succumb to his hair-raising shenanigans. **80m/C VHS, Beta.** Joanna Pettet, Patrick Magee, Max Wall, Eric Flynn. *LIV*

Killer Inside Me **1976 (R)** The inhabitants of a small Western town are unaware that their mild-mannered deputy sheriff is actually becoming a crazed psychotic murderer. From the novel by Jim Thompson. **99m/C VHS, Beta.** Stacy Keach, Susan Tyrrell, Tisha Sterling, Keenan Wynn, John Dehner, John Carradine, Don Stroud; ***D:*** Burt Kennedy; ***W:*** Robert Chandlee. *WAR, OM*

Killer Instinct **1992 (R)** Two brothers do bloody warfare with notorious mobster kingpins in prohibition-era New York City. **101m/C VHS, LV.** Christopher Bradley, Bruce Nozick, Rachel York; ***D:*** Greydon Clark, Ken Stein. *VMK*

Killer Klowns from Outer Space ½ **1988 (PG-13)** Bozo-like aliens resembling demented clowns land on earth and set up circus tents to lure Earthlings in. Visually striking, campy but slick horror flick that'll make you think twice about your next visit to the big top. Mood is heightened by a cool title tune by the Dickies. Definitely has cult potential! **90m/C VHS, Beta, LV.** Grant Cramer, Suzanne Snyder, John Allen Nelson, Royal Dano, John Vernon, Peter Licassi, Michael Siegel; ***D:*** Stephen Chiodo; ***W:*** Charles Chiodo, Stephen Chiodo; ***M:*** John Massari. *MED, CDV*

Killer Likes Candy **1978** An assassin stalks the King of Kafiristan, and a CIA operative tries to stop him. **86m/C VHS, Beta.** Kerwin Mathews, Marilu Tolo; ***D:*** Richard Owens. *GEM, MRV*

Killer Looks ½ **1994 (R)** Phil likes to watch his wife Diane seduce strangers. Then they meet Mickey, a charmer with ideas of his own. Soon Diane and Phil find their kinky world threatened. Unrated version contains 13 minutes of additional footage. **87m/C VHS, LV.** Michael Artura, Sara Suzanne Brown, Len Donato; ***D:*** Toby Phillips. *IMP*

Killer on Board **1977** Folks spending their holiday on a cruise ship are afflicted by a fatal virus and subsequently quarantined. Typical made-for-TV disaster flick. **100m/C VHS, Beta.** Claude Akins, Beatrice Straight, George Hamilton, Patty Duke, Frank Converse, Jane Seymour, William Daniels; ***D:*** Philip Leacock. *LIV*

Killer Party *Woof!* **1986 (R)** Three coeds pledge a sorority and are subjected to a hazing that involves a haunted fraternity house. Standard horror plot; Paul Bartel ("Eating Raoul"; "Lust in the Dust") is the only significant element. **91m/C VHS, Beta.** Elaine Wilkes, Sherry Willis-Burch, Joanna Johnson, Paul Bartel, Martin Hewitt, Ralph Seymour; ***D:*** William Fruet; ***W:*** Barney Cohen; ***M:*** John Beal. *FOX*

The Killer Shrews **1959** Lumet (Sidney's father) creates a serum that causes the humble shrew to take on killer proportions. The creatures are actually dogs in makeup. Goude was 1957's Miss Universe. **70m/B VHS.** James Best, Ingrid Goude, Baruch Lumet, Ken Curtis; ***D:*** Ray Kellogg. *SNC, MRV, HHT*

Killer Tomatoes Eat France ½ **1991** Professor Gangrene takes his tomato fetish to France, where the giant vegetables try to take over the streets. The fourth in the killer-vegetable series. **94m/C VHS, LV.** John Astin, Marc Price, Steve Lundquist; ***D:*** John DeBello. *FXV*

Killer Tomatoes Strike Back **1990** The third "Killer Tomatoes" movie isn't in the league of "The Naked Gun" satires, but it's still bright parody for the Mad Magazine crowd, as tomato-mad scientist Astin harnesses the powers of trash-TV in a planned vegetable invasion. Perhaps due to a 'Killer Tomatoes' cartoon series at the time, this isn't as saucy as its predecessors and is acceptable for family audiences. Followed by "Killer Tomatoes Eat France." **87m/C VHS.** John Astin, Rick Rockwell, Crystal Carson, Steve Lundquist, John Witherspoon; ***D:*** John DeBello. *FXV, IME*

Killer with Two Faces **1974** A woman is terrorized by the evil twin of her boyfriend. Made for television. **70m/C VHS, Beta.** Donna Mills, Ian Hendry, David Lodge, Roddy McMillian. *LIV*

Killer Workout *Aerobicide* **1986 (R)** A murderer stalks the clients of a sweat/sex/muscle-filled gym. **89m/C VHS, Beta.** David James Campbell, Ted Prior; ***D:*** David A. Prior. *ACA*

The Killers *Ernest Hemingway's the Killers* **1964** After two hired assassins kill a teacher, they look into his past and try to find leads to a $1,000,000 robbery. Reagan's last film. Remake of 1946 film of the same name, which was loosely based on a short story by Ernest Hemingway. Originally intended for television, but released to theaters instead due to its violence. **95m/C VHS, Beta.** Lee Marvin, Angie Dickinson, John Cassavetes, Ronald Reagan, Clu Gulager, Claude Akins, Norman Fell; ***D:*** Donald Siegel; ***M:*** John Williams. *MCA*

Killers **1988** Remote jungles of southern Africa are the scene of a military coup. **83m/C VHS, Beta.** Cameron Mitchell, Alicia Hammond, Robert Dix; ***D:*** Ewing Miles Brown. *GHV*

The Killer's Edge ½ *Blood Money* **1990 (R)** Cop is caught between rock and hard place in L.A. when he's forced to confront criminal who once saved his life in 'Nam. Plenty of gut busting and soul wrenching. **90m/C VHS, LV.** Wings Hauser, Robert Z'Dar, Karen Black. *PMH*

Killers from Space *Woof!* **1954** Cheap sci-fi flick in which big-eyed men from beyond Earth bring scientist Graves back to life to assist them with their evil plan for world domination. **80m/B VHS, Beta.** Peter Graves, Barbara Bestar, James Seay; ***D:*** W. Lee Wilder. *NOS, MRV, RHI*

Killer's Kiss ½ **1955** A boxer and a dancer set out to start a new life together when he saves the woman from an attempted rape. Gritty, second feature from Kubrick was financed by friends and family and shows signs of his budding talent. **67m/C VHS.** Frank Silvera, Jamie Smith, Irene Kane, Jerry Jarret; ***D:*** Stanley Kubrick; ***W:*** Stanley Kubrick. *FCT*

Killer's Moon **1984** Four sadistic psychopaths escape from a prison hospital and unleash their murderous rage on anyone who crosses their path. **90m/C VHS, Beta.** *NO*

The Killing **1956** The dirty, harsh, street-level big heist epic that established Kubrick and presented its genre with a new and vivid existentialist aura, as an ex-con engineers the rip-off of a racetrack with disastrous results. Displays characteristic nonsentimental sharp-edged Kubrick vision. Cinematography by Lucien Ballard. Based on the novel "Clean Break" by Lionel White. **83m/B VHS, Beta, LV.** Sterling Hayden, Marie Windsor, Elisha Cook Jr., Jay C. Flippen, Vince Edwards, Timothy Carey, Coleen Gray, Joseph Sawyer, Ted de Corsia; ***D:*** Stanley Kubrick. *MGM*

A Killing Affair **1985 (R)** Set in West Virginia, 1943, this is the story of a widow who takes in a drifter who she believes is the man who killed her husband. She begins to fall for him, but cannot be sure if she should trust him. Vague and melodramatic. From the novel "Monday, Tuesday, Wednesday" by Robert Houston. Saperstein's directorial debut. **100m/C VHS, Beta, LV.** Peter Weller, Kathy Baker, John Glover, Bill Smitrovich; ***D:*** David Saperstein; ***M:*** John Barry. *VTR, PSM*

Killing at Hell's Gate ½ **1981** A made-for-television movie about a group of white-water rafters being picked off by snipers as they travel down river. **96m/C VHS, Beta.** Robert Urich, Deborah Raffin, Lee Purcell; ***D:*** Jerry Jameson; ***M:*** David Bell. *FOX*

The Killing Beach *Turtle Beach* **1992 (R)** Australian photojournalist Judith Wilkes (Scacchi) travels to Malaysia in the late 1970s to report on the plight of the Vietnamese boat people seeking refuge there. She befriends the wife of the Australian ambassador, a former callgirl from Saigon, who hopes to find her own children among the refugees. But the native Malays resent the foreign intrusion and are determined to stop the boat people—no matter what the cost in blood. Based on the novel "Turtle Beach" by Blanche D'Alpuget. **105m/C VHS.** *AU* Greta Scacchi, Joan Chen, Jack Thompson, Art Malik, Norman Kaye; ***D:*** Stephen Wallace; ***W:*** Ann Turner. *COL*

Killing Cars ½ **1985 (R)** A German car designer's pet project, a car that runs without gas, is halted by the influence of an Arab conglomerate. He nevertheless tries to complete it, and is hunted down. **104m/C VHS, Beta.** Juergen Prochnow, Senta Berger, William Conrad, Agnes Soral; ***D:*** Michael Verhoeven. *VMK, HHE, VTR*

The Killing Device ½ **1992** Two government scientists lose their funding on a covert political assassination project and decide to eliminate the government officials responsible. When two journalists attempt to solve the murders they become the next targets. **93m/C VHS.** Clu Gulager, Antony Alda, Gig Rauch. *VCI*

The Killing Edge ½ **1986** In post-nuclear holocaust Earth, a lone warrior seeks justice, and his family, in a lawless land. **85m/C VHS.** Bill French, Marv Spencer; ***D:*** Lindsay Shonteff. *VCD, HHE*

Killing 'em Softly **1985** Segal portrays a down-on-his-luck musician who accidentally murders a music manager during an argument. Cara's boyfriend is accused and to clear his name, the singer moonlights as a detective. She and Segal end up falling in love. Disappointing. **90m/C VHS, Beta.** *CA* George Segal, Irene Cara; ***D:*** Max Fischer. *PSM, HHE*

The Killing Fields ½ **1984 (R)** Based on the New York Times' Sydney Schanberg's account of his friendship with Cambodian interpreter Dith Pran. They separated during the fall of Saigon, when Western journalists fled, leaving behind countless assistants who were later accused of collusion with the enemy by the Khmer Rouge and killed or sent to re-education camps during the bloodbath known as "Year Zero." Schanberg searched for Pran through the Red Cross and U.S. government, while Pran struggled to survive, finally escaping and walking miles to freedom. Ngor's own experiences echoed those of his character Pran. Malkovich's debut is intense. Joffe's directorial debut shows a generally sure hand, with only a bit of melodrama at the end. **142m/C VHS, Beta, LV.** *GB* Sam Waterston, Haing S. Ngor, John Malkovich, Athol Fugard, Craig T. Nelson, Julian Sands, Spalding Gray, Bill Paterson; ***D:*** Roland Joffe; ***W:*** Bruce Robinson; ***C:*** Chris Menges. Academy Awards '84: Best Cinematography, Best Film Editing, Best Supporting Actor (Ngor); Golden Globe Awards '85: Best Supporting Actor (Ngor); Los Angeles Film Critics Association Awards '84: Best Cinematography; New York Film Critics Awards '84: Best Cinematography; National Society of Film Critics Awards '84: Best Cinematography; Writers Guild of America '84: Best Adapted Screenplay; Nominations: Academy Awards '84: Best Actor (Waterston), Best Adapted Screenplay, Best Director (Joffe), Best Picture. *WAR, BTV, HMV*

Killing Floor **1985 (PG)** A black sharecropper during WWI travels to Chicago to get work in the stockyards and becomes a voice in the growing labor movement. Made for television. **118m/C VHS, Beta, LV.** Damien Leake, Alfre Woodard, Moses Gunn, Clarence Felder, Bill Duke; ***D:*** William Duke. *COL, SUE, FCT*

The Killing Game ½ *All Weekend Lovers; Jeu de Massacre* **1967** A husband-wife cartoonist team link up with an unhinged playboy and act out a murder-mystery comic they produce together. In French with subtitles. **90m/C VHS, Beta.** *FR* Jean-Pierre Cassel, Claudine Auger, Michael Duchaussoy, Anna Gaylor; ***D:*** Alain Jessua. *FCT*

The Killing Game **1987** A slew of Californians kill and betray each other for lustful reasons. **90m/C VHS, Beta.** Chad Hayward, Cynthia Killion, Geoffrey Sadwith; ***D:*** Joseph Merhi. *NO*

Killing Heat ½ *The Grass is Singing* **1984 (R)** An independent career woman living in South Africa decides to abandon her career to marry a struggling jungle farmer. Based on Doris Lessing's novel "The Grass is Singing." **104m/C VHS, Beta.** *GB SW* Karen Black, John Thaw, John Kani, John Moulder-Brown; ***D:*** Michael Raeburn. *FOX*

Killing Hour *The Clairvoyant* **1984 (R)** A psychic painter finds that the visions she paints come true in a string of grisly murders. Her ability interests a television reporter and a homicide detective. **97m/C VHS, Beta.** Elizabeth Kemp, Perry King, Norman Parker, Kenneth McMillan; ***D:*** Armand Mastroianni. *FOX*

A Killing in a Small Town **1990 (R)** Candy Morrison seems like the perfect member of her small Texas community—but appearances can be deceiving, particularly after she's charged with killing a fellow church-goer by striking her 41 times with an axe (shades of Lizzie Borden)! Dennehy is her skeptical lawyer who isn't sure if it was self-defense or a peculiar sort of revenge. Good performances by Hershey and Dennehy lift this above the usual tawdry made for TV level. Based on a true story; originally a television miniseries. **95m/C VHS, LV.** Barbara Hershey, Brian Dennehy, Hal Holbrook, Richard Gilliland, John Terry, Lee Garlington; ***D:*** Stephen Gyllenhaal; ***M:*** Richard Gibbs. *VMK*

Killing in the Sun **19?? (R)** Gripping struggle for prosperous smuggling in the Mediterranean consume mobsters from three countries. **90m/C VHS.** Henry Silva, Michael Constantine. *NO*

The Killing Kind ♂♂½ **1973** Man released from prison is obsessed with wreaking vengeance on his daft lawyer and his accuser. His vendetta eventually draws his mother into the fray as well. Fine performance by Savage. **95m/C VHS.** Ann Sothern, John Savage, Ruth Roman, Luana Anders, Cindy Williams; ***D:*** Curtis Harrington; ***M:*** Andrew Belling. *NO*

The Killing Man ♂♂ **1994** Former mobster tries going legit by changing his identity and working for the government. **100m/C VHS.** Jeff Wincott. *APX*

The Killing Mind **1990** A young girl witnesses a grisly murder that is never solved. Twenty years later she (Zimbalist) becomes a cop who specializes in trapping psychos. Haunted by her memories, she and a reporter (Bill) team up to find the killer, never suspecting that she is his next victim. Originally made-for-cable-television. **96m/C VHS.** Stephanie Zimbalist, Tony Bill, Daniel Roebuck; ***D:*** Michael Rhodes. *WOV*

Killing Obsession ♂½ **1994** Albert (Savage) has been locked in the Parkview State Psychiatric Facility for 20 years, ever since he murdered 11-year-old Annie's mother. Annie is Albert's obsession and in his mind she's always remained a young girl. So when Albert is released, he goes looking for Annie—murdering along the way. Now that the real Annie is an adult will Albert finally accept the passage of time or will she be just another victim? **95m/C VHS, LV.** John Savage, Kimberly Chase, John Saxon, Bernie White; ***D:*** Paul Leder; ***W:*** Paul Leder. *TRI*

The Killing of a Chinese Bookie ♂♂ **1976 (R)** Gazzara runs a Sunset Strip nightclub and is in hock to loan sharks. When he can't come up with the cash, he's offered a deal—get rid of a troublesome Chinese bookie and all debts will be forgiven. But it turns out the bookie is highly connected in the Asian mob and nothing goes as planned. Cassavette's improv technique makes for a self-indulgent and endless film. **109m/C VHS, Beta.** Ben Gazzara, Jean-Pierre Cassel, Zizi Johari, Soto Joe Hugh, Robert Phillips, Timothy Carey, Morgan Woodward; ***D:*** John Cassavetes; ***W:*** John Cassavetes. *TOU, FCT*

Killing of Angel Street ♂♂ **1981 (PG)** A courageous young woman unwittingly becomes the central character in an escalating nightmare about saving a community from corrupt politicians and organized crime. **101m/C VHS, Beta.** *AU* Liz Alexander, John Hargreaves; ***D:*** Donald Crombie; ***W:*** Evan Jones. *FCT*

Killing of Randy Webster ♂½ **1981** A father attempts to prove that his son did not die as a criminal when Texas policemen shot him after transporting a stolen van across state lines. **90m/C VHS, Beta.** Hal Holbrook, Dixie Carter, Sean Penn, Jennifer Jason Leigh; ***D:*** Sam Wanamaker. *NO*

The Killing of Sister George ♂♂ **1969 (R)** Racy, sensationalized film based on the Frank Marcus black comedy/melodrama about a lesbian love triangle between a television executive and two soap opera stars. Things get a little uncomfortable when they learn one of their characters is to be written out of the show. Shot in England. **138m/C VHS, Beta.** Beryl Reid, Susannah York, Coral Browne, Ronald Fraser, Patricia Medina, Hugh Paddick, Cyril Elaine Church, Brandan Dillon; ***D:*** Robert Aldrich; ***C:*** Joseph Biroc. *FOX*

Killing Stone ♂♂ **1978** A freelance writer uncovers a small town sheriff's plot to cover up a scandalous homicide. Made for television. **120m/C VHS, Beta.** Gil Gerard, J.D. Cannon, Jim Davis, Nehemiah Persoff; ***D:*** Michael Landon; ***W:*** Michael Landon. *PSM*

Killing Streets ♂♂ **1991** A commando learns that his twin brother is being held hostage in Lebanon and plans a rescue mission. A standard farfetched actioner; noteworthy for a real sense of despair over the endless carnage in the Mideast. Some dialogue in Arabic with subtitles. **109m/C VHS.** Michael Pare, Lorenzo Lamas; ***D:*** Stephen Cornwell; ***W:*** Stephen Cornwell. *VES, LIV*

The Killing Time ♂♂ **1987 (R)** A minor, effective murder thriller about a quiet small resort town suddenly beset by a web of murder, double-crossings, blackmail, and infidelity. They seem to coincide with the appearance of a mysterious stranger posing as the town's deputy sheriff just as the new sheriff is about to take up the badge. **94m/C VHS, Beta, LV.** Kiefer Sutherland, Beau Bridges, Joe Don Baker, Wayne Rogers; ***D:*** Rick King; ***W:*** Dan Bohlinger. *NWV, VTR*

Killing Zoe ♂♂ **1994 (R)** American safecracker travels to Paris for a little rest, recreation, and robbery. At the request of a childhood friend, he involves himself in an ill-conceived daytime bank heist, but not before enjoying a night with a local call girl and participating in some good ol' fashioned heroin-induced debauchery with the other bank robbers on the night before the job. Surprising no one (except maybe the still-stoned crooks), things don't go exactly as planned. Visually impressive debut for Tarantino collaborator Avary, who had his actors read "Beowulf" for its portrayal of Viking excess. **97m/C VHS, LV.** Eric Stoltz, Julie Delpy, Jean-Hugues Anglade, Gary Kemp, Bruce Ramsay, Kario Salem, Carlo Scandiuzzi; ***D:*** Roger Roberts Avary; ***W:*** Roger Roberts Avary; ***C:*** Tom Richmond. *LIV*

The Killing Zone ♂½ **1990** Convict nephew of onetime Drug Enforcement agent rewrites zoning ordinances to hunt for Mexican drug lord south of the border. **90m/C VHS.** Daron McBee, James Dalesandro, Melissa Moore, Armando Silvestre, Augustine Beral, Sydne Squire, Deborah Dare; ***D:*** Addison Randall. *PMH*

Killings at Outpost Zeta ♂ **1980** Earthmen investigate a barren planet where previous expeditions have disappeared, and find hordes of aliens. **92m/C VHS, Beta.** Gordon Devol, Jackie Ray, James A. Watson Jr. *VCI*

Killjoy ♂♂½ *Who Murdered Joy Morgan?* **1981** A sleazy surgeon's daughter is the prey in this television thriller. The plot twists are led by the array of people who become involved. A clever suspense mystery. Made for television. **100m/C VHS, Beta.** Kim Basinger, Robert Culp, Stephen Macht, Nancy Marchand, John Rubinstein, Ann Dusenberry, Ann Wedgeworth; ***D:*** John Llewellyn Moxey; ***M:*** Bruce Broughton. *LIV*

Killpoint ♂½ **1984 (R)** Special task force is assembled to catch the criminals who robbed a National Guard armory for its weapons. **89m/C VHS, Beta, LV.** Leo Fong, Richard Roundtree, Cameron Mitchell; ***D:*** Frank Harris. *LIV, VES*

Killzone ♂ **1985** A brainwashed Vietnam vet breaks down during a training exercise and embarks on a psychotic killing spree. **86m/C VHS, Beta.** Ted Prior, David James Campbell, Richard Massery; ***D:*** David A. Prior. *VES*

Kilma, Queen of the Amazons *Woof!* **1986** A shipwrecked sailor finds himself on an island populated by man-hating Amazons. When a shipload of lusty sailors arrive to rescue him, carnage ensues. **90m/C VHS, Beta.** *NO*

Kim ♂♂♂ **1950** A colorful Hollywood adaptation of the Rudyard Kipling classic about an English boy disguised as a native in 19th Century India, and his various adventures. **113m/C VHS, Beta.** Errol Flynn, Dean Stockwell, Paul Lukas, Cecil Kellaway; ***D:*** Victor Saville; ***M:*** Andre Previn. *MGM*

Kim ♂♂½ **1984** Kim (Sheth) is a 15-year-old boy living by his wits on the streets of 1890s India. Trying to discover his true identity, Kim's befriended by a Buddhist monk who wishes the boy to be his disciple and a British spy, who trains him for a daring mission against the Russians. Rousing TV adaptation of the Rudyard Kipling novel. **135m/C VHS.** Ravi Sheth, Peter O'Toole, Bryan Brown, John Rhys-Davies, Julian Glover; ***D:*** John Davies. *PME*

Kind Hearts and Coronets ♂♂♂½ **1949** Black comedy in which an ambitious young man sets out to bump off eight relatives in an effort to claim a family title. Guinness is wonderful in his role as all eight of the fated relations. Based on Roy Horiman's novel. **104m/B VHS, Beta, LV.** *GB* Alec Guinness, Dennis Price, Valerie Hobson, Joan Greenwood; ***D:*** Robert Hamer. National Board of Review Awards '50: 5 Best Foreign Films of the Year. *REP, FCT, HMV*

A Kind of Loving ♂♂♂ **1962** Two North English young people marry rashly as a result of pregnancy, find they really didn't like each other all that much, but manage to adjust. **107m/B VHS, Beta.** *GB* Alan Bates, Thora Hird, June Ritchie; ***D:*** John Schlesinger. *NO*

Kindergarten ♂♂♂ **1984** Endearing tale based on a true story of a young Russian street violinist. During WWII, the boy meets a variety of interesting people as he travels throughout the Soviet Union. In Russian with English subtitles. **143m/C VHS.** *RU* Klaus Maria Brandauer; ***D:*** Yevgeny Yevtushenko. *KIV*

Kindergarten Cop ♂♂½ **1990 (PG-13)** Pectoral perfect cop Kimble (Schwarzenegger) stalks mama's boy/criminal Crisp (Tyson) by locating the drug lord's ex and his six-year-old son. When the pec man's female partner succumbs to a nasty bout of food poisoning, he's forced to take her place as an undercover kindergarten teacher in the drowsy Pacific northwest community where mother and son reside incognito. A cover all the bases Christmas release, it's got romance, action, comedy and cute. And box office earnings to match Arnie's chest measurements. A bit violent for the milk and cookie set. **111m/C VHS, Beta, LV.** Arnold Schwarzenegger, Penelope Ann Miller, Pamela Reed, Linda Hunt, Richard Tyson, Carroll Baker, Cathy Moriarty, Park Overall, Richard Portnow, Jayne Brook; ***D:*** Ivan Reitman; ***W:*** Murray Salem, Herschel Weingrod, Timothy Harris; ***C:*** Michael Chapman; ***M:*** Randy Edelman. *MCA, CCB*

The Kindred ♂♂½ **1987 (R)** A young student discovers that his mother the biologist has created a hybrid creature using his body tissue. Naturally, he is horrified and begins to search for his test-tube brother; the problem is, this brother likes eating people. Not too bad; boasts some good acting. **92m/C VHS, Beta, LV.** Rod Steiger, Kim Hunter, David Allan Brooks, Timothy Gibbs, Amanda Pays, Talia Balsam, Jeffrey Obrow, Peter Frechette, Julia Montgomery; ***D:*** Jeffrey Obrow, Stephen Carpenter; ***W:*** Jeffrey Obrow, Stephen Carpenter, Joseph Stefano, John Penney, Earl Ghaffari; ***M:*** David Newman. *LIV, VES*

King ♂♂♂ **1978** Docudrama with terrific cast follows the life and career of one of the greatest non-violent civil rights leaders of all time, Martin Luther King. Made for television. **272m/C VHS, Beta.** Paul Winfield, Cicely Tyson, Roscoe Lee Browne, Ossie Davis, Art Evans, Ernie Banks, Howard E. Rollins Jr., William Jordan, Cliff DeYoung; ***D:*** Abby Mann; ***W:*** Abby Mann; ***M:*** Billy Goldenberg. *NO*

The King and Four Queens ♂♂½ **1956** Gable, on the run from the law, happens upon a deserted town, deserted, that is, except for a woman and her three daughters. Clark soon discovers that the women are looking for $100,000 in gold that one of their missing husbands had stolen. True to form, conniving Clark wastes no time putting the moves on each of them to find the whereabouts of the loot. **86m/C VHS, Beta.** Clark Gable, Eleanor Parker, Jo Van Fleet, Jean Wiles, Barbara Nichols, Sara Shane, Roy Roberts, Arthur Shields, Jay C. Flippen; ***D:*** Raoul Walsh; ***M:*** Alex North. *MGM, CCB*

The King and I ♂♂♂♂ **1956** Wonderful adaptation of Rodgers and Hammerstein's Broadway play based on the novel "Anna and the King of Siam" by Margaret Landon. English governess Kerr is hired to teach the King of Siam's many children and bring them into the 20th century. She has more of a job than she realizes, for this is a king, a country, and a people who value tradition above all else. Features one of Rodgers and Hammerstein's best-loved scores. Brynner made this role his, playing it over 4,000 times on stage and screen before his death. Kerr's voice was dubbed when she sang; the voice you hear is Marni Nixon, who also dubbed the star's singing voices in "West Side Story" and "My Fair Lady." ♫Shall We Dance?; Getting To Know You; Hello, Young Lovers; We Kiss in a Shadow; I Whistle a Happy Tune; March of the Siamese Children; I Have Dreamed; A Puzzlement; Something Wonderful. **133m/C VHS, Beta, LV.** Deborah Kerr, Yul Brynner, Rita Moreno, Martin Benson, Terry Saunders, Rex Thompson,

Alan Mowbray, Carlos Rivas; **D:** Walter Lang; **W:** Ernest Lehman; **M:** Richard Rodgers, Oscar Hammerstein, Leon Shamroy. Academy Awards '56: Best Actor (Brynner), Best Art Direction/Set Decoration (Color), Best Costume Design (Color), Best Sound, Best Score; Golden Globe Awards '57: Best Actress—Musical/Comedy (Kerr), Best Film—Musical/Comedy; Nominations: Academy Awards '56: Best Actress (Kerr), Best Color Cinematography, Best Director (Lang), Best Picture. *FOX, BTV, RDG*

King Arthur, the Young Warlord 🦴🦴 **1975 (PG)** The struggle that was the other side of Camelot—the campaign against the Saxon hordes. The early, somewhat violent years of King Art. **90m/C VHS, Beta.** Oliver Tobias, Michael Gothard, Jack Watson, Brian Blessed, Peter Firth; **D:** Sidney Hayers, Pat Jackson, Peter Sasdy. *GEM*

King Boxer 🦴 **1990** A famous martial arts school is taken over by a menacing gang. When a student-to-be finds this out, he enlists himself to take on the best individual of the gang in a deadly match. **106m/C VHS.** Lo Lieh, Wang Ping. *HMD*

King Boxers 🦴🦴 **1980 (R)** Kurate stars in this tale of elephant hunts, warding off Triad Society gangs, and personal combat. Nainam is a former Thailand fists and kick boxing champion. **90m/C VHS, Beta.** Yasuka Kurata, Johnny Nainam. *GEM*

King Creole 🦴🦴½ **1958** The King goes film noir as a teenager with a criminal record who becomes a successful pop singer in New Orleans but is threatened by his ties to crime, represented by Walter Matthau. One of the better Elvis films, based on Harold Robbins' "A Stone for Danny Fisher." Features Elvis' last film appearance before his service in the Army. ♫King Creole; Banana; New Orleans; Turtles, Berries and Gumbo; Crawfish; Don't Ask Me Why; As Long As I Have You; Trouble; Hard-Headed Woman. **115m/B VHS, Beta, LV.** Elvis Presley, Carolyn Jones, Walter Matthau, Dean Jagger, Dolores Hart, Vic Morrow, Paul Stewart; **D:** Michael Curtiz. *MVD, FOX*

King David 🦴½ **1985 (PG-13)** The story of David, the legendary Biblical hero whose acts of bravery paved the way for him to become king of Israel. **114m/C VHS, Beta, LV.** Richard Gere, Alice Krige, Cherie Lunghi, Hurd Hatfield, Edward Woodward; **D:** Bruce Beresford; **W:** Andrew Birkin, James Costigan; **M:** Carl Davis. *PAR*

King Dinosaur 🦴½ **1955** A new planet arrives in the solar system, and a scientific team checks out its giant iguana-ridden terrain. **63m/B VHS, Beta, LV.** Bill Bryant, Wanda Curtis, Patti Gallagher, Douglas Henderson. *MLB*

A King in New York 🦴🦴 **1957** Chaplin plays the deposed king of a European mini-monarchy who comes to the United States in hope of making a new life. Looks critically at 1950s-era America, including Cold War paranoia and over reliance on technology. Containing Chaplin's last starring performance, this film wasn't released in the U.S. until 1973. Uneven but interesting. **105m/B VHS, Beta.** *GB* Charlie Chaplin, Dawn Addams, Michael Chaplin, Oliver Johnston, Maxine Audley, Harry Green; **D:** Charlie Chaplin; **C:** Georges Perinal. *FOX*

King Kelly of the U.S.A. 🦴 **1934** Robertson carries on a forgettable romance with a princess aboard a trans-Atlantic line. **64m/B VHS.** Guy Robertson, Irene Ware, Edgar Kennedy, Franklin Pangborn, Joyce Compton, Ferdinand Gottschalk, William von Brinken, Otis Harlan; **D:** Leonard Fields. *NOS*

King Kong 🦴🦴🦴🦴 **1933** The original beauty and the beast film classic tells the story of Kong, a giant ape captured in Africa and brought to New York as a sideshow attraction. Kong falls for Wray, escapes from his captors and rampages through the city, ending up on top of the newly built Empire State Building. Moody Steiner score adds color, and Willis O'Brien's stop-motion animation still holds up well. Remade numerous times with various theme derivations. Available in a colorized version. The laserdisc, produced from a superior negative, features extensive liner notes and running commentary by film historian Ronald Haver. **105m/B VHS, Beta, LV, 8mm.** Fay Wray, Bruce Cabot, Robert Armstrong, Frank Reicher, Noble Johnson, Sam Hardy, James Flavin; **D:** Ernest B. Schoedsack; **M:** Max Steiner. *TTC, MED, FUS*

King Kong 🦴🦴 **1976 (PG)** Oil company official travels to a remote island to discover it inhabited by a huge gorilla. The transplanted beast suffers unrequited love in classic fashion: monkey meets girl, monkey gets girl and brandishes her while atop the World Trade Center. An updated remake of the 1933 movie classic that also marks the screen debut of Lange. Impressive sets and a believable King Kong romp around New York City in this film. Watch for Joe Piscopo, and quickly for Corbin Bernsen as a reporter. **135m/C VHS, Beta, LV, 8mm.** Jeff Bridges, Charles Grodin, Jessica Lange, Rene Auberjonois, John Randolph, Ed Lauter, Jack O'Halloran; **D:** John Guillermin; **M:** John Barry. Academy Awards '76: Best Visual Effects; Nominations: Academy Awards '76: Best Cinematography, Best Sound. *PAR, HMV*

King Kong Lives 🦴 **1986 (PG-13)** Unnecessary sequel to the 1976 remake of "King Kong," in which two scientists get the big ape, now restored after his asphalt-upsetting fall, together with a lady ape his size and type. **105m/C VHS, Beta, LV.** Brian Kerwin, Linda Hamilton, John Ashton, Peter Michael Goetz; **D:** John Guillermin; **W:** Steven Pressfield. *MED, WAR*

King Kong vs. Godzilla 🦴🦴½ *King Kong Tai Godzilla* **1963** The planet issues a collective shudder as the two mightiest monsters slug it out for reasons known only to themselves. Humankind can only stand by and watch in impotent horror as the tide of the battle sways to and fro, until one monster stands alone and victorious. **105m/C VHS.** *JP* Inoshiro Honda, Michael Keith, Tadao Takashima; **D:** Thomas Montgomery. *GKK*

King Kung Fu 🦴 **1987 (G)** A karate master raises a gorilla, and sends it from Asia to the U.S. There, two out-of-work reporters decide to release it from captivity and then recapture it so they can get the story and some needed recognition. The background they don't have on the gorilla is that its master taught it kung fu. **90m/C VHS.** John Balee, Tom Leahy, Maxine Gray, Bill Schwartz; **D:** Bill Hayes. *NO*

King Lear 🦴🦴🦴½ **1971** Brook's version of Shakespeare tragedy. The king drives away the only decent daughter he has, and when he realizes this, it is too late. Powerful performances and interesting effort at updating the bard. **137m/B VHS.** *GB* Paul Scofield, Irene Worth, Jack MacGowran, Alan Webb, Cyril Cusack, Patrick Magee; **D:** Peter Brook. *NOS, DVT*

King Lear 🦴½ **1987** Loosely adapted from Shakespeare's tragedy of a king who loses everything. A fragmented French existential reading with gangster undercurrent. This updated version is dark, ominous, wandering, strange, and quite unlike the other 1984 remake. Or any other remake, for that matter. **91m/C VHS.** *SI* Peter Sellers, Burgess Meredith, Molly Ringwald, Jean-Luc Godard, Woody Allen; **D:** Jean-Luc Godard; **W:** Norman Mailer. *INJ, CAN*

The King Murder 🦴🦴 **1932** High-society sleuth Tearle tries to solve the mysterious death of a beautiful, yet dangerous extortionist. Looks a lot like murder, although no weapon can be found. **67m/B VHS.** Conway Tearle, Natalie Moorhead, Marceline Day, Dorothy Revier; **D:** Richard Thorpe; **W:** Charles Reed Jones. *SNC*

King of America 🦴 **1980** A Greek sailor and a local labor agent battle over who will become King of America. **90m/C VHS, Beta.** **D:** Dezso Magyar. *NO*

King of Comedy 🦴🦴🦴 **1982 (PG)** An unhinged would-be comedian haunts and eventually kidnaps a massively popular Johnny Carson-type television personality. A cold, cynical farce devised by Scorsese seemingly in reaction to John Hinckley's obsession with his film "Taxi Driver." Controlled, hard-hitting performances, especially by De Niro and Lewis. **101m/C VHS, Beta, LV.** Robert De Niro, Jerry Lewis, Sandra Bernhard, Tony Randall, Diahnne Abbott, Shelley Hack, Liza Minnelli; **D:** Martin Scorsese. British Academy Awards '83: Best Original Screenplay; National Society of Film Critics Awards '83: Best Supporting Actress (Bernhard); Nominations: Cannes Film Festival '83: Best Film. *COL, FCT*

The King of Hearts 🦴🦴🦴 *Le Roi de Coeur* **1966** In WWI, a Scottish soldier finds a battle-torn French town evacuated of all occupants except a colorful collection of escaped lunatics from a nearby asylum. The lunatics want to make him their king, which is not a bad alternative to the insanity of war. Bujold is cute as ballerina wannabe; look for Serrault ("La Cage aux Folles") as, not surprisingly, a would-be effeminate hairdresser. Light-hearted comedy with a serious message; definitely worthwhile. **101m/C VHS, Beta, LV.** *FR GB* Alan Bates, Genevieve Bujold, Adolfo Celi, Francoise Christophe, Micheline Presle; **D:** Philippe de Broca; **M:** Georges Delerue. *MGM, INJ, TVC*

King of Jazz 🦴🦴½ **1930** A lavish revue built around the Paul Whiteman Orchestra with comedy sketches and songs by the stars on Universal Pictures' talent roster. (Though billed as the King of Jazz, Whiteman was never as good as jazz's real royalty.) Filmed in two-color Technicolor with a cartoon segment by Walter Lantz. ♫Rhapsody in Blue; So the Bluebirds and the Blackbirds Got Together; Mississippi Mud; It Happened in Monterey; Ragamuffin Romeo; Happy Feet; Song of the Dawn; A Bench in the Park. **93m/C VHS, Beta.** Paul Whiteman, John Boles, Jeanette Loff, Bing Crosby; **D:** John Murray Anderson. Academy Awards '30: Best Interior Decoration. *MCA, MLB, RXM*

King of Kings 🦴🦴½ **1927** DeMille depicts the life of Jesus Christ in this highly regarded silent epic. The resurrection scene appears in color. Remade by Nicholas Ray in 1961. **115m/B VHS, Beta.** H.B. Warner, Dorothy Cumming, Ernest Torrence, Joseph Schildkraut, Jacqueline Logan, Victor Varconi, William Boyd; **D:** Cecil B. DeMille. *MSP*

The King of Kings 🦴🦴🦴 **1961** The life of Christ is intelligently told, with an attractive visual sense and a memorable score. Remake of Cecil B. DeMille's silent film, released in 1927. Laserdisc format features a special letterboxed edition of this film. **170m/C VHS, Beta, LV.** Jeffrey Hunter, Siobhan McKenna, Hurd Hatfield, Robert Ryan, Rita Gam, Viveca Lindfors, Rip Torn; **D:** Nicholas Ray; **W:** Philip Yordan; **C:** Milton Krasner; **M:** Miklos Rozsa. *MGM, IGP*

King of Kong Island *Woof!* **1978** Intent on world domination, a group of mad scientists implant receptors in the brains of gorillas on Kong Island, and the monster apes run amok. **92m/C VHS, Beta.** *SP* Brad Harris, Marc Lawrence; **D:** Robert Morris. *NO*

The King of Marvin Gardens 🦴🦴½ **1972 (R)** Nicholson stars as a Midwest radio jock who prefers to reminisce about his life and family back in Atlantic City, New Jersey to playing records. When Nicholson returns for a visit he finds brother Dern, king of the get-rich-quick schemers, working for a black crime syndicate. Dern is involved in another scheme which means embezzling money from his boss—not a smart idea although Nicholson can't dissuade him. Talky drama also features Burstyn as Dern's neglected girlfriend. **104m/C VHS.** Jack Nicholson, Bruce Dern, Ellen Burstyn, Scatman Crothers, Julia Anne Robinson, Charles Lavine, Arnold Williams, Josh Mostel; **D:** Bob Rafelson; **W:** Jacob Brackman. *COL, BTV*

King of New York 🦴🦴🦴 **1990 (R)** Drug czar Frank White (Walken), recently returned from a prison sabbatical, regains control of his New York drug empire with the aid of a loyal network of black dealers. How? Call it dangerous charisma, an inexplicable sympatico. Headquartered in Manhattan's chic Plaza hotel, he ruthlessly orchestrates the drug machine, while funneling the profits into a Bronx hospital for the poor. As inscrutable as White himself, Walken makes the drug czar's power tangible, believable, yet never fathomable. **106m/C VHS, LV.** Christopher Walken, Laurence "Larry" Fishburne, David Caruso, Victor Argo, Wesley Snipes, Janet Julian, Joey Chin, Giancarlo Esposito, Steve Buscemi; **D:** Abel Ferrara; **W:** Nicholas St. John; **M:** Joe Delia. *LIV*

King of the Bullwhip 🦴½ **1951** Two undercover U.S. Marshals are sent to Tioga City to stop the killing and looting of a masked bandit, whose whip is as dangerous as his gun. **59m/B VHS, Beta.** Lash LaRue, Al "Fuzzy" St. John, Anne Gwynne, Tom

Neal, Jack Holt, Dennis Moore, Michael Whalen, George Lewis; *D:* Ron Ormond. *NOS, VCN, DVT*

King of the Congo ♂½ **1952** Crabbe, in his last serial, as a pilot who is frantically searching for an important piece of film. In 15 parts. **?m/B VHS.** Buster Crabbe, Gloria Dee; *D:* Spencer Gordon Bennet, Wallace Grissell. *MLB*

King of the Cowboys ♂♂ **1943** Roy fights a gang of saboteurs and saves a defense installation. **54m/B VHS.** Roy Rogers, Smiley Burnette, James Bush. *NOS, VCN, DVT*

King of the Damned ♂ **1936** On an island prison Veidt leads a convict's revolt against the cruel administrator (Hallard), who gets killed. Before he dies, Hallard alerts a convenient warship, which begins shelling the island. Hallard's daughter, who has fallen for Veidt, pleads for the men and everyone is given a fair trial. Miscast and ineptly performed, although Veidt retains some dignity. **81m/B VHS.** *GB* Conrad Veidt, Helen Vinson, C.M. Hallard, Noah Beery Sr., Percy Walsh, Raymond Lovell, Cecil Ramage, Peter Croft; *D:* Walter Forde; *W:* Charles Bennett, Sidney Gilliat, Noel Langley. *HCV*

King of the Forest Rangers 1946 Ranger Steve King must stop an evil archaeologist from finding a treasure whose secret lies within an ancient Indian rug pattern. Edited from an original, 12 episode serial on two cassettes. **167m/B VHS, Beta.** Larry Thompson, Helen Talbot, Stuart Hamblen, Anthony Warde. *REP, MLB*

King of the Grizzlies ♂½ **1969 (G)** The mystical relationship between a Cree Indian and a grizzly cub is put to the acid test when the full grown bear attacks a ranch at which the Indian is foreman. **93m/C VHS, Beta.** Chris Wiggins, John Yesno; *D:* Ron Kelly. *DIS*

King of the Gypsies ♂♂½ **1978 (R)** Interesting drama. A young man, scornful of his gypsy heritage, runs away from the tribe and tries to make a life of his own. He is summoned home to his grandfather's deathbed where he is proclaimed the new king of the gypsies, thus incurring the wrath of his scorned father. From Peter Maas's best-selling novel. **112m/C VHS, Beta, LV.** Sterling Hayden, Eric Roberts, Susan Sarandon, Brooke Shields, Shelley Winters, Annie Potts, Annette O'Toole, Judd Hirsch, Michael V. Gazzo, Roy Brocksmith; *D:* Frank Pierson; *W:* Frank Pierson; *C:* Sven Nykvist. *PAR, CCB*

King of the Hill ♂♂♂½ **1993 (PG-13)** Quiet depression-era drama focuses on Aaron, a 12-year-old who lives in a seedy hotel in St. Louis. The family is barely scraping by: his mother is in a tuberculosis sanitarium, his younger brother has been sent away to live with relatives, and Aaron must fend for himself when his father gets work as a traveling salesman. Aaron excels at school and his efforts there, as well as his hotel friends, manage to provide him with some semblance of a regular life. Soderberg's third directorial effort is unsentimental but admiring of his character's resourcefulness and imagination during difficult times. Based on the book by A.E. Hochner describing his own childhood. **102m/C VHS, LV.** Jesse Bradford, Jeroen Krabbe, Lisa Eichhorn, Karen Allen, Spalding Gray, Elizabeth McGovern, Joseph Chrest, Adrien Brody, Cameron Boyd, Chris Samples, Katherine Heigl, Amber Benson, John McConnell, Ron Vawter, John Durbin, Lauryn Hill, David Jensen; *D:* Steven Soderbergh; *W:* Steven Soderbergh; *M:* Cliff Martinez. Nominations: Cannes Film Festival '93: Best Film. *MCA*

The King of the Kickboxers *Woof!* **1991 (R)** The villains make kung-fu snuff movies with unwitting actors killed on camera. Otherwise, same old junk about a karate cop back in Bangkok to get the dude who squashed his brother. Pretty racist at times. **90m/C VHS.** Loren Avedon, Richard Jaeckel, Billy Blanks, Don Stroud, Keith Cooke; *D:* Lucas Lowe. *IMP*

King of the Kongo ♂♂ **1929** A handsome young man is sent by the government to Nuhalla, deep in the jungle, to break up a gang of ivory thieves. Serial was made in silent and sound versions. **213m/B VHS, Beta.** Jacqueline Logan, Boris Karloff, Richard Tucker; *D:* Richard Thorpe. *VYY, NOS, MLB*

King of the Mountain ♂½ **1981 (PG)** The "Old King" and the "New King" must square off in this tale of daredevil road racers who zoom through the streets of Hollywood. Interesting cast trapped by tired script. **92m/C VHS, Beta.** Richard Cox, Harry Hamlin, Dennis Hopper, Joseph Bottoms, Deborah Van Valkenburgh, Dan Haggerty; *D:* Noel Nosseck; *W:* Roger Christian. *SUE*

King of the Pecos ♂♂½ **1936** A young lawyer (who's also adept at the shootin' iron) exacts revenge on his parents' killers in the courtroom. Well made early Wayne outing, with good character development, taut pacing and beautiful photography. **54m/B VHS.** John Wayne, Muriel Evans, Cy Kendall, Jack Clifford, John Beck, Yakima Canutt; *D:* Joseph Kane. *REP, MLB*

The King of the Roaring '20s: The Story of Arnold Rothstein ♂♂½ *The Big Bankroll* **1961** "True" story of infamous gangster, Arnold Rothstein, a brilliant and ruthless gambler who practically ran New York in the twenties. This version of his life focuses on his rise to power, the dealings with his enemies, and his crumbling personal life. Superficial due mostly to the weak screenplay. Adapted from the book "The Big Bankroll" by Leo Katcher. **106m/B VHS, Beta.** David Janssen, Dianne Foster, Mickey Rooney, Jack Carson, Diana Dors, Dan O'Herlihy, Mickey Shaughnessy, Keenan Wynn; *D:* Joseph M. Newman. *FOX, FCT*

King of the Rocketmen 1949 Jeff King thwarts an attempt by traitors to steal government scientific secrets. Serial in twelve episodes. Later released as a feature titled "Lost Planet Airmen." **156m/B VHS, LV.** Tristram Coffin, Mae Clarke, I. Stanford Jolley; *D:* Fred Brannon. *MED, VCN, REP*

King of the Rodeo ♂♂ **1928** Cowpoke Hoot wins a rodeo and catches a thief in the Windy City. Hoot's final silent ride into the sunset. **54m/B VHS, Beta.** Hoot Gibson, Kathryn Crawford, Slim Summerville, Charles French, Monte Montague, Joseph Girard; *D:* Henry MacRae. *GPV*

King of the Sierras ♂½ **1938** Bosworth tells his nephew the story of a white horse that protected his mares from a black stallion. The acting of the horses is better than that of the humans. **58m/B VHS.** Hobart Bosworth, Harry Harvey, Harry Harvey Jr., Jim Campeau; *D:* Samuel Diege; *W:* W. Scott Darling. *GPV*

King of the Stallions ♂½ **1942** A dangerous stallion is a menacing threat to the herd and the cowboys and Indians and other scattered wildlife. Chief Thundercloud is the only one capable of tackling the matter. Largely Indian cast, including Iron Eyes Cody, famed for the anti-litter campaign. **63m/B VHS.** Chief Thundercloud, Princess Bluebird, Chief Yowlachie, Rick Vallin, Dave O'Brien, Barbara Felker, Iron Eyes Cody; *D:* Edward Finney. *NOS, DVT*

King of the Texas Rangers 1941 Tom King, Texas Ranger, finds that his father's killers are a group of saboteurs who have destroyed American oil fields. This twelve episode serial comes on two tapes. **195m/B VHS.** Sammy Baugh, Neil Hamilton; *D:* William Witney, John English. *REP, MRV, MLB*

King of the Wild Horses ♂♂♂ **1924** Engaging children's story about a wild stallion that comes to the rescue. Terrific action photography of Rex going through his paces. Look for Chase in a rare dramatic role. Silent. **50m/B VHS, Beta.** Rex, Edna Murphy, Leon Barry, Pat Hartigan, Frank Butler, Charley Chase; *D:* Fred Jackman. *NO*

King of the Wind ♂♂½ **1993 (PG)** An epic adventure featuring the true story of a legendary Arabian horse and a poor stable boy who gave the most precious gift of all: love. **101m/C VHS.** Richard Harris, Glenda Jackson. *FHE*

King of the Zombies *Woof!* **1941** Mad scientist creates his own zombies without souls, to be used as the evil tools of a foreign government. Zombie nonsense. **67m/B VHS, Beta.** John Archer, Dick Purcell, Mantan Moreland, Henry Victor, Joan Woodbury; *D:* Jean Yarbrough. Nominations: Academy Awards '41: Best Original Score. *VYY, MRV, SNC*

The King on Main Street ♂♂½ **1925** A king on vacation in America finds romance. **?m/B VHS, Beta.** Adolphe Menjou, Bessie Love. *NO*

King, Queen, Knave ♂♂♂ *Herzbube* **1972** Sexy black comedy about a shy, awkward 19-year-old boy, keenly aware that his interest in girls is not reciprocated. He has to go live with his prosperous uncle and his much younger wife when his parents are killed. Based on the Vladimir Nabokov novel. **94m/C VHS, Beta.** *GE* Gina Lollobrigida, David Niven, John Moulder-Brown; *D:* Jerzy Skolimowski; *W:* David Seltzer. Nominations: Cannes Film Festival '72: Best Film. *SUE*

King Ralph ♂♂ **1991 (PG)** When the rest of the royal family passes away in a freak accident, lounge lizard Ralph finds himself the only heir to the throne. O'Toole is the long-suffering valet who tries to train him for the job. Funny in spots and Goodman is the quintessential good sport, making the whole outing pleasant. Sometimes too forced. **96m/C VHS, Beta, LV.** John Goodman, Peter O'Toole, Camille Coduri, Joely Richardson, John Hurt; *D:* David S. Ward; *W:* David S. Ward; *M:* James Newton Howard. *MCA, CCB*

King Rat ♂♂♂ **1965** Drama set in a WWII Japanese prisoner-of-war camp. Focuses on the effect of captivity on the English, Australian, and American prisoners. An American officer bribes his Japanese captors to live more comfortably than the rest. Based on James Clavell's novel. **134m/B VHS, Beta.** George Segal, Tom Courtenay, James Fox, James Donald, Denholm Elliott, Patrick O'Neal, John Mills; *D:* Bryan Forbes; *C:* Burnett Guffey; *M:* John Barry. Nominations: Academy Awards '65: Best Art Direction/Set Decoration (B & W), Best Black and White Cinematography. *COL*

King Richard and the Crusaders ♂½ **1954** Laughable costume epic with Sanders as Richard the Lionheart, who survives an assassination attempt during the Crusades. Harvey is a loyal knight sworn to find the traitors with Harrison as the noble leader of the Arab forces. Mayo plays Harvey's object of affection. Even the battle scenes are boring. Based on "The Talisman" by Sir Walter Scott. **113m/C VHS.** George Sanders, Rex Harrison, Laurence Harvey, Virginia Mayo, Robert Douglas, Michael Pate, Paula Raymond, Lester Matthews; *D:* David Butler; *W:* John Twist; *M:* Max Steiner. *FCT, MOV, WAR*

King Solomon's Mines ♂♂♂ **1937** The search for King Solomon's Mines leads a safari through the treacherous terrain of the desert, fending off sandstorms, Zulus, and a volcanic eruption. Adapted from the novel by H. Rider Haggard and remade twice. **80m/B VHS, Beta.** Cedric Hardwicke, Paul Robeson, Roland Young, John Loder, Anna Lee; *D:* Robert Stevenson. *SNC, NOS, HMV*

King Solomon's Mines ♂♂♂ **1950** A lavish version of the classic H. Rider Haggard adventures about African explorers searching out a fabled diamond mine. Remake of the 1937 classic; remade again in 1985. **102m/C VHS, Beta.** Stewart Granger, Deborah Kerr, Richard Carlson, Hugo Haas, Lowell Gilmore; *D:* Compton Bennett; *C:* Robert L. Surtees. Academy Awards '50: Best Color Cinematography, Best Film Editing; Nominations: Academy Awards '50: Best Picture. *MGM*

King Solomon's Mines ♂½ **1985 (PG-13)** The third remake of the classic H. Rider Haggard novel about a safari deep into Africa in search of an explorer who disappeared while searching for the legendary diamond mines of King Solomon. Updated but lacking the style of the previous two films. Somewhat imperialistic, racist point of view. **101m/C VHS, Beta.** Richard Chamberlain, John Rhys-Davies, Sharon Stone, Herbert Lom; *D:* J. Lee Thompson; *W:* Gene Quintano; *M:* Jerry Goldsmith. *MGM*

King Solomon's Treasure ♂ **1976** The great white adventurer takes on the African jungle, hunting for hidden treasure in the Forbidden City. Ekland stars as a Phoenician Queen—need we say more?? **90m/C VHS, Beta.** *CA GB* David McCallum, Britt Ekland, Patrick Macnee, Wilfrid Hyde-White; *D:* Alvin Rakoff. *VCI*

The Kingdom ♂♂½ **1995** Danish director von Trier serves up what must be the first four and a half hour-long hospital soap opera/ghost story/comedy/satire. Elderly Mrs. Drusse checks herself into a hospital known as the Kingdom, which is inhabited by the usual medical suspects: Pompous surgeons, incompetent buraucrats, and quirky residents. She hears the ghostly call of a child from an elevator shaft and sticks around to investigate. Made for Danish TV but released theatrically there and in the States, film owes a great deal to "Twin Peaks" and B-movie horror flicks. Doesn't take itself too seriously, but probably can't be watched all in one sitting. Danish and Swedish with subtitles. **279m/C VHS.** *DK* Kirsten Rolffes, Ghita Norby, Udo Kier, Ernst Hugo Jarogard, Soren Pilmark, Holger Juul Hansen, Baard Owe, Birgitte Raabjerg, Peter Mygind; ***D:*** Lars von Trier; ***W:*** Lars von Trier, Tomas Gislason; ***C:*** Eric Kress; ***M:*** Joachim Holbek. *HMK*

Kingdom of the Spiders ♂♂½ **1977 (PG)** A desert town is invaded by swarms of killer tarantulas, which begin to consume townspeople. **90m/C VHS, Beta.** William Shatner, Tiffany Bolling, Woody Strode; ***D:*** John Cardos; ***W:*** Alan Cailou. *FCT*

Kingfish: A Story of Huey P. Long ♂♂½ **1995** Charismatic political kingpin of Louisiana, Huey P. Long is brought to vivid life with Goodman's swaggering portrayal. Story is told in flashback, beginning with Long's assassination in 1935. A champion of the working man, Long parlayed charm and corruption into a Depression-era political career as governor and U.S. Senator. But naturally, the hard-drinking, hard-loving Long makes a lot of enemies along the way. Long's life was also memorably recreated in Robert Penn Warren's "All the King's Men," as was that of his younger brother, Governor Earl Long, in the film "Blaze." **97m/C VHS.** John Goodman, Matt Craven, Anne Heche, Ann Dowd, Jeffery Perry, Bob Gunton, Hoyt Axton, Kirk Baltz, Bill Cobbs; ***D:*** Thomas Schlamme; ***W:*** Paul Monash; ***M:*** Patrick Williams. *TTC*

Kingfisher Caper ♂♂ **1976 (PG)** A power struggle between a businessman, his brother, and a divorced sister is threatening to rip a family-owned diamond empire apart. **90m/C VHS, Beta.** Hayley Mills, David McCallum; ***D:*** Dirk DeVilliers. *MED*

Kingfisher the Killer ♂ **198?** Charles, the Raging Titan of Ninja skill, stalks the bad gang that killed his mother and hits them with nunchakos. **90m/C VHS, Beta.** Sho Kosugi. *TWE*

Kingpin *Woof!* **1996 (PG-13)** It's got an IQ lower than "Dumb & Dumber," which lately has been a good thing, but when no one laughs at a comedy movie's trailer—beware. Roy Munson's (Harrelson) a former bowling champ who, thanks to his sleazy ways, lost a hand and is reduced to selling bowling equipment. That is until he meets innocent Amish phenom Ishamael (Quaid), whom he persuades to hit the road to a big money tournament in Vegas where Roy can confront an old nemesis (Murray). There's lots of stupidity about introducing Quaid to beer, girls, and various debauchery. Wonder if the Amish can sue for defamation of character? **?m/C VHS.** Woody Harrelson, Randy Quaid, Vanessa Angel, Bill Murray; ***D:*** Peter Farrelly, Bobby Farrelly; ***W:*** Bobby Farrelly, Mort Nathan; ***C:*** Mark Irwin; ***M:*** Freedy Johnston. *NYR*

Kings and Desperate Men ♂½ **1983** Apprentice terrorists plea their case at a public forum when they take a rakish talk show host hostage. **118m/C VHS.** *GB* Patrick McGoohan, Alexis Kanner, Andrea Marcovicci, Robin Spry, Frank Moore; ***D:*** Alexis Kanner. *NO*

Kings Go Forth ♂♂½ **1958** Hormones and war rage in this love triangle set against the backdrop of WWII France. Sinatra loves Wood who loves Curtis. When Sinatra asks for her hand in marriage she refuses because she is mixed—half black, half white. He says it doesn't matter, but she still declines because she's in love with Curtis. When Sinatra tells Curtis that Wood is mixed, Curtis says that it doesn't matter to him either because he'd never planned on marrying her. Meanwhile, the war continues. Not particularly satisfying on either the war or race front. Based on a novel by Joe David Brown. **109m/B VHS, Beta.** Frank Sinatra, Tony Curtis, Natalie Wood, Leora Dana; ***D:*** Delmer Daves; ***C:*** Daniel F. Fapp; ***M:*** Elmer Bernstein. *MGM*

Kings of the Road—In the Course of Time ♂♂♂½ **1976** A writer and a film projectionist travel by truck across Germany. The film stands out for its simple and expressive direction, and truly captures the sense of physical and ideological freedom of being on the road. A landmark Wenders epic. In German with English subtitles. **176m/B VHS, Beta.** *GE* Ruediger Vogler, Hanns Zischler, Elisabeth Kreuzer; ***D:*** Wim Wenders; ***W:*** Wim Wenders. Nominations: Cannes Film Festival '76: Best Film. *FCT, GLV, INJ*

Kings, Queens, Jokers **193?** Package includes a foolish lover and ghosts in "Haunted Spooks," an escaped convict in "Dangerous Females," and a search for lost jewels in "Stolen Jools." **60m/B VHS, Beta.** Harold Lloyd, Marie Dressler, Polly Moran, Edward G. Robinson, Gary Cooper, Joan Crawford. *NO*

King's Ransom *Woof!* **1991** When the Japanese Emperor's Pearl is stolen, the underworld is abuzz with excitement. But only the wealthiest individuals are invited to bid for the jewel at Cameron King's secret casino. There, untold pleasures, and dangers, await them. **?m/C VHS.** Miles O'Keeffe, Dedee Pfeiffer, Christopher Atkins; ***D:*** Hugh Parks. *NO*

The King's Rhapsody ♂♂ **1955** Flynn is an heir who abdicates his throne in order to be with the woman he loves. But when the king dies, Flynn sacrifices love for honor and goes back to marry a princess. Very dated and Flynn is long past his swashbuckling-romantic days. **93m/C VHS.** *GB* Errol Flynn, Anna Neagle, Patrice Wymore, Martita Hunt, Finlay Currie, Frank Wolff, Joan Benham, Reginald Tate, Miles Malleson; ***D:*** Herbert Wilcox. *FCT*

Kings Row ♂♂♂ **1941** The Harry Bellamann best-selling Middle American potboiler comes to life. Childhood friends grow up with varying degrees of success, in a decidedly macabre town. All are continually dependent on and inspired by Parris (Cummings) a psychiatric doctor and genuine gentleman. Many cast members worked against type with unusual success. Warner held the film for a year after its completion, in concern for its dark subject matter, but it received wide acclaim. Shot completely within studio settings—excellent scenic design by William Cameron Menzies, and wonderful score. **127m/B VHS, Beta.** Ann Sheridan, Robert Cummings, Ronald Reagan, Betty Field, Charles Coburn, Claude Rains, Judith Anderson, Nancy Coleman, Karen Verne, Maria Ouspenskaya, Harry Davenport, Ernest Cossart, Pat Moriarity, Scotty Beckett; ***D:*** Sam Wood; ***C:*** James Wong Howe; ***M:*** Erich Wolfgang Korngold. Nominations: Academy Awards '42: Best Black and White Cinematography, Best Director (Wood), Best Picture. *MGM, FOX, CCB*

The King's Thief ♂♂½ **1955** Costume swashbuckler with Niven as the bad guy. He's a duke at the court of 17th-century English King Charles II and is involved in a plot to steal the crown jewels. **78m/C VHS.** David Niven, Edmund Purdom, George Sanders, Ann Blyth, Roger Moore, John Dehner, Sean McClory, Melville Cooper, Alan Mowbray; ***D:*** Robert Z. Leonard; ***W:*** Christopher Knopf; ***M:*** Miklos Rozsa. *MGM*

The King's Whore ♂♂ **1990 (R)** Dalton stars as a 17th-century king who falls obsessively in love with the wife of one of his courtiers. His passions lead him to make a decision between the woman and the throne. Good-looking costume epic with obligatory sword fights. **111m/C VHS, LV.** Timothy Dalton, Valeria Golino, Feodor Chaliapin Jr, Margaret Tyzack; ***W:*** Daniel Vigne, Frederic Raphael. *VMK*

Kinjite: Forbidden Subjects ♂♂ **1989 (R)** A cop takes on a sleazy pimp whose specialty is recruiting teenage girls, including the daughter of a Japanese business man. Slimy, standard Bronson fare. **97m/C VHS, Beta, LV.** Charles Bronson, Juan Fernandez, Peggy Lipton; ***D:*** J. Lee Thompson. *MGM, CAN*

A Kink in the Picasso ♂♂ **1990** MTV personality Daddo joins a cast of criminals who chase after a Picasso artwork and a counterfeit. Artless Australian production. **84m/C VHS.** Peter O'Brien, Jon Finlayson, Jane Clifton, Andrew Daddo; ***D:*** Marc Gracie. *ATL*

Kino Pravda/Enthusiasm **1931** Two famous documentaries by Vertov, the first a prime example of his pioneering avant-garde newsreels that helped establish Soviet montage aesthetic, and the second the famous portrait of Don Basin coal miners, augmented by the famous use of sound editing/montage. In Russian with English titles. **120m/B VHS, Beta.** *RU* ***D:*** Dziga Vertov. *FCT, FST*

Kipperbang ♂♂ *Ptang, Yang, Kipperbang* **1982 (PG)** During the summer of 1948, a 13-year-old boy wishes he could kiss the girl of his dreams. He finally gets the chance in a school play. Not unsatisfying, but falls short of being the bittersweet coming-of-age drama it could have been. **85m/C VHS, Beta.** *GB* John Albasiny, Abigail Cruttenden, Alison Steadman; ***D:*** Michael Apted. *MGM*

Kipps ♂♂♂ *The Remarkable Mr. Kipps* **1941** Based on H.G. Wells' satirical novel. A young British shopkeeper inherits a fortune and tries to join high society while neglecting his working-class girlfriend. Set the stage for the musical "Half a Sixpence." **95m/B VHS, Beta.** *GB* Michael Redgrave, Phyllis Calvert, Michael Wilding; ***D:*** Carol Reed. *NOS, HHT, CAB*

The Kirlian Witness ♂ *The Plants Are Watching* **1978 (PG)** A woman uses the power of telepathic communication with house plants to solve her sister's murder. **88m/C VHS, Beta.** Nancy Snyder, Joel Colodner, Ted Leplat; ***D:*** Jonathan Sarno. *NO*

Kismet ♂♂♂ **1920** Original screen version of the much filmed lavish Arabian Nights saga (remade in '30, '44 and '55). A beggar is drawn into deception and intrigue among Bagdad upper-crusters. Glorious sets and costumes; silent with original organ score. **98m/B VHS.** Otis Skinner, Elinor Fair, Herschel Mayall; ***D:*** Louis Gasnier; ***C:*** Gaetano Antonio "Tony" Gaudio. *VYY*

Kismet ♂♂ **1955** A big budget Arabian Nights musical drama of a Baghdad street poet who manages to infiltrate himself into the Wazir's harem. The music was adapted from Borodin by Robert Wright and George Forrest. Original trailer and letterboxed screen available in special laserdisc edition. ♫Fate; Not Since Ninevah; Baubles, Bangles, and Beads; Stranger in Paradise; Bored; Night of My Nights; The Olive Tree; And This Is My Beloved; Sands of Time. **113m/C VHS, Beta, LV.** Howard Keel, Ann Blyth, Dolores Gray, Vic Damone; ***D:*** Vincente Minnelli; ***W:*** Charles Lederer, Luther Davis; ***C:*** Joseph Ruttenberg; ***M:*** Andre Previn. *MGM, FCT*

The Kiss ♂♂♂ **1929** Garbo, the married object of earnest young Ayres' lovelorn affection, innocently kisses him nighty night since a kiss is just a kiss. Or so she thought. Utterly misconstrued, the platonic peck sets the stage for disaster, and murder and courtroom anguish follow. French Feyder's direction is stylized and artsy. Garbo's last silent and Ayres' first film. **89m/B VHS.** Greta Garbo, Conrad Nagel, Holmes Herbert, Lew Ayres, Anders Randolf; ***D:*** Jacques Feyder; ***C:*** William H. Daniels. *MGM, FCT*

The Kiss ♂ **1988 (R)** A kind of "Auntie Mame from Hell" story in which a mysterious aunt visits her teen-age niece in New York, and tries to apprentice her to the family business of sorcery, demon possession, and murder. Aunt Felicity's kiss will make you appreciate the harmless cheek-pinching of your own aunt; your evening would be better spent with her, rather than this movie. **98m/C VHS, Beta, LV.** Pamela Collyer, Peter Dvorsky, Joanna Pacula, Meredith Salenger, Mimi Kuzyk, Nicholas Kilbertus, Jan Rubes; ***D:*** Pen Densham; ***W:*** Tom Ropelewski. *COL, IME*

Kiss and Be Killed ♂½ **1991 (R)** Crazy guy with knife cuts short couple's wedding night. Shortchanged widow is mighty miffed. Will she have to return the wedding gifts? **89m/C VHS, Beta, 8mm.** Caroline Ludvik, Crystal Carson, Tom Reilly, Chip Hall, Ken Norton, Jimmy Baio; ***D:*** Tom Milo. *NO*

Kiss and Kill 🦴🦴 *Blood of Fu Manchu; Against All Odds* **1968 (R)** Lee returns in his fourth outing as Fu Manchu. This time the evil one has injected beautiful girls with a deadly poison that reacts upon kissing. They are then sent out to seduce world leaders. Not on par with the previous movies, but still enjoyable. Sequel to "Castle of Fu Manchu." **91m/C VHS.** Christopher Lee, Richard Greene, Shirley Eaton, Tsai Chin, Maria Rohm, H. Marion Crawford; ***D:*** Jess (Jesus) Franco. *MRV*

A Kiss Before Dying 🦴🦴 **1991 (R)** Botched adaptation of Ira Levin's cunning thriller novel (filmed before in 1956). This flick serves up an exploded head in the first few minutes. So much for subtlety. The highlight is Dillon's chilly role as a murderous opportunist bent on marrying into a wealthy family. Young plays two roles (not very well) as lookalike sisters on his agenda. The ending was hastily reshot and it shows. **93m/C VHS, Beta, LV.** Matt Dillon, Sean Young, Max von Sydow, Diane Ladd, James Russo, Martha Gehman, Ben Browder, Joy Lee, Adam Horovitz; ***D:*** James Dearden; ***W:*** James Dearden. Golden Raspberry Awards '91: Worst Actress (Young), Worst Supporting Actress (Young). *MCA*

Kiss Daddy Goodbye 🦴½ **1981 (R)** A widower keeps his two children isolated in order to protect their secret telekinetic powers. When he is killed by bikers, the kids attempt to raise him from the dead. Also on video as "Revenge of the Zombie" and "The Vengeful Dead." **81m/C VHS, Beta.** Fabian, Marilyn Burns, Jon Cedar, Marvin Miller; ***D:*** Patrick Regan. *MRV, GHV*

Kiss Daddy Goodnight 🦴 **1987 (R)** A Danish-made thriller about a beautiful young girl who seduces men, drugs them and takes their money. One man turns the tables on her, however, and decides that she will only belong to him. **89m/C VHS, Beta.** *DK* Uma Thurman, Paul Dillon, Paul Richards, David Brisbin; ***D:*** P.I. Huemer. *ACA*

A Kiss for Mary Pickford 🦴🦴½ **1927** A rare, hilarious cinematic oddity, a film formulated from Kuleshov montage techniques from footage of the famous American couple's visit to Russia in 1926, wherein a regular guy tries to win a girl through friendship with the stars. Fairbanks and Pickford didn't know of their role in this film, being spliced in later according to montage theory. **70m/B VHS, Beta.** Mary Pickford, Douglas Fairbanks Sr., Igor Ilinsky; ***D:*** Sergei Komarov. *FCT*

A Kiss Goodnight 🦴🦴½ **1994 (R)** Natalie (Trickey) has a romp in the sheets with ad exec Kurt (Corley) when regular beau Michael (Moses) ignores her for work. But when Natalie decides to break things off, Kurt won't take no for an answer. **88m/C VHS.** Paula Trickey, Al Corley, Mark Moses, Lawrence Tierney, Brett Cullen, James Karen, Robert Wuhl, Sydney Walsh; ***D:*** Daniel Raskov; ***W:*** Daniel Raskov; ***C:*** Glenn Kershaw. *ACA*

Kiss Me a Killer 🦴🦴 **1991 (R)** The ancient thriller plot about a young wife and her lover who scheme to kill her middle-aged husband. It's set in L.A.'s Latino community, but extensive shots of salsa music and ethnic cooking hardly raise this above the mediocre. **91m/C VHS, LV.** Julie Carmen, Robert Beltran, Guy Boyd, Ramon Franco, Charles Boswell; ***D:*** Marcus De Leon; ***W:*** Marcus De Leon. *COL*

Kiss Me Deadly 🦴🦴🦴½ **1955** Aldrich's adaptation of Mickey Spillane's private eye tale takes pulp literature high concept. Meeker, as Mike Hammer, is a self interested rough and tumble all American dick (detective, that is). When a woman to whom he happened to give a ride is found murdered, he follows the mystery straight into a nuclear conspiracy. Aldrich, with tongue deftly in cheek, styles a message through the medium; topsy turvy camerawork and rat-a-tat-tat pacing tell volumes about Hammer, the world he orbits, and that special 50s kind of paranoia. Now a cult fave, it's considered to be the American grandaddy to French New Wave. Cinematography by Ernest Laszlo. **105m/B VHS, Beta, LV.** Ralph Meeker, Albert Dekker, Paul Stewart, Wesley Addy, Cloris Leachman, Strother Martin, Marjorie Bennett, Jack Elam; ***D:*** Robert Aldrich; ***C:*** Ernest Laszlo. *MGM, FCT*

Kiss Me Goodbye 🦴🦴 **1982 (PG)** Young widow Fields can't shake the memory of her first husband, a charismatic but philandering Broadway choreographer, who's the antithesis of her boring but devoted professor fiance. She struggles with the charming ghost of her first husband, as well as her domineering mother, attempting to understand her own true feelings. Harmless but two-dimensional remake of "Dona Flor and Her Two Husbands." **101m/C VHS, Beta.** Sally Field, James Caan, Jeff Bridges, Paul Dooley, Mildred Natwick, Claire Trevor; ***D:*** Robert Mulligan; ***W:*** Charlie Peters; ***M:*** Ralph Burns. *FOX*

Kiss Me Kate 🦴🦴🦴 **1953** A married couple can't separate their real lives from their stage roles in this musical-comedy screen adaptation of Shakespeare's "Taming of the Shrew," based on Cole Porter's Broadway show. Bob Fosse bursts from the screen—particularly if you see the 3-D version—when he does his dance number. ♫Out of This World; From This Moment On; Wunderbar; So In Love; I Hate Men; Were Thine That Special Face; I've Come To Wive It Wealthily In Padua; Where Is The Life That Late I Led?; Always True To You Darling In My Fashion. **110m/C VHS, Beta, LV.** Kathryn Grayson, Howard Keel, Ann Miller, Tommy Rall, Bob Fosse, Bobby Van, Keenan Wynn, James Whitmore; ***D:*** George Sidney; ***C:*** Charles Rosher; ***M:*** Andre Previn. Nominations: Academy Awards '53: Best Original Score. *MGM, FCT*

Kiss Me, Kill Me 🦴½ **1969 (R)** Confused woman is on the run after she may have murdered someone. **91m/C VHS, Beta.** Carroll Baker, George Eastman, Isabelle DeFunes, Ely Gallo; ***W:*** Nick Castle. *NO*

Kiss Me, Stupid! 🦴🦴 **1964 (PG-13)** Once condemned as smut, this lesser Billy Wilder effort now seems no worse than an average TV sitcom. Martin basically plays himself as a horny Vegas crooner stranded in the boondocks. A local songwriter wants Dino to hear his tunes but knows the cad will seduce his pretty wife, so he hires a floozy to pose as the tempting spouse. It gets better as it goes along, but the whole thing suffers from staginess, being an adaptation of an Italian play "L'Ora Della Fantasia" by Anna Bonacci. **126m/B VHS, Beta, LV.** Dean Martin, Kim Novak, Ray Walston, Felicia Farr, Cliff Osmond, Barbara Pepper, Doro Merande, Howard McNear, Henry Gibson, John Fiedler, Mel Blanc; ***D:*** Billy Wilder; ***W:*** Billy Wilder, I.A.L. Diamond; ***C:*** Joseph LaShelle; ***M:*** Andre Previn. *MGM*

KISS Meets the Phantom of the Park 🦴½ *Attack of the Phantoms* **1978** The popular '70s rock band is featured in this Dr. Jekyll-esque Halloween horror tale, interspersed with musical numbers. **96m/C VHS, Beta.** Gene Simmons, Paul Stanley, Peter Criss, Ace Frehley, Anthony Zerbe, Deborah Ryan, John Dennis Johnston; ***D:*** Gordon Hessler. *MVD, WOV*

Kiss My Grits 🦴 **1982 (PG)** A good ole boy hightails it to Mexico with his girlfriend and son, chased by mobsters and the law. **101m/C VHS, Beta.** Bruce Davison, Anthony (Tony) Franciosa, Susan George, Bruno Kirby; ***D:*** Jack Starrett. *MED*

Kiss of a Killer 🦴🦴½ **1993** O'Toole is a mousy miss living a dead-end life with her nagging mother. But she has a secret—she spends weekends in a hotel, dressed to entice and picking up strangers. Involved in an auto mishap she's aided by a handsome mechanic, who turns out to be a rapist. When he accidentally kills his latest victim, he realizes our mystery woman can identify him and tries to find her. Based on the novel "The Point of Murder" by Margaret Yorke. Made for television. **93m/C VHS.** Annette O'Toole, Brian Wimmer, Eva Marie Saint, Greg Henry, Vic Polizos; ***D:*** Larry Elikann; ***W:*** David Warfield. *ABC*

Kiss of Death 🦴🦴🦴 **1947** Paroled when he turns state's evidence, Mature must now watch his back constantly. Widmark, in his film debut, seeks to destroy him. Police chief Donlevy tries to help. Filmed on location in New York, this gripping and gritty film is a vision of the most terrifying sort of existence, one where nothing is certain, and everything is dangerous. Excellent. **98m/B VHS.** Victor Mature, Richard Widmark, Anne Grey, Brian Donlevy, Karl Malden, Coleen Gray; ***D:*** Henry Hathaway. Nominations: Academy Awards '47: Best Story, Best Supporting Actor (Widmark). *FXV, FCT*

Kiss of Death 🦴🦴 **1977** Weird comedy about a shy undertaker's assistant and his attempts at first romance. Made for British television. **80m/C VHS.** *GB* David Threlfall, John Wheatley, Kay Adshead, Angela Curran; ***D:*** Mike Leigh; ***W:*** Mike Leigh. *WBF*

Kiss of Death 🦴🦴½ **1994 (R)** Very loose contemporary remake of the 1947 film noir classic of the same name. Jimmy Kilmartin (Caruso) is a paroled car thief turned informant. He soon finds himself trapped in a web of deceit involving corrupt district attorneys and ruthless hoodlums like Little Junior (Cage, pumped up and playing against type), with no one to trust. Crime drama keeps the far-fetched genre conventions in check until the end. Caruso makes the transition from TV cop on "NYPD Blue" by not straying far from his small screen persona. Cage's standout performance may not be as chilling as Widmark's unforgettable debut in the original, but he's able to convey a level of mercilessness and depth that'll make you wince. **100m/C VHS, LV.** David Caruso, Nicolas Cage, Samuel L. Jackson, Helen Hunt, Stanley Tucci, Michael Rapaport, Ving Rhames, Anthony Heald, Anne Meara; ***D:*** Barbet Schroeder; ***W:*** Richard Price; ***M:*** Trevor Jones. Nominations: Golden Raspberry Awards '95: Worst New Star (Caruso). *FXV*

Kiss of the Spider Woman 🦴🦴🦴 **1985 (R)** From the novel by Manuel Puig, an acclaimed drama concerning two cell mates in a South American prison, one a revolutionary, the other a homosexual. Literate, haunting, powerful. **119m/C VHS, Beta, LV, 8mm.** *BR* William Hurt, Raul Julia, Sonia Braga, Jose Lewgoy, Milton Goncalves, Nuno Leal Maia, Denise Dumont; ***D:*** Hector Babenco; ***W:*** Leonard Schrader; ***M:*** John Neschling, Wally Badarou. Academy Awards '85: Best Actor (Hurt); British Academy Awards '85: Best Actor (Hurt); Cannes Film Festival '85: Best Actor (Hurt); Independent Spirit Awards '86: Best Foreign Film; Los Angeles Film Critics Association Awards '85: Best Actor (Hurt); National Board of Review Awards '85: Best Actor (Hurt), Best Actor (Julia); Nominations: Academy Awards '85: Best Adapted Screenplay, Best Director (Babenco), Best Picture. *COL, BTV, NLC*

Kiss of the Tarantula 🦴 **1975 (PG)** Teen girl who lives with her family in a mortuary battles inner torment and vents anxiety by releasing her deadly pet spiders on those whom she despises. Eight-legged "Carrie" rip-off. **85m/C VHS, Beta.** Eric Mason; ***D:*** Chris Munger; ***W:*** Warren Hamilton. *MPI, FCT*

Kiss of the Vampire 🦴🦴½ *Kiss of Evil* **1962** Newlywed couple is stranded in Bavaria near a villa of vampires and are invited in by its charmingly evil owner. Fortunately, hubby manages to escape and finds a knowledgeable professor who unleashes a horde of bats to rout the bloodsuckers. Properly creepy; producer Hinds used the pseudonym John Elder for his screenplay. **88m/C VHS.** *GB* Clifford Evans, Noel Willman, Edward De Souza, Jennifer Daniel, Barry Warren, Jacqueline Wallis; ***D:*** Don Sharp; ***W:*** Anthony John Elder Hinds; ***C:*** Alan Hume; ***M:*** James Bernard. *MCA*

Kiss Shot 🦴🦴 **1989** Goldberg is a struggling single mother who loses her job but still must make the mortgage payments. She takes a job as a waitress but realizes it isn't going to pay the bills so she tries her hand as a pool hustler. Frantz is the promoter who finances her bets and Harewood, the pool-shooting playboy whose romantic advances are destroying her concentration. **88m/C VHS, Beta.** Whoopi Goldberg, Dennis Franz, Dorian Harewood, David Marciano, Teddy Wilson; ***D:*** Jerry London; ***M:*** Stephen Dorff. *ACA, MOV*

Kiss the Night **1987 (R)** An unfortunate hooker falls head over heels for a man she had the pleasure of doing business with. To her chagrin, it is much harder to leave the street than she thought. A dramatic and timely presentation. **99m/C VHS.** Patsy Stephens, Warwick Moss, Gary Aron Cook; ***D:*** James Ricketson. *MCG*

Kiss Tomorrow Goodbye 🦴🦴 **1950** A brutal, murderous escaped convict rises to crime-lord status before his inevitable downfall. Based on a novel by Horace McCoy. **102m/B VHS, LV.** James Cagney,

Barbara Payton, Ward Bond, Luther Adler, Helena Carter, Steve Brodie, Rhys Williams; *D:* Gordon Douglas. *REP*

Kisses **1991** Lauren Bacall hosts an entertaining look at screen kisses from yesterday and today. **47m/C VHS, Beta.** *TTC*

Kisses for My President ½ **1964** Silly comedy about the first woman elected President and her trials and tribulations. MacMurray is the husband who has to adjust to the protocol of being "First Man." Bergen is miscast, but the other performances are just fine. **113m/C VHS.** Fred MacMurray, Polly Bergen, Arlene Dahl, Edward Andrews, Eli Wallach, Donald May; *D:* Curtis Bernhardt. Nominations: Academy Awards '64: Best Costume Design (B & W). *WAR*

Kissin' Cousins ½ **1964** Air Force officer on a secluded base in the South discovers a local hillbilly is his double. Presley quickie that includes country tunes such as "Smokey Mountain Boy" and "Barefoot Ballad" as well as the title song. **96m/C VHS, Beta.** Elvis Presley, Arthur O'Connell, Jack Albertson, Glenda Farrell, Pam Austin, Yvonne Craig, Cynthia Pepper, Donald Woods, Tommy Farrell, Beverly Powers; *D:* Gene Nelson. *MGM*

The Kissing Place **1990** A woman who abducted her "son" years ago tracks the boy to New York City to prevent him from finding his biological family. **90m/C VHS, Beta.** Meredith Baxter, David Ogden Stiers; *D:* Tony Wharmby; *W:* Richard Altabef, Cynthia A. Cherbak. *PAR*

Kissinger and Nixon ½ **1996** Intrigue, ambition, and backbiting politics consume the 18 weeks leading up to the signing of the Vietnam peace accords in Paris in January, 1973. Egotistical Kissinger (Silver) is prepared to sacrifice South Vietnam for the sake of his own ambitions (and an end to the conflict) while a distrustful Nixon (Bridges) lurks uneasily in the background. TV docudrama offers little insight; based on Walter Isaacson's biography "Kissinger." **94m/C VHS.** Ron Silver, Beau Bridges, Matt Frewer, Ron White, George Takei, Kenneth Welsh; *D:* Daniel Petrie; *W:* Lionel Chetwynd. *TTC*

Kit Carson **1940** Frontiersman Kit Carson leads a wagon train to California, fighting off marauding Indians all the way. **97m/B VHS, Beta.** Jon Hall, Dana Andrews, Ward Bond, Lynn Bari; *D:* George B. Seitz. *MED, VTR*

The Kitchen Toto **1987 (PG-13)** Set in 1950 Kenya as British rule was being threatened by Mau Mau terrorists. A young black boy is torn between the British for whom he works and the terrorists who want him to join them. Complex and powerful story of the Kenyan freedom crusade. **96m/C VHS, Beta, LV.** *GB* Bob Peck, Phyllis Logan, Robert Urquhart, Edward Judd, Edwin Mahinda, Kirsten Hughes; *D:* Harry Hook; *W:* Harry Hook; *M:* John Keane. *WAR*

Kitty and the Bagman **1982 (R)** A comedy about two rival madames who ruled Australia in the 1920s. **95m/C VHS, Beta.** *AU* Liddy Clark; *D:* Donald Crombie. *SUE*

Kitty Foyle **1940** From the novel by Christopher Morley, Rogers portrays the white-collar working girl whose involvement with a married man presents her with both romantic and social conflicts. **108m/B VHS, Beta.** Ginger Rogers, Dennis (Stanley Morner) Morgan, James Craig, Gladys Cooper, Ernest Cossart, Eduardo Ciannelli; *D:* Sam Wood. Academy Awards '40: Best Actress (Rogers); Nominations: Academy Awards '40: Best Adapted Screenplay, Best Director (Wood), Best Picture, Best Sound. *MED, CCB, FCT*

The Klansman *Burning Cross; KKK* **1974 (R)** Race relations come out on the short end in this film about a sheriff trying to keep the lid on racial tensions in a southern town. Even the big-name cast can't save what comes off as a nighttime soaper rather than a serious drama. **112m/C VHS.** Lee Marvin, Richard Burton, Cameron Mitchell, Lola Falana, Luciana Paluzzi, Linda Evans, O.J. Simpson; *D:* Terence Young; *W:* Samuel Fuller. *PAR, FCT*

Klondike Annie ½ **1936** West stars as a woman on the lam for a murder (self-defense) who heads out for the Yukon aboard McLaglen's ship. He falls for her, finds out about her problems, and helps her with a scam to pass herself off as a missionary, only she begins to take her saving souls seriously (although in her own risque style). **77m/B VHS.** Mae West, Victor McLaglen, Philip Reed, Helen Jerome Eddy, Harry Beresford, Harold Huber, Conway Tearle, Esther Howard; *D:* Raoul Walsh; *W:* Mae West. *MCA, BTV*

Klondike Fever ½ *Jack London's Klondike Fever* **1979 (PG)** Join the young Jack London as he travels from San Francisco to the Klondike fields during the Great Gold Rush of 1898. **118m/C VHS, Beta.** Rod Steiger, Angie Dickinson, Lorne Greene; *D:* Peter Carter; *M:* Hagood Hardy. *NO*

Klute ½ **1971 (R)** A small-town policeman (Sutherland) comes to New York in search of a missing friend and gets involved with a prostitute/would-be actress (Fonda) being stalked by a killer. Intelligent, gripping drama. **114m/C VHS, Beta, LV.** Jane Fonda, Donald Sutherland, Charles Cioffi, Roy Scheider, Rita Gam, Jean Stapleton; *D:* Alan J. Pakula; *C:* Gordon Willis. Academy Awards '71: Best Actress (Fonda); Golden Globe Awards '72: Best Actress—Drama (Fonda); New York Film Critics Awards '71: Best Actress (Fonda); National Society of Film Critics Awards '71: Best Actress (Fonda); Nominations: Academy Awards '71: Best Story & Screenplay. *WAR, BTV*

The Klutz **1973** A bumbling fool, on the way to visit his girlfriend, becomes accidentally embroiled in a bank robbery and other ridiculous mishaps. Light French comedy; dubbed. **87m/C VHS, Beta.** *FR* Claude Michaud, Louise Portal, Guy Provost; *D:* Pierre Rose. *NWV*

The Knack *The Knack...and How to Get It* **1965** Amusing, fast-paced adaptation of the play by Ann Jellicoe. Schoolteacher Crawford is baffled by his tenant Brooks' extreme luck with the ladies so Brooks decides to teach him the "knack" of picking up women. Crawford promptly falls for the first woman (Tushingham) he meets. Swinging London at its most mod. **84m/B VHS.** *GB* Michael Crawford, Ray Brooks, Rita Tushingham, Donal Donnelly; *D:* Richard Lester; *W:* Charles Wood; *C:* David Watkin; *M:* John Barry. *MGM*

Knife in the Head *Messer Im Kopf* **1978** Biogeneticist Berthold Hoffman (Ganz) is meeting his wife (Winkler) at the left-wing youth centre where she works when there's a police raid and Berthold is shot in the head. He awakens in the hospital having lost both his memory and all physical co-ordination. Determined to battle his disabilities, Berthold also becomes the pawn in a political game between the police and political dissidents. In German with English subtitles. **108m/C VHS.** *GE* Bruno Ganz, Angela Winkler, Hans Honig, Hans Brenner, Udo Samel, Carla Egerer; *D:* Reinhard Hauff; *W:* Peter Schneider. *NYF*

Knife in the Water *Noz w Wodzie* **1962** A journalist, his wife and a hitchhiker spend a day aboard a sailboat. Sex and violence can't be far off. Tense psychological drama. Served as director Polanski's debut. In Polish with English subtitles. **94m/B VHS, Beta, LV.** *PL* Leon Niemczyk, Jolanta Umecka, Zygmunt Malandowicz; *D:* Roman Polanski; *W:* Jerzy Skolimowski, Roman Polanski. Venice Film Festival '62: International Critics Award; Nominations: Academy Awards '63: Best Foreign Language Film. *VYY, FOX, BTV*

Knight Moves **1993 (R)** Suspenseful thriller about a series of murders which take place at an international resort where a championship chess match is underway. The prime suspect is a chess master who has an unlikely affair with a beautiful police psychologist called in to decipher the mind of the murderer. Filmed in the Pacific Northwest. **105m/C VHS, LV.** Christopher Lambert, Diane Lane, Tom Skerritt, Daniel Baldwin; *D:* Carl Schenkel; *W:* Brad Mirman; *M:* Anne Dudley. *REP*

Knight Without Armour **1937** A journalist opposed to the Russian monarchy falls in love with the daughter of a czarist minister in this classic romantic drama. **107m/B VHS, Beta.** *GB* Marlene Dietrich, Robert Donat; *D:* Jacques Feyder; *C:* Harry Stradling; *M:* Miklos Rozsa. *SUE*

Knightriders ½ **1981 (R)** The story of a troupe of motorcyclists who are members of a traveling Renaissance Fair and look and act like modern-day Knights of the Round Table. Their battles center around who is the bravest and strongest, and who deserves to be king. **145m/C VHS, Beta, LV.** Ed Harris, Gary Lahti, Tom Savini, Amy Ingersoll; *D:* George A. Romero; *W:* George A. Romero. *FUS, MED*

Knights ½ **1993 (R)** In a futuristic wasteland a young martial-arts warrior (Long) and a cyborg (Kristofferson) team up to battle rebel cyborgs that have discovered a new source of fuel—human blood. **89m/C VHS, Beta.** Kathy Long, Kris Kristofferson, Lance Henriksen, Scott Paulin, Gary Daniels; *D:* Albert Pyun; *W:* Albert Pyun. *PAR*

Knights & Emeralds ½ **1987 (PG)** Cross-cultural rivalries and romances develop between members of two high school marching bands in a British factory town as the national band championships draw near. **90m/C VHS, Beta.** *GB* Christopher Wild, Beverly Hills, Warren Mitchell; *D:* Ian Emes; *M:* Colin Towns. *WAR*

Knights of the City **1985 (R)** Miami street gangs fight each other over their "turf." One leader decides to opt out, using music. ♫Let the Music Play; Cry of the City; Jailhouse Rap; T.K. and Jessie Rap; Kurtis Blow Rap; Bounce; My Part of Town; Can You Feel It; Love Goes Up and Down. **87m/C VHS, Beta.** Nicholas Campbell, John Mengatti, Wendy Barry, Stoney Jackson, Janine Turner, Michael Ansara; *D:* Leon Isaac Kennedy, Dominic Orlando; *W:* Leon Isaac Kennedy. *NWV, VTR*

Knights of the Range ½ **1940** Vintage western. **66m/B VHS, Beta.** Russell Hayden, Victor Jory, Jean Parker, Britt Wood, J. Farrell MacDonald, Eddie Dean; *D:* Lesley Selander. *VCN, MLB, GPV*

Knights of the Round Table ½ **1953** The story of the romantic triangle between King Arthur, Sir Lancelot and Guinevere during the civil wars of sixth century England. **106m/C VHS, Beta, LV.** Robert Taylor, Ava Gardner, Mel Ferrer, Anne Crawford, Felix Aylmer, Stanley Baker; *D:* Richard Thorpe; *C:* Frederick A. (Freddie) Young; *M:* Miklos Rozsa. Nominations: Academy Awards '53: Best Art Direction/Set Decoration (Color), Best Sound. *MGM*

Knock on Any Door **1949** A young hoodlum from the slums is tried for murdering a cop. He is defended by a prominent attorney who has known him from childhood. **100m/B VHS, Beta, LV.** Humphrey Bogart, John Derek, George Macready; *D:* Nicholas Ray; *W:* Daniel Taradash, John Monks Jr.; *C:* Burnett Guffey. *COL*

Knock Outs **1992** Samantha not only loses her shirt at a sorority strip poker marathon but she loses her tuition money to a gang of biker chicks. Then Samantha and a bevy of bikini-clad friends decide to pose for a swimsuit calendar to earn some cash but are secretly videotaped in the nude by some local sleaze promoters. Tired of being taken advantage of these lovelies take up martial arts and challenge their nefarious girl biker rivals to a winner-take-all wrestling match, not forgetting about the purveyors of the not-so-secret videotape. **90m/C VHS.** Chona Jackson, Sindi Rome, Brad Zutaut; *D:* John Bowen. *HMD*

The Knockout/Dough and Dynamite **1914** Two Chaplin shorts: "The Knockout" (1914), in which Charlie referees a big fight; "Dough and Dynamite" (1914), in which a labor dispute at a bake shop leaves Charlie in charge when the regular baker walks out. **54m/B VHS, Beta.** Charlie Chaplin, Fatty Arbuckle, Mabel Normand, The Keystone Cops; *D:* Charlie Chaplin, Sydney Chaplin. *VYY*

Knute Rockne: All American *A Modern Hero* **1940** Life story of Notre Dame football coach Knute Rockne, who inspired many victories with his powerful speeches. Reagan, as the dying George Gipp, utters that now-famous line, "Tell the boys to win one for the Gipper." **96m/B VHS, Beta.**

Ronald Reagan, Pat O'Brien, Gale Page, Donald Crisp, John Qualen; **D:** Lloyd Bacon. *MGM, FHE*

Kojak: The Belarus File ☠☠ **1985** The bald-headed detective of prime-time television fame searches for a neo-Nazi who is killing Holocaust survivors in New York. Made for television. **95m/C VHS, Beta.** Telly Savalas, Suzanne Pleshette, Max von Sydow, George Savalas; **D:** Robert Markowitz. *MCA*

Kojiro ☠☠☠ **1967** A sprawling epic by prolific Japanese director Inagaki about a dashing rogue's bid for power in feudal times. With English subtitles. **152m/C VHS, Beta.** *JP* Kikunosuke Onoe, Tatsuya Nakadai; **D:** Hiroshi Inagaki. *VDA*

Kolberg ☠☠ *Burning Hearts* **1945** The true story of a Prussian town heroically withstanding Napoleon. Produced by Joseph Goebbels in the last days of the Third Reich, it is best remembered as the film whose expensive production and momentous use of real German soldiers, supplies, and ammunition eventually helped to fell the Axis war machine. In German with English subtitles. **118m/C VHS, Beta.** *GE* Kristina Soderbaum, Heinrich George, Horst Caspar, Paul Wegener; **D:** Veit Harlan. *FCT, IHF, GLV*

Konrad **199?** Konrad, an "instant" child made in a factory, is accidentally delivered to an eccentric woman. The factory wants him back when the mistake is discovered, but Konrad stands up against it. Includes a viewers' guide. Part of the "Wonderworks" series. **110m/C VHS.** Ned Beatty, Polly Holliday, Max Wright, Huckleberry Fox; **D:** Neil Cox; **W:** Malcolm Marmorstein. *PME, HMV, BTV*

Korczak ☠☠☠ **1990** Based on the life of Dr. Janusz Korczak, an outspoken critic of the Nazis, who ran the Jewish orphanage in Warsaw, Poland and accompanied 200 children to to the Treblinka concentration camp. Harshly poetic film quietly details Polish resistance to the Nazi terror. Criticized for end scenes of the children romping in the countryside, implying that they were somehow freed—since the director did not want to show the children actually entering the gas chambers he used this allegory to imply that their souls were freed. In Polish with English subtitles. **118m/C VHS.** *PL* Wojtek Pszoniak, Ewa Dalkowska, Piotr Kozlowski, Marzena Trybala, Wojciech Klata, Adam Siemion; **D:** Andrzej Wajda; **W:** Agnieszka Holland. *NYF, FCT*

Koroshi ☠½ **1967** Secret Agent John Drake is dispatched to Hong Kong to disband a secret society who is killing off international political figures. **100m/C VHS, Beta.** Patrick McGoohan, Kenneth Griffith, Yoko Tani; **D:** Michael Truman, Peter Yates. *MPI*

Kostas ☠☠ **1979 (R)** A migrant Greek taxi driver romantically pursues a wealthy Australian divorcee in England. **88m/C VHS, Beta.** Takis Emmanuel, Wendy Hughes; **D:** Paul Cox. *LIV, VES*

Kotch ☠☠☠ **1971 (PG)** An elderly man resists his children's attempts to retire him. Warm detailing of old age with a splendid performance by Matthau. Lemmon's directorial debut. **113m/C VHS.** Walter Matthau, Deborah Winters, Felicia Farr; **D:** Jack Lemmon; **M:** Marvin Hamlisch. Golden Globe Awards '72: Best Song ("Life Is What You Make It"); Writers Guild of America '71: Best Adapted Screenplay; Nominations: Academy Awards '71: Best Actor (Matthau), Best Film Editing, Best Song ("Life Is What You MaKe It"), Best Sound. *FOX*

Kowloon Assignment ☠ **1977** Comic book superhero Golgo 13 comes to life in this action film dealing with a drug war in the Hong Kong underground. **93m/C VHS, Beta.** Sonny Chiba. *NO*

Koyaanisqatsi ☠☠☠☠ **1983** A mesmerizing film that takes an intense look at modern life (the movie's title is the Hopi word for "life out of balance"). Without dialogue or narration, it brings traditional background elements, landscapes and cityscapes, up front to produce a unique view of the structure and mechanics of our daily lives. Riveting and immensely powerful. A critically acclaimed score by Glass, and Reggio's cinematography prove to be the perfect match to this brilliant film. Followed by "Powaqqatsi." **87m/C VHS, Beta, LV.** **D:** Godfrey Reggio; **M:** Philip Glass. Los Angeles Film Critics Association Awards '83: Best Score. *MVD, FCT, MLB*

Kramer vs. Kramer ☠☠☠½ **1979 (PG)** Highly acclaimed family drama about an advertising executive husband and child left behind when their wife and mother leaves on a quest to find herself, and the subsequent courtroom battle for custody when she returns. Hoffman and Streep give exacting performances as does young Henry. Successfully moves you from tears to laughter and back again. Based on the novel by Avery Corman. **105m/C VHS, Beta, LV.** Dustin Hoffman, Meryl Streep, Jane Alexander, Justin Henry, Howard Duff, JoBeth Williams; **D:** Robert Benton; **W:** Robert Benton; **C:** Nestor Almendros. Academy Awards '79: Best Actor (Hoffman), Best Adapted Screenplay, Best Director (Benton), Best Picture, Best Supporting Actress (Streep); Golden Globe Awards '80: Best Actor—Drama (Hoffman), Best Film—Drama, Best Screenplay, Best Supporting Actress (Streep); National Board of Review Awards '79: 10 Best Films of the Year, Best Supporting Actress (Streep); National Society of Film Critics Awards '79: Best Actor (Hoffman), Best Director (Benton), Best Supporting Actress (Streep); Nominations: Academy Awards '79: Best Cinematography, Best Film Editing, Best Supporting Actor (Henry). *COL, BTV*

The Krays ☠☠☠½ **1990 (R)** An account of British gangsters Reggie and Ronnie Kray, the brothers who ruled London's East End with brutality and violence, making them bizarre celebrities of the sixties. The leads are portrayed by Gary and Martin Kemp, founders of the British pop group Spandau Ballet. **119m/C VHS, LV, 8mm.** *GB* Gary Kemp, Martin Kemp, Billie Whitelaw, Steven Berkoff, Susan Fleetwood, Charlotte Cornwell; **D:** Peter Medak; **W:** Philip Ridley; **M:** Michael Kamen. *COL, FCT*

Kriemhilde's Revenge ☠☠☠☠ *Die Nibelungen* **1924** The second film, following "Siegfried," of Lang's "Die Nibelungen," a lavish silent version of the Teutonic legends Wagner's "Ring of the Nibelungen" was based upon. In this episode, Kriemhilde avenges Siegfried's death by her marriage to the Kings of the Huns, thus fulfilling a prophecy of destruction. **95m/B VHS, LV.** *GE* Paul Richter, Margareta Schoen, Theodore Loos, Hanna Ralph, Rudolf Klein-Rogge; **D:** Fritz Lang. *CCB, IHF, REP*

Kronos ☠☠½ **1957** A giant robot from space drains the Earth of all its energy resources. A good example of this genre from the 50s. Includes previews of coming attractions from classic science fiction films. **78m/B VHS, Beta, LV.** Jeff Morrow, Barbara Lawrence, John Emery; **D:** Kurt Neumann. *MED, MLB*

Krull ☠☠ **1983 (PG)** Likeable fantasy adventure set in a world peopled by creatures of myth and magic. A prince embarks on a quest to find the Glaive (a magical weapon) and then rescues his young bride, taken by the Beast of the Black Fortress. **121m/C VHS, Beta, LV.** *GB* Ken Marshall, Lysette Anthony, Freddie Jones, Francesca Annis, Liam Neeson; **D:** Peter Yates; **M:** James Horner. *GKK*

Krush Groove ☠ **1985 (R)** The world of rap music is highlighted in this movie, the first all-rap musical. ♫King of Rock; Don't You Dog Me; A Love Bizarre; Pick Up the Pace; If I Ruled the World; Holly Rock; It's Like That; Feel the Spin; I Can't Live Without My Radio. **95m/C VHS, Beta, LV.** Blair Underwood, Eron Tabor, Kurtis Blow, Sheila E; **D:** Michael A. Schultz. *WAR*

K2: The Ultimate High ☠☠ **1992 (R)** Two men, one a skirt-chasing lawyer, the other a happily married physicist, tackle the world's second largest mountain—the K-2 in Kashmir, northern Pakistan. They encounter a number of dangers, including an ascent of sheer rock face, an avalanche, and a fall down perpendicular mountain ice, but even the exciting mountain-climbing scenes can't hold up this watered down movie. The film was actually shot on Canada's Mount Waddington. Based on the play by Patrick Meyers. **104m/C VHS, Beta.** Michael Biehn, Matt Craven, Raymond J. Barry, Luca Bercovici, Patricia Charbonneau, Julia Nickson-Soul, Hiroshi Fujioka, Jamal Shah; **D:** Franc Roddam; **W:** Patrick Meyers, Scott Roberts. *PAR*

Kuffs ☠☠ **1992 (PG-13)** Slater stars as George Kuffs, a young guy who reluctantly joins his brother's highly respected private security team in this original action comedy. After his brother is gunned down in the line of duty, George finds himself the new owner of the business. Out to avenge his brother, George pursues a crooked art dealer as he battles crime on the streets of San Francisco. Worthwhile premise is hampered by a predictable plot and mediocre acting. **102m/C VHS, Beta, LV.** Christian Slater, Tony Goldwyn, Milla Jovovich, Bruce Boxleitner, Troy Evans, George de la Pena, Leon Rippy; **D:** Bruce A. Evans; **W:** Bruce A. Evans, Raynold Gideon; **M:** Harold Faltermeyer. *MCA*

Kung Fu ☠☠½ **1972** A fugitive Buddhist quasi-Asian martial arts master accused of murder in his native land, roams across the Old West fighting injustice. Served as a pilot for the successful television series and was reincarnated 14 years later in the sequel, "Kung Fu: The Movie." **75m/C VHS, Beta.** Keith Carradine, David Carradine, Barry Sullivan, Keye Luke; **D:** Jerry Thorpe. *WAR*

Kung Fu Avengers ☠ **1985** On his way to a karate show at Madison Square Garden, our hero Li confronts the abominable Mr. Chin and his deadly henchman. Another foot-stomper. **90m/C VHS, Beta.** Bruce Li, Carl Scott, Jim James, Ku Feng. *PSM*

Kung Fu Commandos ☠ **1980 (R)** Five martial arts masters must face an evil warlord's army to rescue a captured agent. **90m/C VHS, Beta.** John Liu, Shangkuan Ling-Feng. *PSM, GEM*

Kung Fu Massacre ☠ **1982 (R)** Farmers hire hard-handed mercenaries to fight evil war lords. **90m/C VHS, Beta.** Yangzi, Pi Li Lee. *LIV*

Kung Fu Rebels ☠½ **1980** Rebels are fearsome enough, but when they're kung fu masters, the establishment has real trouble on its hands. **90m/C VHS, Beta.** Wang Chung, Wen Ching Lung, Chang Mei. *NO*

Kung Fu: The Movie ☠☠½ **1986** Carradine reprises his role as Kwai Chang Caine from the television show of the '70s. In this made-for-television fare he's hunted by evil warlord Mako, who's involved in the California opium trade. Mako sends assassin Lee (son of martial-arts star Bruce) after Caine. Luke appears in flashbacks as the young Grasshopper's blind mentor, Master Po. **93m/C VHS, Beta.** David Carradine, Mako, Brandon Lee, Keye Luke, Kerrie Keane, Martin Landau, William Lucking, Luke Askew, Benson Fong; **D:** Richard Lang. *WAR*

Kuni Lemel in Tel Aviv ☠☠½ **1977** The bungling folk-hero of the shtetl of 100 years ago is updated to the present. Grandpa Kuni is now 80 and living in Brooklyn. Anxious to see the family line continue, he offers five million dollars to the first of his twin grandsons to marry a nice Jewish girl and settle in Israel. However, the grandsons have plans of their own which conflict with Grandpa's. In Hebrew with English subtitles. **90m/C VHS.** *IS* Mike Burstyn, Mandy Rice-Davies; **D:** Yoel Silberg. *ERG*

Kurt Vonnegut's Harrison Bergeron ☠☠½ *Harrison Bergeron* **1995 (R)** In the year 2053 the American government has gone to absurd lengths to ensure equality. Mediocrity is championed and everyone is forced to wear metallic headbands that stifle intellect through electronic impulses. Too bad for Harrison Bergeron (Astin), a smart young man being punished for his intelligence. But there's a secret undeground elite offering Harrison the chance to think freely, though this power comes with a price. Adapted from Vonnegut's 1961 short story; made for cable TV. **99m/C VHS.** Sean Astin, Christopher Plummer, Miranda de Pencier, Nigel Bennett, Buck Henry, Eugene Levy, Howie Mandel, Andrea Martin; **D:** Bruce Pittman; **W:** Arthur Crimm. *REP*

Kurt Vonnegut's Monkey House ☠☠ **199?** Dramatization of four short stories from Vonnegut's "Welcome to the Monkey House" collection, including a twist on the familiar Frankenstein tale. Made for cable television. **100m/C VHS.** Frank Langella. *PBS*

Kwaidan ☆☆☆☆ **1964** A haunting, stylized quartet of supernatural stories, each with a surprise ending. Adapted from the stories of Lafcadio Hearn, an American author who lived in Japan just before the turn of the century. The visual effects are splendid. In Japanese with English subtitles. **164m/C VHS, Beta, LV.** *JP* Michiyo Aratama, Rentaro Mikuni, Katsuo Makamura, Keiko Kishi, Tatsuya Nakadai, Takashi Shimura; ***D:*** Masaki Kobayashi; ***M:*** Toru Takemitsu. Cannes Film Festival '65: Grand Jury Prize; Nominations: Academy Awards '65: Best Foreign Language Film. *VYY, NOS, SNC*

L.627 ☆☆☆ **1992** Melancholy police procedural about dedicated veteran narcotics cop Lulu (Bezace) who works with a small and ill-equipped Parisian drug squad prone to taking the law into their own hands. Lulu constantly finds himself thwarted by obtuse bureaucrats while his life is disturbed by an informant—a young, drug-addicted prostitute who has disappeared and whom Lulu desires to protect. Film title refers to the French anti-drug statute. French with subtitles. **145m/C VHS.** *FR* Didier Bezace, Jean-Paul Comart, Cecile Garcia-Fogel, Lara Guirao, Charlotte Kady, Jean-Roger Milo, Philippe Torreton, Nils Tavernier; ***D:*** Bertrand Tavernier; ***W:*** Bertrand Tavernier, Michel Alexandre; ***M:*** Philippe Sarde. *KIV*

L.A. Bad ☆ **1985 (R)** A Puerto Rican street thug learns he has cancer, and must come to terms with his own impending death. **101m/C VHS, Beta.** Esai Morales, Janice Rule, John Phillip Law, Chuck Bail, Carrie Snodgress. *VTR, PSM*

La Balance ☆☆☆ **1982 (R)** An underworld stool pigeon is recruited by the Parisian police to blow the whistle on a murderous mob. Baye, as a prostitute in love with the pimp-stoolie, is a standout. Critically acclaimed; French with subtitles. **103m/C VHS, Beta.** *FR* Philippe Leotard, Nathalie Baye, Bob Swaim; ***D:*** Reymond LePlont; ***M:*** Roland Bocquet. Cesar Awards '83: Best Actor (Leotard), Best Actress (Baye), Best Film. *INJ, FOX*

La Bamba ☆☆☆ **1987 (PG-13)** A romantic biography of the late 1950s pop idol Ritchie Valens, concentrating on his stormy relationship with his half-brother, his love for his WASP girlfriend, and his tragic, sudden death in the famed plane crash that also took the lives of Buddy Holly and the Big Bopper. Soundtrack features Setzer, Huntsberry, Crenshaw, and Los Lobos as, respectively, Eddie Cochran, the Big Bopper, Buddy Holly, and a Mexican bordello band. **99m/C VHS, Beta, LV, 8mm.** Lou Diamond Phillips, Esai Morales, Danielle von Zerneck, Joe Pantoliano, Brian Setzer, Marshall Crenshaw, Howard Huntsberry, Rosana De Soto, Elizabeth Pena, Rick Dees; ***D:*** Luis Valdez; ***W:*** Luis Valdez; ***M:*** Carlos Santana, Miles Goodman. *COL*

La Belle Noiseuse ☆☆☆½ *Divertimento* **1990** The connections between art and life are explored in this beautiful (and long) drama. Creatively crippled, an aging painter has left unfinished a masterpiece work, entitled "La Belle Noiseuse," for ten years. When an admiring younger artist and his beautiful lover arrive for a visit, the painter is newly inspired by the young woman and makes her the model and muse for his masterwork. The film details every nuance of the work from the first to the last brushstroke and the battle of wills between artist and model over the symbiotic creative process. Based on a novella by Honore Balzac. French with subtitles. "Divertimento" is actually a recut and shortened version (126 minutes) of the original film. **240m/C VHS.** *FR* Michel Piccoli, Emmanuelle Beart, Jane Birkin, David Bursztein, Marianne Denicourt; ***D:*** Jacques Rivette. Cannes Film Festival '91: Grand Jury Prize; Los Angeles Film Critics Association Awards '91: Best Foreign Film. *NYF, FCT, ING*

La Bete Humaine ☆☆☆½ *The Human Beast* **1938** A dark, psychological melodrama about human passion and duplicity, as an unhinged trainman plots with a married woman to kill her husband. Wonderful performances and stunning photography. Based on the Emile Zola novel. In French with English subtitles. 1954 Hollywood remake, "Human Desire," was directed by Fritz Lang. **90m/B VHS, Beta, 8mm.** *FR* Jean Gabin, Simone Simon, Julien Carette, Fernand Ledoux; ***D:*** Jean Renoir. *NOS, HHT, CAB*

La Boca del Lobo ☆☆ *The Lion's Den* **1989** Peru's civil strife inspired this sluggish drama about government troops occupying a jungle village. Tormented by unseen communist guerillas, the stressed-out soldiers reach the breaking point. **111m/C VHS.** *AR* ***D:*** Francisco J. Lombardi. *CCN, APD, TPV*

La Boum ☆☆½ **1981** A teenager's adjustment to the changes brought about by a move to Paris is compounded by her parents' marital problems. Followed by "La Boum 2." **90m/C VHS, Beta.** *FR* Sophie Marceau, Claude Brasseur, Brigitte Fossey, Denise Grey, Bernard Giraudeau; ***D:*** Claude Pinoteau; ***M:*** Vladimir Cosma. *COL*

L.A. Bounty ☆½ **1989 (R)** A beautiful cop and a bounty hunter go after the same murderer. Hauser steals the show as a psychopath who has completely blown a gasket. **85m/C VHS, Beta, LV.** Sybil Danning, Wings Hauser, Henry Darrow, Lenore Kasdorf, Robert Hanley; ***D:*** Worth Keeter. *NO*

La Cage aux Folles ☆☆☆½ **1978 (R)** Adaption of the popular French play. A gay nightclub owner and his transvestite lover play it straight when Tognazzi's son from a long-ago liaison brings his fiancee and her conservative parents home for dinner. Charming music and lots of fun. So successful, it was followed by two sequels, "La Cage Aux Folles II & III" and also a Broadway musical. In French with English subtitles. **91m/C VHS, Beta, LV.** *FR* Ugo Tognazzi, Michel Serrault, Michel Galabru, Claire Maurier, Remy Laurent, Benny Luke; ***D:*** Edouard Molinaro; ***W:*** Francis Veber; ***M:*** Ennio Morricone. Cesar Awards '79: Best Actor (Serrault); Golden Globe Awards '80: Best Foreign Film; Nominations: Academy Awards '79: Best Adapted Screenplay, Best Costume Design, Best Director (Molinaro). *MGM, FOX, CRC*

La Cage aux Folles 2 ☆☆½ **1981 (R)** Albin sets out to prove to his companion that he still has sex appeal, and gets mixed up in some espionage antics. This sequel to the highly successful "La Cage aux Folles" loses some steam, but is still worth seeing. Followed by "La Cage Aux Folles 3: The Wedding." **101m/C VHS, Beta, LV.** *FR* Ugo Tognazzi, Michel Serrault, Marcel Bozzuffi, Michel Galabru, Benny Luke; ***D:*** Edouard Molinaro; ***W:*** Francis Veber; ***M:*** Ennio Morricone. *MGM, FCT, FOX*

La Cage aux Folles 3: The Wedding ☆½ **1986 (PG-13)** The flamboyant drag queen Albin must feign normalcy by marrying and fathering a child in order to collect a weighty inheritance. Final segment of the trilogy; inferior to the previous films. In French with English subtitles. **88m/C VHS, Beta, LV.** *FR* Michel Serrault, Ugo Tognazzi, Michel Galabru, Benny Luke, Stephane Audran; ***D:*** Georges Lautner; ***M:*** Ennio Morricone. *COL, INJ*

La Ceremonie ☆☆☆ *A Judgment in Stone* **1995** Sullen maid Sophie (Bonnaire) is hired by the rich Lelievre family to work at their country estate. She's befriended by independent postmistress Jeanne (Huppert), who's disliked by Sophie's employers, and who encourages Sophie into small defiant actions. Something's off about the entire situation and there's violence beneath the seemingly calm surface. Based on Ruth Rendell's chiller "Judgement in Stone." French with subtitles. **111m/C VHS.** *FR* Sandrine Bonnaire, Isabelle Huppert, Jacqueline Bisset, Jean-Pierre Cassel; ***D:*** Claude Chabrol; ***W:*** Claude Chabrol, Caroline Eliacheff. Cesar Awards '96: Best Actress (Huppert); Nominations: Cesar Awards '96: Best Actress (Bonnaire), Best Director (Chabrol), Best Film, Best Screenplay, Best Supporting Actor (Cassel), Best Supporting Actress (Bisset).

La Chartreuse de Parme ☆☆½ *Charterhouse at Parma* **1948** Nineteenth century period piece featuring an Archbishop willing to break his vows for the woman he loves, and the aunt who will make sure that if she can't have him only God will. French adaptation of the novel by Stendahl. Available dubbed. **?m/C VHS.** *FR* Gerard Philipe, Maria Casares, Rene Faure. *FRA, FCT*

La Chevre ☆☆☆½ *The Goat* **1981** A screwball French comedy about two policemen (Richard and Depardieu—picture Nick Nolte and Gene Wilder with accents) stumbling along the path of a missing heiress who suffers from chronic bad luck. Contains a hilarious scene with chairs used to test the luck of the investigative team; based on one partner's ability to sit on the only broken chair in a rather large collection, he is judged to be sufficiently jinxed to allow them to recreate the same outrageous misfortunes that befell the heiress in her plight. In French with English subtitles. **91m/C VHS, Beta.** *FR* Gerard Depardieu, Pierre Richard, Corynne Charbit, Michel Robin, Pedro Armendariz Jr.; ***D:*** Francis Veber; ***M:*** Vladimir Cosma. *FCT, INJ, TPV*

La Chienne ☆☆☆☆ *Isn't Life A Bitch?; The Bitch* **1931** Dark, troubling tale of a bedraggled husband whose only excitement is his painting hobby until he becomes consumed by the ever-tempting prostitute Lulu. Director Renoir broke ground with his use of direct sound and Paris shooting locations, and the experiment was a hit. Portrays marriage with acidity; Renoir's own marriage broke up as a result of this film's casting. Mareze died shortly after the filming was complete in a car crash. Based on the novel by Georges de la Fouchardiere. Produced in 1931, but didn't reach American theaters until 1975. In French with English subtitles. Remade in 1945 as "Scarlet Street." **93m/B VHS, Beta, LV.** *FR* Michel Simon, Janie Mareze, Georges Flament, Madeleine Berubet; ***D:*** Jean Renoir; ***W:*** Andre Girard, Jean Renoir. *INT, INJ, TPV*

La Chute de la Maison Usher ☆☆☆½ *The Fall of the House of Usher* **1928** An expressionistic, abstracted adaptation of the Poe story "The Fall of the House of Usher" about an evil mansion and its ruined denizens. Epstein used slow motion, superimpressions, and weird camera angles to obtain the proper atmosphere. **48m/B VHS, Beta.** *FR* Marguerite Gance, Jean Debucourt, Charles Lamy; ***D:*** Jean Epstein. *FCT, GVV, INJ*

La Cicada ☆½ *The Cricket* **1983** The sparks fly when a woman and her seventeen-year-old daughter become rivals for the affections of the same man. **90m/C VHS, Beta.** *IT* Clio Goldsmith, Virna Lisi, Anthony (Tony) Franciosa, Renato Salvatori; ***D:*** Alberto Lattuada. *SUE*

La Collectionneuse ☆☆ **1967** The third of Rohmer's "Moral Tales" finds an artist (Bachau) and an antiques dealer (Pommereulle) vacationing in St. Tropez and sharing a villa with a young woman (Politoff) who picks a different man to sleep with each night. Both try to resist the sexual temptations of being added to her collection of lovers. French with subtitles. **88m/C VHS.** *FR* Patrick Bauchau, Daniel Pommereulle, Haydee Politoff, Alain Jouffroy; ***D:*** Eric Rohmer; ***W:*** Eric Rohmer; ***C:*** Nestor Almendros. *FXL*

L.A. Crackdown ☆ **1987** A ruthless yet compassionate policewoman goes after crack dealers and pimps who are exploiting women. Pretty trashy fare; followed by "L.A. Crackdown 2." Made for video. **90m/C VHS, Beta.** Pamela Dixon, Tricia Parks, Kita Harrison, Jeffrey Olson, Michael Coon; ***D:*** Joseph Merhi. *NO*

L.A. Crackdown 2 ☆ **1988** A woman cop goes undercover as a dancer in a dance hall to try to catch a psychotic killer who stalks hookers in this silly sequel to "L.A. Crackdown." **90m/C VHS, Beta.** Pamela Dixon, Anthony Gates, Joe Vance, Cynthia Miguel, Lisa Anderson, Bo Sabato; ***D:*** Joseph Merhi. *HHE*

La Discrete ☆☆☆ *The Discreet* **1990** Antoine (Luchini) is a cocky writer who is not the lothario he imagines himself to be—in fact his girlfriend has just dumped him. He and his publisher plan a sexist revenge with Antoine advertising for a young female typist whom he will seduce and abandon—all the while keeping a diary of the experience which will be published. The self-possessed Catherine (Henry) answers the ad and even though Antoine protests that she is not his type he finds himself falling in love. Then Catherine discovers Antoine's original scheme. Vincent's directorial debut. In French with English subtitles. **95m/C VHS.** *FR* Fabrice Luchini, Judith Henry, Maurice Garrel, Marie Bunel, Francois Toumarkine; ***D:*** Christian Vincent; ***W:*** Jean-Pierre Ronssin, Christian Vincent; ***M:*** Jay Gottlieb. Cesar Awards '91: Best Writing. *NYF, FCT*

La Dolce Vita ☠☠☠☠ **1960** In this influential and popular work a successful, sensationalistic Italian journalist covers the show-biz life in Rome, and alternately covets and disdains its glitzy shallowness. The film follows his dealings with the "sweet life" over a pivotal week. A surreal, comic tableaux with award-winning costuming; one of Fellini's most acclaimed films. In this film Fellini called his hungry celebrity photographers the Paparazzo—and it is as the paparazzi they have been ever since. In Italian with English subtitles. **174m/B VHS, LV.** *IT* Marcello Mastroianni, Anita Ekberg, Anouk Aimee, Alain Cuny, Lex Barker, Yvonne Furneaux, Barbara Steele, Nadia Gray, Magali Noel, Walter Santesso, Jacques Sernas, Annabelle Ninchi; ***D:*** Federico Fellini; ***W:*** Tullio Pinelli, Ennio Flaiano, Brunello Rondi, Federico Fellini; ***M:*** Nino Rota. Academy Awards '61: Best Costume Design (B & W); Cannes Film Festival '60: Best Film; National Board of Review Awards '61: 5 Best Foreign Films of the Year; New York Film Critics Awards '61: Best Foreign Film; Nominations: Academy Awards '61: Best Art Direction/Set Decoration (B & W), Best Director (Fellini), Best Story & Screenplay. *INJ, REP, APD*

La Femme Nikita ☠☠☠ **1991 (R)** Stylish French noir version of Pygmalion. Having killed a cop during a drugstore theft gone awry, young French sociopath Nikita (Parillaud) is reprieved from a death sentence in order to enroll in a government finishing school, of sorts. Trained in etiquette and assasination, she's released after three years, and starts a new life with a new beau, all the while carrying out agency-mandated assassinations. Parillaud is excellent as the once-amoral street urchin transformed into a woman of depth and sensitivity—a bitterly ironic moral evolution for a contract killer. Remade as "Point of No Return." **117m/C VHS.** *FR* Anne Parillaud, Jean-Hugues Anglade, Tcheky Karyo, Jeanne Moreau, Jean Reno, Jean Bouise; ***D:*** Luc Besson; ***W:*** Luc Besson; ***C:*** Thierry Arbogast; ***M:*** Eric Serra. Cesar Awards '91: Best Actress (Parillaud). *VMK, FCT, BTV*

L.A. Gangs Rising ☠☠ **1989** The streets of Los Angeles run red with blood as a gang war explodes into bloody fury. **87m/C VHS, Beta.** David Kyle, Steve Bond, John Ashton; ***D:*** John Bushelman. *NO*

L.A. Goddess ☠½ **1992 (R)** A hard-living, and drinking, movie star and her beautiful stunt double both fall for a studio head. Both of these women know what they want and the man in the middle hasn't got a clue. Also available in an unrated version. **92m/C VHS.** Kathy Shower, Jeff Conaway, David Heavener, Wendy McDonald, Joe Estevez, James Hong; ***D:*** Jag Mundhra; ***W:*** Jerry Davis. *PSM*

La Grande Bouffe ☠☠☠ *The Blow-Out* **1973** Four middle-aged men, bored with life, meet at a secluded mansion for one last excessive fling and to literally eat themselves to death. Four very fine actors in a vulgar feast. French with subtitles. **125m/C VHS.** *FR* Marcello Mastroianni, Philippe Noiret, Michel Piccoli, Ugo Tognazzi, Andrea Ferreol; ***D:*** Marco Ferreri; ***W:*** Marco Ferreri, Rafael Azcona; ***C:*** Mario Vulpiani; ***M:*** Philippe Sarde. *WBF*

La Grande Bourgeoise ☠☠½ *The Murri Affair* **1974** Historical romance about the clash of aristocratic society and the new bourgeoisie in 1897 Italy. Great cast tries to save the true tale of murder and political intrigue from film's slow pacing, but in the end it's the movie's visual polish that shines forth. In Italian with subtitles. **115m/C VHS, Beta.** *IT* Catherine Deneuve, Giancarlo Giannini, Fernando Rey, Tina Aumont; ***D:*** Mauro Bolognini; ***M:*** Ennio Morricone. *FCT*

La Grande Vadrouille ☠☠☠ *Don't Look Now, We've Been Shot At* **1966** In 1943 German-occupied France, three Allied parachutists drop in on a Paris Opera conductor and a house painter. If the pair wish to find some peace, they must help the trio get to the free zone. France's number one box office hit for almost thirty years. Also available dubbed. **122m/C VHS.** *FR* Louis de Funes, Bourvil, Terry-Thomas; ***D:*** Gerard Oury. *FRA, FCT*

L.A. Heat ☠½ **1988** When a vice cop's partner is killed, he seeks revenge on the murderers, only to find that his own department may have been involved. Followed by "L.A. Vice." **90m/C VHS, Beta.** Jim Brown, Lawrence-Hilton Jacobs; ***D:*** Joseph Merhi. *PAR, HHE*

L.A. Law ☠☠☠ **1986** The pilot episode of the acclaimed dramatic series, in which the staff of a Los Angeles law firm tries a variety of cases. **97m/C VHS, Beta.** Michael Tucker, Jill Eikenberry, Harry Hamlin, Richard Dysart, Jimmy Smits, Alan Rachins, Susan Ruttan, Susan Dey, Corbin Bernsen; ***D:*** Gregory Hoblit. *FOX*

La Lectrice ☠☠½ *The Reader* **1988 (R)** Artesian landscapes, Beethoven sonatas, and a Raymond Jean novel titled "La Lectrice" provide the backdrop for Constance (Miou-Miou) to read aloud to her boyfriend in bed, and from there she imagines herself the novel's heroine, who hires out her services as a reader to various odd characters. She reads from "L'Amant," "Alice," "War and Peace," and "Les Fleurs du Mal." Richly textured and not overly intellectual. In French with English subtitles. **98m/C VHS, Beta, LV.** *FR* Miou-Miou, Christian Ruche, Sylvie Laporte, Michael Raskine, Brigitte Catillon, Regis Royer, Maria Casares, Pierre Dux, Patrick Chesnais; ***D:*** Michel DeVille; ***W:*** Rosalinde DeVille, Michel DeVille. Cesar Awards '89: Best Supporting Actor (Chesnais); Montreal World Film Festival '88: Best Film. *ORI, INJ*

La Marseillaise ☠☠☠½ **1937** Sweeping epic by Renoir made before he hit his stride with "Grand Illusion." It details the events of the French Revolution in the summer of 1789 using a cast of thousands. The opulent lifestyle of the French nobility is starkly contrasted with the peasant lifestyle of poverty and despair. The focus is on two new recruits who have joined the Marseilles division of the revolutionary army as they begin their long march to Paris, the heart of France. As they travel, they adopt a stirring and passionate song that embodies the spirit and ideals of the revolution known as "La Marseillaise," now France's national anthem. In French with English subtitles. **130m/B VHS, Beta.** *FR* Pierre Renoir, Lisa Delamare, Louis Jouvet, Aime Clarimond, Andrex Andrisson, Paul Dullac; ***D:*** Jean Renoir; ***W:*** Jean Renoir; ***C:*** Jean Bourgoin. *NOS, INT, HHT*

La Merveilleuse Visite ☠☠½ *The Marvelous Visit* **1974** Bittersweet fantasy about an angel that falls from the sky and is found unconcious by a priest. He's nursed back to health but causes problems for his host when he wanders into the nearby village and his curiosity is misunderstood. Adapted from a short story by H.G. Wells. In French with English subtitles. **102m/C VHS.** *FR* Gilles Kohler, Deborah Berger, Jean-Pierre Castaldi; ***D:*** Marcel Carne; ***W:*** Marcel Carne. *HTV, FCT*

La Nuit de Varennes ☠☠☠ **1982 (R)** This semi-historical romp is based on an actual chapter in French history when King Louis XVI and Marie Antoinette fled from revolutionary Paris to Varennes in 1791. On the way they meet an unlikely group of characters, including Cassanova and Thomas Paine. At times witty and charming, the melange of history and fiction is full of talk, sometimes profane, punctuated by sex and nudity. Director Scola's imagination stretches to light up this night. In French with English subtitles. **133m/C VHS, Beta, LV.** *FR IT* Marcello Mastroianni, Harvey Keitel, Jean-Louis Barrault, Hanna Schygulla, Jean-Claude Brialy; ***D:*** Ettore Scola; ***W:*** Ettore Scola. Nominations: Cannes Film Festival '82: Best Film. *COL, IME, APD*

La Passante ☠☠☠ *La Passante du Sans Souci; The Passerby* **1983** An otherwise peace-loving man murders the Paraguayan ambassador to France. In somewhat clumsy flashback style the murderer's orphaned childhood and other memories provide motives for the murder. Though posed more slowly than typical intrigue plots, the movie blends love and the legacy of Nazism, passion and politics in an engaging way, spiced with nudity and some violence. In her last screen appearance Schneider movingly portrays dual roles. In French with English subtitles. **106m/C VHS, Beta, LV.** *FR GE* Romy Schneider, Michel Piccoli, Helmut Griem, Gerard Klein, Matthieu Carriere, Maria Schell; ***D:*** Jacques Rouffio; ***M:*** Georges Delerue. Cesar Awards '83: Best Sound. *INJ, TPV*

La Petite Sirene ☠☠ *The Little Mermaid* **1980** Isabelle is a 14-year-old schoolgirl, obssessed with the story of the Little Mermaid, who tries to ingratiate herself to Georges, a 40-year-old garage mechanic. Seeing him as her prince charming, she persists in trying to make him a part of her life, in spite of his resistance. In French with English subtitles. **104m/C VHS.** *FR* Laura Alexis, Philippe Leotard, Evelyne Dress, Marie DuBois; ***D:*** Roger Andrieux; ***W:*** Roger Andrieux. *WAC, FCT, INJ*

La Puritaine ☠☠½ **1986** Before his planned reconciliation with his daughter, the artistic manager of a theater has young actresses portray different sides of the daughter's personality. In French with English subtitles. **90m/C VHS.** Michel Piccoli, Sandrine Bonnaire; ***D:*** Lou Doillon. *FCT*

La Ronde ☠☠☠½ **1951** A classic comedy of manners and sharply witty tour-de-farce in which a group of people in 1900 Vienna keep changing romantic partners until things wind up where they started. Ophuls' swirling direction creates a fast-paced farce of desire and regret with wicked yet subtle style. Based on Arthur Schnitzler's play and remade as "Circle of Love." In French with English subtitles. **97m/B VHS, Beta.** *FR* Simone Signoret, Anton Walbrook, Simone Simon, Serge Reggiani, Daniel Gelin, Danielle Darrieux, Jean-Louis Barrault, Fernand Gravet, Odette Joyeux, Isa Miranda, Gerard Philipe; ***D:*** Max Ophuls. British Academy Awards '51: Best Film; Nominations: Academy Awards '51: Best Art Direction/Set Decoration (B & W), Best Screenplay. *SUE, APD, INJ*

La Rupture ☠☠½ *The Breakup* **1970** Thriller about a wife trying to protect her child from her husband's unsavory family. Audran and her son are attacked by her husband (Drouot), who's high on drugs. She fights back and he winds up in the hospital. Her father-in-law (Bouquet), who wants his grandson to live with him, then hires a seedy investigator (Cassel) to spy on Audran. Based on the Charlotte Armstrong novel. In French with English subtitles. **124m/C VHS.** *FR* Stephane Audran, Jean-Claude Drouot, Michel Bouquet, Jean-Pierre Cassel, Catherine Rouvel, Jean Carmet, Annie Cordy; ***D:*** Claude Chabrol; ***W:*** Claude Chabrol; ***M:*** Pierre Jansen. *CVC, FCT*

La Salamandre ☠☠ *The Salamander* **1971** Non-conformist Rosemonde, suspected of shooting her guardian, is being interviewed by a novelist and a journalist trying to write a television script about the incident. The more they supposedly learn, the more they are both intimately drawn towards her. French with subtitles. **119m/B VHS.** *SI* Bulle Ogier, Jean-Luc Bideau, Jacques Denis; ***D:*** Alain Tanner; ***W:*** Alain Tanner, John Berger; ***M:*** Patrick Moraz. *NYF*

La Scorta ☠☠☠½ *The Bodyguards; The Escorts* **1994** Slick, fact-based political thriller focuses on four carabinieri (state police officers) who struggle to maintain some semblance of their normal lives after they are assigned to protect a judge investigating government corruption and a related murder in a Sicilian town. A crackling alternative to Americanized mobster melodrama, marked by taut direction, meaty characters, and coolly understated performances that seamlessly portray brotherhood, heroism, suspicion, and betrayal amid the battle for power between the Italian state and the Mafia. In Italian with English subtitles. **92m/C VHS.** Claudio Amendola, Enrico Lo Verso, Tony Sperandeo, Ricky Memphis, Carlo Cecchi, Leo Gullotta; ***D:*** Ricardo Tognazzi; ***W:*** Graziano Diana, Simona Izzo; ***M:*** Ennio Morricone. *NYR*

La Signora di Tutti ☠☠☠ **1934** An early Italian biography of Gaby Doriot, a movie star whose professional success is paired by personal misery. Prestigious director Ophuls, working in exile from his native Germany, was unable to complete many projects in the years leading up to and during WWII. This is one of the few. Watch for innovative camera work intended to underscore the film's mood. In Italian with English subtitles. **92m/B VHS, Beta.** *IT* Isa Miranda; ***D:*** Max Ophuls. *CVC, FCT, INJ*

L.A. Story ♪♪♪ **1991 (PG-13)** Livin' ain't easy in the city of angels. Harris K. Telemacher (Martin), a weatherman in a city where the weather never changes, wrestles with the meaning of life and love while consorting with beautiful people, distancing from significant other Henner, cavorting with valley girl Parker, and falling for newswoman Tennant (Martin's real life wife). Written by the comedian, the story's full of keen insights into the everyday problems and ironies of living in the Big Tangerine. (It's no wonder the script's full of so much thoughtful detail: Martin is said to have worked on it intermittently for seven years.) Charming, fault forgiving but not fault ignoring portrait. **98m/C VHS, Beta, LV.** Steve Martin, Victoria Tennant, Richard E. Grant, Marilu Henner, Sarah Jessica Parker, Sam McMurray, Patrick Stewart, Iman, Kevin Pollak; ***D:*** Mick Jackson; ***W:*** Steve Martin; ***M:*** Peter Melnick. *LIV, WAR*

La Strada ♪♪♪♪ *The Road* **1954** Simple-minded girl, played by Fellini's wife, Masina, is sold to a brutal, coarse circus strong-man and she falls in love with him despite his abuse. They tour the countryside and eventually meet up with a gentle acrobat, played by Basehart, who alters their fate. Fellini masterwork was the director's first internationally acclaimed film, and is, by turns, somber and amusing as it demonstrates the filmmaker's sensitivity to the underprivileged of the world and his belief in spiritual redemption. Subtitled in English. **107m/B VHS, Beta, LV.** *IT* Giulietta Masina, Anthony Quinn, Richard Basehart, Aldo Silvani; ***D:*** Federico Fellini; ***W:*** Ennio Flaiano, Brunello Rondi, Tullio Pinelli, Federico Fellini; ***M:*** Nino Rota. Academy Awards '56: Best Foreign Language Film; National Board of Review Awards '56: 5 Best Foreign Films of the Year; New York Film Critics Awards '56: Best Foreign Film; Nominations: Academy Awards '56: Best Original Screenplay. *SUE, IME, APD*

La Symphonie Pastorale ♪♪♪½ **1946** A Swiss pastor takes in an orphan blind girl who grows up to be beautiful. The pastor then competes for her affections with his son. Quiet drama based on the Andre Gide novel, with breathtaking mountain scenery as the backdrop for this tragedy rife with symbolism. **105m/B VHS.** *FR* Pierre Blanchar, Michele Morgan, Jean Desailly, Line Noro, Andree Clement; ***D:*** Jean Delannoy. Cannes Film Festival '46: Best Actress (Morgan). *FLI*

La Terra Trema ♪♪♪½ *Episoda Del Mare; The Earth Will Tremble* **1948** The classic example of Italian neo-realism, about a poor Sicilian fisherman, his family and their village. A spare, slow-moving, profound and ultimately lyrical tragedy, this semi-documentary explores the economic exploitation of Sicily's fishermen. Filmed on location with the villagers playing themselves; highly acclaimed though not commercially successful. In Sicilian with English subtitles. Some radically cut versions may be available, but are to be avoided. Franco Zefferelli was one of the assistant directors. **161m/B VHS, Beta.** *IT* Antonio Pietrangeli; ***D:*** Luchino Visconti. *FCT, INJ*

La Truite ♪♪♪ *The Trout* **1983 (R)** A young woman leaves her family's rural trout farm and a loveless marriage to seek her fortune in high finance and corporate mayhem. The complicated plot, full of intrigue and sexual encounters, sometimes lacks focus. Slickly filmed. **80m/C VHS, Beta.** *FR* Isabelle Huppert, Jean-Pierre Cassel, Daniel Olbrychski, Jeanne Moreau, Jacques Spiesser, Ruggero Raimondi, Alexis Smith, Craig Stevens; ***D:*** Joseph Losey. Cesar Awards '83: Best Cinematography. *COL*

La Vengeance d'une Femme ♪♪ *A Woman's Revenge* **1989** Refined Cecile and sultry Suzy are two sides of a love triangle whose third member, Cecile's husband, has just died. Cecile decides to get to know his mistress better, which naturally has Suzy worried. Is Cecile out for revenge or does she sincerely want to befriend the "other woman." Based on Dostoyevski's "The Eternal Husband." In French with English subtitles. **133m/C VHS.** *FR* Isabelle Huppert, Beatrice Dalle; ***D:*** Jacques Doillon; ***W:*** Jean-Francois Goyet, Jacques Doillon. *INJ, FCT*

L.A. Vice ♪½ **1989** A detective is transferred to the vice squad, where he must investigate a series of murders. Sequel to "L.A. Heat." **90m/C VHS, Beta.** Jim Brown, Lawrence-Hilton Jacobs, William Smith; ***D:*** Joseph Merhi. *PAR*

La Vie Continue ♪♪½ **1982** A middle-aged woman suddenly finds herself widowed after 20 years of marriage and tries to build a new life for herself and her children. Girardot's performance can't quite dispel melodramatic suds. Loosely and more effectively remade as "Men Don't Leave." In French with English subtitles or dubbed. **93m/C VHS, Beta.** *IT* Annie Girardot, Jean-Pierre Cassel, Michel Aumont, Pierre Dux, Guilia Salvatori, Emmanuel Goyet, Rivera Andres; ***D:*** Moshe Mizrahi; ***W:*** Moshe Mizrahi; ***M:*** Georges Delerue. *COL, INJ*

La Vie de Boheme ♪♪♪ *Bohemian Life* **1993** Comedy takes a mocking look at art and romantic love. A trio of hapless but dedicated comrades, Rodolfo (Pellonpaa) the painter, Marcel (Wilms) the poet, and Schaunard (Vaananen), must scrounge around the mealy edges of modern Paris because their art isn't filling their stomachs. Meanwhile, they experience the pangs of love like everyone else, although each is devoutly committed to his art as well. Starkly different from the lush, operatic version by Puccini, but based on the same source, a 19th century novel by Henri Mullet. French with subtitles. **100m/C VHS.** Matti Pellonpaa, Andre Wilms, Kari Vaananen, Jean-Pierre Leaud, Samuel Fuller, Louis Malle, Evelyne Didi, Christine Murillo, Laika, Carlos Salgado, Alexis Nitzer, Sylvie van den Elsen, Gilles Charmant, Dominique Marcas; ***D:*** Aki Kaurismaki; ***W:*** Aki Kaurismaki. *FXL*

La Vie est Belle ♪♪ *Life is Rosy* **1987** The rags to riches story of a poor rural musician from Zaire who goes to the city to break into radio and television. He uses his wit and talent to foil a greedy boss, win a beautiful wife, and make himself a singing sensation. French with subtitles. **85m/C VHS.** ***D:*** Nagangura Mweze, Bernard Lamy. *KIV*

L.A. Wars ♪½ **1994 (R)** A Latin American drug dealer moves into the territory of an Italian mobster, causing a turf war. When a cop rescues the mobster's daughter from the scuzzball, his boss forces him to infiltrate the mobster's organization. Abundant body count, lots of T&A. **94m/C VHS.** Vince Murdocco, Mary Zilba, A.J. Stevens, Rodrigo Obregon; ***D:*** Martin Morris, Tony Kandah. *MNC*

Laboratory ♪ **1980** Things go awry when the earthling subjects of an alien experiment revolt against their captors. **93m/C VHS, Beta.** Camille Mitchell, Corinne Michaels, Garnett Smith. *VCI*

Labyrinth ♪♪♪ **1986 (PG)** While baby-sitting her baby brother Froud, Connelly is so frustrated she asks the goblins to take him away. When the Goblin King, played by Bowie, comes to answer her idle wish, she must try to rescue Froud by solving the fantastic labyrinth. If she does not find him in time, Froud will become one of the goblins forever. During her journey, Connelly is befriended by all sorts of odd creatures created by Henson, and she grows up a little along the way. A fascinating adventure movie for the whole family. **90m/C VHS, Beta, LV, 8mm.** David Bowie, Jennifer Connelly, Toby Froud; ***D:*** Jim Henson; ***W:*** Terry Jones; ***M:*** David Bowie, Trevor Jones. *SUE, NLC*

Labyrinth of Passion ♪♪½ *Laberinto de Pasiones* **1982** A screwball farce, directed by Almodovar, featuring a host of strange characters running around Madrid in search of sex and laughter. They find plenty of both. An early film by an influential director. In Spanish with English subtitles. **100m/C VHS, Beta, LV.** *SP* Antonio Banderas, Imanol Arias, Cecilia Roth; ***D:*** Pedro Almodovar; ***W:*** Pedro Almodovar. *CCN, IME, INJ*

The Lacemaker ♪♪♪½ *La Dentielliere* **1977** Huppert's first shot at stardom, on videodisc with digital sound and a letterboxed print. A young beautician and a university student fall in love on vacation but soon begin to realize the differences in their lives. Adapted from the novel by Pascal Laine. In French with English subtitles. **107m/C LV.** *FR SI GE* Isabelle Huppert, Yves Beneyton, Florence Giorgetti, Anna Marie Duringer; ***D:*** Claude Goretta. Nominations: Cannes Film Festival '77: Best Film. *HMV, CRC, APD*

L'Addition ♪♪½ *The Patsy; Caged Heart* **1985 (R)** According to some cinematic code, the male lead always gets in lots of trouble whenever he tries to help a beautiful stranger. This time, Berry, as Bruno Windler, winds up arrested for shoplifting when he attempts to help Abril. Jailed and on the verge of parole, Windler unwittingly becomes involved in a prison break and is accused of helping a crime don mastermind the escape and of shooting a guard. That's where that gallic flair for capturing the sadomasochistic underbelly of humanity comes in, as Windler is viciously pursued by the malevolent guard. **85m/C VHS, Beta.** Richard Berry, Victoria Abril, Richard Bohringer, Farid Chopel, Fabrice Eberhard; ***D:*** Denis Amar; ***W:*** Jean Curtelin; ***C:*** Robert Fraisse; ***M:*** Jean-Claude Petit. *NWV, MOR*

The Ladies Club ♪½ **1986 (R)** A group of rape victims get together and begin to victimize rapists. **86m/C VHS, Beta.** Bruce Davison, Karen Austin, Diana Scarwid, Shera Danese, Beverly Todd; ***D:*** A.K. Allen. *MED*

The Ladies' Man ♪♪ **1961** Piecemeal Lewis farce, with Jerry playing a clutzy handyman working at a girls' boarding house. Some riotous routines balanced by slow pacing. **106m/C VHS, Beta, LV.** Jerry Lewis, Helen Traubel, Jack Kruschen, Doodles Weaver, Gloria Jean; ***D:*** Jerry Lewis; ***W:*** Jerry Lewis. *PAR*

Ladies Man ♪♪ **1962** Spy adventure with Constantine playing super sleuth/agent, Lemmy Caution, on the French Riviera. **?m/C VHS.** Eddie Constantine. *SNC*

The Ladies of the Bois de Bologne ♪♪ *Les Dames du Bois de Bologne; Ladies of the Park* **1944** Beware the woman scorned—as Jean (Bernard) learns. He ends his longtime relationship with Helene (Casares), although they vow to stay friends, but she secretly plots revenge and finds it in the person of Agnes (Labourdette), a former prostitute. Helene introduces Agnes to Jean, hoping they'll be attracted to one another. They are but after the wedding ceremony Helene reveals the truth about Agnes' sordid past. Updated adaptation of a story in Diderot's "Jacques Le Fatalist." French with subtitles. **83m/B VHS.** *FR* Maria Casares, Paul Bernard, Elina Labourdette; ***D:*** Robert Bresson; ***W:*** Robert Bresson, Jean Cocteau. *HTV*

Ladies of the Chorus ♪♪ **1949** Monroe stars as a burlesque chorus girl who shares the stage with her mom (Jergens) and a handful of other beauties. She meets and falls in love with a wealthy socialite (Brooks), but her mother completely disapproves of the relationship. Monroe later learns that her mother was in love with the same man several years before. Although only her second film appearance, Monroe's talents are already quite apparent in this low-budget musical romance. ♫Every Baby Nees a Da Da Daddy; Anyone Can Tell I Love You; Crazy For You; You're Never Too Old; Ladies of the Chorus. **61m/B VHS.** Adele Jergens, Marilyn Monroe, Rand Brooks, Nana Bryant, Steve Geray, Bill Edwards; ***D:*** Phil Karlson. *COL*

Ladies of the Lotus ♪ **1987** Bloodthirsty Vancouver gangsters raid Lotus, Inc., a modeling agency, and sell beautiful young women into slavery. As bad as it sounds. **120m/C VHS, Beta.** *CA* Richard Dale, Angela Read, Patrick Bermel, Darcia Carnie; ***D:*** Lloyd A. Simanol, Douglas C. Nicolle. *NO*

Ladies on the Rocks ♪♪½ *Koks I Kulissen* **1983** Aspiring comediennes Micha and Laura pack up their van and take their bizarre cabaret act on the road through rural Denmark. They find their private lives disintegrating but turn each disaster into new material for their act. In Danish with English subtitles. **100m/C VHS.** *DK* Helle Ryslinge, Anne Marie Helger, Flemming Quist Moller; ***D:*** Christian Braad Thomsen. *NYF, INJ*

Ladies They Talk About ☆☆½ *Women in Prison* **1933** Stanwyck stars as a tough-talking gun moll who belongs to a gang of bank robbers. They get caught and Stanwyck is sent to the female division of San Quentin. The acting is great in this pre-Code prison movie, but the film gets a bit punchy at times. Based on the true-life experiences of actress Dorothy Mackaye, who went to jail after her husband was killed in a fight with actor Paul Kelley, who was also sent to prison. Adapted from the play "Women in Prison" by Dorothy Mackaye and Carlton Miles. **69m/B VHS.** Barbara Stanwyck, Preston Foster, Lyle Talbot, Dorothy Burgess, Lillian Roth, Maude Eburne, Harold Huber, Ruth Donnelly; ***D:*** Howard Bretherton, William Keighley. *MGM*

Ladies Who Do ☆☆½ **1963** A group of cleaning ladies band together against the unscrupulous businessman who wants to tear down their homes in order to build an office tower. Along with a retired colonel, they use the stock market secrets gleaned from the rubbish they toss away to make a killing in the market and save the day. **90m/B VHS.** *GB* Peggy Mount, Robert Morley, Harry H. Corbett, Miriam Karlin, Avril Elgar, Dandy Nichols, Jon Pertwee, Nigel Davenport; ***D:*** C.M. Pennington-Richards; ***W:*** Michael Pertwee. *FCT*

Lady and the Tramp ☆☆☆☆ **1955 (G)** The animated Disney classic about two dogs who fall in love. Tramp is wild and carefree; Lady is a spoiled pedigree who runs away from home after her owners have a baby. They just don't make dog romances like this anymore. ♫He's a Tramp; La La Lu; Siamese Cat Song; Peace on Earth; Bella Notte. **76m/C VHS, Beta, LV.** ***D:*** Hamilton Luske; ***M:*** Peggy Lee, Sonny Burke; ***V:*** Larry Roberts, Peggy Lee, Barbara Luddy, Stan Freberg, Alan Reed, Bill Thompson, Bill Baucon, Verna Felton, George Givot, Dallas McKennon, Lee Millar. *DIS, APD*

Lady Avenger ☆ **1989 (R)** A woman is bent on getting revenge on her brother's killers. **90m/C VHS, Beta.** Peggie Sanders. *NO*

Lady Be Good ☆☆½ **1941** Adapted from the 1924 Gershwin Broadway hit, the plot's been revamped, much to the critics' distaste ("Variety" called it "molasses paced"). Sothern and Young play a tunesmith duo who excel at musical harmony and marital strife. Applauded for its music (the critics loved Hammerstein's and the Gershwins' tunes), the show's Academy Award winning song was, ironically, written by Jerome Kern. And if that's not enough, levity man Skelton and hoofer Powell are thrown in for good measure. ♫The Last Time I Saw Paris; So Am I; Oh Lady Be Good; Fascinating Rhythm; Hang On To Me; You'll Never Know; You're Words, My Music; Saudades. **111m/B VHS.** Eleanor Powell, Ann Sothern, Robert Young, Lionel Barrymore, John Carroll, Red Skelton, Dan Dailey, Virginia O'Brien, Tom Conway, Phil Silvers, Doris Day; ***D:*** Norman Z. McLeod; ***M:*** Oscar Hammerstein, George Gershwin, Ira Gershwin, Jerome Kern, George Bassman. Academy Awards '41: Best Song ("The Last Time I Saw Paris"). *MGM, TTC, FCT*

Lady Beware ☆☆ **1987 (R)** A psychotic doctor becomes obsessed with a beautiful store-window dresser who specializes in steamy, erotic fantasies. When he wages a campaign of terror against her, she realizes that she must stop him before he kills her. **108m/C VHS, Beta, LV.** Diane Lane, Michael Woods, Cotter Smith, Viveca Lindfors, Tyra Ferrell, Peter Nevargic, Edward Penn; ***D:*** Karen Arthur; ***W:*** Charles Zev Cohen. *LIV*

Lady by Choice ☆☆½ **1934** Lombard stars as a beautiful young fan dancer who is arrested for a lewd public performance. Taking the advice of her press agent, she hires an old bag lady to pose as her mother on Mother's Day. Robson portrays her "mother" and comes to think of Lombard as her own daughter. Robson encourages Lombard to give up fan dancing and to strive for greater things in life. She also pushes her into romance with a wealthy young man (Pryor). Robson is excellent in her role as "mother" and Lombard shows great comic talent in this charming film. **78m/C VHS.** Carole Lombard, May Robson, Roger Pryor, Walter Connolly, Raymond Walburn, James Burke; ***D:*** David Burton; ***W:*** Jo Swerling. *COL*

Lady Caroline Lamb ☆☆ **1973** Lady Caroline is a passionate young lady in 19th-century England, who, although the wife of a member of Parliament, has an affair with Lord Byron and brings about her own downfall. Costume drama that never quite goes anywhere. **123m/C Beta.** *GB IT* Sarah Miles, Richard Chamberlain, Jon Finch, Laurence Olivier, John Mills, Ralph Richardson; ***D:*** Robert Bolt; ***W:*** Robert Bolt; ***C:*** Oswald Morris; ***M:*** Richard Rodney Bennett. *PSM*

Lady Chatterley's Lover ☆½ *L'Amant de Lady Chatterley* **1955** Englishwoman has bad luck to have husband shot up during WWI and sent home paralyzed. In her quest for sexual fulfillment, she takes a new lover, the estate's earthy gamekeeper. Limp adaptation of D.H. Lawrence's novel. In French with English subtitles. **102m/B VHS, Beta, LV.** *FR* Danielle Darrieux, Erno Crisa, Leo Genn; ***D:*** Marc Allegret. *NOS, MRV, HHT*

Lady Chatterley's Lover ☆½ **1981 (R)** Remake of the 1955 film version of D.H. Lawrence's classic novel of an English lady who has an affair with the gamekeeper of her husband's estate. Basically soft-focus soft porn. **107m/C VHS, Beta, LV.** *GB FR* Sylvia Kristel, Nicholas Clay, Shane Briant; ***D:*** Just Jaeckin. *MGM*

Lady Cocoa ☆½ **1975 (R)** Routine story of a young woman who gets released from jail for 24 hours and sets out for Las Vegas to find the man who framed her. **93m/C VHS, Beta.** Lola Falana, Joe "Mean Joe" Greene, Gene Washington, Alex Dreier; ***D:*** Matt Cimber. *UNI*

The Lady Confesses ☆☆ **1945** Average mystery that involves Hughes trying to clear her boyfriend of murder. Independently produced. "Leave it to Beaver" fans will want to watch for "Ward Cleaver" Beaumont. **66m/B VHS.** Mary Beth Hughes, Hugh Beaumont, Edmund MacDonald, Claudia Drake, Emmett Vogan; ***D:*** Sam Newfield. *NOS, SNC*

Lady Dragon ☆☆ **1992 (R)** A woman and her husband are viciously attacked and only she survives. Found by an old man, she learns a number of martial arts tricks and goes out to get her revenge. **89m/C VHS, LV.** Cynthia Rothrock, Richard Norton, Robert Ginty, Bella Esperance, Hengko Tornando; ***D:*** David Worth; ***W:*** David Worth. *IMP*

Lady Dragon 2 ☆☆ **1993 (R)** Martial arts queen Rothrock returns in another saga of kickboxing vengeance. Susan Morgan seeks revenge on the three killers who terrorized her family. When she unleashes the power of the dragon they don't stand a chance. **?m/C VHS.** Cynthia Rothrock, Billy Drago, Sam Jones, Greg Stuart, Bella Esperance, George Rudy, Adisoerya Abdi; ***D:*** David Worth; ***W:*** Clifford Mohr; ***M:*** Jim West. *PSM*

The Lady Eve ☆☆☆☆ **1941** Two con artists, out to trip up wealthy beer tycoon Fonda, instead find themselves tripped up when one falls in love with the prey. Ridiculous situations, but Sturges manages to keep them believable and funny. With a train scene that's every man's nightmare. Perhaps the best Sturges ever. Based on the story "The Faithful Heart" by Monckton Hoffe. Later remade as "The Birds and the Bees." **93m/B VHS, Beta, LV.** Barbara Stanwyck, Henry Fonda, Charles Coburn, Eugene Pallette, William Demarest, Eric Blore, Melville Cooper; ***D:*** Preston Sturges; ***W:*** Preston Sturges; ***C:*** Victor Milner. National Board of Review Awards '41: 10 Best Films of the Year; Nominations: Academy Awards '41: Best Story. *MCA*

Lady for a Day ☆☆☆½ **1933** Delightful telling of the Damon Runyon story, "Madame La Gimp," about an apple peddler (Robson) down on her luck, who is transformed into a lady by a criminal with a heart. "Lady By Choice" is the sequel. **96m/B VHS, Beta, LV.** May Robson, Warren William, Guy Kibbee, Glenda Farrell, Ned Sparks, Jean Parker, Walter Connolly; ***D:*** Frank Capra. Nominations: Academy Awards '33: Best Actress (Robson), Best Adapted Screenplay, Best Director (Capra), Best Picture. *CVC, CRC, MLB*

Lady for a Night ☆☆ **1942** The female owner of a gambling riverboat does her best to break into high society, when murder threatens to spoil her plans. Cast and costumes burdened by pacing. **88m/B VHS.** John Wayne, Joan Blondell, Ray Middleton, Philip Merivale, Blanche Yurka, Edith Barrett, Leonid Kinskey, Montagu Love; ***D:*** Leigh Jason. *REP*

Lady Frankenstein ☆½ *La Figlia di Frankenstein; The Daughter of Frankenstein; Madame Frankenstein* **1972 (R)** Frankenstein's lovely daughter graduates from medical school and returns home. When she sees what her father's been up to, she gets some ideas of her own. Good fun for fans of the genre. **84m/C VHS, Beta.** *IT* Joseph Cotten, Rosalba (Sara Bay) Neri, Mickey Hargitay, Paul Muller; ***D:*** Mel Welles. *SNC, SUE, HEG*

Lady from Louisiana ☆☆ **1942** A lawyer in old New Orleans out to rid the city of corruption falls in love with the daughter of a big-time gambler. Great storm scene. **84m/B VHS.** John Wayne, Ona Munson, Dorothy Dandridge, Ray Middleton, Henry Stephenson, Helen Westley, Jack Pennick; ***D:*** Bernard Vorhaus. *REP*

Lady from Nowhere ☆☆ **1936** A woman is the only witness to a gangland rub-out and is subsequently pursued by both the mob and the police. Unfortunately for her, the gangsters catch up with her first. **60m/B VHS, Beta.** Mary Astor, Charles Quigley, Thurston Hall, Victor Kilian, Spencer Charters; ***D:*** Gordon Wiles. *SNC*

The Lady from Shanghai ☆☆☆½ **1948** An unsuspecting seaman becomes involved in a web of intrigue when a woman hires him to work on her husband's yacht. Hayworth (a one-time Mrs. Orson Welles), in her only role as a villainess, plays a manipulative, sensual schemer. Wonderful and innovative cinematic techniques from Welles, as usual, including a tense scene in a hall of mirrors. Filmed on a yacht belonging to Errol Flynn. **87m/B VHS, Beta, LV.** Orson Welles, Rita Hayworth, Everett Sloane, Glenn Anders, Ted de Corsia, Erskine Sanford, Gus Schilling; ***D:*** Orson Welles; ***W:*** Orson Welles. *COL, MLB*

Lady from Yesterday ☆ **1985** An American couple's life is shattered by the appearance of the husband's Vietnamese mistress and her 10-year-old son. Made for television. **87m/C VHS, Beta.** Wayne Rogers, Bonnie Bedelia, Pat Hingle, Barrie Youngfellow, Blue Dedeort, Tina Chen; ***D:*** Robert Day. *NO*

Lady Godiva Rides **1968** A bad, campy version of the story of Lady Godiva. Godiva comes to the United States with a bevy of scantily clad maidens and winds up in the Old West. When the town villain threatens to compromise her, Tom Jones comes to the rescue. The film (of course) features Godiva's naked ride on horseback through the town. **88m/C VHS.** Marsha Jordan, Forman Shane; ***D:*** A.C. Stephen. *VDM*

Lady Grey ☆ **1982** A poor farmer's daughter rises to the top of the country music charts, but at a price. **111m/C VHS, Beta.** Ginger Alden, David Allen Coe; ***D:*** Worth Keeter. *NO*

Lady Ice ☆☆ **1973 (PG)** Sutherland, as an insurance investigator on the trail of jewel thieves, follows them to Miami Beach and the Bahamas. After stealing a diamond he enters into partnership with a crook's daughter. Worth seeing for the cast. **93m/C VHS, Beta.** Donald Sutherland, Jennifer O'Neill, Robert Duvall, Eric (Hans Gudegast) Braeden; ***D:*** Tom Gries; ***W:*** Alan R. Trustman; ***M:*** Perry Botkin. *NO*

Lady in a Cage ☆☆☆ **1964** A wealthy widow is trapped in her home elevator during a power failure and becomes desperate when hoodlums break in. Shocking violence ahead of its time probably plays better than when first released. Young Caan is a standout among the star-studded cast. **95m/B VHS, Beta.** Olivia de Havilland, Ann Sothern, James Caan, Jennifer Billingsley, Jeff Corey, Scatman Crothers, Rafael Campos; ***D:*** Walter Grauman; ***W:*** Luther Davis. *PAR*

Lady in Cement ☆½ **1968 (R)** The second Tony Rome mystery, in which the seedy Miami dick finds a corpse with cement shoes while swimming. **93m/C VHS, Beta.** Frank Sinatra, Raquel Welch, Richard Conte, Martin Gabel, Lainie Kazan, Pat Henry, Steve Peck, Joe E. Lewis, Dan Blocker; ***D:*** Gordon Douglas; ***C:*** Joseph Biroc. *FOX*

Lady in Distress ꙮꙮ½ *A Window in London* **1939** A British drama about an unhappily married man who witnesses an apparent murder. He discovers, however, it was actually the prank of an illusionist and his flirtatious wife. He soon finds himself becoming increasingly involved with their lives. **59m/B VHS, Beta.** *GB* Michael Redgrave, Paul Lukas, Sally Gray; ***D:*** Herbert Mason. *SNC, VYY, MLB*

The Lady in Question ꙮ½ *It Happened in Paris* **1940** A Parisian shopkeeper, played by Aherne, sits on a jury that acquits Hayworth of murder. His interest doesn't end with the trial, however, and matters heat up when his son also becomes involved. Remake of a melodramatic French release. **81m/B VHS, Beta, LV.** Rita Hayworth, Glenn Ford, Brian Aherne, Irene Rich, Lloyd Corrigan, George Coulouris, Evelyn Keyes, Curt Bois, Edward Norris; ***D:*** Charles Vidor. *COL, CCB*

Lady in Red ꙮꙮ *Guns, Sin and Bathtub Gin* **1979** A story of America in the '30s, and the progress through the underworld of the woman who was Dillinger's last lover. **90m/C VHS, Beta.** Pamela Sue Martin, Louise Fletcher, Robert Conrad, Christopher Lloyd; ***D:*** Lewis Teague; ***W:*** John Sayles; ***M:*** James Horner. *LIV, VES*

Lady in the Death House ꙮꙮ **1944** A framed woman is set to walk the last mile, as a scientist struggles to find the real killer in time. **57m/B VHS, Beta.** Jean Parker, Lionel Atwill, Marcia Mae Jones. *VYY*

Lady in the Lake ꙮꙮ½ **1946** Why is it everyone wants to get artsy with pulp fiction? Actor Montgomery directs himself in this Philip Marlowe goround, using a subjective camera style to imitate Chandler's first person narrative (that means the only time we get to see Marlowe/Montgomery's mug is in a mirror. That pretty well says it all). Having decided to give up eyeing privately, Marlowe turns to the pen to tell the tangled tale of the lady in the lake: once upon a time, a detective was hired to find the wicked wife of a paying client...Some find the direction clever. Others consider MGM chief Louis B. Mayer, who made sure this was Montgomery's last project with MGM, to be a wise man. **103m/B VHS, Beta.** Robert Montgomery, Lloyd Nolan, Audrey Totter, Tom Tully, Leon Ames, Jayne Meadows; ***D:*** Robert Montgomery; ***C:*** Paul Vogel. *MGM, FCT*

Lady in Waiting ꙮꙮ **1994 (R)** Detective Jimmy Scavetti (Nouri) is hunting down a serial kill preying on call girls when he meets the seductive Lori (Whirry). Then he discovers his ex-wife's new hubby was the lawyer for each of the victims—only the lawyer turns up dead and Jimmy becomes a suspect. Also available in an unrated version. **85m/C VHS.** Michael Nouri, Shannon Whirry, William Devane, Karen Kopins, Crystal Chappell, Robert Costanzo, Meg Foster, Charles Grant; ***D:*** Fred Gallo. *AVE*

The Lady in White ꙮꙮꙮ **1988 (PG-13)** Small-town ghost story about murder and revenge. When young Haas is locked in school one night, he's visited by the ghost of a little girl who wants his help in discovering who murdered her. Well-developed characters, interesting style, and suspenseful plot make for a sometimes slow but overall exceptional film. **92m/C VHS, Beta, LV.** Lukas Haas, Len Cariou, Alex Rocco, Katherine Helmond, Jason Presson, Renata Vanni, Angelo Bertolini, Jared Rushton; ***D:*** Frank Laloggia; ***W:*** Frank Laloggia; ***C:*** Russell Carpenter; ***M:*** Frank Laloggia. *NO*

The Lady is Willing ꙮꙮ½ **1942** Dietrich is a stage star who longs for a baby and when an abandoned infant comes her way she decides to keep the child. Only she hasn't a clue about any of the practical aspects. Lucky for her MacMurray is a friendly pediatrician who gives her some advice. Dietrich finds out she can't adopt as a single parent and persuades MacMurray to marry her, in name only, but since this is a romantic comedy the two eventually fall in love. **91m/B VHS.** Marlene Dietrich, Fred MacMurray, Aline MacMahon, Stanley Ridges, Arline Judge, Roger Clark, Ruth Ford, Sterling Holloway, Harvey Stephens, Harry Shannon, Elisabeth Risdon, Charles Halton; ***D:*** Mitchell Leisen; ***W:*** James Edward Grant, Albert McCleery. *FCT*

Lady Jane ꙮꙮꙮ½ **1985 (PG-13)** An accurate account of the life of 15-year-old Lady Jane Grey, who secured the throne of England for 9 days in 1553 as a result of political maneuvering by noblemen and the Church-of-England. A wonderful film even for non-history buffs. Carter's first film. **140m/C VHS, Beta, LV.** *GB* Helena Bonham Carter, Cary Elwes, Sara Kestelman, Michael Hordern, Joss Ackland, Richard Johnson, Patrick Stewart; ***D:*** Trevor Nunn. *PAR, TVC*

Lady Killer ꙮꙮꙮ **1933** Racy, pre-Code comedy with mobster Cagney hiding out in Hollywood. He gets discovered and becomes a big star, but his old gang turns up to blackmail him. Lots of movie "in" jokes and Clarke (of "Public Enemy" fame) is great as a wisecracking moll. Based on the story "The Finger Man" by Rosalind Keating Shaffer. **74m/B VHS.** James Cagney, Mae Clarke, Leslie Fenton, Margaret Lindsay, Henry O'Neill, Raymond Hatton, George Chandler; ***D:*** Roy Del Ruth; ***W:*** Ben Markson, Lillie Hayward. *MGM*

Lady L ꙮ½ **1965** Silly turn-of-the-century farce about a sexy laundress (Loren), married to a French anarchist (Newman!), who also marries the aristocratic Niven (in name only). Elaborate sets and Paris and London backgrounds couldn't overcome the odd casting and weak script. Adapted from the novel by Romain Gary. **107m/C VHS, Beta.** *FR IT* Sophia Loren, Paul Newman, David Niven, Cecil Parker, Claude Dauphin, Marcel Dalio, Philippe Noiret, Michel Piccoli, Daniel Emilfork, Eugene Deckers; ***Cameos:*** Peter Ustinov; ***D:*** Peter Ustinov; ***W:*** Peter Ustinov. *MGM, FCT*

Lady Mobster ꙮ **1988 (PG-13)** When her parents are murdered a young girl is taken in by a Mafia family. She grows up to be a shrewd lawyer but winds up working in her adoptive family's crime syndicate in order to take revenge on her parents' murderers. Exaggerated and silly but watchable for its so-bad-it's-good qualities. Made for television. **94m/C VHS, Beta, LV.** Susan Lucci, Michael Nader, Roscoe Born, Joseph Wiseman; ***D:*** John Llewellyn Moxey. *TTC*

Lady of Burlesque ꙮꙮ½ *Striptease Lady* **1943** Burlesque dancer is found dead, strangled with her own G-string. Clever and amusing film based on "The G-String Murders" by Gypsy Rose Lee. **91m/B VHS, Beta.** Barbara Stanwyck, Michael O'Shea, Janis Carter, Pinky Lee; ***D:*** William A. Wellman. Nominations: Academy Awards '43: Best Original Score. *MRV, NOS, VCN*

Lady of the Evening ꙮꙮ **1979 (PG)** A prostitute and a crook team up to seek revenge against the mob. **110m/C VHS, Beta.** *IT* Sophia Loren, Marcello Mastroianni. *NO*

Lady of the House ꙮꙮ **1978** A true story about a madame who rose from operator of a brothel to become a political force in San Francisco. **100m/C VHS, Beta.** Dyan Cannon, Susan Tyrrell, Colleen Camp, Armand Assante; ***D:*** Ralph Nelson. *PSM*

Lady of the Lake ꙮꙮ **1928** Rare silent adventure film in which an exiled girl saves the king from outlaws in Scotland. Orchestra score. **47m/B VHS.** *GB* Percy Marmont, Benita Hume, Huddon Mason, Lawson Butt; ***D:*** James A. Fitzpatrick. *GPV, FCT, GVV*

Lady On a Train ꙮꙮꙮ **1945** Travelling at Christmas, wealthy young Nicky Collins (Durbin) thinks she sees a murder from her train window but when she arrives in New York she can't get anyone to believe her. But not willing to give up, Nicky turns to Wayne Morgan (Bruce), a mystery writer for help. Recognizing the victim from a newspaper photo, Nicky checks out his family and gets mistaken for a nightclub singer (so Durbin can vamp a torch song). Lots of comedy amidst the mystery and romance, and some surprizes as well. Based on a story by Leslie Charteris. ♫Gimme a Little Kiss, Will You, Huh?; Night and Day; Silent Night. **95m/B VHS.** Deanna Durbin, David Bruce, Ralph Bellamy, Dan Duryea, Edward Everett Horton, Allen Jenkins, Elizabeth Patterson, William Frawley, Jacqueline DeWit, George Coulouris; ***D:*** Charles David; ***W:*** Robert O'Brien, Edmund Beloin; ***C:*** Woody Bredell; ***M:*** Miklos Rozsa. *MCA*

Lady on the Bus ꙮꙮ **1978 (R)** Sexually frustrated newlywed bride rides the city buses looking for men to satisfy her. This bothers her husband. Shot in Rio de Janeiro. In Portuguese with English subtitles. **102m/C VHS, Beta, LV.** *BR* Sonia Braga; ***D:*** Neville D'Almedia. *LIV, VES*

The Lady Refuses ꙮꙮ **1931** A stuffy Victorian father is disappointed in his wastrel son and decides a poor but honest young woman could be the making of him. Problems arise when the girl falls for the father instead. **70m/B VHS, Beta.** Betty Compson, John Darrow, Margaret Livingston, Gilbert Emery; ***D:*** George Archainbaud. *DVT, VYY*

The Lady Says No ꙮꙮ **1951** A photographer must photograph an attractive author who has written a book uncomplimentary toward the male sex. **80m/B VHS.** Joan Caulfield, David Niven, James Robertson Justice, Frances Bavier, Henry Jones, Jeff York, John Wood; ***D:*** Frank Ross. *FCT*

Lady Scarface ꙮꙮ **1941** Murderous mobster queen breaks the law, bats men around, and takes the cops on a merry chase. Cheap, fast-paced action. **66m/B VHS, Beta.** Mildred Coles, Dennis O'Keefe, Frances Neal, Judith Anderson, Eric Blore, Charles Halton; ***D:*** Frank Woodruff. *NO*

Lady Scarface/The Threat **1949** A crime double feature: "Lady Scarface" (1941), a clever cop is on the trail of a dangerous gunwoman; and "The Threat" (1949), a ruthless killer escapes from prison intent on murdering those who convicted him. **132m/B VHS, Beta.** Dennis O'Keefe, Judith Anderson, Robert Knapp, Eric Blore, Charles McGraw, Michael O'Shea, Virginia Grey; ***D:*** Frank Woodruff. *TTC*

Lady Sings the Blues ꙮꙮ½ **1972 (R)** Jazz artist Billie Holiday's life becomes a musical drama depicting her struggle against racism and drug addiction in her pursuit of fame and romance. What could be a typical price-of-fame story is saved by Ross' inspired performance as the tragic singer. ♫My Man; Strange Fruit; God Bless the Child; Don't Explain; T'Ain't Nobody's Business If I Do; Lady Sings the Blues; All Of Me; The Man I Love; Our Love Is Here to Stay. **144m/C VHS, Beta, LV.** Diana Ross, Billy Dee Williams, Richard Pryor, James Callahan, Paul Hampton, Sid Melton; ***D:*** Sidney J. Furie; ***C:*** John A. Alonzo. Nominations: Academy Awards '72: Best Actress (Ross), Best Art Direction/Set Decoration, Best Costume Design, Best Story & Screenplay, Best Original Score. *PAR, FCT*

Lady Stay Dead ꙮ½ **1983** A gory Australian shocker about another faceless, knife-wielding psychotic chasing a girl. **100m/C VHS, Beta.** *AU VCD*

Lady Street Fighter ꙮ **1986** A well-armed female combat fighter battles an organization of assassins to avenge her sister's murder. **73m/C VHS, Beta.** Renee Harmon, Joel McCrea Jr. *UNI*

Lady Takes a Chance ꙮꙮꙮ **1943** A romantic comedy about a New York working girl with matrimonial ideas and a rope-shy rodeo rider who yearns for the wide open spaces. Fine fun on the range. **86m/B VHS, Beta.** John Wayne, Jean Arthur, Phil Silvers, Charles Winninger; ***D:*** William A. Seiter. *REP*

Lady Terminator ꙮ½ **1989 (R)** A student on an anthropology expedition digs up more than she bargained for when she is possessed by an evil spirit and goes on a rampage. **83m/C VHS, Beta.** Barbara Constable, Christopher Hart, Joseph McGlynn, Claudia Rademaker; ***D:*** Jalil Jackson. *NO*

The Lady Vanishes ꙮꙮꙮꙮ **1938** When a kindly old lady disappears from a fast-moving train, her young friend finds an imposter in her place and a spiraling mystery to solve. Hitchcock's first real winner, a smarmy, wit-drenched British mystery that precipitated his move to Hollywood. Along with "39 Steps," considered an early Hitchcock classic. From the novel "The Wheel Spins," by Ethel Lina White. Special edition contains short subject on Hitchcock's cameos in his films. Remade in 1979. **99m/B VHS, Beta, LV.** *GB* Margaret Lockwood, Paul Lukas, Michael Redgrave, May Whitty, Googie Withers, Basil Radford, Naunton Wayne, Cecil Parker, Linden Travers, Catherine Lacey; ***Cameos:*** Alfred Hitchcock; ***D:*** Alfred Hitchcock; ***W:*** Sidney Gilliat,

Frank Launder; **M:** Louis Levy. New York Film Critics Awards '38: Best Director (Hitchcock). *SNC, NOS, SUE*

The Lady Vanishes ♪½ **1979** In this reworking of the '38 Alfred Hitchcock film, a woman on a Swiss bound train awakens from a nap to find that the elderly woman seated next to her was kidnapped. Falls short of the original movie due to the "screwball" nature of the main characters, Gould and Shepherd. Based on Ethel Lina White's novel "The Wheel Spins." **95m/C VHS, Beta, LV.** *GB* Elliott Gould, Cybill Shepherd, Angela Lansbury, Herbert Lom; **D:** Anthony Page; **W:** George Axelrod. *MED, MRV*

Lady Windermere's Fan ♪♪½ **1926** The silent, Lubitsch adaptation of the Oscar Wilde tale concerning an upper-class couple's marriage being almost destroyed by suspected adultery. **66m/B VHS, Beta, 8mm.** Ronald Colman, May McAvoy, Bert Lytell; **D:** Ernst Lubitsch. *VYY, GPV, GVV*

The Lady with the Dog ♪♪♪ **1959** A bittersweet love story based on the Anton Chekhov story, about two married Russians who meet by chance in a park, fall in love, and realize they are fated to a haphazard, clandestine affair. In Russian with English titles. **86m/B VHS, Beta.** *RU* Iya Savvina, Alexei Batalov, Ala Chostakova, N. Alisova; **D:** Yosif Heifitz. *WST, FCT, INJ*

The Lady Without Camelias ♪♪½ **1953** A young woman is discovered by a film producer who casts her in a successful movie and eventually marries her. Convinced that she can sustain a career as a serious actress, the producer is dismayed by the job offers that come her way, usually of a sexually exploitive nature. What follows is a tragic decline for both. **106m/C VHS, Beta.** *IT CIG*

Ladybird, Ladybird ♪♪♪ **1993 (R)** Loach's emotionally bruising look at working-class life and family in the '90s. Maggie (Rock) is a tough unmarried mother of four who's been battered by her lovers and has come under the over-watchful eye of Britain's social services. She meets Jorge (Vega), a gentle Paraguayan, and just when things are looking up, Jorge gets immigration heat, Maggie's insecurities surface, and her baby daughter is taken into care by child welfare. Rock has a no-nonsense manner and acerbic wit that precludes any hand-wringing for her character, even as you hope she'll win out over circumstance. Based on a true story. **102m/C VHS.** *GB* Crissy Rock, Vladimir Vega, Ray Winstone, Sandie Lavelle, Mauricio Venegas, Clare Perkins, Jason Stracey, Luke Brown, Lily Farrell; **D:** Ken Loach; **W:** Rona Munro. Berlin International Film Festival '94: Best Actress (Rock); Nominations: Independent Spirit Awards '95: Best Foreign Language Film. *HMK*

Ladybugs ♪½ **1992 (PG-13)** Hangdog salesman Dangerfield would like to move up the corporate ladder, but must first turn the company-sponsored girl's soccer team into winners. Routine Dangerfield vehicle exploits nearly everything for laughs, including dressing an athletic boy as a girl so he can play on the team. Obvious fluff. **91m/C VHS, Beta.** Rodney Dangerfield, Jackee, Jonathan Brandis, Ilene Graff, Vinessa Shaw, Tom Parks, Jeanetta Arnetta, Nancy Parsons, Blake Clark, Tommy Lasorda; **D:** Sidney J. Furie; **W:** Curtis Burch; **M:** Richard Gibbs. *PAR*

Ladyhawke ♪♪½ **1985 (PG-13)** In medieval times, a youthful pickpocket befriends a strange knight who is on a mysterious quest. This unlikely duo, accompanied by a watchful hawk, are enveloped in a magical adventure. **121m/C VHS, Beta, LV.** Matthew Broderick, Rutger Hauer, Michelle Pfeiffer, John Wood, Leo McKern, Alfred Molina, Ken Hutchison; **D:** Richard Donner; **W:** Edward Khmara, Michael Thomas, Tom Mankiewicz; **M:** Andrew Powell. Nominations: Academy Awards '85: Best Sound. *WAR*

Ladykiller ♪♪ **1992 (R)** Rogers stars as a burned-out cop who goes to a dating service to find a man who'll give her the attention she craves. When she meets wealthy professional Shea she thinks he's the one but her cop's curiosity about her lover's past may cost her her life. **92m/C VHS, LV.** Mimi Rogers, John Shea, Alice Krige, Tom Irwin; **D:** Michael Scott; **W:** Shelley Evans. *MCA*

The Ladykillers ♪♪♪½ *The Lady Killers* **1955** A gang of bumbling bank robbers is foiled by a little old lady. Hilarious antics follow, especially on the part of Guinness, who plays the slightly demented-looking leader of the gang. **87m/C VHS, Beta.** *GB* Alec Guinness, Cecil Parker, Katie Johnson, Herbert Lom, Peter Sellers; **D:** Alexander MacKendrick; **W:** William Rose; **M:** Tristram Cary. British Academy Awards '55: Best Actress (Johnson), Best Screenplay. *REP, FCT, HMV*

Ladykillers ♪♪ **1988** At the glitzy L.A. club Ladykillers, men strip as the women cheer. At the climax of the performance, one of the dancers is brutally murdered, live on stage. In this decadent world of glitter and sex, the women are the hunters and the men are the reward. **97m/C VHS, Beta.** Marilu Henner, Susan Blakely, Lesley-Anne Down, Thomas Calabro; **D:** Robert Lewis; **W:** Greg Dinallo. *PSM*

The Lady's Maid's Bell ♪♪ **1985** Based upon the story by Edith Wharton, this ghost story deals with the new maid in a family estate who discovers the ghost of another past maid. **60m/C VHS, Beta.** *PSM*

The Lady's Not for Burning ♪♪½ **1995** Romantic comedy, set in a medieval English village, finds ex-soldier Thomas Mendip (Branagh) invading the home of querulous Mayor Hebble Tyson (Hepton), demanding to be hanged. He says he's murdered the local rag and bone merchant but the townspeople insist Jennet Jourdemayne (Lunghi), who's seeking refuge at the mayor's, has turned him into a dog. They demand she be burned as a witch (hence the title, since Thomas, unwillingly but strongly, objects to this action). Adapted by Fry from his play; made for TV. **90m/C VHS.** Kenneth Branagh, Cherie Lunghi, Bernard Hepton, Tim Watson, Susannah Harker, Angela Thorne, Shaun Scott; **D:** Julian Amyes; **W:** Christopher Fry. *VCO, FUS*

Lafayette Escadrille ♪♪½ *Hell Bent for Glory* **1958** Action and romance in WWI via the famed flying unit manned by American volunteers. Hunter is banal in the lead role as is his romance with a reformed prostitute (Choreau). Director Wellman actually was a member of the squadron and his son plays him in the film but the director regarded the film as a failure because of studio interference. **92m/B VHS.** Tab Hunter, Etchika Choureau, William Wellman Jr., Joel McCrea, Dennis Devine, Marcel Dalio, David Janssen, Paul Fix, Will Hutchins, Clint Eastwood; **D:** William A. Wellman; **W:** A.S. Fleischman; **C:** William Clothier; **M:** Leonard Rosenman. *WAR*

L'Age D'Or ♪♪♪♪ *Age of Gold* **1930** Bunuel's first full-length film and his masterpiece of sex, repression, and of course, death. A hapless man is prevented from reaching his beloved by middle-class morality, forces of the establishment, the Church, government and every bastion of modern values. Banned for years because of its anti-religious stance. Co-scripted by Dali. A mercilessly savage, surreal satire, the purest expression of Bunuel's wry misanthropy. In French with English subtitles. **62m/B VHS, Beta, LV.** *FR* Gaston Modot, Lya Lys, Max Ernst, Pierre Prevert, Marie Berthe Ernst, Paul Eluard; **D:** Luis Bunuel; **W:** Salvador Dali, Luis Bunuel. *FCT, IME, GVV*

Laguna Heat ♪½ **1987** A tired LA cop investigates a series of murders that are related to an old friend of his father's. Based on a novel by T. Jefferson Parker. Made for television. **110m/C VHS, Beta, LV.** Harry Hamlin, Jason Robards Jr., Catherine Hicks, Rip Torn, Anne Francis; **D:** Simon Langton. *ORI, WAR*

Lai Shi: China's Last Eunuch **1988** A starving Chinese child becomes a eunuch in order to garner wealth in the Emperor's palace. But he is castrated at a historically inopportune moment (as if there's a good time for such modification), just prior to the turbulent 1920s. In Cantonese with English subtitles. **100m/C VHS.** *CH* **D:** Chan Tsi-liang. *FCT*

The Lair of the White Worm ♪♪♪ **1988 (R)** Scottish archaeologist uncovers a strange skull, and then a bizarre religion to go with it, and then a very big worm. An unusual look at the effects of Christianity and paganism on each other, colored with sexual innuendo and, of course, giant worms. A cross between a morality play and a horror film. Adapted from Bram Stoker's last writings, done while he was going mad from Bright's disease. Everything you'd expect from Russell. **93m/C VHS, Beta, LV.** *GB* Amanda Donohoe, Sammi Davis, Catherine Oxenberg, Hugh Grant, Peter Capaldi, Stratford Johns, Paul Brooke, Christopher Gable; **D:** Ken Russell; **W:** Ken Russell; **M:** Stanislas Syrewicz. *VES, LIV, TPV*

Lake Consequence ♪♪ **1992 (R)** Severance plays a suburban housewife who accidentally gets locked in the camper of the tree-trimmer stud (Zane) she's been eyeing while he's been working in her neighborhood. Next thing she knows they wind up at a distant lake where the bored housewife is more than willing to give into her growing sexual fantasies. An unrated version at 90 minutes is also available. **85m/C VHS, LV.** Joan Severance, Billy Zane, May Karasun; **D:** Rafael Eisenman; **W:** Zalman King, Melanie Finn, Henry Cobbold; **M:** George S. Clinton. *REP*

Lakota Woman: Siege at Wounded Knee ♪♪½ **1994** Autobiography of Mary Crow Dog and her coming of age during the American Indian Movement's 1973 occupation of Wounded Knee. Tangled loyalties and the battle between Native Americans and U.S. troops make for strong drama. Bedard is remarkable in her film debut. Based on the book by Mary Crow Dog and Richard Erdoes. Filmed on location in South Dakota. **113m/C VHS.** Irene Bedard, August Schellenberg, Joseph Runningfox, Floyd "Red Crow" Westerman, Tantoo Cardinal, Michael Horse, Lawrence Bayne, Nancy Parsons; **D:** Frank Pierson; **W:** Bill Kerby; **M:** Richard Horowitz. *TTC*

The Lamb ♪♪½ **1915** Intent on proving to his sweetheart that he's not the coward people say he is, a guy heads west to engage in various manly activities, including fisticuffs, karate and Indian kidnapping. Fairbanks' debut on film (he was already an established Broadway star) set the mold for the American leading man: moral, cheerful, physical, and not hard to look at. A popular guy with the public, Fairbanks formed his own film company the following year. Story's based on D.W. Griffith's book, "The Man and the Test." **60m/B VHS, Beta.** Douglas Fairbanks Sr., Seena Owen, Lillian Langdon, Monroe Salisbury, Kate Toncray, Alfred Paget, William E. Lowery; **D:** Christy Cabanne. *GPV, FCT*

Lamb ♪♪ **1985** Troubled 10-year-old Owen Kane (Kane) has been dumped by his abusive mother at a Catholic-run institution for wayward boys in Ireland, run by self-righteous headmaster Brother Benedict (Bannen). Owen becomes Benedict's scapegoat—much to the dismay of Brother Michael Lamb (Neeson). When Lamb claims a small family inheritance, he decides to take Owen and head to London, posing as father and son, where they live in increasingly depressed surroundings while Michael tries painfully to make them into a real family. Based on the novel by MacLaverty, who also wrote the screenplay. **110m/C VHS.** *IR* Liam Neeson, Hugh O'Conor, Ian Bannen, Frances Tomelty; **D:** Colin Gregg; **W:** Bernard MacLaverty; **C:** Mike Garfath; **M:** Van Morrison. *FCT*

Lambada ♪ **1989 (PG)** By day, he's a high school teacher in Beverly Hills; by night, a Latin dirty dancer cum tutor of ghetto teens. The very first of several films based on the short-lived dance craze. **92m/C VHS, Beta, LV.** J. Eddie Peck, Melora Hardin, Adolfo "Shabba Doo" Quinones, Ricky Paull Goldin, Basil Hoffman, Dennis Burkley; **D:** Joel Silberg. *MGM*

Lamerica ♪♪♪ **1995** Two Italian hustlers, Fiore (Placido) and his younger partner Gino (Lo Verso), head for poverty-stricken Albania in 1991, the first year after the collapse of the Communist dictatorship. They intend to set up a phony corporation and scam money from government grants but they need an Albanian figurehead. The duo find simple-minded, elderly Spiro (Di Mazzarelli), who's spent most of his life in prison camps, and stash him in an orphanage for safe keeping. Only when Spiro gets away, Gino heads for the countryside to find him and discovers some secrets about Spiro's past and just how the wily Albanians have been surviving. Italian with subtitles. **120m/C VHS.** *IT* Enrico Lo Verso, Michele Placido, Carmelo Di Mazzarelli, Piro Milkani; ***D:*** Gianni Amelio; ***W:*** Gianni Amelio, Andrea Porporati, Alessandro Sermoneta; ***C:*** Luca Bigazzi; ***M:*** Franco Piersanti. *NYR*

L'Amour en Herbe *Budding Love* **1977** His parents realize Pascal has something on his mind when he fails school. It turns out to be lovely Martine, whom he is then forbidden to see. But Pascal remains true—until betrayed. French with subtitles. **100m/C VHS.** *FR* Pascal Meynier, Guilhaine Dubos; ***D:*** Roger Andrieux. *FCT*

Lamp at Midnight ½ **1966** Presentation from "George Schaefer's Showcase Theatre" deals with three critical periods in the life of Italian astronomer Galileo Galilei, from his invention of the telescope, through his appearance at the Holy Office of the Inquisition, to the publication of his "Dialogue on the Two Systems of the World." For those in a planetary state of mind. **76m/C VHS, Beta.** Melvyn Douglas, David Wayne, Michael Hordern, Hurd Hatfield, Kim Hunter; ***D:*** George Schaefer. *FHS*

Lana in Love **1992** A lonely woman places an ad in the personal section in hopes of finding her Mr. Right. **90m/C VHS, Beta.** Daphna Kastner, Clark Gregg. *NO*

Lancelot of the Lake *Lancelot Du Lac; The Grail; Le Graal* **1974** The Knights of the Round Table return to the court of King Arthur after a long, bloody, and fruitless search for the Holy Grail. Rivalries and jealousies debase the heroes as Lancelot struggles with his feelings for Arthur's Queen Guinevere. Austere acting but the film's rich visuals provide a sensuous air. French with subtitles. **85m/C VHS.** *FR* Luc Simon, Laura Duke Condominas, Vladimir Antolek-Oresek, Humbert Balsan, Patrick Bernard; ***D:*** Robert Bresson; ***W:*** Robert Bresson; ***C:*** Pasqualino de Santis; ***M:*** Philippe Sarde. *NYF*

Land and Freedom **1995** Earnestly talky drama focusing on idealist Liverpudlian communist David Carr (Hart), who heads to Spain in 1937 to fight against Franco's fascists. What David learns is that the Republican forces, made up of independent militia, are bitterly divided, with much infighting and betrayal from the Stalinist forces within David's own party. He falls for socialist Blanca (Pastor) and learns how terrifying and haphazard war can be (with timeout for ideological discussions). Sympathetic characters and sweeping action help to compensate for the political polemics. **109m/C VHS.** *GB SP GE* Ian Hart, Rosana Pastor, Iciar Bollain, Tom Gilroy, Frederic Pierrot, Marc Martinez; ***D:*** Ken Loach; ***W:*** Jim Allen; ***C:*** Barry Ackroyd; ***M:*** George Fenton. Cesar Awards '96: Best Foreign Film; Nominations: British Academy Awards '95: Best Film. *NYR*

The Land Before Time **1988 (G)** Lushly animated children's film about five orphaned baby dinosaurs who band together and try to find the Great Valley, a paradise where they might live safely. Works same parental separation theme as Bluth's "American Tail." Charming, coy, and shamelessly tearjerking; producers included Steven Spielberg and George Lucas. **67m/C VHS, LV.** ***D:*** Don Bluth; ***W:*** Stu Krieger; ***M:*** James Horner; ***V:*** Pat Hingle, Helen Shaver, Gabriel Damon, Candice Houston, Burke Barnes, Judith Barsi, Will Ryan. *MCA, FCT, APD*

The Land Before Time 2: The Great Valley Adventure ½ **1994 (G)** Sequel to 1988's animated adventure finds dinsosaur pals Littlefoot, Cera, Ducky, Petrie, and Spike happily settled in the Great Valley. But their adventures don't stop as they chase two egg-stealing Struthiomimuses and retrieve an egg of unknown origin from the Mysterious Beyond. **75m/C VHS, LV.** *MCA*

The Land Before Time 3: The Time of the Great Giving ½ **1995 (G)** Littlefoot and his pals try to find a new source of water when the Great Valley experiences a severe water shortage. **71m/C VHS, LV.** ***D:*** Roy Allen Smith. *MCA*

Land of Doom **1984** An amazon and a warrior struggle for survival in a post-holocaust fantasy setting. **87m/C VHS, Beta.** Deborah Rennard, Garrick Dowhen; ***D:*** Peter Maris. *LIV*

The Land of Faraway **1987 (G)** A Swedish boy is whisked off to a magical land where he does battle with evil knights and flies on winged horses. Dubbed; based on a novel by Astrid Lindgren. **95m/C VHS, Beta.** Timothy Bottoms, Christian Bale, Susannah York, Christopher Lee, Nicholas Pickard; ***D:*** Vladimir Grammatikov. *PSM*

Land of Fury *The Seekers* **1955** British naval officer Hawkins steps on New Zealand's shore and into trouble when he accidently walks on sacred Maori burial ground. Very British, very dated colonial saga, based on the novel "The Seekers" by John Guthrie. **90m/C VHS.** *GB* Jack Hawkins, Glynis Johns, Noel Purcell, Ian Fleming; ***D:*** Ken Annakin. *NOS*

Land of Hunted Men **1943** The Range Busters are on the case as they track down the hideout of terrorizing gunmen. **58m/B VHS, Beta.** Ray Corrigan, Dennis Moore, Max Terhune. *NOS, DVT*

Land of Promise ½ *Ziemia Obiecana* **1974** At the turn of the century three men build a textile factory in Lodz, Poland. They each represent a particular ethnic group: a Pole (Olbrychski), a German (Seweryn), and a Jew (Pszoniak). Class conflicts threaten to overwhelm as their overworked and underpaid workers plan a revolt. Based on the novel by Wladyslav Reymont. In Polish with English subtitles. **178m/C VHS.** *PL* Daniel Olbrychski, Wojciech Pszoniak, Andrzej Seweryn, Anna Nehrebecka; ***D:*** Andrzej Wajda; ***W:*** Andrzej Wajda; ***M:*** Wojciech Kilar. *FCT*

Land of the Lawless **1947** A group of outlaws rule over a barren wasteland. What's the point? **54m/B VHS.** Rachel Brown, Raymond Hatton, Christine McIntyre, Tristram Coffin; ***D:*** Lambert Hillyer. *NOS, DVT*

Land of the Minotaur *The Devil's Men* **1977 (PG)** Small village is the setting for horrifying ritual murders, demons, and disappearances of young terrorists. Fans of Pleasence and Cushing won't want to miss this. **88m/C VHS, Beta.** *GB* Donald Pleasence, Peter Cushing, Luan Peters; ***D:*** Costa Carayiannis; ***M:*** Brian Eno. *VCI, MRV*

Land of the Pharaohs ½ **1955** An epic about the building of Egypt's Great Pyramid. Hawkins is the extremely talkative pharoah and Collins plays his sugary-sweet yet villainous wife. Sort of campy, but worth watching for the great surprise ending. **106m/C VHS, LV.** Jack Hawkins, Joan Collins, James Robertson Justice, Dewey Martin, Alexis Minotis, Sydney Chaplin; ***D:*** Howard Hawks; ***W:*** Harold Jack Bloom; ***C:*** Lee Garmes. *WAR*

Land Raiders **1969** Savalas plays a man who hates Apaches and wants their land, but is distracted when his brother arrives on the scene, igniting an old feud. **101m/C VHS, Beta.** Telly Savalas, George Maharis, Arlene Dahl, Janet Landgard; ***D:*** Nathan (Hertz) Juran. *GKK*

The Land That Time Forgot **1975 (PG)** A WWI veteran, a beautiful woman, and their German enemies are stranded in a land outside time filled with prehistoric creatures. Based on the 1918 novel by Edgar Rice Burroughs. Followed in 1977 by "The People that Time Forgot." **90m/C VHS, Beta.** *GB* Doug McClure, John McEnery, Susan Penhaligon; ***D:*** Kevin Connor. *LIV, VES*

The Land Unknown ½ **1957** A Naval helicopter is forced down in a tropical land of prehistoric terror, complete with ferocious creatures from the Mesozoic Era. While trying to make repairs, the crew discovers the sole survivor of a previous expedition who was driven to madness by life in the primordial jungle. Good performances from cast, although monsters aren't that believable. Based on a story by Charles Palmer. **78m/B VHS.** Jock Mahoney, Shawn Smith, William Reynolds, Henry Brandon, Douglas Kennedy; ***D:*** Virgil W. Vogel; ***W:*** Laszlo Gorog; ***M:*** Henry Mancini. *MCA*

Landlord Blues **1987** A trashy slumlord without morals or a conscience goes one step too far, and a tenant retaliates with munitions. **96m/C VHS, Beta.** Mark Boone, Raye Dowell, Richard Litt, Bill Rice, Mary Schultz, Gigi Williams; ***D:*** Jacob Burckhardt. *NO*

Landscape in the Mist *Topio Stin Omichli* **1988** A stark Greek landscape in a rainy winter sets the scene for a tragic search by two children for their unknown father. Relies heavily on symbolism to make its point about unfulfilled desire (including the film's imaginary German-Greek border). In Greek with English subtitles. **126m/C VHS.** *GR FR IT* Tania Palaiologou, Michalis Zeke, Stratos Tzortzoglou, Eva Kotamanidou, Alika Georgouli; ***D:*** Theo Angelopoulos; ***W:*** Thanassis Valtinos, Tonino Guerra, Theo Angelopoulos. *NYF, FCT, BTV*

Landslide ½ **1992 (PG-13)** As a geologist, suffering from memory loss, comes closer to discovering his identity his life is endangered by a sinister plot. **95m/C VHS, LV.** Anthony Edwards, Tom Burlinson, Joanna Cassidy, Melody Anderson, Ronald Lacey, Ken James, Lloyd Bochner; ***D:*** Jean-Claude Lord. *REP*

L'Anne Sainte ½ *Pilgrimage to Rome* **1978** In his last film, Gabin is an escaped convict returning to his hidden loot in Rome when his plane is hijacked by international terrorists. Available dubbed. **?m/C VHS.** *FR* Jean Gabin, Jean-Claude Brialy, Paul Giusti, Danielle Darrieux. *FRA, FCT*

L'Annee des Meduses ½ *The Year of the Jellyfish* **1986 (R)** An 18-year-old girl tries to seduce the local Monsieur Beefcake she meets on her vacation. When he doesn't return her interest, she decides to teach him a lesson. In French with English subtitles, or dubbed. **110m/C VHS, Beta.** *FR* Valerie Kaprisky, Barnard Giradeau; ***D:*** Christopher Frank. *FCT, TPV*

Lantern Hill ½ **1990 (G)** During the Depression, a 12-year-old girl attempts to fan the embers between her estranged parents. Made for cable Wonderworks production, filmed partly on Canada's Prince Edward Island. Based on a story by Lucy Maud Montgomery, whose "Anne of Green Gables" is also part of the Wonderworks series. **112m/C VHS, LV.** *CA* Sam Waterston, Colleen Dewhurst, Sarah Polley, Marion Bennett, Zoe Caldwell; ***D:*** Kevin Sullivan. *TOU, FCT*

Lap Dancing *Woof!* **1995 (R)** What hath "Showgirls" wrought? Small town gal Angie Parker moves to Hollywood to become an actress and, when the money runs out, winds up as an exotic dancer. Also available unrated. **90m/C VHS, LV.** Lorissa McComass, Tane McClure, C.T. Miller; ***D:*** Mike Sedan. *TRI*

L'Appat *Fresh Bait; Live Bait; The Bait* **1994** Deglamourizing, if familiar, look at amoral teens and violence. 18-year-old salesgirl Nathalie (Gillain) supports her unemployed boyfriend Eric (Sitruk) and his dim-bulb buddy Bruno (Putzulu). The guys hang out, watch too many gangster videos, and try to be tough, deciding to get rich by dangling Nathalie as bait. She goes to a man's home (presumably for sex) but Eric and Bruno will break in and rob the mark instead. Plan goes awry when their first victim is killed. What's truly disturbing is the trio's blase attitude that crime is a viable way to obtain money or that anything would happen to them should they be caught. Based on the book by Morgan Sportes, which recounted the 1984 crime. French with subtitles. **117m/C VHS.** *FR* Marie Gillain, Olivier Sitruk, Bruno Putzulu, Philippe Duclos, Richard Berry; ***D:*** Bertrand Tavernier; ***W:*** Bertrand Tavernier, Colo Tavernier O'Hagan; ***M:*** Philippe Haim. Berlin International Film Festival '94: Best Film. *NYR*

Laramie Kid **1935** A vintage Tyler sagebrush saga. **60m/B VHS, Beta.** Tom Tyler, Alberta Vaughn, Al Ferguson, Murdock McQuarrie, George Chesebro; ***D:*** Harry S. Webb. *NOS, DVT, RXM*

L'Argent **1983** When a young man's parents refuse to lend him any money a friend helps out by giving him a counterfeit 500-franc note. This sets off a chain of events, with every passing of the money leading to another lie, betrayal, and increasingly violent crime. Austere and stylized vision is not for all tastes. In French with English subtitles. **82m/C VHS.** *FR* Christian Patey, Sylvie van den Elsen, Michel Briguet, Caroline Lang; ***D:*** Robert Bresson; ***W:*** Robert Bresson; ***C:*** Pasqualino de Santis. Cannes Film Festival '83: Best Director (Bresson); National Society of Film Critics Awards '84: Best Director (Bresson). *NYF, FCT*

Larks on a String 🦴🦴🦴½ **1968** Banned for 23 years, this wonderful film is Menzel's masterpiece, even better than his Oscar winning "Closely Watched Trains." Portrays the story of life in labor camps where men and women are re-educated at the whim of the government. No matter what the hardships, these people find humor, hope and love. Their individuality will not be lost, nor their humanity dissolved. Excellent performances, tellingly directed with a beautiful sense of composition and tone. Screenplay written by Menzel and Bohumil Hrabil, author of the short story on which it is based. In Czech with English subtitles. **96m/C VHS.** *CZ* Vaclav Neckar, Jitka Zelenohorska, Jaroslav Satoransky, Rudolf Hrusinsky; ***D:*** Jiri Menzel; ***W:*** Jiri Menzel. *FXL, INJ*

Larry 🦴🦴 **1974** Based on the Nevada State Hospital case history of a 26-year-old man, institutionalized since infancy, who is discovered to be of normal intelligence and must learn to live the life he has always been capable of living. Made for television. **80m/C VHS, Beta.** Frederic Forrest, Tyne Daly, Katherine Helmond, Michael McGuire, Robert Walden; ***D:*** William A. Graham. *LCA*

Larry McMurtry's Streets of Laredo 🦴🦴🦴 *Streets of Laredo* **1995** Texas Ranger-turned-bounty hunter Woodrow F. Call (a splendid Garner) is hired by the railroad to track down ruthless Mexican bandit Joey Garza (Cruz), pitting an old man's skills against a young man's daring, and driving both men across Texas, deep into Mexican territory. Call's old friend Pea Eye Parker (Shepard) reluctantly comes along, with ex-prostitute Lorena (Spacek), who's Parker's wife, and Maria (Braga), Joey's tough-but-deluded mom, providing strong support. Casual cruelty and violence are the norm in the sunset days of both Call's life and that of the west itself. Third in the TV sagas, following "Return to Lonesome Dove." **227m/C VHS.** James Garner, Alexis Cruz, Sam Shepard, Sissy Spacek, Sonia Braga, Wes Studi, Randy Quaid, Charles Martin Smith, Kevin Conway, George Carlin, Ned Beatty, James Gammon, Tristan Tait, Anjanette Comer; ***D:*** Joseph Sargent; ***W:*** Larry McMurtry, Diana Ossana; ***C:*** Eddie Pei; ***M:*** David Shire. *CAF*

Las Vegas Hillbillys 🦴 *Country Music* **1966** A pair of country-singing hillbillies inherit a saloon in Las Vegas and enjoy wine, moonshine, and song. These two make the Clampetts look like high society. Followed, believe it or not, by "Hillbillys in a Haunted House." ♫Money Greases the Wheel. **85m/C VHS, Beta.** Mamie Van Doren, Jayne Mansfield, Ferlin Husky, Sonny James; ***D:*** Arthur C. Pierce. *NLC*

Las Vegas Lady 🦴 **1976 (PG)** Three shrewd casino hostesses plot a multi-million dollar heist in the nation's gambling capital. Non-captivating caper. **90m/C VHS, Beta.** Stella Stevens, Stuart Whitman, George de Cecenzo, Andrew Stevens; ***D:*** Noel Nosseck; ***W:*** Walter Dallenbach; ***M:*** Alan Silvestri. *PSM*

Las Vegas Serial Killer *Woof!* **1986** A serial killer, let out of prison on a technicality, starts killing again. Made for video by Camp. **90m/C VHS, Beta.** Pierre Agostino, Ron Jason, Tara MacGowran, Kathryn Downey. *NO*

The Las Vegas Story *Woof!* **1952** Gambling, colorful sights, and a murder provide the framework for this non-compelling fictional guided-tour of the city. Save your money for the slots. **88m/B VHS, Beta.** Victor Mature, Jane Russell, Vincent Price, Hoagy Carmichael, Brad Dexter; ***D:*** Robert Stevenson. *NO*

Las Vegas Weekend 🦴 **1985** A computer nerd goes to Las Vegas and discovers fun. **83m/C VHS, Beta.** Barry Hickey, Macka Foley, Ray Dennis Steckler; ***D:*** Dale Trevillion; ***W:*** Dale Trevillion. *VTR, NWV*

Laser Mission 🦴🦴½ **1990** When it is discovered that the Soviets have laser weapon capabilities, an agent is given the task of destroying the weapon and kidnapping the scientist who developed it. **83m/C VHS, LV.** Brandon Lee, Debi Monahan, Ernest Borgnine, Werner Pochat, Graham Clarke, Maureen Lahoud, Pierre Knoessen; ***D:*** Beau Davis. *TTC*

Laser Moon 🦴🦴 **1992** A serial killer uses a surgical laser beam to kill his beautiful victims, and he strikes at every full moon. When he announces his next attack on a late-night radio talk show the police call in a beautiful rookie cop (Lords) to use as bait. **90m/C VHS.** Traci Lords, Crystal Shaw, Harrison Leduke, Bruce Carter; ***D:*** Bruce Carter. *HMD*

Laserblast *Woof!* **1978 (PG)** Standard wimp-gets-revenge story in which a frustrated young man finds a powerful and deadly laser which was left near his home by aliens; upon learning of its devastating capabilities, his personality changes and he seeks revenge against all who have taken advantage of him. **87m/C VHS, Beta, LV.** Kim Milford, Cheryl "Rainbeaux" Smith, Keenan Wynn, Roddy McDowall; ***D:*** Michael Raeburn; ***M:*** Richard Band, Joel Goldsmith. *MED*

The Laserman 🦴🦴 **1990 (R)** Exotic black comedy about a Chinese-American scientist who, when not fending off his overbearing Jewish mother or having telepathic orgasms, is contending with a band of political terrorists. **92m/C VHS.** Marc Hayashi, Peter Wang, Tony Leung, Sally Yeh, Maryann Urbano, Joan Copeland; ***D:*** Peter Wang; ***W:*** Peter Wang; ***M:*** Mason Daring. *HTV*

The Lash of the Penitents **1939** An explosive documentary about Southern fundamentalist cults. **70m/B VHS, Beta.** *SNC, NOS, DVT*

Lassie 🦴🦴½ **1994 (PG)** Everyone's favorite collie returns as the Turner family moves to Virginia's Shenandoah Valley to take up sheep ranching. However, because this is the '90s, Dad meets financial disaster, and junior can't stand his stepmom. Can Lassie meet the challenges of dysfunctional family living? "What is it girl? Call a therapist?" This Lassie is a direct descendant of Pal, the original 1943 star. **92m/C VHS, Beta.** Helen Slater, Jon Tenney, Tom Guiry, Brittany Boyd, Richard Farnsworth, Frederic Forrest; ***D:*** Daniel Petrie; ***W:*** Matthew Jacobs, Gary Ross, Elizabeth Anderson. *PAR*

Lassie: Adventures of Neeka **1968** America's best friend joins her Native American buddy, Neeka, for a journey through a forest in the Pacific Northwest. They camp out in a deserted settlement, pull an elderly gentleman out of a frigid pond, and risk their lives to release horses from a stable during a raging wildfire. **75m/B VHS, Beta.** Jed Allan, Mark Miranda, Robert Rockwell, Lassie; ***D:*** Richard Moder, Jack B. Hively. *NO*

Lassie, Come Home 🦴🦴½ **1943 (G)** In first of the Lassie series, the famed collie is reluctantly sold and makes a treacherous cross-country journey back to her original family. **90m/C VHS, Beta, LV.** Roddy McDowall, Elizabeth Taylor, Donald Crisp, Edmund Gwenn, May Whitty, Nigel Bruce, Elsa Lanchester, J. Pat O'Malley, Lassie; ***D:*** Fred M. Wilcox. National Board of Review Awards '43: 10 Best Films of the Year; Nominations: Academy Awards '43: Best Color Cinematography. *MGM*

Lassie from Lancashire 🦴🦴 **1938** Not the famous Collie—but here, a Colleen. A pair of struggling lovebirds try to make it in show biz against all odds, including the girl's lunatic aunt, who locks her away before an audition. **67m/B VHS, Beta.** Marjorie Brown, Hal Thompson, Marjorie Sandford, Lassie, Mark Daly. *VYY*

Lassie: The Miracle 🦴 **1975** A TV-movie featuring the faithful collie saving new-born pups and befriending a mute boy. **90m/C VHS, Beta.** Lassie. *MGM*

Lassie: Well of Love **1990** Various installments of the classic television series featuring the heroic collie are combined to create a movie-length presentation for home video. Lassie takes two young pups under her paw and, in the process, loses her way. As she tries to get home, she brings joy back into the lives of two despondent children. Finally, the old girl faces death when she tumbles into an abandoned well and must depend on humans for rescue. **76m/C VHS, Beta.** Lassie, Mary Gregory, Robert Donner. *NO*

Lassie's Great Adventure 🦴🦴½ **1962** Lassie and her master Timmy are swept away from home by a runaway balloon. After they land in the Canadian wilderness, they learn to rely on each other through peril and adventure. Made for television. **104m/C VHS, Beta.** June Lockhart, Jon Provost, Hugh Reilly, Lassie; ***D:*** William Beaudine. *MGM*

Lassiter 🦴🦴½ **1984 (R)** Selleck plays a jewel thief who is asked to steal diamonds from the Nazis for the FBI. Supporting cast adds value to what is otherwise a fairly ordinary adventure drama. **100m/C VHS, Beta, LV.** Tom Selleck, Jane Seymour, Lauren Hutton, Bob Hoskins, Joe Regalbuto, Ed Lauter, Warren Clarke; ***D:*** Roger Young. *WAR*

Last Action Hero 🦴🦴 **1993 (PG-13)** Newcomer O'Brien finds himself in a movie starring his idol Jack Slater, the kind of guy who never loses a fight and is impervious to gunfire and explosions (and he has a really cool car and a really big gun). Disappointing action/spoof of movies within a movie (rumored to have cost $80 million) was critically maimed and never recovered. The concept isn't new and has been done better before, though Ah-nold possesses his usual self-mocking charm, which is more than can be said for the movie. Look for lots of big stars in small roles and cameos. Cluttered with inside Hollywood gags, the script was given uncredited assistance from William Goldman. **131m/C VHS, Beta, LV, 8mm.** Arnold Schwarzenegger, Austin O'Brien, Mercedes Ruehl, F. Murray Abraham, Charles Dance, Anthony Quinn, Robert Prosky, Tom Noonan, Frank McRae, Art Carney, Brigitte Wilson; ***Cameos:*** Sharon Stone, Hammer, Chevy Chase, Jean-Claude Van Damme, Tori Spelling, Joan Plowright, Adam Ant, James Belushi, James Cameron, Tony Curtis, Timothy Dalton, Tony Danza, Edward Furlong, Little Richard, Damon Wayans, Robert Patrick; ***D:*** John McTiernan; ***W:*** David Arnott, Shane Black; ***C:*** Dean Semler; ***M:*** Michael Kamen. *COL, BTV*

The Last American Hero 🦴🦴🦴 *Hard Driver* **1973 (PG)** The true story of how former moonshine runner Junior Johnson became one of the fastest race car drivers in the history of the sport. Entertaining slice of life chronicling whiskey running and stock car racing, with Bridges superb in the lead. Based on a series of articles written by Tom Wolfe. **95m/C VHS, Beta.** Jeff Bridges, Valerie Perrine, Gary Busey, Art Lund, Geraldine Fitzgerald, Ned Beatty; ***D:*** Lamont Johnson; ***W:*** William Roberts; ***M:*** Charles Fox. National Board of Review Awards '73: 10 Best Films of the Year. *FOX*

Last American Virgin 🦴🦴 **1982 (R)** Usual brainless teen sex comedy about three school buddies who must deal with a plethora of problems in their search for girls who are willing. Music by Blondie, The Cars, The Police, The Waitresses, Devo, U2, Human League, and Quincy Jones. **92m/C VHS, Beta.** Lawrence Monoson, Diane Franklin, Steve Antin, Louisa Moritz; ***D:*** Boaz Davidson; ***W:*** Boaz Davidson. *MGM*

The Last Angry Man 🦴🦴🦴½ **1959** An old, idealistic Brooklyn doctor attracts a television producer wanting to make a documentary about his life and career, and the two conflict. Muni was Oscar-nominated for this, his last film. **100m/B VHS, Beta.** Paul Muni, David Wayne, Betsy Palmer, Luther Adler, Dan Tobin; ***D:*** Daniel Mann; ***C:*** James Wong Howe. Nominations: Academy Awards '59: Best Actor (Muni), Best Art Direction/Set Decoration (B & W). *COL*

The Last Bastion 🦴🦴 **1984** A WWII drama emphasizing the political struggle between Churchill, MacArthur, Roosevelt, and Australia's John Curtin. **160m/C VHS, Beta.** *AU* Robert Vaughn, Timothy West. *ACA*

The Last Best Year 🦴🦴½ **1990 (PG)** Basic TV tearjerker has lonely psychologist Wendy (Moore) befriending patient Jane (Peters), who has a terminal illness. **88m/C VHS.** Mary Tyler Moore, Bernadette Peters, Brian Bedford, Dorothy McGuire, Kate Reid, Kenneth Welsh; ***D:*** John Erman; ***W:*** David W. Rintels. *NHO*

The Last Boy Scout 🦴🦴 **1991 (R)** This formula thriller stars Willis as a private eye and Wayans as an ex-quarterback teaming up against a pro-football team owner who will stop at nothing to get political backing for a bill promoting legalized gambling on sports. Another variation of the violent buddy-picture by "Lethal Weapon" screenwriter Black. **105m/C VHS, LV.** Bruce Willis, Damon Wayans, Halle Berry, Chelsea Field, Noble Willingham, Taylor Negron, Danielle Harris, Bruce McGill; ***D:*** Tony Scott; ***W:*** Shane Black. *WAR*

Last Bullet **1950** A young westerner chases after a band of outlaws to avenge the cold-blooded murder of his parents. **55m/B VHS, Beta, LV.** James Ellison, Russell Hayden, John Cason. *NO*

The Last Butterfly **1992** Quiet Holocaust movie set in Theresienstadt, the Czechoslovak ghetto city used by the Nazis to persuade the outside world of their humane treatment of the Jews. Noted French mime Antoine Moreau (Courtenay) has fallen under suspicion by the Gestapo. He's "persuaded" to give a performance in Theresienstadt for the benefit of the visiting Red Cross but decides to subvert Nazi propaganda with his own version of "Hansel and Gretel." This time the witch feeds the children into her oven. Muted performances and screenplay (adapted from the Michael Jacot novel) heightened the film's surreal calmness. **106m/C VHS, LV.** *CZ* Tom Courtenay, Brigitte Fossey, Freddie Jones, Ingrid Held, Linda Jablonska; ***D:*** Karel Kachyna; ***W:*** Karel Kachyna, Ota Hofman; ***M:*** Alex North. *NLC*

Last Call **1990 (R)** Clearly, Joe Sixpack won't rent this bimbo fest for its subtle plot. Katt, a mafiosi-cheated real estate guy, decides to even the score with the assistance of gal pal/playmate of the year Tweed, who's more than willing to compromise her position. A direct to video release, it also features the talents of playboy emerita Stevens. Available in rated and unrated versions. **90m/C VHS, Beta.** William Katt, Shannon Tweed, Joseph Campanella, Stella Stevens, Matt Roe; ***D:*** Jag Mundhra. *PSM*

The Last Chance **1945** A realistic look at the efforts of three WWII Allied officers to help a group of refugees escape across the Alps from Italy to Switzerland. The officers are played by former pilots who were shot down over Switzerland. In spite of this—or perhaps because of it—the acting is superb. Watch for inspirational scene of refugees singing. **105m/B VHS.** E.G. Morrison, John Hoy, Ray Reagan, Odeardo Mosini, Sigfrit Steiner, Emil Gerber; ***D:*** Leopold Lindtberg. *NOS*

Last Chase ½ **1981 (PG)** Famed race car driver becomes a vocal dissenter against the sterile society that has emerged, in this drama set in the near future. Made for television. Screenplay written by Christopher Crowe under the pseudonym C.R. O'Cristopher. **106m/C VHS, Beta.** *CA* Lee Majors, Burgess Meredith, Chris Makepeace, Alexandra Stewart; ***D:*** Martyn Burke; ***W:*** Christopher Crowe, Martyn Burke. *VES*

Last Command **1928** Famous powerful silent film by Sternberg about a expatriate Czarist general forging out a pitiful living as a silent Hollywood extra, where he is hired by his former adversary to reenact the revolution he just left. Next to "The Last Laugh," this is considered Jannings' most acclaimed performance. Deeply ironic, visually compelling film with a new score by Gaylord Carter. **88m/B VHS, Beta.** Emil Jannings, William Powell, Evelyn Brent, Nicholas Soussanin, Michael Visaroff, Jack Raymond, Fritz Feld; ***D:*** Josef von Sternberg; ***W:*** Warren Duff; ***M:*** Max Steiner, Gaylord Carter. Academy Awards '28: Best Actor (Jannings); Nominations: Academy Awards '28: Best Original Screenplay, Best Picture. *PAR, FCT, BTV*

The Last Command ½ **1955** Jim Bowie and his followers sacrifice their lives in defending the Alamo. A good cast holds its own against a mediocre script; battle scenes are terrific. **110m/C VHS.** Sterling Hayden, Richard Carlson, Ernest Borgnine, J. Carrol Naish, Virginia Grey, Anna Maria Alberghetti; ***D:*** Frank Lloyd. *REP, PAR*

The Last Contract **1986 (R)** An artist who pays his bills by working as a hitman, kills the wrong man. As a result, he must fear for his life since a counterhit is inevitable. **85m/C VHS.** Jack Palance, Rod Steiger, Bo Svenson, Richard Roundtree, Ann Turkel; ***D:*** Allan A. Buckhantz. *ACA*

Last Cry for Help ½ **1979** A psychiatrist helps a seventeen-year-old high school coed who, fearing she has disappointed her parents, attempts suicide. Typical made-for-television melodrama that attempts to make a statement, but falls short. Definitely not the "Partridge Family." **98m/C VHS, Beta.** Linda Purl, Shirley Jones, Tony LoBianco, Murray Hamilton, Grant Goodeve; ***D:*** Hal Sitowitz; ***M:*** Miles Goodman. *UNI*

Last Dance ½ **1991** Five scantily-clad exotic dancers are ready to compete for the title of Miss Dance-TV, but trouble ensues when the dancers start turning up dead. **86m/C VHS, Beta, LV.** Cynthia Bassinet, Elaine Hendrix, Kurt T. Williams, Allison Rhea, Erica Ringston; ***D:*** Anthony Markes. *PSM*

Last Dance **1996 (R)** Following closely on the heels of "Dead Man Walking," this death-row drama suffered from bad timing. Stone plays the convicted murderess condemned to die in an unnamed Southern state. Morrow's the rookie attorney for the state's clemency office assigned to her case. As a bond grows between the two, he uncovers errors in her trial that his bosses would rather have him ignore. The movie makes its big mistake by centering on Morrow's callow lawyer instead of Stone's embittered con. The clock-ticking countdown to the execution (which will amuse fans of "The Player") even fails to hold attention. **103m/C VHS.** Sharon Stone, Rob Morrow, Randy Quaid, Peter Gallagher, Jack Thompson, Jayne Brook, Pamela Tyson, Skeet Ulrich, Don Harvey, Diane Sellers; ***D:*** Bruce Beresford; ***W:*** Ron Koslow; ***C:*** Peter James; ***M:*** Mark Isham. *NYR*

Last Day of the War ½ **1969 (PG)** A German scientist is chased by Americans and Germans as WWII winds to its conclusion. Filmed in Spain. **96m/C VHS, Beta.** *SP* George Maharis, Maria Perschy, James Philbrook, Gerard Herter; ***D:*** Juan Antonio Bardem. *LIV*

The Last Days of Chez Nous ½ **1992 (R)** Armstrong's dramatic comedy about a family falling apart has Ganz as a homesick Frenchman married to controlling, successful Australian writer Harrow. Trouble starts when his wayward sister-in-law Fox returns home to live with them and his wife decides to take an extended holiday with her father. Ganz suddenly finds himself only too involved in Fox's complicated life. Self-involved characters with messy emotional lives leave viewers feeling rather distant, though cast, and particularly Ganz, strive for intimacy. **96m/C VHS, LV.** *AU* Bruno Ganz, Lisa Harrow, Kerry Fox, Kiri Paramore, Bill Hunter, Miranda Otto; ***D:*** Gillian Armstrong; ***W:*** Helen Garner; ***M:*** Paul Grabowsky. Australian Film Institute '92: Best Actress (Harrow); Nominations: Australian Film Institute '92: Best Director (Armstrong), Best Film, Best Supporting Actor (Hunter). *NLC, IME, COL*

The Last Days of Dolwyn ½ *Woman of Dolwyn; Dolwyn* **1949** A man banned for thievery from his Welsh village returns bent upon revenge. He plans to buy the entire district when it is designated part of a water reservoir project, but finds plans thwarted by a dowager and her stepson. Burton's first film was based on a true story. **95m/B VHS.** *GB* Edith Evans, Emlyn Williams, Richard Burton, Anthony James, Barbara Couper, Alan Aynesworth, Hugh Griffith, Roddy Hughes, Tom Jones; ***D:*** Emlyn Williams; ***W:*** Emlyn Williams. *FCT, DVT*

Last Days of Frank & Jesse James ½ **1986** A tired television-movie rehash of the well-known western legend in which the famous brothers try to be like others after their personal war against society ends. **100m/C VHS, Beta.** Johnny Cash, Kris Kristofferson, June Carter Cash, Willie Nelson, Margaret Gibson, Gail Youngs; ***D:*** William A. Graham. *VMK*

The Last Days of Patton ½ **1986** A made-for-television movie depicting the aging general's autumn years as a controversial ex-Nazi defender and desk-bound WWII historian. Scott reprises his feature-film role. **146m/C VHS, Beta.** George C. Scott, Ed Lauter, Eva Marie Saint, Richard Dysart, Murray Hamilton, Kathryn Leigh Scott; ***D:*** Delbert Mann. *FOX*

Last Days of Planet Earth *Woof! Prophecies of Nostradamus; Catastrophe 1999; Nostradamus No Daiyogen* **1974** Really stinky Japanese doomsday movie about a scientist who charges that a build-up of pollution is responsible for giant mutant sea slugs and other environmental disasters. Dubbed. **88m/C VHS.** *JP* Tetsuro Tamba, So Yamamura, Takashi Shimura; ***D:*** Toshio Masuda. *PAR*

Last Days of Pompeii ½ **1935** Vintage DeMille-style epic based on Lord Lytton's book, where the eruption of Vesuvius threatens noblemen and slaves alike. State-of-the-art special effects still look fantastic today. Remade in 1960; available colorized. **96m/B VHS, Beta, LV.** Preston Foster, Alan Hale, Basil Rathbone, George L. Baxt, Louis Calhern, David Holt, Dorothy Wilson, Wryley Birch, Gloria Shea; ***D:*** Ernest B. Schoedsack. *TTC*

The Last Days of Pompeii *Ultimi Giorni di Pompeii* **1960** Superman Reeves plays a gladiator trying to clean up the doomed town of Pompeii in this remake of the 1935 classic. Some spectacular scenes, including the explosive climax when the mountain blows its top. **105m/C VHS.** *IT* Steve Reeves, Christine Kaufmann, Barbara Carroll, Anne Marie Baumann, Mimmo Palmara; ***D:*** Mario Bonnard; ***W:*** Sergio Leone. *GKK*

The Last Detail **1973 (R)** Two hard-boiled career petty officers (Nicholson and Young) are commissioned to transfer a young sailor facing an eight-year sentence for petty theft from one brig to another. In an act of compassion, they attempt to show the prisoner a final good time. Nicholson shines in both the complexity and completeness of his character. Adapted from a Daryl Ponicsan novel. **104m/C VHS, Beta, LV.** Jack Nicholson, Otis Young, Randy Quaid, Clifton James, Michael Moriarty, Carol Kane, Nancy Allen; ***Cameos:*** Gilda Radner; ***D:*** Hal Ashby; ***W:*** Robert Towne; ***C:*** Michael Chapman; ***M:*** Johnny Mandel. British Academy Awards '74: Best Actor (Nicholson), Best Screenplay; Cannes Film Festival '74: Best Actor (Nicholson); National Board of Review Awards '74: 10 Best Films of the Year; New York Film Critics Awards '74: Best Actor (Nicholson); National Society of Film Critics Awards '74: Best Actor (Nicholson); Nominations: Academy Awards '73: Best Actor (Nicholson), Best Adapted Screenplay, Best Supporting Actor (Quaid). *COL, WME*

The Last Dragon ½ *Berry Gordy's The Last Dragon* **1985 (PG-13)** It's time for a Motown kung fu showdown on the streets of Harlem, for there is scarcely enough room for even one dragon. **108m/C VHS, Beta.** Taimak, Vanity, Christopher Murney, Julius J. Carry III, Faith Prince; ***D:*** Michael A. Schultz. *FOX*

Last Embrace **1979 (R)** A feverish thriller in the Hitchcock style dealing with an ex-secret serviceman who is convinced someone is trying to kill him. **102m/C VHS, Beta.** Roy Scheider, Janet Margolin, Christopher Walken, John Glover, Charles Napier, Mandy Patinkin; ***D:*** Jonathan Demme; ***M:*** Miklos Rozsa. *MGM, FOX*

The Last Emperor **1987 (PG-13)** Deeply ironic epic detailing life of Pu Yi, crowned at the age of three as the last emperor of China before the onset of communism. Follows Pu Yi from childhood to manhood (sequestered away in the Forbidden City) to fugitive to puppet-ruler to party proletariat. O'Toole portrays the sympathetic Scot tutor who educates the adult Pu Yi (Lone) in the ways of the western world after Pu Yi abdicates power in 1912. Shot on location inside the People's Republic of China with a cast of thousands; authentic costumes. Rich, visually stunning movie. The Talking Heads' David Byrne contributed to the score. Cinematography by Vittorio Storaro. **140m/C VHS, Beta, LV, 8mm.** *IT* John Lone, Peter O'Toole, Joan Chen, Victor Wong, Ryuichi Sakamoto, Dennis Dun, Maggie Han, Ying Ruocheng, Ric Young; ***D:*** Bernardo Bertolucci; ***W:*** Mark Peploe, Bernardo Bertolucci; ***C:*** Vittorio Storaro; ***M:*** Ryuichi Sakamoto, David Byrne. Academy Awards '87: Best Adapted Screenplay, Best Art Direction/Set Decoration, Best Cinematography, Best Costume Design, Best Director (Bertolucci), Best Film Editing, Best Picture, Best Sound, Best Original Score; British Academy Awards '88: Best Film; Cesar Awards '88: Best Foreign Film; Directors Guild of America Awards '87: Best Director (Bertolucci); Golden Globe Awards '88: Best Director (Bertolucci), Best Film—Drama, Best Screenplay, Best Score; Los Angeles Film Critics Association Awards '87: Best Cinematography; National Board of Review Awards '87: 10 Best Films of the Year; New York Film Critics Awards '87: Best Cinematography. *COL, FCT, BTV*

Last Exit to Brooklyn ☆☆☆½ **1990 (R)** Hubert Selby, Jr.'s shocking book comes to the screen in a vivid film. Leigh gives a stunning performance as a young Brooklyn girl caught between the Mafia, union men, and friends struggling for something better. Set in the 1950s. Fine supporting cast; excellent pacing. **102m/C VHS, LV.** Jennifer Jason Leigh, Burt Young, Stephen Lang, Ricki Lake, Jerry Orbach, Maia Danzinger, Stephen Baldwin; ***D:*** Uli Edel. New York Film Critics Awards '89: Best Supporting Actress (Leigh). *COL, FCT*

The Last Fight ☆½ **1982 (R)** Boxer risks his life and his girlfriend for a shot at the championship title. Watch and see if he could've been a contender. **85m/C VHS, Beta.** Fred Williamson, Willie Colon, Ruben Blades, Joe Spinell, Darlanne Fluegel; ***D:*** Fred Williamson. *NO*

The Last Five Days ☆☆ **1982** Based on the true story of a girl and her brother who, in 1943 Munich, were arrested for distributing anti-Nazi propaganda. The film covers the five days between their capture and execution. In German with English subtitles. **112m/C VHS.** *GE* Lena Stolze, Irm Hermann; ***D:*** Percy Adlon. *CVC, INJ*

The Last Flight of Noah's Ark ☆☆½ **1980 (G)** Disney adventure concerns a high-living pilot, a prim missionary, and two stowaway orphans who must plot their way off a deserted island following the crash landing of their broken-down plane. **97m/C VHS, Beta.** Elliott Gould, Genevieve Bujold, Rick Schroder, Vincent Gardenia, Tammy Lauren; ***D:*** Charles Jarrott; ***W:*** George Arthur Bloom, Steven W. Carabatsos; ***M:*** Maurice Jarre. *DIS*

Last Flight Out: A True Story ☆☆ **1990** Hours before Saigon fell to the Vietcong in 1975, Vietnamese and Americans rushed to board the last commercial flight out of Vietnam. Lukewarm account of a true story. **99m/C VHS, 8mm.** James Earl Jones, Richard Crenna, Haing S. Ngor, Eric Bogosian. *NO*

Last Flight to Hell ☆☆ **19??** When a drug lord is kidnapped, Brown is sent to South America to rescue the slimeball. His interest in the job picks up when the drug lord's 11-on-a-scale-of-ten daughter joins him for the chase. **94m/C VHS.** Reb Brown, Chuck Connors; ***D:*** Paul D. Robinson. *AIP*

The Last Fling ☆½ **1986** When Selleca has her mind set on a romantic fling, Ritter is headed for trouble. She wants love for one night, he wants it forever. Will they solve this difference of opinion? Will true love prevail? Will Ritter consent to being used as a one-night stand? Weakly plotted and poorly acted comedy. Made for television. **95m/C VHS, LV.** John Ritter, Connie Sellecca, Scott Bakula, Shannon Tweed, Paul Sand, John Bennett Perry; ***D:*** Corey Allen; ***M:*** Charles Bernstein. *ACA*

Last Four Days ☆☆ **1977 (PG)** A chronicle of the final days of Benito Mussolini. **91m/C VHS, Beta.** Rod Steiger, Henry Fonda, Franco Nero; ***D:*** Carlo Lizzani. *LIV*

Last Frontier ☆☆½ **1932** Serial of 12 chapters contains shades of spectacular figures in Western history: Custer, Hickok, and others in a background of grazing buffalo, boom towns, and covered wagon trails. **216m/B VHS, Beta.** Lon Chaney Jr., Yakima Canutt, Francis X. Bushman; ***D:*** Spencer Gordon Bennet, Thomas L. Story. *VCN, VYY, DVT*

Last Game ☆☆ **1980** A college student is torn between his devotion to his blind father and going out for the college's football team. **107m/C VHS, Beta.** Howard Segal, Ed L. Grady, Terry Alden; ***D:*** Martin Beck. *NO*

The Last Good Time ☆☆½ **1994 (R)** Old-world violinist Joseph Kopple (Mueller-Stahl), retired and living in a small Brooklyn apartment, has his world turned upside down when his street-smart neighbor Charlotte (d'Abo) seeks refuge from her abusive boyfriend Eddie (Pasdar). An unsentimental friendship develops between the two inspite of the differences in their ages, educations, and lifestyles. Terrific performance from Mueller-Stahl as the lonely but dignified old man. Based on the novel by Richard Bausch. **90m/C VHS.** Armin Mueller-Stahl, Olivia D'Abo, Maureen Stapleton, Lionel Stander, Adrian Pasdar; ***D:*** Bob Balaban; ***W:*** Bob Balaban, John McLaughlin; ***C:*** Claudia Rashke. *HMK*

Last Gun **1964** A legendary gunman on the verge of retirement has to save his town from a reign of terror before turning his gun in. **98m/C VHS, Beta.** Cameron Mitchell. *NO*

The Last Hit ☆☆½ **1993 (R)** Michael Grant (Brown) is a professional assassin, working for the CIA, who's very good at his job. But now he's burned out and ready to retire to New Mexico for some peace and quiet. He buys a house from the widowed Anna (Adams), naturally falling in love with her. Then one last assignment comes along and, wouldn't you know, his target turns out to be Anna's father (Yulin). Based on the novel "The Large Kill" by Patrick Ruell. **93m/C VHS, LV.** Bryan Brown, Brooke Adams, Harris Yulin; ***D:*** Jan Egleson; ***W:*** Walter Klenhard, Alan Sharp; ***M:*** Gary Chang. *MCA*

Last Holiday ☆☆☆ **1950** A man who is told he has a few weeks to live decides to spend them in a posh resort where people assume he is important. **89m/B VHS, Beta.** *GB* Alec Guinness, Kay Walsh, Beatrice Campbell, Wilfrid Hyde-White, Bernard Lee; ***D:*** Henry Cass; ***W:*** J.B. Priestley. *HMV, RXM, LCA*

The Last Horror Film *Woof! The Fanatic* **1982 (R)** Beautiful queen of horror films is followed to the Cannes Film Festival by her number one fan who, unbeknownst to her, is slowly murdering members of her entourage in a deluded and vain attempt to capture her attentions. Title refers to lack of plans for a sequel. **87m/C VHS, Beta.** Caroline Munro, Joe Spinell, Judd Hamilton; ***D:*** David Winters. *MED*

The Last Hour ☆ **1991 (R)** A Wall Street crook crosses a Mafia punk, so the latter holds the former's wife hostage in an unfinished skyscraper. Fortunately the lady's first husband is a gung-ho cop eager to commence the DIE HARD-esque action. Undistinguished fare that gives away the climax in an opening flash-forward. **85m/C VHS, Beta, LV.** Michael Pare, Shannon Tweed, Bobby DiCicco, Robert Pucci; ***D:*** William Sachs. *ACA*

Last House on Dead End Street *Woof! The Fun House* **1977 (R)** Gore galore as actors die for their art in this splatter flick about snuff films. **90m/C VHS.** Steven Morrison, Dennis Crawford, Lawrence Bornman, Janet Sorley; ***D:*** Victor Janos. *SUN*

Last House on the Left ☆☆ **1972 (R)** Two girls are kidnapped from a rock concert by a gang of escaped convicts; the girls' parents exact bloody revenge when the guilty parties pay an intended housecall. Controversial and grim low-budget shocker; loosely based on Bergman's "The Virgin Spring." **83m/C VHS, Beta, LV.** David Hess, Lucy Grantham, Sandra Cassel, Mark Sheffler, Fred J. Lincoln; ***D:*** Wes Craven. *LIV, VES, HHE*

The Last Hunt ☆☆½ **1956** Well-performed western starring Taylor as a seedy buffalo hunter who gains his identity from senseless acts of murder. When personalities clash, he seeks revenge on fellow buffalo hunter Granger. Shot in Custer National Park, the buffalo scenes were real-life attempts at keeping the animals controlled. Based on the novel by Milton Lott. **108m/C VHS.** Robert Taylor, Stewart Granger, Lloyd Nolan, Debra Paget, Russ Tamblyn, Constance Ford, Ainslie Pryor, Ralph Moody, Fred Graham, Dan White, Bill Phillips, Roy Barcroft; ***D:*** Richard Brooks; ***W:*** Richard Brooks; ***M:*** Daniele Amfitheatrof. *MGM*

The Last Hunter ☆ *Hunter of the Apocalypse* **1980 (R)** A soldier fights for his life behind enemy lines during the Vietnam War. **97m/C VHS, Beta.** *IT* Tisa Farrow, David Warbeck, Tony King, Bobby Rhodes, Margit Evelyn Newton, John Steiner, Alan Collins; ***D:*** Anthony (Antonio Margheriti) Dawson. *LIV, VES*

Last Hurrah ☆☆½ **1958** An aging Irish-American mayor battles corruption and political backbiting in his effort to get re-elected for the last time. Semi-acclaimed heart warmer, based on the novel by Edwin O'Connor. **121m/B VHS, Beta, LV.** Spencer Tracy, Basil Rathbone, John Carradine, Jeffrey Hunter, Dianne Foster, Pat O'Brien, Edward Brophy, James Gleason, Donald Crisp, Ricardo Cortez, Wallace Ford, Frank McHugh, Jane Darwell; ***D:*** John Ford. National Board of Review Awards '58: Best Actor (Tracy), Best Director (Ford). *COL*

The Last Innocent Man ☆☆½ **1987** An attorney who quit law due to a guilty conscience is lured into defending a suspected murderer. Things become even more complicated when he begins having an affair with his client's seductive wife. A well-acted and suspense-filled flick. Made for cable television. **113m/C VHS, Beta.** Ed Harris, Roxanne Hart, Bruce McGill, Clarence Williams III, Rose Gregorio, David Suchet, Darrell Larson; ***D:*** Roger Spottiswoode; ***W:*** Dan Bronson; ***M:*** Brad Fiedel. *ORI, WAR*

The Last Laugh ☆☆☆½ *Der Letzte Mann* **1924** An elderly man, who as the doorman of a great hotel was looked upon as a symbol of "upper class," is demoted to washroom attendant due to his age. Important due to camera technique and consuming performance by Jannings. Silent with music score. A 91-minute version is also available. **77m/B VHS, Beta.** *GE* Emil Jannings, Maly Delshaft, Max Hiller; ***D:*** F.W. Murnau. *NOS, FCT, IHF*

Last Light ☆☆ **1993 (R)** A prison guard (Whitaker) on death row forms a tenuous bond with an incorrigible inmate (Sutherland) who's about to be executed. Disturbing, especially the execution scene. Filmed on location at California's Soledad Prison. Sutherland's directorial debut. Made for cable television. **95m/C VHS, LV.** Kiefer Sutherland, Forest Whitaker, Clancy Brown, Lynne Moody, Kathleen Quinlan, Amanda Plummer; ***D:*** Kiefer Sutherland. *VMK*

The Last Man on Earth ☆☆ *L'Ultimo Uomo Della Terra* **1964** Price is the sole survivor of a plague which has turned the rest of the world into vampires, who constantly harass him. Uneven U.S./Italian production manages to convey a creepy atmosphere of dismay. **86m/B VHS.** *IT* Vincent Price, Franca Bettoya, Giacomo "Jack" Rossi-Stuart, Emma Danieli; ***D:*** Ubaldo Ragona, Sidney Salkow. *SNC, MRV*

Last Man Standing ☆ **1987 (R)** A cheap, gritty drama about bare-knuckle fist fighting. Wells stars as a down-on-his-luck prizefighter trying to find work that doesn't involve pugilism. **89m/C VHS, Beta.** William Sanderson, Vernon Wells, Franco Columbo; ***D:*** Damian Lee. *ACA*

Last Man Standing ☆☆ **1995 (R)** L.A. police officer Wincott discovers corruption after his partner Banks is murdered. **96m/C VHS.** Jeff Wincott, Jillian McWhirter, Jonathan Banks, Steve Eastin, Jonathan Fuller, Michael Greene, Ava Fabian; ***D:*** Joseph Merhi; ***W:*** Joseph Merhi; ***M:*** Louis Febre. *PMH*

The Last Married Couple in America ☆☆ **1980 (R)** A couple fight to stay happily married amidst the rampant divorce epidemic engulfing their friends. **103m/C VHS, Beta.** George Segal, Natalie Wood, Richard Benjamin, Valerie Harper, Dom DeLuise, Priscilla Barnes; ***D:*** Gilbert Cates; ***M:*** Charles Fox. *MCA*

Last Mercenary *Woof!* **1984** An angry ex-soldier kills everyone who makes him mad. **90m/C VHS, Beta.** Tony Marsina, Malcolm Duff, Kitty Nichols, Louis Walser. *NO*

The Last Metro ☆☆☆ *Le Dernier Metro* **1980** Truffaut's alternately gripping and touching drama about a theater company in Nazi-occupied Paris. In 1942, Lucas Steiner (Bennent) is a successful Jewish theater director who is forced into hiding. He turns the running of the theater over to his wife, Marion (the always exquisite Deneuve), who must contend with a pro-Nazi theater critic (Richard) and her growing attraction to the company's leading man (Depardieu), who is secretly working with the Resistance. In French with English subtitles. **135m/C VHS, Beta, LV.** *FR* Catherine Deneuve, Gerard Depardieu, Heinz Bennent, Jean-Louis Richard, Jean Poiret, Andrea Ferreol, Paulette Dubost, Sabine Haudepin; ***D:*** Francois Truffaut; ***W:*** Suzanne Schiffman; ***C:*** Nestor Almendros; ***M:*** Georges Delerue. Cesar Awards '81: Best Actor (Depardieu), Best Actress (Deneuve), Best Art Direction/Set Decoration, Best Cinematography, Best Director (Truffaut), Best Film, Best Sound, Best Writing, Best Score; Nominations: Academy Awards '80: Best Foreign Language Film. *HMV, FOX, APD*

The Last Mile 🦴🦴 **1932** The staff of a prison prepares for the execution of a celebrated murderer. **70m/B VHS, Beta.** Preston Foster, Howard Phillips, George E. Stone; ***D:*** Sam Bischoff. *NOS, MRV, BAR*

The Last Movie 🦴½ *Chinchero* **1971 (R)** A movie stunt man stays in a small Peruvian town after his filming stint is over. Hopper's confused, pretentious follow-up to "Easy Rider," has a multitude of cameos but little else. Given an award by the Italians; nobody else understood it. Kristofferson's film debut; he also wrote the music. Based on a story by Hopper and Stern. **108m/C VHS.** Dennis Hopper, Julie Adams, Peter Fonda, Kris Kristofferson, Sylvia Miles, John Phillip Law, Russ Tamblyn, Rod Cameron; ***D:*** Dennis Hopper; ***W:*** Stewart Stern; ***M:*** Kris Kristofferson. *NO*

Last Night at the Alamo 🦴🦴🦴 **1983** Patrons fight to stop the destruction of their Houston bar, the Alamo, which is about to be razed to make room for a modern skyscraper. Insightful comedy written by the author of "The Texas Chainsaw Massacre." **80m/B VHS.** Sonny Carl Davis, Lou Perry, Steve Matilla, Tina Hubbard, Doris Hargrave; ***D:*** Eagle Pennell; ***W:*** Ken Henkel; ***M:*** Wayne Bell. *NO*

The Last of England 🦴🦴🦴½ **1987** A furious non-narrative film by avant-garde filmmaker Jarman, depicting the modern British landscape as a funereal, waste-filled rubble-heap—as depleted morally as it is environmentally. **87m/C VHS, Beta, LV.** *GB* Tilda Swinton, Spencer Leigh; ***D:*** Derek Jarman. *MFV, TPV, INJ*

The Last of His Tribe 🦴🦴 **1992 (PG-13)** In 1911 an anthropologist befriends an Indian and discovers that Ishi is the last surviving member of California's Yahi tribe. Ishi then becomes a media and scientific society darling, spending the remainder of his remaining life in captivity to academia. A good portrayal of the Native American plight. Based on a true story; made for cable television. **90m/C VHS, LV.** Jon Voight, Graham Greene, David Ogden Stiers, Jack Blessing, Anne Archer, Daniel Benzali; ***D:*** Harry Hook. National Academy of Cable Programming ACE Awards '93: Best Actor (Voight). *WAR*

The Last of Mrs. Cheyney 🦴🦴🦴 **1937** Remake of Norma Shearer's 1929 hit, based on the play by Frederick Lonsdale, about a sophisticated jewel thief in England. Crawford stars as the jewel thief who poses as a wealthy woman to get into parties hosted by London bluebloods. Dripping with charm, she works her way into Lord Drilling's mansion where she plans a huge heist. The film is handled well, and the cast gives solid performances throughout. This chic comedy of high society proved to be one of Crawford's most popular films of the '30s. **98m/B VHS.** Joan Crawford, Robert Montgomery, William Powell, Frank Morgan, Nigel Bruce, Jessie Ralph; ***D:*** Richard Boleslawski, George Fitzmaurice. *MGM*

The Last of Mrs. Lincoln 🦴🦴½ **1976** Intimate made for TV portrayal of the famous first lady. Film focuses on Mary Todd Lincoln's life from the assassination of her husband, through her autumn years, and her untimely downfall. **118m/C VHS, Beta.** Julie Harris, Robby Benson, Patrick Duffy. *NO*

The Last of Philip Banter 🦴½ **1987 (R)** An alcoholic writer is terrified to learn events in his life exactly match a mysterious manuscript. **105m/C VHS.** Tony Curtis, Greg Henry, Irene Miracle, Scott Paulin, Kate Vernon; ***D:*** Herve Hachuel. *REP*

The Last of Sheila 🦴🦴½ **1973 (PG)** A movie producer invites six big-star friends for a cruise aboard his yacht, the "Sheila." He then stages an elaborate "Whodunnit" parlor game to discover which one of them murdered his wife. **119m/C VHS, Beta.** Richard Benjamin, James Coburn, James Mason, Dyan Cannon, Joan Hackett, Raquel Welch, Ian McShane; ***D:*** Herbert Ross; ***W:*** Anthony Perkins, Stephen Sondheim; ***M:*** Billy Goldenberg. Edgar Allan Poe Awards '73: Best Screenplay. *WAR*

Last of the Clintons 🦴½ **1935** A range detective tracks an outlaw gang amid spur jinglin', sharp shootin' and cow punchin'. **64m/B VHS, Beta, LV.** Harry Carey Sr. *NOS*

Last of the Comanches 🦴🦴 *The Sabre and the Arrow* **1952** Cavalry and Indians fight for water when both are dying of thirst in the desert. **85m/C VHS, Beta.** Broderick Crawford, Barbara Hale, John Stewart, Lloyd Bridges, Mickey Shaughnessy, George Mathews; ***D:*** Andre de Toth. *GKK*

The Last of the Dogmen 🦴🦴½ **1995 (PG)** Cliched modern western with an intriguing premise and good actors. Montana bounty hunter Lewis Gates (Berenger) is recruited to nab three escaped cons but finds them dead and a Cheyenne arrow nearby. Gates does some investigating (in a library no less!) and discovers that maybe some descendants of the 1864 Sand Creek massacre are existing in the woods. He gets anthropologist Lillian Sloan (Hershey) involved, discovers a tribe of modern-day dog soldiers, and finds a very angry sheriff (Smith) on their trail. Alberta, Canada passes for Big Sky country. **117m/C VHS.** Tom Berenger, Barbara Hershey, Kurtwood Smith, Steve Reevis, Andrew Miller, Gregory Scott Cummins; ***D:*** Tab Murphy; ***W:*** Tab Murphy; ***C:*** Karl Walter Lindenlaub; ***M:*** David Arnold. *HBO*

The Last of the Finest 🦴½ *Street Legal; Blue Heat* **1990 (R)** Overzealous anti-drug task force cops break the rules in trying to put dealer-drug lords in prison; ostensibly a parallel on the Iran-Contra affair. **106m/C VHS, Beta, LV.** Brian Dennehy, Joe Pantoliano, Jeff Fahey, Bill Paxton, Deborra-Lee Furness, Guy Boyd, Henry Darrow, Lisa Jane Persky, Michael C. Gwynne; ***D:*** John MacKenzie; ***W:*** George Armitage, Jere P. Cunningham; ***M:*** Jack Nitzsche. *ORI*

The Last of the Mohicans 🦴🦴🦴 **1920** Color tints enhance this silent version of the James Fenimore Cooper rouser. Beery is the villainous Magua, with Bedford memorable as the lovely Cora and Roscoe as the brave Uncas. Fine action sequences, including the Huron massacre at Fort Henry. Director credit was shared when Tourneur suffered an on-set injury and was off for 3 months. **75m/B VHS, LV.** Wallace Beery, Barbara Bedford, Albert Roscoe, Lillian Hall-Davis, Henry Woodward, James Gordon, George Hackathorne, Harry Lorraine, Nelson McDowell, Theodore Lorch, Boris Karloff; ***D:*** Maurice Tourneur, Clarence Brown; ***W:*** Robert Dillon. *LUM, FCT, MIL*

The Last of the Mohicans **1932** Serial based on James Fenimore Cooper's novel of the life-and-death struggle of the Mohican Indians during the French and Indian War. Twelve chapters, 13 minutes each. Remade as a movie in 1936 and 1992 and as a television movie in 1977. **230m/B VHS, Beta.** Edwina Booth, Harry Carey Sr., Hobart Bosworth, Frank "Junior" Coghlan; ***D:*** Ford Beebe, B. Reeves Eason. *VYY, VCN, NOS*

The Last of the Mohicans 🦴🦴½ **1936** James Fenimore Cooper's classic about the French and Indian War in colonial America is brought to the screen. Remake of the 1932 serial was remade itself in 1977 for television. **91m/B VHS, Beta.** Randolph Scott, Binnie Barnes, Bruce Cabot, Henry Wilcoxon, Heather Angel, Hugh Buckler; ***D:*** George B. Seitz. *LIV, MED, CCB*

The Last of the Mohicans 🦴🦴 **1985 (R)** The classic novel by James Fenimore Cooper about the scout Hawkeye and his Mohican companions, Chingachgook and Uncas during the French and Indian war, comes to life in this made-for-television film. Remake of a 1932 serial and a 1936 film. **97m/C VHS, Beta.** Steve Forrest, Ned Romero, Andrew Prine, Don Shanks, Robert Tessier, Jane Actman; ***D:*** James L. Conway. *VCI*

The Last of the Mohicans 🦴🦴🦴 **1992 (R)** It's 1757, at the height of the French and English war in the American colonies, with various Native American tribes allied to each side. Hawkeye (Day-Lewis), a white frontiersman raised by the Mohicans, wants nothing to do with either "civilized" side, until he rescues the beautiful Cora (Stowe) from the revenge-minded Huron Magua (Studi in a powerful performance). Graphically violent battle scenes are realistic, but not gratuitous. The real pleasure in this adaptation, which draws from both the James Fenimore Cooper novel and the 1936 film, is in its lush look and attractive stars. Means is terrific in his film debut as Hawkeye's foster-father. Released in a letterbox format to preserve the original integrity of the film. **114m/C VHS, LV.** Daniel Day-Lewis, Madeleine Stowe, Wes Studi, Russell Means, Eric Schweig, Jodhi May, Steven Waddington, Maurice Roeves, Colm Meaney, Patrice Chereau; ***D:*** Michael Mann; ***W:*** Christopher Crowe, Michael Mann; ***C:*** Dante Spinotti; ***M:*** Trevor Jones, Randy Edelman. Academy Awards '92: Best Sound. *FXV, BTV*

Last of the Pony Riders 🦴½ **1953** When the telegraph lines linking the East and West Coasts are completed, Gene and the other Pony Express riders find themselves out of a job. Autry's final feature film. **59m/B VHS, Beta.** Gene Autry, Smiley Burnette, Kathleen Case; ***D:*** George Archainbaud. *CCB*

Last of the Red Hot Lovers 🦴½ **1972 (PG)** Not so funny adaptation of Neil Simon's Broadway hit. Middle-aged man decides to have a fling and uses his mother's apartment to seduce three very strange women. **98m/C VHS, Beta, LV.** Alan Arkin, Paula Prentiss, Sally Kellerman, Renee Taylor; ***D:*** Gene Saks; ***W:*** Neil Simon. *PAR*

The Last of the Redmen 🦴½ **1947** An adaptation of James Fenimore Cooper's "The Last of the Mohicans" geared toward youngsters. Hall must lead three children of a British general through dangerous Indian territory. They have a number of adventures including meeting up with Uncas, the last of the Mohicans, who's a villain in this mangled version. **79m/B VHS.** Jon Hall, Michael O'Shea, Evelyn Ankers, Julie Bishop, Buster Crabbe, Rick Vallin, Frederick Worlock, Guy Hedlund; ***D:*** George Sherman; ***W:*** Herbert Dalmas. *COL*

Last of the Warrens 🦴 **1936** A cowboy returns home after WWI to discover that an unscrupulous storekeeper has stolen his property. **56m/C VHS, Beta.** Bob Steele, Charles "Blackie" King, Lafe McKee, Margaret Marquis, Horace Murphy; ***D:*** Robert North Bradbury. *NOS, DVT, GPV*

Last of the Wild Horses 🦴½ **1949** Range war almost starts when ranch owner is accused of trying to force the small ranchers out of business. **86m/B VHS, Beta.** Mary Beth Hughes, James Ellison, Jane Frazee. *NO*

The Last Outlaw 🦴🦴 **1927** Action-packed western with Cooper following his success of "Wings" with Paramount. Most excellent equine stunts. **61m/B VHS, Beta.** Gary Cooper, Jack Luden, Betty Jewel; ***D:*** Arthur Rosson. *GPV, FCT*

Last Outlaw 🦴🦴 **1936** The last of the famous badmen of the old West is released from jail and returns home to find that times have changed. The action climaxes in an old-time blazing shoot-out. **79m/B VHS, Beta.** Harry Carey Sr., Hoot Gibson, Henry B. Walthall, Tom Tyler, Russell Hopton, Alan Curtis, Harry Woods, Barbara Pepper; ***D:*** Christy Cabanne. *VCN*

The Last Outlaw 🦴🦴½ **1993 (R)** Rourke stars as an ex-Confederate officer who leads a gang of outlaws until his violent excesses leave even them disgusted. The gang shoots Rourke but of course he doesn't die and then he sets out for revenge. Made for cable television. **90m/C VHS.** Mickey Rourke, Dermot Mulroney, Ted Levine, John C. McGinley, Steve Buscemi, Keith David; ***D:*** Geoff Murphy; ***W:*** Eric Red. *HBO, FCT*

The Last Picture Show 🦴🦴🦴🦴 **1971 (R)** Slice of life/nostalgic farewell to an innocent age, based on Larry McMurtry's novel. Set in Archer City, a backwater Texas town, most of the story plays out at the local hangout run by ex-cowboy Sam the Lion. Bridges is hooked up with spoiled pretty girl Shepherd, while Bottoms, a sensitive guy, is having an affair with the coach's neglected wife (Leachman). Loss of innocence, disillusionment and confusion are played out against the backdrop of a town about to close its cinema. Shepherd's and Bottoms' film debut. Stunningly photographed in black and white (Bogdanovich claimed he didn't want to "prettify" the picture by shooting in color) by Robert Surtees. Available in a laserdisc special edition with 17 minutes restored. Followed by a weak sequel, "Texasville." A boxed set featuring both films is also available. **118m/B VHS, LV, 8mm.** Jeff Bridges, Timothy Bottoms, Ben Johnson, Cloris Leachman, Cybill Shepherd, Ellen Burstyn, Eileen Brennan, Clu Gulager, Sharon Taggart, Randy Quaid, Sam Bottoms, John Hillerman; ***D:*** Peter Bogdanovich; ***W:*** Larry McMurtry, Peter Bogdanovich; ***C:*** Robert L. Surtees. Academy Awards '71: Best Supporting Actor (Johnson), Best Supporting Actress (Leachman); Golden Globe Awards '72: Best Supporting Actor (Johnson); National Board of Review Awards '71: Best Supporting Actor (Johnson), Best Supporting Actress (Leachman); National Society of Film Critics Awards '71: Best Supporting Actress (Burstyn); Nominations: Academy Awards '71: Best Adapted Screenplay, Best Cinematography, Best Director (Bogdanovich), Best Picture, Best Supporting Actor (Bridges), Best Supporting Actress (Burstyn). *COL, CRC, FCT*

The Last Place on Earth **1994** Saga of bitter hardship and ambition depicting the 1911 race between the British Antarctic Expedition, led by Captain Robert Falcon (Shaw), and his Norwegian rival Roald Amundsen (Ousdal) to conquer the South Pole. On 7 cassettes. **385m/C VHS.** *CA* Martin Shaw, Sverre Anker Ousdal, Max von Sydow, Susan Wooldridge. *TVC, PAP, VCO*

Last Plane Out ½ **1983 (R)** A Texas journalist sent out on assignment to Nicaragua falls in love with a Sandanista rebel. Based on producer Jack Cox's real-life experiences as a journalist during the last days of the Samosa regime. Low-budget propaganda. **90m/C VHS, Beta.** Jan-Michael Vincent, Lloyd Batista, Julie Carmen, Mary Crosby, David Huffman, William Windom; ***D:*** David Nelson. *VTR, FOX*

The Last Polka **1984** SCTV vets Candy and Levy are Yosh and Stan Schmenge, polka kings interviewed for a "documentary" on their years in the spotlight and on the road. Hilarious spoof on Martin Scorsese's "The Last Waltz," about The Band's last concert. Several fellow Second City-ers keep the laughs coming. If you liked SCTV or "This is Spinal Tap," you'll like this. Made for cable (HBO). **54m/C VHS, Beta.** John Candy, Eugene Levy, Rick Moranis, Robin Duke, Catherine O'Hara; ***D:*** John Blanchard. *LIV, VES*

The Last Porno Flick **1974 (PG)** A pornographic movie script winds up in the hands of a couple of goofy cab drivers. The twosome sneak the movie's genre past the producers, families, and police. **90m/C VHS.** Michael Pataki, Marianna Hill, Carmen Zapata, Mike Kellin, Colleen Camp, Tom Signorelli, Antony Carbone; ***D:*** Ray Marsh. *NO*

The Last Prostitute **1991 (PG-13)** Two teenage boys search for a legendary prostitute to initiate them into manhood, only to discover that she has retired. They hire on as laborers on her horse farm, and one of them discovers the meaning of love. Made for cable TV. **93m/C VHS.** Sonia Braga, Wil Wheaton, David Kaufman, Woody Watson, Dennis Letts, Cotter Smith; ***D:*** Lou Antonio; ***W:*** Carmen Culver. *MCA*

The Last Radio Station **1986** A mini-musical with a largely Motown soundtrack about a failing radio station supported by old rock songs: "Reflections," "Nowhere to Run," "Dancing in the Street" and others. **60m/C VHS, Beta, LV.** *MCA, MVD*

The Last Remake of Beau Geste **1977 (PG)** A slapstick parody of the familiar Foreign Legion story from the Mel Brooks-ish school of loud genre farce. Gary Cooper makes an appearance by way of inserted footage from the 1939 straight version. **85m/C VHS, Beta.** Marty Feldman, Ann-Margret, Michael York, Peter Ustinov, James Earl Jones; ***D:*** Marty Feldman; ***W:*** Marty Feldman, Chris Allen. *MCA*

Last Resort *She Knew No Other Way* **1986 (R)** A married furniture executive unknowingly takes his family on vacation to a sex-saturated, Club Med-type holiday spot, and gets more than he anticipated. **80m/C VHS, Beta, LV.** Charles Grodin, Jon Lovitz; ***D:*** Zane Buzby; ***W:*** Jeff Bukai. *LIV, VES*

Last Reunion **1955** Rare British ghost story starring Gough. **?m/C VHS.** *GB* Michael Gough. *NO*

The Last Reunion ½ **1980** The only witness to a brutal killing of a Japanese official and his wife during WWII seeks revenge on the guilty American platoon, thirty-three years later. Violent. **98m/C VHS.** Cameron Mitchell, Leo Fong, Chanda Romero, Vic Silayan, Hal Bokar, Philip Baker Hall; ***D:*** Jay Wertz. *SNC*

The Last Ride **1991** Another movie probing the dark side of hitchhiking. This time our hero thumbs a ride with a truck driver who plans to bypass the next city...for hell. **84m/C VHS.** Dan Ranger, Michael Hilow. *AIP*

The Last Ride *F.T.W* **1994 (R)** Frank T. Wells (Rourke) is out of prison after 10 years and free to try to recapture his former rodeo glory. Hellcat Scarlett Stuart's on the run from a botched bank job/murder perpetrated by her vicious brother Clem (Berg). Scarlett manages to hook up with Frank and decides to help him out financially by robbing convenience stores. Frank's not too happy when he finds out. Rourke is surprisingly subdued and Singer's properly unsympathetic but they don't seem to be working in the same movie. Nice Montana scenery though. **102m/C VHS.** Mickey Rourke, Lori Singer, Brion James, Peter Berg, Rodney Grant, Aaron Neville; ***D:*** Michael Karbelnikoff; ***W:*** Mari Kornhauser; ***M:*** Gary Chang. *HMK*

The Last Ride of the Dalton Gang **1979** A long-winded retelling of the wild adventures that made the Dalton gang legendary among outlaws. **146m/C VHS, Beta.** Larry Wilcox, Jack Palance, Randy Quaid, Cliff Potts, Dale Robertson, Don Collier; ***D:*** Dan Curtis. *WAR, OM*

The Last Riders **1990 (R)** Motorcycle centaur Estrada revs a few motors fleeing from cycle club cronies and crooked cops. Full throttle foolishness. **90m/C VHS, LV.** Erik Estrada, William Smith, Armando Silvestre, Kathrin Lautner; ***D:*** Joseph Merhi. *PMH, HHE*

Last Rites **1988 (R)** A priest at St. Patrick's Cathedral in New York allows a young Mexican woman to seek sanctuary from the Mob, who soon come after both of them. **103m/C VHS, Beta, LV.** Tom Berenger, Daphne Zuniga, Chick Vennera, Dane Clark, Carlo Pacchi, Anne Twomey, Paul Dooley, Vassili Lambrinos; ***D:*** Donald P. Bellisario; ***W:*** Donald P. Bellisario; ***C:*** David Watkin; ***M:*** Bruce Broughton. *FOX*

The Last Safari ½ **1967** A young man on safari in Africa befriends a bitter professional guide in a drama hampered by a poor script. Granger and Garas set out to hunt the rampaging elephant which killed Granger's friend. Granger thinks killing the beast will restore his courage and help him overcome the guilt he feels. Based on the novel "Gilligan's Last Elephant" by Gerald Hanley. **111m/C VHS.** Stewart Granger, Kaz Garas, Gabriella Licudi, Johnny Sekka, Liam Redmond; ***D:*** Henry Hathaway; ***W:*** John Gay; ***C:*** Ted Moore. *PAR*

The Last Samurai **1990 (R)** Arab arms dealer Saxon arranges a fake kidnapping by rebel military leader Cele in order to keep their weapons deal a secret. But among the other hostages is mercenary Hendricksen, who escapes and wrecks havoc on their plotting. **94m/C VHS.** Lance Henriksen, John Saxon, Henry Cele, Arabella Holzbog, John Fujioka, James Ryan, Duncan Regehr, Lisa Eilbacher; ***D:*** Paul Mayersberg. *AVI*

The Last Season *Woof!* **1987** Shoot 'em up involving a bunch of hunters. Their aimless destruction provokes the good guy to save the forest they are demolishing. A battle ensues. **90m/C VHS.** Christopher Gosch, Louise Dorsey, David Cox; ***D:*** Raja Zahr. *NO*

The Last Seduction **1994 (R)** Dahl, the master of modern noir, delivers another stylish hit exploring the darker side of urban life. Fiorentino gives the performance of her life as the most evil, rotten femme fatale to ever hit the big screen. Bridget (Fiorentino) rips off the money her husband Clay (Pullman) made in a pharmaceutical drug deal and leaves Manhattan for a small town in Upstate New York. Once there, she takes nice, naive Mike (Berg) as her lover, while Clay tries to ferret her out and get his money back. Lots of dry humor and a wickedly amusing heroine make for a devilishly entertaining film. **110m/C VHS, LV.** Linda Fiorentino, Peter Berg, J.T. Walsh, Bill Nunn, Bill Pullman; ***D:*** John Dahl; ***W:*** Steve Barancik; ***M:*** Joseph Vitarelli. Independent Spirit Awards '95: Best Actress (Fiorentino); New York Film Critics Awards '94: Best Actress (Fiorentino). *PGV*

The Last Slumber Party *Woof!* **1987** A slumber party is beset by a homicidal maniac. Heavy metal soundtrack. **89m/C VHS, Beta.** Jan Jensen, Nancy Meyer. *VCI*

Last Song ½ **1980 (PG)** A singer's husband discovers a plot to cover up a fatal toxic-waste accident, and is killed because of it. It's up to her to warn the authorities before becoming the next victim. **96m/C VHS, Beta.** Lynda Carter, Ronny Cox, Nicholas Pryor, Paul Rudd, Jenny O'Hara; ***D:*** Alan J. Levi. *FOX*

The Last Starfighter **1984 (PG)** A young man who becomes an expert at a video game is recruited to fight in an inter-galactic war. Listless adventure which explains where all those video games come from. Watch for O'Herlihy disguised as a lizard. **100m/C VHS, Beta, LV.** Lance Guest, Robert Preston, Barbara Bosson, Dan O'Herlihy, Catherine Mary Stewart, Cameron Dye, Kimberly Ross, Wil Wheaton; ***D:*** Nick Castle; ***W:*** Jonathan Betuel. *MCA*

Last Summer ½ **1969 (R)** Three teenagers discover love, sex, and friendship on the white sands of Fire Island, N.Y. The summer vacation fantasy world they create shatters when a sweet but homely female teenager joins their group. Based on a novel by Evan Hunter. **97m/C VHS, Beta.** Barbara Hershey, Richard Thomas, Bruce Davison, Cathy Burns; ***D:*** Frank Perry. Nominations: Academy Awards '69: Best Supporting Actress (Burns). *FOX*

Last Summer In the Hamptons ½ **1996 (R)** In her last film, Viveca Lindfors stars as Helena Mora, the matriarch of a charming three generation theatrical clan that gets together one weekend a year at her spacious, slightly run-down estate to participate in drama workshops and perform plays. When Helena is forced to sell the estate, the family reunites for one last weekend of bickering and performing. Featuring fine performances from the entire ensemble (including Lindfors' son and Jaglom's wife), Jaglom's touching and engaging tribute to his family gives nepotism a good name. **105m/C VHS.** Victoria Foyt, Viveca Lindfors, Jon Robin Baitz, Andre Gregory, Melissa Leo, Martha Plimpton, Roddy McDowall, Nick Gregory, Savannah Smith Boucher, Roscoe Lee Browne, Ron Rifkin, Diane Salinger, Brooke Smith, Kristopher Tabori, Holland Taylor, Henry Jaglom; ***D:*** Henry Jaglom; ***W:*** Victoria Foyt, Henry Jaglom; ***C:*** Hanania Baer; ***M:*** Johnny Mercer, Harold Arlen. *NYR*

The Last Supper **1976** A repentant Cuban slave-owner in the 18th-century decides to cleanse his soul and convert his slaves to Christianity by having twelve of them reenact the Last Supper. Based on a true story. In Spanish with English subtitles. **110m/C VHS, Beta.** *CU* Nelson Villagra, Silvano Rey, Lamberto Garcia, Jose Antonio Rodriguez, Samuel Claxton, Mario Balmasada; ***D:*** Thomas Gutierrez Alea. *NYF, FCT, INJ*

The Last Supper ½ **1996 (R)** First-time feature director Title dishes out an extremely black comedy about a group of liberal roommates who accidentally kill a racist marine they've invited to dinner. This leads to the devious plan of inviting more right wingers over, baiting them into arguments about controversial topics, then killing and burying them in a vegetable garden. Somehow manages to avoid excessive preachiness despite taking on all political comers. Not exactly a great feast, but there's enough tasty snacks to be satisfying. Performances by the roommates are good, but the victims (led by Perlman's Limbaugh turn) really shine. Too bad their characters aren't on screen very long before they become tomato fertilizer. **94m/C VHS.** Cameron Diaz, Annabeth Gish, Ron Eldard, Jonathan Penner, Courtney B. Vance; ***Cameos:*** Ron Perlman, Jason Alexander, Charles Durning, Mark Harmon, Bill Paxton; ***D:*** Stacy Title; ***W:*** Dan Rosen; ***C:*** Paul Cameron; ***M:*** Mark Mothersbaugh. *NYR*

Last Tango in Paris ½ **1973 (R)** Brando plays a middle-aged American who meets a French girl and tries to forget his wife's suicide with a short, extremely steamy affair. Bertolucci proves to be a master; Brando gives one of his best performances. Very controversial when made, still quite explicit. Visually stunning. The X-rated version, at 130 minutes, is also available. **126m/C VHS, Beta, LV.** *IT FR* Marlon Brando, Maria Schneider, Jean-Pierre Leaud; ***D:*** Bernardo Bertolucci; ***W:*** Bernardo Bertolucci; ***C:*** Vittorio Storaro; ***M:*** Gato Barbieri. New York Film Critics Awards '73: Best Actor (Brando); National Society of Film Critics Awards '73: Best Actor (Brando); Nominations: Academy Awards '73: Best Actor (Brando), Best Director (Bertolucci). *MGM, FOX*

The Last Temptation of Christ ½ **1988 (R)** Scorsese's controversial adaptation of the Nikos Kazantzakis novel, portraying Christ in his last year as an ordinary Israelite tormented by divine doubt, human desires and the voice of God. The controversy engulfing the film, as it was heavily protested and widely banned, tended to divert attention from what is an exceptional statement of religious and artistic vision. Excellent score by Peter Gabriel. **164m/C VHS, Beta, LV.** Willem Dafoe, Harvey Keitel, Barbara Hershey, Harry Dean Stanton, Andre Gregory, David Bowie, Verna Bloom, Juliette Caton, John Lurie, Roberts Blossom, Irvin Kershner, Barry Miller, Tomas Arana, Nehemiah Persoff, Paul Herman; ***D:*** Martin Scorsese; ***W:*** Paul Schrader; ***C:*** Michael Ballhaus; ***M:*** Peter Gabriel. Nominations: Academy Awards '88: Best Director (Scorsese). *MCA*

The Last Time I Saw Paris ½ **1954** A successful writer reminisces about his love affair with a wealthy American girl in post-WWII Paris. **116m/C VHS, Beta, LV.** Elizabeth Taylor, Van Johnson, Walter Pidgeon, Roger Moore, Donna Reed, Eva Gabor; ***D:*** Richard Brooks; ***W:*** Richard Brooks, Julius J. Epstein, Philip C. Epstein; ***C:*** Joseph Ruttenberg. *MGM, MRV, NOS*

Last Time Out ½ **1994 (PG-13)** Danny Dolan (Conrad) is a hard-partying college wide receiver who gets a shock when the father who abandoned him enrolls at his school to finish a college degree. Seems Joe (Beck) had his pro quarterback career cut short by a drinking problem and he's worried his son will follow in his unsteady footsteps. **92m/C VHS, LV.** John Beck, Christian Conrad, Lori Werner, Gail Strickland, Betty Buckley; ***D:*** Don Fox Greene. *IMP*

The Last Tomahawk **1965** Colorful and action packed reworking of Cooper's "Last of the Mohicans." **?m/C VHS.** *GE IT* Anthony Steffen, Karin Dor, Dan Martin, Joachim Fuchsberger. *SNC*

The Last Train **1974** Romance most hopeless in the heart of France during zee beeg war. French, very French. **?m/C VHS, Beta.** Romy Schneider, Jean-Louis Trintignant. *NO*

Last Train from Gun Hill **1959** An all-star cast highlights this suspenseful story of a U.S. marshall determined to catch the man who raped and murdered his wife. Excellent action packed western. **94m/C VHS.** Kirk Douglas, Anthony Quinn, Carolyn Jones, Earl Holliman, Brad Dexter, Brian Hutton, Ziva Rodann; ***D:*** John Sturges; ***C:*** Charles B(ryant) Lang. *NO*

The Last Tycoon **1976 (PG)** An adaptation of the unfinished F. Scott Fitzgerald novel about the life and times of a Hollywood movie executive of the 1920s. Confusing and slow moving despite a blockbuster conglomeration of talent. Joan Collins introduces the film. **123m/C VHS, Beta, LV.** Robert De Niro, Tony Curtis, Ingrid Boulting, Jack Nicholson, Jeanne Moreau, Peter Strauss, Robert Mitchum, Theresa Russell, Donald Pleasence, Ray Milland, Dana Andrews, John Carradine, Anjelica Huston; ***D:*** Elia Kazan; ***W:*** Harold Pinter; ***M:*** Maurice Jarre. National Board of Review Awards '76: 10 Best Films of the Year; Nominations: Academy Awards '76: Best Art Direction/Set Decoration. *PAR, FCT*

The Last Unicorn ½ **1982 (G)** Peter Beagle's popular tale of a beautiful unicorn who goes in search of her lost, mythical "family." **95m/C VHS, Beta, LV.** ***D:*** Jules Bass; ***W:*** Peter S. Beagle; ***M:*** Jim Webb; ***V:*** Alan Arkin, Jeff Bridges, Tammy Grimes, Angela Lansbury, Mia Farrow, Robert Klein, Christopher Lee, Keenan Wynn. *FOX, KAR, WTA*

The Last Valley **1971 (PG)** A scholar tries to protect a pristine 17th century Swiss valley, untouched by the Thirty Years War, from marauding soldiers. Historical action with an intellectual twist. **128m/C VHS.** Michael Caine, Omar Sharif, Florinda Bolkan, Nigel Davenport, Per Oscarsson, Arthur O'Connell; ***D:*** James Clavell; ***W:*** James Clavell; ***M:*** John Barry. *NO*

The Last Voyage ½ **1960** Suspenseful disaster film in which Stack and Malone play a married couple in jeopardy while on an ocean cruise. To make the film more realistic, the French liner Ile de France was actually used in the sinking scenes. Although a bit farfetched, film is made watchable because of fine performances and excellent camerawork. **91m/C VHS, LV.** Robert Stack, Dorothy Malone, George Sanders, Edmond O'Brien, Woody Strode, Jack Kruschen; ***D:*** Andrew L. Stone; ***W:*** Andrew L. Stone; ***C:*** Hal Mohr. *MGM*

The Last Waltz **1978 (PG)** Martin Scorsese filmed this rock documentary featuring the farewell performance of The Band, joined by a host of musical guests that they have been associated with over the years. Songs include: "Up On Cripple Creek," "Don't Do It," "The Night They Drove Old Dixie Down," "Stage Fright" (The Band), "Helpless" (Young), "Coyote" (Mitchell), "Caravan" (Morrison), "Further On Up the Road" (Clapton), "Who Do You Love" (Hawkins), "Mannish Boy" (Waters), "Evangeline" (Harris), "Baby, Let Me Follow You Down" (Dylan). **117m/C VHS, Beta, LV.** ***D:*** Martin Scorsese; ***C:*** Michael Chapman. *MVD, MGM*

Last War **1968** A nuclear war between the United States and Russia triggers Armageddon. **79m/C VHS, Beta.** Frankie Sakai, Nobuko Otowa, Akira Takarada, Yuriko Hoshi; ***D:*** Shue Matsubayashi. *GEM*

The Last Warrior ½ *Coastwatcher* **1989 (R)** A good-looking but exploitive "Hell in the Pacific" rip-off, as an American and a Japanese soldier battle it out alone on a remote island during WWII. **94m/C VHS, Beta, LV.** Gary Graham, Cary-Hiroyuki Tagawa, Maria Holvoe; ***D:*** Martin Wragge. *COL*

The Last Wave **1977 (PG)** An Australian attorney takes on a murder case involving an aborigine and he finds himself becoming distracted by apocalyptic visions concerning tidal waves and drownings that seem to foretell the future. Weir's masterful creation and communication of time and place are marred by a somewhat pat ending. **109m/C VHS, Beta.** *AU* Richard Chamberlain, Olivia Hamnett, David Gulpilil, Frederick Parslow; ***D:*** Peter Weir; ***W:*** Peter Weir; ***C:*** John Seale. *FCT, RHI*

The Last Winter **1984 (R)** An American woman fights to find her Israeli husband who has disappeared in the 1973 Yom Kippur War. Trouble is, an Israeli woman thinks the man she's looking for is really her husband too. **92m/C VHS, Beta.** *IS* Kathleen Quinlan, Yona Elian, Zipora Peled, Michael Schnider; ***D:*** Riki Shelach. *COL*

The Last Winter ½ **1989 (PG)** Ten-year-old Will (Murray) has always lived in the country and finds it hard to accept his parents' decision to move to the city. But with the help of his grandfather (Parkes), Will begins to understand about change and growing up. **103m/C VHS.** *CA* Joshua Murray, Gerard Parkes, David Ferry, Wanda Cannon, Marsha Moreau, Nathaniel Moreau, Katie Murray; ***D:*** Aaron Kim Johnston; ***W:*** Aaron Kim Johnston; ***M:*** Victor Davies. *FXV*

The Last Winters ½ **1971** From Jean Charles Tacchella, writer-producer-director of "Cousin Cousine," comes his first short film about an old couple's bittersweet romance. In French with English subtitles. **23m/C VHS, Beta.** *FR* ***D:*** Jean-Charles Tacchella. *INT, MTI*

Last Witness **1988** A man on the run from the government claims that he is innocent and was unjustly persecuted, but the government sees him as a dangerous threat. Nothing will stop the hunt for the escaped man, no matter what it costs. **85m/C VHS, Beta.** Jeff Henderson. *TWE*

The Last Woman on Earth *Woof!* **1961** Two men vie for the affections of the sole surviving woman after a vague and unexplained disaster of vast proportions. Robert Towne, who appears herein under the pseudonym Edward Wain, wrote the script (his first screenwriting effort). You might want to watch this if it were the last movie on earth, although Corman fans will probably love it. **71m/C VHS.** Antony Carbone, Edward Wain, Betsy Jones-Moreland; ***D:*** Roger Corman; ***W:*** Robert Towne. *NOS, MRV, SNC*

The Last Word *Danny Travis* **1980 (PG)** Comedy drama about struggling inventor Harris fighting to protect his home, family, and neighbors from a corrupt real estate deal involving shady politicians, angry policemen, and a beautiful television reporter. **103m/C VHS, Beta.** Richard Harris, Karen Black, Martin Landau, Dennis Christopher, Bill McGuire, Christopher Guest, Penelope Milford, Michael Pataki; ***W:*** Michael Varhol, L.M. Kit Carson. *SUE*

The Last Word **1995 (R)** Journalist Martin (Hutton) writes a newspaper column, often featuring characters based on hometown Detroit mob figures, with info supplied to him by his friend, Doc (Pantoliano), who owes the gangsters some big bucks. Doc also introduces Martin to his latest column subject—stripper Caprice (Burke)—and, thanks again to Doc, a Hollywood studio gets interested in filming her story but wants more sex and violence, which means Martin will be betraying her deepest secrets. Now, he must choose between love, success, or friendship. **95m/C VHS.** Timothy Hutton, Joe Pantoliano, Michelle Burke, Chazz Palminteri, Tony Goldwyn; ***Cameos:*** Richard Dreyfuss, Cybill Shepherd, Jimmy Smits; ***D:*** Tony Spiridakis. *VMK*

Last Year at Marienbad *L'Anee Derniere a Marienbad* **1961** A young man tries to lure a mysterious woman to run away with him from a hotel in France. Once a hit on the artsy circuit, it's most interesting for its beautiful photography. In French with English subtitles. **93m/B VHS, Beta, 8mm.** *FR IT* Delphine Seyrig, Giorgia Albertazzi, Sacha Pitoeff, Luce Garcia-Ville; ***D:*** Alain Resnais. Nominations: Academy Awards '62: Best Story & Screenplay. *VYY, MRV, NOS*

L'Atalante ½ **1934** Vigo's great masterpiece, a slight story about a husband and wife quarreling, splitting, and reuniting around which has been fashioned one of the cinema's greatest poetic films. In French with English subtitles. **82m/B VHS, Beta.** *FR* Dita Parlo, Jean Daste, Michel Simon; ***D:*** Jean Vigo. *NOS, HHT, PMS*

Late Chrysanthemums *Bangiku* **1954** A middle-aged geisha has settled into comfortable retirement as a money lender. When she hears a former lover wants to visit her, she tries to recapture her old glamour only to be disillusioned. Based on a short story by Fumiko Hayashi. In Japanese with English subtitles. **101m/B VHS.** *JP* Haruko Sugimura, Chikako Hosokawa, Sadako Sawahura; ***D:*** Mikio Naruse. *WAC, INJ*

Late Extra **1935** A novice reporter attempts to track down a notorious bank robber and gets some help from a savvy female journalist. Mason's first role of substance. **69m/B VHS, Beta.** *GB* Virginia Cherrill, James Mason, Alastair Sim, Ian Colin, Clifford McLaglen, Cyril Cusack, David Horne, Antoinette Cellier, Donald Wolfit, Michael Wilding; ***D:*** Albert Parker. *SNC*

Late for Dinner **1991 (PG)** In 1962 Willie, a young, married man, and his best friend Frank are framed by a sleazy land developer. On the run, the two decide to become guinea pigs in a cryonics experiment and wind up frozen for 29 years. It's now 1991 and Willie wants to find his family—only his wife is middle-aged and his daughter is all grown-up. Can he make a life with them again or has time indeed passed him by? **93m/C VHS, LV.** Brian Wimmer, Peter Berg, Marcia Gay Harden, Peter Gallagher, Ross Malinger; ***D:*** W.D. Richter; ***W:*** Mark Andrus. *COL, NLC*

The Late Shift ½ **1996 (R)** Cable adaptation of Bill Carter's book chronicling the follies surrounding NBC's "The Tonight Show" succession battle between Jay Leno (Roebuck) and Dave Letterman (Higgins). It's the behind-the-scenes dealmakers that really steal the show, however, including Jay's profane manager Helen Kushnick (Bates) and super-agent Michael Ovitz (Williams), who ultimately orchestrated Dave's move to rival CBS. **96m/C VHS.** Daniel Roebuck, John Michael Higgins, Kathy Bates, Treat Williams, Bob Balaban, Ed Begley Jr., Rich Little, Sandra Bernhard,

Peter Jurasik, Reni Santoni, John Kapelos, John Getz, Lawrence Pressman; **D:** Betty Thomas; **W:** Bill Carter, George Armitage; **C:** Mac Ahlberg; **M:** Ira Newborn. *HBO*

The Late Show 𝒥𝒥𝒥 **1977 (PG)** A veteran private detective finds his world turned upside down when his ex-partner comes to visit and winds up dead, and a flaky woman whose cat is missing decides to become his sidekick. Carney and Tomlin are fun to watch in this sleeper, a tribute to the classic detective film noirs. **93m/C VHS, Beta, LV.** Art Carney, Lily Tomlin, Bill Macy, Eugene Roche, Joanna Cassidy, John Considine; **D:** Robert Benton; **W:** Robert Benton. Edgar Allan Poe Awards '77: Best Screenplay; National Board of Review Awards '77: 10 Best Films of the Year; National Society of Film Critics Awards '77: Best Actor (Carney); Nominations: Academy Awards '77: Best Original Screenplay. *WAR*

Late Spring 𝒥𝒥𝒥𝒥 **1949** An exquisite Ozu masterpiece. A young woman lives with her widowed father for years. He decides to remarry so that she can begin life for herself. Highly acclaimed, in Japanese with English subtitles. Reworked in 1960 as "Late Autumn." **107m/B VHS, Beta.** *JP* Setsuko Hara, Chishu Ryu, Jun Usami, Haruko Sugimura; **D:** Yasujiro Ozu. *NYF, FCT*

Late Summer Blues 𝒥𝒥 *Blues La-Chofesh Ha-Godol* **1987** Experience the life and death decisions of seven teenagers who have finished their finals and face now a more difficult test: serving in the Israeli Armed Forces in the Suez Canal. In Hebrew with English subtitles. **101m/C VHS.** *IS* Dor Zweigenbom, Shahar Segal, Yoav Zafir; **D:** Renen Schorr. *ERG, AUD, HMV*

Lathe of Heaven 𝒥𝒥½ **1980** In a late twentieth century world suffocating from pollution, a young man visits a dream specialist. He then dreams of a world free from war, pestilence, and overpopulation. At times, these dreams have disastrous side effects. Based on futuristic novel by Ursula K. LeGuin; produced for PBS. **120m/C VHS, Beta.** Bruce Davison, Kevin Conway, Margaret Avery; **D:** David Loxton. *WNE*

Latin Lovers 𝒥𝒥½ **1953** Turner plays a wealthy heiress who can't decide if men love her for herself or her money in this festive Brazilian romp. Lund and Montalban portray the suitors vying for her affection. Although not one of MGM's best musicals, the music is good because of the Brodszky-Robin tunes. ♫Night and You; Carlotta, You Gotta Be Mine; A Little More of Your Armor; Come To My Arms; I Had To Kiss You. **104m/C VHS.** Lana Turner, Ricardo Montalban, John Lund, Louis Calhern, Jean Hagen, Eduard Franz, Beulah Bondi; **D:** Mervyn LeRoy; **W:** Isobel Lennart. *MGM*

Latino 𝒥𝒥½ **1985** The self-tortured adventures of a Chicano Green Beret who, while fighting a covert U.S. military action in war-torn Nicaragua, begins to rebel against the senselessness of the war. **108m/C VHS, Beta, LV.** Robert Beltran, Annette Cardona, Tony Plana, James Karen, Ricardo Lopez, Luis Torrentes, Juan Carlos Ortiz, Julio Medina; **D:** Haskell Wexler; **W:** Haskell Wexler; **M:** Diane Louie. *FOX, INJ*

Lauderdale *Woof!* **1989 (R)** Two college schmoes hit the beach looking for beer and babes. Few laughs for the sober and mature. Surf's down in this woofer. **91m/C VHS, Beta, LV.** Darrel Gilbeau, Michelle Kemp, Jeff Greenman, Lara Belmonte; **D:** Bill Milling. *PSM*

Laugh with Linder! **1913** Compilation of Linder shorts, including "Max Learns to Skate" and "Max and His Dog." **70m/B VHS, Beta.** Max Linder. *GVV*

Laughfest **191?** Five classic slapstick shorts: "It's a Gift" (1923), with Snub Pollard, "Barney Oldfield's Race for a Life" (1913), "Kid Auto Races" and "Busy Day" (1914), both with Charlie Chaplin, and "Daredevil" (1923), starring Ben Turpin. **59m/B VHS, Beta.** Ben Turpin, Barney Oldfield, Mabel Normand, Charlie Chaplin, Snub Pollard. *CCB*

Laughing at Danger 𝒥𝒥½ **1924** Talmadge is the supposedly playboy son of a Washington politician. In reality, he's the dashing "Mr. Pep" who comes to the rescue of a scientist who has invented a death ray and is being stalked by agents of a sinister foreign power. Talmadge was a fine silent-screen action star, though his heavy German action proved a barrier with sound films. **45m/B VHS.** Richard Talmadge, Joseph Girard, Eva Novak, Joe Harrington, Stanhope Wheatcroft; **D:** James W. Horne. *GPV*

Laughing at Life 𝒥½ **1933** A mercenary leaves his family to fight in South America. Years later, when he is the leader of said country, he meets a man who turns out to be his son. Rehashed plot has been done better. **72m/B VHS.** Victor McLaglen, William "Stage" Boyd, Lois Wilson, Henry B. Walthall, Regis Toomey; **D:** Ford Beebe. *NOS, DVT, HEG*

The Laughing Policeman 𝒥𝒥½ *An Investigation of Murder* **1974 (R)** Two antagonistic cops embark on a vengeful hunt for a mass murderer through the seamy underbelly of San Francisco. Adapted from the Swedish novel by Per Wahloo and Maj Sjowallo. **111m/C VHS, Beta.** Walter Matthau, Bruce Dern, Louis Gossett Jr.; **D:** Stuart Rosenberg; **M:** Charles Fox. *FOX*

Laughing Sinners 𝒥𝒥 **1931** Society girl Crawford attempts suicide after Hamilton dumps her and is rescued by Gable—a Salvation Army worker! Predictable drama with some unintentionally funny moments. Gable and Crawford were having an off-screen romance at the time which accounts for the sparks generated on-screen. Based on the play "Torch Song" by Kenyon Nicholson. **71m/B VHS.** Joan Crawford, Neil Hamilton, Clark Gable, Marjorie Rambeau, Guy Kibbee, Cliff Edwards, Roscoe Karns; **D:** Harry Beaumont; **C:** Charles Rosher. *MGM*

Laura 𝒥𝒥𝒥𝒥 **1944** A detective assigned to the murder investigation of the late Laura Hunt finds himself falling in love with her painted portrait. Superb collaboration by excellent cast and fine director. Superior suspense yarn, enhanced by a love story. Based on the novel by Vera Caspary. Rouben Mamoulian was the original director, then Preminger finished the film. **85m/B VHS, Beta, LV.** Gene Tierney, Dana Andrews, Clifton Webb, Lane Chandler, Vincent Price, Judith Anderson, Grant Mitchell, Dorothy Adams; **D:** Otto Preminger; **C:** Joseph LaShelle; **M:** David Raksin. Academy Awards '44: Best Black and White Cinematography; Nominations: Academy Awards '44: Best Director (Preminger), Best Interior Decoration, Best Screenplay, Best Supporting Actor (Webb). *FXV, PMS, BTV*

Laurel & Hardy and the Family **1933** Four zany comedies seeing the boys in all kinds of trouble involving homelife. Includes "Brats," "Perfect Day," "Their First Mistake" and "Twice Two." **85m/B VHS.** Stan Laurel, Oliver Hardy. *VTR, FCT*

Laurel & Hardy: Another Fine Mess **1930** The boys find themselves the owners of a magnificent Beverly Hills mansion. Yeah right. Lots of physical comedy and hilarious dialogue with a "special appearance" by Laurel in drag as a maid. Based on a sketch written by Laurel's father. Colorized. **25m/C VHS.** Stan Laurel, Oliver Hardy. *CAF*

Laurel & Hardy: At Work **1932** Three short films collected here. Includes "Towed in a Hole," "Busy Bodies," and "The Music Box." **70m/B VHS.** Oliver Hardy, Stan Laurel. *VTR, FCT*

Laurel & Hardy: Be Big **1931** Stan and Ollie ditch their wives to go to a swinging stag party at their club. Of course everything goes wrong in their quest for lascivious fun. Filled with tons of sight gags. Colorized. **25m/C VHS.** Stan Laurel, Oliver Hardy. *CAF, MOV*

Laurel & Hardy: Below Zero **1930** It's the Great Depression of 1929, and Laurel and Hardy are about as depressed as you can get, working for pennies as street musicians. Their luck changes when they find a full wallet lying in the snow. But, as the saying goes, a fool and his money are soon parted. Colorized. **25m/C VHS.** Stan Laurel, Oliver Hardy. *CAF, MOV*

Laurel & Hardy: Berth Marks **1929** Laurel & Hardy take a hilarious train trip to Pottsville for a vaudeville performance. Colorized. **25m/C VHS.** Stan Laurel, Oliver Hardy. *CAF*

Laurel & Hardy: Blotto **1930** Laurel and Hardy want to get drunk, but they can't get any alcohol and their wives won't let them get away. When they finally do escape, they wind up at the swanky Rainbow Club, where they're drastically out of their element. Colorized. **25m/C VHS.** Stan Laurel, Oliver Hardy. *CAF*

Laurel & Hardy: Brats **1930** Stan and Ollie play not only themselves but also their children when their wives go away and they have to babysit. The children, of course, wreak havoc wherever they go, playing on the hilariously oversized props and sets. One of the few films in which only Laurel and Hardy appear. Colorized. **25m/C VHS.** Stan Laurel, Oliver Hardy. *CAF, MOV*

Laurel & Hardy: Chickens Come Home **1931** Ollie is running for mayor, but things go crazy when an ex-girlfriend shows up and blackmails him with a compromising photo. Stan, acting as Ollie's campaign manager, tries to help, but things just get worse. A remake of their own film "Love 'Em and Weep." Colorized. **25m/C VHS.** Stan Laurel, Oliver Hardy, James Finlayson. *CAF, MOV*

Laurel & Hardy Comedy Classics, Vol. 1 **1933** A collection of four classic comedy shorts starring Laurel and Hardy: "The Music Box," which won an Academy Award for Best Short Subject, "Country Hospital," "The Live Ghost," and "Twice Two," all from 1932-33. **84m/B VHS, Beta.** Stan Laurel, Oliver Hardy, Mae Busch, May Wallace, Charlie Hall, Billy Gilbert. Academy Awards '31: Best Comedy Short ("The Music Box"). *MED*

Laurel & Hardy Comedy Classics, Vol. 2 **1930** A collection of four Laurel and Hardy shorts from 1930 including "Blotto," "Towed in a Hole," "Brats," and "Hog Wild." **75m/B VHS, Beta.** Stan Laurel, Oliver Hardy, Billy Gilbert, Tiny Sandford, Anita Garvin. *MED*

Laurel & Hardy Comedy Classics, Vol. 3 **1934** Laurel and Hardy star in four separate comedy shorts, including "Oliver the 8th," "Busy Bodies," "Their First Mistake," and "Dirty Work," all from 1933-34. **75m/B VHS, Beta.** Stan Laurel, Oliver Hardy, Billy Gilbert, Mae Busch, Tiny Sandford. *MED*

Laurel & Hardy Comedy Classics, Vol. 4 **1932** Laurel and Hardy star in four of their comedy shorts from 1931-32. Included are "Another Fine Mess," "Come Clean," "Laughing Gravy," and "Any Old Part." **75m/B VHS, Beta.** Stan Laurel, Oliver Hardy, Jacqueline Wells, James Finlayson, Thelma Todd. *MED*

Laurel & Hardy Comedy Classics, Vol. 5 **1931** Four classic comedy shorts starring Laurel and Hardy. Included are "Be Big," "The Perfect Day," "Night Owls," and "Help Mates," from 1929-31. **84m/B VHS, Beta.** Stan Laurel, Oliver Hardy, Edgar Kennedy, James Finlayson, Blanche Payson. *MED*

Laurel & Hardy Comedy Classics, Vol. 6 **1935** Laurel and Hardy comedy shorts are presented in this package: "Our Wife," "The Fixer Uppers," "Them Thar Hills," and "Tit for Tat," from 1932-35. **75m/B VHS, Beta.** Stan Laurel, Oliver Hardy, Charlie Hall, Billy Gilbert, Ben Turpin, Mae Busch, James Finlayson. *MED*

Laurel & Hardy Comedy Classics, Vol. 7 **193?** Four Laurel and Hardy two-reelers are combined on this tape: "Me and My Pal" (1933), "The Midnight Patrol" (1933), "Thicker than Water" (1935), and the classic "Below Zero" (1930). **90m/B VHS, Beta.** Stan Laurel, Oliver Hardy, Mae Busch, Daphne Pollard, James Finlayson. *MED*

Laurel & Hardy Comedy Classics, Vol. 8 **193?** Compilation of Laurel and Hardy shorts includes: "Men O' War" (1929), "Scram" (1932), "Laurel and Hardy Murder Case" (1930) and "One Good Turn" (1931). **90m/B VHS, Beta.** Stan Laurel, Oliver Hardy, Lewis R. Foster, James W. Horne, James Parrott. *MED*

Laurel & Hardy Comedy Classics, Vol. 9 193? Includes the shorts: "Beau Hunks" (1931), "Chickens Come Home" (1931), "Going Bye-Bye" (1934), and "Berth Marks" (1929). **100m/B VHS, Beta.** Stan Laurel, Oliver Hardy. *MED*

Laurel & Hardy: Hog Wild 1930 Hilarity ensues when Laurel and Hardy try to fix the radio antenna on Hardy's roof. It may sound easy, but come on, this is Laurel and Hardy. Colorized. **25m/C VHS.** Stan Laurel, Oliver Hardy. *CAF, MOV*

Laurel & Hardy: Laughing Gravy 1931 The boys' pet dog, oddly named Laughing Gravy, gets them into trouble with their landlord who keeps trying to evict them. So funny even the mashed potatos will laugh. Colorized. **25m/C VHS.** Stan Laurel, Oliver Hardy. *CAF, MOV*

Laurel & Hardy: Men O'War 1929 Laurel & Hardy star as two sailors on shore leave trying to impress the ladies. Things go from bad to worse when they take two ladies out on a date. Features the memorable soda fountain and canoe scenes. Colorized. **25m/C VHS.** Stan Laurel, Oliver Hardy, Gloria Greer, Anne Cornwall. *CAF*

Laurel & Hardy: Night Owls 1930 When a cop needs to capture some crooks to save his job, he sets up a fake break-in and catches two bungling burglars—Laurel and Hardy. Lots of sight gags and slapstick. Colorized. **25m/C VHS.** Stan Laurel, Oliver Hardy, Edgar Kennedy. *CAF, MOV*

Laurel & Hardy On the Lam 1930 Four Laurel & Hardy classics are collected, including "Scram," "Another Fine Mess," "One Good Turn," and "Going Bye-Bye." **90m/B VHS.** Oliver Hardy, Stan Laurel. *VTR, FCT*

Laurel & Hardy: Perfect Day 1929 Laurel & Hardy plan a quiet picnic with their wives, but car trouble turns their day into a disaster. Colorized. **25m/C VHS.** Stan Laurel, Oliver Hardy, Edgar Kennedy. *CAF*

Laurel & Hardy Special 🦴🦴½ 19?? A unique program of Laurel and Hardy films including the first film they appeared in together-"Lucky Dog" (1918), "The Soilers," a wild Laurel spoof of The Spoilers, "Kill or Cure," "Near Dublin," "The Sleuths," "Laurel and Hardy's Trip to Britain," and "Stan Visits Ollie," a color home movie of their last visit together. **60m/B VHS, Beta.** Stan Laurel, Oliver Hardy. *GVV*

Laurel & Hardy Spooktacular 1934 Stan and Ollie scream through four spooky comedies, including "The Live Ghost," "The Laurel-Hardy Murder Case," "Oliver the Eighth" and "Dirty Work." **95m/B VHS.** *VTR, FCT*

Laurel & Hardy: Stan "Helps" Ollie 1933 Four Stan and Ollie classics including "County Hospital," "Me and My Pal," "Hog Wild" and "Helpmates." **85m/B VHS.** Stan Laurel, Oliver Hardy. *VTR, FCT*

Laurel & Hardy: The Hoose-Gow 1929 Laurel and Hardy are mistakenly picked up by the police and sent to prison to do hard labor. Hilarity ensues when they try to convince the warden that they're innocent. Colorized. **25m/C VHS.** *CAF, MOV*

Laurel Avenue 🦴🦴½ 1993 Looks at the life of an extended working-class black family in St. Paul, Minnesota, over a busy weekend. Large cast includes family heads Jake and Maggie who live with their basketball coach son, teenage daughter, and elderly uncle. Other children include fraternal twin Yolanda, a cop married to a white man, who knows sister Rolanda's (a recovering drug addict) son is a dealer. Their brother Marcus manages a Mafia-controlled clothing store and is involved in some shady deals while brother Woody is an aspiring musician. The four households are all united at a disasterous Sunday afternoon party. Made for cable television. **156m/C VHS.** Mary Alice, Mel Winkler, Scott Lawrence, Malinda Williams, Jay Brooks, Juanita Jennings, Rhonda Stubbins White, Monte Russell, Vonte Sweet; ***D:*** Carl Franklin; ***W:*** Michael Henry Brown, Paul Aaron. *HBO*

The Lavender Hill Mob 🦴🦴🦴½ 1951 A prim and prissy bank clerk schemes to melt the bank's gold down and re-mold it into miniature Eiffel Tower paper-weights for later resale. The foolproof plan appears to succeed, but then develops a snag. An excellent comedy that is still a delight to watch. Also available with "The Man in the White Suit" on laserdisc. **78m/B VHS, Beta, LV.** *GB* Alec Guinness, Stanley Holloway, Sidney James, Alfie Bass, Marjorie Fielding, John Gregson; ***Cameos:*** Audrey Hepburn; ***D:*** Charles Crichton; ***W:*** T.E.B. Clarke. Academy Awards '52: Best Story & Screenplay; British Academy Awards '51: Best Film; Nominations: Academy Awards '52: Best Actor (Guinness). *REP, FCT, HMV*

L'Avventura 🦴🦴🦴½ *The Adventure* 1960 A stark, dry and minimalist exercise in narrative by Antonioni, dealing with the search for a girl on an Italian island by her lethargic socialite friends who eventually forget her in favor of their own preoccupations. A highly acclaimed, innovative film; somewhat less effective now, in the wake of many film treatments of angst and amorality. Subtitled in English. Laser edition features the original trailer, commentary and a collection of still photographs from Antonioni's work. **145m/C VHS, Beta, LV.** *IT* Monica Vitti, Gabriele Ferzetti, Lea Massari, Dominique Blanchar, James Addams; ***D:*** Michelangelo Antonioni; ***W:*** Tonino Guerra, Michelangelo Antonioni. Cannes Film Festival '60: Special Jury Prize. *CVC, VDM, APD*

Law and Disorder 🦴🦴🦴 1974 (R) Two average Joes, fed up with the rate of rising crime, start their own auxiliary police group. Alternately funny and serious with good performances from the leads. **103m/C VHS.** Carroll O'Connor, Ernest Borgnine, Ann Wedgeworth, Anita Dangler, Leslie Ackerman, Karen Black, Jack Kehoe; ***D:*** Ivan Passer; ***M:*** Angelo Badalamenti. *NO*

The Law and Jake Wade 🦴🦴½ 1958 Gripping western starring Taylor as a former bank robber turned marshal. His old partner (Widmark) turns up and forces Taylor to lead him to buried loot. **86m/C VHS.** Robert Taylor, Richard Widmark, Patricia Owens, Robert Middleton, Henry Silva, DeForest Kelley, Burt Douglas, Eddie Firestone; ***D:*** John Sturges. *MGM*

Law and Lawless 🦴 1933 A roving cowboy brings justice to a gang of cattle thieves in this film. **58m/B VHS, Beta.** Jack Hoxie. *NOS, DVT*

Law and Order 🦴🦴 1942 Billy the Kid impersonates a Cavalry lieutenant in order to swindle his aunt out of her money. Also called "Billy the Kid's Law and Order." **58m/B VHS, Beta.** Buster Crabbe, Al "Fuzzy" St. John. *VDM, MRV*

Law of Desire 🦴🦴🦴½ *La Ley del Deseo* 1986 A wicked, Almodovarian attack-on-decency farce about a love-obsessed gay Madridian and his transsexual brother-sister, among others, getting hopelessly entangled in cross-gender relationships. Unlike the work of any other director; in Spanish with English subtitles. **100m/C VHS, Beta, LV.** *SP* Carmen Maura, Eusebio Poncela, Antonio Banderas, Bibi Andersson; ***D:*** Pedro Almodovar; ***W:*** Pedro Almodovar. *CCN, INJ, TPV*

Law of the Jungle 🦴½ 1942 A lady scientist and a fugitive team up to uncover a secret Nazi radio base in the jungle. **61m/B VHS, Beta.** Arline Judge, John "Dusty" King, Mantan Moreland, Martin Wilkins, Arthur O'Connell; ***D:*** Jean Yarbrough. *SNC*

Law of the Land 🦴 1976 A made-for-television sagebrush epic with the author/artist of "Garfield" portraying an accused but innocent man searching for a murderer. **100m/C VHS, Beta.** Jim Davis, Don Johnson, Barbara Parkins, Charles Martin Smith. *WOV*

Law of the Lash 🦴 1947 Cowboys and rustlers battle it out. **54m/B VHS, Beta.** Lash LaRue, Al "Fuzzy" St. John. *NOS, MRV, VCN*

Law of the Pampas 🦴🦴 1939 Boyd and Hayden ride off to South America to deliver some cattle, but the bad guys intervene. This is Toler's first outing as Hoppy's sidekick, briefly replacing "Gabby" Hayes. **72m/B VHS.** William Boyd, Russell Hayden, Steffi Duna, Sidney Toler, Sidney Blackmer, Pedro de Cordoba, Eddie Dean, Glenn Strange; ***D:*** Nate Watt. *NOS*

Law of the Saddle 🦴½ 1945 The Lone Rider pits himself against a gang of outlaws. **60m/B VHS, Beta.** Bob Livingston. *VCN, MLB*

Law of the Sea 🦴 1938 A family on a sinking ship is rescued by a lecherous sea captain who makes advances on the wife and blinds the husband in a fight. Twenty years later, the husband meets him again, recognizes his laugh and exacts revenge. **63m/B VHS, Beta, LV.** Priscilla Dean, Sally Blane, Ralph Ince, Rex Bell, William Farnum. *VYY*

Law of the Texan 🦴½ 1938 Jones goes undercover to stop Harlan and his gang from stealing a town's store of silver bullion. **54m/B VHS.** Buck Jones, Dorothy Fay, Kenneth Harlan, Don Douglas, Matty Kemp, Robert F. (Bob) Kortman, Dave O'Brien; ***D:*** Elmer Clifton. *GPV*

Law of the Underworld 🦴½ 1938 An innocent couple is framed for the robbery of a jewelry store which resulted in the death of a clerk. When they are arrested, their fate lies in the hands of the gangster responsible for the crime. Will he let them fry in the electric chair, or will his conscience get the better of him? **58m/B VHS, Beta.** Chester Morris, Anne Shirley, Eduardo Ciannelli, Walter Abel, Richard Bond, Lee Patrick, Paul Guilfoyle, Frank M. Thomas Sr., Eddie Acuff, Jack Arnold; ***D:*** Lew (Louis Friedlander) Landers. *SNC*

Law of the Wild 1934 The search for a magnificent stallion that was hijacked by race racketeers before a big sweepstakes race is shown in this 12 chapter serial. **230m/B VHS.** Bob Custer, Ben Turpin, Lucille Browne, Lafe McKee; ***D:*** B. Reeves Eason, Armand Schaefer. *GPV, NOS, VCN*

The Law Rides 🦴 1936 Rush of gold claims causes an outbreak of murder and robbery. **57m/B VHS, Beta.** Bob Steele. *DVT*

The Law Rides Again 🦴 1943 Prairie lawmen bring a cheating Indian agent to justice. **56m/B VHS.** Ken Maynard, Hoot Gibson, Betty Miles, Jack LaRue; ***D:*** William Castle. *NOS, MRV, DVT*

Law West of Tombstone 🦴🦴½ 1938 A former outlaw moves to a dangerous frontier town in order to restore the peace. **73m/B VHS, Beta.** Tim Holt, Harry Carey Sr., Evelyn Brent; ***D:*** Glenn Tryon. *MED*

Lawless Frontier 🦴½ 1935 In the early West, the Duke fights for law and order. **53m/B VHS, Beta.** John Wayne, George "Gabby" Hayes, Sheila Terry, Earl Dwire; ***D:*** Robert North Bradbury. *COL, NOS, VYY*

The Lawless Land 🦴🦴 1988 (R) Post-holocaust America is ruled by a tyrant. Two young lovers who can't take it anymore go on the lam to escape the despotic rule. **81m/C VHS, Beta.** Leon Berkeley, Xander Berkeley, Nick Corri, Amanda Peterson; ***D:*** Jon Hess; ***W:*** Tony Cinciripini, Larry Leahy. *MGM*

The Lawless Nineties 🦴🦴 1936 Wayne plays a government agent sent to guarantee honest elections in the Wyoming territory. Hayes is exceptional as the newspaper editor who backs him up. Re-made in 1940 as "The Dark Command." **55m/B VHS.** John Wayne, Ann Rutherford, Lane Chandler, Harry Woods, George "Gabby" Hayes, Charles "Blackie" King, Sam Flint; ***D:*** Joseph Kane. *REP*

Lawless Range 🦴½ 1935 Wayne and the marshal's posse save the ranchers from trouble. **56m/B VHS.** John Wayne, Sheila Mannors, Jack Curtis, Earl Dwire; ***D:*** Robert North Bradbury. *REP, NOS, MRV*

A Lawless Street 🦴🦴½ 1955 Scott portrays a sheriff who rides the Colorado Territory cleaning up lawless towns. His dedication to duty has caused his wife to leave him and she won't come back until he lays downs his guns forever, which may come sooner than they think after he rides into the corrupt town of Medicine Bend. Based on the novel "Marshal of Medicine Bend" by Brad Ward. **78m/B VHS.** Randolph Scott, Angela Lansbury, Warner Anderson, Jean Parker, Wallace Ford, John Emery, James Bell, Ruth Donnelly, Michael Pate, Don Megowan, Jeanette Nolan; ***D:*** Joseph H. Lewis; ***W:*** Kenneth Gamet; ***C:*** Ray Rennahan. *COL*

Lawman **1971 (PG)** Brutal western about a fanatical U.S. marshall (Lancaster) who rides into town after Cobb and his six ranch hands. The cowboys have accidentally killed a man and Lancaster is determined to bring them to justice no matter what the cost. Though the entire town is against him that doesn't stop his mission. Brooding and relentless with fine performances, particularly by Ryan as the local marshall living on past glories. **95m/C VHS.** Burt Lancaster, Robert Ryan, Lee J. Cobb, Sheree North, Joseph Wiseman, Robert Duvall, Albert Salmi, J.D. Cannon, John McGiver, Richard Jordan, John Beck, Ralph Waite, John Hillerman, Richard Bull; ***D:*** Michael Winner; ***W:*** Gerald Wilson. *MGM*

A Lawman Is Born **1937** A tough-as-nails marshal goes gunning for a pack of no-good, land-stealing varmits in this installment of the Johnny Mack Brown movie serials. Be sure to count the number of bullets each cowboy can fire from a six-shooter before being forced to reload; you may be surprised. **58m/B VHS, Beta.** Johnny Mack Brown, Iris Meredith, Warner Richmond, Mary MacLaren, Dick Curtis, Earle Hodgins, Charles "Blackie" King, Frank LaRue; ***D:*** Sam Newfield. *NOS, MOV, MRV*

Lawmen ½ **1944** Government agents fight to enforce the law in the badlands. **55m/B VHS, Beta.** Johnny Mack Brown, Raymond Hatton. *NOS, DVT*

The Lawnmower Man **1992 (R)** Brosnan is a scientist who uses Fahey, a dim-witted gardener, as a guinea pig to test his experiments in "virtual reality," an artificial computer environment. With the use of drugs and high-tech equipment, Brosnan is able to increase Fahey's mental powers—but not necessarily for the better. Fantastic special effects and a memorable "virtual reality" sex scene. Available in an unrated version which contains 32 more minutes of footage. So minimally based on a short story by Stephen King that the author sued (and won) to have his name removed from the film. **108m/C VHS, LV.** Jeff Fahey, Pierce Brosnan, Jenny Wright, Mark Bringleson, Geoffrey Lewis, Jeremy Slate, Dean Norris; ***D:*** Brett Leonard; ***W:*** Brett Leonard, Gimel Everett; ***C:*** Russell Carpenter. *COL, FCT, MOV*

Lawnmower Man 2: Beyond Cyberspace *Lawnmower Man 2: Jobe's War* **1995 (PG-13)** Resurrecting Jobe (the title character from number one) was easy. So was blowing off his face to explain the new actor (Frewer in for Fahey) playing him. The hard part was tring to make an original movie with a decent script and believable characters. Better luck next time. Corporate baddie Walker (Conway) enlists Jobe to (what else?) take over the world using Virtual Reality. To the rescue comes one burned-out computer expert (Bergin) and a group of VR-addicted kids living in an abandoned subway. Techno-babble abounds but nothing interesting ever happens. Mann and Frewer must've raided their old "Max Headroom" set for the dreary near-future L.A. landscape scenes. **93m/C VHS, LV.** Patrick Bergin, Matt Frewer, Austin O'Brien, Kevin Conway, Ely Pouget, Camille Cooper; ***D:*** Farhad Mann; ***W:*** Farhad Mann; ***C:*** Ward Russell; ***M:*** Robert Folk. *NLC*

Lawrence of Arabia **1962 (PG)** Exceptional biography of T.E. Lawrence, a British military "observer" who strategically aids the Bedouins battle the Turks during WWI. Lawrence, played masterfully by O'Toole in his first major film, is a hero consumed more by a need to reject British tradition than to save the Arab population. He takes on Arab costume and a larger-than-life persona. Stunning photography of the desert in all its harsh reality. Blacklisted co-writer Wilson had his screen credit restored by the Writers Guild of America in 1995. Laser edition contains 20 minutes of restored footage and a short documentary about the making of the film. Available in letterboxed format. **221m/C VHS, Beta, LV.** *GB* Peter O'Toole, Omar Sharif, Anthony Quinn, Alec Guinness, Jack Hawkins, Claude Rains, Anthony Quayle, Arthur Kennedy, Jose Ferrer; ***D:*** David Lean; ***W:*** Robert Bolt, Michael Wilson; ***C:*** Frederick A. (Freddie) Young; ***M:*** Maurice Jarre. Academy Awards '62: Best Art Direction/Set Decoration (Color), Best Color Cinematography, Best Director (Lean), Best Film Editing, Best Picture, Best Sound, Best Original Score; British Academy Awards '62: Best Actor (O'Toole), Best Film, Best Screenplay; Directors Guild of America Awards '62: Best Director (Lean); Golden Globe Awards '63: Best Director (Lean), Best Film—Drama, Best Supporting Actor (Sharif); Nominations: Academy Awards '62: Best Actor (O'Toole), Best Adapted Screenplay, Best Supporting Actor (Sharif). *COL, CRC, BTV*

The Lawrenceville Stories ½ **198?** Chronicles the life and times of a group of young men at the prestigious Lawrenceville prep school in 1905. Galligan plays William Hicks, alias "The Prodigious Hickey," the ringleader of their obnoxious stunts. Based on the stories of Owen Johnson, which originally ran in the Saturday Evening Post. Shown on "American Playhouse" and The Disney Channel. Tapes are available separately or as a set. **180m/C VHS.** Zach Galligan, Edward Herrmann, Nicholas Rowe, Allan Goldstein, Robert Joy, Stephen Baldwin; ***D:*** Robert Iscove. *MON, BTV*

Laws of Gravity **1992 (R)** Critically acclaimed debut film from 29-year-old writer/director Gomez is a three day slice of life set in Brooklyn. Hotheaded Jon (Trese) and married friend Jimmy (Greene) channel violent energy into their relationships and illegal activities. Camera follows "cinema verite" style and captures urban tension as it trails them through a gun heist and subsequent arrest. **100m/C VHS.** Peter Greene, Edie Falco, Adam Trese, Arabella Field, Paul Schulzie; ***D:*** Nick Gomez; ***W:*** Nick Gomez. *TRI*

Lazarillo *El Lazarillo de Tormes* **1959** In 17th-century Castille, a fatherless boy, abandoned by his mother, finds work with a strange succession of employers, including a blind beggar, fake nobleman, and traveling band of performers. They all teach him lessons in survival as well as cunning and deception. Spanish with subtitles. **109m/B VHS.** *SP* Marco Paoletti, Juan Jose Menendez, Carlos Casaravilla, Margarita Lozano; ***D:*** Cesar Ardavin; ***W:*** Cesar Ardavin; ***M:*** Ruiz De Luna. Berlin International Film Festival '60: Best Film. *FCT*

The Lazarus Syndrome **1979** Astute doctor teams up with an ex-patient of the chief of surgery in an effort to expose the chief's unethical surgical procedures. **90m/C VHS, Beta.** Louis Gossett Jr., E.G. Marshall. *NO*

LBJ: A Biography **1991** Produced for the PBS series "The American Experience," this four-hour revisionist look at LBJ is one of the most critically acclaimed political documentaries of our time. Divided into four segments. "Beautiful Texas" chronicles Johnson's rise to power. "My Fellow Americans" focuses on his years as an unelected president. The Great Society and and the escalation of war in Vietnam are covered in "We Shall Overcome." "The Last Believer" highlights events leading to Johnson's withdrawal from politics. **240m/C VHS.** ***D:*** David Grubin; ***W:*** David Grubin. *PBS, SIG*

LBJ: The Early Years **1988** The early years of President Lyndon Baines Johnson's political career are dramatized in this made-for-television movie. Winning performances hoist this above other biographies. **144m/C VHS, Beta.** Randy Quaid, Patti LuPone, Morgan Brittany, Pat Hingle, Kevin McCarthy, Barry Corbin, Charles Frank; ***D:*** Peter Werner. *FRH*

Le Bal **1982** You won't find many films with the music of Paul McCartney and Chopin in the credits, and even fewer without dialogue. With only music and dancing the film uses a French dance hall to illustrate the changes in French society over a fifty-year period. Based on a French play. ♫La Vie en Rose; In the Mood; Michelle; Top Hat White Tie and Tails; Let's Face the Music and Dance; Harlem Nocturne; Shuffle Blues; Tutti Frutti; Only You. **112m/C VHS.** *IT FR* ***D:*** Ettore Scola; ***M:*** Irving Berlin, Paul McCartney, John Lennon, Frederic Chopin, Vladimir Cosma. Cesar Awards '84: Best Director (Scola), Best Film, Best Score; Nominations: Academy Awards '83: Best Foreign Language Film. *WAR, FCT, INJ*

Le Beau Mariage *A Good Marriage; The Well-Made Marriage* **1982 (R)** An award-winning comedy from the great French director about a zealous woman trying to find a husband and the unsuspecting man she chooses to marry. In French with English subtitles. **97m/C VHS, Beta.** *FR* Beatrice Romand, Arielle Dombasle, Andre Dussollier; ***D:*** Eric Rohmer; ***W:*** Eric Rohmer. Venice Film Festival '82: Best Actress (Romand). *INJ*

Le Beau Serge *Handsome Serge* **1958** A convalescing Frenchman returns to his home village and tries to help an old friend, who's become a hopeless drunkard, change his life. Chabrol's first film, and a major forerunner of the nouvelle vague. In French with English subtitles. **97m/B VHS, Beta.** *FR* Gerard Blain, Jean-Claude Brialy, Michele Meritz, Bernadette LaFont; ***D:*** Claude Chabrol; ***W:*** Claude Chabrol. *FCT*

Le Bonheur ½ *Happiness* **1965** A seemingly happily married carpenter (Drouot) takes a vacation with his wife and children where he meets the local postal clerk and the two begin a passionate affair. Unwilling to leave his family, Drouot believes the two women can share him but when his wife discovers his infidelity she kills herself. His grief does not cause Drouot to stop the affair, instead he moves in with his mistress. An uninvolving, unbelievable tale with a lovely Mozart score. In French with English subtitles. **87m/C VHS.** *FR* Jean-Claude Drouot, Claire Drouot, Marie-France Boyer; ***D:*** Agnes Varda; ***W:*** Agnes Varda. *FCT*

Le Boucher *The Butcher* **1969** In a provincial French town a sophisticated schoolmistress is courted by the shy local butcher—who turns out to be a sex murderer. A well-played thriller that looks at sexual frustration. In French with English subtitles. **94m/C VHS, LV.** *FR* Stephane Audran, Jean Yanne, Antonio Passalia; ***D:*** Claude Chabrol; ***W:*** Claude Chabrol. *CVC, INJ*

Le Bourgeois Gentilhomme **1958** Translated "The Would-Be Gentleman." A comedy-ballet in five acts in prose, performed by the Comedie Francaise. Subtitled in English. **97m/C VHS, Beta.** *FR VYY, APD, INJ*

Le Cas du Dr. Laurent **1957** A country doctor in a small French town tries to introduce methods of natural childbirth to the native women, but meets opposition from the superstitious villagers. Fine performance by Gabin. **88m/B VHS, Beta.** *FR* Jean Gabin, Nicole Courcel; ***D:*** Jean-Paul LeChanois. *NOS, VYY, DVT*

Le Cavaleur *Practice Makes Perfect* **1978** A light hearted comedy about a philandering concert pianist. **90m/C VHS, Beta.** *FR* Jean Rochefort, Lila Kedrova, Nicole Garcia, Annie Girardot, Danielle Darrieux; ***D:*** Philippe de Broca; ***M:*** Georges Delerue. *NO*

Le Chat ½ *The Cat* **1975** A middle-aged couple's marriage dissolves into a hate-filled battle of wits, centering around the husband's love for their cat. In French with English subtitles. **88m/C VHS, Beta, LV.** *FR* Jean Gabin, Simone Signoret, Annie Cordy, Jacques Rispal; ***D:*** Pierre Granier-Deferre. Berlin International Film Festival '71: Best Actor (Gabin). *FCT, LUM*

Le Complot *The Conspiracy* **1973** When de Gaulle announces his intention to abandon Algeria, several army officers, feeling that their service has been in vain, stage a coup. There's suspense aplenty as the Gaulists, the leftists, and the police spy and are spied upon. In French with English subtitles. **120m/C VHS, LV.** *FR* Michel Bouquet, Jean Rochefort; ***D:*** Rene Gainville. *CVC, FCT, INJ*

Le Corbeau *The Raven* **1943** A great, notorious drama about a small French village whose everyday serenity is ruptured by a series of poison pen letters that lead to suicide and despair. The film was made within Nazi-occupied France, sponsored by the Nazis, and has been subjected to much misdirected malice because of it. In French with English subtitles. **92m/B VHS, Beta.** *FR* Pierre Fresnay, Noel Roquevort, Ginette LeClerc, Pierre Larquey, Antoine Belpetre; ***D:*** Henri-Georges Clouzot. *NOS, HHT, INJ*

Le Crabe Tambour **1977** Rochefort plays a dying naval captain remembering his relationship with his first officer. Revealed via flashbacks, the recollections concern the adventures which transpired on a North Atlantic supply ship. Great performances from all and award-winning cinematography by Raoul Coutard. Winner of several French Cesars. A French script booklet is available. **120m/C VHS, LV.** *FR* Jean Rochefort, Claude Rich, Jacques Dufilho, Jacques Perrin, Odile Versois, Aurore Clement; ***D:*** Pierre Schoendoerffer. Cesar Awards '78: Best Actor (Rochefort), Best Cinematography, Best Supporting Actor (Dufilho). *INT, IME, APD*

Le Dernier Combat *The Last Battle* **1984 (R)** A stark film about life after a devastating nuclear war marks the directorial debut of Besson. The characters fight to survive in a now speechless world by staking territorial claims and forming new relationships with other survivors. An original and expressive film made without dialogue. **93m/B VHS, Beta.** *FR* Pierre Jolivet, Fritz Wepper, Jean Reno, Jean Bouise, Christiane Kruger; ***D:*** Luc Besson; ***W:*** Luc Besson. *COL, OM*

Le Doulos **1961** Compelling story of an ex-convict and his buddy, a man who may be a police informant. Chronicles the efforts of the snitch (the "doulos" of the title) to bring the criminal element before the law. Melville blends in several plot twists and breathes a new-French life into the cliche-ridden genre. **108m/B VHS, Beta.** *FR* Serge Reggiani, Jean-Paul Belmondo, Michel Piccoli; ***D:*** Jean-Pierre Melville. *INT, TPV, INJ*

Le Gendarme de Saint-Tropez ½ **1967** Officer Ludovic Cruchot's plans for career advancement are on shaky ground after he is transferred to St. Tropez where his daughter has a little too much fun at the beach. Also available dubbed. **?m/C VHS.** *FR* Louis de Funes, Michel Galabru, Genevieve Grad, Jean LeFevre, Christian Marin. *FRA, FCT*

Le Gentleman D'Epsom **1962** A French comedy about a breezy con man who scams everyone around him in order to keep up his upwardly mobile appearance and to put his bets down at the racetrack. Subtitled in English. **83m/B VHS, Beta.** *FR* Jean Gabin, Paul Frankeur. *INJ, BAR*

Le Grand Chemin *The Grand Highway* **1987** A sweet, slice-of-life French film about a young boy's idyllic summer on a family friend's farm while his mother is having a baby. Hubert's son plays the boy Louis in this retelling of the director's own childhood. In French with English subtitles. Remade with an American setting in 1991 as "Paradise." **107m/C VHS, Beta, LV.** *FR* Anemone, Richard Bohringer, Antoine Hubert, Vanessa Guedj, Christine Pascal, Raoul Billerey, Pascale Roberts; ***D:*** Jean-Loup Hubert; ***W:*** Jean-Loup Hubert; ***M:*** Georges Granier. Cesar Awards '88: Best Actor (Bohringer), Best Actress (Anemone). *FCT, INJ, IME*

Le Joli Mai **1962** A famous documentary that established Marker, depicting the everyday life of Paris denizens on the occasion of the end of the Algerian War, May 1962, when France was at peace for the first time since 1939. In French with English subtitles. **180m/B VHS, Beta.** *FR* ***D:*** Chris Marker. *FCT*

Le Jour Se Leve ½ *Daybreak* **1939** The dark, expressionist film about a sordid and destined murder/love triangle that starts with a police stand-off and evolves into a series of flashbacks. The film that put Carne and Gabin on the cinematic map. Highly acclaimed. French with English subtitles. Remade in 1947 as "The Long Night." **89m/B VHS.** *FR* Jean Gabin, Jules Berry, Arletty, Jacqueline Laurent; ***D:*** Marcel Carne. *HMV, APD, INJ*

Le Magnifique *The Magnificent One* **1976** Belmondo is a master spy and novelist who mixes fantasy with reality when he chases women and solves cases. **84m/C VHS, Beta.** *FR* Jean-Paul Belmondo, Jacqueline Bisset; ***W:*** Francis Veber; ***M:*** Claude Bolling. *PSM*

Le Mans **1971 (G)** The famous 24-hour Grand Prix race sets the stage for this tale of love and speed. McQueen (who did his own driving) is the leading race driver, a man who battles competition, fear of death by accident, and emotional involvement. Excellent documentary-style race footage almost makes up for weak plot and minimal acting. **106m/C VHS, LV.** Steve McQueen, Elga Andersen, Ronald Leigh-Hunt, Luc Merenda; ***D:*** Lee H. Katzin; ***C:*** Robert B. Hauser. *FOX, FCT*

Le Million ½ **1931** A comedy/musical masterpiece of the early sound era which centers on an artist's adventures in searching for a winning lottery ticket throughout Paris. Highly acclaimed member of the Clair school of subtle French farce. In French with English subtitles. **89m/B VHS, Beta.** *FR* Annabella, Rene Lefevre, Paul Olivier, Louis Allibert; ***D:*** Rene Clair. National Board of Review Awards '31: 5 Best Foreign Films of the Year. *VYY, NOS, DVT*

Le Petit Amour *Kung Fu Master* **1987 (R)** A popular French comedy about the fateful romance between a 40-year-old divorced woman and a 15-year-old boy obsessed with a kung fu video game. In French with English subtitles. **80m/C VHS, Beta.** *FR* Jane Birkin, Mathieu Demy, Charlotte Gainsbourg, Lou Doillon; ***D:*** Agnes Varda. *PSM*

Le Plaisir ½ *House of Pleasure* **1952** An anthology of three Guy de Maupassant stories, "Le Masque," "Le Modele," and "La Maison Teillier," about the search for pleasure. In French with English subtitles. **97m/B VHS, Beta.** *FR* Claude Dauphin, Simone Simon, Jean Gabin, Danielle Darrieux; ***D:*** Max Ophuls. Nominations: Academy Awards '54: Best Art Direction/Set Decoration (B & W). *NOS, DVT, INJ*

Le Repos du Guerrier *Warrior's Rest* **1962** Star vehicle for Bardot in which she plays a respectable woman who abandons societal norms to pursue an unbalanced lover. In French with English subtitles. **100m/C VHS, Beta.** *FR* Brigitte Bardot, Robert Hossein, James Robertson Justice, Jean-Mark Bory; ***D:*** Roger Vadim. *BAR, INJ*

Le Schpountz *Heartbeat* **1938** Satire on filmmaking and film-loving fans finds a small town grocer (Fernandel) in southern France becoming the victim of a practical joke when a visiting film crew promises to make him a star (signing him to a phony contract) if he'll come to Paris. Naturally, the joke's on them when the naive grocer arrives in the City of Light and becomes a successful movie comic. French with subtitles. **135m/B VHS.** *FR* Fernandel, Charpin, Orane Demazis, Odette Roger, Jean Castan, Leon Belieres; ***D:*** Marcel Pagnol; ***W:*** Marcel Pagnol; ***C:*** Willy; ***M:*** Casimir Oberfeld. *INT*

Le Secret **1974** This classic French thriller with a shocking ending finds an escaped convict seeking shelter with a reclusive couple in the mountains. His tales of abuse and torture create tension for the pair as one believes the woeful story and the other doesn't. Dubbed in English. **103m/C VHS, Beta.** *FR* Jean-Louis Trintignant, Philippe Noiret, Jean-Francois Adam; ***D:*** Robert Enrico; ***M:*** Ennio Morricone. *NO*

Le Sex Shop **1973 (R)** A man turns his little book store into a porn equipment palace, to make ends meet. When his relationship with his wife gets boring, they begin to use their erotic merchandise and adopt a swinging lifestyle. **92m/C VHS, Beta.** *FR* Claude Berri, Juliet Berto, Daniel Auteuil, Nathalie Delon; ***D:*** Claude Berri; ***M:*** Serge Gainsbourg. *COL*

Le Sexe des Etoiles *The Sex of the Stars* **1993** Curiously uninvolving film about 12-year-old Camille who discovers that the father who abandoned her is now a transsexual. Pierre walked out years before and Camille has always dreamed of his return but though they reach a tentative relationship, it's not what Camille hoped for. Title refers to Camille's obsession with astronomy because stars have no sex. Based on the novel by Proulx (who also wrote the screenplay). In French with English subtitles. **104m/C VHS.** *CA* Marianne-Coquelicot Mercier, Denis Mercier, Tobie Pelletier, Sylvie Drapeau; ***D:*** Paule Baillargeon; ***W:*** Monique Proulx. Genie Awards '93: Best Sound. *ICA*

Leader of the Band **1987 (PG)** An out-of-work musician tries to train the world's worst high school band. Landesberg helps this attempted comedy along. **90m/C VHS, Beta, LV.** Steve Landesburg, Gailard Sartain, Mercedes Ruehl, James Martinez, Calvert Deforest; ***D:*** Nessa Hyams; ***M:*** Dick Hyman. *LIV*

The League of Gentlemen ½ **1960** An ex-Army officer plots a daring bank robbery using specially skilled military personnel and irreproachable panache. Hilarious British humor fills the screen. **115m/B VHS, Beta.** *GB* Jack Hawkins, Nigel Patrick, Richard Attenborough, Roger Livesey, Bryan Forbes; ***D:*** Basil Dearden. *HMV, FCT*

A League of Their Own **1992 (PG)** Charming look at sports history and the Rockford Peaches, one of the teams in the real-life All American Girls Professional Baseball League, formed in the 40s when the men were off at war. Main focus is on sibling rivalry between Davis, the beautiful, crackerjack catcher, and Petty, the younger, insecure pitcher. Boozy coach Hanks is wonderful as he reluctantly leads the team; he also gets credit for the classic "There's no crying in baseball" scene. Great cast of supporting characters, including sarcastic talent scout Lovitz, opinionated, sleazy taxi dancer Madonna, loud-mouthed O'Donnell, and shy, homely Cavanagh. Lots of baseball for the sports fan. **127m/C VHS, Beta, LV, 8mm.** Tom Hanks, Geena Davis, Madonna, Lori Petty, Jon Lovitz, David Strathairn, Garry Marshall, Bill Pullman, Rosie O'Donnell, Megan Cavanagh, Tracy Reiner, Bitty Schram, Ann Cusack, Anne Elizabeth Ramsay, Freddie Simpson, Renee Coleman; ***D:*** Penny Marshall; ***W:*** Lowell Ganz, Babaloo Mandel; ***M:*** Hans Zimmer. *COL*

Lean on Me **1989 (PG-13)** The romanticized version of the career of Joe Clark, a tough New Jersey teacher who became the principal of the state's toughest, worst school and, through controversial hard-line tactics, turned it around. **109m/C VHS, Beta, LV, 8mm.** Morgan Freeman, Robert Guillaume, Beverly Todd, Alan North, Lynne Thigpen, Robin Bartlett, Michael Beach, Ethan Phillips, Regina Taylor; ***D:*** John G. Avildsen; ***W:*** Michael Schiffer; ***M:*** Bill Conti. *WAR, FCT*

Leap of Faith ½ **1992 (PG-13)** Jonas Nightengale (Martin) is a traveling evangelist/scam artist whose tour bus is stranded in an impoverished farm town. Nevertheless he sets up his show and goes to work, aided by the technology utilized by accomplice Winger. Both Martin and Winger begin to have a change of heart after experiencing love—Winger with local sheriff Neeson and Martin after befriending a waitress (Davidovich) and her crippled brother (Haas). Martin is in his element as the slick revivalist with the hidden heart but the film is soft-headed as well as soft-hearted. **110m/C VHS, Beta, LV.** Steve Martin, Debra Winger, Lolita Davidovich, Liam Neeson, Lukas Haas, Meat Loaf, Philip S. Hoffman, M.C. Gainey, La Chanze, Delores Hall, John Toles-Bey, Albertina Walker, Ricky Dillard; ***D:*** Richard Pearce; ***W:*** Janus Cercone; ***M:*** Cliff Eidelman. *PAR, BTV*

Leap Year ½ **1921** Made at the apex of the 300 pound comedian's career, "Leap Year" wasn't released in the States until the sixties. Tried for manslaughter in 1921 (with two hung juries), Fatty was forced off camera and his films were taken out of circulation (although he did return to cinema behind the camera using the pseudonym William Goodrich). **60m/B VHS, Beta.** Fatty Arbuckle. *GPV, FCT*

Leapin' Leprechauns ½ **1995 (PG)** John Dennehy's dad Michael has arrived from Ireland for a visit, accompanied by some "wee folk" who are invisible to all non-believers. Seems the little leprechauns are just in time to rescue their ancestral home from a plot by John to turn their Irish land into a theme park and make believers out of a family of skeptics. **84m/C VHS, Beta.** Grant Cramer, John Bluthal, Sharon Lee Jones, Gregory Edward Smith, Sylvester McCoy, James Ellis, Godfrey James, Tina Martin, Erica Nicole Hess; ***D:*** Ted Nicolaou; ***W:*** Ted Nicolaou, Michael McGann. *PAR*

The Learning Tree **1969 (PG)** A beautifully photographed adaptation of Parks' biographical novel about a fourteen-year-old black boy in the 1920s South, living on the verge of manhood, maturity, love, and wisdom. **107m/C VHS, Beta.** Kyle Johnson, Alex Clarke, Estelle Evans, Dana Elcar; ***D:*** Gordon Parks; ***C:*** Burnett Guffey. *WAR, FCT, AFR*

Leather Boys 🦴🦴 **1963** A teen-aged girl marries a mechanic and then begins to look beyond the boundaries of marriage. Considered very controversial in the 60s, but less so now. **103m/C VHS, Beta.** *GB* Rita Tushingham, Dudley Sutton, Colin Campbell; ***D:*** Sidney J. Furie. *NO*

Leather Burners 🦴🦴 **1943** Hoppy goes under cover to get the goods on a suspected rustler. When his cover is blown, the bad guys frame him for murder. Look for Robert Mitchum in his third bit part in this series. **66m/B VHS.** William Boyd, Andy Clyde, Jay Kirby, Victor Jory, George Givot, Bobby Larson, George Reeves, Hal Taliaferro, Forbes Murray, Robert Mitchum; ***D:*** Joseph Henabery. *NOS, MRV*

Leather Jackets 🦴🦴 **1990 (R)** Sweeney plays a nice guy who lets involvement with a childhood pal destroy his life. Elwes is the friend, now gang member, in trouble with both the cops and members of a rival gang, who needs Sweeney's help to escape. Fonda plays Sweeney's girlfriend caught between the two men. Essentially a routine fugitive pic with an attractive cast. **90m/C VHS, LV.** D.B. Sweeney, Bridget Fonda, Cary Elwes, Christopher Penn, Marshall Bell, James LeGros, Jon Polito, Craig Ng, Ginger Lynn Allen; ***D:*** Lee Drysdale; ***W:*** Lee Drysdale. *COL*

Leatherface: The Texas Chainsaw Massacre 3 🦴 **1989 (R)** The human-skin-wearing cannibal is at it again in this, the second sequel to the Tobe Hooper proto-mess. This one sports a bit more humor and is worth seeing for that reason. **81m/C VHS, Beta, LV.** Kate Hodge, William Butler, Ken Foree, Tom Hudson, R.A. Mihailoff; ***D:*** Jeff Burr; ***W:*** David J. Schow. *COL*

The Leatherneck 🦴🦴 **1928** Love unrequited in a faraway place starring soon to be cowboy (Hopalong Cassidy) matinee idol Boyd and Hale, the real life dad of Gilligan Island's skipper. **65m/B VHS, Beta.** William Boyd, Alan Hale, Diane Ellis. Nominations: Academy Awards '29: Best Writing. *GPV, FCT*

Leave 'Em Laughing 🦴🦴 **1981** Rooney plays Chicago clown Jack Thum in this based-on-real-life TV movie. Thum takes in orphans even though he cannot find steady work, and then discovers he has cancer. **103m/C VHS, Beta.** Mickey Rooney, Anne Jackson, Allen (Goorwitz) Garfield, Elisha Cook Jr., William Windom, Red Buttons, Michael Le Clair; ***D:*** Jackie Cooper. *FRH*

Leave Her to Heaven 🦴🦴🦴 **1945** Beautiful neurotic Tierney takes drastic measures to keep hubby all to herself and will do anything to get what she wants. Tierney, in a departure from her usual roles, is excellent as this pathologically possessive creature. Oscar-winner Leon Shamroy's photography (in Technicolor) is breathtaking. Based on the novel by Ben Ames Williams. **110m/C VHS.** Gene Tierney, Cornel Wilde, Jeanne Crain, Vincent Price, Mary Philips, Ray Collins, Darryl Hickman, Gene Lockhart; ***D:*** John M. Stahl; ***W:*** Jo Swerling; ***C:*** Leon Shamroy; ***M:*** Alfred Newman. Academy Awards '45: Best Cinematography; Nominations: Academy Awards '45: Best Actress (Tierney). *FXV*

Leave It to the Marines 🦴½ **1951** A jerky guy wanders into a recruiting office instead of a marriage license bureau and unwittingly signs on for military service. **66m/B VHS, Beta, LV.** Sid Melton, Mara Lynn. *NO*

Leaves from Satan's Book 🦴🦴½ **1919** Impressionistic episodes of Satan's fiddling with man through the ages, from Christ to the Russian Revolution. An early cinematic film by Dreyer, with ample indications of his later brilliance. Silent. **165m/B VHS, Beta.** *DK* Helge Milsen, Halvart Hoft, Jacob Texiere; ***D:*** Carl Theodor Dreyer. *GPV, FCT, GVV*

Leaving Las Vegas 🦴🦴🦴½ **1995 (R)** Ben Sanderson (Cage) is a hopeless alcoholic who goes to Vegas to drink himself to death and meets Sera (Shue), a lonely hooker who loves him enough not to stop him. Definitely as depressing as it sounds, but still manages to have both a subtle sense of humor and compassion. Cage tops his best work and Shue proves she deserves better than the lightweight roles she's had in the past. Not for everyone, but worth the effort for people who like to see honest emotion and hate Hollywood's insistence on happy endings. Based on the semi-autobiographical novel by John O'Brien, who committed suicide shortly before pre-production began. **120m/C VHS, LV.** Nicolas Cage, Elisabeth Shue, Julian Sands, Laurie Metcalf, David Brisbin, Richard Lewis, Valeria Golino, Steven Weber; ***D:*** Mike Figgis; ***W:*** Mike Figgis; ***C:*** Declan Quinn; ***M:*** Mike Figgis. Academy Awards '95: Best Actor (Cage); Golden Globe Awards '96: Best Actor—Drama (Cage); Independent Spirit Awards '96: Best Actress (Shue), Best Cinematography, Best Director (Figgis), Best Film; Los Angeles Film Critics Association Awards '95: Best Actor (Cage), Best Actress (Shue), Best Director (Figgis), Best Film; National Board of Review Awards '95: Best Actor (Cage); New York Film Critics Awards '95: Best Actor (Cage), Best Film; National Society of Film Critics Awards '95: Best Actor (Cage), Best Actress (Shue), Best Director (Figgis); Nominations: Academy Awards '95: Best Actress (Shue), Best Adapted Screenplay, Best Director (Figgis); Directors Guild of America Awards '95: Best Director (Figgis); Golden Globe Awards '96: Best Actress—Drama (Shue), Best Director (Figgis), Best Film—Drama; Independent Spirit Awards '96: Best Actor (Cage), Best Screenplay; Screen Actors Guild Award '95: Best Actress (Shue); Writers Guild of America '95: Best Adapted Screenplay. *MGM*

Leaving Normal 🦴½ **1992 (R)** Darly, a fed-up waitress, and Marianne, an abused housewife, meet at a bus stop in Normal, Wyoming and decide to blow town. They travel across the American West, through Canada, and up to Alaska, where Lahti's ex-boyfriend has left her a house. Because both women have made bad choices all their lives, they decide to leave their futures to chance, and end up finding their nirvana. Plot is similar to "Thelma & Louise," but "Leaving Normal" doesn't come close to the innovativeness of the former. Sappy and sentimental to the point of annoyance at times. **110m/C VHS, LV.** Christine Lahti, Meg Tilly, Lenny Von Dohlen, Maury Chaykin, James Gammon, Patrika Darbo, Eve Gordon, James Eckhouse, Brett Cullen, Rutanya Alda; ***D:*** Edward Zwick; ***W:*** Edward Solomon. *MCA*

L'Ecole Buisoniere 🦴🦴½ **1951** In a provincial French school a teacher with modern ideas inspires his students with a passion for learning until the suspicious parents are aroused. In French with English subtitles. **108m/C VHS.** *FR* ***D:*** Jean-Paul LeChanois. *FCT, INJ, WBF*

The Leech Woman 🦴🦴 **1959** While in Africa, an older woman (Gray) discovers how to restore her youth through a tribal ritual. The only problem is it requires the pineal gland of males, which causes her to go on a killing spree to keep that youthful look. Based on a story by Ben Pivar and Francis Rosenwald. **77m/B VHS.** Coleen Gray, Grant Williams, Gloria Talbot, Phillip Terry; ***D:*** Edward Dein; ***W:*** David Duncan. *MCA*

Left for Dead 🦴½ **1978** A millionaire is accused of brutally killing his wife, and discovers in his search for an alibi that he is the victim of a conspiracy. **82m/C VHS, Beta.** Elke Sommer, Donald Pilon; ***D:*** Murray Markowitz. *LIV, VES*

The Left Hand of God 🦴🦴🦴 **1955** After an American pilot escapes from a Chinese warlord in post-WWII, he disguises himself as a Catholic priest and takes refuge in a missionary hospital. Bogie is great as the flyboy/cleric. **87m/C VHS, Beta.** Humphrey Bogart, E.G. Marshall, Lee J. Cobb, Agnes Moorehead, Gene Tierney; ***D:*** Edward Dmytryk. *FOX*

The Left-Handed Gun 🦴🦴🦴 **1958** An offbeat version of the exploits of Billy the Kid, which portrays him as a 19th-century Wild West juvenile delinquent. Newman's role, which he method-acted, was originally intended for James Dean. Based on a 1955 Philco teleplay by Gore Vidal. **102m/B VHS, Beta.** Paul Newman, Lita Milan, John Dehner; ***D:*** Arthur Penn. *WAR, TLF*

The Legacy 🦴½ *The Legacy of Maggie Walsh* **1979 (R)** An American couple become privy to the dark secrets of an English family gathering in a creepy mansion to inherit an eccentric millionaire's fortune. Death and demons abound. **100m/C VHS, Beta.** *GB* Katharine Ross, Sam Elliott, John Standing, Roger Daltrey, Ian Hogg; ***D:*** Richard Marquand. *MCA*

A Legacy for Leonette *Woof!* **1985** A girl is led into a web of murder and love in this torrid romance novel brought to video. **90m/C Beta.** Loyita Chapel, Michael Anderson Jr., Dinah Anne Rogers. *PSM*

Legacy of Horror *Woof!* **1978 (R)** A weekend at the family's island mansion with two unfriendly siblings sounds bad enough, but when terror, death, and a few family skeletons pop out of the closets, things go from bad to weird. All-round poor effort with substantial gore. A remake of the director's own "The Ghastly Ones." **83m/C VHS, Beta.** Elaine Boies, Chris Broderick, Marilee Troncone, Jeannie Cusik; ***D:*** Andy Milligan. *MPI*

Legacy of Lies 🦴🦴½ **1992 (R)** Zack Resnick is a serious, honest Chicago cop assigned to a murder investigation. He first discovers the killers got the wrong man and then finds out a lot of family secrets he wishes he didn't know. His cop-father is on the take to the Mob, which is really no surprise since Zack's grandfather turns out to be a retired gangland boss, all of which leaves Zack wondering where his loyalties lie. Too intricate plot hampers the story's flow but the cast performances are well worth watching. Made for cable television. **94m/C VHS, LV.** Michael Ontkean, Martin Landau, Eli Wallach, Joe Morton, Patricia Clarkson, Gerry Becker, Chelcie Ross, Ron Dean; ***D:*** Jason Meshover-Iorg; ***W:*** David Black. National Academy of Cable Programming ACE Awards '93: Best Supporting Actor (Landau). *MCA*

Legal Eagles 🦴🦴½ **1986 (PG)** An assistant D.A. faces murder, mayhem, and romance while prosecuting a girl accused of stealing a portrait painted by her father. Redford sparkles in this otherwise convoluted tale from Reitman, while Hannah lacks depth as the daffy thief. **116m/C VHS, Beta, LV.** Robert Redford, Debra Winger, Daryl Hannah, Brian Dennehy, Terence Stamp, Steven Hill, David Clennon, Roscoe Lee Browne, John McMartin, Jennie Dundas, Ivan Reitman; ***D:*** Ivan Reitman; ***W:*** Jim Cash, Jack Epps Jr.; ***M:*** Elmer Bernstein. *MCA*

Legal Tender 🦴½ **1990 (R)** Rude talk-show host Downey as a corrupt S & L chief? Big, menacing Davi as a romantic hero? Give this often-inept thriller credit for creative casting, if little else. Roberts adds steamy sex appeal as a lovely saloon-keeper imperiled by deadly bank fraud. **93m/C VHS, Beta.** Robert Davi, Tanya Roberts, Morton Downey Jr.; ***D:*** Jag Mundhra. *PSM*

Legend 🦴🦴 **1986 (PG)** A colorful, unabashedly Tolkien-esque fantasy about the struggle to save an innocent waif from the Prince of Darkness. Set in a land packed with unicorns, magic swamps, bumbling dwarves and rainbows. Produced in Great Britain. **89m/C VHS, Beta, LV.** *GB* Tom Cruise, Mia Sara, Tim Curry, David Bennent, Billy Barty, Alice Playten; ***D:*** Ridley Scott; ***M:*** Jerry Goldsmith. Nominations: Academy Awards '86: Best Makeup. *MCA*

Legend of Alfred Packer 🦴½ **1980** The true story of how a guide taking five men searching for gold in Colorado managed to be the sole survivor of a blizzard. **87m/C VHS, Beta.** Patrick Dray, Ron Haines, Bob Damon, Dave Ellingson; ***D:*** Jim Roberson. *NO*

Legend of Big Foot 🦴 **1982** Facing a spree of killings, a local town mobilizes to stop the legendary beast. **92m/C VHS, Beta.** Stafford Morgan, Katherine Hopkins. *NO*

Legend of Billie Jean 🦴🦴 **1985 (PG-13)** Billie Jean believed in justice for all. When the law and its bureaucracy landed hard on her, she took her cause to the masses and inspired a generation. **92m/C VHS, Beta.** Helen Slater, Peter Coyote, Keith Gordon, Christian Slater, Richard Bradford, Yeardley Smith, Dean Stockwell; ***D:*** Matthew Robbins; ***W:*** Mark Rosenthal. *FOX*

The Legend of Black Thunder Mountain 🦴½ **1979 (G)** A children's adventure in the mold of "Grizzly Adams" and "The Wilderness Family." **90m/C VHS, Beta.** Holly Beeman, Steve Beeman, Ron Brown, F.A. Milovich; ***D:*** Tom Beeman. *NO*

The Legend of Blood Castle ☠ *The Female Butcher; Blood Ceremony; Ceremonia Sangrienta* **1972 (R)** Another version of the Countess of Bathory legend, in which an evil woman bathes in the blood of virgins in an attempt to keep the wrinkles away. Released hot on the heels of Hammer's "Countess Dracula." **87m/C VHS, Beta.** *IT SP* Lucia Bose, Ewa Aulin; ***D:*** Jorge Grau. *NO*

Legend of Boggy Creek ☠½ **1975 (G)** A dramatized version of various Arkansas Bigfoot sightings. **87m/C VHS, Beta.** Willie E. Smith, John P. Nixon, John W. Gates, Jeff Crabtree, Buddy Crabtree; ***D:*** Charles B. Pierce; ***W:*** Charles B. Pierce. *LIV, MRV*

Legend of Earl Durand ☠½ **1974** In Wyoming 1939, a man spends his life searching for freedom and justice. His Robin Hood actions cause a manhunt of massive proportions. **90m/C VHS.** Martin Sheen, Peter Haskell, Keenan Wynn, Slim Pickens, Anthony Caruso; ***D:*** John D. Patterson. *NO*

The Legend of Frank Woods ☠☠ **1977** Gunslinger returns to the land of the free after an extended holiday south of the border. Mistaken for an expected preacher in a small town, he poses as the padre and signs on the dotted line to take out a new lease on life. **88m/C VHS.** Troy Donahue, Brad Steward, Kitty Vallacher, Michael Christian; ***D:*** Deno Paoli. *SIM*

Legend of Frenchie King ☠½ *Petroleum Girls* **1971** When prospectors discover oil on disputed land, two families feud over their conflicting claims to the property. Adult western still working out the kinks has Bardot heading a band of female outlaws. **96m/C VHS, Beta.** Brigitte Bardot, Claudia Cardinale, Michael J. Pollard, Micheline Presle; ***D:*** Christian-Jaque. *NO*

The Legend of Hell House ☠☠☠ **1973 (PG)** A multi-millionaire hires a team of scientists and mediums to investigate his newly acquired haunted mansion. It seems that the creepy house has been the site of a number of deaths and may hold clues to the afterlife. A suspenseful, scary screamfest. Matheson wrote the screenplay from his novel "Hell House." **94m/C VHS, Beta, LV.** Roddy McDowall, Pamela Franklin, Clive Revill, Gayle Hunnicutt; ***D:*** John Hough; ***W:*** Richard Matheson. *FOX*

The Legend of Hillbilly John ☠ *Who Fears the Devil; My Name is John* **1973 (G)** Hillbilly John holds off the devil with a strum of his six-string. While demons plague the residents of rural America, the hayseed messiah wanders about saving the day. **86m/C VHS, Beta, LV.** Severn Darden, Denver Pyle, Susan Strasberg, Hedge Capers; ***D:*** John Newland. *NWV*

The Legend of Jedediah Carver ☠☠ **197?** A rancher battles desert elements and hostile Indians in a desperate bid for survival. **90m/C VHS.** DeWitt Lee, Joshua Hoffman, Val Chapman, Richard Montgomery, David Terril; ***D:*** DeWitt Lee. *XVC*

Legend of Lobo ☠½ **1962** The story of Lobo, a crafty wolf who seeks to free his mate from the clutches of greedy hunters. A Disney wildlife adventure. **67m/C VHS, Beta.** *DIS*

The Legend of Sea Wolf ☠☠ **1975 (PG)** A sadistic sea captain forcefully rules his crew in this weak version of Jack London's novel. Also known as "Wolf Larsen." **90m/C VHS, Beta.** Chuck Connors, Barbara Bach, Joseph Palmer. *NO*

The Legend of Sleepy Hollow **1949** The story of Ichabod Crane and the legendary ride of the headless horseman by Washington Irving; narrated by Crosby. Also includes two classic short cartoons, "Lonesome Ghosts" (1932) with Mickey Mouse and "Trick or Treat" (1952) with Donald Duck. **45m/C VHS, Beta.** ***D:*** Jack Kinney, Clyde Geronomi, James Algar. *DIS, WTA*

The Legend of Sleepy Hollow ☠☠½ **1979 (G)** Washington Irving's classic tale of the Headless Horseman of Sleepy Hollow is brought to life on the screen. Made for television. **100m/C VHS, Beta, LV.** Jeff Goldblum, Dick Butkus, Paul Sand, Meg Foster, James Griffith, John S. White. *NO*

The Legend of Sleepy Hollow **1986** Classic Washington Irving tale is given the Shelly Duvall treatment in her "Tall Tales and Legends" series. When a snooty teacher goes too far, the town blacksmith decides to play the ultimate Halloween trick on him. Made for cable television. **51m/C VHS.** Ed Begley Jr., Beverly D'Angelo, Charles Durning, Tim Thomerson. *FOX*

The Legend of Suram Fortress ☠☠ *Legenda Suramskoi Kreposti* **1985** Based on a Georgian folktale about a medieval fortress that collapses as soon as it is built. The village soothsayer tells a young man he must sacrifice himself, by bricking himself up alive within the fortress walls, if the building is every to stand. In Russian with English subtitles. **89m/C VHS.** *RU* Levan Outchanechvili, Zourab Kipchidze; ***D:*** Sergei Paradjanov. *KIV*

Legend of the Dinosaurs *Woof!* **1983** Slavering, teeth-gnashing dinosaurs are discovered on Mt. Fuji. **92m/C VHS, Beta.** *CEL*

Legend of the Lone Ranger ☠½ **1981 (PG)** The fabled Lone Ranger (whose voice is dubbed throughout the entire movie) and the story of his first meeting with his Indian companion, Tonto, are brought to life in this weak and vapid version of the famous legend. The narration by Merle Haggard leaves something to be desired as do most of the performances. **98m/C VHS, Beta.** Klinton Spilsbury, Michael Horse, Jason Robards Jr., Richard Farnsworth, Christopher Lloyd, Matt Clark; ***D:*** William A. Fraker; ***W:*** William Roberts, Ivan Goff, Michael Kane; ***M:*** John Barry. Golden Raspberry Awards '81: Worst Actor (Spilsbury), Worst New Star (Spilsbury). *FOX*

Legend of the Lost ☠☠ **1957** Two men vie for desert treasure and desert women. Interesting only because of Wayne, but certainly not one of his more memorable films. **109m/C VHS.** John Wayne, Sophia Loren, Rossano Brazzi, Kurt Kasznar, Sonia Moser; ***D:*** Henry Hathaway; ***C:*** Jack Cardiff. *MGM*

Legend of the Northwest ☠☠ **1978 (G)** The loyalty of a dog is evidenced in the fierce revenge he has for the drunken hunter who shot and killed his master. **83m/C VHS, Beta.** Denver Pyle. *VTR, GEM, HHE*

The Legend of the Sea Wolf ☠☠½ *Wolf Larsen; Larsen, Wolf of the Seven Seas* **1958** Adaptation of Jack London's dramatic adventure novel, "The Sea Wolf." A slave driving ship captain rescues a shipwreck victim and sets to abusing him along with the rest of his crew. A rebellion ensues. Superb musical score benefits the strong acting and good pace. **83m/B VHS.** Barry Sullivan, Peter Graves, Gita Hall, Thayer David; ***D:*** Harmon Jones; ***W:*** Jack DeWitt. *NO*

Legend of the Werewolf ☠☠ **1975 (R)** A child who once ran with the wolves has forgotten his past, except when the moon is full. **90m/C VHS, Beta.** *GB* Peter Cushing, Hugh Griffith, Ron Moody, David Rintoul, Lynn Dalby; ***D:*** Freddie Francis. *MRV*

The Legend of the Wolf Woman ☠☠½ **1977 (R)** The beautiful Daniella assumes the personality of the legendary wolfwoman, leaving a trail of gruesome killings across the countryside. Genre fans will find this one surprisingly entertaining. Also on video as "Werewolf Woman." **84m/C VHS, Beta.** *IT* Anne Borel, Fred Stafford, Tino Carey, Elliot Zamuto, Ollie Reynolds, Andrea Scotti, Karen Carter; ***D:*** Raphael D. Silver. *VIP*

Legend of Tom Dooley ☠☠ **1959** Somber western about three Confederate soldiers who rob a Union stagecoach and kill two soldiers, not knowing that the Civil War has ended. Landon turns in a good performance as the Rebel soldier turned outlaw. Based on the hit song by the Kingston trio. **79m/B VHS.** Michael Landon, Jo Morrow, Jack Hogan, Richard Rust, Dee Pollock, Ken Lynch; ***D:*** Ted Post; ***M:*** Ronald Stein. *COL*

Legend of Valentino **1975** Made-for-television docudrama traces the legendary exploits of one of the silver screen's greatest lovers, Rudolph Valentino. Typical TV-movie fare that lacks the power of the legend's life. **96m/C VHS, Beta.** Franco Nero, Suzanne Pleshette, Lesley Ann Warren, Yvette Mimieux, Judd Hirsch, Milton Berle, Harold J. Stone; ***D:*** Melville Shavelson. *PSM, MRV, NLC*

The Legend of Valentino **1983** A biographical documentary of perhaps the world's greatest lover, beginning with his immigration to America and ending at his unexpected, sudden death. **71m/B VHS, Beta.** *SUE*

Legend of Walks Far Woman ☠ **1982** A made for television film about a proud Sioux woman fighting for survival and her tribe during the American-Indian Wars. Welch is miscast. From Colin Stuart's novel. **120m/C VHS, Beta.** Raquel Welch, Nick Mancuso, Bradford Dillman; ***D:*** Mel Damski. *NO*

The Legend of Wolf Mountain ☠☠½ **1992 (PG)** Three children are held hostage by two prison escapees in the Utah mountains. They are aided in their escape by a Native American "wolf spirit." With the criminals on their trail will the three be able to survive in the wilderness until a search party can find them? **91m/C VHS, LV.** Mickey Rooney, Bo Hopkins, Don Shanks, Vivian Schilling, Robert Z'Dar, David Shark, Nicole Lund, Natalie Lund, Matthew Lewis, Jonathan Best; ***D:*** Craig Clyde; ***W:*** Craig Clyde. *HMD*

Legends of the Fall ☠☠ **1994 (R)** Sweeping, meandering, melodramatic family saga set in Montana (though filmed in Alberta, Canada). Patriarch William Ludlow (Hopkins), a retired Army colonel, is raising three sons: reserved Alfred (Quinn), idealistic Samuel (Thomas), and wild middle son Tristan (Pitt). In 1913, Samuel returns from Boston with a fiancee, the lovely and refined Susannah (Ormond). Only problem is Alfred and Tristan take one look and also desire her—a passion that will carry them through some 20 years of heartbreak. Film loses the spare toughness of the Jim Harrison novella but is a visual feast (and not just because the camera seems to drool every time Pitt appears on screen.) **134m/C VHS, LV, 8mm.** Brad Pitt, Aidan Quinn, Julia Ormond, Anthony Hopkins, Henry Thomas, Gordon Tootoosis, Tantoo Cardinal, Karina Lombard, Paul Desmond, Kenneth Welsh; ***D:*** Edward Zwick; ***W:*** Susan Shilliday, William D. Wittliff; ***C:*** John Toll; ***M:*** James Horner. Academy Awards '94: Best Cinematography; Nominations: Academy Awards '94: Best Art Direction/Set Decoration, Best Sound; Golden Globe Awards '95: Best Actor—Drama (Pitt), Best Director (Zwick), Best Film—Drama, Best Original Score. *COL*

Legends of the North ☠☠½ **1995 (PG)** Crusty prospector Whip Gorman (Quaid) and partner Paul Bel Air are searching for a mythical lake of gold when Paul takes a fall off a mountain. Whip sends for Paul's son Charles so that he can translate his father's diary (it's in French) and get the clues to the gold's whereabouts. Naturally, some rival prospectors, some Indians, and even a feisty gal or two help or hinder our treasure seekers. Based on a story by Jack London. **95m/C VHS.** Randy Quaid. *VMK*

Legion of Iron ☠ **1990 (R)** Adventures in a computer-run, neo-Roman civilization where men and women battle for supremacy. **85m/C VHS, Beta, LV.** Kevin T. Walsh, Erica Nann, Regie De Morton, Camille Carrigan; ***D:*** Yakov Bentsvi. *COL*

Legion of Missing Men ☠½ **1937** Professional soldiers of fortune, the French Foreign Legion, fight the evil sheik Ahmed in the Sahara. **62m/B VHS, Beta.** Ralph Forbes, Ben Alexander, Hala Linda, Roy D'Arcy, Paul Hurst, Jimmy Aubrey; ***D:*** Hamilton MacFadden. *VYY, GPV*

Legion of the Lawless ☠½ **1940** Group of outlaws band together in order to spread terror and confusion among the populace. **59m/B VHS, Beta.** George O'Brien, Virginia Vale. *MED*

Legs ☠☠ **1983** Backstage story of three girls who are competing for a job with Radio City Music Hall's Rockettes. Made for television. **91m/C VHS, Beta.** Gwen Verdon, John Heard, Sheree North, Shanna Reed, Maureen Teefy; ***D:*** Jerrold Freedman. *PSM*

The Lemon Drop Kid ☠☠½ **1951** Second version of the Damon Runyon chestnut about a racetrack bookie who must recover the gangster's money he lost on a bet. As the fast-talking bookie,

Hope sparkles. ♫Silver Bells; It Doesn't Cost a Dime to Dream; They Obviously Want Me to Sing. **91m/B VHS, Beta, LV.** Bob Hope, Lloyd Nolan, Fred Clark, Marilyn Maxwell, Jane Darwell, Andrea King, William Frawley, Jay C. Flippen, Harry Bellaver; ***D:*** Sidney Lanfield; ***W:*** Frank Tashlin, Edmund Hartmann, Robert O'Brien; ***C:*** Daniel F. Fapp. *COL*

The Lemon Sisters 🦴🦴 **1990 (PG-13)** Three women, friends and performance partners since childhood, struggle to buy their own club. They juggle the men in their lives with less success. Great actresses like these should have done more with this interesting premise, and the excellent male cast has much more potential. **93m/C VHS, LV.** Diane Keaton, Carol Kane, Kathryn Grody, Elliott Gould, Ruben Blades, Aidan Quinn; ***D:*** Joyce Chopra. *HBO, FCT*

Lemora, Lady Dracula 🦴 *The Lady Dracula; The Legendary Curse of Lemora* **1973 (PG)** A pretty young church singer is drawn into the lair of the evil Lady Dracula, whose desires include her body as well as her blood. Horror fans will enjoy some excellent atmosphere, particularly in a scence where the girl's church bus is attacked by zombie-like creatures; Smith remains a '70s "B" movie favorite. Perhaps a double feature with "Lady Frankenstein...?" **80m/C VHS.** Leslie Gilb, Cheryl "Rainbeaux" Smith, William Whitton, Steve Johnson, Monty Pyke, Maxine Ballantyne, Parker West, Richard Blackburn; ***D:*** Richard Blackburn. *FRG*

Lena's Holiday 🦴🦴 **1990 (PG-13)** Fluffy comedy about a winsome East German girl visiting L.A. for the first time, and the culture-shock that ensues. Sharp script and performances. **97m/C VHS, Beta, LV.** Felicity Waterman, Chris Lemmon, Noriyuki "Pat" Morita, Susan Anton, Michael Sarrazin, Nick Mancuso, Bill Dana, Liz Torres; ***D:*** Michael Keusch. *PSM*

L'Enfant d'Eau 🦴🦴 *Water Child; Behind the Blue* **1995** Mentally handicapped twentysomething Emile (La Haye) and precocious 12-year-old Cedrine (Monette) must learn to work together to survive after a plane crash strands them on an island in the Bahamas. Familiar story offers no surprises and the script shies away from any sexual implications, negating two excellent performances. French with subtitles. **103m/C VHS.** *CA* David La Haye, Marie-France Monette; ***D:*** Robert Menard; ***W:*** Claire Wojas. Genie Awards '95: Best Actor (La Haye). *NYR*

L'Enfer 🦴🦴🦴 *Jealousy; Torment* **1993** Claustrophobic thriller chronicles the descent into madness of an unstable hotel owner (Cluzet) convinced that his beautiful wife (Beart) is having an affair. Intriguing plot points that blur appearances and reality lead to ambiguous and unsatisfying ending. Clouzot himself began filming his screenplay in 1964, but a heart attack forced him to abandon the project. In French with English subtitles. **103m/C VHS.** *FR* Emmanuelle Beart, Francois Cluzet, Nathalie Cardone, Andre Wilms, Marc Lavoine; ***D:*** Claude Chabrol; ***W:*** Claude Chabrol, Henri-Georges Clouzot, Jose-Andre Lacour. *FXL*

Leningrad Cowboys Go America 🦴🦴½ **1989 (PG-13)** An outlandish Finnish band, the Leningrad Cowboys, pack up their electric accordians and their one dead member and go on tour in America. With matching front-swept pompadours and pointy shoes, the group's appearance is the picture's best joke—and one of its only jokes, as the road trip plods in deadpan fashion that may bore viewers. It's best appreciated by fans of comic minimalist Jim Jarmusch (who has a guest role). In Finnish with English subtitles. **78m/C VHS, LV.** *FI* Jim Jarmusch, Matti Pellonpaa, Kari Vaananen, Nicky Tesco; ***D:*** Aki Kaurismaki; ***W:*** Aki Kaurismaki. *ORI, FCT, INJ*

Lenny 🦴🦴🦴 **1974 (R)** Smoky nightclubs, drug abuse, and obscenities abound in Hoffman's portrayal of the controversial comedian Lenny Bruce, whose use of street language led to his eventual blacklisting. Perrine is a gem as his stripper wife. Adapted from the Julian Barry play, this is a visually compelling piece that sharply divided critics upon release. **111m/B VHS, Beta, LV.** Dustin Hoffman, Valerie Perrine, Jan Miner, Stanley Beck; ***D:*** Bob Fosse; ***W:*** Julian Barry; ***C:*** Bruce Surtees; ***M:*** Ralph Burns. Cannes Film Festival '75: Best Actress (Perrine); National Board of Review Awards '74: 10 Best Films of the Year, Best Supporting Actress (Perrine); Nominations: Academy Awards '74: Best Actor (Hoffman), Best Actress (Perrine), Best Adapted Screenplay, Best Cinematography, Best Director (Fosse), Best Picture; Cannes Film Festival '75: Best Film. *MGM, FOX*

Lenny Bruce Performance Film **1968** A videotape of one of Lenny Bruce's last nightclub appearances at Basin Street West in San Francisco. Also included is "Thank You Masked Man," a color cartoon parody of the Lone Ranger legend, with Lenny Bruce providing all the character voices. **72m/B VHS, Beta.** Lenny Bruce. *VES, RHI, MVD*

Lensman **1984** In the 25th century space pirates known as the Boskande are threatening the civilized universe. Young Kimall Kenison is chosen by a higher power to become a lensman—and live or die for freedom. Based on the E.E. "Doc" Smith novels, this production is a combination of animation and computer graphics. Dubbed in English. **107m/C VHS, LV.** *JP WTA; STP, FUS*

Leolo 🦴🦴 **1992** Deeply disturbing black-comedy about one of the screen's most dysfunctional families. Leo is a 12-year-old French Canadian from Montreal who is determined to remake himself. He's decided to be a Sicilian lad named Leolo, escaping from his horrific family into his fantasies (and potential madness). His parents are obsessed with toilet training, his cowardly brother with body-building, his sisters are demented, and his grandfather is a sadistic, dirty old man. Not for the faint of heart (or stomach). In French with English subtitles. **107m/C VHS, LV.** *CA* Maxime Collin, Julien Guiomar, Ginette Reno, Pierre Bourgault, Yves Montmarquette, Roland Blouin, Giuditta del Vecchio; ***D:*** Jean-Claude Lauzon; ***W:*** Jean-Claude Lauzon. Genie Awards '92: Best Costume Design, Best Film Editing, Best Original Screenplay; Nominations: Cannes Film Festival '92: Best Film. *NLC, ING*

Leon Morin, Priest 🦴🦴½ **1961** A young priest and a widow, who happens to be a Communist, fall in love during the WWII German occupation of France. Based on the novel by Beatrix Beck. In French with English subtitles. **118m/B VHS.** *IT FR* Jean-Paul Belmondo, Emmanuelle Riva; ***D:*** Jean-Pierre Melville. *INT, INJ, FCT*

Leon the Pig Farmer 🦴🦴½ **1993** Dry comedic satire about identity. Leon Geller has never quite fitted into his parents' comfortable Jewish society and no wonder—Leon accidentally discovers he is the product of artificial insemination. And what's more, the lab made a mistake and Leon isn't a true Geller after all. His father is actually a genial (and Gentile) Yorkshire pig farmer named Brian Chadwick, who cheerfully welcomes Leon as his long-lost son. All four parents try to cope while Leon moves bewilderedly amongst them. Film tends to be too timid in its satire but still has its witty moments. **98m/C VHS.** *GB* Mark Frankel, Janet Suzman, Brian Glover, Connie Booth, David DeKeyser, Maryam D'Abo, Gina Bellman; ***D:*** Vadim Jean, Gary Sinyor; ***W:*** Gary Sinyor, Michael Normand. *ORI*

Leonard Part 6 🦴 **1987 (PG)** A former secret agent comes out of retirement to save the world from a crime queen using animals to kill agents. In the meantime, he tries to patch up his collapsing personal life. Wooden and disappointing; produced and co-written by Cosby, who himself panned the film. **83m/C VHS, Beta, LV.** Bill Cosby, Gloria Foster, Tom Courtenay, Joe Don Baker; ***D:*** Paul Weiland; ***W:*** Bill Cosby, Jonathan Reynolds; ***M:*** Elmer Bernstein. Golden Raspberry Awards '87: Worst Picture, Worst Actor (Cosby), Worst Screenplay. *COL*

Leonor 🦴 **1975** Idiotic medieval drivel with Ullmann rising from the dead after husband Piccoli seals her in a tomb. Directed by the son of Luis Bunuel. **90m/C VHS, Beta.** *FR SP IT* Liv Ullmann, Michel Piccoli, Ornella Muti; ***D:*** Juan Bunuel; ***M:*** Ennio Morricone. *FOX*

Leopard Fist Ninja 🦴 **198?** A masked ninja whacks away at American hoodlums in a fit of Maoist, anti-capitalistic fury. Dubbed. **88m/C VHS, Beta.** Willie Freeman, Jack Lam, Chuck Horry. *NO*

Leopard in the Snow 🦴🦴 **1978 (PG)** The romance between a race car driver allegedly killed in a crash and a young woman is the premise of this film. **89m/C VHS, Beta.** Keir Dullea, Susan Penhaligon, Kenneth More, Billie Whitelaw; ***D:*** Gerry O'Hara. *SUE*

The Leopard Man 🦴🦴½ **1943** An escaped leopard terrorizes a small town in New Mexico. After a search, the big cat is found dead, but the killings continue. Minor but effective Jacques Tourneur creepie. Based on Cornell Woolrich's novel "Black Alibi." Another Val Lewton Horror production. **66m/B VHS, Beta, LV.** Jean Brooks, Isabel Jewell, James Bell, Margaret Landry, Dennis O'Keefe, Margo, Rita (Paula) Corday; ***D:*** Jacques Tourneur. *MED*

The Leopard Woman 🦴🦴 **1920** Long before the cat lady cut her first claws, there was the leopard woman. Vamp Glaum finds much trouble to meow about on the Equator. **66m/B VHS, Beta.** Louise Glaum. *GPV, FCT, GVV*

Leper 🦴🦴 **1976** A melodrama of forbidden love between a wealthy nobleman and a beautiful high school teacher. The townspeople try to destroy the love between the two because of their different social classes. In Polish with English subtitles. Also known as "Tredowata." **100m/C VHS.** *PL* Elzbieta Starostecka, Leszek Teleszynski; ***D:*** Jerzy Hoffman. *FCT*

Lepke 🦴🦴½ **1975 (R)** The life and fast times of Louis "Lepke" Buchalter from his days in reform school to his days as head of Murder, Inc. and his execution in 1944. **110m/C VHS, Beta.** Tony Curtis, Milton Berle, Gianni Russo, Vic Tayback, Michael Callan; ***D:*** Menahem Golan. *WAR*

Leprechaun *Woof!* **1993 (R)** A sadistic 600-year-old leprechaun winds up wreaking havoc in North Dakota. If this makes no particular sense, neither does the film which is basic horror story excess. A man goes to Ireland for his mother's funeral, steals the gold belonging to the leprechaun, locks the creature up, and winds up accidentally taking the evil imp back to the States with him. When the leprechaun gets free, he wants a bloodthirsty revenge—and shoes. One of the so-called humorous bits is the leprechaun's shoe fetish. Irish eyes will not be smiling watching this mess. **92m/C VHS, LV.** Warwick Davis, Jennifer Aniston, Ken Olandt, Mark Holton, John Sanderford, Robert Gorman; ***D:*** Mark Jones; ***W:*** Mark Jones. *VMK*

Leprechaun 2 🦴🦴½ **1994 (R)** Sequel to the Irish horror flick about a malevolent gnome. It seems one of his fairy entitlements is that he can possess any woman he wants if she sneezes three times. Thwarted in his attempt to snare a comely lass one thousand years earlier, he returns to present-day California to exact revenge on her descendant Durkin. Contrary to the popular legend that leprechauns are benign kind-hearted sprites, this nasty combines the treachery of a Gestapo officer with the firepower of Rambo in his attempt to harass the unimpressed Durkin into his clutches. **85m/C VHS, LV.** Warwick Davis, Sandy Baron, Adam Biesk, James Lancaster, Clint Howard, Kimmy Robertson, Charlie Heath, Shevonne Durkin; ***D:*** Rodman Flender; ***W:*** Turi Meyer, Al Septien; ***M:*** Jonathan Elias. *VMK*

Leprechaun 3 🦴 **1995 (R)** A student steals the nasty little beastie's gold and he's off to Las Vegas to get it back and to kill the gamblers, also after his magic money, in decidedly disgusting ways. **93m/C VHS, LV.** Warwick Davis, John Gatins, Michael Callan, Caroline Williams; ***D:*** Brian Trenchard-Smith. *VMK*

Les Assassins de L'Ordre 🦴🦴 *Law Breakers* **1971** A righteous French judge faces the case of an innocent man killed by police brutality. Subtitled in English. **100m/C VHS, Beta.** *FR* Jacques Brel, Catherine Rouvel, Michael Lonsdale, Charles Denner; ***D:*** Marcel Carne; ***M:*** Michel Colombier. *INJ*

Les Aventuriers 🦴🦴½ *The Last Adventure* **1977** Two friends find themselves swindled in an insurance scam and set out after the perpetrator who sent them off to Africa in search of a treasure. Available dubbed. **?m/C VHS.** *FR* Alain Delon, Lino Ventura, Joanna Shimkus. *FRA, FCT*

Les Biches ☙☙☙½ *The Heterosexuals* **1968 (R)** An exquisite film that became a landmark in film history with its theme of bisexuality and upper class decadence. A rich socialite picks up a young artist drawing on the streets of Paris, seduces her, and then takes her to St. Tropez. Conflict arises when a suave architect shows up and threatens to come between the two lovers. In French with English subtitles. **95m/C VHS, LV.** *FR* Stephane Audran, Jean-Louis Trintignant, Jacqueline Sassard; ***D:*** Claude Chabrol; ***W:*** Claude Chabrol. *CVC, INJ, LUM*

Les Bonnes Femmes ☙☙☙ *The Good Girls; The Girls* **1960** Four Paris shopgirls dream of escaping the monotony of their lives and finding romance but instead discover broken dreams and danger. Chabrol's New Wave thriller focuses more on character and irony than suspense. French with subtitles. **105m/B VHS.** *FR* Bernadette LaFont, Stephane Audran, Clothilde Joano, Lucile Saint-Simon; ***D:*** Claude Chabrol; ***W:*** Paul Geoauff; ***C:*** Henri Decae; ***M:*** Pierre Jansen, Paul Misraki. *FCT*

Les Bons Debarras ☙☙½ **1981** In French with English subtitles, this Canadian film follows a lonely 13-year-old's effort to win her mother's exclusive love. **114m/C VHS, Beta.** *CA* Marie Tifo, Charlotte Laurier, German Houde; ***D:*** Francis Mankiewicz. Genie Awards '81: Best Actress (Tifo), Best Director (Mankiewicz), Best Film, Best Supporting Actor (Houde). *NO*

Les Carabiniers ☙☙☙ *The Soldiers* **1963** A cynical, grim anti-war tract, detailing the pathetic adventures of two young bums lured into enlisting with promises of rape, looting, torture and battle without justification. Controversial in its day, and typically elliptical and non-narrative. In French with English subtitles. **80m/B VHS, Beta.** *GB IT FR* Anna Karina, Genevieva Galea, Marino Mase; ***D:*** Jean-Luc Godard. *FCT*

Les Comperes ☙☙☙ **1983** A woman suckers two former lovers into finding her wayward son by secretly telling each ex he is the natural father of the punk. Depardieu is a streetwise journalist who teams up with a suicidal hypochondriac/wimp (Richard) to find the little brat. Humorous story full of bumbling misadventures. In French with English subtitles. **92m/C VHS, Beta, LV.** *FR* Pierre Richard, Gerard Depardieu, Anny Duperey, Michel Aumont; ***D:*** Francis Veber; ***W:*** Francis Veber; ***M:*** Vladimir Cosma. *MED, FCT, INJ*

Les Enfants Terrible ☙☙☙ *The Strange Ones* **1950** The classic, lyrical treatment of adolescent deviance adapted by Cocteau from his own play, wherein a brother and sister born into extreme wealth eventually enter into casual crime, self-destruction, and incest. In French with English subtitles. **105m/B VHS, Beta.** *FR* Edouard Dermithe, Nicole Stephane; ***D:*** Jean-Pierre Melville; ***W:*** Jean Cocteau, Jean-Pierre Melville. *FCT, INJ, WBF*

Les Girls ☙☙½ **1957** When one member of a performing troupe writes her memoirs, the other girls sue for libel. Told through a series of flashbacks, this story traces the girls' recollections of their relationships to American dancer Kelly. Cole Porter wrote the score for this enjoyable "Rashomon"-styled musical. Laserdisc features include the original trailer and letterboxed screen. ♫Les Girls; Flower Song; You're Just Too, Too; Ca C'est L'Amour; Ladies In Waiting; La Habanera; Why Am I So Gone (About That Gal?). **114m/C VHS, Beta, LV.** Gene Kelly, Mitzi Gaynor, Kay Kendall, Taina Elg, Henry Daniell, Patrick Macnee; ***D:*** George Cukor; ***C:*** Robert L. Surtees. Academy Awards '57: Best Costume Design; Golden Globe Awards '58: Best Actress—Musical/Comedy (Kendall), Best Film—Musical/Comedy; Nominations: Academy Awards '57: Best Art Direction/Set Decoration, Best Sound. *MGM*

Les Grandes Gueules ☙☙½ *Jailbirds' Vacation* **1965** From the director of the classic "An Occurrence at Owl Creek Bridge," comes this comedy-drama about a sawmill owner dealing with two ex-convicts hired as lumberjacks. In French with English subtitles. **125m/C VHS, Beta.** *FR* Lino Ventura, Bourvil, Marie DuBois; ***D:*** Robert Enrico. *BAR, INJ*

Les Grandes Manoeuvres ☙☙☙ *Summer Manoeuvers; The Grand Maneuvers* **1955** Clair's first film in color depicts the romance between a seductive soldier (Philipe) and a divorcee (Morgan) in a pre-WWI garrison town. Gentle comedy has Philipe falling in love but his reputation as a Don Juan comes between them. French with subtitles. **106m/C VHS.** *FR* Gerard Philipe, Michele Morgan, Yves Robert, Brigitte Bardot, Jean Desailly, Pierre Dux; ***D:*** Rene Clair; ***W:*** Rene Clair; ***M:*** Georges Van Parys. *WBF*

Les Miserables ☙☙☙☙ **1935** Victor Hugo's classic novel about small-time criminal Jean Valjean and 18th-century France. After facing poverty and prison, escape and torture, Valjean is redeemed by the kindness of a bishop. As he tries to mend his ways, he is continually hounded by the policeman Javert, who is determined to lock him away. The final act is set during a student uprising in the 1730s. This version is the best of many, finely detailed and well-paced with excellent cinematography by Gregg Toland. **108m/B VHS, Beta, LV.** Fredric March, Charles Laughton, Cedric Hardwicke, Rochelle Hudson, John Beal, Frances Drake, Florence Eldridge, John Carradine, Jessie Ralph, Leonid Kinskey; ***D:*** Richard Boleslawski; ***W:*** W.P. Lipscomb; ***C:*** Gregg Toland; ***M:*** Alfred Newman. National Board of Review Awards '35: 10 Best Films of the Year; Nominations: Academy Awards '35: Best Cinematography, Best Picture; Academy Awards '36: Best Film Editing. *FOX, APD*

Les Miserables ☙☙½ **1952** Hugo's classic novel done up Italian style with lavish sets and spectacle. Dubbed in English. **119m/B VHS.** *IT* Gino Cervi, Valentina Cortese; ***D:*** Riccardo (Robert Hampton) Freda; ***C:*** Joseph LaShelle; ***M:*** Alex North. *VYY, FCT*

Les Miserables ☙☙☙ **1957** An epic French adaptation of the Victor Hugo standard about Valjean, Javert, and injustice. Although this doesn't reach the level of the 1935 classic, it is still worth watching. Dubbed in English. **210m/C VHS, Beta.** *FR GE* Jean Gabin, Daniele Delorme, Bernard Blier, Bourvil, Gianni Esposito, Serge Reggiani; ***D:*** Jean-Paul LeChanois. *FCT, VEC*

Les Miserables ☙☙☙½ **1978** An excellent made-for-television version of the Victor Hugo classic about the criminal Valjean and the policeman Javert playing cat-and-mouse in 18th-century France. Dauphin's last film role. **150m/C VHS, Beta, LV.** Richard Jordan, Anthony Perkins, John Gielgud, Cyril Cusack, Flora Robson, Celia Johnson, Claude Dauphin; ***D:*** Glenn Jordan. *FOX, FCT*

Les Miserables ☙☙½ **1995 (R)** Clever, modern rendering of the famous Victor Hugo novel, set in World War II. Humble furniture mover Fortin (Belmondo), nicknamed Valjean for displaying the same brutish strength as his Hugo counterpart, helps a Jewish family escape German occupation. The family becomes separated in the attempt, with lawyer, Monsieur Ziman (Boujenah), being hidden by farmers in the country, Madame Ziman (Martines) relegated to a Polish concentration camp, and their daughter Salome (Lelouch, daughter of the director) protected by a nun at a Catholic school. Gump-like, the unusually strong but illiterate Fortin becomes involved with the French resistance and joins in D-Day. Events, though obviously updated, mirror experiences of Hugo's characters. In one sequence, the Ziman's even teach Fortin to read the Hugo's "Les Miserables," with actors playing their counterparts in dramatizations. Reportedly France's most expensive film ever. **174m/C VHS, LV.** Jean-Paul Belmondo, Michel Boujenah, Annie Girardot, Philippe Leotard, Clementine Celarie, Rufus, Alessandra Martines, Salome, Philippe Khorsand; ***D:*** Claude Lelouch; ***W:*** Claude Lelouch; ***C:*** Claude Lelouch; ***M:*** Francis Lai. Golden Globe Awards '96: Best Foreign Language Film; Nominations: British Academy Awards '95: Best Foreign Film; Cesar Awards '96: Best Supporting Actress (Girardot). *WAR*

Les Mistons ☙☙☙ **1957** This study of male adolescence finds five teen-age boys worshiping a beautiful girl from afar, following her everywhere, spoiling her dates, and finally reaching maturity in light of their mistakes. **18m/C VHS, Beta.** *FR* ***D:*** Francois Truffaut. *FLI*

Les Nuits Fauves ☙☙☙ *Savage Nights* **1992** Collard's semi-autobiographical film about the emotional and physical havoc an H.I.V.-positive filmmaker visits on the two objects of his violent affections—an innocent 18-year-old girl and a sadomasochistic 20-year-old boy. As Jean displays increasing desperation with his situation, the life around him shows an equally arbitrary violence and humor. In French with English subtitles. Collard died of AIDS shortly before his film won both best first film and best French film at the 1993 Cesars—a first in the ceremony's history. **129m/C VHS.** *FR* Cyril Collard, Romane Bohringer, Carlos Lopez, Maria Schneider; ***D:*** Cyril Collard; ***W:*** Cyril Collard. Cesar Awards '93: Best Film. *PGV*

Les Patterson Saves the World ☙½ **1990 (R)** An obnoxious ambassador to an anonymous Middle Eastern country teams up with the singularly distastefully named Dr. Herpes to stop a new killer disease about to engulf the world. **105m/C VHS.** Barry Humphries, Pamela Stephenson, Thaao Penghlis, Andrew Clarke, Joan Rivers; ***D:*** George Miller. *HMD*

Les Rendez-vous D'Anna ☙☙ *The Meetings of Anna* **1978** An independent woman travels through Europe and comes face to face with its post-war modernism. In French with English subtitles. **120m/C VHS.** *FR BE GE* Aurore Clement, Helmut Griem, Magali Noel, Hanns Zischler, Lea Massari, Jean-Pierre Cassel; ***D:*** Chantal Akerman; ***W:*** Chantal Akerman. *WAC, INJ*

Les Violons du Bal ☙☙ **1974** Follows the story of a young Jewish boy and his family's attempted escape from Nazi-occupied France during WWII. The boy grows up to be a filmmaker obsessed with making a movie about his childhood experiences. In French with English subtitles. **110m/C VHS.** *FR* Marie-Jose Nat, Jean-Louis Trintignant; ***D:*** Michael Drach. Cannes Film Festival '74: Best Actress (Nat); Nominations: Cannes Film Festival '74: Best Film. *CVC, INJ, PMS*

Les Visiteurs du Soir ☙☙☙½ *The Devil's Envoys* **1942** A beautiful, charming fairy tale about the devil's intrepid interference with a particular love affair in 15th-century France, which he cannot squelch. Purportedly a parable about Hitler's invasion of France. Interestingly, this was released after the Nazi occupation of France, so one assumes that the Germans didn't make the connection. In French with English subtitles. **120m/B VHS.** *FR* Arletty, Jules Berry, Marie Dea, Alain Cuny, Fernand Ledoux, Marcel Herrand; ***D:*** Marcel Carne; ***W:*** Jacques Prevert, Pierre Laroche. *HMV, INJ, FCT*

Less Than Zero ☙ **1987 (R)** An adaptation of Bret Easton Ellis' popular, controversial novel about a group of affluent, drug-abusing youth in Los Angeles. McCarthy and Gertz play friends of Downey who try to get him off his self-destructive path—to no avail. Although it tries, the film fails to inspire any sort of sympathy for this self-absorbed and hedonistic group. Mirrors the shallowness of the characters although Downey manages to rise above this somewhat. Music by the Bangles, David Lee Roth, Poison, Roy Orbison, Aerosmith and more. **98m/C VHS, Beta, LV.** Andrew McCarthy, Jami Gertz, Robert Downey Jr., James Spader; ***D:*** Marek Kanievska; ***M:*** Thomas Newman. *FOX*

Lesson in Love ☙☙½ *En Lektion i Karlek* **1954** A gynecologist's philandering is discovered by his wife, who then starts an affair of her own. Change of pace for Bergman as he does this modest comedy. In Swedish with English subtitles. **95m/B VHS, Beta.** *SW* Gunnar Bjornstrand, Eva Dahlbeck, Harriet Andersson; ***D:*** Ingmar Bergman; ***W:*** Ingmar Bergman. *SUE, INJ, NLC*

Let 'Em Have It ☙☙½ *False Faces* **1935** Exciting action saga loosely based on the newly formed FBI and its bouts with John Dillinger. Car chases and tommy guns abound in this fairly ordinary film. **90m/B VHS.** Richard Arlen, Virginia Bruce, Bruce Cabot, Harvey Stephens, Eric Linden, Joyce Compton, Gordon Jones; ***D:*** Sam Wood. *MGM, NOS, HEG*

Let 'er Go Gallegher ☙☙ **1928** A youngster sees a murder, tells his newspaper buddy about it, and the guy writes an article about the crime. It's a big hit, the guy's ego starts to overinflate, and his life starts to head downwind until he decides its time for him and the little guy to rope themselves a miscreant. **57m/B VHS, Beta.** Frank "Junior" Coghlan, Elinor Fair, Wade Boteler; ***D:*** Elmer Clifton. *GPV, FCT*

Let Freedom Ring 🦴🦴½ **1939** Sappy, yet enjoyable patriotism that has lawyer Eddy returning to small hometown and fighting corruption. Hokey, but it works largely due to Hecht's fine script. ♫Dusty Road; Love Serenade; Home Sweet Home; When Irish Eyes Are Smiling; America; Pat Sez He; Where Else But Here; Funiculi Funicula; Ten Thousand Cattle Straying. **100m/B VHS.** Nelson Eddy, Virginia Bruce, Victor McLaglen, Lionel Barrymore, Edward Arnold, Guy Kibbee, Charles Butterworth, H.B. Warner, Raymond Walburn; ***D:*** Jack Conway; ***W:*** Ben Hecht. *MGM*

Let Him Have It 🦴🦴🦴½ **1991 (R)** Compelling, controversial film about a miscarriage of British justice. In 1952 Christopher Craig, 16, and Derek Bentley, 19, climbed onto the roof of a warehouse in an apparent burglary attempt. The police arrived and captured Bentley; Craig shot and wounded one policeman and killed another. According to testimony Bentley shouted "Let him have it" but did he mean shoot or give the officer the gun? Bentley, whose IQ was 66, was sentenced to death by the British courts—though he didn't commit the murder. The uproar over the sentence was reignited by this release, leading to a request for a reexamination of evidence and sentencing by the British Home Office. **115m/C VHS, LV.** *GB* Christopher Eccleston, Paul Reynolds, Tom Bell, Eileen Atkins, Clare Holman, Michael Elphick, Mark McGann, Tom Courtenay; ***D:*** Peter Medak. *NLC*

Let It Be 🦴🦴 **1970** Documentary look at a Beatles recording session, giving glimpses of the conflicts which led to their breakup. Features appearances by Yoko Ono and Billy Preston. **80m/C VHS, Beta, LV.** John Lennon, Paul McCartney, George Harrison, Ringo Starr, Billy Preston, Yoko Ono; ***D:*** Michael Lindsay-Hogg; ***M:*** The Beatles. Academy Awards '70: Best Original Score. *FOX*

Let It Ride 🦴🦴 **1989 (PG-13)** Dreyfuss is a small-time gambler who finally hits it big at the track. Some funny moments but generally a lame script cripples the cast, although the horses seem unaffected. Garr is okay as his wife who slips further into alcoholism with each race. **91m/C VHS, Beta, LV, 8mm.** Richard Dreyfuss, Teri Garr, David Johansen, Jennifer Tilly, Allen (Goorwitz) Garfield, Ed Walsh, Michelle Phillips, Mary Woronov, Robbie Coltrane, Richard Edson, Cynthia Nixon; ***D:*** Joe Pytka. *PAR*

Let It Rock 🦴 **1986** A maniacal promoter makes superstars out of his new band by staging publicity stunts. Not one of Hopper's better efforts. Filmed in Germany, but Roger Corman bought the U.S. rights and added clips from other movies before it was released here. **75m/C VHS, Beta.** *GE* Dennis Hopper, David Hess; ***D:*** Roland Klick. *MED*

L'Etat Sauvage 🦴🦴🦴½ *The Savage State* **1978** This French political thriller finds its heart in the middle of racism. The story unfolds around a newly independent African republic and a love affair between a black cabinet minister and a white Frenchwoman. Corruption abounds in this film based on George Conchon's award-winning novel. In French with English subtitles. **111m/C VHS, Beta, LV.** *FR* Marie-Christine Barrault, Claude Brasseur, Jacques Dutronc, Doura Mane, Michel Piccoli; ***D:*** Francois Girod. Cesar Awards '79: Best Sound. *INT, INJ, TPV*

Lethal Charm 🦴🦴 **1990** Two power-hungry journalists go head-to-head in the high stakes arena of Washington D.C. **92m/C VHS.** Barbara Eden, Heather Locklear. *LIV*

Lethal Games 🦴🦴 **1990** Stallone and Vaccaro lead a small community against a blood-thirsty band of criminals. **83m/C VHS.** Frank Stallone, Brenda Vaccaro, Dave Adams, Christopher Whalley, Heidi Paine, Karen Russell; ***D:*** John Bowen. *AIP*

Lethal Lolita—Amy Fisher: My Story 🦴🦴 *Amy Fisher: My Story* **1992** The only made-for-television Amy Fisher story out of three whose cast members even remotely resemble the real people—except of course actress Parker is actually pretty. Minor details aside, this account is Amy's story, purchased by NBC for an undisclosed amount, portraying her as an incest victim who gets involved with an opportunistic married jerk who drags her into prostitution, leading her to take out her frustration on his wife. If this is true, the obvious question is "why?"...to which she answers, "He loves me. We have great sex. And he fixes my car." Oh. See also: "The Amy Fisher Story" and "Casualties of Love: The 'Long Island Lolita' Story." **93m/C VHS.** Noelle Parker, Ed Marinaro, Kathleen Lasky, Boyd Kestner, Mary Ann Pascal, Lawrence Dane, Kate Lynch; ***D:*** Bradford May. *TTC*

Lethal Ninja 🦴 **1993 (R)** Kickboxers Joe and Pete set out to rescue Joe's wife from some third-world country overrun by ninjas. Hackneyed but lots of action for martial arts fans. **97m/C VHS, LV.** Ross Kettle, David Webb, Karyn Hill, Frank Notaro. *VMK*

Lethal Obsession 🦴½ *Der Joker* **1987 (R)** Two cops battle street crime and a powerful drug ring. Filmed in Germany. **100m/C VHS, Beta.** *GE* Michael York, Elliott Gould, Tahnee Welch, Peter Maffay, Armin Mueller-Stahl; ***D:*** Peter Patzak; ***M:*** Tony Carey. *VMK*

Lethal Pursuit 🦴 **1988** A popular singer who returns to the town where she grew up is tormented by her ex-boyfriend, a criminal. **90m/C VHS, Beta.** Mitzi Donahue, Blake Gahner, John Wildman; ***D:*** Donald M. Jones. *HMD*

Lethal Weapon 🦴🦴🦴 **1987 (R)** In Los Angeles, a cop nearing retirement (Glover) unwillingly begins work with a new partner (Gibson), a suicidal, semi-crazed risk-taker who seems determined to get the duo killed. Both Vietnam vets, the pair uncover a vicious heroin smuggling ring run by ruthless ex-Special Forces personnel. Packed with plenty of action, violence, and humorous undertones. Clapton's contributions to the musical score are an added bonus. Gibson and Glover work well together and give this movie extra punch. Followed by (so far) two sequels. **110m/C VHS, Beta, LV, 8mm.** Mel Gibson, Danny Glover, Gary Busey, Mitchell Ryan, Tom Atkins, Darlene Love, Traci Wolfe, Steve Kahan; ***D:*** Richard Donner; ***W:*** Shane Black; ***M:*** Michael Kamen, Eric Clapton. Nominations: Academy Awards '87: Best Sound. *WAR*

Lethal Weapon 2 🦴🦴🦴 **1989 (R)** This sequel to the popular cop adventure finds Gibson and Glover taking on a variety of blond South African "diplomats" who try to use their diplomatic immunity status to thwart the duo's efforts to crack their smuggling ring. Gibson finally finds romance, and viewers learn the truth about his late wife's accident. Also features the introduction of obnoxious, fast-talking con artist Leo ("OK, OK") Getz, adeptly played by Pesci, who becomes a third wheel to the crime-fighting team. Followed by a second sequel. **114m/C VHS, Beta, LV, 8mm.** Mel Gibson, Danny Glover, Joe Pesci, Joss Ackland, Derrick O'Connor, Patsy Kensit, Darlene Love, Traci Wolfe, Steve Kahan, Mary Ellen Trainor; ***D:*** Richard Donner; ***W:*** Jeffrey Boam; ***M:*** Michael Kamen, Eric Clapton, David Sanborn. *WAR*

Lethal Weapon 3 🦴🦴½ **1992 (R)** Murtaugh and Riggs return for more action in another slam-bang adventure. Murtaugh hopes his last week before retirement will be a peaceful one, but partner Riggs isn't about to let him go quietly. Not many changes from the successful formula with bickering buddies, lots of adventure, exploding buildings, a little comic relief from Pesci, and the addition of Russo as an Internal Affairs cop who proves to be more than a match for Riggs. **118m/C VHS, LV, 8mm.** Mel Gibson, Danny Glover, Joe Pesci, Rene Russo, Stuart Wilson, Steve Kahan, Darlene Love, Traci Wolfe, Gregory Millar, Jason Meshover-Iorg, Delores Hall; ***D:*** Richard Donner; ***W:*** Jeffrey Boam, Robert Mark Kamen; ***M:*** Michael Kamen, Eric Clapton, David Sanborn. MTV Movie Awards '93: Best On-Screen Duo (Mel Gibson/Danny Glover), Best Action Sequence. *WAR, PMS*

Lethal Woman 🦴½ **1988** A group of beautiful women, all once victimized by rapes, is recruited to an island by the "Lethal Woman," who plots revenge on any man who dares to vacation on the island. **96m/C VHS, Beta, LV.** Shannon Tweed, Merete Van Kamp. *NO*

Let's Dance 🦴🦴½ **1950** A young widow tries to protect her son from his wealthy, paternal grandmother, while Fred dances his way into her heart. More obscure Astaire vehicle, but as charming as the rest. Needless to say, great dancing. ♫Tunnel of Love; The Hyacinth; Piano Dance; Jack and the Beanstalk; Can't Stop Talking; Oh, Them Dudes; Why Fight the Feeling?. **112m/C VHS, Beta, LV.** Betty Hutton, Fred Astaire, Roland Young, Ruth Warrick, Shepperd Strudwick, Lucile Watson, Barton MacLane, Gregory Moffett, Melville Cooper; ***D:*** Norman Z. McLeod. *PAR*

Let's Do It Again 🦴½ **1975 (PG)** Atlanta milkman and his pal, a factory worker, milk two big-time gamblers out of a large sum of money in order to build a meeting hall for their fraternal lodge. Lesser sequel to "Uptown Saturday Night." **113m/C VHS, Beta.** Sidney Poitier, Bill Cosby, John Amos, Jimmie Walker, Ossie Davis, Denise Nicholas, Calvin Lockhart; ***D:*** Sidney Poitier; ***W:*** Richard Wesley. *WAR*

Let's Get Harry 🦴½ *The Rescue* **1987 (R)** Americans led by mercenaries mix it up with a Columbian cocaine franchise in an attempt to rescue their friend, Harry. Never released theatrically, for good reason. **107m/C VHS, Beta, LV.** Robert Duvall, Gary Busey, Michael Schoeffling, Tom Wilson, Glenn Frey, Rick Rossovich, Ben Johnson, Matt Clark, Mark Harmon, Gregory Sierra, Elpidia Carrillo; ***D:*** Alan Smithee; ***W:*** Samuel Fuller, Charles Robert Carner; ***M:*** Brad Fiedel. *HBO*

Let's Get Lost **1988** Absorbing documentary of Chet Baker, the prominent '50s "cool" jazz trumpeter (and occasional vocalist) who succumbed, like many of his peers, to drug addiction. Weber's black-and-white, fashion photography style well suits his subject. Downbeat, but rarely less than worthy. **125m/B VHS.** Chet Baker; ***D:*** Bruce Weber. Nominations: Academy Awards '88: Best Feature Documentary. *MVD, COL*

Let's Get Married 🦴 **1963** A young doctor's weakness under pressure brings him to the brink of babbling idiocy when his wife goes into early labor. **90m/B VHS, Beta.** Anthony Newley, Ann Aubrey. *NO*

Let's Get Tough 🦴 **1942** The East Side Kids, unable to enlist because of their age, harass local Oriental shopkeepers and eventually get involved with a murder. **52m/B VHS, Beta, 8mm.** Leo Gorcey, Bobby Jordan, Huntz Hall, Gabriel Dell, Sammy Morrison; ***D:*** Wallace Fox. *VYY, NOS, RXM*

Let's Go! 🦴½ **1923** The son of a cement company president sets out to prove his worth to the firm by landing a contract with the town of Hillsboro. For some unknown reason, he sets off on an amazing set of stunts. Silent with original organ music. **79m/B VHS, Beta, 8mm.** Richard Talmadge, Hal Clements, Eileen Percy, Tully Marshall; ***D:*** William K. Howard. *VYY, GPV, GVV*

Let's Go Collegiate 🦴½ **1941** Two college rowers promise their girlfriends that they'll win the big race, but their plans are almost frustrated when their best oarsman is drafted. Their only hope lies in replacing him with a truck driver. ♫Look What You've Done To Me; Sweet 16; Let's Do A Little Dreaming. **62m/B VHS.** Frankie Darro, Marcia Mae Jones, Jackie Moran, Keye Luke, Mantan Moreland, Gale Storm; ***D:*** Jean Yarbrough. *NOS*

Let's Kill All the Lawyers 🦴🦴½ **1993** Low-budget satire about one man's angst over whether to become a lawyer is witty, entertaining, and not just for legal eagles. Law-firm intern Foster Merkul (Frederick) is apprenticed to a sleazeball (Vezina) who teaches him that money—not justice—is the name of the game in the law biz. Growing increasingly disillusioned, Foster sets out to reform the system with the help of Satori, a beautiful and mysterious creature of his imagination. Shot at sites in and around Detroit, this independent production features lots of cameos by local media celebrities. **?m/C VHS.** Rick Frederick, James Vezina, Michelle De Vuono, Maggie Patton, Marty Smith; ***D:*** Ron Senkowski; ***W:*** Ron Senkowski. *NYR*

Let's Make It Legal 🦴🦴½ **1951** Amusing comedy of a married couple who decide to get a divorce after 20 years of marriage. Colbert stars as the woman who decides to leave her husband, Carey, because he's a chronic gambler. They part as friends, but soon Colbert's old flame, Scott, is back in town and things get rather complicated. A solid cast serves as the main strength in this film. **77m/B VHS.** Claudette Colbert, MacDonald Carey, Zachary Scott, Barbara Bates, Robert Wagner, Marilyn Monroe; ***D:*** Richard Sale; ***W:*** F. Hugh Herbert. *FXV*

Let's Make Love 🦴🦴½ **1960** An urbane millionaire discovers he is to be parodied in an off-Broadway play, and vows to stop it—until he falls in love with the star of the show. He then ends up acting in the play. ♫My Heart Belongs to Daddy; Let's Make Love; Specialization; Incurably Romantic; Sing Me a Song That Sells; You With the Crazy Eyes; Give Me the Simple Life. **118m/C VHS, Beta.** Yves Montand, Marilyn Monroe, Tony Randall, Frankie Vaughan, Bing Crosby, Gene Kelly, Milton Berle; ***D:*** George Cukor; ***C:*** Daniel F. Fapp. Nominations: Academy Awards '60: Best Original Score. *FOX*

Let's Make Up 🦴🦴 *Lilacs in the Spring* **1955** When it comes to giving her heart, Neagle can't decide between two dashing men. **94m/C VHS.** *GB* Errol Flynn, Anna Neagle, David Farrar, Kathleen Harrison, Peter Graves; ***D:*** Herbert Wilcox. *GKK, MLB, MRV*

Let's Scare Jessica to Death 🦴🦴 **1971 (PG)** A young woman who was recently released from a mental hospital is subjected to unspeakable happenings at a country home with her friends. She encounters murder, vampires, and corpses coming out of nowhere. A supernatural thriller with quite a few genuine scares. **89m/C VHS, Beta.** Zohra Lampert, Barton Heyman, Kevin J. O'Connor, Gretchen Corbett, Alan Manson; ***D:*** John Hancock. *PAR*

Let's Sing Again 🦴🦴 **1936** Eight-year-old singing sensation Bobby Breen made his debut in this dusty musical vehicle, as a runaway orphan who becomes the pal of a washed-up opera star in a traveling show. ♫Let's Sing Again; Lullaby; Farmer in the Dell; La Donna e Mobile. **70m/B VHS.** Bobby Breen, Henry Armetta, George Houston, Vivienne Osborne, Grant Withers, Inez Courtney, Lucien Littlefield; ***D:*** Kurt Neumann. *NOS, LOO, DVT*

The Letter 🦴🦴🦴🦴 **1940** When a man is shot and killed on a Malaysian plantation, the woman who committed the murder pleads self-defense. Her husband and his lawyer attempt to free her, but find more than they expected in this tightly-paced film noir. Based on the novel by W. Somerset Maugham. Davis emulated the originator of her role, Jeanne Eagels, in her mannerisms and line readings, although Eagels later went mad from drug abuse and overwork. **96m/B VHS, Beta, LV.** Bette Davis, Herbert Marshall, James Stephenson, Gale Sondergaard, Bruce Lester, Cecil Kellaway, Victor Sen Yung, Frieda Inescort; ***D:*** William Wyler; ***W:*** Howard Koch; ***C:*** Gaetano Antonio "Tony" Gaudio; ***M:*** Max Steiner. Nominations: Academy Awards '40: Best Actor (Stephenson), Best Actress (Davis), Best Black and White Cinematography, Best Director (Wyler), Best Picture. *FOX, MGM*

Letter from an Unknown Woman 🦴🦴🦴 **1948** A woman falls in love with a concert pianist on the eve of his departure. He promises to return but never does. The story is told in flashbacks as the pianist reads a letter from the woman. A great romantic melodrama. **90m/B VHS, LV.** Joan Fontaine, Louis Jourdan, Mady Christians, Marcel Journet, Art Smith; ***D:*** Max Ophuls. *REP*

Letter of Introduction 🦴🦴½ **1938** A struggling young actress learns that her father is really a well known screen star and agrees not to reveal the news to the public. **104m/B VHS, Beta.** Adolphe Menjou, Edgar Bergen, George Murphy, Eve Arden, Ann Sheridan, Andrea Leeds; ***D:*** John M. Stahl; ***C:*** Karl Freund. *NOS, MRV, HHT*

Letter to Brezhnev 🦴🦴🦴 **1986 (R)** Acclaimed independent film about two working-class Liverpool girls who fall in love with two furloughed Russian sailors. When the men eventually return to the USSR, one of the girls contacts the Russian Secretary General in an effort to rejoin her lover. Amusing tale of different relationships. **94m/C VHS, Beta, LV.** *GB* Margi Clarke, Alexandra Pigg, Peter Firth, Ken Campbell, Tracy Lea, Alfred Molina, Angela Clarke; ***D:*** Chris Bernard; ***W:*** Frank Clarke; ***M:*** Alan Gill. *ORI, IME, WAR*

Letter to My Killer 🦴🦴½ **1995 (PG-13)** Construction worker Nick Parma (Chinlund) finds an unmailed letter in a demolished building, which he and wife Judy (Winningham) discover is 30 years old. The woman letter writer is describing major fraud and when Judy learns that she was murdered, she and Nick decide to blackmail the probable suspects—a powerful business cartel. But if they killed once..... Made for cable movie. **92m/C VHS.** Mare Winningham, Nicholas Chinlund, Rip Torn, Josef Sommer, Eddie Jones, Dey Young; ***D:*** Janet Meyers; ***W:*** Norman Strum; ***C:*** Stephen M. Katz. *MCA*

A Letter to Three Wives 🦴🦴🦴🦴 **1949** Crain, Darnell, and Sothern star as three friends who, shortly before embarking on a Hudson River boat trip, each receive a letter from Holm (who's never shown), the fourth member in their set. The letter tells them that she has run off with one of their husbands but does not specify his identity. The women spend the rest of the trip reviewing their sometimes shaky unions which provides some of the funniest and most caustic scenes, including Douglas (as Sothern's husband) ranting against the advertising business which supports his wife's radio soap opera. Sharp dialogue, moving performances. Based on the novel by John Klempner. Remade for television in 1985. **103m/B VHS, Beta, LV.** Jeanne Crain, Linda Darnell, Ann Sothern, Kirk Douglas, Paul Douglas, Jeffrey Lynn, Thelma Ritter, Barbara Lawrence, Connie Gilchrist, Florence Bates; ***D:*** Joseph L. Mankiewicz; ***W:*** Joseph L. Mankiewicz; ***C:*** Arthur C. Miller; ***M:*** Alfred Newman; ***V:*** Celeste Holm. Academy Awards '49: Best Director (Mankiewicz), Best Screenplay (Mankiewicz); Nominations: Academy Awards '49: Best Picture. *FXV*

Letters from My Windmill 🦴🦴🦴½ **1954** A series of three short stories: "The Three Low Masses," "The Elixir of Father Gaucher," and "The Secret of Master Cornille" from respected director Pagnol. The unique format only enhances this film. In French with English subtitles. **116m/B VHS.** *FR* Henri Velbert, Yvonne Gamy, Robert Vattier, Roger Crouzet; ***D:*** Marcel Pagnol. *NOS, DVT, APD*

Letters from the Park 🦴🦴🦴 **1988** In Cuba, 1913, two taciturn would-be lovers hire a poet, Victor La Place, to write love letters to each other. Normal proboscis aside, the poet follows the fate of Cyrano, and finds himself the unhappy hypotenuse in a triangular romance. Based on an original story by Marquez; made for Spanish television. In Spanish with English subtitles. **85m/C VHS.** *CU* Victor Laplace, Ivonne Lopez, Miguel Paneque; ***D:*** Thomas Gutierrez Alea; ***W:*** Gabriel Garcia Marquez, Thomas Gutierrez Alea. *FXL, FCT, APD*

Letters to an Unknown Lover 🦴🦴½ *Les Louves* **1984** During WWII, a man and woman engage in sexual and emotional combat. **101m/C VHS, Beta.** *GB FR* Cherie Lunghi, Mathilda May, Yves Beneyton, Ralph Bates; ***D:*** Peter Duffell. *ACA*

Letting Go 🦴🦴 **1985 (PG)** Made for television comedy-drama about a broken-hearted career woman and a young widower who fall in love. **94m/C VHS, Beta.** John Ritter, Sharon Gless, Joe Cortese; ***D:*** Jack Bender. *AIP*

Letting the Birds Go Free **1986** When a stranger is caught stealing from a farmer's barn, the farmer and his son decide to let the villain work off his crime. Some very interesting relationships develop from this arrangement. **60m/C VHS.** Lionel Jeffries. *PSM*

Leviathan 🦴🦴 **1989 (R)** A motley crew of ocean-floor miners are trapped when they are accidentally exposed to a failed Soviet experiment that turns humans into insatiable, regenerating fish-creatures. **98m/C VHS, Beta, LV.** Peter Weller, Ernie Hudson, Hector Elizondo, Amanda Pays, Richard Crenna, Daniel Stern, Lisa Eilbacher, Michael Carmine, Meg Foster; ***D:*** George P. Cosmatos; ***W:*** David Peoples, Jeb Stuart; ***M:*** Jerry Goldsmith. *MGM*

L'Homme Blesse 🦴🦴🦴 *The Wounded Man* **1983** A serious erotic film about an 18-year-old boy, cloistered by an overbearing family, and his sudden awakening to his own homosexuality. Anglade's film debut. In French with English subtitles. **90m/C VHS, Beta.** *FR* Jean-Hugues Anglade, Roland Bertin, Vittorio Mezzogiorno; ***D:*** Patrice Chereau. Cesar Awards '84: Best Writing; Nominations: Cannes Film Festival '83: Best Film; Cesar Awards '83: Best Supporting Actor (Anglade). *TPV, INJ, CCN*

Liana, Jungle Goddess 🦴🦴 **1956** A variation on the Greystoke legend featuring a beautiful (and topless) jungle goddess who is discovered living in the wilds of Africa. Thinking that she may be the lost granddaughter of a wealthy English nobleman, she's brought back to London for a reunion. Will civilization prove to be as dangerous as the jungle? **?m/C VHS.** Marion Michael, Hardy Kruger. *SNC*

Lianna 🦴🦴🦴 **1983 (R)** Acclaimed screenwriter/director John Sayles wrote and directed this story of a woman's romantic involvement with another woman. Chronicles an unhappy homemaker's awakening to the feelings of love that she develops for a female professor. Sayles makes an appearance as a family friend. **110m/C VHS, Beta.** Jon DeVries, Linda Griffiths, Jane Hallaren, Jo Henderson, Jessica Wright MacDonald; ***Cameos:*** John Sayles; ***D:*** John Sayles; ***W:*** John Sayles; ***M:*** Mason Daring. *VES*

The Liars 🦴🦴 **1964** Mystery in which a Frenchman strikes it rich in Africa, then returns home to Paris in search of a wife. He advertisies for a mate, but is set up by con artists instead. In French with English subtitles. **92m/C VHS.** Dawn Addams, Jean Servais; ***D:*** Edmond T. Greville. *FCT, INJ*

The Liar's Club 🦴½ **1993 (R)** High-school football teammates try to cover up a rape and wind up involved in murder. **100m/C VHS.** Wil Wheaton, Brian Krause, Soleil Moon Frye, Jennifer Burns, Michael Cudlitz, Bruce Weitz; ***D:*** Jeffrey Porter. *NHO*

Liar's Edge 🦴🦴 **1992 (R)** Tweed portrays a single mother whose teenaged son, Mark, is plagued by violent fantasies. When she remarries and her new husband and sleazy brother-in-law move in, Mark's hallucinations become stronger until he believes he's witnessed a murder. The murder turns out to be a fact and his new stepfather is involved but can Mark prove it. Filmed on location in Niagra Falls. **97m/C VHS, LV.** Shannon Tweed, Nicholas Shields, David Keith, Joseph Bottoms, Christopher Plummer; ***D:*** Ron Oliver; ***W:*** Ron Oliver. *NLC, IME*

Liar's Moon 🦴🦴 **1982 (PG)** A local boy woos and weds the town's wealthiest young lady, only to be trapped in family intrigue. **106m/C VHS, Beta.** Cindy Fisher, Matt Dillon, Christopher Connelly, Susan Tyrrell; ***D:*** David Fisher. *VES*

Libeled Lady 🦴🦴🦴½ **1936** A fast, complicated screwball masterwork, dealing with a newspaper editor's efforts to get something on a bratty heiress with the help of his own fiancee and a reporter he recently fired. One of the era's funniest Hollywood films. Remade in 1946 as "Easy to Wed." **98m/B VHS, Beta, LV.** Myrna Loy, Spencer Tracy, Jean Harlow, William Powell, Walter Connolly, Charley Grapewin, Cora Witherspoon, E.E. Clive, Charles Trowbridge, Dennis O'Keefe, Hattie McDaniel; ***D:*** Jack Conway. Nominations: Academy Awards '36: Best Picture. *MGM*

The Liberation of L.B. Jones 🦴🦴 **1970 (R)** A wealthy black undertaker wants a divorce from his wife, who is having an affair with a white policeman. Wyler's final film. **101m/C VHS, Beta.** Lee J. Cobb, Lola Falana, Barbara Hershey, Anthony Zerbe, Roscoe Lee Browne; ***D:*** William Wyler; ***W:*** Stirling Silliphant; ***M:*** Elmer Bernstein. *COL, FCT*

Liberators 🦴 **1977** Kinski stars as a criminal soldier battling with the American authorities, German troops, and his fugitive partner. **91m/C VHS, Beta.** Klaus Kinski. *UNI*

Liberty & Bash **1990 (R)** Two boyhood friends who served together in Vietnam reunite to rid their neighborhood of drug pushers and save the life of a friend. **92m/C VHS, Beta.** Miles O'Keeffe, Lou Ferrigno, Mitzi Kapture, Richard Eden, Cheryl Paris, Gary Conway; ***D:*** Myrl A. Schreibman. *FRH*

License to Drive **1988 (PG-13)** When teen Haim fails the road test for his all-important driver's license, he steals the family car for a hot date with the girl of his dreams. The evening starts out quietly enough, but things soon go awry. If Haim survives the weekend, he'll definitely be able to pass his driving test on Monday morning. Semi-funny in a demolition derby sort of way. **90m/C VHS, Beta, LV.** Corey Feldman, Corey Haim, Carol Kane, Richard Masur; ***D:*** Greg Beeman; ***C:*** Bruce Surtees; ***M:*** Jay Michael Ferguson. *FOX*

License to Kill **1964** Constantine stars as Agent Nick Carter involved with Oriental spies and a new secret weapon. **100m/C VHS.** *FR* Eddie Constantine, Yvonne Monlaur, Paul Frankeur; ***D:*** Henri Decoin. *SNC*

License to Kill **1984** A young girl is killed by a drunk driver, devastating both families. A made-for-television movie with a strong message against drinking and driving. **96m/C VHS, Beta, LV.** James Farentino, Don Murray, Penny Fuller, Millie Perkins, Donald Moffat, Denzel Washington, Ari Meyers; ***D:*** Jud Taylor. *GEM*

License to Kill **1989 (PG-13)** Dalton's second Bond effort, in which drug lords try to kill 007's best friend and former CIA agent. Disobeying orders for the first time and operating without his infamous "license to kill," Bond goes after the fiends. Fine outing for Dalton (and Bond, too). **133m/C VHS, Beta, LV.** *GB* Timothy Dalton, Carey Lowell, Robert Davi, Frank McRae, Talisa Soto, David Hedison, Anthony Zerbe, Everett McGill, Wayne Newton, Benicio Del Toro, Desmond Llewelyn, Priscilla Barnes; ***D:*** John Glen; ***W:*** Michael G. Wilson, Richard Maibaum; ***M:*** Michael Kamen. *FOX, MGM*

L'Idiot *The Idiot* **1946** Smooth adaptation of Dostoevsky's novel about noble Prince Mishkin's (Philipe) attempts to bring peace to the life of tormented Nastasia Filipovna (Feuillere). First feature for Lampin; French with subtitles. **98m/B VHS.** *FR* Gerard Philipe, Edwige Feuillere, Lucien Coedel, Nathalie Nattier, Marguerite Moreno; ***D:*** Georges Lampin; ***W:*** Charles Spaak; ***C:*** Christian Matras; ***M:*** Maurice Thiriet. *FCT*

Lie Down with Dogs **1995 (R)** You will wake up with fleas if you watch this dull, very low-budget comedy about young Tommie (White), who heads out of New York for some summer fun in the gay-friendly resort of Provincetown, Massachusetts. There's lots of temporary (discreetly filmed) encounters but no lasting romance and Tommie heads back to the Big Apple at season's end satisfied but no wiser. White's debut film. **85m/C VHS.** Wally White, Randy Becker, Darren Dryden; ***D:*** Wally White; ***W:*** Wally White; ***C:*** George Mitas. *TOU*

Lie Down with Lions ½ **1994** Long and dull TV adaptation of the Ken Follett spy novel. American nurse Kate Neeson (Helgenberger) is aghast when she discovers her lover, Jack Carver (Dalton), is a CIA agent. She marries Czech doctor Peter Husak (Havers) on the rebound and the newleyweds travel to Azerbijan to run a clinic, where Kate has a baby. But Jack's not out of the picture since his current assignment takes him into the war-torn region—and back into Kate's life, especially when he discovers Peter is not what he seems. **240m/C VHS.** Timothy Dalton, Marg Helgenberger, Nigel Havers, Omar Sharif, Kabir Bedi, Juergen Prochnow; ***D:*** Jim Goddard; ***W:*** Guy Andrews, Julian Bond; ***C:*** Eddy van der Enden. *NYR*

Liebestraum **1991 (R)** An architectural expert, his old college friend and the friend's wife form a dangerous triangle of passion and lust that strangely duplicates a situation that led to a double murder forty years earlier. The unrated version clocks in at 116 minutes. **109m/C VHS, LV.** Kevin Anderson, Bill Pullman, Pamela Gidley, Kim Novak; ***D:*** Mike Figgis; ***W:*** Mike Figgis. *MGM*

Lies ½ **1983 (PG)** Complicated mystery about a murder/thriller movie plot becoming reality as it is being filmed, revolving around a scam to collect an inheritance from a rich guy in a mental hospital. **93m/C VHS, Beta.** *GB* Ann Dusenberry, Gail Strickland, Bruce Davison, Clu Gulager, Bert Remsen, Dick Miller; ***D:*** Ken Wheat, Jim Wheat. *FOX*

Lies Before Kisses **1992 (PG-13)** A woman finds out her loving husband has been spending time with a beautiful call girl. When the call girl is murdered the husband is accused. His wife decides to help him clear his name but she just may have her own type of revenge in mind. **93m/C VHS, Beta.** Jaclyn Smith, Ben Gazzara, Nick Mancuso, Greg Evigan, Penny Fuller, James Karen; ***D:*** Lou Antonio; ***W:*** Ellen Weston. *TTC, PMS*

Lies My Father Told Me **1975 (PG)** Simple drama about growing up in the 1920s in a Jewish ghetto. The story revolves around a young boy's relationship with his immigrant grandfather. Quiet and moving. **102m/C VHS.** *CA* Yossi Yadin, Len Birman, Marilyn Lightstone, Jeffery Lynas; ***D:*** Jan Kadar; ***W:*** Ted Allan. Golden Globe Awards '76: Best Foreign Film; Nominations: Academy Awards '75: Best Original Screenplay. *NO*

Lies of the Twins **1991** A beautiful model becomes involved with her therapist and his identical, and irresponsible, twin brother. **93m/C VHS.** Isabella Rossellini, Aidan Quinn, Iman, John Pleshette; ***D:*** Tim Hunter. *MCA*

Lt. Robin Crusoe, U.S.N. **1966 (G)** A lighthearted navy pilot crash lands amusingly on a tropical island, falls hard for an island babe and schemes intensely against the local evil ruler. Lackluster Disney debacle. **113m/C VHS, Beta.** Dick Van Dyke, Nancy Kwan, Akim Tamiroff; ***D:*** Byron Paul; ***M:*** Robert F. Brunner. *DIS, OM*

The Life and Adventures of Nicholas Nickleby ½ *Nicholas Nickleby* **1981** Nine-hour performance of the 1838 Dickens' tale by the Royal Shakespeare Company, featuring the work of 39 actors portraying 150 characters. Wonderful performances are characterized by frantic action and smoothly meshing intertwining plots, focusing on the trials and tribulations of the Nickleby family, amidst wealth, poverty, and injustice in Victorian England. Nine cassettes. **540m/C VHS.** *GB* Roger Rees, David Thewlis, Emily Richard, John Woodvine; ***D:*** Jim Goddard; ***W:*** David Edgar; ***M:*** Stephen Oliver. *AAE, FOX, FHS*

The Life and Assassination of the Kingfish **1976** Recommended by the NEA, this story of Louisiana politician Huey Long is riveting. Asner gives a profound performance. **96m/C VHS, Beta.** Ed Asner, Nicholas Pryor, Diane Kagan; ***D:*** Robert Collins. *NO*

The Life and Death of Colonel Blimp *Colonel Blimp* **1943** Chronicles the life of a British soldier who survives three wars (Boer, WWI, and WWII), falls in love with three women (all portrayed by Kerr), and dances a fine waltz. Fine direction and performance abound. **115m/C VHS, Beta, LV.** *GB* Roger Livesey, Deborah Kerr, Anton Walbrook, Ursula Jeans, Albert Lieven; ***D:*** Michael Powell, Emeric Pressburger; ***C:*** Georges Perinal. *NO*

The Life and Loves of Mozart ½ **1959** Despite the title, this is really about the great composer's later life at the time of the premiere of "Die Zauberfloete" ("The Magic Flute"). This is only partly saved by a stellar performance from Werner, as well as the music. Other than that, it gets bogged down in titillation about W.A.M.'s romantic life. In German with English subtitles. **87m/C VHS.** Oskar Werner, Johanna Matz, Angelika Hauff; ***D:*** Karl Hartl; ***V:*** Anton Dermota. *NOS, VEC*

Life and Nothing But ½ *La Vie est Rien d'Autre* **1989 (PG)** Two young women search for their lovers at the end of WWI. They're helped by a French officer brutalized by the war and driven to find all of France's casualties. Romantic, evocative, and saddening. In French with English subtitles. **135m/C VHS, Beta.** *FR* Philippe Noiret, Sabine Azema, Francoise Perrot; ***D:*** Bertrand Tavernier; ***W:*** Bertrand Tavernier. British Academy Awards '89: Best Foreign Film; Cesar Awards '90: Best Actor (Noiret), Best Score; Los Angeles Film Critics Association Awards '90: Best Foreign Film. *ORI, FCT, INJ*

Life & Times of Grizzly Adams **1974 (G)** Lightweight family adventure film based on the rugged life of legendary frontiersman, Grizzly Adams, that served as the launching pad for the TV series. Grizzly is mistakenly chased for a crime he didn't commit and along the way befriends a big bear. **93m/C VHS, Beta.** Dan Haggerty, Denver Pyle, Lisa Jones, Marjorie Harper, Don Shanks; ***D:*** Richard Friedenberg. *NO*

Life & Times of Judge Roy Bean ½ **1972 (PG)** Based on the life of the famed Texas "hanging judge," the film features Newman as the legendary Bean who dispenses frontier justice in the days of the Wild West. Filled with gallows humor. Gardner sparkles as actress Lily Langtry. **124m/C VHS, Beta, LV.** Paul Newman, Stacy Keach, Ava Gardner, Jacqueline Bisset, Anthony Perkins, Roddy McDowall, Victoria Principal; ***D:*** John Huston; ***W:*** John Milius; ***M:*** Maurice Jarre. Nominations: Academy Awards '72: Best Song ("Marmalade, Molasses & Honey"). *WAR*

The Life & Times of the Chocolate Killer ½ **1988** Police turn against the hand that's helped them save property and lives, by framing a good samaritan with deeds done by the "Chocolate Killer." **75m/C VHS.** Michael Adrian, Rod Browning, Tabi Cooper. *VMK*

Life Begins for Andy Hardy **1941** Andy gets a job in New York before entering college and finds the working world to be a sobering experience. Surprisingly downbeat and hard-hitting for an Andy Hardy film. Garland's last appearance in the series. **100m/B VHS, Beta.** Mickey Rooney, Judy Garland, Lewis Stone, Ann Rutherford, Fay Holden, Gene Reynolds, Ralph Byrd; ***D:*** George B. Seitz. *MGM*

A Life in the Theater ½ **1993** Life in the theater as a hammy stage veteran (Lemmon) shares his experiences (and his dressing room) with a callow newcomer (Broderick). Petty squabbles, missed cues, and rare candor are displayed as the two stage scenes from their various repertory. Gentle, slight Mamet play, written when he was 25. Made for television. **78m/C VHS, LV.** Jack Lemmon, Matthew Broderick; ***D:*** Gregory Mosher; ***W:*** David Mamet. *TTC*

Life is a Circus, Charlie Brown/ You're the Greatest, Charlie Brown **1980** Two Peanuts favorites appear on this tape. In the Emmy award-winning "Life Is a Circus, Charlie Brown," Snoopy falls in love with Fifi, a French poodle circus performer, and winds up as a member of the traveling circus. In "You're the Greatest, Charlie Brown," our hero has a chance to win a decathlon in the Junior Olympics. With Peppermint Patty coaching, anything can happen! **60m/C VHS, Beta.** ***D:*** Phil Roman. *SHV, VTR, WTA*

Life Is a Long Quiet River *La Vie Est Une Longue Fleuve Tranquille* **1988** Social comedy about a nurse who, infuriated with her married doctor employer/lover, switches two babies at birth. Twelve years later, after her lover's wife has died and he still refuses to marry her, she reveals the swap. The children are returned to their rightful families causing a multitude of confusion and adjustment. Directorial debut of Chatiliez. In French with English subtitles. **89m/C VHS.** *FR* Benoit Magimel, Helene Vincent, Andre Wilms, Daniel Gelin, Catherine Hiegel, Christine Pignet, Patrick Bouchitey, Valerie Lalande, Tara Romer, Jerome Floch, Sylvie Cubertafon; ***D:*** Etienne Chatiliez; ***W:*** Florence Quentin, Etienne Chatiliez; ***M:*** Gerard Kawczynski. Cesar Awards '89: Best Supporting Actress (Vincent), Best Writing. *NYF, FCT*

Life Is Beautiful ½ **1979** A politically neutral man is arrested and tortured in pre-revolutionary Lisbon, and forced to make, and act on, a political commitment. Dubbed. **102m/C VHS, Beta.** *PT* Giancarlo Giannini, Ornella Muti; ***D:*** Grigorij Ciukhrai. *NWV*

Life Is Sweet ☙☙☙½ **1990 (R)** The consuming passions of food and drink focus the lives of an oddball English working-class family beset by hopeless dreams and passions. Mother is always fixing family meals—in between helping her friend open a gourmet restaurant which features such revolting dishes as pork cyst and prune quiche. Dad is a chef who buys a snack truck and dreams of life on the road. Natalie and Nicola, the grown twins, eat their meals in front of the television but Nicola is also a bulimic who binges and purges on chocolate bars behind her bedroom door. (Note the chocolate scene between Nicola and her boyfriend). An affectionate, if sometimes unattractive, look at a chaotic family. **103m/C VHS, LV.** *GB* Alison Steadman, Jane Horrocks, Jim Broadbent, Claire Skinner, Timothy Spall, Stephen Rea, David Thewlis; ***D:*** Mike Leigh; ***W:*** Mike Leigh. Los Angeles Film Critics Association Awards '91: Best Supporting Actress (Horrocks); National Society of Film Critics Awards '91: Best Actress (Steadman), Best Film, Best Supporting Actress (Horrocks). *REP, BTV*

The Life of Emile Zola ☙☙☙½ **1937** Writer Emile Zola intervenes in the case of Alfred Dreyfus who was sent to Devil's Island for a crime he did not commit. Well-crafted production featuring a handsome performance from Muni. **117m/B VHS, Beta, LV.** Paul Muni, Gale Sondergaard, Gloria Holden, Joseph Schildkraut; ***D:*** William Dieterle; ***C:*** Gaetano Antonio "Tony" Gaudio; ***M:*** Max Steiner. Academy Awards '37: Best Picture, Best Screenplay, Best Supporting Actor (Schildkraut); Nominations: Academy Awards '37: Best Actor (Muni), Best Director (Dieterle), Best Interior Decoration, Best Sound, Best Story, Best Original Score. *MGM, BTV*

A Life of Her Own ☙☙½ **1950** Turner stars as a farm girl who takes her dream of becoming a top model to the Big Apple. She signs with an agency and is befriended by Dvorak, an aging model, who acts as her mentor. Turner finds success and is soon the toast of the town until she gets involved with a married man (Milland) and her life starts to crumble. Average soap opera with flimsy script. Turner is good, but Dvorak steals the show in her role as an over-the-hill fashion plate. **108m/B VHS.** Lana Turner, Ray Milland, Tom Ewell, Louis Calhern, Ann Dvorak, Barry Sullivan, Jean Hagen, Phyllis Kirk, Sara Haden; ***D:*** George Cukor; ***W:*** Isobel Lennart. *MGM*

Life of Oharu ☙☙☙½ *Diary of Oharu; Saikaku Ichidai Onna* **1952** A near masterpiece rivaled only by "Ugetsu" in the Mizoguchi canon, this film details the slow and agonizing moral decline of a woman in feudal Japan, from wife to concubine to prostitute. A scathing portrait of social pre-destination based on a novel by Ibara Saikaku. In Japanese with English subtitles. **136m/B VHS, Beta.** *JP* Kinuyo Tanaka, Toshiro Mifune; ***D:*** Kenji Mizoguchi. *VYY, APD, INJ*

A Life of Sin ☙☙ **1992 (R)** Scandalous drama about an impoverished Caribbean girl who rises to wealth and power as a world-famous madame. Colon stars as the beautiful Isabel, who is betrayed by her childhood friend Paulo (Julia) and rejected by the Catholic bishop (Ferrer) in this tragic story of passion and greed. **112m/C VHS.** Raul Julia, Miriam Colon, Jose Ferrer; ***D:*** Efrain Lopez Neris; ***W:*** Emilio Diaz Valcarcel. *COL, PMS*

Life of Verdi **1984** Epic mini-series biography of the famous composer, with many excerpts of his music sung by Luciano Pavarotti, Renata Telbaldi, and Maria Callas. Made for television. **600m/B VHS, Beta.** *IT* Ronald Pickup, Carla Fracci. *HMV, KUL, MVD*

Life on a String ☙☙ **1990** Set in the distant past, this is a lyrical story of a young boy searching for a cure for his blindness. His possible cure involves a myth which requires him to devote his life to music and the breaking of 1000 strings on a banjo. Adapted from a story by Shi Tiesheng. In Chinese with English subtitles. **110m/C VHS.** *CH* ***D:*** Chen Kaige; ***C:*** Gu Changwei. *FCT, KIV*

Life 101 ☙☙½ **1995** Innocent freshman Haim tries to adjust to college life in the sixties, aided by his hippie roommate Coogan, who introduces Haim to the pleasures of life. Innocuous coming of age comedy. **95m/C VHS.** Corey Haim, Keith Coogan, Ami Dolenz; ***D:*** Redge Mahaffey. *MNC*

Life Stinks ☙ **1991 (PG-13)** So does the film. A grasping tycoon bets he can spend a month living on the street without money, resulting in cheap laughs, heavy-handed sentiment and one musical number. Those expecting the innovative, hilarious Brooks of "Young Frankenstein" or "Blazing Saddles" will be very disappointed—these jokes are stale and the timing is tedious. Those looking for a Chaplinesque tale for modern times should stick with Chaplin. **93m/C VHS, Beta, LV.** Mel Brooks, Jeffrey Tambor, Lesley Ann Warren, Stuart Pankin, Howard Morris, Teddy Wilson, Michael Ensign, Billy Barty, Carmine Caridi, Rudy DeLuca; ***D:*** Mel Brooks; ***W:*** Mel Brooks, Rudy DeLuca; ***C:*** Steven Poster. *MGM*

Life with Father ☙☙☙½ **1947** Based on the writings of the late Clarence Day, Jr., this is the story of his childhood in New York City during the 1880s. A delightful saga about a stern but loving father and his relationship with his knowing wife and four red-headed sons. **118m/C VHS, Beta.** William Powell, Irene Dunne, Elizabeth Taylor, Edmund Gwenn, ZaSu Pitts, Jimmy Lydon, Martin Milner; ***D:*** Michael Curtiz; ***M:*** Max Steiner. Golden Globe Awards '48: Best Score; New York Film Critics Awards '47: Best Actor (Powell); Nominations: Academy Awards '47: Best Actor (Powell), Best Art Direction/Set Decoration (Color), Best Color Cinematography. *CNG, MRV, NOS*

Life with Mikey ☙☙½ **1993 (PG-13)** Michael "Mikey" Chapman (Fox) is a washed-up former child star who now half-heartedly runs a minor talent agency for other pint-sized would-be thespians. Ever mindful of his previous glory, he believes he is doomed to obscurity when a 10-year-old Brooklyn pickpocket reanimates his taste for life. Light, sweet comedy is generally predictable, a typical Fox effort. Unbilled cameo from Reuben Blades as Vidal's father. **92m/C VHS, Beta, LV.** Michael J. Fox, Christina Vidal, Cyndi Lauper, Nathan Lane, David Huddleston, Victor Garber, David Krumholtz, Tony Hendra; ***Cameos:*** Ruben Blades; ***D:*** James Lapine; ***W:*** Marc Lawrence; ***M:*** Alan Menken. *TOU, BTV*

Lifeboat ☙☙☙½ **1944** When a German U-boat sinks a freighter during WWII, the eight survivors seek refuge in a tiny lifeboat. Tension peaks after the drifting passengers take in a stranded Nazi. Hitchcock saw a great challenge in having the entire story take place in a lifeboat and pulled it off with his usual flourish. In 1989, the film "Dead Calm" replicated the technique. From a story by John Steinbeck. Bankhead shines. **96m/B VHS, Beta, LV.** Tallulah Bankhead, John Hodiak, William Bendix, Canada Lee, Walter Slezak, Hume Cronyn, Henry Hull, Mary Anderson; ***D:*** Alfred Hitchcock. National Board of Review Awards '44: 10 Best Films of the Year; New York Film Critics Awards '44: Best Actress (Bankhead); Nominations: Academy Awards '44: Best Director (Hitchcock). *HMV, FOX*

Lifeforce ☙☙½ **1985 (R)** A beautiful female vampire from outer space drains Londoners and before long the city is filled with disintegrating zombies in this hi-tech thriller. Sex was never stranger. **100m/C VHS, Beta, LV.** Steve Railsback, Peter Firth, Frank Finlay, Patrick Stewart, Michael Gothard, Nicholas Ball, Aubrey Morris, Nancy Paul, Mathilda May, John Hallam; ***D:*** Tobe Hooper; ***W:*** Dan O'Bannon, Don Jakoby; ***M:*** Henry Mancini, Michael Kamen. *MGM, LIV, VES*

Lifeguard ☙☙ **1975 (PG)** The lifeguard lives by the credo that work is for people who cannot surf. Aging, he questions whether he should give up the beach life and start selling Porsches. Made for television. **96m/C VHS, Beta.** Sam Elliott, Anne Archer, Stephen Young, Parker Stevenson, Kathleen Quinlan; ***D:*** Daniel Petrie. *PAR*

Lifepod ☙ **1980** A group of intergalactic travelers is forced to evacuate a luxury space liner when a mad computer sabotages the ship. **94m/C VHS, Beta.** Joe Penny, Jordan Michaels, Kristine DeBell. *VCI*

Lifepod ☙☙½ **1993** Trapped on a ship with a killer—only this time it's a space ship. In the year 2169 an interplanetary liner is sabotaged. Nine people escape in a damaged lifepod emergency craft. The survivors are perilously short of food and water and cannot contact Earth. They also face frightening evidence that the terrorist is among their group and is determined to kill the remaining survivors. Very loose adaptation of Alfred Hitchcock's 1944 film "Lifeboat." Made for television. **120m/C VHS, LV.** Ron Silver, Robert Loggia, CCH Pounder, Stan Shaw, Adam Storke, Jessica Tuck, Kelli Williams, Ed Gate; ***D:*** Ron Silver; ***W:*** M. Jay Roach, Pen Densham. *CAF*

Lifespan ☙ **1975** A young American scientist visiting Amsterdam discovers experiments involving a drug that halts aging. **85m/C VHS, Beta.** Klaus Kinski, Hiram Keller, Tina Aumont; ***D:*** Alexander Whitelaw. *VES*

The Lifetaker *Woof!* **1989** A woman lures an unsuspecting young man into her home where she seduces him. Violence and sex ensue. **97m/C VHS.** Lea Dregorn, Peter Duncan, Terence Morgan; ***D:*** Michael Papas. *NO*

The Lift ☙☙ **1985 (R)** Unsuspecting passengers meet an unfortunate fate when they take a ride in a demonic elevator in a highrise. In this film the last stop isn't ladies' lingerie, but death. In Dutch with English subtitles. **95m/C VHS, Beta, LV.** *NL* Huub Stapel, Willeke Van Ammelrooy; ***D:*** Dick Maas. *MED, INJ*

The Light Ahead ☙☙½ **1939** Lovers Fishke and Hodel dream of escaping the poverty and prejudices of their shtetl for the possibilities of big city life in Odessa. They're aided in their quest by enlightened bookseller Mendele who turns the town's superstitions to their advantage. Based on the stories of social satirist Mendele Mokher Seforim. In Yiddish with English subtitles. **94m/B VHS.** David Opatoshu, Isadore Cashier, Helen Beverly; ***D:*** Edgar G. Ulmer. *NCJ, ERG*

Light at the Edge of the World ☙☙ **1971 (PG)** A band of pirates torments a lighthouse keeper near Cape Horn after he sees a shipwreck they caused. **126m/C VHS, Beta.** Kirk Douglas, Yul Brynner, Samantha Eggar; ***D:*** Kevin Billington. *MED*

The Light in the Forest ☙☙½ **1958** Disney adaptation of the classic Conrad Richter novel about a young man, kidnapped by Indians when he was young, who is forcibly returned to his white family. **92m/C VHS, Beta.** James MacArthur, Fess Parker, Carol Lynley, Wendell Corey, Joanne Dru, Jessica Tandy, Joseph Calleia, John McIntire; ***D:*** Herschel Daugherty; ***C:*** Ellsworth Fredericks. *DIS*

The Light in the Jungle ☙☙½ **1991 (PG)** The biography of Nobel Peace Prize winner Dr. Albert Schweitzer. He established a hospital in Africa and had to overcome many obstacles, including tribal superstitions and European bureaucracy to make it successful and bring health care to the area. **91m/C VHS, LV.** Malcolm McDowell, Susan Strasberg, Andrew Davis; ***D:*** Gray Hofmeyr. *LIV*

Light of Day ☙☙ **1987 (PG-13)** A rock 'n roll semi-musical about a working class brother and sister who escape from their parents and aimless lives through their bar band. Script tends to fall flat although both Fox and Jett are believable. Title song written by Bruce Springsteen. **107m/C VHS, Beta, LV.** Michael J. Fox, Joan Jett, Gena Rowlands, Jason Miller, Michael McKean, Michael Rooker, Michael Dolan; ***D:*** Paul Schrader; ***W:*** Paul Schrader; ***C:*** John Bailey; ***M:*** Thomas Newman. *LIV, VES*

The Light of Faith **1922** A sick young woman is cured when she touches the Holy Grail, which a man stole from her former lover in order to help her. Silent. **33m/C VHS, Beta.** Lon Chaney Sr., Hope Hampton; ***D:*** Clarence Brown. *SNC, BFA, CNM*

The Light of Western Stars ☙☙½ **1930** Brian plays a young woman from the east who comes to claim her late brother's ranch. She meets her murdered brother's best friend (Arlen) who is a drunken cowboy, and he falls madly in love with her. Wanting to impress her, he quickly sobers up and prevents a gang from taking over the ranch. This was Paramount's first talking adaptation of a Grey novel and the third version of this particular Grey novel; silent versions were made in 1918 and 1925. **70m/B VHS.** Richard Arlen, Mary Brian, Regis Toomey, Harry Green,

Syd Saylor, George Chandler; ***D:*** Otto Brower, Edwin H. Knopf. *GPV*

The Light of Western Stars ☆ **1940** A proper Eastern woman goes West and falls in love with a drunken lout. **67m/B VHS.** Victor Jory, Jo Ann Sayers, Russell Hayden, Morris Ankrum; ***D:*** Lesley Selander. *GPV, DVT, NOS*

Light Sleeper ☆☆ **1992 (R)** Schrader's moody look at upscale drug dealers in New York. Dafoe is John LaTour, a 40 year-old drug courier to the club scene. Since his boss (Sarandon) is giving up the drug business for the safer world of natural cosmetics, John must look to his own future. His life becomes even more complicated when he runs into a bitter ex-flame (Delany) and finds the attraction is still overpowering. Cynical, contemplative, and menacing. **103m/C VHS, LV.** Willem Dafoe, Susan Sarandon, Dana Delany, David Clennon, Mary Beth Hurt; ***D:*** Paul Schrader; ***W:*** Paul Schrader; ***M:*** Michael Been. *LIV*

Light Years ☆☆½ **1988 (PG)** Garish animated fantasy epic about an idyllic land suddenly beset by evil mutations and death rays. Based on the novel "Robots Against Gondohar" by Jean-Pierre Andrevan. **83m/C VHS, Beta, LV.** ***D:*** Harvey Weinstein; ***W:*** Isaac Asimov, Raphael Cluzel; ***M:*** Gabriel Yared; ***V:*** Glenn Close, Jennifer Grey, Christopher Plummer, Penn Jillette, John Shea, David Johansen, Bridget Fonda, Paul Shaffer, Terrence Mann, Teller. *VMK, WTA, FUS*

Lightblast ☆ **1985** A San Francisco policeman tries to stop a deadly explosive-wielding mad scientist from blowing the city to kingdom come. **89m/C VHS, Beta.** Erik Estrada, Michael Pritchard; ***D:*** Enzo G. Castellari. *LIV*

The Lighthorsemen ☆☆☆ **1987 (PG-13)** Compelling WWI drama follows several battle-hardened men of the Australian Light-Horse mounted infantry stationed in the Middle Eastern desert and the new recruit who joins their ranks and craves acceptance. Superbly filmed, particularly the final battle scene which pits the Aussies against the Turks for control of the wells at Beersheba. Fine performance by Andrews in this epic which contains the essential elements of a good war movie—horses, guns, and more horses. Originally filmed at 140 minutes. Good companion film for another Aussie WWI saga: "Gallipoli." **110m/C VHS, Beta.** *AU* Jon Blake, Peter Phelps, Tony Bonner, Bill Kerr, Nick Wateres, John Walton, Tim McKenzie, Sigrid Thornton, Anthony Andrews; ***D:*** Simon Wincer; ***W:*** Ian Jones; ***M:*** Mario Millo. *WAR*

Lightnin' Carson Rides Again ☆½ **1938** A tough frontier lawman tracks down his payroll-carrying nephew who's been accused of murder and thievery. **58m/B VHS, Beta, 8mm.** Tim McCoy, Joan Barclay, Ted Adams, Forrest Taylor; ***D:*** Sam Newfield. *NOS, VYY*

Lightning Bill ☆ **1935** Bill champions good in battling rustlers. **46m/B VHS, Beta, LV.** Buffalo Bill Jr. *NO*

Lightning Bill Crandall ☆½ **1937** Gunman heads south for the quiet life. Unfortunately, Arizona proves the scene of a fierce battle between various factions of cattlemen. The gunman aids the good guys, and tries to win the daughter's heart. **60m/B VHS.** Bob Steele, Lois January, Charles "Blackie" King, Frank LaRue, Ernie Adams, Earl Dwire, Dave O'Brien; ***D:*** Sam Newfield. *NOS, DVT*

Lightning Bolt ☆ *Operazione Goldman* **1967** Someone is stealing moon rockets from Cape Kennedy, and secret agent Harry Sennet must find out who is doing this devilish deed. It leads him to an evil madman who plots to destroy the world from his underwater hideout. Cheap and unintentionally funny. **96m/C VHS.** *IT SP* Anthony Eisley, Wandisa Leigh, Folco Lulli, Diana Lorys, Ursula Parker; ***D:*** Anthony (Antonio Margheriti) Dawson. *SNC*

The Lightning Incident ☆ **1991 (R)** McKeon plays a young Santa Fe sculptor whose worst nightmares come true when her baby is kidnapped by a devil-worshipping cult. Discovering she has a powerful psychic gift, she pursues the kidnappers across the country in a race to save her baby. Almost as bad as it sounds. **90m/C VHS, Beta.** Nancy McKeon, Polly Bergen, Tantoo Cardinal, Elpidia Carrillo, Tim Ryan; ***D:*** Michael Switzer; ***W:*** Michael J. Murray. *PAR*

Lightning Jack ☆½ **1994 (PG-13)** Western comedy about Lightning Jack Kane (Hogan), an aging second-rate outlaw who desperately wants to become a western legend. Mute store clerk Ben (Gooding) winds up as his partner in crime, while barely eluding criticisms of Stepin Fetchitism. Cliches galore, the running gags (including Kane's surreptitious use of his eyeglasses so he can see his shooting targets) fall flat. **101m/C VHS, LV.** Paul Hogan, Cuba Gooding Jr., Beverly D'Angelo, Kamala Dawson, Pat Hingle, Richard Riehle, Frank McRae, Roger Daltrey, L.Q. Jones, Max Cullen; ***D:*** Simon Wincer; ***W:*** Paul Hogan; ***M:*** Bruce Rowland. *HBO*

Lightning Over Water **1980** An odd, touching documentary co-arranged by Ray and Wenders, all about Ray's last months dying of cancer in his New York loft, his editing of his final film "We Can't Go Home Again," his film corpus and career in general. **91m/C VHS, Beta, LV.** Nicholas Ray, Wim Wenders, Ronee Blakley, Tom Farrel, Gerry Bamman; ***D:*** Wim Wenders; ***W:*** Wim Wenders; ***M:*** Ronee Blakley. *IME, INJ*

Lightning Raiders ☆☆ **1945** When a stage coach filled with mail gets robbed, Billy Carson (Crabbe) and Fuzzy (St. John) set off to avenge the postal system. One of the last Crabbe/St. John efforts; perhaps they should have called it quits a few films earlier. **61m/C VHS.** Buster Crabbe, Al "Fuzzy" St. John, Mady Lawrence, Henry Hall, Steve Darrell, I. Stanford Jolley, Karl Hackett, Roy Brent, Marin Sais, Al Ferguson; ***D:*** Sam Newfield; ***W:*** Elmer Clifton. *HEG*

Lightning Range ☆ **1933** Roosevelt stars as a U.S. Deputy Marshal who continually foils the nefarious plots of a gang of outlaws. **50m/B VHS, Beta.** Buddy Roosevelt, Lafe McKee. *NOS, VYY*

Lightning Strikes West ☆½ **1940** U.S. Marshal trails an escaped convict, eventually catches him, and brings him in to finish paying his debt to society. **57m/B VHS, Beta.** Ken Maynard. *VCN, VCI*

Lightning: The White Stallion ☆½ **1986 (PG)** An old gambler and his two young friends enter a horse race in order to win their beloved white stallion back from thieves. **93m/C VHS, Beta.** Mickey Rooney, Susan George, Isabel Lorca; ***D:*** William A. Levey. *MED*

Lightning Warrior **1931** Western suspense about pioneer life and the unraveling of a baffling mystery. Twelve chapters, 13 minutes each. **156m/B VHS, Beta.** George Brent, Frankie Darro; ***D:*** Armand Schaefer, Ben Kline. *VCN*

Lights! Camera! Murder! ☆☆ **1989** When a twelve-year-old boy witnesses a filmed murder, he becomes the next target. **89m/C VHS.** John Barrett; ***D:*** Frans Nel. *ATL*

Lights of Old Santa Fe ☆½ **1947** A cowboy rescues a beautiful rodeo owner from bankruptcy. The original, unedited version of the film. **78m/B VHS, Beta.** Roy Rogers, Dale Evans, George "Gabby" Hayes, Bob Nolan, The Pioneers. *NOS, DVT, TIM*

The Lightship ☆☆ **1986 (PG-13)** On a stationary lightship off the Carolina coast, the crew rescues three men from a disabled boat, only to find they are murderous criminals. Duvall as a flamboyant homosexual psychopath is memorable, but the tale is pretentious, overdone, and hackneyed. Based on Siegfried Lenz's story. **87m/C VHS, Beta.** Robert Duvall, Klaus Maria Brandauer, Tom Bower, William Forsythe, Arliss Howard; ***D:*** Jerzy Skolimowski. *FOX*

Like Father, Like Son ☆ **1987 (PG-13)** First and worst of a barrage of interchangeable switcheroo movies that came out in '87-'88. Moore is in top form, but the plot is contrived. **101m/C VHS, Beta, LV.** Dudley Moore, Kirk Cameron, Catherine Hicks, Margaret Colin, Sean Astin; ***D:*** Rod Daniel; ***W:*** Steven L. Bloom, Lorne Cameron; ***M:*** Miles Goodman. *COL*

Like Water for Chocolate ☆☆☆½ *Como Agua para Chocolate* **1993 (R)** Magical Mexican fairytale set in the early 1900s about family, love, and the power of food. Formidable Mama Elena is left a widow with three daughters. The youngest, Tita, grows up in the kitchen surrounded by all the magic Nacha, the housekeeper, can impart to her about food. Doomed by tradition to spend her days caring for her mother, Tita escapes by cooking, releasing her sorrows and longings into the food, infecting all who eat it. Wonderfully sensuous and slyly exaggerated. Based on the novel by Esquival who also wrote the screenplay and whose husband, Arau, directed. In Spanish with English subtitles; also available dubbed. **105m/C VHS, LV.** *MX* Lumi Cavazos, Marco Leonardi, Regina Torne, Mario Ivan Martinez, Ada Carrasco, Yareli Arizmendi, Caludette Maille, Pilar Aranda; ***D:*** Alfonso Arau; ***W:*** Laura Esquivel; ***C:*** Steven Bernsein; ***M:*** Leo Brower. Nominations: British Academy Awards '93: Best Foreign Language Film; Independent Spirit Awards '94: Best Foreign Film. *TOU*

Li'l Abner ☆½ *Trouble Chaser* **1940** Al Capp's famed comic strip comes somewhat to life in this low-budget comedy featuring all of the Dogpatch favorites. **78m/C VHS, Beta.** Cranville Owen, Martha Driscoll, Buster Keaton; ***D:*** Albert Rogell. *NOS, MRV, DVT*

Li'l Abner ☆☆½ **1959** High color Dogpatch drama adapted from the Broadway play (with most of the original cast) based on the Al Capp comic strip. When Abner's berg is considered as a site for atomic bomb testing, the natives have to come up with a reason why they should be allowed to exist. Choreography by Michael Kidd and Dee Dee Wood. ♫Jubilation T. Cornpone; Don't Take That Rag Off'n the Bush; A Typical Day; If I Had My Druthers; Room Enuff for Us; Namely You; The Country's in the Very Best of Hands; Unnecessary Town; I'm Past My Prime. **114m/C VHS, Beta.** Peter Palmer, Leslie Parrish, Stubby Kaye, Julie Newmar, Howard St. John, Stella Stevens, Billie Hayes, Joe E. Marks; ***D:*** Melvin Frank; ***W:*** Norman Panama; ***C:*** Daniel F. Fapp; ***M:*** Johnny Mercer, Jean De Paul. Nominations: Academy Awards '59: Best Original Score. *PAR, FCT*

Lili ☆☆☆ **1953** Delightful musical romance about a 16-year-old orphan who joins a traveling carnival and falls in love with a crippled, embittered puppeteer. Heartwarming and charming, if occasionally cloying. Leslie Caron sings the films's song hit, "Hi-Lili, Hi-Lo." **81m/C VHS, Beta.** Leslie Caron, Jean-Pierre Aumont, Mel Ferrer, Kurt Kasznar, Zsa Zsa Gabor; ***D:*** Charles Walters; ***M:*** Bronislau Kaper. Academy Awards '53: Best Score; British Academy Awards '53: Best Actress (Caron); Golden Globe Awards '54: Best Screenplay; National Board of Review Awards '53: 10 Best Films of the Year; Nominations: Academy Awards '53: Best Actress (Caron), Best Art Direction/Set Decoration (Color), Best Color Cinematography, Best Director (Walters), Best Screenplay. *MGM*

Lilies of the Field ☆☆☆ **1963** Five East German nuns enlist the aid of a free-spirited U.S. Army veteran. They persuade him to build a chapel for them and teach them English. Poitier is excellent as the itinerant laborer, holding the saccharine to an acceptable level, bringing honesty and strength to his role. Actress Skala had been struggling to make ends meet in a variety of day jobs until this opportunity. Poitier was the first African-American man to win an Oscar, and the first African-American nominated since Hattie MacDaniel in 1939. Followed by "Christmas Lilies of the Field," (1979). **94m/B VHS, Beta.** Sidney Poitier, Lilia Skala, Lisa Mann, Isa Crino, Stanley Adams; ***D:*** Ralph Nelson; ***M:*** Jerry Goldsmith. Academy Awards '63: Best Actor (Poitier); Berlin International Film Festival '63: Best Actor (Poitier); Golden Globe Awards '64: Best Actor—Drama (Poitier); National Board of Review Awards '63: 10 Best Films of the Year; Nominations: Academy Awards '63: Best Adapted Screenplay, Best Black and White Cinematography, Best Picture, Best Supporting Actress (Skala). *MGM, FOX, BTV*

Liliom ☆☆☆ **1935** Boyer goes to heaven and is put on trial to see if he is deserving of his wings. Lang's first film after leaving Nazi Germany is filled with wonderful ethereal imagery, surprising coming from the man responsible for such grim visions as "Metropolis." In French only. **85m/B VHS, Beta.** *FR* Charles Boyer, Madeleine Ozeray, Florelle, Roland Toutain; ***D:*** Fritz Lang. *SNC, DVT, HEG*

Lilith 🦴🦴🦴 **1964** Therapist-in-training Beatty falls in love with beautiful mental patient Seberg and approaches madness himself. A look at the doctor-patient relationship among the mentally ill and at the nature of madness and love. Doesn't always satisfy, but intrigues. Rossen's swan song. **114m/B VHS, Beta.** Warren Beatty, Jean Seberg, Peter Fonda, Gene Hackman, Kim Hunter; ***D:*** Robert Rossen; ***C:*** Eugene Eugen Shufftan Shuftan. *COL, MLB*

Lillie 🦴🦴🦴 **1979** The life of Edwardian beauty Lillie Langtry, known as "The Jersey Lily," is portrayed in this British made-for-television drama. Defying the morals of the times, Lillie was the first publicly acknowledged mistress of the Prince of Wales, only one of her numerous lovers. On seven cassettes. Shown on "Masterpiece Theatre" on PBS. **690m/C VHS.** *GB* Francesca Annis, Cheryl Campbell, John Castle, Dennis Lili, Peter Egan, Anton Rodgers, Ann Firbank. *SIG, TVC, HMV*

Lily in Love 🦴🦴½ *Playing for Keeps; Jatszani Kell* **1985 (PG-13)** An aging stage star disguises himself as a suave Italian to star in his playwright wife's new play, and woos her to test her fidelity. Charming, warm, and sophisticated. Loosely based on Molnar's "The Guardsman." Made for television. **100m/C VHS, Beta, LV.** *HU* Maggie Smith, Christopher Plummer, Elke Sommer, Adolph Green; ***D:*** Karoly Makk; ***W:*** Frank Cucci. *LIV, VES*

Lily in Winter 🦴🦴½ **1994 (PG)** Christmas story about families and the ties that bind, set in 1957. Black nanny Lily (Cole in her film debut) works for busy showbiz New Yorkers, the Towlers (Hoffmann and Brown), looking after their neglected 10-year-old son Michael (Bonsall). But Lily thinks she's in trouble, thanks to her no-account brother Booker (Russell), and takes off to her rural Alabama roots without realizing Michael has followed her. His parents, however, think Lily has kidnapped him. Made for cable TV. **120m/C VHS.** Natalie Cole, Brian Bonsall, Dwier Brown, Cecil Hoffmann, Marla Gibbs, Monte Russell, Rae'ven Kelly, Salli Richardson, James Pickens Jr., Matthew Faison; ***D:*** Delbert Mann; ***W:*** Robert Eisele; ***C:*** Charles Mills; ***M:*** David Shire. *MCA*

Lily of Killarney 🦴🦴 *The Bride of the Lake* **1934** A musical comedy romance about a British lord who arranges to pay his debts via horse-races, arranged marriages and inheritances. **82m/B VHS, Beta, 8mm.** *GB* Gina Malo, John Garrick, Stanley Holloway; ***D:*** Maurice Elvey. *VYY*

Lily Was Here 🦴½ **1989 (R)** After her fiancee is senselessly murdered, a young woman named Lily is forced to turn to a life of crime in order to survive. A series of petty thefts evolves into a huge crime wave and Lily soon finds herself the object of a massive manhunt. Lily must make the ultimate choice between freedom and motherhood in this shocking thriller. Soundtrack by Dave Stewart features hit instrumental theme "Lily was Here" by saxophonist Candy Dulfur. **110m/C VHS.** Marion Van Thijn, Thom Hoffman, Adrian Brine, Dennis Rudge; ***D:*** Ben Verbong; ***W:*** Ben Verbong, Sytze Van Der Laan, Willem Jan Otten. *INJ*

Limelight 🦴🦴🦴 **1952** A nearly washed-up music hall comedian is stimulated by a young ballerina to a final hour of glory. A subtle if self-indulgent portrait of Chaplin's own life, featuring an historic pairing of Chaplin and Keaton. **120m/B VHS, Beta, LV.** Charlie Chaplin, Claire Bloom, Buster Keaton, Nigel Bruce; ***D:*** Charlie Chaplin; ***C:*** Karl Struss. National Board of Review Awards '52: 10 Best Films of the Year. *FOX*

Limit Up 🦴🦴 **1989 (PG-13)** An ambitious Chicago Trade Exchange employee makes a deal with the devil to corner the market in soybeans. Turgid attempt at supernatural comedy, featuring Charles as God. Catch Sally Kellerman in a cameo as a nightclub singer. **88m/C VHS, Beta, LV.** Nancy Allen, Dean Stockwell, Brad Hall, Danitra Vance, Ray Charles, Luana Anders; ***Cameos:*** Sally Kellerman; ***D:*** Richard Martini. *NO*

The Limping Man 🦴🦴 **1953** Bridges returns to post-WWII London to renew a wartime romance. On the way, he gets caught up in solving a murder. Unexceptional of-its-era thriller. **76m/B VHS, Beta.** *GB* Lloyd Bridges, Moira Lister, Leslie Phillips, Helene Cordet, Alan Wheatley; ***D:*** Charles De Latour. *SNC, RXM, VYY*

Lincoln County Incident 🦴½ **1980** A satiric western starring secondary-school children. **47m/C VHS, Beta.** *NO*

Linda 🦴🦴½ **1929** Linda, a young mountain girl, is forced to marry a much older man though her heart belongs to a young doctor. Her kind husband tries to make the best of the situation. **75m/B VHS.** Helen Foster, Warner Baxter, Noah Beery Sr., Mitchell Lewis, Kate Price, Alan Connor; ***D:*** Dorothy Davenport Reid. *GPV, FCT*

Linda 🦴🦴 **1993 (PG-13)** Madsen in her femme fatale mode as treacherous wife Linda who wants to frame her schlump husband (Thomas) for murder. Whose murder? Why the inconvenient wife (Harrington) of her boyfriend (McGinley). The two homicidal lovebirds want to take the insurance money and run—leaving hubby to face the consequences. Based on the novella "Linda" by John D. MacDonald. **88m/C VHS, Beta.** Virginia Madsen, Richard Thomas, Ted McGinley, Laura Harrington; ***D:*** Nathaniel Gutman; ***W:*** Nevin Schreiner; ***M:*** David Michael Frank. *PAR*

The Lindbergh Kidnapping Case 🦴🦴🦴 **1976** The famous Lindbergh baby kidnapping in 1932 and the trial and execution of Bruno Hauptmann, convincingly portrayed by Hopkins. DeYoung as Lindbergh is blah, but the script is quite good. Made for TV. **150m/C VHS, Beta.** Anthony Hopkins, Joseph Cotten, Cliff DeYoung, Walter Pidgeon, Dean Jagger, Martin Balsam, Laurence Luckinbill, Tony Roberts; ***D:*** Buzz Kulik; ***M:*** Billy Goldenberg. *COL*

The Line 🦴½ **1980 (R)** Not-so-hot anti-war drama about a sit-down strike at a military installation by Vietnam veteran prison inmates. Leans heavily on recycled footage from director Siegel's own "Parade" (1971). **94m/C VHS, Beta.** Russ Thacker, David Doyle, Erik Estrada; ***D:*** Robert Siegel. *NO*

The Linguini Incident 🦴🦴 **1992 (R)** An inept escape artist, a pathological liar, a lingerie designer, a deaf restaurant hostess who throws out one-liners in sign language, and two sinister, yet chic, restaurant owners get together in this marginal comedy about magic and adventure. **99m/C VHS, LV.** Rosanna Arquette, David Bowie, Eszter Balint, Andre Gregory, Buck Henry, Viveca Lindfors, Marlee Matlin, Lewis Arquette; ***Cameos:*** Julian Lennon, Iman; ***D:*** Richard Shepard; ***W:*** Richard Shepard, Tamar Brott; ***M:*** Thomas Newman. *IME*

Link *Woof!* **1986 (R)** A primatologist and his nubile assistant find their experiment has gone—you guessed it—awry, and their hairy charges are running—yep, that's right—amok. Run for your life! **103m/C VHS, Beta.** *GB* Elisabeth Shue, Terence Stamp; ***D:*** Richard Franklin; ***M:*** Jerry Goldsmith. *REP*

The Lion Has Wings 🦴🦴½ **1940** The story of how Britain's Air Defense was set up to meet the challenge of Hitler's Luftwaffe during their "finest hour." Dated, now-quaint but stirring wartime period piece. "Docudrama" style was original at the time. **75m/B VHS, Beta, LV.** Merle Oberon, Ralph Richardson, Flora Robson, June Duprez; ***D:*** Michael Powell, Brian Desmond Hurst; ***C:*** Harry Stradling. *SUE, RXM*

The Lion in Winter 🦴🦴🦴🦴 **1968 (PG)** Medieval monarch Henry II and his wife, Eleanor of Aquitaine, match wits over the succession to the English throne and much else in this fast-paced film version of James Goldman's play. The family, including three grown sons, and visiting royalty are united for the Christmas holidays fraught with tension, rapidly shifting allegiances, and layers of psychological manipulation. Superb dialogue and perfectly realized characterizations. O'Toole and Hepburn are triumphant. Screen debuts for Hopkins and Dalton. Shot on location, this literate costume drama surprised the experts with its box-office success. **134m/C VHS, LV.** Peter O'Toole, Katharine Hepburn, Jane Merrow, Nigel Terry, Timothy Dalton, Anthony Hopkins, John Castle, Nigel Stock; ***D:*** Anthony Harvey; ***W:*** James Goldman; ***M:*** John Barry. Academy Awards '68: Best Actress (Hepburn), Best Adapted Screenplay, Best Score; Directors Guild of America Awards '68: Best Director (Harvey); Golden Globe Awards '69: Best Actor—Drama (O'Toole), Best Film—Drama; National Board of Review Awards '68: 10 Best Films of the Year; New York Film Critics Awards '68: Best Film; Nominations: Academy Awards '68: Best Actor (O'Toole), Best Costume Design, Best Director (Harvey), Best Picture. *COL, BTV, TVC*

A Lion Is in the Streets 🦴🦴🦴 **1953** Cagney stars as a backwoods politician in a southern state who fights on the side of the sharecroppers and wins their support when he exposes the corrupt practices of a powerful businessman. On his way up the political ladder, however, Cagney betrays and exploits the very people who support him. Although this is a familiar storyline, Cagney is riveting as the corrupt politician, and Hale is wonderful as his patient wife. **88m/C VHS.** James Cagney, Barbara Hale, Anne Francis, Warner Anderson, John McIntire, Jeanne Cagney, Lon Chaney Jr., Frank McHugh, Larry Keating, Onslow Stevens; ***D:*** Raoul Walsh. *WAR*

The Lion King 🦴🦴🦴🦴 **1994 (G)** Highest grossing film in Disney history (likely a temporary title) is a winner for kids and their folks. Like his dad Mufasa (Jones), Lion cub Simba (Taylor) is destined to be king of the beasts, until evil uncle Scar (Irons) plots against him and makes him an outcast. Growing up in the jungles of Africa, Simba (now Broderick) learns about life and responsibility, before facing his uncle once again. Supporting characters frequently steal the show, with Sabella's Pumba the warthog and Lane's Timon the meerkat heading the procession (though Chong and Goldberg as hyenas give them a run). Disney epic features heartwarming combo of crowd-pleasing songs, a story with depth, emotion, and politically correct multiculturalism, and stunning animation. The sound quality is equally spectacular; during the 2 1/2 minute wildebeest stampede scene, you'll swear the animals are running amuck in the house. 32nd Disney animated feature is the first without human characters, the first based on an original story, and the first to use the voices of a well-known, ethnically diverse cast. Scenes of violence in the animal kingdom may be too much for younger viewers. ♫Can You Feel the Love Tonight; The Circle of Life; I Just Can't Wait to Be King; Be Prepared; Hakuna Matata. **88m/C VHS.** ***D:*** Rob Minkoff, Roger Allers; ***W:*** Jonathan Roberts, Irene Mecchi; ***M:*** Elton John, Hans Zimmer, Tim Rice; ***V:*** Matthew Broderick, Jeremy Irons, James Earl Jones, Madge Sinclair, Robert Guillaume, Jonathan Taylor Thomas, Richard "Cheech" Marin, Whoopi Goldberg, Rowan Atkinson, Nathan Lane, Ernie Sabella, Niketa Calame, Moira Kelly, Jim Cummings. Academy Awards '94: Best Song ("Can You Feel the Love Tonight"), Best Original Score; Chicago Film Critics Awards '94: Best Score; Golden Globe Awards '95: Best Film—Musical/Comedy, Best Song ("Can You Feel the Love Tonight?"), Best Original Score; Blockbuster Entertainment Awards '95: Family Movie, Theatrical, Best Soundtrack; Nominations: Academy Awards '94: Best Song ("Circle of Life"), Best Song ("Hakuna Matata"); MTV Movie Awards '95: Best Villain (Irons), Best Song ("Can You Feel the Love Tonight"). *DIS*

The Lion Man 🦴🦴 **1936** Arabian tale of a boy raised by lions. **?m/B VHS.** Jon Hall, Ted Adams. *LOO*

Lion Man 🦴 **1979** Raised by wild animals, the son of King Solomon returns to his father's kingdom and roars his way to the throne. **91m/C VHS, Beta.** Steve Arkin. *BFV*

The Lion of Africa 🦴🦴 **1987** A down-to-earth woman doctor and an abrasive diamond dealer share a truck ride across Kenya. Filmed on location in East Africa. Fine lead performances in otherwise nothing-special made-for-cable adventure. **115m/C VHS, Beta.** Brian Dennehy, Brooke Adams, Joseph Shiloal; ***D:*** Kevin Connor; ***M:*** George S. Clinton. *ORI, WAR*

Lion of the Desert 🦴🦴🦴 *Omar Mukhtar* **1981 (PG)** Bedouin horse militias face-off against Mussolini's armored terror in this epic historical drama. Omar Muktar (Quinn as the "Desert Lion") and his Libyan guerrilla patriots kept the Italian troops of Mussolini (Steiger) at bay for 20 years. Outstanding performances enhanced by the desert backdrop. A British-Libyan co-production. **162m/C VHS, Beta.** *GB* Anthony Quinn, Oliver Reed, Irene Papas, Rod Steiger, Raf Vallone,

John Gielgud; **D:** Moustapha Akkad; **W:** H.A.L. Craig; **C:** Jack Hildyard; **M:** Maurice Jarre.

The Lion of Thebes **1964** A muscleman unhesitatingly jumps into the thick of things when Helen of Troy is kidnapped. A superior sword and sandal entry. **?m/C VHS, Beta.** *IT* Mark Forest, Yvonne Furneaux. *SNC*

The Lion of Venice **1982** A kid and an old Venetian gondolier see a stone lion move and uncover a legend of secret treasure. **73m/C VHS, Beta.** *GEM*

Lionheart ½ **1987 (PG)** A romantic portrayal of the famous English King Richard the Lionheart's early years. Meant for kids, but no Ninja turtles herein—and this is just as silly, and slow to boot. **105m/C VHS, Beta, LV.** Eric Stoltz, Talia Shire, Nicola Cowper, Dexter Fletcher, Nicholas Clay, Deborah Barrymore, Gabriel Byrne; **D:** Franklin J. Schaffner; **W:** Richard Outten; **M:** Jerry Goldsmith. *WAR*

Lionheart ½ *A.W.O.L.; Wrong Bet* **1990 (R)** Van Damme deserts the foreign legion and hits the streets when he learns his brother has been hassled. Many fights ensue, until you fall asleep. **105m/C VHS, Beta, LV.** Jean-Claude Van Damme, Harrison Page, Deborah Rennard, Lisa Pelikan, Brian Thompson; **D:** Sheldon Lettich; **W:** Jean-Claude Van Damme, Sheldon Lettich. *MCA*

Lion's Den ½ **1936** A night club performer and a detective head west to fight crime in this film. **59m/B VHS, Beta.** Tim McCoy, Dave O'Brien. *NOS, DVT*

The Lion's Share **1979** A gang of bank robbers have their loot stolen and go after the guy who ripped them off. **105m/C VHS, Beta.** *SP* Julio de Grazia, Luisina Brando, Fernanda Mistral, Ulises Dumont, Julio Chavez. *NO*

Lip Service **1988** Satirical comedy-drama about the TV news industry. An ambitious young newscaster befriends a veteran reporter. He then manipulates his way to replace him on the reporter's morning program. Dooley as the veteran and Dunne as the upstart are fun to watch in this well-done cable rip-off of "Broadcast News." **67m/C VHS, Beta.** Griffin Dunne, Paul Dooley; **D:** William H. Macy. *PSM*

Lipstick *Woof!* **1976 (R)** Fashion model Margaux seeks revenge on the man who brutally attacked and raped her, after he preys on her kid sister (real-life sis Mariel, in her debut). Exquisitely exploitative excuse for entertainment. **90m/C VHS, Beta, LV.** Margaux Hemingway, Anne Bancroft, Perry King, Chris Sarandon, Mariel Hemingway; **D:** Lamont Johnson; **W:** David Rayfiel. *PAR*

Lipstick Camera **1993 (R)** Keats wants a career in television news and seeks out a successful freelance cameraman (Wimmer) to help her out. She also asks to borrow her techno-friend Feldman's mini-camera and then goes after a story on an ex-spy and his sexy companion. Only no one expects what the camera captures. Weak plot but strong cast and high-end production. **93m/C VHS, LV.** Ele Keats, Brian Wimmer, Corey Feldman, Sandahl Bergman, Terry O'Quinn; **D:** Mike Bonifer; **W:** Mike Bonifer. *TRI*

Lipstick On Your Collar **1994** British TV fantasy/drama set in the stuffy confines of the British War Offices during the Suez Crisis of 1956. Two army clerks fantasize about the world outside through daydreams set to original tunes. Last series for the innovative Potter; on 3 cassettes. **360m/C VHS.** *GB* Ewan McGregor, Giles Thomas, Louise Germaine; **D:** Renny Rye; **W:** Dennis Potter. *TVC, NEW*

Liquid Dreams **1992 (R)** In this fast-paced, futuristic thriller, Daly goes undercover as an erotic dancer in a glitzy strip joint to try and solve her sister's murder. She finds that the owner and clientele deal not only in sexual thrills, but also in a strange brain-sucking ritual that provides the ultimate rush. Also available in an unrated version. **92m/C VHS, Beta.** Richard Steinmetz, Candice Daly, Barry Dennen, Juan Fernandez, Tracey Walter, Frankie Thorn, Paul Bartel, Mink Stole; **D:** Mark Manos; **W:** Mark Manos, Zach Davis. *ACA*

Liquid Sky **1983 (R)** An androgynous bisexual model living in Manhattan is the primary attraction for a UFO, which lands atop her penthouse in search of the chemical nourishment that her sexual encounters provide. Low-budget, highly creative film may not be for everyone, but the audience for which it was made will love it. Look for Carlisle also playing a gay male. **112m/C VHS, Beta, LV.** Anne Carlisle, Paula Sheppard, Bob Brady; **D:** Slava Tsukerman; **W:** Anne Carlisle; **C:** Yuri Neyman. *MED*

Lisa **1990 (PG-13)** A young girl develops a crush on the new guy in town and arranges a meeting with him in which she pretends to be her mother. Little does she realize he's a psychotic serial killer. Lock your doors! Don't let anyone in if they have this video! **95m/C VHS.** Staci Keanan, Cheryl Ladd, D.W. Moffett, Tanya Fenmore, Jeffrey Tambor, Julie Cobb; **D:** Gary Sherman; **W:** Karen Clark. *FOX*

Lisa and the Devil *Woof! The House of Exorcism; La Casa Dell' Exorcismo* **1975 (R)** An unfortunate outing for Savalas and Sommer, about devil worship. Poor quality leaves little room for redemption. Just like on the telly, Telly's sucking on a sucker. A shortened version of the director's original 1972 release, re-edited and with additional footage added by producer Alfred Leone. **93m/C VHS.** *IT* Telly Savalas, Elke Sommer, Sylva Koscina, Robert Alda; **D:** Mario Bava. *VDM, MPI*

Lisbon **1956** First film directed by Milland, shot in Portugal, details the adventures of a sea captain entangled in international espionage and crime while attempting to rescue damsel O'Hara's husband from communist doings. A familiar plot told with less-than-average panache. **90m/C VHS, Beta.** Ray Milland, Claude Rains, Maureen O'Hara, Francis Lederer, Percy Marmont; **D:** Ray Milland. *NO*

The List of Adrian Messenger **1963** A crafty murderer resorts to a variety of disguises to eliminate potential heirs to a family fortune. Solid Huston-directed thriller with a twist: you won't recognize any of the name stars. **98m/B VHS, Beta.** Kirk Douglas, George C. Scott, Robert Mitchum, Dana Wynter, Burt Lancaster, Frank Sinatra; **D:** John Huston; **M:** Jerry Goldsmith. *MCA*

Listen, Darling ½ **1938** Garland is appealing in her first big screen role as Pinky Wingate, who decides to find the perfect husband for her widowed mother (Astor). Pinky and her friend Buzz (Bartholomew) manage to find Pidgeon and have him become the engaging objection of everyone's affections. ♫Zing! Went the Strings of My Heart; Ten Pins in the Sky; On the Bumpy Road to Love. **70m/C VHS.** Judy Garland, Freddie Bartholomew, Mary Astor, Walter Pidgeon, Alan Hale, Scotty Beckett; **D:** Edwin L. Marin. *MGM, FCT*

Listen to Me ½ **1989 (PG-13)** A small-town college debate team heads for the big time when they go to a national debate tournament. The usual mutual-distaste-turns-to-romance thing. Cheesy-as-all-get-out climactic abortion debate, in front of supposed real-life Supreme Court justices—yeah, right. And Kirk Cameron: get an accent, will ya? **109m/C VHS, Beta, LV.** Kirk Cameron, Jami Gertz, Roy Scheider, Amanda Peterson, Tim Quill, Christopher Atkins; **D:** Douglas Day Stewart; **C:** Fred W. Koenekamp; **M:** David Foster. Golden Raspberry Awards '89: Worst Supporting Actor (Atkins). *COL*

Listen to Your Heart ½ **1983** Office romance in the '80s! Sounds like a mediocre, forgettable made-for-TV comedy-drama—which is exactly what it is. If Jackson was the brainy one on "Charlie's Angels," why wasn't she smart enough to avoid this one? **90m/C VHS, Beta.** Tim Matheson, Kate Jackson; **D:** Don Taylor. *FOX*

Lisztomania *Woof!* **1975 (R)** Russell's excessive vision of what it must have been like to be classical composer/musician Franz Liszt, who is depicted as the first pop star. Rock opera in the tradition of "Tommy" with none of the sense or music. **106m/C VHS, Beta, LV.** *GB* Roger Daltrey, Sara Kestelman, Paul Nicholas, Fiona Lewis, Ringo Starr; **D:** Ken Russell; **W:** Ken Russell. *WAR*

The Little American ½ **1917** German-American Karl Von Austreim leaves behind sweetheart Angela Moore, returning to Germany to fight in WWI. Angela travels to France to care for her dying aunt and discovers her aunt's chateau has been turned into a hospital. She remains in the face of a German advance and is naturally reunited with her much-changed beau. **80m/B VHS, Beta.** Mary Pickford, Jack Holt, Raymond Hatton, Walter Long, Hobart Bosworth, Ben Alexander, DeWitt Jennings. *GPV*

Little Annie Rooney **1925** A policeman's tomboy daughter spends her time mothering her father and brother while getting into mischief with street punks. Minor melodrama. Silent. **60m/B VHS, Beta, LV.** Mary Pickford, William Haines, Walter James, Gordon Griffith, Vola Vale; **D:** William Beaudine; **C:** Charles Rosher. *NOS, CCB, IME*

Little Ballerina **1947** A young dancer struggles against misfortune and jealousy to succeed in the world of ballet, under the auspices of Fonteyn. **62m/B VHS, Beta.** Margot Fonteyn, Anthony Newley, Martita Hunt, Yvonne Marsh. *VYY*

Little Big Horn ½ *The Fighting Seventh* **1951** Low-budget depiction of Custer et al. at Little Big Horn actually has its gripping moments; solid acting all around helps. **88m/B VHS, Beta.** Marie Windsor, John Ireland, Lloyd Bridges, Reed Hadley, Hugh O'Brian, Jim Davis; **D:** Charles Marquis Warren. *MRV*

Little Big League ½ **1994 (PG)** 12-year-old inherits the Minnesota Twins baseball team from his grandfather, appoints himself manager when everyone else declines, and becomes the youngest owner-manager in history. Nothing new about the premise, but kids and America's favorite pastime add up to good clean family fun. Features real-life baseball players, including the Mariners' Griffey and O'Neil from the Yankees. Good cast features TV's Busfield at first base. Screenwriting debut from Pincus, and directorial debut from the executive producer of "Seinfeld," Scheinman. **120m/C VHS, LV.** Luke Edwards, Jason Robards Jr., Kevin Dunn, Dennis Farina, John Ashton, Jonathan Silverman, Wolfgang Bodison, Timothy Busfield, Ashley Crow, Scott Patterson, Billy L. Sullivan, Miles Feulner, Kevin Elster, Leon "Bull" Durham, Brad "The Animal" Lesley; ***Cameos:*** Don Mattingly, Ken Griffey Jr., Paul O'Neill; **D:** Andrew Scheinman; **W:** Gregory Pincus, Adam Scheinman. *COL*

Little Big Man ½ **1970 (PG)** Based on Thomas Berger's picaresque novel, this is the story of 121-year-old Jack Crabb and his quixotic life as gunslinger, charlatan, Indian, ally to George Custer, and the only white survivor of Little Big Horn. Told mainly through flashbacks. Hoffman provides a classic portrayal of Crabb, as fact and myth are jumbled and reshaped. **135m/C VHS, Beta, LV.** Dustin Hoffman, Faye Dunaway, Chief Dan George, Richard Mulligan, Martin Balsam, Jeff Corey, Aimee Eccles; **D:** Arthur Penn; **W:** Calder Willingham; **C:** Harry Stradling Jr. New York Film Critics Awards '70: Best Supporting Actor (George); National Society of Film Critics Awards '70: Best Supporting Actor (George); Nominations: Academy Awards '70: Best Supporting Actor (George). *FOX, HMV*

Little Boy Lost **1978 (G)** The true story of the disappearance of a young boy in Australia. **92m/C VHS, Beta.** *AU* John Hargreaves, Tony Barry, Lorna Lesley; **D:** Alan Spires. *NO*

Little Buddha **1993 (PG)** Tibetan Lama Norbu informs the Seattle Konrad family that their 10-year-old son Jesse may be the reincarnation of a respected monk. He wants to take the boy back to Tibet to find out and, with some apparently minor doubts, the family head off on their spiritual quest. In an effort to instruct Jesse in Buddhism, this journey is interspersed with the story of Prince Siddhartha, who will leave behind his worldly ways to follow the path towards enlightenment and become the Buddha. The two stories are an ill-fit, the acting awkward (with the exception of Ruocheng as the wise Norbu), but boy, does the film look good (from cinematographer Vittorio Storaro). Filmed on location in Nepal and Bhutan. **123m/C VHS, LV.** Keanu Reeves, Alex Wiesendanger, Ying Ruocheng, Chris Isaak, Bridget Fonda; ***D:*** Bernardo Bertolucci; ***W:*** Mark Peploe, Rudy Wurlitzer; ***C:*** Vittorio Storaro; ***M:*** Ryuichi Sakamoto. *MAX*

Little Caesar ⚲⚲⚲ **1930** A small-time hood rises to become a gangland czar, but his downfall is as rapid as his rise. Still thrilling. The role of Rico made Robinson a star and typecast him as a crook for all time. **80m/B VHS, Beta.** Edward G. Robinson, Glenda Farrell, Sidney Blackmer, Douglas Fairbanks Jr.; ***D:*** Mervyn LeRoy; ***C:*** Gaetano Antonio "Tony" Gaudio. Nominations: Academy Awards '31: Best Adapted Screenplay. *FOX, FCT*

Little Church Around the Corner ⚲⚲½ **1923** Silent small town melodrama about a preacher who falls in love with a mine owner's daughter, but finds he isn't dad's favorite fella when he confronts him about poor mining conditions. When the mine caves in, the preacher man's caught between a rock and hard place when his sweetie's family needs protection from an angry mob. **70m/B VHS, Beta.** Kenneth Harlan, Hobart Bosworth, Walter Long, Pauline Starke, Alec B. Francis, Margaret Seddon, George Cooper; ***D:*** William A. Seiter. *GPV*

The Little Colonel ⚲⚲⚲ **1935 (PG)** After the Civil War, an embittered Southern patriarch turns his back on his family, until his dimple-cheeked granddaughter softens his heart. Hokey and heartwarming. Shirley's first teaming with Bill "Bojangles" Robinson features the famous dance scene. Adapted by William Conselman from the Annie Fellows Johnston best-seller. **80m/B VHS, Beta.** Shirley Temple, Lionel Barrymore, Evelyn Venable, John Lodge, Hattie McDaniel, Bill Robinson, Sidney Blackmer; ***D:*** David Butler; ***C:*** Arthur C. Miller. *FOX*

Little Darlings *Woof!* **1980 (R)** Distasteful premise has summer campers Kristy and Tatum in a race to lose their virginity. Kristy is better (at acting, that is); but who cares? And just who is meant to be the market for this movie, anyway? **95m/C VHS, Beta, LV.** Tatum O'Neal, Kristy McNichol, Matt Dillon, Armand Assante, Margaret Blye; ***D:*** Ronald F. Maxwell; ***M:*** Charles Fox. *PAR*

Little Dorrit, Film 1: Nobody's Fault ⚲⚲⚲ **1988** The mammoth version of the Dickens tome, about a father and daughter trapped interminably in the dreaded Marshalsea debtors' prison, and the good samaritan who works to free them. Told in two parts (on four tapes), "Nobody's Fault," and "Little Dorrit's Story." **369m/C VHS, Beta, LV.** *GB* Alec Guinness, Derek Jacobi, Cyril Cusack, Sarah Pickering, Joan Greenwood, Max Wall, Amelda Brown, Daniel Chatto, Miriam Margolyes, Bill Fraser, Roshan Seth, Michael Elphick, Eleanor Bron, Patricia Hayes, Robert Morley, Sophie Ward; ***D:*** Christine Edzard; ***W:*** Christine Edzard; ***M:*** Giuseppe Verdi. Los Angeles Film Critics Association Awards '88: Best Film, Best Supporting Actor (Guinness); Nominations: Academy Awards '88: Best Adapted Screenplay, Best Supporting Actor (Guinness). *WAR, SIG, TVC*

Little Dorrit, Film 2: Little Dorrit's Story ⚲⚲⚲ **1988** The second half of the monumental adaptation of Dickens' most popular novel during his lifetime tells of Amy Dorrit's rise from debtor's prison to happiness. **369m/C VHS, Beta, LV.** *GB* Alec Guinness, Derek Jacobi, Cyril Cusack, Sarah Pickering, Joan Greenwood, Max Wall, Amelda Brown, Daniel Chatto, Miriam Margolyes, Bill Fraser, Roshan Seth, Michael Elphick, Patricia Hayes, Robert Morley, Sophie Ward, Eleanor Bron; ***D:*** Christine Edzard; ***W:*** Christine Edzard; ***M:*** Giuseppe Verdi. Los Angeles Film Critics Association Awards '88: Best Film, Best Supporting Actor (Guinness). *WAR, SIG, TVC*

Little Dragons ⚲ **1980** A grandfather and two young karate students rescue a family held captive by a backwoods gang. **90m/C VHS, Beta.** Ann Sothern, Joe Spinell, Charles Lane, Chris Petersen, Pat Petersen, Sally Boyden, Rick Lenz, Sharon Weber, Tony Bill; ***D:*** Curtis Hanson; ***W:*** Alan Ormsby. *AHV*

The Little Drummer Girl ⚲⚲⚲ **1984 (R)** An Israeli counterintelligence agent recruits an actress sympathetic to the Palestinian cause to trap a fanatical terrorist leader. Solid performances from Keaton as the actress and Kinski as the Israeli counter-intelligence office sustain interest through a puzzling, sometimes boring and frustrating, cinematic maze of espionage. Keaton is at or near her very best. Based on the bestselling novel by John Le Carre. **130m/C VHS, Beta, LV.** Diane Keaton, Klaus Kinski, Yorgo Voyagis, Sami Frey, Michael Cristofer, Anna Massey, Thorley Walters; ***D:*** George Roy Hill; ***M:*** Dave Grusin. *WAR*

The Little Foxes ⚲⚲⚲½ **1941** A vicious southern woman will destroy everyone around her to satisfy her desire for wealth and power. Filled with corrupt characters who commit numerous revolting deeds. The vicious matriarch is a part made to fit for Davis, and she makes the most of it. Script by Lillian Hellman from her own play. **116m/B VHS, Beta, LV.** Bette Davis, Herbert Marshall, Dan Duryea, Teresa Wright, Charles Dingle, Richard Carlson; ***D:*** William Wyler. Nominations: Academy Awards '41: Best Actress (Davis), Best Director (Wyler), Best Film Editing, Best Interior Decoration, Best Picture, Best Screenplay, Best Supporting Actress (Collinge, Wright), Best Original Score. *SUE*

Little Giant ⚲⚲½ **1946** The duo fly separately in this entry, which highlights Costello's comic talents and leaves Abbott in the supporting role. Costello is a country bumpkin come to the big city to get enough money to marry his sweetheart. He's hired to sell vacuum cleaners by Abbott and becomes the butt of everyone's jokes but the joke's on them when Lou becomes the company's top-selling salesman. **92m/B VHS.** Bud Abbott, Lou Costello, Brenda Joyce, Jacqueline De Wit, George Cleveland, Elena Verdugo, Mary Gordon, Pierre Watkin; ***D:*** William A. Seiter; ***W:*** Walter DeLeon. *MCA*

Little Giants ⚲⚲½ **1994 (PG)** Familiar kids/sport movie about the klutzy coach (Moranis) of an equally woeful pee-wee football team. Coach Danny is up against his overbearing big brother Kevin (O'Neill), former local football hero and the coach of the best team in town. Naturally, there's the big game between the misfit underdogs and the stars. Predictable, of course, but not without some amusing moments. **106m/C VHS, LV.** Rick Moranis, Ed O'Neill, Shawna Waldron, Mary Ellen Trainor, Devon Sawa, Susanna Thompson, John Madden; ***D:*** Duwayne Dunham; ***W:*** Tommy Swerdlow, Michael Goldberg, James Ferguson, Robert Shallcross; ***C:*** Janusz Kaminski; ***M:*** John Debney. *WAR*

Little Girl ... Big Tease ⚲ **1975 (R)** Teen society girl is kidnapped and exploited (along with the viewer) by a group which includes her teacher. **86m/C VHS, Beta.** Jody Ray, Rebecca Brooke; ***D:*** Roberto Mitrotti. *NO*

The Little Girl Who Lives Down the Lane ⚲⚲½ **1976 (PG)** Engrossing, offbeat thriller about a strange 13-year-old girl whose father is never home, and who hides something - we won't say what - in her basement. Very young Foster is excellent, as are her supporters. Then there's a child molester who knows what she's hiding. . . **90m/C VHS, Beta, LV.** *CA* Jodie Foster, Martin Sheen, Alexis Smith, Scott Jacoby; ***D:*** Nicolas Gessner. *LIV, VES*

Little Gloria...Happy at Last ⚲⚲½ **1984** Mini series based on the best-selling book about the custody battle over child heiress Gloria Vanderbilt, and her tumultuous youth. Lansberry leads a fine cast as the poor little rich girl's aunt Gertrude, the matriarchal family power broker. Made for television. **180m/C VHS, Beta.** Bette Davis, Angela Lansbury, Christopher Plummer, Maureen Stapleton, Martin Balsam, Barnard Hughes, John Hillerman; ***D:*** Waris Hussein. *PSM, PAR*

Little Heroes ⚲⚲½ **1991 (G)** An impoverished little girl gets through hard times with the aid of her loyal dog (the Hound can relate). A low-budget family tearjerker that nonetheless works, it claims to be based on a true story. **78m/C VHS.** Raeanin Simpson, Katherine Willis, Keith Christensen; ***D:*** Craig Clyde; ***W:*** Craig Clyde; ***M:*** John McCallum. *HMD*

Little Heroes of Shaolin Temple ⚲ **1972** The "Prince of Blood" attacks the Shaolin temple, but the Master's Ninjas await him. **90m/C VHS, Beta.** Cheng Tain Syh, Hw-Luen, Li Shuen Hwa, Tang Chen Da. *TWE*

Little House on the Prairie ⚲⚲⚲ **1974** The pilot for the television series based on the life of Laura Ingalls Wilder and her family's struggles on the American plains in the 1860s. Other episodes are also available on tape, including one in which Patricia Neal guest stars as a terminally ill widow seeking a home for her children. Neal's performance earned her a best actress Emmy in 1975. **98m/C VHS, Beta.** Michael Landon, Karen Grassle, Victor French, Melissa Gilbert, Melissa Sue Anderson; ***D:*** Michael Landon. *GKK, TLF*

Little Indian, Big City ⚲⚲½ *An Indian in the City; Un Indien dans la Ville* **1995 (PG)** French blockbuster dubbed over with "Americanized" English to give U.S. audiences an appetite for upcoming Disney remake. Lhermitte travels to the Amazon to finalize the divorce of a long-dead marriage, only to find he has a 12-year-old son, Mimi-Siku (Briand). Father and son bond and Dad decides to bring the jungle-bred boy to his home in Paris. Dubbing process unfortunately tomahawks this charming story as loin cloth meets Eiffel Tower, but Lhermitte, Briand and Miou-Miou (as estranged wife Patricia) shine through. Subplot of Russian mobsters who cut the fingers off their victims gives an indication of the French definition of "family fare." **90m/C VHS.** *FR* Thierry Lhermitte, Miou-Miou, Patrick Timsit, Arielle Dombasle, Ludwig Briand; ***D:*** Herve Palud; ***W:*** Thierry Lhermitte, Herve Palud, Philippe Bruneau, Igor Aptekman; ***C:*** Pierre Lorraine; ***M:*** Manu Katche. *NYR*

Little Johnny Jones **1980** George M. Cohan's classic musical is featured in a 1980 revival. Songs include "Yankee Doodle Dandy" and "Give My Regards to Broadway." **93m/C VHS, Beta.** *WAR, OM*

The Little Kidnappers ⚲⚲½ **1990 (G)** Embittered man (Heston) is forced to take in his Scottish grandsons when the two boys are orphaned. They settle in with gramps in Nova Scotia but when the duo decide to adopt the abandoned baby they've found, they are accused of being kidnappers. Cable remake of 1953 British film. **100m/C VHS.** *CA* Charlton Heston, Bruce Greenwood, Leah K. Pinsent, Charles Miller, Leo Wheatley, Patricia Gage; ***D:*** Donald Shebib. *AVE*

Little Ladies of the Night ⚲ *Diamond Alley* **1977** Former pimp tries to save Purl and other teenagers from the world of prostitution. Exploitation posing as "significant drama." **96m/C VHS, Beta.** Linda Purl, David Soul, Clifton Davis, Carolyn Jones, Louis Gossett Jr.; ***D:*** Marvin J. Chomsky. *PSM*

Little Laura & Big John ⚲⚲ **1973** The true-life exploits of the small-time Ashley Gang in the Florida everglades around the turn of the century. Fabian's comeback vehicle, for what it's worth. **82m/C VHS, Beta.** Fabian, Karen Black; ***D:*** Luke Moberly. *NO*

Little Lord Fauntleroy ⚲⚲⚲½ **1936** The vintage Hollywood version of the Frances Hodgson Burnett story of a fatherless American boy who discovers he's heir to a British dukedom. Also available in computer-colorized version. Well cast, charming, remade for TV in 1980. Smith is loveable as the noble tyke's crusty old guardian. **102m/B VHS, Beta.** Freddie Bartholomew, Sir C. Aubrey Smith, Mickey Rooney, Dolores Costello, Jessie Ralph, Guy Kibbee; ***D:*** John Cromwell; ***C:*** Charles Rosher; ***M:*** Max Steiner. *NOS, MRV, VEC*

Little Lord Fauntleroy ⚲⚲½ **1980** A poor boy in New York suddenly finds himself the heir to his grandfather's estate in England. Lavish remake of the 1936 classic, adapted from Frances Hodgson Burnett's novel. Well-deserved Emmy winner for photography; Guinness is his usual old-pro self. Made for TV. **98m/C VHS, Beta.** Rick Schroder, Alec Guinness, Victoria Tennant, Eric Porter, Colin Blakely, Connie Booth, Rachel Kempson; ***D:*** Jack Gold. *FHE*

Little Man Tate ⚲⚲⚲ **1991 (PG)** A seven-year-old genius is the prize in a tug of war between his mother, who wants him to lead a normal life, and a domineering school director who loves him for his intellect. An acclaimed directorial debut for Foster, with overtones of her own extraordinary life as a child prodigy. **99m/C VHS.** Jodie Foster, Dianne Wiest, Harry

Connick Jr., Adam Hann-Byrd, George Plimpton, Debi Mazar, Celia Weston, David Pierce, Danitra Vance, Josh Mostel, P.J. Ochlan; ***D:*** Jodie Foster; ***W:*** Scott Frank; ***M:*** Mark Isham. *ORI, CCB*

Little Marines **1990** Three young boys journey into the wilderness for three days of fun and instead embark on an incredible adventure. **90m/C VHS.** Stephen Baker, Steve Landers Jr., Noah Williams; ***D:*** A.J. Hixon. *MHF*

The Little Match Girl 🦴🦴 **1984** A musical version of the Hans Christian Andersen classic about a girl whose dying grandmother tells her of the magic in the matches she sells. **54m/C VHS, Beta.** Monica McSwain, Nancy Duncan, Matt McKim, Don Hays; ***D:*** Mark Hoeger. *SUE*

The Little Match Girl 🦴🦴 **1987** The Hans Christian Andersen Yuletide classic about an orphan selling magical matches this time set in the 1920's, with the littlest "Cosby" kid in the title role. Ain't she cute? **90m/C VHS, Beta.** *GB* Roger Daltrey, Twiggy, Natalie Morse; ***D:*** Michael Custance. *ACA*

Little Men 🦴½ **1940** A modern version of the classic juvenile story by Louisa May Alcott is too cute for words. **86m/B VHS, Beta.** Jack Oakie, Jimmy Lydon, Kay Francis, George Bancroft; ***D:*** Norman Z. McLeod. *NOS, MRV, VCN*

The Little Mermaid 🦴🦴½ **1978 (G)** An animated version of Hans Christian Andersen's tale about a little mermaid who rescues a prince whose boat has capsized. She immediately falls in love and wishes that she could become a human girl. Not to be confused with the 1989 Disney version. **71m/C VHS, Beta.** ***D:*** Tim Reid. *VTR, GEM*

The Little Mermaid **1984** From "Faerie Tale Theatre" comes an adaptation of the Hans Christian Andersen tale of a little mermaid who makes a big sacrifice to win the prince she loves. **60m/C VHS, Beta.** Karen Black, Brian Dennehy, Helen Mirren, Pam Dawber, Treat Williams; ***D:*** Robert Iscove. *FOX, FCT*

The Little Mermaid 🦴🦴🦴½ **1989 (G)** Headstrong teenage mermaid falls in love with a human prince and longs to be human too. She makes a pact with the evil Sea Witch to trade her voice for a pair of legs; based on the famous Hans Christian Andersen tale. Charming family musical, which harks back to the days of classic Disney animation, and hails a new era of superb Disney animated musicals. Sebastian the Crab nearly steals the show with his wit and showstopping number "Under the Sea." ♫Under the Sea; Kiss the Girl; Daughters of Triton; Part of Your World; Poor Unfortunate Souls; Les Poissons. **82m/C VHS, Beta, LV, 8mm.** ***D:*** John Musker, Ron Clements; ***W:*** John Musker, Ron Clements; ***M:*** Alan Menken, Howard Ashman; ***V:*** Jodi Benson, Christopher Daniel Barnes, Pat Carroll, Rene Auberjonois, Samuel E. Wright, Buddy Hackett, Jason Marin, Edie McClurg, Kenneth Mars, Nancy Cartwright. Academy Awards '89: Best Song ("Under the Sea"), Best Original Score; Golden Globe Awards '90: Best Song ("Under the Sea"), Best Score; Nominations: Academy Awards '89: Best Song ("Kiss the Girl"). *DIS, OM*

Little Minister 🦴🦴🦴 **1934** An adaptation of the James Barrie novel about a prissy Scottish pastor who falls in love with a free-spirited gypsy...he thinks she is, in fact, the local earl's daughter, played to perfection by the young Hepburn. **101m/B VHS, Beta.** Katharine Hepburn, John Beal, Alan Hale, Donald Crisp; ***D:*** Richard Wallace; ***M:*** Max Steiner. *TTC*

Little Miss Broadway 🦴🦴 **1938** Orphan Temple brings the residents of a theatrical boarding house together in hopes of getting them into show business. She and Durante give worthwhile performances. Also available in computer-colorized version. ♫Be Optimistic; How Can I Thank You; I'll Build a Broadway For You; If All the World Were Paper; Thank You For the Use of the Hall; We Should Be Together; Swing Me an Old-Fashioned Song; When You Were Sweet Sixteen; Happy Birthday to You. **70m/B VHS, Beta.** Shirley Temple, George Murphy, Jimmy Durante, Phyllis Brooks, Edna May Oliver, George Barbier, Donald Meek, Jane Darwell; ***D:*** Irving Cummings; ***C:*** Arthur C. Miller. *FOX*

Little Miss Innocence 🦴 **1973** Recording executive tries to survive the amorous advances of the two attractive female hitchhikers that he drove home. **79m/C VHS, Beta.** John Alderman, Sandy Dempsey, Judy Medford; ***D:*** Chris Warfield. *AHV*

Little Miss Marker 🦴🦴🦴 *Girl in Pawn* **1934** Heartwarming story starring Temple, who is the IOU for a gambling debt and steals her way into everyone's heart. Remade three times as "Sorrowful Jones," as "40 Pounds of Trouble," and in 1980 with the original title. **88m/B VHS.** Adolphe Menjou, Shirley Temple, Dorothy Dell, Charles Bickford, Lynne Overman; ***D:*** Alexander Hall. *MCA*

Little Miss Marker 🦴½ **1980 (PG)** Mediocre remake of the often retold story of a bookie who accepts a little girl as a security marker for a $10 bet. Disappointing performance from Curtis adds to an already dull film. **103m/C VHS, Beta.** Walter Matthau, Julie Andrews, Tony Curtis, Bob Newhart, Lee Grant, Sara Stimson, Brian Dennehy; ***D:*** Walter Bernstein; ***W:*** Walter Bernstein; ***M:*** Henry Mancini. *MCA*

Little Miss Millions 🦴🦴½ **1993 (PG)** A 12-year-old has run away from her wicked stepmom who hires a bounty hunter to bring her back—for a half a million bucks. Only when he finds the girl stepmom doesn't want to pay up and she tells anyone who will listen that the bounty hunter actually kidnapped the girl. Bounty hunter turns to friends, including the 12-year-old who isn't a fool and knows stepmom is a lying witch, for help. **90m/C VHS.** Howard Hesseman, Anita Morris, Love Hewitt; ***D:*** Roger Corman. *NHO*

Little Monsters 🦴🦴 **1989 (PG)** A young boy (Savage) discovers a monster (Mandel) under his bed and eventually befriends it. The pair embark on adventures that land them in trouble. Hardworking, talented cast hurdles the weak script, but can't save the film. **100m/C VHS, Beta, LV.** Fred Savage, Howie Mandel, Margaret Whitton, Ben Savage, Daniel Stern, Rick Ducommun, Frank Whaley; ***D:*** Richard Alan Greenberg; ***W:*** Ted Elliot, Terry Rossio; ***M:*** David Newman. *MGM*

Little Moon & Jud McGraw 🦴½ **1978** A wronged Indian woman and a framed cowpoke take their revenge on a small, corrupt town, razing it overnight. Already-weak plot is disabled by too many flashbacks. **92m/C VHS, Beta.** James Caan, Sammy Davis Jr., Stefanie Powers, Aldo Ray; ***D:*** Bernard Girard. *PSM*

Little Murders 🦴🦴🦴 **1971 (PG)** Black comedy set in New York City. A woman convinces a passive photographer to marry her. Gardenia gives an excellent performance as the woman's father. A shadow of crime, depression, and strife seem to hangs over the funny parts of this film; more often depressing than anything else. Adapted by Jules Feiffer from his own play. **108m/C VHS, Beta.** Elliott Gould, Marcia Rodd, Vincent Gardenia, Elizabeth Wilson, Jon Korkes, Donald Sutherland, Alan Arkin, Lou Jacobi; ***D:*** Alan Arkin; ***W:*** Jules Feiffer; ***C:*** Gordon Willis. *FOX*

Little Nellie Kelly 🦴🦴½ **1940** Garland plays both mother and daughter in a film based on a musical comedy by George M. Cohan. Garland is married to Irish cop Murphy but dies in childbirth. The film then advances twenty years to daughter Garland who is trying to make good on the stage and have a romance with a young man her father disapproves of. ♫Nellie Kelly I Love You; Nellie is a Darling; It's a Great Day For the Irish; A Pretty Girl Milking Her Cow; Danny Boy; Singing in the Rain. **100m/B VHS.** Judy Garland, George Murphy, Charles Winninger, Douglas McPhail; ***D:*** Norman Taurog. *MGM, FCT*

Little Nemo: Adventures in Slumberland 🦴🦴½ **1992 (G)** A bland animated tale of a young boy whose dreams take him to Slumberland. There, Nemo unwittingly unleashes a monster from Nightmare Land who kidnaps Slumberland's king. Nemo must then rescue the king—aided by the king's daughter, a comic squirrel sidekick, and a mischievous con-frog. Based on Winsor McCay's 1900 comic strip. Has some cute comic moments for the kiddies and, while the animation is better than Saturday-morning cartoon quality, it's not Disney. **85m/C VHS, LV.** ***D:*** William T. Hurtz, Masami Hata; ***W:*** Chris Columbus, Richard Outten; ***M:*** Tom Chase, Steve Rucker; ***V:*** Gabriel Damon, Mickey Rooney, Rene Auberjonois, Daniel Mann, Laura Mooney, Bernard Erhard, William E. Martin. *HMD, WTA*

A Little Night Music 🦴½ **1977 (PG)** Features four interwoven, contemporary love stories adapted from the Broadway play, and based loosely on Bergman's "Smiles of a Summer Night." Taylor's pathetic rendition of "Send in the Clowns" should be banned. Filmed on location in Austria. **110m/C VHS, Beta, LV.** Elizabeth Taylor, Diana Rigg, Hermione Gingold, Len Cariou, Lesley-Anne Down; ***D:*** Harold Prince. Academy Awards '77: Best Adapted Score; Nominations: Academy Awards '77: Best Costume Design. *SUE*

Little Nikita 🦴🦴 **1988 (PG)** A California boy (Phoenix) discovers that his parents are actually Soviet spies planted as American citizens for eventual call to duty. Poitier's performance as the FBI agent tracking the spies is about the only spark in this somewhat incoherent thriller. **98m/C VHS, Beta, LV.** River Phoenix, Sidney Poitier, Richard Bradford, Richard Lynch, Caroline Kava, Lucy Deakins; ***D:*** Richard Benjamin; ***W:*** Bo Goldman; ***M:*** Marvin Hamlisch. *COL*

Little Ninjas 🦴🦴½ **1992** Three topnotch ninja kids go up against the Sarak to rescue their friend who is being held hostage. **85m/C VHS, LV.** Steven Nelson, Jon Anzaldo, Alan Godshaw; ***D:*** Emmett Alston. *VMK*

Little Noises 🦴🦴 **1991** Glover stars as an artist who seeks not only fame and fortune, but also the love of his best friend (O'Neal). He finally creates a piece that his agent loves, but problems arise. **91m/C VHS, Beta.** Crispin Glover, Tatum O'Neal, Rik Mayall, Tate Donovan, John C. McGinley; ***D:*** Jane Spencer; ***W:*** Jane Spencer. *PSM*

Little Odessa 🦴🦴½ **1994 (R)** Working for the stateside Russian mafia, hitman Joshua Shapira (Roth) returns to his childhood neighborhood to carry out his next assignment. Set in the Russian-Jewish emigre community of Brooklyn's Brighton Beach, Gray's directorial debut explores Joshua's relationship with his family—especially kid brother Reuben (Furlong). Not your typical mob opera, this one focuses more on characters than killing. Relationships between family members are explored to the hilt, but the audience is left with too many unanswered questions. Dimly lit and entirely too ambiguous, this family tragedy could spawn a serious case of depression. **98m/C VHS, LV.** Tim Roth, Edward Furlong, Moira Kelly, Vanessa Redgrave, Maximilian Schell, Paul Guilfoyle; ***D:*** James Gray; ***W:*** James Gray. Nominations: Independent Spirit Awards '96: Best Actor (Roth), Best Cinematography, Best First Feature, Best Supporting Actress (Redgrave). *LIV*

Little Orphan Annie **1918** Surrounded by a group of children, poet James Whitcomb Riley narrates the story of Little Orphant Annie, who loses her mother at an early age and is sent to an orphanage where she charms the other children with her stories of ghosts and elves. **57m/B VHS.** Thomas Santschi, Eugenie Besserer, Ben Alexander, Lillie Hayward, Lafayette McKee, Colleen Moore, Harry Lonsdale, Doris Baker, Lillian Wade, Billy Jacobs, Lillian Wade, James Whitcomb Riley; ***D:*** Colin Campbell. *GPV*

Little Orphan Annie 🦴🦴½ **1932** The unjustly forgotten first sound adaptation of the comic strip. Fun score adds a lot, as does the good cast. **60m/B VHS, Beta.** May Robson, Buster Phelps, Mitzie Green, Edgar Kennedy; ***D:*** John S. Robertson; ***M:*** Max Steiner. *CCB*

The Little Prince 🦴🦴 **1974 (G)** Disappointing adaptation of the classic children's story by Antoine de Saint-Exupery, about a little boy from asteroid B-612. Lousy Lerner and Loewe score underscores a general lack of magic or spontaneity. ♫It's a Hat; I Need Air; I'm On Your Side; Be Happy; You're a Child; I Never Met a Rose; Why Is the Desert (Lovely to See)?; Closer and Closer and Closer; Little Prince (From Who Knows Where). **88m/C VHS, Beta, LV.** *GB* Richard Kiley, Bob Fosse, Steven Warner, Gene Wilder; ***D:*** Stanley Donen; ***W:*** Alan Jay Lerner; ***M:*** Frederick Loewe, Alan Jay Lerner. Golden Globe Awards '75: Best Score; Nominations: Academy Awards '74: Best Song ("Little Prince"), Best Original Score. *PAR*

The Little Princess 🦴🦴🦴½ **1939 (G)** Based on the Frances Hodgson Burnett children's classic; perhaps the best of the moppet's films. Shirley is a young schoolgirl in Victorian London sent to a harsh boarding school when her Army officer father is posted abroad. When her father is declared missing, the penniless girl must work as a servant at the school to pay her keep, all the while haunting the hospitals, never believing her father has died. A classic tearjerker. **91m/B VHS, Beta, LV.** Shirley Temple, Richard Greene, Anita Louise, Ian Hunter, Cesar Romero, Arthur Treacher, Sybil Jason, Miles Mander, Marcia Mae Jones, E.E. Clive; ***D:*** Walter Lang; ***C:*** Arthur C. Miller. *CNG, MRV, NOS*

The Little Princess **1987** A three-cassette adaptation of Frances Hodgson Burnett's book. In Victorian England, kind-hearted Sara is forced into poverty when her father suddenly dies. Can his long-time friend find her and restore her happiness? Originally aired on PBS as part of the "Wonderworks" family movie series. **180m/C VHS.** *GB* Amelia Shankley, Nigel Havers, Maureen Lipman; ***D:*** Carol Wiseman. *FCT, PME, SIG*

A Little Princess 🦴🦴🦴½ **1995 (G)** Compelling fantasy, based on the children's book by Frances Hodgson Burnett, and previously best known for the 1939 Shirley Temple incarnation. Sara (Matthews) has been raised in India by her widowed father (Cunningham). When he's called up to fight in WWI, Sara is taken to New York to be educated at stern Miss Michin's (Bron) school, where her money makes her a favored boarder. However, the irrepressible Sara suffers a severe reversal of fortune when her father is reported killed and Miss Michin promptly makes her a servant to pay her way. But Sara's charm has made her some true friends who become her allies under trying circumstances. Lively script, dazzling visuals, and a welcome lack of sappiness create a classic-in-the-making. **97m/C VHS, LV.** Liesl Matthews, Eleanor Bron, Liam Cunningham, Rusty Schwimmer, Arthur Malet, Vanessa Lee Chester, Errol Sitahal, Heather DeLoach, Taylor Fry; ***D:*** Alfonso Cuaron; ***W:*** Richard LaGravenese, Elizabeth Chandler; ***C:*** Emmanuel Lubezki; ***M:*** Patrick Doyle. Nominations: Academy Awards '95: Best Art Direction/Set Decoration, Best Cinematography. *WAR*

The Little Rascals 🦴🦴½ **1994 (PG)** Alfalfa runs afoul of the membership requirements for the "He-Man Womun Haters Club" when he starts to fall for Darla. Charming remake of the short film series, now set in suburban L.A., from Spheeris, who also redid another television favorite, "The Beverly Hillbillies." **83m/C VHS, LV.** Daryl Hannah, Courtland Mead, Travis Tedford, Brittany Ashton Holmes, Bug Hall, Zachary Mabry, Kevin Jamal Woods, Ross Bagley, Sam Saletta, Blake Collins, Jordan Warkol, Blake Ewing, Juliette Brewer, Heather Karasek; ***Cameos:*** Whoopi Goldberg; ***D:*** Penelope Spheeris; ***W:*** Penelope Spheeris, Paul Guay, Steve Mazur; ***M:*** David Foster, Linda Thompson. *MCA*

Little Rascals, Book 1 **193?** Three "Our Gang" shorts: "Railroadin'" (1929), in which the gang takes off on a runaway train; "A Lad and a Lamp" (1932), wherein they find an Aladdin's lamp; and "Beginner's Luck" (1935), in which Spanky wins a dress for a young actress. Additional volumes are available. **59m/B VHS, Beta.** Farina Hoskins, Joe Cobb, Matthew "Stymie" Beard, George "Spanky" McFarland, Carl "Alfalfa" Switzer, Mary Ann Jackson. *CCB*

Little Rascals Christmas Special **1979** Spanky and the Little Rascals attempt to raise enough money to buy a winter coat for Spanky's mom and learn the true meaning of Christmas along the way. **60m/C VHS, Beta.** Darla Hood, Matthew "Stymie" Beard; ***D:*** Fred Wolf, Charles Swenson. *FHE*

Little Rascals, Vol. 1 **1929** Here is a collection of three uncut "Little Rascals" short subjects. In "Boxing Gloves" (1929), Chubby and Joe decide two settle their differences over who should have Jean Darling's love by staging a winner-take-all boxing match. In "The Kid from Borneo" (1933), Spanky thinks he's met a crazy relative when he confuses an untamed human from Borneo for his uncle from the circus. In "Roamin' Holiday" (1936), Alfalfa and Spanky lead the gang on a journey fit for a hobo. **50m/B VHS.** Darla Hood, George "Spanky" McFarland, Carl "Alfalfa" Switzer, Matthew "Stymie" Beard. *REP, CCB*

Little Rascals, Vol. 2 **1930** Another uncut compilation of three classic episodes featuring the goofy gang. In "The First Seven Years" (1930), Speck and Jackie battle for the attention of a beautiful Mary Ann. In the award-winning "Bored of Education" (1936), Spanky and Alfalfa devise a plan to play hooky from school by developing very acute tooth problems. In "Rushin' Ballet" (1937), Alfalfa and Spanky establish the Secret Revengers Club and liberate Buckwheat and Porky from the bonds of tyranny. **50m/B VHS.** George "Spanky" McFarland, Carl "Alfalfa" Switzer. Academy Awards '36: Best Comedy Short ("Bored of Education"). *REP, CCB*

Little Red Riding Hood **1983** From "Faerie Tale Theatre" comes the retelling of the story about a girl (Mary Steenburgen) off to give her grandmother a picnic basket, only to get stopped by a wicked wolf McDowell. Not particularly faithful, but fun and scary. **60m/C VHS, Beta, LV.** Mary Steenburgen, Malcolm McDowell; ***D:*** Graeme Clifford. *FOX, FCT*

Little Red Schoolhouse 🦴🦴 **1936** A hard-nosed schoolteacher hunts for a truant lad and both of them land in jail. **64m/C VHS, Beta.** Frank "Junior" Coghlan, Dickie Moore, Ann Doran. *NOS, BAR, FCT*

A Little Romance 🦴🦴🦴 **1979 (PG)** An American girl living in Paris falls in love with a French boy; eventually they run away, to seal their love with a kiss beneath a bridge. Olivier gives a wonderful, if not hammy, performance as the old pickpocket who encourages her. Gentle, agile comedy based on the novel by Patrick Cauvin. **110m/C VHS, Beta, LV.** Laurence Olivier, Diane Lane, Thelonious Bernard, Sally Kellerman, Broderick Crawford; ***D:*** George Roy Hill; ***W:*** Allan Burns; ***M:*** Georges Delerue. Academy Awards '79: Best Original Score; Nominations: Academy Awards '79: Best Adapted Screenplay. *WAR, INJ*

A Little Sex 🦴🦴 **1982 (R)** Capshaw, in her screen debut, finds herself the wife of womanizer Matheson. Harmless, but pointless, with a TV-style plot. **94m/C VHS, Beta.** Tim Matheson, Kate Capshaw, Edward Herrmann, Wallace Shawn, John Glover; ***D:*** Bruce Paltrow; ***W:*** Robert De Laurentis; ***C:*** Ralf Bode; ***M:*** Georges Delerue. *MCA*

Little Shop of Horrors 🦴🦴🦴½ **1960** The landmark cheapie classic, which Roger Corman reputedly filmed in three days, about a nebbish working in a city florist shop who unknowingly cultivates an intelligent plant that demands human meat for sustenance. Notable for then-unknown Nicholson's appearance as a masochistic dental patient. Hilarious, unpretentious farce—if you liked this one, check out Corman's "Bucket of Blood" for more of the same. Inspired a musical of the same name, remade as a movie again in 1986. Available colorized. **70m/B VHS, Beta, LV.** Jackie Joseph, Jonathan Haze, Mel Welles, Jack Nicholson, Dick Miller; ***D:*** Roger Corman. *CNG, MRV, NOS*

Little Shop of Horrors 🦴🦴🦴 **1986 (PG-13)** During a solar eclipse, Seymour buys an unusual plant and takes it back to the flower shop where he works. The plant, Audrey 2, becomes a town attraction as it grows at an unusual rate, but Seymour learns that he must feed Audrey fresh human blood to keep her growing. Soon, Audrey is giving the orders ("Feed me") and timid Seymour must find "deserving" victims. Martin's performance as the masochistic dentist is alone worth the price. Song, dance, gore, and more prevail in this outrageous musical comedy. Four Tops Levi Stubbs is the commanding voice of Audrey 2. Based on the Off-Broadway play, which was based on Roger Corman's 1960 horror spoof. ♫Mean Green Mother From Outer Space; Some Fun Now; Your Day Begins Tonight. **94m/C VHS, Beta, LV.** Rick Moranis, Ellen Greene, Vincent Gardenia, Steve Martin, James Belushi, Christopher Guest, Bill Murray, John Candy; ***D:*** Frank Oz; ***M:*** Miles Goodman, Howard Ashman. Nominations: Academy Awards '86: Best Song ("Mean Green Mother from Outer Space"). *WAR, HMV, MVD*

Little Sister 🦴½ **1992 (PG-13)** Prankster Silverman, on a dare, dresses up as a girl and joins a sorority. Problems arise when he falls in love with his "big sister" (Milano) in the sorority. What will happen when she finds out the truth? Will we care? **94m/C VHS.** Jonathan Silverman, Alyssa Milano; ***W:*** Sergio D. Altieri. *LIV*

A Little Stiff 🦴🦴 **1991** Slacker romantic comedy about the unrequited romance between filmmaker Caveh and fellow UCLA student McKim from first meeting, through angst, and grand final gestures. **85m/C VHS.** Erin McKim, Caveh Zahedi; ***D:*** Caveh Zahedi, Greg Watkins; ***M:*** Kath Bloom. *WAC*

Little Sweetheart 🦴½ **1990 (R)** A reworking of "The Bad Seed," with a nine-year-old girl engaging in murder, burglary, and blackmail, ruining the adults around her. Based on "The Naughty Girls" by Arthur Wise. **93m/C VHS, Beta, LV, 8mm.** John Hurt, Karen Young, Barbara Bosson, John McMartin, Cassie Barasch; ***D:*** Anthony Simmons. *SUE*

The Little Theatre of Jean Renoir 🦴🦴🦴 **1971** A farewell by director Jean Renoir featuring three short films. In the first, Renoir's humanist beliefs are apparent in "The Last Christmas Dinner," a Hans Christian Andersen-inspired story. Next, "The Electric Floor Waxer" is a comic opera. The third piece is called "A Tribute to Tolerance." Slight but important late statement by a great director. In French with English subtitles. **100m/C VHS, Beta, LV.** Jean Renoir, Fernand Sardou, Jean Carmet, Francoise Arnoul, Jeanne Moreau; ***D:*** Jean Renoir; ***W:*** Jean Renoir. *INT, FLI, IME*

The Little Thief 🦴🦴🦴 **1989 (PG-13)** Touted as Francois Truffaut's final legacy, this trite minidrama is actually based on a story he co-wrote with Claude de Givray about a post-WWII adolescent girl who reacts to the world around her by stealing and petty crime. Truffaut's hand is markedly absent, but this film is a testament to his abruptly and sadly truncated career. Director Miller was Truffaut's longtime assistant. French with subtitles. **108m/C VHS, Beta, LV.** *FR* Charlotte Gainsbourg, Simon de la Brosse, Didier Bezace, Raoul Billerey, Nathalie Cardone; ***D:*** Claude Miller; ***W:*** Annie Miller, Claude Miller; ***M:*** Alain Jomy. *HBO, INJ*

Little Tough Guys 🦴🦴 **1938** The Little Tough Guys (a.k.a. Dead End Kids) come to the rescue of Halop, a young tough guy gone bad to avenge his father's unjust imprisonment. First of the "Little Tough Guys" series for the former Dead End Kids, who later became the East Side Kids before eventually evolving into the Bowery Boys. **84m/B VHS, Beta.** Helen Parrish, Billy Halop, Leo Gorcey, Marjorie Main, Gabriel Dell, Huntz Hall; ***D:*** Harold Young. *NOS, MRV, VYY*

Little Treasure 🦴½ **1985 (R)** A stripper heads for Mexico to search for her long-lost father, but ends up looking for treasure with an American guy. Disappointing effort of director Sharp. **95m/C VHS, Beta, LV.** Burt Lancaster, Margot Kidder, Ted Danson, Joseph Hacker, Malena Doria; ***D:*** Alan Sharp; ***W:*** Alan Sharp. *COL*

The Little Valentino 🦴🦴 **1979** One day in the aimless life of a young punk who gets by on his wits and petty theft. Jeles' directorial debut. In Hungarian with English subtitles. **102m/B VHS.** *HU* ***D:*** Andras Jeles. *FCT, AUD*

Little Vegas 🦴🦴½ **1990 (R)** Looks like easy street for a young man who inherits a bundle from his girlfriend, but he's forced to wake up and smell the cappucino when her family and the other residents of the tiny desert berg think there's a gigolo in the wodpile. Much strife with siblings as he wages a battle for the bucks with the son while wooing the woman's daughter, with a measure of mob inflicted plot twists. Mildly amusing, cut from vein of you can't get rich quick and get away with it. **90m/C VHS, LV.** Michael Nouri, Jerry Stiller, John Sayles, Anthony John Denison, Catherine O'Hara, Bruce McGill, Anne Francis, Bob(cat) Goldthwait, Jay Thomas, Perry Lang; **D:** Perry Lang; **W:** Perry Lang; **M:** Mason Daring. *COL*

Little Vera *Malenkaya Vera* **1988** Extremely well-done Soviet film chronicles the life of a young working-class woman who loves rock music and who has been profoundly affected by Western civilization. Post-glasnost Soviet production gives Westerners a glimpse into the Russian way of life. A box-office bonanza back home. Russian with subtitles. **130m/C VHS, Beta, LV.** *RU* Natalia Negoda, Andrei Sokolov, Yuri Nazarov, Ludmila Zaisova, Alexander Niegreva; **D:** Vassili Pitchul. *FCT, LUM, WBF*

Little White Lies **1989** Jillian and Matheson meet and fall in love during an exotic vacation. But both are traveling under assumed identities—she's a policewoman tracking a jewel thief and he's an incognito doctor. When they reunite stateside they try to stick to their ruses in humdrum comedic fashion. Made for network TV. **88m/C VHS.** Ann Jillian, Tim Matheson; **D:** Anson Williams. *RHI*

Little Women **1933** Louisa May Alcott's Civil War story of the four March sisters—Jo, Beth, Amy, and Meg—who share their loves, their joys, and their sorrows. Everything about this classic film is wonderful, from the lavish period costumes to the excellent script, and particularly the captivating performances by the cast. A must-see for fans of Alcott and Hepburn, and others will find it enjoyable. Remade in 1949, in 1978 for television, and again in 1994. **107m/B VHS, Beta, 8mm.** Katharine Hepburn, Joan Bennett, Paul Lukas, Edna May Oliver, Frances Dee, Spring Byington, Jean Parker, Douglass Montgomery; **D:** George Cukor; **W:** Victor Heerman, Sarah Y. Mason; **M:** Max Steiner, Max Steiner. Academy Awards '33: Best Adapted Screenplay; Venice Film Festival '34: Best Actress (Hepburn); Nominations: Academy Awards '33: Best Director (Cukor), Best Picture. *MGM, IGP*

Little Women **1949** Stylized color remake of the George Cukor 1933 classic. Top-notch if too obvious cast portrays Louisa May Alcott's story of teenage girls growing up against the backdrop of the Civil War. Remade again, for television in 1978. **121m/C VHS.** June Allyson, Peter Lawford, Margaret O'Brien, Elizabeth Taylor, Janet Leigh, Mary Astor; **D:** Mervyn LeRoy; **W:** Andrew Solt; **M:** Adolph Deutsch. Academy Awards '49: Best Art Direction/Set Decoration (Color); Nominations: Academy Awards '49: Best Color Cinematography. *MGM*

Little Women **1978** The third screen version of Louisa May Alcott's classic story. Lackluster compared to the previous attempts, particularly the sterling 1933 film, but still worthwhile. During the Civil War, four sisters share their lives as they grow up and find romance. Garson's television debut. Followed by a television series. **200m/C VHS.** Meredith Baxter, Susan Dey, Ann Dusenberry, Eve Plumb, Dorothy McGuire, Robert Young, Greer Garson, Cliff Potts, William Shatner; **D:** David Lowell Rich; **M:** Elmer Bernstein. *NO*

Little Women **1994 (PG)** Beloved story of the March women is beautifully portrayed in a solid production that blends a seamless screenplay with an excellent cast, authentic period costumes, and lovely cinematography and music. Ryder, perfectly cast as the unconventional Jo, is also the strongest of the sisters: domestically inclined Meg (Alvarado), the fragile Beth (Danes), and the youngest, mischevious Amy (the delightful Dunst) who grows up into a sedate young lady (Mathis). Charming adaptation remains faithful to the spirit of the Alcott classic while adding contemporary touches. Fittingly brought to the big screen by producer Denise Di Novi, writer/co-producer Swicord, and director Armstrong. **118m/C VHS, LV, 8mm.** Winona Ryder, Gabriel Byrne, Trini Alvarado, Samantha Mathis, Kirsten Dunst, Claire Danes, Christian Bale, Eric Stoltz, John Neville, Mary Wickes, Susan Sarandon; **D:** Gillian Armstrong; **W:** Robin Swicord; **C:** Geoffrey Simpson; **M:** Thomas Newman. Chicago Film Critics Awards '94: Most Promising Actress (Dunst); Nominations: Academy Awards '94: Best Actress (Ryder), Best Costume Design, Best Original Score. *COL*

Little World of Don Camillo *Le Petit Monde de Don Camillo* **1951** A French-made farce based on the beloved novels of Giovanni Guareschi. Earthy priest Don Camillo clashes repeatedly with his friendly enemy, the communist mayor of a tiny Italian village. The hero talks directly to God, whose voice is provided by Orson Welles, also narrator of the English version. Charming, good-natured approach. **106m/B VHS, Beta, 8mm.** *FR IT* Fernandel, Gino Cervi, Sylvia, Vera Talqui; **D:** Julien Duvivier. *VYY, FCT*

The Littlest Angel **1969** Musical about a shepherd boy who dies falling off a cliff and wants to become an angel. He learns a valuable lesson in the spirit of giving. Made for TV. **77m/C VHS, Beta.** Johnny Whitaker, Fred Gwynne, E.G. Marshall, Cab Calloway, Connie Stevens, Tony Randall. *SUE, KAR*

The Littlest Horse Thieves ½ *Escape from the Dark* **1976 (G)** Good Disney film about three children and their efforts to save some ponies who work in mines. The children take it upon themselves to see that the animals escape the abuse and neglect they are put through. Filmed on location in England with excellent photography. **109m/C VHS, Beta.** Alastair Sim, Peter Barkworth; **D:** Charles Jarrott. *DIS*

The Littlest Outlaw ½ **1954** A Mexican peasant boy steals a beautiful stallion to save it from being destroyed. Together, they ride off on a series of adventures. Disney movie filmed on location in Mexico. **73m/C VHS, Beta.** Pedro Armendariz Sr., Joseph Calleia, Andres Velasquez; **D:** Roberto Gavaldon. *DIS*

The Littlest Rebel ½ **1935 (PG)** Temple stars in this well-done piece set during the Civil War in the Old South. She befriends a Union officer while protecting her father at the same time. She even goes to Washington to talk with President Lincoln. Nice dance sequences by Temple and Robinson. Available in computer-colored version. **70m/B VHS, Beta.** Shirley Temple, John Boles, Jack Holt, Bill Robinson, Karen Morley, Willie Best; **D:** David Butler. *FOX*

The Littlest Viking ½ **1994 (PG)** Twelve-year-old Sigurd finds archery practice and mock battles an exciting way to learn to be a Viking. But when his older brother is killed in battle, Sigurd's father expects him to avenge the death, and Sigurd must decide just what being a Viking prince means. Scenic Scandinavian settings; obvious dubbing. **85m/C VHS, LV.** Kristian Tonby, Per Jansen, Terje Stromdahl; **D:** Knut W. Jorfald, Lars Rasmussen, Paul Trevor Bale. *HMD*

Live a Little, Love a Little **1968 (PG)** Itinerant photographer Elvis juggles two different jobs by running around a lot. Sexually more frank than earlier King vehicles. ♫Almost in Love; A Little Less Conversation; Edge of Reality; Wonderful World. **90m/C VHS, Beta.** Elvis Presley, Michele Carey, Rudy Vallee, Don Porter, Dick Sargent, Sterling Holloway, Eddie Hodges; **D:** Norman Taurog. *MGM*

Live and Let Die **1973 (PG)** Agent 007 is out to thwart the villainous Dr. Kananga, a black mastermind who plans to control western powers with voodoo and hard drugs. Moore's first appearance as Bond. Can't we have the real Bond back? Title song by Paul McCartney. **131m/C VHS, Beta, LV.** *GB* Roger Moore, Jane Seymour, Yaphet Kotto, Clifton James, Julius W. Harris, Geoffrey Holder, David Hedison, Gloria Hendry, Bernard Lee, Lois Maxwell, Madeleine Smith; **D:** Guy Hamilton; **W:** Tom Mankiewicz; **C:** Ted Moore; **M:** George Martin. Nominations: Academy Awards '73: Best Song ("Live and Let Die"). *MGM, FOX, TLF*

Live Bait ½ **1995** Canadian-flavored Gen-X comedy features suburban 23-year-old virgin Trevor MacIntosh (Scholte) trying for a little romance (or at least sex) but seemingly doomed to failure. At least until he meets much older artist Charlotte (Maunsell). Sweeney handles his debut writing, directing, and producing skills with equal aplomb. **84m/B VHS.** *CA* Tom Scholte, Micki Maunsell, Kevin McNulty, Babz Chula, David Lovgren, Laara Sadiq, Michelle Beaudoin, Kelly Aisenstat; **D:** Bruce Sweeney; **W:** Bruce Sweeney; **C:** David Pelletier. Toronto-City Award '95: Best Canadian Feature Film. *NYR*

Live! From Death Row **1992** Cassidy plays a tabloid TV host who'll do anything to get ratings. She's set to do a live interview with a condemned serial killer (Davison) shortly before his execution. But Davison and his fellow death-row inmates take Cassidy and her crew hostage as he decides to use the show for his own media message. **94m/C VHS.** Joanna Cassidy, Bruce Davison, Art LaFleur, Calvin Levels, Michael D. Roberts; **D:** Patrick Duncan; **W:** Patrick Duncan. *ABC, PSM*

Live Nude Girls **1995 (R)** Group of thirty-something girlfriends get together to throw a bachelorette party for one of their number and sit around gossiping about sex, relationships, family, and friends. Not much plot but nice ensemble work. **92m/C VHS, LV.** Dana Delany, Kim Cattrall, Cynthia Stevenson, Laila Robins, Olivia D'Abo, Lora Zane, Glenn Quinn, Tim Choate; **D:** Julianna Lavin; **W:** Julianna Lavin; **C:** Christopher Taylor; **M:** Anton Sanko. *REP*

The Live Wire **1934** Stunt-ridden action fare featuring Talmadge at his most daring. This adventure is complete with desert island, lost treasure, stowaways, evil-doers, and a race against the clock. **57m/B VHS, Beta.** Richard Talmadge, George Walsh, Charles French, Alberta Vaughn; **D:** Harry S. Webb. *NOS, DVT, GPV*

Live Wire ½ **1992 (R)** Brosnan is an FBI bomb expert who needs a new line of work. He's up against a terrorist psychopath who has his greedy hands on a new type of explosive. It's liquid, undetectable, looks as innocent as a glass of water, and is capable of blowing up Washington, D.C. Made for cable television. Also available in an unrated version. **85m/C VHS.** Pierce Brosnan, Ben Cross, Ron Silver, Lisa Eilbacher; **D:** Christian Duguay; **W:** Bart Baker. *COL, NLC*

Live Wire: Human Timebomb ½ **1995 (R)** FBI agent Jim Parker is captured by a Cuban general who implants a computer chip into his neck—turning Parker into a human timebomb. **98m/C VHS.** Bryan Genesse, Joe Lara; **D:** Mark Roper; **W:** Jeff Albert; **C:** Rod Stewart; **M:** Itai Haber. *TTC*

The Lives of a Bengal Lancer **1935** One of Hollywood's greatest rousing adventures. Three British Lancers, of varying experience, encounter a vicious revolution against colonial rule. Rivaled only by "Gunga Din" as the ultimate 1930s swashbuckler. Swell plot, lotsa action, great comraderie. Based on the novel by Major Francis Yeats-Brown, and remade in 1939 as "Geronimo." **110m/B VHS, Beta.** Gary Cooper, Franchot Tone, Richard Cromwell, Guy Standing, Sir C. Aubrey Smith, Monte Blue, Kathleen Burke, Noble Johnson, Lumsden Hare, Akim Tamiroff, J. Carrol Naish, Douglass Dumbrille; **D:** Henry Hathaway; **W:** Waldemar Young, John Balderston; **C:** Charles B(ryant) Lang; **M:** Milan Roder. National Board of Review Awards '35: 10 Best Films of the Year; Nominations: Academy Awards '35: Best Adapted Screenplay, Best Director (Hathaway), Best Film Editing, Best Interior Decoration, Best Picture, Best Sound. *MCA*

Livin' Large **1991 (R)** An African-American delivery boy gets the break of his life when a nearby newscaster is shot dead. Grabbing the microphone and continuing the story, he soon finds himself hired by an Atlanta news station as an anchorman, fulfilling a life-long dream. But problems arise when he finds himself losing touch with his friends, his old neighborhood and his roots. Comedy "deals" with the compelling issue of blacks finding success in a white world by trivializing the issue at every turn and resorting to racial stereotypes. **96m/C VHS.** Terrence "T.C." Carson, Lisa Arrindell, Blanche Baker, Nathaniel "Afrika" Hall, Julia Campbell; **D:** Michael A. Schultz; **M:** Herbie Hancock. *HBO*

The Living Coffin ½ *El Grito de la Muerte* **1958** Woman has alarm rigged on her coffin in case she's buried alive. And they called her paranoid. Loosely based on Poe's "Premature Burial." **72m/C VHS.** *MX* Gaston Santos, Maria Duval, Pedro de Aguillon; **D:** Fernando Mendez. *SNC*

The Living Daylights ½ **1987 (PG)** After being used as a pawn in a fake Russian defector plot, our intrepid spy tracks down an international arms and opium smuggling ring. Fine debut by Dalton as 007 in a rousing, refreshing cosmopolitan shoot-em-up. Let's be frank: we were all getting a little fatigued by Roger Moore. **130m/C VHS, Beta, LV.** Timothy Dalton, Maryam D'Abo, Jeroen Krabbe, John Rhys-Davies, Robert Brown, Joe Don Baker, Desmond Llewelyn, Art Malik, Geoffrey Keen, Walter Gotell, Andreas Wisniewski; ***D:*** John Glen; ***W:*** Richard Maibaum, Michael G. Wilson; ***M:*** John Barry. *MGM, TLF, FOX*

The Living Dead *The Scotland Yard Mystery* **1936** An English film about a mad, re-animating scientist. **76m/B VHS, Beta.** *GB* Gerald du Maurier, George Curzan. *NOS, SNC, DVT*

The Living End **1992** Director Araki's radical lovers-on-the-lam story concerns freelance L.A. writer Jon (Gilmore) who has just learned he is H.I.V.-positive. He meets a handsome, violent, hustler named Luke (Dytri) and the two begin a desperate road trip along the California coast which can only end in tragedy. Araki not only wrote and directed the film but also served as cinematographer and editor—all on a $23,000 budget. Stylish, tragic, and filled with black humor and frank homoeroticism. **92m/C VHS.** Craig Gilmore, Mike Dytri, Darcy Marta; ***D:*** Gregg Araki; ***W:*** Gregg Araki. *ACA*

Living Free ½ **1972 (G)** Sequel to "Born Free," based on the nonfictional books by Joy Adamson. Recounts the travails of Elsa the lioness, who is now dying, with three young cubs that need care. Nice and pleasant, but could you pick up the pace? **91m/C VHS, Beta, LV.** Susan Hampshire, Nigel Davenport; ***D:*** Jack Couffer. *COL, GKK*

The Living Head ½ *La Cabeza Viviente* **1959** Archaeologists discover the ancient sepulcher of the great Aztec warrior, Acatl. Ignoring a curse, they steal his severed head and incur the fury of Xitsliapoli. They should have known better. Dubbed in English. **75m/B VHS, Beta.** *MX* Mauricio Garces, Ana Luisa Peluffo, German Robles, Abel Salazar; ***D:*** Chano Urueto. *VYY, SNC*

Living in Oblivion **1994 (R)** Humorous tri-part story is an insiders joke on the problems of low-budget filmmaking, including talent, libido, ego, and pervasive chaos. First, director Nick Reve (Buscemi) tries to film an emotional scene with leading lady Nicole (Keener) only to have everything go wrong; then star Chad (LeGros), a dimwit but a "name," arrives to throw his weight around (and seduce Nicole); and finally the leading lady must deal with an overly sensitive dwarf and Nick's mother. A sleeper. **92m/C VHS, LV.** Steve Buscemi, Catherine Keener, James LeGros, Dermot Mulroney, Danielle von Zerneck, Robert Wightman, Rica Martens, Hilary Gilford; ***D:*** Tom DiCillo; ***W:*** Tom DiCillo; ***C:*** Frank Prinzi; ***M:*** Jim Farmer. Sundance Film Festival '95: Best Screenplay; Nominations: Independent Spirit Awards '96: Best Film, Best Screenplay, Best Supporting Actor (LeGros). *COL*

Living on Tokyo Time ½ **1987** Interesting but often dull, low budget independent comedy about a young Japanese woman who hitches up with a boorish Japanese-American man in order to stay in the United States. An Asian view of Asian-America, filmed on location in San Francisco. **83m/C VHS, Beta.** Minako Ohashi, Ken Nakagawa, Kate Connell, Mitzi Abe, Bill Bonham, Brenda Aoki; ***D:*** Steven Okazaki; ***W:*** Steven Okazaki, John McCormick. *NLC, INJ*

Living Proof: The Hank Williams Jr. Story ½ **1983** TV biopic focusing on the country singer's hell-raising ways as he seeks to get out from under the shadow of his famous father and into the spotlight on his own right. Based on Williams, Jr.'s autobiography; includes 10 songs by Sr. and Jr. **97m/C VHS.** Richard Thomas, Clu Gulager, Allyn Ann McLerie, Naomi Judd, Christian Slater; ***D:*** Dick Lowry; ***W:*** I.C. Rapoport, Stephen Kandel. *WAR*

Living to Die ½ **1991 (R)** Vegas gumshoe is assigned to investigate a blackmailed official, and discovers a woman believed to be dead is alive and beautiful and living incognito. This mystifies him. **84m/C VHS.** Wings Hauser, Darcy Demoss, Asher Brauner, Arnold Vosloo, Jim Williams; ***D:*** Wings Hauser. *PMH, HHE*

The Lizzies of Mack Sennett **1915** Three quick-paced, hilarious Sennett "Tin Lizzie" comedies: "Lizzies of the Field," "Leading Lizzie Astray" and "Love, Speed and Thrills." Plenty of signature slapstick from the master. **51m/C VHS, Beta.** Billy Bevan, Fatty Arbuckle, Mack Swain, Chester Conklin; ***D:*** Mack Sennett. *VYY*

Lloyds of London **1936** If you wonder how the story of a British insurance company can be exciting, just watch this lavish spectacular (which, of course, lacks historical accuracy). Jonathan Blake (Power) has risen in the ranks of the firm, thanks in part to his lifelong friendship with Lord Horatio Nelson (Burton), much to the disgust of haughty Lord Everett Stacy (an ever-supercilious Sanders). As Bonaparte comes to power, Blake travels to France to rescue some friends and saves Elizabeth (Carroll), who turns out to be Stacy's wife. Stacy is also spreading rumors about Lloyds' solvency and Nelson's heroics at Trafalgar and his machinations lead to further trouble with Blake. **115m/B VHS.** Tyrone Power, George Sanders, Madeleine Carroll, John Burton, Guy Standing, Sir C. Aubrey Smith, Freddie Bartholomew, Virginia Field, Montagu Love, Una O'Connor; ***D:*** Henry King; ***W:*** Ernest Pascal, Walter Ferris; ***C:*** Bert Glennon. *FXV*

Loaded **1996 (R)** Writer-director Campion (sister of director Jane) follows a group of teens to an abandoned English mansion as they try to film an amateur horror movie. While there, the group decides to have some fun, with the help of LSD. This leads to some therapeutic and angst-ridden discussions about each of their problems, as well as a tragic accident, which changes the lives of all involved. There's some nice character sketches, unfortunately they're more interesting than the loose plot, which leaves too many questions unanswered. **105m/C VHS.** *GB* Thandie Newton, Catherine McCormack, Oliver Milburn, Nick Patrick, Danny Cunningham, Mathew Eggleton, Biddy Hodson; ***D:*** Anna Campion; ***W:*** Anna Campion; ***C:*** Alan Almond; ***M:*** Simon Fisher Turner. *NYR*

Loaded Guns *Woof!* **1975** Airline stewardess-cum-double agent must totally immobilize a top drug trafficking ring. Pathetic spy tale with plenty of unintended laughs. **90m/C VHS, Beta.** Ursula Andress, Woody Strode; ***D:*** Fernando Di Leo. *LIV*

Loaded Pistols **1948** Story set in the old West starring Gene Autry. **80m/B VHS, Beta.** Gene Autry, Jack Holt, Barbara Britton; ***D:*** John English. *NOS, VCN, DVT*

Loan Shark **1952** An ex-convict gets a job at a tire company, working undercover to expose a loan shark ring. Hackneyed plot moves quickly. **79m/B VHS, Beta, LV.** George Raft, John Hoyt; ***D:*** Seymour Friedman. *NO*

Lobster for Breakfast ½ **1982 (R)** An Italian gag-fest about a toilet salesman infiltrating his friend's confused marital existence just to make a sale. With English subtitles; also available in a dubbed version. **96m/C VHS, Beta.** *IT* Enrico Montesano, Claude Brasseur, Claudine Auger; ***D:*** Giorgio Capitani. *SUE*

Lobster Man from Mars **1989 (PG)** When rich movie producer (Curtis) learns from his accountant that he must produce a flop or be taken to the cleaners by the IRS, he buys a homemade horror movie from a young filmmaker. The film is an ultra-low budget production featuring a kooky lobster man and a screaming damsel. The premise peters out about halfway through, but there are enough yuks to keep you going. **84m/C VHS, Beta, LV.** Tony Curtis, Deborah Foreman, Patrick Macnee, Tommy Sledge, Billy Barty, Phil Proctor; ***D:*** Stanley Shiff. *LIV*

Local Badman **1932** A dim-witted cowhand saves the day in this rip-roaring tale of the old west. **60m/B VHS, Beta.** Hoot Gibson. *NOS, VCI, RXM*

Local Hero **1983 (PG)** Riegert is a yuppie representative of a huge oil company who endeavors to buy a sleepy Scottish fishing village for excavation, and finds himself hypnotized by the place and its crusty denizens. Back in Texas at company headquarters, tycoon Lancaster deals with a psycho therapist and gazes at the stars looking for clues. A low-key, charmingly offbeat Scottish comedy with its own sense of logic and quiet humor, poetic landscapes, and unique characters, epitomizing Forsyth's original style. **112m/C VHS, Beta, LV.** *GB* Peter Riegert, Denis Lawson, Burt Lancaster, Fulton Mackay, Jenny Seagrove, Peter Capaldi, Norman Chancer; ***D:*** Bill Forsyth; ***W:*** Bill Forsyth; ***C:*** Chris Menges; ***M:*** Mark Knopfler. British Academy Awards '83: Best Director (Forsyth); New York Film Critics Awards '83: Best Screenplay; National Society of Film Critics Awards '83: Best Screenplay. *WAR*

The Loch Ness Horror *Woof!* **1982** The famed monster surfaces and chomps on the local poachers—and with good reason. Would that it had munched this movie's producer in, say, 1981. **93m/C VHS, Beta.** Barry Buchanan, Miki McKenzie, Sandy Kenyon; ***D:*** Larry Buchanan. *NO*

Lock 'n' Load **1990 (R)** Why are all the soldiers in the 82nd Airborne stealing vast sums, then committing suicide? One of the guys involved wants to know. **?m/C VHS, LV.** Jack Vogel; ***D:*** David A. Prior. *AIP*

Lock Up ½ **1989 (R)** Peaceful con Stallone, with only six months to go, is harassed and tortured by vicious prison warden Sutherland in retribution for an unexplained past conflict. Lackluster and moronic; semi-color; surely Sutherland can find better roles. **115m/C VHS, Beta.** Sylvester Stallone, Donald Sutherland, Sonny Landham, John Amos, Darlanne Fluegel, Frank McRae; ***D:*** John Flynn; ***W:*** Jeb Stuart; ***M:*** Bill Conti. *LIV*

Lockdown ½ **1990** Charged with his partner's murder, a detective is forced to ponder the perennial puzzle of life. Not a pretty sight. **90m/C VHS.** Joe Estevez, Mike Farrell, Richard Lynch. *VMK*

L'Odeur des Fauves **1966** One of a cynical reporter's scandalous stories gets an innocent man killed, compelling the reporter somehow to make restitution. Subtitled in English. **86m/C VHS, Beta.** *FR* Maurice Ronet, Josephine Chaplin, Vittorio De Sica; ***D:*** Richard Balducci. *BAR*

The Lodger *The Case of Jonathan Drew; The Lodger: A Case of London Fog* **1926** A mysterious lodger is thought to be a rampaging mass murderer of young women. First Hitchcock film to explore the themes and ideas that would become his trademarks. Silent. Climactic chase is memorable. Remade three times. Look closely for the Master in his first cameo. **91m/B VHS, Beta.** *GB* Ivor Novello, Marie Ault, Arthur Chesney, Malcolm Keen; ***Cameos:*** Alfred Hitchcock; ***D:*** Alfred Hitchcock; ***W:*** Alfred Hitchcock. *GPV, NOS, VYY*

Logan's Run ½ **1976** In the 23rd century, a hedonistic society exists in a huge bubble and people are only allowed to live to the age of 30. Intriguing concepts and great futuristic sets prevail here. Based on the novel by William Nolan and George Clayton Johnson. **120m/C VHS, Beta, LV.** Michael York, Jenny Agutter, Richard Jordan, Roscoe Lee Browne, Farrah Fawcett, Peter Ustinov, Camilla Carr, Ann Ford; ***D:*** Michael Anderson Sr.; ***W:*** David Zelag Goodman; ***C:*** Ernest Laszlo; ***M:*** Jerry Goldsmith. Academy Awards '76: Best Visual Effects; Nominations: Academy Awards '76: Best Art Direction/Set Decoration, Best Cinematography. *MGM*

Lois Gibbs and the Love Canal **1982** Mason's television movie debut as Lois Gibbs, a housewife turned activist, fighting the authorities over chemical-dumping in the Love Canal area of Niagara Falls, New York. The script doesn't convey the seriousness of developments in that region. **100m/C VHS.** Marsha Mason, Bob Gunton, Penny Fuller, Roberta Maxwell, Jeremy Licht, Louise Latham; ***D:*** Glenn Jordan. *NO*

Lola **1961** A wonderful tale of a nightclub dancer and her amorous adventures. Innovative film that marked the beginning of French New Wave. In French with English subtitles. **90m/B VHS.** *FR* Anouk

Aimee, Marc Michel, Elina Labourdette, Jacques Harden; *D:* Jacques Demy. *INT, INJ, TPV*

Lola ☙½ *The Statutory Affair; Twinky* **1969 (PG)** A teenaged girl links up romantically with a considerably older writer of pornographic books. One would expect more from such a good cast, but the film never follows through. British release was originally 98 minutes. **88m/C VHS.** *GB IT* Charles Bronson, Susan George, Trevor Howard, Michael Craig, Honor Blackman, Lionel Jeffries, Robert Morley, Jack Hawkins, Orson Bean, Kay Medford, Paul Ford; *D:* Richard Donner. *FCT, MRV*

Lola Montes ☙☙☙☙ **1955** Ophuls' final masterpiece recounts the life and sins of the famous courtesan, mistress of Franz Liszt and the King of Bavaria. Ignored upon release, but hailed later by the French as a cinematic landmark. Presented in its original wide-screen format; in French with English subtitles. Also available in a 110 minute version. Adapted from an unpublished novel by Cecil Saint-Laurent. **140m/C Beta, LV.** *FR* Martine Carol, Peter Ustinov, Anton Walbrook, Ivan Desny, Oskar Werner; *D:* Max Ophuls; *W:* Max Ophuls; *M:* Georges Auric. *CRC, INJ, NLC*

Lolita ☙☙☙ **1962** A middle-aged professor is consumed by his lust for a teenage nymphet in this strange film considered daring in its time. Based on Vladimir Nabokov's novel. Watch for Winters' terrific portrayal as Lolita's sex-starved mother. **152m/B VHS, Beta, LV.** *GB* James Mason, Shelley Winters, Peter Sellers, Sue Lyon; *D:* Stanley Kubrick; *C:* Oswald Morris. Nominations: Academy Awards '62: Best Adapted Screenplay. *MGM, CRC*

London Kills Me ☙☙ **1991 (R)** A slice-of-life story London-style. Set at the end of the Thatcher era, Clint is a homeless drifter dealing drugs to get by. He's trying to get enough money for a new pair of shoes which will enable him to get a job in a fancy restaurant and away from his aimless life. His friend Muffdiver leads the group of drug pushers and is obsessed with money and power. Sylvie is the sultry junkie who drifts between Clint, Muffdiver, and her drug needs. The directorial debut of Kureishi is more a collection of characters and situations than a complete film but there are moments of disturbing intensity and odd sweetness. **105m/C VHS, LV.** *GB* Justin Chadwick, Steven Mackintosh, Emer McCourt, Roshan Seth, Fiona Shaw, Brad Dourif, Gordon Warnecke; *D:* Hanif Kureishi; *W:* Hanif Kureishi. *LIV, PMS*

London Melody ☙½ *Girl in the Street* **1937** Neagle is a spirited Cockney busker who meets a kindly Italian diplomat who decides to finance her musical education. He promptly also falls in love with her. **71m/B VHS, Beta, 8mm.** *GB* Anna Neagle, Tullio Carminati, Robert Douglas, Horace Hodgers; *D:* Herbert Wilcox. *VYY*

The Lone Avenger ☙☙ **1933** Average oater centers around a bank panic, with two-gun Maynard clearing up the trouble. **60m/B VHS, Beta.** Ken Maynard, Muriel Gordon, James Marcus. *NOS, VCN, CAB*

Lone Bandit ☙½ **1933** Vintage western starring Chandler. **57m/B VHS, Beta.** Lane Chandler, Doris Brook, Wally Wales; *D:* J.P. McGowan. *VCN*

The Lone Defender **1932** A dozen episodes of the western serial starring the canine crusader, Rin Tin Tin. **235m/B VHS, Beta.** Walter Miller, June Marlowe, Buzz Barton, Josef Swickard, Frank Lanning, Robert F. (Bob) Kortman; *D:* Richard Thorpe. *VDM, GPV, MLB*

Lone Justice ☙☙½ **1993 (R)** Cowboy Ned Blessing has seen and done it all (from outlaw to sheriff) but his wild ways have caught up with him. Now, he's relating his exploits from a jail cell as he awaits his fate at the end of a rope. Beware—this looks like the first chapter of a series and there's no real ending. **94m/C VHS, LV.** Daniel Baldwin, Luis Avalos, Chris Cooper, Sean Baca, Taylor Fry, Julia Campbell, Rene Auberjonois, Timothy Scott, Bob Gunton, Miguel Sandoval, Jeff Kober; *D:* Peter Werner; *W:* William D. Wittliff; *M:* Basil Poledouris. *ACA*

Lone Justice 2 ☙☙½ *Ned Blessing: The Story of My Life and Times* **1993 (PG-13)** Laconic hero Ned Blessing (Johnson), along with Mexican sidekick Crecencio (Avalos), return to Blessing's hometown after a six year absence and find it ruled by six-shooters and fists. The despicable Borgers clan has murdered the local sheriff (who happens to be Blessing's daddy) and rules by intimidation—until Ned gets involved. Cliched but amusing TV movie. **93m/C VHS.** Brad Johnson, Luis Avalos, Wes Studi, Bill McKinney, Brenda Bakke, Julius Tennon, Richard Riehle, Gregory Scott Cummins, Rob Campbell, Rusty Schwimmer; *D:* Jack Bender; *W:* William D. Wittliff. *TRI*

The Lone Ranger **1938** Western serial about the masked man and his faithful Indian sidekick. From a long-sought print found in Mexico, this program is burdened by a noisy sound track, two completely missing chapters, an abridged episode #15, and Spanish subtitles. **234m/B VHS, Beta.** Lee Powell; *D:* William Witney, John English. *VYY, NOS, VCN*

Lone Ranger **1956** Tonto and that strange masked man must prevent a war between ranchers and Indians in the first of the "Lone Ranger" series. "Hi-ho Silver!" **87m/C VHS, Beta.** Clayton Moore, Jay Silverheels, Lyle Bettger, Bonita Granville; *D:* Stuart Heisler. *MGM*

Lone Ranger and the Lost City of Gold ☙☙ **1958** Three Indian men are found dead, and the Lone Ranger and Tonto set out to discover the killers. **80m/C VHS.** Clayton Moore, Jay Silverheels, Douglas Kennedy; *D:* Lesley Selander; *M:* Les Baxter. *NO*

The Lone Rider in Cheyenne ☙½ **1942** One of the last in the "Lone Rider" series. The Lone Rider is out to clear the name of an innocent man accused of murder. **59m/B VHS.** George Houston, Al "Fuzzy" St. John; *D:* Sam Newfield. *NOS, DVT, HEG*

The Lone Rider in Ghost Town ☙½ **1941** Outlaws "haunt" a ghost town to protect their hidden mine and the Lone Rider and his pal, Fuzzy, are out to solve the mystery. Installment in the short-lived "Lone Rider" series. **64m/B VHS.** George Houston, Al "Fuzzy" St. John, Budd Buster; *D:* Sam Newfield. *NOS, DVT, HEG*

The Lone Runner *Woof!* **1988 (PG)** An adventurer rescues a beautiful heiress from Arab kidnappers in this dud. **90m/C VHS, Beta, LV.** Miles O'Keeffe, Ronald Lacey, Michael J. Aronin, John Steiner, Al Yamanouchi; *D:* Ruggero Deodato. *MED*

Lone Star ☙☙½ **1952** Big stars, big budget western in which Texas fights for independence as good guy Gable and badman Crawford fight each other. Gardner plays a fiery newspaper editor as well as Gable's love interest. Script is chock full of holes, but great action scenes make up for it. Based on the story by Borden Chase. **94m/B VHS.** Clark Gable, Ava Gardner, Broderick Crawford, Lionel Barrymore, Beulah Bondi, Ed Begley Sr., William Farnum, Lowell Gilmore; *D:* Vincent Sherman; *W:* Howard Estabrook, Borden Chase. *MGM*

Lone Star ☙☙☙½ **1995 (R)** Terrific contemporary western set in the border town Frontera, Texas. Sheriff Sam Deeds (Cooper) is still dealing with the legacy of his father, legendary lawman Buddy Deeds (McConaughey) who, 40 years before, wrestled control of the town from his racist, corrupt predecessor Charlie Wade (Kristofferson) and supposedly sent him packing. But when skeletal remains and a sheriff's badge turn up on an abandoned Army rifle range, guess whose bones they turn out to be. Buddy's friends would like Sam to just leave the past lie but he can't and learns some hard home truths. This is only one of the town's stories that Sayles gracefully tells and, as always, his ensemble cast all offer outstanding performances. **134m/C VHS.** Chris Cooper, Matthew McConaughey, Kris Kristofferson, Elizabeth Pena, Joe Morton, Ron Canada, Clifton James, Miriam Colon, Frances McDormand; *D:* John Sayles; *W:* John Sayles; *C:* Stuart Dryburgh; *M:* Mason Daring. *NYR*

Lone Star Kid **1988** 11-year-old Brian Zimmerman lives in Crabb, Texas—population 400. After he witnesses a car accident death because there's no adequate emergency service, he decides to run for mayor and help modernize the town. Based on a true story. Includes a viewers' guide. Presented as part of the "Wonderworks" series. **55m/C VHS.** James Earl Jones, Chad Sheets; *M:* Charlie Daniels. *PME, HMV, BTV*

Lone Star Law Men ☙ **1942** A U.S. marshal has his hands full in a border town overrun with bandits. Keene stars as the deputy marshall who goes undercover and joins the gang in an attempt to foil their crooked plans. **58m/B VHS.** Tom Keene, Frank Yaconelli, Sugar Dawn, Betty Miles; *D:* Robert Emmett Tansey. *NOS, DVT*

The Lone Star Ranger ☙½ **1930** Former outlaw O'Brien is trying to go straight by helping to bring a gang of rustlers to justice. Interesting plot twist in the link between his girlfriend and the head of the gang. **64m/B VHS.** George O'Brien, Sue Carol, Walter McGrail, Warren Hymer, Russell Simpson; *D:* A.F. Erickson. *DVT, HEG*

Lone Wolf ☙ **1988** A werewolf terrorizes a high school, and a few computerniks track it down. **97m/C VHS, Beta.** Dyann Brown, Kevin Hart, Jamie Newcomb, Ann Douglas; *D:* John Callas. *PSM*

Lone Wolf McQuade ☙☙½ **1983** Martial arts action abounds in this modern-day Western which pits unorthodox Texas Ranger Norris against a band of gun-running mercenaries led by Carradine. Oh, and there's a conflict-ridden love interest as well. Violent (and not particularly literary) but worthy entry in chop-socky genre. **107m/C VHS, Beta, LV.** Chuck Norris, Leon Isaac Kennedy, David Carradine, L.Q. Jones, Barbara Carrera; *D:* Steve Carver; *W:* H. Kaye Dyal. *VES*

The Loneliest Runner ☙☙ **1976** Based on the true story of an Olympic track star who, as a teenager, suffered humiliation as a bed-wetter. The real-life experiences of producer-director Landon are presented in a touching and sensitive manner. Made for television. **74m/C VHS, Beta.** Michael Landon, Lance Kerwin, DeAnn Mears, Brian Keith, Melissa Sue Anderson; *D:* Michael Landon. *WAR, OM*

The Loneliness of the Long Distance Runner ☙☙☙ *Rebel with a Cause* **1962** Courtenay, in his film debut, turns in a powerful performance as an angry young man infected by the poverty and hopelessness of the British slums. His first attempt at crime is a bust and lands him in a boys reformatory where he is recruited for the running team. While training for the big event with a rival school, Redgrave's obsession with winning the race and Courtenay's continued indifference to the outcome lock the two in an intriguing, seemingly one-sided power struggle. Though widely overlooked when first released, it has since been praised as one of the finest teenage angst films of the '60s. Riveting depiction on a boy's rite of passage into manhood. **104m/B VHS, Beta.** *GB* Tom Courtenay, Michael Redgrave, Avis Bunnage, Peter Madden, James Bolam, Julia Foster, Topsy Jane, Frank Finlay; *D:* Tony Richardson; *C:* Walter Lassally; *M:* John Addison. *WAR, SNC*

Lonely Are the Brave ☙☙☙ **1962** A free-spirited cowboy out of sync with the modern age tries to rescue a buddy from a local jail, and in his eventual escape is tracked relentlessly by modern law enforcement. A compelling, sorrowful essay on civilized progress and exploitation of nature. Adapted from the novel "Brave Cowboy" by Edward Abbey. **107m/B VHS, Beta, LV.** Kirk Douglas, Walter Matthau, Gena Rowlands, Carroll O'Connor, George Kennedy; *D:* David Miller; *M:* Jerry Goldsmith. *MCA*

The Lonely Guy ☙☙½ **1984 (R)** Romantic comedy with Martin as a jilted writer who writes a best-selling book about being a lonely guy and finds stardom does have its rewards. Based on "The Lonely Guy's Book of Life" by Bruce Jay Friedman. **91m/C VHS, Beta, LV.** Steve Martin, Charles Grodin, Judith Ivey, Steve Lawrence, Robyn Douglass, Merv Griffin, Dr. Joyce Brothers; *D:* Arthur Hiller; *W:* Stan Daniels; *M:* Jerry Goldsmith. *MCA*

Lonely Hearts ☙☙☙ **1982 (R)** An endearing Australian romantic comedy about a piano tuner, who at 50 finds himself alone after years of caring for his mother, and a sexually insecure spinster, whom he meets through a dating service. Wonderful performances and a good script make this a delightful film that touches the human heart. **95m/C VHS, Beta.** *AU* Wendy Hughes, Norman Kaye, Jon Finlayson, Julia Blake, Jonathon Hardy; ***D:*** Paul Cox; ***W:*** John Clarke, Paul Cox. Australian Film Institute '82: Best Film. *SUE*

Lonely Hearts ☙½ **1991 (R)** A handsome con man works his wiles on a lonely woman in this erotic thriller. Standard plot wastes a good cast. **109m/C VHS.** Eric Roberts, Beverly D'Angelo, Joanna Cassidy; ***W:*** R.E. Daniels. *LIV*

Lonely in America ☙☙½ **1990** Charming romantic comedy of a newcomer in New York City. Arun (Chowdhry) has just arrived from India and has quite a few things to learn about life in the Big Apple. **96m/C VHS.** Ranjit Chowdhry, Adelaide Miller, Robert Kessler, Melissa Christopher, David Toney, Tirlok Malik; ***D:*** Barry Brown; ***W:*** Barry Brown, Satyajit Joy Palit. *ACA*

The Lonely Lady *Woof!* **1983 (R)** Young writer comes to Hollywood with dreams of success, gets involved with the seamy side of movie-making, and is driven to a nervous breakdown. Pia needs acting lessons, yet it probably wouldn't have helped this trash. Adapted from the novel by Harold Robbins. **92m/C VHS, Beta, LV.** Pia Zadora, Lloyd Bochner, Bibi Besch, Joseph Cali, Ray Liotta; ***D:*** Peter Sasdy. Golden Raspberry Awards '83: Worst Picture, Worst Actress (Zadora), Worst Director (Sasdy), Worst Screenplay, Worst Song ("The Way You Do It"). *MCA*

Lonely Man ☙☙½ **1957** A gunfighter tries to end his career, but is urged into one last battle. Strong performances and tight direction make up for weak plot. **87m/B VHS, Beta.** Jack Palance, Anthony Perkins, Neville Brand, Elaine Aiken; ***D:*** Henry Levin; ***C:*** Lionel Lindon. *PAR, BAR*

The Lonely Passion of Judith Hearne ☙☙☙ **1987 (R)** A self-effacing Dublin spinster meets a man who gives her his attention, but she must overcome her own self-doubt and crisis of faith. Adapted from Brian Moore's 1955 novel. Excellent performances from both Hoskins and Smith. **116m/C VHS.** *GB* Maggie Smith, Bob Hoskins, Wendy Hiller, Marie Kean, Ian McNeice, Alan Devlin, Rudi Davies, Prunella Scales; ***D:*** Jack Clayton; ***W:*** Peter Nelson; ***M:*** Georges Delerue. British Academy Awards '88: Best Actress (Smith). *CAN*

The Lonely Sex ☙½ **1959** Creepy and bizarre film in which a maniac kidnaps a young girl and is then harassed by her psychotic housemate. **?m/C VHS.** Jean Evans, Karl Light, Mary Gonzales. *SNC, TPV*

Lonely Trail/Three Texas Steers **1939** Double your pleasure with two early Duke operas. In "Lonely Trail," Wayne dukes it out with dastardly carpetbaggers after the Civil War, while "Three Texas Steers," part of the "Three Mesquiteers" series, has Wayne and company spare a gal rancher/major babe from certain peril. **112m/B VHS.** John Wayne, George "Gabby" Hayes, Ray Corrigan, Raymond Hatton; ***D:*** George Sherman. *REP*

Lonely Wives ☙☙ **1931** A lawyer hires an entertainer to serve as his double because of his marital problems. **86m/B VHS, Beta.** Edward Everett Horton, Patsy Ruth Miller, Laura La Plante, Esther Ralston; ***D:*** Russell Mack. *NOS, VYY*

Lonelyhearts ☙☙½ **1958** Clift plays a reporter who is assigned the lovelorn column of his paper and gets too immersed in the problems of his readers. Given the superior cast and excellent material, this is a somewhat disappointing adaptation of the brilliant Nathanael West novel "Miss Lonelyhearts." Film debuts of both Stapleton and director Donehue. **101m/B VHS.** Montgomery Clift, Robert Ryan, Myrna Loy, Dolores Hart, Maureen Stapleton, Frank Maxwell, Jackie Coogan, Mike Kellin; ***D:*** Vincent J. Donehue. Nominations: Academy Awards '58: Best Supporting Actress (Stapleton). *MGM, SUE*

Loners ☙☙ **1972 (R)** Three teenagers run from the Southwest police after they are accused of murdering a highway patrolman. **80m/C VHS, Beta.** Dean Stockwell, Gloria Grahame, Scott Brady, Alex Dreier, Pat Stich; ***D:*** Sutton Roley; ***W:*** Barry Sandler. *NO*

Lonesome Dove ☙☙☙½ **1989** Classic western saga with Duvall and Jones in outstanding roles as two aging ex-Texas Rangers who decide to leave their quiet lives for a last adventure—a cattle drive from Texas to Montana. Along the way they encounter a new love (Lane), a lost love (Huston), and a savage renegade Indian (well-played by Forrest). Based on Larry McMurtry's Pulitzer Prize winning novel, this handsome television miniseries is a finely detailed evocation of the Old West, with a wonderful cast and an equally fine production. Available in a four volume boxed set. Followed by "Return to Lonesome Dove." **480m/C VHS, LV.** Robert Duvall, Tommy Lee Jones, Anjelica Huston, Danny Glover, Diane Lane, Rick Schroder, Robert Urich, D.B. Sweeney, Frederic Forrest; ***D:*** Simon Windsor; ***W:*** William D. Wittliff; ***M:*** Basil Poledouris. *CAF, TVC, IME*

Lonesome Trail ☙½ **1955** Routine Western that differs from the average oater by having the good guys use bows and arrows to fight their battles. **73m/B VHS, Beta.** Jimmy Wakely, Lee White, Lorraine Miller, John James; ***D:*** Richard Bartlett. *NO*

Long Ago Tomorrow ☙☙ *The Raging Moon* **1971 (PG)** A paralyzed athlete enters a church-run home for the disabled rather than return to his family as the object of their pity. A love affair with a woman, who shares the same disability, helps the athlete to adapt. **90m/C VHS, Beta.** *GB* Malcolm McDowell, Nanette Newman, Bernard Lee, Georgia Brown, Gerald Sim; ***D:*** Bryan Forbes. *COL*

The Long Dark Hall ☙☙½ **1951** Courtroom drama in which an innocent man is brought to trial when his showgirl mistress is found dead. **86m/B VHS, Beta.** *GB* Rex Harrison, Lilli Palmer, Denis O'Dea, Raymond Huntley, Patricia Wayne, Anthony Dawson; ***D:*** Anthony Bushell, Reginald Beck. *SNC*

The Long Day Closes ☙☙☙ **1992 (PG)** It's 1956 Liverpool and 11-year-old Bud (McCormack) is part of a working-class Catholic family who longs to escape from his humdrum life. And how? By going to the movies of course and filling his head with pop songs. Nostalgic view of family life filled with sweet, small everyday moments set in a dreary postwar England. Sequel to Davies's also autobiographical film "Distant Voices, Still Lives." **84m/C VHS.** *GB* Leigh McCormack, Marjorie Yates, Anthony Watson, Ayse Owens; ***D:*** Terence Davies; ***W:*** Terence Davies. Nominations: Cannes Film Festival '92: Best Film. *COL*

Long Day's Journey into Night ☙☙☙☙ **1962** A brooding, devastating film based on Eugene O'Neill's most powerful and autobiographical play. Depicts a day in the life of a family deteriorating under drug addiction, alcoholism, and imminent death. Hepburn's performance is outstanding. In 1988, the Broadway version was taped and released on video. **174m/B VHS, LV.** Ralph Richardson, Katharine Hepburn, Dean Stockwell, Jeanne Barr, Jason Robards Jr.; ***D:*** Sidney Lumet; ***W:*** Eugene O'Neill; ***C:*** Boris Kaufman; ***M:*** Andre Previn. Cannes Film Festival '62: Best Actress (Hepburn); National Board of Review Awards '62: 10 Best Films of the Year, Best Supporting Actor (Robards); Nominations: Academy Awards '62: Best Actress (Hepburn). *REP*

Long Day's Journey into Night ☙☙ **1988** A taped version of the Broadway production of the epic Eugene O'Neill play about a Southern family deteriorating under the weight of terminal illness, alcoholism and drug abuse. In 1962 a movie adaptation of the play was released with outstanding performances from its cast. **169m/C VHS, Beta.** Jack Lemmon, Bethel Leslie, Peter Gallagher, Kevin Spacey, Jodie Lynne McLintock; ***D:*** Jonathan Miller. *LIV, VES*

The Long Days of Summer ☙☙ **1980** Set in pre-WWII America, this film portrays a Jewish attorney's struggle against the prejudices of the New England town where he lives. Sequel to "When Every Day Is the Fourth of July." Made for television. **105m/C VHS.** Dean Jones, Joan Hackett, Louanne, Donald Moffat, Andrew Duggan, Michael McGuire; ***D:*** Dan Curtis. *LIV*

Long Gone ☙☙½ **1987** In the fifties, an over-the-hill minor-league player/manager is given a last lease on life and the pennant with two talented rookies and a sexy baseball groupie. Made for cable television. **113m/C VHS, Beta, LV.** William L. Petersen, Henry Gibson, Katy Boyer, Virginia Madsen; ***D:*** Martin Davidson. *ORI, WAR*

The Long Good Friday ☙☙☙½ **1979** Set in London's dockland, this is a violent story of a crime boss who meets his match. Hoskin's world crumbles over an Easter weekend when his buildings are bombed and his men murdered. He thinks its the work of rival gangsters only to discover an even deadlier threat is behind his troubles. One of the best of the crime genre, with an exquisitely charismatic performance by Hoskins. **109m/C VHS, Beta.** *GB* Bob Hoskins, Helen Mirren, Dave King, Bryan Marshall, George Coulouris, Pierce Brosnan, Derek Thompson, Eddie Constantine; ***D:*** John MacKenzie; ***C:*** Phil Meheux. Edgar Allan Poe Awards '82: Best Screenplay. *VTR*

The Long Goodbye ☙☙☙ **1973 (R)** Raymond Chandler's penultimate novel with the unmistakable Altman touch—which is to say that some of the changes to the story have pushed purist noses out of joint. Gould is cast as an insouciant anti-Marlowe, the film noir atmosphere has been transmuted into a Hollywood film neon, genre jibing abounds, and the ending has been rewritten. But the revamping serves a purpose, which is to make Marlowe a viable character in a contemporary world. Handsomely photographed by Vilmos Zsigmond. Don't miss bulky boy Arnold's cameo (his second film appearance). **112m/C VHS, Beta, LV.** Elliott Gould, Nina Van Pallandt, Sterling Hayden, Henry Gibson, Mark Rydell, David Arkin, Warren Berlinger; ***Cameos:*** Arnold Schwarzenegger, David Carradine; ***D:*** Robert Altman; ***W:*** Leigh Brackett; ***C:*** Vilmos Zsigmond; ***M:*** John Williams. National Society of Film Critics Awards '73: Best Cinematography. *MGM, FCT*

The Long Gray Line ☙☙☙ **1955** Power gives an outstanding performance as Marty Maher, a humble Irish immigrant who became an institution at West Point. This is the inspiring story of his rise from an unruly cadet to one of the academy's most beloved instructors. O'Hara does a fine job of playing his wife, who like her husband, adopts the young cadets as her own. Director Ford gracefully captures the spirit and honor associated with West Point in this affectionate drama. **138m/C VHS.** Tyrone Power, Maureen O'Hara, Robert Francis, Donald Crisp, Ward Bond, Betsy Palmer, Phil Carey; ***D:*** John Ford. *COL*

The Long Haul ☙☙ **1957** A truck driver becomes involved with crooks as his marriage sours. **88m/C VHS.** Victor Mature, Diana Dors, Patrick Allen, Gene Anderson; ***D:*** Ken Hughes. *GKK*

The Long, Hot Summer ☙☙☙½ **1958** A tense, well-played adaptation of the William Faulkner story about a wanderer latching himself onto a tyrannical Mississippi family. The first on-screen pairing of Newman and Woodward, and one of the best. Remade for television in 1986. **117m/C VHS, Beta.** Paul Newman, Orson Welles, Joanne Woodward, Lee Remick, Anthony (Tony) Franciosa, Angela Lansbury, Richard Anderson; ***D:*** Martin Ritt; ***W:*** Harriet Frank Jr., Irving Ravetch; ***C:*** Joseph LaShelle; ***M:*** Alex North. Cannes Film Festival '58: Best Actor (Newman). *FOX*

The Long, Hot Summer ☙☙☙½ **1986** A made-for-television version of the William Faulkner story, "The Hamlet," about a drifter taken under a Southern patriarch's wing. He's bribed into courting the man's unmarried daughter. Wonderful performances from the entire cast, especially Ivey and surprisingly, Johnson. Remake of the 1958 film with Paul Newman and Joanne Woodward that is on par with the original. **172m/C VHS, Beta.** Don Johnson, Cybill Shepherd, Judith Ivey, Jason Robards Jr., Ava Gardner, William Russ, Wings Hauser, William Forsythe, Albert Hall; ***D:*** Stuart Cooper; ***M:*** Charles Bernstein. *FOX*

The Long Island Four ☙☙½ **1980** Four Nazi saboteurs are smitten by the decadent nightlife of the Big Apple in 1942. The late Grafstrom's Super-8 film, based on a true story, was an underground hit. **100m/C VHS.** ***D:*** Anders Grafstrom. *MWF*

Long John Silver ☠½ *Long John Silver Returns to Treasure Island* **1953** Famed pirate John Silver plans a return trip to Treasure Island to search for the elusive treasure; unofficial sequel to "Treasure Island" by Disney. **106m/C VHS, Beta.** *AU* Robert Newton, Connie Gilchrist, Kit Taylor, Grant Taylor, Rod Taylor; ***D:*** Byron Haskin. *GEM, MRV, CAB*

Long Journey Back ☠☠ **1978** The biographical story of a young woman's rehabilitation after her injury in a school bus accident. Produced for television. **100m/C VHS.** Mike Connors, Cloris Leachman, Stephanie Zimbalist, Katy Kurtzman; ***D:*** Mel Damski. *LIV*

The Long, Long Trailer ☠☠½ **1954** A couple on their honeymoon find that trailer life is more than they bargained for. Lots of fun with charming direction from Minelli, and Ball's incredible slapstick style. **97m/C VHS, LV.** Desi Arnaz Sr., Lucille Ball, Marjorie Main, Keenan Wynn; ***D:*** Vincente Minnelli. *MGM, FCT, BTV*

The Long Riders ☠☠☠ **1980 (R)** Excellent mythic western in which the Jesse James and Cole Younger gangs raid banks, trains, and stagecoaches in post-Civil War Missouri. Stylish, meticulous and a violent look back, with one of the better slow-motion shootouts in Hollywood history. Notable for the portrayal of four sets of brothers by four Hollywood brother sets. Complimented by excellent Cooder score. **100m/C VHS, Beta, LV.** Stacy Keach, James Keach, Randy Quaid, Dennis Quaid, David Carradine, Keith Carradine, Robert Carradine, Christopher Guest, Nicholas Guest, Pamela Reed, Savannah Smith, James Whitmore Jr., Harry Carey Jr.; ***D:*** Walter Hill; ***W:*** Stacy Keach, James Keach, Bill Bryden; ***M:*** Ry Cooder. Nominations: Cannes Film Festival '80: Best Film. *MGM*

Long Road Home ☠☠½ **1991 (PG)** Migrant family must decide between working under inhumane conditions or risk losing everything by joining the labor movement during the depression. TV movie. **?m/C VHS.** Mark Harmon, John Evans, Adam Horovitz, Lee Purcell, Leon Russom, Donald Sutherland, Morgan Weisser; ***D:*** John Korty. *NHO*

Long Shadows ☠½ **1986** An analysis of how the resonating effects of the Civil War can still be felt on society, via interviews with a number of noted writers, historians, civil rights activists and politicians. **88m/C VHS, Beta.** Robert Penn Warren, Studs Terkel, Jimmy Carter, Robert Coles, Tom Wicker. *JAF*

Long Shot **1981** Two foosball enthusiasts work their way through local tournaments to make enough money to make it to the World Championships in Tahoe. **100m/C VHS, Beta.** Ian Giatti. *NO*

Long Time Gone ☠ **1986** An over-the-hill detective tries to solve a murder while dealing with his bratty, alienated 11-year-old son. Made for television. **97m/C VHS, Beta.** Paul LeMat, Wil Wheaton, Ann Dusenberry, Barbara Stock; ***D:*** Robert Butler. *NO*

The Long Voyage Home ☠☠☠½ **1940** A talented cast performs this must-see screen adaptation of Eugene O'Neill's play about crew members aboard a merchant steamer in 1939. Wayne plays a young lad from Sweden who is trying to get home and stay out of trouble as he and the other seaman get shore leave. **105m/B VHS, Beta, LV.** John Wayne, Thomas Mitchell, Ian Hunter, Barry Fitzgerald, Mildred Natwick, John Qualen; ***D:*** John Ford; ***C:*** Gregg Toland. National Board of Review Awards '40: 10 Best Films of the Year; New York Film Critics Awards '40: Best Director (Ford); Nominations: Academy Awards '40: Best Black and White Cinematography, Best Film Editing, Best Picture, Best Screenplay, Best Original Score. *WAR*

The Long Walk Home ☠☠☠ **1989 (PG)** In Montgomery Alabama, in the mid 1950s, sometime after Rosa Parks refused to sit in the black-designated back of the bus, Martin Luther King Jr. led a bus boycott. Spacek is the affluent wife of a narrow-minded businessman while Goldberg is their struggling maid. When Spacek discovers that Goldberg is supporting the boycott by walking the nine-mile trek to work, she sympathizes and tries to help, antagonizing her husband. The plot marches inevitably toward a white-on-white showdown on racism while quietly exploring gender equality between the women. Outstanding performances by Spacek and Goldberg, and a great 50s feel. **95m/C VHS, LV.** Sissy Spacek, Whoopi Goldberg, Dwight Schultz, Ving Rhames, Dylan Baker; ***D:*** Richard Pearce; ***W:*** John Cork; ***M:*** George Fenton. *LIV, IME, FCT*

A Long Way Home ☠☠ **1981** A television movie about a grown man searching for his long-lost siblings, after the three of them were given up for adoption after birth. **97m/C VHS, Beta.** Timothy Hutton, Brenda Vaccaro, Rosanna Arquette, Paul Regina, George Dzundza, John Lehne, Bonnie Bartlett; ***D:*** Robert Markowitz; ***C:*** Ralf Bode; ***M:*** William Goldstein. *LIV*

The Long Weekend ☠ **1986** When a vacationing couple goes camping and carelessly destroys a forest, Mother Nature turns her powers of retribution on them. **95m/C VHS, Beta.** *AU TWE*

The Longest Day ☠☠☠½ **1962** The complete story of the D-Day landings at Normandy on June 6, 1944, as seen through the eyes of American, French, British, and German participants. Exhaustively accurate details and extremely talented cast make this one of the all-time great Hollywood epic productions. The first of the big budget, all-star war productions; based on the book by Cornelius Ryan. Three directors share credit. Also available in a colorized version. **179m/C VHS, Beta, LV.** John Wayne, Richard Burton, Red Buttons, Robert Mitchum, Henry Fonda, Robert Ryan, Paul Anka, Mel Ferrer, Edmond O'Brien, Fabian, Sean Connery, Roddy McDowall, Arletty, Curt Jurgens, Rod Steiger, Jean-Louis Barrault, Peter Lawford, Robert Wagner, Sal Mineo, Leo Genn, Richard Beymer, Jeffrey Hunter, Stuart Whitman, Eddie Albert, Tom Tryon, Alexander Knox, Ray Danton, Kenneth More, Richard Todd, Gert Frobe, Christopher Lee; ***D:*** Ken Annakin; ***W:*** Bernhard Wicki; ***M:*** Maurice Jarre. Academy Awards '62: Best Black and White Cinematography, Best Special Effects; National Board of Review Awards '62: 10 Best Films of the Year; Nominations: Academy Awards '62: Best Art Direction/Set Decoration (B & W), Best Film Editing, Best Picture. *FXV, TLF, HMV*

The Longest Drive ☠☠ *The Quest* **1976** Two brothers comb the wildest parts of the West for their sister, whom they believe is living with Indians. A made for television movie originally titled "The Quest," which became a brief television series. Highlights include colorful performances from the veteran actors and a unique horse/camel race. A continuation of the series is available on video as "The Captive: The Longest Drive 2." **92m/C VHS, LV.** Kurt Russell, Tim Matheson, Brian Keith, Keenan Wynn, Neville Brand, Cameron Mitchell, Morgan Woodward, Iron Eyes Cody, Luke Askew; ***D:*** Lee H. Katzin. *VMK*

The Longest Yard ☠☠½ **1974 (R)** A one-time pro football quarterback, now an inmate, organizes his fellow convicts into a football team to play against the prison guards. Filmed on location at Georgia State Prison. **121m/C VHS, Beta, LV.** Burt Reynolds, Eddie Albert, Bernadette Peters, Ed Lauter, Richard Kiel; ***D:*** Robert Aldrich; ***W:*** Tracy Keenan Wynn; ***C:*** Joseph Biroc. Golden Globe Awards '75: Best Film—Musical/Comedy; Nominations: Academy Awards '74: Best Film Editing. *PAR*

The Longshot *Woof!* **1986 (PG-13)** Four bumblers try to raise cash to put on a sure-bet racetrack tip in this sorry comedy. Mike Nichols is the executive producer. **89m/C VHS, Beta.** Tim Conway, Harvey Korman, Jack Weston, Ted Wass, Jonathan Winters, Stella Stevens, Anne Meara; ***D:*** Paul Bartel; ***W:*** Tim Conway, John Myhers; ***M:*** Charles Fox. *CNG*

Longtime Companion ☠☠☠½ **1990 (R)** Critically acclaimed film follows a group of gay men and their friends during the 1980s. The closely knit group monitors the progression of the AIDS virus from early news reports until it finally hits home and begins to take the lives of their loved ones. One of the first films to look at the situation in an intelligent and touching manner. Produced by the PBS "American Playhouse" company. **100m/C VHS.** Stephen Caffrey, Patrick Cassidy, Brian Cousins, Bruce Davison, John Dossett, Mark Lamos, Dermot Mulroney, Mary-Louise Parker, Michael Schoeffling, Campbell Scott, Robert Joy; ***D:*** Norman Rene. Golden Globe Awards '91: Best Supporting Actor (Davison); Independent Spirit Awards '91: Best Supporting Actor (Davison); New York Film Critics Awards '90: Best Supporting Actor (Davison); National Society of Film Critics Awards '90: Best Supporting Actor (Davison); Sundance Film Festival '90: Audience Award; Nominations: Academy Awards '90: Best Supporting Actor (Davison). *VMK, FCT, BTV*

Look Back in Anger ☠☠☠½ **1958** Based on John Osbourne's famous play, the first British "angry young man" film, in which a squalor-living lad takes out his anger on the world by seducing his friend's wife. **99m/B VHS, Beta, LV.** *GB* Richard Burton, Claire Bloom, Mary Ure, Edith Evans, Gary Raymond; ***D:*** Tony Richardson; ***W:*** John Osborne; ***C:*** Oswald Morris; ***M:*** John Addison. National Board of Review Awards '59: 10 Best Films of the Year. *SUE*

Look Back in Anger ☠☠ **1980** A working class man angered by society's hypocrisy lashes out at his upper class wife, his mistress, and the world. Inferior remake of 1958 film version starring Richard Burton, based on '50s stage hit. **100m/C VHS, Beta.** Malcolm McDowell, Lisa Banes, Fran Brill, Raymond Hardie, Lindsay Anderson. *WAR, OM*

Look Back in Anger ☠☠☠ **1989** There's something about John Osborne's play that brings out the angry young man in British leads. Richard Burton played Osborne's irascible guy in 1958, Malcom McDowell looked back angrily in '80, and now Branagh convincingly vents his spleen on wife and mistress in this made for British TV production. Director Jones earlier filmed "84 Charing Cross Road" and "Jacknife." **114m/C VHS.** *GB* Kenneth Branagh, Emma Thompson, Gerard Horan, Siobhan Redmond; ***D:*** David Jones. *HBO*

Look for the Silver Lining ☠☠½ **1949** Insipid musical biography of Broadway star Marilyn Miller (Haver). Bolger is the highlight as Miller's mentor from vaudeville to the Great White Way. ♫Look for the Silver Lining; Whip-Poor-Will; A Kiss in the Dark; Pirouette; Just a Memory; Time On My Hands; Wild Rose; Shine On Harvest Moon; Back, Back, Back to Baltimore. **100m/C VHS, Beta.** June Haver, Ray Bolger, Gordon MacRae, Charlie Ruggles, Rosemary DeCamp, S.Z. Sakall; ***D:*** David Butler; ***W:*** Phoebe Ephron, Henry Ephron, Marian Spitzer. *MGM, FCT, BTV*

Look Out Sister ☠☠☠ **1948** Jordan and an all-black cast star in this musical satire of westerns. "Two Gun" Jordan saves a dude ranch from foreclosure and wins the girl. Lots of black culture, slang and music from the '40s. Broad but enjoyable humor. ♫Caldonia; Don't Burn the Candle at Both Ends. **64m/B VHS.** Louis Jordan, Suzette Harbin, Monte Hawley, Maceo B. Sheffield; ***D:*** Bud Pollard. *NOS*

Look Who's Laughing ☠☠ **1941** Bergen's plane lands in a town conveniently populated by radio stars. Not much plot here, but it might be worth a look to fans of the stars including Jim and Marion Jordan, better known as Fibber McGee and Molly. **79m/B VHS, Beta, LV.** Edgar Bergen, Jim Jordan, Marian Jordan, Lucille Ball, Harold Peary, Lee Bonnell, Charles Halton; ***D:*** Allan Dwan. *TTC, MLB*

Look Who's Talking ☠☠☠ **1989 (PG-13)** When Alley bears the child of a married, and quite fickle man, she sets her sights elsewhere in search of the perfect father; Travolta is the cabbie with more on his mind than driving Alley around and babysitting. All the while, the baby gives us his views via the voice of Bruce Willis. A very light comedy with laughs for the whole family. **90m/C VHS, Beta, LV.** John Travolta, Kirstie Alley, Olympia Dukakis, George Segal, Abe Vigoda; ***D:*** Amy Heckerling; ***W:*** Amy Heckerling; ***M:*** David Kitay; ***V:*** Bruce Willis. People's Choice Awards '90: Best Film—Musical/Comedy. *COL, RDG*

Look Who's Talking Now ☠½ **1993 (PG-13)** Continuing to wring revenue from a tired premise, the family dogs throw in their two cents in the second sequel to "Look Who's Talking." For anyone who thinks Diane Keaton's hair makes her look a little like a hound dog, here's a chance to visualize her as a similarly long-eared poodle with an attitude. DeVito is also cast in character as the voice of a rough street-smart mutt, who happens to get thrown into the same household as the bosses' pure-bred poodle. Sparks, Alpo, and butt jokes fly as the dogs mark their territory. Meanwhile, dimwit wife Alley is worried that husband Travolta is having an affair, and is determined to get him back. **95m/C VHS, LV, 8mm.** John Travolta, Kirstie Alley, Olympia Dukakis, George Segal, Lysette Anthony; ***D:*** Tom Ropelewski; ***W:*** Tom Ropelewski, Leslie Dixon; ***M:*** William Ross; ***V:*** Diane Keaton, Danny DeVito. *COL*

Look Who's Talking, Too 🦴 **1990 (PG-13)** If Academy Awards for Stupidest Sequel and Lamest Dialogue existed, this diaper drama would have cleaned up. The second go-round throws the now married accountant-cabbie duo into a marital tailspin when Alley's babysitting brother moves in and the Saturday Night dancer moves out. Meanwhile, Willis cum baby smartasses incessantly. A once-clever gimmick now unencumbered by plot; not advised for linear thinkers. The voice of Arnold, though, is a guarantee you'll get one laugh for your rental. **81m/C VHS, LV, 8mm.** Kirstie Alley, John Travolta, Olympia Dukakis, Elias Koteas; ***D:*** Amy Heckerling; ***V:*** Bruce Willis, Mel Brooks, Damon Wayans, Roseanne. *COL*

The Lookalike 🦴🦴 **1990 (PG-13)** A made for cable adaptation of Kate Wilhelm's novel. Bereaved mother Gilbert questions her sanity when she thinks she sees her daughter after she was killed in an automobile accident. Could this girl provide answers to questions about her past? **88m/C VHS.** Melissa Gilbert, Diane Ladd, Frances Lee McCain, Jason Scott Lee, Thaao Penghlis; ***D:*** Gary Nelson; ***W:*** Linda J. Bergman. *MCA*

Looker 🦴½ **1981 (PG)** Stunning models are made even more beautiful by a plastic surgeon, but one by one they begin to die. Finney plays the Beverly Hills surgeon who decides to investigate when he starts losing all his clients. **94m/C VHS, Beta, LV.** Albert Finney, James Coburn, Susan Dey, Leigh Taylor-Young; ***D:*** Michael Crichton; ***W:*** Michael Crichton. *WAR*

Lookin' to Get Out 🦴🦴½ **1982 (R)** Comedy about two gamblers running from their debts. They wind up at the MGM Grand in Las Vegas trying to get out of a mess. **70m/C VHS, Beta.** Ann-Margret, Jon Voight, Burt Young; ***D:*** Hal Ashby; ***M:*** John Beal, Miles Goodman. *FOX*

Looking for Miracles 🦴🦴½ **1990 (G)** Two brothers, separated during the Depression because of poverty, get a chance to cultivate brotherly love when they're reunited in 1935. A Wonderworks production based on the A.E. Hochner novel. **104m/C VHS, LV.** Zachary Bennett, Greg Spottiswood, Joe Flaherty. *TOU, DIS, FCT*

Looking for Mr. Goodbar 🦴🦴 **1977 (R)** Young teacher Keaton seeks companionship and love by frequenting single's bars and furthers her self-destruction by her aimless intake of drugs and alcohol. In need of a father figure, she makes herself available to numerous men and eventually regrets her hedonistic behavior. Unpleasant, aimless characters do little for this dreary film, whose sexual theme sparked a bit of public conversation when first released. Based on the bestselling novel by Judith Rossner. Oscar nominations for supporting actress Weld, and cinematography. **136m/C VHS, Beta, LV.** Diane Keaton, Tuesday Weld, Richard Gere, Tom Berenger, William Atherton, Richard Kiley; ***D:*** Richard Brooks; ***W:*** Richard Brooks; ***C:*** William A. Fraker. Nominations: Academy Awards '77: Best Cinematography, Best Supporting Actress (Weld). *PAR*

The Looking Glass War 🦴🦴 **1969 (PG)** Polish defector is sent behind the Iron Curtain on a final mission to photograph a rocket in East Berlin. He's guided by frustrated British security officers Rogers and Richardson, who both offer sly turns. An otherwise slow-moving adaptation of John Le Carre's bestselling spy novel. **108m/C VHS, Beta.** *GB* Christopher Jones, Ralph Richardson, Pia Degermark, Anthony Hopkins, Susan George; ***D:*** Frank Pierson; ***W:*** Frank Pierson. *COL, MLB*

Looney Looney Looney Bugs Bunny Movie 🦴🦴🦴 *Friz Freleng's Looney Looney Looney Bugs Bunny Movie* **1981 (G)** A feature-length compilation of classic Warner Brothers cartoons tied together with new animation. Cartoon stars featured include Bugs Bunny, Elmer Fudd, Porky Pig, Yosemite Sam, Duffy Duck and Foghorn Leghorn. **80m/C VHS, Beta.** ***D:*** Isadore "Friz" Freleng, Chuck Jones, Bob Clampett; ***V:*** Mel Blanc, June Foray. *WAR, FCT, WTA*

Loophole 🦴🦴 *Break In* **1983** An out-of-work architect, hard pressed for money, joins forces with an elite team of expert criminals, in a scheme to make off with millions from the most established holding bank's vault. **105m/C VHS, Beta.** *GB* Albert Finney, Martin Sheen, Susannah York, Robert Morley, Colin Blakely, Jonathan Pryce; ***D:*** John Quested. *MED, HHE, MTX*

Loose Cannons 🦴 **1990 (R)** Yet another mismatched-cop-partner comedy, wherein a mystery is ostensibly solved by a veteran cop and a schizophrenic detective. **95m/C VHS, Beta, LV.** Gene Hackman, Dan Aykroyd, Dom DeLuise, Ronny Cox, Nancy Travis, David Alan Grier; ***D:*** Bob (Benjamin) Clark; ***W:*** Bob (Benjamin) Clark, Richard Matheson. *COL*

Loose Connections 🦴🦴 **1987** A feminist driving to a convention in Europe advertises for a travelmate, and gets a hopeless chauvinist who is masquerading as a gay man in this offbeat cult comedy. **90m/C VHS, Beta.** *GB* Lindsay Duncan, Stephen Rea, Robbie Coltrane; ***D:*** Richard Eyre. *TPV*

Loose in New York 🦴🦴 **198?** Much to her surprise, a cynical socialite begins to fall for her computer-arranged mate. **91m/C VHS, Beta.** Rita Tushingham, Aldo Maccione; ***D:*** Gian Polidoro. *NO*

Loose Screws 🦴 **1985 (R)** Four perverted teenagers are sent to a restrictive academy where they continue their lewd ways in this stupid sequel to "Screwballs." **75m/C VHS, Beta.** *CA* Bryan Genesse, Karen Wood, Alan Deveau, Jason Warren; ***D:*** Rafal Zeilinski; ***W:*** Michael Cory. *LIV*

Loose Shoes 🦴🦴 *Coming Attractions* **1980 (R)** A collection of vignettes that satirize movie trailers, teasers and special announcements. Murray's film debut. **84m/C VHS, Beta.** Bill Murray, Howard Hesseman, Jaye P. Morgan, Buddy Hackett, Misty Rowe, Susan Tyrrell; ***D:*** Ira Miller. *FOX*

Loot...Give Me Money, Honey! 🦴🦴½ **1970** Black comedy about a motley crew of greed-driven golddiggers who chase after a heisted fortune in jewels, which is hidden in a coffin belonging to one of the thieves' mother. From Joe Orton's play. **101m/C VHS, Beta.** *GB* Richard Attenborough, Lee Remick, Hywel Bennett, Milo O'Shea, Roy Holder; ***D:*** Silvio Narizzano. *NO*

Lord Jim 🦴🦴🦴 **1965** A ship officer (O'Toole) commits an act of cowardice that results in his dismissal and disgrace, which leads him to the Far East in search of self-respect. Excellent supporting cast. Based on Joseph Conrad's novel. **154m/C VHS, Beta.** Peter O'Toole, James Mason, Curt Jurgens, Eli Wallach, Jack Hawkins, Paul Lukas, Akim Tamiroff, Daliah Lavi, Andrew Keir, Jack MacGowran, Walter Gotell; ***D:*** Richard Brooks; ***W:*** Richard Brooks; ***C:*** Frederick A. (Freddie) Young. *COL, TVC*

Lord of Illusions 🦴🦴½ *Clive Barker's Lord of Illusions* **1995 (R)** New York P.I. Harry D'Amour (Bakula), who has an affinity for the occult, becomes involved with Dorothea (Janssen), the supposed widow of magician Philip Swann (O'Connor). As Harry investigates he discovers some terrifying secrets, including resurrected cult leader Nix (Von Bargen). Gruesome effects rather than excessive gore but you'll feel like you've been dropped in the middle of a plot without a clear idea what's happening. Bakula's Harry obviously has more stories to tell but Janssen's Dorothea, while attractive, is just around to cower. Barker directs from his own short story "The Last Illusion." The unrated director's cut clocks in at 120 minutes. **109m/C VHS, LV.** Scott Bakula, Famke Janssen, Kevin J. O'Connor, Daniel von Bargen, Joel Swetow, Barry Sherman, Jordan Marder, Joseph Latimore, Vincent Schiavelli; ***D:*** Clive Barker; ***W:*** Clive Barker; ***C:*** Ronn Schmidt. *MGM*

Lord of the Flies 🦴🦴🦴½ **1963** Proper English schoolboys stranded on a desert island during a nuclear war are transformed into savages. A study in greed, power, and the innate animalistic/survivalistic instincts of human nature. Based on William Golding's novel, which he described as a journey to the darkness of the human heart. The laser disc version contains outtakes, the film trailer, and additional material. **91m/B VHS, Beta, LV.** *GB* James Aubrey, Tom Chapin, Hugh Edwards, Roger Elwin, Tom Gamen; ***D:*** Peter Brook; ***W:*** Peter Brook. National Board of Review Awards '63: 10 Best Films of the Year. *HMV, FUS*

Lord of the Flies 🦴🦴 **1990 (R)** Inferior second filming of the famed William Golding novel about schoolboys marooned on a desert island who gradually degenerate into savages. Lushly photographed, yet redundant and poorly acted. **90m/C VHS, Beta, LV, 8mm.** Balthazar Getty, Danuel Pipoly, Chris Furrh, Badgett Dale, Edward Taft, Andrew Taft; ***D:*** Harry Hook. *COL, SUE, TVC*

The Lord of the Rings 🦴🦴 **1978 (PG)** An animated interpretation of Tolkien's classic tale of the hobbits, wizards, elves, and dwarfs who inhabit Middle Earth. Animator Ralph Bakshi used live motion animation (roto-scoping) to give his characters more life-like and human motion. Well done in spite of the difficulty of adapting from Tolkien's highly detailed and lengthy works. **128m/C VHS, Beta.** ***D:*** Ralph Bakshi; ***W:*** Peter S. Beagle, J.C. (Chris) Conkling; ***V:*** Christopher Guard, John Hurt. *REP, FCT, WTA*

The Lords of Discipline 🦴🦴½ **1983 (R)** A military academy cadet is given the unenviable task of protecting a black freshman from racist factions at a southern school circa 1964. Based on Pat Conroy's autobiographical novel. **103m/C VHS, Beta, LV.** David Keith, Robert Prosky, Barbara Babcock, Judge Reinhold, G.D. Spradlin, Rick Rossovich, Michael Biehn; ***D:*** Franc Roddam; ***M:*** Howard Blake. *PAR*

The Lords of Flatbush 🦴🦴½ **1974 (PG)** Four street toughs battle against their own maturation and responsibilities in 1950s Brooklyn. Winkler introduces the leather-clad hood he's made a career of and Stallone introduces a character not unlike Rocky. Interesting slice of life. **88m/C VHS, Beta, LV.** Sylvester Stallone, Perry King, Henry Winkler, Susan Blakely, Armand Assante, Paul Mace; ***D:*** Stephen Verona, Martin Davidson; ***M:*** Joseph Brooks. *COL*

Lords of Magick 🦴 **1988 (PG-13)** Two warriors chase an evil sorcerer and the princess he's kidnapped across time to the 20th century. **98m/C VHS, Beta.** Jarrett Parker, Matt Gauthier, Brendan Dillon Jr.; ***D:*** David Marsh. *PSM*

Lords of the Deep *Woof!* **1989 (PG-13)** A Roger Corman cheapie about underwater technicians trapped on the ocean floor with a race of aliens. A film rushed out to capitalize on the undersea sci-fi subgenre highlighted by "The Abyss." **95m/C VHS, Beta.** Bradford Dillman, Priscilla Barnes, Melody Ryane, Eb Lottimer, Daryl Haney; ***D:*** Mary Ann Fisher; ***W:*** Daryl Haney, Howard R. Cohen. *MGM*

Lorenzo's Oil 🦴🦴🦴 **1992 (PG-13)** Based on the true story of Augusto and Michaela Odone's efforts to find a cure for their 5-year-old, Lorenzo, diagnosed with the rare and incurable disease ALD (Adrenoleukodystrophy). Confronted by a slow-moving and clinically cold medical community, the Odones embark on their own quest for a cure. Sarandon delivers an outstanding and emotionally charged performance as Lorenzo's determined mother. Nolte is his equally devoted Italian father, complete with black hair and hand gestures. They are a powerful presence in a film which could have easily degenerated into a made-for-TV movie, but is instead a tribute to what love and hope can accomplish. **135m/C VHS, Beta, LV.** Nick Nolte, Susan Sarandon, Zach O'Malley-Greenberg, Peter Ustinov, Kathleen Wilhoite, Gerry Bamman, Margo Martindale, James Rebhorn, Ann Hearn; ***D:*** George Miller; ***W:*** Nick Enright, George Miller; ***C:*** John Seale. Nominations: Academy Awards '92: Best Actress (Sarandon), Best Original Screenplay. *MCA, MOV, BTV*

The Loretta Young Show **1954** Two enchanting episodes of the popular fifties series "The Loretta Young Show," entitled "Somebody Else's Dream" and "So Bright the Light." Other episodes are also available, two per tape. **60m/C VHS, Beta.** Loretta Young. *MVC*

Lorna Doone **1922** A young girl of royal descent is kidnapped and raised by the bandit Doone family in the highlands of Scotland. Adapted from the novel by R.D. Blackmore. **?m/C VHS, Beta, 8mm.** Madge Bellamy, John Bowers; ***D:*** Maurice Tourneur. *GVV*

Lorna Doone ½ **1934** Early version of the R.D. Blackmore novel about an English farmer who falls in love with the daughter of an outlaw family. Set in rural England in the 1600s; remade in 1951 and 1990. **90m/B VHS.** *GB* Victoria Hopper, John Loder, Margaret Lockwood, Roy Emerton, Mary Clare, Edward Rigby, Roger Livesey; ***D:*** Basil Dean; ***W:*** Miles Malleson. *FCT*

Lorna Doone ½ **1990 (PG)** Classic romance set in 17th-century England and based on the novel by R.D. Blackmore. John Ridd (Bean) vows to destroy the land-grabbing Doone family, whom he blames for the death of his parents. Then he meets, and immediately falls in love with, the beautiful and innocent Lorna Doone (Walker). Made for British television. **90m/C VHS, Beta.** *GB* Sean Bean, Polly Walker, Clive Owen, Billie Whitelaw; ***D:*** Andrew Grieve; ***W:*** Matthew Jacobs. *PAR*

Los Olvidados ½ *The Young and the Damned* **1950** From surrealist Bunuel, a powerful story of the poverty and violence of young people's lives in Mexico's slums. In Spanish with English subtitles. **81m/B VHS, Beta, 8mm.** *MX* Alfonso Mejias, Roberto Cobo; ***D:*** Luis Bunuel. Cannes Film Festival '51: Best Director (Bunuel), Best Film. *VYY, HHT, DVT*

The Losers ½ **1970 (R)** Four motorcyclists are hired by the U.S. Army to rescue a presidential advisor who is being held captive by Asian bad guys. **96m/C VHS, Beta.** William Smith, Bernie Hamilton, Adam Roarke, Houston Savage, Brad Johnson, Vernon Wells; ***D:*** Jack Starrett. *ACA*

Losin' It **1982 (R)** Four teens travel across the Mexican border to Tijuana on a journey to lose their virginity. Cruise meets a married woman who says she is in town for a divorce, while the others become caught up in frenzied undertakings of their own. **104m/C VHS, Beta, LV.** Tom Cruise, John Stockwell, Shelley Long, Jackie Earle Haley; ***D:*** Curtis Hanson. *SUE, NLC*

Losing Isaiah **1994 (R)** "Kramer vs. Kramer" meets the movie-of-the-week in this controversial and emotionally moving story of a social worker (Lange) who adopts the title character, an African American baby abandoned by his drug-addicted mother (Berry). Courtroom battle ensues when four years later mom, now clean and sober, discovers Isaiah is alive. She enlists the aid of a lawyer (Jackson) known for his high-profile, racially charged cases. Lange and Berry lead the parade of fine performances. Taking on some volatile issues, director Gyllenhaal manages (for the most part) to refrain from melodrama. Based on the novel by Seth Margolis. **108m/C VHS, Beta.** Jessica Lange, Halle Berry, David Strathairn, Samuel L. Jackson, Cuba Gooding Jr., Latanya Richardson; ***D:*** Stephen Gyllenhaal; ***W:*** Naomi Foner; ***C:*** Andrzej Bartkowiak; ***M:*** Mark Isham. *PAR*

Lost ½ **1983** A young girl runs away into the wilderness because of the resentment she feels toward her new stepfather. **92m/C VHS, Beta.** Sandra Dee, Don Stewart, Ken Curtis, Jack Elam, Sheila Newhouse. *PSM*

Lost **1986** When their boat capsizes in the Pacific, three sailors desperately cling to life, drifting aimlessly for 74 days. Based on a true story, this film is adult-fare. **93m/C VHS, Beta.** *CA* Michael Hogan, Helen Shaver, Kenneth Welsh; ***D:*** Peter Rowe. *HHE, BMV*

Lost and Found ½ **1979 (PG)** An American professor of English and an English film production secretary fall in love on a skiing vacation. Good cast but Segal and Jackson did romance better in "A Touch of Class." **104m/C VHS, Beta.** George Segal, Glenda Jackson, Maureen Stapleton, Hollis McLaren, John Cunningham, Paul Sorvino, John Candy, Martin Short; ***D:*** Melvin Frank; ***W:*** Jack Rose. *GKK*

Lost Angels ½ **1989 (R)** A glossy "Rebel Without a Cause" '80s reprise providing a no-holds-barred portrait of life in the fast lane. A wealthy, disaffected San Fernando Valley youth immerses himself in sex, drugs and rock 'n' roll. Ultimately he is arrested and sent by his parents to a youth home, where a dedicated therapist assists his tortuous road back to reality. **116m/C VHS, Beta, LV.** Donald Sutherland, Adam Horovitz, Amy Locane, Kevin Tighe, John C. McGinley, Graham Beckel, Park Overall, Don Bloomfield, Celia Weston; ***D:*** Hugh Hudson; ***W:*** Michael Weller; ***M:*** Philippe Sarde. *ORI*

Lost Boundaries ½ **1949** Respected physician Scott Carter (debut role for Ferrer) and his family live and work in a small New Hampshire town, hiding the fact that they are black, passing for white, in their segregated society. But then the truth becomes known. Strong, if slow-moving, and based on a true story; the use of white leads for black roles was common casting. **99m/B VHS.** Mel Ferrer, Beatrice Pearson, Richard Hylton, Susan Douglas, Canada Lee, Carleton Carpenter, Seth Arnold, Wendell Holmes; ***D:*** Alfred Werker; ***W:*** Virginia Shaler, Eugene Ling, Charles A. Palmer, Furland de Kay; ***C:*** William J. Miller; ***M:*** Louis Applebaum. *WAR*

The Lost Boys **1987 (R)** Santa Cruz seems like a dull town when Michael, his younger brother, and their divorced mom move into their eccentric grandfather's home. But when Michael falls for a pretty girl with some hard-living friends he takes on more than he imagines—these partying teens are actually a group of vampires. Some humor, some bloodletting violence, and an attractive cast help out this updated vampire tale. Rock-filled soundtrack. **97m/C VHS, Beta, LV, 8mm.** Jason Patric, Kiefer Sutherland, Corey Haim, Jami Gertz, Dianne Wiest, Corey Feldman, Barnard Hughes, Edward Herrmann, Billy Wirth; ***D:*** Joel Schumacher; ***W:*** Jeffrey Boam; ***M:*** Thomas Newman. *WAR, FUS*

Lost Canyon **1943** Hoppy tries to help a fugitive who's been framed for bank robbery. This is the second installment distributed by United Artists. The song "Jingle, Jangle, Jingle" is sung by the Sportsman Quartet. **61m/B VHS.** William Boyd, Jay Kirby, Andy Clyde, Lola Lane, Douglas Fowley, Herbert Rawlinson; ***D:*** Lesley Selander. *NOS*

The Lost Capone **1990 (PG-13)** Made for cable TV version of the story of Al Capone's youngest brother, a clean living small town sheriff who struggles with his sibling's reputation at every turn. **93m/C VHS, Beta.** Ally Sheedy, Eric Roberts, Adrian Pasdar, Titus Welliver, Jimmie F. Skaggs, Maria Pitillo, Anthony Crivello; ***D:*** John Gray; ***W:*** John Gray. *TTC*

The Lost City **1934** A feature version of the rollicking vintage movie serial about a lost jungle city, adventurers and mad scientists. **74m/B VHS, Beta.** William "Stage" Boyd, Kane Richmond, George "Gabby" Hayes, Claudia Dell; ***D:*** Harry Revier. *NOS, SNC, DVT*

Lost City of the Jungle **1945** 13-chapter serial focusing on a crazed Atwill, in his last screen role, believing that he can rule the world from the heart of a deep, dark jungle by utilizing a special mineral. The final Universal serial. **169m/B VHS, Beta.** Russell Hayden, Lionel Atwill, Jane Adams; ***D:*** Ray Taylor, Lewis D. Collins. *NOS, GPV, DVT*

The Lost Command ½ **1966** A French colonel, relieved of his command, endeavors to regain power by battling a powerful Arab terrorist with his own specially trained platoon of soldiers. Crisp adventure set in post-WWII North Africa. Based on "The Centurions" by Jean Larteguy. **129m/C Beta.** Anthony Quinn, Michele Morgan, George Segal, Alain Delon, Maurice Ronet, Claudia Cardinale; ***D:*** Mark Robson; ***C:*** Robert L. Surtees. *COL*

The Lost Continent ½ **1951** An expedition searching for a lost rocket on a jungle island discovers dinosaurs and other extinct creatures. **82m/B VHS, Beta, LV.** Cesar Romero, Hillary Brooke, Chick Chandler, John Hoyt, Acquanetta, Sid Melton, Whit Bissell, Hugh Beaumont; ***D:*** Sam Newfield. *MRV, MLB*

Lost Diamond **1974** Bumbling spies search for a smuggled gem. **83m/C VHS, Beta.** Juan Ramon, Sonia Rivas, Ricardo Bauleo. *MED*

The Lost Empire **1983 (R)** Three bountiful and powerful women team up to battle the evil Dr. Syn Do. **86m/C VHS, Beta.** Melanie Vincz, Raven De La Croix, Angela Aames, Paul Coufos, Robert Tessier, Angus Scrimm, Angelique Pettyjohn, Kenneth Tobey; ***D:*** Jim Wynorski; ***W:*** Jim Wynorski. *LIV*

Lost Honeymoon **1947** Monkeyshines abound as a soldier marries a girl while in a state of amnesia, and then wakes up to find twin daughters. **70m/B VHS, Beta.** Franchot Tone, Ann Richards; ***D:*** Leigh Jason. *NOS, DVT, HEG*

The Lost Honor of Katharina Blum *Die Verlorene Ehre Der Katharina Blum* **1975 (R)** A woman becomes involved with a man who's under police surveillance and finds her life open to public scrutiny and abuse from the media and the government. Based on Heinrich Boll's prize-winning novel. In German with English subtitles. Remade for television as "The Lost Honor of Kathryn Beck." **97m/C VHS, Beta.** *GE* Angela Winkler, Mario Adorf, Dieter Laser, Juergen Prochnow; ***D:*** Volker Schlondorff, Margarethe von Trotta. *SUE, APD, GLV*

Lost Horizon **1937** A group of strangers fleeing revolution in China are lost in the Tibetan Himalayas and stumble across the valley of Shangri La. The inhabitants of this Utopian community have lived for hundreds of years in kindness and peace—but what will the intrusion of these strangers bring? The classic romantic role for Colman. Capra's directorial style meshed perfectly with the pacifist theme of James Hilton's classic novel, resulting in one of the most memorable films of the 1930s. This version restores more than 20 minutes of footage which had been cut from the movie through the years. **132m/B VHS, Beta, LV.** Ronald Colman, Jane Wyatt, H.B. Warner, Sam Jaffe, Thomas Mitchell, Edward Everett Horton, Isabel Jewell, John Howard, Margo; ***D:*** Frank Capra; ***W:*** Robert Riskin; ***M:*** Dimitri Tiomkin. Academy Awards '37: Best Film Editing, Best Interior Decoration; Nominations: Academy Awards '37: Best Picture, Best Sound, Best Supporting Actor (Warner), Best Original Score. *COL, RDG*

The Lost Idol/Shock Troop **198?** In "The Lost Idol," a lone soldier raids a sacred temple in order to retrieve a golden idol. "Shock Troop" tells of top secret mission to destroy a powerful computer that lies behind enemy lines. **219m/C VHS.** Danny Aiello, Lyle Alzado, Erik Estrada. *NO*

Lost in a Harem ½ **1944** Abbott & Costello play magicians in a theatrical troupe stranded in a desert kingdom ruled by an evil sheik. The sheik's nephew (and rightful heir) hires the two to steal some magic rings and the pretty Maxwell to play footsie with his susceptible uncle in an attempt to regain his kingdom. Average comedy with musical numbers by Jimmy Dorsey and His Orchestra. **89m/B VHS.** Bud Abbott, Lou Costello, Marilyn Maxwell, John Conte, Douglass Dumbrille, Lottie Harrison; ***D:*** Charles Riesner. *MGM*

Lost in Alaska ½ **1952** Up in the Alaskan wilderness, Abbott & Costello save Ewell from a greedy saloon owner and his cohorts who are trying to get their hands on Ewell's fortune. **87m/B VHS.** Bud Abbott, Lou Costello, Tom Ewell, Mitzie Green, Bruce Cabot, Emory Parnell, Jack Ingram, Rex Lease; ***D:*** Jean Yarbrough; ***W:*** Martin Ragaway, Leonard Stern; ***M:*** Henry Mancini. *MCA, FCT*

Lost in America **1985 (R)** After deciding that he can't "find himself" at his current job, advertising executive David Howard and his wife sell everything they own and buy a Winnebago to travel across the country. This Albert Brooks comedy is a must-see for everyone who thinks that there is more in life than pushing papers at your desk and sitting on "Mercedes leather." Available in widescreen on laserdisc. **91m/C VHS, Beta, LV.** Albert Brooks, Julie Hagerty, Michael Greene, Tom Tarpey, Garry Marshall, Art Frankel; ***D:*** Albert Brooks; ***W:*** Albert Brooks, Monica Johnson; ***M:*** Arthur

B. Rubinstein. National Society of Film Critics Awards '85: Best Screenplay. *WAR*

Lost in the Barrens 🦴🦴 **1991** Two young boys, one a Canadian Indian and the other a rich white boy, get lost in the wilderness of the Canadian north. Out of necessity and common need they become close and form a lifelong friendship. Based on the book by Farley Mowat. **95m/C VHS.** *CA* Graham Greene, Nicholas Shields. *NO*

Lost in Yonkers 🦴🦴½ *Neil Simon's Lost in Yonkers* **1993 (PG)** Arty and Jay are two teenage brothers who, while their widowed father looks for work, are sent to live with their stern grandmother, small-time gangster uncle, and childlike aunt in 1942 New York. Ruehl reprises her Tony award-winning performance as Aunt Bella, who loses herself in the movies while trying to find a love of her own, out from under the oppressive thumb of her domineering mother (Worth). Performances by the adults are more theatrical than necessary but the teenagers do well in their observer roles. Based on the play by Neil Simon, which again chronicles his boyhood. **114m/C VHS, LV, 8mm.** Mercedes Ruehl, Irene Worth, Richard Dreyfuss, Brad Stoll, Mike Damus, David Strathairn, Robert Miranda, Jack Laufer, Susan Merson; ***D:*** Martha Coolidge; ***W:*** Neil Simon; ***M:*** Elmer Bernstein. *COL, FCT*

The Lost Jungle **1934** Circus legend Beatty searches for his girl and her dad in the jungle. Animal stunts keep it interesting. Serial in 12 chapters, 13 minutes each. **156m/B VHS, Beta.** Clyde Beatty, Cecilia Parker, Syd Saylor, Warner Richmond, Wheeler Oakman; ***D:*** Armand Schaefer, David Howard. *NOS, VCN, VDM*

The Lost Language of Cranes 🦴🦴🦴 **1992** David Leavitt's novel is transported from New York to present-day London but the wrenching emotional drama remains the same. A family is in crisis as long-hidden secrets concerning homosexuality and infidelity are finally revealed. The title refers to one character's social worker's thesis on a young boy from a dysfunctional family who imitates the movements of the building cranes he sees. Fine performances by all. Adult sexual situations. **90m/C VHS.** *GB* Brian Cox, Eileen Atkins, Angus MacFadyen, Corey Parker, Cathy Tyson; ***Cameos:*** John Schlesinger, Rene Auberjonois; ***D:*** Nigel Finch. *FOX, BTV*

Lost Legacy: A Girl Called Hatter Fox 🦴🦴½ **1977** Tradition and technology are at odds in the life of a young Indian girl. Strong cast makes this work. Made for television and better than average. **100m/C VHS.** Ronny Cox, Joanelle Romero, Conchata Ferrell; ***D:*** George Schaefer. *GEM*

Lost, Lonely, and Vicious 🦴 **1959** Clayton is a suicidal Hollywood actor who spends much of his time indulging his penchant for women, figuring he may as well enjoy what little time he has left. Then he meets Wilson, a drugstore clerk who moves him to reconsider his self-destructive ways. **73m/B VHS.** Ken Clayton, Barbara Wilson, Lilyan Chauvin, Richard Gilden, Carole Nugent, Sandra Giles, Allen Fife, Frank Stallworth, Johnny Erben, Clint Quigley, T. Earl Johnson; ***D:*** Frank Myers; ***W:*** Norman Graham. *SMW, TPV*

The Lost Missile 🦴🦴 **1958** A lost, alien missile circles the Earth, causing overheating and destruction on the planet's surface. A scientist works to find a way to save the planet before it explodes into a gigantic fireball. Director Burke's last film. **70m/B VHS.** Robert Loggia, Ellen Parker, Larry Kerr, Phillip Pine, Marilee Earle; ***D:*** William (Lester Williams) Berke. *FRG*

Lost Moment 🦴🦴 **1947** A publisher travels to Italy to search for a valuable collection of a celebrated author's love letters, but finds a neurotic woman in his way. Based on Henry James' "Aspern Papers." **89m/B VHS.** Robert Cummings, Agnes Moorehead, Susan Hayward; ***D:*** Martin Gabel; ***C:*** Hal Mohr. *REP*

The Lost One 🦴🦴 *Der Verlone* **1951** A German scientist's lover is suspected of selling his findings to England during WWII. Based on a true story; Lorre's only directorial outing. **97m/B VHS.** *GE* Peter Lorre, Karl John, Renate Mannhardt; ***D:*** Peter Lorre. *NO*

The Lost Patrol 🦴🦴🦴½ **1934** WWI British soldiers lost in the desert are shot down one by one by Arab marauders as Karloff portrays a religious soldier convinced he's going to die. The usual spiffy Ford exteriors peopled by great characters with a stirring score. Based on the story, "Patrol" by Philip MacDonald. **66m/B VHS, Beta, LV.** Victor McLaglen, Boris Karloff, Reginald Denny, Wallace Ford, Alan Hale; ***D:*** John Ford; ***M:*** Max Steiner. National Board of Review Awards '34: 10 Best Films of the Year; Nominations: Academy Awards '34: Best Score. *CCB, MED, RXM*

Lost Planet Airmen 🦴½ **1949** A feature-length condensation of the 12-part sci-fi serial "King of the Rocket Men." Rocket Man is pitted against the sinister Dr. Vulcan in this intergalactic battle of good and evil. **65m/B VHS, Beta.** Tristram Coffin, Mae Clarke, Dale Van Sickel; ***D:*** Fred Brannon. *AOV, DVT, RXM*

The Lost Platoon **1989 (R)** A troop of soldiers are transformed into vampires. **120m/C VHS, Beta, LV.** David Parry, William Knight, Sean Heyman; ***D:*** David A. Prior. *AIP*

Lost Squadron 🦴🦴½ **1932** A look at the dangers stuntmen go through in movie-making. **79m/B VHS, Beta, LV.** Richard Dix, Erich von Stroheim; ***D:*** George Archainbaud; ***M:*** Max Steiner. *RXM*

The Lost Stooges **1933** From the trio's one year at MGM, rare clips of them performing their famous slaptick gags. In black and white and color. **68m/B VHS, Beta.** Moe Howard, Curly Howard, Larry Fine, Clark Gable, Joan Crawford, Jimmy Durante, Robert Montgomery. *TTC*

The Lost Tribe 🦴 **1989** A man takes his wife on a trek through the jungle to find his lost brother. **96m/C VHS, Beta.** John Bach, Darien Teakle; ***D:*** John Laing. *MED*

The Lost Weekend 🦴🦴🦴🦴 **1945** The heartrending Hollywood masterpiece about alcoholism, depicting a single weekend in the life of a writer, who cannot believe he's addicted. Except for its pat ending, it is an uncompromising, startlingly harsh treatment, with Milland giving one of the industry's bravest lead performances ever. Acclaimed then and now. **100m/B VHS, Beta, LV.** Ray Milland, Jane Wyman, Phillip Terry, Howard da Silva, Doris Dowling, Frank Faylen, Mary Young; ***D:*** Billy Wilder; ***W:*** Charles Brackett, Billy Wilder; ***M:*** Miklos Rozsa. Academy Awards '45: Best Actor (Milland), Best Director (Wilder), Best Picture, Best Screenplay; Cannes Film Festival '46: Best Actor (Milland), Best Film; Golden Globe Awards '46: Best Actor—Drama (Milland), Best Director (Wilder), Best Film—Drama; National Board of Review Awards '45: 10 Best Films of the Year, Best Actor (Milland); Nominations: Academy Awards '45: Best Black and White Cinematography, Best Film Editing, Best Original Score. *MCA, PAR, BTV*

The Lost World 🦴🦴½ **1925** A zoology professor leads a group on a South American expedition in search of the "lost world," where dinosaurs roam in this silent film. Based on a story by Sir Arthur Conan Doyle. A 90-minute version includes the film's original trailer and a recreation of some of the missing footage (the film was released at 108 minutes). **62m/B VHS, Beta, LV.** Wallace Beery, Lewis Stone, Bessie Love, Lloyd Hughes; ***D:*** Harry Hoyt. *NOS, MIL, VYY*

The Lost World 🦴🦴½ **1992** "Land of the Lost"/"Jurassic Park" themes, based on the story by Sir Arthur Conan Doyle. A scientific team ventures deep into uncharted African jungles where they find themselves confronted by dinosaurs and other dangers. **99m/C VHS.** John Rhys-Davies, David Warner; ***D:*** Timothy Bond. *WOV*

Lost Zeppelin 🦴🦴 **1929** A dirigible becomes lost in the wastes of Antarctica, forcing its passengers to combat the elements. Impressive special effects and miniatures for its time. **73m/B VHS, Beta.** Conway Tearle, Virginia Valli, Ricardo Cortez, Duke Martin, Kathryn McGuire; ***D:*** Edward Sloman. *SNC, GPV*

Lotna 🦴🦴½ **1964** Wadja's first color film serves as a tribute to the Polish calvary who fought against the Germans in WWII. The story is told through the trials of a horse that passes to various military officials until it breaks a leg and must be shot. Wadja himself is the son of a cavalryman killed in the war. Polish with subtitles. **89m/C VHS.** *PL* Bozena Kurowska, Jerzy Pichelski, Jerzy Moes, Adam Pawlikowski; ***D:*** Andrzej Wajda; ***W:*** Andrzej Wajda, Wojciech Zukrowski; ***C:*** Jerzy Lipman; ***M:*** Tadeusz Baird. *FCT*

Lots of Luck 🦴🦴 **1985** A knee-slapping comedy about a family that wins the million-dollar lottery and sees that money doesn't solve all problems. Disney made for cable. **88m/C VHS, Beta.** Martin Mull, Annette Funicello, Fred Willard, Polly Holliday, Hamilton Camp, Vincent Schiavelli; ***D:*** Peter Baldwin; ***M:*** William Goldstein. *DIS*

Lottery Bride 🦴🦴½ **1930** In this charming musical, Jeanette MacDonald is the lottery bride who is won by the brother of the man she really loves. A fine outing for all involved, particularly the supporting cast. ♫You're an Angel; My Northern Lights; Come Drink to the Girl That You Love; Yubla; Round She Whirls; Shoulder to Shoulder; High and Low; Napoli; Two Strong Men. **85m/B VHS, Beta.** Jeanette MacDonald, Joe E. Brown, ZaSu Pitts, John Garrick, Carroll Nye; ***D:*** Paul Stein. *NO*

The Lotus Eaters 🦴🦴 **1993 (PG-13)** Sensitive family drama set in British Columbia in the 1960s about a wife who discovers her husband has fallen in love with their childrens' new teacher. Domestic angst done with naturalism and not without humor. **100m/C VHS.** *CA* Sheila McCarthy, R.H. Thomson, Michelle-Barbara Pelletier, Frances Hyland, Paul Soles; ***D:*** Paul Shapiro; ***W:*** Peggy Thompson. Genie Awards '93: Best Actress (McCarthy), Best Screenplay, Best Sound. *SDE, FCT*

Louisiana 🦴 **1987** A belle of the Old South tries to get back the family plantation by romancing the new owner, even though she loves someone else. Oh, and then the Civil War breaks out. Made for television. **130m/C VHS, Beta.** Ian Charleson, Margot Kidder, Victor Lanoux, Len Cariou, Lloyd Bochner; ***D:*** Philippe de Broca. *PSM*

Louisiana Purchase 🦴🦴½ **1941** Successful screen adaptation of the Broadway musical features several performers from the original cast, lavish costumes, and great musical numbers. As usual, Hope's comedy is extremely funny, especially his famous filibuster scene in Congress. Based on the stage musical by Morrie Ryskind and B. G. DeSylva. **95m/C VHS.** Bob Hope, Vera Zorina, Victor Moore, Dona Drake, Irene Bordoni, Raymond Walburn, Maxie "Slapsie" Rosenbloom, Frank Albertson, Barbara Britton; ***D:*** Irving Cummings. Nominations: Academy Awards '41: Best Color Cinematography, Best Interior Decoration. *MCA, BTV*

Louisiana Story 🦴🦴🦴 **1948** The final effort by the master filmmaker, depicting the effects of oil industrialization on the southern Bayou country as seen through the eyes of a young boy. One of Flaherty's greatest, widely considered a premiere achievement. **77m/B VHS, Beta.** ***D:*** Robert Flaherty; ***M:*** Virgil Thomson. National Board of Review Awards '48: 10 Best Films of the Year; Nominations: Academy Awards '48: Best Story. *HMV, VYY, DVT*

Loulou 🦴🦴🦴½ **1980 (R)** A woman leaves her middle-class husband for a leather-clad, uneducated jock who is more attentive. Romantic and erotic. In French with English subtitles. **110m/C VHS, Beta.** *FR* Isabelle Huppert, Gerard Depardieu, Guy Marchand; ***D:*** Maurice Pialat. Nominations: Cannes Film Festival '80: Best Film. *NYF, INJ*

The Lovable Cheat 🦴🦴 **1949** Pretty lame adapatation of Balzac's play "Mercadet Le Falseur," about a father who cons money from his friends in order to line up a marriage suitable for his daughter. **75m/B VHS.** Charlie Ruggles, Peggy Ann Garner, Richard Ney, Alan Mowbray, Iris Adrian, Ludwig Donath, Fritz Feld; ***D:*** Richard Oswald. *FCT*

Love 🦴🦴🦴½ **1971** Torocsik, touted as Hungary's leading actress in the '70s, plays a young woman whose husband has been imprisoned for political crimes. Living in a cramped apartment with her mother-in-law, she keeps the news from the aged and dying woman (Darvas) by reading letters she's fabricated to keep alive the woman's belief that her son is a successful movie director in America. The story is punctuated by the older woman's dreamy remembrances of things past. Exceptional performances by both women, it was Darvas' final film. Based on two novellas by Tibor Dery, it won a special jury prize at the 1973 Cannes film festival. In Hungarian with English subtitles. **100m/C VHS, LV.** *HU* Lili Darvas, Mari Torocsik, Ivan Darvas; ***D:*** Karoly Makk. Nominations: Cannes Film Festival '71: Best Film. *CVC, IME, INJ*

Love Affair 🦴🦴🦴½ **1939** Multi-kleenex weepie inspired countless romantic dreams of true love atop the Empire State Building. Dunn and Boyer fall in love on a ship bound for NYC, but they're both involved. They agree to meet later at, guess where, to see if their feelings hold true, but tragedy intevenes. Excellent comedy-drama is witty at first, more subdued later, with plenty of romance and melodrama. Remade in 1957 (by McCarey) as "An Affair to Remember," a lesser version whose popularity overshadows the original. Look for fleeting glimpses of Leslie, Beckett, and Mohr. Ignore the public domain video, which replaces the original music. Remade again in 1994 as "Love Affair." **87m/B VHS.** Irene Dunne, Charles Boyer, Maria Ouspenskaya, Lee Bowman, Astrid Allwyn, Maurice Moscovich, Scotty Beckett, Joan Leslie, Gerald Mohr, Dell Henderson, Carol Hughes; ***D:*** Leo McCarey; ***W:*** Delmer Daves, Leo McCarey, Donald Ogden Stewart. Nominations: Academy Awards '39: Best Actress (Dunne), Best Interior Decoration, Best Picture, Best Song ("Wishing"), Best Story, Best Supporting Actress (Ouspenskaya). *NOS, MRV, TTC*

Love Affair 🦴🦴 **1994 (PG-13)** Second remake of the timeless classic has a contemporary look and feel but doesn't justify a new version. The photogenic leads may meet on a plane, but never fear, the Empire State Building and a tragedy are still the main plot devices. The problem is viewers never feel drawn into their lives. Hepburn has a small but moving role as Beatty's aunt. Superb cinematography makes it easy on the eyes and Morricone's lush romantic score makes it easy on the ears, but ultimately, it's all gloss with little substance. Watch this one, but then set aside time to see the superior original (made in 1939) or the better known 1957 attempt "An Affair to Remember." **108m/C VHS, LV.** Warren Beatty, Annette Bening, Katharine Hepburn, Garry Shandling, Chloe Webb, Pierce Brosnan, Kate Capshaw, Paul Mazursky, Brenda Vaccaro, Glenn Shadix, Barry Miller, Harold Ramis; ***D:*** Glenn Gordon Caron; ***W:*** Warren Beatty, Robert Towne; ***M:*** Ennio Morricone. *WAR*

The Love Affair, or The Case of the Missing Switchboard Operator 🦴🦴🦴 *Switchboard Operator; Case of the Missing Switchboard Operator; Ljubarni Slucaj; An Affair of the Heart* **1967** Makavejev's second film, a dissertation on the relationship between sex and politics, involving an affair between a switchboard operator and a middle-aged ex-revolutionary, is told in the director's unique, farcically disjointed manner. In Serbian with English subtitles. **73m/B VHS, Beta.** *YU* Eva Ras, Slobodan Aligrudic, Ruzica Sokic; ***D:*** Dusan Makavejev; ***W:*** Dusan Makavejev. *FCT*

Love Affair: The Eleanor & Lou Gehrig Story 🦴🦴🦴 **1977** The true story, told from Mrs. Gehrig's point of view, of the love affair between baseball great Lou Gehrig and his wife Eleanor from his glory days as a New York Yankee, to his battle with an incurable disease. A television drama that is supported by Herrmann and Danner's convincing portrayals. **96m/C VHS, Beta.** Blythe Danner, Edward Herrmann, Patricia Neal, Ramon Bieri, Lainie Kazan; ***D:*** Fielder Cook. *WOV*

Love After Love 🦴🦴 *Apres l'Amour* **1994** A look at sex and relationships among thirtysomething professionals in Paris. Lola (Huppert), a successful romance novelist, is suffering a crisis in both her career and, ironically, her love life. She is involved with two men who, in turn, are involved with different women who happen to have borne them children. The movie starts off with so much mate switching and secret sexual rendezvous, that by the second half, you really don't care who Lola ends up with. French with English subtitles. **104m/C VHS.** *FR* Isabelle Huppert, Hippolyte Girardot, Lio; ***D:*** Diane Kurys; ***W:*** Diane Kurys, Antoine Lacomblez; ***C:*** Fabio Conversi; ***M:*** Yves Simon, Serge Perathone, Jannick Top. *ORI*

Love Among the Ruins 🦴🦴🦴 **1975** A made-for-television romance about an aging, wealthy widow who, after being scandalously sued for breach of promise by her very young lover, turns for aid to an old lawyer friend who has loved her silently for more than forty years. **100m/C VHS, Beta, LV.** Laurence Olivier, Katharine Hepburn, Leigh Lawson, Colin Blakely; ***D:*** George Cukor; ***M:*** John Barry. *FOX*

Love and a .45 🦴🦴 **1994 (R)** Satirical and violent road movie finds petty career criminal Watty Watts (Bellows) living in a Texas trailer park with gal Starlene (Zellweger), for whom he's just purchased an expensive engagement ring. But he's borrowed the money from some crazed gangster types who want the loan repaid in a timely fashion. Soon, the dippy duo are on the run to Mexico with a trail of dead bodies behind them and the media just delighted to make them the next tabloid darlings. **101m/C VHS, LV.** Gil Bellows, Renee Zellweger, Rory Cochrane, Ann Wedgeworth, Peter Fonda, Jeffrey Combs, Jace Alexander; ***D:*** C.M. Talkington; ***W:*** C.M. Talkington; ***M:*** Tom Verlaine. Nominations: Independent Spirit Awards '95: Debut Performance (Zellweger). *VMK*

Love and Anarchy 🦴🦴🦴 *Film d'Amore et d'Anarchia* **1973** An oppressed peasant vows to assassinate Mussolini after a close friend is murdered. Powerful drama about the rise of Italian facism. In Italian with English subtitles. **108m/C VHS, Beta.** *IT* Giancarlo Giannini, Mariangela Melato; ***D:*** Lina Wertmuller; ***W:*** Lina Wertmuller; ***M:*** Nino Rota. Cannes Film Festival '73: Best Actor (Giannini); Nominations: Cannes Film Festival '73: Best Film. *COL, APD*

Love and Bullets 🦴½ **1979 (PG)** An Arizona homicide detective is sent on a special assignment to Switzerland to bring a mobster's girlfriend back to the United States to testify against him in court. **95m/C VHS, Beta.** *GB* Charles Bronson, Jill Ireland, Rod Steiger, Strother Martin, Bradford Dillman, Henry Silva, Michael V. Gazzo; ***D:*** Stuart Rosenberg; ***W:*** Wendell Mayes; ***C:*** Fred W. Koenekamp; ***M:*** Lalo Schifrin. *FOX*

Love and Death 🦴🦴🦴 **1975 (PG)** In 1812 Russia, a condemned man reviews the follies of his life. Woody Allen's satire on "War and Peace," and every other major Russian novel. **89m/C VHS, Beta, LV.** Woody Allen, Diane Keaton, Georges Adel, Despo Diamantidou, Frank Adu, Harold Gould; ***D:*** Woody Allen; ***W:*** Woody Allen; ***C:*** Ghislan Cloquet. *MGM, FOX*

Love and Faith 🦴🦴🦴 **1978** Two lovers are torn between their love for each other and their faiths during sixteenth-century Japan. English subtitles. **154m/C VHS, Beta.** *JP* Toshiro Mifune, Takashi Shimura, Yoshiko Nakana; ***D:*** Kei Kumai. *VDA*

Love and Hate: A Marriage Made in Hell 🦴🦴½ *Love and Hate: The Story of Colin and Joanne Thatcher* **1990** Marital murder mystery based on a true Canadian case. Joanne (Nelligan), the wife of wealthy rancher-politico Colin (Walsh), leaves her publicly charismatic and privately abusive husband with two thirds of their brood. A bitter battle for custody is waged, and Joanne is soon found savagely slain. The number one suspect: philandering exspouse Colin. Based on Maggie Siggins' "A Canadian Tragedy," the faux biography originally aired in two parts on Canadian TV. **156m/C VHS, Beta, LV.** Kate Nelligan, Ken Walsh, Leon Pownall, John Colicos, Noam Zylberman, Victoria Snow, Cedric Smith, R.H. Thomson, Victoria Wauchope, Doris Petrie, Duncan Ollenenshaw; ***D:*** Francis Mankiewicz; ***W:*** Suzette Couture. *PAR*

Love and Human Remains 🦴🦴🦴 **1993 (R)** Director Arcand's first English-language film features a group of late 20ish urbanites trying to come to grips with their place in the world (and their sexuality). David (Gibson) is an ammoral Lothario who doesn't believe in love and can only manage casual gay relationships. He hangs out with a variety of friends, all of whom are trying to cope with their varying sexual natures. Melodramatic framing story about a serial murderer who may, or may not, be one of the principal characters proves somewhat of a distraction. Lots of caustically witty dialogue and some fine performances (particularly Gibson's); filmed in Montreal. Adaptation of the play "Unidentified Human Remains and the True Nature of Love" by Fraser, who also did the screenplay. **100m/C VHS, LV.** *CA* Thomas Gibson, Ruth Marshall, Cameron Bancroft, Mia Kirshner, Joanne Vannicola, Matthew Ferguson, Rick Roberts; ***D:*** Denys Arcand; ***W:*** Brad Fraser; ***C:*** Paul Sarossy. Genie Awards '94: Best Adapted Screenplay. *COL*

Love & Murder 🦴½ **1991 (R)** Poorly developed tale of a photographer and his bevy of with beautiful models involved with murder and love, not necessarily in that order. **87m/C VHS.** Todd Waring, Kathleen Lasky, Ron White, Wayne Robson; ***D:*** Steven Hilliard Stern. *HMD*

Love and the Frenchwoman 🦴🦴🦴 *La Francaise et L'Amour* **1960** A French tale tracing the nature of love through stages. Deals with a story about where babies come from, puppy love, saving sex for marriage, and the way some men treat women. **135m/B VHS, Beta.** *FR* Jean-Paul Belmondo, Pierre-Jean Vaillard, Marie-Jose Nat, Annie Girardot; ***D:*** Jean Delannoy; ***M:*** Georges Delerue. *DVT, MRV, HEG*

Love at First Bite 🦴🦴½ **1979 (PG)** Intentionally campy spoof of the vampire film. Dracula is forced to leave his Transylvanian home as the Rumanian government has designated his castle a training center for young gymnasts. Once in New York, the Count takes in the night life and falls in love with a woman whose boyfriend embarks on a campaign to warn the city of Dracula's presence. Hamilton of the never-fading tan is appropriately tongue-in-cheek in a role which resurrected his career. **93m/C VHS, Beta, LV.** George Hamilton, Susan St. James, Richard Benjamin, Dick Shawn, Arte Johnson, Sherman Hemsley, Isabel Sanford; ***D:*** Stan Dragoti; ***M:*** Charles Bernstein. *ORI, WAR*

Love at First Sight 🦴 *Love is Blind; At First Sight* **1976** A pre-"Saturday Night Live" hack job for Aykroyd, playing a blind man who falls in love with a girl he bumps into. ♫Love at First Sight. **86m/C VHS, Beta.** Dan Aykroyd, Mary Ann McDonald, George Murray, Barry Morse; ***D:*** Rex Bromfield. *NO*

Love at Large 🦴🦴🦴 **1989 (R)** Hired by a beautiful woman, a private detective accidentally follows the wrong man and winds up being followed himself. He vies with a female detective in solving this case of mistaken identity. **90m/C VHS, Beta, LV.** Tom Berenger, Elizabeth Perkins, Anne Archer, Ann Magnuson, Annette O'Toole, Kate Capshaw, Ted Levine, Kevin J. O'Connor, Ruby Dee, Neil Young, Barry Miller; ***D:*** Alan Rudolph; ***W:*** Alan Rudolph; ***C:*** Elliot Davis. *ORI, FCT*

Love at Stake 🦴🦴½ **1987 (R)** It's condo owners versus the witches in this charming parody that features a hilarious cameo by Dr. Joyce Brothers and a very sexy performance from Carrera. **83m/C VHS, LV.** Patrick Cassidy, Kelly Preston, Bud Cort, Barbara Carrera, Stuart Pankin, Dave Thomas, Georgia Brown, Annie Golden; ***Cameos:*** Dr. Joyce Brothers; ***D:*** John Moffitt; ***M:*** Charles Fox. *SUE, NLC*

Love at the Top 🦴🦴½ **1986** Ladies' foundation designer falls in love with her boss's son-in-law, jeopardizing her career. **90m/C Beta.** Janis Paige, Richard Young, Jim MacKrell; ***D:*** John Bowab. *PSM*

The Love Boat **197?** All aboard! Love's waiting for you in this special movie presentation of the immensely popular television series. Captain Stubeing, Julie, Gopher, Isaac (your bartender) and a whole host of celebrities at the end of their careers, fall in and out of love as they sail back and forth between expensive resorts. **?m/C VHS.** Gavin MacLeod, Bernie Kopell, Ted Lange, Lauren Tewes. *GKK*

The Love Bug 🦴🦴½ **1968 (G)** A race car driver (Jones) is followed home by Herbie, a white Volkswagen with a mind of its own. Eventually, Jones follows the "Love Bug" to a life of madcap fun. Followed by several sequels. **110m/C VHS, Beta, LV.** Dean Jones, Michele Lee, Hope Lange, Robert Reed, Bert Convy; ***D:*** Robert Stevenson; ***C:*** Edward Colman; ***M:*** George Bruns. *DIS*

Love Butcher **1982 (R)** A crippled old gardener kills his female employers with his garden tools and cleans up neatly afterward. **84m/C VHS, Beta.** Erik Stern, Kay Neer, Robin Sherwood; ***D:*** Mikel Angel, Donald M. Jones. *NO*

Love by Appointment 🦴 **1976** An unlikely romantic comedy with a very unlikely cast has two businessmen meeting up with European prostitutes. Made for television. **96m/C VHS, Beta.** Ernest Borgnine, Robert Alda, Francoise Fabian, Corinne Clery. *NLC*

Love Camp 🦴 **1976** A woman is invited to a swinger's holiday camp, frolics for a while, then is told she can never leave. Suspenseful hijinks ensue. **100m/C VHS, Beta.** Laura Gemser, Christian Anders, Gabriele Tinti. *AHV*

Love, Cheat & Steal 🦴🦴 **1993 (R)** Convicted murderer Reno Adams (Roberts) breaks out of prison when he hears that his luscious ex (Amick) has just married another man (Lithgow). He turns up on her door, threatening to destroy her new life, but things aren't exactly what they seem. Faux noir. **95m/C VHS.** Eric Roberts, Madchen Amick, John Lithgow, Richard Edson, Donald Moffat, David Ackroyd, Dan O'Herlihy; ***D:*** William Curran; ***W:*** William Curran. *COL*

Love Child 🦴🦴 **1982 (R)** The story of a young woman in prison who becomes pregnant by a guard and fights to have and keep her baby. **97m/C VHS, Beta.** Amy Madigan, Beau Bridges, MacKenzie Phillips, Albert Salmi; ***D:*** Larry Peerce; ***M:*** Charles Fox. *WAR*

Love Crazy 🦴🦴🦴½ **1941** Powell and Loy team once again for a non-"Thin Man" romp through a married-people farce. Via a nosy mother-in-law and a series of misunderstandings, Powell and Loy squabble almost to the point of divorce. Not the wry wit the team was known for, but zany, high-action comedy at its best. **99m/B VHS.** William Powell, Myrna Loy, Gail Patrick, Jack Carson, Florence Bates, Sidney Blackmer, Sig Rumann; ***D:*** Jack Conway. *MGM*

Love Crimes 🦴 **1992 (R)** A con man (Bergin) poses as a photographer who sexually intimidates women while playing on their erotic fantasies. Young is the Atlanta district attorney who sets out to nail him when none of his victims will testify against him, only she may be enjoying her undercover work more than she realizes. Implausible and sleazy. Also available in an unrated version. **84m/C VHS, LV.** Sean Young, Patrick Bergin, Arnetia Walker, James Read; ***D:*** Lizzie Borden; ***C:*** Phedon Papamichael; ***M:*** Graeme Revell. *HBO*

Love Desperados 🦴 **1986** Cowboys and ranchers' wives mix it up in a lot of softcore hay. **99m/C VHS, Beta.** Virginia Gordon, James Arena. *MED*

Love 'Em and Leave 'Em 🦴🦴🦴 **1926** Two sisters, with opposite personalities, are department store sales clerks. Brent is the "good" girl and Brooks the "bad" flirt who, under the influence of Perkins, bets the store's welfare benefit money on the horses and loses it all. Brent manages to make things right, while keeping boyfriend Gray from her sister's clutches. Brooks' baby vamp (the actress was 19) stole the picture. Introduced the "Black Bottom" shimmy dance to the screen. Remade in 1929 as "The Saturday Night Kid" with Clara Bow and Jean Arthur. **70m/B VHS, Beta.** Louise Brooks, Evelyn Brent, Lawrence Gray, Osgood Perkins; ***D:*** Frank Tuttle. *GPV*

The Love Factor 🦴 **1969** A secret agent tries to foil the plans of a race of topless female aliens in this sleazy softcore sci-fi film. Also known as "Zeta One." **?m/C VHS.** *GB* Robin Hawdon, James Robertson Justice, Yutte Stensgaard. *SNC*

Love Field 🦴🦴½ **1991 (PG-13)** Pfeiffer is a Jackie Kennedy-obsessed hairdresser who decides to travel by bus to D.C. when she hears about President Kennedy's assassination. Along the way she gets involved in an interracial friendship with the secretive Haysbert, who's traveling with his young daughter. Pfieffer's Lurene is basically a sweet dim bulb and Haysbert has an unfortunately written one-note character (mainly exasperation). The 6-year-old McFadden (in her debut) makes the most impact. **104m/C VHS, LV.** Michelle Pfeiffer, Dennis Haysbert, Stephanie McFadden, Brian Kerwin, Louise Latham, Peggy Rea, Beth Grant, Cooper Huckabee, Mark Miller, Johnny Rae McGhee; ***D:*** Jonathan Kaplan; ***W:*** Don Roos; ***M:*** Jerry Goldsmith. Nominations: Academy Awards '92: Best Actress (Pfeiffer). *ORI, MOV*

Love Film 🦴🦴 **1970** A train trip from Budapest, Hungary to Lyon, France leads a young man to recall his past as he journeys to visit a childhood sweetheart. Jancsi and Kata's friendship has been disrupted by the 1956 uprising and Jancsi wonders if the love once developing between them has been broken by distance and time. In Hungarian with English subtitles. **130m/C VHS.** *HU* Andras Balint, Judit Halasz; ***D:*** Istvan Szabo. *INJ, TPV*

Love Finds Andy Hardy 🦴🦴🦴 **1938** Young Andy Hardy finds himself torn between three girls before returning to the girl next door. Garland's first appearance in the acclaimed Andy Hardy series features her singing "In Between" and "Meet the Best of my Heart." Also available with "Andy Hardy Meets Debutante" on Laser Disc. **90m/B VHS, Beta, LV.** Mickey Rooney, Judy Garland, Lana Turner, Ann Rutherford, Fay Holden, Lewis Stone, Marie Blake, Cecilia Parker, Gene Reynolds; ***D:*** George B. Seitz. *MGM*

The Love Flower 🦴🦴½ **1920** A man kills his second wife's lover and escapes with his daughter to a tropical island, pursued by a detective and a young adventurer. Interesting ending wraps things up nicely. Silent. **70m/B VHS, Beta.** Carol Dempster, Richard Barthelmess, George MacQuarrie, Anders Randolf, Florence Short; ***D:*** D.W. Griffith; ***W:*** D.W. Griffith. *NO*

Love for Lydia 🦴🦴🦴 **1979** Made for British television miniseries following wayward beauty Lydia, orphaned heiress to a manufacturing fortune, through the high-spirited 1920s. Set in the industrial Midlands and farming communities of England, Lydia dazzles every man she meets, often to an unhappy end. Based on the novel by H.E. Bates. Available as a seven cassette boxed set. **657m/C VHS.** *GB* Mel Martin, Christopher Blake, Peter Davison, Jeremy Irons, Michael Aldridge, Rachel Kempson, Beatrix Lehmmann. *FCT, SIG*

Love from a Stranger 🦴🦴 **1937** Thriller about a working woman who wins a lottery. Soon she is charmed by and marries a man whom she later suspects may be trying to kill her. Remade in 1947. **90m/B VHS.** *GB* Ann Harding, Basil Rathbone, Binnie Hale, Bruce Seton, Bryan Powley, Jean Cadell; ***D:*** Rowland V. Lee. *NOS, SNC, NWV*

Love from a Stranger 🦴🦴½ *A Stranger Walked In* **1947** In this remake of the 1937 film, a young newlywed bride fears that the honeymoon is over when she suspects that her husband is a notorious killer and that she will be his next victim. **81m/B VHS, Beta, LV.** Sylvia Sidney, John Hodiak, John Howard, Ann Richards, Isobel Elsom, Ernest Cossart; ***D:*** Richard Whorf. *NWV*

The Love God? 🦴½ **1970 (PG-13)** Very silly comedy finds mild-mannered Abner Peacock (Knotts) trying on Hugh Hefner's mantle. With his bird-watcher's magazine in financial trouble, Abner takes on a couple of shifty partners who change it into a different kind of bird watching magazine (the nude female kind) that gets Abner charged with pornography and finds him becoming a (very) unlikely sex symbol. **103m/C VHS.** Don Knotts, Edmond O'Brien, Anne Francis, Maureen Arthur, James Gregory, Margaret (Maggie) Peterson, Marjorie Bennett; ***D:*** Nat Hiken; ***W:*** Nat Hiken; ***C:*** William Margulies; ***M:*** Vic Mizzy. *MCA*

The Love Goddesses **1965** A sixty-year examination of some of the most beautiful women on the silver screen, reflecting with extraordinary accuracy the customs, manners and mores of the times. Released theatrically in 1972. **83m/B VHS, Beta, LV.** Marlene Dietrich, Greta Garbo, Jean Harlow, Gloria Swanson, Mae West, Betty Grable, Rita Hayworth, Elizabeth Taylor, Marilyn Monroe, Theda Bara, Claudette Colbert, Dorothy Lamour; ***D:*** Saul J. Turell. *COL, SUE*

Love Happy 🦴🦴½ **1950** A group of impoverished actors accidentally gain possession of valuable diamonds. Unfortunately for them, detective Groucho is assigned to recover them! **85m/B VHS, LV.** Groucho Marx, Harpo Marx, Chico Marx, Vera-Ellen, Ilona Massey, Marion Hutton, Raymond Burr, Marilyn Monroe; ***D:*** David Miller; ***C:*** William Mellor. *REP*

Love Has Many Faces 🦴½ **1965** Judith Crist was too kind when she said this was for connoisseurs of truly awful movies. Playgal Turner marries beachboy Robertson and many faces come between them. Much melodrama. Filmed on location. **104m/C VHS, Beta.** Lana Turner, Cliff Robertson, Hugh O'Brian, Ruth Roman, Stefanie Powers, Virginia Grey, Ron Husmann; ***D:*** Alexander Singer. *GKK*

Love Hurts 🦴🦴 **1991 (R)** A guy looking for romance finds his hands full with a number of beautiful women. Will he find the love he craves, or will the pain be too much to bear? **110m/C VHS.** Jeff Daniels, Judith Ivey, John Mahoney, Cynthia Sikes, Amy Wright; ***D:*** Bud Yorkin; ***W:*** Ron Nyswaner. *LIV, VES*

A Love in Germany 🦴🦴½ *Un Amour En Allemagne; Eine Liebe in Deutschland* **1984 (R)** A tragic love affair develops between a German shopkeeper's wife and a Polish prisoner-of-war in a small German village during WWII. In German with English subtitles. **110m/C VHS, Beta.** *FR GE* Hanna Schygulla, Piotr Lysak, Elisabeth Trissenaar, Armin Mueller-Stahl; ***D:*** Andrzej Wajda; ***W:*** Andrzej Wajda, Agnieszka Holland, Boleslaw Michalek. *COL, APD, GLV*

Love in the Afternoon 🦴🦴½ **1957** A Parisian private eye's daughter (Hepburn) decides to investigate a philandering American millionaire (Cooper) and winds up falling in love with him. Cooper's a little old for the Casanova role but Hepburn is always enchanting. **126m/B VHS, Beta.** Gary Cooper, Audrey Hepburn, John McGiver, Maurice Chevalier; ***D:*** Billy Wilder; ***W:*** Billy Wilder, I.A.L. Diamond; ***C:*** William Mellor. *FOX, IME*

Love in the City 🦴🦴🦴 **1953** Five stories of life, love and tears in Rome. In Italian with English subtitles and narration. **90m/B VHS, Beta.** *IT* Ugo Tognazzi, Maresa Gallo, Caterina Rigoglioso, Silvia Lillo; ***D:*** Michelangelo Antonioni, Federico Fellini, Dino Risi, Carlo Lizzani, Alberto Lattuada, Francesco Maselli, Cesare Zavattini; ***W:*** Federico Fellini. *NOS, FCT, APD*

Love in the Present Tense 🦴 **1985** A woman's romantic novel on video, dealing with an affair that reawakens the torpid, tragic life of a beautiful ex-model. **90m/C VHS, Beta.** *PSM*

Love Is a Gun 🦴½ **1994 (R)** A police photographer (Roberts) begins having violent and erotic hallucinations that begin to affect his fiancee (Garrett). Things get even weirder when a femme fatale model (Preston) enters the picture. **92m/C VHS, LV.** Eric Roberts, Kelly Preston, Eliza Garrett, R. Lee Ermey; ***D:*** David Hartwell. *VMK*

Love Is a Many-Splendored Thing 🦴🦴½ **1955** A married American war correspondent and a beautiful Eurasian doctor fall in love in post-WWII Hong Kong. They struggle with racism and unhappiness, until he's sent to Korea to observe the Army's activities there. Based on the novel by Han Suyin. The extensive LA Asian acting community got some work out of this film, although the leads are played by Caucasians. Oscar winning song was a very big popular hit. ♫Love is a Many-Splendored Thing. **102m/C VHS, Beta, LV.** William Holden, Jennifer Jones, Torin Thatcher, Isobel Elsom, Jorja Curtright, Virginia Gregg, Richard Loo; ***D:*** Henry King; ***C:*** Leon Shamroy; ***M:*** Alfred Newman. Academy Awards '55: Best Costume Design (Color), Best Song ("Love Is a Many-Splendored Thing"), Best Score; Nominations: Academy Awards '55: Best Actress (Jones), Best Art Direction/Set Decoration (Color), Best Color Cinematography, Best Picture, Best Sound. *FXV, BTV*

Love Is Better Than Ever 🦴🦴½ *The Light Fantastic* **1952** Lightweight romantic-comedy casts Taylor as a dancing instructor who travels to the Big Apple for a convention. Once there, she meets and falls for talent agent Parks. Carefree, bachelor Parks is too busy to be bothered by small town Taylor, but Liz is determined to land her man. Release of this picture was held back because of Parks' blacklisting by the McCarthy committee. **81m/B VHS.** Larry Parks, Elizabeth Taylor, Josephine Hutchinson,

Tom Tully, Ann Doran, Elinor Donahue, Kathleen Freeman; ***Cameos:*** Gene Kelly; ***D:*** Stanley Donen; ***W:*** Ruth Brooks Flippen. *MGM*

Love Kills ✗✗ **1991 (PG-13)** Is the man a beautiful heiress falls in love with actually an assassin hired by her husband to kill her? Find out in this steamy suspenser. **92m/C VHS, Beta, LV.** Virginia Madsen, Lenny Von Dohlen, Erich Anderson, Kate Hodge, Jim Metzler; ***D:*** Brian Grant. *PAR*

Love Laughs at Andy Hardy ✗✗ **1946** Andy Hardy, college boy, is in love and in trouble. Financial and romantic problems come to a head when Andy is paired with a six-foot tall blind date. One in the series. **93m/B VHS, Beta.** Mickey Rooney, Lewis Stone, Sara Haden, Lina Romay, Bonita Granville, Fay Holden; ***D:*** Willis Goldbeck. *NOS, MRV, HHT*

Love Leads the Way ✗✗ **1984** The true story of how Morris Frank established the seeing-eye dog system in the 1930s. **99m/C VHS, Beta.** Timothy Bottoms, Eva Marie Saint, Arthur Hill, Susan Dey, Ralph Bellamy, Ernest Borgnine, Patricia Neal; ***D:*** Delbert Mann. *DIS*

Love Letters ✗✗✗ *Passion Play; My Love Letters* **1983 (R)** A young disc jockey falls under the spell of a box of love letters that her mother left behind which detailed her double life. She, in turn, begins an affair with a married man. Thoughtful treatment of the psychology of infidelity. **102m/C VHS, Beta, LV.** Jamie Lee Curtis, Amy Madigan, Bud Cort, Matt Clark, Bonnie Bartlett, Sally Kirkland, James Keach; ***D:*** Amy Holden Jones. *LIV, VES, IME*

Love, Lies and Murder ✗✗½ **1991 (PG-13)** Shocking psychological thriller in which a businessman convinces his daughter and sister-in-law to murder his wife and then sends his daughter to prison for the crime. The "perfect murder" is not so perfect, however, when the daughter learns that her father has remarried and is now living an insurance-rich lifestyle. She decides to fight back in this true made-for-television story of bizarre murder and deception. **190m/C VHS, LV.** Clancy Brown, John Ashton, Sheryl Lee, Moira Kelly, Ramon Bieri, Ken Walsh, Tom Bower, John M. Jackson; ***D:*** Robert Markowitz. *REP*

The Love Machine ✗½ **1971 (R)** A power-hungry newscaster climbs the corporate ladder by sleeping with many, including the president's wife. An adaptation of Jacqueline Susann's novel. **108m/C VHS, Beta.** John Phillip Law, Dyan Cannon, Robert Ryan, Jackie Cooper, David Hemmings, Jodi Wexler, William Roerick, Maureen Arthur, Shecky Greene, Clinton Greyn, Sharon Farrell, Alexandra Hay, Eve Bruce, Greg Mullavey, Edith Atwater, Gene Baylos, Claudia Jennings, Mary Collinson, Madeleine Collinson, Ann Ford, Gayle Hunnicutt; ***D:*** Jack Haley Jr.; ***C:*** Charles B(ryant) Lang; ***M:*** Artie Butler. *COL, MLB*

Love Matters ✗✗ **1993 (R)** Tom and Julie's fast-track marriage is hovering on the brink when Tom's best friend Geoff, who's also married, shows up on their doorstep with his sexy mistress and announces he's getting a divorce. Reluctantly, Tom and Julie allow the X-rated lovebirds to stay the night but all that heat only shows up the flaws in their own marriage even more. An unrated version at 103 minutes is also available. **97m/C VHS, LV.** Griffin Dunne, Tony Goldwyn, Annette O'Toole, Gina Gershon, Kate Burton; ***D:*** Eb Lottimer; ***W:*** Eb Lottimer; ***M:*** Simon Boswell. *REP*

Love Me Deadly ✗ **1976 (R)** A young woman tries to get her husband interested in her new hobby-necrophilia. **95m/C VHS, Beta.** Mary Wilcox, Lyle Waggoner, Christopher Stone, Timothy Scott. *GEM*

Love Me or Leave Me ✗✗✗ **1955** A hard-hitting biography of '20s torch singer Ruth Etting and her rise and fall at the hand of her abusive, gangster husband, a part just made for Cagney. Day emotes and sings expressively in one of the best performances of her career. ♫I'll Never Stop Loving You; Never Look Back; Shaking the Blues Away; Mean to Me; Love Me or Leave Me; Sam, the Old Accordian Man; At Sundown; Everybody Loves My Baby; Five Foot Two. **122m/C VHS, Beta, LV.** Doris Day, James Cagney, Cameron Mitchell, Robert Keith, Tom Tully, Veda Ann Borg; ***D:*** Charles Vidor. Academy Awards '55: Best Story; Nominations: Academy Awards '55: Best Actor (Cagney), Best Screenplay, Best Song ("I'll Never Stop Loving You"), Best Sound, Best Original Score. *MGM*

Love Me Tender ✗✗ **1956** A Civil War-torn family is divided by in-fighting between two brothers who both seek the affections of the same woman. Presley's first film. Songs include "Poor Boy," "We're Gonna Move," and the title tune. **89m/B VHS, Beta.** Elvis Presley, Richard Egan, Debra Paget, Neville Brand, Mildred Dunnock, James Drury, Barry Coe; ***D:*** Robert D. Webb. *MVD, FOX*

Love Meetings *Comizi d'Amore* **1964** Pasolini acts as director and interviewer to query a wide-range of individuals on their experiences at love, including homosexuality, prostitution, marital and non-marital interludes. In Italian with English subtitles. **90m/B VHS, LV.** *IT* ***D:*** Pier Paolo Pasolini. *WBF, INJ*

Love Nest ✗✗ **1951** Lundigan stars as Jim Scott, the landlord of an apartment building brimming with wacky tenants, including Monroe, Paar, and Fay. He dreams of becoming a famous writer, but his time is always filled with fixing up the building and trying to pay the mortgage. When one of the tenants ends up in jail because he was living off wealthy widows, Scott's luck changes. This moderately funny film is a good look at the early careers of Monroe and Paar. **84m/B VHS.** William Lundigan, June Haver, Frank Fay, Marilyn Monroe, Jack Paar; ***D:*** Joseph M. Newman. *FXV*

Love Notes **1988** Three short vignettes of soft core fantasy, in the life of an ordinary guy. **60m/C VHS, Beta.** Jeff Daniels, Christine Veronica. *AHV*

The Love of Three Queens ✗½ **1954** The loves, on and off stage, of a beautiful actress in a European traveling theatre group. **80m/C VHS, Beta.** Gerard Oury, Massimo Serato, Robert Beatty, Cathy O'Donnell, Terence Morgan, Hedy Lamarr; ***D:*** Marc Allegret. *FCT, VDM*

Love on the Dole ✗✗✗ **1941** In a gloomy industrial section of England during the early '30s a family struggles to survive and maintain dignity. Grim Depression drama salvaged by great acting. **89m/B VHS, Beta.** *GB* Deborah Kerr, Clifford Evans, George Carney; ***D:*** John Baxter. *NOS, VYY*

Love on the Run ✗✗½ **1936** Enjoyable romantic comedy starring Crawford as a rich American heiress and Gable and Tone (Crawford's real husband at the time) as journalists stationed in Europe. Gable and Tone are assigned to cover an international aviator, who turns out to be an evil spy, as well as the upcoming wedding of flighty Crawford. When Crawford asks for help in getting out of her marriage, Gable and Tone steal a plane and the trio is chased across Europe by spies. Wild and farfetched plot, but the stars make it worthwhile. Based on the story "Beauty and the Beast" by Alan Green and Julian Brodie. **80m/B VHS.** Joan Crawford, Clark Gable, Franchot Tone, Reginald Owen, Mona Maris, Ivan Lebedeff, Charles Judels, William Demarest; ***D:*** Woodbridge S. Van Dyke; ***W:*** John Lee Mahin, Manuel Seff, Gladys Hurlbut. *MGM*

Love on the Run ✗✗✗ *L'Amour en Fuite* **1978** The further amorous adventures of Antoine Doinel, hero of "The 400 Blows," "Stolen Kisses," and "Bed and Board." Doinel is now in his thirties and newly divorced. He renews affairs with several women from his past but, after his mother's death, must contend with his emotional immaturity and his inability to sustain a relationship. In French with English subtitles. **95m/C VHS, Beta.** *FR* Jean-Pierre Leaud, Marie-France Pisier, Claude Jade; ***D:*** Francois Truffaut; ***C:*** Nestor Almendros; ***M:*** Georges Delerue. Cesar Awards '80: Best Score. *HMV, WAR*

Love on the Run ✗½ **1985** A beautiful lawyer helps a wrongly-accused convict escape from prison, then they both evade the law. Made for television. **102m/C VHS, Beta.** Stephanie Zimbalist, Alec Baldwin, Constance McCashin, Howard Duff; ***D:*** Gus Trikonis; ***M:*** Billy Goldenberg. *COL*

Love or Money? ✗½ **1988 (PG-13)** A small comedy about a yuppie who must choose between a woman and a real estate deal. **90m/C VHS, Beta, LV.** Timothy Daly, Haviland Morris, Kevin McCarthy, Shelley Fabares, David Doyle, Allen Havey; ***D:*** Todd Hallowell; ***W:*** Bart Davis. *NO*

Love Potion #9 ✗½ **1992 (PG-13)** Two nerdy biochemists procure a love potion that they test on animals. Meeting with success they agree to test it on themselves. Predictably, the scientists are transformed and fall in love with each other. Features a talented young cast, with an amusing cameo by Bancroft, but the script is a real disappointment because of its shallow characters and lame gags. Inspired by the song by Jerry Leiber and Mike Stoller. **96m/C VHS, LV.** Tate Donovan, Sandra Bullock, Mary Mara, Dale Midkiff, Hillary Bailey Smith, Dylan Baker; ***Cameos:*** Anne Bancroft; ***D:*** Dale Launer; ***W:*** Dale Launer. *FXV*

Love Songs ✗✗ **1985 (R)** A mother of two is confronted with her husband's abandonment and a subsequent romance with a younger man. In French with English subtitles or dubbed. ♫Leave It to Me; Psychic Flash; I Am With You Now; Human Race; We Can Dance; One More Moment; From the Heart; This Must Be Heaven. **107m/C VHS, Beta.** *FR CA* Catherine Deneuve, Christopher Lambert; ***D:*** Elie Chouraqui. *LIV, VES, INJ*

Love Story ✗✗✗ **1970 (PG)** Melodrama had enormous popular appeal. O'Neal is the son of Boston's upper crust at Harvard; McGraw's the daughter of a poor Italian on scholarship to study music at Radcliffe. They find happiness, but only for a brief period. Timeless story, simply told, with artful direction from Hiller pulling exceptional performances from the young duo (who have never done as well since). The end result is perhaps better than Segal's simplistic novel, which was produced after he sold the screenplay and became a best-seller before the picture's release—great publicity for any film. Remember: "Love means never having to say you're sorry." **100m/C VHS, Beta, LV.** Ryan O'Neal, Ali MacGraw, Ray Milland, John Marley, Tommy Lee Jones; ***D:*** Arthur Hiller; ***W:*** Erich Segal. Academy Awards '70: Best Original Score; Golden Globe Awards '71: Best Actress—Drama (MacGraw), Best Director (Hiller), Best Film—Drama, Best Screenplay, Best Score; National Board of Review Awards '70: 10 Best Films of the Year; Nominations: Academy Awards '70: Best Actor (O'Neal), Best Actress (MacGraw), Best Director (Hiller), Best Picture, Best Story & Screenplay, Best Supporting Actor (Marley). *PAR*

Love Strange Love ✗½ **1982** A young boy develops a bizarre relationship with his mother who works in a luxurious bordello. Also available in an unedited 120-minute version. **97m/C VHS, Beta.** Vera Fischer, Mauro Mendonca. *LIV, VES*

Love Streams ✗✗½ **1984 (PG-13)** A quirky character drama about a writer and his sister who struggle to find love despite their personal problems. **122m/C VHS, Beta.** Gena Rowlands, John Cassavetes, Diahnne Abbott, Seymour Cassel; ***D:*** John Cassavetes; ***W:*** Ted Allan. Berlin International Film Festival '84: Golden Berlin Bear. *MGM*

Love Thrill Murders *Woof!* **1971 (R)** A film about a Mansonesque lunatic who is worshipped and obeyed by a mob of runaways and dropouts. **89m/C VHS, Beta.** Troy Donahue. *LIV, VES*

Love Under Pressure ✗✗ **198?** Man and woman's marriage starts to evaporate when they realize their son is seriously disturbed. **92m/C VHS.** Karen Black, Keir Dullea. *ACA*

Love with a Perfect Stranger **1986** This Harlequin Romance takes place in Italy where a young widow meets a dashing Englishman. He changes her life forever. **102m/C VHS, Beta.** Marilu Henner, Daniel Massey; ***M:*** John Du Prez. *PAR*

Love with the Proper Stranger ✗✗✗ **1963** A quiet, gritty romance about an itinerant musician and a young working girl in Manhattan awkwardly living through the consequences of their one night stand. Moved Wood well into the realm of adult roles, after years playing teen-agers and innocents. Although the story is about an Italian neighborhood and family, an exceptional number of the cast members were Jewish, as was the screenwriter. Story does not conclude strongly, although this did not hamper the box office returns. **102m/B VHS, Beta, LV.** Natalie Wood, Steve McQueen, Edie Adams, Herschel Bernardi, Tom Bosley, Harvey Lembeck, Penny Santon, Virginia Vincent, Nick Alexander, Augusta Ciolli; ***D:*** Robert Mulligan; ***W:*** Arnold Schulman; ***C:*** Milton Krasner; ***M:*** Elmer Bernstein. Nominations: Academy Awards '63: Best Actress (Wood), Best Art Direction/Set Decoration (B & W), Best Black and White Cinematography, Best Costume Design (B & W), Best Story & Screenplay. *PAR*

Love Without Fear **1990** A dramatic, heart-rendering look at children with AIDS. Story focuses on the lives of three women from completely different backgrounds who adopt babies with AIDS and develop a special love for these children. Also shows their confrontations with a society which fears the disease and the women's strength to reach out and make a difference. **?m/C VHS.** *NO*

Love Without Pity 𝔅𝔅½ **1991** Rochant's theatrical debut is a modern romance, with more distance and alienation than joy. A lovely, successful grad student loses her heart to a jobless, unambitious layabout who wants total commitment from her. Untypical, sardonic love story may be too cynical for sentimental types. In French with English subtitles. **95m/C VHS.** *FR* Hippolyte Girardot, Mireille Perrier, Jean Marie Rollin; ***D:*** Eric Rochant; ***W:*** Eric Rochant; ***M:*** Gerard Torikian. *INJ, ORI*

Love Your Mama 𝔅𝔅½ **1989 (PG-13)** An urban black drama about the strong Dorothy whose faith helps her cope with her many family complications, including her drunken husband, car thief son, and pregnant teenage daughter. Believable role models and good performances help out this amatuer filmmaking effort. **93m/C VHS.** Audrey Morgan, Carol E. Hall, Andre Robinson, Ernest Rayford, Kearo Johnson, Jacqueline Williams; ***D:*** Ruby L. Oliver; ***W:*** Ruby L. Oliver. *HMD, BTV, FCT*

The Loved One 𝔅𝔅𝔅 **1965** A famously outlandish, death-mocking farce based on Evelyn Waugh's satire about a particularly horrendous California funeral parlor/cemetery and how its denizens do business. A shrill, protracted spearing of American capitalism. **118m/B VHS, Beta, LV.** Robert Morse, John Gielgud, Rod Steiger, Liberace, Anjanette Comer, Jonathan Winters, James Coburn, Dana Andrews, Milton Berle, Tab Hunter, Robert Morley, Lionel Stander, Margaret Leighton, Roddy McDowall, Bernie Kopell, Alan Napier; ***D:*** Tony Richardson; ***W:*** Terry Southern, Christopher Isherwood; ***C:*** Haskell Wexler; ***M:*** John Addison. *MGM*

Loveless 𝔅𝔅 **1983 (R)** A menacing glance into the exploits of an outcast motorcycle gang. In the 50s, a group of bikers on their way to the Florida Cycle Races stop for lunch in a small-town diner. While repairs are being made on their motorcycles, they decide to take full advantage of their situation. **85m/C VHS, Beta.** Robert Gordon, Willem Dafoe, J. Don Ferguson; ***D:*** Kathryn Bigelow; ***W:*** Kathryn Bigelow. *MED*

Lovelines 𝔅 **1984 (R)** Two rock singers from rival high schools meet and fall in love during a panty raid. Laughs uncounted ensue. **93m/C VHS, Beta.** Greg Bradford, Michael Winslow, Mary Beth Evans, Don Michael Paul, Tammy Taylor, Stacey Toten, Miguel Ferrer, Shecky Greene, Aimee Eccles, Sherri Stoner; ***D:*** Rod Amateau. *FOX*

Lovely ... But Deadly 𝔅½ **1982 (R)** Young girl wages a war against the drug dealers in her school after her brother dies of an overdose. **95m/C VHS, Beta.** Lucinda Dooling, John Randolph, Richard Herd, Susan Mechsner, Mel Novak; ***D:*** David Sheldon. *LIV, VES*

Lovely to Look At 𝔅𝔅𝔅 **1952** Three wanna-be Broadway producers (Skelton, Keel, Champion) go to gay Paree to peddle Skelton's half interest in Madame Roberta's, a chi chi dress shop. There, they meet the shop's other half interest, two sisters (Champion and Miller), and together they stage a fashion show to finance the floundering hospice of haute couture. Lavish production, light plot. Filmed in Technicolor based on Kern's 1933 Broadway hit (inspired by Alice Duer Miller's "Gowns by Roberta"). Vincent Minelli staged the fashion show, with gowns by Adrian (watch for cop-beater Zsa Zsa as a model). Laserdisc format features the original motion picture trailer. ♫Opening Night; Smoke Gets in Your Eyes; Lovely to Look At; The Touch of Your Hand; Yesterdays; I Won't Dance; You're Devastating; The Most Exciting Night; I'll Be Hard to Handle. **105m/C VHS, LV.** Kathryn Grayson, Red Skelton, Howard Keel, Gower Champion, Marge Champion, Ann Miller, Zsa Zsa Gabor, Kurt Kasznar, Marcel Dalio, Diane Cassidy; ***D:*** Mervyn LeRoy; ***M:*** Jerome Kern. *MGM, TTC, FCT*

The Lover 𝔅𝔅 *L'Amant* **1992 (R)** Portrays the sexual awakening of a French teenager and her older Chinese lover in Indochina in 1929. The characters, who remain nameless, meet on a ferry where the man is smitten by the girl's beauty. Detached, determined, and unromantic (the opposite of her indolent lover), she allows herself to be seduced for the experience, and money, he offers. The film is equally detached, including the beautifully photographed but uninvolving sex scenes. Moreau narrates as an adult looking back on her life. March's debut; filmed on location in Vietnam. Based on the semi-autobiographical novel by Marguerite Duras who reputiated director Annuad's film when it was released in France. Also available in an unrated, letterbox version at 115 minutes. **103m/C VHS, Beta, LV.** *FR* Jane March, Tony Leung, Frederique Meininger, Arnaud Giovanietti, Melvil Poupaud, Lisa Faulkner, Xiem Mang; ***D:*** Jean-Jacques Annaud; ***W:*** Gerard Brach, Jean-Jacques Annaud; ***C:*** Robert Fraisse. Cesar Awards '93: Best Score; Nominations: Academy Awards '92: Best Cinematography. *MGM, BTV*

Lover Come Back 𝔅𝔅½ **1961** More Day-Hudson antics in which an advertising executive falls in love with his competitor but that doesn't stop him from stealing her clients. Is there no shame? **107m/C VHS, Beta.** Rock Hudson, Doris Day, Tony Randall, Edie Adams, Joe Flynn, Ann B. Davis, Jack Oakie, Jack Albertson, Jack Kruschen, Howard St. John; ***D:*** Delbert Mann. Nominations: Academy Awards '61: Best Story & Screenplay. *MCA, MOV*

Loverboy 𝔅 **1989 (PG-13)** A college schnook takes a summer job as a Beverly Hills pizza delivery boy and is preyed upon by many rich and sex-hungry housewives. **105m/C VHS, Beta, LV.** Patrick Dempsey, Kate Jackson, Barbara Carrera, Kirstie Alley, Carrie Fisher, Robert Ginty; ***D:*** Joan Micklin Silver; ***W:*** Tom Ropelewski, Leslie Dixon; ***M:*** Michel Colombier. *COL*

The Lovers 𝔅𝔅𝔅 **1959** Chic tale of French adultery with Moreau starring as a provincial wife whose shallow life changes overnight when she meets a young man. Had a controversial American debut because of the film's tender eroticism and innocent view of adultery. In French with English subtitles. **90m/B VHS.** *FR* Jeanne Moreau, Alain Cuny, Jose-Luis De Villalonga, Jean-Mark Bory; ***D:*** Louis Malle; ***W:*** Louis Malle. Venice Film Festival '59: Special Jury Prize. *NYF, FCT, ING*

Lovers: A True Story 𝔅𝔅𝔅 **1990 (R)** Erotic love triangle in 1950s Madrid, while Spain is under the suffocating dictatorship of Franco. Naive, young Paco has a virginal, hardworking fiancee named Trini. Things would seem to be headed for an average life until Paco rents a room from young widow Luisa and they embark on a sexual affair bordering on obsession. When Trini discovers what's going on she turns out to have a more passionate, and violent, nature than even Paco could imagine. Steamy and highly dramatic with excellent performances. Based on a true story. In Spanish with English subtitles. An unrated version is also available. **105m/C VHS.** *SP* Victoria Abril, Jorge Sanz, Maribel Verdu; ***D:*** Vicente Aranda. Berlin International Film Festival '91: Best Actress (Abril). *REP, INJ*

Lovers and Liars 𝔅𝔅 *Travels with Anita; A Trip with Anita* **1981 (R)** A romantic adventure in Rome turns into a symphony of zany mishaps when the man forgets to tell the woman that he is married!! **93m/C VHS, Beta.** *IT* Goldie Hawn, Giancarlo Giannini, Laura Betti; ***D:*** Mario Monicelli; ***M:*** Ennio Morricone. *SUE*

Lovers and Other Strangers 𝔅𝔅𝔅 **1970 (R)** Two young people decide to marry after living together for a year and a half. Various tensions surface between them and among their families as the wedding day approaches. Good comedy features some charming performances. Keaton's first film. ♫For All We Know. **106m/C VHS.** Gig Young, Beatrice Arthur, Bonnie Bedelia, Anne Jackson, Harry Guardino, Michael Brandon, Richard Castellano, Bob Dishy, Marian Hailey, Cloris Leachman, Anne Meara, Diane Keaton; ***D:*** Cy Howard; ***W:*** Renee Taylor, Joseph Bologna, David Zelag Goodman. Academy Awards '70: Best Song ("For All We Know"); Nominations: Academy Awards '70: Best Adapted Screenplay, Best Supporting Actor (Castellano). *FOX*

Lovers Like Us 𝔅𝔅½ *Le Sauvage; The Savage* **1975** Two people each leave their spouses, meet one another, and fall in love. **103m/C VHS, Beta.** *FR* Catherine Deneuve, Yves Montand, Luigi Vannucchi, Tony Roberts, Dana Wynter; ***D:*** Jean-Paul Rappeneau; ***W:*** Jean-Paul Rappeneau. *NO*

Lovers' Lovers 𝔅½ **1994** All sorts of bizarre and erotic adventures ensue when Blaire the jilted narcissist meets Michael, who doesn't want to commit to girlfriend Teri. Michael plans an affair with Blaire without realizing that Teri is already having a fling with Ray, Blaire's ex. Some funny situations but too many talky scenes stop the film cold. **90m/C VHS, LV.** Serge Rodnunsky, Jennifer Ciesar, Cindy Parker, Ray Bennett; ***D:*** Serge Rodnunsky; ***W:*** Serge Rodnunsky; ***M:*** Pierre Rodnunsky. *TRI*

Lovers of Their Time 𝔅 **1985** A romantic novel on tape, about forbidden love and other problems. **60m/C Beta.** Edward Petherbridge, Cheryl Prime, Lynn Farleigh; ***D:*** Robert Knights. *PSM*

Loves & Times of Scaramouche 𝔅½ *Scaramouche* **1976** Eighteenth-century rogue becomes involved in a plot to assassinate Napoleon and winds up seducing Josephine in the process. Dubbed. **92m/C VHS, Beta.** *IT* Michael Sarrazin, Ursula Andress, Aldo Maccione; ***D:*** Enzo G. Castellari. *SUE, COL*

Loves of a Blonde 𝔅𝔅𝔅½ *A Blonde in Love; Lasky Jedne Plavovlasky* **1965** A shy teenage factory girl falls in love with a visiting piano player when the reservist army comes to her small town. But when she goes to visit his family, she discovers things aren't as she imagined. Touching look at the complications of love and our expectations. Czech with subtitles. **88m/B VHS, Beta.** *CZ* Jana Brejchova, Josef Sebanek, Vladimir Pucholt; ***D:*** Milos Forman. Nominations: Academy Awards '66: Best Foreign Language Film. *HMV, INJ, COL*

The Loves of Carmen 𝔅𝔅½ **1948** Film version of the classic Prosper Merrimee novel about a tempestuous Spanish gypsy and the soldier who loves her. Hayworth is great to look at and the film's main selling point. **98m/C VHS, Beta.** Rita Hayworth, Glenn Ford, Ron Randell, Victor Jory, Arnold Moss, Luther Adler, Joseph Buloff; ***D:*** Charles Vidor. Nominations: Academy Awards '48: Best Color Cinematography. *COL*

The Loves of Edgar Allen Poe 𝔅𝔅 **1942** A bland biographical drama about young Poe's adoption, his treatment at the hands of his foster father, his rejection by a woman for a more well-off man, his marriage to his first cousin, and his early death from alcoholism. **67m/B VHS.** Linda Darnell, Shepperd Strudwick, Virginia Gilmore, Jane Darwell, Mary Howard; ***D:*** Harry Lachman. *TCF*

The Loves of Hercules *Woof! Hercules and the Hydra* **1960** The mythic mesomorph finds a mate with equiponderant chest measurements, and must save her from an evil queen. Somehow it eludes him that both queen and maiden are Miss Jayne in red and black wigs. Kudos for worst dubbing and special effects; a must see for connoisseurs of kitsch. **94m/C VHS.** *IT FR* Jayne Mansfield, Mickey Hargitay; ***D:*** Carlo L. Bragaglia. *SNC, VDM*

The Loves of Irina 𝔅 **198?** Franco's dreamy, sanguine, produced-on-a-dime tale of a vampiress. She cruises the Riviera, seducing and nibbling on a variety of men and women. Spanish release known as "Erotikill," not for most tastes. **95m/C VHS, Beta.** Lina Romay, Monica Swin, Jack Taylor, Alice Arno; ***D:*** Jess (Jesus) Franco. *MED*

Love's Savage Fury *Woof!* **1979** Two escapees from a Union prison camp seek out a hidden treasure that could determine the outcome of the Civil War. A bad made-for-television "Gone With the Wind" rip-off. **100m/C VHS, Beta.** Jennifer O'Neill, Perry King, Robert Reed, Raymond Burr, Connie Stevens, Ed Lauter; ***D:*** Joseph Hardy; ***M:*** John Addison. *PSM*

Lovesick ☙☙ **1983 (PG)** A very-married New York psychiatrist goes against his own best judgment when he falls in love with one of his patients. **98m/C VHS, Beta, LV.** Dudley Moore, Elizabeth McGovern, Alec Guinness, John Huston, Ron Silver; ***D:*** Marshall Brickman; ***W:*** Marshall Brickman. *WAR*

Lovespell ☙ *Tristan and Isolde* **1979** A retelling of the legend of Isolde and Tristan. Stilted direction and writing, but another chance to reminisce on Richard Burton. **91m/C VHS.** Richard Burton, Kate Mulgrew, Nicholas Clay, Cyril Cusack, Geraldine Fitzgerald, Niall Toibin, Diana Van Der Vlis, Niall O'Brien; ***D:*** Tom Donovan. *NO*

Lovey: A Circle of Children 2 ☙☙ **1982** Teacher for special children takes in a terrified girl diagnosed as brain damaged or schizophrenic, and discovers love and intelligence in the girl as well as finding some important insights into her own life. **120m/C VHS, Beta.** Jane Alexander, Kris McKeon; ***D:*** Jud Taylor. *TLF*

Loving ☙☙½ **1984** The full-length, shot-on-video pilot for the daytime television soap opera, with various guest stars. Exteriors shot at C.W. Post Center on Long Island. **120m/C VHS, Beta.** Lloyd Bridges, Geraldine Page. *NO*

Loving Couples ☙☙ **1980 (PG)** Two happily married couples meet at a weekend resort...and switch partners. Tired and predictable but it has its moments. **120m/C VHS, Beta.** Shirley MacLaine, James Coburn, Susan Sarandon, Stephen Collins, Sally Kellerman; ***D:*** Jack Smight. *VES*

Loving You ☙☙ **1957** A small town boy with a musical style all his own becomes a big success thanks to the help of a female press agent. Features many early Elvis hits. ♫Loving You; Teddy Bear; Lonesome Cowboy; Got a Lot of Livin' To Do; Party; Mean Woman Blues; Hot Dog. **101m/C VHS, Beta, LV.** Elvis Presley, Wendell Corey, Lizabeth Scott, Dolores Hart, James Gleason; ***D:*** Hal Kanter; ***W:*** Hal Kanter. *WAR, OM*

Low Blow ☙ **1985** A kung fu expert tracks down a mind-bending cult. **90m/C VHS, Beta.** Cameron Mitchell, Leo Fong; ***D:*** Frank Harris. *LIV, VES*

A Low Down Dirty Shame ☙☙ **1994 (R)** Shame (Wayans) is a down-on-his-luck private eye, with the obligatory wisecracking secretary, Peaches (Pinkett), who's hired by an old friend to find a vicious drug lord, a sultry ex-girlfriend, and $20 million. Lots of fun stunts and one liners can't make up for major plot holes. **100m/C VHS, LV.** Keenen Ivory Wayans, Jada Pinkett, Salli Richardson, Charles S. Dutton, Andrew Divoff, Corwin Hawkins; ***D:*** Keenen Ivory Wayans; ***W:*** Keenen Ivory Wayans. *TOU*

The Lower Depths ☙☙☙½ *Les Bas Fonds; Underground* **1936** Renoir's adaptation of the Maxim Gorky play about a thief and a financially ruined baron learning about life from one another. In French with English subtitles. **92m/B VHS, Beta.** *FR* Jean Gabin, Louis Jouvet, Vladimir Sokoloff, Robert Le Vigan, Suzy Prim; ***D:*** Jean Renoir. National Board of Review Awards '37: 10 Best Films of the Year. *FCT, DVT, GVV*

The Lower Depths ☙☙☙½ **1957** Kurosawa sets the Maxim Gorky play in Edo during the final Tokugawa period, using Noh theatre elements in depicting the lowly denizens of a low-rent hovel. In Japanese with English subtitles. **125m/B VHS, Beta.** *JP* Toshiro Mifune, Isuzu Yamada, Ganjiro Nakamura, Kyoko Kagawa, Bokuzen Hidari; ***D:*** Akira Kurosawa. *FCT, INJ, COL*

Lower Level ☙ **1991 (R)** While working late, an attractive business woman becomes trapped in an office building by her psychotic secret admirer. **88m/C VHS, LV.** David Bradley, Elizabeth Gracen, Jeff Yagher; ***D:*** Kristine Peterson. *REP*

Loyalties ☙☙½ **1986 (R)** A strong treatment of the issue of sexual abuse of girls by men, and of an upper-class woman's willingness to establish a true friendship with a woman of a so-called lower economic class. **98m/C VHS.** *CA* Kenneth Welsh, Tantoo Cardinal, Susan Wooldridge, Vera Martin, Christopher Barrington-Leigh; ***D:*** Anne Wheeler; ***W:*** Sharon Riis; ***M:*** Michael Conway Baker. *NO*

Loyola, the Soldier Saint **1952** A biography of the founder of the Jesuits from his years as a page in the Spanish court to his daring exploits on the battle field and, finally, his spiritual awakening at the University of Paris. Narrated by Father Alfred J. Barrett. **93m/B VHS.** Rafael Duran, Maria Rosa Jiminez; ***D:*** Jose Diaz Morales. *IVY, KEP*

Lucas ☙☙☙ **1986 (PG-13)** A high school brain falls in love with the new girl in town, and tries to win her by trying out for the football team. Genuine film about the perils of coming of age. Thoughtful, noncondescending, and humorous. **100m/C VHS, Beta.** Corey Haim, Kerri Green, Charlie Sheen, Winona Ryder, Courtney Thorne-Smith, Thomas E. Hodges; ***D:*** David Seltzer; ***W:*** David Seltzer; ***M:*** Dave Grusin. *FXV, FOX*

The Lucifer Complex ☙ **1978** Nazi doctors are cloning exact duplicates of such world leaders as the Pope and the President of the United States on a remote South American island in the year 1996. **91m/C VHS, Beta.** Robert Vaughn, Merrie Lynn Ross, Keenan Wynn, Aldo Ray; ***D:*** David L. Hewitt, Kenneth Hartford. *VCI*

Lucky Cisco Kid ☙☙½ **1940** Romero takes over from Warner Baxter in the fourth entry in the series, with Martin as his loyal sidekick. This time a rustler and his gang are stealing cattle and using the Kid's name to place the blame. Fast-paced with Romero appropriately debonair. Andrews screen debut. **67m/B VHS.** Cesar Romero, Chris-Pin Martin, Mary Beth Hughes, Dana Andrews, Evelyn Venable, Joseph Sawyer, Francis Ford; ***D:*** H. Bruce Humberstone; ***W:*** Robert Ellis, Helen Logan. *GPV*

Lucky Devil ☙½ **1925** Lucky devil wins car and motors around the country to the tune of organ music. **63m/B VHS, Beta.** Richard Dix, Esther Ralston, Edna May Oliver, Tom Findley; ***D:*** Frank Tuttle. *GPV, FCT*

Lucky Jim ☙☙½ **1958** A junior lecturer in history at a small university tries to get himself in good graces with the head of his department, but is doomed from the start by doing the wrong things at the worst possible times. Minus the social satire of the Kingsley Amis novel on which it was based; what's left is a cheerful comedy. **91m/B VHS, Beta.** *GB* Ian Carmichael, Terry-Thomas, Hugh Griffith; ***D:*** John Boulting; ***M:*** John Addison. *NO*

Lucky Luciano ☙☙ *A Proposito Luciano; RE: Lucky Luciano* **1974 (R)** A violent depiction of the final years of Lucky Luciano, gangster kingpin. **108m/C VHS, Beta.** *IT FR* Edmond O'Brien, Rod Steiger, Vincent Gardenia, Gian Marie Volonte; ***D:*** Francesco Rosi; ***C:*** Pasqualino de Santis. *NLC*

Lucky Luke ☙☙½ **1994 (PG)** Fastest gun in the west brings the law to Daisy Town, aided by his horse, Jolly Jumper—who can talk. Not exactly John Wayne material but amusing. **91m/C VHS.** Terence Hill, Nancy Morgan, Ron Carey; ***D:*** Terence Hill; ***V:*** Roger Miller. *APX, ACA*

Lucky Luke: The Ballad of the Daltons **1978** Easygoing cowboy hero Lucky Luke gets involved in a wild feud with the bumbling Dalton Brothers gang in this animated feature. **82m/C VHS, Beta, LV.** ***D:*** Rene Goscinny. *DIS, WTA*

Lucky Me ☙☙ **1954** A group of theater entertainers are stranded in Miami and are forced to work in a hotel kitchen. They soon acquire the support of a wealthy oilman (Goodwin) who invests in their show, but not before his spoiled daughter tries to thwart all plans. ♫Lucky Me; Superstition Song; I Speak to the Stars; Take a Memo to the Moon; Love You Dearly; Bluebells of Broadway; Parisian Pretties; Wanna Sing Like an Angel; High Hopes. **100m/C VHS, LV.** Doris Day, Robert Cummings, Phil Silvers, Eddie Foy Jr., Nancy Walker, Martha Hyer, Bill Goodwin, Marcel Dalio, James Burke, Jack Shea, William "Billy" Bakewell, Charles Cane, Ray Teal, Tom Powers, Angie Dickinson, Dolores Dorn; ***D:*** Jack Donohue. *WAR, CCB, MVD*

Lucky Partners ☙☙ **1940** When an artist and an errand girl share a winning lottery ticket, funny complications arise as they embark on a fantasy honeymoon. Although Rogers' innocence and Coleman's savoir faire provide an interesting contrast, the script isn't equal to the status of its stars. **101m/B VHS, Beta.** Ronald Colman, Ginger Rogers, Jack Carson, Spring Byington, Harry Davenport; ***D:*** Lewis Milestone. *TTC*

Lucky Stiff ☙☙ **1988 (PG)** A fat, unpopular dweeb has the shock of his life when a radiant woman falls in love with him, the strangeness of which becomes evident when he meets her very weird family. **93m/C VHS, Beta, LV.** Donna Dixon, Joe Alaskey, Jeff Kober, Elizabeth Arlen, Charles Frank, Barbara Howard; ***D:*** Anthony Perkins; ***W:*** Pat Proft. *COL*

Lucky Terror ☙ **1936** Routine Hoot cowboy drama. **60m/B VHS, Beta.** Hoot Gibson, Kone Andre, Charles "Blackie" King; ***D:*** Alan James. *NOS, GPV, VCN*

Lucky Texan ☙½ **1934** Wayne plays a tough easterner who goes West and finds himself involved in a range war. **61m/B VHS, Beta.** John Wayne, George "Gabby" Hayes, Yakima Canutt; ***D:*** Robert North Bradbury. *COL, REP, MRV*

Lucy and Desi: A Home Movie **1994** Behind the scenes look at the stars of the "I Love Lucy" TV show, with home movies from the '40s and '50s, stills, clips, and interviews. **?m/C VHS.** *KUL*

Lucy and Desi: Before the Laughter ☙☙½ **1991 (PG-13)** The meeting and early married life of actress/comedian Lucille Ball and Cuban bandleader Desi Arnaz is depicted in this routine biopic. Film depicts Desi's womanizing, their struggles with fame, and their efforts to get their television show on the air. Fisher does well as television's favorite redhead but this made-for-television effort is melodramatic. Daughter Lucy Arnaz vehemently opposed this depiction of her parents life. **95m/C VHS, LV.** Frances Fisher, Maurice Benard, John Wheeler, Robin Pearson Rose; ***D:*** Charles Jarrott; ***W:*** William Luce. *REP, PMS*

L'Udienza ☙☙½ **1971** A bizarre black comedy about a guy who does anything he can, at any criminal cost, to obtain an audience with the Pope. In Italian with subtitles. **111m/C VHS, Beta.** *IT* Claudia Cardinale, Ugo Tognazzi; ***D:*** Marco Ferreri. *FCT*

Luggage of the Gods ☙☙ **1987 (G)** A lost tribe of cave people are confronted with civilization when suitcases fall from an airplane. Low-budget comedy reminiscent of "The Gods Must Be Crazy." **78m/C VHS, Beta.** Mark Stolzenberg, Gabriel Barre, Gwen Ellison; ***D:*** David Kendall. *ACA*

Lullaby of Broadway ☙☙½ **1951** Many songs highlight this flimsy musical about a girl (Day) who ventures from England to the Big Apple in search of an acting career. She soon discovers that her mom has become a has-been actress now performing in a Greenwich Village dive. Day struggles to gain her own success while coping with her mother's downfall. ♫Lullaby of Broadway; You're Getting to Be a Habit With Me; Just One of Those Things; Somebody Loves Me; I Love the Way You Say Goodnight; Fine and Dandy; Please Don't Talk About Me When I'm Gone; A Shanty in Old Shanty Town; We'd Like to Go On A Trip. **93m/C VHS.** Doris Day, Gene Nelson, S.Z. Sakall, Billy DeWolfe, Gladys George, Florence Bates; ***D:*** David Butler. *WAR, CCB, MVD*

Lumiere ☙☙½ **1976 (R)** An acclaimed drama about four actresses who, during the course of one night together, make pivotal decisions about their lives and relationships. Moreau's first directorial effort; dubbed. **101m/C VHS, Beta.** *FR* Jeanne Moreau, Lucia Bose, Francine Racette, Caroline Cartier, Keith Carradine; ***D:*** Jeanne Moreau. *SUE*

Luna Park ☙☙ **1991** In contemporary Russia, Andrei (Goutine) is the leader of a gang of bodybuilder, right-wing skinheads who beat up Jews, foreigners, and anyone else they dislike. Then the anti-

Semitic Andrei learns his father is Jewish and he frantically searches through Moscow to find him and discover his past. In Russian with subtitles. **105m/C VHS.** *RU* Oleg Borisov, Andrei Goutine, Natalya Yegorova; ***D:*** Pavel Lounguine; ***W:*** Pavel Lounguine. *NYF*

Lunatic 🦴 **1991** "Some minds should be wasted" according to the film promo and if you're in the mood for an amateur mind (and time) waster, this is for you. High schoolers in the woods encounter mayhem in the best horror tradition as the innocents are slaughtered by an escapee from the local lunatic asylum. **90m/C VHS.** Rocky Tucker, Ondrea Tucker, Brian D'Lawrence, Keith Vallot, Bronwyn St. John, Cameron Derrick, Ernest Jackson, Rookie Macpherson, Susan Spain; ***D:*** James Tucker; ***W:*** James Tucker. *CTD*

The Lunatic 🦴🦴 **1992 (R)** A robust, oversexed, and scheming German tourist travels to Jamaica where she meets the village idiot, a man who regularly holds conversations with the local plants. The two hook up with a butcher, and the three live happily in the hills, that is until the money is gone. The Jamaican scenery, a few bawdy laughs, and a great reggae soundtrack make this one worthwhile. **93m/C VHS, Beta.** *GB* Julie T. Wallace, Paul Campbell, Reggie Carter, Carl Bradshaw; ***D:*** Lol Creme; ***M:*** Wally Badarou. *ACA*

Lunatics: A Love Story 🦴🦴🦴 **1992 (PG-13)** Hank (Raimi) is an ex-mental patient poet suffering from hallucinations and afraid to leave his Los Angeles apartment. For companionship he dials a party-line until, one day, he misdials and insteads gets the number of a local pay telephone, which is answered by a naive woman dumped by her boyfriend. When Nancy (Foreman) decides to visit Hank you learn she's as crazy as he is—so it only makes sense they would fall in love. A well-acted fable of how love fragilely connects even the most unlikely of people. **87m/C VHS, LV.** Theodore (Ted) Raimi, Deborah Foreman, Bruce Campbell, Brian McCree, Eddie Rosmaya, Michele Stacey; ***D:*** Josh Beck; ***W:*** Josh Beck; ***M:*** Joseph Lo Duca. *NO*

Lunatics & Lovers 🦴½ **1976 (PG)** Musician meets a bizarre nobleman who is in love with an imaginary woman. **92m/C VHS, Beta.** *IT* Marcello Mastroianni, Lino Toffalo; ***D:*** Flavio Mogherini. *FOX*

Lunch Wagon 🦴🦴 *Come 'n' Get It; Lunch Wagon Girls* **1981 (R)** Two co-eds are given a restaurant to manage during summer vacation and wind up involved in a hilarious diamond chase and sex romp. **88m/C VHS, Beta.** Rick Podell, Candy Moore, Pamela Bryant, Rosanne Katon; ***D:*** Ernie Pintoff. *MED*

Lupo 🦴🦴 **1970 (G)** When threatened with the loss of his home and the separation of his family, an exuberant Greek man challenges the modern world. **99m/C VHS, Beta.** Yuda Barkan, Gabi Armoni, Esther Greenberg; ***D:*** Menahem Golan. *MGM*

Lure of the Islands 🦴 **1942** Federal agents track wanted criminals to an island retreat in this highly predictable low-budget thriller. **61m/B VHS, Beta.** Margie Hart, Robert Lowery, Guinn "Big Boy" Williams, Warren Hymer, Gale Storm; ***D:*** Jean Yarbrough. *NOS, SNC*

Lure of the Sila 🦴🦴½ **1949** Italian melodrama about a young peasant girl infiltrating a landowner's home in order to avenge the death of her brother and mother. Dubbed and more interesting than it sounds. **72m/B VHS, Beta, 8mm.** *IT* Silvana Mangano, Amedeo Nazzari, Vittorio Gassman; ***D:*** Duilio Coletti. *VYY*

Lurkers *Woof!* **1988 (R)** An unappealing metaphysical morass about a woman who has been haunted throughout her life by...something. **90m/C VHS.** Christine Moore, Gary Warner, Marina Taylor, Carissa Channing, Tom Billett; ***D:*** Roberta Findlay. *MED*

Lurking Fear 🦴🦴 **1994 (R)** The town of Lefferts Corner has suffered from generations of horror thanks to man-eating ghouls that dwell beneath the local graveyard and arise whenever a storm breaks out. The inhabitants prepare to fight back but their plan is hindered by the arrival of a group of criminals who are after a fortune supposedly hidden in one of the graves. Based on a story by H.P. Lovecraft. **78m/C VHS, Beta, LV.** Jon Finch, Blake Bailey, Ashley Lauren, Jeffrey Combs, Paul Mantee, Allison Mackie, Joe Leavengood, Vincent Schiavelli; ***D:*** C. Courtney Joyner; ***W:*** C. Courtney Joyner; ***M:*** Jim Manzie. *PAR*

Lush Life 🦴🦴🦴 **1994 (R)** New York jazz session musicians Al (Goldblum) and Buddy (Whitaker) roam the city's musical scene until dawn, on the prowl for food, women, and ever more music. When trumpeter Buddy is diagnosed with an inoperable brain tumor, saxophonist Al decides on a grand final gesture—a Park Avenue farewell bash, though no one is to know just how final the farewell is to be. Great jazz soundtrack, fine acting, and atmospheric use of the Big Apple. And it avoids overt tearjerking. Made for cable. **96m/C VHS.** Jeff Goldblum, Forest Whitaker, Kathy Baker, Lois Chiles, Don Cheadle; ***D:*** Michael Elias; ***W:*** Michael Elias. *COL*

Lust for a Vampire 🦴🦴 *To Love a Vampire* **1971 (R)** The sanguine tale of a deadly vampire who indiscriminately preys on pupils and teachers when she enrolls at a British finishing school. Moody and erotically charged, with an impressive ending. Quasi-sequel to "The Vampire Lovers." **95m/C VHS, Beta, LV.** *GB* Ralph Bates, Barbara Jefford, Suzanna Leigh, Michael Johnson, Yutte Stensgaard, Pippa Steele; ***D:*** Jimmy Sangster. *MLB*

Lust for Freedom 🦴 **1987** An undercover cop decides to hit the road after she sees her partner gunned down. She winds up near the California-Mexico border, where she is wrongly imprisoned with a number of other young women in a white slavery business. This low-budget film includes lots of steamy women-behind-bars sex scenes. **92m/C VHS.** Melanie Coll, William J. Kulzer; ***D:*** Eric Louzil. *AIP, MOV*

Lust for Gold 🦴🦴 **1949** Ford battles against greedy former lover Lupino and her husband for control of the Lost Dutchman gold mine. **90m/B VHS, Beta.** Ida Lupino, Glenn Ford, Gig Young, William Prince, Edgar Buchanan, Will Geer, Paul Ford, Jay Silverheels; ***D:*** Sylvan Simon; ***M:*** George Duning. *GKK*

Lust for Life 🦴🦴🦴½ **1956** Absorbing, serious biography of Vincent Van Gogh, from his first paintings to his death. Remarkable for Douglas' furiously convincing portrayal. Featuring dozens of actual Van Gogh works from private collections. Based on an Irving Stone novel, produced by John Houseman. **122m/C VHS, Beta, LV.** Kirk Douglas, Anthony Quinn, James Donald, Pamela Brown, Everett Sloane, Henry Daniell, Niall MacGinnis, Noel Purcell, Lionel Jeffries, Jill Bennett; ***D:*** Vincente Minnelli; ***M:*** Miklos Rozsa. Academy Awards '56: Best Supporting Actor (Quinn); Golden Globe Awards '57: Best Actor—Drama (Douglas); National Board of Review Awards '56: 10 Best Films of the Year; New York Film Critics Awards '56: Best Actor (Douglas); Nominations: Academy Awards '56: Best Actor (Douglas), Best Adapted Screenplay, Best Art Direction/Set Decoration (Color). *MGM, BTV*

Lust in the Dust 🦴🦴🦴 **1985 (R)** When part of a treasure map is found on the derriere of none other than Divine, the hunt is on for the other half. This comedy western travels to a sleepy town called Chile Verde (green chili for those who don't speak Spanish) and the utterly ridiculous turns comically corrupt. Deliciously distasteful fun. Features Divine singing a bawdy love song in his/her break from John Waters. **85m/C VHS, Beta, LV.** Tab Hunter, Divine, Lainie Kazan, Geoffrey Lewis, Henry Silva, Cesar Romero, Gina Gallego, Courtney Gains, Woody Strode, Pedro Gonzalez-Gonzalez; ***D:*** Paul Bartel; ***W:*** Philip John Taylor; ***M:*** Peter Matz. *NWV, VTR, HHE*

The Lusty Men 🦴🦴🦴 **1952** Two rival rodeo champions, both in love with the same woman, work the rodeo circuit until a tragic accident occurs. Mitchum turns in a fine performance as the has-been rodeo star trying to make it big again. **113m/B VHS, Beta, LV.** Robert Mitchum, Susan Hayward, Arthur Kennedy, Arthur Hunnicutt; ***D:*** Nicholas Ray; ***C:*** Lee Garmes. *NO*

Luther 🦴🦴½ **1974 (G)** A well-acted characterization of Martin Luther's development from a young seminarian to his leadership of the Reformation Movement. **112m/C VHS.** Stacy Keach, Patrick Magee, Hugh Griffith, Robert Stephens, Alan Badel; ***D:*** Guy Green; ***W:*** Edward Anhalt; ***C:*** Frederick A. (Freddie) Young; ***M:*** John Addison. *NO*

Luther the Geek *Woof!* **1990** Little Luther's visit to the circus is dramatically changed when he sees the geek, a sideshow freak. Since then Luther has taken to biting off chicken's heads and drinking their blood in his small Illinois town; the town will never be the same. (And neither will you if you watch this stupid film.) **90m/C VHS.** Edward Terry, Joan Roth, J. Jerome Clarke, Tom Mills; ***D:*** Carlton J. Albright. *NO*

Luv 🦴½ **1967 (PG)** Although good cast tries hard, they can't do much with this comic farce. Three intellectuals, including one that's suicidal, discuss the trials and tribulations of their middle-class New York existence. **95m/C VHS, Beta, LV.** Jack Lemmon, Peter Falk, Elaine May; ***D:*** Clive Donner; ***W:*** Murray Schisgal; ***C:*** Ernest Laszlo. *GKK*

Luzia 🦴🦴½ **1988** Ohana stars as a tough and sexy Brazilian cowgirl who is caught in the middle of a class struggle where the personal is definitely political. Her horseriding skills and beauty give her options in both lifestyles. Will she choose to side with the squatters or the wealthy landowners? In Portuguese with English subtitles. **112m/C VHS.** *BR* Claudia Ohana, Thales Pan Chacon, Jose de Abreu, Luiza Falcao; ***D:*** Fabio Barreto. *FXL, INJ, FCT*

Lydia 🦴🦴🦴 **1941** Sentimental drama in which an elderly lady (Oberon) gets to relive her romantic past when she has a reunion with four of her lost loves. Well acted and directed, Oberon gives one of her best performances ever. Adapted from the highly regarded French film "Un Carnet de Bal." **98m/B VHS, Beta, LV.** Merle Oberon, Joseph Cotten, Alan Marshal, George Reeves; ***D:*** Julien Duvivier; ***C:*** Lee Garmes; ***M:*** Miklos Rozsa. Nominations: Academy Awards '41: Best Original Score. *SUE*

Lying Lips 🦴½ **1939** All-black detective mystery about a young nightclub singer framed for murder. Her boyfriend then turns detective to clear her name. **60m/B VHS, Beta.** Edna Mae Harris, Carmen Newsome, Earl Jones, Amanda Randolph; ***D:*** Oscar Micheaux. *FCT, VCN, DVT*

M 🦴🦴🦴🦴 **1931** The great Lang dissection of criminal deviance, following the tortured last days of a child murderer, and the efforts of both the police and the underground to bring him to justice. Poetic, compassionate, and chilling. Inspired by real-life serial killer known as "Vampire of Dusseldorf," Lang also borrowed story elements from Jack the Ripper's killing spree. Lorre's screen debut. Lang's personal favorite among his own films. In German with English subtitles. Remade in 1951. **99m/B VHS, Beta, LV, 8mm.** *GE* Peter Lorre, Ellen Widmann, Inge Landgut, Gustav Grundgens; ***D:*** Fritz Lang; ***W:*** Fritz Lang. National Board of Review Awards '33: 10 Best Films of the Year. *SNC, NOS, HHT*

M. Butterfly 🦴🦴 **1993 (R)** Disappointing adaptation of Hwang's award-winning play, which was based on a true story. Irons is Rene Gallimard, a minor French diplomat sent to China in 1964. Taken in by the exoticism of the mysterious east, he falls for a Chinese opera performer, Song Liling (Lone). Only she's no lady and the oblivious diplomat turns out to be a patsy as Song Liling uses him to gather information. The story only works if the passion, however deceptive, between Gallimard and Song Liling is believable, passion which is noticeably lacking between Irons and Lone. Irons comes across as too intelligent to be gullibile and the usually excellent Lone does not make his role believable. **101m/C VHS, Beta, LV.** Jeremy Irons, John Lone, Ian Richardson, Barbara Sukowa, Vernon Dobtcheff, Annabel Leventon, Shizuko Hoshi, Richard McMillan; ***D:*** David Cronenberg; ***W:*** David Henry Hwang; ***M:*** Howard Shore. *WAR*

Ma and Pa Kettle 🦴🦴½ *The Further Adventures of Ma and Pa Kettle* **1949** The hillbilly couple were supporting characters in "The Egg and I" but their popularity found them spun off into their own cornpone series. This first feature finds the couple and their 15 children about to be evicted only to have Pa win a tobacco slogan contest. The prize is a brand-new fully-automated house whose futuristic contraptions get the better of Pa. **76m/B VHS.** Marjorie Main, Percy Kilbride, Richard Long, Meg Randall, Esther

Dale, Barry Kelley, Patricia Alphin; *D:* Charles Lamont; *W:* Al Lewis, Herbert Margolis, Louis Morheim. *MCA*

Ma and Pa Kettle at Home ½ **1954** Elwin, one of the Kettle's 15 children, is a finalist in an essay contest that could win him a college scholarship. Then Pa Kettle hears the two judges plan to visit each of the finalists' homes so he tries to spruce-up the family's tumbled-down farm. **80m/B VHS.** Marjorie Main, Percy Kilbride, Alan Mowbray, Ross Elliott, Brett Halsey, Mary Wickes, Irving Bacon, Emory Parnell; *D:* Charles Lamont; *W:* Kay Lenard. *MCA*

Ma and Pa Kettle at the Fair ½ **1952** The Kettle's eldest daughter Rosie wants to go to college so Ma enters the county fair baking contest to win some money and Pa buys a decrepit old nag to enter in the fair's horse race. Somehow things just have a way of working out for the Kettles. **79m/B VHS.** Marjorie Main, Percy Kilbride, Lori Nelson, James Best, Esther Dale, Russell Simpson, Emory Parnell; *D:* Charles T. Barton; *W:* John Grant, Richard Morris. *MCA*

Ma and Pa Kettle at Waikiki ½ **1955** Ma (Main) and Pa (Kilbride), as well as oldest daughter Rosie (Nelson), head for Hawaii to help out cousin Rodney's (Smith) pineapple factory. Seems he's ill and about to go bankrupt and he thinks Pa is some kind of financial whiz who can bail him out. Pa accidentally does help the business and then gets kidnapped by some sleazy competitors. But it's Ma to the rescue (and the bad guys don't stand a chance). Kilbride retired after his seventh take as Pa in the comedy series. **79m/B VHS.** Marjorie Main, Percy Kilbride, Lori Nelson, Loring Smith, Russell Johnson, Byron Palmer, Mabel Albertson, Hilo Hattie, Fay Roope, Oliver Blake, Lowell Gilmore, Teddy Hart; *D:* Lee Sholem; *W:* Jack Henley, Harry Clork, Elwood Ullman. *MCA*

Ma and Pa Kettle Back On the Farm ½ **1951** First-time grandparents, the Kettles have to deal with their daughter-in-law's snobby Bostonian parents and their parenting ideas. The family's also moved back to their ramshackle farm where Pa thinks he's found uranium, leading to all sorts of problems. **81m/B VHS.** Marjorie Main, Percy Kilbride, Richard Long, Meg Randall, Ray Collins, Barbara Brown, Emory Parnell; *D:* Edward Sedgwick; *W:* Jack Henley. *MCA*

Ma and Pa Kettle Go to Town ½ **1950** Ma and Pa head off for New York City when Pa wins a jingle-writing contest, unknowingly leaving their brood in the care of on the lam mobster Mike, who asks the Kettles to deliver a package to his brother. This gets both the crooks and the cops trailing the hillbilly couple, whose backwoods ways are more than a match for any city slicker. **80m/B VHS.** Marjorie Main, Percy Kilbride, Richard Long, Meg Randall, Charles McGraw, Ray Collins, Esther Dale, Ellen Corby, Barbara Brown; *D:* Charles Lamont; *W:* Martin Ragaway, Leonard Stern. *MCA*

Ma and Pa Kettle on Vacation ½ *Ma and Pa Kettle Go to Paris* **1953** Ma and Pa visit Paris as guests of their son's wealthy in-laws and Pa unwittingly gets involved with spies and shady ladies. **79m/B VHS.** Marjorie Main, Percy Kilbride, Ray Collins, Sig Rumann, Bodil Miller, Barbara Brown, Peter Brocco, Jay Novello; *D:* Charles Lamont; *W:* Jack Henley. *MCA*

Ma Barker's Killer Brood **1960** Biography of the infamous American criminal and her four sons, edited together from a television serial. The shoot-em-up scenes and Tuttle's performance keep the pace from slackening. **82m/B VHS, Beta.** Lurene Tuttle, Tristram Coffin, Paul Dubov, Nelson Leigh, Myrna Dell, Vic Lundin, Donald Spruance; *D:* Bill Karn. *SNC, DVT, HEG*

Mabel & Fatty **1916** Three silent shorts featuring the two stars, made with Mack Sennett: "He Did and He Didn't," "Mabel and Fatty Viewing The World's Fair at San Francisco" (with scenes of the actual 1914 World's Fair) and "Mabel's Blunder." **61m/B VHS, Beta, 8mm.** Mabel Normand, Fatty Arbuckle, Al "Fuzzy" St. John. *VYY*

Mac **1993 (R)** It's a family affair. Immigrant carpenter's funeral is the starting point for the story of his three sons, construction workers who live in Queens, New York in the 1950s. The passionate bros battle, bitch, and build, with Turturro as the eldest summing up the prevailing philosophy: "It's the doing, that's the thing." Turturro's directorial debut is a labor of love and a tribute to his own dad. Filmed on location in New York City. Fine performances from newcomers Badalucco and Capotorto are complemented by smaller roles from Amos, Barkin, and Turturro's real-life wife Borowitz and brother Nick. **118m/C VHS, LV.** John Turturro, Carl Capotorto, Michael Badalucco, Katherine Borowitz, John Amos, Olek Krupa, Ellen Barkin, Joe Paparone, Nicholas Turturro, Dennis Farina; *D:* John Turturro; *W:* John Turturro, Brandon Cole; *M:* Richard Termini, Vin Tese. Nominations: Independent Spirit Awards '94: Best Director (Turturro), Best First Feature. *COL, FCT*

Mac and Me **1988 (PG)** Lost E.T.-like alien stranded on Earth befriends a wheelchair-bound boy. Aimed at young kids, it's full of continual product plugs, most notably for McDonald's. Make the kids happy and stick to the real thing. **94m/C VHS, Beta, LV.** Christine Ebersole, Jonathan Ward, Katrina Caspary, Lauren Stanley, Jade Calegory; *D:* Stewart Raffill; *W:* Stewart Raffill; *M:* Alan Silvestri. Golden Raspberry Awards '88: Worst Director (Raffill). *ORI*

Macabre **1977** A beautiful woman, lustful and precocious, kills her husband and his twin brother. **89m/C VHS, Beta.** Larry Ward, Teresa Gimpera, Giacomo "Jack" Rossi-Stuart. *NO*

Macao **1952** On the lam for a crime he didn't commit, an adventurer sails to the exotic Far East, meets a buxom cafe singer, and helps Interpol catch a notorious crime boss. A strong film noir entry. Russell sneers, Mitchum wise cracks. Director von Sternberg's last film for RKO. **81m/B VHS, Beta, LV.** Robert Mitchum, Jane Russell, William Bendix, Gloria Grahame; *D:* Josef von Sternberg. *MED*

Macaroni ½ *Maccheroni* **1985 (PG)** An uptight American businessman returns to Naples forty years after being stationed there in WWII. Comedic situations abound when he is reunited with his Italian war buddy, brother of his lover. Pleasant acting can't save irritating script. **104m/C VHS, Beta, LV.** *IT* Jack Lemmon, Marcello Mastroianni, Daria Nicolodi, Isa Danieli; *D:* Ettore Scola; *W:* Ettore Scola. *PAR, INJ*

MacArthur **1977 (PG)** General Douglas MacArthur's life from Corregidor in 1942 to his dismissal a decade later in the midst of the Korean conflict. Episodic sage with forceful Peck but weak supporting characters. Fourteen minutes were cut from the original version; intended to be Peck's "Patton," it falls short of the mark. **130m/C VHS, Beta, LV.** Gregory Peck, Ivan Bonar, Ward Costello, Nicolas Coster, Dan O'Herlihy; *D:* Joseph Sargent; *W:* Matthew Robbins, Hal Barwood; *M:* Jerry Goldsmith. *MCA, TLF*

MacArthur's Children **1985** A poignant evocation of life in a Japanese fishing village as it faces the end of WWII and American occupation. Not as good as some of the other Japanese films, but it is an interesting look at the changes in culture caused by their defeat in the war. In Japanese with English subtitles. **115m/C VHS, Beta, LV.** *JP* Masako Natsume, Shima Iwashita, Hiromi Go, Takaya Yamamauchi, Shiori Sakura, Ken Watanabe, Juzo Itami, Yoshiyuka Omori; *D:* Masahiro Shinoda; *W:* Takeski Tamura. *FCT, INJ, TPV*

Macbeth ½ **1948** Shakespeare's classic tragedy is performed with a celebrated lead performance by Welles, who plays the tragic king as a demonic leader of a barbaric society. A low budget adaptation with cheap sets, a three-week shooting schedule, lots of mood, and an attempt at Scottish accents. After making this film, Welles took a 10-year break from Hollywood. **111m/B VHS, LV.** Orson Welles, Jeanette Nolan, Dan O'Herlihy, Roddy McDowall, Robert Coote; *D:* Orson Welles. *REP, TVC*

Macbeth **1971 (R)** Polanski's notorious adaptation of the Shakespearean classic, marked by realistic design, unflinching violence, and fatalistic atmosphere. Contains stunning fight scenes and fine acting. Polanski's first film following the grisly murder of his pregnant wife, actress Sharon Tate, was torn apart by critics. It is in fact a worthy continuation of his work in the horror genre. Very well made. First film made by Playboy Enterprises. Originally rated X. **139m/C VHS, Beta, LV.** Jon Finch, Nicholas Selby, Martin Shaw, Francesca Annis, Terence Baylor; *D:* Roman Polanski. National Board of Review Awards '71: 10 Best Films of the Year. *COL, HMV, PBS*

Macbeth **1976** An extraordinary version of Shakespeare's "Macbeth" in which all the fire, ambition and doom of his text come brilliantly to life. **137m/C** Eric Porter, Janet Suzman. *TLF*

Macbeth **1990** Another production of the classic tragedy by Shakespeare. Produced as part of HBO's Thames Collection. **110m/C VHS, Beta.** Michael Jayston, Leigh Hunt. *HBO*

Machine Gun Blues *Black Rose of Harlem* **1995 (R)** 1920s Black jazz singer falls in love with white mobster amidst a scene of moonshine, gunrunning and racketeering. **?m/C VHS.** Cynda Williams, Nick Cassavetes, Maria Ford, Lawrence Monoson, Joe Viterelli, Billy Dee Williams; *D:* Fred Gallo. *NHO*

Machine Gun Kelly ½ **1958** Corman found Euro-appeal with this thirties style gangster bio. Bronson, who was just gaining a reputation as an action lead, stars as criminal Kelly, who's convinced by his moll to give up bank robbery for kidnapping. Amsterdam, the wisecracking writer from "The Dick Van Dyke Show," is the fink who turns him in. **80m/B VHS.** Charles Bronson, Susan Cabot, Morey Amsterdam, Barboura Morris, Frank De Kova, Jack Lambert, Wally Campo; *D:* Roger Corman; *W:* Mike Werb; *C:* Floyd Crosby. *COL, FCT*

Machine to Kill Bad People *La Macchina Ammazzacattivi* **1948** In a small Italian village, a photographer receives a magical camera that has the power to terrify and kill anyone it photographs. The photographer decides to get rid of all the village's evil people but soon learns the difficulty of distinguishing between the grey areas of good and bad. Italian with subtitles. **80m/B VHS.** *IT* Gennaro Pisano, Giovanni Amato, Marilyn Buferd; *D:* Roberto Rossellini; *W:* Roberto Rossellini. *FCT*

Macho Callahan **1970 (R)** A Civil War convict escapes from a frontier jail bent on tracking down the man who imprisoned him. (The escaped prisoner bit is a recurring theme in Janssen's oeuvre.) Confused script even has a one-armed Carradine! **99m/C VHS, Beta.** David Janssen, Jean Seberg, David Carradine, Lee J. Cobb; *D:* Bernard L. Kowalski. *COL, NLC*

Machoman **197?** The matchless, peerless, Machoman knows all the best killing methods including: Lizard Fists, Crane Kung Fu, and the Drunken Fist. **94m/C VHS, Beta.** Araujo, Enyaw Liew, Jerry Rages. *NO*

Maciste in Hell ½ *Witch's Curse* **1960** Inexplicably living in 17th century Scotland, Italian hero Maciste pursues a witch into the depths of Hell. She's placed a curse on the world and he wants her to remove it. **78m/C VHS.** *IT* Kirk Morris, Helene Chanel, Vira Silenti, Andrea Bosic, Angelo Zanolli, John Karlsen; *D:* Riccardo (Robert Hampton) Freda. *UNI, SNC*

Mack ½ **1973 (R)** The Mack is a pimp who comes out of retirement to reclaim a piece of the action in Oakland, California. Violent blaxploitation flick was a box office dynamite at time of release. Early Pryor appearance. **110m/C VHS, Beta.** Max Julien, Richard Pryor, Don Gordon, Roger E. Mosley, Carol Speed; *D:* Michael Campus. *NLC*

Mack & Carole **1928** Lombard began her screen career, in earnest, as a Mack Sennett comedienne. These three shorts represent her earliest screen work. **60m/B VHS, Beta.** Carole Lombard. *GVV*

Mack Sennett Comedies: Vol. 1 **1921** Four Sennett films are included: "The Eyes Have It," "The Cannon Ball," "The Desperate Scoundrel," and "Pride of Pikeville." Ben Turpin and the Keystone Cops at their manic best. **85m/B VHS.** Ben Turpin, Chester Conklin, Ford Sterling, Minta Durfee; ***D:*** *Mack Sennett. REP*

Mack Sennett Comedies: Vol. 2 **1916** Four more Sennett shorts are featured: "Mabel and Fatty Adrift," "Mabel, Fatty, and the Law," "Fatty's Tin-Type Tangle," and "Our Congressman." The last film features Will Rogers in a lampoon of Capitol Hill. **84m/B VHS.** Fatty Arbuckle, Mabel Normand, Will Rogers, Madge Hunt; ***D:*** Mack Sennett. *REP*

Mack the Knife *Woof! The Threepenny Opera* **1989 (PG-13)** Terrible adaptation of Brecht and Weill's "Threepenny Opera," detailing the adventures of a master thief in love with an innocent girl. Too much music, too much dancing, too much emoting. **121m/C VHS, Beta, LV.** Raul Julia, Roger Daltrey, Richard Harris, Julie Walters, Clive Revill, Erin Donovan, Rachel Robertson, Julia Migenes-Johnson; ***D:*** Menahem Golan. *COL*

MacKenna's Gold 🦴🦴½ **1969 (PG)** Grim desperados trek through Apache territory to uncover legendary cache of gold in this somewhat inflated epic. Subdued stars Peck and Shariff vie for attention here with such overactors as Cobb, Meredith, and Wallach. Meanwhile, Newmar (Catwoman of TV's Batman) swims nude. A must for all earthquake buffs. **128m/C VHS, Beta, LV.** Gregory Peck, Omar Sharif, Telly Savalas, Julie Newmar, Edward G. Robinson, Keenan Wynn, Ted Cassidy, Eduardo Ciannelli, Eli Wallach, Raymond Massey, Lee J. Cobb, Burgess Meredith, Anthony Quayle, John David Garfield; ***D:*** J. Lee Thompson; ***M:*** Quincy Jones. *GKK*

Mackintosh Man 🦴🦴½ **1973 (PG)** An intelligence agent must undo a communist who has infiltrated the free world's network in this solid but somewhat subdued thriller. Good cast keeps narrative rolling, but don't look here for nudity-profanity-violence fix. **100m/C VHS, Beta.** Paul Newman, Dominique Sanda, James Mason, Ian Bannen, Nigel Patrick, Harry Andrews, Leo Genn, Peter Vaughan, Michael Hordern; ***D:*** John Huston; ***W:*** Walter Hill; ***M:*** Maurice Jarre. *WAR*

Macon County Line 🦴🦴½ **1974 (R)** A series of deadly mistakes and misfortunes lead to a sudden turn-around in the lives of three young people when they enter a small Georgia town and find themselves accused of brutally slaying the sheriff's wife. Sequelled by "Return to Macon County" in 1975, starring Don Johnson and Nick Nolte. **89m/C VHS, Beta.** Alan Vint, Jesse Vint, Cheryl Waters, Geoffrey Lewis, Joan Blackman, Max Baer Jr.; ***D:*** Richard Compton. *SUE*

Macumba Love 🦴 **1960** An author journeys to Brazil to prove a connection between mysterious murders and voodoo. A tedious suspense exploitation travelogue with generous servings of cheesecake and calypso music. **86m/C VHS.** Walter Reed, Ziva Rodann, William Wellman Jr., June Wilkinson, Ruth de Souza; ***D:*** Douglas Fowley. *NO*

Mad About Money 🦴🦴 *He Loved an Actress; Stardust* **1930** An early sound comedy about a bespectacled mild-mannered fellow who runs up against a Mexican spitfire. ♫Oh So Beautiful; Perpetual Motion; Little Lost Tune; Dustin' The Stars. **80m/B VHS, Beta.** Lupe Velez, Wallace Ford, Ben Lyon, Harry Langdon, Jean Colin; ***D:*** Melville Brown. *NOS, DVT*

Mad About Music 🦴🦴🦴 **1938** On the advice of her publicist, film star Gwen Taylor (Patrick) sends her teenaged daughter Gloria (Durbin) off to a Swiss boarding school and keeps her identity a secret. So Gloria invents an exciting world-traveler father that envious schoolmate Felice (Parrish) insists upon meeting. Gloria manages to persuade a complete stranger, composer Richard Todd (Marshall), into playing the role (he's charmed by her singing). Naturally, there's lots of confusion, especially when mother and "father" finally meet. ♫I Love to Whistle; Chapel Bells; Serenade to the Stars; There Isn't a Day Goes By. **92m/B VHS.** Deanna Durbin, Herbert Marshall, Gail Patrick, Arthur Treacher, Helen Parrish, William Frawley, Marcia Mae Jones, Jackie Moran; ***D:*** Norman Taurog; ***W:*** Bruce Manning, Felix Jackson; ***C:*** Joseph Valentine. *MCA*

Mad About You *Woof!* **1990 (PG)** Millionaire helps his daughter measure prospective suitors. Adam West is not the fourth man in the Montgomery Clift-James Dean-Marlon Brando chain of American acting greats. **92m/C VHS, Beta, LV.** Claudia Christian, Joseph Gian, Adam West, Shari Shattuck; ***D:*** Lorenzo Doumani. *ACA*

Mad at the Moon 🦴🦴 **1992 (R)** Western thriller in which a young bride (Masterson) discovers that the man she married is less than human with the rising of the full moon. The only one who can protect her is her husband's half-brother played by Bochner. Masterson gives a great performance as a woman torn apart by a terrifying family secret out on the American plains. **98m/C VHS, LV.** Mary Stuart Masterson, Hart Bochner, Fionnula Flanagan, Cec Verrell; ***D:*** Martin Donovan; ***W:*** Martin Donovan, Richard Pelusi. *REP*

The Mad Bomber *Woof! Police Connection; Detective Geronimo* **1972** Grim lawman Edwards tracks deranged bomber Connors, who is determined to blow up anyone who ever offended him. A must for all connoisseurs of acting that is simultaneously overblown and flat. **80m/C VHS, Beta.** Vince Edwards, Chuck Connors, Neville Brand; ***D:*** Bert I. Gordon. *MRV*

Mad Bull 🦴 **1977** Sensitive wrestler finds meaning in life when he falls in love. If you ever cared about Karras, then you probably already saw this. If you never cared about Karras, then you probably never heard of this. If you ever cared about Anspach, rent "Five Easy Pieces" instead. **96m/C VHS, Beta.** Alex Karras, Susan Anspach, Nicholas Colasanto, Tracey Walter; ***D:*** Walter Doniger. *NO*

The Mad Butcher 🦴 **1972 (R)** Typically unhinged mental patient seeks teenage flesh for his various instruments of torture and death. Buono has never been more imposing. **90m/C VHS, Beta.** *IT* Victor Buono, Karin Field, Brad Harris; ***D:*** John Zuru. *GHV, MRV*

Mad Death 🦴🦴 **1985** The British Isles take extreme steps to quarantine themselves against rabies from the European continent. This condensed TV miniseries preys on fears of the worst, as an outbreak of the virus spreads from dogs and other pets to humans, and special commandoes are mobilized. **120m/C VHS.** *GB FCT, VCO*

Mad Doctor of Blood Island *Woof! Tomb of the Living Dead; Blood Doctor* **1969** Dull band of travelers arrive on mysterious tropical island and encounter bloodthirsty creature. Warning: This film is not recognized for outstanding achievements in acting, dialogue, or cinematography. **110m/C VHS, Beta.** John Ashley; ***D:*** Gerardo (Gerry) De Leon. *NO*

Mad Dog *Woof!* **1984** An escaped convict seeks revenge on the cop responsible for his imprisonment. **90m/C VHS, Beta.** Helmut Berger, Marisa Mell; ***D:*** Sergio Grieco. *VDC*

Mad Dog and Glory 🦴🦴🦴 **1993 (R)** Cast against type, Murray and De Niro play each other's straight man in this dark romantic comedy. Meek "Mad Dog" (De Niro) is an off-duty police photographer who happens upon a convenience store robbery and manages to save the life of Frank (Murray), obnoxious gangster by day, obnoxious stand-up comic by night. To settle up, Frank offers him Glory (Thurman), for a week. Eventually, Frank wants Glory back, forcing wimpy Mad Dog to either confront or surrender. Directed by McNaughton, who established himself with "Henry: Portrait of a Serial Killer." Uneven and not of the knee-slapper ilk, but the performances are tight, including "NYPD Blue" Caruso as a cop buddy of De Niro's. **97m/C VHS, LV.** Robert De Niro, Uma Thurman, Bill Murray, David Caruso, Mike Starr, Tom Towles, Kathy Baker, Derek Anunciation, J.J. Johnston, Richard Belzer; ***D:*** John McNaughton; ***W:*** Richard Price; ***M:*** Elmer Bernstein. *MCA, FCT*

Mad Dog Morgan 🦴🦴½ *Mad Dog* **1976 (R)** Hopper delivers as engaging outlaw roaming outlands of nineteenth-century Australia. Quirky and violent G'day man. Based on a true story. **93m/C VHS, Beta.** *AU* Dennis Hopper, David Gulpilil; ***D:*** Philippe Mora. *SIM*

The Mad Executioners 🦴🦴 *Der Henker Von London* **1965** Scotland Yard inspector searches for a sex maniac who decapitates women. In the meantime, a group of vigilantes capture criminals and sentence them without a trial. Confusing film with a predictable ending. Based on the book "White Carpet" by Bryan Edgar Wallace. **92m/B VHS.** *GE* Hansjorg Felmy, Maria Perschy, Dieter Borsche, Rudolph Forster, Chris Howland, Wolfgang Preiss; ***D:*** Edwin Zbonek. *SNC*

The Mad Ghoul 🦴🦴½ **1943** Mad scientist (is there any other kind?) Dr. Morris (Zucco) is researching an ancient Egyptian gas that causes paralysis, turning victims into obedient zombies. Morris exposes his innocent assistant Ted (Bruce) to the gas, making Ted dependent on the antidote serum made from newly dead hearts. Poor Ted's fiance Isabel (Ankers) just can't understand what's the matter. **66m/B VHS.** George Zucco, David Bruce, Evelyn Ankers, Turhan Bey, Robert Armstrong, Milburn Stone, Charles McGraw, Rose Hobart; ***D:*** James Hogan; ***W:*** Brenda Weisberg, Paul Gangelin. *MCA*

Mad Love 🦴🦴🦴 *The Hands of Orlac* **1935** A brilliant surgeon (Lorre) falls madly in love with an actress, but she rebuffs him. When her pianist husband's hands are cut off in a train accident, Lorre agrees to attach new hands, using those of a recently executed murderer. Lorre then kills the man's stepfather, and to drive him crazy uses psychological terror to make the pianist think he killed him. There's also an appearance by the supposedly executed murderer who shows up to reclaim his hands. A real chiller about obsessive love and psychological fear. The only downfall to this one is the unnecessary comic relief by Healy. Lorre's first American film. **70m/B VHS.** Peter Lorre, Colin Clive, Frances Drake, Ted Healy, Edward Brophy, Sara Haden, Henry Kolker; ***D:*** Karl Freund. *MGM*

Mad Love 🦴½ **1995 (PG-13)** Teen love has rarely been so insipid. Impulsive, fragile, and annoyingly melodramatic Casey (Barrymore) bewitches responsible, straightlaced Matt (O'Donnell) with her kewpie-doll charm and penchant for mischief. When Casey's bipolar ways land her in a mental hospital, Matt breaks her out and the unconvincing duo hit the road, where their supposedly free-spirited, passion-filled escapades grow increasingly inconsistent and silly, eventually halted by Casey's clinical crash. Slightly redeemed by a cool soundtrack and decent acting, but otherwise dull and insignificant, with an ending that may induce involuntary eyerolling. You've been warned. **95m/C VHS, LV.** Chris O'Donnell, Drew Barrymore, Joan Allen, Kevin Dunn, Jude Ciccolella, Amy Sakasitz, T.J. Lowther; ***D:*** Antonia Bird; ***W:*** Paula Milne; ***C:*** Fred Tammes. *TOU*

Mad Max 🦴🦴🦴½ **1980 (R)** Set on the stark highways of the post-nuclear future, an ex-cop seeks personal revenge against a rovin' band of vicious outlaw bikers who killed his wife and child. Futuristic scenery and excellent stunt work make for an exceptionally entertaining action-packed adventure. Followed by "The Road Warrior" (also known as "Mad Max 2") in 1981 and "Mad Max Beyond Thunderdome" in 1985. **93m/C VHS, Beta, LV.** Mel Gibson, Joanne Samuel, Hugh Keays-Byrne, Steve Bisley, Tim Burns, Roger Ward; ***D:*** George Miller; ***W:*** George Miller. *LIV, VES*

Mad Max: Beyond Thunderdome 🦴🦴½ **1985 (PG-13)** Max drifts into evil town ruled by Turner and becomes gladiator, then gets dumped in desert and is rescued by band of feral orphans. Third in a bleak, extremely violent, often exhilirating series. **107m/C VHS, Beta, LV, 8mm.** *AU* Mel Gibson, Tina Turner, Helen Buday, Frank Thring Jr., Bruce Spence, Robert Grubb, Angelo Rossitto, Angry Anderson, George Spartels, Rod Zuanic; ***D:*** George Miller, George Ogilvie; ***W:*** George Miller, Terry Hayes; ***M:*** Maurice Jarre. *WAR*

Mad Miss Manton 🦴🦴 **1938** A socialite turns detective to solve murder. Pleasant comedy-mystery provides occasional laughs and suspense. **80m/B VHS, Beta, LV.** Barbara Stanwyck, Henry Fonda, Hattie McDaniel, Sam Levene, Miles Mander, Charles Halton; ***D:*** Leigh Jason. *TTC*

Mad Mission 3 ✌½ **1984** Chinese man vacationing in Paris becomes involved in plot to recover precious jewels stolen from England's royal crown. Has there already been "Mad Mission" and "Mad Mission 2"? **81m/C VHS, Beta.** Richard Kiel, Sam Kui, Karl Muka, Sylvia Chang, Tsuneharu Sugiyama. *NO*

The Mad Monster ✌½ **1942** This "Wolf Man"-inspired cheapie looks like a misty relic today. A mad scientist furthers the war effort by injecting wolf's blood into a handyman, who becomes hairy and anti-social. **77m/B VHS.** Johnny Downs, George Zucco, Anne Nagel, Sarah Padden, Glenn Strange, Gordon DeMain, Mae Busch; ***D:*** Sam Newfield. *NOS, LOO, VCN*

Mad Monster Party ✌✌½ **1968** Frankenstein is getting older and wants to retire from the responsibilities of being senior monster, so he calls a convention of creepy creatures to decide who should take his place—The Wolfman, Dracula, the Mummy, the Creature, It, the Invisible Man, or Dr. Jekyll and Mr. Hyde. Animated feature using the process of "Animagic." **94m/C VHS, Beta.** ***D:*** Jules Bass; ***V:*** Boris Karloff, Ethel Ennis, Phyllis Diller. *COL, SUE*

Mad Wax: The Surf Movie ✌ **1990** A flimsy plot about a window-cleaner who discovers a magical surfing wax serves as a framework for lots and lots of scenes of surfin' dudes. **45m/C VHS, Beta.** Richard Cram, Marvin Foster, Aaron Napolean, Tom Carroll, Bryce Andrews, Ross Clarke-Jones; ***D:*** Michael Hohensee. *FCT*

The Mad Whirl ✌½ **1925** The Roarin' Twenties are a mad mad whirl in this silent silent piece of period period. **80m/B VHS, Beta.** Myrtle Stedman, Barbara Bedford, Alec B. Francis, George Fawcett, Joseph Singleton. *GPV, FCT*

Mad Youth *Woof!* **1940** A teenage girl falls in love with a man whom her slutty, alcoholic mother had been chasing. Bottom of the barrel production provides many unintentional laughs. Extraneous South American dance sequences included as character development. **61m/B VHS, Beta.** Mary Ainslee, Betty Atkinson, Willy Castello, Betty Compson, Tommy Wonder; ***D:*** Melville Shyer; ***W:*** Willis Kent. *SNC*

Madam Satan ✌✌½ **1930** Extremely bizarre DeMille film highlighted by lavish musical numbers and outrageous costumes. Wealthy socialite realizes she's losing her husband to a young showgirl, so she disguises herself as a sultry French tramp and entices her husband at a masquerade party aboard a zeppelin—surely one of the wildest party scenes ever captured on film. Chorus girls perform several exotic dance numbers inside the airship that are nothing short of fantastic. A storm breaks out and the floating dirigible is struck by lightning—leading viewers to wonder if the mad party-goers will make it to safety or crash and burn like this pic did at the box office. **115m/B VHS.** Kay Johnson, Reginald Denny, Lillian Roth, Roland Young, Boyd Irwin, Elsa Peterson; ***D:*** Cecil B. DeMille. *MGM*

Madame Bovary ✌✌✌ **1934** A young adultress with delusions of romantic love finds only despair in this offbeat adaptation of Flaubert's masterpiece. In French with English subtitles. **102m/B VHS, Beta.** *FR* Pierre Renoir, Valentine Tessier, Max Dearly; ***D:*** Jean Renoir. *HTV, INJ*

Madame Bovary ✌✌✌ **1949** Young adultress with delusions of romantic love finds only despair, even in this Hollywood version of Flaubert's classic. Mason/Flaubert is put on trial for indecency following publication of the novel, with the story told from the witness stand. While this device occasionally slows the narrative, astute direction helps the plot along. Minnelli's handling of the celebrated ball sequence is superb. **115m/B VHS, Beta.** Jennifer Jones, Van Heflin, Louis Jourdan, James Mason, Gene Lockhart, Gladys Cooper, George Zucco; ***D:*** Vincente Minnelli; ***M:*** Miklos Rozsa. Nominations: Academy Awards '49: Best Art Direction/Set Decoration (B & W). *MGM, CCB*

Madame Bovary ✌✌✌½ **1991 (PG-13)** Provincial 19th century France is the setting for the tragedy of a romantic woman. Emma Bovary is bored by her marriage to an unsuccessful country doctor and longs for passion and excitement. She allows herself to be seduced (and abandoned) by a local aristocrat and herself seduces a young banker. She also struggles with an increasing burden of debt as she continues her quest for luxury. Realizing she will never find the passion she desires, Emma takes drastic, and tragic, measures. Sumptuous-looking film, with an extraordinary performance by Huppert. In French with English subtitles. Based on the novel by Gustave Flaubert. **130m/C VHS, LV.** *FR* Isabelle Huppert, Jean-Francois Balmer, Christophe MaLavoy, Jean Yanne; ***D:*** Claude Chabrol; ***W:*** Claude Chabrol; ***M:*** Matthieu Chabrol. Nominations: Academy Awards '91: Best Costume Design. *REP, INJ, BTV*

Madame Curie ✌✌✌ **1943** The film biography of Madame Marie Curie, the woman who discovered Radium. A deft portrayal by Garson, who is reteamed with her "Mrs. Miniver" co-star, Pidgeon. Certainly better than most biographies from this time period and more truthful as well. **124m/B VHS, LV.** Greer Garson, Walter Pidgeon, Robert Walker, May Whitty, Henry Travers, Sir C. Aubrey Smith, Albert Basserman, Victor Francen, Reginald Owen, Van Johnson; ***D:*** Mervyn LeRoy; ***C:*** Joseph Ruttenberg. Nominations: Academy Awards '43: Best Actor (Pidgeon), Best Actress (Garson), Best Black and White Cinematography, Best Interior Decoration, Best Picture, Best Sound, Best Original Score. *MGM, CCB*

Madame Rosa ✌✌✌ *La Vie Devant Soi* **1977 (PG)** An aging Jewish prostitute tends prostitutes' offspring in this warmhearted work. A survivor of the Holocaust, the old woman finds her spirit revived by one of her charges—an abandoned Arab boy. In French with English subtitles. **105m/C VHS, Beta.** *FR IS* Simone Signoret, Claude Dauphin; ***D:*** Moshe Mizrahi; ***C:*** Nestor Almendros. Academy Awards '77: Best Foreign Language Film; Cesar Awards '78: Best Actress (Signoret); Los Angeles Film Critics Association Awards '78: Best Foreign Film. *HTV, VES*

Madame Sin ✌✌½ **1971** Aspiring world dominator enlists former CIA agent in scheme to obtain nuclear submarine. Davis is appealing as evil personified, in her first television movie. **91m/C VHS, Beta.** Bette Davis, Robert Wagner; ***D:*** David Greene; ***M:*** Michael Gibbs. *CCB, FOX*

Madame Sousatzka ✌✌✌ **1988 (PG-13)** Eccentric, extroverted piano teacher helps students develop spiritually as well as musically. When she engages a teenage Indian student, however, she finds herself considerably challenged. MacLaine is perfectly cast in this powerful, winning film. **113m/C VHS, Beta, LV.** Shirley MacLaine, Peggy Ashcroft, Shabana Azmi, Twiggy, Leigh Lawson, Geoffrey Bayldon, Navin Chowdhry, Lee Montague; ***D:*** John Schlesinger; ***W:*** Ruth Prawer Jhabvala, John Schlesinger; ***M:*** Gerald Gouriet. Golden Globe Awards '89: Best Actress—Drama (MacLaine); Venice Film Festival '88: Best Actress (MacLaine), Best Actress (MacLaine). *MCA*

Madame X ✌✌½ **1937** Fourth version of this classic tearjerker finds diplomat's wife George having a fling with a playboy. There's a murder and she turns to her nasty mother-in-law for aid. She arranges for daughter-in-law-dearest's "death" in order to prevent a scandal. Then George is on the slippery path to alcoholism and prostitution. Adapted from the play by Alexandre Bisson. Run-of-the-mill; Lana Turner's 1966 version is still the one to watch. **96m/B VHS.** Gladys George, John Beal, Warren William, Reginald Owen, William Henry, Henry Daniell, Philip Reed, Lynne Carver, Emma Dunn, Ruth Hussey; ***D:*** Sam Wood; ***W:*** John Meehan. *MGM*

Madame X ✌✌ *Absinthe* **1966** Turner is perfectly cast in this oft-filmed melodrama about a social outcast who is tried for murder and defended by her unknowing son, who believes her long dead. Bennett's last film. **100m/C VHS, Beta.** Lana Turner, John Forsythe, Ricardo Montalban, Burgess Meredith, Virginia Grey, Constance Bennett, Keir Dullea; ***D:*** David Lowell Rich; ***C:*** Russell Metty. *MCA*

M.A.D.D.: Mothers Against Drunk Driving ✌✌½ **1983** Emotionally gripping television movie recounts the story of Candy Lightner, who, after her daughter was killed in a drunk driving accident, founded M.A.D.D. and built it into a nationwide organization. Similar to "License to Kill," which dramatized the effect that a drunk driving accident can have on the families of those involved. **97m/C VHS, Beta.** Mariette Hartley, Paula Prentiss, Bert Remsen; ***D:*** William A. Graham; ***M:*** Bruce Broughton. *MCA*

The Maddening ✌½ **1995 (R)** When their car breaks down in a remote area, Cassie (Sara) and daughter Samantha find refuge at the home of Roy Scudder (Reynolds) and his wife Georgina (Dickinson). At least Cassie thought it was a refuge—until she realizes the Scudders are crazy killers. **97m/C VHS, LV.** Burt Reynolds, Angie Dickinson, Mia Sara, Brian Wimmer; ***D:*** Danny Huston. *VMK*

Made for Each Other ✌✌✌ **1939** Newlyweds must overcome meddlesome in-laws, poverty, and even serious illness in this classic melodrama. Dated but appealing. **85m/B VHS, Beta.** James Stewart, Carole Lombard, Charles Coburn, Lucile Watson; ***D:*** John Cromwell; ***C:*** Leon Shamroy. *CNG, MRV, NOS*

Made for Love ✌½ **1926** Couple journeys romantically in Egypt until disaster strikes: they fall into a tomb and can't get out. **65m/B VHS, Beta.** Leatrice Joy, Edmund Burns, Ethel Wales, Brandon Hurst, Frank Butler; ***D:*** Paul Sloane. *GPV, FCT*

Made in America ✌✌ **1993 (PG-13)** High-energy, lightweight comedy stars Whoopi as a single mom whose daughter Long discovers her birth was the result of artifical insemination. More surprising is her biological dad: white, obnoxious, country-western car dealer Danson. Overwrought with obvious gags, basically a one-joke movie. Nonetheless, Goldberg and Danson chemically connect onscreen (and for a short time offscreen as well) while supporting actor Smith grabs comedic attention as Teacake, Long's best friend. Both Goldberg and Danson deserve better material. **111m/C VHS, Beta, LV.** Whoopi Goldberg, Ted Danson, Will Smith, Nia Long, Paul Rodriguez, Jennifer Tilly, Peggy Rea, Clyde Kusatsu; ***D:*** Richard Benjamin; ***W:*** Holly Goldberg Sloan; ***M:*** Mark Isham. *WAR*

Made in Argentina ✌✌ **1986** An Argentinean couple living in New York decide to return for a visit. Having left for political reasons, they still harbor bitterness. **90m/C VHS, Beta.** *AR* Luis Brandoni, Marta Bianchi, Leonor Manso; ***D:*** Juan Jose Jusid. *VES*

Made in Heaven ✌✌ **1952** Arid comedy in which British newlyweds try to sustain honeymoon for entire year. The bride, however, eventually suspects her husband of shenanigans with the maid. If this sounds good, then you may like it. **90m/C VHS, Beta.** *GB* Petula Clark, David Tomlinson, Sonja Ziemann, A.E. Matthews; ***D:*** John Paddy Carstairs. *HMV*

Made in Heaven ✌✌½ **1987 (PG)** Two souls in heaven fall in love and must find each other after being reborn on Earth if they are to remain eternal lovers. Contains ethereal interpretations of heaven and several cameo appearances by famous actors and musicians. **105m/C VHS, Beta, LV.** Timothy Hutton, Kelly McGillis, Maureen Stapleton, Mare Winningham, Ann Wedgeworth, Don Murray, Amanda Plummer, Timothy Daly, Marj Dusay; ***Cameos:*** Ellen Barkin, Neil Young, Tom Petty, Ric Ocasek, Tom Robbins, Debra Winger, Gary Larsen, David Rasche; ***D:*** Alan Rudolph; ***W:*** Raynold Gideon, Bruce A. Evans; ***M:*** Mark Isham. *WAR, ORI*

Made in USA ✌½ **1988 (R)** Wayward dudes engage vixen while cruising Midwest. Trouble, however, awaits. Note: This is not Godard's mid-sixties classic. **82m/C VHS, Beta, LV.** Adrian Pasdar, Lori Singer, Christopher Penn; ***D:*** Ken Friedman; ***W:*** Ken Friedman. *SUE, NLC*

Madeleine ✌✌½ *The Strange Case of Madeleine* **1950** Courtroom drama of woman charged with poisoning her French lover in 1850s Scotland. Directed by the same David Lean who made "Bridge on the River Kwai" and "Lawrence of Arabia". Here, though, he was merely trying to provide a vehicle for his wife, actress Todd. Intrigued? **114m/B VHS, Beta.** Ann Todd, Leslie Banks, Ivan Desny; ***D:*** David Lean; ***C:*** Guy Green. *LCA*

Mademoiselle 1966 Moreau is a psychotic, sexually repressed schoolteacher in a small village who manages to keep herself under control until studly woodcutter Manni and his son take up residence. The locals distrust the stranger but Moreau can't wait to get her hands on him. Suddenly, the village is battered by a rash of poisonings, fires, and floods, all of which are blamed on Manni, leading the locals to exact a terrible vengeance. In French with English subtitles. **105m/B VHS.** *FR GB* Jeanne Moreau, Ettore Manni, Umberto Orsini, Keith Skinner, Jane Berretta, Mony Rey; ***D:*** Tony Richardson; ***W:*** Jean Genet. *MGM, FCT*

Mademoiselle Fifi ½ 1944 Simon stars as a French laundress in 1870 France who refuses to give in to her small town's Prussian oppressors. The film title is the nickname of the most brutal of the Prussian officers, played by Kreuger. An unsucessful attempt at political allegory for the devastation of WWII. **69m/B VHS, LV.** Simone Simon, John Emery, Kurt Kreuger, Alan Napier, Jason Robards Sr.; ***D:*** Robert Wise. *FCT*

Mademoiselle Striptease ½ *Please! Mr. Balzac; While Plucking the Daisy; En Effeuillant la Marguerite* 1957 Bardot stars as a young woman who finds a valuable stolen book. Her attempts to disassociate herself from the actual theft are supposed to be funny. Bardot is characteristically appealing. **100m/B VHS, Beta.** Brigitte Bardot, Robert Hirsch, Daniel Gelin; ***D:*** Marc Allegret. *STV, MRV*

Madhouse 1974 A troubled horror film star tries to bring his "Dr. Death" character to television, but during production people begin dying in ways remarkably similar to the script. A strong genre cast should hold the fans' attention during this mild adaptation of Angus Hall's novel "Devilday." **92m/C VHS, Beta.** *GB* Vincent Price, Peter Cushing, Robert Quarry, Adrienne Corri, Natasha Pyne, Linda Hayden, Michael Parkinson; ***D:*** Jim Clark. *HBO*

Madhouse 1987 A woman has bizarre recollections of her twin sister whom she finally meets when she escapes from a mental hospital. Lots of violence and gore, has definite cult potential. **90m/C VHS, Beta.** Trish Everly, Michael MacRae, Dennis Robertson, Morgan Hart; ***D:*** Ovidio G. Assonitis. *NO*

Madhouse 1990 (PG-13) New homeowners find themselves unable to expel loathsome, boorish guests. Presumably, a comedy cashing in on two of sitcom's brightest lights. **90m/C VHS, Beta, LV.** John Larroquette, Kirstie Alley, Alison La Placa, John Diehl, Jessica Lundy, Bradley Gregg, Dennis Miller, Robert Ginty; ***D:*** Tom Ropelewski; ***W:*** Tom Ropelewski; ***M:*** David Newman. *ORI*

Madhouse Mansion ½ *Ghost Story* **1974 (PG)** A horror actor revives his career and becomes embroiled in murder. Plenty of in-jokes and clips from older movies. **86m/C VHS.** *GB* Marianne Faithfull, Leigh Lawson, Anthony Bate, Larry Dann, Sally Grace, Penelope Keith, Vivian Mackerell, Murray Melvin, Barbara Shelley; ***D:*** Stephen Weeks. *NO*

Madigan 1968 Realistic and exciting and among the best of the behind-the-scenes urban police thrillers. Hardened NYC detectives (Widmark and Guardino) lose their guns to a sadistic killer and are given 72 hours to track him down. Fonda is the police chief none to pleased with their performance. Adapted by Howard Rodman, Abraham Polonsky, and Harry Kleiner from Richard Dougherty's "The Commissioner." **101m/C VHS, Beta.** Richard Widmark, Henry Fonda, Inger Stevens, Harry Guardino, James Whitmore, Susan Clark, Michael Dunn, Don Stroud; ***D:*** Donald Siegel; ***W:*** Abraham Polonsky; ***C:*** Russell Metty. *MCA*

Madigan's Millions *Woof!* **1967 (G)** Incompetent Treasury agent treks to Italy to recover funds swiped from deceased gangster. This is Hoffman's first film, and is to his career what "The Last Chalice" was to Paul Newman's and "Studs and Kitty" was Sylvester Stallone. Recommended only to the terminally foolhardy. **89m/C VHS, Beta.** Dustin Hoffman, Elsa Martinelli, Cesar Romero; ***D:*** Stanley Prager. *RHI*

Madman 1979 (R) Deranged Soviet Jew joins Israeli army to more effectively fulfill his desire to kill loathsome Soviets. Good date movie for those nights when you're home alone. Weaver's first starring role. **95m/C VHS, Beta.** *IS* Sigourney Weaver, Michael Beck, F. Murray Abraham; ***D:*** Dan Cohen. *CNG*

Madman 1982 (R) Camp leader prompts terror when he revives legend regarding ax murderer. Seems that when you call his name, he appears. Buffoon does not believe story and calls out madman's name. Madman hears the call and emerges from forest, says hi, and hacks everyone to death. Lesson learned, case closed. Filmed on Long Island. **89m/C VHS, Beta.** Alexis Dubin, Tony Fish. *HHE*

The Madness of King George ½ 1994 (R) Poor King George is a monarch with problems—his 30 years of royal authority are being usurped by Parliament, his American colonies have been lost, and, in 1788, he's begun to periodically lose his mind. So what do you do when a ruler becomes irrational? The royal physicians are baffled, his loving Queen Charlotte (Mirren) is in despair, but the noxious Prince of Wales (Everett) can barely contain his glee at finally having a chance at the throne. A last resort is offered by Dr. Willis (Holm), a former clergyman with some unusual and sadistic ideas about treating the mentally ill (even if they do have royal blood). Brilliant performance by Hawthorne (who originated the stage role in Bennett's 1991 play "The Madness of George III"). Screen note explains that King George suffered from the metabolic disorder known as porphyria. A Tony Award-winner for his Broadway productions of "Miss Saigon" and "Carousel," Hytner makes his feature-film directing debut. **110m/C VHS, LV.** *GB* Nigel Hawthorne, Helen Mirren, Ian Holm, Rupert Everett, Amanda Donohoe, Rupert Graves, Julian Wadham, John Wood, Julian Rhind-Tutt; ***D:*** Nicholas Hytner; ***W:*** Alan Bennett; ***M:*** George Fenton. Academy Awards '94: Best Art Direction/Set Decoration; British Academy Awards '95: Best Actor (Hawthorne); Cannes Film Festival '95: Best Actress (Mirren); Nominations: Academy Awards '94: Best Actor (Hawthorne), Best Adapted Screenplay, Best Supporting Actress (Mirren). *HMK*

Mado 1976 A middle-aged businessman's life is undone when he falls for a mysterious woman. Piccoli and Schneider are, as usual, convincing. Another of underrated director Sautet's effective, lowkey works. In French with subtitles. **130m/C VHS, Beta.** Romy Schneider, Michel Piccoli, Charles Denner; ***D:*** Claude Sautet. Cesar Awards '77: Best Sound. *FCT*

Madonna: Innocence Lost ½ 1995 Tacky TV movie focusing on the ambitious singer and would-be actress who made wearing underwear as outerwear almost acceptable. Tawdry gossip highlights this laughfest as the trash talker hustles her way to the top of the heap, uncaring of whom she steps on along the way. Toronto substitutes for New York City grit. **90m/C VHS.** Terumi Matthews, Wendie Malick, Jeff Yagher, Dean Stockwell, Nigel Bennett, Don Francks, Rod Wilson, Tom Melissis; ***D:*** Bradford May; ***W:*** Michael J. Murray. *FXV*

Madron ½ 1970 (PG) Road western filmed in the Israel desert, complete with menacing Apaches, wagon train massacre, a nun and a gunslinger. **93m/C VHS, Beta.** Richard Boone, Leslie Caron, Paul Smith; ***D:*** Jerry Hopper. Nominations: Academy Awards '70: Best Song ("Till Love Touches Your Life"). *NO*

The Madwoman of Chaillot ½ 1969 (G) Four men conspire to drill for oil which they believe lurks under Paris. Hepburn finds out about their plot and tells each man that oil is bubbling up through her basement. Before the men can arrive at her house to confirm this, she and her three cronies hold a mock trial and sentence the men to death. Features a stellar cast, but this modern-day adaptation of Jean Giraudoux's play "La Folle de Chaillot" falls flat. **142m/C VHS, LV.** Katharine Hepburn, Charles Boyer, Claude Dauphin, Edith Evans, John Gavin, Paul Henreid, Oscar Homolka, Margaret Leighton, Giulietta Masina, Nanette Newman, Richard Chamberlain, Yul Brynner, Donald Pleasence, Danny Kaye, Fernand Gravet; ***D:*** Bryan Forbes; ***W:*** Edward Anhalt. *WAR*

Mae West ½ 1984 This made-for-television film details West's life from her humble beginnings to her racy film stardom. Jillian does a good job bringing the buxom legend back to life. **97m/C VHS, Beta.** Ann Jillian, James Brolin, Piper Laurie, Roddy McDowall; ***D:*** Lee Philips; ***M:*** Brad Fiedel. *ORI*

Maedchen in Uniform ½ *Girls in Uniform* **1931** A scandalous early German talkie about a rebellious schoolgirl who falls in love with a female teacher and commits suicide when the teacher is punished for the relationship. A controversial criticism of lesbianism and militarism that impelled the Nazis, rising to power two years later, to exile its director. It was also banned in the United States. In German with English subtitles. Remade in 1965. **90m/B VHS, Beta.** *GE* Dorothea Wieck, Ellen Schwannecke, Hertha Thiele; ***D:*** Leontine Sagan. National Board of Review Awards '32: 5 Best Foreign Films of the Year. *SUE, MRV, INJ*

Mafia Princess 1986 The daughter of a Mafia boss tries to discover her own identity despite her father's involvement in crime. Based on a best-selling autobiography by a real-life member of a Mob family, Antoinette Giancana. Made for television. **100m/C VHS.** Tony Curtis, Susan Lucci, Kathleen Widdoes, Chuck Shamata, Louie Dibianco; ***D:*** Robert Collins. *NO*

Mafia vs. Ninja ½ 1984 The mob wants to control the city, but the Ninja has other ideas. **90m/C VHS, Beta.** Alexander Lou, Silvio Azzolini, Wang Hsia, Charlema Hsu, Eugene Trammel. *NO*

Magdalene ½ 1988 (PG) Somewhere in medieval Europe, a violent Baron seeks revenge on a beautiful whore that spurned him. Small-budget costumer. **89m/C VHS, Beta, LV.** Steve Bond, Nastassia Kinski, David Warner, Gunter Meisner, Ferdinand "Ferdy" Mayne, Anthony Quayle, Franco Nero, Janet Agren; ***D:*** Monica Teuber. *PAR, FCT*

Magee and the Lady *She'll Be Sweet* **1978 (PG)** The crusty captain of a rusty ship must warm up to a spoiled debutante or lose his ship to a foreclosure firm. Could be better. Made for TV. **92m/C VHS, Beta.** *AU* Tony LoBianco, Sally Kellerman; ***D:*** Gene Levitt. *ACA*

Magic ½ 1978 (R) Ventriloquist Hopkins and his dummy, an all-too-human counterpart, get involved with a beautiful but impressionable woman lost between reality and the irresistible world of illusion. Spine-chilling psycho-drama with a less-than-believable premise. Screenplay by Goldman from his novel. **106m/C VHS, Beta, LV.** Anthony Hopkins, Ann-Margret, Burgess Meredith, Ed Lauter; ***D:*** Richard Attenborough; ***W:*** William Goldman; ***M:*** Jerry Goldsmith. *SUE, NLC*

The Magic Bubble ½ 1993 (PG-13) On her 40th birthday, Julia Cole finds the fountain of youth...inside a bottle of enchanted bubbles. Ageless and timeless, she begins to know the meaning of true happiness. **90m/C VHS.** Diane Salinger, John Calvin, Priscilla Pointer, Colleen Camp, Tony Peck, Wallace Shawn; ***D:*** Alfredo Ringel, Deborah Taper Ringel; ***W:*** Meredith Baer, Geof Pryssir. *MNC*

The Magic Christian 1969 (PG) A series of related skits about a rich man (Sellers) and his son (Starr) who try to prove that anyone can be bought. Raucous, now somewhat dated comedy; music by Badfinger, including Paul McCartney's "Come and Get It." **101m/C VHS, Beta, LV.** *GB* Peter Sellers, Ringo Starr, Isabel Jeans, Wilfrid Hyde-White, Graham Chapman, John Cleese, Peter Graves, John Lennon, Yoko Ono, Richard Attenborough, Leonard Frey, Laurence Harvey, Christopher Lee, Spike Milligan, Yul Brynner, Roman Polanski, Raquel Welch; ***D:*** Joseph McGrath; ***W:*** Terry Southern; ***C:*** Geoffrey Unsworth. *REP, MRV*

The Magic Flute ½ 1973 (G) Bergman's acclaimed version of Mozart's famous comic opera, universally considered one of the greatest adaptations of opera to film ever made. Staged before a live audience for Swedish television. In Swedish with English subtitles. **134m/C VHS, Beta, LV.** *SW* Josef Kostlinger, Irma Urrila, Hakan Hagegard, Elisabeth Erikson; ***D:*** Ingmar Bergman. *HMV, PAR, MVD*

The Magic Fountain ☞☞ **1961** Three princes search for a magic fountain whose waters will cure their ailing father. Two of them, however, take the evil course and are turned into ravens by a wicked dwarf. Based on the fairy tale "Das Wasser des Lebens" by the Brothers Grimm. **82m/C VHS.** Peter Nestler, Helmo Kinderman, Josef Marz, Catherine Hansen, Cedric Hardwicke; ***D:*** Allan David. *SNC*

Magic in the Water ☞½ **1995 (PG)** Divorced, obnoxious radio shrink and neglectful dad Dr. Jack Black (Harmon) takes the kiddies on a summer jaunt to a Canadian lake, where they begin to explore the legend of Orky, Canada's answer to the Loch Ness monster. Dad becomes a believer when Orky possesses his body and (New Age Alert!) releases his inner child. Harmless fun for the kids, but parents will gag at the attempt to provide a meaningful and symbolic message, which arrives with all the subtlety of an Oliver Stone history lesson. Sort of an "E.T." meets "Free Willy" with Orky shilling for the EPA. Beautiful cinematography showcasing the British Columbia landscape helps, but not enough. **100m/C VHS.** Mark Harmon, Joshua Jackson, Harley Jane Kozak, Sarah Wayne, Willie Nark-Orn, Frank S. Salsedo; ***D:*** Rick Stevenson; ***W:*** Icel Dobell Massey, Rick Stevenson; ***C:*** Thomas Burstyn; ***M:*** David Schwartz. Genie Awards '95: Best Cinematography, Best Sound. *COL*

Magic Island ☞☞½ **1995 (PG)** Thirteen-year-old Jack (Bryan) gets sucked into the pages of a pirate book and finds himself with Blackbeard and his scurvy crew. They're on a treasure hunt and figure Jack's book contains some missing clues. Naturally, Jack finds himself in lots of trouble. **88m/C VHS.** Zachery Ty Bryan, Edward Kerr, Lee Armstrong, French Stewart, Abraham Benrubi, Jessie-Ann Friend, Oscar Dillon, Sean O'Kane, Schae Harrison, Ja'net DuBois, Andrew Divoff; ***D:*** Sam Irvin; ***W:*** Neil Ruttenberg, Brent Friedman; ***C:*** James Lawrence Spencer; ***M:*** Richard Band. *PAR*

Magic Kid ☞☞½ *Ninja Dragons* **1992 (PG)** Thirteen-year-old martial-arts champ Kevin and his older sister vacation in L.A., staying with their shady Uncle Bob, a second-rate talent agent. Kevin wants to meet his martial arts movie idol and his sister her favorite soap opera hunk. But they wind up being chased by the mobsters Uncle Bob owes money to. **91m/C VHS, LV.** Ted Jan Roberts, Shonda Whipple, Stephen Furst, Joseph Campanella, Billy Hufsey, Sondra Kerns, Pamela Dixon, Lauren Tewes, Don "The Dragon" Wilson; ***D:*** Joseph Merhi; ***W:*** Stephen Smoke; ***M:*** Jim Halfpenny. *PMH*

Magic Kid 2 ☞☞½ **1994 (PG)** The young star of a popular martial arts program wants to quit and go to high school like a normal teenager. But the studio execs have other ideas. **90m/C VHS, LV.** Ted Jan Roberts, Stephen Furst, Donald Gibb, Jennifer Savidge; ***D:*** Stephen Furst. *PMH*

The Magic Legend of the Golden Goose ☞ **1965** A retelling of the familiar brothers Grimm chestnut. **72m/C VHS, Beta.** *NO*

Magic Moments ☞☞½ **199?** Ambitious British TV exec Melanie James (Seagrove) is about to score the coup of her career. She's persuaded charismatic American illusionist Troy Gardner (Shea) to recreate his death-defying act on TV—but only if Melanie will produce the show herself. Too bad her power-hungry boss is out to cause trouble. Made for British TV. **103m/C VHS.** *GB* Jenny Seagrove, John Shea. *VCO*

Magic of Lassie ☞☞ **1978 (G)** Stewart is engaging as the nice grandpa who refuses to sell his land to mean rich guy Roberts. Innocuous, pleasant remake of "Lassie Come Home." Stewart sings, as do Pat Boone and daughter Debby. **100m/C VHS, Beta.** James Stewart, Mickey Rooney, Stephanie Zimbalist, Alice Faye, Pernell Roberts, Lassie; ***D:*** Don Chaffey. Nominations: Academy Awards '78: Best Song ("When You're Loved"). *MGM*

The Magic of the Golden Bear: Goldy 3 ☞ *Goldy 3* **1994 (G)** Down-on-his-luck magician (Marin) tries to buy Goldy to save his failing act and Jessie (Morgan) is torn between wanting to keep the bear or return her to the wild. An animal-loving holy man (Mr. T:) tries to help her decide. **104m/C VHS.** Bonnie Morgan, Richard "Cheech" Marin, Mr. T; ***D:*** John Quinn. *FHE*

Magic on Love Island ☞ **1980** Romantic misadventures ensue when eight ladies go on vacation to Love Island, a tropical paradise. **96m/C VHS, Beta.** Adrienne Barbeau, Bill Daily, Howard Duff, Dody Goodman, Dominique Dunne, Lisa Hartman Black, Janis Paige; ***D:*** Earl Bellamy. *NO*

Magic Serpent ☞☞☞ **1966** Fantasy set in medieval Japan features a grand duel in magic between a good hero and evil sorcerer who transform into a giant dragon and a giant frog to do battle. **?m/C VHS.** Hiroki Matsukata, Tomoko Ogawa, Ryutaro Otomo, Bin Amatsu; ***D:*** Tetsuya Yamauchi. *SMW*

The Magic Sword ☞☞ **1962** A family-oriented adventure film about a young knight who sets out to rescue a beautiful princess who is being held captive by an evil sorcerer and his dragon. **80m/C VHS, Beta.** Basil Rathbone, Estelle Winwood, Gary Lockwood; ***D:*** Bert I. Gordon. *MGM, MRV, VYY*

Magic Town ☞☞½ **1947** An opinion pollster investigates a small town which exactly reflects the views of the entire nation, making his job a cinch. The publicity causes much ado in the town with ensuing laughs. Uneven but entertaining. **103m/B VHS.** Jane Wyman, James Stewart, Kent Smith, Regis Toomey, Donald Meek; ***D:*** William A. Wellman; ***C:*** Joseph Biroc. *REP*

The Magic Voyage ☞☞½ **1993 (G)** Animated tale of a friendly woodworm named Pico who voyages with Columbus to the new world and convinces him that the world is indeed round. He then comes to the aid of a magical firefly named Marilyn who helps Columbus find gold to bring back to Spain. **82m/C VHS, LV.** ***V:*** Dom DeLuise, Mickey Rooney, Corey Feldman, Irene Cara, Dan Haggerty, Samantha Eggar. *HMD*

The Magic Voyage of Sinbad ☞☞ *Sadko* **1952** Sinbad embarks on a fantastic journey after promising the people of his Covasian home that he will find the elusive Phoenix, the bird of happiness. Unreleased in the U.S. until 1962; rewritten for the American screen by a young Coppola. **79m/C VHS, Beta.** *RU* Sergey Stolyarov, Alla Larionova, Mark Troyanovsky; ***D:*** Alexander Ptushko; ***W:*** Francis Ford Coppola. *SNC*

Magical Mystery Tour **1967** On the road with an oddball assortment of people, the Beatles experience a number of strange incidents around the English countryside. Originally made for British television. ♫Magical Mystery Tour; Blue Jay Way; Your Mother Should Know; The Fool on the Hill. **55m/C VHS, Beta, LV.** *GB* John Lennon, George Harrison, Ringo Starr, Paul McCartney, Victor Spinetti. *MPI, MED, WFV*

Magical Wonderland **1985** Join a handsome prince and his fair young maiden as they venture through such fairy tale classics as "Beauty and the Beast" and "Sleeping Beauty." **90m/C VHS, Beta.** *VCI*

The Magician ☞☞☞ **1958** A master magician in 19th century Sweden (von Sydow) wreaks ill in this darkly comical, supernatural parable. Dark, well photographed early Bergman effort. In Swedish with English subtitles. **101m/B VHS, Beta, LV.** *SW* Max von Sydow, Ingrid Thulin, Gunnar Bjornstrand, Bibi Andersson, Naima Wifstrand; ***D:*** Ingmar Bergman; ***W:*** Ingmar Bergman. Venice Film Festival '59: Special Jury Prize. *SUE, MRV, HHT*

The Magician of Lublin ☞½ **1979 (R)** Based on an unusual story by Issac Bashevis Singer. Follows the exploits of a magician/con man in turn-of-the century Poland whose personal flaws kill his career, until a chance emerges for one last trick. A good example of movie not as good as book; this rendering is superficial, badly acted and unsatisfying. Made soon after Singer won the Nobel Prize for literature in 1978. **105m/C VHS, Beta.** Alan Arkin, Valerie Perrine, Louise Fletcher, Lou Jacobi, Shelley Winters; ***D:*** Menahem Golan; ***M:*** Maurice Jarre. *NO*

Magnificent Adventurer ☞ **1976** Ostensibly a biography of Benvenuto Cellini, the Florentine sculptor, with a concentration on his love life and swordplay. **94m/C VHS, Beta.** Brett Halsey. *UNI*

The Magnificent Ambersons ☞☞☞☞ **1942** Welles' second film. A fascinating, inventive translation of the Booth Tarkington novel about a wealthy turn of the century family collapsing under the changing currents of progress. Pure Welles, except the glaringly bad tacked-on ending that the studio shot (under the direction of the great Robert Wise and Fred Fleck), after taking the film from him. It seems they wanted the proverbial happy ending. Also available on laserdisc, with interviews and the original story boards. **88m/B VHS, Beta, LV.** Joseph Cotten, Anne Baxter, Tim Holt, Richard Bennett, Dolores Costello, Erskine Sanford, Ray Collins, Agnes Moorehead; ***D:*** Freddie Fleck, Robert Wise, Orson Welles; ***W:*** Orson Welles; ***M:*** Bernard Herrmann, Roy Webb. New York Film Critics Awards '42: Best Actress (Moorehead); Nominations: Academy Awards '42: Best Black and White Cinematography, Best Interior Decoration, Best Picture, Best Supporting Actress (Moorehead). *CRC, MLB, TTC*

The Magnificent Dope ☞☞½ **1942** Fonda is likeable, as usual, as the hapless yokel in the big city. A trip to New York to take a course on being successful is his prize for winning a "laziest man" contest. He falls for his teacher; she uses his crush to motivate him. Funny and entertaining. **83m/B VHS.** Henry Fonda, Lynn Bari, Don Ameche, Edward Everett Horton, Hobart Cavanaugh, Pierre Watkin; ***D:*** Walter Lang. *TCF*

The Magnificent Matador ☞☞½ *The Brave and the Beautiful* **1955** The story of an aging matador who faces death in the bullring to win the love of a woman. Quinn is the bullfighter on the horns of a dilemma. Lots of bull in script carried by harried bull in ring. **94m/C VHS, Beta.** Anthony Quinn, Maureen O'Hara, Thomas Gomez; ***D:*** Budd Boetticher. *VHE*

Magnificent Obsession ☞☞½ **1954** A drunken playboy (Hudson) kills a man and blinds his wife in an automobile accident. Plagued by guilt, he devotes his life to studying medicine in order to restore the widow's sight. Well-acted melodrama lifted Hudson to stardom. Faithful to the 1935 original, based on a novel by Lloyd C. Douglas. **108m/C VHS, Beta.** Jane Wyman, Rock Hudson, Barbara Rush, Agnes Moorehead; ***D:*** Douglas Sirk; ***W:*** Robert Blees; ***C:*** Russell Metty. Nominations: Academy Awards '54: Best Actress (Wyman). *MCA*

The Magnificent Seven ☞☞☞☞ **1960** Western remake of Akira Kurosawa's classic "The Seven Samurai." Mexican villagers hire gunmen to protect them from the bandits who are destroying their town. Most of the actors were relative unknowns, though not for long. Sequelled by "Return of the Seven" in 1966, "Guns of the Magnificent Seven" in 1969, and "The Magnificent Seven Ride" in 1972. Excellent score. Uncredited writing by Walter Newman and Walter Bernstein. **126m/C VHS, Beta, LV.** Yul Brynner, Steve McQueen, Robert Vaughn, James Coburn, Charles Bronson, Horst Buchholz, Eli Wallach, Brad Dexter; ***D:*** John Sturges; ***W:*** William Roberts; ***C:*** Charles B(ryant) Lang; ***M:*** Elmer Bernstein. Nominations: Academy Awards '60: Best Original Score. *MGM, FOX, TLF*

The Magnificent Yankee ☞☞☞ *The Man with Thirty Sons* **1950** Adaptation of Emmet Lavery's Broadway play on the life of Supreme Court Justice Oliver Wendell Holmes, starring Calhern (who also did the stage version). America's foremost legal mind was well-served by Calhern, with Harding as his ever-patient wife. **80m/B VHS, Beta.** Louis Calhern, Ann Harding, Eduard Franz, Philip Ober, Ian Wolfe, Edith Evanson, Richard Anderson, Jimmy Lydon, Robert Sherwood, Hugh Sanders; ***D:*** John Sturges; ***W:*** Emmet Lavery. Nominations: Academy Awards '50: Best Actor (Calhern). *MGM, FCT, BTV*

Magnum Force ☞☞ **1973 (R)** Eastwood's second "Dirty Harry" movie. Harry finds a trail leading from a series of gangland killings straight back to the P.D. Less gripping than "Dirty Harry" (1971); followed by "The Enforcer" (1976), "Sudden Impact" (1983), and "The Dead Pool" (1988). Holbrook is cast intriguingly against type, and the premise is good, but little else recommends this too-violent installment. **124m/C VHS, Beta, LV.** Clint Eastwood, Hal Holbrook, Mitchell Ryan, David Soul, Robert Urich, Tim Matheson, Kip Niven; ***D:*** Ted Post; ***W:*** Michael Cimino, John Milius; ***M:*** Lalo Schifrin. *WAR, TLF*

Magnum Killers ☆ **1976** A young man becomes involved in a web of deadly intrigue when he sets out to find who cheated him out of a small fortune during a card game. **92m/C VHS, Beta.** Sombat Methance, Prichela Lee. *UNI*

Magnum P.I.: Don't Eat the Snow in Hawaii **1980** Series pilot finds Vietnam-vet-turned-private-eye Thomas Sullivan Magnum (Selleck) living in Hawaii (in the guest house of never-seen mystery writer Robin Masters) and investigating the death of a wartime buddy. Hillerman excels as autocratic major domo Higgins. **99m/C VHS.** Tom Selleck, John Hillerman, Roger E. Mosley, Larry Manetti; ***D:*** Roger Young; ***W:*** Donald P. Bellisario, Glen Larson. *MCA*

The Mahabharata **1989** Adapted from the myths and folklore of ancient India, the screen version of the original 9 hour stage play is the story of a devastating war between two powerful clans. Initially broadcast on public television, the 6 hour movie is divided into three 2 hour tapes, "The Game of Dice," "Exile in the Forest," and "The War." **318m/C VHS, LV.** *GB FR* Robert Langton-Lloyd, Antonin Stahly-Vishwanadan, Bruce Myers; ***D:*** Peter Brook; ***W:*** Jean-Claude Carriere; ***M:*** Toshi Tsuchitori. *BTV, WSH, FCT*

Mahler ☆☆☆ **1974 (PG)** Strange Russell effort on the life of the great composer Gustav Mahler. Imperfect script is rescued by fine acting. **110m/C VHS, Beta.** Robert Powell, Georgina Hale, Richard Morant, Lee Montague, Terry O'Quinn; ***D:*** Ken Russell; ***W:*** Ken Russell. Nominations: Cannes Film Festival '74: Best Film. *NO*

Mahogany ☆½ **1975 (PG)** Poor girl becomes world-famous high fashion model and designer, ditches boyfriend in the old neighborhood, gets a career boost when she daringly appears in a dress of her own creation at a Roman fashion show, and still yearns for the boy back home. Motown attempt to make mainstream hit that's glossy and predictable. **109m/C VHS, Beta, LV.** Diana Ross, Billy Dee Williams, Jean-Pierre Aumont, Anthony Perkins, Nina Foch; ***D:*** Berry Gordy; ***W:*** John Byrum; ***C:*** David Watkin. Nominations: Academy Awards '75: Best Song ("Theme from Mahogany"). *PAR, CCB, FCT*

The Maid ☆☆½ **1990 (PG)** An offbeat comedy romance with Sheen as the house husband to Bisset's female executive character. Nice acting; charming, if unoriginal, premise. **91m/C VHS, Beta, LV.** Martin Sheen, Jacqueline Bisset, Jean-Pierre Cassel, James Faulkner, Victoria Shalet; ***D:*** Ian Toynton. *MED, VTR*

Maid to Order ☆½ **1987 (PG)** Rich girl Sheedy's fairy godmother puts her in her place by turning her into a maid for a snooty Malibu couple. Good-natured and well-acted if rather mindless Cinderella story. **92m/C VHS, Beta, LV.** Ally Sheedy, Beverly D'Angelo, Michael Ontkean, Dick Shawn, Tom Skerritt, Valerie Perrine; ***D:*** Amy Holden Jones; ***W:*** Perry Howze; ***M:*** Georges Delerue. *LIV*

Maid's Night Out ☆☆ **1938** Pleasant, simple-minded mistaken-identity comedy. Fontaine is an heiress; rich-guy posing-as-milkman Lane thinks she is a maid. They fall in love, of course. **64m/B VHS.** Joan Fontaine, Allan "Rocky" Lane, Hedda Hopper, George Irving, William Brisbane, Billy Gilbert, Cecil Kellaway; ***D:*** Ben Holmes. *MLB*

Maids of Wilko ☆☆ *The Young Ladies of Wilko; Panny z Wilka* **1979** Wajda's adaptation of Jaroslav Iwaszkiewicz's memoirs set in the late '20s. Viktor Ruben (Olbrychski) reexamines his life following the death of a friend. He returns to the home of his aunt and uncle in Wilko where he renews friendships with five sisters on a neighboring estate in an attempt to resurrect a happier past. Lots of fruitless romantic yearning. In French and Polish with English subtitles. **118m/C VHS.** *PL FR* Daniel Olbrychski, Christine Pascal, Maja Komorowska, Anna Seniuk, Krystyna Zachwatowicz, Stanislawa Celinska, Zofia Jaroszewska, Tadeusz Bialoszczynski; ***D:*** Andrzej Wajda; ***W:*** Zbigniew Kaminski. *FCT*

The Main Event ☆☆ **1979 (PG)** Streisand plays a wacky—and bankrupt—cosmetic executive who must depend on the career of washed-up boxer O'Neal to rebuild her fortune. Desperate (and more than a little smitten), she badgers and bullies him back into the ring. Lame, derivative screwball comedy desperate to suggest chemistry of Streisand and O'Neal's "What's Up, Doc?" (1972). Streisand sings the title song. **109m/C VHS, Beta.** Barbra Streisand, Ryan O'Neal; ***D:*** Howard Zieff. *WAR*

Main Street to Broadway ☆☆ **1953** Superficial story of a struggling playwright. Interesting mainly for abundant big-name cameos. Based on a story by Robert E. Sherwood. **102m/B VHS, Beta.** Tom Morton, Mary Murphy, Agnes Moorehead, Herb Shriner, Rosemary DeCamp, Clinton Sundberg; ***Cameos:*** Lionel Barrymore, Ethel Barrymore, Tallulah Bankhead, Shirley Booth, Cornel Wilde, Rex Harrison, Joshua Logan, Helen Hayes, Mary Martin; ***D:*** Tay Garnett. *MPI, MLB*

Maitresse ☆☆½ **1976** An examination of the sexual underworld in the same vein as "Blue Velvet" and "Crimes of Passion." Director Scroeder also created "Reversal of Fortune." In French with English subtitles. **112m/C VHS.** Gerard Depardieu; ***D:*** Barbet Schroeder; ***C:*** Nestor Almendros. *WAR, BTV, FCT*

Major Barbara ☆☆☆½ **1941** A wealthy, idealistic girl joins the Salvation Army against her father's wishes. Based on the play by George Bernard Shaw. The excellent adaptation of the original and the cast make this film a winner. Deborah Kerr's film debut. **90m/B VHS, Beta.** *GB* Wendy Hiller, Rex Harrison, Robert Morley, Sybil Thorndike, Deborah Kerr; ***D:*** Gabriel Pascal. *LCA, FCT, HMV*

Major Dundee ☆☆½ **1965** A Union army officer (Heston) chases Apaches into Mexico with a motley collection of prisoner volunteers. Too long and flawed; would have been better had Peckinpah been allowed to finish the project. Excellent cast. **124m/C VHS, Beta.** Charlton Heston, Richard Harris, James Coburn, Jim Hutton, Ben Johnson, Slim Pickens; ***D:*** Sam Peckinpah; ***C:*** Sam Leavitt. *GKK*

Major League ☆☆½ **1989 (R)** Comedy about a pathetic major league baseball team whose new owner schemes to lose the season and relocate the team to Miami. Sheen is okay as the pitcher with control problems (both on and off the field), while Bernsen seems to be gazing affectionately at "L.A. Law" from a distance. Predictable sports spoof is good for a few laughs, particularly those scenes involving Haysbert as a slugger with voodoo on his mind (and in his locker) and Snipes as a base stealer whose only problem is getting on base. **107m/C VHS, Beta, LV, 8mm.** Tom Berenger, Charlie Sheen, Corbin Bernsen, James Gammon, Margaret Whitton, Bob Uecker, Rene Russo, Wesley Snipes, Dennis Haysbert, Charles Cyphers; ***D:*** David S. Ward; ***W:*** David S. Ward; ***C:*** Reynaldo Villalobos; ***M:*** James Newton Howard. *PAR*

Major League 2 ☆½ **1994 (PG)** It's been five years since they won the series, and this plodding sequel finds the wacky championship Cleveland Indians ruined by success and once again struggling in last place. Limited charm of original is lost; dull and filled with so many lame jokes that you won't care if they manage to make it to the top again. Cast returns, with the exception of Wesley Snipes as Willie Mays Hays (now played by Epps). **105m/C VHS, LV.** Charlie Sheen, Tom Berenger, Corbin Bernsen, James Gammon, Dennis Haysbert, Omar Epps, David Keith, Bob Uecker, Alison Doody, Michelle Burke, Margaret Whitton, Eric Bruskotter, Takaaki Ishibashi; ***D:*** David S. Ward; ***W:*** R.J. Stewart; ***M:*** Michel Colombier. *WAR*

Major Payne ☆ **1995 (PG-13)** When the marines have no more use for killing-machine Major Payne (Wayans), he reluctantly agrees to train the inept junior ROTC cadets at academically-challenged Madison Academy. The misfit brigade contains the usual assortment of stock loser-types who follow the predictable "outcasts get even" plot to the letter. Wayans shows flashes of comic genius, but not nearly enough to make up for the one-dimensional characters and indifferent writing. Most of the showcase jokes involve the humiliation and degradation of the kids, always a laugh-riot. Sub-moronic remake of 1955's "The Private War of Major Benson." **97m/C VHS, LV.** Damon Wayans, Karyn Parsons, William Hickey, Albert Hall, Steven Martini, Andrew Harrison Leeds, Scott "Bam Bam" Bigelow; ***D:*** Nick Castle; ***W:*** Damon Wayans, Dean Lorey, Gary Rosen. *MCA*

The Majorettes ☆ **1987 (R)** Eek! Someone is lurking around a high school murdering the majorettes with their own batons. A bare-bones plot lurks within this otherwise worthless pic. **93m/C VHS, Beta.** Kevin Kindlan, Terrie Godfrey, Mark V. Jevicky; ***D:*** John Russo. *LIV, VES, TEM*

A Majority of One ☆☆½ **1956** Dated comedy about late-in-life romance and prejudice. Russell stars as Jewish Brooklyn widow Mrs. Jacoby, who tags along with her daughter and diplomat son-in-law on their shipboard trip to Japan. She meets the charming Koichi Asano (a surprisingly effective Guinness), who's with the Japanese diplomatic corp, runs into problems with her family, and decides she must give up her chance at romance. Adapted from the play by Leonard Spigelgass. **149m/C VHS.** Rosalind Russell, Alec Guinness, Ray Danton, Madlyn Rhue, Mae Questel, Frank Wilcox, Alan Mowbray; ***D:*** Mervyn LeRoy; ***W:*** Leonard Spigelgass. *WAR*

Make a Million ☆☆ **1935** The Depression is played (successfully) for yuks in this tale of an economics professor fired from his post for advocating radical income redistribution. He doesn't get mad, he gets even: he makes a million by advertising for money. **66m/B VHS, Beta.** Charles Starrett, Pauline Brooks. *VYY*

Make a Wish ☆☆ **1937** A noted composer goes stale in this colorful musical about backstage life. The comic relief provides the films best moments. ♫Music In My Heart; My Campfire Dreams; Make a Wish; Old Man Rip. **80m/B VHS, Beta.** Basil Rathbone, Leon Errol, Bobby Breen, Ralph Forbes; ***D:*** Kurt Neumann; ***M:*** Oscar Straus. Nominations: Academy Awards '37: Best Original Score. *VYY*

Make Haste to Live ☆☆½ **1954** Good, scary thriller. A woman survives attempted murder by her husband; moves far away to raise their infant daughter. He does time, then returns for revenge. McGuire is good as the terrorized wife. **90m/B VHS.** Dorothy McGuire, Stephen McNally, Edgar Buchanan, John Howard; ***D:*** William A. Seiter; ***M:*** Elmer Bernstein. *REP*

Make Me an Offer ☆☆ **1955** Somewhat slow-moving comedy centering on an antique dealer who attempts to buy an expensive vase from an old man. From the novel by Wolf Mankowitz. **88m/C VHS.** *GB* Peter Finch, Adrienne Corri, Rosalie Crutchley, Finlay Currie; ***D:*** Cyril Frankel. *SUE*

Make Me an Offer ☆½ **1980** Made-for-TV movie about selling real estate in Hollywood. Better than similar efforts. **97m/C VHS, Beta.** Susan Blakely, Stella Stevens, Patrick O'Neal; ***D:*** Jerry Paris; ***M:*** Ralph Burns. *NLC*

Make Mine Mink ☆☆☆ **1960** Oft-hilarious British comedy about guests at an elegant but run-down mansion who become unlikely thieves, stealing furs for charity. Good cast headed by Terry-Thomas. **100m/C VHS, Beta.** *GB* Terry-Thomas, Billie Whitelaw, Hattie Jacques; ***D:*** Robert Asher. *NO*

Make Room for Tomorrow ☆☆ **1981 (R)** Subtle, somewhat funny French comedy about generations in a family. A man in mid-life crisis has to cope with his father, son, and grandfather on the grandfather's 90th birthday. **106m/C VHS, Beta.** *FR* Victor Lanoux, Jane Birkin, George Wilson; ***D:*** Peter Kassovitz. *SUE*

Make-Up ☆☆ **1937** A doctor turned circus clown uses his medical skills when an elephant renders a society girl unconscious. After she awakens the two become involved. The clown's daughter objects, but is soon caught up in an accusation that she murdered the lion tamer. Her father the clown tries to save the day. Predictable doctor/clown relationship. **72m/B VHS.** Nils Asther, June Clyde, Judy Kelly, Kenne Duncan, John Turnbull; ***D:*** Alfred Zeisler. *NOS, DVT, HEG*

Making Contact ☆½ **1986 (PG)** A small boy's telekinetic powers enable him to bring to life his favorite toys. The ridicule he endures because of this leads him to set off on terrifying adventures with only his toys and a friend for company. **83m/C VHS, Beta.** Joshua Morrell, Eve Kryll; ***D:*** Roland Emmerich. *NWV, VTR*

Making Love ☆☆ **1982 (R)** A closet homosexual risks his 8-year marriage by getting involved with a carefree writer. What could be a powerful subject gets only bland treatment. **112m/C VHS, Beta.** Kate Jackson, Harry Hamlin, Michael Ontkean, Wendy Hiller, Arthur Hill, Nancy Olson, Terry Kiser, Camilla Carr, Michael Dudikoff; ***D:*** Arthur Hiller; ***W:*** Barry Sandler. *FOX*

Making Mr. Right ☆☆½ **1986 (PG-13)** Under-rated satire about a high-powered marketing and image consultant who falls in love with the android that she's supposed to be promoting. Unbelievable comedy is shaky at times, but Magnuson and Malkovich create some magic. **95m/C VHS, Beta, LV.** John Malkovich, Ann Magnuson, Glenne Headly, Ben Masters, Laurie Metcalf, Polly Bergen, Hart Bochner, Polly Draper, Susan Anton; ***D:*** Susan Seidelman; ***W:*** Floyd Byars. *HBO*

Making the Grade ☆☆ *Preppies* **1984 (PG)** Jersey tough kid owes the mob; attends prep school in place of a rich kid who can't be bothered. Better than similar '80s teen flicks, but not by much. **105m/C VHS, Beta.** Judd Nelson, Joanna Lee, Dana Olsen, Ronald Lacey, Scott McGinnis, Gordon Jump, Carey Scott, Andrew Dice Clay; ***D:*** Dorian Walker; ***W:*** Gene Quintano; ***M:*** Basil Poledouris. *MGM*

The Makioka Sisters ☆☆☆ **1983** Much praised drama centering around the lives of four Japanese sisters who are heiresses to the family fortune and, hence, must be found proper husbands. The efforts of the older sisters to "match" their younger siblings are entwined with a gradual realization on the part of the elders that the quiet way of life representative of their own formative years is passing away with the advent of WWII. The movie is as visually stunning as it is poignant. In Japanese with English subtitles. **140m/C VHS, LV.** *JP* Keiko Kishi, Yoshiko Sakuma, Sayuri Yoshinaga; ***D:*** Kon Ichikawa. *FCT, INJ, TPV*

Malarek ☆☆ **1989 (R)** Tough Montreal journalist Victor Malarek exposed abuse in that city's teen detention center in his book "Hey, Malarek." Compelling lead performance from Koteas in decent though not great screen adaptation. **95m/C VHS, Beta, LV.** Michael Sarrazin, Elias Koteas, Al Waxman, Kerrie Keane; ***D:*** Roger Cardinal. *COL*

Malaya ☆☆½ *East of the Rising Sun* **1949** Hokey adventure tale set in WWII that's based on a true story. Stewart and Tracy are hired to smuggle a huge shipment of rubber out of Malaya to waiting U.S. ships without the Japanese finding out. Greenstreet does his usual shifty role. **98m/B VHS.** Spencer Tracy, James Stewart, Sydney Greenstreet, Valentina Cortese, John Hodiak, Lionel Barrymore, Gilbert Roland, Richard Loo, Roland Winters; ***D:*** Richard Thorpe; ***W:*** Frank Fenton; ***M:*** Bronislau Kaper. *MGM*

Malcolm ☆☆½ **1986 (PG-13)** An offbeat comedy about a slightly retarded young man who is mechanically inclined and his unusual entry into a life of crime. Directorial debut for actress Tass, whose husband Parker wrote the screenplay (and designed the Tinkertoys). Music score performed by The Penguin Cafe Orchestra. **86m/C VHS, Beta, LV.** *AU* Colin Friels, John Hargreaves, Lindy Davies, Chris Haywood, Charles Tingwell, Beverly Phillips, Judith Stratford; ***D:*** Nadia Tass; ***W:*** David Parker; ***M:*** Simon Jeffes. Australian Film Institute '86: Best Actor (Friels), Best Film. *LIV, VES*

Malcolm X ☆☆☆ **1992 (PG-13)** Stirring tribute to the controversial black activist, a leader in the struggle for black liberation. Hitting bottom during his imprisonment in the 50s, he became a Black Muslim and then a leader in the Nation of Islam. His assassination in 1965 left a legacy of black nationalism, self-determination, and racial pride. Marked by strong direction from Lee and good performances (notably Freeman Jr. as Elijah Muhammad), it is Washington's convincing performance in the title role that truly brings the film alive. Based on "The Autobiography of Malcolm X" by Malcolm X and Alex Haley. **201m/C VHS, Beta, LV, 8mm.** Denzel Washington, Angela Bassett, Albert Hall, Al Freeman Jr., Delroy Lindo, Spike Lee, Theresa Randle, Kate Vernon, Lonette McKee, Tommy Hollis, James McDaniel, Ernest Thompson, Jean LaMarre, Giancarlo Esposito, Craig Wasson, John Ottavino, David Patrick Kelly, Shirley Stoler; ***Cameos:*** Christopher Plummer, Karen Allen, Peter Boyle, William Kunstler, Bobby Seale, Al Sharpton; ***D:*** Spike Lee; ***W:*** Spike Lee, Arnold Perl, James Baldwin; ***M:*** Terence Blanchard. Chicago Film Critics Awards '93: Best Actor (Washington), Best Film; MTV Movie Awards '93: Best Male Performance (Washington); New York Film Critics Awards '92: Best Actor (Washington); Nominations: Academy Awards '92: Best Actor (Washington), Best Costume Design. *WAR, MOV, BTV*

Malcolm X: Make It Plain **1995** In-depth portrait of the life of Malcolm X as told through the memories of many of Malcolm's close personal friends and individuals who had worked closely with him. Contains footage of Malcolm X speaking at rallies, meetings, and interviews with Maya Angelou, Ossie Davis, Alex Haley, Mike Wallace, and his family. **136m/C VHS.** *MPI*

Male and Female ☆☆☆☆ **1919** A group of British aristocrats is shipwrecked on an island and must allow their efficient butler (Meighan) to take command for their survival. Swanson is the spoiled rich girl who falls for her social inferior. Their rescue provides a return to the rigid British class system. Based on the play "The Admirable Crichton" by James M. Barrie. **110m/B VHS, Beta.** Gloria Swanson, Thomas Meighan, Lila Lee, Raymond Hatton, Bebe Daniels; ***D:*** Cecil B. DeMille. *GPV*

Malibu Beach ☆½ **1978 (R)** The California beach scene is the setting for this movie filled with bikini clad girls, tanned young men, and instant romances. For connoisseurs of the empty-headed teen beach movie. **93m/C VHS, Beta.** Kim Lankford, James Daughton; ***D:*** Robert J. Rosenthal. *PSM*

The Malibu Beach Vampires **1991 (R)** Three unscrupulous yuppies, Congressman Teri Upstart, Col. Ollie West and Rev. Timmy Fakker, keep beautiful mistresses in their Malibu beach house. What they don't know is, the girls are all really vampires who have injected them with a serum that compels them to tell the truth! Will our "heroes" continue to dupe the American Public, or will the sexy blood suckers cause their downfall? **90m/C VHS.** Angelyne, Becky Le Beau, Joan Rudelstein, Marcus A. Frishman, Rod Sweitzer, Francis Creighton, Anet Anatelle, Yvette Buchanan, Cherie Romaors, Kelly Galindo; ***D:*** Francis Creighton. *NO*

Malibu Bikini Shop ☆ **1986 (R)** Two brothers manage a beachfront bikini shop in Malibu, and spend their time ogling the customers and arguing about running the "business." Just another excuse for parading babes in bathing suits across the naked screen. **90m/C VHS, Beta.** Michael David Wright, Bruce Greenwood, Barbara Horan, Debra Blee, Jay Robinson, Galyn Gorg, Ami Julius, Frank Nelson, Kathleen Freeman, Rita Jenrette; ***D:*** David Wechter; ***W:*** David Wechter. *FOX*

Malibu Express ☆ **1985 (R)** Mystery/adventure plot about a P.I. is the excuse; babes in swimsuits is the reason for this waste of time. **101m/C VHS, Beta.** Darby Hinton, Sybil Danning, Art Metrano, Shelley Taylor Morgan, Niki Dantine, Barbara Edwards; ***D:*** Andy Sidaris. *MCA*

Malibu High ☆ **1979 (R)** The accidental death of a young prostitute's client leads her to a new series of illegal activities of the "sex and hit" variety. Dark, sleazy, and antisocial; belies Beach Boys-esque title. **92m/C VHS, Beta.** Jill Lansing, Stuart Taylor; ***D:*** Irvin Berwick. *NO*

Malibu Hot Summer ☆ *Sizzle Beach U.S.A* **1974 (R)** Three aspiring young actresses want a shot at becoming famous and travel to Los Angeles where they spend their time at the beach with little budget and no particular purchase. Re-released and renamed in 1986 when Costner (in his film debut) became more well-known. **89m/C VHS.** Terry Congie, Leslie Brander, Roselyn Royce, Kevin Costner; ***D:*** Richard Brander. *VHE, VMK, VTR*

Malice ☆☆½ **1993 (R)** In a sleepy little college town, strange things sure do happen. Too bad rumpled college dean Andy Safian (Pullman) didn't see "Pacific Heights." If he did, he would know that sometimes roommates are more trouble than they're worth, even if renovation on that old Victorian is getting expensive. Routine thriller throws out an inventive twist to keep things moving, but manages to be fairly predictable anyway. **107m/C VHS, LV.** Alec Baldwin, Nicole Kidman, Bill Pullman, Bebe Neuwirth, Anne Bancroft, George C. Scott, Peter Gallagher, Josef Sommer; ***D:*** Harold Becker; ***W:*** Aaron Sorkin, Scott Frank; ***C:*** Gordon Willis; ***M:*** Jerry Goldsmith. *NLC*

Malicious ☆☆ *Malizia* **1974 (R)** A housekeeper hired for a widower and his three sons becomes the object of lusty affection of all four men. As Papa makes plans to court and marry her, his fourteen-year-old son plots to have her as a companion on his road to sensual maturity. Dubbed in English. **98m/C VHS, Beta.** *IT* Laura Antonelli, Turi Ferro, Alessandro Momo, Tina Aumont; ***D:*** Salvatore Samperi. *PAR*

Malicious ☆☆ **1995 (R)** College athlete impulsively has what he thinks is a one-nighter with a mystery lady. Only she's not willing to give him up and his rejection sends her on the road to revenge. **92m/C VHS, LV.** Molly Ringwald, Patrick McGaw, John Vernon, Mimi Kuzyk, Rick Henrickson; ***D:*** Ian Corson; ***W:*** George Saunders; ***M:*** Graeme Coleman. *REP*

Mallrats ☆☆½ **1995 (R)** Smith's better-financed follow-up to the legendary "Clerks" (the second in the "Lord of the Rings" trilogy) follows Jersey slackers T.S. (London) and Brodie (Lee) to the mall, where they intend to wallow in food-court cookies and reclaim their girlfriends, who recently dumped them. While wandering the mall in low-key and confused pursuit of their women and self respect, they encounter the usual band of bizarre inhabitants, including Ivannah, the topless psychic, and Silent Bob (Smith) and stoner Jay (Mewes), the guys who hung out in front of the video shop during "Clerks." Dialogue and sightgags are director/writer Smith's strong point; moving the plot forward is not high on the priority list. The ensemble cast, featuring Doherty as the boring babe who spurns Brodie, is up to the often funny sidebits and gen-x references. Ribald humor is not for young teens with virgin ears, unless mom and dad are out for the evening. Slick packaging with alternative soundtrack insures return on investment. **95m/C VHS, LV.** Shannen Doherty, Jeremy London, Jason Lee, Claire Forlani, Michael Rooker, Priscilla Barnes, Renee Humphrey, Ben Affleck, Joey Adams, Jason Mewes, Brian O'Halloran, David Brinkley, Kevin Smith; ***Cameos:*** Stan Lee; ***D:*** Kevin Smith; ***W:*** Kevin Smith; ***C:*** David Klein; ***M:*** Ira Newborn. *MCA*

Malone ☆½ **1987 (R)** A burnt-out secret agent stumbles into a real-estate swindle/murder plot in Oregon and sets out to stop it. Film tries hard but doesn't succeed in being believable. **92m/C VHS, Beta, LV.** Burt Reynolds, Lauren Hutton, Cliff Robertson, Kenneth McMillan, Scott Wilson, Cynthia Gibb; ***D:*** Harley Cokliss; ***M:*** David Newman. *ORI*

Malou ☆☆ **1983 (R)** A young French woman tries to uncover the truth about her late mother's life, sifting through wildly contradictory evidence in the desire to discover her own identity and avoid her mother's mistakes. A feminist story. In German with English subtitles. **95m/C VHS, Beta.** *GE* Grischa Huber, Ingrid Caven, Helmut Griem; ***D:*** Jeanine Meerapfel. *SUE, GLV*

Malta Story ☆☆½ **1953** A British WWII flier becomes involved with the defense of Malta. **103m/B VHS, Beta.** Alec Guinness, Jack Hawkins, Anthony Steel, Flora Robson, Muriel Pavlow; ***D:*** Brian Desmond Hurst. *SUE*

The Maltese Falcon ☆☆☆ *Dangerous Female* **1931** A good first screen version of the Dashiell Hammett story about private detective Sam Spade's search for the elusive Black Bird. Remade five years later as "Satan Met a Lady" with Bette Davis. Its most famous remake, however, occurred in 1941 with Humphrey Bogart in the lead. **80m/B VHS, Beta.** Bebe Daniels, Ricardo Cortez, Dudley Digges, Thelma Todd,

Una Merkel, Dwight Frye, Robert Elliott; ***D:*** Roy Del Ruth. *MLB*

The Maltese Falcon **1941** After the death of his partner, detective Sam Spade finds himself enmeshed in a complicated, intriguing search for a priceless statuette. "It's the stuff dreams are made of," says Bogart of the Falcon. Excellent, fast-paced film noir with outstanding performances, great dialogue, and concentrated attention to details. Director Huston's first film and Greenstreet's talky debut. First of several films by Bogart and Astor. Based on the novel by Dashiell Hammett. Also available colorized. **101m/B VHS, Beta, LV.** Humphrey Bogart, Mary Astor, Peter Lorre, Sydney Greenstreet, Ward Bond, Barton MacLane, Gladys George, Lee Patrick, Elisha Cook Jr., Jerome Cowan; ***Cameos:*** Walter Huston; ***D:*** John Huston; ***W:*** John Huston; ***M:*** Adolph Deutsch. Nominations: Academy Awards '41: Best Picture, Best Screenplay, Best Supporting Actor (Greenstreet). *MGM, FOX, TLF*

Mama Dracula *Woof!* **1980** Fletcher stars in this poor satire of the horror genre. She's a vampire who needs the blood of virgins to stay young. Her son helps out—what good son wouldn't? **90m/C VHS.** *FR* Louise Fletcher, Bonnie Schneider, Maria Schneider, Marc-Henri Wajnberg, Alexander Wajnberg, Jess Hahn; ***D:*** Boris Szulzinger. *TWE*

Mama, There's a Man in Your Bed *Romauld et Juliet* **1989 (PG)** When a powerful executive is framed for insider trading, the only witness to the crime and his only hope is an earthy cleaning woman named Juliette. Together they plot revenge and takeovers in her tiny apartment, filled with children. Soon, he regains his former position of power but realizes his life isn't complete without his co-conspirator. In French with English subtitles. **111m/C VHS, Beta, LV.** *FR* Daniel Auteuil, Firmine Richard, Pierre Vernier, Maxime LeRoux, Gilles Privat, Muriel Combeau, Catherine Salviat, Sambou Tati; ***D:*** Coline Serreau; ***W:*** Coline Serreau. *HBO, FCT, INJ*

Mama Turns a Hundred **1979 (R)** A baronial family (a bizarre set of characters) is celebrating their mother's 100th birthday at her estate. One of the daughter's seduces her brother-in-law, another has a uniform fetish, a religious zealot is desperate to hang-glide, and several of them are trying to kill poor Mama. But of course she prevails, although sick and ailing. Slow-paced yet uproarious film full of inept characters who bumble along. In Spanish with English subtitles. **100m/C VHS, Beta.** *SP* Geraldine Chaplin, Fernando Gomez, Amparo Munoz; ***D:*** Carlos Saura. Nominations: Academy Awards '79: Best Foreign Language Film. *INT, AUD, INJ*

Mama's Dirty Girls **1974 (R)** A gangster mom's daughters take over where their mother left off and have the time of their lives. **82m/C VHS, Beta.** Gloria Grahame, Paul Lambert, Sondra Currie, Candice Rialson, Mary Stoddard; ***D:*** John Hayes; ***M:*** Don Bagley. *TWE*

Mambo ½ **1955** A poor young dancer inspires patronage and lust by dancing the Mambo. Although attracted to Gassman, she marries Rennie for his money. Technically weak but artistically interesting, though Rennie and Mangano have done their roles somewhat better elsewhere. **94m/B VHS.** Silvana Mangano, Michael Rennie, Vittorio Gassman, Shelley Winters, Katherine Dunham, Mary Clare, Eduardo Ciannelli; ***D:*** Robert Rossen; ***M:*** Nino Rota. *NOS, HTV, INJ*

The Mambo Kings **1992 (R)** Armand and Banderas (in his first English speaking role) are Cesar and Nestor Castillo, two brothers who flee Cuba for New York City with dreams of hitting it big with their mambo music. Desi Arnaz Jr. gets to play his own dad in a funny and technical scene that leads to a climactic confrontation between the brothers. Good cast and great music make this one worthwhile. Based on the Pulitzer prizewinning novel "The Mambo Kings Play Songs of Love" by Oscar Hijuelos. **100m/C VHS, LV, 8mm.** Armand Assante, Antonio Banderas, Cathy Moriarty, Maruschka Detmers, Desi Arnaz Jr., Celia Cruz, Roscoe Lee Browne, Vondie Curtis-Hall, Tito Puente, Talisa Soto; ***D:*** Arne Glimcher; ***W:*** Cynthia Cidre; ***C:*** Michael Ballhaus; ***M:*** Robert Kraft, Carlos Franzetti. Nominations: Academy Awards '92: Best Song ("Beautiful Maria of My Soul"). *WAR, FCT, MVD*

Mame **1974 (PG)** In an adaptation of the Broadway musical "Auntie Mame" by Jerry Herman, Ball plays a dynamic woman who takes it upon herself to teach a group of eccentrics how to live life to the fullest. Arthur plays Mame's friend just as splendidly as she did in the Broadway version, but Ball in her last feature film is a lame Mame. Overly ambitious production avoids reaching goal. ♫Mame; We Need a Little Christmas; If He Walked Into My Life; Bosom Buddies; It's Today; Loving You; My Best Girl; What Do I Do Now? (Gooch's Sont); Open a New Window. **132m/C VHS, Beta, LV.** Lucille Ball, Beatrice Arthur, Robert Preston, Joyce Van Patten, Bruce Davison; ***D:*** Gene Saks. *WAR, MVD*

Mamele ½ *Little Mother* **1938** Picon prematurely becomes the "mother" of her seven siblings when their mother dies. Quintessential Yiddish musical with the usual shimmering performance from Picon. In Yiddish with English subtitles. **95m/B VHS, Beta.** *PL* Molly Picon, Max Bozyk, Edmund Zayenda; ***D:*** Joseph Green. *ERG, INJ, TPV*

Mamma Roma ½ **1962** Pasolini's second film is a heartbreaking story of family ties, escaping the past, and dreams of the future. The title character (Magnani) is a former prostitute who attempts respectability for herself and her teenaged son (Garofolo). But her ex-pimp (Citti) threatens her new life and Rome's big-city temptations prove to be a pathway to crime and tragedy for the boy. Magnani gives one of her finest performances. Italian with subtitles. **110m/B VHS.** *IT* Anna Magnani, Ettore Garofolo, Franco Citti, Silvana Corsini, Luisa Loiano; ***D:*** Pier Paolo Pasolini; ***W:*** Pier Paolo Pasolini; ***C:*** Tonino Delli Colli. *MFI*

A Man, a Woman, and a Bank ½ **1979 (PG)** Two con-men plan to rob a bank by posing as workers during the bank's construction. An advertising agency woman snaps their picture for a billboard to show how nice the builders have been, then becomes romantically involved with one of the would-be thieves. Nice performances, but wacky touches aren't plentiful enough or well-timed to sustain comedy. Also called "A Very Big Weekend." **100m/C VHS, Beta.** *CA* Donald Sutherland, Brooke Adams, Paul Mazursky; ***D:*** Noel Black; ***W:*** Bruce A. Evans, Raynold Gideon; ***M:*** Bill Conti. *SUE, NLC*

A Man, a Woman and a Killer ½ **19??** Unusual film within a film shows the actual making of a movie while unfolding a story of a hired killer. A joint project from the directors of the well-received "Emerald Cities" and "Chan is Missing." **75m/C VHS.** ***D:*** Rick Schmidt, Wayne Wang. *FCT*

A Man About the House ½ **1947** Two unmarried English sisters move into the Italian villa they have inherited. There, one marries the caretaker, who secretly plans to regain the property that once belonged to his family. When the newly married sister is found dead, her sibling sets out to solve the murder. **83m/B VHS.** *GB* Kieron Moore, Margaret Johnston, Dulcie Gray, Guy Middleton, Felix Aylmer; ***D:*** Leslie Arliss. *NOS, SNC*

A Man Alone **1955** Man falsely accused of robbing a stagecoach hides not alone but with comely sheriff's daughter. Milland's debut behind the camera. **96m/C VHS.** Ray Milland, Ward Bond, Mary Murphy, Raymond Burr, Lee Van Cleef; ***D:*** Ray Milland; ***C:*** Lionel Lindon. *REP*

A Man and a Woman *Un Homme et Un Femme* **1966** When a man and a woman, both widowed, meet and become interested in one another but experience difficulties in putting their past loves behind them. Intelligently handled emotional conflicts within a well-acted romantic drama, acclaimed for excellent visual detail. Remade in 1977 as "Another Man, Another Chance." Followed in 1986 with "A Man and A Woman: 20 Years Later." Dubbed. **102m/C VHS, Beta.** *FR* Anouk Aimee, Jean-Louis Trintignant, Pierre Barouh, Valerie Lagrange; ***D:*** Claude Lelouch; ***W:*** Claude Lelouch. Academy Awards '66: Best Foreign Language Film, Best Original Screenplay; British Academy Awards '67: Best Actress (Aimee); Cannes Film Festival '66: Best Film; Golden Globe Awards '67: Best Actress—Drama (Aimee), Best Foreign Film; Nominations: Academy Awards '66: Best Actress (Aimee), Best Director (Lelouch). *WAR, APD, INJ*

A Man and a Woman: 20 Years Later ½ *Un Homme Et Une Femme: Vingt Ans Deja* **1986 (PG)** Slouchy sequel to the highly praised "A Man and a Woman" that catches up with a couple after a long separation. The sad romantic complications of the original are more mundane in this sequel, which is burdened by a film-within-a-film script as well as shots from the original. In French with English subtitles. **112m/C VHS, Beta.** *FR* Jean-Louis Trintignant, Anouk Aimee, Richard Berry; ***D:*** Claude Lelouch; ***W:*** Claude Lelouch. *WAR, INJ*

Man & Boy *Ride a Dark Horse* **1971 (G)** A black Civil War veteran, played by Bill Cosby, encounters bigotry and prejudice when he tries to set up a homestead in Arizona. An acceptable family film, some might be disappointed that Cosby is not playing this one for laughs. **98m/C VHS, Beta.** Bill Cosby, Gloria Foster, George Spell, Henry Silva, Yaphet Kotto; ***D:*** E.W. Swackhamer; ***M:*** Quincy Jones. *COL*

The Man and the Monster ½ **1965** When a concert pianist sells his soul to the devil, he fails to realize that part of the deal has him turning into a hideous beast every time he hears a certain piece of music. Maybe it was "Stairway to Heaven." **78m/B VHS.** *MX* Enrique Rambal, Abel Salazar, Martha Roth; ***D:*** Rafael Baledon. *SNC*

Man Bait ½ *The Last Page* **1952** A complex web of intrigue and mystery surrounds a blackmailed book dealer when he allows a blonde woman to catch his eye. A competently made film. **78m/B VHS, Beta, LV.** *GB* George Brent, Marguerite Chapman, Diana Dors; ***D:*** Terence Fisher. *RXM, MLB*

Man Beast **1955** The abominable snowman is sought and found in this grade-Z '50s monster movie. **65m/B VHS, Beta.** Rock Madison, Virginia Maynor, George Skaff, Lloyd Nelson, Tom Maruzzi; ***D:*** Jerry Warren. *NOS, MRV, RHI*

Man Bites Dog **1991 (NC-17)** A pseudo-documentary about a serial killer, filled with ever-mounting violence. Ben is the killer being followed by a two-man camera/sound crew (which he's hired), who record his casual carnage without lifting a finger to stop him. Indeed his continued killing and robbing is to pay for financing the documentary about himself. This satire on film violence, as well as reality-based television shows, is both appalling and humorous in a sick way. In French with English subtitles. Also available in an unrated edited version. **95m/B VHS.** *BE* Benoit Poelvoorde, Remy Belvaux, Andre Bonzel; ***D:*** Benoit Poelvoorde, Remy Belvaux, Andre Bonzel; ***W:*** Benoit Poelvoorde, Remy Belvaux, Andre Bonzel, Vincent Tavier. *FXL, FCT*

A Man Called Adam ½ **1966** A jazz musician is tortured by prejudice and the guilt created by his having accidentally killed his wife and baby years before. Davis is appropriately haunted, but the film is poorly produced. **103m/B VHS, Beta.** Sammy Davis Jr., Louis Armstrong, Ossie Davis, Cicely Tyson, Frank Sinatra Jr., Lola Falana, Mel Torme, Peter Lawford; ***D:*** Leonard Penn; ***C:*** Jack Priestley. *COL, NLC*

A Man Called Horse **1970 (PG)** After a wealthy Britisher is captured and tortured by the Sioux Indians in the Dakotas, he abandons his formal ways and discovers his own strength. As he passes their torture tests, he is embraced by the tribe. In this very realistic and gripping portrayal of American Indian life, Harris provides a strong performance. Sequelled by "Return of a Man Called Horse" (1976) and "Triumphs of a Man Called Horse" (1983). **114m/C VHS, Beta, LV.** Richard Harris, Judith Anderson, Jean Gascon, Stanford Howard, Manu Tupou, Dub Taylor; ***D:*** Elliot Silverstein; ***W:*** Jack DeWitt; ***C:*** Robert B. Hauser. *FOX*

A Man Called Peter **1955** A biographical epic about Peter Marshall, a Scottish chaplain who served the U.S. Senate. Todd does his subject justice by sensitively showing all that was human in Marshall, and a talented supporting cast makes for a thoroughly watchable film. **119m/C VHS, Beta.** Richard Todd, Jean Peters, Marjorie Rambeau, Jill Esmond, Les Tremayne, Robert Burton; ***D:*** Henry Koster. Nominations: Academy Awards '55: Best Color Cinematography. *FOX*

A Man Called Rage *Woof!* **1984** Rage is the only man capable of safely escorting a group of pioneers through a nuclear wasteland infested with mutants and cannibals. **90m/C VHS, Beta.** *IT* Stelio Candelli, Conrad Nichols; ***D:*** Anthony Richmond. *LIV*

A Man Called Sarge 🦴½ **1990 (PG-13)** Sophomoric comedy about a daffy WWII sergeant leading his squad against the Germans at Tobruk. **88m/C VHS, Beta, LV.** Gary Kroeger, Marc Singer, Gretchen German, Jennifer Runyon; ***D:*** Stuart Gillard. *WAR, OM*

A Man Called Sledge 🦴🦴 **1971** Garner fans might be surprised to see the star play a villain in this violent story of a gang of outlaws who wind up fighting each over a cache of gold. This is mainstream Western entertainment. **93m/C VHS.** James Garner, Dennis Weaver, Claude Akins, John Marley, Laura Antonelli; ***D:*** Vic Morrow. *COL, GKK*

A Man Escaped 🦴🦴🦴½ *Un Condamne a Mort s'est Echappe; The Wind Bloweth Where it Listeth* **1957** There's an excruciating realism about Bresson's account of a WWII Resistance fighter's escape from a Nazi prison just before he was to be executed by the Gestapo. It's the sounds and lingering camera shots, not the wham bam variety of action, that create and sustain the film's suspense. Bresson, who had been a Nazi prisoner, solicited the supervision of Andre Devigny, whose true story the film tells. Contributing to the realistic feel was the use of non professional actors. An award-wiining film that fellow director Truffaut lauded as the most crucial French film of the previous ten years. In French with English subtitles. **102m/B VHS.** Francois Leterrier; ***D:*** Robert Bresson. Cannes Film Festival '57: Best Director (Bresson); National Board of Review Awards '57: 5 Best Foreign Films of the Year. *INJ, NYF*

Man Facing Southeast 🦴🦴🦴½ *Hombre Mirando Al Sudeste; Man Looking Southeast* **1986 (R)** The acclaimed Argentinean film about the sudden appearance of a strange man in an asylum who claims to be an extraterrestrial, and a psychologist's attempts to discover his true identity. The sense of mystery intensifies when the new patient indeed seems to have some remarkable powers. Although the pace at times lags, the story intriguingly keeps one guessing about the stranger right to the end. In Spanish, with English subtitles. **105m/C VHS, Beta, LV.** *AR* Lorenzo Quinteros, Hugo Soto, Ines Vernengo; ***D:*** Eliseo Subiela; ***M:*** Pedro Aznar. *VTR, NWV, IME*

A Man for All Seasons 🦴🦴🦴🦴 **1966 (G)** Sterling, heavily Oscar-honored biographical drama concerning the life and subsequent martyrdom of 16th-century Chancellor of England, Sir Thomas More (Scofield). Story revolves around his personal conflict when King Henry VIII (Shaw) seeks a divorce from his wife, Catherine of Aragon, so he can wed his mistress, Anne Boleyn—events that ultimately lead the King to bolt from the Pope and declare himself head of the Church of England. Remade for television in 1988 with Charlton Heston in the lead role. **120m/C VHS, Beta, LV.** *GB* Paul Scofield, Robert Shaw, Orson Welles, Wendy Hiller, Susannah York, John Hurt, Nigel Davenport, Vanessa Redgrave; ***D:*** Fred Zinnemann; ***W:*** Constance Willis, Robert Bolt; ***C:*** Ted Moore; ***M:*** Georges Delerue. Academy Awards '66: Best Actor (Scofield), Best Adapted Screenplay, Best Color Cinematography, Best Costume Design (Color), Best Director (Zinnemann), Best Picture; British Academy Awards '67: Best Actor (Scofield), Best Film, Best Screenplay; Directors Guild of America Awards '66: Best Director (Zinnemann); Golden Globe Awards '67: Best Actor—Drama (Scofield), Best Director (Zinnemann), Best Film—Drama, Best Screenplay; National Board of Review Awards '66: 10 Best Films of the Year, Best Actor (Scofield), Best Director (Zinnemann), Best Supporting Actor (Shaw); Nominations: Academy Awards '66: Best Supporting Actor (Shaw), Best Supporting Actress (Hiller). *COL, BTV, TVC*

A Man for All Seasons 🦴🦴🦴 **1988** Fresh from the London stage, Heston directs and stars in this version of Robert Bolt's play depicting the conflict between Henry VIII and his chief advisor, Sir Thomas More. Strong supporting cast. Made for cable TV. **150m/C VHS, LV.** Charlton Heston, Vanessa Redgrave, John Gielgud, Richard Johnson, Roy Kinnear, Martin Chamberlain; ***D:*** Charlton Heston. *TTC*

Man Friday 🦴🦴 **1975 (PG)** Stranded on a deserted island, a man forces a native from a neighboring island to be his slave. Based on the classic story "Robinson Crusoe" by Daniel Defoe, this adaptation charts the often-brutal treatment the native receives as his captor tries to civilize him. Through his intelligence, the enslaved man regains his freedom and returns home with his former captor, who then seeks acceptance from the native's tribe. A sometimes confusing story line and excessive blood and guts detract from this message-laden effort. **115m/C VHS.** *GB* Peter O'Toole, Richard Roundtree, Peter Cellier, Christopher Cabot, Joel Fluellen; ***D:*** Jack Gold; ***M:*** Carl Davis. Nominations: Cannes Film Festival '75: Best Film. *FOX*

The Man from Atlantis 🦴🦴 **1977** Patrick Duffy stars as the water-breathing alien who emerges from his undersea home, the Lost City of Atlantis. The made-for-TV movie led to a brief television series. **60m/C VHS, Beta.** Patrick Duffy, Belinda J. Montgomery, Victor Buono; ***D:*** Lee H. Katzin. *WOV*

The Man from Beyond 🦴🦴½ **1922** Frozen alive, a man returns 100 years later to try and find his lost love. Silent. **50m/B VHS, Beta.** Harry Houdini, Arthur Maude, Nita Naldi; ***D:*** Burton King. *SNC, VYY, DVT*

Man from Button Willow 🦴🦴 **1965 (G)** Classic animated adventure is the story of Justin Eagle, a man who leads a double life. He is a respected rancher and a shrewd secret agent for the government, but in 1869 he suddenly finds himself the guardian of a four-year-old Oriental girl, leading him into a whole new series of adventures. Strictly for younger audiences. **79m/C VHS, Beta.** ***M:*** George Bruns; ***V:*** Dale Robertson, Edgar Buchanan, Barbara Jean Wong, Howard Keel. *NO*

Man from Cairo 🦴🦴 **1954** An American in Algiers is mistaken for a detective in search of gold lost during WWII and decides to play along. **82m/B VHS, Beta, LV.** *IT* George Raft, Gianna Maria Canale; ***D:*** Ray Enright. *NO*

Man from Cheyenne 🦴 **1942** Cowboy comes home to find his town under a siege of terror from a lawless gang of cattle rustlers. He gets mad and seeks some frontier justice. **54m/B VHS, Beta.** Roy Rogers, Gale Storm, George "Gabby" Hayes, Sally Payne. *NOS, DVT, RXM*

Man from Colorado 🦴🦴½ **1949** An odd Technicolor western about two Civil War vets at odds, one an honest marshall, the other a sadistic judge. Solid Western fare with a quirky performance by Ford. **99m/C VHS, Beta.** William Holden, Glenn Ford, Ellen Drew, Ray Collins, Edgar Buchanan, Jerome Courtland, James Millican, Jim Bannon; ***D:*** Henry Levin; ***M:*** George Duning. *COL*

Man from Deep River *Woof!* **1977 (R)** A photographer is captured by a savage tribe in Thailand and forced to undergo a series of grueling initiation rites. Full of very violent and sickening tortures inflicted on both human and animal victims. **90m/C VHS, Beta.** *IT* Ivan Rassimov; ***D:*** Umberto Lenzi. *NO*

The Man from Gun Town 🦴½ **1936** McCoy comes to the rescue of a woman who has been framed by an evil gang for the murder of her brother. **58m/B VHS.** Tim McCoy, Billie Seward, Rex Lease, Jack Clifford, Wheeler Oakman, Bob McKenzie; ***D:*** Ford Beebe. *NOS, DVT*

Man from Headquarters 🦴🦴 **1928** Good silent mystery in which a U.S. agent takes on a gang of foreign operatives. **?m/B VHS.** Cornelius Keefe, Edith Roberts. *SNC*

The Man from Hell 🦴 **1934** Sheriff Russell goes undercover to expose the head of a gang of outlaws. Low-budget fare. **55m/B VHS.** Reb Russell, Fred Kohler Jr., Ann Darcy, George "Gabby" Hayes, Jack Rockwell, Charles French, Charles "Slim" Whitaker, Yakima Canutt; ***D:*** Lewis D. Collins. *DVT, HEG, GPV*

Man from Hell's Edges 🦴½ **1932** An innocent cowpoke escapes from jail and brings the real baddy to justice. **63m/B VHS, Beta.** Bob Steele, Nancy Drexel, Julian Rivero, Robert E. Homans, George "Gabby" Hayes; ***D:*** Robert North Bradbury. *NOS, DVT*

The Man from Laramie 🦴🦴🦴½ **1955** A ranch baron who is going blind worries about which of his two sons he will leave the ranch to. Into this tension-filled familial atmosphere rides Stewart, a cow-herder obsessed with hunting down the men who sold guns to the Indians that killed his brother. Needless to say, the tension increases. Tough, surprisingly brutal western, the best of the classic Stewart-Mann films. **104m/C VHS, Beta.** James Stewart, Arthur Kennedy, Donald Crisp, Alex Nicol, Cathy O'Donnell, Aline MacMahon, Wallace Ford, Jack Elam; ***D:*** Anthony Mann; ***W:*** Philip Yordan; ***C:*** Charles B(ryant) Lang. *COL*

The Man from Left Field 🦴½ **1993** Homeless man winds up coaching a little league baseball team, inspiring the kids, and turning his life around. Made for TV. **96m/C VHS.** Burt Reynolds, Reba McEntire; ***D:*** Burt Reynolds; ***M:*** Bobby Goldsboro. *CAF*

Man from Montana 🦴½ *Montana Justice* **1941** Brown is a sheriff who battles outlaws trying to stir up trouble between ranchers and homesteaders. **56m/B VHS.** Johnny Mack Brown, Fuzzy Knight, William Gould, Kermit Maynard, Nell O'Day, Billy Lenhart, Kenneth Brown, Murdock McQuarrie, Ray Taylor. *GPV*

Man from Monterey 🦴🦴 **1933** South-of-the-border Western has U.S. Army captain Wayne trying to get Mexican landowners to register their property under Spanish land grants or lose them to public domain. Wayne's last series western for Warner Bros. **59m/B VHS.** John Wayne, Ruth Hall, Luis Alberni, Francis Ford, Lafe McKee, Lillian Leighton, Charles "Slim" Whitaker; ***D:*** Mack V. Wright; ***W:*** Lesley Mason. *MGM*

The Man from Music Mountain 🦴🦴 **1938** Worthless mining stock is sold in a desert mining town, but Gene and Smiley clear that up, with a little singing as well. **54m/B VHS, Beta.** Gene Autry, Smiley Burnette, Carol Hughes, Polly Jenkins. *NOS, VDM, HHT*

Man from Nowhere 🦴🦴½ **1937** A henpecked man gets the break of his life when his domineering wife and mother-in-law believe he's dead. Based on the novel by Luigi Pirandello. In French with English subtitles. **98m/B VHS, Beta.** *FR* Pierre Blanchar, Ginette LeClerc; ***D:*** Pierre Chenal. *FCT, AUD*

The Man from Painted Post 🦴 **1917** Fairbanks plays a Cattlemen's Association detective who comes to the range to stop the cattle rustlers as well as to find the man who murdered his sister. **?m/B VHS.** Douglas Fairbanks Sr., Eileen Percy, Frank Campeau, Monte Blue; ***D:*** Joseph Henabery. *GVV*

The Man from Snowy River 🦴🦴½ **1982 (PG)** Stunning cinematography highlights this otherwise fairly ordinary adventure story set in 1880's Australia. A young man comes of age in the outback while taming a herd of wild horses. In a dual role, Douglas portrays battling brothers, one a rich landowner and the other a one-legged prospector. Based on the epic poem by A.B. "Banjo" Paterson and followed by "Return to Snowy River Part II." A big hit in Australia and not directed by "Mad Max's" Miller, but another Miller named George. **104m/C VHS, Beta, LV.** *AU* Kirk Douglas, Tom Burlinson, Sigrid Thornton, Terence Donovan, Tommy Dysart, Jack Thompson, Bruce Kerr; ***D:*** George Miller. *FOX, TVC, HMV*

Man from Texas 🦴🦴 **1939** Singing and gun-slinging Tex defends a kid accused of horse thieving until the kid turns bad and Tex must bring him in. **55m/B VHS, Beta.** Tex Ritter, Hal Price, Charles B. Wood, Vic Demourelle Sr.; ***D:*** Al(bert) Herman. *NOS, VDM*

Man from the Alamo ⅋⅋⅋ **1953** A soldier sent from the Alamo during its last hours to get help is branded as a deserter, and struggles to clear his name. Well acted, this film will satisfy those with a taste for action. **79m/C VHS.** Glenn Ford, Julie Adams, Chill Wills, Victor Jory, Hugh O'Brian; ***D:*** Budd Boetticher. *MCA*

The Man from the Pru ⅋⅋½ **1989** Shocking 1931 murder case follows insurance agent William Wallace (Pryce) who was sentenced to hang for the murder of his wife, Julia. Wallace insisted he was called from home on a possible insurance sale and returned home to find his wife dead. His case made British legal history when the appeals court overturned the verdict. Made for TV. **90m/C VHS.** *GB* Jonathan Pryce, Anna Massey, Susannah York; ***D:*** Rob Rohrer. *TVC, AAE*

Man from Thunder River ⅋⅋ **1943** A group of cowboys uncover a plot to steal gold ore and wind up saving a young girl's life in the process. Standard western with lots of action. **55m/B VHS, Beta.** Wild Bill Elliott, George "Gabby" Hayes, Anne Jeffreys, Ian Keith, John James; ***D:*** John English. *DVT*

The Man from U.N.C.L.E. **1964** Vaughn and McCallum star as Napoleon Solo and Illya Kuryakin, two super-cool super-agents battling the evil forces of THRUSH. The series ran from 1964-1968. Two epsidoes per tape; additional episodes available. On this tape: "The Project Strigas Affair" has Solo and Illya against a Balkan intelligence agent. In "The Never Never Affair" an innocent translator is captured by a ruthless THRUSH operator who's after some valuable microfilm. **110m/B VHS, Beta.** Robert Vaughn, David McCallum, Leo G. Carroll, Leonard Nimoy, William Shatner, Barbara Feldon, Cesar Romero. *MGM, MOV*

Man from Utah ⅋½ **1934** The Duke tangles with the crooked sponsor of some rodeo events who has killed several of the participants. Also available with "Blue Steel" on laserdisc. **55m/B VHS, Beta, LV.** John Wayne, George "Gabby" Hayes, Polly Ann Young, Yakima Canutt, Lafe McKee; ***D:*** Robert North Bradbury. *COL, NOS, MRV*

The Man I Love ⅋⅋⅋ **1946** Slick drama about nightclub singer Lupino falling for no-good mobster Alda. Enjoyable and well-acted, although script doesn't make sense. Great selection of tunes. This film inspired Scorsese's "New York, New York." Based on the novel "Night Shift" by Maritta Wolff. ♫Body and Soul; Why Was I Born; Bill; The Man I Love; Liza; If I Could Be With You. **96m/B VHS.** Ida Lupino, Robert Alda, Andrea King, Martha Vickers, Bruce (Herman Brix) Bennett, Alan Hale, Dolores Moran, John Ridgely, Don McGuire, Warren Douglas, Craig Stevens; ***D:*** Raoul Walsh, John Maxwell; ***W:*** Catherine Turney, Jo Pagano; ***M:*** Max Steiner. *MGM, FCT*

The Man in Grey ⅋⅋⅋ **1945** In a story of romantic intrigue set in nineteenth-century England, a Marquis's wife is betrayed by her vile husband and the schoolmate she once befriended who has an affair with him. Stunning costumes and fine performances compensate for the overly extravagant production values in a work that helped bring stardom to Mason. **116m/B VHS, Beta.** *GB* James Mason, Margaret Lockwood, Stewart Granger, Phyllis Calvert; ***D:*** Leslie Arliss. *NO*

A Man in Love ⅋⅋⅋ *Un Homme Amoureux* **1987 (R)** An international romantic melodrama set during the Italian filming of a biography of suicidal author Cesar Pavese. The self-important lead actor and a beautiful supporting actress (Coyote and Scacchi) become immersed in the roles and fall madly in love, oblivious to the fact that Coyote is married and Scacchi's engaged. The two make a steamy pair, to the detriment of friends, family, and the movie they're making. Kurys' first English-language film is visually appealing with a lush, romantic score, seamlessly weaving the story lines among vivid characters. **110m/C VHS, Beta, LV.** *FR* Peter Coyote, Greta Scacchi, Jamie Lee Curtis, Peter Riegert, Jean Pigozzi, John Berry, Claudia Cardinale, Vincent Lindon; ***D:*** Diane Kurys; ***W:*** Diane Kurys, Oliver Schatzky, Israel Horovitz; ***M:*** Georges Delerue. *COL, SUE*

The Man in the Attic ⅋½ **1994 (R)** Harris certainly leaves his "Doogie Howser" past behind as he takes a grownup turn in an erotic thriller based on a true case history from the early 20th century, gathered from the book "Sex and the Criminal Mind." Teenaged Edward (Harris) has a blazing affair with married, mature Krista (Archer), who does indeed hide her young lover in the family attic when her clueless husband (Cariou) returns home at night. But such consuming passion can hardly be kept a secret for long—and takes a decidedly deadly turn. Made for cable. **97m/C VHS, Beta.** Anne Archer, Neil Patrick Harris, Len Cariou, Alex Carter; ***D:*** Graeme Campbell; ***W:*** Duane Poole, Tom Swale; ***M:*** Lou Natale. *PAR*

The Man in the Glass Booth ⅋⅋⅋ **1975 (PG)** In this adaptation of a play written by actor Robert Shaw, a successful Jewish businessman is suspected of being a Nazi war criminal. Loosely based on the life of death camp commandant Otto Adolf Eichmann, the film depicts the arrest and subsequent trial of the former Nazi by the Israelis. The film's title is derived from the fact that Eichmann sat in a glass booth during his trial. Schell's performance is outstanding. **117m/C VHS.** Maximilian Schell, Lois Nettleton, Luther Adler, Lawrence Pressman, Henry Brown, Richard Rasof; ***D:*** Arthur Hiller; ***W:*** Edward Anhalt; ***C:*** Sam Leavitt. Nominations: Academy Awards '75: Best Actor (Schell). *NO*

The Man in the Gray Flannel Suit ⅋⅋½ **1956** A very long and serious adaptation of the Sloan Wilson novel about a Madison Avenue advertising exec trying to balance his life between work and family. The Hollywood treatment falls short of the adaptation potential of the original story. **152m/C VHS, Beta, LV.** Gregory Peck, Fredric March, Jennifer Jones, Ann Harding, Arthur O'Connell, Henry Daniell, Lee J. Cobb, Marisa Pavan, Gene Lockhart, Keenan Wynn, Gigi Perreau, Joseph Sweeney, Kenneth Tobey, DeForest Kelley; ***D:*** Nunnally Johnson. *FOX*

The Man in the Iron Mask ⅋⅋⅋ **1939** Swashbuckling tale about twin brothers separated at birth. One turns out to be King Louis XIV of France, and the other a carefree wanderer and friend of the Three Musketeers. Their eventual clash leads to action-packed adventure and royal revenge. Remake of the "The Iron Mask" (1929) with Douglas Fairbanks. Remade for television in 1977 with Richard Chamberlain. **110m/B VHS, Beta.** Louis Hayward, Alan Hale, Joan Bennett, Warren William, Joseph Schildkraut, Walter Kingsford, Marion Martin; ***D:*** James Whale. Nominations: Academy Awards '39: Best Original Score. *CCB, MED*

The Man in the Iron Mask ⅋⅋⅋ **1977** A tyrannical French king kidnaps his twin brother and imprisons him on a remote island. Chamberlain, the king of the miniseries, is excellent in a dual role in this big production swashbuckler. Adapted from the Dumas classic. Made for television. **105m/C VHS, Beta.** Richard Chamberlain, Patrick McGoohan, Louis Jourdan, Jenny Agutter, Ian Holm, Ralph Richardson; ***D:*** Mike Newell. *LIV, FUS, FOX*

The Man in the Mist **1983** Private investigators Tommy and Tuppence Beresford find themselves trying to solve a murder while on vacation in a provincial hotel. Made for British television and based upon the Agatha Christie story. **51m/C VHS, Beta.** *GB* Francesca Annis, James Warwick. *TPV*

The Man in the Moon ⅋⅋⅋½ **1991 (PG-13)** Beautifully rendered coming-of-age tale. On a farm outside a small Louisiana town in the 1950s, 14 year-old Dani wonders if she will ever be as pretty and popular as her 17 year-old sister Maureen. This becomes especially important as Dani is beginning to notice boys, particularly Court, the 17 year-old young man she meets when swimming. Although Dani and Maureen have always been especially close a rift develops between the sisters after Court meets Maureen. Intelligently written, excellent direction, lovely cinematography, and exceptional acting make this a particularly worthwhile and entertaining film. **100m/C VHS.** Reese Witherspoon, Emily Warfield, Jason London, Tess Harper, Sam Waterston, Gail Strickland; ***D:*** Robert Mulligan. *MGM*

The Man in the Raincoat ⅋⅋ **1957** French film about a bumbling clarinet player who is erroneously tracked down as a murderer. Strenuous efforts to evoke laughter usually fail. Dubbed. **97m/B VHS, Beta, 8mm.** *FR* Fernandel, John McGiver, Bernard Blier; ***D:*** Julien Duvivier. *VYY*

Man in the Saddle ⅋⅋½ *The Outcast* **1951** Western star Scott gets roped in a romantic triangle out on the range, leading to some exciting gunplay. As usual, justice triumphs in this above average oater. Based on the novel by Ernest Haycox. **87m/C VHS.** Randolph Scott, Joan Leslie, Ellen Drew, Alexander Knox, Richard Rober, John Russell; ***D:*** Andre de Toth; ***W:*** Kenneth Gamet. *COL*

The Man in the Santa Claus Suit ⅋⅋ **1979** A costume shop owner has an effect on three people who rent Santa Claus costumes from him. Astaire plays seven different roles in this made for television film. Average holiday feel-good movie. **96m/C VHS, Beta.** Fred Astaire, Gary Burghoff, John Byner, Nanette Fabray, Bert Convy; ***D:*** Corey Allen. *MED*

Man in the Silk Hat ⅋⅋ **1915** A collection of the nearly-forgotten French comic's early silent comedy shorts, made in France before his resettlement in America. **96m/B VHS, Beta.** *FR* Max Linder; ***D:*** Maud Linder. *INJ*

Man in the Silk Hat ⅋⅋⅋ **1983** Gabriel-Maximilien Leuvielle, known in films as Max Linder, is now credited with developing the style of silent-movie slapstick comedy that Mack Sennett, Charlie Chaplin, and others became more famous for in their time. Here, Linder's daughter has done a fine job writing and directing a film full of historic footage of her father's work. **99m/B VHS, Beta.** Mack Sennett, Buster Keaton, Charlie Chaplin, Max Linder. *XVC, MED*

The Man in the White Suit ⅋⅋⅋½ **1951** A humble laboratory assistant in a textile mill invents a white cloth that won't stain, tear, or wear out, and can't be dyed. The panicked garment industry sets out to destroy him and the fabric, resulting in some sublimely comic situations and a variety of inventive chases. Also available with "Lavender Hill Mob" on Laser Disc. **82m/B VHS, Beta.** *GB* Alec Guinness, Joan Greenwood; ***D:*** Alexander MacKendrick. National Board of Review Awards '52: 10 Best Films of the Year; Nominations: Academy Awards '52: Best Screenplay. *REP, HMV*

Man in the Wilderness ⅋⅋½ **1971 (PG)** Harris is part of an expedition traveling through the Northwest Territory. He's mauled by a grizzly and left for dead by leader Huston. While Harris fights for survival, he also plots revenge. Blood and violence is somewhat offset by good lead performances. **108m/C VHS.** Richard Harris, John Huston, Henry Wilcoxon, Percy Herbert, Dennis Waterman, Prunella Ransome, Norman Rossington, James Doohan; ***D:*** Richard Sarafian; ***W:*** Jack DeWitt; ***M:*** Johnny Harris. *WAR*

A Man in Uniform ⅋⅋ *I Love a Man in Uniform* **1993 (R)** A look at the making of a sociopath. Henry (McCamus) is a quiet bank employee who moonlights as an actor. Then he gets his big break in the role of a self-righteous cop in a TV series. Only the lines between his make-believe cop and the real world begin to blur and Henry's intensity turns to violence. Fine performances lead to an unsatisfying film conclusion. **99m/C VHS.** *CA* Tom McCamus, Brigitte Bako, Kevin Tighe, David Hemblen, Alex Karzis, Graham McPherson; ***D:*** David Wellington; ***W:*** David Wellington. Genie Awards '93: Best Actor (McCamus), Best Supporting Actor (Tighe). *APX*

The Man Inside ⅋½ **1976** Undercover agent infiltrates a powerful underworld narcotics ring and finds his honesty tested when $2 million is at stake. **96m/C VHS, Beta.** *CA* James Franciscus, Stefanie Powers, Jacques Godin; ***D:*** Gerald Mayer. *TWE*

The Man Inside 1990 (PG) Lukewarm Cold War saga based on the true story of Gunther Wallraff, a West German journalist who risked all to expose the corruption behind a large European newspaper. **93m/C VHS, LV.** *NL GE* Juergen Prochnow, Peter Coyote, Nathalie Baye, Dieter Laser, Monique Van De Ven, Sylvie Granotier; ***D:*** Bobby Roth; ***W:*** Bobby Roth. *COL*

Man Is Not a Bird ½ 1965 Follows the destructive love of a factory engineer and a hairdresser in a small Yugoslavian mining town. In Serbian with English subtitles. **80m/B VHS, Beta.** *YU* Eva Ras, Milena Dravic, Janez Urhovec; ***D:*** Dusan Makavejev; ***W:*** Dusan Makavejev. *FCT*

A Man Like Eva *Ein Mann wie Eva* 1983 A weird, morbid homage to and portrait of Rainer Werner Fassbinder after his inevitable death, detailing his work-obsessed self-destruction. Mattes, one of Fassbinder's favorite actresses, plays him in drag, in an eerie gender-crossing transformation. In German with English subtitles. **92m/C VHS, Beta.** *GE* Eva Mattes, Elisabeth Kreuzer, Charles Regnier, Werner Stocker; ***D:*** Radu Gabrea. *FCT, APD, GLV*

Man Made Monster ½ 1941 Chaney stars as carnival performer "Dynamo" Dan McCormick, whose act has caused Dan to build up an immunity to electrical charges. Dan falls prey to the mad Dr. Rigas (Atwill) who seeks to create a race of electro-men who'll do his bidding. Experiments on the hapless Dan turn him into a glowing monster whose very touch can kill. Chaney's first role in the horror genre led to Universal's casting him in "The Wolf Man" and "The Ghost of Frankenstein." **61m/B VHS.** Lon Chaney Jr., Lionel Atwill, Anne Nagel, Frank Albertson, Samuel S. Hinds; ***D:*** George Waggner; ***W:*** Joseph West. *MCA*

Man of a Thousand Faces ½ 1957 A tasteful and touching portrayal of Lon Chaney, from his childhood with his deaf and mute parents to his success as a screen star. Recreates some of Chaney's most famous roles, including the Phantom of the Opera and Quasimodo in "Notre Dame." Cagney is magnificent as the long-suffering film star who was a genius with makeup and mime. **122m/B VHS, LV.** James Cagney, Dorothy Malone, Jane Greer, Marjorie Rambeau, Jim Backus, Roger Smith, Robert Evans; ***D:*** Joseph Pevney; ***W:*** Ivan Goff; ***C:*** Russell Metty. Nominations: Academy Awards '57: Best Story & Screenplay. *MCA*

Man of Action ½ 1933 Texas Ranger McCoy is out to solve the mystery of what happened to money, recovered from a robbery, which has vanished once again. **56m/B VHS.** Tim McCoy, Wheeler Oakman, Walter Brennan, Stanley Blystone, Charles French; ***D:*** George Melford. *GPV*

Man of Aran 1934 Celebrated account of a fisherman's struggle for survival on a barren island near the west coast of Ireland, featuring amateur actors. Three years in the making, it's the last word in man against nature cinema, and a visual marvel. A former explorer, Flaherty became an influential documentarian. Having first gained fame with "Nanook of the North," he compiled an opus of documentaries made for commercial release. **132m/B VHS.** ***D:*** Robert Flaherty. *HMV, GVV*

Man of Destiny ½ 1973 Bonaparte (Keach) and a mysterious woman battle good-humoredly over a collection of love letters. From a Bernard Shaw story. Charming and well-acted. **60m/C VHS, Beta.** Stacy Keach, Samantha Eggar. *NO*

Man of Evil *Fanny by Gaslight* 1948 The hard times of the illegitimate daughter of a member of the British Parliament in the early 1900s, told with an astonishing number of plot twists and a plodding melodramtic style. Based on the novel "Fanny by Gaslight." **108m/B VHS.** *GB* Phyllis Calvert, James Mason, Wilfred Lawson, Stewart Granger, Margaretta Scott, Jean Kent, John Laurie, Stuart Lindsell, Nora Swinburne, Amy Veness, Ann Wilton, Helen Haye, Cathleen Nesbitt, Guy le Feuvre, John Turnbull, Peter Jones; ***D:*** Anthony Asquith. *FCT*

Man of Flowers ½ 1984 Because of his puritan upbringing, a reclusive art collector has trouble coping with his feelings of sexuality. He pays a woman to disrobe in front of him, but is never able to bring himself to see her naked. A moody piece with overtones of black humor, this work has limited audience appeal. **91m/C VHS, Beta, LV.** *AU* Norman Kaye, Alyson Best, Chris Haywood, Sarah Walker, Julia Blake, Bob Ellis, Werner Herzog; ***D:*** Paul Cox; ***W:*** Bob Ellis, Paul Cox. Australian Film Institute '83: Best Actor (Kaye). *LIV, VES*

Man of Iron *Czlowiek z Zelaza* 1981 (PG) Director Wajda's follow-up to "Man of Marble" deals with a reporter (Odania) who is expected to tow the government line when writing about the Gdansk shipyard strike of 1980. He meets the harassed laborer son (Radziwilowicz) of worker-hero Birkut, against whom Odania is expected to conduct a smear campaign, and finds his loyalties tested. In Polish with English subtitles. **116m/C VHS.** *PL* Jerzy Radziwilowicz, Marian Opania, Krystyna Janda; ***D:*** Andrzej Wajda; ***W:*** Aleksander Scibor-Rylski; ***M:*** Andrezej Korzynski. Cannes Film Festival '81: Best Film. *MGM*

Man of La Mancha ½ 1972 (PG) Arrested by the Inquisition and thrown into prison, Miguel de Cervantes relates the story of Don Quixote. Not nearly as good as the Broadway musical it is based on. ♫It's All the Same; The Impossible Dream; Barber's Song; Man of La Mancha; Dulcinea; I'm Only Thinking of Him; Little Bird, Little Bird; Life as It Really Is; The Dubbing. **129m/C VHS, Beta, LV.** Peter O'Toole, Sophia Loren, James Coco, Harry Andrews, John Castle, Brian Blessed; ***D:*** Arthur Hiller. National Board of Review Awards '72: 10 Best Films of the Year, Best Actor (O'Toole); Nominations: Academy Awards '72: Best Original Score. *FOX, FCT*

Man of Legend 1971 (PG) An adventure-romance filmed in Morocco; a WWI German soldier flees to the Foreign Legion and fights with nomadic rebels, ultimately falling in love with their chief's beautiful daughter. An unoriginal desert saga. **95m/C VHS, Beta.** *IT SP* Peter Strauss, Tina Aumont, Pier Paola Capponi; ***D:*** Sergio Grieco. *NO*

Man of Marble 1976 A satire on life in post-WWII Poland. A young filmmaker sets out to tell the story of a bricklayer who, because of his exceptional skill, once gained popularity with other workers. He became a champion for worker rights, only to then find himself being persecuted by the government. The conclusion was censored by the Polish government. Highly acclaimed and followed by "Man of Iron" in 1981. In Polish with English subtitles. **160m/C VHS.** *PL* Krystyna Janda, Jerzy Radziwilowicz, Tadeusz Lomnicki, Jacek Lomnicki, Krystyna Zachwatowicz; ***D:*** Andrzej Wajda; ***W:*** Aleksander Scibor-Rylski; ***M:*** Andrezej Korzynski. *NYF, FCT, INJ*

A Man of No Importance 1994 (R) Touching and entertaining saga of lovable Alfie Byrne (Finney), a 1960's Dublin bus conductor with a passion for the work of Oscar Wilde, who successfully represses his own homosexuality. He also moonlights as director of a community theatre, where he sets out to produce Wilde's controversial play "Salome" starring fetching new bus passenger Adele (Fitzgerald), who further confuses Alfie's take on his identity. Finney is both delightful and heartbreaking in this character study of an innocent soul whose life is tested by the social code of his day. Equally affecting and charming supporting performances round out this witty but sad tale. **98m/C VHS, LV.** *GB* Albert Finney, Brenda Fricker, Michael Gambon, Tara Fitzgerald, Rufus Sewell, Patrick Malahide, David Kelly; ***D:*** Suri Krishnamma; ***W:*** Barry Devlin; ***M:*** Julian Nott. *COL*

A Man of Passion 199? (R) Quinn plays an aging artist living pleasurably on a Mediterranean isle. His summer guest is his uptight grandson, a classical pianist. Naturally, Gramps is about to teach the kid to loosen up, including appreciating one of his lovely artist's models. Another variation for Quinn on his "Zorba" personality but it works. **90m/C VHS.** Anthony Quinn, Ramon Sheen, Maud Adams, Elizabeth Ashley, R.J. Williams, Ray Walston, Victoria Vera; ***D:*** J. Anthony Loma; ***W:*** J. Anthony Loma. *ATV*

Man of the Forest 1933 A cowboy goes to the aid of a damsel in distress and he winds up being framed for murder for his efforts. Based on Zane Grey's novel. **59m/B VHS.** Randolph Scott, Verna Hillie, Harry Carey Sr., Noah Beery Sr., Barton MacLane; ***D:*** Henry Hathaway. *NOS, DVT, MLB*

Man of the House 1995 (PG) Kids' comedy about a boy's scheme to sabotage his mother's new love interest. Ben (Thomas) concocts a plan to join the YMCA Indian Guides to discourage daddy wannabe Jack (Chase), while mom (Fawcett) stands idly by tolerating her son's bratty behavior. Subplot involves a screwy gangster theme that deteriorates into a "Home Alone-ish" ending. Film attempts to play off of Chase's knack for physical comedy, but falls short. And what's with the mime? Wendt is amusing as the Indian Guide leader. Will probably appeal more to younger crowds as Thomas' scheming teen upstages Chase's deadpan dad-to-be. **97m/C VHS, LV.** Chevy Chase, Farrah Fawcett, Jonathan Taylor Thomas, George Wendt, David Shiner, Art LaFleur, Richard Portnow, Richard Foronjy, Spencer Vrooman, John Disanti, Chief Leonard George, Peter Appel, George Greif, Chris Miranda, Ron Canada, Zachary Browne, Nicholas Garrett; ***D:*** James Orr; ***W:*** James Orr, Jim Cruickshank; ***C:*** Jamie Anderson; ***M:*** Mark Mancina. *DIS*

Man of the West ½ 1958 Reformed bad guy Cooper is asked to deliver a tidy hunk of cash to another city to recruit a school marm. Ambushed en route by his former partners in crime (who are led by his wacko uncle) he's forced to revert to his wanton ways in order to survive and save innocent hostages. There's a raging debate among Cooper fans whether this late effort has been unduly overlooked or duly ignored. A number of things conspire to give it a bad rap: Cooper does little but look mournful until the very end; there's no hiding the fact that he's older than Cobb, who plays his uncle; and the acting is in general more befitting of a B-grade slice and dicer. You be the judge. **100m/C VHS, Beta.** Gary Cooper, Julie London, Lee J. Cobb, Arthur O'Connell, Jack Lord, John Dehner, Royal Dano, Guy Wilkerson, Emory Parnell; ***D:*** Anthony Mann; ***W:*** Reginald Rose. *MGM, FCT*

Man of Violence *The Sex Racketeers* 1971 A vulgar, tasteless man spends the worthless hours of his wasted life lurking about the more wretched entrance-ways of his native land. **107m/C VHS, Beta.** Michael Latimer, Luan Peters; ***D:*** Pete Walker. *NO*

Man on a String ½ 1971 (PG) In order to bring down a Mob boss the feds first frame cop Peter King and send him to the pen. When he gets out, King uses his prison contacts to get in with the Mob and winds up pitting two rival gangs against each other in order to destroy them both. Made for television. **73m/C VHS.** Christopher George, Jack Warden, Keith Carradine, Joel Grey, William Schallert, Kitty Winn; ***D:*** Joseph Sargent. *COL*

Man on Fire 1987 (R) Told via flashback, a cynical ex-CIA man is hired as a bodyguard for the daughter of a wealthy Italian couple, who is soon thereafter kidnapped by terrorists. He goes to her rescue with all the subtlety of a wrecking ball. Decent cast goes down the tubes in this botched thriller. **92m/C VHS, Beta, LV.** *FR* Scott Glenn, Brooke Adams, Danny Aiello, Joe Pesci, Paul Shenar, Jonathan Pryce, Jade Malle; ***D:*** Elie Chouraqui. *LIV, VES*

The Man on the Box ½ 1925 Chaplin is a wealthy bachelor who takes a job as a gardener to be near his girl. He overhears a plot by the butler, who's an enemy agent, to steal the secret plans for a helicopter from his sweetie's father. In order to thwart the dastardedly scheme Chaplin dresses as a maid to infiltrate the household. **58m/B VHS.** Sydney Chaplin, David Butler, Alice Calhoun, Kathleen Calhoun, Helene Costello, Theodore Lorch; ***D:*** Charles F. Reisner. *GPV, GVV*

Man on the Eiffel Tower ☠☠☠ **1948** Laughton plays Inspector Maigret, the detective created by novelist Georges Simenon, in a highly suspenseful and cerebral mystery about a crazed killer who defies the police to discover his identity. This is the first film Meredith directed. **82m/C VHS, Beta.** Charles Laughton, Burgess Meredith, Franchot Tone, Patricia Roc; ***D:*** Burgess Meredith. *NOS, MRV, GEM*

Man on the Run ☠☠ **1949** A robbery takes place in the store where an Army deserter is trying to sell his gun, and he ends up taking the rap. It's up to a lovely lady lawyer to prove his innocence. Efficiently told "B" crime drama. **82m/B VHS, Beta.** *GB* Derek Farr, Joan Hopkins, Edward Chapman, Laurence Harvey, H. Marion Crawford, Alfie Bass, John Bailey, John Stuart, Edward Underdown, Leslie Perrins, Kenneth More, Martin Miller, Eleanor Summerfield; ***D:*** Lawrence Huntington; ***W:*** Lawrence Huntington. *SNC*

Man on the Run ☠½ **1974 (R)** After an unwitting involvement with a small robbery, a teenager finds himself the object of a police manhunt for a murder suspect. **90m/C VHS, Beta.** Kyle Johnson, James B. Sikking, Terry Carter; ***D:*** Herbert L. Strock. *PSM*

Man or Gun ☠½ **1958** Standard western yarn involving a drifter who rides into a town operated by a powerful family and liberates the cowardly townsfolk. **79m/B VHS.** MacDonald Carey, Audrey Totter, James Craig, James Gleason, Warren Stevens, Harry Shannon; ***D:*** Albert C. Gannaway; ***W:*** Vance Skarstedt, James C. Cassity. *MOV*

The Man Outside ☠☠ **1968 (R)** After a CIA agent is fired for allegedly assisting another agent in defecting to the East, he becomes involved in further intrigue. A Russian spy is looking to defect. In the process, the ex-agent is framed for murder. Straightforward espionage tale taken from Gene Stackleborg's novel "Double Agent." **98m/C VHS.** *GB* Van Heflin, Heidelinde Weis, Pinkas Braun, Peter Vaughan, Charles Gray, Ronnie Barker; ***D:*** Samuel Gallu. *NO*

Man Outside ☠ **1988 (PG-13)** Logan is an ex-lawyer who takes to the Arkansas outback after his wife dies. Anthropologist/teacher Quinlan takes a shine to him. He seems like an okay guy, but bad guy Dillman has made it look like he's a child snatcher. Slick on the outside but empty inside independent effort. Look for former members of The Band in supporting roles. **109m/C VHS, LV.** Robert F. Logan, Kathleen Quinlan, Bradford Dillman, Rick Danko, Levon Helm; ***D:*** Mark Stouffer. *NO*

The Man They Could Not Hang ☠☠½ **1939** A good doctor tinkering with artificial hearts is caught by police while experimenting on a willing student. When the doctor is convicted and hanged for a murder, his assistant uses the heart to bring him back to life. No longer a nice guy, he vows revenge against the jurors that sentenced him. Karloff repeated the same story line in several films, and this one is representative of the type. **70m/B VHS, Beta.** Boris Karloff, Adrian Booth, Roger Pryor, Robert Wilcox; ***D:*** Nick Grinde. *GKK*

Man Trouble ☠☠ **1992 (PG-13)** A divorcing opera singer (Barkin) seeks the help of a sleazy attack-dog trainer (Nicholson) when she becomes the victim of a stalker. Nicholson hits on her, first because that's one of his habits, and then because he is being paid to by a billionaire who wants him to steal the manuscript of a tell-all book about him written by Barkin's sister. Although both Nicholson and Barkin are excellent actors, they lack the electricity to make the romance credible, and the jokes are weak. Supporting cast, including D'Angelo, Stanton, and McKean, provide the funny parts in this otherwise dull film. **100m/C VHS, LV.** Jack Nicholson, Ellen Barkin, Harry Dean Stanton, Beverly D'Angelo, Michael McKean, Saul Rubinek, Viveka Davis, Veronica Cartwright, David Clennon, John Kapelos, Paul Mazursky; ***D:*** Bob Rafelson; ***W:*** Adrien (Carole Eastman) Joyce; ***M:*** Georges Delerue. *FXV*

The Man Upstairs ☠☠½ **1993** Escaped con Moony Polaski (O'Neal) hides out in the home of crotchety spinster Victoria Brown (Hepburn). When she finds the crook in her attic, instead of turning him in, Victoria befriends the slob and soon the two are sharing dinner and secrets. Meanwhile, the manhunt for Moony is intensifying and, oh yes, Christmas is coming as well. Made for television cornpone barely saved by some professional performances. Executive producer Burt Reynolds was hoping for a part until scheduling made it impossible. **95m/C VHS.** Katharine Hepburn, Ryan O'Neal, Henry Beckman, Helen Carroll, Brenda Forbes; ***D:*** George Schaefer; ***W:*** James Prideaux. *CAF*

The Man Who Broke 1,000 Chains ☠☠ **1987** A made-for-television movie about a man who is committed to a chain gang after WWII for a petty crime, and his efforts, after escaping, in making a new life for himself. An unimaginative plot is occasionally highlighted by a good scene or two. **113m/C VHS, Beta.** Val Kilmer, Charles Durning, Sonia Braga; ***D:*** Daniel Mann; ***M:*** Charles Bernstein. *ORI, WAR*

The Man Who Came to Dinner ☠☠☠½ **1941** Based on the Moss Hart-George S. Kaufman play, this comedy is about a bitter radio celebrity (Woolley) on a lecture tour (a character based on Alexander Woolcott). He breaks his hip and must stay in a quiet suburban home for the winter. While there, he occupies his time by barking orders, being obnoxious and generally just driving the other residents nuts. Woolley reprises his Broadway role in this film that succeeds at every turn, loaded with plenty of satiric jabs at the Algonquin Hotel Roundtable regulars. **112m/B VHS, Beta, LV.** Monty Woolley, Bette Davis, Ann Sheridan, Jimmy Durante, Reginald Gardiner, Richard Travis, Billie Burke, Grant Mitchell, Mary Wickes, George Barbier, Ruth Vivian, Elisabeth Fraser; ***D:*** William Keighley; ***W:*** Julius J. Epstein, Philip C. Epstein; ***C:*** Gaetano Antonio "Tony" Gaudio. *MGM*

The Man Who Could Work Miracles ☠☠☠½ **1937** A mild-mannered draper's assistant becomes suddenly endowed with supernatural powers to perform any feat he wishes. Great special effects (for an early film) and fine performances result in a classic piece of science fiction. **82m/B VHS, Beta, LV.** Ralph Richardson, Joan Gardner, Roland Young; ***D:*** Lothar Mendes. *SUE*

The Man Who Cried ☠☠½ **1993** Abel Mason (Hinds) is an unhappily married man with a vindictive wife (Walsh) and a young son he's desperate to provide for. When an affair with a married woman ends in murder, Mason and his son travel in search of a new life. Desperate for a home, Mason enters into a bigamous marriage with a widow—only to find himself falling in love with her sister. Based on the novel by Catherine Cookson. Set in the years between England's depression and WW2. **156m/C VHS.** *GB* Ciaran Hinds, Amanda Root, Kate Buffery, Angela Walsh. *VCO*

The Man Who Envied Women ☠½ **1985** The non-narrative feminist story of a smug womanizer: the man "who knows almost too much about women." **125m/C VHS, Beta.** Bill Raymond, Larry Loonin, Trisha Brown; ***D:*** Yvonne Rainer; ***W:*** Yvonne Rainer. *NO*

The Man Who Fell to Earth ☠☠☠½ **1976 (R)** Entertaining and technically adept cult classic about a man from another planet (Bowie, in a bit of typecasting) who ventures to earth in hopes of finding water to save his family and drought-stricken planet. Instead he becomes a successful inventor and businessman, along the way discovering the human vices of booze, sex, and television. Also available in a restored version at 138 minutes. Remade for television in 1987 and based on Walter Tevis' novel. **118m/C VHS, Beta, LV.** *GB* David Bowie, Candy Clark, Rip Torn, Buck Henry, Bernie Casey; ***D:*** Nicolas Roeg. *COL*

The Man Who Guards the Greenhouse **1988** Tracy must come to terms with her attraction for Jeff as well as once again trying to write a meaningful novel. **150m/C VHS.** Christopher Cazenove, Rebecca Dewey. *ORI*

Man Who Had Power Over Women ☠☠ **1970 (R)** Disappointing sex farce about the exploits of a carnally insatiable (and married) talent executive (Taylor) who has an affair with every woman he meets and creates problems aplenty. Adapted from a novel by Gordon Williams. **89m/C VHS, Beta.** *GB* Rod Taylor, James Booth, Carol White, Penelope Horner, Clive Francis; ***D:*** John Krish; ***W:*** Chris Bryant, Allan Scott. *SUE*

The Man Who Haunted Himself ☠☠ **1970** While a man lies in critical condition on the operating table after a car accident, his alter-ego emerges and turns his ideal life into a nightmare until the man recovers and moves toward a fateful encounter. An expanded version of an episode of the television series "Alfred Hitchcock Presents," this was Moore's first movie after having starred in the TV series "The Saint," and it was Dearden's last film; he died in a car accident the following year. Appeals primarily to those fascinated by "Hitchcock" or "The Twilight Zone"—where mystery matters most. Filmed in London. **94m/C VHS, Beta.** *GB* Roger Moore, Hildegarde Neil, Olga Georges-Picot; ***D:*** Basil Dearden. *NO*

The Man Who Knew Too Much ☠☠☠ **1934** Hitchcock's first international success. A British family man on vacation in Switzerland is told of an assassination plot by a dying agent. His daughter is kidnapped to force his silence. In typical Hitchcock fashion, the innocent person becomes caught in a web of intrigue; the sticky situation culminates with surprising events during the famous shootout in the final scenes. Remade by Hitchcock in 1956. **75m/B VHS, Beta.** *GB* Leslie Banks, Edna Best, Peter Lorre, Nova Pilbeam, Pierre Fresnay; ***D:*** Alfred Hitchcock; ***W:*** Emlyn Williams, Charles Bennett. *SNC, MRV, NOS*

The Man Who Knew Too Much ☠☠½ **1956 (PG)** Hitchcock's remake of his 1934 film, this time about an American doctor and his family vacationing in Marrakech. They become involved in a complicated international plot involving kidnapping and murder. While Doris tries to save the day by singing "Que Sera, Sera," Stewart tries to locate his abducted son. More lavish settings and forms of intrigue make this a less focused and, to some, inferior version. ♫Que Sera, Sera. **120m/C VHS, Beta, LV.** James Stewart, Doris Day, Brenda de Banzie, Bernard Miles, Ralph Truman, Daniel Gelin, Alan Mowbray, Carolyn Jones, Hillary Brooke; ***D:*** Alfred Hitchcock; ***W:*** John Michael Hayes; ***C:*** Robert Burks. Academy Awards '56: Best Song ("Que Sera, Sera"). *MCA, HHE*

The Man Who Laughs ☠☠☠½ **1927** Veidt's sensitive performance highlights this silent classic. He plays a young man whose features are surgically altered into a permanent smile because his family are political enemies of the current ruler. The man is befriended by the owner of a sideshow who first exhibits him as a freak but later finds Veidt gaining fame as a clown. A beautiful blind girl in the show loves Veidt for who he is and the two find happiness. **110m/B VHS.** Conrad Veidt, Mary Philbin, Olga Baclanova, Josephine Crowell, George Siegmann, Brandon Hurst; ***D:*** Paul Leni. *GPV*

The Man Who Lived Again ☠☠½ *The Man Who Changed His Mind; The Brainsnatchers; Dr. Maniac* **1936** Boris strives to be a brain-switcher, and suspense builds around the question of whether or not he will change his mind. Shot in England with fine sets and a definite Anglo feel to the proceedings, with Karloff doing one of his better mad scientist routines. **61m/B VHS, Beta, 8mm.** *GB* Boris Karloff, Anna Lee, John Loder, Frank Cellier, Lyn Harding, Cecil Parker; ***D:*** Robert Stevenson. *SNC, VYY, MLB*

Man Who Loved Cat Dancing ☠☠ **1973 (PG)** Reynolds is an outlaw on the run after avenging his wife's murder and robbing a safe with pals Hopkins and Warden, and Miles has recently escaped from her abusive husband. It's love on the run as Burt and Sarah are pursued by bounty hunters and their tragic pasts—coming close to making us care, but close doesn't mean as much in movies as it does in dancing. Based on Marilyn Durham's novel. **114m/C VHS, Beta.** Burt Reynolds, Sarah Miles, Jack Warden, Lee J. Cobb, Jay Silverheels, Robert Donner; *D:* Richard Sarafian; *C:* Harry Stradling Jr.; *M:* John Williams. *MGM, FCT*

The Man Who Loved Women ☙☙☙
L'Homme Qui Aimait les Femmes **1977** An intelligent, sensitive bachelor writes his memoirs and recalls the many, many, many women he has loved. Truffaut couples sophistication and lightheartedness, the thrill of the chase and, when it leads to an accidental death, the wondering what-it's-all-about in the mourning after. In French with English subtitles. Remade in 1983. **119m/C VHS, Beta, LV.** *FR* Charles Denner, Brigitte Fossey, Leslie Caron; *D:* Francois Truffaut; *W:* Suzanne Schiffman; *C:* Nestor Almendros. National Board of Review Awards '77: 5 Best Foreign Films of the Year. *MGM, INJ, BTV*

The Man Who Loved Women ☙☙
1983 (R) A remake of the 1977 French film, this is slower, tries to be funnier, and is less subtle than the original. Reynolds is a Los Angeles sculptor whose reputation as a playboy leads him to a psychoanalyst's couch, where a lot of talk slows the action—though Burt & Julie (the shrink) do share the couch. **110m/C VHS, Beta.** Burt Reynolds, Julie Andrews, Kim Basinger, Marilu Henner, Cynthia Sikes, Jennifer Edwards; *D:* Blake Edwards; *W:* Blake Edwards; *M:* Henry Mancini. *COL*

The Man Who Never Was ☙☙☙ **1955**
Tense true story (with melodramatic embroidery) from WWII shows in step-by-step detail how Britain duped the Axis by letting them find an Allied corpse bearing phony invasion plans. Based on the book by the scheme's mastermind Ewen Montagu, played by Webb; Peter Sellers provides the voice of an offscreen Winston Churchill. **102m/C VHS, Beta.** *GB* Clifton Webb, Gloria Grahame, Robert Flemyng, Josephine Griffin, Stephen Boyd, Andre Morell, Laurence Naismith, Geoffrey Keen, Michael Hordern; *D:* Ronald Neame; *C:* Oswald Morris. British Academy Awards '56: Best Screenplay. *FOX, FCT, TVC*

The Man Who Shot Liberty Valance ☙☙☙ ½ **1962** Tough cowboy Wayne and idealistic lawyer Stewart join forces against dreaded gunfighter Liberty Valance, played leatherly by Marvin. While Stewart rides to Senatorial success on his reputation as the man who shot the villain, he suffers moral crises about the act, but is toughened up by Wayne. Wayne's use of the word "pilgrim" became a standard for his impersonators. Strong character acting, great Western scenes, and value judgements to ponder over make this last of Ford's black and white westerns among his best. **123m/B VHS, Beta, LV.** James Stewart, John Wayne, Vera Miles, Lee Marvin, Edmond O'Brien, Andy Devine, Woody Strode, Ken Murray, Jeanette Nolan, John Qualen, Strother Martin, Lee Van Cleef, John Carradine, Carleton Young; *D:* John Ford; *C:* William Clothier. Nominations: Academy Awards '62: Best Costume Design (B & W). *PAR, HMV*

The Man Who Skied Down Everest ☙☙ ½ **1975 (G)** Documentary about a Japanese athlete who undertakes a demanding downhill run, and the cost (human and financial) of getting there. **86m/C VHS.** Academy Awards '75: Best Feature Documentary. *NO*

The Man Who Wagged His Tail ☙☙ ½ *An Angel Passed Over Brooklyn; Un Angelo e Sceso a Brooklyn* **1957** A mean slumlord is turned into a dog as the result of a curse cast upon him. In order to return to his human form, he must be loved by someone. Despite his attempts to be loved, the dog alienates his only friend and must try to redeem himself. Played for fun, this is a mildly amusing fantasy filmed in Spain and Brooklyn. Not released in the U. S. until 1961. **91m/B VHS.** *IT SP* Peter Ustinov, Pablito Calvo, Aroldo Tieri, Silvia Marco; *D:* Ladislao Vajda. *SNC, VYY*

The Man Who Wasn't There ☙ **1983**
(R) A member of the State department receives a formula from a dying spy that can render him invisible, see? He has to use the formula to protect himself from the police and other spies, becoming a comic "Invisible Man," see? Generally chaotic tale that's bad, but not so bad that it's worth seeing, though you might want to see what invisibility looks like in 3-D. **111m/C VHS, Beta.** Steve Guttenberg, Jeffrey Tambor, Art Hindle, Lisa Langlois; *D:* Bruce Malmuth; *M:* Miles Goodman. *PAR*

The Man Who Would Be King ☙☙☙☙ **1975 (PG)** A grand, old-fashioned adventure based on the classic story by Rudyard Kipling about two mercenary soldiers who travel from India to Kafiristan in order to conquer it and set themselves up as kings. Splendid characterizations by Connery and Caine, and Huston's royal directorial treatment provides it with adventure, majestic sweep, and well-developed characters. **129m/C VHS, Beta, LV.** Sean Connery, Michael Caine, Christopher Plummer, Saeed Jaffrey, Shakira Caine; *D:* John Huston; *W:* Gladys Hill, John Huston; *C:* Oswald Morris; *M:* Maurice Jarre. Nominations: Academy Awards '75: Best Adapted Screenplay, Best Art Direction/Set Decoration, Best Costume Design, Best Film Editing. *FOX*

The Man Who Would Not Die ☙☙
Target in the Sun **1975 (PG)** During his investigation of several deaths, a man discovers that all of the deceased were actually the same man. It seems the deaths were part of a intricate scheme to cover up a million dollar heist. Two of the top three actors are killed early on; it's not very suspenseful. It's more like the mystery that would not die. From Charles Williams' novel "The Sailcloth Shroud." **83m/C VHS, Beta.** Dorothy Malone, Keenan Wynn, Aldo Ray; *D:* Robert Arkless. *WAR, OM*

Man with a Cross ☙☙ **1943** Archaeologists of the cinema may want to unearth this early Rossellini, made by the future father of neo-realist cinema as a propaganda piece for the fascist war effort. A heroic Italian chaplain on the Russian front ministers to foe and friend alike, and even converts a few commies to Christ. Not as awful as it sounds—but never forget where this came from. **88m/B VHS.** *IT* *D:* Roberto Rossellini. *FST*

Man with a Gun ☙☙ ½ **1995 (R)** Hitman John Hardin (Madsen) is asked by mobster employer Jack Rushton (Busey) to kill his ex-girlfriend Rena (Tilly) and get a CD-ROM filled with info he doesn't want to get out. Rena now happens to be John's gal pal but isn't too upset since she figures they'll substitute Rena's goody two-shoes twin sister Kathy for the needed corpse. Too bad John starts to fall for the intended victim, leaving the plan to unravel. It's a connect-the-dots plot with a creditable cast. Based on the novel "The Shroud Society" by Hugh C. Rae. **100m/C VHS.** Michael Madsen, Jennifer Tilly, Gary Busey, Robert Loggia, Ian Tracey, Bill Cobbs; *D:* David Wyles; *W:* Laurie Finstad-Knizhik; *C:* Jan Kiesser; *M:* George Blondheim. *HMK*

A Man with a Maid ☙ **1973** A bizarre British exploitation pic mixes spookhouse cliches and sex, as a young man finds his new bachelor pad haunted by Jack the Ripper. Originally shot in 3-D and known variously as "The Groove Room" and "What the Swedish Butler Saw." It didn't help. **83m/C VHS.** Sue Longhurst, Martin Long, Diana Dors; *D:* Vernon Becker. *VDM*

The Man with a Movie Camera ☙☙☙ ½ **1929** A plotless, experimental view of Moscow through the creative eye of the cameraman Dziga Vertov, founder of the Kino Eye. The editing methods and camera techniques used in this silent film were very influential and still stand up to scrutiny today. **69m/B VHS, Beta.** *RU* *D:* Dziga Vertov. *IHF, MRV, DVT*

The Man with Bogart's Face ☙☙
Sam Marlowe, Private Eye **1980 (PG)** Sacchi is no Bogart, but he does imitate him well. Bogart fans will enjoy this fond tribute to the late great actor, but the story uncertainly wavers between genuine detective story and detective spoof. **106m/C VHS, Beta.** Robert Sacchi, Misty Rowe, Sybil Danning, Franco Nero, Herbert Lom, Victor Buono, Olivia Hussey; *D:* Robert Day; *W:* Andrew J. Fenady; *M:* John Beal, George Duning. Golden Raspberry Awards '80: Worst Song ("The Man with Bogart's Face"). *FOX*

The Man with One Red Shoe ☙☙
1985 (PG) Hanks is a lovable clod of a violinist who ensnares himself in a web of intrigue when CIA agents, both good and evil, mistake him for a contact by his wearing one red shoe. Sporadically funny remake of the French "The Tall Blond Man with One Black Shoe." **92m/C VHS, Beta.** Tom Hanks, Dabney Coleman, Lori Singer, Carrie Fisher, James Belushi, Charles Durning, Edward Herrmann, Tom Noonan, Gerrit Graham, David Lander, David Ogden Stiers; *D:* Stan Dragoti; *M:* Thomas Newman. *FXV, OM*

The Man with the Golden Arm ☙☙☙
1955 A gripping film version of the Nelson Algren junkie melodrama, about an ex-addict who returns to town only to get mixed up with drugs again. Considered controversial in its depiction of addiction when released. Sinatra's performance as Frankie Machine is a stand-out. **119m/B VHS, Beta.** Frank Sinatra, Kim Novak, Eleanor Parker, Arnold Stang, Darren McGavin, Robert Strauss, George Mathews, John Conte, Doro Merande; *D:* Otto Preminger; *C:* Sam Leavitt; *M:* Elmer Bernstein. Nominations: Academy Awards '55: Best Actor (Sinatra), Best Art Direction/Set Decoration (B & W), Best Original Score. *WAR, MRV, NOS*

The Man with the Golden Gun ☙☙ ½ **1974 (PG)** Roger Moore is the debonair secret agent 007 in this ninth James Bond flick. Assigned to recover a small piece of equipment which can be utilized to harness the sun's energy, Bond engages the usual bevy of villains and beauties. **134m/C VHS, Beta, LV.** *GB* Roger Moore, Christopher Lee, Britt Ekland, Maud Adams, Herve Villechaize, Clifton James, Soon-Teck Oh, Richard Loo, Marc Lawrence, Bernard Lee, Lois Maxwell, Desmond Llewelyn; *D:* Guy Hamilton; *W:* Tom Mankiewicz; *C:* Ted Moore; *M:* John Barry. *MGM, FOX*

The Man with the Perfect Swing ☙☙ ½ **1995** Middle-aged ex-baseball player-turned-business entrepreneur Anthony "Babe" Lombardo (Black) is deep in debt and having trouble with the IRS even as he schemes to find success with his latest endeavor—designing specialty golf equipment. But Babe's latest design is a radically new golf swing (combining putting with his baseball expertise) featured in a how-to video with a budding PGA star. Naturally, given Babe's woeful record, the money just doesn't seem to be coming his way. **94m/C VHS.** James Black, Suzanne Savoy, Marco Perella, James Belcher, Richard Bradshaw; *D:* Michael Hovis; *W:* Michael Hovis; *C:* Jim Barham; *M:* Paul English. *MNC*

The Man with Two Brains ☙☙☙ **1983**
(R) Did you hear the one about the brilliant neurosurgeon who falls in love with a woman in his laboratory? He only has two problems: dealing with his covetous wife and finding a body for his cerebral lover. Plenty of laughs in this spoof of mad scientist movies that is redeemed from potential idiocy by the cast's titillating performances. Listen closely and you'll recognize the voice of Spacek as the brain-in-the-jar of Martin's dreams. **91m/C VHS, Beta, LV.** Steve Martin, Kathleen Turner, David Warner, Sissy Spacek; *D:* Carl Reiner; *W:* Steve Martin, George Gipe, Carl Reiner; *C:* Michael Chapman; *M:* Joel Goldsmith. *WAR*

Man with Two Heads ☙ **1972 (R)** Doctor Jekyll gets in touch with his innermost feelings when his muffed experiments turn him into, gasp, Mr. Blood. Another forlorn addition to the Dr. Jekyll retread collection. **80m/C VHS.** *D:* Andy Milligan; *W:* Andy Milligan. *NO*

The Man with Two Lives ☙☙ ½ **1942**
Well done horror thriller about a wealthy young man who's killed in a car accident, then brought back to life by a mad scientist. At precisely the moment his life is restored, a murderous gangster is executed and his soul enters the young man's body. **?m/C VHS.** Edward Norris, Addison Richards, Marlo Dwyer. *SNC*

The Man Without a Face ☙☙ ½ **1993**
(PG-13) Gibson plays a badly scarred recluse in Maine who develops a mentor relationship with a lonely, fatherless boy. Chuck (Stahl) wants to go away to military school, but flunks the extrance exam, and enlists former teacher McLeod as a tutor. First

foray for Gibson into the director's chair tends to be overly melodramatic. Adapted from a novel by Isabelle Holland. **115m/C VHS, Beta, LV.** Mel Gibson, Nick Stahl, Margaret Whitton, Fay Masterson, Richard Masur, Gaby Hoffman, Geoffrey Lewis, Jack DeMave; ***D:*** Mel Gibson; ***W:*** Malcolm MacRury; ***M:*** James Horner. *WAR*

Man Without a Star 🦴🦴🦴 **1955** A cowboy helps ranchers stop a ruthless cattle owner from taking over their land. The conflict between freedom in the wild west and the need for order and settlements is powerfully internalized in Douglas, whose fight for justice will tame the cowboy code he lives by. You'll shed a tear for the fading frontier. **89m/B VHS, Beta.** Kirk Douglas, Jeanne Crain, Claire Trevor, William Campbell; ***D:*** King Vidor. *MCA*

Man, Woman & Child 🦴🦴 **1983 (PG)** A close, upscale California family is shocked when a child from the husband's long-ago affair with a Frenchwoman appears at their door. Pure sentimentalism, as the family confronts this unexpected development. Two hankies—one each for fine performances by Sheen and Danner. Based on a sentimental novel by Erich Segal of "Love Story" fame, who co-wrote the script. **99m/C VHS, Beta.** Martin Sheen, Blythe Danner, Craig T. Nelson, David Hemmings; ***D:*** Dick Richards; ***W:*** Erich Segal; ***M:*** Georges Delerue. *PAR*

Manchurian Avenger 🦴 **1984 (R)** Desperados have wrested control of a Colorado gold rush town from Joe Kim's family, but he'll put an end to that, chop chop. **87m/C VHS, Beta.** Bobby Kim, Bill Wallace; ***D:*** Ed Warnick. *NO*

The Manchurian Candidate 🦴🦴🦴🦴 **1962** Political thriller about an American Korean War vet who suspects that he and his platoon may have been brainwashed during the war, with his highly decorated, heroic friend programmed by commies to be an operational assassin. Loaded with shocks, conspiracy, inventive visual imagery, and bitter political satire of naivete and machinations of the left and right. Excellent performances by an all-star cast, with Lansbury and Gregory particularly frightening. Based on the Richard Condon novel. Featuring a special interview with Sinatra and Frankenheimer in which Sinatra is deified. **126m/B VHS, Beta, LV.** Frank Sinatra, Laurence Harvey, Angela Lansbury, Janet Leigh, James Gregory, Leslie Parrish, John McGiver, Henry Silva, Khigh Deigh; ***D:*** John Frankenheimer; ***W:*** George Axelrod, John Frankenheimer; ***C:*** Lionel Lindon; ***M:*** David Amram. Golden Globe Awards '63: Best Supporting Actress (Lansbury); National Board of Review Awards '62: Best Supporting Actress (Lansbury); Nominations: Academy Awards '62: Best Film Editing, Best Supporting Actress (Lansbury). *MGM*

The Mandarin Mystery 🦴½ **1937** In the process of trying to retrieve a stolen Mandarin stamp, detective Ellery Queen uncovers a counterfeiting ring. Some fine performances, but a muddled script creates a mystery as to whether or not the action is played for laughs. **65m/B VHS, Beta.** Eddie Quillan, Charlotte Henry, Rita La Roy, Wade Boteler, Franklin Pangborn, George Irving, Kay Hughes, William Newell; ***D:*** Ralph Staub. *NOS, SNC*

Mandela 🦴🦴🦴 **1987** A gripping, powerful drama about human rights and dignity, tracing the real-life trials of Nelson and Winnie Mandela. The story focuses on the couple's early opposition to South African apartheid, as well as the events leading up to Nelson's life-imprisonment sentencing in 1964. Excellent, restrained performances from Glover and Woodard. Made for cable television. **135m/C VHS, Beta.** Danny Glover, Alfre Woodard, John Matshikiza, Warren Clarke, Allan Corduner, Julian Glover; ***D:*** Philip Saville. *KUI, FCT*

Mandinga 🦴 **1977** A plantation owner develops an obsession for one of his female slaves. Made to cash in on the already exploitive "Mandingo"; two wrongs don't make a right. **100m/C VHS, Beta.** Anthony Gismond; ***D:*** Mario Pinzauti. *PAR*

Mandingo 🦴🦴 **1975 (R)** Overheated Southern-fried tale of slavery in the Deep South, circa 1840, dealing with the tangled loves and hates of a family and their slaves. Heavyweight boxer Norton made his screen debut in the title role as the slave who makes his master money with his boxing prowess. King is the wastrel son who makes Norton's wife, another slave, his mistress. Followed by 1975's "Drum." Based on the novel by Kyle Onstott. **127m/C VHS, Beta, LV.** James Mason, Susan George, Perry King, Richard Ward, Ken Norton, Ben Masters, Brenda Sykes, Paul Benedict, Ji Tu Cumbuka; ***D:*** Richard Fleischer; ***M:*** Maurice Jarre. *PAR*

Mandroid 🦴½ **1993 (R)** Two scientists design a high-tech robot, Mandroid, to handle a powerful new element they've discovered. Dr. Zimmer and daughter Zanna want to use their creation to help mankind while mad scientist Dr. Drago wants the power Mandroid can give him. When a laboratory accident leaves Drago horribly disfigured it also gives him the chance to steal Mandroid and put his evil plan into action. Filmed on location in Romania. **81m/C VHS, Beta.** Brian Cousins, Jane Caldwell, Michael DellaFemina, Curt Lowens, Patrick Ersgard, Robert Symonds; ***D:*** Joakim Ersgard; ***W:*** Jackson Barr, Earl Kenton. *PAR*

Mandy 🦴🦴🦴 *Crash of Silence* **1953** Poignant drama of a deaf child and the family who must come to terms with her deafness. Well-developed plot and well performed; an intelligent treatment in all. **93m/B VHS, Beta.** *GB* Phyllis Calvert, Jack Hawkins, Mandy Miller; ***D:*** Alexander MacKendrick. *LCA*

Manfish 🦴½ **1956** Two men venture out in a boat, the Manfish, to hunt for sunken treasure in the Caribbean. Only one survives the trip, as his greed destroys the other. The scenes off the Jamaican coast are lovely, but the story fails to take hold. Though there is a star aboard in Chaney, you'll look astern and bow out with a sinking feeling. Derived from two Edgar Allan Poe stories, "The Gold Bug" and "The Tell-Tale Heart." **76m/C VHS.** John Bromfield, Lon Chaney Jr., Victor Jory, Barbara Nichols; ***D:*** W. Lee Wilder. *NOS, SNC*

The Mangler 🦴 **1994 (R)** Laundry machine munches workers in a small-town Maine industrial plant. Bossman Englund's only concern (besides huge workman's comp premiums) is keeping the machine well-fed. Weak attempt at horror by veteran Tobe "If it's worth doing, it's worth overdoing" Hooper ("The Texas Chainsaw Massacre") that tries to capitalize on the popularity of story originator Stephen King. Offers little in plot or scare, but fans of the gore genre will enjoy the overuse of chunky-style blood and guts spewed from the monstrous steam ironer and folder that is apparently possesed by the devil. About 45 minutes too long for anybody to suspend their disbelief. **106m/C VHS, LV.** Robert Englund, Ted Levine, Daniel Matmor, Vanessa Pike, Demetre Phillips, Lisa Morris, Ashley Hayden, Vera Blacker; ***D:*** Tobe Hooper; ***W:*** Tobe Hooper, Peter Welbeck, Stephen Brooks; ***C:*** Amnon Salomon; ***M:*** Barrington Pheloung. *NLC, TTC, IME*

The Mango Tree 🦴🦴½ **1977** A young man comes of age in a small Australian town during the 1920s. Everything is well done, if not dramatic or fascinating. **93m/C VHS, Beta.** *AU* Geraldine Fitzgerald, Robert Helpmann, Diane Craig, Gerald Kennedy, Christopher Pate; ***D:*** Kevin Dobson. *NO*

Manhandled 🦴🦴½ **1924** Department store clerk Swanson is the hit of an artist's party with her impersonations and is asked by Morgan to impersonate a Russian countess to lend some class to his store. She winds up with lots of suitors. **67m/B VHS.** Gloria Swanson, Frank Morgan, Tom Moore, Lilyan Tashman, Ian Keith, Arthur Houseman; ***D:*** Allan Dwan. *GPV*

The Manhandlers 🦴 **1973 (R)** After the uncle of a young woman is killed by the mob, she goes after them for revenge. For your entertainment pleasure, best stick with the soup commercial of the same name. **87m/C VHS, Beta.** Cara Burgess, Judy Brown, Vince Cannon, Rosalind Miles; ***D:*** Lee Madden. *TWE*

Manhattan 🦴🦴🦴🦴 **1979 (R)** Successful TV writer Allen yearns to be a serious writer. He struggles through a series of ill-fated romances, including one with high school senior Hemingway, about 25 years younger, and another with Keaton, who's also having an on-again, off-again affair with Murphy, Allen's best friend. Scathingly serious and comic view of modern relationships in urban America and of the modern intellectual neuroses. Shot in black-and-white to capture the mood of Manhattan and mated with an excellent Gershwin soundtrack, the video version preserves the widescreen effect adding yet another impressive element to the overall production. **96m/B VHS, Beta, LV.** Woody Allen, Diane Keaton, Meryl Streep, Mariel Hemingway, Michael Murphy, Wallace Shawn, Anne Byrne, Tisa Farrow, Mark Linn-Baker, David Rasche, Karen Allen; ***D:*** Woody Allen; ***W:*** Woody Allen, Marshall Brickman; ***C:*** Gordon Willis; ***M:*** George Gershwin. British Academy Awards '79: Best Film, Best Screenplay; Cesar Awards '80: Best Foreign Film; Los Angeles Film Critics Association Awards '79: Best Supporting Actress (Streep); National Board of Review Awards '79: 10 Best Films of the Year; New York Film Critics Awards '79: Best Director (Allen), Best Supporting Actress (Streep); Nominations: Academy Awards '79: Best Original Screenplay, Best Supporting Actress (Hemingway). *MGM*

Manhattan Baby 🦴 **1982** Unscary horror film about an archaeologist who digs up a relic that draws evil into the world and infects an American girl with powers that lead to many deaths. Advice to you that might have saved the archaelogist: don't dig this. **90m/C VHS, Beta.** *IT* Christopher Connelly, Martha Taylor; ***D:*** Lucio Fulci. *LIV*

Manhattan Melodrama 🦴🦴🦴½ **1934** Powell and Gable are best friends from childhood, growing up together in an orphanage. Their adult lives take different paths, however, as Powell becomes a respected prosecuting attorney while Gable becomes a notorious gambler/racketeer. Lovely Loy is Gable's girl who comes between the two. Eventually, Powell must prosecute his life-long friend for murder in order to win the governorship. One of Gable's toughest roles; Powell's character, however, is a bit unbelievable as his ethics seem to extend beyond love and friendship. This is the first film to team Powell and Loy, who would go on to make 13 more films together, including the "Thin Man" series. **93m/B VHS, Beta, LV.** Clark Gable, William Powell, Myrna Loy, Leo Carrillo, Nat Pendleton, George Sidney, Isabel Jewell, Muriel Evans, Claudelle Kaye, Frank Conroy, Jimmy Butler, Mickey Rooney, Edward Van Sloan; ***D:*** Woodbridge S. Van Dyke; ***C:*** James Wong Howe. *MGM, CCB*

Manhattan Merry-Go-Round 🦴🦴 **1937** One of the movies where a corrupt boss—in this case a record producer—threatens a bunch of good people as a pretense for a plot when the movie simply serves as a showcase for stars. Features many singing stars of the thirties ("where have you gone Cab Calloway?") plus Joltin' Joe, who ended up having a hit-streak in another genre. ♫Mama I Wanna Make Rhythm; Manhattan Merry-Go-Round; Heaven?; I Owe You; It's Round Up Time in Reno. **89m/B VHS, Beta.** Cab Calloway, Louis Prima, Ted Lewis, Ann Dvorak, Phil Regan, Kay Thompson, Gene Autry, Joe DiMaggio; ***D:*** Charles Riesner. Nominations: Academy Awards '37: Best Interior Decoration. *NOS, VCN, HHT*

Manhattan Murder Mystery 🦴🦴🦴 **1993 (PG)** Keaton and Allen team up again as two New Yorkers who get involved in a mystery when their neighbor dies under strange circumstances. Light, entertaining comedy steers clear of some of Allen's heavier themes and should keep audiences laughing till the end. Allen, writing with Brickman for the first time since "Annie Hall" and "Manhattan," makes viewers fall in love with the magic of NYC all over again. **105m/C VHS, LV, 8mm.** Woody Allen, Diane Keaton, Anjelica Huston, Alan Alda, Jerry Adler, Ron Rifkin, Joy Behar, Lynn Cohen, Melanie Norris; ***D:*** Woody Allen; ***W:*** Woody Allen, Marshall Brickman. Nominations: Golden Globe Awards '94: Best Actress—Musical/Comedy (Keaton). *COL*

The Manhattan Project 🦴🦴 *Manhattan Project: The Deadly Game* **1986 (PG-13)** An exceptionally bright teenager decides to build a nuclear bomb for his project at the New York City science fair. He's out to prove how dangerously easy it is to build big bombs. When he steals plutonium from a local government installation, the feds attempt to nab the precocious youngster. Light moral overtones abound.

Director Brickman co-wrote similarly titled "Manhattan." **112m/C VHS, Beta, LV.** John Lithgow, Christopher Collet, Cynthia Nixon, Jill Eikenberry, John Mahoney, Sully Boyer, Richard Council, Robert Schenkkan, Paul Austin; ***D:*** Marshall Brickman; ***W:*** Marshall Brickman, Thomas Baum; ***C:*** Billy Williams. *REP*

Manhunt *The Italian Connection; La Mala Ordina* **1973 (R)** A man marked for execution by the mob launches his own assault on the organization's headquarters. Action and Italian food, but not much else. Dubbed. **93m/C VHS, Beta.** *IT* Henry Silva, Mario Adorf, Woody Strode, Luciana Paluzzi; ***D:*** Fernando Di Leo. *MED, AIP*

The Manhunt **1986** A framed cowhand escapes from prison to prove his innocence. Made-for-TV movie. **89m/C VHS, Beta.** Ernest Borgnine, Bo Svenson, John Ethan Wayne; ***D:*** Larry Ludman. *MED*

Manhunt ½ **1995 (R)** Fugitive Jim Trudell (Wilson) rescues a woman from a gang of thugs and winds up in a net of police corruption. Now he needs to survive long enough to figure out what's going on. **?m/C VHS, LV.** Don "The Dragon" Wilson, Jillian McWhirter. *NHO*

Manhunt for Claude Dallas **1986** Mountain man uses game wardens for firing practice, ticks off local sheriff Torn, is tossed behind bars, checks out ahead of schedule and becomes a legend in his own time. Mediocre made-for-TV macho man melodrama. From the novel "Outlaw" by Jeff Long. **93m/C VHS, Beta.** Matt Salinger, Rip Torn, Claude Akins, Pat Hingle, Lois Nettleton, Beau Starr, Frederick Coffin; ***D:*** Jerry London; ***W:*** John Gay; ***M:*** Stephen Dorff. *PSM*

Manhunt in the African Jungle **1954** An American undercover agent battles Nazi forces in Africa. A serial in fifteen episodes. **240m/B VHS, LV.** Rod Cameron, Joan Marsh, Duncan Renaldo. *VCN, REP, MLB*

Manhunt of Mystery Island *Captain Mephisto and the Transformation Machine* **1945** Serial about the super-powered Captain Mephisto. **100m/C VHS, Beta, LV.** Linda Stirling, Roy Barcroft, Richard Bailey, Kenne Duncan; ***D:*** Spencer Gordon Bennet. *MED, MLB*

Manhunter **1974** A made-for-television escapade about a WWI Marine who returns home from China in 1933 to track down a bunch of gangsters headed by his sister. **78m/C VHS, Beta, LV.** Ken Howard, Stefanie Powers, Gary Lockwood, Tim O'Connor, L.Q. Jones; ***D:*** Walter Grauman. *WAR, TWE*

Manhunter ½ **1983** A mercenary sets out to disengage organized crime from high-level politics. Produced by Owensby. **92m/C VHS, Beta.** Earl Owensby, Johnny Popwell, Doug Hale, Elizabeth Upton; ***D:*** Earl Owensby. *MED*

Manhunter *Red Dragon* **1986 (R)** FBI forensic specialist—who retired after a harrowing pursuit of a serial killer—is called back to duty to find a psychotic family killer. His technique: to match the thought processes of serial killers and thus anticipate their moves. Intense thriller, based on the Thomas Harris novel "Red Dragon." Harris also wrote "The Silence of the Lambs," whose most notorious character Hannibal ("The Cannibal") Lecter, appears in this movie as well. Director Mann applies the slick techniques he introduced in the popular television series "Miami Vice," creating a quiet, moody intensity broken by sudden onslaughts of violence. Available in widescreen on laserdisc. **100m/C VHS, Beta, LV.** William L. Petersen, Kim Greist, Joan Allen, Brian Cox, Dennis Farina, Stephen Lang, Tom Noonan; ***D:*** Michael Mann; ***W:*** Michael Mann. *WAR*

Mania ½ *The Flesh and the Fiends; Fiendish Ghouls; Psycho Killers* **1960** Fine adaptation of the Burke and Hare grave robbing legend. Cushing is the doctor who needs corpses and Pleasence and Rose provide them by any means. Highly atmospheric representation of dismal, 19th century Edinburgh. Very graphic for its time. **87m/B VHS.** *GB* Peter Cushing, June Laverick, Donald Pleasence, George Rose, Dermot Walsh, Renee Houston, Billie Whitelaw, John Cairney, Michael Balfour; ***D:*** John Gilling; ***M:*** Stanley Black. *SNC, DVT, MLB*

Mania **198?** Four suspense/murder stories set in a sleazy urban milieu. **120m/C Beta.** Deborah Grover, Stephen Hunter, Lenore Zann, Wayne Robson. *NO*

Maniac *Woof!* **1934** A scientist has designs on raising the dead and searches for victims on which to experiment. Bizarre "adults only" exploitation feature was considered very risque for its time, and includes eaten eyeballs, a cat fight with syringes and a rapist who thinks he's an orangutan. A must for genre aficionados. **67m/B VHS, Beta.** Bill Woods, Horace Carpenter, Ted Edwards, Thea Ramsey, Jennie Dark, Marcel Andre, Celia McGann; ***D:*** Dwain Esper. *VDM, SNC, MRV*

Maniac **1963** An American artist living in France becomes involved with the daughter of a cafe owner, not suspecting that murder will follow. Seems that her old man is locked up in an insane asylum for torching the daughter's rapist several years earlier. **86m/B VHS, Beta.** *GB* Kerwin Mathews, Nadia Gray, Donald Houston, Liliane Brousse; ***D:*** Michael Carreras; ***W:*** Jimmy Sangster; ***M:*** Stanley Black. *COL, MLB*

Maniac *Ransom; Assault on Paradise; The Town That Cried Terror* **1977 (PG)** A New York cop hunts down an arrow-shooting and obviously crazed Vietnam veteran who endeavors to hold an entire Arizona town for ransom. Which is entirely appropriate, since the cast is in it only for the money. **87m/C VHS, Beta.** Oliver Reed, Deborah Raffin, Stuart Whitman, Jim Mitchum, Edward Brett, John Ireland, Richard Compton, Paul Koslo; ***D:*** Richard Compton. *SUE, LIV, VES*

Maniac *Woof!* **1980** A psycho murderer slaughters and scalps his victims, adding the "trophies" to his collection. Carries a self-imposed equivalent "X" rating due to its highly graphic gore quotient. For extremely strong stomachs only. **91m/C VHS, Beta.** Joe Spinell, Caroline Munro, Gail Lawrence, Kelly Piper, Tom Savini; ***D:*** William Lustig; ***W:*** Joe Spinell, C.A. Rosenberg. *MED*

Maniac Cop **1988 (R)** In New York city, a cop goes beyond the realm of sanity and turns vigilante. Low-budget slasher/thriller that too often sags. **92m/C VHS, Beta.** Tom Atkins, Bruce Campbell, Laurene Landon, Richard Roundtree, William Smith, Robert Z'Dar, Sheree North; ***D:*** William Lustig; ***W:*** Larry Cohen. *TWE, HHE*

Maniac Cop 2 **1990 (R)** Everyone thought he was dead but you can't keep a bad guy down so this grossly disfigured policeman forms a one-man vigilante squad, seeking revenge (why never matters—just the body count). Blood and guts fly as any plot shortcomings are cleverly disguised by an array of violent video deaths. Sequel to "Maniac Cop." **90m/C VHS, LV.** Robert Davi, Claudia Christian, Michael Lerner, Bruce Campbell, Laurene Landon, Robert Z'Dar, Clarence Williams III, Leo Rossi; ***D:*** William Lustig; ***W:*** Larry Cohen. *LIV*

Maniac Cop 3: Badge of Silence **1993 (R)** The grossly disfigured policeman returns yet again to exact gory vengeance as the good guys try to get rid of him once and for all. **85m/C VHS.** Robert Z'Dar, Robert Davi, Gretchen Becker, Paul Gleason, Doug Savant, Caitlin Dulany; ***D:*** William Lustig, Joel Soisson; ***W:*** Larry Cohen; ***M:*** Jerry Goldsmith. *ACA*

Maniac Warriors **199?** A nuclear apocalypse has caused some strange changes in the population—and not for the better. Blood-crazed mutants attack the heavily armed inhabitants of New State Idaho and there's lots of mayhem in store. **91m/C VHS.** Tom Schioler, John Wood, Melanie Kilgour. *AIP, MOV*

The Manions of America ½ **1981** The long and sometimes interesting rags-to-riches tale of Rory O'Manion, a feisty Irish patriot who leaves his native land during the potato famine of 1845 to settle in America. Originally a television miniseries. **290m/C VHS, Beta.** Pierce Brosnan, Kate Mulgrew, Linda Purl, David Soul, Kathleen Beller, Simon MacCorkindale; ***D:*** Joseph Sargent, Charles S. Dubin. *PSM, PAR*

Manipulator **1971 (R)** A deranged ex-movie makeup man (Rooney, playing to type) kidnaps a young actress and holds her prisoner in a deserted Hollywood sound stage. **91m/C VHS, Beta.** Mickey Rooney, Luana Anders, Keenan Wynn; ***D:*** Yabo Yablonsky. *LIV, VES*

The Manitou **1978 (PG)** A San Francisco woman suffers from a rapidly growing neck tumor which eventually grows into a 400-year-old Indian witch doctor. (I hate when that happens.) Redeemed only by good special effects, especially those that kept Curtis, Strasberg, and Meredith from laughing. **104m/C VHS, Beta, LV.** Susan Strasberg, Tony Curtis, Stella Stevens, Ann Sothern, Burgess Meredith, Michael Ansara; ***D:*** William Girdler; ***M:*** Lalo Schifrin. *COL, NLC*

Mankillers **1987** A group of tough female convicts are enlisted to hunt down and rub out a psycho drug dealer, all the while displaying their feminine charms. **90m/C VHS, Beta.** Edd Byrnes, Gail Fisher, Edy Williams, Lynda Aldon, William Zipp, Christopher Lunde, Susanne Tegman, Marilyn Stafford, Paul Bruno, Byron Clark; ***D:*** David A. Prior. *COL*

Mannequin ½ **1937** Tracy and Crawford star in this romantic story of a poor girl who finds temporary happiness by marrying a wealthy man after ditching her con-artist husband. Somewhat predictable, the movie reads like a "People" magazine story on The Donald and Ivana. Tracy and Crawford keep the story afloat (in their only film together), with an able assist from Curtis. **95m/B VHS.** Joan Crawford, Spencer Tracy, Alan Curtis, Ralph Morgan, Leo Gorcey, Elisabeth Risdon, Paul Fix; ***D:*** Frank Borzage; ***W:*** Lawrence Hazard. Nominations: Academy Awards '38: Best Song ("Always and Always"). *MGM, MED*

Mannequin **1987 (PG)** A young artist creates a store window display using various mannequins, one of which contains the spirit of an ancient Egyptian woman. She comes to life when he is around, and naturally none of his co-workers believe him. Very light comedy, featuring two pretty stars and music by Jefferson Starship. **90m/C VHS, Beta, LV.** Andrew McCarthy, Kim Cattrall, Estelle Getty, James Spader, Meshach Taylor, Carole Davis, G.W. Bailey; ***D:*** Michael Gottlieb; ***W:*** Ed Rugoff. Nominations: Academy Awards '87: Best Song ("Nothing's Gonna Stop Us Now"). *CCB, MED, VTR*

Mannequin 2: On the Move *Woof!* **1991 (PG)** Less of a sequel, more of a lame rehash proving that the first "Mannequin" could have been even dumber. At this rate part three will be off the scale. Now it's a lovesick Teutonic princess frozen for 1,000 years who revives in a department store. Taylor reprises his grotesque gay role. **95m/C VHS, LV.** Kristy Swanson, William Ragsdale, Meshach Taylor, Terry Kiser, Stuart Pankin; ***D:*** Stewart Raffill; ***W:*** Ed Rugoff. *LIV*

Manny's Orphans *Here Come the Tigers* **1978 (PG)** An out-of-work teacher takes on a lovable home for orphaned boys. Dull remake of "Bad News Bears." **92m/C VHS, Beta.** Richard Lincoln, Malachy McCourt, Sel Skolnick; ***D:*** Sean S. Cunningham. *LIV, VES*

Manon **1950** Tragic tale of a French woman condemned for her affair with a Resistance fighter. They flee to Paris, where her brother forces her into prostitution. Based on the novel "Manon Lescaut" by Abbe Antoine-Francois Prevost. In French with English subtitles. **91m/B VHS.** Cecile Aubry, Michel Auclair, Serge Reggiani, Henri Vilbert, Daniel Ivernel; ***D:*** Henri-Georges Clouzot. *NOS*

Manon of the Spring ½ *Manon des Sources; Jean de Florette 2* **1987 (PG)** In this excellent sequel to "Jean de Florette," the adult daughter of the dead hunchback, Jean, discovers who blocked up the spring on her father's land. She plots her revenge, which proves greater than she could ever imagine. Montand is astonishing. Based on a Marcel Pagnol novel. In French with English subtitles. **113m/C VHS, Beta, LV.** *FR* Yves Montand, Daniel Auteuil, Emmanuelle Beart, Hippolyte Girardot; ***D:*** Claude Berri; ***W:*** Gerard Brach, Claude Berri. National Board of Review Awards '87: 5 Best Foreign Films of the Year. *ORI, APD, INJ*

Manos, the Hands of Fate *Woof!* **1966** Horrible acting and laughable special effects elevate this story of a family ensnared by a satanic cult a notch above your average bad horror film. Highlights include a Satan-like character who can't stop laughing; the dreaded "hounds of hell" (or are those mangy dogs with big ears glued on?); and Torgo the monstrous henchman, who you know is evil because he has giant kneecaps (a sure sign of the devil's work). Notable as the one of the most often requested movies on Comedy Central's satiric "Mystery Science Theatre 3000," this one is good for a laugh. **74m/C VHS.** Tom Nayman, Diane Mahree, Hal P. Warren, John Reynolds; ***D:*** Hal P. Warren; ***W:*** Hal P. Warren. *SNC*

Man's Best Friend 🦴½ **1993 (R)** A guard dog is the object of a genetic experiment that has given him the agressiveness of other creatures, including a cobra and a leopard. Since Max is an enormous Tibetan mastiff this means big trouble for everyone but the reporter (Sheedy) who rescued him—and even she better watch out. **87m/C VHS, LV.** Ally Sheedy, Lance Henriksen, Frederic Lehne, Robert Costanzo, John Cassisi, J.D. Daniels; ***D:*** John Lafia; ***W:*** John Lafia; ***M:*** Joel Goldsmith. *NLC*

Man's Country 🦴🦴 **1938** A rip-roarin' western saga filled with the usual action and danger, as ranger Randall leads the fight against a band of nasties headed by Long, in a dual role as twin brothers. **55m/B VHS, Beta.** Jack Randall, Ralph Peters, Marjorie Reynolds, Walter Long; ***D:*** Robert F. "Bob" Hill. *NOS, DVT*

Man's Favorite Sport? 🦴🦴½ **1963** A slapstick comedy about a renowned fishing expert author who actually hates fishing, but is forced to compete in a major tournament by a romantically inclined publicity agent. Very funny in spots. **121m/C VHS, Beta.** Rock Hudson, Paula Prentiss, Charlene Holt, Maria Perschy, John McGiver; ***D:*** Howard Hawks; ***M:*** Henry Mancini. *MCA, CCB*

Man's Land 🦴½ **1932** A ranch needs savin', and Hoot's the guy to do it in this formulaic Gibson epic. **65m/B VHS, Beta.** Hoot Gibson, Marion Shilling, Skeeter Bill Robbins, Alan Bridge; ***D:*** Phil Rosen. *VCI*

Mansfield Park 🦴🦴½ **1985** Fanny is an impoverished young woman, snubbed by society, who earns the respect and love of her cousin in a BBC mini-series adaptation of the Jane Austen classic set in 19th century England. **261m/C VHS, Beta.** *GB* Sylvestria Le Touzel, Bernard Hepton, Anna Massey, Donald Pleasence; ***D:*** David Giles. *FOX, TVC, HMV*

The Manster 🦴 *The Manster—Half Man, Half Monster; The Split* **1959** Another masterpiece from the director who brought us "Monster from Green Hell." Womanizing, whiskey swilling American journalist receives mysterious injection from crazed scientist and sprouts unsightly hair and extra head. Although shot in the land of the rising sun, lips move in sync with dialogue. **72m/B VHS.** *JP* Peter Dyneley, Jane Hylton, Satoshi Nakamura, Terri Zimmern; ***D:*** Kenneth Crane, George Breakston. *SNC, MRV*

Mantis in Lace 🦴½ *Lila* **1968 (R)** A go-go dancer slaughters men while tripping on LSD. Cinematography by pre-"Easy Rider" Laslo Kovacs. Watch it for the "hep" dialogue. **68m/C VHS.** Susan Stewart, Steve Vincent, M.K. Evans, Vic Lance, Pat Barrington, Janu Wine, Stuart Lancaster, John Carrol, Judith Crane, Cheryl Trepton; ***D:*** William Rotsler. *TPV*

Mantrap 🦴🦴½ **1926** Early silent success by Fleming, who later directed "Gone with the Wind" and "The Wizard of Oz." Fabled flapper Bow tempts a lawyer on retreat in the woods. **66m/B VHS, Beta.** Clara Bow, Ernest Torrence, Percy Marmont, Eugene Pallette, Tom Kennedy; ***D:*** Victor Fleming. *GPV, FCT*

The Manxman 🦴🦴½ **1929** Hitchcock's last silent film, a romantic melodrama about ambition and infidelity on the Isle of Man. **129m/B VHS, Beta.** *GB* Carl Brisson, Anny Ondra; ***D:*** Alfred Hitchcock. *VYY, MRV, MLB*

The Many Adventures of Winnie the Pooh **1977 (G)** Disney's 22nd animated feature offers A.A. Milne's beloved characters and their adventures in the Hundred Acre Wood. Includes a behind-the-scenes featurette with the original creators, animators, and voices. **83m/C VHS.** *TOU*

Many Faces of Sherlock Holmes **1986** A documentary look at the various incarnations of the famous sleuth from A. Conan Doyle's stories to various film portrayals. **58m/C VHS, Beta.** Christopher Plummer, Basil Rathbone, Christopher Lee. *PSM*

Map of the Human Heart 🦴🦴 **1993 (R)** Thirty-year saga told in flashback. Young Eskimo Avik (Lee) and his Metis love interest Albertine (Parillaud) struggle with racism in a white world. They meet and become friends as children and years later meet again in Dresden during WWII, but now Albertine is married to Avik's once close friend, denying her heritage and living in the white world that he has been fighting for so long. Mediocre movie with extraordinary Arctic scenery. Cusack has a small role as a mapmaker. **109m/C VHS.** Jason Scott Lee, Anne Parillaud, Patrick Bergin, Robert Joamie, Annie Galipeau, John Cusack, Jeanne Moreau; ***D:*** Vincent Ward; ***W:*** Vincent Ward, Louis Nowra. *HBO, FCT, BTV*

Marat/Sade 🦴🦴🦴½ *Persecution and Assassination of Jean-Paul Marat as Performed by the Inmates of the Asylum of Charenton Under the Direction of the Marquis De Sade* **1966 (R)** A theatrical production presented by patients at a mental institution is directed by the Marquis de Sade. Well directed and visually effective, featuring Jackson's first film performance. Based on a play by Peter Weiss. Some theaters were forced to add extensions to the marquee when the film was first released. **115m/C VHS, LV.** *GB* Patrick Magee, Clifford Rose, Glenda Jackson, Ian Richardson, Brenda Kempner, Ruth Baker, Michael Williams; ***D:*** Peter Brook; ***C:*** David Watkin. *WBF, MGM, LUM*

Marathon 🦴🦴 **1980** When a middle-aged jogger's ego gets a boost through the attention of a beautiful young woman, he takes up marathon running. Light comedy. Made for television. **100m/C VHS.** Bob Newhart, Leigh Taylor-Young, Herb Edelman, Dick Gautier, Anita Gillette, John Hillerman; ***D:*** Jackie Cooper. *LIV*

Marathon Man 🦴🦴🦴 **1976 (R)** Nightmarish chase-thriller in which a graduate student becomes entangled in a plot involving a murderous Nazi fugitive. As student Hoffman is preparing for the Olympic marathon, he is reunited with his secret-agent brother, setting the intricate plot in motion. Courtesy of his brother, Hoffman becomes involved with Olivier, an old crazed Nazi seeking jewels taken from concentration camp victims. Non-stop action throughout, including a torture scene sure to set your teeth on edge. Goldman adapted the screenplay from his novel. **125m/C VHS, Beta, LV.** Dustin Hoffman, Laurence Olivier, Marthe Keller, Roy Scheider, William Devane, Fritz Weaver; ***D:*** John Schlesinger; ***W:*** William Goldman; ***C:*** Conrad Hall. Golden Globe Awards '77: Best Supporting Actor (Olivier); Nominations: Academy Awards '76: Best Supporting Actor (Olivier). *PAR*

Marauder 🦴🦴 **1965** The prince of Venice leads a sea-faring onslaught against ransacking pirates and enemy fleets. **90m/C VHS, Beta.** *IT* Gordon Scott, Gianna Maria Canale, Franca Bettoya; ***D:*** Luigi Capuano. *NO*

Marbella 🦴½ **1985** A luxury resort in Spain is the setting for a big caper heist of three million dollars from a monarchical tycoon. **96m/C VHS, Beta.** Rod Taylor, Britt Ekland; ***D:*** Miguel Hermoso. *LIV*

March of the Wooden Soldiers 🦴🦴🦴 *Babes in Toyland* **1934** The classic Mother Goose tale about the secret life of Christmas toys, with Laurel and Hardy as Santa's helpers who must save Toyland from the wicked Barnaby. A Yuletide "must see." Also available in a colorized version. **73m/B VHS, LV.** Stan Laurel, Oliver Hardy, Charlotte Henry, Henry Kleinbach (Brandon), Felix Knight, Jean Darling, Johnny Downs, Marie Wilson; ***D:*** Charles R. Rogers, Gus Meins. *NOS, GKK, IME*

March or Die 🦴🦴½ **1977 (PG)** Great potential, unrealized. An American joins the French Foreign Legion during WWI after his dismissal from West Point. Following the brutality of training, he is assigned to guard an archeological expedition in Morocco, where he pulls together a rag-tag outfit for the mission. Hackman proves once again the wide range of his acting abilities, surmounting the cliched and fairly sadistic plot. Shot on location in the Sahara Desert. **104m/C VHS.** *GB* Gene Hackman, Terence Hill, Max von Sydow, Catherine Deneuve, Ian Holm; ***D:*** Dick Richards; ***W:*** David Zelag Goodman; ***M:*** Maurice Jarre. *FOX*

Marciano 🦴🦴 **1979** A made-for-television version of the great boxer's life. Average fight movie. **97m/C VHS, Beta.** Tony LoBianco, Vincent Gardenia; ***D:*** Bernard L. Kowalski; ***M:*** Ernest Gold. *SUE, NLC*

Marco 🦴🦴 **1973** Entertaining musical adventure of Marco Polo's life casts Arnaz as Marco Polo and Mostel as Kublai Khan. A couple of cut-ups, right? One of the first films to combine animation with live action. Shot partially on location in the Orient. ♫By Damn; Walls; A Family Man; Spaghetti. **109m/C VHS, Beta.** Desi Arnaz Jr., Zero Mostel, Jack Weston, Cie Cie Win; ***D:*** Seymour Robbie. *PSM*

Marco Polo, Jr. 🦴 **1972** Marco Polo, Jr., the daring descendant of the legendary explorer, travels the world in search of his destiny in this song-filled, feature-length, but poorly animated, fantasy. **82m/C VHS, Beta.** ***D:*** Eric Porter; ***V:*** Bobby Rydell. *FHE, WTA*

Mardi Gras for the Devil 🦴🦴 **1993 (R)** Black magic and the occult combine as a New Orleans cop tries to catch a killer who strikes only at Mardi Gras. The cop's got his work cut out for him since the killer is no mere mortal but a demon who believes in human sacrifice. **95m/C VHS, Beta.** Robert Davi, Michael Ironside, Lesley-Anne Down, Lydie Denier, Mike Starr, Margaret Avery, John Amos; ***D:*** David A. Prior; ***W:*** David A. Prior. *PSM*

Mardi Gras Massacre *Woof! Crypt of Dark Secrets* **1978** Aztec priest arrives in New Orleans during Mardi Gras to revive the blood ritual of human sacrifice to an Aztec god. A police detective relentlessly pursues him. Much gore and gut-slicing, with no redeeming social value. **92m/C VHS, Beta.** Curt Dawson, Gwen Arment, Wayne Mack, Laura Misch; ***D:*** Jack Weis. *VHE*

Margaret's Museum 🦴🦴½ **1995** The museum of the title is the bizarre shrine Margaret (Bonham Carter) dedicates to the family members who have been killed in the coal mines that dominate her small (1940s) Cape Breton, New Brunswick town. Both Margaret and her mother, Catherine (Nelligan), are embittered by their tragedies and when Margaret finds romance with eccentric bagpiper Neil (Russell), she makes him promise he'll never return to mine work. But with a bad economy, Neil is forced back to the pits and inevitable disaster. It's Bonham Carter's picture all the way and she shows a wide (and welcome) range of emotions and strength. Adapted from a story by Sheldon Currie. **114m/C VHS.** *CA GB* Helena Bonham Carter, Clive Russell, Kate Nelligan, Kenneth Welsh, Craig Olejnik; ***D:*** Mort Ransen; ***W:*** Mort Ransen, Gerald Wexler; ***C:*** Vic Sarin; ***M:*** Milan Kymlicka. Genie Awards '95: Best Actress (Bonham Carter), Best Costume Design, Best Supporting Actor (Welsh), Best Supporting Actress (Nelligan), Best Writing, Best Score. *NYR*

Margin for Murder 🦴🦴 *Mickey Spillane's Margin for Murder* **1981** Mike Hammer investigates a mysterious accident that killed his best friend. Made for television. **98m/C VHS, Beta.** Kevin Dobson, Cindy Pickett, Donna Dixon, Charles Hallahan; ***D:*** Daniel Haller. *PSM*

Maria Candelaria 🦴🦴 *Portrait of Maria; Xochimilco* **1946** Society rejects a woman because people don't like her mother. (She posed nude for an artist, and the town responds by stoning her to death, proving that going against small-town morals can be lethal). Eventually, time and circumstance push daughter onto mother's path in this tragic soaper. Del Rio portrays the scorned young woman, although she was 40 years old. **96m/B VHS, Beta.** *MX* Dolores Del Rio, Pedro Armendariz Sr., Margarita Cortes; ***D:*** Emilio Fernandez. *MAD*

Maria Chapdelaine 🦴🦴🦴 **1934** An early film from the renowned French director, in which a brutish trapper and a sophisticate battle for the love of a girl in the Canadian wilderness. English subtitles. Remade in 1984. **75m/B VHS, Beta.** *FR* Jean Gabin, Jean-Pierre Aumont, Madeleine Renaud; ***D:*** Julien Duvivier. *HHT*

Maria Chapdelaine 🦴🦴½ **1984** Around the turn of the century, a young girl in the Northern Canadian wilderness endures a year of passion, doomed love, and tragedy. In French with subtitles.

Remake of a 1935 French film. **108m/C VHS, Beta.** *FR CA* Nick Mancuso, Carole Laure, Claude Rich, Pierre Curzi; ***D:*** Gilles Carle. *MED*

Marianne and Juliane ☠☠☠½ **1982** Powerful combination of relationships and politics in West Germany as experienced through the lives of two sisters—Juliane, a feminist editor, and Marianne, a political terrorist. Based on the lives of Gudrun and Christiane Ensslin. German with subtitles. **106m/C VHS.** *GE* Jutta Lampe, Barbara Sukowa, Ruediger Vogler, Doris Schade, Franz Rudnick; ***D:*** Margarethe von Trotta. *NYF*

Maria's Child ☠☠½ **1993** Light comedy about a dancer who becomes pregnant and must decide whether or not to keep the baby. When her live-in boyfriend (not the father) admits he cheated on her, she kicks him out. Unable to make up her mind, she imagines a dialogue with the fetus. Second of a trilogy by British television screenwriter Malcolm McKay on the subject of forgiveness. **97m/C VHS.** *GB* Yolanda Vasquez, David O'Hara, Fiona Shaw, Alec McCowen, Sophie Okenado, Linda Davidson, Rudi Davies, Nicholas Woodeson, Anita Zagaria; ***D:*** Malcolm McKay; ***W:*** Malcolm McKay; ***M:*** Philip Appleby. *NYR*

Maria's Day ☠☠☠ **1984** Chronicles the plague-riddled downfall of a formerly aristocratic and wealthy Hungarian family in the years following the failed 1849 Revolution. In Hungarian with English subtitles. **113m/C VHS, Beta.** ***D:*** Judit Elek. *FCT, AUD*

Maria's Lovers ☠☠½ **1984 (R)** The wife (Kinski) of an impotent WWII veteran (Savage) succumbs to the charms of a rakish lady-killer (Spano). Savage turns to the charms of an older woman, finds love again with Kinski, but is still impotent; she gets pregnant by a wandering minstrel (Carradine) and on we go to film climax. Offbeat and uneven, representing Russian director Konchalovsky's first American film and one of Kinski's better roles. **103m/C VHS, Beta.** Nastassia Kinski, John Savage, Robert Mitchum, Keith Carradine, Anita Morris, Bud Cort, Karen Young, Tracy Nelson, John Goodman, Vincent Spano; ***D:*** Andrei Konchalovsky; ***W:*** Marjorie David, Andrei Konchalovsky, Gerard Brach; ***C:*** Juan Ruiz-Anchia. *MGM*

Maricela **1988** Young Maricela Flores and her mother have come to the U.S. from El Salvador to escape the fighting. Living with a Southern Californian family, Maricela has a hard time adjusting to American life and, in particular, dealing with prejudice. An entry in the PBS "Wonderworks" series. **55m/C VHS.** Linda Lavin, Carlina Cruz. *PME, HMV, BTV*

Marie ☠☠☠ **1985 (PG-13)** In this true story, a divorced (and battered) mother works her way through school and the system to become the first woman to head the Parole Board in Tennessee. Finding rampant corruption, she blows the whistle on her bosses, who put her life in jeopardy. Spacek gives a powerful performance, as does first-time actor Thompson, portraying himself as the abused woman's attorney. Based on the book by Peter Maas. **113m/C VHS, Beta.** Sissy Spacek, Jeff Daniels, Keith Szarabajka, John Cullum, Morgan Freeman, Fred Dalton Thompson, Don Hood, Lisa Banes, Vincent Irizarry; ***D:*** Roger Donaldson; ***W:*** John Briley; ***C:*** Chris Menges; ***M:*** Francis Lai. *MGM*

Marie Antoinette ☠☠½ **1938** An elephantine costume drama chronicling the French queen's life from princesshood to her final days before the Revolution. A Shearer festival all the way, and a late example of MGM's overstuffed period style and star-power. Overlong, but engrossing for the wrong reasons. Morley, in his first film, plays Louis XVI. Power's only MGM loan-out casts him as a Swedish count and Marie's romantic dalliance. Based on a book by Stephan Zweig, with script assistance from (among others) F. Scott Fitzgerald. **160m/B VHS, Beta, LV.** Norma Shearer, Tyrone Power, John Barrymore, Robert Morley, Gladys George, Anita Louise, Joseph Schildkraut, Henry Stephenson, Reginald Gardiner, Peter Bull, Albert Dekker, Joseph Calleia, George Zucco, Cora Witherspoon, Barry Fitzgerald, Mae Busch, Harry Davenport, Scotty Beckett; ***D:*** Woodbridge S. Van Dyke; ***W:*** F. Scott Fitzgerald; ***C:*** William H. Daniels. Nominations: Academy Awards '38: Best Actress (Shearer), Best Interior Decoration, Best Supporting Actor (Morley). *MGM*

Marie Galante ☠☠☠ **1934** Fine spy drama has Tracy running into Gallien in Panama (years earlier she had been left there after a kidnapping). He finds her most helpful in his attempt to thwart the bombing of the Panama Canal. It's the performances that raise this otherwise standard thriller up a few notches. **88m/B VHS, Beta.** Spencer Tracy, Katie Galian, Ned Sparks, Helen Morgan, Sig Rumann, Leslie Fenton, Jay C. Flippen; ***D:*** Henry King. *NOS, SNC, HEG*

Marihuana ☠ *Marijuana: The Devil's Weed* **1936** An unintentionally hilarious, "Reefer Madness"-type cautionary film about the exaggerated evils of pot smoking. A real dopey film favored by right-winger zealots. **57m/B VHS, Beta.** Harley Wood, Hugh McArthur, Pat Carlyle; ***D:*** Dwain Esper. *SNC, VYY, HEG*

Marilyn & Bobby: Her Final Affair ☠½ **1994** Sordid account of the alleged romance between movie star Monroe (Anderson) and Attorney General Robert Kennedy (Kelly). Culminates in a silly scene at Marilyn's home, on the night of her death, where various men all try to find her tell-all diary while keeping out of sight of each other. Made for cable TV. **95m/C VHS.** Melody Anderson, James F. Kelly, Richard Dysart, Thomas Wagner, Raymond Serra, Kristopher Tabori, Jonathan Banks, Geoffrey Blake, Ian Buchanan; ***D:*** Bradford May. *AVE*

Marilyn: The Untold Story ☠☠☠ **1980** Nominated for an Emmy, Hicks elevates what could easily have been a dull made-for-TV movie with her remarkable performance as Marilyn Monroe. Based on the book by Norman Mailer. **156m/C VHS.** Catherine Hicks, Richard Basehart, Frank Converse, John Ireland, Sheree North, Anne Ramsey, Viveca Lindfors, Jason Miller, Bill Vint; ***D:*** Jack Arnold, John Flynn, Lawrence Schiller; ***M:*** William Goldstein. *ABC*

Marine Raiders ☠☠ **1943** Marines train and then fight at Guadalcanal. A typical flag-waver, watchable but not particularly engaging. **90m/B VHS, Beta.** Pat O'Brien, Robert Ryan, Ruth Hussey, Frank McHugh, Barton MacLane; ***D:*** Harold Schuster. *TTC*

Marius ☠☠☠☠ **1931** This is the first of Marcel Pagnol's trilogy ("Fanny" and "Cesar" followed), about the lives and adventures of the people of Provence, France. Marius is a young man who dreams of going away to sea. When he acts on those dreams, he leaves behind his girlfriend, Fanny. Realistic dialogue and vivid characterizations. Adapted by Pagnol from his play. The musical play and film "Fanny" (1961) were adapted from this trilogy. **125m/B VHS, Beta, LV.** *FR* Raimu, Pierre Fresnay, Charpin, Orane Demazis; ***D:*** Alexander Korda; ***W:*** Marcel Pagnol; ***M:*** Francis Gromon. *NOS, MRV, INT*

Marjoe **1972 (PG)** Documentary follows the career of rock-style evangelist Marjoe Gortner, who spent 25 years of his life touring the country as a professional preacher. Marjoe later went on to become an actor and professional fundraiser. **88m/C VHS, Beta.** Marjoe Gortner; ***D:*** Howard Smith, Sarah Kernochan. Academy Awards '72: Best Feature Documentary. *COL*

Marjorie Morningstar ☠☠ **1958** A temperate Hollywood adaptation of the Herman Wouk story of a young actress who fails to achieve stardom and settles on being a housewife. Wood slipped a bit in this story. **123m/C VHS.** Natalie Wood, Gene Kelly, Martin Balsam, Claire Trevor, Ed Wynn, Everett Sloane, Carolyn Jones; ***D:*** Irving Rapper; ***C:*** Harry Stradling; ***M:*** Max Steiner. Nominations: Academy Awards '58: Best Song ("A Very Precious Love"). *REP*

The Mark ☠☠☠½ **1961** Story of a convicted child molester who cannot escape his past upon his release from prison. Whitman gives a riveting performance as the convict. **127m/B VHS, Beta.** *GB* Stuart Whitman, Maria Schell, Rod Steiger, Brenda de Banzie, Maurice Denham, Donald Wolfit, Paul Rogers, Donald Houston; ***D:*** Guy Green; ***M:*** Richard Rodney Bennett. Nominations: Academy Awards '61: Best Actor (Whitman). *NO*

Mark of Cain ☠☠½ **1984** Twin brothers, one normal, the other a raving lunatic with murderous tendencies, confuse the authorities who imprison the nice guy, allowing the nutcase to chase after his beautiful sister-in-law. **90m/C VHS, Beta.** Robin Ward, Wendy Crewson, August Schellenberg; ***D:*** Bruce Pittman; ***W:*** Peter Colley. *LIV, VES*

Mark of the Beast ☠ **19??** Two students inadvertently videotape an assassination, and are then relentlessly pursued by the killer. **90m/C VHS.** Carolyn Guillet, David Smulker; ***D:*** Robert Stewart. *NO*

Mark of the Devil ☠ *Burn, Witch, Burn; Brenn, Hexe, Brenn* **1969 (R)** Witchcraft and romance don't mix, as a Medieval witch hunter and a sexy girl accused of witchery discover. Notoriously graphic torture scenes add to the mayhem but the weird part is that this is based on true stories. **96m/C VHS, Beta.** *GB GE* Herbert Lom, Olivera Vuco, Udo Kier, Reggie Nalder, Herbert Fux, Michael Maien, Ingeborg Schoener, Johannes Buzalski, Gaby Fuchs; ***D:*** Michael Armstrong. *VES, LIV, TPV*

Mark of the Devil 2 ☠ **1972 (R)** Sadistic witchhunters torture satan's servants and torch sisters of mercy, whilst trying to horn in on a nobleman's fortune. It's just not as gross without the vomit bags. **90m/C VHS.** *GB GE* Erika Blanc, Anton Diffring, Reggie Nalder; ***D:*** Adrian Hoven. *VDM*

The Mark of the Hawk ☠☠☠ *The Accused* **1957** A uniquely told story of African nations struggling to achieve racial equality after gaining independence. Songs include "This Man Is Mine," sung by Kitt. **83m/C VHS.** *GB* Sidney Poitier, Eartha Kitt, Juano Hernandez, John McIntire; ***D:*** Michael Audley. *MRV*

Mark of the Spur ☠½ **1932** The mark on an injured man's face is used to track down his attacker. **60m/B VHS, Beta.** Bob Custer, Lillian Rich, Franklyn Farnum, Bud Osborne; ***D:*** J.P. McGowan. *NOS, DVT, GPV*

Mark of the Vampire ☠☠☠ **1935** A murder in a small town is solved through the use of vaudeville actors who pose as vampires. Great cast, surprise ending. **61m/B VHS, Beta.** Lionel Barrymore, Bela Lugosi, Elizabeth Allan; ***D:*** Tod Browning; ***C:*** James Wong Howe. *MGM, MLB*

Mark of Zorro ☠☠☠ **1920** Fairbanks plays a dual role as the hapless Don Diego and his dashing counterpart, Zorro, the hero of the oppressed. Silent film. **80m/B VHS, LV.** Douglas Fairbanks Sr., Marguerite de la Motte, Noah Beery Sr.; ***D:*** Fred Niblo. *REP, MRV, GPV*

The Mark of Zorro ☠☠☠½ **1940** The dashing Power swashbuckles his way through this wonderfully acted and directed romp. He plays the foppish son of a 19th-century California aristocrat who is secretly the masked avenger of the oppressed peons. Bromberg plays the wicked governor, with the beautiful niece (Darnell) beloved by Power, and Rathbone is supremely evil as his cruel minion. Lots of swordplay with a particularly exciting duel to the death between Rathbone and Power. Based on the novel "The Curse of Capistrano" by Johnston McCulley. Remake of the 1921 silent film and followed by a number of other Zorro incarnations. **93m/B VHS.** Tyrone Power, Linda Darnell, Basil Rathbone, Gale Sondergaard, Eugene Pallette, J. Edward Bromberg, Montagu Love, Janet Beecher; ***D:*** Rouben Mamoulian; ***W:*** John Taintor Foote; ***C:*** Arthur C. Miller; ***M:*** Alfred Newman. *FXV, BTV*

Mark Twain and Me ☠☠½ **1991** Robards portrays the aging and irascible Mark Twain, attended by a neglected but devoted daughter, and befriended by 11-year-old Dorothy Quick, as they travel on the same ship. Based on a true story. Made for television. **93m/C VHS.** Jason Robards Jr., Talia Shire, Amy Stewart, Chris Wiggins, R.H. Thomson, Fiona Reid; ***D:*** Daniel Petrie. *DIS, BTV*

Marked for Death ☠½ *Screwface* **1990 (R)** Having killed a prostitute, DEA agent Seagal decides it's time to roll out the white picket fence in the 'burbs with the little woman and brood. Trouble is, a bunch of guys with dreadlocks don't approve of his early retirement, and the Jamaican gangsters plan to send him and his family to the great Rasta playground in the sky. Whereupon the Stevester kicks and punches and wags his ponytail. Much blood flows, mon. Tunes by Jimmy Cliff. **93m/C VHS, LV.** Steven Seagal, Joanna Pacula, Basil Wallace, Keith David, Tom Wright, Danielle Harris, Arlen Dean Snyder, Teri Weigel; ***D:*** Dwight Little; ***W:*** Mark Victor, Michael Grais. *FXV, CCB*

Marked for Murder 🦴½ **1945** Another in the Texas Ranger series. In this entry, the Rangers come to the rescue when a rancher war appears inevitable. **58m/B VHS, LV.** Tex Ritter, Dave O'Brien, Guy Wilkerson; ***D:*** Elmer Clifton; ***W:*** Elmer Clifton. *VMK*

Marked for Murder 🦴½ **1989 (R)** Two TV station employees are framed for murder after being sent out to find a missing videocassette. Renee Estevez is part of the Sheen/Estevez dynasty. **88m/C VHS, Beta.** Renee Estevez, Wings Hauser, Jim Mitchum, Ross Hagen, Ken Abraham; ***D:*** Rick Sloane. *VMK*

Marked Money 🦴🦴 **1928** Amiable captain takes in boy who'll soon roll in the dough and swindlers show up on the scene. The captain's courageous girl and her pilot beau step in to right the rookery. **61m/B VHS, Beta.** Frank "Junior" Coghlan, George Duryea, Tom Kennedy, Bert Woodruff, Virginia Bradford, Maurice Black, Jack Richardson; ***D:*** Spencer Gordon Bennet. *GPV, FCT*

Marked Trails 🦴 **1944** One clue stamps out the guilty parties in this wild west saga. **59m/B VHS, Beta.** Hoot Gibson, Bob Steele, Veda Ann Borg. *NOS, DVT*

Marked Woman 🦴🦴🦴 **1937** Gangster drama about crusading District Attorney who persuades a group of clipjoint hostesses to testify against their gangster boss. A gritty studio melodrama loosely based on a true story. **97m/B VHS, Beta, LV.** Bette Davis, Humphrey Bogart, Eduardo Ciannelli, Isabel Jewell, Jane Bryan, Mayo Methot, Allen Jenkins, Lola Lane; ***D:*** Lloyd Bacon; ***C:*** George Barnes. Venice Film Festival '37: Best Actress (Davis). *MGM*

Marlon Brando **1985** Documentary recounting the life and career of Hollywood's most rebellious superstar. **120m/C VHS, Beta.** Marlon Brando; ***D:*** Claudio Masenza. *BAR*

Marlowe 🦴🦴½ **1969 (PG)** Updated telling by Stirling Silliphant of Chandler's "The Little Sister" sports retro guy Garner as Philip Marlowe, gumshoe. Hired by a mystery blonde to find her misplaced brother, rumpled sleuth Marlowe encounters kicking Bruce Lee in his first film. Slick looking, but the story's a bit slippery. **95m/C VHS, Beta.** James Garner, Gayle Hunnicutt, Carroll O'Connor, Rita Moreno, Sharon Farrell, William Daniels, Bruce Lee; ***D:*** Paul Bogart; ***W:*** Stirling Silliphant; ***C:*** William H. Daniels. *MGM, FCT*

Marnie 🦴🦴🦴½ **1964** A lovely blonde with a mysterious past robs her employers and then changes her identity. When her current boss catches her in the act and forces her to marry him, he soon learns the puzzling aspects of Marnie's background. Criticized at the time of its release, the movie has since been accepted as a Hitchcock classic. **130m/C VHS, Beta, LV.** Tippi Hedren, Sean Connery, Diane Baker, Bruce Dern, Louise Latham; ***D:*** Alfred Hitchcock; ***W:*** Jay Presson Allen; ***C:*** Robert Burks. *MCA*

Maroc 7 🦴 **1967** Slow story of a secret agent after a thief suffering from a split personality. **92m/C VHS.** Gene Barry, Elsa Martinelli, Cyd Charisse, Leslie Phillips; ***D:*** Gerry O'Hara. *PAR*

Marooned 🦴🦴 **1969 (G)** Tense thriller casts Crenna, Hackman, and Franciscus as astronauts stranded in space after a retro-rocket misfires and their craft is unable to return to earth. **134m/C VHS, Beta, LV.** Gregory Peck, David Janssen, Richard Crenna, James Franciscus, Gene Hackman, Lee Grant; ***D:*** John Sturges; ***C:*** Daniel F. Fapp. Academy Awards '69: Best Visual Effects; Nominations: Academy Awards '69: Best Cinematography, Best Sound. *GKK*

The Marriage Circle 🦴🦴🦴 **1924** A pivotal silent comedy depicting the infidelity of several married couples in Vienna. Director Lubitsch's first American comedy. Remade as a musical, "One Hour With You," in 1932. Silent. **90m/B VHS.** Florence Vidor, Monte Blue, Marie Prevost, Creighton Hale, Adolphe Menjou, Harry Myers, Dale Fuller; ***D:*** Ernst Lubitsch. *NOS, MOV, GVV*

Marriage Is Alive and Well 🦴 **1980** A wedding photographer reflects on the institution of marriage from his unique perspective. Made for television. **100m/C VHS.** Joe Namath, Jack Albertson, Melinda Dillon, Judd Hirsch, Susan Sullivan, Fred McCarren, Swoosie Kurtz; ***D:*** Russ Mayberry. *LIV*

Marriage Italian Style 🦴🦴🦴 **1964** When an engaged man hears that his mistress is on her death bed, he goes to her side and, in an emotional gesture, promises to marry her if she survives. She does, and holds him to his promise. After they're married, however, she gives him a big surprise—three grown sons. A silly film, but DeSica's direction keeps it from being too fluffy. Lots of fun. Based on the play "Filumena Marturano" by Eduardo De Filippo. **102m/C VHS.** *IT* Sophia Loren, Marcello Mastroianni, Aldo Puglisi, Tecla Scarano, Marilu Tolo; ***D:*** Vittorio De Sica. Golden Globe Awards '65: Best Foreign Film; Nominations: Academy Awards '64: Best Actress (Loren), Best Foreign Language Film. *VTR*

The Marriage of Maria Braun 🦴🦴🦴🦴 *Die Ehe Der Maria Braun* **1979 (R)** In post-WWII Germany, a young woman uses guile and sexuality to survive as the nation rebuilds itself into an industrial power. The first movie in Fassbinder's trilogy about German women in Germany during the post war years, it is considered one of the director's finest films, and an indispensable example of the New German Cinema. In German with English subtitles. **120m/C VHS, Beta.** *GE* Hanna Schygulla, Klaus Lowitsch, Ivan Desny, Gottfried John, Gisela Uhlen; ***D:*** Rainer Werner Fassbinder; ***W:*** Rainer Werner Fassbinder; ***C:*** Michael Ballhaus; ***M:*** Peer Raben. Berlin International Film Festival '79: Best Actress (Schygulla); National Board of Review Awards '79: 5 Best Foreign Films of the Year. *NYF, COL, GLV*

Married? 🦴½ **1926** Couple endures 365 days of marital bliss in order to inherit big bucks. Some do it for less. **65m/B VHS, Beta.** Owen Moore, Constance Bennett; ***D:*** George Terwilliger. *GPV, FCT*

A Married Man 🦴🦴 **1984** Story focusing on a bored British lawyer who begins cheating on his wife. Amid the affair, someone gets murdered. Made for television. **200m/C VHS, Beta.** *GB* Anthony Hopkins, Ciaran Madden, Lise Hilboldt, Yvonne Coulette, John Le Mesurier, Sophie Ashton; ***D:*** John Davies. *LIV*

Married People, Single Sex 🦴🦴½ **1993 (R)** Three couples decide to spread their sexual wings. Shelly takes a new lover; Artie makes obscene phone calls; and Beth and Mike, who end their relationship, still can't keep out of bed. An unrated version is also available. **110m/C VHS.** Chase Masterson, Joseph Pilato, Darla Slavens, Shelley Michelle, Wendi Westbrook, Robert Zachar, Samuel Mongiello, Teri Thompson; ***D:*** Mike Sedan; ***W:*** Catherine Tavel. *TRI*

Married People, Single Sex 2: For Better or Worse 🦴½ **1994 (R)** Three women are faced with sexual unhappiness: Carol's hubby had an affair, Valerie wants a baby but her spouse doesn't, and Karen's husband is just too darn nice (she wants some spice in her life). So, there's lots of sexual encounters to solve their problems. Also available unrated. **93m/C VHS.** Kathy Shower, Monique Parent, Liza Smith, Craig Stepp, Doug Jeffrey; ***D:*** Mike Sedan. *TRI*

Married to It 🦴🦴 **1993 (R)** Three vastly different couples work together to plan a pageant at a private school. The oil and water group includes struggling hippie leftovers Bridges and Channing, '80s-era corporate cutthroats Shepherd and Silver, and starry-eyed newlyweds Masterson and Leonard. Contrived plot offers few humourous moments, with the main focus revolving around coping rather than comedy. And the coping is slow business, done by characters you don't really care about with problems that don't really matter. **112m/C VHS, LV.** Beau Bridges, Stockard Channing, Robert Sean Leonard, Mary Stuart Masterson, Cybill Shepherd, Ron Silver; ***D:*** Arthur Hiller; ***W:*** Janet Kovalcik; ***M:*** Henry Mancini. *ORI*

Married to the Mob 🦴🦴🦴 **1988 (R)** After the murder of her husband, an attractive Mafia widow tries to escape "mob" life, but ends up fighting off amorous advances from the current mob boss while being wooed by an undercover cop. A snappy script and a spry performance by Pfeiffer pepper this easy-to-watch film. **102m/C VHS, Beta, LV.** Michelle Pfeiffer, Dean Stockwell, Alec Baldwin, Matthew Modine, Mercedes Ruehl, Anthony J. Nici, Joan Cusack, Ellen Foley, Chris Isaak, Trey Wilson, Charles Napier, Tracey Walter, Al Lewis, Nancy Travis, David Johansen, Jonathan Demme; ***D:*** Jonathan Demme; ***W:*** Mark Burns, Barry Strugatz; ***C:*** Tak Fujimoto; ***M:*** David Byrne. New York Film Critics Awards '88: Best Supporting Actor (Stockwell); National Society of Film Critics Awards '88: Best Supporting Actor (Stockwell), Best Supporting Actress (Ruehl); Nominations: Academy Awards '88: Best Supporting Actor (Stockwell). *ORI*

Married Too Young 🦴🦴 *I Married Too Young* **1962** High school honeys elope, despite disapproval from the parental units. When the boy groom trades his med school plans for a monkey wrench in order to support the little missus, he finds much trouble with the hot rod heavies. **76m/B VHS.** Harold Lloyd Jr., Jana Lund, Anthony Dexter, Marianna Hill, Trudy Marshall, Brian O'Hara, Nita Loveless; ***D:*** George Moskov. *HHT, SNC*

A Married Woman 🦴🦴🦴 *La Femme Mariee* **1965** Dramatizes a day in the life of a woman who has both a husband and a lover. One of Godard's more mainstream efforts. **94m/B VHS, Beta, 8mm.** *FR* Macha Meril, Phillippe LeRoy, Bernard Noel; ***D:*** Jean-Luc Godard; ***W:*** Jean-Luc Godard. *VYY, MRV, DVT*

Marry Me, Marry Me 🦴🦴🦴 *Mazel Tov Ou le Mariage* **1969 (R)** While in Paris, a Jewish encyclopedia salesman falls in love with a pregnant Belgian woman. A sensitive story about European Jewish families. Berri wrote, produced, directed, and starred in this romantic comedy. **87m/C VHS.** *FR* Elisabeth Wiener, Regine, Claude Berri, Louisa Colpeyn; ***D:*** Claude Berri; ***C:*** Ghislan Cloquet. *NO*

The Marrying Man 🦴½ **1991 (R)** Young man meets his match when his buddies take him to Las Vegas for his bachelor party. He falls like a ton of bricks for the singer, not knowing she belongs to the local crime lord, who catches them together and forces them to marry. They immediately divorce, can't forget each other and eventually re-marry, again and again and again. Silly story supposedly based on the story of Harry Karl (eventual husband of Debbie Reynolds) and Marie MacDonald. Basinger and Baldwin's off-stage romance created quite a stir but their chemistry onscreen is zilch. Ineffective, not funny, poorly paced and acted: a good example of what happens when egotistical stars get their way. **116m/C VHS, LV.** Alec Baldwin, Kim Basinger, Robert Loggia, Armand Assante, Elisabeth Shue, Paul Reiser, Fisher Stevens, Peter Dobson, Gretchen Wyler; ***D:*** Jerry Rees; ***W:*** Neil Simon; ***M:*** David Newman. *HPH*

Mars Needs Women 🦴 **1966** When the Martian singles scene starts to drag, Mars boys cross the galaxy in search of fertile earth babes to help them repopulate the planet. Seems Batgirl Craig, the go-go dancing lady scientist, is at the top of their dance cards. **80m/C VHS.** Tommy Kirk, Yvonne Craig; ***D:*** Larry Buchanan; ***W:*** Larry Buchanan. *SNC*

Marshal Law 🦴🦴 **1996 (R)** Highland Glen is a gated community in L.A. that seems very secure, especially to ex-Texas Marshal Jack Coleman (Smits) and his family. But an earthquake leaves the neighborhood prey to a vicious gang unless Coleman can find a way to outwit them. **96m/C VHS.** Jimmy Smits, James LeGros, Vonte Sweet, Scott Plank, Kristy Swanson, Channon Roe, Michael Cavalieri, Rodney Rowland, Tai Thai; ***D:*** Stephen Cornwell; ***W:*** Stephen Cornwell, Nick Gregory; ***C:*** Levie Isaacks; ***M:*** Tim Truman. *MGM*

Marshal of Cedar Rock 🦴🦴 **1953** Marshal Rocky Lane sets a prisoner free, thinking the guy will lead him to a stash of stolen bank funds. Seems he miscalculates, but by way of consolation, he routs a rotten railroad agent who's rooking innocent people. Features the equine talent of Black Jack. **54m/B VHS.** Allan "Rocky" Lane, Phyllis Coates, Roy Barcroft, William Henry, Robert Shayne, Eddy Waller; ***D:*** Harry Keller. *HEG, DVT, NOS*

Marshal of Heldorado 🦴 **1950** An outlaw-infested town needs an injection of law and order. **53m/B VHS.** James Ellison, Russell Hayden, Raymond Hatton, Fuzzy Knight; ***D:*** Thomas Carr. *NOS, DVT*

The Marshal's Daughter 🦴½ **1953** A father and daughter team up to outwit an outlaw. Features many cowboy songs, including the title track by Tex Ritter. **71m/B VHS.** Tex Ritter, Ken Murray,

Laurie Anders, Preston Foster, Hoot Gibson; **D:** William (Lester Williams) Berke. *NOS, MOV, HEG*

Martha and I ♪♪♪ **1991** In 1934 Czechoslovakia, distinguished Jewish doctor Ernest Paul Fuchs (Piccoli), having divorced his unfaithful wife, impulsively marries his lower-class gentile German maid Martha (Sagebrecht). What turns out to be a true love match is witnessed through the adolescent eyes of nephew Emil (Chalupa), who comes to live with the couple. With the rise of Nazism and increased Jewish persecution the devoted Martha begins to fear for her husband and makes a futile attempt to find a safe haven. Stirring drama based on the director's childhood (he's the semi-fictionalized Emil). German with subtitles. **107m/C VHS.** Marianne Sagebrecht, Michel Piccoli, Vaclov Chalupa, Ondrej Vetchy; **D:** Jiri Weiss; **W:** Jiri Weiss; **C:** Viktor Ruzicka; **M:** Jiri Stivin. *NYR*

Martial Law ♪½ **1990 (R)** A film solely for martial arts fans. Two cops use their hands, feet, and other body parts to fight crime. **90m/C VHS.** Chad McQueen, Cynthia Rothrock, David Carradine, Andy McCutcheon; **D:** S.E. Cohen; **W:** Richard Brandes. *MED, FOX, VTR*

Martial Law 2: Undercover ♪½ **1991 (R)** Two cops, martial arts experts and part of an elite police force called Martial Law, go undercover to investigate the murder of a colleague. They uncover a fast-growing crime ring headed by a bad cop and a nightclub owner. The nightclub is host to the city's rich and powerful, who are treated to a bevy of beautiful women, protected by martial arts experts, and entertained by martial arts fights to the death. Lots of high-kicking action. **92m/C VHS, LV.** Jeff Wincott, Cynthia Rothrock, Paul Johansson, Evan Lurie, L. Charles Taylor, Sherrie Rose, Billy Drago; **D:** Kurt Anderson; **W:** Richard Brando, Jiles Fitzgerald. *MCA*

Martial Outlaw ♪♪ **1993 (R)** DEA man Kevin White (Wincott) has been following a drug-dealing ex-KGB kingpin from Moscow to San Francisco. The Russian's latest move takes him to Los Angeles where Kevin meets up with his older brother Jack (Hudson), a maverick LA cop. Jack persuades Kevin to let him in on the action but Kevin begins to suspect Jack is playing both sides and their sibling rivalry could lead to death. **89m/C VHS, LV.** Jeff Wincott, Gary Hudson, Richard Jaeckel, Krista Errickson, Vladimir Skomarovsky, Liliana Komorowska, Gary Wood; **D:** Kurt Anderson; **W:** Thomas Ritz. *REP*

The Martian Chronicles: Part 1 **1979** Series episode "The Explorers." Adapted from Ray Bradbury's critically acclaimed novel. Futuristic explorations of the planet Mars. Strange fates of the discovery teams make everything more curious. Made for television. **120m/C VHS, Beta.** Rock Hudson, Bernie Casey, Nicholas Hammond, Darren McGavin; **D:** Michael Anderson Sr. *FRH*

The Martian Chronicles: Part 2 ♪½ **1979** Episode following the television movie. This part is called "The Settlers." The planet Mars meets with its first colonization and the settlers watch the Earth explode. **97m/C VHS, Beta.** Rock Hudson, Fritz Weaver, Roddy McDowall, Bernie Casey, Darren McGavin, Gayle Hunnicutt, Barry Morse, Bernadette Peters; **D:** Michael Anderson Sr. *FRH*

The Martian Chronicles: Part 3 ♪♪½ **1979** In the final chapter of this space saga, the Martian's secrets become known and will forever change man's destiny. Adapted from Ray Bradbury's classic novel; made-for-television. **97m/C VHS, Beta.** Rock Hudson, Bernadette Peters, Christopher Connelly, Fritz Weaver, Roddy McDowall, Bernie Casey, Nicholas Hammond, Darren McGavin, Gayle Hunnicutt, Barry Morse; **D:** Michael Anderson Sr. *FRH*

Martians Go Home! ♪½ **1990 (PG-13)** Joke-loving Martians come to earth and pester a nerdy composer. **89m/C VHS, Beta, LV.** Randy Quaid, Margaret Colin, Anita Morris, John Philbin, Ronny Cox, Gerrit Graham, Barry Sobel, Vic Dunlop; **D:** David Odell. *NO*

Martin ♪♪♪ **1977 (R)** Martin is a charming young man, though slightly mad. He freely admits of the need to drink blood. Contemporary vampire has found a new abhorrent means of killing his victims. **96m/C VHS, Beta, LV.** John Amplas, Lincoln Maazel; **D:** George A. Romero; **W:** George A. Romero. *NO*

Martin Luther ♪½ **1953** French-made biography of the 16th century reformer who began the Protestant Reformation. **105m/B VHS, Beta.** *FR* Niall MacGinnis, John Ruddock, Pierre Leeavre, Guy Verney. Nominations: Academy Awards '53: Best Art Direction/Set Decoration (B & W), Best Black and White Cinematography. *NOS, VCI, ECU*

Martin's Day ♪♪ **1985 (PG)** An unusual friendship develops between an escaped convict and the young boy he kidnaps. **99m/C VHS, Beta.** *CA* Richard Harris, Lindsay Wagner, James Coburn, Justin Henry, Karen Black, John Ireland; **D:** Alan Gibson; **W:** Chris Bryant, Allan Scott. *MGM, FOX*

Marty ♪♪♪½ **1955** Marty is a painfully shy bachelor who feels trapped in a pointless life of family squabbles. When he finds love, he also finds the strength to break out of what he feels is a meaningless existence. A sensitive and poignant film from the writer of "Altered States." Remake of a television version that originally aired in 1953. Notable for Borgnine's sensitive portrayal, one of his last quality jobs before sinking into the B-Movie sludge pit. **91m/B VHS, Beta, LV.** Ernest Borgnine, Betsy Blair, Joe De Santis, Esther Minciotti, Jerry Paris, Karen Steele; **D:** Delbert Mann; **W:** Paddy Chayefsky; **C:** Joseph LaShelle. Academy Awards '55: Best Actor (Borgnine), Best Director (Mann), Best Picture, Best Screenplay; British Academy Awards '55: Best Actor (Borgnine), Best Actress (Blair); Golden Globe Awards '56: Best Actor—Drama (Borgnine); National Board of Review Awards '55: 10 Best Films of the Year, Best Actor (Borgnine); Nominations: Academy Awards '55: Best Art Direction/Set Decoration (B & W), Best Black and White Cinematography, Best Supporting Actor (Mantell), Best Supporting Actress (Blair). *MGM, FOX, BTV*

Marvelous Stunts of Kung Fu ♪ **1983** Beautiful woman, fortune teller, and martial arts hero team up to seek vengeance against the evil empire. **86m/C VHS, Beta.** Ling Yun, Wei Ping Line, Lung Fei. *TWE*

Marvin & Tige ♪♪½ **1984 (PG)** A deep friendship develops between an aging alcoholic and a street-wise 11-year-old boy after they meet one night in an Atlanta park. **104m/C VHS, Beta.** John Cassavetes, Gibran Brown, Billy Dee Williams, Fay Hauser, Denise Nicholas-Hill; **D:** Eric Weston; **W:** Eric Weston, Wanda Dell. *SUE*

The Marx Brothers in a Nutshell ♪♪♪½ **1990** A tribute to the Marx Brothers, narrated by Gene Kelly. Contains clips from "Duck Soup," "Horse Feathers," "Animal Crackers," "Cocoanuts," and "Room Service." Also contains rare outakes and interviews with the brothers, plus guest appearances by Dick Cavett, Robert Klein, David Steinberg, and others. Indispensible. **100m/B VHS, LV.** Groucho Marx, Chico Marx, Harpo Marx, Zeppo Marx, Robert Klein, David Steinberg, George Fenneman, Dick Cavett. *FCT*

Mary and Joseph: A Story of Faith ♪½ **1979** A speculative look at the experiences and courtship of Mary and Joseph before the birth of Jesus. Made for television. **100m/C VHS, Beta.** Blanche Baker, Jeff East, Colleen Dewhurst, Stephen McHattie, Lloyd Bochner, Paul Hecht; **D:** Eric Till. *LIV, WAR*

Mary, Mary, Bloody Mary ♪ **1976 (R)** Young beautiful artist ravages Mexico with her penchant for drinking blood. Turns out she's a bisexual vampire. When even her friends become victims, her father steps in to end the bloodbath. **85m/C VHS, Beta.** Christina Ferrare, David Young, Helena Rojo, John Carradine; **D:** Juan Lopez Moctezuma; **M:** Tom Bahler. *NO*

Mary of Scotland ♪♪♪ **1936** The historical tragedy of Mary, Queen of Scots and her cousin, Queen Elizabeth I of England is enacted in this classic film. Traces Mary's claims to the throne of England which ultimately led to her execution. Based on the Maxwell Anderson play. **123m/B VHS, Beta, LV.** Katharine Hepburn, Fredric March, Florence Eldridge, Douglas Walton, John Carradine, Robert Barrat, Gavin Muir, Ian Keith, Moroni Olsen, William Stack, Alan Mowbray; **D:** John Ford. *TTC*

Mary Poppins ♪♪♪½ **1964** Magical English nanny arrives one day on the East Wind and takes over the household of a very proper London banker. She introduces her two charges to her friends and family, including Bert, the chimney sweep (Van Dyke), and eccentric Uncle Albert (Wynn). She also changes the lives of everyone in the family. From her they learn that life can always be happy and joyous if you take the proper perspective. Film debut of Andrews. Based on the books by P.L. Travers. A Disney classic that hasn't lost any of its magic. Look for the wonderful sequence where Van Dyke dances with animated penguins. ♫Chim Chim Cheree; A Spoonful of Sugar; The Perfect Nanny; Sister Suffragette; The Life I Lead; Stay Awake; Feed the Birds; Fidelity Feduciary Bank; Let's Go Fly a Kite. **139m/C VHS, Beta, LV.** Ed Wynn, Hermione Baddeley, Julie Andrews, Dick Van Dyke, David Tomlinson, Glynis Johns; **D:** Robert Stevenson; **C:** Edward Colman. Academy Awards '64: Best Actress (Andrews), Best Film Editing, Best Song ("Chim Chim Cher-ee"), Best Visual Effects, Best Score; Golden Globe Awards '65: Best Actress—Musical/Comedy (Andrews); Nominations: Academy Awards '64: Best Adapted Screenplay, Best Art Direction/Set Decoration (Color), Best Color Cinematography, Best Costume Design (Color), Best Director (Stevenson), Best Picture, Best Sound, Best Original Score. *DIS, APD, BTV*

Mary Reilly ♪♪ **1995 (R)** Mary (Roberts) is an innocent maid whose employer happens to be the infamous Dr. Jekyll (Malkovich). They both seem to be employed by Dr. Freud in this dank, dreary psychosexual thriller. Mary is torn between the repressed affection of the doctor and the oily sexuality of his alter ego, who conjures up images of her abusive father. Reuniting the crew and some of the cast of "Dangerous Liaisons" (Glenn Close also appears as a bawdy brothel owner), they fail to reach their previous heights. Most of the gloomy sets will make you wish you were wearing galoshes. Release date was bumped several times as the ending of the film was reshot (more than once). Based on the novel by Valerie Martin. **118m/C VHS.** Julia Roberts, John Malkovich, George Cole, Michael Gambon, Kathy Staff, Glenn Close, Michael Sheen, Bronagh Gallagher, Linda Bassett, Henry Goodman, Ciaran Hinds, Sasha Hanav; **D:** Stephen Frears; **W:** Christopher Hampton; **C:** Philippe Rousselot; **M:** George Fenton. *NYR*

Mary Shelley's Frankenstein ♪♪½ *Frankenstein* **1994 (R)** Branagh turns from Shakespeare to another form of literary classic with his operatic (and loose) adaptation of the Shelley novel. He also plays Victor, the overwrought medical student who decides that death can be vanquished and sets out to prove his theories by making a man. De Niro is sufficently grisly (though lacking in pathos) as the reanimated corpse with Bonham Carter alternately suffering and excitable as Victor's fiancee Elizabeth. Visually arresting—particularly the Creature's birth scene—pic doesn't engender audience sympathy for the characters' trials and final fates. **123m/C VHS, LV, 8mm.** Kenneth Branagh, Robert De Niro, Helena Bonham Carter, Tom Hulce, Aidan Quinn, John Cleese, Ian Holm, Richard Briers, Robert Hardy, Cherie Lunghi, Celia Imrie, Trevyn McDowell; **D:** Kenneth Branagh; **W:** Frank Darabont, Steph Lady; **M:** Patrick Doyle. Nominations: Academy Awards '94: Best Makeup. *COL*

Mary White ♪♪ **1977** The true story of Mary White, the sixteen-year-old daughter of a newspaper editor who rejects her life of wealth and sets out to find her own identity. **102m/C VHS, Beta.** Ed Flanders, Kathleen Beller, Tim Matheson, Donald Moffat, Fionnula Flanagan; **D:** Jud Taylor. *PAR*

Masada ♪♪♪ **1981** Based on Ernest K. Gann's novel "The Antagonists," this dramatization recreates the first-century A.D. Roman siege of the fortress Masada, headquarters for a group of Jewish freedom fighters. Abridged from the original television presentation. **131m/C VHS, Beta.** Peter O'Toole, Peter Strauss, Barbara Carrera, Anthony Quayle, Giulia Pagano, David Warner; **D:** Boris Sagal; **M:** Jerry Goldsmith. *MCA*

Masala 🦴🦴 **1991** An experiment in a variety of genres, including glitzy musical-comedy numbers, erotic fantasy sequences, and all manner of kitsch. Krishna (who both stars and directs in his feature film debut) is a violence-prone, ex-junkie still trying to recover from the deaths of his family in a plane crash as they travelled from their home in Toronto to a vacation in India. Jaffrey has multi-roles as Krishna's unscrupulous uncle and cousin as well as the blue-skinned Indian deity, Lord Krishna, who appears to an Indian grandmother on her television set. Multicultural confusion. **105m/C VHS.** *CA* Srinivas Krishna, Saeed Jaffrey, Zohra Segal, Sakina Jaffrey; ***D:*** Srinivas Krishna; ***W:*** Srinivas Krishna. *FXL, FCT*

Mascara 🦴🦴 **1987 (R)** A group inspecting a transvestite's death are led into the seedy underground world of Belgian nightlife. **99m/C VHS, Beta.** *BE* Derek De Lint, Charlotte Rampling, Michael Sarrazin; ***D:*** Patrick Conrad. *WAR*

Masculine Feminine 🦴🦴🦴½ *Masculin Feminin* **1966** A young Parisian just out of the Army engages in some anarchistic activities when he has an affair with a radical woman singer. Hailed as one of the best French New Wave films. In French with English subtitles. **103m/B VHS, Beta.** *FR* Jean-Pierre Leaud, Chantal Goya, Marlene Jobert; ***D:*** Jean-Luc Godard. Berlin International Film Festival '66: Best Actor (Leaud). *NYF, DVT, VDM*

M*A*S*H 🦴🦴🦴🦴 **1970 (R)** Hilarious, irreverent, and well-cast black comedy about a group of surgeons and nurses at a Mobile Army Surgical Hospital in Korea. The horror of war is set in counterpoint to their need to create havoc with episodic late-night parties, practical jokes, and sexual antics. An all-out anti-war festival, highlighted by scenes that starkly uncover the chaos and irony of war, and establish Altman's influential style. Watch for real-life football players Fran Tarkenton, Ben Davidson, and Buck Buchanan in the game. Loosely adapted from the novel by the pseudonymous Richard Hooker (Dr. H. Richard Hornberger and William Heinz). Subsequent hit TV series moved even further from the source novel. **116m/C VHS, Beta, LV.** Donald Sutherland, Elliott Gould, Tom Skerritt, Sally Kellerman, JoAnn Pflug, Robert Duvall, Rene Auberjonois, Roger Bowen, Gary Burghoff, Fred Williamson, John Schuck, Bud Cort, G. Wood; ***D:*** Robert Altman; ***W:*** Ring Lardner Jr.; ***M:*** Johnny Mandel. Academy Awards '70: Best Adapted Screenplay; Cannes Film Festival '70: Best Film; Golden Globe Awards '71: Best Film—Musical/Comedy; National Society of Film Critics Awards '70: Best Film; Writers Guild of America '70: Best Adapted Screenplay; Nominations: Academy Awards '70: Best Director (Altman), Best Film Editing, Best Picture, Best Supporting Actress (Kellerman). *FOX*

M*A*S*H: Goodbye, Farewell & Amen 🦴🦴🦴½ **1983** The final two-hour special episode of the television series "M*A*S*H" follows Hawkeye, B.J., Colonel Potter, Charles, Margaret, Klinger, Father Mulcahy, and the rest of the men and women of the 4077th through the last days of the Korean War, the declaration of peace, the dismantling of the camp, and the fond and tearful farewells. **120m/C VHS, Beta, LV.** Alan Alda, Mike Farrell, Harry (Henry) Morgan, David Ogden Stiers, Loretta Swit, Jamie Farr, William Christopher, Allan Arbus. *FOX, OM*

M*A*S*H: The Collector's Edition **1972** Join Hawkeye, Trapper John, Radar, Klinger, and the rest of the loonies of the 4077th Mobile Army Surgical Hospital, located three miles from the frontline of the Korean conflict, as they battle military regulations (and sometimes each other). Three episodes per cassette from the television series which lasted 11 seasons. Additional episodes available. **?m/C VHS.** Alan Alda, Wayne Rogers, McLean Stevenson, Gary Burghoff, Loretta Swit, Larry Linville, Jamie Farr, William Christopher. *CMB*

The Mask 🦴🦴 *Eyes of Hell; The Spooky Movie Show* **1961** A deservedly obscure gory horror film about a masked killer, filmed mostly in 3-D. With special 3-D packaging and limited edition 3-D glasses. **85m/B VHS, Beta, LV.** *CA* Paul Stevens, Claudette Nevins, Bill Walker, Anne Collings, Martin Lavut; ***D:*** Julian Roffman. *RHI, MLB*

Mask 🦴🦴🦴 **1985 (PG-13)** A dramatization of the true story of a young boy afflicted with craniodiaphyseal dysplasia (elephantiasis). The boy overcomes his appearance and revels in the joys of life in the California bikers' community. Well acted, particularly the performances of Stoltz and Cher. A touching film, well-directed by Bogdanovich, that only occasionally slips into maudlin territory. **120m/C VHS, Beta, LV.** Cher, Sam Elliott, Eric Stoltz, Estelle Getty, Richard Dysart, Laura Dern, Harry Carey Jr., Lawrence Monoson, Marsha Warfield, Barry Tubb, Andrew (Andy) Robinson, Alexandra Powers; ***D:*** Peter Bogdanovich; ***W:*** Anna Hamilton Phelan. Academy Awards '85: Best Makeup; Cannes Film Festival '85: Best Actress (Cher). *MCA*

The Mask 🦴🦴🦴 **1994 (PG-13)** Adolescent supernatural comedy with lollapalooza special effects is Carrey's follow-up to "Ace Ventura." Mild-mannered bank clerk Carrey discovers an ancient mask that has supernatural powers. Upon putting on the mask, he turns into one truly animated guy. He falls for a dame mixed up with gangsters and from there on, our hero deals not only with the incredible powers of the mask, but with hormones and bad guys as well. Based on the Dark Horse comic book series and originally conceived as a horror flick, director Russell, who gave Freddy Krueger a sense of humor, recast this one as a hellzapoppin' cartoon-action black comedy. Carrey's rubber face is an asset magnified by the breakthrough special effects courtesy of Industrial Light and Magic. **100m/C VHS.** Jim Carrey, Cameron Diaz, Peter Greene, Peter Riegert, Amy Yasbeck, Orestes Matacena, Richard Jeni; ***D:*** Chuck Russell; ***W:*** Mike Werb; ***M:*** Randy Edelman. Blockbuster Entertainment Awards '95: Comedy Actor, Theatrical (Carrey), Female Newcomer, Theatrical (Diaz); Nominations: Academy Awards '94: Best Visual Effects; Golden Globe Awards '95: Best Actor—Musical/Comedy (Carrey); MTV Movie Awards '95: Breakthrough Performance (Diaz), Most Desirable Female (Diaz), Best Comedic Performance (Carrey), Best Dance Sequence (Jim Carrey/Cameron Diaz). *NLC*

The Mask of Dijon 🦴🦴½ **1946** A mad magician suspects that his wife is cheating on him and tries to hypnotize her into killing her supposed paramour. The plan goes awry when the wife uses a gun loaded with blanks. Von Stroheim's performance makes it worthwhile. **73m/B VHS.** Erich von Stroheim, Jeanne Bates, William Wright, Edward Van Sloan, Denise Vernac; ***D:*** Lew (Louis Friedlander) Landers. *NOS*

The Mask of Fu Manchu 🦴🦴½ **1932** The evil Dr. Fu Manchu and his equally evil daughter set out to capture the scimitar and golden mask of Genghis Khan. With them, they will be able to destroy all white men and rule the world. Although a detective from Scotland Yard tries to stop them, the pair obtain the treasures and begin sadistically torturing their victims to death. Can they be stopped before they destroy the earth? One of the creepiest entries in the Fu Manchu series, and Loy's last oriental role. Based on the novel by Sam Rohmer. **72m/B VHS.** Boris Karloff, Lewis Stone, Karen Morley, Charles Starrett, Myrna Loy, Jean Hersholt, Lawrence Grant, David Torrence; ***D:*** Charles Brabin; ***C:*** Gaetano Antonio "Tony" Gaudio. *MGM*

Mask of the Dragon 🦴 **1951** A soldier's friend and girlfriend track down his killer after he delivers a golden curio to a shop in Los Angeles. **54m/B VHS, Beta, LV.** Richard Travis, Sheila Ryan, Richard Emory, Jack Reitzen. *NO*

The Masked Marvel *Sakima and the Masked Marvel* **1943** The Masked Marvel saves America's war industries from sabotage. Serial in twelve episodes. **195m/B VHS.** William Forrest, Louise Currie, Johnny Arthur; ***D:*** Spencer Gordon Bennet. *VCN, REP, MLB*

The Masked Rider 🦴🦴½ **1941** Drifters Brown and Knight head south of the border and find themselves trying to solve crimes committed by a mysterious masked rider. Latin American dancers and singers provide a nice change of pace from the usual cowpoke musical relief. Based on a story by Sam Robins. **57m/B VHS.** Johnny Mack Brown, Fuzzy Knight, Nell O'Day, Grant Withers; ***D:*** Ford Beebe; ***W:*** Sherman Lowe, Victor McLeod. *MOV*

Masks of Death 🦴🦴 **1986** New adventure for Sherlock Holmes, as he is pulled from retirement to find the murderer of three unidentified corpses found in London's East End. **80m/C VHS, Beta, LV.** Peter Cushing, John Mills, Anne Baxter, Ray Milland; ***D:*** Roy Ward Baker. *ORI, IME, WAR*

Mason of the Mounted 🦴🦴 **1932** Harmless enough western in which a Canadian Mountie tracks down a murderer in the U.S. **58m/B VHS.** Bill Cody, Nancy Drexel, Art Mix, Nelson McDowell; ***D:*** Harry Fraser. *NOS, DVT, HEG*

Masque of the Red Death 🦴🦴🦴 **1965** An integral selection in the famous Edgar Allan Poe/Roger Corman canon, it deals with an evil prince who traffics with the devil and playfully murders any of his subjects not already dead of the plague. Photographed by Nicholas Roeg. Remade in 1989 with Corman as producer. **88m/C VHS, Beta.** *GB* Vincent Price, Hazel Court, Jane Asher, Patrick Magee; ***D:*** Roger Corman. *ORI, LIV, MLB*

Masque of the Red Death 🦴🦴 **1989 (R)** Roger Corman's second attempt at Edgar Allan Poe's horror tale pales compared to his Vincent Price version made 25 years earlier. Under-aged cast adds youth appeal but subtracts credibility from the fable of a sadistic prince and his sycophants trying to ignore the plague outside castle walls. Only late in the plot does veteran actor Macnee add proper note of doom. **90m/C VHS, Beta, LV.** Patrick Macnee, Jeffery Osterhage, Adrian Paul, Tracy Reiner, Maria Ford; ***D:*** Larry Brand; ***W:*** Larry Brand, Daryl Haney. *MGM, IME*

Masque of the Red Death 🦴½ **1990 (R)** Unrecognizable Poe mutation has guests invited to the mansion of a dying millionaire, only to be murdered by an unknown stalker. One scene features a pendulum, and that's it for literary faithfulness. **94m/C VHS, LV.** Frank Stallone, Brenda Vaccaro, Herbert Lom, Michelle McBride, Christine Lunde; ***D:*** Alan Birkinshaw. *COL*

Masque of the Red Death/Premature Burial **1965** Double feature of horror classics adapted from Edgar Allan Poe's work. Price stars in "Masque of the Red Death" as a satan worshipper. Millard plays a man obsessed with the fear of catastrophe in "Premature Burial." **175m/C VHS, LV.** Vincent Price, Hazel Court, Jane Asher, Patrick Magee, Nigel Green, Ray Milland; ***D:*** Roger Corman. *IME*

Masquerade 🦴🦴🦴 **1988 (R)** A lonely young heiress meets a handsome "nobody" with a mysterious background and it is love at first sight. The romance distresses everyone in the circle of the elite because they assume that he is after her money and not her love. At first it seems decidedly so, then definitely not, and then nothing is certain. A real romantic thriller, with wonderful scenes of the Hamptons. **91m/C VHS, Beta, LV.** Rob Lowe, Meg Tilly, John Glover, Kim Cattrall, Doug Savant, Dana Delany, Eric Holland; ***D:*** Bob Swaim; ***W:*** Dick Wolf; ***C:*** David Watkin; ***M:*** John Barry. *FOX*

Mass Appeal 🦴🦴 **1984 (PG)** An adaptation of the Bill C. Davis play about the ideological debate between a young seminarian and a complacent but successful parish pastor. Lemmon has had better roles and done better acting. **99m/C VHS, Beta, LV.** Jack Lemmon, Zeljko Ivanek, Charles Durning, Louise Latham, James Ray, Sharee Gregory, Talia Balsam; ***D:*** Glenn Jordan; ***W:*** Bill Davis; ***M:*** Bill Conti. *MCA*

Massacre at Central High 🦴🦴½ **1976 (R)** A new student takes matters into his own hands when gang members harass other students at a local high school. Other than some silly dialogue, this low-budget production is above average. **85m/C VHS.** Derrel Maury, Andrew Stevens, Kimberly Beck, Robert Carradine, Roy Underwood, Steve Bond; ***D:*** Renee Daalder; ***W:*** Renee Daalder. *MPI*

Massacre in Dinosaur Valley 🦴½ **1985** A dashing young paleontologist and his fellow explorers go on a perilous journey down the Amazon in search of the Valley of the Dinosaur. **98m/C VHS, Beta.** Michael Sopkiw, Suzanne Carvall. *LIV*

Massacre in Rome 🦴🦴½ **1973 (PG)** A priest opposes a Nazi colonel's plan to execute Italian civilians in retaliation for the deaths of 33 German soldiers. Strong drama based on a real event. **110m/C VHS, Beta.** Richard Burton, Marcello Mastroianni, Leo McKern, John Steiner, Anthony Steel; ***D:*** George P. Cosmatos; ***W:*** George P. Cosmatos; ***M:*** Ennio Morricone. *NO*

Masseuse 🦴 **1995 (R)** Kristy (Drew) decides to get back at cheating fiance Jack (Abell), who's out of town on a business trip, by turning their house into a massage parlor. **90m/C VHS.** Griffin Drew, Monique Parent, Tim Abell; ***D:*** Daniel Peters. *TRI*

Massive Retaliation 🦴 **1985** Hordes of pesky villagers seek refuge within the secluded safety of a family's country house as WWIII approaches. **90m/C VHS, Beta, LV.** Tom Bower, Peter Donat, Karlene Crockett, Jason Gedrick, Michael Pritchard; ***D:*** Thomas A. Cohen. *LIV, VES*

Master Blaster 🦴½ **1985 (R)** Friendly game of survival with paintball guns goes awry when one of the contestants exchanges the play guns for deadly weapons. **94m/C VHS.** Jeff Moldovan, Donna Rosae, Joe Hess, Peter Lunblad; ***D:*** Glenn Wilder. *MVD, PSM*

Master Harold and the Boys 🦴🦴🦴 **1984** Stagey cable presentation of South African Athol Fugard's play about relationship between white man and two black servants. Occasionally provocative. **90m/C VHS, Beta.** Matthew Broderick; ***D:*** Michael Lindsay-Hogg. *ORI, WAR*

Master Key 🦴½ **1944** Federal agents battle Nazis in this action-packed 12-chapter serial. **169m/B VHS, Beta.** Jan Wiley, Milburn Stone, Lash LaRue, Dennis Moore; ***D:*** Ray Taylor, Lewis D. Collins. *NOS, DVT, MLB*

Master Killer 🦴 *The Thirty-Sixth Chamber* **1984 (R)** Master Killers are made, not born. Liu trains as he readies himself for an attack on the brutal Manchu assassins. **109m/C VHS, Beta.** Liu Chia Hui; ***D:*** Liu Chia Liang. *SUE, FXL*

Master Mind 🦴🦴 **1973** A renowned Japanese super sleuth attempts to solve the theft of a sophisticated midget android. **86m/C VHS, Beta.** Zero Mostel, Keiko Kishi, Bradford Dillman, Herbert Berghof, Frankie Sakai; ***D:*** Alex March. *UNI*

Master Minds 🦴½ **1949** The Bowery Boys run into trouble when Hall gets a toothache and can suddenly predict the future. He takes a job at a carnival where a mad scientist wants to transplant his brain into that of a monster ape man. **64m/B VHS.** Leo Gorcey, Huntz Hall, Glenn Strange, Gabriel Dell, Alan Napier, Billy Benedict, Bennie Bartlett, David Gorcey; ***D:*** Jean Yarbrough. *GPV*

Master Ninja 🦴½ *The Master* **1978** First in the continuing adventures of the Master and Max (Van Cleef and Van Patten) follow the pair across the US in their search for the Master's long-lost daughter. They're pursued by Kosugi. Originally filmed for television; each tape includes two programs. **93m/C VHS, Beta.** Lee Van Cleef, Sho Kosugi, Timothy Van Patten. *QVD, TWE*

The Master of Ballantrae 🦴🦴 **1953** Flynn plays James Durrisdear, the heir to a Scottish title, who gets involved in a rebellion with Bonnie Prince Charlie against the English crown. When the rebellion fails, Flynn heads for the West Indies where he and his partner amass quite a fortune through piracy. Flynn eventually returns to Scotland where he finds that his brother has taken over his title as well as his longtime love. Based on the novel by Robert Louis Stevenson. Flynn's riotous life had put him long past his peak swashbuckling days, as this film unfortunately demonstrates. **89m/C VHS, Beta, LV.** Errol Flynn, Roger Livesey, Anthony Steel, Beatrice Campbell, Yvonne Furneaux, Jacques Berthier, Felix Aylmer, Mervyn Johns; ***D:*** William Keighley; ***C:*** Jack Cardiff. *WAR*

Master of Dragonard Hill 🦴½ **1989** A low-rent swashbuckling romance-novel pastiche. **92m/C VHS, Beta.** Oliver Reed, Eartha Kitt; ***W:*** R.J. Marx. *MED*

Master of Kung Fu 🦴 **1977** A Kung Fu instructor calls upon his former teacher to help him fend off loan sharks who want to take over his school. **88m/C VHS, Beta.** Yu Chan Yuan, Chi Hsiao Fu. *FOX*

Master of the House 🦴🦴🦴 *Thou Shalt Honour Thy Wife* **1925** Story of a spoiled husband, a type extinct in this country but still in existence abroad. Silent with titles in English. **118m/B VHS, Beta.** ***D:*** Carl Theodor Dreyer. *VYY, INJ, FCT*

Master of the World 🦴🦴½ **1961** Visionary tale of a fanatical 19th century inventor who uses his wonderous flying fortress as an antiwar weapon. Adapted from "Robur, the Conqueror" and "Master of the World," both by Jules Verne. **95m/C VHS, Beta.** Vincent Price, Charles Bronson, Henry Hull; ***D:*** William Witney; ***W:*** Richard Matheson; ***M:*** Les Baxter. *ORI, WAR*

Master Race 🦴🦴½ **1944** Absorbing cautionary tale of a German officer who escapes retribution when the Nazis collapse, continuing to hold control over the inhabitants of a small town through intimidation. **98m/B VHS, Beta.** George Coulouris, Lloyd Bridges, Osa Massen, Nancy Gates, Stanley Ridges; ***D:*** Herbert Biberman; ***C:*** Russell Metty. *TTC*

Master Touch 🦴½ *Hearts and Minds; Un Uomo da Rispettare* **1974 (PG)** When a legendary safecracker is released from prison, he attempts one last heist at a Hamburg insurance company. **96m/C VHS, Beta.** *GE IT* Kirk Douglas, Florinda Bolkan, Giuliano Gemma; ***D:*** Michele Lupo; ***M:*** Ennio Morricone. *PSM*

The Masters of Menace 🦴½ **1990 (PG-13)** The men in blue are mighty miffed when a bunch of bikers break parole to pay their last respects to a comrade in leather. Comic bits by Candy, Belushi, Aykroyd and Wendt provide little relief. **97m/C VHS, LV.** David Rasche, Catherine Bach, Dan Aykroyd, James Belushi, John Candy, George Wendt, Tino Insana; ***D:*** Daniel Raskov; ***W:*** Tino Insana. *COL*

Masters of the Universe 🦴🦴 **1987 (PG)** A big-budget live-action version of the cartoon character's adventures, with He-Man battling Skeletor for the sake of the universe. **109m/C VHS, Beta, LV.** Dolph Lundgren, Frank Langella, Billy Barty, Courteney Cox, Meg Foster; ***D:*** Gary Goddard; ***M:*** Bill Conti. *WAR*

Masters of Venus 🦴½ **1959** Eight-part serial about spaceships, space maidens and the like. **121m/B VHS, Beta.** Ferdinand "Ferdy" Mayne. *SNC, VDM*

Master's Revenge 🦴½ **1971** When a girl is kidnapped by a violent motorcycle gang, martial artists are called in to rescue her. Originally released as "Devil Rider." **78m/C VHS.** Sharon Mahon, Ridgely Abele, Johnny Pachivas. *ACA*

Mata Hari 🦴🦴🦴 **1932** During WWI, a lovely German spy steals secrets from the French through her involvement with two military officers. Lavish production and exquisite direction truly make this one of Garbo's best. Watch for her exotic pseudo-strip tease. **90m/B VHS, Beta.** Greta Garbo, Ramon Novarro, Lionel Barrymore, Lewis Stone, C. Henry Gordon, Karen Morley, Alec B. Francis; ***D:*** George Fitzmaurice; ***C:*** William H. Daniels. *MGM, FCT*

Mata Hari 🦴🦴 **1985 (R)** Racy, adventure-prone story of WWI's most notorious spy, Mata Hari, who uses her seductive beauty to seduce the leaders of Europe. Stars "Emmanuelle" Kristel. **105m/C VHS, Beta.** Sylvia Kristel, Christopher Cazenove, Oliver Tobias, Gaye Brown, Gottfried John; ***D:*** Curtis Cunningham. *MGM*

Matador 🦴🦴½ **1986** Bizarre, entertaining black comedy about a retired matador who satiates his desire to kill by appearing in snuff films. He meets his match in an equally deadly woman and the two are drawn closer together by a young bullfighting student who confesses to a series of murders. Not for all tastes, but fine for those who like the outrageous. In Spanish with English subtitles. **90m/C VHS, Beta, LV.** *SP* Assumpta Serna, Antonio Banderas, Nacho Martinez, Eva Cobo, Carmen Maura, Julieta Serrano, Chus Lampreave; ***D:*** Pedro Almodovar; ***W:*** Pedro Almodovar, Jesus Ferrere; ***M:*** Bernardo Bonazzi. *CCN, INJ, TPV*

The Match Factory Girl 🦴🦴🦴 *Tulitikkutehtaan Tytto* **1990** Kaurismak's final segment of his "working class" trilogy. Iris, a plain, shy outsider shares a drab dwelling with her one-dimensional mother and stepfather, works in a match factory, and hopes desperately for romantic love. Her world is transformed when the extraordinary occurs—she spots a brightly colored party dress in a shop window, buys it, wears it to a bar, and meets the Scandinavian creep who will soon get her pregnant and dump her. Angry at the world, Iris seeks revenge, and in so doing the audience learns that she has become very real and human. Kaurismaki makes his point that beauty can exist in ugly places. In Finnish with English subtitles. **70m/C VHS.** *SW FI* Kati Outinen, Elina Salo, Esko Nikkari, Vesa Vierikko; ***D:*** Aki Kaurismaki; ***W:*** Aki Kaurismaki. *KIV, BTV, FCT*

The Matchmaker 🦴🦴🦴 **1958** An adaptation of the Thornton Wilder play concerning two young men in search of romance in 1884 New York. Later adapted as "Hello Dolly." An amusing diversion. **101m/B VHS, Beta, LV.** Shirley Booth, Anthony Perkins, Shirley MacLaine, Paul Ford, Robert Morse, Perry Wilson, Wallace Ford, Russell Collins, Rex Evans, Gavin Gordon, Torben Meyer; ***D:*** Joseph Anthony; ***W:*** John Michael Hayes; ***C:*** Charles B(ryant) Lang. *PAR, FCT*

Matewan 🦴🦴🦴½ **1987 (PG-13)** An acclaimed dramatization of the famous Matewan massacre in the 1920s, in which coal miners in West Virginia, reluctantly influenced by a young union organizer, rebelled against terrible working conditions. Complex and imbued with myth, the film is a gritty, moving, powerful drama with typically superb Sayles dialogue and Haskell Wexler's beautiful and poetic cinematography. Jones delivers an economical yet intense portrayal of the black leader of the miners. The director makes his usual on-screen appearance, this time as an establishment-backed reactionary minister. Partially based on the Sayles novel "Union Dues." **130m/C VHS, Beta, LV.** Chris Cooper, James Earl Jones, Mary McDonnell, William Oldham, Kevin Tighe, David Strathairn; ***D:*** John Sayles; ***W:*** John Sayles; ***C:*** Haskell Wexler; ***M:*** Mason Daring. Independent Spirit Awards '88: Best Cinematography; Nominations: Academy Awards '87: Best Cinematography. *ORI, WAR*

Matilda 🦴🦴 **1978 (PG)** Family fare about a entrepreneur who decides to manage a boxing kangaroo, which nearly succeeds in defeating the world heavyweight champion. Uneven and occasionally engaging. Based on Paul Gallico's novel. **103m/C VHS, Beta.** Elliott Gould, Robert Mitchum, Harry Guardino, Clive Revill; ***D:*** Daniel Mann. *LIV, VES*

Matilda 🦴🦴½ **1996** Intelligent child Matilda is oppressed by both her monstrous parents and awful school principal but her first grade teacher, Miss Honey, believes in her, which is enough to make Matilda plot an appropriate fate for the miserable people in her life. Based on the book by Roald Dahl. Director DeVito, who wanted to create the illusion of a live-action cartoon, built among other things a "Carrot-cam" to capture the flying food of a food fight. **?m/C VHS.** Danny DeVito, Rhea Perlman, Embeth Davidtz, Mara Wilson, Pam Ferris; ***D:*** Danny DeVito; ***W:*** Robin Swicord, Nicholas Kazan. *NYR*

Matinee 🦴🦴½ **1992 (PG)** "MANT: Half-man, Half-ant, All Terror!" screams from the movie marquee after Lawrence Woolsey, promoter extraordinare, and Ruth Corday, his leading lady, roll into Key West circa 1962. Meanwhile, teen Gene Loomis listens to his health teacher push the benefits of red meat and his girlfriend question life, while worrying about his dad, stationed in Cuba. Builds sly parallels between real life and movie horror by juxtaposing Woolsey (modeled after B-movie king William Castle) hyping his schlock, shown in "Atomo-Vision," against JFK solemnly announcing the Russian's approach. Fun, nostalgic look at days gone by—and the matinees that died with them. **98m/C VHS, Beta, LV.** John Goodman, Cathy Moriarty, Simon Fenton, Omri Katz, Lisa Jakub, Kellie Martin, Jesse Lee, Lucinda Jenney, James Villemaire, Robert Picardo, Dick Miller, John Sayles,

Mark McCracken, Jesse White, David Clennon, Luke Halpin; *D:* Joe Dante; *M:* Jerry Goldsmith. *MCA, BTV*

The Mating Game ☠☠☠ **1959** A fast-paced comedy about a tax collector, a beautiful girl, and a wily farm couple. Randall is the straitlaced IRS agent who finds out that the farming Larkins have never paid taxes and use a complicated barter system to get along. Randall falls for farm daughter Reynolds, gets drunk with her Pa, and decides to help the family out of their government dilemma—to the dismay of his superiors. Randall has a terrific drunk scene among his many comedic capers and Reynolds is a highlight. **96m/C VHS.** Tony Randall, Debbie Reynolds, Paul Douglas, Una Merkel, Fred Clark, Philip Ober, Charles Lane; *D:* George Marshall; *W:* William Roberts. *MGM*

Mating Season ☠☠½ **1981** Successful female attorney Arnaz meets good-natured laundromat owner Luckinbill at a bird-watching retreat. Romance ensues. Made for television. **96m/C VHS, Beta.** Lucie Arnaz, Laurence Luckinbill; *D:* John Llewellyn Moxey. *LCA*

Matrimaniac ☠☠ **1916** A man goes to great lengths to marry a woman against her father's wishes. Silent with music score. **48m/B VHS, Beta.** Douglas Fairbanks Sr., Constance Talmadge. *VYY, GPV*

A Matter of Degrees ☠☠ **1990 (R)** Weeks before his graduation, a beatnik-type college senior finally acquires a goal: romancing a mystery girl...or maybe saving the student radio station...or not. The hero's aimlessness permeates the script, which never goes anywhere in its exploration of campus ennui. Good photography and a great stratum of alternative music groups on the soundtrack: Dream Syndicate, Pere Ubu, Schooly D, Pixies, Poi Dog Pondering, Minutemen, and Throwing Muses. **89m/C VHS, Beta.** Arye Gross, Judith Hoag, Tom Sizemore, John Doe; *Cameos:* John F. Kennedy Jr., Fred Schneider, Kate Pierson; *D:* W.T. Morgan. *PSM*

A Matter of Dignity ☠☠ **1957** Young girl, forced into marriage with millionaire, eventually brings ruin to the entire family. Why? In Greek with English subtitles. **104m/B VHS, Beta.** *GR* Georges Pappas, Ellie Lambetti, Athena Michaelidou, Eleni Zafirou; *D:* Michael Cacoyannis. *FCT*

A Matter of Honor ☠☠ **1995 (PG)** Rugby player is killed during match and his coach gets blamed. So, to clear his name, said coach takes up an unusual challenge with the captain of the opposing team. **95m/C VHS.** Jackson Bostwick, Alan Arkus, Rebecca Gray, David Michie; *D:* Frederick P. Watkins. *AVI*

A Matter of Life and Death ☠☠ **1981** True story follows the real-life experiences of nurse Joy Ufema who has devoted her life to helping terminally ill patients. Exceptional work from Lavin. Made for television. **98m/C VHS.** Linda Lavin, Salome Jens, Gail Strickland, Gerald S. O'Loughlin, Ramon Bieri, Tyne Daly, Larry Breeding, John Bennett Perry; *D:* Russ Mayberry. *NO*

A Matter of Love ☠ **1978 (R)** Two couples indulge in spouse swapping while vacationing at the beach. **89m/C VHS, Beta.** Michelle Harris, Mark Anderson, Christy Neal, Jeff Alin; *D:* Chuck Vincent. *LIV, VES*

A Matter of Principle **1983** The perennial Christmas special about a Scrooge-like character's yuletide change of heart. He decides it's time to shape up when he realizes he may lose his family permanently. **60m/C VHS, Beta.** Alan Arkin, Barbara Dana, Tony Arkin; *D:* Gwen Arner. *ACA*

A Matter of Time *Woof!* **1976 (PG)** Maid is taught to enjoy life by an eccentric, flamboyant contessa, then finds the determination to become an aspiring actress. Often depressing and uneven, arguably Minnelli's worst directing job and his last film. Also Boyer's last appearance and first bit for Bergman's daughter Rosellini, in a small part as a nun. **97m/C VHS, Beta.** Liza Minnelli, Ingrid Bergman, Charles Boyer, Tina Aumont, Spiros Andros, Anna Proclemer, Isabella Rossellini; *D:* Vincente Minnelli; *C:* Geoffrey Unsworth. *VES*

A Matter of WHO ☠☠ **1962** A detective for the World Health Organization, or WHO, investigates the disease related deaths of several oil men. Traveling to the Middle East, he uncovers a plot by an unscrupulous businessman to control the oil industry by killing off its most powerful members. Although intended as a comedy, the subject matter is too grim to be taken lightly. **92m/B VHS, Beta.** *GB* Terry-Thomas, Alex Nicol, Sonja Ziemann, Richard Briers, Clive Morton, Vincent Ball, Honor Blackman, Carol White, Martin Benson, Geoffrey Keen; *D:* Don Chaffey; *M:* Edwin Astley. *SNC*

Matters of the Heart ☠☠ **1990** Young pianist searches for an opportunity to display his talents, much to the disapproval of his veteran father. He meets a successful but embittered musician who takes him under her wing and passion between the two soon flares. Made for cable TV and based on "The Country of the Heart" by Barbara Wershba. **94m/C VHS.** Jane Seymour, Christopher Gartin, James Stacy, Geoffrey Lewis, Nan Martin, Allen Rich, Clifford David, Kathy Cannon; *D:* Michael Rhodes; *W:* Linda J. Bergman. *MCA*

Maurice ☠☠☠ **1987 (R)** Based on E.M. Forster's novel about a pair of Edwardian-era Cambridge undergraduates who fall in love, but must deny their attraction and abide by British society's strict norms regarding homosexuality. Maurice finds, however, that he cannot deny his nature, and must come to a decision regarding family, friends, and social structures. A beautiful and stately film of struggle and courage. **139m/C VHS, Beta, LV.** *GB* James Wilby, Hugh Grant, Rupert Graves, Mark Tandy, Ben Kingsley, Denholm Elliott, Simon Callow, Judy Parfitt, Helena Bonham Carter, Billie Whitelaw, Phoebe Nicholls, Barry Foster; *D:* James Ivory; *W:* James Ivory, Kit Hesketh-Harvey; *M:* Richard Robbins. Nominations: Academy Awards '87: Best Costume Design. *ORI, IME, WAR*

Mausoleum ☠☠ **1983 (R)** Only one man can save a woman from eternal damnation. **96m/C VHS, Beta, LV.** Marjoe Gortner, Bobbie Bresee, Norman Burton, LaWanda Page, Shari Mann; *D:* Michael Dugan. *SUE*

Maverick ☠☠½ **1994 (PG)** Entertaining remake of the popular ABC series is fresh and funny, with sharp dialogue and a good cast. Everybody looks like they're having a great time, not difficult for the charming Gibson, but a refreshing change of pace for the usually serious Foster and Greene. In a fun bit of casting, Garner, the original Maverick, shows up as Marshal Zane Cooper. Lightweight, fast-paced comedy was reportedly highly improvised, though Donner retained enough control to keep it coherent. The end is left wide open so a sequel seems likely. Keep your eyes peeled for cameos from country stars, old time Western actors, and an unbilled appearance from Glover. **127m/C VHS, LV.** Mel Gibson, Jodie Foster, James Garner, Graham Greene, James Coburn, Alfred Molina, Paul Smith, Geoffrey Lewis, Max Perlich; *Cameos:* Dub Taylor, Dan Hedaya, Robert Fuller, Doug McClure, Bert Remsen, Denver Pyle, Will Hutchins, Waylon Jennings, Kathy Mattea, Danny Glover, Clint Black; *D:* Richard Donner; *W:* William Goldman; *C:* Vilmos Zsigmond; *M:* Randy Newman. Blockbuster Entertainment Awards '95: Comedy Actress, Theatrical (Foster); Nominations: Academy Awards '94: Best Costume Design. *WAR*

The Maverick Queen ☠☠½ **1955** Barbara Stanwyck, owner of a gambling casino and a member of the "Wild Bunch" outlaw gang, is torn between going straight for the love of a lawman or sticking with the criminals. Stanwyck is perfectly cast in this interesting Western. **90m/C VHS.** Barbara Stanwyck, Barry Sullivan, Wallace Ford, Scott Brady, Jim Davis, Mary Murphy; *D:* Joseph Kane. *REP*

Maverick: The Collector's Edition **195?** Offbeat television western starring Garner as conniving gambler Bret Maverick. The premiere show, "War of the Silver Kings," finds Maverick falling out with the richest man in town over a card game. "Point Blank" features Connors as a conniving bank clerk. Additional episodes are available. **100m/B VHS.** James Garner, Mike Connors. *WAR, MOV*

Max **1922** Compilation of hilarious Linder shorts plus two features, "Seven Years Bad Luck" and "The Three Must-Get-Theres" **90m/B VHS, Beta.** Max Linder. *GVV*

Max ☠☠ **1979** A night watchman watches an aspiring actress who is working on her performance in a Broadway play. He tells her she would be better off marrying a doctor. **20m/C VHS, Beta.** Jack Gilford, Lynn Lipton; *D:* Joseph Gilford, Jennifer Lax. *NO*

Max and Helen ☠☠½ **1990** Uneven, but sensitive and at times highly moving made for TV story of two lovers who are victims of the holocaust. Max (Williams) survives both Nazi and Stalinist camps out of both love for his fiancee and guilt for having lived while she did not. **94m/C VHS, Beta.** *GB* Treat Williams, Alice Krige, Martin Landau, Jodhi May, John Phillips, Adam Kotz; *D:* Philip Saville; *W:* Corey Blechman. *TTC*

Max Dugan Returns ☠☠ **1983 (PG)** A Simon comedy about an ex-con trying to make up with his daughter by showering her with presents bought with stolen money. Sweet and light, with a good cast. **98m/C VHS, Beta, LV.** Jason Robards Jr., Marsha Mason, Donald Sutherland, Matthew Broderick, Kiefer Sutherland; *D:* Herbert Ross; *W:* Neil Simon; *M:* David Shire. *FOX*

Max Fleischer's Documentary Features **1923** Two scientific films, "Evolution" and "Einstein's Theory of Relativity," from Fleischer's early studio were made to finance their cartoons. Features animated sequences. **60m/B VHS, Beta.** *D:* Max Fleischer. *GVV*

Max Headroom, the Original Story ☠☠½ **1986** The computer-generated, British Channel-4 comedy personality stars in his first film, actually a shot-on-video feature about an innocent reporter who is transformed by an evil futuristic TV station into Headroom, the perfect (read: artificial) talk show host. **60m/C VHS, Beta, LV.** *GB* Matt Frewer, Nickolas Grace, Hilary Tindall, Amanda Pays, Rocky Morton, Annabel Jankel. *ORI, WAR*

Max is Missing ☠☠½ **1995 (PG)** 12-year-old boy (Caudell) gets separated from his father, is given a priceless Incan artifact by a dying man, and joins with a local lad to guard it from fortune hunters. Set in the ruins of Machu Picchu in the Peruvian Andes. Made for cable. **95m/C VHS.** Toran Caudell, Victor Rojas, Matthew Sullivan, Rick Dean, Charles Napier; *D:* Mark Griffiths. *HMK*

Max, Mon Amour ☠☠ *Max, My Love* **1986** A very refined British diplomat in Paris discovers his bored wife has become involved with Max, who happens to be a chimpanzee. Instead of being upset, the husband decides Max should live with them. Very strange menage a trois manages to avoid the obvious vulgarities. In French with English subtitles. **97m/C VHS.** *FR* Anthony Higgins, Charlotte Rampling, Victoria Abril, Christopher Hovik, Anne-Marie Besse, Pierre Etaix; *D:* Nagisa Oshima; *W:* Jean-Claude Carriere; *M:* Michel Portal. *CVC, ING*

Maxie ☠☠ **1985 (PG)** Highly predictable, and forgettable, comedy where a ghost of a flamboyant flapper inhabits the body of a modern-day secretary, and her husband is both delighted and befuddled with the transformations in his spouse. Close is okay, but the film is pretty flaky. **98m/C VHS, Beta, LV.** Glenn Close, Ruth Gordon, Mandy Patinkin, Barnard Hughes, Valerie Curtin, Harry Hamlin; *D:* Paul Aaron; *W:* Patricia Resnick; *M:* Georges Delerue. *NO*

Maxim Xul *Woof!* **1991** A professor of the occult is forced to tangle with a beast from Hell that possesses enormous strength and an insatiable appetite for human blood. **90m/C VHS.** Adam West, Jefferson Leinberger, Hal Strieb, Mary Schaeffer; *D:* Arthur Egeli. *NO*

Maximum Breakout ☠½ **1991** A beautiful and wealthy girl is kidnapped, her boyfriend left for dead. But he recovers and leads a posse of mercenaries to the rescue. **93m/C VHS.** Sydney Coale Phillips; *D:* Tracy Lynch Britton. *AIP*

Maximum Force ☆½ **1992 (R)** Three renegade cops join together to infiltrate the underworld and bring to justice both the city's leading crime king and their own corrupt chief of police. **90m/C VHS, LV.** Sam Jones, Sherrie Rose, Jason Lively, John Saxon, Richard Lynch, Mickey Rooney, Jeff Langton; ***D:*** Joseph Merhi. *PMH*

Maximum Overdrive ☆ **1986 (R)** Based upon King's story "Trucks," recounts what happens when a meteor hits Earth and machines run by themselves, wanting only to kill people. Score by AC/DC. **97m/C VHS, Beta, LV.** Emilio Estevez, Pat Hingle, Laura Harrington, Christopher Murney, Yeardley Smith; ***D:*** Stephen King; ***W:*** Stephen King. *ORI, WAR*

Maximum Security ☆ **1987** A small-budget prison film detailing the tribulations of a model prisoner struggling to resist mental collapse. **113m/C VHS, LV.** Geoffrey Lewis, Jean Smart, Robert Desiderio; ***D:*** Bill Duke. *VTR, NWV*

Maximum Thrust *Woof! Waldo Warren: Private Dick Without a Brain* **1988** A few white men confront a deadly Caribbean voodoo tribe. **80m/C Beta.** Rick Gianasi, Joe Derrig, Jennifer Kanter, Mizan Nunes; ***D:*** Tim Kincaid. *NO*

May Fools ☆☆☆ *Milou en Mai; Milou in May* **1990 (R)** Malle portrays individuals collectively experiencing personal upheaval against the backdrop of unrelated social upheaval. An upper-crust family gathers at a country estate for the funeral of the clan's matriarch, while the May of '68 Parisian riots unfold. Few among the family members mourn the woman's passing, save her son Milou (Piccoli) who leads a pastoral existence tending grapes on the estate. Milou's daughter (Miou-Miou), like the others, is more concerned with her personal gain, suggesting, to her father's horror, that they divide the estate in three. Touching, slow, keenly observed. In French with English subtitles. **105m/C VHS, LV.** *FR* Michel Piccoli, Miou-Miou, Michael Duchaussoy, Dominique Blanc, Harriet Walter, Francois Berleand, Paulette Dubost, Bruno Carette, Martine Gautier; ***D:*** Louis Malle; ***W:*** Jean-Claude Carriere, Louis Malle; ***M:*** Stephane Grappelli. Cesar Awards '91: Best Supporting Actress (Blanc). *ORI, FXL, FCT*

May Wine ☆☆ **1990 (R)** A sexy, romantic comedy starring "Twin Peaks" alumna, Boyle. **85m/C VHS, LV.** Guy Marchand, Lara Flynn Boyle, Joanna Cassidy. *MED, VTR*

Maya ☆½ **1966** After the death of his mother, young Terry (North) goes to join his big-game hunting father in India. After a quarrel Terry runs off and meets an Indian boy who has promised his dying father he will deliver a sacred white elephant to a jungle temple. The two lads join forces for the trek and have all sorts of adventures along the way. Basis for a short-lived television series. **91m/C VHS.** Jay North, Clint Walker, Sajid Kahn, I.S. Johar; ***D:*** John Berry; ***W:*** John Fante. *MGM, FCT*

Maya *Woof!* **1982** A teacher of fashion in a high school becomes the object of a student's devotion and another teacher's insane jealousy. **114m/C VHS, Beta.** Berta Dominguez, Joseph D. Rosevich; ***D:*** Agust Agustsson. *NO*

Mayalunta **1986** A young artist is emotionally tortured by a dying older couple. **90m/C VHS.** *SP* Federico Luppi, Miguel Angel Sola, Barbara Mujica. *VES*

Maybe I'll Be Home in the Spring ☆☆½ *Deadly Desire* **1970 (PG)** Denise (Field) is estranged from her family and decides to leave home for life on a commune where she becomes involved with drugs. When she decides to return home everyone finds it hard to adjust. Made for television. **90m/C VHS.** Sally Field, Jackie Cooper, Eleanor Parker, David Carradine, Lane Bradbury; ***D:*** Joseph Sargent. *VTR*

Maybe...Maybe Not ☆☆ *Der Bewegte Mann; The Most Desired Man* **1994 (R)** The German title refers to a man who moves between both sexual preferences although the film takes a straighter line. Hunky-but-dumb Axel (Schweiger) has cheated on girlfriend Dorothy (Riemann) once too often and she kicks him out. Axel winds up staying with gay pal Norbert (Krol), who would like to go from friendship to lovers, which Axel doesn't pick up on. Dorothy does, however, and wonders if Axel is really gay, but when she discovers she's pregnant, Dorothy decides to marry him anyway. Warm-hearted and campy, with some blatantly sexual dialogue. Based on two gay comic books by Ralf Koenig. German with subtitles. **93m/C VHS.** *GE* Til Schweiger, Katja Riemann, Joachim Krol, Rufus Beck; ***D:*** Soenke Wortmann; ***W:*** Soenke Wortmann; ***C:*** Gernot Roll; ***M:*** Torsten Breuer. *NYR*

Mayerling ☆☆☆½ **1936** Considered one of the greatest films about doomed love. Story of the tragic and hopeless affair between Crown Prince Rudolf of Hapsburg and young Baroness Marie Vetsera. Heart wrenching and beautiful, with stupendous acting. Remade in 1968. In French with English subtitles. **95m/B VHS, Beta, LV.** Charles Boyer, Danielle Darrieux; ***D:*** Anatole Litvak. New York Film Critics Awards '37: Best Foreign Film. *VYY, MRV, FCT*

Mayerling ☆☆½ **1968 (PG-13)** Based on the tragic romance between Crown Prince Rudolf of Hapsburg (Sharif) and the teenaged Baroness Maria Vetsera (Deneuve). Set in 1888, the royal Rudolf defies his father, the Emperor Franz Josef (Mason), to take part in a student revolt for the liberation of Hungary and to fall for the common-born Maria (despite his political marriage). No doubt meant to be a sweeping combo of politics and love ala "Doctor Zhivago," it's mostly tedious; see the 1936 version instead. **140m/C VHS.** *GB FR* Omar Sharif, Catherine Deneuve, James Mason, Ava Gardner, James Robertson Justice, Genevieve Page, Ivan Desny, Fabienne Dali; ***D:*** Terence Young; ***W:*** Terence Young; ***C:*** Henri Alekan; ***M:*** Francis Lai. *MGM*

Mayflower Madam ☆☆ **1987 (R)** Fairly unsexy and uninteresting made-for-TV movie recounting the business dealings and court battles of the real-life Sydney Biddle Barrows. Barrows/Bergen is a prominent New York socialite and madam of an exclusive escort service whose clientele includes businessmen and dignitaries. **93m/C VHS, Beta.** Candice Bergen, Chris Sarandon, Chita Rivera; ***D:*** Lou Antonio; ***M:*** David Shire. *VMK*

Mayhem ☆ **1987** Two loners in Hollywood confront all types of urban low-life murderers, drug pushers, and child molesters. **90m/C VHS, Beta.** Raymond Martino, Pamela Dixon, Robert Gallo, Wendy MacDonald. *NO*

Maytime ☆☆☆ **1937** Lovely story of an opera star (MacDonald) and penniless singer (Eddy) who fall in love in Paris, but her husband/teacher (Barrymore) interferes. One of the best films the singing duo ever made. ♫Maytime Finale; Virginia Ham and Eggs; Vive l'Opera; Student Drinking Song; Carry Me Back to Old Virginny; Reverie; Jump Jim Crow; Road to Paradise; Page's Aria. **132m/B VHS, LV.** Jeanette MacDonald, Nelson Eddy, John Barrymore, Herman Bing, Tom Brown, Lynne Carver; ***D:*** Robert Z. Leonard; ***W:*** Noel Langley. Nominations: Academy Awards '37: Best Sound, Best Original Score. *MGM*

Maytime in Mayfair ☆☆ **1952** A dress shop owner's rival is getting all the goodies first, for which he takes the heat from his partner. When he finds out how the rival is doing it, the partners up and head for a vacation in the south of France. Overly simplistic but charming kitsch, helped along by Technicolor shots of the fashions and sets. **94m/C VHS.** Anna Neagle, Michael Wilding, Peter Graves, Nicholas Phipps, Tom Walls, Tom Walls Jr.; ***D:*** Herbert Wilcox. *NOS*

The Maze ☆☆☆ **1985** Made-for-British-television mystery about a young girl who meets the ghost of her mother's first love in her garden estate. **60m/C VHS, Beta.** *GB* Francesca Annis, James Bolam, Sky McCatskill. *PSM*

Mazes and Monsters ☆☆½ *Rona Jaffe's Mazes and Monsters; Dungeons and Dragons* **1982** A group of university students becomes obsessed with playing a real life version of the fantasy role-playing game, Dungeons and Dragons (known in the film as Mazes & Monsters since D&D is trademarked). Early Hanks appearance is among the film's assets. Adapted for television from the book by Rona Jaffe. **100m/C VHS, Beta.** *CA* Tom Hanks, Wendy Crewson, David Wallace, Chris Makepeace, Lloyd Bochner, Peter Donat, Murray Hamilton, Vera Miles, Louise Sorel, Susan Strasberg, Anne Francis; ***D:*** Steven Hilliard Stern; ***M:*** Hagood Hardy. *ORI, HHE, WAR*

McBain ☆☆☆ **1991 (R)** In this exciting fast-paced action-thriller, POW Robert McBain (Walken) leads a group of veterans into battle against the Columbian drug cartel. Stunning cinematography and superb performances combine to make this a riveting action film you won't soon forget. **104m/C VHS.** Christopher Walken, Maria Conchita Alonso, Michael Ironside, Steve James, Jay Patterson, Thomas G. Waites; ***D:*** James Glickenhaus; ***W:*** James Glickenhaus. *MCA*

McCabe & Mrs. Miller ☆☆☆☆ **1971 (R)** Altman's characteristically quirky take on the Western casts Beatty as a self-inflated entrepreneur who opens a brothel in the Great North. Christie is the madame who helps stabilize the haphazard operation. Unfortunately, success comes at a high price, and when gunmen arrive to enforce a business proposition, Beatty must become the man he has, presumably, merely pretended to be. A poetic, moving work, and a likely classic of the genre. Based on the novel by Edmund Naughton. **121m/C VHS, Beta, LV.** Warren Beatty, Julie Christie, William Devane, Keith Carradine, John Schuck, Rene Auberjonois, Shelley Duvall, Bert Remsen, Michael Murphy, Hugh Millais, Jack Riley; ***D:*** Robert Altman; ***W:*** Robert Altman; ***C:*** Vilmos Zsigmond; ***M:*** Leonard Cohen. Nominations: Academy Awards '71: Best Actress (Christie). *WAR*

The McConnell Story ☆☆½ *Tiger in the Sky* **1955** True story of ace flyer McConnell, his heroism during WWII and the Korean conflict, and his postwar aviation pioneer efforts. Fine acting from Allyson and Ladd, with good support from Whitmore and Faylen. **107m/C VHS, Beta, LV.** Alan Ladd, June Allyson, James Whitmore, Frank Faylen; ***D:*** Gordon Douglas; ***M:*** Max Steiner. *WAR, FCT*

The McGuffin ☆☆ **1985** A film critic's inquisitiveness about the activities of his neighbors gets him caught up in murder and a host of other problems. A takeoff of Alfred Hitchcock's 1954 classic "Rear Window." **95m/C VHS.** *GB* Charles Dance, Ritza Brown, Francis Matthews, Brian Glover, Phyllis Logan, Jerry Stiller, Anna Massey; ***D:*** Colin Bucksey. *NO*

McKenzie Break ☆☆☆ **1970** Irish intelligence agent John Connor (Keith) is sent to Scotland to Camp McKenzie, a prison for German POWs during WWII. Captured U-boat commander Schluetter (Griem) is suspected of planning a mass escape and Connor is supposed to stop the action. The battle of wills between the hard-headed Connor and wily Schluetter provides taut, suspenseful drama. Adapted from "The Bowmanville Break" by Sidney Shelley. **106m/C VHS.** Brian Keith, Helmut Griem, Ian Hendry, Jack Watson, Horst Janson, Patrick O'Connell; ***D:*** Lamont Johnson; ***W:*** William W. Norton Sr. *MGM*

McLintock! ☆☆☆ **1963** Rowdy western starring Wayne as a tough cattle baron whose refined wife (O'Hara) returns from the east after a two-year separation. She wants a divorce and custody of their 17-year-old daughter (Powers), who's been away at school. In the meantime, he's hired a housekeeper (De Carlo), whose teenage son (real-life son Patrick) promptly falls for Powers. It's a battle royal between the feisty wife and cantankerous husband but no one out-dukes the Duke. Other Wayne family members involved in the production include daughter Aissa (as the housekeeper's daughter) and son Michael who produced the film. **127m/C VHS, LV.** John Wayne, Maureen O'Hara, Yvonne De Carlo, Patrick Wayne, Stefanie Powers, Jack Kruschen, Chill Wills, Jerry Van Dyke, Edgar Buchanan, Bruce Cabot, Perry Lopez, Michael Pate, Strother Martin, Gordon Jones; ***D:*** Andrew V. McLaglen; ***W:*** James Edward Grant; ***C:*** William Clothier. *MPI, GKK, ING*

The McMasters ☆☆ *The Blood Crowd; The McMasters...Tougher Than the West Itself* **1970 (PG)** Set shortly after the Civil War, the film tells the story of the prejudice faced by a black soldier who returns to the southern ranch on which he was raised. Once there, the rancher gives him half of the property, but the ex-soldier has difficulty finding men who will work for him. When a group of Native Americans assist him, a band of bigoted men do their best to stop it. The movie was released in two versions with different endings: in one, prejudice prevails; in the other, bigotry is defeated. **89m/C VHS.** Burl Ives, Brock Peters, David Carradine, Nancy Kwan, Jack Palance, Dane Clark, L.Q. Jones, Alan Vint, John Carradine; ***D:*** Alf Kjellin. *VTR, XVC*

McQ 🦴🦴½ **1974 (PG)** After several big dope dealers kill two police officers, a lieutenant resigns to track them down. Dirty Harry done with an aging Big Duke. **116m/C VHS, Beta, LV.** John Wayne, Eddie Albert, Diana Muldaur, Clu Gulager, Colleen Dewhurst, Al Lettieri, Julie Adams, David Huddleston; ***D:*** John Sturges; ***C:*** Harry Stradling Jr.; ***M:*** Elmer Bernstein. *WAR*

McVicar 🦴🦴½ **1980 (R)** A brutish and realistic depiction of crime and punishment based on the life of John McVicar, who plotted to escape from prison. From the book by McVicar. **90m/C VHS, Beta, LV.** *GB* Roger Daltrey, Adam Faith, Cheryl Campbell; ***D:*** Tom Clegg; ***W:*** Tom Clegg. *VES*

Me and Him 🦴½ *Ich und Er* **1989 (R)** An unsuspecting New Yorker finds himself jockeying for position with his own instincts when his libido decides it wants a life of its own. **94m/C VHS, LV.** *GE* Griffin Dunne, Carey Lowell, Ellen Greene, Craig T. Nelson; ***D:*** Doris Dorrie; ***M:*** Klaus Doldinger; ***V:*** Mark Linn-Baker. *COL*

Me and the Colonel 🦴🦴½ **1958** Average satire finds Jewish refugee S.L. Jacobowsky (Kaye) trying to get out of Paris to Spain before the Nazis occupy the city. He gets stuck travelling with anti-Semitic Polish colonel Prokoszny (Jurgens), who's also not eager to fall into German hands. If the trip went smoothly, there wouldn't be a story, so naturally the men are forced to put aside their differences to survive. Adapted from Franz Werfel's play "Jacobowsky and the Colonel." **110m/B VHS.** Danny Kaye, Curt Jurgens, Akim Tamiroff, Nicole Maurey, Francoise Rosay, Martita Hunt, Alexander Scourby, Liliane Montevecchi; ***D:*** Peter Glenville; ***W:*** S.N. Behrman, George Froeschel; ***C:*** Burnett Guffey; ***M:*** George Duning. *COL*

Me and the Kid 🦴🦴½ **1993 (PG)** Minor career criminals Aiello and Pantoliano try a robbery on a ruthless financier's (Dukes) home and wind up kidnapping his 10-year-old son instead. But dad doesn't want to pay the ransom and Aiello dumps his partner (who wants to kill the kid) and heads out on the road with the boy. **97m/C VHS, LV.** Danny Aiello, Joe Pantoliano, Alex Zuckerman, Cathy Moriarty, David Dukes, Anita Morris; ***D:*** Dan Curtis. *ORI*

Me and the Mob 🦴🦴½ **1994 (R)** Writer Jimmy Corona (Lorinz) thinks the way to get some colorful stories is to join up with his mobster uncle (Darrow). But Jimmy's no tough guy and the feds coerce him into wearing a wire to bust the local godfather. Deadpan comedy. **85m/C VHS.** James Lorinz, Tony Darrow, John Costelloe, Sandra Bullock, Anthony Michael Hall, Stephen Lee, Ted Sorel; ***Cameos:*** Steve Buscemi; ***D:*** Frank Rainone; ***W:*** James Lorinz, Frank Rainone. *AVI*

Me & Veronica 🦴🦴 **1993 (R)** Two estranged sisters try to come to terms with each other and their dead end lives. Good sister Fanny (McGovern) is a divorced waitress living in a run-down seaside town in New Jersey. One day bad sister Veronica (Wettig) shows up, announcing she's about to be sent to jail for welfare fraud. Veronica asks Fanny to look after her two kids while she's in jail and it is while visiting Veronica in prison that Fanny comes to realize her seemingly flamboyant sister is actually mentally ill and possibly suicidal. Grim little film with good lead performances. **97m/C VHS.** Elizabeth McGovern, Patricia Wettig, Michael O'Keefe, John Heard; ***D:*** Don Scardino; ***W:*** Leslie Lyles; ***M:*** David Mansfield. *COL*

Me, Myself & I 🦴🦴½ **1992 (R)** Segal is a successful New York writer who falls in love with next-door neighbor Williams. But the road to romance is never smooth—particularly when your paranoid gal suffers from multiple personality disorder. Fun leads, dumb movie. **97m/C VHS.** George Segal, JoBeth Williams, Shelley Hack, Don Calfa, Bill Macy, Betsey Lynn George, Sharon McNight, Ruth Gilbert; ***D:*** Pablo Fero; ***W:*** Julian Barry. *COL*

The Meal 🦴🦴 *Deadly Encounter* **1975 (R)** During a dinner party held by a wealthy woman, the rich and powerful guests divulge each others' secrets with reckless disregard for the consequences. **90m/C VHS.** Dina Merrill, Carl Betz, Leon Ames, Susan Logan, Vicki Powers, Steve Potter; ***D:*** R. John Hugh. *MOV*

Mean Dog Blues 🦴🦴½ **1978 (PG)** A musician is convicted of hit-and-run driving after hitching a ride with an inebriated politician. **108m/C VHS, Beta.** George Kennedy, Kay Lenz, Scatman Crothers, Greg Henry, Gregory Sierra, Tina Louise, William Windom; ***D:*** Mel Stuart; ***C:*** Robert B. Hauser. *LIV, VES*

Mean Frank and Crazy Tony 🦴🦴 **1975 (R)** A mobster and the man who idolizes him attempt a prison breakout in this fun, action-packed production. **92m/C VHS, Beta.** *IT* Lee Van Cleef, Tony Lo-Bianco, Jean Rochefort, Jess Hahn; ***D:*** Michele Lupo. *LIV*

Mean Johnny Barrows 🦴½ **1975** When Johnny Barrows returns to his home town after being dishonorably discharged from the Army he is offered a job as a gang hitman. **83m/C VHS, Beta.** Fred Williamson, Roddy McDowall, Stuart Whitman, Luther Adler, Jenny Sherman, Elliott Gould; ***D:*** Fred Williamson. *UNI*

Mean Machine 🦴🦴 **1973 (R)** A man and his beautiful cohort plot revenge on organized crime for the murder of his father. **89m/C VHS, Beta.** Chris Mitchum, Barbara Bouchet, Arthur Kennedy. *NO*

Mean Season 🦴🦴 **1985 (R)** A vicious mass murderer makes a Miami crime reporter his confidante in his quest for publicity during his killing spree. In time, the madman's intentions become clear as the tensions and headlines grow with each gruesome slaying. Then the reporter must come to terms with the idea that he is letting himself be used due to the success that the association is bringing him. Suspenseful story with a tense ending. Good performance from Russell as the reporter. Screenplay written by Christopher Crowe under the pseudonym Leon Piedmont. **106m/C VHS, Beta, LV.** Kurt Russell, Mariel Hemingway, Richard Jordan, Richard Masur, Andy Garcia, Joe Pantoliano, Richard Bradford, William Smith; ***D:*** Phillip Borsos; ***W:*** Christopher Crowe; ***M:*** Lalo Schifrin. *NO*

Mean Streets 🦴🦴🦴🦴 **1973 (R)** A grimy slice of street life in Little Italy among lower echelon Mafiosos, unbalanced punks, and petty criminals. A riveting, free-form feature film, marking the formal debut by Scorsese (five years earlier he had completed a student film, "Who's That Knocking At My Door?"). Unorthodox camera movement and gritty performances by De Niro and Keitel, with underlying Catholic guilt providing the moral conflict. Excellent early '60s soundtrack. **112m/C VHS, Beta, LV.** Harvey Keitel, Robert De Niro, David Proval, Amy Robinson, Richard Romanus, David Carradine, Robert Carradine, Cesare Danova, George Memmoli; ***D:*** Martin Scorsese; ***W:*** Mardik Martin, Martin Scorsese. National Society of Film Critics Awards '73: Best Supporting Actor (De Niro). *WAR*

The Meanest Men in the West 🦴 **1976 (PG)** Two criminal half-brothers battle frontier law and each other. **92m/C VHS, Beta.** Charles Bronson, Lee Marvin, Lee J. Cobb, James Drury, Albert Salmi, Charles Grodin; ***D:*** Samuel Fuller; ***W:*** Charles S. Dubin. *MCA*

Meatballs 🦴🦴 **1979 (PG)** The Activities Director at a summer camp who is supposed to organize fun for everyone prefers his own style of "fun." If you enjoy watching Murray blow through a movie, you'll like this one even as it lapses into box office sentimentality. **92m/C VHS, Beta, LV.** *CA* Bill Murray, Harvey Atkin, Kate Lynch; ***D:*** Ivan Reitman; ***W:*** Len Blum, Harold Ramis, Janis Allen; ***M:*** Elmer Bernstein. Genie Awards '80: Best Actress (Lynch). *PAR*

Meatballs 2 🦴½ **1984 (PG)** The future of Camp Sasquatch is in danger unless the camp's best fighter can beat Camp Patton's champ in a boxing match. The saving grace of Bill Murray is absent in this one. **87m/C VHS, Beta, LV, 8mm.** Archie Hahn, John Mengatti, Tammy Taylor, Kim Richards, Ralph Seymour, Richard Mulligan, Hamilton Camp, John Larroquette, Paul (Pee Wee Herman) Reubens, Misty Rowe, Elayne Boosler; ***D:*** Ken Wiederhorn. *COL*

Meatballs 3 *Woof!* **1987 (R)** Second sequel to the teen-age sex/summer camp comedy. Enough is enough! **95m/C VHS, Beta.** Sally Kellerman, Shannon Tweed, George Buza, Isabelle Mejias, Al Waxman, Patrick Dempsey; ***D:*** George Mendeluk. *LIV*

Meatballs 4 🦴½ **1992 (R)** Feldman stars as a water skier hired to serve as recreation director of Lakeside Water Ski Camp. His enemy is Monica (Douglas) of a nearby rival camp who wants to buy out Lakeside's owner and use the land for real estate development. Lame plot only serves to showcase some good water skiing stunts. **87m/C VHS.** Corey Feldman, Jack Nance, Sarah Douglas, Bojesse Christopher; ***D:*** Bob Logan. *HBO*

The Meateater *Woof!* **1979** Disgusting horror flick of a disfigured hermit who inhabits a closed-up movie house. When it is reopened he turns into a stereotypical slasher. Vegetarians beware: references throughout about eating meat. **84m/C VHS, Beta.** Arch Jaboulian, Diane Davis, Emily Spendler; ***D:*** Derek Savage. *NO*

The Mechanic 🦴🦴 *Killer of Killers* **1972 (R)** Bronson stars as Arthur Bishop, a wealthy professional killer for a powerful organization. He has innumerable ways to kill. **100m/C VHS, Beta, LV.** Charles Bronson, Jan-Michael Vincent, Keenan Wynn, Jill Ireland, Linda Ridgeway; ***D:*** Michael Winner; ***W:*** Lewis John Carlino. *MGM, FOX*

Medea **1959** Medea, who betrayed her homeland for Jason, is becoming wary of his boredom with her. The classic story of love and revenge ensues thereafter in unbridled fury and passion. **107m/B VHS.** Colleen Dewhurst, Zoe Caldwell, Judith Anderson; ***D:*** Jose Quintero. *IVY, FHS*

Medea **1970** Cinema poet Pasolini directs opera diva Callas in this straightforward adaptation of Euripides's classic about a sorceress whose escapades range from assisting in the theft of the Golden Fleece to murdering her own children. Not Pasolini at his best, but still better than most if what you're looking for is something arty. In Italian with English subtitles. **118m/C VHS, Beta.** *IT* Maria Callas, Guiseppi Gentile, Laurent Terzieff; ***D:*** Pier Paolo Pasolini. *HMV, VAI, APD*

Medicine Man 🦴½ **1930** Benny stars as a con-man who fronts a medicine show in this early talkie comedy. **57m/B VHS, Beta.** Jack Benny, Betty Bronson, E. Alyn Warren, George E. Stone, Tom Dugan; ***D:*** Scott Pembroke. *NOS, DVT, VYY*

Medicine Man 🦴🦴 **1992 (PG-13)** Connery's usual commanding presence and the beautiful scenery are the only things to recommend in this lame effort. Dr. Robert Campbell (Connery) is a biochemist working in the Amazon rain forest on a cancer cure. Bracco is Dr. Rae Crane, a fellow researcher sent by the institute sponsoring Campbell to see how things are going. Although Crane is uptight and Campbell is gruff, they fall in love (supposedly), but they're sorely lacking in chemistry. Oh, Campbell's cancer cure is made from a rare flower being eradicated by the destruction of the rain forest. This politically correct cause meets romance falls short of ever being truly entertaining. **105m/C VHS, Beta.** Sean Connery, Lorraine Bracco, Jose Wilker, Rodolfo de Alexandra, Francisco Tsirene Tsere Rereme, Elias Monteiro da Silva; ***D:*** John McTiernan; ***M:*** Jerry Goldsmith. *HPH*

Medicine River 🦴🦴½ **1994 (PG)** A Native American photojournalist returns to his hometown after a 20-year absence and winds up in hot water with newfound friend Harlen Bigbear. **96m/C VHS.** Graham Greene, Tom Jackson, Sheila Tousey, Jimmy Herman, Raoul Trujillo; ***D:*** Stuart Margolin. *ACA*

The Mediterranean in Flames 🦴½ **1972** In Nazi-occupied Greece, a small but brave resistance is formed to fight its captors. One of the women within the group is forced to seduce a Nazi officer in an attempt to learn enemy secrets. **85m/C VHS, Beta.** *GR* Costas Karras, Costas Precas; ***D:*** Dimis Dadiras. *NO*

Mediterraneo 1991 (R) Languid, charming comedy based on the premise that love does make the world go 'round—especially in wartime. In 1941, eight misfit Italian soldiers are stranded on a tiny Greek island and are absorbed into the life of the island, finding love and liberty in the idyllic setting. Lighthearted fun. In Italian with English subtitles. **90m/C VHS, Beta, LV.** *IT* Diego Abatantuono, Giuseppe Cederna, Claudio Bigagli, Vanna Barba, Claudio Bisio, Luigi Alberti, Ugo Conti, Memo Dini, Vasco Mirandola, Luigi Montini, Irene Grazioli, Antonio Catania; ***D:*** Gabriele Salvatores. Academy Awards '91: Best Foreign Language Film. *TOU, IME*

The Medium 1951 A phony medium is done in by her own trickery in this filmed version of the Menotti opera. **80m/B VHS, Beta.** Marie Powers, Anna Maria Alberghetti, Leo Coleman; ***D:*** Gian-Carlo Menotti; ***W:*** Gian-Carlo Menotti. Nominations: Academy Awards '52: Best Original Score. *MVD, VAI*

Medium Cool ½ 1969 Commentary on life in the '60s focuses on a television news cameraman and his growing apathy with the events around him. His involvement with a Appalachian woman and her young son reawakens his conscience, leading to the three getting caught up in the turbulence of the 1968 Chicago Democratic convention. A frightening depiction of detachment in modern society. **111m/C VHS, Beta.** Robert Forster, Verna Bloom, Peter Bonerz, Marianna Hill, Peter Boyle; ***D:*** Haskell Wexler; ***W:*** Haskell Wexler; ***C:*** Haskell Wexler. *PAR*

Medusa *Twisted* 1974 A bizarre series of events occur when an abandoned yacht containing two lifeless bodies is found on the Aegean Sea. **103m/C VHS, Beta.** George Hamilton, Cameron Mitchell, Luciana Paluzzi, Theodore Roubanis; ***D:*** Gordon Hessler. *SNC, PSM*

Medusa Against the Son of Hercules *Perseus the Invincible* 1962 This time the strongman takes on the evil Medusa and her deadly army of rock men. **?m/C VHS, Beta.** *IT* Richard Harrison. *SNC*

The Medusa Touch 1978 (R) A man is struck over the head and is admitted to a hospital. Meanwhile, strange disasters befall the surrounding city. It seems that despite his unconscious state, the man is using his telekinetic powers to will things to happen.... **110m/C VHS.** *GB* Richard Burton, Lino Ventura, Lee Remick, Harry Andrews, Alan Badel, Marie-Christine Barrault, Michael Hordern, Derek Jacobi, Jeremy Brett; ***D:*** Jack Gold; ***W:*** Jack Gold, John Briley. *FOX*

Meet Danny Wilson ½ 1952 Talented New York singer Wilson (Siantra) and his pianist buddy Mike Ryan (Nicol) head out to Hollywood to try their luck. Danny meets club singer Joy Carroll (Winters) who introduces him to gangster owner Nick Driscoll (Burr). Nick manages Danny for a hefty percentage and makes him a star at his club but Danny's lovelife goes south when Joy picks Mike over him. Then Driscoll demands his money. Sinatra gets to croon some great tunes. ♫I've Got a Crush on You; How Deep Is the Ocean; When You're Smiling; All of Me; She's Funny That Way; That Old Black Magic; You're a Sweetheart; Lonesome Man Blues; A Good Man Is Hard to Find. **88m/B VHS.** Frank Sinatra, Alex Nicol, Shelley Winters, Raymond Burr, Tommy Farrell, Vaughn Taylor, Jack Kruschen, Donald MacBride; ***D:*** Joseph Pevney; ***W:*** Don McGuire. *MCA*

Meet Dr. Christian ½ 1939 The good old doctor settles some problems. Part of a series. **72m/B VHS, Beta.** Jean Hersholt, Robert Baldwin, Paul Harvey; ***D:*** Bernard Vorhaus. *NOS, DVT, VYY*

Meet John Doe 1941 A social commentary about an unemployed, down-and-out man selected to be the face of a political goodwill campaign. Honest and trusting, he eventually realizes that he is being used to further the careers of corrupt politicians. Available in colorized version. **123m/B VHS, LV.** Gary Cooper, Barbara Stanwyck, Edward Arnold, James Gleason, Walter Brennan, Spring Byington, Gene Lockhart, Regis Toomey, Ann Doran, Rod La Rocque; ***D:*** Frank Capra; ***C:*** George Barnes. Nominations: Academy Awards '41: Best Story. *NOS, MRV, PSM*

Meet Me in Las Vegas 1956 Compulsive gambler/cowboy Dailey betters his luck when he hooks up with hoofer girlfriend Charisse. Much frolicking and dancing and cameo appearances by a truckload of stars. A little more entertaining than a game of solitaire. ♫The Girl With the Yaller Shoes; If You Can Dream; Hell Hath No Fury; Lucky Charm; I Refuse to Rock 'n Roll; Rehearsal Ballet; Sleeping Beauty Ballet; Frankie and Johnny. **112m/C VHS, LV.** Dan Dailey, Cyd Charisse, Agnes Moorehead, Lili Darvas, Jim Backus, Cara Williams, Betty Lynn, Oscar Karlweis, Liliane Montevecchi, Jerry Colonna, Frankie Laine; ***Cameos:*** Debbie Reynolds, Frank Sinatra, Peter Lorre, Vic Damone, Tony Martin, Elaine Stewart; ***D:*** Roy Rowland; ***W:*** Isobel Lennart. Nominations: Academy Awards '56: Best Original Score. *MGM, TTC, FCT*

Meet Me in St. Louis ½ 1944 Wonderful music in this charming tale of a St. Louis family during the 1903 World's Fair. One of Garland's better musical performances. ♫You and I; Skip to My Lou; Over the Bannister; Meet Me In St. Louis; Brighten the Corner; Summer In St. Louis; All Hallow's Eve; Ah, Love; The Horrible One. **113m/C VHS, Beta, LV, 8mm.** Judy Garland, Margaret O'Brien, Mary Astor, Lucille Bremer, Tom Drake, June Lockhart, Harry Davenport; ***D:*** Vincente Minnelli. National Board of Review Awards '44: 10 Best Films of the Year; Nominations: Academy Awards '44: Best Color Cinematography, Best Screenplay, Best Song ("The Trolley Song"), Best Original Score. *MGM, TLF, HMV*

Meet Sexton Blake 1944 A detective is hired to find a ring and some secret papers that were stolen from the corpse of a man killed in an air raid. He discovers that the papers contained the plans for a new metal alloy to be used in planes. Entertaining for its melodramatic elements. **80m/B VHS, Beta.** *GB* David Farrar, John Varley, Magda Kun, Gordon McLeod, Manning Whiley; ***D:*** John Harlow; ***W:*** John Harlow. *SNC*

Meet the Feebles 1989 Sex and violence gorefest perpetuated by puppets—and the dementia of director Jackson. A TV variety show, populated by animal puppets and humans in costume, is the setting for backstage mayhem, including sex, drugs, and a shooting spree. Among the characters are a sleazy walrus producer, his slinky Siamese cat mistress, a junkie frog, and a manic-depressive elephant. There's also several musical production numbers, if things aren't strange enough for you already. **94m/C VHS.** *NZ* ***D:*** Peter Jackson; ***W:*** Peter Jackson, Danny Mulheron, Frances Walsh. *MTH*

Meet the Hollowheads ½ 1989 (PG-13) Family situation comedy set in a futuristic society. **89m/C VHS, LV.** John Glover, Nancy Mette, Richard Portnow, Matt Shakman, Juliette Lewis, Anne Ramsey; ***D:*** Tom Burman; ***W:*** Tom Burman. *MED, IME*

Meet the Mob 1942 A country spinster visits her son in the big city and is mistaken for a notorious murderess. Complications arise when she tries to keep the boy honest. Could have worked better. **62m/B VHS.** ZaSu Pitts, Roger Pryor, Warren Hymer, Gwen Kenyon, Douglas Fowley, Elizabeth Russell, Tristram Coffin, Lester Dorr, Wheeler Oakman, Bud McTaggart; ***D:*** Jean Yarbrough. *NOS*

Meet the Navy 1946 Post-war musical revue about a pianist and a dancer. **81m/B VHS, Beta.** Joan Pratt, Margaret Hurst, Lionel Murton. *VYY*

Meet the Parents 1991 A young man visits his fiance's parents and every nightmare, every tragedy that can possibly happen, does. From the minds of "National Lampoon," with an appearance by beyond-bizarre comedian Emo Phillips. **?m/C VHS.** Greg Glionna, Jacqueline Cahill, Dick Galloway, Carol Wheeler, Mary Ruth Clarke, Emo Phillips; ***D:*** Greg Glionna; ***W:*** Mary Ruth Clarke. *NO*

Meeting at Midnight 1944 Charlie Chan is invited to a seance to solve a perplexing mystery. Chan discovers that they use mechanical figures and from there on solving the murder is easy. **67m/B VHS, Beta.** Sidney Toler, Joseph Crehan, Mantan Moreland, Frances Chan, Ralph Peters, Helen Beverly; ***D:*** Phil Rosen. *MGM, VCN, MRV*

The Meeting: Eddie Finds a Home 1990 Ben Davidson finds an orphan pup rummaging through the trash and cautiously begins a relationship of trust. **?m/C VHS.** *SPW*

Meeting Venus ½ 1991 (PG-13) Backstage drama featuring Close as Karin Anderson, a world-famous Swedish opera diva. An international cast of characters adds to this sophisticated film of romance, rivalry and political confrontation set amidst a newly unified Europe. **121m/C VHS, Beta, LV.** Glenn Close, Niels Arestrup, Erland Josephson, Johanna Ter Steege, Maria De Medeiros, Ildiko Bansagi, Macha Meril, Dorottya Udvaros, Jay O. Sanders, Victor Poletti; ***D:*** Istvan Szabo; ***W:*** Istvan Szabo, Michael Hirst; ***C:*** Lajos Koltai; ***V:*** Kiri Te Kanawa. *WAR*

Meetings with Remarkable Men ½ 1979 An acclaimed, visually awesome film version of the memoir by Gurdjieff, about his wanderings through Asia and the Middle East searching for answers and developing his own spiritual code. Mildly entertaining but only of true interest to those familiar with the subject. **108m/C VHS, Beta.** Terence Stamp, Dragan Maksimovic, Mikica Dmitrijevic; ***D:*** Peter Brook. *INJ, WSH*

Megaforce *Woof!* 1982 (PG) Futuristic thriller directed by stuntman Needham follows the adventures of the military task force, Megaforce, on its mission to save a small democratic nation from attack. Bostwick leads the attack. 'Nuff said. **99m/C VHS, Beta.** Barry Bostwick, Persis Khambatta, Edward Mulhare, Henry Silva, Michael Beck, Ralph Wilcox; ***D:*** Hal Needham. *FOX*

Megaville 1991 (R) Set in the not too distant future, corrupt politician Travanti struggles to corner the market on the evil technology "Dream-a-Life," which aims to control the rebellious "riff-raff" of Megaville. He does all of his dealings while up against a hitman who has a defective memory chip in his brain. **96m/C VHS.** Billy Zane, Daniel J. Travanti, J.C. Quinn, Grace Zabriskie; ***D:*** Peter Lehner; ***W:*** Peter Lehner. *LIV*

Mein Kampf: Hitler's Rise and Fall 1960 The rise and fall of German fascism and its impact upon the world is examined in this documentary. **120m/C VHS, Beta, LV.** ***D:*** Erwin Leiser. *SUE, MRV, CCP*

Melanie ½ 1982 (PG) Drama tells the tale of one poor woman's courage, determination, and optimism, as she tries to regain her child from her ex-husband. She befriends musician Cummings (a founding member of "Guess Who" rock band) who helps. Usual cliches balanced by good performances. **109m/C VHS, Beta.** *CA* Glynnis O'Connor, Paul Sorvino, Don Johnson, Burton Cummings; ***D:*** Rex Bromfield. *VES*

Melodie en Sous-Sol *Any Number Can Win* 1963 Two ex-convicts, one old and one young, risk their lives and freedom for one last major heist: a gambling casino. In French with English subtitles. **118m/B VHS, Beta.** *FR* Jean Gabin, Alain Delon, Viviane Romance; ***D:*** Henri Verneuil. *BAR, INJ*

Melody 1971 (G) Sensitive but slow study of a special friendship which enables two pre-teens to survive in a regimented and impersonal world. Features music by the Bee Gees. **106m/C VHS, Beta.** *GB* Tracy Hyde, Jack Wild, Mark Lester, Colin Barrie, Roy Kinnear; ***D:*** Waris Hussein; ***W:*** Alan Parker. *SUE*

Melody Cruise 1932 Boring musical romantic comedy that can't stay with any one of those three things for more than a minute without careening into one of the other two. ♫I Met Her at a Party; He's Not the Marrying Kind; Isn't This a Night For Love; This is the Hour. **75m/B VHS, Beta.** Phil Harris, Charlie Ruggles, Greta Nissen, Helen Mack, Chick Chandler; ***D:*** Mark Sandrich; ***M:*** Max Steiner. *TTC*

Melody for Three 1941 In the tradition of matchmaker, Doctor Christian aids in the reuniting of music-teacher mother and great-conductor father, who have been divorced for years, in order to help the couple's son, a violin prodigy. **69m/B VHS, Beta,**

8mm. Jean Hersholt, Fay Wray; ***D:*** Erle C. Kenton. *NOS, VYY, DVT*

Melody in Love 🦴 **1978** A young girl visits her cousin and her swinging friends on a tropical island. Dubbed. **90m/C VHS, Beta.** Melody O'Bryan, Sasha Hehn; ***D:*** Hubert Frank. *FOX*

Melody Master 🦴🦴 *New Wine* **1941** Romanticized biography of composer Franz Schubert, chronicling his personal life and loves, along with performances of his compositions. If you just have to know what drove the composer of "Ave Maria" it may hold your interest, but otherwise not very compelling. **80m/B VHS, Beta.** Alan Curtis, Ilona Massey, Binnie Barnes, Albert Basserman, Billy Gilbert, Sterling Holloway; ***M:*** Miklos Rozsa. *NOS, VYY, DVT*

Melody of the Plains 🦴 **1937** Singing cowpoke teams up with a young girl for some cattle-rustlin' adventure. Substandard horse opry due to poor direction and haphazard lensing. **53m/B VHS.** Fred Scott, Louise Small, Al "Fuzzy" St. John, David Sharpe, Lafe McKee, Charles "Slim" Whitaker, Hal Price, Lew Meehan; ***D:*** Sam Newfield; ***W:*** Bennett Cohen. *MOV*

Melody Ranch 🦴½ **1940** Gene returns to his home town as an honored guest and appointed sheriff. But gangster MacLane is determined to drive him out of town. ♫Melody Ranch; Call of the Canyon; We Never Dream the Same Dream Twice; Vote for Autry; My Gal Sal; Torpedo Joe; What Are Cowboys Made Of?; Rodeo Rose; Back in the Saddle Again. **84m/C VHS, Beta.** Gene Autry, Jimmy Durante, George "Gabby" Hayes, Ann Miller, Barton MacLane, Joseph Sawyer, Horace McMahon, Veda Ann Borg; ***D:*** Joseph Santley. *CCB, VCN*

Melody Trail 🦴 **1935** Autry wins $1000 in a rodeo, loses the money to a gypsy, gets a job, falls for his employer's daughter...and in the end captures a kidnapper and cattle rustlers. ♫Hold On, Little Doggie, Hold On; On the Prairie; Lookin for the Lost Chord; The Hurdy Gurdy Man; My Prayer For Tonight; End of the Trail; I'd Love a Home in the Mountains. **60m/B VHS, Beta.** Gene Autry, Smiley Burnette, Ann Rutherford; ***D:*** Joseph Kane. *CCB, VCN*

Melvin and Howard 🦴🦴🦴½ **1980 (R)** Story of Melvin Dummar, who once gave Howard Hughes a ride. Dummar later claimed a share of Hughes's will. Significant for Demme's direction and fine acting from Steenburgen/LeMat, and Robards in a small role as Hughes. Offbeat and very funny. **95m/C VHS, Beta, LV.** Paul LeMat, Jason Robards Jr., Mary Steenburgen, Michael J. Pollard, Dabney Coleman, Elizabeth Cheshire, Pamela Reed, Cheryl "Rainbeaux" Smith; ***D:*** Jonathan Demme; ***W:*** Bo Goldman. Academy Awards '80: Best Original Screenplay, Best Supporting Actress (Steenburgen); Los Angeles Film Critics Association Awards '80: Best Supporting Actress (Steenburgen); National Board of Review Awards '80: 10 Best Films of the Year; New York Film Critics Awards '80: Best Director (Demme), Best Screenplay, Best Supporting Actress (Steenburgen); Writers Guild of America '80: Best Original Screenplay; Nominations: Academy Awards '80: Best Supporting Actor (Robards). *MCA, BTV*

Melvin Purvis: G-Man 🦴🦴 *The Legend of Machine Gun Kelly* **1974** Mediocre action film has dedicated federal agent tracking killer Machine Gun Kelly across American Midwest during Depression. Made for television. **78m/C VHS.** Dale Robertson, Harris Yulin, Margaret Blye, Matt Clark, Elliot Street, Dick Sargent, John Karlen, David Canary; ***D:*** Dan Curtis. *HBO*

The Member of the Wedding 🦴🦴🦴 **1952** While struggling through her adolescence, a twelve-year-old girl growing up in 1945 Georgia seeks solace from her family's cook. Based on Carson McCullers's play, this story of family, belonging, and growth is well acted and touching. **90m/C VHS, Beta.** Ethel Waters, Julie Harris, Brandon de Wilde, Arthur Franz; ***D:*** Fred Zinnemann; ***W:*** Edward Anhalt; ***C:*** Hal Mohr; ***M:*** Alex North. Nominations: Academy Awards '52: Best Actress (Harris). *NO*

The Member of the Wedding 🦴🦴 **1983** TV rehash of Carson McCuller's play about a young girl who finds she's got some growing up to do when big brother marries. No match for Zinnemann's '52 version, or for Mann's earlier "All Quiet on the Western Front" and "Marty." **90m/C VHS.** Dana Hill, Pearl Bailey, Howard E. Rollins Jr.; ***D:*** Delbert Mann. *VHE*

Memoirs of an Invisible Man 🦴½ **1992 (PG-13)** Nick Halloway, a slick and shallow stock analyst, is rendered invisible by a freak accident. When he is pursued by a CIA agent-hit man who wants to exploit him, Nick turns for help to Alice, a documentary filmmaker he has just met. Naturally, they fall in love along the way. Effective sight gags, hardworking cast can't overcome pitfalls in script, which indecisively meanders between comedy and thrills. **99m/C VHS, LV.** Chevy Chase, Daryl Hannah, Sam Neill, Michael McKean, Stephen Tobolowsky, Jim Norton, Patricia Heaton, Rosalind Chao; ***D:*** John Carpenter; ***W:*** Robert Collector. *WAR*

Memorial Day 🦴🦴 **1983** Good cast highlights this made-for-television outing covering a Vietnam veterans reunion. With the old memories come new problems for the men and their families. **120m/C VHS.** Mike Farrell, Shelley Fabares, Keith Mitchell, Bonnie Bedelia, Robert Walden, Edward Herrmann, Danny Glover; ***D:*** Joseph Sargent; ***M:*** Billy Goldenberg. *NO*

Memorial Valley Massacre 🦴 **1988 (R)** When campers settle for a weekend in a new, unfinished campground, they're slaughtered in turn by a nutty hermit. **93m/C VHS, Beta, LV.** Cameron Mitchell, William Smith, John Kerry, Mark Mears, Lesa Lee, John Caso; ***D:*** Robert C. Hughes. *SUE, NLC*

Memories of a Marriage 🦴🦴🦴 **1990** A nostalgic look at a couple's many years of marriage, from the husband's point of view, as they face their most trying times. Touchingly reminiscent as it spans the youthful years of new love and marriage to the more quiet, solid years of matured love. In Danish with English subtitles. **90m/C VHS.** *DK* Ghita Norby, Frits Helmuth, Rikke Bendsen, Henning Moritzen; ***D:*** Kaspar Rostrup. *ORI, INJ, FXL*

Memories of Hell **1987** Examines the special bonds of friendship that have been maintained among the New Mexicans who survived one of WWII's most brutal battles and subsequent prisoner experiences. **57m/C VHS, Beta.** *NO*

Memories of Me 🦴🦴 **1988 (PG-13)** A distraught doctor travels to L.A. to see his ailing father and make up for lost time. Both the doctor and his father learn about themselves and each other. Story of child/parent relationships attempts to pull at the heartstrings but only gets as far as the liver. Co-written and co-produced by Crystal, this film never quite reaches the potential of its cast. **103m/C VHS, Beta, LV.** Billy Crystal, Alan King, JoBeth Williams, David Ackroyd, Sean Connery, Janet Carroll; ***D:*** Henry Winkler; ***W:*** Billy Crystal, Eric Roth; ***M:*** Georges Delerue. *FOX*

Memories of Murder **1990** A woman suffering from amnesia is stalked by a merciless killer, apparently seeking revenge. Can she regain her memory and understand why she is being hunted, before it's too late? **104m/C VHS, Beta.** Vanity, Nancy Allen, Robin Thomas; ***D:*** Robert Lewis; ***W:*** John Kent Harrison, Nevin Schreiner. *PSM*

Memories of Underdevelopment 🦴🦴½ **1968** Set in the early 1960s. An anti-revolutionary, Europeanized intellectual takes a stand against the new government in Cuba. In Spanish with English subtitles. **97m/B VHS.** *CU* Sergio Corrieri, Daisy Granados; ***D:*** Thomas Gutierrez Alea; ***W:*** Thomas Gutierrez Alea. *NYF, FCT, INJ*

Memory of Us 🦴🦴 **1974 (PG)** Still-relevant story of a married, middle-aged woman who starts to question her happiness as a wife and mother. Written by its star Geer, whose father, Will, plays a bit part. **93m/C VHS.** Ellen Geer, Jon Cypher, Barbara Colby, Peter Brown, Robert Hogan, Rose Marie, Will Geer; ***D:*** H. Kaye Dyal. *ACA*

Memphis 🦴🦴½ **1991 (PG-13)** In 1957 three white drifters (two men and a woman) decide to secure some easy money by kidnapping the young grandson of the richest black businessman in Memphis. They think it's an easy job since, given the prejudice of the times, the police will do little or nothing but they reckon without the resources of the black community itself. Based on the novel "September, September" by Shelby Foote. Originally made for cable. **92m/C VHS, Beta, LV.** Cybill Shepherd, John Laughlin, J.E. Freeman, Richard Brooks, Moses Gunn, Vanessa Bell, Martin C. Gardner; ***D:*** Yves Simoneau; ***W:*** Cybill Shepherd, Larry McMurtry; ***M:*** David Bell. *TTC*

Memphis Belle 🦴🦴🦴 **1990 (PG-13)** Satisfying Hollywood version of the documentary of the same name captures the true story of the final mission of a WWII bomber crew stationed in England. The boys of the Memphis Belle were the first group of B-17 crewmen to complete a 25 mission tour—no small feat in an air war that claimed many lives. Good ensemble cast of up and coming young actors; Lithgow has a nice turn as an army PR guy determined to exploit their boyish good looks on the homefront. Caton-Jones effectively uses 1940s film techniques and some original footage, making up for a rather hokey script. Film debut of singer Connick. Produced by Catherine Wyler, whose father made the original. **107m/C VHS, Beta, LV, 8mm.** Matthew Modine, John Lithgow, Eric Stoltz, Sean Astin, Harry Connick Jr., Reed Edward Diamond, Tate Donovan, D.B. Sweeney, Billy Zane, David Strathairn, Jane Horrocks, Courtney Gains, Neil Giuntoli; ***D:*** Michael Caton-Jones; ***W:*** Monte Merrick; ***C:*** David Watkin; ***M:*** George Fenton. *WAR, VYY, FCT*

Memphis Belle: A Story of a Flying Fortress **1944** The entire final mission of the B-25 bomber "Memphis Belle" and its daring daylight attack on the submarine pens at Wilhelmshaven, Germany is captured through newsreel footage. The crew was the first to complete a 25 run mission. A film version of the story was released in 1990 as "Memphis Belle." Produced by William Wyler. **43m/C VHS, Beta.** *TPV, NOS, HHT*

The Men 🦴🦴🦴½ *Battle Stripe* **1950** A paraplegic WWII veteran sinks into depression until his former girlfriend manages to bring him out of it. Marlon Brando's first film. A thoughtful story that relies on subtle acting and direction. **85m/B VHS.** Marlon Brando, Teresa Wright, Everett Sloane, Jack Webb; ***D:*** Fred Zinnemann. National Board of Review Awards '50: 10 Best Films of the Year; Nominations: Academy Awards '50: Best Story & Screenplay. *REP*

Men... 🦴🦴🦴½ **1985** A funny and insightful satire about a man who discovers his loving wife has been having an affair with a young artist. In a unique course of revenge, the husband ingratiates himself with the artist and gradually turns him into a carbon copy of himself. In German with English subtitles or dubbed. **96m/C VHS.** *GE* Heiner Lauterbach, Uwe Ochsenknecht, Ulrike Kriener, Janna Marangosoff; ***D:*** Doris Dorrie. *ING, NYF*

Men Are Not Gods 🦴🦴½ **1937** Verbose film (precursor to "A Double Life") about an actor playing Othello who nearly kills his wife during Desdemona's death scene. **90m/B VHS, Beta, LV.** *GB* Rex Harrison, Miriam Hopkins, Gertrude Lawrence; ***D:*** Walter Reisch. *SUE*

Men at Work 🦴🦴 **1990 (PG-13)** Garbage collectors Sheen and Estevez may not love their work, but at least it's consistent from day to day. That is, until they get wrapped up in a very dirty politically-motivated murder. And who will clean up the mess when the politicians are through trashing each other? A semi-thrilling semi-comedy that may leave you semi-satisfied. **98m/C VHS, Beta, LV.** Charlie Sheen, Emilio Estevez, Leslie Hope, Keith David; ***D:*** Emilio Estevez; ***W:*** Emilio Estevez. *COL, FOX*

Men Don't Leave 🦴🦴½ **1989 (PG-13)** A recent widow tries to raise her kids single-handedly, suffers big city life, and takes a chance at a second love. Good performances by all, especially Cusack as the sweet seducer of teenaged O'Donnell. By the director of "Risky Business." **115m/C VHS, Beta, LV, 8mm.** Jessica Lange, Arliss Howard, Joan Cusack, Kathy Bates, Charlie Korsmo, Corey Carrier, Chris O'Donnell, Tom Mason, Jim Haynie; ***D:*** Paul Brickman; ***W:*** Barbara Benedek, Paul Brickman; ***C:*** Bruce Surtees; ***M:*** Thomas Newman. *WAR*

Men in Love ♂♂ **1990** A young San Franciscan travels to Hawaii with the cremated remains of his lover, who has succumbed to AIDS. There he encounters a supportive group of men who nurse him back to sexual and spiritual wholeness. **93m/C VHS.** Doug Self, Joe Tolbe, Emerald Starr, Kutira Decosterd, Scott Catamas; ***D:*** Marc Huestis. *WBF, FCT, INJ*

Men in War ♂♂½ **1957** Korean War drama about a small platoon trying to take an enemy hill by themselves. A worthwhile effort with some good action sequences. **100m/B VHS, Beta.** Robert Ryan, Robert Keith, Aldo Ray, Vic Morrow; ***D:*** Anthony Mann; ***W:*** Philip Yordan; ***M:*** Elmer Bernstein. *FGF, MRV, BMV*

Men of Boys Town ♂♂½ **1941** Sequel to 1938's "Boys Town" has the same sentimentality, even more if that's possible. Father Flanagan's reformatory faces closure, while the kids reach out to an embittered new inmate. Worth seeing for the ace cast reprising their roles. **106m/B VHS.** Spencer Tracy, Mickey Rooney, Darryl Hickman, Henry O'Neill, Lee J. Cobb, Sidney Miller; ***D:*** Norman Taurog. *MGM, FCT*

Men of Ireland ♂♂ **1938** A Dublin medical student cavorts with islanders off the Irish coast. Uninspired programmer with authentic native folk of the Blasket Islands, plus their songs and dances. **62m/B VHS, Beta, 8mm.** *IR* Cecil Ford, Eileen Curran, Brian O'Sullivan, Gabriel Fallon; ***D:*** Richard Bird. *VYY*

Men of Respect ♂♂ **1991 (R)** Shakespeare meets the mafia in this misbegotten gangster yarn. Turturro, a gangster MacBeth, is prodded by wife and psychic to butcher his way to the top o' the mob. Well acted but ill conceived, causing Bard's partial roll over in grave. **113m/C VHS, LV, 8mm.** John Turturro, Katherine Borowitz, Peter Boyle, Dennis Farina, Chris Stein, Steven Wright, Stanley Tucci; ***D:*** William Reilly; ***W:*** William Reilly. *COL*

Men of Sherwood Forest ♂♂½ **1957** Robin Hood and his band take it to the sheriff et al in this colorful Hammer version of the timeless legend. **77m/C VHS.** *GB* Don Taylor, Reginald Beckwith, Eileen Moore, Davis King-Wood, Patrick Holt, John Van Eyssen, Douglas Wilmer; ***D:*** Val Guest. *NOS, SNC, DVT*

Men of Steel ♂ **1988 (PG)** Two Canadian military officers, one French and one English, must struggle to survive when their plane crashes in the wilderness. Besides contending with the surroundings, they must deal with one another's instilled bitterness and underlying prejudices. **91m/C VHS, Beta.** Allan Royal, Robert Lalonde, David Ferry, Mavor Moore, Yvan Ponton; ***D:*** Donald Shebib. *TWE*

Men of the Fighting Lady ♂♂♂½ **1954** Action-adventure offers plenty of exciting battle footage. Features the stories of selected pilots stationed on a U.S. aircraft carrier in the Pacific during the Korean War. The stories, told to Calhern as writer James A. Michener, center around the lead pilot Johnson. Dramatic airflights include a scene in which Johnson helps a blinded Martin land his plane safely on the carrier deck. Gene Ruggerio's editing of the war footage was so expertly done that he was questioned by the Pentagon when they had a hard time believing the scenes were achieved by skillful editing and painted backdrops. Look for "Beaver" Mathers as one of Wynn's sons. **81m/C VHS, Beta.** Van Johnson, Walter Pidgeon, Louis Calhern, Dewey Martin, Keenan Wynn, Frank Lovejoy, Robert Horton, Bert Freed, Jerry Mathers; ***D:*** Andrew Marton; ***M:*** Miklos Rozsa. *MGM*

Men of Two Worlds ♂♂ *Witch Doctor; Kisenga, Man of Africa* **1946** Classical musician raised in Africa is the toast of Europe until he finds out he's got a voodoo curse, and suddenly he's got the heebie jeebies too bad to play chopsticks. **90m/C VHS, Beta.** *GB* Robert Adams, Eric Portman, Orlando Martins, Phyllis Calvert, Arnold Marle, Cathleen Nesbitt, David Horne, Cyril Raymond; ***D:*** Thorold Dickinson. *SNC*

Men of War ♂½ **1994 (R)** Ex-Special Forces mercenaries decide to defend, rather than destroy, the inhabitants of an exotic island, whose land is wanted by a suspicious company interested in mining rights. **102m/C VHS, LV.** Dolph Lundgren, Charlotte Lewis, B.D. Wong, Anthony John Denison, Tim Guinee, Don Harvey, Tiny Lister, Tom Wright, Kevin Tighe; ***D:*** Perry Lang; ***W:*** John Sayles, Ethan Reiff, Cyrus Voris; ***C:*** Ronn Schmidt; ***M:*** Gerald Gouriet. *TOU*

The Men Who Tread on the Tiger's Tail ♂♂½ **1945** Twelfth-century Japan is the setting for this struggle of power between two brothers, one a reigning shogun, the other on the run. English subtitles. **60m/B VHS, Beta.** *JP* ***D:*** Akira Kurosawa. *IHF*

Menace on the Mountain ♂♂ **1970 (G)** Family-oriented drama about a father and son who battle carpetbagging Confederate deserters during the Civil War. **89m/C VHS, Beta.** Patricia Crowley, Albert Salmi, Charles Aidman; ***D:*** Vincent McEveety. *DIS*

Menace II Society ♂♂♂½ **1993 (R)** Portrayal of black teens lost in inner-city hell is realistically captured by 21-year-old twin directors, in their big-screen debut. Caine (Turner) lives with his grandparents and peddles drugs for spending money, from the eve of his high school graduation to his decision to escape south-central Los Angeles for Atlanta. Bleak and haunting, with some of the most unsettling, bloodiest violence ever shown in a commercial film. Disturbing to watch, but critcally acclaimed. The Hughes' make their mark on contemporary black cinema with intensity, enhanced by an action-comics visual flair. Based on a story by the Hughes' and Tyger Williams. **104m/C VHS, LV.** Tyrin Turner, Larenz Tate, Samuel L. Jackson, Glenn Plummer, Julian Roy Doster, Bill Duke, Charles S. Dutton, Jada Pinkett; ***D:*** Allen Hughes, Albert Hughes; ***W:*** Tyger Williams. Independent Spirit Awards '94: Best Cinematography; MTV Movie Awards '94: Best Film; Nominations: Independent Spirit Awards '94: Best Actor (Turner), Best First Feature. *COL, NLC, IME*

Menage ♂♂♂ *Tenue de Soiree* **1986** Depardieu is the homosexual crook who breaks into the home of an impoverished couple—the dominating Miou-Miou and her submissive husband, Blanc. An unrepentant thief, he begins to take over their lives, introducing them to the wonderful world of crime, among other, more kinky, pastimes. Gender-bending farce that doesn't hold up to the end but is worth watching for sheer outrageousness. In French with English subtitles. **84m/C VHS.** *FR* Gerard Depardieu, Michel Blanc, Miou-Miou, Bruno Cremer, Jean-Pierre Marielle; ***D:*** Bertrand Blier; ***W:*** Bertrand Blier; ***M:*** Serge Gainsbourg. Cannes Film Festival '86: Best Actor (Blanc). *TRI, INJ, FCT*

The Men's Club ♂½ **1986 (R)** Seven middle-aged buddies get together for a single night, and bare their respective souls and personal traumas, talking about women and eating and drinking. Banal. Based on novel by Leonard Michael. **100m/C VHS, Beta, LV.** Harvey Keitel, Roy Scheider, Craig Wasson, Frank Langella, David Dukes, Richard Jordan, Treat Williams, Stockard Channing, Jennifer Jason Leigh, Ann Dusenberry, Cindy Pickett, Gwen Welles; ***D:*** Peter Medak. *PAR*

Menschenfrauen ♂♂½ **1980** A philandering journalist is put in his place by the four women with whom he is simultaneously having relationships. In German with English subtitles. **100m/C VHS, Beta.** *GE* ***D:*** Valie Export. *FCT*

Mephisto ♂♂♂½ **1981** An egomaniacal actor, compellingly played by Brandauer, sides with the Nazis to further his career, with disastrous results. The first of three brilliant films by Szabo and Brandauer exploring the price of power and personal sublimation in German history. Critically hailed. In German with English subtitles. From the novel by Klaus Mann. Followed by "Colonel Redl" and "Hanussen." **144m/C VHS, Beta.** *HU* Klaus Maria Brandauer, Krystyna Janda, Ildiko Bansagi, Karin Boyd, Rolf Hoppe, Christine Harbort, Gyorgy Cserhalmi, Christiane Graskoff, Peter Andorai, Ildiko Kishonti; ***D:*** Istvan Szabo; ***C:*** Lajos Koltai. Academy Awards '81: Best Foreign Language Film; Nominations: Cannes Film Festival '81: Best Film. *REP, INJ, SWC*

The Mephisto Waltz ♂♂♂ **1971 (R)** Journalist gets more than a story when he is granted an interview with a dying pianist. It turns out that he is a satanist and the cult he is a part of wants the journalist. Chilling adaptation of the Fred Mustard Stewart novel features a haunting musical score. **108m/C VHS.** Alan Alda, Jacqueline Bisset, Barbara Parkins, Curt Jurgens, Bradford Dillman, William Windom, Kathleen Widdoes; ***D:*** Paul Wendkos; ***M:*** Jerry Goldsmith. *FOX*

The Mercenaries ♂½ **1965** Romantic warrior fights to save the lives and honor of his people who are under attack from mercenaries murdering and raping their way across Europe. **98m/C Beta.** Debra Paget. *AIP*

The Mercenaries ♂ *Cuba Crossing; Kill Castro; Assignment: Kill Castro; Key West Crossing; Sweet Dirty Tony* **1980** A tough guy, given the assignment to kill Fidel Castro, encounters all sorts of adversity along the way. Key West scenery is the only thing of interest. **92m/C VHS, Beta.** Stuart Whitman, Robert Vaughn, Caren Kaye, Raymond St. Jacques, Woody Strode, Sybil Danning, Albert Salmi, Michael V. Gazzo; ***D:*** Chuck Workman. *ACA, JEF*

Mercenary Fighters ♂½ **1988 (R)** An American soldier-of-fortune fights for both sides of an African revolution. Shot in South Africa. **90m/C VHS, Beta, LV.** Peter Fonda, Reb Brown, Ron O'Neal, Jim Mitchum; ***D:*** Riki Shelach. *MED, VTR*

The Merchant of Four Seasons ♂♂♂ **1971** Story focuses on the depression and unfulfilled dreams of an average street merchant. Direction from Fassbinder is slow, deliberate, and mesmerizing. In German with English subtitles. **88m/C VHS, Beta.** Hans Hirschmuller, Irm Hermann, Hanna Schygulla, Andrea Schober, Gusti Kreissl; ***D:*** Rainer Werner Fassbinder; ***W:*** Rainer Werner Fassbinder. *NYF, INJ*

The Merchant of Venice ♂♂♂ **1973** Shakespeare's tragedy of prejudice, vengeance, and sacrifice stars Olivier as the persecuted money lender Shylock, who demands his payment of a pound of flesh for a defaulted loan. **131m/C VHS.** *GB* Laurence Olivier, Joan Plowright, Jeremy Brett. *FUS, FCT*

Merchants of War ♂ **1990 (R)** Sent out by the CIA on a mission, two best friends are soon the target of one of the most dangerous terrorists in the world. The fanatical Islamic terrorist soon casts his wrath upon the two men. **100m/C VHS.** Asher Brauner, Jesse Vint, Bonnie Beck; ***D:*** Peter M. MacKenzie. *VMK*

Mercy Mission ♂♂½ **1993** Young pilot Bakula runs into trouble over the Pacific with his small plane and it's upto Air New Zealand airline pilot Loggia, who risks the lives of his passengers and crew, to come to his rescue. **92m/C VHS.** Scott Bakula, Robert Loggia; ***D:*** Roger Young. *HMK*

Meridian: Kiss of the Beast ♂½ **1990 (R)** A beautiful heiress is courted, kidnapped and loved by a demonic man-beast. **90m/C VHS, Beta, LV.** Sherilyn Fenn, Malcom Jamieson, Hilary Mason, Alex Daniels, Phil Fondacaro; ***D:*** Charles Band; ***W:*** Dennis Paoli; ***M:*** Pino Donaggio. *PAR*

Merlin ♂♂½ **1992 (PG-13)** In a remote California town reporter Christy Lake is stunned to discover her ancient heritage. Turns out she's the reincarnated daughter of legendary Merlin the magician and it is her duty to protect the Sword of Power from the evil sorcerer Pendragon. And aided by a handsome warrior and an ancient sage, that's just what she intends to do. **112m/C VHS.** Nadia Cameron, Peter Phelps, Richard Lynch, James Hong, Ted Markland, Desmond Llewelyn; ***D:*** Paul Hunt; ***W:*** Nick McCarty. *HMD*

Merlin and the Sword ♂ *Arthur the King* **1985** Poor use of a good cast in this treatment of the legend of Merlin, Arthur and Excalibur. **94m/C VHS, Beta.** Malcolm McDowell, Edward Woodward, Candice Bergen, Dyan Cannon; ***D:*** Clive Donner. *LIV, VES*

Merlin of the Crystal Cave ♂♂½ **1991** Depicts the adventures of the young boy Merlin as he learns the ways of magic in the days before Camelot and King Arthur. Made for British television. **159m/C VHS.** *GB FOX*

Mermaids ♂♂♂ **1990 (PG-13)** Mrs. Flax (Cher) is the flamboyant mother of two who hightails out of town every time a relationship threatens to turn serious. Having moved some eighteen times, her daughters, Charlotte (Ryder), 15, and Kate (Ricci), 8, are a little worse for the wear, psychologically speaking.

One aspires to be a nun though not Catholic, and the other holds her breath under water. Now living in Massachusetts, Mrs. Flax starts having those "I got you, babe" feelings for Hoskins, a shoestore owner. Amusing, well-acted multi-generational coming of ager based on a novel by Patty Dann. **110m/C VHS, Beta, LV.** Cher, Winona Ryder, Bob Hoskins, Christina Ricci, Michael Schoeffling, Caroline McWilliams, Jan Miner; ***D:*** Richard Benjamin; ***W:*** June Roberts; ***M:*** Jack Nitzsche. National Board of Review Awards '90: Best Supporting Actress (Ryder). *ORI*

The Mermaids of Tiburon 🦴 *The Aqua Sex* **1962** A marine biologist and a criminal travel to a remote island off Mexico in search of elusive, expensive "fire pearls." There they encounter a kingdom of lovely mermaids who promptly liven things up. Filmed in "Aquascope" for your viewing pleasure. **77m/C VHS.** Diane Webber, George Rowe, Timothy Carey, Jose Gonzalez-Gonzalez, John Mylong, Gil Baretto, Vicki Kantenwine, Nani Morrissey, Judy Edwards, Jean Carroll, Diana Cook, Karen Goodman, Nancy Burns; ***D:*** John Lamb; ***W:*** John Lamb. *FRG*

Merrill's Marauders 🦴🦴½ **1962** Chandler is the commander of a battle-hardened regiment fighting in the jungles of Burma in 1944. The exhausted unit gains their latest objective and expects to be relieved, only to be continuously pushed into more fighting down the line. Director Fuller excels at showing the confusion of battle; Chandler's last film role (he died before the film was released). **98m/C VHS.** Jeff Chandler, Ty Hardin, Peter Brown, Andrew Duggan, Will Hutchins, Claude Akins; ***D:*** Samuel Fuller; ***W:*** Milton Sperling, Samuel Fuller; ***C:*** William Clothier; ***M:*** Howard Jackson. *WAR*

Merry Christmas, Mr. Lawrence 🦴🦴🦴 **1983 (R)** An often overlooked drama about a WWII Japanese POW camp. Taut psychological drama about clashing cultures and physical and emotional survival focusing on the tensions between Bowie as a British POW and camp commander Sakamato, who also composed the outstanding score. A haunting and intense film about the horrors of war. Based on the novel by Laurens van der Post. **124m/C VHS, Beta.** *JP GB* David Bowie, Tom Conti, Ryuichi Sakamoto, Takeshi, Jack Thompson; ***D:*** Nagisa Oshima. National Board of Review Awards '83: Best Actor (Conti); Nominations: Cannes Film Festival '83: Best Film. *MCA*

Merry-Go-Round 🦴🦴🦴 **1923** A handsome Austrian count is engaged to a woman of his class when he meets the beautiful Agnes, who works as an organ grinder for the local merry-go-round. He disguises himself to woo her but finally decides to marry his fiance, although Agnes continues to love him. But the story doesn't end for the two lovers who are destined to be together. Producer Thalberg and director von Stroheim battled over the expense and length of the film until Thalberg had the director replaced. However, much of the film still shows the von Stroheim brillance and attention to lavish detail. **110m/B VHS.** Norman Kerry, Mary Philbin, Cesare Gravina, Edith Yorke, George Hackathorne; ***D:*** Rupert Julian, Erich von Stroheim. *FCT, HEG*

The Merry Widow 🦴🦴🦴½ *The Lady Dances* **1934** The first sound version of the famous Franz Lehar operetta, dealing with a playboy from a bankrupt kingdom who must woo and marry the land's wealthy widow or be tried for treason. A delightful musical comedy, with a sterling cast and patented Lubitschian gaiety. Made as a silent in 1912 and 1925; remade in color in 1952. ♫Girls, Girls, Girls; Vilia; Tonight Will Teach Me to Forget; Melody of Laughter; Maxim's; The Girls at Maxim's; The Merry Widow Waltz; If Widows are Rich; Russian Dance. **99m/B VHS, Beta, LV.** Maurice Chevalier, Jeanette MacDonald, Edward Everett Horton, Una Merkel, George Barbier, Minna Gombell, Ruth Channing, Sterling Holloway, Henry Armetta, Barbara Leanard, Donald Meek, Akim Tamiroff, Herman Bing; ***D:*** Ernst Lubitsch; ***M:*** Franz Lehar, Lorenz Hart. Academy Awards '34: Best Interior Decoration. *MGM*

The Merry Widow 🦴🦴½ **1952** Rich widow Turner travels to her husband's homeland of Marshovia to dedicate a statue to his memory. The country is deeply in debt and the king would like the widow to marry a local count and remain (along with her fortune). Lamas is charming as the intended bridegroom but Turner, though lovely looking, is miscast; her singing was dubbed by Erwin. Uninspired remake of the 1934 film only benefits from being shot in color and the lavish production values. Based on the operetta by Lehar. ♫The Merry Widow Waltz; Can-Can; Girls, Girls, Girls; I'm Going to Maxim's. **105m/C VHS.** Lana Turner, Fernando Lamas, Una Merkel, Richard Haydn, Thomas Gomez, John Abbott, Marcel Dalio, King Donovan, Robert Coote, Joi Lansing; ***Cameos:*** Gwen Verdon; ***D:*** Curtis Bernhardt; ***W:*** Sonya Levien, William Ludwig; ***C:*** Robert L. Surtees; ***M:*** Franz Lehar; ***V:*** Trudy Erwin. Nominations: Academy Awards '52: Best Art Direction/Set Decoration (Color), Best Costume Design (Color). *MGM*

Merton of the Movies 🦴🦴½ **1947** Skelton stars as star-struck, small town theater usher Merton Gill who wins a trip to Hollywood. He's befriended by stunt double Phyllis (O'Brien) who recognizes his comedic talents and works to get him that big break. Based on the play by George S. Kaufman and Marc Connelly and previously filmed in 1924 and 1932 (as "Make Me a Star"). **82m/B VHS, Beta.** Red Skelton, Virginia O'Brien, Gloria Grahame, Leon Ames, Alan Mowbray, Charles D. Brown, Hugo Haas, Harry Hayden; ***D:*** Robert Alton; ***W:*** George Wells, Lou Breslow. *MGM, FCT*

Mesa of Lost Women *Woof! Lost Women; Lost Women of Zarpa* **1952** Mad scientist creates brave new race of vicious women with long fingernails. So bad it's a wanna-B. Addams Family buffs will spot the Fester in Coogan. **70m/B VHS.** Jackie Coogan, Richard Travis, Allan Nixon, Mary Hill, Robert Knapp, Tandra Quinn, Lyle Talbot, Katherine Victor, Angelo Rossitto; ***D:*** Herbert Tevos, Ron Ormond; ***W:*** Herbert Tevos; ***C:*** Gilbert Warrenton, Karl Struss. *NOS, MRV, SNC*

Mesmerized 🦴🦴 *Shocked* **1984** Based on the work by Jerzy Skolimowski, the film is a dramatization of the Victoria Thompson murder case in 1880's New Zealand. A teenaged orphaned girl marries an older man and decides after years of abuse to kill him through hypnosis. An unengaging drama, though the lovely New Zealand landscape serves as a fitting contrast to the film's ominous tone. **90m/C VHS, Beta.** *GB NZ AU* John Lithgow, Jodie Foster, Michael Murphy, Dan Shor, Harry Andrews; ***D:*** Michael Laughlin. *LIV, VES*

Mesquite Buckaroo 🦴 **1939** Two cowboys bet over who is the better bronco buster, but one of them gets kidnapped. **59m/B VHS, Beta.** Bob Steele, Carolyn Curtis, Frank LaRue, Juanita Fletcher, Charles "Blackie" King; ***D:*** Harry S. Webb. *NOS, DVT*

Messalina, Empress of Rome 🦴 **1980** Ancient Rome is torn to bits in the zaniest manner possible in this Italian-French coproduction. **100m/C VHS, Beta.** *VCD*

Messalina vs. the Son of Hercules 🦴 **1964** A Roman slave leads a rebellion against the emperor Messalina. Italian; dubbed into English. **105m/C VHS, Beta.** *IT* Richard Harrison, Marilu Tolo, Lisa Gastoni; ***D:*** Umberto Lenzi. *SNC, NLC*

The Messenger 🦴 **1987 (R)** A man right out of prison sets out to avenge his wife's murder by an Italian drug syndicate. **95m/C VHS, Beta.** Fred Williamson, Sandy Cummings, Christopher Connelly, Cameron Mitchell. *FCT*

Messenger of Death 🦴🦴½ **1988 (R)** A tough detective investigates the slaughter of a Mormon family, and uncovers a conspiracy centering around oil-rich real estate. **90m/C VHS, Beta, LV.** Charles Bronson, Trish Van Devere, Laurence Luckinbill, Daniel Benzali, Marilyn Hassett, Jeff Corey, John Ireland, Penny Peyser, Gene Davis; ***D:*** J. Lee Thompson; ***W:*** Paul Jarrice; ***M:*** Robert O. Ragland. *MED, VTR*

The Messenger of the Blessed Virgin 🦴🦴 **1930** When his beloved niece Dorothy is tragically paralyzed Uncle John makes a trip to the shrine at Lourdes to pray for a miracle. The story of the original vision of Bernadette and the blessed virgin in 1856 is also related to Uncle John for inspiration. **105m/B VHS.** *VYY*

The Messiah 🦴🦴🦴½ **1975** Rossellini's final film, a rarely-seen version of the life of Christ, completely passed over any notions of divinity to portray him as a morally perfect man. In Italian with subtitles. **145m/C VHS, Beta.** *IT* ***D:*** Roberto Rossellini. *FCT, MVD*

Messiah of Evil 🦴 *Dead People; Return of the Living Dead; Revenge of the Screaming Dead; The Second Coming* **1974 (R)** California coastal town is invaded by zombies. Confusing low-rent production from the writers of "American Graffiti." **90m/C VHS, Beta.** Marianna Hill, Joy Bang, Royal Dano, Elisha Cook Jr., Michael Greer; ***D:*** Gloria Katz, Willard Huyck; ***W:*** Gloria Katz, Willard Huyck. *GEM, MRV*

Messidor 🦴🦴 **1977** Bored university student Jeanne (Amouroux) and shop assistant Marie (Retore) meet while hitchhiking and decide to travel together through Europe—committing robberies when they run out of money. French with subtitles. **118m/C VHS.** *SI* Clementine Amouroux, Catherine Retore, Franziskus Abgottspon, Gerald Battiaz, Hansjorg Bedschard; ***D:*** Alain Tanner; ***W:*** Alain Tanner; ***C:*** Renato Berta; ***M:*** Arie Dzierlatka. *NYF, FCT*

Metallica 🦴 **1985** Alien warmongers endeavor to conquer Earth and scientists try to stop them. **90m/C VHS, Beta.** Anthony Newcastle, Sharon Baker; ***D:*** Al Bradley. *NO*

Metalstorm: The Destruction of Jared Syn 🦴 **1983 (PG)** It's the science fiction battle of the ages with giant cyclopes and intergalactic magicians on the desert planet of Lemuria. **84m/C VHS, Beta, LV.** Jeffrey Byron, Mike Preston, Tim Thomerson, Kelly Preston, Richard Moll; ***D:*** Charles Band; ***W:*** Alan J. Adler; ***M:*** Richard Band. *MCA*

Metamorphosis 🦴 **1990 (R)** Novice scientist foolishly uses himself as the guinea pig for his anti-aging experiments. He quickly loses control of the project. **90m/C VHS, Beta.** Gene Le Brock, Catherine Baranov, Stephen Brown, Harry Cason, Jason Arnold; ***D:*** G.L. Eastman. *IMP, VMK*

Metamorphosis: The Alien Factor 🦴🦴½ **1993 (R)** Gerard is a genetic engineer who is bitten by a frog injected with a mutation sample from outer space. He turns into a slimy virus that infects everything he touches. **92m/C VHS.** George Gerard, Tony Gigante, Katharine Romaine; ***D:*** Glen Takakjian. *VMK*

Meteor *Woof!* **1979 (PG)** American and Soviet scientists attempt to save the Earth from a fast-approaching barrage of meteors from space in this disaster dud. Destruction ravages parts of Hong Kong and the Big Apple. **107m/C VHS, Beta, LV.** Sean Connery, Natalie Wood, Karl Malden, Brian Keith, Martin Landau, Trevor Howard, Henry Fonda, Joseph Campanella, Richard Dysart; ***D:*** Ronald Neame. Nominations: Academy Awards '79: Best Sound. *WAR, OM*

The Meteor Man 🦴🦴½ **1993 (PG)** Townsend is a school teacher who reluctantly becomes a hero when he acquires semi-super powers after being hit by a meteor. Meteor Man flies only four feet off the ground (because he's afraid of heights) and wears costumes fashioned by his mother. Funny premise satires "superhero" movies, but is inconsistent with some hilarious gags and others that fall flat. Includes interesting cameos by Cosby, Sinbad, Vandross, and Page. **100m/C VHS, LV.** Robert Townsend, Robert Guillaume, Marla Gibbs, James Earl Jones, Frank Gorshin; ***Cameos:*** Bill Cosby, Sinbad, Luther Vandross, LaWanda Page; ***D:*** Robert Townsend; ***W:*** Robert Townsend; ***C:*** John A. Alonzo. *MGM*

Meteor Monster *Woof! Teenage Monster* **1957** A young boy is hit by a meteor and is somehow transformed into a raving, slime-covered maniac. **73m/C VHS, Beta.** Anne Gwynne, Stuart Wade, Gloria Castillo, Chuck Courtney; ***D:*** Jacques Marquette. *SNC*

Metropolis 🦴🦴🦴🦴 **1926** Now a classic meditation on futurist technology and mass mentality, this fantasy concerns mechanized society. Original set design and special effects made this an innovative and influential film in its day. Is now considered one of the hippest films of the sci-fi genre. Silent, with musical score. The 1984 re-release features some color tinting, reconstruction, and a digital score with songs by Pat Benatar, Bonnie Tyler, Giorgio Moroder, and Queen. **115m/B VHS, Beta, LV.** *GE* Brigitte Helm, Alfred Abel, Gustav Froehlich, Rudolf Klein-Rogge, Fritz Rasp; ***D:*** Fritz Lang. *SNC, NOS, MRV*

Metropolitan **1990 (PG-13)** The Izod set comes of age on Park Avenue during Christmas break. Tom Townsend (Clements), a member of the middle class, finds himself drawn into a circle of self-proclaimed urban haute bourgeoisie types. They're embarrassingly short on male escorts for the holiday season's parties so he stands in and gets an inside look at life with the brat pack. Intelligently written and carefully made, it transcends the flirting-with-adulthood genre. **98m/C VHS, LV.** Carolyn Farina, Edward Clements, Taylor Nichols, Christopher Eigeman, Allison Rutledge-Parisi, Dylan Hundley, Isabel Gillies, Bryan Leder, Will Kempe, Elizabeth Thompson; ***D:*** Whit Stillman; ***W:*** Whit Stillman; ***M:*** Mark Suozzo. Independent Spirit Awards '91: Best First Feature; New York Film Critics Awards '90: Best Director (Stillman); Nominations: Academy Awards '90: Best Original Screenplay. *COL, FCT*

Mexican Bus Ride ½ *Ascent to Heaven; Subida Al Cielo* **1951** A good-natured Bunuel effort about a newlywed peasant who travels to the big city to attend to his mother's will. While en route, he encounters a diversity of people on the bus and some temptation. In Spanish with English subtitles. **85m/B VHS, Beta.** *MX* Lilia Prado, Esteban Marquez, Carmelita Gonzalez; ***D:*** Luis Bunuel. *FCT, APD, AUD*

Mexican Hayride **1948** Bud heads a gang of swindlers and Lou is the fall guy. When things up north get too hot, the boys head south of the border to cool off and start a mining scam. Watch for the hilarious bullfighting scene. Believe it or not, this is based on a Cole Porter musical—minus the music. **77m/B VHS.** Bud Abbott, Lou Costello, Virginia Grey, Luba Malina, John Hubbard, Pedro de Cordoba, Fritz Feld, Tom Powers, Pat Costello, Frank Fenton; ***D:*** Charles T. Barton; ***W:*** Oscar Brodney. *MCA*

Mexican Spitfire at Sea ½ **1942** The feisty wife from South of the Border heads for Hawaii to close a deal for her husband. He goes along to help her, impersonating nobility. The thin story line keeps it from being quite as good as the first "Mexican Spitfire" film. Most of the action takes place aboard ship. **73m/B VHS.** Lupe Velez, Leon Errol, Charles "Buddy" Rogers, ZaSu Pitts, Elisabeth Risdon, Florence Bates, Marion Martin, Eddie Dunn, Harry Holman; ***D:*** Leslie Goodwins. *NOS*

Mexican Spitfire/Smartest Girl in Town **1940** A comedy double feature: In "Mexican Spitfire," a man impersonates an English lord in order to save a contract for the spitfire's husband. In "The Smartest Girl in Town," a photographer's model mistakes a millionaire for a fellow magazine model. **125m/B VHS, Beta.** Lupe Velez, Leon Errol, Donald Woods, Ann Sothern, Gene Raymond. *TTC*

MGM: When the Lion Roars **1992** Three-part documentary covers the history and films of the Metro-Goldwyn-Mayer (MGM) studio from its beginnings in 1924 with the release of the studio's first film ("He Who Gets Slapped"), through its glory years, to the studio's gradual decline and ever-changing leadership. MGM brought out such films as "The Wizard of Oz," "Gone With the Wind," the Andy Hardy series, and the Thin Man films. Features clips of films and stars as well as footage of studio executives, including Louis B. Mayer and legendary studio chief and producer Irving Thalberg. Tapes are also available individually for $19.98. Originally made for cable TV. **360m/C VHS, LV.** *MGM*

MGM's The Big Parade of Comedy **1992** An anthology of more than 50 of MGM's stars and comedians in some of their funniest screen moments. Looks at Laurel & Hardy, the Marx Brothers, W.C. Fields, Clark Gable, Jean Harlow, Greta Garbo, and others. **100m/C VHS.** *MGM*

Mi Vida Loca *My Crazy Life* **1994 (R)** Looks at the lives of Latina gang members from L.A.'s Echo Park. The women talk about their romantic dreams, friendships, families, and raising children amidst the pervasive violence and despair of their tough neighborhood. Small budget and some unpolished performances don't lessen film's impact—about the stupidity of violence and how "average" the hopes and dreams of these women are. **92m/C VHS.** Angel Aviles, Jacob Vargas, Jesse Borrego, Seidy Lopez, Marlo Marron, Neilida Lopez, Bertilla Damas, Art Esquer, Christina Solis, Salma Hayek, Magali Alvarado, Julian Reyes, Panchito Gomez; ***D:*** Allison Anders; ***W:*** Allison Anders; ***M:*** John Taylor. *HBO*

Miami Beach Cops ½ **1993** Two vets return home expecting life to be routine when they become sheriff's deputies. But when bad guys murder a local merchant things heat up fast. **97m/C VHS.** Frank Maldonatti, Salvatore Rendino, William Childers, Joyce Geier, Raff Baker, Dan Preston, Deborah Daniels; ***D:*** James R. Winburn. *AIP*

Miami Blues ½ **1990 (R)** Cold-blooded killer plays cat-and-mouse with bleary cop while diddling with an unflappable prostitute. Violent and cynical, with appropriate performances from three leads. Based on the novel by Charles Willeford. **97m/C VHS, Beta, LV.** Fred Ward, Alec Baldwin, Jennifer Jason Leigh, Nora Dunn, Charles Napier, Jose Perez, Paul Gleason, Obba Babatunde, Martine Beswick; ***D:*** George Armitage; ***W:*** George Armitage; ***M:*** Gary Chang. New York Film Critics Awards '90: Best Supporting Actress (Leigh). *ORI, IME*

Miami Cops **1989** When a cop's father is killed by a drug smuggler, he and his partner pursue the murderer over two continents. Italian-made adventure is a bit drawn-out. **103m/C VHS, Beta.** *IT* Richard Roundtree, Harrison Muller, Dawn Baker, Michael J. Aronin; ***D:*** Al Bradley. *CAN*

Miami Horror **1987** A Florida scientist is experimenting with bacteria from space, trying to recreate a human only to have his efforts stolen by a crook. His intentions for the use of the experiment are not exactly for the furtherance of science. **85m/C VHS, Beta.** *IT* David Warbeck, Laura Trotter, Lawrence Loddi, John Ireland; ***D:*** Martin Herbert. *NO*

Miami Rhapsody **1995 (PG-13)** Woody Allen-ish romantic comedy about a young, neurotic copywriter who becomes disillusioned with the idea of marriage as she discovers every member of her family is having an affair. Parker plays the newly-engaged Gwyn who is not entirely sure if she wants to marry her cute, zoologist boyfriend. Most of the characters come across as annoying, self-absorbed whiners, except for Banderas, who charms as a sexy Cuban nurse. Film moves along with its light-hearted narrative, but never reaches the comic or emotional depth of Allen's work. Director/writer Frankel shows promise, but should come out from behind the Woodman's shadow. Filmed on location in Miami. **95m/C VHS, LV.** Sarah Jessica Parker, Gil Bellows, Antonio Banderas, Mia Farrow, Paul Mazursky, Kevin Pollak, Barbara Garrick, Carla Gugino, Bo Eason, Naomi Campbell, Jeremy Piven, Kelly Bishop; ***D:*** David Frankel; ***W:*** David Frankel; ***C:*** Jack Wallner; ***M:*** Mark Isham. *TOU*

Miami Supercops ½ **1985** Two goofy policemen strike out against such threats as a gang that hassles buses, the attempted kidnapping of an Orange Bowl quarterback, and a multi-million-dollar robbery. **97m/C VHS, Beta.** Terence Hill, Bud Spencer, Jackie Castellano, C.V. Wood Jr.; ***D:*** Bruno Corbucci. *WAR*

Miami Vendetta **1987** L.A. vice cop risks it all to avenge his friend's death at the hands of Cuban drug smugglers. **90m/C VHS, Beta.** Sandy Brooke, Frank Gargani, Maarten Goslins, Barbara Pilavin; ***D:*** Steven Seemayer. *NO*

Miami Vice ½ **1984** Pilot for the popular television series paired Crockett and Tubbs for the first time on the trail of a killer in Miami's sleazy underground. Music by Jan Hammer and other pop notables. **99m/C VHS, Beta, LV.** Don Johnson, Philip Michael Thomas, Saundra Santiago, Michael Talbott, John Diehl, Gregory Sierra; ***D:*** Thomas Carter. *MCA*

Miami Vice 2: The Prodigal Son **1985** The second full-length television movie spawned by the popular series, following the laconic Floridians to the gritty streets of New York. **99m/C VHS, Beta, LV.** Don Johnson, Philip Michael Thomas, Edward James Olmos, Penn Jillette. *MCA*

The Michigan Kid **1928** Two boys fight for the same girl in this silent love triangle set in Alaska. Film's most notable scene is of a raging forest fire, considered a classic even today. **62m/B VHS, Beta.** Conrad Nagel, Renee Adoree, Fred Esmelton, Virginia Grey, Adolph Milar, Lloyd Whitlock; ***D:*** Irvin Willat. *GPV*

Mickey **1917** Spoof on high society as a penniless young woman moves in with relatives and works as the family's maid. Silent film. **105m/B VHS, Beta.** Mabel Normand, Lew Cody, Minta Durfee; ***D:*** Mack Sennett. *NOS, VYY, DVT*

Mickey **1948** A tomboy becomes a woman even as she plays matchmaker for her own father and sings a few songs. Not too exciting; you may fall alseep if you're slipped this "Mickey." Based on the novel "Clementine," by Peggy Goodin. **87m/C VHS.** Lois Butler, Bill Goodwin, Irene Hervey, John Sutton, Hattie McDaniel; ***D:*** Ralph Murphy. *NOS*

Mickey One ½ **1965** Nightclub comic Mickey (Beatty) gets into trouble when he can't pay his gambling debts. So he hides out in Chicago under an assumed name, working as a janitor, but can't live without the applause. His agent finds him a club job but Mickey panics, thinking the place is under mob control, and spends a lot of time running around, trying to clear his debts. Finally, returning to the club, Mickey resigns himself to a bleak fate. Beatty's jumpy character is an acquired taste—as is the film. **93m/B LV.** Warren Beatty, Hurd Hatfield, Alexandra Stewart, Franchot Tone, Teddy Hart, Jeff Corey; ***D:*** Arthur Penn; ***W:*** Alan M. Surgal; ***C:*** Ghislan Cloquet; ***M:*** Jack Shaindlin, Eddie Sauter. *FCT*

Mickey the Great **1939** Stitched together from several late 20's Mickey McGuire shorts, starring 10-year-old Rooney. **70m/B VHS, Beta.** Billy Barty, Mickey Rooney. *VYY, DVT, NOS*

Mickey's Christmas Carol **1983 (G)** Mickey Mouse returns along with all the other Disney characters in this adaptation of the Charles Dickens classic. Includes a documentary on how the featurette was made. **25m/C VHS, Beta, LV.** ***V:*** Alan Young, Hal Smith, Will Ryan, Wayne Alline, Clarence Nash, Eddie Carroll, Pat Parris, Susan Sheridan. *DIS, MTI, DSN*

Micki & Maude **1984 (PG-13)** When a man longs for a baby, he finds that his wife, Micki, is too busy for motherhood. Out of frustration, he has an affair with Maude that leads to her pregnancy. Still shocked by the news of his upcoming fatherhood, the man learns that his wife is also expecting. **117m/C VHS, Beta, LV.** Dudley Moore, Amy Irving, Ann Reinking, Richard Mulligan, Wallace Shawn, George Gaynes, Andre the Giant; ***D:*** Blake Edwards; ***W:*** Jonathan Reynolds; ***C:*** Harry Stradling Jr. Golden Globe Awards '85: Best Actor—Musical/Comedy (Moore). *COL*

Microwave Massacre **1983 (R)** Killer kitchen appliances strike again as late lounge comic Vernon murders nagging wife and 'waves her. Overcome by that Betty Crocker feeling, he goes on a microwave murdering/feeding spree of the local ladies. Lots of Roger Corman copying. **80m/C VHS.** Jackie Vernon, Loren Schein, Al Troupe; ***D:*** Wayne Berwick. *RHI, FCT*

Mid-Channel ½ **1920** A married couple become bored with each other and the wife seeks diversion with other men. Surprise ending. **70m/B VHS, Beta.** Clara Kimball Young, J. Frank Glendon, Edward M. Kimball, Bertram Grassby, Eileen Robinson, Helen Sullivan, Katherine Griffith, Jack Livingston; ***D:*** Harry Garson. *NOS, MRV, GPV*

Mid Knight Rider **1984** Penniless actor becomes a male prostitute at the service of bored, rich women. At an all-night orgy, he suddenly goes on a rampage, nearly killing one of his customers. **76m/C VHS, Beta.** Michael Christian, Keenan Wynn. *TWE*

The Midas Touch ♧♧ **1989** A flea market merchant in 1956 Budapest has the ability to turn items into gold. In Hungarian with English subtitles. **100m/C VHS, Beta.** *HU* ***D:*** Geza Beremenyi; ***W:*** Geza Beremenyi. *EVD, FCT, INJ*

Middle Age Crazy ♧½ **1980 (R)** Story of a Texas building contractor who takes life pretty lightly until his own father dies. Then he becomes immersed in a mid-life crisis and has an affair with a Dallas Cowboys' cheerleader. Ann-Margaret plays the victim wife of the middle aged swingin' guy. **95m/C VHS.** *CA* Bruce Dern, Ann-Margret, Graham Jarvis, Eric Christmas, Deborah Wakeham; ***D:*** John Trent. *FOX*

Middlemarch ♧♧♧ **1993** Stylish British TV costume drama, adapted from George Eliot's 1872 novel, finds idealistic Dorothea Brooke (Aubrey) determined to be a helpmate to the older scholar, the Rev. Edward Casaubon (Malahide), whom she marries. Too bad that he takes so little interest in her ability (or in Dorothea herself). This leads Casaubon's distant cousin, young and handsome Will Ladislaw (Sewell), to discreetly make his interest clear. Naturally, Eliot has a number of other plots (some dealing with the impact of the Industrial Revolution on 19th-century life) and romances worked into the mix. Filmed in Stamford, England. On 3 cassettes. **360m/C VHS.** *GB* Juliet Aubrey, Patrick Malahide, Rufus Sewell, Douglas Hodge, Trevyn McDowell, Michael Hordern, Robert Hardy, John Savident, Jonathan Firth, Peter Jeffrey, Simon Chandler, Julian Wadham; ***D:*** Anthony Page; ***W:*** Andrew Davies, Stanley Myers; ***C:*** Brian Tufano. *FOX, TVC*

Midnight ♧♧½ *Call it Murder* **1934** A jury foreman's daughter is romantically involved with a gangster who is interested in a particular case before it appears in court. The foreman, who sentenced a girl to death, faces a dilemma when his own daughter is arrested for the same crime. An early Bogart appearance in a supporting role led to a re-release of the film as "Call it Murder" after Bogart made it big. Weak melodrama. **74m/B VHS, Beta.** Humphrey Bogart, Sidney Fox, O.P. Heggie, Henry Hull, Richard Whorf, Margaret Wycherly, Lynne Overman; ***D:*** Chester Erskine. *CCB, DVT, BAR*

Midnight ♧♧♧½ **1939** Struggling showgirl Colbert masquerades as Hungarian countess in sophisticated comedy of marital conflicts. Near-classic film scripted by Wilder and Brackett. Based on a story by Edwin Justus Mayer and Franz Schulz. Remade as "Masquerade in Mexico." **94m/B VHS.** Claudette Colbert, Don Ameche, John Barrymore, Francis Lederer, Mary Astor, Hedda Hopper, Rex O'Malley; ***D:*** Mitchell Leisen; ***W:*** Billy Wilder, Charles Brackett; ***C:*** Charles B(ryant) Lang. *MCA*

Midnight ♧ *Backwoods Massacre* **1981 (R)** Russo, who cowrote the original "Night of the Living Dead," wrote and directed this film about a runaway girl who is driven out of her home by a lecherous stepfather and meets two young thieves and then a family of cultists. Russo adapted his own novel. He also attains some of "Night of the Living Dead's" low-budget ambience. **88m/C VHS, Beta.** Lawrence Tierney, Melanie Verliin, John Hall, John Amplas; ***D:*** John Russo. *VMK*

Midnight ♧ **1989 (R)** Murder-thriller involving the vampirish hostess of a television horror movie showcase and a fanatical fan. **90m/C VHS, Beta, LV.** Lynn Redgrave, Tony Curtis, Steve Parrish, Rita Gam, Gustav Vintas, Karen Witter, Frank Gorshin, Wolfman Jack; ***D:*** Norman Thaddeus Vane. *VTR*

Midnight 2: Sex, Death, and Videotape ♧ **1993** Sequel to "Midnight" finds the sole surviving member of the crazed family stalking a beautiful unsuspecting teller with a video camera. Only she's teamed up with a detective to solve the murder of her best friend—even if it means she's bait for a psycho. **70m/C VHS.** Matthew Jason Walsh, Jo Norcia; ***D:*** John Russo. *TEM, MOV*

Midnight at the Wax Museum ♧ *Midnight at Madame Tussaud's* **1936** A man attempts to spend an evening in a wax museum's chamber of horrors, only to find that he is the target of a murder plot. **66m/B VHS.** Lucille Lisle, James Carew, Charles Oliver, Kim Peacock; ***D:*** George Pearson. *NOS, DVT, SNC*

Midnight Auto Supply ♧½ **1978** Dealers in hot car parts, working out of the garage behind the local brothel, become persuaded to donate some of their profits to the cause of Mexican farm workers. Also called "Love and the Midnight Auto Supply." **91m/C VHS.** Michael Parks, Rory Calhoun, Scott Jacoby, Rod Cameron, Colleen Camp, Linda Cristal, John Ireland; ***D:*** James Polakof. *NO*

Midnight Cabaret *Woof!* **1990 (R)** A New York nightclub-based Satanic cult selects a child actress to bear Satan's child. **94m/C VHS, Beta, LV.** Michael Des Barres, Thom Mathews, Carolyn Seymour, Leonard Termo, Norbert Weisser, Lydie Denier; ***D:*** Pece Dingo; ***W:*** Pece Dingo; ***M:*** Michel Colombier. *WAR*

A Midnight Clear ♧♧♧ **1992 (PG)** Sensitive war drama that takes place in the Ardennes Forest, near the French-German border in December 1944. It's Christmastime and six of the remaining members of a 12-member squad are sent on a dangerous mission to an abandoned house to locate the enemy. Filmed in a dreamy surreal style, the setting is somewhat reminiscent of a fairytale, although a sense of anguish filtrates throughout the picture. A solid script, excellent direction, and a good cast make this a worthwhile film that pits the message of peace against the stupidity of war. Adapted from the novel by William Wharton. **107m/C VHS, LV.** Peter Berg, Kevin Dillon, Arye Gross, Ethan Hawke, Gary Sinise, Frank Whaley, John C. McGinley, Larry Joshua, Curt Lowens; ***D:*** Keith Gordon; ***W:*** Keith Gordon; ***M:*** Mark Isham. *COL, PMS*

Midnight Confessions ♧ **1995 (R)** Provocative night-time DJ Vannesse (Hoyt) lures her listeners into revealing their sexual fantasies. But when an obsessed fan begins killing women just how deeply is she involved? **98m/C VHS, LV.** Carol Hoyt, Julie Strain, Monique Parent, Richard Lynch. *TRI*

Midnight Cop ♧ **1988 (R)** A young woman gets tangled up in a web of murder, intrigue, prostitution and drugs, and she enlists the aid of a cop to help get her out of it. **100m/C VHS, Beta, LV.** Michael York, Morgan Fairchild, Frank Stallone, Armin Mueller-Stahl; ***D:*** Peter Patzak. *VMK, HHE*

Midnight Cowboy ♧♧♧½ **1969 (R)** Drama about the relationship between a naive Texan hustler and a seedy derelict, set in the underbelly of New York City. Graphic and emotional character study is brilliantly acted and engaging. Shocking and considered quite risque at the time of its release, this film now carries an "R" rating. It is the only film carrying an "X" rating ever to win the Best Picture Oscar. From James Leo Herlihy's novel. Laserdisc version features: audio commentary by director John Schlesinger and producer Jereome Hellman, behind the scenes production photos, and original movie trailer. **113m/C VHS, Beta, LV.** Dustin Hoffman, Jon Voight, Sylvia Miles, Brenda Vaccaro, John McGiver, Bob Balaban, Barnard Hughes; ***D:*** John Schlesinger; ***W:*** Waldo Salt; ***C:*** Adam Holender; ***M:*** John Barry. Academy Awards '69: Best Adapted Screenplay, Best Director (Schlesinger), Best Picture; British Academy Awards '69: Best Actor (Hoffman), Best Director (Schlesinger), Best Film, Best Screenplay; Directors Guild of America Awards '69: Best Director (Schlesinger); New York Film Critics Awards '69: Best Actor (Voight); National Society of Film Critics Awards '69: Best Actor (Voight); Writers Guild of America '69: Best Adapted Screenplay; Nominations: Academy Awards '69: Best Actor (Hoffman), Best Actor (Voight), Best Film Editing, Best Supporting Actress (Miles). *MGM, CRC, BTV*

Midnight Crossing ♧♧ **1987 (R)** Two married couples are subjected to jealousy, betrayal and uncloseted-skeletons as their pleasure cruise on a yacht turns into a ruthless search for sunken treasure. **96m/C VHS, Beta, LV.** Faye Dunaway, Daniel J. Travanti, Kim Cattrall, John Laughlin, Ned Beatty; ***D:*** Roger Holzberg. *LIV, VES*

Midnight Dancer ♧♧ **1987** A young ballerina is forced to work as an erotic dancer. **97m/C VHS, Beta.** *AU* Deanne Jeffs, Mary Regan; ***D:*** Pamela Gibbons. *ACA*

Midnight Dancers ♧♧ **1994** Seamy look at Manila's gay subculture and male prostitution. Sonny and his older brothers Dennis and Joel work as dancers at a sleazy club whose upstairs apartments are used for prostitution. The boys need the money to help their impoverished family survive in the slums but the emotional wear and tear (not to mention police raids and assorted brutalities) provide lots of melodrama. Filipino with subtitles. **115m/C VHS.** *PH* Alex Del Rosario, Gandong Cervantes, Laurence David, Perla Bautista, Soxy Topacio; ***D:*** Mel Chionglo; ***W:*** Ricardo Lee; ***C:*** George Tutanes; ***M:*** Nonong Buenoamino. *ICA*

Midnight Edition ♧♧ **1993 (R)** Investigative reporter Jack Travers (Patton) returns to his Georgia hometown newspaper just in time to write the story of his life. Nineteen-year-old Darryl Weston (DeLuise) massacres a local family for no apparent reason, is tried, convicted, and sentenced to die. Jack's death row interviews with Darryl become hot news but his reporter's objectivity is lost and he becomes a pawn in an escape plan. Good interplay between the charming sociopath and the self-deluded reporter in a sometimes confusing thriller. Based on the autobiography "Escape of My Dead Men" by Charles Postell. **98m/C VHS.** Will Patton, Michael DeLuise, Clare Wren, Nancy Moore Atchison, Sarabeth Tucek, Judson Vaughn, Ji Tu Cumbuka, Jay Bernard; ***D:*** Howard Libov; ***W:*** Howard Libov, Yuri Zeltser, Michael Stewart; ***M:*** Murray Attaway. *MCA*

Midnight Express ♧♧♧ **1978 (R)** Gripping and powerful film based on the true story of Billy Hayes. Davis plays Hayes as a young American in Turkey who is busted trying to smuggle hashish. He is sentenced to a brutal and nightmarish prison for life. After enduring tremendous mental and physical torture, he seeks escape along the "Midnight Express." Not always easy to watch, but the overall effect is riveting and unforgettable. **120m/C VHS, Beta, LV, 8mm.** John Hurt, Randy Quaid, Brad Davis, Paul Smith, Bo Hopkins, Oliver Stone; ***D:*** Alan Parker; ***W:*** Oliver Stone; ***M:*** Giorgio Moroder. Academy Awards '78: Best Adapted Screenplay, Best Score; British Academy Awards '78: Best Director (Parker), Best Supporting Actor (Hurt); National Board of Review Awards '78: 10 Best Films of the Year; Writers Guild of America '78: Best Adapted Screenplay; Nominations: Academy Awards '78: Best Director (Parker), Best Film Editing, Best Picture, Best Supporting Actor (Hurt). *COL*

Midnight Faces ♧♧ **1926** Mysterious doings abound in a house in the Florida bayous, recently inherited by Bushman. Silent, with original organ music. **72m/B VHS, Beta, 8mm.** Francis X. Bushman, Jack Perrin, Kathryn McGuire. *SNC, VYY, LSV*

Midnight Fear ♧½ **1990** When a sexually demented killer skins a woman alive, Sheriff Hanley sets out to find whodunit. He suspects two weird brothers, who turn out to be holding a woman hostage, but the situation may not be so simple. Carradine plays the good-guy sheriff in this creeper. **90m/C VHS.** David Carradine, Craig Wasson; ***D:*** William Crain. *RHI*

Midnight Girl ♧½ **1925** A fading opera impresario plots to steal a family's fortune. Lugosi before he became Dracula. Silent. **84m/B VHS, Beta, 8mm.** Bela Lugosi, Lila Lee. *GPV, VYY, DVT*

Midnight Heat ♧♧½ **1995 (R)** Football player is the prime suspect when his lover's husband (who happens to be the team owner) is murdered. **97m/C VHS.** Tim Matheson, Stephen Mendel, Mimi Craven; ***D:*** Harvey Frost. *AVE*

The Midnight Hour ♧½ **1986** A group of high schoolers stumbles upon a vintage curse that wakes up the dead. Made for television. More humor than horror. **97m/C VHS.** Shari Belafonte, LeVar Burton, Lee Montgomery, Dick Van Patten, Kevin McCarthy, Jonelle Allen, Peter DeLuise, Dedee Pfeiffer, Mark Blankfield; ***D:*** Jack Bender; ***M:*** Brad Fiedel. *VMK*

Midnight Kiss ♧♧½ **1993 (R)** When a woman police detective investigates a mysterious series of deaths—women whose blood has been drained—she gets more than she bargains for. She's attacked by a vampire and is herself turned into a reluctant bloodsucker. Quick moving and some gross special effects. Also available in an unrated version. **85m/C VHS.** Michelle Owens, Gregory A. Greer; ***D:*** Joel Bender; ***W:*** John Weidner, Ken Lamplugh. *ACA*

Midnight Lace 🦴🦴½ **1960** Acceptable thriller about a woman in London who is being harassed by a telephone creep. Day is at her frantic best, and Harrrison is suitably charming. Handsome Gavin later became American ambassador to Mexico. Adapted from the play "Matilda Shouted Fire." **108m/C VHS, Beta.** Doris Day, Rex Harrison, John Gavin, Myrna Loy, Roddy McDowall; ***D:*** David Miller; ***W:*** Ivan Goff; ***C:*** Russell Metty. Nominations: Academy Awards '60: Best Costume Design (Color). *MCA*

Midnight Limited 🦴🦴 **1940** A detective sets out to thwart the criminals who would rob the "Midnight Limited" train on its route from New York to Montreal. **61m/B VHS, Beta.** John "Dusty" King, Marjorie Reynolds, George Cleveland, Edward Keane, Pat Flaherty, Monty Collins, I. Stanford Jolley; ***D:*** Howard Bretherton. *SNC*

Midnight Madness 🦴 **1980 (PG)** Five teams of college students search the city of Los Angeles for clues leading to hundreds and thousands of dollars in buried treasure. **110m/C VHS, Beta.** David Naughton, Stephen Furst, Debra Clinger, Eddie Deezen, Michael J. Fox, Maggie Roswell; ***D:*** David Wechter; ***W:*** David Wechter. *TOU, OM*

Midnight Movie Massacre 🦴🦴½ **1988** Retro splatterama has really gross alien land outside a movie theater in 1956, and the really weird movie patrons try to terminate it. **86m/C VHS.** Robert Clarke, Ann Robinson; ***D:*** Mark Stock. *NO*

Midnight Murders 🦴🦴½ *Manhunt in the Dakotas* **1991 (R)** Steiger stars as a farmer and Posse Commitatus member whose paramilitary pretensions lead to a bloody confrontation with federal marshals. Gross is the FBI agent sent to hunt him down. Made for TV. **95m/C VHS.** Rod Steiger, Michael Gross, Gary Basaraba, Christopher Rich, Henderson Forsythe; ***D:*** Dick Lowry. *NHO*

The Midnight Phantom 🦴🦴 **1935** Incredibly rare horror film featuring a bizarre murder at a midnight lecture. **?m/B VHS.** Reginald Denny. *SNC*

Midnight Ride 🦴½ **1992** Lots of silly action fails to save this slight tale of a cop (Dudikoff) chasing after his runaway wife (Gersak), who has made the mistake of picking up a psycho hitchhiker (Hamill, gleefully overacting). **95m/C VHS.** Michael Dudikoff, Mark Hamill, Savina Gersak; ***Cameos:*** Robert Mitchum; ***D:*** Robert Bralver. *CAN*

Midnight Run 🦴🦴🦴 **1988 (R)** An ex-cop, bounty hunter must bring in an ex-mob accountant who has embezzled big bucks from his former boss. After he catches up with the thief, the hunter finds that bringing his prisoner from New York to Los Angeles will be very trying, especially when it is apparent that the Mafia and FBI are out to stop them. The friction between the two leads—De Niro and Grodin—is fun to watch, while the action and comic moments are enjoyable. **125m/C VHS, Beta, LV.** Robert De Niro, Charles Grodin, Yaphet Kotto, John Ashton, Dennis Farina, Joe Pantoliano, Richard Foronjy, Wendy Phillips; ***D:*** Martin Brest; ***W:*** George Gallo; ***C:*** Donald E. Thorin; ***M:*** Danny Elfman. *MCA*

Midnight Tease 🦴½ **1994** Strip bar, the Club Fugazi, is having trouble with its help—the dancers keep getting murdered. Dancer Samantha (Leigh) actually dreams about the murders before they occur, so naturally she becomes the prime suspect. Leigh can actually do more than look fetching but plot is barely apparent. **87m/C VHS, LV.** Cassandra Leigh, Rachel Reed, Edmund Halley, Ashlie Rhey, Todd Joseph; ***D:*** Scott Levy. *NHO*

Midnight Tease 2 🦴 **1995 (R)** Woman poses as a stripper to find her sister's killer. **?m/C VHS.** Kimberly Kelly, Tane McClure, Ross Hagen; ***D:*** Richard Styles. *NHO*

Midnight Warning 🦴🦴½ **1932** A woman thinks she's going off the deep-end when her brother and all records of his existence disappear. Based on an urban legend that appeared somewhere around the time of the 1893 World's Fair. Remade in 1952 as "So Long at the Fair." **63m/B VHS.** William Boyd, Claudia Dell, Henry Hall, John Harron, Hooper Atchley; ***D:*** Spencer Gordon Bennet. *SNC, NOS, DVT*

Midnight Warrior 🦴 **1989** A reporter strikes it big when he investigates the underside of L.A. nightlife, but things go terribly wrong when he becomes wrapped up in the sleaze. **90m/C VHS, Beta.** Bernie Angel, Michelle Berger, Kevin Bernhardt, Lilly Melgar; ***D:*** Joseph Merhi. *PAR*

Midnight Witness 🦴½ **1993 (R)** Guy finds himself on the run when after he videotapes the beating of a young drug dealer by corrupt cops. Plot bears more than a little resemblance to the Rodney King incident, but according to writer Foldy it was written before it took place. Low budget thriller went direct to video. **90m/C VHS.** Maxwell Caulfield, Jan-Michael Vincent, Paul Johansson, Karen Moncrieff, Mark Pellegrino, Virginia Mayo; ***D:*** Peter Foldy; ***W:*** Peter Foldy; ***M:*** Graydon Hillock. *ACA*

Midnight's Child 🦴½ **1993** Another Nanny-from-Hell story, only this time it's literal. D'Abo is the Nanny in question, who belongs to a Satanic cult. Her mission is to select the young daughter in her care as a bride for the devil, even if the girl's parents don't approve of the match. **89m/C VHS, Beta.** Olivia D'Abo, Marcy Walker, Cotter Smith, Elissabeth Moss, Jim Norton, Judy Parfitt, Roxann Biggs, Mary Larkin; ***D:*** Colin Bucksey; ***W:*** David Chaskin. *PSM*

Midnite Spares 🦴🦴 **1985** A young man's search for the men who kidnapped his father leads him into the world of car thieves and chop-shops. **90m/C VHS, Beta.** Bruce Spence, Gia Carides, James Laurie; ***M:*** Cameron Allan. *NO*

A Midsummer Night's Dream 🦴🦴🦴 **1935** Famed Reinhardt version of the Shakespeare classic, featuring nearly every star on the Warner Brothers lot. The plot revolves around the amorous battle between the king and queen of a fairy kingdom, and the humans who are drawn into their sport. Features de Havilland's first film role. Classic credit line: Dialogue by William Shakespeare. **117m/B VHS, Beta.** James Cagney, Dick Powell, Joe E. Brown, Hugh Herbert, Olivia de Havilland, Ian Hunter, Mickey Rooney, Victor Jory, Arthur Treacher, Billy Barty; ***D:*** Max Reinhardt, William Dieterle; ***C:*** Hal Mohr. Academy Awards '35: Best Cinematography, Best Film Editing; Nominations: Academy Awards '35: Best Picture. *MGM, FOX, FCT*

A Midsummer Night's Dream 🦴🦴½ **1968** Fine acting from the Royal Shakespeare Company cast in this filmed version of the play. Makes very little use of the Athens, Greece scenery. **124m/C VHS.** *GB* David Warner, Diana Rigg, Ian Richardson, Judi Dench, Ian Holm, Barbara Jefford, Nicholas Selby, Helen Mirren, Michael Jayston, Derek Godfrey, Hugh Sullivan, Paul Rogers, Sebastian Shaw, Bill Travers; ***D:*** Peter Hall. *WBF, WAR, BTV*

A Midsummer Night's Sex Comedy 🦴🦴🦴½ **1982 (PG)** Allen's homage to Shakespeare, Renoir, Chekhov, Bergman, and who knows who else is an engaging ensemble piece about hijinks among friends and acquaintances gathered at a country house at the turn of the century. Standouts include Ferrer as pompous professor and Steenburgen as Allen's sexually repressed wife. Mia's first for the Woodman. **88m/C VHS, Beta.** Woody Allen, Mia Farrow, Mary Steenburgen, Tony Roberts, Julie Hagerty, Jose Ferrer; ***D:*** Woody Allen; ***W:*** Woody Allen; ***C:*** Gordon Willis. *WAR*

Midway 🦴🦴 **1976 (PG)** The epic WWII battle of Midway, the turning point in the war, is retold through Allied and Japanese viewpoints by a big all-star cast saddled with dumpy dialogue and enough weaponry to seize Hollywood on any given Wednesday. **132m/C VHS, Beta, LV.** Charlton Heston, Henry Fonda, James Coburn, Glenn Ford, Hal Holbrook, Robert Mitchum, Cliff Robertson, Robert Wagner, Kevin Dobson, Christopher George, Toshiro Mifune, Tom Selleck; ***D:*** Jack Smight; ***C:*** Harry Stradling Jr.; ***M:*** John Williams. *MCA, TLF*

A Midwinter's Tale 🦴🦴½ *In the Bleak Midwinter* **1995 (R)** Branagh assembles a largely unknown cast in this low-budget backstage saga about an out-of-work thesp, Joe Harper (Maloney), who assembles a shaggy crew of actors to stage an alternative "Hamlet" in a small English country church. The diverse cast squabble, stumble, and emote their way through rehearsals, finally pulling together for the big show. Funny and interesting performances manage to show through the dense and somewhat cliched script. Maloney's Joe, who exhibits the proper frustration of being forced to deal with amateurs and Sessions as a camp queen playing the Queen (Gertrude, that is) stand out. **100m/B VHS.** *GB* Michael Maloney, Richard Briers, Mark Hadfield, Nicholas Farrell, Gerard Horan, John Sessions, Celia Imrie, Hetta Charnley, Julia Sawalha, Joan Collins, Jennifer Saunders; ***D:*** Kenneth Branagh; ***C:*** Roger Lanser; ***M:*** Jimmy Yuill. *NYR*

Mighty Aphrodite 🦴🦴½ **1995 (R)** Neurotic (Surprise!) New York sportswriter Lenny Weinrib (Allen) is trapped in an unhappy marriage to art dealer Amanda (Bonham-Carter), who talks him into adopting a child. Film comes alive when Lenny tracks down his son's biological mother, consummate dumb blond and hooker/porno actress Linda, played with over-the-top (in a good way) gusto by Sorvino. Lenny attempts to reform his son's real mother while a Greek chorus (including Abraham and Dukakis) provide a running commentary on the tragedy/comedy of Lenny's predicaments. Allen's 31st film treads into familiar Woodman waters but falls short of his past comic genius. **95m/C VHS, LV.** Woody Allen, Helena Bonham Carter, Mira Sorvino, F. Murray Abraham, Michael Rapaport, Jack Warden, Olympia Dukakis, Peter Weller, Claire Bloom, David Ogden Stiers; ***D:*** Woody Allen; ***W:*** Woody Allen; ***C:*** Carlo DiPalma; ***M:*** Dick Hyman. Academy Awards '95: Best Supporting Actress (Sorvino); Golden Globe Awards '96: Best Supporting Actress (Sorvino); National Board of Review Awards '95: Best Supporting Actress (Sorvino); New York Film Critics Awards '95: Best Supporting Actress (Sorvino); Nominations: Academy Awards '95: Best Screenplay; British Academy Awards '95: Best Supporting Actress (Sorvino); Screen Actors Guild Award '95: Best Supporting Actress (Sorvino); Writers Guild of America '95: Best Original Screenplay. *TOU*

The Mighty Ducks 🦴🦴½ **1992 (PG)** Bad News Bears on skates. Selfish yuppie lawyer is arrested for drunk driving and as part of his community service sentence, he is forced to coach an inner-city hockey team full of the usual misfits and underachievers. Although sarcastic and skeptical, Coach Gordon Bombay (Estevez) eventually bonds with the Ducks and learns to treat them with respect. Dual themes of teamwork and redemption are repeated constantly, and it gets a bit hokey at times, but the kids won't mind with this fun Disney film, while adults will appreciate the sarcasm. Followed by "D2: The Mighty Ducks." **114m/C VHS, Beta, LV.** Emilio Estevez, Joss Ackland, Lane Smith, Heidi Kling, Josef Sommer, Matt Doherty, Steven Brill, Joshua Jackson, Elden Ratliff, Shaun Weiss; ***D:*** Stephen Herek; ***W:*** Steven Brill, Brian Hohlfield; ***M:*** David Newman. *TOU, BTV*

Mighty Joe Young 🦴🦴½ **1949** Tongue-in-cheek King Kong variation features giant ape brought to civilization and exploited in a nightclub act, whereupon things get darned ugly. Bullied and given the key to the liquor cabinet, mild-mannered Joe goes on a drunken rampage, but eventually redeems himself by rescuing orphans from a fire. Special effects (courtesy of Willis O'Brien and the great Ray Harryhausen) probably film's greatest asset. Also available colorized. **94m/B VHS, Beta, LV.** Terry Moore, Ben Johnson, Robert Armstrong, Frank McHugh; ***D:*** Ernest B. Schoedsack. Academy Awards '49: Best Special Effects. *TTC*

Mighty Jungle 🦴🦴 **1964** Lost in the Amazon jungle, a hunter must fight off killer iguanas, man-eating crocodiles and bloodthirsty natives who perform human sacrifices. **90m/C VHS, Beta.** Marshall Thompson, David Dalie. *NO*

Mighty Morphin Power Rangers: The Movie 🦴🦴 **1995 (PG)** From the living room onto the big screen, these six surburban teenagers with super powers battle the evil Ivan Ooze to save Earth. Offers more special effects, new Zord animals, more ooze and more growth to the retail toy industry than the small screen could provide. A child's dream come true, but a parent's nightmare. **93m/C VHS.** Paul Freeman, Jason Harold Yost, Amy Jo Johnson, Jason David Frank, John Yong Bosch, Stephen Antonio Cardenas; ***D:*** Bryan Spicer; ***W:*** Arne Olsen, John Camps; ***C:*** Paul Murphy; ***M:*** Graeme Revell. *FXV*

The Mighty Pawns **1987** Inner-city kids turn to chess when their teacher inspires them to stay off the streets. Originally aired on PBS as part of the "Wonderworks" family movie series. **58m/C VHS.** Paul Winfield, Alfonso Ribeiro, Terence Knox, Rosalind Cash, Teddy Wilson; ***D:*** Eric Laneuville. *PME, HMV, FCT*

The Mighty Quinn 🦴🦴½ **1989 (R)** While investigating the local murder of a rich white guy, the black Jamaican head of police becomes convinced that the prime suspect, a childhood friend, is innocent. As the police chief, Denzel is good in this offbeat comedy mystery. **98m/C VHS, Beta, LV.** Denzel Washington, Robert Townsend, James Fox, Mimi Rogers, M. Emmet Walsh, Sheryl Lee Ralph, Esther Rolle, Art Evans, Norman Beaton, Keye Luke; ***D:*** Carl Schenkel; ***W:*** Hampton Fancher; ***M:*** Anne Dudley. *MGM, FOX*

The Migrants 🦴🦴🦴 **1974** Adaptation of the Tennessee Williams play about the hard-scrabble world of a migrant family yearning for a better life. Made for TV. **83m/C VHS.** Cloris Leachman, Ron Howard, Sissy Spacek, Cindy Williams, Ed Lauter, Lisa Lucas, Mills Watson, Claudia McNeil, Dolph Sweet; ***D:*** Tom Gries; ***W:*** Lanford Wilson. *MON*

Mike's Murder 🦴½ **1984 (R)** Disjointed drama about a shy bank teller who falls for a slick tennis player. When he is murdered, she investigates the circumstances, placing herself in dangerously close contact with his seedy, drug-involved buddies. The twists and confused plot leave the viewer bewildered. **109m/C VHS, Beta.** Debra Winger, Mark Keyloun, Paul Winfield, Darrell Larson, Dan Shor, William Ostrander; ***D:*** James Bridges; ***W:*** James Bridges; ***M:*** John Barry. *WAR*

Mikey 🦴½ **1992 (R)** Mikey seems like such a sweet little boy—but these awful things keep happening all around him. At every foster home and every school people have such dreadful, and deadly, accidents. But innocent Mikey couldn't be to blame—or could he. **92m/C VHS.** Brian Bonsall, John Diehl, Lyman Ward, Josie Bissett; ***D:*** Dennis Dimster. *IMP*

Mikey & Nicky 🦴🦴½ **1976 (R)** Quirky, uneven film about longtime friends dodging a hit man during one long night. Bears little evidence of time and money invested. Cassavetes and Falk, however, provide some salvation. **105m/C VHS, Beta.** John Cassavetes, Peter Falk, Ned Beatty, Oliver Clark, William Hickey; ***D:*** Elaine May; ***W:*** Elaine May. *WAR, OM*

The Milagro Beanfield War 🦴🦴🦴½ **1988 (R)** Redford's endearing adaptation of John Nichols's novel about New Mexican townfolk opposing development. Seemingly simple tale provides plenty of insight into human spirit. Fine cast, with especially stellar turns from Blades, Braga, and Vennera. **118m/C VHS, Beta, LV.** Chick Vennera, John Heard, Ruben Blades, Sonia Braga, Daniel Stern, Julie Carmen, Christopher Walken, Richard Bradford, Carlos Riqueline, James Gammon, Melanie Griffith, Freddy Fender, M. Emmet Walsh; ***D:*** Robert Redford; ***W:*** David S. Ward; ***C:*** Robbie Greenberg; ***M:*** Dave Grusin. Academy Awards '88: Best Original Score. *MCA*

Mildred Pierce 🦴🦴🦴½ **1945** Gripping melodrama features Crawford as hard-working divorcee rivaling daughter for man's love. Things, one might say, eventually get ugly. Adaptation of James M. Cain novel is classic of its kind. **113m/B VHS, Beta, LV.** Joan Crawford, Jack Carson, Zachary Scott, Eve Arden, Ann Blyth, Bruce (Herman Brix) Bennett; ***D:*** Michael Curtiz; ***W:*** Ranald MacDougall; ***M:*** Max Steiner. Academy Awards '45: Best Actress (Crawford); Nominations: Academy Awards '45: Best Black and White Cinematography, Best Picture, Best Screenplay, Best Supporting Actress (Arden, Blyth). *MGM, FOX, BTV*

Miles from Home 🦴🦴 *Farm of the Year* **1988 (R)** Times are tough for farmers Frank and Terry Roberts. The brothers are about to have another bad harvest and the bank is threatening to foreclose. In a symbolic last ditch effort to save their pride, they decide to burn the farm and leave. On their journey, they meet strangers who recognize the pair and help them escape the police. A melodrama with many members of Chicago's Steppenwolf Theater. **113m/C VHS, Beta, LV.** Richard Gere, Kevin Anderson, John Malkovich, Brian Dennehy, Judith Ivey, Penelope Ann Miller, Laurie Metcalf, Laura San Giacomo, Daniel Roebuck, Helen Hunt; ***D:*** Gary Sinise; ***W:*** Chris Gerolmo; ***M:*** Robert Folk. *WAR*

Miles to Go 🦴½ **1986** A successful businesswoman tries to enjoy her last days after learning she has terminal cancer. **88m/C VHS, Beta.** Mimi Kuzyk, Tom Skerritt, Jill Clayburgh; ***D:*** David Greene. *NO*

Miles to Go before I Sleep 🦴🦴½ **1974** A retired, lonely man and a delinquent girl distrust each other but eventually reach out in mutual need. **78m/C VHS, Beta.** Martin Balsam, MacKenzie Phillips, Kitty Winn, Elizabeth Wilson; ***D:*** Fielder Cook. *LCA*

Milk Money 🦴½ **1994 (PG-13)** Twelve year-old Frank (Carter) talks his pals into pooling their milk money and heading to the big city so they can get a look at a naked woman. They find a prostitute (Griffith) for the job, whom Frank decides would be perfect to bring home to his widower dad (Harris). Although Griffith is generally adorable and the movie is actually less salacious than the premise might suggest, overall, it's sappy and another in the long line of cute-hooker/Cinderella fairytales. **110m/C VHS, Beta.** Michael Patrick Carter, Melanie Griffith, Ed Harris, Malcolm McDowell, Casey Siemaszko, Anne Heche, Philip Bosco; ***D:*** Richard Benjamin; ***W:*** John Mattson; ***M:*** Michael Convertino. *PAR*

Milky Way 🦴🦴½ **1936** Loopy comedy about milkman who finds unhappiness after accidentally knocking out champion boxer. Adequate, but not equal to Lloyd's fine silent productions. **89m/B VHS, Beta, LV.** Harold Lloyd, Adolphe Menjou, Verree Teasdale, Helen Mack, William Gargan; ***D:*** Leo McCarey. *VYY, MRV, NOS*

The Milky Way 🦴🦴🦴 **1968** Wicked anticlerical farce. Two bums team on religious pilgrimage and encounter seemingly all manner of strangeness and sacrilege in this typically peculiar Bunuel work. Perhaps the only film in which Jesus is encouraged to shave. In French with English subtitles. **102m/C VHS, Beta, LV.** *FR* Laurent Terzieff, Paul Frankeur, Delphine Seyrig, Alain Cuny, Bernard Verley, Michel Piccoli, Edith Scob; ***D:*** Luis Bunuel; ***W:*** Jean-Claude Carriere. *XVC, MED, FCT*

Mill of the Stone Women 🦴🦴½ *Il Mulino Delle Donne di Pietra; Horror of the Stone Women; The Horrible Mill Women* **1960** Sculpture-studying art student encounters strange carousel with beautiful babes rather than horsies, and soon finds out that the statues contain shocking secrets. Filmed in Holland, it's offbeat and creepy. **94m/C VHS.** *FR IT* Pierre Brice, Scilla Gabel, Danny Carrel, Wolfgang Preiss, Herbert Boenne, Liana Orfei; ***D:*** Giorgio Ferroni. *SNC*

The Mill on the Floss 🦴🦴 **1937** Based on George Eliot's classic novel, this film follows the course of an ill-fated romance and family hatred in rural England. Underwhelming, considering the source. **77m/B VHS, Beta.** *GB* James Mason, Geraldine Fitzgerald, Frank Lawton, Victoria Hopper, Fay Compton, Griffith Jones, Mary Clare; ***D:*** Tim Whelan. *NOS, MRV, DVT*

Millenium 🦴🦴½ **1989 (PG-13)** The Earth of the future is running out of time. The people are sterile and the air is terrible. To keep the planet viable, Ladd and company must go back in time and yank people off planes that are doomed to crash. Great special effects and well-thought out script make this a ball of fun. **108m/C VHS, Beta, LV.** Kris Kristofferson, Cheryl Ladd, Daniel J. Travanti, Lloyd Bochner, Robert Joy, Brent Carver, Maury Chaykin, David McIlwraith, Al Waxman; ***D:*** Michael Anderson Sr.; ***W:*** John Varley; ***M:*** Eric N. Robertson. *CCB*

Miller's Crossing 🦴🦴🦴½ **1990 (R)** From the Coen brothers (makers of "Blood Simple" and "Raising Arizona") comes this extremely dark entry in the gangster movie sweepstakes of 1990. Jewish, Italian, and Irish mobsters spin webs of deceit, protection, and revenge over themselves and their families. Byrne is the protagonist, but no hero, being as deeply flawed as the men he battles. Harden stuns as the woman who sleeps with Byrne and his boss, Finney, in hopes of a better life and protection for her small-time crook brother. Visually exhilarating, excellently acted and perfectly paced. **115m/C VHS, Beta, LV.** Albert Finney, Gabriel Byrne, Marcia Gay Harden, John Turturro, Jon Polito, J.E. Freeman; ***D:*** Joel Coen; ***W:*** Ethan Coen, Joel Coen; ***M:*** Carter Burwell. *FXV, FCT*

Millie 🦴½ **1931** Creaky melodrama about a divorcee who wants every man but one. He pursues her teenage daughter instead, leading to tragedy and courtroom hand-wringing. Twelvetrees still stands out in this hokum, based on a Donald Henderson novel considered daring in its day. **85m/B VHS.** Helen Twelvetrees, Robert Ames, Lilyan Tashman, Joan Blondell, John Halliday, James Hall, Anita Louise, Frank McHugh; ***D:*** John Francis Dillon. *NOS*

Million Dollar Duck 🦴½ **1971 (G)** A family duck is doused with radiation and begins to lay gold eggs. Okay Disney family fare, especially for youngsters. **92m/C VHS, Beta.** Dean Jones, Sandy Duncan, Joe Flynn, Tony Roberts; ***D:*** Vincent McEveety; ***M:*** Buddy Baker. *DIS, OM*

Million Dollar Haul 🦴 **1935** Tarzan sniffs out a ring of warehouse thieves. **60m/B VHS, Beta, LV.** Reed Howes, Janet Chandler, William Farnum. *NO*

Million Dollar Kid 🦴🦴 **1944** When a group of thugs wreak havoc in the neighborhood, the East Side Kids try to help a wealthy man put a stop to it. They face an even greater dilemma when they discover that the man's son is part of the gang. Part of the "Bowery Boys" series. **65m/B VHS.** Leo Gorcey, Huntz Hall, Gabriel Dell, Louise Currie, Noah Beery Jr., Iris Adrian, Mary Gordon; ***D:*** Wallace Fox. *VYY, DVT, NOS*

Million Dollar Mermaid 🦴🦴 **1952** The prototypical Williams aquashow, with the requisite awesome Berkeley dance numbers. As a biography of swimmer Annette Kellerman it isn't much, but as an MGM extravaganza, it fits the bill. **115m/C VHS, Beta.** Esther Williams, Victor Mature, Walter Pidgeon, Jesse White, David Brian, Maria Tallchief, Howard Freeman, Busby Berkeley; ***D:*** Mervyn LeRoy. Nominations: Academy Awards '52: Best Color Cinematography. *MGM*

Million Dollar Mystery 🦴🦴 **1927** Silent suspense film involving an old house, a secret society, and a million dollars in missing money. **?m/B VHS.** *SNC*

Million Dollar Mystery 🦴½ **1987 (PG)** A dying man's last words indicate that several million dollars have been stashed near a diner. Chaos breaks out as nearly everyone in town tries to dig up the loot. **95m/C VHS, LV.** Eddie Deezen, Penny Baker, Tom Bosley, Rich Hall, Wendy Sherman, Rick Overton, Mona Lyden; ***D:*** Richard Fleischer; ***W:*** Rudy DeLuca, Tim Metcalfe; ***C:*** Jack Cardiff. *HBO, CNG*

A Million to Juan 🦴🦴½ **1994 (PG)** Familiar rags-to-riches tale, this time set in a Los Angeles barrio, centers on Juan Lopez (Rodriguez), an uneducated good guy struggling to raise his son. Juan gets his lucky break when a stranger hands him a check for one million dollars, explains it's a loan, and if Juan can use the money properly for a month, he'll get a reward. Juan remains incredibly noble; the movie remains mushy. Loose adaptation of the Mark Twain story "The Million Pound Bank Note." Directorial debut for Rodriguez. **97m/C VHS.** Paul Rodriguez, Polly Draper, Pepe Serna, Bert Rosario, Jonathan Hernandez, Gerardo, Victor Rivers, Edward James Olmos, Paul Williams; ***Cameos:*** Tony Plana, Ruben Blades, Richard "Cheech" Marin, David Rasche, Liz Torres; ***D:*** Paul Rodriguez; ***W:*** Francisca Matos, Robert Grasmere. *PSM*

A Million to One 🦴½ **1937** An athlete trains for the Olympic decathlon, and catches the eye of an upper-class woman in the process. The lead Bennett was actually a shot-putter in the 1932 Olympic Games. **60m/B VHS.** Bruce (Herman Brix) Bennett, Joan Fontaine, Monte Blue, Kenneth Harlan, Reed Howes; ***D:*** Lynn Shores. *VYY*

The Millionairess 🦴🦴½ **1960** Loren is an incredibly rich woman who has ended a bad marriage, and feels that the only thing she still needs to fulfill her life is a good husband. She meets a humble doctor from India, in the person of Sellers, and finds he evades her every effort to snare him. In the process she learns that money can't buy everything. From a play by George Bernard Shaw. **90m/C VHS.** *GB* Sophia Loren, Peter Sellers, Alastair Sim, Vittorio De Sica, Dennis Price; ***D:*** Anthony Asquith; ***C:*** Jack Hildyard. *FXL*

Millions 🦴½ **1990 (R)** To a family of millionaires, money is everything, and the heir to the family fortune is willing to do anything to get his hands on all that money. Even if it means sleeping with his sister-in-law and cousin! Lucky for him they happen to be beautiful models. **118m/C VHS, Beta.** *IT* Billy Zane, Lauren Hutton, Carol Alt, Alexandra Paul, Catherine Hickland, Donald Pleasence; ***D:*** Carlo Vanzina. *PSM*

Milo & Otis 🦴🦴½ **1989 (G)** Charming tale of a kitten named Milo and his best friend, a puppy named Otis. The two live on a farm and, when exploring the countryside, Milo is swept down a rushing river. Otis goes after to rescue his friend and the two begin a series of adventures as they try to return home. **76m/C VHS.** *COL*

Milo Milo 🦴🦴 **196?** Comedy about some very silly French people who propose to steal the Venus de Milo from the Louvre. **110m/C VHS, Beta.** Antonio Fargas, Joe Higgins. *VCD*

The Milpitas Monster 🦴 **1975 (PG)** Creature spawned in a Milpitas, California, waste dump terrorizes the town residents. **80m/C VHS, Beta.** Doug Hagdahl, Scott A. Henderson, Scott Parker; ***D:*** Robert L. Burrill. *VCI*

Mimi 🦴🦴 **1935** Melodrama with a down-on-his-luck playwright falling for a poor lass who provides him with the needed inspiration to be a winner. The question is, will she die before he hits the big time? Loosely based on "La Vie de Boheme" by Henri Murger. **98m/B VHS.** *GB* Douglas Fairbanks Jr., Gertrude Lawrence, Diana Napier, Harold Warrender, Carol Goodner, Richard Bird, Austin Trevor, Lawrence Hanray, Paul Graetz, Martin Walker; ***D:*** Paul Stein. *VYY, FCT*

Min & Bill 🦴🦴 **1930** Patchy early talkie about two houseboat dwellers fighting to preserve their waterfront lifestyle and keep their daughter from being taken to a "proper" home. **66m/B VHS, Beta.** Marie Dressler, Wallace Beery, Marjorie Rambeau, Dorothy Jordan; ***D:*** George Roy Hill. Academy Awards '31: Best Actress (Dressler). *MGM, BTV, FHE*

Mina Tannenbaum 🦴🦴 **1994** Touching but unsentimental look at the 25-year friendship between two Jewish women in Paris. Mina (Bohringer) and Ethel (Zylberstein) meet as seven-year-olds and go through various childhood and teenage tramas together, including the desperate pangs of first love. Mina becomes an intense artist while flirty Ethel works as a freelance journalist. And, naturally, their friendship undergoes its own relentless changes. Pacing problems cause something of a letdown. Directorial debut for cinematographer Dugowson. French with subtitles. **128m/C VHS.** *FR* Romane Bohringer, Elsa Zylberstein, Nils Tavernier, Florence Thomassin, Jean-Philippe Ecoffey, Stephane Slima; ***D:*** Martine Dugowson; ***W:*** Martine Dugowson; ***C:*** Dominique Chapuis. *NYR*

Minbo—Or the Gentle Art of Japanese Extortion 🦴🦴 **1992** Satire on Japanese mobsters, known as the Yakuza, focusing on the blackmail and intimidation that gives these criminals a great deal of their power. The ill-mannered group like to congregate at a local hotel—much to the detriment of business—and hotel management finally hire a hardball-playing female lawyer to solve their problems with the thugs. Japanese with subtitles. **123m/C VHS.** *JP* Nobuko Miyamoto, Akira Takarada, Takehiro Murata, Yasuo Daichi, Hideji Otaki; ***D:*** Juzo Itami; ***W:*** Juzo Itami; ***C:*** Yonezo Maeda; ***M:*** Toshiyuki Honda. *HMV*

Mind, Body & Soul 🦴🦴 **1992 (R)** When a woman witnesses a human sacrifice performed by her boyfriend's satanic cult, she goes to the police. The cops, however, believe she is part of the cult, so she is forced to rely on the public defender to protect her from angry cult members. Pretty dull, but Hauser and Allen add some spice to this hokey thriller. **93m/C VHS.** Wings Hauser, Ginger Lynn Allen, Jay Richardson, Ken Hill, Jesse Kaye, Tami Bakke; ***D:*** Rick Sloane. *AIP*

Mind Games 🦴½ **1989 (R)** A young couple and their ten-year-old son pick up a hitcher in their mobile home, never suspecting that he's a deranged psychology student ready to pit the family against each other as an experiment. **93m/C VHS, Beta.** Edward Albert, Shawn Weatherly, Matt Norero, Maxwell Caulfield; ***D:*** Bob Yari. *FOX, HHE*

Mind Snatchers 🦴🦴½ **1972 (PG)** An American G.I. becomes involved in U.S. Army experimental psychological brain operations when he is brought into a western European hospital for treatment. Also know as "The Happiness Cage." **94m/C VHS, Beta.** Christopher Walken, Ronny Cox, Ralph Meeker, Joss Ackland; ***D:*** Bernard Girard. *PSM*

A Mind to Kill 🦴🦴 **1995** When a murdered girl is found in a small English seaside town, the crime is linked to a previous death. Police call on a university professor for help but then a new victim, with ties to the professor, is discovered and the police detective in charge finds that his own loved ones are now in danger. **95m/C VHS.** *GB* Hywel Bennett, Philip Madoc, Sue Jones-Davies, Nicola Beddoe; ***D:*** Peter Edwards. *FCT*

Mind Trap 🦴½ **1991** A beautiful movie star's family is killed due to her father's involvement with naval research. The government wants no part of her troubles so she is forced to take the law into her own hands. **90m/C VHS.** Dan Haggerty, Lyle Waggoner, Martha Kincare, Thomas Elliot, Samuel Steven; ***D:*** Eames Demetrios. *NO*

Mind Twister 🦴½ **1993 (R)** Erotic thriller finds a tough police detective on the trail of a sadistic killer with a twist. An unrated version is available at 94 minutes. **87m/C VHS.** Telly Savalas, Gary Hudson, Richard Roundtree, Erica Nann, Suzanne Slater; ***D:*** Fred Olen Ray. *VCI*

Mind Warp 🦴½ *Grey Matter; The Brain Machine* **1972 (R)** A future society exercises mental control and torture over its citizens. **92m/C VHS, Beta.** James Best, Barbara Burgess, Gil Peterson, Gerald McRaney, Marcus J. Grapes, Doug Collins, Anne Latham; ***D:*** Joy Houck Jr. *COL*

Mindfield 🦴½ **1989 (R)** An innocent man gets trapped by the CIA and is used by them in mind control experiments. **91m/C VHS, Beta, LV.** *CA* Michael Ironside, Lisa Langlois, Christopher Plummer, Stefan Wodoslowsky, Sean McCann; ***D:*** Jean-Claude Lord. *NO*

Mindkiller 🦴½ **1987** A tongue-in-cheek gore-fest about a shy young guy who develops his brain in an effort to be socially accepted. Unfortunately, he overdoes it and his brain mutates, bursts from his head and runs around on its own. An aspiring cult classic. **84m/C VHS, Beta.** Joe McDonald, Christopher Wade, Shirley Ross, Kevin Hart; ***D:*** Michael Krueger. *PSM*

Mindwalk: A Film for Passionate Thinkers 🦴🦴🦴 **1991 (PG)** A feature-length intellectual workout; a physicist, poet and politician stroll the ancient grounds of Mont St. Michel monastery in France and discuss the need to change mankind's view of the universe. Uncinematic? Perhaps, but it entertainingly conveys the epochal ideas of scientist/author Fritjof Capra (whose book was adapted for the screen by younger brother Bernt). **111m/C VHS, Beta.** Liv Ullmann, Sam Waterston, John Heard, Ione Skye; ***D:*** Bernt Capra; ***W:*** Fritjof Capra, Floyd Byars; ***M:*** Philip Glass. *PAR, WSH*

Mindwarp 🦴🦴 **1991 (R)** After an ecological disaster, residents of Earth move to a sterile haven known as "Inworld." When survivor Judy (Alicia) seeks answers about her missing father (accidentally killing her mother in the process), she is cast from "Inworld" into Earth's wasteland, where she and human compatriot Stover (Campbell) are left to fight the elements and learn the awful truth about Judy's father. **91m/C VHS, LV.** Marta Alicia, Bruce Campbell, Angus Scrimm, Elizabeth Kent, Mary Becker; ***D:*** Steve Barnett; ***W:*** Henry Dominick. *COL*

Mine Own Executioner 🦴🦴🦴 **1947** Determined but unstable psychologist in postwar London struggles to treat schizophrenic who suffered torture by Japanese while wartime prisoner. Strong, visually engrossing fare. **102m/B VHS.** *GB* Burgess Meredith, Kieron Moore, Dulcie Gray, Christine Norden, Barbara White, John Laurie, Michael Shepley; ***D:*** Anthony Kimmins. *FCT, DVT, HHT*

Mines of Kilimanjaro 🦴½ **1987 (PG-13)** An archaeology student heads for Africa to investigate his professor's murder and comes up with a heap of trouble. **88m/C VHS, Beta.** Christopher Connelly, Tobias Hoels, Gordon Mitchell, Elena Pompei; ***D:*** Mino Guerrini. *IMP*

Ministry of Vengeance 🦴 **1989 (R)** A psychotic murderer who hates grapes of any kind finds the woman of his dreams—she's a psychotic murderer who hates grapes! Together they find bliss—until the plumber discovers their secret! **90m/C VHS, Beta, LV.** John Schneider, Ned Beatty, George Kennedy, Yaphet Kotto, James Tolkan, Apollonia. *LIV, VTR*

The Miniver Story 🦴🦴 **1950** Weepy sequel to "Mrs. Miniver" reunites the family in post-WWII England, but clearly lacks the inspiration of the original. Garson is again Mrs. Miniver and she's secretly suffering from a never-named fatal disease. She decides to straighten out the family troubles before her time is up, including her daughter's love life and her husband's plan to move to Brazil. Depressing and glum. **104m/B VHS.** *GB* Greer Garson, Walter Pidgeon, John Hodiak, Leo Genn, Cathy O'Donnell, Reginald Owen, Anthony Bushell; ***D:*** H.C. Potter; ***W:*** Ronald Millar, George Froeschel; ***C:*** Joseph Ruttenberg; ***M:*** Miklos Rozsa. *MGM*

Minnesota Clay 🦴½ *L'Homme du Minnesota* **1965** A blind gunman, who aims by sound and smell, is marked by two rival gangs and a tempestuous tramp. **89m/C VHS, Beta, LV.** *FR IT* Cameron Mitchell, Diana Martin; ***D:*** Sergio Corbucci. *NO*

A Minor Miracle 🦴🦴 **1983 (G)** Tender family fare about a group of orphaned children who band together under the loving guidance of their guardian (Huston) to save St. Francis School for boys from the town planners. Warms the cockles. **100m/C VHS, Beta, LV.** John Huston, Pele, Peter Fox; ***D:*** Terrell Tannen. *COL, SUE*

Minsky's Follies **1983** Recreation of an old time burlesque revue complete with strippers. **60m/C VHS, Beta.** Phyllis Diller, Rip Taylor, Stubby Kaye. *NO*

A Minute to Pray, A Second to Die 🦴🦴 *Un Minuto Per Pregare, Un Istante Per Morire; Dead or Alive; Outlaw Gun* **1967** A notorious, wanted-dead-or-alive gunman retreats to the amnesty of the New Mexico Territory, but finds he cannot shake his past. **100m/C VHS, Beta.** *IT* Robert Ryan, Arthur Kennedy, Alex Cord; ***D:*** Franco Giraldi. *FOX*

The Miracle 🦴🦴🦴 *Ways of Love* **1948** An innocent peasant woman is seduced by a shepherd and becomes convinced that her pregnancy will produce a second Christ. Controversial, compelling film derived from a story by Federico Fellini. In Italian with English subtitles. **43m/B VHS, Beta.** *IT* Anna Magnani, Federico Fellini; ***D:*** Roberto Rossellini. *NOS, FCT, APD*

The Miracle 🦴🦴½ **1991 (PG)** Irish teens, whose strong friendship is based upon their equally unhappy home lives, find both tested when a secretive American woman turns up in town. Excellent debuts from Byrne and Pilkington but tedious pacing in a dreamy script that tells too much too soon. Worth watching just for D'Angelo's smouldering rendition of

"Stardust." **97m/C VHS, LV.** *GB* Beverly D'Angelo, Donal McCann, Niall Byrne, Lorraine Pilkington, J.G. Devlin; ***D:*** Neil Jordan; ***W:*** Neil Jordan; ***C:*** Philippe Rousselot; ***M:*** Anne Dudley. *LIV*

Miracle at Moreaux **1986** Three Jewish children fleeing from Nazis find sanctuary with a nun and her wards. Based on Clare Huchet Bishop's book "Twenty and Ten." Originally aired on PBS as part of the "Wonderworks" family movie series. **58m/C VHS.** Loretta Swit, Marsha Moreau, Robert Joy, Ken Pogue, Robert Kosoy, Talya Rubin; ***D:*** Paul Shapiro. *PME, HMV, IGP*

Miracle Beach ½ **1992 (PG-13)** Scotty McKay has lost his job, his apartment, and his girl. Then he gets rejected by Dana, the super model he's secretly adored. Can things get any worse? Scotty decides to take a walk along the beach and sort things out when he stumbles across a girl genie, named Jeanie, who has been sent to Earth on a good will mission. Scotty gets Jeanie to grant his every material wish in order to dazzle model Dana. But when Jeanie falls in love with Scotty can she get him to recognize the difference between true love and fantasy? **88m/C VHS, LV.** Dean Cameron, Felicity Waterman, Ami Dolenz, Alexis Arquette, Martin Mull, Noriyuki "Pat" Morita, Vincent Schiavelli; ***D:*** Skott Snider. *COL*

Miracle Down Under **1987** A family endures arduous times in 1890s Australia before a Christmas miracle changes their fortunes. Inoffensive Disney-produced drama. Australia has two directors named George Miller—one directs Mad Max movies; the other directs family fare such as "The Man from Snowy River." This Miller is the latter. **101m/C VHS, Beta.** *AU* Dee Wallace Stone, John Waters, Charles Tingwell, Bill Kerr, Andrew Ferguson; ***D:*** George Miller. *TOU, IGP*

Miracle in Harlem **1948** A gang tries to take over a candy shop and when the gang leader is killed, the evidence points to the foster daughter of the shop owner. The script suffers from cliched dialog and less-than-believable situations, but the all-black cast turns in good performances. **69m/B VHS.** Sheila Guyse, Stepin Fetchit, Hilda Offley, Lawrence Criner, Monte Hawley; ***D:*** Jack Kemp. *NOS*

Miracle in Milan *Miracolo a Milano* **1951** An innocent, child-like fantasy about heavenly intervention driving capitalists out of a Milanese ghetto and helping the poor to fly to a new Utopia. Happy mixture of whimsy and neo-realism. In Italian with English subtitles. **95m/B VHS, Beta, LV.** *IT* Francesco Golisano, Brunella Bova, Emma Gramatica, Paolo Stoppa; ***D:*** Vittorio De Sica; ***W:*** Cesare Zavattini. Cannes Film Festival '51: Best Film; National Board of Review Awards '51: 5 Best Foreign Films of the Year; New York Film Critics Awards '51: Best Foreign Film. *HMV, FCT, APD*

Miracle in Rome ½ *Milagro en Roma* **1988** Margarito Duarte digs up his dead daughter and finds her body in perfect condition despite 12-year internment. Attempting to convince the local clergy that she's miracle material, he finds them less than eager to elect her to sainthood. Based on a story by Gabriel Garcia marquez; made for Spanish TV. In Spanish with English subtitles. **76m/C VHS, LV.** *SP* Frank Ramirez, Gerardo Arellano, Amalia Duque Garcia, Lisandro Duque, Daniel Priolett; ***D:*** Lisandro Duque Naranjo; ***W:*** Lisandro Duque Naranjo, Gabriel Garcia Marquez. *FXL, FCT, APD*

Miracle in the Wilderness ½ **1991** A Christmas western based on Paul Gallico's novella, "The Snow Goose." Kristofferson stars as Jericho Adams, a former Indian fighter, who turns to farming to support his wife and child. When they are captured by a raiding party of Blackfeet, Adams discovers they have never heard the story of the Nativity. **88m/C VHS, LV.** Kris Kristofferson, Kim Cattrall, John Dennis Johnston, Joanelle Romero, Dennis Olvers, Sheldon Peters Wolfchild; ***D:*** Kevin Dobson; ***W:*** Jim Byrnes. *TTC, FCT*

Miracle Kid **1942** Standard story of a young boxer who'd rather be something else. His romance is interrupted when he becomes successful in the ring. **66m/B VHS.** Tom Neal, Carol Hughes, Betty Blythe, Minta Durfee, Gertrude Messinger; ***D:*** William Beaudine. *NOS*

Miracle Mile **1989 (R)** A riveting, apocalyptic thriller about a mild-mannered misfit who, while inadvertently standing on a street corner at 2 a.m., answers a ringing pay phone. The caller is a panicked missile-silo worker who announces that the bombs have been launched for an all-out nuclear war. With about an hour left before the end, he decides to head into the city and rendezvous with his new girlfriend. A surreal, wicked farce sadly overlooked in theatrical release. Music by Tangerine Dream. **87m/C VHS, Beta, LV.** Anthony Edwards, Mare Winningham, John Agar, Denise Crosby, Lou Hancock, Mykelti Williamson, Kelly Jo Minter, Kurt Fuller, Robert DoQui, Danny De La Paz; ***D:*** Steve DeJarnatt; ***W:*** Steve DeJarnatt; ***M:*** Tangerine Dream. *HBO*

Miracle of Morgan's Creek **1944** The breakneck comedy that stands as Sturges' premier achievement. Details the misadventures of a wartime floozy who gets drunk, thinks she marries a soldier on leave, gets pregnant by him, forgets the whole thing, and then tries to evade scandal by getting a local schnook to marry her again. And she's expecting sextuplets. Hilarious, out-to-make-trouble farce that shouldn't have, by all rights, made it past the censors of the time. Sturges' most scathing assault on American values earned him an Oscar nomination for writing. Remade as "Rock-A-Bye Baby" in 1958. **98m/B VHS, Beta.** Eddie Bracken, Betty Hutton, Diana Lynn, Brian Donlevy, Akim Tamiroff, Porter Hall, Emory Parnell, Alan Bridge, Julius Tannen, Victor Potel, Almira Sessions, Chester Conklin, William Demarest, Jimmy Conlin; ***D:*** Preston Sturges; ***W:*** Preston Sturges; ***M:*** Leo Shuken, Charles Bradshaw. Nominations: Academy Awards '44: Best Original Screenplay. *PAR, CCB*

Miracle of Our Lady of Fatima *The Miracle of Fatima* **1952** Slick cold-war version of the supposedly true events surrounding the sighting of a holy vision by three children in Portugal during WWI. **102m/C VHS, Beta, LV.** Gilbert Roland, Susan Whitney, Sherry Jackson, Sammy Ogg, Angela Clark, Frank Silvera, Jay Novello; ***D:*** John Brahm; ***M:*** Max Steiner. Nominations: Academy Awards '52: Best Original Score. *WAR, IGP, KEP*

The Miracle of the Bells **1948** A miracle occurs after a dead movie star is buried in the cemetary of her modest hometown. Given the premise, the casting is all the more peculiar. Adapted by Ben Hecht from Russell Janney's novel. **120m/B VHS, Beta.** Fred MacMurray, Alida Valli, Frank Sinatra, Lee J. Cobb; ***D:*** Irving Pichel. *REP, IGP*

Miracle of the Heart: A Boys Town Story **1986** A television movie based on the story of Boys Town, and an old priest who sticks up for Boys Town's principles in the face of a younger priest with rigid ideas. **100m/C VHS, Beta.** Art Carney, Casey Siemaszko, Jack Bannon; ***D:*** Georg Stanford Brown. *COL*

The Miracle of the White Stallions ½ *The Flight of the White Stallions* **1963** A disappointing Disney adventure about the director of a Viennese riding academy who guides his prized Lipizzan stallions to safety when the Nazis occupy Austria in WWII. **92m/C VHS, Beta.** Robert Taylor, Lilli Palmer, Eddie Albert, Curt Jurgens; ***D:*** Arthur Hiller; ***W:*** A.J. Carothers. *DIS*

Miracle on Ice ½ **1981** Occasionally stirring television film recounts the surprise triumph of the American hockey team over the touted Soviet squad during the 1980 Winter Olympics at Lake Placid. **150m/C VHS, Beta.** Karl Malden, Steve Guttenberg, Andrew Stevens, Lucinda Dooling, Jessica Walter; ***D:*** Steven Hilliard Stern. *NO*

Miracle on 34th Street *The Big Heart* **1947** The actual Kris Kringle is hired as Santa Claus for the Macy's Thanksgiving parade but finds difficulty in proving himself to the cynical parade sponsor. When the boss's daughter also refuses to acknowledge Kringle, he goes to extraordinary lengths to convince her. Holiday classic equal to "It's a Wonderful Life," with Gwenn and Wood particularly engaging. Also available colorized. **97m/B VHS, Beta, LV.** Maureen O'Hara, John Payne, Edmund Gwenn, Natalie Wood, William Frawley, Porter Hall, Gene Lockhart, Thelma Ritter, Jack Albertson; ***D:*** George Seaton; ***W:*** George Seaton; ***M:*** Cyril Mockridge. Academy Awards '47: Best Story & Screenplay, Best Supporting Actor (Gwenn); Nominations: Academy Awards '47: Best Picture. *CCB, FOX, HMV*

Miracle on 34th Street ½ **1994 (PG)** Updated remake of the 1947 Christmas classic in which a jolly, bearded gent (Attenborough) claiming to be Santa Claus brings happiness to a doubting girl (Wilson) and her jaded mother (Perkins). Before he can prove himself to the precocious child, he must prove himself in a court of law with the help of Perkins's impossibly perfect neighbor (McDermott), a lawyer with a heart of gold (talk about your Christmas miracles!). This version can't compete with the original's "classic" status, but Attenborough and Wilson bring soul and substance to this otherwise average adaptation. **114m/C VHS.** Richard Attenborough, Elizabeth Perkins, Dylan McDermott, J.T. Walsh, Mara Wilson, Joss Ackland, James Remar, Jane Leeves, Simon Jones, Robert Prosky, William Windom; ***D:*** Les Mayfield; ***W:*** John Hughes, George Seaton; ***M:*** Bruce Broughton. *FXV*

The Miracle Rider **1935** A 15-chapter serial finds the bad guys trying to run the Indians off their lands in this saga of the old west. **295m/B VHS.** Tom Mix, Joan Gale, Charles Middleton, Jason Robards Sr., Pat O'Malley, Robert Frazer, Wally Wales, Tom London, George Chesebro, Lafe McKee; ***D:*** B. Reeves Eason, Armand Schaefer. *GPV, MRV, VCN*

The Miracle Worker ½ **1962** Depicts the unconventional methods that teacher Anne Sullivan used to help the deaf and blind Helen Keller adjust to the world around her and shows the relationship that built between the two courageous women. An intense, moving experience. William Gibson adapted his own play for the screen. **107m/B VHS, Beta.** Anne Bancroft, Patty Duke, Victor Jory, Inga Swenson, Andrew Prine, Beah Richards; ***D:*** Arthur Penn. Academy Awards '62: Best Actress (Bancroft), Best Supporting Actress (Duke); National Board of Review Awards '62: 10 Best Films of the Year, Best Actress (Bancroft); Nominations: Academy Awards '62: Best Adapted Screenplay, Best Costume Design (B & W), Best Director (Penn). *MGM, BTV, CCB*

The Miracle Worker **1979** Remade for television story of blind, deaf and mute Helen Keller and her teacher, Annie Sullivan, whose patience and perseverance finally enable Helen to learn to communicate with the world. Duke was Keller in the 1962 original, but plays the teacher in this version. **98m/C VHS, Beta.** Patty Duke, Melissa Gilbert; ***D:*** Paul Aaron; ***M:*** Billy Goldenberg. *WAR, OM*

Miracles ½ **1986 (PG)** Comedic misfire pairs a recently divorced couple as reluctant adventurers dodging jewel thieves and peculiar tribes in South America. In a desperate move to create a plot, Mexican jewel thieves, strange tribal rites, and some outrageously unlikely coincidences reunite the family. If this sounds good, see "Romancing the Stone" instead. **90m/C VHS, Beta, LV.** Tom Conti, Teri Garr, Paul Rodriguez, Christopher Lloyd, Jorge Russek, Charles Rocket, Bob Nelson; ***D:*** Jim Kouf; ***M:*** Peter Bernstein. *IME*

Mirage **1966** An amnesiac finds himself the target of a dangerous manhunt in New York City in this offbeat thriller. Peck is particularly sympathetic in the lead, and McCarthy, Matthau, and Kennedy all shine in supporting roles. Worth it just to hear thug Kennedy grunt, "I owe this man some pain!" **108m/B VHS, Beta.** Gregory Peck, Diane Baker, Walter Matthau, Jack Weston, Kevin McCarthy, Walter Abel, George Kennedy; ***D:*** Edward Dmytryk; ***M:*** Quincy Jones. *BAR, MLB*

Mirage ½ **1994 (R)** Neo-noir with plot problems has former Palm Springs cop Matteo Juarez (Olmos) hired to protect Jennifer (Young), the wife of wealthy environmentalist Donald Gale (Williams). But Jennifer just happens to suffer from multiple personality disorder, leading a not-so-secret second life as a stripper and having trouble always on her heels. **106m/C VHS.** Edward James Olmos, Sean Young, James Andronica, Paul W. Williams; ***D:*** Paul W. Williams; ***W:*** James Andronica. *MCA*

Mirele Efros ☊☊½ **1938** A widowed but successful businesswoman finds herself at odds with her daughter-in-law in this film set in the turn of the century. In Yiddish with English subtitles. **80m/B VHS, Beta.** Berta Gersten, Michael Rosenberg, Ruth Elbaum, Albert Lipton, Sarah Krohner, Moishe Feder; ***D:*** Joseph Berne. *ERG, INJ*

The Mirror ☊☊☊ *Zerkalo; A White White Boy* **1975** Wonderful child's view of life in Russia during WWII. Black and white flashbacks of important events in the country's history are interspersed with scenes of day-to-day family life. In Russian with English subtitles. **106m/C VHS.** *RU* Margarita Terekhova, Philip Yankovsky, Ignat Daniltsev, Oleg Yankovsky; ***D:*** Andrei Tarkovsky. *INJ, TPV, KIV*

The Mirror Crack'd ☊☊ **1980 (PG)** While filming a movie in the English countryside, an American actress is murdered and Miss Marple must discover who the killer is. Based on the substantially better Agatha Christie novel. **105m/C VHS, Beta, LV.** *GB* Elizabeth Taylor, Rock Hudson, Kim Novak, Tony Curtis, Edward Fox, Geraldine Chaplin, Charles Gray, Pierce Brosnan; ***D:*** Guy Hamilton; ***W:*** Barry Sandler. *REP*

Mirror Images ☊½ **1991 (R)** Although sexy twins Kaitlin and Shauna may look alike, they couldn't have more diverse personalities. Yet the gorgeous twins find their lives thrown together in a mad tornado of passion and danger when they each encounter a handsome, mysterious stranger. Could it be that this guy has something more on his mind than love, something like... murder? Also available in an even steamier unrated version. **94m/C VHS.** Delia Sheppard, Jeff Conaway, Richard Arbolino, John O'Hurley, Korey Mall, Julie Strain, Nels Van Patten; ***D:*** Alexander Gregory Hippolyte. *ACA*

Mirror Images 2 ☊☊ **1993** Direct-to-video erotic thriller features identical twins Carrie and Terrie (Whirry in a dual role). Carrie's Miss Goody Two-Shoes and Terrie's a murderous nympho who likes Carrie's guys. Terrie dies in a mysterious fire and Carrie sets out to investigate. Sex and nudity sells. **92m/C VHS.** Shannon Whirry, Luca Bercovici, Tom Reilly; ***D:*** Alexander Gregory Hippolyte. *ACA*

Mirror, Mirror ☊☊ **1990 (R)** The prolific Ms. Black turns on the ol' black magic when her daughter's classmates decide it's open season for taunting shrinking violets. Thanks to a magical mirror on the wall, the cheerleading classmates are willed to the great pep rally in the sky. **105m/C VHS, LV.** Karen Black, Rainbow Harvest, Kristin Datillo, Ricky Paull Goldin, Yvonne De Carlo, William Sanderson; ***D:*** Marina Sargenti. *ACA*

Mirror, Mirror 2: Raven Dance ☊½ **1994 (R)** Teenaged Marlee (Wells) and her brother are temporarily housed in a convent after the death of their parents. The mystery mirror is discovered and looking into it causes Marlee to become partially blind. Meanwhile, her inheritance is threatened and a mysterious stranger, living in the convent's basement, may be Marlee's only hope. **91m/C VHS, LV.** Tracy Wells, Roddy McDowall, Sally Kellerman, Veronica Cartwright, William Sanderson, Lois Nettleton; ***D:*** Jimmy Lifton; ***W:*** Jimmy Lifton, Virginia Perfili. *ORP*

Mirror of Death ☊ **1987** A woman subject to physical abuse gets more than she bargains for when she seeks revenge by unleashing the gruesome Queen of Hell. Watch this if you dare! **85m/C VHS, Beta.** Julie Merrill, Kuri Browne, John Reno, Deryn Warren. *NO*

Mirrors ☊ **1978** Woman finds that her dreams lead to death and destruction in New Orleans. **83m/C VHS, Beta.** Kitty Winn, Peter Donat, William Swetland, Mary-Robin Redd, William Burns; ***D:*** Noel Black. *NO*

Mirrors ☊☊½ **1985** A Detroit-born ballerina goes to the Big Apple in search of fame and glory, leaving behind her journalist boyfriend. This upbeat love story features some spectacular dance routines and a behind-the-scenes look at a Broadway dancer's lifestyle. Originally made for television. **99m/C VHS.** Timothy Daly, Marguerite Hickey, Antony Hamilton; ***D:*** Harry Winer. *VMK*

The Misadventures of Merlin Jones ☊½ **1963 (G)** A pair of college sweethearts become embroiled in a rollicking chimp-napping scandal. Disney pap done appropriately. A sequel, "The Monkey's Uncle," followed. **90m/C VHS, Beta.** Tommy Kirk, Annette Funicello, Leon Ames, Stuart Erwin, Connie Gilchrist; ***D:*** Robert Stevenson; ***C:*** Edward Colman; ***M:*** Buddy Baker. *DIS*

The Misadventures of Mr. Wilt ☊☊ *Wilt* **1990 (R)** Bumbling college lecturer has to convince inept inspector that he murdered a blowup doll, not his mean missing wife. Based on Tom Sharpe's bestseller. **84m/C VHS.** *GB* Griff Rhys Jones, Mel Smith, Alison Steadman, Diana Quick; ***D:*** Michael Tuchner; ***M:*** Anne Dudley. *VMK*

Misbehaving Husbands ☊½ **1941** Weak story finds store-owner Langton suspected of being untrue by wife Blythe—thanks to rumors spread by a shyster lawyer only to happy to console the lady after the divorce. **65m/B VHS.** Harry Langdon, Betty Blythe, Ralph Byrd, Esther Muir, Luana Walters; ***D:*** William Beaudine. *GPV*

Mischief ☊☊ **1985 (R)** Alienated youths form a friendship during James Dean's heydey. Warning: this film offers a fairly convincing recreation of the 1950s. **97m/C VHS, Beta, LV.** Doug McKeon, Catherine Mary Stewart, Kelly Preston, Chris Nash, D.W. Brown, Jami Gertz, Margaret Blye, Graham Jarvis, Terry O'Quinn; ***D:*** Mel Damski; ***W:*** Noel Black. *FOX*

Misery ☊☊☊ **1990 (R)** Author Caan decides to chuck his lucrative but unfulfilling pulp novels and write seriously by finishing off his most popular character, Misery Chastain. However, fate intervenes when he crashes his car near the home of Bates, his "biggest fan ever," who saves his life, but then tortures him into resurrecting her favorite character. Bates is chillingly glib and and calmly brutal—watch your ankles. Based on the novel by Stephen King. **107m/C VHS, Beta, LV.** James Caan, Kathy Bates, Lauren Bacall, Richard Farnsworth, Frances Sternhagen, Graham Jarvis; ***D:*** Rob Reiner; ***W:*** William Goldman; ***M:*** Marc Shaiman. Academy Awards '90: Best Actress (Bates); Golden Globe Awards '91: Best Actress—Drama (Bates). *COL, NLC, BTV*

The Misfit Brigade ☊☊ *Wheels of Terror* **1987 (R)** Variation on the "Dirty Dozen" finds German misfits recruited for warfare by desperate Nazis during WWII. **99m/C VHS, Beta.** Bruce Davison, Oliver Reed, David Carradine, David Patrick Kelly, D.W. Moffett, Keith Szarabajka; ***D:*** Gordon Hessler. *TWE*

The Misfits ☊☊☊ **1961** A cynical floozy befriends grim cowboys in this downbeat drama. Compelling performances from leads Clift, Monroe (screenwriter Miller's wife), and Gable. Last film for the latter two performers, and nearly the end for Clift. **124m/B VHS, Beta, LV.** Clark Gable, Marilyn Monroe, Montgomery Clift, Thelma Ritter, Eli Wallach, James Barton, Estelle Winwood; ***D:*** John Huston; ***W:*** Arthur Miller; ***C:*** Russell Metty; ***M:*** Alex North. *MGM, FOX, FCT*

Misfits of Science ☊ **1985** Pilot for a failed television series about a group of teens with special powers who fight to save the world. **96m/C VHS, Beta.** Dean Paul Martin, Kevin Peter Hall, Mark Thomas Miller, Kenneth Mars, Courteney Cox; ***D:*** Philip DeGuere. *MCA*

Mishima: A Life in Four Chapters ☊☊☊ **1985 (R)** Somewhat detached account and indulgent portrayal of the narcissistic Japanese author (and actor, filmmaker, and militarist) alternates between stylized interpretations of his books and a straightforward account of his life. Culminates in a pseudo-military operation that, in turn, resulted in Mishima's ritualistic suicide. A U.S./Japanese production. Innovative design by Eiko Ishioka. In Japanese with English subtitles. **121m/C VHS, Beta.** Ken Ogata, Kenji Sawada, Yasosuke Bando; ***D:*** Paul Schrader; ***W:*** Leonard Schrader, Paul Schrader; ***C:*** John Bailey; ***M:*** Philip Glass. *WAR, INJ*

Miss A & Miss M **1986** A young girl is shocked when she realizes that two teachers she has befriended also live together. **60m/C VHS.** Kika Markham, Jennifer Hilary. *PSM*

Miss All-American Beauty ☊½ **1982** A behind-the-scenes look at a smalltime Texas beauty pageant. Lane stars as a contestant who comes to realize her self-respect is more important than winning an award. Meadow's mean pageant director adds an ironic edge that the movie as a whole lacks. Made for television. **96m/C VHS, Beta.** Diane Lane, Cloris Leachman, David Dukes, Jayne Meadows, Alice Hirson, Brian Kerwin; ***D:*** Gus Trikonis. *LIV*

Miss Annie Rooney ☊☊ **1942 (G)** Intended to bill the child star in a more mature role, Temple receives her first screen kiss in this story about a poor Irish girl who falls in love with a wealthy young man. The well-worn plot is weighed down by lifeless dialogue. **86m/B VHS, Beta.** Shirley Temple, Dickie Moore, William Gargan, Guy Kibbee, Peggy Ryan, June Lockhart; ***D:*** Edwin L. Marin. *LIV, MED*

Miss Firecracker ☊☊☊ **1989 (PG)** Hunter, longing for love and self-respect, decides to change her promiscuous image by entering the local beauty pageant in her conservative southern hometown. The somewhat drippy premise is transformed by a super script and cast into an engaging and upbeat film. Henley's script was adapted from her own Off-Broadway play where Hunter created the role. Actress Lahti, wife of director Schlamme, makes a brief appearance. **102m/C VHS, Beta, LV.** Holly Hunter, Scott Glenn, Mary Steenburgen, Tim Robbins, Alfre Woodard, Trey Wilson, Bert Remsen, Ann Wedgeworth, Christine Lahti, Amy Wright; ***D:*** Thomas Schlamme; ***W:*** Beth Henley; ***M:*** David Mansfield. *HBO*

Ms. 45 ☊☊☊ *Angel of Vengeance* **1981 (R)** Rough, bristling cult favorite about a mute girl who, in response to being raped and beaten twice in one night, goes on a man-killing murder spree. Wild ending. **84m/C VHS, Beta, LV.** Zoe Tamerlis, Steve Singer, Jack Thibeau, Peter Yellen, Darlene Stuto, Editta Sherman, Albert Sinkys, Jimmy Laine; ***D:*** Abel Ferrara. *LIV, FCT*

Miss Grant Takes Richmond ☊☊ *Innocence is Bliss* **1949** Zipperhead secretary finds herself in hot water a la Lucy when she finds out the company she's been working for is really the front for a gambling getup. Only Lucy fans need apply. **87m/B VHS.** Lucille Ball, William Holden, Janis Carter, James Gleason, Gloria Henry, Frank McHugh, George Cleveland, Arthur Space, William Wright, Jimmy Lloyd; ***D:*** Lloyd Bacon. *COL, FCT*

Miss Julie ☊☊ **1950** Melodramatic stew adapted from from the August Strindberg play about a confused noblewoman who disgraces herself when she allows a servant to seduce her. In Swedish with English subtitles. **90m/B VHS, Beta.** *SW* Anita Bjork, Ulf Palme, Anders Henrikson; ***D:*** Alf Sjoberg. Cannes Film Festival '51: Best Film. *COL, SUE, INJ*

Miss Mary ☊☊½ **1986 (R)** A compassionate English governess in Buenos Aires conflicts with the honor-obsessed family she works for and Argentina's tumultuous history. Christie gives a wonderful performance. **100m/C VHS, Beta.** *AR* Julie Christie, Donald McIntire, Sofia Viruboff, Luisina Brando; ***D:*** Maria-Luisa Bemberg; ***W:*** Jorge Goldenberg, Maria-Luisa Bemberg. *VTR, NWV*

Miss Melody Jones ☊ **1973** A beautiful young black woman's dreams of stardom unravel as she is forced to pander to prurient men by disrobing publicly for financial recompense. **86m/C VHS.** Philomena Nowlin, Ronald Warren, Jacqueline Dalya, Peter Jacob; ***D:*** Bill Brame; ***W:*** Bill Brame. *XVC*

Miss Right ☊ **1981 (R)** A young man determines to find the ideal woman for himself and casts aside his other romantic interests. Sputtering lightweight comedy. **98m/C VHS, LV.** William Tepper, Karen Black, Virna Lisi, Margot Kidder, Marie-France Pisier; ***D:*** Paul Williams. *IME*

Miss Rose White ☊☊☊ **1992 (PG)** Sedgwick is Rose, a modern young career woman in post-WWII New York, as American as apple pie, who lives two very separate lives. Born Rayzel Weiss, a Polish Jew, she immigrated to the U.S. with her father as a very young girl, before the holocaust devastated her remaining family in Poland. After the war her older sister, thought dead, comes to America. The haunted

Luisa causes Rose to question whether she can ever leave her past behind. Above average Hallmark Hall of Fame presentation has a good cast, particularly Plummer as Luisa. Based on the play "A Shayna Maidel" by Barbara Lebow. **95m/C VHS.** Kyra Sedgwick, Amanda Plummer, Maximilian Schell, D.B. Sweeney, Penny Fuller, Milton Selzer, Maureen Stapleton; ***D:*** Joseph Sargent; ***W:*** Anna Sandor. *REP, BTV*

Miss Sadie Thompson **1953** Based on the novel "Rain" by W. Somerset Maugham. Promiscuous tart Hayworth arrives on a Pacific island occupied by a unit of Marines and a sanctimonious preacher played by Ferrer While Hayworth parties with the Marines and becomes involved with Ray's Sgt. O'Hara, Ferrer moralizes and insists she return to the mainland to face moral charges. Quasi-musical with a scattering of dubbed songs by Hayworth includes a memorable erotic dance scene complete with tight dress and dripping sweat. Hayworth's strong performance carries the picture with Ferrer and Ray turning in cardboard versions of their Maugham characters. Originally filmed in 3-D. **91m/C VHS, Beta, LV.** Rita Hayworth, Jose Ferrer, Aldo Ray, Charles Bronson; ***D:*** Curtis Bernhardt. Nominations: Academy Awards '53: Best Song ("Sadie Thompson's Song (Blue Pacific Blues)"). *COL*

Missile to the Moon ½ **1959** First expedition to the moon encounters not acres of dead rock but a race of gorgeous women in lingerie and high heels. A bad but entertaining remake of "Cat Women of the Moon," featuring a bevy of beauty contest winners from New Hampshire to Yugoslavia. Who says truth is stranger than fiction. **78m/B VHS, Beta.** Gary Clarke, Cathy Downs, K.T. Stevens, Laurie Mitchell, Michael Whalen, Nina Bara, Richard Travis, Tommy Cook, Marjorie Hellen; ***D:*** Richard Cunha. *RHI, SNC, CNM*

Missiles of October **1974** Telling the story of the October 1962 Cuban Missile crisis, this made-for-TV drama keeps you on the edge of your seat while unfolding the sequence of events within the U.S. government. Well written, with a strong cast including Devane, who turns in a convincing performance as—guess who—J.F.K. **155m/C VHS, Beta.** William Devane, Ralph Bellamy, Martin Sheen, Howard da Silva; ***D:*** Anthony Page. *MPI, LCA*

Missing ½ **1982 (PG)** At the height of a military coup in Chile (never named in the movie), a young American writer (Shea) disappears. His right-wing father Lemmon tries to get to the bottom of his disappearance while bickering with Shea's wife, played by Spacek, a bohemian who is the political opposite of her father-in-law. Outstanding performances by Spacek and Lemmon along with excellent writing and direction result in a gripping and thought-provoking thriller. Based on the book by Thomas Hauser from the true story of Charles Horman. **122m/C VHS, Beta, LV.** Jack Lemmon, Sissy Spacek, John Shea, Melanie Mayron, David Clennon, Charles Cioffi, Joe Regalbuto, Richard Venture, Janice Rule; ***D:*** Constantin Costa-Gavras; ***W:*** Constantin Costa-Gavras, Donald Stewart; ***M:*** Vangelis. Academy Awards '82: Best Adapted Screenplay; British Academy Awards '82: Best Screenplay; Cannes Film Festival '82: Best Actor (Lemmon), Best Film; Writers Guild of America '82: Best Adapted Screenplay; Nominations: Academy Awards '82: Best Actor (Lemmon), Best Actress (Spacek), Best Picture. *MCA*

The Missing Corpse **1945** When a newspaper publisher's worst rival is murdered, he fears that he will be implicated. He decides the only thing to do is hide the body to prevent its being discovered. Enjoyable, light comedy/mystery. **62m/B VHS.** J. Edward Bromberg, Eric Sinclair, Frank Jenks, Isabelle Randolph, Paul Guilfoyle, John Shay, Lorell Sheldon; ***D:*** Al(bert) Herman. *NOS, MRV, SNC*

Missing in Action ½ **1984 (R)** An army colonel returns to the Vietnam jungle to settle some old scores and rescue some POWs while on an MIA fact-finding mission. Box office smash. **101m/C VHS, Beta, LV.** Chuck Norris, M. Emmet Walsh; ***D:*** Joseph Zito; ***W:*** James Bruner. *MGM, TLF*

Missing in Action 2: The Beginning **1985 (R)** Set in Vietnam, this prequel to the original "Missing in Action" provides some interesting background on Norris's rocky relationship with communism. Packed with violence, bloodshed and torture. **96m/C VHS, Beta, LV.** Chuck Norris, Soon-Teck Oh, Cosie Costa, Steven Williams; ***D:*** Lance Hool; ***W:*** Steve Bing. *MGM*

Missing Link ½ **1988 (PG)** A strange, meditative quasi-documentary depicting the singular adventures of a humanoid silently transversing the African wilderness and confronting various natural phenomena. Beautifully photographed. Make-up by Rick Baker. **92m/C VHS, Beta.** Peter Elliott, Michael Gambon; ***D:*** David Hughes. *MCA*

Missing Pieces ½ **1983** A woman takes a job as a private investigator in order to find her journalist husband's killer. Effective made-for-television mystery taken from the novel "A Private Investigation" by Karl Alexander. **96m/C VHS.** Elizabeth Montgomery, Louanne, John C. Reilly, Ron Karabatsos, Robin Gammell, Julius W. Harris; ***D:*** Mike Hodges. *LIV*

The Mission **1986 (PG)** Sweeping, cinematically beautiful historical drama about an 18th-century Jesuit mission in the Brazilian jungle. The missionaries struggle against the legalized slave trade of Portugal and political factions within the church. Written by Bolt (of "A Man for All Seasons" fame), its visual intensity is marred by length and so much overt symbolism that an emotional coolness surfaces when the action slows. Nonetheless, epic in ambition and nearly in quality. Magnificent musical score. **125m/C VHS, Beta, LV, 8mm.** Robert De Niro, Jeremy Irons, Ray McAnally, Philip Bosco, Aidan Quinn, Liam Neeson, Cherie Lunghi, Rev. Daniel Berrigan, Ronald Pickup; ***D:*** Roland Joffe; ***W:*** Robert Bolt; ***C:*** Chris Menges; ***M:*** Ennio Morricone. Academy Awards '86: Best Cinematography; British Academy Awards '86: Best Supporting Actor (McAnally); Cannes Film Festival '86: Best Film; Golden Globe Awards '87: Best Screenplay, Best Score; Los Angeles Film Critics Association Awards '86: Best Cinematography; Nominations: Academy Awards '86: Best Art Direction/Set Decoration, Best Costume Design, Best Director (Joffe), Best Film Editing, Best Picture, Best Original Score. *WAR*

Mission Batangas ½ **1969** Unremarkable adventure-war-heist movie tells the story of a shallow American WWII pilot (Weaver) and a missionary nurse (Miles), who team up to steal the Philippine government's entire stock of gold bullion from the Japanese who captured it. Beautiful scenery, shot in the Philippines, adds something to an otherwise vacant effort. **100m/C VHS, Beta, LV.** Dennis Weaver, Vera Miles, Keith Larsen; ***D:*** Keith Larsen. *VTR, NWV*

Mission Corbari **197?** One heavily armed and ill-tempered hombre takes on the Nazis, with indifferent results. **88m/C VHS, Beta.** *NO*

Mission Galactica: The Cylon Attack **1979** Spaceship Battlestar Galactica is stranded in space without fuel and open to attack from the chrome-plated Cylons. Adama (Greene) is forced to stop Commander Cain's (Bridges) efforts to launch an attack against the Cylons, while countering the attacks of the Cylon leader. Warmed over made-for-television sci-fi. **108m/C VHS, Beta, LV.** Lorne Greene, Lloyd Bridges, Richard Hatch, Dirk Benedict. *MCA*

Mission: Impossible **1996 (PG-13)** Cruise and director DePalma did not completely succeed or fail in their mission to create a blockbuster hit based on the popular '60's TV series. Cruise (one of the film's producers) is Ethan Hunt, pointman extraordinaire of the IMF team headed by Jim Phelps (Jon Voight). Their team is sent to recover a computer disk with devastating information from a mercenary Russian spy. Smelling a double cross, Hunt confronts his conniving agency boss Kitteridge (the perfectly cast Czerny) and creates his own team of crack agents to get to the truth, mind-boggling plot twists and crazy train rides be damned. The plotline may have self-destructed two-thirds into the movie and the absence of a truly sinister villain causes some damage, but with solid acting talent, tight pacing, alluring European locales, and tension-inducing special effects, who has time to notice? $100 million gross in the first two weeks would seem to indicate a sequel is in order. **110m/C VHS.** Tom Cruise, Jon Voight, Emmanuelle Beart, Ving Rhames, Henry Czerny, Emilio Estevez, Vanessa Redgrave; ***D:*** Brian DePalma; ***W:*** Robert Towne, David Koepp; ***C:*** Stephen Burum; ***M:*** Danny Elfman. *NYR*

Mission in Morocco **1959** When an oilman scouting for oil fields in the Sahara is killed, his partner, Barker, hops a jet to Morocco to find the whereabouts of a microfilm that gives the location of a valuable oil deposit. The search for the secret microfilm is complicated by competing parties also interested in the black gold. Ho-hum action adventure. **79m/C VHS.** Lex Barker, Juli Reding. *REP*

Mission Inferno **1984** The ups and downs of a hot-blooded Korean War commando taking revenge, escaping prison, fighting and just plain making war. **90m/C VHS, Beta.** *VCD*

Mission Manila **1987 (R)** An ex-CIA operative and Manila-based drug addict is called by his ex-lover to return to Manila to help his brother, who has gotten in much the same trouble he had. **98m/C VHS, Beta, LV.** Larry Wilcox. *NO*

Mission Mars **1967** American astronauts McGavin and Adams, on a mission to the red planet, discover the bodies of two cosmonauts floating in space. After landing on the planet's surface, they find a third cosmonaut, this one in a state of suspended animation. While putting the viewer to sleep, they proceed to revive the third cosmonaut and have at it with the sinister alien force responsible for all the trouble. **87m/C VHS, Beta.** Darren McGavin, Nick Adams, George DeVries; ***D:*** Nicholas Webster. *UNI*

Mission: Monte Carlo **1975** An episode from the television series "The Persuaders," wherein our two vacationing adventurers discover a girl's drowned body and try to solve the case. **102m/C VHS, Beta.** Roger Moore, Tony Curtis, Susan George, Annette Andre, Alfred Marks, Laurence Naismith; ***D:*** Basil Dearden, Roy Ward Baker. *FOX*

Mission of Justice **1992 (R)** Revel in non-stop martial arts action with this tale of a cop who goes undercover to get the goods on a corrupt female politico, who also happens to run her own ruthless private army. **?m/C VHS, LV.** Jeff Wincott, Brigitte Nielsen, Matthias Hues, Luca Bercovici, Cyndi Pass, Billy "Sly" Williams, Tony Burton; ***D:*** Steve Barnett; ***W:*** John Bryant. *REP*

Mission of the Shark **1991** A top secret naval mission leads to a scandal-ridden court martial in this true WWII saga, based on the worst sea disaster in naval history. The U.S.S. Indianapolis has just completed a secret mission when it is torpedoed by enemy subs. The survivors spend five days in shark-infested waters awaiting rescue and, when the Navy points fingers, the ship's highly decorated and well-respected Captain McVay accepts responsibility for the good of the service. Contains some harrowing scenes of sailors versus sharks. Made for television. **92m/C VHS.** Stacy Keach, Richard Thomas, Steve Landesburg, Carrie Snodgress, Bob Gunton, Andrew Prine, Stacy Keach Sr., Don Harvey; ***D:*** Robert Iscove. *TRI*

Mission Phantom **1979** A group of spies on a mission in Russia plans to steal some diamonds and help a woman get to the United States. **90m/C VHS, Beta.** Andrew Ray, Ingrid Sholder, Peter Martell; ***D:*** James Reed. *NO*

Mission Stardust ½ *4...3...2...1...Morte* **1968** An internationally produced but thoroughly unambitious adaptation of the once-popular Perry Rhodan sci-fi serial, in which Rhodan and his team bring ill aliens back to Earth and defend them against evil spies. Dubbed. **90m/C VHS, Beta.** *GE IT SP* Essy Persson, Gianni Rizzo, Lang Jeffries, Pinkas Braun; ***D:*** Primo Zeglio. *RHI*

Mission to Death 1966 An adventure extravaganza in which a group of friends must risk their very lives. **76m/C VHS.** Jim Brewer, James E. McLarty, Jim Westerbrook, Robert Stolper, Dudley Hafner, Jerry Lasater. *LBD*

Mission to Glory ♂♂ *The Father Kino Story* **1980 (PG)** This dozer tells the story of Father Francisco "Kino" Kin, a tough, seventeenth-century priest in California who took on the Apaches and murderous Conquistadors in defense of his people. **100m/C VHS, Beta.** Richard Egan, John Ireland, Cesar Romero, Ricardo Montalban, Rory Calhoun, Michael Ansara, Keenan Wynn, Aldo Ray; ***D:*** Ken Kennedy. *IGP*

Mission to Kill ♂½ **1985 (R)** An American demolitions expert, Ginty, joins a Latin American guerrilla force in battling tyrannical junta forces. This action-packed, fast-paced thriller is big on revenge and violence but not much else. **97m/C VHS, Beta.** Robert Ginty, Olivia D'Abo, Cameron Mitchell; ***D:*** David Winters. *MED*

Mission to Venice ♂♂ **1963** Flynn plays a sleuth attempting to find a missing husband when he accidentally stumbles upon a ring of spies. **?m/C VHS.** Sean Flynn, Madeleine Robinson. *SNC*

The Missionary ♂♂½ **1982 (R)** A mild-mannered English missionary returns to London from his work in Africa and is recruited into saving the souls of a group of prostitutes. Aspiring to gentle comedy status, it's often formulaic and flat, with Palin and Smith fighting gamely to stay above script level. Still, good for some laughs, particularly during the near classic walking butler sequence. **86m/C VHS, Beta.** *GB* Michael Palin, Maggie Smith, Trevor Howard, Denholm Elliott, Michael Hordern; ***D:*** Richard Loncraine; ***W:*** Michael Palin. *PAR, TVC, FCT*

Mississippi Burning ♂♂♂ **1988 (R)** Hard-edged social drama centers around the civil rights movement in Mississippi in 1964. When three activists turn up missing, FBI agents Hackman and Dafoe are sent to head up the investigation. Unfortunately, this is another example of a "serious" film about racial conflict in which white characters predominate and blacks provide background. **127m/C VHS, Beta, LV.** Gene Hackman, Willem Dafoe, Frances McDormand, Brad Dourif, R. Lee Ermey, Gailard Sartain, Stephen Tobolowsky, Michael Rooker, Pruitt Taylor Vince, Badja Djola, Kevin Dunn, Frankie Faison, Tom Mason, Park Overall; ***D:*** Alan Parker; ***W:*** Chris Gerolmo; ***C:*** Peter Biziou; ***M:*** Trevor Jones. Academy Awards '88: Best Cinematography; Berlin International Film Festival '88: Best Actor (Hackman); National Board of Review Awards '88: 10 Best Films of the Year, Best Actor (Hackman), Best Director (Parker), Best Supporting Actress (McDormand); Nominations: Academy Awards '88: Best Actor (Hackman), Best Director (Parker), Best Film Editing, Best Picture, Best Sound, Best Supporting Actress (McDormand). *ORI*

Mississippi Masala ♂♂♂ **1992 (R)** "Masala" is an Indian seasoning blending different-colored spices, as this film is a blend of romance, comedy, and social conscience. An interracial romance sets off a cultural collision and escalates racial tensions in a small Southern town when Mina, a sheltered young Indian woman, falls in love with Demetrius, an ambitious black man with his own carpet-cleaning business. Washington and Choudhury are engaging as the lovers with Seth, as Mina's unhappy father, especially watchable. **118m/C VHS, LV.** Denzel Washington, Sarita Choudhury, Roshan Seth, Sharmila Tagore, Charles S. Dutton, Joe Seneca, Ranjit Chowdhry; ***Cameos:*** Mira Nair; ***D:*** Mira Nair; ***W:*** Sooni Taraporevala; ***M:*** L. Subramaniam. NAACP Image Awards '93: Best Actor (Washington). *COL, FCT*

Mississippi Mermaid ♂♂♂ **1969 (PG)** Truffaut generally succeeds in merging his own directorial style with Hitchcockian suspense, but this is not considered one of his best. Millionaire tobacco planter Belmondo looks for a bride in the personals and finds Deneuve. Belmondo feels lucky landing this beauty until she leaves him and takes his money with her. A lookalike, also played by Deneuve, takes over his wife's role and attempts to poison Belmondo. Look for numerous references to the movies, including Bogart, Balzac and Cocteau. Based on the Cornell Woolrich novel "Waltz into Darkness." In French with English subtitles. **110m/C VHS, LV.** *FR IT* Jean-Paul Belmondo, Catherine Deneuve, Michel Bouquet, Nelly Borgeaud, Marcel Berbert, Martine Ferriere; ***D:*** Francois Truffaut; ***W:*** Francois Truffaut; ***M:*** Antoine Duhamel. *MGM, FCT, INJ*

Missouri Breaks ♂♂ **1976 (PG)** Thomas McGuane wrote the screenplay for this offbeat tale of Montana ranchers and rustlers fighting over land and livestock in the 1880s. Promising combination of script, cast and director unfortunately yields rather disappointing results, though both Brando and Nicholson chew up scenery to their hearts' content. **126m/C VHS, Beta.** Jack Nicholson, Marlon Brando, Randy Quaid, Kathleen Lloyd, Frederic Forrest, Harry Dean Stanton; ***D:*** Arthur Penn; ***W:*** Thomas McGuane; ***M:*** John Williams. *FOX*

Missouri Traveler ♂♂♂ **1958** An orphan boy struggles to get his own farm in Missouri. Family fare based on John Buress' novel. **103m/C VHS, Beta.** Lee Marvin, Gary Merrill, Brandon de Wilde, Paul Ford. *MRV*

Missourians ♂♂½ **1950** Small-town sheriff Hale helps a Polish rancher overcome ethnic prejudice among the townspeople. The situation worsens with the arrival in town of the rancher's outlaw brother. Strong direction and engaging storyline. **60m/B VHS, Beta.** Monte Hale, Paul Hurst. *DVT*

Mrs. 'Arris Goes to Paris ♂♂½ **1992** Ada Harris (Lansbury) is a widowed charwoman, living in '50s London, whose one dream is to visit Paris and buy a Christian Dior gown at the designer's own salon. Naturally, her dream comes true—and she even finds a little romance too. Adapted from the Paul Gallico novel; made for TV. **90m/C VHS.** Angela Lansbury, Omar Sharif, Diana Rigg, Lothaire Bluteau, Lila Kaye, John Savident. *TVC, CCB*

Mrs. Brown, You've Got a Lovely Daughter ♂½ **1968 (G)** The Herman's Hermits gang inherits a greyhound and attempts to make a racer out of him while singing their songs. For the Brit group's diehard fans only. ♫It's Nice To Be Out in the Morning; Ooh, She's Done It Again; Lemon and Lime; The World is for the Young; Holiday Inn; The Most Beautiful Thing in My Life; Daisy Chain; Mrs. Brown, You've Got a Lovely Daughter; There's a King of Hush. **95m/C VHS, Beta.** Peter Noone, Stanley Holloway, Mona Washbourne; ***D:*** Saul Swimmer. *MGM*

Mrs. Doubtfire ♂♂½ **1993 (PG-13)** Williams is an unemployed voiceover actor going through a messy divorce. When his wife gets custody, the distraught father decides to dress up as a woman and become a nanny to his own children. He also has to deal with the old flame who re-enters his ex-wife's life. Williams schtick extraordinaire with more than a little sugary sentimentality. Based on the British children's book "Madame Doubtfire" by Anne Fine. **120m/C VHS, LV.** Robin Williams, Sally Field, Pierce Brosnan, Harvey Fierstein, Robert Prosky, Mara Wilson; ***D:*** Chris Columbus; ***W:*** Randi Mayem Singer, Leslie Dixon; ***M:*** Howard Shore. Academy Awards '93: Best Makeup; Golden Globe Awards '94: Best Actor—Musical/Comedy (Williams), Best Film—Musical/Comedy; MTV Movie Awards '94: Best Comedic Performance (Williams); Nominations: MTV Movie Awards '94: Best Actor (Williams). *FXV*

Mrs. Miniver ♂♂♂♂ **1942** A moving tale of a courageous, gentle middle-class British family and its struggle to survive during WWII. A classic that garnered six Academy Awards, it's recognized for contributions to the Allied effort. Contains one of the most powerful orations in the film history, delivered by Wilcoxon, who portrayed the vicar. Followed by "The Miniver Story." Adapted from Jan Struther's book. **134m/B VHS, Beta, LV.** Greer Garson, Walter Pidgeon, Teresa Wright, May Whitty, Richard Ney, Henry Travers, Reginald Owen, Henry Wilcoxon, Helmut Dantine, Aubrey Mather, Rhys Williams, Tom Conway, Peter Lawford; ***D:*** William Wyler; ***W:*** George Froeschel, James Hilton, Arthur Wimperis, Claudine West; ***C:*** Joseph Ruttenberg; ***M:*** Herbert Stothart. Academy Awards '42: Best Actress (Garson), Best Black and White Cinematography, Best Director (Wyler), Best Picture, Best Screenplay, Best Supporting Actress (Wright); Nominations: Academy Awards '42: Best Actor (Pidgeon), Best Film Editing, Best Sound, Best Supporting Actor (Travers), Best Supporting Actress (Whitty). *MGM, BTV*

Mrs. Munck ♂♂ **1995 (R)** Creepy cable thriller finds widowed Rose Munck (Ladd) agreeing to care for bitter father-in-law Patrick Leary (Dern, Ladd's real-life ex-hubby), who's suffered a debilitating stroke. But they share a nasty past—seems he seduced a teenaged Rose (played by Preston), she had a child, Patrick refused any responsibilty, and the child died. So whacked-out Rose is really out for revenge. Based on a novel by Ella Leffland. Ladd's debut as writer/director. **99m/C VHS.** Diane Ladd, Bruce Dern, Kelly Preston, Shelley Winters; ***D:*** Diane Ladd; ***W:*** Diane Ladd; ***C:*** James Glennon; ***M:*** Leonard Rosenman. *REP*

Mrs. Parker and the Vicious Circle ♂♂½ *Mrs. Parker and the Round Table* **1994 (R)** Bio of witty, suicidal writer Dorothy Parker and her equally witty friends, including theater critics, playwrights, and novelists, who lunched together at New York's Algonquin Hotel for most of the 1920's. An irreverant band known as the Algonquin Round Table, their numerous bon mots were regularly reported in the papers. Their private lives were often less than happy with alcohol, drug addiction and depression prominent factors. Parker's downward spiral is depressing though compelling to watch, thanks to Leigh's performance (in spite of much criticism for her lockjawed accent) but many of the characters come and go so quickly they make little impression. **124m/C VHS, LV.** Jennifer Jason Leigh, Matthew Broderick, Andrew McCarthy, Campbell Scott, Jennifer Beals, Tom McGowan, Nick Cassavetes, Sam Robards, Rebecca Miller, Wallace Shawn, Martha Plimpton, Gwyneth Paltrow; ***D:*** Alan Rudolph; ***W:*** Rudolph Coburn, Randy Sue Coburn; ***C:*** Jan Kiesser. Chicago Film Critics Awards '94: Best Actress (Leigh); National Society of Film Critics Awards '94: Best Actress (Leigh); Nominations: Golden Globe Awards '95: Best Actress—Drama (Leigh); Independent Spirit Awards '95: Best Actor (Scott), Best Actress (Leigh), Best Director (Rudolph), Best Film, Best Screenplay. *NLC, IME*

Mrs. Parkington ♂♂½ **1944** Overblown epic drama spanning six decades tells the story of the rise and fall of an American dynasty made on easy money. Garson plays the woman who goes from working as a maid in a boarding house to living a life of luxury when she marries a multimillionaire. This was the fifth pairing of Garson and Pidgeon and although it's not one of their best, it proved to be a big hit with audiences. Lavish costumes and good performances by Garson and Moorehead. Based on the novel by Louis Bromfield. **124m/B VHS.** Greer Garson, Walter Pidgeon, Edward Arnold, Frances Rafferty, Agnes Moorehead, Selena Royle, Gladys Cooper, Lee Patrick; ***D:*** Tay Garnett; ***W:*** Robert Thoeren, Polly James; ***C:*** Joseph Ruttenberg. Golden Globe Awards '45: Best Supporting Actress (Moorehead); Nominations: Academy Awards '44: Best Actress (Garson), Best Supporting Actress (Moorehead). *MGM*

Mrs. R's Daughter ♂♂ **1979** An outraged mother fights the judicial systems in order to bring her daughter's rapist to trial. Based on a true story and made for television. **97m/C VHS, Beta.** Cloris Leachman, Season Hubley, Donald Moffat, John McIntire, Stephen Elliott, Ron Rifkin; ***D:*** Dan Curtis. *WAR, OM*

Mrs. Silly ♂ **1985** Romance novel on tape, following the exploits of an aging woman who in losing material wealth, gains contentment. **60m/C Beta.** Maggie Smith, James Villiers, Cyril Luckham. *PSM*

Mrs. Soffel ♂♂½ **1984 (PG-13)** Falling in love with a convicted murderer and helping him flee confinement occupies the time of the prison warden's wife. Effectively captures the 1901 setting, yet a dark pall fairly strangles any emotion. Based on a true story. **110m/C VHS, Beta, LV.** Diane Keaton, Mel Gibson, Matthew Modine, Edward Herrmann, Trini Alvarado, Terry O'Quinn, Jennie Dundas, Danny Corkill, Maury Chaykin, Dana Wheeler-Nicholson; ***D:*** Gillian Armstrong; ***W:*** Ron Nyswaner; ***M:*** Mark Isham. *MGM*

Mrs. Wiggs of the Cabbage Patch ♂♂½ **1942** A warm, funny, and altogether overdone story of a mother whose husband abandons her, leaving the woman to raise their four children alone. It's Thanksgiving, so the rich visit the poor household to deliver a turkey dinner, and in the end all live happily ever after. Not one of Fields' larger roles; he doesn't even make an appearance until midway through the scmaltz. **80m/B VHS.** Pauline Lord, ZaSu Pitts, W.C. Fields, Evelyn Venable, Donald Meek, Barbara Britton; ***D:*** Norman Taurog. *GKK*

Mrs. Winterbourne ☠☠ **1996 (PG-13)** Pregnant loser Connie Doyle (Lake) is whisked into the lap of luxury when she's assumed to be the widowed Patricia Winterbourne after a train wreck. The grieving family (who had never met the bride) take her in and accept her and her baby as part of the household. Since her life is now going well, Connie decides to keep her true identity a secret while she falls for faux-brother-in-law Bill (Fraser). MacLaine is brilliant as the spirited matriarch of the family. Retooled as a comedy, the story is actually based on the noirish novel "I Married a Dead Man" by Cornell Woolrich and a remake of the equally dark "No Man of Her Own" from 1950. **104m/C VHS.** Ricki Lake, Brendan Fraser, Shirley MacLaine, Miguel Sandoval, Loren Dean, Susan Haskell, Paula Prentiss; ***D:*** Richard Benjamin; ***W:*** Phoef Sutton, Lisa-Marie Rodano; ***C:*** Alex Nepomniaschy; ***M:*** Patrick Doyle. *NYR*

Mistaken Identity ☠½ **1936** A swank hotel is the setting for this so-so comedy about three con men who wind up conning each other as much as their supposed victims. A couple of light romances are also thrown in for good measure. **75m/B VHS.** Chick Chandler, Evalyn Knapp, Berton Churchill, Patricia Farr, Richard Carle, Bradley Page, Lew Kelly; ***D:*** Phil Rosen. *VYY*

Mistaken Identity ☠½ **1941** All-black mystery set against the background of a nightclub, and featuring a production number, "I'm a Bangi from Ubangi." **60m/B VHS, Beta.** Nellie Hill, George Oliver. *VCN, DVT, RXM*

Mr. Ace ☠½ **1946** A congresswoman decides to run for governor without the approval of the loyal political kingpin, Mr. Ace. **85m/B VHS, Beta, LV.** George Raft, Sylvia Sidney, Sara Haden, Stanley Ridges; ***D:*** Edwin L. Marin. *COL*

Mr. & Mrs. Bridge ☠☠☠☠ **1990 (PG-13)** Set in the thirties and forties in Kansas City, Ivory's adaptation of Evan S. Connell's novels painstakingly portrays an upper middle-class family struggling to survive within an emotional vacuum. Newman and Woodward, together for the first time in many years as Walter and Ivory Bridge, bring a wealth of experience and insight to their characterizations. Many consider this to be Newman's best, most subtle and nuanced performance. **127m/C VHS, LV.** Joanne Woodward, Paul Newman, Kyra Sedgwick, Blythe Danner, Simon Callow, Diane Kagan, Robert Sean Leonard, Saundra McClain, Margaret Welsh, Austin Pendleton, Gale Garnett, Remak Ramsay; ***D:*** James Ivory; ***W:*** Ruth Prawer Jhabvala; ***C:*** Tony Pierce-Roberts. New York Film Critics Awards '90: Best Actress (Woodward), Best Screenplay; Nominations: Academy Awards '90: Best Actress (Woodward). *FCT*

Mr. & Mrs. Loving ☠☠☠ **1996 (PG-13)** Fact-based cable movie, set in the 1960s, follows the romance, marriage, and struggle of Richard Loving (Hutton) and Mildred "Bean" Jeter (Rochon). Growing up in rural Central Point, Viriginia, their interracial relationship isn't considered uncommon. But when Bean gets pregnant, they won't be allowed to marry and live together because of Virginia's racial laws. Instead, the Lovings start a life in Washington, DC, but desperately homesick and increasingly aware of the civil rights movement, Bean writes a letter to the Attorney General's office. What results is young ACLU lawyer Bernie Cohen (Parker) taking on their case—which eventually leads to a landmark Supreme Court decision about miscegenation laws. **95m/C VHS, LV.** Timothy Hutton, Lela Rochon, Corey Parker, Ruby Dee, Isaiah Washington, Bill Nunn, Charles Gray; ***D:*** Richard Friedenberg; ***W:*** Richard Friedenberg; ***C:*** Kenneth Macmillan; ***M:*** Branford Marsalis. *HMK*

Mr. & Mrs. Smith ☠☠☠½ **1941** Hitchcock's only screwball comedy, an underrated, endearing farce about a bickering but happy modern couple who discover their marriage isn't legitimate and go through courtship all over again. Vintage of its kind, with inspired performances and crackling dialogue. **95m/B VHS, Beta, LV.** Carole Lombard, Robert Montgomery, Gene Raymond, Jack Carson, Lucile Watson, Charles Halton; ***D:*** Alfred Hitchcock; ***W:*** Norman Krasna. *MED, TTC*

Mr. Arkadin ☠☠☠ *Confidential Report* **1955** Screenwriter, director, star Welles, adapting from his own novel, gave this plot a dry run on radio during early 1950s. Welles examines the life of yet another ruthless millionaire, but this one can't seem to remember the sordid source of all that cash. Investigator Arden follows the intriguing and descending trail to a surprise ending. As in "Citizen Kane," oblique camera angles and layered dialogue prevail, but this time only serve to confuse the story. Shot over two years around Europe, required seven years of post production before finding distribution in 1962. **99m/B VHS, Beta, LV.** *GB* Orson Welles, Akim Tamiroff, Michael Redgrave, Patricia Medina, Mischa Auer; ***D:*** Orson Welles; ***C:*** Jean Bourgoin. *VDM, HTV, HEG*

Mr. Baseball ☠☠ **1992 (PG-13)** Washed-up American baseball player tries to revive his career by playing in Japan and experiences cultures clashing under the ballpark lights. Semi-charmer swings and misses often enough to warrant return to minors. Film drew controversy during production when Universal was bought by the Japanese Matsushita organization and claims of both Japan- and America-bashing were thrown about. **109m/C VHS, Beta, LV.** Tom Selleck, Ken Takakura, Toshi Shioya, Dennis Haysbert, Aya Takanashi; ***D:*** Fred Schepisi; ***W:*** Gary Ross, Kevin Wade, Monte Merrick; ***C:*** Ian Baker; ***M:*** Jerry Goldsmith. *MCA*

Mr. Billion ☠☠ **1977 (PG)** Engaging chase adventure comedy about an Italian mechanic who stands to inherit a billion dollar fortune if he can travel from Italy to San Francisco in twenty days. Of course, things get in his way. Hill made his American debut in this film. **89m/C VHS, Beta.** Jackie Gleason, Terence Hill, Valerie Perrine, Slim Pickens, Chill Wills; ***D:*** Jonathan Kaplan; ***W:*** Jonathan Kaplan, Ken Friedman; ***M:*** Dave Grusin. *FOX*

Mr. Bill's Real Life Adventures **1986** A made-for-television live-action adventure for the "Saturday Night Live" clay star, portrayed by Scolari, who is victimized as usual by his nemesis, Mr. Sluggo. **43m/C VHS, Beta.** Peter Scolari, Valerie Mahaffey, Lenore Kasdorf, Michael McManus; ***D:*** Jim Drake. *PAR*

Mr. Blandings Builds His Dream House ☠☠☠½ **1948** Classic comedy features Grant as an adman who tires of city life and moves his family to the country, where his troubles really begin. Grant is at his funniest. Loy and Douglas provide strong backup. A must for all homeowners. **93m/B VHS, Beta, LV.** Cary Grant, Myrna Loy, Melvyn Douglas, Lex Barker, Reginald Denny, Louise Beavers; ***D:*** H.C. Potter; ***W:*** Norman Panama. *TTC, MED, MLB*

Mr. Boggs Steps Out ☠½ **1938** A pencil-pusher wins a bundle and invests it in a barrel factory. Trouble arises when a slickster tries to close it down. Even with the usual romantic entanglements, the film has trouble staying interesting. **68m/B VHS.** Stuart Erwin, Helen Chandler, Toby Wing, Tully Marshall, Spencer Charters, Otis Harlan, Walter Byron, Milburn Stone; ***D:*** Gordon Wiles. *NOS, VYY*

Mr. Corbett's Ghost ☠☠ **1990** A young man, displeased with his boss's managerial finesse, cuts a deal with a soul collector who pink slips the guy to the great unemployment line in the sky. Once a boss always a boss, and the guy's ghost stops in to say boo, while the soul collector is hot to get his hands on his part of the bargain. Huston's final film appearance. Made for television. **60m/C VHS.** John Huston, Paul Scofield, Burgess Meredith. *MON, KAR*

Mr. Deeds Goes to Town ☠☠☠½ **1936** Typical Capra fare offers Cooper as philanthropic fellow who inherits $20 million and promptly donates it to the needy. He also manages to find time to fall in love with a beautiful reporter. Arthur is the hard-edged reporter determined to fathom the good guy's motivation. Superior entertainment. Based on Clarence Budington Kelland's play "Opera Hut." **118m/B VHS, Beta, LV.** Gary Cooper, Jean Arthur, Raymond Walburn, Walter Catlett, Lionel Stander, George Bancroft, H.B. Warner, Ruth Donnelly, Douglass Dumbrille, Margaret Seddon, Margaret McWade; ***D:*** Frank Capra; ***W:*** Robert Riskin. Academy Awards '36: Best Director (Capra); National Board of Review Awards '36: 10 Best Films of the Year; New York Film Critics Awards '36: Best Film; Nominations: Academy Awards '36: Best Actor (Cooper), Best Picture, Best Screenplay, Best Sound. *COL, BTV*

Mr. Destiny ☠☠ **1990 (PG-13)** Mid-level businessman Belushi has a mid-life crisis of sorts when his car dies. Wandering into an empty bar, he encounters bartender Caine who serves cocktails and acts omniscient before taking him on the ten-cent tour of life as it would've been if he hadn't struck out in a high school baseball game. Less than wonderful rehash of "It's a Wonderful Life." **110m/C VHS, Beta, LV.** James Belushi, Michael Caine, Linda Hamilton, Jon Lovitz, Bill McCutcheon, Hart Bochner, Rene Russo, Jay O. Sanders, Maury Chaykin, Pat Corley, Douglas Seale, Courteney Cox, Kathy Ireland; ***D:*** James Orr; ***W:*** James Orr, Jim Cruickshank. *TOU, FCT*

Mr. Emmanuel ☠☠½ **1944** An elderly Jewish widower leaves his English home in 1935 in quest of the mother of a German refugee boy, and is subjected to shocking treatment in Germany. **97m/B VHS, Beta.** Felix Aylmer, Greta Gynt, Walter Rilla, Jean Simmons. *LCA*

Mr. Frost ☠ **1989 (R)** Goldblum feigns fascination in this lackluster tale of the devil incarnate, who is imprisoned after owning up to a series of grisly murders, and who hides his true identity until approached by a woman psychiatrist. **92m/C VHS.** Jeff Goldblum, Kathy Baker, Alan Bates, Roland Giraud, Jean-Pierre Cassel; ***D:*** Phillip Setbon; ***W:*** Phillip Setbon, Brad Lynch. *FCT, IME*

Mister Halpren & Mister Johnson ☠☠ **1983** Gleason attends the funeral of a longtime friend and one time flame, and becomes acquainted with the woman's husband (Olivier). Heavyweight cast wasted on flimsy script...and away we go! **57m/C VHS, Beta.** Laurence Olivier, Jackie Gleason; ***D:*** Alvin Rakoff. *NO*

Mr. Hobbs Takes a Vacation ☠☠☠ **1962** Good-natured comedy in which beleaguered parents try to resolve family squabbles while the entire brood is on a seaside vacation. Stewart and O'Hara are especially fine and funny as the well-meaning parents. **116m/C VHS, Beta.** James Stewart, Maureen O'Hara, Fabian, John Saxon, Marie Wilson, John McGiver, Reginald Gardiner; ***D:*** Henry Koster; ***M:*** Henry Mancini. Berlin International Film Festival '62: Best Actor (Stewart). *FOX, HMV*

Mr. Holland's Opus ☠☠☠ **1995 (PG)** Well-done Disney tearjerker begins in 1965 as musician Glenn Holland (Dreyfuss) takes a teaching job to get himself off the wedding reception circuit and help support his wife, Iris (Headley), and their deaf son. Spanning three decades, with actual newsreel footage thrown in to highlight time passing, Holland sets aside his dream of composing a great symphony and finds his true calling—mentoring and inspiring young minds. Holland's son being deaf might have proved corny, but their rocky relationship is deeply rooted to the storyline. Dreyfuss turns in his most vibrant performance in years and, while sentimental buttons are definitely pushed, director Herek avoids falling into sappiness. **142m/C VHS, LV.** Richard Dreyfuss, Glenne Headly, Jay Thomas, Olympia Dukakis, William H. Macy, Alicia Witt, Jean Louisa Kelly, Anthony Natale; ***D:*** Stephen Herek; ***W:*** Patrick Sheane Duncan; ***C:*** Oliver Wood; ***M:*** Michael Kamen. Nominations: Academy Awards '95: Best Actor (Dreyfuss); Golden Globe Awards '95: Best Actor—Drama (Dreyfuss), Best Screenplay. *TOU*

Mr. Horn ☠☠ **1979** Based on the William Goldman western novel, this slow-paced film about folk-hero Scott Tom Horn capturing the famous Apache warrior, Geronimo, is average at best. **200m/C VHS.**

David Carradine, Richard Widmark, Karen Black, Jeremy Slate, Enrique Lucero, Jack Starrett; ***D:*** Jack Starrett. *LIV*

Mr. Hulot's Holiday 🦴🦴🦴½ *Les Vacances de Monsieur Hulot; Monsieur Hulot's Holiday* **1953** Superior slapstick details the misadventures of a dullard's seaside holiday. Inventive French comedian Tati at his best. Light-hearted and natural, with magical mime sequences. Followed by "Mon Oncle." **86m/B VHS, Beta, LV, 8mm.** *FR* Jacques Tati, Natalie Pascaud, Michelle Rolia; ***D:*** Jacques Tati. National Board of Review Awards '54: 5 Best Foreign Films of the Year; Nominations: Academy Awards '55: Best Story & Screenplay. *NOS, MRV, VYY*

Mr. Inside, Mr. Outside 🦴½ **1974** A television movie about two New York City cops, one undercover, one not, trying to infiltrate a tough diamond-smuggling ring. **74m/C VHS, Beta.** Tony LoBianco, Hal Linden; ***D:*** William A. Graham. *VMK*

Mister Johnson 🦴🦴🦴 **1991 (PG-13)** In 1923 Africa, an educated black man working for the British magistrate constantly finds himself in trouble, thanks to backfiring schemes. This highly enjoyable film from the director of "Driving Miss Daisy" suffers only from the underdevelopment of the intriguing lead character. Based on the novel by Joyce Cary. **105m/C VHS.** Pierce Brosnan, Edward Woodward, Maynard Eziashi, Beatie Edney, Denis Quilley, Nick Reding; ***D:*** Bruce Beresford; ***W:*** Bruce Beresford, William Boyd; ***M:*** Georges Delerue. *VES, LIV*

Mr. Jones 🦴½ **1993 (R)** Psychiatrist (Olin) falls in love with her manic-depressive patient (Gere). Head case Mr. Jones (Gere) is a charmer who gets a rush from tightrope walking a high beam on a construction site, yet is prone to bad moods when he fails to remember his own name. He can't resist flirting with the seductive Dr. Bowen, who eagerly leaps past professional boundaries while trying to coax him out of his illness. Wastes the talents of its stars with Gere showy, Olin brittle, and the whole story as contrived as their prefunctory love affair. Psychiatrists are getting as bad a rep professionally as lawyers in their recent film appearances. **110m/C VHS, LV.** Richard Gere, Lena Olin, Anne Bancroft, Tom Irwin, Delroy Lindo, Bruce Altman, Lauren Tom; ***D:*** Mike Figgis; ***W:*** Michael Cristofer, Eric Roth; ***M:*** Maurice Jarre. *COL*

Mr. Kingstreet's War 🦴🦴½ *Heroes Die Hard* **1971** An idealistic game warden and his wife defend the wildlife of Africa against the fighting Italian and British armies at the dawn of WWII. **92m/C VHS, Beta.** John Saxon, Tippi Hedren, Rossano Brazzi, Brian O'Shaughnessy; ***D:*** Percival Rubens. *VCI*

Mr. Klein 🦴🦴🦴 **1975 (PG)** Cleverly plotted script and fine direction in this dark and intense film about a French-Catholic merchant who buys valuables from Jews trying to escape Nazi occupied France in 1942, paying far less than what the treasures are worth. Ironically, he is later mistaken for a Jew by the same name who has been using this man's reputation as a cover. **122m/C VHS, Beta.** Alain Delon, Jeanne Moreau; ***D:*** Joseph Losey. Nominations: Cannes Film Festival '76: Best Film. *COL, SWC*

Mr. Love 🦴🦴½ **1986 (PG-13)** A meek gardener is perceived by neighbors as a fool until he dies and numerous women arrive for his funeral. Is it his cologne? The radishes? **91m/C VHS, Beta.** *GB* Barry Jackson, Maurice Denham, Margaret Tyzack, Linda Marlowe; ***D:*** Roy Battersby; ***M:*** Willy Russell. *WAR*

Mr. Lucky 🦴🦴🦴 **1943** Likeable wartime drama about a gambler who hopes to swindle a philanthropic organization, but then falls in love and determines to help the group in a fundraising effort. Grant is, no surprise, excellent as the seemingly cynical con artist who actually has a heart of gold. Cliched, but nonetheless worthwhile. Later developed into a television series. **99m/B VHS, Beta, LV.** Cary Grant, Laraine Day, Charles Bickford, Gladys Cooper, Paul Stewart, Henry Stephenson, Florence Bates; ***D:*** H.C. Potter; ***C:*** George Barnes. *MED, RXM, TTC*

Mr. Majestyk 🦴🦴½ **1974 (PG)** When a Vietnam veteran's attempt to start an honest business is thwarted by Mafia hitmen and the police, he goes after them with a vengeance. **103m/C VHS, Beta.** Charles Bronson, Al Lettieri, Linda Cristal, Lee Purcell; ***D:*** Richard Fleischer; ***W:*** Elmore Leonard; ***M:*** Charles Bernstein. *MGM*

Mister Mean 🦴 **1977** A man who once worked for a mafia don is now given the task of rubbing him out. For Cosa Nostra diehards and gluttons for Roman scenery. **98m/C VHS, Beta.** *IT* Fred Williamson; ***D:*** Fred Williamson. *NO*

Mr. Mike's Mondo Video 🦴🦴 **1979 (R)** A bizarre, outrageous comedy special declared too wild for television conceived by the "Saturday Night Live" alumnus Mr. Mike. **75m/C VHS, Beta.** Michael O'Donoghue, Dan Aykroyd, Jane Curtin, Carrie Fisher, Teri Garr, Joan Haskett, Deborah Harry, Margot Kidder, Bill Murray, Laraine Newman, Gilda Radner, Julius LaRosa, Paul Shaffer, Sid Vicious; ***W:*** Mitch Glazer. *NO*

Mr. Mom 🦴🦴🦴 **1983 (PG)** A tireless auto exec loses his job and stays home with the kids while his wife becomes the breadwinner. He's forced to cope with the rigors of housework and child care, resorting to drugs, alcohol and soap operas. Keaton's hilarious as the homebound dad chased by killer appliances and poker buddy to the ladies in the neighborhood. **92m/C VHS, Beta, LV.** Michael Keaton, Teri Garr, Christopher Lloyd, Martin Mull, Ann Jillian, Jeffrey Tambor, Edie McClurg, Valri Bromfield; ***D:*** Stan Dragoti; ***W:*** John Hughes. *LIV, VES*

Mr. Moto's Last Warning 🦴🦴🦴 **1939** One of the better in the series of Mr. Moto, the wily detective! Lorre is convincing in the title role and gets good support from character villains Carradine and Sanders in this story of saboteurs converging on the Suez Canal plotting to blow up the French Fleet. **71m/B VHS, Beta.** Peter Lorre, George Sanders, Ricardo Cortez, John Carradine, Virginia Field, Robert Coote; ***D:*** Norman Foster. *SNC, NOS, CAB*

Mr. Moto's Last Warning/Meeting at Midnight **1944** The first film finds Moto at the Suez Canal trying to save France's flotilla from a deadly conspiracy. The second feature is classic Charlie Chan fare. This time his driver, Birmingham, gets Chan caught in the midst of the occult. **130m/B VHS, Beta.** Sidney Toler, Peter Lorre, Mantan Moreland. *AOV*

Mr. Music 🦴🦴½ **1950** Crosby is a successful songwriter who would rather enjoy life on the golf course than pen any more tunes. He's persuaded by his secretary to help out an old-time producer who's fallen on hard times by writing a new Broadway show. Light-hearted fluff. Based on the play "Accent on Youth" by Samson Raphaelson which had been filmed in 1935. ♫Life is So Precious; Accidents Will Happen; High on the List; Wouldn't It Be Funny; Wasn't I There?; Mr. Music; Once More the Blue and White; Milady; Then You'll Be Home. **113m/B VHS.** Bing Crosby, Nancy Olson, Charles Coburn, Robert Stack, Tom Ewell, Ruth Hussey, Charles Kemper, Donald Woods, Gower Champion, Marge Champion; ***Cameos:*** Groucho Marx, Peggy Lee; ***D:*** Richard Haydn. *PAR*

Mr. Nanny 🦴🦴 **1993 (PG)** For those who fear change, this predictable plot should serve as comforting assurance that Hollywood will still sacrifice substance for the quick buck. Basic story line has the child-hating Hulkster playing nanny/bodyguard to a couple of bratty kids. Meanwhile, his arch rival (Johansen) hatches a scheme to gain world dominance by kidnapping the kids for the ransom of their father's top secret computer chip. Never fear—in this world, the good guys kick butt, naturally, and everyone learns a lesson. **85m/C VHS.** Hulk Hogan, Sherman Hemsley, Austin Pendleton, Robert Gorman, Madeline Zima, Mother Love, David Johansen; ***D:*** Michael Gottlieb; ***W:*** Ed Rugoff, Michael Gottlieb; ***M:*** David Johansen, Brian Koonin. *COL*

Mr. Nice Guy 🦴 **1986 (PG-13)** In the near future, a hired gun strives for national recognition as the best of his now legitimate profession. Comedy with few laughs. **92m/C VHS, Beta.** Michael MacDonald, Jan Smithers, Joe Silver. *VTR, NWV*

Mr. North 🦴🦴½ **1988 (PG)** Capra-corn fable about a charming, bright Yale graduate who encounters admiration and disdain from upper-crust Rhode Island residents when news of his miraculous "cures" spreads. Marks the directorial debut of Danny Huston, son of John Huston, who co-wrote the script and served as executive producer before dying several weeks into shooting. Set in the 1920s and adapted from Thornton Wilder's "Theophilus North." **90m/C VHS, Beta, LV.** Anthony Edwards, Robert Mitchum, Lauren Bacall, Harry Dean Stanton, Anjelica Huston, Mary Stuart Masterson, Virginia Madsen, Tammy Grimes, David Warner, Hunter Carson, Christopher Durang, Mark Metcalf, Katharine Houghton; ***D:*** Danny Huston; ***W:*** John Huston, Janet Roach, James Costigan; ***M:*** David McHugh. *NO*

Mr. Peabody & the Mermaid 🦴🦴½ **1948** Lightweight fish story about a middle-aged married man who hooks a beautiful mermaid while fishing in the Caribbean and eventually falls in love with her. Powell is smooth as always, though hampered by the unrestrained absurdity of it all. Based on the novel by Guy and Constance Jones. Also available colorized. **89m/B VHS.** William Powell, Ann Blyth, Irene Hervey, Andrea King, Clinton Sundberg, Art Smith; ***D:*** Irving Pichel; ***W:*** Nunnally Johnson. *REP*

Mr. Peek-A-Boo 🦴🦴½ *Garou Garou le Passe Muraille* **1950** A French clerk discovers he has the ability to walk through walls. Although friends try to coax him into a life of crime, he instead comes to the aid of an English girl who is being blackmailed. Good-natured French comedy was shot with English dialogue for the American market. **74m/B VHS, Beta.** *FR* Joan Greenwood, Bourvil, Marcel Arnold, Roger Treville; ***D:*** Jean Boyer. *SNC*

Mr. Reeder in Room 13 🦴🦴 **1938** Based on the mystery stories created by Edgar Wallace, Mr. Reeder (a cultured English gentleman who fights crime) enlists the aid of a young man to get evidence on a gang of counterfeiters. **66m/B VHS, Beta.** Gibb McLaughlin. *VYY*

Mister Roberts 🦴🦴🦴🦴 **1955** Crew of a Navy cargo freighter in the South Pacific during WWII relieves the boredom of duty with a series of elaborate practical jokes, mostly at the expense of their long-suffering and slightly crazy captain, who then determines that he will get even. The ship's cargo officer, Mr. Roberts, longs to be transferred to a fighting vessel and see some action. Originally a hit Broadway play (based on the novel by Thomas Heggen) which also featured Fonda in the title role. Great performance from Lemmon as Ensign Pulver. Powell's last film. Sequelled in 1964 by "Ensign Pulver," and later a short-lived TV series as well as a live TV special. Newly transferred in 1988 from a pristine stereo print. **120m/C VHS, Beta.** Henry Fonda, James Cagney, Jack Lemmon, William Powell, Betsy Palmer, Ward Bond, Harry Carey Jr., Nick Adams, Phil Carey, Ken Curtis, Martin Milner, Jack Pennick, Perry Lopez, Patrick Wayne; ***D:*** John Ford, Mervyn LeRoy; ***W:*** Frank Nugent, Joshua Logan; ***C:*** Winton C. Hoch; ***M:*** Franz Waxman. Academy Awards '55: Best Supporting Actor (Lemmon); National Board of Review Awards '55: 10 Best Films of the Year; Nominations: Academy Awards '54: Best Picture; Academy Awards '55: Best Sound. *WAR, BTV*

Mr. Robinson Crusoe 🦴🦴½ **1932** Rollicking adventure in the South Seas as Fairbanks makes a bet that he can live on a desert island for a year without being left any refinements of civilization. Lucky for him, a woman arrives. Also written by Fairbanks. **76m/B VHS, Beta, LV.** Douglas Fairbanks Sr., William Farnum, Maria Alba, Earle Brown; ***D:*** Edward Sutherland; ***W:*** Douglas Fairbanks Sr.; ***M:*** Alfred Newman. *NOS, GPV, CCB*

Mr. Saturday Night 🦴🦴½ **1992 (R)** Crystal, in his directorial debut, stars as Buddy Young, Jr., a self-destructive comedian whose career spans five decades. His nasty one-liners and witty jokes combine with poignancy in this satisfying comedy/drama. Paymer is excellent as Young's long-suffering, faithful brother and manager. Watch for Lewis in a cameo role. Expectations were very high and the box office results were disappointing, but fans of Crystal shouldn't miss this one. The video also includes additional footage and outtakes selected and hosted by Crystal. **118m/C VHS, LV.** Billy Crystal, David Paymer, Julie Warner, Helen Hunt, Mary Mara, Jerry Orbach, Ron Silver,

Sage Allen, Jackie Gayle, Carl Ballantine, Slappy (Melvin) White, Conrad Janis; ***Cameos:*** Jerry Lewis; ***D:*** Billy Crystal; ***W:*** Billy Crystal, Babaloo Mandel, Lowell Ganz; ***M:*** Marc Shaiman. Nominations: Academy Awards '92: Best Supporting Actor (Paymer). *COL, IME, MOV*

Mr. Scarface 𝄞½ **1977 (R)** A young man searches for the man who murdered his father years earlier in a dark alley. **85m/C VHS, Beta.** Jack Palance, Edmund Purdom, Al Cliver, Harry Baer, Gisela Hahn; ***D:*** Fernando Di Leo. *CNG*

Mr. Skeffington 𝄞𝄞𝄞 **1944** A super-grade soap opera spanning 26 years in the life of a ravishing, spoiled New York socialite. The beauty with a fondness for bedrooms marries for convenience, abuses her husband, then enjoys a highly equitable divorce settlement. Years later when diphtheria leaves her totally deformed and no man will have her, she is saved by her former husband. Based on the novel by "Elizabeth" (Mary Annette Beauchamp Russell) and adapted by "Casablanca's" Julius and Philip Epstein. **147m/B VHS, Beta, LV.** Bette Davis, Claude Rains, Walter Abel, Richard Waring, George Coulouris, John Alexander; ***D:*** Vincent Sherman. Nominations: Academy Awards '44: Best Actress (Davis), Best Supporting Actor (Rains). *MGM*

Mr. Skitch 𝄞𝄞 **1933** Weak Rogers offering. Couple loses their farm and begins cross country jaunt with mishaps at every turn. All ends well when their daughter meets an Army cadet, but few laughs and lots of loose ends. **70m/B VHS.** Will Rogers, ZaSu Pitts, Rochelle Hudson, Charles Starrett; ***D:*** James Cruze. *FOX, FCT*

Mr. Smith Goes to Washington 𝄞𝄞𝄞𝄞 **1939** Another classic from Hollywood's golden year of 1939. Jimmy Stewart is an idealistic and naive young man selected to fill in for an ailing Senator. Upon his arrival in the Capitol, he is inundated by a multitude of corrupt politicians. He takes a stand for his beliefs and tries to denounce many of those he feels are unfit for their positions, meeting with opposition from all sides. Great cast is highlighted by Stewart in one of his most endearing performances. Quintessential Capra tale sharply adapted from Lewis Foster's story. Outstanding in every regard. **130m/B VHS, Beta, LV.** James Stewart, Jean Arthur, Edward Arnold, Claude Rains, Thomas Mitchell, Beulah Bondi, Eugene Pallette, Guy Kibbee, Harry Carey Sr., H.B. Warner, Porter Hall, Jack Carson, Charles Lane; ***D:*** Frank Capra; ***W:*** Sidney Buchman; ***M:*** Dimitri Tiomkin. Academy Awards '39: Best Story; National Board of Review Awards '39: 10 Best Films of the Year; New York Film Critics Awards '39: Best Actor (Stewart); Nominations: Academy Awards '39: Best Actor (Stewart), Best Director (Capra), Best Interior Decoration, Best Picture, Best Screenplay, Best Sound, Best Supporting Actor (Rains, Carey), Best Score. *COL, HMV*

Mr. Stitch 𝄞 **1995 (R)** Demented scientist (Hauer) plays Frankenstein and makes a creature, named Lazarus (Wheaton), from the body parts of more than 80 men and women. Unfortunately, the sensitive Lazarus has retained the collective memories of all these people and becomes obsessed with finding the reason for his existence. He receives compassion from a shrink (Peeples) but his maker has less-than-honorable plans for Lazarus. **98m/C VHS.** Rutger Hauer, Wil Wheaton, Nia Peeples, Taylor Negron, Ron Perlman, Michael Harris; ***Cameos:*** Tom Savini; ***D:*** Roger Roberts Avary. *AVE*

Mr. Superinvisible 𝄞𝄞 *Mr. Invisible; L'Inafferrabile Invincible* **1973 (G)** Searching to cure the common cold, a bumbling scientist invents a bizarre virus, then strives with his loyal (of course) sheepdog to keep it from falling into the wrong hands. The Disney-like plot, featuring enemy agents and invisibility may appeal to youngsters. **90m/C VHS, Beta.** *IT GE SP* Dean Jones, Ingeborg Schoener, Gastone Moschin; ***D:*** Anthony (Antonio Margheriti) Dawson. *NO*

Mr. Sycamore 𝄞½ **1974** A sappy mail carrier escapes his badgering wife by sprouting into a tree. A potentially whimsical piece that wilts. **90m/C VHS, Beta.** Jason Robards Jr., Jean Simmons, Sandy Dennis; ***D:*** Pancho Kohner; ***M:*** Maurice Jarre. *WOV*

Mr. Walkie Talkie 𝄞𝄞 **1952** Tired of a sargeant's jabber-jaws, a soldier requests to be relocated to the front lines, only to find his catty comrade has followed. Set during the Korean War and featuring some truly amusing escapades set between the lulls in the war. **65m/B VHS, Beta, LV.** William Tracy, Joseph Sawyer; ***D:*** Fred Guiol. *NO*

Mr. Winkle Goes to War 𝄞𝄞 **1944** A weak, nerdy former banker is drafted for service during WWII and proves himself a hero by bulldozing a Japanese foxhole. Bits of genuine war footage add a measure of realism to an otherwise banal flag-waving comedy that is based on a novel by Theodore Pratt. **80m/B VHS, Beta.** Edward G. Robinson, Ruth Warrick, Richard Lane, Robert Armstrong; ***D:*** Alfred E. Green. *COL*

Mr. Wise Guy 𝄞𝄞 **1942** The East Side Kids break out of reform school to clear one of the Kids' brother of a murder charge. Typical pre-Bowery Boys vehicle. **70m/B VHS, Beta.** Leo Gorcey, Huntz Hall, Billy Gilbert, Guinn "Big Boy" Williams, Benny Rubin, Douglas Fowley, Ann Doran, Jack Mulhall, Warren Hymer, David Gorcey; ***D:*** William Nigh. *NOS, DVT, HEG*

Mr. Wonderful 𝄞𝄞½ **1993 (PG-13)** Bittersweet (rather than purely romantic) look at love and romance. Divorced Con Ed worker Gus (Dillon) is hard up for cash and tries to marry off ex-wife Lee (Sciorra) so he can use her alimony to invest in a bowling alley with his buddies. Routine flick's saved by the cast, who manage to bring a small measure of believability to a transparent plot. Minghella was a hit with his first film "Truly, Madly, Deeply" but may find that fame can be fleeting with this second effort. **99m/C VHS, Beta, LV.** Matt Dillon, Annabella Sciorra, William Hurt, Mary-Louise Parker, Luis Guzman, Dan Hedaya, Vincent D'Onofrio; ***D:*** Anthony Minghella; ***W:*** Amy Schor, Vicki Polon; ***M:*** Michael Gore. *WAR*

Mr. Wong, Detective 𝄞𝄞 **1938** The first in the Mr. Wong series, the cunning detective traps a killer who feigns guilt to throw suspicion away from himself. The plot is loaded with the usual twists and villains. However, Karloff is a standout. **69m/B VHS, Beta.** Boris Karloff, Grant Withers; ***D:*** William Nigh. *NOS, MRV, HHT*

Mr. Wong in Chinatown 𝄞½ **1939** Third of the Mr. Wong series finds James Lee Wong investigating the murder of a wealthy Chinese woman. She had been helping to fund the purchase of airplanes to equip China in its 1930s' struggle with Japan. **70m/B VHS.** Boris Karloff, Grant Withers, William Royle, Marjorie Reynolds, Peter George Lynn, Lotus Long, Richard Loo; ***D:*** William Nigh. *VYY, MRV, SNC*

Mr. Write 𝄞𝄞 **1992 (PG-13)** Modest advertising satire mixed with romance. Aspiring writer Charlie (Reiser) decides to make some money by acting in commercials. He falls for ad exec Nicole (Tuck) but there are some complications to be overcome first, including her dim bulb boyfriend and obnoxious father. Adapted from the play by Howard J. Morris. **89m/C VHS, LV.** Paul Reiser, Jessica Tuck, Doug Davidson, Martin Mull, Wendie Jo Sperber, Eddie Barth, Darryl M. Bell, Tom Wilson, Jane Leeves, Calvert Deforest; ***D:*** Charles Loventhal; ***W:*** Howard J. Morris. *MCA*

Mr. Wrong 𝄞𝄞 **1995 (PG-13)** In her feature film debut, DeGeneres plays Martha, a thirtysomething single woman with wacky friends who's being pressured by parents toward marriage while having little luck in the dating scene. Hmm...sounds familiar. Pullman plays Whitman, her dreamboat who quickly turns into the Titanic. Along the relationship road to ruin she is forced to deal with bad poetry, charades and...gum in her hair!! The usually entertaining DeGeneres is given little to do but react lamely to the wild events going on around her. Those that have had an experience with "the ex that would not go away" might want to rent something more calming, such as "Psycho." **92m/C VHS.** Ellen DeGeneres, Bill Pullman, Joan Cusack, Dean Stockwell, Joan Plowright, John Livingston, Robert Goulet, Ellen Cleghorne, Brad Henke, Polly Holliday, Briant Wells; ***D:*** Nick Castle; ***W:*** Chris Matheson, Kerry Ehrin, Craig Munson; ***C:*** John Schwartzman; ***M:*** Craig Safan. *TOU*

Mistral's Daughter 𝄞½ **1984** Frothy miniseries, based on the Judith Krantz novel, about a French artist and his relationship with three beautiful women. Formulaic TV melodrama offers sexual scenes and revealing glimpses. Produced, like other Krantz miniseries, by author's hubby, Steve. **390m/C VHS, Beta.** Stefanie Powers, Lee Remick, Stacy Keach, Robert Urich, Timothy Dalton; ***D:*** Douglas Hickox; ***M:*** Vladimir Cosma. *LIV*

Mistress 𝄞𝄞𝄞 *Wild Geese* **1953** A classic Japanese period piece about an innocent woman who believes she's married to a ruthless industrialist, only to find he is already married and she is but his mistress. Her love for a medical student unleashes tragedy. Subtly moving in a low-key way; starkly beautiful in black and white. In Japanese, with English subtitles. **106m/B VHS, Beta.** *JP* Hideko Takamine, Hiroshi Akutagawa; ***D:*** Shiro Toyoda. *SUE, INJ*

Mistress 𝄞½ **1987** Weepy made-for-television melodrama about a woman who makes a living as a mistress. When her lover dies, she must learn to stand on her own two feet. **96m/C VHS.** Victoria Principal, Alan Rachins, Don Murray; ***D:*** Michael Tuchner; ***M:*** Michael Convertino. *REP*

Mistress 𝄞𝄞 **1991 (R)** A weak script does in a formidable cast in a behind-the-scenes look at movie making. Wuhl plays Marvin Landisman, a failed director/screenwriter, who's approached by has-been producer Jack Roth (Landau) who says he's found a backer to finance a movie from one of Marvin's old scripts. It turns out Roth has three men (De Niro, Aiello, and Wallach) ready to finance the film as long as each of their mistresses, who all have acting ambitions, gets the starring role. Double-dealing at a bargain basement level sets up the rest of this lifeless comedy. **100m/C VHS, LV.** Robert Wuhl, Martin Landau, Robert De Niro, Eli Wallach, Danny Aiello, Sheryl Lee Ralph, Jean Smart, Tuesday Weld, Jace Alexander, Laurie Metcalf; ***Cameos:*** Christopher Walken, Ernest Borgnine; ***D:*** Barry Primus; ***W:*** J.F. Lawton, Barry Primus. *LIV, PMS*

Mistress of the Apes *Woof!* **1979 (R)** A woman searches for her missing husband in Africa with a group of scientists and discovers a tribe of near-men, who may be the missing link in evolution (or perhaps, a professional football team). Into their little group she is accepted, becoming their queen. Buchanan earned his reputation as a maker of horrible films honestly. Includes the songs "Mistress of the Apes" and "Ape Lady." **88m/C VHS, Beta.** Jenny Neumann, Barbara Leigh, Garth Pillsbury, Walt Robin, Stuart Lancaster, Suzy Mandel; ***D:*** Larry Buchanan; ***W:*** Larry Buchanan. *MON*

Mistress of the World 𝄞𝄞 **1959** A scientist, aided by Swedish Intelligence agent Ventura, works to protect his gravity-altering invention from Chinese agents. Partly based on a German serial from the silent film era, but not up to director Dieterle's usual fare. A must-see for Ventura fans and Mabuse mavens. **107m/C VHS, Beta.** Martha Hyer, Micheline Presle, Gino Cervi, Lino Ventura, Sabu, Wolfgang Preiss; ***D:*** William Dieterle. *VMK*

Mistress Pamela 𝄞½ **1974 (R)** When young Pamela goes to work in the household of handsome Lord Devonish, he sets about in wild pursuit of her virginity. Loosely based on the 1740 work "Pamela" by Samuel Richardson, considered the first modern English novel. Read the book unless you only have 95 minutes to spend finding out who gets what. **95m/C VHS, Beta.** Anne Michelle, Julian Barnes, Anna Quayle, Rosemary Dunham; ***D:*** Jim O'Connor. *NO*

Misty 𝄞𝄞½ **1961** Ladd and Smith are two kids who capture a wild pony and teach it to run around in circles and step over things. Based on Marguerite Henry's bestselling "Misty of Chincoteague," and filmed on an island off the coast of Virginia. **92m/C VHS.** David Ladd, Arthur O'Connell, Pam Smith; ***D:*** James B. Clark. *PAR, WAX, FCT*

Misunderstood 𝄞𝄞½ **1984 (PG)** A former black market merchant has to learn how to relate to his sons after his wife dies. The father, now a legitimate businessman, is more concerned with running his shipping business than growing closer to his boys. Fine acting can't overcome a transparent plot. **92m/C VHS, Beta.** Gene Hackman, Susan Anspach, Henry Thomas, Rip Torn, Huckleberry Fox; ***D:*** Jerry Schatzberg; ***C:*** Pasqualino de Santis. *MGM*

Misunderstood **1987** A father learns his lonely son is full of love and sensitivity when a tragedy reveals that it is this son who takes the blame for all the wrongs his brother commits. **101m/C VHS, Beta.** Anthony Quayle, Stefano Colagrande, Simone Gianozzi, John Sharp; ***D:*** Luigi Comencini. *IMP*

Mitchell **1975 (R)** Tough cop battles drug traffic and insipid script. Big screen release with that certain TV look. **90m/C VHS.** Joe Don Baker, Linda Evans, Martin Balsam, John Saxon, Merlin Olsen, Harold J. Stone; ***D:*** Andrew V. McLaglen. *VTR*

Mixed Blood ½ **1984 (R)** From the renowned underground film-maker, a dark comedy that examines the seedy drug subculture in New York. Violent, fast, and funny. **98m/C VHS, Beta.** Marilia Pera, Richard Vlacia, Linda Kerridge, Geraldine Smith, Angel David; ***D:*** Paul Morrissey; ***W:*** Paul Morrissey. *MED*

Mixed Nuts *Lifesavers* **1994 (PG-13)** Misfits man a suicide hotline on Christmas Eve in this unfunny, pathetic comedy that's a real downer. Director/writer Ephron (along with her co-writer sister Delia) try way too hard to fashion a hip, racy, madcap farce reminiscent of the screwball comedies that Hollywood churned out in the 1930s and '40s. Film never finds its style and the story line is very weak. Most of the performances are over the top, although Martin, Shandling, and Kahn are good for a few amusing scenes. Ephron and the cast are capable of doing so much better, it's a shame their talents are virtually wasted here. Adapted from the French film "Le Pere Noel Est Une Ordure." **97m/C VHS, LV.** Steve Martin, Madeline Kahn, Robert Klein, Anthony LaPaglia, Juliette Lewis, Rob Reiner, Adam Sandler, Rita Wilson, Garry Shandling, Liev Schreiber; ***D:*** Nora Ephron; ***W:*** Nora Ephron, Delia Ephron; ***M:*** George Fenton. *COL*

M'Lady's Court **198?** A lawyer searching for an heiress in a convent of lusty maidens has loads of fun. None too captivating. **92m/C VHS, Beta.** Sonia Jeanine, Maja Hoppe. *MED*

Mo' Better Blues ½ **1990 (R)** Not one of his more cohesive or compelling works, Lee's fourth feature is on the surface a backstage jazz biopic. But all Lee features are vitally concerned with complicated racial issues, and though subtle, this is no exception. Bleek Gilliam is a handsome, accomplished jazz trumpeter who divides his limited extra-curricular time between Clarke (newcomer Williams) and Indigo (junior Lee sibling Joie). What's interesting is not so much the story of self-interested musician and ladies' man Gilliam, but the subtle racial issues his life draws into focus. The Branford Marsalis Quartet provides the music for Bleek's group, scored by Lee's dad Bill (on whose life the script is loosely based). **129m/C VHS, Beta, LV.** Denzel Washington, Spike Lee, Joie Lee, Wesley Snipes, Cynda Williams, Giancarlo Esposito, Robin Harris, Bill Nunn, John Turturro, Dick Anthony Williams, Ruben Blades, Nicholas Turturro, Samuel L. Jackson, Abbey Lincoln, Tracy C. Johns, Joe Seneca; ***D:*** Spike Lee; ***W:*** Spike Lee; ***M:*** Branford Marsalis, Bill Lee. *MCA, FCT*

Mo' Money ½ **1992 (R)** Damon Wayans is a small-time con-artist who is inspired to go straight by a beautiful woman (Dash). He lands a job at the credit card company she works for, but temptation overcomes him, he swipes some plastic, and the scamming begins anew. With the help of his younger brother (played by real-life younger brother Marlon), they get involved in an even bigger, more dangerous scam being operated by the credit card company's head of security. Crude formula comedy driven by energetic, inventive performances by the brothers Wayans. Needless to say, will be especially enjoyed by fans of TV's "In Living Color." **97m/C VHS, Beta, LV, 8mm.** Damon Wayans, Marlon Wayans, Stacey Dash, Joe Santos, John Diehl, Harry J. Lennix, Mark Beltzman, Quincy Wong, Larry Brandenburg, Almayvonne; ***D:*** Peter Macdonald; ***W:*** Damon Wayans; ***C:*** Don Burgess; ***M:*** Jay Gruska. *COL*

Moana, a Romance of the Golden Age ½ **1926** An early look through American eyes at the society of the people of Samoa, in the Pacific Islands. Picturesque successor to Flaherty's "Nanook of the North." **76m/B VHS.** Ta'avale, Fa'amgase, Moana; ***D:*** Robert Flaherty. *GPV, FCT*

Mob Boss **1990 (R)** Gangster films spoof starring Hickey as the head of a successful California crime ring. When his beautiful wife conspires to have him killed, he is left just breaths away from his demise. He calls his nerdy son to his bedside to ask him to take over the family business. But this kid thinks that money laundering requires detergent! Take this one down for a walk by the river in its new cement shoes. **93m/C VHS.** Eddie Dezen, Morgan Fairchild, William Hickey, Stuart Whitman; ***D:*** Fred Olen Ray. *VMK*

Mob Story ½ **1990 (R)** Vernon stars as a big-wig mob boss on the run from the government and a few of his "closest" friends. He plans to disappear into Canada, but if his girl (Kidder) and best friend (Waxman) find him first he'll be traveling in a body-bag. Very silly, but fun. **98m/C VHS, Beta, LV.** John Vernon, Margot Kidder, Al Waxman, Kate Vernon; ***D:*** Gabriel Markiw, Jancarlo Markiw. *IME*

Mob War *Woof!* **1978** A bloody Mafia adventure in which a sausage factory plays a large role. **102m/C VHS, Beta, LV.** *VCD*

Mob War ½ **1988 (R)** A war breaks out between the head of New York's underworld and a media genius. After deciding to become partners, the "family" tries to take over. For fun, count how many times the word "respect" pops up in the script. Tries hard but fails. **96m/C VHS, Beta.** John Christian, David Henry Keller, Jake La Motta, Johnny Stumper; ***D:*** J. Christian Ingvordsen. *MCG*

Mobsters ½ **1991 (R)** It sounded like a great idea, casting the hottest young actors of the '90s as youthful racketeers "Lucky" Luciano, Meyer Lansky, Bugsy Siegel, and Frank Costello. But it would take an FBI probe to straighten out the blood-choked plot, as the pals' loyalties get tested the hard way in a dismembered narrative. Sicker than the violence is a seeming endorsement of the glamorous hoods. **104m/C VHS, Beta, LV.** Christian Slater, Patrick Dempsey, Richard Grieco, Costas Mandylor, Anthony Quinn, F. Murray Abraham, Lara Flynn Boyle, Michael Gambon, Christopher Penn; ***D:*** Michael Karbelnikoff; ***W:*** Nicholas Kazan; ***C:*** Lajos Koltai. *MCA, CCB*

Moby Dick **1956** This adaptation of Herman Melville's high seas saga features Peck as Captain Ahab. His obsession with desire for revenge upon the great white whale, Moby Dick, isn't always believable, but the moments that click, however, make the film more than worthwhile. **116m/C VHS, Beta, LV.** Gregory Peck, Richard Basehart, Orson Welles, Leo Genn, Harry Andrews, Friedrich Ledebur; ***D:*** John Huston; ***W:*** Ray Bradbury, John Huston; ***C:*** Oswald Morris. National Board of Review Awards '56: 10 Best Films of the Year, Best Director (Huston). *FOX, BMV, HMV*

Mockery ½ **1927** Chaney plays a peasant working for a Russian countess. He becomes involved in a peasant revolution against the rich and threatens the countess but eventually saves her from the mob. **75m/B VHS.** Lon Chaney Sr., Barbara Bedford, Ricardo Cortez, Emily Fitzroy; ***D:*** Benjamin Christiansen. *FCT*

The Mod Squad **1968** The ultimate sixties series features a trio of young misfits who are recruited by a gruff police captain in Southern California. Their undercover assignments take them into the counter-culture. The series was created by former L.A. police officer Bud Ruskin, and was based on his own experiences. Two episodes per tape: "Teeth of the Barracuda" explains the formation of the Mod Squad, while "Mother of Sorrow" finds a generation gap leading to murder. Additional episodes are available. **60m/C VHS.** Michael Cole, Clarence Williams III, Peggy Lipton, Tige Andrews, Lee Grant, Richard Dreyfuss. *MOV*

Model Behavior ½ **1982** Fresh from college, an aspiring photographer pines for a glamorous model. **86m/C VHS, Beta.** Richard Bekins, Bruce Lyons, Cindy Harrel; ***D:*** Bud Gardner. *LIV*

Model by Day ½ **1994 (R)** When New York model Janssen's father is murdered, she takes up martial arts training and becomes the vengeful "Lady X." Then she becomes the prime suspect in a murder and finds herself falling for a plainsclothes cop. Fair amount of action, somewhat less exploitive than usual for the genre. **89m/C VHS, Beta, LV.** Famke Janssen, Stephen Shellan, Shannon Tweed, Sean Young; ***D:*** Christian Duguay. *ACA*

Modern Girls ½ **1986 (PG-13)** Teen comedy about three bubble-headed LA rock groupies and their various wild adventures during a single night on the town. Surprising in that the three lead actresses waste their talents in this lesson in exploitation. Bruce Springsteen's younger sister portrays a drug user. **82m/C VHS, Beta, LV.** Cynthia Gibb, Daphne Zuniga, Virginia Madsen; ***D:*** Jerry Kramer; ***W:*** Laurie Craig; ***M:*** Eddie Arkin. *PAR*

Modern Love **1990 (R)** An average slob realizes that marriage, fatherhood and in-law-ship isn't quite what he expected. Benson stars, directs and produces as well as co-starring with real-life wife DeVito. A plotless hodgepodge of bits that were more successful in "Look Who's Talking" and "Parenthood." **89m/C VHS, Beta.** Robby Benson, Karla DeVito, Rue McClanahan, Kaye Ballard, Frankie Valli, Cliff Bemis, Louise Lasser, Burt Reynolds, Lyric Benson; ***D:*** Robby Benson; ***W:*** Robby Benson. *NO*

Modern Problems **1981 (PG)** A man involved in a nuclear accident discovers he has acquired telekinetic powers, which he uses to turn the tables on his professional and romantic rivals. A fine cast but an unsuccessful fission trip. **93m/C VHS, Beta.** Chevy Chase, Patti D'Arbanville, Mary Kay Place, Brian Doyle-Murray, Nell Carter, Dabney Coleman; ***D:*** Ken Shapiro. *FOX*

Modern Romance **1981 (R)** The romantic misadventures of a neurotic film editor who is hopelessly in love with his girlfriend but can't seem to maintain a normal relationship with her. Smart and hilarious at times and always simmering with anxiety. Offers an honest look at relationships as well as an accurate portrait of filmmaking. **102m/C VHS, Beta, LV.** Albert Brooks, Kathryn Harrold, Bruno Kirby, George Kennedy, James L. Brooks, Bob Einstein; ***D:*** Albert Brooks; ***W:*** Albert Brooks, Monica Johnson. *COL*

Modern Times **1936** This "mostly" silent film finds Chaplin playing a factory worker who goes crazy from his repetitious job on an assembly line and his boss' demands for greater speed and efficiency. Ultimately encompassing the tyranny of machine over man, this cinematic masterpiece has more relevance today than ever. Chaplin wrote the musical score which incorporates the tune "Smile." Look for a young Gloria De Haven as one of Goddard's sisters; she's the real-life daughter of Chaplin's assistant director. **87m/B VHS, Beta, LV.** Charlie Chaplin, Paulette Goddard, Henry Bergman, Stanley Sandford, Gloria De Haven, Chester Conklin; ***D:*** Charlie Chaplin; ***W:*** Charlie Chaplin; ***M:*** Charlie Chaplin. National Board of Review Awards '36: 10 Best Films of the Year. *FOX, HMV*

The Moderns **1988 (R)** One of the quirkier directors around, this time Rudolph tries a comedic period piece about the avant-garde art society of 1920s Paris. Fleshed out with some familiar characters (Ernest Hemingway, Gertrude Stein) and some strange art-world types. The tone is not consistently funny but, instead, romantic as the main characters clash over art and love. **126m/C VHS, Beta, LV, 8mm.** Keith Carradine, Linda Fiorentino, John Lone, Genevieve Bujold, Geraldine Chaplin, Wallace Shawn, Kevin J. O'Connor; ***D:*** Alan Rudolph; ***W:*** Alan Rudolph; ***M:*** Mark Isham. Los Angeles Film Critics Association Awards '88: Best Supporting Actress (Bujold). *SUE, NLC*

Modigliani ½ *Montparnasse 19; The Lovers of Montparnasse; Modigliani of Montparnasse* **1958** Life of dissolute 19th-century painter Modigliani (Philipe), which tracks his affairs with British poet Beatrice Hastings (Palmer) and later mistress Jeanne (Aimee), who commits suicide shortly before his death. Female performances make up for the lackluster lead. Becker inherited the film from director Max Ophuls, who co-wrote the screenplay but who died before the start of production. In French with English subtitles. **110m/B VHS.** *FR* Gerard Philipe, Lilli Palmer, Anouk Aimee, Gerard Sety, Lino Ventura, Lila Kedrova, Lea Padovani; ***D:*** Jacques Becker; ***W:*** Max Ophuls, Henri Jeanson, Jacques Becker. *FCT*

Mogambo ☙☙☙ **1953** Remake of "Red Dust," this is the steamy story of a love triangle between an African game hunter, a proper British lady, and an American showgirl in the jungles of Kenya. **115m/C VHS, Beta.** Clark Gable, Ava Gardner, Grace Kelly; ***D:*** John Ford; ***C:*** Robert L. Surtees. Golden Globe Awards '54: Best Supporting Actress (Kelly); National Board of Review Awards '53: 10 Best Films of the Year; Nominations: Academy Awards '53: Best Actress (Gardner), Best Supporting Actress (Kelly). *MGM, FCT, CCB*

Mohammed: Messenger of God ☙☙ *The Message; Al-Ris-Alah* **1977 (PG)** Sprawling saga of the genesis of the religion of Islam, with Quinn portraying Mohammad's uncle, Hamza, an honored warrior. The story behind the movie might prove much more successful as a sequel than did the movie itself. The filming itself created a religious controversy. **180m/C VHS.** *GB* Damien Thomas, Anthony Quinn, Irene Papas, Michael Ansara, Johnny Sekka, Michael Forest, Neville Jason; ***D:*** Moustapha Akkad; ***C:*** Jack Hildyard; ***M:*** Maurice Jarre. Nominations: Academy Awards '77: Best Original Score. *NO*

Mohawk ☙½ **1956** A cowboy and his Indian maiden try to stop a war between Indian tribes and fanatical landowners. **80m/C VHS, Beta.** Rita Gam, Neville Brand, Scott Brady, Lori Nelson; ***D:*** Kurt Neumann; ***C:*** Karl Struss. *NOS, MRV, GEM*

Mole Men against the Son of Hercules ☙ **1961** Italian muscleman Maciste battles the pale-skinned denizens of an underground city. **?m/C VHS, Beta.** *IT* Mark Forest. *SNC*

The Mole People ☙ **1956** A really bad fifties creature feature which finds two archeologists accidentally discovering an underground civilization of albinos who shun all forms of light. They've also enslaved the local populace of half-human, half-mole creatures who decide to help the good guys escape by rising up in a revolt against their evil masters. When the weapon of choice is a flashlight you know not to expect much. **78m/B VHS.** John Agar, Cynthia Patrick, Hugh Beaumont, Alan Napier, Nestor Paiva, Phil Chambers; ***D:*** Virgil W. Vogel; ***W:*** Laszlo Gorog. *MCA*

Moll Flanders ☙☙☙ **1996 (PG-13)** Writer/director Densham takes only the title character and the 18th-century London setting from Daniel Defoe's 1722 novel in telling of spirited heroine Moll Flanders' (Wright) life. Orphaned Moll eventually finds herself working at the brothel of greedy, scheming Mrs. Allworthy (Channing). Her life as a prostitute leads her to drink and near suicide—despite the unwavering friendship of Hibble (Freeman), Allworthy's dignified servant—until she falls for an impoverished artist (Lynch) and briefly finds happiness. Wright's heartfelt performance holds everything together (with help from a talented supporting cast and a strong story). **123m/C VHS.** Robin Wright, Morgan Freeman, Stockard Channing, John Lynch, Brenda Fricker, Aisling Corcoran, Geraldine James, Jim Sheridan, Jeremy Brett, Britta Smith, Ger Ryan; ***D:*** Pen Densham; ***W:*** Pen Densham; ***C:*** David Tattersall; ***M:*** Mark Mancina. *NYR*

Molly and Gina ☙☙ **1994 (R)** The very different lives of Molly and Gina intersect suddenly when their boyfriends are killed in the street by gunfire. They are drawn into the underworld of gun-runners and violence, as they seek justice for the men they loved. **90m/C VHS.** Frances Fisher, Natasha Gregson Wagner, Bruce Weitz, Stella Stevens, Peter Fonda; ***D:*** Paul Leder; ***W:*** Reuben Leder; ***M:*** Dana Walden. *APX*

Molly & Lawless John ☙☙ **1972** Average western, with Miles the wife of a sadistic sheriff who helps a prisoner escape the gallows so they can run away together. Enough cliches for the whole family to enjoy. **90m/C VHS, Beta.** Sam Elliott, Vera Miles; ***D:*** Gary Nelson. *NO*

Molly Maguires ☙☙½ **1970 (PG)** Dramatization based on a true story, concerns a group of miners called the Molly Maguires who resort to using terrorist tactics in their fight for better working conditions during the Pennsylvania Irish coal mining rebellion in the 1870s. During their reign of terror, the Mollies are infiltrated by a Pinkerton detective who they mistakenly believe is a new recruit. It has its moments but never fully succeeds. Returned less than fifteen percent of its initial eleven million dollar investment. **123m/C VHS, Beta.** Sean Connery, Richard Harris, Samantha Eggar, Frank Finlay; ***D:*** Martin Ritt; ***W:*** Walter Bernstein; ***C:*** James Wong Howe; ***M:*** Henry Mancini. Nominations: Academy Awards '70: Best Art Direction/Set Decoration. *PAR, CCB*

Mom *Woof!* **1989 (R)** When his mother is bitten by a flesh-eater, Clay Dwyer is at a loss as to what to do. How do you tell your own mother that she must be destroyed, lest she continue to devour human flesh? A campy horror/comedy. **95m/C VHS, LV.** Mark Thomas Miller, Art Evans, Mary McDonough, Jeanne Bates, Brion James, Stella Stevens, Claudia Christian; ***D:*** Patrick Rand. *COL*

Mom & Dad ☙☙ **1947** An innocent young girl's one night of passion leads to an unwanted pregnancy. Stock footage of childbirth and a lecture on the evils of syphilis concludes this campy schlock that features the national anthem. Banned or denied release for years, this movie is now a cult favorite for its time-capsule glimpse at conventional 1940s sexual attitudes. **97m/B VHS, Beta.** Hardie Albright, Sarah Blake, George Eldridge, June Carlson, Jimmy Clark, Bob Lowell; ***D:*** William Beaudine. *VDM*

Mom and Dad Save the World ☙½ **1992 (PG)** A suburban housewife (Garr) is transported along with her husband in the family station wagon to the planet Spengo, ruled by King Tod Spengo (Lovitz), who has fallen in love with her and wants to save her from his plans to blow up Earth. While trying to prevent the king from marrying her and killing him, Garr and Jones wind up in many goofy situations and wind up saving the Earth from its imminent doom. Uninspired comedy just isn't funny, and the excellent cast is misused, especially Idle and Shawn. Save this one for the kiddies. **87m/C VHS, LV.** Teri Garr, Jeffrey Jones, Jon Lovitz, Eric Idle, Wallace Shawn, Dwier Brown, Kathy Ireland, Thalmus Rasulala; ***D:*** Greg Beeman; ***M:*** Jerry Goldsmith. *HBO*

Mom, the Wolfman and Me ☙☙½ **1980** An 11-year-old girl arranges and manages the love affair of her mother, an ultra-liberated photographer, and an unemployed teacher, who is also the owner of an Irish wolfhound. Charming adaptation of a novel by Norma Klein. **100m/C VHS, Beta.** Patty Duke, David Birney, Danielle Brisebois, Keenan Wynn, Viveca Lindfors, John Lithgow; ***D:*** Edmond Levy. *TLF*

Moment in Time ☙ **1984** A romantic novel on tape, about a guy, a girl, and their various troubles. **60m/C Beta.** Jean Simmons. *PSM*

Mommie Dearest ☙☙ **1981 (PG)** Film based on Christina Crawford's memoirs of her incredibly abusive and violent childhood at the hands of her adoptive mother, actress Joan Crawford. The story is controversial and sometimes trashy, but fairly well done nevertheless. **129m/C VHS, Beta, LV.** Faye Dunaway, Diana Scarwid, Steve Forrest, Mara Hobel, Rutanya Alda, Harry Goz, Howard da Silva; ***D:*** Frank Perry; ***W:*** Robert Getchell; ***M:*** Henry Mancini. Golden Raspberry Awards '81: Worst Picture, Worst Actress (Dunaway), Worst Supporting Actor (Forrest), Worst Supporting Actress (Scarwid), Worst Screenplay. *PAR*

Mommy ☙☙½ **1995** Schoolteacher is stalked by murderous mom who'll do anything for her daughter. Mommy McCormack was the original "Bad Seed" child. Filmed in Muscatine, Iowa. **89m/C VHS.** Patty McCormack, Majel Barrett, Jason Miller, Brinke Stevens, Rachel Lemieux, Mickey Spillane, Michael Cornelison, Sarah Jane Miller; ***D:*** Max Allan Collins; ***W:*** Max Allan Collins; ***C:*** Phillip W. Dingeldein; ***M:*** Richard Lowry. *MNC*

Mon Oncle ☙☙☙☙ *My Uncle; My Uncle, Mr. Hulot* **1958** Tati's celebrated comedy contrasts the simple life of Monsieur Hulot with the technologically complicated life of his family when he aids his nephew in war against his parents' ultramodern, push-button home. An easygoing, delightful comedy, this is the director's first piece in color. Sequel to "Mr. Hulot's Holiday," followed by "Playtime." In French with English subtitles. **110m/C VHS, Beta, LV, 8mm.** *FR* Jacques Tati, Jean-Pierre Zola, Adrienne Serrantie, Alain Bacourt; ***D:*** Jacques Tati; ***C:*** Jean Bourgoin. Academy Awards '58: Best Foreign Language Film; Cannes Film Festival '58: Grand Jury Prize; National Board of Review Awards '58: 5 Best Foreign Films of the Year; New York Film Critics Awards '58: Best Foreign Film. *HMV, MRV, SUE*

Mon Oncle Antoine ☙☙☙½ **1971** A splendid tale of young Benoit, who learns about life from a surprisingly compassionate uncle, who works as everything from undertaker to grocer in the depressed area where they live. **104m/C VHS.** *CA* Jean Duceppe, Olivette Thibault; ***D:*** Claude Jutra. *HMV, FLI, APD*

Mon Oncle D'Amerique ☙☙☙½ *Les Somnambules* **1980 (PG)** Three French characters are followed as they try to find success of varying kinds in Paris, interspersed with ironic lectures by Prof. Henri Laborit about the biology that impels human behavior. Their disappointments lead them to dream of a legendary American uncle, who could make their desires come true. An acclaimed, witty comedy by former Nouvelle Vague filmmaker, dubbed into English. **123m/C VHS, Beta.** *FR* Gerard Depardieu, Nicole Garcia, Roger-Pierre, Marie DuBois; ***D:*** Alain Resnais; ***W:*** Jean Gruault. Cannes Film Festival '80: Grand Jury Prize; New York Film Critics Awards '80: Best Foreign Film; Nominations: Academy Awards '80: Best Original Screenplay; Cannes Film Festival '80: Best Film. *NYF, BTV*

Mona Lisa ☙☙☙½ **1986 (R)** Jordan's wonderful, sad, sensitive story of a romantic, small-time hood who gets personally involved with the welfare and bad company of the high-priced whore he's been hired to chauffeur. Hoskins is especially touching and Caine is chilling as a suave gangster. Fine film debut for Tyson. Brilliantly filmed and critically lauded. **104m/C VHS, Beta, LV.** *GB* Bob Hoskins, Cathy Tyson, Michael Caine, Clarke Peters, Kate Hardie, Robbie Coltrane, Zoe Nathenson, Sammi Davis, Rod Bedall, Joe Brown, Pauline Melville; ***D:*** Neil Jordan; ***W:*** Neil Jordan; ***M:*** Michael Kamen. British Academy Awards '86: Best Actor (Hoskins); Cannes Film Festival '86: Best Actor (Hoskins); Golden Globe Awards '87: Best Actor—Drama (Hoskins); Los Angeles Film Critics Association Awards '86: Best Actor (Hoskins), Best Supporting Actress (Tyson); National Society of Film Critics Awards '86: Best Actor (Hoskins); Nominations: Academy Awards '86: Best Actor (Hoskins). *VTR*

Monaco Forever ☙☙ **1983** An enigmatic American meets a mysterious Frenchwoman and they set off on a string of unusual romantic adventures. Set around the 1956 marriage of Grace Kelly to Prince Rainier of Monaco. Film debut of Van Damme. **79m/C VHS.** Charles Pitt, Martha Farris, Sydney Lassick, Jean-Claude Van Damme; ***D:*** William A. Levey; ***W:*** C. William Pitt, William A. Levey. *VHE, FCT*

Mondo Balardo ☙ **1964** Translated as "Crazy World," this is crude sensationalism masked as a horror story. Karloff guides the viewer through a curious mixture of society's fringe elements. A loosely connected series of sketches includes portraits of a reincarnated Rudolph Valentino, practitioners of transvestism, Roman coke whores, and an Italian-Japanese rock 'n roll midget (Drago) in director Montero's unusual vision of an anti-paradise. Includes standard lesbian club scene. Volume 11 of Frank Henenlotter's Sexy Shockers. **86m/C VHS.** Franz Drago; ***D:*** Robert Montero; ***W:*** Albert T. Viola. *SMW, TPV*

Mondo Cane ☙☙ **1963 (R)** A documentary showcasing the eccentricities of human behavior around the world, including cannibalism, pig killing and more. Dubbed in English. Inspired a rash of "shockumentaries" over the next several years. The song "More" made its debut in this film. **105m/C VHS, Beta.** *IT* ***D:*** Gualtiero Jacopetti. Nominations: Academy Awards '63: Best Song ("More"). *SNC, VDC, VDM*

Mondo Cane 2 🦴 *Mondo Pazzo* **1964 (R)** More documentary-like views of the oddities of mankind and ethnic rituals around the world. Enough, already. **94m/C VHS, Beta.** *IT* ***D:*** Gualtiero Jacopetti. *VDC, HHE, TPV*

Mondo Magic 🦴½ **1976** A compilation of tribal rituals offering viewers a look on the darker side of matters magical. **100m/C VHS, Beta.** ***D:*** Melvin Ashford. *NO*

Mondo Trasho *Woof!* **1969** A major trasho film of the last day in the life of a most unfortunate woman, complete with sex and violence. First full length effort from cult filmmaker Waters, who was also writer, producer, and editor. **95m/B VHS, Beta.** Divine, Mary Vivian Pearce, John Leisenring, Mink Stole, David Lochary, Chris Atkinson; ***D:*** John Waters; ***W:*** John Waters. *NO*

The Money 🦴🦴 **1975 (R)** The quest for money drives a young man to kidnap the child that his girlfriend is baby-sitting. Average but Workman's direction is right on the money. **88m/C VHS.** Laurence Luckinbill, Elizabeth Richards, Danny DeVito, Graham Beckel; ***D:*** Chuck Workman. *GHV, VTR*

Money for Nothing 🦴🦴 **1993 (R)** $1.2 million falls off a truck in the warehouse district of Philadelphia where a simple-minded unemployed longshoreman (Cusack) finds the chance of a lifetime. Indiscreetly leaving behind a trail of spending, he soon has a detective (Madsen) snooping around dangerously close. But he only digs himself deeper by enlisting the assistance of the mob to help him launder the money. At this point the film disintegrates into a limp diatribe on the injustice of capitalism on society's downtrodden. Mazar plays Joey's ex-girlfriend who double-times it back to the fold after his find. Based on a true story. **100m/C VHS, LV.** John Cusack, Michael Madsen, Benicio Del Toro, Michael Rapaport, Debi Mazar, Fionnula Flanagan, Maury Chaykin, James Gandolfini, Elizabeth Bracco, Ashleigh Dejon, Lenny Venito; ***D:*** Ramon Menendez; ***W:*** Ramon Menendez, Carol Sobieski, Tom Musca; ***M:*** Craig Safan. *TOU*

Money Madness 🦴🦴 **1947** Beaumont (Ward Cleaver) plays a taxi driver turned thief in this curiosity. **?m/C VHS.** Hugh Beaumont, Frances Rafferty. *SNC*

Money Movers 🦴🦴 **1978** Aussie thieves plan megabuck bank robbery but heist and plot go sour. An oft told tale based on a true story. Features early appearance from burly boy Brown. **94m/C VHS.** *AU* Terence Donovan, Ed Devereaux, Tony Bonner, Lucky Grills, Charles Tingwell, Candy Raymond, Bryan Brown, Alan Cassell; ***D:*** Bruce Beresford; ***W:*** Bruce Beresford. *IMP*

The Money Pit 🦴🦴 **1986 (PG)** A young yuppie couple encounter sundry problems when they attempt to renovate their newly purchased, seemingly self-destructive, Long Island home. However, the collapse of their home leads directly to the collapse of their relationship as well. Somewhat modeled after "Mr. Blandings Builds His Dream House." Hanks and Long fail to jell as partners and the many sight gags are on the predictable side. A Spielberg production. **91m/C VHS, Beta, LV.** Tom Hanks, Shelley Long, Alexander Godunov, Maureen Stapleton, Philip Bosco, Joe Mantegna, Josh Mostel; ***D:*** Richard Benjamin; ***C:*** Gordon Willis; ***M:*** Michel Colombier. *MCA*

Money to Burn 🦴🦴 **1983** Aging high school counselor and two senior citizens develop a plan to steal $50 million dollars from the Federal Reserve Bank. Harmless bit of fun. **90m/C VHS, Beta.** Jack Kruschen, Meegan King, David Wallace, Phillip Pine; ***D:*** Virginia Lively Stone. *NO*

Money to Burn 🦴½ **1994 (R)** Two buddies go off on a wild spending spree when $2 million in cash falls into their laps. Only one problem—a crazy cop who's determined to stop them squandering the money. **96m/C VHS, LV.** Chad McQueen, Don Swayze, Joe Estevez, Julie Strain, Sydney Lassick; ***D:*** John Sjogren; ***W:*** John Sjogren, Scott Ziehl. *NLC, COL*

Money Train 🦴½ **1995 (R)** Snipes and Harrelson team up again, this time as New York City transit cops (and foster brothers) who decide to rob the money train—a subway car that collects all the cash accrued from the transit system each day. To complicate matters, they're both in love with their new Latina partner (Lopez). Lame attempt to cash in on the Snipes and Harrelson chemistry leaves out one important ingredient—a competent script. The movie is almost over before the train actually becomes part of the plot line. Film came under criticism when it was blamed for a series of "copycat" arsons in which a New York City subway clerk was killed. **110m/C VHS, LV, 8mm.** Woody Harrelson, Wesley Snipes, Jennifer Lopez, Robert (Bobby) Blake, Chris Cooper, Joe Grifasi; ***D:*** Joseph Ruben; ***W:*** Doug Richardson, David Loughery; ***C:*** John Lindley; ***M:*** Mark Mancina. *COL*

The Moneytree 🦴½ **1993** A carefree would-be actor decides to make some money by harvesting a huge marijuana crop in the California hills, all the while fending off his girlfriend, the cops, and some wild boars. **92m/C VHS.** Christopher Dienstag; ***D:*** Alan Dienstag. *TPV*

A Mongolian Tale 🦴🦴 *Hei Ma* **1994** Nai Nai has raised her granddaughter Somiya and the abandoned Bayingbulag among the Mongolian steppes. Eventually, Bayingbulag leaves to get an education but promises to return and marry Somiya. Away three years, he comes back only to discover Somiya pregnant, so he takes off, finds success as a folk singer, and doesn't return for 12 years. Somiya now has a drunken husband, four sons, and an illegitimate 12-year-old daughter who is desperate for a father. Mongolian dialogue. Adapted by Chengzhi from his story "A Song of the Grassland." **105m/C VHS.** *CH HK* Narenhua, Tengger; ***D:*** Xie Fei; ***W:*** Zhang Chengzhi. Montreal World Film Festival '95: Best Director (Fei). *NYR*

The Mongols 🦴🦴½ *Les Mongols* **1960** Splashy Italian production has Genghis Khan's son repelling invading hordes while courting buxom princess. Pairing of Palance and Ekberg makes this one worthy of consideration. **105m/C VHS.** *IT FR* Jack Palance, Anita Ekberg, Antonella Lualdi, Franco Silva, Gianni "John" Garko, Roldano Lupi, Gabriella Pallotti; ***D:*** Andre de Toth, Leopoldo Savona, Riccardo (Robert Hampton) Freda. *SNC*

Mongrel *Woof!* **1983** El-cheapo kennel horror about a man who dreams he's a wild murderous mutt. His relief upon waking up is short-lived, however, when he discovers the people he killed in his dreams are actually dead. Flick will make you want to gnaw on a bone. **90m/C VHS, Beta.** Aldo Ray, Terry Evans; ***D:*** Robert Burns. *NO*

Monika 🦴🦴½ *Summer with Monika* **1952** Two teenagers who run away together for the summer find the winter brings more responsibility than they can handle when the girl becomes pregnant and gives birth. Lesser, early Bergman, sensitively directed, but dull. Adapted by Bergman from a Per Anders Fogelstrom novel. In Swedish with English subtitles. **96m/B VHS.** *SW* Harriet Andersson, Lars Ekborg, John Harryson, Georg Skarstedt, Dagmar Ebbesen, Ake Gronberg; ***D:*** Ingmar Bergman; ***W:*** Ingmar Bergman; ***M:*** Les Baxter. *HMV, CVC, TPV*

Monique 🦴 **1983** A sophisticated career woman is about to unleash a terrifying secret on her new husband. **96m/C VHS, Beta.** Florence Giorgetti, John Ferris. *NO*

Monkey Boy 🦴🦴½ **1990** Decent sci-fi horror from Britain, about a cunning human-ape hybrid that escapes from a genetics lab after massacring the staff. Not excessively gruesome or vulgar, and some sympathy is aroused for the killer mutant. Based on the novel "Chimera." **104m/C VHS, Beta.** John Lynch, Christine Kavanagh, Kenneth Cranham; ***D:*** Lawrence Gordon Clark. *PSM*

Monkey Business 🦴🦴🦴½ **1931** Marx Brothers run amok as stowaways on ocean liner. Fast-paced comedy provides seemingly endless amount of gags, quips, and pratfalls, including the fab four imitating Maurice Chevalier at Immigration. This film, incidentally, was the group's first to be written—by noted humorist Perelman—directly for the screen. **77m/B VHS, Beta, LV.** Groucho Marx, Harpo Marx, Chico Marx, Zeppo Marx, Thelma Todd, Ruth Hall, Harry Woods; ***D:*** Norman Z. McLeod. *MCA*

Monkey Business 🦴🦴🦴 **1952** A scientist invents a fountain-of-youth potion, a lab chimpanzee mistakenly dumps it into a water cooler, and then grown-ups start turning into adolescents. Top-flight crew occasionally labors in this screwball comedy, though comic moments shine. Monroe is the secretary sans skills, while absent-minded Grant and sexy wife Rogers race hormonally as teens. **97m/B VHS, Beta, LV.** Cary Grant, Ginger Rogers, Charles Coburn, Marilyn Monroe, Hugh Marlowe, Larry Keating, George Winslow; ***D:*** Howard Hawks; ***W:*** Ben Hecht, Charles Lederer, I.A.L. Diamond; ***C:*** Milton Krasner. *FOX*

Monkey Grip 🦴🦴🦴 **1982** An unmarried woman copes with parenthood and a drug-addicted boyfriend while working on the fringe of Australia's music business. Grim but provocative, based on Helen Graham's novel. **101m/C VHS.** *AU* Noni Hazlehurst, Colin Friels, Alice Garner, Harold Hopkins, Candy Raymond; ***D:*** Ken Cameron; ***W:*** Ken Cameron. Australian Film Institute '82: Best Actress (Hazlehurst). *SUE*

Monkey Hustle 🦴 **1977 (PG)** Vintage blaxploitation has trouble hustling laffs. The Man plans a super freeway through the ghetto, and law abiding do gooders join forces with territorial lords of vice to fight the project. Shot in the Windy City. **90m/C VHS.** Yaphet Kotto, Rudy Ray Moore, Rosalind Cash, Debbi Morgan, Thomas Carter; ***D:*** Arthur Marks. *ORI, FCT*

Monkey Shines 🦴🦴 *Monkey Shines: An Experiment in Fear* **1988 (R)** Based on the novel by Michael Stuart, this is a sick, scary yarn about a quadriplegic who is given a specially trained capuchin monkey as a helpmate. However, he soon finds that the beast is assuming and acting on his subconscious rages. **108m/C VHS, Beta, LV.** Jason Beghe, John Pankow, Melanie Parker, Christine Forrest, Stephen Root, Kate McNeil, Joyce Van Patten, Stanley Tucci, Janine Turner; ***D:*** George A. Romero; ***W:*** George A. Romero; ***M:*** David Shire. *ORI*

Monkey Trouble 🦴🦴½ **1994 (PG)** Lonely schoolgirl Birch is feeling abandoned when mom and stepdad shower attention on her new baby brother. Then a monkey trained as a pickpocket enters her life. Keitel is the organ grinder turned bad who must answer to the mob when the monkey scampers off to suburbia. Stakes a lot of its entertainment wallop on the considerable talents of the slippery-fingered monkey, who steals the show. Birch is amusing as the youngster caught in all sorts of uncomfortable situations. Formula abounds, but the milk and cookies set won't notice; fine family fare. **95m/C VHS, LV.** Thora Birch, Harvey Keitel, Mimi Rogers, Christopher McDonald; ***D:*** Franco Amurri; ***W:*** Franco Amurri, Stu Krieger; ***M:*** Mark Mancina. *COL*

Monkeys, Go Home! 🦴½ **1966** Dumb Disney yarn about young American who inherits a badly neglected French olive farm. When he brings in four chimpanzees to pick the olives, the local townspeople go on strike. People can be so sensitive. Based on "The Monkeys" by G. K. Wilkinson. Chevalier's last film appearance. **89m/C VHS, Beta.** Dean Jones, Yvette Mimieux, Maurice Chevalier, Clement Harari, Yvonne Constant; ***D:*** Andrew V. McLaglen; ***M:*** Robert F. Brunner. *DIS*

Monkey's Uncle 🦴½ **1965** A sequel to Disney's "The Misadventures of Merlin Jones" and featuring more bizarre antics and scientific hoopla, including chimps and a flying machine. **90m/C VHS, Beta.** Tommy Kirk, Annette Funicello, Leon Ames, Arthur O'Connell; ***D:*** Robert Stevenson; ***C:*** Edward Colman; ***M:*** Buddy Baker. *DIS*

The Monocle 🦴🦴 **1964** Steele plays a seductive villainess in this rare, spy/comedy thriller. **?m/C VHS.** *FR* Paul Meurisse, Barbara Steele, Marcel Dalio. *SNC*

Monolith 🦴🦴½ **1993 (R)** Tucker (Paxton) and Flynn (Frost) are unlikely partners on the LAPD. But they're teamed up on an unlikely case: a Russian scientist commits a seemingly senseless murder and is taken away by a mystery man (Hurt) before she can be interrogated. What the curious duo discover is a lethal alien force capable of posessing any living creature and whose objective is the destruction of the planet. **96m/C VHS, LV.** Bill Paxton, Lindsay Frost, John Hurt, Louis Gossett Jr.; ***D:*** John Eyres; ***W:*** Stephen Lister. *MCA*

The Monolith Monsters ☠☠ **1957** A geologist investigates a meteor shower in Arizona and discovers strange crystals. The crystals attack humans and absorb their silicone, causing them to grow into monsters. Good "B" movie fun. **76m/B VHS.** Grant Williams, Lola Albright, Les Tremayne, Trevor Bardette; ***D:*** John Sherwood; ***W:*** Norman Jolley, Robert M. Fresco; ***M:*** Joseph Gershenson. *MCA, MLB, FRG*

Monsieur Beaucaire ☠½ **1924** The Duke of Chartres ditches France posing as a barber, and once in Britain, becomes a lawman. Not a classic Valentino vehicle. **100m/B VHS, Beta.** Rudolph Valentino, Bebe Daniels, Lois Wilson, Doris Kenyon, Lowell Sherman, John Davidson; ***D:*** Sidney Olcott. *GPV*

Monsieur Beaucaire ☠☠☠ **1946** Entertaining Hope vehicle that casts him as a barber impersonating a French nobleman in the court of Louis XV. He's set to wed a Spanish princess in order to prevent a full-scale war from taking place. However, he really wants to marry social-climber chambermaid Caulfield. Director Marshall was at his best here. Based on the novel by Booth Tarkington. **93m/B VHS.** Bob Hope, Joan Caulfield, Patric Knowles, Marjorie Reynolds, Cecil Kellaway, Joseph Schildkraut, Reginald Owen, Constance Collier; ***D:*** George Marshall; ***W:*** Melvin Frank, Norman Panama; ***C:*** Lionel Lindon. *MCA, BTV*

Monsieur Hire ☠☠☠½ *M. Hire* **1989 (PG-13)** The usual tale of sexual obsesssion and suspense. Mr. Hire spends much of his time trying to spy on his beautiful young neighbor woman, alternately alienated and engaged by her love affairs. The voyeur soon finds his secret desires have entangled him in a vicious intrigue. Political rally set-piece is brilliant. Excellent acting, intense pace, elegant photography. Based on "Les Fiancailles de M. Hire" by Georges Simenone and adapted by Leconte and Patrick Dewolf. In French with English subtitles. **81m/C VHS, LV.** *FR* Michel Blanc, Sandrine Bonnaire, Luc Thuillier, Eric Berenger, Andre Wilms; ***D:*** Patrice Leconte; ***W:*** Patrice Leconte. Cesar Awards '90: Best Sound. *FXL, FCT, IME*

Monsieur Verdoux ☠☠☠ **1947** A thorough Chaplin effort, as he produced, directed, wrote, scored and starred. A prim and proper bank cashier in Paris marries and murders rich women in order to support his real wife and family. A mild scandal in its day, though second-thought pacifism and stale humor date it. A bomb upon release (leading Chaplin to shelve it for 17 years) and a cult item today, admired for both its flaws and complexity. Raye fearlessly chews scenery and croissants. Initially based upon a suggestion from Orson Welles. **123m/B VHS, Beta, LV.** Charlie Chaplin, Martha Raye, Isobel Elsom, Mady Correll, Marilyn Nash, Irving Bacon, William Frawley, Allison Roddan, Robert Lewis; ***D:*** Charlie Chaplin; ***W:*** Charlie Chaplin. National Board of Review Awards '47: 10 Best Films of the Year; Nominations: Academy Awards '47: Best Original Screenplay. *FOX*

Monsieur Vincent ☠☠☠ **1948** True story of 17th century French priest who became St. Vincent de Paul. He forsakes worldly possessions and convinces members of the aristocracy to finance his charities for the less fortunate. Inspirational. In French with English subtitles or dubbed. **100m/B VHS, Beta.** *FR* Pierre Fresnay, Lisa Delamare, Aime Clarimond; ***D:*** Maurice Cloche. *HTV, MRV, DVT*

Monsignor *Woof!* **1982 (R)** Callow, ambitious priest befriends mobsters and even seduces a nun while managing Vatican's business affairs. No sparks generated by Reeve and Bujold (who appears nude in one scene), and no real conviction related by most other performers. Absurd, ludicrous melodrama best enjoyed as unintentional comedy. Based on Jack Alain Leger's book. **121m/C VHS, Beta.** Christopher Reeve, Fernando Rey, Genevieve Bujold, Jason Miller; ***D:*** Frank Perry; ***W:*** Abraham Polonsky, Wendell Mayes; ***C:*** Billy Williams; ***M:*** John Williams. *FOX*

Monsignor Quixote ☠☠½ **1991** A small town priest takes on the persona of his ancestor, Don Quixote, and prepares to battle the evil he sees around him. Based on the novel by Graham Greene. **118m/C VHS.** Alec Guinness, Ian Richardson, Graham Crowden, Maurice Denham, Philip Stone, Rosalie Crutchley, Valentine Pelka, Don Fellows, Leo McKern; ***D:*** Rodney Bennett. *FCT, INJ*

The Monster ☠☠☠ **1925** This silent horror film has all the elements that would become genre standards. A mad scientist (Chaney), working in an asylum filled with lunatics, abducts strangers to use in his fiendish experiments to bring the dead back to life. There's the obligatory dungeon and even a lovely heroine that needs rescuing. Great atmosphere and Chaney's usual spine-tingling performance. **86m/B VHS.** Lon Chaney Sr., Gertrude Olmsted, Johnny Arthur, Charles Sellon; ***D:*** Roland West. *FCT*

Monster ☠ **1978 (R)** Bloodthirsty alien indiscriminately preys on gaggle of teens in wilds of civilization. Performers struggle with dialogue and their own self-esteem. **98m/C VHS, Beta.** Jim Mitchum, Diane McBain, Roger Clark, John Carradine, Phil Carey, Anthony Eisley, Keenan Wynn; ***D:*** Herbert L. Strock. *GHV, MRV*

Monster a Go-Go! *Woof!* **1965** Team of go-go dancers battle a ten-foot monster from outer-space whose mass is due to a radiation mishap. He can't dance, either. **70m/B VHS, Beta.** Phil Morton, June Travis, Bill Rebane, Sheldon Seymour; ***D:*** Herschell Gordon Lewis. *VCI*

The Monster and the Girl ☠☠½ **1941** It's the mob vs. the ape in this tale of revenge. Scott (Terry) discovers innocent sister Susan (Drew) is being lead down the path to prostitution by suave mobster Reed (Paige). But Reed manages to frame Scott for murder and he's executed, although not before donating his brain to science. Then scientist Parry (Zucco) decides to transplant the brain into the body of an ape who goes on a rampage aimed at the mobster. **65m/B VHS.** Ellen Drew, Robert Paige, Phillip Terry, Paul Lukas, Joseph Calleia, Onslow Stevens, Rod Cameron, George Zucco, Marc Lawrence, Gerald Mohr; ***D:*** Stuart Heisler; ***W:*** Stuart Anthony; ***C:*** Victor Milner. *MCA*

The Monster and the Stripper ☠ **1973 (R)** A bayou creature is pursued by a gangster who foolishly hopes to realize considerable profits from the venture. **90m/C VHS, Beta.** *NO*

The Monster Club ☠☠ **1985** Price and Carradine star in this music-horror compilation, featuring songs by Night, B.A. Robertson, The Pretty Things and The Viewers. Soundtrack music by John Williams, UB 40 and The Expressos. **104m/C VHS, Beta, LV.** *GB* Vincent Price, Donald Pleasence, John Carradine, Stuart Whitman, Britt Ekland, Simon Ward, Patrick Magee; ***D:*** Roy Ward Baker. *LIV*

The Monster Demolisher ☠☠ **1960** Nostradamus' descendent shares the family penchant for sanguine cocktails, and threatens a professor who protects himself with an electronic wonder of modern technology. Edited from a sombrero serial; if you make it through this one, look up its Mexican siblings, "Curse of Nostradamus" and "Genie of Darkness." **?m/B VHS.** *MX* German Robles; ***D:*** Frederick Curiel. *NOS, LOO*

Monster Dog *Woof!* **1982** A rock band is mauled, threatened, and drooled upon by an untrainable mutant canine. Rock star Cooper plays the leader of the band. No plot, but the German shepherd is worth watching. **88m/C VHS, Beta.** Alice Cooper, Victoria Vera; ***D:*** Clyde Anderson. *TWE*

Monster from Green Hell ☠ **1958** An experimental rocket containing radiation-contaminated wasps crashes in Africa, making giant killer wasps that run amok. Stinging big bug horror. **71m/B VHS, Beta.** Jim Davis, Robert Griffin, Barbara Turner, Eduardo Cianelli; ***D:*** Kenneth Crane. *NOS, MRV, SNC*

Monster from the Ocean Floor ☠ *It Stalked the Ocean Floor; Monster Maker* **1954** An oceanographer in a deep-sea diving bell is threatened by a multi-tentacled creature. Roger Corman's first production. **66m/C VHS, Beta.** Anne Kimball, Stuart Wade; ***D:*** Wyott Ordung. *VMK*

Monster High ☠ **1989 (R)** Bloodthirsty alien indiscriminately preys on gaggle of teens in wilds of civilization. Even the people who made this one may not have seen it all the way through. **89m/C VHS, Beta, LV.** David Marriott, Dean Iandoli, Diana Frank, D.J. Kerzner; ***D:*** Rudiger Poe. *COL*

Monster in a Box ☠☠☠ **1992 (PG-13)** Master storyteller Gray spins a wonderful tale about his life, including stories about his adventures at a Moscow film festival, a trip to Nicaragua, and his first experience with California earthquakes. Filled with wit, satire, and hilarity. Filmed before an audience, this is based on Gray's Broadway show of the same title. By the way, the monster in the box is a 1,900-page manuscript of his autobiography and the box in which he lugs it around. **88m/C VHS, LV.** Spalding Gray; ***D:*** Nick Broomfield; ***W:*** Spalding Gray; ***M:*** Laurie Anderson. *NLC, COL, BTV*

Monster in the Closet ☠☠ **1986 (PG)** A gory horror spoof about a rash of San Francisco murders that all take place inside closets. A news reporter and his scientist friend decide they will be the ones to protect California from the evil but shy creatures. From the makers of "The Toxic Avenger." **87m/C VHS, Beta.** Donald Grant, Claude Akins, Denise DuBarry, Stella Stevens, Howard Duff, Henry Gibson, Jesse White, John Carradine; ***D:*** Bob Dahlin; ***W:*** Bob Dahlin. *ORI, WAR*

The Monster Maker ☠☠ **1944** Low-budget gland fest in which deranged scientist develops serum that inflates heads, feet, and hands. He recklessly inflicts others with this potion, then must contend with deformed victims while courting a comely gal. **65m/B VHS, Beta.** J. Carrol Naish, Ralph Morgan, Wanda McKay, Terry Frost; ***D:*** Sam Newfield. *NOS, MRV, SNC*

The Monster of London City ☠½ *Das Ungeheuer von London City* **1964** During a stage play about Jack the Ripper, murders occur paralleling those in the production. The lead actor finds himself to be the prime suspect. Lightweight horror from Germany. **87m/B VHS, Beta.** *GE* Hansjorg Felmy, Marianne Koch, Dietmar Schoenherr, Hans Nielsen; ***D:*** Edwin Zbonek. *SNC*

The Monster of Piedras Blancas *Woof!* **1957** During a seaside festival, two fisherman are killed by a bloodthirsty oceanic critter with no respect for holidays. The fishing village is determined to find it and kill it. Low-budget, with amateurish effects and poor acting. **72m/B VHS.** Les Tremayne, Jeanne Carmen, Forrest Lewis; ***D:*** Irvin Berwick. *VDM, MRV, REP*

Monster on the Campus ☠☠½ **1959** Science-fiction thriller about the blood of a prehistoric fish turning college professor into murderous beast. Will the halls of Dunsfield University ever be safe again? **76m/B VHS.** Arthur Franz, Joanna Moore, Judson Pratt, Nancy Walters, Troy Donahue; ***D:*** Jack Arnold; ***W:*** David Duncan. *MCA*

The Monster Squad ☠½ **1987 (PG-13)** Youthful monster enthusiasts find their community inundated by Dracula, Frankenstein creature, Wolf Man, Mummy, and Gill Man(!?!), who are all searching for a life-sustaining amulet. Somewhat different, but still somewhat mediocre. **82m/C VHS, Beta, LV.** Andre Gower, Stephen Macht, Tom Noonan, Duncan Regehr; ***D:*** Fred Dekker; ***W:*** Fred Dekker, Shane Black; ***M:*** Bruce Broughton. *LIV, VES*

The Monster That Challenged the World ☠☠½ **1957** Huge, ancient eggs are discovered in the Salton Sea and eventually hatch into killer, crustaceous caterpillars. Superior monster action. **83m/B VHS.** Tim Holt, Audrey Dalton, Hans Conried, Harlen Ward, Max Casey Adams Showalter, Mimi Gibson, Gordon Jones; ***D:*** Arnold Laven. *MGM, FRG, MLB*

The Monster Walks ☠☠ *The Monster Walked* **1932** A whodunit thriller, complete with stormy nights, suspicious cripples, weird servants, a screaming gorilla, and a spooky house. Not unique but entertaining. **60m/B VHS, Beta.** Rex Lease, Vera Reynolds, Mischa Auer, Willie Best; ***D:*** Frank Strayer. *SNC, NOS, CCB*

Monsters Crash the Pajama Party 🦴🦴 **1965** Mad scientist is discovered conducting weird experiments by a group of teens who enter a supposedly haunted house. This one was much better in the theater, because "monsters" would run through the audience and select a victim. Then the monsters and the victim would magically appear on the screen. Weird. **?m/C VHS.** Peter J. D'Noto; ***D:*** David L. Hewitt. *SNC*

Montana 🦴🦴½ **1990 (PG)** Hoyce and Bess Guthrie are long-married and strong-willed ranchers who are at odds over the family ranch in Montana. He wants to sell the land to a power company for oil drilling but she wants to keep the land in the family. Made for cable television. **91m/C VHS, Beta.** Gena Rowlands, Richard Crenna, Lea Thompson, Justin Deas, Elizabeth Berridge, Scott Coffey, Darren Dalton; ***D:*** William A. Graham; ***W:*** Larry McMurtry. *TTC, FCT*

Montana Belle 🦴🦴 **1952** A buxom bandit teams with the notorious Dalton Brothers before embarking on a life of reform. In the cardgame of life, Russell is always holding a pair. **81m/C VHS, Beta.** Jane Russell, George Brent, Scott Brady, Forrest Tucker, Andy Devine, Jack Lambert, John Litel, Ray Teal; ***D:*** Allan Dwan. *TTC*

Monte Carlo 🦴🦴 **1986** A sexy Russian woman aids the Allies by relaying important messages during WWII. Fun, made for television production featuring Collins at her seductive best. **200m/C VHS, Beta.** Joan Collins, George Hamilton, Lisa Eilbacher, Lauren Hutton, Robert Carradine, Malcolm McDowell; ***D:*** Anthony Page. *VTR, NWV*

Monte Carlo Nights 🦴½ **1934** Wrongly convicted murderer determines to prove his innocence even as he is tracked by police. **60m/B VHS, Beta.** Mary Brian, John Darrow, Kate Campbell, Robert Frazer, Astrid Allwyn, George "Gabby" Hayes, George Cleveland; ***D:*** William Nigh. *SNC*

Monte Walsh 🦴🦴🦴 **1970 (PG)** Aging cowboy sees declining of Old West, embarks on mission to avenge best friend's death. Subdued, moving western worthy of genre greats Marvin and Palance. Cinematographer Fraker proves himself a proficient director in this, his first venture. Based on Jack Schaefer's novel. **100m/C VHS, Beta.** Lee Marvin, Jack Palance, Jeanne Moreau, Jim Davis, Mitchell Ryan; ***D:*** William A. Fraker; ***W:*** David Zelag Goodman; ***M:*** John Barry. *FOX*

Montenegro 🦴🦴🦴½ *Montenegro—Or Pigs and Pearls* **1981** Offbeat, bawdy comedy details experiences of bored, possibly mad housewife who lands in a coarse, uninhibited ethnic community. To its credit, this film remains unpredictable to the end. And Anspach, an intriguing, resourceful—and attractive—actress, delivers what is perhaps her greatest performance. **97m/C VHS, Beta.** *SW* Susan Anspach, Erland Josephson; ***D:*** Dusan Makavejev; ***W:*** Dusan Makavejev. Nominations: Cannes Film Festival '81: Best Film. *NO*

Monterey Pop 🦴🦴🦴½ **1968** This pre-Woodstock rock 'n roll festival in Monterey, California features landmark performances by some of the most popular sixties rockers. Compelling for the performances, and historically important as the first significant rock concert film. Appearances by Jefferson Airplane, Janis Joplin, Jimi Hendrix, Simon and Garfunkel, The Who, and Otis Redding. **72m/C VHS, Beta, LV, 8mm.** *MVD, COL*

A Month by the Lake 🦴🦴½ **1995 (PG)** Redgrave takes the plunge into highly familiar romantic comedy of the Proper English sort and glides effortlessly through this slow-moving but often charming adaptation of an H. E. Bates short story. Set in pre-WWII northern Italy, Miss Bentley (Redgrave) sets her spinster's eye on the somewhat wooden, but gradually warming, English Major Wilshaw (Fox). Petulant American nanny Thurman arrives to provide an arresting diversion for Wilshaw, while Gassman proves an unwitting pawn for Miss Bentley's game of "get the major." Touching and lighthearted performances, especially by heavyweight Redgrave, are complemented by glorious cinematography. **92m/C VHS, LV.** Vanessa Redgrave, Edward Fox, Uma Thurman, Alida Valli, Alessandro Gassman, Carlo Cartier; ***D:*** John Irvin; ***W:*** Trevor Bentham; ***C:*** Pasqualino de Santis; ***M:*** Nicola Piovani. Nominations: Golden Globe Awards '96: Best Actress—Musical/Comedy (Redgrave). *TOU*

A Month in the Country 🦴🦴🦴 **1987** The reverently quiet story of two British WWI veterans, one an archaeologist and the other a church painting restorer, who are working in a tiny village while trying to heal their emotional wounds. Based on the novel by J.L. Carr. **92m/C VHS, Beta, LV.** *GB* Colin Firth, Natasha Richardson, Kenneth Branagh, Patrick Malahide, Tony Haygarth, Jim Carter; ***D:*** Pat O'Connor; ***W:*** Simon Gray; ***M:*** Howard Blake. *ORI, WAR*

Monty Python and the Holy Grail 🦴🦴🦴½ **1975 (PG)** Britain's famed comedy band assaults the Arthurian legend in a cult classic replete with a Trojan rabbit and an utterly dismembered, but inevitably pugnacious, knight. Fans of manic comedy—and graphic violence—should get more than their fill here. **90m/C VHS, Beta, LV, 8mm.** *GB* Graham Chapman, John Cleese, Terry Gilliam, Eric Idle, Terry Jones, Michael Palin, Carol Cleveland, Connie Booth, Neil Innes, Patsy Kensit; ***D:*** Terry Gilliam, Terry Jones; ***W:*** Graham Chapman, John Cleese, Terry Gilliam, Eric Idle, Terry Jones, Michael Palin. *COL, SIG, TVC*

Monty Python Live at the Hollywood Bowl 🦴🦴🦴 **1982** The revered comedy group perform many of their most celebrated routines in this uproarious performance documentary. A must-see for all Python aficionados. **78m/C VHS, Beta, LV.** *GB* Eric Idle, Michael Palin, John Cleese, Terry Gilliam, Terry Jones, Graham Chapman; ***D:*** Terry Hughes; ***W:*** John Cleese, Terry Gilliam; ***M:*** John Du Prez. *PAR*

Monty Python's Flying Circus **1971** The original classic irreverant BBC comedy series that introduced the gang of six comics to the world. Two episodes per tape. Four skits: "The Architect's Sketch," "The Naughty Chemist," "Ministry of Silly Walks," and "The Piranha Brothers." **60m/C VHS, Beta, LV.** *GB* Michael Palin, Graham Chapman, Eric Idle, John Cleese, Terry Jones, Terry Gilliam, Carol Cleveland, Connie Booth, Neil Innes; ***D:*** Ian MacNaughton. *MOV, PAR*

Monty Python's Life of Brian 🦴🦴🦴½ *Life of Brian* **1979 (R)** Often riotous spoof of Christianity tracks hapless peasant mistaken for the messiah in 32 A.D. Film reels from routine to routine, and only the most pious will remain unmoved by a chorus of crucifixion victims. Probably the group's most daring, controversial venture. **94m/C VHS, Beta, LV.** *GB* Graham Chapman, John Cleese, Terry Gilliam, Eric Idle, Michael Palin, George Harrison, Terry Jones; ***D:*** Terry Jones; ***W:*** Graham Chapman, John Cleese, Terry Gilliam, Eric Idle, Michael Palin, Terry Jones; ***M:*** Geoffrey Burgon. *PAR, SIG*

Monty Python's Parrot Sketch Not Included **1990** To celebrate their 20th anniversary, the crazy guys of Monty Python put together this collection of some of their funniest sketches. The parrot was pretty disappointed that he wasn't included. **75m/C VHS, LV.** Graham Chapman, John Cleese, Terry Gilliam, Eric Idle, Terry Jones, Michael Palin. *PAR, SIG, TVC*

Monty Python's The Meaning of Life 🦴🦴🦴 **1983 (R)** Funny, technically impressive film conducts various inquiries into the most profound questions confronting humanity. Notable among the sketches here are a live sex enactment performed before bored schoolboys, a student-faculty rugby game that turns quite violent, and an encounter between a physician and a reluctant, untimely organ donor. Another sketch provides a memorable portrait of a glutton prone to nausea. And at film's end, the meaning of life is actually revealed. **107m/C VHS, Beta, LV.** *GB* Graham Chapman, John Cleese, Terry Gilliam, Eric Idle, Terry Jones, Michael Palin, Carol Cleveland; ***D:*** Terry Jones; ***W:*** Graham Chapman, John Cleese, Terry Gilliam, Eric Idle, Terry Jones, Michael Palin; ***M:*** John Du Prez. Cannes Film Festival '83: Grand Jury Prize; Nominations: Cannes Film Festival '93: Best Film. *MCA, CCB, SIG*

The Moon and Sixpence 🦴🦴🦴 **1943** Stockbroker turns ambitious painter in this adaptation of W. Somerset Maugham's novel that was, in turn, inspired by the life of artist Paul Gauguin. Fine performance from Sanders. Filmed mainly in black and white, but uses color sparingly to great advantage. Compare this one to "Wolf at the Door," in which Gauguin is played by Donald Sutherland. **89m/B VHS.** George Sanders, Herbert Marshall, Steve Geray, Doris Dudley, Eric Blore, Elena Verdugo, Florence Bates, Albert Basserman, Heather Thatcher; ***D:*** Albert Lewin. Nominations: Academy Awards '43: Best Original Score. *MGM, IVY*

Moon 44 🦴🦴½ **1990 (R)** A space prison is overrun by thugs who terrorize their fellow inmates. Fine cast, taut pacing. Filmed in Germany. **102m/C VHS, LV.** *GE* Malcolm McDowell, Lisa Eichhorn, Michael Pare, Stephen Geoffreys, Roscoe Lee Browne, Brian Thompson, Dean Devlin, Mechmed Yilmaz, Leon Rippy; ***D:*** Roland Emmerich. *LIV, IME, BTV*

Moon in Scorpio 🦴½ **1986** Three Vietnam-vet buddies go sailing and are attacked by the back-from-the-dead victims of a bloody war crime. **90m/C VHS, Beta.** John Phillip Law, Britt Ekland, William Smith; ***D:*** Gary Graver. *TWE*

Moon in the Gutter 🦴½ *La Lune Dans le Caniveau* **1983 (R)** In a ramshackle harbor town, a man searches despondently for the person who killed his sister years before. Various sexual liaisons and stevedore fights intermittently spice up the action. Nasty story that doesn't make much sense on film; adapted from a book by American pulp writer David Goodis. In French with English subtitles. **109m/C VHS, Beta.** *IT FR* Gerard Depardieu, Nastassia Kinski, Victoria Abril, Vittorio Mezzogiorno, Dominique Pinon; ***D:*** Jean-Jacques Beineix; ***W:*** Jean-Jacques Beineix; ***C:*** Philippe Rousselot. Cesar Awards '84: Best Art Direction/Set Decoration; Nominations: Cannes Film Festival '83: Best Film. *COL*

The Moon Is Blue 🦴🦴½ **1953** A young woman flaunts her virginity in this stilted adaptation of F. Hugh Herbert's play. Hard to believe that this film was once considered risque. Good performances, though, from Holden and Niven. **100m/B Beta, LV.** William Holden, David Niven, Maggie McNamara, Tom Tully; ***D:*** Otto Preminger; ***C:*** Ernest Laszlo. Golden Globe Awards '54: Best Actor—Musical/Comedy (Niven); Nominations: Academy Awards '53: Best Actress (McNamara), Best Film Editing, Best Song ("The Moon is Blue"). *WAR*

Moon of the Wolf 🦴 **1972** A small town in bayou country is terrorized by a modern-day werewolf that rips its victims to shreds. Made-for-television. **74m/C VHS, Beta.** David Janssen, Barbara Rush, Bradford Dillman, John Beradino; ***D:*** Daniel Petrie. *WOV, GKK*

Moon over Harlem 🦴½ **1939** A musical melodrama about a widow who unwittingly marries a fast-talking gangster involved in the numbers racket. The film features 20 chorus girls, a choir, and a 60-piece orchestra. **67m/B VHS, Beta.** Bud Harris, Cora Green, Alec Lovejoy, Sidney Bechet; ***D:*** Edgar G. Ulmer. *FCT, DVT, NOS*

Moon over Miami 🦴🦴🦴 **1941** Manhunting trio meet their match in this engaging musical. A remake of 1938's "Three Blind Mice," this was later remade in 1946 as "Three Little Girls in Blue." ♫Moon Over Miami; I've Got You All To Myself; What Can I Do For You?; Kindergarten Congo; You Started Something; Oh Me Oh Mi-Am-Mi; Solitary Seminole; Is That Good?; Loveliness and Love. **91m/C VHS, Beta.** Don Ameche, Betty Grable, Robert Cummings, Carole Landis, Charlotte Greenwood, Jack Haley; ***D:*** Walter Lang; ***W:*** Mitch Glazer; ***C:*** Leon Shamroy. *FOX*

Moon over Parador 🦴🦴½ **1988 (PG-13)** An uneven comedy about a reluctant American actor who gets the role of his life when he gets the chance to pass himself off as the recently deceased dictator of a Latin American country. A political strongman wants to continue the charade until he can take over, but the actor begins to enjoy the benefits of dictatorship. Look for a cameo by director/writer Mazursky in drag. **103m/C VHS, Beta, LV.** Richard Dreyfuss, Sonia Braga, Raul Julia, Jonathan Winters, Fernando Rey, Ed Asner, Dick Cavett, Michael Greene, Sammy Davis Jr., Polly Holliday, Charo, Marianne Sagebrecht, Dana Delany, Ike Pappas;

Cameos: Paul Mazursky; ***D:*** Paul Mazursky; ***W:*** Leon Capetanos, Paul Mazursky; ***M:*** Maurice Jarre. *MCA*

Moon Pilot **1962** An astronaut on his way to the moon encounters a mysterious alien woman who claims to know his future. **98m/C VHS, Beta.** Tom Tryon, Brian Keith, Edmond O'Brien, Dany Saval, Tommy Kirk; ***D:*** James Neilson. *DIS*

The Moon-Spinners **1964 (PG)** Lightweight Disney drama featuring Mills as a young tourist traveling through Crete who meets up with a young man, accused of being a jewel thief, and the two work together to find the real jewel thieves. Watch for silent film star Pola Negri. **118m/C VHS, Beta.** Hayley Mills, Peter McEnery, Eli Wallach, Pola Negri; ***D:*** James Neilson. *DIS, OM*

The Moon Stallion ½ **1985** A charming tale of mystery and fantasy for children and adults. Professor Purwell is researching King Arthur. His blind daughter soon becomes involved with supernatural events and a white horse that appears to lead her into adventures not of this age. **95m/C VHS.** *GB* Sarah Sutton, David Haig, James Greene, John Abineri, Caroline Goodall; ***D:*** Dorothea Brooking. *VCO, HMV*

Mooncussers ½ **1962** A children's film detailing the exploits of a precocious 12-year-old determined to exact revenge upon a band of ruthless pirates. **85m/C VHS, Beta.** Kevin Corcoran, Rian Garrick, Oscar Homolka; ***D:*** James Neilson. *DIS*

Moonfleet ½ **1955** Follows the adventures of an 18th century buccaneer who tries to swindle a young lad in his charge of a valuable diamond. From J. Meade Falkner's novel. **89m/C VHS, LV.** Stewart Granger, Jon Whiteley, George Sanders, Viveca Lindfors, Joan Greenwood, Ian Wolfe; ***D:*** Fritz Lang; ***M:*** Miklos Rozsa. *MGM*

Moonlight and Valentino **1995 (R)** To help her recover from the death of her husband, Rebecca turns to the comfort of flaky neighbor Sylvie (Goldberg), self-destructive sis Lucy (Paltrow) and overbearing ex-stepmother Alberta (Turner). Together they sit around and talk some of the more contrived and cliched "women talk" ("Chicken soup is the most womanly thing on the face of the planet") in recent film history. The finale, a hokey ritual in a cemetery, will have you pulling out hair rather than hankies. Rock star Bon Jovi makes his screen debut as the beefcake (discussion of his butt takes up about two-thirds of the dialogue) who puts the fire back into Rebecca's life. Not for the estrogen impaired. **104m/C VHS, LV.** Elizabeth Perkins, Whoopi Goldberg, Gwyneth Paltrow, Kathleen Turner, Jon Bon Jovi, Jeremy Sisto, Josef Sommer, Peter Coyote; ***D:*** David Anspaugh; ***W:*** Ellen Simon; ***C:*** Julio Macat; ***M:*** Howard Shore. *PGV*

Moonlight Sonata ½ **1938** Professional concert pianist Paderewski performs his way through a confusing soap-opera of a film. Includes performances of Franz Liszt's "Second Hungarian Rhapsody" and Frederic Chopin's "Polonaise." **80m/B VHS.** *GB* Ignace Jan Paderewski, Charles Farrell, Marie Tempest, Barbara Greene, Eric Portman; ***D:*** Lothar Mendes. *NOS, DVT*

Moonlighting ½ **1982 (PG)** Compelling drama about Polish laborers illegally hired to renovate London flat. When their country falls under martial law, the foreman conceals the event and pushes workers to complete project. Unlikely casting of Irons as foreman is utterly successful. **97m/C VHS, Beta, LV.** *PL GB* Jeremy Irons, Eugene Lipinski, Jiri Stanislay, Eugeniusz Haczkiewicz; ***D:*** Jerzy Skolimowski; ***C:*** Tony Pierce-Roberts; ***M:*** Hans Zimmer. Nominations: Cannes Film Festival '82: Best Film. *MCA*

Moonlighting ½ **1985** The television-pilot for the popular detective show, where Maddie and David, the daffy pair of impetuous private eyes, meet for the first time and solve an irrationally complex case. **93m/C VHS, Beta.** Cybill Shepherd, Bruce Willis, Allyce Beasley; ***D:*** Robert Butler. *WAR, OM*

The Moonraker ½ **1958** Compelling action scenes highlight this tale set at the end of the English Civil War, as the Royalists attempt to sneak the king out of England and into France. **82m/C VHS.** *GB* George Baker, Sylvia Syms, Peter Arne, Marius Goring, Clive Morton, Gary Raymond, Richard Leech, Patrick Troughton; ***D:*** David MacDonald. *NOS*

Moonraker **1979 (PG)** Uninspired Bond fare has 007 unraveling intergalactic hijinks. Bond is aided by a female CIA agent, assaulted by a giant with jaws of steel, and captured by Amazons when he sets out to protect the human race. Moore, Chiles, and Lonsdale all seem to be going through the motions only. **136m/C VHS, Beta, LV.** *GB* Roger Moore, Lois Chiles, Richard Kiel, Michael Lonsdale, Corinne Clery, Geoffrey Keen, Emily Bolton, Walter Gotell, Bernard Lee, Lois Maxwell, Desmond Llewelyn; ***D:*** Lewis Gilbert; ***M:*** John Barry. *MGM, TLF*

Moonrise **1948** A melodramatic tale about the son of an executed murderer who becomes the object of derision in the small town where he lives. One tormentor finally attacks him, and the young man must make a split-second decision that may affect his own mortality. **90m/B VHS, LV.** Dane Clark, Gail Russell, Ethel Barrymore, Allyn Joslyn, Harry (Henry) Morgan, Lloyd Bridges, Selena Royle, Rex Ingram, Harry Carey Jr.; ***D:*** Frank Borzage. *REP*

The Moon's Our Home ½ **1936** A fast-paced, breezy, screwball comedy about an actress and adventurer impulsively marrying and then bickering through the honeymoon. Silliness at its height. Fonda and Sullavan were both married and then divorced before filming this movie. **80m/B VHS, Beta.** Margaret Sullavan, Henry Fonda, Beulah Bondi, Charles Butterworth, Margaret Hamilton, Walter Brennan; ***D:*** William A. Seiter; ***C:*** Joseph Valentine. *BAR*

Moonshine County Express ½ **1977 (PG)** Three sexy daughters of a hillbilly moonshiner set out to run the still and avenge their father's murder. **97m/C VHS, Beta.** John Saxon, Susan Howard, William Conrad, Morgan Woodward, Claudia Jennings, Jeff Corey, Dub Taylor, Maureen McCormick, Albert Salmi, Candice Rialson; ***D:*** Gus Trikonis. *WAR*

Moonshine Highway **1996 (PG-13)** Redneck alert! Moonshiner Jed Muldoon (MacLachlan) clashes with sheriff (Quaid), who's not only aggrieved about Jed's illegal liquor running but is not happy that his estranged wife has taken up with the miscreant. Lots of backwoods car chases. Made for cable. **96m/C VHS, Beta.** Kyle MacLachlan, Randy Quaid, Gary Farmer, Jeremy Ratchford; ***D:*** Andy Armstrong; ***W:*** Andy Armstrong; ***C:*** Dick Quinlan. *PAR*

Moonshine Mountain *Woof! White Trash on Moonshine Mountain* **1964** A country-western star travels with his girlfriend to the singer's home in backwoods Carolina. When the girl is killed by a lusting resident, all hell breaks loose. One of gore-meister Lewis' excursions into the dramatic. **90m/C VHS, Beta.** Chuck Scott, Adam Sorg, Jeffrey Allen, Bonnie Hinson, Carmen Sotir, Ben Moore, Pat Patterson, Mark Douglas; ***D:*** Herschell Gordon Lewis. *SNC*

Moonstruck ½ **1987 (PG-13)** Winning romantic comedy about widow engaged to one man but falling in love with his younger brother in Little Italy. Excellent performances all around, with Cher particularly fetching as attractive, hapless widow. Unlikely casting of usually dominating Aiello, as unassuming mama's boy also works well, and Cage is at his best as a tormented one-handed opera lover/baker. **103m/C VHS, Beta, LV.** Cher, Nicolas Cage, Olympia Dukakis, Danny Aiello, Vincent Gardenia, Julie Bovasso, Louis Guss, Anita Gillette, Feodor Chaliapin Jr, John Mahoney; ***D:*** Norman Jewison; ***W:*** John Patrick Shanley; ***C:*** David Watkin. Academy Awards '87: Best Actress (Cher), Best Original Screenplay, Best Supporting Actress (Dukakis); Golden Globe Awards '88: Best Actress—Musical/Comedy (Cher), Best Supporting Actress (Dukakis); National Board of Review Awards '87: Best Supporting Actress (Dukakis); Writers Guild of America '87: Best Original Screenplay; Nominations: Academy Awards '87: Best Director (Jewison), Best Picture, Best Supporting Actor (Gardenia). *MGM, BTV, HMV*

Moontrap **1989** An astronaut discovers an alien frozen in space and returns to Earth with it. Once thawed, the creature reveals its horrible secret. **92m/C VHS, LV.** Walter Koenig, Bruce Campbell, Leigh Lombardi; ***D:*** Robert Dyke. *MOV, IME*

Morals for Women ½ **1931** This soap-opera's so old it almost predates soap. A secretary becomes the Kept Woman of her boss in the Big Bad City. She escapes, but not for long. **65m/B VHS.** Bessie Love, Conway Tearle, John Holland, Natalie Moorhead, Emma Dunn, June Clyde; ***D:*** Mort Blumenstock. *NOS, LOO*

Moran of the Lady Letty ½ **1922** Seaweed saga of Ramon Laredo (Valentino), a high society guy who's kidnapped aboard a pirate barge. When the salty dogs rescue/capture Moran (a theme ahead of its time?) from a ship fuming with burning coal, Ramon is smitten in a big way with the boyish girl and battles contagiously to prevent the pirates from selling her as a slave. Excellent fight scenes with much hotstepping over gangplanks and swinging from masts, with a 60-foot death dive from above. Little known Dalton was a celluloid fave in the 'teens and twenties, and Valentino is atypically cast as a man's man. The sheik himself is said not to have like this one because it undermined his image as a ladies' man. **71m/B VHS, Beta.** Dorothy Dalton, Rudolph Valentino, Charles Brinley, Walter Long, Emil Jorgenson; ***D:*** George Melford. *GPV, FCT*

More ½ **1969** Smells like teen angst in the sixties when a German college grad falls for an American in Paris, to the tune of sex, drugs, and Pink Floyd. Schroeder's first effort as director, it's definitely a sixties pic. In French with English subtitles. **110m/C VHS, Beta.** Mimsy Farmer, Klaus Grunberg, Heinz Engelmann, Michel Chanderli; ***D:*** Barbet Schroeder; ***C:*** Nestor Almendros. *WAR, BTV, FCT*

More American Graffiti ½ **1979 (PG)** Sequel to 1973's acclaimed '50s homage "American Graffiti" charts various characters' experiences in the more radical '60s. George Lucas didn't direct, Richard Dreyfuss didn't reprise. Ron Howard doesn't direct, he acts. B.W.L. Norton doesn't direct either, though he's credited. Pass on this one and have that root canal done instead. **111m/C VHS, LV.** Candy Clark, Bo Hopkins, Ron Howard, Paul LeMat, MacKenzie Phillips, Charles Martin Smith, Anna Bjorn, Richard Bradford, Cindy Williams, Scott Glenn; ***D:*** Bill W.L. Norton; ***C:*** Caleb Deschanel. *MCA*

More! Police Squad **1982** More episodes from the seminal spoof of television cop shows, episodes entitled "Revenge and Remorse," "The Butler Did It" and "Testimony of Evil." **75m/C VHS, Beta, LV.** Leslie Nielsen, Alan North, Rex Hamilton, Peter Lupus. *PAR*

The More the Merrier **1943** Likeable romantic comedy in which working girl must share apartment with two bachelors in Washington, D.C., during WWII. Arthur is especially endearing as a young woman in male company. **104m/B VHS, Beta, LV.** Joel McCrea, Jean Arthur, Charles Coburn, Richard Gaines, Bruce (Herman Brix) Bennett, Ann Savage, Ann Doran, Frank Tully, Grady Sutton; ***D:*** George Stevens. Academy Awards '43: Best Supporting Actor (Coburn); New York Film Critics Awards '43: Best Director (Stevens); Nominations: Academy Awards '43: Best Actress (Arthur), Best Director (Stevens), Best Picture, Best Story. *COL, BTV*

More Wild, Wild West **1980** Another feature-length continuation of the satirical television western series, with Winters taking on Conrad and Martin. Made for television. **94m/C VHS, Beta.** Robert Conrad, Ross Martin, Jonathan Winters, Victor Buono; ***D:*** Burt Kennedy. *FOX*

Morgan! ½ *Morgan: A Suitable Case for Treatment; A Suitable Case for Treatment* **1966** Offbeat comedy in which deranged artist copes with divorce by donning ape suit. Some laughs ensue. Based on David Mercer's play. **93m/B VHS, Beta, LV.** *GB* Vanessa Redgrave, David Warner, Robert Stephens, Irene Handl; ***D:*** Karel Reisz. British Academy Awards '66: Best Screenplay; Cannes Film Festival '66: Best Actress (Redgrave); Nominations: Academy Awards '66: Best Actress (Redgrave), Best Costume Design (B & W). *NO*

Morgan Stewart's Coming Home *Home Front* **1987 (PG-13)** When Dad needs a good family image in his political race, he brings Morgan home from boarding school. Fortunately, Morgan can see how his parents are using him and he doesn't approve at all. He decides to turn his family's life upside down while pursuing the love of his life. **96m/C VHS, Beta, LV.** Jon Cryer, Lynn Redgrave, Nicholas Pryor, Viveka Davis, Paul Gleason, Andrew Duncan, Savely Kramorov, John Cullum, Robert Sedgwick, Waweru Njenga, Sudhir Rad; ***D:*** Alan Smithee; ***M:*** Peter Bernstein. *NO*

Morgan the Pirate ☠☠ *Capitaine Morgan; Morgan il Pirata* **1960** Steve Reeves is at his finest as Morgan, an escaped slave who becomes a notorious pirate in the Caribbean and is wrongly condemned to death in this brisk, sea-going adventure. **93m/C VHS, Beta, LV.** *FR IT* Steve Reeves, Valerie Lagrange; ***D:*** Andre de Toth. *SUE, FCT*

Morituri ☠☠☠ *Saboteur: Code Name Morituri; The Saboteur* **1965** Gripping wartime drama in which an Allied spy tries to persuade German gunboat captain to surrender his vessel. Brando is—no surprise—excellent. **123m/C VHS, Beta.** Marlon Brando, Yul Brynner, Trevor Howard, Janet Margolin, Wally Cox, William Redfield; ***D:*** Bernhard Wicki; ***W:*** Daniel Taradash; ***C:*** Conrad Hall; ***M:*** Jerry Goldsmith. Nominations: Academy Awards '65: Best Black and White Cinematography, Best Costume Design (B & W). *FOX*

Mork & Mindy **1978** Williams struts his comedic stuff in this 1978-1981 sitcom as a mixed-up alien from the planet Ork who lands in Boulder, Colorado and manages to convince Mindy McConnell (Dawber) to let him stay with her while he studies human behavior (and tries to adapt). And a good "Nanu, nanu" to you too! Two episodes per tape. **50m/C VHS.** Robin Williams, Pam Dawber, Conrad Janis. *PAR*

A Mormon Maid ☠½ **1917** Young woman and her family, after being saved from an Indian attack by a Mormon group, come to live among them without converting to their beliefs. Considered a shocking expose of controversial Mormon practices, including polygamy. **78m/B VHS, Beta.** Mae Murray, Frank Borzage, Hobart Bosworth, Noah Beery Sr.; ***D:*** Robert Z. Leonard. *VYY, GVV*

The Morning After ☠☠ **1986 (R)** A predictable suspense-thriller about an alcoholic actress who wakes up one morning with a corpse in bed next to her, but cannot remember anything about the night before. She evades the police, accidentally meets up with an ex-cop, and works with him to unravel an increasingly complicated mystery. **103m/C VHS, Beta, LV.** Jane Fonda, Jeff Bridges, Raul Julia, Diane Salinger, Richard Foronjy, Geoffrey Scott, Kathleen Wilhoite, Frances Bergen, Rick Rossovich, Kathy Bates; ***D:*** Sidney Lumet; ***W:*** James Cresson. Nominations: Academy Awards '86: Best Actress (Fonda). *ORI, WAR*

Morning Glory ☠☠½ **1933** Small-town girl finds love and fame in the big city. Predictable fare nonetheless boasts fine performances from Hepburn and Fairbanks. Adapted from Zoe Atkins' stage play. **74m/B VHS, Beta, LV.** Katharine Hepburn, Douglas Fairbanks Jr., Adolphe Menjou, Mary Duncan; ***D:*** Lowell Sherman; ***M:*** Max Steiner. Academy Awards '33: Best Actress (Hepburn). *CCB, MED, BTV*

Morning Glory ☠☠½ **1993 (PG-13)** Sappy romance, set during the Depression, about a pregnant widow (Raffin) trying to survive on her hardscrabble farm in Georgia. Elly Dinsmore advertises for a husband, not for romance but to help with the work, and is answered by Will Parker (Reeve), an ex-con trying to live down his past. When a local floozy who has been eyeing Will is killed the sheriff (Walsh) is only too happy to go after the stranger in town. Light-weight with some unbelievable plot twists. Based on the novel "Morning Glory" by LaVyrle Spencer. **90m/C VHS.** Deborah Raffin, Christopher Reeve, Lloyd Bochner, Nina Foch, Helen Shaver, J.T. Walsh; ***D:*** David Hillard Stern; ***W:*** Deborah Raffin, Charles Jarrott; ***M:*** Jonathan Elias. *ACA*

Morocco ☠☠☠½ **1930** A foreign legion soldier falls for a world-weary chanteuse along the desert sands. Cooper has never been more earnest, and Dietrich has never been more blase and exotic. In her American film debut, Dietrich sings "What am I Bid?" A must for anyone drawn to improbable, gloriously well-done kitsch. Based on Benno Vigny's novel, "Amy Jolly." **92m/B VHS, Beta, LV.** Marlene Dietrich, Gary Cooper, Adolphe Menjou, Ullrich Haupt, Francis McDonald, Eve Southern, Paul Porcasi; ***D:*** Josef von Sternberg; ***C:*** Lee Garmes. Nominations: Academy Awards '31: Best Actress (Dietrich), Best Cinematography, Best Director (von Sternberg), Best Interior Decoration. *MCA, FCT*

Morons from Outer Space ☠☠ **1985 (PG)** Slow-witted aliens from elsewhere in the universe crash onto Earth, but unlike other sci-fis, these morons become internationally famous, despite them acting like intergalactic stooges. Plenty of sight gags. **87m/C VHS.** *GB* Griff Rhys Jones, Mel Smith, James B. Sikking, Dinsdale Landen, Jimmy Nail, Joanne Pearce, Paul Brown; ***D:*** Mike Hodges; ***C:*** Phil Meheux; ***M:*** Peter Brewis. *MGM*

Mortal Danger ☠☠½ *Turn Your Pony Around* **1994 (PG-13)** Kathy and Phil are suicidal teens finding different solutions to their difficulties over the same weekend. Comes across like a TV movie but does maintain an honest message with affecting performances. **86m/C VHS, LV.** Ami Dolenz, Noah Hathaway, Paul Coufos, Larry Gatlin, Charles Napier; ***D:*** Brianne Murphy. *IMP, BPG*

Mortal Kombat: The Movie ☠☠ **1995 (PG-13)** Inevitable film version of mega popular arcade game intended to cash in fast on the game's popularity. Shameless nirvana for youngin's with permanent joystick scars on their hands. Grown-ups forced to sit through it may get into some of the eye-popping special effects and nifty martial arts sequences if they can block out the contrived plot, lame acting, and Lambert's presence as Thunder God. **101m/C VHS.** Christopher Lambert, Talisa Soto, Cary-Hiroyuki Tagawa, Brigitte Wilson; ***D:*** Paul Anderson. *NLC*

Mortal Passions ☠½ **1990 (R)** Another "Double Indemnity" rip-off, with a scheming tramp manipulating everyone around her with betrayal, sex, and murder. Her dead husband's brother eventually ignites old flames to steer her away from his money. **96m/C VHS, Beta.** Zach Galligan, Krista Errickson, Michael Bowen, Luca Bercovici, Sheila Kelley, David Warner; ***D:*** Andrew Lane. *FOX*

Mortal Sins ☠ **1990 (R)** A TV evangelist finds more than salvation at the altar, when bodies begin to turn up. The detective he hires is close-mouthed, but more than a little interested in the preacher's daughter. A tense psycho-sexual thriller. **85m/C VHS.** Brian Benben, Anthony LaPaglia, Debrah Farentino; ***D:*** Yuri Sivo. *ACA, FXV*

Mortal Sins ☠☠ **1992 (PG-13)** Reeve stars as parish priest Thomas Cusack, who hears the confession of a serial killer. What's worse is that the killer is preying on the women of Cusack's parish. Since he can't break the seal of the confessional, the good Father tries to stop the killer himself before another murder takes place. **93m/C VHS, LV.** Christopher Reeve; ***D:*** Bradford May. *FXV*

The Mortal Storm ☠☠☠½ **1940** Phyllis Bottome's famous novel comes to life in this extremely well acted film about the rise of the Nazi regime. Stewart and Sullavan are young lovers who risk everything to escape the country after their families are torn apart by the Nazi takeover. Although Germany is never identified as the country, it is obvious in this story about the early days of WWII. Hitler took one look at this and promptly banned all MGM movies in Nazi Germany. **100m/B VHS.** Margaret Sullavan, James Stewart, Robert Young, Frank Morgan, Robert Stack, Bonita Granville, Irene Rich; ***D:*** Frank Borzage; ***W:*** Claudine West, George Froeschel, Anderson Ellis; ***C:*** William H. Daniels. *MGM*

Mortal Thoughts ☠☠½ **1991 (R)** Best friends find their relationship tested when the brutal husband of one of them is murdered. Moore and Headly are exceptional, capturing the perfect inflections and attitudes of the hard-working New Jersey beauticians sure of their friendship. Excellent pacing, fine supporting cast, with Keitel and Willis stand-outs. **104m/C VHS, Beta, LV, 8mm.** Demi Moore, Bruce Willis, Glenne Headly, Harvey Keitel, John Pankow, Billie Neal; ***D:*** Alan Rudolph; ***W:*** William Reilly, Claude Kerven; ***C:*** Elliot Davis; ***M:*** Mark Isham. National Society of Film Critics Awards '91: Best Supporting Actor (Keitel). *COL*

Mortuary ☠ **1981 (R)** Young woman's nightmares come startlingly close to reality. **91m/C VHS, Beta.** Christopher George, Lynda Day George, Paul Smith; ***D:*** Howard (Hikmet) Avedis; ***W:*** Howard (Hikmet) Avedis. *LIV, VES*

Mortuary Academy ☠ **1991 (R)** To win an inheritance two brothers must attend the family mortician school, a situation paving the way for aggressively tasteless jokes on necrophilia. An attempt to recapture the successful black humor of the earlier Bartel/Woronov teaming "Eating Raoul," this one's dead on arrival. **86m/C VHS, LV.** Christopher Atkins, Perry Lang, Paul Bartel, Mary Woronov, Tracey Walter, Lynn Danielson, Cesar Romero, Wolfman Jack; ***D:*** Michael Schroeder. *COL*

The Mosaic Project ☠½ **1995 (R)** Action junkies should be happy with the chases, explosions, and other mayhem engendered by this story of two buddies who find themselves the victims of a mad scientist. Now they have experimental computer chips implanted in their brains that make them skilled in 25 martial arts forms (and some other stuff that doesn't matter much). **89m/C VHS.** Jon Tabler, Ben Marley, Joe Estevez; ***D:*** John Sjogren. *MNC*

Mosby's Marauders ☠☠ **1966** A young boy joins a Confederate raiding company during the Civil War and learns about bravery, war, and love. **79m/C VHS, Beta.** Kurt Russell, James MacArthur, Jack Ging, Peggy Lipton, Nick Adams; ***D:*** Michael O'Herlihy. *DIS*

Moscow Does Not Believe in Tears ☠☠☠ *Moscow Distrusts Tears; Moskwa Sljesam Nje Jerit* **1980** Three Soviet women realize very different fates when they pursue their dreams in 1950's Moscow. Bittersweet, moving fare that seems a somewhat surprising production from pre-Glasnost USSR. Brief nudity and violence. In Russian with English subtitles. A 150-minute version has also been released. **115m/C VHS, Beta, LV.** *RU* Vera Alentova, Irina Muravyova, Raisa Ryazanova, Natalie Vavilova, Alexei Batalov; ***D:*** Vladimir Menshov. Academy Awards '80: Best Foreign Language Film. *COL, IME, INJ*

Moscow on the Hudson ☠☠☠ **1984 (R)** Good-natured comedy has Williams as Soviet defector trying to cope with new life of freedom in fast-paced, freewheeling melting pot of New York City. Williams is particularly winning as naive jazzman, though Alonso also scores as his Hispanic love interest. Be warned though, it's not just played for laughs. **115m/C VHS, Beta, LV, 8mm.** Robin Williams, Maria Conchita Alonso, Cleavant Derricks, Alejandro Rey, Elya Baskin; ***D:*** Paul Mazursky; ***W:*** Leon Capetanos, Paul Mazursky. *COL*

Moses *Woof!* **1976 (PG)** Lancaster goes biblical as Moses, the man with the tablets. Edited from the 360-minute British television series, with no improvement obvious from the economy, except that the bad parts are shorter. Poor chatter and scattered bouts of acting are surpassed in inadequacy only by special effects. **141m/C VHS, Beta.** Burt Lancaster, Anthony Quayle, Ingrid Thulin, Irene Papas, William Lancaster; ***D:*** Gianfranco DeBosio; ***W:*** Anthony Burgess, Vittorio Bonicelli; ***M:*** Ennio Morricone. *FOX, LIV, VES*

Mosquito ☠ **1995 (R)** Alien forces transform the annoying insects into monstrous mutants. Schlocky special effects are good for laughs. **92m/C VHS.** Gunnar Hansen, Ron Asheton, Steve Dixon, Rachel Loiselle, Tim Loveface; ***D:*** Gary Jones; ***W:*** Gary Jones, Steve Hodge, Tom Chaney; ***C:*** Tom Chaney; ***M:*** Allen Lynch, Randall Lynch. *HMD*

The Mosquito Coast ☠☠½ **1986 (PG)** Ambitious adaptation of Paul Theroux's novel about an asocial inventor who transplants his family to a rainforest to realize his utopian dream. A nightmare ensues. Ford tries hard, but supporters Mirren and Phoenix are main appeal of only intermittently successful drama. **119m/C VHS, Beta, LV.** Harrison Ford, Helen Mirren, River Phoenix, Andre Gregory, Martha Plimpton, Conrad Roberts, Butterfly McQueen, Jadrien Steele, Hilary Gordon, Rebecca Gordon, Dick O'Neill, Jason Alexander;

D: Peter Weir; ***W:*** Paul Schrader; ***C:*** John Seale; ***M:*** Maurice Jarre. *WAR*

The Most Dangerous Game *The Hounds of Zaroff* **1932** Shipwrecked McRae washed ashore on the island of Banks's Count Zaroff, a deranged sportsman with a flair for tracking humans. Guess who becomes the mad count's next target. Oft-told tale is compellingly related in this, the first of many using Richard Connell's famous short story. If deja vu sets in, don't worry. This production uses most of the scenery, staff, and cast from its studio cousin, "King Kong." Remade in 1945 as "A Game of Death" and in 1956 as "Run for the Sun." **78m/B VHS, Beta.** Joel McCrea, Fay Wray, Leslie Banks, Robert Armstrong; ***D:*** Ernest B. Schoedsack, Irving Pichel; ***M:*** Max Steiner. *SNC, NOS, MED*

Most Wanted ½ **1976** A psychopath with a penchant for raping nuns and collecting crucifixes is tracked down by a special police unit in this made-for-television film. Became a TV series. **78m/C VHS, Beta.** Robert Stack, Shelly Novack, Leslie Charleson, Tom Selleck, Sheree North; ***D:*** Walter Grauman. *WOV*

Motel Hell ½ **1980 (R)** A completely tongue-in-cheek gore-fest about a farmer who kidnaps tourists, buries them in his garden, and reaps a human harvest to grind into his distinctive brand of smoked, preservative-free sausage. **102m/C VHS, Beta, LV.** Rory Calhoun, Nancy Parsons, Paul Linke, Nina Axelrod, Wolfman Jack, Elaine Joyce, Dick Curtis; ***D:*** Kevin Connor. *MGM*

Mother ½ **1926** Pudovkin's innovative classic about a Russian family shattered by the uprising in 1905. A masterpiece of Russian cinema that established Pudovkin, and rivaled only Eisenstein for supremacy in montage, poetic imagery, and propagandistic ideals. Based on Maxim Gorky's great novel, it's one of cinematic history's seminal works. Striking cinematography, stunning use of montage make this one important. Silent with English subtitles. **70m/B VHS, Beta.** *RU* Vera Baranovskaya, Nikolai Batalov; ***D:*** Vsevolod Pudovkin. *NOS, IHF, DVT*

Mother ½ *Okasan* **1952** A Japanese family is undone after the devastation of WWII. An uncharacteristically dramatic, and thus more accessible, film from one of the Japanese cinema's greatest masters. In Japanese with English subtitles. **98m/B VHS, Beta, LV.** *JP* Kinuyo Tanaka, Kyoko Kagawa, Eiji Okada, Akihiko Katayama; ***D:*** Mikio Naruse. *FCT, IME, INJ*

Mother ½ **1994 (R)** Olivia Hendrix (Ladd) is a very over-protective mom—even though son Tom (Weisser) is nineteen and anxious to untie the apron strings. But Mom thinks she knows best and she's willing to kill to made certain Tom stays home where he belongs. **90m/C VHS, LV.** Diane Ladd, Olympia Dukakis, Morgan Weisser, Ele Keats; ***D:*** Frank Laloggia. *TRI*

Mother & Daughter: A Loving War ½ **1980** A made-for-television film about three women experiencing motherhood. Special appearance by Harry Chapin as himself. **96m/C VHS, Beta.** Tuesday Weld, Frances Sternhagen, Kathleen Beller, Jeanne Lang, Ed Winter; ***D:*** Burt Brinckerhoff. *NLC*

Mother and Son **1931** Melodrama finds the wayward Young shielding her son from the fact that she runs a gambling hall. He grows up to be a society lad before discovering the devastating truth. **67m/B VHS.** Clara Kimball Young, Bruce Warren, Mildred Golden, John Elliott, Gordon Wood, Ernest Hilliard; ***D:*** John P. McCarthy. *GPV*

Mother Doesn't Always Know Best ½ **196?** A strange relationship between a young count and his widowed mother initiates a strange series of events. **95m/C VHS, Beta.** Senta Berger; ***D:*** Alfredo Gianelli. *NO*

Mother Goose Rock 'n' Rhyme **1990** Duvall follows the success of her "Faerie Tale Theatre" series with a new comedic fable, starring some of Hollywood's top names. Great fun for the whole family. **96m/C VHS, Beta.** Shelley Duvall, Teri Garr, Howie Mandel, Jean Stapleton, Ben Vereen, Bobby Brown, Art Garfunkel, Dan Gilroy, Deborah Harry, Cyndi Lauper, Little Richard, Paul Simon, Harry Anderson, Elayne Boosler, Woody Harrelson, Richard "Cheech" Marin, Garry Shandling. *MED*

Mother Joan of the Angels *The Devil and the Nun; Matka Joanna Od Aniolow* **1960** A priest investigating demonic possession among nuns in a 17th-century Polish convent becomes involved in a mutual attraction with the Mother Superior. A powerful allegory complemented by the stylized narrative and performances. Polish with subtitles. Based on actual events at Loudun and also the subject of a play by John Whiting, an opera by Krzysztof Penderecki, "The Devils of Loudon" novel by Aldous Huxley, and Ken Russell's movie "The Devils." **108m/B VHS.** *PL* Lucyna Winnicka, Mieczyslaw Voit, Anna Ciepielewska, Maria Chwalibog; ***D:*** Jerzy Kawalerowicz; ***W:*** Jerzy Kawalerowicz, Tadeusz Konwicki; ***M:*** Adam Walacinski. Cannes Film Festival '61: Grand Jury Prize. *FCT*

Mother, Jugs and Speed ½ **1976 (PG)** Black comedy about the day-to-day tragedies encountered by a group of ambulance drivers. Interesting mix of stars. **95m/C VHS.** Bill Cosby, Raquel Welch, Harvey Keitel, Allen (Goorwitz) Garfield, Larry Hagman, Bruce Davison, Dick Butkus, L.Q. Jones, Toni Basil; ***D:*** Peter Yates; ***W:*** Tom Mankiewicz. *FOX*

Mother Kusters Goes to Heaven *Mutter Kusters Fahrt Zum Himmel* **1976** Mrs. Kusters's husband is a frustrated factory worker who goes over the edge and kills the factory owner's son and himself. Left alone, she learns that everyone is using her husband's death to further their own needs, including her daughter, who uses the publicity to enhance her singing career. A statement that you should trust no one, not even your family and friends. This film was banned from the Berlin Film Festival because of its political overtones. In German with English subtitles. **108m/C VHS.** *GE* Brigitte Mira, Ingrid Caven, Armin Meier, Irm Hermann, Gottfried John, Margit Carstensen; ***D:*** Rainer Werner Fassbinder; ***W:*** Rainer Werner Fassbinder; ***C:*** Michael Ballhaus. *NYF*

Mother Lode ½ *Search for the Mother Lode; The Last Great Treasure* **1982 (PG)** The violent conflict between twin brothers (played by Heston) is intensified by greed, near madness, and the all-consuming lust for gold in this action-adventure. Heston's son, Fraser Clarke Heston, wrote as well as produced the film. **101m/C VHS, Beta.** Charlton Heston, Nick Mancuso; ***D:*** Charlton Heston. *VES*

Mother of Kings **1982** Livin' ain't easy for a widowed charwoman thanks to WWII and Stalinism. Innovative use of newsreel scenes. In Polish with English subtitles. **126m/C VHS.** *PL* Magda Teresa Wojcik. *FCT*

Mother's Boys **1994 (R)** Estranged mother Curtis attempts to reunite with the family she abandoned only to be snubbed, inspiring in her a ruthless effort to win back the children and oust father Gallagher's new live-in girlfriend Whalley-Kilmer. With an almost psychotic devotion, she terrorizes everyone in the family, including enticing her 12-year-old son Edwards into a nude bathtub game of peek-a-boo. Film lacks the tension necessary to carry suspense. Based on the novel by Bernard Taylor. **96m/C VHS, LV.** Jamie Lee Curtis, Peter Gallagher, Joanne Whalley, Luke Edwards, Vanessa Redgrave, Colin Ward, Joss Ackland, Paul Guilfoyle, John C. McGinley, J.E. Freeman, Ken Lerner, Lorraine Toussaint, Joey Zimmerman, Jill Freedman; ***D:*** Yves Simoneau; ***W:*** Richard Hawley, Barry Schneider; ***M:*** George S. Clinton. *MAX, TOU*

Mother's Day ½ **1980** Three women who were former college roommates plan a reunion together in the wilderness. All goes well until they are dragged into an isolated house by two insane boys who constantly watch television, ardently consume the products advertised, and then terrorize and torture people to please their mom. Sanitized gore with black satiric intentions. **98m/C VHS, Beta.** Tiana Pierce, Nancy Hendrickson, Deborah Luee, Holden McGuire, Billy Ray McQuade, Rose Ross; ***D:*** Charles Kaufman; ***W:*** Warren Leight, Charles Kaufman. *MED*

A Mother's Prayer ½ **1995 (PG-13)** Fact-based story about young mom Rosemary Holmstrom (Hamilton), who has AIDS, and is determined to find a home for her 8-year-old son T.J. (Fleiss) before she dies. Guaranteed to make the tear ducts flow, with a determined performance from Hamilton that lessens the sentimentality. Made for cable TV. Holmstrom died at the age of 36 in 1994. **90m/C VHS.** Linda Hamilton, Noah Fleiss, Bruce Dern, Kate Nelligan, S. Epatha Merkerson, Corey Parker, Jenny O'Hara, RuPaul; ***D:*** Larry Elikann; ***W:*** Lee Rose. *MCA*

Mothra **1962** Classic Japanese monster shenanigans about an enraged giant caterpillar that invades Tokyo while searching for the Alilenas, a set of very tiny, twin princesses who've been kidnapped by an evil nightclub owner in the pursuit of big profits. After tiring of crushing buildings and wreaking incidental havoc, the enormous crawly thing zips up into a cocoon and emerges as Mothra, a moth distinguished by both its size and bad attitude. Mothra and the wee babes make appearances in later Godzilla epics. **101m/C VHS, Beta.** *JP* Yumi Ito, Frankie Sakai, Lee Kresel, Emi Ito; ***D:*** Inoshiro Honda. *GKK*

Motor Patrol ½ **1950** A cop poses as a racketeer to infiltrate a car-stealing ring. **66m/B VHS, Beta, LV.** Don Castle, Jane Nigh, Charles Victor. *NO*

Motor Psycho *Woof!* **1965** When a motorcycle gang rapes a woman, she and her husband pursue them into the desert to seek their brutal revenge. **73m/B VHS.** Haji, Alex Rocco, Stephen Oliver, Holle K. Winters, Joseph Cellini, Thomas Scott, Coleman Francis, Sharon Lee; ***D:*** Russ Meyer. *RMF*

Motorama **1991 (R)** A 10-year-old juvenile delinquent becomes obsessed with winning a gas station contest which involves collecting game cards. So he steals a car and hits the road where he gets his first tattoo and encounters a beautiful "older" woman (Barrymore) and lots of trouble. **89m/C VHS.** Jordan Christopher Michael, Martha Quinn, Flea, Michael J. Pollard, Meat Loaf, Drew Barrymore, Garrett Morris, Robin Duke, Sandy Baron, Mary Woronov, Susan Tyrrell, John Laughlin, John Diehl, Robert Picardo, Jack Nance, Vince Edwards, Dick Miller, Allyce Beasley, Shelley Berman; ***D:*** Barry Shils; ***W:*** Joe Minion; ***M:*** Andy Summers. *COL, BTV*

Motorcycle Gang **1957** It's the summer of '57, and Randy plans to bring home the title at the Pacific Motorcycle Championships for his club, the "Skyriders." But first his old rival Nick, who's just out of jail, turns up and challenges Randy to an illegal street race. Will Randy succumb to peer pressure and race? Lame plot + lame acting = lame movie. **78m/B VHS.** Steven Terrell, John Ashley, Anne Neyland, Carl "Alfalfa" Switzer, Raymond Hatton; ***D:*** Edward L. Cahn; ***W:*** Lou Rusoff. *COL*

Motorcycle Squad ½ **1937** A policeman is dishonorably discharged so he can get the "inside" dope on a gang of crooks in this 'B' thriller. **?m/C VHS.** Kane Richmond, Wynne Gibson. *SNC*

Mouchette ½ **1967** A lonely 14-year-old French girl, daughter of a drunk father and dying mother, eventually finds spiritual release by committing suicide. Typically somber, spiritual fare from unique master filmmaker Bresson. Perhaps the most complete expression of Bresson's austere, Catholic vision. In French with English subtitles. **80m/B VHS, Beta.** *FR* Nadine Nortier, Maria Cardinal, Paul Hebert; ***D:*** Robert Bresson; ***C:*** Ghislan Cloquet. *FCT, INJ, TPV*

Moulin Rouge ½ **1952** Colorful, entertaining portrait of acclaimed Impressionist painter Toulouse-Lautrec, more famous for its production stories than on-screen drama, Ferrer delivers one of his most impressive performances as the physically stunted, cynical artist who basked in the seamy Montmartre nightlife. **119m/C VHS, Beta, LV.** Jose Ferrer, Zsa Zsa Gabor, Christopher Lee, Peter Cushing, Colette Marchand, Katherine Kath, Michael Balfour, Eric Pohlmann; ***D:*** John Huston; ***C:*** Oswald Morris. Academy Awards '52: Best Art Direction/Set Decoration (Color), Best Costume Design (Color); National Board of Review Awards '53: 5 Best Foreign Films of the Year; Nominations: Academy Awards '52: Best Actor (Ferrer), Best Director (Huston), Best Film

Editing, Best Picture, Best Supporting Actress (Marchand). *MGM*

The Mountain 🦴🦴 **1956** A man and his shady younger brother set out to inspect a Paris-routed plane that crashed in the French Alps. After some harrowing experiences in climbing the peak, it becomes evident that one brother has designs to save whatever he can, while the other intends to loot it. Many real, as well as staged, climbing scenes. Based on Henri Troyat's novel. **105m/C VHS, Beta.** Spencer Tracy, Robert Wagner, Claire Trevor, William Demarest, Richard Arlen, E.G. Marshall; ***D:*** Edward Dmytryk. *PAR*

Mountain Charlie 🦴½ **1980** Mountain girl's life is destroyed by three drifters. **96m/C VHS, Beta.** Denise Neilson, Dick Robinson, Rick Guinn, Lynn Seus; ***D:*** George Stapleford. *NO*

Mountain Family Robinson 🦴🦴 **1979 (G)** An urban family, seeking escape from the hassles of city life, moves to the Rockies, determined to get back to nature. They soon find that nature may be more harsh than rush-hour traffic and nasty bosses when a bear comes calling. More "Wilderness Family"-type adventures. **102m/C VHS, Beta.** Robert F. Logan, Susan Damante Shaw, Heather Rattray, Ham Larsen, William Bryant, George Flower; ***D:*** John Cotter. *MED, VTR*

Mountain Fury **1990 (R)** A spoof based on the novel by Alexandre Dumas wherein two brothers separated at birth are reunited and battle against an evil French baron. **90m/C VHS.** *NO*

Mountain Justice 🦴🦴½ *Kettle Creek* **1930** Maynard's first all-talkie western finds our hero in search of his father's murderer. Good action sequences (with stunts performed by Maynard), including those aboard a moving train and a buckboard. **73m/B VHS.** Ken Maynard, Otis Harlan, Kathryn Crawford, Paul Hurst; ***D:*** Harry Joe Brown. *GPV*

Mountain Man 🦴🦴½ *Guardian of the Wilderness* **1977** Historically accurate drama about Galen Clark's successful fight in the 1860s to save the magnificent wilderness area that is now Yosemite National Park. Together with naturalist John Muir, he fought a battle against the lumber companies who wanted the timber and won President Lincoln's support for his cause. **96m/C VHS, Beta.** Denver Pyle, John Dehner, Ken Berry, Cheryl Miller, Don Shanks, Cliff Osmond, Jack Kruschen, Ford Rainey; ***D:*** David O'Malley; ***W:*** David O'Malley. *LME*

The Mountain Men 🦴½ **1980 (R)** Dull adventure drama set in the American West of the 1880s. Two trappers argue about life and have trouble with Indians. **102m/C VHS, Beta, LV.** Charlton Heston, Brian Keith, John Glover, Seymour Cassel, Victor Jory; ***D:*** Richard Lang. *COL*

The Mountain Road 🦴½ **1960** Listless drama of an American squadron stationed in China during the last days of WWII. Only Stewart makes this drab film worthwile. **102m/B VHS.** James Stewart, Harry (Henry) Morgan, Glenn Corbett, Mike Kellin; ***D:*** Daniel Mann. *COL*

Mountains of the Moon 🦴🦴🦴½ **1990 (R)** Sprawling adventure detailing the obsessive search for the source of the Nile conducted by famed Victorian rogue/explorer Sir Richard Burton and cohort John Hanning Speke in the late 1800s. Spectacular scenery and images. Director Rafelson, better known for overtly personal films such as "Five Easy Pieces" and "The King of Marvin Gardens," shows considerable skill with this epic. Cinematography by Roger Deakins. From William Harrison's novel "Burton and Speke." **140m/C VHS, Beta, LV.** Patrick Bergin, Iain Glen, Fiona Shaw, Richard E. Grant, Peter Vaughan, Roger Rees, Bernard Hill, Anna Massey, Leslie Phillips, John Savident, James Villiers, Delroy Lindo, Roshan Seth; ***D:*** Bob Rafelson; ***W:*** Bob Rafelson; ***C:*** Roger Deakins. *LIV*

Mountaintop Motel Massacre *Woof!* **1986 (R)** A resort motel's hostess is a raving lunatic who regularly slaughters her guests. **95m/C VHS, Beta.** Bill Thurman, Anna Chappell, Will Mitchell; ***D:*** Jim McCullough. *VTR, NWV*

Mouse and His Child 🦴🦴 **1977** A gentle animated fantasy adventure about a toy wind-up mouse and his child who fall into the clutches of a villainous rat when they venture into the outside world. **83m/C VHS, Beta.** ***D:*** Fred Wolf; ***V:*** Peter Ustinov, Cloris Leachman, Andy Devine. *COL, WTA*

The Mouse That Roared 🦴🦴🦴 **1959** With its wine export business going down the drain, a tiny, desperate country decides to declare war on the United States in hopes that the U.S., after its inevitable triumph, will revive the conquered nation. So off to New York go 20 chain-mail clad warriors armed with bow and arrow. Featured in three roles, Sellers is great as the duchess, less effective (though still funny) as the prime minister, and a military leader. A must for Sellers' fans; maintains a sharp satiric edge throughout. Based on the novel by Leonard Wibberley. **83m/C VHS, Beta.** *GB* Peter Sellers, Jean Seberg, Leo McKern, David Kossoff, William Hartnell, Timothy Bateson, MacDonald Parke, Monte Landis; ***D:*** Jack Arnold; ***W:*** Roger MacDougall, Stanley Mann; ***M:*** Edwin Astley. *COL*

Mouth to Mouth 🦴🦴 *Boca a Boca* **1995 (R)** Budding actor Victor (Bardem) is working in Madrid as a phone sex operator while waiting to hear about his big break on an American picture. Victor's regularly called by repressed gay surgeon Ricardo (Flotats) and Amanda (Sanchez-Gijon), who says she's Ricardo's wife. Naive Victor falls for Amanda—who of course isn't Ricardo's wife but seems to be involved in a plot to kill Ricardo masterminded by his real wife Angela (Barranco) and her lover David (Gutierrez Caba). The plot's a little tangled but there's lots of visual gags and bedroom farce and the virile Bardem turns out to be a gifted comedian. Spanish with subtitles. **105m/C VHS.** *SP* Javier Bardem, Aitana Sanchez-Gijon, Josep Maria Flotats, Maria Barranco, Emilio Gutierrez Caba, Fernando Guillen, Myriam Meziere; ***D:*** Manuel Gomez Pereira; ***W:*** Manuel Gomez Pereira, Joaquin Oristrell, Naomi Wise, Juan Luis Iborra; ***C:*** Juan Amoros; ***M:*** Bernardo Bonezzi. *NYR*

Movers and Shakers 🦴½ **1985 (PG)** An irreverent spoof of Hollywood depicting a filmmaker's attempt to render a best-selling sex manual into a blockbuster film. Fails to live up to its potential and wastes a star-studded cast. **100m/C VHS, Beta.** Walter Matthau, Charles Grodin, Gilda Radner, Vincent Gardenia, Bill Macy, Tyne Daly, Steve Martin, Penny Marshall, Luana Anders; ***D:*** William Asher; ***W:*** Charles Grodin. *MGM*

The Movie House Massacre 🦴 **1978** A psychopath runs rampant in a theatre killing and maiming moviegoers. No refunds are given. **80m/C VHS, Beta.** Mary Woronov. *AHV, MRV*

Movie ... In Your Face 🦴 **1990** Japanese mobsters want to take over a movie studio. This supposed comedy comes with a "PU-13" rating—"Stinks to anyone with an I.Q. over 13," make of that what you will and be forewarned that it's also sophomoric and tasteless. **85m/C VHS.** Tommy Sledge. *HTV*

Movie Maker 🦴 *Smart Alec* **1986** A young filmmaker ineptly raises money for his next film. **87m/C VHS, Beta.** Zsa Zsa Gabor, Antony Alda, Orson Bean, Bill Henderson; ***D:*** Jim Wilson. *LIV*

Movie, Movie 🦴🦴½ **1978 (PG)** Acceptable spoof of 1930s films features Scott in twin-bill of black and white "Dynamite Hands," which lampoons boxing dramas, and "Baxter's Beauties," a color send-up of Busby Berkeley musicals. There's even a parody of coming attractions. Wholesome, mildly entertaining. **107m/B VHS.** Stanley Donen, George C. Scott, Trish Van Devere, Eli Wallach, Red Buttons, Barbara Harris, Barry Bostwick, Harry Hamlin, Art Carney; ***D:*** Stanley Donen; ***W:*** Larry Gelbart; ***M:*** Ralph Burns. Writers Guild of America '78: Best Original Screenplay. *FOX*

A Movie Star's Daughter **1979** The daughter of a famous movie star moves to a new town and school. She is afraid her popularity is due to her famous father. She must make choices and learn the real meaning of friendship. Also available in a 33-minute edited version. **46m/C VHS, Beta.** Frank Converse, Trini Alvarado; ***D:*** Robert Fuest. *LCA*

Movie Stuntmen 🦴 *Hollywood Thrillmakers; Hollywood Stunt Man* **1953** A retired Hollywood stunt man takes a job for a dead friend so that the friend's widow can receive the fee. Good stunt work taken mostly from old Richard Taldmadge movies almost makes up for poor production. **56m/B VHS.** James Gleason, William Henry; ***D:*** Bernard B. Ray. *NOS*

Moving 🦴 **1988 (R)** An engineer must relocate his family from New Jersey to Idaho in order to get his dream job. Predictable calamities ensue. Not apt to move you. **89m/C VHS, Beta, LV, 8mm.** Richard Pryor, Randy Quaid, Dana Carvey, Dave Thomas, Rodney Dangerfield, Stacey Dash; ***D:*** Alan Metter; ***W:*** Andy Breckman; ***M:*** Howard Shore. *WAR*

Moving Out 🦴🦴 **1983** Adolescent migrant Italian boy finds it difficult to adjust to his new surroundings in Melbourne, Australia. **91m/C VHS, Beta.** Vince Colosimo, Sally Cooper, Maurice Devincentis, Tibor Gyapjas; ***D:*** Michael Pattinson. *NO*

Moving Target 🦴½ **1989 (R)** A young woman witnesses the brutal murder of her boyfriend by mobsters and flees to Florida. Unbeknownst to her, the thugs are still after her. Although top-billed, Blair's role is actually a supporting one. **85m/C VHS, Beta.** *IT* Linda Blair, Ernest Borgnine, Stuart Whitman, Charles Pitt, Jainine Linde, Kurt Woodruff; ***D:*** Marius Mattei. *HMD*

Moving Targets 🦴🦴 **1987** A young girl and her mother find themselves tracked by a homicidal maniac. **95m/C VHS, Beta.** *AU* Michael Aitkens, Carmen Duncan, Annie Jones, Shane Briant; ***D:*** Chris Langman. *ACA*

Moving Violation 🦴🦴 **1976 (PG)** Crooked cops chase two young drifters who have witnessed the local sheriff commit a murder. Corman car chase epic. **91m/C VHS, Beta, LV.** Eddie Albert, Kay Lenz, Stephen McHattie, Will Geer, Lonny Chapman; ***D:*** Charles S. Dubin; ***W:*** William W. Norton Sr. *FOX*

Moving Violations 🦴 **1985 (PG-13)** This could be entitled "Adventures in Traffic Violations School." A wise-cracking tree planter is sent to traffic school after accumulating several moving violations issued to him by a morose traffic cop. Bill Murray's little brother in feature role. **90m/C VHS, Beta, LV.** John Murray, Jennifer Tilly, James Keach, Brian Backer, Sally Kellerman, Fred Willard, Clara Peller, Wendie Jo Sperber; ***D:*** Neal Israel; ***W:*** Pat Proft; ***M:*** Ralph Burns. *FOX*

Mozart: A Childhood Chronicle 🦴🦴🦴 **1976** An experimental, semi-narrative portrait of the immortal composer, from the ages of seven to twenty, filmed on authentic locations and with the original instruments of the era. Entire soundtrack is composed of Mozart's music. In German with English subtitles. **224m/B VHS, Beta, LV.** *GE* ***D:*** Klaus Kirschner. *KIV, IME, GLV*

The Mozart Brothers 🦴🦴🦴 **1986** An angst-ridden Swedish opera director decides to break all the rules while doing an innovative production of Mozart's "Don Giovanni." At first he horrifies his conservative opera company but as his vision is gradually realized their resistance breaks down. A wonderful look at behind-the-scenes chaos and not just for opera aficionados. In Swedish with English subtitles. **111m/C VHS.** *SW* Etienne Glaser, Philip Zanden, Henry Bronett; ***D:*** Suzanne Osten. *TPV, INJ*

The Mozart Story 🦴🦴 **1948** After Mozart's death, music minister to the Emperor, Antonio Salieri, reflects on how his jealousy and hatred of the musical genius held the great composer back and contributed to his death. Originally filmed in Austria in 1937, scenes were added for the U.S. release in 1948. **91m/B VHS, Beta.** Hans Holt, Winnie Markus, Irene von Meyendorf, Rene Deltgen, Edward Vedder, Wilton Graff, Walther Jansson, Curt Jurgens, Paul Hoerbiger; ***D:*** Karl Hartl. *VYY, GLV*

Much Ado about Nothing 🦴🦴🦴½ **1993 (PG-13)** Shakespeare for the masses details romance between two sets of would-be lovers—the battling Beatrice and Benedick (Thompson and Branagh) and the ingenuous Hero and Claudio (Beckinsdale and Leonard). Washington is the noble warrior leader, Reeves his evil half-dressed half-brother, and

Keaton serves comic relief as the officious, bumbling Dogberry. Sunlit, lusty, and revealing about all the vagaries of love, Branagh brings passion to his quest of making Shakespeare more approachable. His second attempt after "Henry V" at breaking the stuffy Shakespearean tradition. Filmed on location in Tuscany, Italy. **110m/C VHS, LV.** *GB* Kenneth Branagh, Emma Thompson, Robert Sean Leonard, Kate Beckinsale, Denzel Washington, Keanu Reeves, Michael Keaton, Brian Blessed, Phyllida Law, Imelda Staunton, Gerard Horan, Jimmy Yuill, Richard Clifford, Ben Elton; ***D:*** Kenneth Branagh; ***W:*** Kenneth Branagh; ***M:*** Patrick Doyle. Nominations: Cannes Film Festival '93: Best Film; Golden Globe Awards '94: Best Film—Musical/Comedy; Independent Spirit Awards '94: Best Actress (Thompson), Best Film. *COL*

Mugsy's Girls 🦴 *Delta Pi* **1985 (R)** A messy comedy about six sorority women, educated in the refined skills of bar mud wrestling, who wallow in a Las Vegas championship tournament. Features pop singer Laura Branigan. **87m/C VHS, Beta.** Ruth Gordon, Laura Branigan, Eddie Deezen; ***D:*** Kevin Brodie. *LIV, VES*

Mulholland Falls 🦴🦴½ **1995 (R)** Noir meets the nuclear age in this stylish period piece from New Zealand director Tamahori. Nolte plays the leader of the Hat Squad, a vicious group of fedora-sporting detectives assigned to bust organized crime in '50s L.A. at all costs. While investigating the murder of his ex-mistress, Nolte and cohorts Madsen, Palminteri and Penn discover evidence linking the murder to a general (Malkovich) in charge of the top secret nuclear program. Although the cast is dripping with big name stars, the best performance is put in by the glossy set design of Richard Sylbert, who probably had a strong case of deja vu, having previously done "Chinatown." **107m/C VHS, LV.** Nick Nolte, Melanie Griffith, Chazz Palminteri, Michael Madsen, Christopher Penn, Treat Williams, Jennifer Connelly, Andrew McCarthy, John Malkovich, Daniel Baldwin, Bruce Dern, Ed Lauter; ***Cameos:*** William L. Petersen, Rob Lowe; ***D:*** Lee Tamahori; ***W:*** Pete Dexter; ***C:*** Haskell Wexler; ***M:*** Dave Grusin. *MGM*

Multiple Maniacs 🦴 **1970** Waters at his most perverse. Divine's travelling freak show, filled with disgusting side-show sex acts, is the vehicle used for robbing and killing hapless spectators. One of the best scenes of a sordid lot is Divine being raped by Lobstora, a 15-foot broiled lobster. **90m/B VHS.** Divine, David Lochary, Mary Vivian Pearce, Edith Massey, Mink Stole; ***D:*** John Waters. *NO*

Multiplicity 🦴🦴½ **1996 (PG-13)** With too many business and personal responsibilities, Doug Kinney (Keaton) decides to have himself cloned. Since the cloning process isn't exactly perfect, each clone has a different dominant personality trait. Confusion reigns as his wife (McDowell) deals with separation anxiety on a grand scale. Pleasant comedy shows Keaton can still be funny given the chance. Keaton had his choice of cloning comedies and chose this one over Chris Columbus's "More." **?m/C VHS.** Michael Keaton, Andie MacDowell; ***D:*** Harold Ramis; ***W:*** Harold Ramis, Chris Miller, Lowell Ganz, Babaloo Mandel. *NYR*

The Mummy 🦴🦴🦴½ **1932** Eerie chills mark this classic horror tale of an Egyptian priest, buried alive nearly 4000 years earlier, who comes back to life after a 1921 archaeological dig. Eight hours of extraordinary makeup transformed Karloff into the macabre mummy, who believes the soul of the long-deceased (and probably long-decayed) lover resides in the body of a young woman. Marked the directing debut of famed German cinematographer Freund. **72m/B VHS, Beta, LV.** Boris Karloff, Zita Johann, David Manners, Edward Van Sloan; ***D:*** Karl Freund. *MCA, TLF*

The Mummy 🦴🦴🦴 **1959** A group of British archaeologists discover they have made a grave mistake when a mummy kills off those who have violated his princess' tomb. A summation of all the previous "mummy" films, this one has a more frightening mummy (6'4" Lee) who is on screen much of the time. Additionally, there is pathos in this monster, not merely murder and revenge. An effective remake of the 1932 classic. **88m/C VHS, Beta, LV.** *GB* Peter Cushing, Christopher Lee, Felix Aylmer, Yvonne Furneaux; ***D:*** Terence Fisher; ***W:*** Jimmy Sangster. *WAR, MLB*

Mummy & Curse of the Jackal *Woof!* **1967** Upon opening the tomb of female mummy, a man is cursed to roam the streets of Las Vegas as a werejackal. Impossibly inept. **86m/C VHS.** Anthony Eisley, Martina Pons, John Carradine, Saul Goldsmith; ***D:*** Oliver Drake. *ACA*

The Mummy's Curse 🦴🦴 **1944** Sequel to "The Mummy's Ghost" and Chaney's last outing as Kharis. Construction by a government order causes Kharis and Ananka to be dug up in a Louisiana bayou and taken to Cajun country for study by archaeologists. The usual havoc ensues. Includes lots of stock footage from earlier mummy movies. Based on a story by Leon Abrams and Dwight V. Babcock. **61m/B VHS.** Lon Chaney Jr., Peter Coe, Virginia Christine, Kay Harding, Dennis Moore, Martin Kosleck, Kurt Katch; ***D:*** Leslie Goodwins; ***W:*** Bernard Schubert. *MCA, FCT*

The Mummy's Ghost 🦴🦴 **1944** Sequel to "The Mummy's Tomb" has Chaney, Jr. searching for the reincarnation of his ancient love, Princess Ananka. The least interesting entry in the series. Based on a story by Griffith Jay and Henry Sucher. **61m/B VHS.** Lon Chaney Jr., John Carradine, Ramsay Ames, Robert Lowery, Barton MacLane, George Zucco; ***D:*** Reginald LeBorg; ***W:*** Griffin Jay, Henry Sucher, Brenda Weisberg. *MCA, FCT*

The Mummy's Hand 🦴🦴½ **1940** Two archaeologists (Foran and Ford) searching for the tomb of ancient Egyptian Princess Ananka discover more than they bargained for when they find that an evil and deadly mummy is the tomb's guardian. From there the plot unravels, but the good cast and a mix of scares and comedy make this worth watching. **70m/B VHS.** Dick Foran, Wallace Ford, Peggy Moran, Cecil Kellaway, George Zucco, Tom Tyler, Eduardo Ciannelli, Charles Trowbridge; ***D:*** Christy Cabanne. *MCA*

The Mummy's Revenge 🦴 **1973** A fanatic revives a mummy with virgin blood. The first mummy movie to feature open gore. **91m/C VHS, Beta.** *SP* Paul Naschy, Jack Taylor, Maria Silva, Helga Line; ***D:*** Carlos Aured; ***W:*** Paul Naschy. *UNI*

The Mummy's Tomb 🦴🦴 **1942** Chaney, Jr. is in wraps for the first time in this sequel to "The Mummy's Hand." Kharis is transported to America by a crazed Egyptian high priest to kill off surviving members of the expedition. Weakened by a lame script and too much stock footage. Based on a story by Neil P. Varnick. **71m/B VHS.** Lon Chaney Jr., Dick Foran, John Hubbard, Elyse Knox, George Zucco, Wallace Ford, Turhan Bey; ***D:*** Harold Young; ***W:*** Griffin Jay, Henry Sucher. *MCA, FCT*

Munchie 🦴½ **1992 (PG)** A forgotten alien critter is discovered in a mine shaft by young Gage. Munchie turns out to be a good friend, protecting Gage from bullies and granting other wishes. Frequent sight gags help keep the film moving but it's still awfully slow. Sequel to "Munchies" (1987). **80m/C VHS.** Loni Anderson, Andrew Stevens, Arte Johnson, Jamie McEnnan; ***D:*** Jim Wynorski; ***V:*** Dom DeLuise. *NHO*

Munchies 🦴 **1987 (PG)** "Gremlins" rip-off about tiny aliens who love beer and fast food, and invade a small town. Lewd and ribald. **83m/C VHS, Beta.** Harvey Korman, Charles Stratton, Nadine Van Der Velde; ***D:*** Bettina Hirsch. *MGM*

The Munsters' Revenge 🦴🦴 **1981** Television movie based on the continuing adventures of the 1960s comedy series characters. Herman, Lily, and Grandpa have to contend with robot replicas of themselves that were created by a flaky scientist. **96m/C VHS, Beta.** Fred Gwynne, Yvonne De Carlo, Al Lewis, Jo McDonnel, Sid Caesar, Ezra Stone, Howard Morris, Bob Hastings, K.C. Martel; ***D:*** Don Weis. *MCA*

The Muppet Christmas Carol 🦴🦴½ **1992 (G)** Christmas classic features all the muppet favorites together and in Victorian garb. Storyline is more or less faithful to Dickens original, with pleasant special effects. Gonzo the Great as Dickens narrates the tale as Scrooge (Caine) takes his legendary Christmas Eve journey escorted by three (flannel) spirits. The Cratchits are led by Kermit and Miss Piggy. Directed by Brian Henson, Jim's son, the film is as heartwarming as the Cratchit's crackling fire, but doesn't quite achieve the former muppet magic. Also features some sappy songs by Williams, including "Love is Like a Heatwave" and "Island in the Sun." **120m/C VHS, Beta.** Michael Caine; ***D:*** Brian Henson; ***M:*** Paul Williams, Miles Goodman; ***V:*** Dave Goelz, Steve Whitmire, Jerry Nelson, Frank Oz. *JHV*

The Muppet Movie 🦴🦴🦴½ **1979 (G)** Seeking fame and footlights, Kermit the Frog and his pal Fozzie Bear travel to Hollywood, and along the way are joined by sundry human and muppet characters, including the lovely Miss Piggy. A delightful cult favorite filled with entertaining cameos, memorable (though somewhat pedestrian) songs and crafty special effects—Kermit rides a bike and rows a boat! A success for the late Jim Henson. ♫The Rainbow Connection; Frog's Legs So Fine; Movin Right Along; Can You Picture That?; Never Before; Something Better; This Looks Familiar; I'm Going Back There Someday. **94m/C VHS, Beta, LV.** *GB* Jim Henson's Muppets; ***Cameos:*** Edgar Bergen, Milton Berle, Mel Brooks, Madeline Kahn, Steve Martin, Carol Kane, Paul Williams, Charles Durning, Bob Hope, James Coburn, Dom DeLuise, Elliott Gould, Cloris Leachman, Telly Savalas, Orson Welles; ***D:*** James Frawley; ***W:*** Jack Burns; ***M:*** Paul Williams; ***V:*** Jim Henson, Frank Oz. Nominations: Academy Awards '79: Best Song ("The Rainbow Connection"), Best Original Score. *JHV, FOX*

Muppet Treasure Island 🦴🦴½ **1996 (G)** Literary classic gets its first coat of felt as Kermit the Frog, Miss Piggy and all the Muppet gang hit the high seas in an adaptation of Robert Louis Stevenson's 1883 well-worn adventure tale. Delightful settings, from an old English tavern to an exotic south sea island, frame the journey of young Jim Hawkins (flesh and blood Bishop), who along with tavern owners Rizzo the Rat (Whitmire) and the Great Gonzo (Goelz) search for buried treasure. Long John Silver is played to the hilt by Curry, master of the over-the-top villain. Helmer Henson steers a steady ship, with over 400 Muppet critters making an appearance. **99m/C VHS.** Tim Curry, Kevin Bishop, Billy Connolly, Jennifer Saunders; ***D:*** Brian Henson; ***W:*** Jerry Juhl, Jim V. Hart, Kirk R. Thatcher; ***C:*** John Fenner; ***M:*** Hans Zimmer; ***V:*** Steve Whitmire, Frank Oz, Dave Goelz. *TOU*

The Muppets Take Manhattan 🦴🦴🦴 **1984 (G)** Following a smashing success with a college musical, the Muppets take their show and talents to Broadway, only to face misfortune in the form of an unscrupulous producer. A less imaginative script than the first two Muppet movies, yet an enjoyable experience with numerous major stars making cameo appearances. **94m/C VHS, Beta, LV.** Jim Henson's Muppets; ***Cameos:*** Dabney Coleman, James Coco, Art Carney, Joan Rivers, Gregory Hines, Linda Lavin, Liza Minnelli, Brooke Shields, John Landis; ***D:*** Frank Oz; ***M:*** Ralph Burns; ***V:*** Jim Henson, Frank Oz. Nominations: Academy Awards '84: Best Original Score. *FOX, HMV*

Murder 🦴🦴🦴 **1930** Believing in a young woman's innocence, one jurist begins to organize the pieces of the crime in order to save her. Fine early effort by Hitchcock based on play "Enter Sir John," by Clemense Dane and Helen Simpson. **92m/B VHS, Beta.** *GB* Herbert Marshall, Nora Baring, Phyllis Konstam, Miles Mander; ***D:*** Alfred Hitchcock; ***W:*** Alfred Hitchcock. *REP, NOS, HHT*

Murder Ahoy 🦴🦴½ **1964** Miss Marple looks perplexed when dead bodies surface on a naval cadet training ship. Dame Marge is the dottie detective in the final, and least appealing, of her four Agatha Christie films of the sixties (although it was released in the States prior to "Murder Most Foul"). **74m/B VHS, Beta.** Margaret Rutherford, Lionel Jeffries, Charles Tingwell, William Mervyn, Francis Matthews; ***D:*** George Pollock. *MGM, FCT*

Murder at 45 R.P.M. 🦴🦴 *Meurtre en 45 Tours* **1965** A singer and her lover suspect each other of their husband's murder. Things become sticky when she receives a recorded message from her dead husband. Average. **98m/C VHS.** *FR* Danielle Darrieux, Michel Auclair, Jean Servais, Henri Guisol; *D:* Etienne Perier. *SNC*

Murder at Midnight 🦴🦴 **1931** The killings begin with a game of charades in which the gun wasn't supposed to be loaded, and continue as members of English high society die one by one. "Blondie" director Strayer still working on his change of pace. **69m/B VHS, Beta, 8mm.** Alice White, Leslie Fenton, Aileen Pringle, Hale Hamilton, Robert Elliott, Clara Blandick, Brandon Hurst; *D:* Frank Strayer. *SNC, NOS, DVT*

Murder at the Baskervilles 🦴🦴 *Silver Blaze* **1937** Sherlock Holmes is invited to visit Sir Henry Baskerville at his estate, but then finds that Baskerville's daughter's fiance is accused of stealing a race horse and murdering its keeper. Based on Sir Arthur Conan Doyle's story "Silver Blaze." **67m/B VHS, Beta.** *GB* Arthur Wontner, Ian Fleming, Lyn Harding; *D:* Thomas Bentley. *SNC, CCB, REP*

Murder at the Gallop 🦴🦴🦴½ **1963** Snooping Miss Marple doesn't believe a filthy rich old-timer died of natural causes, despite the dissenting police point of view. Wheedling her way into the police investigation, she discovers the secret of the Gallop club, a place where people bounce up and down on top of horses. Much mugging between Dame Margaret and Morley. Marple's assistant, Mr. Stringer, is the real life Mr. Dame Margaret. Based on Christie's Poirot mystery "After the Funeral." **81m/B VHS, Beta.** Margaret Rutherford, Robert Morley, Flora Robson, Charles Tingwell, Duncan Lamont; *D:* George Pollock. *MGM, FCT*

Murder at the Vanities 🦴🦴½ **1934** Vintage murder mystery set against a musical revue format, in which a tough detective must find a killer before the Earl Carroll-based cabaret ends and he or she will escape with the exiting crowd. Also featured is a mind-boggling production number based on the song "Marijuana." ♫Marijuana; Lovely One; Where Do They Come From Now; Live and Love Tonight; Cokctails for Two; Ebony Rhapsody. **91m/B VHS, Beta.** Victor McLaglen, Kitty Carlisle Hart, Jack Oakie, Duke Ellington, Carl Brisson; *D:* Mitchell Leisen. *MCA*

Murder by Death 🦴🦴½ **1976 (PG)** Capote is an eccentric millionaire who invites the world's greatest detectives to dinner, offering one million dollars to the one who can solve the evening's murder. Entertaining and hammy spoof of Agatha Christie's "And Then There Were None" and the earlier "Ten Little Indians." **95m/C VHS, Beta, LV.** Peter Falk, Alec Guinness, David Niven, Maggie Smith, Peter Sellers, Eileen Brennan, Elsa Lanchester, Nancy Walker, Estelle Winwood, Truman Capote, James Coco; *D:* Robert Moore; *W:* Neil Simon; *M:* Dave Grusin. *COL, TVC*

Murder by Decree 🦴🦴🦴 **1979 (PG)** Realistic and convincing version of the Jack the Ripper story. Sherlock Holmes and Dr. Watson find a vast web of conspiracy when they investigate the murders of Whitechapel prostitutes. Based partially on facts, it's a highly detailed suspenser with interesting camera work and fine performances. **120m/C VHS, Beta.** *CA* Christopher Plummer, James Mason, Donald Sutherland, Genevieve Bujold, Susan Clark, David Hemmings, Frank Finlay, John Gielgud, Anthony Quayle; *D:* Bob (Benjamin) Clark; *W:* John Hopkins. Genie Awards '80: Best Actor (Plummer), Best Director (Clark), Best Supporting Actress (Bujold). *SUE, NLC*

Murder by Moonlight 🦴🦴 **1991 (PG-13)** Rival agents investigate a mysterious murder in a prosperous mining colony on the moon. Not only do they discover a dastardly trail that leads all the way back to Earth, but a strange romantic attraction for each other. Originally broadcast on British TV. **94m/C VHS.** *GB* Julian Sands, Brigitte Nielsen, Gerald McRaney, Jane Lapotaire, Brian Cox; *D:* Michael Lindsay-Hogg; *M:* Trevor Jones. *VMK*

Murder by Natural Causes 🦴🦴🦴 **1979** A made-for-TV brain teaser in which a woman and her lover plot to kill her mind-reader husband. Lots of twists make this fun for viewers who enjoy a challenge. **96m/C VHS, Beta.** Hal Holbrook, Barry Bostwick, Katharine Ross, Richard Anderson; *D:* Robert Day. *NO*

Murder by Night 🦴🦴½ **1989 (PG-13)** Amnesia victim Urich is found next to a dead body, the result of a gruesome murder. Urich is the only witness and thinks he may be the next victim. Others think he's the killer. Made for cable mystery with enough twists to make it worthwhile. **95m/C VHS, Beta.** Robert Urich, Kay Lenz, Jim Metzler, Richard Monette, Michael Ironside, Michael Williams; *D:* Paul Lynch. *MCA*

Murder by Numbers 🦴½ **1989 (PG-13)** Murder in the art world stumps a detective. What might have been a good suspense story is ruined by bad editing and a lack of continuity, resulting in confusion rather than suspense. **91m/C VHS, Beta, LV.** Sam Behrens, Shari Belafonte, Ronee Blakley, Stanley Kamel, Jayne Meadows, Debra Sandlund, Dick Sargent, Cleavon Little; *D:* Paul Leder; *W:* Paul Leder. *NO*

Murder by Phone 🦴🦴 *Bells; The Calling* **1982 (R)** A deranged technician has turned his phone into an instrument of electronic death. Chamberlain is the visiting professor trying to discover who's permanently disconnecting the numbers of his students. Good cast decides to test schlock meter. **79m/C VHS, Beta.** *CA* Richard Chamberlain, John Houseman, Sara Botsford; *D:* Michael Anderson Sr.; *W:* Michael Butler, John Kent Harrison; *M:* John Barry. *WAR*

Murder by Television 🦴½ *The Houghland Murder Case* **1935** Low-budget murder mystery with Lugosi in a dual role as twins—one good, one not so. When a professor and the evil twin are murdered, the instrument of death suspected is...television. Still an exotic and misunderstood invention when this was made, TV sometimes invoked fear and suspicion in the general public. Historically interesting and Lugosi fans will appreciate seeing him in a non-vampiric role. **55m/B VHS, Beta.** Bela Lugosi, George Meeker; *D:* Clifford Sanforth. *VYY, SNC, NOS*

Murder by the Book 🦴🦴½ *Alter Ego* **1987** A mystery writer finds that his fictional character, a hard-boiled private eye, has taken control of his life. With his new macho persona the writer solves a crime and saves the obligatory dame. Based on the novel "Alter Ego" by Mel Arrighi. Made for television. **100m/C VHS, Beta.** Robert Hays, Catherine Mary Stewart, Celeste Holm, Fred Gwynne, Christopher Murney; *D:* Mel Damski. *NO*

Murder Elite 🦴½ **1986** A murdering maniac terrorizes the rural English countryside, where MacGraw has returned after losing all her money in America. Poor acting and direction make this one a dust-gatherer. **98m/C VHS, Beta.** Ali MacGraw, Billie Whitelaw, Hywel Bennett; *D:* Claude Whatham. *LIV, VES*

Murder for Sale 🦴 **1970** Secret Agent 117 stages an elaborate scam in order to infiltrate a ring of terrorists and criminals. Ask for Bond next time. **90m/C VHS, Beta.** John Gavin, Margaret Lee, Curt Jurgens. *MED*

Murder in Coweta County 🦴🦴½ **1983** Griffith and Cash are strong in this true-crime drama based on the book by Margaret Anne Barnes. Griffith is a Georgia businessman who thinks he's gotten away with murder; Cash is the lawman who tenaciously pursues him. Based on an actual 1948 case. Made for television. **100m/C VHS, Beta.** Johnny Cash, Andy Griffith, Earl Hindman, June Carter Cash, Cindi Knight, Ed Van Nuys; *D:* Gary Nelson; *M:* Brad Fiedel. *LIV*

Murder-in-Law 🦴 **1992 (R)** Graphic slasher flick about a mother-in-law from hell who escapes from an insane asylum and terrorizes her son-in-law (Estevez) and his family in a series of gruesome killings. **97m/C VHS.** Marilyn Adams, Joe Estevez, Sandy Snyder, Darrel Guilbeau; *D:* Tony Jiti Gill. *MNC*

Murder in New Hampshire: The Pamela Smart Story 🦴🦴½ **1991 (PG-13)** A sleazy true story about a young high school teacher who seduces an impressionable student into murdering her husband. Hunt's fine as the seductress but this made-for-television fare is just average. **93m/C VHS, Beta.** Helen Hunt, Chad Allen, Larry Drake, Howard Hesseman, Ken Howard, Michael Learned; *D:* Joyce Chopra; *M:* Gary Chang. *TTC, PMS*

Murder in Space 🦴½ **1985** Nine multinational astronauts are stranded aboard a space station when they discover one of them is a murderer. This creates anxiety, particularly since the killer's identity is unknown. Oatmeal salesman Brimley is the earthbound mission control chief trying desperately to finger a spaceman while the bodies pile up. Made for television. **95m/C VHS, Beta.** Wilford Brimley, Martin Balsam, Michael Ironside; *D:* Steven Hilliard Stern. *VMK*

Murder in Texas 🦴🦴🦴 **1981** Made for television docudrama looks at the strange but true events surrounding the death of society woman Joan Robinson Hill, first wife of prominent plastic surgeon, Dr. John Hill, and daughter of wealthy oilman Ash Robinson. Well-crafted script and effective performances keep your interest. Griffith was Emmy nominated. From the book "Prescription Murder," written by the doctor's second wife. **200m/C VHS, Beta.** Farrah Fawcett, Katharine Ross, Andy Griffith, Sam Elliott, Craig T. Nelson, Barbara Sammeth; *D:* William Hale. *VHE, HHE*

Murder in the Doll House 🦴½ **1979** Private detective must find out who is systematically killing off the family of a Japanese toy executive. With English subtitles. **92m/C VHS, Beta.** *JP* Yusaku Matsuda, Hiroko Shino, Yoko Nosaki. *VDA*

Murder In the First 🦴🦴½ **1995 (R)** Hours after leaving a three-year stint in solitary confinement at Alcatraz, petty thief Henri Young (Bacon) kills the inmate he thinks ratted him out. Young, eager-puppy lawyer James Stamphill (Slater) defends Young by claiming that inhumane and brutal prison treatment turned him into a murderer. Heavy-handed and uneven despite excellent performances by top-notch cast. Oldman does his usual fine job with yet another unsympathetic character, the sadistic warden. Major professional landmark for both Slater and Bacon. Loosely based on a true story that led to the closing of Alcatraz. **123m/C VHS, LV.** Christian Slater, Kevin Bacon, Gary Oldman, Embeth Davidtz, Bill Macy, Stephen Tobolowsky, Brad Dourif, R. Lee Ermey, Mia Kirshner, Stefan Gierasch, Kyra Sedgwick; *D:* Marc Rocco; *W:* Dan Gordon; *C:* Fred Murphy; *M:* Christopher Young. Nominations: Screen Actors Guild Award '95: Best Supporting Actor (Bacon). *WAR*

Murder in the Footlights 🦴🦴 **1951** Murder drama involving a socialite and a vaudeville team. **?m/C VHS.** *GB* Lesley Brook, David Hutcheson. *SNC*

Murder in the Old Red Barn 🦴 *Maria Marten* **1936** Based on the real murder of an unassuming girl by a randy squire. Stiff, melodramatic performances are bad enough, but the play-style production, unfamiliar to modern viewers, is the last nail in this one's coffin. **67m/B VHS, Beta.** *GB* Tod Slaughter, Sophie Stewart, D.J. Williams, Eric Portman; *D:* Milton Rosmer. *NOS, MRV, SNC*

A Murder Is Announced 🦴🦴 *Agatha Christie's Miss Marple: A Murder Is Announced* **1987** From the critically acclaimed BBC television series. While on holiday, super-sleuth Marple encounters a murder that was advertised in the local newspaper one week prior to its occurrence. Based on the 1952 Agatha Christie novel, Hickson shines once again as Christie's detective extraordinaire. **155m/C VHS, Beta.** *GB* Joan Hickson; *D:* David Giles. *FOX, HMV, VCO*

Murder Mansion 🦴½ **1970** Some decent scares ensue when a group of travelers is stranded in an old haunted mansion. **84m/C VHS, Beta.** *SP* Evelyn Stewart, Analia Gade; *D:* Francisco Lara Polop. *UNI, SNC, FCT*

Murder Most Foul 🦴🦴🦴 **1965** Erstwhile school marm Dame Margaret is excellent as the only jury member to believe in the accused's innocence. Posing as a wealthy actress to insinuate herself into the local acting troupe, she sniffs out the true culprit. Based on the Poirot mystery "Mr. McGinty's Dead." **90m/B VHS, Beta.** Margaret Rutherford, Ron Moody, Charles Tingwell, Megs Jenkins, Dennis Price, Ralph Michael; *D:* George Pollock. *MGM, FCT*

Murder Motel 🦴 **1974** Inept made-for-television spine-tingler about a motel keeper who makes a practice of killing his customers. There's always a vacancy at the Murder Motel, at least until the fiancee of one of his victims decides to look into the matter. **80m/C VHS, Beta.** Robyn Millan, Derek Francis, Ralph Bates, Edward Judd. *LIV*

Murder, My Sweet 🦴🦴🦴½ *Farewell, My Love* **1944** Down-on-his-luck private detective Philip Marlowe (Powell) searches for an ex-convict's missing girlfriend through a dark world of murder, mayhem and ever-twisting directions. Classic film noir screen version of Raymond Chandler's tense novel "Farewell, My Lovely," which employs flashback fashion using that crisp Chandler narrative. A breakthrough dramatically for singer Powell; Chandler's favorite version. Remade using the novel's title in 1975. **95m/B VHS, Beta, LV.** Dick Powell, Claire Trevor, Mike Mazurki, Otto Kruger, Anne Shirley, Miles Mander; ***D:*** Edward Dmytryk. Edgar Allan Poe Awards '45: Best Screenplay. *MED, CCB*

Murder of a Moderate Man 🦴½ **197?** An Interpol agent sets out for the Alps to apprehend an assassin gunning down political leaders. A British-made effort based on a novel by John Howlett. **165m/C VHS.** *GB* Denis Quilley, Susan Fleetwood. *FCT, MOV, VCO*

The Murder of Mary Phagan 🦴🦴🦴½ **1987 (PG)** Lemmon stars as John Slaton, governor of Georgia during one of America's most notorious miscarriages of justice. In 1913, timid, Jewish factory manager Leo Frank is accused of the brutal murder of a female worker. Prejudice and a power hungry prosecuting attorney conspire to seal the man's fate at the end of the hangman's noose. Sensing the injustice, Slaton re-opens the case, causing riots in Atlanta. Top notch television drama, featuring a superb recreation of turn of the century atmosphere and a compelling, true story which was not finally resolved until the 1970s. **251m/C VHS.** Jack Lemmon, Peter Gallagher, Richard Jordan, Robert Prosky, Paul Dooley, Rebecca Miller, Kathryn Walker, Charles S. Dutton, Kevin Spacey, Wendy J. Cooke; ***D:*** Billy Hale; ***M:*** Maurice Jarre. *ORI*

Murder on Approval 🦴 *Barbados Quest* **1956** Conway is a carbon-copy Sherlock Holmes, called in to verify the authenticity of a stamp and finds himself involved in murder. Slow-paced, weak and transparent. **70m/B VHS.** Tom Conway, Delphi Lawrence, Brian Worth, Michael Balfour, John Colicos; ***D:*** Bernard Knowles. *NOS*

Murder on Flight 502 🦴🦴 **1975** A crisis arises on a 747 flight from New York to London when a terrorist runs amuck. Big cast of TV stars and Stack as the pilot keep this stale television flick from getting lost in the ozone. **97m/C VHS, Beta.** Farrah Fawcett, Sonny Bono, Ralph Bellamy, Theodore Bikel, Dane Clark, Polly Bergen, Laraine Day, Fernando Lamas, George Maharis, Hugh O'Brian, Molly Picon, Walter Pidgeon, Robert Stack; ***D:*** George McCowan. *PSM*

Murder on Lenox Avenue 🦴🦴½ **1941** When the leader of the Harlem Better Business Bureau is overthrown, he swears revenge. **60m/C VHS.** Alec Lovejoy. *BBE, MOV*

Murder on Line One 🦴🦴 **1990** A London murderer films his crimes for his later viewing pleasure. The police arrest a suspect, but the killings continue. Both the police and viewer are soon aware that they've made a mistake. **103m/C VHS, Beta.** Emma Jacobs, Peter Blake, Simon Shepherd, Allan Surtees, Andrew Wilde, Dirkan Tulane, Neil Duncan, Brett Forrest; ***D:*** Anders Palm; ***W:*** Anders Palm. *ACA, TTC*

Murder on the Bayou 🦴🦴🦴 *A Gathering of Old Men* **1991 (PG)** Down on the L'siana bayou, a white guy who thinks civil rights are color coded is murdered, and an elderly black man is accused of the crime. Made for TV, well performed, engaging. From the novel by Ernest J. Gaines. **91m/C VHS, LV.** Louis Gossett Jr., Richard Widmark, Holly Hunter, Woody Strode, Joe Seneca, Papa John Creach, Julius W. Harris, Will Patton; ***D:*** Volker Schlondorff. *VMK*

Murder on the Campus 🦴🦴 *Out of the Shadow* **1952** A reporter investigates the apparant suicide of his brother at Cambridge University. He discovers that a number of other mysterious deaths have occurred as well. Interesting characterizations hampered by predictability. **61m/B VHS, Beta.** *GB* Terence Longden, Donald Gray, Diane Clare, Robertson Hare, Dermot Walsh; ***D:*** Michael Winner; ***W:*** Michael Winner. *NOS, MRV, SNC*

Murder on the High Seas 🦴🦴 **1932** Infidelity and murder aboard a cruise ship. **?m/C VHS.** Natalie Moorhead, Jack Mulhall. *SNC*

Murder on the Midnight Express 🦴½ **1974** Made-for-television mystery about spies, thieves, honeymooners and a corpse aboard an all-night train. All aboard. **70m/C VHS, Beta.** Judy Geeson, James Smilie, Charles Gray. *LIV*

Murder on the Orient Express 🦴🦴🦴 **1974 (PG)** An Agatha Christie mystery lavishly produced with an all-star cast. In 1934, a trainful of suspects and one murder victim make the trip from Istanbul to Calais especially interesting. Super-sleuth Hercule Poirot sets out to solve the mystery. An entertaining whodunit, ably supported by the remarkable cast. Followed by "Death on the Nile." **128m/C VHS, Beta, LV.** *GB* Albert Finney, Martin Balsam, Ingrid Bergman, Lauren Bacall, Sean Connery, Richard Widmark, Anthony Perkins, John Gielgud, Jacqueline Bisset, Jean-Pierre Cassel, Wendy Hiller, Rachel Roberts, Vanessa Redgrave, Michael York, Colin Blakely, George Coulouris; ***D:*** Sidney Lumet; ***C:*** Geoffrey Unsworth; ***M:*** Richard Rodney Bennett. Academy Awards '74: Best Supporting Actress (Bergman); British Academy Awards '74: Best Supporting Actor (Gielgud), Best Supporting Actress (Bergman); Nominations: Academy Awards '74: Best Actor (Finney), Best Adapted Screenplay, Best Cinematography, Best Costume Design, Best Original Score. *PAR, BTV*

Murder on the Yukon 🦴½ **1940** An installment in the "Renfrew of the Royal Mounted" series. Newill and O'Brien's vacation plans are ruined when they find a corpse in a canoe and must investigate. Lots of action, but a somewhat threadbare production. Based on "Renfrew Rides North" by Lauri York Erskine. **57m/B VHS, Beta.** James Newill, Dave O'Brien, Polly Ann Young; ***D:*** Louis Gasnier. *VDM*

Murder Once Removed 🦴½ **1971** A private eye discovers that a respectable doctor has a bedside manner that women are dying for. Made for television. **74m/C VHS, Beta.** John Forsythe, Richard Kiley, Barbara Bain, Joseph Campanella; ***D:*** Charles S. Dubin. *ORI*

Murder One 🦴 **1988 (R)** Two half-brothers escape from a Maryland prison and go on a killing spree, dragging their younger brother with them. Low-budget and it shows. Based on a true story. **83m/C VHS, Beta, LV.** Henry Thomas, James Wilder, Stephen Shellan, Errol Slue; ***D:*** Graeme Campbell. *SUE, NLC*

Murder 101 🦴🦴 **1991 (PG-13)** Brosnan plays Charles Lattimore, an author and English professor who specializes in murder mysteries. He gives his students a rather unique assignment of planning the perfect murder. When a student is killed right before his eyes and a fellow teacher turns up dead, Lattimore realizes he's being framed for murder. Surprising twists abound in this stylish thriller. **93m/C VHS.** Pierce Brosnan, Dey Young, Raphael Sbarge, Kim Thomson; ***D:*** Bill Condon; ***W:*** Bill Condon. *MCA*

Murder or Mercy 🦴🦴½ **1974** Still timely story of a famous doctor accused of killing his terminally ill wife. Focuses on the morality of mercy killing. Made for television. **78m/C VHS.** Melvyn Douglas, Bradford Dillman, David Birney, Denver Pyle, Mildred Dunnock; ***D:*** Harvey Hart. *WOV*

Murder Ordained 🦴🦴½ **1987** Yet another true-crime network miniseries, this time about a Kansas minister and her lover plotting the demise of their spouses. Good acting for this sort of thing. In two-cassette package. **183m/C VHS.** Keith Carradine, JoBeth Williams, Terry Kinney, Guy Boyd, Terence Knox, Darrell Larson, M. Emmet Walsh, Kathy Bates; ***D:*** Mike Robe. *FRH*

Murder over New York 🦴🦴 **1940** Episode in the Charlie Chan mystery series. Chan visits New York City and becomes involved in an investigation at the airport. With the aid of his klutzy son, he sleuths his way through a slew of suspects until the mystery is solved. Standard fare for the Chan fan. **65m/B VHS, Beta.** Sidney Toler, Marjorie Weaver, Robert Lowery, Ricardo Cortez, Donald MacBride, Melville Cooper, Victor Sen Yung; ***D:*** Harry Lachman. *FOX*

Murder Rap 🦴 **1987** An aspiring musician/sound technologist becomes involved with a mysterious woman and her plot to kill her husband. Complications galore, especially for the viewer. **90m/C VHS, Beta.** John Hawkes, Seita Kathleen Feigny; ***D:*** Kliff Keuhl. *VCI*

Murder She Said 🦴🦴½ *Meet Miss Marple* **1962** Dame Margaret, playing the benign Miss M for the first time, witnesses a murder on board a train, but the authorities don't seem inclined to believe her. Posing as a maid at an estate near where she thought the body was dropped, she solves the murder and lands three more Miss Marple movies. Based on Christy's "4:50 From Paddington," it features Marple-to-be Hickson as the cook. **87m/B VHS, Beta.** Margaret Rutherford, Arthur Kennedy, Muriel Pavlow, James Robertson Justice, Thorley Walters, Charles Tingwell, Conrad Phillips; ***D:*** George Pollock. *MGM, FCT*

Murder So Sweet 🦴🦴½ *Poisoned by Love: The Kern County Murders* **1993** Hamlin stars as a slick small-town loser, with an apparently limitless appeal to women. He marries five of them but two wives and his mother mysteriously die of poisoning. Then an ex gets suspicious and tries to make certain it'll never happen again. Based on a true story. Made for television. **94m/C VHS.** Harry Hamlin, Helen Shaver, Faith Ford, Daphne Ashbrook, Eileen Brennan, K.T. Oslin, Terence Knox, Ed Lauter. *ACA*

Murder Story 🦴🦴½ **1989 (PG)** An aspiring mystery writer finds himself mixed up in a real murder and winds up involving his mentor as well. An overdone story, but a reasonably enjoyable film. **90m/C VHS, Beta, LV.** Christopher Lee, Bruce Boa; ***D:*** Eddie Arno, Markus Innocenti; ***W:*** Eddie Arno. *FHS, ACA*

Murder: Ultimate Grounds for Divorce 🦴 **1985** A quiet weekend of camping turns into a night of horror for two couples when one of them plans an elaborate murder scheme. **90m/C VHS, Beta.** Roger Daltrey, Toyah Wilcox, Leslie Ash, Terry Raven. *ORI, WAR*

Murder with Music 🦴🦴 **1945** A musical drama featuring an all-black cast. **60m/B VHS, Beta.** Bob Howard, Noble Sissle, Nellie Hill; ***D:*** George P. Quigley. *NOS, DVT, VDM*

Murder without Motive 🦴🦴½ **1992** When two African American teenagers harrass an undercover cop, a struggle ensues and one teen ends up dead. Was the struggle racially motivated, or did the police act justifiably? **93m/C VHS.** Curtis McClaren, Anna Maria Horsford, Carla Gugino, Christopher Daniel Barnes, Cuba Gooding Jr., Georg Stanford Brown; ***D:*** Kevin Hooks. *TTC*

Murdered Innocence 🦴🦴 **1994 (R)** In 1972, a rookie New York cop is called to a crime scene where a woman has been stabbed to death. Her young son is hysterical and her husband is holding the knife. When the husband panics and tries to flee, the cop shoots him in the back. Now, it's 1992, the convicted killer is out of prison and out for revenge (seems the son said his mother's lover committed the crime but there was a police coverup). **88m/C VHS.** Jason Miller, Ellen Greene, Fred Carpenter; ***D:*** Frank Coraci; ***W:*** Diego Matamoros. *COL*

Murderers among Us: The Simon Wiesenthal Story 🦴🦴🦴 **1989** Powerful reenactment of concentration camp survivor Simon Wiesenthal's search for war criminals. Kingsley's gripping performance drives this made-for-cable film. Be prepared for disturbing death camp scenes. **157m/C VHS.** Ben Kingsley, Renee Soutendijk, Craig T. Nelson, Paul Freeman, Louisa Haigh, Jack Shepherd; ***D:*** Brian Gibson; ***W:*** Abby Mann; ***M:*** Bill Conti. *HBO, FCT*

Murderer's Keep *Woof!* **1988** Secret ingredients used in the Central Meat Market's hamburger are discovered by a young, deaf girl. Beware of filler, she learns, particularly if it's someone you know. **89m/C VHS, Beta.** Vic Tayback, Talia Shire, Robert Walden; ***D:*** Paulmichel Miekhe. *GHV*

Murderers' Row ✗½ **1966** Daredevil bachelor and former counter-espionage agent Matt Helm is summoned from his life of leisure to ensure the safety of an important scientist. Martin's attempt as a super-spy doesn't wash, and Margret is implausible as the kidnapped scientist's daughter. Unless you want to hear Martin sing "I'm Not the Marrying Kind," don't bother. Second in the "Matt Helm" series. **108m/C VHS, Beta.** Dean Martin, Ann-Margret, Karl Malden, Beverly Adams, James Gregory; ***D:*** Henry Levin; ***M:*** Lalo Schifrin. *COL*

Murderlust *Woof!* **1986** Employers in search of a security guard make a poor choice in offering the position to a sexually frustrated man whose hobbies include strangling prostitutes. Poor hiring decisions come into play later when he secures a job at an adolescent crisis center. **90m/C VHS, Beta.** Eli Rich, Rochelle Taylor, Dennis Gannon, Bonnie Schneider, Lisa Nichols; ***D:*** Donald M. Jones. *PSM*

Murderous Vision ✗✗ **1991 (R)** Television fixture Boxleitner is a bored detective in this outing. But one day, while tracking a young mother in the missing persons bureau, he stumbles upon the trail of a serial killer. Enter a beautiful psychic who wants to help, add a race to catch the murderer, and Bruce suddenly has his hands full. Made for television. **93m/C VHS, LV.** Bruce Boxleitner, Laura Johnson, Robert Culp; ***D:*** Gary Sherman. *PAR*

Murders at Lynch Cross **1985** Made-for-British-television mystery about a weird, isolated hotel on the Yorkshire moors. **60m/C VHS, Beta.** *GB* Jill Bennett, Joanna David, Barbara Jefford, Sylvia Syms. *PSM*

Murders in the Rue Morgue ✗✗½ **1932** Lugosi stars as a deranged scientist (what a stretch) who wants to find a female companion for his pet gorilla. He kidnaps a beautiful woman and prepares to make her the gorilla's bride. Very loosely based on the story by Edgar Allan Poe, which has been remade several times. **61m/B VHS.** Bela Lugosi, Sidney Fox, Leon Ames, Brandon Hurst, Arlene Francis; ***D:*** Robert Florey; ***C:*** Karl Freund. *MCA*

Murders in the Rue Morgue ✗✗½ **1971 (PG)** A young woman has frightening dreams inspired by a play that her father is producing in Paris at the turn of the century. After many people associated with the production become murder victims, the girl becomes involved with one of her father's former associates, a man who killed her mother years ago and then faked his own suicide. The fourth film based on Edgar Allan Poe's classic horror story. **87m/C VHS, Beta.** Jason Robards Jr., Lilli Palmer, Herbert Lom, Michael Dunn, Christine Kaufmann, Adolfo Celi; ***D:*** Gordon Hessler. *NO*

The Murders in the Rue Morgue ✗✗✗ **1986 (PG)** The fifth filmed version of the Edgar Allan Poe story. Set in 19th-century Paris; actors in a mystery play find their roles coming to life. Scott is terrific, with good supporting help. Made for television. **92m/C VHS.** George C. Scott, Rebecca DeMornay, Val Kilmer, Ian McShane, Neil Dickson; ***D:*** Jeannot Szwarc. *VMK*

Murders in the Zoo ✗✗½ **1933** Zoologist Atwill has a reason to be insanely jealous since his wife (Burke) has been having lots of extramarital affairs. But his way of dealing with these other men is certainly unique—he feeds them to various zoo animals (after first sewing the victims' lips shut). Censors were outraged and the film underwent various edits for its theatrical release. **62m/B VHS.** Lionel Atwill, Kathleen Burke, Charlie Ruggles, Randolph Scott, Gail Patrick, John Lodge, Harry Beresford; ***D:*** Edward Sutherland; ***W:*** Philip Wylie, Seton I. Miller. *MCA*

Muriel ✗✗✗½ *Muriel, Ou le Temps d'Un Retour; The Time of Return; Muriel, Or the Time of Return* **1963** A complex, mosaic drama about a middle-aged woman who meets an old lover at Boulogne, and her stepson who cannot forget the needless suffering he caused a young woman named Muriel while he was a soldier at war. Throughout, director Alain Resnais plumbs the essential meanings of memory, age, and the anxieties created from the tension between personal and public actions. Acclaimed; in French with subtitles. **115m/C VHS, Beta.** *FR IT* Delphine Seyrig, Jean-Pierre Kerien, Nita Klein, Jean-Baptiste Thierree; ***D:*** Alain Resnais; ***M:*** Georges Delerue. Venice Film Festival '63: Best Actress (Seyrig). *HTV, FCT*

Muriel's Wedding ✗✗✗ **1994 (R)** Muriel (Collette) can catch a bridal bouquet, but can she catch a husband? Her blonde, bitch-goddess friends don't think so. But dowdy, pathetic, overweight Muriel dreams of a fairy tale wedding anyway. How she fulfills her obsessive fantasy is the basis for this quirky, hilarious, and often touchingly poignant ugly duckling tale with the occasional over-the-top satiric moment. Strong cast is led by sympathetic and engaging performances from Collette (who gained 40-plus pounds for the role) and Griffiths as her best friend, Rhonda. '70s pop supergroup ABBA lends its kitschy but catchy tunes to the plot and soundtrack. Not released in the U.S. until 1995. **105m/C VHS, LV.** *AU* Toni Collette, Bill Hunter, Rachel Griffiths, Jeanie Drynan, Gennie Nevinson Brice, Matt Day, Daniel Lapaine; ***D:*** P.J. Hogan; ***W:*** P.J. Hogan; ***M:*** Peter Best. Australian Film Institute '94: Best Actress (Collette), Best Film, Best Sound, Best Supporting Actress (Griffiths); Nominations: Australian Film Institute '94: Best Director (Hogan), Best Screenplay, Best Supporting Actor (Hunter), Best Supporting Actress (Drynan); Golden Globe Awards '96: Best Actress—Musical/Comedy (Collette); Writers Guild of America '95: Best Original Screenplay. *MAX*

Murmur of the Heart ✗✗✗½ **1971 (R)** Honest treatment of a fourteen-year-old's coming of age. After his older brothers take him to a prostitute for his first sexual experience, he comes down with scarlet fever. He then travels to a health spa with his mom to recover. There they find that their mother-son bond is stronger than most. Music by Charlie Parker is featured in the score. In French with English subtitles. **118m/C VHS, Beta, LV.** *FR* Benoit Ferreux, Daniel Gelin, Lea Massari, Corinne Kersten, Jacqueline Chauveau, Marc Wincourt, Michael Lonsdale; ***D:*** Louis Malle; ***W:*** Louis Malle. Nominations: Academy Awards '72: Best Story & Screenplay; Cannes Film Festival '71: Best Film. *ORI, INJ*

Murph the Surf ✗✗½ *Live a Little, Steal a Lot; You Can't Steal Love* **1975 (PG)** Fact-based, engrossing story of two beach bums turned burglars who grow bored with small-time robbery and plan a trip to New York City to steal the Star of Africa sapphire. Notable among the many action scenes is a boat chase through the inland waterways of Miami, Florida. **102m/C VHS, Beta.** Robert Conrad, Don Stroud, Donna Mills, Luther Adler, Robyn Millan, Paul Stewart; ***D:*** Marvin J. Chomsky. *WAR, OM*

Murphy's Fault ✗✗ **1988 (PG-13)** Dark comedy about a night watchman/writer plagued by a series of bad luck incidents. **94m/C VHS, Beta, LV.** Patrick Dollaghan, Anne Curry, Stack Pierce; ***D:*** Robert J. Smawley. *VMK*

Murphy's Law ✗ **1986 (R)** A hard-headed cop gets framed for his ex-wife's murder and embarks on a mission to find the actual killer. He is slowed down by a smart-mouthed prostitute who is handcuffed to him during his search. Casting a female in the role of a psycho-killer is unique to the genre. **101m/C VHS, Beta, LV.** Charles Bronson, Carrie Snodgress, Kathleen Wilhoite, Robert F. Lyons, Richard Romanus, Angel Tompkins, Bill Henderson, James Luisi, Janet MacLachlan, Lawrence Tierney; ***D:*** J. Lee Thompson; ***M:*** Mark Donohue. *MED, VTR*

Murphy's Romance ✗✗✗ **1985 (PG-13)** A young divorced mother with an urge to train horses pulls up the stakes and heads for Arizona with her son. There she meets a pharmacist who may be just what the doctor ordered to help her build a new life. **107m/C VHS, Beta, LV.** James Garner, Sally Field, Brian Kerwin, Corey Haim, Dennis Burkley, Charles Lane, Georgann Johnson; ***D:*** Martin Ritt; ***W:*** Harriet Frank Jr., Irving Ravetch; ***M:*** Carole King. Nominations: Academy Awards '85: Best Actor (Garner), Best Cinematography. *COL, HMV*

Murphy's War ✗✗ **1971 (PG)** In WWII, the Germans sink an English ship and gun down most of its crew. An Irishman, however, survives and returns to health with the help of a nurse. He then seeks revenge on those who killed his crewmates, even after he learns the war has ended. O'Toole is interesting as the revenge-minded seaman though saddled with a mediocre script. **106m/C VHS, Beta.** *GB* Peter O'Toole, Sian Phillips, Philippe Noiret; ***D:*** Peter Yates; ***W:*** Stirling Silliphant; ***M:*** John Barry. *PAR, CCB*

Murrow ✗✗½ **1986** A cable television biography of the renowned chain-smoking journalist who changed broadcasting history by fearlessly voicing his liberal ideas on the air waves. His life was more interesting though Travanti does his best to breathe some life into the script. **114m/C VHS, Beta.** Daniel J. Travanti, Dabney Coleman, Edward Herrmann, David Suchet, John McMartin, Robert Vaughn, Kathryn Leigh Scott; ***D:*** Jack Gold; ***W:*** Ernest Kinoy; ***M:*** Carl Davis. *FCT, LIV*

Muscle Beach Party ✗✗ **1964** Sequel to "Beach Party" finds Frankie and Annette romping in the sand again. Trouble invades teen nirvana when a new gym opens and the hardbodies try to muscle in on surfer turf. Meanwhile, Paluzzi tries to muscle in on Funicello's turf. Good clean corny fun, with the usual lack of script and plot. Lorre appeals in a cameo, his final screen appearance. Watch for "Little" Stevie Wonder in his debut. Rickles' first appearance in the "BP" series; Lupus was credited as Rock Stevens. Followed by "Bikini Beach." ♫Muscle Beach Party; Runnin' Wild; Muscle Bustle; My First Love; Surfin' Woodie; Surfer's Holiday; Happy Street; A Girl Needs a Boy; A Boy Needs a Girl. **94m/C VHS, Beta, LV.** Frankie Avalon, Annette Funicello, Buddy Hackett, Luciana Paluzzi, Don Rickles, John Ashley, Jody McCrea, Morey Amsterdam, Peter Lupus, Candy Johnson, Dolores Wells, Stevie Wonder, Donna Loren, Amadee Chabot; ***Cameos:*** Peter Lorre; ***D:*** William Asher; ***W:*** William Asher, Robert Dillon; ***M:*** Les Baxter. *NO*

Music Box ✗✗½ **1989 (R)** An attorney defends her father against accusations that he has committed inhumane Nazi war crimes. If she loses, her father faces deportation. As the case progresses, she must struggle to remain objective in the courtroom and come to terms with the possibility that her father is guilty. Lange's portrayal of an ethnic character is highly convincing. **126m/C VHS, Beta, LV.** Jessica Lange, Frederic Forrest, Lukas Haas, Armin Mueller-Stahl, Michael Rooker, Donald Moffat, Cheryl Lynn Bruce; ***D:*** Constantin Costa-Gavras; ***W:*** Joe Eszterhas; ***M:*** Philippe Sarde. Nominations: Academy Awards '89: Best Actress (Lange). *JCF*

Music Box/Helpmates **1932** These two classic, award-winning comedy shorts by the dynamic duo have been color-enhanced by Colorization. **50m/B VHS, Beta.** Stan Laurel, Oliver Hardy. *VTR*

Music in My Heart ✗½ **1940** Two taxi cabs crash and spur the love of Martin and Hayworth. She proceeds to break off her engagement to save Martin from deportation. Hayworth's last low-budget film before becoming a Hollywood goddess. **69m/B VHS.** Rita Hayworth, Tony Martin, Edith Fellows, Alan Mowbray, Eric Blore, George Tobias, Joseph Crehan, George Humbert, Phil Tead; ***D:*** Joseph Santley; ***M:*** Robert Wright, Chet Forrest. Nominations: Academy Awards '40: Best Song ("It's a Blue World"). *COL, CCB*

The Music Lovers ✗✗½ **1971 (R)** Russell's version of Tchaikovsky's tormented life and glorious achievements is a shocker, a movie that infuriates professed music lovers but, nonetheless, has introduced many a neophyte to the world of classical music via its sensationalism. Homosexual Tchaikovsky marries an admirer to appease the Russian government and his financial benefactor. Stunned when he discovers his wife is a nymphomaniac, he banishes her to a netherworld of prostitution and eventual insanity which Russell mercilessly explores. Tchaikovsky's own squalid life is hardly better, though he does enjoy success before the bottom falls out. **122m/C VHS, LV.** *GB* Richard Chamberlain, Glenda Jackson, Max Adrian, Christopher Gable, Kenneth Colley, Izabella Telezynska, Maureen Pryor; ***D:*** Ken Russell; ***W:*** Melvin Bragg. *MGM, MLB, FCT*

The Music Man ♀♀♀♀ **1962 (G)** Con man in the guise of a traveling salesman gets off the train in River City, Iowa. After hearing about plans to build a pool hall, he argues it would be the gateway to hell for the young, impressionable males of the town. He then convinces the River Cityians to look toward the future of the community and finance a wholesome children's marching band. Although the huckster plans to take their money and run before the instruments arrive, his feelings for the town librarian cause him to think twice about fleeing the Heartland. This isn't just a slice of Americana; it's a whole pie. Acting and singing are terrific "with a capital 'T' and that rhymes with 'P' and that stands for" Preston, who epitomizes the charismatic pitchman. ♫Seventy-six Trombones; Trouble; If You Don't Mind; Till There Was You; The Wells Fargo Wagon; Being in Love; Goodnight, My Someone; Rock Island; Iowa Stubborn. **151m/C VHS, Beta, LV.** Robert Preston, Shirley Jones, Buddy Hackett, Hermione Gingold, Paul Ford, Pert Kelton, Ron Howard; ***D:*** Morton DaCosta; ***W:*** Marion Hargrove; ***C:*** Robert Burks. Academy Awards '62: Best Adapted Score; Golden Globe Awards '63: Best Film—Musical/Comedy; Nominations: Academy Awards '62: Best Art Direction/Set Decoration (Color), Best Costume Design (Color), Best Film Editing, Best Picture, Best Sound. *WAR, MVD, TLF*

The Music of Chance ♀♀½ **1993 (R)** Convoluted story about a smalltime gambler (Spader) and a drifter (Patinkin) who wind up involved in a bizarre high stakes poker game with a Laurel and Hardyish pair (Durning and Grey) who live in an isolated mansion. When Spader and Patinkin lose, their debt forces them into an indentured servitude where they must construct a brick wall around their new masters' estate. Bloated with symbolism, this adaptation from cult fave novelist Auster (who has a small part), loses its eclectic significance in the translation to the big screen. Nonetheless, valiant effort by rookie director Haas. **98m/C VHS, LV.** James Spader, Mandy Patinkin, Joel Grey, Charles Durning, M. Emmet Walsh, Samantha Mathis, Christopher Penn, Pearl Jones, Paul Auster; ***D:*** Philip Haas; ***W:*** Philip Haas, Belinda Haas; ***C:*** Bernard Zitzermann; ***M:*** Philip Johnston. *COL, BTV*

Music Shoppe ♀♀ **1982 (G)** Four teenagers form a rock band with the assistance of the local music store proprietor. Interesting cast. **93m/C VHS, Beta.** Gary Crosby, Nia Peeples, Benny Medina, Stephen Schwartz, David Jackson, Jesse White, Doug Kershaw, Giselle MacKenzie. *GEM*

The Music Teacher ♀♀½ *Le Maitre de Musique* **1988 (PG)** A Belgian costume drama dealing with a famed singer who retires to devote himself to teaching two students exclusively. In time, he sees his prized pupils lured into an international competition by an old rival of his. Although the singing is sharp, the story is flat. In French with yellow English subtitles. **95m/C VHS, Beta, LV.** *BE* Patrick Bauchau, Sylvie Fennec, Phillipe Volter, Jose Van Dam, Johan Leysen, Anne Roussel; ***D:*** Gerard Corbiau. Nominations: Academy Awards '88: Best Foreign Language Film. *ORI, INJ*

Musica Proibita ♀♀½ **1943** A serious opera-spiced drama about a young romance crushed by adultery in the teenage couple's ancestry. In Italian with English subtitles. **93m/B VHS, Beta.** Tito Gobbi, Maria Mercader. *VYY, APD, INJ*

Mussolini & I ♀♀½ *Mussolini: The Decline and Fall of Il Duce* **1985** Docudramatization of the struggle for power between Italy's Benito Mussolini and his son-in-law, Galeazzo Ciano. Narrated by Sarandon in the role of Il Duce's daughter. Made for cable television. **130m/C VHS, Beta.** Bob Hoskins, Anthony Hopkins, Susan Sarandon, Annie Girardot, Barbara DeRossi, Fabio Testi, Kurt Raab; ***D:*** Alberto Negrin. *NLC*

Mutant ♀½ *Night Shadows* **1983 (R)** Another argument for the proper disposal of toxic waste. Hazardous materials transform the people of a southern town into monsters. **100m/C VHS, Beta, LV.** Wings Hauser, Bo Hopkins, Jennifer Warren, Lee Montgomery; ***D:*** John Cardos; ***M:*** Richard Band. *LIV, VES*

Mutant Hunt *Woof! Matt Riker* **1987** Made for video movie about a battle between robots gone haywire and an all-American hero. The detective cyborgs are set free while high on a sexual stimulant called Euphoron to wreak their technological havoc on a rampage in Manhattan. **90m/C VHS, Beta.** Rick Gianasi, Mary-Anne Fahey; ***D:*** Tim Kincaid; ***W:*** Tim Kincaid. *NO*

Mutant on the Bounty ♀½ **1989** A musician, lost in space as a beam of light for 23 years, is transported aboard a spaceship. Once he materializes, it becomes apparent that he has undergone some incredible physical changes. As if that's not enough, the crew then must flee from a couple of thugs who are trying to steal a vial of serum they have on board. A space spoof that never gets into orbit. **93m/C VHS.** John Roarke, Deborah Benson, John Furey, Victoria Catlin, John Fleck, Kyle T. Heffner; ***D:*** Robert Torrance. *HMD*

Mutant Species ♀ *Bio-Force I* **1995 (R)** Soldier is accidentally exposed to altered DNA and begins to mutate into a remorseless and terrifying killer. **100m/C VHS, LV.** Leo Rossi, Ted Prior, Grant Gelt, Denise Crosby, Powers Boothe, Wilford Brimley; ***D:*** David A. Prior; ***W:*** David A. Prior, William Vigil; ***C:*** Carlos Gonzalez. *LIV*

Mutant Video **1976** Six comedic, award-winning short-subject films from Jim Belushi and Rob Riley. Outrageous humor. **60m/B VHS, Beta.** James Belushi, Rob Riley. *LIV*

Mutants In Paradise *Woof!* **1988** Comedy about a human guinea-pig who always gets involved in some sort of mishap. **78m/C VHS, Beta.** Brad Greenquist, Robert Ingham, Anna Nicholas. *TWE*

Mutator ♀♀ *Time of the Beast* **1990 (R)** A corporation makes a tiny genetic mistake and winds up creating a new life form...a demonic pussycat who preys on humans. **91m/C VHS, Beta.** Brion James, Carolyn Ann Clark, Milton Raphiel Murrill; ***D:*** John R. Bowey; ***W:*** Lynn Rose Higgins. *PSM*

Mute Witness ♀♀½ **1995 (R)** Low-budget British thriller, lensed in Moscow film studio, about U.S. filmers making a cheap thriller in Moscow film studio. Billy (Sudina) is the mute make-up artist of the title who, returning to the studio for a forgotten item, witnesses some of the crew shooting a snuff film with a real-life stabbing. First-timer Waller mocks both thriller genre and film biz, sometimes relying on, rather than spoofing, cliched elements. Highlight is 20-minute long chase scene with the killers pursuing Billy in the cavernous studio. Guinness makes a surprise appearance in a cameo. **100m/C VHS, LV.** *GB* Marina Sudina, Fay Ripley, Evan Richards, Oleg Jankowskij, Igor Volkow, Sergei Karlenkov; ***Cameos:*** Alec Guinness; ***D:*** Anthony Waller; ***W:*** Anthony Waller; ***C:*** Egon Werdin; ***M:*** Wilbert Hirsch. *COL*

The Muthers ♀♀ **1976 (R)** Women prisoners escape from their confinement in a South American jungle. **101m/C VHS, Beta.** Jeanne Bell, Rosanne Katon, Jayne Kennedy, Trina Parks; ***D:*** Cirio H. Santiago. *NO*

The Mutilator *Woof! Fall Break* **1985 (R)** After accidentally bumping off his mother, a young man stalks five high school students wanting to cut them up into tiny bits. An unedited version is also available. Bloody boredom. **85m/C VHS, Beta, LV.** Jack Chatham, Trace Cooper, Frances Raines, Bill Hitchcock; ***D:*** Buddy Cooper. *LIV, VES*

Mutiny ♀♀ **1952** In the War of 1812, the crew of an American ship carrying $10 million in gold fight among themselves for a part of France's donation to the war effort. The beautiful photography doesn't make up for the predictability of the storyline. **76m/C VHS, Beta.** Mark Stevens, Gene Evans, Angela Lansbury, Patric Knowles; ***D:*** Edward Dmytryk; ***W:*** Philip Yordan. *NOS, VCI*

Mutiny in the Big House ♀♀½ **1939** A man is sent to prison for writing a bad ten dollar check and must choose between seeking salvation with the prison chaplain or toughing it out with a hardened convict. Suprisingly good low-budget programmer. **83m/B VHS, Beta.** Charles Bickford, Barton MacLane, Pat Moriarity, Dennis Moore, William Royle, Charles Foy, George Cleveland; ***D:*** William Nigh. *SNC*

The Mutiny of the Elsinore ♀ **1939** A writer on board an old sailing ship fights mutineers and wins back both the helm and the captain's daughter. Tedious British flotsam that made hash of an oft-filmed Jack London tale, and made news even in 1939 for its use of modern-day slang and clothing in the period setting. **74m/B VHS.** Paul Lukas, Lyn Harding, Kathleen Kelly, Clifford Evans, Ben Soutten, Jiro Soneya; ***D:*** Roy Lockwood. *NOS, DVT, FCT*

Mutiny on the Bounty ♀♀♀♀ **1935** Compelling adaptation of the true story of sadistic Captain Bligh, Fletcher Christian and their turbulent journey aboard the HMS Bounty. No gray here: Laughton's Bligh is truly a despicable character and extremely memorable in this MGM extravaganza. Remade twice, in 1962 and again in 1984 as "The Bounty." Much, much better than the 1962 remake. **132m/B VHS, Beta, LV, 8mm.** Clark Gable, Franchot Tone, Charles Laughton, Donald Crisp, Dudley Digges, Spring Byington, Henry Stephenson, Eddie Quillan, Herbert Mundin, Movita, Ian Wolfe; ***D:*** Frank Lloyd; ***W:*** Talbot Jennings, Jules Furthman, Carey Wilson; ***M:*** Herbert Stothart. Academy Awards '35: Best Picture; National Board of Review Awards '35: 10 Best Films of the Year; New York Film Critics Awards '35: Best Actor (Laughton); Nominations: Academy Awards '35: Best Actor (Gable), Best Actor (Tone, Laughton), Best Adapted Screenplay, Best Director (Lloyd), Best Film Editing, Best Score. *MGM, BMV, BTV*

Mutiny on the Bounty ♀♀ **1962** Based on the novel by Charles Nordhoff and James Norman Hall, this account of the 1789 mutiny led by Fletcher Christian against Captain Bligh of the Bounty is highlighted by lavish photography. Can't navigate the same perfect course set by the 1935 classic. Marlon Brando seems miscast, giving a choppy performance as the mutiny leader. **177m/C VHS, Beta, LV.** Marlon Brando, Trevor Howard, Richard Harris, Hugh Griffith; ***D:*** Lewis Milestone; ***C:*** Robert L. Surtees. Nominations: Academy Awards '61: Best Picture; Academy Awards '62: Best Art Direction/Set Decoration (Color), Best Color Cinematography, Best Song ("Love Song (Follow Me)"), Best Original Score. *MGM*

Mutual Respect ♀½ **1977 (PG)** A dying wealthy man sets out to find the son he never knew. **88m/C VHS, Beta.** Lloyd Bridges, Beau Bridges. *ACA*

My African Adventure *Woof!* **1987** Silly tale of an ambassador's son discovering a talking monkey in Africa and meeting a slew of opportunistic misfits in his travels. A comedy unfortunately short on laughs. Based on Tamar Burnstein's book. **93m/C VHS, Beta.** Dom DeLuise, Jimmie Walker; ***D:*** Sam Firstenberg. *MED*

My American Cousin ♀♀♀ **1985 (PG)** Award-winning Canadian coming-of-age comedy about a 12-year-old girl who falls for her rebellious, fun-loving 17-year-old American cousin over summer vacation. Followed by "American Boyfriends." **94m/C VHS, Beta, LV.** *CA* Margaret Langrick, John Wildman, Richard Donat, Jane Mortifee; ***D:*** Sandy Wilson; ***W:*** Sandy Wilson. Genie Awards '86: Best Actor (Wildman), Best Actress (Langrick), Best Director (Wilson), Best Film. *MED, VTR*

My Antonia ♀♀½ **1994 (PG)** Orphaned teenaged farm boy Jim Burden (Harris) discovers first romance with poor immigrant girl Antonia (Lowensohn) in 1886 Nebraska. They fall in love, separate, but maintain a 30-year friendship. Based on the book by Willa Cather. **92m/C VHS, Beta.** Neil Patrick Harris, Jason Robards Jr., Eva Marie Saint, Elina Lowensohn, Norbert Weisser, Travis Fine, Jan Triska, Anne Tremko, Mira Furlan, Boris Krutonog; ***D:*** Joseph Sargent; ***C:*** Robert Primes. *PAR*

My Apprenticeship **1939** The second film of Donskoi's trilogy on Maxim Gorky has the writer earning his living, at the age of eight, as an apprentice to a bourgeois family. Although they promise him an education, Gorky is forced to learn to read on his own and eventually sets off on a series of land and sea voyages. He recognizes that the poverty and abuse he has suffered is typical of the lives of most Russians and he encounters the beginnings of revolution. In Russian with English subtitles. Preceded by "My Childhood" and followed by "My Universities." **100m/C VHS.** *RU* ***D:*** Mark Donskoi. *FCT*

My Beautiful Laundrette **1985 (R)** Omar (Warnecke), the nephew of a Pakistani businessman, is given the opportunity to better himself by turning his uncle's run-down laundry into a profitable business. He reunites with Johnny (Day Lewis), a childhood friend and a working-class street punk, and they go into the business together. They find themselves battling the prejudice of each other's families and friends in order to succeed. An intelligent look at the sexuality, race relations and economic problems of Thatcher's London. Great performances by a relatively unknown cast (for contrast, note Day Lewis' performance in "Room with a View," released in the same year.) **93m/C VHS, Beta, LV.** Gordon Warnecke, Daniel Day-Lewis, Saeed Jaffrey, Roshan Seth, Shirley Anne Field, Derrick Branche; ***D:*** Stephen Frears; ***W:*** Hanif Kureishi; ***M:*** Ludus Tonalis. National Board of Review Awards '86: Best Supporting Actor (Day-Lewis); New York Film Critics Awards '86: Best Screenplay, Best Supporting Actor (Day-Lewis); Nominations: Academy Awards '86: Best Original Screenplay. *ORI, WAR*

My Best Friend Is a Vampire **1988 (PG)** Another teenage vampire story, about trying to cope with certain changes that adolescence and bloodsucking bring. Good supporting cast. **90m/C VHS.** Robert Sean Leonard, Evan Mirand, Cheryl Pollak, Rene Auberjonois, Cecilia Peck, Fannie Flagg, Kenneth Kimmins, David Warner, Paul Wilson; ***D:*** Jimmy Huston; ***M:*** Stephen Dorff. *HBO*

My Best Friend's Girl ½ *La Femme De Mon Pote* **1984** Coy, sardonic French romance about a woman who slaloms between two buddies working at a ski resort. Despite fine performances from all, it never quite makes it to the top of the hill. In French with English subtitles. **99m/C VHS, Beta.** *FR* Isabelle Huppert, Thierry Lhermitte, Coluche, Francoise Perrot; ***D:*** Bertrand Blier; ***W:*** Bertrand Blier, Gerard Brach. *COL, INJ, SUE*

My Best Girl **1927** Mary attempts to bring her new sweetheart home for dinner, with disastrous results. A gentle satire on middle-American life in the 1920s. Includes organ score. **78m/B VHS, Beta, LV.** Mary Pickford, Charles "Buddy" Rogers; ***D:*** Sam Taylor; ***C:*** Charles Rosher; ***M:*** Gaylord Carter. Nominations: Academy Awards '28: Best Cinematography. *CCB*

My Bloody Valentine **1981 (R)** Psychotic coal miner visits the peaceful little town of Valentine Bluffs on the night of the yearly Valentine Ball. Many of the townspeople have their hearts removed with a pick axe and sent to the sheriff in candy boxes. The bloodiest scenes were cut out to avoid an X-rating. **91m/C VHS, Beta, LV.** *CA* Paul Kelman, Lori Hallier; ***D:*** George Mihalka. *PAR*

My Blue Heaven **1990 (PG-13)** After agreeing to rat on the Mafia, Martin is dropped into suburbia as part of the witness protection program. Moranis plays the FBI agent assigned to help the former mobster become an upstanding citizen. Adjusting to life in the slow lane isn't easy for an ex con who has grown accustomed to the big time. Not the typical role for Martin, who plays a brunette with a New York accent and is handcuffed by bad writing. **96m/C VHS, Beta, LV.** Steve Martin, Rick Moranis, Joan Cusack, Melanie Mayron, Carol Kane, Bill Irwin, William Hickey, Daniel Stern; ***D:*** Herbert Ross; ***W:*** Nora Ephron; ***C:*** John Bailey; ***M:*** Ira Newborn. *WAR, BTV*

My Bodyguard **1980 (PG)** An undersized high school student fends off attacking bullies by hiring a king-sized, withdrawn lad as his bodyguard. Their "business" relationship, however, develops into true friendship. An adolescent coming of age with more intelligence and sensitivity than most of its ilk, and a pack of up and coming stars as well as old stand-bys Houseman and Gordon. **96m/C VHS, Beta.** Chris Makepeace, Adam Baldwin, Martin Mull, Ruth Gordon, Matt Dillon, John Houseman, Joan Cusack, Craig Richard Nelson; ***D:*** Tony Bill; ***W:*** Alan Ormsby; ***M:*** Dave Grusin. National Board of Review Awards '80: 10 Best Films of the Year. *FOX*

My Boy ½ **1921** Coogan stars as a foreign orphan who faces deportation. Instead he escapes and follows an old man home. This rare film includes an organ score. **56m/B VHS, Beta.** Jackie Coogan, Claude Gillingwater, Mathilde Brundage; ***D:*** Albert Austin. *GPV*

My Boyfriend's Back *Johnny Zombie* **1993 (PG-13)** Embarassingly dumb flick about a teenage boy who wants to take the prettiest girl in the school to the prom. The only problem is that he's become a zombie. Bits of him keep falling off (his girl thoughtfully glues them back on) and if he wants to stay "alive" long enough to get to the dance he has to munch on human flesh. Yuck. **85m/C VHS, LV.** Andrew Lowery, Traci Lind, Edward Herrmann, Mary Beth Hurt, Danny Zorn, Austin Pendleton, Jay O. Sanders, Paul Dooley, Bob Dishy, Matthew Fox, Paxton Whitehead; ***D:*** Bob Balaban; ***W:*** Dean Lorey. *TOU*

My Boys Are Good Boys **1978 (PG)** A young foursome steal from an armored car and have to face the consequences. Quirky with an implausible storyline. **90m/C VHS, Beta.** Ralph Meeker, Ida Lupino, Lloyd Nolan, David Doyle; ***D:*** Bethel Buckalew. *NO*

My Breakfast with Blassie **1983** Kaufman and professional wrestler Blassie meet for breakfast and carry on a comical dialogue. **60m/C VHS, Beta.** Andy Kaufman, Freddie Blassie; ***D:*** Johnny Legend, Linda Lautrec. *RHI*

My Brilliant Career ½ **1979 (G)** A headstrong young woman spurns the social expectations of turn-of-the-century Australia and pursues opportunities to broaden her intellect and preserve her independence. Davis is wonderful as the energetic and charismatic community trendsetter. Based on an autobiographical novel by Miles Franklin which has been marvelously transferred to the screen. Armstrong deserves credit for her fine direction. **101m/C VHS, Beta.** *AU* Judy Davis, Sam Neill, Wendy Hughes; ***D:*** Gillian Armstrong. Australian Film Institute '79: Best Film; British Academy Awards '80: Best Actress (Davis); Nominations: Academy Awards '80: Best Costume Design; Cannes Film Festival '79: Best Film. *VES*

My Brother Has Bad Dreams **1988** Young man with sibling tosses and turns in bed. **97m/C VHS.** Nick Kleinholz, Marlena Lustic. *VCI*

My Brother's Wife ½ **1989 (PG)** Barney (Ritter), the black sheep of a wealthy family, spends two decades pursuing Eleanor (Harris), the woman of his dreams. Unfortunately, she's already married—to the brother he despises. Adapted from the play "The Middle Ages" by A.R. Gurney. Made for television. **94m/C VHS.** John Ritter, Mel Harris, Polly Bergen, Dakin Matthews, David Byron, Lee Weaver; ***D:*** Jack Bender; ***W:*** Percy Granger. *APX, TPV*

My Champion **1984** Chance meeting propels Mike Gorman and Miki Tsuwa into a relationship based on the strong bonds of love and athletic competition. **101m/C VHS, Beta.** Yoko Shimada, Chris Mitchum. *MED*

My Chauffeur ½ **1986 (R)** When a wisecracking female is hired on as a chauffeur at an all-male chauffeur service, sparks fly. And when the owner takes a definite liking to her work, things take a turn for the worse. As these sort of sexploitation flicks go, this is one of the better ones. **94m/C VHS, Beta, LV.** Deborah Foreman, Sam Jones, Howard Hesseman, E.G. Marshall, Sean McClory; ***D:*** David Beaird; ***W:*** David Beaird. *LIV, VES*

My Childhood **1938** The first of director Donskoi's trilogy on the life of Maxim Gorky, based on Gorky's autobiographical stories. In this first film, Donskoi depicts Gorky's childhood of abuse and poverty with his grandparents in the 1870s. Eventually, Gorky is forced into the streets and he becomes a wandering beggar. In Russian with English subtitles. Followed by "My Apprenticeship" and "My Universities." **100m/C VHS.** *RU* ***D:*** Mark Donskoi. *FCT*

My Cousin Vinny **1992 (R)** Vinny Gambini (Pesci), a lawyer who took the bar exam six times before passing, goes to Wahzoo City, Alabama to get his cousin and a friend off the hook when they're accused of killing a store clerk. Leather jackets, gold chains, Brooklyn accents, and his fiancee Tomei's penchant for big hair and bold clothing don't go over well with conservative judge Gwynne, causing plenty of misunderstandings. Surprising hit with simplistic story reaches popular heights via entertaining performances by the entire cast. Tomei in particular steals every scene she's in and has an Oscar to prove it. **120m/C VHS.** Joe Pesci, Ralph Macchio, Marisa Tomei, Mitchell Whitfield, Fred Gwynne, Lane Smith, Austin Pendleton, Bruce McGill; ***D:*** Jonathan Lynn; ***W:*** Dale Launer; ***M:*** Randy Edelman. Academy Awards '92: Best Supporting Actress (Tomei); MTV Movie Awards '93: Breakthrough Performance (Tomei). *FXV, MOV, PMS*

My Darlin' Clementine **1986** Shelly Duvall gives the famous song about a miner who bemoans the loss of his daughter and her size nine shoes her own touch in this entry from the "Tall Tales and Legends" series. Made for cable television. **49m/C VHS.** Shelley Duvall, Ed Asner, David Dukes, John Matuszak. *FOX*

My Darling Clementine ½ **1946** One of the best Hollywood westerns ever made, this recounts the precise events leading up to and including the gunfight at the O.K. Corral. Ford allegedly knew Wyatt Earp and used his stories to recount the details vividly, though not always accurately. Remake of 1939's "Frontier Marshal." **97m/B VHS, Beta, LV.** Henry Fonda, Victor Mature, Walter Brennan, Linda Darnell, Tim Holt, Ward Bond, John Ireland; ***D:*** John Ford. *FOX, TLF*

My Daughter's Keeper **1993 (R)** The apparently perfect nanny of an unsuspecting family reveals her deadly agenda of murder, adultery, and more. **94m/C VHS.** Nicholas Guest, Jocelyn Broderick, Ana Padrao. *LIV*

My Dear Secretary ½ **1949** After she marries her boss, a woman grows jealous of the secretary that replaces her. Comedic dialogue and antics result. **94m/C VHS, Beta.** Kirk Douglas, Laraine Day, Keenan Wynn, Rudy Vallee, Florence Bates, Alan Mowbray, Charles Halton; ***D:*** Charles Martin; ***W:*** Charles Martin. *NOS, MRV, BAR*

My Demon Lover **1987 (PG-13)** This sex comedy is complicated by the hero's transformation into a demon whenever he is aroused. Saved from complete mediocrity by Family Ties's Valentine in a likable performance. **90m/C VHS, Beta, LV.** Scott Valentine, Michelle Little, Arnold Johnson, Gina Gallego; ***D:*** Charles Loventhal; ***M:*** David Newman, Ed Alton. *COL*

My Dinner with Andre ½ **1981** Two friends talk about their lives and philosophies for two hours over dinner one night. A wonderful exploration into storytelling, the conversation juxtaposes the experiences and philosophies of nerdish, bumbling Shawn and the globe-trotting spiritual pilgrimage of Gregory, in this sometimes poignant, sometimes comic little movie that starts you thinking. **110m/C VHS, Beta, LV.** Andre Gregory, Wallace Shawn; ***D:*** Louis Malle. *INJ, HMV, TPV*

My Dog Shep ½ **1946** An orphan and his dog run away and are pursued diligently when it is discovered that he is a wealthy heir. **71m/B VHS, Beta, LV.** Tom Neal, William Farnum, Lannie Rees; ***D:*** Ford Beebe. *NOS, VYY*

My Dog, the Thief **1969** A helicopter weatherman is unaware that the lovable St. Bernard he has adopted is a kleptomaniac. When the dog steals a valuable necklace from a team of professional jewel thieves, the fun begins. **88m/C VHS, Beta.** Joe Flynn, Elsa Lanchester, Roger C. Carmel, Mickey Shaughnessy, Dwayne Hickman, Mary Ann Mobley; ***D:*** Robert Stevenson. *DVT*

My Dream Is Yours 🦴🦴½ **1949** Day plays an up and coming radio star in this Warner Brothers musical comedy with a cameo from Bugs Bunny in a dream sequence. This fresh, fun remake of "Twenty Million Sweethearts" is often underrated, but is well worth a look. ♫My Dream is Yours; Some Like You; Tic, Tic, Tic; Love Finds a Way; I'll String Along with You; Canadian Capers; Freddie Get Ready; You Must Have Been a Beautiful Baby; Jeepers, Creepers. **101m/C VHS.** Jack Carson, Doris Day, Lee Bowman, Adolphe Menjou, Eve Arden, S.Z. Sakall, Selena Royle, Edgar Kennedy; ***D:*** Michael Curtiz. *FOX, FCT, MLB*

My Fair Lady 🦴🦴🦴½ **1964 (G)** Colorful production of Lerner and Loewe's musical version of "Pygmalion," about an ill-mannered cockney girl who is plucked from her job as a flower girl by Professor Henry Higgins. Higgins makes a bet with a colleague that he can turn this rough diamond into a "lady." Winner of eight Academy Awards. Hepburn's singing voice is dubbed by Marni Nixon, who was also responsible for the singing in "The King and I" and "West Side Story;" the dubbing may have undermined her chance at an Oscar nomination. Typecasting role for Harrison as the crusty, egocentric Higgins. A timeless classic. ♫Why Can't the English?; Wouldn't It Be Loverly?; I'm an Ordinary Man; With a Little Bit of Luck; Just You Wait, 'Enry 'Iggins; The Servant's Chorus; The Rain in Spain; I Could Have Danced all Night; Ascot Gavotte. **170m/C VHS, Beta, LV.** Audrey Hepburn, Rex Harrison, Stanley Holloway, Wilfrid Hyde-White, Theodore Bikel, Mona Washbourne, Jeremy Brett, Robert Coote, Gladys Cooper; ***D:*** George Cukor; ***C:*** Harry Stradling; ***M:*** Frederick Loewe, Alan Jay Lerner. Academy Awards '64: Best Actor (Harrison), Best Adapted Score, Best Art Direction/Set Decoration (Color), Best Color Cinematography, Best Costume Design (Color), Best Director (Cukor), Best Picture, Best Sound; British Academy Awards '65: Best Film; Directors Guild of America Awards '64: Best Director (Cukor); Golden Globe Awards '65: Best Actor—Musical/Comedy (Harrison), Best Director (Cukor), Best Film—Musical/Comedy; National Board of Review Awards '64: 10 Best Films of the Year; New York Film Critics Awards '64: Best Actor (Harrison), Best Film; Nominations: Academy Awards '64: Best Adapted Screenplay, Best Film Editing, Best Supporting Actor (Holloway), Best Supporting Actress (Cooper). *FOX, FCT, BTV*

My Family 🦴🦴🦴½ **1994 (R)** Patriarch Jose Sanchez (Rojas) comes to America in the early 1900's from Mexico and soon finds that the grass is not always greener on the other side. Thus begins the multigenerational saga of the Sanchez family in L.A., which chronicles their struggles and hopes over a time span of sixty years. Overlooked in the glut of Hispanic-themed movies released, featuring soulful performances from the ensemble cast, especially Smits and Morales as troubled men from separate generations. Their deep-seated need to assimilate matched by a disdain for authority provide most of the family's heartaches. English and Spanish dialogue. **126m/C VHS, LV.** Jimmy Smits, Esai Morales, Eduardo Lopez Rojas, Jenny Gago, Elpidia Carrillo, Lupe Ontiveros, Jacob Vargas, Jennifer Lopez, Scott Bakula, Edward James Olmos; ***D:*** Gregory Nava; ***W:*** Anna Thomas, Gregory Nava; ***C:*** Edward Lachman; ***M:*** Pepe Avila, Mark McKenzie. Nominations: Academy Awards '95: Best Makeup; Independent Spirit Awards '96: Best Actor (Smits), Best Supporting Actress (Lopez). *NLC, TTC*

My Family Treasure 🦴🦴½ **1993** Mother tells her children about her dangerous trip into Russia to recover a family legacy—a priceless Faberge egg. **95m/C VHS.** Dee Wallace Stone, Theodore Bikel, Alex Vincent, Bitty Schram; ***D:*** Rolfe Kanefsky, Edward Staroselsky. *AVI*

My Father Is Coming 🦴🦴 **1991** German immigrant, Vicky, is trying to get an acting career off the ground in New York. She shares her apartment with Ben, a gay man, and generally does more work as a waitress than actress. Vicky's alarmed when her father, Hans, arrives for a visit. She's told him she's married (Vicky's also gay), so Ben agrees to pose as her husband. The rest of the film details Vicky's complicated love life, unsuccessful career tryouts, and her father's increasing bewilderment. It's meant as a sort of reverse, and perverse, innocents abroad, with the two Germans adrift in zany New York but this only works fitfully. **82m/C VHS.** *GE* Shelley Kastner, Alfred Edel, David Bronstein, Mary Lou Graulau, Michael Massee, Annie Sprinkle, Bruce Benderson; ***D:*** Monika Treut; ***W:*** Monika Treut. *NO*

My Father, My Rival 🦴 **1985** A high school student's crush on his teacher leads to emotional complications when his widowed father becomes romantically involved with her. **60m/C VHS, Beta.** Lance Guest. *NO*

My Father the Hero 🦴🦴 **1993 (PG)** Another adaptation of a French film ("Mon Pere, Ce Heroes") finds 14-year-old Heigl on an island paradise with divorced dad Depardieu, passing him off as her boyfriend (without his knowledge) to impress a cute boy, causing obvious misunderstandings. Depardieu shows a flair for physical comedy, but his talent is wasted in a role that's vaguely disturbing; one of the few funny moments finds him unwittingly singing "Thank Heaven For Little Girls" to a horrified audience. For the pre-teen set only, others will probably find it a waste of time. Top notch actress Thompson's surprising (uncredited) cameo is due to her friendship with Depardieu. **90m/C VHS, LV.** Gerard Depardieu, Katherine Heigl, Dalton James, Lauren Hutton, Faith Prince; ***Cameos:*** Emma Thompson; ***D:*** Steve Miner; ***W:*** Francis Veber, Charlie Peters; ***M:*** David Newman. *TOU*

My Father's Glory 🦴🦴🦴 *La Gloire de Mon Pere* **1991 (G)** Based on Marcel Pagnol's tales of his childhood, this is a sweet, beautiful memory of a young boy's favorite summer in the French countryside of the early 1900s. Not much happens, yet the film is such a perfect evocation of the milieu that one is carried swiftly into the dreams and thoughts of all the characters. One half of a duo, followed by "My Mother's Castle." In French with English subtitles. **110m/C VHS.** *FR* Julien Ciamaca, Philippe Caubere, Nathalie Roussel, Therese Liotard, Didier Pain; ***D:*** Yves Robert; ***W:*** Lucette Andrei; ***M:*** Vladimir Cosma. *INJ, ORI, BTV*

My Father's House 🦴🦴 **1975** Magazine editor recounts his youth while recovering from a heart attack. He measures his own quality of life against the life that his father led and begins to question his own choices with regard to his family. **96m/C VHS, Beta.** Cliff Robertson, Robert Preston, Eileen Brennan, Rosemary Forsyth. *WOV*

My Father's Nurse 🦴 **1985** While father convalesces upstairs, the family frolics about the house and plots his dispatch. When his new nurse secretly cures him, he takes to a wheelchair and mounts a comedic covert counter offensive. **97m/C VHS, Beta.** *VCD, MOV*

My Favorite Blonde 🦴🦴🦴 **1942** Beautiful British spy Carroll convinces Hope to aid her in carrying out a secret mission. Lots of fun as Hope and his trained penguin, along with Carroll, embark on a cross-country chase to elude the Nazis. Hope's behavior is hilarious and the pacing of the film is excellent. Based on a story by Melvin Frank and Norman Panama. **78m/B VHS.** Bob Hope, Madeleine Carroll, Gale Sondergaard, George Zucco, Lionel Royce, Walter Kingsford, Victor Varconi; ***Cameos:*** Bing Crosby; ***D:*** Sidney Lanfield; ***W:*** Frank Butler, Don Hartman; ***C:*** William Mellor. *MCA, BTV*

My Favorite Brunette 🦴🦴½ **1947** Detective parody starring Hope as a photographer turned grumbling private eye. He becomes involved with a murder, a spy caper, and a dangerous brunette (Lamour). **85m/B VHS, Beta, LV.** Bob Hope, Dorothy Lamour, Peter Lorre, Lon Chaney Jr., Alan Ladd, Reginald Denny, Bing Crosby; ***D:*** Elliott Nugent; ***C:*** Lionel Lindon. *CNG, MRV, NOS*

My Favorite Wife 🦴🦴🦴 **1940** Handsome widower Grant remarries only to discover that first wife Dunne, shipwrecked seven years earlier and presumed dead, has reappeared. Eventually, a judge must decide what to do in this most unusual situation, completely lacking precedent. Farcical and hilarious story filled with a clever cast. The 1963 remake "Move Over Darling" lacks the style and wit of this presentation. Also available colorized. **88m/B VHS, Beta, LV.** Irene Dunne, Cary Grant, Randolph Scott, Gail Patrick, Scotty Beckett; ***D:*** Garson Kanin; ***W:*** Samuel Spewack, Bella Spewack, Leo McCarey. Nominations: Academy Awards '40: Best Story, Best Original Score. *MED, MLB, TTC*

My Favorite Year 🦴🦴🦴 *My Favourite Year* **1982 (PG)** A young writer on a popular live television show in the 1950s is asked to keep a watchful eye on the week's guest star—his favorite swashbuckling movie hero. Through a series of misadventures, he discovers his matinee idol is actually a drunkard and womanizer who has trouble living up to his cinematic standards. Sterling performance from O'Toole, with memorable portrayal from Bologna as the show's host, King Kaiser (a take-off of Sid Caesar from "Your Show of Shows"). **92m/C VHS, Beta, LV.** Peter O'Toole, Mark Linn-Baker, Joseph Bologna, Jessica Harper, Lainie Kazan, Bill Macy, Anne DeSalvo, Lou Jacobi, Adolph Green, Cameron Mitchell, Gloria Stuart; ***D:*** Richard Benjamin; ***W:*** Norman Steinberg; ***M:*** Ralph Burns. Nominations: Academy Awards '82: Best Actor (O'Toole). *MGM*

My First Wife 🦴🦴½ **1984 (PG)** Strong drama about a self-indulgent man's devastation when his wife abruptly leaves him after ten years of marriage. Realistic and well-acted. **95m/C VHS.** *AU* John Hargreaves, Wendy Hughes, Lucy Angwin, Anna Jemison, David Cameron; ***D:*** Paul Cox; ***W:*** Paul Cox, Bob Ellis. Australian Film Institute '84: Best Actor (Hargreaves). *NO*

My Forbidden Past 🦴🦴½ **1951** Melodrama set in 1890 New Orleans centers on a young woman (Gardner) with an unsavory past who unexpectedly inherits a fortune and vows to break up the marriage of the man (Mitchum) she loves. His wife is murdered and he is charged with doing the deed until Gardner, exposing her past, wins his love and helps to extricate him. **81m/B VHS, Beta.** Ava Gardner, Melvyn Douglas, Robert Mitchum; ***D:*** Robert Stevenson. *MED*

My Friend Flicka 🦴🦴🦴 **1943** Boy makes friends with four-legged beast. Dad thinks the horse is full of wild oats, but young Roddie trains it to be the best gosh darned horse in pre-Disney family faredom. Based on Mary O'Hara book, followed by "Thunderhead, Son of Flicka," and TV series. **89m/C VHS, Beta.** Roddy McDowall, Preston Foster, Rita Johnson, James Bell, Jeff Corey; ***D:*** Harold Schuster. *FXV, FCT, HMV*

My Friend Irma 🦴½ **1949** An adaptation of the radio series, featuring Wilson as the dumb blonde with boyfriend trouble and Lynn as her sensible pal. The film debut of Martin (singing) and Lewis (mugging) as juice-bar operators. Followed by a sequel, "My Friend Irma Goes West," and later by a television series. **103m/B VHS, LV.** Marie Wilson, Diana Lynn, John Lund, Don DeFore, Dean Martin, Jerry Lewis, Hans Conried; ***D:*** George Marshall. *PAR*

My Friend Walter 🦴🦴½ **1993** Bess Throckmorten attends a family reunion in London with her Aunt Ellie and discovers one of her ancestors is Sir Walter Raleigh. Visiting the Tower of London, Bess finds Sir Walter's ghost who wants to follow her home to Devon to see how the family is doing. He finds that the Throckmorten's are about to lose the family farm but Sir Walter comes up with a plan to restore their fortunes. Shot on location in England and based on the book by Michael Morpurgo. **87m/C VHS.** *GB* Polly Grant, Ronald Pickup, Prunella Scales, Louise Jameson, James Hazeldine, Lawrence Cooper, Constance Chapman; ***D:*** Gavin Millar. *PME, BTV*

My Geisha 🦴🦴½ **1962** MacLaine and husband experience bad karma because she wants to be in his new film. In pancake makeup and funny shoes, she poses as a geisha girl and is cast as Madame Butterfly. Her husband, however, is one sharp cookie. Filmed in Japan. **120m/C VHS.** Shirley MacLaine, Yves Montand, Edward G. Robinson, Robert Cummings; ***D:*** Jack Cardiff. Nominations: Academy Awards '62: Best Costume Design (Color). *PAR, WAX, FCT*

My Girl ☙☙½ **1991 (PG)** Chlumsky is delightful in her film debut as an 11-year old tomboy who must come to grips with the realities of life. Culkin plays her best friend Thomas, who understands her better than anyone else, including her father, a mortician, and his girlfriend, the makeup artist at the funeral parlor. Some reviewers questioned whether young children would be able to deal with some unhappy occurrences in the film, but most seemed to classify it as a movie the whole family would enjoy. **102m/C VHS, LV, 8mm.** Dan Aykroyd, Jamie Lee Curtis, Macaulay Culkin, Anna Chlumsky, Griffin Dunne, Raymond Buktenica, Richard Masur, Ann Nelson, Peter Michael Goetz, Tom Villard; ***D:*** Howard Zieff; ***W:*** Laurice Elehwany; ***M:*** James Newton Howard. MTV Movie Awards '92: Best Kiss (Macaulay Culkin/Anna Chlumsky). *COL*

My Girl 2 ☙☙½ **1994 (PG)** It's 1974 and Chlumsky is back as Vada (this time without Culkin, given the killer bee attack in MG1) in this innocent coming-of-ager. Portly Ackroyd and flaky Curtis return as parental window dressing who encourage Vada's search for information on her long-dead mother. She tracks down old friends of her mom's (Masur and Rose) who are having difficulties with their obnoxious adolescent son (O'Brien). Predictable, but enjoyable. Certain to fail the credibility test of nit-pickers who may wonder why the only thing Ackroyd can remember of his first wife is that she left behind a paper bag with a date scribbled on it. **99m/C VHS, LV, 8mm.** Anna Chlumsky, Dan Aykroyd, Jamie Lee Curtis, Austin O'Brien, Richard Masur, Christine Ebersole; ***D:*** Howard Zieff; ***W:*** Janet Kovalcik; ***M:*** Cliff Eidelman. *COL*

My Girl Tisa ☙☙½ **1948** Chronicles the experiences of a young immigrant woman who struggles to survive in the U.S. at the turn of the century and hopes to bring her father over from their home country. Based on a play by Lucille S. Prumbs and Sara B. Smith. **95m/B VHS.** Lilli Palmer, Sam Wanamaker, Akim Tamiroff, Alan Hale, Hugo Haas, Gale Robbins, Stella Adler; ***D:*** Elliott Nugent; ***M:*** Max Steiner. *REP*

My Grandpa is a Vampire ☙½ **1992 (PG)** When 12 year-old Lonny and his pal visit Grandpa Cooger in New Zealand Lonny discovers a long-hidden family secret—Grandpa's a vampire! This doesn't stop either boy from joining with Grandpa in lots of scary adventures. **90m/C VHS.** Al Lewis, Justin Gocke, Milan Borich, Noel Appleby; ***D:*** David Blyth. *REP*

My Heroes Have Always Been Cowboys ☙☙½ **1991 (PG)** An aging rodeo rider returns to his hometown to recuperate and finds himself forced to confront his past. His ex-girlfriend, his dad and his sister all expect something from him. He learns how to give it, and gains the strength of purpose to get back on the bull that stomped him. Excellent rodeo footage, solid performances, but the story has been around the barn too many times to hold much interest. **106m/C VHS, Beta, LV.** Scott Glenn, Kate Capshaw, Ben Johnson, Balthazar Getty, Mickey Rooney, Gary Busey, Tess Harper, Clarence Williams III, Dub Taylor, Clu Gulager, Dennis Fimple; ***D:*** Stuart Rosenberg; ***W:*** Joel Don Humphreys; ***M:*** James Horner. *VTR, FXV, COL*

My Lady of Whims ☙ **1925** Clara Bow's dad disapproves of debutante daughter's desire to hang out with the girls who just want to have fun. **42m/B VHS, Beta.** Clara Bow, Betty Baker, Carmelita Geraghty, Donald Keith, Lee Moran. *GPV, FCT*

My Left Foot ☙☙☙☙ **1989 (R)** A gritty, unsentimental drama based on the life and autobiography of cerebral-palsy victim Christy Brown. Considered an imbecile by everyone but his mother (Fricker, in a stunning award-winning performance) until he teaches himself to write. He survives his impoverished Irish roots to become a painter and writer using his left foot, the only appendage over which he has control. He also falls in love and finds some heartaches along the way. Day-Lewis is astounding; the supporting cast, especially Shaw and Cusack, match him measure for measure. **103m/C VHS, Beta, LV.** *IR* Daniel Day-Lewis, Brenda Fricker, Ray McAnally, Cyril Cusack, Fiona Shaw, Hugh O'Conor, Adrian Dunbar, Ruth McCabe, Alison Whelan; ***D:*** Jim Sheridan; ***W:*** Shane Connaughton, Jim Sheridan; ***M:*** Elmer Bernstein. Academy Awards '89: Best Actor (Day-Lewis), Best Supporting Actress (Fricker); Independent Spirit Awards '90: Best Foreign Film; Los Angeles Film Critics Association Awards '89: Best Actor (Day-Lewis), Best Supporting Actress (Fricker); New York Film Critics Awards '89: Best Actor (Day-Lewis), Best Film; National Society of Film Critics Awards '89: Best Actor (Day-Lewis); Nominations: Academy Awards '89: Best Adapted Screenplay, Best Director (Sheridan), Best Picture. *HBO, BTV, HMV*

My Life ☙☙½ **1993 (PG-13)** Maudlin, sometimes depressing production preaches the power of a well-examined life. Public relations exec Keaton is diagnosed with cancer and the doctors predict he will most likely die before the birth of his first child. Film follows his transition from uncommunicative and angry to acceptance, a role to which Keaton brings a sentimental strength. Kidman is window dressing as the ever-patient, nobly suffering wife, a cardboard character notable mainly for her beauty. **114m/C VHS, LV, 8mm.** Michael Keaton, Nicole Kidman, Haing S. Ngor, Bradley Whitford, Queen Latifah, Michael Constantine, Toni Sawyer, Rebecca Schull, Lee Garlington; ***D:*** Bruce Joel Rubin; ***W:*** Bruce Joel Rubin; ***M:*** John Barry. *COL*

My Life and Times with Antonin Artaud ☙☙☙ *En Compagnie d'Antonin Artaud* **1993** Postwar Parisian bohemia is depicted in the obsessive friendship between ambitious young poet Jacques Prevel (Barbe) and famed intellectual/poet/impressario Antonin Artaud (Frey), who founded the Theatre of Cruelty. Artaud has returned to Paris after spending nine years in an asylum and is suffering from terminal cancer, the misery of which is partially alleviated by the opiates that Prevel can provide. Delusional and paranoid, Artaud makes his self-destruction into genius while Prevel documents Artaud's last two years in diaries, hoping to gain some measure of fame for himself. French with subtitles. Based on Prevel's "En Compagnie d'Antonin Artaud." **93m/B VHS.** *FR* Sami Frey, Marc Barbe, Valerie Jeannet, Julie Jezequel; ***D:*** Gerard Mordillat; ***W:*** Gerard Mordillat, Jerome Prieur; ***C:*** Francois Catonne; ***M:*** Jean-Claude Petit. *FXL*

My Life as a Dog ☙☙☙☙ *Mitt Liv Som Hund* **1985** A troublesome boy is separated from his brother and is sent to live with relatives in the country when his mother is taken ill. Unhappy and confused, he struggles to understand sexuality and love and tries to find security and acceptance. Remarkable Swedish film available with English subtitles or dubbed. **101m/C VHS, Beta, LV.** *SW* Anton Glanzelius, Tomas Van Bromssen, Anki Liden, Melinda Kinnaman, Kicki Rundgren, Ing-mari Carlsson; ***D:*** Lasse Hallstrom. Golden Globe Awards '88: Best Foreign Film; Independent Spirit Awards '88: Best Foreign Film; New York Film Critics Awards '87: Best Foreign Film; Nominations: Academy Awards '87: Best Adapted Screenplay, Best Director (Hallstrom). *PAR, INJ, HMV*

My Life to Live ☙☙☙☙ *Vivre Savie; It's My Life* **1962** A woman turns to prostitution in this probing examination of sexual, and social, relations. Idiosyncratic Godard has never been more starstruck than in this vehicle for the endearing Karina, his wife at the time. A classic. In French with English subtitles. **85m/B VHS, Beta.** *FR* Anna Karina, Sady Rebbot, Andre S. Labarthe, Guylaine Schlumberger; ***D:*** Jean-Luc Godard; ***W:*** Jean-Luc Godard; ***M:*** Michel Legrand. Venice Film Festival '62: Special Jury Prize. *NOS, NYF, DVT*

My Life's In Turnaround ☙☙ **1994 (R)** Amusing low-budget comedy takes a behind-the-scenes, semi-autobiographical look at the lives of two would-be filmmakers. They try for cool but manage only goofy. **84m/C VHS.** Eric Schaeffer, Donal Lardner Ward, Lisa Gerstein, Dana Wheeler-Nicholson, Debra Clein, Sheila Jaffe; ***Cameos:*** Casey Siemaszko, John Sayles, Martha Plimpton, Phoebe Cates; ***D:*** Eric Schaeffer, Donal Lardner Ward; ***W:*** Eric Schaeffer, Donal Lardner Ward; ***M:*** Reed Hays. *AVI*

My Little Chickadee ☙☙☙ **1940** Classic comedy about a gambler and a fallen woman who marry for convenience so they can respectably enter an unsuspecting town. Sparks fly in their adventures together. Fields and West are both at their best playing their larger-than-life selves. **91m/B VHS, Beta, LV.** W.C. Fields, Mae West, Joseph Calleia, Dick Foran, Margaret Hamilton, Donald Meek; ***D:*** Eddie Cline; ***C:*** Joseph Valentine. *MCA, MLB, BTV*

My Little Girl ☙☙ **1987 (R)** A rich Philadelphia girl idealistically volunteers her time to help local institutionalized orphans, but meets with opposition. **118m/C VHS, Beta, LV.** Mary Stuart Masterson, James Earl Jones, Geraldine Page, Anne Meara, Peter Gallagher, George Newbern; ***D:*** Connie Kaiserman. *PSM*

My Little Pony: The Movie ☙☙½ **1986** Animated tale about the siege of Ponyland by malevolent witches. **87m/C VHS, Beta.** ***D:*** Michael Joens; ***V:*** Danny DeVito, Cloris Leachman, Tony Randall, Madeline Kahn. *WTA*

My Love For Yours ☙☙½ *Honeymoon in Bali* **1939** The romantic tale of a young man hoping to win the love of a beautiful but icy girl. A tad silly in parts, but the clever dialogue moves the story along. **99m/B VHS, Beta.** Fred MacMurray, Madeleine Carroll; ***D:*** Edward H. Griffith. *NOS, CAB*

My Lucky Star ☙☙½ **1938** Skating star Henie plays a department store clerk that gets sent off to college to model clothes from the store's sports line. She somehow manages to convince school officials to stage their winter ice show in the department store, where she gets to show off her stuff. Don't miss the grand finale, a performance of "Alice in Wonderland Ice Ballet." Based on the story "They Met in Chicago" by Karl Tunberg and Don Ettlinger. ♫I've Got a Date With a Dream; Could You Pass in Love; This May Be the Night; The All-American Swing; Plymouth University Song. **81m/B VHS.** Sonja Henie, Richard Greene, Joan Davis, Cesar Romero, Buddy Ebsen, Arthur Treacher, George Barbier, Gypsy Rose Lee; ***D:*** Roy Del Ruth; ***W:*** Harry Tugend, Jack Yellen. *FXV*

My Man Adam ☙☙ **1986 (R)** A dreamy, Mitty-esque high schooler falls in love with a girl (Daryl's auburn-haired sister, Page Hannah), and becomes ensnared in a real life crime, leaving his friend to bail him out. Typical boy-meets-girl, boy-gets-in-trouble yarn. **84m/C VHS, Beta.** Raphael Sbarge, Veronica Cartwright, Page Hannah, Larry B. Scott, Charlie Barnett, Arthur Pendleton, Dave Thomas; ***D:*** Roger L. Simon. *FOX*

My Man Godfrey ☙☙☙☙ **1936** A spoiled rich girl picks up someone she assumes is a bum as part of a scavenger hunt and decides to keep him on as her butler. In the process, he teaches her about life, money, and happiness. Top-notch screwball comedy defines the genre. Lombard is a stunner alongside the equally charming Powell. Watch for Jane Wyman as an extra in the party scene. Remade in 1957 with June Allyson and David Niven. From the novel by Eric Hatch, who also co-scripted. **95m/B VHS, Beta.** William Powell, Carole Lombard, Gail Patrick, Alice Brady, Mischa Auer, Eugene Pallette, Alan Mowbray, Franklin Pangborn, Jane Wyman; ***D:*** Gregory La Cava; ***W:*** Morrie Ryskind, Gregory La Cava. Nominations: Academy Awards '36: Best Actor (Powell), Best Actress (Lombard), Best Director (La Cava), Best Screenplay, Best Supporting Actor (Auer), Best Supporting Actress (Brady). *CNG, MRV, NOS*

My Man Godfrey ☙☙½ **1957** Inferior remake of the sophisticated screwball comedy of the 30's about a butler who brings a touch of the common man to the filthy rich. Niven stars as the butler and Allyson plays the rich girl, but nothing compares to the original roles created by Powell and Lombard. **92m/C VHS.** June Allyson, David Niven, Martha Hyer, Jessie Royce Landis, Robert Keith, Eva Gabor, Jay Robinson, Jeff Donnell; ***D:*** Henry Koster; ***W:*** Everett Freeman, Peter Berneis, William Bowers; ***C:*** William H. Daniels. *MCA*

My Michael ☙☙☙ **1975** Sensitive adaptation of Amos Oz's novel set in Jerasalem in the late 1950s. A young woman is stifled by marriage and the conventions of her bourgeois life and her fantasies begin to take over. In Hebrew with English subtitles. **90m/C VHS, Beta.** *IS* Efrat Lavie, Oded Kotler; ***D:*** Dan Wolman. *ERG, FCT, INJ*

My Mom's a Werewolf ✂✂½ **1989 (PG)** An average suburban mother gets involved with a dashing stranger and soon, to her terror, begins to turn into a werewolf. Her daughter and companion must come up with a plan to regain dear, sweet mom. **90m/C VHS, Beta, LV.** Susan Blakely, John Saxon, John Schuck, Katrina Caspary, Ruth Buzzi, Marilyn McCoo, Marcia Wallace, Diana Barrows; ***D:*** Michael Fischa; ***W:*** Mark Pirro. *PSM*

My Mother's Castle ✂✂✂½ *Le Chateau de Ma Mere* **1991 (PG)** The second half of the two part film series based on the autobiography of Marcel Pagnol. Picking up where "My Father's Glory" left off, the family begins a series of vacations in a beautiful country home. Dynamically acted and tenderly directed, charming and suitable for the entire family. In French with English subtitles. **98m/C VHS.** *FR* Philippe Caubere, Nathalie Roussel, Didier Pain, Therese Liotard, Julien Ciamaca, Victorien Delmare; ***D:*** Yves Robert; ***M:*** Vladimir Cosma. *INJ, ORI, BTV*

My Mother's Secret Life ✂½ **1984** Dull drama focusing on a long-forgotten daughter who suddenly appears on her mother's doorstep and discovers that mom makes a living as a high-priced hooker. **100m/C VHS, Beta.** Loni Anderson, Paul Sorvino, Amanda Wyss, James Sutorius, Sandy McPeak; ***D:*** Robert Markowitz; ***M:*** Brad Fiedel. *PSM*

My Name Called Bruce **198?** When the unstoppable "Bruce" is teamed with a sexy secret agent, the criminals of Hong Kong issue a collective shudder. **90m/C VHS, Beta.** Bruce Le. *BFV*

My Name is Ivan ✂✂✂½ *Ivan's Childhood; The Youngest Spy* **1962** Tarkovsky's first feature film is a vivid, wrenching portrait of a young Soviet boy surviving as a spy behind enemy lines during WWII. Technically stunning, heralding the coming of modern cinema's greatest formalist. In Russian with English subtitles. **84m/B VHS, Beta, LV.** *RU* Kolya Burlyayev, Valentin Zubkov, Ye Zharikov, S. Krylov; ***D:*** Andrei Tarkovsky. Venice Film Festival '62: Best Film. *FXL, FCT, INJ*

My Name is Nobody ✂✂½ *Il Mio Nome e Nessuno* **1974 (PG)** Fast-paced spaghetti-western wherein a cocky, soft-hearted gunfighter is sent to kill the famous, retired outlaw he reveres, but instead they band together. **115m/C VHS, Beta.** Henry Fonda, Terence Hill, R.G. Armstrong; ***D:*** Tonino Valerii; ***M:*** Ennio Morricone. *BAR, HHE*

My Neighbor Totoro ✂✂½ **1993 (G)** Rather gooey Japanese animated movie about Satsuki and her younger sister Lucy, whose new house in the country is filled with magic, including a friendly creature named Totoro. Totoro is a cuddly, if weird, mix of bear, owl, and seal, with whiskers and a gentle roar. He can fly, has a magic bus, and can only be seen by children. Naturally, every time the two girls get into mischief Totoro is there to rescue them. Dubbed into English. **76m/C VHS, LV.** *JP* ***D:*** Hayao Miyazaki; ***W:*** Hayao Miyazaki. *FXV*

My Neighborhood **1984** A debonair bar-owner leads a double life as a knife wielding psychopath. **35m/C VHS, Beta.** *NO*

My New Gun ✂✂½ **1992 (R)** Uneven, restless dark comedy about Debbie and Gerald Bender, yuppified suburban couple whose lives are disrupted by a gun. When their newly engaged friends get a gun, Gerry decides they need a gun as well. Debbie is very uncomfortable about having a weapon in the house and doesn't want anything to do with it. When mysterious neighbor LeGros steals the gun, it sets off a bizarre chain of events that culminate at the wedding of their friends. Impressive first effort for writer/director Cochran. **99m/C VHS, LV.** Diane Lane, Stephen Collins, James LeGros, Tess Harper, Bill Raymond, Bruce Altman, Maddie Corman; ***D:*** Stacy Cochran; ***W:*** Stacy Cochran; ***M:*** Pat Irwin. Cannes Film Festival '92: Best Film. *COL*

My New Partner ✂✂½ *Les Ripoux* **1984 (R)** Amiable French comedy in which cynical veteran cop is saddled with straight arrow rookie partner. French Cesars for best film and best director, but remember: They like Jerry Lewis too. In French with English subtitles. **106m/C VHS, Beta, LV.** *FR* Philippe Noiret, Thierry Lhermitte, Regine, Grace de Capitani, Claude Brosset, Julien Guiomar; ***D:*** Claude Zidi; ***W:*** Claude Zidi. *MED, IME*

My Night at Maud's ✂✂✂ *My Night with Maud; Ma Nuit Chez Maud* **1969** Typically subtle Rohmer entry concerns quandary of upright fellow who finds himself drawn to comparatively carefree woman. Talky, somewhat arid film is one of director's Six Moral Tales. You'll either find it fascinating or wish you were watching "Rocky XXIV" instead. Cinematography by Nestor Almendros; in French with English subtitles. **111m/B VHS, Beta, LV.** *FR* Jean-Louis Trintignant, Francoise Fabian, Marie-Christine Barrault, Antoine Vitez; ***D:*** Eric Rohmer; ***W:*** Eric Rohmer; ***C:*** Nestor Almendros. New York Film Critics Awards '70: Best Screenplay; National Society of Film Critics Awards '70: Best Cinematography, Best Screenplay; Nominations: Academy Awards '69: Best Foreign Language Film; Cannes Film Festival '69: Best Film. *MED, INJ, APD*

My Old Man ✂✂½ **1979** Plucky teen and her seedy horsetrainer father come together over important horse race. Oates makes this one worth watching on a slow evening. A Hemingway story made for television. **102m/C VHS, Beta.** Kristy McNichol, Warren Oates, Eileen Brennan; ***D:*** John Erman. *CAF*

My Old Man's Place ✂½ **1971 (R)** A veteran, with two war buddies and a girl, returns to his father's run-down farm, hoping to fix it up. Sexual tensions arise and violence erupts. **93m/C VHS, Beta.** Arthur Kennedy, Michael Moriarty, Mitchell Ryan, William Devane, Topo Swope; ***D:*** Edwin Sherin. *PSM*

My Other Husband ✂✂½ *Attention! Une Femme Peut en Cacher une Autre* **1985 (PG-13)** A woman has two husbands and families, one in Paris and one in Trouville, who eventually meet each other. Seems silly but grows into a sensitive and sad portrait of married life. In French with English subtitles. **110m/C VHS, Beta.** *FR* Miou-Miou, Rachid Ferrache, Roger Hanin; ***D:*** Georges Lautner. *COL, INJ*

My Outlaw Brother ✂✂ *My Brother, the Outlaw* **1951** A man travelling West to visit his brother in Mexico meets a Texas Ranger on the train. The man discovers that his brother is an outlaw, and teams up with the Ranger to capture him. **82m/B VHS.** Mickey Rooney, Wanda Hendrix, Robert Preston, Robert Stack, Jose Torvay; ***D:*** Elliott Nugent. *MOV, MRV, VYY*

My Own Private Idaho ✂✂✂ **1991 (R)** Director Van Sant of "Drugstore Cowboy" returns to the underworld to examine another group of outsiders, this time young, homosexual hustlers. On the streets of Seattle, narcoleptic hustler Mike meets slumming rich boy Scott, and together they begin a search for Mike's lost mother, which leads them to Idaho and Italy. Stunning visuals, an elliptical plot, and a terrific performance by Phoenix highlight this search for love, the meaning of life, and power. Van Sant couples these activities with scenes from Shakespeare's "Henry IV" for a sometimes inscrutable, but always memorable film. Look for director Richert's Falstaff role as an aging chickenhawk. **105m/C VHS, LV.** River Phoenix, Keanu Reeves, James Russo, William Richert, Rodney Harvey, Michael Parker, Flea, Chiara Caselli, Udo Kier, Grace Zabriskie, Tom Troupe; ***D:*** Gus Van Sant; ***W:*** Gus Van Sant. Independent Spirit Awards '92: Best Actor (Phoenix), Best Screenplay; National Society of Film Critics Awards '91: Best Actor (Phoenix). *COL, NLC*

My Pal, The King ✂✂½ **1932** Amusing western with Rooney as the boy king of Ruritania, who's bored with his official duties. He meets Mix, the proprietor of a traveling wild west show which just happens to be performing in the country. Good thing too because Rooney has an evil prime minister who wants the throne for himself and kidnaps the kid. Naturally, Mix and his friends arrive to save him in the nick of time. **62m/B VHS.** Tom Mix, Mickey Rooney, Stuart Holmes, Paul Hurst, Noel Francis, James Kirkwood, Jim Thorpe; ***D:*** Kurt Neumann. *GPV*

My Pal Trigger ✂✂ **1946** Roy is unjustly imprisoned in this high adventure on the plains. Better than usual script and direction makes this is one of the more entertaining of the singing cowboy's films. **79m/B VHS, Beta.** Roy Rogers, George "Gabby" Hayes, Dale Evans, Jack Holt; ***D:*** Frank McDonald. *NOS, MRV, HHT*

My Pleasure Is My Business **1974 (R)** Cinematic autobiography of Xaveria Hollander, the world's most renowned prostitute of the seventies, and the zany occurrences which abound in her profession. **85m/C VHS.** *CA* Xaviera Hollander, Henry Ramer, Colin Fox, Ken Lynch, Jayne Eastwood; ***D:*** Al Waxman. *NO*

My Samurai ✂½ **1992 (R)** When young Peter McCrea witnesses a gang murder he turns to his martial-arts expert friend Young Park to help him. On the run from both the gang and the police Peter learns self-defense and the courage to face his fears. **87m/C VHS, LV.** Julian Lee, Mako, Terry O'Quinn, Bubba Smith, Jim Turner, Carlos Palomino, John Kallo; ***D:*** Fred Dresch. *IMP*

My Science Project ✂½ **1985 (PG)** Teenager Stockwell stumbles across a crystal sphere with a funky light. Unaware that it is an alien time-travel device, he takes it to school to use as a science project in a last-ditch effort to avoid failing his class. Chaos follows and Stockwell and his chums find themselves battling gladiators, mutants, and dinosaurs. Plenty of special effects and a likeable enough, dumb teenage flick. **94m/C VHS, Beta, LV.** John Stockwell, Danielle von Zerneck, Fisher Stevens, Raphael Sbarge, Richard Masur, Barry Corbin, Ann Wedgeworth, Dennis Hopper, Candace Silvers, Beau Dremann, Pat Simmons, Pamela Springsteen; ***D:*** Jonathan Betuel; ***W:*** Jonathan Betuel; ***M:*** Peter Bernstein. *TOU*

My Side of the Mountain ✂✂½ **1969 (G)** A thirteen-year-old boy decides to emulate his idol, Henry David Thoreau, and gives up his home and his family to live in the Canadian mountains. **100m/C VHS, Beta.** *CA* Teddy Eccles, Theodore Bikel; ***D:*** James B. Clark. *PAR*

My Sister Eileen ✂✂✂ **1955** Ruth and Eileen are two small-town Ohio sisters who move to Manhattan seeking excitement. They live in a basement apartment in Greenwich Village with an assortment of oddball tenants as they pursue success and romance. Everyone is daffy and charming, as is the film. Fun, but unmemorable songs, however the terrific choreography is by Fosse, who also appears as one sister's suitor. Remake of a 1942 film which was based on a Broadway play, which was based on a series of autobiographical stories published in the New Yorker. The play was later turned into a Broadway musical known as "Wonderful Town," which has nothing to do with this version of the original stories. ♫Give Me a Band and My Baby; It's Bigger Than You and Me; There's Nothing Like Love; As Soon As They See Eileen; I'm Great; Conga; Atmosphere. **108m/C VHS.** Janet Leigh, Betty Garrett, Jack Lemmon, Bob Fosse, Kurt Kasznar, Dick York, Lucy Marlow, Tommy Rall, Barbara Brown, Horace McMahon; ***D:*** Richard Quine; ***W:*** Blake Edwards, Richard Quine; ***M:*** Jule Styne. *COL, MOV, MVD*

My Sister, My Love ✂½ *The Cage; The Mafu Cage* **1978 (R)** Odd tale of two sisters' incestuous relationship and what happens when one of them takes another lover. The cage of the alternate titles refers to the place where their pet apes are kept and seems to symbolize the confining nature of their life together. **102m/C VHS.** Lee Grant, Carol Kane, Will Geer, James Olson; ***D:*** Karen Arthur. *NO*

My Son, the Vampire ✂½ *Old Mother Riley Meets the Vampire; The Vampire and the Robot; Vampire Over London; Mother Riley Meets the Vampire* **1952** Last of Britain's Old Mother Riley series in which Lucan plays the Irish housekeeper in drag. Lugosi is a crazed scientist who thinks he's a vampire and wants to take over the world with his giant robot. Mother Riley interferes. Theme song by Alan Sherman. **72m/B VHS.** *GB* Bela Lugosi, Arthur Lucan, Dora Bryan, Richard Wattis; ***D:*** John Gilling. *NOS, SNC*

My Song Goes Round the World ☆½ **1934** Chronicles the romantic foibles of a singing trio and the one girl they decide they all love. **68m/B VHS.** Joseph Schmidt, John Loder, Charlotte Ander; ***D:*** Richard Oswald. *NOS, DVT*

My Stepmother Is an Alien ☆☆ **1988 (PG-13)** When eccentric physicist Aykroyd sends a message beam to another galaxy on a stormy night, the last thing he expects is a visit from beautiful alien Basinger. Unfortunately, he does not realize that this gorgeous blonde is an alien and he continues to court her despite her rather odd habits. Only the daughter seems to notice the strange goings on, and her dad ignores her warnings, enabling Basinger's evil sidekick to continue in its plot to take over the Earth. **108m/C VHS, Beta, LV.** Dan Aykroyd, Kim Basinger, Jon Lovitz, Alyson Hannigan, Joseph Maher, Seth Green, Wesley Mann, Adrian Sparks, Juliette Lewis, Tanya Fenmore; ***D:*** Richard Benjamin; ***W:*** Herschel Weingrod, Timothy Harris, Jonathan Reynolds; ***M:*** Alan Silvestri. *COL*

My Summer Story ☆☆½ *It Runs in the Family* **1994 (PG)** Humorist Shepherd and director Clark re-team for another period family comedy in the tradition of their first collaboration, "A Christmas Story," now a video classic. This time the Parkers find themselves battling their crazy new neighbors, the Bumpus family, Ralphie (Kieran Culkin) has troubles with a neighborhood bully and tries to bond with his dad (Grodin) while fishing, and mom (Steenburgen) goes loopy over gravy boats. Charming family fun. Based on Shepherd's novels "In God We Trust, All Others Pay Cash" and "Wanda Hickey's Night of Golden Memories and Other Disasters." **85m/C VHS, LV.** Charles Grodin, Mary Steenburgen, Kieran Culkin, Chris Culkin, Al Mancini, Troy Evans, Glenn Shadix, Dick O'Neill, Wayne Grace; ***D:*** Bob (Benjamin) Clark; ***W:*** Jean Shepherd, Bob (Benjamin) Clark, Leigh Brown; ***C:*** Stephen M. Katz; ***M:*** Paul Zaza. *MGM*

My Sweet Charlie ☆☆½ **1970** Unwed, pregnant white woman hides out with black lawyer in backwater Texas. Better than it sounds, with nice performances by Duke and Freeman. Made for television. **97m/C VHS, Beta.** Patty Duke, Al Freeman Jr., Ford Rainey, William Hardy, Chris Wilson, Archie Moore, Noble Willingham; ***D:*** Lamont Johnson. *MCA*

My Sweet Little Village ☆☆½ *Vesnicko Ma Strediskova* **1986** Gentle comedy set in a rural village and dealing with everyday events, including a romantic teenager who develops a crush on a schoolteacher, an adulterous wife and her boyfriend, the accident-prone doctor, a Laurel and Hardy duo of truck drivers, and others. Czech with subtitles. **100m/C VHS.** *CZ* Rudolf Hrusinsky, Janos Ban, Marian Labuda, Milena Dvorska, Ladislav Zupanic, Petr Cepek; ***D:*** Jiri Menzel; ***W:*** Zdenek Sverak; ***C:*** Jaromir Sofr; ***M:*** Jiri Sust. Nominations: Academy Awards '86: Best Foreign Language Film. *HTV*

My Sweet Victim ☆☆ **1985** A young couple who recently moved to the United States from Poland try to make a go of their own business. The business fails, and so does their marriage. Will it end in murder? **92m/C VHS.** Candice Bergen, Juergen Prochnow. *QVD*

My Therapist *Woof!* **1984** A sex therapist's boyfriend cannot bear the thought of her having intercourse with other men as part of her work. Soft core. **81m/C VHS, Beta.** Marilyn Chambers; ***D:*** Gary Legon. *NO*

My Tutor ☆½ **1982 (R)** When a high school student is in danger of flunking French, his parents hire a private tutor to help him learn the lessons. It becomes clear that his studies will involve many more subjects, however. Standard teen sex comedy. **97m/C VHS, Beta, LV.** Caren Kaye, Matt Lattanzi, Kevin McCarthy, Clark Brandon, Bruce Bauer, Arlene Golonka, Crispin Glover, Shelley Taylor Morgan, Francesca "Kitten" Natividad, Jewel Shepard, Marilyn Tokuda; ***D:*** George Bowers. *MCA*

My Twentieth Century ☆☆☆ *Az en XX. Szazadom* **1990** This quirky gem of a movie is a charming, sentimental journey through the early 1900s. Twins Dora and Lili are separated in early childhood. They reunite as grown, very different women on the Orient Express after they both (unknowingly) have sex with the same man. Dora is a sex kitten, while Lili is a radical equipped with explosives. When the two sisters come together, they both lose their destructive, dependent selves (Dora on men, Lili on politics) and become independent women. Lots of sidelights and subplots that are sure to amuse the viewer. In Hungarian with English subtitles. **104m/B VHS.** *HU CA* Dortha Segda, Oleg Jankowskij, Peter Andorai, Gabor Mate, Paulus Manker, Laszlo Vidovszky; ***D:*** Ildiko Enyedi; ***W:*** Ildiko Enyedi. *FXL, INJ*

My Universities ☆☆☆ **1940** In the final part of Donskoi's trilogy on Maxim Gorky, Gorky is a young man at university who is introduced to radical politics by several liberal intellectuals. He makes his first attempts at writing and joins the revolution as he leaves his painful past behind. In Russian with English subtitles. Preceded by "My Childhood" and "My Apprenticeship." **100m/C VHS.** *RU* ***D:*** Mark Donskoi. *FCT*

My Wicked, Wicked Ways ☆☆½ **1984** Cleverly cast, low-budget television drama based on the autobiography of Errol Flynn. **95m/C VHS, Beta.** Duncan Regehr, Barbara Hershey, Hal Linden, Darren McGavin; ***D:*** Don Taylor. *FOX*

My Wonderful Life ☆ **1990 (R)** Softcore gristle about a beautiful tramp climbing the social ladder via the boudoir. **107m/C VHS, Beta, LV.** *IT* Pierre Cosso, Jean Rochefort, Massimo Venturiello, Carol Alt, Elliott Gould; ***D:*** Carlo Vanzina. *COL*

Myra Breckinridge *Woof!* **1970 (R)** A tasteless version of the Gore Vidal novel. An alleged satire of a film critic who undergoes a sex change operation and then plots the destruction of the American male movie star stereotype. Created an outcry from all sides, and hung out to dry by studio where it's reportedly still blowing in the wind. **94m/C VHS, Beta.** Mae West, John Huston, Raquel Welch, Rex Reed, Farrah Fawcett, Jim Backus, John Carradine, Andy Devine, Tom Selleck; ***D:*** Michael Sarne. *FOX*

The Mysterians ☆☆½ *Earth Defense Forces; Chikyu Boelgun* **1958** A race of gigantic scientific intellects from a doomed planet attempts to conquer Earth. They want to rebuild their race by reproducing with earth women. Earth fights back. From the director of "Godzilla." Dubbed in English from Japanese. **85m/C VHS, Beta.** *JP* Kenji Sahara, Yumi Shirakawa, Takashi Shimura; ***D:*** Inoshiro Honda. *MLB*

Mysteries ☆½ **1984** A rich tourist becomes obsessed by a beautiful local girl. As his obsession grows, his behavior becomes stranger. Interesting and well-acted. The film is an adaptation of the famous love story by Nobel-laureate Knut Hamsun. Suffers from poor dubbing. **100m/C VHS, Beta.** Rutger Hauer, Sylvia Kristel, David Rappaport, Rita Tushingham; ***D:*** Paul de Lussanet. *NO*

Mysterious Desperado ☆½ **1949** Young man, about to inherit a large estate, is framed on a murder charge by land grabbers. **61m/B VHS, Beta.** Tim Holt, Richard Martin. *NO*

Mysterious Desperado/Rider From Tucson ☆☆½ **1949** A western double feature. In "Mysterious Desperado," a young man is framed for a crime he did not commit. In "Rider From Tucson," evil claim jumpers will resort to murder to gain control of a gold mine. **121m/B VHS, Beta.** Tim Holt, Richard Martin. *TTC*

Mysterious Doctor Satan ☆☆ **1940** A mad satanic scientist builds an army of mechanical robots to rob and terrorize the nation. In 15 episodes. **250m/B VHS.** Eduardo Ciannelli, Robert Wilcox, Ella Neal; ***D:*** William Witney. *REP, VCN, MLB*

Mysterious Island ☆☆☆½ **1961** Exhilarating sci-fi classic adapted from Jules Verne's novel about escaping Civil War soldiers who go up in Verne balloon and come down on a Pacific island populated by giant animals. They also encounter two shipwrecked English ladies, pirates, and Captain Nemo (and his sub). Top-rate special effects by master Ray Harryhausen. **101m/C VHS, Beta, LV.** *GB* Michael Craig, Joan Greenwood, Michael Callan, Gary Merrill, Herbert Lom, Beth Rogan, Percy Herbert, Dan Jackson, Nigel Green; ***D:*** Cy Endfield; ***M:*** Bernard Herrmann. *COL, MLB*

Mysterious Island of Beautiful Women ☆ **1979** A male sextet is stranded on a South Sea island, where they must endure the trials of an angry tribe of conveniently bikini-clad women. **100m/C VHS.** Jamie Lyn Bauer, Jayne Kennedy, Kathryn Davis, Deborah Shelton, Susie Coelho, Peter Lawford, Steven Keats, Clint Walker; ***D:*** Joseph Pevney. *LIV*

Mysterious Jane ☆ **198?** Amid soft-focus nudity, a husband and his lover conspire to institutionalize his wife. **90m/C VHS, Beta.** Amber Lee, Sandy Carey. *MED*

The Mysterious Lady ☆☆½ **1928** Pre-Ninotchka Garbo plays Russian spy who betrays her mother country because she does not want to be alone. **99m/B VHS.** Greta Garbo, Conrad Nagel, Gustav von Seyffertitz, Richard Alexander, Albert Pollet, Edward Connelly; ***C:*** William H. Daniels. *MGM, FCT*

The Mysterious Magician ☆☆½ **1965** Entertaining suspense story of the mad murderer known as "The Wizard," who was thought by Scotland Yard to be dead, but the current murderwave in London suggests otherwise. Based on an Edgar Wallace story. **95m/C VHS.** *GE* Joachim Fuchsberger, Eddi Arent, Sophie Hardy, Karl John, Heinz Drache; ***D:*** Alfred Vohrer. *SNC*

Mysterious Mr. Wong ☆½ **1935** The Thirteen Coins of Confucius put San Francisco's Chinatown in a state of terror until Mr. Wong arrives. **56m/B VHS, Beta.** Arline Judge, Wallace Ford; ***D:*** William Nigh. *VYY, MRV, SNC*

Mysterious Planet ☆ **1984** Humans fight off alien hordes in this space flick. **90m/C VHS, Beta.** *VCD*

The Mysterious Rider ☆☆½ *The Fighting Phantom* **1933** A cowboy tries to prevent unscrupulous homesteaders from cheating farmers out of their land. **59m/B VHS.** Kent Taylor, Lona Andre, Gail Patrick, Warren Hymer, Berton Churchill; ***D:*** Fred Allen. *SNC, DVT*

The Mysterious Rider ☆½ *Mark of the Avenger* **1938** A man framed for murder must help innocent homesteaders from being cheated out of their land. **75m/B VHS.** Douglass Dumbrille, Sidney Toler, Russell Hayden, Charlotte Field; ***D:*** Lesley Selander. *NOS, DVT, RXM*

The Mysterious Rider ☆☆ **1942** Routine oater has Crabbe and St. John helping a couple of kids protect their inheritance. **56m/B VHS.** Buster Crabbe, Al "Fuzzy" St. John, Caroline Burke, John Merton, Kermit Maynard, Jack Ingram, Charles "Slim" Whitaker; ***D:*** Sam Newfield. *DVT, HEG*

The Mysterious Stranger ☆☆ **1982** Printer's apprentice is given to bouts of daydreaming about a magic castle in Austria. Based on Twain tale. **89m/C VHS.** Chris Makepeace, Lance Kerwin, Fred Gwynne; ***D:*** Peter H. Hunt. *MCA*

Mysterious Two ☆☆½ **1982** Two aliens visit the Earth in an effort to enlist converts to travel the universe with them. **100m/C VHS, Beta.** John Forsythe, Priscilla Pointer, Noah Beery Jr., Vic Tayback, James Stephens, Karen Werner, Robert Englund, Robert Pine; ***D:*** Gary Sherman. *LIV*

Mystery at Castle House **1982** Three precocious children stumble onto a mystery when their friends disappear at a neighborhood castle. **80m/C VHS, Beta.** *NO*

Mystery at Fire Island ☆ **1981** A clever young girl and her cousin encounter some strange people as they try to find out why their fisherman friend mysteriously vanished. **52m/C VHS, Beta.** Frank Converse, Barbara Byrne, Beth Ehlers, Eric Gurry. *NO*

Mystery Date ☆☆ **1991 (PG-13)** A sort of teen version of "After Hours," in which a shy college guy gets a date with the girl of his dreams, only to be mistaken for a master criminal and pursued by gangsters, police and a crazed florist. Not terrible, but if you're old enough to drive you're probably too old to watch with amusement. **98m/C VHS.** Ethan Hawke, Teri Polo, Brian McNamara, Fisher Stevens, B.D. Wong; ***D:*** Jonathan Wacks; ***W:*** Terry Runte, Parker Bennett; ***M:*** John Du Prez. *ORI*

Mystery in Swing **1940** An all-black mystery with music, about a trumpet player who has snake venom put on his mouthpiece. **66m/B VHS, Beta.** F.E. Miller, Monte Hawley, Marguerite Whitten, Tom Moore, Ceepee Johnson; ***D:*** Arthur Dreifuss. *VYY*

Mystery Island ½ **1981** Beautifully filmed underwater scenes in this children's film about four youths who discover a deserted island which they name Mystery Island, and a retired pirate who lives there. When the children find counterfeit money and the bad guys return for it, the old pirate's clever plans keep the kids safe. **75m/C VHS, Beta.** *NO*

Mystery Liner ½ *The Ghost of John Holling* **1934** Dead bodies are found aboard ocean liner and passengers are concerned about it. Slow-moving sea cruise. **62m/B VHS, Beta.** Noah Beery Sr., Astrid Allwyn, Cornelius Keefe, Gustav von Seyffertitz, Edwin Maxwell, Boothe Howard, George "Gabby" Hayes; ***D:*** William Nigh. *NOS, SNC*

The Mystery Man ½ **1935** A Chicago reporter goes on a drinking binge and ends up in St. Louis. There he stumbles upon a mystery which may involve the paper for which he works. He teams up with a beautiful woman to try to crack the case. **65m/B VHS, Beta.** Robert Armstrong, Maxine Doyle, Henry Kolker, Leroy Mason, James Burke; ***D:*** Ray McCarey. *SNC*

Mystery Man ½ **1944** Below-average episode has rancher Hoppy being bothered by rustlers. Boyd solves things in the usual way, while Clyde provides the laughs. **58m/B VHS.** William Boyd, Andy Clyde, Jimmy Rogers, Don Costello, Francis McDonald, Forrest Taylor, Eleanor Stewart; ***D:*** George Archainbaud. *NOS*

Mystery Mansion **1983 (PG)** Fortune in gold and a hundred-year-old mystery lead three children into an exciting treasure hunt. Family fare. **95m/C VHS, Beta.** Dallas McKennon, Greg Wynne, Jane Ferguson. *MED*

Mystery Mountain ½ **1934** Twelve episodes depict the villain known as the "Rattler" attempting to stop the construction of a railroad over Mystery Mountain. **156m/B VHS, Beta.** Ken Maynard, Gene Autry, Smiley Burnette; ***D:*** Otto Brower, B. Reeves Eason. *NOS, VCN, CAB*

The Mystery of Alexina ½ *Mystere Alexina* **1986** True story of Herculine Adelaide Barbin, a 19th-century French hermaphrodite, who, after growing up a woman, fell in love with another woman and was actually revealed to be a man. Subtitled. **86m/C VHS, Beta.** *FR* Vuillemin, Valeri Stroh; ***D:*** Rene Feret; ***W:*** Jean Gruault. *SUE, NLC*

The Mystery of Edwin Drood ½ **1993** When Edwin Drood vanishes on Christmas Eve, his disappearance leads to a terrifying mystery that unfolds amidst the slums of Victorian England. Adapted from Charles Dickens' last novel, which was left unfinished at his death. **98m/C VHS.** *GB* Robert Powell, Michelle Evans, Jonathan Phillips, Finty Williams, Rupert Rainsford, Nanette Newman, Freddie Jones, Rosemary Leach, Ronald Fraser; ***D:*** Timothy Forder; ***W:*** Timothy Forder. *AAE, TVC*

Mystery of Mr. Wong ½ **1939** The largest star sapphire in the world, the "Eye of the Daughter of the Moon," is stolen from a museum in its home country of China. Mr. Wong becomes involved in trying to trace its trail and the perpetrator of the murders that follow in its wake. One in the series of detective films. **67m/B VHS.** Boris Karloff, Grant Withers, Dorothy Tree, Lotus Long; ***D:*** William Nigh. *VYY, MRV, DVT*

The Mystery of Rampo **1994 (R)** Visually dazzling fantasy that propels mystery writer Edogawa Rampo (Takenaka) into his own stories. Set just before WWII, Rampo is despondent when his latest novel (about a woman suffocating her husband in a trunk) is censored by the government and then amazed when a newspaper story reveals a similar crime. So Rampo decides to meet the widow Shizuko (Hada) and discovers she's a double for his fictional character. He then writes a sequel, again featuring Shizuko, and once again finds reality and fiction blending into the bizarre. Rampo was the pseudonym for renowned writer Hirai Taro, regarded as the Japanese Edgar Allan Poe. The film had its own complications when the version filmed by original director Rentaro Mayusumi was rejected by producer Okuyama, who then reshot much of the film himself. Japanese with subtitles. **96m/C VHS.** *JP* Naoto Takenaka, Michiko Hada, Masahiro Motoki, Teruyuki Kagawa, Mikijiro Hira; ***D:*** Kazuyoshi Okuyama; ***W:*** Kazuyoshi Okuyama, Yuhei Enoki; ***C:*** Yasushi Sasakibara; ***M:*** Akira Senju. *HMK*

Mystery of the Hooded Horseman **1937** Tex finds himself pitted against a very strange adversary. **61m/B VHS, Beta.** Tex Ritter, Iris Meredith, Charles "Blackie" King, Joseph Girard, Lafe McKee; ***D:*** Ray Taylor. *NOS, VDM, DVT*

Mystery of the Leaping Fish/Chess Fever ½ **1925** Two silent shorts. The first, filmed in 1916, is a surreal comedy-mystery about a doped-up detective named Coke Ennyday and his hallucinatory, sped-up adventures. The second, made in 1925 during the Moscow Chess Tournament, is a parody of professional chess playing and the fever with which it grips a country. Pudovkin's second directorial credit. **64m/B VHS, Beta, 8mm.** Douglas Fairbanks Sr., Bessie Love, Alma Rubens; ***D:*** John Emerson, Vsevolod Pudovkin; ***W:*** Tod Browning. *VYY, MRV*

The Mystery of the Mary Celeste *The Phantom Ship; The Mystery of the Marie Celeste* **1937** Tale of terror based on the bizarre case of the "Marie Celeste," an American ship found adrift off the coast of England with her sails set but minus any of her crew on December 5, 1872. **64m/B VHS, Beta.** Bela Lugosi, Shirley Grey, Edmund Willard, Arthur Margetson. *NOS, MRV, VYY*

Mystery of the Million Dollar Hockey Puck ½ **198?** Sinister diamond smugglers learn a lesson on ice from a pair of orphan lads. Features the National Hockey League's Montreal Canadians in one of their few film appearances. **88m/C VHS, Beta.** Michael MacDonald, Angele Knight; ***D:*** Jean LaFleur, Peter Svatek. *NO*

Mystery of the Riverboat ½ **1944** Louisiana and the Mississippi River are the background for these 13 episodes of mystery and murder. **90m/B VHS, Beta.** Robert Lowery, Eddie Quillan, Lyle Talbot, Francis McDonald, Arthur Hohl; ***D:*** Ray Taylor, Lewis D. Collins. *VCI, MLB, GPV*

Mystery of the Wax Museum **1933** Rarely seen, vintage horror classic about a wax-dummy maker who, after a disfiguring fire, resorts to murder and installs the wax-covered bodies of his victims in his museum. Famous for its pioneering use of two-strip Technicolor. Remade in 1953 in 3-D as "House of Wax." **77m/C VHS, Beta, LV.** Lionel Atwill, Fay Wray, Glenda Farrell; ***D:*** Michael Curtiz; ***C:*** Ray Rennahan. *MGM, MLB*

Mystery Plane ½ **1939** An inventor devises a new bomb-dropping mechanism, and must evade secret agents on his way to deliver it to the government. **60m/B VHS, Beta.** John Trent, Marjorie Reynolds, Milburn Stone, Peter George Lynn, Polly Ann Young; ***D:*** George Waggner. *NOS, DVT, HEG*

Mystery Ranch ½ **1934** A cowboy finds himself in strange predicaments out on the range. **52m/B VHS, Beta.** George O'Brien, Charles Middleton, Cecilia Parker; ***D:*** David Howard. *NOS, DVT, GPV*

Mystery Science Theater 3000: The Movie ½ **1996 (PG-13)** Mad scientist Dr. Clayton Forrester (Beaulieu) maroons Mike Nelson on the Satellite of Love, forces him to watch bad movies, and monitors his reactions. Mike and his robotic pals, Tom Servo and Crow T. Robot, save their sanity by wisecracking their way through the movies. Today's experiment is "This Island Earth," an uncharacteristically semi-respectable flick. As regular viewers know, the jokes and snide remarks come fast and in bunches. Not all of them work, but the ones that do will be remembered and repeated often. Audience participation is inevitable. Weekend theme-party status is virtually assured. **73m/C VHS.** Trace Beaulieu, James Mallon, Michael J. Nelson, Kevin Murphy, John Brady; ***D:*** James Mallon; ***W:*** Trace Beaulieu, James Mallon, Michael J. Nelson, Kevin Murphy, Mary Jo Pehl, Paul Chaplin, Bridget Jones; ***C:*** Jeff Stonehouse; ***M:*** Billy Barber. *NYR*

Mystery Squadron **1933** Twelve chapters, 13 minutes each. Daredevil air action in flight against the masked pilots of the Black Ace. **240m/B VHS, Beta.** Bob Steele, Guinn "Big Boy" Williams, Lucille Browne, Jack Mulhall, J. Carrol Naish, Jack Mower; ***D:*** Colbert Clark. *GPV, VCN, DVT*

Mystery Train **1989 (R)** A run down hotel in Memphis is the scene for three vignettes concerning the visit of foreigners to the U.S. Themes of mythic Americana, Elvis, and life on the fringe pervade this hip and quirky film. The three vignettes all tie together in clever and funny overlaps. Waits fans should listen for his performance as a DJ. **110m/C VHS, LV.** Masatoshi Nagase, Youki Kudoh, Jay Hawkins, Cinque Lee, Joe Strummer, Nicoletta Braschi, Elizabeth Bracco, Steve Buscemi, Tom Noonan, Rockets Redglare, Rick Aviles, Rufus Thomas; ***D:*** Jim Jarmusch; ***W:*** Jim Jarmusch; ***M:*** John Lurie; ***V:*** Tom Waits. *ORI*

Mystery Trooper *Trail of the Royal Mounted* **1932** Adventures in the great wilderness full of prospecting, greed, and Indians all being observed by the Royal Mounties. Ten chapters of the serial at 20 minutes each. **200m/B VHS, Beta.** Robert Frazer, Buzz Barton. *GPV, NOS, CAB*

Mystic Circle Murder **1939** Reporter sets out to uncover phony mediums, particularly the Great La Gagge, whose fake apparitions are so convincing that it caused one of his clients to have a heart attack. Cheaply made, and it's obvious. Watch for a cameo by Harry Houdini's wife, who talks about life after death. Also known as "Religious Racketeers." Based on a story by director O'Connor. **69m/B VHS.** Betty Compson, Robert Fiske, Helene Le Berthon, Arthur Gardner; ***D:*** Frank O'Connor. *SNC*

Mystic Pizza **1988 (R)** Intelligent coming of age drama centers on two sisters and their best friend as they struggle with their hopes, loves, and family rivalries in the small town of Mystic, Connecticut. At times predictable, there are enough unexpected moments to keep interest high; definite appeal to young women, but others may not relate. The relatively unknown Roberts got most of the attention, but is the weakest of the three leads, so watch this one for the strong performances from Gish and Taylor. **101m/C VHS, Beta, LV.** Annabeth Gish, Julia Roberts, Lili Taylor, Vincent D'Onofrio, William R. Moses, Adam Storke, Conchata Ferrell, Joanna Merlin; ***D:*** Donald Petrie; ***W:*** Amy Holden Jones, Perry Howze, Alfred Uhry; ***M:*** David McHugh. Independent Spirit Awards '89: Best First Feature. *VTR*

Nabonga *Gorilla; Jungle Woman* **1944** The daughter of an embezzler, whose plane crashes in the jungle, befriends a gorilla who protects her. Soon a young man comes looking for the embezzler's cash, meets the woman and the ape, and together they go on a wonderful journey. **72m/B VHS.** Buster Crabbe, Fifi d'Orsay, Barton MacLane, Julie London, Herbert Rawlinson; ***D:*** Sam Newfield. *SNC, NOS, MOV*

Nadia ½ **1984** Entertaining account of the life of Nadia Comaneci, the Romanian gymnast who earned six perfect tens with her stunning performance at the 1976 Olympic Games. Made for television. **100m/C VHS, Beta.** Talia Balsam, Jonathan Banks, Simone Blue, Johann Carlo, Carrie Snodgress; ***D:*** Alan Cooke. *FHE, STP*

Nadine ½ **1987 (PG)** In Austin circa 1954, an almost divorced beautician witnesses a murder and goes undercover with her estranged husband to track down the murderer, before he finds her. Plenty of low-key humor. Well-paced fun; Basinger is terrific. **83m/C VHS, Beta, LV.** Jeff Bridges, Kim Basinger, Rip Torn, Gwen Verdon, Glenne Headly, Jerry Stiller, Jay Patterson; ***D:*** Robert Benton; ***W:*** Robert Benton; ***C:*** Nestor Almendros; ***M:*** Howard Shore. *FOX*

Nadja 🦴🦴🦴 **1995 (R)** Fresh, modern comic take on the vampire tale is about family ties and the power of home, with the required AIDS analogy and lesbian sex scenes. Tired of nightly blood-letting, the daughter of the now-deceased Count, Nadja (Lowensohn), lives in New York's East Village, hoping to change her life. She seduces and falls in love with Lucy (Craze), whose husband is the nephew of old family nemesis Van Helsing (Fonda, in a surprisingly comedic role). Manic Fonda Van Helsing sets out to save Lucy and steal the film. Meanwhile, Nadja finds her long lost twin brother (Harris, son of Richard) and Lucy discovers sex with Nadja is draining. Innovative camera work (vampire point-of-view scenes shot with a toy Pixelvision camera and blown up to 35mm for a moody, grainy look) and a great score keep "Nadja" very watchable despite some missteps in the plot. (Director Almereyda pioneered use of the Pixel-vision camera in "Another Girl, Another Planet.") Executive producer David Lynch contributes a cameo as a guard at the morgue where Nadja claims her father's body. **92m/B VHS.** Elina Lowensohn, Suzy Amis, Galaxy Craze, Martin Donovan, Peter Fonda, Karl Geary, Jared Harris; ***Cameos:*** David Lynch; ***D:*** Michael Almereyda; ***W:*** Michael Almereyda; ***C:*** Jim Denault; ***M:*** Simon Fisher Turner. Nominations: Independent Spirit Awards '96: Best Actress (Lowensohn), Best Cinematography, Best Director (Almereyda). *HMK*

Nail Gun Massacre *Woof!* **1986** A crazed killer with a penchant for nailing bodies to just about anything goes on a hammering spree. In horrific, vivid color. **90m/C VHS, Beta.** Rocky Patterson, Ron Queen, Beau Leland, Michelle Meyer; ***D:*** Bill Lesley. *NO*

Nails 🦴½ **1992 (R)** Harry "Nails" Niles (Hopper) is a tough, experienced cop whose partner has been killed by drug dealers. Harry doesn't take this well and decides to go on a violent search for revenge. Archer is wasted as Harry's estranged wife and Hopper can sleepwalk through this type of cliched wildman role. Made for cable television. **96m/C VHS, Beta, LV.** Dennis Hopper, Anne Archer, Tomas Milian, Cliff DeYoung; ***D:*** John Flynn. *FXV, VTR*

Nairobi Affair 🦴🦴 **1988 (PG)** Savage and Heston fight poachers and each other in Kenya, when the father has an affair with his son's ex-wife. Mediocre, derivative script, but beautiful scenery. Made for television. **95m/C VHS, Beta.** Charlton Heston, John Savage, Maud Adams, John Rhys-Davies, Connie Booth; ***D:*** Marvin J. Chomsky. *VMK*

Nais 🦴🦴🦴 **1945** Vintage Pagnolian peasant drama. A hunchback sacrifices himself for the girl he loves. She escapes to another man's arms. Adapted from the Emile Zola novel "Nais Micoulin." In French with English subtitles. **105m/B VHS, Beta, 8mm.** *FR* Fernandel; ***D:*** Fernand Lauterier; ***W:*** Marcel Pagnol. *VYY, FCT, DVT*

Naked 🦴🦴🦴 *Mike Leigh's Naked* **1993 (R)** Existential angst in a '90s London filled with Leigh's usual eccentrics. The unemployed Johnny (Thewlis) comes to London and bunks with former girlfriend Louise (Sharp). After seducing her flatmate Sophie (Cartlidge), Johnny leaves to wander the streets, exchanging philosophical, if foul-mouthed, dialogues with a variety of odd characters. Thewlis gives an explosive performance as the calculatingly brutal and desolate Johnny. Chaotic shifts in mood from comedy to violence to love prove a challenge and the pervasive abuse of all the women characters is very disturbing. Critically acclaimed; see it as a reflection on the mess of modern England. **131m/C VHS, LV.** *GB* David Thewlis, Lesley Sharp, Katrin Cartlidge, Greg Cruttwell, Claire Skinner, Peter Wight, Ewen Bremmer, Susan Vidler; ***D:*** Mike Leigh; ***W:*** Mike Leigh; ***M:*** Andrew Dickinson. Cannes Film Festival '93: Best Actor (Thewlis), Best Director (Leigh); National Society of Film Critics Awards '93: Best Actor (Thewlis); Nominations: British Academy Awards '93: Best Film; Cannes Film Festival '93: Best Film; Independent Spirit Awards '94: Best Foreign Film. *COL, IME*

The Naked and the Dead 🦴🦴½ **1958** Sanitized adaptation of Norman Mailer's bestselling novel about army life in the Pacific during WWII. Resentment between officers and enlisted men proves to be almost as dangerous as the Japanese. Uneven acting and cliched characterizations make this an average outing. Don't expect to hear the profane language that sensationalized the book, because most of it was edited out of the screenplay. **131m/C VHS, Beta.** Aldo Ray, Cliff Robertson, Joey Bishop, Raymond Massey, Lili St. Cyr, James Best; ***D:*** Raoul Walsh; ***C:*** Joseph LaShelle. *NO*

The Naked Angels 🦴 **1969 (R)** Rape, mayhem, beatings, and road-hogging streetbikes highlight this biker film, acted, in part, by actual bikers, and in part by others who were actually (almost) actors. The gang war rages from Los Angeles to Las Vegas. Roger Corman was the executive producer. **83m/C VHS, Beta.** Michael Greene, Richard Rust, Felicia Guy; ***D:*** Bruce Clark; ***W:*** Bruce Clark. *CRV*

Naked Cage *Woof!* **1986 (R)** Brutal women's prison film that is borderline soft-core, about an innocent country woman, a horseriding fanatic, who is framed for a robbery and sent to the slammer. There, she contends with lesbian wardens and inmates. Disgusting. **97m/C VHS, Beta.** Shari Shattuck, Angel Tompkins, Lucinda Crosby, Christina Whitaker; ***D:*** Paul Nicholas. *COL*

The Naked City 🦴🦴🦴½ **1948** Film noir classic makes spectacular use of its NYC locations. Beautiful playgirl is murdered and police detectives Fitzgerald and Taylor are left without clues. They spend most of their time running down weak leads and interviewing various suspects and witnesses. When they finally get a break, it leads to playboy Duff. Spectacular ending on the Brooklyn Bridge between cops and killer. Producer Hellinger provided the hard-boiled narration, patterned after the tabloid newspaper stories he once wrote. Served as the impetus for the TV show of the same name, where Hellinger's film postscript also became the show's noted tagline: "There are eight million stories in the naked city, this has been one of them." **96m/B VHS.** Barry Fitzgerald, Don Taylor, Howard Duff, Ted de Corsia, Dorothy Hart; ***D:*** Jules Dassin; ***C:*** William H. Daniels; ***M:*** Miklos Rozsa. Academy Awards '48: Best Black and White Cinematography, Best Film Editing; Nominations: Academy Awards '48: Best Story. *IVY*

The Naked Civil Servant 🦴🦴🦴½ **1975** Remarkable film, based on the life of flamboyant homosexual Quentin Crisp, who came out of the closet in his native England, long before his lifestyle would be tolerated by Britains. For mature audiences. **80m/C VHS, Beta.** John Hurt; ***D:*** Jack Gold; ***M:*** Carl Davis. *HBO*

The Naked Country 🦴½ **1985 (R)** In the untamed frontier of Australia rancher bigoted Lance Dillion and his sensual wife Mary are determined to make their way. But when Lance finds out that the neglected Mary is fooling around with a local cop, he goes on a killing spree on land sacred to the Aborigines. Plodding plot. **90m/C VHS.** *AU* John Stanton, Rebecca Gilling, Ivar Kants; ***D:*** Tim Burstall; ***M:*** Bruce Smeaton. *HMD*

The Naked Edge 🦴🦴 **1961** Cooper stars as a middle-aged businessman whose wife suspects him of murder after she begins snooping into his business affairs. Cooper's last film and far from his best. Poor direction and holes in the screenplay divert from what could have been a tight thriller. **99m/C VHS.** *GB* Gary Cooper, Deborah Kerr, Eric Portman, Diane Cilento, Hermione Gingold, Peter Cushing, Michael Wilding, Ronald Howard; ***D:*** Michael Anderson Sr.; ***W:*** Joseph Stefano. *MGM, MOV*

The Naked Face 🦴🦴 **1984 (R)** A psychiatrist tries to find out why his patients are being killed. He gets no help from police, who suspect he is the murderer. A dull affair featuring unusual casting of Moore, while Steiger's suspicious police captain character provides spark. From the novel by Sidney Sheldon. **105m/C VHS, Beta.** Roger Moore, Rod Steiger, Elliott Gould, Art Carney, Anne Archer, David Hedison; ***D:*** Bryan Forbes. *MGM*

The Naked Flame *Woof!* **1968 (R)** O'Keefe plays an investigator in a strange town inhabited by weird, religious fanatics. After he arrives, the womenfolk shed their clothes in this pitiful, pathetic hilarity. **?m/C VHS.** Dennis O'Keefe, Linda Bennett, Kasey Rogers. *SNC*

The Naked Gun: From the Files of Police Squad 🦴🦴🦴 **1988 (PG-13)** More hysterical satire from the creators of "Airplane!" The short-lived television cop spoof "Police Squad" moves to the big screen and has Lt. Drebin uncover a plot to assassinate Queen Elizabeth while she is visiting Los Angeles. Nearly nonstop gags and pratfalls provide lots of laughs. Nielsen is perfect as Drebin and the supporting cast is strong; cameos abound. **85m/C VHS, Beta, LV, 8mm.** Leslie Nielsen, Ricardo Montalban, Priscilla Presley, George Kennedy, O.J. Simpson, Nancy Marchand, John Houseman; ***Cameos:*** Weird Al Yankovic, Reggie Jackson, Dr. Joyce Brothers; ***D:*** David Zucker; ***W:*** Jerry Zucker, Jim Abrahams, Pat Proft, David Zucker; ***M:*** Ira Newborn. *PAR*

Naked Gun 33 1/3: The Final Insult 🦴🦴 **1994 (PG-13)** Ever dumb, crass, and crude, Lt. Drebin returns to the force from retirement to lead an investigation into terrorist activities in Hollywood. Lots of current events jokes—dated as soon as they hit the screen. Sure to satisfy genre fans with a taste for bad puns. Watch for the cameos, especially at the "Oscars." **90m/C VHS, Beta, LV.** Leslie Nielsen, Priscilla Presley, O.J. Simpson, Fred Ward, George Kennedy, Gary Cooper, Kathleen Freeman, Raquel Welch; ***Cameos:*** Pia Zadora, James Earl Jones, Weird Al Yankovic, Ann B. Davis; ***D:*** Peter Segal; ***W:*** Robert Locash, David Zucker, Pat Proft; ***M:*** Ira Newborn. Golden Raspberry Awards '94: Worst Supporting Actor (Simpson), Worst New Star (Smith). *PAR*

Naked Gun 2 1/2: The Smell of Fear 🦴🦴½ **1991 (PG-13)** Lt. Drebin returns to rescue the world from a faulty energy policy devised by the White House and oil-lords. A notch down from the previous entry but still hilarious cop parody. Nielsen has this character down to a tee, and there's a laugh every minute. Laserdisc version is letterboxed and features dolby surround sound. **85m/C VHS, Beta, LV, 8mm, CD-I.** Leslie Nielsen, Priscilla Presley, George Kennedy, O.J. Simpson, Robert Goulet, Richard Griffiths, Jacqueline Brookes, Lloyd Bochner, Tim O'Connor, Peter Mark Richman; ***Cameos:*** Mel Torme, Eva Gabor, Weird Al Yankovic; ***D:*** David Zucker; ***W:*** David Zucker, Pat Proft; ***M:*** Ira Newborn. *PAR*

Naked Hills 🦴½ **1956** Meandering tale about a man (Wayne) who, suffering from gold fever, searches for 40 years in 19th Century California and ends up out of luck, losing his wife and family. **72m/C VHS.** David Wayne, Keenan Wynn, James Barton, Marcia Henderson, Jim Backus, Denver Pyle, Myrna Dell, Frank Fenton, Fuzzy Knight; ***D:*** Josef Shaftel; ***W:*** Josef Shaftel. *NO*

Naked in New York 🦴🦴½ **1993 (R)** Aspiring New York playwright Jake Briggs (Stoltz) and his girlfriend Joanne (Parker), an aspiring photographer, find their relationship in jeopardy when their respective careers start to take off. Offspring from the "Annie Hall" school of neurotic romance examines a number of issues, including ambition, commitment, and the societal dynamics of theatre and art. Celebrity appearances abound, including Styron as himself and Goldberg as a tragedy mask on a wall. Directorial debut of Scorsese protege Algrant is uneven but charming. Parker is particularly strong, and Turner's a riot as a sexpot soap star on the prowl for Jake. **89m/C VHS, LV.** Eric Stoltz, Mary-Louise Parker, Ralph Macchio, Jill Clayburgh, Tony Curtis, Kathleen Turner, Timothy Dalton, Lynne Thigpen, Roscoe Lee Browne; ***Cameos:*** Whoopi Goldberg, William Styron, Eric Bogosian, Quentin Crisp; ***D:*** Dan Algrant; ***W:*** Dan Algrant, John Warren; ***M:*** Angelo Badalamenti; ***V:*** David Johansen. *COL*

Naked in the Night 🦴 **1958** Cheap German exploitation film about the dangers of promiscuous women. Dubbed in English. **?m/C VHS.** *GE* Eva Bartok, Alexander Kerst. *SNC, TPV*

Naked in the Sun **1957** The true story of events leading to the war between the Osceola and Seminole Indians and a slave trader. Somewhat slow. **95m/C VHS.** James Craig, Lita Milan, Barton MacLane, Tony Hunter; ***D:*** R. John Hugh. *REP*

Naked Is Better **1973** A couple of buffoons pose as hospital workers so they can play doctor with a hospitalized actress. **93m/C VHS, Beta.** Alberto Olmedo, Jorge Porcel, Jorge Barreiro, Maria Casan. *MED*

Naked Jungle **1954** Suspenseful, well-done jungle adventure of a plantation owner (Heston) in South America and his North American mail-order bride (Parker), who do battle with a deadly, miles-long siege of red army ants. Realistic and worth watching. Produced by George Pal, shot by Ernest Laszlo and based on the story "Leiningen vs. the Ants" by Carl Stephenson. **95m/C VHS, Beta, LV.** Charlton Heston, Eleanor Parker, Abraham Sofaer, William Conrad; ***D:*** Byron Haskin; ***W:*** Philip Yordan; ***C:*** Ernest Laszlo. *PAR*

Naked Killer **1992** Kitty (Ching) turns to a female assassin to learn the art of killing so that she may avenge her father's death. When her teacher is herself unceremoniously murdered, Kitty and her policeman boyfriend (Yam) have two scores to settle. Sex and violence. Subtitled in English. **86m/C VHS.** *CN* My Yau Ching, Simon Yam; ***D:*** Clarence Fok Yiu Leung. *WVE*

Naked Kiss ½ *The Iron Kiss* **1964** Fuller's most savage, hysterical film noir. A brutalized prostitute escapes her pimp and tries to enter respectable small-town society. She finds even more perversion and sickness there. **92m/B VHS, LV.** Constance Towers, Anthony Eisley, Michael Dante, Virginia Grey, Patsy Kelly, Betty Bronson; ***D:*** Samuel Fuller. *HMV*

Naked Lie **1989** A District Attorney and a judge engage in an ultra-steamy affair and inevitably clash when she is assigned as a prosecutor on the politically explosive case over which he is presiding. **89m/C VHS.** Victoria Principal, James Farentino, Glenn Withrow, William Lucking, Dakin Matthews; ***D:*** Richard A. Colla; ***M:*** Robert Alcivar. *ING*

Naked Lunch **1991 (R)** Whacked-out movie based on William S. Burroughs's autobiographical account of drug abuse, homosexuality, violence, and weirdness set in the drug-inspired land called Interzone. Hallucinogenic images are carried to the extreme: typewriters metamorphose into beetles, bloblike creatures with sex organs scurry about, and characters mainline insecticide. Some of the characters are clearly based on writers of the Beat generation, including Jane and Paul Bowles, Allen Ginsberg, and Jack Kerouac. **117m/C VHS.** Peter Weller, Judy Davis, Ian Holm, Julian Sands, Roy Scheider, Monique Mercure, Nicholas Campbell, Michael Zelniker, Robert A. Silverman, Joseph Scorsiani; ***D:*** David Cronenberg; ***W:*** David Cronenberg; ***M:*** Howard Shore. Genie Awards '92: Best Adapted Screenplay, Best Art Direction/Set Decoration, Best Cinematography, Best Director (Cronenberg), Best Film, Best Sound, Best Supporting Actress (Mercure); National Society of Film Critics Awards '91: Best Director (Cronenberg), Best Screenplay. *TCF, INJ*

The Naked Maja **1959** Elaborate, yet dull drama about the tumultous romance between a Spanish duchess and the legendary painter Francisco Goya. Even the gorgeous costumes and spectacular sets can't overcome the weak script and poor direction that plague the film. Based on a story by Oscar Saul and Talbot Jennings. **111m/C VHS.** Ava Gardner, Anthony (Tony) Franciosa, Amedeo Nazzari, Gino Cervi, Lea Padovani, Massimo Serato, Carlo Rizzo, Renzo Cesana; ***D:*** Henry Koster, Mario Russo; ***W:*** Norman Corwin, Giorgio Prosperi. *MGM, FCT*

Naked Massacre **198?** A maniac kills nurses, leaving no clues for the police to follow. **90m/C VHS, Beta.** Matthieu Carriere, Carol Laurie; ***D:*** Denis Heroux. *VDC*

Naked Obsession ½ **1991 (R)** A city councilman running for mayor is mugged in one of the seedier parts of the city. He's found by a homeless man who takes him to a kinky nightclub where the councilman is promptly seduced by a topless bar hostess with secrets of her own. Also available in an unrated version. **93m/C VHS.** William Katt, Maria Ford, Rick Dean; ***D:*** Dan Golden. *VES, MOV*

Naked Paradise **1978 (R)** A young woman moves in with her mother and step-sister and finds difficulty in adjusting. **86m/C VHS, Beta.** Laura Gemser, Annie Belle. *NO*

The Naked Prey **1966** Unnerving African adventure which contains some unforgettably brutal scenes. A safari guide (Wilde), leading a hunting party, must watch as an indigenous tribe murders all his companions, and according to their customs, allows him to be set free, sans clothes or weapons, to be hunted by the best of the tribe. **96m/C VHS, Beta, LV.** Cornel Wilde, Gertrude Van Der Berger, Ken Gampu; ***D:*** Cornel Wilde. Nominations: Academy Awards '66: Best Story & Screenplay. *PAR*

Naked Souls **1995 (R)** Anderson must save fiance Krause from the evil experiments of murderous doctor Warner. Like you'll care as long as the Anderson bod is on display. **90m/C VHS.** Pamela Anderson Lee, Brian Krause, Clayton Rohner, Justina Vail, David Warner; ***Cameos:*** Dean Stockwell; ***D:*** Lyndon Chubbuck; ***W:*** Frank Dietz; ***C:*** Eric Goldstein; ***M:*** Nigel Holton. *WEA*

The Naked Spur ½ **1953** A compulsive bounty hunter tracks down a vicious outlaw and his beautiful girlfriend. An exciting film from the Mann-Stewart team and considered one of their best, infusing the traditional western with psychological confusion. Wonderful use of Rockies locations. **93m/C VHS, Beta.** James Stewart, Robert Ryan, Janet Leigh, Millard Mitchell; ***D:*** Anthony Mann; ***C:*** William Mellor. Nominations: Academy Awards '53: Best Story & Screenplay. *MGM, TLF*

The Naked Sword of Zorro **1969** Deadly Don Luis taxes the town by day and violates the women by night, but Zorro takes a stand and saves the town. When he's not dressed as Zorro, he is Don Diego, an inept fool, but when he puts that suit on, look out. The ladies can't keep their hands off of him. There are more lusty females than villains, but there's still lots of swordplay and action. **94m/C VHS.** *VDM*

The Naked Truth ½ *Your Past is Showing* **1958** A greedy publisher tries to get rich quick by publishing a scandal magazine about the "lurid" lives of prominent citizens. Well-drawn characters in an appealing offbeat comedy. **92m/C VHS, Beta.** *GB* Peter Sellers, Terry-Thomas, Shirley Eaton, Dennis Price; ***D:*** Mario Zampi. *SUE*

Naked Vengeance *Woof! Satin Vengeance* **1985 (R)** A woman's husband is murdered, she is beaten and raped, and she becomes a vengeful, vicious killing machine. Gratuitous violence, distasteful to the max. **97m/C VHS, Beta.** Deborah Tranelli, Kaz Garas, Bill McLaughlin; ***D:*** Cirio H. Santiago. *LIV*

Naked Venus ½ **1958** Ulmer's last film is a slow-paced tale about an American artist, married to a model who poses in the nude and belongs to a nudist camp, whose wealthy mother tries to tear the marriage apart. Discrimination and intolerance of nudist camps is explored. **80m/B VHS, Beta.** Patricia Conelle; ***D:*** Edgar G. Ulmer. *VDM, TPV*

Naked Warriors *The Arena* **1973 (R)** Ancient Romans capture beautiful women from around the world and force them to compete in gladiatorial games. New World exploitation gem featuring mostly Italian cast, including Bay, who starred in the previous year's "Lady Frankenstein." **75m/C VHS, Beta.** Margaret Markov, Pam Grier, Lucretia Love, Paul Muller, Daniel Vargas, Marie Louise, Mary Count, Rosalba (Sara Bay) Neri, Vic Karis, Sid Lawrence, Peter Cester, Anna Melita; ***D:*** Steve Carver. *MGM*

The Naked Witch *The Naked Temptress* **1964** College student researching witchcraft digs up the grave of a long-dead witch. She comes back to life and takes revenge on the village that killed her years earlier. The nude shots feature someone's finger over the camera lens to cover the witch's vital organs. **60m/C VHS.** Beth Porter, Robert Burgos, Bryarly Lee, Lee Forbes; ***D:*** Andy Milligan. *SNC*

Naked Youth *Woof! Wild Youth* **1959** Seedy drive-in cheapie about two punks breaking out of juvenile prison and heading south of the border on a trail filled with crime, drugs, and loose women. **80m/B VHS, Beta.** Robert Hutton, John Goddard, Carol Ohmart, Jan Brooks, Robert Arthur, Steve Rowland, Clancy Cooper; ***D:*** John F. Schreyer. *RHI, SNC*

Nam Angels **1988 (R)** Hell's Angels enter Southeast Asia and rescue POWs. **91m/C VHS, Beta.** Brad Johnson, Vernon Wells, Kevin Duffis; ***D:*** Cirio H. Santiago. *MED*

A Name for Evil **1970 (R)** Having grown tired of city living, a couple moves to an old family estate out in the country near the Great Lakes. Strange sounds in the night are the first signs of the terror to come. **74m/C VHS, Beta.** Robert Culp, Samantha Eggar, Sheila Sullivan, Mike Lane; ***D:*** Bernard Girard. *NO*

The Name of the Rose ½ **1986 (R)** An exhaustive, off-center adaptation of the bestselling Umberto Eco novel about violent murders in a 14th-century Italian abbey. An English monk struggles against religious fervor in his quest to uncover the truth. **128m/C VHS, Beta, LV.** *IT GE FR* Sean Connery, F. Murray Abraham, Christian Slater, Ron Perlman, William Hickey, Feodor Chaliapin Jr, Elya Baskin, Michael Lonsdale; ***D:*** Jean-Jacques Annaud; ***W:*** Andrew Birkin, Gerard Brach, Howard Franklin; ***C:*** Tonino Delli Colli; ***M:*** James Horner. British Academy Awards '87: Best Actor (Connery); Cesar Awards '87: Best Foreign Film. *NLC*

Namu, the Killer Whale ½ **1966** Based on the true story of a marine biologist (Lansing) who gets the perfect opportunity to study killer whales when one is confined to a small cove. The local fisherman want to kill the creature because it feeds on the salmon they catch but they are persuaded against their baser instincts. Filmed on location in the San Juan Islands of Puget Sound. The real Namu lived at the Seattle Public Aquarium. **89m/C VHS.** Robert Lansing, John Anderson, Robin Mattson, Richard Erdman, Lee Meriwether, Joe Higgins; ***D:*** Laslo Benedek. *MGM, FCT*

Nana **1955** French version of Emile Zola's novel about an actress-prostitute who seduces the high society of Paris in the late 1880s, and suffers a heart-breaking downfall and death. Film has three remakes of the original 1926 version. **118m/C VHS, Beta.** *FR* Charles Boyer, Martine Carol. *NOS, DVT, HEG*

Nana ½ **1982** A lavishly photographed, graphic adaptation of the Emile Zola novel about a Parisian whore who acquires power by seducing the richest and politically formidable men. Dubbed. **92m/C VHS, Beta.** *IT* Katya Berger, Jean-Pierre Aumont; ***D:*** Dan Wolman; ***W:*** Marc Behm; ***M:*** Ennio Morricone. *FCT, MGM*

Nancy Astor **1982** A portrait of the beautiful, spirited Virginian who became a member of the British Parliament. **55m/C VHS, Beta.** *GB* Lisa Harrow, James Fox, Dan O'Herlihy, Sylvia Syms. *TLF*

Nancy Drew, Reporter **1939** The young sleuth gets to play reporter after winning a newspaper contest. In no time at all, she's involved in a murder mystery. **68m/B VHS.** Bonita Granville, John Litel, Frankie Thomas Jr., Mary Lee, Sheila Bromley, Betty Amann, Dick Jones, Olin Howlin, Charles Halton; ***D:*** William Clemens. *HTV, NOS*

Nancy Goes to Rio ½ **1950** Actresses Powell and Sothern compete for the same part in a play and for the same man. Catch is, they're mother and daughter. Zany consequences ensue. Sothern's last film for MGM. ♫Time and Time Again; Shine On Harvest Moon; Cha Bomm Pa Pa; Yipsee-I-O; Magic is the Moonlight; Musetta's Waltz; Love is Like This; Nancy Goes to Rio. **99m/C VHS.** Ann Sothern, Jane Powell, Barry Sullivan, Carmen Miranda, Louis Calhern, Scotty Beckett, Hans Conried, Glenn Anders; ***D:*** Robert Z. Leonard; ***W:*** Sidney Sheldon. *MGM, MLB, CCB*

The Nanny ½ **1965** Creepfest stars Davis as a seemingly proper nameless nanny who's been accused by her young charge Joey (Dix) of drowning his sister in the bathtub. But it's Joey who's sent away to a home for disturbed children and when he returns two years later (and just why is the nanny still around a childless home?) it's a battle of wills between the duo over who's responsible for some evil goings-on. Based on a novel by Evelyn Piper. **93m/B VHS.** *GB* Bette Davis, William Dix, Wendy Craig, Jill Bennett, James Villiers, Pamela Franklin, Jack Watling, Alfred Burke, Maurice Denham; ***D:*** Seth Holt; ***W:*** Jimmy Sangster; ***C:*** Henry Waxman; ***M:*** Richard Rodney Bennett. *FXV*

Napoleon **1927** A vivid, near-complete restoration of Gance's epic silent masterpiece about the famed conqueror's early years, from his youth through the Italian Campaign. An innovative, spectacular achievement with its use of multiple split screens, montage, color, and triptychs. Given a gala theatrical re-release in 1981. Remade in 1955. **235m/B VHS, Beta, LV.** *FR* Albert Dieudonne, Antonin Artaud, Pierre Batcheff, Gina Manes, Armand Bernard, Harry Krimer, Albert Bras, Abel Gance, Georges Cahuzac; ***D:*** Abel Gance; ***M:*** Carmine Coppola. *MCA, INJ*

Napoleon **1955** Depicts life story of Napoleon from his days as a soldier in the French army to his exile on the Island of Elba. Falls short of the fantastic 1927 silent classic as it attempts to delve into Napoleon the man, as opposed to his conquests. Some might find it too slow for their tastes. **123m/C VHS, Beta, LV.** *FR* Raymond Pellegrin, Orson Welles, Maria Schell, Yves Montand, Erich von Stroheim, Jean Gabin, Jean-Pierre Aumont; ***D:*** Sacha Guitry. *NOS, MRV, MPI*

Napoleon and Samantha **1972** Disney adventure about Napoleon, an orphan (Whitaker), who is befriended by Danny, a college student (Douglas). After the death of his grandfather, Napoleon decides to take Major, his elderly pet lion, and follow Danny, who is herding goats for the summer, across the American northwest mountains and they are joined by Samantha (Foster in her film debut). Worth watching. **91m/C VHS, Beta.** Jodie Foster, Johnny Whitaker, Michael Douglas, Will Geer, Henry Jones; ***D:*** Bernard McEveety; ***W:*** Stewart Raffill; ***M:*** Buddy Baker. Nominations: Academy Awards '72: Best Original Score. *DIS*

The Narcotics Story *Woof! The Dreaded Persuasion* **1958** Bad film on the same vein as "Reefer Madness." Originally intended as a police training film, this shows the evils and destruction of heroin addiction. Portrayals of drug addicts are hilarious. **75m/C VHS.** Sharon Strand, Darlene Hendricks, Herbert Crisp, Fred Marratto; ***D:*** Robert W. Larsen. *SNC, TPV*

The Narrow Margin **1952** Well-made, harrowing adventure about a cop who is in charge of transporting a gangster's widow to a trial where she is to testify. On the train he must try to keep her safe from the hit-men who would murder her. A real cat and mouse game—one of the best suspense movies of the '50s. **71m/B VHS.** Charles McGraw, Marie Windsor, Jacqueline White, Queenie Leonard, Gordon Gebert, Don Beddoe, Harry Harvey; ***D:*** Richard Fleischer. Nominations: Academy Awards '52: Best Story. *TTC, MLB, TTC*

Narrow Margin **1990 (R)** Archer reluctantly agrees to testify against the mob after witnessing a murder, and Los Angeles D.A. Hackman is assigned to protect her on the train through the Rockies back to L.A. Bad idea, she finds out. No match for its '52 predecessor. **99m/C VHS, LV.** Gene Hackman, Anne Archer, James B. Sikking, J.T. Walsh, M. Emmet Walsh; ***D:*** Peter Hyams; ***W:*** Peter Hyams; ***M:*** Bruce Broughton. *LIV*

Narrow Trail ½ **1917** A silent classic that still stands as one of the best Westerns ever made. A tough cowboy with a troubled past hopes a good woman can save him. But she's seen trouble, too. They meet up again in San Francisco's Barbary Coast. A horse race might hold the answer. **56m/B VHS, Beta.** William S. Hart, Sylvia Bremer, Milton Ross; ***D:*** William S. Hart. *NOS, GPV, CCB*

Nashville **1975 (R)** Altman's stunning, brilliant film tapestry that follows the lives of 24 people during a political campaign/music festival in Nashville. Seemingly extemporaneous vignettes, actors playing themselves (Elliott Gould and Julie Christie), funny, touching, poignant character studies concerning affairs of the heart and despairs of the mind. Repeatedly blurs reality and fantasy. ♫I'm Easy; Two Hundred Years; Keep A'Goin'; One, I Love You; Let Me Be the One; The Day I Looked Jesus in the Eye; For the Sake of the Children; I Never Get Enough; It Don't Worry Me. **159m/C VHS, Beta, LV.** Keith Carradine, Lily Tomlin, Henry Gibson, Ronee Blakley, Keenan Wynn, David Arkin, Geraldine Chaplin, Lauren Hutton, Shelley Duvall, Barbara Harris, Allen (Goorwitz) Garfield, Karen Black, Christina Raines, Michael Murphy, Ned Beatty, Barbara Baxley, Scott Glenn, Jeff Goldblum, Gwen Welles, Bert Remsen, Robert DoQui; ***Cameos:*** Elliott Gould, Julie Christie; ***D:*** Robert Altman; ***W:*** Joan Tewkesbury; ***M:*** Richard Baskin. Academy Awards '75: Best Song ("I'm Easy"); Golden Globe Awards '76: Best Song ("I'm Easy"); National Board of Review Awards '75: 10 Best Films of the Year, Best Director (Altman), Best Supporting Actress (Blakley); National Society of Film Critics Awards '75: Best Director (Altman), Best Film, Best Supporting Actor (Gibson), Best Supporting Actress (Tomlin); Nominations: Academy Awards '75: Best Director (Altman), Best Picture, Best Supporting Actress (Blakley, Tomlin). *PAR*

Nashville Beat **1989** Gang targets the citizens of Nashville, Tennessee, until two tough cops stomp the gang's delusion that Southern folk are easy marks. **110m/C VHS.** Kent McCord, Martin Milner; ***D:*** Bernard L. Kowalski. *NO*

Nashville Girl *Country Music Daughter; New Girl in Town* **1976 (R)** Innocent country girl who wants to make good in the country music scene, rises to the top of the Nashville success ladder, by compromising everything and hanging out with stereotyped no-goods in the show biz world. It's as good as a yawn. **90m/C VHS, Beta.** Monica Gayle, Johnny Rodriguez; ***D:*** Gus Trikonis. *NLC*

The Nasty Girl ½ **1990 (PG-13)** A bright young German model plans to enter a national essay contest on the topic of her hometown's history during the Third Reich. While researching the paper, she's harassed and even brutalized, but refuses to cease her sleuthing. Excellent performances, tight direction, with comedic touches that charmingly imparts an important message. Based on a true story. In German with English subtitles. **93m/C VHS.** *GE* Lena Stolze, Monika Baumgartner, Michael Gahr; ***D:*** Michael Verhoeven; ***W:*** Michael Verhoeven. British Academy Awards '91: Best Foreign Film; New York Film Critics Awards '90: Best Foreign Film; Nominations: Academy Awards '90: Best Foreign Language Film. *INJ, HBO*

Nasty Habits **1977 (PG)** Broad farce depicting a corrupt Philadelphia convent as a satiric parallel to Watergate, with nuns modeled on Nixon, Dean and Mitchell. Includes cameo appearances by various media personalities. Based on the British novel "The Abbess of Crewe" by Muriel Spark. **92m/C VHS, Beta.** *GB* Glenda Jackson, Geraldine Page, Anne Jackson, Melina Mercouri, Sandy Dennis, Susan Penhaligon, Anne Meara, Edith Evans, Rip Torn, Eli Wallach, Jerry Stiller; ***Cameos:*** Mike Douglas, Bill Jorgensen, Jessica Savitch, Howard K. Smith; ***D:*** Michael Lindsay-Hogg. *MED*

Nasty Hero ½ **1989 (PG-13)** Hard-boiled ex-con comes to Miami to avenge the car thieves who framed him and got him sent to the slammer. This is car-chase scene heaven—little plot or drama. **79m/C VHS, Beta, LV.** Robert Sedgwick, Carlos Palomino, Scott Feraco, Mike Starr, Rosanna DaVon; ***D:*** Nick Barwood. *COL*

Nasty Rabbit *Spies-A-Go-Go* **1964** Ridiculous spoof about Soviet spies intent on releasing a rabbit with a hideous Communist disease into the U.S. Everyone gets in on the chase: Nazi forces, cowboys and indians, sideshow freaks, banditos—what is the point? **88m/C VHS, Beta.** Arch Hall Jr., Micha Terr, Melissa Morgan, John Akana; ***D:*** James Landis. *RHI*

Natas...The Reflection **1983 (PG)** A reporter persists in validating an Indian demon myth. **90m/C VHS, Beta.** Randy Mulkey, Pat Bolt, Craig Hensley, Kelli Kuhn. *LIV*

Nate and Hayes ½ **1983 (PG)** Set during the mid-1800s in the South Pacific, the notorious real-life swashbuckler Captain "Bully" Hayes ("good pirate") helps young missionary Nate recapture his fiancee from a cutthroat gang of evil slave traders. Entertaining "jolly rogers" film. **100m/C VHS, Beta, LV.** *NZ* Tommy Lee Jones, Michael O'Keefe, Max Phipps, Jenny Seagrove; ***D:*** Ferdinand Fairfax; ***M:*** Trevor Jones. *PAR*

A Nation Aflame ½ **1937** Anti-Klan film is based on a story by Thomas L. Dixon, the author of "The Clansman," from which D.W. Griffith made "The Birth of a Nation." In this story, a con man gains control of the state's government through an ultra-nationalistic secret society, and eventually pays for his corruption. **70m/B VHS, Beta.** Lila Lee, Noel Madison, Snub Pollard, Norma Trelvar; ***D:*** Victor Halperin. *SNC, NOS, GVV*

National Lampoon Goes to the Movies **1981** Parodies of popular Hollywood genres, including cop thrillers, melodramas, and inspirational biographies, done in goofy "Lampoon" style. **89m/C VHS.** Robby Benson, Candy Clark, Diane Lane, Christopher Lloyd, Peter Riegert, Richard Widmark, Henny Youngman; ***D:*** Henry Jaglom. *MOV*

National Lampoon's Animal House ½ *Animal House* **1978 (R)** Classic Belushi vehicle running amuck. Set in 1962 and responsible for launching Otis Day and the Knights and defining cinematic food fights. Every college tradition from fraternity rush week to the homecoming pageant is irreverently and relentlessly mocked in this wild comedy about Delta House, a fraternity on the edge. Climaxes with the homecoming parade from hell. Sophomoric, but very funny, with a host of young stars who went on to more serious work. Remember: "Knowledge is good." **109m/C VHS, Beta, LV.** John Belushi, Tim Matheson, John Vernon, Donald Sutherland, Peter Riegert, Stephen Furst, Bruce McGill, Mark Metcalf, Verna Bloom, Karen Allen, Tom Hulce, Mary Louise Weller, Kevin Bacon; ***D:*** John Landis; ***W:*** Harold Ramis; ***M:*** Elmer Bernstein. People's Choice Awards '79: Best Film. *MCA*

National Lampoon's Attack of the 5 Ft. 2 Women *Attack of the 5 Ft. 2 Women* **1994 (R)** Brown parodies two of 1994's most notorious tabloid queens in "Tonya: The Battle of Wounded Knee" and "He Never Give Me Orgasm: The Lenora Babbitt Story." Made for cable TV. **82m/C VHS.** Julie Brown, Sam McMurray, Adam Storke, Priscilla Barnes, Lauren Tewes, Dick Miller, Rick Overton, Stanley DeSantis, Anne DeSalvo, Liz Torres, Vicki Lawrence, Stella Stevens, Peter DeLuise; ***D:*** Julie Brown, Richard Wenk; ***W:*** Julie Brown, Charlie Coffey; ***M:*** Christopher Tyng. *PAR*

National Lampoon's Christmas Vacation ½ *Christmas Vacation* **1989 (PG-13)** The third vacation for the Griswold family finds them hosting repulsive relatives for Yuletide. The sight gags, although predictable, are sometimes on the mark. Quaid is a standout as the slovenly cousin. **93m/C VHS, Beta, LV, 8mm.** Chevy Chase, Beverly D'Angelo, Randy Quaid, Diane Ladd, John Randolph, E.G. Marshall, Doris Roberts, Julia Louis-Dreyfus, Mae Questel, William Hickey, Brian Doyle-Murray, Juliette Lewis, Johnny Galecki, Nicholas Guest, Miriam Flynn; ***D:*** Jeremiah S. Chechik; ***W:*** John Hughes; ***M:*** Angelo Badalamenti. *WAR*

National Lampoon's Class of '86 *Class of '86* **1986** This is a live stage comedy show written and sponsored by the infamous adult humor magazine, featuring a new cast of comics. **86m/C VHS, Beta.** Rodger Bumpass, Veanne Cox, Annie Golden, John Michael Higgins, Tommy Koenig. *PAR*

National Lampoon's Class Reunion *Woof! Class Reunion* **1982 (R)** Class reunion with some very wacky guests and a decided lack of plot or purpose. Things go from bad to worse when a crazed killer decides to join in on the festivities. Disappointing with very few laughs. **85m/C VHS, Beta, LV.** Shelley Smith, Gerrit Graham, Michael Lerner; ***D:*** Michael Miller; ***W:*** John Hughes; ***M:*** Peter Bernstein. *PAR, VES*

National Lampoon's European Vacation ½ *European Vacation* **1985 (PG-13)** Sappy sequel to "Vacation" that has witless Chase and his family bumbling around in the land "across the pond." The Griswolds nearly redefine the term "ugly American." Stonehenge will never be the same. **94m/C VHS, Beta, LV, 8mm.** Chevy Chase, Beverly D'Angelo, Dana Hill, Jason Lively, Victor Lanoux, John Astin;

D: Amy Heckerling; *W:* John Hughes, Robert Klane, Eric Idle; *M:* Charles Fox. *WAR*

National Lampoon's Favorite Deadly Sins ♪♪½ **1995 (R)** Three sketches about greed, anger, and lust. In "Lust," Leary plays a security guard who spies on a neighbor; "Anger" finds Clay as an irate convenience store shopper; and Mantegna, in "Greed," stars as a sleazoid producer who helps a young woman kill her wicked stepmother and stepsisters in order to make a movie about it. **99m/C VHS.** Joe Mantegna, Denis Leary, Annabella Sciorra, Andrew Dice Clay, Cassidy Rae, Brian Keith, William Ragsdale, Farrah Forke, Tanya Pohlkotte; *D:* Denis Leary, David Jablin; *W:* Michael Barrie, Jim Mulholland, Lee Biondi, Ann Lembeck. *REP*

National Lampoon's Last Resort ♪½ **1994 (PG-13)** Retired film actor finds his long-time movie nemesis can't separate screen life from the real thing anymore and is planning an invasion of the actor's private island. So, he calls on his nephew (who brings along a friend) to help him out. **91m/C VHS, LV.** Corey Feldman, Corey Haim, Geoffrey Lewis, Robert Mandan; *D:* Rafal Zielinksi. *VMK*

National Lampoon's Loaded Weapon 1 ♪½ *Loaded Weapon 1* **1993 (PG-13)** Cop Jack Colt (Estevez) and partner Wes Luger (Jackson) attempt to recover a microfilm which contains a formula for turning cocaine into cookies. Essentially a sendup of the popular "Lethal Weapon" series, although other movies and themes make an appearance, well sort of. Short on plot and long on slapstick, but that's the whole point. Tired formula creates nostalgia for the granddaddy of them all, "Airplane." Lots of cameos, including one from sibling spoof star Sheen. The magazine folded while the movie was in production, an ominous sign. **83m/C VHS, LV.** Emilio Estevez, Samuel L. Jackson, Jon Lovitz, Tim Curry, Kathy Ireland, William Shatner; ***Cameos:*** Dr. Joyce Brothers, James Doohan, Richard Moll, F. Murray Abraham, Denis Leary, Corey Feldman, Phil Hartman, J.T. Walsh, Erik Estrada, Larry Wilcox, Allyce Beasley, Charlie Sheen; *D:* Gene Quintano; *W:* Gene Quintano, Don Holley. *COL, IME*

National Lampoon's Senior Trip ♪ *Senior Trip* **1995 (R)** According to the promotion, "they came, they saw, they passed out." Good dumb fun is hard to come by, particularly here. Latest lesser "Lampoon" effort in a long line of lesser Lampoons is about midwestern high school seniors who take a bus trip to Washington to meet the President. Along the way they have hijinks, including manipulation by a stereotypically corrupt senator out to embarrass his politcal opponent. Frewer is the inept principal who leads the hopelessly cliched group of misfits through the dopey corridors of power. Somehow, even the Coreys avoided this one. **91m/C VHS, LV.** Matt Frewer, Valerie Mahaffey, Lawrence Dane, Thomas Chong, Kevin McDonald; *D:* Kelly Makin; *W:* I. Marlene King, Roger Kumble. *NLC*

National Lampoon's Vacation ♪♪♪ *Vacation* **1983 (R)** The Clark Griswold (Chase) family of suburban Chicago embarks on a westward cross-country vacation via car to the renowned "Wally World." Ridiculous and hysterical misadventures, including a falling asleep at the wheel sequence and the untimely death of Aunt Edna. **98m/C VHS, Beta, LV.** Chevy Chase, Beverly D'Angelo, Imogene Coca, Randy Quaid, Christie Brinkley, James Keach, Anthony Michael Hall, John Candy, Eddie Bracken, Brian Doyle-Murray, Eugene Levy; *D:* Harold Ramis; *W:* John Hughes, Harold Ramis; *M:* Ralph Burns. *WAR*

National Velvet ♪♪♪♪ **1944 (G)** A young English girl wins a horse in a raffle and is determined to train it to compete in the famed Grand National race. Taylor, only 12 at the time, is superb in her first starring role. Rooney also gives a fine performance. Filmed with a loving eye on lushly decorated sets, this is a masterpiece version of the story of affection between a girl and her pet. Based on the novel by Enid Bagnold and followed by "International Velvet" in 1978. **124m/C VHS, LV.** Elizabeth Taylor, Mickey Rooney, Arthur Treacher, Donald Crisp, Anne Revere, Angela Lansbury, Reginald Owen, Norma Varden, Jackie "Butch" Jenkins, Terence Kilburn; *D:* Clarence Brown; *W:* Helen Deutsch, Theodore Reeves; *M:* Herbert Stothart. Academy Awards '45: Best Film Editing, Best Supporting Actress (Revere); Nominations: Academy Awards '45: Best Color Cinematography, Best Director (Brown). *MGM, TLF, BTV*

Native Son ♪♪½ **1951** A young black man from the ghettos of Chicago is hired as a chauffeur by an affluent white family. His job is to drive their head-strong daughter anywhere she wants to go. Unintentionally, he kills her, tries to hide, and is ultimately found guilty. Based on the classic novel by Richard Wright, who also stars. Remade in 1986. Unprofessional direction and low budget work against the strong story. **91m/B VHS.** Richard Wright, Jean Wallace, Nicholas Joy, Gloria Madison, Charles Cane; *D:* Pierre Chenal. *NOS, XVC, FCT*

Native Son ♪♪½ **1986 (R)** This second film adaptation of the classic Richard Wright novel is chock full of stars and tells the story of a poor black man who accidentally kills a white woman and then hides the body. Changes in the script soft-soap some of the novel's disturbing truths and themes—so-so drama for those who have not read the book. **111m/C VHS, Beta, LV.** Geraldine Page, Oprah Winfrey, Matt Dillon, John Karlen, Elizabeth McGovern, Akosua Busia, Carroll Baker, Victor Love, John McMartin, Art Evans, Willard Pugh, David Rasche; *D:* Jerrold Freedman; *W:* Richard Wesley; *M:* James Mtume. *MON, KUI, LIV*

Nativity ♪♪ **1978** Unmemorable, made-for-TV portrayal of the romance between Mary and Joseph (of the Bible story), Joseph's response to Mary's pregnancy, and the birthing of Jesus. Not exactly a Bible epic, the direction and acting are uninspired. **97m/C VHS, Beta.** John Shea, Madeleine Stowe, Jane Wyatt, John Rhys-Davies, Kate O'Mara; *D:* Bernard L. Kowalski. *FOX*

The Natural ♪♪♪ **1984 (PG)** A beautifully filmed movie about baseball as myth. A young man, whose gift for baseball sets him apart, finds that trouble dogs him, particularly with a woman. In time, as an aging rookie, he must fight against his past to lead his team to the World Series, and win the woman who is meant for him. From the Bernard Malamud story. **134m/C VHS, Beta, LV.** Robert Redford, Glenn Close, Robert Duvall, Kim Basinger, Wilford Brimley, Barbara Hershey, Richard Farnsworth, Robert Prosky, Darren McGavin, Joe Don Baker, Michael Madsen; *D:* Barry Levinson; *C:* Caleb Deschanel; *M:* Randy Newman. Nominations: Academy Awards '84: Best Art Direction/Set Decoration, Best Cinematography, Best Supporting Actress (Close). *COL*

Natural Born Killers ♪♪ **1994 (R)** An old script by (Graphic Screen Violence) Tarantino is resurrected by (Damn the Torpedoes) Stone and invested with its own unique subtle nuance and style. Controversial (natch, considering the director and writer) look at the way the media portrays criminals. Harrelson and Lewis are the lovestruck, white-trash serial killers who become tabloid-TV darlings, thanks to a sensationalistic press led by Downey, Jr. Stone's dark and manic comment on America's fascination and revulsion with violence is strictly of the love it or leave it variety. Bloodshed galore, dazzling photography, and a dynamite soundtrack (with over 75 selections) add up to sensory overload. **119m/C VHS, LV.** Woody Harrelson, Robert Downey Jr., Juliette Lewis, Tommy Lee Jones, Ashley Judd, Tom Sizemore, Rodney Dangerfield, Rachel Ticotin, Arliss Howard, Russell Means, Denis Leary, Steven Wright, Pruitt Taylor Vince; *D:* Oliver Stone; *W:* Oliver Stone; *C:* Robert Richardson; *M:* Trent Reznor. Nominations: Golden Globe Awards '95: Best Director (Stone); MTV Movie Awards '95: Best On-Screen Duo (Woody Harrelson/Juliette Lewis), Best Kiss (Woody Harrelson/Juliette Lewis). *WAR, VMK*

Natural Causes ♪½ **1994 (PG-13)** Muddled political thriller finds Dr. Jessie McCarthy (Purl) traveling to Thailand to visit her estranged mother Rachel (Paige), only to discover she's just been murdered. Then Jessie learns Rachel had a secret life aiding Vietnamese refugees and a scheme is afoot to sabotage a reconciliation treaty between the U.S. and Vietnam. However, none of this makes much sense, though the Bangkok settings provide a pleasant distraction. **90m/C VHS.** Linda Purl, Cary-Hiroyuki Tagawa, Will Patton, Tim Thomerson, Janis Paige, Ali MacGraw; *D:* James Becket; *W:* Jake Raymond Needham; *C:* Denis Maloney; *M:* Nathan Wang. *COL*

Natural Enemies ♪♪½ **1979 (R)** A successful publisher begins to consider suicide and murder as the cure for his family's increasing alienation and despair. Dark and depressing drama. **100m/C VHS, Beta.** Hal Holbrook, Louise Fletcher, Jose Ferrer, Viveca Lindfors; *D:* Jeff Kanew; *W:* Jeff Kanew. *COL*

The Natural History of Parking Lots ♪♪ **1994** What's a rich L.A. father to do when his teenage son hot-wires antique cars for kicks? Why pay his gun-running older brother to keep an eye on him. And the whackiness is just beginning. **92m/C VHS.** *D:* Everet Lewis. *FCT*

Nature of the Beast ♪♪ **1994 (R)** A businessman and a drifter are both hiding deadly secrets as police search for both a serial killer and the million dollars missing in a Vegas casino robbery. Just which man is involved in which crime? **91m/C VHS, LV.** Eric Roberts, Lance Henriksen, Brion James; *D:* Victor Salva; *W:* Victor Salva. *NLC*

Nature's Playmates ♪ **1962** A beautiful private eye tours Florida nudist camps in search of a missing man with a distinctive tattoo on his posterior. One of H.G. Lewis' obscure "nudie" flicks, sexually tame by modern standards, awful by any standards. **56m/B VHS.** Vicki Miles, Scott Osborne; *D:* Herschell Gordon Lewis. *VDM, TPV*

Naughty Knights ♪ *Up the Chastity Belt* **1971 (PG)** Soft-core romp in a medieval setting. Toss it in the moat. **94m/C VHS, Beta.** Frankie Howerd, Graham Crowden, Bill Fraser, Roy Hudd, Hugh Paddick, Anna Quayle, Eartha Kitt, Dave King, Fred Emney; *D:* Bob Kellett; *M:* Carl Davis. *ACA*

Naughty Marietta ♪♪½ **1935** A French princess switches identities with a mail-order bride to escape from her arranged marriage, and is captured by pirates. When she's saved by a dashing Indian scout, it's love at first sight. The first MacDonald-Eddy match-up and very popular in its day. ♫Italian Street Song; Chansonette; Antoinette and Anatole; Prayer; Tramp, Tramp, Tramp; The Owl and the Bobcat; Neath the Southern Moon; Mon Ami Pierrot; Ship Ahoy. **106m/B VHS, Beta, LV.** Jeanette MacDonald, Nelson Eddy, Frank Morgan, Elsa Lanchester, Douglass Dumbrille, Cecilia Parker; *D:* Woodbridge S. Van Dyke; *C:* William H. Daniels. Academy Awards '35: Best Sound; Nominations: Academy Awards '35: Best Picture. *MGM*

The Naughty Nineties ♪♪ **1945** Bud and Lou help a showboat owner fend off crooks in the 1890s. Usual slapstick shenanigans, but highlighted by verbal banter. Includes the first on-screen rendition of the classic "Who's on First?" routine. ♫Rolling Down the River; Uncle Tom's Cabin; I Can't Get You Out of My Mind; On a Sunday Afternoon; I'd Leave My Happy Home for You; Nora Malone; Ma Blushin' Rosie; The Showboat's Comin' to Town; A Blarney from Killarney. **72m/B VHS, Beta.** Bud Abbott, Lou Costello, Henry Travers, Alan Curtis, Joseph Sawyer, Rita Johnson, Joe Kirk, Lois Collier; *D:* Jean Yarbrough. *MCA, MLB*

Navajo Joe ♪½ **1967** The sole survivor of a massacre single-handedly kills each person involved in the atrocity, and aids a terrorized, though unappreciative, town in the process. Low-budget Spanish-Italian western only worth watching because of Reynolds. Filmed in Spain. **89m/C VHS.** *IT SP* Burt Reynolds, Aldo Sambrel, Tanya Lopert, Fernando Rey; *D:* Sergio Corbucci; *M:* Ennio Morricone. *MGM*

The Navigator ♪♪♪ **1924** Ever the quick thinker, Keaton actually bought a steamer headed for the scrap heap and used it to film an almost endless string of sight gags. Rejected by a socialite, millionaire Keaton finds himself alone with her on the abandoned boat. As he saves her from various and sundry perils, the gags and thrills abound—including one stunt that was inspired by a near-accident on the set. Too bad they don't make 'em like this anymore. Silent. **60m/B VHS.** Buster Keaton, Kathryn McGuire, Frederick Vroom, Noble Johnson, Clarence Burton, H. M. Clugston; ***D:*** Buster Keaton, Donald Crisp. *NO*

The Navigator ☙☙☙ **1988 (PG)** A creative time-travel story of a 14th-century boy with visionary powers who leads the residents of his medieval English village away from a plague by burrowing through the earth's core and into late-20th-century New Zealand. Quite original and refreshing. **92m/C VHS.** *NZ* Hamish McFarlane, Bruce Lyons, Chris Haywood, Marshall Napier, Noel Appleby, Paul Livingston, Sarah Pierse; ***D:*** Vincent Ward; ***W:*** Vincent Ward. Australian Film Institute '88: Best Cinematography, Best Director (Ward), Best Film. *HTV*

Navy Blue and Gold ☙☙½ **1937** Three football-playing midshipmen (Young, Stewart, and Brown) at Annapolis share a friendship. Stewart has registered under a false name since his dad was unfairly cashiered from the service. When he hears some slander about his old man he stands up and tells the truth and gets suspended, just before the big game with Army. Naturally, he's reinstated just in time to make the big play and carry the team to victory. Well-done, old-fashioned hokum. **94m/B VHS.** James Stewart, Robert Young, Tom Brown, Lionel Barrymore, Florence Rice, Billie Burke, Samuel S. Hinds, Paul Kelly, Frank Albertson, Minor Watson; ***D:*** Sam Wood; ***W:*** George Bruce. *MGM, MOV*

The Navy Comes Through ☙☙ **1942** Salty sailors aboard a mangy freighter beat the odds and sink Nazi warships and subs with the greatest of ease. Boy meets girl subplot is added for good measure. Morale booster includes newsreel footage. **81m/B VHS.** Pat O'Brien, George Murphy, Jane Wyatt, Jackie Cooper, Carl Esmond, Max Baer Sr., Desi Arnaz Sr., Ray Collins, Lee Bonnell, Frank Jenks, Helmut Dantine; ***D:*** Edward Sutherland. *TTC*

Navy SEALS ☙½ **1990 (R)** A group of macho Navy commandos, whose regular work is to rescue hostages from Middle Eastern underground organizations, finds a stash of deadly weapons. They spend the balance of the movie attempting to destroy the arsenal. Sheen chews the scenery as a crazy member of the commando team. Lots of action and violence, but simplistic good guys - bad guys philosophy and plot weaknesses keep this from being more than below average. **113m/C VHS, Beta, LV.** Charlie Sheen, Michael Biehn, Joanne Whalley, Rick Rossovich, Cyril O'Reilly, Bill Paxton, Dennis Haysbert, Paul Sanchez, Ron Joseph, Nicholas Kadi; ***D:*** Lewis Teague; ***W:*** Gary Goldman; ***C:*** John A. Alonzo. *ORI*

Navy vs. the Night Monsters *Woof!* **1966** When horrifying, acid-secreting plant monsters try to take over the world, Van Doren and the Navy must come to the rescue, with the action taking place in a tropical South Pole setting. Amazing deployment of talents. **87m/C VHS, Beta.** Mamie Van Doren, Anthony Eisley, Pamela Mason, Bobby Van, Russ Bender; ***D:*** Michael Hoey; ***W:*** Michael Hoey. *NO*

Navy Way ☙ **1944** Hurriedly produced war propaganda film in which a boxer gets inducted into the Navy just before his title shot. **74m/B VHS.** Robert Lowery, Jean Parker; ***D:*** William (Lester Williams) Berke, William C. Thomas. *NOS, DVT, HEG*

Nazarin ☙☙☙ **1958** Bunuel's scathing indictment of Christianity finds its perfect vehicle in the adventures of a defrocked priest attempting to relive Christ's life. Gathering a group of disciples, he wanders into the Mexican desert as a cross between Christ and Don Quixote. Filmed in Mexico, this is Bunuel at his grimmest. In Spanish with English subtitles. **92m/B VHS, Beta, LV.** *MX* Francesco Rabal, Rita Macedo, Margo Lopez, Rita McLedo, Ignacio Lopez Tarso, Jesus Fernandez; ***D:*** Luis Bunuel. *MAD, INJ, CVC*

Nea ☙☙½ **1978 (R)** Comic drama about a young girl from a privileged home who writes a best selling pornographic novel anonymously. When her book writing talents are made public through betrayal, she gets even in a most unique way. Subtitled "A Young Emmanuelle." Kaplan also performs. Appealing and sophisticated. **101m/C VHS, Beta.** Sami Frey, Ann Zacharias, Heinz Bennent; ***D:*** Nelly Kaplan. *COL*

Near Dark ☙☙☙ **1987 (R)** A farm boy falls in unwillingly with a family of thirsty, outlaw-fringe vampires who roam the West in a van. The first mainstream effort by Bigelow, and a rollicking, blood-saturated, slaughterhouse of a movie, with enough laughs and stunning imagery to revive the genre. **95m/C VHS, Beta, LV.** Adrian Pasdar, Jenny Wright, Bill Paxton, Jenette Goldstein, Lance Henriksen, Tim Thomerson, Joshua Miller; ***D:*** Kathryn Bigelow; ***W:*** Kathryn Bigelow, Eric Red; ***M:*** Tangerine Dream. *HBO, IME*

Near Misses ☙½ **1991** Missable farce with Reinhold as a bigamist in the foreign service. To make time for a mistress he swaps identities with a young Marine in Paris, but then the KGB kidnaps the imposter. Doors slam in hallways all over the place as the performers crank up the mixups to maximum frenzy, but with little effect since you really don't care much about these fools. **93m/C VHS, Beta, LV.** Judge Reinhold, Casey Siemaszko; ***D:*** Baz Taylor; ***W:*** Peter Baloff, Dave Wollert. *FXV, VTR*

Near the Rainbow's End ☙½ **1930** Cattle rancher Steele (in his first talking western) finds out that rustlers are aggravating the trouble between the cattlemen and the sheep herders. So he goes after the bad guys and then settles the feud by marrying a sheep herder's daughter. **57m/B VHS.** Bob Steele, Lafe McKee, Louise Lorraine, Al Ferguson, Al Hewston; ***D:*** J.P. McGowan. *GPV*

'Neath Brooklyn Bridge ☙☙ **1942** The Boys from the Bowery get tangled up in crime when they try to help a young girl whose guardian was murdered. **61m/B VHS.** Leo Gorcey, Huntz Hall, Bobby Jordan, Sammy Morrison, Ann Gillis, Noah Beery Jr., Marc Lawrence, Gabriel Dell; ***D:*** Wallace Fox. *NOS, MRV, PME*

'Neath Canadian Skies ☙ **1946** Mounted lawman who says "eh" a lot tracks murdering gang of mine looters. **41m/B VHS, Beta, LV, 8mm.** *CA* Russell Hayden, Inez Cooper, Cliff Nazarro, Kermit Maynard, Jack Mulhall. *VYY*

'Neath the Arizona Skies ☙☙ **1934** Low budget oater epic about a cowhand who finds all the action he and his friends can handle as they try to rescue a young Indian girl (and oil heiress) who has been kidnapped. 'Nuff said. **54m/B VHS.** John Wayne, George "Gabby" Hayes, Sheila Terry; ***D:*** Harry Fraser. *COL, NOS, REP*

Necessary Parties **1988** Based on Barbara Dana's book that has a 15-year-old boy filing a lawsuit to stop his parents' divorce. Originally aired on PBS as part of the "Wonderworks" family movie series. **120m/C VHS.** Alan Arkin, Mark Paul Gosselaar, Barbara Dana, Adam Arkin, Donald Moffat, Julie Hagerty, Geoffrey Pierson, Taylor Fry; ***D:*** Gwen Arner. *PME, WNE, HMV*

Necessary Roughness ☙☙ **1991 (PG-13)** After losing their NCAA standing, the Texas Southern University (passing for the real Texas State) Armadillos football team looks like it's headed for disaster. The once proud football factory is now composed of assorted goofballs instead of stud players. But hope arrives in the form of a 34-year-old farmer with a golden arm, ready to recapture some lost dreams as quarterback. Can this unlikey team rise above itself and win a game, or will their hopes be squashed all over the field? **108m/C VHS, Beta, LV.** Scott Bakula, Robert Loggia, Harley Jane Kozak, Sinbad, Hector Elizondo, Kathy Ireland, Jason Bateman; ***D:*** Stan Dragoti; ***M:*** Bill Conti. *PAR*

Necromancer: Satan's Servant ☙☙ **1988 (R)** After a woman is brutally raped, she contacts a sorceress and makes a pact with the devil to ensure her successful revenge. Plenty of graphic violence and nudity. **90m/C VHS, Beta, LV.** Elizabeth Cayton, Russ Tamblyn, Rhonda Dorton; ***D:*** Dusty Nelson. *MCG, IME*

Necropolis ☙ **1987 (R)** A witch burned at the stake 300 years ago is brought back to life as a motorcycle punkette in New York searching for a sacrificial virgin (in New York?). New wave horror should have been watchable. **77m/C VHS, Beta.** Leeanne Baker, Michael Conte, Jacquie Fritz, William Reed, Paul Ruben; ***D:*** Tim Kincaid. *LIV, VES*

Ned Kelly ☙☙½ *Ned Kelly, Outlaw* **1970 (PG)** Dramatizes the life of Australia's most notorious outlaw. Kelly (Jagger) and his family start off as horse thieves and proceed from there. A manhunt results in death and the eventual capture and execution of Kelly. The very contemporary British Jagger was miscast as a period Australian and British director Richardson seems to have lacked an empathy for the material, given his lethargic direction. **100m/C VHS.** *GB* Mick Jagger, Allen Bickford, Geoff Gilmour, Mark McManus, Serge Lazareff, Peter Sumner, Ken Shorter, James Elliott, Diane Craig, Sue Lloyd, Clarissa Kaye; ***D:*** Tony Richardson; ***W:*** Ian Jones, Tony Richardson; ***M:*** Shel Silverstein. *MGM*

Needful Things ☙☙½ **1993 (R)** Stephen King film adaptations are becoming as prolific as his novels, though few seem to improve in the transition from page to screen. This time a scheming Maine shopkeeper (Von Sydow) sells unsuspecting small towners peculiar items that, not surprisingly, begin to cause horror and mayhem. Harris is the town sheriff who tries to warn everyone that he's the devil in disguise. Big screen directorial debut for Heston (yes, Charlton's son). **120m/C VHS, LV.** Ed Harris, Bonnie Bedelia, Max von Sydow, Amanda Plummer, J.T. Walsh; ***D:*** Fraser Heston; ***W:*** W.D. Richter; ***M:*** Patrick Doyle. *COL*

Nefertiti, Queen of the Nile ☙☙ **1964** Woman, married against her will, turns into Nefertiti. For fans of Italo-Biblical epics only. **97m/C VHS.** *IT* Jeanne Crain, Vincent Price, Edmund Purdom, Amedeo Nazzari, Liana Orfei; ***D:*** Fernando Cerchio. *NO*

Negatives ☙☙ **1968** A couple indulge in sexual fantasies to dangerous extremes, with the man first impersonating Dr. Crippen, the early 1900s murderer, and later a WWI flying ace. When a photographer friend joins the fun, the action careens off the deep end. **90m/C VHS.** *GB* Peter McEnery, Diane Cilento, Glenda Jackson, Maurice Denham, Norman Rossington; ***D:*** Peter Medak. *NO*

The Neighbor ☙☙½ **1993 (R)** See nice city couple John and Mary move to small town Vermont. See their nice retired obstetrician neighbor Myron welcome them. See Mary get pregnant and Myron take an obsessional interest. See John arrested for murder. See Mary left alone—except for Myron's tender care. **93m/C VHS.** Linda Kozlowski, Ron Lea, Rod Steiger, Francis Bay, Bruce Boa, Jane Wheeler; ***D:*** Rodney Gibbons; ***W:*** Kurt Wimmer. *ACA*

Neighbors ☙☙ **1981 (R)** The Keeses (Belushi and Walker) live in a quiet, middle-class suburban neighborhood where life is calm and sweet. But their new neighbors, Ramona and Vic (Aykroyd and Moriarty), prove to be loud, obnoxious, crazy, and freeloading. Will Earl and Enid Keese mind their manners as their neighborhood disintegrates? Some funny moments, but as the script fades, so do the laughs. Belushi's last waltz is based on Thomas Berger's novel. **90m/C VHS, Beta, LV.** John Belushi, Dan Aykroyd, Kathryn Walker, Cathy Moriarty; ***D:*** John G. Avildsen; ***W:*** Larry Gelbart; ***M:*** Bill Conti. *GKK*

Nell ☙☙½ **1994 (R)** "Wild child" story—adult version. When illiterate, barely verbal backwoods Nell (Foster) is discovered after her stroke-afflicted mother's death, she's placed in the care of a doctor (Neeson) and psychologist (Richardson) who have different ideas about how to bring her into society. Unfairly dismissed by some as self-indulgent, Foster's raw, physical performance is truly mesmerizing; dull script, unconvincingly tidy ending, and gross over-sentimentality are what disappoint. From the play "Idioglossia" by Mark Handley. **114m/C VHS.** Jodie Foster, Liam Neeson, Natasha Richardson, Richard Libertini; ***D:*** Michael Apted; ***W:*** William Nicholson. Screen Actors Guild Award '94: Best Actress (Foster); Nominations: Academy Awards '94: Best Actress (Foster); Golden Globe Awards '95: Best Actress—Drama (Foster), Best Film—Drama, Best Original Score; MTV Movie Awards '95: Best Female Performance (Foster). *FXV*

Nelly et Monsieur Arnaud 🦴🦴🦴 *Nelly and Mr. Arnaud* **1995** Chatty adult May/December would-be romance between 25-year-old secretary Nelly (Beart) and Pierre Arnaud (Serrault), the mid-60s retired magistrate for whom she's working. The arrogant divorced Arnaud is intrigued by the independent Nelly, whom he finds he can't control, while she comes to appreciate their emotional ties (altogether different from the selfishness of the younger men she knows). Conclusion avoids a neat resolution to a situation beset by bad timing. French with subtitles. **105m/C VHS.** *IT GE FR* Emmanuelle Beart, Michel Serrault, Jean-Hugues Anglade, Francoise Brion, Claire Nadeau, Michael Lonsdale, Charles Berling, Michele Laroque; ***D:*** Claude Sautet; ***W:*** Jacques Fieschi, Claude Sautet; ***C:*** Jean-Francois Robin; ***M:*** Philippe Sarde. Cesar Awards '96: Best Actor (Serrault), Best Director (Sautet); Nominations: Cesar Awards '96: Best Actress (Beart), Best Film, Best Film Editing, Best Screenplay, Best Sound, Best Supporting Actor (Anglade, Lonsdale), Best Supporting Actress (Nadeau), Best Score. *NYR*

Nemesis 🦴½ **1993 (R)** Futuristic thriller that combines cybernetics and cyborgs in post-nuclear Los Angeles. Gruner plays a human (although he's mostly composed of mechanical replacement parts) in a world overwrought with system cowboys, information terrorists, bio-enhanced gangsters, and cyborg outlaws. Film's biggest flaw is the extremely confusing script that makes no attempt at logic whatsoever. Special visual effects are good despite the obviously low f/x budget. **95m/C VHS, LV.** Olivier Gruner, Tim Thomerson, Cary-Hiroyuki Tagawa, Merele Kennedy, Yuji Okumoto, Marjorie Monaghan, Nicholas Guest, Vincent Klyn; ***D:*** Albert Pyun; ***W:*** Rebecca Charles; ***M:*** Michael Rubini. *IMP, UND*

Nemesis 3: Time Lapse 🦴½ **1996 (R)** Superhuman mutant Alex is the last hope for mankind as the cyborgs once again prepare to destroy civilization. **?m/C VHS.** Sue Price, Tim Thomerson, Norbert Weisser, Xavier DeClie, Sharon Bruneau, Debbie Muggli; ***D:*** Albert Pyun; ***W:*** Albert Pyun; ***C:*** George Mooradian; ***M:*** Tony Riparetti. *IMP*

The Neon Bible 🦴🦴 **1995** Beautifully crafted, yet thin telling of the struggles of a rural family in 1940's Georgia. The stories unfold in a series of flashbacks, as a 15-year old boy travels alone on a train, reflecting on his dysfunctional early adolescence. An abusive father (Leary) who dies in the war, suicidal mom (Scarwid), and ex-showgirl visiting aunt (Rowlands) provide plenty of opportunities for familial angst. Starts out strong, with some stunning scenes sprinkled throughout, but director Davies never ventures far from the narrative territory he's covered thoroughly in his other films ("Distant Voices, Still Lives" and "The Long Day Closes"). Adapted from the novel by Pulitzer Prize winning author John Kennedy Toole. **92m/C VHS.** Gena Rowlands, Jacob Tierney, Diana Scarwid, Drake Bell, Denis Leary, Leo Burmester, Frances Conroy, Peter McRobbie, Joan Glover, Dana Dick, Virgil Graham Hopkins; ***D:*** Terence Davies; ***W:*** Terence Davies; ***C:*** Michael Coulter. *NYR*

Neon City 🦴🦴 **1991 (R)** Title refers to a rumored city of refuge in the year 2053, where eight misfit adventurers in an armored transport seek safety from the Earth's toxic environment and "Mad Max" cliches. **99m/C VHS.** Michael Ironside, Vanity, Lyle Alzado, Valerie Wildman, Nick Klar, Juliet Landau, Arsenio "Sonny" Trinidad, Richard Sanders; ***D:*** Monte Markham. *VMK*

The Neon Empire 🦴½ **1989 (R)** Tepid tale of two gangsters battling inner mob opposition and backstabbing to build Las Vegas. Ostensibly based on the story of Bugsy Siegel and Meyer Lansky. Made for cable. **120m/C VHS, Beta, LV.** Martin Landau, Ray Sharkey, Gary Busey, Harry Guardino, Julie Carmen, Linda Fiorentino, Dylan McDermott; ***D:*** Larry Peerce; ***W:*** Pete Hamill. *FRH*

Neon Maniacs *Woof!* **1986 (R)** An even half-dozen fetish-ridden zombies stalk the streets at night, tearing their victims into teensy weensy bits. Brave teenagers try to stop the killing. Brave viewers will stop the tape. **90m/C VHS, Beta.** Allan Hayes, Leilani Sarelle Ferrer, Bo Sabato, Donna Locke, Victor Elliot Brandt; ***D:*** Joseph Mangine. *LIV, VES*

Neptune Factor 🦴 *The Neptune Disaster; An Underwater Odyssey* **1973 (G)** Scientists board a special new deep-sea sub to search for their colleagues lost in an undersea earthquake. Diving ever deeper into the abyss that swallowed their friend's Ocean Lab II, they end up trapped themselves. The plot's many holes sink it. **94m/C VHS, Beta.** Ben Gazzara, Yvette Mimieux, Walter Pidgeon, Ernest Borgnine; ***D:*** Daniel Petrie; ***W:*** Jack DeWitt. *FOX*

Neptune's Daughter 🦴🦴 **1949** A swim-happy bathing suit designer finds romance and deep pools of studio water to dive into. Typically lavish and ridiculous Williams aqua-parade. ♫Baby It's Cold Outside; I Love Those Men; My Heart Beats Faster. **92m/C VHS, Beta, LV.** Esther Williams, Red Skelton, Ricardo Montalban, Betty Garrett, Keenan Wynn, Xavier Cugat, Ted de Corsia, Mike Mazurki, Mel Blanc, Juan Duvall, George Mann, Joi Lansing; ***D:*** Edward Buzzell; ***C:*** Charles Rosher. Academy Awards '49: Best Song ("Baby It's Cold Outside"). *MGM*

Nervous Ticks 🦴🦴½ **1993 (R)** Ninety minutes in the life of airline employee York Daley. All he needs to do is get off work, go home, grab his luggage, pick up his married girfriend, and get back to the airport for a flight to Rio De Janeiro. Simple, right? Not in this movie. **95m/C VHS.** Bill Pullman, Julie Brown, Peter Boyle, James LeGros, Brent Jennings; ***D:*** Rocky Lang; ***W:*** David Frankel. *COL*

The Nervous Wreck 🦴🦴🦴 **1926** Harrison Ford (not the one from "Indiana Jones") heads West, seeking a cure for what he believes is a terminal illness. Once there, he becomes romantically entangled with the sheriff's fiancee, uses a wrench to hold up a gas station, and gets involved in other shenanigans. And then he discovers he's going to live after all. **70m/B VHS, Beta.** Harrison Ford, Phyllis Haver, Chester Conklin, Mack Swain, Hobart Bosworth, Charles Gerrard; ***D:*** Scott Sidney. *NO*

The Nest 🦴🦴½ **1980** Tragic romance of an elderly man and a 13-year-old girl is helped along by superior script and directing. **109m/C VHS, Beta.** *SP* Ana Torrent, Hector Alterio, Patricia Adriani; ***D:*** Jaime de Arminan. Nominations: Academy Awards '80: Best Foreign Language Film. *SUE, APD*

The Nest 🦴🦴½ **1988 (R)** A small island is overcome by giant cockroaches created by, you guessed it, a scientific experiment gone wrong. Special effects make it watchable. **89m/C VHS, Beta.** Robert Lansing, Lisa Langlois, Franc Luz, Terri Treas, Stephen Davies, Diana Bellamy, Nancy Morgan; ***D:*** Terence H. Winkless; ***W:*** Robert King; ***M:*** Rick Conrad. *MGM*

The Nesting 🦴½ **1980 (R)** Too-long tale of a neurotic author who rents a haunted Victorian manor and finds herself a pawn in a ghostly plan for revenge. Features Grahame's last performance. **104m/C VHS, Beta.** Robin Groves, John Carradine, Gloria Grahame, Christopher Loomis, Michael Lally; ***D:*** Armand Weston. *WAR*

The Net 🦴🦴½ **1995 (PG-13)** The ever-spunky Bullock gets stuck behind a computer screen rather than the wheel of a bus as reclusive computer systems analyst Angela Bennett. She's puzzled by a mysterious Internet program, which Angela finds can easily access highly classified databases. It's soon apparent that someone knows she knows because every record of her identity has been erased and the conspirators decide to take care of one last detail by eliminating her as well. Miller's the ex she turns to for help and Northam's a seductive British hacker. Techno paranoia. **114m/C VHS, LV, 8mm.** Sandra Bullock, Jeremy Northam, Dennis Miller, Diane Baker, Ken Howard, Wendy Gazelle, Ray McKinnon; ***D:*** Irwin Winkler; ***W:*** John Brancato, Michael Ferris; ***C:*** Jack N. Green; ***M:*** Mark Isham. *COL*

Netherworld 🦴½ **1990 (R)** A young man investigating his mysterious, dead father travels to his ancestral plantation in the bayou. To his horror, he discovers that his father was involved in the black arts. Now two beautiful young witches are after him. Can he possibly survive this madness? **87m/C VHS, LV.** Michael C. Bendetti, Denise Gentile, Anjanette Comer, Holly Floria, Robert Burr; ***D:*** David Schmoeller; ***W:*** Billy Chicago; ***M:*** Edgar Winter. *PAR*

Network 🦴🦴🦴½ **1976 (R)** As timely now as it was then; a scathing indictment of the television industry and its propensity towards self-prostitution. A television newscaster's mental breakdown turns him into a celebrity when the network tries to profit from his illness. The individual characters are startlingly realistic and the acting is excellent. **121m/C VHS, Beta, LV.** Faye Dunaway, Peter Finch, William Holden, Robert Duvall, Wesley Addy, Ned Beatty, Beatrice Straight; ***D:*** Sidney Lumet; ***W:*** Paddy Chayefsky; ***C:*** Owen Roizman. Academy Awards '76: Best Actor (Finch), Best Actress (Dunaway), Best Original Screenplay, Best Supporting Actress (Straight); Golden Globe Awards '77: Best Actor—Drama (Finch), Best Actress—Drama (Dunaway), Best Director (Lumet), Best Screenplay; Los Angeles Film Critics Association Awards '76: Best Director (Lumet), Best Film; National Board of Review Awards '76: 10 Best Films of the Year; New York Film Critics Awards '76: Best Screenplay; Writers Guild of America '76: Best Original Screenplay; Nominations: Academy Awards '76: Best Actor (Holden), Best Cinematography, Best Director (Lumet), Best Film Editing, Best Picture, Best Supporting Actor (Beatty). *MGM, BTV*

Neurotic Cabaret 🦴½ **1990** Would-be actress dances exotically and finds more exotic ways to roll in dough. **90m/C VHS.** Edwin Neal, Tammy Stone. *AIP*

Neutron and the Black Mask 🦴 **1961** Man wears mask with lightning bolts and gains comic book style powers to do deathly battle with a scientist with a neutron bomb up his sleeve. First Neutron feature. **80m/B VHS.** *MX* Wolf Ruvinskis, Julio Aleman, Armando Silvestre, Rosita Arenas, Claudio Brook; ***D:*** Frederick Curiel. *SNC*

Neutron vs. the Amazing Dr. Caronte 🦴 **1961** Dr. Caronte from "Neutron and the Black Mask" just won't give up that neutron bomb and let the series die. **80m/B VHS.** *MX* Wolf Ruvinskis, Julio Aleman, Armando Silvestre, Rosita Arenas, Rodolfo Landa; ***D:*** Frederick Curiel. *SNC*

Neutron vs. the Death Robots 🦴 **1962** Guy with a mask takes on army of killer robots and neutron bomb to protect the world from future sequels. **80m/B VHS.** *MX* Wolf Ruvinskis, Julio Aleman, Armando Silvestre, Rosita Arenas; ***D:*** Frederick Curiel. *SNC*

Neutron vs. the Maniac 🦴 **1962** Man in mask hunts guys who kill people. **80m/B VHS.** *MX* Wolf Ruvinskis. *SNC*

Nevada 🦴🦴½ **1927** Entertaining silent western with a great cast finds gunslinger Cooper running from the law and winding up on a ranch where he falls for Todd, the rancher's daughter. Naturally, Cooper redeems himself by going after a gang of cattle rustlers, led by Powell. Based on a novel by Zane Grey. **67m/B VHS.** Gary Cooper, Thelma Todd, William Powell, Ernie Adams, Philip Strange; ***D:*** John Waters. *GPV*

Nevada 🦴🦴½ **1944** Cowpoke Mitchum is mistaken for the killer of a homesteader and narrowly escapes the rope by finding the real killer. First leading role for Mitchum as the tough but laconic hero. Based on a story by Zane Grey. **62m/B VHS.** Robert Mitchum, Anne Jeffreys, Nancy Gates, Craig Reynolds, Guinn "Big Boy" Williams, Richard Martin, Harry Woods; ***D:*** Edward Killy. *GPV*

Nevada City 🦴½ **1941** Roy outwits a financier who is trying to monopolize transportation in California. **54m/B VHS, Beta.** Roy Rogers. *VCN*

Nevada Smith 🦴🦴 **1966** The half-breed Nevada Smith (previously introduced in Harold Robbins' story "The Carpetbaggers" and film of same name) seeks the outlaws who killed his parents. Standard western plot, characters. Later remade as a TV movie. **135m/C VHS, Beta, LV.** Steve McQueen, Karl Malden, Brian Keith, Arthur Kennedy, Raf Vallone, Suzanne Pleshette; ***D:*** Henry Hathaway; ***W:*** John Michael Hayes. *PAR*

The Nevadan 🦴½ *The Man From Nevada* **1950** A marshal goes in search of an outlaw's gold cache, only to be opposed by a crooked rancher. Good scenery and action, but not one of Scott's best. **81m/C VHS, Beta.** Randolph Scott, Dorothy Malone, Forrest Tucker, Frank Faylen, George Macready, Charles Kemper, Jeff Corey, Tom Powers, Jock Mahoney; ***D:*** Gordon Douglas. *GKK*

Never a Dull Moment 🦴🦴 **1950** New York songwriter falls for rodeo Romeo, moves out West, and finds welcome wagon deficient. Mediocre songs; many dull moments. ♫Once You Find Your Guy; Sagebrush Lullaby; The Man With the Big Felt Hat. **89m/B VHS.** Irene Dunne, Fred MacMurray, William Demarest, Andy Devine, Gigi Perreau, Natalie Wood, Philip Ober, Jack Kirkwood, Ann Doran, Margaret Gibson; ***D:*** George Marshall. *TTC, FCT*

Never a Dull Moment 🦴🦴 **1968 (G)** Mobsters mistake an actor for an assassin in this gag-filled adventure. They threaten the thespian into thievery, before the trouble really starts when Ace, the actual assassin, arrives. **90m/C VHS, Beta, LV.** Dick Van Dyke, Edward G. Robinson, Dorothy Provine, Henry Silva, Joanna Moore, Tony Bill, Slim Pickens, Jack Elam; ***D:*** Jerry Paris; ***W:*** A.J. Carothers; ***M:*** Robert F. Brunner. *DIS*

Never Cry Wolf 🦴🦴🦴½ **1983 (PG)** A young biologist is sent to the Arctic to study the behavior and habitation of wolves, then becomes deeply involved with their sub-society. Based on Farley Mowat's book. Beautifully photographed. **105m/C VHS, Beta, LV.** Charles Martin Smith, Brian Dennehy, Samson Jorah; ***D:*** Carroll Ballard; ***W:*** Curtis Hanson, Sam Hamm. National Society of Film Critics Awards '83: Best Cinematography; Nominations: Academy Awards '83: Best Sound. *DIS*

Never Forget 🦴🦴 **1991** Made-for-cable-TV true story of California resident Mel Mermelstein (played by Nimoy), a survivor of Hitler's death camps who accepted a pro-Nazi group's challenge to prove in court that the Holocaust of six million Jews really happened. A sincere, well-meaning courtroom drama that just can't surmount the uncinematic nature of the source material. **94m/C VHS, Beta.** Leonard Nimoy, Blythe Danner, Dabney Coleman; ***D:*** Joseph Sargent; ***M:*** Henry Mancini. *TTC*

Never Give a Sucker an Even Break 🦴🦴🦴½ *What a Man* **1941** An almost plotless comedy, based on an idea reputedly written on a napkin by Fields (he took screenplay credit as Otis Criblecoblis), and features Fields at his most unleashed. It's something of a cult favorite, but not for all tastes. Classic chase scene ends it. Fields' last role in a feature-length film. **71m/B VHS, Beta, LV.** W.C. Fields, Gloria Jean, Franklin Pangborn, Leon Errol, Margaret Dumont; ***D:*** Eddie Cline. *MCA, BAR*

Never Let Go 🦴🦴 **1960** A man unwittingly tracks down the mastermind of a gang of racketeers. Sellers sheds his comedic image to play the ruthless and brutal gang boss, something he shouldn't have done. **91m/C VHS, Beta.** *GB* Peter Sellers, Richard Todd, Elizabeth Sellars, Carol White; ***D:*** John Guillermin; ***M:*** John Barry. *SUE*

Never Let Me Go 🦴🦴½ **1953** Implausible yet entertaining account of American newsman Gable trying to smuggle ballerina wife Tierney out of Russia. Hard to believe Gable as a one-man assault force infiltrating Russia, but enjoyable nonetheless. Based on the novel "Came the Dawn" by Roger Bax. **94m/B VHS.** Clark Gable, Gene Tierney, Richard Haydn, Bernard Miles, Kenneth More, Karel Stepanek, Theodore Bikel; ***D:*** Delmer Daves; ***W:*** Ronald Millar, George Froeschel. *MGM*

Never Love a Stranger 🦴🦴 **1958** A young man becomes a numbers runner for a mobster and ultimately winds up heading his own racket. Later he finds himself in conflict with his old boss and the district attorney. No surprises here. Based on the Harold Robbins' novel. **93m/B VHS.** John Blythe Barrymore Jr., Steve McQueen, Lita Milan, Robert Bray; ***D:*** Robert Stevens. *REP*

Never on Sunday 🦴🦴🦴 **1960** An American intellectual tries to turn a Greek prostitute into a refined woman. Fine performances and exhilarating Greek photography. Fun all around. ♫Never on Sunday. **91m/B VHS, Beta.** *GR* Melina Mercouri, Titos Vandis, Jules Dassin, Mitsos Liguisos; ***D:*** Jules Dassin; ***W:*** Jules Dassin; ***M:*** Manos Hadjidakis. Academy Awards '60: Best Song ("Never on Sunday"); Cannes Film Festival '60: Best Actress (Mercouri); Nominations: Academy Awards '60: Best Actress (Mercouri), Best Costume Design (B & W), Best Director (Dassin), Best Story & Screenplay. *MGM, HMV*

Never on Tuesday 🦴½ **1988 (R)** Two jerks from Ohio head to California and find themselves stuck midway in the desert with a beautiful girl, who has plans of her own. **90m/C VHS, Beta, LV.** Claudia Christian, Andrew Lauer, Peter Berg; ***Cameos:*** Charlie Sheen, Emilio Estevez; ***D:*** Adam Rifkin; ***W:*** Adam Rifkin. *PAR*

Never Pick Up a Stranger 🦴½ **1979** When a local hooker is murdered, her cop boyfriend, who never gives up on a case, hunts her killer with a vengeance. Extremely graphic. Also on video as "Bloodrage." **82m/C VHS, Beta.** Ian Scott, Judith-Marie Bergan, James Johnston, Lawrence Tierney; ***D:*** Joseph Bigwood. *LIV, BFV*

Never Say Die 🦴½ **1990** Two innocents are thrown into a web of international intrigue and acquit themselves rather well. Lots of explosions and car crashes for a film shot in New Zealand. **98m/C VHS, Beta.** *NZ* George Wendt, Lisa Eilbacher; ***D:*** Geoff Murphy. *JTC*

Never Say Die 🦴🦴 **1994 (R)** Ex-Special Forces soldier John Blake (Zagarino), ambushed and left to die, returns to seek vengeance on the renegade commander who betrayed him. And he has the perfect opportunity when his nemesis kidnaps a general's daughter. **99m/C VHS, LV.** Frank Zagarino, Billy Drago, Todd Jensen, Jennifer Miller, Robin Smith; ***D:*** Yossi Wein; ***W:*** Jeff Albert; ***M:*** Wendy Oldfield, Adrian Levy. *TTC, NLC*

Never Say Goodbye 🦴🦴 **1946** Cliche-ridden story about a man trying to win back his divorce-bound wife. Flynn tries hard, but the material just isn't up to par. Based on the story "Don't Ever Leave Me" by Ben and Norma Barzman. Co-screenwriter Diamond later became famous when he teamed up with Billy Wilder to script "Some Like it Hot" and "The Apartment." **97m/B VHS.** Errol Flynn, Eleanor Parker, Lucile Watson, S.Z. Sakall, Forrest Tucker, Donald Woods, Peggy Knudsen, Tom D'Andrea, Hattie McDaniel; ***D:*** James V. Kern; ***W:*** James V. Kern, I.A.L. Diamond, Lewis R. Foster. *MGM*

Never Say Never Again 🦴🦴½ **1983 (PG)** James Bond matches wits with a charming but sinister tycoon who is holding the world nuclear hostage as part of a diabolical plot by SPECTRE. Connery's return to the world of Bond after 12 years is smooth in this remake of "Thunderball" hampered by an atrocious musical score. Carrera is stunning as Fatima Blush. Although Connery is back, purists will have qualms considering this part of the "official" Bond series since longtime Bond producer, Albert "Cubby" Broccoli, had nothing to do with this endeavor. **134m/C VHS, Beta, LV.** Sean Connery, Klaus Maria Brandauer, Max von Sydow, Barbara Carrera, Kim Basinger, Edward Fox, Bernie Casey, Pamela Salem, Rowan Atkinson, Valerie Leon, Prunella Gee, Saskia Cohen Tanugi; ***D:*** Irvin Kershner. *WAR, TLF*

Never So Few 🦴🦴½ **1959** A military commander and his outnumbered troops overcome incredible odds against the Japanese. There is a lot of focus on romance, but the script and acting make a strong impression nonetheless. Based on the novel by Tom T. Chamales. **124m/C VHS, LV.** Frank Sinatra, Gina Lollobrigida, Peter Lawford, Steve McQueen, Richard Johnson, Paul Henreid, Charles Bronson; ***D:*** John Sturges; ***C:*** William H. Daniels. *MGM*

Never Steal Anything Small 🦴½ **1959** A tough union boss pushes everyone as he battles the mob for control of the waterfront. A strange musical-drama combination that will be of interest only to the most ardent Cagney and Jones fans. Based on the Maxwell Anderson/Rouben Mamoulian play "The Devil's Hornpipe." Largely forgettable songs. ♫I'm Sorry, I Want a Ferrari; I Haven't Got a Thing to Wear; It Takes Love to Make a Home; Never Steal Anything Small; Helping Out Friends. **94m/C VHS, Beta.** James Cagney, Shirley Jones, Cara Williams; ***D:*** Charles Lederer; ***M:*** Henry Mancini. *MCA*

Never Talk to Strangers 🦴🦴 **1995 (R)** Sarah Taylor (DeMornay) is an uptight criminal psychologist who gets involved with handsome stranger Tony Ramirez (Banderas) while working on the case of a serial killer (Stanton). Then Sarah finds herself the target of an increasingly malevolent stalker—and she has lots of suspects to choose from. Typical woman-in-peril film with equally standard frights but the leads certainly look good (and Banderas is a fine sex object in a bit of role reversal). Filmed in Toronto. **86m/C VHS, LV.** Rebecca DeMornay, Antonio Banderas, Harry Dean Stanton, Dennis Miller, Len Cariou, Beau Starr; ***D:*** Peter Hall; ***W:*** Lewis Green, Jordan Rush; ***C:*** Elemer Ragaly; ***M:*** Pino Donaggio. *COL*

Never Too Late to Mend 🦴🦴 **1937** Victorian British play about the abuses of the penal system which had, upon its initial London West End run, caused Queen Victoria to institute a sweeping program of prison reform. The movie caused considerably less stir. **67m/B VHS, Beta, 8mm.** *GB* Tod Slaughter, Marjorie Taylor, Jack Livesey, Ian Colin; ***D:*** David MacDonald. *VYY, MRV, SNC*

Never Too Young to Die 🦴 **1986 (R)** A young man is drawn into a provocative espionage adventure by his late father's spy associates. Together they try to discover who killed the young man's father. High point may be Simmons as a crazed hermaphrodite plotting to poison L.A. **97m/C VHS, Beta, LV.** John Stamos, Vanity, Gene Simmons, George Lazenby; ***D:*** Gil Bettman; ***W:*** Gil Bettman; ***M:*** James Newton Howard, Lennie Niehaus. *COL, NLC*

Never Wave at a WAC 🦴🦴½ *The Private Wore Skirts* **1952** A Washington socialite joins the Women's Army Corps hoping for a commission that never comes. She has to tough it out as an ordinary private. A reasonably fun ancestor of "Private Benjamin," with a cameo by Gen. Omar Bradley as himself. **87m/B VHS.** Rosalind Russell, Paul Douglas, Marie Wilson, William Ching, Arleen Whelan, Leif Erickson, Hillary Brooke, Regis Toomey; ***Cameos:*** Omar Bradley; ***D:*** Norman Z. McLeod; ***M:*** Elmer Bernstein. *NOS, DVT, HEG*

Never Weaken/Why Worry? 🦴🦴🦴 **1923** Silent comedy shorts from Harold. In "Never Weaken" (1921), Lloyd hustles customers. In "Why Worry?" (1923), he plays a wealthy young man who journeys to South America for his health and gets caught in the middle of a revolution. **78m/B VHS, Beta.** Harold Lloyd. *TLF*

The NeverEnding Story 🦴🦴🦴½ **1984 (PG)** A lonely young boy helps a warrior save the fantasy world in his book from destruction by the Nothing. A wonderful, intelligent family movie about imagination, with swell effects and a sweet but not overly sentimental script. Petersen's first English-language film, based on the novel by Michael Ende. **94m/C VHS, Beta, LV, 8mm.** Barret Oliver, Noah Hathaway, Gerald McRaney, Moses Gunn, Tami Stronach, Patricia Hayes, Sydney Bromley; ***D:*** Wolfgang Petersen; ***W:*** Wolfgang Petersen; ***M:*** Klaus Doldinger, Giorgio Moroder. *WAR, GLV, APD*

NeverEnding Story 2: The Next Chapter 🦴🦴 **1991 (PG)** Disappointing sequel to the first story that didn't end. Boy Oliver staves off life of couch potatodom reading books and escaping into fantasy land. Even the kids may wander away. But wait: contains the first Bugs Bunny theatrical cartoon in 26 years, "Box Office Bunny." **90m/C VHS, LV, 8mm.** Jonathan Brandis, Kenny Morrison, Clarissa Burt, John Wesley Shipp, Martin Umbach; ***D:*** George Miller; ***M:*** Robert Folk. *WAR, APD*

The Neverending Story 3 🦴🦴 **1994 (G)** The third time was not the charm in this case. Bastian, on the edge of puberty, is being bullied by a group at school called the Nasties. He seeks refuge in the library and enters the world of Fantasia through the "Neverending Story" tome. When the book is stolen by the Nasties, it is up to Bastian to return it. Unfortunately, the story does not have the charm of the original, trying to incorporate too much reality and not enough of dreamland. **95m/C VHS.** Jason James

Richter, Melody Kay, Freddie Jones, Jack Black, Ryan Bollman, Tracey Ellis, Kevin McNulty; ***D:*** Peter Macdonald. *NYR*

Nevil Shute's The Far Country 🦴🦴½ *The Far Country* **1985** Carl Zlintner (York), once a doctor in Hitler's army, escapes to Australia from postwar Europe to begin a new life with a new identity. Falling in love with the beautiful Jennifer Morton (Thornton), Carl hopes he's left his past behind. But nothing is every that simple. Made-for-television adaptation of the Shute novel. **120m/C VHS, Beta.** *AU* Michael York, Sigrid Thornton; ***D:*** George Miller. *NO*

The New Adventures of Pippi Longstocking 🦴½ **1988 (G)** Decent cast is trapped in another musical rehashing of the Astrid Lindgren children's books about a precocious redheaded girl and her fantastic adventures with horses, criminals, and pirates. **100m/C VHS, Beta, LV.** Tami Erin, Eileen Brennan, Dennis Dugan, Dianne Hull, George DiCenzo, John Schuck, Dick Van Patten; ***D:*** Ken Annakin; ***W:*** Ken Annakin. *COL, TVC*

The New Adventures of Tarzan **1935** Twelve episodes, each 22 minutes long, depict the adventures of Edgar Rice Burrough's tree-swinging character—Tarzan. Also known as "Tarzan and the Green Goddess." **260m/B VHS, Beta.** Bruce (Herman Brix) Bennett, Ula Holt, Frank Baker, Dale Walsh, Lewis Sargent; ***D:*** Edward Kull. *SNC, NOS, VCN*

The New Age 🦴🦴 **1994 (R)** Illusions in L.A. centering on talent agent Peter (Weller) and art designer Katherine (Davis) Witner. Katherine loses her job the same day Peter decides to quit his and suddenly the caustic duo are dependent upon each other. The trendy couple decide to open a boutique and quickly find themselves in a fiscal sinkhole and on a downhill slide. The acting is fine but the story is empty. **106m/C VHS, LV.** Peter Weller, Judy Davis, Adam West, Patrick Bauchau, Corbin Bernsen, Jonathan Hadary, Samuel L. Jackson, Patricia Heaton, Audra Lindley, Paula Marshall, Maureen Mueller, Bruce Ramsay, Sandra Seacat, Susan Traylor; ***D:*** Michael Tolkin; ***W:*** Michael Tolkin, Mark Mothersbaugh. *WAR*

The New Centurions 🦴🦴½ **1972 (R)** Rookies training for the Los Angeles Police Department get the inside info from retiring cops. Gritty and realistic drama based on the novel by former cop Joseph Wambaugh. Tends to be disjointed at times, but overall is a good adaptation of the bestseller. Scott, excellent as the retiring beat-walker, is supported well by the other performers. **103m/C VHS, Beta, LV.** George C. Scott, Stacy Keach, Jane Alexander, Scott Wilson, Erik Estrada, James B. Sikking; ***D:*** Richard Fleischer; ***W:*** Stirling Silliphant; ***M:*** Quincy Jones. *COL, FCT*

New Crime City: Los Angeles 2020 🦴½ **1994 (R)** Prisoner Tony Ricks (Rossovich) is executed and then revived thanks to technology. But there's a price to pay for his life and freedom—he must retrieve a biowarfare weapon from a prison gang and he only has 24 hours to do it. **95m/C VHS, LV.** Rick Rossovich, Stacy Keach, Sherrie Rose; ***W:*** Rick Rossovich. *NHO*

New Eden 🦴🦴 **1994 (R)** In the year 2237 wartime prisoners are condemned to a desert planet where they are preyed upon by brutal Sand Pirates. An idealistic engineer falls in love and seeks to protect his new family from a deadly confrontation. **89m/C VHS, LV.** Stephen Baldwin, Lisa Bonet, Tobin Bell, Michael Bowen, Janet Hubert-Whitten; ***D:*** Alan Metzger; ***W:*** Dan Gordon. *MCA*

New Faces of 1952 🦴🦴½ **1954** Based on the hit Broadway revue. The plot revolves around a Broadway show that is about to be closed down, and the performers who fight to keep it open. Lots of hit songs. Mel Brooks is credited as a writer, under the name Melvin Brooks. ♫C'est Si Bon; Santa Baby; Uskadara; Monotonous; Bal Petit Bal; Boston Beguine; I'm in Love with Miss Logan; Penny Candy; Time for Tea. **98m/C VHS, Beta.** Ronny Graham, Eartha Kitt, Robert Clary, Alice Ghostley, June Carroll, Carol Lawrence, Paul Lynde; ***D:*** Harry Horner. *FCT, NOS, VAI*

New Fist of Fury 🦴 **1985** During WWII, a former pickpocket becomes a martial arts whiz with the assistance of his fiancee, and fights the entire Imperial Army. **120m/C VHS, Beta.** Jackie Chan; ***D:*** Jackie Chan. *NO*

The New Frontier 🦴½ **1935** Wayne is a small-town sheriff whose predecessor, his father, was murdered. The local saloon-keeper and his gang do everything they can to prevent Wayne from bringing the culprit to justice. **59m/B VHS.** John Wayne, Muriel Evans, Murdock McQuarrie, Mary MacLaren, Warner Richmond; ***D:*** Carl Pierson. *NOS, MLB*

The New Gladiators *Woof!* **1987** In the future, criminals try to kill each other on television for public entertainment. Two such gladiators discover that the network's computer is using the games in order to take over mankind, and they attempt to stop it. Even if the special effects were any good, they couldn't save this one. **90m/C VHS, Beta.** *IT* Jared Martin, Fred Williamson, Eleanor Gold, Howard Ross, Claudio Cassinelli; ***D:*** Lucio Fulci. *MED*

The New Invisible Man 🦴🦴 **1958** A so-so Mexican adaptation of the popular H.G. Wells novel has a prisoner receiving a vanishing drug from his brother, who created it—perhaps to aid an escape attempt. Also called "H.G. Wells' New Invisible Man." **95m/B VHS.** *MX* Arturo de Cordova, Ana Luisa Peluffo, Jorge Mondragon; ***D:*** Alfredo B. Crevenna. *SNC*

New Jack City 🦴🦴½ **1991 (R)** Just say no ghetto-melodrama. Powerful performance by Snipes as wealthy Harlem drug lord sought by rebel cops Ice-T and Nelson. Music by Johnny Gill, 2 Live Crew, Ice-T and others. **101m/C VHS, LV.** Wesley Snipes, Ice-T, Mario Van Peebles, Chris Rock, Judd Nelson, Tracy C. Johns, Allen Payne, Kim Park, Vanessa Williams, Nick Ashford, Thalmus Rasulala, Michael Michele, Bill Nunn, Russell Wong; ***D:*** Mario Van Peebles; ***W:*** Keith Critchlow, Barry Michael Cooper; ***M:*** Roger Bourland, Michel Colombier. *WAR, CCB*

New Jersey Drive 🦴🦴½ **1995 (R)** Jason (Corley) has dreams of life outside the mean streets of Newark, but he jeopardizes his future by stealing cars and joyriding around the neighborhood with his friends. Unblinking realism, provided by credible actors (especially Corley, a former gang member), dialogue, and filming in the projects of Brooklyn and Queens, is nuetralized by stereotypical characters (especially the lily-white, sadistically brutal cops) and lack of a sympathetic point of view. Loosely based on a series of articles by Michel Mariott, a reporter for the "New York Times." **98m/C VHS, LV.** Sharron Corley, Gabriel Casseus, Saul Stein, Andre Moore, Donald A. Faison, Conrad Meertin Jr., Deven Eggleston; ***D:*** Nick Gomez; ***W:*** Nick Gomez; ***C:*** Adam Kimmel; ***M:*** Wendy Blackstone. Nominations: Independent Spirit Awards '96: Debut Performance (Casseus). *MCA*

The New Kids 🦴🦴 **1985 (R)** An orphaned brother and sister find out the limitations of the good neighbor policy. A sadistic gang terrorizes them after their move to a relatives' home in Florida. They go after expected revenge. **90m/C VHS, Beta, LV.** Shannon Presby, Lori Loughlin, James Spader, Eric Stoltz; ***D:*** Sean S. Cunningham; ***W:*** Brian Taggert, Stephen Gyllenhaal. *COL*

A New Kind of Love 🦴🦴½ **1963** Romantic fluff starring real-life couple Newman and Woodward who meet en route to Paris and end up falling in love. Newman plays a reporter and Woodward is a fashion designer in this light comedy set amidst the sights of Paris. **110m/C VHS, Beta.** Paul Newman, Joanne Woodward, Thelma Ritter, Eva Gabor, Maurice Chevalier, George Tobias; ***D:*** Melville Shavelson; ***W:*** Melville Shavelson; ***C:*** Daniel F. Fapp. Nominations: Academy Awards '63: Best Costume Design (Color), Best Original Score. *PAR*

The New Land 🦴🦴🦴 *Nybyggarna* **1973 (PG)** Sequel to "The Emigrants" follows Von Sydow and his family as they struggle to make their new home in the new world. Hardships include severe weather which devastates the farm, a Sioux indian uprising, and a disastrous trek to the Southwest to search for gold. Sensitive performances and direction. Based on the novels by Vilhelm Moberg. Dubbed into English. **161m/C VHS.** *SW* Max von Sydow, Liv Ullmann, Allan Edwall, Eddie Axberg, Hans Alfredson, Halvar Bjork, Peter Lindgren, Monica Zetterlund, Pierre Lindstedt, Per Oscarsson; ***D:*** Jan Troell; ***W:*** Jan Troell, Bengt Forslund; ***M:*** Bengt Ernryd, George Oddner. National Board of Review Awards '73: Best Actress (Ullmann); National Society of Film Critics Awards '73: Best Actress (Ullmann). *WAR, MOV*

A New Leaf 🦴🦴½ **1971 (G)** A playboy who has depleted his financial resources tries to win the hand of a clumsy heiress. May was the first woman to write, direct and star in a movie. She was unhappy with the cuts that were made by the studio, but that didn't seem to affect its impact with the public. Even with the cuts, the film is still funny and May's performance is worth watching. **102m/C VHS.** Walter Matthau, Elaine May, Jack Weston, George Rose, William Redfield, James Coco; ***D:*** Elaine May; ***W:*** Elaine May. *PAR, CCB*

A New Life 🦴🦴½ **1988 (PG-13)** An uptight stockbroker is abandoned by his wife. The New York singles scene beckons both of them to a new chance at life. Appealing performances cannot completely mask the old story line, but it's definitely worth a look. **104m/C VHS, Beta, LV.** Alan Alda, Ann-Margret, Hal Linden, Veronica Hamel, John Shea, Mary Kay Place, Cynthia Belliveau, Beatrice Alda; ***D:*** Alan Alda; ***W:*** Alan Alda; ***M:*** Joseph Turrin. *PAR*

New Mafia Boss 🦴½ *Crime Boss* **1972 (PG)** Italian-made plodder has Savalas taking over a huge Mafia family and all hell breaking loose. **90m/C VHS, Beta.** *IT* Telly Savalas, Lee Van Cleef, Antonio Sabato, Paolo Tedesco; ***D:*** Alberto De Martino. *VCD*

New Moon 🦴🦴½ **1940** An adaptation of the operetta by Sigmund Romberg and Oscar Hammerstein II. A French heiress traveling on a boat that is captured by pirates falls in love with their leader. Remake of the 1930 film. Includes the 1935 Robert Benchley MGM short "How to Sleep." ♫Dance Your Cares Away; Stranger in Paris; The Way They Do It in Paris; Lover Come Back; Shoes; Softly as in a Morning Sunrise; One Kiss; Troubles of the World; No More Weeping. **106m/B VHS, Beta.** Jeanette MacDonald, Nelson Eddy, Buster Keaton, Joe Yule, Jack Perrin, Mary Boland; ***D:*** Robert Z. Leonard. *MGM*

New Orleans After Dark 🦴🦴 **1958** A pair of New Orleans detectives tour the city, crime-buster style, and bag a dope ring. Average crime tale, shot on location in the Big Easy. **69m/B VHS.** Stacy Harris, Louis Sirgo, Ellen Moore; ***D:*** John Sledge. *NOS, LOO*

New Pastures 🦴🦴½ **1962** Three ex-convicts run into some humorous situations when they go back to their small hometown. A semi-acclaimed Czech comedy, with subtitles. **92m/B VHS, Beta.** *CZ* ***D:*** Vladimir Cech. *IHF*

New Year's Day 🦴🦴🦴 **1989 (R)** Jaglom continues his look at modern relationships in this story of a man reclaiming his house from three female tenants. Introspective character study lightened by humor and insight. **90m/C VHS, Beta.** Maggie Jakobson, Gwen Welles, Melanie Winter, Milos Forman, Michael Emil, David Duchovny, Tracy Reiner, Henry Jaglom; ***D:*** Henry Jaglom; ***W:*** Henry Jaglom. *PAR, BTV, FCT*

New Year's Evil *Woof!* **1978 (R)** Every hour during a New Year's Eve concert, a madman kills an unsuspecting victim. After each killing, the murderer informs a local disc jockey of his deed. Little does the disc jockey know that she will soon be next on his list. No suspense, bad music makes this slash and crash a holiday wrecker. **88m/C VHS, Beta.** Roz Kelly, Kip Niven, Chris Wallace, Louisa Moritz, Grant Kramer, Jed Mills; ***D:*** Emmett Alston; ***W:*** Emmett Alston. *CAN*

New York Cop 🦴½ **1994 (R)** Japanese martial arts expert Toshi (Nakamura) joins the NYPD and is given an undercover assignment to infiltrate a gun-running gang that supplies both drug lords and Japanese mobsters. But internal rivalries force Toshi to bond with gang leader Hawk (McQueen) and the duo to do battle together. **88m/C VHS.** Toru Nakamura, Chad McQueen, Mira Sorvino; ***D:*** Toru Murakawa. *COL*

New York, New York 🦴🦴🦴 **1977 (PG)** Tragic romance evolves between a saxophonist and an aspiring singer/actress in this salute to the big-band era. A love of music isn't enough to hold them together through career rivalries and life on the road. Fine performances by De Niro and Minnelli and the supporting cast. Re-released in 1981 with the "Happy Endings" number, which was cut from the original. Look for "Big Man" Clarence Clemons on sax. ♫New York, New York; There Goes the Ball Game; Happy Endings; But the World Goes 'Round; Night in Tunisia; Opus One; Avalon; You Brought a New Kind of Love to Me; I'm Getting Sentimental Over You. **163m/C VHS, Beta, LV.** Robert De Niro, Liza Minnelli, Lionel Stander, Barry Primus, Mary Kay Place, Dick Miller, Diahnne Abbott; ***D:*** Martin Scorsese; ***W:*** Mardik Martin; ***M:*** Ralph Burns. *FOX*

New York Nights 🦴 **1984 (R)** The lives of nine New Yorkers intertwine in a treacherous game of passion and seduction. Liberal borrowing from plot of "La Ronde." **104m/C VHS, Beta.** Corinne Alphen, George Auyer, Bobbi Burns, Peter Matthey, Cynthia Lee, Willem Dafoe; ***D:*** Simon Nuchtern. *LIV*

New York Ripper *Woof!* **1982** A New York cop tracks down a rampaging murderer in this dull, mindless slasher flick. **88m/C VHS, Beta.** *IT* Fred Williamson; ***D:*** Lucio Fulci. *VMK*

New York Stories 🦴🦴🦴 **1989 (PG)** Entertaining anthology of three separate short films by three esteemed directors, all set in New York. In "Life Lessons" by Scorsese, an impulsive artist tries to prevent his live-in girlfriend from leaving him. "Life Without Zoe" by Coppola involves a youngster's fantasy about a wealthy 12-year-old who lives mostly without her parents. Allen's "Oedipus Wrecks," generally considered the best short, is about a 50-year-old man who is tormented by the specter of his mother. **124m/C VHS, Beta, LV.** Nick Nolte, Rosanna Arquette, Woody Allen, Mia Farrow, Mae Questel, Julie Kavner, Talia Shire, Giancarlo Giannini, Don Novello, Patrick O'Neal, Peter Gabriel, Paul Herman, Deborah Harry, Steve Buscemi, Heather McComb, Chris Elliott, Carole Bouquet, Edward I. Koch; ***D:*** Woody Allen, Martin Scorsese, Francis Ford Coppola; ***W:*** Woody Allen, Francis Ford Coppola, Richard Price, Sofia Coppola; ***C:*** Sven Nykvist, Nestor Almendros; ***M:*** Carmine Coppola. *TOU*

New York's Finest 🦴 **1987 (R)** Three prostitutes are determined to leave their calling and marry very eligible millionaires. But becoming society ladies is more difficult than they thought. Would-be sophisticated comedy misfires. **80m/C VHS, Beta.** Ruth Collins, Jennifer Delora, Scott Thompson Baker, Heidi Paine, Jane Hamilton, Alan Naggar, John Altamura, Alan Fisler, Josey Duval; ***D:*** Chuck Vincent. *ACA*

The Newlydeads 🦴½ **1987** An uptight, conservative, honeymoon resort owner murders one of his guests and finds out that "she" is really a he. Fifteen years later, on his wedding night, all of his guests are violently murdered by the transvestite's vengeful ghost. Oddball twist to the usual slasher nonsense. **84m/C VHS, Beta.** Scott Kaske, Jim Williams, Jean Levine, Jay Richardson; ***D:*** Joseph Merhi. *NO*

Newman's Law 🦴🦴 **1974 (PG)** A city detective is implicated in a corruption investigation. While on suspension, he continues with his own investigation of a large drug ring and finds corruption is closer than he thought. Director Heffron's first feature film. **98m/C VHS, Beta.** George Peppard, Roger Robinson, Eugene Roche, Gordon Pinsent, Louis Zorich, Abe Vigoda; ***D:*** Richard T. Heffron. *MCA*

News at Eleven 🦴🦴 **1986** A fading news anchorman is pressured by his ambitious young boss to expose a touchy local sex scandal, forcing him to consider the public's right to know versus the rights of the individual. About average for made-for-television drama. **95m/C VHS, Beta, LV.** Martin Sheen, Peter Riegert, Barbara Babcock, Sheree J. Wilson, Sydney Penny, David S. Sheiner, Christopher Allport; ***D:*** Mike Robe. *TTC*

News from Home 🦴🦴 **1976** Scenes of life in New York are juxtaposed with voiceover from the letters of a mother to her young daughter. Plotless narrative deals with the small details of life. **85m/C VHS.** ***D:*** Chantal Akerman; ***W:*** Chantal Akerman. *WAC, FCT*

Newsfront 🦴🦴🦴 **1978** A story about two brothers, both newsreel filmmakers, and their differing approaches to life and their craft in the 1940s and '50s. Tribute to the days of newsreel film combines real stories and fictionalized accounts with color and black and white photography. Noyce's feature film debut. **110m/C VHS, LV.** *AU* Bill Hunter, Gerard Kennedy, Angela Punch McGregor, Wendy Hughes, Chris Haywood, John Ewart, Bryan Brown; ***D:*** Phillip Noyce. Australian Film Institute '78: Best Actor (Hunter), Best Film. *SUE*

Newsies 🦴½ **1992 (PG)** An unfortunate attempt at an old-fashioned musical with a lot of cute kids and cardboard characters and settings. The plot, such as it is, concerns the 1899 New York newsboys strike against penny-pinching publisher Joseph Pulitzer. Bale plays the newsboy's leader and at least shows some charisma in a strictly cartoon setting. The songs are mediocre but the dancing is lively. However, none of it moves the story along. Add a bone for viewers under 12. Choreographer Ortega's feature-film directorial debut. **121m/C VHS, Beta.** Christian Bale, Bill Pullman, Robert Duvall, Ann-Margret, Michael Lerner, Kevin Tighe, Charles Cioffi, Luke Edwards, Max Casella, David Moscow; ***D:*** Kenny Ortega; ***M:*** Alan Menken, Jack Feldman. Golden Raspberry Awards '92: Worst Song ("High Times, Hard Times"). *DIS*

Next Door 🦴🦴½ **1994 (R)** Matt and Karen have the perfect suburban home—complete with the perfect suburban garden. Then their boorish neighbor Lenny takes to enthusiastic lawn watering and ruins their flowers. One thing leads to a full-scale feud. Made for cable TV. **95m/C VHS.** James Woods, Randy Quaid, Kate Capshaw; ***D:*** Tony Bill; ***W:*** Barney Cohen. *COL*

The Next Karate Kid 🦴🦴½ **1994 (PG)** Fourth installment in the "Kid" series finds martial arts expert Miyagi (Morita) training Julie Pierce (Swank), the orphaned tomboy daughter of an old war buddy who saved his life 50 years earlier. He even teaches her the waltz, just in time for the prom, but she's still tough enough to scrap with a guy. A must-see for "Karate Kid" fans, if there are any left. **107m/C VHS, LV.** Noriyuki "Pat" Morita, Hilary Swank; ***D:*** Christopher Cain; ***W:*** Mark Lee; ***M:*** Bill Conti. *COL*

Next of Kin 🦴 **1982** A daughter moves into her dead mother's retirement home and discovers an unspeakable evil that lurks there. Typical horror stuff has some very creepy moments; filmed in New Zealand. **90m/C VHS, Beta, LV, 8mm.** *AU* Jackie Kerin, John Jarratt, Gerida Nicholson, Alex Scott; ***D:*** Tony Williams. *NO*

Next of Kin 🦴🦴 **1984** A young man experiencing familial difficulties undergoes experimental video therapy where he views a videotape of an Armenian family who gave their son up for adoption. When he discovers the actual family he insinuates himself into their life, determined to be their long-lost son. **72m/C VHS.** *CA* Patrick Tierney; ***D:*** Atom Egoyan; ***W:*** Atom Egoyan. *CVC, FCT, INJ*

Next of Kin 🦴🦴 **1989 (R)** A Chicago cop returns to his Kentucky home to avenge his brother's brutal murder. Swayze's return to action films after his success in "Dirty Dancing" is unimpressive. **108m/C VHS, Beta, LV, 8mm.** Patrick Swayze, Adam Baldwin, Bill Paxton, Helen Hunt, Andreas Katsulas, Ben Stiller, Michael J. Pollard, Liam Neeson; ***D:*** John Irvin; ***C:*** Steven Poster; ***M:*** Jack Nitzsche. *WAR*

Next One 🦴½ **1984** Mysterious visitor from another time winds up on an isolated Greek island as the result of a magnetic storm. The local inhabitants are amazed when the visitor displays some Christ-like characteristics. **105m/C VHS, Beta.** Keir Dullea, Adrienne Barbeau, Jeremy Licht, Peter Hobbs; ***D:*** Nico Mastorakis. *VES*

Next Stop, Greenwich Village 🦴🦴🦴 **1976 (R)** An affectionate, autobiographical look by Mazursky at a Brooklyn boy with acting aspirations, who moves to Greenwich Village in 1953. Good performances, especially by Winters as the overbearing mother. **109m/C VHS.** Lenny Baker, Christopher Walken, Ellen Greene, Shelley Winters, Lou Jacobi, Mike Kellin; ***D:*** Paul Mazursky; ***W:*** Paul Mazursky; ***M:*** Bill Conti. Nominations: Cannes Film Festival '76: Best Film. *FXV*

Next Summer 🦴🦴🦴 *L'Ete Prochain* **1984** A large, character-studded French family pursues power, love and beauty. Excellent performances. In French with English subtitles. **120m/C VHS, Beta.** *FR* Jean-Louis Trintignant, Claudia Cardinale, Fanny Ardant, Philippe Noiret, Marie Trintignant; ***D:*** Nadine Trintignant. *TPV, FCT, INJ*

Next Time I Marry 🦴½ **1938** Lucy fraternizes with ditch digger Ellison because she needs to hitch a Yankee in order to inherit $20 mill. Seems she really loves a foreigner, though. Not much to bobaloo about. Director Kanin's second effort. **65m/B VHS.** Lucille Ball, James Ellison, Lee Bowman, Granville Bates, Mantan Moreland, Florence Lake; ***D:*** Garson Kanin. *TTC, FCT, MLB*

The Next Victim 🦴 *Lo Strano Vizio Della Signora Wardh* **1971 (PG)** The unfaithful wife of an Austrian diplomat attempts to find out who has been slicing up beautiful jet-setters. Tepid mystery. **87m/C VHS, Beta.** George Hilton, Edwige French, Christina Airoldi, Ivan Rassimov; ***D:*** Sergio Martino. *GEM, CNG*

Next Victim 🦴 **1974** A beautiful woman confined to a wheelchair is stalked by a lunatic killer. You've seen it before, and done better. **80m/C VHS, Beta.** *GB* Carroll Baker, T.P. McKenna, Ronald Lacey, Maurice Kaufman; ***D:*** James Ormerod. *LIV*

The Next Voice You Hear 🦴🦴½ **1950** Lives are changed forever when a group of people hear the voice of God on the radio. Interesting premise presented seriously. **84m/B VHS, Beta.** James Whitmore, Nancy Davis, Gary Gray, Lillian Bronson, Art Smith, Tom D'Andrea, Jeff Corey, George Chandler; ***D:*** William A. Wellman. *MGM*

Next Year If All Goes Well 🦴🦴½ **1983** Two young lovers struggle to overcome insecurities while establishing a relationship. Dubbed. **95m/C VHS, Beta.** *FR* Isabelle Adjani, Thierry Lhermitte, Mariann Chazel; ***D:*** Jean-Loup Hubert. *VTR*

Niagara 🦴🦴½ **1952** During their honeymoon in Niagara Falls, a scheming wife (Monroe) plans to kill her crazed war-vet husband (Cotten). Little does she know that he is plotting to double-cross her. Steamy, quasi-Hitchcockian mystery ably directed, with interesting performances. Monroes sings "Kiss." **89m/B VHS, Beta, LV.** Joseph Cotten, Jean Peters, Marilyn Monroe, Max Casey Adams Showalter, Don Wilson; ***D:*** Henry Hathaway. *FOX*

Nice Girl Like Me 🦴🦴 **1969 (PG)** An orphaned young girl roams Europe, getting pregnant twice by two different men. She eventually finds love in the form of a kind caretaker. Harmless fluff. Based on Anne Piper's novel "Marry At Leisure." **91m/C VHS, Beta.** *GB* Harry Andrews, Barbara Ferris, Gladys Cooper, Bill Hinnant, James Villiers; ***D:*** Desmond Davis. *NLC*

Nice Girls Don't Explode 🦴🦴 **1987 (PG)** A girl telekinetically starts fires when sexually aroused. This puts a bit of a damper on her relationship with O'Leary, much to her mother's delight. Matchless entertainment. **92m/C VHS, Beta.** Barbara Harris, Wallace Shawn, Michelle Meyrink, William O'Leary; ***D:*** Chuck Martinez; ***M:*** Brian Banks. *VTR, NWV*

Nice Neighbor 🦴🦴🦴 **1979** An acclaimed film about an outwardly self-sacrificing neighbor who cold-bloodedly manipulates his fellow rooming house tenants for his own ends. In Hungarian with English subtitles. **90m/C VHS, Beta.** *HU* Laszlo Szabo, Margit Dayka, Agi Margittay; ***D:*** Zsolt Kedzi-Kovacs. *FCT*

Nicholas and Alexandra 🦴🦴½ **1971 (PG)** Epic chronicling the final years of Tsar Nicholas II, Empress Alexandra and their children. Their lavish royal lifestyle gives way to imprisonment and eventual execution under the new Lenin government. Beautiful, but overlong costume epic that loses steam in the second half. Based on the biography by Robert Massie. Available in widescreen format on laserdisc. **183m/C VHS, Beta, LV.** Michael Jayston, Janet Suzman, Tom Baker, Laurence Olivier, Michael Redgrave, Harry Andrews, Jack Hawkins, Alexander Knox, Curt Jurgens; ***D:*** Franklin J. Schaffner; ***C:*** Frederick A. (Freddie) Young; ***M:*** Richard Rodney Bennett. Academy Awards '71: Best Art Direction/Set Decoration, Best Costume Design; National Board of Review Awards '71: 10 Best Films of the Year; Nominations: Academy Awards '71: Best Actress (Suzman), Best Cinematography, Best Picture, Best Original Score. *COL, TVC*

Nicholas Nickleby ♥♥♥ *The Life and Adventures of Nicholas Nickleby* **1946** An ensemble cast works hard to bring to life Charles Dickens' novel about an impoverished family dependent on their wealthy but villainous uncle. Young Nicholas is an apprentice at a school for boys, and he and a student run away to a series of exciting adventures. An enjoyable film, though it is hard to tell the entire story in such a small amount of time. **108m/B VHS, Beta.** *GB* Cedric Hardwicke, Stanley Holloway, Derek Bond, Alfred Drayton, Sybil Thorndike, Sally Ann Howes, Bernard Miles, Mary Merrall, Cathleen Nesbitt; ***D:*** Alberto Cavalcanti; ***C:*** Georges Perinal. *MRV, PSM, DVT*

Nick Knight ♥♥ **198?** An L.A. cop on the night beat is really a good-guy vampire, who quaffs cattle blood as he tracks down another killer who's draining humans of their plasma. A gimmicky pilot for a would-be TV series that never bit. **92m/C VHS.** Rick Springfield, Michael Nader, Laura Johnson. *VTR*

Nick of Time ♥½ **1995 (R)** A malicious stranger (Walken) and his cohort give ordinary accountant Gene Watson (Depp) 90 minutes to assassinate the governor of California (Mason) or his little girl will be killed. Walken as an evil psycho...now there's a stretch. On the other hand, Depp as a button-down, conservative widower is a bit off a switch after his usually quirky roles of the recent past. This may be the first time Depp's picked up a gun since "21 Jump Street." Illogical scenarios (even for an action flick) and curiously uneven pacing do this one in. Shot almost entirely in L.A's Bonaventure Hotel in real time with a handheld camera. **98m/C VHS, Beta.** Johnny Depp, Christopher Walken, Charles S. Dutton, Peter Strauss, Roma Maffia, Gloria Reuben, Marsha Mason, Courtney Chase, Bill Smitrovich, G.D. Spradlin; ***D:*** John Badham; ***W:*** Patrick Duncan; ***C:*** Roy Wagner; ***M:*** Arthur B. Rubinstein. *PAR*

Nickel & Dime ♥♥ **1992 (PG)** A con artist's luck turns bad when the IRS catches up with him, impounds all his worldly goods, and sticks him with an officious auditor. But if Jack can find the heiress to a fortune, within 48 hours, he can claim a hefty finder's fee and his money worries will be a thing of the past. **96m/C VHS.** C. Thomas Howell, Wallace Shawn, Lise Cutter, Lynn Danielson, Roy Brocksmith; ***D:*** Ben Moses; ***W:*** Seth Front, Eddy Polon, Ben Moses. *COL*

Nickel Mountain ♥♥½ **1985** Heartwarming story of a suicidal 40-year-old man who finds a new reason to live when he falls in love with a pregnant 16-year-old girl who works at his diner. Langenkamp particularly appealing. Based on a John Gardner novel. **88m/C VHS, Beta.** Michael Cole, Heather Langenkamp, Ed Lauter, Brian Kerwin, Patrick Cassidy, Grace Zabriskie, Don Beddoe; ***D:*** Drew Denbaum. *ORI*

Nicole ♥ **1972 (R)** The downfall of a wealthy woman who is able to buy everything she wants except love. **91m/C VHS, Beta.** Leslie Caron, Catherine Bach, Ramon Bieri; ***D:*** Itsvan Ventilla. *GHV*

The Night After Halloween ♥ **1983 (R)** A young woman gets the shock of her life when she discovers that her boyfriend is a crazed killer. **90m/C VHS, Beta.** *IT* Chantal Contouri, Robert Bruning, Sigrid Thornton. *NO*

Night After Night ♥♥½ **1932** West's screen debut finds her in an unaccustomed secondary role, although a prime scene-stealer. In Raft's first starring role, he's a monied low-life who opens a fancy nightclub and becomes infatuated with Park Avenue beauty Cummings. His problems are compounded by the arrival of raucous ex-flames West and Gleason. When a hatcheck girl cries "Goodness!" over West's diamonds, she replies, in suggestive West-style, "Goodness had nothing to do with it, dearie." Adapted from the novel "Single Night" by Louis Bromfield. **73m/B VHS.** George Raft, Constance Cummings, Mae West, Wynne Gibson, Alison Skipworth, Roscoe Karns, Louis Calhern; ***D:*** Archie Mayo; ***W:*** Mae West, Kathryn Scola, Vincent Lawrence. *MCA*

Night Ambush ♥♥½ *Ill Met By Moonlight* **1957** A Nazi general is kidnapped on Crete by British agents, who embark on a dangerous trip to the coast where a ship awaits to take them to Cairo. The general tries to thwart their plans, but they outwit him at every turn. Based on a novel by W. Stanley Moss that details a similar real-life event. **100m/B VHS.** *GB* Dirk Bogarde, Marius Goring, David Oxley, Cyril Cusack, Christopher Lee; ***D:*** Michael Powell, Emeric Pressburger. *NO*

Night and Day ♥♥½ **1946** Sentimental musical about the life of bon-vivant composer-extraordinaire Cole Porter. His intensity and the motivations for his music are dramatized, but this film succeeds best as a fabulous showcase for Porter's songs. ♫Begin the Beguine; My Heart Belongs to Daddy; You're the Top; I've Got You Under My Skin; Just One of Those Things; I Get a Kick Out of You; Night and Day; What Is This Thing Called Love; Do I Love You. **128m/C VHS, Beta.** Cary Grant, Alexis Smith, Jane Wyman, Eve Arden, Mary Martin, Alan Hale, Monty Woolley, Ginny Simms, Dorothy Malone; ***D:*** Michael Curtiz; ***M:*** Max Steiner. Nominations: Academy Awards '46: Best Original Score. *MGM, FCT*

Night and Day ♥♥♥ *Nuit et Jour* **1991** Charming adult romance about Jack and Julie, young lovers newly arrived in Paris. When Jack gets a night job driving a cab, Julie finds her evenings lonely. But not for long. She meets Joseph, a cab driver on the day shift. Soon, Julie is juggling sexual affairs with both men and everything gets increasingly complicated. Her lovers find out about each other but Julie doesn't want to fully commit to either of them. In French with English subtitles. **90m/C VHS.** *FR BE SI* Guilaine Londez, Thomas Langmann, Francois Negret; ***D:*** Chantal Akerman; ***W:*** Pascal Bonitzer, Chantal Akerman; ***M:*** Marc Herouet. *FXL, ORI, FCT*

Night and the City ♥♥♥½ **1950** A film noir classic about a hustler's money-making schemes. Widmark is Harry Fabian, a small-time promoter working for slimy nightclub owner Sullivan, whose job is to hustle the marks into the club where his girlfriend Tierney is the singer. Widmark also happens to be romancing Sullivan's wife, Withers, and wants her to back his latest con. But his schemes go awry and Fabian's on the run for his life. Widmark gives a riveting performance of a lowlife whose brains don't match his ambitions. Filmed in London with appropriate brooding tawdriness. Adapted from the novel by Gerald Kersh; remade in 1992. **95m/B VHS.** *GB* Richard Widmark, Gene Tierney, Googie Withers, Francis L. Sullivan, Hugh Marlowe, Herbert Lom, Mike Mazurki, Charles Farrell; ***D:*** Jules Dassin; ***W:*** Jo Eisinger; ***M:*** Franz Waxman. *FXV, MOV, RXM*

Night and the City ♥♥♥ **1992 (R)** Harry Fabian (De Niro), a con-artist/ambulance-chaser, concocts a scheme to make it big, and approaches an old boxing great (Warden) to come out of retirement and revive a local boxing night. Problem is, although Harry has energy and ambition, he also has a talent for making enemies out of the wrong people, like the boxer's brother (King), a neighborhood mobster. Filled with details more interesting than the plot; more about fast-living, fast-talking New Yorkers, a fine showcase for De Niro's talent. Winkler's remake of the 1950 Jules Dassin film. **98m/C VHS, LV.** Robert De Niro, Jessica Lange, Cliff Gorman, Alan King, Jack Warden, Eli Wallach, Barry Primus, Gene Kirkwood, Pedro Sanchez; ***Cameos:*** Regis Philbin, Joy Philbin, Richard Price; ***D:*** Irwin Winkler; ***W:*** Richard Price; ***C:*** Tak Fujimoto; ***M:*** James Newton Howard. *FXV*

Night Angel ♥ **1990 (R)** A beautiful seductress lures men into a deadly trap from which only true love can free them. **90m/C VHS, Beta, LV.** Isa Anderson, Linda Ashby, Debra Feuer, Helen Martin, Karen Black; ***D:*** Dominique Othenin-Girard; ***W:*** Joe Augustyn. *FRH*

A Night at the Opera ♥♥♥♥ **1935** The Marx Brothers get mixed up with grand opera in their first MGM-produced epic and their first without Zeppo. Jones, as a budding opera singer warbles "Alone" and "Cosi Cosa." One of their best films, blessed with a big budget—used to reach epic anarchic heights. Some scenes were tested on live audiences before inclusion, including the Groucho/Chico paper-tearing contract negotiation and the celebrated stateroom scene, in which the boys are joined in a small closet by two maids, the ship's engineer, his assistant, a manicurist, a young woman, a cleaning lady, and four food-laden waiters. Laserdisc includes letterboxing, digital sound, original trailers, production photos, memorabilia, and soundtrack commentary by film critic Leonard Maltin. **92m/B VHS, Beta, LV.** Groucho Marx, Chico Marx, Harpo Marx, Allan Jones, Kitty Carlisle Hart, Sig Rumann, Margaret Dumont, Walter Woolf King; ***D:*** Sam Wood; ***W:*** George S. Kaufman, Morrie Ryskind, Bert Kalmar, Harry Ruby, Al Boasberg; ***M:*** Herbert Stothart. *MGM, CRC, CCB*

Night Beast ♥ **1983** Alien creature lands his spaceship near a small town and begins a bloody killing spree. Recycled plot. **90m/C VHS, Beta.** Tom Griffith, Dick Dyszel, Jaimie Zemarel; ***D:*** Donald M. Dohler. *NO*

Night Beat ♥½ **1948** A labored crime drama from postwar Britain. Two army pals pursue diverging careers. One becomes a cop, the other a crook. Want to bet that they meet again? **95m/B VHS.** *GB* Anne Crawford, Maxwell Reed, Ronald Howard, Christine Norden; ***D:*** Harold Huth. *LOO*

The Night Before ♥♥½ **1988 (PG-13)** Snobby high school beauty Loughlin loses a bet and has to go to the prom with the school geek Reeves. On the way, they get lost on the wrong side of the tracks, and become involved with pimps, crime and the police. A drunken Reeves loses Loughlin as well as his father's car. Typical teen farce. **90m/C VHS, Beta.** Keanu Reeves, Lori Loughlin, Trinidad Silva, Michael Greene, Theresa Saldana, Suzanne Snyder, Morgan Lofting, Gwil Richards; ***D:*** Thom Eberhardt; ***W:*** Gregory Scherick, Thom Eberhardt. *HBO*

Night Birds ♥ **1931** Early British thriller about a notorious crook named "Flash Jack," who heads a gang of top-hatted criminals that rob the wealthy. Poor production quality and Raine's standoffish screen presence contribute to this below-average film. **76m/B VHS.** *GB* Jameson Thomas, Jack Raine, Muriel Angelus, Eve Gray; ***D:*** Richard Eichberg; ***W:*** Miles Malleson. *SNC*

Night Breed ♥½ **1990 (R)** A teenager flees a chaotic past to slowly become a member of a bizarre race of demons that live in a huge, abandoned Canadian graveyard; a place where every sin is forgiven. Based on Barker's novel "Cabal," and appropriately gross, nonsensical and strange. Good special effects almost save this one. **102m/C VHS, Beta, LV.** *CA* Craig Sheffer, Anne Bobby, David Cronenberg, Charles Haid; ***D:*** Clive Barker; ***W:*** Clive Barker. *MED*

The Night Brings Charlie ♥½ **1990** A disfigured tree surgeon is the prime suspect in some grisly murders committed with a tree trimming saw. Obviously, everyone in the town fears him as a result. Not a sequel to "Roots." **90m/C VHS.** Kerry Knight, Joe Fishback, Aimee Tenalia, Monica Simmons; ***D:*** Tom Logan. *NO*

Night Call Nurses ♥♥ **1972 (R)** Three gorgeous nurses find danger and intrigue on the night shift at a psychiatric hospital. Third in the "nurse" quintet is back on target, shrugging off the previous film's attempts at "serious" social commentary. Miller provides comic relief. Preceded by "The Student Nurses" and "Private Duty Nurses" and followed by "The Young Nurses," and "Candy Stripe Nurses." Also on video as "Young L.A. Nurses 2." **85m/C VHS, Beta.** Patricia T. Byrne, Alana Collins, Mittie Lawrence, Clinton Kimbrough, Felton Perry, Stack Pierce, Richard Young, Dennis Dugan, Dick Miller; ***D:*** Jonathan Kaplan; ***W:*** George Armitage. *NLC*

Night Caller from Outer Space 🦴½ *Blood Beast from Outer Space; The Night Caller* **1966** When a woman-hunting alien arrives in London, women begin to disappear. At first, incredibly, no one makes the connection, but then the horrible truth comes to light. **84m/B VHS, Beta, LV.** *GB* John Saxon, Maurice Denham, Patricia Haines, Alfred Burke, Jack Watson, Aubrey Morris; ***D:*** John Gilling. *COL*

Night Children 🦴 **1989 (R)** Tough L.A. cop teams with a parole officer to battle a nasty gang leader. The battle is quite violent and senseless. **90m/C VHS, Beta.** David Carradine, Nancy Kwan, Griffin O'Neal, Tawny Fere; ***D:*** Norbert Meisel. *VMK*

The Night Club 🦴🦴½ **1925** Swinging single stands to gain fortune if he weds a certain girl, and, as luck would have it, he falls for her. When the usual hearts and roses don't convince her he's earnest, he tries to prove his love is true by attempting suicide and hiring a hit man. **62m/B VHS, Beta.** Raymond Griffith, Vera Reynolds, Wallace Beery, Louise Fazenda; ***D:*** Frank Urson. *GPV*

Night Creature 🦴 *Out of the Darkness; Fear* **1979 (PG)** A tough, Hemingway-type writer is determined to destroy the man-eating black leopard which nearly killed him once before. Filmed in Thailand. **83m/C VHS, Beta.** Donald Pleasence, Nancy Kwan, Ross Hagen; ***D:*** Lee Madden. *VCI*

Night Cries 🦴🦴½ **1978** After a woman's baby dies at birth, she has persistent dreams that he is alive and in trouble. No one will believe her when she tells them that something is wrong. Made for television. **100m/C VHS, Beta.** Susan St. James, Michael Parks, William Conrad; ***D:*** Richard Lang. *WOV*

Night Crossing 🦴🦴½ **1981 (PG)** The fact-based story of two East German families who launch a daring escape to the West in a homemade hot air balloon. Exciting action for the whole family. **106m/C VHS, Beta.** John Hurt, Jane Alexander, Glynnis O'Connor, Doug McKeon, Beau Bridges; ***D:*** Delbert Mann; ***W:*** John McGreevey; ***M:*** Jerry Goldsmith. *DIS*

The Night Cry 🦴🦴 **1926** Silent canine melodrama has sheep-murdering dog sentenced to death row until he saves little girl from unbelievably big bird. **65m/B VHS, Beta.** John Harron, June Marlowe, Mary Louise Miller; ***D:*** Herman C. Raymaker. *GPV, GVV*

The Night Evelyn Came Out of the Grave 🦴½ *La Notte Che Evelyn Usca Dalla Tomba* **1971 (R)** A wealthy Italian playboy, obsessed with his dead, flame-haired wife, lures living redheads into his castle, where he tortures and kills them. Standard '70s Euro/horror/sex stuff enlivened by the presence of the incredible Erika Blanc as a stripper who works out of a coffin. **99m/C VHS.** *IT* Anthony Steffen, Marina Malfatti, Rod Murdock, Erika Blanc, Giacomo "Jack" Rossi-Stuart, Umberto Raho; ***D:*** Emilio P. Miraglio. *FRG*

Night Eyes 🦴 *Hidden Vision* **1990 (R)** Surveillance can be a dangerous profession, especially when your boss happens to be the jealous husband of a very sexy woman. Watching turns to yearning for this professional peeper, but he may just get more than he bargained for. Roberts is worth watching. **95m/C VHS, Beta, LV.** Andrew Stevens, Tanya Roberts, Warwick Sims, Cooper Huckabee; ***D:*** Emilio P. Miraglio; ***W:*** Tom Citrano. *PSM*

Night Eyes 2 🦴½ **1991 (R)** A security expert assigned to protect the sultry wife of a foreign diplomat finds himself spending a little too much time eyeing her through his hidden cameras. Soon he can no longer control his desire and he makes a move on her that may have international implications. Also available in an unrated version. **97m/C VHS, Beta.** Andrew Stevens, Shannon Tweed, Tim Russ, Richard Chaves, Geno Silva; ***D:*** Rodney McDonald. *PSM*

Night Eyes 3 🦴🦴 **1993 (R)** Night Eyes Security boss Stevens' latest assignment is to protect the superstar lead (Shannon Tweed) of a top TV cop show from a stalker. They wind up in very close contact but someone is videotaping their private moments which don't stay private for long. Maybe onscreen partner Tracy (Shannon's sister) has something to do with it. Also available in an unrated version. **97m/C VHS, Beta.** Andrew Stevens, Shannon Tweed, Tracy Tweed, Tristan Rogers; ***D:*** Andrew Stevens; ***W:*** Andrew Stevens, Michael W. Potts. *PSM*

Night Eyes 4: Fatal Passion 🦴½ **1995 (R)** Beverly Hills shrink gets involved with the bodyguard hired to protect her from a stalker. Also available unrated. **101m/C VHS.** Paula Barbieri, Jeff Trachta, Andrew Stevens; ***D:*** Rodney McDonald; ***W:*** John Eubanks, Henry Krinkle; ***C:*** Gary Graver; ***M:*** Patrick Seymour. *PSM*

Night Fire 🦴½ **1994 (R)** Barry wants wife Lydia to try to rekindle the passion in their marriage by getting away for the weekend at their remote ranch. But they're interrupted in their leisure by the stranded Cal and Gwen. Only it turns out Barry has hired the duo, who like kinky games, to peak Lydia's interest. She's merely disgusted and Barry gets nasty. Also available unrated. **93m/C VHS.** Shannon Tweed, John Laughlin, Martin Hewitt, Rochelle Swanson; ***D:*** Mike Sedan; ***W:*** Catherine Tavel, Helen Haxton. *TRI*

Night Flight from Moscow 🦴🦴½ *The Serpent* **1973 (PG)** A Soviet spy defects with a fistful of secret documents that implicate every free government. Then the CIA must decide if he's telling the truth. Complex espionage thriller. **113m/C VHS, Beta.** *FR IT GE* Yul Brynner, Henry Fonda, Dirk Bogarde, Virna Lisi, Philippe Noiret, Farley Granger, Robert Alda, Marie DuBois, Elga Andersen; ***D:*** Henri Verneuil; ***M:*** Ennio Morricone. *NLC*

A Night for Crime 🦴🦴 **1942** A movie star disappears during the filming of a movie. When she turns up dead, a bumbling cop suspects everyone on the set. **75m/B VHS.** Glenda Farrell, Lyle Talbot, Lena Basquette, Donald Kirke, Ralph Sanford; ***D:*** Alexis Thurn-Taxis. *NOS, DVT*

Night Friend 🦴 **1987 (R)** A priest sets out to help a young woman caught up in a world of drug abuse and prostitution. Exploitation morality flick. **94m/C VHS, Beta.** Art Carney, Chuck Shamata, Jayne Eastwood, Heather Kjollesdal; ***D:*** Peter Gerretsen. *PSM*

A Night Full of Rain 🦴½ *End of the World (in Our Usual Bed in a Night Full of Rain)* **1978 (R)** Italian communist tries unsuccessfully to seduce vacationing American feminist. They meet again in San Francisco and wedding bells chime. They argue. They argue more. They put all but rabid Wertmuller fans to sleep. The director's first English-language film. **104m/C VHS.** *IT* Giancarlo Giannini, Candice Bergen, Anne Byrne, Flora Carabella; ***D:*** Lina Wertmuller; ***W:*** Lina Wertmuller. *WAR, FCT*

Night Gallery 🦴🦴🦴 **1969** Serling is the tour guide through an unusual art gallery consisting of portraits that reflect people's greed, desire and guilt. Made for television pilot for the series, which ran from 1969 to 1973. Three stories, including "Eyes," which saw novice Spielberg directing veteran Crawford. **95m/C VHS, Beta.** Joan Crawford, Roddy McDowall, Tom Bosley, Barry Sullivan, Ossie Davis, Sam Jaffe, Kate Greenfield; ***D:*** Steven Spielberg, Boris Sagal. *MCA*

Night Game 🦴½ **1989 (R)** A cop links a string of serial killings to the night games won by the Houston Astros. Brave cast tries hard, but is retired without a hit. **95m/C VHS, Beta, LV.** Roy Scheider, Karen Young, Paul Gleason, Lane Smith, Carlin Glynn; ***D:*** Peter Masterson; ***M:*** Pino Donaggio. *HBO*

Night Games 🦴 **1980 (R)** Raped as a child, California girl Pickett has trouble relating to her husband. To overcome her sexual anxieties, she engages in a number of bizarre fantasies. **100m/C VHS, Beta, LV.** Cindy Pickett, Joanna Cassidy, Barry Primus, Gene Davis; ***D:*** Roger Vadim; ***M:*** John Barry. *SUE*

The Night God Screamed *Woof! Scream* **198? (PG)** A fanatical cult leader is convicted of murder and the cult goes wild. **85m/C VHS, Beta.** Michael Sugich, Jeanne Crain, James B. Sikking; ***D:*** Lee Madden. *TWE*

The Night Has Eyes 🦴🦴½ *Terror House* **1942** Tense melodrama concerns a young teacher who disappears on the Yorkshire moors at the same spot where her girlfriend had vanished the previous year. Early film appearance for Mason. **79m/B VHS, Beta.** *GB* James Mason, Joyce Howard, Wilfred Lawson, Mary Clare; ***D:*** Leslie Arliss. *NOS, SNC, DVT*

Night Hunter 🦴🦴 **1995 (R)** Jack Cutter's (Wilson) vampire-hunting parents were killed by a group of bloodsuckers so he teams up with a tabloid reporter (Smith) to eliminate the last nine vampires who have gathered together in Los Angeles and plan to multiply. **86m/C VHS.** Don "The Dragon" Wilson, Melanie Smith, Nicholas Guest, Maria Ford; ***D:*** Rick Jacobson. *NHO*

A Night in Casablanca 🦴🦴🦴 **1946** Groucho, Harpo and Chico find themselves in the luxurious Hotel Casablanca, going after some leftover Nazis searching for treasure. One of the later Marx Brothers' films, but still loaded with the familiar wisecracks and mayhem. **85m/B VHS, Beta.** Groucho Marx, Harpo Marx, Chico Marx, Charles Drake, Dan Seymour, Sig Rumann; ***D:*** Archie Mayo. *NO*

A Night in Heaven *Woof!* **1983 (R)** A college teacher gets involved with one of her students, who moonlights as a male stripper. Will he earn that extra credit he needs to pass? Uninspired, overly explicit. Look for Denny Terrio of "Dance Fever" fame. **85m/C VHS, Beta.** Christopher Atkins, Lesley Ann Warren, Carrie Snodgress, Andy Garcia; ***D:*** John G. Avildsen; ***W:*** Joan Tewkesbury. Golden Raspberry Awards '83: Worst Actor (Atkins). *FOX*

A Night in the Life of Jimmy Reardon 🦴½ **1988 (R)** A high school Casanova watches his friends leave for expensive schools while he contemplates a trip to Hawaii with his rich girlfriend, a ruse to avoid the dull business school his father has picked out. Well photographed, but acting leaves something to be desired. Based on Richert's novel "Aren't You Even Going to Kiss Me Goodbye?" **95m/C VHS, Beta, LV.** River Phoenix, Meredith Salenger, Matthew L. Perry, Louanne, Ione Skye, Ann Magnuson, Paul Koslo, Jane Hallaren, Jason Court; ***D:*** William Richert; ***M:*** Elmer Bernstein, Bill Conti. *FOX*

Night Is My Future 🦴🦴½ *Music in Darkness* **1947** A young musician, blinded in an accident, meets a girl who tries to bring him happiness. Usual somber Bergman, but unimportant story. In Swedish with English subtitles. **89m/B VHS, Beta.** *SW* Mai Zetterling, Birger Malmsten, Naima Wifstrand, Olof Winnerstrand, Hilda Borgstrom; ***D:*** Ingmar Bergman. *VYY, DVT, INJ*

Night Life 🦴🦴 **1990 (R)** A teenager gets the all-out, high-stakes ride of his life when four cadavers are re-animated in his uncle's mortuary. **92m/C VHS, LV.** Scott Grimes, John Astin, Cheryl Pollak, Alan Blumenfeld; ***D:*** David Acomba; ***W:*** Keith Critchlow; ***M:*** Roger Bourland. *COL*

Night Life in Reno 🦴🦴 **1931** When a man leaves his wife, she sets out for Reno and falls in love with a married man. When her new love is killed by his jealous wife, the woman returns to her husband and they begin their marriage anew. Watchable melodrama. **58m/B VHS, Beta, LV.** Jameson Thomas, Dorothy Christy, Virginia Valli, Carmelita Geraghty. *NO*

Night Master 🦴 **1987** A handful of karate students practice their homework with much higher stakes away from the classroom. For them, deadly Ninja games are the only way to study. **87m/C VHS, Beta.** Tom Jennings, Nicole Kidman, Vince Martin; ***D:*** Mark Joffe. *ACA*

Night Monster 🦴🦴½ *House of Mystery* **1942** A maniac wears artifical limbs to hunt down and murder the doctors responsible for amputating his legs. Picture was shot in 11 days. Fire scene was stock footage from "The Ghost of Frankenstein." **80m/B VHS.** Ralph Morgan, Lionel Atwill, Leif Erickson, Don Porter, Irene Hervey, Nils Asther, Bela Lugosi; ***D:*** Ford Beebe. *MCA*

'night, Mother 🦴🦴½ **1986 (PG-13)** A depressed woman, living with her mother, announces one evening that she is going to kill herself. Her mother spends the evening reliving their lives and trying to talk her out of it, but the outcome seems inevitable. Well acted, though depressing. Based on Marsha Norman's Pulitzer Prize-winning novel. **97m/C VHS, Beta, LV.** Sissy Spacek, Anne Bancroft, Ed Berke, Carol Robbins, Jennifer Roosendahl; ***D:*** Tom Moore; ***W:*** Marsha Norman; ***M:*** David Shire. *MCA*

Night Moves ½ **1975 (R)** While tracking down a missing teenager, a Hollywood detective uncovers a bizarre smuggling ring in the Florida Keys. Hackman is realistic as the detective whose own life is unraveling and in one of her early roles, Griffith plays the teenager. The dense, disjointed plot reaches a shocking end. Underrated when released and worth a view. **100m/C VHS, Beta.** Gene Hackman, Susan Clark, Jennifer Warren, Melanie Griffith, Harris Yulin, Edward Binns, Kenneth Mars, James Woods, Dennis Dugan, Max Gail; ***D:*** Arthur Penn; ***C:*** Bruce Surtees. *WAR*

Night Nurse **1931** Stanwyck is a nurse who uncovers a sordid plot involving the murder of two young children for an inheritance. An entertaining, overlooked crime-drama, initially notorious for Stanwyck and roommate Blondell's continual on-screen dressings and undressings. Gable is compelling in an early, villainous role. **72m/B VHS, LV.** Barbara Stanwyck, Ben Lyon, Joan Blondell, Charles Winninger, Charlotte Merriam, Eddie Nugent, Blanche Frederici, Allan "Rocky" Lane, Walter McGrail, Ralf Harolde, Clark Gable; ***D:*** William A. Wellman. *MGM*

Night Nurse **1977** Young nurse signs on to care for an aging, wheelchair-ridden opera star, only to find that the house is haunted. **80m/C VHS, Beta.** Davina Whitehouse, Kay Taylor, Gary Day, Kate Fitzpatrick; ***D:*** Igor Auzins. *NO*

Night of a Thousand Cats *La Noche de Los Mil Gatos; Blood Feast* **1972 (R)** A reclusive playboy cruises Mexico City in his helicopter, searching for beautiful women. It seems he needs their bodies for his cats who, for some reason, eat only human flesh. He keeps the heads, for some reason, for his private collection. A really odd '70s cannibal cat entry, but it moves along nicely and features some truly groovy fashions (floppy hats, translucent blouses, etc.). Not to be confused with the 1963 film of the same name. From the director of "Night of the Bloody Apes" and "Survive!" **83m/C VHS, Beta.** *MX* Anjanette Comer, Zulma Faiad, Hugo Stiglitz, Christa Linder, Teresa Velasquez, Barbara Ange; ***D:*** Rene Cardona Jr. *ACA, JEF*

Night of Bloody Horror ½ **1976 (R)** Tale of a former mental patient who is believed to be responsible for the brutal murders of his ex-girlfriends. A night of bloody horror indeed, as the gore is liberally spread. **89m/C VHS, Beta.** Gaye Yellen, Evelyn Hendricks, Gerald McRaney. *NO*

Night of Dark Shadows *Woof! Curse of Dark Shadows* **1971 (PG)** An abominable film which even fans of the TV show have a hard time liking. The last of the Collins family and his new bride are sent 150 years into the past. Sequel to "House of Dark Shadows." **97m/C VHS, Beta.** David Selby, Lara Parker, Kate Jackson, Grayson Hall, John Karlen, Nancy Barrett, James Storm; ***D:*** Dan Curtis. *MGM*

Night of Evil ½ **1962** Girl is released from reform school and promptly wins a beauty contest. Her bid to win the Miss America title is blown to smithereens however, when it is discovered that she has been secretly married all along. From there she resorts to working in strip joints and attempts to pull off an armed robbery. As exploitation fare goes, a winner. **88m/B VHS, Beta.** Lisa Gaye, William Campbell; ***D:*** Richard Galbreath. *SNC*

Night of Horror ½ **198? (R)** Zombies attack four young people stranded in the wilderness. **76m/C VHS, Beta.** Steve Sandkuhler, Gae Schmitt, Rebecca Bach, Jeff Canfield. *GHV, MRV*

A Night of Love ½ *Manifesto* **1987 (R)** Because of an assassination threat on the new king, Inspector Avanti (Molina) is charged with rounding up the town's troublemakers. Among them is a beguiling debutante (Soeberg) whose sexual appetites are matched only by her passion to kill the king. Based on a story by Emile Zola. **97m/C VHS.** Alfred Molina, Camilla Soeberg, Eric Stoltz, Gabrielle Anwar; ***D:*** Dusan Makavejev. *ORI, FXL*

Night of Terror ½ *He Lived to Kill* **1933** A swami, a couple of Hindu servants, a pretty heroine, a reporter, and all stalked by a killer who's after a formula that can put people in a state of suspended animation. Lame chiller. **64m/B VHS.** Bela Lugosi, Sally Blane, Wallace Ford, Tully Marshall, George Meeker, Edwin Maxwell; ***D:*** Ben Stoloff; ***C:*** Joseph Valentine. *GPV*

Night of Terror **1987** A bizarre family conducts brain experiments on themselves and then begins to kill each other. Bloodshed for the whole family. **105m/C VHS.** Renee Harmon, Henry Lewis. *IME*

Night of the Assassin **1977** Priest leaves his pulpit to become a terrorist. He plans a surprise for a U.N. secretary visiting Greece that would put the U.S. and Greek governments in the palm of his hand. Hard to believe. **98m/C VHS, Beta.** Klaus Kinski, Michael Craig, Eva Renzi; ***D:*** Robert McMahon. *LIV*

Night of the Blood Beast ½ **1958** An astronaut comes back from space with an alien growing inside his body. The low budget defeats a valiant attempt at a story. Alternative title: "Creature from Galaxy 27." **65m/B VHS.** Michael Emmet, Angela Greene, John Baer, Ed Nelson; ***D:*** Bernard L. Kowalski. *SNC, MRV*

Night of the Bloody Apes *Woof! Gomar the Human Gorilla; La Horriplante Bestia Humana* **1968 (R)** When a doctor transplants an ape's heart into his dying son's body, the son goes berserk. Gory Mexican-made horror at its finest. **84m/C VHS, Beta.** *MX* Jose Elias Moreno, Armando Silvestre, Norma Lazarendo, Augustin Martinez Solares, Gina Moret, Noelia Noel, Gerard Zepeda; ***D:*** Rene Cardona Jr. *MPI*

Night of the Bloody Transplant *Woof!* **1986 (R)** A lunatic scientist switches hearts from one person to another in this bloody gorefest. Footage of real surgery adds authenticity, but not believeability. **90m/C VHS, Beta.** Dick Grimm; ***D:*** David W. Hanson. *NO*

Night of the Cobra Woman **1972 (R)** A woman who can turn herself into a cobra needs constant sex and snake venom to keep her eternally young. Shot on location in the Philippines. One-time underground filmmaker Meyer co-wrote the script, for the Corman factory. **85m/C VHS, Beta.** *PH* Joy Bang, Marlene Clark, Roger Garrett, Slash Marks, Vic Diaz; ***D:*** Andrew Meyer; ***W:*** Andrew Meyer. *NO*

Night of the Comet ½ **1984 (PG-13)** After surviving the explosion of a deadly comet, two California girls discover that they are the last people on Earth. When zombies begin to chase them, things begin to lose their charm. Cute and funny, but the script runs out before the movie does. **90m/C VHS, Beta.** Catherine Mary Stewart, Kelli Maroney, Robert Beltran, Geoffrey Lewis, Mary Woronov, Sharon Farrell, Michael Bowen; ***D:*** Thom Eberhardt; ***W:*** Thom Eberhardt. *FOX*

Night of the Creeps ½ **1986 (R)** In 1958 an alien organism lands on earth and infects a person who is then frozen. Thirty years later he is accidentally unfrozen and starts spreading the infection throughout a college town. B-movie homage contains every horror cliche there is. Director Dekker's first film. **89m/C VHS, Beta, LV.** Jason Lively, Jill Whitlow, Tom Atkins, Dick Miller, Steve Marshall; ***D:*** Fred Dekker; ***W:*** Fred Dekker. *NO*

Night of the Cyclone **1990 (R)** A complex but not overly interesting thriller about a big city cop who goes to an island paradise in search of his missing daughter and finds murder. **90m/C VHS, LV.** Kris Kristofferson, Jeffrey Meek, Marisa Berenson, Winston Ntshona, Gerrit Graham; ***D:*** David Irving. *REP*

Night of the Death Cult *Night of the Seagulls* **1975** After moving to a quiet seaside community, a young couple is plagued by cult practising human sacrifice in order to appease the Templars, a zombie-like pack of ancient clergymen who rise from the dead and torture the living. Last in a four film series about the Templars. **90m/C VHS, Beta.** *SP* Victor Petit, Julie James, Maria Kosti, Sandra Mozarowsky; ***D:*** Armando de Ossorio. *NO*

Night of the Demon *Woof!* **1980** Anthropology students are attacked by the legendary Bigfoot. Later they discover that he has raped and impregnated a young woman. Gore and sex prevail. **97m/C VHS, Beta.** Jay Allen, Michael J. Cutt, Bob Collins, Jodi Lazarus; ***D:*** James C. Watson. *VHE*

Night of the Demons **1988 (R)** A gory, special-effects-laden horror farce about teenagers calling up demons in a haunted mortuary. On Halloween, of course. **92m/C VHS, LV.** Linnea Quigley, Cathy Podewell, Alvin Alexis, William Gallo, Mimi Kinkade, Lance Fenton; ***D:*** Kevin S. Tenney; ***W:*** Joe Augustyn. *REP*

Night of the Demons 2 **1994 (R)** Some humor and reasonable special effects help this rise above the usual teen-slasher horror sequels. The demonic Angela (complete with her skull-shaped lollipops) lives on in legend, handily haunting her creepy old house where a group of dumb teens end up on Halloween (and soon wind up dead). With each casualty, a new victim also joins the ranks of the undead. Funniest parts come with heroic rescuer, yardstick-wielding Sister Gloria, who's not about to let any of Satan's helpers get the better of her. **96m/C VHS, LV.** Amelia Kinkade, Jennifer Rhodes, Merele Kennedy, Bobby Jacoby, Rod McCary, Zoe Trilling, Cristi Harris, Johnny Moran, Rick Peters, Christine Taylor, Ladd York, Darin Heames; ***D:*** Brian Trenchard-Smith; ***W:*** Joe Augustyn; ***M:*** Jim Manzie. *REP*

The Night of the Following Day **1969 (R)** Four professional criminals kidnap a young girl at France's Orly airport, demanding a large ransom from her wealthy father. Each kidnapper turns out to be beset by personal demons, hindering their plans and leading to a bloody climax. Then, there's a final twist to the entire story. Brando and Boone are properly chilling but the plot is muddled and melodramatic. From the novel "The Snatchers" by Lionel White. **93m/C VHS.** Marlon Brando, Richard Boone, Rita Moreno, Pamela Franklin, Jess Hahn, Jacques Marin, Gerard Buhr, Hughes Wanner; ***D:*** Hubert Cornfield; ***W:*** Robert Phippeny, Hubert Cornfield. *MCA, FCT*

Night of the Fox **1990 (R)** An American officer with top secret knowledge is captured by Germans on the brink of D-day. His home team plans to kill him if he cannot be rescued before spilling the beans. On-location filming adds much. Made for cable. **95m/C VHS, LV.** Michael York, Deborah Raffin, George Peppard; ***D:*** Charles Jarrott. *VMK*

Night of the Generals *La Nuit de Generaux* **1967 (R)** A Nazi intelligence officer is pursuing three Nazi generals who may be involved in the brutal murder of a Warsaw prostitute. Dark and sinister, may be too slow for some tastes. Based on Hans Helmut Kirst's novel. **148m/C VHS, Beta, LV.** Peter O'Toole, Omar Sharif, Tom Courtenay, Joanna Pettet, Donald Pleasence, Christopher Plummer, Philippe Noiret, John Gregson; ***D:*** Anatole Litvak; ***M:*** Maurice Jarre. *COL, MOV*

Night of the Ghouls *Woof! Revenge of the Dead* **1959** Second to last in Wood's celebrated series of inept horror films that began with "Bride of the Monster" and "Plan 9 from Outer Space." This one tells of a phony spiritualist who swindles the grieving by pretending to raise the dead. To his great surprise he actually does enliven some cadavers, who then go after him. Unreleased for over 20 years because Wood couldn't pay the film lab. Not quite as classically bad as his other films, but still a laugh riot. **69m/B VHS, Beta.** Paul Marco, Tor Johnson, Duke Moore, Kenne Duncan, John Carpenter; ***D:*** Edward D. Wood Jr. *RHI, SNC, MED*

Night of the Grizzly **1966** An ex-lawman's peaceful life as a rancher is threatened when a killer grizzly bear goes on a murderous rampage terrorizing the residents of the Wyoming countryside. **99m/C VHS, Beta.** Clint Walker, Martha Hyer; ***D:*** Joseph Pevney. *PAR*

Night of the Howling Beast *The Werewolf and the Yeti* **1975 (R)** The selling point of this one is an epic, first-time battle between a werewolf and a Yeti. Unfortunately it lasts about fifteen seconds. Naschy's eighth stint as the wolfman. **87m/C VHS, Beta.** *SP* Paul Naschy, Grace Mills, Castillo Escalona, Silvia Solar, Gil Vidal; ***D:*** Miguel Iglesias. *REP*

The Night of the Hunter **1955** The nightmarish story of a psychotic preacher who marries a lonely widow with two children in the hopes of finding the cache of money her thieving husband had stashed. A dark, terrifying tale, completely unique in Hollywood's history. Mitchum is terrific. From novel by Davis Grubb and, sadly, Laughton's only directorial effort. **93m/B VHS, Beta, LV.** Robert Mitchum, Shelley Winters, Lillian Gish, Don Beddoe, Evelyn Varden, Peter Graves, James Gleason, Billy Chapin, Sally Jane Bruce; ***D:*** Charles Laughton; ***W:*** James Agee. *MGM*

The Night of the Iguana **1964** An alcoholic ex-minister acts as a tour guide in Mexico, becoming involved with a spinster and a hotel owner. Based on Tennessee Williams' play. Excellent performances from Burton and Gardner. **125m/B VHS, Beta, LV.** Richard Burton, Deborah Kerr, Ava Gardner, Grayson Hall, Sue Lyon; ***D:*** John Huston. Academy Awards '64: Best Costume Design (B & W); Nominations: Academy Awards '64: Best Art Direction/Set Decoration (B & W), Best Black and White Cinematography, Best Supporting Actress (Hall). *MGM*

Night of the Juggler ½ **1980 (R)** An ex-cop encounters countless obstacles in trying to track down his daughter's kidnapper in New York City. Just a tad too complicated for some tastes. **101m/C VHS, Beta.** James Brolin, Cliff Gorman, Richard Castellano, Mandy Patinkin, Julie Carmen; ***D:*** Robert Butler; ***W:*** William W. Norton Sr. *MED*

Night of the Kickfighters **1991** A mighty band of martial artists takes on a terrorist group that has in their possession a secret weapon that could destroy the world. **87m/C VHS.** Andy Bauman, Adam West, Marcia Karr; ***D:*** Buddy Reyes. *AIP*

Night of the Laughing Dead ½ *Crazy House; House in Nightmare Park* **1975** Veteran British comedy cast perform unthinkable spoof. Man stands to inherit lotsa money as his family members kick the bucket one by one. **90m/C VHS, LV.** *GB* Ray Milland, Frankie Howerd, Rosalie Crutchley, Kenneth Griffith; ***D:*** Peter Sykes. *MGM*

Night of the Living Babes *Woof!* **1987** Two yuppie men go looking for fun at a brothel. They get their just deserts in the form of sex-seeking female zombies. **60m/C VHS.** Michelle (McClellan) Bauer, Connie Woods, Andrew Nichols, Louie Bonanno; ***D:*** Jon Valentine. *NO*

Night of the Living Dead ½ *Night of the Flesh Eaters* **1968** Cult favorite is low budget but powerfully frightening. Space experiments set off a high level of radiation that makes the newly dead return to life, with a taste for human flesh. Handful of holdouts find shelter in a farmhouse. Claustrophobic, terrifying, gruesome, extreme, and yes, humorous. Followed by "Dawn of the Dead" (1979) and "Day of the Dead" (1985). Romero's directorial debut. Available in a colorized version. **90m/B VHS, LV.** Judith O'Dea, Duane Jones, Russell Streiner, Karl Hardman; ***D:*** George A. Romero. *REP, MRV, NOS*

Night of the Living Dead **1990 (R)** A bunch of people are trapped in a farmhouse and attacked by ghouls with eating disorders. Remake of the '68 classic substitutes high tech blood 'n' guts for bona fide frights. **92m/C VHS, LV.** Tony Todd, Patricia Tallman, Tom Towles; ***D:*** Tom Savini; ***W:*** George A. Romero. *COL*

Night of the Living Dead, 25th Anniversary Documentary **1993** Features behind the scenes look at low-budget 1968 classic film about legions of dead people who stalk the earth looking for live humans to feed on. **83m/C VHS, LV.** *MTH*

Night of the Running Man ½ **1994 (R)** Las Vegas cab driver McCarthy finds $1 million stolen from a casino and goes on the run from hit man Glenn, who's been hired to recover the loot. **93m/C VHS, LV.** Scott Glenn, Andrew McCarthy, John Glover; ***D:*** Mark L. Lester. *VMK*

Night of the Scarecrow ½ **1995 (R)** Hundreds of years before a small town makes a pact with a warlock (Lazar) to ensure prosperity. After regretting the deal, the townspeople kill him and bury the body in a field where it's eventually uncovered. Now the warlock's ghost inhabits the frame of a scarecrow and is off on a murderous rampage. Formula horror with some decent production values. Based on a comic book. **90m/C VHS.** Elizabeth Barondes, John Mese, Stephen Root, Bruce Glover, Dirk Blocker, Howard Swain, Gary Lockwood, John Lazar, John Hawkes; ***D:*** Jeff Burr; ***W:*** Reed Steiner, Dan Mazur; ***C:*** Tom Calloway; ***M:*** Jim Manzie. *REP*

Night of the Sharks *Woof!* **1989** Mercenaries in a downed plane go after a jewel-ridden shipwreck despite a plethora of sharks. **87m/C VHS, Beta, LV.** Treat Williams, Christopher Connelly, Antonio Fargas, Janet Agren; ***D:*** Anthony Richmond. *LIV, VTR*

The Night of the Shooting Stars *The Night of San Lorenzo; La Notte di San Lorenzo* **1982 (R)** Set in an Italian village during the last days of WWII, this film highlights the schism in the village between those who support the fascists and those who sympathize with the Allies. This division comes to a head in the stunning final scene. A poignant, deeply moving film. **106m/C VHS, Beta.** *IT* Omero Antonutti, Margarita Lozano, Claudio Bigagli, Massimo Bonetti, Norma Martel; ***D:*** Paolo Taviani, Vittorio Taviani; ***W:*** Tonino Guerra, Giuliani G. De Negri, Paolo Taviani, Vittorio Taviani; ***M:*** Nicola Piovani. Cannes Film Festival '82: Grand Jury Prize; National Society of Film Critics Awards '83: Best Director (Taviani), Best Director (Taviani), Best Film; Nominations: Cannes Film Festival '82: Best Film. *MGM, APD, AUD*

Night of the Sorcerers *Woof!* **1970** An expedition to the Congo uncovers a bizarre tribe of vampire leopard women who lure young girls to their deaths. **85m/C VHS, Beta.** Jack Taylor, Simon Andrew, Kali Hansa; ***D:*** Armando de Ossorio. *UNI*

Night of the Strangler **1973 (R)** A love affair between a white society girl and a young black man causes a chain of events that end with brutal murders in New Orleans. **88m/C VHS, Beta.** Mickey Dolenz, James Ralston, Susan McCullough; ***D:*** Joy Houck Jr. *NO*

Night of the Twisters ½ **1995** A teenager and his new stepfather must work together to protect the family when tornadoes rip through their small Nebraska town. Based on the book by Ivy Ruckman. Made for cable. **?m/C VHS.** John Schneider, Devon Sawa, Lori Hallier, Helen Hughes. *GKK*

Night of the Warrior **1991 (R)** Music videos and martial arts don't mix...not here, anyway. A hunky exotic-dance-club owner pays his disco bills by fighting in illegal, underground blood matches, but not enough to make it exciting. Lamas stars with real life wife Kinmont and mom Dahl. **96m/C VHS, LV.** Lorenzo Lamas, Anthony Geary, Kathleen Kinmont, Arlene Dahl. *VMK*

Night of the Wilding **1990** Very, very loosely based on the story of the female jogger who was gang-raped and left for dead in New York's Central Park. Made for television, soon after the actual incident occurred. **90m/C VHS, Beta, LV.** Erik Estrada, Kathrin Lautner; ***D:*** Joseph Merhi. *NO*

Night of the Zombies *Gamma 693; Night of the Wehrmacht Zombies* **1981 (R)** WWII soldiers with eating disorders shuffle through 88 minutes of gratuitous gore, while pursued by porn star cum intelligence agent. From the director of "Bloodsucking Freaks." **88m/C VHS.** James Gillis, Ryan Hilliard, Samantha Grey, Joel M. Reed; ***D:*** Joel M. Reed; ***W:*** Joel M. Reed. *PSM*

Night of the Zombies *Woof! Apocalipsis Canibal; Hell of the Living Dead; Zombie Creeping Flesh* **1983** Staff of a scientific research center are killed and then resurrected as cannibals who prey on the living. The living will suffer again if trapped into watching. Mattel is pseudonym for director Vincent Dawn. Cheap, dubbed, and possessing minimal coherence. **101m/C VHS, Beta.** *IT SP* Margit Evelyn Newton, Frank Garfield, Selan Karay; ***D:*** Bruno Mattei. *VES, PSM*

Night on Earth **1991 (R)** Jarmusch's "road" movie comprises five different stories taking place on the same night in five different cities—Los Angeles, New York, Paris, Rome, and Helsinki—between cabbies and their passengers. As with any anthology some stories work better than others but all have their moments in this ambitious film with its outstanding international cast. Subtitled in English for the three foreign segments. **125m/C VHS, LV.** Winona Ryder, Gena Rowlands, Giancarlo Esposito, Armin Mueller-Stahl, Rosie Perez, Beatrice Dalle, Roberto Benigni, Paolo Bonacelli, Matti Pellonpaa, Kari Vaananen, Sakari Kuosmanen, Tomi Salmela; ***D:*** Jim Jarmusch; ***W:*** Jim Jarmusch; ***M:*** Tom Waits. Independent Spirit Awards '93: Best Cinematography. *NLC, INJ, FAF*

Night Partners ½ **1983** Bored housewives assist the police to patrol the streets after the kids have gone to bed. Originally made for television with the intention of turning it into a series, but the script doesn't hold water. **100m/C VHS, Beta.** Yvette Mimieux, Diana Canova, Arlen Dean Snyder, M. Emmet Walsh, Patricia Davis, Larry Linville; ***D:*** Noel Nosseck. *NWV*

The Night Patrol ½ **1926** Talmadge is a cop who winds up arresting his girlfriend's brother for murder. Convinced the boy is innocent, Talmadge disguises himself in order to infiltrate the gang he thinks is actually responsible for the crime. Lots of derring-do and a last-minute rescue from the electric chair. **53m/B VHS.** Richard Talmadge, Mary Carr, Rose Blossom, Josef Swickard, Gardner James; ***D:*** Noel Mason Smith. *GPV*

Night Patrol *Woof!* **1985 (R)** The streets of Hollywood will never be the same after the night patrol runs amuck in the town. Crude imitation of "Police Academy." **87m/C VHS, Beta, LV.** Linda Blair, Pat Paulsen, Jaye P. Morgan, Jack Riley, Murray Langston, Billy Barty, Noriyuki "Pat" Morita, Sydney Lassick, Andrew Dice Clay; ***D:*** Jackie Kong. Golden Raspberry Awards '85: Worst Actress (Blair). *NWV, VTR*

The Night Porter *Il Portiere de Notte* **1974 (R)** Max, an ex-SS concentration camp officer, unexpectedly meets his former lover-victim at the Viennese hotel where he works as the night porter. After they get reacquainted, the couple must hide from the porter's ex-Nazi friends who want the women dead because they fear she will disclose their past. A sado-masochistic voyage not for the fainthearted. **115m/C VHS, Beta, LV.** *IT* Dirk Bogarde, Charlotte Rampling, Phillippe LeRoy, Gabriele Ferzetti, Isa Miranda; ***D:*** Liliana Cavani. *SUE, GLV, INJ*

Night Rhythms ½ **1992 (R)** Nick West is a radio talk show host with a sexy voice that causes his women listeners to reveal their most intimate fantasies and problems to him on the air. When one listener goes too far, it's murder, and Nick must work to prove his innocence in the crime if he intends to save his career—and his life. Also available in an unrated version. **?m/C VHS, LV.** Martin Hewitt, Delia Sheppard, David Carradine, Terry Tweed, Sam Jones, Deborah Driggs, Julie Strain; ***D:*** Alexander Gregory Hippolyte. *IMP, MOV*

Night Rider **1932** A cowboy posing as a gunman ends a trail of murder and violence in a small western town. **54m/B VHS, Beta.** Harry Carey Sr., George "Gabby" Hayes. *NOS, DVT*

Night Riders of Montana **1950** A state ranger helps a group of ranchers to fight off a band of rustlers. **60m/B VHS, Beta.** Allan "Rocky" Lane. *DVT*

Night Ripper **1986** A psychopathic killer stalks high fashion models and kills them by carving them up. Lots of violence. **88m/C VHS, Beta.** James Hansen, April Anne, Larry Thomas; ***D:*** Jeff Hathcock. *NO*

Night School *Terror Eyes* **1981 (R)** A police detective must find out who has been decapitating the women attending night school at Wendell College. Ward's first film. **89m/C VHS, Beta.** Edward Albert,

Rachel Ward, Leonard Mann, Drew Snyder, Joseph R. Sicari; ***D:*** Ken Hughes; ***W:*** Ruth Avergon; ***M:*** Brad Fiedel. *FOX*

Night Screams **1987** Violent scare-monger about two escaped convicts who crash a high school house party. Kids and convicts start getting killed, one by one. **85m/C VHS, Beta.** Joe Manno, Ron Thomas, Randy Lundsford, Megan Wyss; ***D:*** Allen Plone. *PSM*

Night Shadow **1990 (R)** A woman, returning home after being away for years, picks up a hitchhiker. Soon after her arrival, terrible serial killings begin, and only she has the nerve to track down the killer. **90m/C VHS.** Brenda Vance, Dana Chan, Tom Boylan; ***D:*** Randolph Cohlan; ***W:*** Randolph Cohlan. *NO*

Night Shift **1982 (R)** Two morgue attendants, dull Winkler and manic Keaton, decide to spice up their latenight shift by running a call-girl service on the side. Keaton turns in a fine performance in his film debut, and Howard's sure-handed direction almost overcome the silly premise. **106m/C VHS, Beta, LV.** Henry Winkler, Michael Keaton, Shelley Long, Kevin Costner, Pat Corley, Bobby DiCicco, Nita Talbot, Richard Belzer, Shannen Doherty; ***D:*** Ron Howard; ***W:*** Babaloo Mandel, Lowell Ganz; ***M:*** Burt Bacharach. *WAR*

Night Siege Project: Shadowchaser 2 ½ *Project Shadowchaser 2* **1994 (R)** Smooth actioner finds a terrorist android taking over a nuclear arsenal and threatening to make Washington, D.C. a mushroom cloud. Naturally, there's a hero (and a heroine) to take care of the evildoers. **97m/C VHS, LV.** Bryan Genesse, Frank Zagarino, Beth Toussaint; ***D:*** John Eyres; ***W:*** Nick Davis; ***M:*** Steve Edwards. *TTC, NLC*

Night Slasher **1984** A madman enjoys spilling the innards of London prostitutes with his dagger. **87m/C VHS, Beta.** Jack May, Linda Marlowe. *UNI*

Night Stage to Galveston ½ **1952** Autry leads his Texas Rangers on a mission to uncover corruption in the Texas State Police during the turbulent post-Civil War era. **61m/B VHS, Beta.** Gene Autry, Pat Buttram, Virginia Huston, Thurston Hall; ***D:*** George Archainbaud. *CCB*

Night Stalker **1987 (R)** A bloodthirsty serial killer is tracked by a detective through the streets in New York. The usual rigamarole of fisticuffes, gunplay, and car chases ensure. Impressive acting from Napier raises the film from the run-of-the-mill. **91m/C VHS, Beta.** Charles Napier, John Goff, Robert Viharo, Robert Z'Dar, Joseph Gian, Gary Crosby, Joan Chen, Michelle Reese; ***D:*** Max Cleven. *VES*

The Night Stalker: Two Tales of Terror **1974** Two episodes from the television series "Kolchak: The Night Stalker" in which McGavin plays a nosy newspaper reporter who constantly stumbles upon occult phenomenon. Episodes are "Jack the Ripper" and "The Vampire." **98m/C VHS, Beta.** Darren McGavin, Simon Oakland. *MCA*

Night Terror **1976** Everyone's after a hausfrau who saw a highway patrolman murdered on an expressway...including the psychotic murderer. Pretty standard fare. Made for television. **73m/C VHS, Beta.** Valerie Harper, Richard Romanus, Michael Tolan, Beatrice Manley, John Quade, Quinn Cummings, Nicholas Pryor; ***D:*** E.W. Swackhamer. *WOV*

Night Terror **1989** A man wakes up from a nightmare only to find that his terrors are still present. **90m/C VHS, Beta.** Lloyd B. Mote, Jeff Keel, Guy Ecker, Jon Hoffman, Michael Coopet; ***D:*** Michael Weaver, Paul Howard. *NO*

The Night the City Screamed ½ **1980 (PG)** It's the hottest day of the year, the city experiences a massive blackout, and nighttime brings out less-than-noble emotions amongst the citizenry. Made for television. **96m/C VHS.** Raymond Burr, Georg Stanford Brown, Linda Purl, Robert Culp, Clifton Davis, David Cassidy, George DiCenzo, Gary Frank, Don Meredith, Shelley Smith, Vic Tayback, Dick Anthony Williams; ***D:*** Harry Falk; ***W:*** Larry Brody. *COL*

The Night the Lights Went Out in Georgia **1981 (PG)** Loosely based on the popular hit song, the film follows a brother and sister as they try to cash in on the country music scene in Nashville. McNichol is engaging. **112m/C VHS, Beta.** Kristy McNichol, Dennis Quaid, Mark Hamill, Don Stroud; ***D:*** Ronald F. Maxwell; ***W:*** Bob Bonney; ***M:*** David Shire. *SUE, TWE*

The Night They Raided Minsky's *The Night They Invented Striptease* **1969 (PG)** Chaotic but interesting period comedy about a young Amish girl who leaves her tyrannical father to come to New York City in the 1920s. She winds up at Minsky's Burlesque and accidentally invents the striptease. Lahr's last performance—he died during filming. ♫The Night They Raided Minsky's; Take Ten Terrific Girls But Only 9 Costumes; How I Love Her; Perfect Gentleman; You Rat, You; Penny Arcade; Wait For Me. **97m/C VHS, Beta.** Jason Robards Jr., Britt Ekland, Elliott Gould, Bert Lahr, Norman Wisdom, Denholm Elliott; ***D:*** William Friedkin; ***W:*** Norman Lear, Arnold Schulman. *FOX*

The Night They Robbed Big Bertha's **1983** Bungling burglar attempts to knock off Big Bertha's massage parlor. **83m/C VHS, Beta.** Robert Nichols. *NO*

The Night They Saved Christmas ½ **1987** A Christmas special in which Santa's North Pole headquarters are endangered by the progress of an expanding oil company. Will the attempts of three children be enough to save the day? **94m/C VHS, Beta.** Art Carney, Jaclyn Smith, Paul Williams, Paul LeMat; ***D:*** Jackie Cooper. *CAF, PSM*

Night Tide ½ **1963** Hopper in another off the wall character study, this time as a lonely sailor. He falls for a mermaid (Lawson) who works at the dock. She may be a descendent of the man-killing Sirens. Interesting and different little love story, sometimes advertised as horror, which it is not. **84m/B VHS.** Dennis Hopper, Gavin Muir, Luana Anders, Marjorie Eaton, Tom Dillon; ***D:*** Curtis Harrington. *SNC, FRG, TPV*

Night Time in Nevada ½ **1948** Young woman heads West to claim $50,000 trust left by dear old dad, but his crooked lawyer and associate have their hands in the pot. Cowboy Roy rides horse and flexes dimples while helping helpless girl. **67m/B VHS, Beta, 8mm.** Roy Rogers, Adele Mara, Andy Devine, Grant Withers, Joseph Crehan; ***D:*** William Witney. *NOS, HEG, VYY*

A Night to Remember **1942** A murder-mystery writer's wife convinces him to move to a new apartment because she thinks the change might help him finish a novel he started long ago. When they find a dead body behind their new building, they try their hands at sleuthing. A clever and witty mystery, indeed, supported by likeable performances. **91m/B VHS.** Loretta Young, Brian Aherne, Sidney Toler, Gale Sondergaard, William Wright, Donald MacBride, Blanche Yurka; ***D:*** Richard Wallace. *COL*

A Night to Remember **1958** Gripping tale of the voyage of the Titanic with an interesting account of action in the face of danger and courage amid despair. Large cast is effectively used. Adapted by Eric Ambler from the book by Walter Lord. **119m/B VHS, Beta, LV.** Kenneth More, David McCallum, Anthony Bushell, Honor Blackman, Michael Goodliffe, George Rose, Laurence Naismith, Frank Lawton, Alec McCowen; ***D:*** Roy Ward Baker; ***W:*** Eric Ambler; ***C:*** Geoffrey Unsworth. Golden Globe Awards '59: Best Foreign Film; National Board of Review Awards '58: 5 Best Foreign Films of the Year. *PAR, HMV*

The Night Train to Kathmandu **1988** A young girl accompanies her parents on a research expedition to Nepal, where her head is turned by an exotically handsome young Sherpa. Old story without much help from actors or director. Made for cable. **102m/C VHS, Beta, LV.** Milla Jovovich, Pernell Roberts, Eddie Castrodad; ***D:*** Robert Wiemer. *PAR*

Night Train to Munich *Night Train; Gestapo* **1940** There's Nazi intrigue galore aboard a big train when a scientist's daughter joins allied intelligence agents in retrieving some secret documents. From the book "Report on a Fugitive" by Gordon Wellesley. **93m/B VHS, Beta.** *GB* Margaret Lockwood, Rex Harrison, Paul Henreid; ***D:*** Carol Reed. *NOS, DVT, HEG*

Night Train to Terror *Woof!* **1984 (R)** Strange things start happening on the train where a rock band makes its last appearance. Clips from other horror flicks were pieced together to make this film that's so bad it's almost good. **98m/C VHS, Beta.** John Phillip Law, Cameron Mitchell, Marc Lawrence, Charles Moll, Ferdinand "Ferdy" Mayne; ***D:*** Jay Schlossberg-Cohen. *PSM*

Night Train to Venice ½ **1993 (R)** Martin (Grant) is aboard the Orient Express on his way to Venice to deliver his book about the rise of neo-Nazism. He meets a mystery man (McDowell) and an actress (Welch) with ties to a neo-Nazi group, who also happen to be aboard the train and anxious to stop Martin from delivering his expose. Extended dream sequences and flashbacks tend to stop the story cold but Grant is a draw (and probably the only reason this mishmash has been released to video). **98m/C VHS, LV.** Hugh Grant, Malcolm McDowell, Tahnee Welch, Kristina Soderbaum; ***D:*** Carlo U. Quinterio; ***W:*** Leo Tichat, Toni Hirtreiter; ***M:*** Alexander Bubenheim. *LIV, WEA*

Night Vision **1987** A young writer in the big city is given a video monitor by a street thief which is equipped with some remarkable features, including the ability to present scenes of future murders and demon worship. **102m/C VHS, Beta.** Ellie Martins, Stacy Carson, Shirley Ross, Tony Carpenter; ***D:*** Michael Krueger. *PSM*

The Night Visitor ½ **1970 (PG)** A man in a prison for the criminally insane seeks violent vengeance on those he believes have set him up. Heavily detailed, slow moving. Ullman and von Sydow can do better. **106m/C VHS, Beta.** *GB DK* Max von Sydow, Liv Ullmann, Trevor Howard, Per Oscarsson, Andrew Keir; ***D:*** Laslo Benedek; ***M:*** Henry Mancini. *VCI*

Night Visitor *Never Cry Devil* **1989 (R)** A retired police detective teams up with a teenage peeping tom to disclose the identity of a satanic serial killer. The killer, of course, is one of the youth's teachers. **95m/C VHS, Beta.** Derek Rydell, Shannon Tweed, Elliott Gould, Allen (Goorwitz) Garfield, Michael J. Pollard, Richard Roundtree, Henry Gibson; ***D:*** Rupert Hitzig; ***W:*** Randal Viscovich. *MGM*

The Night Walker ½ **1964** Stanwyck is always worth watching and she has the best moments in this psycho-thriller which suffers from a low-budget and confused script. The basic story has Stanwyck as a rich widow with a recurring nightmare featuring a faceless lover. There's also a too-helpful lawyer (Taylor), a suspicious private detective (Bochner)—and maybe her husband isn't so dead after all. Taylor and Stanwyck, who had once been married, worked together for the first time in 27 years. **86m/B VHS.** Barbara Stanwyck, Robert Taylor, Lloyd Bochner, Hayden Rorke, Judith Meredith, Rochelle Hudson; ***D:*** William Castle; ***W:*** Robert Bloch. *MCA, GPV*

Night Warning *Nightmare Maker; Butcher Baker (Nightmare Maker)* **1982 (R)** A slasher gorefest redeemed by Tyrrell's go-for-broke performance. She plays a sexually repressed aunt who makes up for her problems by going on murderous rampages. Hide the kitchen knives! **96m/C VHS, Beta.** Bo Svenson, Jimmy McNichol, Susan Tyrrell, Julia Duffy; ***D:*** William Asher; ***W:*** Stephen Breimer. *NO*

Night Wars ½ **1988** Two ex-POWs who are plagued by their memories turn to dream therapy to relive their escape. Eventually, they rescue a buddy they left behind. **90m/C VHS, Beta.** Dan Haggerty, Brian O'Connor, Cameron Smith; ***D:*** David A. Prior. *COL*

Night Watch ½ *Le Trou; Il Buco* **1972** A woman recovering from a nervous breakdown witnesses a murder, but no one will believe her. **100m/C VHS, Beta.** *GB* Elizabeth Taylor, Laurence Harvey, Billie Whitelaw; ***D:*** Brian G. Hutton; ***C:*** Billy Williams. *MED*

The Night We Never Met ☠☠½ **1993 (R)** Three yuppies bring different visions of romance and a case of mistaken identity to a time-share apartment in New York's Greenwich Village. Sam (Broderick) needs a quiet space to get over being dumped by a flaky performance artist (Tripplehorn). Ellen (Sciorra) is looking for space to paint away from the confines of her thick-headed spouse (Mantell). Brian, the organizer of the living arrangement, wants a space where he can be one of the boys and escape from his cloying fiancee (Bateman). Fairly predictable but enjoyable romantic comedy. **98m/C VHS.** Matthew Broderick, Jeanne Tripplehorn, Kevin Anderson, Justine Bateman, Annabella Sciorra, Christine Baranski, Doris Roberts, Dominic Chianese, Michael Mantell, Tim Guinee, Greg Germann, Dana Wheeler-Nicholson, Louise Lasser, Bill Campbell, Ranjit Chowdhry, Garry Shandling, Katharine Houghton, Brooke Smith; ***D:*** Warren Leight; ***W:*** Warren Leight; ***M:*** Evan Lurie. *HBO*

Night Zoo ☠☠ *Un Zoo, La Nuit* **1987** A confusing story about a father/son reconciliation and the lurid underworld of drugs and sex in Montreal. The graphic sex and violence undermines the sensitive aspects of the film. **115m/C VHS, Beta, LV.** *CA* Gilles Maheu, Roger Le Bel, Lynne Adams, German Houde; ***D:*** Jean-Claude Lauzon. Genie Awards '88: Best Actor (Le Bel), Best Director (Lauzon), Best Film, Best Supporting Actor (Houde). *VTR, NWV, IME*

Nightbreaker ☠☠☠ **1989** Revelation of the U.S. government's deliberate exposure of servicemen to atomic bomb tests and the resulting radiation, in order to observe the effects on humans. Sheen and his son, Estevez, portray a U.S. doctor in the 1980s and the 1950s, respectively. **100m/C VHS.** Martin Sheen, Emilio Estevez, Lea Thompson, Melinda Dillon, Nicholas Pryor, Joe Pantoliano; ***D:*** Peter Markle; ***W:*** T.S. Cook; ***M:*** Peter Bernstein. *TTC*

The Nightcomers ☠ **1972 (R)** A pretend "prequel" to Henry James's "The Turn of the Screw," wherein an Irish gardener trysts with the nanny of two watchful children who believe that lovers unite in death. Don't be fooled: stick to the original. **96m/C VHS, Beta, LV.** *GB* Marlon Brando, Stephanie Beacham, Thora Hird; ***D:*** Michael Winner. *COL, NLC*

Nightfall ☠☠☠ **1956** Ray, accused of a crime he didn't commit, is forced to flee from both the law and the underworld. Classic example of film noir, brilliantly filmed by Tourneur. **78m/B VHS.** Aldo Ray, Brian Keith, Anne Bancroft, Jocelyn Brando, James Gregory, Frank Albertson; ***D:*** Jacques Tourneur; ***W:*** Stirling Silliphant. *GKK*

Nightfall ☠☠ **1988 (PG-13)** Television adaptation of the classic Isaac Asimov short story. A planet that has two suns (and therefore no night) experiences an eclipse and its inhabitants go mad. **87m/C VHS, Beta.** David Birney, Sarah Douglas, Alexis Kanner, Andra Millian; ***D:*** Paul Mayersberg. *MGM*

Nightflyers ☠½ **1987 (R)** Aboard a weathered space freighter, the crew experience a series of deadly accidents caused by an unknown evil presence. From a novella by George R.R. Martin; T.C. Blake is better known as Robert Collector. **88m/C VHS, Beta, LV.** Michael Praed, Michael Des Barres, Catherine Mary Stewart, John Standing, Lisa Blount; ***D:*** T.C. Blake. *NO*

Nightforce ☠ **1986 (R)** Five buddies plunge into Central American jungles to rescue a young girl held by terrorists. **87m/C VHS, Beta.** Linda Blair, James Van Patten, Chad McQueen, Richard Lynch, Cameron Mitchell; ***D:*** Lawrence Foldes. *NO*

Nighthawks ☠☠½ **1981 (R)** New York City cops scour Manhattan to hunt down an international terrorist on the loose. They race from disco to subway to an airborne tramway. Exciting and well paced. Hauer's American film debut. **100m/C VHS, Beta, LV.** Sylvester Stallone, Billy Dee Williams, Rutger Hauer, Lindsay Wagner, Nigel Davenport, Persis Khambatta, Catherine Mary Stewart, Joe Spinell; ***D:*** Bruce Malmuth; ***M:*** Keith Emerson. *MCA*

The Nightingale **1983** From "Faerie Tale Theatre" comes the story of an Emperor who discovers the value of true friendship and loyalty from his palace kitchen maid who gives him a nightingale. **60m/C VHS, Beta, LV.** Mick Jagger, Barbara Hershey, Bud Cort, Mako; ***D:*** Ivan Passer. *KUI, FOX, FCT*

Nightkill ☠☠½ **1980 (R)** Simple love affair turns into a deadly game of cat and mouse when a bored wife plots to do away with her wealthy, powerful husband with the aid of her attractive lover. Mitchum is the reluctant investigator pulled into the game. **104m/C VHS, Beta.** Jaclyn Smith, Mike Connors, James Franciscus, Robert Mitchum, Sybil Danning; ***D:*** Ted Post. *SUE, NLC*

Nightlife ☠☠½ **1990** An ancient vampiress who rises from the dead spends her time haunting a blood clinic, where the Jewish hematologist starts to fall for her. Made for cable. **93m/C VHS, Beta, LV.** Ben Cross, Maryam D'Abo, Keith Szarabajka, Jesse Corti, Oliver Clark, Glenn Shadix, Camille Saviola; ***D:*** Daniel Taplitz. *MCA*

The Nightman ☠☠ **1993 (R)** Ex-soldier Marcoux becomes the night manager of a failing southern resort, run by sexy, and lonely, Kerns. They begin an affair, which turns sour when Roberston, Kerns' teenaged daughter, also falls for the stud. Then mom is murdered and Marcoux goes to prison. But 18 years later Robertson's past comes back to haunt her. Just what did happen all those years ago? Made for television thriller with additional footage. **96m/C VHS, LV.** Ted Marcoux, Jenny Robertson, Joanna Kerns; ***D:*** Charles Haid; ***W:*** James Poe; ***M:*** Gary Chang. *APX*

Nightmare ☠☠½ **1963** As a child, Janet sees her insane mother stab her father to death. Left in the care of two guardians, the now-grown Janet has recurring nightmares and fears she's inherited her mother's madness. Routine, with red herrings galore. **83m/B VHS.** *GB* Jennie Linden, David Knight, Moira Redmond, Brenda Bruce; ***D:*** Freddie Francis; ***W:*** Jimmy Sangster; ***C:*** John Wilcox; ***M:*** Don Banks. *MCA*

Nightmare *Woof! Blood Splash* **1982 (R)** Boring splatterthon has a young boy hacking his father and his aggressive mistress to pieces when he discovers them in bed. He grows up to be a psycho who continues along the same lines. Humorless and dreadful, the original ads claimed Tom Savini did the special effects. He had nothing to do with it. **97m/C VHS, Beta.** Baird Stafford, Sharon Smith, C.J. Cooke, Mik Cribben, Kathleen Ferguson, Danny Ronan; ***D:*** Romano Scavolini; ***W:*** Romano Scavolini. *NO*

Nightmare at Bittercreek ☠☠ **1991 (PG-13)** Four babes and a tour guide are pursued by psycho gang in the Sierra mountains. Made for television nightmare in your living room. **92m/C VHS.** Tom Skerritt, Joanna Cassidy, Lindsay Wagner, Constance McCashin, Janne Mortil; ***D:*** Tim Burstall. *VMK*

Nightmare at 43 Hillcrest **1974** A family's life becomes a living hell when the police mistakenly raid their house. Based on a true story. **72m/C VHS, Beta.** Jim Hutton, Mariette Hartley. *NO*

Nightmare at Noon ☠ **1987 (R)** Watered-down thriller about a small desert town beset by violent terrorists (who are really locals gone mad from a chemical experiment dumped into the water system). Only the sheriff's small staff is there to stop them. **96m/C VHS.** Wings Hauser, George Kennedy, Bo Hopkins, Brion James, Kimberly Beck, Kimberly Ross; ***D:*** Nico Mastorakis. *REP*

The Nightmare Before Christmas ☠☠☠ *Tim Burton's The Nightmare Before Christmas* **1993 (PG)** Back when he was a animator trainee at Disney, Burton came up with this adventurous idea but couldn't get it made; subsequent directorial success brought more clout. Relies on a painstaking stop-motion technique that took more than two years to film and is justifiably amazing. The story revolves around Jack Skellington, the Pumpkin King of the dangerously weird Halloweentown. Suffering from ennui, he accidentally discovers the wonders of Christmastown and decides to kidnap Santa and rule over this peaceable holiday. Fast pace is maintained by the equally breathless score. Not cuddly, best appreciated by those with a feel for the macabre. **75m/C VHS, LV.** ***D:*** Henry Selick; ***W:*** Caroline Thompson, Tim Burton; ***M:*** Danny Elfman; ***V:*** Danny Elfman, Chris Sarandon, Catherine O'Hara, William Hickey, Ken Page, Ed Ivory, Paul (Pee Wee Herman) Reubens, Glenn Shadix. Nominations: Academy Awards '93: Best Visual Effects; Golden Globe Awards '94: Best Original Score. *TOU*

Nightmare Castle ☠☠ *Amanti d'Oltretomba; Night of the Doomed; The Faceless Monsters; Lovers From Beyond the Tomb* **1965** Jealous mad scientist murders his wife and her lover. Then he conducts a bizarre experiment, using the dead couple's blood to rejuvenate an old servant. Not quite satisfied with his revenge, he then seeks to marry his late wife's sister after realizing that she has been left the inheritance. In time, the perturbed ghosts of the late lovers appear and seek revenge. A real nightmare. **90m/B VHS, Beta.** *IT* Barbara Steele, Paul Muller, Helga Line; ***D:*** Allan Grunewald; ***M:*** Ennio Morricone. *SNC, HHT*

Nightmare in Badham County ☠ *Nightmare* **1976** Two girls get arrested on trumped-up charges in a small backwoods town. They soon discover that the prison farm is a front for a slavery ring. Made for television. **100m/C VHS, Beta.** Deborah Raffin, Lynne Moody, Chuck Connors, Della Reese, Robert Reed, Ralph Bellamy, Tina Louise; ***D:*** John Llewellyn Moxey; ***M:*** Charles Bernstein. *VMK*

Nightmare in Blood ☠½ *Horror Convention* **1975** Vampires lurk in San Francisco and wreak havoc on the night life. **90m/C VHS, Beta.** Kerwin Mathews, Jerry Walter, Barrie Youngfellow; ***D:*** John Stanley. *VCD*

Nightmare in Red China *Woof!* **1955** A campy film examining life in communist China with an all-Indian cast. **67m/B VHS, Beta.** *NO*

Nightmare in Wax ☠½ *Crimes in the Wax Museum* **1969** After suffering disfigurement in a fight with a studio boss, a former make-up man starts a wax museum. For fun, he injects movie stars with a formula that turns them into statues. **91m/C VHS, Beta.** Cameron Mitchell, Anne Helm; ***D:*** Bud Townsend. *MRV*

A Nightmare on Elm Street ☠☠½ **1984 (R)** Feverish, genuinely frightening horror film about Freddy Krueger (Englund), a scarred maniac in a fedora and razor-fingered gloves who kills neighborhood teens in their dreams and, subsequently, in reality. Of the children-fight-back genre, in which the lead victim (Langenkamp) ingeniously goes to great lengths to destroy Freddy. In the tradition of "Friday the 13th" and "Halloween;" spawned a "Freddy" phenomenon: five sequels (to date); a TV series ("Freddy's Nightmares," a horror anthology show hosted by Englund capitalized on his character); and an army of razor-clawed trick or treaters at Halloween. **92m/C VHS, Beta, LV.** John Saxon, Heather Langenkamp, Ronee Blakley, Robert Englund, Amanda Wyss, Nick Corri, Johnny Depp, Charles Fleischer; ***D:*** Wes Craven; ***W:*** Wes Craven; ***M:*** Charles Bernstein. *MED, CDV, IME*

A Nightmare on Elm Street 2: Freddy's Revenge ☠½ **1985 (R)** Mediocre sequel to the popular horror film. Freddy, the dream-haunting psychopath with the ginsu knife hands, returns to possess a teenager's body in order to kill again. Nothing new here, however praise is due for the stunning high-tech dream sequence. **87m/C VHS, Beta, LV.** Mark Patton, Hope Lange, Clu Gulager, Robert Englund, Kim Myers; ***D:*** Jack Sholder; ***W:*** David Chaskin. *MED, CDV, IME*

A Nightmare on Elm Street 3: Dream Warriors ☠☠ **1987 (R)** Chapter three in this slice and dice series. Freddy Krueger is at it again, haunting the dreams of unsuspecting suburban teens. Langenkamp, the nightmare-freaked heroine from the first film, returns to counsel the latest victims of Freddy-infested dreams. Noted for the special effects wizardry but little else, Part Three was produced on a $4.5 million shoe string and took in more than $40 million, making it one of the most successful independently produced films in Hollywood. Followed by "Nightmare on Elmstreet 4: Dream Master." **96m/C VHS, Beta, LV.** Patricia Arquette, Robert Englund, John Saxon, Craig Wasson, Heather Langenkamp, Dick Cavett, Priscilla Pointer, Laurence "Larry" Fishburne; *D:* Chuck Russell; *W:* Chuck Russell, Bruce Wagner, Wes Craven, Frank Darabont; *C:* Roy Wagner; *M:* Angelo Badalamenti. *MED, CDV, IME*

A Nightmare on Elm Street 4: Dream Master ✓✓½ **1988 (R)** Freddy Krueger is still preying on people in their dreams, but he may have met his match as he battles for supremacy with a telepathically talented girl. What Part 4 lacks in substance, it makes up for in visual verve, including scenes of a kid drowning in his waterbed, and a pizza covered with pepperoni-like faces of Freddy's previous victims. This box office bonanza set a new record as the most successful opening weekend of any independently released film. Followed by "A Nightmare on Elm Street: A Dream Child." **99m/C VHS, Beta, LV.** Robert Englund, Rodney Eastman, Danny Hassel, Andras Jones, Tuesday Knight, Lisa Wilcox, Ken Sagoes, Toy Newkirk, Brooke Theiss, Brooke Bundy; *D:* Renny Harlin; *W:* Scott Pierce, Brian Helgeland; *M:* Craig Safan. *MED, CDV, IME*

A Nightmare on Elm Street 5: Dream Child ✓✓ **1989 (R)** The fifth installment of Freddy Krueger's never-ending adventures. Here, America's favorite knife-wielding burn victim, unable to best the Dream Master from the previous film, haunts the dreams of her unborn fetus. Gore fans may be disappointed to discover that much of the blood and guts ended up on the cutting room floor. **90m/C VHS, Beta, LV.** Robert Englund, Lisa Wilcox, Kelly Jo Minter, Danny Hassel; *D:* Stephen Hopkins; *W:* Leslie Bohem; *M:* Jay Michael Ferguson. Golden Raspberry Awards '89: Worst Song ("Bring Your Daughter to the Slaughter"). *IME, MED, VTR*

Nightmare on the 13th Floor ✓ **1990 (PG-13)** A travel writer at an old hotel glimpses murder on a supposedly non-existent floor. Nasty devil-worshippers are afoot, but the chills in this mild made-for-cable throwaway seldom dip below room temperature. **85m/C VHS, Beta.** Michael Greene, John Karlen, Louise Fletcher, Alan Fudge, James Brolin; *D:* Walter Grauman. *PAR*

Nightmare Sisters *Woof!* **1987 (R)** Three sorority sisters become possessed by a demon and then sexually ravage a nearby fraternity. **83m/C VHS, Beta.** Brinke Stevens, Michelle (McClellan) Bauer, Linnea Quigley; *D:* David DeCoteau. *TWE*

Nightmare Weekend ✓ **1986 (R)** A professor's evil assistant lures three young women into his lab and performs cruel and vicious experiments that transform the girls and their dates into crazed zombies. **86m/C VHS, Beta.** Dale Midkiff, Debbie Laster, Debra Hunter, Lori Lewis; *D:* Henry Sala. *LIV*

The Nightmare Years **1989** An American reporter in Nazi Germany dares to report the truth to an unbelieving world. Based on a true story. Two cassettes. **237m/C VHS, Beta.** Sam Waterston, Marthe Keller, Kurtwood Smith; *D:* Anthony Page; *M:* Vladimir Cosma. *TTC*

Nightmares ✓✓ **1983 (PG)** A less-than-thrilling horror anthology featuring four tales in which common, everyday occurrences take on the ingredients of a nightmare. In the same vein as "Twilight Zone" and "Creepshow." **99m/C VHS, Beta.** Christina Raines, Emilio Estevez, Moon Zappa, Lance Henriksen, Richard Masur, Veronica Cartwright; *D:* Joseph Sargent; *W:* Jeffrey Bloom, Christopher Crowe. *MCA*

Nights and Days ✓✓½ **1976** Adaptation of writer Maria Dabrowska's tale about a Polish family chronicles the persecution, expulsions, and land grabbing that occurred after the unsuccessful Uprising of 1864. In Polish with English subtitles. **255m/C VHS.** *PL* Jadwiga Baranska, Jerzy Binczycki; *D:* Jerzy Antczak. Nominations: Academy Awards '76: Best Foreign Language Film. *FCT*

Nights in White Satin ✓½ **1987** A made-for-video Cinderella story about the growing love between a fashion photographer and a young model whose boyfriend has just been murdered. **96m/C VHS, Beta.** Kenneth Gilman, Priscilla Harris; *D:* Michael Bernard. *PSM, PAR*

Nights of Cabiria ✓✓✓½ *Le Notti de Cabiria; Cabiria* **1957** Fellini classic which details the personal decline of a naive prostitute who thinks she's found true love. In Italian with English subtitles or dubbed. Basis for the musical "Sweet Charity." **111m/B VHS, Beta.** *IT* Giulietta Masina, Amedeo Nazzari; *D:* Federico Fellini; *W:* Federico Fellini, Tullio Pinelli, Ennio Flaiano; *M:* Nino Rota. Academy Awards '57: Best Foreign Language Film; Cannes Film Festival '57: Best Actress (Masina). *NOS, VYY, APD*

Nightscare ✓✓ *Night Scare; Beyond Bedlam* **1993 (R)** When Dr. Stephanie Lyell's (Hurley) drug behavior-modification experiment goes wrong it allows serial killer Marc Gilmour (Allen) to get to his victims through their dreams. The doc tries to prove to Detective Inspector Terry Hamilton (Fairbrass) that the drug is safe by injecting them both but things get out of hand. Adapted from the novel by Harry Adam Knight. **89m/C VHS, LV.** *GB* Craig Fairbrass, Elizabeth Hurley, Keith Allen, Jesse Birdsall, Craig Kelly; *D:* Vadim Jean; *W:* Vadim Jean. *LIV*

Nightstalker *Woof!* **1979** A brother and sister who were condemned to eternal death 12,000 years ago must eat virgins to keep their bodies from rotting. Trouble is, while they search for dinner, the movie decomposes. For mature audiences with no fantasies of celluloid nirvana. **90m/C VHS, Beta.** Aldo Ray. *LIV*

Nightstick ✓½ *Calhoun* **1987 (R)** New York vigilante cop fights nasties who threaten to blow the lid off the city. Worse, they kidnap super cop's girl forcing him to save her along with the city. Lots of violence, predictable plot, and mediocre acting leave this one without much bang. **90m/C VHS, Beta.** Bruce Fairbairn, Kerrie Keane, John Vernon, Robert Vaughn, Isaac Hayes, Leslie Nielsen; *D:* Joseph L. Scanlan. *COL*

Nightwing ✓½ **1979 (PG)** Suspense drama about three people who risk their lives to exterminate a colony of plague-carrying vampire bats in New Mexican Indian community. From the novel by Martin Cruz Smith and adapted by Smith, Steve Shagan, and Bud Shrake. OK viewing for the undiscriminating palate. **103m/C VHS, Beta, LV.** Nick Mancuso, David Warner, Kathryn Harrold, Strother Martin; *D:* Arthur Hiller; *M:* Henry Mancini. *COL*

Nightwish ✓½ **1989 (R)** Students do more than homework when a professor leads them into their own horrifying dreams. Soon it becomes impossible to distinguish dreams from reality. **96m/C VHS, LV.** Jack Starrett, Robert Tessier; *D:* Bruce Cook Jr. *VES*

Nijinsky ✓✓ **1980 (R)** An opulent biography of the famous ballet dancer. His exciting and innovative choreography gets little attention. The film concentrates on his infamous homosexual lifestyle and his relationship with impresario Sergei Diaghilev (Bates, in a tour-de-force performance). Lovely to look at, but slow and unconvincing. **125m/C VHS, Beta.** Alan Bates, George de la Pena, Leslie Browne, Alan Badel, Carla Fracci, Colin Blakely, Ronald Pickup, Ronald Lacey, Vernon Dobtcheff, Jeremy Irons, Frederick Jaeger, Janet Suzman, Sian Phillips; *D:* Herbert Ross. *PAR*

Nikki, the Wild Dog of the North ✓½ **1961 (G)** When a Malemute pup is separated from his Canadian trapper master, he teams up with a bear cub for a series of adventures. Later the pup is reunited with his former master for still more adventures. Adapted from a novel by James Oliver Curwood for Disney. **73m/C VHS, Beta.** *CA* Jean Coutu; *D:* Jack Couffer, Don Haldane. *DIS*

Nina Takes a Lover ✓✓ **1994 (R)** Romantic comedy finds Nina (San Giacomo) deciding that the passion is gone from her three-year marriage so, while her husband is out of town, she picks up a nameless Welsh photographer (Rhys) and begins an affair. The affair is over as the movie begins but Nina tells her story to a tabloid journalist (O'Keefe) who's writing about adultery. Gimmicky, with shallow if attractive characters and an equally attractive San Francisco setting. **100m/C VHS, LV.** Laura San Giacomo, Paul Rhys, Michael O'Keefe, Cristi Conaway, Fisher Stevens; *D:* Alan Jacobs; *W:* Alan Jacobs; *C:* Phil Parmet; *M:* Todd Boekelheide. *COL*

Nine Ages of Nakedness ✓ **1969** The story of a man whose ancestors have been plagued by a strange problem: beautiful, naked women who create carnal chaos. **88m/C VHS, Beta.** Harrison Marks. *VDM, MED, MRV*

9 1/2 Ninjas ✓✓½ **1990 (R)** A cautious and disciplined martial artist trains a young and flirtatious woman in the ways of the ninja. His life becomes exciting in more ways than one, when he realizes she's being followed by ninjas with more on their minds than her training—they want to assassinate her! Crazy mixture of sex, kung fu and humor make this film one surprise after another. **88m/C VHS, Beta, LV.** Michael Phenicie, Andee Gray, Tiny Lister; *D:* Aaron Worth; *W:* Bill Crounse. *REP*

9 1/2 Weeks ✓✓½ **1986 (R)** Chance meeting between a Wall Street exec and an art gallery employee evolves into an experimental sexual relationship bordering on sado-masochism. Video version is more explicit than the theatrical release, but not by much. Strong characterizations by both actors prevent this from being strictly pornography. Well-written, with strength of male and female personalities nicely balanced. Intriguing, but not for all tastes. **114m/C VHS, Beta, LV.** Mickey Rourke, Kim Basinger, Margaret Whitton, Karen Young, David Margulies, Christine Baranski, Roderick Cook, Dwight Weist; *D:* Adrian Lyne; *W:* Patricia Louisianna Knop, Zalman King; *M:* Jack Nitzsche. *MGM*

Nine Days a Queen ✓✓✓ *Lady Jane Grey; Tudor Rose* **1934** An historical drama based on the life of Lady Jane Grey, proclaimed Queen of England after the death of Henry VIII of England and summarily executed for treason by Mary Tudor after a nine-day reign. An obscure tragedy with good performances and absorbing storyline. Remade as "Lady Jane" (1985). **80m/B VHS, Beta.** *GB* John Mills, Cedric Hardwicke, Nova Pilbeam, Sybil Thorndike, Leslie Perrins, Felix Aylmer, Miles Malleson; *D:* Robert Stevenson. *HHT, DVT*

Nine Deaths of the Ninja *Woof!* **1985 (R)** Faceless ninja warrior Kosugi leads a team of commandos on a mission to rescue a group of political prisoners held captive in the Philippine jungles. Features Ozone-depleted plot, incongruous performances, and inane dialogue, not to mention two main villains—a neurotic Nazi in a wheelchair and a black lesbian amazon—who chew jungle and bring bad art to a new level of appreciation. Amazing in its total badness. Produced by Cannon. **93m/C VHS, Beta.** Sho Kosugi, Brent Huff, Emelia Lesniak, Regina Richardson; *D:* Emmett Alston; *W:* Emmett Alston. *MED*

The Nine Lives of Elfego Baca ✓✓ **1958** Venerable Western hero Loggia faces a veritable army of gunfighters and bandits. Action-packed but not too violent; family fun. **78m/C VHS, Beta.** Robert Loggia, Robert Simon, Lisa Montell, Nestor Paiva; *D:* Norman Foster. *DIS*

Nine Lives of Fritz the Cat ✓✓ **1974** Fritz feels that life's too square in the 70's, so he takes off into some of his other lives for more adventure. Cleaner but still naughty sequel to the X-rated "Fritz the Cat," featuring neither the original's writer/director Ralph Bakshi nor cartoonist Robert Crumb. Tame and lame. Animated. **77m/C VHS, LV.** *D:* Robert Taylor. Nominations: Cannes Film Festival '74: Best Film. *VES*

Nine Months ✓✓½ **1995 (PG-13)** Happily single Samuel (Grant) gets girlfriend Rebecca (Moore) pregnant and promptly wigs out. He makes amends to the lovely Rebecca, they marry, and true to writer/director Columbus' style, live happily ever after. Bachelor pal Sean (Goldblum) and an expectant couple (Arnold and Cusack) with three kids round out the cast, with Williams offering his usual manic flair as a Russian obstetrician, improvising his scenes with glee. Grant's knack for clumsy befuddlement fits well with the warm, fuzzy style of Columbus. "Nine" doesn't go out on any limbs, but is a pleasant diversion anyway. Film may well have gotten lost in the mega-box office summer of '95, till Grant guaranteed publicity when his dalliance with Divine Brown threw him into jail and the headlines. His faux pas causes unintended laughs during a few key scenes.

The trailer clip showing Grant during a mug shot is gone—producers claim the segment was deleted before his real-life arrest. Remake of the French film "Neuf Mois." **103m/C VHS, LV.** Hugh Grant, Julianne Moore, Tom Arnold, Joan Cusack, Jeff Goldblum; ***Cameos:*** Robin Williams; ***D:*** Chris Columbus; ***W:*** Chris Columbus; ***C:*** Donald McAlpine; ***M:*** Hans Zimmer. *TCF*

9 to 5 ☠☠½ **1980 (PG)** In this caricature of large corporations and women in the working world, Coleman plays the male chauvinist boss who calls the shots and keeps his employees, all female, under his thumb. Three of the office secretaries daydream of Coleman's disposal and rashly kidnap him after a silly set of occurrences threaten their jobs. While they have him under lock and key, the trio take office matters into their own hands and take a stab at running things their own way, with amusing results. The basis for a television series. **111m/C VHS, Beta, LV.** Jane Fonda, Lily Tomlin, Dolly Parton, Dabney Coleman, Sterling Hayden, Norma Donaldson; ***D:*** Colin Higgins; ***W:*** Patricia Resnick; ***C:*** Reynaldo Villalobos; ***M:*** Charles Fox. Nominations: Academy Awards '80: Best Song ("Nine to Five"). *FOX*

976-EVIL ☠☠ **1988 (R)** Englund (the infamous Freddy from the Nightmare on Elm Street epics) directs this horror movie where a lonely teenager dials direct to demons from hell. **102m/C VHS, Beta, LV.** Stephen Geoffreys, Jim Metzler, Maria Rubell, Sandy Dennis, Robert Picardo, Leslie Deane, Pat O'Bryan; ***D:*** Robert Englund; ***M:*** Tom Chase, Steve Rucker. *COL*

976-EVIL 2: The Astral Factor ☠½ **1991 (R)** Satan returns the call in this supernatural thriller that sequels the original film. **93m/C VHS.** Pat O'Bryan, Rene Assa, Debbie James; ***D:*** Jim Wynorski; ***W:*** Erik Anjou. *LIV, VES*

984: Prisoner of the Future *The Tomorrow Man* **1984** A shocking, futuristic tale of human self-destruction. **70m/C VHS, Beta.** Don Francks, Stephen Markle; ***D:*** Tibor Takacs. *NO*

1900 ☠☠☠ **1976 (R)** Bertolucci's impassioned epic about two Italian families, one land-owning, the other, peasant. Shows the sweeping changes of the 20th century begun by the trauma of WWI and the onslaught of Italian socialism. Edited down from its original 360-minute length and dubbed in English from three other languages, the film suffers somewhat from editing and from its nebulous lack of commitment to any genre. Elegantly photographed by Vittorio Storaro. Also titled "Novecento." **255m/C VHS, Beta, LV.** *FR IT GE* Robert De Niro, Gerard Depardieu, Burt Lancaster, Donald Sutherland, Dominique Sanda, Sterling Hayden, Laura Betti, Francesca Bertini, Werner Bruhns, Stefania Sandrelli, Anna Henkel, Alida Valli; ***D:*** Bernardo Bertolucci; ***W:*** Giuseppe Bertolucci, Bernardo Bertolucci; ***C:*** Vittorio Storaro. *PAR, INJ*

1918 ☠☠½ **1985** An adaptation of the Horton Foote play about the effects of WWI and an influenza epidemic on a small Texas town. Slow-moving but satisfying. Score by Willie Nelson. Originally produced for PBS's "American Playhouse." Prequelled by "On Valentine's Day." **89m/C VHS, Beta.** Matthew Broderick, Hallie Foote, William Converse-Roberts, Rochelle Oliver, Michael Higgins, Horton Foote Jr., William Bill McGhee, Jeannie McCarthy; ***D:*** Ken Harrison; ***W:*** Horton Foote; ***M:*** Willie Nelson. *FOX*

1931: Once Upon a Time in New York ☠☠ **1972** Prohibition-era gangsters war, beat each other up, make headlines, and drink bathtub gin. **90m/C VHS, Beta.** Richard Conte, Adolfo Celi, Lionel Stander, Irene Papas. *VCD*

1941 ☠☠½ **1979 (PG)** Proved to be the most expensive comedy of all time with a budget exceeding $35 million. The depiction of Los Angeles in the chaotic days after the bombing of Pearl Harbor combines elements of fantasy and black humor. **120m/C VHS, Beta, LV.** John Belushi, Dan Aykroyd, Patti LuPone, Ned Beatty, Slim Pickens, Murray Hamilton, Christopher Lee, Tim Matheson, Toshiro Mifune, Warren Oates, Robert Stack, Nancy Allen, Elisha Cook Jr., Lorraine Gary, Treat Williams, Mickey Rourke, John Candy; ***D:*** Steven Spielberg; ***W:*** Robert Zemeckis, Bob Gale; ***C:*** William A. Fraker; ***M:*** John Williams. Nominations: Academy Awards '79: Best Cinematography, Best Sound. *MCA, CCB*

1969 ☠☠☠½ **1989 (R)** Three teenage friends during the 1960s become radicalized by the return of one of their friends from Vietnam in a coffin. Critically lambasted directorial debut for "On Golden Pond" author Ernest Thompson. **96m/C VHS, Beta, LV.** Kiefer Sutherland, Robert Downey Jr., Winona Ryder, Bruce Dern, Joanna Cassidy, Mariette Hartley; ***D:*** Ernest Thompson. *MED*

1984 ☠☠☠½ **1984 (R)** A very fine adaptation of George Orwell's infamous novel, this version differs from the overly simplistic and cautionary 1954 film because of fine casting and production design. The illegal love affair of a government official becomes his attempt to defy the crushing inhumanity and lack of simple pleasures of an omniscient government. Filmed in London, it skillfully visualizes our time's most central prophetic nightmare. **117m/C VHS, Beta, LV.** *GB* John Hurt, Richard Burton, Suzanna Hamilton, Cyril Cusack, Gregory Fisher, Andrew Wilde, Rupert Baderman; ***D:*** Michael Radford; ***C:*** Roger Deakins. *LIV*

1990: The Bronx Warriors *Woof! 1990 I Guerrieri del Bronx; Bronx Warriors* **1983 (R)** Good street gang members combat evil corporate powers in a semi-futuristic South Bronx. Lame copy of "Escape from New York." **86m/C VHS, Beta.** *IT* Vic Morrow, Christopher Connelly, Fred Williamson; ***D:*** Enzo G. Castellari. *MED*

1991: The Year Punk Broke **1992** Documents a grunge rock tour of European festivals in 1991 when the alternative bands were largely unknown to all but hardcore fans. Follows Sonic Youth, Nirvana, Dinosaur Jr., Babes in Toyland, Gumball, and grandaddy punk idols, The Ramones, behind-the-scenes and through their performances. **95m/C VHS.** ***D:*** David Markey. *MOV*

90 Days ☠☠☠ **1986** Charming independently made Canadian comedy about two young men handling their respective romantic dilemmas—one awaiting an oriental fiancee he's never met, the other who is being kicked out of his house by his wife. **99m/C VHS, Beta.** *CA* Stefan Wodoslowsky, Sam Grana, Christine Pak; ***D:*** Giles Walker. *FOX*

92 in the Shade ☠☠☠ **1976 (R)** Based upon McGuane's novel, the film deals with a bored, wealthy rogue who becomes a fishing guide in the Florida Keys, and battles against the competition of two crusty, half-mad codgers. Sloppy, irreverent comedy as only a first-time writer-turned-director can fashion. **91m/C VHS, Beta.** Peter Fonda, Warren Oates, Margot Kidder, Burgess Meredith, Harry Dean Stanton; ***D:*** Thomas McGuane; ***W:*** Thomas McGuane. *FOX*

99 & 44/100 Dead ☠ *Call Harry Crown* **1974 (PG)** Frankenheimer falters with this silly gangster flick. Harris is hired to kill Dillman, by local godfather O'Brien. Originally written as a satirical look at gangster movies, but it doesn't stick to satire, and as a result is disappointing. **98m/C VHS.** Richard Harris, Chuck Connors, Edmond O'Brien, Bradford Dillman, Ann Turkel; ***D:*** John Frankenheimer; ***W:*** Robert Dillon; ***M:*** Henry Mancini. *FOX*

99 Women ☠½ *Isle of Lost Women* **1969 (R)** Sympathetic prison warden attempts to investigate conditions at a women's prison camp. Thin and exploitative view of lesbianism behind bars that sensationalizes the subject. **90m/C VHS, Beta.** *GB SP GE IT* Maria Schell, Herbert Lom, Mercedes McCambridge, Luciana Paluzzi; ***D:*** Jess (Jesus) Franco. *NO*

Ninja 3: The Domination ☠☠ **1984 (R)** Ninja master must remove the spirit of a deadly ninja assassin from a young woman intent on wreaking havoc among the Phoenix police department. Extremely silly super ninja epic utterly uninhibited by the usual plot conventions. **92m/C VHS, Beta.** Lucinda Dickey, Sho Kosugi; ***D:*** Sam Firstenberg; ***W:*** James R. Silke. *MGM*

Ninja Academy ☠½ **1990 (R)** Seven wimps, losers, and spoiled brats come to the Ninja Academy to learn the art. Will they make it? **93m/C VHS.** Will Egan, Kelly Randall, Gerald Okomura, Michael David, Robert Factor, Jeff Robinson; ***D:*** Nico Mastorakis. *NO*

Ninja: American Warrior ☠½ **1990** An evil ninja takes on the U.S. Drug Enforcement Agency when the authorities threaten to shut him down. **90m/C VHS, Beta.** Joff Houston, John Wilford; ***D:*** Tommy Cheng. *IMP*

Ninja Brothers of Blood ☠ **1989** A guy falls for a rival gang member's girl. Neither the gang nor the guy's former girlfriend take kindly to this! **90m/C VHS, Beta, LV.** Marcus Gibson, Fonda Lynn, Brian McClave, Jonathan Soper; ***D:*** Raymond Woo. *IMP*

Ninja Champion *Woof!* **198?** White-clad and masked ninja heros come to the aid of some Interpol agents tracking down a sleazy diamond smuggler. Invisible storyline features very little actual ninja. Extremely unconvincing and poorly dubbed. **90m/C VHS, Beta.** *HK* Bruce Baron, Richard Harrison; ***D:*** Godfrey Ho; ***W:*** Godfrey Ho. *TWE*

Ninja Checkmate ☠ **1990** An evil ninja seems indestructible, but finally he meets his match. **90m/C VHS, Beta.** Simon Lee, Jack Long, Jeanie Chang. *MGI*

Ninja Commandments ☠ **1987** Everything is at stake when an evil warrior takes on the greatest fighter in the land: the winner will rule the empire! **90m/C VHS, Beta.** Richard Harrison, Dave Wheeler; ***D:*** Joseph Lai. *IMP*

Ninja Condors ☠ **1987** A young man grows up to avenge the murder of his father. **85m/C VHS, Beta.** Alexander Lou, Stuart Hugh; ***D:*** James Wu. *TWE*

Ninja Connection ☠ **1990** Ninja terrorism is employed as a scare tactic to deter a group who wants to break up an international drug ring. **90m/C VHS, Beta.** Patricia Greenford, Jane Kingsly, Joe Nelson, Louis Roth, Henry Steele, Stuart Steen; ***D:*** York Lam. *IMP*

Ninja Death Squad ☠ **1987** A team specializing in political assassinations is hunted down by a special agent. **89m/C VHS, Beta.** Glen Carson, Patricia Goodman, Joff Houston, Billy Jones, Wallace Jones, John Wilford; ***D:*** Tommy Cheng. *IMP*

Ninja Demon's Massacre ☠ **198?** Ninja named Willie responds to federal investigations into his spying business by wearing a black robe and slashing feds with long swords. **89m/C VHS, Beta.** Ted Brooke, James Lear. *TWE*

Ninja Destroyer ☠ **197? (R)** Ninja warriors battle over an emerald mine. **92m/C VHS, Beta.** *HK* Bruce Baron, Stuart Smith; ***D:*** Godfrey Ho; ***W:*** Godfrey Ho. *TWE*

Ninja Dragon ☠ **198?** Two Ninjas are hired in a gang war and dazzle all those who watch by kicking their enemies to death. **92m/C VHS, Beta.** Richard Harrison. *TWE*

Ninja Exterminators *Woof!* **1981** Low-grade kung-fu antics mascarading as ninja rib-kicking bonanza. Dubbed. **85m/C VHS, Beta.** *HK* Jacky Cheng, Ko Shou Liang, Tai Chen. *NO*

Ninja Fantasy *Woof!* **1986** Ninja drug smugglers and government officials battle over a large drug shipment. Everybody go chop socky. Not much in way of ninja fantasy. Dubbed. **95m/C VHS, Beta.** *HK* Adam Nell, Ian Frank, Jordan Heller, Ken Ashley, Jenny Mills, Jack Rodman; ***D:*** Bruce Lambert; ***W:*** Anthony Green. *TWE*

Ninja Hunt *Woof!* **198?** This time, ninjas kick international terrorists in the head while searching for secret formula. Poorly dubbed pseudo ninja developed by Godfrey Ho. **92m/C VHS, Beta.** *HK* Bruce Baron, Stuart Smith; ***D:*** Joseph Lai; ***W:*** Stephen Saul. *TWE*

Ninja Massacre ☠ **1984** Gangsters covet a secret manual of kung fu techniques. Heel-splintering battles break out as a result. **87m/C VHS, Beta.** Lo Lieh, Pai Ying, Lung Jun Ehr, Tiki Shirtee. *GEM, MRV*

Ninja Masters of Death ☠ **1985** Terrorists reign supreme until the white ninja saves the city. **90m/C VHS, Beta.** Mick Jones, Chris Petersen, Daniel Wells, Richard Young; ***D:*** Bruce Lambert. *IMP*

Ninja Mission ☠½ **1984 (R)** First Scandinavian ninja epic follows CIA agent and his group of ninja fighters as they embark on a hazardous mission to rescue two people from a Soviet prison. They use their fighting skills (Swedish ninjas favor guns more than ninjutsu) against Russian soldiers. Dubbed. **95m/C VHS, Beta.** *SW* Christopher Kohlberg, Curt Brober, Hanna Pola; ***D:*** Mats Helge. *MED*

Ninja Nightmare **1988 (R)** A man seeks revenge for his family's death. **98m/C VHS, Beta.** Leo Fong. *PSM*

Ninja of the Magnificence ½ **1989** When the ninja master is killed, factions within his group battle for control. **90m/C VHS, Beta.** Sam Baker, Patrick Frbezar, Clive Hadwen, Tim Michael, Renato Sala; ***D:*** Charles Lee. *IMP*

Ninja Operation: Licensed to Terminate **1987** Two warriors risk broken noses and twisted limbs to take on the Black Ninja Empire. **89m/C VHS, Beta.** Richard Harrison, Paul Marshall, Jack McPeat, Grant Temple; ***D:*** Joseph Lai. *IMP*

Ninja Phantom Heroes **1987** Two Vietnam vets are imprisoned for war crimes. One escapes and forms his own secret ninja society. **90m/C VHS, Beta.** Glen Carson, George Dickson, Allen Leung, Christine Wells; ***D:*** Bruce Lambert. *TWE*

The Ninja Pirates ½ **1990** In the Sung Dynasty, a group of bloodthirsty pirates are hunted down after stealing a golden treasure. **90m/C VHS, Beta.** Chi Lan, Lo Lieh, Carter Wong, Nancy Yan. *MGI*

Ninja Powerforce ½ **1990** Two childhood friends end up as members of rival ninja gangs in the midst of a bloody war. Usual assortment of ninja-inflicted injuries result. **90m/C VHS, Beta.** Jonathan Bould, Richard Harrison; ***D:*** Joseph Lai. *IMP*

Ninja Showdown **1990** A warrior must take on a number of vicious bandits in order to defend his small town. He vows revenge on anyone who threatens his people. **92m/C VHS, Beta.** Richard Harrison; ***D:*** Joseph Lai. *TWE*

Ninja Squad **198?** Empires, families, and honor are at stake in a fierce battle of heel-to-head action. **92m/C VHS, Beta.** Dave Wheeler, Richard Harrison, Timalden. *TWE*

Ninja Strike Force ½ **1988** The Black Ninjas steal the powerful "spirit sword," and go on a bloody rampage. **89m/C VHS, Beta.** Richard Harrison, Gary Carter; ***D:*** Joseph Lai. *IMP*

Ninja Supremo ½ **1990** A rebellious teenager studies Kung-fu, and then returns to his village a hero after he gains expertise in his chosen field. **100m/C VHS, Beta.** David Tao, Yueh Wah, Sun Yueh. *MGI*

Ninja Swords of Death ½ **1990** A noble warrior challenges a vicious assassin who uses a spur-sword. He is nearly decapitated in the process. **90m/C VHS, Beta.** Chang Ying Chun, Chia Ling, Tien Pang, Kong Pun. *MGI*

Ninja Terminator *Woof!* **1969** Possession of all three pieces of the Golden Warrior turns the holder into the magically super-powered "Ninja Terminator." Three students battle for that honor. Very bad indeed. **92m/C VHS.** *TWE, VTR*

Ninja the Battalion **1990** Agents from America, the Soviet Union, and China try to recover germ warfare secrets stolen by the Japanese secret service. **90m/C VHS, Beta.** Roger Crawford, Sam Huxley, Alexander Lou, Dickson Warn; ***D:*** Victor Sears. *TWE*

Ninja the Protector **198?** A ninja tracks down and kicks the ninja head of a counterfeiting ring. **92m/C VHS, Beta.** Richard Harrison. *TWE*

Ninja, the Violent Sorcerer ½ **1986** Murderer, with the help of Chinese vampires, does battle with the ghost of a dead gambling lord's wife and the gambling lord's living brother. Often tedious even with above average production and incredible plot. **90m/C VHS, Beta.** ***D:*** Bruce Lambert; ***W:*** Daniel Clough. *TWE*

Ninja Turf *L.A. Streetfighters* **1986 (R)** Teenage kick artists rip off a Hollywood drug dealer and are pursued by a swarm of ninja hitmen. **83m/C VHS, Beta, LV.** Jun Chong, Bill Wallace, Rosanna King, James Lew, Phillip Rhee. *COL*

Ninja Vengeance ½ **1993 (R)** The corrupt sheriff of a small Texas town, who also leads the KKK, is terrorizing a young African-American local. Then our lone hero rides into town on his trusty motorcycle to save the day. Only this time instead of your average gunman, he's a ninja. **87m/C VHS.** Stephen K. Hayes, Janet K. Pawlak, Craig Boyett, David Paul Lord; ***D:*** Karl Armstrong; ***W:*** Carrie Armstrong, Karl Armstrong. *COL*

Ninja vs. Ninja ½ **1990** A scientist has found a cure for heroin addiction, but ninja drug lords won't let his discovery see the light of day! **90m/C VHS, Beta.** Hui Hsiao Chiang, Callan Leong. *MGI*

Ninja vs. the Shaolin ½ **1984** Savage fighting between priests and ninjas results in one of the bloodiest pages in history. **90m/C VHS, Beta.** Alexander Lou, John Wu; ***D:*** Jacky Hwong. *MGI*

Ninja Wars *Woof!* **1984** One ninja takes on five ninja assassins who, along with an evil ninja sorcerer, have kidnapped his ninja girlfriend. Medieval ninja nonsense that's essentially incoherent. In Japanese with English dubbing. **95m/C VHS, Beta.** *PSM*

Ninja's Extreme Weapons ½ **1990** Blue Ninja takes it to the streets when his brother is killed by the underworld. **90m/C VHS, Beta.** James Gray, Donald Muir; ***D:*** Victor Sears. *TWE, HHE*

Ninotchka ½ **1939 (R)** Delightful romantic comedy. Garbo is a cold Russian agent sent to Paris to check up on her comrades, who are being seduced by capitalism. She inadvertently falls in love with a playboy, who melts her communist heart. Garbo talks and laughs. Satirical, energetic, and witty. Later a Broadway musical called "Silk Stockings." **110m/B VHS, Beta, LV, 8mm.** Greta Garbo, Melvyn Douglas, Ina Claire, Sig Rumann, Felix Bressart, Bela Lugosi; ***D:*** Ernst Lubitsch; ***W:*** Billy Wilder; ***C:*** William H. Daniels. National Board of Review Awards '39: 10 Best Films of the Year; Nominations: Academy Awards '39: Best Actress (Garbo), Best Picture, Best Screenplay, Best Story. *MGM*

The Ninth Configuration *Twinkle, Twinkle, Killer Kane* **1979 (R)** Based on Blatty's novel "Twinkle, Twinkle, Killer Kane" (also the film's alternate title), this is a weird and surreal tale of a mock rebellion of high-ranking military men held in a secret base hospital for the mentally ill. Keach is good as the commander who is just as insane as the patients. Available in many different lengths, this is generally considered to be the best. **115m/C VHS, Beta, LV.** Stacy Keach, Scott Wilson, Jason Miller, Ed Flanders, Neville Brand, Alejandro Rey, Robert Loggia, George DiCenzo; ***D:*** William Peter Blatty; ***W:*** William Peter Blatty. Golden Globe Awards '81: Best Screenplay. *NWV*

Nitti: The Enforcer **1988 (PG-13)** Made-for-TV saga about Al Capone's brutal enforcer and right hand man, Frank Nitti. Diversified cast, (Moriarty in particular) do their best to keep things moving along, and the atmosphere is consistently and appropriately violent. Made to capitalize on the success of 1987's "The Untouchables." **94m/C VHS.** Anthony LaPaglia, Vincent Guastaferro, Trini Alvarado, Michael Moriarty, Michael Russo, Louis Guss, Bruno Kirby; ***D:*** Michael Switzer. *ACA*

Nixon **1995 (R)** Stone again "interprets" historical events of the 60s and 70s with a sprawling, bold bio of Richard Nixon. Covering all the highlights of Nixon's public life, and speculating on his private one, Hopkins convincingly portrays "Tricky Dick" as an embattled, lonely political genius. Gigantic all-star cast is lead by Oscar-caliber performance of Joan Allen as Pat Nixon. Even at over three hours, there isn't nearly enough time to explore the significance of all the events covered here. As usual, Stone has taken some creative license, which lead to the Nixon daughters publicly trashing the film, and Walt Disney's daughter expressing "shame" at being affiliated with it. **190m/C VHS.** Anthony Hopkins, Joan Allen, Ed Harris, Bob Hoskins, David Paymer, Paul Sorvino, J.T. Walsh, James Woods, Madeline Kahn, Brian Bedford, Mary Steenburgen, Powers Boothe, E.G. Marshall, David Hyde Pierce, Kevin Dunn, Annabeth Gish, Tony Goldwyn, Larry Hagman, Edward Herrmann, Saul Rubinek, Tony LoBianco; ***D:*** Oliver Stone; ***W:*** Christopher Wilkinson, Stephen J. Rivele, Oliver Stone; ***C:*** Robert Richardson; ***M:*** John Williams. Los Angeles Film Critics Association Awards '95: Best Supporting Actress (Allen); National Society of Film Critics Awards '95: Best Supporting Actress (Allen); Nominations: Academy Awards '95: Best Actor (Hopkins), Best Screenplay, Best Score; Academy Awards '96: Best Supporting Actress (Allen); British Academy Awards '95: Best Supporting Actress (Allen); Golden Globe Awards '95: Best Actor—Drama (Hopkins); Screen Actors Guild Award '95: Best Actor (Hopkins), Best Actress (Allen), Cast. *TOU*

No Big Deal ½ **1983 (PG-13)** Dillon is a streetwise teenager who makes friends at his new school. Blah promise; bad acting makes this no big deal. **86m/C VHS.** Kevin Dillon, Sylvia Miles, Tammy Grimes, Jane Krakowski, Christopher Gartin, Mary Joan Negro; ***D:*** Robert Charlton. *BTV*

No Comebacks **1985** Two British mysteries, made for television from stories by Frederick Forsyth: "A Careful Man," about a dying millionaire who cheats his heirs, and "Privilege," about a clever stamp dealer who exacts revenge upon a libelous gossip columnist. **60m/C VHS, Beta.** *GB* Milo O'Shea, Cyril Cusack, Dan O'Herlihy, Gayle Hunnicutt. *PSM*

No Contest **1994 (R)** International terrorists, lead by Oz (Clay), hold the TV host (Tweed) and contestants of the Ms. Galaxy beauty pageant hostage with a $10 million ransom demand. **98m/C VHS.** Andrew Dice Clay, Shannon Tweed, Robert Davi, Roddy Piper, Nicholas Campbell; ***D:*** Paul Lynch; ***W:*** Robert Cooper. *COL*

No Dead Heroes **1987** Green Beret Vietnam war hero succumbs to Soviet scheming when they plant a computer chip in his brain. Unoriginal and unworthy. **86m/C VHS, Beta.** Max Thayer, John Dresden, Toni Nero; ***D:*** J.C. Miller. *NO*

No Deposit, No Return *Double Trouble* **1976 (G)** Tedious,. silly, pointless Disney action comedy. Rich brats persuade bumbling crooks to kidnap them, offer them for ransom to millionaire grandfather. **115m/C VHS, Beta.** David Niven, Don Knotts, Darren McGavin, Barbara Feldon, Charles Martin Smith; ***D:*** Norman Tokar; ***W:*** Arthur Alsberg; ***M:*** Buddy Baker. *DIS*

No Dessert Dad, 'Til You Mow the Lawn ½ **1994 (PG)** Suburban parents Ken and Carol Cochran (Robert Hays and Joanna Kerns) are harassed at home by their annoying offspring, Justin, Monica, and Tyler. When they try hypnosis tapes to quit smoking, the kids discover by doctoring the tapes, they can plant suggestions resulting in parental perks. **80m/C VHS.** Robert Hays, Joanna Kerns, Joshua Schaefer, Allison Meek, Jimmy Marsden, Richard Moll, Larry Linville; ***D:*** Howard McCain. *NHO*

No Drums, No Bugles ½ **1971 (G)** A West Virginia farmer and conscientious objector leaves his family to live alone in a cave for three years during the Civil War. Bad direction spoils Sheen's good performance. **85m/C VHS, Beta.** Martin Sheen, Davey Davidson, Denine Terry, Rod McCary; ***D:*** Clyde Ware. *VTR*

No End *Bez Konca* **1984** The ghost of a dead lawyer watches as his wife and young son struggle to survive without him, including the widow getting involved in her husband's last case about a worker arrested for organizing a strike. Well-acted but overly solemn and slow; set during Poland's martial law in 1982. In Polish with English subtitles. **108m/C VHS.** *PL* Grazyna Szapolowska, Jerzy Radziwilowicz, Maria Pakulnis, Aleksander Bardini, Artur Barcis, Michal Bajor; ***D:*** Krzysztof Kieslowski; ***W:*** Krzysztof Piesiewicz, Krzysztof Kieslowski. *NYF, FCT, ING*

No Escape ½ **1994 (R)** In 2022, Captain Robbins (Liotta) has been banished to a prison colony island inhabited by the most dangerous criminals. With no walls and no guards, the prisoners are left to kill each other. Then Robbins discovers a relatively peaceful community of prisoners who help each other. But this group is soon bedeviled by the evil nasties on the other side of the island. Attempts at escape define the plot, so the film is filled with superhuman feats of sheer courage, determination, and guts.

Adapted from the book "The Penal Colony" by Richard Herley. **118m/C VHS, LV.** Ray Liotta, Lance Henriksen, Stuart Wilson, Kevin Dillon, Kevin J. O'Connor, Michael Lerner, Ernie Hudson, Ian McNeice, Jack Shepherd; ***D:*** Martin Campbell; ***W:*** Joel Gross; ***M:*** Graeme Revell. *HBO*

No Escape, No Return ☆☆½ **1993 (R)** An FBI agent (Nouri) and a police captain (Saxon) force three renegade cops (Nguyen, Caulfield, and Loveday) to infiltrate a drug syndicate. But things go from bad to worse when a war breaks out between rival drug gangs, leaving a lot of bodies, and a large chunk of money gone missing. Now the trio is sought by both the cops and the crooks. **93m/C VHS, LV.** Maxwell Caulfield, Dustin Nguyen, Denise Loveday, John Saxon, Michael Nouri, Kevin Benton; ***D:*** Charles Kanganis; ***W:*** Charles Kanganis; ***M:*** Jim Halfpenny. *PMH*

No Fear, No Die ☆☆ **1990** To make some quick cash two black immigrants in France train and sell birds for illegal cockfights at a roadside restaurant. Jocelyn, who trains the cocks, pays them lavish, obsessive attention. But cultural conflicts and repressed passions are just waiting to explode. In French with English subtitles. **97m/C VHS.** *FR* Alex Descas, Isaach de Bankole, Jean-Claude Brialy, Solveig Dommartin, Christopher Buchholz; ***D:*** Claire Denis; ***W:*** Claire Denis, Jean-Pol Fargeau; ***M:*** Abdullah Ibrahim. *ICA*

No Greater Love ☆☆½ **1943** Capraesque Soviet war movie. A peasant woman mobilizes her village against the Nazis to avenge her family's death. Dubbed into English by the Soviets for Western circulation during WWII. **74m/B VHS, Beta.** *RU* Vera Maretskaya; ***D:*** Frederic Ermler. *FCT, IHF*

No Grumps Allowed! **1969** A package of episodes of the children's fantasy series. **90m/C VHS, Beta.** *SUE*

No Highway in the Sky ☆☆☆ **1951** Eccentric scientist Theodore Honey (Stewart) works for the Royal Aircraft Establishment, which has just produced a new plane, the Reindeer. But Honey tells his boss Dennis Scott (Hawkins) that the plane has a serious defect. While flying to examine a Reindeer crash site, Honey befriends Monica (Dietrich), a musical star, and stewardess Marjorie (Johns), who support him when his company accuses him of maliciously damaging the aircraft's reputation. Dietrich steals every scene with her Christian Dior wardrobe and star attitude. Based on the novel "No Highway" by Nevil Shute. **98m/B VHS.** *GB* James Stewart, Marlene Dietrich, Glynis Johns, Jack Hawkins, Ronald Squire, Niall MacGinnis, Elizabeth Allan, Kenneth More, David Hutcheson; ***D:*** Henry Koster; ***W:*** R.C. Sherriff, Oscar Millard; ***M:*** Malcolm Arnold. *FXV*

No Holds Barred ☆½ **1989 (PG-13)** Cheesy, campy remake of cheesy, campy 1952 wrestling movie. Hulk Hogan on the big screen, at last. **98m/C VHS, Beta, LV.** Hulk Hogan, Kurt Fuller, Joan Severance, Tiny Lister; ***D:*** Thomas J. Wright. *COL*

No Love for Johnnie ☆☆☆ **1960** Well acted if unoriginal political drama. Finch is a British M.P. who fails in both public and private life. Based on the novel by Wilfred Fienburgh. **105m/B VHS, Beta.** *GB* Peter Finch, Stanley Holloway, Donald Pleasence, Mary Peach, Mervyn Johns, Dennis Price, Oliver Reed, Billie Whitelaw; ***D:*** Ralph Thomas; ***W:*** Mordecai Richler; ***M:*** Malcolm Arnold. British Academy Awards '61: Best Actor (Finch). *NO*

No Man of Her Own ☆☆½ **1932** Gable and Lombard in their only screen pairing. Gambler Babe Stewart (Gable) marries small town librarian (Lombard) on a bet and attempts to hide his secret life from her. Neither star's best film. **81m/B VHS, Beta, LV.** Carole Lombard, Clark Gable, Grant Mitchell, Elizabeth Patterson, Dorothy Mackaill; ***D:*** Wesley Ruggles. *MCA, BAR*

No Man's Land ☆☆ **1987 (R)** Undercover cop Sweeney tails playboy Sheen but is seduced by wealth and glamour. Flashy surfaces, shiny cars, little substance. **107m/C VHS, Beta, LV.** Charlie Sheen, D.B. Sweeney, Lara Harris, Randy Quaid; ***D:*** Peter Werner; ***W:*** Dick Wolf; ***M:*** Basil Poledouris. *ORI*

No Man's Law ☆☆½ **1927** Hardy plays the depraved villian desperate to get the goldmine owned by an old prospector and his beautiful daughter. But the mine is protected by Rex the Wonder Horse! **?m/B VHS.** Oliver Hardy, Barbara Kent, James Finlayson, Theodore von Eltz; ***D:*** Fred Jackman. *NO*

No Man's Range ☆ *No Man's Land* **1935** Unremarkable, typical, predictable Western: good guys, bad guys, guns, bullets, horses. **56m/B VHS, Beta.** Bob Steele. *NO*

No Mercy ☆☆ **1986 (R)** A Chicago cop (Gere) plunges into the Cajun bayou in order to avenge the murder of his partner. He falls for a beautiful girl enslaved by the killer, but that doesn't stop him from using her to flush out the powerful swamp-inhabiting crime lord. Absurd story without much plot. **108m/C VHS, Beta, LV.** Richard Gere, Kim Basinger, Jeroen Krabbe, George Dzundza, William Atherton, Ray Sharkey, Bruce McGill; ***D:*** Richard Pearce; ***W:*** Jim Carabatsos; ***M:*** Alan Silvestri. *COL*

No, No Nanette ☆½ **1940** Lackluster filming of the Broadway production which fared better on the stage. Stock story of a young woman (Neagle) who rescues her uncle from financial ruin and finds romance in the process. **96m/B VHS.** Anna Neagle, Richard Carlson, Victor Mature, Roland Young, ZaSu Pitts, Eve Arden, Billy Gilbert, Keye Luke; ***D:*** Herbert Wilcox; ***C:*** Russell Metty. *NOS*

No One Cries Forever *Woof!* **1985** When a prostitute breaks away from a gangster-madam after finding love, she is tracked down and disfigured. Swedish; dubbed. **96m/C Beta.** Elke Sommer, Howard Carpendale, Zoli Marks; ***D:*** Jans Rautenbach. *NO*

No Place to Hide ☆½ **1981** A girl's father drowns and she blames herself. Her mother and psychologist try to convince the girl that her father's spirit isn't stalking her. She doesn't believe them. Made for television. **120m/C VHS, Beta.** Keir Dullea, Mariette Hartley, Kathleen Beller, Arlen Dean Snyder, Gary Graham, John Llewellyn Moxey; ***D:*** John Llewellyn Moxey. *PSM*

No Place to Hide ☆☆½ **1993 (R)** Barrymore is the target of a psycho who's already killed her sister. Kristofferson plays the hard-edged cop who's out to protect her and trap the killer. **90m/C VHS.** Drew Barrymore, Kris Kristofferson, Martin Landau, O.J. Simpson, Dey Young, Bruce Weitz; ***D:*** Richard Danus; ***W:*** Richard Danus. *CAN*

No Place to Run ☆☆ **1972** An elderly man fights for custody of his grandson, then kidnaps him and flees with him to Canada. Made for TV. **78m/C VHS, Beta.** Herschel Bernardi, Larry Hagman, Stefanie Powers, Neville Brand; ***D:*** Delbert Mann. *VMK*

No Prince for My Cinderella **1978** A schizophrenic girl who has turned to prostitution is sought desperately by her social worker. **100m/C VHS, Beta.** Robert Reed. *WOV*

No Problem ☆☆ **197?** A man is pursued, shot, and drops dead in the apartment of an unsuspecting man who doesn't know what to do with the body. Dubbed in English. **94m/C VHS, Beta.** *FR* Miou-Miou. *NO*

No Regrets for Our Youth ☆☆☆ **1946** A feminist saga depicting the spiritual growth of a foolish Japanese girl during the tumultuous years of WWII. In Japanese with English subtitles. **110m/B VHS.** *JP* Setsuko Hara; ***D:*** Akira Kurosawa. *CVC, INJ*

No Retreat, No Surrender ☆ **1986 (PG)** A young American kick-boxer battles a formidable Russian opponent and wins, quite improbably, after having been tutored by the ghost of Bruce Lee in an abandoned house. Notable as Van Damme's debut, but little else recommends this silly "Rocky" rehash. Followed by "No Retreat, No Surrender II." **85m/C VHS, Beta, LV.** Kurt McKinney, J.W. Fails, Jean-Claude Van Damme; ***D:*** Corey Yuen. *NWV, VTR*

No Retreat, No Surrender 2 ☆ **1989 (R)** With help from two karate experts, a man sets out to find his girlfriend who has been kidnapped by Soviets. Has little or nothing to do with the movie to which it is ostensibly a sequel. High level kick-boxing action sequences. **92m/C VHS, Beta.** Loren Avedon, Max Thayer, Cynthia Rothrock; ***D:*** Corey Yuen; ***W:*** Maria Elene Cellino. *MCG*

No Retreat, No Surrender 3: Blood Brothers ☆ **1991 (R)** Sibling martial arts rivals decide to bond in a manly way when CIA agent dad is most heinously slain by terrorists. Answers the burning question: "Whatever became of Joseph Campanella?" **97m/C VHS.** Keith Vitali, Loren Avedon, Joseph Campanella. *IMP*

No Room to Run ☆½ **1978** Concert promoter's life turns into a nightmare of deadly corporate intrigue when he arrives in Australia. Luckily, he finds time to fall in love. Made for television hokum. **101m/C VHS, Beta.** *AU* Richard Benjamin, Paula Prentiss, Barry Sullivan; ***D:*** Robert Lewis. *ACA*

No Safe Haven ☆ **1987 (R)** A government agent seeks revenge for his family's death. **92m/C VHS, Beta.** Wings Hauser, Marina Rice, Robert Tessier; ***D:*** Ronnie Rondell; ***M:*** Joel Goldsmith. *MCG*

No Secrets ☆½ **1991 (R)** A young man on the run seeks refuge with three girls in an isolated house. His dread secret isn't so dread, leaving this mild teen-oriented thriller starved for lack of menace. **92m/C VHS, LV.** Adam Coleman Howard, Amy Locane, Heather Fairfield, Traci Lind; ***D:*** Dezso Magyar. *COL*

No Small Affair ☆☆ **1984 (R)** A 16-year-old aspiring photographer becomes romantically involved with a sultry 22-year-old rock star. **102m/C VHS, Beta, LV.** Jon Cryer, Demi Moore, George Wendt, Peter Frechette, Elizabeth Daily, Tim Robbins, Jennifer Tilly, Rick Ducommun, Ann Wedgeworth; ***D:*** Jerry Schatzberg; ***M:*** Rupert Holmes. *COL*

No Surrender ☆☆☆ **1986 (R)** An unpredictable, darkly charming comedy about a Liverpool nightclub newly managed by Angelis. On New Year's Eve, a small drunken war is triggered when two groups of irate senior citizens are booked into the club and clash over their beliefs. The group is made up of Protestants and Catholics and the fight resembles the ongoing conflicts in modern-day Northern Ireland, although most of the action takes place in the loo. Watch for Costello as an inept magician. **100m/C VHS, Beta.** *GB* Ray McAnally, Michael Angelis, Avis Bunnage, James Ellis, Tom Georgeson, Mark Mulholland, Joanne Whalley, Elvis Costello, Bernard Hill, Michael Ripper; ***D:*** Peter Smith; ***W:*** Alan Bleasdale; ***M:*** Daryl Runswick. *PSM*

No Survivors, Please ☆½ *Der Chef Wuenscht Keine Zeugen; The Chief Wants No Survivors* **1963** Aliens from Orion take over politicians in order to rule the Earth. Bizarre, obscure, based on true story. **92m/B VHS.** *GE* Maria Perschy, Uwe Friedrichsen, Robert Cunningham, Karen Blanguernon, Gustavo Rojo; ***D:*** Hans Albin, Peter Berneis. *MOV*

No Time for Romance ☆☆ **1948** A sprightly musical with an all-black cast. First such film to be shot in color. **?m/C VHS.** Bill Walker. *FCT*

No Time for Sergeants ☆☆☆ **1958** Hilarious film version of the Broadway play by Ira Levin. Young Andy Griffith is excellent as the Georgia farm boy who gets drafted into the service and creates mayhem among his superiors and colleagues. Story also told on an earlier television special and later in a series. Note Don Knotts and Benny Baker in small roles along with Jameel Farah who went on to star in TV's M*A*S*H after changing his name to Jamie Farr. **119m/B VHS, Beta, LV.** Andy Griffith, Nick Adams, Murray Hamilton, Don Knotts, Jamie Farr, Myron McCormick; ***D:*** Mervyn LeRoy. *WAR*

No Time to Die ☆ **1978** In Indonesia, two corporate pawns and a beautiful reporter battle for the possession of a new laser cannon. **87m/C VHS, Beta.** Chris Mitchum, John Phillip Law, Grazyna Dylong. *TWE*

No Trace ☆☆ **1950** A writer who broadcasts his crime stories as part of a radio show is the victim of blackmail. It seems a former associate is aware that the stories are all based in fact. A Scotland Yard detective investigates when murder rears its ugly head. **76m/B VHS, Beta.** *GB* Hugh Sinclair, Dinah Sheridan, John Laurie, Barry Morse, Michael Brennan, Dora Bryan; ***D:*** John Gilling. *SNC*

No Way Back 🦴🦴 **1974 (R)** Way. Writer, director, and producer Williamson portrays Jess Crowder, a man-for-hire who is an expert with guns, fists, and martial arts. An angry look at the white establishment. **92m/C VHS, Beta.** Fred Williamson, Charles Woolf, Tracy Reed, Virginia Gregg, Don Cornelius; ***D:*** Fred Williamson. *UNI*

No Way Out 🦴🦴🦴 **1987 (R)** Career Navy man Costner is involved with a beautiful, sexy woman who is murdered. Turns out she was also the mistress of the Secretary of Defense, Costner's boss. Assigned to investigate the murder, he suddenly finds himself the chief suspect. A tight thriller based on 1948's "The Big Clock," with a new surprise ending. **114m/C VHS, Beta, LV.** Kevin Costner, Sean Young, Gene Hackman, Will Patton, Howard Duff, George Dzundza, Iman, Chris D, Marshall Bell, Jason Bernard, Fred Dalton Thompson, David Paymer; ***D:*** Roger Donaldson; ***W:*** Robert Garland; ***M:*** Maurice Jarre. *HBO*

No Way to Treat a Lady 🦴🦴🦴 **1968** Steiger is a psychotic master of disguise who stalks and kills various women in this suspenseful cat-and-mouse game. Segal, as the detective assigned to the case, uncovers clues, falls in love, and discovers that his new girl may be the killer's next victim. **108m/C VHS, Beta.** Rod Steiger, Lee Remick, George Segal, Eileen Heckart, Murray Hamilton; ***D:*** Jack Smight; ***W:*** John Gay; ***C:*** Jack Priestley. *PAR*

Noa at Seventeen 🦴🦴🦴 **1982** The political/social turmoil of Israel in 1951 is allegorically depicted by the school vs. kibbutz debate within a young girl's middle-class family. In Hebrew with English subtitles. **86m/C VHS, Beta.** *IS* Dalia Shimko, Idit Zur, Shmuel Shilo, Moshe Havazelet; ***D:*** Isaac Yeshurun. *ERG, FCT, INJ*

Noble House **1988** Continuation of James Clavell's Hong Kong series, following "Tai-Pan," and set in the present day. Ian Dunross (Brosnan) is the head of Struan and Company, Hong Kong's leading trading company, which is being undermined by the nefarious Quillan Gornt (Rhys-Davies) who plots to destroy his archrival. American businesswoman Casey Tcholok (the bland Raffin) serves as Dunross' love interest. Originally a four-part TV miniseries partially filmed on location. **350m/C VHS.** Pierce Brosnan, John Rhys-Davies, Deborah Raffin, Ben Masters, Julia Nickson-Soul, Khigh Dheigh, Tia Carrere, Gordon Jackson. *TVC*

The Noble Ninja 🦴🦴 **1990** In a fantastic prehistoric world, a ninja does battle with foes both real and supernatural. **90m/C VHS, Beta.** Tsui Fung, Lo Lieh. *MGI*

Nobody's Daughter 🦴🦴½ **1976** The tragedy of an eight-year-old orphan shuttled from one family to another, all of whom are only interested in the money the government will pay for her care. In Hungarian with English subtitles. **90m/C VHS.** *HU* Zsuzsi Czinkoczi; ***D:*** Lazlo Ranody. *EVD, INJ*

Nobody's Fool 🦴🦴 **1986 (PG-13)** Another entry in the genre of quirky Americana, this romantic comedy concerns a hapless Midwestern waitress suffering from low-self esteem who falls in love with a traveling stage-hand. **107m/C VHS, Beta, LV.** Rosanna Arquette, Eric Roberts, Mare Winningham, Louise Fletcher, Jim Youngs; ***D:*** Evelyn Purcell; ***W:*** Beth Henley; ***M:*** James Newton Howard. *ORI, WAR*

Nobody's Fool 🦴🦴🦴½ **1994 (R)** Newman shines as 60-year-old Donald "Sully" Sullivan, a construction worker who, in spite of himself, begins mending his many broken relationships over the course of the holiday season. Seemingly plotless scenario is sprinkled with enough humor, hope, and understated inspiration to become a delightfully modest celebration of a perfectly ordinary man. Character-driven story is blessed with commendable performances by supporting players—obviously inspired by Newman's brilliant portrayal. Based on the novel by Richard Russo. **110m/C VHS, Beta.** Paul Newman, Jessica Tandy, Bruce Willis, Melanie Griffith, Dylan Walsh, Pruitt Taylor Vince, Gene Saks, Josef Sommer, Philip S. Hoffman, Philip Bosco, Margo Martindale, Jay Patterson; ***D:*** Robert Benton; ***W:*** Robert Benton; ***C:*** Roger Deakins; ***M:*** John Bloom. Berlin International Film Festival '94: Best Actor (Newman); New York Film Critics Awards '94: Best Actor (Newman); National Society of Film Critics Awards '94: Best Actor (Newman); Nominations: Academy Awards '94: Best Actor (Newman), Best Adapted Screenplay; Golden Globe Awards '95: Best Actor—Drama (Newman); Screen Actors Guild Award '94: Best Actor (Newman). *PAR*

Nobody's Perfect 🦴 **1990 (PG-13)** Where "Tootsie" and "Some Like it Hot" collide (or more likely crash and burn). A lovesick teenager masquerades as a girl and joins the tennis team to be near his dream girl. Takes its title from Joe E. Brown's famous last line in "Some Like it Hot." **90m/C VHS, Beta, LV.** Chad Lowe, Gail O'Grady, Patrick Breen, Kim Flowers, Robert Vaughn; ***D:*** Robert Kaylor; ***W:*** Joel Block. *MED, VTR*

Nobody's Perfekt *Woof!* **1979 (PG)** Supposed comedy about three psychiatric patients who decide to extort $650,000 from the city of Miami when their car is wrecked. Lacks laughs and generally considered a turkey. **95m/C VHS, Beta.** Gabe Kaplan, Robert Klein, Alex Karras, Susan Clark; ***D:*** Peter Bonerz. *COL*

Nocturna *Woof! Nocturna, Granddaughter of Dracula* **1979 (R)** Hard times have fallen upon the house of Dracula. To help pay the taxes on the castle, the owners have converted it to the Hotel Transylvania. In order to increase business and the blood supply at the hotel, Nocturna books a disco group to entertain the guests. Hard times fell on this script, too. It's no wonder that director Tampa hid behind the alias Harry Hurwitz. **82m/C VHS, Beta, LV.** Yvonne De Carlo, John Carradine, Tony Hamilton, Nai Bonet; ***D:*** Harry Tampa. *MED*

Nocturne 🦴🦴½ **1946** A police lieutenant investigates the supposed suicide of a famous composer and uncovers dark secrets that suggest murder is afoot. An overlooked RKO production shines thanks to Raft's inimitable tough guy performance and some offbeat direction. For film noir completists. **88m/B VHS, Beta, LV.** George Raft, Lynn Bari, Virginia Huston, Joseph Pevney, Myrna Dell, Edward Ashley, Walter Sande, Mabel Paige; ***D:*** Edwin L. Marin. *TTC*

Noir et Blanc 🦴🦴 **1986** Antoine (Frappat) is a shy accountant who takes a job in a health club and begins an increasingly sado-masochistic relationship with black masseur, Jacques (Martial). The violence is inferred not actually shown but still makes for some kinky adult fare. Based on a short story by Tennessee Williams; debut film for director Devers. French with subtitles. **82m/B VHS.** *FR* Francis Frappat, Jacques Martial, Josephine Fresson, Marc Berman, Claire Rigollier; ***D:*** Claire Devers; ***W:*** Claire Devers. *CCN*

Noises Off 🦴🦴½ **1992 (PG-13)** An Americanization of a British farce about a group of second-rate actors touring in a sex comedy and their convoluted private lives. Wretched rehersals and equally disasterous preformances, backstage sniping, lovers' quarrels, and a beleaguered director all bumble along together. It worked better on stage, where it was a Broadway hit, but the actors at least have some fun with the material. Based on the play by Michael Frayn. **101m/C VHS, Beta, LV.** Michael Caine, Carol Burnett, Denholm Elliott, Julie Hagerty, Marilu Henner, Mark Linn-Baker, Christopher Reeve, John Ritter, Nicolette Sheridan; ***D:*** Peter Bogdanovich; ***W:*** Marty Kaplan; ***M:*** Phil Marshall. *TOU, PMS*

Nomad Riders 🦴 **1981** A la "Mad Max," (though with an even smaller budget and a decided lack of originality) one rugged man goes after the bikers who killed his wife and daughter. **82m/C VHS, Beta.** Wayne Chema, Richard Cluck, Ron Gregg; ***D:*** Frank Roach. *LIV, VES*

Nomads 🦴🦴½ **1986 (R)** A supernatural thriller set in Los Angeles about a French anthropologist who is mysteriously killed, and the woman doctor who investigates and becomes the next target of a band of strange street people with nomadic spirits. Nomad notables include pop stars Adam Ant and Josie Cotton. **91m/C VHS, Beta, LV.** Pierce Brosnan, Lesley-Anne Down, Adam Ant, Anna Maria Monticelli, Mary Woronov; ***D:*** John McTiernan; ***M:*** Bill Conti. *IME, PAR*

Nomads of the North 🦴½ **1920** Vintage silent melodrama set in the North Woods with the requisite young girl beset by evil villians, a climactic forest fire, and a dashing Mountie who allows a man wrongly sought by the law to be reunited with the woman he secretly loves. Also available at 75 minutes. **109m/B VHS, Beta, 8mm.** Lon Chaney Sr., Lewis Stone, Betty Blythe; ***D:*** David M. Hartford. *SNC, GPV, VYY*

Nomugi Pass 🦴🦴½ **1979** A young woman working in a Japanese silk mill in the early 1900s must endure hardship and abuse. English subtitles. **154m/C VHS, Beta.** *JP* Shinobu Otake, Meiko Harada, Rentaro Mikuni, Takeo Jii. *VDA*

Non-Stop New York 🦴🦴½ **1937** Mystery tale with interesting twist. A wealthy woman can give an alibi for a murder suspect, but no one will listen, and she is subsequently framed. Pays homage to Hitchcock with its photography and humor. Quick and charming. **71m/B VHS.** Anna Lee, John Loder, Francis L. Sullivan, Frank Cellier; ***D:*** Robert Stevenson. *NOS, SNC*

None But the Brave 🦴🦴 **1965** During WWII, an American bomber plane crash-lands on an island already inhabited by stranded Japanese forces. After a skirmish, the two groups initiate a fragile truce, with the understanding that fighting will resume if one or the other sends for help. The Americans repair their radio unit and must decide on their next actions. Sinatra's directorial debut is a poor effort. **105m/C VHS, Beta, LV.** Frank Sinatra, Clint Walker, Tommy Sands, Brad Dexter, Tony Bill, Tatsuya Mihashi, Takeshi Kato, Sammy Jackson; ***D:*** Frank Sinatra; ***M:*** John Williams. *WAR, FCT*

None But the Lonely Heart 🦴🦴🦴 **1944** In the days before WWII, a Cockney drifter (Grant) wanders the East End of London. When his get-rich-quick schemes fail, his dying shopkeeper-mother tries to help and lands in prison. Interesting characterization of life in the slums. Odets not only directed, but wrote the screenplay. **113m/B VHS, Beta.** Cary Grant, Ethel Barrymore, Barry Fitzgerald, Jane Wyatt, Dan Duryea, George Coulouris, June Duprez; ***D:*** Clifford Odets; ***W:*** Clifford Odets; ***C:*** George Barnes. Academy Awards '44: Best Supporting Actress (Barrymore); National Board of Review Awards '44: 10 Best Films of the Year; Nominations: Academy Awards '44: Best Actor (Grant), Best Film Editing, Best Original Score. *MED, BTV*

Noon Sunday 🦴 **1971 (PG)** A cold war situation in the Pacific islands explodes into an orgy of death. **104m/C VHS, Beta.** Mark Lenard, John Russell, Linda Avery, Keye Luke. *ACA*

Noon Wine 🦴🦴🦴 **1984** Dramatization of Katherine Anne Porter's classic story about a Swedish worker on a Texas farm who becomes the center of a family battle. Made for PBS' American Playhouse. **60m/C VHS, Beta.** Fred Ward, Lise Hilboldt, Stellan Skarsgard, Jon Cryer; ***D:*** Michael Fields. *MON, FCT, KAR*

The Noose Hangs High 🦴🦴🦴 **1948** This broad comedy has our heroes as window washers mistaken for gamblers and getting involved with a bunch of gangsters. Much physical and verbal shenanigans as only these two can do it. The bits may be a bit old, but they're done with a fresh twist. Some good word play with the phrase "You can't be here" runs in the same vein as their classic "Who's on first?" routine. Genuinely funny. **77m/B VHS.** Bud Abbott, Lou Costello, Cathy Downs, Joseph Calleia, Leon Errol, Mike Mazurki, Jack Overman, Fritz Feld, Vera Martin, Joe Kirk, Matt Willis, Benny Rubin; ***D:*** Charles T. Barton. *MGM, NOS*

Norma Rae 🦴🦴🦴 **1979 (PG)** A poor, uneducated textile worker joins forces with a New York labor organizer to unionize the reluctant workers at a Southern mill. Field was a surprise with her fully developed character's strength, beauty, and humor; her Oscar was well-deserved. Ritt's direction is top-notch. Jennifer Warnes sings the theme song, "It Goes Like It Goes," which also won an Oscar. ♫It Goes Like It Goes. **114m/C VHS, Beta, LV.** Sally Field, Ron Leibman, Beau Bridges, Pat Hingle; ***D:*** Martin Ritt; ***W:*** Harriet Frank Jr., Irving Ravetch; ***C:*** John A. Alonzo; ***M:*** David Shire. Academy Awards '79: Best Actress (Field), Best Song

("It Goes Like It Goes"); Golden Globe Awards '80: Best Actress—Drama (Field); Los Angeles Film Critics Association Awards '79: Best Actress (Field); National Board of Review Awards '79: Best Actress (Field); New York Film Critics Awards '79: Best Actress (Field); National Society of Film Critics Awards '79: Best Actress (Field); Nominations: Academy Awards '79: Best Adapted Screenplay, Best Picture; Cannes Film Festival '79: Best Film. *FOX, BTV*

Normal Life **1996 (R)** Straight-arrow, smalltown Illinois rookie cop Chris Anderson (Perry) comes to the aid of sexy, impetuous biker chick Pam (Judd) and they impulsively marry. Fast forward two years and the willfully irresponsible Pam has turned their lives into a disaster but for some reason Chris (now a security guard) sticks it out, even pulling bank jobs to afford Pam's luxuries. When she finds out what Chris has been doing, Pam insists on joining in, leading to a bitter end. Based on the true story of Jeffrey and Jill Erickson, who went on a bank robbing spree and were killed in 1991. Great lead performances though character motivation is lacking. **101m/C VHS.** Luke Perry, Ashley Judd, Bruce A. Young, Jim True, Dawn Maxey, Penelope Milford, Tom Towles; ***D:*** John McNaughton; ***W:*** Bob Schneider, Peg Haller; ***C:*** Jean De Segonzac. *NLC*

Norman Conquest *Park Plaza* **1953** Conway finds himself drugged and framed for murder in this bargain-basement thriller. Bartok is the leader of a diamond-smuggling operation who may be involved. **75m/B VHS.** *GB* Tom Conway, Eva Bartok, Joy Shelton, Sidney James, Richard Wattis, Robert Adair, Ian Fleming; ***D:*** Bernard Knowles; ***W:*** Bernard Knowles. *NOS, SNC*

The Norman Conquests, Part 1: Table Manners **1980** Part one of playwright Alan Ayckbourn's comic trilogy of love unfulfilled, as the charmingly unreliable Norman (Conti) works his amorous wiles on three women. **108m/C VHS, Beta.** *GB* Tom Conti, Richard Briers, Penelope Keith. *TVC*

The Norman Conquests, Part 2: Living Together **1980** Part two concerns the happenings in the living room during Norman's disastrous weekend of unsuccessful seduction. **93m/C VHS, Beta.** *GB* Tom Conti, Penelope Keith, Richard Briers. *TVC*

The Norman Conquests, Part 3: Round and Round the Garden **1980** Part three concerns Norman's furtive appearance in the garden, which suggests that the weekend is going to misfire. **106m/C VHS, Beta.** *GB* Tom Conti, Penelope Keith, Richard Briers. *TVC*

Norman, Is That You? ½ **1976** Unsuccessful film adaptation based on the unsuccessful Broadway play about one family's sexual revolution. Revamped by a host of black stars, it's basically a one-joke affair when Foxx discovers his son is gay and living with his white lover. Shot on videotape and transferred to film. **91m/C VHS.** Redd Foxx, Pearl Bailey, Dennis Dugan, Michael Warren, Tamara Dobson, Vernee Watson-Johnson, Jayne Meadows, George Furth; ***D:*** George Schlatter; ***W:*** George Schlatter, Ron Clark, Sam Bobrick; ***M:*** William Goldstein. *MGM*

Norman Loves Rose ½ **1982 (R)** A precocious 13-year-old and his married sister-in-law join forces in this substandard comedy. When Rose tries to help Norman by teaching him about sex, she learns a little too—she's pregnant. **95m/C VHS, Beta.** *AU* Carol Kane, Tony Owen, Warren Mitchell, Myra de Groot; ***D:*** Henri Safran. *LIV, VES*

Norman's Awesome Experience *Woof!* **1988 (PG-13)** Three adolescents are transported back in time to the Roman Empire. Bill and Ted, anyone? **90m/C VHS, Beta.** Tom McCamus, Laurie Paton, Jaques Lussier; ***D:*** Paul Donovan. *NO*

Norseman ½ **1978 (PG)** Leader of a band of Norsemen sets sail for the New World in search of his missing royal father. Low-budget Viking adventure. **90m/C VHS, Beta.** Lee Majors, Cornel Wilde, Mel Ferrer, Christopher Connelly, Jack Elam; ***D:*** Charles B. Pierce; ***W:*** Charles B. Pierce. *LIV, VES*

North ½ **1994 (PG)** Some laughs with a message in family fare from Reiner. Eleven-year old ace kid actor Wood divorces his workaholic parents Alexander and Louis-Dreyfus and searches the world for a functional family (good luck). Willis, who's a treat in a pink bunny suit, acts as guardian angel/narrator and shows the kid what's really important. Illustrious comedic cast inhabits story based on a book by original "Saturday Night Live" screenwriter (and "Gary Shandling Show" co-creator) Zweibel, who put things in motion ten years ago when he asked Reiner to write a book jacket quote for the novel. **87m/C VHS, LV.** Elijah Wood, Jason Alexander, Julia Louis-Dreyfus, Bruce Willis, Jon Lovitz, Alan Arkin, Dan Aykroyd, Kathy Bates, Faith Ford, Graham Greene, Reba McEntire, John Ritter, Abe Vigoda, Kelly McGillis, Alexander Godunov, Noriyuki "Pat" Morita; ***D:*** Rob Reiner; ***W:*** Andrew Scheinman, Alan Zweibel; ***M:*** Marc Shaiman. Nominations: Golden Raspberry Awards '94: Worst Picture, Worst Actor (Willis). *NLC*

North and South Book 1 **1985** Lavish spectacle about a friendship tested by the turbulent times leading up to Civil War. Orry Main (Swayze) is a South Carolina plantation owner while his best friend George Hazard (Read) comes from a Pennsylvania industrial family. Orry is also involved in a doomed romance with the beautiful Madeline (Down), who's forced to marry the odious Justin LaMotte (Carradine). Lots of intrigue and excitement. Based on the novel by John Jakes. Filmed on location in Charleston, South Carolina. Originally broadcast as a six-part TV miniseries. Available on six cassettes. **561m/C VHS, Beta.** Patrick Swayze, James Read, Lesley-Anne Down, David Carradine, Kirstie Alley, Jean Simmons, Inga Swenson, Jonathon Frakes, Genie Francis, Terri Garber, Georg Stanford Brown, Olivia Cole, David Ogden Stiers, Robert Guillaume, Hal Holbrook, Gene Kelly, Robert Mitchum, Johnny Cash, Elizabeth Taylor; ***M:*** Bill Conti. *WAR, FUS, TVC*

North and South Book 2 **1986** Equally dramatic sequel follows the southern Main clan and the northern Hazard family into the Civil War as friendship and romance struggle to survive the fighting. Casnoff is a notable presence as the aptly-named Bent, who will go to any length to settle old scores with both families. Based on the John Jakes novel "Love and War." Originally broadcast as a six-part TV miniseries; on six cassettes. The last of the Jakes trilogy, "Heaven and Hell," was finally filmed for TV in '94 but proved a major disappointment. **570m/C VHS.** Patrick Swayze, James Read, Lesley-Anne Down, Terri Garber, Genie Francis, Jean Simmons, Kirstie Alley, Philip Casnoff, Hal Holbrook, Lloyd Bridges, James Stewart, Morgan Fairchild, Nancy Marchand, Parker Stevenson, Lewis Smith; ***M:*** Bill Conti. *WAR, TVC*

The North Avenue Irregulars ½ **1979 (G)** Slapstick Disney comedy along the same lines as some of their earlier laugh-fests. A priest and three members of the local ladies' club try to bust a crime syndicate. Though the premise is silly, there are still lots of laughs in this family film. **99m/C VHS.** Edward Herrmann, Barbara Harris, Susan Clark, Karen Valentine, Michael Constantine, Cloris Leachman, Melora Hardin, Alan Hale Jr., Ruth Buzzi, Patsy Kelly, Virginia Capers; ***D:*** Bruce Bilson; ***M:*** Robert F. Brunner. *DIS*

North by Northwest **1959** Self-assured Madison Avenue ad exec Grant inadvertently gets involved with international spies when they mistake him for someone else. His problems are compounded when he's framed for murder. The movie where Grant and Saint dangle from the faces of Mount Rushmore and a plane chases Grant through farm fields. Exceptional performances, particularly Grant's. Plenty of plot twists are mixed with tongue-in-cheek humor. Considered by many to be one of Hitchcock's greatest films. Laserdisc includes letterboxing, digital soundtrack, Hitchcock interview, production and publicity photos, storyboards, and the original trailer. **136m/C VHS, Beta, LV.** Cary Grant, Eva Marie Saint, James Mason, Leo G. Carroll, Martin Landau, Jessie Royce Landis, Philip Ober, Adam Williams, Josephine Hutchinson, Edward Platt; ***D:*** Alfred Hitchcock; ***W:*** Ernest Lehman; ***C:*** Robert Burks; ***M:*** Bernard Herrmann. Edgar Allan Poe Awards '59: Best Screenplay; Nominations: Academy Awards '59: Best Art Direction/Set Decoration (Color), Best Film Editing, Best Story & Screenplay. *MGM, CRC, TLF*

North Dallas Forty ½ **1979 (R)** Based on the novel by former Dallas Cowboy Peter Gent, the film focuses on the labor abuses in pro-football. One of the best football movies ever made, it contains searing commentary and very good acting, although the plot is sometimes dropped behind the line of scrimmage. **119m/C VHS, Beta, LV.** Nick Nolte, Mac Davis, Charles Durning, Bo Svenson, Brian Dennehy, John Matuszak, Dayle Haddon, Steve Forrest, Dabney Coleman, G.D. Spradlin; ***D:*** Ted Kotcheff. National Board of Review Awards '79: 10 Best Films of the Year. *PAR*

North of the Border ½ **1946** A cowboy in Canada gets involved with back-stabbing and treachery in and around Alberta. **40m/B VHS, Beta, LV.** *CA* Russell Hayden, Lyle Talbot, Inez Cooper, Douglas Fowley, Jack Mulhall; ***D:*** B. Reeves Eason. *VYY*

North of the Great Divide ½ **1950** Standard Rogers programmer, with Roy as a half-breed mediator between salmon fisherman and Indians. **67m/C VHS.** Roy Rogers, Penny Edwards, Gordon Jones, Roy Barcroft, Jack Lambert, Douglas Evans, Noble Johnson; ***D:*** William Witney. *REP*

North Shore ½ **1987 (PG)** A young surfer from Arizona hits the beaches of Hawaii and discovers love, sex, and adventure. Only redeeming quality is surfing footage. **96m/C VHS, Beta.** Matt Adler, Nia Peeples, John Philbin, Gregory Harrison, Christina Raines; ***D:*** Will Phelps. *MCA*

The North Star *Armored Attack* **1943** Gripping war tale of Nazis over-running an eastern Russian city, with courageous villagers fighting back. Colorized version available. **108m/B VHS, Beta.** Dana Andrews, Walter Huston, Anne Baxter, Farley Granger, Walter Brennan, Erich von Stroheim, Jack Perrin, Dean Jagger; ***D:*** Lewis Milestone; ***M:*** Aaron Copland. Nominations: Academy Awards '43: Best Black and White Cinematography, Best Interior Decoration, Best Original Screenplay, Best Sound, Best Original Score. *NOS, MRV, VYY*

North to Alaska **1960** A gold prospector encounters many problems when he agrees to pick up his partner's fiancee in Seattle to bring her home to Nome, Alaska, in the 1890s. Overly slapstick at times, but great fun nonetheless. Loosely based on Laszlo Fodor's play "The Birthday Gift." **120m/C VHS, Beta, LV.** John Wayne, Stewart Granger, Ernie Kovacs, Fabian, Capucine; ***D:*** Henry Hathaway; ***C:*** Leon Shamroy. *FOX*

Northanger Abbey ½ **1987** Catherine is a young woman whose head is turned by her romance readings of dark secrets, sinister castles, dashing heroes, and helpless women. When the handsome Henry Tilney invites her to visit his ancestral home, Northanger Abbey, it seems all her fancies have come to life. A somewhat tepid adaptation of Jane Austen's parody of the popular Gothic romances of her day. **90m/C VHS.** *GB* Peter Firth, Katherine Schlesinger, Googie Withers, Robert Hardy. *TVC, VCO, FUS*

Northeast of Seoul **1972 (PG)** Three people will stop at nothing to steal a legendary jewel-encrusted sword out of Korea. **84m/C VHS, Beta.** Anita Ekberg, John Ireland, Victor Buono; ***D:*** David Lowell Rich. *MGM*

Northern Extremes ½ *Buried on Sunday* **1993 (PG)** Silly comedy about an eccentric Canadian island village whose fishing livelihood is threatened. So the town mayor captures an errant nuclear submarine and uses it as a big bargaining chip. Filmed in Nova Scotia, Canada. **80m/C VHS.** *CA* Paul Gross, Denise Virieux, Henry Czerny, Jeff Leder, Tommy Sexton, Louis Del Grande, Maury Chaykin; ***D:*** Paul Donovan; ***W:*** Bill Fleming. *ACA*

Northern Lights **1979** A small, black-and-white independent drama depicting the struggle of a lowly farmer combating governmental forces in the 1915 heartland. Subtitled. **85m/B VHS, Beta.** Robert

Behling, Susan Lynch, Joe Spano, Rob Nilsson, Henry Martinson, Marianne Astrom-DeFina, Ray Ness, Helen Ness; **D:** Rob Nilsson, John Hanson; **W:** Rob Nilsson. *VTR, NWV*

Northern Passage ♂♂½ **1995 (PG-13)** Cowboy tries to protect a young Native American woman from harm in the wilderness. **97m/C VHS.** Jeff Fahey, Neve Campbell. *VMK*

Northern Pursuit ♂♂½ **1943** A Canadian Mountie disguises himself to infiltrate a Nazi spy ring in this exciting adventure film. Based on Leslie White's "Five Thousand Trojan Horses." **94m/B VHS, Beta.** Errol Flynn, Helmut Dantine, Julie Bishop, Gene Lockhart, Tom Tully; **D:** Raoul Walsh. *MGM, MLB*

Northville Cemetery Massacre ♂ *The Northfield Cemetery Massacre* **1976 (R)** Gang of bikers comes to town and all hell breaks loose. The result is a horribly bloody war between the townsfolk and the gang. Yup, it was a massacre. **81m/C VHS, Beta.** David Hyry, Craig Collicott, Jan Sisk; **W:** William Dear. *NO*

Northwest Outpost ♂½ *End of the Rainbow* **1947** Eddy is a California cavalry officer in this light-weight operetta. He helps a young woman who is trying to free her husband from jail, and after his death they are able to pursue their relationship. Eddy's last film. ♫Weary; Raindrops on a Drum; Tell Me With Your Eyes; One More Mile to Go; Russian Easter Hymn; Love is the Time; Nearer and Dearer. **91m/B VHS.** Nelson Eddy, Ilona Massey, Hugo Haas, Elsa Lanchester, Lenore Ulric; **D:** Allan Dwan. *REP*

Northwest Passage ♂♂♂ **1940** The lavish first half of a projected two-film package based on Kenneth Roberts' popular novel, depicting the troop of Rogers' Rangers fighting the wilderness and hostile Indians. Beautifully produced; the second half was never made and the passage itself is never seen. **126m/C VHS, Beta.** Spencer Tracy, Robert Young, Ruth Hussey, Walter Brennan, Nat Pendleton, Robert Barrat, Lumsden Hare; **D:** King Vidor. Nominations: Academy Awards '40: Best Color Cinematography. *MGM*

Northwest Trail ♂♂ **1946** Royal Canadian Mountie Steele's assignment is to escort Woodbury across the wilderness. She's carrying a large sum of money to save her uncle's business. Problem is, killers are on their trail. **75m/C VHS, Beta.** Bob Steele, Joan Woodbury, John Litel, Raymond Hatton, Madge Bellamy, Charles Middleton; **D:** Derwin Abrahams. *NOS, HHT, VCN*

Nosferatu ♂♂♂♂ *Nosferatu, Eine Symphonie des Grauens; Nosferatu, A Symphony of Terror; Nosferatu, A Symphony of Horror; Nosferatu, The Vampire* **1922** The first film adaptation of Bram Stoker's "Dracula" remains one of the creepiest and most atmospheric versions. Murnau knew how to add just the right touches to make this one of the best vampire films ever made. All it lacks is the name of Dracula, which was changed due to copyright problems with Stoker's widow. Filmed in Bavaria. Silent with music and English titles. Remade by Werner Herzog in 1979. **63m/B VHS, Beta, LV.** *GE* Max Schreck, Alexander Granach, Gustav von Wagenheim, Greta Schroeder; **D:** F.W. Murnau. *GPV, MRV, NOS*

Nostradamus ♂♂ **1993 (R)** Historical soap opera about unconventional 16th-century French physician and astrologer Michel de Nostradame. Persecuted by the Inquisition, he comes under the protection of Queen Catherine de Medici of France, although his visions of destruction and death continue to haunt him. Nostradamus' prophecies, first published in 1555, have continued to fascinate, being used to predicate everything from the death of historical leaders to WWI. The film, however, is slow going and fails to hold much interest. **118m/C VHS, LV.** *FR* Tcheky Karyo, F. Murray Abraham, Julia Ormond, Rutger Hauer, Amanda Plummer, Assumpta Serna, Anthony Higgins, Diana Quick, Michael Gough; **D:** Roger Christian; **W:** Knut Boeser, Piers Ashworth. *ORI*

The Nostradamus Kid ♂♂ **1992 (R)** Young man, convinced the world is about to end, decides his last goal will be to make love (for the first time) with his girlfriend. **120m/C VHS.** Noah Taylor, Miranda Otto, Arthur Dignam; **D:** Bob Ellis. *LIV*

Not as a Stranger ♂♂½ **1955** Glossy film about the medical profession and the varying degrees of dedication shown by doctors. Mitchum stars as an medical student who can't afford to pay his tuition, so he marries nurse de Havilland and continues going to school on her money, although their relationship is far from being a loving one. Producer Kramer's directorial debut. Based on the book by Morton Thompson. **135m/B VHS.** Olivia de Havilland, Robert Mitchum, Frank Sinatra, Gloria Grahame, Broderick Crawford, Charles Bickford, Myron McCormick, Lon Chaney Jr.; **D:** Stanley Kramer; **W:** Edward Anhalt. Nominations: Academy Awards '55: Best Sound. *MGM*

Not for Publication ♂♂ **1984 (R)** A woman working as both a tabloid reporter and a mayoral campaign worker uncovers governmental corruption with the help of a shy photographer and a midget. Meant to be on par with older screwball comedies but lacking the wit and subtlety. **87m/C VHS, Beta.** Nancy Allen, David Naughton, Richard Paul, Alice Ghostley, Laurence Luckinbill; **D:** Paul Bartel; **W:** Paul Bartel. *NO*

Not My Kid ♂♂½ **1985** The 15-year-old daughter of a surgeon brings turmoil to her family when she becomes heavily involved in drugs. Producer Polson, along with Dr. Miller Newton, wrote the original book for this emotional story that is one of the better treatments of this important subject. Made for television. **120m/C VHS, Beta.** George Segal, Stockard Channing, Viveka Davis, Andrew (Andy) Robinson, Gary Bayer, Nancy Cartwright, Tate Donovan; **D:** Michael Tuchner; **W:** Christopher Knopf. *SVE*

Not of This Earth ♂½ **1988 (R)** In a remake of the 1957 Roger Corman quickie, an alien wearing sunglasses makes an unfriendly trip to Earth. In order to save his dying planet he needs major blood donations from unsuspecting Earthlings. Not a match for the original version, some may nevertheless want to see ex-porn star Lords in her role as the nurse. **92m/C VHS, Beta.** Traci Lords, Arthur Roberts, Lenny Juliano, Rebecca Perle, Ace Mask, Roger Lodge; **D:** Jim Wynorski; **W:** Jim Wynorski, R.J. Robertson. *MGM*

Not Quite Human ♂♂ **1987** When Jonas Carson builds himself an android teenage son, he must keep the technology from falling into the hands of an evil toy manufacturer with plans of his own. Humorous hijinks abound. Based on the book series "Not Quite Human" by Seth McEvoy. Made for cable television; followed by two sequels. **91m/C VHS, Beta.** Alan Thicke, Robin Lively, Robert Harper, Joseph Bologna, Jay Underwood; **D:** Steven Hilliard Stern. *DIS*

Not Quite Human 2 ♂♂½ **1989** In this sequel, Dr. Jonas Carson sends his cyber-son off to college where Chip meets the not-quite-human girl of his dreams. Followed by "Still Not Quite Human." Made for cable television. **91m/C VHS, Beta.** Alan Thicke, Jay Underwood, Robin Lively, Greg Mullavey, Katie Barberi, Mark Arnott; **D:** Eric Luke. *DIS*

Not Quite Love ♂♂ **1988** Pre-pubescent ghetto waif and a self-appointed prophet seek love in uncaring city. Much music, singing and foot-stomping. **30m/C VHS.** **D:** David Scmidlapp. *FCT, MWF*

Not Quite Paradise ♂ *Not Quite Jerusalem* **1986 (R)** A young American medical student falls in love with a young Israeli girl living on a kibbutz. **106m/C VHS, Beta.** Sam Robards, Joanna Pacula; **D:** Lewis Gilbert. *VTR, NWV*

Not Tonight Darling ♂ **1972 (R)** A bored suburban housewife becomes involved with a fast-talking businessman who leads her into a web of deceit and blackmail. **70m/C VHS, Beta.** Luan Peters, Vincent Ball, Jason Twelvetrees. *GEM*

Not Without My Daughter ♂♂½ **1990 (PG-13)** Overwrought drama shot in Israel about American Field, who travels with her Arab husband and their daughter to his native Iran, where (he must have forgotten to tell her) she has no rights. He decides the family will stay, using beatings and confinement to persuade his uncooperative wife, but she risks all to escape with daughter. Based on the true story of Betty Mahmoody. **116m/C VHS, Beta, LV, 8mm.** Sally Field, Alfred Molina, Sheila Rosenthal, Roshan Seth, Sarah Badel, Mony Rey, Georges Corraface; **D:** Brian Gilbert. *MGM, FCT*

Notes for an African Orestes ♂♂ **1970** Director Pasolini's insight into how a filmmaker works and what motivates him, as the camera reveals his plans to film a modern day version of Aeschylus' "Orestes" in Africa. **75m/B VHS.** **D:** Pier Paolo Pasolini; **M:** Gato Barbieri. *MFV, CIG, INJ*

Nothing But a Man ♂♂½ **1964** Duff Anderson (Dixon) is a black laborer trying to make a life in a small Alabama town. He falls for the daughter of a minister, they marry, and he gets a job at a local sawmill. When he won't bend to his racist white employers, he's fired and labeled a troublemaker. Unsentimental depiction of the times. **95m/B VHS.** Ivan Dixon, Abbey Lincoln, Gloria Foster, Julius W. Harris, Martin Priest, Yaphet Kotto; **D:** Michael Roemer; **W:** Michael Roemer. *NEW, BTV, AAE*

Nothing But the Night ♂½ *The Devil's Undead; The Resurrection Syndicate* **1972 (PG)** Lee's company produced this convoluted story of orphans who are victims of a cult that uses them in their quest for immortality. **90m/C VHS.** *GB* Christopher Lee, Peter Cushing, Diana Dors, Georgia Brown, Keith Barron, Fulton Mackay, Gwyneth Strong; **D:** Peter Sasdy. *SNC*

Nothing But Trouble ♂♂½ **1944** Laurel & Hardy's last film for MGM is a complicated tale of two servants who wind up protecting an exiled boy king from the machinations of his power-mad uncle. **70m/B VHS.** Stan Laurel, Oliver Hardy, Henry O'Neill, Mary Boland, David Leland, John Warburton, Connie Gilchrist, Philip Merivale; **D:** Sam Taylor. *MGM*

Nothing But Trouble ♂ **1991 (PG-13)** Yuppie couple out for weekend drive find themselves smoldering in small town hell thanks to a traffic ticket. Horror and humor mix like oil and water in Aykroyd's debut as director. **93m/C VHS, Beta, LV, 8mm.** Dan Aykroyd, Demi Moore, Chevy Chase, John Candy, Taylor Negron, Bertila Demas, Valri Bromfield; **D:** Dan Aykroyd; **W:** Dan Aykroyd, Peter Aykroyd. Golden Raspberry Awards '91: Worst Supporting Actor (Aykroyd). *WAR*

Nothing in Common ♂♂½ **1986 (PG)** In his last film, Gleason plays the abrasive, diabetic father of immature advertising agency worker Hanks. After his parents separate, Hanks learns to be more responsible and loving in caring for his father. Comedy and drama are blended well here with the help of satirical pokes at the ad business and Hanks turns in a fine performance, but the unorganized, lengthy plot may lose some viewers. **119m/C VHS, Beta, LV.** Tom Hanks, Jackie Gleason, Eva Marie Saint, Bess Armstrong, Hector Elizondo, Barry Corbin, Sela Ward, John Kapelos, Jane Morris, Dan Castellaneta, Tracy Reiner; **D:** Garry Marshall; **W:** Rick Podell; **C:** John A. Alonzo; **M:** Patrick Leonard. *WAR*

Nothing Personal ♂½ **1980 (PG)** Confused mix of romantic comedy and environmental themes. Lawyer (?) Somers attempts to help college professor Sutherland prevent the slaughter of seals. Enter romance (hey, but what about the baby seals?). Enlivened by appearances of Canadian SCTV vets and Somers's first starring theatrical role. **96m/C VHS, Beta, LV.** Donald Sutherland, Suzanne Somers, Dabney Coleman, John Dehner, Roscoe Lee Browne, Catherine O'Hara; **D:** George Bloomfield. *LIV, VES*

Nothing Sacred ♂♂♂½ **1937** Slick, overzealous reporter takes advantage of a small-town girl's situation. As a publicity stunt, his newspaper brings her to the Big Apple to distract her from her supposedly imminent death in order to manipulate the public's sentiment as a means to sell more copy. Innocent young Lombard, however, is far from death's door, and deftly exploits her exploitation. Scathing indictment of the mass media and bovine mentality of the masses. Both hysterically funny and bitterly cynical; boasts Lombard's finest performance as the small-town rube who orchestrates the ruse. Remade in 1954 as "Living It Up." **75m/C VHS, Beta, LV.** Fredric March, Carole Lombard, Walter Connolly, Sig Rumann, Charles Winninger, Margaret Hamilton; **D:** William

A. Wellman; *W:* Ben Hecht; *C:* William Howard Greene; *M:* Oscar Levant. *NOS, MRV, VYY*

Nothing Underneath ♂½ **1985** An American guy goes to Rome to search for his model twin sister, who may be one of the victims of a series of scissor killings. **95m/C VHS, Beta.** Tom Schanley, Renee Simonsen, Nicola Perring, Donald Pleasence; *D:* Carlo Vanzina. *NO*

Notorious ♂♂♂♂ **1946** Post-WWII story of a beautiful playgirl sent by the US government to marry a suspected spy living in Brazil. Grant is the agent assigned to watch her. Duplicity and guilt are important factors in this brooding, romantic spy thriller. Suspenseful throughout, with a surprise ending. The acting is excellent all around and Hitchcock makes certain that suspense is maintained throughout this classy and complex thriller. Laser edition contains original trailer, publicity photos, and additional footage. **101m/B VHS, Beta, LV.** Cary Grant, Ingrid Bergman, Claude Rains, Louis Calhern, Madame Konstantin, Reinhold Schunzel, Moroni Olsen; *D:* Alfred Hitchcock; *W:* Ben Hecht. Nominations: Academy Awards '46: Best Original Screenplay, Best Supporting Actor (Rains). *FOX, CRC, MLB*

The Notorious Lady ♂♂½ **1927** Englishman Stone kills the man he finds in Bedford's room, believing him to be his wife's lover. He's mistaken but she lies to save him and Stone takes off for the diamond mines in Africa. Bedford hears he's dead and sets out, seeking the truth. **79m/B VHS.** Lewis Stone, Barbara Bedford, Earl Metcalfe, Francis McDonald; *D:* King Baggot; *C:* Gaetano Antonio "Tony" Gaudio. *FCT*

Nous N'Irons Plus au Bois ♂♂ **1969** On the outskirts of a forest held by the Germans, a small group of French resistance fighters capture a German soldier during WWII. He actually wants to join forces with them, however, after falling in love with a lovely young French girl. In French; subtitled in English. **98m/C VHS, Beta.** *FR* Marie-France Pisier, Siegfried Rauch, Richard Leduc; *D:* Georges Dumoulin. *NO*

Nouvelle Vague ♂♂½ *New Wave* **1990** Delon is a philosopher king and Giordano a wealthy countess involved in Godard's usual sexual and political themes, which has society geared toward support of the rich. Dialogue is composed entirely of quotations. In French with English subtitles. **89m/C VHS.** *SI FR* Alain Delon, Domiziana Giordano, Roland Amstutz, Laurence Cote, Christophe Odent; *D:* Jean-Luc Godard; *W:* Jean-Luc Godard. *INJ, FCT*

Novel Desires ♂½ **1992 (R)** Brian Freedman is a best-selling author who teams up with his writing rival, Vicky Chance. But it isn't just their imaginations they give free reign to, it's all their desires as well. **80m/C VHS.** Tyler Gains, Caroline Monteith, Mitchell Clark, Lisa Hayland; *D:* Lawrence Unger. *CEL*

Now and Forever ♂½ **1982 (R)** Young wife's life is shattered when her unfaithful husband is wrongly accused and convicted of rape. After he is sent to prison, she begins drinking and taking drugs. From the novel by Danielle Steel, it will appeal most to those who like their romances a la Harlequin. **93m/C VHS, Beta, LV.** *AU* Cheryl Ladd, Robert Coleby, Carmen Duncan, Christine Amor, Aileen Britton; *D:* Adrian Carr. *MCA*

Now and Then ♂♂ **1995 (PG-13)** Four women hold a reunion 25 years after their most eventful childhood summer to relive the good ol' days of prepubescent triumphs and tragedies. Flashback, which thankfully comprises about 85% of the movie, explores first kisses, budding breasts, death and divorce. Despite good intentions, this nostalgic coming-of-ager for the girls is a jumbled mass of borrowed formulas that just can't shake that feeling of forced sentimentality. The young actresses are talented and charming, but their less convincing adult counterparts serve mostly as big names to draw crowds and studio support. **97m/C VHS, LV.** Rosie O'Donnell, Melanie Griffith, Demi Moore, Rita Wilson, Christina Ricci, Thora Birch, Gaby Hoffman, Ashleigh Aston Moore, Cloris Leachman, Lolita Davidovich, Bonnie Hunt, Brendan Fraser; *D:* Lesli Linka Glatter; *W:* I. Marlene King; *C:* Ueli Steiger; *M:* Cliff Eidelman. *NLC*

Now, Voyager ♂♂♂½ **1942** Davis plays a lonely spinster who is transformed into a vibrant young woman by therapy. She comes out of her shell to have a romantic affair with a suave European (who turns out to be married) but still utters the famous phrase "Oh, Jerry, we have the stars. Let's not ask for the moon." Definitely melodramatic, but an involving story nonetheless. Based on a novel by Olive Higgins Prouty. **117m/B VHS, Beta, LV.** Bette Davis, Gladys Cooper, Claude Rains, Paul Henreid, Bonita Granville; *D:* Irving Rapper; *M:* Max Steiner. Academy Awards '42: Best Score; Nominations: Academy Awards '42: Best Actress (Davis), Best Supporting Actress (Cooper). *MGM*

Now You See Him, Now You Don't ♂♂ **1972 (G)** Light Disney comedy involving a gang of crooks who want to use a college student's invisibility formula to rob a local bank. Sequel to Disney's "The Computer Wore Tennis Shoes." **85m/C VHS, Beta.** Kurt Russell, Joe Flynn, Cesar Romero, Jim Backus; *D:* Robert Butler; *M:* Robert F. Brunner. *DIS*

Nowhere to Hide ♂♂ **1987 (R)** A widow whose Marine officer husband has been assassinated is chased by some bad guys who are after a helicopter part (say what?) and she must fight for survival for herself and her 6-year-old son. **91m/C VHS, Beta.** Amy Madigan, Daniel Hugh-Kelly, Michael Ironside; *D:* Mario Azzopardi; *M:* Brad Fiedel. *ORI, HHE, WAR*

Nowhere to Hide ♂♂ **19??** A hitman is hired to kill a young boy who witnesses a brutal murder. The hitman, however, decides he's already killed too many people and wants to get out of the business. Will he become the next murder target? **80m/C VHS.** Paul Winfield, Rod Taylor. *QVD*

Nowhere to Run ♂ **1988 (R)** Slipshod version of a true story about a series of murders in Caddo, Texas in 1960. Carradine, parolled from prison, murders for revenge while six high school seniors get involved in the chase and in the seedy side of politics, police, and their own puberty. **87m/C VHS, Beta.** David Carradine, Jason Priestley, Kieran Mulroney, Henry Jones; *D:* Carl Franklin. *MGM*

Nowhere to Run ♂½ **1993 (R)** Kickboxer with heart seeks cross-over movie to establish real acting career. Unfortunately, even if such a movie existed, Van Damme wouldn't know what to do with it. Arquette plays the damsel in distress, facing eviction from the family farm with her two small children. Fortunately for Van Damme's escaped convict character, she is also a very lonely widow (nudge, nudge). He saves the day by abusing the daylights out of the big bad bankers, yet also finds time to play surrogate dad. Whatta guy. **95m/C VHS, LV, 8mm.** Jean-Claude Van Damme, Rosanna Arquette, Kieran Culkin, Tiffany Taubman, Joss Ackland, Ted Levine; *D:* Robert Harmon; *W:* Joe Eszterhas, Leslie Bohem, Randy Feldman; *M:* Mark Isham. *COL*

Nuclear Conspiracy ♂½ **1985** A reporter disappears while investigating a huge nuclear waste shipment, and his wife searches for him. **115m/C VHS, Beta.** Birgit Doll, Albert Fortell. *VMK*

The Nude Bomb ♂♂½ *The Return of Maxwell Smart* **1980 (PG)** Proof that old TV shows never die—they just get made into big screen movies. Maxwell Smart from "Get Smart" (would you believe?) tries to save the world from a bomb intended to destroy clothing and leave everyone in the buff. Old hat lines. Followed by the TV movie "Get Smart, Again!" **94m/C VHS, LV.** Don Adams, Dana Elcar, Pamela Hensley, Sylvia Kristel, Norman Lloyd, Rhonda Fleming, Joey Forman; *D:* Clive Donner; *W:* Bill Dana; *M:* Lalo Schifrin. *MCA*

Nude on the Moon *Woof!* **1961** Lunar expedition discovers moon inhabited by people who bare skin as hobby. Groovy theme song, "I'm Mooning Over You, My Little Moon Doll." Part of Joe Bob Brigg's "Sleaziest Movies in the History of the World" series. **83m/C VHS.** *D:* Doris Wishman. *VTR*

Nudity Required ♂ **1990** Two pals use the casting couch, pretending to be Hollywood producers, to seduce young women. Silly comedy with gratuitous nudity (Ms. Newmar included). Hardly a laugh to be found. **90m/C VHS.** Julie Newmar, Troy Donahue, Brad Zutaut, Billy Frank, Ty Randolph, Alvin Silver, Eli Rich, Phil Hock; *D:* John Bown. *NO*

Nudo di Donna ♂♂♂ *Portrait of a Woman, Nude* **1983** A witty comedy about a Venetian bookseller who is becoming tired of marital struggles with his sexy wife of 16 years. He wanders into a fashion photography shop, sees a backside nude photo of a model who looks like his wife, and he takes off in fiery pursuit to find the subject of the photo. Venetian location photography is quite nice. In Italian with English subtitles. **112m/C VHS, Beta, LV.** *IT* Nino Manfredi, Jean-Pierre Cassel, George Wilson, Elenora Giorgi; *D:* Nino Manfredi. *APD, TPV*

Nukie ♂♂½ **1993 (G)** Brothers from another planet crash land on Earth. The first one is subjected to a dizzying array of scientific experiments in Florida involving electric cattle prods. The other one, Nukie, lands in Africa and is befriended by twins from a remote tribal village. They join him in his quest to free his brother from the sadistic clutches of suntanned professionals who have lost all compassion. Important message for our youth about the dangers of a runaway technocracy. **99m/C VHS, LV.** Glynis Johns, Steve Railsback; *D:* Sias Odendal. *VMK*

Number One Fan ♂½ **1994 (R)** Hollywood star is stalked by woman with whom he had a brief romance. She resorts to murder to make sure she's the only woman in his life. **93m/C VHS.** Chad McQueen, Catherine Mary Stewart, Renee Ammann, Hoyt Axton, Paul Bartel, Eric Da Re, Charles Matthau; *D:* Jane Simpson; *W:* Anthony Lawrence Green. *ORI*

Number 1 of the Secret Service ♂♂ **1977 (PG)** A handsome secret agent must foil the plans of a millionaire industrialist to destroy the economy. Spy spoof that's marginally interesting. **87m/C VHS, Beta.** *GB* Nicky Henson, Geoffrey Keen, Sue Lloyd, Aimi MacDonald, Richard Todd; *D:* Lindsay Shonteff. *MGM*

Number One with a Bullet ♂♂ **1987 (R)** Two unorthodox "odd couple" detectives are demoted after losing a key witness, but still set out on their own to unearth a drug czar. Carradine and Williams are better than this standard action material. **103m/C VHS, Beta.** Robert Carradine, Billy Dee Williams, Peter Graves, Valerie Bertinelli; *D:* Jack Smight; *W:* James Belushi, Andrew Kurtzman, Rob Riley. *MGM*

No. 17 ♂♂♂ **1932** A humorous early thriller by the Master Hitchcock, filmed before the likes of "The 39 Steps." An unsuspecting hobo accidentally discovers a jewel thief's cache. The chase is on—superb final chase sequence involving a bus and a train. Based on the play by J. Jefferson Farjeon. **64m/B VHS, Beta, 8mm.** *GB* Leon M. Lion, Anne Grey, John Stuart, Donald Calthrop; *D:* Alfred Hitchcock; *W:* Alfred Hitchcock. *REP, NOS, HHT*

Numero Deux ♂♂ *Number Two* **1975** Godard explores politics, sex, and the trials of the modern family. A dissatisfied wife suffers from chronic constipation, her exhausted husband is impotent, they, their children, and grandparents all try to cope with daily life. For nine-tenths of the film Godard only used small portions of the screen (the upper left and lower right corners) to manipulate his message of frustration. It's only at the end that the full-screen is used to offer some sort of relief. In French with English subtitles. **90m/C VHS.** *FR* Sandrine Battistella, Pierre Oudry, Alexandre Rignault, Rachel Stefanopol; *D:* Jean-Luc Godard; *W:* Anne-Marie Mieville, Jean-Luc Godard. *FCT*

The Nun ♂♂½ **1966** A young woman, unable to meet financial obligations, is forced into a convent. Victimized by the mother superior and betrayed by a clergyman who befriends her, she escapes from the convent and eventually ends up in a bordello, despairing and suicidal. Not a cheery story. Banned in France for two years. In French with English subtitles. **155m/C VHS.** *FR* Anna Karina, Lilo (Liselotte) Pulver, Micheline Presle, Christine Lenier, Francine Berge, Francesco Rabal, Wolfgang Reichmann, Catherine Diamant, Yori Bertin; *D:* Jacques Rivette. *INT, FCT, INJ*

Nuns on the Run ☠☠ **1990 (PG-13)** Idle and Coltrane are two nonviolent members of a robbery gang who double-cross their boss during a hold-up and disguise themselves as nuns while on the run from both the Mob and the police. Catholic humor, slapstick, and much fun with habits dominate. Idle and Coltrane do their best to keep the so-so script moving with its one-joke premise. **95m/C VHS, Beta, LV.** Eric Idle, Robbie Coltrane, Janet Suzman, Camille Coduri, Robert Patterson, Tom Hickey, Doris Hare, Lila Kaye; ***D:*** Jonathan Lynn; ***W:*** Jonathan Lynn. *FOX*

The Nun's Story ☠☠☠½ **1959** The melancholy tale of a young nun working in the Congo and Belgium during WWII, and struggling to reconcile her free spirit with the rigors of the order. Highly acclaimed; from the Kathryn Hulme novel. **152m/C VHS, Beta, LV.** Audrey Hepburn, Peter Finch, Edith Evans, Peggy Ashcroft, Mildred Dunnock, Dean Jagger, Beatrice Straight, Colleen Dewhurst; ***D:*** Fred Zinnemann; ***W:*** Robert Anderson. British Academy Awards '59: Best Actress (Hepburn); National Board of Review Awards '59: 10 Best Films of the Year, Best Director (Zinnemann), Best Supporting Actress (Evans); Nominations: Academy Awards '59: Best Actress (Hepburn), Best Adapted Screenplay, Best Color Cinematography, Best Director (Zinnemann), Best Film Editing, Best Picture, Best Sound, Best Original Score. *WAR*

Nurse ☠☠½ **1980** A recently widowed woman resumes her career as a nurse in a large urban hospital, after her son leaves for college. Based on Peggy Anderson's book. Made for television; became a weekly series. **105m/C VHS, Beta.** Michael Learned, Robert Reed, Antonio Fargas; ***D:*** David Lowell Rich. *LIV*

Nurse Edith Cavell ☠☠☠ **1939** Fine performances in this true story of Britain's famous nurse who aided the Belgian underground during WWI, transporting wounded soldiers out of the German-occupied country. Decidedly opposes war and, ironically, was released just as WWII began to heat up in 1939. **95m/B VHS, Beta.** George Sanders, Edna May Oliver, ZaSu Pitts, Robert Coote, May Robson, Anna Neagle; ***D:*** Herbert Wilcox. Nominations: Academy Awards '39: Best Original Score. *NOS, CAB, BAR*

Nurse on Call ☠ **1988** A bevy of trampy nurses cavort throughout a big city hospital. Softcore. **80m/C VHS, Beta.** Anne Tilson, Jennie Martinez, Christopher Floyd. *MED*

The Nut ☠☠½ **1921** Charlie Jackson (Fairbanks) is a wacky, wealthy inventor who falls for Estrell Wynn (De La Motte), a society gal dedicated to improving the lives of underprivileged children. He tries to aid her in a variety of ways—none of which work out as he expects. The usually swashbuckling Fairbanks does get to rescue the heroine. **61m/B VHS.** Douglas Fairbanks Sr., Marguerite de la Motte, William E. Lowery; ***D:*** Theodore Reed; ***W:*** William Parker. *FCT*

Nutcase ☠ **1983** A trio of young children in New Zealand attempt to thwart a group of terrorists who threaten to reactivate a large city's volcanoes unless they are given a large sum of money. Novel twist there. **49m/C VHS, Beta.** *NZ* Nevan Rowe, Ian Watkin, Michael Wilson; ***D:*** Roger Donaldson. *NO*

Nutcracker, A Fantasy on Ice **1983** An ice-skating version of the famed story and Tchaikovsky ballet aired as a television special in 1983. **85m/C VHS, Beta.** Dorothy Hamill. *VMK*

The Nutcracker Prince ☠☠ **1991** The classic children's Christmas tale comes alive in this feature-length animated special. **75m/C VHS, LV, 8mm.** *CA* ***D:*** Paul Schibli; ***V:*** Kiefer Sutherland, Megan Follows, Michael MacDonald, Phyllis Diller, Peter O'Toole. *WAR, WTA*

Nutcracker Sweet ☠ **1984** Ridiculous drama about a beautiful and powerful socialite (Collins) who runs a renowned ballet company with an iron fist. A Russian ballerina defects and infiltrates Collins's company to try out her own treacherous motives. **101m/C VHS, Beta.** Joan Collins, Finola Hughes, Paul Nicholas; ***D:*** Anwar Kawadri. *LIV, VES*

Nutcracker: The Motion Picture ☠☠½ **1986** A lavish, stage-bound filmization of the Tchaikovsky ballet, designed by Maurice Sendak. **82m/C VHS, Beta.** ***D:*** Carroll Ballard. *PAR, BAR, KAR*

Nuts ☠☠☠ **1987 (R)** A high-priced prostitute attempts to prove her sanity when she's accused of manslaughter. Ashamed of her lifestyle, and afraid of her reasons for it, her parents attempt to institutionalize her. A filmed version of Tom Topor's play that manages to retain its mesmerizing qualities. Fine performances, although the funnygirl goes over the top on several occasions. **116m/C VHS, Beta, LV, 8mm.** Barbra Streisand, Richard Dreyfuss, Maureen Stapleton, Karl Malden, James Whitmore, Robert Webber, Eli Wallach, Leslie Nielsen, William Prince, Dakin Matthews, Hayley Taylor Block; ***D:*** Martin Ritt; ***W:*** Tom Topor, Darryl Ponicsan, Alvin Sargent; ***M:*** Barbra Streisand. *WAR*

Nuts in May ☠☠ **1976** Two smug, middle-aged, middle-class vegetarians go on a camping trip and totally alienate their cynical, working-class fellow campers. Made for British television. **84m/C VHS.** *GB* Alison Steadman; ***D:*** Mike Leigh. *WBF, BTV*

The Nutt House ☠½ **1995 (PG-13)** Identical twins—separated at birth— grow up to be a slimy politician and a nutcase (living up to the family name) with multiple personalities. Naturally, when the two are reunited it makes for lots of outrageous complications. **90m/C VHS, LV.** Stephen Kearney, Traci Lords, Amy Yasbeck; ***Cameos:*** Stella Stevens, Robert Mandan, Catherine Bach; ***D:*** Adam Rifkin. *TRI*

The Nutty Professor ☠☠☠ **1963** A mild-mannered chemistry professor creates a potion that turns him into a suave, debonair, playboy type with an irresistible attraction to women. Lewis has repeatedly denied the slick character is a Dean Martin parody, but the evidence is quite strong. Easily Lewis's best film. **107m/C VHS, Beta, LV.** Jerry Lewis, Stella Stevens, Howard Morris, Kathleen Freeman; ***D:*** Jerry Lewis; ***W:*** Jerry Lewis. *PAR*

The Nutty Professor ☠☠☠ **1996 (PG-13)** In this remake of the Jerry Lewis 1963 comedy, Murphy stars as Professor Sherman Klump, a severely overweight but bright man whose heft gets in the way of his love life. He takes a swig of his own secret potion and is transformed into the slim and suave Buddy Love. Only the formula isn't perfect and seems to wear off at the worst possible times. After a string of bad movies, Murphy may have stumbled upon his own formula for a comeback by relinquishing creative control and concentrating on the comedy. Reminiscent of "Coming to America", Murphy plays eight different roles. The fat jokes and the fart jokes are plentiful and so are the laughs. **?m/C VHS.** Eddie Murphy, Jada Pinkett, James Coburn, Dave Chappelle; ***D:*** Tom Shadyac; ***W:*** David Sheffield, Barry W. Blaustein, Steve Oedekerk, Tom Shadyac; ***C:*** Julio Macat; ***M:*** David Newman. *NYR*

Nyoka and the Tigermen *Nyoka and the Lost Secrets of Hippocrates; Perils of Nyoka* **1942** The adventures of the jungle queen Nyoka and her rival Vultura in their search for the lost tablets of Hippocrates. In 15 episodes. **250m/B VHS, LV.** Kay Aldridge, Clayton Moore; ***D:*** William Witney. *VCN, REP, MLB*

O Lucky Man! ☠☠☠☠ **1973 (R)** Surreal, black comedy following the rise and fall and eventual rebirth of a modern British coffee salesman. Several actors play multiple roles with outstanding performances throughout. Price's excellent score combines with the hilarity for an extraordinary experience. **178m/C VHS, Beta.** *GB* Malcolm McDowell, Ralph Richardson, Rachel Roberts, Arthur Lowe, Alan Price, Helen Mirren, Mona Washbourne, Warren Clarke; ***D:*** Lindsay Anderson; ***M:*** Alan Price. British Academy Awards '73: Best Supporting Actor (Lowe); National Board of Review Awards '73: 10 Best Films of the Year; Nominations: Cannes Film Festival '73: Best Film. *WAR*

O Pioneers! ☠☠½ **1991 (PG)** Lange plays Alexandra Bergson, an unmarried woman at the turn of the century, who inherits her family's Nebraska homestead because her father knows how much she loves the land. Although the family has prospered through Alexandra's smart investments, her brothers come to resent her influence. When her first love returns after fifteen years and the romance is rekindled, family resentments surface once again. Based on the novel by Willa Cather. A Hallmark Hall of Fame presentation. **99m/C VHS, LV.** Jessica Lange, David Strathairn, Tom Aldredge, Reed Edward Diamond, Anne Heche, Heather Graham, Josh Hamilton, Leigh Lawson, Graham Beckel; ***D:*** Glenn Jordan; ***W:*** Glenn Jordan. *REP, FCT*

O Quatrilho ☠☠ **1995** Two young couples from Italy immigrate to southern Brazil in the 1910s, hoping to find their fortunes. Thrifty peasant Angelo (Paternost) marries romantic Teresa (Pillar) and goes into business with the equally romantic Massimo (Campos), who's married to the thrifty Pierina (Pires). The grain mill thrives but the romantic half of each couple delve into some illicit amore and decide to flee while their left-behind spouses discover their own attractions. A happy ending is had by all (this must be a fairytale). Lots of high-gloss gush. Based on the novel by Jose Clemente Pozenat. Portuguese and Italian with subtitles. **120m/C VHS.** *BR* Gloria Pires, Patricia Pillar, Bruno Campos, Alexandre Paternost; ***D:*** Fabio Barreto; ***W:*** Leopoldo Serran; ***C:*** Felix Monti; ***M:*** Caetano Veloso. Nominations: Academy Awards '95: Best Foreign Language Film. *NYR*

The Oak ☠☠½ **1993** Morgenstern grieves over the loss of her father until she realizes she can't get rid of the body. Her difficulties in locating adequate medical facilities reflect the nightmarish realities of pre-1990 communist Romania. Potentially farcical aspects of storyline are successfully removed by violence in following scene involving Morgenstern and a band of roaming soldiers. A tragicomic look at obstinate communist bureaucrats and the wily, willful peasants who overcome them. Based on a novel by Ion Baiesu. In Romanian with English subtitles. **105m/C VHS.** *RO* Maia Morgenstern, Razvan Vasilescu, Victor Rebengiuc, Dorel Visan, Mariana Mihut, Dan Condurache, Virgil Andriescu, Leopoldina Balanuta, Matei Alexandru, Gheorghe Visu, Magda Catone, Ionel Mahailescu; ***D:*** Lucian Pintilie; ***W:*** Lucian Pintilie. *NYF*

Oasis of the Zombies ☠ **1982** European students set out to find buried treasure in Saharan oasis but instead find bevy of hungry Nazis with eating disorders. **75m/C VHS, Beta.** *SP FR* Manuel Gelin, France Jordan, Jeff Montgomery, Miriam Landson, Eric Saint-Just, Caroline Audret, Henry Lambert; ***D:*** A.M. Frank. *NO*

Oath of Vengeance ☠½ **1944** Billy the Kid rides the West once more. **50m/B VHS, Beta.** Buster Crabbe, Al "Fuzzy" St. John, Jack Ingram, Charles "Blackie" King; ***D:*** Sam Newfield. *VCN, RXM*

The Object of Beauty ☠☠☠ **1991 (R)** Two Americans, trapped in Europe by their love of pleasure and their lack of money, bicker over whether to sell their one object of value - a tiny Henry Moore sculpture. When it disappears, their relationship is challenged. Excellent acting and telling direction. Forces an examination of one's own value placement. **105m/C VHS, LV.** Andie MacDowell, John Malkovich, Joss Ackland, Lolita Davidovich, Peter Riegert, Bill Paterson, Rudi Davies, Ricci Harnett; ***D:*** Michael Lindsay-Hogg; ***W:*** Michael Lindsay-Hogg; ***C:*** David Watkin; ***M:*** Tom Bahler. *LIV*

Object of Obsession ☠½ **1995 (R)** One wrong phone call propels divorcee Margaret into an affair with a stranger that leads to kinky psycho/sexual games and revenge. **91m/C VHS, LV.** Erika Anderson, Scott Valentine; ***D:*** Alexander Gregory Hippolyte. *APX*

Objective, Burma! ☠☠☠☠ **1945** Deemed by many to be the greatest and most moving WWII production released during the war. American paratroopers are dropped over Burma where their mission is to destroy a Japanese radar station. The Americans led by Flynn are successful in wiping out the station, but they are spotted and descended upon by Japanese forces. Impeded from returning to Allied lines, the American soldiers must try to survive enemy encounters, exhaustion, starvation, and the elements until they are rescued. Splendid performance by Flynn and exceptional direction from Walsh; excellent performances enhanced by energetic score. **142m/B VHS, Beta.** Errol Flynn, James Brown, William Prince, George Tobias, Henry Hull, Warner Anderson, Richard Erdman, Mark Stevens, Anthony Caruso, Hugh Beaumont; ***D:*** Raoul Walsh; ***W:*** Ranald MacDougall, Lester Cole; ***C:*** James Wong Howe; ***M:*** Franz Waxman. Nominations: Academy Awards '45: Best Film Editing, Best Story, Best Original Score. *MGM*

Oblivion ✗✗½ **1994 (PG-13)** In this sci-fi western, set in the year 3031, its cowboys versus the aliens. A sheriff's son (Paul) returns to the town of Oblivion to avenge his father's murder and finds a reptilian extraterrestrial (Divoff) terrorizing the community. **94m/C VHS, Beta.** Richard Joseph Paul, Andrew Divoff, Jackie Swanson, Meg Foster, Isaac Hayes, Julie Newmar, Carel Struycken, George Takei; ***D:*** Sam Irvin; ***W:*** Peter David; ***M:*** Pino Donaggio. *PAR*

Oblomov ✗✗✗½ *A Few Days in the Life of I.I. Oblomov; Neskolko Dnel iz Zhizni I.I. Oblomov* **1981** A production of the classic Goncharov novel about a symbolically inert Russian aristocrat whose childhood friend helps him find a reason for action. Well made, with fine performances. In Russian with English subtitles. **145m/C VHS, Beta.** *RU* Oleg Tabakov, Elena Solovei; ***D:*** Nikita Mikhalkov. *TPV, KIV, AUD*

The Oblong Box ✗✗ *Edgar Allen Poe's The Oblong Box* **1969 (PG)** Coffins, blood, and live corpses fill drawn-out and lifeless adaptation of Edgar Allan Poe story. English aristocrat Price attempts to hide his disfigured brother in an old tower. Brother predictably escapes and rampages through town before being killed. **91m/C VHS, Beta.** *GB* Vincent Price, Christopher Lee, Alastair Williamson, Hilary Dwyer, Peter Arne, Harry Baird, Carl Rigg, Sally Geeson, Maxwell Shaw; ***D:*** Gordon Hessler. *NO*

The Obsessed ✗✗ *The Late Edwina Black* **1951** Uninspiring story with Farrar suspected of murdering his wife. Competent performances, but this mystery isn't developed with any sense of style and the killer's real identity will be obvious to anyone watching. Cliches and stereotyped situations don't add anything. **77m/B VHS, LV.** *GB* David Farrar, Geraldine Fitzgerald, Roland Culver, Jean Cadell, Mary Merrall; ***D:*** Maurice Elvey. *SNC, NOS, MOV*

Obsessed ✗½ **1988 (PG-13)** Semi-realistic tale of a woman's exhausting desire for revenge against hit-and-run driver who killed her son. Cast acceptable but lack of psychological foundation weakens plot. **100m/C VHS, Beta, LV.** Kerrie Keane, Alan Thicke, Colleen Dewhurst, Saul Rubinek, Daniel Pilon, Lynne Griffin; ***D:*** Robin Spry. Genie Awards '89: Best Supporting Actress (Dewhurst). *NO*

Obsession ✗✗½ **1976 (PG)** A rich, lonely businessman meets a mysterious young girl in Italy, the mirror image of his late wife who was killed by kidnappers. Intriguing suspense film that's not quite up to comparisons with Hitchcock thrillers. Music by Hitchcock-collaborator Herrmann. **98m/C VHS, Beta, LV.** Cliff Robertson, Genevieve Bujold, John Lithgow; ***D:*** Brian DePalma; ***W:*** Paul Schrader; ***M:*** Bernard Herrmann. National Board of Review Awards '76: 10 Best Films of the Year; Nominations: Academy Awards '76: Best Original Score. *COL, HHE*

Obsession: A Taste for Fear ✗½ **1989 (R)** Diane's high fashion models are being killed and although there are plenty of suspects, she can't find the killer. **90m/C VHS, Beta.** Virginia Hey, Gerard Darmon, Carlo Mucari; ***D:*** Piccio Raffanini. *IMP*

Obsessive Love ✗✗½ **1984** A lonely, mentally unstable typist (Mimieux) becomes obsessed with her soap opera hero and decides to go to Hollywood to seduce him. She transforms herself into a sleek and stunning Hollywood temptress to woo him, and at first he goes along with her—until he realizes that she is insane. An average made-for-TV movie of the older woman/younger man genre. **97m/C VHS.** Yvette Mimieux, Simon MacCorkindale, Kin Shriner, Constance McCashin, Allan Miller, Lainie Kazan; ***D:*** Steven Hilliard Stern. *LIV*

O.C. and Stiggs ✗½ **1987 (R)** Two teens spend a summer harassing a neighbor and his family. Flimsy attempts at comedy fall flat. A failed adaptation of a National Lampoon short story, it was held for three years before release. **109m/C VHS, Beta.** Daniel H. Jenkins, Neill Barry, Jane Curtin, Tina Louise, Jon Cryer, Dennis Hopper, Paul Dooley, Ray Walston, Louis Nye, Martin Mull, Melvin Van Peebles; ***D:*** Robert Altman; ***W:*** Donald Cantrell. *FOX*

The Occult Experience **1984** An engrossing study into the world of devil-worshippers, shamans, and the like. This documentary actually records exorcisms and other rituals. Not for the faint hearted. **87m/C VHS, LV.** *COL*

The Occultist *Woof!* **1989** Satan worshippers do the dance of death as they skin men alive for their evil purposes. **82m/C VHS, Beta.** Rick Gianasi; ***D:*** Tim Kincaid; ***W:*** Tim Kincaid. *UNI*

An Occurrence at Owl Creek Bridge/Coup de Grace **1962** "Occurrence at Owl Creek Bridge" (1962), from a story by Ambrose Bierce documents the last moments of a man about to be hanged for sabotage. "Coup de Grace" (1978) tells the story of a group of friends who are caught up amongst the turmoil of the Bolshevik revolution. **123m/B VHS, Beta.** Margarethe von Trotta, Matthias Habich, Rudiger Kirschstein, Matthieu Carriere, Valeska Gert; ***D:*** Volker Schlondorff, Robert Enrico. *NO*

Ocean Drive Weekend *Woof!* **1985 (PG-13)** Several college students congregate at "Ocean Drive" for a weekend of beer, sex, and dancing. Stereotypical characters, lack of plot, and poor versions of 1960 classics combine for boring and inane comedy. **98m/C VHS, Beta.** Robert Peacock, Charles Redmond, Tony Freeman; ***D:*** Brian Thomas Jones. *LIV, VES*

Ocean's 11 ✗✗½ **1960** A gang of friends plans to rob five Las Vegas casinos simultaneously. Part of the "A Night at the Movies" series, this tape simulates a 1960 movie evening, with Bugs Bunny cartoon, "Person to Bunny;" a newsreel; and coming attractions for "The Sundowners" and "Sunrise at Campobello." **148m/C VHS, Beta, LV.** Frank Sinatra, Dean Martin, Sammy Davis Jr., Angie Dickinson, Peter Lawford; ***D:*** Lewis Milestone; ***C:*** William H. Daniels. *WAR*

Oceans of Fire ✗ **1986 (PG)** Average rehash of the tension-filled world of oil riggers. Lives of two ex-cons are threatened when they hire on as divers for world's deepest undersea oil rig. **100m/C VHS, Beta, LV.** Gregory Harrison, Billy Dee Williams, Cynthia Sikes, Lyle Alzado, Tony Burton, Ray "Boom Boom" Mancini, David Carradine, Ken Norton; ***D:*** Steve Carver. *VMK*

Octagon ✗✗ **1980 (R)** Norris protects a woman from threatening Ninja warriors in average kung-fu adventure. Enough action and violence for fans of the genre. **103m/C VHS, Beta, LV.** Chuck Norris, Karen Carlson, Lee Van Cleef, Kim Lankford, Art Hindle, Jack Carter; ***D:*** Eric Karson; ***W:*** Paul Aaron, Leigh Chapman. *MED*

Octaman ✗½ **1971** Comical thriller featuring non-threatening octopus-man discovered by scientists in Mexico. Rip-off of director Essex's own "Creature from the Black Lagoon." Not without its curiosity factor: young Rick Baker designed the octopus man, while actress Angeli died of a drug overdose during filming. **79m/C VHS, Beta.** Kerwin Mathews, Pier Angeli, Harry Guardino, David Essex, Jeff Morrow, Norman Fields; ***D:*** Harry Essex. *GEM, CNG, PSM*

Octavia ✗ **1982 (R)** A contemporary fable about a blind girl who befriends a convict and learns about life and love. **93m/C VHS, Beta.** Susan Curtis; ***D:*** David Beaird; ***W:*** David Beaird. *NLC*

The October Man ✗✗✗ **1948** When a model is found murdered, a stranger with mental problems must prove his innocence to others and himself. Strong characters make good, suspenseful mystery reminiscent of Hitchcock. **95m/B VHS.** *GB* John Mills, Joan Greenwood, Edward Chapman, Joyce Carey, Kay Walsh, Felix Aylmer, Juliet Mills; ***D:*** Roy Ward Baker. *FCT*

Octopussy ✗✗ **1983 (PG)** The Bond saga continues as Agent 007 is on a mission to prevent a crazed Russian general from launching a nuclear attack against the NATO forces in Europe. Lots of special effects and gadgets keep weak plot moving. **140m/C VHS, Beta, LV.** *GB* Roger Moore, Maud Adams, Louis Jourdan, Kristina Wayborn, Kabir Bedi; ***D:*** John Glen; ***W:*** Michael G. Wilson; ***M:*** John Barry. *MGM, FOX, TLF*

The Odd Angry Shot ✗✗½ **1979** Australian soldiers fighting in Vietnam discover the conflict is not what they expected. Ironic perspective of men struggling with their feelings about the war. More of an unremarkable drama with comic overtones than a combat film, it will appeal to those who prefer good direction to bloodshed. **90m/C VHS, Beta.** *AU* ***D:*** Tom Jeffrey. *LIV, VES*

Odd Birds ✗✗½ **1985** Coming of age drama set in 1965 California. Shy 15 year old Joy Chan is a Chinese-American dreaming of becoming an actress. Her widowed immigrant mother wants Joy to have a practical profession—like nursing. Longing for someone to understand Joy meets Brother Murphy, a math teacher at the local boys school. Murphy's been trying to reconcile his religious commitment with his unorthodox views. It isn't long before these two individualists recognize a fellow kindred spirit. **87m/C VHS.** Michael Moriarty, Donna Lai Ming Lew, Nancy Lee, Bruce Gray, Karen Maruyama, Scott Crawford; ***D:*** Jeanne Collachia; ***W:*** Jeanne Collachia. *WAC*

The Odd Couple ✗✗✗½ **1968 (G)** Two divorced men with completely opposite personalities move in together. Lemmon's obsession with neatness drives slob Matthau up the wall, and their inability to see eye-to-eye results in many hysterical escapades. A Hollywood rarity, it is actually better in some ways than Neil Simon's original Broadway version. Basis for the hit television series. **106m/C VHS, Beta, LV.** Jack Lemmon, Walter Matthau, Herb Edelman, John Fiedler, Monica Evans, Carol Shelley; ***D:*** Gene Saks; ***W:*** Neil Simon; ***C:*** Robert B. Hauser. Nominations: Academy Awards '68: Best Adapted Screenplay, Best Film Editing. *PAR*

The Odd Job ✗✗ **1978** Insurance salesman Chapman, depressed after his wife leaves him, hires a hit man to kill him. Chapman then has a hard time shaking his stalker after deciding he wants to live. Monty Python fans will enjoy seeing ex-troupe member Chapman again, but the comic's heart isn't in this unoriginal story. **100m/C VHS, Beta.** *GB* Graham Chapman; ***D:*** Peter Medak; ***M:*** Howard Blake. *VES*

Odd Jobs ✗✗ **1985 (PG-13)** When five college friends look for jobs during summer break, they wind up running their own moving business with the help of the mob. Good comic talent, but a silly slapstick script results in only a passable diversion. **89m/C VHS, Beta.** Paul Reiser, Scott McGinnis, Rick Overton, Robert Townsend; ***D:*** Mark Story; ***W:*** Robert Conte; ***M:*** Robert Folk. *NO*

Odd Man Out ✗✗✗½ *Gang War* **1947** An Irish revolutionary is injured during a robbery attempt. Suffering from gunshot wounds and closely pursued by the police, he must rely on the help of others who could betray him at any moment. A gripping tale of suspense and intrigue that will keep the proverbial seat's edge warm until the final credits. Adapted from F.L. Green's novel, previously filmed as "The Last Man." **111m/B VHS, Beta, LV.** *GB* James Mason, Robert Newton, Dan O'Herlihy, Kathleen Ryan, Cyril Cusack; ***D:*** Carol Reed; ***C:*** Robert Krasker. British Academy Awards '47: Best Film; National Board of Review Awards '47: 10 Best Films of the Year; Nominations: Academy Awards '47: Best Film Editing. *PAR*

Odd Obsession ✗✗½ *The Key* **1960** One of Ichikawa's first films, about an elderly Japanese gentleman with a young wife whose feelings of jealousy and impotence eventually wreak havoc on the marriage. In Japanese with English subtitles. **96m/C VHS, Beta.** *JP* Machiko Kyo, Ganjiro Nakamura; ***D:*** Kon Ichikawa. Golden Globe Awards '60: Best Foreign Film. *COL, SUE, INJ*

The Odd Squad 🦴 **1986 (R)** Five GIs in WWII defend a bridge from the enemy, and manage in doing so to have loads of laughs. **82m/C VHS, Beta.** Johnny Dorelli, Vincent Gardenia; ***D:*** E.B. Clucher. *VTR, PSM*

Oddball Hall 🦴🦴 **1991 (PG)** Two aging jewel thieves hide out in the African wilds, masquerading as powerful "wizards." When they head back to civilization, an African tribe beseeches the phony sorcerers to cure their long drought. **87m/C VHS.** Don Ameche, Burgess Meredith; ***D:*** Jackson Hunsicker; ***W:*** Jackson Hunsicker. *WAR, CAN*

Oddballs *Woof!* **1984 (PG-13)** In another attempt to capitalize on the success of Bill Murray's "Meatballs," this summer camp story follows three campers and their pathetic attempts to lose their virginity. Brooks has his moments, but there is little else to recommend here. **92m/C VHS, Beta.** Foster Brooks, Jason Sorokin, Wally Wodchis, Konnie Krome; ***D:*** Miklos Lente. *LIV*

Odds and Evens 🦴½ **1978 (PG)** Italian supercops pretend they don't have badges in order to clean up illegal betting and gambling rings in sunny Miami. Odds are this spaghetti cop-o-rama won't keep Morpheus at bay. **109m/C VHS, Beta.** *IT* Terence Hill, Bud Spencer; ***D:*** Sergio Corbucci. *WAR*

Ode to Billy Joe 🦴🦴 **1976 (PG)** The 1967 Bobby Gentry hit song of the same title is expanded to tell why a young man jumped to his death off the Tallahatchie Bridge. The problems of growing up in the rural South and teenage romance do not match the appeal of the theme song. Benson and O'Connor, however, work well together. **106m/C VHS, Beta.** Robby Benson, Glynnis O'Connor, Joan Hotchkis, Sandy McPeak, James Best; ***D:*** Max Baer Jr. *CCB, WAR*

The Odessa File 🦴🦴½ **1974 (PG)** During 1963, a German journalist attempts to track down some SS war criminals who have formed a secret organization called ODESSA. The story, from Frederick Forsyth's novel, drags in some places, but the scene where bad guy Schell and reporter Voight finally confront each other is a high point. **128m/C VHS, Beta, LV.** *GB* Jon Voight, Mary Tamm, Maximilian Schell, Maria Schell, Derek Jacobi; ***D:*** Ronald Neame; ***C:*** Oswald Morris; ***M:*** Andrew Lloyd Webber. *GKK*

The Odyssey of the Pacific 🦴🦴½ *The Emperor of Peru* **1982** Three young Cambodian refugees encounter retired train engineer Rooney living in the woods where a railway station once thrived. Together they work to restore an old locomotive. The ordinary, inoffensive script will not endanger quality family time. **82m/C VHS, Beta.** *CA* Mickey Rooney, Monique Mercure; ***D:*** Fernando Arrabal. *MCA*

Oedipus Rex 🦴🦴🦴 *Edipo Re* **1967** A new twist on the famous tragedy as Pasolini gives the story a modern prologue and epilogue. The classic plot has Oedipus spiraling downward into moral horror as he tries to avoid fulfulling the prophecy that he will murder his father and sleep with his mother. Cross-cultural curiosities include Japanese music and Lenin-inspired songs, some written by Pasolini, who also stars as the high priest. In Italian with English subtitles. **110m/C VHS.** *IT* Franco Citti, Silvana Mangano, Alida Valli, Julian Beck, Pier Paolo Pasolini; ***D:*** Pier Paolo Pasolini. *FST, INJ, FCT*

Of Cooks and Kung-Fu 🦴🦴 **198?** A martial arts culinary adventure. **90m/C VHS, Beta.** Jacky Cheng, Chia Kai, Lee Kuen. *MGI*

Of Human Bondage 🦴🦴🦴 **1934** The first movie version of W. Somerset Maugham's classic novel in which a young, handicapped medical student falls in love with a crude cockney waitress, in a mutually destructive affair. Established Davis's role as the tough, domineering woman. Remade in 1946 and 1964. **84m/B VHS, Beta, LV.** Bette Davis, Leslie Howard, Frances Dee, Reginald Owen, Reginald Denny, Alan Hale; ***D:*** John Cromwell; ***M:*** Max Steiner. *CNG, MRV, NOS*

Of Human Bondage 🦴🦴 **1964** An essentially decent man falls fatally in love with an alluring but heartless waitress, who subtly destroys him. Based on the W. Somerset Maugham novel. Miscast and least interesting of the three film versions, although Novak gives a good performance. **100m/B VHS, Beta.** *GB* Kim Novak, Laurence Harvey, Robert Morley, Roger Livesey, Siobhan McKenna; ***D:*** Henry Hathaway, Ken Hughes; ***W:*** Bryan Forbes; ***C:*** Oswald Morris. *MGM*

Of Human Hearts 🦴🦴½ **1938** Rural life just before the Civil War sets up this cornpone tale of family strife. Huston is a stern preacher who has his family living in near poverty as an example of sacrifice to his flock. Son Stewart wants to study medicine and Bondi, defying her husband, manages to fund his dream. Only Stewart becomes so engrossed by his ambitions that he ignores the family, even after his father dies and his mother is left poor and alone. Then Stewart joins the Civil War as a doctor where he meets President Lincoln (Carradine), who tells him he should never neglect his mother. Oy. Well, the cast is good. Adapted from the story "Benefits Forgot" by Honore Morrow. **100m/B VHS.** James Stewart, Beulah Bondi, Walter Huston, John Carradine, Guy Kibbee, Charles Coburn, Ann Rutherford, Charley Grapewin, Gene Lockhart; ***D:*** Clarence Brown; ***W:*** Bradbury Foote; ***C:*** Clyde De Vinna. *MGM, MOV*

Of Love and Shadows 🦴🦴 **1994 (R)** Political photojournalist Francisco (Banderas) begins investigating the disappearance of a self-proclaimed saint after the bloody 1973 coup in Chile. He's aided by aristocratic Chilean Irene (Connelly), who's engaged to her Army captain cousin Gustavo (Gallardo) but can't resist Francisco's ever-smoldering charms. The intrepid duo naturally find lots of corruption. Based on the novel by Isabel Allende; shot on location in Argentina. **109m/C VHS.** Antonio Banderas, Jennifer Connelly, Stefania Sandrelli, Camillo Gallardo, Patricio Contreras; ***D:*** Betty Kaplan; ***W:*** Donald Freed; ***C:*** Felix Monti; ***M:*** Jose Nieto. *NYR*

Of Mice and Men 🦴🦴🦴🦴 **1939** A powerful adaptation of the classic Steinbeck tragedy about the friendship between two itinerant Southern ranch hands during the Great Depression. Chaney is wonderful as the gentle giant and mentally retarded Lenny, cared for by migrant worker Meredith. They both get into an irreversible situation when a woman is accidentally killed. **107m/C VHS, Beta.** Lon Chaney Jr., Burgess Meredith, Betty Field, Bob Steele, Noah Beery Jr., Charles Bickford; ***D:*** Lewis Milestone; ***M:*** Aaron Copland. Nominations: Academy Awards '39: Best Picture, Best Sound, Best Score. *NO*

Of Mice and Men 🦴🦴🦴 **1981** Made-for-television remake of the classic Steinbeck tale, casting TV's Baretta (Blake) as George and Quaid as Lenny. Worth watching. **150m/C VHS, Beta.** Robert (Bobby) Blake, Randy Quaid, Lew Ayres, Mitchell Ryan, Ted Neeley, Cassie Yates, Pat Hingle, Whitman Mayo, Dennis Fimple, Pat Corley; ***D:*** Reza Badiyi. *PSM*

Of Mice and Men 🦴🦴🦴½ **1992 (PG-13)** Set on the migratory farms of California, John Steinbeck's novel covers the friendship of the simple-minded Lenny, his protector George, and a flirtatious farm wife who doesn't know Lenny's strength. Director Sinise got permission from Steinbeck's widow to film the novel (actually the third adaptation). **110m/C VHS, LV.** John Malkovich, Sherilyn Fenn, Casey Siemaszko, Joe Morton, Ray Walston, Gary Sinise, John Terry, Richard Riehle; ***D:*** Gary Sinise; ***W:*** Horton Foote. Nominations: Cannes Film Festival '92: Best Film. *MGM, PMS, BTV*

Of Unknown Origin 🦴🦴½ **1983 (R)** Weller encounters a mutated rampaging rat in his New York townhouse while his family is away on vacation. His house becomes the battleground in a terror-tinged duel of survival. A well-done rat thriller not for those with a delicate stomach. **88m/C VHS, Beta.** *CA* Peter Weller, Jennifer Dale, Lawrence Dane, Kenneth Welsh, Louis Del Grande, Shannon Tweed; ***D:*** George P. Cosmatos; ***W:*** Brian Taggert. *WAR*

Off Beat 🦴½ **1986 (PG)** A shy librarian unluckily wins a spot in a police benefit dance troupe, and then falls in love with a tough police woman. With a screenplay by playwright Medoff, and a good supporting cast, it still manages to miss the mark. **92m/C VHS, Beta, LV.** Judge Reinhold, Meg Tilly, Cleavant Derricks, Fred Gwynne, John Turturro, Jacques D'Amboise, James Tolkan, Joe Mantegna, Harvey Keitel, Amy Wright, Christopher Noth; ***D:*** Michael Dinner; ***W:*** Mark Medoff; ***M:*** James Horner. *TOU*

Off Limits 🦴🦴½ **1953** When a boxing manager is drafted into the Army, he freely breaks regulations in order to train a fighter as he sees fit. Hope and Rooney, while not in peak form, make a snappy duo in this amusing romp. **89m/B VHS, Beta, LV.** Bob Hope, Mickey Rooney, Marilyn Maxwell, Marvin Miller; ***D:*** George Marshall. *BAR*

Off Limits 🦴½ **1987 (R)** A spree of murders involving Vietnamese hookers draws two cops from the Army's Criminal Investigation Department into the sleazy backstreets of 1968 Saigon. There is little mystery as to who the killer is in this tale that seems written more for the sake of foul language and gratuitous gunfights than actual plot. **102m/C VHS, Beta, LV.** Willem Dafoe, Gregory Hines, Fred Ward, Scott Glenn, Amanda Pays, Keith David, David Alan Grier; ***D:*** Christopher Crowe; ***W:*** Christopher Crowe, Jack Thibeau; ***M:*** James Newton Howard. *FOX*

Off on a Comet **1979** An animated adaptation of the Jules Verne story about a group of people carried through the cosmos on a comet. In HiFi. **52m/C VHS, Beta.** *MGM*

Off the Mark 🦴🦴 **1987 (R)** Neely is a young athlete suffering from a childhood affliction that causes spasms in his legs. Facing the ultimate challenge, he must overcome his handicap and defeat a talented woman athlete and a Russian student in a triathalon competition. An unremarkable effort, it had a limited one-week run in theaters. **89m/C VHS, Beta.** Mark Neely, Terry Farrell, Jon Cypher, Clarence Gilyard Jr.; ***D:*** Bill Berry. *FRH*

Off the Wall 🦴 **1982 (R)** Two hitchhikers wind up in a southern maximum security prison after being accused of a crime they did not commit. What follows is a series of shenanigans as they try to escape. This supposed comedy falls flat in every way with the possible exception of Arquette's portrayal of the governor's daughter. **86m/C VHS, Beta.** Paul Sorvino, Rosanna Arquette, Patrick Cassidy, Billy Hufsey, Monte Markham, Mickey Gilley; ***D:*** Rick Friedberg. *LIV, VES*

Off Your Rocker 🦴½ **1980** Representatives of a corporate conglomerate find that the residents of Flo Adler's Mapleview Nursing Home can still muster stiff resistance to a threatened takeover. **99m/C VHS, Beta.** Milton Berle, Red Buttons, Lou Jacobi, Dorothy Malone, Helen Shaver, Sharon Acker, Helen Hughes; ***D:*** Morley Markson, Larry Pall. *NO*

The Offence 🦴🦴🦴 *Something Like the Truth* **1973 (R)** Connery plays a London detective who beats a suspected child molester to death during a police interrogation. Turns out he's reacting to a long-buried molestation incident from his own childhood. A chilling psycho-drama highlighted by a strong lead performance by Connery. **108m/C VHS.** *GB* Sean Connery, Trevor Howard, Vivien Merchant, Ian Bannen, Derek Newark, John Hallam, Peter Bowles; ***D:*** Sidney Lumet; ***W:*** John Hopkins. *MGM*

Offerings 🦴 **1989 (R)** After a boy is tormented by a gang of children who cause him to fall down a well, his resulting brain injuries turn him into a psychopathic killer. Seeking revenge ten years later, he systematically murders his oppressors, offering bits of their anatomy to the one girl who treated him kindly. A typical slasher movie, the plot is only slightly better than the worst examples of the genre. **96m/C VHS, Beta.** G. Michael Smith, Loretta L. Bowman; ***D:*** Christopher Reynolds. *HMD*

Office Romances 🦴🦴 **1986** A woman who has moved to London from the country is seduced by her employer. Because of her plain appearance, she is flattered by his attention even though he is married and has no real feelings for her. Competently made, nonetheless hard to watch because of the slow pace. **60m/C VHS, Beta.** *GB* Judy Parfitt, Ray Brooks, Suzanne Burden. *PSM*

An Officer and a Gentleman ☊☊☊½ **1982 (R)** Young drifter Gere, who enters Navy Officer Candidate School because he doesn't know what else to do with his life, becomes a better person almost despite himself. Winger is the love interest who sets her sights on marrying Gere, and Gossett is the sergeant who whips him into shape. Strong performances by the whole cast made this a must-see in 1982 that is still appealing, despite the standard Hollywood premise. ♫Up Where We Belong; Hungry for Your Love; An Officer and a Gentleman; Treat Me Right; Tunnel of Love. **126m/C VHS, Beta, LV, 8mm.** Richard Gere, Louis Gossett Jr., David Keith, Lisa Eilbacher, Debra Winger, David Caruso, Robert Loggia, Lisa Blount; ***D:*** Taylor Hackford; ***C:*** Donald E. Thorin; ***M:*** Jack Nitzsche. Academy Awards '82: Best Song ("Up Where We Belong"), Best Supporting Actor (Gossett); Nominations: Academy Awards '82: Best Actress (Winger), Best Film Editing, Best Original Screenplay, Best Original Score. *PAR, FCT, BTV*

Official Denial ☊☊½ **1993** A victim of an alien abduction becomes the only hope for a captured space being. Can Paul help the alien escape from a special Air Force UFO group and what secrets will he uncover if he does? Made for television. **86m/C VHS, Beta.** Parker Stevenson, Erin Gray, Dirk Benedict, Chad Everett; ***D:*** Brian Trenchard-Smith; ***W:*** Bruce Zabel; ***M:*** Garry McDonald, Laurie Stone. *PAR*

The Official Story ☊☊☊½ *La Historia Oficial; The Official History; The Official Version* **1985 (R)** A devastating drama about an Argentinian woman who realizes her young adopted daughter may be a child stolen from one of the thousands of citizens victimized by the country's repressive government. A powerful, important film. In Spanish with English subtitles or dubbed. **112m/C VHS, Beta, LV.** *AR* Norma Aleandro, Hector Alterio, Chunchuna Villafane, Patricio Contreras; ***D:*** Luis Puenzo; ***W:*** Luis Puenzo, Aida Bortnik. Academy Awards '85: Best Foreign Language Film; Cannes Film Festival '85: Best Actress (Aleandro); Golden Globe Awards '86: Best Foreign Film; Los Angeles Film Critics Association Awards '85: Best Foreign Film; New York Film Critics Awards '85: Best Actress (Aleandro); Nominations: Academy Awards '85: Best Original Screenplay. *APD, INJ, TPV*

Offnight ☊½ **1984** When a man is put on the day shift for the first time in fifteen years, his life turns to chaos. **47m/C VHS, Beta.** *NO*

The Offspring ☊☊ *From a Whisper to a Scream* **1987 (R)** In four stories of past evils Price reveals his hometown can force folks to kill. Not the usual Price material: dismemberment, cannibalism, and necrophilia clash with his presence. Strong yuk factor. **99m/C VHS, Beta, LV.** Vincent Price, Cameron Mitchell, Clu Gulager, Terry Kiser, Susan Tyrrell, Harry Caesar, Rosalind Cash, Martine Beswick, Angelo Rossitto, Lawrence Tierney; ***D:*** Jeff Burr; ***W:*** C. Courtney Joyner, Jeff Burr; ***M:*** John Beal. *LIV*

Oh, Alfie ☊☊ *Alfie Darling* **1975 (R)** In every man's life, there comes a time to settle down... but never when you're having as much fun as Alfie! Inadequate sequel to "Alfie." **99m/C VHS, Beta.** *GB* Joan Collins, Alan Price, Jill Townsend; ***D:*** Ken Hughes; ***W:*** Ken Hughes. *HHE*

Oh, Bloody Life! ☊☊½ **1988** Young actress faces deportation during the Stalin era in Hungary because of her aristocratic family ties. In Hungarian with English subtitles. **115m/C VHS.** *HU* Udvaros Dorottya, Szacsvay Laszlo, Kern Andras, Bezeredi Zoltan, Oze Lajos, Lukacs Margit; ***D:*** Peter Bacso; ***W:*** Peter Bacso. Montreal World Film Festival '88: Best Actress (Dorottya). *EVD, INJ, TPV*

Oh! Calcutta! ☊½ **1972** Film version of the first nude musical to play on Broadway, which caused a sensation in the late 1960s. It's really a collection of skits, some of which were written by such notables as John Lennon, Sam Shepard, and Jules Feiffer. And it's really not that funny or erotic. **105m/C VHS, Beta.** Bill Macy, Mark Dempsey, Raina Barrett, Samantha Harper, Patricia Hawkins, Mitchell McGuire; ***D:*** Guillaume Martin Aucion. *NO*

Oh Dad, Poor Dad (Momma's Hung You in the Closet & I'm Feeling So Sad) ☊☊ **1967** Cult fave black comedy about a bizarre family on a vacation in Jamaica. The domineering mother travels with a coffin containing the stuffed body of her late husband. Additional corpses abound. Based on the play by Arthur L. Kopit. **86m/C VHS, Beta.** Rosalind Russell, Robert Morse, Barbara Harris, Hugh Griffith, Lionel Jeffries, Jonathan Winters; ***D:*** Richard Quine. *PAR*

Oh, God! ☊☊½ **1977 (PG)** God, in the person of Burns, recruits Denver as his herald in his plan to save the world. Despite initial skepticism, Denver, in his film debut, keeps faith and is rewarded. Sincere performances and optimistic end make for satisfying story. Followed by "Oh God! Book 2" and "Oh God! You Devil." **104m/C VHS, Beta, LV.** George Burns, John Denver, Paul Sorvino, Ralph Bellamy, Teri Garr, William Daniels, Donald Pleasence, Barnard Hughes, Barry Sullivan, Dinah Shore, Jeff Corey, David Ogden Stiers; ***D:*** Carl Reiner; ***W:*** Larry Gelbart. Writers Guild of America '77: Best Adapted Screenplay; Nominations: Academy Awards '77: Best Adapted Screenplay. *WAR*

Oh, God! Book 2 ☊ **1980 (PG)** Burns returns as the "Almighty One" in strained sequel to "Oh God!" This time he enlists the help of a young girl to remind others of his existence. The slogan she concocts saves God's image, but not the movie. Followed by "Oh, God! You Devil." **94m/C VHS, Beta.** George Burns, Suzanne Pleshette, David Birney, Louanne, Conrad Janis, Wilfrid Hyde-White, Hans Conried, Howard Duff; ***D:*** Gilbert Cates; ***M:*** Charles Fox. *WAR*

Oh, God! You Devil ☊☊ **1984 (PG)** During his third trip to earth, Burns plays both the Devil and God as he first takes a struggling musician's soul, then gives it back. A few zingers and light atmosphere save unoriginal plot. The second sequel to "Oh, God!" **96m/C VHS, Beta, LV.** George Burns, Ted Wass, Roxanne Hart, Ron Silver, Eugene Roche, Robert Desiderio; ***D:*** Paul Bogart; ***W:*** Andrew Bergman; ***M:*** David Shire. *WAR*

Oh, Heavenly Dog! ☊☊ **1980 (PG)** A private eye returns from the dead as a dog to solve his own murder. Man's best friend and intelligent to boot. The famous dog Benji's third film, and his acting improves with each one. Adults may find this movie slow, but kids will probably love it. **104m/C VHS, Beta.** Chevy Chase, Jane Seymour, Omar Sharif, Robert Morley, Susan Kellerman; ***D:*** Joe Camp; ***W:*** Joe Camp, Rod Browning. *FOX*

Oh, Mr. Porter ☊☊ **1937** Billeted at an obscure railway post, the stationmaster hero renovates the place and hires a special train to transport the area soccer team. Trouble arises when the train is hijacked by gun smugglers. **85m/B VHS.** *GB* Will Hay, Moore Marriott, Graham Moffatt, Frederick Piper; ***D:*** Marcel Varnel. *NOS*

Oh Susannah ☊½ **1938** Robbed and thrown from a train, Autry and the two drifters who rescue him follow the thieves to Mineral Springs. Their journey is plagued by too many songs and the bad guys are predictably punished in the end. **59m/B VHS, Beta.** Gene Autry, Boothe Howard, Smiley Burnette, Frances Grant, Donald Kirke, Clara Kimball Young; ***D:*** Joseph Kane. *NOS, VDM, HHT*

Oh, What a Night ☊☊ **1992 (PG-13)** Bittersweet coming of age tale about a lonely 17-year-old (Haim) who has moved with his father and stepmother to a chicken farm in 1955 Ontario. After struggling with the untimely death of his mother, Haim falls in love with an older woman who has a husband and two kids. Features a great fifties soundtrack and beautiful scenes of the Canadian countryside. **93m/C VHS, LV.** *CA* Corey Haim, Barbara Williams, Keir Dullea, Genevieve Bujold, Robbie Coltrane; ***D:*** Eric Till. *COL, NLC*

O'Hara's Wife ☊½ **1982** Loving wife Harley continues to care for her family even after her untimely death. Only husband Asner, however, can see her ghost. Lightweight, made-for-television drama traps good cast. **87m/C VHS, Beta.** Ed Asner, Mariette Hartley, Jodie Foster, Tom Bosley, Perry Lang, Ray Walston; ***D:*** William S. Bartman; ***W:*** William S. Bartman; ***M:*** Artie Butler. *VES*

O.H.M.S. ☊½ **1937** Convoluted story about a New York hood (Ford) who flees to England where he joins the British Army by posing as a Canadian. He buddies up with Mills and they both fall for Lee. His regiment is sent to China, via ship, and Lee just happens to be a stowaway. In China, Ford manages to prove his worth by saving Lee from bandits. Maybe it's not supposed to make sense. **71m/B VHS.** *GB* Wallace Ford, John Mills, Anna Lee, Frank Cellier, Frederick Leister, Peter Croft; ***D:*** Raoul Walsh. *HCV*

Oil ☊ **1978 (PG)** Seven men fight a raging oil fire that threatens to destroy an entire country. Unfortunately, the movie is unable to ignite any interest at all. **95m/C VHS, Beta.** Ray Milland, Woody Strode, Stuart Whitman, Tony Kendall, William Berger; ***D:*** Mircea Dragan. *VCI*

The O.J. Simpson Story ☊ **1994** Tacky tabloid TV movie follows incredibly exploited story about former gridiron star Simpson (Hosea) who's accused of murdering blonde babe ex-wife Nicole (Tuck). Mainly stolid performances though Weitz is slick as Simpson lawyer Robert Shapiro. Told in flashbacks, the actual murder is never depicted. Director Jerry Friedman took his name off the credits, leaving the standard Smithee pseudonym as a replacement. **90m/C VHS.** Bobby Hosea, Jessica Tuck, James Handy, Kimberly Russell, David Roberson, Bruce Weitz; ***D:*** Alan Smithee; ***W:*** Stephen Harrigan; ***M:*** Harald Kloser. *FXV*

Oklahoma! ☊☊☊½ **1955 (G)** Jones's film debut; a must-see for musical fans. A cowboy and country girl fall in love, but she is tormented by another unwelcomed suitor. At over two hours, cuteness wears thin for some. Actually filmed in Arizona. Adapted from Rodgers and Hammerstein's broadway hit with original score; choreography by Agnes de Mille. ♫Oh, What a Beautiful Morning; Surrey with the Fringe on Top; I Cain't Say No; Many a New Day; People Will Say We're in Love; Poor Jud Is Dead; All 'Er Nuthin'; Everything's Up to Date in Kansas City; The Farmer and the Cowman. **145m/C VHS, Beta, LV.** Gordon MacRae, Shirley Jones, Rod Steiger, Gloria Grahame, Eddie Albert, Charlotte Greenwood, James Whitmore, Gene Nelson, Barbara Lawrence, Jay C. Flippen; ***D:*** Fred Zinnemann; ***W:*** Sonya Levien, William Ludwig; ***C:*** Robert L. Surtees; ***M:*** Richard Rodgers, Oscar Hammerstein. Academy Awards '55: Best Sound, Best Score; Nominations: Academy Awards '55: Best Color Cinematography, Best Film Editing. *FOX, RDG, HMV*

Oklahoma Annie ☊ **1951** Storekeeper Canova joins the new sheriff in booting undesirables out of town, and tries to sing her way into his heart. Amazingly, it works—not for delicate ears. **90m/C VHS, Beta.** Judy Canova, Fuzzy Knight, Grant Withers, John Russell, Denver Pyle, Allen Jenkins, Almira Sessions; ***D:*** R.G. Springsteen. *MLB*

Oklahoma Badlands ☊½ **1948** Lane and his horse outsmart a corrupt newspaper publisher trying to steal land from a female rancher. An early directorial work for veteran stuntman Canutt. **59m/B VHS, Beta.** Allan "Rocky" Lane, Mildred Coles; ***D:*** Yakima Canutt. *DVT*

Oklahoma Bound ☊ **1981** A feisty farmer tries to save his failing farm through a series of ostensibly comedic, unsuccessful schemes. **92m/C VHS, Beta.** F.E. Bowling, Dan Jones; ***D:*** Patrick C. Poole. *NO*

Oklahoma Crude ☊☊½ **1973 (PG)** Sadistic oil trust rep Palence battles man-hating Dunaway for her well. Drifter Scott helps her resist on the promise of shared profits. In this 1913 setting, Dunaway tells Scott she wishes she could avoid men altogether, but later settles for him. **108m/C VHS.** George C. Scott, Faye Dunaway, John Mills, Jack Palance, Harvey Jason, Woodrow Parfrey; ***D:*** Stanley Kramer; ***W:*** Marc Norman; ***C:*** Robert L. Surtees; ***M:*** Henry Mancini. *FOX*

Oklahoma Cyclone ☊½ **1930** A group of bronco busters find action and adventure on the prairie. Second of eight talkies in Steele series, includes his first of few singing roles. **64m/B VHS.** Bob Steele, Al "Fuzzy" St. John, Nita Ray, Charles "Blackie" King; ***D:*** John P. McCarthy. *NOS, GPV, DVT*

Oklahoma Kid ♪♪♪ **1939** Offbeat, hilarious western with Bogie as the villain and gunfighter Cagney seeking revenge for his father's wrongful death. Highlight is Cagney's rendition of "I Don't Want To Play In Your Yard," complete with six-shooter accompaniment. **82m/B VHS, Beta.** James Cagney, Humphrey Bogart, Rosemary Lane, Ward Bond, Donald Crisp, Charles Middleton, Harvey Stephens; ***D:*** Lloyd Bacon; ***C:*** James Wong Howe; ***M:*** Max Steiner. *MGM, FCT*

The Oklahoman ♪♪ **1956** A routine western with some trivia value. Town doc McCrea helps Indian Pate keep his land. Talbott plays Indian maiden in same year as her title role in Daughter of Jekyll. Continuity buffs will note Hale wears the same outfit in m ost scenes. **80m/C VHS, Beta.** Joel McCrea, Barbara Hale, Brad Dexter, Gloria Talbott, Verna Felton, Douglas Dick, Michael Pate, Scotty Beckett; ***D:*** Francis D. Lyon. *FOX*

Okoge ♪♪ **1993** Rueful sexual comedy about a triangular friendship. Sayoko is a single young working woman living in a tiny Tokyo apartment. She meets the gay Noh and his older married lover Tochi and when they become friendly, Sayoko lets them use her apartment as their love nest—to the complications of all concerned. Title is a slang term used to refer to women who prefer the company of gay men. In Japanese with English subtitles. **120m/C VHS.** *JP* Misa Shimizu, Takehiro Murata, Takeo Nakahara, Masayuki Shionoya, Noriko Songoku, Kyozo Nagatsuka, Toshie Nogishi; ***D:*** Takehiro Nakajima; ***W:*** Takehiro Nakajima. *FCT*

Old Barn Dance ♪½ **1938** Autry and his singing cowboys are selling horses until a crooked tractor company puts them out of business. They join a radio program, discovers that it is owned by the same company that put them out of the horse-selling business, and runs the crooks out of town. **54m/B VHS, Beta.** Gene Autry, Smiley Burnette, Roy Rogers; ***D:*** Joseph Kane. *NOS, VCN, DVT*

Old Boyfriends ♪♪ **1979 (R)** Shire is weak as a psychologist searching for old boyfriends in order to analyze her past. Strange combination of Carradine and Belushi may draw curious fans. **103m/C VHS, Beta, LV.** Talia Shire, Richard Jordan, John Belushi, Keith Carradine, John Houseman, Buck Henry; ***D:*** Joan Tewkesbury; ***W:*** Leonard Schrader, Paul Schrader; ***M:*** David Shire. *NLC*

Old Corral ♪♪ *Texas Serenade* **1936** Sheriff Autry protects his love interest, a girl fleeing the Mob. **54m/B VHS, Beta.** Gene Autry, Roy Rogers, Smiley Burnette; ***D:*** Joseph Kane. *NOS, MRV, VTR*

The Old Curiosity Shop ♪♪½ **1935** Webster and Benson are an old gambler and his daughter in this well-made film adaptation of the Dickens tale. Their miserly landlord tries to ruin their lives by evicting them and forcing them into a life of poverty. Remade as "Mr. Quilp" in 1957. **90m/B VHS.** Ben Webster, Elaine Benson, Hay Petrie, Beatrix Thompson, Gibb McLaughlin, Reginald Purdell; ***D:*** Thomas Bentley. *NOS*

The Old Curiosity Shop ♪♪ *Mr. Quilp* **1975 (G)** Flat musical version of the Charles Dickens story about an evil man who wants to take over a small antique shop run by an elderly man and his granddaughter. ♫When a Felon Needs a Friend; Somewhere; Love Has the Longest Memory; Happiness Pie; The Sport of Kings; What Shouldn't Happen to a Dog; Quilp. **118m/C VHS, Beta.** *GB* Anthony Newley, David Hemmings, David Warner, Jill Bennett, Peter Duncan, Michael Hordern; ***D:*** Michael Tuchner; ***M:*** Elmer Bernstein. *REP, SUE*

The Old Curiosity Shop **1984 (G)** An animated adaptation of the classic Dickens story about a young girl and her grandfather who are evicted from their curiosity shop by an evil man. **72m/C VHS, Beta.** ***V:*** John Benton, Jason Blackwell, Wallas Easton, Pennie Hackforth-Jones, Brian Harrison. *LIV*

The Old Curiosity Shop ♪♪½ **1994 (PG)** Another adaptation of Charles Dickens' 1840 tale about Grandfather Trent (Ustinov), an antiques dealer who has lost his fortune through gambling and makes matters worse by borrowing money from the miserable Mr. Quilp (Courtenay). Unable to repay the debt, Trent and young granddaughter Sally (Walsh) try to escape London, which turns Quilp's wrath upon them. Fine performances and a colorful production; made for cable TV. **280m/C VHS.** Peter Ustinov, Tom Courtenay, James Fox, Sally Walsh, William Mannering, Christopher Ettridge, Julia McKenzie, Anne White, Jean Marlow, Cornelia Hayes O'Herlihy, Michael Mears; ***D:*** Kevin Connor; ***W:*** John Goldsmith; ***C:*** Doug Milsome; ***M:*** Mason Daring. *HMK*

The Old Dark House ♪♪♪ **1932** An atmospheric horror film, with more than a touch of comedy, well-directed by Whale. In an old haunted house live the bizarre Femm family: the 102 year-old patriarch, an atheist son, a religious fanatic daughter, and a crazed pyromanic son, all watched over by the mute, scarred, and psychotic butler (Karloff's first starring role). Into this strange group wander five unsuspecting, stranded travelers who set all sorts of dastardly plots in motion. Based on the novel "Benighted" by J.B. Priestley. **71m/B VHS.** Boris Karloff, Melvyn Douglas, Charles Laughton, Gloria Stuart, Ernest Thesiger, Raymond Massey, Lillian Bond, Eva Moore, Brember Wills, John Dudgeon; ***D:*** James Whale; ***W:*** Robert Dillon. *KIV, FCT*

Old Enough ♪♪ **1984 (PG)** Slow-moving coming-of-age comedy on the rich kid-poor kid friendship theme. Silver's directing debut. **91m/C VHS, Beta.** Sarah Boyd, Rainbow Harvest, Neill Barry, Danny Aiello, Susan Kingsley, Roxanne Hart, Alyssa Milano, Fran Brill, Anne Pitoniak; ***D:*** Marisa Silver; ***W:*** Marisa Silver. Sundance Film Festival '84: Grand Jury Prize. *MED*

Old Explorers ♪♪½ **1990 (PG)** Two old friends refuse to let old age lessen their want for excitement, so they get together on a regular basis to set out on dangerous, imaginary adventures. They search for Atlantis, explore the Himalayan Mountains, and visit the Bermuda Triangle. After one of the men survives a stroke, the two set out on a real-life adventure on a tugboat cruising down the Mississippi River. Although the leads put in strong performances, they can't hide the slow-moving plot or the thin action sequences. Based on the play by James Cada and Mark Keller. **91m/C VHS, LV.** Jose Ferrer, James Whitmore, Jeffrey Gadbois, Caroline Kaiser, William Warfield, Christopher Pohlad, Storm Richardson, William M. Pohlad. *ACA*

Old Gringo ♪♪½ **1989 (R)** Adapted from Carlos Fuentes' novelization of writer Ambrose Bierce's mysterious disappearance in Mexico during the revolution of 1913. Features Fonda in the unlikely role of a virgin schoolteacher, Smits as her revolutionary lover, and Peck as her hero. Soggy acting by all but Peck, whose presence is wasted in a sketchy character. Technical problems and cheesy sets and costumes—look for the dusk backdrop in the dance scene and Smits' silly moustache. Better to read the book. **119m/C VHS, Beta, LV, 8mm.** Jane Fonda, Gregory Peck, Jimmy Smits, Patricio Contreras, Jenny Gago, Gabriela Roel, Sergio Calderon, Guillermo Rios, Anne Pitoniak, Pedro Armendariz Jr., Jim Metzler; ***D:*** Luis Puenzo; ***W:*** Aida Bortnik, Luis Puenzo; ***M:*** Lee Holdridge. *COL*

Old Gun ♪♪♪ **1976** A grief-plagued doctor finds he must seek out and kill each Nazi involved in the slaughter of his wife and child to ease his pain. Excellent directing and a fully formed main character. **141m/C VHS, Beta.** Philippe Noiret, Romy Schneider, Jean Bouise; ***D:*** Robert Enrico. *MED*

Old Ironsides ♪♪♪ **1926** Silent, black-and-white version of the big budget/important director and stars action-adventure. Merchant marines aboard the famous Old Ironsides battle 19th century Barbary pirates in rousing action scenes. Home video version features an engaging organ score by Gaylord Carter. Based on the poem "Constitution" by Oliver Wendell Holmes. **111m/B VHS, Beta.** Esther Ralston, Wallace Beery, Boris Karloff, Charles Farrell, George Bancroft; ***D:*** James Cruze; ***M:*** Gaylord Carter. *PAR*

The Old Lady Who Walked in the Sea ♪♪ *La Vieille qui Marchait dans la Mer* **1991** Eccentric Lady M (Moreau) and her equally aging exlover Pompilius (Serrault) have spend their lives conning the rich. Summering on the French Riviera, Lady M spots handsome beach boy/thief Lambert (Thuiller) and decides to groom him for their latest caper, a jewel heist. Meanwhile, Pompilius pursues the young Noemie (Danon) and brings her into their menage, where Lambert is instantly smitten. Their lust leads to some unexpected complications but the real drama in the film is watching old pros Moreau and Serrault at work. Based on the novel by San Antonio; French with subtitles. **95m/C VHS.** *FR* Jeanne Moreau, Michel Serrault, Luc Thuillier, Geraldine Danon; ***D:*** Laurent Heynemann; ***W:*** Dominique Roulet; ***C:*** Robert Alazraki; ***M:*** Philippe Sarde. *HMK*

The Old Maid ♪♪♪ **1939** After her beau is killed in the Civil War, a woman allows her cousin to raise her illegitimate daughter, and therein begins a years-long struggle over the girl's affections. High grade soaper based on Zoe Adkin's stage adaptation of Edith Wharton's novel. **96m/B VHS, Beta.** Bette Davis, Miriam Hopkins, George Brent, Donald Crisp, Jane Bryan, Louise Fazenda, Henry Stephenson; ***D:*** Edmund Goulding; ***C:*** Gaetano Antonio "Tony" Gaudio; ***M:*** Max Steiner. *MGM*

The Old Man and the Sea ♪♪½ **1990** Quinn is wonderful as Hemingway's aging Cuban fisherman, Santiago, who battles a band of marauding sharks for a giant marlin in the Gulf Stream. Unfortunately, this made for TV adaptation is ordinary. **97m/C VHS.** Anthony Quinn, Gary Cole, Alexis Cruz, Patricia Clarkson, Francesco Quinn; ***D:*** Jud Taylor; ***W:*** Roger O. Hirson; ***C:*** James Wong Howe; ***M:*** Bruce Broughton. *VCO*

Old Mother Riley's Ghosts ♪♪ **1941** A group of spies "haunt" Mother Riley's castle home in a futile attempt to scare her out; she turns the tables. Some good scares and laughs. Part of the Old Mother Riley series. Look for similarities to later Monty Python films. **82m/B VHS, Beta.** *GB* Arthur Lucan, Kitty McShane, John Stuart; ***D:*** John Baxter. *NOS, SNC*

Old Spanish Custom ♪ *The Invader* **1936** Only a Keaton fan could love this comedy, set in Spain and filmed in England. One of his rarest—and poorest—sound films. He plays a bumbling rich yachtsman smitten with Tovar, a Spanish maiden who uses him to make her lover jealous. **58m/B VHS, Beta.** *GB* Buster Keaton, Lupita Tovar, Lyn Harding, Esme Percy; ***D:*** Adrian Brunel. *VYY, GPV, VDM*

Old Swimmin' Hole ♪♪ *When Youth Conspires* **1940** Small-town friends Moran and Jones try to bring their single parents together; his mother can't afford to finance his dream to be a doctor. Dull, melodramatic ode to heartland America, reminiscent of "Our Town." **78m/B VHS, Beta.** Marcia Mae Jones, Jackie Moran, Leatrice Joy, Charles D. Brown; ***D:*** Robert McGowan. *VYY*

Old Yeller ♪♪♪½ **1957 (G)** Disney Studios' first and best boy-and-his-dog film. Fifteen-year-old Kirk is left in charge of the family farm while Parker is away. When his younger brother brings home a stray dog, Kirk is displeased but lets him stay. Yeller saves Kirk's life, but contracts rabies in the process. Kirk is forced to kill him. Keep tissue handy, especially for the kids. Stong acting, effective scenery—all good stuff. Based on the novel by Fred Gipson. Sequel "Savage Sam" released in 1963. **84m/C VHS, Beta, LV.** Dorothy McGuire, Fess Parker, Tommy Kirk, Kevin Corcoran, Jeff York, Beverly Washburn, Chuck Connors; ***D:*** Robert Stevenson. *DIS*

Oldest Confederate Widow Tells All ♪♪♪ **1995** TV drama starts with the recollections of 99-year-old Lucy Marsden (Bancroft), the widow of the title, as she revisits her marriage to troubled Civil War veteran Capt. William Marsden (Sutherland, sporting an impressive set of whiskers). In 1899, the teenaged Lucy (played by Lane) marries the eccentric 50-year-old, who constantly relives battlefield horrors and the loss of his boyhood friend, while she deals with family and various domestic crises. Somewhat meandering story with fine performances and subtle details. Based on Allan Gurganus' novel. **180m/C VHS.** Diane Lane, Donald Sutherland, Anne Bancroft, Cicely Tyson, Blythe Danner, E.G. Marshall, Gwen Verdon, Maureen Mueller, Wil Horneff; ***D:*** Ken Cameron; ***W:*** Joyce Eliason; ***M:*** Mark Snow. *CAF*

Oldest Living Graduate ☠☠☠½ **1982** Fonda is memorable in his last stage role as the oldest graduate of a Texas military academy. He and his son clash when Fonda refuses to give up his land. Teleplay features strong performances from Leachman and other big-name cast members. **75m/C VHS, Beta.** Cloris Leachman, Henry Fonda, John Lithgow, Timothy Hutton, Harry Dean Stanton, David Ogden Stiers, George Grizzard, Penelope Milford. *VHE*

Oldest Profession ☠ *Le Plus Vieux Metier du Monde* **1967** A study of prostitution from prehistoric times to the future. Generally unexciting and unfunny. In six segments meant as vehicles for their directors. **97m/C VHS, Beta, LV.** *FR GE IT* Raquel Welch, Jeanne Moreau, Elsa Martinelli, Michele Mercier; ***D:*** Jean-Luc Godard, Philippe de Broca, Claude Autant-Lara, Franco Indovina, Mauro Bolognini, Michael Pfleghar; ***W:*** Jean-Luc Godard. *NWV, IME*

Oleanna ☠½ **1994** Mamet directs the big-screen version of his controversial play about political correctness, sexual harrassment, and the gender gap. Pompous, burned-out college professor (Macy) is accused of sexual harassment by dense, shrill, academically weak student (Eisenstadt) after she misconstrues a self-important speech as a come-on. Unbalanced perspective, obvious stereotyping of unsympathetic characters, and weak performances remove any hint of the intended drama. **90m/C VHS, LV.** William H. Macy, Debra Eisenstadt; ***D:*** David Mamet; ***W:*** David Mamet; ***M:*** Rebecca Pidgeon. Nominations: Independent Spirit Awards '95: Best Actor (Macy). *HMK*

Oliver! ☠☠☠½ **1968 (G)** Splendid big-budget musical adaptation of Dickens' "Oliver Twist." An innocent orphan is dragged into a life of crime when he is befriended by a gang of pickpockets. ♫Food, Glorious Food; Oliver; Boy For Sale; Where Is Love?; Consider Yourself; Pick a Pocket or Two; I'd Do Anything; Be Back Soon; As Long As He Needs Me. **145m/C VHS, Beta, LV.** *GB* Mark Lester, Jack Wild, Ron Moody, Shani Wallis, Oliver Reed, Hugh Griffith; ***D:*** Carol Reed; ***C:*** Oswald Morris. Academy Awards '68: Best Art Direction/Set Decoration, Best Director (Reed), Best Picture, Best Sound, Best Score; Golden Globe Awards '69: Best Actor—Musical/Comedy (Moody), Best Film—Musical/Comedy; National Board of Review Awards '68: 10 Best Films of the Year; Nominations: Academy Awards '68: Best Actor (Moody), Best Adapted Screenplay, Best Cinematography, Best Costume Design, Best Film Editing, Best Supporting Actor (Wild). *COL, BTV, HMV*

Oliver & Company ☠☠½ **1988 (G)** Animated animal retelling of Dicken's "Oliver Twist"—Disney style. Kitten Oliver (Lawrence) is left to fend for himself on the mean streets of New York until he's taken under the paw of Dodger (Joel) the dog. Dodger heads up a gang of doggy thieves, who help down-and-out human Fagin (DeLuise), who owes money to ruthless loan shark Sykes (Loggia). Out on his first job, Oliver's found by rich little Jenny (Gregory) and happily adopted. But his pals think he's been kidnapped and are off to rescue him. **72m/C VHS.** ***D:*** George Scribner; ***W:*** Jim Cox, James Mangold; ***V:*** Joey Lawrence, Billy Joel, Richard "Cheech" Marin, Bette Midler, Dom DeLuise, Roscoe Lee Browne, Richard Mulligan, Sheryl Lee Ralph, Robert Loggia, Taurean Blacque, Carl Weintraub, Natalie Gregory, William Glover. *TOU*

Oliver Twist ☠☠☠ **1922** Silent version of the Dickens classic is a vehicle for young Jackie Coogan. As orphan Oliver Twist, he is subjected to many frightening incidents before finding love and someone to care for him. Remade numerous times, most notably in 1933 and 1948 and as the musical "Oliver!" in 1968. **77m/B VHS, Beta.** Jackie Coogan, Lon Chaney Sr., Gladys Brockwell, George Siegmann, Esther Ralston; ***D:*** Frank Lloyd. *NOS, CCB, KIV*

Oliver Twist ☠☠ **1933** The first talking version of Dickens' classic about an ill-treated London orphan involved with youthful gang of pickpockets. Moore was too young—at five—to be very credible in the lead role. The 1948 version is much more believable. **70m/B VHS, Beta.** Dickie Moore, Irving Pichel, William "Stage" Boyd, Barbara Kent; ***D:*** William J. Cowen. *NOS, MRV, HHT*

Oliver Twist ☠☠☠☠ **1948** Charles Dickens' immortal story of a workhouse orphan who is forced into a life of crime with a gang of pickpockets. The best of many film adaptations, with excellent portrayals by the cast. **116m/C VHS, Beta, LV.** *GB* Robert Newton, John Howard Davies, Alec Guinness, Francis L. Sullivan, Anthony Newley, Kay Walsh, Diana Dors, Henry Stephenson; ***D:*** David Lean; ***W:*** David Lean; ***C:*** Guy Green. *PAR, DVT, FHS*

Oliver Twist ☠☠☠ **1982** Good made-for-television version of the classic Dicken's tale of a boy's rescue from a life of crime. Scott's Fagin is a treat, and period details are on the mark. **100m/C VHS.** George C. Scott, Tim Curry, Michael Hordern, Timothy West, Lysette Anthony, Eileen Atkins, Cherie Lunghi; ***D:*** Clive Donner; ***W:*** James Goldman; ***M:*** Nick Bicat. *TVC, VES, REP*

Oliver Twist **1985** A British television miniseries adaptation of the Charles Dickens classic about an orphan boy plunging into the underworld of 19th-century London. On two tapes. **333m/C VHS, Beta.** *GB* Ben Rodska, Eric Porter, Frank Middlemass, Gillian Martell. *FOX, SIG, HMV*

Oliver's Story ☠ **1978 (PG)** A "not so equal" sequel to "Love Story", where widower O'Neal wallows in grief untils rich heiress Bergen comes along. He falls in love again, this time with money. **90m/C VHS, Beta.** Ryan O'Neal, Candice Bergen, Ray Milland, Edward Binns, Nicola Pagett, Charles Haid; ***D:*** John Korty; ***W:*** Erich Segal. *PAR*

Olivia ☠½ **1983** Abused housewife moonlights as a prostitute and begins killing her customers. She falls in love with an American businessman and flees to America when her husband finds out about the affair. Revenge and murder are the result. **90m/C VHS, Beta.** Suzanna Love, Robert Walker Jr., Jeff Winchester; ***D:*** Ulli Lommel. *VHE*

Olivier, Olivier ☠☠☠ **1992 (R)** Holland's directorial follow-up to "Europa, Europa" is based on a 1984 French newspaper story and evokes "The Return of Martin Guerre" and its update, "Sommersby." Beloved nine-year-old boy disappears from his home in a small French town and his dysfunctional family falls apart. Mom obsesses and falls into trances, dad escapes to North Africa, and sister Nadine develops telekinetic powers in order to cope. Six years later a detective brings an amnesiac teenager, who has been working as a hustler in Paris, to the boy's family. Is it the missing Olivier? Spooky, provocative, and emotionally resonate. In French with English subtitles. **110m/C VHS, LV.** *FR* Francois Cluzet, Brigitte Rouan, Gregoire Colin, Marina Golovine, Jean-Francois Stevenin, Emmanuel Morozof, Faye Gatteau, Frederic Quiring; ***D:*** Agnieszka Holland; ***W:*** Agnieszka Holland. Los Angeles Film Critics Association Awards '93: Best Score. *COL*

Ollie Hopnoodle's Haven of Bliss ☠☠½ **1988** Humorist Jean Shepherd (of "A Christmas Story" fame) spins another tale of frantic family life with his alter ego, Ralphie. This time the family is off on a summer vacation—with all its inherent problems. Made for cable television. **90m/C VHS, Beta.** James B. Sikking, Dorothy Lyman, Jerry O'Connell; ***D:*** Dick Bartlett. *DIS*

Olly Olly Oxen Free ☠☠ *The Great Balloon Adventure* **1978** Junkyard owner Hepburn helps two boys fix up and fly a hot-air balloon, once piloted by McKenzie's grandfather, as a surprise for the man's birthday. Beautiful airborne scenes over California and a dramatic landing to the tune of the "1812 Overture," but not enough to make the whole film interesting. **89m/C VHS, Beta.** Katharine Hepburn, Kevin McKenzie, Dennis Dimster, Peter Kilman; ***D:*** Richard A. Colla; ***M:*** Robert Alcivar. *TLF*

Olongape: The American Dream ☠½ **1989** A young woman works in a cheap bar while waiting for the chance to come to America. **97m/C VHS, Beta.** Jacklyn Jose, Susan Africa, Chanda Romero, Joel Torre, Marilou Sadiua; ***D:*** Chito Rono. *TWE*

Omar Khayyam ☠☠ **1957** In medieval Persia, Omar (Wilde) becomes involved in a romance with the Shah of Persia's fiancee, while trying to fight off a faction of assassins trying to overthrow the Shah. Although this film has a great cast, the script is silly and juvenile, defeating the cast's fine efforts. **101m/C VHS.** Cornel Wilde, Michael Rennie, Debra Paget, Raymond Massey, John Derek, Yma Sumac, Margaret Hayes, Joan Taylor, Sebastian Cabot; ***D:*** William Dieterle. *PAR*

Omega Cop ☠ *John Travis, Solar Survivor* **1990 (R)** In a post-apocalyptic future, there's only one cop left. He uses his martial arts skills and tons of guns attempting to rescue three women, but the violence doesn't cover the poor acting and shoddy production. Fans of TV's Batman might enjoy this for West's presence. **89m/C VHS.** Ron Marchini, Adam West, Stuart Whitman, Troy Donahue, Meg Thayer, Jennifer Jostyn, Chrysti Jimenez, D.W. Landingham, Chuck Katzakian; ***D:*** Paul Kyriazi. *HMD*

Omega Man ☠☠½ **1971 (PG)** In post-holocaust Los Angeles, Heston is immune to the effects of a biologically engineered plague and battles those who aren't—an army of albino victims bent on destroying what's left of the world. Strong suspense with considerable violence, despite the PG rating. Based on the science fiction thriller "I Am Legend" by Richard Matheson, which is also the basis for the film "The Last Man on Earth." **98m/C VHS, Beta, LV.** Charlton Heston, Anthony Zerbe, Rosalind Cash, Paul Koslo; ***D:*** Boris Sagal; ***C:*** Russell Metty. *WAR*

Omega Syndrome ☠½ **1987 (R)** Neo-Nazis kidnap Wahl's daughter. He and Vietnam buddy DiCenzo get her back. Ho hum. DiCenzo's is the best performance. Tolerable for vigilante film fans. **90m/C VHS, Beta.** Ken Wahl, Ron Kuhlman, George DiCenzo, Doug McClure; ***D:*** Joseph Manduke. *NWV, VTR*

The Omen ☠☠½ *Birthmark* **1976 (R)** American diplomat's family adopts a young boy who always seems to be around when bizarre and inexplicable deaths occur. Of course, what else would you expect of Satan's son? The shock and gore prevalent in "The Exorcist" is replaced with more suspense and believable effects. Well-done horror film doesn't insult the viewer's intelligence. Followed by three sequels: "Damien: Omen 2," "The Final Conflict," and "Omen 4." **111m/C VHS, Beta, LV.** Gregory Peck, Lee Remick, Billie Whitelaw, David Warner, Holly Palance, Richard Donner; ***D:*** Richard Donner; ***W:*** David Seltzer; ***M:*** Jerry Goldsmith. Academy Awards '76: Best Original Score; Nominations: Academy Awards '76: Best Song ("Ave Satani"). *FOX*

Omen 4: The Awakening ☠☠ **1991** It turns out Damien of Omens past had a daughter, Delia, who takes up where dear old devilish Dad left off. Delia is adopted by your basic clueless couple and proceeds to wreak havoc wherever she goes, including getting rid of several interfering adults. She also plans to make her adoptive father, a U.S. senator, President, so that his delightful child anti-Christ can have him carry out all her evil plans. **97m/C VHS.** Faye Grant, Michael Woods, Michael Lerner, Asia Vieira; ***D:*** Jorge Montesi, Dominique Othenin-Girard. *FXV*

Omoo Omoo, the Shark God ☠ **1949** A sea captain is cursed when he removes the black pearls from a stone shark god in this extremely cheap adventure. **58m/B VHS.** Ron Randell, Devera Burton, Trevor Bardette, Pedro de Cordoba, Richard Benedict, Rudy Robles, Michael Whalen, George Meeker; ***D:*** Leo Leonard. *SNC*

On a Clear Day You Can See Forever ☠☠ **1970 (G)** A psychiatric hypnotist helps a girl stop smoking and finds that in trances she remembers previous incarnations. He falls in love with one of the women she used to be. Alan Jay Lerner of "My Fair Lady" and "Camelot" wrote the lyrics and the book. Based on a musical by Lerner and Burton Lane. ♫On a Clear Day, You Can See Forever; Come Back to Me; What Did I Have That I Don't Have?; He Isn't You; Hurry, It's Lovely Up Here; Go To Sleep; Love with All the Trimmings; Melinda. **129m/C VHS, Beta, LV.** Barbra Streisand, Yves Montand,

Bob Newhart, Jack Nicholson, Simon Oakland; ***D:*** Vincente Minnelli; ***C:*** Harry Stradling. *PAR*

On an Island with You 🦴🦴½ **1948** Williams plays a movie star who finds romance on location in Hawaii in this musical extravaganza. Contains many of Williams' famous water ballet scenes and a bevy of bathing beauties. ♫On an Island with You; If I Were You; Taking Miss Mary to the Ball; Dog Song; Buenas Noches, Buenos Aires; Wedding Samba; I Can Do Without Broadway, But Can Broadway Do Without Me?. **107m/C VHS.** Esther Williams, Peter Lawford, Ricardo Montalban, Jimmy Durante, Cyd Charisse, Leon Ames; ***D:*** Richard Thorpe. *MGM*

On Approval 🦴🦴🦴 **1944** Hilarious British farce in which two women trade boyfriends. Lillie's performace provides plenty of laughs. Brook runs the show as leading man, co-author, director, and co-producer. Based on the play by Frederick Lonsdale. **80m/B VHS, Beta.** *GB* Clive Brook, Beatrice Lillie, Googie Withers, Roland Culver; ***D:*** Clive Brook. *NOS, MRV, HHT*

On Borrowed Time 🦴🦴🦴 **1939** Engrossing tale of Death (Hardwicke) coming for an old man (Barrymore) who isn't ready to die so he traps him in his backyard apple tree. Performances are first rate in this good adaptation of the stage success (originally by Eugene O'Neill). Hardwicke is especially a standout; he gave up theatre for Hollywood after making this film. **99m/B VHS.** Lionel Barrymore, Cedric Hardwicke, Beulah Bondi, Una Merkel, Bobs Watson, Henry Travers; ***D:*** Harold Bucquet; ***C:*** Joseph Ruttenberg. *MGM*

On Dangerous Ground 🦴🦴🦴 **1951** A world-weary detective is sent to the countryside to investigate a murder. He encounters the victim's revenge-hungry father and the blind sister of the murderer. In the hateful father the detective sees a reflection of the person he has become, in the blind woman, he learns the redeeming qualities of humanity and compassion. A well-acted example of film noir that features the composer Herrman's favorite score. **82m/B VHS, Beta, LV.** Robert Ryan, Ida Lupino, Ward Bond, Ed Begley Sr., Cleo Moore, Charles Kemper; ***D:*** Nicholas Ray; ***M:*** Bernard Herrmann. *TTC*

On Deadly Ground *Woof!* **1994 (R)** Seagal nearly destroys Alaska in an effort to save it in this inane, preachy story of an oil-rig roughneck out to protect the landscape from an evil oil company's drilling habits. Directorial debut for Seagal lumbers from scene to scene. Violence is expected, as is silly dialogue—just try to keep from laughing when stoney-faced Steven intones "What does it take to change the essence of man?" A better script, for one. **102m/C VHS, LV.** Steven Seagal, Michael Caine, Joan Chen, John C. McGinley; ***D:*** Steven Seagal; ***W:*** Ed Horowitz; ***M:*** Basil Poledouris. Golden Raspberry Awards '94: Worst Director (Seagal); Nominations: Golden Raspberry Awards '94: Worst Picture. *WAR*

On Golden Pond 🦴🦴🦴½ **1981 (PG)** Henry Fonda won his first, and long overdue, Oscar for his role as the curmudgeonly patriarch of the Thayer family. He and his wife have grudgingly agreed to look after a young boy while at their summer home in Maine. Through his gradually affectionate relationship with the boy, Fonda learns to allay his fears of mortality. He also gains an understanding of his semi-estranged daughter. Jane Fonda plays his daughter and Hepburn is his loving wife in this often funny adaptation of Ernest Thompson's 1978 play. Predictable but deeply moving. Henry Fonda's final screen appearance. **109m/C VHS, Beta, LV.** Henry Fonda, Jane Fonda, Katharine Hepburn, Dabney Coleman, Doug McKeon, William Lanteau; ***D:*** Mark Rydell; ***W:*** Ernest Thompson; ***C:*** Billy Williams; ***M:*** Dave Grusin. Academy Awards '81: Best Actor (Fonda), Best Actress (Hepburn), Best Adapted Screenplay; British Academy Awards '82: Best Actress (Hepburn); Golden Globe Awards '82: Best Actor—Drama (Fonda), Best Film—Drama, Best Screenplay; National Board of Review Awards '81: Best Actor (Fonda); Writers Guild of America '81: Best Adapted Screenplay; Nominations: Academy Awards '81: Best Actor (Fonda), Best Cinematography, Best Director (Rydell), Best Film Editing, Best Sound, Best Supporting Actress (Fonda), Best Original Score. *FHE, KAR, BTV*

On Her Majesty's Secret Service 🦴🦴🦴 **1969 (PG)** In the sixth 007 adventure, Bond again confronts the infamous Blofeld, who is planning a germ-warfare assault on the entire world. Australian Lazenby took a crack at playing the super spy, with mixed results. Many feel this is the best-written of the Bond films and might have been the most famous, had Sean Connery continued with the series. Includes the song "We Have All the Time In the World," sung by Louis Armstrong. **144m/C VHS, Beta, LV.** *GB* George Lazenby, Diana Rigg, Telly Savalas, Gabriele Ferzetti, Ilse Steppat, Bernard Lee, Lois Maxwell, Desmond Llewelyn, Catherine Schell, Julie Ege, Joanna Lumley, Mona Chong, Anouska Hempel, Jenny Hanley; ***D:*** Peter Hunt; ***M:*** John Barry. *MGM, FOX, TLF*

On Moonlight Bay 🦴🦴½ **1951** Set in small-town Indiana in 1917 with Day as the tomboyish Marjorie who falls for college man MacRae. Her father (Ames) doesn't approve but the trouble really begins when Marjorie's younger brother gets into trouble at school. The incorrigible Wesley (Gray) blames everything on dear old dad and MacRae feels he must come to Marjorie's rescue! Gray steals the movie as the bratty brother—otherwise its business as usual. Based on Booth Tarkington's "Penrod" stories and followed by "By the Light of the Silvery Moon." ♫Love Ya; On Moonlight Bay; Till We Meet Again; Pack Up Your Troubles In Your Old Kit Bag; I'm Forever Blowing Bubbles; Christmas Story; Tell Me Why Nights Are Lonely; Cuddle Up a Little Closer; Every Little Movement Has a Meaning All Its Own. **95m/C VHS, LV.** Doris Day, Gordon MacRae, Leon Ames, Billy Gray, Rosemary DeCamp, Mary Wickes, Ellen Corby, Esther Dale; ***D:*** Roy Del Ruth; ***W:*** Melville Shavelson, Jack Rose; ***M:*** Max Steiner. *WAR, MVD*

On the Air Live with Captain Midnight 🦴½ *Captain Midnight* **1979** Socially challenged teen finds hipness as a rebel DJ operating an illegal radio station from his van. Leading actor is the son of the director/writer/producer but nepotism does not a good film make. **90m/C VHS, Beta.** Tracy Sebastian; ***D:*** Ferd Sebastian. *NO*

On the Avenue 🦴🦴🦴 **1937** Broadway showman Powell opens up a new musical, starring Faye as the richest girl in the world, in this musical-comedy satirizing upper-crust society. Debutante Carroll is outraged because she realizes it's mocking her actual life. Carroll tries to get Powell to change the show, they fall in love, Faye gets her nose out of joint, and after lots of fuss everything ends happily. Fine Berlin score. ♫He Ain't Got Rhythm; You're Laughing at Me; This Year's Kisses; Slumming on Park Avenue; The Girl on the Police Gazette; I've Got My Love to Keep Me Warm. **90m/B VHS.** Dick Powell, Madeleine Carroll, Alice Faye, George Barbier, The Ritz Brothers, Alan Mowbray, Cora Witherspoon, Walter Catlett, Stepin Fetchit, Sig Rumann, Douglas Fowley, Joan Davis; ***D:*** Roy Del Ruth; ***W:*** Gene Markey; ***M:*** Irving Berlin. *FXV*

On the Beach 🦴🦴🦴½ **1959** A group of survivors attempt to live normal lives in post-apocalyptic Australia, waiting for the inevitable arrival of killer radiation. Astaire is strong in his first dramatic role. Though scientifically implausible, still a good anti-war vehicle. Based on the best-selling novel by Nevil Shute. **135m/B VHS, Beta, LV.** Gregory Peck, Anthony Perkins, Donna Anderson, Ava Gardner, Fred Astaire; ***D:*** Stanley Kramer; ***C:*** Daniel F. Fapp; ***M:*** Ernest Gold. Golden Globe Awards '60: Best Score; National Board of Review Awards '59: 10 Best Films of the Year; Nominations: Academy Awards '59: Best Film Editing, Best Original Score. *FOX, FCT*

On the Comet 🦴🦴🦴 *Na Komete; Hector Servadac's Ark* **1968** Zeman's fourth fantasy based on Jules Verne stories, about a chunk of the Earth's crust suddenly becoming a comet and giving its passengers a ride through the galaxy. Complete with Zeman's signature animation fantasias. In English. **76m/C VHS, Beta.** *CZ* Emil Horvath Jr., Magda Vasarykova, Frantisek Filipovsky; ***D:*** Karel Zeman. *FCT, MRV*

On the Edge 🦴 **1982** A narcotics agent tracks down a wealthy Brazilian drug kingpin. **82m/C VHS, Beta.** Anthony Steffen. *NO*

On the Edge 🦴🦴½ **1986 (PG-13)** A drama about the inevitable Rocky-esque triumph of Dern as an aging marathon runner. Simultaneous to his running endeavor, Dern is trying to make up for lost time with his father. Available in two versions, one rated, the other unrated with a racy appearance by Pam Grier as the runner's interracial lover. **86m/C VHS, Beta.** Bruce Dern, John Marley, Bill Bailey, Jim Haynie, Pam Grier; ***D:*** Rob Nilsson; ***W:*** Rob Nilsson. *NO*

On the Edge: The Survival of Dana 🦴 **1979** Another entry from the world of low-quality made-for-TV films. A young girl moves with her family to a new town. When she falls in with the "bad" crowd, her ethical standards are challenged. A stinker that may appeal to those with campy tastes. Not for the discriminating palate. **92m/C VHS, Beta.** Melissa Sue Anderson, Robert Carradine, Marion Ross, Talia Balsam, Michael Pataki, Kevin Breslin, Judge Reinhold, Barbara Babcock; ***D:*** Jack Starrett. *GEM*

On the Line 🦴½ **1983** Two Mexico-US border guards, one hard-bitten, the other sympathetic to the illegal immigrants' plight, battle it out over a beautiful Mexican whore. Disjointed and confusing. **95m/C VHS, Beta.** *SP* David Carradine, Victoria Abril, Scott Wilson, Sam Jaffe, Jesse Vint; ***D:*** Jose Luis Borau; ***W:*** Jose Luis Borau. *SUE, NLC*

On the Nickel 🦴🦴 **1980 (R)** An ex-alcoholic returns to Fifth Street in Los Angeles to save his friend from a life of despair. Waits' musical score enhances this sentimental skid row drama. Scripted, directed and produced by "The Waltons'" Waite. **96m/C VHS, Beta.** Ralph Waite, Donald Moffat, Hal Williams, Jack Kehoe; ***D:*** Ralph Waite; ***W:*** Ralph Waite; ***M:*** Tom Waits. *VES*

On the Night Stage 🦴🦴 **1915** Gruff bandit (legendary Hart) loses his girl-of-questionable-values to town preacher. One of the first feature length westerns. **83m/B VHS, Beta, 8mm.** William S. Hart, Robert Edeson, Rhea Mitchell, Shorty Hamilton; ***D:*** Reginald Barker. *GPV, VYY*

On the Old Spanish Trail 🦴½ **1947** Rogers becomes a singing cowboy with a traveling tent show in order to pay off a note signed by the Sons of the Pioneers. **56m/B VHS, Beta.** Roy Rogers, Jane Frazee, Andy Devine, Tito Guizar; ***D:*** William Witney. *NOS, MRV, VCN*

On the Right Track 🦴½ **1981 (PG)** Young orphan living in Chicago's Union Station has the gift of being able to pick winning race horses. May be appealing to fans of Coleman and "Different Strokes" television show, but lacks the momentum to keep most viewers from switching tracks. **98m/C VHS, Beta.** Gary Coleman, Lisa Eilbacher, Michael Lembeck, Norman Fell, Maureen Stapleton, Herb Edelman; ***D:*** Lee Philips. *FOX*

On the Run 🦴 **1985 (R)** An ex-con and his gal cut a law-defying swath through the Bayou. **96m/C VHS, Beta.** Jack Conrad, Rita George, Dub Taylor, David Huddleston. *GEM*

On the Third Day 🦴 **1983** A headmaster finds a mysterious stranger in his house who turns out to be his long-lost illegitimate son. **101m/C VHS, Beta.** Richard Marant, Catherine Schell, Paul Williamson. *ORI*

On the Town 🦴🦴🦴½ **1949** Kelly's directorial debut features three sailors on a one day leave search for romance in the Big Apple. Filmed on location in New York City, with uncompromisingly authentic flavor. Based on the successful Broadway musical, with a score composed by Leonard Bernstein, Betty Comden, and Adolph Green. Additional songs by Roger Edens. Available in a deluxe collector's laserdisc edition. ♫New York, New York; I Feel Like I'm Not Out of Bed Yet; Come Up to My Place; Miss Turnstiles Ballet; Main Street; You're Awful; On the Town; You Can Count on Me; Pearl of the Persian Sea. **98m/C VHS, Beta, LV.** Gene Kelly, Frank Sinatra, Vera-Ellen, Ann Miller, Betty Garrett; ***D:*** Gene Kelly, Stanley Donen; ***W:*** Betty Comden, Adolph Green. Academy Awards '49: Best Score. *MGM*

On the Town ½ **1991** Bernstein's first big Broadway success in 1944, recorded in a live performance June 1992, at London's Barbican Centre. Follows the story of three sailors on a 24-hour leave in New York City during WWII. This version includes numbers which never made it into the original Broadway show. **110m/C VHS, LV.** Frederica von Stade, Tyne Daly, Marie McLaughlin, David Garrison, Thomas Hampson, Kurt Ollman, Evelyn Lear, Samuel Ramey, Cleo Laine; ***M:*** Leonard Bernstein, Betty Comden, Adolph Green. *PGV, FCT*

On the Waterfront **1954** A trend-setting, gritty portrait of New York dock workers embroiled in union violence. Cobb is the gangster union boss, Steiger his crooked lawyer, and Brando, Steiger's ex-fighter brother who "could've been a contender!" Intense performances and excellent direction stand up well today. The picture was a huge financial success. **108m/B VHS, Beta, LV.** Marlon Brando, Rod Steiger, Eva Marie Saint, Lee J. Cobb, Karl Malden, Pat Henning, Leif Erickson, Tony Galento, John Hamilton, Nehemiah Persoff; ***D:*** Elia Kazan; ***W:*** Budd Schulberg; ***C:*** Boris Kaufman; ***M:*** Leonard Bernstein. Academy Awards '54: Best Actor (Brando), Best Art Direction/Set Decoration (B & W), Best Black and White Cinematography, Best Director (Kazan), Best Film Editing, Best Picture, Best Story & Screenplay, Best Supporting Actress (Saint); Directors Guild of America Awards '54: Best Director (Kazan); Golden Globe Awards '55: Best Actor—Drama (Brando), Best Director (Kazan), Best Film—Drama; National Board of Review Awards '54: 10 Best Films of the Year; New York Film Critics Awards '54: Best Actor (Brando), Best Director (Kazan), Best Film; Nominations: Academy Awards '54: Best Supporting Actor (Cobb), Best Supporting Actor (Malden, Steiger), Best Original Score. *COL, BTV*

On the Yard **1979 (R)** An attempt to realistically portray prison life. Focuses on a murderer who runs afoul of the leader of the prisoners and the system. A fairly typical prison drama with above average performances from Heard and Kellin. **102m/C VHS, Beta.** John Heard, Thomas G. Waites, Mike Kellin, Joe Grifasi; ***D:*** Raphael D. Silver; ***W:*** Malcolm Braly. *MED*

On Top of Old Smoky ½ **1953** Autry and the Cass County Boys are mistaken for Texas Rangers by a gang of land poachers. **59m/B VHS, Beta.** Gene Autry, Smiley Burnette, Gail Davis, Sheila Ryan; ***D:*** George Archainbaud. *CCB*

On Top of the Whale **1982** Two scholars move onto the estate of strange but wealthy benefactor to conduct research on the few survivors of a disappearing clan of Indians. Two tribesmen speak bizarre dialect which utilizes only one word while others confound the researchers with stories of ghosts and graveyards. Dutch comedy subtitled in English. **93m/C VHS.** *NL* ***D:*** Raul Ruiz. *KIV, FCT, INJ*

On Valentine's Day ½ *Story of a Marriage* **1986 (PG)** Author Horton Foote based this story loosely on his parents' lives. A wealthy young Southern girl marries a poor but decent young man and finds herself ostracized from her family. A prequel to the same author's "1918." Produced with PBS for "American Playhouse." **106m/C VHS, Beta.** Hallie Foote, Matthew Broderick, Michael Higgins, Steven Hill, William Converse-Roberts, Rochelle Oliver, Richard Jenkins, Horton Foote Jr., Carol Goodheart; ***D:*** Ken Harrison; ***W:*** Horton Foote; ***M:*** Jonathan Sheffer. *ORI*

On Wings of Eagles ½ **1986** During the 1979 Iranian revolution two American executives are imprisoned by Islamic radicals. Help arrives in the form of covert agents of their boss—Texas tycoon H. Ross Perot (played by Crenna). Don't expect strict historical veracity or insight from this network miniseries (based on the "nonfiction novel" by Ken Follett), an okay but lengthy "mission impossible." It came out in a two-cassette set, just in time for Perot's 1992 presidential campaign. **221m/C VHS.** Burt Lancaster, Richard Crenna, Paul LeMat, Esai Morales, Constance Towers, Jim Metzler, James Sutorius, Lawrence Pressman, Karen Carlson, Cyril O'Reilly; ***D:*** Andrew V. McLaglen. *WOV*

Onassis ½ *The Richest Man in the World: The Story of Aristotle Onassis* **1988** Romanticized biography of Greek shipping magnate Aristotle Onassis, from the poverty of his youth to his later wealth and family and romantic liaisons and tragedies. Julia is adequate as the title character but English actress Annis is badly miscast as Jackie Kennedy Onassis. However, Seymour is terrific as Onassis' lover, opera star Maria Callas. Quinn, who played Onassis in "The Greek Tycoon," plays Onassis' father in this one. Based on the novel by Peter Evans. Originally a made for television miniseries. **120m/C VHS, LV.** Raul Julia, Jane Seymour, Francesca Annis, Anthony Quinn, Anthony Zerbe, Lorenzo Quinn; ***D:*** Waris Hussein. *TTC*

Once a Hero **1988** The dregs of society, the Cicero Gang, have taken Captain Justice's number one fan and his mother hostage. Is it really curtains for rosy cheeks, bubble gum, and apple pie? But wait, it's Captain Justice, the man, the myth, to the rescue! **74m/C VHS.** Jeff Lester, Robert Forster, Milo O'Shea; ***D:*** Claudia Weill. *NWV, VTR*

Once Around ½ **1991 (R)** 30ish, lonely Renata Bella (Hunter) meets boisterous, self-assured (read utterly obnoxious) Lithuanian salesman Sam Sharpe (Dreyfuss). He sweeps her off her feet, showers her with affection and gifts, and then tries hard—too hard—to please her close-knit Italian family. Casting doesn't get much better than the group assembled here and Hallstrom steers everyone to wonderful performances in his American directorial debut. The major flaw is the script, a light romantic comedy that sometimes swerves into heavy drama, so much so that you may need kleenex. **115m/C VHS, Beta, LV.** Richard Dreyfuss, Holly Hunter, Danny Aiello, Gena Rowlands, Laura San Giacomo, Roxanne Hart, Danton Stone, Tim Guinee, Greg Germann, Griffin Dunne; ***D:*** Lasse Hallstrom; ***W:*** Malia Scotch Marmo; ***M:*** James Horner. *MCA, FCT*

Once Before I Die ½ **1965** Army soldiers caught in the Philippines during WWII struggle to survive and elude the Japanese. A single woman traveling with them becomes the object of their spare time considerations. A brutal, odd, and gritty war drama. Director/actor Derek was Andress' husband at the time. **97m/C VHS.** *PH* Ursula Andress, John Derek, Richard Jaeckel, Rod Lauren, Ron Ely; ***D:*** John Derek. *MOV*

Once Bitten **1985 (PG-13)** Centuries-old though still remarkably youthful vampiress comes to LA to stalk male virgins. That may be the wrong city, but she needs their blood to retain her young countenance. Vampire comedy theme was more effectively explored in 1979s "Love at First Bite," notable, however for the screen debut of comic Carrey who would later gain fame for TV's "In Living Color" and "Ace Ventura, Pet Detective." **94m/C VHS, Beta, LV.** Lauren Hutton, Jim Carrey, Cleavon Little, Karen Kopins, Thomas Balltore, Skip Lackey; ***D:*** Howard Storm; ***W:*** Jonathan Roberts; ***M:*** John Du Prez. *LIV, VES*

Once in Paris... ½ **1979 (PG)** A bittersweet romance about a scriptwriter working in Paris, the chauffeur who befriends him, and the aristocratic British woman with whom the writer falls in love. Beautiful French scenery and the engaging performance of Lenoir as the chauffeur make this film a diverting piece of entertainment. **100m/C VHS, Beta.** Wayne Rogers, Gayle Hunnicutt, Jack Lenoir; ***D:*** Frank D. Gilroy; ***W:*** Frank D. Gilroy. *SUE, MED*

Once is Not Enough ½ *Jacqueline Susann's Once is Not Enough* **1975 (R)** Limp trash-drama concerning the young daughter of a has-been movie producer who has a tempestuous affair with a writer who reminds her of her father. Based on the novel by Jacqueline Susann. **121m/C VHS, Beta.** Kirk Douglas, Deborah Raffin, David Janssen, George Hamilton, Brenda Vaccaro, Alexis Smith, Melina Mercouri; ***D:*** Guy Green; ***W:*** Julius J. Epstein, Philip C. Epstein; ***C:*** John A. Alonzo; ***M:*** Henry Mancini. Golden Globe Awards '76: Best Supporting Actress (Vaccaro); Nominations: Academy Awards '75: Best Supporting Actress (Vaccaro). *PAR*

Once Upon a Brothers Grimm **1977** An original musical fantasy in which the Brothers Grimm meet a succession of their most famous storybook characters including Hansel and Gretel, the Gingerbread Lady, Little Red Riding Hood, and Rumpelstiltskin. **102m/C VHS, Beta.** Dean Jones, Paul Sand, Cleavon Little, Ruth Buzzi, Chita Rivera, Teri Garr. *VCI*

Once Upon a Crime ½ **1992 (PG)** Extremely disappointing comedy featuring a high profile cast set in Europe. The plot centers around Young and Lewis finding a dachshund and travelling from Rome to Monte Carlo to return the stray and collect a $5,000 reward. Upon arrival in Monte Carlo, they find the dog's owner dead and they end up getting implicated for the murder. Other prime suspects include Belushi, Candy, Hamilton, and Shepherd. Weak script is made bearable only by the comic genius of Candy. **94m/C VHS.** John Candy, James Belushi, Cybill Shepherd, Sean Young, Richard Lewis, Ornella Muti, Giancarlo Giannini, George Hamilton, Joss Ackland, Elsa Martinelli; ***D:*** Eugene Levy; ***M:*** Richard Gibbs. *MGM*

Once Upon a Forest **1993 (G)** Animated tale of three woodland creatures in a daring race against time when their young friend's life is at stake. Ecologically correct story by "American Tail" creator David Kirschner is light on humor and heavy on gloom, as little animals encounter oppressive human society and their big, bad machines. Servicable animation, though not up to Don Bluth standards (and a long, long way from Disney). Crawford, the voice of the wise old uncle, has a song, while Vereen breaks into a fervent gospel number as a marsh bird with a yen for preaching. For an evening of anti-pollution, treat the earth kindly animation, see it with "Ferngully." **80m/C VHS, LV.** ***D:*** Charles Grosvenor; ***W:*** Mark Young, Kelly Ward; ***V:*** Michael Crawford, Ben Vereen. *FXV, FUS, WTA*

Once Upon a Honeymoon ½ **1942** Set in 1938, Grant is an American radio broadcaster reporting on the oncoming war. Rogers is the ex-showgirl who unknowingly marries a Nazi. In this strange, uneven comedy, Grant tries to get the goods on him and also rescue Rogers. The plot is basic and uneven with Grant attempting to expose the Nazi and save Rogers. However, the slower moments are offset by some fairly surreal pieces of comedy. **116m/B VHS, Beta, LV.** Ginger Rogers, Cary Grant, Walter Slezak, Albert Dekker; ***D:*** Leo McCarey; ***C:*** George Barnes. Nominations: Academy Awards '42: Best Sound. *CCB, TTC, FCT*

Once Upon a Midnight Scary **1990** Price narrates a collection of three tales of terror, "The Ghost Belonged to Me," "The Legend of Sleepy Hollow," and "The House with a Clock in Its Walls." Aimed at the kiddies. **50m/C VHS.** Rene Auberjonois, Severn Darden; ***D:*** Neil Cox. *GEM, MRV*

Once Upon a Scoundrel ½ **1973 (G)** A ruthless Mexican land baron arranges to have a young woman's fiancee thrown in jail so he can have her all to himself. **90m/C VHS, Beta.** Zero Mostel, Katy Jurado, Titos Vandis, Priscilla Garcia, A. Martinez; ***D:*** George Schaefer; ***M:*** Alex North. *PSM*

Once Upon a Time **1976 (G)** A pretty girl, her puppy, a charming prince, and a grinch combine for a magical, wondrous animated fantasy. **83m/C VHS, Beta.** *GEM*

Once Upon a Time **1987** Two rival tribes spoil the love of a prince and princess in ancient times. Animated. **92m/C VHS, Beta.** *MED*

Once Upon a Time in America ½ **1984 (R)** The uncut original version of director Leone's saga of five young men growing up in Brooklyn during the '20s who become powerful mob figures. Also available in a 143-minute version. Told from the perspective of De Niro's Noodles as an old man looking back at 50 years of crime, love, and death, told with a sweeping and violent elegance. **225m/C VHS, Beta, LV.** Robert De Niro, James Woods, Elizabeth McGovern, Treat Williams, Tuesday Weld, Burt Young, Joe Pesci, Danny Aiello, Darlanne Fluegel, Jennifer Connelly; *D:* Sergio Leone; *C:* Tonino Delli Colli; *M:* Ennio Morricone. *WAR*

Once Upon a Time in the West ♪♪♪½ **1968 (PG)** The uncut version of Leone's sprawling epic about a band of ruthless gunmen who set out to murder a mysterious woman waiting for the railroad to come through. Filmed in John Ford's Monument Valley, it's a revisionist western with some of the longest opening credits in the history of the cinema. Fonda is cast against type as an extremely cold-blooded villain. Brilliant musical score. **165m/C VHS, Beta, LV.** *IT* Henry Fonda, Jason Robards Jr., Charles Bronson, Claudia Cardinale, Keenan Wynn, Lionel Stander, Woody Strode, Jack Elam; *D:* Sergio Leone; *W:* Sergio Leone, Bernardo Bertolucci, Dario Argento; *C:* Tonino Delli Colli; *M:* Ennio Morricone. *PAR*

Once Upon a Time in Vietnam ♪ *How Sleep the Brave* **198?** This politically irksome drama about Vietnam was filmed in Georgia. **90m/C VHS, Beta.** *VCD*

Once Upon a Time...When We Were Colored ♪♪♪ **1995 (PG)** Actor Reid makes a fine directorial debut with the story of a black youngster growing up parentless in 50's Mississippi. His family faces the usual troubles of the time, including poor wages and white bigotry, but manages to provide a positive and loving home life for him. Nostalgic, sensitive, and heartwarming adaptation of Clifton Taulbert's autobiographical book. **112m/C VHS.** Al Freeman Jr., Paula Kelly, Phylicia Rashad, Polly Bergen, Richard Roundtree, Charles Taylor, Willie Norwood, Jr., Damon Hines, Leon; *D:* Tim Reid; *W:* Paul Cooper; *C:* Johnny Simmons; *M:* Steve Tyrell. *REP*

Once Were Warriors ♪♪♪ **1994 (R)** Violent story of the struggling Maori Heke family, who have left their rural New Zealand roots to live in the city. Feisty mom Beth (Owen) is struggling with five kids and volatile hubby Jake (Heke), who's continuously out of work, boozing, and fighting. Eldest son Nig (Arahanga) has left home and joined a street gang and the rest of the kids hate Jake for beating up on their mother. They also fall victim to his temper and his habit of bringing his brawling, drunk buddies home-leading to further tragedy. Intense drama showcases great performances, with Owen honored as best actress at the Montreal World Film Festival. Based on the novel by Alan Duff. Feature-film directorial debut of Tamahori. **102m/C VHS, LV.** *NZ* Rena Owen, Temuera Morrison, Mamaengaroa Kerr-Bell, Julian (Sonny) Arahanga, Taungaroa Emile, Rachael Morris, Joseph Kairau, Pete Smith; *D:* Lee Tamahori; *W:* Riwia Brown; *M:* Murray Grindlay, Murray McNabb. Australian Film Institute '95: Best Foreign Film; Montreal World Film Festival '94: Best Actress (Owen), Best Film. *NLC*

One Against the Wind ♪♪♪ **1991 (PG)** A true story of one woman's courage against great odds. British Mary Liddell and her children are living in Paris during the WWII Nazi occupation. Mary's secret agenda is to smuggle downed Allied pilots out of the country to safety without arousing Nazi suspicions. Great performances by Davis as the resourceful Mary and Neill as one of the pilots she rescues. A Hallmark Hall of Fame presentation. **96m/C VHS.** Judy Davis, Sam Neill, Denholm Elliott, Anthony Higgins, Christien Anholt, Kate Beckinsale, Frank Middlemass; *D:* Larry Elikann. *REP*

One A.M. **1916** Charlie is a drunk who must first battle a flight of stairs in order to get to bed. Silent with music track. **20m/B VHS, Beta.** Charlie Chaplin. *CAB, GVV*

The One and Only ♪♪½ **1978 (PG)** An egotistical young man is determined to make it in show business. Instead, he finds himself in the world of professional wrestling. Most of the humor comes from the wrestling scenes, with Winkler and Darby's love story only serving to dilute the film. **98m/C VHS, Beta.** Henry Winkler, Kim Darby, Gene Saks, William Daniels, Harold Gould, Herve Villechaize; *D:* Carl Reiner. *PAR*

The One and Only, Genuine, Original Family Band ♪♪♪ **1968 (G)** A harmonious musical family becomes divided when various members take sides in the presidential battle between Benjamin Harrison and Grover Cleveland, a political era that has been since overlooked. **110m/C VHS, Beta, LV.** Walter Brennan, Buddy Ebsen, Lesley Ann Warren, Kurt Russell, Goldie Hawn, Wally Cox, Richard Deacon, Janet Blair; *D:* Michael O'Herlihy. *DIS*

One Arabian Night ♪♪♪ *Sumurun* **1921** When an exotic dancer in a traveling carnival troupe is kidnapped into a harem, a dwarf acts on his unrequited love and avenges her death by murdering the sheik who killed her. Secured a place in American filmmaking for director Lubitsch. **85m/B VHS, Beta.** *GE* Pola Negri, Ernst Lubitsch, Paul Wegener; *D:* Ernst Lubitsch. *VYY, GPV, GLV*

The One Arm Swordsmen ♪ **1972** Many one-armed men are persecuted for the murder committed by one fugitive one-armed man, and they decide to group together to track him down themselves. **109m/C VHS, Beta.** *UNI*

One Armed Executioner ♪♪ **1980 (R)** An Interpol agent seeks revenge on his wife's murderers. **90m/C VHS, Beta.** Franco Guerrero, Jody Kay; *D:* Bobby A. Auarez. *NO*

One Away ♪ **1980 (PG)** Gypsy escapes from a South African prison and the police are in hot pursuit. **83m/C VHS, Beta.** Elke Sommer, Bradford Dillman, Dean Stockwell. *NO*

One Body Too Many ♪♪ **1944** A mystery spoof about a wacky insurance salesman who's mistaken for a detective. The usual comedy of errors ensues. A contrived mish-mash—but it does have Lugosi going for it. **75m/B VHS, Beta.** Jack Haley, Jean Parker, Bela Lugosi, Lyle Talbot; *D:* Frank McDonald. *NOS, SNC, HHT*

One Brief Summer *Woof!* **1970 (R)** Love triangles and intrigues abound on a spectacular country manor. An aging woman is mortified by her father's interest in a young seductress, who finds herself attracted to the old man, but not only him. **86m/C VHS.** Clifford Evans, Felicity Gibson, Jennifer Hilary, Jan Holden, Peter Egan; *D:* John MacKenzie. *NO*

One Cooks, the Other Doesn't ♪♪ **1983** A most unlikely story of a man's ex-wife and his son moving back into his house, where he's now living with his new wife. Made for television. **96m/C VHS, Beta.** Suzanne Pleshette, Joseph Bologna, Rosanna Arquette, Oliver Clark; *D:* Richard Michaels. *LIV*

One Crazy Night ♪♪½ **1993 (PG-13)** In 1964, five Australian teenagers try to get into the Melbourne hotel where the Beatles are staying on tour. They wind up trapped in the basement, swapping secrets, and finding out how much they have in common. **92m/C VHS.** *AU* Noah Taylor, Beth Champion, Malcolm Kennard, Danni Minogue, Malcolm Braly; *D:* Michael Pattinson. *VMK*

One Crazy Summer ♪♪½ **1986 (PG)** A group of wacky teens spend a fun-filled summer on Nantucket Island in New England. This follow-up to "Better Off Dead" is offbeat and fairly charming, led by Cusack's perplexed cartoonist and with comic moments delivered by Goldthwait. **94m/C VHS, Beta, LV.** John Cusack, Demi Moore, William Hickey, Curtis Armstrong, Bob(cat) Goldthwait, Mark Metcalf, Joel Murray, Tom Villard, Joe Flaherty; *D:* Steve Holland; *W:* Steve Holland; *M:* Cory Lerios. *WAR*

One Dark Night ♪½ **1982 (R)** Two high school girls plan an initiation rite for one of their friends who is determined to shed her "goody-goody" image. West is the caped crusader of TV series "Batman" fame. **94m/C VHS, Beta.** Meg Tilly, Adam West, David Mason Daniels, Robin Evans; *D:* Tom McLoughlin. *NO*

One Day in the Life of Ivan Denisovich ♪♪♪ **1971** The film version of Nobel Prize-winner Alexander Solzhenitsyn's novel about a prisoner's experiences in a Soviet labor camp. A testament to human endurance. Photography be Sven Nykvist. **105m/C VHS, LV.** *NO GB* Tom Courtenay, Alfred Burke, Espen Skjonberg, James Maxwell, Eric Thompson; *D:* Caspar Wrede; *W:* Ronald Harwood; *C:* Sven Nykvist. *INJ*

One Deadly Owner ♪ **1974** A made-for-television film about a possessed Rolls-Royce torturing its new owner. Quite a vehicle for the usually respectable set of wheels. **80m/C VHS, Beta.** Donna Mills, Jeremy Brett, Robert Morris, Laurence Payne. *LIV*

One Deadly Summer ♪♪♪ *L'Ete Meurtrier* **1983 (R)** Revenge drama about a young girl who returns to her mother's home village to ruin three men who had assaulted her mother years before. Very well acted. From the novel by Sebastien Japrisot. In French with English subtitles. **134m/C VHS, Beta.** *FR* Isabelle Adjani, Alain Souchon, Suzanne Flon; *D:* Jean Becker; *M:* Georges Delerue. Cesar Awards '84: Best Actress (Adjani), Best Supporting Actress (Flon), Best Writing; Nominations: Cannes Film Festival '83: Best Film. *MCA, INJ*

One Down, Two to Go! *Woof!* **1982 (R)** When the mob is discovered to be rigging a championship karate bout, two dynamic expert fighters join in a climactic battle against the hoods. Example of really bad "blaxploitation" that wastes talent, film, and the audience's time. **84m/C VHS, Beta.** Jim Brown, Fred Williamson, Jim Kelly, Richard Roundtree; *D:* Fred Williamson. *MED, RHI, HHE*

One-Eyed Jacks ♪♪♪½ **1961** An often engaging, but lengthy, psychological western about an outlaw who seeks to settle the score with a former partner who became a sheriff. Great acting by all, particularly Brando, who triumphed both as star and director. Stanley Kubrick was the original director, but Brando took over mid-way through the filming. The photography is wonderful and reflects the effort that went into it. **141m/C VHS, Beta, LV.** Marlon Brando, Karl Malden, Katy Jurado, Elisha Cook Jr., Slim Pickens, Ben Johnson, Pina Pellicer, Timothy Carey; *D:* Marlon Brando; *W:* Calder Willingham; *C:* Charles B(ryant) Lang. Nominations: Academy Awards '61: Best Color Cinematography. *PAR*

One-Eyed Soldiers ♪ **1967** Young woman, criminal, and dwarf follow trail to mysterious key to unlock $15 million treasure. Much cheesy intrigue. **83m/C VHS.** *GB YU* Dale Robertson, Luciana Paluzzi; *D:* Jean Christopher. *NO*

One-Eyed Swordsman ♪ **1963** A handicapped samurai battles shogun warriors. With English subtitles. **95m/C VHS, Beta.** *JP* Tetsuro Tamba, Haruko Wanibuchi; *D:* Seiichiro Uchikawa. *VDA*

One False Move ♪♪♪ **1991 (R)** Black psycho Pluto, his white-trash partner Ray, and Ray's biracial lover Fantasia are three low-level drug dealers on the streets of Los Angeles who get involved in murder. Fleeing the city for Fantasia's small hometown in Arkansas, they come up against the local sheriff and two L.A. cops sent to bring them back. Not a typical crime thriller, first-time feature director Franklin is more interested in a psychological character study of racism and smalltown mores than in your average shoot 'em up action picture. Good performances, especially by Williams as the deceptive bad girl. **105m/C VHS, LV.** Bill Paxton, Cynda Williams, Michael Beach, Jim Metzler, Earl Billings, Billy Bob Thornton, Natalie Canderday, Robert Ginnaven, Robert Anthony Bell, Kevin Hunter; *D:* Carl Franklin; *W:* Billy Bob Thornton, Tom Epperson. Independent Spirit Awards '93: Best Director (Franklin); MTV Movie Awards '93: Best New Filmmaker Award (Franklin). *COL, FCT*

One Flew Over the Cuckoo's Nest ♪♪♪♪ **1975 (R)** Touching, hilarious, dramatic, and completely effective adaptation of Ken Kesey's novel. Nicholson is a two-bit crook, who, facing a jail sentence, feigns insanity to be sentenced to a cushy mental hospital. The hospital is anything but cushy, with a tyrannical head nurse out to squash any vestige of the patients' independence. Nicholson proves to be a crazed messiah and catalyst for these mentally troubled patients and a worthy adversary for the head nurse. Classic performs superbly on numerous levels. **129m/C VHS, Beta, LV.** Jack Nicholson, Brad Dourif, Louise Fletcher, Will Sampson,

William Redfield, Danny DeVito, Christopher Lloyd, Scatman Crothers, Vincent Schiavelli, Michael Berryman, Peter Brocco, Louisa Moritz; *D:* Milos Forman; *W:* Ken Kesey, Bo Goldman; *C:* Haskell Wexler; *M:* Jack Nitzsche. Academy Awards '75: Best Actor (Nicholson), Best Actress (Fletcher), Best Adapted Screenplay, Best Director (Forman), Best Picture; British Academy Awards '76: Best Actor (Nicholson), Best Actress (Fletcher), Best Director (Forman), Best Film, Best Supporting Actor (Dourif); Golden Globe Awards '76: Best Actor—Drama (Nicholson), Best Actress—Drama (Fletcher), Best Director (Forman), Best Film—Drama, Best Screenplay; National Board of Review Awards '75: 10 Best Films of the Year, Best Actor (Nicholson); National Society of Film Critics Awards '75: Best Actor (Nicholson); People's Choice Awards '77: Best Film; Writers Guild of America '75: Best Adapted Screenplay; Nominations: Academy Awards '75: Best Cinematography, Best Film Editing, Best Supporting Actor (Dourif), Best Original Score. *REP, BTV, FCT*

One Frightened Night 🦴🦴½ **1935** An eccentric millionaire informs his family members that he is leaving each of them one million dollars...as long as his long-lost granddaughter doesn't reappear. Guess who comes to dinner. **69m/B VHS, Beta.** Mary Carlisle, Wallace Ford, Hedda Hopper, Charley Grapewin; *D:* Christy Cabanne. *NOS, BAR, VYY*

One from the Heart 🦴🦴 **1982 (R)** The film more notable for sinking Coppola's Zoetrope Studios than for its cinematic context. Garr and Forrest are a jaded couple who seek romantic excitement with other people. An extravagant (thus Coppola's finance problems) fantasy Las Vegas set, pretty to look at but does little to enhance the weak plot. Score by Waits, a much-needed plus. **100m/C VHS, Beta, LV.** Teri Garr, Frederic Forrest, Nastassia Kinski, Raul Julia, Lainie Kazan, Rebecca DeMornay, Harry Dean Stanton; *D:* Francis Ford Coppola; *W:* Armyan Bernstein, Francis Ford Coppola; *M:* Tom Waits, Robert Alcivar. Nominations: Academy Awards '82: Best Original Score. *COL*

One Good Cop 🦴🦴½ **1991 (R)** A noble, inconsistent attempt to do a police thriller with a human face, as a young officer and his wife adopt the three little daughters of his slain partner from the force. But it reverts to a routine action wrapup, with 'Batman' Keaton even donning a masked-avenger getup to get revenge. **105m/C VHS, Beta, LV.** Michael Keaton, Rene Russo, Anthony LaPaglia, Kevin Conway, Rachel Ticotin, Grace Johnston, Blair Swanson, Rhea Silver-Smith, Tony Plana, Benjamin Bratt, Charlaine Woodard; *D:* Heywood Gould; *W:* Heywood Gould; *C:* Ralf Bode; *M:* William Ross. *HPH*

100 Men and a Girl 🦴🦴🦴 **1937** Charming musical features Durbin as the daughter of an unemployed musician, who decides she will try to persuade Leopold Stokowski to help her launch an orchestra that will employ her father and his musician friends. Beautiful mix of classical and pop music. Based on a story by Hans Kraly. ♫Hungarian Rhapsody No. 2; Symphony No. 5; Alleluja; It's Raining Sunbeams; A Heart That's Free. **85m/B VHS.** Deanna Durbin, Leopold Stokowski, Adolphe Menjou, Alice Brady, Eugene Pallette, Mischa Auer, Billy Gilbert, Alma Kruger, Christian Rub, Jed Prouty, Jack Mulhall; *D:* Henry Koster; *C:* Joseph Valentine. Academy Awards '37: Best Score; Nominations: Academy Awards '37: Best Film Editing, Best Picture, Best Story. *MCA*

100 Rifles 🦴🦴 **1969 (R)** Native American bank robber and Black American lawman join up with a female Mexican revolutionary to help save the Mexican Indians from annihilation by a despotic military governor. What it lacks in political correctness it makes up for in fits of action. Although quite racy in its day for its interracial sex sizzle of Brown and Rachel, it's tame and overblown by today's standards. **110m/C VHS, Beta.** Jim Brown, Raquel Welch, Burt Reynolds, Fernando Lamas; *D:* Tom Gries; *M:* Jerry Goldsmith. *FOX, FXV*

101 Dalmatians 🦴🦴🦴½ **1961 (G)** Disney classic is one of the highest-grossing animated films in the history of Hollywood. Dogowners Roger and Anita, and their spotted pets Pongo and Perdita are shocked when their puppies are kidnapped by Cruella de Vil, villainess extraordinaire, to make a simply fabulous spotted coat. The aid of various animals including a dog named Colonel, a horse, a cat, and a goose is enlisted to rescue the doomed pups. Imagine their surprise when they find not only their own puppies, but 84 more as well. You can expect a happy ending and lots of spots—6,469,952 to be exact. Based on the children's book by Dodie Smith. Technically notable for the first time use of the Xerox process to transfer the animator's drawings onto celluloid, which made the film's opening sequence of dots evolving into 101 barking dogs possible. ♫Remember When; Cruella de Vil; Dalmation Plantation; Kanine Krunchies Kommercial. **79m/C VHS, Beta.** *D:* Clyde Geronomi, Wolfgang Reitherman, Hamilton Luske; *M:* George Bruns; *V:* Rod Taylor, Betty Lou Gerson, Lisa Davis, Ben Wright, Frederick Worlock, J. Pat O'Malley. *DIS, OM*

125 Rooms of Comfort 🦴🦴 **1983** A mental patient has bizarre fantasies that create havoc among those who stand in his way. **82m/C VHS, Beta.** Tim Henry, Jackie Burroughs, Bob Warner, Bob Silverman, Les Barker; *D:* Patrick Loubert; *W:* Patrick Loubert, Bill Freut. *TWE*

One in a Million 🦴🦴🦴 **1936** Debut film of Norwegian skating star Henie centers around a Swiss girl whose father is training her for the Olympics. Features good comedy by the Ritz Brothers and Sparks, as well as the beautiful skating of Henie. ♫One in a Million; We're Back in Circulation Again; Who's Afraid of Love; Lovely Lady in White; The Moonlight Waltz. **95m/B VHS.** Sonja Henie, Adolphe Menjou, Jean Hersholt, The Ritz Brothers, Arline Judge, Don Ameche, Ned Sparks, Montagu Love, Leah Ray; *D:* Sidney Lanfield; *W:* Leonard Praskins, Mark Kelly. *FXV*

One in a Million: The Ron LeFlore Story 🦴🦴½ **1978** The true story of Detroit Tigers' star Ron LeFlore, who rose from the Detroit ghetto to the major leagues. Adaptation of LeFlore's autobiography, "Breakout." A well-acted and compelling drama with Burton in a standout performance. **90m/C VHS, Beta.** LeVar Burton, Madge Sinclair, Billy Martin, James Luisi; *D:* William A. Graham. *NO*

One Last Run 🦴½ **1989** It's drama on the slopes as a variety of individuals confront their pasts/fears/personal demons via extreme skiing. Features the performances of champion skiers Franz Weber and Scot Schmidt. **82m/C VHS, Beta.** Russell Todd, Ashley Laurence, Craig Branham, Jimmy Aleck, Tracy Scoggins, Nels Van Patten, Chuck Connors; *D:* Peter Winograd, Glenn Gebhard; *W:* Peter Winograd, Glenn Gebhard. *PSM*

One Little Indian 🦴🦴 **1973** An AWOL cavalry man and his Indian ward team up with a widow and her daughter in an attempt to cross the New Mexican desert. A tepid presentation from the usually high quality Disney studio. **90m/C VHS, Beta.** James Garner, Vera Miles, Jodie Foster, Clay O'Brien, Andrew Prine, Bernard McEveety; *D:* Bernard McEveety; *M:* Jerry Goldsmith. *DIS*

One Magic Christmas 🦴🦴½ **1985 (G)** Disney feel-good film about a disillusioned working woman whose faith in Christmas is restored when her guardian angel descends to Earth and performs various miracles. Somewhat cliched and tiresome, but partially redeemed by Stanton and Steenburgen's presence. **88m/C VHS, Beta, LV.** Mary Steenburgen, Harry Dean Stanton, Gary Basaraba, Michelle Meyrink, Arthur Hill, Elisabeth Harnois, Robbie Magwood; *D:* Phillip Borsos; *W:* Thomas Meehan; *M:* Michael Conway Baker. *DIS*

One Man Army 🦴½ **1993 (R)** Kickboxer goes to visit gramps in small town, only to discover the old guy has been murdered and corruption and cover-ups abound. So he decides to kick some butt and set things right. **95m/C VHS.** Jerry Trimble; *D:* Cirio H. Santiago. *NHO*

One Man Force 🦴🦴 **1989 (R)** L.A. narcotics cop Jake Swan goes on a vigilante spree. Huge in body and vengeful in spirit, he makes his partner's murderers pay! **92m/C VHS, Beta, LV.** John Matuszak, Ronny Cox, Charles Napier, Sharon Farrell, Sam Jones, Chance Boyer, Richard Lynch, Stacey Q; *D:* Dale Trevillion; *W:* Dale Trevillion; *M:* Charles Fox. *ACA*

One Man Jury 🦴 **1978 (R)** LAPD lieutenant, wearied by an ineffective justice system, becomes a one-man vigilante avenger. Pale Dirty Harry rip-off with over acting and an overdose of violence. **95m/C VHS, Beta.** Jack Palance, Chris Mitchum, Joe Spinell, Pamela Shoop; *D:* Charles Martin. *VCI*

One Man Out 🦴 **1989 (R)** An ex-CIA agent diverts his psychological problems into his new job: assassin for a South American despot. His jaded view of life changes when he meets and falls in love with an American journalist. Trouble in paradise when he is ordered to kill her. One man out was not enough, they should have done away with the entire crew of this stinker. **90m/C VHS, Beta, LV.** Stephen McHattie, Deborah Van Valkenburgh, Aharon Ipale, Ismael Carlo, Michael Champion, Dennis A. Pratt; *D:* Michael Kennedy. *COL*

One Man's Justice 🦴🦴½ **1995 (R)** Army drill sergeant John North (Bosworth) heads for the streets of Venice, California to get the drug-dealing, gun-running scum who killed his wife and daughter. And a streetwise 10-year-old may be his best chance for finding them. **100m/C VHS, LV.** Brian Bosworth, Bruce Payne, Jeff Kober, DeJuan Guy, Hammer; *D:* Kurt Wimmer; *W:* Steven Selling; *M:* Anthony Marinelli. *LIV*

One Man's War 🦴🦴½ **1990 (PG-13)** A human-rights crusader in repressive Paraguay won't be silenced, even after government thugs torture and murder his son. He fights obsessively to bring the killers to justice. The true story of the Joel Filartiga family is heartfelt but ultimately a dramatic letdown; an epilogue proves that full story hasn't been told. **91m/C VHS.** Anthony Hopkins, Norma Aleandro, Fernanda Torres, Ruben Blades; *D:* Sergio Toledo. *HBO*

One Man's Way 🦴🦴½ **1963** Murray is appropriately devout as charasmatic religious leader Norman Vincent Peale. With the support of his wife (Hyland), he survives the adulations and accusations of blasphemy for his rather unorthodox theological ideas and his book, "The Power of Positive Thinking." Based on the book "Norman Vincent Peale: Minister to Millions" by Arthur Gordon. **105m/B VHS, Beta.** Don Murray, Diana Hyland, William Windom, Virginia Christine, Carol Ohmart, Veronica Cartwright, Liam Sullivan, June Dayton, Ian Wolfe; *D:* Denis Sanders; *W:* Eleanore Griffin, John W. Bloch. *MGM, FCT, BTV*

One Million B.C. 🦴🦴½ *The Cave Dwellers; Cave Man; Man and His Mate* **1940** The strange saga of the struggle of primitive cavemen and their battle against dinosaurs and other monsters. Curiously told in flashbacks, this film provided stock footage for countless dinosaur movies that followed. Portions of film rumored to be directed by cinematic pioneer D. W. Griffith. **80m/B VHS, Beta.** Victor Mature, Carole Landis, Lon Chaney Jr.; *D:* Hal Roach, Hal Roach Jr. Nominations: Academy Awards '40: Best Original Score. *MED, RXM*

One Million Years B.C. 🦴🦴½ **1966 (R)** It's Welch in a fur bikini and special FX expert Ray Harryhausen doing dinosaurs so who cares about a plot (which involves Welch and her boyfriend, who's from a rival clan). Remake of the 1940 film "One Million B.C." **100m/C VHS.** *GB* Raquel Welch, John Richardson, Percy Herbert, Robert Brown, Martine Beswick; *D:* Don Chaffey. *FXV*

One Minute Before Death 🦴 **1988** A woman is buried in a catatonic state, and returns from the grave to exact retribution. Supposedly based loosely on Poe. **87m/C VHS, Beta.** Giselle MacKenzie. *NO*

One Minute to Zero 🦴🦴 **1952** Korean War action film divides its time between an army romance and war action. The lukwarm melodrama features Mitchum as a colonel in charge of evacuating American civilians but who ends up bombing refugees. **105m/B VHS, Beta.** Robert Mitchum, Ann Blyth, William Talman, Charles McGraw, Margaret Sheridan, Richard Egan, Eduard Franz, Robert Osterloh, Robert Gist; *D:* Tay Garnett. *TTC*

One More Chance 🦴½ **1990** While he was in jail, an ex-con's family moves away without leaving a forwarding address. When he's released he strikes up a friendship with a woman from the neighborhood who knows where they've gone. **102m/C VHS, Beta.** Kirstie Alley, John Lamotta, Logan Clarke, Michael Pataki, Hector Maisonette; ***D:*** Sam Firstenberg. *WAR, OM*

One More Saturday Night 🦴 **1986 (R)** Franken and Davis, "Saturday Night Live" alumni, wrote this film about a small town going wild on the weekend. Dry, taxing, and unfunny. Averages about 1 laugh per 1/2 hour—at 1 1/2 hours, it's way too long. **96m/C VHS, Beta, LV.** Al Franken, Tom Davis, Nan Woods, Dave Reynolds; ***D:*** Dennis Klein; ***W:*** Al Franken, Tom Davis. *NO*

One Night in the Tropics 🦴🦴½ **1940** The film debut of radio stars Abbott & Costello who play secondary roles to a love triangle (set to music). Jones is an insurance salesman who falls in love with Kelly, the fiance of Cummings. Based on the novel "Love Insurance" by Earl Derr Biggers. ♫Back in My Shell; Remind Me; You and Your Kiss; Your Dream is the Same as My Dream. **83m/B VHS.** Allan Jones, Robert Cummings, Nancy Kelly, Bud Abbott, Lou Costello, Mary Boland, Peggy Moran, William Frawley, Leo Carrillo; ***D:*** Edward Sutherland; ***W:*** Kathryn Scola, Gertrude Purcell, Charles Grayson, Francis Martin. *MCA, FCT*

One Night of Love 🦴🦴🦴½ **1934** Moore's best quasi-operetta, about a young American diva rebelling in response to her demanding Italian teacher. "Pygmallion"-like story has her falling in love with her maestro. Despite being nearly 60 years old, this film is still enchanting and fresh. ♫One Night of Love; Ciri-Biri-Bin; Sempre Libera; Sextet; Indian Love Call; 'Tis the Last Rose of Summer; Habanera; Un bel di; None But the Lonely Heart. **95m/B VHS, Beta, LV.** Grace Moore, Tullio Carminati, Lyle Talbot, Jane Darwell, Nydia Westman, Mona Barrie, Jessie Ralph, Luis Alberni; ***D:*** Victor Schertzinger. Academy Awards '34: Best Sound, Best Score; Nominations: Academy Awards '34: Best Actress (Moore), Best Director (Schertzinger), Best Film Editing, Best Picture. *COL*

One Night Only **1984** A gorgeous law student decides to make big money by hiring herself and her friends out as hookers to the school football team. **87m/C VHS, Beta.** Lenore Zann, Jeff Braunstein, Grant Alianak; ***D:*** Timothy Bond. *FOX*

One Night Stand 🦴🦴 **1977** Woman's chance encounter with a man in a singles bar leads to an evening of unexpected terror. Adapted from a play for Canadian television. Billed as a horror flick, it is really more of a drama. **90m/C VHS, Beta.** *CA* Chapelle Jaffe, Brent Carver. *TWE*

One Night Stand 🦴🦴🦴 **1984** Four young people attempt to amuse themselves at the empty Sydney Opera House on the New Year's Eve, that night WWIII begins. An odd commentary on nuclear war that sees the bomb as the ultimate bad joke. Features an appearance by alternative rock group Midnight Oil. **94m/C VHS, Beta.** Tyler Coppin, Cassandra Delaney, Jay Hackett, Saskia Post; ***D:*** John Duigan. *SUE*

One Night Stand 🦴🦴½ **1995** Lonely Michelle (Sheedy) visits a nightclub and allows herself to be picked up by your basic handsome stranger, Jack (Martinez) in this case. She wakes up alone and learns from building owner Josslyn (Forrest) that the apartment is up for lease. Obsessed with finding her mystery man, Michelle discovers Jack's wife was murdered—possibly by him or maybe by Josslyn, who turns out to be the dead woman's father. Debut feature for director Shire covers familiar territory, with Sheedy giving a strong performance. **92m/C VHS.** Ally Sheedy, A. Martinez, Frederic Forrest, Don Novello, Diane Salinger, Millie Slavin; ***D:*** Talia Shire; ***W:*** Marty Casella; ***C:*** Arthur Albert; ***M:*** David Shire. *NHO*

One of My Wives Is Missing 🦴🦴½ **1976** An ex-New York cop tries to solve the mysterious disappearance of a newlywed socialite. Things become strange when she reappears but is discovered as an imposter. Above average acting in a film adapted from the play, "The Trap for a Lonely Man." **97m/C VHS, Beta.** Jack Klugman, Elizabeth Ashley, James Franciscus; ***D:*** Glenn Jordan. *ORI*

One of Our Aircraft Is Missing 🦴🦴🦴½ **1941** The crew of an R.A.F. bomber downed in the Netherlands, struggle to escape Nazi capture. A thoughtful study of wars and the men who fight them, with an entertaining melodramatic plot. Look for the British version, which runs 106 minutes. Some of the American prints only run 82 minutes. **103m/B VHS.** *GB* Godfrey Tearle, Eric Portman, Hugh Williams, Pamela Brown, Googie Withers, Peter Ustinov; ***D:*** Emeric Pressburger, Michael Powell. National Board of Review Awards '42: 10 Best Films of the Year; Nominations: Academy Awards '42: Best Original Screenplay. *NOS, MRV, REP*

One of Our Dinosaurs Is Missing 🦴🦴 **1975 (G)** An English nanny and her cohorts help British Intelligence retrieve a microfilm—concealing dinosaur fossil from the bad guys that have stolen it. Disney film was shot on location in England. **101m/C VHS, Beta.** Peter Ustinov, Helen Hayes, Derek Nimmo, Clive Revill, Robert Stevenson, Joan Sims; ***D:*** Robert Stevenson. *DIS*

One on One 🦴🦴½ **1977 (PG)** A Rocky-esque story about a high school basketball star from the country who accepts an athletic scholarship to a big city university. He encounters a demanding coach and intense competition. Light weight drama that is economically entertaining. **100m/C VHS, Beta.** Robby Benson, Annette O'Toole, G.D. Spradlin, Gail Strickland, Melanie Griffith; ***D:*** Lamont Johnson; ***W:*** Robby Benson; ***M:*** Charles Fox. *WAR*

One Plus One 🦴 *Exploring the Kinsey Report* **1961** A dramatization, believe it or not, of the Kinsey sex survey of the 1950s. Participants in a sex lecture talk about and demonstrate various "risque" practices, such as premarital sex and extramarital affairs. Despite this film, the sexual revolution went on as planned. **114m/B VHS, Beta.** *CA* Leo G. Carroll, Hilda Brawner, William Traylor, Kate Reid, Ernest Graves; ***D:*** Arch Oboler; ***W:*** Arch Oboler. *SNC*

One-Punch O'Day 🦴 **1926** Boxing boy tries to buy back hometown's oil livelihood by winning prizefight. Much patient waiting by his honey. **60m/B VHS, Beta.** Billy Sullivan, Jack Herrick, Charlotte Merriam; ***D:*** Harry Joe Brown. *GPV, FCT, GVV*

One Rainy Afternoon 🦴🦴 **1936** A bit-player kisses the wrong girl in a Paris theater causing a massive uproar that brands him as a notorious romantic "monster." Patterned after a German film, the story lacks depth and zest. **80m/B VHS, Beta.** Francis Lederer, Ida Lupino, Hugh Herbert, Roland Young, Donald Meek; ***D:*** Rowland V. Lee. *NOS, MRV, VYY*

One Russian Summer *Woof!* **1973 (R)** During the Russian Revolution, a cripple seeks revenge on the corrupt land baron who murdered his parents. An unfortunate attempt to dramatize a novel by M. Lermontov. **112m/C VHS, Beta.** Oliver Reed, Claudia Cardinale, John McEnery, Carole Andre, Ray Lovelock; ***D:*** Antonio Calenda. *VCI*

One Shoe Makes It Murder 🦴🦴 **1982** A shady casino owner hires ex-cop Mitchum to investigate the disappearance of his unfaithful wife. Adapted from Eric Bercovici's novel, the story does little to enhance Mitchum's TV debut. **100m/C VHS, Beta.** Robert Mitchum, Angie Dickinson, Mel Ferrer, Howard Hesseman, Jose Perez; ***D:*** William Hale; ***M:*** Bruce Broughton. *LIV*

One Sings, the Other Doesn't 🦴🦴½ *L'Une Chante L'Autre Pas* **1977** Seeking contentment, a conservative widow and a liberal extrovert help each other cope in a man's world. Endearing characters, but a superficial treatment of dated feminist issues. In French with English subtitles. **105m/C VHS, Beta.** *FR BE* Valerie Mairesse, Therese Liotard; ***D:*** Agnes Varda; ***W:*** Agnes Varda. *COL, INJ*

One Step Beyond **1959** This creepy anthology series featured stories of the occult and supernatural which were supposedly based on true incidents. Two episodes per tape. Includes "Message from Clara" starring Barbara Baxley and Robert Ellenstein and "The Sorcerer" with Christopher Lee and Martin Benson. **60m/B VHS.** ***D:*** John Newland. *MOV, HEG*

One Step to Hell 🦴½ *Caccia Ai Violenti; King of Africa* **1968** Good cop rescues gold-miner's widow from three escaped convicts. Beautiful African scenery helps save an otherwise mediocre film. **90m/C VHS, Beta.** Ty Hardin, Rossano Brazzi, Pier Angeli, George Sanders, Tab Hunter, Sandy Howard. *NO*

One Summer Love 🦴½ *Dragonfly* **1976** Man checks out from loony bin, searches for family ties and befriends beautiful woman who works in a moviehouse. **95m/C VHS.** Beau Bridges, Susan Sarandon, Mildred Dunnock, Ann Wedgeworth, Michael B. Miller, Linda Miller, James Noble, Frederick Coffin; ***D:*** Gilbert Cates; ***W:*** N. Richard Nash. *HBO*

One That Got Away 🦴🦴🦴 **1957** A loyal German Luftwaffe pilot captured by the British becomes obsessed with escape. Fast paced and exciting. Based on a true story. **111m/B VHS, Beta.** Hardy Kruger, Colin Gordon, Alec Gordon; ***D:*** Roy Ward Baker. *NO*

One Third of a Nation 🦴🦴½ **1939** Depression era film contrasts the conditions of slum life with those in high society. A young entrepreneur inherits a city block in ruins, only to fall in love with a young woman who lives there and help her crippled brother. Timely social criticism. **79m/B VHS.** Sylvia Sidney, Leif Erickson, Myron McCormick, Sidney Lumet; ***D:*** Dudley Murphy. *NOS, PAR, MLB*

1001 Arabian Nights 🦴🦴½ **1959** In this Arabian nightmare, the nearsighted Mr. Magoo is known as "Azziz" Magoo, lamp dealer and uncle of Aladdin. **76m/C VHS, Beta.** ***D:*** Jack Kinney; ***M:*** George Duning; ***V:*** Jim Backus, Kathryn Grant, Hans Conried, Herschel Bernardi. *COL*

One Too Many 🦴 *The Important Story of Alcoholism; Killer With a Label* **1951** Exploitation film depicting the evils of alcoholism. Campy, but slick. **?m/C VHS.** Ruth Warrick, Richard Travis, Victor Kilian, Onslow Stevens, Lyle Talbot. *SNC*

One Touch of Venus 🦴🦴½ **1948** Love fills a department store when a window dresser kisses a statue of the goddess Venus—and she comes to life. Appealing adaptation of the Broadway musical. ♫Speak Low; The Trouble with Women; That's Him; Don't Look Now But My Heart Is Showing; My Week. **82m/B VHS.** Ava Gardner, Robert Walker, Eve Arden, Dick Haymes, Olga San Juan, Tom Conway; ***D:*** William A. Seiter; ***M:*** Kurt Weill, Ogden Nash. *REP, MLB*

One Trick Pony 🦴🦴½ **1980 (R)** Once-popular rock singer/songwriter struggles to keep his head above water in a turbulent marriage and in the changing currents of popular taste. Simon wrote the autobiographical screenplay and score, but let's hope he is more sincere in real life. A good story. **100m/C VHS, Beta.** Paul Simon, Blair Brown, Rip Torn, Joan Hackett, Mare Winningham, Lou Reed, Harry Shearer, Allen (Goorwitz) Garfield, Daniel Stern; ***D:*** Robert M. Young. *WAR*

One, Two, Three 🦴🦴🦴½ **1961** Cagney, an American Coca-Cola exec in Germany, zealously pursues any opportunity to run Coke's European operations. He does the job too well and loses his job to a Communist hippie turned slick capitalist. Fast-paced laughs, wonderful cinematography, and a fine score. **110m/B VHS, Beta, LV.** James Cagney, Horst Buchholz, Arlene Francis; ***D:*** Billy Wilder; ***W:*** Billy Wilder, I.A.L. Diamond; ***C:*** Daniel F. Fapp; ***M:*** Andre Previn. National Board of Review Awards '61: 10 Best Films of the Year; Nominations: Academy Awards '61: Best Black and White Cinematography. *MGM*

One Wild Moment 🦴🦴½ **1978 (R)** Comic complications arise when a divorced man is seduced by his best friend's daughter while vacationing. Warm and charming. Later re-made as "Blame It on Rio." In French with English subtitles. **88m/C VHS, Beta.** *FR* Jean-Pierre Marielle, Victor Lanoux, Agnes Soral, Christine Dejoux, Martine Sarcey; ***D:*** Claude Berri; ***W:*** Claude Berri. *COL, INJ*

One Wish Too Many 🦴🦴½ **1955** A young boy finds a marble that grants wishes. He has the time of his life with his teachers and the school bullies, but runs into trouble when he creates a giant steam roller which overruns London. Winner of Best Children's Film, 1956 Venice Film Festival, but it is hard to say why. **55m/B VHS, Beta.** *GB* Anthony Richmond, Rosalind Gourgey, John Pike; ***D:*** John Durst. *SNC*

One Woman or Two 🦴🦴½ *Une Femme ou Deux* **1985 (PG-13)** Paleontologist Depardieu is duped by beautiful ad-exec who plans to use his findings to push perfume. Remake of "Bringing Up Baby," this screwball comedy has a few screws loose. Dubbed. **100m/C VHS, Beta.** *FR* Gerard Depardieu, Sigourney Weaver, Dr. Ruth Westheimer, Michel Aumont, Zabou; ***D:*** Daniel Vigne; ***W:*** Elisabeth Rappeneau, Daniel Vigne. *LIV, VES, INJ*

Onibaba 🦴🦴🦴 *The Demon; The Devil Woman* **1964** A brutal parable about a mother and her daughter-in-law in war-ravaged medieval Japan who subsist by murdering stray soldiers and selling their armor. One soldier beds the daughter, setting the mother-in-law on a vengeful tirade. Review of the film varied widely, hailed by some as a masterpiece and by others as below average; in Japanese with subtitles. **103m/B VHS, Beta.** *JP* Nobuko Otowa, Yitsuko Yoshimura, Kei Sato; ***D:*** Kaneto Shindo. *CVC, INJ, TPV*

The Onion Field 🦴🦴🦴½ **1979 (R)** True story about the mental breakdown of an ex-cop who witnessed his partner's murder. Haunted by the slow process of justice and his own feelings of insecurity, he is unable to get his life together. Based on the novel by Joseph Wambaugh, who also wrote the screenplay. Compelling script and excellent acting. **126m/C VHS, Beta, LV.** John Savage, James Woods, Ronny Cox, Franklyn Seales, Ted Danson; ***D:*** Harold Becker. *SUE, NLC*

Only Angels Have Wings 🦴🦴🦴🦴 **1939** Melodramatic adventure about a broken-down Peruvian air mail service. Large cast adds to the love tension between Grant, a pilot, and Arthur, a showgirl at the saloon. Nominated for special effects, a category recognized by the academy that year for the first time. William Rankin and Eleanor Griffin are uncredited writers. **121m/B VHS, Beta.** Cary Grant, Thomas Mitchell, Richard Barthelmess, Jean Arthur, Noah Beery Jr., Rita Hayworth, Sig Rumann, John Carroll, Allyn Joslyn; ***D:*** Howard Hawks; ***W:*** Jules Furthman; ***M:*** Dimitri Tiomkin. Nominations: Academy Awards '39: Best Black and White Cinematography, Best Special Effects. *COL*

Only Once in a Lifetime 🦴 **1983** A love story about an Hispanic immigrant painter looking for success in America. **90m/C VHS, Beta.** Miguel Robelo, Estrellita Lopez, Sheree North. *VHE, MOV*

Only One Night 🦴🦴 *En Enda Natt* **1942** Upon finding out that he's the illegitimate son of an aristocrat, a happy-go-lucky carousel operator in a circus joins high society and is promptly matched with a beautiful but repressed woman. In Swedish with English subtitles. **87m/B VHS, Beta, LV.** *SW* Ingrid Bergman, Edvin Adolphson, Alno Taube, Olof Sandborg, Erik Berglund, Marianne Lofgren, Magnus Kesster; ***D:*** Gustaf Molander. *WAC, LUM, INJ*

Only the Brave 🦴🦴 **1994** Gay coming-of-age story about two teenaged, working-class girls living on the seedy fringes of Melbourne. Alex (Manadalis), her wild best friend Vicki (Kaskanis), and their equally tough girlfriends seem to spend most of their time hanging out, smoking dope, and getting into trouble. But Alex slowly recognizes her feelings for Vicki are also sexual, and their friendship drastically changes. **62m/C VHS.** *AU* Elena Mandalis, Dora Kaskanis, Moudo Davey, Bob Bright; ***D:*** Ana Kokkinos; ***W:*** Ana Kokkinos, Mira Robertson. *ICA*

Only the Lonely 🦴🦴½ **1991 (PG)** Middle-aged cop, Candy, falls in love with a shy undertaker's assistant, Sheedy, and is torn between love and dear old Mom, O'Hara, in her first role in years. Candy is an unlikely leading man and even the jokes are forced. But the restaurant scene makes the whole thing well worth seeing. **104m/C VHS, Beta, LV.** John Candy, Ally Sheedy, Maureen O'Hara, Anthony Quinn, Kevin Dunn, James Belushi, Milo O'Shea, Bert Remsen, Macaulay Culkin, Joe V. Greco; ***D:*** Chris Columbus; ***W:*** Chris Columbus; ***M:*** Maurice Jarre. *FXV, OM*

Only the Strong 🦴½ **1993 (PG-13)** Louis (Dacascos) is a special forces officer who has mastered capoeira, a Brazilian form of kung fu. In Miami, he works with his old teacher (Lewis) to instill discipline in the 12 toughest punks in school by teaching them his martial arts skills. A neighborhood drug lord, related to two of the students, decides to cause trouble for Louis. Dascascos displays some charm along with his physical abilities but the story's ridiculous and the movie hastily put together. **96m/C VHS, LV.** Mark Dacascos, Stacy Travis, Todd Susman, Geoffrey Lewis, Paco Christian Prieto; ***D:*** Sheldon Lettich; ***W:*** Sheldon Lettich, Luis Esteban; ***M:*** Harvey W. Mason. *FXV*

Only the Valiant 🦴🦴 **1950** Action-packed story of a cavalry officer who struggles to win his troops respect while warding off angry Apaches. Fast-paced Western fun requires little thought. **105m/B VHS, LV.** Gregory Peck, Ward Bond, Gig Young, Lon Chaney Jr., Barbara Payton, Neville Brand; ***D:*** Gordon Douglas; ***C:*** Lionel Lindon. *REP*

Only Two Can Play 🦴🦴🦴 **1962** Sellers is a hilarious Casanova librarian who puts the moves on a society lady to get a promotion. Funny, of course, and based on Kingsley Amis' novel "That Uncertain Feeling." **106m/C VHS, Beta.** *GB* Peter Sellers, Virginia Maskell, Mai Zetterling, Richard Attenborough; ***D:*** Sidney Gilliat; ***M:*** Richard Rodney Bennett. *COL*

The Only Way 🦴🦴½ **1970 (G)** A semi-documentary account of the plight of the Jews in Denmark during the Nazi occupation. Despite German insistence, the Danes succeeded in saving most of their Jewish population from the concentration camps. **86m/C VHS, Beta.** Jane Seymour, Martin Potter, Benjamin Christiansen; ***M:*** Carl Davis. *VCI*

The Only Way Home 🦴🦴 **1972 (PG)** Two bikers end up in big trouble when one of them kills a wealthy man, and they kidnap his wife. Filmed entirely in Oklahoma. **86m/C VHS, Beta.** Bo Hopkins, Beth Brickell, Steve Sandor, G.D. Spradlin; ***D:*** G.D. Spradlin. *NO*

Only When I Laugh 🦴🦴🦴 *It Hurts Only When I Laugh* **1981 (R)** Neil Simon reworked his Broadway flop "The Gingerbread Lady" to produce this poignant comedy about the relationship between an aging alcoholic actress and her teenage daughters. **120m/C VHS, Beta, LV.** Marsha Mason, Kristy McNichol, James Coco, Joan Hackett, David Dukes, Kevin Bacon, John Bennett Perry; ***D:*** Glenn Jordan; ***W:*** Neil Simon; ***M:*** David Shire. Golden Globe Awards '82: Best Supporting Actress (Hackett); Nominations: Academy Awards '81: Best Actress (Mason), Best Supporting Actor (Coco), Best Supporting Actress (Hackett). *COL*

Only with Married Men 🦴 **1974** Carne's hassle-free dating routine is disrupted when a sly bachelor pretends that he's married to get a date. A middle-aged persons answer to a teenage sex comedy. Pretty bad. **74m/C VHS, Beta.** David Birney, Judy Carne, Gavin MacLeod, John Astin; ***D:*** Jerry Paris. *ORI*

Only You 🦴½ **1992 (PG-13)** A shy guy has always searched for true romance. But his cup runneth over when he meets, and must choose between, two beautiful women—your basic beach babe and a sensible beauty. What's a guy to do? **85m/C VHS.** Andrew McCarthy, Kelly Preston, Helen Hunt; ***M:*** Wendy Blackstone. *LIV*

Only You 🦴🦴½ *Him; Just in Time* **1994 (PG)** According to her ouija board, young Faith's (Tomei) soul mate is named Damon Bradley. But as the years pass, Faith is about to settle for a podiatrist—until an old school friend of her fiance's calls from Venice, Italy, with best wishes. Guess what his name is. So Faith and best friend Kate (Hunt) hop on a plane in search of Mr. Right. Then Faith meets charming shoe salesman Peter Wright (Downey) and wonders if ouija got things wrong. Slight romantic comedy with Jewison creating satisfactory chemistry with charming Downey and the somewhat miscast Tomei (and the Venetian scenery is gorgeous). **108m/C VHS, LV.** Marisa Tomei, Robert Downey Jr., Bonnie Hunt, Fisher Stevens, Billy Zane, Joaquim de Almeida; ***D:*** Norman Jewison; ***W:*** Diane Drake. *COL*

Open All Hours 🦴 **1983** A British television comedy about a small corner shop and its viciously greedy, opportunistic owner. **85m/C VHS, Beta.** *GB* Ronnie Barker, Lynda Baron, David Jason, Stephenie Cole. *FOX*

Open City 🦴🦴🦴🦴 *Roma, Citta Aperta; Rome, Open City* **1945** A leader in the Italian underground resists Nazi control of the city. A stunning film, making Rossellini's realistic style famous. In Italian with English subtitles. **103m/B VHS, Beta, 8mm.** *IT* Anna Magnani, Aldo Fabrizi, Marcel Pagliero, Maria Michi, Vito Annichiarico, Nando Bruno, Harry Feist; ***D:*** Roberto Rossellini; ***W:*** Federico Fellini, Sergio Amidei. National Board of Review Awards '46: 5 Best Foreign Films of the Year; New York Film Critics Awards '46: Best Foreign Film; Nominations: Academy Awards '46: Best Screenplay. *VYY, MRV, NOS*

Open Doors 🦴🦴🦴½ *Porte Aperte* **1989 (R)** Bitter review of Fascist rule and justice. The Fascist regime promises security, safety, and tranquility. So, on the morning that a white collar criminal murders his former boss, murders the man who got his job, and then rapes and murders his wife, tensions rise and the societal structures are tested. The people rally for his death. A judge and a juror struggle to uphold justice rather than serve popular passions. Winner of 4 Donatello Awards, Italian Golden Globes for Best Film, Best Actor, and Best Screenplay, and many international film awards. In Italian with English subtitles. **109m/C VHS.** *IT* Gian Marie Volonte, Ennio Fantastichini, Lidia Alfonsi; ***D:*** Gianni Amelio; ***W:*** Gianni Amelio. Nominations: Academy Awards '90: Best Foreign Language Film. *ORI, FCT, INJ*

Open Fire 🦴🦴 **1994 (R)** Alex McNeil (Wincott) is an ex-FBI agent, haunted by the death of his partner. But when a group of terrorists threaten to release a cloud of nerve gas over L.A. and hold McNeil's father hostage, he comes back full force. **93m/C VHS, LV.** Jeff Wincott, Patrick Kilpatrick, Lee DeBroux, Mimi Craven, Arthur Taxier. *REP*

Open House 🦴 **1986** Radio psychologist and beautiful real estate agent search for the killer of real estate agents and their clients. A mystery-thriller for the very patient. **95m/C VHS, Beta.** Joseph Bottoms, Adrienne Barbeau, Mary Stavin, Rudy Ramos; ***D:*** Jag Mundhra. *PSM*

Open Secret 🦴🦴 **1948** Jewish residents are plagued by a gang of anti-semitic thugs. Violence and destruction escalate until a fed up police lieutenant, tenaciously played by Ireland, and a victimized shop owner (Tyne) join forces to just say no more. When the gang learns the shopkeeper has caught their dastardly deeds on camera, the battle begins in earnest. Fast-paced and intriguing suspense. **70m/B VHS, Beta.** John Ireland, Jane Randolph, Roman Bohnen, Sheldon Leonard, George Tyne, Morgan Farley, Ellen Lowe, Anne O'Neal, Arthur O'Connell; ***D:*** John Reinhardt. *SNC*

Opening Night 🦴🦴½ **1977 (PG-13)** Very long study about an actress (Rowlands) and the play she's about to open in on Broadway. Backstage turmoil increases her own insecurities and the bad luck persists when an adoring fan dies in an accident on opening night. Performances carry this neurotic epic along, including Cassavettes as Rowland's co-star and Blondell as the playwright. **144m/C VHS, Beta.** Gena Rowlands, John Cassavetes, Joan Blondell, Ben Gazzara, Paul Stewart, Zohra Lampert, Laura Johnson; ***D:*** John Cassavetes; ***W:*** John Cassavetes. *TOU, BTV*

Opera do Malandro **1987** A lavish Brazilian take off of "The Threepenny Opera." Married hustler falls for a beautiful entrepreneur longing to get rich off of American goods. Based on Chico Buarque's musical play. In Portuguese, with subtitles. **106m/C VHS, Beta, LV.** *BR* Edson Celulari, Claudia Ohana, Elba Ramalho, Ney Latorraca; ***D:*** Ruy Guerra. *NO*

Operation Amsterdam 🦴🦴 **1960** Four agents have fourteen hours to snare $10 million in diamonds from under the noses of local Nazis. Based on a true story. Full of 1940s wartime action and suspense. **103m/B VHS, Beta.** Peter Finch, Eva Bartok, Tony Britton, Alexander Knox; ***D:*** Michael McCarthy. *SUE*

Operation C.I.A. 🦴🦴 *Last Message From Saigon* **1965** A plot to assassinate the U.S. ambassador in Saigon inspires brave CIA agent Reynolds to wipe out the bad guys. Action-packed and somewhat exciting. **90m/C VHS, Beta.** Burt Reynolds, John Hayt, Kieu Chinh, Danielle Aubry; ***D:*** Christian Nyby. *FOX, DVT, HEG*

Operation Cross Eagles 🦴🦴 *Unakrsna Vatra* **1969** Routine WWII military thriller with Conte and Calhoun on a mission to rescue an American general in exchange for their German prisoner. Their mission is complicated by a traitor in the group. Conte's only directorship. **90m/C VHS.** *YU* Richard Conte, Rory Calhoun, Aili King, Phil Brown; ***D:*** Richard Conte. *NO*

Operation Crossbow 🦴🦴🦴 *The Great Spy Mission; Code Name: Operation Crossbow* **1965** Action-packed espionage tale in which a trio of agents are assigned to destroy a Nazi munitions installation. Exciting ending and sensational pyrotechnics. **116m/C VHS.** Sophia Loren, George Peppard, Trevor Howard, John Mills, Richard Johnson, Tom Courtenay, Jeremy Kemp, Anthony Quayle, Helmut Dantine; ***D:*** Michael Anderson Sr. *MGM*

Operation Dames 🦴½ **1959** A squadron of soldiers must go behind Korean enemy lines to locate a missing U.S.O. troupe and bring them to safety. Low budget and not very funny for a supposed comedy. **73m/B VHS.** Eve Meyer, Chuck Henderson, Don Devlin, Ed Craig, Cindy Girard; ***D:*** Louis Clyde Stouman. *COL*

Operation Dumbo Drop 🦴🦴½ *Dumbo Drop* **1995 (PG)** It's 1968 and tough Green Beret captain (Glover), rescued by Vietnamese villagers, promises to replace their prized elephant, which was killed during his mission. He and a group of commandos use land, sea, and air to transport the reluctant beast, learning way more about elephant hygiene and eating habits than they ever wanted to know in the process. Wincer, who also directed "Free Willy," seems to be going for the title of "greatest large mammal director of all time." Anything with good-guy U.S. troops, a paratrooper elephant, and a family-friendly plot should be a Bob Dole favorite. **107m/C VHS, LV.** Danny Glover, Ray Liotta, Doug E. Doug, Denis Leary, Corin "Corky" Nemec, Thein Le Dihn; ***D:*** Simon Wincer; ***W:*** Jim Kouf, Gene Quintano; ***C:*** Russell Boyd; ***M:*** David Newman. *DIS*

Operation Golden Phoenix 🦴 **1994 (R)** A security specialist (Mehri) is betrayed in his assignment is to protect one half of a valuable medallion. Seems the medal reveals the location in Lebanon of a ancient mountain of gold—desired by a ruthless warlord (Hong). Martial arts fights are well done in this routine actioner. **95m/C VHS, LV.** Jalal Merhi, James Hong, Al Waxman, Loren Avedon; ***D:*** Jalal Merhi. *MCA*

Operation Haylift 🦴🦴 **1950** The true story of the U.S. Air Force's efforts to rescue starving cattle and sheep herds during Nevada's blizzards of 1949. The Air Force provided realism for the film with planes, equipment, and servicemen. **73m/B VHS, Beta, LV.** Bill Williams, Tom Brown, Ann Rutherford, Jane Nigh; ***D:*** William (Lester Williams) Berke. *NO*

Operation Inchon 🦴 **1981** A foreign film depicting the battle in Devil Ridge during the Korean War. **90m/C VHS, Beta.** *VCD*

Operation Intercept 🦴½ **1995 (R)** Woman suspects that the government is behind her father's murder after he develops technology that causes enemy planes to crash. So she threatens to destroy civilian aircraft until the killer is brought to justice. **94m/C VHS.** Lance Henriksen, Corbin Bernsen, Dennis Christopher; ***D:*** Paul Levine. *VMK*

Operation Julie 🦴½ **1985** A detective searches out a huge drug ring that manufactures LSD. **100m/C VHS, Beta.** Colin Blakely, Lesley Nightingale, Clare Powney; ***D:*** Bob Mahoney. *LIV*

Operation 'Nam 🦴🦴 **1985** A group of bored Vietnam vets return to 'Nam to rescue their leader from a POW camp. Nothing special, but features John Wayne's son. **85m/C VHS.** Oliver Tobias, Christopher Connelly, Manfred Lehman, John Steiner, Ethan Wayne, Donald Pleasence; ***D:*** Larry Ludman. *IMP*

Operation Orient 🦴½ **19??** A statue laden with drugs is stolen when an international drug smuggler tries to bring it to the U.S. **94m/C VHS, Beta.** Gianni Gori, Gordon Mitchell; ***D:*** Elia Milonakos. *MED*

Operation Petticoat 🦴🦴🦴½ **1959** Submarine captain Grant teams with wheeler-dealer Curtis to make his sub seaworthy. They're joined by a group of Navy women, and the gags begin. Great teamwork from Grant and Curtis keeps things rolling. Jokes may be considered sexist these days. Later remake and TV series couldn't hold a candle to the original. **120m/C VHS, LV.** Cary Grant, Tony Curtis, Joan O'Brien, Dina Merrill, Gene Evans, Arthur O'Connell, Virginia Gregg; ***D:*** Blake Edwards. Nominations: Academy Awards '59: Best Story & Screenplay. *REP*

Operation Thunderbolt 🦴🦴½ *Entebbe: Operation Thunderbolt* **1977** Israeli-produced depiction of Israel's July 14, 1976 commando raid on Entebbe, Uganda to rescue the passengers of a hijacked plane. Better than the American versions "Raid on Entebbe" and "Victory at Entebbe" in its performances as well as the information provided, much of it unavailable to the American filmmakers. **120m/C VHS, Beta.** Yehoram Gaon, Assaf Dayan, Ori Levy, Klaus Kinski; ***D:*** Menahem Golan. Nominations: Academy Awards '77: Best Foreign Language Film. *MGM*

Operation War Zone 🦴 **1989** A platoon of soldiers uncovers a plot by corrupt officers to continue the Vietnam war and sell weapons. **86m/C VHS, Beta.** Joe Spinell. *AIP*

The Oppermann Family 🦴🦴½ **1982** On two tapes, the long epic made for German television about a family trying to survive in Berlin during the rise of Hitler. In German with subtitles. **238m/C VHS, Beta.** *GE* ***D:*** Egon Monk. *FCT, APD*

The Opponent 🦴🦴 **1989 (R)** A young boxer saves a young woman's life, not realizing that she has mob connections, thus embroiling him in a world of crime. **102m/C VHS, LV.** *IT* Daniel Greene, Ernest Borgnine, Julian Gemma, Mary Stavin, Kelly Shaye Smith; ***D:*** Sergio Martino. *VMK*

Opportunity Knocks 🦴🦴½ **1990 (PG-13)** Carvey's first feature film has him impersonating a friend of a rich suburbanite's family while hiding from a vengeful gangster. They buy it, and give him a job and the daughter. Not hilarious, but not a dud either. **105m/C VHS, Beta, LV.** Dana Carvey, Robert Loggia, Todd Graff, Milo O'Shea, Julia Campbell, James Tolkan, Doris Belack, Sally Gracie, Del Close; ***D:*** Donald Petrie; ***W:*** Mitchel Katlin, Nat Bernstein; ***M:*** Miles Goodman. *MCA*

Opposing Force 🦴🦴½ *Hellcamp* **1987 (R)** The commander of an Air Force camp simulates prisoner-of-war conditions for realistic training, but he goes too far, creating all too real torture situations. He preys on the only female in the experiment, raping her as part of the training. A decent thriller. **97m/C VHS, Beta.** Tom Skerritt, Lisa Eichhorn, Anthony Zerbe, Richard Roundtree, Robert Wightman, John Considine, George Kee Chueng, Paul Joynt, Jay Louden, Ken Wright, Dan Hamilton; ***D:*** Eric Karson; ***W:*** Gil Cowan; ***M:*** Mark Donohue. *HBO*

The Opposite Sex 🦴🦴 **1956** Bevy of women battle mediocre script in adaptation of 1939's "The Women." Laserdisc includes original trailer and letterboxed screen. ♫The Opposite Sex; Dere's Yellow Gold on de Trees (De Banana); A Perfect Love; Rock and Roll Tumbleweed; Now! Baby, Now; Jungle Red; Young Man with a Horn. **115m/C VHS, LV.** June Allyson, Joan Collins, Dolores Gray, Ann Sheridan, Ann Miller, Leslie Nielsen, Agnes Moorehead, Joan Blondell; ***D:*** David Miller; ***W:*** Fay Kanin, Michael Kanin. *MGM, FCT*

The Opposite Sex and How to Live With Them 🦴 **1993 (R)** Yuppies (Gross and Cox) from different backgrounds (he's Jewish, she's a WASP) meet, fall in love, fight, break up, and reunite, inspiring yawning disinterest. All this while their two best buddies (Pollak and Brown) offer what are meant to be "candid insights" delivered directly to the camera. Flat and formulaic romantic comedy wants to sparkle, but script lacks both purpose and point, and worse, takes way too much time not getting there. Winner of the annual Grammar Police award for the worst example of a semantically incorrect title in recent years. **86m/C VHS.** Arye Gross, Courteney Cox, Kevin Pollak, Julie Brown, Mitchell Ryan, Philip Bruns, Mitzi McCall, B.J. Ward; ***D:*** Matthew Meshekoff; ***W:*** Noah Stern; ***M:*** Ira Newborn. *HBO*

Options 🦴🦴 **1988 (PG)** Nerdy Hollywood agent Salinger treks to Africa to "option" a princess's life story—hence the title. He gets mixed up with her kidnapping and with her. Misplaced cameos by Roberts and Anton drag down the overall comedy content, which isn't to high to begin with. **105m/C VHS, LV.** Matt Salinger, Joanna Pacula, John Kani, James Keach; ***Cameos:*** Susan Anton, Eric Roberts; ***D:*** Camilo Vila; ***W:*** Edward Decter. *LIV, VES*

The Oracle 🦴 **1985** A woman takes a new apartment only to find that the previous occupant's spirit is still a resident. The spirit tries to force her to take revenge on his murderers. Not bad for a low-budget thriller, but bad editing is a distraction. **94m/C VHS, Beta.** Caroline Capers Powers, Roger Neil; ***D:*** Roberta Findlay. *LIV*

Orca *Woof! Orca—Killer Whale* **1977 (PG)** Ridiculous premise has a killer whale chasing bounty hunter Harris to avenge the murder of its pregnant mate. Great for gore lovers, especially when the whale chomps Derek's leg off. **92m/C VHS, Beta, LV.** Richard Harris, Charlotte Rampling, Bo Derek, Keenan Wynn, Will Sampson; ***D:*** Michael Anderson Sr.; ***C:*** Ted Moore; ***M:*** Ennio Morricone. *PAR*

Orchestra Wives 🦴🦴🦴 **1942** A drama bursting with wonderful Glenn Miller music. A woman marries a musician and goes on the road with the band and the other wives. Trouble springs up with the sultry singer who desperately wants the woman's new husband. The commotion spreads throughout the group. ♫People Like You and Me; At Last; Serenade in Blue; I've Got a Gal in Kalamazoo. **98m/B VHS, Beta, LV.** George Montgomery, Glenn Miller, Lynn Bari, Carole Landis, Jackie Gleason, Cesar Romero, Ann Rutherford, Virginia Gilmore, Mary Beth Hughes, Harry (Henry) Morgan; ***D:*** Archie Mayo. Nominations: Academy Awards '42: Best Song ("I've Got a Gal in Kalamazoo"). *FXV, FCT*

Ordeal by Innocence 🦴½ **1984 (PG-13)** Sutherland is an amateur sleuth in 1950s England convinced he has proof that a convicted murderer is innocent, but no one wishes to reopen the case. Big-name cast is essentially wasted. Based on an Agatha Christie story. **91m/C VHS, Beta, LV.** Donald Sutherland, Christopher Plummer, Faye Dunaway, Sarah Miles, Ian McShane, Diana Quick, Annette Crosbie, Michael Elphick; ***D:*** Desmond Davis; ***C:*** Billy Williams; ***M:*** Pino Donaggio. *MGM*

The Ordeal of Dr. Mudd 🦴🦴🦴 **1980** His name was Mudd—a fitting moniker after he unwittingly aided President Lincoln's assassin. Dr. Mudd set John Wilkes Boothe's leg, broken during the assassination, and was jailed for conspiracy. He became a hero in prison for his aid during yellow fever epidemics and was eventually released. A strong and intricate performance by Weaver keeps this made-for-television drama interesting. Mudd's descendants are still trying to completely clear his name of any wrongdoing in the Lincoln assassination. **143m/C VHS, Beta.** Dennis Weaver, Susan Sullivan, Richard Dysart, Michael McGuire, Nigel Davenport, Arthur Hill; ***D:*** Paul Wendkos. *LIV*

Order of the Black Eagle 🦴½ **1987 (R)** A Bond-ish spy and his sidekick, Typhoon the Baboon, battle neo-Nazis planning to bring Hitler back to life in this silly tongue-in-cheek thriller. **93m/C VHS, Beta.** *GB* Ian Hunter, Charles K. Bibby, William T. Hicks, Jill Donnellan; ***D:*** Worth Keeter. *CEL*

Order of the Eagle 🦴½ **1989** An innocent scouting trip turns into a non-stop nightmare when an Eagle Scout uncovers some dangerous information. **88m/C VHS, Beta.** Frank Stallone. *AIP*

Order to Kill 🦴🦴½ **1973** A gambling boss puts out a contract on a hit man. **110m/C VHS, Beta.** Jose Ferrer, Helmut Berger, Sydne Rome, Kevin McCarthy; ***D:*** Jose Maesso. *NO*

Ordet ♂♂♂½ *The Word* **1955** A man who believes he is Jesus Christ is ridiculed until he begins performing miracles, which result in the rebuilding of a broken family. A statement on the nature of religious faith vs. fanaticism by the profoundly religious Dreyer, and based on the play by Kaj Munk. In Danish with English subtitles. **126m/B VHS, Beta.** *DK* Henrik Malberg; ***D:*** Carl Theodor Dreyer. Golden Globe Awards '56: Best Foreign Film; National Board of Review Awards '57: 5 Best Foreign Films of the Year; Venice Film Festival '55: Best Film. *NOS, WFV, INJ*

Ordinary Heroes ♂♂½ **1985** The story is familiar but the leads make it worthwhile. Anderson is strong as a blinded Vietnam vet readjusting to life at home. Bertinelli's portrayal of his former girlfriend is eloquent. Nice work on an overdone story. **105m/C VHS.** Richard Dean Anderson, Doris Roberts, Valerie Bertinelli; ***D:*** Peter H. Cooper. *HBO*

Ordinary Magic ♂♂½ **1993** Teenaged Jeffrey was raised in India, picking up more than a little eastern wisdom along the way. After the death of his parents Jeffrey comes to the U.S. to live with his aunt where he sticks out not only as the new kid but as a decided oddball. But he manages to make some new friends and teach a few lessons about individuality along the way. Adapted from the novel by Malcolm Bosse. **96m/C VHS.** David Fox, Glenne Headly, Heath Lamberts, Ryan Reynolds; ***Cameos:*** Paul Anka; ***D:*** Giles Walker; ***W:*** Jefferson Lewis. *TRI*

Ordinary People ♂♂♂½ **1980 (R)** Powerful, well-acted story of a family's struggle to deal with one son's accidental death and the other's subsequent guilt-ridden suicide attempt. Features strong performances by all, but Moore is especially believable as the cold and rigid mother. McGovern's film debut as well as Redford's directorial debut. Based on the novel by Judith Guest. **124m/C VHS, Beta, LV.** Mary Tyler Moore, Donald Sutherland, Timothy Hutton, Judd Hirsch, M. Emmet Walsh, Elizabeth McGovern, Adam Baldwin, Dinah Manoff, James B. Sikking; ***D:*** Robert Redford; ***W:*** Alvin Sargent; ***C:*** John Bailey; ***M:*** Marvin Hamlisch. Academy Awards '80: Best Adapted Screenplay, Best Director (Redford), Best Picture, Best Supporting Actor (Hutton); Golden Globe Awards '81: Best Actress—Drama (Moore), Best Director (Redford), Best Film—Drama, Best Supporting Actor (Hutton); National Board of Review Awards '80: 10 Best Films of the Year, Best Director (Redford); Writers Guild of America '80: Best Adapted Screenplay; Nominations: Academy Awards '80: Best Actress (Moore), Best Supporting Actor (Hirsch). *PAR, BTV*

Oregon Trail **1939** A western serial in 15 chapters, each 13 minutes long. **195m/B VHS, Beta.** Johnny Mack Brown, Fuzzy Knight; ***D:*** Ford Beebe. *VCN, DVT, MLB*

The Organization ♂♂♂ **1971 (PG)** Poitier's third and final portrayal of Detective Virgil Tibbs, first seen in "In the Heat of the Night." This time around he battles a drug smuggling ring with a vigilante group. Good action scenes and a realistic ending. **108m/C VHS, Beta.** Sidney Poitier, Barbara McNair, Sheree North, Raul Julia; ***D:*** Don Medford; ***C:*** Joseph Biroc. *MGM, FOX*

Organized Crime & Triad Bureau ♂♂ *Chungon Satluk Linggei* **1993** Determined Lee and his cop team seal off crowded Hong Kong island Cheung Chai to trap mob boss Tung and his tootsie. And the bystanders better just get out of the way. Lots of action; Chinese with subtitles. **91m/C VHS, LV.** *HK* Danny Lee, Anthony Wong, Cecilia Yip; ***D:*** Kirk Wong. *TAI*

Orgy of the Dead *Woof!* **1965** Classic anticanon film scripted by Ed Wood, Jr. from his own novel. Two innocent travelers are forced to watch an even dozen nude spirits dance in a cardboard graveyard. Hilariously bad. **90m/C VHS, Beta.** Criswell, Fawn Silver, William Bates, Pat Barringer; ***D:*** A.C. Stephen; ***W:*** Edward D. Wood Jr. *RHI*

Orgy of the Vampires ♂ *Vampire's Night Orgy* **1973 (R)** Tourists wander into village during cocktail hour. **86m/C VHS.** *SP IT* Jack Taylor, Charo Soriano, Dianik Zurakowska, John Richard; ***D:*** Leon Klimovsky. *SNC*

Oriane ♂♂ **1985** A troubled Venezuelan woman must leave France for her native soil when her aunt dies. Once there, in the place where she spent youthful summers, she begins to recall her incestuous past. **88m/C VHS.** Deniela Sliverio, Doris Wells, Philippe Rouleau, David Crotto; ***D:*** Fina Torres. *NO*

The Original Fabulous Adventures of Baron Munchausen ♂♂½ *The Fabulous Baron Munchausen* **1961** An adventure fantasy that takes the hero all over, from the belly of a whale, eventually landing him on the surface of the moon. **84m/C VHS, LV.** *CZ* Milos Kopecky, Jana Brejchova, Rudolph Jelinek, Jan Werich; ***D:*** Karel Zeman. *NO*

The Original Flash Gordon Collection **1991** Four vintage Flash Gordon serials from the 1930s were recently re-edited into feature length films and released as this collection. Great stuff, including "Spaceship to the Unknown," "Deadly Ray From Mars," "Peril From Planet Mongo," and "Purple Death From Outer Space." **366m/B VHS.** Buster Crabbe. *QHV, FCT*

Original Gangstas ♂♂ **1996 (R)** In Hollywood everything old eventually becomes new again. John Bookman (Williamson) returns to his old neighborhood in Gary, Indiana after his father is brutally shot by a gang leader. Things have changed from Bookman's days of gang banging, with the streets swarming with young machine gun-toting lowlifes. Bent on revenge, cigar chewing Bookman, aided by childhood friends Jake (Jim Brown), Slick (Richard Roundtree) and Bubba (Ron O'Neal), decide to take back their streets with a little help from Foxy Brown herself (Grier), as a greiving mother. The nostalgia quotient is high watching these '70's blaxploitation stars together in one movie, older, more gray and a little wider, but still able to kick butt. Serious topic (gang violence) is lost in a conventional vigilante vehicle, which sacrifices a message for an all-too-familiar and bloody showdown. **98m/C VHS.** Jim Brown, Fred Williamson, Pam Grier, Ron O'Neal, Richard Roundtree, Paul Winfield; ***D:*** Larry Cohen; ***W:*** Aubrey Rattan; ***C:*** Carlos Gonzalez; ***M:*** Vladimir Horunzhy. *NYR*

Original Intent ♂♂ **1991 (PG)** A successful lawyer, facing a mid-life crisis, jeopardizes both his family and career when he decides to defend a homeless shelter from eviction proceedings. What might have been a powerful drama about one man's crusade to help the homeless instead merely melodramtic. Actor/activist Sheen appears briefly as a homeless man. **97m/C VHS, Beta.** Jay Richardson, Candy Clark, Kris Kristofferson, Vince Edwards, Cindy Pickett, Robert DoQui, Joseph Campanella; ***Cameos:*** Martin Sheen; ***D:*** Robert Marcarelli; ***W:*** Robert Marcarelli. *PAR*

Orion's Belt ♂♂ **1985 (PG)** Three Norwegian adventurers must flee through the wilderness when they discover a secret Soviet base on the Europe/Russia/Greenland border. **87m/C VHS, Beta.** *VTR, NWV*

Orlando ♂♂♂ **1992 (PG-13)** Potter's sumptuous film adaptation of Virginia Woolf's 1928 novel, which covers 400 years in the life of an English nobleman, who not only defies death but evolves from a man to a woman in the intervening years. Orlando (Swinton) is first seen as a young man in the court of Queen Elizabeth I (Crisp) but after a deep sleep it's suddenly 40 years later. Things like this just keep happening and by 1750 he is now a she (and remains so), finding and losing love, and eventually gaining fulfillment in the 20th century. Elaborate productions never overwhelm Swinton's serene, self-assured performance. **93m/C VHS, LV.** *GB* Tilda Swinton, Charlotte Valandrey, Billy Zane, Lothaire Bluteau, John Wood, Quentin Crisp, Heathcote Williams, Dudley Sutton, Thom Hoffman; ***D:*** Sally Potter; ***W:*** Sally Potter. Nominations: Academy Awards '93: Best Art Direction/Set Decoration, Best Costume Design; Independent Spirit Awards '94: Best Foreign Film. *COL*

The Orphan ♂½ **1979** A young orphaned boy seeks revenge against his cruel aunt who is harassing him with sadistic discipline. **80m/C VHS, Beta.** Mark Evans, Joanna Miles, Peggy Feury; ***D:*** John Ballard. *PSM, RHI*

An Orphan Boy of Vienna ♂½ **1937** A homeless street urchin with a beautiful singing voice is accepted into the wonderful world of the Choir, but is later unjustly accused of stealing. Performances by the Vienna Boys' Choir redeem the melodramatic plot. In German with English subtitles. **87m/B VHS, Beta.** *GE* ***D:*** Max Neufeld. *VYY, IHF, GLV*

Orphan Train ♂♂♂ **1979** A woman realizes her New York soup kitchen can't do enough to help the neighborhood orphans, so she takes a group of children out West in hopes of finding families to adopt them. Their journey is chronicled by a newspaper photographer and a social worker. Based on the actual "orphan trains" of the mid- to late 1800s. From the novel by Dorothea G. Petrie. Made for television. **150m/C VHS.** Jill Eikenberry, Kevin Dobson, Glenn Close, Linda Manz; ***D:*** William A. Graham. *PSM, KAR, HHE*

Orphans ♂♂♂ **1983** A sensitive edge-of-glasnost portrait of a young boy's discovery of love, friendship, and literature. In Russian with English subtitles. **97m/C VHS, Beta.** ***D:*** Nikolai Gubenko. *FCT*

Orphans ♂♂♂ **1987 (R)** A gangster on the run is kidnapped by a tough New York orphan but soon takes control by befriending his abductor's maladjusted brother. Eventually each brother realizes his need for the older man, who has become a father figure to them. This very quirky film is salvaged by good performances. Based on the play by Lyle Kessler. **116m/C VHS, Beta, LV.** Albert Finney, Matthew Modine, Kevin Anderson; ***D:*** Alan J. Pakula; ***W:*** Lyle Kessler; ***M:*** Michael Small. *ORI, WAR*

Orphans of the North ♂ **1940** The story of Bedrock Brown's search for gold and his lost partner. Filmed on location in Alaska with non-professional actors. Impressive footage of America's "last frontier," including the flora and fauna. **56m/C VHS, Beta, 8mm.** ***D:*** Norman Dawn; ***W:*** Susan Denis. *VYY*

Orphans of the Storm ♂♂♂½ **1921** Two sisters are separated and raised in opposite worlds—one by thieves, the other by aristocrats. Gish's poignant search for her sister is hampered by the turbulent maelstrom preceding the French Revolution. Silent. Based on the French play "The Two Orphans." **190m/B VHS, LV.** Lillian Gish, Dorothy Gish, Monte Blue, Joseph Schildkraut; ***D:*** D.W. Griffith. *NOS, MRV, CCB*

Orpheus ♂♂½ *Orphee* **1949** Cocteau's fascinating, innovative retelling of the Orpheus legend in a modern, though slightly askew, Parisian setting. Classic visual effects and poetic imagery. In French with English subtitles. **95m/B VHS, Beta, 8mm.** Jean Marais, Francois Perier, Maria Casares; ***D:*** Jean Cocteau. *SNC, NOS, SUE*

Orpheus Descending ♂♂½ **1991** Lust and hatred in small Southern town. Confusing, poorly paced, but interesting for Anderson as Elvis-style drifter and Redgrave as woman addicted to love. Made-for-cable version of the 1989 Broadway revival of Tennessee Williams play. **117m/C VHS.** Vanessa Redgrave, Kevin Anderson, Anne Twomey, Miriam Margolyes, Brad Sullivan, Sloane Shelton, Patti Allison; ***D:*** Peter Hall; ***W:*** Peter Hall, Tennessee Williams. *TTC, FCT*

Osa ♂½ **1985** Yet another post-nuke flick with the usual devastated landscape, leather-clad survivors, and hokey dialog. It's sometimes funny, despite everyone's effort to make it dramatic. The supposed plot centers on one woman's efforts to break up a man's monopoly on clean water. **94m/C VHS.** Kelly Lynch, Daniel Grimm, Phillip Vincent, Etienne Chicot, John Forristal, Pete Walker, David Hausman, Bill Moseley; ***D:*** Oleg Egorov; ***M:*** Mason Daring. *NO*

Osaka Elegy ♂♂½ *Woman of Osaka* **1936** A study of Japanese cultural rules when society condemns a woman for behavior that is acceptable for a man. In Japanese with English subtitles. **71m/B VHS.** *JP* Isuzu Yamada; ***D:*** Kenji Mizoguchi. *INJ*

The Oscar ♂½ **1966 (R)** Unless you enjoy razzing bad acting, this is not for you. Meant as a comeuppance for Hollywood, by Hollywood, this story of a star climbing the ladder of success and squashing fingers on every rung is too schlocky to succeed. The climax, when the scumbag star thinks he's won an Oscar and stands up, only to find it's for someone else, was based on Frank Capra's embarrassing experience with the same situation. **119m/C VHS, Beta.** Stephen Boyd, Elke Sommer, Jill St. John, Tony Bennett, Milton Berle, Eleanor Parker, Joseph Cotten, Edie Adams, Ernest Borgnine, Ed Begley Sr., Walter Brennan, Broderick Crawford, James Dunn, Peter Lawford, Merle Oberon, Bob Hope, Frank Sinatra; ***D:*** Russel Rouse; ***C:*** Joseph Ruttenberg. Nominations: Academy Awards '66: Best Art Direction/Set Decoration (Color), Best Costume Design (Color). *SUE*

Oscar ꗃꗃ **1991 (PG)** The improbable casting of Stallone in a 1930s style crime farce (an attempt to change his image) is hard to imagine, and harder to believe. Stallone has little to do as he plays the straight man in this often ridiculous story of a crime boss who swears he'll go straight. Cameos aplenty, with Curry's the most notable. Based on a French play by Claude Magnier. **109m/C VHS, LV.** Sylvester Stallone, Ornella Muti, Peter Riegert, Vincent Spano, Marisa Tomei, Kirk Douglas, Art LaFleur, Ken Howard, Chazz Palminteri, Tim Curry, Don Ameche, Richard Romanus; ***D:*** John Landis; ***W:*** Michael Barrie, Jim Mulholland; ***M:*** Elmer Bernstein. *COL, IME, TOU*

Oscar's Greatest Moments: 1971-1991 **1992** Collection of highlights from the Oscar ceremonies, featuring footage from the past 21 years. Proceeds from video sales benefit the Center for Motion Picture Study. **110m/C VHS, LV, 8mm.** ***D:*** Jeff Margolis. *COL, BTV*

Ossessione ꗃꗃꗃ½ **1942** An adaptation of "The Postman Always Rings Twice," transferred to Fascist Italy, where a drifter and an innkeeper's wife murder her husband. Visconti's first feature, which initiated Italian neo-realism, was not released in the U.S. until 1975 due to a copyright dispute. In Italian with English subtitles. **135m/B VHS, Beta.** *IT* Massimo Girotti, Clara Calamai, Juan deLanda, Elio Marcuzzo; ***D:*** Luchino Visconti. *FCT, INJ, TPV*

The Osterman Weekend ꗃꗃ **1983 (R)** Peckinpah was said to have disliked the story and the script in this, his last film, which could account for the convoluted and confusing end result. Adding to the problem is the traditional difficulty of adapting Ludlum's complex psychological thrillers for the screen. The result: cast members seem to not quite "get it" as they portray a group of friends, one of whom has been convinced by the CIA that the others are all Soviet spies. **102m/C VHS, Beta, LV.** Burt Lancaster, Rutger Hauer, Craig T. Nelson, Dennis Hopper, John Hurt, Chris Sarandon, Meg Foster, Helen Shaver; ***D:*** Sam Peckinpah; ***M:*** Lalo Schifrin. *NO*

Otaku no Video *Fan's Video* **1991** Fictionalized animated history of the famed Japanese animation studio Gainax, including strange interviews with rabid fans who want to "Otakunize" the human race. Contains both episodes: "Otaku no Video" (1982) and "More Otaku no Video" (1985). In Japanese with English subtitles. **100m/C VHS.** *JP ANI*

Otello ꗃꗃꗃ½ **1986 (PG)** An uncommon film treat for opera fans, with a stellar performance by Domingo as the troubled Moor who murders his wife in a fit of jealous rage and later finds she was never unfaithful. Be prepared, however, for changes from the Shakespeare and Verdi stories, necessitated by the film adaptation. Highly acclaimed and awarded; in Italian with English subtitles. **123m/C VHS, Beta, LV.** *IT* Placido Domingo, Katia Ricciarelli, Justino Diaz; ***D:*** Franco Zeffirelli. Nominations: Academy Awards '86: Best Costume Design. *HMV, MED, MVD*

Othello ꗃꗃ½ **1922** A silent version of Shakespeare's tragedy, featuring Jannings as the tragic Moor. Titles are in English; with musical score. **81m/B VHS, Beta.** *GE* Emil Jannings, Lya de Putti, Werner Krauss; ***D:*** Dimitri Buchowetzki. *VYY, NOS, DVT*

Othello ꗃꗃꗃ **1952** Welles' striking adaptation of the Shakespeare tragedy casts him as the self-deluding Moor, with MacLiammoir as the despicable Iago and Cloutier as innocent victim, Desdemona. Welles filmed his epic over a four-year period due to budget difficulties, which also resulted in his filming in a number of different countries and settings. The film underwent a $1 million restoration, supervised by Welles' daughter, prior to its limited theatrical re-release in 1992. **90m/B VHS, LV.** Orson Welles, Michael MacLiammoir, Suzanne Cloutier, Robert Coote, Hilton Edwards, Michael Lawrence, Nicholas Bruce, Fay Compton, Doris Dowling, Jean Davis, Joseph Cotten, Joan Fontaine; ***D:*** Orson Welles. Cannes Film Festival '52: Best Film. *ACA*

Othello ꗃꗃ½ **1995 (R)** Fishburne stars as Shakespeare's tragic Moor, with Branagh as silken agitator Iago, and Jacob as the tragic Desdemona. First time director Oliver Parker (brother Nathaniel is also in the film) drastically cut the play, rearranging scenes (and even adding material)—purists will no doubt scream, but performances carry the production. Through the clever use of asides directed at the camera, Branagh's Iago makes the viewer feel like an accomplice in the plot. French-speaking Jacob, however, seems to have a hard time pronouncing the Shakespearean dialogue. Fishburne's imposing performance as Othello is the first by an actor of African descent in a major motion picture. **125m/C VHS, LV.** Laurence "Larry" Fishburne, Irene Jacob, Kenneth Branagh, Nathaniel Parker, Michael Maloney, Anna Patrick, Nicholas Farrell, Indra Ove, Michael Sheen, Andre Oumansky, Philip Locke, John Savident, Gabriele Ferzetti, Pierre Vaneck; ***D:*** Oliver Parker; ***W:*** Oliver Parker; ***C:*** David Johnson; ***M:*** Charlie Mole. Nominations: Screen Actors Guild Award '95: Best Supporting Actor (Branagh). *COL*

The Other ꗃꗃꗃ **1972 (PG)** Eerie, effective thriller adapted by Tyron from his supernatural novel. Twin brothers represent good and evil in a 1930s Connecticut farm town beset with gruesome murders and accidents. A good scare. **100m/C VHS, Beta.** Martin Udvarnoky, Chris Udvarnoky, Uta Hagen, Diana Muldaur, Christopher Connelly, Victor French, John Ritter; ***D:*** Robert Mulligan; ***C:*** Robert L. Surtees; ***M:*** Jerry Goldsmith. *FOX*

Other Hell ꗃ **1985 (R)** Schlocky Italian-made chiller has the devil inhabiting a convent where he does his damnest to upset the nuns. Gross, but not scary—lots of cliche dark-hallway scenes and fright music. **88m/C VHS, Beta.** *IT* Carlo De Meyo, Francesca Carmeno; ***D:*** Stefan Oblowsky. *LIV, VES*

Other People's Money ꗃꗃ½ **1991 (R)** DeVito is "Larry the Liquidator," a corporate raider with a heart of stone and a penchant for doughnuts. When he sets his sights on a post-smokestack era, family-owned cable company, he gets a taste of love for the first time in his life. He and Miller, the daughter of the company president and also its legal advisor, court one another while sparring over the fate of the company. Unbelievably clipped ending mars otherwise enterprising comedy about the triumph of greed in corporate America. Based on the off-Broadway play by Jerry Sterner. **101m/C VHS, LV, 8mm.** Danny DeVito, Penelope Ann Miller, Dean Jones, Gregory Peck, Piper Laurie, Tom Aldredge, R.D. Call; ***D:*** Norman Jewison; ***W:*** Alvin Sargent; ***C:*** Haskell Wexler; ***M:*** David Newman. *WAR, CCB*

The Other Side of Midnight *Woof!* **1977 (R)** The dreary, depressingly shallow life story of a poor French girl, dumped by an American GI, who sleeps her way to acting stardom and a profitable marriage, then seeks revenge for the jilt. Based on Sidney Sheldon's novel, it's not even titillating—just a real downer. **160m/C VHS, Beta, LV.** Susan Sarandon, Marie-France Pisier, John Beck, Raf Vallone, Clu Gulager, Sorrell Booke; ***D:*** Charles Jarrott; ***W:*** Daniel Taradash; ***C:*** Fred W. Koenekamp. Nominations: Academy Awards '77: Best Costume Design. *FOX*

The Other Side of the Law ꗃꗃ **1995 (R)** Man makes a wilderness hideout with his son after killing his wife's murderer. But when the boy grows up, dad decides to send him back into civilization for education, leading to nothing but trouble. **96m/C VHS.** Juergen Prochnow; ***D:*** Gilles Carle. *VMK*

The Other Side of the Mountain ꗃꗃ *A Window to the Sky* **1975 (PG)** Tear-jerking true story of Olympic hopeful skier Jill Kinmont, paralyzed in a fall. Bridges helps her pull her life together. A sequel followed two years later. Based on the book "A Long Way Up" by E. G. Valens. **102m/C VHS, Beta.** Marilyn Hassett, Beau Bridges, Dabney Coleman, John David Garfield, Griffin Dunne; ***D:*** Larry Peerce; ***W:*** David Seltzer; ***M:*** Charles Fox. Nominations: Academy Awards '75: Best Song ("Richard's Window"). *MCA*

The Other Side of the Mountain, Part 2 ꗃꗃ **1978 (PG)** Quadriplegic Jill Kinmont, paralyzed in a skiing accident that killed her hopes for the Olympics, overcomes depression and the death of the man who helped her to recover. In this chapter, she falls in love again and finds happiness. More tears are jerked. **99m/C VHS, Beta.** Marilyn Hassett, Timothy Bottoms; ***D:*** Larry Peerce. *MCA*

Oubliette **1914** A peripheral version of Francois Villon, in what is a recently discovered and restored film, the earliest extant Chaney film. **35m/B VHS, Beta.** Lon Chaney Sr. *GVV, LSV*

Our Daily Bread ꗃꗃꗃ *Miracle of Life* **1934** Vidor's sequel to the 1928 "The Crowd." A young couple inherit a farm during the Depression and succeed in managing the land. A near-classic, with several sequences highly influenced by directors Alexander Dovshenko and Sergei Eisenstein. Director Vidor also co-scripted this film, risking bankruptcy to finance it. **80m/B VHS, Beta, LV.** Karen Morley, Tom Keene, John Qualen, Barbara Pepper, Addison Richards; ***D:*** King Vidor; ***W:*** King Vidor. *NOS, SUE, BAR*

Our Dancing Daughters ꗃꗃ½ **1928** Flapper (Crawford on the brink of stardom) falls hard for millionaire who's forced into arranged marriage, but obliging little missus kicks bucket so Crawford can step in. **98m/B VHS, Beta.** Joan Crawford, Johnny Mack Brown, Nils Asther, Dorothy Sebastian, Anita Page; ***D:*** Harry Beaumont; ***C:*** George Barnes. Nominations: Academy Awards '29: Best Cinematography, Best Writing. *MGM, FCT*

Our Family Business ꗃꗃ **1981** Made for television and meant as a series pilot, this generally plodding "Godfather"-type story is saved by good performances by Wanamaker and Milland. **74m/C VHS.** Sam Wanamaker, Vera Miles, Ray Milland, Ted Danson, Chip Mayer; ***D:*** Robert Collins. *LIV*

Our Gang **1926** Two silent "Our Gang" comedies, including "Thundering Fleas" and "Shivering Spooks." **57m/B VHS, Beta, 8mm.** Joe Cobb, Farina Hoskins, Mary Kornman, Mickey Daniels, Scooter Lowry. *VYY*

Our Gang Comedies **194?** The five shorts on this cassette show the gang at their comedic best. They include "The Big Premiere," "Bubbling Troubles," "Clown Princes," "Don't Lie" and "Farm Hands." **53m/B VHS, Beta, LV.** Robert (Bobby) Blake, Billie "Buckwheat" Thomas, George "Spanky" McFarland, Darla Hood, Carl "Alfalfa" Switzer, Tommy "Butch" Bond, Eugene "Porky" Lee, Shirley "Muggsy" Coates, Joe "Corky" Geil, Billy "Froggy" Laughlin. *MGM, VTR*

Our Gang Comedy Festival **1988** A 20-year span of comedy from the Little Rascals, including rare silent features. **45m/B VHS.** Joe Cobb, Farina Hoskins, Mary Kornman, Mickey Daniels, Scooter Lowry. *GKK*

Our Gang Comedy Festival 2 **1989** More riotous good times with The Little Rascals, including silent footage. **45m/B VHS.** Joe Cobb, Farina Hoskins, Mary Kornman, Mickey Daniels, Scooter Lowry. *GKK*

Our Hospitality ꗃꗃꗃꗃ **1923** One of Keaton's finest silent films, with all the elements in place. William McKay (Keaton) travels to the American South on a quaint train (a near-exact replica of the Stephenson Rocket), to claim an inheritance as the last survivor of his family. En route, a young woman traveler informs him that her family has had a long, deadly feud with his, and that they intend to kill him. McKay resolves to get the inheritance, depending on the Southern rule of hospitality to guests to save his life until he can make his escape. Watch for the river scene where, during filming, Keaton's own life was really in danger. By the way, Keaton married his leading lady in real life. **74m/B VHS, LV.** Buster Keaton, Natalie Talmadge, Joe Keaton, Buster Keaton Jr., Kitty Bradbury, Joe Roberts; ***D:*** Buster Keaton, John Blystone. *HBO*

Our Little Girl ☠☠ **1935 (PG)** A precocious little tyke tries to reunite her estranged parents by running away to their favorite vacation spot. Sure to please Shirley Temple fans, despite a lackluster script. **65m/B VHS, Beta.** Shirley Temple, Joel McCrea, Rosemary Ames, Lyle Talbot, Erin O'Brien Moore; ***D:*** John S. Robertson. *FOX*

Our Man Flint ☠☠ **1966** James Bond clone Derek Flint uses gadgets and his ingenuity to save the world from an evil organization, GALAXY, that seeks world domination through control of the weather. The plot moves quickly around many bikini-clad women, but still strains for effect. Spawned one sequel: "In Like Flint." **107m/C VHS, Beta, LV.** James Coburn, Lee J. Cobb, Gila Golan, Edward Mulhare, Benson Fong, Shelby Grant, Sigrid Valdis, Gianna Serra, James Brolin, Helen Funai, Michael St. Clair; ***D:*** Daniel Mann; ***C:*** Daniel F. Fapp; ***M:*** Jerry Goldsmith. *FOX*

Our Miss Brooks ☠☠½ **1956** Quietly pleasing version of the television series. Miss Brooks pursues the "mother's boy" biology professor. The father of the child she begins tutoring appears taken with her. The professor takes notice. **85m/B VHS.** Eve Arden, Gale Gordon, Nick Adams, Richard Crenna, Don Porter; ***D:*** Al Lewis. *WAR*

Our Modern Maidens ☠☠½ **1929** Scandalous jazz-age drama in which Crawford and Fairbanks both fall in love with other people before their wedding is to take place. This sequel to "Our Dancing Daughters" features beautiful gowns and lush, opulent Art Deco interiors. Based on a story by Josephine Lovett. **75m/B VHS.** Joan Crawford, Rod La Rocque, Douglas Fairbanks Jr., Anita Page, Josephine Dunn; ***D:*** Jack Conway; ***W:*** Josephine Lovett. *MGM*

Our Relations ☠☠☠½ **1936** Confusion reigns when Stan and Ollie meet the twin brothers they never knew they had, a pair of happy-go-lucky sailors. Laurel directs the pair through madcap encounters with their twins' wives and the local underworld. One of the pair's best efforts, though not well-remembered. Based on a story by W.W. Jacobs. **94m/B VHS, Beta.** Stan Laurel, Oliver Hardy, Alan Hale, Sidney Toler, James Finlayson, Daphne Pollard; ***D:*** Harry Lachman. *MED, CCB, MLB*

Our Sons ☠☠½ **1991** Two middle-aged moms strike up an unlikely friendship over their gay sons in this TV weeper. Arkansas waitress Luanna (Ann Margret) hasn't talked to son Donald (Ivanek) in years—now he's dying of AIDS. Successfull career woman Audrey (Andrews in her TV-movie debut) has seemingly accepted son James' (Grant) life with Donald and it's James who urges his mother to make contact with Luanna and persuade her to see Donald one last time. **100m/C VHS.** Julie Andrews, Ann-Margret, Hugh Grant, Zeljko Ivanek, Tony Roberts; ***D:*** John Erman; ***W:*** John Erman, William Hanley. *AEL*

Our Time ☠☠½ *Death of Her Innocence* **1974** An exclusive girls finishing school in the fifties is the setting for the friendship of Abby (Martin) and Muffy (Slade) and their first stirrings of romance. But when Muffy gets pregnant, tragedy awaits. Sappy. **91m/C VHS.** Pamela Sue Martin, Betsey Slade, Parker Stevenson, George O'Hanlon Jr., Roderick Cook, Edith Atwater, Meg Wyllie, Debralee Scott, Nora Heflin, Kathryn Holcomb, Robert Walden; ***D:*** Peter Hyams; ***W:*** Jane C. Stanton. *WAR*

Our Town ☠☠☠ **1940** Small-town New England life in Grover's Corners in the early 1900s is celebrated in this well-performed and directed adaptation of the Pulitzer Prize-winning play by Thornton Wilder. Film debut of Scott. **90m/B VHS, Beta.** Martha Scott, William Holden, Thomas Mitchell, Fay Bainter, Guy Kibbee, Beulah Bondi, Frank Craven; ***D:*** Sam Wood; ***M:*** Aaron Copland. National Board of Review Awards '40: 10 Best Films of the Year; Nominations: Academy Awards '40: Best Actress (Scott), Best Interior Decoration, Best Picture, Best Sound, Best Original Score. *CNG, MRV, NOS*

Our Town ☠☠☠ **1977** Television version of Thornton Wilder's classic play about everyday life in Grovers Corners, a small New England town at the turn of the century. It hews more closely to the style of the stage version than the earlier film version. **120m/C VHS, Beta, LV.** Ned Beatty, Sada Thompson, Ronny Cox, Glynnis O'Connor, Robby Benson, Hal Holbrook, John Houseman; ***D:*** Franklin J. Schaffner. *MAS*

Our Town ☠☠½ **1989** Filmed TV version of the Tony Award-winning Lincoln Center production of the Thornton Wilder play focusing on small-town life in Grover's Corners, New Hampshire. Gray is the omniscient Stage Manager, with Stolz and Miller as the young couple brought together by the everyday cycle of happiness and hardship. **104m/C VHS.** Eric Stoltz, Penelope Ann Miller, Spalding Gray; ***D:*** Gregory Mosher. *MAS*

Our Vines Have Tender Grapes ☠☠☠½ **1945** A change of pace role for the volatile Robinson who plays a kind Norwegian farmer, living in Wisconsin with his daughter, the spunky O'Brien. The film is made-up of small-town moments as O'Brien learns a few of life's lessons, eased by the thoughtful compassion of Robinson. Based on the novel "For Our Vines Have Tender Grapes" by George Victor Martin. **105m/B VHS.** Edward G. Robinson, Margaret O'Brien, James Craig, Agnes Moorehead, Jackie "Butch" Jenkins, Morris Carnovsky, Frances Gifford, Sara Haden, Louis Jean Heydt; ***D:*** Roy Rowland; ***W:*** Dalton Trumbo; ***C:*** Robert L. Surtees. *MGM, MOV, BTV*

Out ☠☠½ **1988** A drifter's travels throughout the U.S. from the sixties to the eighties. Successfully manages to satirize just about every conceivable situation but keeps from posturing by not taking itself too seriously. Adapted from an experimental novel by Ronald Sukenick. **88m/C VHS.** Peter Coyote, Danny Glover, O-Lan Shepard, Jim Haynie, Scott Beach, Semu Haute; ***D:*** Eli Hollander; ***W:*** Eli Hollander; ***M:*** David Cope. *NO*

Out Cold ☠½ **1989 (R)** Black comedy follows the misadventures of a butcher who believes he has accidentally frozen his business partner; the iced man's girlfriend, who really killed him; and the detective who tries to solve the crime. Too many poor frozen body jokes may leave the viewer cold. **91m/C VHS, Beta, LV.** John Lithgow, Teri Garr, Randy Quaid, Bruce McGill; ***D:*** Malcolm Mowbray; ***M:*** Michel Colombier. *HBO*

Out for Blood ☠☠ **1993 (R)** Attorney John Decker is living a happy life until his family is murdered by drug dealers. He turns vigilante, dubbed "Karateman" by the press, and finds himself hunted by the cops and the criminals. **?m/C VHS.** Don "The Dragon" Wilson, Shari Shattuck, Michael Delano, Kenneth McLeod, Todd Curtis, Timothy Baker, Howard Jackson, Bob Schott, Eric Lee; ***D:*** Richard W. Munchkin; ***W:*** David S. Green. *PMH*

Out for Justice ☠½ **1991 (R)** A psycho Brooklyn hood goes on a murder spree, and homeboy turned lone-wolf cop Seagal races other police and the mob to get at him. Bloodthirsty and profane, it does try to depict N.Y.C.'s Italian-American community—but 90 percent of them are dead by the end so what's the point? Better yet, why does it open with a quote from Arthur Miller? Better still, what's Daffy Duck doing on this tape peddling Warner Brothers T-shirts to kid viewers?! **91m/C VHS, Beta, LV, 8mm.** Steven Seagal, William Forsythe, Jerry Orbach. *WAR*

Out of Africa ☠☠☠ **1985 (PG)** An epic film of the years spent by Danish authoress Isak Dinesen (her true name is Karen Blixen) on a Kenya coffee plantation. She moved to Africa to marry, and later fell in love with Denys Finch-Hatten, a British adventurer. Based on several books, including biographies of the two lovers. Some critics loved the scenery and music; others despised the acting and the script. A definite "no" for those who love action. **161m/C VHS, Beta, LV.** Meryl Streep, Robert Redford, Klaus Maria Brandauer, Michael Kitchen, Malick Bowens, Michael Gough, Suzanna Hamilton, Rachel Kempson, Graham Crowden, Shane Rimmer, Donal McCann, Iman, Joseph Thiaka, Stephen Kinyanjui; ***D:*** Sydney Pollack; ***W:*** Kurt Luedtke; ***C:*** David Watkin; ***M:*** John Barry. Academy Awards '85: Best Adapted Screenplay, Best Art Direction/Set Decoration, Best Cinematography, Best Director (Pollack), Best Picture, Best Sound, Best Original Score; British Academy Awards '86: Best Adapted Screenplay; Golden Globe Awards '86: Best Film—Drama, Best Supporting Actor (Brandauer), Best Score; Los Angeles Film Critics Association Awards '85: Best Actress (Streep), Best Cinematography; National Board of Review Awards '85: Best Supporting Actor (Brandauer); New York Film Critics Awards '85: Best Cinematography, Best Supporting Actor (Brandauer); Nominations: Academy Awards '85: Best Actress (Streep), Best Costume Design, Best Supporting Actor (Brandauer). *MCA, BTV*

Out of Annie's Past ☠☠½ **1994 (R)** Successful career woman has managed to hide a dreadful secret from family and co-workers for some 10 years. But now the past is back to haunt her—seems Annie was once the prime suspect in a murder. Made for cable. **91m/C VHS.** Catherine Mary Stewart, Dennis Farina, Scott Valentine. *MCA*

Out of Bounds ☠½ **1986 (R)** An Iowa farmboy picks up the wrong bag at the Los Angeles airport, and is plunged into a world of crime, drugs, and murder. Plenty of action, but the fast pace can't hide huge holes in the script or the silliness of Hall playing a tough kid on the run from the law. **93m/C VHS, Beta, LV.** Anthony Michael Hall, Jenny Wright, Jeff Kober; ***D:*** Richard Tuggle; ***C:*** Bruce Surtees; ***M:*** Stewart Copeland. *COL*

Out of Control ☠ **1985 (R)** A plane full of rich teenagers crash on a secluded island and must battle a gang of vicious smugglers to survive. A teen sex theme keeps working its way in, leaving the viewer as confused as the actors and actresses appear to be. **78m/C VHS, Beta, LV.** Betsy Russell, Martin Hewitt, Claudia Udy, Andrew J. Lederer; ***D:*** Allan Holzman; ***W:*** Vicangelo Bullock; ***C:*** John A. Alonzo. *NWV, VTR*

Out of Order ☠½ **1984** A German-made film about people stuck in an office building's malevolent, free-thinking elevator. Dubbed. **87m/C VHS, Beta.** *GE* Renee Soutendijk, Goetz George, Wolfgang Kieling, Hannes Jaenicke; ***D:*** Carl Schenkel. *LIV, VES*

Out of Season ☠☠ *Winter Rates* **1975 (R)** Mother and teenage daughter compete for the attentions of the mother's mysterious ex-lover. We never know who wins the man in this enigmatic drama set in an English village, and hints of incest make the story even murkier. Had only a short run in the U.S. **90m/C VHS, Beta.** *GB* Cliff Robertson, Vanessa Redgrave, Susan George; ***D:*** Alan Bridges. *VCI*

Out of Sight, Out of Her Mind ☠☠ **1989 (R)** After witnessing her daughter burned alive, Alice is released from a mental institution. She tries to start a new life, but her daughter won't let her—she keeps appearing, crying out for help. **94m/C VHS, Beta, LV.** Susan Blakely, Eddie Albert, Wings Hauser. *PSM, PAR*

Out of Sync ☠½ **1995 (R)** Deejay Jason St. Julian gets in trouble with his bookies and L.A. detectives, one of whom forces him into an undercover job with a drug-dealing club owner. Then Jason falls for the dealer's girlfriend. Hip-hop soundtrack may provide the only interest. **105m/C VHS, LV.** L.L. Cool J., Victoria Dillard, Howard Hesseman, Ramy Zada, Don Yesso, Yaphet Kotto; ***D:*** Debbie Allen; ***W:*** Robert E. Dorn; ***M:*** Steve Tyrell. *LIV*

Out of the Blue ☠☠½ **1947** There's trouble in paradise for a married man when a shady lady passes out in his apartment. Thinking she is dead, he tries to get rid of the body. The antics with his neighbor and wife provide plenty of laughs. **86m/B VHS, Beta, LV.** George Brent, Virginia Mayo, Carole Landis, Turhan Bey, Ann Dvorak; ***D:*** Leigh Jason. *NWV*

Out of the Blue ☠☠☠ **1980 (R)** A harsh, violent portrait of a shattered family. When an imprisoned father's return fails to reunite this Woodstock-generation family, the troubled teenage daughter takes matters into her own hands. "Easy Rider" star Hopper seems to have reconsidered the effects of the 1960s. **94m/C VHS, Beta.** Dennis Hopper, Linda Manz, Raymond Burr; ***D:*** Dennis Hopper. Nominations: Cannes Film Festival '80: Best Film. *MED*

Out of the Body 🦴 **1988 (R)** A man is possessed by a spirit that likes to kill young, beautiful women. This makes him (and the viewer) uncomfortable. **91m/C VHS, LV.** Mark Hembrow, Tessa Humphries; ***D:*** Brian Trenchard-Smith. *NO*

Out of the Dark 🦴½ **1988 (R)** The female employees of a telephone-sex service are stalked by a killer wearing a clown mask in this tongue-in-cheek thriller. A few laughs amid the slaughter. Look for Divine. **98m/C VHS, Beta, LV.** Cameron Dye, Divine, Karen Black, Bud Cort, Lynn Danielson, Geoffrey Lewis, Paul Bartel, Tracey Walter, Silvania Gallardo, Starr Andreeff, Lainie Kazan, Tab Hunter; ***D:*** Michael Schroeder; ***W:*** James DeFelice; ***M:*** Paul Antonelli. *COL*

Out of the Darkness 🦴🦴🦴 **1985 (R)** A television movie about the personal life of the New York detective who hunted and arrested sexual killer Son of Sam. Sheen shines in a tight suspenser. **96m/C VHS, Beta, LV.** Martin Sheen, Hector Elizondo, Matt Clark, Jennifer Salt, Eddie Egan, Robert Trebor; ***D:*** Jud Taylor; ***W:*** T.S. Cook. *VTR, VMK*

Out of the Past 🦴🦴🦴½ *Build My Gallows High* **1947** A private detective gets caught in a complex web of love, murder, and money in this film noir classic. The plot is torturous but clear thanks to fine directing. Mitchum became an overnight star after this film, which was overlooked but now considered one of the best in its genre. Based on Geoffrey Homes' novel "Build My Gallows High." Remade in 1984 as "Against All Odds." **97m/B VHS, Beta, LV.** Robert Mitchum, Kirk Douglas, Jane Greer, Rhonda Fleming, Steve Brodie, Dickie Moore; ***D:*** Jacques Tourneur; ***W:*** Geoffrey Homes. *MED, TTC*

Out of the Rain 🦴🦴½ **1990 (R)** A small town becomes a hotbed of deceit and lies due to the influence of drugs. A man and and a woman engage in a passionate struggle to free themselves from the town's grip. **91m/C VHS, Beta, LV.** Bridget Fonda, Michael O'Keefe, John E. O'Keefe, John Seitz, Georgine Hall, Al Shannon; ***D:*** Gary Winick; ***W:*** Shem Bitterman. *CCB, LIV*

The Out-of-Towners 🦴🦴🦴 **1970 (G)** A pair of Ohio rubes travels to New York City and along the way everything that could go wrong does. Lemmon's performance is excellent and Simon's script is, as usual, both wholesome and funny. **98m/C VHS, Beta, LV.** Jack Lemmon, Sandy Dennis, Anne Meara, Sandy Baron, Billy Dee Williams; ***D:*** Arthur Hiller; ***W:*** Neil Simon. Writers Guild of America '70: Best Original Screenplay. *PAR*

Out on a Limb 🦴🦴 **1987** MacLaine plays herself in this made-for-television miniseries based on her best-selling book by the same name. In the midst of love affairs with an unnamed British politician and a mysterious teacher, she learns about her past, present, and future through meditation and her beliefs in reincarnation. Features footage of psychics performing spiritual channeling. Beautiful scenery filmed on location in California, Hong Kong, London, Hawaii, Sweden, and Peru, but the acting is just average, and the movie is slow in some parts. A 234-minute special collector's edition is also available. **160m/C VHS, Beta.** Shirley MacLaine, Charles Dance, John Heard, Anne Jackson, Jerry Orbach; ***D:*** Robert Butler. *PSM, WSH*

Out on a Limb 🦴 **1992 (PG)** Lame comedy follows the misadventures of financial whiz Bill Campbell (Broderick). His young sister is convinced their stepfather is a criminal and persuades her brother to return home. On his way, Bill is robbed and abandoned by a woman hitchhiker, then found by two moronic brothers. It also turns out his stepfather has a twin brother who wants revenge for past crimes. Frantic chase scenes and lots of noise do not a comedy make. Broderick and Jones also appeared together in "Ferris Bueller's Day Off." **82m/C VHS, Beta, LV.** Matthew Broderick, Jeffrey Jones, Heidi Kling, John C. Reilly, Marian Mercer, Larry Hankin, David Margulies; ***D:*** Francis Veber. *MGM*

Out on Bail 🦴½ **1989 (R)** A law-abiding citizen witnesses a murder, only to discover the crooked town council is behind the slaying. **102m/C VHS, Beta.** Robert Ginty, Kathy Shower, Tom Badal, Sydney Lassick; ***D:*** Gordon Hessler; ***W:*** Tom Badal, Jason Booth. *TWE*

Out There 🦴🦴½ **1995 (PG-13)** Cable sci-fi comedy finds photographer Delbert Mosley (Campbell) buying a Brownie camera at a garage sale and discovering the 25-year-old film shows pictures of a UFO encounter. Mosley then tries to verify the photos with a supermarket tabloid, the military, and UFO fanatics all on his trail. Fast-paced amusement with appealing performances. **98m/C VHS, Beta.** Bill Campbell, Wendy Schaal, Julie Brown, David Rasche, Paul Dooley, Bill Cobbs, Bob(cat) Goldthwait, Rod Steiger, June Lockhart, Jill St. John, Carel Struycken, Billy Bob Thornton, P.J. Soles; ***D:*** Sam Irvin; ***W:*** Thomas Strelich, Alison Nigh; ***C:*** Gary Tieche; ***M:*** Deborah Holland, Frankie Blue. *PAR*

Outbreak 🦴🦴🦴 **1994 (R)** Smuggled African monkey spits on someone who kisses someone else who sneezes on a bunch of people, thus initiating the spread of a highly infectious mystery disease in a northern California 'burb. Hoffman leads a team of scientists in a search for the anti-serum, but it's a secret government plot to exterminate the victims that literally sends Hoffman and crew into action movie cliche overdrive (add "helicopter" to the list of chase scene vehicles). Not that that's so bad—if the beat-the-clock tempo doesn't grab you, paranoia certainly will. But Hoffman's hardly a threat to Arnold or Sylvester as the next action hero, and the talented Russo remains suspiciously ravishing even with festering pustules. Based on two books: Richard Preston's "The Hot Zone" and Laurie Garrett's "The Coming Plague." **128m/C VHS, LV.** Dustin Hoffman, Rene Russo, Morgan Freeman, Donald Sutherland, Cuba Gooding Jr., Kevin Spacey, J.T. Walsh; ***D:*** Wolfgang Petersen; ***W:*** Robert Roy Pool, Laurence Dworet; ***C:*** Michael Ballhaus; ***M:*** James Newton Howard. New York Film Critics Awards '95: Best Supporting Actor (Spacey). *WAR*

The Outcast 🦴🦴 **1954** A young tough heads west to seize the family ranch wrongfully held by a conniving uncle. Of course he finds love as well, and enjoys gun and fistfights in this exciting though unspectacular western. **90m/C VHS.** John Derek, Jim Davis, Joan Davis; ***D:*** William Witney. *REP*

The Outcast 🦴½ **1984** Story of three brothers who live by the ax, love from the heart, hate with passion, and die violently. Trouble is they have to recite from a script written in crayon. **86m/C VHS.** Ben Dekker, Sandra Prinsloo. *REP*

The Outcasts 🦴🦴🦴 **1986** A Taiwanese film about young gay boys in an urban jungle who are given shelter and protection by an aging photographer. In Chinese with English subtitles. **102m/C VHS, Beta.** *TW* ***D:*** Yu Kan-Ping. *FCT*

Outcasts of the City 🦴🦴 **1958** The sort of negligible film filler that TV killed off. An American officer in post-WWII Germany romances a German girl, then gets blamed for the death of her Boche beau. **61m/B VHS.** Osa Massen, Robert Hutton, Maria Palmer, Nestor Paiva, John Hamilton, George Neise, Norbert Schiller, George Sanders; ***D:*** Boris L. Petroff. *NOS*

The Outer Limits: Galaxy Being **1963** "There is nothing wrong with your TV set..." in this sci-fi series which ran from 1963-1965. In the show's pilot episode an obsessed scientist transmits a pure-energy being from Andromeda into our universe, and chaos ensues. Additional episodes are available. **53m/B VHS, Beta.** Cliff Robertson, Jacqueline Scott, Lee Philips, William O. Douglas Jr.; ***D:*** Leslie Stevens. *MGM, MOV*

The Outer Limits: Sandkings 🦴🦴🦴 *Sandkings* **1995** Made-for-cable revival of the '60s sci-fi series is creepier than ever with this tale of loony scientist Simon Kress (Bridges). He discovers tiny alien eggs while doing an analysis of Martian soil samples and decides to take his research home with him when the government cuts off funding. Big mistake—the critters he successfully hatches in his barn are mean and hungry. Features both dad Lloyd and Beau's 10-year-old son, Dylan, in roles. **93m/C VHS.** Beau Bridges, Lloyd Bridges, Helen Shaver, Dylan Bridges, Kim Coates; ***D:*** Stuart Gillard; ***W:*** Melinda M. Snodgrass. *MGM*

The Outfit 🦴🦴½ **1993 (R)** It's the 1930s and a mob war is brewing between Lucky Luciano, Legs Diamond and Dutch Schultz. A maverick FBI agent gets in good with Diamond and works to end their reign of crime—only he winds up being the spark to light a war between the rival bosses. **92m/C VHS, LV.** John Christian, Billy Drago, Lance Henriksen, Martin Kove, Josh Moby, Rick Washburne; ***D:*** J. Christian Ingvordsen; ***W:*** J. Christian Ingvordsen, Steven Kaman, Whitney Ransick. *MCA, SGE*

The Outing 🦴🦴 *The Lamp* **1987 (R)** A group of high school kids sneaks into a museum at night to party, and get hunted down by a 3,000-year-old genie-in-a-lamp. The genie idea is original enough to make things interesting. Mediocre special effects and run-of-the-mill acting. **87m/C VHS, Beta.** Deborah Winters, James Huston; ***D:*** Tom Daley. *LIV*

Outland 🦴🦴 **1981 (R)** On a volcanic moon of Jupiter, miners begin suffering from spells of insanity. A single federal marshal begins an investigation that threatens the colony's survival. No more or less than a western in space, and the science is rather poor. Might make an interesting double feature with "High Noon," though. **109m/C VHS, Beta, LV.** Sean Connery, Peter Boyle, Frances Sternhagen, James B. Sikking; ***D:*** Peter Hyams; ***W:*** Peter Hyams; ***M:*** Jerry Goldsmith. Nominations: Academy Awards '81: Best Sound. *WAR*

The Outlaw 🦴🦴 **1943** Hughes's variation on the saga of Billy the Kid, which spends more time on Billy's relationship with girlfriend Rio than the climactic showdown with Pat Garrett. The famous Russell vehicle isn't as steamy as it must have seemed to viewers of the day, but the brouhaha around it served to keep it on the shelf for six years. Also available colorized. **123m/B VHS, Beta, LV.** Jane Russell, Jack Beutel, Walter Huston, Thomas Mitchell; ***D:*** Howard Hughes. *CNG, MRV, NOS*

The Outlaw and His Wife 🦴🦴½ **1917** An early silent film about a farmer, accused of a petty crime, who flees with his wife into the mountains to escape the police. This powerful drama was a breakthrough film for the early Swedish movie industry. **73m/B VHS, Beta, LV.** *SW* Victor Sjostrom, Edith Erastoff; ***D:*** Victor Sjostrom. *KIV, FCT, INJ*

The Outlaw Bikers—Gang Wars 🦴 **1970** The original road warriors take it to the streets as rival biker gangs square off. **90m/C VHS, Beta.** Clancy Syrko, Des Roberts, King John III, Linda Jackson; ***D:*** Lawrence Merrick. *PSM*

Outlaw Blues 🦴🦴 **1977 (PG)** An ex-convict becomes a national folk hero when he sets out to reclaim his stolen hit song about prison life. St. James is charming in her first major movie role. A grab bag of action, drama, and tongue-in-cheek humor. **101m/C VHS, Beta.** Peter Fonda, Susan St. James, Johnny Crawford, Michael Lerner, James Callahan; ***D:*** Richard T. Heffron; ***M:*** Charles Bernstein. *WAR*

Outlaw Country 🦴🦴½ **1949** LaRue has a dual role as the marshal who is after a band of counterfeiters and an outlaw who's part of the gang. **72m/B VHS.** Lash LaRue, Al "Fuzzy" St. John, House Peters Jr., Ted Adams, Dan White, Steve Dunhill; ***D:*** Ray Taylor. *GPV*

The Outlaw Deputy 🦴½ **1935** The law-abiding McCoy as an outlaw! It's really a mistake and Lane helps him clear his name. Based on the story "King of Cactusville" by Johnston McCulley. **55m/B VHS.** Tim McCoy, Nora Lane, Bud Osborne, Si Jenks, George Offerman Jr.; ***D:*** Otto Brower. *GPV*

Outlaw Express 🦴½ **1938** After the annexing of California, a U.S. marshall is sent to stop a gang of outlaws who have been raiding Spanish landowners. **57m/B VHS, Beta.** Bob Baker, Cecilia Callejo, Leroy Mason, Don Barclay, Carleton Young; ***D:*** George Waggner. *DVT*

Outlaw Force 🦴 **1987 (R)** A Vietnam veteran country singer tracks down the vicious rednecks that kidnapped his daughter and raped and killed his wife. Heavener did all the work in this low-budget, low-quality take-off on "Death Wish." **95m/C VHS, Beta.** David Heavener, Frank Stallone, Paul Smith, Robert Bjorklund, Devin Dunsworth; ***D:*** David Heavener. *TWE*

Outlaw Fury 🦴½ **1950** Another Shamrock Ellison epic, this time dealing with a coward proving himself by killing the bad guys. **55m/B VHS, Beta, LV.** James Ellison, Russell Hayden. *NO*

Outlaw Gang 🦴½ **1949** A marshal investigates a rash of rancher killings, leading to a conflict between Indians and local land and water companies. **59m/B VHS, Beta, LV.** Donald (Don "Red") Barry, Robert Lowery, Betty Adams. *NO*

The Outlaw Josey Wales 🦴🦴🦴½ **1976 (PG)** Eastwood plays a farmer with a motive for revenge—his family was killed and for years he was betrayed and hunted. His desire to play the lone killer is, however, tempered by his need for family and friends. He kills plenty, but in the end finds happiness. Considered one of the last great Westerns, with many superb performances. Eastwood took over directorial chores during filming from Kaufman, who co-scripted. Adapted from "Gone To Texas" by Forest Carter. **135m/C VHS, Beta, LV.** Clint Eastwood, Chief Dan George, Sondra Locke, Matt Clark, John Vernon, Bill McKinney, Sam Bottoms; ***D:*** Clint Eastwood; ***W:*** Philip Kaufman; ***C:*** Bruce Surtees. Nominations: Academy Awards '76: Best Original Score. *WAR, TLF*

Outlaw Justice 🦴🦴 **1932** Worn oater plot has our hero infiltrating a gang of outlaws to bring them to justice and save the heroine. **56m/C VHS, Beta.** Jack Hoxie, Dorothy Gulliver, Donald Keith, Kermit Maynard, Charles "Blackie" King, Tom London; ***D:*** Armand Schaefer. *GPV*

Outlaw of Gor 🦴½ **1987 (PG)** Once again, the mild professor is transported to Gor, where he has new, improved, bloody adventures. Lots of sword-play, but no magic. Sequel to "Gor." From the novel by John Norman. **89m/C VHS, Beta.** Rebecca Ferratti, Urbano Barberini, Jack Palance, Donna Denton; ***D:*** John Cardos; ***W:*** R.J. Marx. *WAR*

Outlaw of the Plains 🦴 **1946** Another of Crabbe's cowboy pictures in which he played hero Billy Carson, now bailing his trouble-prone sidekick out of a land swindle. Very plain indeed. **56m/B VHS.** Buster Crabbe, Al "Fuzzy" St. John, Patti McCarty, Charles "Blackie" King, Karl Hackett, John Cason, Bud Osborne, Budd Buster, Charles "Slim" Whitaker; ***D:*** Sam Newfield. *NOS*

Outlaw Riders 🦴 **1972 (PG)** Three outlaw bikers take it on the lam after committing a series of disastrous bank robberies. **84m/C VHS, Beta.** Sonny West, Darlene Duralia, Bambi Allen, Bill Bonner; ***D:*** Tony Houston. *NO*

Outlaw Roundup 🦴 **1944** The Texas Rangers battle an outlaw gang. Guess who wins. **51m/B VHS, Beta.** Tex O'Brien, James Newill, Guy Wilkerson, Helen Chapman, Jack Ingram, I. Stanford Jolley; ***D:*** Harry Fraser. *NOS, MRV, VDM*

Outlaw Rule 🦴½ **1936** Standard action-packed western adventure pitting outlaws against the law of the West. **61m/B VHS, Beta.** Reb Russell, Betty Mack, Yakima Canutt, Jack Rockwell, John McGuire, Alan Bridge; ***D:*** S. Roy Luby. *NOS, VCN, HEG*

The Outlaw Tamer 🦴 **1933** Even though Chandler is on the run he still helps capture some horse thieves. **56m/B VHS, Beta.** Lane Chandler, J.P. McGowan, Janet Morgan, George "Gabby" Hayes; ***D:*** J.P. McGowan. *GPV, VCN*

Outlaw Trail 🦴½ **1944** The Trail Blazers put an end to a counterfeiter's evil ways. **53m/B VHS, Beta.** Hoot Gibson, Bob Steele, Chief Thundercloud, Jennifer Holt, Cy Kendall; ***D:*** Robert Emmett Tansey. *NOS, DVT*

Outlaw Women 🦴 **1952** A western town is run by a woman who won't let male outlaws in—until one wins her heart. **76m/C VHS, Beta.** Marie Windsor, Jackie Coogan, Carla Balenda; ***D:*** Sam Newfield. *NO*

The Outlaws is Coming! 🦴🦴½ **1965** Three magazine staffers (Larry, Moe, and Curly Joe) and their editor (West) encounter Wyatt Earp, Wild Bill Hickock, Jesse James, and Annie Oakley when they journey out West to save the buffalo. Last, and one of the best, of the Three Stooges feature films. **90m/B VHS.** Moe Howard, Larry Fine, Joe DeRita, Adam West, Nancy Kovack, Emil Sitka, Henry Gibson; ***D:*** Norman Maurer. *COL*

Outlaws of Sonora 🦴½ **1938** A man transports money to a neighboring town while his outlaw double tries to steal it from him. **58m/B VHS.** Bob Livingston, Ray Corrigan, Max Terhune, Jack Mulhall, Otis Harlan; ***D:*** George Sherman. *NOS, DVT*

Outlaws of the Desert 🦴½ **1941** Having run out of bad guys in the Old West, Hoppy and his pals head to Arabia to buy some horses. Once there, they get involved in a kidnapping. Russell Hayden is replaced as Hoppy's sidekick by Brad King. Duncan ("The Cisco Kid") Renaldo plays the sheik. **66m/B VHS.** William Boyd, Brad King, Andy Clyde, Forrest Stanley, Jean Phillips, Duncan Renaldo, George Lewis; ***D:*** Howard Bretherton. *NOS*

Outlaws of the Range 🦴½ **1936** Action western featuring outlaws who terrorize the countryside. **60m/B VHS, Beta.** Bill Cody, Catherine Cotter, William McCall, Gordon Griffith; ***D:*** Al(bert) Herman. *VCN*

Outlaw's Paradise 🦴🦴 **1939** Cowboy hero McCoy plays not only a lawman out to catch mail thieves, but also the chief outlaw he's hunting! That's one way to keep the budget low. **62m/B VHS.** Tim McCoy, Benny Corbett, Joan Barclay, Ted Adams, Forrest Taylor, Bob Terry; ***D:*** Sam Newfield. *NOS, LOO, RXM*

Outpost in Morocco 🦴½ **1949** A desert soldier is sent to quiet the restless natives and falls for the rebel leader's daughter. The good guys win, but the love interest is sacrificed. Glory before love boys, and damn the story. **92m/B VHS.** George Raft, Marie Windsor, Akim Tamiroff, John Litel, Eduard Franz; ***D:*** Robert Florey. *NOS, MRV, MGM*

Outrage! 🦴🦴½ **1986** An upstanding citizen guns down his daughter's killer and turns himself in to police. His ambitious lawyer fights an open-and-shut homicide case with both fair and foul means. Not a shootout like the cassette box suggests, but an okay courtroom drama attacking excesses of the legal system. From a novel by Henry Denker, made for TV by producer Irwin Allen. **96m/C VHS.** Robert Preston, Beau Bridges, Anthony Newley, Mel Ferrer, Burgess Meredith, Linda Purl, William Allen Young; ***D:*** Walter Grauman. *VMK*

Outrage 🦴🦴 *Dispara* **1993 (R)** Journalist Marco Vallez's (Banderas) latest assignment is a story about a traveling circus. Bored with the usual acts, he's intrigued by equestrian/sharpshooter Anna (Neri) and asks her for an interview, which leads to passion. While Marco is on assignment in Barcelona, Anna is attacked and raped in her trailer. Rather than calling the police, Anna decides to take her own revenge. Spanish with subtitles or dubbed. **108m/C VHS.** *SP* Antonio Banderas, Francesca Neri; ***D:*** Carlos Saura. *APX*

Outrageous! 🦴🦴🦴 **1977 (R)** An offbeat, low-budget comedy about the strange relationship between a gay female impersonator and his pregnant schizophrenic friend. The pair end up in New York, where they feel right at home. Russell's impersonations of female film stars earned him the best actor prize at the Berlin Film Festival. **100m/C VHS, Beta.** *CA* Craig Russell, Hollis McLaren, Richard Easley, Allan Moyle, Helen Shaver; ***D:*** Richard Benner. *COL*

Outrageous Fortune 🦴🦴 **1987 (R)** Two would-be actresses - one prim and innocent and one wildly trampy - chase after the same two-timing boyfriend and get involved in a dangerous CIA plot surrounding a deadly bacteria. Tired plot. Mediocre acting and formula jokes, but somehow still funny. Disney's first foray into comedy for grown-ups. **112m/C VHS, Beta, LV.** Shelley Long, Bette Midler, George Carlin, Peter Coyote; ***D:*** Arthur Hiller; ***W:*** Leslie Dixon; ***M:*** Alan Silvestri. *TOU*

Outside Chance 🦴 **1978** A soapy, sanitized remake of Mimieux's film, "Jackson County Jail," wherein an innocent woman is persecuted in a small Southern jail. Made for television. **92m/C VHS, Beta.** Yvette Mimieux, Royce D. Applegate; ***D:*** Michael Miller. *NLC*

Outside Chance of Maximillian Glick 🦴🦴 **1988 (G)** A sentimental Canadian comedy about a boy's dreams and his tradition-bound Jewish family. **94m/C VHS, Beta.** *CA* Noam Zylberman, Fairuza Balk, Saul Rubinek; ***D:*** Allan Goldstein. Toronto-City Award '88: Best Canadian Feature Film. *HMD*

The Outside Man 🦴🦴 *Un Homme Est Mort* **1973 (PG)** A French hit man is called to Los Angeles to knock off a crime boss, which he does. But then an American hit man is hired to do in the Frenchman. The climatic showdown is set around the crime boss' body, which happens to be embalmed in a sitting position. Decidely offbeat. **104m/C VHS.** *FR* Jean-Louis Trintignant, Roy Scheider, Ann-Margret, Angie Dickinson, Georgia Engel, Carlo De Meyo, Umberto Orsini, Ted de Corsia, Felice Orlandi, John Hillerman; ***D:*** Jacques Deray. *MGM*

Outside the Law 🦴🦴 **1921** Lon Chaney plays dual roles of the underworld hood in "Black Mike Sylva," and a Chinese servant in "Ah Wing." Silent. **77m/B VHS.** Lon Chaney Sr., Priscilla Dean, Ralph Lewis, Wheeler Oakman; ***D:*** Tod Browning. *KIV, CCB, VYY*

Outside the Law 🦴½ **1995 (R)** Maverick cop Brad Kingsbury (Bradley) crosses the line when he falls for luscious Tanya Borgman (Thomson), who's the prime suspect in a murder investigation. Also available unrated. **94m/C VHS, LV.** David Bradley, Anna Thomson, Ashley Laurence; ***D:*** Boaz Davidson; ***W:*** Dennis Dimster Denk; ***C:*** Avi Karpik; ***M:*** Blake Leyh. *TTC, NLC, IME*

The Outsiders 🦴🦴½ **1983 (PG)** Based on the popular S.E. Hinton book, the story of a teen gang from the wrong side of the tracks and their conflicts with society and each other. Melodramatic and over-done, but teen-agers still love the story. Good soundtrack and cast ripples with up and coming stars. Followed by a television series. Coppola adapted another Hinton novel the same year, "Rumble Fish." **91m/C VHS, Beta, LV.** C. Thomas Howell, Matt Dillon, Ralph Macchio, Patrick Swayze, Diane Lane, Tom Cruise, Emilio Estevez, Rob Lowe, Tom Waits, Leif Garrett; ***D:*** Francis Ford Coppola; ***W:*** Kathleen Rowell; ***C:*** Stephen Burum; ***M:*** Carmine Coppola. *WAR*

Outtakes 🦴½ **1985 (R)** A piecemeal compilation of comedy skits, concentrating on sex and genre parody. **85m/C VHS, Beta.** Forrest Tucker, Bobbi Wexler, Joleen Lutz; ***D:*** Jack M. Sell. *NO*

The Oval Portrait 🦴½ **1988** An adaptation of the Edgar Allan Poe suspense tale about a Civil War-era maiden, her illicit love for a Confederate soldier and her eventual death. **89m/C VHS, Beta.** Giselle MacKenzie, Barry Coe; ***D:*** Regelio A. Gonzalez Jr. *NO*

Over Indulgence 🦴🦴 **1987 (R)** A young woman witnesses a murder in an affluent society in British East Africa. **95m/C VHS, Beta.** Denholm Elliott, Holly Aird, Michael Byrne, Kathryn Pogson; ***D:*** Ross Devenish. *MCG*

Over the Brooklyn Bridge 🦴🦴 *My Darling Shiksa* **1983 (R)** A young Jewish man (Gould) must give up his Catholic girlfriend (Hemingway) in order to get his uncle (Caesar) to lend him the money he needs to buy a restaurant in Manhattan. Nowhere near as funny as it should be, and potentially offensive to boot. **100m/C VHS, Beta.** Elliott Gould, Sid Caesar, Shelley Winters, Margaux Hemingway, Carol Kane, Burt Young; ***D:*** Menahem Golan; ***M:*** Pino Donaggio. *MGM*

Over the Edge 🦴🦴🦴½ **1979 (PG)** The music of Cheap Trick, The Cars, and The Ramones highlights this realistic tale of alienated suburban youth on the rampage. Dillon makes his screen debut in this updated, well-done "Rebel Without a Cause." Shelved for several years, the movie was finally released after Dillon made it big. Sleeper with excellent direction and dialogue. **91m/C VHS, Beta.** Michael Kramer, Matt Dillon, Pamela Ludwig, Vincent Spano; ***D:*** Jonathan Kaplan. *WAR*

Over the Hill 🦴🦴½ **1993 (PG)** Dukakis stars as Alma, an eccentric widow who decides to leave her well-meaning son's restrictive home in Maine to visit her estranged daughter Elizabeth in Sydney, Australia. Embarassed by her peculiarities Elizabeth arranges a holiday away but Mom has her own plans. She wants to "loop the loop," and make a complete circuit around the Australian continent. Soon Alma is on the road, meeting fellow eccentrics and experiencing a variety of adventures. **102m/C VHS, LV.** Olympia Dukakis, Sigrid Thornton, Derek Fowlds, Pippa Grandison; **D:** George Miller; **W:** Robert Caswell. *NLC, COL, IME*

Over the Summer ☠☠½ **1985** Strong drama about a troubled teen who escapes the city for a summer with her grandparents. No cliches here—the grandfather lusts after the granddaughter and eventually kills himself, and problems remain at the end. Intelligent and entertaining, though marred by needless nude scenes. **97m/C VHS, Beta.** Laura Hunt, Johnson West, Catherine Williams, David Romero; **D:** Teresa Sparks. *LIV, VES*

Over the Top ☠½ **1986 (PG)** The film that started a nationwide arm-wrestling craze. A slow-witted trucker decides the only way he can retain custody of his estranged son, as well as win the boy's respect, is by winning a big arm-wrestling competition. Stallone is an expert at grinding these movies out by now, and the kid (General Hospital's Mikey) is all right, but the end result is boredom, as it should be with an arm-wrestling epic. **94m/C VHS, Beta, LV.** Sylvester Stallone, Susan Blakely, Robert Loggia, David Mendenhall; **D:** Menahem Golan; **W:** Sylvester Stallone, Gary Conway, Stirling Silliphant. Golden Raspberry Awards '87: Worst Supporting Actor (Mendenhall), Worst New Star (Mendenhall). *WAR*

Over the Wire ☠½ **1995** Telephone lineman accidentally overhears a conversation where a woman hires a hitman to kill her sister. He finds out that the sisters live together and tries to figure out just who the target is before it's too late (of course, he has to seduce both of them to accomplish this). **90m/C VHS.** Shauna O'Brien, Griffin Drew, Tim Abell. *TRI*

Overboard ☠☠ **1987 (PG)** A wealthy, spoiled woman falls off of her yacht and into the arms of a low-class carpenter who picks her up and convinces her she is in fact his wife, and mother to his four brats. Just when she learns to like her life, the tables are turned again. Even though it's all been done before, you can't help but laugh at the screwy gags. **112m/C VHS, Beta, LV.** Goldie Hawn, Kurt Russell, Katherine Helmond, Roddy McDowall, Edward Herrmann; **D:** Garry Marshall; **W:** Leslie Dixon; **C:** John A. Alonzo; **M:** Alan Silvestri. *MGM, HMV, FOX*

The Overcoat ☠☠☠½ **1959** An adaptation of Nikolai Gogol's classic story about the dehumanizing life endured in 20th-century bureaucracy. All a menial civil servant wants is a new overcoat. When he finally gets one, this treasured article not only keeps him warm but makes him feel self-satisfied as well. In Russian with English subtitles. **93m/B VHS, Beta.** *RU* Rolan Bykov; **D:** Alexei Batalov. National Board of Review Awards '65: 5 Best Foreign Films of the Year. *HTV, INJ*

Overdrawn at the Memory Bank ☠☠ **1983** In a futuristic tyranny, a romantic rebel becomes somehow fused with the spirit of Humphrey Bogart in the milieu of "Casablanca," and lives out a cliched version of the film character's adventures. **84m/C VHS, Beta.** Raul Julia, Linda Griffiths; **D:** Douglas Williams. *VTR, NWV*

Overexposed ☠☠ **1990 (R)** All the wackos love the sultry soap star Oxenburg; one is a killer. Eighty minutes and a bunch of bodies later the killer is unmasked. Plenty of suspense and some original gore. Based on the true stories of fans who stalk celebrities. **83m/C VHS.** Catherine Oxenberg, David Naughton, Jennifer Edwards, Karen Black; **D:** Larry Brand; **W:** Larry Brand. *MGM*

Overkill ☠ **1986 (R)** A detective and the vengeance-minded brother of a dead Japanese-American can fight back against the controlling Yakuza in Little Tokyo. **81m/C Beta.** Steve Rally, John Nishio, Laura Burkett, Roy Summerset; **D:** Ulli Lommel. *NO*

Overland Mail **1941** Fifteen episodes of the vintage serial filled with western action. **225m/B VHS, Beta.** Lon Chaney Jr., Helen Parrish. *NOS, VCN, MLB*

Overland Stage Raiders ☠☠☠ **1938** The "Three Mesquiteers" ride again, this time to guard a Greyhound bus! The trio must protect a shipment of gold from hijackers. This is the last film for Brooks, who had starred in the German masterpiece "Pandora's Box" in 1929. **55m/B VHS.** John Wayne, Ray Corrigan, Max Terhune, Louise Brooks, John Archer, Frank LaRue, Yakima Canutt; **D:** George Sherman. *REP, NOS*

Overlanders ☠☠☠ **1946** The Japanese may invade, but rather than kill 1,000 head of cattle, these Aussies drive the huge herd across the continent, facing danger along the way. Beautifully photographed, featuring the "Australian Gary Cooper" and a stampede scene to challenge "Dances with Wolves." **91m/B VHS, Beta.** *AU* Chips Rafferty, Daphne Campbell, Jean Blue, John Nugent Hayward; **D:** Harry Watt. *NOS, DVT, HEG*

The Overlanders ☠☠ **1979** A group of nine men, two women and a boy challenge the forbidding Canadian Northwest circa 1862. **76m/C VHS, Beta.** *TWE*

Overnight Sensation ☠☠ **1983** A modern adaptation of the W. Somerset Maugham story about a traditional marriage being tested by the wife's sudden literary success. **30m/C VHS, Beta.** Louise Fletcher, Robert Loggia, Shari Belafonte. *PYR*

Overseas: Three Women with Man Trouble ☠☠☠ **1990** Three beautiful sisters in French colonial Algeria surround themselves in a life of luxury to avoid the incredible social changes going on around them. Each sister has a different perspective on her life, and the perspectives are graphically revealed. Lush photography set in the Mediterranean. In French with English subtitles. **96m/C VHS.** *FR* Nicole Garcia, Marianne Basler, Philippe Galland, Pierre Doris, Brigitte Rouan; **D:** Brigitte Rouan; **W:** Brigitte Rouan. Cannes Film Festival '90: Best Film. *FXL, BTV, BFV*

Overthrow ☠½ **1982 (R)** American sportswriter finds himself caught up in violence and intrigue in Buenos Aires. **90m/C VHS, Beta.** John Phillip Law, Lewis Van Bergen, Roger Wilson; **D:** Larry Ludman. *IMP, HHE, VTR*

Overture **1975** An episode of "The Persuaders." Brett and Danny are tricked into helping a retired judge. This adventure leads them to the Mediterranean and a gorgeous gal. **52m/C VHS.** *GB* Roger Moore, Tony Curtis. *NO*

Overture to Glory ☠☠½ *Der Vilner Shtot Khazn* **1940** A Jewish cantor longs for the world of opera. He leaves his wife and son to fulfill his passion, but eventually he loses his voice and humbly returns home on Yom Kippur, the Jewish Day of Atonement. He learns that his son has passed away. Grief-stricken, he goes to the synagogue. There, the cantor regains his voice as he performs Kol Nidre in a passionate and melodious rendering. In Yiddish with English subtitles. **85m/B VHS, Beta.** Helen Beverly, Florence Weiss. *ERG, INJ, TPV*

The Owl and the Pussycat ☠☠☠ **1970 (PG)** Nerdy author gets the neighborhood hooker evicted from her apartment. She returns the favor, and the pair hit the street—and the sack—in Buck Henry's hilarious adaptation of the Broadway play. Streisand's first non-singing role. **96m/C VHS, Beta, LV.** Barbra Streisand, George Segal, Robert Klein, Allen (Goorwitz) Garfield; **D:** Herbert Ross; **W:** Buck Henry; **C:** Harry Stradling, Andrew Laszlo. *GKK*

The Ox ☠☠½ **1991** Slow-moving, simple tale, set in rural Sweden in the 1860's during a famine. Desperate to feed his family a tenant farmer kills his employer's ox. Consumed by guilt, the man is quickly found out and sentenced to life imprisonment. Pardoned after six years, the farmer returns to his family, to find out his wife has survived by doing things he finds difficult to forgive. Based on a true story. Directorial debut of Nykvist, the longtime cinematographer for Ingmar Bergman, well displays his familiarity with composition and lighting to heighten mood. In Swedish with English subtitles. **93m/C VHS.** *SW* Stellan Skarsgard, Ewa Froling, Lennart Hjulstrom, Max von Sydow, Liv Ullmann, Bjorn Granath, Erland Josephson; **D:** Sven Nykvist; **W:** Lasse Summanen, Sven Nykvist. Nominations: Academy Awards '91: Best Foreign Language Film. *ACA, ICA, FCT*

The Ox-Bow Incident ☠☠☠☠ *Strange Incident* **1943** A popular rancher is murdered, and a mob of angry townspeople can't wait for the sheriff to find the killers. They hang the young man, despite the protests of Fonda, a cowboy with a conscience. Excellent study of mob mentality with strong individual characterizations. A brilliant western based on a true story by Walter Van Tilburg Clark. Also see "Twelve Angry Men"—less tragic but just as moving. **75m/B VHS, Beta, LV.** Henry Fonda, Harry (Henry) Morgan, Dana Andrews, Anthony Quinn, Frank Conroy, Harry Davenport, Jane Darwell, William Eythe, Mary Beth Hughes; **D:** William A. Wellman; **W:** Lamar Trotti; **C:** Arthur C. Miller; **M:** Cyril Mockridge. National Board of Review Awards '43: 10 Best Films of the Year, Best Director (Wellman); Nominations: Academy Awards '43: Best Picture. *FOX*

Oxford Blues ☠☠ **1984 (PG-13)** An American finagles his way into England's Oxford University and onto the rowing team in pursuit of the girl of his dreams. Beautiful scenery, but the plot is wafer-thin. Remake of "Yank at Oxford." **98m/C VHS, Beta, LV.** Rob Lowe, Ally Sheedy, Amanda Pays, Julian Sands, Michael Gough, Gail Strickland, Cary Elwes; **D:** Robert Boris; **W:** Robert Boris; **M:** John Du Prez. *FOX*

Pace That Kills ☠ **1928** An anti-drug cautionary drama from the Roaring '20s, one of many now marketed on cassette as campy fun. Beware, though, a little bit of this stuff goes a long way. A young man goes to the big city to find his missing sister and winds up hooked on heroin. **87m/B VHS, Beta, 8mm.** Owen Gorin, Virginia Roye, Florence Turner. *GVV*

Pacific Heights ☠☠☠ **1990 (R)** Young San Francisco couple takes on mammoth mortgage assuming tenants will write their ticket to the American dream, but psychopathic tenant Keaton moves in downstairs and redecorates. He won't pay the rent and he won't leave. Creepy psycho-thriller has lapses but builds to effective climax. It's a treat to watch mother/daughter actresses Hedren and Griffith work together. Watch for D'Angelo as Keaton's lover. **103m/C VHS, LV.** Melanie Griffith, Matthew Modine, Michael Keaton, Mako, Nobu McCarthy, Laurie Metcalf, Carl Lumbly, Dorian Harewood, Luca Bercovici, Tippi Hedren, Sheila McCarthy, Dan Hedaya, Beverly D'Angelo, Nicholas Pryor, Miriam Margolyes; **D:** John Schlesinger; **W:** Daniel Pyne; **M:** Hans Zimmer. *FOX*

Pacific Inferno ☠☠ **1985** During WWII, American POWs endeavor to break out of a Japanese prison camp in the Philippines. Their goal is to prevent their captors from retrieving millions of dollars worth of sunken U.S. gold. Made for cable television. **90m/C VHS, Beta.** Jim Brown, Richard Jaeckel, Tim Brown; **D:** Rolf Bayer. *NO*

The Pack ☠☠½ *The Long, Dark Night* **1977 (R)** A group of dogs become wild when left on a resort island. A marine biologist leads the humans who fight to keep the dogs from using vacationers as chew toys. Fine production valves keep it from going to the dogs. Made with the approval of the American Humane Society who helped with the treatment of stage hands. **99m/C VHS, Beta.** Joe Don Baker, Hope Alexander-Willis, R.G. Armstrong, Richard B. Shull; **D:** Robert Clouse; **W:** Robert Clouse. *WAR*

The P.A.C.K. ☠☠ **1996** The P.A.C.K. are alien warriors who mistakenly land on earth, which doesn't prevent them from killing all but one of a team of government agents sent to investigate. Now lone agent Rachel (Bergman) reluctantly teams up with a second alien who's been sent to destroy the P.A.C.K. **90m/C VHS.** Sandahl Bergman, Ted Prior, Red West. *SWI*

Pack Up Your Troubles ☠☠½ *We're In the Army Now* **1932** Laurel and Hardy make good on a promise to help find the grandfather of a girl whose father was killed in WWI. All they know is the grandfather's last name though—Smith. Wholesome R and R. **68m/B VHS, Beta.** Stan Laurel, Oliver Hardy, James Finlayson, Jacquie Lyn; **D:** George Marshall. *MED, FCT, MLB*

The Package 🦴🦴½ **1989 (R)** An espionage thriller about an army sergeant who loses the prisoner he escorts into the U.S. When he tries to track him down, he uncovers a military plot to start WWIII. Hackman is believable in his role as the sergeant. **108m/C VHS, Beta, LV.** Gene Hackman, Tommy Lee Jones, Joanna Cassidy, Dennis Franz, Pam Grier, John Heard, Reni Santoni, Thalmus Rasulala, Ike Pappas, Kevin Crowley; ***D:*** Andrew Davis; ***W:*** John Bishop; ***M:*** James Newton Howard. *ORI*

Packin' It In 🦴🦴 **1983** A Los Angeles family is in for a rude awakening when they leave the city for a quieter life in the Oregon woods. There they encounter a band of survivalists with semi-comedic results. **92m/C VHS, Beta.** Richard Benjamin, Paula Prentiss, Molly Ringwald, Tony Roberts, Andrea Marcovicci; ***D:*** Jud Taylor. *NO*

Paco 🦴½ **1975 (G)** A young, South American boy heads for the city, where he meets his uncle. He discovers his uncle is the leader of a gang of youthful thieves. Predictable and sluggish. **89m/C VHS, Beta.** Jose Ferrer, Panchito Gomez, Allen (Goorwitz) Garfield, Pernell Roberts, Andre Marquis; ***D:*** Robert Vincent O'Neil. *GHV*

Paddy 🦴🦴 *Goodbye to the Hill* **1970 (PG)** A young Irish lad realizes his sexual potential by seducing every woman he can find. Freudians will have a field day. **97m/C VHS, Beta.** *IR* Des Cave, Milo O'Shea, Darbnia Molloy, Peggy Cass; ***D:*** Daniel Haller. *NO*

Padre Nuestro 🦴🦴½ **1985** Religious satire about a dying priest who wishes to reunite his family, who include an atheist brother, a mistress from his youth, and his illegitimate daughter who's a notorious prostitute. In Spanish with English subtitles. **91m/C VHS.** *SP* Fernando Rey, Francesco Rabal, Victoria Abril; ***D:*** Francisco Regueiro. *CVC, FCT*

Padre Padrone 🦴🦴🦴½ *Father Master; My Father, My Master* **1977** The much acclaimed adaptation of the Gavino Ledda autobiography about his youth in agrarian Sardinia with a brutal, tyrannical father. Eventually he overcomes his handicaps, breaks the destructive emotional ties to his father and successfully attends college. Highly regarded although low budget; in an Italian dialect (Sardinian) with English subtitles. **113m/C VHS, Beta.** *IT* Omero Antonutti, Saverio Marconi, Marcella Michelangeli, Fabrizio Forte, Salverio Marioni; ***D:*** Paolo Taviani, Vittorio Taviani; ***W:*** Paolo Taviani, Vittorio Taviani. Cannes Film Festival '77: Best Film. *COL, INJ*

Pagan Island 🦴 **1960** A man is stranded on a desert island with 30 beautiful girls who tie him up and abandon him. Maki, to be sacrificed by the rest, saves Dew and they fall in love. They go off in search of a reputed treasure, which they find, but at a deadly cost. **67m/B VHS.** Eddie Dew, Nani Maka; ***D:*** Barry Mahon; ***W:*** Clelle Mahon. *SMW, TPV*

Pagan Love Song 🦴🦴 **1950** A dull musical which finds Keel in Tahiti taking over his uncle's coconut plantation and falling in love with Williams. Surprise! Williams performs one of her famous water ballets, which is the only saving grace in this lifeless movie. ♫The House of Singing Bamboo; Singing in the Sun; Etiquette; Why is Love So Crazy; Tahiti; The Sea of the Moon; Pagan Love Song; Coconut Milk. **76m/C VHS.** Esther Williams, Howard Keel, Minna Gombell, Rita Moreno; ***D:*** Robert Alton. *MGM*

The Pagemaster 🦴½ **1994 (G)** Timid Richard (Macauley) is basically scared of his own shadow but, during a storm, he's forced to take refuge in a mysterious library with an even odder librarian, Mr. Dewey (Lloyd). Richard's intrigued by the library's mural, which turns out to be the doorway to an animated universe where the wizardlike Pagemaster (voiced by Lloyd) and other literary characters help Richard discover his strengths and overcome his fears. Mildly amusing but kids may not know who the characters refer to unless they're readers (a good intro, perhaps?) **76m/C VHS, LV.** Macaulay Culkin, Christopher Lloyd, Ed Begley Jr., Mel Harris; ***D:*** Joe Johnston, Maurice Hunt; ***W:*** David Casci, David Kirschner, Ernie Contreras; ***M:*** James Horner; ***V:*** Christopher Lloyd, Whoopi Goldberg, Patrick Stewart, Frank Welker, Leonard Nimoy. Nominations: Golden Raspberry Awards '94: Worst Actor (Culkin). *FXV*

Paid to Kill 🦴🦴 *Five Days* **1954** A failing businessman hires a thug to kill him in order to leave his family insurance money, but when the business picks up, he can't contact the thug to cancel the contract. The actors' lack of talent is matched only by the characters' lack of motivation. **71m/B VHS, Beta, LV.** *GB* Dane Clark, Paul Carpenter, Thea Gregory; ***D:*** Montgomery Tully. *RXM*

Pain in the A— 🦴🦴🦴 **1977 (PG)** A hit man helps a suicidal shirt salesman solve his marital problems in this black comedy that was later Americanized as "Buddy, Buddy." Not for all tastes, but has acquired a reputation for its dark wit. In French with English subtitles. **90m/C VHS, Beta.** *FR IT* Lino Ventura, Jacques Brel, Caroline Cellier; ***D:*** Edouard Molinaro; ***W:*** Francis Veber, Edouard Molinaro. *COL, INJ*

Paint It Black 🦴🦴½ **1989 (R)** A violent/steamy mystery and action flick from the director of "River's Edge," in which a young man from the silver-spoon set develops a fascination for an artist. **101m/C VHS, Beta, LV.** Sally Kirkland, Rick Rossovich, Martin Landau, Doug Savant, Peter Frechette, Julie Carmen, Jason Bernhard, Monique Van De Ven; ***D:*** Tim Hunter. *LIV, VES*

The Paint Job 🦴🦴 **1993 (R)** Wesley, the lonely house painter, falls in love with his neighbor, Margaret. Unfortunately, Margaret is married—to Wesley's boss Willy. Margaret is drawn to Wesley and bored with Willy. But one of the men turns out to be a serial killer. What's a gal in love to do? **90m/C VHS.** Will Patton, Bebe Neuwirth, Robert Pastorelli; ***D:*** Micheal Taav; ***W:*** Micheal Taav; ***M:*** John Wesley Harding. *COL*

Paint Your Wagon 🦴🦴½ **1969 (PG)** Big-budget western musical-comedy about a gold mining boom town, and two prospectors sharing the same Mormon wife complete with a classic Lerner and Lowe score. Marvin chews up the sagebrush and Eastwood attempts to sing, although Seberg was mercifully dubbed. Overlong, with patches of interest, pretty songs, and plenty of panoramic scenery. Adapted from the L & L play. ♫I Talk To the Trees; I Still See Elisa; I'm On My Way; Hand Me Down That Can O' Beans; Whoop-Ti-Ay; They Call the Wind Maria; There's a Coach Comin' In; Wandrin' Star; Best Things. **164m/C VHS, Beta, LV.** Lee Marvin, Clint Eastwood, Jean Seberg, Harve Presnell; ***D:*** Joshua Logan; ***W:*** Paddy Chayefsky; ***M:*** Frederick Loewe, Andre Previn, Alan Jay Lerner. Nominations: Academy Awards '69: Best Original Score. *PAR*

Painted Desert 🦴🦴 **1931** Gable's first film role of any consequence came in this early sound western. Gable plays a villain opposite "good guy" William Boyd. **80m/B VHS, Beta.** William Boyd, Helen Twelvetrees, George O'Brien, Clark Gable, William Farnum; ***D:*** Howard Higgin. *NOS, MRV, HHT*

Painted Hero 🦴🦴½ **1995 (R)** Rodeo clown Yoakum has to watch out for more than rampaging bulls when he returns to Waco, where he's accused of murder and reunites with the mother of his dead son. **105m/C VHS.** Dwight Yoakam, Bo Hopkins, Cindy Pickett, Michelle Joyner; ***D:*** Terry Benedict. *CAF*

The Painted Hills 🦴🦴½ **1951 (G)** Lassie outsmarts crooked miners and rescues her friends. Surprise, Surprise! Overly sentimental, but action packed and beautifully shot. Lassie's last outing with MGM. **70m/C VHS, Beta.** Paul Kelly, Bruce Cowling, Gary Gray, Art Smith, Ann Doran, Lassie; ***D:*** Harold F. Kress. *MGM, BPG, FCT*

The Painted Stallion **1937** This 12-chapter serial features a mysterious figure on a painted stallion who attempts to maintain peace between Mexicans and Indians. **212m/B VHS, LV.** Ray Corrigan, Hoot Gibson, Duncan Renaldo, Leroy Mason, Yakima Canutt; ***D:*** William Witney, Ray Taylor. *NOS, VDM, REP*

The Painted Veil 🦴🦴½ **1934** Adaptation of a W. Somerset Maugham story. Garbo, once again the disillusioned wife turning to the affections of another man, is magnificent, almost eclipsing the weak script. Lost money at the box office, but for Garbo fans, an absolute must. **83m/B VHS, Beta.** Greta Garbo, Herbert Marshall, George Brent, Warner Oland, Jean Hersholt; ***D:*** Richard Boleslawski; ***C:*** William H. Daniels. *MGM, FCT*

Pair of Aces 🦴🦴½ **1990** Kristofferson is a Texas Ranger who's on the trail of a serial killer. His only other problem is being saddled with Nelson, a philosophical safecracker who's awaiting trial and in the reluctant cop's custody. Low-key western with good buddy pairing of Nelson and Kristofferson. Made for television. **94m/C VHS.** Willie Nelson, Kris Kristofferson, Rip Torn, Helen Shaver, Jane Cameron, Sonny Carl Davis, Lash LaRue, Emily Warfield, Michael Marich; ***D:*** Aaron Lipstadt. *WAR*

Paisan 🦴🦴🦴 **1946** Six episodic tales of life in Italy, several featuring Allied soldiers and nurses during WWII. One of the stories tells of a man who tries to develop a relationship without being able to speak Italian. Another focuses on a young street robber who is confronted by one of his victims. Strong stories that covers a wide range of emotions. In Italian with English subtitles. **90m/B VHS, Beta, 8mm.** *IT* Maria Michi, Carmela Sazio, Gar Moore, William Tubbs, Harriet White, Robert Van Loon, Dale Edmonds, Carla Pisacane, Dots Johnson; ***D:*** Roberto Rossellini; ***W:*** Federico Fellini, Roberto Rossellini. National Board of Review Awards '48: 5 Best Foreign Films of the Year, Best Director (Fellini); Nominations: Academy Awards '49: Best Story & Screenplay. *NOS, HHT, CAB*

The Pajama Game 🦴🦴🦴½ **1957** A spritely musical about the striking workers of a pajama factory and their plucky negotiator, who falls in love with the boss. Based on the hit Broadway musical, which was based on Richard Bissell's book "Seven and a Half Cents" and adapted for the screen by Bisell and Abbott. Bob Fosse choreographed the dance numbers. ♫I'm Not at All in Love; Small Talk; There Once Was a Man; Steam Heat; Hernando's Highway; Hey There; Once-a-Year Day; Seven and a Half Cents; I'll Never Be Jealous Again. **101m/C VHS, Beta, LV.** Doris Day, John Raitt, Eddie Foy Jr., Reta Shaw, Carol Haney; ***D:*** Stanley Donen, George Abbott; ***C:*** Harry Stradling. *WAR*

Pajama Party 🦴🦴 **1964** Followup to "Bikini Beach" takes the party inside in this fourth entry in the popular "Beach Party" series. Plot is up to beach party realism. Funicello is Avalon-less (although he does have a cameo) so she falls for Martian Kirk instead. He's scouting for an alien invasion, but after he falls into Annette's lap decides to save the planet instead. Typical fluff with the usual beach movie faces present; look for a young Garr as a dancer. Followed by the classic "Beach Blanket Bingo." ♫It's That Kind of Day; There Has to Be a Reason; Where Did I Go Wrong?; Pajama Party; Beach Ball; Among the Young; Stuffed Animal. **82m/C VHS, LV.** Tommy Kirk, Annette Funicello, Elsa Lanchester, Harvey Lembeck, Jesse White, Jody McCrea, Donna Loren, Susan Hart, Bobbi Shaw, Cheryl Sweeten, Luree Holmes, Candy Johnson, Dorothy Lamour, Toni Basil, Teri Garr, Ben Lessy; ***Cameos:*** Buster Keaton, Frankie Avalon, Don Rickles; ***D:*** Don Weis; ***W:*** Louis M. Heyward; ***C:*** Floyd Crosby; ***M:*** Les Baxter. *NO*

Pajama Tops 🦴🦴½ **1983** A stage production of the classic French bedroom farce, taped live at the Music Hall Theatre in Toronto, Canada. Includes all the trials of marriage including adultery and deceit. **105m/C VHS.** Robert Klein, Susan George, Pia Zadora. *NO*

Pal Joey 🦴🦴🦴 **1957** Musical comedy about an opportunistic singer who courts a wealthy socialite in hopes that she will finance his nightclub. His play results in comedic complications. Stellar choreography, fine direction, and beautiful costumes complement performances headed by Hayworth and Sinatra. Oscar overlooked his pal Joey when awards were handed out. Songs include some of Rodgers and Hart's best. Based on John O'Hara's book and play. ♫Zip; Bewitched, Bothered and Bewildered; I Could Write a Book; That Terrific Rainbow; Whad Do I Care for a Dame?; Happy Hunting Horn; Plant You Now, Dig You Later; Do It the Hard Way; Take Him. **109m/C VHS, Beta, LV.** Frank Sinatra, Rita Hayworth, Kim

Novak; *D:* George Sidney; *M:* Richard Rodgers, Lorenz Hart. Golden Globe Awards '58: Best Actor—Musical/Comedy (Sinatra); Nominations: Academy Awards '57: Best Art Direction/Set Decoration, Best Costume Design, Best Film Editing, Best Sound. *COL*

Palais Royale ½ **1988** Craven plays an ad exec who gets involved in the world of gangsters in the late 50s. **100m/C VHS.** *CA* Matt Craven, Kim Cattrall, Dean Stockwell; *D:* Martin Lavut. *REP*

Pale Blood ½ **1991 (R)** A serial killer in Los Angeles is leaving his victims drained of blood. Could it be that a vampire is stalking the modern American metropolis, or is this merely the workings of a bloodthirsty psychopath? **93m/C VHS, LV.** George Chakiris, Wings Hauser, Pamela Ludwig, Diana Frank, Darcy Demoss; *D:* VV Dachin Hsu. *NO*

Pale Rider **1985 (R)** A mysterious nameless stranger rides into a small California gold rush town to find himself in the middle of a feud between a mining syndicate and a group of independent prospectors. Christ-like Eastwood evokes comparisons to "Shane." A classical western theme treated well complemented by excellent photography and a rock-solid cast. **116m/C VHS, Beta, LV, 8mm.** Clint Eastwood, Michael Moriarty, Carrie Snodgress, Sydney Penny, Richard Dysart, Richard Kiel, Christopher Penn, John Russell, Charles Hallahan, Douglas McGrath, Fran Ryan; *D:* Clint Eastwood; *W:* Michael Butler, Dennis Shryack; *C:* Bruce Surtees; *M:* Lennie Niehaus. *WAR, TLF*

The Paleface **1948** A cowardly dentist becomes a gunslinging hero when Calamity Jane starts aiming for him. A rip-roarin' good time as the conventions of the Old West are turned upside down. Includes the Oscar-winning song "Buttons and Bows." The 1952 sequel is "Son of Paleface." Remade in 1968 as "The Shakiest Gun in the West." ♫Buttons and Bows; Get a Man!; Meetcha 'Round the Corner. **91m/C VHS, Beta, LV.** Jane Russell, Bob Hope, Robert Armstrong, Iris Adrian, Robert Watson; *D:* Norman Z. McLeod; *C:* Ray Rennahan. Academy Awards '48: Best Song ("Buttons and Bows"). *MCA*

The Palermo Connection **1991 (R)** Not the action-thriller the cassette box claims, but a cynical study of a crusading N.Y.C. mayoral candidate who honeymoons in Mafia-haunted Sicily and learns that the war on crime has already been lost. Remote adaptation of "To Forget Palermo" by Edmonde Charles-Roux. **100m/C VHS, LV.** James Belushi, Mimi Rogers, Joss Ackland, Philippe Noiret, Vittorio Gassman, Caroline Rosi; *D:* Francesco Rosi; *W:* Gore Vidal. *LIV*

The Pallbearer ½ **1995 (PG-13)** You probably liked this one better when it was called "The Graduate," as this one shares some key plot points with, but lacks the edge and cultural impact of the 1967 classic. Basset-faced Schwimmer plays Tom, who is asked to be a pallbearer for an old high school classmate whom he can't quite remember. He is then seduced by the mother (Hershey) of the deceased, while trying to kindle a romance with the fabulous Julie DeMarco (Paltrow), an old classmate who can't quite remember him. The spurned older woman then begins to exact her revenge, while Tom tries to figure out how to court Julie while living at home with his mom. Good performances make it watchable. **107m/C VHS.** David Schwimmer, Gwyneth Paltrow, Barbara Hershey, Michael Rapaport, Carol Kane, Toni Collette, Michael Vartan; *D:* Matt Reeves; *W:* Matt Reeves, Jason Katims; *C:* Robert Elswit; *M:* Stewart Copeland. *NYR*

Palm Beach **1979** The lives of two petty thieves, a runaway, and a private detective intertwine at Palm Beach Down Under. Best appreciated by fans of things Aussie. **90m/C VHS, Beta.** *AU* Bryan Brown, Nat Young, Ken Brown, Amanda Berry; *D:* Albie Thomas. *AHV*

The Palm Beach Story **1942** Colbert and McCrea play a married couple who have everything—except money. The wife decides to divorce her current husband, marry a rich man, and finance her former husband's ambitions. She decides the best place to husband-hunt is Palm Beach. A Sturges classic screwball comedy. **88m/B VHS, Beta, LV.** Claudette Colbert, Joel McCrea, Mary Astor, Rudy Vallee, William Demarest, Franklin Pangborn; *D:* Preston Sturges; *C:* Victor Milner. *MCA*

Palm Springs Weekend ½ **1963** A busload of love-hungry kids head south and get involved in routine hijinks. Actually shot in Palm Springs with adove average performances by a handful of stars. **100m/C VHS, Beta, LV.** Troy Donahue, Ty Hardin, Connie Stevens, Stefanie Powers, Robert Conrad, Jack Weston, Andrew Duggan; *D:* Norman Taurog. *WAR*

Palombella Rossa **1989** Political comedy about the fate of Italian communism. When communist politician Michele loses his memory in a car crash, he finds himself trying to reconstruct his life during a game of water polo as well as trying to answer political questions and keep track of the people from his life who randomly appear and disappear. In Italian with English subtitles. **87m/C VHS.** *IT* *D:* Nanni Moretti. *FXL, ORI, FCT*

Palooka ½ *Joe Palooka; The Great Schnozzle* **1934 (G)** Based on the comic strip, this film portrays a fast-talking boxing manager and his goofy, lovable protege. The young scrapper fights James Cagney's little brother. Durante sings his classic tune, "Inka-Dinka-Doo," and packs a punch in the lead. A two-fisted comedy with a witty dialogue and fine direction. Not a part of the Palooka series of the 1940s. **86m/B VHS, Beta.** Jimmy Durante, Stuart Erwin, Lupe Velez, Robert Armstrong, Thelma Todd, William Cagney; *D:* Ben Stoloff. *NOS, RXM, VYY*

Pals **1987** Old friends stumble across $3 million in cash and learn the predictable lesson that money can't buy happiness. A terribly trite TV-movie with an exceptional cast. **90m/C VHS.** Don Ameche, George C. Scott, Sylvia Sidney, Susan Rinell, James Greene; *D:* Lou Antonio. *VMK*

Pals of the Range **1935** A framed ranch owner breaks out of jail in order to catch the real cattle thieves. Ho hum in the Old West. **55m/B VHS, Beta.** Rex Lease. *NOS*

Pals of the Saddle ½ **1938** The intrepid trio go after enemy agents who are trying to smuggle chemicals for poisonous gas into Mexico. This is the first of the series in which the Duke played the part of Stony Brooke. Somewhat convoluted plot, but nevertheless enjoyable. **55m/B VHS.** John Wayne, Ray Corrigan, Max Terhune, Doreen McKay, Josef Forte, Ted Adams, Curly Dresden; *D:* George Sherman. *NOS*

The Pamela Principle **1991 (R)** A bored, middle-aged man thinks his prayers are answered when he meets a sexy 20-year-old model and begins a sordid affair with her. Soon, however, he finds himself in a tense situation when he must choose between his family or his fantasy. Also available in an unrated version. **?m/C VHS, LV.** J.K. Dumont, Veronica Cash, Shelby Lane, Troy Donahue, Frank Pesce; *D:* Toby Phillips. *IMP*

Panama Hattie **1942** Screen adaptation of Cole Porter's delightful Broadway musical. Unfortunately, something (like a plot) was lost in transition. Southern runs a saloon for our boys down in Panama. Among the musical numbers and vaudevillian acts some spies show up. Several screenwriters and directors, including Vincente Minnelli, worked uncredited on this picture, to no avail. Horne's second screen appearance. ♫It Was Just One of Those Things; Fresh as a Daisy; I've Still Got My Health; Let's Be Buddies; Make It Another Old Fashioned; Hattie from Panama; Good Neighbors; I'll Do Anything for You; The Son of a Gun Who Pick on Uncle Sam. **79m/B VHS.** Ann Sothern, Dan Dailey, Red Skelton, Virginia O'Brien, Rags Ragland, Alan Mowbray, Ben Blue, Carl Esmond, Lena Horne; *D:* Norman Z. McLeod; *M:* George Bassman, Cole Porter. *MGM, CCB*

Panama Lady ½ **1939** Ball stars as the sexy, sultry "Panama Lady" in this old-fashioned romance. She gets involved in some shady business south of the border. A lackluster remake of "Panama Flo." **65m/B VHS, Beta.** Lucille Ball, Evelyn Brent. *NO*

Panama Menace *South of Panama* **1941** An agent heads to Panama to thwart spies who are after a special paint that makes things invisible. Poor effort all around, in spite of Beaumont's presence. **68m/B VHS, Beta.** Roger Pryor, Virginia Vale, Lionel Royce, Lucien Prival, Duncan Renaldo, Lester Dorr, Hugh Beaumont; *D:* Jean Yarbrough. *SNC, VYY*

Panama Patrol ½ **1939** Just as they are about to be married, two Army officers are called to duty in Panama. It seems that the Chinese have infiltrated the area with spies and something's got to be done. Too much attention to minor parts of the plot slows the story occasionally, but performances and photography compensate for some of the sluggishness. **67m/B VHS, Beta.** Leon Ames, Charlotte Wynters, Weldon Heyburn, Adrienne Ames, Abner Biberman, Hugh McArthur, Donald (Don "Red") Barry; *D:* Charles Lamont. *SNC*

Panamint's Bad Man **1938** Ballaw is a poor man's Gary Cooper fighting for justice against stagecoach robbers. Almost as much flavor as tumbleweed. **59m/B VHS, Beta.** Smith Ballew, Evelyn Daw, Noah Beery Sr.; *D:* Ray Taylor. *NOS, VDM, DVT*

Pancho Barnes ½ **1988 (PG)** Routine biography of one of the first female pilots of the 1920s. Barnes is a bored debutante who finds her challenge in life when she learns to fly, becoming a barnstormer and movie stunt pilot. Her ambitions naturally get in the way of her romantic life. Good flying scenes. Made for television. **150m/C VHS.** Valerie Bertinelli, Ted Wass, Sam Robards, James Stephens, Cynthia Harris, Geoffrey Lewis; *D:* Richard T. Heffron; *W:* John Michael Hayes. *ORI*

Pancho Villa ½ **1972 (PG)** Savalas has the lead in this fictional account of the famous Mexican, He leads his men in a raid on an American fort after being hoodwinked in an arms deal. Connors tries to hold the fort against him. The finale, in which two trains crash head on, is the most exciting event in the whole darn movie. **92m/C VHS.** *SP* Telly Savalas, Clint Walker, Anne Francis, Chuck Connors, Angel Del Pozo, Luis Davila; *D:* Eugenio Martin. *NO*

Pancho Villa Returns **1950** It's 1913, and noble Mexican General Pancho Villa leads his merry men against the assassins of President Madera. This Mexican production (filmed in English) paints a partisan portrait of title character as a good-hearted revolutionary folk hero, not the roving bandit later notorious north of the border. **95m/B VHS.** *MX* Leo Carrillo, Esther Fernandez, Jeanette Comber, Rodolfo Acosta; *D:* Miguel Contreras Torres; *W:* Miguel Contreras Torres. *NOS, LOO*

Pandemonium ½ *Thursday the 12th* **1982 (PG)** A spoof of teen slasher films involving murder at Bambi's Cheerleading School. Seems that nationwide, cheerleaders have been brutally eliminated from their squads, leaving Bambi's as the last resort for the terminally perky. Smothers is interesting and more intelligent than his TV persona (although not by much) as the Mountie hero, assisted by Paul Reubens in a pre-Pee-Wee role. Kane steals the show as Candy, a pleasant lass with hyperkinetic powers. **82m/C VHS, Beta.** *CA* Tom Smothers, Carol Kane, Miles Chapin, Paul (Pee Wee Herman) Reubens, Judge Reinhold, Tab Hunter, Marc McClure, Donald O'Connor, Eve Arden, Eileen Brennan, Edie McClurg; *D:* Alfred Sole. *MGM*

Pandora and the Flying Dutchman ½ **1951** Feverish romantic fantasy has playgirl/nightclub singer Pandora Reynolds (Gardner) living in '30s Spain and being romanced by every man in sight. Naturally, she cares for none of them until she meets enigmatic Dutch captain Hendrick van der Zee (Mason) who is, in fact, the legendary Flying Dutchman—condemned to wander the seas forever unless a woman is willing to give up her life for him. Gardner is, as usual, exotically lovely. **123m/C VHS.** Ava Gardner, James Mason, Nigel Patrick, Sheila Sim, Harold Warrender, Mario Cabre; *D:* Albert Lewin; *W:* Albert Lewin; *C:* Jack Cardiff; *M:* Alan Rawsthorne. *KIV*

Pandora's Box ☊☊☊☊ *Die Buechse Der Pandora* **1928** This silent classic marked the end of the German Expressionist era and established Brooks as a major screen presence. She plays the tempestuous Lulu, who destroys everyone she comes in contact with, eventually sinking to prostitution and a fateful meeting with Jack the Ripper. Silent with orchestral score. **110m/B VHS, Beta.** *GE* Louise Brooks, Fritz Kortner, Francis Lederer, Carl Goetz; ***D:*** G.W. Pabst; ***W:*** G.W. Pabst. *GPV, MRV, VDM*

Panic ☊½ **1983** A scientist terrorizes a small town when he becomes hideously deformed by one of his bacteria experiments. He should have known better. **90m/C VHS, Beta.** David Warbeck, Janet Agren. *MPI*

Panic Button ☊½ **1962** Mel Brooks took the plot from this film and made "The Producers," which was much better. Italian gangsters produce a television show and stack the deck so that it will fail. Unbeknownst to them, the star has figured out what they are doing and works to make it a success. Shot in Italy, mainly in Venice and Rome. **90m/B VHS.** *IT* Maurice Chevalier, Eleanor Parker, Jayne Mansfield, Mike Connors, Akim Tamiroff; ***D:*** George Sherman. *NO*

Panic in Echo Park ☊☊ **1977** A doctor races against time to find the cause of an epidemic that is threatening the health of a city. Good performances compensate for a predictable plot. Made for television. **78m/C VHS.** Dorian Harewood, Robin Gammell, Catlin Adams, Ramon Bieri, Movita; ***D:*** John Llewellyn Moxey. *NO*

Panic in Needle Park ☊☊☊ **1975 (R)** Drugs become an obsession for a young girl who goes to New York for an abortion. Her new boyfriend is imprisoned for robbery in order to support both their habits. She resorts to prostitution to continue her drug habit, and trouble occurs when her boyfriend realizes she was instrumental in his being sent to jail. Strikes a vein in presenting an uncompromising look at drug use. May be too much of a depressant for some. Pacino's first starring role. **90m/C VHS, LV.** Al Pacino, Kitty Winn, Alan Vint, Richard Bright, Kiel Martin, Warren Finnerty, Raul Julia, Paul Sorvino; ***D:*** Jerry Schatzberg; ***W:*** Joan Didion, John Gregory Dunne; ***C:*** Adam Holender. Cannes Film Festival '71: Best Actress (Winn); Nominations: Cannes Film Festival '71: Best Film. *FOX*

Panic in the Streets ☊☊☊ **1950** The Black Death threatens New Orleans in this intense tale. When a body is found on the waterfront, a doctor (Widmark) is called upon for a diagnosis. The carrier proves to be deadly in more ways than one. Fine performances, taut direction (this was one of Kazan's favorite movies). Filmed on location in New Orleans. **96m/B VHS, LV.** Richard Widmark, Jack Palance, Barbara Bel Geddes, Paul Douglas, Zero Mostel; ***D:*** Elia Kazan; ***W:*** Edward Anhalt. Academy Awards '50: Best Story. *FOX, FCT*

Panic in the Year Zero! ☊☊½ *End of the World* **1962** Milland and family leave Los Angeles for a fishing trip just as the city is hit by a nuclear bomb. Continuing out into the wilderness for safety, the family now must try to survive as their world crumbles around them. Generally considered the best of Milland's five directorial efforts. **92m/B VHS.** Ray Milland, Jean Hagen, Frankie Avalon, Mary Mitchell, Joan Freeman, Richard Garland, Rex Holman; ***D:*** Ray Milland; ***M:*** Les Baxter. *FRG*

Panic on the 5:22 ☊☊ **1974** Wealthy commuters are kidnapped and held hostage by terrorist hoodlums in a suburban train club car. Standard made for television vehicle. **78m/C VHS, Beta.** Lynda Day George, Laurence Luckinbill, Ina Balin, Bernie Casey; ***D:*** Harvey Hart. *WOV*

Panic Station ☊☊ *The Plains of Heaven* **1982** Two guys get lonely at remote satellite relay station. **90m/C VHS.** *AU* Richard Moir, Reg Evans, Gerard Kennedy; ***D:*** Ian Pringle. *ACA*

Panique ☊☊☊ *Panic* **1947** A study of mob psychology in slums of post-WWII Paris. Two lovers frame a stranger for murder. Dark and tautly paced thriller taken from the novel by Georges Simenon. In French with English subtitles. **87m/B VHS, Beta.** *FR* Michel Simon, Viviane Romance; ***D:*** Julien Duvivier. *NOS, HHT, CAB*

Pantaloons ☊☊ **1957** A man who fancies himself to be irresistible chases women for sport. A quaint and lively period film. **93m/C VHS.** *FR* Fernandel, Carmen Sevilla, Fernando Rey; ***D:*** John Berry. *VYY*

Panther ☊☊ **1995 (R)** The Van Peebles family teaches Oliver Stone History 101 with a fictionalized account of the Black Panthers' emergence as a voice for African Americans and as a fixture on the FBI's most wanted list in the late '60's. Judge (Hardison), a Vietnam vet forced by the FBI to become an informant, chronicles the activities of leaders Bobby Seale (Vance) and Huey P. Newton (Chong) and serves as witness to the Panthers' rise and subsequent fall into corruption and disintegration. Scatter-shot editing is meant to signify the chaos of the times, but instead adds to the action-flick feel and further detracts from the professed intent of being a message movie. **124m/C VHS.** Kadeem Hardison, Marcus Chong, Courtney B. Vance, Bokeem Woodbine, Joe Don Baker, Anthony Griffith, Nefertiti, James Russo, Richard Dysart, M. Emmet Walsh, Mario Van Peebles; ***D:*** Mario Van Peebles; ***W:*** Melvin Van Peebles; ***C:*** Eddie Pei; ***M:*** Stanley Clarke. *PGV*

Panther Squad ☊ **1984** Litter of sex kittens led by Danning get into major scraps to save world. **77m/C VHS.** Sybil Danning. *NO*

The Panther's Claw ☊☊ **1942** Murder befalls an opera troupe, but a sleuth with the memorable name of Thatcher Colt is on the case. A quick-moving mystery quickie that delivers on its own modest terms. **72m/B VHS.** Sidney Blackmer, Byron Foulger, Rick Vallin, Herbert Rawlinson; ***D:*** William Beaudine. *NOS, LOO*

Papa's Delicate Condition ☊☊☊ **1963** Based on the autobiographical writings of silent screen star Corinne Griffith. Gleason is Papa whose "delicate condition" is a result of his drinking. His antics provide a constant headache to his family. A paean to turn-of-the-century family life. No I.D.s required as the performances are enjoyable for the whole family. Features the Academy Award-winning song "Call Me Irresponsible." ♫Call Me Irresponsible; Bill Bailey, Won't You Please Come Home?. **98m/C VHS, Beta.** Jackie Gleason, Glynis Johns, Charlie Ruggles, Laurel Goodwin, Elisha Cook Jr., Murray Hamilton; ***D:*** George Marshall; ***W:*** Jack Rose; ***C:*** Loyal Griggs. Academy Awards '63: Best Song ("Call Me Irresponsible"). *BAR*

The Paper ☊☊☊ **1994 (R)** Another crowd pleaser from director Howard follows a red letter day in the life of an editor at the tabloid New York Sun (modeled on the trashy Post). Fresh, fast-moving script by the Koepp brothers (who appear as reporters) offers a fairly accurate portrayal of the business of journalism (including the "brisk" language), with a few Hollywood exceptions. Pace suffers from cutaways to life outside, while script and direction sometimes coast past targets. Propelled by a fine cast, with cola-swigging editor Keaton the focus as he juggles his personal and professional lives. As a managing editor married to her work and ready to run over anyone in her way, Close is both funny and scary. Duvall contributes salt as the old newsroom warhorse. Tons of cameos, though those outside of the business may not notice them. **112m/C VHS, LV.** Michael Keaton, Robert Duvall, Marisa Tomei, Glenn Close, Randy Quaid, Jason Robards Jr., Jason Alexander, Spalding Gray, Catherine O'Hara, Lynne Thigpen; ***D:*** Ron Howard; ***W:*** David Koepp, Steven Koepp; ***M:*** Randy Newman. Nominations: Academy Awards '94: Best Song ("Make Up Your Mind"). *MCA*

The Paper Chase ☊☊☊ **1973 (PG)** Students at Harvard Law School suffer and struggle through their first year. A realistic, sometimes acidly humorous look at Ivy League ambitions, with Houseman stealing the show as the tough professor. Wonderful adaptation of the John Jay Osborn novel which later became the basis for the acclaimed television series. **111m/C VHS, Beta, LV.** Timothy Bottoms, Lindsay Wagner, John Houseman, Graham Beckel, Edward Herrmann, James Naughton, Craig Richard Nelson, Bob Lydiard; ***D:*** James Bridges; ***W:*** James Bridges; ***C:*** Gordon Willis; ***M:*** John Williams. Academy Awards '73: Best Supporting Actor (Houseman); Golden Globe Awards '74: Best Supporting Actor (Houseman); National Board of Review Awards '73: Best Supporting Actor (Houseman); Nominations: Academy Awards '73: Best Adapted Screenplay, Best Sound. *FOX, BTV*

Paper Lion ☊☊½ **1968** A comedy "documentary" about bestselling writer George Plimpton's tryout game as quarterback with the Detroit Lions. Film debut of Alan Alda. Helped Karras make the transition from the gridiron to the silver screen. Moves into field goal range but doesn't quite score. **107m/C VHS, Beta.** Alan Alda, Lauren Hutton, Alex Karras, Ann Turkel, John Gordy, Roger Brown, "Sugar Ray" Robinson, Roy Scheider, David Doyle; ***D:*** Alex March. *NO*

Paper Man ☊☊ **1971** A group of college students create a fictitious person in a computer for a credit card scam. The scheme snowballs, resulting in murder and hints of possible artificial intelligence. But it's just standard network TV fare, with a creepy performance by Stockwell as a computer whiz. **90m/C VHS.** Dean Stockwell, Stefanie Powers, James Stacy, Elliot Street, Tina Chen, James Olson, Ross Elliott; ***D:*** Walter Grauman. *XVC, VTR*

Paper Marriage ☊½ **1988** In Canada, a less than successful Chinese boxer agrees to marry a Hong Kong girl for a promise of payment in order that she may become a citizen. The money never comes, but the nearly betrothed pair discover that they love each other, after all. In Cantonese with English subtitles. **102m/C VHS.** *CH* Samo Hung, Maggie Cheung; ***D:*** Alfred Cheung. *FCT, MOV, ACA*

Paper Marriage ☊☊½ **1993** Yet another variation on the marriage in order to gain citizenship but yes we're going to fall in love films. A young Polish woman has fallen for an upper-crust English doctor she's met in Warsaw. When Alicja arrives in England, she's promptly dumped by the cad. She's ambitious and wants to stay in England so Alicja arranges a marriage of convenience with small-time crook Aiden, who finds his new bride is more than he bargained for. **88m/C VHS.** *GB PL* Gary Kemp, Joanna Trepechinska, Rita Tushingham, Richard Hawley, David Horovitch, William Ilkley, Mark McKellen, Ann Mitchell, Sadie Frost; ***D:*** Krzysztof Lang; ***W:*** Marek Kreutz, Krzysztof Lang. *ACA*

Paper Mask ☊☊½ **1991 (R)** When a promising young doctor is killed in an auto accident, an unscrupulous, psychotic porter assumes his identity. He uses said identity to, among other things, initiate an affair with a sultry co-worker. How long will this madman play his unholy game, and at what cost? **105m/C VHS.** *GB* Paul McGann, Amanda Donohoe, Frederick Treves, Barbara Leigh-Hunt, Jimmy Yuill, Tom Wilkinson; ***D:*** Christopher Morahan; ***W:*** John Collee; ***M:*** Richard Harvey. *ACA*

Paper Moon ☊☊☊½ **1973 (PG)** Award-winning story set in depression-era Kansas with Ryan O'Neal as a Bible-wielding con who meets up with a nine-year-old orphan. During their travels together, he discovers that the orphan (his daughter, Tatum) is better at "his" game than he is. Irresistible chemistry between the O'Neals, leading to Tatum's Oscar win (she is the youngest actor ever to take home a statue). Cinematically picturesque and cynical enough to keep overt sentimentalism at bay. Based on Joe David Brown's novel, "Addie Pray." The director's version contains a prologue by director Bogdanovich. **102m/B VHS, Beta, LV.** Ryan O'Neal, Tatum O'Neal, Madeline Kahn, John Hillerman, Randy Quaid; ***D:*** Peter Bogdanovich; ***W:*** Alvin Sargent. Academy Awards '73: Best Supporting Actress (O'Neal); National Board of Review Awards '73: 10 Best Films of the Year; Writers Guild of America '73: Best Adapted Screenplay; Nominations: Academy Awards '73: Best Adapted Screenplay, Best Sound, Best Supporting Actress (Kahn). *PAR, BTV*

Paper Tiger ☊☊ **1974** Niven plays an imaginative English tutor who fabricates fantastic yarns fictionalizing his past in order to impress his student, the son of the Japanese ambassador to a Southeast

Asian country. Poorly executed karate, misdirection, and a simplistic storyline work against it. **104m/C VHS, Beta.** *GB* David Niven, Toshiro Mifune, Eiko Ando, Hardy Kruger; ***D:*** Ken Annakin; ***W:*** Jack Davies. *SUE, OM*

A Paper Wedding 🦴🦴🦴 *Les Noces de Papier* **1989** A middle-aged literature professor with a dead-end career and equally dead-end romance with a married man is persuaded by her lawyer sister to marry a Chilean political refugee to avoid his deportation. Of course, they must fool an immigration official and their fake marriage does turn into romance, but this is no light-hearted "Green Card." Bujold shines. In French and Spanish with English subtitles. **90m/C VHS, LV.** *CA* Genevieve Bujold, Manuel Aranguiz, Dorothee Berryman; ***D:*** Michel Brault. *CTL, INJ, LUM*

Paperback Hero 🦴🦴 **1973** A hot-shot hockey player turns to crime when his team loses its financial backing. Choopy storyline could use a Zamboni, while Dullea should be penalized for occasionally losing his rustic accent. Still the supporting actors skate through their roles and, for periods, it works. A slapshot that ultimately clangs off the goal post. **94m/C VHS.** *CA* Keir Dullea, Elizabeth Ashley, John Beck, Dayle Haddon; ***D:*** Peter Pearson. *NO*

The Paperboy 🦴🦴 **1994 (R)** Melissa Thorpe (Paul) returns to her small hometown to settle her mother's estate, only to become the obsession of Johnny (Marut), the 12-year-old paperboy she mistakenly befriends. Seems he becomes psychotically jealous when Melissa takes up with an old flame (Katt) and dead bodies become as common as old newspapers. **93m/C VHS, LV.** Alexandra Paul, Marc Marut, William Katt, Brigid Tierney; ***D:*** Douglas Jackson; ***W:*** David Peckinpah; ***M:*** Milan Kymlicka. *REP*

Paperhouse 🦴🦴🦴 **1989** An odd fantasy about a young girl plagued by recurring dreams that begin to influence real life. Very obtuse, British-minded film with "Twilight Zone" feel that manages to capture genuine dream-ness. Not for all audiences, but intriguing nontheless. Based on the novel "Marianne Dreams" by Catherine Storr. **92m/C VHS, Beta, LV.** *GB* Glenne Headly, Ben Cross, Charlotte Burke, Elliott Spiers, Gemma Jones, Sarah Newbold; ***D:*** Bernard Rose; ***W:*** Matthew Jacobs; ***M:*** Hans Zimmer, Stanley Myers. *LIV, VES*

Papillon 🦴🦴🦴 **1973 (PG)** McQueen is a criminal sent to Devil's Island in the 1930s determined to escape from the Lemote prison. Hoffman is the swindler he befriends. A series of escapes and recaptures follow. Box-office winner based on the autobiographical writings of French thief Henri Charriere. Excellent portrayal of prison life and fine performances from the prisoners. Certain segments would have been better left on the cutting room floor. The film's title refers to the lead's butterfly tattoo. **150m/C VHS, Beta, LV.** Steve McQueen, Dustin Hoffman, Victor Jory, George Coulouris, Anthony Zerbe; ***D:*** Franklin J. Schaffner; ***C:*** Fred W. Koenekamp; ***M:*** Jerry Goldsmith. Nominations: Academy Awards '73: Best Original Score. *FOX, WAR*

Parade 🦴🦴🦴 **1974** A series of vignettes in a circus, "Parade" is actually a play within a play, meshing the action with events offstage. The laser disc edition includes Rene Clement's 1936 "Soigne Ton Gauche," Tati's inspiration. **85m/C VHS, LV.** *FR* Jacques Tati; ***D:*** Jacques Tati; ***W:*** Jacques Tati. *HMV, CRC, FCT*

The Paradine Case 🦴🦴½ **1947** A passable Hitchcock romancer about a young lawyer who falls in love with the woman he's defending for murder, not knowing whether she is innocent or guilty. Script could be tighter and more cohesive. Seventy thousand dollars of the three million budget were spent recreating the original Bailey courtroom. Based on the novel by Robert Hichens. **125m/B VHS, Beta, LV.** Gregory Peck, Alida Valli, Ann Todd, Louis Jourdan, Charles Laughton, Charles Coburn, Ethel Barrymore, Leo G. Carroll; ***D:*** Alfred Hitchcock; ***C:*** Lee Garmes. Nominations: Academy Awards '47: Best Supporting Actress (Barrymore). *FOX*

Paradise 🦴🦴 **1982 (R)** Young American boy and beautiful English girl on a 19th-century jaunt through the Middle East are the sole survivors when their caravan is massacred. Left to their own devices, they discover a magnificent oasis and the joys of frolicking naked and experience (surprise) their sexual awakening. Do a double-take: it's the "Blue Lagoon" all over, with a bit more nudity and a lot more sand. **96m/C VHS, Beta, LV.** Phoebe Cates, Willie Aames, Richard Curnock, Tuvio Tavi; ***D:*** Stuart Gillard. *COL*

Paradise 🦴🦴🦴 **1991 (PG-13)** Young boy is sent to the country to live with his pregnant mother's married friends (real life husband and wife Johnson and Griffith). From the outset it is clear that the couple are experiencing marital troubles, making the boy's assimilation all the more difficult. Help arrives in the form of a sprightly ten-year-old girl, with whom he forms a charming relationship. Largely predictable, this remake of the French film "Le Grand Chemin" works thanks to the surprisingly good work of its ensemble cast, and the gorgeous scenery of South Carolina, where the movie was filmed. **112m/C VHS, Beta.** Melanie Griffith, Don Johnson, Elijah Wood, Thora Birch, Sheila McCarthy, Eve Gordon, Louise Latham, Greg Travis, Sarah Trigger; ***D:*** Mary Agnes Donoghue; ***W:*** Mary Agnes Donoghue; ***M:*** David Newman. *TOU*

Paradise Alley 🦴🦴 **1978 (PG)** Rocky tires of boxing, decides to join the WWF. Three brothers brave the world of professional wrestling in an effort to strike it rich and move out of the seedy Hell's Kitchen neighborhood of New York, circa 1946. Stallone wrote, stars in, and makes his directorial debut in addition to singing the title song. He makes a few good moves as director, but is ultimately pinned to the canvas. **109m/C VHS, Beta, LV.** Sylvester Stallone, Anne Archer, Armand Assante, Lee Canalito, Kevin Conway; ***D:*** Sylvester Stallone; ***W:*** Sylvester Stallone; ***M:*** Bill Conti. *MCA*

Paradise Canyon 🦴½ **1935** Early Wayne "B" thriller, in which he plays an undercover government agent sent to track down a group of counterfeiters. **59m/B VHS.** John Wayne, Yakima Canutt, Marion Burns. *COL, NOS, REP*

Paradise, Hawaiian Style 🦴½ **1966** Out-of-work pilot returns to Hawaii, where he and a buddy start a charter service with two helicopters. Plenty of gals are wooed by "the Pelvis." Filmed four years after Elvis's first Pacific piece, "Blue Hawaii." Presley, showing the first signs of slow-down, displays no surprises here. ♫Paradise, Hawaiian Style; Scratch My Back (Then I'll Scratch Yours); Stop Where You Are; This Is My Heaven; House of Sand; Queenie Wahine's Papaya; Datin'; Drums of the Islands; A Dog's Life. **91m/C VHS, Beta.** Elvis Presley, Suzanna Leigh, James Shigeta, Donna Butterworth, Irene Tsu, Julie Parrish, Philip Ahn, Mary Treen, Marianna Hill, John Doucette, Grady Sutton; ***D:*** Michael Moore. *FOX, MVD*

Paradise in Harlem 🦴½ **1940** All-black musical in which a cabaret performer witnesses a gangland murder, sees his sick wife die, and is pressured into leaving town by the mob. Have a nice day. **83m/B VHS, Beta.** Frank Wilson, Mamie Smith, Edna Mae Harris, Juanita Hall; ***D:*** Joseph Seiden. *VYY, FCT, VCN*

Paradise Island 🦴 **1930** Down-scale musical romance about an ingenue on her way to join her fiance in the South Seas, only to find that he has gambled away his money. The opportunistic saloon owner tries to put the moves on her. Will the two lovers be reunited? ♫I've Got a Girl In Every Port; Drinking Song; Lazy Breezes; Just Another Dream. **68m/B VHS.** Kenneth Harlan, Marceline Day, Thomas Santschi, Paul Hurst, Victor Potel, Gladden James, Will Stanton; ***D:*** Bert Glennon. *GPV, NOS*

Paradise Motel 🦴½ **1984 (R)** Teen exploitation film centered around a local motel predominantly used for one-night rendezvous. High school heroes and jocks battle for the affections of a beautiful classmate. **87m/C VHS, Beta.** Bob Basso, Gary Hershberger, Jonna Leigh Stack, Robert Krantz; ***D:*** Cary Medoway. *FOX*

Paradise Park 🦴🦴½ **199?** A whimsical comedy about the inhabitants of a West Virginia trailer park who dream of better lives while coping with their depressing surroundings. An English teacher (Groce) wishes he was a writer, an elderly woman (Basquette) dreams of winning a TV quiz show, and a mechanic wants to be a race car driver. Director Boyd sprinkles in appearances of non-Hollywood notables Porter Waggoner, Johnny Paycheck, Webb Wilder, and wrestler Dusty Rhodes. Includes some black and white fantasy sequences. **100m/C VHS.** Lena Basquette, Larry Groce, Jennifer Gurney; ***Cameos:*** Johnny Paycheck, Webb Wilder, Dusty Rhodes, Porter Waggoner; ***D:*** Daniel Boyd. *MTH*

Paradisio 🦴½ **1961 (R)** Dying inventor wills Oxford professor an authentic pair of X-ray specs. Spies come gunning for the professor, chasing him through Europe. Doc keeps forgetting he's being chased while using the special specs to see (sometimes in 3-D) through the clothing of young women. Meager plot does not get in way of 3-D nudie exploitation. **82m/C VHS, Beta.** Arthur Howard, Eva Waegner. *NWV, VDM*

The Parallax View 🦴🦴🦴½ **1974 (R)** A reporter tries to disprove a report which states that a presidential candidate's assassination was not a conspiracy. As he digs deeper and deeper, he uncovers more than he bargained for and becomes a pawn in the conspirators' further plans. Beatty is excellent and the conspiracy is never less than believable. A lesser-known, compelling political thriller that deserves to be more widely seen. **102m/C VHS, Beta.** Warren Beatty, Hume Cronyn, William Daniels, Paula Prentiss, Kenneth Mars, Bill McKinney, Anthony Zerbe, Walter McGinn; ***D:*** Alan J. Pakula; ***C:*** Gordon Willis. National Society of Film Critics Awards '74: Best Cinematography. *PAR*

Parallel Corpse 🦴 **1983** A mortuary attendant finds a murder victim hidden in a coffin and blackmails the remorseless killer. **89m/C VHS, Beta.** Buster Larsen, Jorgen Kiil, Agneta Ekmanner, Masja Dessau. *MED*

Parallel Lives 🦴🦴½ **1994 (R)** Sorority sisters and frat brothers (and their various spouses and lovers) , from the classes of both 1948 and 1973, gather for an on-campus weekend reunion and discover old and new jealousies, rivalries, and lots of lust (requited and not). There's also an unexpected death and a police investigation as well. Director Yellen had her cast improvise much of their dialogue—the same method she used in "Chantilly Lace." Made for cable TV. **105m/C VHS, Beta.** James Belushi, James Brolin, LeVar Burton, Lindsay Crouse, Jill Eikenberry, Ben Gazzara, Jack Klugman, David Lansbury, Liza Minnelli, Dudley Moore, Gena Rowlands, Ally Sheedy, Helen Slater, Mira Sorvino, Paul Sorvino, Robert Wagner, Patricia Wettig, JoBeth Williams, Treat Williams; ***D:*** Linda Yellen; ***W:*** Gisella Bernice; ***M:*** Patrick Seymour. *PAR*

Paralyzed 🦴🦴 **197?** An unconscious journalist, mistaken for dead in a hospital emergency room, flashes back to the investigation that embroiled him in his predicament. **90m/C VHS, Beta.** Ingrid Thulin, Jean Sorel, Mario Adorf; ***D:*** Aldo Lado; ***W:*** Aldo Lado. *MPI*

Paramedics 🦴½ **1988 (PG-13)** A motley crew of cavorting paramedics battle their evil captain. Another parody of people in uniform. A comedy with little pulse. **91m/C VHS, Beta, LV.** George Newbern, Christopher McDonald, John P. Ryan, Ray Walston, Lawrence-Hilton Jacobs; ***D:*** Stuart Margolin. *LIV, VES*

Paranoia 🦴 *Orgasmo; A Beautiful Place to Kill; A Quiet Place to Kill* **1969** Beautiful jet-set widow is trapped in her own Italian villa by a young couple who drug her to get her to perform in various sex orgies, which are probably the most interesting part of this muddled affair. **94m/C VHS, Beta.** *IT* Carroll Baker, Lou Castel, Colette Descombes; ***D:*** Umberto Lenzi. *REP*

Paranoiac 🦴🦴½ **1962** Greed and terror set in a country mansion. Simon (Reed) wants the family inheritance all to himself even if it means driving sister Eleanor (Scott) insane. This may not be so hard—she's claiming to see their dead brother Tony. Surprise! Tony (Davion) shows up (really throwing Simon for a loop). Reed's evil is tinged with humor although the numerous plot twists can get confusing. First directorial effort for cinematographer Francis. **80m/B VHS.** *GB* Oliver Reed, Janette Scott, Alex Davion, Liliane Brousse, Sheila Burell, Maurice Denham; ***D:*** Freddie Francis; ***W:*** Jimmy Sangster; ***C:*** Arthur Grant; ***M:*** Elisabeth Lutyens. *MCA*

Parasite *Woof!* **1982 (R)** A small town is beset by giant parasites. An "Alien" ripoff originally filmed in 3-D, during that technique's brief return in the early '80s. Bad films like this killed it both the first and second times. An unpardonable mess that comes off as a stinky sixth-grade film project. **90m/C VHS, Beta, LV.** Demi Moore, Luca Bercovici, Cherie Currie, Gale Robbins, James Davidson, Al Fann, Cheryl "Rainbeaux" Smith, Vivian Blaine; ***D:*** Charles Band; ***W:*** Alan J. Adler; ***M:*** Richard Band. *PAR*

Pardners 🦴🦴½ **1956** Spoiled New York millionaire (Lewis) becomes the sheriff of small western town, with Martin as a ranch foreman. The two team up to rid the town of bad guys and romance two local cuties. Western spoof (with music) is a remake of 1936's "Rhythm on the Range." ♫Buckskin Beauty; Pardners; The Wind! The Wind!; Me 'N You 'N the Moon. **88m/C VHS.** Jerry Lewis, Dean Martin, Lori Nelson, Jackie Loughery, Jeff Morrow, John Baragrey, Agnes Moorehead, Lon Chaney Jr., Milton Frome, Lee Van Cleef, Jack Elam, Bob Steele, Emory Parnell; ***D:*** Norman Taurog; ***W:*** Sidney Sheldon, Jerry Davis. *PAR*

Pardon Mon Affaire 🦴🦴🦴 *Un Elephant a Trompe Enormement* **1976 (PG)** When a middle-aged civil servant gets a look at a model in a parking garage, he decides it's time to cheat on his wife. Enjoyable French farce. Re-made as in the United States "The Woman in Red" and followed by "Pardon Mon Affair, Too!" Subtitled. **107m/C VHS, Beta, LV.** *FR* Jean Rochefort, Claude Brasseur, Guy Bedos, Victor Lanoux, Daniele Delorme, Martine Sarcey, Anny Duperey; ***D:*** Yves Robert; ***M:*** Vladimir Cosma. Cesar Awards '77: Best Supporting Actor (Brasseur). *SUE*

Pardon Mon Affaire, Too! 🦴🦴½ *We Will All Meet in Paradise* **1977** Pale sequel to the first popular French comedy, "Pardon Mon Affair." This time the four fantasy-minded buddies withstand the trials of marriage and middle-class life. With English subtitles or dubbed. **105m/C VHS, Beta.** *FR* Jean Rochefort, Claude Brasseur, Guy Bedos; ***D:*** Yves Robert; ***M:*** Vladimir Cosma. *SUE*

Pardon My Gun 🦴½ **1930** Cowpoke falls for the boss' daughter but has a rival in a wealthy rancher, who isn't above sabotage to get the girl. **64m/B VHS.** George Duryea, Harry Woods, Sally Starr, Lee Moran, Mona Ray; ***D:*** Robert De Lacy; ***W:*** Hugh Cummings. *GPV*

Pardon My Sarong 🦴🦴½ **1942** Bud and Lou star as Chicago bus drivers who end up shipwrecked on a South Pacific island when they get involved with notorious jewel thieves. The island natives think Lou is a god! Standard Abbott & Costello fare. **83m/B VHS.** Bud Abbott, Lou Costello, Virginia Bruce, Robert Paige, Lionel Atwill, Leif Erickson, William Demarest, Samuel S. Hinds; ***D:*** Erle C. Kenton; ***C:*** Milton Krasner. *MCA*

Pardon My Trunk 🦴🦴 *Hello Elephant; Buongiorno, Elefante* **1952** Struggling against poverty on his teacher's salary, a man and his family receive a gift from a Hindu prince—an elephant. De Sica carries this silly premise beyond mere slapstick. Dubbed. **85m/B VHS, Beta.** *IT* Sabu, Vittorio De Sica; ***D:*** Gianni Franciolini. *VYY*

Pardon Us 🦴🦴½ *Jail Birds* **1931** Laurel and Hardy are thrown into prison for bootlegging. Plot meanders along aimlessly, but the duo have some inspired moments. The first Laurel and Hardy feature. **78m/B VHS, Beta.** Stan Laurel, Oliver Hardy, June Marlowe, James Finlayson; ***D:*** James Parrott. *MED, CCB, MLB*

The Parent Trap 🦴🦴½ **1961** Mills plays a dual role in this heartwarming comedy as twin sisters who conspire to bring their divorced parents together again. Well-known Disney fluff. Followed by several made-for-television sequels featuring the now grown-up twins. **127m/C VHS, Beta, LV.** Hayley Mills, Maureen O'Hara, Brian Keith, Charlie Ruggles, Una Merkel, Leo G. Carroll; ***D:*** David Swift. Nominations: Academy Awards '61: Best Film Editing, Best Sound. *DIS*

Parenthood 🦴🦴🦴 **1989 (PG-13)** Four grown siblings and their parents struggle with various levels of parenthood. From the college drop-out, to the nervous single mother, to the yuppie couple raising an overachiever, every possibility is explored, including the perspective from the older generation, portrayed by Robards. Genuinely funny with dramatic moments that work most of the time, with an affecting performance from Martin and Wiest. Director Howard has four kids and was inspired to make this film when on a European jaunt with them. **124m/C VHS, Beta, LV.** Steve Martin, Mary Steenburgen, Dianne Wiest, Martha Plimpton, Keanu Reeves, Tom Hulce, Jason Robards Jr., Rick Moranis, Harley Jane Kozak, Joaquin Rafael (Leaf) Phoenix, Paul Linke, Dennis Dugan; ***D:*** Ron Howard; ***W:*** Lowell Ganz, Babaloo Mandel, Ron Howard; ***M:*** Randy Newman. Nominations: Academy Awards '89: Best Song ("I Love to See You Smile"), Best Supporting Actress (Wiest). *MCA*

Parents 🦴🦴🦴 **1989 (R)** Dark satire of middle class suburban life in the '50s, centering on a young boy who discovers that his parents aren't getting their meat from the local butcher. Gives new meaning to leftovers and boasts a very disturbing barbecue scene. Balaban's debut is a strikingly visual and creative gorefest with definite cult potential. The eerie score is by Badalamenti, who also composed the music for "Blue Velvet," "Wild at Heart," and the television series "Twin Peaks." **81m/C VHS, Beta, LV.** Randy Quaid, Mary Beth Hurt, Sandy Dennis, Kathryn Grody, Deborah Rush, Graham Jarvis, Bryan Madorsky, Juno Mills-Cockell; ***D:*** Bob Balaban; ***W:*** Christopher Hawthorne; ***M:*** Angelo Badalamenti, Jonathan Elias. *LIV, VES, HHE*

Paris Belongs to Us 🦴🦴½ *Paris Nous Appartient; Paris is Ours* **1960** An early entry in the French "new wave" of naturalistic cinema, this psychological mystery drama has a woman investigating a suicide linked to a possible worldwide conspiracy. Interesting, if somewhat dated by Cold War elements. **120m/B VHS.** *FR* Jean-Claude Brialy, Betty Schneider, Gianni Esposito, Francoise Prevost; ***D:*** Jacques Rivette; ***W:*** Jacques Rivette, Jean Gruault. *VDM*

Paris Blues 🦴🦴½ **1961** Two jazz musicians, one white, one black, strive for success in Paris and become involved with American tourists who want to take them back to the States. Score by Duke Ellington and an appearance by Armstrong make it a must-see for jazz fans. **100m/B VHS, Beta.** Paul Newman, Sidney Poitier, Joanne Woodward, Diahann Carroll, Louis Armstrong, Barbara Lange; ***D:*** Martin Ritt; ***W:*** Jack Sher, Walter Bernstein; ***M:*** Duke Ellington. Nominations: Academy Awards '61: Best Original Score. *MGM, FCT*

Paris Express 🦴🦴½ *The Man Who Watched Trains Go By* **1953** When a man steals money from his employer, he boards the Paris Express to escape from the police. A bit convoluted, but well acted. Based on the George Simenon novel. **82m/C VHS, Beta.** Claude Rains, Herbert Lom, Felix Aylmer, Marius Goring, Anouk Aimee, Marta Toren; ***D:*** Harold French. *SNC, NOS, MRV*

Paris, France 🦴🦴 **1994 (NC-17)** Lucy (Hope) is a frustrated writer, living in Toronto, who decides the pursuit of sexual passion will unleash her blocked creative urges. Her main partner is poet Sloan (Outerbridge), the young man Lucy is trying to fashion in the image of a deceased Parisian lover, and also the man whose poetry her husband (and publisher) Michael (Ertmanis) is promoting. Lots of self-delusion and literary pretensions as well as erotic grappling. Adapted from the novel by Tom Walmsley. **96m/C VHS.** *CA* Leslie Hope, Peter Outerbridge, Victor Ertmanis, Raoul Trujillo, Dan Lett; ***D:*** Gerard Ciccoritti; ***W:*** Tom Walmsley; ***M:*** John McCarthy. *APX*

Paris Holiday 🦴🦴½ **1957** An actor heading for Paris to buy a noted author's latest screenplay finds mystery and romance. Entertaining chase scenes as the characters try to find the elusive script. **100m/C VHS, Beta.** Bob Hope, Fernandel, Anita Ekberg, Martha Hyer, Preston Sturges; ***D:*** Gerd Oswald. *UNI*

Paris is Burning 🦴🦴🦴 **1991 (R)** Livingston's documentary portrayal of New York City's transvestite balls where men dress up, dance, and compete in various categories. Filmed between 1985 and 1989, this is a compelling look at a subculture of primarily black and Hispanic men and the one place they can truly be themselves. Madonna noted this look and attitude (much watered down) in her song "Vogue." **71m/C VHS.** Dorian Corey, Pepper Labeija, Venus Xtravaganza, Octavia St. Laurant, Willi Ninja, Anji Xtravaganza, Freddie Pendavis, Junior Labeija; ***D:*** Jennie Livingston. National Society of Film Critics Awards '91: Best Feature Documentary; Sundance Film Festival '91: Grand Jury Prize. *ACA, FCT*

Paris, Texas 🦴🦴🦴½ **1983 (PG)** After four years a drifter returns to find his son is being raised by his brother because the boy's mother has also disappeared. He tries to reconnect with the boy. Introspective script acclaimed by many film critics, but others found it to be too slow. **145m/C VHS, Beta, LV.** *FR GE* Harry Dean Stanton, Nastassia Kinski, Dean Stockwell, Hunter Carson, Aurore Clement; ***D:*** Wim Wenders; ***W:*** Sam Shepard, L.M. Kit Carson; ***M:*** Ry Cooder. British Academy Awards '84: Best Director (Wenders); Cannes Film Festival '84: Best Film. *FOX*

Paris Trout 🦴🦴½ **1991 (R)** Believing himself above the law, southern Trout (Hopper) shoots the mother and sister of a young black man who reneged on his IOU. Lawyer Harris is forced to defend a man he knows deserves to be punished, and wife Hershey suffers long. Adapted by Pete Dexter from his National Book Award-winning novel. Made for cable. **98m/C VHS, Beta, LV.** Dennis Hopper, Barbara Hershey, Ed Harris, Tina Lifford, Darnita Henry, Eric Ware, Ray McKinnon; ***D:*** Stephen Gyllenhaal; ***W:*** Pete Dexter. *MED, FXV, FCT*

Paris When It Sizzles 🦴🦴 **1964** A screenwriter and his secretary fall in love while working on a film in Paris, confusing themselves with the script's characters. Star-studded cast deserves better than this lame script. Shot on location in Paris. Holden's drinking—he ran into a brick wall while under the influence—and some unresolved romantic tension between him and Hepburn affected shooting. Dietrich, Sinatra, Astaire, Ferrer, and Curtis show up for a party on the set. **110m/C VHS, Beta.** William Holden, Audrey Hepburn, Gregoire Aslan, Raymond Bussieres, Tony Curtis, Fred Astaire, Frank Sinatra, Noel Coward, Marlene Dietrich, Mel Ferrer; ***D:*** Richard Quine; ***W:*** George Axelrod. *PAR*

Park Avenue Logger 🦴½ **1937** Silly story has blue-blood Ingraham believing son O'Brien is a panty-waist, so he sends him to a lumber camp to prove his manhood. But junior is actually a wrestling champ (known as The Masked Marvel) and manages just fine, even winning the gal. **65m/B VHS.** George O'Brien, Beatrice Roberts, Lloyd Ingraham, Ward Bond, Willard Robertson, Bert Hanlon; ***D:*** David Howard. *GPV*

The Park is Mine 🦴🦴 **1985** A deranged and desperate Vietnam vet takes hostages in Central Park. Semi-infamous film, notable for being the first movie made for HBO on cable and for being filmed in Toronto, before the inexpensive practice of filming in Canada became widespread. **102m/C VHS, Beta.** Tommy Lee Jones, Yaphet Kotto, Helen Shaver; ***D:*** Steven Hilliard Stern; ***M:*** Tangerine Dream. *FOX*

Parker 🦴🦴 **1984** An executive is kidnapped, then released, but does not know why. Unable to live with the mystery, he tracks his kidnappers down into a world of blackmail, drugs, and intrigue. **100m/C VHS, Beta.** Bryan Brown, Kurt Raab. *ORI*

Parlor, Bedroom and Bath 🦴🦴 *Romeo in Pyjamas* **1931** A family tries to keep a young woman from seeing that her love interest is flirting with other prospects. Doesn't live up to the standard Keaton set in his silent films. Keaton spoke French and German for foreign versions. **75m/B VHS, Beta.** Buster Keaton, Charlotte Greenwood, Cliff Edwards, Reginald Denny; ***D:*** Edward Sedgwick. *NOS, VYY, VDM*

Parole, Inc. ☊☊ **1949** FBI takes on the underground in this early crime film. Criminals on parole have not served their sentences, and the mob is responsible. A meagerly financed yawner. **71m/B VHS.** Michael O'Shea, Evelyn Ankers, Turhan Bey, Lyle Talbot; ***D:*** Alfred Zeisler. *NOS, SNC*

Paroled to Die ☊½ **1937** A man frames a young rancher for a bank robbery and a murder he committed in this wild west saga. Predictable and bland. **66m/B VHS, Beta.** Bob Steele, Kathleen Elliott. *NOS, DVT*

Parrish ☊½ **1961** Parrish McLean (Donohue) is a very ambitious young man, determined to make it in the rich world of the tobacco growers of the Connecticut River Valley. But his ruthless tobacco king stepfather (Malden) would like to thwart his plans. As befits Donohue's teen idol status, he also gets to romance three beautiful girls. Very silly and much too long. Based on the novel by Mildred Savage. **138m/C VHS.** Troy Donahue, Claudette Colbert, Karl Malden, Dean Jagger, Diane McBain, Connie Stevens, Sharon Hugueny, Dub Taylor, Hampton Fancher, Bibi Osterwald, Madeline Sherwood, Sylvia Miles, Carroll O'Connor, Vincent Gardenia; ***D:*** Delmer Daves; ***W:*** Delmer Daves; ***C:*** Harry Stradling; ***M:*** Max Steiner. *WAR*

Parting Glances ☊☊☊ **1986 (R)** Low-budget but acclaimed film shows the relationship between two gay men and how they deal with a close friend's discovery of his exposure to the AIDS virus. Touching and realistic portrayals make this a must see. In 1990 Sherwood died of AIDS without completing any other films. **90m/C VHS, Beta.** John Bolger, Richard Ganoung, Steve Buscemi, Adam Nathan, Patrick Tull; ***D:*** Bill Sherwood; ***W:*** Bill Sherwood. *FOX, INJ*

Partner ☊☊☊ **1968** An extremely shy young man invents a strong alter ego to cope with the world but this second personality comes to dominate—with tragic results. In Italian with English subtitles. **110m/C VHS.** *IT* Pierre Clementi, Stefania Sandrelli, Tina Aumont; ***D:*** Bernardo Bertolucci; ***M:*** Ennio Morricone. *INJ, TPV*

Partners ☊☊ **1982 (R)** A straight, macho cop must pose as the lover of a gay cop to investigate the murder of a gay man in Los Angeles' homosexual community. Sets out to parody "Cruising"; unfortunately, the only source of humor the makers could find was in ridiculous homosexual stereotypes that are somewhat offensive and often unfunny. **93m/C VHS, Beta.** Ryan O'Neal, John Hurt, Kenneth McMillan, Robyn Douglass, Jay Robinson, Rick Jason; ***D:*** James Burrows; ***W:*** Francis Veber; ***M:*** Georges Delerue. *PAR*

Partners of the Trail ☊½ **1944** U.S. marshals Brown and Hatton try to find out who's murdering ranchers which leads them to gunplay with Ingraham's band of outlaws. **57m/B VHS.** Johnny Mack Brown, Raymond Hatton, Lloyd Ingraham, Christine McIntyre, Robert Frazer; ***D:*** Lambert Hillyer. *GPV*

The Party ☊☊☊ **1968** Disaster-prone Indian actor wreaks considerable havoc at a posh Hollywood gathering. Laughs come quickly in this quirky Sellers vehicle. **99m/C VHS.** Peter Sellers, Claudine Longet, Marge Champion, Sharron Kimberly, Denny Miller, Gavin MacLeod, Carol Wayne; ***D:*** Blake Edwards; ***W:*** Blake Edwards; ***M:*** Henry Mancini. *MGM, TVC*

Party Animal ☊ **1983 (R)** A college stud teaches a shy farm boy a thing or two about the carnal aspects of campus life. **78m/C VHS, Beta.** Timothy Carhart, Matthew Causey, Robin Harlan; ***D:*** David Beaird; ***W:*** David Beaird. *LIV*

Party Camp ☊ **1987 (R)** A rowdy summer camp counselor endeavors to turn a tame backwoods camp into a non-stop party. Late entry in the "Meatballs"-spawned genre fails to do anything of even minor interest. **96m/C VHS, Beta.** Andrew Ross, Billy Jacoby, April Wayne, Kirk Cribb; ***D:*** Gary Graver. *LIV*

Party Favors *Woof!* **1989 (R)** Erotic dancing, strip tease acts, and general hilarity are featured in this party tape. **83m/C VHS, Beta.** Jeannie Winters, Marjorie Miller, Gail Thackray; ***D:*** Ed Hansen. *LIV, VES*

Party Girl ☊☊☊½ **1958** A crime drama involving an attorney representing a 1920s crime boss and his henchmen when they run afoul of the law. The lawyer falls in love with a nightclub dancer who successfully encourages him to leave the mob, but not before he is wounded in a gang war attack, arrested, and forced to testify against the mob as a material witness. The mob then takes his girlfriend hostage to prevent his testifying, leading to an exciting climax. Must-see viewing for Charisse's steamy dance numbers. **99m/C VHS, Beta, LV.** Robert Taylor, Cyd Charisse, Lee J. Cobb, John Ireland, Kent Smith, Claire Kelly, Corey Allen; ***D:*** Nicholas Ray. *MGM*

Party Girl ☊☊½ **1994 (R)** In the "girls just wanna have fun" category comes this spritely saga of twenty-something Manhattan club gal Mary (Posey), who needs some steady income after the cops bust her for throwing an illegal rent party. So, since Mary's godmother is a librarian, she gets a job as a library clerk and discovers the wonders of the Dewey Decimal system (no, I'm not joking but presumably director Mayer is). Parker's Mary is a properly flaunting poseur but a little nightlife tends to go a long way. **94m/C VHS, LV.** Parker Posey, Omar Townsend, Anthony De Sando, Guillermo Diaz, Sasha von Scherler, Liev Schreiber; ***D:*** Daisy von Scherler Mayer; ***W:*** Harry Birckmayer, Daisy von Scherler Mayer; ***C:*** Michael Slovis; ***M:*** Anton Sanko. *COL*

Party Girls ☊½ **1929** Escort service girls run afoul of the law in this hokey melodrama. **67m/B VHS, Beta.** Douglas Fairbanks Jr., Jeanette Loff, Judith Barrie, Marie Prevost, John St. Polis, Lucien Prival; ***D:*** Victor Halperin. *NOS, LOO, SNC*

Party Girls for Sale ☊☊ **1954** Mystery thriller in which a young girl's body is found on the beach in Rio de Janeiro. Also known as "Violated." **?m/C VHS.** Raymond Burr, Scott Brady, Johanna Matz. *SNC*

Party Incorporated ☊☊ *Party Girls* **1989 (R)** Marilyn Chambers (of "Behind the Green Door" fame) stars as a young widow with a huge tax load who gives parties to pay it off. Also known as "Party Girls." **80m/C VHS, LV.** Marilyn Chambers, Kurt Woodruff, Christine Veronica, Kimberly Taylor; ***D:*** Chuck Vincent. *VTR, NWV, IME*

Party Line ☊ **1988 (R)** A veteran police captain and a district attorney team up to track down a pair of killers who find their victims through party lines. **90m/C VHS, Beta.** Richard Hatch, Shawn Weatherly, Richard Roundtree, Leif Garrett, Greta Blackburn; ***D:*** William Webb; ***W:*** Richard Brandes. *NO*

Party! Party! **1983** A bunch of kids go nuts and have a party when their parents leave. **100m/C VHS.** *GB* ***M:*** Sting, David Bowie, Joe Jackson, Elvis Costello. *ACA*

Party Plane ☊ **1990** Softcore fun-fest about a plane full of oversexed stewardesses. **81m/C VHS, Beta, LV.** Kent Stoddard, Karen Annarino, John Goff, Jill Johnson; ***D:*** Ed Hansen. *VES*

Pascali's Island ☊☊☊½ **1988 (PG-13)** A Turkish spy becomes involved with an adventurer's plot to steal rare artifacts, then finds himself ensnared in political and personal intrigue. Superior tragedy features excellent performances from Kingsley, Dance, and Mirren. **106m/C VHS, Beta, LV.** *GB* Ben Kingsley, Helen Mirren, Charles Dance, Sheila Allen, Vernon Dobtcheff; ***D:*** James Dearden; ***W:*** James Dearden; ***M:*** Loek Dikker. *LIV*

Pass the Ammo ☊☊½ **1988 (R)** Entertaining comedy about a young couple who attempt to steal back $50,000 of inheritance money that a televangelist swindled from the family. One of the more creative satires on this religious TV phenomenon. **93m/C VHS, Beta, LV.** Bill Paxton, Tim Curry, Linda Kozlowski, Annie Potts, Anthony Geary, Dennis Burkley, Glenn Withrow, Richard Paul; ***D:*** David Beaird; ***W:*** Neil Cohen, Joel Cohen; ***M:*** Carter Burwell. *LIV*

A Passage to India ☊☊☊ **1984 (PG)** An ambitious adaptation of E.M. Forster's complex novel about relations between Brits and Indians in the 1920s. Drama centers on a young British woman's accusations that an Indian doctor raped her while serving as a guide in some rather ominous caves. Film occasionally flags, but is usually compelling. Features particularly strong performances from Banerjee, Fox, and Davis. **163m/C VHS, Beta, LV.** *GB* Peggy Ashcroft, Alec Guinness, James Fox, Judy Davis, Victor Banerjee, Nigel Havers; ***D:*** David Lean; ***M:*** Maurice Jarre. Academy Awards '84: Best Supporting Actress (Ashcroft), Best Original Score; British Academy Awards '85: Best Actress (Ashcroft); Golden Globe Awards '85: Best Foreign Film, Best Supporting Actress (Ashcroft), Best Score; Los Angeles Film Critics Association Awards '84: Best Supporting Actress (Ashcroft); National Board of Review Awards '84: Best Actor (Banerjee), Best Actress (Ashcroft), Best Director (Lean); Nominations: Academy Awards '84: Best Adapted Screenplay, Best Art Direction/Set Decoration, Best Cinematography, Best Costume Design, Best Director (Lean), Best Film Editing, Best Picture, Best Sound; Academy Awards '87: Best Actress (Davis). *COL, BTV, HMV*

Passage to Marseilles ☊☊☊ **1944** Hollywood propaganda in which convicts escape from Devil's Island and help French freedom fighters combat Nazis. Routine but entertaining. What else could it be with Bogart, Raines, Greenstreet, and Lorre, who later made a pretty good film set in Casablanca? **110m/B VHS, Beta.** Humphrey Bogart, Claude Rains, Sydney Greenstreet, Peter Lorre, Helmut Dantine, George Tobias, John Loder, Eduardo Ciannelli, Michele Morgan; ***D:*** Michael Curtiz; ***C:*** James Wong Howe; ***M:*** Max Steiner. *FOX*

Passed Away ☊½ **1992 (PG-13)** Family patriarch Jack Scanlan dies and his entire family gets together for the funeral and a big Irish wake. The family, of course, is made up of a weird group of characters, good steadfast son Hoskins, dim-witted but good-looking son Petersen, rebellious daughter Reed, and a left-wing nun who works in Central America and is accompanied by an illegal alien (McDormand). Throw in a mysterious female mourner and a pregnant granddaughter who goes into labor at the graveside and you come up with a movie that manages to use every comic death cliche ever imagined. Talented cast is wasted in a movie that should have passed away. **96m/C VHS, Beta.** Bob Hoskins, Jack Warden, William L. Petersen, Helen Lloyd Breed, Maureen Stapleton, Pamela Reed, Tim Curry, Peter Riegert, Blair Brown, Patrick Breen, Nancy Travis, Teri Polo, Frances McDormand; ***D:*** Charlie Peters; ***W:*** Charlie Peters; ***M:*** Richard Gibbs. *HPH*

The Passenger ☊☊☊½ *Profession: Reporter* **1975 (PG)** A dissatisfied television reporter changes identities with a dead man while on assignment in Africa, then learns that he is posing as a gunrunner. Mysterious, elliptical production from Italian master Antonioni, who co-wrote. Nicholson is fine in the low-key role, and Schneider is surprisingly winning as the woman drawn to him. The object of much debate, hailed by some as quintessential cinema and by others as slow and unrewarding. **119m/C VHS, Beta.** *IT* Jack Nicholson, Maria Schneider, Ian Hendry, Jenny Runacre, Steven Berkoff; ***D:*** Michelangelo Antonioni; ***W:*** Mark Peploe, Michelangelo Antonioni; ***M:*** Claude Bolling. National Board of Review Awards '75: 10 Best Films of the Year. *WAR*

Passenger 57 ☊ **1992 (R)** Classic movie-of-the-week fare. Anti-terrorist specialist John Cutter (Snipes) leaves his profession because of his wife's murder, and coincidentally boards the same plane as Charles Rane (Payne), an apprehended evil terrorist headed to trial in L.A. Somehow, Rane's thugs have also sneaked aboard with plans to hijack the plane, and it's up to Cutter to use his skills and save the day. Athletic Snipes is convincing in his role but can't make up for the plot's lack of premise. **84m/C VHS, LV.** Wesley Snipes, Bruce Payne, Tom Sizemore, Alex Datcher, Bruce Greenwood, Robert Hooks, Elizabeth Hurley, Michael Horse; ***D:*** Kevin Hooks; ***W:*** David Loughery, Dan Gordon; ***M:*** Stanley Clarke. *WAR*

The Passing ☊☊½ **1988** Two men find themselves trapped in the darker vicissitudes of life. The two lead almost parallel lives until an extraordinary event unites them. **96m/C VHS.** James Plaster, Welton Benjamin Johnson, Lynn Dunn, Albert B. Smith; ***D:*** John Huckert. *NO*

The Passing of Evil 🦴🦴½ *The Grasshopper; Passions* **1970 (R)** Bisset is a starstruck Canadian undone by the bright lights and big cities of America. By age 22, she's a burnt-out prostitute in Las Vegas. Cheerless but compelling. **96m/C VHS.** Jacqueline Bisset, Jim Brown, Joseph Cotten, Corbett Monica, Ramon Bieri, Christopher Stone, Roger Garrett, Stanley Adams, Dick Richards, Tim O'Kelly, Ed Flanders; ***D:*** Jerry Paris; ***C:*** Sam Leavitt; ***M:*** Billy Goldenberg. *WAR*

The Passing of the Third Floor Back 🦴🦴 **1936** Boarding house tenants improve their lives after being inspired by a mysterious stranger. They revert, though, when he leaves. Now you know. Based on a Victorian morality play. **80m/B VHS, Beta.** *GB* Conrad Veidt, Rene Ray, Frank Cellier, Anna Lee, John Turnbull, Cathleen Nesbitt; ***D:*** Berthold Viertel. *SNC*

Passion 🦴🦴½ **1919** Paris, and the decadent Louis XV falls for the lovely Jeanne, making her his mistress, much to the scandal of the nation. Respectable silent version of "Madame DuBarry" is a relatively realistic costume drama, but it doesn't rate with the best German films of this period. **135m/B VHS, Beta.** *GE* Pola Negri, Emil Jannings, Harry Liedtke; ***D:*** Ernst Lubitsch. *VYY, GLV, GVV*

Passion 🦴🦴 **1954** When a rancher's young family falls victim to rampaging desperadoes, he enlists an outlaw's aid to avenge the murders of his loved ones. **84m/C VHS, Beta.** Raymond Burr, Cornel Wilde, Yvonne De Carlo, Lon Chaney Jr., John Qualen; ***D:*** Allan Dwan. *NO*

Passion 🦴½ **1992** Linda decides she married the wrong brother. So she plots to kill her husband and marry her in-law instead. **90m/C VHS.** Kristine Rose, Robert Labrosse, Kristine Frischhertz, Jack Ciolini; ***D:*** Joe D'Amato. *TSR*

Passion Fish 🦴🦴🦴 **1992 (R)** McDonnell plays May-Alice, a soap opera actress who is paralyzed after a taxi accident in New York. Confined to a wheelchair, the bitter woman moves back to her Louisiana home and alienates a number of live-in nurses until Chantelle (Woodard), who has her own problems, comes along. Blunt writing and directing by Sayles overcome the story's inherent sentimentality as do the spirited performances of the leads, including Curtis-Hall as the rogue romancing Chantelle and Strathairn as the Cajun bad boy McDonnell once loved. The laserdisc is available in letterbox format. **136m/C VHS, LV.** Mary McDonnell, Alfre Woodard, David Strathairn, Vondie Curtis-Hall, Nora Dunn, Sheila Kelley, Angela Bassett, Mary Portser, Maggie Renzi, Leo Burmester; ***D:*** John Sayles; ***W:*** John Sayles; ***C:*** Roger Deakins; ***M:*** Mason Daring. Independent Spirit Awards '93: Best Supporting Actress (Woodard); Nominations: Academy Awards '92: Best Actress (McDonnell), Best Original Screenplay. *COL, MOV, BTV*

Passion Flower 🦴🦴 **1986 (PG-13)** A tropical romantic melodrama made for network TV and set in Singapore, where an ambitious banker falls in love with the daughter of island's wealthiest smuggler. The mixture of high finance, low-dealing and lust only proves moderately passionate. **95m/C VHS.** Bruce Boxleitner, Barbara Hershey, Nicol Williamson; ***D:*** Joseph Sargent; ***M:*** Miles Goodman. *VMK*

Passion for Life 🦴🦴½ *L'Ecole Buissonniere; I Have a New Master* **1948** A new teacher uses revolutionary methods to engage students, but draws ire from staid parents in rural France. Worthwhile drama. In French with English subtitles. **89m/B VHS, Beta.** Bernard Blier, Julliette Faber, Edouard Delmont; ***D:*** Jean-Paul LeChanois. *FCT*

Passion for Power **1985** Two men involved in a drug-smuggling syndicate attempt to take over the business. Complications arise when they both fall for a beautiful, deceitful woman who turns them against one another. **94m/C VHS.** *SP* Hector Suarez, Sasha Montenegro, Manuel Capetillo, Alejandra Peniche. *NO*

Passion in Paradise 🦴🦴½ **1989** Fact-based mystery set in the Bahamas in 1943. Stewart is a spoiled rich girl who marries a handsome gigolo (Assante), much to daddy big bucks' (Steiger) displeasure. Then daddy is murdered and the son-in-law becomes the key suspect. Trashy, but Assante's fine. Made for television. **100m/C VHS, LV.** Armand Assante, Catherine Mary Stewart, Rod Steiger, Mariette Hartley, Wayne Rogers; ***D:*** Harvey Hart. *APX*

The Passion of Anna 🦴🦴🦴 **1970 (R)** A complicated psychological drama about four people on an isolated island. Von Sydow is an ex-con living a hermit's existence when he becomes involved with a crippled widow (Ullmann) and her two friends—all of whom have secrets in their pasts. Brutal and disturbing. Wonderful cinematography by Sven Nykvist. Filmed on the island of Faro. In Swedish with English subtitles. **101m/C VHS.** *SW* Max von Sydow, Liv Ullmann, Bibi Andersson, Erland Josephson, Erik Hell; ***D:*** Ingmar Bergman; ***W:*** Ingmar Bergman; ***C:*** Sven Nykvist. National Society of Film Critics Awards '70: Best Director (Bergman). *MGM, BTV*

The Passion of Joan of Arc 🦴🦴🦴🦴 **1928** Masterful silent film relates the events of St. Joan's trial and subsequent martyrdom. Moving, eloquent work features legendary performance by Falconetti. Also rates among master Dreyer's finest efforts. A classic. Silent with music. **114m/B VHS, Beta.** *FR* Maria Falconetti, Eugena Sylvaw, Maurice Schultz, Antonin Artaud; ***D:*** Carl Theodor Dreyer. *VYY, MRV, NOS*

Passion of Love 🦴🦴🦴 *Passione d'Amore* **1982** Military captain becomes the obsession of his commander's mysterious cousin when he reports to an outpost far from home. Daring and fascinating. An unrelentingly passionate historical romance guaranteed to heat up the VCR. Available dubbed or with subtitles. **117m/C VHS, Beta.** *IT FR* Laura Antonelli, Bernard Giraudeau, Valeria D'Obici, Jean-Louis Trintignant; ***D:*** Ettore Scola; ***W:*** Ettore Scola. Nominations: Cannes Film Festival '81: Best Film. *VES, INJ, CIG*

A Passion to Kill 🦴½ *Rules of Obsession* **1994 (R)** Formulaic thriller finds psychologist David (Bakula) getting sexually involved with his best friend Jerry's (Getz) wife, who has a lurid past. Seems Diana (Field) stuck a kitchen knife into her abusive first husband and now Jerry's prospects don't look too good. **93m/C VHS.** Scott Bakula, Chelsea Field, Sheila Kelly, John Getz, Rex Smith, France Nuyen, Michael Warren; ***D:*** Rick King; ***W:*** William F. Delligan. *APX*

Passionate Thief 🦴🦴½ *Risate de Gioia* **1960** Two pickpockets and a bumbling actress plan to rip off the guests at a posh New Year's Eve party with slightly comic results. Not much to recommend in this slow moving flick. **100m/C VHS, Beta.** *IT* Anna Magnani, Ben Gazzara, Fred Clark; ***D:*** Mario Monicelli. *NLC*

The Passover Plot 🦴🦴 **1975 (PG)** A controversial look at the crucifixion of Christ which depicts him as a Zealot leader who, aided by his followers, faked his death and then "rose" to win new converts. **105m/C VHS, Beta.** Harry Andrews, Hugh Griffith, Zalman King, Donald Pleasence, Scott Wilson; ***D:*** Michael Campus; ***M:*** Alex North. Nominations: Academy Awards '76: Best Costume Design. *CAN*

Passport to Pimlico 🦴🦴½ **1949** Farce about a London neighborhood's residents who discover an ancient charter proclaiming their right to form their own country within city limits. Passable comedy. **81m/B VHS, Beta.** *GB* Stanley Holloway, Margaret Rutherford, Hermione Baddeley, Naunton Wayne, Basil Radford; ***D:*** Henry Cornelius. Nominations: Academy Awards '49: Best Story & Screenplay. *NOS, PSM, DVT*

Past Midnight 🦴🦴 **1992 (R)** Richardson plays a social worker who believes recently paroled killer Hauer was wrongly convicted. She attempts to prove his innocence while also falling in love—a dangerous combination. Richardson's beautiful and Hauer's making a successful career out of playing handsome psychos. **100m/C VHS, LV.** Natasha Richardson, Rutger Hauer, Clancy Brown, Guy Boyd; ***D:*** Jan Eliasberg; ***W:*** Frank Norwood; ***M:*** Steve Bartek. *COL*

Past Tense 🦴🦴½ **1994 (R)** Complicated thriller about a cop with a gorgeous but mysterious neighbor, a murder to solve, and problems separating reality from his nightmares. Made for cable television. **91m/C VHS, LV.** Scott Glenn, Lara Flynn Boyle, Anthony LaPaglia, David Ogden Stiers, Sheree J. Wilson, Marita Geraghty, Stephen Graziano; ***D:*** Graeme Clifford. *REP*

Past the Bleachers 🦴🦴½ **1995 (PG)** Sentimental TV movie finds Anderson starring as Bill Parish—a man still lost by the death of his 11-year-old son. Reluctantly, he agrees to coach the Little League team his son had played on, with the help of an opinionated senior citizen (scene-stealer Hughes), and is drawn to the boy who turns out to be the team's star player. The appropriately named Lucky Diamond (Fricke) is both mute and of a mysterious family background, and bonding proves therapeutic for both Bill and the youngster. Based on a novel by Christopher A. Bohjalian. **120m/C VHS, LV.** Richard Dean Anderson, Barnard Hughes, Grayson Fricke, Glynnis O'Connor, Ken Jenkins; ***D:*** Michael Switzer; ***W:*** Don Rhymer; ***M:*** Stewart Levin. *HMK*

Pastime 🦴🦴🦴 *One Cup of Coffee* **1991 (PG)** A bittersweet baseball elegy set in the minor leagues in 1957. A boyish 41-year-old pitcher can't face his impending retirement and pals around with the team pariah, a 17-year-old black rookie. Splendidly written and acted, it's a melancholy treat whether you're a fan of the game or not, and safe for family attendance. The only drawback is a grungy, low-budget look. **94m/C VHS, LV.** William Russ, Scott Plank, Glenn Plummer, Noble Willingham, Jeffrey Tambor, Deidre O'Connell; ***D:*** Robin B. Armstrong; ***W:*** Robin B. Armstrong. Sundance Film Festival '91: Audience Award. *COL*

Pat and Mike 🦴🦴🦴 **1952** War of the sexes rages in this comedy about a leathery sports promoter who futilely attempts to train a woman for athletic competition. Tracy and Hepburn have fine chemistry, but supporting players contribute too. Watch for the first on-screen appearance of Bronson (then Charles Buchinski) as a crook. **95m/B VHS, Beta, LV.** Spencer Tracy, Katharine Hepburn, Aldo Ray, Jim Backus, William Ching, Sammy White, Phyllis Povah, Charles Bronson, Chuck Connors, Mae Clarke, Carl "Alfalfa" Switzer; ***D:*** George Cukor; ***W:*** Ruth Gordon, Garson Kanin; ***C:*** William H. Daniels. Nominations: Academy Awards '52: Best Story & Screenplay. *MGM*

Pat Garrett & Billy the Kid 🦴🦴🦴 **1973** Coburn is Garrett, one-time partner of Billy the Kid (Kristofferson), turned sheriff. He tracks down and eventually kills the outlaw. The uncut director's version which was released on video is a vast improvement over the theatrically released and television versions. Dylan's soundtrack includes the now famous "Knockin' on Heaven's Door." **106m/C VHS, Beta, LV.** Kris Kristofferson, James Coburn, Bob Dylan, Richard Jaeckel, Katy Jurado, Chill Wills, Charles Martin Smith, Slim Pickens, Harry Dean Stanton; ***D:*** Sam Peckinpah; ***W:*** Rudy Wurlitzer; ***M:*** George Duning. *MGM*

A Patch of Blue 🦴🦴½ **1965** A kind-hearted blind girl falls in love with a black man without acknowledging racial differences. Good performances from Hartman and Poitier are film's strongest assets. **108m/C VHS, Beta.** Sidney Poitier, Elizabeth Hartman, Shelley Winters, Wallace Ford, Ivan Dixon, John Qualen, Elisabeth Fraser, Kelly Flynn; ***D:*** Guy Green; ***C:*** Robert Burks; ***M:*** Jerry Goldsmith. Academy Awards '65: Best Supporting Actress (Winters); Nominations: Academy Awards '65: Best Actress (Hartman), Best Art Direction/Set Decoration (B & W), Best Black and White Cinematography. *MGM, BTV*

Patchwork Girl of Oz 🦴🦴 **1914** A very early silent film production by Baum that brought his own Oz books to the screen. **80m/B VHS, Beta.** ***D:*** L. Frank Baum. *NOS, DVT, VYY*

Paternity 🦴🦴 **1981 (PG)** Routine comedy about middle-aged manager of Madison Square Gardens (Reynolds) who sets out to find a woman to bear his child, no strings attached. The predictability of the happy ending makes this a yawner. Steinberg's directorial debut. **94m/C VHS, Beta, LV.** Burt Reynolds, Beverly D'Angelo, Lauren Hutton, Norman Fell, Paul Dooley, Elizabeth Ashley; ***D:*** David Steinberg; ***W:*** Charlie Peters; ***M:*** David Shire. Golden Raspberry Awards '81: Worst Song ("Baby Talk"). *PAR*

Pather Panchali 🦴🦴🦴🦴 *The Song of the Road; The Saga of the Road; The Lament of the Path* **1954** Somber, moving story of a young Bengali boy growing up in impoverished India. Stunning debut from India's master filmmaker Ray, who continued the story in "Aparajito" and "World of Apu." A truly great work. In Bengali with English subtitles. **112m/B VHS, Beta.** *IN* Kanu Banerjee, Karuna Banerjee, Uma Das Gupta, Subir Banerji, Runki Banerji, Chunibala Devi; ***D:*** Satyajit Ray; ***W:*** Satyajit Ray; ***M:*** Ravi Shankar. *NOS, FCT, MRV*

Pathfinder 🦴🦴🦴½ **1987** A young boy in Lapland of 1,000 years ago comes of age prematurely after he falls in with cutthroat nomads who already slaughtered his family and now want to wipe out the rest of the village. Gripping adventure in the ice and snow features stunning scenery. In Lappish with English subtitles and based on an old Lapp fable. **88m/C VHS.** *NO* Mikkel Gaup, Nils Utsi, Svein Scharffenberg, Helgi Skulason, Sara Marit Gaup, Sverre Porsanger; ***D:*** Nils Gaup; ***W:*** Nils Gaup. Nominations: Academy Awards '87: Best Foreign Language Film. *FXL, FCT, INJ*

Paths of Glory 🦴🦴🦴🦴 **1957** Classic anti-war drama set in WWI France. A vain, ambitious officer imposes unlikely battle strategy on his hapless troops, and when it fails, he demands that three soldiers be selected for execution as cowards. Menjou is excellent as the bloodless French officer, with Douglas properly heroic as the French officer who knows about the whole disgraceful enterprise. Fabulous, wrenching fare from filmmaking great Kubrick, who co-wrote. Based on a true story from Humphrey Cobb's novel of the same name. **86m/B VHS, Beta, LV.** Kirk Douglas, Adolphe Menjou, George Macready, Ralph Meeker, Richard Anderson, Wayne Morris, Timothy Carey, Susanne Christian, Bert Freed; ***D:*** Stanley Kubrick; ***W:*** Calder Willingham, Stanley Kubrick. *MGM, FOX*

Paths to Paradise 🦴🦴🦴 **1925** Compson and Griffith share criminal past, reunite at gala event to snatch priceless necklace and head south of the border. World- class chase scene. **78m/B VHS, Beta.** Raymond Griffith, Betty Compson, Thomas Santschi, Bert Woodruff, Fred Kelsey; ***D:*** Clarence Badger. *GPV*

Patrick 🦴½ **1978 (PG)** Coma patient suddenly develops strange powers and has a weird effect on the people he comes in contact with. **115m/C VHS, Beta.** *AU* Robert Helpmann, Susan Penhaligon, Rod Mullinar; ***D:*** Richard Franklin. *NO*

The Patriot 🦴½ **1986 (R)** An action film about an ex-Navy commando who battles a band of nuclear-arms smuggling terrorists. Edited via George Lucas' electronic editor, Edit Droid. **88m/C VHS, Beta, LV.** Jeff Conaway, Michael J. Pollard, Leslie Nielsen, Greg Henry, Simone Griffeth; ***D:*** Frank Harris; ***W:*** Andy Ruben, Katt Shea Ruben; ***M:*** Jay Michael Ferguson. *LIV, VES*

Patriot Games 🦴🦴🦴 **1992 (R)** Jack Ryan, retired CIA analyst, takes his wife and daughter to England on a holiday and ends up saving a member of the Royal Family from assassination by IRA extremists. Ryan, who has killed one of the terrorists, then becomes the target of revenge by the dead man's brother. Good action sequences but otherwise predictable adaptation of the novel by Tom Clancy. Companion to "The Hunt for Red October," with Ford taking over the role of Ryan from Alec Baldwin. Since this movie did well, we can probably expect two more from Ford, who's becoming the king of trilogies. Followed by "Clear and Present Danger." **117m/C VHS, Beta, CD-I.** Harrison Ford, Anne Archer, Patrick Bergin, Thora Birch, Sean Bean, Richard Harris, James Earl Jones, James Fox, Samuel L. Jackson, Polly Walker; ***D:*** Phillip Noyce; ***W:*** W. Peter Iliff, Donald Stewart; ***M:*** James Horner. *PAR*

The Patriots 🦴🦴🦴 **1933** A German prisoner works as a shoemaker in a small village during WWI. A lyrical drama in German and Russian with English titles. **82m/B VHS, Beta.** *RU* ***D:*** Boris Barnet. *FCT, IHF*

The Patsy 🦴🦴 **1964** Shady producers attempt to transform a lowly bellboy into a comedy superstar. Not one of Lewis's better efforts; Lorre's last film. **101m/C VHS, Beta.** Jerry Lewis, Ina Balin, Everett Sloane, Phil Harris, Keenan Wynn, Peter Lorre, John Carradine, Hans Conried, Richard Deacon, Scatman Crothers, Del Moore, Neil Hamilton, Buddy Lester, Nancy Kulp, Norman Alden, Jack Albertson; ***D:*** Jerry Lewis; ***W:*** Jerry Lewis. *IME*

Pattern for Plunder 🦴½ *The Bay of Saint Michel* **1962** Ex-commando leader rounds up his former comrades to head back to Normandy in search of buried Nazi plunder. **73m/B VHS.** *GB* Keenan Wynn, Mai Zetterling, Ronald Howard, Edward Underdown; ***D:*** John Ainsworth; ***W:*** Christopher Davis. *SNC*

Patterns 🦴🦴🦴 *Patterns of Power* **1956** Realistic depiction of big business. Heflin starts work at a huge New York office that is under the ruthless supervision of Sloane. Serling's astute screenplay (adapted from his TV play) is adept at portraying ruthless, power-struggling executives and the sundry workings of a large corporation. Film has aged slightly, but it still has some edge to it. Originally intended for television. **83m/B VHS.** Van Heflin, Everett Sloane, Ed Begley Sr., Beatrice Straight, Elizabeth Wilson; ***D:*** Fielder Cook; ***W:*** Rod Serling; ***C:*** Boris Kaufman. *NOS, MGM, MRV*

Pattes Blanches 🦴🦴½ *White Paws* **1949** A reclusive aristocrat always wears white spats, causing ridicule in the small fishing village where he lives. Trouble comes when a local saloon-keeper becomes resentful of the rich man's advances on his girlfriend. Moody, sensual French melodrama exploring class, money and sex. Adaptation of a play by Jean Anouilh. In French with English subtitles. **92m/B VHS.** *FR* Suzy Delair, Fernand Ledoux, Paul Bernard, Michel Bouquet; ***D:*** Jean Gremillon. *INT, FCT*

Patti Rocks 🦴🦴🦴 **1988 (R)** Offbeat, realistic independent effort concerns a foul chauvinist who enlists a friend to accompany him on a visit to a pregnant girlfriend who turns out to be less than the bimbo she's portrayed as en route. Mulkey shines as the sexist. Same characters featured earlier in "Loose Ends." **86m/C VHS, Beta, LV.** Chris Mulkey, John Jenkins, Karen Landry, David L. Turk, Stephen Yoakam; ***D:*** David Burton Morris; ***W:*** Chris Mulkey, John Jenkins, Karen Landry, David Burton Morris; ***M:*** Doug Maynard. *NO*

Patton 🦴🦴🦴½ *Patton—Lust for Glory; Patton: A Salute to a Rebel* **1970 (PG)** Lengthy but stellar bio of the vain, temperamental American general who masterminded significant combat triumphs during WWII. "Old Blood and Guts," who considered himself an 18th-century commander living in the wrong era, produced victory after victory in North Africa and Europe, but not without a decided impact upon his troops. Scott is truly magnificent in the title role, and Malden shines in the supporting role of General Omar Bradley. Not a subtle film, but neither is its subject. Interesting match-up with the 1986 made-for-TV movie "The Last Days of Patton," also starring Scott. **171m/C VHS, Beta, LV.** George C. Scott, Karl Malden, Stephen Young, Michael Strong, Frank Latimore, James Edwards, Lawrence Dobkin, Michael Bates, Tim Considine; ***D:*** Franklin J. Schaffner; ***W:*** Francis Ford Coppola, Edmund H. North; ***C:*** Fred W. Koenekamp; ***M:*** Jerry Goldsmith. Academy Awards '70: Best Actor (Scott), Best Art Direction/Set Decoration, Best Director (Schaffner), Best Film Editing, Best Picture, Best Sound, Best Story & Screenplay; Directors Guild of America Awards '70: Best Director (Schaffner); Golden Globe Awards '71: Best Actor—Drama (Scott); National Board of Review Awards '70: 10 Best Films of the Year, Best Actor (Scott); National Society of Film Critics Awards '70: Best Actor (Scott); Writers Guild of America '70: Best Original Screenplay; Nominations: Academy Awards '70: Best Original Score. *FXV, TLF, BTV*

Patty Hearst 🦴½ **1988 (R)** Less than fascinating, expressionistic portrait of Hearst from her kidnapping through her brainwashing and eventual criminal participation with the SLA. An enigmatic film that seems to only make Hearst's transformation into a Marxist terrorist all the more mysterious. Based on Hearst's book, "Every Secret Thing." **108m/C VHS, Beta, LV.** Natasha Richardson, William Forsythe, Ving Rhames, Frances Fisher, Jodi Long, Dana Delany; ***D:*** Paul Schrader; ***W:*** Nicholas Kazan. *MED*

Paul and Michelle 🦴 **1974 (R)** The equally dull sequel to "Friends" finds the two lovers a little older but no wiser. Paul has graduated from his British school and returns to France to seek out Michelle and their child. They try to rekindle their romance but the stresses of everyday life cause them problems. **102m/C VHS.** *GB FR* Sean Bury, Anicee Alvina, Keir Dullea, Ronald Lewis, Catherine Allegret, Georges Beller; ***D:*** Lewis Gilbert; ***M:*** Michel Colombier. *PAR*

Paul Bartel's The Secret Cinema 🦴🦴½ **1969** A woman cannot determine whether her life is real or a film by a maniacal director. Offbeat, creative, and a little disturbing. Followed by Bartel's short "Naughty Nurse." **37m/B VHS, Beta.** ***D:*** Paul Bartel. *RHI*

Paul Robeson 🦴🦴 **197?** Major events in the life of the popular actor are recounted in this one-man performance. Originally staged by Charles Nelson Reilly. **118m/C VHS, Beta.** James Earl Jones; ***D:*** Lloyd Richards. *KAR*

Pauline at the Beach 🦴🦴🦴½ *Pauline a la Plage* **1983 (R)** A young woman accompanies her more experienced cousin to the French coast for a summer of sexual hijinks. Contemplative, not coarse, though the leads look great in—and out—of their swimsuits. Breezy, typically talky fare from small-film master Rohmer. Cinematography by Nester Almendro. In French with English subtitles. **95m/C VHS, Beta, LV.** *FR* Amanda Langlet, Arielle Dombasle, Pascal Greggory, Rosette; ***D:*** Eric Rohmer; ***W:*** Eric Rohmer; ***C:*** Nestor Almendros. *XVC, MED, INJ*

The Pawnbroker 🦴🦴🦴½ **1965** A Jewish pawnbroker in Harlem is haunted by his grueling experiences in a Nazi camp during the Holocaust. Powerful and well done. Probably Steiger's best performance. Adapted from a novel by Edward Lewis Wallant. **120m/B VHS, LV.** Rod Steiger, Brock Peters, Geraldine Fitzgerald, Jaime Sanchez, Thelma Oliver; ***D:*** Sidney Lumet; ***C:*** Boris Kaufman; ***M:*** Quincy Jones. Berlin International Film Festival '65: Best Actor (Steiger); British Academy Awards '66: Best Actor (Steiger); Nominations: Academy Awards '65: Best Actor (Steiger). *REP*

Pawnshop **1916** Charlie is employed as a pawnbroker's assistant. Silent with music track. **20m/B VHS, Beta.** Charlie Chaplin. *CAB, GVV*

Pay Off 🦴 **1989** A lunatic psychiatrist seeks murderous revenge on his ex-patient/girlfriend and her family. **87m/C VHS, Beta.** Michael Fitzpatrick, Veronika Mattson, Margareta Krook; ***D:*** George Tirl. *TWE*

Pay or Die **1983 (R)** A crime boss' men turn on him and kidnap his daughter. **92m/C VHS, Beta.** Dick Adair, Johnny Wilson; ***D:*** Bobby Suarez. *LIV*

Payback 🦴 **1989** A brawny young man uses firepower to avenge those who have wronged him. **90m/C VHS, Beta.** Jean Carol. *NO*

Payback 🦴½ **1990 (R)** A convict sets out to avenge his brother's death, and creates all sorts of mayhem in the process. Produced by Bob "Newlywed Game" Eubanks and scored by Daryl "Captain and Tenille" Dragon. **94m/C VHS.** Corey Michael Eubanks, Michael Ironside, Teresa Blake, Bert Remsen, Vincent Van Patten, Don Swayze; ***D:*** Russell Solberg; ***M:*** Daryl Dragon. *REP*

Payback 🦴🦴½ **1994 (R)** An old, dying con tells a fellow inmate the whereabouts of a fortune if he'll promise to kill the cruel jail guard who made the geezer's life a misery. Years later, the now ex-con finds the ex-guard running a diner near the spot where the money is buried and decides to carry out his plan for revenge. Also available in an unrated version. **92m/C VHS, LV.** C. Thomas Howell, Joan Severance, Marshall Bell, R.G. Armstrong; ***D:*** Anthony Hickox. *VMK*

Payday 🦴🦴½ **1972** Torn stars as a declining country music star on tour in this portrayal of the seamy side of show business, from groupies to grimy motels. Well-written script and fine performances make this an engaging, if rather draining, drama not easily found on the big screen. **98m/C VHS, Beta.** Rip Torn, Ahna Capri, Michael C. Gwynne, Jeff Morris; ***D:*** Daryl Duke. *NO*

The Payoff 🦴½ **1943** The old-fashioned newspaper-reporter-as-crime-fighter routine. When the city's special prosecutor is murdered a daring newshawk investigates and tracks the bad guys. But will he spell their names right? **74m/B VHS.** Lee Tracy, Tom Brown, Tina Thayer, Evelyn Brent, Jack LaRue, Ian Keith, John Maxwell; ***D:*** Arthur Dreifuss. *NOS, LOO*

Payoff **1991 (R)** An ex-cop discovers the identity of gangsters who killed his parents. He traces them to a Lake Tahoe resort and plots revenge. Familiar crime story with a good cast. **111m/C VHS, Beta, LV.** Keith Carradine, Kim Greist, Harry Dean Stanton, John Saxon, Jeff Corey; ***D:*** Stuart Cooper; ***W:*** Douglas S. Cook; ***M:*** Charles Bernstein. *FXV*

P.C.U. **1994 (PG-13)** Satire on campus political correctness follows freshman Tom Lawrence's (Young) adventures as he navigates the treacherous waters of Port Chester University (PCU). He falls in with the gang from the Pit, the militantly non-PC dorm, who encourage bizarre and offensive behavior. Essentially a modern update of "National Lampoon's Animal House," but without the brilliance; add half a bone for tackling the thorny sensitivity issue in a humorous way that parodies, but shouldn't offend. Actor Bochner's directorial debut. **81m/C VHS, LV.** Jeremy Piven, Chris Young, David Spade, Sarah Trigger, Jessica Walter, Jon Favreau, Megan Ward, Jake Busey; ***Cameos:*** George Clinton; ***D:*** Hart Bochner; ***W:*** Adam Leff, Zak Penn; ***M:*** Steve Vai. *FXV*

Peacekillers ½ **1971** A mean bunch of bikers visit a commune to kidnap a young woman. The gang has a big surprise in store for them when the girl escapes. **86m/C VHS, Beta.** Michael Ontkean, Clint Ritchie, Paul Krokop; ***D:*** Douglas Schwartz. *NWV, VTR*

Peacemaker **1990 (R)** Two aliens masquerading as human cops stalk each other through a major city. **90m/C VHS, Beta, LV.** Robert Forster, Lance Edwards, Hilary Shepard, Bert Remsen, Robert Davi; ***D:*** Kevin S. Tenney; ***W:*** Kevin S. Tenney. *FRH*

The Peacock Fan ½ **1929** The Peacock Fan is protected by a deadly curse, with certain death to anyone who possesses it. **50m/B VHS, Beta.** Lucian Preval. *SNC, VYY*

The Peanut Butter Solution ½ **1985 (PG)** An imaginative 11-year-old boy investigates a strange old house which is haunted by friendly ghosts who are in possession of a magic potion. **96m/C VHS, Beta.** Matthew Mackay, Siluck Saysanasy, Alison Podbrey, Michael Maillot, Griffith Brewer, Michael Hogan, Helen Hughes; ***D:*** Michael Rubbo; ***W:*** Michael Rubbo; ***M:*** Lewis Furey. *NWV, VTR, HHE*

The Pearl **1948** Based on a John Steinbeck story, a Mexican fisherman, living in poverty, finds a magnificent pearl and he thinks it will improve the lives of his family. He is bewildered by what this pearl really brings—liars and thieves. Simple, yet larger-than-life film, beautifully photographed; a timeless picture capturing human nature. **77m/B VHS.** *MX* Pedro Armendariz Sr., Maria Elena Marques, Fernando Wagner, Charles Rooner; ***D:*** Emilio Fernandez. *FCT, MAS*

The Pearl of Death ½ **1944** Holmes and Watson investigate the theft of a precious pearl. **69m/B VHS, Beta.** Basil Rathbone, Nigel Bruce, Dennis Hoey, Miles Mander, Rondo Hatton, Evelyn Ankers; ***D:*** Roy William Neill. *FOX*

Pearl of the South Pacific *South Sea Woman* **1955** A trio of adventurers destroy a quiet and peaceful island when they ransack it for pearl treasures. **85m/C VHS, Beta.** Dennis (Stanley Morner) Morgan, Virginia Mayo, David Farrar; ***D:*** Allan Dwan; ***W:*** Edwin Blum. *NO*

The Pebble and the Penguin ½ **1994 (G)** Animated musical about a shy, romantic penguin named Hubie (Short), who must present his lady love Marina (Golden) with a beautiful pebble to win her hand forever before the villainous Drake (Curry) can claim her. Hubie is helped along the way by a cantankerous new friend (Belushi) he meets when stranded on a boat to Tahiti. Together the two race back to Antarctica fighting enemies and the elements along the way. Based on a true mating custom of the Adeli penguins, the story is satisfying for younger viewers, but does not have the animation magic of other recents films to keep adults interested. Beware of the sugary Manilow tunes. **74m/C VHS, LV.** ***W:*** Rachel Koretsky, Steve Whitestone; ***M:*** Barry Manilow, Bruce Sussman, Mark Watters; ***V:*** Martin Short, Annie Golden, Tim Curry, James Belushi. *MGM*

Peck's Bad Boy **1921** Impudent, precocious brat causes his parents considerable grief. Someone should lock this kid in a room with W.C. Fields or the Alien. Silent film based on the stories by George Wilbur Peck. **51m/B VHS, Beta, LV.** Jackie Coogan, Thomas Meighan, Raymond Hatton, Wheeler Oakman, Lillian Leighton; ***D:*** Sam Wood. *NOS, MRV, CCB*

Peck's Bad Boy ½ **1934** A wedge is driven between a young boy and his adoptive father when the man's sister and her son move in. The aunt wants her son to be number one, causing much discord. Cooper is excellent in his role as the adopted son. **70m/B VHS.** Thomas Meighan, Jackie Cooper, Dorothy Peterson, Jackie Searl, O.P. Heggie, Harvey Clark, Lloyd Ingraham; ***D:*** Eddie Cline. *NOS, MLB*

Peck's Bad Boy with the Circus **1938** The circus will never be the same after the mischievous youngster and his buddies get done with it. Gilbert and Kennedy provide the high points. **67m/B VHS, Beta.** Tommy Kelly, Ann Gillis, George "Spanky" McFarland, Edgar Kennedy, Billy Gilbert; ***D:*** Eddie Cline. *NOS, VYY, DVT*

Pecos Bill **1986** Meet the man who used the Grand Canyon for a swimmin' hole, dug the Rio Grande and used the Texas panhandle for a fryin' pan. From Shelly Duvall's "Tall Tales and Legends" series. Originally made for cable television. **50m/C VHS.** Steve Guttenberg, Martin Mull, Claude Akins, Rebecca DeMornay. *FOX, COL*

Pecos Kid **1935** A child has his parents killed, and grows up embittered, vengeful and thirsty for blood. **56m/B VHS, Beta, LV.** Fred Kohler Jr. *NOS*

Peddlin' in Society *Da Bancarella a Bancarotta* **1947** A fruit vendor makes it big on the black market and lives the good life, until poor investments force her back to her old means. Strong perfomances by Magnani and De Sica. In Italian with English subitiles. **85m/B VHS.** *IT* Anna Magnani, Vittorio De Sica, Virgilio Riento, Laura Gore; ***D:*** Gennaro Righelli. *DVT, HEG*

The Pedestrian ½ *Der Fussgaenger* **1973 (PG)** A prominent German industrialist is exposed as a Nazi officer who supervised the wholesale devastation of a Greek village during WWII. Impressive debut for director Schell, who also appears in a supporting role. **97m/C VHS, Beta.** *GE SI* Maximilian Schell, Peggy Ashcroft, Lil Dagover, Francoise Rosay, Elisabeth Bergner; ***D:*** Maximilian Schell; ***M:*** Manos Hadjidakis. Golden Globe Awards '74: Best Foreign Film; National Board of Review Awards '74: 5 Best Foreign Films of the Year; Nominations: Academy Awards '73: Best Foreign Language Film. *SUE, GLV, SWC*

The Pee Wee Herman Show **1982** The original HBO special which introduced Pee Wee to the world. Hilarious stuff, with help from Captain Carl (Hartman), Miss Yvonne, and other assorted pals. Warning: Not to be confused with Pee Wee's children's show. **60m/C VHS.** Paul (Pee Wee Herman) Reubens, Phil Hartman, John Paragon. *NO*

Pee Wee's Big Adventure ½ **1985 (PG)** Zany, endearing comedy about an adult nerd's many adventures while attempting to recover his stolen bicycle. Chock full of classic sequences, including a barroom encounter between Pee Wee and several ornery bikers, and a tour through the Alamo. A colorful, exhilerating experience. **92m/C VHS, Beta, LV.** Paul (Pee Wee Herman) Reubens, Elizabeth Daily, Mark Holton, Diane Salinger, Judd Omen, Cassandra Peterson, James Brolin, Morgan Fairchild, Tony Bill, Jan Hooks; ***D:*** Tim Burton; ***W:*** Paul (Pee Wee Herman) Reubens, Phil Hartman, Michael Varhol; ***M:*** Danny Elfman. *WAR*

Pee Wee's Playhouse Festival of Fun **1988** Five fun-filled episodes of the playhouse! **123m/C VHS, Beta.** Paul (Pee Wee Herman) Reubens. *MED*

Peephole **1993** Prison psychiatrist is asked by the DA to keep Rick, who committed a sex crime against a little girl, in jail any way he can. So he visits Rick's prostitute girlfriend Sheena for info but instead winds up one of her clients. Meanwhile, Rick has been released and a little girl has been found dead, but nothing's that clear cut. Based on director/writer Bitterman's play. **90m/C VHS.** Patrick Husted, Rick Dean, William Dennis Hunt, Kristen Trucksess; ***D:*** Shem Bitterman; ***W:*** Shem Bitterman. *LEO*

Peeping Tom ½ **1963** Controversial, unsettling thriller in which a psychopath lures women before his film camera, then records their deaths at his hand. Unnerving subject matter is rendered impressively by British master Powell. A classic of its kind, but definitely not for everyone. This is the original uncut version of the film, released in the U.S. in 1979 with the assistance of Martin Scorsese. **88m/C VHS, Beta, LV.** Karl-Heinz Boehm, Moira Shearer, Anna Massey, Maxine Audley, Esmond Knight, Shirley Anne Field, Brenda Bruce, Pamela Green, Jack Watson, Nigel Davenport, Susan Travers, Veronica Hurst; ***D:*** Michael Powell. *HMV, AOV*

Peg O' My Heart **1922** Taylor portrays the motherless Irish charmer sent to live with her mother's English relatives during the Irish rebellion. Of course, she must overcome their upper-class English snobbery to become a part of the family. **85m/B VHS.** Laurette Taylor, Mahlon Hamilton, Russell Simpson, Ethel Grey; ***D:*** King Vidor; ***C:*** George Barnes. *NO*

Peggy Sue Got Married ½ **1986 (PG-13)** Uneven but entertaining comedy about an unhappily married woman seemingly unable to relive her life when she falls unconscious at a high school reunion and awakens to find herself back in school. Turner shines, but the film flags often, and Cage isn't around enough to elevate entire work. O'Connor scores, though, as a sensitive biker. Look for musician Marshall Crenshaw as part of the reunion band. **103m/C VHS, Beta, LV.** Kathleen Turner, Nicolas Cage, Catherine Hicks, Maureen O'Sullivan, John Carradine, Helen Hunt, Lisa Jane Persky, Barbara Harris, Joan Allen, Kevin J. O'Connor, Barry Miller, Don Murray, Leon Ames, Sofia Coppola, Sachi Parker, Jim Carrey; ***D:*** Francis Ford Coppola; ***W:*** Jerry Leichtling, Arlene Sarner; ***M:*** John Barry. National Board of Review Awards '86: Best Actress (Turner); Nominations: Academy Awards '86: Best Actress (Turner), Best Cinematography, Best Costume Design. *FOX*

The Peking Blond ½ *The Blonde From Peking; Le Blonde de Pekin* **1968** French-fried spyfilm boasts lousy acting unencumbered by plot. Amnesiac may or may not hold secrets coveted by Americans, Russians and Chinese. **80m/C VHS.** *FR* Mireille Darc, Claudio Brook, Edward G. Robinson, Pascale Roberts; ***D:*** Nicolas Gessner; ***W:*** Nicolas Gessner, Marc Behm. *MRV*

The Pelican Brief ½ **1993 (PG-13)** Tulane law student Darby Shaw (Roberts) writes a speculative brief on the murders of two Supreme Court justices that results in more murder and sends her running for her life. Fairly faithful to the Grisham bestseller, but the multitude of characters is confusing. Pakula adds style and star-power, but much will depend on your tolerance for paranoid political thrillers and ability to accept Roberts as the smart cookie who hits on the right answer and then manages to keep herself alive while bodies are dropping all around her. Washington is sharp as reporter Gray Grantham, the guy Roberts looks like she falls hard for (but the book's romance is nowhere to be seen). **141m/C VHS, LV, 8mm.** Julia Roberts, Denzel Washington, John Heard, Tony Goldwyn, Stanley Tucci, James B. Sikking, William Atherton, Robert Culp, John Lithgow, Sam Shepard; ***Cameos:*** Hume Cronyn; ***D:*** Alan J. Pakula; ***W:*** Alan J. Pakula; ***C:*** Stephen Goldblatt; ***M:*** James Horner. Nominations: MTV Movie Awards '94: Best Actress (Roberts), Most Desirable Male (Washington). *WAR*

Pelle the Conqueror **1988** Overpowering tale of a Swedish boy and his widower father who serve landowners in late 19th-century Denmark. Compassionate saga of human spirit contains numerous memorable sequences. Hvenegaard is wonderful as young Pelle, but von Sydow delivers what is probably his finest performance as a sympathetic weakling. American distributors foolishly trimmed the film by some 20 minutes (140 minute version). From the novel by Martin Anderson Nexo. In Swedish with English subtitles. **160m/C VHS, Beta, LV.** *SW DK* Max von Sydow, Pelle Hvenegaard, Erik Paaske,

Bjorn Granath, Axel Strobye, Astrid Villaume, Troels Asmussen, John Wittig, Anne Lise Hirsch Bjerrum, Kristina Tornqvist, Morten Jorgensen; *D:* Bille August; *W:* Bille August. Academy Awards '88: Best Foreign Language Film; Cannes Film Festival '88: Best Film; Golden Globe Awards '89: Best Foreign Film; Nominations: Academy Awards '88: Best Actor (von Sydow). *HBO, INJ*

The Penalty ☆☆½ **1920** Legless madman Blizzard (Chaney) is after revenge on his family, doctor, and society. Chaney's properly creepy. **60m/B VHS.** Lon Chaney Sr., Claire Adams, Kenneth Harlan, Charles Clary; *D:* Wallace Worsley. *FCT*

Penalty Phase ☆☆ **1986** An up-for-election judge must decide a murder case in which his future, as well as the defendant's, is in question. Made for television. **94m/C VHS, Beta.** Peter Strauss, Melissa Gilbert, Jonelle Allen; *D:* Tony Richardson; *M:* Ralph Burns. *VTR, NWV*

Pendulum ☆☆ **1969 (PG)** A police captain struggles to prove himself innocent of his wife's—and his wife's lover's—murders. Wow. **106m/C VHS, Beta, LV.** George Peppard, Jean Seberg, Richard Kiley, Madeline Sherwood, Charles McGraw, Marj Dusay; *D:* George Schaefer; *C:* Lionel Lindon. *COL*

The Penitent ☆☆ **1988 (PG-13)** A remote village's annual reenactment of the crucifixion of Christ serves as the backdrop for Assante's affair with his friend's (Julia) wife. Quirky little tale that focuses a shade too much on the romantic problems of the trio rather than the intriguing religious practices going on around them. **94m/C VHS, Beta.** Raul Julia, Armand Assante, Rona Freed, Julie Carmen; *D:* Cliff Osmond; *M:* Alex North. *LIV*

Penitentiary ☆☆½ **1979 (R)** A realistic story of a black fighter who survives his prison incarceration by winning bouts against the other prisoners. Well-made and executed, followed by two progressively worse sequels. **99m/C VHS, Beta.** Leon Isaac Kennedy, Jamaa Fanaka; *D:* Jamaa Fanaka; *W:* Jamaa Fanaka. *UNI, FCT*

Penitentiary 2 ☆ **1982 (R)** A welterweight fighter is after the man who murdered his girlfriend, who, luckily, is incarcerated in the same prison as Our Hero. Sometimes things just work out right. **108m/C VHS, Beta.** Leon Isaac Kennedy, Mr. T, Leif Erickson, Ernie Hudson, Glynn Turman; *D:* Jamaa Fanaka; *W:* Jamaa Fanaka. *MGM, HHE*

Penitentiary 3 ☆½ **1987 (R)** Once again, Kennedy as the inmate boxer extraordinaire punches his way out of various prison battles. Another punch-drunk sequel. **91m/C VHS, Beta.** Leon Isaac Kennedy, Anthony Geary, Steve Antin, Ric Mancini, Kessler Raymond, Jim Bailey; *D:* Jamaa Fanaka; *W:* Jamaa Fanaka. *WAR*

Penn and Teller Get Killed ☆☆ **1990 (R)** The comedy team with a cult following are pursued by an assassin through dozens of pratfalls in this dark comedy. **91m/C VHS, Beta, LV.** Penn Jillette, Teller, Caitlin Clarke, Leonardo Cimino, David Patrick Kelly; *D:* Arthur Penn. *WAR*

Pennies From Heaven ☆☆☆½ **1981 (R)** Underrated, one-of-a-kind musical about a horny sheet-music salesman in Chicago and his escapades during the Depression. Extraordinary musical sequences have stars lip-synching to great effect. Martin is only somewhat acceptable as the hapless salesman, but Peters and Harper deliver powerful performances as the women whose lives he ruins. Walken brings down the house in a stunning song-and-dance sequence. Adapted by Dennis Potter from his British television series. ♫The Clouds Will Soon Roll By; Did You Ever See A Dream Walking?; Yes, Yes; Pennies From Heaven; Love Is Good for Anything That Ails You; I Want to Be Bad; Let's Misbehave; Life Is Just a Bowl of Cherries; Let's Face the Music and Dance. **107m/C VHS, Beta, LV.** Steve Martin, Bernadette Peters, Christopher Walken, Jessica Harper, Vernel Bagneris; *D:* Herbert Ross; *W:* Dennis Potter; *C:* Gordon Willis; *M:* Ralph Burns, Marvin Hamlisch. Golden Globe Awards '82: Best Actress—Musical/Comedy (Peters); National Society of Film Critics Awards '81: Best Cinematography; Nominations: Academy Awards '81: Best Adapted Screenplay, Best Costume Design, Best Sound. *MGM, FCT*

Penny Serenade ☆☆☆ **1941** Newlyweds adopt a child, but tragedy awaits. Simplistic story nonetheless proves to be a moving experience. They don't make 'em like this anymore, and no one plays Grant better than Grant. Dunne is adequate. Also available colorized. **120m/B VHS, LV.** Cary Grant, Irene Dunne, Beulah Bondi, Edgar Buchanan; *D:* George Stevens. Nominations: Academy Awards '41: Best Actor (Grant). *CNG, NOS, PSM*

Pentathlon ☆☆½ **1994 (R)** An East German Olympic athlete defects to the U.S. a year before the crash of the Berlin Wall, causing embarassed German authorities to seek revenge on him and his family. **101m/C VHS, LV.** Dolph Lundgren, David Soul, Roger E. Mosley, Renee Coleman; *D:* Bruce Malmuth. *LIV*

Penthouse ☆☆☆ *Crooks in Clover* **1933** Baxter is a corporation lawyer who, for a change of pace, defends a gangland boss (Pendleton). His success loses him his high-society clientele but wins him Pendleton's respect and protection. But Baxter then gets involved in a further series of gang-related crimes, which nearly cost him his life. Also aiding Baxter is Loy, playing a smart-cookie gun moll, who would take her wisecracks to "The Thin Man" the following year. Good combo of melodrama, suspense, and humor. **90m/B LV.** Warner Baxter, Myrna Loy, Nat Pendleton, C. Henry Gordon, Mae Clarke, Charles Butterworth, Phillips Holmes; *D:* Woodbridge S. Van Dyke. *MGM*

The Penthouse ☆☆ **1992** Givens stars as a wealthy young woman stalked by an old boyfriend who just happens to have escaped from a mental institution. When he traps her in her home, she has two choices—love him or die. Based on the novel by Elleston Trevor. **93m/C VHS.** Robin Givens, David Hewlett, Cedric Smith, Donnelly Rhodes, Robert Guillaume; *D:* David Greene. *TTC*

The People ☆☆½ **1971** A young teacher takes a job in a small town and finds out that her students have telepathic powers and other strange qualities. Adapted from a novel by Zenna Henderson. Good atmosphere, especially for a TV movie. **74m/C VHS, Beta.** Kim Darby, Dan O'Herlihy, Diane Varsi, William Shatner; *D:* John Korty; *M:* Carmine Coppola. *PSM*

People Are Funny ☆☆ **1946** Battling radio producers vie to land the big sponsor with an original radio idea. Comedy ensues when one of them comes up with a great idea—stolen from a local station. **94m/B VHS, Beta.** Jack Haley, Rudy Vallee, Ozzie Nelson, Art Linkletter, Helen Walker; *D:* Sam White. *NO*

The People Next Door ☆☆ **1970** Seventies attempt at exposing the drug problems of suburban youth. Typical middle-class parents Wallach and Harris are horrified to discover that daughter Winters is strung out on LSD. They fight to expose the neighborhood pusher while struggling to understand their now-alien daughter. Based on J.P. Miller's television play. **93m/C VHS.** Deborah Winters, Eli Wallach, Julie Harris, Stephen McHattie, Hal Holbrook, Cloris Leachman, Nehemiah Persoff; *D:* David Greene. *NO*

The People That Time Forgot ☆☆½ **1977 (PG)** Sequel to "The Land That Time Forgot," based on the Edgar Rice Burroughs novel. A rescue team returns to a world of prehistoric monsters to rescue a man left there after the first film. **90m/C VHS, Beta.** *GB* Doug McClure, Patrick Wayne, Sarah Douglas, Dana Gillespie, Thorley Walters, Shane Rimmer; *D:* Kevin Connor. *SUE*

The People Under the Stairs ☆☆½ **1991 (R)** Adams is part of a scheme to rob a house in the slums owned by a mysterious couple (Robie and McGill, both of "Twin Peaks" fame). After his friends are killed off in a gruesome fashion, he discovers that the couple aren't the house's only strange inhabitants—homicidal creatures also lurk within. **102m/C VHS, Beta, LV.** Everett McGill, Wendy Robie, Brandon Adams, Ving Rhames, A.J. Langer, Sean Whalen; *D:* Wes Craven; *W:* Wes Craven; *C:* Sandi Sissel; *M:* Don Peake. *MCA*

The People vs. Jean Harris ☆☆☆ **1981** Follows the trial of Jean Harris. Shortly before this film was released, she had been convicted of murder in the death of Dr. Herman Tarnower, the author of "The Scarsdale Diet." Harris was headmistress in a private school all the while. Made for television. Burstyn was nominated for an Emmy Award for best actress. **147m/C VHS, Beta.** Ellen Burstyn, Martin Balsam, Richard Dysart, Peter Coyote, Priscilla Morrill, Sarah Marshall, Millie Slavin; *D:* George Schaefer; *M:* Brad Fiedel. *NO*

People Who Own the Dark *Woof!* **1975 (R)** A group of wealthy men and a coterie of call girls are having an orgy in the basement of an old home when a nuclear war breaks out. Everyone outside is blinded by the blast but some survivors manage to make their way to the house where they try to attack the inhabitants. Don't bother. **87m/C VHS.** Paul Naschy, Tony Kendall, Maria Perschy, Terry Kemper, Tom Weyland, Anita Brock, Paul Mackey; *D:* Armando de Ossorio; *W:* Armando de Ossorio. *SUN, MRV*

People Will Talk ☆☆☆½ **1951** Grant plays Dr. Noah Praetorius, a doctor and educator who believes that the mind is a better healer than medicine. Archenemy Cronyn is the fellow instructor with a vengeance. Sickened by Grant's goodwill and the undying attention he receives, Cronyn reports Grant's unconventional medical practices to the higher-ups in hopes of ruining his reputation as doctor/educator. Witty and satirical, this well-crafted comedy-drama is chock-full of interesting characters and finely tuned dialogue. Adapted from the play "Dr. Praetorius" by Curt Goetz. **110m/B VHS.** Cary Grant, Jeanne Crain, Finlay Currie, Hume Cronyn, Walter Slezak, Sidney Blackmer, Basil Ruysdael, Katherine Locke, Margaret Hamilton, Carleton Young, Billy House, Stuart Holmes; *D:* Joseph L. Mankiewicz; *W:* Joseph L. Mankiewicz; *C:* Milton Krasner. *FXV*

People's Choice ☆☆ **1946** A small town boy suffers laryngitis, becomes a radio personality via his new huskiness, and claims he's a notorious criminal. **68m/B VHS, Beta, LV.** Drew Kennedy, Louise Arthur, George Meeker, Rex Lease, Fred Kelsey. *NO*

Pepe Le Moko ☆☆☆ **1937** An influential French film about a notorious gangster holed up in the Casbah, emerging at his own peril out of love for a beautiful woman. Stirring film established Gabin as a matinee idol. Cinematography is particularly fine too. Based upon the D'Ashelbe novel. The basis for both "Algiers," the popular Boyer-Lamarr melodrama, and the musical "The Casbah." In French with English subtitles. **87m/B VHS, Beta, 8mm.** *FR* Jean Gabin, Mireille Balin, Gabriel Gabrio, Lucas Gridoux; *D:* Julien Duvivier. National Board of Review Awards '41: 5 Best Foreign Films of the Year. *VYY, NOS, HHT*

Pepi, Luci, Bom and Other Girls on the Heap ☆½ *Pepi, Luci, Bom y Otras Chicas del Monton* **1980** Almodovar's low-budget directorial debut will be of interest primarily to the director's aficionadoes. Pepi (Maura's debut role) is a Madrid heiress who gets in trouble when her neighbor, a policeman, notices her marijuana plants. She offers sexual favors in return for silence but is raped instead. Pepi later decides on revenge by seducing Luci, the policeman's wife, aided by her girlfriend, Bom. There's lots of partying, drugs, promiscuity, and violence, none of it very involving. In Spanish with English subtitles. **80m/C VHS.** *SP* Carmen Maura, Eva Siva, Olivido Gara, Felix Rotaeta; *D:* Pedro Almodovar; *W:* Pedro Almodovar. *FCT, INJ, CCN*

Pepper and His Wacky Taxi ☆½ **1972 (G)** Father of four buys a '59 Cadillac and starts a cab company. Time-capsule fun. **79m/C VHS, Beta.** John Astin, Frank Sinatra Jr., Jackie Gayle, Alan Sherman; *D:* Alex Grasshof. *UNI*

Peppermint Soda ☆☆☆ **1977** Kurys' affecting directorial debut is a semi-autobiographical tale of two teenaged sisters set in 1963 Paris. Seen through the eyes of the 13-year-old Anne, who lives with 15-year-old sister Frederique and their divorced mother, this is the year of first loves, strict teachers, dreaded family vacations, and a general awareness of growing up. Sweet look at adolescence and all its embarassing tribulations. In French with English subtitles. **97m/C VHS.** *FR* Eleonore Klarwein, Odile Michel, Anouk Ferjac, Tsilla Chelton, Coralie Clement, Marie-Veronique Maurin, Puterflam; ***D:*** Diane Kurys; ***W:*** Diane Kurys; ***C:*** Philippe Rousselot. *NYF, BTV, FCT*

Percy & Thunder ½ **1993** Percy Banks (Jones) is an old-school boxing trainer who believes in hard work and he sees a likely prospect in Wayne "Thunder" Carter (Vance), a middleweight with a chance to be a champ. That is, if big time boxing promotion doesn't get in the way. **90m/C VHS.** James Earl Jones, Billy Dee Williams, Courtney B. Vance; Robert Wuhl, Gloria Foster, Zakes Mokae, Gloria Reuben; ***D:*** Ivan Dixon; ***W:*** Art Washington; ***M:*** Tom Scott. *TTC*

The Perez Family ½ **1994 (R)** Juan Paul Perez (Molina) has spent 20 years in Cuban jails, dreaming of being reunited with wife Carmela (Huston) and daughter Teresa (Alvarado) who successfully escaped to Miami. Part of the 1980 Mariel exodus, Juan meets exuberant Dottie (Tomei), who learns families get sponsored first at the refugee camps. She convinces Juan to pose as her husband, while Carmela, who's being wooed by cop Pirelli (Palminteri), mistakenly believes Juan has literally missed the boat. Tomei's spunky (but with a garish accent), Huston's regal, Palminteri courtly, and Molina morose. The film's inconsistently whimsical, wistful, and clunky. From the novel by Christine Bell. **135m/C VHS.** Marisa Tomei, Alfred Molina, Anjelica Huston, Chazz Palminteri, Trini Alvarado, Celia Cruz; ***D:*** Mira Nair; ***W:*** Robin Swicord; ***C:*** Stuart Dryburgh; ***M:*** Alan Silvestri. *HMK*

Perfect ½ **1985 (R)** A "Rolling Stone" reporter goes after the shallowness of the Los Angeles health club scene, and falls in love with the aerobics instructor he is going to write about. "Rolling Stone" publisher Wenner plays himself. As bad as it sounds. **120m/C VHS, Beta, LV.** John Travolta, Jamie Lee Curtis, Carly Simon, Marilu Henner, Laraine Newman, Jann Wenner, Anne DeSalvo; ***D:*** James Bridges; ***W:*** James Bridges, Aaron Latham; ***C:*** Gordon Willis; ***M:*** Ralph Burns. *COL*

Perfect Alibi ½ **1994** Woman's suspicions of her husband's affair leads to murder. **90m/C VHS.** Teri Garr, Hector Elizondo, Kathleen Quinlan, Anne Ramsey; ***D:*** Kevin Meyer. *AVE*

The Perfect Bride ½ **1991 (R)** A pretty young nurse prepares to marry her fiance, but his sister thinks she is hiding a secret. Could the bride-to-be have murder on her mind? Made for cable. **95m/C VHS, Beta, LV.** Sammi Davis, Kelly Preston, Linden Ashby, Marilyn Rockafellow, Ashley Tillman; ***D:*** Terrence O'Hara; ***M:*** Richard Bronskill. *FXV, VTR*

Perfect Crime **1978** A Scotland Yard inspector must find out who has been killing off executives of a powerful world trust. **90m/C VHS, Beta.** Joseph Cotten, Anthony Steel, Janet Agren. *NO*

Perfect Family **1992 (R)** Standard woman-and-kids-in-peril-from-psycho tale. Maggie is a recent widow with two young daughters who's looking for a nanny and a handyman. She hires brother and sister combo Janice and Alan, who, of course, are too good to be true. One is a sociopath who has murdered a family once before. Guess along with Maggie who the nut might be. **92m/C VHS, Beta.** Jennifer O'Neill, Bruce Boxleitner, Joanna Cassidy, Juliana Hansen, Shiri Appleby; ***D:*** E.W. Swackhamer; ***W:*** Christian Stoianovich, Phoebe Dorin; ***M:*** Nicholas Pike. *PAR*

Perfect Furlough ½ *Strictly for Pleasure* **1959** A corporal wins a week in Paris with a movie star, accompanied by a female Army psychologist. Pretty bizarre, but it works. **93m/C VHS, Beta.** Tony Curtis, Janet Leigh, Keenan Wynn, Linda Cristal, Elaine Stritch; ***D:*** Blake Edwards. *BAR, MLB*

The Perfect Gift **1995 (R)** Suzanne decides to fulfill her boyfriend's menage-a-trois fantasy and discovers that the partner they involve just may be the woman of her dreams. **90m/C VHS.** John McCafferty, Kim Dawson, Monique Parent. *SWI*

Perfect Harmony ½ **1991** Racial conflict at an exclusive Southern boys school in 1950s South Carolina is overcome through friendship and the love of music in this sentimental tale. Made for cable television. **93m/C VHS, Beta.** Peter Scolari, Darren McGavin, Catherine Mary Stewart, Moses Gunn, Cleavon Little, Justin Whalin, David Faustino, Richie Havens, Eugene Boyd; ***D:*** Will MacKenzie. *DIS*

Perfect Killer ½ *Satanic Mechanic* **1977 (R)** Van Cleef stars as a world weary Mafia hit-man who is double-crossed by his girl, set up by his best friend, and hunted by another hired assassin. **85m/C VHS, Beta.** Lee Van Cleef, Tita Barker, John Ireland, Robert Widmark; ***D:*** Marlon Sirko. *PSM*

A Perfect Little Murder ½ *A Quiet Little Neighborhood, A Perfect Little Murder* **1990** Marsha is expecting an uneventful life of barbecues and Little League when her family settles down in the suburbs. But then she overhears a murder plot and someone finds out she knows. Made for television. **94m/C VHS.** Teri Garr, Robert Urich, Susan Ruttan, Jeffrey Tambor, Tom Poston, Florence Stanley, Gail Edwards, Alex Rocco; ***D:*** Anson Williams; ***W:*** Mark Stein. *TTC*

The Perfect Marriage **1946** Tired comedy about a perfect couple who decide they can't stand each other anymore after ten years of marriage. Good cast makes the most of weak script. Based on the play by Samuel Raphaelson. **88m/B VHS.** Loretta Young, David Niven, Eddie Albert, Charlie Ruggles, ZaSu Pitts, Jerome Cowan, Rita Johnson; ***D:*** Lewis Allen; ***W:*** Leonard Spigelgass. *MCA*

Perfect Match **1988 (PG)** A timid young woman and an unambitious young man meet each other through the personal ads and then lie to each other about who they are and what they do for a living. **93m/C VHS, Beta.** Marc McClure, Jennifer Edwards, Diane Stilwell, Rob Paulsen, Karen Witter; ***D:*** Mark Deimel. *MCG*

A Perfect Spy ½ *John Le Carre's A Perfect Spy* **1988** In this BBC miniseries, John Le Carre takes a break from the world of George Smiley to take a look at spying from a personal view. Magnus Pym (Evan) would seem to be the perfect English gentleman; having gone to the right schools he proceeds to join the covert world of espionage. But Magnus hides the secret that his estranged father is a con man par excellence and it leads him to his own betrayals. Adapted from the novel, which Le Carre is said to have drawn from his own past. On three cassettes. **360m/C VHS.** *GB* Peter Egan, Ray McAnally, Frances Tomelty, Benedict Taylor, Tim Healy; ***W:*** Arthur Hopcraft. *FOX, SIG, VCO*

Perfect Strangers *Blind Alley* **1984 (R)** Thriller develops around a murder and the child who witnesses it. The killer attempts to kidnap the young boy, but problems arise when he falls in love with the lad's mother. **90m/C VHS, Beta.** Anne Carlisle, Brad Rijn, John Woehrle, Matthew Stockley, Ann Magnuson, Stephen Lack; ***D:*** Larry Cohen; ***W:*** Larry Cohen. *SUE, NLC*

Perfect Timing *Woof!* **1984** Soft-core film about a fledgling photographer who can't turn his orgy-like photo sessions into anything profitable. **87m/C VHS, Beta.** Stephen Markle, Michelle Scarabelli; ***D:*** Rene Bonniere. *LIV*

Perfect Victims **1987 (R)** Beautiful models are being hunted by a killer, and a police officer wants to catch the psychopath before he strikes again. **100m/C VHS, Beta, LV.** Deborah Shelton, Clarence Williams III, Lyman Ward; ***D:*** Shuki Levy. *ACA*

The Perfect Weapon **1991 (R)** Kenpo karate master Speakman severs family ties and wears funny belt in order to avenge underworld murder of his teacher. **85m/C VHS, Beta, LV.** Jeff Sanders, Jeff Speakman; ***D:*** Mark DiSalle; ***W:*** David Wilson; ***M:*** Gary Chang. *PAR*

Perfect Witness ½ **1989** A restaurant owner witnesses a mob slaying and resists testifying against the culprit to save his family and himself. Made for cable television. Filmed in New York City. **104m/C VHS, Beta, LV.** Brian Dennehy, Aidan Quinn, Stockard Channing, Laura Harrington, Joe Grifasi; ***D:*** Robert Mandel; ***M:*** Brad Fiedel. *HBO*

A Perfect World ½ **1993 (PG-13)** Butch Haynes (Costner) is an escaped con who takes 8-year-old fatherless Phillip (Lowther) as a hostage in 1963 Texas and is pursued by Texas Ranger Red Garnett (Eastwood). Butch is a bad guy and the film never tries to make him heroic but it also allows him to grow attached to Phillip and acknowledge him as a surrogate son. Costner gives a quiet and strong performance and the remarkable Lowther never goes wrong in his role as the needy little boy. Eastwood's role is strictly secondary as the well-tested lawman who understands justice without seeking vengeance. Somewhat draggy—especially the protracted final scene. **138m/C VHS, LV.** Kevin Costner, T.J. Lowther, Clint Eastwood, Laura Dern, Keith Szarabajka, Leo Burmester, Paul Hewitt, Bradley Whitford, Ray McKinnon, Wayne Dehart, Jennifer Griffin, Linda Hart; ***D:*** Clint Eastwood; ***W:*** John Lee Hancock; ***C:*** Jack N. Green; ***M:*** Lennie Niehaus. *WAR*

Perfectly Normal **1991 (R)** Two friends end up in hilarious situations when one opens an eccentric restaurant with a mysterious, newly found fortune. **106m/C VHS, Beta, LV.** Michael Riley, Robbie Coltrane, Kenneth Welsh, Eugene Lipinski; ***D:*** Yves Simoneau; ***W:*** Eugene Lipinski, Paul Quarrington. *ACA*

Performance ½ **1970 (R)** Grim and unsettling psychological account of a criminal who hides out in a bizarre house occupied by a peculiar rock star and his two female companions. Entire cast scores high marks, with Pallenberg especially compelling as a somewhat mysterious and attractive housemate to mincing Jagger. A cult favorite, with music by Nitzsche under the direction of Randy Newman. **104m/C VHS, Beta, LV.** *GB* James Fox, Mick Jagger, Anita Pallenberg; ***D:*** Donald Cammell, Nicolas Roeg; ***W:*** Donald Cammell; ***M:*** Jack Nitzsche. *WAR*

Perfume ½ **1991** Five beautiful, black childhood friends join together to conquer the cosmetics industry with their new perfume, Sassy. But can they resist all the temptations success brings and keep both their company and their friendship? **98m/C VHS.** Cheryl Francis Harrington, Kathleen Bradley Overton, Shy Jefferson, Lynn Marlin, Eugina Wright, Ted Lange; ***D:*** Roland S. Jefferson. *XVC*

Perfumed Nightmare **1989** Unique, appealing fable about a Filipino youth who discovers the drawbacks of social and cultural progress when he moves to Paris. Director Tahimik also plays the lead role. Imaginative, yet remarkably economical, this film was produced for $10,000 and received the International Critics Award at the Berlin Film Festival. In Tagalog with English dialogue and subtitles. **93m/C VHS.** *PH* Kidlat Tahimik, Dolores Santamaria, Georgette Baudry, Katrin Muller, Harmut Lerch; ***D:*** Kidlat Tahimik. *UWA*

Peril ½ *Peril en la Demeure* **1985 (R)** From the novel "Sur La Terre Comme Au Ciel" by Rene Belletto. Deals with a music teacher's infiltration into a wealthy family and the sexually motivated, back-stabbing murder plots that ensue. DeVille does poorly with avant-garde technique. In French with English subtitles. **100m/C VHS, Beta.** *FR* Michel Piccoli, Christophe MaLavoy, Richard Bohringer, Nicole Garcia, Anais Jeanneret; ***D:*** Michel DeVille; ***W:*** Michel DeVille. Cesar Awards '86: Best Director (DeVille). *INJ*

The Perils of Gwendoline ½ *Gwendoline; The Perils of Gwendoline in the Land of the Yik-Yak* **1984 (R)** A young woman leaves a convent to search for her long-lost father, in this adaptation of a much funnier French comic strip of the same name. What ends up on the screen is merely a very silly rip-off of the successful "Raiders of the Lost Ark," and of primary interest for its numerous scenes of amply endowed Kitaen in the buff. **88m/C VHS, Beta, LV.** *FR* Tawny Kitaen, Brent Huff, Zabou, Bernadette LaFont, Jean Rougerie; ***D:*** Just Jaeckin; ***M:*** Pierre Bachelet. *LIV, VES*

The Perils of Pauline ½ **1934** All 12 episodes of this classic melodrama/adventure serial in one package, featuring dastardly villains, cliff-hanging predicaments, and worldwide chases. **238m/B**

VHS, Beta. Evalyn Knapp, Robert Allen, James Durkin, Sonny Ray, Pat O'Malley; ***D:*** Ray Taylor. *NOS, VYY, MLB*

The Perils of Pauline **1947** A musical biography of Pearl White, the reigning belle of silent movie serials. Look for lots of silent film stars. **96m/C VHS, Beta.** Betty Hutton, John Lund, Constance Collier, William Demarest, Billy DeWolfe; ***D:*** George Marshall; ***C:*** Ray Rennahan; ***M:*** Frank Loesser. Nominations: Academy Awards '47: Best Song ("I Wish I Didn't Love You So"). *NOS, PSM, HHT*

Perils of the Darkest Jungle ½ *The Tiger Woman; Jungle Gold* **1944** Tiger Woman battles money-mad oil profiteers to protect her tribe. This twelve episode serial comes on two tapes. **180m/B VHS, LV.** Linda Stirling, Allan "Rocky" Lane, Duncan Renaldo, George Lewis; ***D:*** Spencer Gordon Bennet. *REP, MLB*

Period of Adjustment **1962** Heart-warming comedy about young newlyweds adjusting to the pressures of domestic life and trying to help the troubled marriage of an older couple. Based on the play by Tennessee Williams. **112m/B VHS.** Anthony (Tony) Franciosa, Jane Fonda, Jim Hutton, Lois Nettleton, John McGiver, Jack Albertson; ***D:*** George Roy Hill; ***W:*** Isobel Lennart. Nominations: Academy Awards '62: Best Art Direction/Set Decoration (B & W). *MGM*

Periphery ½ **1986** Shot in Berlin, this fictional narrative tells the story of a group of refugees from WWII who build their own society in which they communicate telepathically. They are hunted down by the press and the police. The film raises questions about the inability of society to deal with alternative lifestyles. **29m/C VHS.** *NO*

Permanent Record ½ **1988 (PG-13)** Hyper-sincere drama about a popular high schooler's suicide and the emotional reactions of those he left behind. Great performance from Reeves. Cinematography by Frederick Elmes. **92m/C VHS, Beta, LV.** Alan Boyce, Keanu Reeves, Michelle Meyrink, Jennifer Rubin, Pamela Gidley, Michael Elgart, Richard Bradford, Barry Corbin, Kathy Baker; ***D:*** Marisa Silver; ***W:*** Jarre Fees, Alice Liddle, Larry Ketron; ***M:*** Joe Strummer. *PAR*

Permanent Vacation ½ **1984** A young man disenchanted with New York City decides to escape to Europe to forget about his problems. **80m/C VHS, Beta.** John Lurie, Chris Parker; ***D:*** Jim Jarmusch; ***W:*** Jim Jarmusch; ***M:*** John Lurie. *NO*

Permission To Kill ½ **1975 (PG)** Grim spy drama features Bogard as an agent determined to prevent the return of a third-world radical to a totalitarian state. **96m/C VHS, Beta.** *GB* Dirk Bogarde, Ava Gardner, Timothy Dalton, Frederic Forrest; ***D:*** Cyril Frankel; ***C:*** Frederick A. (Freddie) Young; ***M:*** Richard Rodney Bennett. *SUE*

Perry Mason Returns **1985** Perry Mason returns to solve another baffling mystery. This time he must help his longtime assistant, Della Street, when she is accused of killing her new employer. **95m/C VHS, Beta.** Raymond Burr, Barbara Hale, William Katt, Patrick O'Neal, Richard Anderson, Cassie Yates, Al Freeman Jr.; ***D:*** Ron Satlof. *MCG*

Perry Mason: The Case of the Lost Love ½ **1987** Super-lawyer Mason defends the husband of a former lover he hadn't seen in 30 years. The solution to the mystery may catch viewer off guard. **98m/C VHS.** Raymond Burr, Barbara Hale, William Katt, Jean Simmons, Gene Barry, Robert Walden, Stephen Elliott, Robert Mandan, David Ogden Stiers; ***D:*** Ron Satlof. *VTR*

Persona **1966** A famous actress turns mute and is treated by a talkative nurse at a secluded cottage. As their relationship turns increasingly tense, the women's personalitites begin to merge. Memorable, unnerving—and atypically avant garde—fare from cinema giant Bergman. First of several collaborations between the director and leading lady Ullman. In Swedish with English subtitles. **100m/C VHS, Beta, 8mm.** *SW* Bibi Andersson, Liv Ullmann, Gunnar Bjornstrand, Margareta Krook; ***D:*** Ingmar Bergman; ***W:*** Ingmar Bergman; ***C:*** Sven Nykvist. National Board of Review Awards '67: 5 Best Foreign Films of the Year; National Society of Film Critics Awards '67: Best Actress (Andersson), Best Director (Bergman), Best Film. *MGM, VYY, VDM*

Personal Best **1982 (R)** Lesbian lovers compete while training for the 1990 Olympics. Provocative fare often goes where few films have gone before, but overly stylized direction occasionally overwhelms characterizations. It gleefully exploits locker-room nudity, with Hemingway in her pre-implant days. Still, an ambitious, often accomplished production. Towne's directorial debut. **126m/C VHS, Beta.** Mariel Hemingway, Scott Glenn, Patrice Donnelly; ***D:*** Robert Towne; ***W:*** Robert Towne; ***C:*** Michael Chapman; ***M:*** Jack Nitzsche. *WAR*

Personal Exemptions ½ **1988 (PG)** In this stock comedy a frenzied IRS auditor learns that her daughter is smuggling aliens into the country, her son is brokering with some businessmen she's targeted for tax fraud, and her husband is having an affair with a high-school girl. **100m/C VHS, Beta.** Nanette Fabray, John Cotton; ***D:*** Peter Rowe. *HMD*

Personal Property ½ *The Man in Possession* **1937** Taylor tries every trick in the book to win Harlow over in this MGM romantic fluff. Not that big on laughs, but plenty of good shots of Harlow and a beefcake scene of Taylor in a bathtub, who was the darling of the MGM lot and worked with every leading lady. This was the only film Harlow and Taylor made together. Remake of the 1931 film "The Man in Possession." **84m/B VHS.** Robert Taylor, Jean Harlow, Reginald Owen, Una O'Connor, E.E. Clive, Henrietta Crosman, Cora Witherspoon; ***D:*** Woodbridge S. Van Dyke; ***W:*** Hugh Mills. *MGM*

Personal Services ½ **1987 (R)** A bawdy satire loosely based on the life and times of Britain's modern-day madam, Cynthia Payne, and her rise to fame in the world of prostitution. Payne's earlier years were featured in the film "Wish You Were Here." **104m/C VHS, Beta, LV.** *GB* Julie Walters, Alec McCowen, Shirley Stelfox, Tim Woodward, David Atkins, Danny Schiller, Victoria Hardcastle; ***D:*** Terry Jones; ***W:*** David Leland; ***M:*** John Du Prez. *LIV, VES*

The Personals ½ **1983 (PG)** A recently divorced young man takes out a personal ad in a newspaper to find the woman of his dreams. But it isn't quite that simple in this independent comedy shot entirely in Minneapolis. **90m/C VHS, Beta.** Bill Schoppert, Karen Landry, Paul Eiding, Michael Laskin, Vickie Dakil; ***D:*** Peter Markle. *SUE*

Personals **1990** Chilling drama that casts O'Neill as an unnoticed librarian, until she begins to meet (and kill) the men who answer her ads. Zimbalist is a widow who is determined to learn the truth. Made for television. **93m/C VHS, Beta, LV.** Stephanie Zimbalist, Jennifer O'Neill, Robin Thomas, Clark Johnson, Gina Gallego, Rosemary Dunsmore, Colm Feore; ***D:*** Steven Hilliard Stern. *PAR*

The Persuaders **1971** The first two episodes of Moore and Curtis as international playboy crime fighters. **52m/C VHS, Beta.** *GB* Roger Moore, Tony Curtis, Alex Scott, Joan Collins, Robert Hutton; ***D:*** Basil Dearden. *NO*

Persuasion ½ **1995 (PG)** Charming British costume romance, based on Jane Austen's final novel, deals with the constricted life of practical, plain, put-upon Anne Elliot (Root). Thanks to well-meaning interference, Anne refused the marriage proposal of the manly Frederick Wentworth (Hinds) and instead stuck by her snobbish and demanding family. Eight years later, Anne is given a second chance at love when the now-wealthy Wentworth happens back into her life—but she still has her obnoxious relations to contend with. It's wonderful to see Anne blossom from mouse to lioness although the swirl of supporting players (and settings) provide some confusion. **104m/C VHS, LV.** *GB* Amanda Root, Ciaran Hinds, Susan Fleetwood, Corin Redgrave, Fiona Shaw, John Woodvine, Phoebe Nicholls, Sam West, Sophie Thompson, Judy Cornwell, Felicity Dean, Simon Russell Beale, Victoria Hamilton, Emma Roberts; ***D:*** Roger Mitchell; ***W:*** Nick Dear, Jeremy Sams; ***C:*** John Daly. *COL*

The Perverse Countess *La Comtesse Perverse* **1973** Romay is a bored tourist who spends a free weekend on a fling with Woods, who procures human flesh for the cannibalistic Count and Countess Zaroff (Vernon and Arno). Romay accompanies her lover to the haunted castle on a delivery, not realizing she is the package. When the Countess sees what a succulent bon-bon Romay is, she faces difficult choices. Subtitled in English. **86m/C VHS.** *FR* Lina Romay, Robert Woods, Howard Vernon, Alice Arno, Caroline Riviere; ***D:*** Jess (Jesus) Franco. *VSM*

Pet Sematary **1989 (R)** A quirky adaptation of Stephen King's bestseller about a certain patch of woods in the Maine wilderness that rejuvenates the dead, and how a newly located college MD eventually uses it to restore his dead son. Mildly creepy. **103m/C VHS, Beta, LV, 8mm.** Dale Midkiff, Fred Gwynne, Denise Crosby, Stephen King; ***D:*** Mary Lambert; ***W:*** Stephen King; ***M:*** Elliot Goldenthal. *PAR*

Pet Sematary 2 ½ **1992 (R)** Lame sequel to original Stephen King flick. After seeing his mother electrocuted, a teen and his veterinarian father move to the Maine town where the legendary Pet Sematary is located. Horror begins when the boy's friend's dog is shot by his stepfather, and the boys bury the dog in the "sematary." King wasn't involved with this film, so the story isn't very coherent, but shock value and special effects are great. Not recommended for those with a weak stomach. **102m/C VHS, Beta, LV.** Anthony Edwards, Edward Furlong, Clancy Brown, Jared Rushton, Darlanne Fluegel, Lisa Waltz, Jason McGuire, Sarah Trigger; ***D:*** Mary Lambert; ***W:*** Richard Outten. *PAR*

Pet Shop ½ **1994 (PG)** Pair of evil, galaxy-travelling aliens take over the local pet store in a remote desert town and plan to abduct all the kids by bewitching them with a spaceship full of intergalactic creatures. Only Dena (aided by the good alien furballs) can stop the bad guys from making space pets of the earthlings. **88m/C VHS, Beta.** Leigh Ann Orsi, Spencer Vrooman, David Wagner, Joannne Baron, Jane Morris, Terry Kiser, Jeff Michalski, Shashawnee Hall, Sabrina Wiener, Cody Burger; ***D:*** Hope Perello; ***W:*** Mark Goldstein, Greg Suddeth, Brent Friedman; ***M:*** Reg Powell. *PAR*

Pete Kelly's Blues **1955** A jazz musician in a Kansas City speakeasy is forced to stand up against a brutal racketeer. The melodramatic plot is brightened by a nonstop flow of jazz tunes sung by Lee and Fitzgerald and played by an all-star lineup that includes Dick Cathcart, Matty Matlock, Eddie Miller and George Van Eps. ♫Sugar; Sombody Loves Me; Bye Bye Blackbird; What Can I Say After I Say I'm Sorry?; He Needs Me; Sing a Rainbow; Pete Kelly's Blues. **96m/C VHS, Beta, LV.** Jack Webb, Janet Leigh, Edmond O'Brien, Lee Marvin, Martin Milner, Peggy Lee, Ella Fitzgerald, Jayne Mansfield; ***D:*** Jack Webb. Nominations: Academy Awards '55: Best Supporting Actress (Lee). *WAR*

Pete 'n' Tillie ½ **1972 (PG)** Amiable comedy turns to less appealing melodrama as couple meets, marries, and endures tragedy. Film contributes little to director Ritt's hitt-and-miss reputation, but Matthau and Burnett shine in leads. Adapted by Julius J. Epstein from a Peter de Vries' story. **100m/C VHS, Beta.** Walter Matthau, Carol Burnett, Geraldine Page, Barry Nelson, Rene Auberjonois, Lee Montgomery, Henry Jones, Kent Smith; ***D:*** Martin Ritt; ***W:*** Julius J. Epstein; ***C:*** John A. Alonzo; ***M:*** John Williams. British Academy Awards '73: Best Actor (Matthau); Nominations: Academy Awards '72: Best Adapted Screenplay, Best Supporting Actress (Page). *MCA*

Pete Townshend: White City **1985** The Who guitarist portrays a musician who helps bring a close friend and and his estranged wife back together. This semi-autobiographical film includes music from Townsend. **60m/C VHS, Beta, LV.** Pete Townshend, Andrew Wilde, Frances Barber; ***D:*** Richard Lowenstein. *MVD, VES*

Peter Gunn **1989** Detective Peter Gunn returns, only to find himself being hunted by both the mob and the Feds. A TV movie reprise of the vintage series that has none of the original cast members. **97m/C VHS.** Peter Strauss, Barbara Williams, Jennifer Edwards, Charles Cioffi, Pearl Bailey, Peter Jurasik, David Rappaport; ***D:*** Blake Edwards; ***M:*** Henry Mancini. *VTR*

Peter Lundy and the Medicine Hat Stallion ½ *The Medicine Hat Stallion; Pony Express* **1977** A teenaged Pony Express rider must outrun the Indians and battle the elements in order to carry mail from the Nebraska Territory to the West Coast in this made-for-television film. Good family entertainment. **85m/C VHS, Beta.** Leif Garrett, Mitchell Ryan, Bibi Besch, John Quade, Milo O'Shea; ***D:*** Michael O'Herlihy. *LIV, VES*

Peter Pan **1953 (G)** Disney classic about a boy who never wants to grow up. Based on J.M. Barrie's book and play. Still stands head and shoulders above any recent competition in providing fun family entertainment. Terrific animation and lovely hummable music. **76m/C VHS, Beta, LV.** ***D:*** Hamilton Luske; ***V:*** Bobby Driscoll, Kathryn Beaumont, Hans Conried, Heather Angel, Candy Candido. *DIS, APD, HMV*

Peter Pan ½ **1960** A TV classic, this videotape of a performance of the 1954 Broadway musical adapted from the J.M. Barrie classic features Mary Martin in one of her most famous incarnations, as the adolescent Peter Pan. Songs include "I'm Flying," "Neverland," and "I Won't Grow Up." **100m/C VHS, Beta, LV.** Mary Martin, Cyril Ritchard, Sondra Lee, Heather Halliday, Luke Halpin; ***D:*** Vincent J. Donehue. *GKK, COL, MLT*

Peter the First: Part 1 **1937** The first half of Petrov's Soviet epic about the early years of Tsar Peter I's reign. Lavish, in Russian with English subtitles. **95m/B VHS, Beta.** *RU* ***D:*** Vladimir Petrov. *FCT, INJ*

Peter the First: Part 2 **1938** The second half of Petrov's epic, also titled "The Conquests of Peter the Great," covering the triumphs and final years of the famous Tsar. In Russian with English subtitles. **104m/B VHS, Beta.** *RU* ***D:*** Vladimir Petrov. *FCT, INJ*

Peter the Great **1986** Dry but eye-pleasing TV mini-series follows the life of Russia's colorful, very tall ruler from childhood on. Much of the interesting cast is wasted in tiny roles. **371m/C VHS.** Maximilian Schell, Laurence Olivier, Omar Sharif, Vanessa Redgrave, Ursula Andress. *VTR*

Peter's Friends ½ **1992 (R)** Peter has recently inherited a grand manor house located outside London and invites some chums to celebrate a New Year's Eve weekend, ten years after they've been at university together. So begins another nostalgic trip down memory lane ala "The Big Chill," but unlike other clones, this one can stand on its own, with a lightweight and sly script by talented comedienne Rudner (in her film debut) and her husband Bergman. If the script sometimes falls a little flat, the fine cast will make up for it. Thompson's mother, actress Law, plays the housekeeper. **102m/C VHS, LV.** *GB* Kenneth Branagh, Rita Rudner, Emma Thompson, Stephen Fry, Hugh Laurie, Imelda Staunton, Alphonsia Emmanuel, Tony Slattery, Alex Lowe, Alex Scott, Phyllida Law, Richard Briers; ***D:*** Kenneth Branagh; ***W:*** Rita Rudner, Martin Bergman; ***M:*** Jacques Offenbach. *HBO, BTV*

Pete's Dragon ½ **1977 (G)** Elliot, an enormous, bumbling dragon with a penchant for clumsy heroics, becomes friends with poor orphan Pete. Combines brilliant animation with the talents of live actors for an interesting effect. **128m/C VHS, Beta, LV.** Helen Reddy, Shelley Winters, Mickey Rooney, Jim Dale, Red Buttons, Sean Marshall, Jim Backus, Jeff Conaway; ***D:*** Don Chaffey; ***W:*** Malcolm Marmorstein; ***V:*** Charlie Callas. Nominations: Academy Awards '77: Best Song ("Candle on the Water"), Best Original Score. *DIS, FCT, WTA*

Petit Con ½ **1984 (R)** A live-action version of the popular French comic strip wherein a young rebel drops out of society to live with aging hippies. With English subtitles. **90m/C VHS, Beta.** *FR* Guy Marchand, Michel Choupon, Caroline Cellier, Bernard Brieux, Soudad Amidou; ***D:*** Gerard Lauzier. *ORI*

Petrified Forest **1936** Patrons and employees are held captive by a runaway gangster's band in a desert diner. Often gripping, with memorable performances from Davis, Howard, and Bogart. Based on the play by Robert Sherwood with Howard and Bogart recreating their stage roles. **83m/B VHS, Beta.** Bette Davis, Leslie Howard, Humphrey Bogart, Dick Foran, Charley Grapewin, Porter Hall; ***D:*** Archie Mayo. *FOX, MGM*

Petulia **1968 (R)** Overlooked, offbeat drama about a flighty woman who spites her husband by dallying with a sensitive, recently divorced surgeon. Classic '60s document and cult favorite offers great performance from the appealing Christie, with Scott fine as the vulnerable surgeon. On-screen performances by the Grateful Dead and Big Brother. Among idiosyncratic director Lester's best. Photographed by Nicholas Roeg. From the novel "Me and the Arch Kook Petulia" by John Haase. **105m/C VHS, Beta.** George C. Scott, Richard Chamberlain, Julie Christie, Shirley Knight, Arthur Hill, Joseph Cotten, Pippa Scott, Richard Dysart, Kathleen Widdoes, Austin Pendleton, Rene Auberjonois; ***D:*** Richard Lester; ***W:*** Lawrence B. Marcus; ***M:*** John Barry. *WAR*

Peyton Place **1957** Passion, scandal, and deception in a small New England town set the standard for passion, scandal, and deception in soap operadom. Shot on location in Camden, Maine. Performances and themes now seem dated, but produced a blockbuster in its time. Adapted from Grace Metalious' popular novel and followed by "Return to Peyton Place." **157m/C VHS, LV.** Lana Turner, Hope Lange, Lee Philips, Lloyd Nolan, Diane Varsi, Lorne Greene, Russ Tamblyn, Arthur Kennedy, Terry Moore, Barry Coe, David Nelson, Betty Field, Mildred Dunnock, Leon Ames, Alan Reed Jr.; ***D:*** Mark Robson; ***W:*** John Michael Hayes; ***C:*** William Mellor. Nominations: Academy Awards '56: Best Director (Robson), Best Supporting Actress (Lange). *FOX, FCT*

Phaedra **1961** Loose and updated adaptation of Euripides' "Hipploytus." Mercouri, the second wife of a rich Greek shipping magnate, is dispatched to London to convince her husband's adult son (Perkins) to come home to Greece. Mercouri and Perkins immediately begin a steamy affair but their return home brings problems for all. Dubbed. **116m/B VHS.** *GR FR* Melina Mercouri, Anthony Perkins, Raf Vallone, Elizabeth Ercy; ***Cameos:*** Jules Dassin; ***D:*** Jules Dassin; ***W:*** Jules Dassin, Margarita Liberaki; ***M:*** Mikis Theodorakis. *FCT*

Phantasm ½ **1979 (R)** A small-budgeted, hallucinatory horror fantasy about two parentless brothers who discover weird goings-on at the local funeral parlor, including the infamous airborne, brain-chewing chrome ball. Creepy, unpredictable nightmare fashioned on a shoestring by young independent producer Coscarelli. Scenes were cut out of the original film to avoid "X" rating. Followed by "Phantasm II." **90m/C VHS, Beta, LV.** Michael Baldwin, Bill Thornbury, Reggie Bannister, Kathy Lester, Terrie Kalbus, Ken Jones, Susan Harper, Lynn Eastman, David Arntzen, Angus Scrimm, Bill Cone; ***D:*** Don A. Coscarelli; ***W:*** Don A. Coscarelli. *COL, SUE*

Phantasm II **1988 (R)** Teen psychic keeps flashing on villainous Tall Man. A rehash sequel to the original, cultishly idiosyncratic fantasy, wherein more victims are fed into the inter-dimensional abyss and Mike discovers that the horror is not all in his head. Occasional inspired gore; bloodier than its predecessor. More yuck for the buck. **97m/C VHS, Beta, LV.** James LeGros, Reggie Bannister, Angus Scrimm; ***D:*** Don A. Coscarelli; ***W:*** Don A. Coscarelli. *MCA*

Phantasm III: Lord of the Dead ½ **1994 (R)** Murderous mortician The Tall Man and his killer silver spheres return once again in this continuing gore fest. Mike, whose brother Jody was one of The Tall Man's victims, teams up with the cynical Reggie and martial arts expert Rocky to try to defeat the creep. That's if they can get past his zombie cohorts and flesh-eating ghouls. **91m/C VHS, LV.** Reggie Bannister, A. Michael Baldwin, Bill Thornbury, Gloria Henry, Kevin Connor, Angus Scrimm; ***D:*** Don A. Coscarelli; ***W:*** Don A. Coscarelli. *MCA*

The Phantom **1931** Rare cheapie of a hooded killer terrorizing a group of people in a haunted house. **62m/C VHS.** Guinn "Big Boy" Williams, Wilfrid Lucas, Sheldon Lewis, Tom O'Brien, William Gould; ***D:*** Alan James. *SNC, GPV*

The Phantom ½ **1996 (PG)** Based on the Lee Falk comic created in 1936. Deep in the Bengalla jungle, a mysterious costumed figure honors a 400 year old legacy by fighting piracy, greed, and cruelty. With the help of a beautiful newspaper heiress (Swanson), the latest guardian (Zane) must keep an American industrialist (Williams) and a secret brotherhood of pirates from finding three sacred skulls that contain the power to dominate the world. Old-fashioned swashbuckling story is helped along by Zane's enthusiastic portrayal of the stalwart hero. Action set pieces, while done more dynamically elsewhere, are fun and exciting. Older kids (read: teenagers) may find the proceedings a bit hokey, but everyone seems to be having a good time. **100m/C VHS.** Billy Zane, Kristy Swanson, Treat Williams, Catherine Zeta Jones, James Remar, Jon Tenney, Patrick McGoohan, Samantha Eggar, Cary-Hiroyuki Tagawa, Robert Coleby, David Proval; ***D:*** Simon Wincer; ***W:*** Jeffrey Boam; ***C:*** David Burr; ***M:*** David Newman. *NYR*

The Phantom Broadcast ½ *Phantom of the Air* **1933** A popular radio crooner is murdered. The main suspect is his hunchbacked accompanist and manager, who had all along secretly prerecorded his own velvet voice for the crooner to lip-sync along with. A tightly plotted minor thriller that holds up surprisingly well. **63m/B VHS, Beta, 8mm.** Ralph Forbes, Gail Patrick, Vivienne Osborne, Guinn "Big Boy" Williams, George "Gabby" Hayes; ***D:*** Phil Rosen. *VYY, NOS, FCT*

Phantom Brother ½ **1988** A semi-spoof about a teenager left orphaned by a car crash that wiped out his entire family, and who is subsequently haunted by his dead brother. Even thinner than it sounds. **92m/C VHS, Beta.** Jon Hammer, Patrick Molloy, John Gigante, Mary Beth Pelshaw; ***D:*** William Szarka. *HMD*

The Phantom Bullet ½ **1926** Hoot wants to holler at his father's murderers. **60m/B VHS, Beta.** Hoot Gibson. *GPV*

The Phantom Chariot ½ **1920** A fantasy depicting the Swedish myth about how Death's coach must be driven by the last man to die each year. Silent. **89m/B VHS, Beta.** *SW* ***D:*** Victor Sjostrom. *SNC, FCT, GVV*

The Phantom Creeps **1939** Evil Dr. Zorka, armed with a meteorite chunk which can bring an army to a standstill, provides the impetus for this enjoyable serial in 12 episodes. **235m/B VHS, Beta.** Bela Lugosi, Dorothy Arnold, Robert Kent, Regis Toomey; ***D:*** Ford Beebe, Saul Goodkind. *NOS, SNC, VCN*

The Phantom Empire *Radio Ranch* **1935** Autry faces the futuristic "Thunder Riders" from the subterranean city of Murania, located 20,000 feet beneath his ranch. A complete serial in twelve episodes. If you only see one science fiction western in your life, this is the one. Also available in an edited theatrical version at 80 minutes. **245m/B VHS, Beta.** Gene Autry, Frankie Darro, Betsy King Ross, Smiley Burnette; ***D:*** B. Reeves Eason, Otto Brower. *NOS, SNC, VYY*

Phantom Empire **1987 (R)** A woman who rules over a lost city takes a bunch of scientists prisoner and forces them to be slaves. **85m/C VHS, Beta.** Ross Hagen, Jeffrey Combs, Dawn Wildsmith, Robert Quarry, Susan Stokey, Michelle (McClellan) Bauer, Russ Tamblyn, Sybil Danning; ***D:*** Fred Olen Ray. *PSM*

Phantom Express **1932** Experienced old engineer is dismissed from his job because no one believes his explanation that a mysterious train caused the wreck of his own train. He aims to find justice. **65m/B VHS, Beta.** J. Farrell MacDonald, Sally Blane, William Collier Jr., Hobart Bosworth; ***D:*** Emory Johnson. *NO*

Phantom Fiend ½ **1935** A gentle musician becomes a suspect when a series of Jack-the-Ripper type murders terrorize London. Is he the nice guy known by his girlfriend and the people in his lodging house, or is the musician really JTR? Based on the novel "The Lodger" by Marie Belloc-Lowndes. **70m/B VHS.** *GB* Ivor Novello, Elizabeth Allan, A.W. Baskcomb, Jack Hawkins, Barbara Everest, Peter Gawthorne, P. Kynaston Reeves; ***D:*** Maurice Elvey. *FCT, RXM*

The Phantom Flyer 🦴½ **1928** Stunt pilot helps out a cattle-owning frontier family bedeviled by rustlers. Silent. **54m/B VHS, Beta, 8mm.** Al Wilson. *VYY, GPV, RXM*

Phantom from Space 🦴½ **1953** An invisible alien lands on Earth, begins killing people, and is pursued by a pair of scientists. **72m/B VHS, Beta.** Ted Cooper, Rudolph Anders, Noreen Nash, James Seay, Harry Landers; ***D:*** W. Lee Wilder; ***C:*** William Clothier. *VYY, SNC, NOS*

The Phantom from 10,000 Leagues 🦴 **1956** Slimy sea monster attacks swimmers and fishermen; investigating oceanographer pretends not to notice monster is hand puppet. Early AIP release, when still named American Releasing Company. **80m/B VHS.** Kent Taylor, Cathy Downs, Michael Whalen, Helene Stanton, Phillip Pine; ***D:*** Dan Milner. *VYY, SNC, MLB*

Phantom Gold 🦴½ **1938** The wicked Whitaker claims to have struck it rich but it's really a scam to lure unsuspecting miners to the claim and then rob and murder them. Luden's suspicious and proves Whitaker's a bad guy. **56m/B VHS.** Jack Luden, Charles "Slim" Whitaker, Beth Marion, Hal Taliaferro, Art Davis; ***D:*** Joseph Levering. *GPV*

The Phantom in the House 🦴🦴 **1929** A woman commits a murder and has her inventor husband take the rap. While he's in prison, she gets rich off of his work. Things get hairy when he is released fifteen years later and is introduced to his daughter as a friend of the family. Melodramatic film was originally made with and without sound. **64m/B VHS, Beta.** Ricardo Cortez, Nancy Welford, Henry B. Walthall, Grace Valentine; ***D:*** Phil Rosen. *SNC*

Phantom Killer 🦴🦴 **1942** A district attorney tries to hang a murder rap on a most improbable suspect. When the man is aquitted, the DA quits his job to find the truth, which takes a disturbing twist. The plot is a thinly veiled rehash of "The Sphinx" (1933). **61m/B VHS.** Dick Purcell, Joan Woodbury, John Hamilton, Warren Hymer, Kenneth Harlan, J. Farrell MacDonald, Mantan Moreland; ***D:*** William Beaudine. *NOS*

The Phantom Light 🦴🦴½ **1935** A lighthouse keeper is murdered under strange circumstances and a mysterious light keeps appearing at the scene. Detective Hale joins up with a navy man and another lighthouse keeper to solve the crime. A low-budget mystery with good atmosphere and some humor. **75m/B VHS.** *GB* Binnie Hale, Gordon Harker, Ian Hunter, Donald Calthrop; ***D:*** Michael Powell. *HCV*

Phantom of Chinatown 🦴 **1940** Mr. Wong is called in to solve another murder in the final entry in the series. The first to have an Asian actor portray the lead, as Luke replaced Boris Karloff. **61m/B VHS.** Keye Luke, Lotus Long, Grant Withers, Paul McVey, Charles Miller; ***D:*** Phil Rosen. *NOS, SNC, HEG*

Phantom of Death 🦴½ **1987 (R)** A brilliant pianist, stricken by a fatal disease that causes rapid aging, goes on a murderous rampage. **95m/C VHS, Beta.** *IT* Michael York, Donald Pleasence, Edwige Fenech; ***D:*** Ruggero Deodato; ***M:*** Pino Donaggio. *VMK*

The Phantom of 42nd Street 🦴🦴 **1945** An actor and a cop team up to find the killer of a wealthy uncle. **58m/B VHS.** Dave O'Brien, Kay Aldridge, Alan Mowbray, Frank Jenks; ***D:*** Al(bert) Herman. *SNC, NOS, MRV*

Phantom of Liberty 🦴🦴🦴½ *Le Fantome de la Liberte; The Specter of Freedom* **1968** Master surrealist Bunuel's episodic film wanders from character to character and from event to event. Animals wander through a man's bedroom, soldiers conduct military exercises in an inhabited area, a missing girl stands before her parents even as they futilely attempt to determine her whereabouts, and an assassin is found guilty, then applauded and led to freedom. They don't get much more surreal than this. If you think you may like it, you'll probably love it. Bunuel, by the way, is among the firing squad vicitms in the film's opening enactment of Goya's May 3, 1808. In French with English subtitles. **104m/C VHS, Beta, LV.** *FR* Adrianna Asti, Jean-Claude Brialy, Michel Piccoli, Adolfo Celi, Monica Vitti; ***D:*** Luis Bunuel. National Board of Review Awards '74: 5 Best Foreign Films of the Year. *XVC, INJ, APD*

The Phantom of Soho 🦴🦴 *Das Phantom von Soho* **1964** A Scotland Yard detective investigates the murders of several prominent businessmen and is assisted by a beautiful mystery writer. **92m/B VHS, Beta.** *GE* Dieter Borsche, Barbara Rutting, Hans Sohnker, Peter Vogel, Helga Sommerfeld, Werner Peters; ***D:*** Franz Gottlieb. *SNC*

Phantom of the Air **1933** Twelve chapters of high-flying adventure with Tom Tyler! **230m/B VHS.** Tom Tyler, Gloria Shea, William Desmond, Leroy Mason, Walter Brennan; ***D:*** Ray Taylor. *GPV, MLB*

Phantom of the Mall: Eric's Revenge 🦴 **1989** A murderous spirit haunts the local mall. Gore flows like water. **91m/C VHS, Beta, LV.** Morgan Fairchild, Kari Whitman, Jonathan Goldsmith, Derek Rydell; ***D:*** Richard S. Friedman. *FRH*

The Phantom of the Opera 🦴🦴🦴 **1925** Deranged, disfigured music lover haunts the sewers of a Parisian opera house and kills to further the career of an unsuspecting young soprano. First of many film versions still packs a wallop, with fine playing from Chaney, Sr. Silent with two-color Technicolor "Bal Masque" sequence. Versions with different running times are also available, including 79 and 88 minutes. **101m/B VHS.** Lon Chaney Sr., Norman Kerry, Mary Philbin, Gibson Gowland; ***D:*** Rupert Julian. *KIV, NOS, FUS*

The Phantom of the Opera 🦴🦴🦴 **1943** Second Hollywood version—the first with talking—of Gastron Leroux novel about a madman who promotes fear and mayhem at a Paris opera house. Raines is good in lead; Eddy warbles away. **92m/C VHS, Beta, LV.** Claude Rains, Nelson Eddy, Susanna Foster, Edgar Barrier, Leo Carrillo, Hume Cronyn, J. Edward Bromberg; ***D:*** Arthur Lubin; ***C:*** Hal Mohr. Academy Awards '43: Best Color Cinematography, Best Interior Decoration; Nominations: Academy Awards '43: Best Sound. *MCA*

The Phantom of the Opera 🦴🦴½ **1962** Hammer version of the Gaston Leroux novel transfers the action from Paris to London but keeps the basic story of a young singer (Sears) and her masked benefactor (Lom), who lives in the sewers beneath the opera house. There's also the wimpy fiance (De Souza) to come between them. Good gothic melodrama. Sears' singing was dubbed by opera performer Pat Clark; producer Hinds used the pseudonym John Elder for his screenplay. **85m/C VHS.** Herbert Lom, Heather Sears, Edward De Souza, Thorley Walters, Michael Gough, Martin Miller, Ian Wilson; ***D:*** Terence Fisher; ***W:*** Anthony John Elder Hinds; ***C:*** Arthur Grant; ***M:*** Edwin Astley. *MCA*

The Phantom of the Opera 🦴½ **1989 (R)** A gory, "Elm Street"-ish version of the Gaston Leroux classic, attempting to cash in on the success of the Broadway musical. **93m/C VHS, Beta, LV.** Robert Englund, Jill Schoelen, Alex Hyde-White, Bill Nighy, Terence Harvey, Stephanie Lawrence; ***D:*** Dwight Little. *COL*

The Phantom of the Opera 🦴🦴½ **1990** Yet another version of the tragic tale of a disfigured mask-wearing opera lover, who lurks in the depths of the Paris Opera House, and his desire for lovely young singer, Christine. Dance plays the Phantom as doomed romantic, with Lancaster his protective father. Kopit adapted from his 1983 play. Made for TV drama, originally shown in two parts. **200m/C VHS.** *GB* Charles Dance, Burt Lancaster, Teri Polo, Ian Richardson, Andrea Ferreol, Adam Storke, Jean-Pierre Cassel; ***D:*** Tony Richardson; ***W:*** Arthur Kopit; ***M:*** John Addison. *AVE*

Phantom of the Paradise 🦴🦴 **1974 (PG)** A rock 'n roll parody of "Phantom of the Opera." Splashy, only occasionally horrific spoof in which cruel music executive Williams, much to his everlasting regret, swindles a songwriter. Violence ensues. Not for most, or even many, tastes. Graham steals the film as rocker Beef. A failure at the box office, and now a cult item (small enthusiastic cult with few outside interests) for its oddball humor and outrageous rock star parodies. Williams also wrote the turgid score. ♫Goodbye, Eddie, Goodbye; Faust; Upholstery; Special to Me; Old Souls; Somebody Super Like You; Life At Last; The Hell of It; The Phantom's Theme (Beauty and the Beast). **92m/C VHS, Beta, LV.** Paul Williams, William Finley, Jessica Harper, Gerrit Graham; ***D:*** Brian DePalma; ***W:*** Brian DePalma; ***M:*** Paul Williams. Nominations: Academy Awards '74: Best Original Score. *FOX*

The Phantom of the Range 🦴½ **1938** Marion is trying to sell her grandfather's ranch only his "ghost" is scaring everyone away. She and cowpoke Tyler find out a group of evil treasure hunters are searching the property for hidden gold. **59m/B VHS.** Tom Tyler, Beth Marion, Charles "Blackie" King, Forrest Taylor, John Elliott, Soledad Jiminez, Sammy Cohen; ***D:*** Robert F. "Bob" Hill. *GPV*

Phantom of the Ritz 🦴🦴 **1988 (R)** Bizarre accidents begin to take place when Ed Blake and his girlfriend start renovating the old Ritz Theater. It seems the theater is inhabited by a rather angry ghost and somebody's got to deal with it before the Ritz can rock and roll. Featuring the fabulous sounds of the Fifties. **89m/C VHS, Beta.** Peter Bergman, Deborah Van Valkenburgh; ***D:*** Allen Plone. *PSM*

Phantom of the West 🦴🦴 **1931** Ten-episode serial about a rancher who becomes "The Phantom of the West" in order to smoke out his father's killer. **166m/B VHS, Beta.** William Desmond, Thomas Santschi, Tom Tyler; ***D:*** David Ross Lederman. *VYY, NOS, VCN*

Phantom Patrol 🦴½ **1936** A mystery writer is kidnapped and someone impersonates him. Mountie Maynard must come to the rescue. **60m/B VHS, Beta.** Kermit Maynard, Joan Barclay, Paul Fix, Julian Rivero, Eddie Phillips, Roger Williams; ***D:*** Charles Hutchinson. *DVT, NOS*

The Phantom Planet 🦴½ **1961** An astronaut crash-lands on an asteroid and discovers a race of tiny people living there. Having breathed the atmosphere, he shrinks to their dimunitive size and aids them in their war against brutal invaders. Infamously peculiar. **82m/B VHS, Beta.** Dean Fredericks, Coleen Gray, Tony Dexter, Dolores Faith, Francis X. Bushman, Richard Kiel; ***D:*** William Marshall. *NOS, SNC*

Phantom Rancher 🦴½ **1939** Roaring melodrama finds Maynard donning a mask to find the real Phantom, who is causing havoc. **61m/B VHS, Beta.** Ken Maynard. *VCI, VCN*

Phantom Ranger 🦴½ **1938** A federal agent masquerades as a crook to catch a band of counterfeiters. **54m/B VHS.** Tim McCoy, Suzanne Kaaren, Karl Hackett, John St. Polis, John Merton, Harry Strang; ***D:*** Sam Newfield. *NOS, DVT*

The Phantom Rider **1937** Mystery fills the old West in this serial composed of fifteen chapters. **152m/B VHS, Beta.** Buck Jones, Marla Shelton. *REP, MLB, VCN*

The Phantom Rider 🦴½ **1946** The masked do-gooder rides the plains protecting the local Indians from some surly settlers. A 12-episode serial. **167m/C VHS.** Robert Kent, Peggy Stewart, Leroy Mason, Chief Thundercloud. *MOV*

Phantom Thunderbolt 🦴½ **1933** A man who has falsely spread the rumor that he's a gunfighter is hired to chase away some good-for-nothings. **62m/B VHS, Beta.** Ken Maynard, Frances Lee, Frank Rice, William Gould, Robert F. (Bob) Kortman; ***D:*** Alan James. *NOS, DVT, MTX*

Phantom Tollbooth 🦴🦴🦴 **1969 (G)** A young boy drives his car into an animated world, where the numbers are at war with the letters and he has been chosen to save Rhyme and Reason, to bring stability back to the Land of Wisdom. Completely unique and typically Jonesian in its intellectual level and interests. Bright children will be interested, but this is really for adults who will understand the allegory. Based on Norman Justers' metaphorical novel. **89m/C VHS, Beta.** ***D:*** Chuck Jones; ***V:*** Mel Blanc, Hans Conried. *MGM, WTA*

Phantom 2040 Movie: The Ghost Who Walks 🦴🦴½ **1995** Teenager Kit Walker discovers his destiny when a mysterious stranger tells him about his late father and how Kit must carry on his father's legacy as a superhero called the Phantom. A purple suit renders Kit invisible and he finds himself battling his dad's old nemesis, Rebecca Madison, who's out to destroy the Earth's resources. Based on the television and comic book series. **97m/C VHS.** ***V:*** Scott Valentine, Margot Kidder, Ron Perlman, Carrie Snodgress, Mark Hamill. *FHE, LIV*

Phar Lap 🦴🦴½ *Phar Lap: Heart of a Nation* **1984 (PG)** Saga of a legendary Australian racehorse who rose from obscurity to win nearly 40 races in just three years before mysteriously dying in 1932. American version runs 10 minutes shorter than the Aussie one. **107m/C VHS, Beta.** *AU* Ron Leibman, Tom Burlinson, Judy Morris, Celia de Burgh; ***D:*** Simon Wincer; ***W:*** David Williamson. *FOX*

Pharaoh 🦴🦴 **1966** An expensive Polish epic about the power plays of royalty in ancient Egypt. Dubbed. **125m/B VHS, Beta.** *PL* Jerzy Zelnick; ***D:*** Jerzy Kawalerowicz. *FCT*

Pharmacist 🦴🦴½ **1932** A day in the life of a hapless druggist undone by disgruntled customers and robbers. Typical Fields effort. **19m/B VHS, Beta.** Elise Cavanna, Babe Kane, W.C. Fields, Grady Sutton. *CCB*

Pharoah's Army 🦴🦴½ **1995 (PG-13)** Five Union soldiers are foraging for food at a small Kentucky farm when one young soldier (Fox) is badly injured and his captain, John Abston (Cooper), is forced to stay put while he treats the wounds. The farm is home to Sarah Anders (Clarkson) and her young son (Lucas), while her husband is off fighting for the Confederates. Sarah isn't happy about the arrangement but the decent Alston, a farmer himself in peacetime, begins slowly to win her over. Their friendship, however, doesn't sit well with either his men nor Sarah's son. Fine performances in a restrained drama. **90m/C VHS.** Chris Cooper, Patricia Clarkson, Kris Kristofferson, Richard Tyson, Huckleberry Fox, Will Lucas; ***D:*** Robby Henson; ***W:*** Robby Henson; ***C:*** Doron Schlair. *ORI*

Phase 4 🦴🦴 **1974 (PG)** A tale of killer ants retaliating against the humans attempting to exterminate them. **84m/C VHS, Beta, LV.** Nigel Davenport, Michael Murphy, Lynne Frederick; ***D:*** Saul Bass. *PAR*

Phedre 🦴½ **1968** Jean Racine's adaptation of the Greek legend involving Phedre, Theseus, and Hippolyte. Bell is the only one worth watching in this weak and stagy picture. In French with English subtitles. **93m/C VHS, Beta.** Marie Bell; ***D:*** Pierre Jourdan. *VYY, APD, INJ*

Phenomenal and the Treasure of Tutankamen 🦴🦴 **197? (R)** Fiendish criminal genius steals priceless golden mask of King Tut. Superhero Phenomenal is less than dry spaghetti sci-fi. **90m/C VHS.** *IT* Mauro Parenti, Lucretia Love. *NO*

Phenomenon 🦴🦴½ **1996 (PG)** Average small town schmo George Malley (Travolta) is turned into a genius when he's struck by a bright light on his 37th birthday. This development brings him to the attention of the scientific community and, of course, the military. The locals scorn him, thus fulfilling the Hollywood stereotype of rural folks fearing anything they don't understand. Good-natured weeper plays the Gump card and wins as Travolta gets to be the nice guy. **124m/C VHS.** John Travolta, Robert Duvall, Kyra Sedgwick, Forest Whitaker, Richard Kiley, Brent Spiner; ***D:*** Jon Turteltaub; ***W:*** Gerald DiPego; ***C:*** Phedon Papamichael; ***M:*** Thomas Newman. *NYR*

Phffft! 🦴🦴½ **1954** Holliday and Lemmon are a bored couple who decide to divorce, date others, and take mambo lessons. By no stretch of plausibility, they constantly run into each other and compete in the same mambo contest. **91m/B VHS.** Judy Holliday, Jack Lemmon, Jack Carson, Kim Novak, Luella Gear, Merry Anders; ***D:*** Mark Robson; ***W:*** George Axelrod; ***C:*** Charles B(ryant) Lang. *GKK*

Philadelphia 🦴🦴🦴½ **1993 (PG-13)** AIDS goes Hollywood as hot-shot corporate attorney Andrew Beckett (Hanks), fired because he has the disease, hires brilliant but homophobic personal injury attorney Washington as his counsel when he sues for discrimination. Box office winner was criticized by some gay activists as too mainstream, which is the point. It doesn't probe deeply into the gay lifestyle, focusing instead on justice and compassion. Boasts a good script, make-up that transforms Hanks, sure direction, great soundtrack, and a strong supporting cast, but all would mean little without Hanks' superb performance, his best to date. ♫Streets of Philadelphia. **125m/C VHS, LV, 8mm.** Tom Hanks, Denzel Washington, Antonio Banderas, Jason Robards Jr., Joanne Woodward, Mary Steenburgen, Ron Vawter, Robert Ridgely, Obba Babatunde, Robert Castle, Daniel Chapman, Roger Corman, John Bedford Lloyd, Roberta Maxwell, Warren Miller, Anna Deavere Smith, Kathryn Witt, Andre B. Blake, Ann Dowd, Bradley Whitford, Chandra Wilson, Charles Glenn, Peter Jacobs, Paul Lazar, Dan Olmstead, Joey Perillo, Lauren Roselli, Bill Rowe, Lisa Talerico, Daniel von Bargen, Tracey Walter; ***Cameos:*** Karen Finley, David Drake, Quentin Crisp; ***D:*** Jonathan Demme; ***W:*** Ron Nyswaner; ***C:*** Tak Fujimoto; ***M:*** Howard Shore. Academy Awards '93: Best Actor (Hanks), Best Song ("Streets of Philadelphia"); Golden Globe Awards '94: Best Actor—Drama (Hanks), Best Song ("Streets of Philadelphia"); Blockbuster Entertainment Awards '95: Drama Actor, Video (Hanks); Nominations: Academy Awards '93: Best Makeup, Best Original Screenplay, Best Song ("Philadelphia"); MTV Movie Awards '94: Best Film, Best On-Screen Duo (Tom Hanks/Denzel Washington), Best Song ("Streets of Philadelphia"). *COL*

The Philadelphia Experiment 🦴🦴½ **1984 (PG)** A WWII sailor falls through a hole in time and lands in the mid-1980s, whereupon he woos a gorgeous woman. Sufficient chemistry between Pare and Allen, but PG rating is an indication of the film's less-than-graphic love scenes. **101m/C VHS, Beta, LV.** Michael Pare, Nancy Allen, Eric Christmas, Bobby DiCicco; ***D:*** Stewart Raffill; ***W:*** Don Jakoby. *VTR*

Philadelphia Experiment 2 🦴🦴½ **1993 (PG-13)** Melodramatic sci-fi what-ifer has Germany winning WWII by dropping a bomb on Washington. So southern California is now one big labor camp with an evil mad scientist (Graham) and a beleagured hero (Johnson) who must time-travel back to 1943 to prevent the Germans from dropping that bomb. **98m/C VHS, LV.** Brad Johnson, Gerrit Graham, Marjean Holden, James Greene, Geoffrey Blake, John Christian Grass, Cyril O'Reilly; ***D:*** Stephen Cornwell; ***W:*** Kevin Rock, Nick Paine; ***M:*** Gerald Gouriet. *VMK*

The Philadelphia Story 🦴🦴🦴🦴 **1940** A woman's plans to marry again go awry when her dashing ex-husband arrives on the scene. Matters are further complicated when a loopy reporter—assigned to spy on the nuptials—falls in love with the blushing bride. Classic comedy, with trio of Hepburn, Grant, and Stewart all serving aces. Based on the hit Broadway play by Philip Barry, and remade as the musical "High Society" in 1956 (stick to the original). Also available colorized. **112m/B VHS, Beta, LV.** Katharine Hepburn, Cary Grant, James Stewart, Ruth Hussey, Roland Young, John Howard, John Halliday, Virginia Weidler, Henry Daniell, Hillary Brooke, Mary Nash; ***D:*** George Cukor; ***W:*** Donald Ogden Stewart; ***C:*** Joseph Ruttenberg; ***M:*** Franz Waxman. Academy Awards '40: Best Actor (Stewart), Best Screenplay; New York Film Critics Awards '40: Best Actress (Hepburn); Nominations: Academy Awards '40: Best Actress (Hepburn), Best Director (Cukor), Best Picture, Best Supporting Actress (Hussey). *MGM, BTV, HMV*

Philby, Burgess and MacLean: Spy Scandal of the Century 🦴🦴½ **1984** The true story of the three infamous British officials who defected to the Soviet Union in 1951, after stealing some vital British secrets for the KGB. **83m/C VHS, Beta.** *GB* Derek Jacobi, Anthony Bate, Michael Culver; ***D:*** Gordon Flemyng. *MTI*

Phobia *Woof!* **1980 (R)** Patients at a hospital are mysteriously being murdered. Stupid and unpleasant story that lasts too long and probably should never have started. **91m/C VHS, Beta.** *CA* Paul Michael Glaser, Susan Hogan; ***D:*** John Huston; ***W:*** Peter Bellwood, Lew Lehman, Gary Sherman, Ronald Shusett, Jimmy Sangster. *PAR*

Phoenix 🦴½ **1978** Aging queen summons her marksman to find the Phoenix, a mythical bird that she believes will bring her eternal life. With English subtitles. **137m/C VHS, Beta.** *JP* Tatsuya Nakadai, Tomisaburo Wakayama, Raoru Yumi, Reiko Ohara. *VDA*

Phoenix 🦴🦴 **1995** The Titus 4 deep-space outpost has problems when the creators of a killing machine are targeted for death by their creation, which has begun to think for itself. **?m/C VHS.** Stephen Nichols, Billy Drago, William Sanderson, Brad Dourif. *MNC*

The Phoenix and the Magic Carpet 🦴🦴½ **1995 (PG)** Visiting England to settle her father's estate, Mrs. Wilson and her three children discover an egg from which a phoenix emerges. This mythical firebird proceeds to take the children on a magic adventure. Adapted from the book by Edith Nesbit. **80m/C VHS.** Dee Wallace Stone, Timothy Hegeman, Nick Klein, Laura Kamrath, Peter Ustinov; ***D:*** Zoran Perisic; ***W:*** Florence Fox; ***M:*** Alan Parker. *PAR*

Phoenix Team 🦴 **1980** Two agents discover their mutual attraction can be deadly in the spy business. **90m/C VHS, Beta.** Don Francks, Elizabeth Shepherd. *TWE*

Phoenix the Ninja 🦴 **198?** A young girl grows up to be a ninja warrior and battles everyone who would deign to impede her. **92m/C VHS, Beta.** Sho Kosugi. *TWE*

Phoenix the Warrior 🦴 **1988** Sometime in the future, female savages battle each other for control of the now ravaged earth. A newcomer seeks the tribe most worthy of receiving the last man on the planet, thereby continuing the human race. **90m/C VHS.** Persis Khambatta, James H. Emery, Peggy Sands, Kathleen Kinmont; ***D:*** Robert Hayes. *NO*

The Phone Call 🦴🦴 **1989 (R)** 900-number morality tale about high-powered executive who calls phone sex line and is connected with escaped homicidal maniac who takes a toll on him and his family. **95m/C VHS.** Michael Sarrazin, Linda Smith, Ron Lea, Lisa Jakub; ***D:*** Allan Goldstein. *NO*

Phone Call from a Stranger 🦴🦴½ **1952** After a plane crash, a survivor visits the families of three of the victims whom he met during the flight. **96m/B VHS, Beta.** Bette Davis, Gary Merrill, Michael Rennie, Shelley Winters, Hugh Beaumont, Keenan Wynn, Eve Arden, Craig Stevens; ***D:*** Jean Negulesco; ***W:*** Nunnally Johnson; ***C:*** Milton Krasner. *FOX*

Photographer 🦴 **1975 (PG)** A photographer turns into a murderer, showing the negative side of his personality. **94m/C VHS, Beta.** Michael Callan; ***D:*** William B. Hillman. *NLC*

Physical Evidence 🦴🦴 **1989 (R)** A lawyer finds herself falling for an ex-cop turned murder suspect while she tries to defend him for a crime he doesn't remember committing. **99m/C VHS, Beta, LV.** Burt Reynolds, Theresa Russell, Ned Beatty, Kay Lenz, Ted McGinley; ***D:*** Michael Crichton; ***W:*** Bill Phillips; ***C:*** John A. Alonzo; ***M:*** Henry Mancini. *LIV, VES, HHE*

P.I. Private Investigations 🦴 **1987 (R)** Corrupt, drug-dealing cops stalk another cop who can finger them. **91m/C VHS, Beta.** Martin Balsam. *FOX*

Piaf **1981 (PG)** Musical drama chronicles the life of Edith Piaf, France's legendary singer of the Roaring '20s. Her rise from the streets, bout with temporary blindness, and many self-destructive attempts at experiencing life are retold in music. **114m/C VHS, Beta.** Jane Lapotaire. *FOX*

The Piano 🦴🦴🦴½ **1993 (R)** In the 1850s, Ada (Hunter), a mute Scottish widow with a young daughter, agrees to an arranged marriage with Stewart (Neill), a colonial landowner in New Zealand. The way she expresses her feelings is by playing her cherished piano, left behind on the beach by her new husband. Another settler, George, (Keitel) buys it, arranges for lessons with Ada, and soon the duo begin a grand passion leading to a cruelly calculated revenge. Fiercely poetic and well acted (with Keitel in a notably romantic role), though the film may be too dark and intense for some. Fine original score with Hunter doing her own piano playing. **120m/C VHS, LV.** *AU* Holly Hunter, Harvey Keitel, Sam Neill, Anna Paquin, Kerry Walker, Genevieve Lemon; ***D:*** Jane Campion; ***W:*** Jane Campion; ***C:*** Stuart Dryburgh; ***M:*** Michael Nyman. Academy Awards '93: Best Actress (Hunter), Best Original Screenplay, Best Supporting Actress (Paquin); British Academy Awards '93: Best Actress (Hunter); Cannes Film Festival '93: Best Actress (Hunter), Best Film; Golden Globe Awards '94: Best Actress—Drama (Hunter); Independent Spirit Awards '94: Best Foreign Film; Los Angeles Film Critics Association Awards '93: Best Actress (Hunter), Best Cinematography, Best Director (Campion), Best Screenplay, Best Supporting Actress (Paquin); New York Film Critics Awards '93: Best Actress (Hunter), Best Director (Campion), Best Screenplay; National Society of Film Critics Awards '93: Best Actress (Hunter), Best Screenplay; Writers Guild of America '93: Best Original Screenplay; Nominations: Academy Awards '93: Best Cinematography, Best Costume Design, Best Director (Campion), Best Film Editing, Best Picture; British Academy Awards '94: Best Director (Campion), Best Film, Best Original Screenplay, Best Original Score; Directors Guild of America Awards '93: Best Director (Campion); Golden Globe Awards '94: Best Director (Campion), Best Film—Drama, Best Screenplay, Best Supporting Actress (Paquin), Best Original Score. *LIV*

A Piano for Mrs. Cimino **1982** Declared senile and incompetent, a widowed woman fights for control of her own life. Good script helps this made for TV soaper. **100m/C VHS, Beta.** Bette Davis, Keenan Wynn, Alexa Kenin, Penny Fuller, Christopher Guest, George Hearn; ***D:*** George Schaefer; ***M:*** James Horner. *GEM*

The Piano Lesson **1994 (PG)** The prized heirloom of the Charles family is an 80-year-old, ornately carved upright piano, jealously guarded by widowed Berniece (Woodard), and housed in the Pittsburgh home of Uncle Doaker (Gordon). When Berniece's brother Willie Boy (Dutton) visits from Mississippi, it's to persuade her to sell the piano in order to buy some land that their grandfather had worked as a slave. But the past, carved into the piano's panels, has a strong hold—one that Berniece refuses to give up. Set in 1936. Adaptation by Wilson of his 1990 Pulitzer Prize-winning play. **99m/C VHS, LV.** Alfre Woodard, Charles S. Dutton, Courtney B. Vance, Carl Gordon, Tommy Hollis, Zelda Harris, Lou Myers, Rosalyn Coleman, Tommy La Fitte; ***D:*** Lloyd Richards; ***W:*** August Wilson; ***M:*** Stephen James Taylor, Dwight Andrews. *REP*

Picasso Trigger **1989 (R)** An American spy tries to catch an elusive murderer. The sequel to "Hard Ticket to Hawaii" and "Malibu Express." **99m/C VHS.** Steve Bond, Dona Speir, John Aprea, Hope Marie Carlton, Guich Koock, Roberta Vasquez, Bruce Penhall; ***D:*** Andy Sidaris. *WAR*

Pick a Star *Movie Struck* **1937** Lawrence is a small-town girl who wins a contest and is off to Hollywood. Only no one pays any attention to her except for publicity man Haley, who arranges her screen test. Naturally, she knocks the studio bosses for a loop and becomes a star. Laurel & Hardy are featured in a couple of comedy segments showing the newcomer some backstage silliness and movie business on the set of a Western they're filming (with Finlayson, better known as a director, cast as the duo's director). **70m/B VHS.** Rosina Lawrence, Jack Haley, Patsy Kelly, Mischa Auer, Stan Laurel, Oliver Hardy, Charles Halton, Tom Dugan, Russell Hicks, James Finlayson; ***D:*** Edward Sedgwick. *MGM, NOS, CAB*

The Pick-Up Artist ½ **1987 (PG-13)** The adventures of a compulsive Don Juan who finds he genuinely loves the daughter of an alcoholic who's in debt to the mob. Standard story with no surprises. **81m/C VHS, Beta, LV.** Robert Downey Jr., Molly Ringwald, Dennis Hopper, Harvey Keitel, Danny Aiello, Vanessa Williams, Robert Towne, Mildred Dunnock, Lorraine Bracco, Joe Spinell, Victoria Jackson, Polly Draper, Brian Hamill; ***D:*** James Toback; ***W:*** James Toback; ***C:*** Gordon Willis; ***M:*** Georges Delerue. *FOX*

Pick-Up Summer *Pinball Summer; Pinball Pick-Up* **1979 (R)** Two suburban boys cruise their town after school lets out, chasing a pair of voluptuous sisters. **99m/C VHS, Beta.** *CA* Michael Zelniker, Carl Marotte; ***D:*** George Mihalka. *NWV*

The Pickle **1993 (R)** Self-indulgent comedy about a midlife crisis. Aiello stars as a middle-aged manic-depressive director certain that his new film is going to be an abysmal flop (as have all his recent pictures). He seeks comfort and reassurance from various ex-wives, children, lovers, and others, though he abuses them all. This dispirited tale also shows clips of the director's dreadful film about children who launch a giant pickle into space. It couldn't possibly be worse that what Mazursky actually put up on the screen. **103m/C VHS, LV.** Danny Aiello, Dyan Cannon, Clothilde Courau, Shelley Winters, Barry Miller, Jerry Stiller, Christopher Penn, Rebecca Miller; ***Cameos:*** Ally Sheedy, Little Richard, Spalding Gray, Griffin Dunne, Isabella Rossellini, Dudley Moore; ***D:*** Paul Mazursky; ***W:*** Paul Mazursky; ***M:*** Michel Legrand. *COL*

Pickpocket ½ **1959** Slow moving, documentary-like account of a petty thief's existence is a moral tragedy inspired by "Crime and Punishment." Ending is particularly moving. Classic filmmaking from Bresson, France's master of austerity. In French with English subtitles. **75m/B VHS, Beta.** *FR* Martin LaSalle, Marika Green, Pierre Leymarie; ***D:*** Robert Bresson. *FCT, INJ, TPV*

Pickup on South Street **1953** Petty thief Widmark lifts woman's wallet only to find it contains top secret Communist micro-film for which pinko agents will stop at nothing to get back. Intriguing look at the politics of the day. The creme of "B" movies. **80m/B VHS, Beta.** Richard Widmark, Jean Peters, Thelma Ritter, Murvyn Vye, Richard Kiley, Milburn Stone; ***D:*** Samuel Fuller; ***W:*** Samuel Fuller. Nominations: Academy Awards '53: Best Supporting Actress (Ritter). *FOX, FCT*

The Pickwick Papers ½ **1954** Comedy based on the Dickens classic wherein Mrs. Bardell sues the Pickwick Club for breach of promise. **109m/B VHS, Beta.** *GB* James Hayter, James Donald, Nigel Patrick, Hermione Gingold, Hermione Baddeley, Kathleen Harrison; ***D:*** Noel Langley. Nominations: Academy Awards '55: Best Costume Design (B & W). *VCI*

Picnic ½ **1955** A wanderer arrives in a small town and immediately wins the love a his friend's girl. The other women in town seem interested too. Strong, romantic work, with Holden excelling in the lead. Novak provides a couple pointers too. Lavish Hollywood adaptation of the William Inge play, including the popular tune "Moonglow/Theme from Picnic." **113m/C VHS, Beta, LV.** William Holden, Kim Novak, Rosalind Russell, Susan Strasberg, Arthur O'Connell, Cliff Robertson, Betty Field, Verna Felton, Reta Shaw, Nick Adams, Phyllis Newman, Raymond Bailey; ***D:*** Joshua Logan; ***W:*** Daniel Taradash; ***C:*** James Wong Howe; ***M:*** George Duning. Academy Awards '55: Best Art Direction/Set Decoration (Color), Best Film Editing; Golden Globe Awards '56: Best Director (Logan); National Board of Review Awards '55: 10 Best Films of the Year; Nominations: Academy Awards '54: Best Picture, Best Supporting Actor (O'Connell). *COL*

Picnic at Hanging Rock **1975 (PG)** School outing in 1900 into a mountainous region ends tragically when three girls disappear. Eerie film is strong on atmosphere, as befits mood master Weir. Lambert is extremely photogenic—and suitable subdued—as one of the girls to disappear. Otherwise beautifully photographed on location. From the novel by Joan Lindsey. **110m/C VHS, Beta.** *AU* Margaret Nelson, Rachel Roberts, Dominic Guard, Helen Morse, Jacki Weaver; ***D:*** Peter Weir; ***C:*** John Seale; ***M:*** Bruce Smeaton. *VES, OM*

Picnic on the Grass *Le Dejeuner Sur l'Herbe; Lunch on the Grass* **1959** A strange, whimsical fantasy heavily evocative of the director's Impressionist roots; a science-minded candidate for the president of Europe throws a picnic as public example of his earthiness, and falls in love with a peasant girl. In French with English subtitles. **92m/C VHS, Beta.** *FR* Paul Meurisse, Catherine Rouvel, Fernand Sardou, Jacqueline Morane, Jean-Pierre Granval; ***D:*** Jean Renoir. *FCT, INT, INJ*

Picture Bride ½ **1994 (PG-13)** Familiar immigrant saga finds 17-year-old Japanese Riyo (Kudoh) setting off for Hawaii in 1918 as a "picture bride" to a husband she's never met but with whom she's exchanged photos (hence the title). Riyo's shocked to discover her intended, sugar-cane worker Matsuji (Takayama), has deceived her with an out-of-date picture and is at least 25 years older than she. She refuses to consummate the marriage and goes to work in the fields, intending to earn money for her passage home but of course things don't work out quite as Riyo intends. Japanese with subtitles. **95m/C VHS, LV.** *JP* Youki Kudoh, Akira Takayama, Tamlyn Tomita, Cary-Hiroyuki Tagawa; ***Cameos:*** Toshiro Mifune; ***D:*** Kayo Hatta; ***W:*** Mari Hatta, Kayo Hatta. Sundance Film Festival '95: Audience Award; Nominations: Independent Spirit Awards '96: Best First Feature. *TOU*

Picture Mommy Dead **1966** Well acted melodrama involving a scheming shrew who struggles to drive her mentally disturbed stepdaughter insane for the sake of cold, hard cash. **85m/C VHS, Beta.** Don Ameche, Zsa Zsa Gabor, Martha Hyer, Susan Gordon; ***D:*** Bert I. Gordon; ***C:*** Ellsworth Fredericks. *NLC*

Picture of Dorian Gray **1945** Hatfield plays the rake who stays young while his portrait ages in this adaptation of Oscar Wilde's classic novel. Lansbury steals this one. **110m/B VHS, Beta, LV.** Hurd Hatfield, George Sanders, Donna Reed, Angela Lansbury, Peter Lawford, Lowell Gilmore; ***D:*** Albert Lewin; ***C:*** Harry Stradling. Academy Awards '45: Best Black and White Cinematography; Golden Globe Awards '46: Best Supporting Actress (Lansbury); Nominations: Academy Awards '45: Best Interior Decoration, Best Supporting Actress (Lansbury). *MGM, FHE, TVC*

Picture of Dorian Gray **1974** Another version of Wilde's renowned novel about a man who retains his youthful visage while his portrait shows the physical ravages of aging. Davenport is particularly appealing in the lead. Made for television. **130m/C VHS, Beta.** Shane Briant, Nigel Davenport, Charles Aidman, Fionnula Flanagan, Linda Kelsey, Vanessa Howard; ***D:*** Glenn Jordan. *LIV, MPI*

Picture Windows **1995 (R)** Three short cable movies inspired by works of art. "Lightning," based on Frederic Remington sketches and a Zane Grey short story, finds western codger Keith striking gold with the help of his trusty mule. A David Hockney painting suggested "Armed Response," which features a confrontation between a wealthy lawyer (Loggia) and a burglar (Zahn). And an anonymous 16th-century canvas "Two Nudes Bathing" is given an imaginative history. **?m/C VHS.** Brian Keith, Robert Loggia, Steve Zahn, Charley Boorman; ***D:*** Joe Dante, Bob Rafelson, John Boorman. *HMK*

Pictures ½ **198?** The silent-film era in England is spoofed in this look at ambitious waitress Ruby Sears, who's determined to be a film star, and writer Bill Trench, who winds up a novice screenwriter. Bill's first movie script is based on Ruby's life and she desperately wants to star in the production, if only she can convince the producer and the drunken male lead that she has the talent. Made for British television; 7 episodes on 4 cassettes. **208m/C VHS.** *GB* Wendy Morgan, Peter McEnery, Harry Towb, Anton Rodgers, Annette Badland, Malcom Jamieson, Marc Smith; ***W:*** Roy Clarke. *TVC, SIG, VCO*

Piece of Cake ½ **1990** Adaptation of the Derek Robinson novel follows the flyboys of the RAF Hornet Squadron during the early years of WWII. They have trouble taking the war seriously but tangles with the Luftwaffe and increasing casualties put a strain on everyone. Great aerial photography and the British planes are vintage Spitfires not repros. Made for British TV miniseries on 6 cassettes. **312m/C VHS.** *GB* Tom Burlinson, Tim Woodward, Boyd Gaines, Nathaniel Parker, Neil Dudgeon, David Horovitch, Richard Hope, Jeremy Wortham, Michael Elwyn, Corinne Dacla, Helena Michell. *SIG, PAP, VCO*

A Piece of Pleasure 🦴🦴🦴 **1970** Marriage declines due to a domineering husband in this familiar domestic study from French master Chabrol. Good, but not among the director's best efforts. In French with English subtitles. **100m/C VHS, Beta.** ***D:*** Claude Chabrol. *FCT*

Piece of the Action 🦴🦴½ **1977 (PG)** An ex-cop beats two con men at their own game when he convinces them to work for a Chicago community center. **135m/C VHS, Beta.** Sidney Poitier, Bill Cosby, James Earl Jones, Denise Nicholas, Hope Clarke, Tracy Reed, Titos Vandis, Ja'net DuBois; ***D:*** Sidney Poitier; ***M:*** Curtis Mayfield. *WAR*

Pieces *Woof!* **1983 (R)** Chain-saw wielding madman roams a college campus in search of human parts for a ghastly jigsaw puzzle. Gory and loathsome. **90m/C VHS, Beta.** *IT SP* Christopher George, Lynda Day George, Paul Smith; ***D:*** J. Piquer Simon. *VES*

The Pied Piper of Hamelin 🦴🦴 **1957** The evergreen classic of the magical piper who rids a village of rats and then disappears with the village children into a mountain when the townspeople fail to keep a promise. **90m/C VHS, Beta.** Van Johnson, Claude Rains, Jim Backus, Kay Starr, Lori Nelson; ***D:*** Bretaigne Windust. *KAR, NOS, MED*

The Pied Piper of Hamelin **1984** From Shelley Duvall's "Faerie Tale Theatre" comes the story of how a man with a magic flute charmed the rats out of Hamelin. **60m/C VHS, Beta.** Eric Idle; ***D:*** Nicholas Meyer. *FOX, FCT*

Pier 23 🦴🦴 **1951** A private eye is hired to bring a lawless ex-convict to a priest's custody, but gets an imposter instead. A web of intrigue follows. **57m/B VHS, Beta, LV.** Hugh Beaumont, Ann Savage, David Bruce, Raymond Greenleaf, Joi Lansing. *NO*

Pierrot le Fou 🦴🦴🦴½ **1965** A woman fleeing a gangster joins a man leaving his wife in this stunning, occasionally confusing classic from iconoclast Godard. A hallmark in 1960s improvisational filmmaking, with rugged Belmondo and always-photogenic Karina effortlessly excelling in leads. In French with English subtitles. **110m/C VHS, LV.** *FR IT* Samuel Fuller, Jean-Pierre Leaud, Jean-Paul Belmondo, Anna Karina, Dirk Sanders; ***D:*** Jean-Luc Godard; ***M:*** Antoine Duhamel. *INT, FCT, IME*

Pigs 🦴½ *Daddy's Deadly Darling; The Killers* **1973** Young woman who has escaped from a mental hospital teams up with an evil old man to go on a murdering spree. They complement each other beautifully. She kills them and he disposes of the bodies by making pig slop out of them. **90m/C VHS, Beta.** Toni Lawrence, Marc Lawrence, Jesse Vint, Katharine Ross; ***D:*** Marc Lawrence; ***W:*** Marc Lawrence; ***M:*** Charles Bernstein. *MRV*

A Pig's Tale 🦴½ **1994 (PG)** Rich kids rule at Kamp Kipperman but one 13-year-old forms the Pig Pen club and the club members decide to turn the tables on their overbearing rivals. **94m/C VHS.** Joe Flaherty, Graham Sack; ***D:*** Paul Tassie. *PGV*

Pilgrim, Farewell 🦴🦴½ **1982** Dramatic story about a dying woman who needs to tie up loose ends before her death and goes looking for her estranged teenage daughter. Made for television for PBS' "American Playhouse." **110m/C VHS, Beta.** Elizabeth Huddle, Christopher Lloyd, Laurie Pranage, Lesley Paxton, Shelley Wyant, Robert Brown; ***D:*** Michael Roemer. *FLI*

Pillow Talk 🦴🦴🦴½ **1959** Sex comedy in which a man woos a woman who loathes him. By the way, they share the same telephone party line. Narrative provides minimal indication of the film's strengths, which are many. Classic '50's comedy with masters Day and Hudson exhibiting considerable rapport, even when fighting. Lighthearted, constantly funny. **102m/C VHS, Beta, LV.** Rock Hudson, Doris Day, Tony Randall, Thelma Ritter, Nick Adams, Lee Patrick; ***D:*** Michael Gordon. Academy Awards '59: Best Story & Screenplay; Nominations: Academy Awards '59: Best Actress (Day), Best Art Direction/Set Decoration (Color), Best Supporting Actress (Ritter). *MCA, CCB*

Pilot 🦴½ **1984** Young girl discovers the debilitating effects of dishonesty when she becomes a break-dancing champion. **27m/C VHS, Beta.** Kelly Jo Minter, Adolph "Oz" Alvarez, Katie Rich. *PAU*

Pimpernel Smith 🦴🦴½ *Mister V* **1942** Seemingly scatterbrained archaeology professor is actually a dashing agent rescuing refugees from evil Nazis in WWII France. Howard is well cast, but the film is somewhat predictable, and it's too long. Wonderful scene, though, in which a Nazi officer champions Shakespeare as Aryan. **121m/B VHS, Beta.** *GB* Leslie Howard, Mary Morris, Francis L. Sullivan, David Tomlinson; ***D:*** Leslie Howard. *VYY*

Pin 🦴🦴½ **1988 (R)** A boy's imaginary friend assists in the slaying of various enemies. Horror effort could be worse. **103m/C VHS, Beta, LV.** Cyndy Preston, David Hewlett, Terry O'Quinn; ***D:*** Sandor Stern. *VTR, NWV, IME*

Pin Down Girls 🦴 **1951** Great schlock about girl wrestlers. Also known as "Racket Girls." **?m/C VHS.** Clara Mortensen, Rita Martinez. *SNC*

Pin-Up Girl 🦴🦴 **1944** Grable plays a secretary who becomes an overnight sensation during WWII. Loosely based on her famous pinup poster that was so popular at the time, the movie didn't even come close to being as successful. The songs aren't particularly memorable, although Charlie Spivak and his Orchestra perform. ♫Once Too Often; Yankee Doodle Dandy; I'll Be Marching to a Love Song; You're My Little Pin Up Girl; Story of the Very Merry Widow; Time Alone Will Tell; Don't Carry Tales Out of School; Red Robins, Bob Whites and Blue Birds. **83m/C VHS, LV.** Betty Grable, Martha Raye, Jon Harvey, Joe E. Brown, Eugene Pallette, Mantan Moreland; ***D:*** H. Bruce Humberstone; ***C:*** Ernest Palmer. *FOX, FXV*

The Pinchcliffe Grand Prix 🦴 **1981 (G)** Master inventor designs the ultimate race car. **88m/C VHS, Beta.** *GEM*

Ping Pong 🦴🦴½ **1987 (PG)** A Chinese patriarch drops dead in London's Chinatown, leaving a young law student to disentangle his will, and get mixed up with his cross-cultured family. **100m/C VHS, Beta, LV.** David Yip, Lucy Sheen, Robert Lee, Lam Fung, Victor Kan, Ric Young; ***D:*** Po Chich Leong. *NO*

Pink Cadillac 🦴🦴½ **1989 (PG-13)** A grizzled, middle-aged bondsman is on the road, tracking down bail-jumping crooks. He helps the wife and baby of his latest target escape from her husband's more evil associates. Eastwood's performance is good and fun to watch, in this otherwise lightweight film. **121m/C VHS, Beta, LV, 8mm.** Clint Eastwood, Bernadette Peters, Timothy Carhart, Michael Des Barres, William Hickey, John Dennis Johnston, Geoffrey Lewis, Jim Carrey, Tiffany Gail Robinson, Angela Louise Robinson; ***D:*** Buddy Van Horn; ***W:*** John Eskow; ***M:*** Stephen Dorff. *WAR*

The Pink Chiquitas 🦴 **1986 (PG-13)** Sci-fi spoof about a detective battling a mob of meteorite-traveling Amazons. **86m/C VHS, Beta.** Frank Stallone, Eartha Kitt, Bruce Pirrie, McKinlay Robinson, Elizabeth Edwards, Claudia Udy; ***D:*** Anthony Currie. *PSM*

Pink Flamingos 🦴🦴 **1972** Divine, the dainty 300-pound transvestite, faces the biggest challenge of his/her career when he/she competes for the title of World's Filthiest Person. Tasteless, crude, and hysterical film; this one earned Waters his title as "Prince of Puke." If there are any doubts about this honor—or Divine's rep—watch through to the end to catch Divine chewing real dog excrement, all the time wearing a you-know-what grin. **95m/C VHS, Beta, LV.** Divine, David Lochary, Mary Vivian Pearce, Danny Mills, Mink Stole, Edith Massey; ***D:*** John Waters; ***W:*** John Waters. *NO*

Pink Floyd: The Wall 🦴🦴½ **1982 (R)** Film version of Pink Floyd's 1979 LP, "The Wall." A surreal, impressionistic tour-de-force about a boy who grows up numb from society's pressures. The concept is bombastic and overwrought, but Geldof manages to remain somewhat likeable as the cynical rock star and the Gerald Scarfe animation perfectly complements the film. Laserdisc edition includes the original theatrical trailer and the letterboxed format of the film. **95m/C VHS, Beta, LV.** *GB* Bob Geldof, Christine Hargreaves, Bob Hoskins; ***D:*** Alan Parker; ***M:*** Michael Kamen. *MVD, MGM*

Pink Motel *Woof! Motel* **1982 (R)** Several people spend a night meant to be romantic at a pink stucco motel which caters to couples. Comic stiff with Diller and Pickens as the owners of said pink motel. **90m/C VHS, Beta.** Phyllis Diller, Slim Pickens, Terri Berland, Squire Fridell; ***D:*** Mike MacFarland. *NO*

Pink Nights 🦴 **1987 (PG)** A high school nebbish is suddenly pursued by three beautiful girls, and his life gets turned upside-down. **87m/C VHS, Beta, LV.** Shaun Allen, Kevin Anderson, Larry King, Johnathan Jamcovic Michaels; ***D:*** Philip Koch. *VTR, NWV*

The Pink Panther 🦴🦴🦴 **1964** Bumbling, disaster-prone inspector invades a Swiss ski resort and becomes obsessed with capturing a jewel thief hoping to lift the legendary "Pink Panther" diamond. Said thief is also the inspector's wife's lover, though the inspector doesn't know it. Slick slapstick succeeds on strength of Sellers' classic portrayal of Clouseau, who accidentally destroys everything in his path while speaking in a funny French accent. Followed by "A Shot in the Dark," "Inspector Clouseau" (without Sellers), "The Return of the Pink Panther," "The Pink Panther Strikes Again," "Revenge of the Pink Panther," "Trail of the Pink Panther," and "Curse of the Pink Panther." Memorable theme supplied by Mancini. **113m/C VHS, Beta, LV.** *GB* Peter Sellers, David Niven, Robert Wagner, Claudia Cardinale, Capucine, Brenda de Banzie; ***D:*** Blake Edwards; ***W:*** Blake Edwards; ***M:*** Henry Mancini. Nominations: Academy Awards '64: Best Original Score. *MGM, FOX, TVC*

The Pink Panther Strikes Again 🦴🦴🦴 **1976 (PG)** Fifth in the series has the incompetent inspector tracking his former boss, who has gone insane and has become preoccupied with destroying the entire world. A must for Sellers buffs and anyone who appreciates slapstick. **103m/C VHS, Beta, LV.** *GB* Peter Sellers, Herbert Lom, Lesley-Anne Down, Colin Blakely, Leonard Rossiter, Burt Kwouk; ***D:*** Blake Edwards; ***W:*** Edwards Waldman, Frank Waldman; ***M:*** Henry Mancini. Writers Guild of America '76: Best Adapted Screenplay; Nominations: Academy Awards '76: Best Song ("Come to Me"). *FOX, TVC*

Pink Strings and Sealing Wax 🦴🦴 **1945** A brutish pub owner in Victorian England is poisoned by his abused wife. She tries to involve the son of a chemist with the idea of blackmailing the father. Fine period flavor. **75m/B VHS, Beta.** *GB* Mervyn Johns, Mary Merrall, Gordon Jackson, Googie Withers, Sally Ann Howes, Catherine Lacey, Garry Marsh; ***D:*** Robert Hamer. *SNC*

Pinky 🦴🦴🦴 **1949** Early Hollywood treatment of the tragic choice made by some black Americans to pass as white in order to attain a better life for themselves and their families. The story is still relevant today. Waters and Barrymore also star, but the lead black character is portrayed by a white actress. Based on the novel "Quality" by Cyd Ricketts Sumner. **102m/B VHS.** Jeanne Crain, Ethel Barrymore, Ethel Waters, Nina Mae McKinney, William Lundigan; ***D:*** Elia Kazan; ***W:*** Philip Dunne, Dudley Nichols; ***M:*** Alfred Newman. Nominations: Academy Awards '49: Best Actress (Crain), Best Supporting Actress (Barrymore, Waters). *FXV*

Pinocchio 🦴🦴🦴🦴 **1940 (G)** Second Disney animated film featuring Pinocchio, a little wooden puppet, made with love by the old woodcarver Geppetto, and brought to life by a good fairy. Except Pinocchio isn't content to be just a puppet—he wants to become a real boy. Lured off by a sly fox, Pinocchio undergoes a number of adventures as he tries to return safely home. Has some scary scenes, including Geppetto, Pinocchio, and their friend Jiminy Cricket getting swallowed by a whale, and Pleasure Island, where naughty boys are turned into donkeys. An example of animation at its best and a Disney classic that has held up over time. ♫When You Wish Upon a Star; Give a Little Whistle; Turn on the Old Music Box; Hi-Diddle-Dee-Dee (An Actor's Life For Me); I've Got No Strings. **87m/C VHS, Beta, LV.** ***D:*** Ben Sharpsteen; ***V:*** Dick Jones, Cliff Edwards, Evelyn Venable,

Walter Catlett, Frankie Darro, Charles Judels, Don Brodie, Christian Rub. Academy Awards '40: Best Song ("When You Wish Upon a Star"), Best Original Score. *DIS, WTA*

Pinocchio **1976** Classic Pinocchio story in musical form. **76m/C VHS, Beta.** Danny Kaye, Sandy Duncan. *VCI*

Pinocchio **1983** Pee Wee Herman is the puppet who wants to be a real little boy in this "Faerie Tale Theatre" adaptation of this children's classic. **60m/C VHS, Beta.** Paul (Pee Wee Herman) Reubens, James Coburn, Carl Reiner, Lainie Kazan; ***D:*** Peter Medak. *FOX, FCT*

Pinocchio's Storybook Adventures ½ **1979** Pinocchio takes over for an ailing puppet master and puts on a show for a group of children. **80m/C VHS, Beta.** ***D:*** Ron Merk. *VTR*

Pinto Canyon ½ **1940** An honest sheriff does away with a band of cattle rustlers. **55m/B VHS.** Bob Steele, Louise Stanley, Kenne Duncan, Ted Adams, Steve Clark, Budd Buster; ***D:*** Raymond K. Johnson. *NOS, DVT*

Pinto Rustlers ½ **1936** A cowboy left orphaned by a gang of rustlers seeks revenge. **52m/C VHS, Beta.** Tom Tyler, Catherine Cotter. *NOS, DVT*

Pioneer Marshal **1949** Lawman Hale disguises himself as a criminal to track down an embezzler. **60m/B VHS, Beta.** Monte Hale, Paul Hurst. *DVT*

Pioneer Woman *Pioneers* **1973** A family encounters hostility when they set up a frontier homestead in Nebraska in 1867. Told from the feminine perspective, the tale is strewn with hurdles, both personal and natural. **74m/C VHS, Beta.** Joanna Pettet, William Shatner, David Janssen; ***D:*** Buzz Kulik. *WOV*

The Pioneers ½ **1941** Ritter sets out to protect a wagon train. **59m/B VHS, Beta.** Tex Ritter. *VCN*

Pipe Dreams **1976 (PG)** A couple tries to repair their broken marriage against the backdrop of the Alaskan pipeline's construction. **89m/C VHS, Beta.** Gladys Knight, Barry Hankerson, Bruce French, Sally Kirkland, Sherry Bain; ***D:*** Stephen Verona. *COL, SUE*

Pippi Goes on Board ½ **1975 (G)** The fourth and last film in the Swedish series finds Pippi's father arriving one day to take her sailing to Taka-Kuka, his island kingdom. She can't bear to leave her friends and jumps off the ship to return home. The series is poorly dubbed and technically flawed, which the kids probably won't notice. Based on the books by Astrid Lindgren. Preceded by "Pippi Longstocking," "Pippi in the South Seas," and "Pippi on the Run." **83m/C VHS, Beta.** *SW* Inger Nilsson; ***D:*** Olle Hellbron. *GEM, MOV, TPV*

Pippi in the South Seas ½ *Pippi Langstrump Pa de Sju Haven* **1974 (G)** Pippi, a fun-loving, independent, red haired little girl, and her two friends decide to rescue her father, who is being held captive by a band of pirates on a South Sea island. Naturally, clever Pippi saves the day. Poorly dubbed and edited. Based on the children's book by Astrid Lindgren. Follows "Pippi Longstocking" and precedes "Pippi on the Run" and "Pippi Goes on Board." **99m/C VHS, Beta.** *SW* Inger Nilsson; ***D:*** Olle Hellbron. *GEM, MOV, TPV*

Pippi Longstocking ½ **1973 (G)** This little red-headed, pigtailed terror is left alone by her sailor father as he heads out to sea. Not that Pippi minds, since it gives her the chance to create havoc in her town through the antics of her pets, a monkey and a horse. Pippi's antics may amuse the kiddies but adults will find her obnoxious. Poorly dubbed and technically somewhat shaky. Based on the children's book by Astrid Lindgren. Followed by "Pippi in the South Seas," "Pippi on the Run," and "Pippi Goes on Board." **99m/C VHS, Beta.** *SW* Inger Nilsson; ***D:*** Olle Hellbron. *GEM, MOV, TPV*

Pippi on the Run ½ **1974 (G)** The third film in the series finds Pippi on the trail of two friends who have run away from home. The three have many adventures before deciding home is best. Preceded by "Pippi Longstocking" and "Pippi in the South Seas," followed by "Pippi Goes on Board." Films lacks technical and dubbing skills. Based on the children's book by Astrid Lindgren. **99m/C VHS, Beta.** *SW GEM, MOV, TPV*

Pippin **1981** Video version of the stage musical about the adolescent son of Charlemagne finding true love. Adequate record of Bob Fosse's Broadway smash. Features Vereen recreating his original Tony Award-winning role. **120m/C VHS, Beta, LV.** Ben Vereen, William Katt, Martha Raye, Chita Rivera. *VCI, FHE, FCT*

Piranha ½ **1978 (R)** A rural Texas resort area is plagued by attacks from ferocious man-eating fish which a scientist created to be used as a secret weapon in the Vietnam War. Spoofy horror film features the now-obligatory Dante film in-jokes in the background. **90m/C VHS, Beta.** Bradford Dillman, Heather Menzies, Kevin McCarthy, Keenan Wynn, Barbara Steele, Dick Miller, Paul Bartel; ***D:*** Joe Dante; ***W:*** John Sayles; ***M:*** Pino Donaggio. *WAR, OM*

Piranha 2: The Spawning ½ *Piranha 2: Flying Killers* **1982 (R)** Diving instructor and a biochemist seek to destroy piranha mutations that are murdering tourists at a club. Early Cameron exercise in gore tech that's a step down from original "Piranha." **88m/C VHS, Beta, LV.** Steve Marachuk, Lance Henriksen, Ricky Paul; ***D:*** James Cameron. *SUE, NLC*

The Pirate **1948** A traveling actor poses as a legendary pilot to woo a lonely woman on a remote Caribbean island. Minnelli always scores with this type of fare, and both Garland and Kelly make the most of the Cole Porter score. ♫Be a Clown; Nina; Mack the Black; You Can Do No Wrong; Sweet Ices, Papayas, Berry Man; Sea Wall; Serafin; The Ring; Judy Awakens. **102m/C VHS, Beta, LV.** Judy Garland, Gene Kelly, Walter Slezak, Gladys Cooper, George Zucco, Reginald Owen, Nicholas Brothers; ***D:*** Vincente Minnelli; ***C:*** Harry Stradling. Nominations: Academy Awards '48: Best Original Score. *MGM*

Pirate Movie ½ **1982 (PG)** Gilbert and Sullivan's "The Pirates of Penzance" is combined with new pop songs in this tale of fantasy and romance. Feeble attempt to update a musical that was fine the way it was. **98m/C VHS, Beta.** Kristy McNichol, Christopher Atkins, Ted Hamilton, Bill Kerr, Garry McDonald; ***D:*** Ken Annakin; ***M:*** Tony Britten. Golden Raspberry Awards '82: Worst Director (Annakin), Worst Song ("Pumpin' and Blowin'"). *FOX*

Pirate Ship ½ *The Mutineers* **1949** Slow-moving story has sailor Hall discovering new captain Reeves is involved with a gang of gun-runners and counterfeiters. **60m/C VHS.** Jon Hall, George Reeves, Adele Jergens, Noel Cravat, Tom Kennedy, Lyle Talbot; ***D:*** Jean Yarbrough. *GPV*

Pirate Warrior **1964** Grade-B pirate flick about slavery and the evil Tortuga. **86m/C VHS, Beta.** Ricardo Montalban, Vincent Price, Liana Orfei; ***D:*** Mary Costa. *NO*

Pirates ½ **1986 (PG-13)** Blustery, confused effort at a big-budgeted retro-adventure, about a highly regarded pirate and his gains and losses on the high seas. Broad comedy, no story to speak of. **124m/C VHS, Beta.** Walter Matthau, Cris Campion, Damien Thomas, Richard Pearson, Charlotte Lewis, Olu Jacobs, David Patrick Kelly, Roy Kinnear, Bill Fraser, Jose Santamaria; ***D:*** Roman Polanski; ***W:*** Gerard Brach, Roman Polanski. Cesar Awards '87: Best Art Direction/Set Decoration, Best Costume Design; Nominations: Academy Awards '86: Best Costume Design. *LIV*

The Pirates of Penzance **1983 (G)** Gilbert and Sullivan's comic operetta is the story of a band of fun-loving pirates, their reluctant young apprentice, the "very model of a modern major general," and his lovely daughters. An adaptation of Joseph Papp's award-winning Broadway play. **112m/C VHS, Beta, LV.** Kevin Kline, Angela Lansbury, Linda Ronstadt, Rex Smith, George Rose; ***D:*** Wilford Leach. *MCA, FOX*

Pirates of the Coast ½ **1961** A Spanish naval commander teams up with a group of pirates to even the score with an evil governor during the 1500s. **102m/C VHS, Beta.** Lex Barker, Estella Blain, Livio Lorenzon, Liana Orfei; ***D:*** Domenico Paolella. *UNI*

Pirates of the High Seas ½ **1950** Crabbe helps a friend save his shipping line from sabotage. A serial in fifteen chapters. **?m/C VHS.** Buster Crabbe, Lois Hall, Tommy Farrell, Gene Roth, Tristram Coffin; ***D:*** Spencer Gordon Bennet, Thomas Carr. *MLB*

Pirates of the Seven Seas ½ **1962** In the further tales of "Sandokan the Great," the pirate hero helps save the heroine's father from an evil English Imperialist. **90m/C VHS, Beta.** Steve Reeves, Jacqueline Sassard, Andrea Bosic; ***D:*** Umberto Lenzi. *NO*

Pistol: The Birth of a Legend ½ **1990 (G)** Biography of "Pistol" Pete Maravich, the basketball star who defied age limitations in the 1960s to play on his varsity team. **104m/C VHS, Beta.** Adam Guier, Nick Benedict, Boots Garland, Millie Perkins; ***D:*** Frank C. Schroeder; ***W:*** Darrel A. Campbell. *COL*

Pistoleros Asesinos **1987** Plenty of action, plus a little romance, when a man falls in love with a crooked landowner's daughter and must battle her father's henchmen for her hand. **83m/C VHS, Beta.** *SP* Maria de Lourdes, Federico Villa, Victor Alcocer, Arturo Benavides, Polo Ortin, Rosa Gloria. *MAD*

The Pit ½ **1981 (R)** Autistic boy gets his chance for revenge. The townspeople who humiliate him are in for a surprise after he stumbles across a huge hole in the forest, at the bottom of which are strange and deadly creatures. **96m/C VHS, Beta.** Sammy Snyders, Sonja Smits, Jeannie Elias, Laura Hollingsworth; ***D:*** Lew Lehman. *VTR, SUE*

The Pit and the Pendulum **1961** A woman and her lover plan to drive her brother mad, and he responds by locking them in his torture chamber, which was built by his loony dad, whom he now thinks he is. Standard Corman production only remotely derived from the classic Poe tale, with the cast chewing on a loopy script. A landmark in Gothic horror. **80m/C VHS, Beta.** Vincent Price, John Kerr, Barbara Steele, Luana Anders; ***D:*** Roger Corman; ***W:*** Richard Matheson; ***C:*** Floyd Crosby; ***M:*** Les Baxter. *WAR, OM*

The Pit & the Pendulum ½ **1991 (R)** Retelling of the classic Poe short story, mixed with his "A Cask of Amantillado" and set during the Spanish Inquisition. Great special effects and professional scary guy, Lance Henriksen. **97m/C VHS, LV.** Lance Henriksen, Rona De Ricci, Jonathan Fuller, Jeffrey Combs, Tom Towles, Stephen Lee, Francis Bay, Oliver Reed; ***D:*** Stuart Gordon; ***W:*** Dennis Paoli; ***M:*** Richard Band. *PAR*

Pitfall **1948** Gritty tale in which an insurance salesman, bored with his routine suburban life and family, follows his less noble instincts—and finds himself up to his ears in stolen goods, adultery and murder. **85m/B VHS, LV.** Dick Powell, Jane Wyatt, Lizabeth Scott, Raymond Burr, John Litel, Byron Barr, Ann Doran; ***D:*** Andre de Toth. *REP, FCT*

Pittsburgh **1942** Slow-moving drama about a love triangle combined with class differences. Dietrich loves Wayne, but he's more interested in the coal and steel business, so rival Scott steps in. Although limited by standard plot, picture works because of excellent performances by leads. Based on a screen story by George Owen and Tom Reed. **98m/B VHS.** Marlene Dietrich, Randolph Scott, John Wayne, Frank Craven, Louise Allbritton, Shemp Howard, Thomas Gomez, Ludwig Stossel; ***D:*** Lewis Seiler; ***W:*** Kenneth Gamet, Tom Reed, John Twist. *MCA, FCT*

Pixote **1981** Wrenching, documentary-like account of an orphan-boy's life on the streets in a Brazil metropolis. Graphic and depressing, it's not for all tastes but nonetheless masterfully done. In Portuguese with English subtitles. **127m/C VHS, Beta.** *BR* Fernando Ramos Da Silva, Marilia Pera, Jorge Juliao, Gilberto Moura, Jose Nilson dos Santos, Edilson Lino; ***D:*** Hector Babenco; ***W:*** Hector Babenco; ***M:*** John Neschling. Los Angeles Film Critics Association Awards '81: Best Foreign Film; New York Film Critics Awards '81: Best Foreign Film; National Society of Film Critics Awards '81: Best Actress (Pera). *COL*

Pizza Man ½ **1991 (PG-13)** Pizza deliveryman Elmo Bunn is minding his own business, delivering an extra large with anchovies and sausage, when he finds himself mixed up in a political scandal. Lawton directed under alias "J.D. Athens." **90m/C VHS.**

Bill Maher, Annabelle Gurwitch; *D:* J.F. Lawton; *W:* J.F. Lawton. *MNC*

P.K. and the Kid 🦴🦴 **1985** A runaway kid meets up with a factory worker on his way to an arm wrestling competition and they become friends. **90m/C VHS, Beta, LV.** Molly Ringwald, Paul LeMat, Alex Rocco, John Madden, Esther Rolle; *D:* Lou Lombardo; *W:* Neal Barbera; *M:* James Horner. *ORI, WAR*

A Place Called Glory 🦴🦴 *Die Holle von Manitoba* **1966** Barker comes to the aid of the local townsfolk in Glory city who have their hands full with a gang of bloodthirsty outlaws. **92m/C VHS.** Lex Barker, Pierre Brice, Marianne Koch. *SNC*

A Place Called Today 🦴 **1972** Sordid tale of big city politics where violence and fear in the streets is at the heart of the campaign. Also called "City in Fear." **105m/C VHS, Beta.** Cheri Caffaro, J. Herbert Kerr Jr., Lana Wood, Richard Smedley, Tim Brown; *D:* Don Schain. *NO*

A Place for Annie 🦴🦴½ **1994 (PG)** Lots of tears in this drama of devoted pediatrics nurse Susan Lansing (Spacek) who decides to become the foster mother of abandoned baby girl Annie, who's been diagnosed as HIV-positive. Then Annie's destitute birth mom (Parker), a former junkie dying of AIDS, resurfaces and decides she wants her daughter back. Sputters into melodrama but good performances by strong women, including Plowright as the nanny and Merkerson as a concerned hospital social worker. Based on a true story. Made for television. **98m/C VHS.** Sissy Spacek, Mary-Louise Parker, Joan Plowright, S. Epatha Merkerson, Jack Noseworthy; *D:* John Gray; *W:* Cathleen Young, Lee Guthrie. *REP*

Place in Hell 🦴½ **1965** The Japanese armed forces camouflage a Pacific island beach which they are holding and invite the American forces to invade it during WWII. **106m/C VHS, Beta.** Guy Madison, Helene Chanel, Monty Greenwood. *UNI*

A Place in the Sun 🦴🦴🦴 **1951** Melodramatic adaptation of "An American Tragedy," Theodore Dreiser's realist classic about an ambitious laborer whose aspirations to the high life with a gorgeous debutante are threatened by his lower-class lover's pregnancy. Clift is magnificent in the lead, and Taylor and Winters also shine in support. Burr, however, grossly overdoes his role of the vehement prosecutor. Still, not a bad effort from somewhat undisciplined director Stevens. **120m/B VHS, Beta, LV.** Montgomery Clift, Elizabeth Taylor, Shelley Winters, Raymond Burr, Anne Revere; *D:* George Stevens; *C:* William Mellor; *M:* Franz Waxman. Academy Awards '51: Best Black and White Cinematography, Best Costume Design (B & W), Best Director (Stevens), Best Film Editing, Best Screenplay, Best Score; Directors Guild of America Awards '51: Best Director (Stevens); Golden Globe Awards '52: Best Film—Drama; National Board of Review Awards '51: 10 Best Films of the Year; Nominations: Academy Awards '51: Best Actor (Clift), Best Actress (Winters), Best Picture. *PAR, BTV*

A Place in the World 🦴🦴🦴 **1995** Returning from exile to their native Argentina during a military dictatorship, Mario and Ana (Luppi and Roth) work to help the less advantaged in their society, determined to make a difference. Story is seen as a flashback from point-of-view of the couples' son Ernesto (Batyi). Well-crafted, finely acted piece exploring political, social, and interpersonal themes. 1993 Oscar bid retracted due to controversy over country of film's origin. **120m/C VHS.** *AR* Jose Sacristan, Federico Luppi, Cecilia Roth, Leonor Benedetto, Gaston Batyi, Lorena Del Rio; *D:* Adolfo Aristarain; *W:* Alberto Lecchi, Adolfo Aristarain; *C:* Ricardo De Angelis; *M:* Emilio Kauderer. *NYR*

Place of Weeping 🦴🦴½ **1986 (PG)** Early entry in the anti-apartheid sweepstakes (made in South Africa, no less). A South African woman opposes her nation's racist policies. A reporter supports her. **88m/C VHS, Beta.** *SA* James Whylie, Geini Mhlophe; *D:* Darrell Roodt. *VTR, NWV, FCT*

Places in the Heart 🦴🦴🦴 **1984 (PG)** A young widow determines to make the best of a bad situation on a small farm in Depression-era Texas, fighting poverty, racism, and sexism while enduring back-breaking labor. Support group includes a blind veteran and a black drifter. Hokey but nonetheless moving film is improved significantly by strong performances by virtually everyone in the cast. In his debut, Malkovich shines through this stellar group. Effective dust-bowl photography by Nestor Almendros. **113m/C VHS, Beta, LV.** Sally Field, John Malkovich, Danny Glover, Ed Harris, Lindsay Crouse, Amy Madigan, Terry O'Quinn; *D:* Robert Benton; *W:* Robert Benton; *C:* Nestor Almendros; *M:* Howard Shore. Academy Awards '84: Best Actress (Field), Best Original Screenplay; Golden Globe Awards '85: Best Actress—Drama (Field); National Board of Review Awards '84: Best Supporting Actor (Malkovich); New York Film Critics Awards '84: Best Screenplay; National Society of Film Critics Awards '84: Best Supporting Actor (Malkovich); Nominations: Academy Awards '84: Best Costume Design, Best Director (Benton), Best Picture, Best Supporting Actor (Malkovich), Best Supporting Actress (Crouse). *FOX, BTV, HMV*

The Plague 🦴½ **1992 (R)** An outbreak of bubonic plague has turned the South American city of Oran into a prison, with no one permitted to leave until the disease has run its course. Hurt is the doctor trying to balance his duties with his own fears. Necessarily bleak adaptation of the Albert Camus novel is also slow-moving and long-winded—an equally deadly combination for the viewer. **105m/C VHS.** *FR SP* William Hurt, Robert Duvall, Raul Julia, Sandrine Bonnaire, Jean-Marc Barr; *D:* Luis Puenzo. *LIV, FCT, BTV*

The Plague Dogs 🦴🦴½ **1982** Two dogs carrying a plague escape from a research center and are tracked down in this unlikely animated film. A bit ponderous. And yes, that is Hurt's voice. From the novel by Richard Adams, author of "Watership Down." **99m/C VHS, Beta.** *D:* Martin Rosen; *W:* Martin Rosen; *M:* Patrick Gleeson; *V:* John Hurt, Christopher Benjamin, Judy Geeson, Barbara Leigh-Hunt, Patrick Stewart. *NLC*

Plain Clothes 🦴🦴½ **1988 (PG)** An undercover cop masquerades as a high school student to solve the murder of a teacher. He endures all the trials that made him hate high school the first time around. **98m/C VHS, Beta.** Arliss Howard, George Wendt, Suzy Amis, Diane Ladd, Seymour Cassel, Larry Pine, Jackie Gayle, Abe Vigoda, Robert Stack; *D:* Martha Coolidge; *M:* Scott Wilk. *PAR*

The Plainsman 🦴🦴½ **1937** Western legends Wild Bill Hickock, Buffalo Bill, and Calamity Jane team up for adventure in this big, empty venture. Just about what you'd expect from splashy director DeMille. **113m/B VHS, Beta, LV.** Gary Cooper, Jean Arthur, Charles Bickford, Anthony Quinn, George "Gabby" Hayes, Porter Hall, James Mason; *D:* Cecil B. DeMille; *C:* Victor Milner. *MCA, MLB*

Plan 9 from Outer Space *Woof! Grave Robbers from Outer Space* **1956** Two or three aliens in silk pajamas conspire to resurrect several slow-moving zombies from a cardboard graveyard in order to conquer the Earth. Spaceships that look suspiciously like paper plates blaze across the sky. Pitiful, inadvertently hilarious fright worth a look if you're desperate to kill time since it's in the running for the "dumbest movie ever made" award. Lugosi's actual screen time is under two minutes, since he had the good sense to die before the film was complete. Enjoy the taller and younger replacement (the chiropractor of Wood's wife) they found for Lugosi, who remains hooded to protect his identity. **78m/B VHS, Beta, LV.** Bela Lugosi, Tor Johnson, Lyle Talbot, Vampira, Gregory Walcott; *D:* Edward D. Wood Jr. *NOS, SNC, MED*

Plan 10 from Outer Space 🦴½ **1995** The play on the infamous Ed Wood title is the only connection between the two fringe features as director Harris takes aim at his hometown of Salt Lake City, Utah. Heroine Lucinda (Russell) discovers a mysterious bronze plaque buried near the Great Salt Lake and uncovers a UFO conspiracy loosely conforming to Mormon mythology. There's a basic mass hysteria/alien invasion scene, cheesy special effects, dumb sexual humor, and not much else. **82m/C VHS.** Stefene Russell, Pat Collins, Curtis James, Karen Black; *D:* Trent Harris; *W:* Trent Harris; *C:* Bryan Duggan; *M:* Fred Myrow. *LEO*

Planes, Trains & Automobiles 🦴🦴½ **1987 (R)** One-joke Hughes comedy saved by Martin and Candy. A straight-laced businessman (played straight by Martin) on the way home for Thanksgiving meets up with a oafish, bad-luck-ridden boor who turns his efforts to get home upside down. Martin and Candy both turn in fine performances, and effectively straddle a thin line between true pathos and hilarious buffoonery. Bacon and McClurg, both Hughes alumni, have small but funny roles. **93m/C VHS, Beta, LV, 8mm.** Steve Martin, John Candy, Edie McClurg, Kevin Bacon, Michael McKean, William Windom, Laila Robins, Martin Ferrero, Charles Tyner, Dylan Baker; *D:* John Hughes; *W:* John Hughes; *M:* Ira Newborn. *PAR*

Planet Burg 🦴🦴½ **1962** A classic Soviet sci-fi flick about a space exploration team landing on Venus. Their job becomes a rescue mission when one of the crew is stranded. Although there are some silly moments, some good plot twists and acting make up for them. In Russian with English subtitles. **90m/C VHS, Beta.** *RU* Vladimir Temelianov, Gennadi Vernov, Kyunna Ignatova; *D:* Pavel Klushantsev. *SNC*

Planet Busters 🦴 **1985** Japanimation feature. Haphazardly developed swift-paced science fiction adventure about a magic sword, a royal heir apparent, a couple of bounty hunters, and evil robots. **80m/C VHS.** *JP STP, TPV*

Planet Earth 🦴🦴½ **1974** In the year 2133, a man who has been in suspended animation for 154 years is revived to lead the troops against a violent group of women (and mutants, too!). **78m/C VHS.** John Saxon, Janet Margolin, Ted Cassidy, Diana Muldaur, Johana DeWinter, Christopher Gary; *D:* Marc Daniels. *UNI*

Planet of Blood 🦴🦴 *Queen of Blood* **1966** Space opera about an alien vampire discovered on Mars by a rescue team. If you've ever seen the Soviet film "Niebo Zowiet," don't be surprised if some scenes look familiar; the script was written around segments cut from that film. **81m/C VHS.** John Saxon, Basil Rathbone, Judi Meredith, Dennis Hopper, Florence Marly; *D:* Curtis Harrington. *SNC, NOS, MRV*

Planet of Dinosaurs 🦴½ **1980 (PG)** Survivors from a ruined spaceship combat huge savage dinosaurs on a swampy uncharted planet. **85m/C VHS, Beta.** James Whitworth; *D:* James K. Shea. *AHV, VTR*

Planet of the Apes 🦴🦴🦴½ **1968 (G)** Astronauts crash land on a planet where apes are masters and humans are merely brute animals. Superior science fiction with sociological implications marred only by unnecessary humor. Heston delivers one of his more plausible performances. Superb ape make-up creates realistic pseudo-simians of McDowall, Hunter, Evans, Whitmore, and Daly. Adapted from Pierre Boulle's novel "Monkey Planet." Followed by four sequels and two television series. **112m/C VHS, Beta, LV.** Charlton Heston, Roddy McDowall, Kim Hunter, Maurice Evans, Linda Harrison, James Whitmore, James Daly; *D:* Franklin J. Schaffner; *W:* Rod Serling, Michael G. Wilson; *C:* Leon Shamroy; *M:* Jerry Goldsmith. National Board of Review Awards '68: 10 Best Films of the Year; Nominations: Academy Awards '68: Best Costume Design, Best Original Score. *FOX, FUS*

Planet of the Vampires 🦴🦴½ *Terror in Space; Terreur dans l'Espace; Space Mutants; The Demon Planet* **1965** Astronauts search for missing comrades on a planet dominated by mind-bending forces. Acceptable atmospheric filmmaking from genre master Bava, but it's not among his more compelling ventures. **86m/C VHS, Beta.** *IT* Barry Sullivan, Norman Bengell, Angel Aranda, Evi Marandi; *D:* Mario Bava. *ORI*

Planet on the Prowl 🦴 *War Between the Planets* **1965** A fiery planet causes earthly disasters, so a troop of wily astronauts try to destroy it with the latest technology. They fail, leading one sacrificial soul to do it himself. **80m/C VHS, Beta.** *IT* Giacomo "Jack" Rossi-Stuart, Amber Collins, Peter Martell, John Bartha, Halina Zalewska, James Weaver; *D:* Anthony (Antonio Margheriti) Dawson. *NO*

Planets Against Us ½ *I Pianeti Contro di Noi; The Man with the Yellow Eyes; Hands of a Killer; The Monster with Green Eyes* **1961** Science fiction tale of escaped alien humanoid robots who take refuge on Earth, but whose touch is fatal. Good special effects. **85m/B VHS.** *IT FR* Michel Lemoine, Maria Pia Luzi, Jany Clair; ***D:*** Romano Ferrara. *SNC*

Platinum Blonde **1931** Screwball comedy in which a newspaper journalist (Williams) marries a wealthy girl (Harlow) but finds that he doesn't like the restrictions and confinement of high society. Yearning for a creative outlet, he decides to write a play and hires a reporter (Young) to collaborate with him. The results are funny and surprising when Young shows up at the mansion flanked by a group of hard-drinking, fun-loving reporters. **86m/B VHS.** Loretta Young, Robert Williams, Jean Harlow, Louise Closser Hale; ***D:*** Frank Capra; ***W:*** Jo Swerling, Dorothy Howell. *COL*

Platinum High School ½ *Trouble at 16; Rich, Young, and Deadly* **1960** Divorced father Rooney is appalled when his son is "accidentally" killed while off at an exclusive military academy. His suspicions are aroused by the prevaricating school commander and he discovers some horrible truths about his son's death and life at the school. **91m/B VHS.** Mickey Rooney, Terry Moore, Dan Duryea, Conway Twitty, Warren Berlinger, Yvette Mimieux, Jimmy Boyd, Richard Jaeckel, Harold Lloyd Jr., Elisha Cook Jr., Jimmy Murphy; ***D:*** Charles Haas; ***W:*** Robert Smith; ***M:*** Van Alexander. *REP*

Platoon ½ **1986 (R)** A grunt's view of the Vietnam War is provided in all its horrific, inexplicable detail. Sheen is wooden in the lead, but both Dafoe and Berenger are resplendent as, respectively, good and bad soldiers. Strong, visceral filmmaking from fearless director Stone, who based the film on his own GI experiences. Highly acclaimed; considered by many to be the most realistic portrayal of the war on film. **113m/C VHS, Beta, LV.** Charlie Sheen, Willem Dafoe, Tom Berenger, Francesco Quinn, Forest Whitaker, John C. McGinley, Kevin Dillon, Richard Edson, Reggie Johnson, Keith David, Johnny Depp; ***D:*** Oliver Stone; ***W:*** Oliver Stone; ***C:*** Robert Richardson; ***M:*** Georges Delerue. Academy Awards '86: Best Director (Stone), Best Film Editing, Best Picture, Best Sound; British Academy Awards '87: Best Director (Stone); Directors Guild of America Awards '86: Best Director (Stone); Golden Globe Awards '87: Best Director (Stone), Best Film—Drama, Best Supporting Actor (Berenger); National Board of Review Awards '86: 10 Best Films of the Year; Nominations: Academy Awards '86: Best Cinematography, Best Original Screenplay, Best Supporting Actor (Berenger, Dafoe). *LIV, BTV*

Platoon Leader **1987 (R)** A battle-drenched portrait of a West Point lieutenant in Vietnam. When he first arrives, he must win the trust of his men, who have been on their tours for a much longer time. As time goes on, he slowly becomes hardened to the realities of the brutal life in the field. Made on the heels of the widely acclaimed "Platoon," but it doesn't have the same power. Norris is martial arts king Chuck Norris' brother. **97m/C VHS, Beta, LV.** Michael Dudikoff, Brian Libby, Robert F. Lyons, Rick Fitts, Jesse Dabson, William Smith, Michael De Lorenzo; ***D:*** Aaron Norris; ***W:*** R.J. Marx; ***M:*** George S. Clinton. *MED, VTR*

Platoon the Warriors **1988** The underworld rages with violence when two kingpins, Rex and Bill, become bitter and declare war over a botched drug deal. **90m/C VHS, Beta.** David Coley, Dick Crown, James Miller, Don Richard, Alex Sylvian; ***D:*** Philip Ko. *NO*

Platypus Cove **1986** An adopted boy tracks down the culprits responsible for the sabotage of his family's boat, a crime for which he was suspected. Australian. **72m/C VHS, Beta.** Paul Smith; ***D:*** Peter Maxwell. *SUE*

Play Dead *Satan's Dog* **1981** Poor Yvonne De Carlo plays a psychotic woman who trains a dog to rip people to shreds. **89m/C VHS.** Yvonne De Carlo, Stephanie Dunham, David Cullinane, Glenn Kezer, Ron Jackson, Carolyn Greenwood; ***D:*** Peter Wittman. *ACA*

Play It Again, Charlie Brown **1970** The Peanuts gang goes bananas when Lucy enlists Schroeder to play rock music at a PTA meeting. **25m/C VHS, Beta.** Charles M. Schulz. *SHV, VTR, WTA*

Play It Again, Sam ½ **1972 (PG)** Allen is—no surprise—a nerd, and this time he's in love with his best friend's wife. Modest storyline provides a framework of endless gags, with Allen borrowing heavily from "Casablanca." Bogey even appears periodically to counsel Allen on the ways of wooing women. Superior comedy isn't hurt by Ross directing instead of Allen, who adapted the script from his own play. **85m/C VHS, Beta, LV, 8mm.** Woody Allen, Diane Keaton, Tony Roberts, Susan Anspach, Jerry Lacy, Jennifer Salt, Joy Bang, Viva, Herbert Ross; ***D:*** Herbert Ross; ***W:*** Woody Allen; ***C:*** Owen Roizman; ***M:*** Billy Goldenberg. *PAR*

Play Misty for Me **1971 (R)** A radio deejay obliges a psychotic woman's song request and suddenly finds himself the target of her obsessive behavior, which rapidly turns from seductive to murderous. Auspicious directorial debut for Eastwood, borrowing from the Siegel playbook (look for the director's cameo as a barkeep). Based on a story by Heims. **102m/C VHS, Beta, LV.** Jessica Walter, Donna Mills, John Larch, Irene Hervey, Jack Ging, Clint Eastwood; ***Cameos:*** Donald Siegel; ***D:*** Clint Eastwood; ***W:*** Jo Heims, Dean Riesner; ***C:*** Bruce Surtees; ***M:*** Dee Barton. *MCA, TLF*

Play Murder for Me **1991 (R)** Saxophonist performing in a seedy Buenos Aires nightclub has his world turned upside down when a former lover suddenly re-enters his life. She still has her eye on him, but she's now the woman of a notorious mobster. Soon the musician finds himself drawn into the usual deadly world of crime, deceit, and unharnessed passion. **80m/C VHS.** Jack Wagner, Tracy Scoggins; ***D:*** Hector Olivera. *NHO*

Play Nice ½ **1992 (R)** A detective hunts down a murderous psychopath but is shocked when he discovers his suspect is a woman—and someone he knows. Also available in an unrated version. **90m/C VHS.** Ed O'Ross. *VMK*

Play Time **1994** Jeannie, Lindsay, and their husbands are on vacation in Palm Springs where they get up to some naughty sexual games that test the limits of friendship. Available in an unedited version at 95 minutes. **90m/C VHS.** Monique Parent, Craig Stepp. *TRI*

Playback ½ **1995 (R)** Young couple think they've finally captured the gold ring when hubby David (Grant) gets a chance at a million dollar merger deal. But David's set-up by a sexy co-worker (Whirry) and his slimy boss (Hamilton) tries to seduce his wife. **91m/C VHS, Beta.** Charles Grant, Shannon Whirry, George Hamilton, Tawny Kitaen, Harry Dean Stanton; ***D:*** Oley Sassone; ***W:*** Oley Sassone, David DuBos. *PAR*

Playboy of the Western World ½ **1962** An innkeeper's daughter is infatuated with a young man who says he murdered his father. Adapted from the classic play by John Millington Synge. **96m/C VHS, Beta.** *IR* Siobhan McKenna, Gary Raymond; ***D:*** Brian Desmond Hurst. *NO*

The Playboys **1992 (PG-13)** In 1957 in a tiny Irish village, unmarried Tara Maguire causes a scandal by having a baby. Her beauty attracts lots of men—there's a former beau who kills himself, the obsessive, middle-aged Sergeant Hegarty, and the newest arrival, Tom Castle, an actor with a rag-tag theatrical troupe called the Playboys. Slow-moving and simple story with particularly good performances by Wright as the strong-willed Tara and Finney as Hegarty, clinging to a last chance at love and family. The Playboys' hysterically hammy version of "Gone With the Wind" is a gem. Directorial debut of Mackinnon. Filmed in the village of Redhills, Ireland, the hometown of co-writer Connaughton. **114m/C VHS.** Albert Finney, Aidan Quinn, Robin Wright, Milo O'Shea, Alan Devlin, Niamh Cusack, Ian McElhinney, Niall Buggy, Adrian Dunbar; ***D:*** Gilles Mackinnon; ***W:*** Shane Connaughton, Kerry Crabbe; ***M:*** Jean-Claude Petit. *HBO, FCT*

The Player ½ **1992 (R)** Clever, entertaining, and biting satire of the movie industry and the greed that controls it. Robbins is dead-on as Griffin Mill, a young studio exec who becomes the chief suspect in a murder investigation. He personifies Hollywood's ethics (or lack thereof) in a performance both cold and vulnerable, as he looks for the right buttons to push and the proper back to stab. Strong leading performances are supplemented by 65 star cameos. Some viewers may be put off by the inside-Hollywood jokes, but Altman fans will love it. The laserdisc version includes commentary by Altman, interviews with 20 screenwriters, and celebrity cameos that didn't make the final cut. **123m/C VHS, LV.** Tim Robbins, Greta Scacchi, Fred Ward, Whoopi Goldberg, Peter Gallagher, Brion James, Cynthia Stevenson, Vincent D'Onofrio, Dean Stockwell, Richard E. Grant, Dina Merrill, Sydney Pollack, Lyle Lovett, Randall Batinkoff, Gina Gershon; ***Cameos:*** Burt Reynolds, Cher, Nick Nolte, Jack Lemmon, Lily Tomlin, Marlee Matlin, Julia Roberts, Bruce Willis, Anjelica Huston, Elliott Gould, Sally Kellerman, Steve Allen, Richard Anderson, Harry Belafonte, Shari Belafonte, Karen Black, Gary Busey, Robert Carradine, James Coburn, Cathy Lee Crosby, John Cusack, Brad Davis, Peter Falk, Teri Garr, Leeza Gibbons, Scott Glenn, Jeff Goldblum, Joel Grey, Buck Henry, Kathy Ireland, Sally Kirkland, Andie MacDowell, Martin Mull, Mimi Rogers, Jill St. John, Susan Sarandon, Rod Steiger, Joan Tewkesbury, Robert Wagner, Michael Tolkin; ***D:*** Robert Altman; ***W:*** Michael Tolkin; ***M:*** Thomas Newman. British Academy Awards '92: Best Adapted Screenplay; Cannes Film Festival '92: Best Actor (Robbins), Best Director (Altman); Golden Globe Awards '93: Best Actor—Musical/Comedy (Robbins), Best Film—Musical/Comedy; Independent Spirit Awards '93: Best Film; New York Film Critics Awards '92: Best Cinematography, Best Director (Altman), Best Film; Writers Guild of America '92: Best Adapted Screenplay; Nominations: Academy Awards '92: Best Adapted Screenplay, Best Director (Altman), Best Film Editing; Cannes Film Festival '92: Best Film. *NLC, CRC, MOV*

Players **1979 (PG)** Young tennis hustler touring Mexico hooks up with beautiful and mysterious older woman. They seem to be from different worlds yet their love grows. She inspires him enough to enter Wimbledon. Several tennis pros appear, including Guillermo Vilas, John McEnroe, and Ilie Nastase. Almost as boring as watching a real tennis game. **120m/C VHS, Beta.** Ali MacGraw, Dean Paul Martin, Maximilian Schell, Pancho Gonzales; ***D:*** Anthony Harvey; ***W:*** Arnold Schulman; ***M:*** Jerry Goldsmith. *PAR*

Playgirl Killer *Decoy for Terror* **1966** After impulsively murdering a restless model, an artist continues to kill indiscriminately, keeping his spoils on ice. Sedaka croons between kills and luxuriates poolside—seemingly oblivious to the plot of the film—while a female decoy is sent to bait the killer for the police. For adult viewers. **86m/C VHS, Beta.** *CA* William Kerwin, Jean Christopher, Andree Champagne, Neil Sedaka; ***D:*** Erick Santamaria. *NWV*

Playing Away **1987** A team of Caribbean cricket players meet a team of stuffy Brits on the field in a clash of the cultures. **100m/C VHS, Beta, LV.** *GB* Norman Beaton, Robert Urquhart; ***D:*** Horace Love. *NLC*

Playing Dead ½ **1915** Drew and his wife portray a married couple in this silent farce. The insecure husband decides to fake his death so his wife can be with the man he thinks she loves. **58m/B VHS.** Sidney Drew, Lucille Drew, Alice Lake, Donald Hall, Harry English, Isadore Marcil; ***D:*** Sidney Drew. *GPV*

Playing for Keeps **1986 (PG-13)** Three high school grads turn a dilapidating hotel into a rock 'n roll resort. Music by Pete Townshend, Peter Frampton, Phil Collins, and others. **103m/C VHS, Beta, LV.** Daniel Jordano, Matthew Penn, Leon Grant, Harold Gould, Jimmy Baio; ***D:*** Bob Weinstein. *MCA*

Playing for Time **1980** Compelling, award-winning television drama based on actual experiences of a Holocaust prisoner who survives by leading an inmate orchestra. Strong playing from Redgrave and Mayron. Pro-Palestinian Redgrave's political beliefs made her a controversial candidate for the role of Jewish Fania Fenelon, but her stunning performance is on the mark. **148m/C VHS, Beta.** Vanessa Redgrave, Jane Alexander, Maud Adams, Verna Bloom, Melanie Mayron; ***D:*** Daniel Mann; ***M:*** Brad Fiedel. *NO*

Playing with Fire 🦴 **197?** A young girl gets caught up in drugs, casual sex, and murder. **87m/C VHS, Beta.** Karen Tungay, Danny Keogh, Sam Marais; ***D:*** Alan Nathanson. *NO*

Playmaker 🦴½ **1994 (R)** Jaime (Rubin) is a struggling actress whose coach Talbert (Firth) guarantees success as long as she follows his bizarre training methods, which include seduction, abuse, and betrayal. Good chemistry between the leads but a mishmash of a script. **91m/C VHS.** Jennifer Rubin, Colin Firth, John Getz, Jeffery Perry; ***D:*** Yuri Zeltser; ***W:*** Yuri Zeltser; ***C:*** Ross Berryman; ***M:*** Mark Snow. *ORI*

Playmates 🦴 **1941** Barrymore is practically wasted in his last film as a down-on-his-luck actor who agrees to turn bandleader Kyser into a Shakespearean actor. Bizarre comedy is funny at times, but leaves the audience wondering what Barrymore thought he was doing. ♫Humpty Dumpty Heart; How Long Did I Dream?; Que Chica?; Romeo Smith and Juliet Jones; Thank Your Lucky Stars and Stripes. **96m/B VHS, Beta.** Kay Kyser, John Barrymore, Ginny Simms, Lupe Velez, May Robson, Patsy Kelly, Peter Lind Hayes, George Cleveland; ***D:*** David Butler. *TTC*

Playmates 🦴🦴½ **1972** Two divorced buddies fall in love with each other's ex-wives in this made for television flick. Typical Alda vehicle isn't bad. **78m/C VHS, Beta.** Doug McClure, Alan Alda, Connie Stevens, Barbara Feldon, Eileen Brennan, Tiger Williams, Severn Darden; ***D:*** Theodore J. Flicker. *VMK*

Playroom 🦴🦴 **1990 (R)** Archaeologist McDonald is completing his father's search for the tomb of a medieval boy-prince. But someone, or something, has been waiting for him for a long, long time. When he finally reaches the long-sought-after tomb, he discovers that it is a torture chamber where his worst nightmares become realities. The demonic prince who was buried in the tomb has picked Chris as his playmate, and the rest of the staff as his personal toys. **87m/C VHS, LV.** Lisa Aliff, Aron Eisenberg, Christopher McDonald, James Purcell, Jamie Rose, Vincent Schiavelli; ***D:*** Manny Coto. *REP*

Playtime 🦴🦴🦴 **1967** Occasionnally enterprising comedy in which the bemused Frenchman Hulot tries in vain to maintain an appointment in an urban landscape of glass and steel. The theme of cold, unfeeling civilization is hardly unique, but the film is nonetheless enjoyable. The third in the Hulot trilogy, preceded by "Mr. Hulot's Holiday" and "Mon Oncle." In French with English subtitles. **108m/C VHS, Beta.** *FR* Jacques Tati, Barbara Dennek, Jacqueline Lecomte, Jack Gautier; ***D:*** Jacques Tati. *SUE, INJ, NLC*

Plaza Suite 🦴🦴🦴 **1971 (PG)** Three alternating skits from Neil Simon's play about different couples staying at the New York hotel. Matthau shines in all three vignettes. Some of Simon's funnier stuff, with the first sketch being the best: Matthau and Stapleton are a couple celebrating their 24th anniversary. She's sentimental, while he's yearning for his mistress. Number two has producer Matthau putting the make on old flame Harris, while the finale has father Matthau coaxing his anxious daughter out of the bathroom on her wedding day. **114m/C VHS, Beta, LV.** Walter Matthau, Maureen Stapleton, Barbara Harris, Lee Grant, Louise Sorel; ***D:*** Arthur Hiller; ***W:*** Neil Simon; ***M:*** Maurice Jarre. *PAR*

Please Don't Eat My Mother *Woof!* *Hungry Pets; Glump* **1972** A softcore remake of "Little Shop of Horrors" in which a lonely voyeur plays host to a human-eating plant. **95m/C VHS.** Buck Kartalian, Renee Bond; ***D:*** Carl Monson. *MOV, VDM, TPV*

Please Don't Eat the Daisies 🦴🦴½ **1960** City couple and kids leave the Big Apple for the country and are traumatized by flora and fauna. Goofy sixties fluff taken from Jean Kerr's book and the basis for the eventual TV series. **111m/C VHS, Beta, LV.** Doris Day, David Niven, Janis Paige, Spring Byington, Richard Haydn, Patsy Kelly, Jack Weston, Margaret Lindsay; ***D:*** Charles Walters. *MGM, FCT*

Pleasure 🦴🦴 **1931** A saga of love, treachery, and melodrama in English society where self-indulgence held priority and good manners were the rule. **53m/B VHS, Beta, LV.** Conway Tearle, Roscoe Karns, Carmel Myers, Lena Basquette. *NOS*

A Pleasure Doing Business 🦴 **1979 (R)** Three high school buddies, now in their 40s, are reunited at a stag party, where they decide to go into business as managers in "the oldest profession." **86m/C VHS, Beta.** Conrad Bain, John Byner, Alan Oppenheimer, Misty Rowe, Phyllis Diller, Tom Smothers; ***D:*** Steve Vagnino. *VHE*

Pleasure Palace 🦴🦴 **1980** A gambling lady's-man (Sharif) meets his match when he helps a woman casino owner (Lange). Made for television. **96m/C VHS, Beta.** Omar Sharif, Victoria Principal, J.D. Cannon, Gerald S. O'Loughlin, Jose Ferrer, Hope Lange, Alan King; ***D:*** Walter Grauman. *LIV*

Pledge Night 🦴🦴 **1990 (R)** Tale of horror and revenge. Killed years before in a fraternity hazing, Sid returns for the brothers who did him in. Gory and violent. **90m/C VHS, LV.** Will Kempe, Shannon McMahon, Todd Eastland; ***D:*** Paul Ziller. *IMP*

Plenty 🦴🦴½ **1985 (R)** Difficult but worthwhile film with Streep in top form as a former member of the French Resistance, who upon returning to England finds life at home increasingly tedious and banal and begins to fear her finest hours may be behind her. Gielgud is flawless as the aging career diplomat. Adapted by David Hare from his play, an allegory to British decline. **119m/C VHS, Beta, LV.** Meryl Streep, Tracey Ullman, Sting, John Gielgud, Charles Dance, Ian McKellen, Sam Neill, Burt Kwouk; ***D:*** Fred Schepisi; ***W:*** David Hare; ***M:*** Bruce Smeaton. Los Angeles Film Critics Association Awards '85: Best Supporting Actor (Gielgud); National Society of Film Critics Awards '85: Best Supporting Actor (Gielgud). *REP*

The Plot Against Harry 🦴🦴🦴 **1969** Jewish racketeer Harry Plotnik checks out of prison, and finds the outside world ain't what it used to be. Attempting to lead an honest life only makes matters worse. Completely overlooked when first released in 1969 (and quickly shelved) because it was considered to have no commercial potential, Roemer's crime comedy found an enthusiastic audience when it was rediscovered twenty years later. **81m/B VHS.** Martin Priest, Ben Lang, Maxine Woods, Henry Nemo; ***D:*** Michael Roemer; ***W:*** Michael Roemer. *NYF, FCT*

The Ploughman's Lunch 🦴🦴🦴 **1983** A BBC news reporter claws and lies his way to the top. He then discovers that he is the victim of a far more devious plan. Engrossing and well made, although some of the political views are simplistic. **107m/C VHS, Beta.** Jonathan Pryce, Charlie Dore, Tim Curry, Rosemary Harris, Frank Finlay, Bill Paterson; ***D:*** Richard Eyre. *SUE*

Plughead Rewired: Circuitry Man 2 🦴🦴 *Circuitry Man 2* **1994 (R)** Earth's atmosphere has been destroyed and survivors are forced underground, where they're terrorized by the humanoid Plughead, who likes to literally plug into the minds of his victims. Plughead wants to rule what's left of life on Earth and all that stands in his way is the android Circuitry Man and FBI agent Kyle. Special effects are strictly bargain basement level. **97m/C VHS.** Vernon Wells, Deborah Shelton, Jim Metzler, Dennis Christopher, Nicholas Worth, Traci Lords; ***D:*** Steven Lovy, Robert Lovy; ***W:*** Steven Lovy, Robert Lovy. *COL*

Plumber 🦴🦴½ **1979** A plumber who makes a house call extends his stay to psychologically torture the woman of the house. Originally made for Australian television. **76m/C VHS, Beta.** *AU* Judy Morris, Ivar Kants, Robert Coleby; ***D:*** Peter Weir; ***W:*** Peter Weir. *MED*

Plunder Road 🦴🦴½ **1957** A pair of crooks cook up a plan to rob a train bound for the San Francisco Mint that's carrying a fortune in gold bullion. Top notch B-film noir. **76m/B VHS.** Gene Raymond, Jeanne Cooper, Wayne Morris, Elisha Cook Jr.; ***D:*** Hubert Cornfield. *REP*

Plunge Into Darkness 🦴½ **1977** Quiet weekend in the mountains turns into a nightmare for an ex-Olympic runner and his family. **77m/C VHS, Beta.** Bruce Barry, Olivia Hamnett, Ashley Greenville, Wallace Eaton, Tom Richards; ***D:*** Peter Maxwell. *NO*

Plutonium Baby 🦴 **1987** A mutated kid, whose mother was killed by the same radiation exposure that infected him, tracks down the guilty party in New York in this comic-book style film. **85m/C VHS, Beta.** Patrick Molloy, Danny Guerra; ***D:*** Ray Hirschman. *TWE*

Plutonium Incident 🦴🦴 **1982** A female technician at a nuclear power plant suspects the facility to be less safe than it appears, and faces a diabolical plan of harassment when she attempts to bring attention to the hazards. **90m/C VHS, Beta.** Janet Margolin, Powers Boothe, Bo Hopkins, Joseph Campanella; ***D:*** Richard Michaels. *TLF*

Pocahontas 🦴🦴🦴 **1995 (G)** It's 1607 and spirited Powhatan maiden Pocahontas and British settler Captain John Smith strike an unlikely but doomed romance in Disney's 33rd animated feature, its first based on the life of a historical figure. Lovely Poca, a virtual post-adolescent Native American superbabe, introduces the roguish captain (spoken and sung by Gibson) to the wonders of unspoiled nature and serves as peacemaker in the clash of European and Native American cultures. Disney puts its spin on history but maintains cultural sensitivity: several characters are voiced by Native American performers, including Chief Powhatan, spoken by American Indian activist Means, who led the 1973 siege at Wounded Knee, and Bedard as Pocahantas. Just don't tell the kids the real Pocahontas married someone else, moved to England, and died of smallpox at 21. Stunningly animated, but its mediocre soundtrack and decidedly somber tone leave it lacking in typical Disney majesty and charm. Premiered at New York's Central Park, for the usual theater crowd of 100,000 or so. **90m/C VHS.** ***D:*** Mike Gabriel, Eric Goldberg; ***W:*** Carl Binder, Susannah Grant, Philip LaZebnik; ***M:*** Alan Menken, Stephen Schwartz; ***V:*** Irene Bedard, Judy Kuhn, Mel Gibson, Joe Baker, Christian Bale, Billy Connolly, James Apaumut Fall, Linda Hunt, John Kassir, Danny Mann, Bill Cobbs, David Ogden Stiers, Michelle St. John, Gordon Tootoosis, Frank Welker. Academy Awards '95: Best Song ("Colors of the Wind"), Best Score; Golden Globe Awards '96: Best Song ("Colors of the Wind"); Nominations: Golden Globe Awards '96: Best Score. *DIS*

Pocahontas: The Legend 🦴🦴½ **1995** Live-action version of the increasingly familiar story of the Native American girl who aids Virginia settler, John Smith. **101m/C VHS.** Sandrine Holt, Miles O'Keeffe, Tony Goldwyn, Gordon Tootoosis; ***D:*** Daniele Suissa; ***W:*** Daniele Suissa. *GKK*

The Pocatello Kid 🦴½ **1931** Maynard stretches in a dual role as the wrongly convicted Kid and the Kid's no-good sheriff brother. **60m/B VHS, Beta.** Ken Maynard, Marceline Day, Charles "Blackie" King, Lafe McKee; ***D:*** Phil Rosen. *NOS, VCN, VDM*

Pocket Money 🦴🦴 **1972 (PG)** Down-on-their-luck cowpokes foolishly do business with crooked rancher in attempt to make comeback in faltering acting careers. Star-powered, moderately entertaining modern western-comedy based on the novel "Jim Kane" by J.K.S. Brown. **100m/C VHS, Beta.** Paul Newman, Lee Marvin, Strother Martin, Christine Belford, Wayne Rogers, Hector Elizondo, Gregory Sierra; ***D:*** Stuart Rosenberg; ***W:*** Terence Malick; ***M:*** Alex North. *WAR, FCT*

Pocketful of Miracles 🦴🦴🦴 **1961** Capra's final film, a remake of his 1933 "Lady for a Day," is just as corny and sentimental but doesn't work quite as well. Davis is delightful as Apple Annie, a down-on-her-luck street vendor who will go to any extreme to hide her poverty from the well-married daughter she adores. Ford is terrific as the man who transforms Annie into a lady in time for her daughter's visit. Touching. Maybe too touching. Also marks Ann-Margret's film debut. **136m/C VHS, Beta, LV.** Bette Davis, Glenn Ford, Peter Falk, Hope Lange, Arthur O'Connell, Ann-Margret, Thomas Mitchell, Jack Elam, Edward Everett Horton, David Brian, Mickey Shaughnessy; ***D:*** Frank Capra. Golden Globe Awards '62: Best Actor—Musical/Comedy

(Ford); Nominations: Academy Awards '61: Best Costume Design (Color), Best Song ("Pocketful of Miracles"), Best Supporting Actor (Falk). *MGM, FOX, CCB*

A Pocketful of Rye ℒℒ *Agatha Christie's Miss Marple: A Pocketful of Rye* **1987** Based on Agatha Christie's novel featuring the sleuthing Miss Marple. She faces another murderous puzzle, this one based on an old nursery rhyme. Made for British television. **101m/C VHS, Beta.** *GB* Joan Hickson; ***D:*** Guy Slater. *FOX, HMV, VCO*

Poco ℒ **1977** The story of Poco, a shaggy little dog who travels across the country to search for the young girl who owns him. **88m/C VHS, Beta.** Chill Wills, Michelle Ashburn, John Steadman. *LIV, VES*

Poetic Justice ℒℒ½ **1993 (R)** Justice (Jackson in her movie debut, for better or worse) gives up college plans to follow a career in cosmetology after her boyfriend's brutal murder. She copes with her loss by dedicating herself to poetry writing (provided by no less than poet Maya Angelou) and meets postal worker Shakur. Singleton's second directorial effort is about the girlz n the hood and boasts a lighter script (well, it is about a hairdresser) focusing less on the Boyz-style morality and more on the trials and tribulations of Justice. Production stopped on the South Central L.A. set during the '92 riots, but the aftermath provided poignant pictures for later scenes. **109m/C VHS, LV, 8mm.** Janet Jackson, Tupac Shakur, Tyra Ferrell, Regina King, Joe Torry, Norma Donaldson; ***D:*** John Singleton; ***W:*** John Singleton; ***M:*** Stanley Clarke. MTV Movie Awards '94: Best Female Performance (Jackson), Most Desirable Female (Jackson); Nominations: Academy Awards '93: Best Song ("Again"); Golden Globe Awards '94: Best Song ("Again"). *COL, BTV*

Pogo for President: "I Go Pogo" ℒℒ½ **1984 (PG)** Animated adventure with Walt Kelly's Pogo Possum becoming an unlikely presidential candidate when Howland Owl proclaims him the winner of a election. **120m/C VHS, Beta.** ***V:*** Jonathan Winters, Vincent Price, Ruth Buzzi, Stan Freberg, Jimmy Breslin, Arnold Stang. *DIS, WTA*

Poil de Carotte ℒℒ½ *The Red Head* **1931** A semi-famous French melodrama about a young boy harassed by his overbearing mother to the point of disaster, redeemed finally by the love of his father. In French with English subtitles. **90m/B VHS, Beta.** *FR* Harry Baur, Robert Lynen, Catherine Fontenoy; ***D:*** Julien Duvivier. *NOS, FCT, MRV*

The Point **1971** Charming and sincere made-for-television animated feature about the rejection and isolation of a round-headed child in a world of pointy-headed people. Excellent score. **74m/C VHS, Beta, LV.** ***D:*** Fred Wolf; ***M:*** Harry Nilsson; ***V:*** Paul Frees. *FHE, VES, WTA*

Point Blank ℒℒ½ **1967** Adapted from Stark's "The Hunter." The film's techniques are sometimes compared to those of Resnais and Godard. Double-crossed and believed dead, gangster Marvin returns to claim his share of the loot from the Organization. Hard-nosed examination of the depersonalization of a mechanized urban world. **92m/C VHS, Beta.** Lee Marvin, Angie Dickinson, Keenan Wynn, Carroll O'Connor, Lloyd Bochner, Michael Strong, James B. Sikking; ***D:*** John Boorman. *MGM*

Point Break ℒℒ½ **1991 (R)** If you can suspend your disbelief—and you'd need a crane—then this crime adventure is just dandy. Reeves is a young undercover FBI kid sent to infiltrate a gang of bank-robbing surfer dudes. Swayze is the leader of the beach subculture, a thrillseeker who plays cat-and-mouse with the feds in a series of excellent action scenes. Silly brain candy. **117m/C VHS, LV.** Patrick Swayze, Keanu Reeves, Gary Busey, Lori Petty, John C. McGinley, Chris Pederson, Bojesse Christopher, Julian Reyes, Daniel Beer, Sydney Walsh, Vincent Klyn, James LeGros, John Philbin; ***D:*** Kathryn Bigelow; ***W:*** W. Peter Iliff; ***M:*** Mark Isham. MTV Movie Awards '92: Most Desirable Male (Reeves). *FXV*

Point of Impact ℒℒ **1993 (R)** A Miami customs officer is killed in an explosion and his partner is blamed. He knows a Cuban crime boss was actually behind it and goes undercover to bring the criminal organization down. But there's also the temptation of the the criminal's sexy ladyfriend. Also available in an unrated version. **96m/C VHS, LV.** Michael Pare, Barbara Carrera, Michael Ironside. *VMK*

Point of No Return ℒℒ½ **1993 (R)** Fonda is Maggie, a drugged-out loser condemned to death for her part in a murder spree, but if she agrees to work as a government assassin, she'll be given a reprieve. Fonda displays a certain perkiness as the assassin and is better in her early surly scenes; Keitel is creepy as another assassin. Flashy, exacting, but ultimately innocuous remake of the 1990 French thriller "La Femme Nikita." **108m/C VHS, Beta, LV.** Bridget Fonda, Gabriel Byrne, Dermot Mulroney, Miguel Ferrer, Anne Bancroft, Olivia D'Abo, Harvey Keitel, Richard Romanus, Lorraine Toussaint, Geoffrey Lewis, Calvin Levels; ***D:*** John Badham; ***W:*** Robert Getchell, Alexandra Seros; ***C:*** Michael Watkins; ***M:*** Hans Zimmer. *WAR*

Point of Terror ℒ **1971 (R)** A handsome rock singer seduces a record company executive's wife in order to further his career. **88m/C VHS, Beta.** Peter Carpenter, Dyanne Thorne, Lory Hansen, Leslie Simms; ***D:*** Alex Nicol. *NO*

The Pointsman ℒℒ½ *De Wisselwachter* **1986 (R)** A quirky, small film based on the novel by Jean Paul Franssens. A beautiful Scandinavian woman accidentally gets off a train in Northern Scotland, where the only shelter is a small railway outpost, and the only company is a mysterious pointsman who lives by the comings and goings of the trains. The couple's increasing isolation as winter falls and their lack of a common language persists is portrayed with both humor and poignancy. **95m/C VHS, Beta, LV.** *NL* Jim Van Der Woude, Stephane Excoffier, John Kraaykamp, Josse De Pauw, Ton Van Dort; ***D:*** Jos Stelling. *LIV, VES*

Poison ℒℒℒ **1991 (R)** A controversial, compelling drama weaving the story of a seven year-old boy's murder of his father with two other tales of obsessive, fringe behavior. From the director of the underground hit "Superstar: The Karen Carpenter Story," which was shot using only a cast of "Barbie" dolls. **85m/C VHS.** Edith Meeks, Larry Maxwell, Susan Norman, Scott Renderer, James Lyons; ***D:*** Todd Haynes; ***W:*** Todd Haynes; ***M:*** James Bennett. Sundance Film Festival '91: Grand Jury Prize. *FXL, INJ*

Poison Ivy ℒℒ **1985** A routine, made for television comedy about a chaotic and lusty summer camp. **97m/C VHS, Beta.** Michael J. Fox, Nancy McKeon, Robert Klein, Caren Kaye; ***D:*** Larry Elikann; ***M:*** Miles Goodman. *NO*

Poison Ivy ℒℒ **1992 (R)** Barrymore is right on target as a junior femme fatale in this trashy tale of a wayward teenager and her takeover of her best friend's family. Ivy has no discernable family life and quickly attaches herself to the lonely, neglected Cooper (Gilbert) who ends up watching as she systematically seduces both her mother (emotionally) and her father (physically). But when Ivy's homewrecking turns lethal, Cooper must fight her "friend" to save herself. Glossy, over-done pulp. An unrated version is also available. **91m/C VHS.** Drew Barrymore, Sara Gilbert, Tom Skerritt, Cheryl Ladd; ***D:*** Katt Shea Ruben; ***W:*** Katt Shea Ruben, Andy Ruben; ***C:*** Phedon Papamichael. *COL, NLC, PMS*

Poison Ivy 2: Lily ℒ½ **1995 (R)** Art student Lily (Milano) finds the provocative Ivy's diary and becomes intrigued enough to decide to take a walk on the wild side herself. Also available unrated. **110m/C VHS, LV.** Alyssa Milano, Xander Berkeley, Johnathon Schaech, Belinda Bauer; ***D:*** Anne Goursaud; ***W:*** Chloe King; ***M:*** Joseph Williams. *NLC*

Poker Alice ℒℒ **1987** A lively Western starring Elizabeth Taylor as a sometime gambler who wins a brothel in a poker game. **100m/C VHS, Beta.** Elizabeth Taylor, George Hamilton, Tom Skerritt, Richard Mulligan, David Wayne, Susan Tyrrell, Pat Corley; ***D:*** Arthur Seidelman; ***W:*** James Lee Barrett. *VTR, NWV*

The Polar Bear King ℒℒ½ **1994 (PG)** When a handsome prince refuses to marry the evil witch of Summerland, the wicked woman uses her power to turn him into a polar bear. The polar bear prince embarks on a journey to Winterland where he meets and falls in love with a beautiful princess. Together they return to Summerland and try to break the witch's spell. Filmed on location in Norway and Sweden. **87m/C VHS, LV.** Maria Bonnerie, Jack Fjeldstad, Tobias Hoesl, Anna-Lotta Larsson; ***D:*** Ola Solum. *HMD*

Poldark ℒℒℒ **1975** Tempestuous love, political intrigue, and family struggles all set in 18th-century Cornwall, then the copper-producing center of England. Heroic Ross Poldark has just returned from fighting upstart Americans in the Revolutionary War only to discover that his father has died and the family mines are about to be sold to the scheming Warleggan family. Ross struggles to pay off family debts, reclaim his heritage, resolve his feelings for an old love, and fight his attraction to the beguiling, but completely unsuitable, Demelza. Adapted from the novels by Winston Graham. Made for British television; 12 episodes on 6 cassettes. **720m/C VHS.** *GB* Robin Ellis, Angharad Rees, Jill Townsend, Judy Geeson, Ralph Bates, Richard Morant, Clive Francis, John Baskcomb, Paul Curran, Tilly Tremayne, Mary Wimbush; ***D:*** Paul Annett, Christopher Barry, Kenneth Ives; ***W:*** Paul Wheeler, Jack Russell, Peter Draper, Jack Pulman. *TVC, SIG, PAP*

Poldark 2 ℒℒℒ **1975** The further adventures of Ross Poldark, wife Demelza, and assorted family, friends, and enemies, all set in 18th-century Cornwall. Demelza's two meddlesome younger brothers come to live at Nampara, enemy George Warleggan and Ross' old love Elizabeth move too close for comfort, and the uncertainties of the copper mining economy all bring their share of trouble. Adapted from the novels by Winston Graham. Made for British TV; 6 cassettes. **720m/C VHS.** *GB* Robin Ellis, Angharad Rees, Jill Townsend, Judy Geeson, Ralph Bates, Kevin McNally, Brian Stirner, Michael Cadman, Jane Wymark, David Delve, Christopher Biggins, Trudie Styler; ***D:*** Philip Dudley, Roger Jenkins; ***W:*** Alexander Baron, John Wiles, Martin Worth. *TVC*

Police ℒℒ½ **1985** French police drama with the intense Depardieu as a cop hunting an Algerian drug boss. Matters grow complicated when he falls for the elusive crook's girlfriend. Sometimes gripping, but unveven; the actors were encouraged to improvise. Inspired by the novel "Bodies Are Dust" by P.J. Wolfson. In French with English subtitles. **113m/C VHS.** *FR* Gerard Depardieu, Sophie Marceau, Sandrine Bonnaire, Richard Anconina, Pascale Rocard; ***D:*** Maurice Pialat; ***W:*** Catherine Breillat. Venice Film Festival '85: Best Actor (Depardieu). *NYF, FCT, INJ*

Police Academy ℒ½ **1984 (R)** In an attempt to recruit more cops, a big-city police department does away with all its job standards. The producers probably didn't know that they were introducing bad comedy's answer to the "Friday the 13th" series, but it's hard to avoid heaping the sins of its successors on this film. Besides, it's just plain dumb. **96m/C VHS, Beta, LV, 8mm.** Steve Guttenberg, Kim Cattrall, Bubba Smith, George Gaynes, Michael Winslow, Leslie Easterbrook, Georgina Spelvin, Debralee Scott; ***D:*** Hugh Wilson; ***W:*** Hugh Wilson, Pat Proft, Neal Israel; ***M:*** Robert Folk. *WAR*

Police Academy 2: Their First Assignment ℒ **1985 (PG-13)** More predictable idiocy from the cop shop. This time they're determined to rid the precinct of some troublesome punks. No real story to speak of, just more high jinks in this mindless sequel. **87m/C VHS, Beta, LV.** Steve Guttenberg, Bubba Smith, Michael Winslow, Art Metrano, Colleen Camp, Howard Hesseman, David Graf, George Gaynes; ***D:*** Jerry Paris; ***W:*** Barry W. Blaustein. *WAR*

Police Academy 3: Back in Training ℒ **1986 (PG)** In yet another sequel, the bumbling cops find their alma mater is threatened by a budget crunch and they must compete with a rival academy to see which school survives. The "return to school" plot allowed the filmmakers to add new characters to replace those who had some scruples about picking up yet another "Police Lobotomy" check. Followed by three more sequels. **84m/C VHS, Beta, LV.** Steve Guttenberg, Bubba Smith, David Graf, Michael Winslow, Marion Ramsey, Art Metrano, Bob(cat) Goldthwait, Leslie Easterbrook, Tim Kazurinsky, George Gaynes, Shawn Weatherly; ***D:*** Jerry Paris; ***W:*** Gene Quintano; ***M:*** Robert Folk. *WAR*

Police Academy 4: Citizens on Patrol **1987 (PG)** The comic cop cutups from the first three films aid a citizen's patrol group in their unnamed, but still wacky, hometown. Moronic high jinks ensue. Fourth in the series of five (or is it six?) that began with "Police Academy". **88m/C VHS, Beta, LV.** Steve Guttenberg, Bubba Smith, Michael Winslow, David Graf, Tim Kazurinsky, George Gaynes, Colleen Camp, Bob(cat) Goldthwait, Sharon Stone; ***D:*** Jim Drake; ***W:*** Gene Quintano; ***M:*** Robert Folk. *WAR*

Police Academy 5: Assignment Miami Beach *Woof!* **1988 (PG)** The fourth sequel, wherein the misfits-with-badges go to Miami and bumble about in the usual manner. It's about time these cops were retired from the force. **89m/C VHS, Beta, LV.** Bubba Smith, David Graf, Michael Winslow, Leslie Easterbrook, Rene Auberjonois, Marion Ramsey, Janet Jones, George Gaynes, Matt McCoy; ***D:*** Alan Myerson; ***W:*** Stephen J. Curwick; ***M:*** Robert Folk. *WAR*

Police Academy 6: City Under Siege **1989 (PG)** In what is hoped to be the last in a series of bad comedies, the distinguished graduates pursue three goofballs responsible for a crime wave. **85m/C VHS, LV.** Bubba Smith, David Graf, Michael Winslow, Leslie Easterbrook, Marion Ramsey, Matt McCoy, Bruce Mahler, G.W. Bailey, George Gaynes; ***D:*** Peter Bonerz; ***W:*** Stephen J. Curwick; ***M:*** Robert Folk. *WAR*

Police Academy: Mission to Moscow **1994 (PG)** The seventh in the series is another inept comedy, which finds the chaotic crew tackling a Russian mobster on his Moscow turf—all because of a popular computer game with some sinister software. Like you'll care about the plot anyway. **83m/C VHS.** George Gaynes, Michael Winslow, David Graf, Leslie Easterbrook, G.W. Bailey, Charlie Schlatter, Ron Perlman, Christopher Lee; ***D:*** Alan Metter; ***W:*** Michele S. Chodos, Randolph Davis; ***M:*** Robert Folk. *WAR*

Police Court **1937** The son of a faded, alcoholic screen star tries to bring the old fellow back to prominence. **62m/B VHS, Beta, LV.** Nat Barry, Henry B. Walthall, Leon Janney. *NO*

Police Squad! Help Wanted! **1982** Three episodes from the brilliant, short-lived television spoof, with the patented pun-a-second style of humor typical of the makers of "Airplane!" and "The Naked Gun," which was based on this show. Episodes included: "A Substantial Gift," "Ring of Fear," and "Rendezvous at Big Gulch." See also "More! Police Squad." **75m/C VHS, Beta, LV.** Leslie Nielsen, Alan North, Ed Williams, William Duell; ***D:*** Jerry Zucker, David Zucker, Jim Abrahams; ***W:*** Jerry Zucker, David Zucker, Jim Abrahams. *PAR*

Policewoman Centerfold **1983** Exploitative rendering based on the true story of a cop who posed for a pornographic magazine. Anderson is appealing in the lead. **100m/C VHS, Beta.** Melody Anderson, Ed Marinaro, Donna Pescow, Bert Remsen, David Spielberg; ***D:*** Reza Badiyi. *NO*

Policewomen ½ **1973 (R)** Female undercover agent must stop a ring of gold smugglers. **99m/C VHS, Beta.** Sondra Currie, Tony Young, Phil Hoover, Elizabeth Stuart, Jeanne Bell; ***D:*** Lee Frost. *NO*

A Polish Vampire in Burbank **1980** A shy vampire in Burbank tries again and again to find blood and love. Wacky. **84m/C VHS, Beta.** Mark Pirro, Lori Sutton, Eddie Deezen; ***D:*** Mark Pirro. *NO*

Pollyanna ½ **1920** A young orphan girl is adopted by her cold, embittered aunt and does her best to bring joy and gladness to all the new people she meets. Silent with music score. **60m/B VHS, Beta, LV.** Mary Pickford; ***C:*** Charles Rosher. *CCB*

Pollyanna ½ **1960** Based on the Eleanor Porter story about an enchanting young girl whose contagious enthusiasm and zest for life touches the hearts of all she meets. Mills is perfect in the title role and was awarded a special Oscar for outstanding juvenile performance. A distinguished supporting cast is the icing on the cake in this delightful Disney confection. Original version was filmed in 1920 with Mary Pickford. **134m/C VHS, Beta, LV.** Hayley Mills, Jane Wyman, Richard Egan, Karl Malden, Nancy Olson, Adolphe Menjou, Donald Crisp, Agnes Moorehead, Kevin Corcoran; ***D:*** David Swift. *DIS, BTV*

Poltergeist **1982 (PG)** This production has Stephen Spielberg written all over it. A young family's home becomes a house of horrors when they are terrorized by menancing spirits who abduct their five-year-old daughter...through the TV screen! Roller-coaster thrills and chills, dazzling special effects, and perfectly timed humor highlight this stupendously scary ghost story. **114m/C VHS, Beta, LV.** JoBeth Williams, Craig T. Nelson, Beatrice Straight, Heather O'Rourke, Zelda Rubinstein, Dominique Dunne, Oliver Robbins, Richard Lawson, James Karen; ***D:*** Tobe Hooper; ***W:*** Steven Spielberg, Michael Grais, Mark Victor; ***M:*** Jerry Goldsmith. Nominations: Academy Awards '82: Best Original Score. *MGM*

Poltergeist 2: The Other Side ½ **1986 (PG-13)** Adequate sequel to the Spielburg-produced venture into the supernatural, where demons follow the Freeling family in their efforts to recapture the clairvoyant young daughter Carol Anne. The film includes sojourns into Indian lore and a four-foot high agave worm designed by H.R. Giger. The movie was followed by "Poltergeist 3" in 1988. **92m/C VHS, Beta, LV.** Craig T. Nelson, JoBeth Williams, Heather O'Rourke, Will Sampson, Julian Beck, Geraldine Fitzgerald, Oliver Robbins, Zelda Rubinstein; ***D:*** Brian Gibson; ***W:*** Mark Victor, Michael Grais; ***M:*** Jerry Goldsmith. *MGM*

Poltergeist 3 ½ **1988 (PG-13)** Wrestling with the supernatural has finally unnerved Carol Ann and she's sent to stay with her aunt and uncle in Chicago where she attends a school for gifted children with emotional disorders. Guess who follows her? Uninspired acting, threadbare premise, and one ghastly encounter too many. Oddly, O'Rourke died suddenly four months before the film's release. **97m/C VHS, Beta, LV.** Tom Skerritt, Nancy Allen, Heather O'Rourke, Lara Flynn Boyle, Zelda Rubinstein; ***D:*** Gary Sherman; ***W:*** Brian Taggert. *MGM*

Polyester ½ **1981 (R)** Amusing satire on middle-class life, described by producer, director and writer Waters as "'Father Knows Best' gone berserk." Forlorn housewife Divine pines for the man of her dreams while the rest of her life is falling apart at the seams. Filmed in "Odorama," a hilarious gimmick in which theatre goers were provided with scratch-n-sniff cards, containing specific scents corresponding to key scenes. Video watchers will have to use their imagination in experiencing a wide range of smells. The first of Waters' more mainstream films. Features songs by Murray and Harry. **86m/C VHS, Beta, LV.** Divine, Tab Hunter, Edith Massey, Mink Stole, Stiv Bators, David Samson, Mary Garlington, Kenneth King, Joni-Ruth White; ***D:*** John Waters; ***W:*** John Waters; ***M:*** Bill Murray, Deborah Harry, Michael Kamen. *NLC*

Pom Pom Girls ½ **1976 (R)** High school seniors, intent on having one last fling before graduating, get involved in crazy antics, clumsy romances, and football rivalries. **90m/C VHS, Beta.** Robert Carradine, Jennifer Ashley, Michael Mullins, Cheryl "Rainbeaux" Smith, Dianne Lee Hart, Lisa Reeves, Bill Adler; ***D:*** Joseph Ruben. *NO*

Pontiac Moon ½ **1994 (PG-13)** Danson plays a high school teacher who takes his son on a road trip to Spires of the Moon National Park hoping to arrive simultaneously with the astronauts' first lunar landing. His wife (Steenburgen) decides to follow them, although she's phobic about leaving the house and hasn't set foot outside in seven years. Sincere yet tedious film about father-son bonding has a few heartfelt moments, but not enough to sustain interest for entire viewing period. Best (and only) reason for watching: Monument Valley scenery. **108m/C VHS, Beta.** Ted Danson, Mary Steenburgen, Ryan Todd, Eric Schweig, Cathy Moriarty, Max Gail, Lisa Jane Persky; ***D:*** Peter Medak; ***W:*** Finn Taylor, Jeffrey Brown; ***M:*** Randy Edelman. *PAR*

The Pony Express ½ **1925** Melodramatic western about an evil senator (Hart) who's out to establish his own empire. His scheme is thwarted by pony express rider Cortez. Based on the novel by Henry James Forman and Walter Woods. **67m/B VHS.** Ricardo Cortez, Al Hart, Betty Compson, Ernest Torrence, Wallace Beery, George Bancroft, Frank Lackteen; ***D:*** James Cruze; ***W:*** Walter Woods. *GPV*

Pony Express **1953** Buffalo Bill Cody and Wild Bill Hickok join forces to extend the Pony Express mail route west to California through rain and sleet, snow and hail. Far from a factual account but good for extending the myth of the Old West. **101m/C VHS, Beta.** Charlton Heston, Rhonda Fleming, Jan Sterling, Forrest Tucker; ***D:*** Jerry Hopper; ***C:*** Ray Rennahan. *PAR, BAR, HHE*

Pony Express Rider **1976 (G)** Young man with a mission joins up with the Pony Express hoping to bag the male responsible for killing his pa. The well-produced script boasts a bevy of veteran western character actors, all lending, solid, rugged performances. **100m/C VHS.** Stewart Peterson, Henry Wilcoxon, Buck Taylor, Maureen McCormick, Joan Caulfield, Ken Curtis, Slim Pickens, Dub Taylor, Jack Elam; ***D:*** Robert Totten. *TPI*

Pony Post ½ **1940** Standard horse opera has Brown running a pony express station where he battles Indians and typical villains. **59m/B VHS.** Johnny Mack Brown, Fuzzy Knight, Nell O'Day, Dorothy Short, Kermit Maynard, Lane Chandler; ***D:*** Ray Taylor; ***W:*** Sherman Lowe. *GPV*

Pool Hustlers ½ **1983** A romantic comedy about an amateur billiards whiz who finds love and successfully defeats the national champ. In Italian with English subtitles. **101m/C VHS, Beta.** *IT* Francesco Nuti, Guiliana de Sio, Marcello Loti; ***D:*** Maurizio Ponzi. *XVC, MED, INJ*

Pool Sharks ½ **1915** W.C. Fields' first film features the comedian's antics while playing a pool game to win the love of a woman. Silent. **10m/B VHS, Beta.** W.C. Fields. *FLI, GVV*

Poor Girl, A Ghost Story **1974** A young girl takes a job as a governess at an English mansion and is besieged by all manner of strange goings-on. **52m/C VHS, Beta.** *AU* Lynn Miller, Angela Thorne; ***D:*** Michael Apted. *PSM*

A Poor Little Rich Girl **1917** Mary Pickford received raves in this film, in which she portrayed Gwendolyn, with everything money could buy, except the attention of her family. Gwendolyn has a bizarre dream in which she sees a number of horrors and is tempted by death. Elaborate sets and special effects, as well as Pickford's delicate performance, make this one special. Organ score. **64m/B VHS, Beta.** Mary Pickford, Madeline Traverse, Charles Wellesley, Gladys Fairbanks; ***D:*** Maurice Tourneur. *CCB, VYY*

The Poor Little Rich Girl ½ **1936** A motherless rich girl wanders away from home and is "adopted" by a pair of struggling vaudevillians. With her help, they rise to the big time. Also available with "Heidi" on laserdisc. ♫Oh My Goodness; Buy a Bar of Barry's; Wash Your Neck With a Cake of Peck's; Military Man; When I'm with You; But Definitely; You've Gotta Eat Your Spinach, Baby. **79m/B VHS, Beta.** Shirley Temple, Jack Haley, Alice Faye, Gloria Stuart, Michael Whalen, Sara Haden, Jane Darwell; ***D:*** Irving Cummings. *FOX*

Poor Little Rich Girl: The Barbara Hutton Story ½ **1987** Bio-drama of the one-time richest woman in America, Woolworth heiress Hutton (Fawcett), and her extravagant lifestyle. She married seven times (including actor Cary Grant) until falling into self-destructive alcohol and drug addictions. Lavishly presented but superficial. Based on the book by C. David Heymann. Originally a two-part television movie. **98m/C VHS.** Farrah Fawcett, Bruce Davison, Kevin McCarthy, Burl Ives, James Read, Stephane Audran, Anne Francis, David Ackroyd, Tony Peck, Zoe

Wanamaker, Amadeus August; *D:* Charles Jarrott; *W:* Dennis Turner; *M:* Richard Rodney Bennett. *LIV*

Poor Pretty Eddie ½ **1973 (R)** A young black singer gets waylaid and taken in by a twisted white Southern clan. An incredibly sleazy movie which boasts Shelly Winters performing a strip act. Also on video as "Black Vengeance," "Redneck County," and "Heartbreak Motel." **90m/C Beta.** Leslie Uggams, Shelley Winters, Michael Christian, Ted Cassidy, Slim Pickens, Dub Taylor; *D:* Richard Robinson. *MRV*

Poor White Trash ½ *Bayou* **1957** An architect arrives in bayou country with plans to design a new building. He meets with resistance from the locals but falls for the sensual daughter of one of his staunchest detractors. **83m/B VHS, Beta.** Peter Graves, Lita Milan, Douglas Fowley, Timothy Carey, Jonathan Haze; *D:* Harold Daniels. *NO*

Poor White Trash 2 *Scum of the Earth* **1975 (R)** A young couple, vacationing in Louisiana's bayou country, are introduced to an unusual brand of southern hospitality by the eponymous group of locals. **90m/C VHS, Beta.** Gene Ross, Ann Stafford, Norma Moore, Camilla Carr; *D:* S.F. Brownrigg. *TPV*

Pop Always Pays **1940** A father gets in a jam when he has to make good on a bet with his daughter's boyfriend. **67m/B VHS, Beta.** Walter Catlett, Dennis O'Keefe, Leon Errol, Adele Pearce; *D:* Leslie Goodwins. *MLB*

Pop Goes the Cork **1922** Three films by the man Chaplin referred to as his "professor," Max Linder: "Be My Wife," "Seven Years Bad Luck," and "The Three Must-Get-Theres." Linder was the foremost film comedian in early twentieth-century France, and made these three films during a stay in America. **87m/B VHS, Beta.** Max Linder. *CCB*

Popcorn **1989 (R)** A killer stalks a movie audience who is unaware that his crimes are paralleling those in the very film they are watching. **93m/C VHS, LV, 8mm.** Jill Schoelen, Tom Villard, Dee Wallace Stone, Derek Rydell, Elliott Hurst, Kelly Jo Minter, Malcolm Danare, Ray Walston, Tony Roberts; *D:* Mark Herrier; *W:* Alan Ormsby. *COL*

Pope John Paul II **1984** A made-for-television biography of the Pontiff, from childhood to world eminence. **150m/C VHS, Beta.** Albert Finney, Michael Crompton, Nigel Hawthorne, John McEnery, Brian Cox; *D:* Herbert Wise. *PSM, IGP*

The Pope Must Diet ½ *The Pope Must Die* **1991 (R)** Coltrane stars as a misfit who accidentally becomes Pope Dave I. Living up to the benevolence suggested by his title, Pope Dave proposes to use Vatican money to create a children's fund. But there are those in the organization who have different, less noble plans for the cash, and soon Dave finds himself the target of a mob hit. Frantic comedy caused a stir with its original title "The Pope Must Die," with many newspapers refusing to run ads for the film. This, coupled with lukewarm critical reviews, led to a very brief stint at the box office. **87m/C VHS, Beta, LV.** *GB* Robbie Coltrane, Alex Rocco, Beverly D'Angelo, Herbert Lom, Paul Bartel, Salvatore Cascio, Balthazar Getty; *D:* Peter Richardson; *M:* Anne Dudley. *MED, VTR*

The Pope of Greenwich Village ½ **1984 (R)** A film about two Italian-American cousins who struggle to escape the trap of poverty in New York's Greenwich Village. When a small crime goes wrong in a big way, the two must learn about deception and loyalty. Mostly character study; Page is exceptional. Inferior re-run of the "Mean Streets" idea. **122m/C VHS, Beta, LV.** Eric Roberts, Mickey Rourke, Daryl Hannah, Geraldine Page, Tony Musante, M. Emmet Walsh, Kenneth McMillan, Burt Young; *D:* Stuart Rosenberg; *W:* Vincent Patrick; *C:* John Bailey; *M:* Dave Grusin. Nominations: Academy Awards '84: Best Supporting Actress (Page). *CCB, MGM*

Popeye **1980 (PG)** The cartoon sailor brought to life is on a search to find his long-lost father. Along the way, he meets Olive Oyl and adopts little Sweet Pea. Williams accomplishes the near-impossible feat of physically resembling the title character, and the whole movie does accomplish the maker's stated goal of "looking like a comic strip," but it isn't anywhere near as funny as it should be. **114m/C VHS, Beta, LV.** Robin Williams, Shelley Duvall, Ray Walston, Paul Dooley, Bill Irwin, Paul Smith, Linda Hunt, Richard Libertini; *D:* Robert Altman; *W:* Jules Feiffer; *M:* Harry Nilsson. *PAR*

Popi **1969 (G)** Arkin is the heart and soul of this poignant charmer in his role as a Puerto Rican immigrant hell-bent on securing a better life outside the ghetto for his two sons. His zany efforts culminate in one outrageous scheme to set them adrift off the Florida coast in hopes they will be rescued and raised by a wealthy family. Far fetched, but ultimately heartwarming. **115m/C VHS, Beta.** Alan Arkin, Rita Moreno, Miguel Alejandro, Ruben Figueroa; *D:* Arthur Hiller. *NO*

The Poppy Is Also a Flower ½ *Poppies Are Also Flowers; Opium Connection* **1966 (PG)** A star-laden, antidrug drama produced by the United Nations. Filmed on location in Iran, Monaco, and Italy. Based on a drug trade thriller by Ian Fleming that explains how poppies, converted into heroin, are brought into the United States. Made for television. **100m/C VHS, Beta.** E.G. Marshall, Trevor Howard, Gilbert Roland, Eli Wallach, Marcello Mastroianni, Angie Dickinson, Rita Hayworth, Yul Brynner, Trini Lopez, Bessie Love; *D:* Terence Young. *NO*

Porcile *Pigsty* **1969** Pasolini intertwines the story of a soldier cannibal living in a medieval age with the son of an ex-Nazi industrialist in present day Germany. Both the soldier and the young German (who prefers pigs to his fiance) become sacrificial victims of their differing societies. A grotesque fable on Pasolini's hatred of middle class mores and the 20th century. In Italian with English subtitles. **90m/C VHS, LV.** *IT* Pierre Clementi, Franco Citti, Jean-Pierre Leaud, Anna Wiazemsky, Ugo Tognazzi, Alberto Lionello; *D:* Pier Paolo Pasolini; *W:* Pier Paolo Pasolini; *C:* Tonino Delli Colli. *WBF*

Pork Chop Hill **1959** A powerful, hard-hitting account of the last hours of the Korean War. Peck is totally believable as the man ordered to hold his ground against the hopeless onslaught of Chinese Communist hordes. A chilling, stark look in the face of a no-win situation. Top notch cast and masterful directing. **97m/B VHS, Beta, LV.** Gregory Peck, Harry Guardino, Rip Torn, George Peppard, James Edwards, Bob Steele, Woody Strode, Robert (Bobby) Blake, Martin Landau, Norman Fell, Bert Remsen; *D:* Lewis Milestone; *C:* Sam Leavitt. *MGM*

Porky's ½ **1982 (R)** Investigation of teen horniness set in South Florida during the fab '50s. Irreverent comedy follows the misadventures of six youths imprisoned in Angel Beach High School who share a common interest: girls. Their main barrier to sexual success: the no-touch babes they lust after and the incredibly stupid adults who run the world. Fairly dumb and tasteless with occasional big laughs that earned mega bucks at the drive-in and created perceived popular outcry for more porky: "Porky's II: The Next Day" (1983) and "Porky's Revenge" (1985). **94m/C VHS, Beta, LV.** *CA* Dan Monahan, Wyatt Knight, Scott Colomby, Tony Ganios, Mark Herrier, Cyril O'Reilly, Roger Wilson, Bob (Benjamin) Clark, Kim Cattrall, Kaki Hunter; *D:* Bob (Benjamin) Clark; *W:* Bob (Benjamin) Clark. *FXV, FOX*

Porky's 2: The Next Day **1983 (R)** More tame tomfoolery about teenage sex drives, Shakespeare, fat high school teachers, the Ku Klux Klan, and streaking in the Florida high school where it all began. Outright caricature shares the stage with juvenile humor, some of which may induce laughter. **100m/C VHS, Beta, LV.** *CA* Bill Wiley, Dan Monahan, Wyatt Knight, Cyril O'Reilly, Roger Wilson, Tony Ganios, Mark Herrier, Scott Colomby; *D:* Bob (Benjamin) Clark; *W:* Alan Ormsby, Bob (Benjamin) Clark. *FOX*

Porky's Revenge **1985 (R)** The Angel Beach High School students are out to get revenge against Porky who orders the school basketball coach to throw the championship game. The second of the "Porky's" sequels. **95m/C VHS, Beta, LV.** *CA* Dan Monahan, Wyatt Knight, Tony Ganios, Nancy Parsons, Chuck "Porky" Mitchell, Kaki Hunter, Kimberly Evenson, Scott Colomby; *D:* James Komack. *FOX*

The Pornographers **1966** Bizzare, black comedy focuses on a part-time porno filmmaker lusting after the daughter of the widow he lives with and trying to cope with his family, the world, and himself. A perversely fascinating exploration of contemporary Japanese society and the many facets of sexual emotion. In Japanese with English subtitles. **128m/B VHS.** *JP* Shoichi Ozawa, Massaomi Konda, Sumiko Sakamota, Haruo Tanaka, Keiko Sagowa; *D:* Shohei Imamura. *CVC, INJ, TPV*

Porridge *Doing Time* **1991** A British comedy inspired by the popular BBC situation comedy of the title, about a habitual criminal and convict who makes the most of his time in prison. **105m/C VHS.** *GB* Ronnie Barker, Fulton Mackay, Peter Vaughan, Julian Holloway, Geoffrey Bayldon; *D:* Dick Clement. *VCO*

Port Arthur ½ **1983** A sweeping Japanese film describing the Russo-Japanese Wars in the early 1900's. **140m/C VHS, Beta.** *JP VCD*

Port of Call **1948** Early Bergman drama about a seaman on the docks who falls for a troubled woman whose wild, unhappy past has earned her an unsavory reputation. The hopeful, upbeat tone seems incongruous with the grim harbor/slum setting. It's minor Bergman but the seeds of his trademark themes can be seen taking shape, making it a must-see for avid fans. In Swedish with English subtitles. **100m/B VHS, Beta.** *SW* Ivine-Christine Jonsson, Bengt Eklund, Erik Hell, Berta Hall, Mimi Nelson; *D:* Ingmar Bergman. *SUE, INJ, NLC*

The Port of Missing Girls **1938** A young woman implicated in a murder stows away on a freighter. There she becomes caught up in a waterfront world of pirates, smugglers and other assorted undesirables. **56m/B VHS, Beta, 8mm.** Harry Carey Sr., Judith Allen, Milburn Stone, Betty Compson; *D:* Karl Brown. *VYY*

Port of New York **1949** A narcotics gang is smuggling large quantities of drugs into New York. A government agent poses as a gang member in order to infiltrate the mob and get the goods on them. Brynner's film debut. **82m/B VHS, Beta.** Scott Brady, Yul Brynner, K.T. Stevens; *D:* Laslo Benedek. *NOS, VYY, DVT*

Portfolio **1988 (R)** Real-life models star in this gritty drama about rising to the top of the fashion heap. Music by Eurythmics, Fun Boy Three and others. **83m/C VHS, LV.** Paulina Porizkova, Julie Wolfe, Carol Alt, Kelly Emberg. *NO*

Portnoy's Complaint ½ **1972 (R)** Limp screen adaptation of Philip Roth's novel follows the frustrating experiences of a sexually obsessed young man as he relates them to his psychiatrist. **101m/C VHS, Beta.** Richard Benjamin, Karen Black, Lee Grant, Jeannie Berlin, Jill Clayburgh; *D:* Ernest Lehman; *W:* Ernest Lehman. *WAR*

The Portrait **1993** Longtime real-life friends Bacall and Peck on-screen together for the first time in 37 years prove they are still shining stars as they play aging parents to Peck's real-life daughter, Cecilia Peck. The younger Peck is an artist preparing for a exhibition and asks her parents to sit for a portrait. This is the pole around which their relationships and reconciliations swing in this emotional made-for-cable-tv drama based loosely on Tina Howe's 1983 off-Broadway play, "Painting Churches." **89m/C VHS, LV.** Lauren Bacall, Gregory Peck, Cecilia Peck, Paul McCrane, Joyce O'Connor, Donna Mitchell, Mitchell Laurance, William Prince, Augusta Dabney; *D:* Arthur Penn; *W:* Lynn Roth, Jack Darcus; *M:* Michael Conway Baker. *TTC, BTV*

Portrait in Terror ½ **1966** A master thief and a deranged artist plan a heist of a Titian painting in an oddball suspense piece. Not a great success, but atmospheric and weird. **81m/B VHS.** Patrick Magee, William Campbell, Anna Pavane; *D:* Jack Hill. *SMW*

Portrait of a Hitman 🦴 *Jim Buck* **1977** Aspiring painter leads a double life as a professional hitman. Ragged feature feels more abandoned than finished, as if most of the movie had been shot and then the money ran out. All leads turn in paycheck performances, no more. **85m/C VHS, Beta.** Jack Palance, Rod Steiger, Richard Roundtree, Bo Svenson, Ann Turkel; ***D:*** Allan A. Buckhantz. *NO*

Portrait of a Lady 🦴🦴½ **1967** A spirited young American woman is taken to England and insists on complete freedom to choose her own future and make her own choices. Based on the 1881 novel by Henry James. On 2 cassettes. **240m/C VHS.** *GB* Richard Chamberlain, Suzanne Neve, Edward Fox. *VCO, TVC*

Portrait of a Rebel: Margaret Sanger 🦴🦴½ **1982** TV docudrama about the struggle of Margaret Sanger to repeal the Comstock Act of 1912, which prohibited the distribution of birth control information. **96m/C VHS, Beta.** Bonnie Franklin, David Dukes, Milo O'Shea; ***D:*** Virgil W. Vogel. *TLF*

Portrait of a Showgirl 🦴🦴 **1982** Inexperienced showgirl learns the ropes of Las Vegas life from a veteran of the Vegas stages. Made for television. **100m/C VHS, Beta.** Lesley Ann Warren, Rita Moreno, Tony Curtis, Dianne Kay, Howard Morris; ***D:*** Steven Hilliard Stern. *PSM*

Portrait of a Stripper 🦴 **1979** A widowed mother works part-time as a stripper to support her son. Trouble arises when her father-in-law attempts to prove that she is an unfit mother. **100m/C VHS, Beta.** Lesley Ann Warren, Edward Herrmann, Vic Tayback, Sheree North; ***D:*** John Alonzo. *VES*

Portrait of a White Marriage 🦴🦴½ **1988** An extended made-for-cable comedy special revamping certain old "Mary Hartman, Mary Hartman" and "Fernwood 2-Night" conventions; a moronic talk show host moves his cheap show to his hometown of Hawkins Falls in order to boost the ratings. **81m/C VHS, Beta.** Martin Mull, Mary Kay Place, Fred Willard, Michael McKean, Harry Shearer, Jack Riley, Conchata Ferrell; ***D:*** Harry Shearer. *MCA*

Portrait of Grandpa Doc 🦴½ **1977** As a young artist prepares for his first one-man show, he struggles to complete a painting which he especially wants to have ready for the show—a portrait of his grandfather, who died seven years earlier. Well, okay. **28m/C VHS, Beta.** Melvyn Douglas, Bruce Davison, Barbara Rush, Anne Seymour, Keith Blanchard. *BFA, ECU*

Portrait of Jennie 🦴🦴🦴½ *Jennie; Tidal Wave* **1948** In this haunting, romantic fable, a struggling artist is inspired by and smitten with a strange and beautiful girl who he also suspects may be the spirit of a dead woman. A fine cast works wonders with what could have been a forgettable story. The last reel was tinted green in the original release with the last scene shot in technicolor. Oscar-winning special effects. **86m/B VHS, Beta, LV.** Joseph Cotten, Jennifer Jones, Cecil Kellaway, Ethel Barrymore, David Wayne, Lillian Gish, Henry Hull, Florence Bates, Felix Bressart, Anne Francis; ***D:*** William Dieterle. Academy Awards '48: Best Special Effects; Venice Film Festival '49: Best Actor (Cotten); Nominations: Academy Awards '48: Best Black and White Cinematography. *FOX*

Portrait of Teresa 🦴🦴🦴 **1979** Havana housewife has to balance motherhood, textile job, and cultural group activities without the cooperation of her husband. Vega skillfully portrays the lingering archaic attitudes and insulting assumptions that still confront post-revolution women. A fine eye for the revealing moments and movements of everyday life. In Spanish with English subtitles. **115m/C VHS.** Daisy Granados, Aldolfo Llaurado, Alina Sanchez, Alberto Molina; ***D:*** Pastor Vega. *NYF, FCT, INJ*

Portraits of a Killer 🦴🦴 **1995** Attorney Elaine Taylor (Grey) is getting all hot and bothered by her client—photographer George Kendell (Mandylor), who's suspected in the murders of five hookers. But the detective (Ironside) on the case thinks she's just asking for trouble. **93m/C VHS, LV.** Jennifer Grey, Costas Mandylor, Michael Ironside, Patricia Charbonneau, Kenneth Welsh, M. Emmet Walsh; ***D:*** Bill Corcoran. *LIV*

Posed For Murder 🦴🦴 **1989 (R)** A young centerfold is stalked by a psycho who wants her all for himself. **90m/C VHS, Beta.** Charlotte J. Helmkamp, Carl Fury, Rick Gianasi, Michael Merrins; ***D:*** Brian Thomas Jones. *ACA*

The Poseidon Adventure 🦴🦴½ **1972 (PG)** The cruise ship Poseidon is on its last voyage from New York to Athens on New Year's Eve when it is capsized by a tidal wave. The ten survivors struggle to escape the water-logged tomb. Oscar-winning special effects, such as Shelley Winters floating in a boiler room. Created an entirely new genre of film making—the big cast disaster flick. ♫The Morning After. **117m/C VHS, Beta, LV.** Gene Hackman, Ernest Borgnine, Shelley Winters, Red Buttons, Jack Albertson, Carol Lynley, Roddy McDowall; ***D:*** Ronald Neame; ***W:*** Wendell Mayes, Stirling Silliphant; ***M:*** John Williams. Academy Awards '72: Best Song ("The Morning After"), Best Visual Effects; Golden Globe Awards '73: Best Supporting Actress (Winters); Nominations: Academy Awards '72: Best Art Direction/Set Decoration, Best Cinematography, Best Costume Design, Best Film Editing, Best Sound, Best Supporting Actress (Winters), Best Original Score. *FOX*

Positive I.D. 🦴🦴 **1987 (R)** A troubled housewife learns that the man who raped her years before is getting released on parole. She devises a second persona for herself with which to entrap him and get her revenge. **96m/C VHS, Beta.** Stephanie Rascoe, John Davies, Steve Fromholz; ***D:*** Andy Anderson; ***W:*** Andy Anderson. *MCA*

The Positively True Adventures of the Alleged Texas Cheerleader-Murdering Mom 🦴🦴🦴½ **1993 (R)** Satirical melodrama about Texas housewife Wanda Holloway (Hunter), accused of hiring a hitman to murder the mother of her daughter's chief cheerleading rival. She figures the girl will be so distraught that her own daughter can easily replace her. Ruthless and hilarious, this fact-based made-for-cable movie goes way over the top in satirizing suburban life-style excess and media overkill. Hunter, complete with whiney Texas twang, is perfect in her role as self-absorbed Wanda and Bridges is great as her loopy ex-brother-in-law and partner in planned homicide. A riot compared to the usual dramatic movies served up by the networks. **99m/C VHS.** Holly Hunter, Beau Bridges, Swoosie Kurtz, Greg Henry, Matt Frewer, Frankie Ingrassia, Elizabeth Ruscio, Megan Berwick; ***D:*** Michael Ritchie; ***W:*** Jane Anderson; ***M:*** Lucy Simon. National Academy of Cable Programming ACE Awards '93: Best Movie/Miniseries, Best Actress (Hunter). *HBO, FCT, BTV*

Posse 🦴🦴🦴 **1975 (PG)** There's a hidden agenda, fueled by political ambition, in a lawman's (Douglas) dauntless pursuit of an escaped bandit (Dern). An interesting contrast between the evil of corrupt politics and the honesty of traditional lawlessness. Well performed, well photographed, and almost insightful. **94m/C VHS, Beta, LV.** Kirk Douglas, Bruce Dern, James Stacy, Bo Hopkins, Luke Askew, David Canary, Alfonso Arau, Kate Woodville, Mark Roberts; ***D:*** Kirk Douglas; ***W:*** William Roberts; ***M:*** Maurice Jarre. *PAR*

Posse 🦴🦴🦴 **1993 (R)** Big, brawny western shot with MTV in mind that tells the tale in part of how more than 8,000 black cowboys helped tame the American frontier. Or, as the advertising put it, "The untold story of the wild West." Or, spaghetti western meets blaxploitation meets the magnificent seven meets the L.A. riots, with characters actually saying, "No justice, no peace" and "Can't we all get along." However categorized, the intent is to show a side of Americana seldom seen, a goal realized. Strode, perhaps the greatest black Western star, appears at both the beginning and ending, while several other veteran black performers, including Russell, appear in cameos. Hunky Van Peebles is the leader of the usual misfits in the "Dirty Dozen" tradition, infantry deserters holding a load of gold. Between them and freedom is a gang of goons led by Zane. Lots of flash and dash, but lacking soul. **113m/C VHS, LV.** Mario Van Peebles, Stephen Baldwin, Charles Lane, Tiny Lister, Big Daddy Kane, Billy Zane, Blair Underwood, Tone Loc, Salli Richardson, Reginald Hudlin, Richard Edson, Reginald Vel Johnson, Warrington Hudlin; ***Cameos:*** Melvin Van Peebles, Pam Grier, Isaac Hayes, Robert Hooks, Richard Jordan, Paul Bartel, Nipsey Russell, Woody Strode, Aaron Neville, Stephen J. Cannell; ***D:*** Mario Van Peebles; ***W:*** Sy Richardson, Dario Scardapane; ***M:*** Michel Colombier. *PGV, FCT*

Possessed 🦴🦴½ **1931** A poor factory girl becomes a wealthy Park Avenue sophisticate when she falls in love with a rich lawyer who wants to be governor. Not to be confused with Crawford's 1947 movie of the same name, but worth a look. Gable and Crawford make a great couple! **77m/B VHS, Beta.** Joan Crawford, Clark Gable, Wallace Ford, Richard "Skeets" Gallagher, John Miljan; ***D:*** Clarence Brown. *MGM*

The Possessed 🦴🦴🦴 **1947** Crawford is at her melodramatic best as a crazed gal who can't find happiness with either hunk Heflin or bland Massey. First film for Brooks. From the story "One Man's Secret" by Rita Weiman. **109m/B VHS, LV.** Joan Crawford, Van Heflin, Raymond Massey, Geraldine Brooks, Stanley Ridges, John Ridgely, Nana Bryant, Moroni Olsen; ***D:*** Curtis Bernhardt; ***C:*** Joseph Valentine. Nominations: Academy Awards '47: Best Actress (Crawford). *MGM*

The Possessed 🦴½ **1977 (PG-13)** Farentino is a priest who loses his faith, but regains it after an apparently fatal auto accident. Hackett is the headmistress of a private girls' school which is in need of an exorcist, since one of her student's appears to be possessed, and Farentino seems just the man for the job. Fairly tame, since originally made for TV. **75m/C VHS, Beta.** James Farentino, Joan Hackett, Diana Scarwid, Claudette Nevins, Eugene Roche, Ann Dusenberry, Dinah Manoff, P.J. Soles; ***D:*** Jerry Thorpe. *UNI*

Possessed by the Night 🦴🦴 **1993 (R)** Kinky sex games ensue between a married writer and a sexy other woman thanks to a mysterious fetish object. Unrated version also available. **84m/C VHS, LV.** Ted Prior, Shannon Tweed, Sandahl Bergman, Chad McQueen, Henry Silva; ***D:*** Fred Olen Ray. *COL*

Possession 🦴 **1981 (R)** Returned from a long mission, a secret agent notices that his wife is acting very strangely. She's about to give birth to a manifestation of the evil within her! Gory, hysterical, over-intellectual and often unintelligible. Originally shown in a longer version in Europe. **97m/C VHS, Beta.** *FR GE* Isabelle Adjani, Sam Neill, Heinz Bennent, Margit Carstensen, Shaun Lawtor; ***D:*** Andrzej Zulawski. Cesar Awards '82: Best Actress (Adjani); Nominations: Cannes Film Festival '81: Best Film. *LIV, VES*

The Possession of Joel Delaney 🦴🦴½ **1972 (R)** Blend of occult horror and commentary on social mores works for the most part, but some viewers may be put off by the low production values and spottiness of the script. MacLaine is a wealthy divorcee who must deal with the mysterious transformations affecting her brother. Skeptical at first, she begins to suspect he is the victim of Caribbean voodoo. **105m/C VHS.** Shirley MacLaine, Perry King, Michael Hordern, David Elliott, Robert Burr; ***D:*** Waris Hussein. *PAR*

Possession: Until Death Do You Part 🦴 **1990** When one man's attraction for a beautiful young woman becomes an obsession, a bizarre series of inexplicable events unravels a terrifying account of passion and revenge. **93m/C VHS.** Monica Marko, John R. Johnston, Sharlene Martin, Cat Williamson; ***D:*** Michael Mazo, Lloyd A. Simanol. *NO*

Postal Inspector 🦴🦴 **1936** An extraordinary tale of a postal inspector's life. Crime, romance, and natural disaster all overtake this civil servant. Catch the song "Let's Have Bluebirds On All Our Wallpaper." **58m/B VHS.** Carlos Cortez, Patricia Ellis, Michael Loring, Bela Lugosi, David Oliver, Wallis Clark; ***D:*** Otto Brower. *SNC, LSV*

Postcards from America 🦴🦴 **1995 (R)** Traces the non-artistic aspects of the life of writer/artist David Wojnarowicz, who died of AIDS. Neophyte McLean concentrates on troubled childhood with an abusive father and teen years spent as a street hustler years. Choppy narrative uses little of

Wojnarowicz's dialogue, save the voice-over narration by the lead character. Based on two semi-autobiographical novels by the artist. **93m/C VHS.** James Lyons, Michael Tighe, Olmo Tighe, Michael Imperioli, Michael Ringer, Maggie Low; ***D:*** Steve McLean; ***W:*** Steve McLean; ***C:*** Ellen Kuras; ***M:*** Stephen Endelman. *NYR*

Postcards from the Edge 🦴🦴🦴½ **1990 (R)** Fisher adapted her best-selling novel, tamed and tempered, for the big screen with a tour-de-force of talent. Streep very fine as a delightfully harried actress struggling with her career, her drug dependence, and her competitive, overwhelming show-biz mother. Autobiographical script is bitingly clever and filled with refreshingly witty dialogue. Lots of cameos by Hollywood's hippest. **101m/C VHS, Beta, LV, 8mm.** Meryl Streep, Shirley MacLaine, Dennis Quaid, Gene Hackman, Richard Dreyfuss, Rob Reiner, Mary Wickes, Conrad Bain, Annette Bening, Michael Ontkean, Dana Ivey; ***Cameos:*** Robin Bartlett, Anthony Heald, Oliver Platt, CCH Pounder; ***D:*** Mike Nichols; ***W:*** Carrie Fisher; ***C:*** Michael Ballhaus. Nominations: Academy Awards '90: Best Actress (Streep), Best Song ("I'm Checkin' Out"). *COL, FCT*

The Postman 🦴🦴🦴½ *Il Postino* **1994 (PG)** Bittersweet, charming film about Mario (Troisi), a shy villager who winds up the personal postman of poet Pablo Neruda (Noiret), who is exiled from his beloved Chile in 1952, granted asylum by the Italian government, and who finds himself living in the tiny Italian community of Isla Negra. The tongue-tied Mario has fallen in love with barmaid Beatrice (Cucinotta) and asks the poet's help in wooing the dark-eyed beauty, striking up an unlikely friendship with the worldly Neruda. Based on the novel "Burning Patience" by Antonio Skarmeta. Italian with subtitles. Troisi, a beloved comic actor in his native Italy, was gravely ill, needing a heart transplant, during the making of the film (all-too apparent from his gaunt appearance) and died the day after filming was completed. **115m/C VHS.** *IT* Massimo Troisi, Philippe Noiret, Maria Grazia Cucinotta, Linda Moretti, Renato Scarpa, Anna Buonaiuto, Mariana Rigillo; ***D:*** Michael Radford; ***W:*** Massimo Troisi, Michael Radford, Furio Scarpelli, Anna Pavignano, Giacomo Scarpelli; ***C:*** Franco Di Giacomo; ***M:*** Luis Bacalov. Academy Awards '95: Original Dramatic Score; British Academy Awards '95: Best Director (Radford), Best Foreign Film, Best Score; Nominations: Academy Awards '95: Best Actor (Troisi), Best Adapted Screenplay, Best Director (Radford), Best Picture; British Academy Awards '95: Best Actor (Troisi), Best Adapted Screenplay; Directors Guild of America Awards '95: Best Director (Radford); Screen Actors Guild Award '95: Best Actor (Troisi). *TOU*

The Postman Always Rings Twice 🦴🦴🦴½ **1946** Even without the brutal sexuality of the James M. Cain novel, Garfield and Turner sizzle as the lust-laden lovers in this lurid tale of fatal attraction. Garfield steals the show as the streetwise drifter who blows into town and lights a fire in Turner. As their affair steams up the two conspire to do away with her husband and circumstances begin to spin out of control. Tense and compelling. A classic. **113m/B VHS, Beta, LV.** Lana Turner, John Garfield, Cecil Kellaway, Hume Cronyn, Leon Ames, Audrey Totter, Alan Reed; ***D:*** Tay Garnett; ***M:*** George Bassman. *MGM*

The Postman Always Rings Twice 🦴🦴 **1981 (R)** It must be true because he's ringing again in Mamet's version of James M. Cain's depression-era novel. This time Nicholson plays the drifter and Lange the amoral wife with an aged husband. Truer to the original story than the 1946 movie in its use of brutal sex scenes, it nevertheless lacks the power of the original. Nicholson works well in this time era and Lange adds depth and realism to the character of Cora. But in the end it remains dreary and easily forgettable. **123m/C VHS, Beta, LV.** Jack Nicholson, Jessica Lange, John Colicos, Anjelica Huston, Michael Lerner, John P. Ryan, Christopher Lloyd; ***D:*** Bob Rafelson; ***W:*** David Mamet; ***C:*** Sven Nykvist. *FOX, WAR*

Postmark for Danger 🦴🦴½ *Portrait of Alison* **1956** Detectives do their best to smash a diamond smuggling ring that operates between Britain and the U.S. Along the way a number of people are killed. **84m/B VHS, Beta.** *GB* Terry Moore, Robert Beatty, William Sylvester, Josephine Griffin, Geoffrey Keen, Henry Oscar; ***D:*** Guy Green. *SNC*

Postmark for Danger/Quicksand 🦴🦴 **1956** A "film noire" double feature. In "Postmark for Danger," a young actress returns from the dead to find a criminal, while in "Quicksand," a mechanic becomes indebted to the mob when he borrows extra money for a date. **155m/B VHS, Beta.** *GB* Terry Moore, Robert Beatty, Mickey Rooney, Jeanne Cagney, Peter Lorre; ***D:*** Guy Green. *SNC*

Pot O' Gold 🦴🦴 *The Golden Hour* **1941** Stewart plays a wealthy young man who signs on with a struggling band. He convinces his uncle, who has a radio program, to let the band perform during a radio giveaway show he has concocted. Slight comedy, Stewart notwithstanding. **87m/B VHS, Beta.** Paulette Goddard, James Stewart, Charles Winninger, Horace Heidt, Art Carney; ***D:*** George Marshall. *NOS, CCB, VYY*

Pot, Parents, and Police 🦴 **1971** A 13-year-old boy goes crazy when his dog dies and soon gets in with a hippie crowd, drops acid, and gets in trouble with the cops. **m/C VHS.** Phillip Pine, Robert Mantell, Madelyn Keen; ***D:*** Phillip Pine; ***W:*** Phillip Pine. *SMW, MOV, TPV*

Pound Puppies and the Legend of Big Paw **1988** The Pound Puppies, known for breaking dogs out of pounds and delivering them to safe and secure homes, are featured in their first full-length musical (and merchandising effort). Fifties music. **76m/C VHS.** ***D:*** Pierre de Celles; ***W:*** Jim Carlson; ***V:*** Nancy Cartwright, George Rose, B.J. Ward, Ruth Buzzi, Brennan Howard. *FHE, WTA*

Pouvoir Intime 🦴🦴½ **1987 (PG-13)** What happens when robbers of an armored car lock the guard in the vehicle, and he decides to fight back? This film offers one possible scenario. Available in dubbed or subtitled versions. **86m/C VHS.** *FR* Marie Tifo, Pierre Curzi, Yvan Ponton, Jaques Lussier; ***D:*** Yves Simoneau. *TPV*

P.O.W. Deathcamp 🦴🦴 **1989** A combat unit is captured and tortured by the Vietcong in this typical Vietnam story. **92m/C VHS.** Charles Black, Bill Balbridge, Rey Malonzo; ***D:*** Jett C. Espirtu. *ATL*

The P.O.W. Escape 🦴½ *Behind Enemy Lines* **1986 (R)** The adventures of a surly American commander captured as a POW during the final days of the Vietnam War. **90m/C VHS, Beta, LV.** David Carradine, Mako, Charles R. Floyd, Steve James; ***D:*** Gideon Amir; ***W:*** Malcolm Barbour, James Bruner, Jeremy Lipp, John Langley. *VTR*

Powaqqatsi: Life in Transformation 🦴🦴🦴½ **1988 (G)** Director Reggio's follow-up to "Koyaanisqatsi" doesn't pack the wallop of its predecessor. Still, the cinematography is magnificent and the music of Philip Glass is exquisitely hypnotic as we are taken on a spellbinding video collage of various third world countries and see the price they've paid in the name of progress. Part 2 of a planned trilogy. **95m/C VHS, Beta.** ***D:*** Godfrey Reggio; ***M:*** Philip Glass. *CAN*

Powder 🦴🦴 **1995 (PG-13)** An electromagnetic albino with an I.Q. off the charts is discovered living in his grandparents' cellar and brought to live in a school for troubled teens. Despite harrassment from the crude locals, Powder (Flanery) manages to exude compassion and electricity all over the place with the help of sensitive school director Steenbergen and wacky science teacher Goldblum. Hyper-sentimentality, convoluted and contradictory writing, absurd messianic overtones, and a cop-out climax barely scratch the surface of film's problems. Revelations of Salva's criminal conviction for child molestation cast some scenes in a disturbing light and caused major headaches for Disney's publicity department. **111m/C VHS.** Sean Patrick Flanery, Mary Steenburgen, Lance Henriksen, Jeff Goldblum, Brandon Smith, Bradford Tatum, Susan Tyrrell, Missy Crider, Ray Wise, Esteban Louis Powell; ***D:*** Victor Salva; ***W:*** Victor Salva; ***C:*** Jerzy Zielinski; ***M:*** Jerry Goldsmith. Nominations: MTV Movie Awards '96: Breakthrough Performance (Flanery). *TOU*

Powder Keg 🦴🦴 **1970** Railroad company hires a rowdy team of investigators to retrieve a hijacked train. Action never quits. The idea for the television pilot "The Bearcats" came from this movie. **93m/C VHS, Beta.** Rod Taylor, Dennis Cole, Michael Ansara, Fernando Lamas, Tisha Sterling; ***D:*** Douglas Heyes. *SIM, WOV*

Powdersmoke Range 🦴½ **1935** Crooked frontier politician plots to steal valuable ranch property. The new owners, however, have other ideas. First in "The Three Mesquiteer" series. **71m/B VHS, Beta.** Harry Carey Sr., Hoot Gibson, Tom Tyler, Guinn "Big Boy" Williams, Bob Steele, Sam Hardy, Patricia "Boots" Mallory, Franklyn Farnum, William Desmond, William Farnum, Buzz Barton, Wally Wales, Art Mix, Buffalo Bill Jr., Buddy Roosevelt; ***D:*** Wallace Fox. *MED, RXM*

Power 🦴🦴½ **1928** Two dam-building construction workers vie with each other for the local girls. Silent. **60m/B VHS, Beta.** William Boyd, Alan Hale, Carole Lombard, Joan Bennett; ***D:*** Howard Higgin. *FCT, GPV, GVV*

Power 🦴🦴½ *Jew Suss* **1934** A Jewish ghetto inhabitant in 18th-century Wurtemburg works his way out of the gutter and into some authority by pleasing the whims of an evil duke. Based on the novel by Leon Fuechtwangler. **105m/B VHS.** *GB* Conrad Veidt, Benita Hume, Frank Vosper, Cedric Hardwicke, Gerald du Maurier, Pamela Ostrer, Joan Maude, Paul Graetz, Mary Clare, Percy Parsons, Dennis Hoey, Gibb McLaughlin, Francis L. Sullivan; ***D:*** Lothar Mendes. *DVT*

The Power 🦴½ **1980 (R)** An ancient clay idol that was created by the Aztecs and possesses incredible destructive power is unleashed on modern man. **87m/C VHS.** Warren Lincoln, Susan Stokey, Lisa Erickson, Jeffrey Obrow; ***D:*** Stephen Carpenter; ***W:*** Stephen Carpenter, John Penney. *LIV, VES*

Power 🦴🦴½ **1986 (R)** A study of corporate manipulations. Gere plays a ruthless media consultant working for politicians. Fine cast can't find the energy needed to make this great, but it's still interesting. Lumet did better with same material in "Network." **111m/C VHS, Beta, LV.** Richard Gere, Julie Christie, E.G. Marshall, Gene Hackman, Beatrice Straight, Kate Capshaw, Denzel Washington, Fritz Weaver, Michael Learned, E. Katherine Kerr, Polly Rowles, Matt Salinger, J.T. Walsh; ***D:*** Sidney Lumet; ***W:*** David Himmelstein; ***M:*** Cy Coleman. *ORI, WAR*

Power of Attorney 🦴🦴 **1994 (R)** Ambitious lawyer Paul Dell (Koteas) is forced to defend Mafia don Joseph Scassi (Aiello) against federal charges of murder and extortion. **97m/C VHS.** Danny Aiello, Elias Koteas, Nina Siemaszko, Rae Dawn Chong; ***D:*** Howard Himelstein; ***W:*** George Erschbamer, Jeff Barmash; ***M:*** Hal Beckett. *TTC*

The Power of One 🦴🦴 **1992 (PG-13)** Good cast is generally wasted in liberal white look at apartheid. Set in South Africa during the 1940s, P.K. is a white orphan of British descent who is sent to a boarding school run by Afrikaaners (South Africans of German descent). Humiliated and bullied, particularly when England and Germany go to war, P.K. is befriended by a German pianist and a black boxing coach who teach him to box and stand up for his rights. Preachy and filled with stereotypes. Based on the novel by Bryce Courtenay. **126m/C VHS, LV.** Stephen Dorff, Armin Mueller-Stahl, Morgan Freeman, John Gielgud, Fay Masterson, Marius Weyers, Tracy Brooks Swope, John Osborne, Daniel Craig, Dominic Walker, Alois Mayo, Ian Roberts, Maria Marais; ***D:*** John G. Avildsen; ***W:*** Robert Mark Kamen. *WAR*

The Power of the Ninjitsu 🦴 **1988** A young man inherits the leadership of a martial arts crime gang, the Scorpions, but the elder members muscle him out of his place. He returns for revenge and has the old ones running scared. Power to the Ninjitsu! **90m/C VHS, Beta.** Britton Lee, Adam Frank, Peter Ujaer; ***D:*** Joseph Lai. *IME*

Power, Passion & Murder 🦴½ **1983** A young, glamorous movie star has an affair with a married man which begins the end of her career in 1930s Hollywood. **104m/C VHS, Beta, LV.** Michelle Pfeiffer, Darren McGavin, Stella Stevens; ***D:*** Paul Bogart, Leon Ichaso. *VMK, IME, HHE*

Power Play 🦴½ *Operation Overthrow* **1981** Young army colonel from a small European country joins forces with rebels to overthrow the government. After the coup, the group discovers that in their midst is a traitor. So who is it? Suspense never builds adequately. **95m/C VHS, Beta.** *CA GB* Peter O'Toole, David Hemmings, Donald Pleasence, Barry Morse; ***D:*** Martyn Burke; ***W:*** Martyn Burke. *MED*

The Power Within 🦴½ **1979** An electrified stuntman finds he can send electrical shocks from his hands and becomes the victim of a kidnapping plot. **90m/C VHS, Beta.** Eric (Hans Gudegast) Braeden, David Hedison, Susan Howard, Art Hindle; ***D:*** John Llewellyn Moxey. *PSM*

The Power Within 🦴🦴½ **1995 (PG-13)** Evil Raymond Vonn has stolen an ancient ring of power but to acquire its complete strength he needs to find a second, matching ring. This is in the possession of teenaged Stan Dryer (Roberts), who must discover the ring's power if he expects to defeat Vonn. **97m/C VHS.** Ted Jan Roberts, Karen Valentine, Keith Coogan, John O'Hurley, Gary Morgan, Sean Fitzgerald; ***D:*** Art Camacho; ***W:*** Susan Bowen, Jacobsen Hart; ***M:*** Jim Halfpenny. *PMH*

Powwow Highway 🦴🦴🦴½ **1989 (R)** Remarkably fine performances in this unusual, thought-provoking, poorly-titled foray into the plight of Native Americans. Farmer shines as the unassuming, amiable Cheyenne traveling to New Mexico in a beat-up Chevy with his Indian activist buddy, passionately portrayed by Martinez. On the journey they are constantly confronted with the tragedy of life on a reservation. A sobering look at government injustice and the lingering spirit of a people lost inside their homeland. **105m/C VHS, Beta.** Gary Farmer, A. Martinez, Amanda Wyss, Rene Handren-Seals, Graham Greene; ***D:*** Joanelle Romero, Jonathan Wacks; ***M:*** Barry Goldberg. Sundance Film Festival '89: Filmmakers Trophy. *WAR, OM*

The Practice of Love 🦴🦴 **1984** A woman journalist's investigation of a murder casts suspicion on her two male lovers. The film raises the question of whether love is even possible in a world dominated by men's struggles for power. In German with English subtitles. **90m/C VHS.** *GE* ***D:*** Valie Export. *FCT, MOV*

Prairie Badmen 🦴½ **1946** Outlaws are after a treasure map in the possession of the owner of a medicine show. It's up to our hero to stop them. One of the "Billy Carson" western series. **55m/B VHS, Beta.** Buster Crabbe. *VCN*

The Prairie King 🦴½ **1927** Will grants three people the same gold mine but stipulates only one may own it. Silent quandary. **58m/B VHS, Beta.** Hoot Gibson, Barbara Worth, Charles Sellon, Albert Priscoe. *GPV*

Prairie Moon 🦴½ **1938** Autry becomes the guardian of three tough kids from Chicago after they inherit a ranch. The kids help Autry round up a gang of rustlers. **58m/B VHS, Beta.** Gene Autry, Smiley Burnette. *CCB, VCN, DVT*

Prairie Pals 🦴½ **1942** Deputies go undercover to rescue a kidnapped scientist. **60m/B VHS, Beta.** William Boyd, Lee Powell, Art Davis, Charles "Blackie" King, John Merton, Kermit Maynard, Al "Fuzzy" St. John; ***D:*** Sam Newfield. *GPV, VCN*

The Prairie Pirate 🦴🦴½ **1925** Carey is the western hero tracking down the dirty dogs who murdered his sister. Fast-paced. **59m/B VHS.** Harry Carey Sr., Lloyd Whitlock, Jean Dumas, Trilby Clark; ***D:*** Edmund Mortimer. *GPV*

Prancer 🦴🦴 **1989 (G)** An eight-year-old girl whose mother has recently died thinks an injured reindeer she has found belongs to Santa. She lovingly nurses him back to health. Harmless family entertainment. **102m/C VHS, Beta, LV, 8mm.** Sam Elliott, Rebecca Harrell, Cloris Leachman, Rutanya Alda, John Joseph Duda, Abe Vigoda, Michael Constantine, Ariana Richards, Mark Rolston; ***D:*** John Hancock; ***M:*** Maurice Jarre. *COL, ORI, FCT*

Pray for Death 🦴🦴 **1985 (R)** When a mild-mannered Japanese family is victimized by a crime syndicate in L.A., a master ninja comes to the rescue. Higher quality production than most ninja adventures. **93m/C VHS, Beta.** James Booth, Robert Ito, Sho Kosugi, Shane Kosugi, Kane Kosugi, Donna Kei Benz; ***D:*** Gordon Hessler; ***W:*** James Booth. *NO*

Pray for the Wildcats 🦴½ **1974** Three advertising executives' promotional trip from (or to?) Hell. Anything to please a client. **96m/C VHS, Beta.** Andy Griffith, William Shatner, Angie Dickinson, Janet Margolin, Marjoe Gortner, Lorraine Gary; ***D:*** Robert Lewis. *REP*

Pray TV 🦴🦴 *KGOD* **1980 (PG)** A sly con man turns a failing television station into a profitable one when the station starts to broadcast around-the-clock religious programming. Made for television. **92m/C VHS, Beta, LV.** Dabney Coleman, Archie Hahn, Joyce Jameson, Nancy Morgan, Roger E. Mosley, Marcia Wallace; ***D:*** Rick Friedberg; ***W:*** Nick Castle. *VES*

Pray TV 🦴🦴 **1982** A television movie expose of broadcast religion in which a young preacher chooses between orthodox religion and lots of money. Not as cutting an indictment as it could have been. **100m/C VHS, Beta.** John Ritter, Ned Beatty, Madolyn Smith, Richard Kiley, Louise Latham, Jonathan Prince, Michael Currie, Lois Areno; ***D:*** Robert Markowitz. *SUE*

A Prayer for Katarina Horovitzova 🦴🦴🦴½ **1969** Stunning tale of a Polish singer who struggles to find the meaning and beauty of life while working to trade Nazi prisoners in U.S. jails for Jews hoping to emigrate. Based on the Arnost Lustig novel. Confiscated by the Czech Communist government and kept from the screen for 21 years. In Czechoslovakian with English subtitles. **60m/C VHS.** *CZ* Jiri Adamira, Lenka Fiserova, Cestmir Randa. *FCT*

Prayer for the Dying 🦴🦴½ **1987 (R)** An IRA hitman longs to quit, but he has to complete one last assignment. The hit is witnessed by a priest who becomes an unwitting associate when the hitman hides out at the church. Fine performances from Bates and Rourke, though Hodges and Rourke were not satisfied with finished film. **104m/C VHS, Beta, LV.** Mickey Rourke, Alan Bates, Bob Hoskins, Sammi Davis, Liam Neeson, Alison Doody, Christopher Fulford; ***D:*** Mike Hodges; ***W:*** Edmund Ward, Martin Lynch; ***M:*** Bill Conti. *NO*

Prayer of the Rollerboys 🦴🦴½ **1991 (R)** Violent, futuristic, funky action as Haim infiltrates a criminal gang of syncopated roller-blading neo-nazi youth with plans for nationwide domination. Though routinely plotted and predictable, it's got great skating stunts and a wry vision of tomorrow's shattered USA—broke, drug-soaked, homeless, foreign-owned; even sharper when you realize this is a Japanese-American co-production. **94m/C VHS, LV.** Corey Haim, Patricia Arquette, Christopher Collet, Julius W. Harris, J.C. Quinn, Jake Dengel, Devin Clark, Mark Pellegrino, Morgan Weisser; ***D:*** Rick King. *ACA*

Praying Mantis 🦴🦴 **1983 (PG-13)** The professor's scheming nurse murdered his family and plans to marry him for his money. She enlists the aid of the professor's assistant in her evil plot. **119m/C VHS, Beta.** Jonathan Pryce, Cherie Lunghi, Ann Cropper, Carmen Du Sautoy, Pinkas Braun; ***D:*** Jack Gold; ***M:*** Carl Davis. *NO*

Praying Mantis 🦴🦴½ **1993 (PG-13)** Seymour stars as a femme fatale who likes to get married and then, in a rage against her own abusive childhood, kill her new husbands off. So far her total is five dead hubbies with number six (Bostwick) in her sights. Only this time, her almost-sister-in-law (Fisher) is very suspicious of the bride-to-be. Made for cable television. **90m/C VHS, Beta.** Jane Seymour, Barry Bostwick, Frances Fisher, Chad Allen; ***D:*** James Keach; ***W:*** Duane Poole, William F. Delligan; ***M:*** John Debney. *PAR*

Pre-Madonnas: Rebels Without a Clue 🦴🦴½ **1995 (PG-13)** Kim Sterling (Sturges) decides to rig the Beverly Hills Las Madonnas debutante ball to teach the snobs a lesson. **98m/C VHS, LV.** Shannon Sturges, Bobbie Bresee, Peter Anthony Elliott, Kenn Cooper; ***D:*** Lawrence Foldes. *AVE*

Preacherman 🦴½ **1983 (R)** Phony preacher travels through the South, fleecing gullible congregations (and providing for their sexual desires) wherever he goes. **90m/C VHS.** Amos Huxley, Marian Brown, Adam Hesse, Ilene Kristen, W. Henry Smith; ***D:*** Albert T. Viola; ***W:*** Albert T. Viola, Harvey Flaxman; ***M:*** W. Henry Smith, Roland Pope. *TTV*

Predator 🦴🦴½ **1987 (R)** Schwarzenegger leads a team of CIA-hired mercenaries into the Central American jungles to rescue hostages. They encounter an alien force that begins to attack them one by one. Soon it's just Arnold and the Beast in this attention-grabbing, but sometimes silly, suspense film. **107m/C VHS, Beta, LV.** Arnold Schwarzenegger, Jesse Ventura, Sonny Landham, Bill Duke, Elpidia Carrillo, Carl Weathers, R.G. Armstrong, Richard Chaves, Shane Black, Kevin Peter Hall; ***D:*** John McTiernan; ***W:*** Jim Thomas, John Thomas; ***M:*** Alan Silvestri. *FXV*

Predator 2 🦴🦴 **1990 (R)** Tough cop takes time away from battling drug dealers to deal with malicious extraterrestrial who exterminated Arnold's band of commandos in "Predator." Miss-billed as sequel, its only resemblance to the original is that the predator has inexplicably returned (this time to the thick of L.A.). Gory action aplenty, little logic. Fine cast dominated by minority performers can't save this one. **105m/C VHS, Beta, LV.** Danny Glover, Gary Busey, Ruben Blades, Maria Conchita Alonso, Bill Paxton, Robert Davi, Adam Baldwin, Kent McCord, Morton Downey Jr., Calvin Lockhart, Teri Weigel; ***D:*** Stephen Hopkins; ***W:*** John Thomas, Jim Thomas. *FXV, CCB*

Prehistoric Bimbos in Armageddon City *Woof!* **1993** Trianna and her tribe of Prehistoric Bimbos must prevent post-nuclear domination in Old Chicago City, the last remaining civilization after WWIII, by defeating the evil ruler Nemesis and his cyborgs. "Enough bimbos to fill two post-nuclear action comedies." So bad its gotta be good. **70m/C VHS.** Robert Vollrath, Tonia Monahan, Deric Bernier. *TEM*

Prehistoric Women *Woof! Slave Girls* **1950** A tribe of prehistoric women look for husbands the old-fashioned way—they drag them back to their caves from the jungle. So bad it's almost good. **74m/C VHS, Beta.** Laurette Luez, Allan Nixon, Mara Lynn, Joan Shawlee, Judy Landon; ***D:*** Greg Tallas. *FHE, NOS, RHI*

Prehysteria 🦴🦴½ **1993 (PG)** Fantasy/adventure about a widower, his 11-year-old son and teenage daughter, and what happens when some mysterious eggs from South America accidentally wind up at their farm. Imagine their surprise when the eggs hatch and out pop a brood of pygmy dinosaurs. The dinosaurs are cute (as is the family), the villain is dumb, and the violence minimal. **84m/C VHS, Beta, LV.** Brett Cullen, Austin O'Brien, Samantha Mills, Colleen Morris, Tony Longo, Stuart Fratkin, Stephen Lee; ***D:*** Albert Band, Charles Band; ***W:*** Greg Suddeth, Mark Goldstein. *PAR*

Prehysteria 2 🦴🦴½ **1994 (PG)** While their adoptive family is on vacation the pygmy dinosaurs get loose and aid a lonely rich boy whose governess is plotting to send him to military boarding school. **81m/C VHS, Beta.** Kevin R. Connors, Jennifer Harte, Dean Scofield, Bettye Ackerman, Larry Hankin, Greg Lewis, Alan Palo, Michael Hagiwara, Owen Bush; ***D:*** Albert Band; ***W:*** Brent Friedman, Michael Paul Davis; ***M:*** Richard Band. *PAR*

Prehysteria 3 🦴🦴½ **1995 (PG)** The mini-dinos take up miniature golf. Seems Thomas MacGregor's (Willard) putt-putt business is about to sink when his daughter Ella (Anderson) finds the pygmy dinosaurs and a promotional bonanza is born. But Thomas' evil brother Hal (Weitz) hatches a plot to take over the now-successful enterprize. **85m/C VHS.** Fred Willard, Bruce Weitz, Whitney Anderson, Pam Matteson; ***D:*** Julian Breen; ***W:*** Michael Paul Davis, Neil Ruttenberg. *PAR*

Prelude to a Kiss 🦴🦴 **1992 (PG-13)** Disappointing screen adaptation of Craig Lucas' hit play features Baldwin and Ryan as young lovers in this romantic fantasy. Ryan is Rita, a free-spirited bartender and Baldwin is Peter, a conservative writer, who decide to marry after a whirlwind courtship. At their wedding reception, Rita obligingly kisses one of their guests, an old man (Walker). Then, on their honeymoon, Peter begins to notice a number of changes to Rita's character and comes to realize this is truly not the girl he married. The delicate fantasy which worked on stage struggles to survive the "opening up" of the screen adaptation though Baldwin (who reprises his stage role) and Ryan are appealing. **106m/C VHS, LV.** Alec Baldwin, Meg Ryan, Sydney Walker, Ned Beatty, Patty Duke, Kathy Bates, Stanley Tucci; ***D:*** Norman Rene; ***M:*** Howard Shore. *FXV, PMS*

Prelude to War **1942** A compact look at the events of 1931-39; includes a series of contrasts between free societies and totalitarian governments. From the "Why We Fight" series. **53m/B VHS, Beta.** ***D:*** Frank Capra. Academy Awards '42: Best Feature Documentary. *REP, MPI, HHT*

Premature Burial 🦴🦴 **1962** A cataleptic Englishman's worst fears come true when he is buried alive. He escapes and seeks revenge on his doctor and his greedy wife. Based upon the story by Edgar Allan Poe. **81m/C VHS, Beta, LV.** Ray Milland, Richard Ney, Hazel Court, Heather Angel; ***D:*** Roger Corman; ***C:*** Floyd Crosby. *LIV, VES, MLB*

Premonition 🦴½ **1971 (PG)** Three drug-riddled '60s college students experience similar premonitions of death, and subsequently either die or become tormented. **83m/C VHS, Beta.** Carl Crow, Tim Ray, Winfrey Hester Hill, Victor Izay; ***D:*** Alan Rudolph; ***W:*** Alan Rudolph; ***C:*** John Bailey. *NO*

The Premonition 🦴🦴½ **1975 (PG)** Parapsychologist searching for a missing child is drawn into a frightening maze of dream therapy and communication with the dead. Well-done paranorm tale filmed in Mississippi. **94m/C VHS, Beta.** Richard Lynch, Sharon Farrell, Jeff Corey, Ellen Barber, Edward Bell, Danielle Brisebois; ***D:*** Robert Allen Schnitzer; ***W:*** Anthony Mahon. *SUE*

Prep School 🦴 **1981 (PG-13)** A very proper New England prep school is turned topsy-turvy by two rambunctious co-eds. They're determined to break every one of the school's cardinal rules. **97m/C VHS, Beta.** Leslie Hope, Andrew Sabiston; ***D:*** Paul Almond. *PSM*

The Preppie Murder 🦴🦴½ **1989** Made for TV crime drama based on the killing of Jennifer Levin in New York City's Central Park in 1987, with Baldwin cast as prep school grad Robert Chambers. Amid sensational headlines, the story told of drugs, sexual games, and idle and disaffected youth. **100m/C VHS.** William Baldwin, Lara Flynn Boyle, Danny Aiello, Joanna Kerns, Dorothy Fielding, James Handy, William Devane; ***D:*** John Herzfeld. *TTC*

Preppies 🦴½ **1982 (R)** Yet another teen sex comedy, but this time Ivy Leaguer Drake must pass his exams to receive his $50 million inheritance. Lots of skirt chasing as his conniving cousin leads him astray. **83m/C VHS, Beta.** Dennis Drake, Peter Brady Reardon, Steven Holt, Nitchie Barrett, Cindy Manion, Katt Shea Ruben, Lynda Wiesmeier; ***D:*** Chuck Vincent. *LIV, VES*

Prescott Kid 🦴🦴 **1936** Legendary western star McCoy plays a law-abiding cowboy mistaken for the new Marshall in the outlaw town of San Lorenzo, which has been targeted by a gang of cattle rustling killers. **58m/B VHS.** Tim McCoy, Sheila Mannors, Alden Chase, Hooper Atchley, Walter Brennan; ***D:*** David Selman; ***W:*** Ford Beebe. *COL*

Presenting Lily Mars 🦴🦴 **1943** A small-town girl comes to New York to make it on Broadway. Based on the Booth Tarkington novel. ♫When I Look at You; Three O'Clock in the Morning; Kulebiaka; Is It Love? (Or The Gypsy in Me); Broadway Rhythm; Sweethearts of America; Where There's Music; Every Little Movement Has a Meaning All Its Own; Tom, Tom the Piper's Son. **105m/B VHS, Beta.** Judy Garland, Van Heflin, Fay Bainter, Richard Carlson, Tommy Dorsey; ***D:*** Norman Taurog; ***C:*** Joseph Ruttenberg. *MGM*

The President's Analyst 🦴🦴🦴½ **1967** A superbly written, brilliantly executed satire from the mind of Theodore J. Flicker, who wrote as well as directed. Coburn steals the show as a psychiatrist who has the dubious honor of being appointed "secret shrink" to the President of the U.S. Pressures of the job steadily increase his paranoia until he suspects he is being pursued by agents and counter agents alike. Is he losing his sanity or...? Vastly entertaining. **104m/C VHS.** James Coburn, Godfrey Cambridge, Severn Darden, Joan Delaney, Pat Harrington, Will Geer, William Daniels; ***D:*** Theodore J. Flicker; ***W:*** Theodore J. Flicker; ***M:*** Lalo Schifrin. *PAR*

President's Mistress 🦴½ **1978** A security agent searches for his sister's murderer, while trying to obscure the fact that she was having an affair with the President. **97m/C VHS, Beta.** Beau Bridges, Susan Blanchard, Larry Hagman, Joel Fabiani, Karen Grassle; ***D:*** John Llewellyn Moxey. *NO*

The President's Mystery 🦴½ *One For All* **1936** A lawyer decides to turn his back on society by giving up his practice and his marriage. Eventually he meets and falls in love with another woman. The most interesting aspect of the film is that it is based on a story by Franklin D. Roosevelt, which was published in "Liberty" magazine. The story was supposedly better than its screen adaptation. **80m/B VHS, Beta.** Henry Wilcoxon, Betty Furness, Sidney Blackmer, Evelyn Brent; ***D:*** Phil Rosen. *SNC*

The President's Plane is Missing 🦴🦴 **1971** When Air Force One disappears, the less than trustworthy Vice President takes control. Could there be a dire plot in the making? Based on a novel by Rod Serling's brother Robert J. Serling. **100m/C VHS.** Buddy Ebsen, Peter Graves, Arthur Kennedy, Rip Torn, Louise Sorel, Raymond Massey, James Wainwright, Mercedes McCambridge, Dabney Coleman, Joseph Campanella; ***D:*** Daryl Duke. *REP*

President's Target 🦴🦴 **1993** An anti-drug mission in South America is ambushed and CIA operative Peter Caine is the only survivor. Now he's out to see who planned the double-cross and how best to get his revenge. **82m/C VHS.** John Coleman, Martin Kove, Bo Hopkins, Brigitte Audrey; ***D:*** Yvan Chiffre. *HMD*

The Presidio 🦴🦴 **1988 (R)** An easy going police detective must investigate a murder on a military base where he and the base commander have sparred before. The commander becomes downright nasty when his daughter shows an interest in the detective. Good action scenes in San Francisco almost covers up script weaknesses, but not quite. **97m/C VHS, Beta, LV, 8mm.** Sean Connery, Mark Harmon, Meg Ryan, Jack Warden, Mark Blum, Jenette Goldstein; ***D:*** Peter Hyams; ***W:*** Larry Ferguson; ***M:*** Bruce Broughton. *PAR*

Pressure Point 🦴🦴🦴 **1962** Poitier stars as a prison psychiatrist treating an inmate who is a racist and a member of the Nazi party. Darin gives an excellent performance as the Nazi patient in this intelligent drama based on a true case. **87m/B VHS.** Sidney Poitier, Bobby Darin, Peter Falk, Carl Benton Reid, Barry Gordon, Howard Caine, Mary Munday; ***D:*** Hubert Cornfield; ***M:*** Ernest Gold. *MGM*

Presumed Guilty 🦴 **1991** An innocent man is released from prison only to find he is once again a wanted man! So he gets his gal, who happens to be the sheriff's daughter, is beaten up and in the end winds up living happily ever after. **91m/C VHS, LV.** Jack Vogel, Holly Floria, Sean Holton, Wayne Zanelotti, Bradley Rockwell, Sharon Young, Al Schuerman; ***D:*** Lawrence L. Simeone; ***W:*** Lawrence L. Simeone. *AIP*

Presumed Innocent 🦴🦴🦴 **1990 (R)** Assistant district attorney is the prime suspect when a former lover turns up brutally murdered. Cover-ups surround him, the political climate changes, and friends and enemies switch sides. Slow-paced courtroom drama with excellent performances from Ford, Julia, and Bedelia. Skillfully adapted from the bestseller by Chicago attorney Scott Turow. **127m/C VHS, Beta, LV, 8mm.** Harrison Ford, Brian Dennehy, Bonnie Bedelia, Greta Scacchi, Raul Julia, Paul Winfield, John Spencer, Joe Grifasi, Anna Maria Horsford, Sab Shimono, Christine Estabrook, Michael Tolan, Tom Mardirosian; ***D:*** Alan J. Pakula; ***W:*** Frank Pierson, Alan J. Pakula; ***C:*** Gordon Willis; ***M:*** John Williams. *WAR, FCT*

Pretty Baby 🦴🦴🦴 **1978 (R)** Shield's launching pad and Malle's first American film is a masterpiece of cinematography and style, nearly upstaged by the plodding storyline. Carradine manages to be effective but never succeeds at looking comfortable as the New Orleans photographer besotted with, and subsequently married to, an 11-year old prostitute (Shields). Low key, disturbingly intriguing story, beautifully photographed by Sven Nykist. **109m/C VHS, Beta, LV.** Brooke Shields, Keith Carradine, Susan Sarandon, Barbara Steele, Diana Scarwid, Antonio Fargas; ***D:*** Louis Malle; ***C:*** Sven Nykvist. National Board of Review Awards '78: 10 Best Films of the Year; Nominations: Academy Awards '78: Best Original Score; Cannes Film Festival '78: Best Film. *PAR*

Pretty in Pink 🦴🦴½ **1986 (PG-13)** More teen angst from the pen of Hughes. Poor girl falls for a rich guy. Their families fret, their friends are distressed, and fate conspires against them. If you can suspend your disbelief that a teenager with her own car and answering machine is financially inferior, then you may very well be able to accept the entire premise. Slickly done and adequately, if not enthusiastically, acted. In 1987, Hughes essentially remade this film and put himself in the director's chair with "Some Kind of Wonderful," the same story with the rich/pauper characters reversed by gender. **96m/C VHS, Beta, LV, 8mm.** Molly Ringwald, Andrew McCarthy, Jon Cryer, Harry Dean Stanton, James Spader, Annie Potts, Andrew Dice Clay, Margaret Colin, Alexa Kenin, Gina Gershon, Dweezil Zappa; ***D:*** Howard Deutch; ***W:*** John Hughes; ***C:*** Tak Fujimoto; ***M:*** Michael Gore. *PAR*

Pretty Poison 🦴🦴🦴½ **1968** You won't need an antidote for this one. Original, absorbing screenplay, top-notch acting, and on target direction combine to raise this low-budget, black comedy above the crowd. Perkins at his eerie best as a burned-out arsonist who cooks up a crazy scheme and enlists the aid of a hot-to-trot high schooler, only to discover too late she has some burning desires of her own. Weld is riveting as the turbulent teen. **89m/C VHS.** Anthony Perkins, Tuesday Weld, Beverly Garland, John Randolph, Dick O'Neill; ***D:*** Noel Black. New York Film Critics Awards '68: Best Screenplay. *ING, MLB*

Pretty Smart *Woof!* **1987 (R)** Two diametrically opposed sisters at a European finishing school team up against a drug-dealing, voyeuristic teacher. Pretty lame. **84m/C VHS, Beta.** Tricia Leigh Fisher, Patricia Arquette, Dennis Cole, Lisa Lorient; ***D:*** Dimitri Logothetis; ***M:*** Eddie Arkin. *VTR, NWV*

Pretty Woman 🦴🦴🦴 **1990 (R)** An old story takes a fresh approach as a successful but stuffy business man hires a fun-loving, energetic young hooker to be his companion for a week. The film caused some controversy over its upbeat portrayal of prostitution, but its popularity at the box office catapulted Roberts to stardom. **117m/C VHS, Beta, LV.** Richard Gere, Julia Roberts, Ralph Bellamy, Jason Alexander, Laura San Giacomo, Hector Elizondo, Alex Hyde-White, Elinor Donahue, Larry Miller, Jane Morris; ***D:*** Garry Marshall; ***W:*** J.F. Lawton; ***M:*** James Newton Howard. Golden Globe Awards '91: Best Actress—Musical/Comedy (Roberts); People's Choice Awards '91: Best Film, Best Film—Musical/Comedy; Nominations: Academy Awards '90: Best Actress (Roberts). *TOU*

Prettykill *Woof!* **1987 (R)** A confusing storyline with numerous subplots involves detective with a paramour/prostitute (Hubley) attempting to stalk a mad killer while contending with her split personality. **95m/C VHS, Beta, LV.** David Birney, Susannah York, Season Hubley, Yaphet Kotto, Suzanne Snyder, Germane Honde; ***D:*** George Kaczender; ***W:*** Sandra K. Bailey. *WAR*

The Prey 🦴 **1980 (R)** Poorly done horror show about a predator who is looking for a mate in the Colorado Rockies and kills five campers in the process. **80m/C VHS, Beta.** Debbie Thurseon, Steve Bond, Lori Lethin, Jackie Coogan; ***D:*** Edwin Scott Brown; ***W:*** Edwin Scott Brown, Summer Brown. *NO*

Prey for the Hunter 🦴 **1992 (R)** Four businessmen on a big-game hunt decide they're bored with their usual prey. They persuade a photojournalist to join them in a game with paint pellet guns except they decide to use real bullets and the journalist becomes their new target. An old and tired plot with nothing new to distinguish it. **90m/C VHS.** Todd Jensen, Andre Jacobs, Michelle Bestbier, Evan J. Klisser, David Butler, Allan Granville; ***D:*** John H. Parr. *COL*

Prey of the Chameleon 🦴 **1991 (R)** A female serial killer escapes from her asylum, ready to rip more men to shreds. However a tough lady cop has other ideas and goes all out to put an end to the madwoman's doings. Can she stop this fiend before the man she loves becomes the next victim? **91m/C VHS, Beta.** Daphne Zuniga, James Wilder, Alexandra Paul, Don Harvey; ***D:*** Fleming Fuller. *PSM*

Priceless Beauty 🦴🦴½ **1990 (R)** Musician Lambert was only looking when he spotted the bottle which changed his life. Beautiful genie (Lane) lives inside, and is waiting just for him! Fun premise, good score, nice chemistry between the actors. **94m/C VHS, LV.** Christopher Lambert, Diane Lane, Francesco Quinn, J.C. Quinn, Claudia Ohana, Monica Scattini, Joaquin D'Almeida; ***D:*** Charles Finch. *REP*

Prick Up Your Ears 🦴🦴🦴 **1987 (R)** Film biography of popular subversive playwright Joe Orton depicts his rise to fame and his eventual murder at the hands of his homosexual lover in 1967. Acclaimed for its realistic and sometimes humorous portrayal of the relationship between two men in a society that regarded homosexuality as a crime, the film unfortunately pays scant attention to Orton's theatrical success. The occasional sluggishness of the script detracts a bit from the three leads' outstanding performances. **110m/C VHS, Beta, LV.** *GB* Gary Oldman, Alfred Molina, Vanessa Redgrave, Julie Walters, Lindsay Duncan, Wallace Shawn, James Grant, Frances Barber, Janet Dale, David Atkins; ***D:*** Stephen Frears; ***W:*** Alan Bennett; ***M:*** Stanley Myers. New York Film Critics Awards '87: Best Supporting Actress (Redgrave). *NO*

Pride and Prejudice 🦴🦴🦴½ **1940** Classic adaptation of Austen's classic novel of manners as a young marriageable woman spurns the suitor her parents choose for her. Excellent cast vividly recreates 19th century England, aided by the inspired set design that won the film an Oscar. **114m/B VHS, Beta, LV.** Greer Garson, Laurence Olivier, Edmund Gwenn, Edna May Oliver, Mary Boland, Maureen O'Sullivan, Ann Rutherford, Frieda Inescort; ***D:*** Robert Z. Leonard; ***C:*** Karl Freund. Academy Awards '40: Best Interior Decoration. *MGM*

Pride and Prejudice 🦴🦴½ **1985** BBC mini-series adaptation of Jane Austen's novel about 19th century British mores and the attempts of five sisters to get married. **226m/C VHS, Beta, LV.** *GB* Elizabeth Garvie, David Rintoul; ***D:*** Cyril Coke. *FOX, SIG, TVC*

Pride and Prejudice 🦴🦴🦴 **1995** Lavish TV adaptation of the Jane Austen novel finds bright Elizabeth Bennet (Ehle) unwillingly smitten by the wealthy, mysterious, and arrogant Mr. Darcy (Firth). Her family, filled with unmarried daughters, is rather silly and, of course, Elizabeth should be looking to get married (or at least not hinder her sisters' chances). Filmed on location in Derbyshire. On 6 cassettes. **300m/C VHS.** *GB* Jennifer Ehle, Colin Firth, Susannah Harker, Alison Steadman, Julia Sawalha, Benjamin Whitrow, Crispin Bonham Carter, Anna Chancellor, David Bamber, David Bark-Jones, Polly Maberly, Lucy Briers, Barbara Leigh-Hunt, Adrian Lukis; ***D:*** Simon Langton; ***W:*** Andrew Davies; ***C:*** John Kenway; ***M:*** Carl Davis. *AAE, PBS*

The Pride and the Passion 🦴🦴 **1957** A small group of resistance fighters battling for Spanish independence in 1810 must smuggle a 6-ton cannon across the rugged terrain of Spain. Miscasting, especially of Sinatra as a Spanish peasant, hurts this film. **132m/C VHS, Beta.** Cary Grant, Frank Sinatra, Sophia Loren; ***D:*** Stanley Kramer; ***W:*** Edward Anhalt. *MGM*

Pride of Jesse Hallum 🦴½ **1981** A made-for-television film about an illiterate man, played by country singer Cash, who learns, after much trial and tribulation, to read. **105m/C VHS, Beta.** Johnny Cash, Brenda Vaccaro, Eli Wallach; ***D:*** Gary Nelson. *FOX*

Pride of St. Louis 🦴🦴 **1952** A romanticized and humorous portrait of famed baseball player-turned-commentator Dizzy Dean. **93m/B VHS, Beta.** Dan Dailey, Joanne Dru, Richard Crenna, Richard Haydn, Hugh Sanders; ***D:*** Harmon Jones; ***W:*** Herman J. Mankiewicz. Nominations: Academy Awards '52: Best Story. *FOX*

Pride of the Bowery 🦴 *Here We Go Again* **1941** The Dead End Kids versus a boxing hopeful in training camp. **60m/B VHS, Beta.** Leo Gorcey, David Gorcey, Huntz Hall, Gabriel Dell, Billy Halop, Bobby Jordan; ***D:*** Joseph H. Lewis. *NOS, CAB, DVT*

Pride of the Clan 🦴🦴½ **1918** Silent drama with Pickford and Moore as Scottish sweethearts battling a bit of adversity. When Pickford's father is lost at sea, she moves onto his fishing boat. She meets Moore, a fishing boy, and falls in love. But, he inherits a fortune and his parents forbid him to see Pickford. He goes off to live the good life but comes back to dramatically rescue Pickford. **80m/B VHS, Beta.** Mary Pickford, Matt Moore; ***D:*** Maurice Tourneur. *GPV*

The Pride of the Yankees 🦴🦴🦴½ **1942** Excellent portrait of baseball great Lou Gehrig. Beginning as he joined the Yankees in 1923, the film follows this great American through to his moving farewell speech as his career was tragically cut short by the disease that bears his name. Cooper is inspiring in the title role. **128m/B VHS, Beta, LV.** Gary Cooper, Teresa Wright, Babe Ruth, Walter Brennan, Dan Duryea; ***D:*** Sam Wood. Academy Awards '42: Best Film Editing; Nominations: Academy Awards '41: Best Actress (Wright); Academy Awards '42: Best Actor (Cooper), Best Black and White Cinematography, Best Interior Decoration, Best Picture, Best Sound, Best Story, Best Original Score. *FOX*

Priest 🦴🦴 **1994 (R)** Father Greg (an intense performance by Roache) is a young, idealistic priest who gets a rude awakening when he's assigned to a tough inner-city Liverpool parish. His superior, Father Matthew (Wilkinson), is a middle-aged rabble rouser who's openly having an affair with their black housekeeper Maria (Tyson). But Father Greg has a secret of his own—despite struggles with his sexuality he gets involved with Graham (Carlyle), a man he meets in the local gay bar. Greg's inner turmoil is heightened when a young parishoner confesses that her father is sexually abusing her but, because of the seal of the confessional, the priest cannot report the problem. Director Bird walks a fine line between criticism and condemnation of Catholic doctrine. British TV feature provoked a storm of controversy in the U.S.; originally released at 105 minutes. **98m/C VHS.** *GB* Linus Roache, Tom Wilkinson, Cathy Tyson, Robert Carlyle, James Ellis, John Bennett, Rio Fanning, Jimmy Coleman, Lesley Sharp, Robert Pugh, Christine Tremarco; ***D:*** Antonia Bird; ***W:*** Jimmy McGovern; ***C:*** Fred Tammes; ***M:*** Andy Roberts. Nominations: Australian Film Institute '95: Best Foreign Film. *TOU*

Priest of Love 🦴🦴½ **1981 (R)** Arty account of the final years of the life of then-controversial author D.H. Lawrence, during which time he published "Lady Chatterly's Lover." A slow-moving but interesting portrayal of this complex man and his wife as they grapple with his imminent death from tuberculosis. **125m/C VHS, Beta.** *GB* Ian McKellen, Janet Suzman, John Gielgud, Helen Mirren, Jorge Rivero; ***D:*** Christopher Miles; ***W:*** Alan Plater; ***C:*** Ted Moore. *HBO*

Primal Fear 🦴🦴 **1996 (R)** Chicago defense attorney Martin Vail (Gere) is torn between the fight for justice and the lure of fame. He seems to have found the spotlight when a gentle altar boy (newcomer Norton is a standout) is accused of savagely murdering an archbishop. This leads to some courtroom fireworks due, in part, to the fact that the prosecutor (Linney) is Vail's former lover. Gere turns in a satisfying performance but, except when he's with his client, can't keep the script afloat. Lame plot revelations and an obvious "shocker" ending don't help matters. Feature directorial debut of Gregory Hoblit, Emmy winner for TV's "Hill Street Blues," "L.A. Law," and "NYPD Blue." **130m/C VHS.** Richard Gere, Laura Linney, Edward Norton, John Mahoney, Alfre Woodard, Frances McDormand, Terry O'Quinn, Andre Braugher, Steven Bauer, Joe Spano, Tony Plana, Stanley Anderson, Maura Tierney, John Seda; ***D:*** Gregory Hoblit; ***W:*** Steve Shagan, Ann Biderman; ***C:*** Michael Chapman; ***M:*** James Newton Howard. *NYR*

Primal Impulse 🦴½ **1974** An astronaut, stranded on the moon because of a sinister experimental double-cross, unleashes a mental scream which possesses a young woman's mind back on earth. **90m/C VHS, Beta.** Klaus Kinski. *NO*

Primal Rage 🦴 **1990 (R)** A student is bitten by an experimental monkey, and begins to manifest his primal urges physically. Special effects by Carlo Rimbaldi. **92m/C VHS, Beta.** Bo Svenson, Patrick Lowe, Mitch Watson, Cheryl Arutt, Sarah Buxton; ***D:*** Vittoria Rambaldi. *WAR*

Primal Scream 🦴½ *Hellfire* **1987 (R)** The Year is 1993. Earth's fuel sources are rapidly decaying and the top secret project to mine a revolutionary new energy source is underway—independently managed by a corrupt corporation. **95m/C VHS.** Kenneth John McGregor, Sharon Mason, Julie Miller, Jon Maurice, Mickey Shaughnessy; ***D:*** William Murray. *NO*

Primal Secrets 🦴🦴½ *Trick of the Eye* **1994** Artist Tilly, who specializes in illusionary trompe l'oeil paintings, is commissioned to paint a mural for reclusive socialite/widow Burstyn but there's a lot of mystery surrounding the job, especially when Burstyn begins to take an overly avid interest in Tilly's life. Based on the novel by Jane Stanton Hitchcock. Made for TV. **93m/C VHS.** Meg Tilly, Ellen Burstyn, Barnard Hughes; ***D:*** Ed Kaplan. *HMK*

Primary Motive 🦴🦴 **1992 (R)** Taut political thriller with Nelson as Andy Blumenthal, a press secretary who finds that an opposing candidate's campaign is covered by a web of lies. Blumenthal exposes the lies, but the candidate denies them and pulls further ahead in the polls. When the candidate's wife gives Blumenthal an extremely damaging piece of information, will the polls finally turn against him? **93m/C VHS, Beta, LV.** Judd Nelson, Richard Jordan, Sally Kirkland, Justine Bateman, John Savage; ***D:*** Daniel Adams; ***W:*** William Snowden III, Daniel Adams; ***M:*** John Cale. *FXV, VTR*

Primary Target 🦴 **1989 (R)** A mercenary reunites his 'Nam guerilla unit to rescue a diplomat's wife kidnapped by a Laotian jungle lord. **85m/C VHS, Beta.** John Calvin, Miki Kim, Joey Aresco, Chip Lucio, John Ericson, Colleen Casey; ***D:*** Clark Henderson. *MGM*

Prime Cut 🦴🦴½ **1972 (R)** Veritable orgy of drug trafficking, prostitution, extortion, loan sharking, fisticuffs and gangsters getting ground into mincemeat. Sleazy but well-made crime melodrama has its followers, but is best known as Spacek's film debut. **86m/C VHS, Beta.** Lee Marvin, Gene Hackman, Sissy Spacek, Angel Tompkins, Gregory Walcott; ***D:*** Michael Ritchie; ***W:*** Robert Dillon; ***M:*** Lalo Schifrin. *FOX*

Prime Evil 🦴🦴 **1988 (R)** A brave and determined nun infiltrates a sect of devil worshipping monks in an attempt to end their demonic sacrifices. The question is, will this sister slide beneath Satan's cleaver? **87m/C VHS, LV.** William Beckwith, Christine Moore; ***D:*** Roberta Findlay. *VTR*

The Prime of Miss Jean Brodie 🦴🦴🦴 **1969 (PG)** Oscar-winning performance by Smith as a forward-thinking teacher in a Scottish Girls' school during the 1920s. She captivates her impressionable young students with her fascist ideals and free-thinking attitudes in this adaptation of the play taken from Muriel Spark's novel. **116m/C VHS, Beta.** *GB* Maggie Smith, Pamela Franklin, Robert Stephens, Celia Johnson, Gordon Jackson, Jane Carr; ***D:*** Ronald Neame; ***W:*** Jay Presson Allen; ***C:*** Ted Moore. Academy Awards '69: Best Actress (Smith); British Academy Awards '69: Best Actress (Smith), Best Supporting Actress (Johnson); National Board of Review Awards '69: Best Supporting Actress (Franklin); Nominations: Academy Awards '69: Best Song ("Jean"); Cannes Film Festival '69: Best Film. *FOX, BTV*

Prime Risk 🦴½ **1984 (PG-13)** A young engineer who discovers an electronic method to break into automated teller machines finds that it leads to more trouble when she discovers that foreign agents are hot on her trail. **98m/C VHS, Beta.** Toni Hudson, Lee Montgomery, Sam Bottoms; ***D:*** W. Farkas. *LIV*

Prime Suspect 🦴🦴 **1982** An honest citizen becomes the prime suspect after the coverage of a murder by an over-ambitious television reporter. **100m/C VHS, Beta.** Mike Farrell, Teri Garr, Veronica Cartwright, Lane Smith, Barry Corbin, James Sloyan, Charles Aidman; ***D:*** Noel Black. *NO*

Prime Suspect 🦴🦴 **1988** A young man escapes from a mental institution to clear his name after being wrongfully accused of murdering his girlfriend. **89m/C VHS.** Susan Strasberg, Frank Stallone, Billy Drago, Doug McClure; ***D:*** Mark Rutland. *NO*

Prime Suspect 🦴🦴🦴 **1992** Mirren stars as Detective Chief Inspector Jane Tennison in this British television police procedural. When a male inspector dies of a heart attack while investigating a rape-murder, Tennison, the only women of senior police status, wants the case. But she runs into multiple obstructions, not the least being the smug male police system. Then the case really takes a turn when it appears Tennison is searching for a serial killer. But Jane is no quitter and she has both the brains and the guts to back up her orders. Adapted from the book by Lynda La Plante, who also wrote the teleplay. **240m/C VHS.** *GB* Helen Mirren, Tom Bell, Zoe Wanamaker, John Bowe, Tom Wilkinson, Ralph Fiennes; ***D:*** Christopher Menaul; ***W:*** Lynda La Plante. *SIG, FXL, PAP*

Prime Suspect 2 🦴🦴🦴 **1993** DCI Jane Tennison (Mirren) returns in another British made for TV police drama. Jane has been off at a police seminar where she has a brief liaison with a black police detective, Robert Oswalde (Salmon). She is recalled to investigate the decomposed body of a young woman found in one of London's Afro-Caribbean neighborhoods and must deal with their resentment of the police. When detective Oswalde is reassigned to Jane's department, she begins having trouble separating her public and private feelings, while trying to obtain a confession from her most likely suspect. Based on a story by Lynda La Plante. **240m/C VHS.** *GB* Helen Mirren, Colin Salmon, Tom Watson, Ian Fitzgibbon, Philip Wright, Jack Ellis, Craig Fairbrass; ***D:*** John Strickland; ***W:*** Allan Cubitt. *SIG, FXL, PAP*

Prime Suspect 3 🦴🦴🦴 **1993** The BBC returns Jane Tennison to the beat (as does her portrayer Mirren) in another intriguing police drama. Tennison has transferred from homicide to the vice squad but still can't escape murder investigations—or male chauvinists. Oh yes, Tennison has a new team of macho colleagues to contend with and she's still getting heat from her bosses about her job. Still, this is one copper who lets nothing stand in her way. Made for British TV; on 3 cassettes. **205m/C VHS.** *GB* Helen Mirren, Tom Bell, Peter Capaldi, David Thewlis, Ciaran Hinds, Terrence Hardiman, Mark Strong, Karen Tomlin, Struan Rodger, Liza Sadovy, Andrew Woodall, Kelly Hunter; ***D:*** David Drury; ***W:*** Lynda La Plante; ***M:*** Stephen Warbeck. *TVC, PBS*

Prime Suspect: Inner Circles 🦴🦴½ **1995** Jane Tennison (Mirren) finds herself caught up in suburban fraud and murder and once again on the outs with her bosses. Two drugged-up youths are accused of murdering a country club manager. The powers that be are satisfied but Tennison isn't—and rightly so because the murder is merely the tip of a very large and nasty iceberg. TV movie. **102m/C VHS.** *GB* Helen Mirren, Jill Baker, Anthony Bate, John Benfield, Richard Hawley, James Laurenson, Kelly Reilly, Sophie Stanton, Nick Patrick, Tom Russell; ***D:*** Sarah Pia Anderson; ***W:*** Eric Deacon; ***C:*** David Odd; ***M:*** Stephen Warbeck. *VTR*

Prime Suspect: The Lost Child 🦴🦴🦴 **1994** Jane Tennison (Mirren), promoted to Detective Chief Inspector, is caught up in a drama that strikes a little too close to her well-schooled emotions. A young mother's (Edney) 14-month-old daughter has been abducted—has the child been kidnapped for ransom or is this the work of a pedophile? Suspicion falls on released sex offender Chris (Glenister) but things aren't that simple—even as tensions rise among Tennison's own detectives. Made for TV. **102m/C VHS.** *GB* Helen Mirren, Beatie Edney, Robert Glenister, Lesley Sharp, Jack Ellis, Stuart Wilson, John Benfield, Richard Hawley; ***D:*** John Madden; ***W:*** Paul Billing; ***M:*** Stephen Warbeck. *VTR*

Prime Suspect: The Scent of Darkness 🦴🦴🦴 **1995** Could this be curtains for the career of the irascible Jane Tennison? Not bloody likely but she's got more than her fair share of trouble when a new wave of murders are in the same modus operandi as multiple killer George Marlow—whom Tennison put away four years before (in "Prime Suspect"). Now Marlow's conviction is called into question, as are Jane's methods, so she's placed on suspension. But that isn't going to stop her from getting to the truth. **102m/C VHS.** *GB* Helen Mirren, Tim Woodward, Stuart Wilson, Richard Hawley, John Benfield, Christopher Fulford, Joyce Redman, Stephen Boxer; ***D:*** Paul Marcus. *VTR*

Prime Target 🦴🦴 **1991 (R)** Small-town cop John Bloodstone (Heavener) is recruited by the FBI to transfer a mafia boss (Curtis) from a safehouse to the courthouse. He has to keep the former mobster alive long enough to testify against the "family." Their cross-country adventure is heightened by a murderous confrontation with evil forces that want them both dead. **87m/C VHS.** David Heavener, Tony Curtis, Isaac Hayes, Jenilee Harrison, Robert Reed, Andrew (Andy) Robinson, Don Stroud; ***D:*** David Heavener; ***W:*** David Heavener; ***M:*** Chris Boardman. *HMD*

The Prime Time *Woof!* **1960** Horrid film about a teen girl who leaves home and gets involved with a teen gang and a slimy detective. She's also kidnapped by a weird beatnik artist who forces her to pose nude. Black's film debut. Also known as "Hellkitten." **76m/B VHS.** JoAnn LeCompte, Frank Roche, James Brooks, Ray Gronwold, Maria Pavelle, Robert Major, Karen Black; ***D:*** Herschell Gordon Lewis. *SNC*

Prime Time 🦴½ **1980 (R)** Forgotten satirical comedy about what would happen if the censors took a day off from American television. **73m/C VHS, Beta.** Warren Oates, David Spielberg. *NO*

Prime Time Murder 🦴½ **1992 (R)** Freelance TV journalist hooks up with eccentric ex-cop to trail a psycho stalking street people. **95m/C VHS.** Tim Thomerson, Sally Kirkland, Anthony Finetti, Laura Reed; ***D:*** Gary Skeen Hall. *ACA*

The Primitive Lover 🦴🦴 **1916** Early silent comedy about young wife who decides she deserves more than her marriage is giving her. **67m/B VHS, Beta.** Constance Talmadge, Kenneth Harlan, Harrison Ford; ***D:*** Sidney Franklin. *GPV*

Primo Baby 🦴🦴½ **1988** A troublesome 15-year-old girl learns responsibility when she must care for a crippled racehorse. They both have a chance at success when she enters the thoroughbred in a race. **97m/C VHS.** *WOV*

Primrose Path 🦴🦴½ **1940** Melodramatic soaper with comedic touches about a wrong-side-of-the-tracks girl falling for and then losing an ambitious young go-getter running a hamburger stand. **93m/B VHS, Beta.** Ginger Rogers, Joel McCrea, Marjorie Rambeau, Henry Travers, Miles Mander, Queenie Vasser, Joan Carroll, Vivienne Osborne; ***D:*** Gregory La Cava. Nominations: Academy Awards '40: Best Supporting Actress (Rambeau). *TTC*

Prince and the Great Race 🦴🦴 **1983** Three Australian children search the outback to find their kidnapped horse who is scheduled to run in the big New Year's Day Race. **91m/C VHS, Beta.** *AU* John Ewart, John Howard, Nicole Kidman. *LIV*

The Prince and the Pauper 🦴🦴🦴 **1937** Satisfying adaptation of the classic Mark Twain story of a young street urchin who trades places with the young king of England. Wonderful musical score by noted composer Korngold who provided the music for many of Flynn's adventure films. Also available in a computer-colorized version. **118m/B VHS, Beta, LV.** Errol Flynn, Claude Rains, Alan Hale, Billy Mauch, Montagu Love, Henry Stephenson, Barton MacLane; ***D:*** William Keighley; ***M:*** Erich Wolfgang Korngold. *FOX, MLB, CCB*

The Prince and the Pauper 🦴🦴 **1962** A prince and a poor young boy swap their clothes and identities, thus causing a lot of confusion for their families. Based on the story by Mark Twain. **93m/C VHS, Beta.** Guy Williams, Laurence Naismith, Donald Houston, Jane Asher, Walter Hudd. *DIS*

The Prince and the Pauper 🦴🦴½ *Crossed Swords* **1978 (PG)** Remake of the 1937 Errol Flynn film employing lavish sets and a tongue-in-cheek attitude among the all-star cast, who occasionally wander adrift when the director stops for tea. When an English prince and a pauper discover that they have identical appearances, they decide to trade places with each other. From Mark Twain's classic. **113m/C VHS, Beta.** *GB* Oliver Reed, Raquel Welch, Mark Lester, Ernest Borgnine, George C. Scott, Rex Harrison, Charlton Heston, Sybil Danning; ***D:*** Richard Fleischer; ***C:*** Jack Cardiff; ***M:*** Maurice Jarre. *MED*

The Prince and the Showgirl 🦴🦴½ **1957** An American showgirl in 1910 London is wooed by the Prince of Carpathia. Part of the "A Night at the Movies" series, this tape simulates a 1957 movie evening, with a Sylvester the Cat cartoon, "Greedy for Tweety," a newsreel and coming attractions for "Spirit of St. Louis." **127m/C VHS, Beta, LV.** Laurence Olivier, Marilyn Monroe, Sybil Thorndike, Jeremy Spenser, Richard Wattis; ***D:*** Laurence Olivier; ***W:*** Terence Rattigan; ***C:*** Jack Cardiff. *WAR*

Prince Brat and the Whipping Boy 🦴🦴🦴 *The Whipping Boy* **1995 (G)** Orphaned Jemmy (Munro) is living on the streets of the 18th-century German town of Brattenburg with his younger sister Annyrose (Salt). Neglected, spoiled Prince Horace (Knight) has been causing mischief in the castle but instead of being punished himself, the king's men catch Jemmy and use him as a punishment stand-in. Jemmy escapes the castle to go get back to his sister and the Prince decides to go along for the adventure. Filmed on location in North Rhine-Westphalia and Burgundy, Germany. Adventurous TV movie with spunky leads; adapted from Sid Fleischman's novella. **96m/C VHS, LV.** Truan Munro, Nic Knight, Karen Salt, George C. Scott, Kevin Conway, Vincent Schiavelli, Andrew Bicknell, Jean Anderson, Mathilda May; ***D:*** Syd Macartney; ***W:*** Max Brindle; ***M:*** Lee Holdridge. *COL*

Prince Jack 🦴🦴 **1983** Profiles the turbulent political career of President John F. Kennedy. **100m/C VHS, Beta.** Lloyd Nolan, Dana Andrews, Robert Guillaume, Cameron Mitchell; ***D:*** Bert Lovitt; ***M:*** Elmer Bernstein. *LIV*

Prince of Bel Air 🦴½ **1987 (R)** A pool-cleaning playboy who makes a habit of one night stands meets a woman and starts falling in love with her. Originally a made-for-television movie. **95m/C VHS, Beta, LV.** Mark Harmon, Kirstie Alley, Robert Vaughn, Patrick Laborteaux, Deborah Harmon; ***D:*** Charles Braverman; ***M:*** Robert Folk. *ACA*

The Prince of Central Park 🦴🦴🦴 **1977** Two young orphans are forced by circumstance to live in a tree in New York's Central Park until they are befriended by a lonely old woman. An above-average made for television adaptation of the novel by Evan H. Rhodes, the story was later used for a Broadway play. **76m/C VHS, Beta.** Ruth Gordon, T.J. Hargrave, Lisa Richards, Brooke Shields, Marc Vahanian, Dan Hedaya; ***D:*** Harvey Hart. *LIV*

Prince of Darkness 🦴½ **1987 (R)** University students release Satan, in the form of a mysterious chemical, unwittingly on the world. Written by Martin Quatermass (a pseudonym of Carpenter). Strong personnel does not save this dreary and slow-moving cliche plot. **102m/C VHS, Beta, LV.** Donald Pleasence, Lisa Blount, Victor Wong, Jameson Parker, Dennis Dun; ***Cameos:*** Alice Cooper; ***D:*** John Carpenter; ***W:*** John Carpenter; ***M:*** John Carpenter. *MCA*

Prince of Pennsylvania 🦴½ **1988 (R)** A mild comedy about a spaced-out youth who kidnaps his own father in hopes of nabbing a family inheritance. **113m/C VHS, Beta, LV.** Keanu Reeves, Fred Ward, Amy Madigan, Bonnie Bedelia, Jeff Hayenga; ***D:*** Ron Nyswaner; ***W:*** Ron Nyswaner; ***M:*** Thomas Newman. *COL*

Prince of the City ♂♂♂ **1981 (R)** Docudrama of a police officer who becomes an informant in an effort to end corruption within his narcotics unit, but finds he must pay a heavy price. Based on the true story told in Robert Daly's book, the powerful script carries the tension through what would otherwise be an overly long film. Excellent performances make this a riveting character study. **167m/C VHS, Beta, LV.** Treat Williams, Jerry Orbach, Richard Foronjy, Don Billett, Kenny Marino, Lindsay Crouse, Lance Henriksen; ***D:*** Sidney Lumet; ***W:*** Jay Presson Allen, Sidney Lumet. New York Film Critics Awards '81: Best Director (Lumet); Nominations: Academy Awards '81: Best Adapted Screenplay. *WAR*

The Prince of Thieves ♂♂ **1948** Robin Hood helps Lady Marian extricate herself from a forced marriage in this adventure made with younger audiences in mind. **72m/C VHS.** Jon Hall, Patricia Morison, Adele Jergens, Alan Mowbray, Michael Duane; ***D:*** Howard Bretherton. *COL*

The Prince of Tides ♂♂♂½ **1991 (R)** Conroy's sprawling southern-fried saga is neatly pared down to essentials in this tale of the dysfunctional Wingo family, whose dark tragedies are gradually revealed as twins Tom and Savannah come to grips with personal demons under the ministering aid of psychiatrist Streisand. Bravura performance by Nolte in what may be his best role to date; Streisand is restrained in both her performance and direction although a subplot dealing with her bad marriage and rebellious son is a predictable distraction. The South Carolina low country, and even New York City, never looked better. Conroy adapted the screenplay from his novel of the same name with Johnston's help. **132m/C VHS, Beta, LV, 8mm.** Nick Nolte, Barbra Streisand, Blythe Danner, Kate Nelligan, Jeroen Krabbe, Melinda Dillon, George Carlin, Jason Gould, Brad Sullivan; ***D:*** Barbra Streisand; ***W:*** Pat Conroy, Becky Johnston; ***M:*** James Newton Howard. Golden Globe Awards '92: Best Actor—Drama (Nolte); Los Angeles Film Critics Association Awards '91: Best Actor (Nolte); Nominations: Academy Awards '91: Best Actor (Nolte), Best Adapted Screenplay, Best Art Direction/Set Decoration, Best Cinematography, Best Picture, Best Supporting Actress (Nelligan), Best Original Score. *COL*

Prince Valiant ♂♂½ **1954** When his royal dad is exiled by an evil tyrant, brave young Wagner brushes aside bangs and journeys to Camelot to seek the help of King Arthur. Based on Harold Foster's classic comic strip. **100m/C VHS, Beta.** James Mason, Janet Leigh, Robert Wagner, Debra Paget, Sterling Hayden, Victor McLaglen, Donald Crisp, Brian Aherne, Barry Jones, Mary Philips; ***D:*** Henry Hathaway; ***W:*** Dudley Nichols. *FXV, FCT*

Princes in Exile ♂♂½ **1990 (PG-13)** Young people struggle with their life-threatening illnesses at a special summer camp. They find that love and friendship hold the key to dreams about the future. Excellent cast of newcomers. Based on a novel of the same name by Mark Schreiber. **103m/C VHS, Beta, LV.** *CA* Zachary Ansley, Nicholas Shields, Stacy Mistysyn, Alexander Chapman, Chuck Shamata; ***D:*** Giles Walker. *FRH, FCT*

Princess Academy ♂ **1987 (R)** A self-respecting young debutante battles the ways of her elitist finishing school. **91m/C VHS, Beta.** *FR* Eva Gabor, Lu Leonard, Richard Paul, Lar Park Lincoln, Carole Davis; ***D:*** Bruce Block; ***M:*** Paul Antonelli, Roger Bellon. *LIV*

The Princess & the Call Girl ♂♂ **1984** A call girl asks her look-alike roommate to take her place in Monaco for a lavishly erotic weekend. **90m/C VHS, Beta.** Carol Levy, Shannah Hall, Victor Bevine; ***D:*** Radley Metzger. *MON*

The Princess and the Goblin ♂♂½ **1994 (G)** Little kiddies may enjoy this animated adventure but it's a bland story with mediocre animation. Groups of ugly, underground-dwelling goblins like nothing better than to scare humans, especially castle-dwelling Princess Irene. Brave working-class Curdie helps to save the day. Based on a book by George MacDonald. **82m/C VHS.** *GB HU* ***V:*** Sally Ann Marsh, Peter Murray, Claire Bloom. *HMD*

The Princess and the Pea **1983** From "Faerie Tale Theatre" comes the story of a princess who tries to prove that she's a blueblood by feeling the bump of a tiny pea under the thickness of twenty mattresses. **60m/C VHS, Beta, LV.** Liza Minnelli, Tom Conti, Tim Kazurinsky, Pat McCormick, Beatrice Straight; ***D:*** Tony Bill. *FOX, FCT*

The Princess and the Pirate ♂♂♂ **1944** Hope at his craziest as a vaudvillian who falls for a beautiful princess while on the run from buccaneers on the Spanish Main. Look for Crosby in a closing cameo performance. Available in digitally remastered stereo with original movie trailer. **94m/C VHS, Beta, LV.** Bob Hope, Walter Slezak, Walter Brennan, Virginia Mayo, Victor McLaglen; ***Cameos:*** Bing Crosby; ***D:*** David Butler; ***C:*** Victor Milner. Nominations: Academy Awards '44: Best Interior Decoration, Best Original Score. *HBO, SUE*

The Princess and the Swineherd ♂½ **1960** A German adaptation of the Brothers Grimm fairy tale about a young suitor who tries to please a materialistic princess. **82m/B VHS, Beta.** *GE VYY*

The Princess Bride ♂♂♂½ **1987 (PG)** A modern update of the basic fairy tale crammed with all the cliches, this adventurously irreverent love story centers around a beautiful maiden and her young swain as they battle the evils of the mythical kingdom of Florin to be reunited with one another. Great dueling scenes and offbeat satire of the genre make this fun for adults as well as children. Based on William Goldman's cult novel. **98m/C VHS, Beta, LV, 8mm.** Cary Elwes, Mandy Patinkin, Robin Wright, Wallace Shawn, Peter Falk, Andre the Giant, Chris Sarandon, Christopher Guest, Billy Crystal, Carol Kane, Fred Savage, Peter Cook, Mel Smith; ***D:*** Rob Reiner; ***W:*** William Goldman; ***M:*** Mark Knopfler. Nominations: Academy Awards '87: Best Song ("Storybook Love"). *COL, SUE, HMV*

Princess Caraboo ♂♂½ **1994 (PG)** Fluffy quasi-fairy tale (but based on a true story) finds an exotic beauty (Cates) appearing in an English village in 1817. She speaks a language no one understands and is taken under the wing of the local gentry, the Worralls, who believe she is an Asian princess washed ashore during a shipwreck. Meanwhile, the local jouralist (Rea) is suspicious but protective, an Oxford linguist (Lithgow) is determined to prove her a fraud, and she must put up with the Worrall family's pompous Greek butler (Cate's husband Kline at his showy best). **97m/C VHS, LV.** Phoebe Cates, Stephen Rea, John Lithgow, Kevin Kline, Jim Broadbent, Wendy Hughes, Peter Eyre, Jacqueline Pearce, John Lynch, John Sessions, Arkie Whiteley, John Wells; ***D:*** Michael Austin; ***W:*** John Wells, Michael Austin; ***M:*** Richard Hartley. *COL*

Princess Cinderella ♂♂ **193?** A live-action dramatization of the famous fantasy. Dubbed in English. **75m/B VHS, Beta.** *SP* Silvana Jachino, Roberto Villa. *JEF*

The Princess Comes Across ♂♂♂ **1936** Deft comedy-mystery finds Brooklyn actress Lombard deciding to take an ocean voyage and pass herself off as a Swedish princess in the hopes of furthering her career. Bandleader MacMurray is smitten but an old beau recognizes the ruse and demands hush money. Then he turns up dead and the duo fall under the suspicious eye of a German passenger (Rumann) who happens to be a detective. From the novel by Louis Lucien Rogger. **77m/B VHS.** Carole Lombard, Fred MacMurray, Alison Skipworth, Sig Rumann, Douglass Dumbrille, William Frawley, Porter Hall, George Barbier, Lumsden Hare, Mischa Auer, Tetsu Komai; ***D:*** William K. Howard; ***W:*** Walter DeLeon, Francis Martin, Frank Butler, Don Hartman; ***C:*** Ted Tetzlaff. *MCA*

Princess Daisy ♂ **1983** Made for television movie about a beautiful model who claws her way to the top of her profession while trying to find true love and avoid the clutches of her rotten half-brother. Adapted from Judith Krantz's glitzy best-selling novel. **200m/C VHS, Beta.** Merete Van Kamp, Lindsay Wagner, Claudia Cardinale, Stacy Keach, Ringo Starr, Barbara Bach; ***D:*** Waris Hussein. *VTR, FOX, MOV*

Princess Tam Tam ♂♂♂ **1935** Pleasing French adaptation of Shaw's "Pygmalion," as a beautiful native African woman is "westernized" by a handsome writer and then introduced to high society as an exotic princess. A musical notable for its spectacular choreography and on-location Tunisian scenery. Story by Pepito Abatino, who was then Baker's husband. In French with English subtitles. **77m/B VHS, Beta, LV.** *FR* Josephine Baker, Albert Prejean, Germaine Aussey, Viviane Romance; ***D:*** Edmond T. Greville. *MVD, TPV, KIV*

The Princess Who Never Laughed **1984** A stern king holds a laugh-off contest to make his morose daughter happy in this adaptation of the Brothers Grimm story from the "Faerie Tale Theatre" series. **60m/C VHS, Beta.** Ellen Barkin, Howard Hesseman, Howie Mandel, Mary Woronov. *FOX, FCT*

Princess Yang Kwei Fei ♂♂♂ *Yokihi; The Empress Yang Kwei Fei* **1955** Set in 8th-century China and based on the life of the last T'ang emperor and the beautiful servant girl he loves and makes his bride. She falls victim to court jealousies and he to his greedy family, though even death cannot end their love. Beautifully filmed and acted romantic tragedy. In Japanese with English subtitles. **91m/C VHS.** *JP* Machiko Kyo, Masayuki Mori, Sakae Ozawa, So Yamamura; ***D:*** Kenji Mizoguchi. *NYF*

The Principal ♂♂½ **1987 (R)** A tough, down-on-his-luck high school teacher is hired as the principal of a relentlessly violent, uncontrollable high school. Naturally he whips it into shape. **109m/C VHS, Beta, LV.** James Belushi, Louis Gossett Jr., Rae Dawn Chong, Michael Wright, Esai Morales, J.J. Cohen, Troy Winbush; ***D:*** Christopher Cain; ***W:*** Frank Deese; ***M:*** Jay Gruska. *COL*

Prison ♂½ **1988 (R)** The zombified body of an unjustly executed inmate haunts Creedmore Prison, stalking the guard that killed him. His search is aided by the terrified inmates. **102m/C VHS, Beta, LV.** Lane Smith, Chelsea Field, Viggo Mortensen, Lincoln Kilpatrick, Tom Everett, Tiny Lister; ***D:*** Renny Harlin; ***W:*** C. Courtney Joyner; ***M:*** Richard Band. *NWV*

Prison Break ♂♂ **1938** A convict plans a daring prison escape in order to clear his name for a murder he did not commit. **72m/B VHS, Beta.** Barton MacLane, Glenda Farrell, Ward Bond. *SNC, NOS, MRV*

Prison for Children ♂♂½ **1993** Sixteen year old Chris is orphaned and put into a boys home where a supervisor sees his potential and helps him achieve it. **96m/C VHS.** Raphael Sbarge, Kenny Ransom, Jonathan Chapin, Josh Brolin, James Callahan, Betty Thomas, John Ritter; ***D:*** Larry Peerce. *MCA*

Prison Planet ♂½ **1992 (R)** In the year 2200 Earth is under the dictatorship of an evil king, with only a band of intrepid rebels to oppose him. Blaine, one of the rebels, gets himself arrested and sent to prison in search of the true ruler, the king's brother. But the prison is protected by a brutal warlord and his equally sadistic warriors, whom Blaine must battle if he ever hopes to find truth and justice. **90m/C VHS.** James Phillips, Jack Willcox, Michael Foley, Deborah Thompson-Carlin; ***D:*** Armand Gazarian; ***W:*** Armand Gazarian. *COL*

Prison Shadows ♂ **1936** Contrived programmer about a fighter (Nugent) who attempts to make a comeback after having served three years of a five-year sentence for killing an opponent in the boxing ring. He makes his comeback, but deals yet another mortal blow. Turns out that a gambling ring is behind the bizarre murders of the fighters and Nugent is their next victim. **67m/B VHS.** Eddie Nugent, Lucille Lund, Joan Barclay, Forrest Taylor, Syd Saylor, Monte Blue; ***D:*** Robert F. "Bob" Hill; ***W:*** Al Martin. *SNC*

Prison Stories: Women on the Inside ♂♂♂ **1991** Three short dramatic stories depict the life of women inside prison walls. "New Chicks," directed by Spheeris, tells the story of two lifelong friends and partners in crime. "Esperanza," directed by Deitch, tells the story of a woman on the inside trying to prevent her family from following the same destructive path. Silver's "Parole Board" features Davidovich as a murderess up for parole but reluctant to leave the security of the prison. Blunt and gritty portrayal of prison gangs, the lifestyle of female inmates, and their fears of returning to life on the outside. Originally produced for cable TV. **94m/C VHS, Beta.** Rae Dawn Chong, Annabella Sciorra, Lolita Davidovich, Talisa Soto, Rachel Ticotin, Grace Zabriskie, Silvania Gallardo, Francesca Roberts; ***D:*** Donna Deitch, Penelope Spheeris, Joan Micklin Silver; ***W:*** Dick Beebe. *PSM*

Prison Train ☠☠½ *People's Enemy* **1938** Travelogue of a convicted murderer's cross-country journey to begin his prison sentence at Alcatraz. **84m/B VHS.** Fred Keating, Linda (Dorothy Comingore) Winters, Clarence Muse, Faith Bacon, Alexander Leftwich, Nestor Paiva, Franklyn Farnum; ***D:*** Gordon Wiles. *VYY, MOV*

The Prisoner ☠☠☠ **1955** Gritty drama about a Cardinal imprisoned in a Soviet bloc country as his captors attempt to break his determination not to be used as a propaganda tool. Interactions between the prisoner and his interogator are riveting. Based on the real-life experiences of Cardinal Mindszenty, a Hungarian activist during and after WWII. **91m/B VHS.** *GB* Alec Guinness, Jack Hawkins, Raymond Huntley, Wilfred Lawson; ***D:*** Peter Glenville. *COL*

The Prisoner: Arrival **1968** Introductory episode of the cult television series. McGoohan stars as a former British spy abducted and held captive in a mysterious village where everyone is assigned a number. As Number 6 he tries to figure out what's going on and how he can get out. Additional episodes available. **52m/C VHS, Beta, LV.** *GB* Patrick McGoohan, Virginia Maskell, Guy Doleman, Paul Eddington, George Baker, Angelo Muscat, Barbara Yu Ling, Stephanie Randall; ***D:*** Don Chaffey. *MPI, MOV, TVC*

Prisoner Cell Block H **1980** Popular Australian television soap opera set in Wentworth Detention Center, a women's prison. Primary characters include Franky, a violent lesbian biker in for armed robbery; Karen, who murdered her husband and is the object of Franky's affection; and naive Lynn, accused of kidnapping and attempted murder. Two episodes per cassette. **95m/C VHS.** *AU* Carol Burns, Kerry Armstrong, Patsy King, Gerard Maguire, Barry Quin, Mary Ward, Monica Maughan, Fiona Spence, Val Lehman, Pieta Tommano. *MPI, MOV*

Prisoner in the Middle ☠☠ **1974 (PG)** Janssen is the only man who can stop a nuclear warhead from falling into the hands of rival Middle East factions. Originally released as "Warhead." **87m/C VHS, Beta, LV, 8mm.** David Janssen, Karin Dor, Christopher Stone, Turia Tan, David Semadar, Art Metrano; ***D:*** John O'Conner. *ACA, MTX*

Prisoner of Honor ☠☠☠ **1991 (PG)** A made-for-cable-TV retelling of notorious Dreyfus Affair, in which a Jewish officer in the 19th-century French military was accused of treason based on little evidence and lots of bigotry. George Piquart (Dreyfuss), the anti-semitic counterintelligence head, grows to realize Dreyfuss' innocence and fights zealously for the truth. Russell's flamboyant direction takes the heroic tale into the realm of the surreal; this may not be a thoroughly accurate account, but it's one of the more eye-filling. **90m/C VHS.** Richard Dreyfuss, Oliver Reed, Peter Firth, Jeremy Kemp, Brian Blessed, Peter Vaughan, Kenneth Colley, Lindsay Anderson; ***D:*** Ken Russell. *HBO*

Prisoner of Rio ☠☠ **1989** The made-for-cable-TV satire about scruple-less television evangelists and their nefarious schemes at acquiring their audience's money. **90m/C VHS, Beta, LV.** Steven Berkoff, Paul Freeman; ***D:*** Lech Majewski; ***M:*** Hans Zimmer. *MOV*

Prisoner of Second Avenue ☠☠½ **1974 (PG)** A New Yorker in his late forties faces the future, without a job or any confidence in his ability, with the help of his understanding wife. Based on the Broadway play by Neil Simon. **98m/C VHS, Beta, LV.** Jack Lemmon, Anne Bancroft, Gene Saks, Elizabeth Wilson, Sylvester Stallone, F. Murray Abraham; ***D:*** Melvin Frank; ***W:*** Neil Simon; ***M:*** Marvin Hamlisch. *WAR*

Prisoner of Zenda ☠☠☠½ **1937** An excellent cast and splendid photography make this the definitive film adaptation of Anthony Hope's swashbuckling novel. A British commoner is forced to pose as his cousin, the kidnapped king of a small European country, to save the throne. Complications of the romantic sort ensue when he falls in love with the queen. Excellent acting, robust sword play, and beautifully designed costumes make this an enjoyable spectacle. **101m/B VHS, Beta, LV.** Ronald Colman, Douglas Fairbanks Jr., Madeleine Carroll, David Niven, Raymond Massey, Mary Astor, Sir C. Aubrey Smith, Montagu Love, Byron Foulger, Alexander D'Arcy, Charles Halton; ***D:*** John Cromwell; ***W:*** Donald Ogden Stewart, John Balderston, Wells Root; ***C:*** James Wong Howe. Nominations: Academy Awards '36: Best Original Score; Academy Awards '37: Best Interior Decoration. *MGM*

Prisoner of Zenda ☠☠½ **1952** Less-inspired remake of the 1937 version of Anthony Hope's novel, of a man resembling the monarch of a small country who is forced to pose as King during the coronation ceremony, becomes enamored with the queen, and finds himself embroiled in a murder plot. Worth watching for the luxurious costumes and lavish sets. Cast as a Cardinal here, Stone starred in the 1922 version. **101m/C VHS, Beta, LV.** Stewart Granger, Deborah Kerr, Louis Calhern, James Mason, Jane Greer, Lewis Stone; ***D:*** Richard Thorpe; ***C:*** Joseph Ruttenberg. *MGM*

Prisoner of Zenda ☠☠ **1979 (PG)** Flat comedic interpretation of Anthony Hope's swashbuckling tale of two identical men who switch places, only to find things complicated by a murder. Sellers stars in the double role of Prince Rudolph of Ruritania and Syd, the cockney cab driver who doubles for Rudolph when the Prince is imprisoned by his jealous brother Michael. **108m/C VHS, Beta.** Peter Sellers, Jeremy Kemp, Lynne Frederick, Lionel Jeffries, Elke Sommer; ***D:*** Richard Quine; ***W:*** Dick Clement, Ian LaFrenais; ***M:*** Henry Mancini. *MCA*

Prisoners of Inertia ☠☠½ **1989 (R)** Two newlyweds travel to New York city and find themselves caught up in a whirlwind adventure in this well-acted but lazily scripted comedy drama. **92m/C VHS.** Amanda Plummer, Christopher Rich, John C. McGinley; ***D:*** Jay Noyles Seles. *BTV*

Prisoners of the Lost Universe ☠½ **1984** Talk-show hostess and her buddy are transported to a hostile universe by a renegade scientist. The two terrified humans search desperately for the dimensional door that is their only hope of escape. Made for television. **94m/C VHS, Beta.** Richard Hatch, Kay Lenz, John Saxon; ***D:*** Terry Marcel. *NO*

Prisoners of the Sun ☠☠☠ *Blood Oath* **1991 (R)** Right after WWII an Australian captain fights to convict Japanese officers for atrocities against Allied POWs, but he's stonewalled by both the U.S. military and still-defiant enemy prisoners. This fiery drama from Down Under packs a punch as it questions whether wartime justice even exists; similar in that way to Brown's earlier "Breaker Morant." Takei (Sulu of the original "Star Trek") makes an imposing Japanese admiral. **109m/C VHS, Beta.** *AU* Bryan Brown, George Takei, Terry O'Quinn, John Back, Toshi Shioya, Deborah Unger; ***D:*** Stephen Wallace. *PAR*

Private Affairs ☠ **1989 (R)** The mistress of a well-known surgeon becomes jealous when the doctor decides to have a fling with a gorgeous young swim instructor. Italian-made cheapie. **83m/C VHS, Beta.** *IT* Guiliana de Sio, Kate Capshaw, David Naughton, Luca Barbareschi, Michele Placido; ***D:*** Francesco Massaro. *ACA*

The Private Affairs of Bel Ami ☠☠☠ **1947** "This is the story of a scoundrel," proclaims the opening. Sanders is ideally cast as a suave cad who rises in 1880s Parisian society, largely through the strategic seduction of prominent women. Moralistically minded Old Hollywood toned down the talky adaptation of the Guy de Maupassant novel, but it's still drama of a high order. **112m/B VHS.** George Sanders, Angela Lansbury, Ann Dvorak, Frances Dee, John Carradine, Susan Douglas, Hugo Haas, Marie Wilson, Albert Basserman, Warren William, Katherine Emery, Richard Fraser; ***D:*** Albert Lewin; ***W:*** Albert Lewin. *REP, FCT*

Private Benjamin ☠☠½ **1980 (R)** Lighthearted fare about a pampered New York Jewish princess who impulsively enlists in the U.S. Army after her husband dies on their wedding night. Hawn, who also produced, creates a character loveable even at her worst moments and brings a surprising amount of depth to this otherwise frivolous look at high society attitudes. The basis for the television series. **110m/C VHS, Beta, LV.** Goldie Hawn, Eileen Brennan, Albert Brooks, Robert Webber, Armand Assante, Barbara Barrie, Mary Kay Place, Sally Kirkland, Craig T. Nelson, Harry Dean Stanton, Sam Wanamaker; ***D:*** Howard Zieff; ***W:*** Nancy Meyers, Charles Shyer, Harvey Miller; ***M:*** Bill Conti. Writers Guild of America '80: Best Original Screenplay; Nominations: Academy Awards '80: Best Actress (Hawn), Best Original Screenplay, Best Supporting Actress (Brennan). *WAR*

Private Buckaroo ☠☠ **1942** War time entertainment in which Harry James and his orchestra get drafted. They decide to put on a show for the soldiers and get help from the Andrews Sisters. ♫Don't Sit Under the Apple Tree with Anyone Else But Me; Three Little Sisters; Private Buckaroo; Johnny Get Your Gun Again; We've Got a Job to Do; You Made Me Love You; Six Jerks in a Jeep; That's the Moon My Son; I Love the South. **70m/B VHS, Beta.** The Andrews Sisters, Harry James, Joe E. Lewis, Dick Foran, Shemp Howard, Mary Wickes, Donald O'Connor; ***D:*** Eddie Cline. *NOS, HEG, CAB*

Private Contentment ☠☠ **1983** This is a drama about a young soldier's experiences before he goes off to war in 1945. **90m/C VHS, Beta.** Trini Alvarado, Peter Gallagher, John McMartin, Kathryn Walker; ***D:*** Vivian Matalon. *FLI*

Private Duty Nurses ☠½ **1971 (R)** Three nurses take on racism, war wounds, and a menage-a-trois (between one nurse, a doctor, and a drug addict). Second in Roger Corman's "nurse" quintet takes itself too seriously to be entertaining, but the gals make good use of those exciting new inventions, waterbeds. Preceded by "The Student Nurses" and followed by "Night Call Nurses," "The Young Nurses," and "Candy Stripe Nurses." Also on video as "Young L.A. Nurses 1." **80m/C VHS, Beta.** Kathy Cannon, Joyce Williams, Pegi Boucher, Joseph Kaufmann, Dennis Redfield, Herbert Jefferson Jr., Paul Hampton, Paul Gleason; ***D:*** George Armitage; ***W:*** George Armitage. *NLC, SUE*

The Private Eyes ☠½ **1980 (PG)** Light and uneven comedic romp with Knotts and Conway as bungling sleuths engaged to investigate two deaths. They're led on a merry chase through secret passages to a meeting with a ghostly adversary. **91m/C VHS, Beta, LV.** Don Knotts, Tim Conway, Trisha Noble, Bernard Fox; ***D:*** Lang Elliott; ***W:*** Tim Conway, John Myhers. *VES*

The Private Files of J. Edgar Hoover ☠☠½ **1977 (PG)** Scandal-mongering "biography" of J. Edgar Hoover's private, sex-filled life. **112m/C VHS.** Broderick Crawford, Dan Dailey, Jose Ferrer, Rip Torn, Michael Parks, Raymond St. Jacques, Ronee Blakley; ***D:*** Larry Cohen; ***W:*** Larry Cohen. *HBO*

A Private Function ☠☠½ **1984 (PG)** A ribald gag-fest dealing with Palin as a Yorkshireman who steals and fattens a wily contraband pig against the backdrop of post-WWII rationing. The satire ranges from biting to downright nasty, but Palin is always likeable in the center of it all. **96m/C VHS, Beta.** *GB* Michael Palin, Maggie Smith, Denholm Elliott, Bill Paterson, Liz Smith; ***D:*** Malcolm Mowbray; ***W:*** Alan Bennett; ***C:*** Tony Pierce-Roberts; ***M:*** John Du Prez. British Academy Awards '84: Best Actress (Smith), Best Supporting Actor (Elliott), Best Supporting Actress (Smith). *PAR, TVC, FCT*

Private Hell 36 ☠☠ **1954** Two detectives become guilt-ridden after keeping part of some stolen money recovered after a robbery. Co-produced by Lupino. **81m/B VHS, LV.** Ida Lupino, Howard Duff, Steve Cochran; ***D:*** Donald Siegel; ***W:*** Ida Lupino. *REP*

The Private History of a Campaign That Failed 🦴½ **1987** Adaptation of the Mark Twain story about a cowardly troop of Confederate soldiers. **89m/C VHS, Beta.** Pat Hingle, Edward Herrmann. *MCA*

Private Investigations 🦴½ **1987 (R)** A made-for-video thriller about a nosey reporter who gets himself and his adult son in trouble while investigating drug-pushing cops. **91m/C VHS, Beta.** Ray Sharkey, Clayton Rohner, Talia Balsam, Anthony Zerbe, Paul Le-Mat; ***D:*** Nigel Dick; ***W:*** John Dahl, David Warfield. *MGM, FOX*

Private Lessons 🦴🦴 **1981 (R)** Teenage boy is left alone for the summer in the care of an alluring maid and a scheming chauffeur. **83m/C VHS, Beta, LV.** Eric Brown, Sylvia Kristel, Howard Hesseman; ***D:*** Alan Myerson; ***C:*** Jan De Bont. *MCA*

Private Lessons **19??** A boy can't concentrate on his piano lessons when he gets a beautiful new teacher. You won't be able to concentrate on anything but comedy. **90m/C VHS, Beta.** Carroll Baker. *JEF*

Private Lessons, Another Story 🦴½ **1994 (R)** A New York photographer (Morgan) is sick of her philandering husband and decides to experience some sexual excitement of her own by heading off to Miami. All that tropical heat inspires passion with her Cuban chauffeur (Garaza). **86m/C VHS.** Mariana Morgan, Ray Garaza, Theresa Morris; ***D:*** Dominique Othenin-Girard; ***W:*** William Mernit. *PAR*

Private Life 🦴🦴½ *Chastnaya Zhizn* **1982** Suddenly with time on his hands, a Soviet official scrutinizes his relationships. After a number of revelations, he is forced to make new choices based on what he has learned. Oscar nominee in 1983. In Russian with English subtitles. **103m/C VHS.** *RU* Mikhail Ulyanov, Ita Sanvina, Irina Gubanova; ***D:*** Edgar Ryazanov; ***W:*** Andrew Davies. Nominations: Academy Awards '82: Best Foreign Language Film. *KIV, FCT*

Private Life of Don Juan 🦴🦴 *Don Juan* **1934** Appropriately slow-moving British costume drama set in 17th-century Spain finds an aging Don Juan struggling to maintain his usual antics in the pursuit of beautiful women. Furthermore, his reputation is being upstaged by a young imposter. Notable only as the last film appearance by Douglas Fairbanks Sr., and based on the play by Henri Bataille. **87m/B VHS, Beta.** *GB* Douglas Fairbanks Sr., Merle Oberon, Binnie Barnes, Melville Cooper, Joan Gardner, Benita Hume, Athene Seyler; ***D:*** Alexander Korda; ***C:*** Georges Perinal. *CNG, NOS, GPV*

The Private Life of Henry VIII 🦴🦴🦴🦴 **1933** Lavish historical spectacle lustily portraying the life and lovers of notorious British Monarch, King Henry VIII. A tour de force for Laughton as the robust 16th-century king, with outstanding performances by the entire cast. **97m/B VHS, Beta, LV.** *GB* Charles Laughton, Binnie Barnes, Elsa Lanchester, Robert Donat, Merle Oberon, Miles Mander, Wendy Barrie, John Loder; ***D:*** Alexander Korda; ***W:*** Arthur Wimperis, Lajos Biro; ***C:*** Georges Perinal. Academy Awards '33: Best Actor (Laughton); Nominations: Academy Awards '33: Best Picture. *HBO, NOS, PSM*

The Private Life of Sherlock Holmes 🦴🦴🦴½ **1970 (PG-13)** A unique perspective on the life of the famous detective reveals a complex character. Beautifully photographed, with fine performances by the supporting cast, the film boasts a haunting musical score but received suprisingly little recognition despite Wilder's high caliber direction. **125m/C VHS, LV.** *GB* Robert Stephens, Colin Blakely, Genevieve Page, Irene Handl, Stanley Holloway, Christopher Lee, Clive Revill; ***D:*** Billy Wilder; ***W:*** I.A.L. Diamond, Billy Wilder; ***M:*** Miklos Rozsa. *FOX*

Private Lives 🦴🦴🦴½ **1931** Stylish adaptation of Noel Coward play starring Shearer and Montgomery as a couple with a tempestuous relationship. Although once married, they have since divorced and married other mates. While honeymooning at the same french hotel (Quelle coincidence!), they have trouble showing affection to their new spouses and realize they still feel passionately about one another. Excellent acting combined with Coward's witty dialogue makes this film a treat. **92m/B VHS, LV.** Norma Shearer, Robert Montgomery, Reginald Denny, Una Merkel, Jean Hersholt; ***D:*** Sidney Franklin. *MGM*

The Private Lives of Elizabeth & Essex 🦴🦴🦴 **1939** Cast reads like a Who's Who in Hollywood in this lavishly costumed dramatization of the love affair between Queen Elizabeth I and the Second Earl of Essex. Forced to choose between her Kingdom and her lover, Davis' monarch is the epitome of a regal women. Fobray made her first film appearance as an adult in the adaptation of Maxwell Anderson's "Elizabeth the Queen." **106m/C VHS, Beta.** Bette Davis, Errol Flynn, Vincent Price, Nanette Fabray, Olivia de Havilland, Alan Hale, Donald Crisp, Leo G. Carroll; ***D:*** Michael Curtiz. Nominations: Academy Awards '39: Best Color Cinematography, Best Special Effects, Best Score. *FOX*

Private Manoeuvres *Woof!* **1983** A comely Swiss military adviser gives her all to uplift the morale of the men at Camp Samantha. **79m/C VHS, Beta.** Zachi Noy, Yoseph Shiloah, Dvora Bekon. *MGM*

A Private Matter 🦴🦴🦴 **1992 (PG-13)** Based on the true story of Sherri Finkbine (hostess of TV's "Romper Room") and the controversy surrounding her decision to terminate her pregnancy in 1962. Pregnant with her fifth child, she discovered her sleeping medication contained thalidomide, known to cause severe birth defects. Although technically illegal, her doctor agreed to quietly perform an abortion. Sherri warned a local newspaper reporter about the drug's dangers and her identity was mistakenly revealed. A storm of adverse publicity forced her to Sweden for the abortion. Great performances highlight this complex and traumatic issue. Made for cable television. **89m/C VHS, LV.** Sissy Spacek, Aidan Quinn, Estelle Parsons, Sheila McCarthy, Leon Russom, William H. Macy; ***D:*** Joan Micklin Silver; ***W:*** William Nicholson. *HBO*

Private Obsession 🦴½ **1994 (R)** Model Emanuelle Griffith (Whirry) is missing—kidnapped by obsessed admirer Richard (Christian) who wants the beauty for himself alone. Emanuelle may be blonde but she's not dumb and she decides to turn the tables on her captor. **93m/C VHS.** Shannon Whirry, Michael Christian, Bo Svenson, Rip Taylor; ***D:*** Lee Frost. *TRI*

Private Parts 🦴🦴 **1972 (R)** A bizarre first attempt at feature length for Bartel. Black comedy featuring a runaway, a voyeuristic photographer and a hotel full of strange people who participate in murder and a variety of freakish sexual acts. **87m/C VHS.** Ayn Ruymen, Lucille Benson, John Ventantonio, Laurie Main, Stanley Livingston, Charles Woolf; ***D:*** Paul Bartel. *FRG, MGM*

Private Passions 🦴 **1985** A sultry woman gives her teenaged cousin a lesson in love during his European vacation. **86m/C VHS, Beta.** Sybil Danning. *PSM*

Private Resort 🦴🦴 **1984 (R)** Curious house detective and a bumbling thief interrupt the highjinks of two girl-crazy teens on a quest for fun at an expensive Miami hotel. Occasionally funny plodder. **82m/C VHS, Beta, LV.** Johnny Depp, Rob Morrow, Karyn O'Bryan, Emily Longstreth, Tony Azito, Hector Elizondo, Dody Goodman, Leslie Easterbrook, Andrew Dice Clay; ***D:*** George Bowers. *COL*

Private Road: No Trespassing **1987 (R)** A stock car racer and a top engineer compete over a military project, cars and a rich heiress. **90m/C VHS, Beta.** George Kennedy, Greg Evigan, Mitzi Kapture; ***D:*** Raphael Nussbaum. *TWE*

Private School 🦴½ **1983 (R)** Two high school girls from the exclusive Cherryvale Academy for Women compete for the affections of a young man from nearby Freemount Academy for Men, while Cherryvale's headmistress is trying to raise funds to build a new wing. Banal teen sexploitation comedy with better-than-average cast. **89m/C VHS, Beta, LV.** Phoebe Cates, Betsy Russell, Kathleen Wilhoite, Sylvia Kristel, Ray Walston, Matthew Modine, Michael Zorek, Fran Ryan, Jonathan Prince, Kari Lizer, Richard Stahl; ***D:*** Noel Black; ***C:*** Walter Lassally. *MCA*

The Private Secretary 🦴½ **1935** Horton is a mild-mannered clergyman who finds out his identity has been usurped by a young man with a great many angry creditors. Horton has some amusing comic bits but the film, based on a popular Victorian farce "Der Bibliotheker" by Van Moser, did not translate well to the screen. **70m/B VHS.** *GB* Edward Everett Horton, Barry Mackay, Oscar Asche, Judy Gunn, Michael Shepley, Alastair Sim; ***D:*** Henry Edwards. *HCV*

Private War 🦴½ **1990 (R)** Training for an elite force turns deadly when the commanding officer makes the rules. Now it's a private war between two brutal fighting machines. Adapted from a Jan Guillou story. **95m/C VHS.** Martin Hewitt, Joe Dallesandro, Kimberly Beck; ***D:*** Frank De Palma; ***W:*** Frank De Palma, Terry Borst. *REP*

Private Wars 🦴🦴 **1993 (R)** A law-abiding community falls victim to gangland violence until the inhabitants hire a down-and-out private eye (Railsback) to show them how to fight back. He finds out that a greedy land developer (Whitman) has bribed the Chief of Police (Champion) to let his goons do anything to get the people out so he can redevelop the land. **94m/C VHS, LV.** Steve Railsback, Michael Champion, Stuart Whitman, Holly Floria, Dan Tullis Jr., Michael Delano, James Lew, Brian Patrick Clark; ***D:*** John Weidner; ***W:*** Ken Lamplugh, John Weidner. *PMH, IME*

Privates on Parade 🦴🦴½ **1984 (R)** Film centering around the comic antics of an Army song-and-dance unit entertaining the troops in the Malayan jungle during the late '40s. Occasionally-inspired horseplay based on Peter Nichols play. **107m/C VHS, Beta.** *GB* John Cleese, Denis Quilley, Simon Jones, Joe Melia, Nicola Pagett, Julian Sands; ***D:*** Michael Blakemore. *PAR, TVC*

Prix de Beaute 🦴½ *Miss Europe* **1930** A woman's boyfriend does not know that she has won a beauty contest. Brooks' last starring role and the only film she did in France. In French with English subtitles. **93m/B VHS, Beta.** *FR* Louise Brooks, Jean Bradin, George Charlia, Gaston Jacquet; ***D:*** Augusto Genina. *INT, INJ*

The Prize 🦴🦴🦴 **1963** Gripping spy story laced with laughs based on a novel by Irving Wallace (adapted by Lehman). In Stockholm, writer accepts the Nobel prize for dubious reasons and then finds himself in the midst of political intrigue. Newman and Sommer turn in great performances in this action drama. **136m/C VHS.** Paul Newman, Edward G. Robinson, Elke Sommer, Leo G. Carroll, Diane Baker, Micheline Presle, Gerard Oury, Sergio Fantoni; ***D:*** Mark Robson; ***W:*** Ernest Lehman; ***C:*** William H. Daniels; ***M:*** Jerry Goldsmith. *MGM, REP, MLB*

Prize Fighter 🦴🦴 **1979 (PG)** Comedy team of Knotts and Conway take on Depression-era boxing. Fight manager Knotts and his pugilistic protege Conway unknowingly get involved with a powerful gangster, who convinces them to fight in a fixed championship match. Most enjoyable if intelligence is suspended at onset. **99m/C VHS, Beta.** Tim Conway, Don Knotts; ***D:*** Michael Preece; ***W:*** Tim Conway. *MED*

Prize of Peril 🦴🦴 **1984** A French television game show rewards it winners with wealth and its losers with execution. Not always the best policy to learn what's behind Door #1. **95m/C VHS, Beta.** *FR* Michel Piccoli, Marie-France Pisier; ***D:*** Yves Boisset. *LIV*

The Prize Pulitzer 🦴🦴 **1989** Watered-down, made-for-television account of the scandalous divorce between publishing heir Herbert "Pete" Pulitzer and his young wife Roxanne. Based on the book "The Prize Pulitzer" by Roxanne Pulitzer. Also known as "Roxanne: The Prize Pulitzer." **95m/C VHS.** Perry King, Chynna Phillips, Courteney Cox, Betsy Russell, Sondra Blake, Caitlin Brown; ***D:*** Richard A. Colla. *CAF*

The Prizefighter and the Lady 🦴🦴🦴 *Every Woman's Man* **1933** In his first film role boxer Baer (who won the heavyweight boxing crown in 1934) is a natural as a fighter who falls for a beautiful nightclub singer (Loy). Baer and Loy get, but don't stay, together but she does turn out to be his lucky charm in the big fight finale. Fellow professional boxer Carnera, Baer's opponent in the climatic fight scene, refused to lose as the script indicated and the film ending was eventually rewritten. The likeable Baer later earned his living as an actor. **102m/B LV.** Max Baer Sr., Myrna Loy, Otto Kruger, Primo Carnera, Walter Huston, Vince Barnett, Muriel Evans; ***D:*** Woodbridge S. Van Dyke. Nominations: Academy Awards '33: Best Original Screenplay. *MGM*

Prizzi's Honor **1985 (R)** Highly stylized, sometimes leaden black comedy about an aging and none-to-bright hit man from a New York mob family who breaks with family loyalties when he falls for an upwardly mobile tax consultant who's also a hired killer. Skirting caricature in every frame, Nicholson is excellent in his portrayal of the thick-skulled mobster, as are Angelica Huston as the hot-to-trot Mafia daughter and Hickey as the Don. Adapted by Richard Condon and Janet Roach from Condon's novel. **130m/C VHS, Beta, LV.** Jack Nicholson, Kathleen Turner, Robert Loggia, John Randolph, Anjelica Huston, Lawrence Tierney, William Hickey, Lee Richardson, Michael Lombard, Joseph Ruskin, CCH Pounder; ***D:*** John Huston; ***W:*** Richard Condon, Janet Roach; ***M:*** Alex North. Academy Awards '85: Best Supporting Actress (Huston); British Academy Awards '85: Best Adapted Screenplay; Golden Globe Awards '86: Best Actor—Musical/Comedy (Nicholson), Best Actress—Musical/Comedy (Turner), Best Director (Huston), Best Film—Musical/Comedy; Los Angeles Film Critics Association Awards '85: Best Supporting Actress (Huston); New York Film Critics Awards '85: Best Actor (Nicholson), Best Director (Huston), Best Film, Best Supporting Actress (Huston); Writers Guild of America '85: Best Adapted Screenplay; Nominations: Academy Awards '85: Best Actor (Nicholson), Best Adapted Screenplay, Best Costume Design, Best Director (Huston), Best Film Editing, Best Picture, Best Supporting Actor (Hickey). *PAR, VES, BTV*

Probable Cause **1995 (R)** A knife-wielding serial killer specializes in murdering cops and the clues seem to point to a troubled veteran cop (Ironside), newly-paired with a beautiful detective (Vernon). Some unexpected twists and a surprise ending. **90m/C VHS.** Michael Ironside, Kate Vernon, Kirk Baltz, Craig T. Nelson, M. Emmet Walsh; ***D:*** Paul Ziller; ***W:*** Hal Salwen; ***C:*** Danny Nowak. *LIV*

Probation *Second Chances* **1932** A dashing young man in trouble with the law receives an unusual sentence; he must become a chauffeur for a spoiled society girl. Grable's first film role is a small one. **60m/B VHS, Beta.** Sally Blane, J. Farrell MacDonald, Eddie Phillips, Clara Kimball Young, Betty Grable; ***D:*** Richard Thorpe. *NOS, SNC*

Probe ½ **1972** A detective uses computer-age technology to apprehend criminals. Pilot for the television series "Search." **95m/C VHS.** Hugh O'Brian, Elke Sommer, John Gielgud, Burgess Meredith, Angel Tompkins, Lilia Skala, Kent Smith, Alfred Ryder, Jaclyn Smith; ***D:*** Russ Mayberry; ***W:*** Leslie Stevens. *UNI*

Problem Child ½ **1990 (PG)** Ritter decides to adopt Oliver out of the goodness of his heart, but it seems young Oliver's already got a father figure named Beelzebub. Potential for laughs is unmet. **81m/C VHS, LV.** John Ritter, Michael Oliver, Jack Warden, Amy Yasbeck, Gilbert Gottfried, Michael Richards, Peter Jurasik; ***D:*** Dennis Dugan; ***W:*** Scott Alexander, Larry Karaszewski; ***M:*** Miles Goodman. *MCA*

Problem Child 2 **1991 (PG-13)** Ritter and his nasty adopted son are back, but this time there's an equally malevolent little girl. They team up to prevent Ritter's upcoming marriage to a socialite. Low slapstick junk. **91m/C VHS, Beta, LV.** John Ritter, Michael Oliver, Laraine Newman, Amy Yasbeck, Jack Warden, Ivyann Schwan, Gilbert Gottfried, James Tolkan, Charlene Tilton, Alan Blumenfeld, Paul Sutera; ***D:*** Brian Levant; ***W:*** Scott Alexander, Larry Karaszewski. *MCA*

The Prodigal ½ **1955** Luke's New Testament Bible story of the son seduced by greed slickly transfered to the silver screen by MGM. A colorful cast is the main attraction. **113m/C LV.** Lana Turner, Edmund Purdom, Louis Calhern, Audrey Dalton, Neville Brand, Walter Hampden, Taina Elg, Francis L. Sullivan, Joseph Wiseman, Sandy Descher, John Dehner, Cecil Kellaway, Henry Daniell, Paul Cavanagh, Tracey Roberts, Jay Novello, Dorothy Adams, Richard Devon; ***D:*** Richard Thorpe; ***C:*** Joseph Ruttenberg. *MGM*

The Prodigal **1983 (PG)** A born-again family drama in which a sundered family is brought together by the return of a once-estranged son. **109m/C VHS, Beta, LV.** John Hammond, Hope Lange, John Cullum, Morgan Brittany, Ian Bannen, Arliss Howard, Joey Travolta, Billy Graham; ***M:*** Bruce Broughton. *LIV*

Prodigal Boxer: The Kick of Death **1973 (R)** A son must avenge his father's death by facing two kung fu masters. **90m/C VHS, Beta, LV.** Meng Fei, Pa Hung, Suma Wah Lung. *GEM, MRV*

The Prodigal Planet **1988** Small group of believers continue their struggle against the world government UNTIE by disrupting their communication network. Sequel to "Thief in the Night," "A Distant Thunder," and "Image of the Beast." **67m/C VHS, Beta.** William Wellman Jr., Linda Beatie, Cathy Wellman, Thom Rachford; ***D:*** Donald W. Thompson. *HHE*

The Producers ½ **1968** Considered one of Brooks' best films, this hilarious farce follows an attempted swindle by a con artist and his accountant who attempt to stage a Broadway flop only to have it backfire. Achieving cult status, the film is known for musical interlude "Springtime for Hitler." The phony play was later actually produced by Alan Johnson. **90m/C VHS, Beta, LV, 8mm.** Zero Mostel, Gene Wilder, Dick Shawn, Kenneth Mars, Estelle Winwood; ***D:*** Mel Brooks; ***W:*** Mel Brooks. Academy Awards '68: Best Story & Screenplay; Writers Guild of America '68: Best Original Screenplay; Nominations: Academy Awards '68: Best Supporting Actor (Wilder). *COL, CRC*

The Professional *Leon* **1994 (R)** Leon (Reno) is an eccentric French hit man, working New York's mean streets, when his 12-year-old neighbor Mathilda (Portman) comes knocking. Seems her family has been murdered by minions of crooked drug enforcement agent Stansfield (Oldman) and she'd like Leon to teach her how to be a "cleaner" so she can get revenge. And Leon obliges. The lovely young Portman (in her film debut) is a little too Lolita-ish for comfort as she manipulates the stolid Reno, with Oldman suitably extravagant in the role of sadistic psycho. **109m/C VHS, LV.** *FR* Jean Reno, Natalie Portman, Gary Oldman, Danny Aiello, Michael Badalucco, Ellen Greene; ***D:*** Luc Besson; ***W:*** Luc Besson; ***C:*** Thierry Arbogast; ***M:*** Eric Serra. Nominations: Cesar Awards '94: Best Actor (Reno), Best Director (Besson), Best Film. *COL*

The Professional: Golgo 13 **1983** Animated mystery & suspense film. Leonard Dawson vows revenge for his son's death and must battle Duke Togo, a professional hitman better known as "Golgo 13." Dubbed. **94m/C VHS.** *JP WTA*

Professional Killers 1 **1973** Trio of hired assassins wanders about the countryside killing people during Japan's Feudal Era. **87m/C VHS, Beta.** Jiro Tamiya, Koji Takahashi. *NO*

The Professionals ½ **1966 (PG)** Action and adventure count for more than a storyline in this exciting western about four mercenaries hired by a wealthy cattle baron to rescue his young wife from Mexican kidnappers. Breathtaking photography recreates turn-of-the-century Mexico in this adaptation of the Frank O'Rourke novel. **117m/C VHS, Beta, LV.** Burt Lancaster, Lee Marvin, Claudia Cardinale, Jack Palance, Robert Ryan, Woody Strode, Ralph Bellamy; ***D:*** Richard Brooks; ***W:*** Richard Brooks; ***C:*** Conrad Hall; ***M:*** Maurice Jarre. Nominations: Academy Awards '66: Best Color Cinematography, Best Director (Brooks), Best Story & Screenplay. *COL*

Professionals **1976** When the daily rigors of cocaine smuggling begin to dampen their spirits, the "Professionals" plan an exciting plutonium heist. From the British Action Show. **104m/C VHS, Beta, LV.** Gordon Jackson, Martin Shaw, Lewis Collins. *TWE*

The Professor **1958** Rare sci-fi thriller featuring a werewolf, an eccentric scientist and a communist plot. Also includes several 'werewolf' oriented movie trailers. **30m/C VHS.** Doug Hobart, John Copeland, Irene Barr. *SNC*

Profile ½ **1954** A newsman gets an editorial job for a magazine called "Profile," and promptly falls in love with the boss's daughter. Complications arise when the boss's wife puts the moves on him. As if that isn't trouble enough, he finds himself accused of embezzlement. Average entertainment with some notable performances and an interesting chase scene. **65m/B VHS, Beta.** John Bentley, Kathleen Byron, Thea Gregory, Stuart Lindsell; ***D:*** Francis Searle. *SNC*

The Program ½ **1993 (R)** Sensitive tearjerker about college football players getting caught up in the drive for a championship. As the season takes its toll on both mind and body, players prepare for the Big Game. Caan is the team's gruff coach, who's willing to look the other way as long as his boys are winning. Film sparked controversy when the Disney studio pulled and recut it after release because one scene, where Sheffer's character lies down in traffic, sparked copy-cat actions and several deaths. The scene was not restored for the video version. **110m/C VHS, Beta, LV.** James Caan, Craig Sheffer, Kristy Swanson, Halle Berry, Omar Epps, Duane Davis, Abraham Benrubi, Jon Maynard Pennell, Andrew Bryniarski; ***D:*** David S. Ward; ***W:*** Aaron Latham, David S. Ward; ***M:*** Michel Colombier. *TOU*

Programmed to Kill *Retaliator* **1986 (R)** A beautiful terrorist is captured by the CIA and transformed into a buxom bionic assassin. **91m/C VHS, Beta.** Robert Ginty, Sandahl Bergman, James Booth, Louise Caire Clark; ***D:*** Allan Holzman. *MED*

Project A-ko **1986** Set in the near future, this Japanese animated feature, which is intended for adults, concerns teenagers with strange powers, an alien spaceship, and lots of action. Seventeen year-old A-ko possesses superhuman strength and a ditzy sidekick, C-ko. B-ko, the spoiled and rich daughter of a business tycoon, decides to fight A-ko for C-ko's companionship. Meanwhile, an alien spaceship is headed toward Earth with unknown intentions. Somehow, everything ties together—watch and see how. In Japanese with English subtitles. **86m/C VHS, LV.** *JP CPM, INJ, WTA*

Project: Alien **1989 (R)** Science fiction fans in search of a good extraterrestrial flick should avoid this teaser, for it has nothing to do with aliens. As the film begins, Earth is allegedly being attacked by beings from space, and a vast array of scientists, militia and journalists track the aliens. What's actually happening revolves around the testing of deadly biological weapons. Shot in Yugoslavia. **92m/C VHS, LV.** Michael Nouri, Darlanne Fluegel, Maxwell Caulfield, Charles Durning; ***D:*** Frank Shields; ***W:*** Anthony Able. *VMK*

Project: Eliminator ½ **1991 (R)** A group of terrorists kidnap a designer of "smart" weapons, and it's up to a hard-hitting special forces unit to get him back. Filmed in New Mexico. **89m/C VHS.** David Carradine, Frank Zagarino, Drew Snyder, Hilary English, Vivian Schilling; ***D:*** H. Kaye Dyal; ***W:*** H. Kaye Dyal, Morris Asgar. *HMD*

Project: Genesis ½ **1993** Pascal and a beautiful Alien Woman are shipwrecked on a desolate planet in the 23rd century. As they watch the worlds around them clash in war, they know it is up to them to create a new beginning at the end of the Universe. **79m/C VHS, LV.** David Ferry, Olga Prokhorova; ***D:*** Philip Jackson; ***W:*** Philip Jackson; ***M:*** Andy McNeill. *PSM*

Project: Kill! **1977** Head of a murder-for-hire squad suddenly disappears and his former assistant is hired to track him down dead or alive. **94m/C VHS, Beta.** Leslie Nielsen, Gary Lockwood, Nancy Kwan. *QVD*

Project Metalbeast: DNA Overload ½ **1994 (R)** A CIA agent, cryogenically frozen for 10 years, becomes the guinea pig when a group of scientists decide to unthaw him for a DNA experiment involving living metallic skin. Too bad he turns into a metal beast by the light of the full moon. Sci-fi take on the werewolf saga. **92m/C VHS.** Kim Delaney, Barry Bostwick; ***D:*** Allessandro DeGaetano; ***W:*** Timothy E. Sabo; ***M:*** Conrad Pope. *PSM*

Project Moon Base 🦴½ **1953** Espionage runs rampant on a spaceship headed by a female officer. Eventually the ship is stranded on the moon. Actually filmed for a television series "Ring Around the Moon." A cold-war sexist relic. **64m/C VHS, Beta.** Donna Martell, Hayden Rourke; ***D:*** Richard Talmadge. *VMK*

Project: Nightmare 🦴½ **1985** Seems not all dreams are wish fulfillment, when these nightmares start coming t rue. **75m/C VHS.** Elly Koslo, Lance Dickson; ***D:*** Donald M. Jones. *ACA, MOV*

Project: Shadowchaser 🦴½ **1992 (R)** Action-packed would-be thriller about a billion dollar android who escapes from a top secret government laboratory. Programmed with superhuman strength and no human emotions the android and five terrorists take over a hospital (located in a skyscraper no less). Their hostages include the President's daughter and the terrorists demand a $50 million ransom. With a four-hour deadline the FBI calls in the hospital architect to advise them—only they've got the wrong man—and the android's creator, who wants his creation back—no matter what the cost. A low budget Terminator clone. **97m/C VHS.** Martin Kove, Meg Foster, Frank Zagarino, Paul Koslo, Joss Ackland; ***D:*** John Eyres. *PSM*

Project Shadowchaser 3000 🦴½ **1995 (R)** Deep space satellite station collides with a mining vessel carrying a killer android. The seven surviving crew are then hunted by the android as the ship's nuclear core is also threatening to explode. **99m/C VHS, LV.** Frank Zagarino, Sam Bottoms, Christopher Atkins, Musetta Vander, Christopher Neame; ***D:*** John Eyres; ***W:*** Nick Davis; ***M:*** Steve Edwards. *TTC, NLC*

Project Vampire 🦴½ **1993** Vampire concocts a serum that will change humans into vampires withing three days. His first guinea pig fights to stop the evil from succeeding. **90m/C VHS.** Brian Knudson, Mary-Louise Gemmill, Christopher Cho, Myron Natwick; ***D:*** Peter Flynn. *AIP*

Project X 🦴🦴½ **1987 (PG)** A bemused Air Force pilot is assigned to a special project involving chimpanzees. He must decide where his duty lies when he realizes the semi-intelligent chimps are slated to die. **107m/C VHS, Beta, LV.** Matthew Broderick, Helen Hunt, William Sadler, Johnny Rae McGhee, Jonathan Stark, Robin Gammell, Stephen Lang, Jean Smart, Dick Miller; ***D:*** Jonathan Kaplan; ***W:*** Stanley Weiser, Lawrence Lasker; ***C:*** Dean Cundey; ***M:*** James Horner. *FOX*

The Projectionist 🦴🦴🦴 **1971 (PG)** A must-see for movie buffs, Dangerfield made his screen debut in this story about a projectionist in a seedy movie house whose real-life existence begins to blur into the films he continuously watches. Made on a limited budget, this creative effort by Hurwitz was the first film to utilize the technique of superimposition. **84m/C VHS, Beta.** Rodney Dangerfield, Chuck McCann, Ina Balin; ***D:*** Harry Hurwitz; ***W:*** Harry Hurwitz. *LIV, VES*

Prom Night 🦴🦴 **1980 (R)** A masked killer stalks four high school girls during their senior prom as revenge for a murder which occurred six years prior. Sequelled by "Hello Mary Lou: Prom Night II" and "Prom Night III: The Last Kiss." **91m/C VHS, Beta, LV.** *CA* Jamie Lee Curtis, Leslie Nielsen; ***D:*** Paul Lynch. *NLC*

Prom Night 3: The Last Kiss 🦴 **1989 (R)** The second sequel, in which the reappearing high school ghoul beguiles a lucky teenager. **97m/C VHS, Beta, LV.** Tim Conlon, Cyndy Preston, Courtney Taylor; ***D:*** Ron Oliver, Peter Simpson. *LIV*

Prom Night 4: Deliver Us From Evil 🦴 **1991 (R)** Yet another gory entry in the Prom series (one would hope it will be the last). Another group of naive teens decide that they can have more fun at a private party than at the prom. They host the party in a summer home that was once a monastery, but the festive affair soon turns into a night of terror when an uninvited guest crashes the party. For true fans of slasher flicks. **95m/C VHS.** Nikki DeBoer, Alden Kane, Joy Tanner, Alle Ghadban; ***D:*** Clay Borris. *LIV*

The Promise 🦴½ *Face of a Stranger* **1978 (PG)** Weepie outdated story about star-crossed lovers Michael (Collins) and Nancy (Quinlan). A car accident leaves Michael comatose and Nancy badly disfigured. Michael's mother (Straight), who loathes Nancy, sees her chance to finally break them up. She offers to pay for Nancy's plastic surgery if she'll leave Michael forever, then Mom tells her son his girlfriend's dead. A year later Nancy, with her new face and new identity, and Michael meet. From the novel by Danielle Steele. **97m/C VHS.** Stephen Collins, Kathleen Quinlan, Beatrice Straight, Laurence Luckinbill, William Prince, Michael O'Hare; ***D:*** Gilbert Cates; ***W:*** Garry Michael White; ***M:*** David Shire. *MCA*

The Promise 🦴🦴½ *Das Versprechen* **1995 (R)** Young lovers Konrad (Zoller and Zirner) and Sophie (Harfouch and Becker) find themselves separated by the Berlin Wall after a botched escape attempt in 1961. The estranged lovers meet only four times during the next three decades as they adjust to the systems under which they're forced to live. Somewhat contrived and cliched, this bittersweet romance uses Konrad and Sophie as symbols of the social and political turmoil and triumphs of the divided Germany. Received some criticism from East Germans who found the film's severe portrayal of Communist rule too harsh. Gets points for being the first post-fall film to explore the Wall's legacy. **115m/C VHS, LV.** *GE* Corinna Harfouch, Meret Becker, August Zirner, Anian Zollner, Jean-Yves Gaultier, Eva Mattes, Suzanne Uge, Hans Kremer, Pierre Besson, Tina Engel, Otto Sander, Hark Bohm; ***D:*** Margarethe von Trotta; ***W:*** Peter Schneider, Margarethe von Trotta; ***C:*** Franz Rath; ***M:*** Jurgen Knieper. *NLC*

Promise Her Anything 🦴🦴 **1966** A widow (Caron) with a baby decides to make her boss (Cummings), a child psychologist who hates kids, her new husband. So she stashes the kid with her upstairs neighbor (Beatty), a would-be filmmaker who earns his living making blue movies. But the filmmaker has romantic designs on the widow and decides the baby may be his way to make a good impression. Beatty isn't very believable in this type of light-romantic comedy and the farcical situations are forced. **98m/C VHS.** *GB* Warren Beatty, Leslie Caron, Robert Cummings, Hermione Gingold, Lionel Stander, Keenan Wynn, Cathleen Nesbitt; ***D:*** Arthur Hiller; ***W:*** William Peter Blatty. *PAR*

Promise to Murder 🦴½ **1956** An early murder-drama episode from the "Climax" television series. **60m/B VHS, Beta.** Peter Lorre, Louis Hayward, Ann Harding. *NOS, DVT*

Promised a Miracle 🦴🦴½ **1988 (PG)** Based on the true story of a religious couple who sought help for their diabetic son through prayer rather than conventional medical means. Following the boy's death in 1974 the couple were charged with manslaughter. From the non-fiction account "We Let Our Son Die" by Larry Parker. Made for television. **94m/C VHS, LV.** Rosanna Arquette, Judge Reinhold, Tom Bower, Gary Bayer, Maria O'Brien, Vonni Ribisi; ***D:*** Stephen Gyllenhaal; ***W:*** David Hill. *REP*

Promised Land 🦴🦴🦴 *Young Hearts* **1988 (R)** Two high school friends from the rural northwestern U.S. come together several years after graduation under tragic circumstances. Writer Hoffman's semi-autobiographical, disillusioned look at the American Dream was re-discovered by movie goers due to its excellent dramatic performances, notable also as the first film produced by Robert Redford's Sundance Institute. **110m/C VHS, Beta, LV.** Kiefer Sutherland, Meg Ryan, Tracy Pollan, Jason Gedrick, Googy Gress, Deborah Richter, Sandra Seacat, Jay Underwood, Oscar Rowland; ***D:*** Michael Hoffman; ***W:*** Michael Hoffman; ***M:*** James Newton Howard. *LIV, VES*

Promises in the Dark 🦴🦴½ **1979 (PG)** Drama focusing on the complex relationship between a woman doctor and her 17-year-old female patient who is terminally ill with cancer. Hellman's directorial debut. **118m/C VHS, Beta.** Marsha Mason, Ned Beatty, Kathleen Beller, Susan Clark, Paul Clemens, Donald Moffat, Michael Brandon; ***D:*** Jerome Hellman. *WAR*

Promises! Promises! 🦴½ *Promise Her Anything* **1963** Having difficulty getting pregnant, a woman goes on a cruise with her husband. While on board, they meet another couple, all get drunk, and change partners. Of course, both women find themselves pregnant, leaving the paternity in doubt. Famous primarily as the movie Mansfield told "Playboy" magazine she appeared "completely nude" in. **90m/B VHS, Beta.** Jayne Mansfield, Marie McDonald, Tommy Noonan, Fritz Feld, Claude Stroud. *NO*

The Promoter 🦴🦴🦴 *The Card* **1952** Horatio Alger comedy stars Guinness as an impoverished student who gives himself a surreptitious leg up in life by altering his school entrance exam scores. Outstanding performances enliven this subtle British comedy of morals. **87m/B VHS, Beta.** *GB* Alec Guinness, Glynis Johns, Petula Clark, Valerie Hobson, Michael Hordern; ***D:*** Ronald Neame. Nominations: Academy Awards '52: Best Sound. *HMV*

Proof 🦴🦴🦴 **1991 (R)** Directorial debut of Moorhouse tells a tale of manipulation, friendship, and obsessive love between a blind photographer, Martin, his housekeeper, and the young man he befriends. Martin, mistrustful of the world around him, takes photographs as "proof" of the reality of his life. A chance meeting with Andy provides Martin with his "eyes" and the opportunity to expand his world and emotions—something his housekeeper, Celia, would be only too happy to help him with. Unhealthy triangle leads all three to a re-evaluation of their lives. Propelled by terrific performances and enough humor to balance its emotional content. **90m/C VHS, LV.** *AU* Hugo Weaving, Genevieve Picot, Russell Crowe, Heather Mitchell, Jeffrey Walker, Frank Gallacher; ***D:*** Jocelyn Moorhouse; ***W:*** Jocelyn Moorhouse. Australian Film Institute '91: Best Actor (Weaving), Best Director (Moorhouse), Best Film, Best Film Editing, Best Supporting Actor (Crowe), Best Writing. *NLC, COL, INJ*

Proof of the Man 🦴 **1984** A Japanese co-production about a murder in Tokyo that takes on international importance. **100m/C VHS, Beta.** *JP* George Kennedy, Broderick Crawford, Toshiro Mifune. *VCD*

Property 🦴½ **1978** A comedy about a group of leftover '60s radicals adjusting to 1970s corporate America. **92m/C VHS.** *NO*

Prophecy 🦴½ **1979 (PG)** A doctor and his wife travel to Maine to research the effects of pollution caused by the lumber industry. They encounter several terrifying freaks of nature and a series of bizarre human deaths. Laughable horror film. **102m/C VHS, Beta.** Talia Shire, Robert Foxworth, Armand Assante, Victoria Racimo, Richard Dysart; ***D:*** John Frankenheimer; ***W:*** David Seltzer; ***C:*** Harry Stradling Jr. *PAR*

The Prophecy 🦴🦴½ **1995 (R)** Modern variation of "Paradise Lost" carries a heavy load including possession, Native American mythology, and Walken as the archangel Gabriel. Not surprisingly, it stumbles under the weight. Gabriel is at odds with good angel Simon (Stolz) over the souls of humans, a battle that has its final showdown in a small Arizona community and crosses the paths of homicide detective Thomas Dagget (Koteas) and school teacher Katherine (Madsen). Successfully mixes humor and horror, but biblical jargon can lose horror fans just looking for a cheap thrill. Directorial debut of screenwriter Widen. **97m/C VHS, LV.** Christopher Walken, Eric Stoltz, Elias Koteas, Virginia Madsen, Amanda Plummer, Viggo Mortensen; ***D:*** Gregory Widen; ***W:*** Gregory Widen; ***C:*** Bruce Douglas Johnson, Richard Clabaugh; ***M:*** David Williams. *MAX*

A Propos de Nice 🦴🦴🦴 **1929** First film by French director Vigo, the silent film parodies French travelogues in a manner that indicates the director's later brilliance. **25m/B VHS, Beta.** *FR* ***D:*** Jean Vigo. *FST, MRV*

Prospero's Books 🦴🦴🦴 **1991 (R)** Greenaway's free-ranging adaptation of Shakespeare's "The Tempest" has all his usual hallmarks of the bizarre. Gielgud is the aged Propsero, exiled to a magical island with his innocent daughter Miranda, and 24 beloved books containing the magician's recipe for life, each of which becomes a separate chapter in the film. Greenaway mixes film and high-definition video to create, with cinematographer Sacha Vierny, dazzling visuals that threaten to overwhelm but don't quite, thanks to both Greenaway's skill and the astonishing performance of the then 87-year-old Gielgud. **129m/C VHS, Beta, LV.** John Gielgud, Michel Blanc, Erland Josephson, Isabelle Pasco, Tom Bell, Kenneth Cranham, Michael Clark, Mark Rylance; ***D:*** Peter Greenaway; ***W:*** Peter Greenaway; ***M:*** Michael Nyman. *FXV, FCT, VTR*

Protect Your Daughters **1932** Hilarious schlock featuring good girls getting involved with sex and alcohol. Also known as "Reckless Decision." **?m/B VHS.** *SNC*

Protector **1985 (R)** A semi-martial arts cops 'n' robbers epic about the cracking of a Hong Kong-New York heroin route. **94m/C VHS, Beta, LV.** Jackie Chan, Danny Aiello; ***D:*** James Glickenhaus. *WAR*

Protocol **1984 (PG)** A series of comic accidents lead a Washington cocktail waitress into the U.S. State Department's employ as a protocol official. Once there she is used as a pawn to make an arms deal with a Middle Eastern country. Typical Hawn comedy with an enjoyable ending. **100m/C VHS, Beta, LV.** Goldie Hawn, Chris Sarandon, Andre Gregory, Cliff DeYoung, Ed Begley Jr., Gail Strickland, Richard Romanus, Keith Szarabajka, James Staley, Kenneth Mars, Kenneth McMillan, Archie Hahn, Amanda Bearse; ***D:*** Herbert Ross; ***W:*** Charles Shyer, Buck Henry, Nancy Meyers, Harvey Miller; ***M:*** Basil Poledouris. *WAR*

Prototype **1983** Made-for-television revision of the Frankenstein legend has award-winning scientist Plummer as the creator of the first android. Fearful of the use the military branch of government has in mind for his creation, he attempts to steal back his discovery, in this suspenseful adventure. **100m/C VHS, LV.** Christopher Plummer, David Morse, Frances Sternhagen, James Sutorius; ***D:*** David Greene; ***M:*** Billy Goldenberg. *LIV*

Prototype X29A ½ **1992 (R)** The year is 2057 in a desolate, lawless Los Angeles. A research scientist is conducting experiments on a crippled ex-soldier named Hawkins when they suddenly go awry, turning him into a half-man, half-machine robot. Known as Prototype, the creature goes on a hunting and killing spree. Lame "Terminator" & "Robocop" takeoff. **98m/C VHS, LV.** Brenda Swanson, Robert Tossberg, Lane Lenhart; ***D:*** Phillip J. Roth; ***W:*** Phillip J. Roth. *VMK*

The Proud and the Damned *Proud, Damned, and Dead* **1972 (PG)** Five Civil-War-veteran mercenaries wander into a Latin American war and get manipulated by both sides. **95m/C VHS, Beta.** Chuck Connors, Aron Kincaid, Cesar Romero; ***D:*** Ferde Grofe Jr. *NOS, VCI, MRV*

Proud Men **1987** A cattle rancher and his expatriate son are separated by bitterness toward each other. Good acting from Heston and Strauss, and good action sequences, but ordinary script. **95m/C VHS.** Charlton Heston, Peter Strauss, Nan Martin, Alan Autry, Belinda Balaski, Red West; ***D:*** William A. Graham. *TTC*

The Proud Ones ½ *Les Orgueilleux* **1953** An aristocratic French woman and her husband are traveling through Mexico when he suddenly dies of a mysterious illness. Left penniless in a decaying seaside town, she falls for the local doctor who is mourning the death of his wife. Adaptation of the Satre novel "L'Amour Redempteur." In French with English subtitles. **105m/B VHS.** *FR* Gerard Philipe, Michele Morgan, Victor Manuel Mendoza; ***D:*** Yves Allegret. Nominations: Academy Awards '56: Best Story. *FCT, INT*

Proud Rebel **1958** A character study of a stubborn widower who searches for a doctor to aid him in dealing with the problems of his mute son, and of the woman who helps to tame the boy. Ladd's real-life son makes his acting debut. **99m/C VHS, Beta.** Alan Ladd, Olivia de Havilland, Dean Jagger, Harry Dean Stanton; ***D:*** Michael Curtiz. *SUE*

Providence **1977 (R)** An interesting score highlights this British fantasy drama of a dying writer envisioning his final novel as a fusion of the people from his past with the circumstances he encounters on a daily basis. The first English-language effort by French director Resnais. **104m/C VHS, Beta.** *GB* John Gielgud, Dirk Bogarde, Ellen Burstyn, David Warner, Elaine Stritch; ***D:*** Alain Resnais; ***M:*** Miklos Rozsa. Cesar Awards '78: Best Art Direction/Set Decoration, Best Director (Resnais), Best Film, Best Sound, Best Writing, Best Score; New York Film Critics Awards '77: Best Actor (Gielgud). *COL*

Provincial Actors **1979** Ambitious Christopher is the leading actor of a rural theater troupe, who dreams of moving to the city and becoming a star. But his wife Anna is fed up with his dreams and leaves him and Christopher must make a choice between his career and his marriage. Polish with subtitles. **104m/C VHS.** *PL* Tadeysz Huk, Halina Labonarska, Ewa Dalkowska, Jerzy Stuhr; ***D:*** Agnieszka Holland. *NYF*

Provoked ½ **1989** What would you do if your husband were being held hostage by a gang of ruthless, but stupid, escaped cons? Well, Maranne actually wants her husband back (maybe 'cause they're newleyweds) and no by-the-book police chief (Jones) is gonna stop her. This bride gets her hands on some automatic weaponry and look out! Shot in eight days with a $130,000 budget. **90m/C VHS, Beta.** Cindy Maranne, McKeiver Jones III, Harold W. Jones, Sharon Blair, Bob Fall, Joe Sprosty, Phyllis Durant, Tara Untiedt; ***D:*** Rick Pamplin; ***W:*** Tara Untiedt, Steve Pake. *VTR, HHE*

Prowler ½ **1951** Heflin is a cop who responds to a prowler scare and finds the beautiful married Keyes worried about an intruder. He learns she will inherit a lot of money if anything happens to her husband so he seduces her and then "accidentally" kills her husband, supposedly mistaking him for a prowler. Keyes then marries Heflin but when she learns the truth her own life is in danger. Tidy thriller with Heflin doing a good job as the unpredictable villain. **92m/B VHS, Beta.** Van Heflin, Evelyn Keyes, Katherine Warren, John Maxwell; ***D:*** Joseph Losey; ***C:*** Arthur C. Miller. *NO*

The Prowler *Rosemary's Killer* **1981 (R)** A soldier returns from duty during WWII, only to find his girl in bed with another guy. He kills them, and for unclear reasons, returns to the same town 35 years later to kill more people. An effects-fest for Tom Savini. **87m/C VHS.** Vicky Dawson, Christopher Goutman, Cindy Weintraub, Farley Granger, John Seitz, Lawrence Tierney; ***D:*** Joseph Zito; ***W:*** Neal Barbera; ***M:*** Richard Einhorn. *VHE*

Prudential Family Playhouse **1950** Presentation of Sinclair Lewis' "Dodsworth." Tells the story of a wealthy American couple who travel from their small town to Europe. **53m/B VHS, Beta.** Ruth Chatterton, Walter Abel, Cliff Hall, Eva Marie Saint. *VYY*

Prurient Interest **1974** A video play revolving around a movie producer's battle with the Board of Censors for approval of his feature "Eat Me in St. Louis." **20m/B VHS, Beta.** *EAI*

PSI Factor ½ **1980** A civilian researcher working at the NASA space track station observes and records signals coming from planet Serius B. **91m/C VHS.** Peter Mark Richman, Gretchen Corbett, Tommy Martin; ***D:*** Bryan Trizers; ***W:*** Quentin Masters. *NO*

Psych-Out ½ **1968** A deaf girl searches Haight-Ashbury for her runaway brother. She meets hippies and flower children during the Summer of Love. Psychedelic score with Strawberry Alarm Clock and The Seeds. Somewhere in the picture, Nicholson whangs on lead guitar. **95m/C VHS, Beta, LV.** Jack Nicholson, Bruce Dern, Susan Strasberg, Dean Stockwell, Henry Jaglom; ***D:*** Richard Rush; ***W:*** Richard Rush. *HBO*

Psychedelic Fever **1990 (R)** A swinging look at the free-love decade of the 1960s. **80m/C VHS.** ***D:*** William Rotsler. *NO*

The Psychic *Woof!* **1968** An ad executive gains psychic powers after he falls off a ladder and tries to conquer the world. A later effort by gore-king Lewis, notable only for sex scenes inserted by Lewis to make the movie salable. **90m/C VHS, Beta.** Dick Genola, Robin Guest, Bobbi Spencer; ***D:*** Herschell Gordon Lewis. *NO*

The Psychic **1978 (R)** A psychic envisions her own death and attempts to alter the prediction. **90m/C VHS, Beta.** Jennifer O'Neill, Marc Porel, Evelyn Stewart, Gabriele Ferzetti, Gianni "John" Garko; ***D:*** Lucio Fulci. *NO*

Psychic ½ **1991 (R)** A college student with psychic powers believes he knows who the next victim of a demented serial killer will be. The problem is: no one will believe him. And the victim is the woman he loves. **92m/C VHS.** Michael Nouri, Catherine Mary Stewart, Zach Galligan. *VMK*

Psychic Killer ½ **1975 (PG)** A wrongfully committed asylum inmate acquires psychic powers and decides to use them in a deadly revenge. Good cast in cheapie horror flick. **89m/C VHS, Beta.** Jim Hutton, Paul Burke, Julie Adams, Neville Brand, Aldo Ray, Rod Cameron, Della Reese; ***D:*** Ray Danton. *SUE*

Psycho **1960** Hitchcock counted on his directorial stature and broke all the rules in this story of violent murder, transvestism, and insanity. Based on Robert Bloch's novelization of an actual murder, Leigh plays a fleeing thief who stops at the secluded Bates Motel where she meets her death in Hitchcock's classic "shower scene." Shot on a limited budget in little more than a month, "Psycho" changed the Hollywood horror film forever. Followed by "Psycho II" (1983), "Psycho III" (1986), and a made-for-television movie. **109m/B VHS, Beta, LV.** Anthony Perkins, Janet Leigh, Vera Miles, John Gavin, John McIntire, Martin Balsam, Simon Oakland, Ted Knight, John Anderson, Frank Albertson, Patricia Hitchcock; ***D:*** Alfred Hitchcock; ***W:*** Joseph Stefano; ***M:*** Bernard Herrmann. Edgar Allan Poe Awards '60: Best Screenplay; Golden Globe Awards '61: Best Supporting Actress (Leigh); Nominations: Academy Awards '60: Best Art Direction/Set Decoration (B & W), Best Black and White Cinematography, Best Director (Hitchcock), Best Supporting Actress (Leigh). *MCA, TLF*

Psycho 2 **1983 (R)** This sequel to the Hitchcock classic finds Norman Bates returning home after 22 years in an asylum to find himself haunted by "mother" and caught up in a series of murders. In a surprisingly good horror film, Perkins and Miles reprise their roles from the original "Psycho." Perkins went on to direct yet another sequel, "Psycho 3." **113m/C VHS, Beta, LV.** Anthony Perkins, Vera Miles, Meg Tilly, Robert Loggia, Dennis Franz; ***D:*** Richard Franklin; ***W:*** Tom Holland; ***C:*** Dean Cundey; ***M:*** Jerry Goldsmith. *MCA*

Psycho 3 **1986 (R)** The second sequel to Hitchcock's "Psycho" finds Norman Bates drawn into his past by "mother" and the appearance of a woman who reminds him of this original victim. Perkins made his directorial debut in this film that stretches the plausibility of the storyline to its limits, but the element of parody throughout makes this an entertaining film for "Psycho" fans. **93m/C VHS, Beta, LV.** Anthony Perkins, Diana Scarwid, Jeff Fahey, Roberta Maxwell, Robert Alan Browne; ***D:*** Anthony Perkins; ***W:*** Charles Edward Pogue; ***C:*** Bruce Surtees; ***M:*** Carter Burwell. *MCA*

Psycho 4: The Beginning **1990 (R)** Prequels "Psycho" when, at the behest of a radio talk show host, Norman Bates recounts his childhood and reveals the circumstances that aided in the development of his peculiar neuroses. Stefano wrote the original screenplay and the original score is used, but this doesn't even come close to the original. **96m/C VHS, LV.** Anthony Perkins, Henry Thomas, Olivia Hussey, CCH Pounder, Warren Frost, Donna Mitchell; ***D:*** Mick Garris; ***W:*** Joseph Stefano; ***M:*** Bernard Herrmann. *MCA*

Psycho Cop ½ **1988** Six college undergrads on a weekend retreat are menaced and picked off one at a time by a crazed local cop. **89m/C VHS, Beta.** Bobby Ray Shafer; ***D:*** Wallace Potts. *NO*

Psycho Cop 2 ½ **1994 (R)** Four buddies plan a raunchy bachelor party, commandeering the company conference room for an after-hours orgy. Only Psycho Cop is on their case. Gore. **80m/C VHS.** Bobby Ray Shafer, Barbara Lee Alexander, Julie Strain; ***D:*** Rif Coogan. *COL*

Psycho from Texas 🦴 *The Butcher* **1983 (R)** Quiet Southern town is disrupted by the kidnapping of a wealthy oil man, followed by a string of meaningless murders. **85m/C VHS, Beta.** King John III, Candy Dee, Janel King. *NO*

Psycho Girls 🦴 **1986 (R)** Very low budget horror flick redeemed by spurts of weird black humor. Crazed woman is released from institution to seek out sister who should have been put away in the first place. She crashes anniversary celebration and, well, let's just say she's not the life of the party. Never released theatrically. **87m/C VHS, Beta.** *CA* John Haslett Cuff, Darlene Mignacco, Agi Gallus, Rose Graham, Silvio Oliviero, Michael Hoole, Pier Giorgia DiCicco, Fernne Kane; ***D:*** Gerard Ciccoritti; ***W:*** Gerard Ciccoritti, Michael Boekner. *MGM*

Psychomania 🦴½ *Violent Midnight* **1963** Semi-limpid mystery thriller about a former war hero and painter who is suspected of being the demented killer stalking girls on campus. To prove his innocence, he tracks the killer himself. **95m/C VHS, Beta.** Lee Philips, Shepperd Strudwick, Jean Hale, Dick Van Patten, Sylvia Miles, James Farentino; ***D:*** Richard Hilliard. *SNC, HHT*

Psychomania 🦴🦴 *The Death Wheelers* **1973 (R)** A drama of the supernatural, the occult, and the violence which lies just beyond the conventions of society for a group of dead motorcyclists, the Living Dead, who all came back to life after committing suicide with the help of the devil. **89m/C VHS, Beta.** *GB* George Sanders, Beryl Reid, Nicky Henson, Mary Laroche, Patrick Holt; ***D:*** Don Sharp. *MED, MRV*

Psychopath 🦴½ **1968** A film about a modern-day, slightly unhinged, Robin Hood and his escapades, stealing from other thieves and giving to the victimized. **90m/C VHS, Beta.** *GB* Klaus Kinski, George Martin, Ingrid Schoeller; ***D:*** Guido Zurli. *NO*

Psychopath 🦴 *An Eye for an Eye* **1973 (PG)** A nutso children's television personality begins to murder abusive parents. Fairly gory, and definitely not for family viewing. **85m/C VHS, Beta.** Tom Basham, Gene Carlson, Gretchen Kanne; ***D:*** Larry G. Brown; ***M:*** John Williams. *MED*

Psychos in Love *Woof!* **1987** A psychotic murderer who hates grapes of any kind finds the woman of his dreams—she's a psychotic murderer who hates grapes! Together they find bliss—until the plumber discovers their secret! **90m/C VHS, Beta.** Carmine Capobianco, Debi Thibeault, Frank Stewart; ***D:*** Gorman Bechard. *NO*

The Psychotronic Man 🦴½ **1991** An innocent man suddenly finds he possesses amazing and dangerous powers, enabling him to control outside events with a thought. **88m/C VHS.** Peter Spelson, Christopher Carbis, Curt Colbert, Robin Newton, Paul Marvel; ***D:*** Jack M. Sell. *UNI*

PT 109 🦴🦴 **1963** The WWII exploits of Lieutenant (j.g.) John F. Kennedy in the South Pacific. Part of the "A Night at the Movies" series, this tape simulates a 1963 movie evening, with a Foghorn Leghorn cartoon ("Banty Raids"), a newsreel on the JFK assassination, and coming attractions for "Critic's Choice" and "Four for Texas." **159m/C VHS, Beta, LV.** Cliff Robertson, Ty Hardin, Ty Hardin, Robert (Bobby) Blake, Robert Culp, James Gregory; ***D:*** Leslie Martinson. *WAR*

Puberty Blues 🦴🦴½ **1981 (R)** Two Australian girls become part of the local surfing scene in order to be accepted by the "in crowd" at their high school. **86m/C VHS, Beta.** *AU* Neil Schofield, Jad Capelja; ***D:*** Bruce Beresford. *MCA*

Public Access 🦴🦴 **1993 (R)** Newcomer Whitley Pritcher (Marquette) manages to cause trouble in the small town of Brewster when he begins broadcasting a call-in program over a public-access cable station that encourages complaining about the town's problems. Skeletons start falling out of closets, leading to unexpected tragedy. Feature-film directorial debut of Singer. **90m/C VHS.** Ron Marquette, Dina Brooks, Burt Williams, Charles Kavanaugh, Larry Maxwell, Brandon Boyce; ***D:*** Bryan Singer; ***W:*** Bryan Singer, Christopher McQuarrie, Michael Feit Dougan; ***C:*** Bruce Douglas Johnson; ***M:*** John Ottman. Sundance Film Festival '93: Grand Jury Prize. *TRI*

A Public Affair 🦴½ **1962** Exposes the evils and abuses of collection agencies without even a shred of humor. Certainly gets its point across, but will bore any audience to tears or spontaneous naps. **71m/B VHS, Beta.** Myron McCormick, Edward Binns, Harry Carey Jr. *VYY*

Public Cowboy No. 1 🦴½ **1937** Cattle thieves use a radio, airplanes, and refrigerator trucks in their updated rustling schemes. **54m/B VHS, Beta.** Gene Autry, William Farnum. *NOS, VCN, DVT*

Public Enemy 🦴🦴🦴½ *Enemies of the Public* **1931** Cagney's acting career was launched by this story of two Irish boys growing up in a Chicago shantytown to become hoodlums during the prohibition era. Cagney and Woods hook up with molls Clarke and Blondell on their rise to the top. Considered the most realistic "gangster" film, Wellman's movie is also the most grimly brutal due to its release prior to Hollywood censorship. The scene where Cagney smashes a grapefruit in Clarke's face was credited with starting a trend in abusing film heroines. **85m/B VHS, Beta, LV.** James Cagney, Edward Woods, Leslie Fenton, Joan Blondell, Mae Clarke, Jean Harlow; ***D:*** William A. Wellman. Nominations: Academy Awards '31: Best Original Screenplay. *MGM, FOX*

The Public Eye 🦴🦴🦴½ **1992 (R)** Underappreciated film noir homage casts Pesci as a crime photographer with an unsuspected romantic streak. It's 1942 in NYC and cynical freelancer Leon "Bernzy" Bernstein's always looking for the perfect shot. Hershey's the recent widow whose nightclub-owner husband had mob ties and decides Pesci would be a likely patsy for helping her out. Hershey seems decorative and the romantic angle never quite develops, but Pesci delivers a rich, low-key performance as the visionary, hard-boiled artist. Climatic mob shootout is cinematic bullet ballet. Based loosely on the career of '40s photog Weegee, who defined New York and its times in his work. **98m/C VHS, Beta, LV.** Joe Pesci, Barbara Hershey, Stanley Tucci, Richard Foronjy, Richard Riehle, Jared Harris, Jerry Adler, Dominic Chianese, Gerry Becker; ***D:*** Howard Franklin; ***W:*** Howard Franklin; ***M:*** John Barry. *MCA*

Pucker Up and Bark Like a Dog 🦴 **1989 (R)** A young artist and his inspirationally lovely actress girl-friend find themselves in strange and crazy situations. Good cast gives this potential. **94m/C VHS.** Lisa Zane, Jonathan Gries, Paul Bartel, Robert Culp; ***D:*** Paul S. Parco. *FRH, BTV*

Pudd'nhead Wilson 🦴½ **1987** An adaptation of a Mark Twain story about a small-town lawyer who discovers the illicit exchange of a white infant for a light-skinned negro infant by a slave woman. Made for television as an "American Playhouse" presentation on PBS. **87m/C VHS, Beta.** Ken Howard; ***D:*** Alan Bridges. *MCA*

Pueblo Affair 🦴🦴🦴 **1973** A dramatization of the capture of the American spy ship "Pueblo" by the North Koreans, during which time the crew was tortured, imprisoned, and all intelligence documents were confiscated. **99m/C VHS, Beta.** Hal Holbrook, Andrew Duggan, Richard Mulligan, George Grizzard, Gary Merrill, Mary Fickett; ***D:*** Anthony Page. *NO*

Pulp 🦴🦴½ **1972 (PG)** Caine, playing a mystery writer, becomes a target for murder when he ghostwrites the memoirs of a movie gangster from the 1930s, played deftly by Rooney. **95m/C VHS, Beta.** *GB* Michael Caine, Mickey Rooney, Lionel Stander, Lizabeth Scott, Nadia Cassini, Dennis Price, Al Lettieri; ***D:*** Mike Hodges; ***W:*** Mike Hodges. *NO*

Pulp Fiction 🦴🦴🦴🦴 **1994 (R)** Tarantino moves into the cinematic mainstream with his trademark violence and '70s pop culture mindset intact in this stylish crime trilogy. A day in the life of a criminal community unexpectedly shifts from outrageous, esoteric dialogue to violent mayhem with solid scripting that takes familiar stories to unexplored territory. Offbeat cast offers superb performances, led by Travolta, who ditches the baby talk for his best role to date as a hit man whose adventures with partner Jackson tie the seemingly unrelated stories together. Clever, almost gleeful look at everday life on the fringes of mainstream society. Inspired by "Black Mask" magazine. A special collector's edition includes never-before-seen footage and commentary by Tarantino. **154m/C VHS, LV.** John Travolta, Samuel L. Jackson, Uma Thurman, Harvey Keitel, Tim Roth, Amanda Plummer, Maria De Medeiros, Ving Rhames, Eric Stoltz, Rosanna Arquette, Christopher Walken, Bruce Willis, Frank Whaley, Steve Buscemi, Quentin Tarantino; ***D:*** Quentin Tarantino; ***W:*** Roger Roberts Avary, Quentin Tarantino; ***C:*** Andrzej Sekula. Academy Awards '94: Best Original Screenplay; British Academy Awards '94: Best Original Screenplay, Best Supporting Actor (Jackson); Chicago Film Critics Awards '94: Best Director (Tarantino), Best Screenplay; Golden Globe Awards '95: Best Screenplay; Independent Spirit Awards '95: Best Actor (Jackson), Best Director (Tarantino), Best Film, Best Screenplay; Los Angeles Film Critics Association Awards '94: Best Actor (Travolta), Best Director (Tarantino), Best Film, Best Screenplay; MTV Movie Awards '95: Best Film, Best Dance Sequence (John Travolta/Uma Thurman); New York Film Critics Awards '94: Best Director (Tarantino), Best Screenplay; National Society of Film Critics Awards '94: Best Director (Tarantino), Best Film, Best Screenplay; Nominations: Academy Awards '94: Best Actor (Travolta), Best Director (Tarantino), Best Film Editing, Best Original Screenplay, Best Picture, Best Supporting Actor (Jackson), Best Supporting Actress (Thurman); Directors Guild of America Awards '94: Best Director (Tarantino); Golden Globe Awards '95: Best Actor—Drama (Travolta), Best Director (Tarantino), Best Film—Drama, Best Supporting Actor (Jackson), Best Supporting Actress (Thurman); MTV Movie Awards '95: Best Male Performance (Travolta), Best Female Performance (Thurman), Best On-Screen Duo (John Travolta/Samuel L. Jackson), Best Song ("Girl, You'll Be A Woman Soon"). *MAX*

Pulse 🦴🦴 **1988 (PG-13)** Electricity goes awry in this science-fiction thriller about appliances and other household devices that become super-charged and destroy property and their owners. **90m/C VHS, Beta, LV.** Cliff DeYoung, Roxanne Hart, Joey Lawrence, Charles Tyner, Dennis Redfield, Robert Romanus, Myron Healey; ***D:*** Paul Golding; ***M:*** Jay Michael Ferguson. *COL*

Pulsebeat *Woof!* **1985** Flick about warring health club owners. As boring as it sounds unless you're in the mood for lots of on-screen aerobics. If so, rent Jane Fonda instead. Dubbed. **92m/C VHS, Beta.** *SP* Daniel Greene, Lee Taylor Allen, Bob Small, Alice Moore, Helga Line, Alex Intriago, Peter Lupus; ***D:*** Marice Tobias. *LIV*

The Puma Man *Woof!* **1980** Puma Man is a super hero who must stop the evil Dr. Kobras from using an ancient mask in his attempt to become ruler of the world. Unreleased theatrically in the U.S., this low budget Sci fi/ horror mix is so bad one wonders why an actor like Pleasence would sign on. Special effects these days are so extraordinary that the ones employed here are laughable. **80m/C VHS, Beta.** *IT* Donald Pleasence, Walter George Alton, Sydne Rome, Miguel Angel Fuentes; ***D:*** Alberto De Martino. *PSM*

Pump Up the Volume 🦴🦴½ **1990 (R)** High school newcomer leads double life as Hard Harry, sarcastic host of an illegal radio broadcast and Jack Nicholson soundalike. Anonymously popular with his peers, he invites the wrath of the school principal due to his less than flattering comments about the school administration. Slater seems to enjoy himself as defiant deejay while youthful cast effectively supports. **105m/C VHS, LV, 8mm.** Christian Slater, Scott Paulin, Ellen Greene, Samantha Mathis, Cheryl Pollak, Annie Ross, Andy Romano, Mimi Kennedy; ***D:*** Allan Moyle; ***W:*** Allan Moyle. *COL, FCT, MVD*

Pumping Iron **1976 (PG)** A widely acclaimed documentary look at the sport of bodybuilding, following the behind-the-scenes action surrounding the competition for the Mr. Olympia title. The grueling training ritual and the constant striving for perfection are all explored. **90m/C VHS, Beta, LV.** Arnold Schwarzenegger, Mike Katz, Franco Columbo, Lou Ferrigno; ***D:*** George Butler. *COL, SCH, RHI*

Pumping Iron 2: The Women **1985** This sequel to "Pumping Iron" takes an in-depth look at the world of female body building. The documentary also follows the ladies to a competition held at

Caesar's Palace in Las Vegas. **107m/C VHS, Beta, LV.** Lori Bowen, Bev Francis, Rachel McLish, Carla Dunlap, Lydia Cheng; ***D:*** George Butler. *VES*

The Pumpkin Eater **1964** British housewife Jo (Bancroft) has seemingly found contentment with her third husband, famous and wealthy writer Jake (Finch), and her eight children. But as Jo struggles to face middle age she discovers Jake is chronically unfaithful and goes into an emotional tailspin. Last film for Hardwicke. Slow-paced film with fine performances; based on the novel by Penelope Mortimer. **110m/C VHS.** *GB* Anne Bancroft, Peter Finch, James Mason, Richard Johnson, Cedric Hardwicke, Maggie Smith, Alan Webb, Eric Porter; ***D:*** Jack Clayton; ***W:*** Harold Pinter; ***C:*** Oswald Morris; ***M:*** Georges Delerue. British Academy Awards '64: Best Screenplay; Nominations: Academy Awards '64: Best Actress (Bancroft). *COL*

Pumpkinhead ½ **1988 (R)** A farmer evokes a demon from the earth to avenge his son's death. When it continues on its murdering rampage, the farmer finds he no longer has any control over the vicious killer. **89m/C VHS, Beta, LV.** Lance Henriksen, John DiAquino, Kerry Remsen, Matthew Hurley, Jeff East, Kimberly Ross, Cynthia Bain, Joel Hoffman, Florence Schauffler, Buck Flower, Tom Woodruff Jr.; ***D:*** Stan Winston; ***W:*** Gary Gerani, Mark Patrick Carducci; ***M:*** Richard Stone. *MGM*

Pumpkinhead 2: Blood Wings ½ **1994 (R)** Five typically stupid teenagers resurrect a demon and the creature goes on a bloodthirsty rampage. His leaves his signature, a calling card in the shape of wings, at each murder scene. **88m/C VHS, LV.** Ami Dolenz, Andrew (Andy) Robinson, Kane Hodder, R.A. Mihailoff, Linnea Quigley; ***D:*** Jeff Burr. *LIV*

Punch the Clock **1990 (R)** Attractive female thief finds her bail bondsman very exciting; he's ready to help her any way he can. **88m/C VHS.** Michael Rogan, Chris Moore, James Lorinz; ***D:*** Eric L. Schlagman. *NO*

Punchline **1988 (R)** A look at the lives of stand-up comics, following the career ups-and-downs of an embittered professional funny-man and a frustrated housewife hitting the stage for the first time. Some very funny and touching moments and some not-so-funny and touching as the movie descends into melodrama without a cause. **100m/C VHS, Beta, LV.** Tom Hanks, Sally Field, John Goodman, Mark Rydell, Kim Greist, Barry Sobel, Paul Mazursky, Pam Matteson, George Michael McGrath, Taylor Negron, Damon Wayans; ***D:*** David Seltzer; ***W:*** David Seltzer; ***C:*** Reynaldo Villalobos. Los Angeles Film Critics Association Awards '88: Best Actor (Hanks). *COL*

The Punisher **1990 (R)** Lundgren portrays Frank Castle, the Marvel Comics anti-hero known as the Punisher. When his family is killed by the mob Castle set his eyes on revenge. Filmed in Australia. **92m/C VHS, Beta, LV.** Dolph Lundgren, Louis Gossett Jr., Jeroen Krabbe, Kim Miyori; ***D:*** Mark Goldblatt. *LIV*

Punk Rock Movie **1978** The musical explosion known as punk rock is documented here in its early days (circa 1977) at the Roxy in England. Includes a look at leading punk rock artists such as the Sex Pistols, the Clash, Slits, and others, and at the entire counterculture that was punk. **80m/C VHS, Beta.** *MVD, SUN*

Punk Vacation **1990** A gang of motorcycle mamas terrorize a small town. The usual biker stuff. **90m/C VHS, Beta, LV.** Stephen Falchi, Roxanne Rogers, Don Martin, Sandra Bogan; ***D:*** Stanley Lewis. *NO*

Puppet Master ½ **1989 (R)** Four psychics are sent to investigate a puppet maker who they think may have discovered the secret of life. Before they know it, they are stalked by evil puppets. Great special effects, not-so-great script. **90m/C VHS, Beta, LV.** Paul LeMat, Jimmie F. Skaggs, Irene Miracle, Robin Rates, Barbara Crampton, William Hickey; ***D:*** David Schmoeller; ***M:*** Richard Band. *PAR*

Puppet Master 2 **1990 (R)** Puppets on a rampage turn hotel into den of special effects. Less effective string pulling than in original. Long live Pinocchio. **90m/C VHS, Beta, LV.** Elizabeth MacLellan, Collin Bernsen, Greg Webb, Charlie Spradling, Nita Talbot, Steve Welles, Jeff Weston; ***D:*** David Allen; ***W:*** David Pabian; ***M:*** Richard Band. *PAR*

Puppet Master 3: Toulon's Revenge **1990 (R)** Prequel about the origin of the whole gory Puppet Master shebang, set in Nazi Germany. The weapon-hungry Third Reich tries to wrest secrets of artificial life from sorceror Andre Toulon, who sics his deadly puppets on them. Toulon's a good guy here, one of many contradictions in the series. Fine cast, but strictly for the followers. **86m/C VHS, LV.** Guy Rolfe, Ian Abercrombie, Sarah Douglas, Richard Lynch, Walter Gotell; ***D:*** David DeCoteau; ***M:*** Richard Band. *PAR*

Puppet Master 4 **1993 (R)** It's the puppets versus the totems, equally loathsome midget creatures who derive their power from the same eternal force as the puppets. No one wants to share and there's lots of gore while they battle for supremacy. **80m/C VHS, Beta.** Gordon Currie, Chandra West, Jason Adams, Teresa Hill, Guy Rolfe; ***D:*** Jeff Burr; ***W:*** Todd Henschell, Steven E. Carr, Jo Duffy, Dough Aarniokoski, Keith Payson; ***M:*** Richard Band. *PAR*

Puppet Master 5: The Final Chapter ½ **1994** Greedy Dr. Jennings has come to Bodega Bay Inn to capture the puppets and discover the secret formula for their animation so he can sell it to the highest bidder. But he's not the only threat, it seems the demonic Eyad, a being from another dimension, also wants the secret and has sent his own evil puppet to kill the puppet master and steal their magic. **81m/C VHS, Beta, LV.** Gordon Currie, Chandra West, Ian Ogilvy, Teresa Hill, Nicholas Guest, Willard Pugh, Diane McBain, Kaz Garas, Guy Rolfe; ***D:*** Jeff Burr; ***M:*** Richard Band. *PAR*

The Puppet Masters ½ *Robert A. Heinlein's The Puppet Masters* **1994 (R)** Government official (Sutherland) discovers aliens are taking over the bodies of humans and if he doesn't find a way to stop the parasites they'll soon rule the Earth. Yes, it does sound like "Invasion of the Body Snatchers" but the film is based on Robert A. Heinlein's 1951 novel, written five years before. The parasites are sufficiently yucky but, unfortunately, this adaptation is mediocre and generally wastes a talented cast. **109m/C VHS, LV.** Donald Sutherland, Eric Thal, Julie Warner, Keith David, Will Patton, Richard Belzer, Yaphet Kotto; ***D:*** Stuart Orme; ***W:*** Terry Rossio, David S. Goyer, Ted Elliott; ***M:*** Colin Towns. *HPH*

Puppet on a Chain **1972 (PG)** American narcotics officer busts an Amsterdam drug ring and the leader's identity surprises him. Slow-moving thriller based on the Alistair MacLean novel. **97m/C VHS, Beta.** *GB* Sven-Bertil Taube, Barbara Parkins, Alexander Knox, Patrick Allen, Geoffrey Reeve; ***D:*** Geoffrey Reeve; ***C:*** Jack Hildyard. *PSM*

The Puppetoon Movie **1987 (G)** A compilation of George Pal's famous Puppetoon cartoons from the 1940s, marking his stature as an animation pioneer and innovator. Hosted by Gumby, Pokey, Speedy Alka Seltzer and Arnie the Dinosaur in newly directed scenes. **80m/C VHS, Beta, LV.** ***D:*** Arnold Leibovit; ***M:*** Buddy Baker. *FHE, WTA*

The Purchase Price **1932** After a less than amorous beginning, farmer Brent and mail order bride Stanwyck fall into love and financial despair in this drama bordering on comedy. Good neighbor Landau is willing to help the poor agriculturalist out in exchange for Stanwyck. Tragedy strikes a_ain when Stanwyck's bootlegger ex-boyfriend shows up and further disasters continue to test the couple's commitment. Based on the story "The Mud Lark" by Arthur Stringer. **70m/B VHS.** Barbara Stanwyck, George Brent, Lyle Talbot, Hardie Albright, David Landau; ***D:*** William A. Wellman; ***W:*** Robert Lord. *MGM*

Pure Country ½ **1992 (PG)** An easygoing movie about a familiar subject is held together by the charm of Strait (in his movie debut) and the rest of the cast. Strait plays a country music superstar, tired of the career glitz, who decides to get out and go back to his home in Texas. He falls in love with the spunky Glasser and decides to run his career his own way. Warren is effective as his tough manager and old-time cowboy Calhoun is finely weathered as Glasser's gruff dad. **113m/C VHS, Beta, LV.** George Strait, Isabel Glasser, Lesley Ann Warren, Rory Calhoun, Kyle Chandler, Molly McClure, John Doe; ***D:*** Christopher Cain; ***W:*** Rex McGee; ***M:*** Stephen Dorff. *WAR, MVD*

A Pure Formality *Una Pura Formalita; Une Pure Formalite* **1994 (PG-13)** Murky psycho-drama finds a disheveled man (Depardieu) winding up at an isolated police station in a nameless country (in the middle of a rainstorm, no less). The Inspector (Polanski) suspects him of a local murder, especially after he claims to be a famous writer named Onoff, yet, can remember nothing. The Inspector wants a confession and spends the night trying to exact one from his guileful suspect. French with subtitles. Film is rated at a much younger level than will possibly understand or enjoy it. **111m/C VHS, LV.** *FR IT* Gerard Depardieu, Roman Polanski, Sergio Rubini; ***D:*** Giuseppe Tornatore; ***W:*** Giuseppe Tornatore, Pascal Quignard; ***C:*** Basco Giurato; ***M:*** Ennio Morricone. *COL*

The Pure Hell of St. Trinian's ½ **1961** In this sequel to "Blue Murder at St. Trinian's," a sheik who desires to fill out his harem tries recruiting at a rowdy girls' school. Although it isn't as funny as the first, due to the lack of Alistair Sim, it is still humorous. Followed by "The Great St. Trinian's Train Robbery." Based on the cartoon by Ronald Searle. **94m/B VHS.** *GB* Cecil Parker, Joyce Grenfell, George Cole, Thorley Walters; ***D:*** Frank Launder; ***M:*** Malcolm Arnold. *FCT*

Pure Luck ½ **1991 (PG)** A who-asked-for-it remake of a 1981 Franco-Italian film called "La Chevre." The premise is the same: an accident-prone heiress disappears in Mexico, and her father tries to locate her using an equally clumsy accountant. The nebbish and an attendant tough private eye stumble and bumble south of the border until the plot arbitrarily ends. Pure awful. **96m/C VHS, Beta, LV.** Martin Short, Danny Glover, Sheila Kelley, Scott Wilson, Sam Wanamaker, Harry Shearer; ***D:*** Nadia Tass; ***W:*** Herschel Weingrod, Timothy Harris. *MCA*

Purgatory **1989** While travelling abroad, two innocent women find themselves unjustly jailed. During their confinement they are tortured and raped. **90m/C VHS, Beta, LV.** Tanya Roberts, Julie Pop; ***D:*** Ami Artzi; ***W:*** Paul Aratow. *NO*

Purlie Victorious **1963** Presentation of the award-winning Broadway hit, which takes a look at racial integration. **93m/C VHS, Beta.** Ossie Davis, Ruby Dee, Godfrey Cambridge, Alan Alda; ***D:*** Nicholas Webster. *NO*

The Purple Heart ½ **1944** An American Air Force crew is shot down over Tokyo and taken into brutal POW camps. Intense wartime melodramatics. **99m/B VHS, Beta.** Dana Andrews, Richard Conte, Farley Granger, Donald (Don "Red") Barry, Sam Levene, Kevin O'Shea, Tala Birell, Nestor Paiva, Benson Fong, Marshall Thompson, Richard Loo; ***D:*** Lewis Milestone; ***C:*** Arthur C. Miller. *FOX*

Purple Hearts ½ **1984 (R)** Wahl stars as a Navy doctor who falls in love with nurse Ladd against the backdrop of the Vietnam war. Overlong and redundant. **115m/C VHS, Beta.** Cheryl Ladd, Ken Wahl, Stephen Lee, Annie McEnroe, Paul McCrane, Cyril O'Reilly; ***D:*** Sidney J. Furie; ***W:*** Sidney J. Furie, Ron Nyswaner; ***M:*** Robert Folk. *WAR*

The Purple Monster Strikes **1945** A martian plots to conquer Earth to save his dying planet. Serial in fifteen episodes. **188m/B VHS.** Dennis Moore, Linda Stirling, Roy Barcroft; ***D:*** Spencer Gordon Bennet. *REP, VCN, MLB*

Purple People Eater **1988 (PG)** The alien of the title descends to earth to mix with young girls and rock 'n roll. Based on the song of the same name whose performer, Sheb Wooley, appears in the film. Harmless, stupid fun for the whole family. **91m/C VHS, Beta, LV.** Ned Beatty, Shelley Winters, Neil Patrick Harris, Kareem Abdul-Jabbar, Little Richard, Chubby Checker, Peggy Lipton; ***D:*** Linda Shayne. *MED, VTR*

Purple Rain ½ **1984 (R)** A quasi-autobiographical video showcase for the pop-star Prince. Film tells the tale of his struggle for love, attention, acceptance, and popular artistic recognition in Minneapolis. Not a bad film, for such a monumentally egotistical movie. **113m/C VHS, Beta, LV.** Prince, Apollonia, Morris Day, Olga Karlatos, Clarence Williams III; ***D:*** Albert Magnoli; ***W:*** William Blinn; ***C:*** Donald E. Thorin; ***M:*** Michel Colombier. Academy Awards '84: Best Original Score. *MVD, WAR*

The Purple Rose of Cairo **1985 (PG)** A diner waitress, disillusioned by the Depression and a lackluster life, escapes into a film playing at the local movie house where a blond film hero, tiring of the monotony of his role, makes a break from the celluloid to join her in the real world. The ensuing love story allows director-writer Allen to show his knowledge of old movies and provide his fans with a change of pace. Farrow's film sister is also her real-life sister Stephanie, who went on to appear in Allen's "Zelig." **82m/C VHS, Beta, LV.** Mia Farrow, Jeff Daniels, Danny Aiello, Dianne Wiest, Van Johnson, Zoe Caldwell, John Wood, Michael Tucker, Edward Herrmann, Milo O'Shea, Glenne Headly, Karen Akers, Deborah Rush; ***D:*** Woody Allen; ***W:*** Woody Allen; ***C:*** Gordon Willis; ***M:*** Dick Hyman. British Academy Awards '85: Best Film, Best Original Screenplay; Cesar Awards '86: Best Foreign Film; Golden Globe Awards '86: Best Screenplay; New York Film Critics Awards '85: Best Screenplay; Nominations: Academy Awards '85: Best Original Screenplay. *LIV, VES, HMV*

The Purple Taxi ½ **1977 (R)** Romantic drama revolving around several wealthy foreigners who have taken refuge in beautiful southern Ireland. From Michel Deon's bestselling novel. **93m/C VHS, Beta.** *FR* Fred Astaire, Charlotte Rampling, Peter Ustinov, Philippe Noiret, Edward Albert; ***D:*** Yves Boisset. Nominations: Cannes Film Festival '77: Best Film. *COL*

Purple Vigilantes ½ *The Purple Riders* **1938** The Three Mesquiteers uncover a gang of vigilantes. Part of the series. **54m/B VHS, Beta.** Bob Livingston, Ray Corrigan, Max Terhune. *VCN, DVT*

Pursued **1947** Excellent performances by Mitchum and Wright mark this suspenseful Western drama of a Spanish-American war veteran in search of his father's killer. **105m/B VHS.** Teresa Wright, Robert Mitchum, Judith Anderson, Dean Jagger, Alan Hale, Harry Carey Jr., John Rodney; ***D:*** Raoul Walsh; ***C:*** James Wong Howe; ***M:*** Max Steiner. *REP, HEG*

Pursuit **1972** A terrorist threatens to release a toxic nerve gas throughout a city hosting a political convention. Tension mounts as federal agents must beat the extremists' countdown to zero. Based on the novel by Crichton. **73m/C VHS, Beta.** Ben Gazzara, E.G. Marshall, Martin Sheen, Joseph Wiseman, William Windom; ***D:*** Michael Crichton; ***M:*** Jerry Goldsmith. *REP*

Pursuit **1990 (R)** A mercenary comes out of retirement to join a renegade team recovering stolen gold. But they turn on him, stealing the treasure and taking a hostage. Now he must track them down, or there's no movie. **94m/C VHS.** James Ryan, Andre Jacobs; ***D:*** John H. Parr. *HBO*

The Pursuit of D.B. Cooper **1981 (PG)** Based on an actual hijacking that occurred on Thanksgiving Eve in 1971 in which J.R. Meade (alias D.B. Cooper) parachuted out of an airliner with $200,000 of stolen money. Although his fate and whereabouts have remained a mystery, this story speculates about what may have happened. **100m/C VHS, Beta, LV.** Robert Duvall, Treat Williams, Kathryn Harrold, Ed Flanders; ***D:*** Roger Spottiswoode; ***C:*** Harry Stradling Jr.; ***M:*** James Horner. *LIV, VES*

The Pursuit of Happiness ½ **1970 (PG)** An idealistic man is convicted of manslaughter after accidentally running down a woman. Once in prison, he's faced with the decision to try to escape. **85m/C VHS, Beta.** Michael Sarrazin, Arthur Hill, E.G. Marshall, Barbara Hershey, Robert Klein; ***D:*** Robert Mulligan. *NO*

Pursuit of the Graf Spee ½ *The Battle of the River Plate* **1957** Three small British ships destroy the mighty Graf Spee, a WWII German battleship. **106m/C VHS, Beta.** *GB* Anthony Quayle, Peter Finch, Ian Hunter; ***D:*** Michael Powell. *NO*

Pursuit to Algiers ½ **1945** The modernized Holmes and Watson guard over the King of fictional Rovenia during a sea voyage, during which assassins close in. **65m/B VHS, Beta.** Basil Rathbone, Nigel Bruce, Martin Kosleck, Marjorie Riordan, Rosalind Ivan, John Abbott; ***D:*** Roy William Neill. *FOX*

Pushed to the Limit ½ **1992 (R)** Harry Lee, the most feared gangster in Chinatown, is about to meet his match in martial-arts queen Lesseos. She's out for revenge when she learns that Lee is responsible for her brother's murder but first she must get by Lee's lethal bodyguard, the equally skilled Inga. **88m/C VHS, LV.** Mimi Lesseos. *IMP*

Pushing Hands ½ **1992** Aging tai chi master Mr. Chu (Lung) leaves Beijing to live with his son Alex (Wang) and daughter-in-law Martha (Snyder) in suburban New York. High-strung Martha doesn't understand her tranquilly stubborn father-in-law, nor does Chu find disposable American society much to his liking. Naturally, and slowly, some accomodations are made. The title is a tai chi reference to keeping your opponent off-balance while maintaining your own equilibrium. Director Lee's debut feature is also the first in his trilogy of family films—followed by the more accomplished "The Wedding Banquet" and "Eat Drink Man Woman." English and Mandarin Chinese with subtitles. **100m/C VHS, LV.** Sihung Lung, Deb Snyder, Bo Z. Wang, Lai Wang; ***D:*** Ang Lee; ***W:*** Ang Lee; ***C:*** Jong Lin; ***M:*** Xiao-Song Qu. *TRI*

Puss 'n Boots **1984** From "Faerie Tale Theatre" comes the story of a cat who makes his poor master a rich land-owning nobleman. **60m/C VHS, Beta.** Ben Vereen, Gregory Hines; ***D:*** Robert Iscove. *FOX, FCT*

Putney Swope **1969 (R)** Comedy about a token black ad man mistakenly elected Chairman of the board of a Madison Avenue ad agency who turns the company upside-down. A series of riotous spoofs on commercials is the highpoint in this funny, though somewhat dated look at big business. **84m/B VHS, Beta.** Arnold Johnson, Laura Greene, Stanley Gottlieb, Mel Brooks; ***D:*** Robert Downey. *COL*

Puzzle ½ **1978** Franciscus searches for the urn that contains the remains of Buddha but instead finds danger and intrigue. Made for television. **90m/C VHS.** *AU* James Franciscus, Wendy Hughes, Robert Helpmann, Peter Gwynne, Gerald Kennedy, Kerry McGuire; ***D:*** Gordon Hessler. *ACA*

Pygmalion ½ **1938** Oscar-winning film adaptation of Shaw's play about a cockney flower-girl who is transformed into a "lady" under the guidance of a stuffy phonetics professor. Shaw himself aided in writing the script in this superbly acted comedy that would be adapted into the musical, "My Fair Lady," first on Broadway in 1956 and for the screen in 1964. **96m/B VHS, Beta, LV.** *GB* Leslie Howard, Wendy Hiller, Wilfred Lawson, Marie Lohr; ***D:*** Leslie Howard, Anthony Asquith; ***C:*** Harry Stradling. Academy Awards '38: Best Adapted Screenplay; Venice Film Festival '38: Best Actor (Howard); Nominations: Academy Awards '38: Best Actor (Howard), Best Actress (Hiller), Best Picture. *COL, NOS, SUE*

Pyrates **1991 (R)** Real life husband-wife team of Bacon and Sedgwick try to provide fireworks as hot, hot lovers in the forgettable one. For the price of this one you can buy a newspaper and chewing gum instead. Use both at the same time and you'll be ahead of everyone involved in this senseless hoot. **98m/C VHS.** Kevin Bacon, Kyra Sedgwick, Bruce Martyn Payne, Kristin Datillo; ***D:*** Noah Stern. *VES, LIV*

A Pyromaniac's Love Story **1995 (PG)** Offbeat tale of romance has a neigborhood bakery burning down and every major character confessing to the crime. Earnest working stiffs, snotty rich kids, and kindly old shop owners all have really confusing reasons for wanting to take the heat, most of which have to do with unrequited love. At times charming, but ultimately too whimsical for its own good. The quirky characters and goofy plot twists sabotage any attempt to ignite much interest. **99m/C VHS, LV.** John Leguizamo, Sadie Frost, William Baldwin, Erika Eleniak, Michael Lerner, Joan Plowright, Armin Mueller-Stahl, Richard Crenna; ***D:*** Joshua Brand; ***W:*** Morgan Ward; ***C:*** John Schwartzman; ***M:*** Rachel Portman. *TOU*

Python Wolf *C.A.T. Squad: Python Wolf* **1988 (R)** It's non-stop action in South Africa as a counter-terrorist group sets out to thwart a drug smuggler's plans to export plutonium. As usual, intense pacing from director Friedkin. Made for television. Sequel to "C.A.T. Squad" (1986). **100m/C VHS, LV.** Joe Cortese, Jack Youngblood, Steve James, Deborah Van Valkenburgh, Miguel Ferrer, Alan Scarfe; ***D:*** William Friedkin; ***M:*** Ennio Morricone. *VMK*

The Pyx *The Hooker Cult Murders* **1973 (R)** Canadian suspense thriller about the murder of a prostitute with satanic overtones. Poice sergeant investigates the crime and enters a world of devil worship and decadence. Based on the novel by John Buell. **111m/C VHS.** *CA* Karen Black, Christopher Plummer, Donald Pilon; ***D:*** Harvey Hart. *PSM*

Q & A **1990 (R)** Semi-taut thriller with Nolte playing a totally corrupt, hair-trigger cop trying to make his murder of a drug dealer look like self-defense. Assigned to the case is an ex-cop turned assistant DA (Hutton) who's supposed to sweep the case under the rug. Then he finds out another dealer (Assante) is a witness and he happens to be romancing Hutton's former girlfriend (film debut of director Lumet's daughter). Lots of violence and raw language. **132m/C VHS, Beta, LV.** Nick Nolte, Timothy Hutton, Armand Assante, Patrick O'Neal, Lee Richardson, Luis Guzman, Charles S. Dutton, Jenny Lumet, Paul Calderone, Fyvush Finkel; ***D:*** Sidney Lumet; ***W:*** Sidney Lumet; ***M:*** Ruben Blades. *HBO, WAR*

Q Ships ½ **1928** Silent German drama about a submarine commander who has inner conflicts with his country's war effort. Uses actual WWI footage. **78m/B VHS, Beta.** *GE* J.P. Kennedy, Roy Travers, Johnny Butt, Philip Hewland; ***D:*** Geoffrey Barkas, Michael Barringer. *GPV, DVT, GLV*

Q (The Winged Serpent) **1982 (R)** A cult of admirers surrounds this goony monster flick about dragonlike Aztec god Quetzlcoatl, summoned to modern Manhattan by gory human sacrifices, and hungry for rooftop sunbathers and construction teams. Direction and special effects are pretty ragged, but witty script helps the cast shine, especially Moriarty as a lowlife crook who's found the beast's hidden nest. Also called "Q: The Winged Serpent." **92m/C VHS, Beta.** Michael Moriarty, Candy Clark, David Carradine, Richard Roundtree; ***D:*** Larry Cohen; ***W:*** Larry Cohen. *MCA*

QB VII ½ **1974** A knighted physician brings a suit for libel against a novelist for implicating him in war crimes. Hopkins as the purportedly wronged doctor and Gazzara as the writer are both superb. Ending is stunning. Adapted from the novel by Leon Uris. Over five hours long; made for TV. Available only as a three-cassette set. **313m/C VHS, Beta, LV.** Anthony Hopkins, Ben Gazzara, Lee Remick, Leslie Caron, Juliet Mills, John Gielgud, Anthony Quayle; ***D:*** Tom Gries; ***M:*** Jerry Goldsmith. *COL, SWC*

Quackser Fortune Has a Cousin in the Bronx *Fun Loving* **1970 (R)** An Irish fertilizer salesman meets an exchange student from the U.S., who finds herself attracted to this unlearned, but not unknowing, man. An original love story with drama and appeal. **88m/C VHS, Beta, LV.** *IR* Gene Wilder, Margot Kidder; ***D:*** Waris Hussein. *VCI*

Quadrophenia **1979 (R)** Pete Townshend's excellent rock opera about an alienated youth looking for life's meaning in Britain's rock scene circa 1963. Music by The Who is powerful and apt. Fine performance by Sting in his acting debut. **115m/C VHS, Beta, LV.** *GB* Phil Daniels, Mark Wingett, Philip Davis, Leslie Ash, Sting; ***D:*** Franc Roddam. *MVD, COL, RHI*

Quake 🦴½ **1992 (R)** Railsback stars as a stalker who takes advantage of the 1990 San Francisco earthquake to finally obtain the woman of his dreams. A surveillance expert, he's after a beautiful lawyer (Anderson) and when the earthquake leaves her trapped he rushes to rescue her—only to hold her captive himself. **83m/C VHS.** Steve Railsback, Erika Anderson, Eb Lottimer, Dick Miller; ***D:*** Louis Morneau; ***W:*** Mark Evan Schwartz. *COL*

Quality Street 🦴🦴 **1937** English lovers Tone and Hepburn are separated when he leaves to fight in the Napoleonic Wars. When Tone returns years later, he's forgotten his erstwhile heartthrob. He also fails to recognize that the 16-year old coquette who's caught his eye is his old beloved in disguise. Cast works hard to overcome the absurd premise, based on the play by Sir James Barrie. **84m/B VHS, LV.** Katharine Hepburn, Franchot Tone, Fay Bainter, Eric Blore, Cora Witherspoon, Estelle Winwood, Florence Lake, Bonita Granville; ***D:*** George Stevens; ***W:*** J.M. Barrie. Nominations: Academy Awards '37: Best Original Score. *NOS, FCT, TTC*

Quarantine 🦴🦴½ **1989 (R)** Quarantine camps for carriers of a fatal virus are the serious measures taken by the nation. The solution is clear to a rebel and an inventor; all must be liberated or exterminated. **92m/C VHS.** Beatrice Boepple, Garwin Sanford, Jerry Wasserman, Charles Wilkinson; ***D:*** Charles Wilkinson; ***W:*** Charles Wilkinson. *REP*

The Quarrel 🦴🦴½ **1993** Chaim Kovler is a New York poet visiting Montreal in 1948. In a park he notices a group of Orthodox Jews and discovers one is his childhood friend Hersh. Fifteen years earlier their friendship broke over Chaim's decision to give up the religious life for his writing. Having lost their families to the Holocaust in Poland, both men have immigrated to new lives in North America. They immediately pick up their quarrel over religious faith and its value, particularly in light of the Holocaust. The two characters serve too much as careful ideologues to be compelling and the story turns cloyingly sentimental. Based on a short story by Yiddish writer Chaim Grade. **88m/C VHS.** *CA* Saul Rubinek, R.H. Thomson; ***D:*** Eli Cohen; ***W:*** David Brandes; ***M:*** William Goldstein. *BMG*

Quarterback Princess 🦴🦴 **1985** Workaday made-for-TV telling of the real-life girl who goes out for football and becomes homecoming queen. Heartwarming, if you like that kinda stuff, but not exciting. **96m/C VHS, Beta.** Helen Hunt, Don Murray, John Stockwell, Daphne Zuniga; ***D:*** Noel Black. *FOX*

Quartet 🦴🦴🦴 **1981 (R)** A young French woman is taken in by an English couple after her husband goes to prison. The husband seduces her, and she becomes trapped emotionally and socially. Superbly acted, claustrophobic drama based on a Jean Rhys novel. **101m/C VHS, Beta.** *GB FR* Isabelle Adjani, Alan Bates, Maggie Smith, Anthony Higgins; ***D:*** James Ivory; ***W:*** Ruth Prawer Jhabvala. Cannes Film Festival '81: Best Actress (Adjani); Nominations: Cannes Film Festival '81: Best Film. *WAR*

Quartier Mozart 🦴🦴 **1992** Sexual farce presenting the assimilation of African American pop-culture into African traditions. A local sorceress uses witchcraft to give Queen of the 'Hood a first-hand look at sexual politics. The young girl enters the body of a boy struggling to find his place in the male hierarchy established by neighborhood Casanovas. In French with English subtitles. **80m/C VHS.** ***D:*** Jean-Pierre Bekolo. *KIV*

Quatermass 2 🦴🦴🦴 *Enemy from Space* **1957** In the well-made sequel to "Quatermass Experiment," (also known as "The Creeping Unknown") Professor Quatermass battles blobs and brain-washed zombies to rescue government officials whose bodies have been invaded by aliens. "Five Million Years to Earth" concluded the trilogy. **84m/B VHS, Beta, LV.** *GB* Brian Donlevy, John Longden, Sidney James, Bryan Forbes, William Franklyn, Vera Day, John Van Eyssen, Michael Ripper, Michael Balfour; ***D:*** Val Guest; ***M:*** James Bernard. *FCT, CTH, SNC*

Quatermass and the Pit 🦴🦴½ **1958** From the original BBC production. Professor Quatermass is up to his ears in trouble as a Martian spacecraft is found by subway workers. Not long after a monster stalks the streets of London. Remade cinematically in 1968 as "Five Million Years to Earth." **180m/B VHS.** *GB* Andre Morell, Cec Linder. *SNC, MRV*

Quatermass Conclusion 🦴🦴 **1979** An elderly British scientist comes out of retirement to stop an immobilizing death ray from outer space from destroying Earth. Edited version of a television miniseries continues earlier adventures of Quatermass on film and television. **105m/C VHS, Beta.** *GB* John Mills, Simon MacCorkindale, Barbara Kellerman, Margaret Tyzack; ***D:*** Piers Haggard. *NO*

The Quatermass Experiment 🦴🦴🦴 *The Creeping Unknown* **1956** Excellent British production about an astronaut who returns to Earth carrying an alien infestation that causes him to turn into a horrible monster. Competent acting and tense direction. Followed by "Enemy From Space." **78m/B VHS.** *GB* Brian Donlevy, Margia Dean, Jack Warner, Richard Wordsworth; ***D:*** Val Guest; ***M:*** James Bernard. *MGM, SNC, NOS*

Quatorze Juliet 🦴🦴½ **1932** A taxi driver and a flower girl meet on Bastille Day and fall in love. When he becomes involved with gangsters, she steers him back to virtue in this minor French relic from director Clair. **85m/B VHS.** *FR* Anabella Rigaud, Jorge Rigaud; ***D:*** Rene Clair. *VDM, FCT*

Que Viva Mexico 🦴🦴🦴 **1932** Eisenstein's grand unfinished folly on the history of Mexico, reconstructed and released in 1979 by his protege, Grigori Alexandrov. Divided into four sections: "Sandunga" covers the Tehuantepec jungles and its inhabitants; "Manguei" is about a peasant and his bride; "Fiesta" devotes itself to bullfighting and romance; and "Soldadera" depicts the 1910 Mexican revolution through frescoes. Along with "Greed" and "Napoleon," it remains as one of cinema's greatest irrecoverable casualties. Russian narration with English subtitles. **85m/B VHS, Beta.** *RU* ***D:*** Sergei Eisenstein, Grigori Alexandrov. *KIV*

Queen Bee 🦴🦴½ **1955** Crawford is at her manipulative best as Southern belle Eva Phillips, married to wealthy Georgia mill owner Avery (Sullivan). The ruthless Eva is despised by her bitter, tippling husband who finds a chance at romance when cousin Jennifer (Marlow) comes to visit. Naturally, Eva can't stand any competition, though she doesn't care about Avery, and tries to break up the duo even as she seeks to renew her own affair with a former lover (Ireland). Based on the novel by Edna Lee. **94m/B VHS.** Joan Crawford, Barry Sullivan, John Ireland, Lucy Marlow, Betsy Palmer, Fay Wray; ***D:*** Ranald MacDougall; ***W:*** Ranald MacDougall; ***C:*** Charles B(ryant) Lang; ***M:*** George Duning. Nominations: Academy Awards '55: Best Black and White Cinematography. *COL*

Queen Boxer 🦴 **1973 (R)** A female kick-boxer beats up those who reprehensibly enslaved her family. **92m/C VHS, Beta.** Judy Lee, Peter Yang Kwan. *LIV*

Queen Christina 🦴🦴🦴½ **1933** A stylish, resonant star vehicle for Garbo, portraying the 17th-century Swedish queen from ascension to the throne to her romance with a Spanish ambassador. Alternately hilarious and moving, it holds some of Garbo's greatest and most memorable moments. Gilbert's second to last film and his only successful outing after the coming of sound. **101m/B VHS, Beta, LV.** Greta Garbo, John Gilbert, Lewis Stone, Sir C. Aubrey Smith, Ian Keith, Reginald Owen, Elizabeth Young; ***D:*** Rouben Mamoulian; ***C:*** William H. Daniels. *MGM*

Queen for a Day 🦴🦴½ *Horsie* **1951** Three differing vignettes, based on a rather notorious radio and TV game show of the time, in which "deserving" (or sufficiently pathetic) working-class women were rewarded for their selflessness. Part one concerns a perfect suburban family whose son contracts polio. Part two has a teen spooking his immigrant parents by working as a carnival high diver to earn college cash. The finale is a Dorothy Parker farce about a homely but kindhearted nurse caring for the child of an unappreciative couple. So popular was this segment that the film was retitled after the main character. Overall, not bad considering the source. **107m/B VHS.** Phyllis Avery, Darren McGavin, Tristram Coffin, Adam Williams, Tracey Roberts, Jack Bailey, Jim Morgan, Fort Pearson; ***D:*** Arthur Lubin. *NOS*

Queen Kelly 🦴🦴🦴 **1929** The popularly known, slapdash version of von Stroheim's famous final film, in which an orphan goes from royal marriage to white slavery to astounding wealth. Never really finished, the film is the edited first half of the intended project, prepared for European release after von Stroheim had been fired. Even so, a campy, extravagant and lusty melodrama. Silent. **113m/B VHS, Beta, LV, 8mm.** Gloria Swanson, Walter Byron, Seena Owen, Tully Marshall, Madame Sul Te Wan; ***D:*** Erich von Stroheim. *NOS, KIV, VYY*

Queen Margot 🦴🦴🦴½ *La Reine Margot* **1994 (R)** Blood-soaked period of French history is duly rendered on screen in big-budget costume epic. Beautiful Catholic, Marguerite de Valois (Adjani), is the pawn of her devious mother, the widowed queen Catherine de Medici (Lisi) who skillfully manipulates unstable son Charles IX (Anglade), the nominal ruler of 1570's France, while she plots to marry Margot off to Protestant Henri de Navarre (Auteuil). Margot is contemptuous of her new husband, preferring to find her amatory amusements in the Paris streets, where she takes a handsome lover (Perez). But both Margot and Henri are united against the Queen when Catherine's minions order the murder of the rival Huguenots—a notably violent affair known as the St. Bartholomew's Day Massacre. The history's confusing, the violence graphic, the acting flamboyant, and the visuals top-notch. Based on the novel by Alexandre Dumas. French with subtitles; originally released at 161 minutes. **135m/C VHS, LV.** *FR* Isabelle Adjani, Daniel Auteuil, Virna Lisi, Jean-Hugues Anglade, Vincent Perez, Pascal Greggory, Miguel Bose, Dominique Blanc, Claudio Amendola, Asia Argento, Julien Rassam, Jean-Claude Brialy; ***D:*** Patrice Chereau; ***W:*** Patrice Chereau, Daniele Thompson; ***M:*** Goran Bregovic. Cannes Film Festival '94: Special Jury Prize, Best Actress (Lisi); Nominations: Academy Awards '94: Best Costume Design; British Academy Awards '95: Best Foreign Film; Cesar Awards '95: Best Director (Chereau), Best Film, Best Supporting Actress (Blanc). *MAX*

Queen of Diamonds 🦴🦴 **198?** A woman pulls off the biggest diamond heist of all time. **90m/C VHS, Beta.** Claudia Cardinale, Stanley Baker, Henri Charriere. *NO*

Queen of Diamonds 🦴🦴 **1991** The "Queen of Diamonds" is an alienated blackjack dealer in Vegas who, in between dealing cards, casually searches for her missing husband and looks after an old man in a motel. **77m/C VHS.** Tinka Menkes; ***D:*** Nina Menkes; ***W:*** Nina Menkes. *FCT*

Queen of Hearts 🦴🦴🦴½ **1989 (PG)** Excellent, original romantic comedy is a directorial triumph for Amiel in his first feature. An Italian couple defy both their families and marry for love. Four children later, we find them running a diner in England. Humorous, dramatic, sad—everything a movie can and should be. Fine performances. **112m/C VHS, Beta, LV.** *GB* Anita Zagaria, Joseph Long, Eileen Way, Vittorio Duse, Vittorio Amandola, Ian Hawkes; ***D:*** Jon Amiel; ***M:*** Michael Convertino. *NO*

The Queen of Mean 🦴½ *Leona Helmsley: The Queen of Mean* **1990** Tabloid TV-movie based on Ransdell Pierson's scandal-sheet bio of the hotel magnate and convicted tax cheat. See Leona connive. See Leona bitch. See Leona get hers. What's the point? If you ask that you're too bright to watch. **94m/C VHS.** Suzanne Pleshette, Lloyd Bridges, Bruce Weitz, Joe Regalbuto; ***D:*** Richard Michaels. *FRH*

Queen of Outer Space *Woof!* **1958** Notorious male-chauvinist sci-fi cheapie starts out slow, but then the laughs keep coming as the cast plays the hyperdumb material straight. Space cadets crash on Venus, find it ruled by women—and the dolls have wicked plans in store for mankind. Don't be surprised if you've seen the sets before since they were borrowed from "Forbidden Planet," "World Without End," and "Flight to Mars." **80m/C VHS, Beta.** Zsa Zsa Gabor, Eric Fleming, Laurie Mitchell, Paul Birch, Barbara Darrow, Dave Willcock, Lisa Davis, Patrick Waltz, Marilyn Buferd, Marjorie Durant, Lynn Cartwright, Gerry Gaylor; ***D:*** Edward L. Bernds. *FXV*

The Queen of Spades 🦴🦴🦴 **1949** Mystical drama about a Russian soldier who ruins his life searching for winning methods of card playing. Well-made version of the Pushkin story. **95m/B VHS, LV.** *GB* Anton Walbrook, Edith Evans, Ronald Howard, Mary Jerrold, Yvonne Mitchell, Anthony Dawson; ***D:*** Thorold Dickinson. *NO*

Queen of the Amazons 🦴½ **1947** A girl searches for her fiance and finds him reluctantly held captive by a tribe of women who rule the jungle. **60m/B VHS, Beta, LV.** Robert Lowery, Patricia Morison, J. Edward Bromberg, John Miljan. *SNC, NOS*

Queen of the Jungle 🦴 **1935** Re-edited adventure serial featuring a white woman cast off in a hot-air balloon and landing in Africa, where she is hailed as a Queen. High camp, starring ex-Our Ganger Kornman. **85m/B VHS, Beta, 8mm.** Mary Kornman, Reed Howes; ***D:*** Robert F. "Bob" Hill. *VYY, NOS, MLB*

Queen of the Road 🦴🦴 **1984** A feisty Aussie schoolteacher starts a new life as a tractor-trailer driver. **96m/C VHS, Beta.** *AU* Joanne Samuel, Amanda Muggleton; ***D:*** Bruce Best. *LIV, VES*

Queen of the Stardust Ballroom 🦴🦴🦴 **1975** Well-made television drama about a lonely widow who goes to a local dance hall, where she meets a man and begins an unconventional late love. **98m/C Beta.** Maureen Stapleton, Charles Durning, Michael Strong, Charlotte Rae, Sam O'Steen; ***D:*** Michael Brandon; ***M:*** Billy Goldenberg. *PSM*

Queenie 🦴🦴½ **1987** Television miniseries loosely based on the life of actress Merle Oberon, exploring her rise to stardom. Based on the best-selling novel by Michael Korda, Oberon's nephew by marriage. Many long, dry passages fit for leaving the room for snacks. **233m/C VHS.** Mia Sara, Kirk Douglas, Martin Balsam, Claire Bloom, Chaim Topol, Joel Grey, Sarah Miles, Joss Ackland; ***D:*** Larry Peerce; ***M:*** Georges Delerue. *VTR, NWV*

Queens Logic 🦴🦴½ **1991 (R)** Ensemble comedy in the tradition of "The Big Chill" featuring the trials and tribulations of the "old-neighborhood" gang, who gather again on hometurf and reminisce. Most of the film centers around Olin and girlfriend Webb and whether or not he will chicken out of their wedding. Not bad comedy, with Mantegna delivering most of the good lines. **116m/C VHS, LV.** John Malkovich, Kevin Bacon, Jamie Lee Curtis, Linda Fiorentino, Joe Mantegna, Ken Olin, Tom Waits, Chloe Webb, Ed Marinaro, Kelly Bishop, Tony Spiridakis; ***D:*** Steve Rash; ***W:*** Tony Spiridakis; ***M:*** Joe Jackson. *LIV*

Querelle 🦴🦴½ **1983 (R)** Querelle, a handsome sailor, finds himself involved in a bewildering environment of murder, drug smuggling, and homosexuality in the port of Brest. Highly stylized and erotic sets, along with a dark look, give the film an interesting feel. Nice performances by Davis, Nero, and Moreau. Fassbinder's controversial last film, based on the story by Jean Genet. Strange, difficult narrative (such as it is), alternately boring and engrossing. **106m/C VHS, Beta.** *GE* Brad Davis, Jeanne Moreau, Franco Nero, Laurent Malet; ***D:*** Rainer Werner Fassbinder; ***M:*** Peer Raben. *COL, APD, GLV*

The Quest 🦴🦴 **1986 (PG)** Australian film never released theatrically in the United States. A young boy (Thomas, of "E.T." fame) raised in the outback investigates a local Aboriginal superstition about a monster living in an ancient cemetery. Not bad, just dull. **94m/C VHS, Beta.** *AU* Henry Thomas, Tony Barry, John Ewart, Rachel Friend, Tamsin West, Dennis Miller, Katya Manning; ***D:*** Brian Trenchard-Smith. *NLC*

The Quest 🦴🦴 **1996 (PG-13)** In his directorial debut, Van Damme plays pickpocket Christopher Dubois, who finds his adventures just beginning when he hops a freighter heading for the far east in order to escape police trouble. He learns about a prestigious martial arts competition, where the prize could set him up for life, if he can manage to get into the invitation-only event. After many films set in the future, Van Damme chose to set this one in the 20's, with fairly good results. He piles on the beautiful location shots until the inevitable martial arts melee toward the end. Pacing is sketchy but Van Damme does display directorial talent. **95m/C VHS.** Jean-Claude Van Damme, Roger Moore, Aki Aleong, James Remar, Jack McGee, Janet Gunn, Abdel Qissi, Louis Mandylor; ***D:*** Jean-Claude Van Damme; ***W:*** Stuart Klein, Paul Mones; ***C:*** David Gribble; ***M:*** Randy Edelman. *NYR*

Quest for Fire 🦴🦴🦴 **1982 (R)** An interesting story sans the usual dialogue thing. A group of men during the Ice Age must wander the land searching for fire after they lose theirs fending off an attack. During their quest, they encounter and battle various animals and tribesmen in order to survive. The special language they speak was developed by Anthony Burgess, while the primitive movements were Desmond "The Naked Ape" Morris. Perlman went on to become the Beast in TV's "Beauty and the Beast"; Chong is the daughter of Tommy Chong of the comic duo Cheech and Chong. **75m/C VHS, Beta, LV.** *FR* Everett McGill, Ron Perlman, Nameer El-Kadi, Rae Dawn Chong; ***D:*** Jean-Jacques Annaud; ***W:*** Gerard Brach. Academy Awards '82: Best Makeup; Genie Awards '83: Best Actress (Chong). *FOX, INJ*

Quest for Love 🦴🦴½ **1971** Quirky sci-fi story of a man who passes through a time warp and finds himself able to maintain two parallel lives. Based on John Wyndham's short story. **90m/C VHS, Beta.** *GB* Joan Collins, Tom Bell, Denholm Elliott, Laurence Naismith; ***D:*** Ralph Thomas. *NO*

Quest for the Mighty Sword 🦴 **1990 (PG-13)** A warrior battles dragons, demons and evil wizards. **94m/C VHS, Beta, LV.** Eric Allen Kramer, Margaret Lenzey, Donald O'Brien, Dina Marrone, Chris Murphy; ***D:*** David Hills. *COL*

Quest of the Delta Knights 🦴🦴½ **1993 (PG)** Swashbuckling fantasy about a kingdom suffering under an evil ruler and his equally sinister queen. They are opposed by the heroic Delta Knights whose only chance to defeat the fiendish powers of darkness is by unearthing a legendary storehouse containing technology from the age of Atlantis and all the powers of the Ancients. **97m/C VHS.** David Warner, Olivia Hussey, Corbin Allred, Brigid Conley Walsh, David Kriegel; ***D:*** James Dodson. *HMD*

A Question of Attribution 🦴🦴½ **1991** Sir Anthony Blunt (Fox) is an internationally respected art expert who also serves as an art adviser to Queen Elizabeth II. His life unravels when an on-going British Intelligence investigation reveals him to be the fourth man in the Burgess-Maclean-Philby scandal involving Englishmen who spied for, and eventually defected to, the USSR. The investigation of Blunt's covert past is paralleled with his own art investigation of a painting attributed to Titian. Three men are depicted in the art work—with a fourth male figure discovered to have been painted over. Alan Bennett adapted his play for the television drama. **90m/C VHS.** *GB* James Fox, David Calder, Geoffrey Palmer, Prunella Scales, Mark Payton, Jason Flemyng, Edward De Souza, Ann Beach; ***D:*** John Schlesinger; ***W:*** Alan Bennett. *FOX*

Question of Faith 🦴🦴½ **1993** A happily married woman is diagnosed with a rare form of cancer. Much to her family's dismay, she turns to some unconventional medical therapies in order to heal herself. Based on a true story. Basically noble, Archer and Neill lift this tearjerker out of most of its maudlin aspects. **90m/C VHS.** Anne Archer, Sam Neill, Frances Lee McCain, James Tolkan, James Hong, CCH Pounder, Louis Giambalvo, Norman Parker, Michael Constantine; ***D:*** Stephen Gyllenhaal; ***W:*** Bruce Hart. *WOV*

A Question of Guilt 🦴🦴 **1978** When her child turns up dead, a free-wheeling divorcee is the prime suspect. Made-for-television soaper. **100m/C VHS.** Tuesday Weld, Ron Leibman, Peter Masterson, Alex Rocco, Viveca Lindfors, Lana Wood; ***D:*** Robert Butler. *LIV*

Question of Honor 🦴🦴½ **1980** Under governmental pressures, an honest narcotics cop decides to inform on his department's corruption. Co-written and produced by ex-cop Sonny Grosso, on whom "The French Connection" was based. Made for television and based on the book, "Point Blank," by Grosso and Philip Rosenberg. **134m/C VHS, Beta.** Ben Gazzara, Paul Sorvino, Robert Vaughn, Tony Roberts, Danny Aiello, Anthony Zerbe; ***D:*** Jud Taylor; ***W:*** Budd Schulberg. *NO*

A Question of Love 🦴🦴🦴 **1978** Fine performances in this well-done television movie about two lesbians—one of whom is fighting her ex-husband for custody of their child. **100m/C VHS.** Gena Rowlands, Jane Alexander, Ned Beatty, Clu Gulager, Bonnie Bedelia, James Sutorius, Jocelyn Brando; ***D:*** Jerry Thorpe; ***M:*** Billy Goldenberg. *NO*

Question of Silence 🦴🦴🦴 *De Stilte Rond Christine M* **1983 (R)** Three women, strangers to each other, stand trial for a murdering a man. Intricately analyzed courtroom drama with much to say about male domination. In Dutch with English subtitles or dubbed. **92m/C VHS, Beta.** *NL* Cox Habrema, Nelly Frijda, Henriette Tol, Edda Barends; ***D:*** Marleen Gorris. *SUE, INJ*

Question 7 *Frage 7* **1963** The fifteen-year-old son of a pastor who lives behind the iron curtain faces a dilemma: should he answer a political question the way his teacher wants or the way he believes? **107m/B VHS, Beta.** *NO*

Qui Etes Vous, Mr. Sorge? 🦴🦴 **1961** The story of German journalist Richard Sorge, who was hanged by the Japanese in 1944 for being a Soviet spy. Uninteresting docudrama which focuses on the opinions of various witnesses as to the accuracy of the espionage charge. In French with English subtitles. **130m/B VHS, Beta.** *FR* Thomas Holtzman, Keiko Kishi; ***D:*** Andre Girard. *BAR, INJ*

Quick 🦴🦴½ **1993 (R)** Polo stars as Quick, a professional assassin whose latest job is Herschel (Donovan), a mob accountant turned federal witness. When Quick is double-crossed, she takes off with Herschel as her insurance and a couple of bad guys (Fahey and Davi) on her trail. Not too much sex and lots of violence to go along with the fast pacing. **99m/C VHS.** Teri Polo, Martin Donovan, Jeff Fahey, Robert Davi, Tia Carrere; ***D:*** Rick King; ***W:*** Frederick Bailey; ***M:*** Robert Springberry. *ACA*

The Quick and the Dead 🦴🦴 **1987** Based on a Louis L'Amour story, this made-for-cable western features a lone gunslinger who protects a defenseless settler's family from the lawless West, only to become a source of sexual tension for the wife. **91m/C VHS, Beta.** Sam Elliott, Tom Conti, Kate Capshaw, Kenny Morrison, Matt Clark; ***D:*** Robert Day; ***M:*** Stephen Dorff. *ORI, WAR*

The Quick and the Dead 🦴🦴 **1994 (R)** Stone is a tough gal gunslinger (ala a female Clint Eastwood) out to avenge the murder of her father. Ellen arrives in the frontier town of Redemption where arch-villain Herod (Hackman) rules by means of violence and intimidation. Director Raimi packs in so many cliches that you're amazed that it's not a parody of the spaghetti westerns it tries to emulate. Maybe if Stone and Raimi didn't take this film so seriously, it would have been a better movie. One redeeming quality of the film is its wildly staged gunfights. **105m/C VHS, LV, 8mm.** Sharon Stone, Gene Hackman, Leonardo DiCaprio, Russell Crowe, Kevin Conway, Lance Henriksen, Roberts Blossom, Pat Hingle, Keith David, Michael Stone; ***Cameos:*** Gary Sinise; ***D:*** Sam Raimi; ***W:*** Simon Moore; ***C:*** Dante Spinotti. *COL*

Quick Change 🦴🦴½ **1990 (R)** Murray, Davis, and Quaid form bumbling trio of New York bank robbers who can't seem to exit the Big Apple with loot. Based on Jay Cronley's book, it's Murray's directing debut (with help from screenwriter Franklin). Engaging minor caper comedy displaying plenty of NYC dirty boulevards. **89m/C VHS, Beta, LV, 8mm.** Bill Murray, Geena Davis, Randy Quaid, Jason Robards Jr., Bob Elliott, Victor Argo, Kathryn Grody, Philip Bosco, Phil Hartman, Kurtwood Smith, Jamey Sheridan; ***D:*** Bill Murray, Howard Franklin; ***W:*** Howard Franklin; ***C:*** Michael Chapman; ***M:*** Randy Edelman, Howard Shore. *WAR*

Quick, Let's Get Married *Woof! Seven Different Ways; The Confession* **1971** Quick, let's not watch this movie. Even the people who made it must have hated it: they waited seven years to release it. Rogers runs a whorehouse; Eden is a gullible, pregnant prostitute; Gould in his big-screen debut(!) is a deaf-mute. A must-not see. **96m/C VHS, Beta, LV.** Ginger Rogers, Ray Milland, Barbara Eden, Carl Schell, Michael Ansara, Walter Abel, Scott Meyer, Cecil Kellaway, Elliott Gould; ***D:*** William Dieterle. *NO*

Quicker Than the Eye ☌☌ **1988** When a magician gets mixed up in an assassination plot, he must use his wit, cunning, and magic to get out of it. **94m/C VHS, Beta.** Ben Gazzara, Mary Crosby, Catherine Jarrett, Ivan Desny, Eb Lottimer, Sophie Carle, Wolfram Berger, Dinah Hinz, Jean Yanne; ***D:*** Nicolas Gessner. *ACA*

Quicksand ☌☌½ **1950** Mechanic Rooney borrows $20 from his boss's cash register, intending to return it. One thing leads to another, the plot thickens, and it's downhill (for Rooney) from there. Good, tense suspense drama. **79m/B VHS, Beta.** Mickey Rooney, Peter Lorre, Jeanne Cagney; ***D:*** Irving Pichel. *NOS, MRV, SNC*

Quicksand: No Escape ☌☌ **1991 (PG-13)** Scott Reinhardt (Matheson) is a successful architect whose partner decides to secure a building contract by bribing a city official. When his partner is murdered Reinhardt is approached by a former cop (Sutherland) asking a lot of money for some incriminating evidence. Reinhardt is then drawn ever deeper into the illicit dealings, endangering his life. **93m/C VHS, Beta, LV.** Tim Matheson, Donald Sutherland, Jay Acovone, Timothy Carhart, John Finn, Marc Alaimo, Felicity Huffman, Al Pugliese; ***D:*** Michael Pressman; ***W:*** Peter Baloff, Dave Wollert. *MCA*

Quicksilver ☌½ **1986 (PG)** A young stockbroker loses all, then quits his job to become a city bicycle messenger. Pointless, self-indulgent yuppie fantasy. **106m/C VHS, Beta, LV.** Kevin Bacon, Jami Gertz, Paul Rodriguez, Rudy Ramos, Andrew Smith, Gerald S. O'Loughlin, Laurence "Larry" Fishburne, Louie Anderson; ***D:*** Tom Donnelly; ***W:*** Tom Donnelly; ***M:*** Tony Banks. *COL*

Quiet Cool ☌ **1986 (R)** When his former girlfriend's family is killed, a New York cop travels to a sleepy California town run by a pot-growing tycoon. He subsequently kills the bad guys in a Rambo-like fit of vengeance. Dopey exercise in sleepy-eyed bloodshed. **80m/C VHS, Beta, LV.** James Remar, Daphne Ashbrook, Adam Coleman Howard, Jared Martin, Fran Ryan; ***D:*** Clay Borris; ***W:*** Clay Borris; ***M:*** Jay Michael Ferguson. *COL*

Quiet Day In Belfast ☌☌☌ **1974** Tragedy occurs when northern Irish patriots and British soldiers clash in an Irish betting parlor. Kidder plays a duel role: an Irish woman in love with a British soldier and the woman's twin sister. Convincingly adapted from a Canadian stage play. **92m/C VHS, Beta.** *CA* Barry Foster, Margot Kidder; ***D:*** Milad Bessada. *MED*

A Quiet Duel ☌☌ *A Silent Duel; Shizuka Naru Ketto* **1949** Kyoji (Mifune), a young, idealistic doctor working as an army surgeon, contracts syphillis from the blood of a patient during an operation. Because the disease was virtually incurable at the time, the tormented Kyoji abandons his fiance and decides to dedicate himself to his work. Based on a play by Kazuo Kikuta. Japanese with subtitles. **95m/B VHS.** *JP* Toshiro Mifune, Takashi Shimura, Kenjiro Uemura; ***D:*** Akira Kurosawa; ***W:*** Senkichi Taniguhi, Akira Kurosawa; ***M:*** Akira Ifukube. *FCT*

The Quiet Earth ☌☌☌ **1985 (R)** Serious science fiction film about a scientist who awakens to find himself seemingly the only human left on earth as the result of a misfired time/space government experiment. He later finds two other people, a girl and a Maori tribesman, and must try to repair the damage in order to save what's left of mankind. **91m/C VHS, Beta, LV.** *NZ* Bruno Lawrence, Alison Routledge, Peter Smith; ***D:*** Geoff Murphy; ***W:*** Bruno Lawrence, Sam Pillsbury, Bill Baer; ***M:*** John Charles. *FOX*

Quiet Fire ☌½ **1991 (R)** A health-club owner tries to get the goods on the arms-dealing congressman who killed his best friend. Hilton-Jacobs looks properly pumped up since his sweathog days on TV's "Welcome Back Kotter." **100m/C VHS.** Lawrence-Hilton Jacobs, Robert Z'Dar, Nadia Marie, Karen Black, Lance Lindsay; ***D:*** Lawrence-Hilton Jacobs. *PMH*

The Quiet Man ☌☌☌☌ **1952** The classic incarnation of Hollywood Irishness, and one of Ford's best, and funniest films. Wayne is Sean Thornton, a weary American ex-boxer who returns to the Irish hamlet of his childhood and tries to take a spirited lass as his wife, despite the strenuous objections of her brawling brother (McLaglen). Thornton's aided by the leprechaun-like Fitzgerald and the local parish priest, Bond. A high-spirited and memorable film filled with Irish stew, wonderful banter, and shots of the lush countryside. Listen for the Scottish bagpipes at the start of the horse race, a slight geographic inaccuracy. **129m/C VHS, LV.** John Wayne, Maureen O'Hara, Barry Fitzgerald, Victor McLaglen, Arthur Shields, Jack MacGowran, Ward Bond, Mildred Natwick, Ken Curtis, Mae Marsh, Sean McClory, Francis Ford; ***D:*** John Ford; ***W:*** Frank Nugent; ***C:*** Archie Stout; ***M:*** Victor Young. Academy Awards '52: Best Color Cinematography, Best Director (Ford); National Board of Review Awards '52: 10 Best Films of the Year; Venice Film Festival '52: Best Director (Ford); Nominations: Academy Awards '52: Best Art Direction/Set Decoration (Color), Best Picture, Best Screenplay, Best Sound, Best Supporting Actor (McLaglen). *REP, TLF, CCB*

Quiet Thunder ☌ **1987 (PG-13)** A hard-drinking bush pilot in Africa and a beautiful senator's wife are thrown together on the run after both witness an assassination. Mindless, thoroughly derivative "adventure." **94m/C VHS, Beta, LV.** Wayne Crawford, June Chadwick, Victor Steinbach; ***D:*** David Rice. *LIV*

Quigley Down Under ☌☌½ **1990 (PG-13)** A Western sharpshooter moves to Australia in search of employment. To his horror, he discovers that he has been hired to kill aborigines. Predictable action is somewhat redeemed by the terrific chemistry between Selleck and San Giacomo and the usual enjoyable theatrics from Rickman as the landowner heavy. **121m/C VHS, Beta, LV, 8mm.** *AU* Tom Selleck, Laura San Giacomo, Alan Rickman, Chris Haywood, Ron Haddrick, Tony Bonner, Roger Ward, Ben Mendelsohn, Jerome Ehlers, Conor McDermottroe; ***D:*** Simon Wincer; ***W:*** John Hill; ***M:*** Basil Poledouris. *MGM*

The Quiller Memorandum ☌☌☌ **1966** An American secret agent travels to Berlin to uncover a deadly neo-Nazi gang. Refreshingly different from other spy tales of its era. Good screenplay adapted from Adam Hall's novel, "The Berlin Memorandum." **103m/C VHS, Beta.** George Segal, Senta Berger, Alec Guinness, Max von Sydow, George Sanders; ***D:*** Michael Anderson Sr.; ***W:*** Harold Pinter; ***M:*** John Barry. *FOX*

Quilombo ☌☌½ **1984** The title refers to a legendary settlement of runaway slaves in 17th-century Brazil; an epic chronicles its fortunes as leadership passes from a wise ruler to a more militant one who goes to war against the government. Stunning scenery, tribal images, and folk songs, but the numerous characters seldom come to life as personalities. One of Brazil's most expensive films, in Portuguese with English subtitles. **114m/C VHS.** *BR* Vera Fischer, Antonio Pompeo, Zeze Motta, Toni Tornado; ***D:*** Carlos Diegues; ***W:*** Carlos Diegues. Nominations: Cannes Film Festival '84: Best Film. *NYF, FCT, INJ*

Quintet ☌☌ **1979** Atypical Altman sci-fi effort. The stakes in "Quintet," a form of backgammon, are high—you bet your life. Set during the planet's final ice age. Newman and wife Fossey wander into a dying city and are invited to play the game, with Fossey losing quickly. Bizarre and pretentious, with heavy symbolic going. **118m/C VHS, Beta.** Paul Newman, Bibi Andersson, Fernando Rey, Vittorio Gassman, David Langton, Nina Van Pallandt, Brigitte Fossey; ***D:*** Robert Altman; ***W:*** Lionel Chetwynd, Patricia Resnick, Robert Altman, Frank Barhydt. *FOX*

Quiz Show ☌☌☌☌ **1994 (PG-13)** Redford's intelligent, entertaining, and morally complex film about the TV game show scandals of the late '50s is his most accomplished work to date. At the center of the film is Charles Van Doren (Fiennes), an intellectual, golden boy who dethrones Herbert Stempel (Turturro), the reigning champion of the rigged "Twenty-One." The program's sponsor felt Stempel, a nerdy Jewish grad's everyman qualities were wearing thin and wanted a more polished image, which they found in handsome, sophisticated Van Doren. Federal investigator Goodwin (Morrow) suspects Van Doren's reign is a sham and sets out to expose him as a fraud. Acting is of the highest caliber with Fiennes, Turturro, and Morrow all giving beautiful performances. Notable among supporting cast is Scofield as Van Doren's Pulitzer prize-winning father. With strong script and gorgeous lensing, this modern Faust story is a brilliant reflection on corporate greed, class rivalry, and the powers of television. Based on the book "Remembering America: A Voice From the Sixties" by Richard N. Goodwin. **133m/C VHS, LV.** John Turturro, Rob Morrow, Ralph Fiennes, Paul Scofield, David Paymer, Hank Azaria, Christopher McDonald, Johann Carlo, Elizabeth Wilson, Mira Sorvino, Griffin Dunne, Martin Scorsese, Barry Levinson; ***D:*** Robert Redford; ***W:*** Paul Attanasio; ***M:*** Mark Isham. British Academy Awards '94: Best Adapted Screenplay; New York Film Critics Awards '94: Best Film; Nominations: Academy Awards '94: Best Adapted Screenplay, Best Director (Redford), Best Picture, Best Supporting Actor (Scofield); Golden Globe Awards '95: Best Director (Redford), Best Film—Drama, Best Screenplay, Best Supporting Actor (Turturro). *HPH*

Quo Vadis ☌☌½ **1912** One of the first truly huge Italian silent epics. The initial adaptation of the Henryk Sienkiewicz novel about Nero and ancient Rome. Probably the cinema's first great financial success. **45m/B VHS, Beta.** ***D:*** Enrico Guazzoni. *FCT*

Quo Vadis ☌☌☌ **1951** Larger-than-life production about Nero and the Christian persecution. Done on a giant scale: features exciting fighting scenes, romance, and fabulous costumes. Definitive version of the classic novel by Henryk Siekiewicz. Remade for Italian television in 1985. **171m/C VHS, Beta.** Robert Taylor, Deborah Kerr, Peter Ustinov, Patricia Laffan, Finlay Currie, Abraham Sofaer, Marina Berti, Buddy Baer, Felix Aylmer, Nora Swinburne; ***Cameos:*** Sophia Loren, Elizabeth Taylor; ***D:*** Mervyn LeRoy; ***C:*** Robert L. Surtees; ***M:*** Miklos Rozsa. Golden Globe Awards '52: Best Supporting Actor (Ustinov); Nominations: Academy Awards '51: Best Art Direction/Set Decoration (Color), Best Color Cinematography, Best Costume Design (Color), Best Film Editing, Best Picture, Best Supporting Actor (Genn, Ustinov), Best Original Score. *MGM, APD, IGP*

Quo Vadis ☌☌½ **1985 (R)** Third screen version of Henryk Sienkiewicz's book. See the other two first. This one is slow and perfunctory. Brandauer is memorable as Nero; Quinn (in the lead) is the son of Anthony. **122m/C VHS, Beta, LV.** *IT* Klaus Maria Brandauer, Frederic Forrest, Christina Raines, Maria Therese Relin, Francesco Quinn, Barbara DeRossi, Phillippe LeRoy, Max von Sydow, Gabriele Ferzetti, Massimo Girotti, Leopoldo Trieste; ***D:*** Franco Rossi. *PSM, APD*

Rabbit Test ☌½ **1978 (PG)** In Rivers' first directorial effort, a clumsy virginal guy becomes the world's first pregnant man. So irreverent it's almost never in good taste, and so poorly written it's almost never funny. **86m/C VHS, Beta, LV.** Billy Crystal, Roddy McDowall, Imogene Coca, Paul Lynde, Alex Rocco, George Gobel; ***D:*** Joan Rivers. *COL, SUE*

Rabid ☌☌½ *Rage* **1977 (R)** A young girl undergoes a radical plastic surgery technique and develops a strange and unexplained lesion in her armpit. She also finds she has an unusual craving for human blood. **90m/C VHS, Beta.** *CA* Marilyn Chambers, Frank Moore, Joe Silver; ***D:*** David Cronenberg; ***W:*** David Cronenberg. *WAR*

Rabid Grannies *Woof!* **1989 (R)** Wicked satire about two aging sisters who receive a surprise birthday gift from their devilworshipping nephew. The gift turns their party into a gorefest as they rip into various family members—literally. Any humor will be lost on any but the most diehard Troma fans. Dubbed. **89m/C VHS, Beta, LV.** *BE* Catherine Aymerie, Caroline Brackman, Danielle Daven, Raymond Lescot, Anne Marie Fox, Richard Cotica, Patricia Davie; ***D:*** Emmanuel Kervyn; ***W:*** Emmanuel Kervyn. *MED, VTR*

Race for Glory 🦴½ **1989 (R)** A young motorcyclist builds a super-bike he hopes will help him win a world championship race. Will he win? Can you stand the suspense? Let's just say there's a happy ending. **102m/C VHS, Beta.** Alex McArthur, Peter Berg, Pamela Ludwig; ***D:*** Rocky Lang; ***M:*** Jay Michael Ferguson. *HBO*

Race for Life 🦴½ *Mask of Dust* **1955** A race car driver attempts to make a comeback despite objections from his wife. He races around Europe (great scenery); she leaves him; he tries to win her back and salvage his career. Standard, un-gripping story. Car scenes are great. **69m/B VHS, Beta, LV.** *GB* Richard Conte, Mari Aldon, George Coulouris; ***D:*** Terence Fisher. *NO*

Race for Your Life, Charlie Brown 🦴🦴½ **1977 (G)** Another in the popular series of "Peanuts" character films. This one features Charlie Brown, Snoopy, and all the gang spending an exciting summer in the American wilderness. **76m/C VHS, Beta, LV.** ***D:*** Bill Melendez, Phil Roman; ***W:*** Charles M. Schulz; ***M:*** Ed Bogas; ***V:*** Gail Davis, Melanie Kohn, Duncan Watson, Gregory Felton, Stuart Brotman, Liam Martin, Ed Bogas. *PAR, WTA*

Race the Sun 🦴🦴 **1996 (PG)** There's nothin' new under this sun. Tired story of a group of young losers who band together to beat the odds and compete in an unusual contest is trotted out once again for populist amusement. This time it's a Hawaiian high school solar car team traveling to Australia to go for the prize against the big shots and snobs. Based on true events, it features some nice scenery from Berry and the main locations, but not much else. Uninspired but basically harmless, this one's fine for the kids. **105m/C VHS.** Halle Berry, James Belushi, Casey Affleck, Eliza Dushku, Kevin Tighe, Anthony Michael Ruivivar, J. Moki Cho, Dion Basco, Sara Tanaka, Nadja Pionilla, Steve Zahn, Bill Hunter; ***D:*** Charles Kanganis; ***W:*** Barry Morrow; ***C:*** David Burr; ***M:*** Graeme Revell. *NYR*

Race to Freedom: The Story of the Underground Railroad 🦴🦴½ **1994** Story of four fugitive slaves, in 1850, who struggle to get from North Carolina to the safety of Canada through a network of safe-houses and people willing to risk smuggling them to asylum. Made for cable TV. **90m/C VHS.** Courtney B. Vance, Janet Bailey, Glynn Turman, Michael Riley, Dawnn Lewis, Ron White; ***Cameos:*** Tim Reid; ***D:*** Don McBrearty; ***W:*** Nancy Trite Botkin, Diana Braithwaite. *XVC*

Race with the Devil 🦴½ **1975 (PG)** Vacationers are terrorized by devil worshippers after they witness a sacrificial killing. Heavy on car chases; light on plot and redeeming qualities. Don't waste your time. **88m/C VHS, Beta.** Peter Fonda, Warren Oates, Loretta Swit, Lara Parker; ***D:*** Jack Starrett. *FOX, FCT*

The Racers 🦴🦴½ *Such Men are Dangerous* **1955** Douglas brings power to the role of a man determined to advance to the winners' circle. Exciting European location photography, but not much plot. **112m/C VHS.** Gilbert Roland, Kirk Douglas, Lee J. Cobb, Cesar Romero, Bella Darvi; ***D:*** Henry Hathaway; ***M:*** Alex North. *FOX, FCT*

Rachel and the Stranger 🦴🦴🦴 **1948** A God-fearing farmer declares his love for his wife when a handsome stranger (Mitchum) nearly woos her away. Well-cast, well-paced, charming Western comedy-drama. **93m/B VHS, Beta, LV.** Loretta Young, Robert Mitchum, William Holden, Gary Gray; ***D:*** Norman Foster. *MED, TTC*

The Rachel Papers 🦴🦴🦴 **1989 (R)** Based on the Martin Amis novel, this is the funny/sad tale of an Oxford youth who plots via his computer the seduction of a beautiful American girl. For anyone who has ever loved someone just out of their reach. **92m/C VHS, Beta.** Dexter Fletcher, Ione Skye, James Spader, Jonathan Pryce, Bill Paterson, Michael Gambon, Lesley Sharp; ***D:*** Damian Harris; ***W:*** Damian Harris; ***M:*** Chaz Jankel. *FOX*

Rachel, Rachel 🦴🦴🦴½ **1968 (R)** Rachel teaches by day, wearing simple, practical dresses and her hair up. By night she caters to her domineering mother by preparing refreshments for her parties. This sexually repressed, spinster schoolteacher, however, gets one last chance at romance in her small Connecticut town. Woodward mixes just the right amounts of loneliness and sweetness in the leading role. A surprising award-winner that was an independent production of Newman. Based on Margaret Laurence's "A Jest of God." **102m/C VHS, Beta.** Joanne Woodward, James Olson, Estelle Parsons, Geraldine Fitzgerald, Donald Moffat; ***D:*** Paul Newman; ***W:*** Stewart Stern. Golden Globe Awards '69: Best Actress—Drama (Woodward), Best Director (Newman); New York Film Critics Awards '68: Best Actress (Woodward), Best Director (Newman); Nominations: Academy Awards '68: Best Actress (Woodward), Best Adapted Screenplay, Best Picture, Best Supporting Actress (Parsons). *WAR*

Rachel River 🦴🦴½ **1987 (PG-13)** A divorced radio personality struggles to make something of her life in her small Minnesota town. **88m/C VHS, LV.** Pamela Reed, Craig T. Nelson, Viveca Lindfors, James Olson, Zeljko Ivanek, Jo Henderson, Alan North, Jon DeVries; ***D:*** Sandy Smolan; ***W:*** Judith Guest; ***M:*** Arvo Part. *ACA*

Rachel's Man 🦴 **1975** A big-screen version of the Biblical love story of Jacob and Rachel. **115m/C VHS, Beta.** Mickey Rooney, Rita Tushingham, Leonard Whiting; ***D:*** Moshe Mizrahi. *LIV*

Racing Luck 🦴🦴 *Red Hot Tires* **1935** While working at a race track, a man is framed and forced to work for another stable. **56m/B VHS, Beta.** William Boyd, Barbara Worth, George Ernest, Esther Muir, Dick Curtis; ***D:*** Sam Newfield. *GPV*

Racing with the Moon 🦴🦴🦴 **1984 (PG)** Sweet, nostalgic film about two buddies awaiting induction into the Marines in 1942. They have their last chance at summer romance. Benjamin makes the most of skillful young actors and conventional story. Great period detail. Keep your eyes peeled for glimpses of many rising young stars including Hannah and Carvey. **108m/C VHS, Beta, LV.** Sean Penn, Elizabeth McGovern, Nicolas Cage, John Karlen, Rutanya Alda, Max Casey Adams Showalter, Crispin Glover, Suzanne Adkinson, Page Hannah, Michael Madsen, Dana Carvey, Carol Kane, Michael Talbott; ***D:*** Richard Benjamin; ***W:*** Steven Kloves; ***C:*** John Bailey; ***M:*** Dave Grusin. *PAR*

The Racket 🦴🦴🦴 **1951** Police captain Mitchum tries to break up mob racket of gangster Ryan. Internecine strife on both sides adds complexity. Mitchum and especially Ryan are super; fine, tense melodrama. **88m/B VHS, Beta, LV.** Robert Ryan, Robert Mitchum, Lizabeth Scott, Ray Collins, William Conrad, Don Porter; ***D:*** John Cromwell. *MED, TTC*

The Racketeer 🦴🦴½ **1929** A racketeer falls in love with a pretty girl and attempts to win her over. As part of his plan, the gangster arranges to help the girl's boyfriend begin his musical career in exchange for the girl's promise to marry him. **68m/B VHS, Beta.** Carole Lombard, Robert Armstrong, Hedda Hopper; ***D:*** Howard Higgin. *SNC, NOS, CAB*

Racketeers of the Range 🦴½ **1939** Cattleman fights a crooked attorney who wants to sell his client's stock to a large meat packing company. **62m/B VHS, Beta.** George O'Brien, Marjorie Reynolds, Chill Wills, Ray Whitley; ***D:*** David Ross Lederman. *MED*

Racquet 🦴 **1979** Tennis pro Convy searches for true love and a tennis court of to call his own in Beverly Hills. Lame, sophomoric, and unfunny. **87m/C VHS, Beta.** Bert Convy, Edie Adams, Lynda Day George, Phil Silvers, Bobby Riggs, Bjorn Borg, Tanya Roberts; ***D:*** David Winters. *NO*

Rad 🦴½ **1986 (PG)** Teenage drama revolving around BMX racing and such dilemmas as: can the good guys beat the bad guys, who's got the fastest bike, must you cheat to win, and should our hero miss his SAT tests to compete in "the big race.." Directed by stunt-expert Needham. **94m/C VHS, Beta, LV.** Bill Allen, Bart Conner, Talia Shire, Jack Weston, Lori Loughlin; ***D:*** Hal Needham; ***W:*** Sam Bernard. *SUE, NLC*

Radar Men from the Moon *Retik, the Moon Menace* **1952** Commando Cody, with his jet-pack, fights to defend the earth from invaders from the moon. Twelve-episode serial on two tapes. Silly sci-fi. **152m/B VHS, LV.** George Wallace, Aline Towne, Roy Barcroft, William "Billy" Bakewell, Clayton Moore; ***D:*** Fred Brannon. *NOS, REP, SNC*

Radar Secret Service 🦴½ **1950** Two servicemen witness the hijacking of a truck loaded with nuclear material. **59m/B VHS, Beta, LV.** John Howard, Adele Jergens, Tom Neal, Ralph Byrd. *NO*

Radio Days 🦴🦴🦴 **1987 (PG)** A lovely, unpretentious remembrance of the pre-television radio culture. Allen tells his story in a series of vignettes centering around his youth in Brooklyn, his eccentric extended family, and the legends of radio they all followed. The ubiquitous Farrow is a young singer hoping to make it big. **96m/C VHS, Beta, LV.** Mia Farrow, Dianne Wiest, Julie Kavner, Michael Tucker, Wallace Shawn, Josh Mostel, Tony Roberts, Jeff Daniels, Kenneth Mars, Seth Green, William Magerman, Diane Keaton, Renee Lippin, Danny Aiello, Gina DeAngelis, Kitty Carlisle Hart, Mercedes Ruehl, Tito Puente; ***D:*** Woody Allen; ***W:*** Woody Allen. Nominations: Academy Awards '87: Best Art Direction/Set Decoration, Best Original Screenplay. *HBO*

Radio Flyer 🦴🦴 **1992 (PG-13)** It's 1969 and Mike and Bobby have just moved to northern California with their divorced mom. Everything would be idyllic if only their mother hadn't decided to marry a drunken child abuser who beats Bobby whenever the mood strikes him. Mike decides to help Bobby escape by turning their Radio Flyer wagon into a magic rocketship that will carry Bobby to safety, but ultimately proves tragic. Appealing version of childhood dreams sans the child abuse angle (toned down though it was), which is abruptly and unsatisfactorily handled. **114m/C VHS, LV.** Elijah Wood, Joseph Mazzello, Lorraine Bracco, Adam Baldwin, John Heard, Ben Johnson; ***D:*** Richard Donner. *COL*

Radio Inside 🦴🦴½ **1994** Aimless younger brother Matthew (McNamara) comes to live with older brother Michael (Walsh) after their dad's death. Matthew needs someone to listen to him but, unfortunately, his picks his brother's neglected girlfriend Natalie (Shue). Aimless story, as well. Made for cable TV. **91m/C VHS, LV.** William McNamara, Dylan Walsh, Elisabeth Shue, Gil Goldstein; ***D:*** Jeffrey Bell; ***W:*** Jeffrey Bell. *MGM*

Radio Patrol **1937** Plenty of action and thrills abound in this 12-chapter serial. Pinky Adams, radio cop, is assisted by his trusty canine partner, Irish (Silverwolf). A cop's best friend is his dog. **235m/B VHS, Beta.** Mickey Rentschler, Adrian Morris, Monte Montague, Jack Mulhall, Grant Withers, Catherine Hughes; ***D:*** Ford Beebe, Cliff Smith. *NOS, VDM, MLB*

Radioactive Dreams 🦴🦴 **1986 (R)** Surreal, practically senseless fantasy wherein two men, trapped in a bomb shelter for 15 years with nothing to read but mystery novels, emerge as detectives into a post-holocaust world looking for adventure. **94m/C VHS, Beta, LV.** John Stockwell, Michael Dudikoff, Lisa Blount, George Kennedy, Don Murray, Michelle Little; ***D:*** Albert Pyun; ***W:*** Albert Pyun. *LIV, VES*

Radioland Murders 🦴½ **1994 (PG)** Looks overwhelm weak plot in this mystery-comedy about 1939 Chicago radio station WBN. Lots of stock types (befuddled director, preening announcer, lusty vamp) with Masterson as Penny, the secretary holding everything together except for her marriage to head writer Roger (Benben). Then bodies start piling up during the live broadcast and everyone runs around frantically trying to solve the crimes and keep the broadcast going. Tiring and cliched. **112m/C VHS, LV.** Brian Benben, Mary Stuart Masterson, Ned Beatty, George Burns, Brion James, Michael Lerner, Michael McKean, Jeffrey Tambor, Scott Michael Campbell, Anita Morris, Stephen Tobolowsky, Christopher Lloyd, Larry Miller, Corbin Bernsen; ***Cameos:*** Robert Klein, Harvey Korman, Peter MacNicol, Joey Lawrence, Bob(cat) Goldthwait; ***D:*** Mel Smith; ***W:*** Willard

Huyck, Gloria Katz, Jeff Reno, Ron Osborn; **C:** David Tattersall; **M:** Joel McNeely. *MCA*

Rafferty & the Gold Dust Twins 🦴½ *Rafferty and the Highway Hustlers* **1975 (R)** Two women kidnap a motor vehicle inspector at gunpoint in Los Angeles and order him to drive to New Orleans. En route, they become pals. Wandering, pointless female buddy flick. **91m/C VHS, Beta.** Alan Arkin, Sally Kellerman, MacKenzie Phillips, Charles Martin Smith, Harry Dean Stanton; **D:** Dick Richards; **M:** Artie Butler. *WAR*

The Raffle 🦴🦴½ **1994 (R)** Frank and David travel the globe to find the world's most beautiful woman, who'll be the prize date of the lucky guy with the winning raffle ticket. **100m/C VHS, LV.** Nicholas Lea, Bobby Dawson, Jennifer Clement, Teri-Lynn Rutherford, Jay Underwood, Mark Hamill; **D:** Gavin Wilding; **W:** John Fairley; **M:** Robert O. Ragland. *APX*

Rage 🦴🦴 **1972 (PG)** Scott's directorial debut. A military helicopter sprays peace-loving rancher Scott and his son with nerve gas. The son's death is covered up; the rancher embarks on a vengeful rampage. Scott's sudden transformation to avenging killer is implausible and overwrought. **100m/C VHS, Beta.** George C. Scott, Richard Basehart, Martin Sheen, Barnard Hughes, Kenneth Tobey, Ed Lauter, Nicholas Beauvy, Dabbs Greer; **D:** George C. Scott; **C:** Fred W. Koenekamp. *WAR*

Rage 🦴🦴🦴 **1980** Well-acted, well-written, nerve-wracking drama about a convicted rapist who finds help through difficult therapy. Focuses on how the sex-offender discovers the "whys" behind his assaults. Made for television. **100m/C VHS, Beta.** David Soul, James Whitmore, Yaphet Kotto, Caroline McWilliams, Vic Tayback, Sharon Farrell, Craig T. Nelson, Garry Walberg; **D:** William A. Graham. *WAR*

Rage 🦴½ **1995 (R)** When Alex Gainer is kidnapped he becomes the target of a high-tech lab experiment. Injected with chemicals that induce blind and killing rages, Alex escapes and unwillingly goes on a murderous rampage. Now he must find the antidote and clear his name before it happens again. **94m/C VHS.** Gary Daniels, Ken Tigar, Jillian McWhirter, Fiona Hutchinson. *PMH*

Rage and Honor 🦴🦴 **1992 (R)** Rothrock stars as Kris Fairfield, a high-school teacher who spends her spare time tutoring students in the martial-arts. Her present students are a group of cops, including Aussie visitor Preston Michaels. When Michaels witnesses a drug deal, he gets set-up by the dealers for a murder he didn't commit and only Kris can help him prove his innocence. **93m/C VHS, LV.** Cynthia Rothrock, Richard Norton, Brian Thompson, Terri Treas, Catherine Bach, Alex Datcher; **D:** Terence H. Winkless; **W:** Terence H. Winkless. *COL, PMS*

Rage and Honor 2: Hostile Takeover 🦴🦴½ **1993 (R)** Rothrock returns as black-belt CIA operative Kris Fairfield, whose latest assignment takes her to Jakarta where a banker is involved in a large-scale drug money laundering operation. She teams up with Preston Michaels (Norton), a renegade Australian cop, and winds up following a trail that leads to a fortune in diamonds and lots of trouble. **98m/C VHS.** Cynthia Rothrock, Richard Norton, Patrick Muldoon, Frans Tumbuan, Ron Vreeken, Alex Tumundo; **D:** Guy Norris; **W:** Louis Sun, Steven Reich. *COL*

Rage at Dawn 🦴🦴½ *Seven Bad Men* **1955** An outlaw gang is tracked by a special agent who must "bend" the rules a little in order to get the bad guys. Not surprisingly, he gets his girl as well. A solid standard of the genre, with some clever plot twists. **87m/C VHS.** Randolph Scott, Forrest Tucker, Mala Powers, J. Carrol Naish, Edgar Buchanan; **D:** Tim Whelan. *NOS, GHV, MRV*

A Rage in Harlem 🦴🦴🦴 **1991 (R)** The crime novels of Chester A. Himes were translated into the best movies of the early '70s blaxploitation era. Now, a Himes story gets the big budget Hollywood treatment with juice and aplomb. A voluptuous lady crook enters Harlem circa 1950 with a trunkful of stolen gold sought by competing crooks, and the chase is on, with one virtuous soul (Whitaker) who only wants the girl. Great cast and characters, much humor, but unsparing in its violence. **108m/C VHS, LV.** Forest Whitaker, Gregory Hines, Robin Givens, Zakes Mokae, Danny Glover, Tyler Collins, Ron Taylor, T.K. Carter, Willard Pugh, Samm-Art Williams, Jay Hawkins, Badja Djola, John Toles-Bey, Stack Pierce, George Wallace; **D:** Bill Duke; **W:** John Toles-Bey, Bobby Crawford; **M:** Elmer Bernstein. *HBO, FCT*

Rage of Angels 🦴🦴 **1983** Lengthy television miniseries adaptation of the Sidney Sheldon novel about an ambitious female attorney, her furs, and her men. Followed by "Rage of Angels: The Story Continues" (1986). **192m/C VHS, Beta.** Jaclyn Smith, Ken Howard, Armand Assante, Ronald Hunter, Kevin Conway, George Coe, Deborah May; **D:** Buzz Kulik; **M:** Billy Goldenberg. *COL*

Rage of Angels: The Story Continues 🦴🦴½ **1986** In this sequel to the Sidney Sheldon trash-with-flash television miniseries, Smith reprises her role as the beautiful lady lawyer who always gets involved with the wrong men. This time she tries to hide the fact of her illegitimate son from his father, who's about to become Vice President of the United States. **200m/C VHS.** Jaclyn Smith, Ken Howard, Michael Nouri, Susan Sullivan, Brad Dourif, Angela Lansbury, Mason Adams; **D:** Paul Wendkos; **C:** Jack Priestley; **M:** Billy Goldenberg. *VTR*

Rage of Honor 🦴 **1987 (R)** A high-kicking undercover cop seeks vengeance on bad guys for his partner's murder. Standard of its type; why bother? **92m/C VHS, Beta.** Sho Kosugi, Lewis Van Bergen, Robin Evans, Gerry Gibson; **D:** Gordon Hessler; **W:** Wallace C. Bennett. *MED, VTR*

The Rage of Paris 🦴🦴🦴 **1938** Scheming ex-actress and head waiter hope to gain by helping a beautiful French girl (Darrieux) snag a rich hubby. She comes to her senses, realizing that love, true love, matters more than wealth. Well-acted, quaint comedy. **78m/B VHS, Beta.** Danielle Darrieux, Douglas Fairbanks Jr., Mischa Auer, Helen Broderick; **D:** Henry Koster; **C:** Joseph Valentine. *NOS, DVT, CAB*

Rage of Wind 🦴 **1982** Master boxer seeks revenge on a Japanese commandant who kidnaps his wife during WWII. **97m/C VHS, Beta.** Chen Hsing, Yasuka Kurata, Irene Ryder. *WVE*

Rage to Kill 🦴½ **1988 (R)** Jingoistic retelling of the 1982 Grenada invasion, complete with helpless American med students. Good-guy race car driver whips them into shape to fight the Soviet-supplied general (he's the bad guy). Guess who wins. **94m/C VHS, Beta.** Oliver Reed, James Ryan, Henry Cele, Cameron Mitchell; **D:** David Winters. *AIP*

Raggedy Ann and Andy: A Musical Adventure **1977 (G)** Here are the fun-filled exploits of America's favorite fictional dolls, transformed into an enchanting animated musical. Includes 16 songs by Joe Raposo. **87m/C VHS, Beta.** **D:** Richard Williams; **V:** Didi Conn, Joe Silver. *FOX*

Raggedy Man 🦴🦴🦴 **1981 (PG)** Spacek in her signature role as a lonely small-town woman. Here she's raising two sons alone in a small Texas town during WWII. Spacek's strong acting carries a well-scripted story, unfortunately marred by an overwrought ending. **94m/C VHS, Beta, LV.** Sissy Spacek, Eric Roberts, Sam Shepard, Tracey Walter, William Sanderson, Henry Thomas; **D:** Jack Fisk; **W:** William D. Wittliff; **C:** Ralf Bode; **M:** Jerry Goldsmith. *MCA*

The Raggedy Rawney 🦴🦴½ **1990 (R)** A young Army deserter dresses in women's clothing and hides out as a mad woman with a band of gypsies. Good first directing effort by English actor Bob Hoskins. Unpretentious and engaging. **102m/C VHS.** Bob Hoskins, Dexter Fletcher, Zoe Nathenson, David Hill, Ian Dury, Zoe Wanamaker, J.G. Devlin, Perry Fenwick; **D:** Bob Hoskins; **W:** Bob Hoskins, Nicole De Wilde; **M:** Michael Kamen. *CAN*

Ragin' Cajun 🦴 **1990** Retired kickboxer is forced into a death match to save his girlfriend. **91m/C VHS.** David Heavener, Charlene Tilton, Sam Bottoms, Samantha Eggar; **D:** William B. Hillman. *AIP, HHE*

Raging Angels 🦴 **1995 (R)** L.A. couple Chris (Flanery) and Lila (Mazur) are struggling rock 'n' rollers when Lila gets a job as a backup singer to star Colin (Pare), who's part of a cult called the Coalition for World Unity. Turns out they're a recruiting org for Satan and are looking for new souls. Our young duo are aided by flamboyant evangelist Sister Kate (Ladd) but it all comes down to a sky battle over downtown L.A. between a good angel and a satanic creature. Lots of unintentional laughs. The director wisely opted for the industry's Smithee pseudonym. **97m/C VHS.** Sean Patrick Flanery, Monet Mazur, Michael Pare, Diane Ladd, Shelley Winters, Arielle Dombasle; **D:** Alan Smithee; **W:** Kevin Rock, David Markov, Chris Bittler; **C:** Bryan England; **M:** Terry Plumeri. *VMK*

Raging Bull 🦴🦴🦴🦴 **1980 (R)** Scorsese's depressing but magnificent vision of the dying American Dream and suicidal macho codes in the form of the rise and fall of middleweight boxing champ Jake LaMotta, a brutish, dull-witted animal who can express himself only in the ring and through violence. A photographically expressive, brilliant drama, with easily the most intense and brutal boxing scenes ever filmed. De Niro provides a vintage performance, going from the young LaMotta to the aging has-been, and is ably accompanied by Moriarty as his girl and Pesci as his loyal, much beat-upon bro. **128m/B VHS, Beta, LV, 8mm.** Robert De Niro, Cathy Moriarty, Joe Pesci, Frank Vincent, Nicholas Colasanto, Theresa Saldana; **D:** Martin Scorsese; **W:** Paul Schrader, Mardik Martin; **C:** Michael Chapman. Academy Awards '80: Best Actor (De Niro), Best Film Editing; Golden Globe Awards '81: Best Actor—Drama (De Niro); Los Angeles Film Critics Association Awards '80: Best Actor (De Niro), Best Film; National Board of Review Awards '80: Best Actor (De Niro), Best Supporting Actor (Pesci); National Society of Film Critics Awards '80: Best Cinematography, Best Director (Scorsese), Best Supporting Actor (Pesci); Nominations: Academy Awards '80: Best Cinematography, Best Director (Scorsese), Best Picture, Best Sound, Best Supporting Actor (Pesci), Best Supporting Actress (Moriarty). *MGM, FOX, BTV*

Rags to Riches 🦴 **1987** A wealthy Beverly Hills entrepreneur decides to improve his public image by adopting six orphan girls. TV pilot. **96m/C VHS, Beta.** Joseph Bologna, Tisha Campbell. *VTR, NWV*

Ragtime 🦴🦴🦴 **1981 (PG)** The lives and passions of a middle class family weave into the scandals and events of 1906 America. A small, unthinking act represents all the racist attacks on one man, who refuses to back down this time. Wonderful period detail. From the E.L. Doctorow novel, but not nearly as complex. Features Cagney's last film performance. **156m/C VHS, Beta, LV.** Howard E. Rollins Jr., Kenneth McMillan, Brad Dourif, Mary Steenburgen, James Olson, Elizabeth McGovern, Pat O'Brien, James Cagney, Debbie Allen, Jeff Daniels, Moses Gunn, Donald O'Connor, Mandy Patinkin, Norman Mailer; **D:** Milos Forman; **W:** Michael Weller; **M:** Randy Newman. Nominations: Academy Awards '81: Best Adapted Screenplay, Best Art Direction/Set Decoration, Best Cinematography, Best Costume Design, Best Song ("One More Hour"), Best Supporting Actor (Rollins), Best Supporting Actress (McGovern), Best Original Score. *PAR, FCT*

Raid on Entebbe 🦴🦴🦴 **1977 (R)** Dramatization of the Israeli rescue of passengers held hostage by terrorists at Uganda's Entebbe Airport in 1976. A gripping actioner all the more compelling because true. Finch received an Emmy nomination in this, his last film. Made for television. **113m/C VHS, Beta.** Charles Bronson, Peter Finch, Horst Buchholz, John Saxon, Martin Balsam, Jack Warden, Yaphet Kotto, Sylvia Sidney; **D:** Irvin Kershner; **M:** David Shire. *NO*

Raid on Rommel 🦴½ **1971 (PG)** A British soldier (Burton) poses as a Nazi and tries to infiltrate Rommel's team with his rag-tag brigade of misfits. Predictable drivel. Contains action footage from the 1967 film "Tobruk." **98m/C VHS, Beta.** Richard Burton, John Colicos, Clinton Greyn, Wolfgang Preiss; **D:** Henry Hathaway. *MCA*

Raiders in Action 🦴 **1971** Tale following the activities of a band of allied commandos in the closing days of the war. **89m/C VHS, Beta.** Paul Smith. *TWE*

Raiders of Atlantis ☆ *The Atlantis Interceptors* **1983** Battles break out when the lost continent surfaces in the Caribbean. The warriors in these apocalyptic frays deploy atomic arsenals. **100m/C VHS, Beta.** Christopher Connelly; ***D:*** Roger Franklin. *PSM*

Raiders of Ghost City ☆½ **1944** Serial in 13 chapters involves a Union Secret Service Agent after a ring of gold robbers who are posing as Confederate soldiers during the end of the Civil War. **?m/C VHS.** Dennis Moore, Lionel Atwill, Regis Toomey, Wanda McKay. *MOV*

Raiders of Red Gap ☆½ **1943** A cattle company tries running homesteaders off their land to get control of it. The Lone Rider saves the day. **56m/B VHS, Beta.** Al "Fuzzy" St. John, Bob Livingston. *DVT, VYY, VCN*

Raiders of Sunset Pass ☆☆ **1943** Wartime western quickie makes an interesting novelty today. With most cowboys off fighting the Axis, the ladies form the Women's Army of the Plains to watch out for 4-F rustlers. **57m/B VHS.** Eddie Dew, Smiley Burnette, Jennifer Holt, Roy Barcroft, Mozelle Cravens, Beverly Aadland, Nancy Worth, Kenne Duncan, Jack Rockwell, Budd Buster, Jack Ingram; ***D:*** John English. *NOS, HEG*

Raiders of the Border ☆ **1944** A white-hatted cowboy must prevent the takeover of a trading post. **55m/B VHS, Beta.** Johnny Mack Brown, Raymond Hatton, Ellen Hall. *VDM*

Raiders of the Lost Ark ☆☆☆☆ **1981 (PG)** Classic '30s-style adventure reminiscent of early serials spawned two sequels and numerous rip-offs. Made Ford a household name as dashing hero and intrepid archeologist Indiana Jones. He battles mean Nazis, decodes hieroglyphics, fights his fear of snakes, and even has time for a little romance in his quest for the biblical Ark of the Covenant. Allen is perfectly cast as his feisty ex-flame, more than a little irritated with the smooth talker who dumped her years earlier. Asks viewers to suspend belief as every chase and stunt tops the last. Unrelated opening sequence does a great job of introducing the character. Followed by "Indiana Jones and the Temple of Doom." **115m/C VHS, Beta, LV, 8mm.** Harrison Ford, Karen Allen, Wolf Kahler, Paul Freeman, John Rhys-Davies, Denholm Elliott, Ronald Lacey, Anthony Higgins, Alfred Molina; ***D:*** Steven Spielberg; ***W:*** George Lucas, Philip Kaufman; ***M:*** John Williams. Academy Awards '81: Best Art Direction/Set Decoration, Best Film Editing, Best Sound, Best Visual Effects; People's Choice Awards '82: Best Film; Nominations: Academy Awards '81: Best Cinematography, Best Director (Spielberg), Best Picture, Best Original Score. *PAR*

Raiders of the Sun ☆ **1992 (R)** After the Earth has been ruined in a biological disaster, a futuristic warrior arrives to help restore world peace and order. Cheap "Mad Max" ripoff. **80m/C VHS.** Richard Norton, Rick Dean, William Steis, Blake Boyd, Brigitta Stenberg; ***D:*** Cirio H. Santiago. *NHO*

Railroaded ☆☆ **1947** The police seek a demented criminal who kills his victims with perfumed-soaked bullets. Tense, excellent noir Anothony Mann crime drama. **72m/B VHS, Beta, LV.** John Ireland, Sheila Ryan, Hugh Beaumont, Ed Kelly; ***D:*** Anthony Mann. *NOS, NWV, DVT*

Railrodder ☆☆☆ **1965** Buster Keaton as the railroader in this slapstick short fumbles his way across Canada. As in the days of the silents, he speaks not a word. **25m/C VHS, Beta.** Buster Keaton. *NFB*

The Railway Children ☆☆☆½ **1970** At the turn of the century in England, the father of three children is framed and sent to prison during Christmas. The trio and their mother must survive on a poverty stricken farm near the railroad tracks. They eventually meet a new friend who helps them prove their father's innocence. Wonderfully directed by Jeffries. From the classic Edith Nesbitt children's novel. **104m/C VHS, Beta.** *GB* Jenny Agutter, William Mervyn, Bernard Cribbins, Dinah Sheridan, Iain Cuthbertson; ***D:*** Lionel Jeffries. *NO*

The Railway Station Man ☆☆☆ **1992** Set in present-day Ireland. Christie plays a widowed artist struggling to put her life back together after her husband's death in a terrorist bombing. She meets a mysterious American (Sutherland) who's working on restoring the local railway station and finds herself falling in love. When she stumbles upon an IRA bombing plot she also finds out some unpleasant truths about her new lover. Wonderful performances, tragic story. Shot on location in County Donegal, Northern Ireland. Based on the novel by Jennifer Johnston. Made for cable television. **93m/C VHS, Beta, LV.** Julie Christie, Donald Sutherland, John Lynch, Mark Tandy, Frank McCusker, Niall Cusack; ***D:*** Michael Whyte; ***W:*** Shelagh Delaney. *TTC*

Rain ☆☆½ **1932** W. Somerset Maugham's tale of a puritanical minister's attempt to reclaim a "lost woman" on the island of Pago Pago. Crawford and Huston work up some static. Remake of the 1928 silent film "Sadie Thompson." Remade again in 1953 as "Miss Sadie Thompson." **92m/B VHS, Beta.** Joan Crawford, Walter Huston, William Gargan, Guy Kibbee, Beulah Bondi, Walter Catlett; ***D:*** Lewis Milestone. *CNG, NOS, DVT*

The Rain Killer ☆ **1990 (R)** Big city cop and fed don goloshes to track serial killer who slays rich ladies during heavy precipitation. Soggy story. **94m/C VHS, LV.** Ray Sharkey, David Beecroft, Maria Ford, Woody Brown, Tania Coleridge; ***D:*** Ken Stein; ***W:*** Ray Cunneff. *COL*

Rain Man ☆☆☆½ **1988 (R)** When his father dies, ambitious and self-centered Charlie Babbit finds he has an older autistic brother who's been institutionalized for years. Needing him to claim an inheritance, he liberates him from the institution and takes to the road, where both brothers undergo subtle changes. The Vegas montage is wonderful. Critically acclaimed drama and a labor of love for the entire cast. Cruise's best performance to date as he goes from cad to recognizing something wonderfully human in his brother and himself. Hoffman is exceptional. **128m/C VHS, Beta, LV, 8mm.** Dustin Hoffman, Tom Cruise, Valeria Golino, Jerry Molen, Jack Murdock, Michael D. Roberts, Ralph Seymour, Lucinda Jenney, Bonnie Hunt, Kim Robillard, Beth Grant; ***D:*** Barry Levinson; ***W:*** Ronald Bass, Barry Morrow; ***C:*** John Seale; ***M:*** Hans Zimmer. Academy Awards '88: Best Actor (Hoffman), Best Director (Levinson), Best Original Screenplay, Best Picture; Berlin International Film Festival '88: Golden Berlin Bear; Directors Guild of America Awards '88: Best Director (Levinson); Golden Globe Awards '89: Best Actor—Drama (Hoffman), Best Film—Drama; People's Choice Awards '89: Best Film—Drama; Nominations: Academy Awards '88: Best Art Direction/Set Decoration, Best Cinematography, Best Film Editing, Best Original Score. *MGM, OM*

The Rain People ☆☆☆ **1969 (R)** Pregnant housewife Knight takes to the road in desperation and boredom; along the way she meets retarded ex-football player Caan. Well directed by Coppola from his original script. Pensive drama. **102m/C VHS, Beta.** Shirley Knight, James Caan, Robert Duvall; ***D:*** Francis Ford Coppola; ***W:*** Francis Ford Coppola. *WAR*

Rain Without Thunder ☆☆½ **1993 (PG-13)** Imagine the year 2042, a time when abortion is illegal and a fertilized egg has full Constitutional rights. Now imagine sitting through an 87 minute fake documentary that follows the story of a mother and daughter team who have been jailed for trying to go to Sweden so that the daughter can get an abortion. A one-sided, militant pro-choice effort that is neither entertaining nor informational. **87m/C VHS.** Betty Buckley, Jeff Daniels, Ali Thomas, Frederic Forrest, Carolyn McCormick, Linda Hunt, Robert Earl Jones, Graham Greene, Iona Morris, Austin Pendleton; ***D:*** Gary Bennett; ***W:*** Gary Bennett; ***M:*** Randall Lynch, Allen Lynch. *ORI*

Rainbow ☆☆ **1978** Broadway's "Annie" is badly miscast as Judy Garland from her early years in vaudeville to her starring years at M.G.M. Based on the book by Christopher Finch. Made for television; directed by sometime Garland flame Jackie Cooper. **100m/C VHS, Beta, LV.** Andrea McArdle, Jack Carter, Don Murray; ***D:*** Jackie Cooper; ***M:*** Charles Fox. *NO*

The Rainbow ☆☆☆ **1989 (R)** Mature, literate rendering of the classic D.H. Lawrence novel about a young woman's sexual awakening. Beautiful cinematography. Companion/prequel to director Russell's earlier Lawrence adaptation, "Women in Love" (1969). **104m/C VHS, LV.** *GB* Sammi Davis, Amanda Donohoe, Paul McGann, Christopher Gable, David Hemmings, Glenda Jackson, Kenneth Colley; ***D:*** Ken Russell; ***W:*** Vivian Russell, Ken Russell; ***C:*** Billy Williams; ***M:*** Carl Davis. *VES, IME*

Rainbow Bridge ☆ **1971 (R)** The adventures of a group of hippies searching for their consciousness in Hawaii. Features concert footage from Jimi Hendrix's final performance. **74m/C VHS, Beta.** ***D:*** Chuck Wein. *RHI, FCT*

Rainbow Drive ☆☆½ **1990 (R)** Made for cable tv cop thriller promises great things but fails to deliver. Weller is a good cop trapped in the political intrigues of Hollywood. He discovers five dead bodies; when the official count is four, he detects funny business. From the novel by Roderick Thorp. **93m/C VHS.** Peter Weller, Sela Ward, Bruce Weitz, David Caruso, James Laurenson, Chris Mulkey, Kathryn Harrold; ***D:*** Bobby Roth; ***W:*** Roderick Thorp, Bill Phillips, Bennett Cohen; ***M:*** Tangerine Dream. *BTV, VMK*

The Rainbow Gang ☆ **1973** A trio of unlikely prospectors heads into a legendary mine in search of riches and fame. **90m/C VHS, Beta.** Donald Pleasence, Don Calfa, Kate Reid. *NWV*

Rainbow Over Broadway **1933** A former Broadway star mother is set against having her son and daughter try their luck on Broadway. **52m/C VHS.** Joan Marsh, Frank Albertson, Lucien Littlefield, Grace Hayes, Dell Henderson, Harry Myers, Gladys Blake, Glen Boles, Nat Carr; ***D:*** Richard Thorpe. *GPV*

Rainbow Ranch ☆½ **1933** A Navy boxer returns home to his ranch to find murder and corruption. Needless to say, he rides off to seek revenge. **54m/B VHS.** Rex Bell, Cecilia Parker, Robert F. (Bob) Kortman, Henry Hall, Gordon DeMain; ***D:*** Harry Fraser. *NOS, DVT, HEG*

Rainbow Warrior ☆☆½ **1994 (PG)** True story of the bombing of the Greenpeace vessel and the two men who set out to solve the crime. **90m/C VHS.** Sam Neill, Jon Voight, Kerry Fox, Bruno Lawrence; ***D:*** Michael Tuchner. *ABC*

Rainbow's End ☆☆ **1935** Gibson must defend Gale, the female rancher, from an evil adversary who is trying to run Gale and her invalid father off of their land. Things get complicated when Gibson discovers that Stark works for his father! **54m/B VHS.** Hoot Gibson, June Gale, Oscar Apfel, Ada Ince, Charles Hill, Warner Richmond; ***D:*** Norman Spencer. *NOS, DVT*

Raining Stones ☆☆ **1993** A hard-up plumber becomes obsessed with buying an expensive first communion dress for his daughter and gets involved in numerous misadventures trying to get the money. Another of Loach's comedy-dramas about the British working class and their struggle to survive with dignity. **90m/C VHS.** *GB* Bruce Jones, Julie Brown, Ricky Tomlinson, Tom Hickey, Gemma Phoenix, Jonathan James; ***D:*** Ken Loach; ***W:*** Jim Allen; ***M:*** Stewart Copeland. Cannes Film Festival '93: Special Jury Prize; Nominations: British Academy Awards '93: Best Film. *ORI*

The Rainmaker ☆☆☆ **1956** Reminiscent of "Elmer Gantry" in his masterful performance, Lancaster makes it all believable as a con man who comes to a small midwestern town and works miracles not only on the weather but on spinster Hepburn, although both were a little long in the tooth for their roles. Written by Nash from his own play. **121m/C VHS, LV.** Burt Lancaster, Katharine Hepburn, Wendell Corey, Lloyd Bridges, Earl Holliman, Cameron Prudhomme, Wallace Ford; ***D:*** Joseph Anthony; ***W:*** N. Richard Nash; ***C:*** Charles B(ryant) Lang; ***M:*** Alex North. Golden Globe Awards '57: Best Supporting Actor (Holliman); Nominations: Academy Awards '56: Best Actress (Hepburn), Best Original Score. *PAR, CCB*

The Rains Came 🦴🦴½ **1939** Living within a loveless marriage in the mythical Indian city of Ranchipur, English socialite Loy pursues extramarital love interests, including the compassionate doctor Power, potential heir to the maharajah's throne. When an earthquake hits and brings major destruction to the city, Loy aids the doctor in helping the injured. Hankies should be kept handy. Adapted from the Louis Bromfield novel. **104m/B VHS.** Myrna Loy, Tyrone Power, George Brent, Brenda Joyce, Nigel Bruce, Maria Ouspenskaya, Joseph Schildkraut, Laura Hope Crews, Marilyn Nash, Jane Darwell, Marjorie Rambeau, Henry Travers, H.B. Warner, William Royle, Montague Shaw, Harry Hayden, Abner Biberman, George Regas; ***D:*** Clarence Brown; ***W:*** Philip Dunne, Julien Josephson; ***C:*** Arthur C. Miller; ***M:*** Alfred Newman. Academy Awards '40: Best Special Effects (Sersen). *FXV*

Raintree County 🦴🦴½ **1957** A lavish, somewhat overdone epic about two lovers caught up in the national turmoil of the Civil War. An Indiana teacher (Clift) marries a southern belle (Taylor) just after the outbreak of war. The new wife battles mental illness. Producers had hoped this would be another "Gone With the Wind." Adapted from the novel by Ross Lockridge, Jr. Film was delayed in mid-production by Clift's near-fatal and disfiguring car crash. **175m/C VHS, Beta, LV.** Elizabeth Taylor, Montgomery Clift, Eva Marie Saint, Lee Marvin, Nigel Patrick, Rod Taylor, Agnes Moorehead, Walter Abel; ***D:*** Edward Dmytryk; ***C:*** Robert L. Surtees. Nominations: Academy Awards '57: Best Actress (Taylor), Best Art Direction/Set Decoration, Best Costume Design, Best Original Score. *MGM*

Rainy Day 🦴🦴 **1979** A successful actress' return home for her father's funeral brings back unpleasant childhood memories that force her to face the truth about herself. **35m/C VHS, Beta.** Mariette Hartley. *LCA*

Raise the Red Lantern 🦴🦴🦴½ **1991 (PG)** Set in 1920s China, Zhang explores its claustrophobic world of privilege and humiliation. Songlian, an educated 19-year-old beauty, is forced into marriage as the fourth wife of a wealthy and powerful old man. She discovers that the wives have their own separate quarters and servants, and spend most of their time battling to attract their husband's attention. Over the course of a year, Songlian's fury and resentment grow until self-defeating rebellion is all she has. Gong Li is exquisite as the young woman struggling for dignity in a portrayal which is both both haunting and tragic. **125m/C VHS, LV.** *CH* Gong Li, Ma Jingwu, He Caifei, Cao Cuifeng, Jin Shuyuan, Kong Lin, Ding Weimin; ***D:*** Zhang Yimou. British Academy Awards '92: Best Foreign Film; Los Angeles Film Critics Association Awards '92: Best Cinematography; New York Film Critics Awards '92: Best Foreign Film; National Society of Film Critics Awards '92: Best Cinematography, Best Foreign Film; Nominations: Academy Awards '91: Best Foreign Language Film. *ORI, INJ, BTV*

Raise the Titanic *Woof!* **1980 (PG)** A disaster about a disaster. Horrible script cannot be redeemed by purported thrill of the ship's emergence from the deep after 70 years. It's a shame, because the free world's security hangs in the balance. Based on Clive Cussler's best seller. **112m/C VHS, Beta, LV.** Jason Robards Jr., Richard Jordan, Anne Archer, Alec Guinness, J.D. Cannon; ***D:*** Jerry Jameson; ***M:*** John Barry. *FOX*

A Raisin in the Sun 🦴🦴🦴🦴 **1961** Outstanding story of a black family trying to make a better life for themselves in an all-white neighborhood in Chicago. The characters are played realistically and make for a moving story. Each person struggles with doing what he must while still maintaining his dignity and sense of self. Based on the Broadway play by Hansberry, who also wrote the screenplay. **128m/B VHS, Beta, LV.** Diana Sands, John Fiedler, Ivan Dixon, Louis Gossett Jr., Sidney Poitier, Claudia McNeil, Ruby Dee; ***D:*** Daniel Petrie; ***W:*** Lorraine Hansberry. National Board of Review Awards '61: 10 Best Films of the Year, Best Supporting Actress (Dee). *COL, HMV*

A Raisin in the Sun 🦴🦴🦴 **1989** An "American Playhouse," made for television presentation of the Lorraine Hansberry play about a black family threatened with dissolution by the outside forces of racism and greed when they move into an all-white neighborhood in the 1950s. **171m/C VHS, Beta.** Danny Glover, Esther Rolle, Starletta DuPois; ***D:*** Bill Duke. *FRH*

Raising Arizona 🦴🦴🦴½ **1987 (PG-13)** Hi's an ex-con and the world's worst hold-up man. Ed's a policewoman. They meet, fall in love, marry, and kidnap a baby (one of a family of quints). Why not? Ed's infertile and the family they took the baby from has "more than enough," so who will notice? But unfinished furniture tycoon Nathan Arizona wants his baby back, even if he has to hire an axe-murderer on a motorcycle to do it. A brilliant, original comedy narrated in notorious loopy deadpan style by Cage. Innovative camerawork by Barry Sonnenfeld. Wild, surreal and hilarious. **94m/C VHS, Beta, LV.** Nicolas Cage, Holly Hunter, John Goodman, William Forsythe, Randall "Tex" Cobb, Trey Wilson, M. Emmet Walsh, Frances McDormand; ***D:*** Joel Coen; ***W:*** Ethan Coen, Joel Coen; ***M:*** Carter Burwell. *FOX*

Raising Cain 🦴🦴 **1992 (R)** Thriller evoking poor man's Hitchcock about a child psychiatrist who just happens to be nuts features Lithgow in five roles. Seems his supposedly dead Norwegian father has come to the United States and needs his son's help to steal babies for a child development experiment, so the son's alter ego, Cain, shows up to commit the nasty deed. Unfortunately Lithgow also catches his wife with another man, and that's when the bodies start piling up. **95m/C VHS, Beta, LV.** John Lithgow, Lolita Davidovich, Steven Bauer, Frances Sternhagen, Cindy Girard, Tom Bower, Mel Harris, Gabrielle Carteris, Barton Heyman; ***D:*** Brian DePalma; ***W:*** Brian DePalma; ***C:*** Stephen Burum; ***M:*** Pino Donaggio. *MCA*

Rambling Rose 🦴🦴🦴 **1991 (R)** Dern is Rose, a free-spirited, sexually liberated before her time young woman taken in by a Southern family in 1935. Rose immediately has an impact on the male members of the clan, father Duvall and son Haas, thanks to her insuppressible sexuality. This causes consternation with the strait-laced patriarch, who attempts to control his desire for the girl. Eventually Rose decides she must try to stick to one man, but this only causes further problems. Dern gives her best performance yet in this excellent period piece, and solid support is offered from the rest of the cast, in particular Duvall and Dern's real-life mother Ladd. **115m/C VHS, LV.** Laura Dern, Diane Ladd, Robert Duvall, Lukas Haas, John Heard, Kevin Conway, Robert Burke, Lisa Jakub, Evan Lockwood; ***D:*** Martha Coolidge; ***W:*** Calder Willingham; ***M:*** Elmer Bernstein. Independent Spirit Awards '92: Best Director (Coolidge), Best Film, Best Supporting Actress (Ladd); Nominations: Academy Awards '91: Best Actress (Dern), Best Supporting Actress (Ladd). *LIV*

Rambo: First Blood, Part 2 🦴🦴 **1985 (R)** If anyone can save Our Boys still held prisoner in Asia it's John Rambo. Along the way he's tortured, flexes biceps, grunts, and then disposes of the bad guys by the dozen in one of filmdom's bigger dead body parades. Mindless action best enjoyed by testosterone-driven fans of the genre. Sequel to "First Blood" (1982); followed by "Rambo 3" (1988). **93m/C VHS, Beta, LV.** Sylvester Stallone, Richard Crenna, Charles Napier, Steven Berkoff, Julia Nickson-Soul, Martin Kove; ***D:*** George P. Cosmatos; ***W:*** Sylvester Stallone, James Cameron; ***C:*** Jack Cardiff; ***M:*** Jerry Goldsmith. Golden Raspberry Awards '85: Worst Picture, Worst Actor (Stallone), Worst Screenplay, Worst Song ("Peace In Our Life"). *LIV*

Rambo 3 🦴½ **1988 (R)** John Rambo, the famous Vietnam vet turned Buddhist monk, this time invades Afghanistan to rescue his mentor. Meets up with orphan and fights his way around the country. Typically exploitative, kill now, ask questions later Rambo attack, lacking the sheer volume of no-brainer action of the first two Rambos. At the time, the most expensive film ever made, costing $58 million. Filmed in Israel. **102m/C VHS, Beta, LV.** Sylvester Stallone, Richard Crenna, Marc De Jonge, Kurtwood Smith, Spiros Focas; ***D:*** Peter McDonald; ***W:*** Sylvester Stallone; ***M:*** Jerry Goldsmith. Golden Raspberry Awards '88: Worst Actor (Stallone). *LIV*

Rampage 🦴🦴 **1987 (R)** Seemingly all-American guy Charles Reece (McArthur) goes on a murder spree, killing and then mutiliating his victims. Fraser (Biehn) is a liberal district attorney who questions his own views as he argues during the trial that Reece was sane when he committed the murders and deserves the death penalty. Director Friedkin makes no bones about his concerns that the criminal insanity defense often spares the perpetrator while denying justice to the victims. Adapted from the book by William P. Wood and loosely based on killer Richard Chase. Filmed in 1987, the movie wasn't released until 1992 due to the production company's financial difficulties. **92m/C VHS, Beta, LV.** Michael Biehn, Alex McArthur, Nicholas Campbell, Deborah Van Valkenburgh, John Harkins, Art LaFleur; ***D:*** William Friedkin; ***W:*** William Friedkin; ***M:*** Ennio Morricone. *PAR, BTV*

Ramparts of Clay 🦴🦴🦴 **1971 (PG)** A young woman in Tunisia walks the line between her village's traditional way of life and the modern world just after her country's independence from France. Brilliantly shot on location; exquisitely poignant. In Arabic with English subtitles. **87m/C VHS, Beta.** *FR* ***D:*** Jean-Louis Bertucelli. *COL, INJ*

Ramrod 🦴🦴 **1947** Lake is a tough ranch owner at odds with her father, who is being manipulated by a big-time cattleman into trying to put them out of business. She fights back, and McCrea is caught in the middle as the only good guy. Nothing special. **94m/B VHS.** Veronica Lake, Joel McCrea, Arleen Whelan, Don DeFore, Preston Foster, Charlie Ruggles, Donald Crisp, Lloyd Bridges; ***D:*** Andre de Toth. *REP*

The Ramrodder 🦴 *Ramrodders* **1969** An adult western spoof. **92m/C VHS, Beta.** *VDM, TPV*

Ran 🦴🦴🦴🦴 **1985 (R)** The culmination of Kurosawa's career stands as his masterpiece. Loosely adapting Shakespeare's "King Lear," with plot elements from "Macbeth," he's fashioned an epic, heartbreaking statement about honor, ambition, and the futility of war. Aging medieval warlord Hidetora gives control of his empire to his oldest son, creating conflict with two other sons. Soon he's an outcast, as ambition and greed seize the two sons. Stunning battle scenes illuminate the full-blown tragedy of Kurosawa's vision. Superb acting with a scene-stealing Harada as the revenge-minded Lady Kaede; period costumes took three years to create. Japanese with English subtitles. **160m/C VHS, Beta, LV.** *JP FR* Tatsuya Nakadai, Akira Terao, Jinpachi Nesu, Daisuke Ryu, Meiko Harada, Hisashi Igawa, Peter; ***D:*** Akira Kurosawa; ***W:*** Akira Kurosawa, Hideo Oguni, Masato Ide; ***M:*** Toru Takemitsu. Academy Awards '85: Best Costume Design; British Academy Awards '86: Best Foreign Film; Los Angeles Film Critics Association Awards '85: Best Foreign Film; National Board of Review Awards '85: Best Director (Kurosawa); New York Film Critics Awards '85: Best Foreign Film; National Society of Film Critics Awards '85: Best Cinematography, Best Film; Nominations: Academy Awards '85: Best Art Direction/Set Decoration, Best Cinematography, Best Director (Kurosawa). *FOX, APD, INJ*

Rana: The Legend of Shadow Lake 🦴 **1975** Gold at the bottom of a lake is guarded by a frog-monster, but treasure hunters try to retrieve it anyway. **96m/C VHS, Beta.** Alan Ross, Karen McDiarmid, Jerry Gregoris. *AHV*

The Ranch 🦴🦴 **1988 (PG-13)** An executive who loses everything inherits a dilapidated ranch and renovates it into a health spa. **97m/C VHS, Beta.** Andrew Stevens, Gary Fjellgaard, Lou Ann Schmidt, Elizabeth Keefe; ***D:*** Stella Stevens. *HMD*

Rancho Deluxe 🦴🦴🦴 **1975** Off-beat western spoof starring Bridges and Waterston as two carefree cowpokes. Cult favorite featuring music by Buffett, who also appears in the film. **93m/C VHS.** Jeff Bridges, Sam Waterston, Elizabeth Ashley, Charlene Dallas, Clifton James, Slim Pickens, Harry Dean Stanton, Richard Bright, Jimmy Buffett; ***D:*** Frank Perry; ***W:*** Thomas McGuane; ***M:*** Jimmy Buffett. *MGM*

Rancho Notorious ☙☙☙ **1952** Kennedy, on the trail of his girlfriend's murderer, falls for dance hall girl Dietrich. Fine acting. A "period" sample of 50's westerns, but different. A must for Dietrich fans. **89m/C VHS, Beta, LV.** Marlene Dietrich, Arthur Kennedy, Mel Ferrer, William Frawley, Jack Elam, George Reeves; ***D:*** Fritz Lang; ***W:*** Daniel Taradash; ***C:*** Hal Mohr. *NO*

Random Harvest ☙☙☙ **1942** A masterful, tearjerking film based on the James Hilton novel. A shell-shocked WWI amnesiac meets and is made happy by a beautiful music hall dancer. He regains his memory and forgets about the dancer and their child. This is Garson's finest hour, and a shamelessly potent sobfest. **126m/B VHS, Beta.** Greer Garson, Ronald Colman, Reginald Owen, Philip Dorn, Susan Peters, Henry Travers, Margaret Wycherly, Bramwell Fletcher; ***D:*** Mervyn LeRoy; ***C:*** Joseph Ruttenberg. Nominations: Academy Awards '42: Best Actor (Colman), Best Adapted Screenplay, Best Director (LeRoy), Best Interior Decoration, Best Picture, Best Supporting Actress (Peters). *MGM*

Randy Rides Alone ☙☙ **1934** Very young Wayne is good in this slappable but pleasant B effort. Wayne single-handedly cleans up the territory and rids the land of a passel o'bad guys. **53m/B VHS, Beta.** John Wayne, Alberta Vaughn, George "Gabby" Hayes; ***D:*** Harry Fraser. *COL, NOS, VCN*

Range Busters ☙ **1940** Range Busters are called in to find the identity of the phantom killer. **55m/B VHS, Beta.** Ray Corrigan, Max Terhune. *NOS, VCN, DVT*

Range Feud ☙½ **1931** Wayne is a ranch owner's son falsely accused of murder. Just as he's about to hang, Jones, as the heroic sheriff, saves the day and reveals the real killer's identity. **58m/B VHS.** Buck Jones, John Wayne, Susan Fleming, William Walling, Wallace MacDonald, Harry Woods, Ed LeSaint; ***D:*** David Ross Lederman. *COL*

The Range Feud/Two Fisted Law ☙☙ **1931** Two early, short Wayne oaters which reveal the Duke developing the drawl, gait and pleasingly profane style that would carry him to fame. In "Feud" he is a young rancher accused of murdering a cattle rustler. "Law" finds him playing a character named Duke who loses his land and girl to a neighboring land grabber. **112m/C VHS.** Buck Jones, Tim McCoy, John Wayne, Susan Fleming, Alice Faye, Walter Brennan; ***D:*** David Ross Lederman. *COL*

Range Law ☙ **1931** Another entry in the infamous Maynard series of horseplay, cliche, and repetitive plot elements. **60m/B VHS, Beta.** Ken Maynard, Charles "Blackie" King, Lafe McKee. *GPV, VCI, DVT*

Range Law ☙½ **1944** Ranchers are being terrorized for their silver mine and its up to Brown and Hatton to catch the villains. **59m/B VHS.** Johnny Mack Brown, Raymond Hatton, Lloyd Ingraham, Sarah Padden, Ellen Hall, Steve Clark, Jack Ingram, Bud Osborne; ***D:*** Lambert Hillyer. *GPV*

Range Renegades ☙½ **1948** Sheriff Wakely and his pals have their hands full when his deputy gets involved with the leader of a gang of outlaw women. Predictable B oater reflects the then developing trend of using wicked female characters in westerns. Paved the way for films like "Johnny Guitar" and "Rancho Notorious." **54m/B VHS.** Jimmy Wakely, Dub Taylor, Dennis Moore, Jennifer Holt, John James, Steve Clark, Frank LaRue; ***D:*** Lambert Hillyer; ***W:*** Ronald Davidson, William Lively. *MOV*

Range Rider **1952** Eight episodes of the series are on four tapes, including "Greed Rides the Range," "Silver Blade" and "Fatal Bullet." **60m/B VHS, Beta.** Jock Mahoney. *DVT*

Range Riders **1935** A gunman poses as a wimp and cleans out an outlaw gang. **46m/B VHS, Beta.** Buddy Roosevelt. *NO*

Rangeland Empire ☙ **1950** Shamrock and Lucky are at it again, implicated as being members of an outlaw gang until that gang attacks them. **59m/B VHS, Beta, LV.** James Ellison, Russell Hayden, Stanley Price, John Cason. *NO*

Rangeland Racket ☙½ **1941** The Lone Rider (Houston) has been wrongly accused of a crime. **60m/B VHS, Beta.** George Houston, Hillary Brooke, Al "Fuzzy" St. John. *VYY*

Ranger and the Lady ☙½ **1940** Texas Ranger Rodgers romances the woman who is the leader of a wagon train. **54m/B VHS, Beta.** Roy Rogers, George "Gabby" Hayes; ***D:*** Joseph Kane. *NOS, DVT*

Ranger's Roundup ☙ **1938** The Rangers prove their courage by rounding up an outlaw gang. **57m/B VHS, Beta.** Fred Scott, Al "Fuzzy" St. John. *NOS, DVT*

The Rangers Step In ☙½ **1937** Allen leaves the Texas Rangers when a feud between his family and that of the girl he loves heats up again. Turns out rustlers are stirring things up in order to get some of the disputed land. **56m/B VHS.** Robert Allen, Eleanor Stewart, John Merton, Hal Taliaferro, Jack Ingram, Jack Rockwell, Lafe McKee, Robert F. (Bob) Kortman; ***D:*** Spencer Gordon Bennet. *GPV*

Rangers Take Over ☙½ **1943** Gunlords are driven out by the Texas Rangers. **62m/B VHS, Beta.** Dave O'Brien, James Newill. *NOS, VYY, DVT*

Ransom Money ☙½ **1988** A kidnapping scheme involving millions of dollars, in and around the Grand Canyon, backfires. **87m/C VHS, Beta.** Broderick Crawford, Rachel Romen, Gordon Jump, Randy Whipple; ***D:*** DeWitt Lee. *NO*

Ranson's Folly ☙☙½ **1926** Barthelmess makes a wager that he can impersonate a famous outlaw well enough to rob a stage with only a pair of scissors. When the army paymaster is killed, guess who gets caught with his swash unbuckled? **80m/B VHS, Beta.** Richard Barthelmess, Dorothy Mackaill, Anders Randolf, Pat Hartigan, Brooks Benedict; ***D:*** Sidney Olcott. *GPV*

Rapa Nui ☙☙½ **1993 (R)** The title refers to the Polynesian name for Easter Island, with the film set in the 17th-century (before Dutch explorers discovered the island). It depicts the annual rituals of the mysterious people who built the Island's moai—the famous giant stone statues. Lee plays the heroic Noroinia, with Morales as his rival Make, and Holt as Ramana, the object of their desires. Faux primitive but with some great on-location filming. **107m/C VHS, LV.** Jason Scott Lee, Esai Morales, Sandrine Holt; ***D:*** Kevin Reynolds; ***W:*** Kevin Reynolds, Tim Rose Price; ***M:*** Stewart Copeland. *WAR*

Rape ☙ **198?** Two guys investigate a third pal's mysterious death. They discover that his supernatural-power-imbued girlfriend is at the root of the matter. **90m/C VHS, Beta.** Rick Joss, Gil Vidal. *NO*

Rape and Marriage: The Rideout Case ☙☙½ **1980** The true story of an Oregon wife who accused her husband of rape. Thoughtfully explores the legal and moral questions raised by the case. Interpreted well enough, though not superbly, by a decent cast. although Rourke is a little too intense. Made for television. **96m/C VHS, Beta.** Mickey Rourke, Linda Hamilton, Rip Torn, Eugene Roche, Conchata Ferrell, Gail Strickland, Bonnie Bartlett, Alley Mills; ***D:*** Peter Levin. *LIV*

Rape of Love ☙☙½ **1979** The story begins with one of the most chilling rape scenes on film and then attempts to analyze the emotional impact of rape on its victim. Well-acted and directed. In French with English subtitles. **117m/C VHS, Beta.** *FR* Nathalie Nell, Alain Foures; ***D:*** Yannick Bellon. *COL, INJ*

The Rape of the Sabines *Woof! El Rapto de las Sabinas; The Mating of the Sabine Women; Shame of the Sabine Women* **1961** The story of Romulus, king of Rome, and how he led the Romans to capture the women of Sabina. The battles rage, the women plot, and Romulus fights and lusts. Dubbed in English. **101m/C VHS, Beta.** *IT FR* Roger Moore, Mylene Demongeot, Jean Marais; ***D:*** Richard Pottier. *UNI*

Rapid Fire ☙ **1989** Cheap, made-for-video quickie about a good guy U.S. agent who battles terrorists. Easy to skip. **90m/C VHS, Beta.** Joe Spinell, Michael Wayne, Ron Waldron; ***D:*** David A. Prior. *AIP*

Rapid Fire ☙☙½ **1992 (R)** Lee (son of martial arts cult film star Bruce Lee) is a Chinese-American art student who also happens to be a martial arts expert. He's tapped by the police to help stem the violence between the Asian and Italian gangs fighting for control over Chicago's drug trade. Typical martial arts movie is made better by uniquely choreographed action sequences and Lee's attractive presence. **96m/C VHS, LV.** Brandon Lee, Powers Boothe, Nick Mancuso, Raymond J. Barry, Kate Hodge, Tzi Ma, Tony Longo, Michael Paul Chan, Dustin Nguyen, John Vickery; ***D:*** Dwight Little; ***W:*** Alan B. McElroy, Cindy Cirile, Paul Attanasio; ***M:*** Christopher Young. *FXV*

Rappin' ☙ **1985 (PG)** Ex-con Van Peebles gets into it with the landlord and a street gang leader. Forgettable action/music drivel. ♫Rappin'; Two of a Kind; Call Me; Born to Love; Killer; Itching for a Scratch; Snack Attack; Dodge; Golly Gee. **92m/C VHS, Beta.** Mario Van Peebles, Tasia Valenza, Harry Goz, Charles Flohe; ***D:*** Joel Silberg. *MGM*

The Rapture ☙☙ **1991 (R)** A beautiful telephone operator engages in indiscrimate sexual adventures to relieve the boredom of her job and life. She becomes curious by, and eventually converted to, evangelical Christianity, which leads her to a contented marriage and the birth of a daughter. When her husband is tragically killed she becomes convinced that she and her child will be taken by God into heaven if she only waits for the proper sign. **100m/C VHS, LV.** Mimi Rogers, David Duchovny, Patrick Bauchau, Will Patton; ***D:*** Michael Tolkin; ***W:*** Michael Tolkin; ***C:*** Bojan Bazelli. *COL*

Rapunzel **1982** A beautiful young woman locked in a tall tower is saved by the handsome prince who climbs her golden tresses. Part of Shelly Duvall's "Faerie Tale Theatre" series. **60m/C VHS, Beta, LV.** Shelley Duvall, Gena Rowlands, Jeff Bridges. *KUI, FOX, FCT*

The Rare Breed ☙☙½ **1966** Plodding but pleasant Western. A no-strings ranch hand (Stewart) agrees to escort a Hereford Bull to Texas, where the widow of an English breeder plans to crossbreed the bull with longhorn cattle. The widow (O'Hara) insists that she and her daughter accompany Stewart on the trip, which features every kind of western calamity imaginable. When all others believe the attempt to crossbreed has failed, Stewart sets out to prove them wrong. **97m/C VHS, Beta.** James Stewart, Maureen O'Hara, Brian Keith, Juliet Mills, Jack Elam, Ben Johnson; ***D:*** Andrew V. McLaglen; ***C:*** William Clothier; ***M:*** John Williams. *MCA*

A Rare Breed ☙½ **1981 (PG)** Real-life story of a kidnapped horse in Italy and a young girl's quest to retrieve it. Directed by David Nelson of television's "Ozzie and Harriet" fame, this movie is cute and old-fashioned. **94m/C VHS, Beta.** George Kennedy, Forrest Tucker, Tracy Vaccaro, Tom Hallick, Don DeFore; ***D:*** David Nelson. *VTR, LIV*

Rascal Dazzle **1981** Montage-like tribute to that best-loved group of children, the Our Gang kids. Narrated by Jerry Lewis. Includes scenes with Spanky, Alfalfa, Darla and the rest of the gang. **100m/B VHS, Beta, LV.** *SUE*

The Rascals ☙☙½ **1981 (R)** An irrepressible youth at a rural Catholic boys' school comes of age. **93m/C VHS, Beta.** *FR* Thomas Chabrol; ***D:*** Bernard Revon. *SUE*

Rashomon ☙☙☙☙ *In the Woods* **1951** In 12th century Japan, two travelers attempt to discover the truth about an ambush/rape/murder. They get four completely different versions of the incident from the three people involved in the crime and the single witness. An insightful masterpiece that established Kurosawa and Japanese cinema as major artistic forces. Fine performances, particularly Mifune as the bandit. Visually beautiful and rhythmic. Remade as a western, "The Outrage," in 1964. In Japanese with English subtitles. **83m/B VHS, Beta, LV.** *JP* Machiko Kyo, Toshiro Mifune, Masayuki Mori, Takashi Shimura; ***D:*** Akira Kurosawa; ***W:*** Akira Kurosawa. Academy Awards '51: Best Foreign Language Film; National Board of Review Awards '51: 5 Best Foreign Films of the Year, Best Director (Kurosawa); Nominations: Academy Awards '52: Best Art Direction/ Set Decoration (B & W). *SUE, CRC, INJ*

Rasputin ☠☠☠ *Agoniya* **1985** The long-censored and banned film of the story of the mad monk and his domination of the royal family before the Russian Revolution. Petrenko is superb. First released in the United States in 1988. In Russian with English subtitles. **104m/C VHS, Beta.** *RU* Alexei Petrenko, Anatoly Romashin, Velta Linne, Alice Freindlikh; ***D:*** Elem Klimov; ***W:*** Semyon Lunghin, Ilya Nusinov; ***M:*** Alfred Shnitke. *INJ*

Rasputin and the Empress ☠☠☠ *Rasputin: The Mad Monk* **1932** Lavish historical epic teamed the three Barrymore sibs for the first and only time, as they vied for scene-stealing honors. Ethel is Empress Alexandra of Russia, tied to the weak-willed Nicholas II (Morgan) and under the spell of Rasputin, played by Lionel. John is a nobleman who seeks to warn the Russian rulers of their perilous perch on the throne, made only worse by Rasputin's spreading power and corruption. Ethel's first talkie and Wyngard's first film role. Uncredited director Charles Brabin was replaced by Boleslawski due to his incompatability with the imperious Ethel. **123m/B VHS.** Ethel Barrymore, John Barrymore, Lionel Barrymore, Ralph Morgan, Diana Wynyard, Tad Alexander, C. Henry Gordon, Edward Arnold, Gustav von Seyffertitz, Anne Shirley, Jean Parker, Henry Kolker; ***D:*** Richard Boleslawski; ***W:*** Charles MacArthur; ***C:*** William H. Daniels. Nominations: Academy Awards '33: Best Original Screenplay. *MGM, MOV*

Rat Pfink a Boo-Boo *Woof!* **1966** Parody on "Batman" in which a bumbling superhero and his sidekick race around saving people. Notoriously inept. Title story is legendary—it was misspelled accidentally and Steckler didn't have the cash to fix it. **72m/B VHS, Beta.** Vin Saxon, Carolyn Brandt, Titus Moede, Mike Kannon; ***D:*** Ray Dennis Steckler. *NO*

The Rat Race ☠☠☠ **1960** A dancer and a musician venture to Manhattan to make it big, and end up sharing an apartment. Their relationship starts pleasantly and becomes romantic. Enjoyable farce. Well photographed and scripted, with the supporting characters stealing the show. **105m/C VHS.** Tony Curtis, Debbie Reynolds, Jack Oakie, Kay Medford, Don Rickles, Joe Bushkin; ***D:*** Robert Mulligan; ***C:*** Robert Burks; ***M:*** Elmer Bernstein. *PAR*

Ratboy ☠☠½ **1986 (PG-13)** An unscrupulous woman attempts to transform a boy with a rat's face into a celebrity, with tragic results. First directorial effort by Locke that gradually loses steam. **105m/C VHS, Beta.** Sondra Locke, Sharon Baird, Robert Townsend; ***D:*** Sondra Locke; ***W:*** Rob Thompson; ***C:*** Bruce Surtees; ***M:*** Lennie Niehaus. *WAR*

Rate It X **1986 (R)** Sexism in a variety of national institutions, from pornography to consumerism, is revealed through the average man on the street via microphone interviews. **95m/C VHS, Beta.** ***D:*** Lucy Winer, Paula de Koenigsberg. *LIV*

Ratings Game ☠☠ *The Mogul* **1984** A bitter, out-of-work actor and a woman who works at the ratings service manage to mess up the television industry. Early directorial effort by DeVito is uneven but funny. Made for cable television. **102m/C VHS, Beta, LV.** Danny DeVito, Rhea Perlman, Gerrit Graham, Kevin McCarthy, Jayne Meadows, Steve Allen, Ronny Graham, George Wenolt; ***D:*** Danny DeVito; ***W:*** Michael Barrie, Jim Mulholland. *PAR*

Rats ☠☠ **1983** In 2225, the beleaguered survivors of a nuclear holocaust struggle with a mutant rodent problem. **100m/C VHS, Beta.** Richard Raymond, Richard Cross; ***D:*** Vincent Dawn. *NO*

The Rats are Coming! The Werewolves are Here! *Woof!* **1972 (R)** Low budget schlock revolves around a family of werewolves and the daughter who decides to put an end to the curse. Imaginative title promises much more than movie delivers. The killer rats were thrown in as an afterthought to increase the run time. **92m/C VHS, Beta.** Hope Stansbury, Jackie Skarvellis, Noel Collins, Joan Ogden, Douglas Phair, Bernard Kaler; ***D:*** Andy Milligan; ***W:*** Andy Milligan. *NO*

Rattle of a Simple Man ☠☠½ **1964** A naive, chaste, middle-aged bachelor (Corbett) who lives in London must spend the night with a waitress (Cilento) to win a bet. She knows of the bet and kindly obliges. Enjoyable sex comedy. **91m/B VHS, Beta.** *GB* Harry H. Corbett, Diane Cilento, Michael Medwin, Thora Hird; ***D:*** Muriel Box. *NO*

Rattled ☠☠½ **1996 (PG-13)** Indiana Jones won't be the only snake-hater after seeing what hundreds of rattlesnakes can do. When their den is disturbed by construction on a new water project, hundreds of rattlers slither down the mountainside ready to attack anyone in their path. Based on the book "Rattlers" by Joseph Gilmore. **90m/C VHS.** William Katt, Shanna Reed, Michael Galeota, Monica Creel, Clint Howard, Ian Abercrombie, Ed Lauter, Bibi Besch, Zack Eginton; ***D:*** Tony Randel; ***W:*** Jim Wheat, Ken Wheat. *MCA*

Rattler Kid ☠ **197?** Cavalry sergeant wrongly accused of murdering his commanding officer escapes from prison and finds the real killer. **86m/C VHS, Beta.** Richard Wyler, Brad Harris. *UNI*

Rattlers ☠ **1976 (PG)** Made for television movie featuring poisonous rattlesnakes who attack at random. **82m/C VHS, Beta.** Sam Chew, Elizabeth Chauvet, Dan Priest; ***D:*** John McCauley. *NO*

Rave Review ☠☠ **1995** Desperate L.A. theatrical director wants to scare a powerful critic into giving his latest production a glowing review so that his small theater company can remain in business. Too bad he scares the critic to death. **91m/C VHS.** Jeff Seymour, Ed Begley Jr., Leo Rossi, Joe Spano, Bruce Kirby, James Handy; ***D:*** Jeff Seymour; ***W:*** Jeff Seymour. *HMD*

The Raven ☠☠ **1915** An early, eccentric pseudo-biography of author Edgar Allan Poe. The film opens with a look at Poe's ancestors and follows the author to maturity when he turns to alcohol for solace. His drunken stupor produces hallucinations that lead to his tale of "The Raven." Silent with added music track. **80m/B VHS.** Henry B. Walthall, Wanda Howard; ***D:*** Charles Brabin. *GPV, HEG, GVV*

The Raven ☠☠☠ **1935** A lunatic surgeon (Lugosi), who has a dungeon full of torture gadgets inspired by Edgar Allan Poe's stories, is begged by a man to save his daughter's life. The surgeon does, and then falls in love with the girl. But when she rejects his love (she's already engaged), he plans revenge in his chamber of horrors. Karloff plays the criminal who winds up ruining the mad doctor's plans. Lugosi is at his prime in this role, and any inconsistencies in the somewhat shaky script can be overlooked because of his chilling performance. **62m/B VHS, LV.** Boris Karloff, Bela Lugosi, Irene Ware, Lester Matthews, Samuel S. Hinds; ***D:*** Lew (Louis Friedlander) Landers. *MCA*

The Raven ☠☠☠ **1963** This could-have-been monumental teaming of horror greats Karloff, Lorre and Price is more of a satire than a true horror film. One of the more enjoyable of the Corman/Poe adaptations, the movie takes only the title of the poem. As for the storyline: Price and Karloff play two rival sorcerers who battle for supremacy, with Lorre as the unfortunate associate turned into the bird of the title. **86m/C VHS, Beta, LV.** Vincent Price, Boris Karloff, Peter Lorre, Jack Nicholson, Hazel Court; ***D:*** Roger Corman; ***W:*** Richard Matheson; ***C:*** Floyd Crosby; ***M:*** Les Baxter. *MLB*

Ravishing Idiot ☠☠ *Agent 38-24-36; Adorable Idiot; The Warm-Blooded Spy; Bewitching Scatterbrain* **1964** An unemployed bank clerk becomes mixed up with Soviet spies. **99m/B VHS, Beta.** *FR* Brigitte Bardot, Anthony Perkins; ***D:*** Edouard Molinaro. *NO*

Raw Courage ☠ *Courage* **1984** Three long-distance runners relax in New Mexico, but are kidnapped by vigilantes. Loosely based on a James Dickey novel. **90m/C VHS, Beta, LV.** Ronny Cox, Lois Chiles, Art Hindle, Tim Maier, M. Emmet Walsh; ***D:*** Robert L. Rosen. *NWV, VTR*

Raw Deal ☠½ **1986 (R)** Don't ever give Schwarzenegger a raw deal! FBI agent Schwarzie infiltrates the mob and shoots lots of people. **106m/C VHS, Beta, LV.** Arnold Schwarzenegger, Kathryn Harrold, Darren McGavin, Sam Wanamaker, Paul Shenar, Steven Hill; ***D:*** John Irvin; ***W:*** Gary De Vore, Patrick Edgeworth. *TLF*

Raw Force ☠ *Shogun Island* **1981 (R)** Three karate buffs visit an island inhabited by a sect of cannibalistic monks who have the power to raise the dead (it could happen). They fix the villains by kicking them all in the head. **90m/C VHS, Beta.** *PH* Cameron Mitchell, Geoffrey Binney, John Dresden, John Locke, Ralph Lombardi; ***D:*** Edward Murphy. *MED*

Raw Justice ☠☠ **1993 (R)** When the daughter of a powerful Southern mayor is murdered, tough ex-cop Mace (Keith) is hired to get the killer. Mace enlists the reluctant help of call girl Sarah (Anderson) to help him trap Mitch (Hayes), his prime suspect. Only things don't work out as Mace planned and the wary threesome must work together to save themselves from certain death. **92m/C VHS, LV.** David Keith, Pamela Anderson Lee, Robert Hayes, Leo Rossi, Charles Napier, Stacy Keach; ***D:*** David A. Prior; ***W:*** David A. Prior. *REP*

Raw Nerve ☠ **1991 (R)** A cast with possibilities can't overcome this poorly reasoned suspenser. A young man has visions of the local serial killer, but when he reports them to police he becomes the suspect. There are a few twists beyond that, none too thrilling. **91m/C VHS, Beta, LV.** Glenn Ford, Traci Lords, Sandahl Bergman, Randall "Tex" Cobb, Ted Prior, Jan-Michael Vincent; ***W:*** David A. Prior. *AIP*

Rawhead Rex ☠½ **1987 (R)** An ancient demon is released from his underground prison in Ireland by a plowing farmer, and begins to decapitate and maim at will. Adapted by Clive Barker from his own short story. But Barker later disowned the film, so make your own judgment. **89m/C VHS, Beta, LV.** David Dukes, Kelly Piper; ***D:*** George Pavlou; ***W:*** Clive Barker; ***M:*** Colin Towns. *LIV, VES*

Rawhide ☠☠ **1938** Rancher's Protection Association forces landowners to knuckle under resulting in friction. Lou Gehrig plays a rancher in a western released the year before he died. Bandleader Ballew could be more gripping in the lead. **60m/B VHS, Beta.** Lou Gehrig, Smith Ballew, Evalyn Knapp; ***D:*** Ray Taylor. *NOS, CCB, DVT*

Rawhide ☠☠☠ *Desperate Siege* **1950** Four escaped convicts hijack a stagecoach way station and hold hostages while waiting for a shipment of gold. A suspenseful B-grade western with a bang-up ending. Well paced and cast with an abundance of good talent. A remake of "Show Them No Mercy" (1938). **86m/B VHS, Beta.** Tyrone Power, Susan Hayward, Hugh Marlowe, Jack Elam, Dean Jagger, George Tobias, Edgar Buchanan, Jeff Corey; ***D:*** Henry Hathaway; ***C:*** Milton Krasner. *FOX*

Rawhide Mail ☠☠ **193?** Extremely rare "B" western. **?m/C VHS.** Jack Perrin. *LOO*

Rawhide Romance ☠ **1934** Bill finds justice and love in this chap-slappin' opus, which finds him neglecting the thieves operating on the ranch as he romances his girl. Naturally he comes to his senses and goes after the crooks. **47m/B VHS, Beta, LV.** Buffalo Bill Jr., Genee Boutell, Lafe McKee, Si Jenks; ***D:*** Victor Adamson. *VYY*

Razorback ☠ **1984 (R)** Young American travels to the Australian outback in search of his missing journalist wife. During his quest, he encounters a giant killer pig that has been terrorizing the area. Firmly establishes that pigs, with little sense of natural timing, make lousy movie villains. **95m/C VHS, Beta.** *AU* Gregory Harrison, Bill Kerr, Arkie Whiteley, Judy Morris, Chris Haywood; ***D:*** Russell Mulcahy. *WAR*

The Razor's Edge ☠☠☠ **1946** Adaptation of the W. Somerset Maugham novel. A rich young man spends his time between WWI & WWII searching for essential truth, eventually landing in India. A satisfying cinematic version of a difficult novel, supported by an excellent cast. Remade in 1984 with Bill Murray in the lead role. **146m/B VHS, Beta, LV.** Tyrone Power, Gene Tierney, Anne Baxter, Clifton Webb, Herbert Marshall, John Payne, Elsa Lanchester; ***D:*** Edmund Goulding; ***C:*** Arthur C. Miller. Academy Awards '46: Best Supporting Actress (Baxter); Golden Globe Awards '47: Best Supporting Actor (Webb), Best Supporting Actress (Baxter); Nominations: Academy Awards '46: Best Interior Decoration, Best Picture, Best Supporting Actor (Webb). *FXV, BTV*

The Razor's Edge 🦴🦴½ **1984 (PG-13)** A beautifully filmed but idiosyncratic version of the W. Somerset Maugham novel. WWI-ravaged Larry Darrell combs the world in search of the meaning of life. Murray is a little too old and sardonic to seem really tortured. Russell is great as the loser he rescues. Subtly unique, with real shortcomings. **129m/C VHS, Beta, LV.** Bill Murray, Catherine Hicks, Theresa Russell, Denholm Elliott, James Keach, Peter Vaughan, Saeed Jaffrey, Brian Doyle-Murray; ***D:*** John Byrum; ***W:*** John Byrum; ***M:*** Jack Nitzsche. *COL*

Re-Animator 🦴🦴🦴 **1984** Based on an H.P. Lovecraft story, this grisly film deals with a medical student who re-animates the dead. It has quickly turned into a black humor cult classic. Also available in an "R" rated version, and followed by "Bride of Re-Animator." **86m/C VHS, Beta, LV.** Jeffrey Combs, Bruce Abbott, Barbara Crampton, David Gale, Robert Sampson; ***D:*** Stuart Gordon; ***W:*** Stuart Gordon, Dennis Paoli, William J. Norris; ***M:*** Richard Band. *LIV, VES*

Reach for the Sky 🦴🦴½ **1956** WW II flying ace loses both legs in an accident and learns to fly again. He becomes a hero during the Battle of Britain, then is shot down over France and held prisoner by the Germans. At war's end he returns to England to lead 3,000 planes over London in a victory flight. Inspirationaly told true story. **136m/B VHS, Beta.** *GB* Kenneth More, Alexander Knox, Nigel Green; ***D:*** Lewis Gilbert; ***M:*** John Addison. British Academy Awards '56: Best Film. *NO*

Reaching for the Moon 🦴🦴½ **1917** A day-dreaming department store employee finds himself in the unlikely position of ruling a kingdom. Vintage Fairbanks fun, based on a story by Anita Loos. Silent. **62m/B VHS, Beta.** Douglas Fairbanks Sr., Eileen Percy, Millard Webb; ***D:*** John Emerson. *VYY, GPV, GVV*

Reaching for the Moon 🦴🦴½ **1931** Fairbanks is a businessman who falls for liquor and Daniels on a transatlantic cruise. Dull and cruel; not as light-hearted as it intends. One Irving Berlin song sung by Crosby. **62m/B VHS, Beta, 8mm.** Douglas Fairbanks Sr., Bebe Daniels, Bing Crosby, Edward Everett Horton; ***D:*** Edmund Goulding. *NOS, VYY, CAB*

Reactor 🦴 **1985** A low-budget sci-fi film about kidnapped scientists, alien ships and an activated nuclear reactor. **90m/C VHS, Beta.** Yanti Somer, Melissa Long, James R. Stuart, Robert Barnes, Nick Jordan. *NO*

Ready to Wear 🦴🦴 *Pret-a-Porter* **1994 (R)** Altman travels to Paris to take on the fashion industry with his trademark satire, ensemble cast, and cameo players in tow. The untimely death of a major industry player begins a swirl of random subplots involving a head-spinning array of fashion industry stereotypes. Loren and Mastroianni recreate their "Yesterday, Today and Tomorrow" boudoir striptease scene. Coterie of one-dimensional characters is set adrift with no discernable plot, which might make for interesting people watching, but results in a tedious movie. Altman did it better with "The Player" and "Short Cuts." **132m/C VHS, LV.** Sophia Loren, Marcello Mastroianni, Julia Roberts, Tim Robbins, Kim Basinger, Stephen Rea, Anouk Aimee, Lauren Bacall, Lili Taylor, Sally Kellerman, Tracey Ullman, Linda Hunt, Rupert Everett, Forest Whitaker, Richard E. Grant, Danny Aiello, Teri Garr, Lyle Lovett, Jean Rochefort, Michel Blanc, Anne Canovos, Jean-Pierre Cassel, Francois Cluzet, Rossy de Palma, Kaisa Figura, Sam Robards; ***Cameos:*** Cher, Harry Belafonte, Issey Miyake, Sonia Rykiel, Jean-Paul Gaultier, Thierry Mugler; ***D:*** Robert Altman; ***W:*** Barbara Shulgasser, Robert Altman; ***M:*** Michel Legrand. Nominations: Golden Globe Awards '95: Best Film—Musical/Comedy, Best Supporting Actress (Loren). *MAX*

A Real American Hero 🦴½ *Hard Stick* **1978** Made for television story of Tennessee sheriff Buford Pusser, the subject of three "Walking Tall" films. Here, he battles moonshiners, with the usual violence. **94m/C VHS, Beta.** Brian Dennehy, Brian Kerwin, Forrest Tucker; ***D:*** Lou Antonio. *VTR, PSM*

Real Bruce Lee **1979 (R)** Contains actual early films of Bruce Lee, once feared lost but recently discovered in the Chinese film archives, (the movies, not Bruce). **108m/C VHS, Beta.** Bruce Lee. *GEM, SUN, VTR*

The Real Buddy Holly Story **1987** Documentary serves as a tribute to the rock 'n' roll legend who met an untimely death in 1959. **90m/C VHS, Beta, LV.** *SMV, IME, MVD*

Real Bullets 🦴 **1990** Stunt team performs the real thing when two members get imprisoned in a bad guy's desert castle. **86m/C VHS, Beta, LV.** John Gazarian, Martin Landau; ***D:*** Lance Lindsay. *VMK*

Real Genius 🦴🦴🦴 **1985 (PG)** Brainy kids in California work with lasers on a class project that is actually intended for use as an offensive military weapon. When they learn of the scheme, they use their brilliant minds to mount an amusingly elaborate strategic defense initiative of their own. Eccentric characters and an intelligent script provide a bevy of laughs for the family. **108m/C VHS, Beta, LV.** Val Kilmer, Gabe Jarret, Jonathan Gries, Michelle Meyrink, William Atherton, Patti D'Arbanville, Severn Darden; ***D:*** Martha Coolidge; ***W:*** Peter Torokvei, Neal Israel, Pat Proft; ***M:*** Thomas Newman. *COL*

The Real Glory 🦴🦴🦴 **1939** After the U.S. capture of the Philippine islands during the Spanish-American war, an uprising of Moro tribesmen spreads terror. After most of the islands are evacuated only a small group of Army officers is left to lead the Filipino soldiers against the rebels. Cooper plays the heroic doctor, who is not afraid to fight, especially when he comes to the rescue of the beseiged Army fort. Great action sequences and paticularly good performances by Cooper and Niven. **95m/B VHS.** Gary Cooper, Andrea Leeds, David Niven, Reginald Owen, Broderick Crawford; ***D:*** Henry Hathaway. *MGM, WAR*

Real Life 🦴🦴🦴 **1979 (R)** Writer/comedian Brooks's first feature sags in places, but holds its own as a vehicle for his peculiar talent. Brooks plays a pompous director whose ambition is to make a documentary of a "typical" American family. Good, intelligent comedy. **99m/C VHS, Beta.** Charles Grodin, Frances Lee McCain, Albert Brooks; ***D:*** Albert Brooks; ***W:*** Monica Johnson, Harry Shearer, Albert Brooks. *PAR*

The Real McCoy 🦴½ **1993 (PG-13)** Generally awful crime-caper film about female bank robber Karen McCoy (Basinger). Just out of prison, all Karen wants to do is go straight and raise her young son but her plans are thwarted by former associates who kidnap the child to force her into one last heist. Kilmer is the small-time thief, with a crush on Karen, who tries to help her out. Dumb, slow-moving story with a vapid performance by Basinger. **104m/C VHS, LV.** Kim Basinger, Val Kilmer, Terence Stamp, Zach English, Gailard Sartain; ***D:*** Russell Mulcahy; ***W:*** William Davies, William Osborne. *MCA*

Real Men 🦴½ **1987 (PG-13)** The junior Belushi brother is a spy forced to recruit ordinary guy Ritter to help him negotiate with aliens to save the world. Bizarre premise shows promise, but spy spoof doesn't fire on all comedic pistons. Nice try. **86m/C VHS, Beta, LV.** James Belushi, John Ritter, Barbara Barrie; ***D:*** Dennis Feldman; ***M:*** Miles Goodman. *FOX*

Reality Bites 🦴🦴½ **1994 (PG-13)** Humorous look at four recent college grads living, working, and slacking in Houston. Script by newcomer Childress is at its best when highlighting the trends: 7-Eleven Big Gulps, tacky '70s memorabilia, and games revolving around episodes of old TV shows like "Good Times," to name a few. Definite appeal for those in their early 20s, but anyone over 25 may encounter a "Generation X-er" gap, a noticeable problem since "Reality" claims to speak for the entire twentysomething generation. Decent directorial debut for Stiller; good cast, particularly Garofalo, in her film debut. **99m/C VHS, LV.** Winona Ryder, Ethan Hawke, Ben Stiller, Janeane Garofalo, Steve Zahn, Swoosie Kurtz, Joe Don Baker, John Mahoney; ***Cameos:*** David Pirner, Anne Meara, Jeanne Tripplehorn, Karen Duffy, Evan Dando; ***D:*** Ben Stiller; ***W:*** Helen Childress; ***M:*** Karl Wallinger. Nominations: MTV Movie Awards '94: Best Kiss (Ethan Hawke/Winona Ryder). *MCA*

Really Weird Tales 🦴🦴½ **1986** Several SCTV alumni highlight this three-story movie, which is science fiction with a satirical edge. **85m/C VHS, Beta.** John Candy, Martin Short, Joe Flaherty, Catherine O'Hara. *VTR*

Reap the Wild Wind 🦴🦴½ **1942** DeMille epic about salvagers off the Georgia coast in the 1840s featuring Wayne as the captain and Massey and a giant squid as the villains. Good cast, lesser story, fine underwater photography. **123m/C VHS, Beta.** Ray Milland, John Wayne, Paulette Goddard, Raymond Massey, Robert Preston, Lynne Overman, Susan Hayward, Charles Bickford, Walter Hampden, Louise Beavers, Martha O'Driscoll, Elisabeth Risdon, Hedda Hopper, Raymond Hatton, Barbara Britton; ***D:*** Cecil B. DeMille; ***C:*** Victor Milner. Academy Awards '42: Best Special Effects; Nominations: Academy Awards '42: Best Color Cinematography, Best Interior Decoration. *MCA*

Rear Window 🦴🦴🦴🦴 **1954** A newspaper photographer with a broken leg (Stewart) passes the time recuperating by observing his neighbors through the window. When he sees what he believes to be a murder, he decides to solve the crime himself. With help from his beautiful girlfriend and his nurse, he tries to catch the murderer without getting killed himself. Top-drawer Hitchcock blends exquisite suspense with occasional on-target laughs. Based on the story by Cornell Woolrich. **112m/C VHS, Beta, LV.** James Stewart, Grace Kelly, Thelma Ritter, Wendell Corey, Raymond Burr, Judith Evelyn; ***D:*** Alfred Hitchcock; ***W:*** John Michael Hayes; ***C:*** Robert Burks; ***M:*** Franz Waxman. Edgar Allan Poe Awards '54: Best Screenplay; Nominations: Academy Awards '54: Best Director (Hitchcock), Best Screenplay, Best Sound. *MCA, TLF, HMV*

A Reason to Believe 🦴🦴 **1995 (R)** Campus date rape drama filmed at writer/director Tirola's alma mater, Miami University. Charlotte (Smith) goes to her boyfriend Wesley's (Quinn) big frat party, even though he's away and asked her not to. She drinks and flirts (a lot) with his best friend Jim (Underwood) and eventually leaves to collapse in a stupor on Wesley's bed. Jim follows and rapes her, though he'll tell his buddies Charlotte was a willing participant, which Wesley angrily believes. Meanwhile, the traumatized Charlotte is taken up by Linda (Emelin), the leader of the student feminist organization who wants the fraternities disbanded. Somewhat preachy and predicatable. **109m/C VHS.** Allison Smith, Jay Underwood, Daniel Quinn, Georgia Emelin, Obba Babatunde; ***D:*** Douglas Tirola; ***W:*** Douglas Tirola; ***C:*** Sarah Cawley. *VMK*

Reason to Die 🦴 **1990 (R)** Bounty hunter uses his own girlfriend as a decoy to trap a psychotic prostitute killer. **86m/C VHS, LV.** Liam Cundill, Wings Hauser, Anneline Kriel, Arnold Vosloo; ***D:*** Tim Spring. *VMK*

A Reason to Live, A Reason to Die 🦴🦴 *Massacre at Fort Holman; Una Ragione Per Vivere e Una Per Morire* **1973** A bland Italian-French-German-Spanish western in which a group of condemned men attempt to take a Confederate fort. **90m/C VHS, Beta.** James Coburn, Telly Savalas, Bud Spencer, Robert Burton; ***D:*** Tonino Valerii. *NO*

Rebecca 🦴🦴🦴🦴 **1940** Based on Daphne Du Maurier's best-selling novel about a young unsophisticated girl who marries a moody and prominent country gentleman haunted by the memory of his first wife. Fontaine and Olivier turn in fine performances as the unlikely couple. Suspenseful and surprising. Hitchcock's first American film and only Best Picture Oscar. Laserdisc features: rare screen tests of Vivien Leigh, Anne Baxter, Loretta Young, and Joan Fontaine, footage from Rebecca's winning night at the Academy Awards, original radio broadcasts of film by Orson Welles and David O. Selznick, and commentary of film with interview excerpts with Hitchcock. **130m/B VHS, Beta, LV.** Joan Fontaine, Laurence Olivier, Judith Anderson, George Sanders, Nigel Bruce, Florence Bates, Gladys Cooper, Reginald Denny, Leo G. Carroll, Sir C. Aubrey Smith, Melville Cooper; ***D:*** Alfred Hitchcock; ***W:*** Joan Harrison, Robert Sherwood; ***C:*** George Barnes; ***M:*** Franz Waxman. Academy Awards '40: Best Black and White

Cinematography, Best Picture; National Board of Review Awards '40: 10 Best Films of the Year; Nominations: Academy Awards '40: Best Actor (Olivier), Best Actress (Fontaine), Best Adapted Screenplay, Best Director (Hitchcock), Best Film Editing, Best Interior Decoration, Best Supporting Actress (Anderson), Best Original Score. *FOX, HMV, BTV*

Rebecca of Sunnybrook Farm 🦴🦴 **1917** The original film version of the tale about an orphan who spreads sunshine and good cheer to all those around her. Silent with organ score. Based on the popular novel by Kate Douglas Wiggin; remade with Shirley Temple in 1938. **77m/B VHS, Beta, LV.** Mary Pickford, Eugene O'Brien, Marjorie Daw, Helen Jerome Eddy; ***D:*** Marshall Neilan; ***M:*** Gaylord Carter. *CCB*

Rebecca of Sunnybrook Farm 🦴🦴½ **1938** Temple becomes a radio star over her aunt's objections in this bouncy musical that has nothing to do with the famous Kate Douglas Wiggin novel. Temple sings a medley of her hits, and dances the finale with Bill "Bojangles" Robinson. ♫On the Good Ship Lollipop/When I'm With You/Animal Crackers medley; Crackly Corn Flakes; Alone With You; Happy Ending; Au Revoir; An Old Straw Hat; Come and Get Your Happiness; Parade of the Wooden Soldiers. **80m/B VHS, Beta, LV.** Shirley Temple, Randolph Scott, Jack Haley, Phyllis Brooks, Gloria Stuart, Slim Summerville, Bill Robinson, Helen Westley, William Demarest; ***D:*** Allan Dwan; ***C:*** Arthur C. Miller. *FOX, MLB, MLT*

Rebel 🦴½ **1973 (PG)** Mumbling student radical must decide between his love for a country girl and his loyalty to an underground terrorist organization. Notable (or not) for display of early Stallone. **80m/C VHS, Beta.** Sylvester Stallone, Anthony Page, Rebecca Grimes. *NO*

Rebel 🦴½ **1985 (R)** A U.S. Marine falls in love with a Sydney nightclub singer and goes AWOL during WWII. Stylish but empty and badly cast. **93m/C VHS, Beta, LV.** *AU* Matt Dillon, Debbie Byrne, Bryan Brown, Bill Hunter, Ray Barrett; ***D:*** Michael Jenkins. *LIV, VES*

Rebel High 🦴½ **1988 (R)** Hijinks occur at a high school where youngsters study guerilla warfare and teachers wear bullet-proof vests. **92m/C VHS, Beta.** Harvey Berger, Stu Trivax, Larry Gimple, Shawn Goldwater; ***D:*** Harry Jacobs. *ACA*

Rebel Love 🦴 **1985** Love grows between a northern widow and a Confederate spy. In better hands it might have been a good story. Here, it's overwrought and embarrassing historical melodrama. **84m/C VHS, Beta.** Terence Knox, Jamie Rose, Fred Ryan; ***D:*** Milton Bagby Jr.; ***W:*** Milton Bagby Jr. *LIV, VES*

Rebel Rousers 🦴🦴 **1969** A motorcycle gang wreaks havoc in a small town where a drag-race is being held to see who will get the pregnant girlfriend of Dern's high-school buddy as the prize. Young Nicholson in striped pants steals the show. **81m/C VHS, Beta.** Jack Nicholson, Cameron Mitchell, Diane Ladd, Bruce Dern, Harry Dean Stanton; ***D:*** Martin B. Cohen. *MED*

The Rebel Set 🦴🦴½ *Beatsville* **1959** The owner of a beat generation coffeehouse plans an armed robbery with the help of some buddies. Genuinely suspenseful, competently directed. **72m/B VHS, Beta.** Gregg Palmer, Kathleen Crowley, Edward Platt, John Lupton, Ned Glass, Don Sullivan, Vicki Dougan, I. Stanford Jolley; ***D:*** Gene Fowler Jr.; ***C:*** Karl Struss. *SNC*

Rebel Storm 🦴 **1990 (R)** A group of freedom fighters team up to rescue America from the totalitarian rulers that are in charge in 2099 A.D. **99m/C VHS, Beta, LV.** Zach Galligan, Wayne Crawford, June Chadwick, Rod McCary, John Rhys-Davies, Elizabeth Kiefer; ***D:*** Francis Schaeffer. *ACA*

Rebel Vixens *Woof!* **1985** Even though the war is over, ex-confederate soldiers continue looting and raping, until a brothel-full of prostitutes concoct a plan that has a lot to do with softcore sex. **94m/C VHS, Beta.** Maria Lease, Roda Spain. *MED*

Rebel Without a Cause 🦴🦴🦴🦴 **1955** James Dean's most memorable screen appearance. In the second of his three films, he plays a troubled teenager from the right side of the tracks. Dean's portrayal of Jim Stark, a teen alienated from both his parents and peers, is excellent. He befriends outcasts Wood and Mineo in a police station and together they find a commonground. Superb young stars carry this in-the-gut story of adolescence. All three leads met with real-life tragic ends. **111m/C VHS, Beta, LV.** James Dean, Natalie Wood, Sal Mineo, Jim Backus, Nick Adams, Dennis Hopper, Ann Doran, William Hopper, Rochelle Hudson, Corey Allen, Edward Platt; ***D:*** Nicholas Ray; ***W:*** Stewart Stern; ***M:*** Leonard Rosenman. Nominations: Academy Awards '54: Best Supporting Actor (Mineo); Academy Awards '55: Best Story, Best Supporting Actress (Wood). *WAR*

The Rebels 🦴🦴 **1979** In the sequel to the television mini series "The Bastard," Philip Kent (Stevens) continues his Revolutionary War battle on the side of American independence. He is assisted by Southerner Judson Fletcher (Johnson) in thwarting an assassination attempt on George Washington. In addition to Bosley's Ben Franklin, "The Rebels" offers Backus as John Hancock. Followed by "The Seekers;" based on the novel by John Jakes. **190m/C VHS.** Andrew Stevens, Don Johnson, Doug McClure, Jim Backus, Richard Basehart, Joan Blondell, Tom Bosley, Rory Calhoun, MacDonald Carey, Kim Cattrall, William Daniels, Anne Francis, Peter Graves, Pamela Hensley, Wilfrid Hyde-White, Nehemiah Persoff, William Smith, Forrest Tucker, Tanya Tucker, Robert Vaughn, Deborah Richter; ***D:*** Russ Mayberry. *MCA*

Reborn 🦴🦴 **1978** A faith healer and a talent scout hire actors to be cured of fake ailments. **91m/C VHS, Beta.** Dennis Hopper, Michael Moriarty, Francesco Rabal, Antonella Murgia. *VES*

Reckless 🦴🦴 **1935** Harlow, in a role originally intended for Joan Crawford, plays a showgirl coveted by a millionaire and secretly loved by her manager. Unfortunately, Harlow couldn't pull off the acting (much less the singing and dancing), although the plot strangely paralleled her own life. Songs include "Reckless," "Ev'rything's Been Done Before," "Trocadero," "Hear What My Heart Is Saying" and "Cyclone." **96m/B VHS, LV.** Jean Harlow, William Powell, Franchot Tone, May Robson, Ted Healy, Nat Pendleton, Rosalind Russell; ***D:*** Victor Fleming. *MGM*

Reckless 🦴🦴½ **1984 (R)** A sincere movie about a "good" girl who finds herself obsessed with a rebel from the wrong side of her small town. Differs from 1950s' wrong-side-of-the-track flicks only in updated sex and music. **93m/C VHS, Beta, LV.** Aidan Quinn, Daryl Hannah, Kenneth McMillan, Cliff DeYoung, Lois Smith, Adam Baldwin, Dan Hedaya, Jennifer Grey, Pamela Springsteen; ***D:*** James Foley; ***W:*** Chris Columbus; ***M:*** Thomas Newman. *MGM*

Reckless 🦴🦴 **1995 (PG-13)** Rachel (Farrow) thinks she has a happy marriage and family but her husband (Goldwyn) informs her that he's hired a hit man to kill her. This startling revelation sends her on a 15-year journey in which she meets many other people who are not what they seem. Rene and Lucas go for an ultra-stylized fable theme, exploring Rachel's (and America's) aversion to dealing with the world as it really is. Quirky characters and situations are at turns amusing and annoying. Adapted by Lucas from his own play. **91m/C VHS, LV.** Mia Farrow, Scott Glenn, Mary-Louise Parker, Tony Goldwyn, Stephen Dorff, Eileen Brennan, Giancarlo Esposito, Deborah Rush; ***D:*** Norman Rene; ***W:*** Craig Lucas; ***C:*** Frederick Elmes; ***M:*** Stephen Endelman. *HMK*

Reckless Disregard 🦴½ **1984** A doctor whose career is ruined by a news report accusing him of involvement in a drug scam sues the newscaster. Made for television saga based on Dan Rather's "60 Minutes" story and ensuing lawsuit. **92m/C VHS, Beta.** Leslie Nielsen, Tess Harper, Ronny Cox, Kate Lynch; ***D:*** Harvey Hart. *LIV, VES*

Reckless Kelly 🦴🦴½ **1993 (PG)** Australian bank robber, pop culture hero, and local video store owner Kelly is upset when his gang's island retreat is about to be sold to a Japanese conglomerate, unless he can come up with a higher offer. So he prepares for a last-ditch defense of his home. Slapstick homage to legendary Australian outlaw Ned Kelly. **81m/C VHS.** *AU* Yahoo Serious, Hugo Weaving, Melora Hardin, Alexei Sayle, Bob Maza, Kathleen Freeman; ***D:*** Yahoo Serious; ***W:*** Yahoo Serious. *WAR*

Reckless Moment 🦴🦴🦴 **1949** A mother commits murder to save her daughter from an unsavory older man, and finds herself blackmailed. Gripping, intense thriller. **82m/B VHS, Beta.** James Mason, Joan Bennett, Geraldine Brooks; ***D:*** Max Ophuls; ***C:*** Burnett Guffey. *LCA*

The Reckless Way 🦴½ **1936** A young woman struggles for her big break into the movies. **72m/B VHS, Beta.** Marion Nixon, Kane Richmond, Inez Courtney, Malcolm McGregor, Harry Harvey, Arthur Howard; ***D:*** Raymond K. Johnson. *GPV*

Record of a Tenement Gentleman 🦴🦴 **1947** An abandoned child picks a grumpy, middle-aged widow as a surrogate mother and she and her crazy neighbors come to love the little boy. Surprise ending. Japanese with subtitles. **72m/B VHS.** *JP* Choko Iida, Hohi Aoki, Chishu Ryu, Eitaro Ozawa; ***D:*** Yasujiro Ozu. *NYF*

Recruits 🦴 **1986 (R)** Sophomoric gagfest about an inept Californian police force. Typical 80's-style mindless "comedy:" dumb gags ensue from perfunctory premise. **81m/C VHS, Beta, LV.** Alan Deveau, Annie McAuley, Lolita Davidovich; ***D:*** Rafal Zeilinski. *LIV, VES*

The Rector's Wife 🦴🦴 **1994** Anna Bouverie (Duncan) has spent 20 years as a clergyman's wife, scrimping and slaving to raise a family, serve God, and work for the parish on limited means. Tired of the financial strain she takes a job at a local supermarket causing additional disturbances in her already shaky marriage, disapproval of the parish, and the sudden interest of three different men. Based on the novel by Joanna Trollope; on four cassettes. **208m/C VHS.** *GB* Lindsay Duncan, Jonathan Coy, Simon Fenton, Lucy Dawson, Joyce Redman, Stephen Dillane, Ronald Pickup, Miles Anderson, Prunella Scales, Jonathan Cecil; ***D:*** Giles Foster; ***W:*** Hugh Whitemore; ***M:*** Richard Hartley. *SIG, AAE, PAP*

Red Alert 🦴🦴½ **1977** Good, suspenseful, topical made for televison thriller about nuclear meltdown. Will Minneapolis be saved? Usually Barbeau's name in the credits is a red alert, but this one is better than most. **95m/C VHS, Beta.** William Devane, Ralph Waite, Michael Brandon, Adrienne Barbeau; ***D:*** Billy Hale. *PAR*

The Red and the Black 🦴🦴🦴 *Le Rouge et le Noir* **1957** A big budgeted French adaptation of the classic Stendhal novel. A young man from the country seeks success, first in the Church and later in the employment and seduction of the gentry. In French with English subtitles. **134m/B VHS, Beta.** *FR* Danielle Darrieux, Gerard Philipe; ***D:*** Claude Autant-Lara. *INJ, IVY, MRV*

The Red and the White 🦴🦴🦴 *Csillagosok, Katonak* **1968** Epic war drama about the civil war between the Red Army and the non-communist Whites in Russia in 1918. Told from the perspective of Hungarians who fought alongside the Reds. Little dialogue. In Hungarian with English subtitles. **92m/B VHS, LV.** *HU* ***D:*** Miklos Jancso. *KIV, INJ*

The Red Badge of Courage 🦴🦴🦴½ **1951** John Huston's adaptation of the Stephen Crane Civil War novel is inspired, despite cutting room hatchet job by the studio. A classic study of courage and cowardice. Sweeping battle scenes and intense personal drama. **69m/B VHS, Beta.** Audie Murphy, Bill Mauldin, Douglas Dick, Royal Dano, Andy Devine; ***D:*** John Huston. National Board of Review Awards '51: 10 Best Films of the Year. *KUI, MGM, HMV*

Red Ball Express 🦴🦴½ **1952** Fast-paced action highlights this WWII story about the transportation corp that must supply the gas, food, and ammunition necessary for General Patton's tank assault on Nazi-held Paris. Tough company leader Lt. Campbell (Chandler) must get the cooperation of both his first sergeant (Nicol), who holds a pre-war grudge, and a black corporal (Poitier), who believes he's the target of racism, in order to accomplish his mission. **84m/B VHS.** Jeff Chandler, Alex Nicol, Sidney Poitier, Charles Drake, Hugh O'Brian, Jack Kelly, Judith Braun, Jacqueline Duval; ***D:***

Budd Boetticher; ***W:*** John Michael Hayes; ***C:*** Maury Gertsman. *MCA*

The Red Balloon ½ **1956** The story of Pascal, a lonely French boy who befriends a wondrous red balloon which follows him everywhere. Lovely, finely done parable of childhood, imagination and friendship. **34m/C VHS, Beta, LV, 8mm.** *FR* Pascal Lamorisse; ***D:*** Albert Lamorisse. Academy Awards '56: Best Original Screenplay; National Board of Review Awards '57: 5 Best Foreign Films of the Year. *HMV, HHT, DVT*

Red Balloon/Occurrence at Owl Creek Bridge ½ **1962** Two classic award-winning shorts have been combined on one tape: "The Red Balloon" (color, 1956) and "An Occurrence at Owl Creek Bridge." The former is a children's story about a balloon on the loose; the latter is a perfectly rendered adaptation of the Ambrose Bierce short story of the same title, a taut narration of a Civil War hanging. **60m/C VHS, Beta.** *FR* Pascal Lamorisse, Roger Jacquet; ***D:*** Robert Enrico, Albert Lamorisse. *SUE, VYY, WFV*

Red Barry **1938** A comic strip detective tries to track down criminals who threaten the world. Thirteen episodes on one videotape. **?m/B VHS.** Buster Crabbe, Frances Robinson, Edna Sedgwick, Cyril Delevanti, Frank Lackteen; ***D:*** Ford Beebe, Alan James. *NOS, MLB*

Red Beard *Akahige* **1965** An uncharacteristic drama by Kurosawa, about a young doctor in Japan awakening to life and love under the tutelage of a compassionate old physician. Highly acclaimed; in Japanese with English subtitles. **185m/B VHS, Beta, LV.** *JP* Toshiro Mifune, Yuzo Kayama, Yoshio Tsuchiya, Reiko Dan; ***D:*** Akira Kurosawa. *INJ, CRC, FCT*

Red Blooded American Girl **1990 (R)** A scientist develops a virus that turns people into vampires. Those infected hit the streets in search of blood. **89m/C VHS, Beta, LV.** *CA* Christopher Plummer, Andrew Stevens, Heather Thomas, Kim Coates; ***D:*** David Blyth. *PSM*

Red Dawn ½ **1984 (PG-13)** During WWIII, Russian invaders overrun America's heartland and take over the country. Eight small-town teenagers, calling themselves the Wolverines, hide out in the rugged countryside and fight the Russians. Swayze and Grey met again in "Dirty Dancing." **114m/C VHS, Beta, LV.** Patrick Swayze, C. Thomas Howell, Harry Dean Stanton, Powers Boothe, Lea Thompson, Charlie Sheen, Ben Johnson, Jennifer Grey, Ron O'Neal, William Smith; ***D:*** John Milius; ***W:*** John Milius, Kevin Reynolds; ***M:*** Basil Poledouris. *MGM*

Red Desert **1950** The Pecos Kid is sent to track down the theft of a shipment of gold. **60m/B VHS, Beta, LV.** Jack Holt, Donald (Don "Red") Barry, Tom Neal, Joseph Crehan, Tom London; ***D:*** Charles Marquis Warren. *NO*

The Red Desert **1964** Antonioni's first color film, depicting an alienated Italian wife who searches for meaning in the industrial lunar landscape of northern Italy, to no avail. Highly acclaimed, and a masterpiece of visual form. Cinematography by Carlo di Palma. In Italian with English subtitles. **120m/C VHS, Beta.** *IT* Monica Vitti, Richard Harris, Carlos Chionetti; ***D:*** Michelangelo Antonioni; ***W:*** Michelangelo Antonioni, Tonino Guerra; ***C:*** Carlo DiPalma. Venice Film Festival '64: International Critics Award, Best Film. *FCT, INJ, CVC*

Red Desert Penitentiary **1983** A spoof of movie-making featuring caricatures of industry-types. **104m/C VHS, Beta.** James Michael Taylor, Cathryn Bissell, Will Rose; ***D:*** George Sluizer. *NO*

Red Dust **1932** The overseer of a rubber plantation in Indochina causes all kinds of trouble when he falls in love with a young engineer's wife. Filled with free-spirited humor and skillfully directed; remarkably original. Remade in 1940 as "Congo Maisie" and in 1954 as "Mogambo." **83m/B VHS, Beta.** Clark Gable, Jean Harlow, Mary Astor, Gene Raymond, Donald Crisp; ***D:*** Victor Fleming. *MGM*

Red Earth **197?** A satire about life under Hungarian socialism. Szanto is a bauxite mixer whose pigs have rooted out high quality bauxite from his backyard. Only the local bauxite prospectors don't want to believe in luck (and pigs) and credit, instead, careful planning. When Szanto's village is turned into a vast open mine, he's blamed. In Hungarian with English subtitles. **105m/C VHS.** *HU* Imre Nemeth, Sandor Kocsis, Kalman Toronyi, Ferenc Togh, Vilmos Gadori; ***D:*** Laszlo Vitezy; ***W:*** Istvan Darday. *FCT*

Red Firecracker, Green Firecracker ½ *Paoda Shuang Deng* **1993 (R)** Set in northern China before the 1911 revolution, this gorgeous saga focuses on the fortunes of the Cai family. The family, whose wealth depends on their fireworks business, has no male heirs and is headed by daughter Chun Zhi (Jing). To assume this lofty position, Chun Zhi must dress like a man and is forbidden to marry but that doesn't stop her from falling in love with bold young travelling artist Nie Bao (Gang). The household is thrown into a frenzy by their affair and it's decided that all Chun Zhi's potential suitors must undergo a firecracker ritual in order to win her hand. Mandarin Chinese with subtitles. **111m/C VHS.** *HK CH* Ning Jing, Wu Gang, Zhao Xiaorui, Gai Yang; ***D:*** He Ping; ***W:*** Da Ying; ***C:*** Yang Lun. *HMK*

Red Flag: The Ultimate Game ½ **1981** Pilots rival for success in battle simulation training with terrible consequences. Fine performances cover plot weaknesses. Well-written dialogue. Made for television. **100m/C VHS, Beta.** Barry Bostwick, William Devane, Joan Van Ark, Fred McCarren, Debra Feuer, George Coe, Linden Chiles, Arlen Dean Snyder; ***D:*** Don Taylor. *LIV*

The Red Fury **197?** Young Indian boy struggles to overcome prejudice and caring for his horse shows him the way. Good family viewing. **105m/C VHS.** William Jordan, Kathy Cannon. *TPV, HHE, BPG*

Red Garters ½ **1954** A musical parody of old-time westerns which doesn't quite come off. Mitchell palys the cowpoke who comes to town to avenge the death of his brother with Clooney as the saloon singer who uses him to make boyfriend Carson jealous. The adequate songs include "Red Garters," "Man and Woman," "A Dime and a Dollar," and "Vaquero." **91m/C VHS.** Guy Mitchell, Rosemary Clooney, Jack Carson, Gene Barry, Pat Crowley, Joanne Gilbert, Frank Faylen, Reginald Owen, Buddy Ebsen; ***D:*** George Marshall; ***W:*** Michael Fessier; ***M:*** Jay Livingston, Ray Evans. Nominations: Academy Awards '54: Best Art Direction/Set Decoration (Color). *PAR*

The Red Half-Breed ½ **1970** A lonely half-breed Indian, wrongly accused of murder, discovers the real killer while running from the law. **103m/C VHS, Beta.** Daniel Pilon, Genevieve Deloir; ***D:*** Gilles Carle. *NWV*

Red Headed Stranger ½ **1987 (R)** Willie Nelson vehicle based on his 1975 album. Nelson is a gun-totin' preacher who kills his wife and is led to salvation by a good farm woman. But honestly: Morgan Fairchild as Willie Nelson's wife? Please. **108m/C VHS, Beta, LV.** Willie Nelson, Katharine Ross, Morgan Fairchild; ***D:*** William D. Wittliff; ***W:*** William D. Wittliff. *NLC*

Red Headed Woman **1932** Harlow plays an unscrupulous woman who charms her way into the lives of influential men. She causes her boss to divorce his wife and marry her while she sleeps with the chauffeur (Boyer) and others. Audiences loved the scandalous material, but the Hays Office objected to the fact that the immoral woman goes unpunished. Boyer's small but important role salvaged his floundering American film career. Harlow is sultry and funny. **79m/B VHS, Beta.** Jean Harlow, Chester Morris, Lewis Stone, Leila Hyams, Una Merkel, Henry Stephenson, May Robson, Charles Boyer, Harvey Clark; ***D:*** Jack Conway. *MGM, FCT*

Red Heat ½ **1985** Blair is a tourist in East Germany mistakenly arrested and sent to a rough women's prison. Her fiance tries to free her. Meanwhile, she has to deal with tough-lady fellow jail bird Kristel. Familiar and marginal. **104m/C VHS, Beta, LV.** Linda Blair, Sylvia Kristel, Sue Kiel, William Ostrander; ***D:*** Robert Collector. *LIV, VES*

Red Heat **1988 (R)** Two cops—one from the Soviet Union, one from Chicago—team up to catch the Eastern Bloc's biggest drug czar. Lots of action, but at times it seems too similar to Hill's earlier hit "48 Hours." Film claims to be the first major U.S. production shot in Red Square, Moscow. **106m/C VHS, Beta, LV.** Arnold Schwarzenegger, James Belushi, Peter Boyle, Ed O'Ross, Laurence "Larry" Fishburne, Gina Gershon, Richard Bright; ***D:*** Walter Hill; ***W:*** Walter Hill; ***M:*** James Horner. *LIV, TLF*

Red Hot ½ **1995 (PG)** Alexi (Getty), a young Russian classical musician, is secretly smuggled American rock 'n' roll music (it's 1959) by his uncle. He immediately decides to form a band and plots the first underground Soviet rock concert. Too bad girlfriend Valentina's (Gugino) dad is a disapproving highly ranked Communist Party official and the KGB are giving Alexi the evil eye. **95m/C VHS, LV.** Balthazar Getty, Carla Gugino, Donald Sutherland, Armin Mueller-Stahl; ***D:*** Paul Haggis; ***W:*** Paul Haggis, Michael Maurer. *COL*

The Red House **1947** Robinson plays a crippled farmer who, after his daughter brings home a suitor, attempts to keep everyone from a mysterious red house located on his property. Madness and murder prevail. Strange film noir about tangled relationships and unsuccessful attempts to bury the horrid past. Based on the novel by George Agnew Chamberlain. **100m/B VHS, Beta.** Edward G. Robinson, Lon McCallister, Judith Anderson, Allene Roberts, Rory Calhoun, Ona Munson, Julie London; ***D:*** Delmer Daves; ***M:*** Miklos Rozsa. *CNG, NOS, SNC*

The Red Inn *L'Auberge Rouge* **1951** Yes, it is a comedy. An innkeeper and his wife have a second career involving the robbery and murder of stagecoach travellers staying at their isolated inn. And it's up to a monk (Fernandel) to stop the mayhem. French with subtitles. Yves Montand sings on the soundtrack. **95m/B VHS.** *FR* Fernandel, Francoise Rosay, Julien Carette, Gregoire Aslan, Marie-Claire Olivia, Lud Germain; ***D:*** Claude Autant-Lara; ***W:*** Jean Aurenche, Pierre Bost; ***C:*** Andre Bac; ***M:*** Rene Cloerec. *FCT*

Red Kimono **1925** Exploitative silent melodrama about a young woman ditched by her husband. She becomes a prostitute, but is redeemed by true love. Interesting slice of its period. **95m/B VHS, Beta.** Tyrone Power Sr., Priscilla Boner, Nellie Bly Baker, Mary Carr; ***D:*** Walter Lang. *NOS, VYY, DVT*

Red King, White Knight ½ **1989 (R)** An assassin tries to kill Mikhail Gorbachev during superpower peace talks. Ex-s pook Skerritt returns to duty to thwart him. Better than most "topical" thrill ers. Made for cable television. **106m/C VHS, Beta.** Tom Skerritt, Max von Sydow, Helen Mirren; ***D:*** Geoff Murphy. *HBO*

Red Kiss *Rouge Baiser* **1985** In 1952 Paris, Nadia, a 15-year-old French-Jewish Stalinist of Polish descent falls in love with Stephane, an older, apolitical photographer. She's torn between love and politics; he's worried (rightly) about her being underage; and to make matters more complicated, her Polish mother has been reunited with her first love and Nadia's family may be split apart. The sensual Valandrey is a real find in her difficult coming-of-age role. In French with English subtitles. **110m/C VHS, LV.** *FR* Charlotte Valandrey, Lambert Wilson, Marthe Keller, Gunter Lamprecht, Laurent Terzieff; ***D:*** Vera Belmont; ***W:*** Vera Belmont. Berlin International Film Festival '86: Best Actress (Valandrey). *FXL, FCT, INJ*

The Red Light Sting **1984** A Justice Department rookie (Bridges) and a call girl (Fawcett) reluctantly team up to con the Mafia in order to convict a San Francisco rackets czar. Goes down easy, but also easily forgotten or skipped. **96m/C VHS, Beta.** Farrah Fawcett, Beau Bridges, Harold Gould, Paul Burke, Sunny Johnson; ***D:*** Rod Holcomb. *MCA*

Red Lights Ahead **1936** Grandpa tries to save the day as he fights against spiritualism and crystal balls to help a friend prove that he is not running a scam. **63m/C VHS.** Andy Clyde, Paula Stone, Roger Imhof, Frank "Junior" Coghlan, Ben Alexander, Matty

Kemp, Sam Flint, Addison Randall, Lucile Gleason, Dann Doran; **D:** Roland D. Reed. *GPV.*

Red Line 7000 ✗✗ **1965** High stakes auto racers drive fast cars and date women. Excellent racing footage in otherwise routine four-wheel fest. **110m/C VHS, LV.** James Caan, Laura Devon, Gail Hire, Charlene Holt, John Crawford, Marianna Hill, George Takei; **D:** Howard Hawks; **C:** Milton Krasner. *PAR, FCT*

Red Lion ✗✗½ *Akage* **1969** A bumbling horse-tender in feudal Japan impersonates a military officer to impress his family, only to be swept into leading a liberating revolution. In Japanese with English subtitles. **115m/C VHS, Beta.** *JP* Toshiro Mifune, Shima Iwashita; **D:** Kihachi Okamoto. *INJ, VDA*

The Red Menace *Woof!* **1949** Anti-Communist propaganda, made with unknown actors in documentary style has little to offer today's viewers other than unintentional laughs. Picture the Commies offering naive Americans money and sex to join the party, and you'll have an idea of the intellectual talent that went into this one. **87m/B VHS, LV.** Robert Rockwell, Hanne Axman, Shepard Menken, Betty Lou Gerson, Barbara Fuller; **D:** R.G. Springsteen. *REP, FCT*

Red Nightmare ✗½ **1962** Anti-communist propaganda produced for the Department of Defense by Warner Brothers features the cast of "Dragnet." The story dramatizes the Red Menace, with communists conspiring to take over America, and shows what would happen to life in a small American town if the Commies took over. **30m/B VHS, Beta.** Jack Webb, Jack Kelly, Jeanne Cooper, Peter Brown. *VYY, IHF*

Red Nights ✗ **1987** A country boy goes to Hollywood seeking success and finds instead corruption, decadence, and dishonesty. Excellent soundtrack by Tangerine Dream. **90m/C VHS, Beta.** Christopher Parker, Jack Carter, Brian Matthews; **D:** Izhak Hanooka. *TWE*

Red Planet Mars ✗✗ **1952** Anti-communist, pro-Christianity story about scientists discovering that the Voice of Radio Free Mars belongs to God. Incoherent film overburdened with messages about politics, religion, and science was ahead of its time. Based on the play "Red Planet" by John L. Balderson and John Hoare. **87m/B VHS.** Peter Graves, Andrea King, Marvin Miller, Herbert Berghof, House Peters Jr., Vince Barnett; **D:** Harry Horner; **W:** Anthony Veiller, John Balderston. *MGM, FCT*

The Red Pony ✗✗✗ **1949** A young boy escapes from his family's fighting through his love for a pet pony. Based on the novel by John Steinbeck. Remade for television in 1976. Timeless classic that the whole family can enjoy. **89m/C VHS, LV.** Myrna Loy, Robert Mitchum, Peter Miles, Louis Calhern, Shepperd Strudwick, Margaret Hamilton, Beau Bridges; **D:** Lewis Milestone; **C:** Gaetano Antonio "Tony" Gaudio; **M:** Aaron Copland. *REP, KUI*

The Red Pony ✗✗✗ **1976** Excellent TV remake of a classic 1949 adaptation of John Steinbeck. Fonda is superb as a troubled young boy's difficult father. **101m/C VHS, Beta, LV.** Henry Fonda, Maureen O'Hara, Clint Howard, Jack Elam, Ben Johnson; **D:** Robert Totten. *BFA*

The Red Raven Kiss-Off ✗ **1990 (R)** A seedy Hollywood detective becomes the key suspect in a movie-making murder. Based on the 1930s' Dan Turner mystery stories. Made for video. **93m/C VHS, Beta.** Marc Singer, Tracy Scoggins, Nicholas Worth, Arte Johnson; **D:** Christopher Lewis. *FRH*

Red Riding Hood ✗✗½ **1988** Musical version of story of wolf who has little girl fetish. **81m/C VHS, Beta.** Isabella Rossellini, Craig T. Nelson, Rocco Sisto. *MGM, CAN*

Red River ✗✗✗✗ **1948** The classic Hawks epic about a gruelling cattle drive and the battle of wills between father and son. Generally regarded as one of the best westerns ever made, and Wayne's shining moment as a reprehensible, obsessive man. Featuring Clift in his first film. Restored version has eight minutes of previously edited material. Remade for television in 1988 with James Arness and Bruce Boxleitner. **133m/B VHS, Beta, LV.** John Wayne, Montgomery Clift, Walter Brennan, Joanne Dru, John Ireland, Noah Beery Jr., Paul Fix, Coleen Gray, Harry Carey Jr., Harry Carey Sr., Chief Yowlachie, Hank Worden; **D:** Howard Hawks; **W:** Borden Chase, Charles Schnee; **M:** Dimitri Tiomkin. Nominations: Academy Awards '48: Best Film Editing, Best Story. *MGM, TLF, RDG*

Red River Valley ✗✗ *Man of the Frontier* **1936** Autry and partner Burnette go undercover to find out who's plaguing a dam construction site with explosions. Not to be confused with a 1941 Roy Rogers pic bearing the same title. **60m/B VHS.** Gene Autry, Smiley Burnette, Frances Grant, Boothe Howard, Sam Flint, George Chesebro, Charles "Blackie" King, Eugene Jackson, Frank LaRue, Lloyd Ingraham; **D:** B. Reeves Eason. *NOS, VDM, VCN*

Red Rock Outlaw ✗ **1947** A sleazy character tries to kill his twin brother and takes his place as an honest rancher. **56m/B VHS, Beta, LV.** Lee White. *NO*

Red Rock West ✗✗✗½ **1993 (R)** Nothing is what it seems in this stylish and entertaining film noir set in a desolate Wyoming town. Perennial loser and nice guy Michael (Cage) is headed to a job at oil rig, but blows his chance by admitting he has a bad leg. Landing in the tiny burg of Red Rock, he's mistaken for the hit man hired by local barkeep Walsh to kill his pretty wife (Boyle). Then Boyle doubles Walsh's offer—what's a film noir boy to do? And Hopper, the real killer, strides into town. Full of twists, turns, and shades of "El Mariachi," this enjoyable, well-acted thriller is a real gem that escaped directly to cable before being rescued by a San Francisco exhibitor. **98m/C VHS, LV.** Nicolas Cage, Dennis Hopper, Lara Flynn Boyle, J.T. Walsh, Timothy Carhart, Dan Shor, Dwight Yoakam, Bobby Joe McFadden; **D:** John Dahl; **W:** John Dahl, Rick Dahl; **M:** William Olvis. Nominations: Independent Spirit Awards '95: Best Director (Dahl), Best Screenplay. *COL*

The Red Rope ✗½ **1937** A Western hero cuts his honeymoon short to track down some villains. **56m/B VHS.** Bob Steele, Lois January, Forrest Taylor, Charles "Blackie" King, Karl Hackett, Bobby Nelson; **D:** S. Roy Luby. *NOS, DVT*

Red Scorpion ✗ **1989 (R)** A Soviet soldier journeys to Africa where he is to assassinate the leader of a rebel group. Will he succeed or switch allegiances? Poor acting and directing abound. **102m/C VHS, LV.** Dolph Lundgren, M. Emmet Walsh, Al White, T.P. McKenna, Carmen Argenziano, Brion James, Regopstann; **D:** Joseph Zito; **W:** Arne Olsen, Jack Abramoff, Robert Abramoff. *VTR*

Red Scorpion 2 ✗½ **1994 (R)** Another "Dirty Dozen" rip-off finds your average ethnically-mixed good guys brought together by a government agency to be heroic. In this case the enemy is a neo-fascist businessman who uses skinheads to cause mayhem in minority communities. **90m/C VHS, LV.** Matt McColm, John Savage, Jennifer Rubin, Michael Ironside, Michael Covert, Real Andrews, George Touliatos; **D:** Michael Kennedy; **W:** Troy Bolotnick, Barry Victor; **M:** George Blondheim. *MCA*

Red Shoe Diaries ✗✗ **1992 (R)** After a woman's suicide her grieving lover discovers her diaries and finds out she led a secret erotic life, revolving around her shoe-salesman lover and a pair of sexy red shoes. Made for cable television; also available in an unrated version. **105m/C VHS, LV.** David Duchovny, Billy Wirth, Brigitte Bako; **D:** Zalman King. *REP*

Red Shoe Diaries 2: Double Dare ✗✗ **1992 (R)** The erotic sequel to "Red Shoe Diaries" follows the libidinous fancies of three women. Severance begins a sexual affair with a stranger only be torn between love and lust. Johnson gets naked to tease an office worker in the building next door. Crosby is a cop who is rejected by the man she desires—so she arrests and handcuffs him in order to play some kinky games. Also available in an unrated version. **92m/C VHS, LV.** Joan Severance, Laura Johnson, Denise Crosby, Steven Bauer, Arnold Vosloo, David Duchovny; **D:** Zalman King, Tibor Takacs. *REP, PMS*

Red Shoe Diaries 3: Another Woman's Lipstick ✗✗ **1993 (R)** Another sexual anthology focusing on three stories of desire from the made for cable television series. In "Another Woman's Lipstick" Zoey finds out her husband is having an affair and follows him to his liaison—only to become intrigued with his lover herself. "Just Like That" finds the up-tight Trudie falling for two very opposite men. "Talk to Me Baby" finds Ida and her lover Bud caught up in a very obsessional relationship. Also available in an unrated version. **90m/C VHS, LV.** Nina Siemaszko, Matthew LeBlanc, Tcheky Karyo, Maryam D'Abo, Richard Tyson, Lydie Denier, Christina Fulton, Kevin Haley, David Duchovny; **D:** Ted Kotcheff, Rafael Eisenman, Zalman King; **W:** Zalman King, Chloe King. *REP*

Red Shoe Diaries 4: Auto Erotica ✗✗ **1993 (R)** Yet another compilation of erotic tales courtesy of the Zalman King series. The first story finds a maid finding her employer's secret chamber and uncovering a very private fantasy. The second has an architect lured by a mystery woman into a game of seduction and the third finds a couple engaged in competitive obsessions. Also available in an unrated version. **83m/C VHS.** Ally Sheedy, Scott Plank, David Duchovny, Sheryl Lee, Nicholas Chinlund; **D:** Zalman King. *REP*

Red Shoe Diaries 5: Weekend Pass ✗✗ **1995 (R)** Yet another erotic saga from the cable series that features a model (Barbieri) hustling a pool hustler, a bounty hunter (Stansfield) becoming captivated by her prey, and an army recruit (Pouget) whose furlough involves a sexy drifter. **85m/C VHS.** Paula Barbieri, Claire Stansfield, Ely Pouget, Francesco Quinn, Ron Marquette, Tony Addabbo; **D:** Ted Kotcheff. *REP*

Red Shoe Diaries 6: How I Met My Husband ✗✗ **1995 (R)** Three more erotic vignettes from the cable series. "How I Met My Husband" finds Alice enrolling in a course on becoming a domanitrix and falling for Giuseppe, who's one of the training objects. Camille has inherited her father's vast fortune in "Naked in the Moonlight" on the condition that she take special care of his '57 Cadillac convertible—and the one mechanic allowed to work on the car. In "Midnight Bells," Claire reminisces about the mystery lover she meets on only one night of the year—New Year's Eve. **85m/C VHS.** Luigi Amodeo, Neith Hunter, Raven Snow, Carsten Norgaard, John Enos, Charlotte Lewis, David Duchovny; **D:** Anne Goursaud, Philippe Angers, Bernard Auroux. *REP*

The Red Shoes ✗✗✗✗ **1948** British classic about a young ballerina torn between love and success. Inspired by the Hans Christian Andersen fairy tale. Noted for its lavish use of Technicolor. **136m/C VHS, Beta, LV.** *GB* Anton Walbrook, Moira Shearer, Marius Goring, Leonide Massine, Robert Helpmann, Albert Basserman, Ludmila Tcherina, Esmond Knight; **D:** Emeric Pressburger, Michael Powell; **W:** Emeric Pressburger, Michael Powell; **C:** Jack Cardiff. Academy Awards '48: Best Art Direction/Set Decoration (Color), Best Score; Golden Globe Awards '49: Best Score; National Board of Review Awards '48: 10 Best Films of the Year; Nominations: Academy Awards '48: Best Film Editing, Best Picture, Best Story. *PAR, HMV*

The Red Shoes **1983** The Children's Theatre Company and School of Minneapolis perform their own unique interpretation of the Hans Christian Andersen story. **79m/C VHS, Beta.** *MCA*

Red Signals ✗✗ **1927** Mystery criminal makes trains collide. **70m/B VHS, Beta.** Wallace MacDonald, Earl Williams, Eva Novak, J.P. McGowan, Frank Rice; **D:** J.P. McGowan. *GPV, FCT*

Red Snow ✗ **1991** High in the Cascade Mountains, Kyle Lewis is the new snowboard instructor for the Hurricane Ridge Ski Resort. The job is fine in the beginning, until Kyle learns of the tragic fate of the last instructor. Before he knows it, Kyle is the next target and is framed for two murders. He secures the help of his fellow snowboard buddies in hopes of solving the mystery and getting the girl, too. High speed ski scenes and dangerous stunts are the film's only redeeming qualities. **86m/C VHS.** Carlo Scandiuzzi, Scott Galloway, Darla Slavens, Mitchell Cox, Tamar Tibbs, Brian Mahoney; ***D:*** Phillip J. Roth. *VHE*

Red Sonja ♪½ **1985 (PG-13)** Two warriors join forces against an evil queen in this sword and sorcery saga. Big, beautiful bodies everywhere, with Bergman returning from her Conan adventures. Little humor, few special effects, and weak acting make this a poor outing. **89m/C VHS, Beta, LV.** Arnold Schwarzenegger, Brigitte Nielsen, Sandahl Bergman, Paul Smith; ***D:*** Richard Fleischer; ***M:*** Ennio Morricone. Golden Raspberry Awards '85: Worst New Star (Nielsen). *MGM, FOX*

Red Sorghum ♪♪♪½ **1987** A stunning visual achievement, this new wave Chinese film (and Yimou's directorial debut) succeeds on many levels—as an ode to the color red, as dark comedy, and as a sweeping epic with fairy tale overtones. Set in rural China in the 1920s, during the period of the Japanese invasion. The sorghum plot nearby is a symbolic playing field in the movie's most stunning scenes. Here, people make love, murder, betray, and commit acts of bravery, all under the watchful eye of nature. In Mandarin with English subtitles. **91m/C VHS.** *CH* Gong Li, Jiang Wen, Ji Cun Hua; ***D:*** Zhang Yimou; ***C:*** Gu Changwei. *NYF, INJ*

The Red Stallion ♪½ **1947** Good film for animal lovers, but it loses something when it comes to human relationships. A young boy raises his pony into an award-winning racehorse that saves the farm when it wins the big race. Good outdoor photography. **82m/B VHS.** Robert Paige, Noreen Nash, Ted Donaldson, Jane Darwell; ***D:*** Lesley Selander. *NOS, MOV, HEG*

Red Sun ♪♪ **1971** A gunfighter, a samurai, and a French bandit fight each other in various combinations in the 1860s. Ludicrous and boring. **115m/C VHS, Beta.** *FR IT SP* Charles Bronson, Toshiro Mifune, Alain Delon, Ursula Andress; ***D:*** Terence Young; ***W:*** William Roberts; ***M:*** Maurice Jarre. *GEM*

Red Sun Rising ♪½ **1994 (R)** A detective tries to stop a turf war between Japanese mafia and Los Angeles street gangs. **95m/C VHS.** Don "The Dragon" Wilson, Terry Farrell, Michael Ironside, Mako; ***D:*** Francis Megahy. *IMP*

Red Surf ♪♪ **1990 (R)** Action abounds in this surfer film. A couple of hard-nosed wave-riders get involved with big money drug gangs and face danger far greater than the tide. **104m/C VHS, Beta, LV.** George Clooney, Doug Savant, Dedee Pfeiffer, Gene Simmons, Rick Najera, Philip McKeon; ***D:*** H. Gordon Boos. *ACA*

Red Tent ♪♪♪ *Krasnaya Palatka* **1969 (G)** A robust, sweeping man-versus-nature epic based on the true story of the Arctic stranding of Italian explorer Umberto Nobile's expedition in 1928. A Russian-Italian co-production. **121m/C Beta, LV.** Sean Connery, Claudia Cardinale, Peter Finch, Hardy Kruger, Massimo Girotti, Luigi Vannucchi; ***D:*** Mikhail Kalatozov; ***M:*** Ennio Morricone. *PAR*

Red, White & Busted ♪ *Outside In* **1975** Amnesty or prison? That is the scorching, virtually unanswerable question asked by indictment of America. We follow three friends during the Vietnam War and see how they were affected by the events, whether or not they went. **85m/C VHS, Beta, LV.** Darrell Larson, Heather Menzies, Dennia Oliveri, John Bill. *NO*

Red Wind ♪♪ **1991 (R)** Kris Morrow is a psychotherapist whose latest patient, Lila, has a number of disturbing sadomasochistic fantasies. When Kris feels she's getting too close to the situation, she refers Lila to another therapist. But Lila calls and tells Kris she's already acted out one of her fantasies by killing her husband. In order to stop Lila from killing again, Kris goes on a dangerous search for her deadly patient. **93m/C VHS.** Lisa Hartman Black, Deanna Lund, Philip Casnoff, Christopher McDonald; ***D:*** Alan Metzger. *MCA*

The Redeemer ♪ **1976** Group of adults at their high school reunion play the children's game of hide-and-seek, with deadly results. **80m/C VHS, Beta.** F.G. Finkbinder, Damien Knight, Jeanetta Arnetta; ***D:*** Constantine S. Gochis. *GHV*

The Redhead from Wyoming ♪♪½ **1953** Spirited sagebrush adventure with fiery-tempered O'Hara as a saloon proprietress with feelings for both a local cattle rustler and the town's sheriff. Based on a story by James. **81m/C VHS.** Maureen O'Hara, Alex Nicol, William Bishop, Robert Strauss, Alexander Scourby, Jack Kelly, Jeanne Cooper, Dennis Weaver, Stacy Harris; ***D:*** Lee Sholem; ***W:*** Polly James, Herb Meadow. *MCA*

Redneck ♪ **1973** Implausible, distasteful purported "thriller" about criminals on the run. **92m/C VHS, Beta.** *IT GB* Telly Savalas, Franco Nero, Mark Lester, Ely Galleani, Dulio Del Prete, Maria Michi; ***D:*** Silvio Narizzano. *NO*

Redneck Zombies ♪ **1988 (R)** A bunch of backwoods rednecks become zombies after chug-a-lugging some radioactive beer. Eating local tourists becomes a hard habit to break. Betcha can't have just one! **83m/C VHS, Beta.** Floyd Piranha, Lisa DeHaven, W.E. Benson, William W. Decker, James Housely, Zoofoot, Tyrone Taylor, Perieles Lewnes. *TWE*

Reds ♪♪♪ **1981 (PG)** The recreation of the life of author John Reed ("Ten Days that Shook the World"), his romance with Louise Bryant, his efforts to start an American Communist party, and his reporting of the Russian Revolution. A sweeping, melancholy epic using dozens of "witnesses" who reminisce about what they saw. See director Sergei Eisenstein's silent masterpiece "Ten Days that Shook the World," based on Reed's book, for the Russian view of some of the events depicted in Beatty's film. **195m/C VHS, Beta, LV.** Warren Beatty, Diane Keaton, Jack Nicholson, Edward Herrmann, Maureen Stapleton, Gene Hackman, Jerzy Kosinski, George Plimpton, Paul Sorvino, William Daniels, M. Emmet Walsh, Dolph Sweet, Josef Sommer; ***D:*** Warren Beatty; ***W:*** Warren Beatty, Warren Beatty; ***M:*** Dave Grusin, Stephen Sondheim. Academy Awards '81: Best Cinematography, Best Director (Beatty), Best Supporting Actress (Stapleton); Directors Guild of America Awards '81: Best Director (Beatty); Golden Globe Awards '82: Best Director (Beatty); Los Angeles Film Critics Association Awards '81: Best Cinematography, Best Director (Beatty), Best Supporting Actress (Stapleton); New York Film Critics Awards '81: Best Film; National Society of Film Critics Awards '81: Best Supporting Actress (Stapleton); Writers Guild of America '81: Best Original Screenplay; Nominations: Academy Awards '81: Best Actor (Beatty), Best Actress (Keaton), Best Art Direction/Set Decoration, Best Costume Design, Best Film Editing, Best Original Screenplay, Best Picture, Best Sound, Best Supporting Actor (Nicholson). *PAR, BTV*

Redwood Curtain ♪♪½ **1995 (PG)** Geri Riordan (Salonga) is an Amerasian teenager, with a brilliant future as a concert pianist before her, until she becomes obsessed with learning about her past. Her wealthy adoptive father, Laird Riordan (Lithgow), provides understanding but no answers so she turns to her sympathetic Aunt Geneva (Monk), who lives in the redwood forest area of northern California. There Geri encounters homeless Vietnam vet Lyman Fellers (Daniels) and becomes convinced the troubled man is her birth father. Adapted from the play by Lanford Wilson; made for TV. **99m/C VHS.** Lea Salonga, John Lithgow, Jeff Daniels, Debra Monk, Catherine Hicks; ***D:*** John Korty; ***W:*** Ed Namzug; ***M:*** Lawrence Shragge. *REP*

Redwood Forest Trail ♪♪ **1950** Environmental-themed oater about a camp for underprivileged city boys. The boys of the camp are blamed for the death of a landowner whose daughter then refuses to renew the camp's mortgage. Allen and Switzer set out to prove that the real culprits are sawmill workers out to control the area timber. Smokey the Bear also makes an appearance to lecture about careless forest fires and the need to preserve the woods. **67m/B VHS.** Rex Allen, Jeff Donnell, Carl "Alfalfa" Switzer, Jane Darwell, Marten Lamont, Pierre Watkin; ***D:*** Philip Ford; ***W:*** Bradford Ropes. *MOV*

Reefer Madness *Tell Your Children* **1938 (PG)** Considered serious at the time of its release, this low-budget depiction of the horrors of marijuana has become an underground comedy favorite. Overwrought acting and lurid script contribute to the fun. **67m/B VHS, Beta.** Dave O'Brien, Dorothy Short, Warren McCollum, Lillian Miles, Thelma White, Carleton Young; ***D:*** Louis Gasnier. *SNC, NOS, HHT*

Reet, Petite and Gone ♪♪♪ **1947** All-Black musical featuring the music of neglected jive singer Louis Jordan, and his band, The Tympany Five. A girl's mother dies; sneaky lawyer tries to cheat her. Slick and enjoyable. **75m/B VHS, Beta.** Louis Jordan, June Richmond; ***D:*** William Forest Crouch. *MVD, NOS, VYY*

The Ref ♪♪♪ **1993 (R)** The couple from hell turn the tables on Gus (Leary), a hard-nosed fugitive who takes Caroline (Davis) and her husband Lloyd (Spacey) hostage. Gus then finds himself trapped in the traditional Christmas ordeal of a family suffering from industrial-strength dysfunction. He plots his getaway while masquerading as the couple's marriage counselor, hence the film's title. This sometimes brutal, frequently hysterical satire of male-female relationships, family ties, and compulsory holiday rituals uses consistently sharp dialogure and superb acting to tell an absurd but convincing tale. **97m/C VHS, LV.** Denis Leary, Judy Davis, Kevin Spacey, Glynis Johns, Robert J. Steinmiller Jr., Christine Baranski; ***D:*** Ted Demme; ***W:*** Richard LaGravenese, Marie Weiss; ***M:*** David A. Stewart. *TOU*

The Reflecting Skin ♪♪ **1991** In a 1950s prairie town a small boy sees insanity, child-murder, and radiation sickness, leading him to fantasize that the tormented young widow next door is a vampire. The pretentious drama/freak show rationalizes its ghastly events as symbolizing the hero's loss of youthful innocence. But the Hound knows the score; this is "Faces of Death" for the arts crowd, a grotesque menagerie that dares you to watch. The exploding-frog opener is already notorious. Beautiful photography, with vistas inspired by the painting of Andrew Wyeth. **116m/C VHS, LV.** Viggo Mortensen, Lindsay Duncan, Jeremy Cooper; ***D:*** Philip Ridley; ***W:*** Philip Ridley; ***M:*** Nick Bicat. *NO*

A Reflection of Fear ♪♪ *Labyrinth* **1972 (PG)** Lame psycho-thriller about a young girl's jealously of her father's girlfriend, with family members dying of supernatural causes. **90m/C VHS, Beta.** Robert Shaw, Sally Kellerman, Sondra Locke, Mary Ure; ***D:*** William A. Fraker; ***W:*** Lewis John Carlino. *COL*

Reflections in a Golden Eye ♪♪½ **1967** Huston's film adaptation of Carson McCullers novel about repressed homosexuality, madness, and murder at a Southern Army base in 1948. Star-studded cast cannot consistently pull off convoluted lives of warped characters; not for everyone, though it holds some interest. **109m/C VHS, Beta.** Elizabeth Taylor, Marlon Brando, Brian Keith, Julie Harris; ***D:*** John Huston; ***C:*** Oswald Morris. *WAR*

Reflections in the Dark ♪♪ *Reflections on a Crime* **1994 (R)** Beautiful Regina (Rogers) is on death row for murdering her overbearing husband James (Terry). On execution-eve, she relates her tale to young guard Colin (Zane), dispatching hubby by a different method each time she varies her story. Takes itself too seriously though Rogers gives a star performance. **83m/C VHS, LV.** Mimi Rogers, Billy Zane, John Terry, Kurt Fuller, Lee Garlington, Nancy Fish; ***D:*** Jon Purdy; ***W:*** Jon Purdy. *NHO*

Reflections of Murder ♪♪½ **1974** Evil schoolteacher's wife and mistress decide to kill him off and then are plagued by his phantom. Well done made for television remake of the French film "Diabolique." Suspenseful, with a great ending. **97m/C VHS.** Tuesday Weld, Joan Hackett, Sam Waterston, Lucille Benson, R.G. Armstrong, Michael Lerner, Ed Bernard, Lance Kerwin; ***D:*** John Badham; ***M:*** Billy Goldenberg. *REP*

Reform School Girl ♪ **1957** A young girl ends up behind bars when her boyfriend steals a car to go joy-riding and is involved in a hit-and-run murder. Extremely cheap production and incredulous story. Look for Kellerman in a bit part in her first screen appearance. **71m/B VHS.** Gloria Castillo, Ross Ford, Edward Byrnes, Ralph Reed, Jack Kruschen, Sally Kellerman; ***D:*** Edward L. Bernds; ***W:*** Edward L. Bernds. *NLC*

Reform School Girls ☆ **1986 (R)** Satiric raucous women's prison film, complete with tough lesbian wardens, brutal lesbian guards, sadistic lesbian inmates, and a single, newly convicted heterosexual heroine. Wendy O. Williams as a teenager? Come on. Overdone, over-campy, exploitative. **94m/C VHS, Beta, LV.** Linda Carol, Wendy O. Williams, Pat Ast, Sybil Danning, Charlotte McGinnis, Sherri Stoner; ***D:*** Tom De Simone. *VTR, NWV*

The Refrigerator ☆½ **1993** Filmed on a miniscule budget, this comic/horror flick tells the story of the innocent Batemans of Ohio who move into a grubby New York apartment where they discover their battered Norge refrigerator is actually a doorway to hell. The fridge has a taste for flesh and tends to eat the unwary visitor as well as defrosting blood (very messy). All the previous tenants disappeared without a trace—will the Batemans be next? Cartoon satire is too amateurish to be successful. **86m/C VHS.** David Simonds, Julia McNeal, Angel Caban, Nena Segal, Jaime Rojo, Michelle DeCosta; ***D:*** Nicholas A.E. Jacobs; ***W:*** Nicholas A.E. Jacobs. *NO*

Refuge of Fear ☆ **198?** Drama set in a post-nuclear-holocaust world. **90m/C VHS, Beta.** *NO*

Regarding Henry ☆☆☆ **1991 (PG-13)** A cold-hearted lawyer gets shot in the head during a holdup and survives with memory and personality erased. During recovery the new Henry displays compassion and conscience the old one never had. Though too calculated in its yuppie-bashing ironies, the picture works thanks to splendid acting and low-key, on-target direction. **107m/C VHS, Beta, LV.** Harrison Ford, Annette Bening, Bill Nunn, Mikki Allen, Elizabeth Wilson, Robin Bartlett, John Leguizamo, Donald Moffat, Nancy Marchand; ***D:*** Mike Nichols; ***W:*** Jeffrey Abrams; ***C:*** Giuseppe Rotunno; ***M:*** Hans Zimmer. *PAR*

Regeneration ☆☆ **1915** Irish hoodlum Owen (Fellowes) is saved from his life of crime by social worker Mamie Rose (Nilsson). Walsh filmed on location in New York's Bowery district and used actual gangsters in roles. Also features the 10-minute 1910 short "The Police Force of New York City," produced by Thomas Edison. **72m/B VHS.** Rockliffe Fellowes, Anna Q. Nilsson; ***D:*** Raoul Walsh. *KIV*

Reggie Mixes In ☆☆☆ **1916** Wealthy man brawls in bar room and falls for barmaid. Taking a job to be near his beloved, he wipes out local thugs while tending to her welfare. Exhilarating fight scenes in which Fairbanks fists it out with real life boxers. **58m/B VHS, Beta.** Douglas Fairbanks Sr., Bessie Love, Joseph Singleton, William E. Lowery, Wilbur Higby, Frank Bennett; ***D:*** Christy Cabanne. *GPV, FCT*

Regina ☆☆½ **1983** A woman controls all the activities of her husband and son. At age 36, her son is ready to leave home and she refuses to let him. Fine performances in this strange and disturbing film. **86m/C VHS, Beta.** *IT* Anthony Quinn, Ava Gardner, Ray Sharkey, Anna Karina; ***D:*** Jean-Yves Prate. *VMK*

Reg'lar Fellers ☆☆ **1941** A gang of kids save the town and soften the heart of their grandmother, too. Production is sloppy. Based on a comic strip by Gene Byrnes. **66m/B VHS.** Billy Lee, Carl "Alfalfa" Switzer, Buddy Boles, Janet Dempsey, Sarah Padden, Roscoe Ates; ***D:*** Arthur Dreifuss. *NOS, FMT, VYY*

Rehearsal for Murder ☆☆½ **1982** Movie star Redgrave is murdered on the night of her Broadway debut. Seems it might have been someone in the cast. Brought to you by the creative team behind "Columbo." Challenging made for television whodunit a twist. Good cast. **96m/C VHS, Beta.** Robert Preston, Lynn Redgrave, Patrick Macnee, Lawrence Pressman, Madolyn Smith, Jeff Goldblum, William Daniels; ***D:*** David Greene; ***M:*** Billy Goldenberg. *REP*

Reign of Terror ☆☆ *The Black Book* **1949** British-made adventure set during the French Revolution, with everyone after the black book that holds the names of those arch-fiend Robespierre plans to guillotine in his ruthless bid for power. Well-mounted, but historical personages and events are reduced to cartoon form. **89m/B VHS.** Robert Cummings, Arlene Dahl, Richard Hart, Arnold Moss, Richard Basehart; ***D:*** Anthony Mann; ***W:*** Philip Yordan; ***C:*** John Alton. *NOS, MRV, DVT*

Reilly: Ace of Spies ☆☆☆ **1987** Covers the exploits of the real-life superspy and womanizer Sydney Reilly who uncovers Russian secrets in 1901, allowing the Japanese to sink the Russian fleet and invade China. After a lively spying career for the British, Reilly eventually plots against the Bolsheviks and comes close to overthrowing Lenin and installing himself as the new leader of the Russian government. Eleven episodes on four cassettes. **572m/C VHS, Beta, LV.** *GB* Sam Neill, Sebastian Shaw, Jeananne Crowley; ***D:*** Jim Goddard. *SIG, HBO, FCT*

The Reincarnate ☆ **1971 (PG)** Cult guarantees lawyer will live forever if he can find a new body. Enter gullible sculptor; lawyer uses skill at persuasion. **89m/C VHS, Beta.** *CA* Jack Creley, Jay Reynolds, Trudy Young, Terry Tweed; ***D:*** Don Haldane. *NO*

The Reincarnation of Golden Lotus ☆☆☆☆ **1989** In this highly erotic story of love and revenge, Wong escapes China for decadent Hong Kong by marrying a wealthy but foolish man. She has numerous sadomasochistic affairs and begins having flashbacks, revealing her to be the reincarnation of Golden Lotus, a courtesan of ancient China. In Mandarin Chinese with English subtitles. **99m/C VHS.** *HK* Joi Wong, Eric Tsang, Lam Chen Yen; ***D:*** Clara Law. *CVC, INJ*

The Reincarnation of Peter Proud ☆☆ **1975 (R)** A college professor has nightmares which lead him to believe the spirit of a murdered man is now possessing him. Kinda scary, but predictable. Screenplay by Ehrlich from his novel. **105m/C VHS, Beta, LV.** Michael Sarrazin, Jennifer O'Neill, Margot Kidder, Cornelia Sharpe; ***D:*** J. Lee Thompson; ***W:*** Max Ehrlich; ***M:*** Jerry Goldsmith. *LIV, VES*

The Reivers ☆☆☆½ **1969 (PG)** Young boy and two adult pals journey from small town Mississippi (circa 1905) to the big city of Memphis in a stolen car. Picaresque tale is delightful onscreen, as in William Faulkner's enjoyable last novel. **107m/C VHS, Beta.** Steve McQueen, Sharon Farrell, Will Geer, Michael Constantine, Rupert Crosse; ***D:*** Mark Rydell; ***W:*** Harriet Frank Jr., Irving Ravetch; ***M:*** John Williams. Nominations: Academy Awards '69: Best Supporting Actor (Crosse), Best Original Score. *FOX*

The Rejuvenator ☆☆½ *Rejuvenatrix* **1988 (R)** Also known as "Rejuvenatrix." An oft-told film story: an aging actress discovers a "youth" serum but finds out that the serum affects things other than her aging. Well-done. **90m/C VHS, LV.** Marcus Powell, John MacKay, James Hogue, Vivian Lanko, Jessica Dublin; ***D:*** Brian Thomas Jones; ***W:*** Simon Nuchtern; ***M:*** Larry Juris. *NO*

Relative Fear ☆½ **1995 (R)** Little Adam has bad luck with his friends and relatives—they keep getting murdered all around him. His mother begins to suspect something unnatural is going on, and discovers Adam is not her natural child, but the son of a homicidal madwoman. Has Adam inherited some deadly traits? **94m/C VHS.** Darlanne Fluegel, M. Emmet Walsh, James Brolin, Denise Crosby, Martin Neufeld, Linda Sorensen, Matthew Dupuis; ***D:*** George Mihalka; ***W:*** Kurt Wimmer. *REP*

Relentless ☆☆ **1989 (R)** Twisted psycho Nelson, once rejected by the LAPD Academy on psychological grounds takes his revenge by murdering people and using his police training to cover his tracks. Good acting keeps sporadically powerful but cliched thriller afloat. **92m/C VHS, Beta, LV.** Judd Nelson, Robert Loggia, Meg Foster, Leo Rossi, Pat O'Bryan, Mindy Seeger, Angel Tompkins, Ken Lerner, George Flower; ***D:*** William Lustig. *COL*

Relentless 2: Dead On ☆☆ **1991 (R)** Rossi, the detective from the first film, tracks yet another murderer whose occult-style mutilations mask an international political conspiracy. So-so slaughter with artsy camerawork. Honestly, how many "Relentless" fans can you name who've been waiting with anticipation? **93m/C VHS, LV.** Leo Rossi, Ray Sharkey, Meg Foster, Miles O'Keeffe; ***D:*** Michael Schroeder. *COL*

Relentless 3 ☆☆ **1993 (R)** A serial killer (Forsythe) likes to carve up his women victims and send various body parts to taunt the police. Then this sicko decides to really drive the cops crazy by stalking the beautiful girlfriend of the detective (Rossi) investigating the crimes. **84m/C VHS.** William Forsythe, Leo Rossi, Tom Bower, Robert Costanzo, Signy Coleman; ***D:*** James Lemmo; ***W:*** James Lemmo. *NLC*

Relentless 4 ☆½ **1994 (R)** A psychiatrist with a secret (Janssen) is the only clue Detective Sam Dietz (Rossi) has to a serial killer. Seems all the victims knew the shrink but what does she know? **91m/C VHS, LV.** Leo Rossi, Famke Janssen, Ken Lerner, Colleen Coffey; ***D:*** Oley Sassone; ***W:*** Mark Sevi, Terry Plumeri. *NLC*

The Reluctant Agent ☆☆ **1995** Waitress Linda (Jackee) is persuaded to take the place of injured twin sister Charlene, an FBI agent hot on the trail of shady-but-attractive businessman C. Gabriel Dash (Lawson). So, she goes undercover with the questionable assistance of agent John Fraser (Hedaya) to bring their criminal to justice. **94m/C VHS.** Jackee, Richard Lawson, Dan Hedaya, Bill Fagerbakke, Harold Sylvester, Cynthia Stevenson, Sharon Barr, Eda Reiss Merin; ***D:*** Paul Lynch; ***W:*** Jeff Cohn, Kristi Kane; ***M:*** Tim Truman. *AEL*

The Reluctant Astronaut ☆½ **1967** Roy Fleming (Knotts) is a carnvial worker who operates the spaceship ride. Dad's upset the kid has no ambition and sends an application for Roy to NASA. Everyone's surprised when Roy gets accepted and he heads off to Florida but it turns out the job is janitorial. Still Roy does make friends with astronaut Red (Nielsen), who persuades NASA that Roy would be the perfect civilian to send up in an experimental capsule. Too bad Roy's terrified to fly in anything. **103m/C VHS.** Don Knotts, Leslie Nielsen, Joan Freeman, Arthur O'Connell, Jesse White, Jeanette Nolan, Joan Shawlee; ***D:*** Edward J. Montagne; ***W:*** James Fritzell, Everett Greenbaum; ***C:*** Rexford Wimpy; ***M:*** Vic Mizzy. *MCA*

The Reluctant Debutante ☆☆☆ **1958** Harrison and Kendall are the urbane parents of Dee who are trying to find a suitable British husband for their girl. It seems their choices just won't do however, and Dee falls for American bad boy musician Saxon. A very lightweight yet extremely enjoyable romantic comedy thanks to Harrison and in particular his real-life wife Kendall, who unfortunately died the following year. **96m/C VHS, Beta, LV.** Rex Harrison, Kay Kendall, John Saxon, Sandra Dee, Angela Lansbury, Diane Clare; ***D:*** Vincente Minnelli; ***C:*** Joseph Ruttenberg. *MGM*

The Reluctant Dragon **1941** Classic Disney short about a fun-loving dragon, based on the Kenneth Grahame story; accompanied also by the Disney short "Morris, the Midget Moose." Not to be confused with the full-length 1941 Disney feature film. **28m/C VHS, Beta.** ***D:*** Alfred Werker. *DIS, KUI, WTA*

The Remains of the Day ☆☆☆ **1993 (PG)** If repression is your cup of tea then this is the film for you. Others may want to shake British butler par excellence Stevens (Hopkins) and tell him to express an emotion. In the 1930s, Stevens is the rigidly traditional butler to Lord Darlington (Fox). When Miss Kenton (Thompson) the almost vivacious new housekeeper expresses a quietly personal interest in Stevens his loyalty to an unworthy master prevents him from a chance at happiness. A quiet movie, told in flashback. Hopkins' impressive performance gets by strictly on nuance with Thompson at least allowed a small amount of natural charm. Based on the novel by Kazuo Ishiguro. **135m/C VHS, LV, 8mm.** *GB* Anthony Hopkins, Emma Thompson, James Fox, Christopher Reeve, Peter Vaughan, Hugh Grant, Michael Lonsdale, Tim Pigott-Smith; ***D:*** James Ivory; ***W:*** Ruth Prawer Jhabvala; ***C:*** Tony Pierce-Roberts; ***M:*** Richard Robbins. British Academy Awards '93: Best Actor (Hopkins); Los Angeles Film Critics Association Awards '93: Best Actor (Hopkins); National Board of Review Awards '93: Best Actor (Hopkins); Nominations: Academy Awards '93: Best Actor (Hopkins), Best Actress (Thompson), Best Adapted Screenplay, Best Art Direction/Set Decoration, Best Costume Design, Best Director (Ivory), Best Original Screenplay, Best Picture; British Academy

Awards '94: Best Actress (Thompson), Best Adapted Screenplay, Best Director (Ivory), Best Film; Directors Guild of America Awards '93: Best Director (Ivory); Golden Globe Awards '94: Best Actor—Drama (Hopkins), Best Actress—Drama (Thompson), Best Director (Ivory), Best Film—Drama, Best Screenplay. *COL*

Rembrandt 🦴🦴🦴 **1936** Necessarily very visual biography of the great Dutch painter, Rembrandt. Superb acting by Laughton. **86m/B VHS, Beta, LV.** *GB* Charles Laughton, Elsa Lanchester, Gertrude Lawrence, Walter Hudd; ***D:*** Alexander Korda; ***C:*** Georges Perinal. National Board of Review Awards '36: 10 Best Films of the Year. *SUE*

Rembrandt—1669 🦴🦴 **1977** A recreation of the controversial artist's last year, with his egotism clashing with his artistic impulses. In Dutch with English subtitles. **114m/C VHS.** *NL* Frans Stelling, Tom de Koff, Aye Fil; ***D:*** Jos Stelling. *CVC, INJ*

Remedy for Riches 🦴🦴 **1940** The fourth "Dr. Christian" comedy, has the small-town doctor trying to uncover a real estate fraud before it bankrupts his community. Mildly funny. **66m/B VHS, Beta, 8mm.** Jean Hersholt, Dorothy Lovett, Edgar Kennedy, Jed Prouty, Walter Catlett; ***D:*** Erle C. Kenton. *NOS, VYY*

Remember Me 🦴 **1985** Just as a woman is starting to gain control of her life, her husband returns home from the mental hospital. **95m/C VHS, Beta.** Robert Grubb, Wendy Hughes, Richard Moir; ***D:*** Lex Marinos. *NO*

Remember the Night 🦴🦴🦴 **1940** Another Sturges-scripted winner in which assistant D.A. MacMurray falls for sophiticated shoplifter Stanwyck, who has stolen a diamond bracelet amidst the Christmas holiday bustle. On a promise that she will return for the trial MacMurray postpones the trial and offers her a ride home for the holidays. Stanwyck is turned away by her mother and MacMurray brings her home for a real family Christmas, where love blooms. A sentimental, funny romance that boisters holiday cheer any time of year. **94m/B VHS.** Barbara Stanwyck, Fred MacMurray, Beulah Bondi, Elizabeth Patterson, Willard Robertson, Sterling Holloway; ***D:*** Mitchell Leisen; ***W:*** Preston Sturges; ***C:*** Ted Tetzlaff; ***M:*** Frederick Hollander. *MCA*

Remington Steele, Vol. 1: License to Steele **1982** Pilot episode to the light-hearted detective TV series starring Zimbalist as Laura Holt, a female PI who sets up her agency under the name of her fictitious male boss. Then a mystery man appears claiming to be the real Remington Steele (Brosnan) and the two decide to join forces. Also in the first episode are Read as Laura's suspicious assistant, Murphy Michaels, and DeMay as Bernice Fox, the agency secretary. **60m/C VHS.** Stephanie Zimbalist, Pierce Brosnan, James Read, Janet DeMay. *MOV, MTM*

Remo Williams: The Adventure Begins 🦴🦴 **1985 (PG-13)** Adaptation of "The Destroyer" adventure novel series with a Bond-like hero who can walk on water and dodge bullets after being instructed by a Korean martial arts master. Funny and diverting, and Grey is excellent (if a bit over the top) as the wizened oriental. The title's assumption is that the adventure will continue. **121m/C VHS, Beta, LV.** Fred Ward, Joel Grey, Wilford Brimley, Kate Mulgrew; ***D:*** Guy Hamilton. Nominations: Academy Awards '85: Best Makeup. *NO*

Remolina de Pasiones 🦴🦴 **1987** A young woman is driven to suicide after succumbing to her mother's persistent lover. **89m/C VHS, Beta.** *SP* Amparo Rivelles, Carlos Pinar, Susana Dosamantes. *MAD*

Remote 🦴🦴½ **1993 (PG)** Thirteen-year-old Randy is a whiz designing high-tech remote-control gadgets. When one of his toys wipes out a friend's science project, Randy's parents try to put a halt to his tinkering but the kid has other plans. Innocuous rip-off of "Honey, I Shrunk the Kids" with some "Home Alone" thrown in as well. **80m/C VHS, Beta.** Chris Carrara, Jessica Bowman, John Diehl, Derya Ruggles, Tony Longo, Stuart Fratkin; ***D:*** Ted Nicolaou; ***W:*** Mike Farrow; ***M:*** Richard Band. *PAR*

Remote Control 🦴½ **1988 (R)** A circulating videotape of a 1950's sci-fi flick is turning people into murderous zombies, thanks to some entrepreneurial aliens. Silly, but performed by young actors with gusto. **88m/C VHS, Beta, LV.** Kevin Dillon, Deborah Goodrich, Christopher Wynne, Jennifer Tilly; ***D:*** Jeff Lieberman; ***M:*** Peter Bernstein. *LIV, HHE*

Remote Control 🦴🦴½ **1994** Quiet Axel lives with his mom, whose life revolves around the TV set, and his sister Maeja, who spends most of her time partying in a seedy club called Sodoma. Sodoma is run by three amateur gangsters who are anxious to get rid of a rival, Moli. Meanwhile, Axel falls in love with Moli's sister Unnur (who also happens to be Maeja's best friend). Then the gangsters kidnap Unnur and Axel sets out to rescue her. Icelandic with English subtitles. **85m/C VHS.** *IC* Bjorn Fridbjornsson, Margret H. Gustavsdottir, Helgi Bjornsson, Soley Eliasdottir; ***D:*** Oskar Jonasson; ***W:*** Oskar Jonasson. *COL*

Renaissance Man 🦴🦴½ **1994 (PG-13)** Skeptical new teacher inspires a classroom of underachievers and finds his true calling. Based loosely on the experiences of screenwriter Burnstein at a base in Michigan. Civilian Bill Rago (DeVito) is an unemployed ad exec assigned to teach Shakespeare to a group of borderline Army recruits led by Hardison. Add half a bone for the recruits and their Hamlet rap, a breath of fresh air in an otherwise stale plot. Some funny moments, reminiscent of "Stripes," but not quite as wacky. On the other hand, Marshall does endearing well. Look for rapper Marky Mark with his shirt on (hard to recognize). Shot with the cooperation of the Army. **128m/C VHS, LV.** Danny DeVito, Gregory Hines, James Remar, Stacey Dash, Ed Begley Jr., Mark Wahlberg, Lillo Brancato, Kadeem Hardison, Richard T. Jones, Khalil Kain, Peter Simmons, Jenifer Lewis; ***Cameos:*** Cliff Robertson; ***D:*** Penny Marshall; ***W:*** Jim Burnstein, Ned Mauldin; ***M:*** Hans Zimmer. *TOU*

Rendez-Moi Ma Peau 🦴🦴½ **1981** A modern-day witch transposes two people's personalities with comic results. In French with subtitles. **82m/C VHS, Beta.** *FR* ***D:*** Patrick Schulmann. *FCT*

Rendez-vous 🦴🦴🦴 **1985 (R)** A racy, dark film about the sensitive balance between sex and exploitation, the real world and the stage world. Some may be disturbed by chillingly explicit scenes. Impressive tour de force of imagination, direction, and cinematography. In French with English subtitles. **82m/C VHS, LV.** *FR* Juliette Binoche, Lambert Wilson, Wadeck Stanczak, Jean-Louis Trintignant; ***D:*** Andre Techine; ***W:*** Olivier Assayas. Cannes Film Festival '85: Best Director (Techine). *CVC, INJ, TPV*

Renegade Girl 🦴 **1946** A special agent is sent west to capture the female head of a band of outlaws. **65m/B VHS, Beta, LV.** Alan Curtis, Ann Savage, Edward Brophy, Ray Corrigan, Jack Holt; ***D:*** William (Lester Williams) Berke. *NOS, RXM, VYY*

Renegade Monk 🦴½ **1982 (R)** Invincible warrior-monk dispenses his own brand of justice with his fists of aluminum foil. **90m/C VHS, Beta.** Liu Chang Liang, Huang Hsing Shaw, Ko Shou Liang, Lang Shih Chia, Hsu Chung Hsing. *GEM*

Renegade Ninja 🦴 **1983** A man whose father was murdered kicks everyone within reach in his quest for revenge. **109m/C VHS, Beta.** Kensaku Marita; ***D:*** Sadao Nakajima. *PSM*

Renegade Ranger/Scarlet River 🦴½ **1938** A western double feature: A Texas Ranger and his singing sidekick attempt to help out a woman accused of murder in the "The Renegade Ranger," and a cowboy tries to free his sweetheart from a band of cattle rustlers in "Scarlet River." **113m/B VHS, Beta.** Rita Hayworth, Tim Holt, George O'Brien, Ray Whitley, Tom Keene, Lon Chaney Jr., Myrna Loy, Bruce Cabot, Betty Furness; ***D:*** David Howard. *TTC*

Renegade Trail 🦴🦴 **1939** Hopalong Cassidy helps a marshall and a pretty widow round up excons and rustlers. The King's Men, radio singers of the era, perform a fistful of songs. **61m/B VHS.** William Boyd, George "Gabby" Hayes, Russell Hayden, Charlotte Wynters, Russell Hopton, Sonny Bupp, Jack Rockwell, Roy Barcroft, Eddie Dean; ***D:*** Lesley Selander. *NOS*

Renegades 🦴🦴 **1989 (R)** A young cop from Philadelphia and a Lakota Indian begrudgingly unite to track down a gang of ruthless crooks. Good action, and lots of it; not much story. **105m/C VHS, Beta, LV.** Kiefer Sutherland, Lou Diamond Phillips, Rob Knepper, Jami Gertz, Bill Smitrovich; ***D:*** Jack Sholder; ***C:*** Phil Meheux; ***M:*** Michael Kamen. *MCA*

Renfrew of the Royal Mounted 🦴🦴 **1937** A Canadian Mountie goes after counterfeiters and sings a few songs in this mild adaptation of a popular kids' radio serial. Newill was a popular tenor of the day, but the Hound thinks Renfrew's dog 'Lightning' should have been the star. **57m/B VHS, Beta.** Carol Hughes, James Newill, Kenneth Harlan; ***D:*** Al(bert) Herman. *DVT, GPV, HEG*

Renfrew on the Great White Trail 🦴½ *On the Great White Trail; Renfrew of the Royal Mounted on the Great White Trail* **1938** A frustrated fur trader takes off after a pack of thieves. **58m/B VHS.** James Newill, Terry Walker, Robert Frazer, Richard Alexander; ***D:*** Al(bert) Herman. *NOS, DVT*

Reno and the Doc 🦴🦴½ **1984** Enjoyable comedy about two endearingly cranky middle-aged men battling mid-life crises join together and test their mettle in the world of professional skiing. **88m/C VHS, Beta.** *CA* Ken Walsh, Henry Ramer, Linda Griffiths; ***D:*** Charles Dennis. *NWV*

Renoir Shorts 🦴🦴🦴 **1927** Two early silent Renoir fantasies: "The Little Matchgirl," a lyrical adaptation of the Hans Christian Anderson fairy tale, and "Charleston," in which a space-traveling African and Parisian girl dance comically. **50m/B VHS, Beta.** Catherine Hessling; ***D:*** Jean Renoir. *NOS, FCT*

Rent-A-Cop 🦴🦴 **1988 (R)** A cop (Reynolds) is bounced from the force after he survives a drug-bust massacre under suspicious circumstances. He becomes a security guard and continues to track down the still-at-large killer with help from call girl Minnelli. **95m/C VHS, Beta, LV.** Burt Reynolds, Liza Minnelli, James Remar, Richard Masur, Bernie Casey, John Stanton, John P. Ryan, Dionne Warwick, Robby Benson; ***D:*** Jerry London; ***W:*** Michael Blodgett; ***M:*** Jerry Goldsmith. Golden Raspberry Awards '88: Worst Actress (Minnelli). *HBO*

Rent-A-Kid 🦴🦴½ **1995 (G)** Businessman Harry Haber (Nielsen) is asked by his son to keep an eye out on the Mid-Valley Orphanage for a week. Then Harry meets a young couple who are unsure about having a family so, since Harry's business is renting all sorts of things, he decides to rent the couple three orphans so they can get a taste of parenting. **89m/C VHS, LV.** Leslie Nielsen, Christopher Lloyd, Matt McCoy, Sherry Miller, Amos Crawley, Cody Jones, Tabitha Lupien, Tony Rosato; ***D:*** Fred Gerber; ***W:*** Paul Bernbaum; ***C:*** Rene Ohashi; ***M:*** Ron Ramin. *REP*

Rentadick 🦴🦴 **1972** A precursor to the Monty Python masterpieces, written by future members Chapman and Cleese. Private eye spoof isn't as funny as later Python efforts; but it is an indication of what was yet to come and fans should enjoy it. **94m/C VHS.** *GB* James Booth, Julie Ege, Ronald Fraser, Donald Sinden, Michael Bentine, Richard Briers, Spike Milligan; ***D:*** Jim Clark; ***W:*** Graham Chapman, John Cleese; ***M:*** Carl Davis. *NO*

Rented Lips 🦴 **1988 (R)** Two documentary film makers sell out, taking over the production of a porno film at the request of a public television producer who promises to help their careers. Mull and Shawn are well supported by an impressive cast, but everyone's effort is wasted in unfunny attempt at comedy. **82m/C VHS, Beta, LV.** Martin Mull, Dick Shawn, Jennifer Tilly, Kenneth Mars, Edy Williams, Robert Downey Jr., June Lockhart, Shelley Berman, Mel Welles, Pat McCormick, Eileen Brennan; ***D:*** Robert Downey. *NO*

Repentance 🦴🦴🦴 *Pokayaniye; Confession* **1987 (PG)** A popular, surreal satire of Soviet and Communist societies. A woman is arrested for repeatedly digging up a dead local despot, and put on trial. Wickedly funny and controversial; released under the auspices of glasnost. In Russian with English subtitles. **151m/C VHS, Beta, LV.** *RU* Avtandil Makharadze, Zeinab Botsvadze, Ia Ninidze, Edisher Giorgobiani, Ketevan

Abuladze, Kakhi Kavsadze; ***D:*** Tengiz Abuladze. Cannes Film Festival '87: Grand Jury Prize. *MED*

Replikator: Cloned to Kill 🦴½ **1994 (R)** In the 21st century, a ruthless criminal gets hold of replication techology that can duplicate anything, including people. So it's up to a cop and two cyberpunks to stop the destruction. **96m/C VHS.** Michael St. Gerard, Brigitte Bako, Ned Beatty; ***D:*** G. Philip Jackson; ***W:*** Tony Johnston, Michelle Bellerose, John Dawson. *PSM*

Repo Jake 🦴½ **1990** Jake Baxter learns the myth of the carefree life of a repossession man in this action thriller. His illusion is destroyed by angry clients, pornography, a deadly underworld racetrack, and a sinister crime boss. **90m/C VHS.** Dan Haggerty, Robert Axelrod. *PMH*

Repo Man 🦴🦴🦴½ **1983 (R)** An inventive, perversely witty portrait of sick modern urbanity, following the adventures of a punk rocker taking a job as a car repossessor in a barren city. The landscape is filled with pointless violence, no-frills packaging, media hypnosis and aliens. Executive producer: none other than ex-Monkee Michael Nesmith. **93m/C VHS, Beta, LV.** Emilio Estevez, Harry Dean Stanton, Sy Richardson, Tracey Walter, Olivia Barash, Fox Harris, Jennifer Balgobin, Vonetta McGee, Angelique Pettyjohn; ***D:*** Alex Cox; ***W:*** Alex Cox. *MCA*

The Report on the Party and the Guests 🦴🦴🦴🦴 **1966** A controversial, widely banned political allegory, considered a masterpiece from the Czech new wave. A picnic/lawn party deteriorates into brutality, fascist intolerance and persecution. Many Czech film makers, some banned at the time, appear. Based on a story by Ester Krumbachova, who also co-wrote the screenplay. In Czech with English subtitles. **71m/B VHS, Beta.** *CZ* Jiri Nemec, Evald Schorm, Ivan Vyskocil, Jan Klusak, Zdena Skvorecka, Pavel Bosek; ***D:*** Jan Nemec; ***W:*** Jan Nemec. *FCT*

Report to the Commissioner 🦴🦴🦴 *Operation Undercover* **1974 (R)** A rough, energetic crime-in-the-streets cop thriller. A young detective accidentally kills an attractive woman who turns out to have been an undercover cop, then is dragged into the bureaucratic cover-up. **112m/C VHS, Beta.** Michael Moriarty, Yaphet Kotto, Susan Blakely, Hector Elizondo, Richard Gere, Tony King, Michael McGuire, Stephen Elliott; ***D:*** Milton Katselas; ***W:*** Abby Mann; ***M:*** Elmer Bernstein. *MGM*

Repossessed 🦴🦴 **1990 (PG-13)** A corny, occasionally funny takeoff on the human-possessed-by-the-devil films with Blair, as usual, as the afflicted victim. Nielsen, in another typecast role, plays the goofy man of the cloth who must save the day. Numerous actors appear in brief comedy sequences which lampoon current celebrities and constitute the film's highlights. For fans of "Airplane" and "The Naked Gun"; not necessarily for others. **89m/C VHS, LV.** Linda Blair, Ned Beatty, Leslie Nielsen, Anthony Starke, Jesse Ventura; ***D:*** Bob Logan; ***W:*** Bob Logan; ***M:*** Charles Fox. Golden Raspberry Awards '90: Worst Song ("He's Comin' Back (The Devil!)"). *LIV*

Repulsion 🦴🦴🦴½ **1965** Character study of a young French girl who is repulsed and attracted by sex. Left alone when her sister goes on vacation, her facade of stability begins to crack, with violent and bizarre results. Polanski's first film in English and his first publicly accepted full-length feature. Suspenseful, disturbing and potent. **105m/B VHS, Beta, LV.** *GB* Catherine Deneuve, Yvonne Furneaux, Ian Hendry, John Fraser, Patrick Wymark, James Villiers; ***D:*** Roman Polanski; ***W:*** Roman Polanski, Gerard Brach. *VDM, VCN, MRV*

Requiem for a Heavyweight 🦴🦴🦴 **1956** The original television version of the story about an American Indian heavyweight boxer played by Palance who risks blindness in order to help his manager pay off bookies. Highly acclaimed teleplay written for "Playhouse 90." **90m/B VHS, Beta.** Jack Palance, Keenan Wynn, Ed Wynn, Kim Hunter, Ned Glass; ***D:*** Ralph Nelson; ***W:*** Rod Serling. *WKV, FUS, BTV*

Requiem for Dominic 🦴🦴🦴½ *Requiem fur Dominic* **1991 (R)** A Communist-bloc country in the midst of revolution accuses a man of terrorist activities. Can his friend, exiled for years, help him discover the truth? Interesting and timely premise matched with outstanding ensemble acting make for a superior thriller. Amnesty International receives partial proceeds from all sales of this video. In German with English subtitles. **88m/C VHS, LV.** *GE* Felix Mitterer, Viktoria Schubert, August Schmolzer, Angelica Schutz; ***D:*** Robert Dornhelm. *HMD, INJ*

The Rescue 🦴½ **1988 (PG)** An elite team of U.S. Navy Seals is captured after destroying a disabled submarine. When the U.S. government writes off the men, their children decide to mount a rescue. Puerile, empty-headed trash for teens. **97m/C VHS, Beta, LV.** Marc Price, Charles Haid, Kevin Dillon, Christina Harnos, Edward Albert; ***D:*** Ferdinand Fairfax; ***W:*** Jim Thomas, John Thomas; ***M:*** Bruce Broughton. *TOU, HHE*

Rescue Force 🦴🦴 **1990** A crack team of anti-terrorists, led by Lt. Col. Steel, takes on the kidnappers of an American ambassador. Action filled excitement. **85m/C VHS.** Richard Harrison. *NO*

Rescue Me 🦴🦴½ **1993 (PG-13)** Geek photographer Fraser carries a torch for high school honey Ginny and just happens to be on the scene (with camera) when she's kidnapped. So he persuades a scruffy Vietnam vet to help him rescue his damsel in distress. Likeable adventure with lots of chases. **99m/C VHS, LV.** Michael Dudikoff, Stephen Dorff, Peter DeLuise, Ami Dolenz, William Lucking, Dee Wallace Stone; ***D:*** Arthur Seidelman; ***W:*** Michael Snyder; ***M:*** Al Kasha, Joel Hirschhorn, David Waters. *WAR*

The Rescuers 🦴🦴🦴 **1977 (G)** Bernard and Miss Bianca, two mice who are members of the Rescue Aid Society, attempt to rescue an orphan named Penny from the evil Madame Medusa, who's after the world's biggest diamond. They are aided by comic sidekick, Orville the albatross, and a group of lovable swamp creatures. Very charming in the best Disney tradition. Based on the stories of Margery Sharp. Followed by "The Rescuers Down Under." **76m/C VHS, LV.** ***D:*** Wolfgang Reitherman, John Lounsbery; ***M:*** Artie Butler; ***V:*** Bob Newhart, Eva Gabor, Geraldine Page, Jim Jordan, Joe Flynn, Jeanette Nolan, Pat Buttram. Nominations: Academy Awards '77: Best Song ("Someone's Waiting for You"). *DIS, OM*

The Rescuers Down Under 🦴🦴½ **1990 (G)** "Crocodile" Dundee goes Disney; the followup to "The Rescuers" places its characters in Australia with only mild results for a Magic Kingdom product. Heroic mice Bernard and Bianca protect a young boy and a rare golden eagle from a poacher. The great bird closely resembles the logo of Republic Pictures. **77m/C VHS, Beta, LV.** ***D:*** Hendel Butoy, Mike Gabriel; ***W:*** Jim Cox, Karey Kirkpatrick, Joe Ranft, Byron Simpson; ***M:*** Bruce Broughton; ***V:*** Bob Newhart, Eva Gabor, John Candy, Tristan Rogers, George C. Scott, Frank Welker, Adam Ryen. *DIS, OM*

Reservoir Dogs 🦴🦴🦴½ **1992 (R)** Ultraviolent tale of honor among thieves. Six professional criminals known by code names to protect their identities (Misters Pink, White, Orange, Blonde, Blue, and Brown) are assembled by Tierney to pull off a diamond heist. But two of the gang are killed in a police ambush. The survivors regroup in an empty warehouse and try to discover the informer in their midst. In probably the most stomach-churning scene (there is some competition here), a policeman is tortured just for the heck of it to the tune of the Stealers Wheel "Stuck in the Middle with You." Unrelenting; auspicious debut for Tarantino with strong ensemble cast anchored by Keitel as the very professional Mr. White. **100m/C VHS, LV.** Harvey Keitel, Tim Roth, Michael Madsen, Steve Buscemi, Christopher Penn, Lawrence Tierney, Kirk Baltz, Quentin Tarantino; ***D:*** Quentin Tarantino; ***W:*** Quentin Tarantino. Independent Spirit Awards '93: Best Supporting Actor (Buscemi). *LIV, BTV*

The Respectful Prostitute 🦴🦴½ **1952** Sartre's tale of hooker who is cajoled into providing false testimony as a witness in the trial of a member of a prominent family. English language version of French drama. **75m/B VHS.** *FR* Ivan Desny, Barbara Laage, Walter Bryan; ***D:*** Marcel Pagliero, Charles Brabant; ***W:*** Jean-Paul Sartre. *XVC, FCT, INJ*

Rest In Pieces 🦴 **1987 (R)** A young woman inherits a Spanish mansion, and weird things begin to happen. It seems a cult of Satan worshippers is already living on the estate. As one might infer from the title, quite a bit of hacking and slashing ensues. **90m/C VHS, Beta.** Scott Thompson Baker, Lorin Jean, Dorothy Malone; ***D:*** Joseph Braunstein. *LIV*

Restless 🦴 *The Beloved* **1972** A restless homemaker begins an affair with a childhood friend. Director Cosmatos later oversaw "Rambo." **75m/C VHS, Beta.** *GR* Raquel Welch, Richard Johnson, Jack Hawkins, Flora Robson; ***D:*** George P. Cosmatos. *VMK*

The Restless Breed 🦴 **1958** Son is restless after dad, a secret service agent, is slain by gunrunners. Routine oater-revenge epic done in by listless script. **81m/C VHS, LV.** Scott Brady, Anne Bancroft, Jay C. Flippen, Rhys Williams, Jim Davis; ***D:*** Allan Dwan. *FRH, IME*

Restoration 🦴🦴🦴 **1994 (R)** Set in the 17th century after Charles II is restored to the British throne, the title may instead refer to the restoration of one man's values. After curing one of the king's dogs, physician Downey is elevated to courtier and falls into drunken debauchery. He is soon forced to marry (but not touch) the king's favorite mistress. Unfortunately, he is caught trespassing on his majesty's main squeeze and banished from the court. Cast among the common rabble, he encounters the plague and the Great Fire of London while trying to redeem himself. Strong cast and sumptuous set design help to propel Downey's performance. Adapted from Rose Tremain's 1989 novel. Release was delayed a year because no one could seem to come up with a marketing strategy. **118m/C VHS.** Robert Downey Jr., Meg Ryan, Sam Neill, Hugh Grant, David Thewlis, Polly Walker, Ian McKellen; ***D:*** Michael Hoffman; ***W:*** Rupert Walters; ***C:*** Oliver Stapleton; ***M:*** James Newton Howard. Academy Awards '95: Best Art Direction/Set Decoration, Best Costume Design. *TOU*

The Resurrected 🦴🦴½ **1991 (R)** One of the best recent H.P. Lovecraft horror adaptations, a fairly faithful try at "The Case of Charles Dexter Ward." Ward learns he has a satanic ancestor who possessed the secret of resurrection and eternal life—but, as the warlock says, it is very messy. Surprisingly tasteful even with occasional gore and truly ghastly monsters; in fact this pic could have used a bit more intensity. **108m/C VHS.** John Terry, Jane Sibbett, Chris Sarandon; ***D:*** Dan O'Bannon; ***M:*** Richard Band. *LIV*

Resurrection 🦴🦴🦴½ **1980 (PG)** After a near-fatal car accident, a woman finds she has the power to heal others by touch. She denies that God is responsible, much to her Bible Belt community's dismay. Acclaimed and well-acted. **103m/C VHS, Beta.** Ellen Burstyn, Sam Shepard, Roberts Blossom, Eva LeGallienne, Clifford David, Richard Farnsworth, Pamela Payton-Wright; ***D:*** Daniel Petrie; ***W:*** Lewis John Carlino; ***M:*** Maurice Jarre. National Board of Review Awards '80: 10 Best Films of the Year, Best Supporting Actress (LeGallienne); Nominations: Academy Awards '80: Best Actress (Burstyn), Best Supporting Actress (LeGallienne). *MCA*

Resurrection of Zachary Wheeler 🦴🦴½ **1971 (G)** A presidential candidate, who narrowly escaped death in an auto crash, is brought to a mysterious clinic in New Mexico. A reporter sneaks into the clinic and discovers the horrors of cloning. **100m/C VHS, Beta.** Angie Dickinson, Bradford Dillman, Leslie Nielsen, Jack Carter, James Daly; ***D:*** Bob Wynn. *NO*

Retreat, Hell! 🦴🦴 **1952** Korean War drama about the retreat from the Changjin Reservoir. Standard gun-ho military orientation with dismal results. **95m/B VHS.** Frank Lovejoy, Richard Carlson, Russ Tamblyn, Anita Louise; ***D:*** Joseph H. Lewis. *REP*

Retribution 🦴½ **1988 (R)** Struggling artist survives suicide attempt only to find himself possessed by the spirit of a criminal who was tortured to death. Seeing the hood's gruesome demise in his dreams, the survivor sets out to bring his murderers face-to-face with their maker. **106m/C VHS, Beta, LV.** Dennis

Lipscomb, Hoyt Axton, Leslie Wing, Suzanne Snyder; ***D:*** Guy Magar. *NO*

Retrievers ☠ **1982** Young man and a former CIA agent team up to expose the unsavory practices of the organization. **90m/C VHS, Beta.** Max Thayer, Roselyn Royce. *VES*

The Return *Woof! The Alien's Return* **1980 (PG)** Vincent and Shepherd meet as adults and discover that they had both, as children, been visited by aliens who had given technology to a cattle-mutilating prospector. A mess with no idea of what sort of film it wants to be. **91m/C VHS, Beta.** Cybill Shepherd, Raymond Burr, Jan-Michael Vincent, Martin Landau, Vincent Schiavelli, Zachary Vincent, Farah Bunch, Neville Brand, Susan Kiger; ***D:*** Greydon Clark. *NO*

Return ☠☠ **1988 (R)** A woman believes that the man she loves is the reincarnation of her dead grandfather. Interesting concept, but overall, a disappointing mystery. **78m/C VHS, Beta, LV.** Frederic Forrest, Anne Francis, Karlene Crockett, John Walcutt, Lisa Richards; ***D:*** Andrew Silver. *ACA*

Return Engagement ☠½ **1978** A lonely middle-aged ancient history professor falls in love with one of her students. **76m/C VHS, Beta.** Elizabeth Taylor, Joseph Bottoms, Peter Donat, James Ray; ***D:*** Joseph Hardy. *NO*

Return Fire ☠½ **1991 (R)** A former employee of the government finds that he must now fight the system if he wants to save his son. Trivial action fare. **97m/C VHS.** Adam West, Ron Marchini. *AIP*

Return from Witch Mountain ☠½ **1978 (G)** A pair of evil masterminds use a boy's supernatural powers to place Los Angeles in nuclear jeopardy. Sequel to Disney's ever-popular "Escape to Witch Mountain." **93m/C VHS, Beta.** Christopher Lee, Bette Davis, Ike Eisenmann, Kim Richards, Jack Soo; ***D:*** John Hough; ***W:*** Malcolm Marmorstein. *DIS*

The Return of a Man Called Horse ☠☠ **1976 (PG)** Sequel to "A Man Called Horse" tells the story of an English aristocrat who was captured and raised by Sioux Indians, and then returned to his native homeland. Contains more of the torture scenes for which this series is famous, but not much of Harris. **125m/C VHS, Beta.** Richard Harris, Gale Sondergaard, Geoffrey Lewis; ***D:*** Irvin Kershner; ***W:*** Jack DeWitt; ***C:*** Owen Roizman. *FOX*

The Return of Boston Blackie ☠½ **1927** The oft-filmed crook/detective tries to retrieve an heiress's stolen jewels. Silent. **77m/B VHS, Beta.** Raymond Glenn, Corliss Palmer, Strongheart, Rosemary Cooper, Coit Albertson; ***D:*** Harry Hoyt. *VYY, GPV, FCT*

Return of Captain Invincible ☠☠½ *Legend in Leotards* **1983 (PG)** Arkin is a derelict superhero persuaded to fight crime again in this unique spoof. One liners fly faster than a speeding bullet. Lee gives one of his best performances as the mad scientist. Musical numbers by Rocky Horror's O'Brien and Hartley sporadically interrupt. Made on a shoestring budget, offbeat film is entertaining but uneven. **90m/C VHS, Beta, LV.** *AU* Alan Arkin, Christopher Lee, Kate Fitzpatrick, Bill Hunter, Graham Kennedy, Michael Pate, Hayes Gordon, Max Phipps, Noel Ferrier; ***D:*** Philippe Mora; ***W:*** Steven E. de Souza. *NO*

The Return of Casey Jones ☠☠ *Train 2419* **1934** Early adventure film featuring lots of great railroad action. **64m/B VHS.** Charles Starrett, Ruth Hall, George "Gabby" Hayes, Robert Elliott, Margaret Seddon, Jackie Searl; ***D:*** John P. McCarthy. *GPV*

Return of Chandu ☠☠ **1934** This serial in 12 chapters features Bela Lugosi as Chandu, who exercises his magical powers to conquer a religious sect of cat worshippers inhabiting the island of Lemuria. In the process, he fights to save the Princess Nadji from being sacrificed by them. **156m/B VHS, Beta.** Bela Lugosi, Maria Alba, Clara Kimball Young; ***D:*** Ray Taylor. *DVT, NOS, SNC*

The Return of Count Yorga ☠☠ **1971 (R)** The vampire Count returns, taking up residence in a decrepit mansion nearby an orphanage. There he spies the toothsome Cynthia and Yorga decides to make her a vampiric bride. But the Count reckons without Cynthia's noble boyfriend who wants to keep his honey on this side of the grave. Preceded by "Count Yorga, Vampire." **97m/C VHS.** Robert Quarry, Mariette Hartley, Roger Perry, Yvonne Wilder, Rudy DeLuca, George Macready, Walter Brooke; ***D:*** Bob Kelljan; ***W:*** Yvonne Wilder, Bob Kelljan. *ORI*

The Return of Dr. Mabuse ☠☠½ *Im Stahlnetz Des Dr. Mabuse; Phantom Fiend* **1961** The evil doctor is back, this time sending his entranced slaves to attack a nuclear power plant. Frobe, the inspector, and Barker, the FBI man, team up to thwart him. Fun for fans of serial detective stories. **88m/B VHS, Beta.** *GE FR IT* Gert Frobe, Lex Barker, Daliah Lavi, Wolfgang Preiss, Fausto Tozzi, Rudolph Forster; ***D:*** Harald Reinl. *SNC*

Return of Dracula ☠☠ *The Curse of Dracula* **1958** Low-budget film about the Count killing a Czech artist and assuming his identity as he makes his way to the States. Once there, he moves in with the dead man's family and begins acting rather strangely. Retitled "The Curse of Dracula" for TV. **77m/C VHS.** Francis Lederer, Norma Eberhardt, Ray Stricklyn, Jimmie Baird; ***D:*** Paul Landres. *MGM, FCT*

Return of Draw Egan ☠½ **1916** Vintage silent western wherein Hart is an outlaw-turned-greenhorn sheriff of a lawless town. Music score. **64m/B VHS, Beta, 8mm.** William S. Hart, Louise Glaum; ***D:*** William S. Hart. *VYY, GPV, GVV*

The Return of Eliot Ness ☠☠½ **1991** Ness comes out of retirement in 1947 Chicago to track down a friend's killer. And with Al Capone dead, Chicago mob bosses are fighting for their piece of illegal turf. Stack reprises his "The Untouchables" TV role from the early '60s in this made for TV movie. **94m/C VHS.** Robert Stack, Charles Durning, Philip Bosco, Jack Coleman, Lisa Hartman Black, Anthony De Sando; ***D:*** James A. Contner. *APX*

Return of Frank Cannon ☠☠ **1980** Portly private eye Frank Cannon comes out of retirement to investigate the alleged suicide of an old friend. Made for television. **96m/C VHS, Beta.** William Conrad, Diana Muldaur, Joanna Pettet, Allison Argo, Arthur Hill, Ed Nelson; ***D:*** Corey Allen; ***M:*** Bruce Broughton. *WOV*

Return of Frank James ☠☠☠ **1940** One of Lang's lesser Hollywood works, this is nonetheless an entertaining sequel to 1939's "Jesse James." Brother Frank tries to go straight, but eventually has to hunt down the culprits who murdered his infamous outlaw sibling. Tierney's first film. **92m/C VHS, Beta, LV.** Henry Fonda, Gene Tierney, Jackie Cooper, Henry Hull, John Carradine, Donald Meek, J. Edward Bromberg; ***D:*** Fritz Lang. *FOX*

The Return of Grey Wolf ☠☠ **1922** A wild dog must fight for survival in Northern Quebec and is befriended by a fur trapper. An intelligent hound, he repays the trapper's generosity by helping him put the moves on some fur thieves. Silent. **62m/B VHS, Beta, 8mm.** Helen Lynch, Henry Pierce. *VYY*

The Return of Jafar **1994 (G)** Clumsy thief Abis Mal inadvertently releases evil sorcerer Jafar from his lamp prison and now the powerful "genie Jafar" plots his revenge. So it's up to Aladdin and friends to save the Sultan's kingdom once again. Contains five new songs. ♫Just Forget About Love; Nothing In the World (Quite Like a Friend); I'm Looking Out for Me; You're Only Second Rate; Arabian Nights. **66m/C VHS, LV.** ***W:*** Kevin Campbell, Mirith J.S. Colao; ***V:*** Scott Weinger, Linda Larkin, Gilbert Gottfried, Val Bettin, Dan Castellaneta. *DIS*

Return of Jesse James ☠☠ **1950** Look-alike of dead outlaw Jesse James joins in with some former members of the James Gang, leading townsfolk to believe the notorious bank robber never died. It's up to brother Frank James, now an upstanding citizen, to set the record straight. A little slow moving at times, but still worth viewing. **77m/B VHS, Beta.** John Ireland, Ann Dvorak, Reed Hadley, Henry Hull, Hugh O'Brian, Tommy Noonan, Peter Marshall; ***D:*** Arthur Hilton. *NO*

The Return of Josey Wales ☠ **1986 (R)** No match for the original featuring Clint Eastwood, the title character is played woodenly by Parks. This installment finds Wales pitted against a bumbling lawman. Sequel to 1976's "The Outlaw Josey Wales." **90m/C VHS.** Michael Parks, Rafael Campos, Bob Magruder, Paco Vela, Everett Sifuentes, Charlie McCoy; ***D:*** Michael Parks. *HHE*

The Return of Martin Guerre ☠☠☠½ *Le Retour de Martin Guerre* **1983** In this medieval tale, a dissolute village husband disappears soon after his marriage. Years later, someone who appears to be Martin Guerre returns, allegedly from war, and appears much kinder and more educated. Starring in a love story of second chances, Depardieu does not disappoint, nor does the rest of the cast. In French with English subtitles. Based on an actual court case. Remade in 1993 as "Sommersby." **111m/C VHS, Beta, LV.** *FR* Gerard Depardieu, Roger Planchon, Maurice Jacquemont, Barnard Pierre Donnadieu, Nathalie Baye; ***D:*** Daniel Vigne; ***W:*** Daniel Vigne, Jean-Claude Carriere. Cesar Awards '83: Best Writing, Best Score; National Society of Film Critics Awards '83: Best Actor (Depardieu); Nominations: Academy Awards '83: Best Costume Design. *SUE, APD, HMV*

The Return of Our Gang ☠½ **1925** Contains three vintage silent Pathe "Our Gang" shorts: "The School Play (Stage Fright)," "Summer Daze (The Cobbler)," and "Dog Days." **57m/B VHS, Beta, 8mm.** Joe Cobb, Ernie Morrison, Mickey Daniels, Farina Hoskins, Mary Kornman, Jackie Condon, Jack Davis, Jannie Hoskins, Andy Samuels, Eugene Jackson. *VYY*

The Return of Peter Grimm ☠☠½ **1935** Man returns from death to try to tidy up the mess he left behind. Enjoyable if trite fantasy based on a play by David Belasco. **82m/B VHS.** Lionel Barrymore, Helen Mack, Edward Ellis, Donald Meek, George Breakston, James Bush; ***D:*** George Nicholls Jr. *TTC, FCT*

The Return of Spinal Tap ☠☠½ **1992** Cult-fave mock rock group Spinal Tap is back with a feature-length video of performance and backstage footage from its recent reunion concert tour promoting their album "Break Like the Wind." Sequel to "This is Spinal Tap" features lots of heavy metal songs including the title track, "Majesty of Rock," "Bitch School," "Diva Fever," "Clam Caravan," and "Stinkin' Up the Great Outdoors." Not as great as the original satire, but will appeal to Spinal Tap fans. **110m/C VHS, LV.** Christopher Guest, Michael McKean, Harry Shearer, Rick Parnell, C.J. Vanston; ***Cameos:*** Paul Anka, Jeff Beck, Jamie Lee Curtis, Richard Lewis, Martha Quinn, Kenny Rogers, Martin Short, Mel Torme; ***W:*** Christopher Guest, Michael McKean, Harry Shearer. *MPI, MVD*

Return of Superfly ☠ **1990 (R)** Man with insect moniker pesters drug dealers and cops in Harlem. Long-awaited sequel to urban epic "Superfly," scored again by Mayfield. **94m/C VHS.** Margaret Avery, Nathan Purdee, Sam Jackson; ***M:*** Ice-T, Curtis Mayfield. *VMK*

The Return of Swamp Thing ☠½ **1989 (PG-13)** The DC Comics creature rises again out of the muck to fight mutants and evil scientists. Tongue-in-cheek, and nothing at all like the literate, ecologically-oriented comic from which it was derived. **95m/C VHS, Beta, LV.** Louis Jourdan, Heather Locklear, Sarah Douglas, Dick Durock; ***D:*** Jim Wynorski. *COL*

Return of the Aliens: The Deadly Spawn ☠ *The Deadly Spawn* **1983 (R)** Aliens infect the earth and violently destroy humans. Extremely violent and gory. Watch out for those officious offspring. **90m/C VHS.** Charles George Hildebrandt; ***D:*** Douglas McKeown. *NO*

Return of the Ape Man ☠☠ **1944** Campy fun with Carradine and Lugosi. A mad scientist transplants Carradine's brain into the body of the "missing link." Hams galore. **51m/B VHS.** Bela Lugosi, John Carradine, George Zucco, Judith Gibson, Michael Ames, Frank Moran, Mary Currier; ***D:*** Phil Rosen. *MED*

Return of the Bad Men ☠☠ **1948** Scott is a retired marshall who must fight against a gang of outlaws lead by the Sundance Kid. Sequel to "Badman's Territory." **90m/C VHS, Beta.** Randolph Scott, Robert Ryan, Anne Jeffreys, George "Gabby" Hayes, Jason Robards Sr., Jacqueline White; ***D:*** Ray Enright. *CCB, MED, TTC*

Return of the Chinese Boxer ☠ **1974** Samurai and ninja warriors fight, usually to the death. **93m/C VHS, Beta.** Jimmy Wang Yu, Lung Fei, Cheung Ying Chen, Chin Kang. *UNI*

Return of the Dinosaurs **1983** A comet is about to collide with the Earth. Never fear! The dinosaur patrol will interfere (and ultimately save the planet). **82m/C VHS, Beta.** *TWE*

Return of the Dragon ☠☠½ **1973 (R)** In Lee's last picture, a Chinese restaurant in Rome is menaced by gangsters who want to buy the property. On behalf of the owners, Lee duels an American karate champ in the Roman forum. The battle scenes between Lee and Norris are great and make this a must-see for martial arts fans. **91m/C VHS, Beta, LV.** *CH* Bruce Lee, Nora Miao, Chuck Norris; ***D:*** Bruce Lee. *FOX, GEM*

Return of the Evil Dead ☠ *Return of the Blind Dead* **1975** The sightless dead priests return to attack still more 1970s' Europeans in this second installment of the "blind dead" trilogy. Preceded by "Tombs of the Blind Dead" and followed by "Horror of the Zombies." Not to be confused with Raimi's "Evil Dead" slasher flicks. **85m/C VHS.** *SP PT* Tony Kendall, Esther Roy, Frank Blake; ***D:*** Armando de Ossorio. *JEF*

Return of the Family Man ☠ **1989** A mass murderer seems unstoppable as he continues to slash whole families at a time...the family man is redefined in this bloody gore-fest. **90m/C VHS.** Ron Smerczak, Liam Cundill, Terence Reis, Michelle Constant; ***D:*** John Murlowski. *NO*

Return of the Fly ☠☠ **1959** The son of the scientist who discovered how to move matter through space decides to continue his father's work, but does so against his uncle's wishes. He soon duplicates his dad's experiments with similar results. This sequel to "The Fly" doesn't buzz like the original. Followed by "Curse of the Fly." **80m/B VHS, Beta, LV.** Vincent Price, Brett Halsey, John Sutton, Dan Seymour, David Frankham; ***D:*** Edward L. Bernds. *FOX, FCT*

Return of the Jedi ☠☠☠½ **1983 (PG)** Third film in George Lucas' popular space saga. Against seemingly fearsome odds, Luke Skywalker battles such worthies as Jabba the Hut and heavy-breathing Darth Vader to save his comrades and triumph over the evil Galactic Empire. Han and Leia reaffirm their love and team with C3PO, R2-D2, Chewbacca, Calrissian, and a bunch of furry Ewoks to aid in the annihilation of the Dark Side. The special effects are still spectacular, even the third time around. Sequel to "Star Wars" (1977) and "The Empire Strikes Back" (1980). **132m/C VHS, Beta, LV.** Mark Hamill, Carrie Fisher, Harrison Ford, Billy Dee Williams, David Prowse, James Earl Jones, Kenny Baker, Denis Lawson, Anthony Daniels, Peter Mayhew; ***D:*** Richard Marquand; ***W:*** George Lucas, Lawrence Kasdan; ***M:*** John Williams; ***V:*** Alec Guinness, Frank Oz. Academy Awards '83: Best Visual Effects; People's Choice Awards '84: Best Film; Nominations: Academy Awards '83: Best Art Direction/Set Decoration, Best Sound, Best Original Score. *FOX, RDG, HMV*

Return of the Killer Tomatoes! ☠ **1988 (PG)** The man-eating plant-life from 1977's "Attack of the Killer Tomatoes" is back, able to turn into people due to the slightly larger budget. Astin is mad as the scientist. Not as bad as "Attack," representing a small hurdle in the history of filmdom. Followed by "Killer Tomatoes Strike Back." **98m/C VHS, Beta, LV.** Anthony Starke, George Clooney, Karen Mistal, Steve Lundquist, John Astin, Charlie Jones, Rock Peace, Frank Davis, C.J. Dillon, Teri Weigel; ***D:*** John DeBello; ***W:*** John DeBello. *VTR, NWV*

The Return of the King **1980** The third and final animated episode of J.R.R Tolkien's Middle Earth Trilogy. This saga features Frodo, relative to Hobbit Bilbo Baggins, and his faithful servant, making middle Earth safe from Orcs, Gollums and other ooky creatures. **120m/C VHS.** ***D:*** Arthur Rankin Jr., Jules Bass; ***V:*** Orson Bean, Roddy McDowall, John Huston, Theodore Bikel, William Conrad, Glen Yarborough, Paul Frees, Casey Kasem, Sonny Melendrez. *XVC, VTR, FAF*

Return of the Lash ☠ **1947** Lash LaRue once again defends settlers' rights from ruthless outlaws. **53m/B VHS, Beta.** Lash LaRue, Al "Fuzzy" St. John, Mary Maynard, George Chesebro; ***D:*** Ray Taylor. *COL*

Return of the Living Dead ☠☠½ **1985 (R)** Poisonous gas revives a cemetery and a morgue rendering an outrageous spoof on the living-dead sub-genre with fast-moving zombies, punk humor, and exaggerated gore. Its humor does not diminish the fear factor, however. Sequel follows. Directed by "Alien" writer O'Bannon. **90m/C VHS, Beta, LV.** Clu Gulager, James Karen, Linnea Quigley, Don Calfa, Jewel Shepard; ***D:*** Dan O'Bannon. *NO*

Return of the Living Dead 2 ☠½ **1988 (R)** An inevitable sequel to the original Dan O'Bannon satire about George Romero-esque brain-eating zombies attacking suburbia with zest and vigor. **89m/C VHS, Beta, LV.** Dana Ashbrook, Marsha Dietlein, Philip Bruns, James Karen, Thom Mathews; ***D:*** Ken Wiederhorn. *ORI, WAR*

Return of the Living Dead 3 ☠½ **1993 (R)** When Curt's girlfriend Julie dies in a motorcycle accident you'd think that would be the end of romance. But not when your dad heads a secret project that involves reviving corpses. Only problem is now Julie's a zombie with long metal claws and glass spikes sticking out of various body parts. Hey, if it's true love Curt will get over it. Macabre special effects. Also available unrated. **97m/C VHS, LV.** Mindy Clarke, J. Trevor Edmond, Kent McCord, Basil Wallace, Fabio Urena; ***D:*** Brian Yuzna; ***W:*** John Penney; ***M:*** Barry Goldberg. *VMK*

Return of the Man from U.N.C.L.E. ☠☠ **1983** Those dashing super agents Napoleon Solo and Illya Kuryakin come out of retirement to settle an old score with their nemesis THRUSH. Made for television. **96m/C VHS, Beta.** Robert Vaughn, David McCallum, Patrick Macnee, Gayle Hunnicutt, Geoffrey Lewis; ***D:*** Ray Austin. *TWE*

The Return of the Musketeers ☠☠½ **1989 (PG)** Lester's third Musketeers film (after his successful double-act in the '70s) is a good-natured but average costume/comedy/buddy film. Twenty years after D'Artagnan, Athos, Porthos, and Aramis saved the French queen from scandal it's time to do it all over again. Milady DeWinter, who hatched the first plot, is dead but her equally devious daughter Justine is more than able to take mama's scheming place. Just to add a little more excitement Athos' adopted son Raoul meets Justine and passions fly amidst the swordplay. Based on the Alexandre Dumas novel "Twenty Years After." **103m/C VHS, LV.** *GB FR SP* Michael York, Oliver Reed, Frank Finlay, Richard Chamberlain, Kim Cattrall, C. Thomas Howell, Geraldine Chaplin, Roy Kinnear, Christopher Lee, Philippe Noiret, Jean-Pierre Cassel, Billy Connolly, Eusebio Lazaro; ***D:*** Richard Lester; ***W:*** George MacDonald Fraser. *MCA, BTV, FCT*

The Return of the Native ☠☠½ **1994 (PG)** Wind-swept moors, a tempestuous heroine, two loves, and requisite tragedy all courtesy of Thomas Hardy's 1878 novel. Beautiful Eustacia Vye (Jones) longs to leave the boredom of Egdon Heath—even though she's involved with the roguish Damon Wildeve (Owen). Then businessman Clym Yeobright (Stevenson) returns from Paris and captures Eustacia's fancy. She marries him in the hope they'll return to the continent but she's bitterly disappointed when Clym wants to remain in Egdon. Meanwhile, Damon has married Clym's gentle cousin Thomasin (Skinner) but he and Eustacia can't seem to stay away from each other, leading to storms for all. **99m/C VHS.** Catherine Zeta Jones, Clive Owen, Ray Stevenson, Claire Skinner, Joan Plowright, Steven Mackintosh, Celia Imrie, Paul Rogers; ***D:*** Jack Gold; ***W:*** Robert W. Lenski; ***M:*** Carl Davis. *REP*

Return of the Pink Panther ☠☠½ **1974 (G)** Bumbling Inspector Clouseau is called upon to rescue the Pink Panther diamond stolen from a museum. Sellers manages to produce mayhem with a vacuum cleaner and other devices that, in his hands, become instruments of terror. Clever opening credits. Fourth installment in the Pink Panther series but the first with Sellers since 1964's "A Shot In The Dark." **113m/C VHS, Beta, LV.** Peter Sellers, Christopher Plummer, Catherine Schell, Herbert Lom, Victor Spinetti; ***D:*** Blake Edwards; ***W:*** Frank Waldman, Blake Edwards; ***C:*** Geoffrey Unsworth; ***M:*** Henry Mancini. *FOX, FHE, FCT*

Return of the Rebels ☠☠ **1981** Made for television fluff with Eden as a motorcycle matron whose campground is rid of riff-raff by the crow-lined participants in a 25-year reunion of a biker gang. **100m/C VHS.** Barbara Eden, Robert Mandan, Jamie Farr, Patrick Swayze, Don Murray, Christopher Connelly; ***D:*** Noel Nosseck. *NO*

Return of the Scorpion ☠ **1980** Big trouble abounds as that crazy kung fu guy, the "Scorpion," comes back to town. **90m/C VHS, Beta.** Yang Pan Pan, Lam Men Wei, Philip Ko. *NO*

Return of the Secaucus 7 ☠☠☠½ **1980** Centers around a weekend reunion of seven friends who were activists during the Vietnam War in the turbulent '60s. Now turning 30, they evaluate their present lives and progress. Writer and director Sayles plays Howie in this excellent example of what a low-budget film can and should be. A less trendy predecessor of "The Big Chill" (1983) which, perhaps, was a few years ahead of its time. **110m/C VHS, Beta.** Mark Arnott, Gordon Clapp, Maggie Cousineau-Arndt, David Strathairn; ***D:*** John Sayles; ***W:*** John Sayles; ***M:*** Mason Daring. Los Angeles Film Critics Association Awards '80: Best Screenplay. *COL*

Return of the Seven ☠☠ *Return of the Magnificent Seven* **1966** The first sequel to "The Magnificent Seven" features the group liberating a compatriot who is held hostage. Yawn. **97m/C VHS, Beta.** Yul Brynner, Warren Oates, Robert Fuller, Claude Akins; ***D:*** Burt Kennedy; ***W:*** Larry Cohen; ***C:*** Paul Vogel; ***M:*** Elmer Bernstein. Nominations: Academy Awards '66: Best Original Score. *MGM*

Return of the Soldier ☠☠☠ **1982** A shell-shocked WWI veteran has no memory of his marriage, leaving his wife, his childhood flame, and an unrequited love to vie for his affections. Adapted from the novel by Rebecca West. **101m/C VHS, Beta.** *GB* Glenda Jackson, Julie Christie, Ann-Margret, Alan Bates, Ian Holm, Frank Finlay; ***D:*** Alan Bridges; ***M:*** Richard Rodney Bennett. Nominations: Cannes Film Festival '82: Best Film. *NO*

Return of the Street Fighter ☠½ **197?** Sequel to "The Street Fighter," finds Terry Tsuguri (Chiba) hired by a gang to silence a jailed informer. So, Terry gets arrested, practices his karate and does the guy in, and finds out the gang now wants to silence him. Big mistake! Notice a pattern yet? Followed by "The Street Fighter's Last Revenge" and "Sister Street Fighter." **88m/C VHS.** Sonny Chiba. *NLC*

Return of the Tall Blond Man With One Black Shoe ☠☠½ **1974** Sequel to 1972's "The Tall Blond Man With One Black Shoe." Again a "klutz" is mistaken for a master spy and becomes unknowingly involved in the world of international intrigue. In French with English subtitles. Not quite as good as the original. **84m/C VHS, Beta.** *FR* Pierre Richard, Mireille Darc, Michael Duchaussoy, Jean Rochefort, Jean Carmet; ***D:*** Yves Robert; ***W:*** Francis Veber; ***M:*** Vladimir Cosma. *CVC, PSM, INJ*

Return of the Tiger ☠½ **1978** The Hover Night Club in Bangkok fronts the operations of an international narcotics group headed by an American. When a rival Chinese gang tries to dominate the drug market, conflict and lots of kicking ensue. **95m/C VHS, Beta.** Bruce Li, Paul Smith, Chaing I, Angela Mao; ***D:*** Jimmy Shaw. *MED*

Return of the Vampire ☠☠ **1943** A Hungarian vampire and his werewolf servant seek revenge on the family who drove a spike through his heart two decades earlier. **69m/B VHS, Beta, LV.** Bela Lugosi, Nina Foch, Miles Mander, Matt Willis, Frieda Inescort, Roland Varno; ***D:*** Lew (Louis Friedlander) Landers, Kurt Neumann. *GKK, MLB*

Return of Wildfire ½ **1948** Two sisters are left to run the family horse ranch when their brother is killed. A drifter aids the sisters in bringing the murderer to justice. **83m/B VHS, Beta.** Richard Arlen, Patricia Morison, Mary Beth Hughes. *NO*

Return to Africa **1989** Rebels threaten the familial paradise of the tightknit Mallory clan. **95m/C VHS, Beta.** Stan Brock, Anne Collings, David Tors, Ivan Tors, Peter Tors, Steven Tors; ***D:*** Leslie Martinson. *PSM*

Return to Boggy Creek **1977 (PG)** Townspeople in a small fishing village learn from a photographer that a "killer" beast, whom they thought had disappeared, has returned and is living in Boggy Creek. Some curious children follow the shutterbug into the marsh, despite hurricane warnings, and the swamp monster reacts with unusual compassion. OK for the kiddies. Fictitious story unlike other "Boggy Creek" films, which are billed as semi-documentaries. Sequel to "Legend of Boggy Creek" and features Mary Ann from "Gilligan's Island." **87m/C VHS, Beta.** Dawn Wells, Dana Plato, Louise Belaire, John Hofeus; ***D:*** Tom Moore. *FOX*

Return to Earth **1976** Made for television drama deals with the self-doubts faced by Apollo 11 astronaut Buzz Aldrin after his triumphant return to Earth. Based on Aldrin's own novel. **74m/C VHS, Beta.** Cliff Robertson, Shirley Knight, Ralph Bellamy, Stefanie Powers, Charles Cioffi; ***D:*** Jud Taylor. *TWE*

Return to Eden **1989** A young woman falls in love with her philosophy tutor, but he can't return her affections. An interesting comparison between the passion of the primitive and the tangle of modern-day romance. **90m/C VHS.** Sam Bottoms, Edward Binns, Renee Coleman; ***D:*** William Olsen. *NO*

Return to Fantasy Island ½ **1977** Boss, boss, it's da plane! The second full-length television treatment of the once popular series wherein three couples get their most cherished fantasy fulfilled by Mr. Roarke. and company. **100m/C VHS, Beta.** Ricardo Montalban, Herve Villechaize, Adrienne Barbeau, Pat Crowley, Joseph Campanella, Karen Valentine, Laraine Day, George Maharis, Horst Buchholz, France Nuyen, Joseph Cotten, Cameron Mitchell, George Chakiris; ***D:*** George McCowan. *PSM*

Return to Horror High **1987 (R)** A horror movie producer makes a film in an abandoned and haunted high school, where a series of murders occurred years earlier. As in most "return" flicks, history repeats itself. **95m/C VHS, Beta.** Alex Rocco, Vince Edwards, Philip McKeon, Brendan Hughes, Lori Lethin, Scott Jacoby; ***D:*** Bill Froelich. *VTR, NWV*

Return to Lonesome Dove ½ **1993** Routine sequel to successful western saga "Lonesome Dove" picks up after the burial of Gus McCrae in Texas by his friend, ex-Texas Ranger Woodrow F. Call (now played by Voight). The original dealt with a cattle drive, this one with horses. Along the way you'll run into the usual sidewinders as well as McCrae's lost love Clara (now Hershey) and Schroder, returning as Call's unacknowledged son Newt. Filmed on loction in Montana. TV production was already underway when author Larry McMurtry gave the producers his then unpublished sequel "Streets of Laredo" which differed from the script. Some changes were made but the book and miniseries don't match. **330m/C VHS, LV.** Jon Voight, William L. Petersen, Rick Schroder, Barbara Hershey, Louis Gossett Jr., Oliver Reed, Reese Witherspoon, Nia Peeples, Dennis Haysbert, Timothy Scott, Barry Tubb, Chris Cooper, CCH Pounder, William Sanderson; ***D:*** Mike Robe; ***W:*** John Wilder. *CAF, FUS*

Return to Macon County **1975** Tale of three young, reckless youths who become involved with drag racing and a sadistic law enforcement officer. Nolte turns in a good performance in his first film, as does Johnson, despite a mediocre script and dialogue. Sequel to 1974's "Macon County Line." **90m/C VHS, Beta.** Nick Nolte, Don Johnson, Robin Mattson; ***D:*** Richard Compton; ***W:*** Richard Compton. *LIV, VES*

Return to Mayberry **1985** Andy Taylor returns to Mayberry after 20 years to obtain his old job as sheriff. Sixteen of the original actors reappeared for this nostalgia-fest. Made for television. **95m/C VHS, Beta.** Andy Griffith, Ron Howard, Don Knotts, Jim Nabors, Aneta Corsaut, Jack Dodson, George Lindsey, Betty Lynn; ***D:*** Bob Sweeney. *MCG*

Return to Oz ½ **1985 (PG)** Picking up where "The Wizard of Oz" left off, Auntie Em and Uncle Ed place Dorothy in the care of a therapist to cure her "delusions" of Oz. A natural disaster again lands her in the land of the yellow brick road, where the evil Nome King and Princess Mombi are spreading terror and squalor. Based on a later L. Frank Baum book. Enjoyable for the whole family although some scenes may frighten very small children. **109m/C VHS, Beta, LV.** Fairuza Balk, Piper Laurie, Matt Clark, Nicol Williamson, Jean Marsh; ***D:*** Walter Murch; ***C:*** David Watkin; ***M:*** David Shire. *DIS*

Return to Paradise **1953** Cooper is a soldier of fortune wandering through the Polynesian islands in the late 1920s. On a remote atoll he comes across a crazy missionary intent upon subduing the native population. Cooper falls in love with a native beauty (Haynes in her screen debut) and leads the natives in a revolt against authority. Cliched but with nice scenery from the location shoot in Samoa. Loose adaptation of the short story "Mr. Morgan" by James Michener. **100m/C VHS, Beta.** Gary Cooper, Roberta Haynes, Barry Jones, John Hudson, Moira MacDonald; ***D:*** Mark Robson; ***W:*** Charles Kaufman. *MGM, FCT*

Return to Peyton Place ½ **1961** A young writer publishes novel exposing town as virtual Peyton Place, and the townsfolk turn against her and her family. Sequel to the scandalously popular '50s original and inspiration for the just-as-popular soap opera. Astor is excellent as the evil matriarch. **122m/C VHS.** Carol Lynley, Jeff Chandler, Eleanor Parker, Mary Astor, Robert Sterling, Luciana Paluzzi, Tuesday Weld, Brett Halsey, Bob Crane; ***D:*** Jose Ferrer. *FOX, FCT*

Return to Salem's Lot **1987 (R)** Enjoyable camp sequel to the Stephen King tale, this time involving a cynical scientist and his son returning to the town only to find it completely run by vampires. **101m/C VHS, Beta.** Michael Moriarty, Ricky Addison Reed, Samuel Fuller, Andrew Duggan, Evelyn Keyes, Jill Gatsby, June Havoc, Ronee Blakley, James Dixon, David Holbrook; ***D:*** Larry Cohen; ***W:*** James Dixon, Larry Cohen. *WAR*

Return to Snowy River **1988 (PG)** Continues the love story of the former ranch hand and the rancher's daughter in Australia's Victoria Alps that began in "The Man From Snowy River." Dennehy takes over from Kirk Douglas as the father who aims to keep the lovers apart. The photography of horses and the scenery is spectacular, making the whole film worthwhile. **99m/C VHS, Beta, LV.** *AU* Tom Burlinson, Sigrid Thornton, Brian Dennehy, Nicholas Eadie, Mark Hembrow, Bryan Marshall; ***D:*** Geoff Burrowes; ***W:*** Geoff Burrowes. *DIS, TVC*

Return to the Blue Lagoon **1991 (PG-13)** Neither the acting nor the premise has improved with age. Another photogenic adolescent couple experiences puberty on that island; for continuity, the young man is the son of the lovers in the first "Blue Lagoon." Breathtaking scenery—just turn down the sound. **102m/C VHS, LV.** Milla Jovovich, Brian Krause, Lisa Pelikan; ***D:*** William A. Graham; ***C:*** Robert Steadman. *COL*

Return to the Lost World ½ **1993 (PG)** Rival scientists Challenger and Summerlee set out for the Lost World and find it threatened by oil prospectors. With a volcano about to explode the scientists set out to save their prehistoric paradise and its dinosaur inhabitants. Based on a story by Sir Arthur Conan Doyle. Sequel to "The Lost World." **99m/C VHS.** John Rhys-Davies, David Warner, Darren Peter Mercer, Geza Kovacs; ***D:*** Timothy Bond. *WOV*

Return to Two Moon Junction ½ **1993 (R)** New York supermodel Savannah (Clarke) returns to her family's riverfront home in Georgia and promptly sheds her clothing for local sculptor Jake (Schafer). Must be something about the southern heat. This sequel should have the same video success as its predecessor since it keeps to the minimal plot/maximum teasing sex scenes outline. **96m/C VHS, LV.** Mindy Clarke, John Clayton Schafer, Louise Fletcher; ***D:*** Farhad Mann. *VMK*

Reuben, Reuben **1983 (R)** Brilliant, but drunken poet Conti turns himself around when he falls in love with earthy college girl McGillis in her film debut. The student's dog Reuben unwittingly alters Conti's progress, however, in the film's startling conclusion. Based on the writings of Peter DeVries. **100m/C VHS, Beta.** Tom Conti, Kelly McGillis, Roberts Blossom, E. Katherine Kerr, Cynthia Harris, Joel Fabiani, Kara Wilson, Lois Smith; ***D:*** Robert Ellis Miller; ***W:*** Julius J. Epstein; ***M:*** Billy Goldenberg. National Board of Review Awards '83: Best Actor (Conti); Writers Guild of America '83: Best Adapted Screenplay; Nominations: Academy Awards '83: Best Actor (Conti), Best Adapted Screenplay. *FOX*

Reunion **1988 (PG-13)** Robards stars as a Jewish businessman, living in the U.S., who returns to his boyhood home of Stuttgart, Germany some 50 years after his leaving in 1933. He hopes to find out what happened to a boyhood school chum—the son of an artistocractic (and Aryan) German family. Film uses extensive flashbacks to show the the rise of anti-Semitism and how it affects the friendship of both youths. Thoughtfull and well-acted though occasionally plodding drama based on Fred Uhlman's novel. **120m/C VHS, Beta, LV.** *FR GE GB* Jason Robards Jr., Christien Anholt, Sam West, Francoise Fabian, Maureen Kerwin, Barbara Jefford, Alexander Trauner; ***D:*** Jerry Schatzberg; ***W:*** Harold Pinter. *FRH, IME, FCT*

Reunion in France *Mademoiselle France; Reunion* **1942** Parisian dress designer sacrifices her lifestyle to help an American flier flee France after the Nazis invade. Dated patriotic flag-waver. **104m/B VHS, Beta.** Joan Crawford, John Wayne, Philip Dorn, Reginald Owen, Albert Basserman, John Carradine, Ann Ayars, J. Edward Bromberg, Henry Daniell, Moroni Olsen, Howard da Silva, Ava Gardner, John Considine; ***D:*** Jules Dassin. *MGM*

Revenge ½ *Terror under the House; After Jenny Died; Inn of the Frightened People* **1971** The parents of a girl who was brutally killed take the law into their own hands in this bloody, vengeful thriller. **89m/C VHS, Beta.** *GB* Joan Collins, James Booth, Ray Barrett, Sinead Cusack, Kenneth Griffith; ***D:*** Sidney Hayers. *SUE, MRV*

Revenge *Woof!* **1986 (R)** Sequel to "Blood Cult" about a cult led by horror king Carradine. Seems these dog worshippers want McGowan's land and Senator Carradine will stop at nothing to get it. Woofer filled with gratuitous violence. **104m/C VHS, Beta.** Patrick Wayne, John Carradine, Bennie Lee McGowan, Josef Hanet, Stephanie Kropke; ***D:*** Christopher Lewis. *VCI*

Revenge **1990 (R)** Retired pilot Costner makes the mistake of falling in love with another man's wife. Quinn gives a first-rate performance as the Mexican crime lord who punishes his spouse and her lover, beginning a cycle of vengeance. Sometimes contrived, but artfully photographed with tantalizing love scenes. Based on the Jim Harrison novel. **123m/C VHS, Beta, LV, 8mm.** Kevin Costner, Anthony Quinn, Madeleine Stowe, Sally Kirkland, Joe Santos, Miguel Ferrer, James Gammon, Tomas Milian; ***D:*** Tony Scott; ***W:*** Jim Harrison; ***M:*** Jack Nitzsche. *COL*

Revenge in the House of Usher **1982** House holds grudge. **90m/C VHS.** Howard Vernon, Dan Villers; ***D:*** Jess (Jesus) Franco. *MOV*

Revenge of a Kabuki Actor **1963** When Kabuki actor Kazuo Hasegawa's parents are vicously murdered, he seeks their killer with a vengeance. In Japanese with English subtitles. **114m/C VHS.** *JP* ***D:*** Kon Ichikawa. *FST, FCT*

Revenge of Doctor X *Woof!* **198?** A man/beast lies waiting for the pretty reporter who seeks her shipwrecked father in the jungles of an uncharted island. **90m/C VHS, Beta.** John Ashley, Ronald Remy, Angelique Pettyjohn. *NO*

The Revenge of Frankenstein 🦴🦴½ **1958** Frankenstein (Cushing) is rescued from the guillotine by his dwarf servant and decides to relocate to Carlsbruck where he becomes the popular society physician, Dr. Stein. But the misunderstood doc just can't stop his ghoulish experiments and plans to transfer his servant's brain into another sewn together creature. Nicely macabre sequel to "The Curse of Frankenstein;" followed by "The Evil of Frankenstein." **89m/C VHS.** *GB* Peter Cushing, Michael Gwynn, Francis Matthews, Oscar Quitak, Lionel Jeffries, Eunice Gayson, John Welsh; ***D:*** Terence Fisher; ***W:*** Jimmy Sangster. *COL*

Revenge of the Barbarians 🦴 **1964** As the barbarians descend on Rome, Olympus must decide whether to save the empire or the beautiful Gallo, the woman he loves. Decisions, decisions. **99m/C Beta.** Robert Alda, Anthony Steele. *AIP*

Revenge of the Barbarians 🦴 **1985** A Scandinavian adventure about a young Celt seeking revenge against the Viking hordes that killed his family. **95m/C Beta.** ***D:*** Hrafn Gunnlaugsson. *NO*

Revenge of the Cheerleaders 🦴 **1976 (R)** The cheerleaders pull out all the stops to save their school from a ruthless land developer. What spirit. **86m/C VHS, Beta.** Jerii Woods, Cheryl "Rainbeaux" Smith, Helen Lang, Patrice Rohmer, Susie Elene, Eddra Gale, William Bramley, Carl Ballantine, David Hasselhoff; ***D:*** Richard Lerner. *LIV*

Revenge of the Creature 🦴🦴 **1955** In this follow up to "The Creature From the Black Lagoon," the Gill-man is captured in the Amazon and taken to a Florida marine park. There he is put on display for visitors and subjected to heartless experiments. Growing restless in his captive surroundings, the creature breaks free and makes for the ocean. Includes screen debut of Clint Eastwood as a lab technician. Originally shot in 3-D. Based on a story by William Alland. Available on laserdisc as part of a special Encore Edition Double Feature with "The Creature Walks Among Us." **82m/B VHS, LV.** John Agar, Lori Nelson, John Bromfield, John Wood, Nestor Paiva, Clint Eastwood; ***D:*** Jack Arnold; ***W:*** Martin Berkeley. *MCA, FCT*

Revenge of the Dead 🦴 **1984 (R)** European archeological team discovers the existence of a powerful force that allows the dead to return to life. **100m/C VHS, Beta.** *IT* Gabriele Lavia, Anne Canoras; ***D:*** Pupi Avati. *LIV*

Revenge of the Living Zombies 🦴 **1988 (R)** Teens on a Halloween hayride run headlong into flesh-craving zombies. Available in a slightly edited version. **85m/C VHS, Beta.** Bill Hinzman, John Mowod, Leslie Ann Wick, Kevin Kindlan; ***D:*** Bill Hinzman. *NO*

Revenge of the Nerds 🦴🦴½ **1984 (R)** When nerdy college freshmen are victimized by jocks, frat boys and the school's beauties, they start their own fraternity and seek revenge. Carradine and Edwards team well as the geeks in this better than average teenage sex comedy. Guess who gets the girls? Sequel was much worse. **89m/C VHS, Beta, LV.** Robert Carradine, Anthony Edwards, Timothy Busfield, Andrew Cassese, Curtis Armstrong, Larry B. Scott, Brian Tochi, Julia Montgomery, Michelle Meyrink, Ted McGinley, John Goodman, Bernie Casey; ***D:*** Jeff Kanew; ***W:*** Tim Metcalfe, Jeff Bukai; ***M:*** Thomas Newman. *FOX*

Revenge of the Nerds 2: Nerds in Paradise 🦴 **1987 (PG-13)** The nerd clan from the first film (minus Edwards who only makes a brief appearance) travels to Fort Lauderdale for a fraternity conference. They fend off loads of bullies and jocks with raunchy humor. Boy can Booger belch. Not as good as the first Nerds movie; a few laughs nonetheless. **89m/C VHS, Beta, LV.** Robert Carradine, Curtis Armstrong, Timothy Busfield, Andrew Cassese, Ed Lauter, Larry B. Scott, Courtney Thorne-Smith, Anthony Edwards, James Hong; ***D:*** Joe Roth. *FOX*

Revenge of the Nerds 3: The Next Generation 🦴½ **1992** Adams College has nerd-loathing trustee Downey, Jr. mobilizing those frat boys against the bespectacled geeks, who turn to founding nerd Carradine to save them. Cookie-cutter characters and the gags won't hold your attention. Let's hope this is the last in the series. **?m/C VHS.** Robert Carradine, Curtis Armstrong, Ted McGinley, Morton Downey Jr., Julia Montgomery. *FXV*

Revenge of the Nerds 4: Nerds in Love 🦴🦴½ **1994** Yes, even nerds deserve a little love. This time the gang get together for Booger's (Armstrong) wedding—complete with nerd bachelor party and wedding shower. Too bad Booger's future father-in-law is so reluctant to have a nerd in the family that he hires a sleazy detective to dig up some dirt. Made for TV. **90m/C VHS.** Curtis Armstrong, Robert Carradine, Ted McGinley, Larry B. Scott, Donald Gibb, Joseph Bologna, Julia Montgomery, Corinne Bohrer, Christina Pickles, Jessica Tuck, Robert Picardo; ***D:*** Steve Zacharias; ***W:*** Steve Zacharias, Steve Buhai. *FXV*

Revenge of the Ninja 🦴🦴½ **1983 (R)** Ninja Kosugi hopes to escape his past in Los Angeles. A drug trafficker, also ninja-trained, prevents him. The two polish off a slew of mobsters before their own inevitable showdown. Better-than the standard chop-socky fest from Cannon with amusing surreal touches like a battling grandma ninja. Sequel to "Enter the Ninja," followed by "Ninja III." **90m/C VHS, Beta.** Sho Kosugi, Arthur Roberts, Keith Vitali, Virgil Frye, Ashley Ferrare, Kane Kosugi, John Lamotta, Grace Oshita, Melvin C. Hampton, Mario Gallo; ***D:*** Sam Firstenberg; ***W:*** James R. Silke; ***M:*** Rob Walsh. *MGM*

Revenge of the Pink Panther 🦴🦴½ **1978 (PG)** Inspector Clouseau survives his own assassination attempt, but allows the world to think he is dead in order to pursue an investigation of the culprits in his own unique, bumbling way. The last "Pink Panther" film before Sellers died, and perhaps the least funny. **99m/C VHS, Beta, LV.** Peter Sellers, Herbert Lom, Dyan Cannon, Robert Webber, Burt Kwouk, Robert Loggia; ***D:*** Blake Edwards; ***W:*** Blake Edwards, Ron Clark, Frank Waldman; ***M:*** Henry Mancini. *FOX, FCT*

Revenge of the Radioactive Reporter 🦴🦴 **1991** Nuclear plant honchos don't like journalist who's about to hang their dirty laundry, so they toss him into vat of nuclear waste. He returns as a reporter with a cosmetic peel. **90m/C VHS.** David Scammell, Kathryn Boese, Randy Pearlstein, Derrick Strange; ***D:*** Craig Pryce. *NO*

Revenge of the Red Baron 🦴🦴½ **1993 (PG-13)** Jim Spencer (Rooney) is the WWI pilot who shot down Germany's fearsome Red Baron. Now aged and infirm he's tormented by what he thinks is his enemy's ghost. A vengeful ghost who takes after Spencer's family. **90m/C VHS, LV.** Mickey Rooney, Toby Maguire, Laraine Newman, Cliff DeYoung; ***D:*** Robert Gordon; ***W:*** Michael James McDonald; ***C:*** Christian Sebaldt. *NHO*

Revenge of the Stepford Wives 🦴½ **1980** Made for television sequel to the Ira Levin fantasy about suburban husbands who create obedient robot replicas of their wives. In this installment, the wives are not robots, but are simply made docile by drugs. Strange casting pairs Johnson and Kavner as husband and stepford wife. Begat "The Stepford Children." **95m/C VHS, Beta.** Sharon Gless, Julie Kavner, Don Johnson, Audra Lindley, Mason Adams, Arthur Hill; ***D:*** Robert Fuest. *SUE, NLC*

Revenge of the Teenage Vixens from Outer Space 🦴🦴 **1986** A low-budget film about three sex starved females from another planet who come to earth to find men. When the ones they meet do not live up to their expectations, the frustrated females turn the disappointing dudes are turned into vegetables. **84m/C VHS, Beta.** Lisa Schwedop, Howard Scott; ***D:*** Jeff Ferrell. *NO*

Revenge of the Virgins 🦴 **1962** A tribe of topless 'Indian' women protect their sacred land from the white men. Exhumed exploitation for bad-film junkies, narrated by Kenne Duncan, an Ed Wood cohort. **53m/B VHS.** Jewell Morgan, Charles Veltman, Jodean Russo, Stanton Pritchard; ***D:*** Paul Perri. *NOS, SMW, VDM*

Revenge of the Zombies 🦴½ **1943** In this sequel of sorts to "King of the Zombies," Carradine is creating an army of the undead for use by an evil foreign entity. **61m/B VHS.** John Carradine, Robert Lowery, Gale Storm, Veda Ann Borg, Mantan Moreland; ***D:*** Steve Sekely. *MLB*

Revenge of the Zombies 🦴½ **1981 (R)** Kung-fu exploitation film featuring man-eating alligators, zombies, mad magicians, and more. **?m/C VHS.** Ti Lung, Lily Tu. *LOO*

The Revenge Rider 🦴🦴 **1935** Orphan McCoy goes after the villains who killed his parents. Good performance from McCoy in an otherwise average film. **60m/B VHS.** Tim McCoy, Robert Allen, Billie Seward, Edward Earle, Jack Clifford, Lafe McKee; ***D:*** David Selman. *DVT, HEG*

The Revenger 🦴 **1990** A framed man returns from prison and finds that a mobster has kidnapped his wife and wants $50,000 to give her back. **91m/C VHS, Beta.** Oliver Reed, Frank Zagarino; ***D:*** Cedric Sundstrom. *AIP*

Reversal of Fortune 🦴🦴🦴½ **1990 (R)** True tale of wealthy socialite Claus von Bulow (Irons) accused of deliberately giving his wife Sunny (Close) a near-lethal overdose of insulin. Comatose Close narrates history of the couple's courtship and married life, a saga of unhappiness and substance abuse, while Silver (as lawyer Dershowitz) et al prepare von Bulow's defense. An unflattering picture of the idle rich that never spells out what really happened. Irons is excellent as the eccentric and creepy defendant and richly deserved his Best Actor Oscar. From the novel by Dershowitz. **112m/C VHS, Beta, LV, 8mm.** Jeremy Irons, Glenn Close, Ron Silver, Annabella Sciorra, Uta Hagen, Fisher Stevens, Julie Hagerty, Jack Gilpin, Christine Baranski; ***D:*** Barbet Schroeder; ***W:*** Nicholas Kazan. Academy Awards '90: Best Actor (Irons); Golden Globe Awards '91: Best Actor—Drama (Irons); Los Angeles Film Critics Association Awards '90: Best Actor (Irons), Best Screenplay; National Society of Film Critics Awards '90: Best Actor (Irons); Nominations: Academy Awards '90: Best Adapted Screenplay, Best Director (Schroeder). *WAR, FCT, BTV*

The Revolt of Job 🦴🦴🦴 *Job Lazadasa* **1984** An elderly Jewish couple adopts an 8-year-old Gentile boy although it is illegal in WWII-torn Hungary and against the beliefs of the orthodox community. Moving story with fine performances. **98m/C VHS, Beta.** *GE HU* Fereno Zenthe, Hedi Tenessy; ***D:*** Imre Gyongyossy, Barna Kabay. *MGM, SWC*

Revolt of the Barbarians 🦴 **1964** Ancient Rome is plagued by barbarian invasion and piracy. A consul travels to Gaul to try to put an end to their misdeeds. **?m/C VHS, Beta.** *IT* Roland Carey, Grazia Maria Spina, Mario Feliciani. *SNC*

Revolt of the Dragon 🦴 **1975 (R)** Martial arts expert visits friends in his hometown and finds himself battling a ruthless gang that terrorizes the people. **90m/C VHS, Beta.** *HHT*

Revolt of the Zombies 🦴 **1936** A mad scientist learns the secret of bringing the dead to life and musters the zombies into an unique, gruesome military unit during WWI. Strange early zombie flick looks silly by today's standards. **65m/B VHS, Beta.** Dorothy Stone, Dean Jagger, Roy D'Arcy, Robert Noland, George Cleveland; ***D:*** Victor Halperin; ***W:*** Howard Higgin. *SNC, MLB, MRV*

Revolution **1969** Documentary of hippie life in San Francisco during the turbulent '60s. **90m/C VHS.** Today Malone; ***D:*** Jack O'Connell. *WAR*

Revolution 🦴 **1985 (R)** The American Revolution is the setting for this failed epic centering on an illiterate trapper and his son who find themselves caught up in the fighting. Long and dull, which is unfortunate, because the story had some potential. The cast is barely believable in their individual roles. Where did you get that accent, Al? **125m/C VHS, Beta, LV.** *GB* Al Pacino, Donald Sutherland, Nastassia Kinski, Annie Lennox, Joan Plowright, Steven Berkoff, Dave King; ***D:*** Hugh Hudson; ***W:*** Robert Dillon. *WAR*

Revolution! A Red Comedy 𝄞𝄞𝄞
1991 A group of students are lured away from their revolutionary tendencies by materialistic indulgences. This satirical comedy is in color and black and white. **84m/B VHS.** Kimberly Flynn, Christopher Renstrom, Georg Osterman; ***D:*** Jeff Kahn; ***W:*** Jeff Kahn. *INJ*

Revolver 𝄞𝄞 **1992 (R)** FBI agent Nick Sastro is paralyzed by an assassin's bullet when he tries to stop Aldo Testi, an arms and drug smuggler. But Nick decides to come out of retirement when a chance to nail Testi comes his way. **96m/C VHS.** Robert Urich, Dakin Matthews, Steven Williams, Assumpta Serna; ***D:*** Gary Nelson. *COL*

Rhapsody 𝄞𝄞½ **1954** Taylor plays a wealthy woman torn between a famous young violinist and an equally talented pianist in this long and overdrawn soap opera. Although Taylor gives a superb performance, it's not enough to save this sugarcoated musical romance. Includes lush European scenery and sequences of classical music dubbed in by Claudio Arrau and Michael Rabin. Based on the adaptation of the Henry Handel Richardson novel "Maurice Guest." **115m/C VHS.** Elizabeth Taylor, Vittorio Gassman, John Ericson, Louis Calhern, Michael Chekhov, Barbara Bates, Celia Lovsky; ***D:*** Charles Vidor; ***W:*** Michael Kanin, Fay Kanin. *MGM*

Rhapsody in August 𝄞𝄞½ **1991 (PG)**
Talky family drama has four children spending the summer with their grandmother Kane in Nagasaki. They become obsessed with the memorials and bomb sites commemorating the dropping of the atomic bomb in 1945 and their grandmother's experiences. Then Kane's Eurasian nephew (Gere) comes for a visit, inciting more family discussions. Adapted from the novel "Nabe-no-Naka" by Kiyoko Murata. Minor Kurosawa; in Japanese with English subtitles. **98m/C VHS, LV.** *JP* Sachiko Murase, Narumi Kayashima, Hisashi Igawa, Richard Gere; ***D:*** Akira Kurosawa; ***W:*** Akira Kurosawa. *ORI*

Rhapsody in Blue 𝄞𝄞𝄞 **1945** Standard Hollywood biography of the great composer features whitewashed and non-existent characters to deal with the spottier aspects of Gershwin's life. Still, the music is the main attraction and it doesn't disappoint. ♫Rhapsody in Blue; Concerto in F; The Cuban Overture; Fascinatin' Rhythm; The Man I Love; Yankee Doodle Blues; Somebody Loves Me; Swanee; Mine. **139m/B VHS, LV.** Robert Alda, Joan Leslie, Alexis Smith, Charles Coburn, Julie Bishop, Albert Basserman, Morris Carnovsky, Rosemary DeCamp, Herbert Rudley, Charles Halton, Robert Shayne, Johnny Downs, Al Jolson; ***D:*** Irving Rapper; ***W:*** Howard Koch; ***M:*** George Gershwin, Max Steiner, Ira Gershwin. Nominations: Academy Awards '45: Best Sound, Best Original Score. *MGM, FCT*

Rhinestone 𝄞 **1984 (PG)** A country singer claims she can turn anyone, even a cabbie, into a singing sensation. Stuck with Stallone, Parton prepares her protege to sing at New York City's roughest country-western club, The Rhinestone. Only diehard Dolly and Rocky fans need bother with this bunk. Some may enjoy watching the thick, New York accented Stallone learn how to properly pronounce dog ("dawg") in country lingo. Yee-haw. **111m/C VHS, Beta, LV.** Sylvester Stallone, Dolly Parton, Ron Leibman, Richard Farnsworth, Tim Thomerson; ***D:*** Bob (Benjamin) Clark; ***W:*** Sylvester Stallone, Phil Alden Robinson. Golden Raspberry Awards '84: Worst Actor (Stallone), Worst Song ("Drinkenstein"). *FOX, OM*

Rhodes 𝄞𝄞½ *Rhodes of Africa* **1936** The story of Cecil Rhodes, a man who was instrumental in the Boer War in Africa and established the Rhodes Scholarships with $10 million, is told in this biography. Fine performance by Huston and Homolka. **91m/B VHS.** *GB* Walter Huston, Oscar Homolka, Basil Sydney, Frank Cellier, Peggy Ashcroft, Renne De Vaux, Percy Parsons, Bernard Lee, Ndanisa Kumalo; ***D:*** Berthold Viertel. *NOS, SNC*

Rhythm on the Range 𝄞𝄞½ **1936**
Crosby stars as a singing cowboy who befriends freight car stowaway Farmer while transporting his prize steer back to his ranch in California. He invites her to his domicile and she falls in love with life on the range and with the rancher himself. Filled with lots of musical numbers, including an appearance from the Sons of the Pioneers featuring Roy Rogers. Comedy from Burns and Raye, who makes her feature film debut here, is as entertaining as always. Remade by Dean Martin and Jerry Lewis in 1956 as "Pardners." ♫I'm an Old Cowhand; Empty Saddles; I Can't Escape From You; The House That Jack Built for Jill; If You Can't Sing It You'll Have to Swing It; Roundup Lullaby; Drink It Down; Memories; Hang Up My Saddle. **88m/B VHS.** Bing Crosby, Frances Farmer, Bob Burns, Martha Raye, Samuel S. Hinds, Warren Hymer, Lucile Watson; ***D:*** Norman Taurog; ***W:*** John Moffitt, Sidney Salkow, Walter DeLeon, Francis Martin; ***C:*** Karl Struss. *MCA*

Rhythm on the River 𝄞𝄞½ **1940** Famous Broadway songwriter Rathbone has lost his magic touch so he hires melody maker Crosby to ghost for him while also hiring Martin to be the wordsmith. When the two fall in love they decide to strike off on their own but can't get their music heard since everyone assumes they've been copying Rathbone. Lots of backstage jokes with Rathbone terrific as an insecure egomaniac. ♫Rhythm on the River; When the Moon Comes Over Madison Square; Ain't It a Shame About Mame?; What Would Shakespeare Have Said?; Only Forever; That's for Me; I Don't Want to Cry Anymore. **94m/B VHS.** Bing Crosby, Mary Martin, Basil Rathbone, Oscar Levant, Oscar Shaw, Charley Grapewin, William Frawley, Charles Lane; ***D:*** Victor Schertzinger; ***W:*** Dwight Taylor; ***M:*** Victor Young. *MCA*

Rhythm Parade 𝄞𝄞 **1943** A woman takes off for Hawaii, leaving her infant in the care of an L.A. nightclub singer. A jealous rival of the singer takes the opportunity to cause problems. The thin plot serves as a vehicle for lots of singing. ♫Tootin' My Own Horn; Petticoat Army; Mimi From Tahiti; You're Drafted; Wait Till the Sun Shines Nellie; Sweet Sue; 'Neath the Yellow Moon In Old Tahiti. **68m/B VHS.** Nils T. Granlund, Gale Storm, Robert Lowery, Margaret Dumont, Chick Chandler, Cliff Nazarro, Jan Wiley, Candy Candido, Yvonne De Carlo; ***D:*** Howard Bretherton. *NOS, MLB*

Rhythm Thief 𝄞𝄞 **1994** No-budget independent film finds alienated New York hustler Simon (Andrews) eking out a living selling tapes of local underground bands he has illegally recorded. He wants to be left alone but circumstances won't allow it. He's got one of the enraged bands after him, he's pestered by local "admirers," and his eccentric former girlfriend Marty (Daniels) suddenly turns up—severely shaking Simon's emotionally barren existence. Quirky character study gets lots of impact from tiny bucks. **88m/B VHS.** Jason Andrews, Eddie Daniels, Kimberly Flynn, Kevin Corrigan, Sean Haggerty; ***D:*** Matthew Harrison; ***W:*** Matthew Harrison, Christopher Grimm; ***C:*** Howard Krupa. Sundance Film Festival '95: Special Jury Prize; Nominations: Independent Spirit Awards '96: Debut Performance (Andrews). *NYR*

Ricco 𝄞𝄞 *Summertime Killer* **1974 (PG)** A young man swears vengeance against the mobsters who killed his father. He kidnaps the daughter of a mafia kingpin and the battle begins. **90m/C VHS, Beta.** *FR IT SP* Chris Mitchum, Karl Malden, Olivia Hussey, Raf Vallone, Claudine Auger, Gerard Tichy; ***D:*** Antonio Isasi. *NO*

Rich and Famous 𝄞𝄞 **1981 (R)** The story of the 25-year friendship of two women, through college, marriage, and success. George Cukor's last film. **117m/C VHS, Beta, LV.** Jacqueline Bisset, Candice Bergen, David Selby, Hart Bochner, Meg Ryan, Steven Hill, Michael Brandon, Matt Lattanzi; ***D:*** George Cukor; ***W:*** Gerald Ayres; ***M:*** Georges Delerue. Writers Guild of America '81: Best Adapted Screenplay. *MGM*

Rich and Strange 𝄞𝄞½ *East of Shanghai* **1932** Early Hitchcock movie is not in the same class as his later thrillers. A couple inherits a fortune and journeys around the world. Eventually the pair gets shipwrecked. **92m/B VHS, LV.** *GB* Henry Kendall, Joan Barry, Betty Amann, Percy Marmont, Elsie Randolph; ***D:*** Alfred Hitchcock; ***W:*** Alfred Hitchcock. *REP, SNC, MLB*

Rich Girl 𝄞 **1991 (R)** A winsome, wealthy wench hides her millions by going to work in a rock'n'roll bar and falls in love with the local Bruce Springsteen wannabee. Despite the thick coating of music, sex, drugs and profanity, this consists of cliches that were old before talkies. Too earnestly-acted to be campy fun. Poor movie. **96m/C VHS, LV.** Jill Schoelen, Don Michael Paul, Ron Karabatsos, Sean Kanan, Willie Dixon, Paul Gleason; ***D:*** Joel Bender. *COL*

Rich Hall's Vanishing America **1986**
Funnyman Hall travels across the country looking for the mail-order company that promised to give him a genuine Wilt Chamberlain basketball hoop. **50m/C VHS, Beta.** Rich Hall, M. Emmet Walsh, Peter Isacksen, Harry Anderson, Wilt Chamberlain; ***D:*** Steve Rash. *PAR*

Rich in Love 𝄞𝄞½ **1993 (PG-13)** Lighthearted look at the changes in a Southern family after matriarch Helen Odom leaves to pursue her own life, shattering the peaceful existence of those around her. Seen through the eyes of 17-year-old daughter Lucille who assumes the role of "mother" for her sister and father while trying to come to terms with her own confused feelings. Nice performances by newcomer Erbe and Finney can't overcome a mediocre script. Based on the novel by Josephine Humphreys. **105m/C VHS, LV.** Albert Finney, Jill Clayburgh, Kathryn Erbe, Kyle MacLachlan, Piper Laurie, Ethan Hawke, Suzy Amis, Alfre Woodard; ***D:*** Bruce Beresford; ***W:*** Alfred Uhry; ***M:*** Georges Delerue. *MGM, BTV, FCT*

Rich Kids 𝄞𝄞½ **1979 (PG)** A young girl trying to cope with the divorce of her parents is aided by a boyfriend whose parents have already split. **97m/C VHS, Beta.** John Lithgow, Kathryn Walker, Trini Alvarado, Paul Dooley, David Selby, Jill Eikenberry, Olympia Dukakis; ***D:*** Robert M. Young; ***C:*** Ralf Bode. *MGM*

Rich Man, Poor Man 𝄞𝄞𝄞 **1976** Classic television miniseries covers 20, sometimes bitter, years in the lives of the two Jordache brothers. It's 1945 in quiet Port Phillip, New York with embittered German baker Axel (Asner), his unfulfilled wife Mary (McGuire), and sons Tom (Nolte) and Rudy (Strauss). Tom is wild and irresponsible, Rudy is ambitious and college-bound, and Julie Prescott (Blakely), Rudy's girl, overshadows both their lives. Based on the novel by Irwin Shaw. The first series contained 12 episodes. A second series, of 21 episodes, primarily followed the tribulations of the next generation, although Strauss returned as Rudy. **720m/C VHS.** Peter Strauss, Nick Nolte, Susan Blakely, Ed Asner, Dorothy McGuire, Bill Bixby, Robert Reed, Ray Milland, Kim Darby, Talia Shire, Lawrence Pressman, Kay Lenz; ***M:*** Alex North. *CMB*

Rich, Young and Pretty 𝄞𝄞½ **1951**
Light-hearted, innocuous musical starring Powell as a Texas gal visiting Paris with her rancher father (Corey). Powell finds romance with Damone (in his screen debut) and a secret—the mother she has never known (Darrieux). Lamas (in his American screen debut) plays Darrieux's new heartthrob. ♫Dark is the Night; L'Amour Toujours, Tonight For Sure; Wonder Why; I Can See You; Paris; We Never Talk Much; How Do You Like Your Eggs in the Morning?; There's Danger in Your Eyes, Cherie; The Old Piano Roll Blues. **95m/C VHS.** Jane Powell, Danielle Darrieux, Wendell Corey, Vic Damone, Fernando Lamas, Marcel Dalio, Una Merkel, Richard Anderson, Jean Murat, Hans Conried; ***D:*** Norman Taurog; ***W:*** Sidney Sheldon, Dorothy Cooper; ***M:*** Sammy Cahn, Nicholas Brodszky. Nominations: Academy Awards '51: Best Song ("Wonder Why"). *MGM, FCT*

Richard III 𝄞𝄞𝄞½ **1955** This landmark film version of the Shakespearean play features an acclaimed performance by Laurence Olivier, who also directs. The plot follows the life of the mentally and physically twisted Richard of Gloucester and his schemes for the throne of England. **138m/C VHS, Beta, LV.** *GB* Laurence Olivier, Cedric Hardwicke, Ralph Richardson, John Gielgud, Stanley Baker, Michael Gough, Claire Bloom; ***D:*** Laurence Olivier. British Academy Awards '55: Best Actor (Olivier), Best Director (Olivier), Best Film; Golden Globe Awards '57: Best Foreign Film; Nominations: Academy Awards '56: Best Actor (Olivier). *COL, SUE, HMV*

Richard III 🦴🦴🦴½ **1995 (R)** The Brits once again bring the Bard's most notorious monarch to the screen, this time in a new setting. McKellen stars in the title role of the deformed and ruthless English king, now in an imagined 1930s London of swanky Art Deco, Black Shirt thugs and modern media. Purists may resent major dialogue cuts, but famous speeches (such as the "winter of our discontent" opener) are amusingly staged in this modern take. Gorgeously polished visuals are perfect foil for the slimy, evil goings-on. Based on both Shakespeare's play and Richard Eyre's stage adaptation (in which McKellen also starred). **105m/C VHS, LV.** *GB* Ian McKellen, Annette Bening, Jim Broadbent, Robert Downey Jr., Nigel Hawthorne, Kristin Scott Thomas, Maggie Smith, John Wood; ***D:*** Richard Loncraine; ***W:*** Ian McKellen, Richard Loncraine; ***C:*** Peter Biziou; ***M:*** Trevor Jones. Nominations: Academy Awards '95: Best Art Direction/Set Decoration, Best Costume Design; Golden Globe Awards '96: Best Actor—Drama (McKellen). *MGM*

Richard Petty Story 🦴 **1972 (G)** The biography of race car driver Petty, played by himself, and his various achievements on the track. **83m/C VHS, Beta.** Richard Petty, Darren McGavin, Kathie Browne, Lynn Marta, Noah Beery Jr., L.Q. Jones. *GEM*

Richard's Things 🦴🦴 **1980 (R)** A man's wife and his girlfriend find love and comfort in each other after his death. Screenplay by Frederic Raphael, from his novel. Very slow and dreary, with a weak performance from Ullman. **104m/C VHS, Beta.** *GB* Liv Ullmann, Amanda Redman; ***D:*** Anthony Harvey; ***W:*** Frederic Raphael; ***C:*** Frederick A. (Freddie) Young; ***M:*** Georges Delerue. *SUE*

Richie Rich 🦴🦴½ **1994 (PG)** Yet another adaptation from the comics. Richie (Culkin), the world's richest boy, takes over the family business when his madcap parents Richard (Herrmann) and Regina (Ebersole) disappear thanks to the devious Laurence Van Dough (Larroquette). But there's kindly valet Cadbury (Hyde) and eccentric live-in inventor Keenbean (McShane) to help Richie save the day. Some silliness but Culkin has clearly outgrown this type of kid role. Biltmore, the 8,000 acre Vanderbilt estate in Asheville, North Carolina, serves as the Rich family home. **94m/C VHS, LV.** Macaulay Culkin, John Larroquette, Edward Herrmann, Christine Ebersole, Jonathan Hyde, Micheal McShane, Stephi Lineburg; ***Cameos:*** Reggie Jackson, Claudia Schiffer; ***D:*** Donald Petrie; ***W:*** Tom S. Parker, Jim Jennewein; ***C:*** Don Burgess; ***M:*** Alan Silvestri. Nominations: Golden Raspberry Awards '94: Worst Actor (Culkin). *WAR*

Ricky 1 🦴½ **1988** Mumbling pugilist spoof. Da Mob wants to make Ricky da fall guy, but uh, he's not as dumb as he looks. **90m/C VHS.** Michael Michaud, Maggie Hughes, James Herbert, Lane Montano; ***D:*** Bill Naud; ***M:*** Joel Goldsmith. *TPV, HHE*

Ricochet 🦴🦴🦴 **1991 (R)** Rookie cop Washington causes a sensation when he singlehandedly captures notorious psychopath Lithgow. But this particular criminal is a twisted genius, and from his prison cell he comes up with a plan to destroy the young cop. Teaming up with old friend Ice-T, the rookie tries to outwit his evil arch-nemesis, but to do so may cost him his very life. A genuinely scary, tense and violent thriller. **104m/C VHS, LV, 8mm.** Denzel Washington, John Lithgow, Ice-T, Jesse Ventura, Kevin Pollak, Lindsay Wagner, Mary Ellen Trainor, Josh Evans, Victoria Dillard, John Amos, John Cothran Jr.; ***D:*** Russell Mulcahy; ***W:*** Steven E. de Souza; ***M:*** Alan Silvestri. *HBO, CCB*

Riddance 🦴🦴🦴 **1973** The second of Meszaros' trilogy, about a Hungarian couple, an upper-class male student, and a factory-working young woman, and their difficulties in meshing their lives together. In Hungarian with English subtitles. **84m/B VHS, Beta.** *HU* ***D:*** Marta Meszaros. *KIV, INJ*

The Riddle of the Sands 🦴🦴½ **1979** Two English yachtsmen in 1903 inadvertently stumble upon a German plot to invade England by sea. British film based on the Erskine Childers spy novel. **99m/C VHS, Beta.** *GB* Michael York, Jenny Agutter, Simon MacCorkindale, Alan Badel; ***D:*** Tony Maylam; ***M:*** Howard Blake. *MOV, BMV*

Ride a Wild Pony 🦴🦴🦴 **1975 (G)** A poor Australian farmer's son is allowed to pick a horse of his own from a neighboring rancher's herd. After he trains and grows to love the pony, the rancher's daughter, a handicapped rich girl, decides to claim it for herself. Enjoyable Disney story is based on the tale "Sporting Proposition," by James Aldridge. **86m/C VHS, Beta.** *AU* John Meillon, Michael Craig, Robert Bettles, Eva Griffith, Graham Rouse; ***D:*** Don Chaffey; ***M:*** John Addison. *DIS*

Ride 'Em Cowboy 🦴🦴½ **1942** Two peanut and hotdog vendors travel west to try their hand as cowpokes. Usual Abbott and Costello fare with a twist—there are lots of great musical numbers. ♫A Tisket, A Tasket; I'll Remember April; Wake Up Jacob; Beside the Rio Tonto; Rock 'n' Reelin'; Give Me My Saddle; Cow Boogie. **86m/B VHS.** Bud Abbott, Lou Costello, Anne Gwynne, Samuel S. Hinds, Dick Foran, Richard Lane, Johnny Mack Brown, Ella Fitzgerald, Douglass Dumbrille; ***D:*** Arthur Lubin. *MCA*

Ride 'Em Cowgirl 🦴🦴 **1941** Singing cowgirl, Page, enters a horse race to expose the crook who cheated her father. **51m/B VHS.** Dorothy Page, Vince Barnett, Milton Frome; ***D:*** Samuel Diege. *VCN*

Ride Him, Cowboy 🦴🦴🦴 **1932** Entertaining oater has Wayne saving horse Duke from being sentenced to death. This was the first of six series films Wayne made for Warner's, all of which costarred his white wonder horse, Duke. Remake of the 1926 Ken Maynard silent "The Unknown Cavalier." Based on the story by Kenneth Perkins. **55m/B VHS.** John Wayne, Ruth Hall, Henry B. Walthall, Harry Gribbon, Otis Harlan, Charles Sellon; ***D:*** Fred Allen; ***W:*** Scott Mason. *MGM, GPV*

Ride in a Pink Car 🦴 **1974 (R)** When a Vietnam vet returns home, he discovers that his welcoming committee is really a lynch mob. **83m/C VHS, Beta.** Glenn Corbett, Morgan Woodward, Ivy Jones; ***D:*** Robert Emery. *ACA*

Ride in the Whirlwind 🦴🦴 **1967** Three cowboys are mistaken for members of a gang by a posse. Screenplay for the offbeat western by Nicholson. **83m/C Beta, LV.** Jack Nicholson, Cameron Mitchell, Millie Perkins, Katherine Squire, Harry Dean Stanton; ***D:*** Monte Hellman; ***W:*** Jack Nicholson. *MED, HHT, DVT*

Ride Lonesome 🦴🦴½ **1959** The heroic Scott is a bounty hunter looking for a killer (Best). It's not just the money, Scott hopes Best will lead him to the man who murdered Scott's wife. Along the trail he meets a pretty widow and two outlaws who hope if they capture Best, they'll get a pardon. A well-done example of a "B" western with good performances; Coburn's film debut. **73m/C VHS.** Randolph Scott, James Best, Karen Steele, Pernell Roberts, Lee Van Cleef, James Coburn; ***D:*** Budd Boetticher; ***W:*** Burt Kennedy. *MOV*

Ride, Ranger, Ride 🦴½ **1936** Texas Ranger Autry is out to stop a group of Comanches from raiding a wagon train. **56m/B VHS, Beta.** Gene Autry, Smiley Burnette, Kay Hughes, Max Terhune, Monte Blue, Chief Thundercloud; ***D:*** Joseph Kane. *NOS, MED, VYY*

Ride the High Country 🦴🦴🦴🦴 *Guns in the Afternoon* **1962** The cult classic western about two old friends who have had careers on both sides of the law. One, Joel McCrea, is entrusted with a shipment of gold, and the other, Randolph Scott, rides along with him to steal the precious cargo. Although barely promoted by MGM, became a critics' favorite. Grimacing and long in the tooth, McCrea and Scott enact a fitting tribute and farewell to the myth of the grand ol' West. Wonderfully photographed by Lucien Ballard. The laserdisc edition carries the film in widescreen format along with the original movie trailer. **93m/C VHS, Beta, LV.** Randolph Scott, Joel McCrea, Mariette Hartley, Edgar Buchanan, R.G. Armstrong, Ronald Starr, John Anderson, James Drury, L.Q. Jones, Warren Oates; ***D:*** Sam Peckinpah; ***C:*** Lucien Ballard; ***M:*** George Bassman. *MGM*

Ride the Man Down 🦴½ **1953** Story of a murderous land war between neighboring landowners tells the same old story: Greed knows no boundaries. **90m/C VHS.** Brian Donlevy, Chill Wills, Jack LaRue, Rod Cameron, Ella Raines, Barbara Britton; ***D:*** Joseph Kane. *REP*

Ride the Wild Surf 🦴🦴½ **1964** It's fun in the sun when surfers Fabian, Hunter, and Brown head to Hawaii in search of the ultimate waves. Throw in a little romance and a cool title song by Jan and Dean and you've got your better than average beach movie. The surfing footage is excellent. Cowabunga! **101m/C VHS.** Fabian, Tab Hunter, Barbara Eden, Peter Brown, Susan Hart, Shelley Fabares, Jim Mitchum; ***D:*** Don Taylor. *COL*

Ride the Wind 🦴🦴 **1966** "Bonanza" gang goes to the aid of the Pony Express. **120m/C VHS, Beta.** Michael Landon, Lorne Greene, Dan Blocker. *REP*

Ride to Glory 🦴🦴 *The Deserter; La Spina Dorsale del Diavolo* **1971** In 1886, a cavalry officer deserts his troops to seek revenge on the Apaches that brutally killed his family. Hearing this, a general offers to pardon him if he will lead a dangerous group of men on a mission against the Apaches. Fast-paced and very bloody. **90m/C VHS.** Bekim Fehmiu, Richard Crenna, Chuck Connors, Ricardo Montalban, Ian Bannen, Slim Pickens, Woody Strode, Patrick Wayne, John Huston; ***D:*** Burt Kennedy. *SIM, PAR, HHE*

Rider from Tucson 🦴🦴 **1950** Two rodeo riders head out to Colorado for a friend's wedding. They find out the bride has been kidnapped by a bunch of claim jumpers after control of a gold mine. **60m/B VHS, Beta.** Tim Holt, Richard Martin, Elaine Riley, Douglas Fowley, Veda Ann Borg; ***D:*** Lesley Selander. *NO*

Rider of the Law 🦴 **1935** A government agent poses as a greenhorn easterner to nab a gang of outlaws. **56m/B VHS, Beta.** Bob Steele. *NO*

Rider on the Rain 🦴🦴🦴 *Lepassager de la Pluie* **1970** A young housewife is viciously raped by an escaped sex maniac. She kills him and disposes of his body, not knowing that he is being relentlessly pursued by mysterious American Bronson. Suspenseful, French-made thriller featuring one of Bronson's best performances. **115m/C VHS, Beta.** *FR* Marlene Jobert, Charles Bronson, Jill Ireland; ***D:*** Rene Clement. Golden Globe Awards '71: Best Foreign Film. *FCT*

Riders of Death Valley 🦴🦴½ **1941** Splendid western action serial in 15 episodes. Foran, Jones, and Carillo head a passel o'men watching for thieves and claim jumpers in a mining area. **320m/B VHS, Beta.** Dick Foran, Buck Jones, Leo Carrillo, Lon Chaney Jr.; ***D:*** Ford Beebe, Ray Taylor. *NOS, VCN, DVT*

Riders of Destiny 🦴🦴½ **1933** Wayne plays a government agent sent to find out who is stealing water from the local farmers. Very early Wayne has the Duke looking awfully young as an agent securing water rights for ranchers. **59m/B VHS.** John Wayne, George "Gabby" Hayes, Cecilia Parker, Forrest Taylor, Al "Fuzzy" St. John; ***D:*** Robert North Bradbury. *COL, NOS, REP*

Riders of Pasco Basin 🦴½ **1940** Outlaws are tricking ranchers out of their money by falsely promising to build a dam. So Brown and his cohorts come to set things right. **56m/B VHS.** Johnny Mack Brown, Fuzzy Knight, Bob Baker, Frances Robinson, Arthur Loft, Frank LaRue, Lafe McKee, Kermit Maynard; ***D:*** Ray Taylor; ***W:*** Ford Beebe. *GPV*

Riders of the Desert 🦴½ **1932** Steele tracks down the loot from a stagecoach robbery. **57m/B VHS, Beta.** Bob Steele. *VYY, VCN*

Riders of the Purple Sage 🦴🦴½ **1925** When Texas Ranger Jim Lassiter's (Mix) sister and niece are kidnapped by the evil Walters (Oland), he devotes his life to finding them. While working on a ranch (and falling in love with the beautiful ranch owner), he learns Walters has changed his name and is passing himself off as a judge. Promptly shooting the skunk dead, Lassiter and his sweetie must run from a posse. Based on the Zane Grey novel. **63m/B VHS.** Tom Mix, Warner Oland, Mabel Ballin, Beatrice Burnham, Arthur Morrison, Fred Kohler Sr.; ***D:*** Lynn F. Reynolds; ***W:*** Edfrid Bingham. *GPV*

Riders of the Purple Sage 🦴🦴½ **1996** Legendary gunman (are there any other kind?) Lassiter (Harris) helps save Bern (Thomas) from a beating in a town run by a conservative religious sect, lead by Deacon Tull (Weisser). Seems Bern's befriended ranch owner (and nonmember) Jane (Madigan) and the Deacon is not only after Jane but her considerable land and cattle holdings. Lassiter rides to the rescue. Properly brooding TV adaptation of the 1912 Zane Grey novel (the Grey novel specifies that the sect are Mormons but this caused considerable fuss). Filmed in Utah. **90m/C VHS.** Ed Harris, Amy Madigan, Henry Thomas, Norbert Weisser, Robin Tunney, G.D. Spradlin; ***D:*** Charles Haid; ***W:*** Gill Dennis; ***C:*** William Wages; ***M:*** Arthur Kempel. *TTC*

Riders of the Range 🦴🦴 **1924** Sheep invade the cattle range and a range war flares up between those who would herd and the ranchers. Silent flick of interest because of the stars. **62m/B VHS, Beta.** Edmund Cobb, Dolly Dale; ***D:*** Otis Thayer. *GPV*

Riders of the Range 🦴 **1949** Cowboy rides into town just in time to save a girl's brother from gamblers. **60m/B VHS, Beta.** Tim Holt, Richard Martin. *NO*

Riders of the Range/Storm Over Wyoming 🦴½ **1950** A double feature package of Tim Holt Westerns. **120m/B VHS, Beta.** Tim Holt, Richard Martin, Jacqueline Wells. *TTC*

Riders of the Rockies 🦴🦴½ **1937** An honest cowboy turns rustler in order to trap a border gang. One of Ritter's very best cowboy outings; good fun, and a very long fistfight with King. **60m/B VHS, Beta.** Tex Ritter, Yakima Canutt, Louise Stanley, Charles "Blackie" King, Snub Pollard; ***D:*** Robert North Bradbury. *NOS, VCI, VCN*

Riders of the Storm 🦴½ *The American Way* **1988 (R)** A motley crew of Vietnam vets runs a covert television broadcasting station from an in-flight B-29, jamming America's legitimate airwaves. Interesting premise with boring result. **92m/C VHS, Beta, LV.** Dennis Hopper, Michael J. Pollard, Eugene Lipinski, James Aubrey, Nigel Pegram; ***D:*** Maurice Phillips; ***W:*** Scott Roberts. *SUE, NLC*

Riders of the Timberline 🦴🦴 **1941** Unusual for a Hopalong Cassidy programmer in that it puts him in timber country. Yes, he's a lumberjack and he's okay, as he fights against land-grabbing crooks all day. **59m/B VHS.** William Boyd, Brad King, Andy Clyde, J. Farrell MacDonald, Elaine Stewart, Anna Q. Nilsson, Hal Taliaferro, Tom Tyler, Victor Jory; ***D:*** Lesley Selander. *NOS*

Riders of the West 🦴 **1942** An honest cowpoke fights off a band of rustlers. **58m/B VHS.** Buck Jones, Tim McCoy, Raymond Hatton, Sarah Padden, Harry Woods; ***D:*** Howard Bretherton. *NOS, DVT*

Riders of the Whistling Pines 🦴🦴 **1949** Our ever-so-bland hero solves a murder perpetrated by a passel of lumber thieves and saves the day for yet another damsel in distress. **70m/B VHS, Beta.** Gene Autry, Patricia White, Jimmy Lloyd; ***D:*** John English. *NOS, MED, DVT*

Riders of the Whistling Skull 🦴🦴½ *The Golden Trail* **1937** The Three Mesquiteers are guiding an expedition to an ancient Indian city. A gang of rustlers looting the city are holding an archeology professor hostage, and the Mesquiteers must rescue him. Swell cast; nifty, creepy plot; solid-as-usual leads. **58m/B VHS, Beta.** Bob Livingston, Ray Corrigan, Max Terhune, Yakima Canutt, Roland Winters; ***D:*** Mack V. Wright. *SNC, NOS, VCN*

Riders to the Sea 🦴½ **1988** A mother envisions the death of her last son in the same manner her other sons died—by drowning. Based on the play by Irish dramatist John Millington Synge. **90m/C VHS, Beta.** Geraldine Page, Amanda Plummer, Sachi Parker, Barry McGovern; ***D:*** Ronan O'Leary. *NO*

Ridin' Down the Canyon 🦴🦴½ **1942** Standard but entertaining entry in Rogers' popular series. It's Rogers to the rescue when a gang of outlaws are rustling cattle and selling to the government for wartime profits. Roy, along with the Sons of the Pioneers, also manages to croon a few tunes. Based on a story by Robert Williams and Norman Houston. **54m/B VHS.** Roy Rogers, George "Gabby" Hayes, Linda Hayes, Addison Richards, Adrian Booth, James Seay; ***D:*** Joseph Kane; ***W:*** Albert De Mond. *MOV*

Ridin' on a Rainbow 🦴½ **1941** Has-been performer on a steamboat decides to rob a bank in the hopes of starting a new life for himself and his daughter. The money he robs had just been deposited by some cattlemen, one of whom joins the steamboat's crew, wins the daughter's heart, and gets to the father. Slow and dull, with too much singing, and too little plot and scenery. **79m/B VHS, Beta.** Gene Autry, Smiley Burnette, Mary Lee; ***D:*** Lew (Louis Friedlander) Landers. Nominations: Academy Awards '41: Best Song ("Be Honest With Me"). *REP, CCB, VCN*

Ridin' the California Trail 🦴½ **1947** The Cisco Kid is wanted dead or alive in several states. **40m/B VHS, Beta.** Gilbert Roland. *DVT*

Ridin' the Lone Trail *Woof!* **1937** Steele attempts to stop some criminals who've been harassing a stagecoach line. Republic was better than this weak western would lead us to believe. Steele, who went on to better things, is a bright spot in a film that sounds and looks bad. Keep your ears open for the sound of airplanes—apparently Newfield forgot they hadn't been invented in the time of the wild west. From a story by E.B. Mann. **56m/B VHS.** Bob Steele, Claire Rochelle, Charles "Blackie" King, Ernie Adams, Lew Meehan, Julian Rivero; ***D:*** Sam Newfield; ***W:*** Charles Francis Royal. *NOS, DVT*

Ridin' the Trail 🦴 **1940** Scott stars as a cowboy out to rid the countryside of bad guys in this western. **60m/B VHS, Beta.** Fred Scott, Iris Lancaster, Harry Harvey, Jack Ingram, John Ward; ***D:*** Raymond K. Johnson. *NOS, DVT*

Ridin' Thru 🦴🦴 **1935** Another Tom Tyler western, in which the hero does battle with unscrupulous villains. **60m/B VHS, Beta.** Tom Tyler, Ruth Hiatt, Lafe McKee, Philo McCullough, Lew Meehan, Bud Osborne; ***D:*** Harry S. Webb. *NOS, DVT, HEG*

The Riding Avenger 🦴½ **1936** To gain the love of a beautiful lady, a cowboy vows never to fight again, but is forced to break his promise when the town is terrorized. Aw, shucks. **56m/B VHS, Beta.** Hoot Gibson, Ruth Mix, Buzz Barton; ***D:*** Harry Fraser. *VCN*

Riding High 🦴🦴½ **1950** Capra remade his 1934 film "Broadway Bill" as this light-hearted musical. Horse trainer Crosby falls for the wealthy Gray who demands he choose between her and his horse. Bing chooses the horse who proves his loyalty by winning the big race and making Crosby a rich man. ♫Someplace on Anywhere Road; Sunshine Cake; We've Got a Sure Thing; The Horse Told Me; The Whiffenpoof Song; De Camptown Races. **112m/B VHS, Beta.** Bing Crosby, Coleen Gray, Charles Bickford, William Demarest, Frances Gifford, Raymond Walburn, James Gleason, Ward Bond, Percy Kilbride, Harry Davenport, Margaret Hamilton, Douglass Dumbrille, Gene Lockhart, Charles Lane, Frankie Darro, Paul Harvey, Marjorie Lord, Dub Taylor, Max Baer Sr., Oliver Hardy; ***D:*** Frank Capra; ***W:*** Robert Riskin, Melville Shavelson, Jack Rose; ***C:*** George Barnes. *MCA*

Riding High 🦴 **1978** It's a battle for supremacy between the kings of the motorcycle stunt world. Made for television movie's soundtrack includes songs from The Police, Dire Straits, Jerry Lee Lewis, and more. **92m/C VHS, Beta.** Murray Salem, Marella Oppenheim, Eddie Kidd, Irene Handl; ***D:*** Ross Cramer. *LIV*

Riding On 🦴🦴 **1937** Hayseed falls for the daughter of his father's arch rival. While his father battles it out over cattle, he pines for his enemy's daughter. Lots of action which is typical fare in mediocre western production. **59m/B VHS.** Tom Tyler, Germaine Greer, Rex Lease, John Elliott, Earl Dwire; ***D:*** Harry S. Webb. *NOS, DVT*

Riding on Air 🦴🦴 **1937** Small-town newspaper editor Brown discovers that his bumbling methods get him the right results. Smugglers and crazy inventions in a ho-hum Brown entry. **58m/B VHS, Beta.** Joe E. Brown; ***D:*** Edward Sedgwick. *NOS, BAR, FCT*

Riding Speed 🦴 **1935** Our hero breaks up a gang of smugglers along the Mexican border. **50m/B VHS, Beta, LV.** Buffalo Bill Jr. *NO*

Riding the Edge 🦴 **1990 (R)** Teenage motocross rider rescues his scientist dad from Middle Eastern terrorists. Thoroughly unoriginal. **100m/C VHS, LV.** *HBO*

Riding the Sunset Trail 🦴🦴🦴 **1941** Top-notch tale of Keene trying to stop a con from cashing in on his dead half-brother's fortune. Solid production values and an enthusiastic performance by Keene make this one of his best films after a string of flops. **56m/B VHS.** Tom Keene, Betty Miles, Frank Yaconelli, Sugar Dawn, Slim Andrews, Kenne Duncan; ***D:*** Robert Emmett Tansey; ***W:*** Robert Emmett, Frances Kavanaugh. *MOV*

The Riding Tornado 🦴🦴½ **1932** Bronc rider McCoy takes a job on Grey's ranch, promptly falling for her. Ranch foreman Oakman, who's really the leader of a gang of rustlers, kidnaps Grey and McCoy goes after them. **63m/B VHS.** Tim McCoy, Shirley Grey, Wheeler Oakman, Wallace MacDonald, Russell Simpson, Montagu Love, Lafe McKee, Bud Osborne; ***D:*** David Ross Lederman. *GPV*

Riding with Death **1976** A man who can become invisible, thanks to a military experiment, uses his power to uncover a dastardly plot by a mad scientist. So-so TV pilot. **97m/C VHS, Beta.** Ben Murphy, Andrew Prine, Katherine Crawford, Richard Dysart; ***D:*** Alan J. Levi. *MCA*

Riel 🦴🦴 **1979** The story of Louis Riel, a half-French, half-Indian visionary who challenged the Canadian army in his fight for equality and self-rule. **150m/C VHS, Beta.** Raymond Cloutier, Arthur Hill, William Shatner, Christopher Plummer, Leslie Nielsen; ***D:*** George Bloomfield. *PSM*

Riff Raff 🦴🦴 *Riffraff* **1935** Melodramatic story about the relationship of two waterfront workers in the tuna fishing business. Confusing script saddled with too many characters, but there is some good sharp dialogue between the leads. Also features the scenic California waterfront. **80m/B VHS.** Jean Harlow, Spencer Tracy, Joseph Calleia, Una Merkel, Mickey Rooney, Victor Kilian, J. Farrell MacDonald, Roger Imhof; ***D:*** J. Walter Ruben. *MGM*

Riff-Raff 🦴🦴½ **1947** Various dramatic and comic complications arise when a dying man gives Panama City con man O'Brien a map to oil deposits. Interesting and quick-moving melodrama. **80m/B VHS, Beta.** Pat O'Brien, Walter Slezak, Anne Jeffreys, Jason Robards Sr., Percy Kilbride, Jerome Cowan; ***D:*** Ted Tetzlaff. *TTC*

Riff Raff 🦴🦴🦴 **1992** Unsparing black comedy about the British working-class by director Loach. Ex-con Stevie comes to London from Scotland to look for work and escape his thieving past. He finds a nonunion job on a construction site, takes up squatter's rights in an abandoned apartment, and finds a girlfriend in equally struggling singer Susie, who turns out to be a junkie. Loach's characters deal with their unenviable lot in life through rough humor and honest sentiment. Regional accents are so thick that the film is subtitled. **96m/C VHS, LV.** *GB* Robert Carlyle, Emer McCourt, Jimmy Coleman, George Moss, Ricky Tomlinson, David Finch, Bill Jesse; ***D:*** Ken Loach; ***W:*** Bill Jesse; ***M:*** Stewart Copeland. *NLC, COL, IME*

Rififi 🦴🦴🦴½ *Du Rififi Chez les Hommes* **1954** Perhaps the greatest of all "heist" movies. Four jewel thieves pull off a daring caper, only to fall prey to mutual distrust. The long scene of the actual theft, completely in silence, will have your heart in your throat. In French with English subtitles. **115m/B VHS, Beta.** *FR* Jean Servais, Carl Mohner, Robert Manuel, Jules Dassin; ***D:*** Jules Dassin; ***W:*** Jules Dassin. Cannes Film Festival '55: Best Director (Dassin); National Board of Review Awards '56: 5 Best Foreign Films of the Year. *VYY, NOS, HHT*

The Right Hand Man 🦴½ **1987 (R)** A brother and sister must deal with their crusty patriarch's demise in the Victorian-era Australian outback. Disappointing and overwrought. **101m/C VHS,**

Beta. *AU* Rupert Everett, Hugo Weaving, Arthur Dignam; ***D:*** Di Drew. *VTR, NWV*

Right of Way 🦴🦴½ **1984** Stewart plays an elderly man who makes a suicide pact with his wife (Davis) when he learns of her terminal illness. Davis and Stewart's first film together is disappointing and stodgy, with an abrupt ending that looks like bad editing by a frightened studio. Made for TV. **102m/C VHS, Beta.** James Stewart, Bette Davis, Priscilla Morrill, Melinda Dillon; ***D:*** George Schaefer; ***M:*** Brad Fiedel. *NO*

The Right Stuff 🦴🦴🦴 **1983 (PG)** A rambunctious adaptation of Tom Wolfe's nonfiction book about the beginnings of the U.S. space program, from Chuck Yeager's breaking of the sound barrier to the last of the Mercury missions. Featuring an all-star cast and an ambitious script. Rowdy, imaginative, and thrilling, though broadly painted and oddly uninvolving. Former astronaut John Glenn was running for president when this was out. **193m/C VHS, Beta, LV.** Ed Harris, Dennis Quaid, Sam Shepard, Scott Glenn, Fred Ward, Charles Frank, William Russ, Kathy Baker, Barbara Hershey, Levon Helm, David Clennon, Kim Stanley, Mary Jo Deschanel, Veronica Cartwright, Pamela Reed, Jeff Goldblum, Harry Shearer, Donald Moffat, Scott Paulin, Lance Henriksen, Scott Wilson, John P. Ryan, Royal Dano; ***D:*** Philip Kaufman; ***W:*** Philip Kaufman; ***C:*** Caleb Deschanel; ***M:*** Bill Conti. Academy Awards '83: Best Film Editing, Best Sound, Best Original Score; Nominations: Academy Awards '83: Best Art Direction/Set Decoration, Best Cinematography, Best Picture, Best Supporting Actor (Shepard). *WAR*

The Right to Remain Silent 🦴🦴 **1995 (R)** Rookie cop Christine Paley (Thompson) learns all about human foibles in her job processing incoming suspects. Based on a play by Brent Briscoe and Mark Fauser. **96m/C VHS.** Lea Thompson, Amanda Plummer, Christopher Lloyd, Laura San Giacomo, Judge Reinhold, Carl Reiner, L.L. Cool J., Patrick Dempsey, Fisher Stevens, Robert Loggia; ***D:*** Hubert de la Bouillerie. *REP*

Rikisha-Man 🦴🦴🦴½ *Rickshaw Man; Muhomatsu no Issho* **1958** A tragic melodrama about a rickshaw puller who helps raise a young boy after his father has died, and loves the boy's mother from afar. Inagaki's remake of his original 1943 version. In Japanese with English subtitles. **105m/B VHS, Beta.** *JP* Toshiro Mifune; ***D:*** Hiroshi Inagaki. *FCT*

Rikky and Pete 🦴🦴½ **1988 (R)** An engaging Australian comedy about a bizarre, precociously eccentric brother and sister. He's a Rube Goldberg-style mentor; she's a scientist-cum-country singer. They move together to the outback and meet a score of weird characters. A worthy follow-up to director Tass's "Malcolm." **103m/C VHS, Beta, LV.** *AU* Nina Landis, Stephen Kearney, Tetchie Agbayani, Bruce Spence, Bruno Lawrence, Bill Hunter, Dorothy Allison, Don Reid, Lewis Fitz-gerald; ***D:*** Nadia Tass; ***W:*** David Parker; ***M:*** Phil Judd. *MGM, FOX*

Rikyu 🦴🦴🦴 **1990** Set in 16th century Japan, Rikyu is a Buddhist priest who elevated the tea ceremony to an art form. To him it is a spiritual experience, to his master, Lord Hideyoshi Toilyotomi, the ruler of Japan, mastery of the ceremony is a matter of prestige. Conflict arises between Rikyu's ideal of profound simplicity, symbolized by the ceremony, and Toilyotomi's planned conquest of China, which Rikyu opposes. In Japanese with English subtitles. **116m/C VHS, LV.** *JP* Rentaro Mikuni, Tsutomu Yamazaki; ***D:*** Hiroshi Teshigahara. *CTL, INJ, LUM*

Rim of the Canyon 🦴½ **1949** Autry has a dual role as a lawman tracking villains who were jailed by his father years before. **70m/B VHS, Beta.** Gene Autry, Nan Leslie, Thurston Hall, Clem Bevans, Walter Sande, Jock Mahoney, Alan Hale Jr., Denver Pyle; ***D:*** John English. *NOS, DVT, TIM*

Rimfire 🦴🦴½ **1949** An undercover agent tracks down some stolen U.S. Army gold, aided by the ghost of a wrongly-hanged gambler. Fun B western. **65m/B VHS, Beta, LV.** Mary Beth Hughes, Henry Hull, Fuzzy Knight, James Millican, Victor Kilian, Margia Dean, Jason Robards Sr., Reed Hadley; ***D:*** B. Reeves Eason. *NO*

Rin Tin Tin, Hero of the West 🦴🦴 **1955** In one of his last adventures, the famous German Shepherd proves his courage and hyper-canine intelligence. Colorized. **75m/C VHS, Beta.** James Brown, Lee Aaker. *MON*

The Ring 🦴🦴½ **1927** Very early Hitchcock about boxer who marries carnival girl, loses carnival girl, and wins carnival girl back again. Standard romantic punch and roses yarn interesting as measure of young director's developing authority. **82m/B VHS.** *GB* Carl Brisson, Lillian Hall-Davis, Ian Hunter, Gordon Harker; ***D:*** Alfred Hitchcock; ***W:*** Alfred Hitchcock. *VEC, MLB*

The Ring 🦴🦴½ **1952** Poignant early fight movie that gives a lesson in prejudice against Chicanos. The main character feels that the only way to get respect from the world is to fight for it. Well-directed and perceptive. **79m/B VHS.** Gerald Mohr, Rita Moreno, Kiri Te Kanawa, Robert Arthur, Art Aragon, Jack Elam; ***D:*** Kurt Neumann. *MOV, DVT, HEG*

Ring of Bright Water 🦴🦴🦴 **1969 (G)** Well done story of a pet otter from Gavin Maxwell's autobiography. The film stars the couple that made the delightful "Born Free." Beautiful Scottish Highlands photography adds to this captivating and endearing tale of a civil servant who purchases an otter from a pet store and moves to the country. **107m/C VHS, Beta.** *GB* Bill Travers, Virginia McKenna, Peter Jeffrey, Archie Duncan; ***D:*** Jack Couffer. *FXV, FCT, SIG*

Ring of Death 🦴½ **1972** A tough cop investigating a routine case becomes a hunted man after someone kills the man he is following. **93m/C VHS, Beta.** Franco Nero, Florinda Bolkan, Adolfo Celi. *CNG, MRV, GEM*

Ring of Fire 🦴½ **1991 (R)** Wilson is one of very few modern American kung-fu heroes of Asian descent, and he works messages against prejudice into this interracial Romeo-and-Juliet chopsocky tale. What foot through yonder window breaks? **100m/C VHS, LV.** Don "The Dragon" Wilson, Maria Ford, Vince Murdocco, Dale Jacoby, Michael Delano, Eric Lee; ***D:*** Richard W. Munchkin. *IMP, HMV*

Ring of Fire 2: Blood and Steel 🦴½ **1992 (R)** Wilson returns as Dr. Johnny Wu in this martial-arts actioner which finds the good doctor the witness to a robbery. When one of the robbers is killed, the gang's leader kidnaps Johnny's fiance and holds her for ransom. He decides to bypass the police and use his own expertise to rescue her. **94m/C VHS.** Don "The Dragon" Wilson, Maria Ford, Sy Richardson, Michael Delano, Dale Jacoby, Vince Murdocco, Evan Lorie, Gary Robbins, Charlie Ganis, Ron Yuan; ***D:*** Richard W. Munchkin. *PMH*

Ring of Fire 3: Lion Strike 🦴½ **1994 (R)** Johnny Wu is supposed to be on vacation with his son and a beautiful forest ranger when they find themselves in the way of a violent group known as the Global Mafia. Seems Johnny has a computer disk that the gangsters want. **90m/C VHS, LV.** Don "The Dragon" Wilson, Bobbie Phillips, Robert Costanzo; ***D:*** Rick Jacobson. *PMH*

Ring of Steel 🦴🦴 **1994 (R)** Alex, a one-time Olympic hopeful in fencing, is enticed into combat by the mysterious owner of a decadent nightclub where gladiator-type matches are staged for the thrill of the bored and jaded super-rich. Unaware of the high stakes, Alex wins a duel and is showered with money and the attention of a beautiful, yet dangerous woman. When Alex discovers the club's dark secret, he no longer wants to fight, but blackmail draws him in even deeper. **94m/C VHS, LV.** Joe Don Baker, Carol Alt, Robert Chapin, Gary Kasper, Darlene Vogel; ***D:*** David Frost; ***W:*** Robert Chapin; ***M:*** Jeff Beal. *MCA*

Ring of Terror 🦴 **1962** College boy who wants to join a fraternity must survive the initiation rights, which include stealing a ring from a corpse. Unfortunately, this seemingly invincible guy has a deadly terror of the dead. Cheaply made flop allegedly based on a composite of actual hazing incidents. **72m/B VHS.** George Mather, Esther Furst, Austin Green, Joseph Conway; ***D:*** Clark Paylow. *NOS, SNC*

Ring of the Musketeers 🦴🦴½ **1993 (PG-13)** Contemporary spoof of the Musketeers saga finds three descendants of the swashbuckling heroes carrying on the family tradition of protecting the weak and innocent. They even get stuck with a Musketeer-wannabe when they come to the resuce of a young boy who is kidnapped to prevent his dad from testifying against mobsters. **86m/C VHS.** David Hasselhoff, Alison Doody, Thomas Gottschalk, Richard "Cheech" Marin, Corbin Bernsen, John Rhys-Davies; ***D:*** John Paragon; ***W:*** Joel Surnow. *COL*

Ringside 🦴½ **1949** A concert pianist turns boxer to avenge his brother who was blinded in a fight. **64m/B VHS, Beta, LV.** Donald (Don "Red") Barry, Sheila Ryan, Tom Brown. *SNC*

The Rink 🦴🦴🦴 **1916** Chaplin plays a waiter who spends his lunch hour on roller skates. Silent with musical soundtrack added. **20m/B VHS, Beta.** Charlie Chaplin; ***D:*** Charlie Chaplin. *CAB, GVV*

Rink/Immigrant **191?** Two Chaplin shorts: "The Rink" (1916), in which Charlie defends his girlfriend's honor at a local roller skating rink; "The Immigrant" (1917), features Charlie as a newcomer to America. **56m/B VHS, Beta.** Charlie Chaplin, Mack Swain, Edna Purviance. *VYY*

Rio Bravo 🦴🦴🦴½ **1959** The sheriff of a Texas border town (Wayne) takes a brutal murderer into custody and faces a blockade of hired gunmen determined to keep his prisoner from being brought to justice. Long, but continually entertaining. Generally regarded as an American film classic, with an all-star cast, didn't impress the critics at the time. Sequel: "El Dorado." Semi-remake was called "Assault on Precinct 13." **140m/C VHS, Beta.** John Wayne, Dean Martin, Angie Dickinson, Ricky Nelson, Walter Brennan, Ward Bond, Claude Akins, Bob Steele, John Russell; ***D:*** Howard Hawks. *WAR, TLF*

Rio Conchos 🦴🦴🦴 **1964** Nifty nonstop action in this western set in Texas after the Civil War. Three Army buddies search for 2,000 stolen rifles. Boone is understated, O'Brien is good, and Brown memorable in his debut. **107m/C VHS, Beta.** Richard Boone, Stuart Whitman, Edmond O'Brien, Anthony (Tony) Franciosa, Jim Brown; ***D:*** Gordon Douglas; ***M:*** Jerry Goldsmith. *FOX*

Rio Diablo 🦴🦴½ **1993** Country Western singers abound in—what else—a made-for-TV Western movie. A bounty hunter (Rogers) and newlywed groom (Tritt) set off after a gang of thieving kidnappers who have snatched the young bride (Harring). Judd shows up as the owner of a desert hostelry, who happens to cross paths with the hunters. Watch out—this could be more fun than a Partridge Family reunion. **120m/C VHS.** Kenny Rogers, Travis Tritt, Naomi Judd, Stacy Keach, Brion James, Bruce Greenwood, Laura Harring; ***M:*** Larry Brown. *CAF, MVD*

Rio Grande 🦴🦴🦴 **1950** The last entry in Ford's cavalry trilogy following "Fort Apache" and "She Wore a Yellow Ribbon." A U.S. cavalry unit on the Mexican border conducts an unsuccessful campaign against marauding Indians. The commander (Wayne) faces an unhappy wife and is estranged from his son, a new recruit. Featuring an excellent Victor Young score and several songs by the Sons of the Pioneers. **105m/B VHS, LV.** John Wayne, Maureen O'Hara, Ben Johnson, Claude Jarman Jr., Harry Carey Jr., Victor McLaglen, Chill Wills, J. Carrol Naish; ***D:*** John Ford. *REP, TLF, RXM*

Rio Grande Raiders 🦴 **1946** A Stagecoach driver discovers that his kid brother is working for a crooked rival stage company. **54m/B VHS, Beta.** Sunset Carson, Linda Stirling, Bob Steele. *DVT, RXM*

Rio Lobo 🦴🦴½ **1970 (G)** Hawks's final film takes place after the Civil War, when Union Colonel Wayne goes to Rio Lobo to take revenge on two traitors. Disappointing. The Duke has to carry weak supporting performances on his brawny shoulders—and nearly does. **114m/C VHS, Beta, LV.** John Wayne, Jorge Rivero, Jennifer O'Neill, Jack Elam, Chris Mitchum, David Huddleston, George Plimpton; ***D:*** Howard Hawks; ***C:*** William Clothier; ***M:*** Jerry Goldsmith. *FOX*

Rio Rattler ½ **1935** Tyler takes the place of a murdered lawman in order to find his killer. **60m/B VHS, Beta.** Tom Tyler, Marion Shilling, Eddie Gribbon, William Gould, Tom London; ***D:*** Franklin Shamray. *VCN, GPV*

Rio Rita ½ **1942** Abbott & Costello are working on a ranch and somehow become involved with Nazi spies. Provides a few original comic bits for the duo but is otherwise mediocre. An updated remake of the 1929 Wheeler & Woolsey comedy. **91m/B VHS.** Bud Abbott, Lou Costello, Kathryn Grayson, John Carroll, Patricia Dane, Tom Conway, Peter Whitney; ***D:*** Sylvan Simon. *MGM*

Riot ½ **1969 (R)** Men in cages throw tantrums until warden returns from vacation. Filmed in Arizona State Prison with real convicts as extras. Strong performances by fullback Brown and durable Hackman. Based on story by ex-con Frank Elli. Too oft-played theme song sung by Bill Medley of the Righteous Brothers. **97m/C VHS.** Gene Hackman, Jim Brown, Mike Kellin, Ben Carruthers, Frank Eyman; ***D:*** Buzz Kulik; ***W:*** James Poe. *PAR*

Riot in Cell Block 11 **1954** A convict leads four thousand prisoners in an uprising to improve prison conditions. Based on producer/ex-con Walter Wanger's own experience. Powerful and still timely. Filmed at Folsom Prison. **80m/B VHS, Beta.** Neville Brand, Leo Gordon, Emile Meyer, Frank Faylen; ***D:*** Donald Siegel. *REP*

Riot Squad **1941** An intern poses as a doctor in order to find out who was responsible for putting a mob hit on a police captain. **55m/B VHS, Beta.** Richard Cromwell, Rita Quigley, John Miljan, Mary Ruth, Herbert Rawlinson, Mary Gordon, Arthur Space; ***D:*** Edward Finney. *SNC, RXM*

Rip-Off **1977** Two Greek wanderers enter the American way of life via sex, drugs, syndicated crime, and terrorism. **78m/C VHS, Beta.** Michael Benet, Michelle Simone, James Masters, Johnny Dark; ***D:*** Manolis Tsafos. *UNI*

The Rip Off **1978 (R)** A colorful gang of hoodlums goes for the biggest heist of their lives—six million bucks in diamonds! **99m/C VHS, Beta.** Lee Van Cleef, Karen Black, Robert Alda, Edward Albert; ***D:*** Anthony (Antonio Margheriti) Dawson. *WOV*

Rip Roarin' Buckaroo **1936** A fighter sets out to avenge himself when he is framed in a dishonest fight. **51m/B VHS, Beta.** Tom Tyler, B.J. Quinn Jr., Beth Marion, Charles "Blackie" King; ***D:*** Robert F. "Bob" Hill. *NOS, DVT, RXM*

Rip van Winkle **1985** Sleepy Coppola adaptation of the Washington Irving story about a man who falls asleep for twenty years after a group of ghosts get him drunk. From the "Faerie Tale Theatre" series. **60m/C VHS, Beta.** Harry Dean Stanton, Talia Shire; ***D:*** Francis Ford Coppola. *KUI, FOX, FCT*

The Ripper *Woof!* **1986** The spirit of Jack-the-Ripper possesses a university professor's body. Ultra-violent. Shot on videotape for the video market. **90m/C VHS, Beta.** Wade Tower, Tom Schreir, Mona Van Pernis, Andrea Adams; ***D:*** Christopher Lewis. *NO*

Ripping Yarns **1975** Three episodes of the popular British comedy series written by Monty Python's Terry Jones and Michael Palin: "Tomkinson's Schooldays," "Escape from Stalag Luft 112B," and "Golden Gordon." The subsequent episodes are released as "More Ripping Yarns" and "Even More Ripping Yarns." **90m/C VHS, Beta.** *GB* Michael Palin, Gwen Watford, Ian Ogilvy, Roy Kinnear, Bill Fraser; ***D:*** Terry Hughes, Jimmy Franklin, Alan Bell; ***W:*** Michael Palin, Terry Jones. *FOX, VCO*

Riptide **1934** Shearer is a carefree American married to stuffy English lord Marshall. He goes off to America on a business trip, she's bored and goes to a costume party (everyone dresses as insects!) where she meets old flame Montgomery. He gets drunk, follows her home in an effort to rekindle their passion, and winds up in the hospital after a drunken fall. The returning Marshall is appalled by the scandalous press and instigates divorce proceedings. Eventually, they come to their senses and decide they do love each other. Quality production with an entertaining cast. **90m/B VHS.** Norma Shearer, Herbert Marshall, Robert Montgomery, Richard "Skeets" Gallagher, Ralph Forbes, Lilyan Tashman; ***D:*** Edmund Goulding; ***W:*** Edmund Goulding. *MGM*

The Rise and Fall of Legs Diamond ½ **1960** Not quite historically accurate but fast-paced and entertaining gangster bio of legendary booze trafficker Legs Diamond. Danton's debut. **101m/B VHS, LV.** Ray Danton, Karen Steele, Jesse White, Simon Oakland, Robert Lowery, Elaine Stewart; ***D:*** Budd Boetticher. Nominations: Academy Awards '60: Best Costume Design (B & W). *WAR, FCT*

The Rise & Rise of Daniel Rocket **1986** A exceptional young boy believes he can fly without the aid of a flying machine. From the "American Playhouse" series. **90m/C VHS, Beta.** Tom Hulce, Timothy Daly, Valerie Mahaffey; ***D:*** Emile Ardolino. *ACA, PBS*

The Rise of Louis XIV *La Prise de Pouvoir Par Louis XIV* **1966** A masterful docudrama detailing the life and court intrigues of Louis XIV of France. Successfully captures the attitudes and mores of the royalty at the time. One of a series of historical films directed by Rossellini. Made for French television. In French with English subtitles. **100m/C VHS.** *FR* Jean-Marie Patte, Raymond Jourdan, Dominique Vincent, Silvagni, Pierre Barrat; ***D:*** Roberto Rossellini. *HTV, INJ, FCT*

Rising Son **1990** A family man who loves his job faces trauma when his factory closes at the same time his son informs him he's quitting medical school. Solid family drama and parable of economic hard times of the early '80s, sustained by top-drawer performances by Dennehy, Damon, and Laurie. Well directed by Coles. Made for cable. **92m/C VHS, Beta.** Brian Dennehy, Matt Damon, Piper Laurie, Graham Beckel, Ving Rhames, Jane Adams, Richard Jenkins, Emily Longstreth; ***D:*** John David Coles; ***W:*** Bill Phillips. *TTC*

Rising Sun **1993 (R)** When a prostitute is found murdered in the boardroom of a powerful Japanese-owned corporation, seasoned cop (and Japanese expert) Connery and new partner Snipes are sent to investigate. Complicated yarn about business, prejudice, cops, and the differences between east and west. Filmed with stylized camera techniques, quick action, and good rapport between the two leads. Based on the book by Crichton, which offered ominous theories about international politics and business. These aspects had the film labeled as Japan-bashing, one of the reasons the script was rewritten to focus more on the murder mystery. **129m/C VHS, LV.** Sean Connery, Wesley Snipes, Tia Carrere, Harvey Keitel, Kevin Anderson, Stan Egi, Mako, Cary-Hiroyuki Tagawa, Ray Wise, Tatjana Patitz; ***D:*** Philip Kaufman; ***W:*** Michael Backes, Michael Crichton, Philip Kaufman; ***M:*** Toru Takemitsu. *FXV, BTV, FCT*

Risk **1994** Maya (Sillas) is a struggling, emotionally distant, New York artist when she meets overly-friendly Joe (Ilku) on a bus. He follows her home and manages to entice Maya into letting him spend the night but Joe has some psychological problems, including criminal behavior, which manifests itself when he steals a car. Maya, nevertheless, agrees to drive with him to his older sister's home in rural Connecticut and finds bad blood and more mental anguish that she knows how to deal with. Terrifically honest performance by Sillas and an equally touching one by Ilku are highlights of this adult attempt at romance. **85m/C VHS.** Karen Sillas, David Ilku, Molly Price, Jack Gwaltney; ***D:*** Deirdre Fishel; ***W:*** Deirdre Fishel; ***C:*** Peter Pearce; ***M:*** John Paul Jones. *LEO*

Risky Business **1928** Fortune-seeking mother disapproves of daughter's doctor fiance, and educates girl in marital woes. Video includes early Pollard short "Sold at Auction." **104m/B VHS, Beta, LV.** Vera Reynolds, ZaSu Pitts, Ethey Clayton; ***D:*** Alan Hale. *GPV, FCT, WAR*

Risky Business **1983 (R)** With his parents out of town and awaiting word from the college boards, a teenager becomes involved in unexpected ways with a quick-thinking prostitute, her pimp, and assorted others. Cruise is likeable, especially when dancing in his underwear. Funny, well-paced, stylish prototypical '80s teen flick reintroduced Ray-Bans as the sunglasses for the wannabe hip. What a party! **99m/C VHS, Beta, LV, 8mm.** Tom Cruise, Rebecca DeMornay, Curtis Armstrong, Bronson Pinchot, Joe Pantoliano, Kevin Anderson, Richard Masur, Raphael Sbarge, Nicholas Pryor, Janet Carroll; ***D:*** Paul Brickman; ***W:*** Paul Brickman; ***C:*** Reynaldo Villalobos; ***M:*** Tangerine Dream. *WAR*

Rita Hayworth: The Love Goddess ½ **1983** Made for television drama details the tragic life of the beautiful film star. Carter, lovely though she is, plays Rita weakly and without depth. **100m/C VHS, Beta.** Lynda Carter, Michael Lerner, Alejandro Rey, John Considine; ***D:*** James Goldstone. *LIV*

Rita, Sue & Bob Too **1987 (R)** A middle-aged Englishman gets involved in a menage a trois with two promiscuous teenagers, until the whole town gets wind of it. A raunchy, amoral British comedy. **94m/C VHS, Beta, LV.** *GB* Michelle Holmes, George Costigan, Siobhan Finneran, Lesley Sharp, Willie Ross, Patti Nicholls, Kulvinder Ghir; ***D:*** Alan Clarke; ***W:*** Andrea Dunbar; ***M:*** Michael Kamen. *ORI, WAR*

The Rite *The Ritual; Riten* **1969** Members of a famous theatrical troupe are called before a judge to answer charges that a production is obscene. The judge's interrogation exposes their private and painful neuroses until the performers decide to turn on their accuser. Pessimistic even by Bergman standards and the first film the director made specifically for TV. Swedish with subtitles. **75m/B VHS.** *SW* Ingrid Thulin, Gunnar Bjornstrand, Erik Hell, Anders Ek; ***D:*** Ingmar Bergman; ***W:*** Ingmar Bergman; ***C:*** Sven Nykvist. *HMV*

Rituals ½ *The Creeper* **1979** Group of five calm, rational men suddenly turn desperate after a chain of nightmarish events on a camping trip. Yet another low-budget "Deliverance" rip off. **100m/C VHS, Beta.** *CA* Hal Holbrook, Lawrence Dane; ***D:*** Peter Carter. *SUE, VTR*

The Ritz **1976 (R)** Weston tries to get away from his gangster brother-in-law by hiding out in a gay bathhouse in New York. Moreno plays a talentless singer Googie Gomez, who performs in the bathhouse while waiting for her big break. Moreno is great reprising her Tony-winning stage role, and Lester's direction is spiffy. Written by Terence McNally from his play. **91m/C VHS, Beta, LV.** Rita Moreno, Jack Weston, Jerry Stiller, Kaye Ballard, Treat Williams, F. Murray Abraham; ***D:*** Richard Lester. *WAR*

Rivals ½ *Deadly Rivals* **1972 (R)** Shallow, unconvincing drama about a stepfather challenged by his stepson, who wants to kill this new contender for his mother's love. Nice handling of cast credits, but other details—like acting, directing and photography—leave much to be desired. **103m/C VHS, Beta.** Robert Klein, Joan Hackett, Scott Jacoby; ***D:*** Krishna Shah. *TPI*

Rivals of the Silver Fox ½ **1980** Young kickers prove no match for their hoary, hard-chopping elder. **90m/C VHS, Beta.** Casanova Wong, Barry Lam, Chen Shao Ping, Lee Fat Yuen. *NO*

The River **1951** A massively lauded late film by Renoir about three British girls growing up in Bengal, India, all developing crushes on a one-legged American vet. Lyrical and heartwarming, with hailed cinematography by Claude Renoir. Rumer Godden wrote the novel, and co-scripted the screenplay with director Renoir. Satyajit Ray, one of India's greatest filmmakers, assisted Renoir. **99m/C VHS, Beta, LV.** *FR* Patricia Walters, Adrienne Corri, Nora Swinburne, Radha, Arthur Shields, Thomas E. Breen, Esmond Knight; ***D:*** Jean Renoir; ***W:*** Jean Renoir. National Board of Review Awards '51: 5 Best Foreign Films of the Year. *HMV, CRC, INJ*

The River **1984 (PG)** Farmers battle a river whose flood threatens their farm. Spacek, as always, is strong and believable as the wife and mother, but Gibson falters. Beautiful photography. The third in an onslaught of films in the early '80s that dramatized the plight of the small American farmer. "The River" isn't as strong as "Country" and "Places in the

Heart" which managed to convey important messages less cloyingly. **124m/C VHS, Beta, LV.** Mel Gibson, Sissy Spacek, Scott Glenn, Billy Green Bush; ***D:*** Mark Rydell; ***W:*** Julian Barry, Robert Dillon; ***C:*** Vilmos Zsigmond; ***M:*** John Williams. Nominations: Academy Awards '84: Best Actress (Spacek), Best Cinematography, Best Sound, Best Original Score. *MCA*

River Beat 🦴🦴 **1954** A woman aboard an American freighter is unwittingly used as diamond smuggler, and is arrested when the ship docks in London. An inspector does his best to clear the hapless woman. **70m/B VHS, Beta.** Phyllis Kirk, John Bentley, Robert Ayres, Lenny White, Glyn Houston, Charles Lloyd Pack; ***D:*** Guy Green. *SNC*

The River Niger 🦴🦴½ **1976 (R)** Jones is riveting, and Tyson is good in an otherwise muddling adaptation of the Tony-award winning play about black ghetto life. Realistic emotions and believable characters. **105m/C VHS.** James Earl Jones, Cicely Tyson, Glynn Turman, Louis Gossett Jr., Roger E. Mosley, Jonelle Allen; ***D:*** Krishna Shah. *NO*

River of Death 🦴½ **1990 (R)** Absurd adventure, based on an Alistair McLean novel, about a white man entering the Amazon jungle world of a forgotten tribe in search of wealth, tripping over Neo-Nazi scientists and war criminals. Too complex to be harmlessly enjoyable; too mindless for the complexity to be worth unraveling. **103m/C VHS, Beta, LV.** Michael Dudikoff, Robert Vaughn, Donald Pleasence, Herbert Lom, L.Q. Jones, Cynthia Erland, Sarah Maur-Thorp; ***D:*** Steve Carver. *MGM, WAR*

River of Diamonds 🦴 **1990** A daring adventurer, with the standard beautiful woman at his side, battles evil curses and Nazis buried alive to find a fortune in diamonds. Yeah, sure. Another miserable "Indiana Jones" rip off. **88m/C VHS, Beta.** Dack Rambo, Angela O'Neill, Ferdinand "Ferdy" Mayne, Graham Clark, David Sherwood, Tony Caprari, Dominique Tyawa; ***D:*** Robert J. Smawley. *TTC*

River of Evil 🦴½ **1964** Action/adventure in which a young girl travels through the Amazon jungle searching for clues to her father's death. **?m/C VHS.** Barbara Rutting, Harald Leipnitz. *SNC*

River of No Return 🦴🦴½ **1954** During the gold rush, an itinerant farmer and his young son help a heart-of-gold saloon singer search for her estranged husband. Rather crummy script is helped by the mere presence of Mitchum and Monroe. Marilyn sings the title song, "Down in the Meadow," and "I'm Going to File My Claim." **91m/C VHS, Beta, LV.** Robert Mitchum, Marilyn Monroe, Tommy Rettig, Rory Calhoun, Murvyn Vye, Douglas Spencer; ***D:*** Otto Preminger; ***C:*** Joseph LaShelle. *FOX*

River of Unrest 🦴🦴½ *Ourselves Alone* **1937** Remarkable visual expressiveness and emotional power mark this depiction of terrorism and open warfare during the Irish Rebellion. Based on a play, hence slow; but good acting pulls it up half a bone. **69m/B VHS, Beta.** John Lodge, John Loder, Antoinette Cellier. *VYY*

The River Pirates 🦴🦴½ **1994 (PG)** Mississippi boy discovers a lot about life over the summer of his 12th birthday in 1942. He finds the secret hiding place of a band of river thieves, endures a tornado, has some adventures with his friends, and finds out that his crush on the prettiest girl in town is reciprocated. Based on a novel by Willie Morris. **108m/C VHS, LV.** Ryan Francis, Richard Farnsworth, Gennie James, Doug Emerson, Anne Ramsey, Maureen O'Sullivan; ***D:*** Tom G. Robertson. *VMK*

The River Rat 🦴🦴½ **1984 (PG)** Ex-con Jones is reunited with his daughter after spending thirteen years in prison. There's something in there about stashed loot that should have been jettisonned in favor of more getting-to-know-you father-daughter drama, which is good. **93m/C VHS, Beta, LV.** Tommy Lee Jones, Brian Dennehy, Martha Plimpton, Shawn Smith, Melissa Davis; ***D:*** Tom Rickman. *PAR*

A River Runs Through It 🦴🦴🦴½ **1992 (PG)** Contemplative exploration of family ties and coming of age with impact falling just short of the novel's is another well-crafted American tale directed by Redford. Set in Montana during the early part of the century, a Presbyterian minister teaches his two sons, one troubled and one on his way to success, about life and religion via fly-fishing. Based on the novel by Norman Maclean. The laser disc version includes commentary by Redford. **123m/C VHS, LV, 8mm.** Craig Sheffer, Brad Pitt, Tom Skerritt, Brenda Blethyn, Emily Lloyd, Edie McClurg, Stephen Shellan, Susan Taylor; ***D:*** Robert Redford; ***W:*** Richard Friedenberg; ***C:*** Philippe Rousselot; ***M:*** Mark Isham. Academy Awards '92: Best Cinematography; Nominations: Academy Awards '92: Best Adapted Screenplay, Best Original Score. *COL, CRC, BTV*

The River Wild 🦴🦴½ **1994 (PG-13)** Dissatisfied wife Gail (Streep) plans a family white-water rafting vacation with 10-year-old son Roarke (Mazzello) and workaholic husband Tom (Strathairn). A former guide (and white-water expert) Gail comes to the aid of river novices Wade (boyishly menacing Bacon) and Terry (Reilly), who quickly turn out to be violent criminals needing Gail's help with their escape. Slow start leads to nonstop thrills with Streep an adept action heroine, though undercut by the flic's need to do something with Strathairn's thankless role. Beautiful Montana and Oregon settings. **111m/C VHS, LV.** Meryl Streep, David Strathairn, Joseph Mazzello, Kevin Bacon, John C. Reilly, Benjamin Bratt; ***D:*** Curtis Hanson; ***W:*** Raynold Gideon; ***M:*** Jerry Goldsmith. Nominations: Golden Globe Awards '95: Best Actress—Drama (Streep), Best Supporting Actor (Bacon). *MCA*

Riverbend 🦴🦴 **1989 (R)** A renegade black Army major escapes a rigged court martial only to be persecuted by racist whites in a small Southern town. Made for television. **106m/C VHS, Beta.** Steve James, Tony Frank, Julius Tennon, Margaret Avery; ***D:*** Sam Firstenberg. *PAR*

River's Edge 🦴🦴🦴 **1987 (R)** Drug-addled high school student strangles his girlfriend and casually displays the corpse to his apathetic group of friends, who leave the murder unreported for days. Harrowing and gripping; based on a true story. Aging biker Hopper is splendid. **99m/C VHS, Beta, LV, 8mm.** Keanu Reeves, Crispin Glover, Daniel Roebuck, Joshua Miller, Dennis Hopper, Ione Skye, Roxana Zal, Tom Bower, Constance Forslund, Leo Rossi, Jim Metzler; ***D:*** Tim Hunter; ***W:*** Neal Jimenez; ***M:*** Jurgen Knieper. Independent Spirit Awards '88: Best Film, Best Screenplay; Sundance Film Festival '87: Special Jury Prize. *SUE, NLC*

Road Agent 🦴½ *Texas Road Agent* **1926** Hoxie is the Kansas Kid, a fugitive hired by a crooked lawyer to pose as the long-lost heir to a ranching fortune. Only the Kid develops a soft spot for his "family" and may not be able to go through with the evil plot. **70m/B VHS, Beta.** Al Hoxie; ***D:*** J.P. McGowan. *NOS, DVT, MLB*

Road Games 🦴🦴 **1981 (PG)** Trucker Keach is drawn into a web of intrigue surrounding a series of highway "Jack the Ripper"-style murders. Curtis is a hitchhiker. Nothing special. Director Franklin later helmed "Psycho II." **100m/C VHS, Beta.** *AU* Stacy Keach, Jamie Lee Curtis; ***D:*** Richard Franklin. *COL, SUE, NLC*

The Road Home 🦴🦴½ **1995 (PG)** Depression-era heart-tugger features two orphaned brothers who ride the rails from New York to Nebraska in search of a new home at Father Flanagan's Boys Town. **90m/C VHS.** Keegan Macintosh, Will Estes, Kris Kristofferson, Charles Martin Smith, Danny Aiello, Dee Wallace Stone, Mickey Rooney; ***D:*** Dean Hamilton. *REP*

Road House 🦴🦴½ **1948** Nightclub singer Lupino inspires noir feelings between jealous road house owner Widmark and his partner Wilde. Widmark sets up Wilde to take the fall for a faked robbery, convinces the law to release him into his custody, then dares him to escape. **95m/B VHS, Beta.** Richard Widmark, Ida Lupino, Cornel Wilde, Celeste Holm, O.Z. Whitehead; ***D:*** Jean Negulesco. *FOX, FCT*

Road House 🦴½ **1989 (R)** Bouncer Swayze is hired to do the impossible: clean up the toughest bar in Kansas City. When he lays down his rules he makes a lot of enemies, including ex-bar employees and local organized crime. Ample violence; an example of formula filmmaking at its most brain-numbing, with a rock soundtrack. **115m/C VHS, Beta, LV, 8mm.** Patrick Swayze, Sam Elliott, Kelly Lynch, Ben Gazzara, Kevin Tighe, Marshall Teague, Julie Michaels, Jeff Healey; ***D:*** Rowdy Herrington; ***C:*** Dean Cundey; ***M:*** Michael Kamen. *MGM*

Road Kill USA 🦴🦴½ **1993** Two sleazy drifters on a cross-country murder spree pick up a hitchhiking college student and expect him to join in the fun. When he refuses, he has two choices: kill or be killed. **98m/C VHS.** Andrew Porter, Sean Bridges, Deanna Perry; ***D:*** Tony Elwood. *AIP*

The Road Killers 🦴🦴 **1995 (R)** Sickening psycho Cliff (well-played by Sheffer) is head of a brutal quartet that terrorizes a family driving along a remote desert highway. Cliff kidnaps the family daughter and her mild-mannered dad (Lambert) must rescue her. **89m/C VHS, LV.** Christopher Lambert, Craig Sheffer, Adrienne Shelly; ***D:*** Deran Sarafian; ***W:*** Tedi Sarafian. *WEA, LIV*

Road Lawyers and Other Briefs 🦴🦴½ **1989** Several recent comedic shorts. "Road Lawyers," the title short, is a hilarious look at lawyers in a post-apocalyptic world that won major awards at film festivals in New York, Houston, Australia, and Chicago. Also included are: "Escape from Heaven," about a nun with an attitude problem; "Radar Men on the Moon," a comic reworking of an old "Commander Cody" serial; and "Hairline." **79m/C VHS.** *AIP*

Road Racers 🦴🦴 **1959** The roar of the engine, fast cars, and family ties combine in this movie about the thrill of speed. **73m/B VHS.** Joel Lawrence, Marian Collier, Skip Ward; ***D:*** Arthur Swerdloff; ***W:*** Stanley Kallis, Ed Lasko. *COL*

Road Show 🦴🦴½ **1941** Menjou stars as a young man wrongfully committed to an insane asylum. He escapes and joins a bankrupt carnival owned by Landis. Some really zany stuff keeps this from being just standard fare. Co-written by silent film comic Langdon. **87m/B VHS.** Adolphe Menjou, Carole Landis, John Hubbard, Charles Butterworth, Patsy Kelly, George E. Stone, Polly Ann Young, Edward Norris, Marjorie Woodworth, Florence Bates; ***D:*** Hal Roach; ***W:*** Harry Langdon. *NOS*

The Road to Bali 🦴🦴🦴 **1953** Sixth Bob-n-Bing road show, the only one in color, is a keeper. The boys are competing for the love of—that's right—Lamour. She must be some gal, cuz they chase her all the way to Bali, where they meet cannibals and other perils, including the actual Humphrey Bogart. Jones's debut, in a bit role. ♫Moonflowers; Chicago Style; Hoots Mon; To See You; The Merry-Go-Runaround; Chorale for Brass, Piano, and Bongo (instrumental). **90m/C VHS, Beta.** Bob Hope, Bing Crosby, Dorothy Lamour, Murvyn Vye, Ralph Moody, Jane Russell, Jerry Lewis, Dean Martin, Carolyn Jones; ***D:*** Hal Walker. *UNI, DVT, MLB*

The Road to Galveston 🦴🦴🦴 **1996 (PG-13)** Texas widow Jordan Roosevelt (Tyson) needs to pay her mortgage so she turns her home into a residence for three Alzheimer patients. When her financial problems only worsen, Jordan decides to fulfill her lifetime goal and takes everyone on a trip to Galveston to see the ocean. Sentimental, fact-based TV movie cuts the sacharine through compelling performances. **93m/C VHS, Beta.** Cicely Tyson, Piper Laurie, Tess Harper, Salle Ellis, Starletta DuPois, James McDaniel, Penny Johnson, Clarence Williams III, Stephen Root; ***D:*** Michael Toshiyuki Uno; ***W:*** Tony Lee; ***M:*** Stanley Clarke. *PAR*

The Road to Hong Kong 🦴🦴½ **1962** Last of the Crosby/Hope team-ups shows some wear, but still manages charm and humor. Lamour appears only briefly in this twisted comedy of hustlers caught in international espionage and cosmic goings-on. ♫Teamwork; Let's Not Be Sensible; It's The

Only Way to Travel; We're On the Road to Hong Kong; Warmer Than a Whisper. **91m/B VHS, LV.** Bob Hope, Bing Crosby, Joan Collins, Dorothy Lamour, Peter Sellers; ***D:*** Norman Panama; ***W:*** Norman Panama; ***C:*** Jack Hildyard. *MGM, BTV, FCT*

The Road to Lebanon 🦴🦴 **1960** An original musical comedy featuring many stars, spoofing the famous Hope-Crosby "Road" films. **50m/B VHS, Beta.** Danny Thomas, Bing Crosby, Bob Hope, Hugh Downs, Claudine Auger, Sheldon Leonard. *NOS, VYY, DVT*

The Road to Life 🦴🦴 *Putyovka V Zhizn* **1931** In the turmoil caused by Russia's Revolutionary and Civil wars, thousands of orphans roam the countryside resorting to petty crime to survive. One group is sent to a collective as part of an experimental program where they can be reformed and learn a trade but their criminal pasts seem inescapable. Russian with subtitles. **100m/B VHS.** *RU* Nikolai Batalov, Maria Gonfa, Tsifan Kyria; ***D:*** Nicolai Ekk; ***W:*** Nicolai Ekk; ***M:*** Yakov Stollyar. *FCT*

The Road to Morocco 🦴🦴🦴 ½ **1942** The third in the road movie series finds Hope and Crosby in Morocco, stranded and broke. To get some money, Crosby sells Hope into slavery to be the princess's (Lamour) personal plaything. Feeling guilty, Crosby returns to the palace to rescue Hope, only to find that he and the princess are getting married because the royal astrologer said it was in the stars. Crosby then tries to woo Lamour and, when the astrologer discovers the stars were mistaken, those two decide to marry. Quinn, however, also wants her and hilarious scenes ensue when the boys rescue Lamour from him. One of the funniest in the series. Watch for the camel at the end. ♫Constantly; Moonlight Becomes You; Ain't Got a Dime to My Name; Road to Morocco. **83m/C VHS, LV.** Bing Crosby, Bob Hope, Dorothy Lamour, Anthony Quinn, Dona Drake, Vladimir Sokoloff, Yvonne De Carlo; ***D:*** David Butler; ***C:*** William Mellor. Nominations: Academy Awards '42: Best Original Screenplay, Best Sound. *MCA*

Road to Nashville 🦴🦴 **1967 (G)** An agent travels to Nashville to enlist talent for a new musical. Why do so many of these semi-musicals insist on having a plot? Good music. **110m/C VHS, Beta.** Marty Robbins, Johnny Cash, Doodles Weaver, Connie Smith, Richard Arlen; ***D:*** Robert Patrick. *NO*

The Road to Rio 🦴🦴🦴 ½ **1947** The wisecracking duo travel to Rio De Janeiro to prevent Spanish beauty Lamour (there she is again) from going through with an arranged marriage. Top-notch entry; fifth in the "Road" series. ♫But Beautiful; You Don't Have To Know the Language; For What?; Experience; Apalachicola, Florida; Cavaquinho; Brazil. **100m/B VHS, Beta.** Bing Crosby, Bob Hope, Dorothy Lamour, Gale Sondergaard, Frank Faylen, The Andrews Sisters; ***D:*** Norman Z. McLeod; ***W:*** Jack Rose; ***C:*** Ernest Laszlo. Nominations: Academy Awards '47: Best Original Score. *COL*

The Road to Ruin 🦴🦴 **1928** The evils of smoking and drinking plummet a girl into a life of prostitution in this melodramatic, moralistic tale. An unintentional laugh-riot right up there with "Reefer Madness." Silent. **45m/B VHS, Beta.** Helen Foster, Grant Withers, Virginia Roye; ***D:*** Norton S. Parker; ***W:*** Erik Anjou. *SNC, NOS, VYY*

Road to Ruin 🦴🦴 **1991 (R)** A rich playboy pretends to lose all his money to see if his girlfriend loves him for himself or for his wealth. But when his business partner embezzles his fortune, he must regain both his money and his girlfriend's trust. **94m/C VHS.** Peter Weller, Carey Lowell, Michael Duchaussoy; ***D:*** Charlotte Brandstrom. *LIV*

Road to Salina 🦴🦴🦴 **1968 (R)** A drifter is mistaken for (and might actually be) a desert-restaurant owner's long-lost son. He plays along, eventually seducing the family's daughter, who might be his sister. **97m/C VHS, Beta.** *FR* Robert Walker Jr., Rita Hayworth, Mimsy Farmer, Ed Begley Sr.; ***D:*** Georges Lautner. *NLC*

The Road to Singapore 🦴🦴 ½ **1940** This is the movie that started it all. Crosby and Hope decide to swear off women and escape to Singapore to enjoy the free life. There they meet Lamour, a showgirl who is abused by Quinn. The boys rescue Lamour, but soon find they are both falling for her. She's in love with one of them, but won't reveal her feelings. Who will get the girl? Not as funny as some of the other road movies, but it's great for a first try. ♫Captain Custard; The Moon and the Willow Tree; Sweet Potato Piper; Too Romantic; Kaigoon. **84m/C VHS, LV.** Bing Crosby, Bob Hope, Dorothy Lamour, Charles Coburn, Judith Barrett, Anthony Quinn, Jerry Colonna, Johnny Arthur, Pierre Watkin; ***D:*** Victor Schertzinger; ***C:*** William Mellor. *MCA*

The Road to Utopia 🦴🦴🦴 **1946** Fourth of the "Road" films, wherein the boys wind up in Alaska posing as two famous escaped killers in order to locate a secret gold mine. One of the series' funniest and most spontaneous entries, abetted by Benchley's dry, upper-crust comments. ♫Put It There, Pal; Welcome to My Dreams; Would You?; Personality; Sunday, Monday, or Always?; Goodtime Charlie; It's Anybody's Spring. **90m/B VHS, Beta, LV.** Bing Crosby, Bob Hope, Dorothy Lamour, Jack LaRue, Robert Benchley, Douglass Dumbrille, Hillary Brooke; ***D:*** Hal Walker; ***W:*** Norman Panama; ***C:*** Lionel Lindon. Nominations: Academy Awards '46: Best Original Screenplay. *MCA*

The Road to Wellville 🦴🦴 **1994 (R)** Corn flake magnate John Harvey Kellogg takes good health to an intestine-invading extreme in this spa satire featuring Hopkins as the buck-toothed Kellogg. Broderick and Fonda portray a wealthy couple who visit the turn-of-the-century sanitarium in search of Kellogg's cure, but receive only sexual frustration and anal humiliations. Bowel jokes and an essentially plotless scenario overshadow a gifted, but helpless cast. Adapted from T. Coraghessan Boyle's not-so-easily-adaptable novel. **120m/C VHS, LV.** Anthony Hopkins, Bridget Fonda, Matthew Broderick, John Cusack, Dana Carvey, Michael Lerner, Colm Meaney, John Neville, Lara Flynn Boyle, Traci Lind, Roy Brocksmith, Norbert Weisser; ***D:*** Alan Parker; ***W:*** Alan Parker; ***M:*** Rachel Portman. *COL*

The Road to Yesterday 🦴🦴 ½ **1925** Two couples together on a crashing train are somehow thrown into the eighteenth century in roles parallel to their own lives. DeMille's first independent film; intriguing action/melodrama. Silent with musical soundtrack. **136m/B VHS, Beta.** Joseph Schildkraut, William Boyd, Jetta Goudal, Vera Reynolds, Iron Eyes Cody; ***D:*** Cecil B. DeMille. *GPV, VYY*

Road to Yesterday/The Yankee Clipper 🦴🦴 ½ **1927** Four train passengers are transported back to previous lives in "The Road to Yesterday." "The Yankee Clipper" races the British Lord of the Isles from China to New England to capture the tea trade. Both of these pictures are abridged versions. Silent. **56m/B VHS, Beta.** William Boyd, Elinor Fair, Joseph Schildkraut, Jetta Goudal, Vera Reynolds; ***D:*** Cecil B. DeMille. *CCB*

The Road to Zanzibar 🦴🦴🦴 **1941** After selling a fake diamond mine to a criminal, Crosby and Hope flee to Zanzibar, where they meet up with Lamour and Merkel. The guys put up the money for a safari, supposedly to look for Lamour's brother, but they soon discover that they too have been tricked. Deciding to head back to Zanzibar, Crosby and Hope find themselves surrounded by hungry cannibals. Will they survive, or will they be someone's dinner? Not as funny as the other road movies, but amusing nonetheless. ♫It's Always You; You're Dangerous; On the Road to Zanzibar; You Lucky People You; Birds of a Feather; African Etude. **92m/C VHS, LV.** Bing Crosby, Bob Hope, Dorothy Lamour, Una Merkel, Eric Blore, Iris Adrian, Lionel Royce; ***D:*** Victor Schertzinger. *MCA*

The Road Warrior 🦴🦴🦴 ½ **1982 (R)** The first sequel to "Mad Max" takes place after nuclear war has destroyed Australia. Max helps a colony of oil-drilling survivors defend themselves from the roving murderous outback gangs and escape to the coast. The climactic chase scene is among the most exciting ever filmed; this film virtually created the "action-adventure" picture of the 1980s. **95m/C VHS, Beta, LV.** Mel Gibson, Bruce Spence, Emil Minty, Vernon Wells; ***D:*** George Miller; ***W:*** George Miller; ***C:*** Dean Semler. Los Angeles Film Critics Association Awards '82: Best Foreign Film. *WAR*

Roadhouse Girl 🦴 *Marilyn* **1953** A sexy woman kindles a romance with one of her husband's employees and the result is murder. Reminiscent of "The Postman Always Rings Twice," but with poor production values and performances. **70m/B VHS, Beta.** *GB* Maxwell Reed, Sandra Dorne, Leslie Dwyer, Vida Hope, Ferdinand "Ferdy" Mayne; ***D:*** Wolf Rilla; ***W:*** Wolf Rilla. *SNC*

Roadhouse 66 🦴 ½ **1984 (R)** Utterly unoriginal broke-down-in-a-hick-town nonsense. Snooty Reinhold and scruffy Dafoe go through the motions, and of course find a pair of female companions. Soundtrack features Los Lobos, the Pretenders, and Dave Edmunds. **90m/C VHS, Beta.** Willem Dafoe, Judge Reinhold, Karen Lee, Kate Vernon, Stephen Elliott; ***D:*** John Mark Robinson. *FOX*

Roadie 🦴 ½ **1980 (PG)** Supposedly a look at the back-stage world of rock n' roll, but the performances and direction leave a lot to be desired. Meatloaf is a roadie who desperately wants to meet Alice Cooper, and spends the movie trying to do so. Features Art Carney, and musical names like Blondie, Roy Orbison, Hank Williams, Jr. and Don Cornelius (of "Soul Train" fame). **105m/C VHS.** Meat Loaf, Kaki Hunter, Art Carney, Art Carney, Gailard Sartain, Alice Cooper, Roy Orbison, Hank Williams Jr., Ramblin' Jack Elliot; ***D:*** Alan Rudolph; ***W:*** Alan Rudolph, Michael Ventura. *MVD, MGM*

Roadkill 🦴 **1989** Cheap thriller about Ramona (Buhagiar), a concert promoter who tries to find a lost band, "The Children of Paradise," in the Canadian north woods. Along the way, she meets a would-be serial killer and other assorted weirdos. **85m/B VHS.** *CA* Valerie Buhagiar, Don McKellar, Bruce McDonald; ***D:*** Bruce.McDonald; ***W:*** Don McKellar. Toronto-City Award '89: Best Canadian Feature Film. *NO*

Roads to the South 🦴🦴 ½ **1978** One-time Spanish revolutionary turned screenwriter returns to his homeland to fight fascism, but finds himself attracted to his son's beautiful girlfriend. Much soul searching. In French with English subtitles. **100m/C VHS, LV.** *FR* Yves Montand, Miou-Miou; ***D:*** Joseph Losey. *CVC, IME, FCT*

Roadside Prophets 🦴🦴 **1992 (R)** Counterculture road trip, striving to be the '90s version of "Easy Rider," follows factory worker/biker Joe (Doe) on his mission to transport the ashes of a fellow biker to Nevada. He is accompanied by the pesky younger Sam (Horovitz), and together they meet up with lots of eccentrics and stay at lots of cheap motels. Interesting cast meanders through sentimental and slow-moving buddy flick from debut director Wool, who wrote "Sid and Nancy." Cusack completes the cameo hat trick, with appearances here and in 1992's "The Player" and "Shadows and Fog." **96m/C VHS, LV.** John Doe, Adam Horovitz, David Carradine, Timothy Leary, Arlo Guthrie, Barton Heyman, Jennifer Balgobin; ***Cameos:*** John Cusack; ***D:*** Abbe Wool; ***W:*** Abbe Wool. *NLC*

The Roamin' Cowboy 🦴🦴 **1937** In a town where the local ranchers are being threatened, a drifter comes to their rescue and wins both a girl and a job. **56m/B VHS.** Fred Scott, Al "Fuzzy" St. John, Lois January, Forrest Taylor, Roger Williams; ***D:*** Robert F. "Bob" Hill. *NOS, DVT*

Roamin' Wild 🦴🦴 ½ **1936** Exciting, action-packed early western with marshal Tyler saving a lady's stagecoach line from unsavory varmints. **60m/B VHS, Beta.** Tom Tyler, Carol Wyndham, Al Ferguson, George Chesebro, Max Davidson, Fred Parker; ***D:*** Bernard B. Ray. *NOS, DVT*

Roanoak 🦴🦴 ½ **1986** A dramatization in three parts of the mysterious fate of the early English settlement of Roanoak in North Carolina, which disappeared without a trace. Long, but intriguing. Made for PBS: "American Playhouse." **180m/C Beta.** Will Sampson, Victoria Racimo, Porky White, Adrian Sparks, Patrick Kilpatrick; ***D:*** Jan Egleson. *PBS*

Roarin' Lead 🦴½ **1937** Three Mesquiteers fight with a gang of rustlers while helping the orphans' and cattlemen's associations. **54m/B VHS, Beta.** Bob Livingston, Ray Corrigan, Max Terhune. *VCN*

Roaring City 🦴½ **1951** A hard-boiled detective searches for the person behind the murders of gangsters and prize fighters. **58m/B VHS, Beta, LV.** Hugh Beaumont, Edward Brophy, Richard Travis; ***D:*** William (Lester Williams) Berke. *NO*

Roaring Guns 🦴🦴½ **1936** An unflappable McCoy rides in to thwart a despicable landowner trying to drive all the small ranchers out of business. Low-budget fun. **66m/B VHS, Beta.** Tim McCoy, Rex Lease, Wheeler Oakman; ***D:*** Sam Newfield. *NOS, VCN, DVT*

Roaring Ranch 🦴½ **1930** Gibson is trying to protect his ranch from the evil Oakman while attempting to care for a baby as well. **65m/B VHS.** Hoot Gibson, Wheeler Oakman, Sally Eilers, Bobby Nelson, Frank Clark; ***D:*** B. Reeves Eason; ***W:*** B. Reeves Eason. *GPV*

The Roaring Road 🦴🦴½ **1919** Romantic comedy about a car salesman named Toodles, who drives for his company in a big race. Vintage racing footage; silent with original organ music. **57m/B VHS, Beta, 8mm.** Wallace Reid, Ann Little, Theodore Roberts; ***D:*** James Cruze. *VYY, GPV, GVV*

Roaring Roads 🦴 **1935** An heir to a fortune acquires a lust for race car driving, and his family thinks, a reckless death wish. **60m/B VHS, Beta, LV.** Gertrude Messinger, David Sharpe. *NO*

Roaring Six Guns 🦴½ **1937** Maynard protects his property against his crooked partner and his fiancee's father. **60m/B VHS, Beta.** Kermit Maynard, Mary Hayes, John Merton, Edward Cassidy. *NOS, DVT, VCN*

Roaring Speedboats 🦴 *Mile a Minute Love* **1937** Bakewell is a speedboat racer up against crooks who want to con him out of his money by tinkering with his invention. **62m/B VHS, Beta, 8mm.** William "Billy" Bakewell, Arletta Duncan, Duncan Renaldo, Vivien Oakland, Wilfrid Lucas; ***D:*** Elmer Clifton. *VYY*

The Roaring Twenties 🦴🦴🦴½ **1939** Three WWI buddies find their lives intersecting unexpectedly in Prohibition-era New York. Cagney becomes a bootlegger and vies with Bogart for status as crime boss. Lynn is the attorney working to prosecute them. Greatest of all gangster flicks. Cheesy script delivered with zest by top pros. **106m/B VHS, Beta, LV.** James Cagney, Humphrey Bogart, Jeffrey Lynn, Priscilla Lane, Gladys George, Frank McHugh; ***D:*** Raoul Walsh. National Board of Review Awards '39: 10 Best Films of the Year. *MGM, FOX*

Rob Roy 🦴🦴🦴 **1995 (R)** Kilt-raising though overlong tale of legendary Scot Robert Roy MacGregor mixes love and honor with bloodlust and revenge. Neeson's rugged clan leader fends off a band of dastardly nobles led by Cunningham (Roth), a foppish twit with an evil bent. Misty highland scenery and intense romantic interplay between Neeson and Lange as the spirited Mary MacGregor lend a passionate twist to an otherwise earthy, robust adventure of lore capped by one of the best sword fights in years. Both Neeson and Lange provide a gutsy substance to their characters: Neeson's Celtic hero is sexy and steadfast (and generally sports an Irish accent), while Lange inhabits a soulful and tenacious Mary. Roth's delightfully hammy performance as MacGregor's loathsome, bewigged nemesis delivers zip amid the high-minded speeches, plot lulls, and separated body parts. Visually stunning, with on-location shooting in the Scottish Highlands. More ambience is provided by Buswell's evocative score. **144m/C VHS, LV.** Liam Neeson, Jessica Lange, Tim Roth, John Hurt, Eric Stoltz, Andrew Keir, Brian Cox, Brian McCardie, Gilbert Martin, Vicki Masson, David Hayman; ***D:*** Michael Caton-Jones; ***W:*** Alan Sharp; ***C:*** Karl Walter Lindenlaub. British Academy Awards '95: Best Supporting Actor (Roth); Nominations: Academy Awards '95: Best Supporting Actor (Roth); Golden Globe Awards '96: Best Supporting Actor (Roth). *MGM*

Rob Roy—The Highland Rogue 🦴½ *Rob Roy* **1953** In the early 18th century, Scottish Highlander Rob Roy must battle against the King of England's secretary, who would undermine the MacGregor clan to enact his evil deeds. Dull Disney drama. **84m/C VHS, Beta.** Richard Todd, Glynis Johns, James Robertson Justice, Michael Gough; ***D:*** Harold French. *DIS*

Robbers of the Sacred Mountain 🦴🦴 *Falcon's Gold* **1983** TV rip-off of "Raiders of the Lost Ark," loosely based on Arthur Conan Doyle's story "Challenger's Gold." Adventurers seek meteorites in the Mexican jungle. Billed as the first made for cable movie. **95m/C VHS, Beta.** John Marley, Simon MacCorkindale, Louise Vallance, George Touliatos; ***D:*** Bob Schulz. *PSM*

Robbery 🦴🦴½ **1967** Unoriginal but competent rendition of the hackneyed British Royal Mail robbery. Thieves plan and execute a heist of a late-night mail train carrying $10 million. **113m/C VHS, Beta.** *GB* Stanley Baker, James Booth, Joanna Pettet, Frank Finlay, Barry Foster; ***D:*** Peter Yates. *NLC*

Robbery 🦴 **1985** A six-man platoon of Vietnam war veterans endeavors to assault and rob a mob of shiftless bookies. **91m/C VHS, Beta.** John Sheerin, Tony Rickards, Tim Hughes; ***D:*** Michael Thornhill. *LIV*

Robbery Under Arms 🦴🦴½ **1957** From Australia in the 1800s, similar to the American wild west, comes a tale of love and robbery. Finch is the leader of a band of outlaws. Rather dull story redeemed by excellent photography of beautiful landscape. **83m/C VHS.** *GB* Peter Finch, Ronald Lewis, Laurence Naismith, Maureen Swanson, David McCallum, Jill Ireland; ***D:*** Jack Lee. *IMP*

Robby 🦴🦴 **1968** A young white boy and a young black boy shipwrecked on an island form a strong friendship that sees them through a series of adventures. **60m/C VHS, Beta.** Warren Raum, Ryp Siani, John Garces; ***D:*** Ralph Blumke. *FCT*

The Robe 🦴🦴½ **1953** This moving, religious portrait follows the career and religious awakening of drunken and dissolute Roman tribune Marcellus (Burton), after he wins the robe of the just-crucified Christ in a dice game. Mature plays Burton's slave surprisingly well, and reprised the role in the sequel, "Demetrius and the Gladiators"; Burton is wooden. "The Robe" was the first movie to be filmed in CinemaScope. Based on the novel by Lloyd C. Douglas. **133m/C VHS, Beta, LV.** Richard Burton, Jean Simmons, Victor Mature, Michael Rennie, Richard Boone, Dean Jagger, Jeff Morrow, Jay Robinson, Dawn Addams, Ernest Thesiger; ***D:*** Henry Koster; ***C:*** Leon Shamroy. Academy Awards '53: Best Art Direction/Set Decoration (Color), Best Costume Design (Color); Golden Globe Awards '54: Best Film—Drama; National Board of Review Awards '53: 10 Best Films of the Year, Best Actress (Simmons); Nominations: Academy Awards '53: Best Actor (Burton), Best Color Cinematography, Best Picture. *FOX, IGP*

Robert et Robert 🦴🦴🦴 **1979** Two 'ineligible' bachelors resort to using a computerized matrimonial agency to find the girls of their dreams. They become friends while they wait for their dates. Sensitive tale of loneliness and friendship. Warm and witty with fine performances throughout. French with English subtitles. **95m/C VHS, Beta.** *FR* Charles Denner, Jacques Villeret, Jean-Claude Brialy; ***D:*** Claude Lelouch; ***W:*** Claude Lelouch. Cesar Awards '79: Best Supporting Actor (Villeret). *COL*

Robert Kennedy and His Times 🦴🦴½ **1990** Another look at the Kennedy clan, this time from the Bobby angle. Good acting. Based on the book by Arthur Schlesinger. **309m/C VHS.** Brad Davis, Veronica Cartwright, Cliff DeYoung, Ned Beatty, Beatrice Straight, Jack Warden; ***D:*** Marvin J. Chomsky. *COL, PBS*

Roberta 🦴🦴🦴 **1935** A football player inherits his aunt's Parisian dress shop and finds himself at odds with an incognito Russian princess. Dumb plot aside, this is one of the best Astaire-Rogers efforts. A later remake was titled "Lovely to Look At." ♫Let's Begin; Yesterdays; Smoke Gets in Your Eyes; I'll Be Hard to Handle; I Won't Dance; Lovely to Look At; Back Home Again in Indiana; The Touch of Your Hand; You're Devasting. **85m/B VHS, Beta.** Fred Astaire, Ginger Rogers, Irene Dunne, Lucille Ball, Randolph Scott; ***D:*** William A. Seiter; ***M:*** Max Steiner. Nominations: Academy Awards '35: Best Song ("Roberta"). *MGM*

Robin and Marian 🦴🦴 **1976 (PG)** After a separation of twenty years, Robin Hood is reunited with Maid Marian, who is now a nun. Their dormant feelings for each other are reawakened as Robin spirits her to Sherwood Forest. In case you wanted to see Robin Hood robbed of all magic, spontaneity, and fun. Connery is dull, dull, dull, working with an uninspired script. **106m/C VHS, Beta, LV.** *GB* Sean Connery, Audrey Hepburn, Robert Shaw, Richard Harris, Denholm Elliott, Ian Holm, Nicol Williamson, Ronnie Barker; ***D:*** Richard Lester; ***C:*** David Watkin; ***M:*** John Barry. *COL, FOX*

Robin and the 7 Hoods 🦴🦴½ **1964** Runyon-esque Rat Pack version of 1920s Chicago, with Frank and the boys as do-good gangsters in their last go-round. Fun if not unforgettable. ♫Bang! Bang!; Style; Mister Booze; Don't Be a Do-Badder; My Kind of Town. **124m/C VHS, Beta, LV.** Frank Sinatra, Bing Crosby, Dean Martin, Sammy Davis Jr., Peter Falk, Barbara Rush, Allen Jenkins; ***D:*** Gordon Douglas. Nominations: Academy Awards '64: Best Song ("My Kind of Town"), Best Original Score. *WAR*

Robin Hood 🦴🦴🦴½ **1922** Extravagant production casts Fairbanks as eponymous gymnastic swashbuckler who departs for Crusades as Earl of Huntington and returns as the hooded one to save King Richard's throne from the sinister Sheriff of Nottingham. Best ever silent swashbuckling. **110m/B VHS, Beta.** Douglas Fairbanks Sr., Wallace Beery, Sam DeGrasse, Enid Bennett, Paul Dickey, William E. Lowery, Roy Coulson, Bill Bennett, Merrill McCormick, Wilson Benge, Willard Louis, Alan Hale, Maine Geary, Lloyd Talman; ***D:*** Allan Dwan. *NOS, GPV, FCT*

Robin Hood 🦴🦴🦴 **1973** This time the Sherwood Forest crew are portrayed by appropiate cartoon animals, hence, Robin is a fox, Little John a bear, etc. Good family fare, but not as memorable as other Disney features. **83m/C VHS, Beta, LV.** ***D:*** Wolfgang Reitherman; ***M:*** George Bruns; ***V:*** Roger Miller, Brian Bedford, Monica Evans, Phil Harris, Andy Devine, Carol Shelley, Peter Ustinov, Terry-Thomas, Pat Buttram, George Lindsey, Ken Curtis. Nominations: Academy Awards '73: Best Song ("Love"). *DIS, FCT, RDG*

Robin Hood 🦴🦴🦴 **1991** Dark version of the medieval tale. Bergin's Prince of Thieves is well developed and Thurman is a graceful Marion. Three studios announced plans to remake "Robin Hood" in 1990 and two were completed, including this one which was scaled down for cable television. **116m/C VHS, Beta, LV.** Patrick Bergin, Uma Thurman, Juergen Prochnow, Edward Fox, Jeroen Krabbe, Jeff Nuttal, David Morrisey, Owen Teale; ***D:*** John Irvin; ***M:*** Geoffrey Burgon. *FXV, FCT*

Robin Hood: Men in Tights 🦴🦴½ *Men in Tights* **1993 (PG-13)** Brooksian rendition of the classic legend inspires guffaws, but doesn't hit the bullseye on all it promises. Hood afficionados will appreciate the painstaking effort taken to spoof the 1938 Errol Flynn classic while leaving plenty of room to poke fun at the more recent Costner non-classic "Robin Hood: Prince of Thieves." Elwes, last seen swinging swords in "The Princess Bride," is well cast as the Flynn look-alike. Expect the usual off-color humor that's so prevalent in all Brooks outings. **105m/C VHS.** Cary Elwes, Richard Lewis, Roger Rees, Amy Yasbeck, Dave Chappelle, Isaac Hayes, Tracey Ullman, Mark Blankfield, Megan Cavanagh, Eric Allen Kramer, Tony Griffin, Dick Van Patten, Mel Brooks; ***D:*** Mel Brooks; ***W:*** Mel Brooks, J. David Shapiro, Evan Chandler; ***M:*** Hummie Mann. *FXV*

Robin Hood of Texas 🦴🦴½ **1947** Autry finds his calm life disturbed when he is falsely accused of robbing a bank. Pretty good plot for once, in Autry's last Republic western, and plenty of action. **71m/B VHS, Beta.** Gene Autry, Lynn (Mary Hart) Roberts, Sterling Holloway, Adele Mara; ***D:*** Lesley Selander. *NO*

Robin Hood of the Pecos ☠☠½ **1941** Ex-Confederate soldier takes on northern post-war politicians and carpetbaggers. Decent Rogers/Hayes outing. **56m/B VHS, Beta.** Roy Rogers, George "Gabby" Hayes, Marjorie Reynolds, Jay Novello, Roscoe Ates; ***D:*** Joseph Kane. *NOS, DVT, VYY*

Robin Hood: Prince of Thieves ☠☠½ **1991 (PG-13)** Costner is the politically correct Rebel with a Cause, but a thinker, not a doer—and therein lies the problem. His quiet thoughtfulness doesn't add up to leadership and Rickman easily overpowers him as the wicked, crazed Sheriff of Nottingham. Freeman is excellent as a civilized Moor who finds England, and its people, inhospitable, dangerous, and not a little stupid. Mastrantonio, a last minute choice, excels as the lovely Lady Marian. Great action sequences, a gritty and morbid picture of the Middle Ages, and some fun scenes with the Merry Men. Revisionist in its ideas about the times and people, critics generally disapproved of the changes in the story and Costner's performance, though their comments about his lack of an English accent seem nitpicky in light of some basic plot problems. Still has lots of fun for lovers of action, romance and fairy tales. **144m/C VHS, LV.** Kevin Costner, Morgan Freeman, Mary Elizabeth Mastrantonio, Christian Slater, Alan Rickman, Geraldine McEwan, Micheal McShane, Brian Blessed, Michael Wincott, Nick Brimble, Jack Wild, Harold Innocent, Jack Wild; ***Cameos:*** Sean Connery; ***D:*** Kevin Reynolds; ***W:*** Pen Densham, John Watson; ***M:*** Michael Kamen. British Academy Awards '91: Best Supporting Actor (Rickman); MTV Movie Awards '92: Best Song ("(Everything I Do) I Do for You"); Golden Raspberry Awards '91: Worst Actor (Costner); Nominations: Academy Awards '91: Best Song ("(Everything I Do) I Do It for You"). *WAR, RDG*

Robin Hood: The Movie **1955** A colorized and re-mixed version of several episodes of the British television series adds up to a fine version of the classic tale. Excellent cast, clever editing and stunning colorization. **90m/C VHS.** *GB* Richard Greene, Bernadette O'Farrell, Alan Wheatley; ***D:*** Ralph Smart, Daniel Birt, Terence Fisher. *GKK*

Robin Hood...The Legend: Herne's Son ☠☠½ **1985** When Robin Hood is killed by the Sheriff of Nottingham, he begs Robert of Huntington (Connery) to continue his work. Connery refuses, the band dissolves, Maid Marion is kidnapped, and they reunite to save her. Good entry in the BBC series. **101m/C VHS, Beta.** *GB* Jason Connery, Oliver Cotton, Michael Craig, Nickolas Grace, George Baker; ***D:*** Robert M. Young. *FOX, FCT, TVC*

Robin Hood...The Legend: Robin Hood and the Sorcerer ☠☠½ **1983** Robin Hood is chosen by the mystical Herne the Hunter to thwart the evil Sheriff of Nottingham and protect the English peasantry. He must defeat the supernatural powers of a sorcerer and gather together his men in this introduction to the made for British television series. **115m/C VHS.** *GB* Michael Praed, Anthony Valentine, Nickolas Grace, Clive Mantle, Peter Williams; ***D:*** Ian Sharp. *FOX, FCT, TVC*

Robin Hood...The Legend: The Swords of Wayland ☠☠½ **1983** A wicked sorceress provides a supernatural threat to Robin and his merry men. Second entry in the BBC series. Convoluted, breathless plot makes for swashbuckling fun and much derring-do. **115m/C VHS, Beta.** *GB* Michael Praed, Rula Lenska, Nickolas Grace; ***D:*** Robert M. Young. *FOX, FCT*

Robin Hood...The Legend: The Time of the Wolf ☠☠½ **1985** Robin Hood finds out that an old enemy is about to release his evil doings on the world and only he can stop him, while Maid Marian comes to a momentous decision. **105m/C VHS, Beta.** *GB* Jason Connery, Nickolas Grace, Richard O'Brien; ***D:*** Syd Roberson. *FOX, FCT, TVC*

Robin of Locksley ☠☠½ **1995 (PG)** A modern-day, teenaged Robin Hood (Sawa) battles the bullies at his private boys school (thanks to his archery prowess), meets a girl named Marian, and takes on sinister FBI agent Nottingham. **97m/C VHS.** Devon Sawa, Sarah Chalke, Joshua Jackson; ***D:*** Michael Kennedy. *HMK*

Robinson Crusoe ☠☠ **1936** A real oddity: a British silent film originally made in 1927, re-edited ten years later. Music and sound effects were added, along with a narration by children's radio personality Carney. Follows the plot of the famous adventure story by Daniel Defoe. **34m/B VHS, Beta.** *VYY*

Robinson Crusoe & the Tiger ☠½ **1972 (G)** A tiger tells the famous story of how Robinson Crusoe became stranded on a desert island. **109m/C VHS, Beta.** Hugo Stiglitz, Ahui; ***D:*** Rene Cardona Jr. *SUE*

Robinson Crusoe of Clipper Island ☠☠ **1936** Fourteen-episodes serial featuring the investigative expertise of Mala, a Polynesian in the employ of the U.S. Intelligence Service. Each episode runs 16 minutes. Shortened version titled "Robinson Crusoe of Mystery Island." **256m/B VHS, LV.** Mala, Rex, Buck, Kate Greenfield, John Ward, Tracy Lane, Robert F. (Bob) Kortman, Herbert Rawlinson; ***D:*** Mack V. Wright. *SNC, NOS, REP*

Robinson Crusoe of Mystery Island ☠☠ **1936** A Polynesian employed by the U.S. Intelligence Service investigates saboteurs on a mysterious island. Would-be cliffhanger is a yawner; where are the chills and thrills? Edited from the serial "Robinson Crusoe of Clipper Island." **100m/B VHS, Beta.** Mala, Rex, Buck, Herbert Rawlinson, Ray Taylor; ***D:*** Mack V. Wright. *VCN*

Robinson Crusoe on Mars ☠ **1964** Sci-fi interpretation of Defoe classic. West is one of two daring scientists who take a monkey with them on a mission to outer space. When a meteor strikes their ship, it hurtles out of control towards the red planet and only Mantee and Mona survive the wreckage. They meet Lundin, an escaped slave and teach him English until evil slave traders spoil the fun. **109m/C LV.** Adam West, Vic Lundin, Paul Mantee; ***D:*** Byron Haskin; ***W:*** Ib Melchior, John C. Higgins; ***C:*** Winton C. Hoch; ***M:*** Nathan Van Cleave. *IME*

Robo-Chic *Cyber-Chic* **1989** A woman who is part cop, part machine, becomes a defender of justice. **90m/C VHS, Beta.** Kathy Shower, Jack Carter, Burt Ward, Lyle Waggoner; ***D:*** Ed Hansen, Jeffrey Mandel. *AIP*

RoboCop ☠☠☠ **1987 (R)** A nearly dead Detroit cop is used as the brain for a crime-fighting robot in this bleak vision of the future. Humor, satire, action, and violence keep this moving in spite of its underlying sadness. Slick animation techniques from Phil Tippet. Verhoeven's first American film. **103m/C VHS, Beta, LV.** Peter Weller, Nancy Allen, Ronny Cox, Kurtwood Smith, Ray Wise, Miguel Ferrer, Dan O'Herlihy, Robert DoQui, Felton Perry, Paul McCrane, Del Zamora; ***D:*** Paul Verhoeven; ***W:*** Michael Miner, Edward Neumeier; ***C:*** Jan De Bont; ***M:*** Basil Poledouris. Nominations: Academy Awards '87: Best Film Editing, Best Sound. *ORI*

RoboCop 2 ☠☠ **1990 (R)** Grimer, more violent sequel to the initial fascinating look at the future, where police departments are run by corporations hungry for profit at any cost. A new and highly addictive drug has made Detroit more dangerous than ever. Robocop is replaced by a stronger cyborg with the brain of a brutal criminal. When the cyborg goes berserk, Robocop battles it and the drug lords for control of the city. Dark humor and graphic savagery, with little of the tenderness and emotion of the original. **117m/C VHS, Beta, LV.** Peter Weller, Nancy Allen, Belinda Bauer, Dan O'Herlihy, Tom Noonan, Gabriel Damon, Galyn Gorg, Felton Perry, Patricia Charbonneau; ***D:*** Irvin Kershner; ***W:*** Walon Green. *ORI*

RoboCop 3 ☠½ **1991 (PG-13)** Robocop's new Japanese owners plan to build a huge, new, ultra-modern city (in place of the decrepit 21st-century Detroit) but first must evict thousands of people in this third installment of the "Robocop" films (which sat on the studio shelf before finally being released in 1993). There's an android Ninja warrior to do battle with Robo who's gone over to the rebel underground but the plot and action sequences are rehashed from better films. Watch the original. **104m/C VHS, LV.** Robert Burke, Nancy Allen, John Castle, CCH Pounder, Bruce Locke, Rip Torn, Remi Ryan, Felton Perry; ***D:*** Fred Dekker; ***W:*** Fred Dekker, Frank Miller; ***M:*** Basil Poledouris. *ORI*

RoboCop the Series: The Future of Law Enforcement **1994** Premiere episode of the TV series, based on the movie about the unstoppable 21st-century Detroit robocop with the human touch. A murderous corporate creep and a mad doctor team up for nefarious corporate shenanigans. Helping out our hero is a murdered secretary who is merged into the city's central computer as Neuro-Brain. **?m/C VHS, LV.** Richard Eden, Andrea Roth, Cliff DeYoung, John Rubinstein. *ORI*

Roboman ☠☠½ *Who?* **1975 (PG)** American scientist gets in car crash in Soviet Union. When he returns to the States as a cyborg, his friends seem to notice a change. **91m/C VHS.** *GB GE* Elliott Gould, Trevor Howard, Joe Bova, Ed Grover, James Noble, John Lehne; ***D:*** Jack Gold. *ACE, MTX*

Robot Holocaust ☠☠ **1987** Somewhere in the doomed future, after the Earth is laid waste by robots with superior intelligence, a human survivor dares to challenge them. If you're doomed to watch this, you just might survive; it's so-so, unsurprisingly sci-fi. **79m/C VHS, Beta.** Norris Culf, Nadine Hart, Joel von Ornsteiner, Jennifer Delora, Andrew Howarth, Angelika Jager, Rick Gianasi; ***D:*** Tim Kincaid; ***W:*** Tim Kincaid. *NO*

Robot in the Family ☠☠ **1994** Slapstick comedy about Alex and his wacky but endearing robot who embark on a race against time through the streets of New York to track down a priceless antique that could save Alex's family from financial ruin. **92m/C VHS.** Joe Pantoliano, John Rhys-Davies, Danny Gerard, Amy Wright, Tom Signorelli, Peter Maloney, John Wylie, David Shuman, Matthew Locricchio; ***D:*** Mark Richardson, Jack Shaoul; ***W:*** Jack Shaoul; ***M:*** Papo Gely, Ted Mason; ***V:*** Don Peoples. *APX*

Robot Jox ☠½ **1990 (PG)** Two futuristic warriors battle to the finish in giant mechanical robots. Preteen fare. **84m/C VHS, LV.** Gary Graham, Anne-Marie Johnson, Paul Koslo, Robert Sampson, Danny Kamekona, Hilary Mason, Michael Alldredge; ***D:*** Stuart Gordon; ***W:*** Joe Haldeman. *COL*

Robot Monster ☠☠½ *Monsters From the Moon* **1953** Ludicrous cheapie is widely considered one of the worst films of all time, as a single alien dressed in a moth-eaten gorilla suit and diving helmet conspires to take over the Earth from his station in a small, bubble-filled California cave. Available in original 3-D format. **62m/B VHS, Beta, LV.** George Nader, Claudia Barrett, Gregory Moffett, Selena Royle; ***D:*** Phil Tucker; ***M:*** Elmer Bernstein. *RHI, FCT, COL*

Robot Pilot ☠ *Emergency Landing* **1941** Tucker stars as a WWII test pilot trying to promote a friend's invention. Along the way, he's involved in a subplot with enemy agents who steal a bomber. He also finds time to become romantically entangled with the boss' spoiled daughter. **68m/B VHS, Beta, 8mm.** Forrest Tucker, Carol Hughes, Evelyn Brent, Emmett Vogan, William Halligan; ***D:*** William Beaudine. *VYY, SNC*

The Robot vs. the Aztec Mummy *Woof! El Robot Humano; La Momia Azteca Contra el Robot Humano* **1959** Grade-Z Mexican horror film pits a jealous mummy who guards a tomb against tomb robbers and the robot they invent. Special effects are laughable today—the robot's ears are lightbulbs—but true mummy movie fans might want to watch this one. Everyone else will probably be better off skipping it. **65m/B VHS, Beta.** *MX* Ramon Gay, Rosita Arenas, Crox Alvarado, Luis Aceves Cantaneda, Emma Rolden; ***D:*** Rafael Portillo; ***W:*** Alfredo Salazar. *SNC, AOV, MRV*

Robot Wars ☠☠ **1993 (PG)** When what seems to be the last mega-robot on earth falls into enemy hands, a renegade pilot unearths another with the help of an engineer and archeologist to fight for the future of mankind. **106m/C VHS, Beta, LV.** Don Michael Paul, Barbara Crampton, James Staley, Lisa Rinna, Danny Kamekona, Yuji Okumoto, J. Downing, Peter Haskell; ***D:*** Albert Band. *PAR*

Rocco and His Brothers 🦴🦴🦴½ *Rocco et Ses Freres* **1960** A modern classic from top director Visconti, about four brothers who move with their mother from the Italian countryside to Milan. Very long, sometimes ponderous, but engrossing, complex drama. Available shortened to 90 minutes, but the unedited version is much more rewarding. In Italian with English subtitles. **175m/B VHS, LV.** *IT* Alain Delon, Renato Salvatori, Annie Girardot, Katina Paxinou, Claudia Cardinale, Roger Hanin; ***D:*** Luchino Visconti; ***M:*** Nino Rota. *VDM, CVC, INJ*

The Rock 🦴🦴🦴 **1996 (R)** Cage follows up his Oscar win with a big-budget action hero turn, with great results. In an attempt to get benefits for the families of soldiers killed in various covert operations, a decorated general (Harris) and his commando squad occupy Alcatraz island, taking hostages and threatening to unleash a deadly gas bomb on San Francisco. Biochemical weapons expert Stanley Goodspeed (Cage) is called in to disarm the rockets, aided by John Patrick Mason (Connery), only man to successfully escape from the island prison. Like most Simpson/Bruckheimer productions, credibility is stretched to the limit, but the action scenes and crisp pacing don't leave much time for pondering details, anyway. Connery, cool as ever, hasn't lost a step. Cage effectively plays up his character's inexperience at being the hero. Co-producer Don Simpson died of drug overdose during production. **136m/C VHS.** Nicolas Cage, Sean Connery, Ed Harris, Michael Biehn, William Forsythe, David Morse, John Spencer, John C. McGinley, Tony Todd, Bokeem Woodbine, Danny Nucci, Vanessa Marcil, Claire Forlani, Gregory Sporleder; ***D:*** Michael Bay; ***W:*** Jonathan Hensleigh; ***C:*** John Schwartzman; ***M:*** Nick Glennie-Smith. *NYR*

Rock-a-Doodle 🦴🦴½ **1992 (G)** Little Edmond is knocked out during a storm and has an Elvis-influenced vision. He sees Chanticleer, the sun-raising rooster, tricked into neglecting his duties by an evil barnyard owl. Humiliated and scorned, the earnest young fowl leaves the farm and winds up in a Las Vegas-like city as an Elvis-impersonating singer (complete with pompadour) where he meets with success and all its trappings. Mildly amusing, but bland by today's standards of animation, with music which is certainly nothing to crow about. **77m/C VHS, LV.** ***D:*** Don Bluth; ***W:*** David A. Weiss; ***M:*** Robert Folk; ***V:*** Glen Campbell, Christopher Plummer, Phil Harris, Sandy Duncan, Ellen Greene, Charles Nelson Reilly, Eddie Deezen, Toby Scott Granger, Sorrell Booke. *HBO, MVD*

Rock All Night 🦴🦴 **1957** Typically trashy Corman quickie (filmed in five days on one set) about some wild fifties teens and, in this case, a couple of murderers. Seems Cloud Nine, the local teen hangout, is invaded by a couple of murderers who hold the kids hostage. It's up to the hipster bartender, known as Shorty because he's five-foot-one, to save the day. Unrelated concert footage of The Platters and The Blockbusters opens the film. **62m/B VHS.** Dick Miller, Abby Dalton, Russell Johnson, Jonathan Haze, Robin Morse; ***D:*** Roger Corman. *COL, MOV, MVD*

Rock & Roll Cowboys 🦴 **1992** Set in the near-future. Mickey LaGrange is a roadie who has dreams of playing his own songs and becoming a rock and roll star himself. When he meets the mysterious Damien Shard he just may get the opportunity and a lot more besides. Shard is the inventor of an instrument that taps directly into the brain to transform thought into music. When Mickey uses the instrument he becomes an instant success—until he notices some horrifying side effects. **83m/C VHS.** Peter Phelps, David Franklin, John Doyle; ***D:*** Robert Stewart. *MOV*

Rock & Rule 🦴🦴 **1983** Animated sword & sorcery epic with a rock soundtrack. Voices are provided by Deborah Harry, Cheap Trick, Lou Reed, and Iggy Pop. **85m/C VHS, Beta, LV.** ***D:*** Clive A. Smith; ***M:*** Deborah Harry, Lou Reed, Iggy Pop; ***V:*** Paul LeMat, Susan Roman, Don Francks, Dan Hennessey, Chris Wiggins, Catherine Gallant, Catherine O'Hara. *MGM*

Rock & the Money-Hungry Party Girls 🦴 **1989** A struggling musician battles against Gabor-sister-worshipping bimbos in an effort to find unpublished songs by a '50s music legend. **90m/C VHS, Beta.** Paul Sercu, Adam Small, Judi Durand, Mary Baldwin, Debra Lamb; ***D:*** Kurt MacCarley. *NO*

Rock, Baby, Rock It 🦴 **1957** Weak and silly rock-and-roll crime drama about teens trying to fight the Mafia in Dallas in 1957. Features performances by many regional bands including Kay Wheeler, the Cell Block Seven, Johnny Carroll, Preacher Smith and the Deacons, and the Five Stars. If you grew up in Dallas in the '50s, the musical groups may bring back some fond memories; otherwise, this obscure film probably isn't worth your time. **84m/B VHS, Beta.** Kay Wheeler, John Carroll; ***D:*** Murray Douglas Sporup. *RHI*

Rock House 🦴🦴 **1992 (R)** When an L.A. narcotics officer's wife is murdered by drug runners he goes on an obsessive revenge mission to destroy the city's cocaine operations. **98m/C VHS.** Joseph Jennings, Michael Robbin, Alan Shearer; ***D:*** Jack Vacek; ***W:*** Jack Vacek. *HMD*

Rock Hudson's Home Movies **1992** Farr re-creates the character of the late actor over numerous film clips used to suggest homoerotic themes in Hudson's movies. Low-budget and high camp. **58m/C VHS.** Eric Farr; ***D:*** Mark Rappaport; ***W:*** Mark Rappaport. *WBF*

Rock 'n' Roll High School 🦴🦴🦴 **1979 (PG)** The music of the Ramones highlights this non-stop high-energy cult classic about a high school out to thwart the principal at every turn. If it had been made in 1957, it would have been the ultimate rock 'n' roll teen movie. As it is, its 1970s' milieu works against it, but the performances are perfect for the material and the Ramones are great. Songs include "Teenage Lobotomy," "Blitzkrieg Bop," "I Wanna Be Sedated" and the title track, among others. Followed less successfully by "Rock 'n' Roll High School Forever." **94m/C VHS, Beta.** The Ramones, P.J. Soles, Vincent Van Patten, Clint Howard, Dey Young, Mary Woronov, Alix Elias, Dick Miller, Paul Bartel; ***D:*** Allan Arkush; ***C:*** Dean Cundey. *MVD*

Rock 'n' Roll High School Forever 🦴 **1991 (PG-13)** Jesse Davis and his band just want to rock 'n' roll, but the new principal doesn't share their enthusiasm. Way late, way lame sequel to "Rock 'n' Roll High School" doesn't come close to the originality that made it a cult classic. Soundtrack includes music from The Divinyls, Dee Dee Ramone, Mojo Nixon, Will and the Bushmen, The Pursuit of Happiness, and more. **94m/C VHS, Beta, LV.** Corey Feldman, Mary Woronov, Mojo Nixon, Evan Richards, Michael Ceveris, Patrick Malone, Larry Linville, Sarah Buxton; ***D:*** Deborah Brock; ***W:*** Deborah Brock. *LIV, IME*

Rock 'n' Roll Nightmare 🦴½ *The Edge of Hell* **1985 (R)** A rock band is pursued by demons from another dimension. The usual lame garbage. **89m/C VHS, Beta.** *CA* Jon Mikl Thor, Paula Francescatto, Rusty Hamilton; ***D:*** John Fasano. *ACA*

Rock, Pretty Baby 🦴 **1956** Early rock-'n'-roll movie about a teenage band and high school riots. **89m/B VHS, Beta.** Sal Mineo, John Saxon, Rod McKuen, Luana Patten, Fay Wray, Edward Platt, Alan Reed Jr.; ***D:*** Richard Bartlett; ***M:*** Henry Mancini. *BAR*

Rock River Renegades 🦴 **1942** The Range Busters capture a band of renegades and restore peace to the territory once more. **59m/B VHS, Beta.** Ray Corrigan, John "Dusty" King. *NOS, DVT*

Rock, Rock, Rock 🦴🦴½ **1956** A young girl tries to earn enough money for a prom gown after her father closes her charge account. Screen debut of Tuesday Weld. Ultra-low-budget, but a classic after a fashion. Includes classic musical numbers performed by Chuck Berry and other rock'n'roll pioneers. **78m/B VHS, Beta.** Alan Freed, Chuck Berry, Fats Domino, Tuesday Weld; ***D:*** Will Price. *MVD, MED, MRV*

Rocket Attack U.S.A. *Woof!* **1958** Antiquated and ridiculous tale of nuclear warfare about the time of Sputnik, with Russia's first strike blowing up New York City and environs. Mercifully short, with time for a little romance. Everything about this movie is so bad it's good for a laugh. **70m/B VHS, Beta.** Monica Davis, John McKay, Dan Kern, Edward Czerniuk, Art Metrano; ***D:*** Barry Mahon. *NO*

Rocket Gibraltar 🦴🦴🦴 **1988 (PG)** On the occasion of a crusty patriarch's birthday, a large family unites on his remote estate to carry out his special birthday wish. Fine performance by Lancaster. Supported by a solid cast, overcomes a slim story. Culkin, later of "Home Alone," is loveable as the precocious five-year-old. Picturesque Long Island scenery. **92m/C VHS, Beta.** Burt Lancaster, Bill Pullman, John Glover, Suzy Amis, Macaulay Culkin, Patricia Clarkson, Frances Conroy, Sinead Cusack, Bill Martin, Kevin Spacey; ***D:*** Daniel Petrie; ***W:*** Amos Poe; ***M:*** Andrew Powell. *COL*

Rocket to the Moon 🦴🦴 **1986** An adaptation of the Clifford Odets story about the mundane life of a 30-year-old Manhattan dentist and how he comes to terms with his life. From the PBS "American Playhouse" series. **118m/C VHS, Beta.** Judy Davis, John Malkovich, Eli Wallach; ***D:*** John Jacobs. *ACA, PBS*

The Rocketeer 🦴🦴🦴 **1991 (PG)** Lightheaded fun. A stunt flyer in the 1930s finds a prototype jet backpack sought by Nazi spies. Donning a mask, he becomes a flying superhero. Breezy family entertainment with stupendous effects; even better if you know movie trivia, as it brims with Hollywood references, like a great villain (Dalton) clearly based on Errol Flynn. **109m/C VHS, Beta, LV.** Bill Campbell, Jennifer Connelly, Alan Arkin, Timothy Dalton, Paul Sorvino, Melora Hardin, Tiny Ron, Terry O'Quinn, Ed Lauter, James Handy; ***D:*** Joe Johnston; ***W:*** Danny Bilson, Paul DeMeo; ***M:*** James Horner. *DIS, CCB, IME*

Rocketship 🦴🦴 **1936** Flash Gordon battles sea monsters, ray guns, and robots in this sci-fi adventure, which is an edited version of a Flash serial. **?m/B VHS.** Buster Crabbe, Jean Rogers, Charles Middleton. *LOO, HEG*

Rocketship X-M 🦴🦴½ *Expedition Moon* **1950** A lunar mission goes awry and the crew lands on Mars, where they discover ancient ruins. Well acted and nicely photographed. Contains footage, a tinted sequence and previews of coming attractions from classis science fiction files. **77m/B VHS, Beta, LV.** Lloyd Bridges, Osa Massen, John Emery, Hugh O'Brian, Noah Beery Jr.; ***D:*** Kurt Neumann. *MED, RXM*

The Rockford Files: Backlash of the Hunter **1974** The two-part episode which launched the TV series about ex-con turned PI Jim Rockford, who lives (and works) in a beach trailer and only takes clients who have real trouble and real money. His first is a seemingly simple investigation into a man's death. His daughter wants to know if dad was murdered or really did commit suicide. **90m/C VHS.** James Garner, Lindsay Wagner, William Smith, Nita Talbot, Joe Santos; ***D:*** Richard T. Heffron; ***W:*** Stephen J. Cannell. *MCA*

Rockin' Road Trip 🦴 **1985 (PG-13)** A guy meets a girl in a Boston bar, and finds himself on a drunken, slapstick road trip down the Eastern seaboard with a rock band. **101m/C VHS, Beta.** Garth McLean, Katherine Harrison, Margeret Currie, Steve Boles. *FOX*

The Rocking Horse Winner 🦴🦴½ **1949** Poignant tale of a young boy who discovers he can predict racehorse winners by riding his rocking horse. His spendthrift mother's greed leads to tragedy. Based on the short story by D.H. Lawrence. **91m/B VHS.** *GB* John Howard Davies, Valerie Hobson, Hugh Sinclair; ***D:*** Anthony Pelissier. *HMV*

Rocktober Blood 🦴½ **1985 (R)** A convicted and executed rock star comes back from the grave and starts killing people all over again. Yet another gorefest. **88m/C VHS, Beta.** Donna Scoggins, Tray Loren, Nigel Benjamin, Beverly Sebastian; ***D:*** Ferd Sebastian. *LIV, VES*

Rockula ♪½ **1990 (PG-13)** Teen rock comedy about a young-yet-300-year-old vampire looking to lose his virginity. Recommended only for hard-core Diddley fans. **90m/C VHS, Beta, LV.** Dean Cameron, Bo Diddley, Tawny Fere, Susan Tyrrell, Thomas Dolby, Toni Basil; ***D:*** Luca Bercovici; ***W:*** Luca Bercovici. *MGM, WAR*

Rockwell: A Legend of the Wild West ♪♪½ **1993** Black heroics in the wild west. U.S. Marshall Porter Rockwell and his posse of sharp shooters are after a vicious gang murdering supposed claim jumpers who just happen to be Rockwell's friends. **?m/C VHS, LV.** Randy Gleave, Karl Malone, Michael Rudd, George Sullivan. *IMP*

Rocky ♪♪♪½ **1976 (PG)** Box office smash about a young man from the slums of Philadelphia who dreams of becoming a boxing champion. Stallone plays Rocky, the underdog hoping to win fame and self-respect. Rags-to-riches story seems to parallel Stallone's life; he had been previously virtually unknown before this movie. Intense portrayal of the American Dream; loses strength in the subsequent (and numerous) sequels. **125m/C VHS, Beta, LV, 8mm.** Sylvester Stallone, Talia Shire, Burgess Meredith, Burt Young, Carl Weathers; ***D:*** John G. Avildsen; ***W:*** Sylvester Stallone; ***M:*** Bill Conti. Academy Awards '76: Best Director (Avildsen), Best Film Editing, Best Picture; Directors Guild of America Awards '76: Best Director (Avildsen); Golden Globe Awards '77: Best Film—Drama; Los Angeles Film Critics Association Awards '76: Best Film; National Board of Review Awards '76: 10 Best Films of the Year, Best Supporting Actress (Shire); Nominations: Academy Awards '76: Best Actor (Stallone), Best Actress (Shire), Best Original Screenplay, Best Song ("Gonna Fly Now"), Best Sound, Best Supporting Actor (Meredith, Young). *MGM, FOX, BTV*

Rocky 2 ♪♪ **1979 (PG)** Time-marking sequel to the box office smash finds Rocky frustrated by the commercialism which followed his match to Apollo, but considering a return bout. Meanwhile, his wife fights for her life. The overall effect is to prepare you for the next sequel. **119m/C VHS, Beta, LV.** Sylvester Stallone, Talia Shire, Burt Young, Burgess Meredith, Carl Weathers; ***D:*** Sylvester Stallone; ***W:*** Sylvester Stallone; ***M:*** Bill Conti. People's Choice Awards '80: Best Film. *MGM, FOX*

Rocky 3 ♪♪½ **1982 (PG)** Rocky is beaten by big, mean Clubber Lang (played to a tee by Mr. T). He realizes success has made him soft, and has to dig deep to find the motivation to stay on top. Amazingly, Stallone regains his underdog persona here, looking puny next to Mr. T, who is the best thing about the second-best "Rocky" flick. **103m/C VHS, Beta, LV.** Sylvester Stallone, Talia Shire, Burgess Meredith, Carl Weathers, Mr. T, Leif Erickson, Burt Young; ***D:*** Sylvester Stallone; ***W:*** Sylvester Stallone; ***M:*** Bill Conti. Nominations: Academy Awards '82: Best Song ("Eye of the Tiger"). *MGM, FOX*

Rocky 4 ♪½ **1985 (PG)** Rocky travels to Russia to fight the Soviet champ who killed his friend during a bout. Will Rocky knock the Russkie out? Will Rocky get hammered on the head a great many times and sag around the ring? Will Rocky ever learn? Lundgren isn't nearly as much fun as some of Rocky's former opponents and Stallone overdoes the hyper-patriotism and relies too heavily on uplifting footage from earlier "Rocky" movies. **91m/C VHS, Beta, LV.** Sylvester Stallone, Talia Shire, Dolph Lundgren, Brigitte Nielsen, Michael Pataki, Burt Young, Carl Weathers; ***D:*** Sylvester Stallone; ***W:*** Sylvester Stallone. Golden Raspberry Awards '85: Worst Actor (Stallone), Worst Supporting Actress (Nielsen), Worst Director (Stallone), Worst Screenplay, Worst New Star (Nielsen). *MGM, FOX*

Rocky 5 ♪♪ **1990 (PG)** Brain damaged and broke, Rocky finds himself back where he started on the streets of Philadelphia. Boxing still very much in his blood, Rocky takes in a protege, training him in the style that made him a champ (take a lickin' and keep on tickin'). However an unscrupulous promoter has designs on the young fighter and seeks to wrest the lad from under the former champ's wing. This eventually leads to a showdown between Rocky and the young boxer in a brutal streetfight. Supposedly the last "Rocky" film, it's clear the formula has run dry. **105m/C VHS, Beta, LV, 8mm.** Sylvester Stallone, Talia Shire, Burt Young, Sage Stallone, Tom Morrison, Burgess Meredith; ***D:*** John G. Avildsen; ***W:*** Sylvester Stallone; ***C:*** Steven Poster; ***M:*** Bill Conti. *MGM*

The Rocky Horror Picture Show ♪♪♪ **1975 (R)** When a young couple take refuge in a haunted castle, they find themselves the unwilling pawns in a warped scientist's experiment. Cult camp classic has been a midnight movie favorite for years and has developed an entire subculture built around audience participation. The tape includes a seven-minute short detailing the story behind the movie's popularity. May not be as much fun watching it on the little screen unless you bring the rice and squirt guns. ♫The Time Warp; Science Fiction Double Feature; Wedding Song; Sweet Transvestite; The Sword of Damocles; Charles Atlas Song; Whatever Happened to Saturday Night; Touch-a Touch-a Touch-a Touch Me; Eddie's Teddy. **105m/C VHS, LV.** Tim Curry, Susan Sarandon, Barry Bostwick, Meat Loaf, Little Nell, Richard O'Brien; ***D:*** Jim Sharman; ***M:*** John Barry. *FOX, FCT, PMS*

Rocky Jones, Space Ranger **1954** This syndicated space series followed the adventures of Rocky Jones, commander of the spaceship Orbit Jet, who worked for the United Worlds. The first three half-hour television episodes chronicle the story of how Rocky met his beautiful assistant Vena. Entitled "Beyond the Curtain of Space." Additional episodes available. **78m/B VHS, Beta.** Richard Crane, Sally Mansfield, Scotty Beckett. *MVC, MOV*

Rocky Jones, Space Ranger: Renegade Satellite ♪½ **1954** Nostalgia freaks may embrace this revived edition of the infamous early live-TV space cadet show. Rocky squares off against enemies of the United Solar System like Dr. Reno and Rudy DeMarco. Really cheap. **69m/B VHS.** Richard Crane, Sally Mansfield, Maurice Cass. *VDM*

Rocky Mountain Rangers ♪♪ **1940** The Three Mesquiteers do what they do best: save a town from bad guys. **58m/B VHS.** Bob Livingston, Raymond Hatton, Duncan Renaldo, Leroy Mason, Dennis Moore, John St. Polis; ***D:*** George Sherman. *NOS*

Rodan ♪♪ *Radon; Radon the Flying Monster* **1956** A gigantic prehistoric bird is disturbed from his slumber by H-bomb tests. He awakens to wreak havoc on civilization. Big bugs also run amok. From the director of "Godzilla" and a host of other nuclear monster movies. **74m/C VHS, Beta, LV.** *JP* Kenji Sahara, Yumi Shirakawa; ***D:*** Inoshiro Honda. *PAR, MLB, VES*

Rodeo Girl ♪♪½ **1980** Ross is a restless housewife who joins the rodeo in this television drama based on the life of cowgirl Sue Pirtle. Particularly strong supporting cast of Hopkins, Clark, and Brimley. **100m/C VHS, Beta.** Katharine Ross, Bo Hopkins, Candy Clark, Jacqueline Brookes, Wilford Brimley, Parley Baer; ***D:*** Jackie Cooper. *LIV*

Rodrigo D.: No Future ♪♪ **1991** Gritty, realistic portrayal of the youth-killing culture of Medellin, Columbia. Minimal plot involves a young drummer and his drug-running friends. The actors used are actual untrained street kids, several of whom died after the film's completion. In Spanish with English subtitles. **92m/C VHS.** Ramiro Meneses, Carlos Mario Resrepo; ***D:*** Victor Gaviria. *KIV, INJ*

Roe vs. Wade ♪♪♪ **1989** Hunter is excellent as the single woman from Texas who successfully challenged the nation's prohibitive abortion laws in a landmark Supreme Court case. Television drama based on the actual 1973 case of Norma McCorvey. **92m/C VHS, Beta, LV.** Holly Hunter, Amy Madigan, Terry O'Quinn, Stephen Tobolowsky, Dion Anderson, Kathy Bates, James Gammon, Chris Mulkey; ***D:*** Gregory Hoblit. *PAR*

Roger & Me ♪♪♪½ **1989 (R)** Hilarious, controversial and atypical semi-documentary details Moore's protracted efforts to meet General Motors president Roger Smith and confront him with the poverty and despair afflicting Flint, Michigan, after GM closed its plants there. Includes some emotionally grabbing scenes: a Flint family is evicted just before Christmas; a woman makes a living by selling rabbits for food or pets; and a then soon-to-be Miss America addresses the socioeconomic impact of GM's decision. One of the highest-grossing non-fiction films ever released, and Moore's first. **91m/C VHS, Beta, LV.** Michael Moore, Bob Eubanks, Pat Boone, Anita Bryant; ***D:*** Michael Moore; ***W:*** Michael Moore. *WAR*

RoGoPaG ♪♪ **1962** Four episodic films by four European masters (the title refers to their last names), satirizing the human condition. Rossellini's "Virginity" finds an airline stewardess (Schiaffino) fending off an amorous passenger (Balabin). Godard's "The New World" features a post-nuclear Paris and its effect on romance. "La Ricotta" is Pasolini's controversial take on religion with Welles as the director of a religious epic. Gregoretti's "The Range Grown Chicken" finds Tognazzi the frazzled head of a family beset by consumerism. A mixed bag with Pasolini and Godard offering the most disturbing essays. **122m/B VHS.** *IT* Orson Welles, Ugo Tognazzi, Rosanna Schiaffino, Alexandra Stewart, Jean-Mark Bory, Renato Salvatori, Lisa Gastoni, Bruce Balabin; ***D:*** Roberto Rossellini, Jean-Luc Godard, Pier Paolo Pasolini, Ugo Gregoretti; ***W:*** Roberto Rossellini, Jean-Luc Godard, Pier Paolo Pasolini, Ugo Gregoretti; ***M:*** Carlo Ristichelli. *KIV*

Rogue ♪ **1976 (R)** The Rogue is a ruthless man who can make beautiful women do anything that he desires; so, of course, he does. **87m/C VHS, Beta.** Milan Galvonic, Barbara Bouchet, Margaret Lee; ***D:*** Gregory Simpson. *NO*

Rogue Lion ♪½ **1975** A quasi-incompetent game warden more than meets his match when a voraciously carnivorous lion begins stalking an African community. **89m/C VHS, Beta.** *VCI*

Rogue Male ♪♪½ **1976** TV movie finds '30s British aristocrat O'Toole plotting to assassinate Hitler. When his plan fails, he's on the run from both the Gestapo and the British police. Based on the novel by Geoffrey Household. **100m/C VHS.** *GB* Peter O'Toole, Alastair Sim, John Standing, Cyd Hayman; ***D:*** Clive Donner; ***W:*** Frederic Raphael. *FCT*

Rogue of the Range ♪ **1936** A lawman pretends that he is a bandit in order to track down an outlaw gang. **60m/B VHS, Beta.** Johnny Mack Brown. *NOS, DVT, RXM*

Rogue of the Rio Grande ♪½ **1930** Musical western in which the renowned bandit El Malo arrives in the peace-loving town of Sierra Blanca. One of Loy's earlier films. ♫Argentine Moon; Carmita; Song of the Bandoleros. **60m/B VHS, Beta.** Myrna Loy, Jose Bohr, Raymond Hatton, Carmelita Geraghty. *VCN*

Rogue's Gallery ♪♪ **1944** A reporter and photographer covering the story of an inventor and his latest device are caught up in intrigue when he is found murdered. **60m/B VHS, Beta.** Frank Jenks, Robin Raymond, H.B. Warner, Ray Walker, Davison Clark, Robert E. Homans, Frank McGlynn, Pat Gleason, Edward Keane; ***D:*** Al(bert) Herman. *SNC, RXM*

Rogue's Tavern ♪♪ **1936** In this grade B curio, a blood-thirsty killer stalks the occupants of a country inn, bodies are found with their throats crushed, and a psycho psychic is on the loose. Surprise ending. **70m/B VHS, Beta.** Wallace Ford, Joan Woodbury, Clara Kimball Young, Barbara Pepper, Jack Mulhall, John Elliott; ***D:*** Robert F. "Bob" Hill. *NOS, DVT, HEG*

Rogue's Yarn ♪♪ **1956** An investigator probes the death of a woman, ostensibly the result of a boating accident. Gradually he uncovers a plot involving the woman's husband and his mistress in this semi-entertaining British mystery. **80m/B VHS, Beta.** *GB* Nicole Maurey, Derek Bond, Elwyn Brook-Jones, Hugh Latimer; ***D:*** Vernon Sewell. *SNC*

Roland the Mighty ♪½ **1958** Muscular, Herculeanesque hero takes on all comers in this sword and sandal epic set in the Asian steppes. **?m/C VHS, Beta.** *IT* Rick Battaglia. *SNC*

Roll Along Cowboy ♪½ **1937** A vintage sagebrush saga about a cowboy caught by love. Based on Zane Grey's "The Dude Ranger." **55m/B VHS, Beta.** Smith Ballew, Cecilia Parker; ***D:*** Gus Meins. *NOS, CCB, VDM*

Roll of Thunder, Hear My Cry 🦴🦴½ **1978** A black family struggles to survive in Depression-era Mississippi in this inspiring, if somewhat predictable, television production. Look for the always impressive Freeman in a supporting role. Set in the South of 1933 and based on the novels of Mildred Taylor. **110m/C VHS, Beta.** Claudia McNeil, Janet MacLachlan, Morgan Freeman; ***D:*** Jack Smight. *LIV, LCA*

Roll on Texas Moon 🦴 **1946** A cowpoke is hired to prevent a feud between the sheep men and the cattle ranchers. **68m/B VHS.** Roy Rogers, George "Gabby" Hayes, Dale Evans, Dennis Hoey; ***D:*** William Witney. *NOS, DVT, MTX*

Roll, Wagons, Roll 🦴½ **1939** Tex Ritter leads a wagon train to Oregon. **52m/B VHS, Beta.** Tex Ritter; ***D:*** Al(bert) Herman. *NOS, VCN*

Roller Blade 🦴 **1985** In a post-holocaust world a gang of Amazon-style nuns, who worship a "have a nice day" happy face, battle the forces of evil with martial arts and mysticism. Has to be seen to be believed. Extremely low-budget outing. **88m/C VHS, Beta.** Suzanne Solari, Jeff Hutchinson, Shaun Mitchelle; ***D:*** Donald G. Jackson. *NWV*

Roller Blade Warriors: Taken By Force 🦴🦴 **1990** Roller babes battle evil mutant while balancing on big boots with small wheels. **90m/C VHS.** Kathleen Kinmont, Rory Calhoun, Abby Dalton, Elizabeth Kaitan. *NO*

Roller Boogie *Woof!* **1979 (PG)** A truly awful film made at the time of the mercifully brief roller-disco craze. Blair runs away from home and winds up helping some friends thwart a businessman looking to close the local roller rink. Everything about this one reeks amateur. **103m/C VHS.** Linda Blair, Jim Bray, Beverly Garland, Roger Perry, James Van Patten, Kimberly Beck, Mark Goddard, Stoney Jackson, Sean McClory; ***D:*** Mark L. Lester; ***W:*** Barry Schneider. *MGM*

Rollerball 🦴🦴½ **1975 (R)** Caan is utterly convincing in this futuristic tale in which a brutal sport assumes alarming importance to a sterile society. Flashy, violent, sometimes exhilirating. **123m/C VHS, Beta, LV.** James Caan, John Houseman, Maud Adams, Moses Gunn, John Beck; ***D:*** Norman Jewison; ***M:*** Andre Previn. *MGM*

Rollercoaster 🦴🦴 **1977 (PG)** A deranged extortionist threatens to sabotage an amusement park ride. Plucky Segal must stop him. Video renters will be spared the nauseating effects of film's original "Sensurround." **119m/C VHS, Beta, LV.** George Segal, Richard Widmark, Timothy Bottoms, Henry Fonda, Susan Strasberg, Harry Guardino; ***D:*** James Goldstone; ***W:*** William Link; ***M:*** Lalo Schifrin. *MCA*

Rollin' Plains 🦴 **1938** A Texas Ranger tries to settle a feud between cattlemen and sheepmen over water rights. **60m/B VHS, Beta.** Tex Ritter; ***D:*** Al(bert) Herman. *NOS, VCN, VCI*

Rolling Home 🦴🦴 **1948** Tame tale about aging cowpoke, his grandson, and a really swell horse. Saddle up and snooze. **71m/B VHS, Beta, LV.** Jean Parker, Russell Hayden, Pamela Blake, Buss Henry, Raymond Hatton. *VYY*

Rolling Thunder 🦴🦴½ **1977 (R)** Vietnam vet turns vigilante when he arrives home from POW camp and sees his family slaughtered. Graphically violent, potentially cathartic. Typical of screenwriter Paul Schrader. **99m/C VHS, Beta, LV.** William Devane, Tommy Lee Jones, Linda Haynes; ***D:*** John Flynn; ***W:*** Paul Schrader, Heywood Gould. *LIV, VES*

Rolling Vengeance 🦴½ **1987 (R)** Enterprising fellow constructs powerful truck to better facilitate the extermination of gang members who earlier slaughtered his family. Keep on truckin'. **90m/C VHS, Beta, LV.** Don Michael Paul, Ned Beatty, Lawrence Dane, Lisa Howard; ***D:*** Steven Hilliard Stern. *NLC*

Rollover 🦴½ **1981 (R)** Turgid big-budget drama about Arab undermining of American economy. Kristofferson is lifeless, Fonda is humorless. Supporting players Sommer and Cronyn fare better. **117m/C VHS, Beta.** Jane Fonda, Kris Kristofferson, Hume Cronyn, Bob Gunton, Josef Sommer, Martha Plimpton; ***D:*** Alan J. Pakula. *WAR*

Roman Holiday 🦴🦴🦴½ **1953** Hepburn's first starring role is a charmer as a princess bored with her official visit to Rome who slips away and plays at being an "average Jane." A reporter discovers her little charade and decides to cash in with an exclusive story. Before they know it, love calls. Blacklisted screenwriter Trumbo was "fronted" by Ian McLellan Hunter, who accepted screen credit and the Best Story Oscar in Trumbo's stead. The Academy voted to posthumously award Trumbo his own Oscar in 1993. **118m/B VHS, Beta, LV, 8mm.** Audrey Hepburn, Gregory Peck, Eddie Albert, Tullio Carminati; ***D:*** William Wyler; ***W:*** Dalton Trumbo. Academy Awards '53: Best Actress (Hepburn), Best Costume Design (B & W), Best Story; British Academy Awards '53: Best Actress (Hepburn); Golden Globe Awards '54: Best Actress—Drama (Hepburn); New York Film Critics Awards '53: Best Actress (Hepburn); Nominations: Academy Awards '53: Best Art Direction/Set Decoration (B & W), Best Black and White Cinematography, Best Director (Wyler), Best Film Editing, Best Picture, Best Screenplay, Best Supporting Actor (Albert). *PAR, BTV, HMV*

Roman Scandals 🦴🦴½ **1933** A penniless young man daydreams himself back to ancient Rome with uproarious results. Lucille Ball appears as one of the Goldwyn Girls. Dance sequences were choreographed by Busby Berkeley. ♫No More Love; Build A Little Home; Keep Young and Beautiful; Rome Wasn't Built in a Day; Put a Tax on Love. **91m/B VHS, Beta.** Eddie Cantor, Ruth Etting, Gloria Stuart, Edward Arnold, Lucille Ball, Busby Berkeley; ***D:*** Frank Tuttle; ***C:*** Gregg Toland. *SUE, HBO*

Roman Spring of Mrs. Stone 🦴🦴🦴 *The Widow and the Gigolo* **1961** An aging actress determines to revive her career in Rome but finds romance with a gigolo instead in this adaptation of Tennessee Williams's novella. Leigh and Beatty are compelling, but Lenya nearly steals the show as Leigh's distinctly unappealing confidant. **104m/C VHS, Beta.** Warren Beatty, Vivien Leigh, Lotte Lenya, Bessie Love, Jill St. John; ***D:*** Jose Quintero; ***W:*** Gavin Lambert. Nominations: Academy Awards '61: Best Supporting Actress (Lenya). *WAR, FHE*

Romance 🦴🦴 **1930** In only her second talkie, Garbo stars as an Italian opera star who seduces a young priest. Poor story and weak acting from everyone with the exception of Garbo. Even she can't save this one. Adapted from the play "Signora Caccini." **77m/B VHS.** Greta Garbo, Lewis Stone, Gavin Gordon, Elliott Nugent, Florence Lake, Clara Blandick; ***D:*** Clarence Brown; ***C:*** William H. Daniels. Nominations: Academy Awards '30: Best Actress (Garbo), Best Director (Brown). *MGM*

Romance in Manhattan 🦴🦴 **1934** Recent immigrant to New York struggles to build new life, in spite of unemployment, language barriers, and loneliness. He meets Broadway chorine Rogers and song and dance ensues. America, ain't it a great place? **78m/B VHS.** Ginger Rogers, Francis Lederer, J. Farrell MacDonald; ***D:*** Stephen Roberts; ***M:*** Max Steiner. *TTC, FCT*

Romance of a Horsethief 🦴🦴½ **1971 (PG)** Brynner leads this entertaining but slow-paced "Fiddler on the Roof" comedic romp without the music. In 1904 Poland, a Cossack captain takes horses for the Russo-Japanese war. The residents of the town rise up, goaded on by Birkin. **100m/C VHS.** *YU* Yul Brynner, Eli Wallach, Jane Birkin, Oliver Tobias, Lainie Kazan, David Opatoshu; ***D:*** Abraham Polonsky. *ACE, MOV*

Romance on the High Seas 🦴🦴🦴 **1948** A woman is scheduled to take a cruise vacation but skips the boat when she believes her husband is cheating on her. Her husband believes she is taking the cruise to cheat on him and hires a private detective to follow her. Pleasant comedy features the film debut of Doris Day. ♫It's Magic; It's You or No One; The Tourist Trade; Put 'Em in a Box, Tie 'Em with a Ribbon, and Throw 'Em in the Deep Blue Sea; Two Lovers Met in the Night; Run, Run, Run; I'm in Love; Cuban Rhapsody. **99m/C VHS, LV.** Jack Carson, Janis Paige, Don DeFore, Doris Day, Oscar Levant, S.Z. Sakall, Eric Blore, Franklin Pangborn, Leslie Brooks, William "Billy" Bakewell; ***D:*** Michael Curtiz; ***W:*** Julius J. Epstein. Nominations: Academy Awards '48: Best Song ("It's Magic"), Best Original Score. *FOX, FCT*

Romance on the Orient Express 🦴½ **1989** Sparks fly when former lovers meet again on the Orient Express. Don't expect any flesh, though, as film was made for television. **96m/C VHS, Beta.** Cheryl Ladd, Stuart Wilson, John Gielgud; ***D:*** Lawrence Gordon Clark. *TTC*

Romance on the Range 🦴½ **1942** Rogers sets out to trap a gang of fur thieves and finds romance. **60m/B VHS.** Roy Rogers, George "Gabby" Hayes, Sally Payne. *NOS, VCN, REP*

Romance with a Double Bass 🦴🦴🦴 **1974** When a musician and a princess take a skinny dip in the royal lake and get their clothes stolen, comic complications arise. Reminiscent of Cleese's sojourn as a Monty Python member, with surreal, frequently raunchy humor. **40m/C VHS, Beta, LV.** *GB* John Cleese, Connie Booth, Graham Crowden, Desmond Jones, Freddie Jones, Andrew Sachs; ***D:*** Robert M. Young. *FCT, SIG*

Romancing the Stone 🦴🦴🦴 **1984 (PG)** Uptight romance novelist lives out her fantasies after she receives a mysterious map from her murdered brother-in-law and her sister is kidnapped in South America—the ransom being the map. Out to rescue her sister, she's helped and hindered by an American soldier of fortune (Douglas) whose main concern is himself and the hidden treasure described in the map. Great chemistry between the stars and loads of clever dialogue in this appealing adventure comedy. First outing with Turner, Douglas, and DeVito. Followed by "The Jewel of the Nile." **106m/C VHS, Beta, LV.** Michael Douglas, Kathleen Turner, Danny DeVito, Zack Norman, Alfonso Arau, Ron Silver; ***D:*** Robert Zemeckis; ***C:*** Dean Cundey; ***M:*** Alan Silvestri. Golden Globe Awards '85: Best Actress—Musical/Comedy (Turner), Best Film—Musical/Comedy; Los Angeles Film Critics Association Awards '84: Best Actress (Turner); Nominations: Academy Awards '84: Best Film Editing. *FOX, HMV*

Romantic Comedy 🦴🦴 **1983 (PG)** Writing duo never seem to synchronize their desires for each other in this dull comedy. Engaging stars don't inspire each other much, and supporting cast can't make up the difference. Adapted from the Bernard Slade play. **102m/C VHS, Beta.** Dudley Moore, Mary Steenburgen, Frances Sternhagen, Ron Leibman; ***D:*** Arthur Hiller; ***M:*** Marvin Hamlisch. *MGM, FOX*

Romantic Englishwoman 🦴🦴🦴 **1975 (R)** Literate comedy-drama about the intertwined lives of several sophisticated and restrained Brits. Caine is a successful novelist with writer's block whose wife falls for another man while on a trip alone. He then invites his wife's lover to stay with them in order to generate ideas for his writing until his jealousy begins to surface. **117m/C VHS, Beta.** *GB* Glenda Jackson, Michael Caine, Helmut Berger, Kate Nelligan; ***D:*** Joseph Losey; ***W:*** Tom Stoppard, Thomas Wiseman. *WAR, OM*

Rome Adventure 🦴🦴 *Lovers Must Learn* **1962** Spinster librarian Pleshette takes Roman vacation hoping to meet handsome prince. Donahue takes shine to her while girlfriend Dickinson is away, as does suave Roman Brazzi. Soapy, ill-paced romance. **119m/C VHS, LV.** Troy Donahue, Angie Dickinson, Suzanne Pleshette, Rossano Brazzi, Constance Ford, Al Hirt, Chad Everett; ***D:*** Delmer Daves; ***W:*** Delmer Daves; ***M:*** Max Steiner. *PAR, FCT, WAR*

Rome '78 🦴🦴½ **1978** Acclaimed underground film centered around Caligula and the Queen of Sheba in ancient Rome. **60m/C VHS.** Eric Mitchell; ***D:*** James Nares. *MWF*

Romeo and Juliet 🦴🦴🦴½ **1936** One of MGM producer Irving Thalberg's pet projects (and starring Thalberg's wife, Norma Shearer), this Shakespeare classic was given the spare-no-expense MGM treatment. Physically too old to portray teenage lovers, both Howard and Shearer let their acting ability supply all necessary illusions. Also notable is Barrymore's over-the-top portrayal of Mercutio. **126m/B VHS, LV.** Leslie Howard, Norma Shearer, John Barrymore,

Basil Rathbone, Edna May Oliver; ***D:*** George Cukor; ***C:*** William H. Daniels. Nominations: Academy Awards '36: Best Actress (Shearer), Best Interior Decoration, Best Picture, Best Supporting Actor (Rathbone). *MGM, CCB*

Romeo and Juliet 🦴🦴 **1954** Unfulfilling adaptation of Shakespeare's timeless drama of young love cast against family antagonisms. Peculiar supporting cast features both Cabot and ubiquitous master Gielgud. **138m/C VHS, Beta.** *IT* Laurence Harvey, Susan Shantall, Aldo Zollo, Sebastian Cabot, Flora Robson, Mervyn Johns, Bill Travers, John Gielgud; ***D:*** Renato Castellani; ***C:*** Robert Krasker. National Board of Review Awards '54: 5 Best Foreign Films of the Year, Best Director (Castellani). *SUE, LCA*

Romeo and Juliet 🦴🦴🦴½ **1968 (PG)** Young couple share love despite prohibitive conflict between their families in this adaptation of Shakespeare's classic play. Director Zeffirelli succeeds in casting relative novices Whiting and Hussey in the leads, but is somewhat less proficient in lending air of free-wheeling sixties appeal to entire enterprise. Kudos, however, to cinematographer Pasquale de Santis and composer Nina Rota. Also available in a 45-minute edited version. **138m/C VHS, Beta, LV.** *GB IT* Olivia Hussey, Leonard Whiting, Michael York, Milo O'Shea; ***D:*** Franco Zeffirelli; ***C:*** Pasqualino de Santis; ***M:*** Nino Rota. Academy Awards '68: Best Cinematography, Best Costume Design; Golden Globe Awards '69: Best Foreign Film; National Board of Review Awards '68: 10 Best Films of the Year, Best Director (Zeffirelli); Nominations: Academy Awards '68: Best Director (Zeffirelli), Best Picture. *PAR, HMV, PBC*

Romeo Is Bleeding 🦴🦴½ **1993 (R)** Jack (Oldman) is a police detective accepting mobster payoffs from boss Falcone (Scheider) for fingering federally protected witnesses. But the next target proves Jack's undoing—hitwoman Mona (Olin), who's more than a match for any man. Oldman's character is played for a patsy by everyone while Olin's is a kinky psycho-villainess with an enjoyment of violence, red lipstick, and a constant, maniacal laugh. Sciorra is generally wasted as Jack's unhappy wife while Lewis is annoying as his young and vacuous mistress. Part homage, part satire of film noir is overly stylized with intrusive narration but some effective shocks. **110m/C VHS, LV.** Gary Oldman, Lena Olin, Annabella Sciorra, Juliette Lewis, Roy Scheider, Michael Wincott, David Proval, Paul Butler, Will Patton, Larry Joshua, James Cromwell, Ron Perlman; ***D:*** Peter Medak; ***W:*** Hilary Henkin; ***M:*** Mark Isham. Nominations: MTV Movie Awards '94: Best Action Sequence. *PGV*

Romero 🦴🦴½ **1989** Julia is riveting as the Salvadoran archbishop who championed his destitute congregation despite considerable political opposition. A stirring biography financed by the United States Roman Catholic Church. **102m/C VHS, Beta, LV.** Raul Julia, Richard Jordan, Ana Alicia, Eddie Velez, Alejandro Bracho, Tony Plana, Lucy Reina, Harold Gould, Al Ruscio, Robert Viharo; ***D:*** John Duigan; ***W:*** John Sacret Young; ***M:*** Gabriel Yared. *VMK*

Romola 🦴🦴½ **1925** Silent adventure. After Powell and his father are attacked by pirates, Powell escapes. But instead of rescuing his father, he opts for a life of corruption. Dad eventually escapes and returns to exact vengeance. A rather expensive film in its day, troubled by modern-day sights in what was supposed to be old Florence. Gish's drowning scene had to be re-shot because she wouldn't sink. Colman arranged for his then-wife Raye to have a bit part, but they were divorced soon after the film was finished. **120m/B VHS, Beta.** Lillian Gish, Dorothy Gish, William Powell, Ronald Colman, Charles Lane, Herbert Grimwood, Bonaventure Ibanez, Frank Puglia, Thelma Raye; ***D:*** Henry King. *NO*

Romper Stomper 🦴🦴 **1992 (R)** Violent confrontations between Australian skinheads and the Vietnamese community mixed in with a disturbed love story. Suburban rich girl Gabe (McKenzie) is drawn to the charasmatic Hando (Crowe), the certifiably loony leader of a group of Melbourne's skinheads. Any romance takes a backseat to the carnage brought by the skinheads' attacks on the local Asian community, who fight back with equal force. Disquieting look at a brutal world which can't be ignored. Film caused a furor upon its Australian release with debates about whether the extreme violence was intended to titilate or explicate the plot. An unrated version at 89 minutes is also available. **85m/C VHS.** *AU* Russell Crowe, Jacqueline McKenzie, Daniel Pollock; ***D:*** Geoffrey Wright; ***W:*** Geoffrey Wright. Australian Film Institute '92: Best Actor (Crowe), Best Sound, Best Score. *ACA, FCT*

The Roof 🦴🦴 **1956** Uninteresting outing about a young couple who married against their families' wishes and find that setting up a home of their own is more difficult than they thought. In Italian with English subtitles. **98m/B VHS, Beta.** *IT* Gabriella Pallotti, Giorgio Listuzzi; ***D:*** Vittorio De Sica. *NOS, HHT, APD*

Rooftops 🦴½ **1989 (R)** Peculiar but predictable, centering on love between Hispanic girl and white youth who has mastered martial arts dancing. Director Wise is a long way from his earlier "West Side Story." See this one and be the only person you know who has. **108m/C VHS, Beta, LV.** Jason Gedrick, Troy Beyer, Eddie Velez, Tisha Campbell; ***D:*** Robert Wise; ***W:*** Allan Goldstein, Terrence (Terry) Brennan; ***M:*** Michael Kamen. *LIV*

The Rookie 🦴🦴 **1990 (R)** Routine cop drama has worldly veteran and wide-eyed newcomer team to crack stolen-car ring managed by Germans. Eastwood and Sheen are reliable, but Hispanics Julia and Braga, though miscast, nonetheless steal this one as the German villains. **121m/C VHS, Beta, LV, 8mm.** Clint Eastwood, Charlie Sheen, Raul Julia, Sonia Braga, Lara Flynn Boyle, Pepe Serna, Marco Rodriguez, Tom Skerritt, Roberta Vasquez; ***D:*** Clint Eastwood. *WAR*

Rookie of the Year 🦴🦴½ **1993 (PG)** Kid's fluff fantasy come true. Twelve-year-old baseball fanatic Henry has dreams of making it to the big league. He falls, breaks his arm, and when it heals strangely is blessed with a pitching arm so spectacular he finds himself not only playing for the Chicago Cubs, but leading them to the World Series. Enjoyable family outing for first-time director Stern (who also plays a seasoned and very incredulous ballplayer). Keep your eyes peeled for appearances by real-live sluggers Pedro Guerrero, Barry Bonds, and others. **103m/C VHS, LV.** Thomas Ian Nicholas, Daniel Stern, Gary Busey, Dan Hedaya; ***D:*** Daniel Stern; ***W:*** Sam Harper; ***C:*** Jack N. Green; ***M:*** Bill Conti. Blockbuster Entertainment Awards '95: Family Movie, Video. *FXV*

The Room 🦴🦴 **1987** Altman takes on Pinter in this brooding mini-play about two young strangers who try to rent the room already occupied by a disconnected woman and her semi-catatonic husband. Made for television. **48m/C VHS, Beta.** Julian Sands, Linda Hunt, Annie Lennox, David Hemblen, Donald Pleasence; ***D:*** Robert Altman; ***W:*** Harold Pinter. *PSM*

Room at the Top 🦴🦴🦴½ **1959** Ambitious factory man forsakes true love and marries boss's daughter instead in this grim drama set in industrial northern England. Cast excels, with Harvey and Sears as the worker and his wife. Signoret is also quite compelling as the abandoned woman. Adapted from John Braine's novel and followed by "Life at the Top" and "Man at the Top." **118m/B VHS.** *GB* Laurence Harvey, Simone Signoret, Heather Sears, Hermione Baddeley, Anthony Elgar, Donald Wolfit; ***D:*** Jack Clayton. Academy Awards '59: Best Actress (Signoret), Best Adapted Screenplay; British Academy Awards '58: Best Actress (Signoret), Best Film; Cannes Film Festival '59: Best Actress (Signoret); Nominations: Academy Awards '59: Best Actor (Harvey), Best Director (Clayton), Best Picture, Best Supporting Actress (Baddeley). *NO*

Room 43 🦴½ *Passport to Shame* **1958** Campy fable about a British cab driver who falls in love with a French girl, and stumbles onto a white-slavery ring when she falls victim to it. Features a young Caine and future novelist Collins in bit parts. **93m/B VHS, Beta.** Diana Dors, Herbert Lom, Eddie Constantine, Michael Caine, Jackie Collins; ***D:*** Alvin Rakoff. *VDM, TPV*

Room Service 🦴🦴½ **1938** The Marx Brothers provide less than the usual mayhem here with Groucho as penniless theatrical producer determined to remain in his hotel room until he can secure funds for his next play. Ball doesn't help matters much either. Not bad, but certainly not up to the zany Marx clan's usual stuff. **78m/B VHS, Beta, LV.** Groucho Marx, Harpo Marx, Chico Marx, Lucille Ball, Ann Miller, Frank Albertson, Donald MacBride, Charles Halton; ***D:*** William A. Seiter. *CCB, MED, TTC*

Room to Let 🦴🦴 **1949** An elderly woman and her daughter take in boarders in Victorian England. They rent a room to a man who claims to be a doctor, but the two women eventually become prisoners of fear, believing the man is actually Jack the Ripper. Will there be a vacancy soon? Somewhat disturbing and suspenseful. **68m/B VHS, Beta.** *GB* Jimmy Hanley, Valentine Dyall, Christine Silver, Merle Tottenham, Charles Hawtrey, Connie Smith, Laurence Naismith; ***D:*** Godfrey Grayson. *NOS, SNC*

A Room with a View 🦴🦴🦴🦴 **1986** Engaging adaptation of E.M. Forster's novel of requited love. Carter stars as the feisty British idealist who rejects dashing Sands for supercilious Day Lewis, then repents and finds (presumably) eternal passion. A multi-Oscar nominee, with great music (courtesy of Puccini), great scenery (courtesy of Florence), and great performances (courtesy of practically everybody, but supporters Smith, Dench, Callow, and Elliott must be particularly distinguished). Truly romantic, and there's much humor too. **117m/C VHS, Beta, LV.** *GB* Helena Bonham Carter, Julian Sands, Denholm Elliott, Maggie Smith, Judi Dench, Simon Callow, Daniel Day-Lewis, Rupert Graves, Rosemary Leach; ***D:*** James Ivory; ***W:*** Ruth Prawer Jhabvala; ***C:*** Tony Pierce-Roberts. Academy Awards '86: Best Adapted Screenplay, Best Art Direction/Set Decoration, Best Costume Design; British Academy Awards '86: Best Actress (Smith), Best Film, Best Supporting Actress (Dench); Independent Spirit Awards '87: Best Foreign Film; National Board of Review Awards '86: 10 Best Films of the Year, Best Supporting Actor (Day-Lewis); Writers Guild of America '86: Best Adapted Screenplay; Nominations: Academy Awards '86: Best Cinematography, Best Director (Ivory), Best Picture, Best Supporting Actor (Elliott), Best Supporting Actress (Smith). *FOX, HMV*

Roommate **1984** A valedictorian church-goer and a rebellious iconoclast room together at Northwestern University in 1952, with the expected humorous results. Public television presentation based on a John Updike story. **96m/C VHS, Beta.** Lance Guest, Barry Miller, Elaine Wilkes, Melissa Ford, David Bachman; ***D:*** Neil Cox. *LIV, VES*

Roommates 🦴🦴½ **1995 (PG)** Rocky Holeczek (Falk) is a cantankerous coot who, at age 75, decides to care for orphaned 7-year-old grandson Michael. Over the 30 years they are together, they fight over Rocky's old school ways and a grown-up Michael's (Sweeney) attempt to have a family of his own. But despite their bickering, Michael soon realizes that his 107-years-old grandfather's words are truly pearls of wisdom when faced with tragedy. Film hits the right sentimental buttons without going overboard with the tissues and Falk's performance, underneath the layers of latex make-up, is charmingly irascible. Based on co-writer Apple's own grandfather. **108m/C VHS, LV.** Peter Falk, D.B. Sweeney, Julianne Moore, Ellen Burstyn; ***D:*** Peter Yates; ***W:*** Max Apple, Stephen Metcalfe; ***C:*** Mike Southon; ***M:*** Elmer Bernstein. Nominations: Academy Awards '95: Best Makeup. *TOU*

Rooster Cogburn 🦴🦴½ **1975 (PG)** A Bible-thumping schoolmarm joins up with a hard-drinking, hard-fighting marshal in order to capture a gang of outlaws who killed her father. Tired sequel to "True Grit" but the chemistry between Wayne and Hepburn is right on target. **107m/C VHS, Beta, LV.** John Wayne, Katharine Hepburn, Richard Jordan, Anthony Zerbe, John McIntire, Strother Martin, Paul Koslo; ***D:*** Stuart Millar; ***C:*** Harry Stradling Jr. *MCA, TLF*

Rooster: Spurs of Death! *Woof!* **1983 (PG)** An expose on cock fighting, in which a young idealist tries to stop the thriving sport in a small southern town. Dog of a movie that (not surprisingly) went straight to video. **90m/C VHS, Beta.** Vincent Van Patten, Ty Hardin, Kristine DeBell, Ruta Lee. *NO*

Roosters ☙☙½ **1995 (R)** Gallo Morales (Olmos) is returning home, after serving seven years in prison for manslaughter, anxiously awaited by wife Juana (Braga), 20-year-old rebellious son Hector (Nucci), neglected adolescent daughter Angela (Lassez), and sexy sister Chata (Alonso). Gallo is a noted breeder of fighting cocks, which for him represent machismo and power but, to his resentment, it's Hector who owns a potential prize-winning bird, precipitating some explosive family conflicts. Adapted by Sanchez-Scott from her 1987 play. **93m/C VHS.** Edward James Olmos, Sonia Braga, Maria Conchita Alonso, Danny Nucci, Sarah Lassez; ***D:*** Robert M. Young; ***W:*** Milcha Sanchez-Scott; ***C:*** Reynaldo Villalobos; ***M:*** David Kilay. *CAF*

Rootin' Tootin' Rhythm ☙ *Rhythm on the Ranch* **1938** All's not quiet on the range, but Autry comes along to sing things back to normal. Goofy, clumsy, ubiquitous sidekick Burnette is a symbol for this whole effort. **55m/B VHS, Beta.** Gene Autry, Smiley Burnette, Monte Blue; ***D:*** Mack V. Wright. *NOS, VYY, DVT*

Roots ☙☙☙☙ **1977** The complete version of Alex Haley's made for television saga following a black man's search for his heritage, revealing an epic panorama of America's past. Available on six tapes, complete at 570 minutes. **90m/C VHS, Beta.** Ed Asner, Lloyd Bridges, LeVar Burton, Chuck Connors, Lynda Day George, Lorne Greene, Burl Ives, O.J. Simpson, Cicely Tyson, Ben Vereen, Sandy Duncan; ***D:*** David Greene; ***M:*** Quincy Jones. *WAR, MOV, PBS*

Roots of Evil ☙½ **1991 (R)** This erotic thriller follows a cop on the trail of a murderer who specializes in killing Hollywood's most beautiful prostitutes. Also available in unrated and Spanish-language versions. **?m/C VHS.** Alex Cord, Delia Sheppard, Charles Dierkop, Jillian Kesner; ***D:*** Gary Graver. *CAN*

Roots: The Gift ☙☙ **1988** It's Christmas, 1770, and Kunte Kinte (Burton) and Fiddler (Gossett) try to escape slavery via the Underground Railroad. In their attempt, they wind up giving the gift of freedom to several of their fellow slaves. A made for television movie based on the Alex Haley characters. **94m/C VHS.** Louis Gossett Jr., LeVar Burton, Michael Learned, Avery Brooks, Kate Mulgrew, Shaun Cassidy, John McMartin; ***D:*** Kevin Hooks. *WAR, FCT*

Roots: The Next Generation ☙☙☙ **1979** Sequel to the landmark television miniseries continuing the story of author Alex Haley's ancestors from the Reconstruction era of the 1880s to 1967, culminating with Haley's visit to West Africa where he is told the story of Kunta Kinte. On seven tapes. **685m/C VHS.** Georg Stanford Brown, Lynne Moody, Henry Fonda, Richard Thomas, Marc Singer, Olivia de Havilland, Paul Koslo, Beah Richards, Stan Shaw, Harry (Henry) Morgan, Irene Cara, Dorian Harewood, Ruby Dee, Paul Winfield, James Earl Jones, Debbie Allen; ***Cameos:*** Al Freeman Jr., Marlon Brando. *MOV*

Rope ☙☙☙½ **1948 (PG)** In New York City, two gay college students murder a friend for kicks and store the body in a living room trunk. They further insult the dead by using the trunk as the buffet table and inviting his parents to the dinner party in his honor. Very dark humor is the theme in Hitchcock's first color film, which he innovatively shot in uncut ten-minute takes, with the illusion of a continuous scene maintained with tricky camera work. Based on the Patrick Hamilton play and on the Leopold-Laeb murder case. **81m/C VHS, Beta, LV.** James Stewart, John Dall, Farley Granger, Cedric Hardwicke, Constance Collier; ***D:*** Alfred Hitchcock; ***W:*** Arthur Laurents. *MCA*

Rorret ☙☙☙ **1987** "Rorret" is "terror" spelled backwards—a good indication of the psychological and physical terror Mr. Rorret, the owner of the Peeping Tom Cinema, inflicts upon his female patrons. The Cinema is devoted to the horror film and Rorret himself dresses like Peter Lorre in "M;" lives behind the movie screen, watching the films in mirror image; and enjoys the frightened reactions of his female patrons. He enjoys their reactions so much that he later stalks the women for real. Highlighted by recreated sequences from such psycho-terror classics as "Psycho," "Dial M for Murder," "Strangers on a Train," and "Peeping Tom." In Italian with English subtitles. **105m/C VHS.** *IT* Lou Castel, Anna Galiena, Massimo Venturiello; ***D:*** Fulvio Wetzl; ***W:*** Fulvio Wetzl. *NYF, INJ*

Rosa Luxemburg ☙☙ **1986** Based on the life of the Jewish political radical, murdered in 1919. Involving herself with the German Social Democratic Party, Luxemburg undergoes numerous imprisonments and maintains a tempestuous personal life. Based primarily on Luxemburg's letters and speeches; charismatic performance by Sukowa. In German with English subtitles. **122m/C VHS.** *GE* Barbara Sukowa, Daniel Olbrychski, Otto Sander, Adelheid Arndt; ***D:*** Margarethe von Trotta; ***W:*** Margarethe von Trotta. Cannes Film Festival '86: Best Actress (Sukowa). *NYF, FCT*

Rosalie ☙☙½ **1938** A gridiron great from West Point falls for a mysterious beauty from Vassar. He soon learns that her father reigns over a tiny Balkan nation. Expensive, massive, imperfect musical; exotic romantic pairing fails to conceal plot's blah-ness. Oh well, at least Porter's music is good. ♫I've a Strange New Rhythm in My Heart; Why Should I Care?; Spring Love Is in the Air; Rosalie; It's All Over But the Shouting; Who Knows?; In the Still of the Night; To Love or Not to Love; Close (instrumental). **118m/B VHS, Beta.** Nelson Eddy, Eleanor Powell, Frank Morgan, Ray Bolger, Ilona Massey, Reginald Owen, Edna May Oliver, Jerry Colonna; ***D:*** Woodbridge S. Van Dyke; ***M:*** Cole Porter. *MGM*

Rosalie Goes Shopping ☙☙☙ **1989 (PG-13)** Satire about American consumerism hiding behind slapstick comedy, and it works, most of the time. Misplaced Bavarian (Sagebrecht) moves to Arkansas and begins spending wildly and acquiring "things." Twisty plot carried confidently by confident wackiness from Sagebrecht and supporters. **94m/C VHS, LV.** *GE* Marianne Sagebrecht, Brad Davis, Judge Reinhold, Willie Harlander, Alex Winter, Erika Blumberger, Patricia Zehentmayr; ***D:*** Percy Adlon; ***W:*** Eleonore Adlon, Percy Adlon; ***M:*** Bob Telson. *VMK, INJ*

The Rosary Murders ☙☙ **1987 (R)** Based on the William X. Kienzle mystery about a serial killer preying on nuns and priests. Father Koesler (Sutherland) must betray the confessional to stop him. Interesting, though sometimes muddled and too rarely tense. Filmed on location in Detroit. **105m/C VHS, Beta, LV.** Donald Sutherland, Charles Durning, Belinda Bauer, Josef Sommer; ***D:*** Fred Walton; ***W:*** Elmore Leonard, Fred Walton. *VTR*

The Rose ☙☙☙ **1979 (R)** Modeled after the life of Janis Joplin, Midler plays a young, talented and self-destructive blues/rock singer. Professional triumphs don't stop her lonely restlessness and confused love affairs. The best exhibition of the rock and roll world outside of documentaries. Electrifying film debut for Midler features an incredible collection of songs. ♫Fire Down Below; I've Written A Letter to Daddy; Let Me Call You Sweetheart; The Rose; Stay With Me; Camellia; Sold My Soul To Rock 'n' Roll; Keep On Rockin'; When A Man Loves a Woman. **134m/C VHS, Beta, LV.** Bette Midler, Alan Bates, Frederic Forrest, Harry Dean Stanton, David Keith; ***D:*** Mark Rydell; ***C:*** Vilmos Zsigmond. Golden Globe Awards '80: Best Actress—Musical/Comedy (Midler), Best Song ("The Rose"); Nominations: Academy Awards '79: Best Actress (Midler), Best Film Editing, Best Sound, Best Supporting Actor (Forrest). *FOX*

The Rose and the Jackal ☙☙ **1990** Fun, intriguing fictionalization about the founder of the Pinkerton detective agency. During the Civil War, bearded, Scottish Reeve tries to persuade a wealthy Southern lady to help save the Union. Made for cable television. **94m/C VHS, Beta.** Christopher Reeve, Madolyn Smith, Granville Van Dusen, Carrie Snodgress, Kevin McCarthy; ***D:*** Jack Gold. *TTC*

The Rose Garden ☙☙½ **1989 (PG-13)** In modern Germany, a Holocaust survivor is put on trial for assaulting an elderly man. The victim, it turns out, was a Nazi guilty of heinous war crimes. Ullmann and Schell lend substance, though treatment of a powerful theme is inadequate. **112m/C VHS, Beta, LV.** Liv Ullmann, Maximilian Schell, Peter Fonda, Jan Niklas, Kurt Hubner; ***D:*** Fons Rademakers; ***W:*** Paul Hengge; ***M:*** Egisto Macchi. *CAN*

Rose Marie ☙☙☙ *Indian Love Call* **1936** An opera star falls in love with the mountie who captured her escaped convict brother. Hollywood legend has it that when a British singer was presented with the first line in "Indian Love Song," which is "When I'm calling you-oo-oo-oo-oo-oo-oo," the confused performer sang, "When I'm calling you, double oh, double oh, double oh..." Maybe true, maybe not, but funny anyway. Classic MacDonald-Eddy operetta. Remade in 1954. ♫Indian Love Call; Pardon Me, Madame; The Mounties; Rose Marie; Totem Tom Tom; Just for You; Tex Yeux; St. Louis Blues; Dinah. **112m/B VHS, Beta, LV.** Jeanette MacDonald, Nelson Eddy, James Stewart, Allan Jones, David Niven, Reginald Owen; ***D:*** Woodbridge S. Van Dyke; ***C:*** William H. Daniels; ***M:*** Rudolf Friml. *MGM*

Rose Marie ☙☙☙ **1954 (G)** Blyth is a lonely Canadian woman wooed by a mean spirited fur trapper and a gallant mountie. Unremarkable remake of the Eddy/MacDonald musical is saved by specatular technicolor and CinemaScope photography. Choreography by Busby Berkeley. ♫Rose Marie; Indian Love Call; Totem Tom Tom; The Mounties; I Have the Love; The Right Place For A Girl; Free to be Free; The Mountie Who Never Got His Man. **115m/C VHS, LV.** Ann Blyth, Howard Keel, Fernando Lamas, Bert Lahr, Marjorie Main, Joan Taylor, Chief Yowlachie, Abel Fernandez, Al Ferguson, Dabbs Greer, Lumsden Hare; ***D:*** Mervyn LeRoy; ***C:*** Paul Vogel. *MGM, MLB*

Rose of Rio Grande ☙ **1938** A western musical about a Mexican gang that avenges the deaths of members of the upper strata. **60m/B VHS, Beta.** John Carroll, Movita, Antonio Moreno, Lena Basquette, Duncan Renaldo; ***D:*** William Nigh. *GPV*

Rose of Washington Square ☙☙½ **1939** Singer Faye gets involved with the no-account Power, much to the dismay of her friend Jolson. They marry, and she becomes a singing sensation in the Ziegfeld Follies while he becomes an embarassment, eventually winding up on the wrong side of the law. Jolson stole the movie, singing some of his best numbers. This thinly-disguised portrait of Fanny Brice caused the performer to sue for defamation of character; she eventually settled out of court. ♫California, Here I Come; My Mammy; Pretty Baby; Toot Toot Tootsie Goodbye; Rock-A-Bye Your Baby with a Dixie Melody; My Man; I'm Just Wild About Harry; I Never Knew Heaven Could Speak; Rose of Washington Square. **86m/B VHS.** Alice Faye, Tyrone Power, Al Jolson, William Frawley, Joyce Compton, Hobart Cavanaugh, Moroni Olsen; ***D:*** Gregory Ratoff; ***W:*** Nunnally Johnson; ***C:*** Karl Freund. *FXV*

The Rose Tattoo ☙☙☙½ **1955** Magnani, in her U.S. screen debut, is just right as a Southern widow who cherishes her husband's memory, but falls for virile trucker Lancaster. Williams wrote this play and screenplay specifically for Magnani, who was never as successful again. Interesting character studies, although Lancaster doesn't seem right as an Italian longshoreman. **117m/B VHS, Beta, LV.** Anna Magnani, Burt Lancaster, Marisa Pavan, Ben Cooper, Virginia Grey, Jo Van Fleet; ***D:*** Daniel Mann; ***W:*** Tennessee Williams, Hal Kanter; ***C:*** James Wong Howe; ***M:*** Alex North. Academy Awards '55: Best Actress (Magnani), Best Art Direction/Set Decoration (B & W), Best Black and White Cinematography; British Academy Awards '56: Best Actress (Magnani); Golden Globe Awards '56: Best Actress—Drama (Magnani), Best Supporting Actress (Pavan); Nominations: Academy Awards '55: Best Costume Design (B & W), Best Film Editing, Best Picture, Best Supporting Actress (Pavan). *PAR, FCT, BTV*

Roseanne: An Unauthorized Biography ☙ **1994** Boring TV movie about the boorish (ex-)duo of Tom Arnold and Roseanne Barr Pentland Arnold. Recounts her troubled upbringing in Salt Lake City, her stormy marriage, and her long slog toward fame as a "domestic goddess" stand-up comedienne and TV series star. Miscasting of both leads hurts any chance this poor substitute had. **90m/C VHS.** Denny Dillon, David Graf, John Walcutt, John Karlen, Judith Scarpone, Danielle Harris. *PGV*

Rosebud 🦴 **1975 (PG)** Embarassingly dull film finds a group of PLO terrorists kidnapping five young women who were vacationing aboard O'Toole's yacht. He's supposedly a journalist but actually works for the CIA. Action ping-pongs between the plight of the victims and what's being done to rescue them but it's so boring you won't care. "Rosebud" is the name of the yacht. Based on a novel by Joan Hemingway and Paul Bonnecarrere. **126m/C VHS.** Peter O'Toole, Richard Attenborough, Kim Cattrall, Brigitte Ariel, Isabelle Huppert, Lalla Ward, Deborah Berger, Cliff Gorman, Claude Dauphin, Peter Lawford, Raf Vallone, Adrienne Corri; ***D:*** Otto Preminger; ***W:*** Eric Lee Preminger, Marjorie Kellogg. *MGM*

Rosebud Beach Hotel 🦴 *The Big Lobby; The No-Tell Hotel* **1985 (R)** Wimpy loser tries his hand at managing a run-down hotel in order to please his demanding girlfriend. Camp is okay, but this soft-porn excuse is horrible in every other way. **82m/C VHS, Beta, LV.** Colleen Camp, Peter Scolari, Christopher Lee, Fran Drescher, Eddie Deezen, Chuck McCann, Hank Garrett, Hamilton Camp, Cherie Currie; ***D:*** Harry Hurwitz. *LIV, VES*

Roseland 🦴🦴🦴 **1977 (PG)** Three interlocking stories, set at New York's famous old Roseland Ballroom, about lonely people who live to dance. Not fully successful, but strong characters, especially in the second and third stories, make it worth watching, although it lacks energy. **103m/C VHS, Beta, LV.** Christopher Walken, Geraldine Chaplin, Joan Copeland, Teresa Wright, Lou Jacobi; ***D:*** James Ivory; ***W:*** Ruth Prawer Jhabvala. *VES, CVC, INJ*

Rosemary's Baby 🦴🦴🦴🦴 **1968 (R)** A young woman, innocent and religious, and her husband, ambitious and agnostic, move into a new apartment. Soon the woman is pregnant, but she begins to realize that she has fallen into a coven of witches and warlocks, and that they claim the child as the antichrist. Gripping and powerful, subtle yet utterly horrifying, with luminous performances by all. Polanski's first American film; from Levin's best-seller. **134m/C VHS, Beta, LV.** Mia Farrow, John Cassavetes, Ruth Gordon, Maurice Evans, Patsy Kelly, Elisha Cook Jr., Charles Grodin, Sidney Blackmer, William Castle, Ralph Bellamy; ***D:*** Roman Polanski; ***W:*** Roman Polanski; ***C:*** William A. Fraker; ***M:*** Krzysztof Komeda. Academy Awards '68: Best Supporting Actress (Gordon); Golden Globe Awards '69: Best Supporting Actress (Gordon); Nominations: Academy Awards '68: Best Adapted Screenplay. *PAR, MLB, BTV*

Rosencrantz & Guildenstern Are Dead 🦴🦴🦴 **1990 (PG)** Playwright Stoppard adapted his own absurdist 1967 play to film—which at first look makes as much sense as a "Swan Lake" ballet on radio. Patience is rewarded for those who stick with it. Two tragicomic minor characters in "Hamlet" squabble rhetorically and misperceive Shakespeare's plot tightening fatally around them. Uprooted from the stage environment, it's arcane but hilarious if you're paying attention. Roth and Oldman are superb as the doomed duo. **118m/C VHS, Beta, LV.** Gary Oldman, Tim Roth, Richard Dreyfuss, Iain Glen; ***D:*** Tom Stoppard; ***W:*** Tom Stoppard. Venice Film Festival '91: Best Picture. *TOU, FCT*

Roses Bloom Twice 🦴½ **1977** When a middle-aged widow decides to make up for some of the wild living that she missed during her marriage, she shocks her children. **87m/C VHS, Beta.** Glynis McNicoll, Michael Craig, Diane Craig, John Allen, Jennifer West; ***D:*** David Stevens. *NO*

Rosie: The Rosemary Clooney Story 🦴🦴½ **1982** Above average biography of Clooney's up-and-down career. Locke lip-synches Clooney's voice in songs. Orlando doesn't help matters portraying Jose Ferrer. Made for television. **100m/C VHS, Beta.** Sondra Locke, Tony Orlando, Penelope Milford, Katherine Helmond, Kevin McCarthy, John Karlen, Cheryl Anderson, Robert Ridgely, Joey Travolta; ***D:*** Jackie Cooper; ***Performed by:*** Rosemary Clooney. *LIV*

Roswell: The U.F.O. Cover-Up 🦴🦴½ **1994 (PG-13)** Fact-based drama finds intelligence officer Major Jesse Marcel (McLachlan) investigating the wreckage of a craft near his Roswell, New Mexico air base in the summer of 1947. Marcel believes the craft is extraterrestrial—as are the strange bodies recovered from the wreckage. An Air Force press release announces a UFO but is quickly retracted and Marcel's suspicions ridiculed. A 30-year reunion still finds him obsessed and seeking to clear his name but this time Marcel's investigations may finally lead to the truth. Made for TV; based on the book "UFO Crash at Roswell" by Kevin D. Randle and Donald R. Schmitt. **91m/C VHS, LV.** Kyle MacLachlan, Dwight Yoakam, Kim Greist, Martin Sheen, Xander Berkeley, J.D. Daniels, Doug Wert, John M. Jackson, Peter MacNicol, Bob Gunton, Charles Martin Smith; ***D:*** Jeremy Paul Kagan; ***W:*** Jeremy Paul Kagan, Arthur Kopit, Paul Davids; ***C:*** Steven Poster; ***M:*** Elliot Goldenthal. *REP*

R.O.T.O.R. 🦴 **1988** R.O.T.O.R. (Robotic Officer of Tactical Operations Research) is a law enforcement robot that is supposed to stop criminals. But watch out! It might go beserk and wreck your town. **90m/C VHS, LV.** Richard Gesswein, Margaret Trigg, Jayne Smith; ***D:*** Cullen Blaine. *IMP*

Rough Cut 🦴🦴 **1980 (PG)** American diamond thief Reynolds lives in London, pursued by an aging Scotland Yard detective who wants to end his career in a blaze of glory. A beautiful lady is the decoy. Good chemistry; lousy script. **112m/C VHS, Beta, LV.** Burt Reynolds, Lesley-Anne Down, David Niven, Timothy West, Joss Ackland, Patrick Magee; ***D:*** Donald Siegel; ***W:*** Larry Gelbart; ***C:*** Frederick A. (Freddie) Young. *PAR*

Rough Justice 🦴½ **1987** Spaghetti western about a lone gunfighter tracking down three killers. Kinski is a sexually aroused bad guy in this miserable excuse. What could he have been thinking? **95m/C VHS, Beta.** *IT* Klaus Kinski, Steven Tedd; ***D:*** Mario Costa. *TWE*

Rough Night in Jericho 🦴½ **1967** Martin plays unredeemable scum in this cliched western. He's an ex-lawman trying to take over the town of Jericho and all that's left to own is the stagecoach line run by Simmons and McIntire. Coming to Simmons aid is Peppard, a former deputy marshall turned gambler. Predicatably violent. **104m/C VHS.** Dean Martin, Jean Simmons, George Peppard, John McIntire, Slim Pickens, Don Galloway; ***D:*** Arnold Laven; ***W:*** Sydney Boehm, Marvin H. Albert. *MCA, FCT*

Rough Riders of Cheyenne 🦴½ **1945** Sunset Carson ends the feud between the Carsons and the Sterlings. **54m/B VHS, Beta.** Sunset Carson, Peggy Stewart. *MED*

Rough Riders' Roundup 🦴🦴 **1939** Roy and the boys rid a mining town of its crooked manager. Less yodeling than later Roger's outings; also better all around. **54m/B VHS, Beta.** Roy Rogers, Raymond Hatton, Lynn (Mary Hart) Roberts, Dorothy Sebastian, Duncan Renaldo, George Montgomery; ***D:*** Joseph Kane. *NOS, VDM, DVT*

Rough Ridin' Rhythm 🦴½ **1937** Wallace is kidnapped to care for the orphaned child of a bandit's sister with Maynard being accused of having murdered the woman. But he's innocent and fights the gang to clear his name. Based on the story "Getting a Start in Life" by James Oliver Curwood. **58m/B VHS.** Kermit Maynard, Beryl Wallace, Ralph Peters, Betty Mack, Curly Dresden; ***D:*** J.P. McGowan. *GPV*

Rough Riding Rangers 🦴½ *The Secret Stranger* **1935** Threatening letters plague a western ranch family. **57m/B VHS, Beta.** Rex Lease, Janet Chandler. *VCN*

Roughnecks 🦴½ **1980** A team of Texas oil drillers attempt to dig the deepest oil well in history and chase women on the side. Too long, and not particularly action-packed or gripping. Made for television. **240m/C VHS, Beta.** Sam Melville, Cathy Lee Crosby, Vera Miles, Harry (Henry) Morgan, Steve Forrest, Stephen McHattie, Wilford Brimley; ***D:*** Bernard McEveety. *PSM*

Round Midnight 🦴🦴🦴 **1986 (R)** An aging, alcoholic black American jazz saxophonist comes to Paris in the late 1950s seeking an escape from his self-destructive existence. A devoted young French fan spurs him to one last burst of creative brilliance. A moody, heartfelt homage to such expatriate bebop musicians as Bud Powell and Lester Young. In English and French with English subtitles. Available in a Spanish-subtitled version. **132m/C VHS, Beta, LV.** *FR* Dexter Gordon, Lonette McKee, Francois Cluzet, Martin Scorsese, Herbie Hancock, Sandra Reaves-Phillips; ***D:*** Bertrand Tavernier; ***W:*** Bertrand Tavernier, David Rayfiel; ***M:*** Herbie Hancock. Academy Awards '86: Best Original Score; Nominations: Academy Awards '86: Best Actor (Gordon). *MVD, WAR, INJ*

Round Numbers 🦴½ **1991 (R)** Judith Schweitzer believes her husband "Big Al the Muffler King" is having an affair with the gorgeous Muffler Mate of the Month, Mitzi (Playboy Playmate Hope Marie Carlton). Determined to get revenge, Judith books herself into the same health spa that Mitzi attends and the result is pure comedy. **98m/C VHS.** Kate Mulgrew, Samantha Eggar, Marty Ingels, Hope Marie Carlton, Shani Wallis, Natalie Barish, Debra Christofferson; ***D:*** Nancy Zala; ***W:*** Nancy Zala. *HMD*

Round Trip to Heaven 🦴🦴 **1992 (R)** Party guy Larry (Feldman) and his innocent cousin (Galligan) take off in a borrowed Rolls Royce to go meet Larry's dream centerfold in a super model contest. Unfortunately, the Rolls' trunk is loaded with stolen money and Stoneface (Sharkey), the felon who stashed the cash, wants the money back. With Stoneface in pursuit these guys are in for the ride of their lives. For the teen set only. Also available with Spanish subtitles. **97m/C VHS, LV.** Corey Feldman, Zach Galligan, Julie McCullough, Rowanne Brewer, Ray Sharkey; ***D:*** Alan Roberts. *PSM*

The Round Up 🦴🦴½ *Szegenylegenyek Nehezeletuck; The Hopeless Ones; The Poor Outlaws* **1966** Brutal tale spins a realistic political web of fear. Set in 1868 in a prison camp, suspected Hungarian subversives, largely peasants and herdsmen, are thrown into jail and tortured. A direct and shocking exploration of life under dehumanizing, totalitarian rule. In Hungarian with English subtitles. **90m/B VHS.** *HU* Janos Gorbe, Tibor Molnar, Andras Kozak; ***D:*** Miklos Jancso; ***W:*** Gyula Hernadi. *FST, HTV*

Round-Up Time in Texas 🦴🦴 **1937** Autry delivers a herd of horses to his diamond-prospector brother in South Africa and has to deal with bandits after the jewels. Typical early Autry entry, with singin' on the side. **54m/B VHS, Beta.** Gene Autry, Smiley Burnette; ***D:*** Joseph Kane. *NOS, VCN, VYY*

The Rounders 🦴🦴½ **1965** Two aging, no-account cowboys (Ford and Fonda) dream of giving up their bronco-busting ways to open a bar in Tahiti where they can watch the world go by. But they have a habit of blowing all their money on women, whiskey, and bad bets. An ornery unbreakable horse may be the key to changing their luck. Mild-mannered comedy with beautiful Arizona scenery. **85m/C VHS.** Glenn Ford, Henry Fonda, Sue Ane Langdon, Hope Holiday, Chill Wills, Edgar Buchanan, Kathleen Freeman, Joan Freeman, Denver Pyle; ***D:*** Burt Kennedy; ***W:*** Burt Kennedy; ***C:*** Paul Vogel. *MGM*

Rounding Up the Law 🦴🦴½ **1922** Good guy dupes bad guy while organ plays. **62m/B VHS, Beta, 8mm.** Russell Gordon, Chet Ryan, Patricia Palmer, William McCall, Guinn "Big Boy" Williams; ***D:*** Charles Seeling. *VYY, GPV*

Roustabout 🦴🦴½ **1964** A roving, reckless drifter joins a carnival and romances the owner's daughter. Elvis rides on good support from Stanwyck et al. Welch has a bit part in her film debut; look for Terri Garr as a dancer. ♫Roustabout; Poison Ivy League; One Track Heart; Little Egypt; Wheels on My Heels; It's a Wonderful World; It's Carnival Time; Hard Knocks; There's a Brand New Day on the Horizon. **101m/C VHS, Beta.** Elvis Presley, Barbara Stanwyck, Joan Freeman, Leif Erickson, Sue Ane Langdon, Pat Buttram, Joan Staley, Dabbs Greer, Steve Brodie, Jack Albertson, Marianna Hill, Beverly Adams, Billy Barty, Richard Kiel, Raquel Welch; ***D:*** John Rich. *FOX, MVD*

The Rousters 🦴🦴½ **1990 (PG)** Descendants of Wyatt Earp run a carnival in a small Western town. Comic misadventures arise when a modern varmint named Clayton comes looking for action.

Cannell (of "The A-Team" and "Riptide" fame) co-wrote and produced—with his usual extraordinary mix of the absurd and the dangerous. Unusual vehicle for Rogers, but she keeps her style and humor. Made for TV. **72m/C VHS, LV.** Jim Varney, Mimi Rogers, Chad Everett, Maxine Stuart, Hoyt Axton; ***D:*** E.W. Swackhamer; ***W:*** E.W. Swackhamer, Stephen J. Cannell. *VMK*

Rover Dangerfield **1991 (G)** Lovable Las Vegas hound Rover Dangerfield searches for respect but finds none. The results are hilarious. Quality animation from a project developed by Rodney Dangerfield and Harold Ramis. **78m/C VHS, LV, 8mm.** ***D:*** Jim George; ***W:*** Harold Ramis; ***M:*** David Newman; ***V:*** Rodney Dangerfield. *WAR*

Roxanne **1987 (PG)** A modern comic retelling of "Cyrano de Bergerac." The romantic triangle between a big nosed, small town fire chief, a shy fireman and the lovely astronomer they both love. Martin gives his most sensitive and believable performance. Don't miss the bar scene where he gets back at a heckler. A wonderful adaptation for the modern age. **107m/C VHS, Beta, LV, 8mm.** Steve Martin, Daryl Hannah, Rick Rossovich, Shelley Duvall, Michael J. Pollard, Fred Willard, John Kapelos, Max Alexander, Damon Wayans, Matt Lattanzi, Kevin Nealon; ***D:*** Fred Schepisi; ***W:*** Steve Martin; ***C:*** Ian Baker; ***M:*** Bruce Smeaton. Los Angeles Film Critics Association Awards '87: Best Actor (Martin); National Society of Film Critics Awards '87: Best Actor (Martin); Writers Guild of America '87: Best Adapted Screenplay. *COL*

Roxie Hart ½ **1942** Sassy '20s Chicago dance hall girl Roxie (Rogers) decides to take the fall when hubby (Chandler) murders a man. (She sees it as a publicity boost to her career). Slick lawyer Billy Flynn (Menjou) knows he can get the tootsie off if she justs flashes the jury her considerable sex appeal. Montgomery's a smitten reporter who catches Roxie's eye. Based on the play "Chicago" by Maurine Watkins and previously filmed in 1927. Bob Fosse later adapted the play for a Broadway musical. **75m/B VHS.** Ginger Rogers, Adolphe Menjou, George Montgomery, Lynne Overman, Nigel Bruce, Phil Silvers, Sara Allgood, William Frawley, Spring Byington, George Chandler; ***D:*** William A. Wellman; ***W:*** Nunnally Johnson; ***C:*** Leon Shamroy; ***M:*** Alfred Newman. *FXV*

The Royal Bed ½ *The Queen's Husband* **1931** King Eric's queen really wears the pants in the family, and when she leaves on a trip, he's left helpless and hapless. A revolution erupts, and his daughter announces she plans to marry a commoner. What's a king to do? **74m/B VHS, Beta.** Lowell Sherman, Nance O'Neil, Mary Astor, Anthony Bushell, Gilbert Emery, Robert Warwick, J. Carrol Naish; ***D:*** Lowell Sherman. *VYY*

Royal Flash **1975 (PG)** Satirical adventure picture, witty and fast paced, with a few real life period characters thrown in for good measure. Cowardly swashbuckler Flashman, wanting to enter high society, is used to advance a political cause when he is forced to impersonate a Prussian nobleman and marry a duchess. Script by Fraser and based on his series of novels featuring the Flashman character. **98m/C VHS.** *GB* Malcolm McDowell, Alan Bates, Florinda Bolkan, Oliver Reed, Britt Ekland, Lionel Jeffries, Tom Bell, Alastair Sim, Michael Hordern, Joss Ackland, Christopher Cazenove, Bob Hoskins; ***D:*** Richard Lester; ***W:*** George MacDonald Fraser; ***C:*** Geoffrey Unsworth. *NO*

Royal Wedding *Wedding Bells* **1951** Astaire and Powell play a brother-and-sister dance team who go to London during the royal wedding of Princess Elizabeth, and find their own romances. Notable for the inspired songs and Astaire's incredible dancing on the ceiling and walls; Lerner's first screenplay. The idea came from Adele Astaire's recent marriage to a British Lord. ♫Too Late Now; Sunday Jumps; How Can You Believe Me When I Said I Love You When You Know I've Been A Liar All My Life?; You're All the World to Me; The Happiest Day of My Life; Open Your Eyes; Ev'ry Night at Seven; I Left My Hat in Haiti; What A Lovely Day For A Wedding. **93m/C VHS, Beta, LV.** Fred Astaire, Jane Powell, Peter Lawford, Keenan Wynn, Sarah Churchill; ***D:*** Stanley Donen; ***W:*** Alan Jay Lerner. Nominations: Academy Awards '51: Best Song ("Too Late Now"). *MGM, NOS, CAB*

Royce **1993 (R)** After a successful mission, Royce's CIA team is disbanded. But some former agents aren't happy with early retirement and decide to go into business for themselves. **98m/C VHS.** James Belushi, Chelsea Field, Miguel Ferrer, Peter Boyle; ***D:*** Rod Holcomb; ***W:*** Paul Bernbaum. *PAR*

R.P.M.* (*Revolutions Per Minute) ½ **1970 (R)** Another chance to relive the sixties. Student activists force the university hierarchy to appoint their favorite radical professor president. Hip prof-turned-prez Quinn is between a rock and a hard place, and allows police to crack down. Could have been intriguing, but loses steam; in any case, the script and direction both stink. **90m/C VHS, Beta.** Anthony Quinn, Paul Winfield, Gary Lockwood, Ann-Margret; ***D:*** Stanley Kramer; ***W:*** Erich Segal; ***M:*** Perry Botkin. *COL*

R.S.V.P. ½ **1984 (R)** Hollywood party honoring a writer turns tragic when a body is found in the guest of honor's pool. Most interesting part is watching the porn stars who make up most of the cast fail at acting while dressed. **87m/C VHS, Beta, LV.** Harry Reems, Lynda Wiesmeier; ***D:*** Lem Amero. *LIV, VES*

Rubberface **1981 (PG)** Tony Maroni (Carrey) is a very bad but very determined comedian. And he may just catch a break when he teams up with joke writer Janet (Glassbourg). Made for Canadian TV. **48m/C VHS.** *CA* Jim Carrey, Adah Glassbourg; ***D:*** Glen Salzman, Rebecca Yates. *VMK*

Rubdown **1993** An ex-baseball player, turned Beverly Hills masseur, finds himself the victim of a frame-up when one of his clients is murdered. **88m/C VHS, Beta.** Jack Coleman, Michelle Phillips, Kent Williams, Alan Thicke, Catherine Oxenberg, William Devane; ***D:*** Stuart Cooper; ***W:*** Clyde Allen Hayes; ***M:*** Gerald Gouriet. *PAR*

Rubin & Ed **1992 (PG-13)** Ed is a real estate groupie who bribes the eccentric Rubin to attend a get-rich-quick seminar. Rubin decides to cash in on the favor by taking Ed on the road in search of the perfect gravesite for Rubin's long-dead feline. If that sounds wacky, just wait—the fun really begins when the duo is stranded in Death Valley and begins to suffer from sunstroke and hallucinations. Those who dream of weirdos bonding in the desert may be enthused but other viewers may thirst for something more. **82m/C VHS, LV.** Crispin Glover, Howard Hesseman, Karen Black, Michael Greene, Brittney Lewis; ***D:*** Trent Harris; ***W:*** Trent Harris. *COL, FCT*

Ruby **1977 (R)** A young woman, christened in blood and raised in sin, has a love affair with the supernatural and murders up a storm at a drive-in. Confused, uneven horror a step up from most similar flicks. **85m/C VHS, Beta.** Roger Davis, Janet Baldwin, Piper Laurie, Stuart Whitman; ***D:*** Curtis Harrington; ***W:*** Barry Schneider. *NO*

Ruby ½ **1992 (R)** Another in the increasing number of Kennedy assassination and conspiracy dramas—this one told from the viewpoint of Jack Ruby, Lee Harvey Oswald's killer. Confusing plot, somewhat redeemed by the performances of Aiello and Fenn. Combines actual footage of Ruby shooting Oswald with black-and-white filmed scenes. Based on the play "Love Field" by Stephen Davis. **111m/C VHS, LV.** Danny Aiello, Sherilyn Fenn, Arliss Howard, Tobin Bell, David Duchovny, Richard Sarafian, Joe Cortese, Marc Lawrence; ***D:*** John MacKenzie; ***W:*** Stephen Davis; ***C:*** Phil Meheux; ***M:*** John Scott. *COL*

Ruby Gentry ½ **1952** White-trash girl Jones, cast aside by man-she-loves Heston, marries wealthy Malden to spite him, then seeks revenge. Classic Southern theme of comeuppance, good direction and acting lift it a notch. **82m/B VHS, Beta.** Charlton Heston, Jennifer Jones, Karl Malden; ***D:*** King Vidor. *FOX*

Ruby in Paradise **1993 (R)** Leaving her dead-end life in Tennessee, Gissing (Judd) moves to Panama City, Florida and lands a job selling souvenirs for no-nonsense Mildred Chambers (Lyman). Although pursued by two very different men, Ruby concentrates more on self-exploration, recording her thoughts in a journal. A seemingly effortless portrayal of Ruby Lee by Judd (daughter of Naomi and sister of Wynonna Judd) makes for a pleasurable character study of a young woman on her own. **115m/C VHS, LV.** Ashley Judd, Todd Field, Bentley Mitchum, Allison Dean, Dorothy Lyman, Betsy Dowds; ***D:*** Victor Nunez; ***W:*** Victor Nunez; ***M:*** Charles Engstrom. Independent Spirit Awards '94: Best Actress (Judd); Sundance Film Festival '93: Grand Jury Prize; Nominations: Independent Spirit Awards '94: Best Cinematography, Best Director (Nunez), Best Film, Best Screenplay, Best Supporting Actor (Field). *REP*

Ruby's Dream **1992** A bowling alley and nightclub owner dreams of making it big in Las Vegas. After his dreams crash to the ground, however, he realizes what is truly important in life. **100m/C VHS.** Joe Pesci. *QVD*

Ruckus *The Loner* **1981 (PG)** A Vietnam vet uses his training to defend himself when he runs into trouble in a small Alabama town. Less obnoxious than "First Blood," (which came later), but basically the same movie. **91m/C VHS, Beta.** Dirk Benedict, Linda Blair, Ben Johnson, Richard Farnsworth, Matt Clark; ***D:*** Max Kleven. *NO*

Ruddigore **197?** The Lords of Ruddigore have been bound for centuries by a terribly inconvenient curse; they must commit a crime every day or die a horribly painful death. When the Lord of Ruddigore passes his mantle on to the new heir, the young heir loses both his good reputation and his very proper fiancee. A new version of Gilbert and Sullivan's opera. **112m/C VHS, Beta.** Vincent Price, Keith Michell, Sandra Dugdale. *FOX*

Rude Awakening ½ **1981** A real estate agent is tortured by bizarre nightmares which lead to an unusual series of events. Part of the "Thriller Video" series. **60m/C VHS, Beta.** Denholm Elliott, James Laurenson, Pat Heywood; ***D:*** Peter Sasdy. *LIV*

Rude Awakening **1989 (R)** Hippies Cheech and Roberts (where's Chong?) settled in a South American commune 20 years ago. Now they're back, and don't know what to make of old pals Carradine and Hagerty who have become - that's right - yuppies. Rip Van Winkle-ian farce draws a few yuks, but could have been much funnier. Points for trying. **100m/C VHS, Beta, LV.** Eric Roberts, Richard "Cheech" Marin, Julie Hagerty, Robert Carradine, Buck Henry, Louise Lasser, Cindy Williams, Andrea Martin, Cliff DeYoung; ***D:*** Aaron Russo, David Greenwalt; ***W:*** Richard LaGravenese; ***M:*** Jonathan Elias. *HBO*

Rudolph & Frosty's Christmas in July **1982** More animated adventures of Rudolph and friends. This time they are transported to a glittering, sunny seashore for a magical summer weekend that almost turns into tragedy. **97m/C VHS, Beta.** ***V:*** Red Buttons, Ethel Merman, Mickey Rooney, Jackie Vernon, Shelley Winters. *LIV, TLF, WTA*

Rudolph the Red-Nosed Reindeer **1964** The durable Christmas story of the nasally enhanced reindeer who saved the holiday; colorful stop-motion animation and character voices bring it to life, with a memorable guest visit from an abominable snowman. Made for television. **53m/C VHS, Beta, LV, 8mm.** ***D:*** Larry Roemer. *FHE, WTA, LME*

Rudy ½ **1993 (PG)** Likeable, true story about a little guy who triumphs over big odds. Daniel "Rudy" Ruettiger (Astin) dreams of playing football for Notre Dame, no matter how farfetched the dream. He's a mediocre student, physically unsuitable for big time college ball, but sheer determination helps him attain his dream. Astin delivers an engaging performance and is backed up by a good supporting cast. Sentimental story stretches the truth with typical shameless Hollywood manipulation, but is still entertaining. From the director and writer of another David beats Goliath sports film, "Hoosiers." **112m/C VHS, LV, 8mm.** Sean Astin, Ned Beatty, Charles S. Dutton, Lili Taylor, Robert Prosky, Jason Miller, Ron Dean, Chelcie Ross, Jon Favreau, Greta Lind, Scott Benjaminson, Christopher Reed; ***D:*** David Anspaugh; ***W:*** Angelo Pizzo; ***M:*** Jerry Goldsmith. *COL*

Rudyard Kipling's Classic Stories **1970** Three Kipling stories come to animated life: "How the Elephant Got His Trunk," "How the Whale Got His Throat" and "How the First Letter Was Written." **25m/C VHS, Beta.** *NWV*

Rudyard Kipling's The Jungle Book ☠☠½ *The Jungle Book* **1994 (PG)** Respectable live-action version from Disney of the Rudyard Kipling tale of Mowgli (Lee), the boy who's raised by a wolf pack after getting lost in an Indian jungle. This time around Mowgli gets to grow up—enough to have a romantic interest in the lovely Kitty (Headey), the daughter of British officer, Major Brydon (Neill). His rival is the supercilious Captain Boone (Elwes), who learns Mowgli knows the location of a hidden jungle treasure. Now Mowgli must count on his friends, Grey Brother the wolf, Baloo the bear, and Bagheera the black panther, to defeat the greedy Boone and win Kitty. Filmed in India. **111m/C VHS, LV.** Jason Scott Lee, Cary Elwes, Sam Neill, Lena Headey, John Cleese; ***D:*** Stephen Sommers; ***W:*** Stephen Sommers. *DIS*

The Rue Morgue Massacres ☠½ **1973 (R)** A modern reprise of the Poe story with touches of Frankensteinia thrown in; plenty of gore. **90m/C VHS, Beta.** *SP* Paul Naschy, Rossana Yanni, Maria Perschy, Vic Winner, Mary Ellen Arpon; ***D:*** Javier Aguirre. *NO*

Ruggles of Red Gap ☠☠☠☠ **1935** Classic comedy about an uptight British butler who is "won" by a barbarous American rancher in a poker game. Laughton as the nonplussed manservant is hilarious; supporting cast excellent. Third and far superior filming of Harry Leon Wilson story. One of the all-time great comedies, the film was remade musically with Bob Hope and Lucille Ball as "Fancy Pants" (1950). **90m/B VHS, Beta.** Charles Laughton, Mary Boland, Charlie Ruggles, ZaSu Pitts, Roland Young, Leila Hyams, James Burke, Maude Eburne; ***D:*** Leo McCarey; ***W:*** Walter DeLeon; ***M:*** Ralph Rainger. National Board of Review Awards '35: 10 Best Films of the Year; New York Film Critics Awards '35: Best Actor (Laughton); Nominations: Academy Awards '35: Best Picture. *MCA*

Rule #3 ☠☠ **1993** "Never believe everything you see." That's the rule con artist Travis West lives by. This time he's got two scams planned—a Las Vegas real estate swindle and a cash ripoff of a former nemesis. Double- and triple-crosses abound. Based on the true story of West, who swindled more than $9 million in 15 years. **93m/C VHS.** Mitchell Cox, Marcia Swayze; ***D:*** Mitchell Cox. *AVI*

Rulers of the City ☠ **1971** Young gangster avenges his father's death. **91m/C VHS, Beta.** Jack Palance, Edmund Purdom, Al Cliver, Harry Baer. *VDC*

The Rules of the Game ☠☠☠☠ *Le Regle du Jeu* **1939** Renoir's masterpiece, in which a group of French aristocrats, gathering for a weekend of decadence and self-indulgence just before WWII, becomes a metaphor for human folly under siege. The film was banned by the French government, pulled from distribution by the Nazis, and not restored to its original form until 1959, when it premiered at the Venice Film Festival. A great, subtle, ominous film landmark. In French with English subtitles. The laserdisc version includes a commentary by director Peter Bogdanovich. Heavily copied and poorly remade in 1989 as "Scenes from the Class Struggle in Beverly Hills." **110m/B VHS, Beta, LV, 8mm.** Marcel Dalio, Nora Gregor, Jean Renoir, Mila Parely, Julien Carette, Gaston Modot, Roland Toutain, Paulette Dubost, Odette Talazac; ***D:*** Jean Renoir; ***W:*** Jean Renoir. *NOS, SUE, HHT*

The Ruling Class ☠☠☠½ **1972 (PG)** The classic cult satire features O'Toole as the unbalanced 14th Earl of Gurney, who believes that he is either Jesus Christ or Jack the Ripper. Tongue-in-cheek look, complete with dance and music, at eccentric upper-class Brits and their institutions. Uneven, chaotic, surreal and noteworthy. **154m/C VHS, Beta, LV.** *GB* Peter O'Toole, Alastair Sim, Arthur Lowe, Harry Andrews, Coral Browne, Nigel Green; ***D:*** Peter Medak. National Board of Review Awards '72: 10 Best Films of the Year, Best Actor (O'Toole); Nominations: Academy Awards '72: Best Actor (O'Toole); Cannes Film Festival '72: Best Film. *SUE, NLC*

Rumble Fish ☠☠☠ **1983 (R)** A young street punk worships his gang-leading older brother, the only role model he's known. Crafted by Coppola into an important story of growing up on the wrong side of town, from the novel by S.E. Hinton. Ambitious and experimental, with an atmospheric music score; in black and white. **94m/B VHS, Beta, LV.** Matt Dillon, Mickey Rourke, Dennis Hopper, Diane Lane, Vincent Spano, Nicolas Cage, Diana Scarwid, Christopher Penn, Tom Waits; ***D:*** Francis Ford Coppola; ***W:*** Francis Ford Coppola; ***C:*** Stephen Burum; ***M:*** Stewart Copeland. *MCA*

Rumble in the Bronx ☠☠½ **1996 (R)** Singapore action star Chan plays a Hong Kong cop who comes to the South Bronx to attend his uncle's wedding and winds up caught in a crime war between the mob and a vicious motorcycle gang. Living special effect Chan choreographed and performed all of his own stunts, and they are remarkable (pay special attention to the hovercraft scene). Over-the-top cheesy dubbing and streets that are obviously not New York (filmed in Vancouver) add to the cartoonish fun. After several attempts to break into the American market, this is Chan's first release in the United States. **87m/C VHS, LV.** *HK* Jackie Chan, Anita Mui, Francoise Yip, Bill Tung, Morgan Lam, Marc Akerstream; ***D:*** Stanley Tong; ***W:*** Edward Tang, Fibe Ma; ***C:*** Jingle Ma; ***M:*** J. Peter Robinson. *TTC*

The Rumor Mill ☠☠½ *Malice in Wonderland* **1986** The careers and titanic rivalry of influential Hollywood gossip writer Hedda Hopper and Louella Parsons, played with verve by Taylor and Alexander. Fictionalized script based on the book "Hedda and Louella" by George Eels. Made for TV. **94m/C VHS, Beta, LV.** Elizabeth Taylor, Jane Alexander, Richard Dysart, Joyce Van Patten; ***D:*** Gus Trikonis; ***W:*** Jaqueline Feather, David Seidler; ***M:*** Charles Bernstein. *VMK*

A Rumor of War ☠☠☠½ **1980** The first big Vietnam drama for TV is a triumph, portraying the real-life experience of author Philip Caputo (based on his bestseller), from naive youth to seasoned soldier to bitter murder suspect at court martial. Succeeds where Stone's later, much-ballyhooed "Born on the Fourth of July" fails. Adapted by John Sacret Young. **195m/C VHS, Beta.** Brad Davis, Keith Carradine, Michael O'Keefe, Stacy Keach, Steve Forrest, Richard Bradford, Brian Dennehy, John Friedrich, Perry Lang, Chris Mitchum, Dan Shor, Jeff Daniels; ***D:*** Richard T. Heffron. *FRH*

Rumpelstiltskin **1982** From "Faerie Tale Theatre" comes the story of a woman who can spin straw into gold (Duvall) and the strange man who saves her life (Villechaize). Enjoyable for the whole family. **60m/C VHS, Beta, LV.** Bud Cort, Ned Beatty, Shelley Duvall, Herve Villechaize, Paul Dooley. *FOX, FCT*

Rumpelstiltskin ☠☠ **1986 (G)** Musical retelling of the classic Brother Grimm fairy tale. Irving plays a young girl who says she can spin straw into gold. Barty is a dwarf who helps her. The catch: she must give up her first born to pay him. Lackluster direction and uninspired acting make this version a yawner. Irving's real-life mother (Pointer) and brother have roles too. **84m/C VHS, Beta, LV.** Amy Irving, Billy Barty, Robert Symonds, Priscilla Pointer, Clive Revill, John Moulder-Brown; ***D:*** David Irving. *MED*

Rumpole of the Bailey **198?** John Mortimer's famed British barrister comes to life in McKern's portrait in two episodes taken from the television series. In "Rumpole and the Genuine Article," Rumpole is called on to defend an embittered artist in a forgery case. "Rumpole and the Old Boy Network" has the barrister drawn into blackmail and deception when a brothel is discovered in a respectable London neighborhood. Additional episodes available. **104m/C VHS.** *GB* Leo McKern. *MOV, SIG, TVC*

Rumpole of the Bailey: Rumpole's Return ☠☠☠ **1990** A feature-length film based on the popular British television series. A middle aged barrister refuses to settle for less than justice. Based on the character created by John Mortimer. **106m/C VHS.** *GB* Leo McKern. *FCT, INJ*

Run ☠½ **1991 (R)** A high energy action cartoon, with little plot but lots of stunts. Dempsey is a super-smart law student hired to drive a car to Atlantic City. A stop on the way starts trouble. Instant romance with a local girl balances mayhem from crime boss. Expect no more than physical feats and you'll be happy with this lightweight fare. **91m/C VHS, Beta, LV.** Patrick Dempsey, Kelly Preston, Ken Pogue, Alan C. Peterson, Sean McCann; ***D:*** Geoff Burrowes; ***W:*** Michael Blodgett; ***C:*** Bruce Surtees. *HPH*

Run, Angel, Run! ☠½ **1969 (R)** Ex-biker Angel is on the run from his former gang after he helps expose them in a magazine article. He settles on a sheep ranch with his girl and then the gang shows up with revenge in mind. Prime drive-in fare with title song sung by none other than Ms. Tammy Wynette. **90m/C VHS, Beta.** William Smith, Margaret Markov, Valerie Starrett; ***D:*** Jack Starrett. *NO*

Run for the Roses ☠½ *Thoroughbred* **1978 (PG)** "National Velvet" clone about a young Puerto Rican boy and a champion race horse in Kentucky. Cheery family fare. **93m/C VHS, Beta.** Lisa Eilbacher, Vera Miles, Stuart Whitman, Sam Groom; ***D:*** Henry Levin. *LIV*

Run If You Can ☠ **1987 (R)** A woman sees a brutal murderer killing his victims on her television. Will she be next? **92m/C Beta.** Martin Landau, Yvette Nipar, Jerry Van Dyke; ***D:*** Virginia Lively Stone. *ALL*

Run of the Arrow ☠☠ *Hot Lead* **1956** Rather than surrender to the North at the end of the Civil War, an ex-Confederate soldier (Steiger) joins the Sioux nation, engaged in war against the white man. Steiger's Irish brogue is weird and distracting, and the intriguing premise fails to satisfy, but the cast is competent and interesting. **85m/C VHS, Beta, LV.** Rod Steiger, Brian Keith, Charles Bronson, Ralph Meeker, Tim McCoy; ***D:*** Samuel Fuller; ***W:*** Samuel Fuller. *NO*

The Run of the Country ☠☠☠ **1995 (R)** Amid the scenic splendor of a small town south of the North Irish border in County Cavan, Danny (Keeslar) comes of age, sometimes the hard way. His relationship with his bullying dad (Finney), the local Garda officer, begins to crumble after the tragic death of his mum. So he runs away to live with the town malcontent Prunty (Brophy) and falls in love with the beautiful Annagh (Smurfit), who lives north of the border. Life gets even more complicated when Annagh learns she's pregnant. Director Yates, reunited with Finney for the first time since they won Oscars for "The Dresser," sometimes digs too deep into a big crock of standard Irish stew, occasionally delivering Celtic melodrama instead of poignant slice of life. The usual themes of family dysfunction, religious rebellion and moral dilemma are augmented by the occasional appearance of the IRA. As the frustrated, violent father, Finney shines. In their debut, Keeslar and Smurfit are fine, but Brophy's Prunty is the one you'll remember. Adapted by Connaughton (who used similar geography for "The Playboys") from his novel. **109m/C VHS, LV.** Albert Finney, Matt Keeslar, Victoria Smurfit, Anthony Brophy, David Kelly; ***D:*** Peter Yates; ***W:*** Shane Connaughton; ***C:*** Mike Southon; ***M:*** Cynthia Millar. *COL*

Run, Rebecca, Run ☠☠½ **1981** Interesting family adventure yarn for the family about a South American refugee who tries to stop a young girl from leaving from an Australian island where they are both stranded. She eventually befriends him, and attempts to get permission for him to enter the country. **90m/C VHS, Beta.** *AU* Simone Buchanan, Henri Szeps; ***D:*** Peter Maxwell. *NO*

Run Silent, Run Deep ☠☠☠ **1958** Submarine commander Gable battles his officers, especially the bitter Lancaster who vied for the same command, while stalking the Japanese destroyer that sunk his former command. Top-notch WWII sub action, scripted from Commander Edward L. Beach's novel. **93m/B VHS, Beta.** Burt Lancaster, Clark Gable, Jack Warden, Don Rickles, Brad Dexter; ***D:*** Robert Wise; ***W:*** John Gay. *FOX, FCT, MGM*

Run, Stranger, Run *Happy Mother's Day, Love, George* **1973 (PG)** The inhabitants of a seaside house in Nova Scotia are paralyzed with fear when a number of brutal murders occur. A couple of sicko slasher scenes, but hard to swallow. **110m/C VHS.** Ron Howard, Patricia Neal, Cloris Leachman, Bobby Darin; ***D:*** Darren McGavin; ***C:*** Walter Lassally. *COL*

Runaway ½ **1984 (PG-13)** A cop and his sidekick track down a group of killer robots wreaking havoc. Self-serious, sorry sci-fi. Features Simmons of the rock group KISS. **100m/C VHS, Beta, LV.** Tom Selleck, Cynthia Rhodes, Gene Simmons, Stan Shaw, Kirstie Alley; ***D:*** Michael Crichton; ***W:*** Michael Crichton; ***M:*** Jerry Goldsmith. *COL*

Runaway **1989** A boy blames himself for his friend's accidental death and runs away to live in the subway tunnels of New York City. After four months of life underground, a disabled veteran and a waitress lend the boy a hand. Adapted from the novel "Slake's Limbo" by Felice Holman. Made for PBS and aired as part of the "Wonderworks" series. **58m/C VHS.** Charles S. Dutton, Jasmine Guy, Gavin Allen; ***D:*** Gilbert Moses. *PME, HMV, COL*

The Runaway Barge **1975** Tiresomely ordinary TV yarn about three adventurers earning their living on a riverboat. The usual cliches are present, including a gang of bad guys. **78m/C VHS.** Bo Hopkins, Tim Matheson, Jim Davis, Nick Nolte, Devon Ericson, Christina Hart, James Best; ***D:*** Boris Sagal. *LIV*

The Runaway Bus **1954** Filled with the requisite motley crew of passengers, including a gold-carrying thief and the ever-befuddled Margaret Rutherford, a bus gets lost between airports and ends up in a deserted village. Would-be wacky comedy. **78m/B VHS, Beta.** *GB* Frankie Howerd, Margaret Rutherford, Petula Clark, George Coulouris; ***D:*** Val Guest. *VYY, FCT*

Runaway Father ½ **1991** Pat Bennett's husband fakes his own death in an attempt to abandon his family. When Bennett discovers he's alive she works to set a legal precedent—17 years worth of back child support. Based on a true story. Made for television. **94m/C VHS.** Donna Mills, Jack Scalia, Chris Mulkey, Jenny Lewis; ***D:*** John Nicolella. *WOV*

Runaway Nightmare **1984** Two western worm ranchers are kidnapped by a female gang whose members torture and initiate them, then talk about their plan to steal from organized criminals. Just another typical worm rancher flick. **104m/C VHS.** Michael Cartel, Al Valletta; ***D:*** Michael Cartel. *NO*

Runaway Train **1985 (R)** A tough jailbird and his sidekick break out of the hoosegow and find themselves trapped aboard a brakeless freight train heading for certain derailment in northwestern Canada. Harrowing existential action drama based on a screenplay by Akira Kurosawa. Voigt is superb. **112m/C VHS, Beta, LV.** Jon Voight, Eric Roberts, Rebecca DeMornay, John P. Ryan, T.K. Carter, Kenneth McMillan; ***D:*** Andrei Konchalovsky; ***W:*** Andrei Konchalovsky, Djordje Milicevic, Edward Bunker; ***M:*** Trevor Jones. Golden Globe Awards '86: Best Actor—Drama (Voight); Nominations: Academy Awards '85: Best Actor (Voight), Best Film Editing, Best Supporting Actor (Roberts). *MGM*

The Runaways **1975** A boy runs away from an unhappy foster home situation and becomes friends with a leopard that has escaped from an animal park. Sentimental but well-done family fun. **76m/C VHS, Beta.** Dorothy McGuire, John Randolph, Neva Patterson, Josh Albee; ***D:*** Harry Harris. *NO*

Runaways **1984** A corrupt politician's wife falls in love with the man who saved her when she attempted suicide. The two try to escape her husband's wrathful vengeance. **95m/C VHS, Beta.** Steve Oliver, Sondra Currie, John Russell. *NO*

The Runestone **1991 (R)** After the eponymous viking relic is unearthed, an archaeologist's meddling frees a long-imprisoned wolf-beast that terrorizes New York. An adequate horror flick that taps the seldom-explored vein of Norse mythology. Based on a novel by Mark E. Rogers. **105m/C VHS, LV.** Peter Riegert, Joan Severance, William Hickey, Tim Ryan, Chris Young, Alexander Godunov; ***D:*** Willard Carroll; ***W:*** Willard Carroll; ***M:*** David Newman. *LIV*

The Runner Stumbles ½ **1979 (R)** Dated melodrama about a priest who goes on trial for murdering the nun with whom he fell in love in a mining town in the 1920s. Based on a true incident, from the play by Milan Stiff. Van Dyke in an unwanted serious role is miserably grim and wooden. **109m/C VHS, Beta.** Dick Van Dyke, Kathleen Quinlan, Maureen Stapleton, Ray Bolger, Beau Bridges, Tammy Grimes; ***D:*** Stanley Kramer; ***M:*** Ernest Gold. *FOX*

The Runnin' Kind ½ **1989 (R)** A yuppie expecting to inherit his father's Ohio law firm goes on a wild spree with an all-girl rock band. Sexy drummer Howard shows him the sights of certain parts of L.A. Original, fun comedy. Independent. **89m/C VHS, Beta.** David Packer, Pleasant Gehman, Brie Howard, Susan Strasberg; ***D:*** Max Tash. *FOX*

Running Against Time ½ **1990 (PG)** A teacher tries to change history (and erase his brother's Vietnam War death) by time-warping back to 1963 and preventing JFK's murder. The made for cable TV movie takes an offhanded gee-whiz approach to a tantalizing premise, as temporal paradoxes multiply in "Back to the Future" style. No assassination-conspiracy theories, by the way, but Lyndon Johnson fans may not like his portrayal here. Based on the novel "A Time to Remember" by Stanley Shapiro. **93m/C VHS.** Robert Hays, Catherine Hicks, Sam Wanamaker, James DiStefano, Brian Smiar; ***D:*** Bruce Seth Green; ***W:*** Robert Glass. *MCA*

Running Away **1989 (PG-13)** Bittersweet story of WWII romance, with a twist of adventure. Strong cast creates good chemistry, but somehow the story is not engaging. Loren and Penny are mother and daughter, leaving Rome for the hills and encountering dangers. **101m/C VHS, LV.** Sophia Loren, Sydney Penny, Robert Loggia, Andrea Occhipinti; ***D:*** Dino Risi. *PSM, PAR, FCT*

Running Blind **197?** Espionage/adventure thriller has a double agent and a beautiful woman on the run in Iceland. **120m/C VHS.** *GB* Stuart Wilson, Heidi Steindorsottir. *FCT, VCO*

Running Brave **1983 (PG)** The true story of Billy Mills, a South Dakota Sioux Indian who won the Gold Medal in the 10,000 meter run at the 1964 Tokyo Olympics. Not bad, but hokey in the way of many of these plodding true-story flicks. **90m/C VHS, Beta, LV.** Robby Benson, Claudia Cron, Pat Hingle, Denis Lacroix; ***D:*** D.S. Everett; ***W:*** Henry Bean. *DIS*

Running Cool **1993 (R)** Two easy-going bikers join up with an old friend to protect his wetlands property from a lowlife developer and his stooges. Chicks (there's a romance with a local biker babe), motorcycles, fighting, and saving the environment—what more could you want? **106m/C VHS, Beta.** Andrew Divoff, Tracy Sebastian, Dedee Pfeiffer, James Gammon, Paul Gleason, Arlen Dean Snyder, Bubba Baker; ***D:*** Beverly Sebastian, Ferd Sebastian; ***W:*** Beverly Sebastian, Ferd Sebastian. *PAR*

Running Delilah ½ **1993** Delilah (Cattrall) is a secret agent who is apparently killed by a vicious arms dealer. Only her fellow agent (Zane) resurrects her and Delilah is transformed into a cybernetic super agent. And her assignment is to go after a terrorist who's building a nuclear weapon with plutonium supplied by Delilah's killer. **85m/C VHS.** Kim Cattrall, Billy Zane, Diana Rigg. *ABC*

Running Free ½ **1994 (PG)** Sullen Garrett joins his naturalist mother in the Alaskan wilderness and establishes a friendship with a wolverine cub (who's smarter than the kid). **90m/C VHS, LV.** Jesse Montgomery Sythe, Jayme Lee Misfeldt, Michael Pena; ***D:*** Steve Kroschel. *VMK*

Running Hot ½ *Highway to Hell; Lucky 13* **1983 (R)** Seventeen-year-old convicted murderer Stoltz gets love letter in prison from older woman Carrico. When he escapes, they flee the law together. Quick-paced and entertaining. **88m/C VHS, Beta.** Monica Carrico, Eric Stoltz, Stuart Margolin, Virgil Frye, Richard Bradford, Sorrels Pickard, Juliette Cummins; ***D:*** Mark Griffiths; ***W:*** Mark Griffiths. *LIV, VES*

The Running Man ½ **1987 (R)** Special-effects-laden adaptation of the Stephen King novel about a futuristic television game show. Convicts are given a chance for pardon—all they have to do is survive an on going battle with specially-trained assassins in the bombed-out sections of Los Angeles. Sci-fi with an attitude. **101m/C VHS, Beta, LV.** Arnold Schwarzenegger, Richard Dawson, Maria Conchita Alonso, Yaphet Kotto, Mick Fleetwood, Dweezil Zappa, Jesse Ventura; ***D:*** Paul Michael Glaser; ***W:*** Steven E. de Souza; ***M:*** Harold Faltermeyer. *LIV, VES*

Running Mates **1986 (PG-13)** Occasionally intriguing drama of two teens who fall in love, but are kept apart by their fathers' local political rivalry. Could have been better, but cardboard characters abound. **90m/C VHS, Beta.** Greg Webb, Barbara Howard, J. Don Ferguson, Clara Dunn; ***D:*** Thomas L. Neff. *VTR, NWV*

Running Mates **1992 (PG-13)** Cynically amusing political satire about a bachelor politician and his too intelligent lady love. Harris is Hugh, a U.S. senator looking forward to the presidential primaries when he meets widowed children's novelist Aggie (Keaton). She hates politics and he's Mr. Slick, although decent enough behind the political expediency. Aggie, however, has a potentially damaging secret in her past which causes the scandal-scenting pack of press hounds to bay in salivating anticipation. Will Hugh stick by Aggie and will Aggie overcome her natural political distaste for everything to end happily? A well-played romp. Made for cable television. **88m/C VHS, LV.** Ed Harris, Diane Keaton, Ed Begley Jr., Ben Masters, Robert Harper, Brandon Maggart, Russ Tamblyn; ***D:*** Michael Lindsay-Hogg; ***W:*** A.L. Appling. *HBO*

Running on Empty **1988 (PG-13)** Two 1960s radicals are still on the run in 1988 for a politically motivated Vietnam War-era crime. Though they have managed to stay one step ahead of the law, their son wants a "normal" life, even if it means never seeing his family again. Well-performed, quiet, plausible drama. **116m/C VHS, Beta, LV, 8mm.** Christine Lahti, River Phoenix, Judd Hirsch, Martha Plimpton, Jonas Arby, Ed Crowley, L.M. Kit Carson, Steven Hill, Augusta Dabney, David Margulies, Sidney Lumet; ***D:*** Sidney Lumet; ***W:*** Naomi Foner; ***M:*** Tony Mottola. Golden Globe Awards '89: Best Screenplay; Los Angeles Film Critics Association Awards '88: Best Actress (Lahti); National Board of Review Awards '88: Best Supporting Actor (Phoenix); Nominations: Academy Awards '88: Best Original Screenplay, Best Supporting Actor (Phoenix). *WAR*

Running Out of Luck ½ **1986 (R)** A light, song-packed story about a rock star very much like Jagger who is abandoned in South America and believed dead, until he returns to his world. Features songs from Jagger's solo album "She's the Boss". **88m/C VHS, Beta, LV.** Mick Jagger, Dennis Hopper, Jerry Hall, Rae Dawn Chong; ***D:*** Julien Temple. *MVD, FOX*

Running Scared **1979 (PG)** Two young men, returning from military service as stowaways aboard an Army cargo plane, are caught by an intelligence agent and thought to be spies, because Reinhold has unknowingly photographed a secret U.S. base with his stolen Army-issue camera. Not-bad spy thriller with a twist—the "spies" are hapless nobodies, now on the lam. **92m/C VHS, Beta, LV.** Ken Wahl, Judge Reinhold, John Saxon, Annie McEnroe, Bradford Dillman, Pat Hingle; ***D:*** Paul Glickler. *NO*

Running Scared ½ **1986 (R)** Hip, unorthodox Chicago cops Hines and Crystal have to handle an important drug arrest before taking an extended vacation in Key West. Not as relentless as "48 Hrs," but more enjoyable in some ways. Ever wonder what it's like to ride in a car at high speed on the tracks? Find out here. **107m/C VHS, Beta, LV.** Gregory Hines, Billy Crystal, Dan Hedaya, Jimmy Smits, Darlanne Fluegel, Joe Pantoliano, Steven Bauer; ***D:*** Peter Hyams; ***W:*** Gary De Vore. *MGM*

Running Wild 🦴🦴 **1927** Early silent comedy starring mustachioed Fields as an eternal coward who suddenly turns into a lion by hypnosis. Odd, often unfunny Fields entry sometimes hits the mark. He's awfully mean, though. **68m/B VHS, Beta.** W.C. Fields, Mary Brian, Claud Buchanan; ***D:*** Gregory La Cava; ***M:*** Gaylord Carter. *PAR*

Running Wild 🦴🦴½ **1973 (G)** A free-lance photographer becomes involved in a dispute to save a corral of wild mustang horses. The usual great Colorado scenery enhances a good, family-view story. **102m/C VHS, Beta.** Lloyd Bridges, Dina Merrill, Pat Hingle, Gilbert Roland, Morgan Woodward; ***D:*** Robert McCahon; ***W:*** Robert McCahon. *MED*

Running Wild 🦴 **1994 (R)** Beautiful woman abandons her much older fiance to go on a wild road trip with his son that includes sex and crime. **91m/C VHS, LV.** Jennifer Barker, Daniel Dupont, Daniel Spector, Eliot Keener; ***D:*** Philippe Blot. *APX*

Rush 🦴 **1984** A post-nuclear world war movie in which a rebel named Rush battles the rulers of a slave colony. **83m/C VHS.** *IT* Conrad Nichols, Gordon Mitchell, Laura Trotter, Rita Furlan; ***D:*** Tonino Ricci. *NO*

Rush 🦴🦴🦴 **1991 (R)** Texas drug culture, circa 1975, is portrayed in this bleak cop drama. Rookie narcotics officer Kristen Cates (Leigh) goes undercover with the experienced Raynor (Patric) to catch a big-time dealer, menancingly played by Allman, and their bosses don't much care how they do it. Cates falls in love with Raynor and is drawn ever deeper into the drug-addicted world they are supposed to destroy. Fine performances and a great blues score by Clapton. The directorial debut of Zanuck. Based on ex-narcotics cop Kim Wozencraft's autobiographical novel. **120m/C VHS.** Jason Patric, Jennifer Jason Leigh, Gregg Allman, Max Perlich, Sam Elliott, Tony Frank, William Sadler; ***D:*** Lili Fini Zanuck; ***W:*** Pete Dexter; ***M:*** Eric Clapton. *MGM*

Rush It 🦴½ **1977** Scriptwriters ponder possible plots over capucino: "I've got it! 'Bike Messengers in Love'!" "Nah. The title's too obvious. Why don't we call it 'Rush It'?" Much hard work and many months later, the result is forgettable. **78m/C VHS, Beta.** Tom Berenger, Jill Eikenberry. *UNI*

Rush Week 🦴 **1988 (R)** Dead coeds populate campus during frat week. Greg Allman has bit part and the Dickies perform two songs. **93m/C VHS, LV.** Dean Hamilton, Gregg Allman, Kathleen Kinmont, Roy Thinnes, Pamela Ludwig; ***D:*** Bob Bravler. *COL*

The Russia House 🦴🦴½ **1990 (R)** Russian scientist Brandauer attempts to publish book debunking Soviet Union's claims of military superiority by passing it through ex-lover Pfeiffer to British editor Connery, apparently unaware of impending glasnost. Star-studded spy thriller aspires to heights it never quite reaches. Adapted from John Le Carre's novel, Stoppard's screenplay is very fine, actually making some aspects of the novel work better. **122m/C VHS, LV, 8mm.** Sean Connery, Michelle Pfeiffer, Roy Scheider, James Fox, John Mahoney, Klaus Maria Brandauer, Ken Russell, J.T. Walsh, Michael Kitchen, David Threlfall, Ian McNeice, Christopher Lawford; ***D:*** Fred Schepisi; ***W:*** Tom Stoppard; ***C:*** Ian Baker; ***M:*** Jerry Goldsmith. *MGM, FCT*

Russian Roulette 🦴🦴 **1975** The Russian premier is visiting Vancouver in 1970, and the Mounties must prevent a dissident KGB terrorist from assassinating him. Un-thrilling spy yarn fails to deliver on intriguing premise. **100m/C VHS, Beta.** George Segal, Christina Raines, Bo Brundin, Denholm Elliott, Louise Fletcher; ***D:*** Lou Lombardo. *FOX*

Russian Roulette 🦴🦴½ **1993** Routine story about an American woman on vacation in Russia who finds herself in the middle of a plot to locate a hidden Czarist artifact and smuggle it out of the country. Everyone on her tour group is suspect, an American businessman becomes involved, and a killer starts eliminating the number of players. Great location scenery. **89m/C VHS.** Susan Blakely, Barry Bostwick, E.G. Marshall, Jeff Altman; ***D:*** Greydon Clark. *MNC*

The Russian Terminator 🦴 **1990 (R)** An FBI agent is up against a one-man "death squad." **90m/C VHS.** Helena Michaelson, Frederick Offrein, Harley Melin, Tina Tjung; ***D:*** Mats Helge; ***W:*** Mats Helge. *XVC, DMP*

The Russians are Coming, the Russians are Coming 🦴🦴🦴 **1966** Based on the comic novel "The Off-Islanders" by Nathaniel Benchley, this is the story of a Russian sub which accidentally runs aground off the New England coast. The residents falsely believe that the nine-man crew is the beginning of a Soviet invasion, though the men are only looking for help. A memorable set of silly events follows the landing, engineered by a gung-ho police chief and a town filled with overactive imaginations. **126m/C VHS, Beta.** Alan Arkin, Carl Reiner, Theodore Bikel, Eva Marie Saint, Brian Keith, Paul Ford, Jonathan Winters, Ben Blue, Tessie O'Shea, Doro Merande, John Phillip Law; ***D:*** Norman Jewison; ***C:*** Joseph Biroc. Golden Globe Awards '67: Best Actor—Musical/Comedy (Arkin), Best Film—Musical/Comedy; National Board of Review Awards '66: 10 Best Films of the Year; Nominations: Academy Awards '66: Best Actor (Arkin), Best Picture, Best Story & Screenplay. *FOX, MLB*

Russkies 🦴½ **1987 (PG)** A jolly comedy about three adorable American kids who capture, and eventually grow to like, a stranded Russian sailor. Friendly and peace-loving, but dull. **98m/C VHS, Beta, LV.** Joaquin Rafael (Leaf) Phoenix, Whip Hubley, Peter Billingsley, Stefan DeSalle; ***D:*** Rick Rosenthal; ***M:*** James Newton Howard. *ORI, WAR*

Rustler's Hideout 🦴 *Rustler's Roundup* **1944** One of numerous westerns starring Crabbe as cowboy do-gooder Billy Carson, here plodding through standard histrionics against rustlers, a cardsharp, and a business fraud. **60m/C VHS, Beta.** Buster Crabbe, Al "Fuzzy" St. John, Charles "Blackie" King, John Merton, Lane Chandler, Hal Price, Edward Cassidy, Bud Osborne; ***D:*** Sam Newfield. *GPV*

Rustlers of Red Dog 🦴🦴½ **1935** A 12-chapter western serial about Indian wars and cattle rustlers. **235m/B VHS.** Johnny Mack Brown, Raymond Hatton, Joyce Compton, Walter Miller, Harry Woods, William Desmond, Wally Wales, Chief Thundercloud, Art Mix, Bill Patton, Bud Osborne, Lafe McKee; ***D:*** Lew (Louis Friedlander) Landers. *GPV*

Rustler's Paradise 🦴 **1935** Carey seeks revenge on the man who stole his wife and daughter. **59m/B VHS, Beta, LV.** Harry Carey Sr., Gertrude Messinger, Edmund Cobb; ***D:*** Harry Fraser. *NOS*

Rustler's Rhapsody 🦴🦴 **1985 (PG)** A singing cowboy rides into a small western town and encounters all kinds of desperados in this earnest would-be satire of '40s B-movie westerns. **89m/C VHS, Beta, LV.** Tom Berenger, Patrick Wayne, G.W. Bailey, Andy Griffith, Marilu Henner; ***D:*** Hugh Wilson; ***W:*** Hugh Wilson; ***M:*** Stephen Dorff. *PAR*

Rustler's Roundup 🦴½ **1933** Mix rides to the rescue of Sinclair, whose daddy has been murdered by villains out to steal the ranch. **58m/B VHS.** Tom Mix, Diane Sinclair, Noah Beery Jr., Douglass Dumbrille, Roy Stewart, Nelson McDowell, William Desmond, Frank Lackteen, Pee Wee Holmes, Bud Osborne; ***D:*** Henry MacRae. *GPV*

Rustler's Valley 🦴🦴 **1937** Hopalong Cassidy is a ranch foreman who tries to save his employer from the clutches of a crooked lawyer. Pretty fun ordinary range-ridin' saga. **59m/B VHS, Beta.** William Boyd, George "Gabby" Hayes, Lee J. Cobb; ***D:*** Nate Watt. *VYY*

Rusty's Birthday 🦴🦴½ **1949** Danny searches for the lost Rusty who's been taken in by a family of transient workers. When Danny discovers his pal, he finds the young son of the family doesn't want to give Rusty up. **61m/B VHS.** Ted Donaldson, John Litel, Ann Doran, Jimmy Hunt, Ray Teal; ***D:*** Seymour Friedman; ***W:*** Brenda Weisberg. *COL*

The Rutanga Tapes 🦴½ **1990 (R)** Soviet bloc country has representatives in Africa producing deadly chemicals used for war and a dissident has taped evidence of native deaths. Reporter babe Simpson wants an exclusive, Petersen wants the dissident, Libyan agents want the tapes, and you'll want to fast forward to the end. **88m/C VHS.** Henry Cele, Arnold Vosloo, Wilson Dunster, David Dukes, Susan Anspach; ***D:*** David Lister. *NO*

The Rutherford County Line 🦴 **1987** A tough small-town sheriff searches for the killer of his deputies. **98m/C VHS, Beta.** Earl Owensby; ***D:*** Thom McIntyre. *MCA*

The Ruthless Four 🦴🦴 *Every Man For Himself; Each One For Himself; Sam Cooper's Gold; Each Man For Himself* **1970** Quartet of unlikely mining partners match wills and wits and battle the elements. Not-so-hot spaghetti western, with good lead from Heflin. **97m/C VHS, Beta.** *IT* Van Heflin, Klaus Kinski, Gilbert Roland, George Hilton; ***D:*** Giorgio Capitani. *MON*

Ruthless People 🦴🦴🦴 **1986 (R)** DeVito and his mistress spend a romantic evening plotting his obnoxious wife's untimely demise. Before he can put his plan into action, he's delighted to discover she's been kidnapped by some very desperate people—who don't stand a chance with Bette. High farcical entertainment is a variation on the story "The Ransom of Red Chief," by O. Henry. **93m/C VHS, Beta, LV.** Bette Midler, Danny DeVito, Judge Reinhold, Helen Slater, Anita Morris, Bill Pullman; ***D:*** David Zucker, Jim Abrahams, Jerry Zucker; ***W:*** Dale Lanner; ***C:*** Jan De Bont; ***M:*** Michel Colombier. *TOU*

Ruyblas 🦴🦴 **1948** Revenge and romance beset the court of Charles II in this tale of mistaken identity (with Marais in a dual role). Based on the novel by Victor Hugo. **90m/B VHS.** *FR* Jean Marais, Danielle Darrieux; ***D:*** Pierre Billon; ***W:*** Jean Cocteau. *FCT*

Ryan's Daughter 🦴🦴½ **1970 (PG)** Irish woman (Miles) marries a man she does not love and then falls for a shell-shocked British major who arrives during the 1916 Irish uprising to keep the peace. Not surprisingly, she is accused of betraying the local IRA gunrunners to her British lover. Tasteful melodrama with lots of pretty scenery that goes on a bit too long. **194m/C VHS, Beta, LV.** *GB* Sarah Miles, Robert Mitchum, John Mills, Trevor Howard, Christopher Jones, Leo McKern; ***D:*** David Lean; ***W:*** Robert Bolt; ***C:*** Frederick A. (Freddie) Young; ***M:*** Maurice Jarre. Academy Awards '70: Best Cinematography, Best Supporting Actor (Mills); National Board of Review Awards '70: 10 Best Films of the Year; Nominations: Academy Awards '70: Best Actress (Miles), Best Sound. *MGM, BTV*

Ryder P.I. **1988 (PG-13)** P.I Ryder and his sidekick fight crime and solve weird cases in the big city. **92m/C VHS, Beta.** Bob Nelson. *MOV, VTR*

Sabaka 🦴🦴 *The Hindu* **1955** Adventure set in India about a scary religious cult. Karloff and the cast of stalwart "B" movie performers have fun with this one, and you should, too. **81m/C VHS.** Boris Karloff, Reginald Denny, Victor Jory, Lisa Howard, Jeanne Bates, Jay Novello, June Foray; ***D:*** Frank Ferrin. *SNC*

Sabotage 🦴🦴🦴 *Woman Alone* **1936** Early Hitchcock thriller based on Conrad's "The Secret Agent." A woman who works at a movie theater (Sidney) suspects her quiet husband (Homolka) might be the terrorist planting bombs around London. Numerous sly touches of the Master's signature humor. **81m/B VHS, Beta, LV, 8mm.** Oscar Homolka, Sylvia Sidney, John Loder; ***D:*** Alfred Hitchcock; ***W:*** Charles Bennett. *SNC, NOS, HHT*

Saboteur 🦴🦴🦴 **1942** A man wrongly accused of sabotaging an American munitions plant during WWII sets out to find the traitor who framed him. Hitchcock uses his locations, including Boulder Dam, Radio City Music Hall, and the Statue of Liberty, to greatly intensify the action. Stunning resolution. **108m/B VHS, Beta, LV.** Priscilla Lane, Robert Cummings, Otto Kruger, Alan Baxter, Norman Lloyd, Charles Halton; ***D:*** Alfred Hitchcock; ***W:*** Alfred Hitchcock, Peter Viertel; ***C:*** Joseph Valentine. *MCA*

Sabre Jet 🦴🦴 **1953** Run-of-the-mill wartime drama of hubbies flying combat missions in Korea and long-suffering spouses on the home front. **90m/C VHS, Beta.** Robert Stack, Amanda Blake, Louis King; ***D:*** Louis King. *NO*

Sabrina 🦴🦴🦴 *Sabrina Fair* **1954** Two wealthy brothers, one an aging businessman (Bogart) and the other a dissolute playboy (Holden), vie for the attention of their chauffeur's daughter (Hepburn), who has just returned from a French cooking school. Typically acerbic, in the Wilder manner, with Bogart and Holden cast interestingly against type (but it's Hepburn's picture anyway). Based on the play "Sabrina Fair" by Samuel Taylor. **113m/B VHS, Beta, LV.** Audrey Hepburn, Humphrey Bogart, William Holden, Walter Hampden, Francis X. Bushman, John Williams, Martha Hyer, Marcel Dalio; ***D:*** Billy Wilder; ***W:*** Billy Wilder, Ernest Lehman; ***C:*** Charles B(ryant) Lang. Academy Awards '54: Best Costume Design (B & W); Directors Guild of America Awards '54: Best Director (Wilder); Golden Globe Awards '55: Best Screenplay; National Board of Review Awards '54: 10 Best Films of the Year, Best Supporting Actor (Williams); Nominations: Academy Awards '54: Best Actress (Hepburn), Best Art Direction/Set Decoration (B & W), Best Black and White Cinematography, Best Director (Wilder), Best Screenplay. *PAR*

Sabrina 🦴🦴½ **1995 (PG)** Updated version of Billy Wilder's 1954 fairytale that starred a luminous Audrey Hepburn. This time around the pretty Ormond is the chauffeur's daughter who gets closely involved with the wealthy Larrabees. And this time the emphasis is more on workaholic business mogul Linus (Ford), who plays a dangerous game when he decides to transfer Sabrina's affections from his feckless engaged brother David (Kinnear) to himself in order to protect a business merger. Ford's a little too stodgy (you'll wonder why Sabrina bothers except she's probably just too nice to say no) but Kinnear's suitably charming (in his film debut) and Marchand properly matriarchal. **127m/C VHS, Beta.** Harrison Ford, Julia Ormond, Greg Kinnear, Nancy Marchand, John Wood, Richard Crenna, Angie Dickinson, Lauren Holly, Fanny Ardant, Dana Ivey, Patrick Bruel, Miriam Colon, Elizabeth Franz; ***D:*** Sydney Pollack; ***W:*** David Rayfiel, Barbara Benedek; ***C:*** Giuseppe Rotunno; ***M:*** John Williams. Nominations: Academy Awards '95: Best Song ("Moonlight"), Best Score; Golden Globe Awards '96: Best Actor—Musical/Comedy (Ford), Best Film—Musical/Comedy, Best Song ("Moonlight"). *PAR*

Sabrina the Teenage Witch 🦴🦴½ **1996 (PG)** Based on the Archie Comics, this lighthearted cable movie finds 16-year-old Sabrina (Hart) being told by her two eccentric aunts, Hilda (Miller) and Zelda (Fernetz), that she is a witch, descended from a long line of good witches and warlocks. Sabrina's having enough trouble fitting in at Riverdale High without this kind of news but she does find that her magical powers have their advantages. **90m/C VHS.** Melissa Joan Hart, Charlene Fernetz, Sherry Miller, Michelle Beaudoin, Ryan Reynolds, Tobias Mehler, Lalainia Lindbjerg; ***D:*** Tibor Takacs; ***W:*** Barney Cohen, Kathryn Wallack, Nicholas Factor. *HMK*

Sacco & Vanzetti 🦴🦴 *Sacco e Vanzetti* **1971 (PG)** Two Italian immigrants and acknowledged anarchists are caught amidst communist witch-hunts and judicial negligence when they are tried and executed for murder in 1920s America. Based on the true-life case, considered by some a flagrant miscarriage of justice and political martyrdom, by others, honest American judicial-system proceedings. Well-made and acted. Joan Baez sings the title song "The Ballad of Sacco and Vanzetti." **120m/C VHS, Beta.** Gian Marie Volonte, Riccardo Cucciolla, Milo O'Shea, Cyril Cusack, Geoffrey Keen; ***D:*** Guiliano Montaldo; ***M:*** Ennio Morricone. Cannes Film Festival '71: Best Actor (Cucciolla); Nominations: Cannes Film Festival '71: Best Film. *NO*

The Sacketts 🦴🦴½ **1979** Follows the adventures of three Tennessee brothers who migrate to the West after the Civil War. Based on two Louis L'Amour novels. Made for television. **198m/C VHS, Beta.** Jeffery Osterhage, Tom Selleck, Sam Elliott, Glenn Ford, Ben Johnson, Mercedes McCambridge, Ruth Roman, Jack Elam, Gilbert Roland; ***D:*** Robert Totten. *WAR, HHE*

Sacred Ground 🦴🦴 **1983 (PG)** A trapper and his pregnant Apache wife unknowingly build shelter on the Paiute Indians' sacred burial ground. When the wife dies in childbirth, the pioneer is forced to kidnap a Paiute woman who has just buried her own deceased infant. Average western drama. **100m/C VHS, Beta.** Tim McIntire, Jack Elam, L.Q. Jones, Mindi Miller; ***D:*** Charles B. Pierce; ***W:*** Charles B. Pierce. *FOX*

Sacred Mountain/White Flame 🦴🦴🦴 **1931** Two short films starring Riefenstahl, featuring mostly fluid dance sequences and Teutonic mountain boy/girl plots. Silent. **60m/B VHS, Beta.** *GE* Leni Riefenstahl. *FCT, GLV, MRV*

The Sacrifice 🦴🦴🦴 **1986 (PG)** Tarkovsky's enigmatic final film, released after his death. Deals with a retired intellectual's spiritually symbolic efforts at self-sacrifice in order to save his family on the eve of a nuclear holocaust. Stunning cinematography by Sven Nykvist. Acclaimed, but sometimes slow going; not everyone will appreciate Tarkovsky's visionary spiritualism. In Swedish with English subtitles. **145m/C VHS, Beta, LV.** *FR SW* Erland Josephson, Susan Fleetwood, Valerie Mairesse, Allan Edwall, Gudrun Gisladottir, Sven Wollter, Filippa Franzen; ***D:*** Andrei Tarkovsky; ***C:*** Sven Nykvist. British Academy Awards '87: Best Foreign Film. *INJ, TPV*

Sacrilege 🦴½ **1986** A nun and a nobleman engage in a hot love affair that fosters scandal, murder and, revenge. Cynical use of religious theme masks otherwise ordinary sex/romance flick. Controversial Italian-made erotic drama. **104m/C VHS, Beta.** *IT* Myriem Roussel, Alessandro Gassman; ***D:*** Luciano Odorisio. *PSM*

The Sad Sack 🦴🦴 **1957** A bumbling hero with a photographic memory winds up in Morocco as a member of the French Foreign Legion. Although a success at the box office, Lewis's second movie (without partner Dean Martin) seems jerky and out of sorts today. Based on the comic strip character by George Baker, but not effectively. **98m/B VHS.** Jerry Lewis, Phyllis Kirk, David Wayne, Peter Lorre, Gene Evans, Mary Treen; ***D:*** George Marshall; ***C:*** Loyal Griggs; ***M:*** Burt Bacharach, Hal David. *COL*

Sadat 🦴🦴½ **1983 (PG)** Gossett, Jr. well plays his title role of Egyptian leader and Nobel Peace Prize winner, Anwar el Sadat. But the controversial life and peace efforts of the president (assassinated in 1981) are given a quick overview in this average drama. Made for television. **195m/C VHS.** Louis Gossett Jr., John Rhys-Davies, Jeremy Kemp, Nehemiah Persoff, Madolyn Smith, Anne Heywood, Jeffrey Tambor, Barry Morse; ***D:*** Richard Michaels; ***M:*** Charles Bernstein. *COL*

Saddle Buster 🦴🦴 **1932** A rodeo cowboy loses his nerve after being thrown by a tough horse, but gets it back again by the end of the hour. Actual rodeo footage is incorporated into this low-budget bronco saga. **59m/B VHS.** Tom Keene, Helen Foster, Charles Quigley, Marie Quillen, Robert Frazer, Charles "Slim" Whitaker; ***D:*** Fred Allen. *NOS, HEG*

Saddle Mountain Round-Up 🦴 **1941** The Range Busters are on the trail again as they smoke out a murderer. **61m/B VHS, Beta.** Ray Corrigan, John "Dusty" King, Max Terhune. *NOS, DVT, RXM*

Sadie McKee 🦴🦴🦴 **1934** A melodrama with Crawford as a maid searching for love in the big city. She falls for a self-destructive ne'er-do-well, marries an alcoholic millionaire, and eventually finds true love with the wealthy Tone (who would become Crawford's third husband). Professional acting and directing elevate the story. **90m/B VHS.** Joan Crawford, Franchot Tone, Gene Raymond, Edward Arnold; ***D:*** Clarence Brown. *BTV*

Sadie Thompson 🦴🦴🦴 **1928** Swanson plays a harlot with a heart of gold, bawdy and good-natured, in the South Seas. A zealot missionary (Barrymore) arrives and falls in love with her. The last eight minutes of footage have been recreated by using stills and the original title cards, to replace the last reel which had decomposed. Remade as "Rain," "Dirty Gertie From Harlem," and "Miss Sadie Thompson." Based on W. Somerset Maugham's "Rain." **97m/B VHS, LV.** Gloria Swanson, Lionel Barrymore, Raoul Walsh, Blanche Frederici, Charles Lane, James Marcus; ***D:*** Raoul Walsh. Nominations: Academy Awards '28: Best Actress (Swanson), Best Cinematography. *KIV, MOV*

The Sadist 🦴🦴½ *The Profile of Terror* **1963** Three teachers on their way to Dodger Stadium find themselves stranded at a roadside garage and terrorized by a snivelling lunatic. Tense and plausible. Cinematography by Vilmos Zsigmond. **95m/B Beta.** Arch Hall Jr., Helen Hovey, Richard Alden, Marilyn Manning; ***D:*** James Landis; ***W:*** James Landis. *SNC, RHI*

Safari 3000 🦴½ **1982 (PG)** "Playboy" writer is assigned to do a story on a three-day, 3,000 kilometer car race in Africa. Doesn't take itself too seriously, and neither should we. Dumb, dull, and disjointed. **91m/C VHS, Beta.** Stockard Channing, David Carradine, Christopher Lee; ***D:*** Harry Hurwitz; ***M:*** Ernest Gold. *MGM*

Safe 🦴🦴🦴 **1995 (R)** Surburban California housewife Carol (Moore) literally becomes allergic to her environment and winds up seeking relief in a holistic center in Albuquerque, where director Haynes takes a shot at the New Age and finds a link to the AIDS crisis. Serious, stylistically detached look at a near future riddled with environmental toxins is led by Moore's performance as the sunny suburbanite undone by the unseen. **119m/C VHS, LV.** Julianne Moore, Peter Friedman, Xander Berkeley, Susan Norman, James LeGros, Mary Carver, Kate McGregor Stewart; ***D:*** Todd Haynes; ***W:*** Todd Haynes; ***C:*** Alex Nepomniaschy; ***M:*** Ed Tomney. Nominations: Independent Spirit Awards '96: Best Actress (Moore), Best Director (Haynes), Best Film, Best Screenplay. *COL*

Safe Passage 🦴🦴 **1994 (PG-13)** Grueling family drama with Sarandon and Shepherd portraying an unhappily married couple who are the parents of seven sons, one of whom is missing and presumed dead in the Sinai Desert war. One by one the grown boys arrive home to await any further news. They rehash memories, watch old videos, open old wounds, and generally affirm life. None of the performances, with the exception of Sarandon, are truly believable. She is the only one that brings any depth to her character as the tough matriarch that holds the family together. Feels like a TV movie, albeit one with classier names. Based on the novel by Ellyn Bache. **98m/C VHS, LV.** Susan Sarandon, Sam Shepard, Robert Sean Leonard, Sean Astin, Marcia Gay Harden, Nick Stahl, Jason London, Philip Bosco, Matt Keeslar; ***D:*** Robert Ackerman; ***W:*** Deena Goldstone; ***M:*** Mark Isham. *TTC, NLC*

Saga of Death Valley 🦴🦴½ **1939** Rogers battles a band of outlaws and discovers that their leader is his own brother. Exciting and likeable early Rogers western. **56m/B VHS, Beta.** Roy Rogers, George "Gabby" Hayes, Donald (Don "Red") Barry, Doris Day; ***D:*** Joseph Kane. *NOS, VDM, VCN*

The Saga of the Draculas 🦴 *Dracula Saga; Dracula: The Bloodline Continues...; The Saga of Dracula* **1972 (R)** An aging vampire wishes to continue his bloodline and seeks to convert his niece's baby to his bloodsucking ways. **90m/C VHS.** *SP* Narciso Ibanez Menta, Tina Sainz, Tony Isbert, Maria Koski, Cristina Suriani, Helga Line; ***D:*** Leon Klimovsky. *SNC*

Saga of the Vagabond 🦴🦴½ *Sengoku Gunto-Den* **1959** Arranged by master director Akira Kurosawa. A band of ruthless outlaws careen across a civil war-torn countryside. With English subtitles. **115m/C VHS, Beta.** *JP* Toshiro Mifune, Michiyo Aratama; ***D:*** Toshio Sugie. *VDA*

Sagebrush Law 🦴½ **1943** Western yarn has Holt playing a young man trying to clear the name of his bank president father. Barclay serves as the love interest and "Ukulele Ike" Edwards provides needed comic and music relief. **56m/B VHS.** Tim Holt, Cliff Edwards, Joan Barclay, Edward Cassidy, Karl Hackett, Roy Barcroft, Ernie Adams; ***D:*** Sam Nelson; ***W:*** Bennett Cohen. *MOV*

Sagebrush Trail 🦴🦴🦴 **1933** Wayne's second-ever western, complete with all sorts of tumbleweed and white-hat cliches. Our hero is wrongly accused of killin' a man, and busts out of the hoosegow to clear his name. Interesting plot twists makes for fun, compelling viewing. **53m/B VHS, LV.** John Wayne, Yakima Canutt, Wally Wales; ***D:*** Armand Schaefer. *COL, REP, NOS*

Sahara 🦴🦴🦴 **1943** A British-American unit must fight the Germans for their survival in the Libyan desert during WWII. Plenty of action and suspense combined with good performances makes this one a step above the usual war movie. **97m/B VHS, Beta.** Humphrey Bogart, Dan Duryea, Bruce (Herman Brix) Bennett, Lloyd Bridges, Rex Ingram, J. Carrol Naish, Richard Nugent, Miklos Rozsa; ***D:*** Zoltan Korda. Nominations: Academy Awards '43: Best Black and White Cinematography, Best Sound, Best Supporting Actor (Naish). *COL*

Sahara *Woof!* **1983 (PG)** Disappointing "Perils of Pauline" type adventure. Shields disguises herself as a man (sure) to complete a race across the desert in honor of her late father, and a sheik captures her. **111m/C VHS, Beta, LV.** Brooke Shields, Lambert Wilson, Horst Buchholz, John Rhys-Davies, Ronald Lacey, John Mills, Steve Forrest, Perry Lang, Cliff Potts; ***D:*** Andrew V. McLaglen; ***W:*** James R. Silke; ***M:*** Ennio Morricone. *MGM*

Saigon Commandos 🦴 **1988 (R)** Commandos, on the eve of the fall of Saigon in the 1970s, attempt to prevent heroin dealers from toppling the already-shaky government. So-so war/action flick. **84m/C VHS, Beta, LV.** Richard Young, P.J. Soles, John Allen Nelson, Jimi B Jr.; ***D:*** Clark Henderson. *MED*

Saigon: Year of the Cat 🦴 **1987** A made for British television drama about an American ambassador, a CIA operative, and a British bank clerk who try to leave Saigon in 1974 before the Vietcong enter the city. **106m/C VHS, Beta.** *GB* Frederic Forrest, E.G. Marshall, Judi Dench; ***D:*** Stephen Frears; ***W:*** David Hare; ***M:*** George Fenton. *HBO*

Sailing Along 🦴🦴 **1938** British musical about a young starlet who sacrifices her career for true love. **80m/B VHS.** *GB* Jessie Matthews, Barry Mackay, Jack Whiting, Roland Young, Noel Madison, Athene Seyler, Patrick Barr; ***D:*** Sonnie Hale. *FCT*

Sailor-Made Man/Grandma's Boy 🦴🦴🦴 **192?** Silent comedy shorts. In "A Sailor-Made Man" (1921) Lloyd joins the Navy. As shy "Grandma's Boy" (1922), he is given courage and good advice to win the hand of a girl and defeat a bully. **83m/B VHS, Beta.** Harold Lloyd. *TLF*

The Sailor Who Fell from Grace with the Sea 🦴🦴 **1976 (R)** Perverse tale of a disillusioned sailor who rejects the sea for the love of a lonely young widow and her troubled son. Graphic sexual scenes. Based on the novel by Yukio Mishima, the film suffers from the transition of Japanese culture to an English setting. **105m/C VHS, Beta, LV.** *GB* Sarah Miles, Kris Kristofferson, Jonathan Kahn, Margo Cunningham; ***D:*** Lewis John Carlino; ***W:*** Lewis John Carlino. *FOX, SUE*

The Saint 🦴🦴 **1968** Moore is Simon Templar, Leslie Charteris' mysterious British detective/hero in this adventure tale that takes him to Naples. Revival of and improvement on earlier movie series, and based on the very popular British television show. **98m/C VHS.** *GB* Roger Moore, Ian Hendry. *FOX*

St. Benny the Dip 🦴🦴½ *Escape If You Can* **1951** Three con-men evade police by posing as clergymen, and end up going straight after a series of adventures in a skid row mission. Funny in parts but extremely predictable. Still, good for a few laughs. **80m/B VHS.** Dick Haymes, Nina Foch, Roland Young, Lionel Stander, Freddie Bartholomew; ***D:*** Edgar G. Ulmer. *NOS, FCT, HEG*

St. Elmo's Fire 🦴🦴½ **1985 (R)** Seven Georgetown graduates confront adult problems during their first post-graduate year. Reminiscent of "The Big Chill," but a weak story wastes lots of talent and time. **110m/C VHS, Beta, LV.** Rob Lowe, Demi Moore, Andrew McCarthy, Judd Nelson, Ally Sheedy, Emilio Estevez, Mare Winningham, Martin Balsam, Jenny Wright, Joyce Van Patten, Andie MacDowell, Anna Maria Horsford; ***D:*** Joel Schumacher; ***W:*** Joel Schumacher; ***C:*** Stephen Burum; ***M:*** David Foster. Golden Raspberry Awards '85: Worst Supporting Actor (Lowe). *COL*

St. Helen's, Killer Volcano 🦴🦴½ **1982** A young man and an old man develop a deep friendship amid the devastation, fear, greed, and panic surrounding the eruption of the Mt. St. Helen's volcano. Based on the true story of Harry Truman (!), who refused to leave his home. Pretty good. **95m/C VHS, Beta.** Art Carney, David Huffman, Cassie Yates, Bill McKinney, Ron O'Neal, Albert Salmi, Cesare Danova; ***D:*** Ernie Pintoff. *VES*

The Saint in London 🦴🦴 **1939** The Saint investigates a gang trying to pass counterfeit banknotes. The third in "The Saint" series. **72m/B VHS, Beta.** George Sanders, Sally Gray; ***D:*** John Paddy Carstairs. *MED*

The Saint in New York 🦴🦴 **1938** The Saint, Simon Templar, turns Robin Hood to help the Civic Committee clean up a gang of desperados. First of "The Saint" series. **71m/B VHS, Beta.** Louis Hayward, Kay Sutton, Jack Carson, Charles Halton; ***D:*** Ben Holmes. *MED*

St. Ives 🦴🦴 **1976 (PG)** Former police reporter Bronson agrees to recover some stolen ledgers and finds himself dealing with betrayal and murder. Bisset is sultry and the tale is slickly told, but dumb. Costars Travanti, later of TV's "Hill Street Blues." **94m/C VHS, Beta.** Charles Bronson, Jacqueline Bisset, John Houseman, Harry Guardino, Maximilian Schell, Harris Yulin, Elisha Cook Jr., Daniel J. Travanti; ***D:*** J. Lee Thompson; ***W:*** Barry Beckerman; ***M:*** Lalo Schifrin. *WAR*

Saint Jack 🦴🦴🦴 **1979 (R)** The story of a small-time pimp with big dreams working the pleasure palaces of late-night Singapore. Engrossing and pleasant. Based on Paul Theroux's novel. **112m/C VHS, Beta.** Ben Gazzara, Denholm Elliott, Joss Ackland, George Lazenby; ***D:*** Peter Bogdanovich; ***W:*** Peter Bogdanovich. *LIV, VES*

Saint Joan 🦴🦴 **1957** Film of the George Bernard Shaw play, adapted by Graham Greene, about the French Maid of Orleans at her trial. Otto Preminger went on a nationwide talent hunt for his leading actress and chose the inexperienced Seberg (her screen debut). A good thing for her career, but not for this ill-begotten, overambitious opus. Seberg doesn't fit. Also available colorized. **131m/B VHS, Beta.** Jean Seberg, Anton Walbrook, Richard Widmark, John Gielgud, Harry Andrews, Felix Aylmer, Richard Todd; ***D:*** Otto Preminger; ***C:*** Georges Perinal. *WAR*

The Saint of Fort Washington 🦴🦴½ **1993 (R)** Sweetly naive and schizophrenic Matthew (Dillon) is homeless and through government screw-ups is sent to the Fort Washington Armory, which houses more than 700 homeless men. Harassed by others, Matthew is befriended by Jerry, a kindly Vietnam vet, who tries to care for him. Subject is taken seriously but slips into mawkishness; good performances by the leads. **104m/C VHS, Beta, LV.** Danny Glover, Matt Dillon, Rick Aviles, Nina Siemaszko, Ving Rhames, Joe Seneca; ***D:*** Tim Hunter; ***W:*** Lyle Kessler; ***M:*** James Newton Howard. *WAR*

The Saint Strikes Back 🦴🦴 **1939** Sanders debuts as the mysterious Simon Templar in this competent series. On a trip to San Francisco, the Saint aims to clear the name of a murdered man. The second in the series. **67m/B VHS.** George Sanders, Wendy Barrie, Jonathan Hale, Jerome Cowan, Neil Hamilton, Barry Fitzgerald, Edward Gargan, Robert Strange; ***D:*** John Farrow. *MOV*

The Saint Strikes Back: Criminal Court 🦴🦴 **1946** A suspense double feature: The Saint helps a daughter clear the name of her murdered father, a San Francisco police commissioner in "The Saint Strikes Back," and a young lawyer becomes involved in murder in "Criminal Court." **127m/B VHS, Beta.** George Sanders, Wendy Barrie, Barry Fitzgerald, Tom Conway, Steve Brodie; ***D:*** John Farrow. *TTC*

The Saint Takes Over 🦴🦴 **1940** More adventures with the British mystery man; this time involving racetrack gambling. An original story that wasn't based on a Leslie Charteris novel as were the others. **69m/B VHS.** George Sanders, Jonathan Hale, Wendy Barrie, Paul Guilfoyle, Morgan Conway, Cy Kendall; ***D:*** Jack Hively. *MOV*

The St. Tammany Miracle 🦴🦴½ **1994** Predictable, good-natured sports film about young coach Lootie Pfannder (Luner) who takes a job at a prep school and turns the losing girls basketball team into winners. Her broadcaster boyfriend Carl (Gosselaar) thinks she's crazy but aided by her assistant (Frye), Lootie is determined to prove everyone wrong. **90m/C VHS.** Jamie Luner, Mark Paul Gosselaar, Soleil Moon Frye, Jeffrey Meek, Julie McCullough; ***Cameos:*** Steve Allen; ***D:*** Joy Houck Jr.; ***W:*** Jim McCullough Jr.; ***M:*** Jay Weigel. *VCI*

The St. Valentine's Day Massacre 🦴🦴½ **1967** Corman's big studio debut recreates the events leading to one of the most violent gangland shootouts in modern history: the bloodbath between Chicago's Capone and Moran gangs on February 14, 1929. Uninspired and unremittingly violent. Watch for Jack Nicholson's bit part. **100m/C VHS, Beta.** Jason Robards Jr., Ralph Meeker, Jean Hale, Joseph Campanella, Bruce Dern, Clint Ritchie, Richard Bakalayan, George Segal; ***D:*** Roger Corman; ***C:*** Milton Krasner. *FOX, FCT*

Saints and Sinners 🦴½ **1995 (R)** Street-smart "Pooch" Puccia (Chapa) returns to his 'hood as an undercover cop to set up childhood buddy, drug dealer Big Boy Baynes (Plank), and winds up getting involved with seductive bad girl Eve (Rubin), who's also bedding Baynes. Then Pooch discovers his police contact is in the pay of the mob, so does he go through with the deal or not? Lots of macho posturing (attractive actors). **99m/C VHS, LV.** Damian Chapa, Scott Plank, Jennifer Rubin, Damon Whitaker, Panchito Gomez, William Atherton; ***D:*** Paul Mones; ***W:*** Paul Mones; ***C:*** Michael Bonvillain. *LIV*

The Saint's Double Trouble 🦴🦴 **1940** Leslie Charteris' suave detective becomes embroiled in another mystery, this one involving jewel thieves. Sanders plays a dual role as the hero and the crook. The fourth in the series. **68m/B VHS.** George Sanders, Helene Whitney, Jonathan Hale, Bela Lugosi, Donald MacBride, John Hamilton; ***D:*** Jack Hively. *MED*

The Saint's Vacation/The Narrow Margin **1952** A mystery double feature. In "The Saint's Vacation," Simon Templar prevents a valuable secret from getting into the wrong hands, and in "The Narrow Margin," strange things happen to a detective when he takes a train ride with a witness to Chicago. Sinclair took over the sleuth's role from George Sanders in this series. **148m/B VHS, Beta.** Hugh Sinclair, Sally Gray, Charles McGraw, Marie Windsor, Jacqueline White. *TTC*

Sakharov 🦴🦴🦴 **1984** The true story of the Russian physicist who designed the H-bomb and then rose to lead the Soviet dissident movement and win the Nobel Peace Prize. Robards is excellent. Made for cable; topical and powerful. **120m/C VHS, Beta.** Glenda Jackson, Jason Robards Jr., Michael Bryant; ***D:*** Jack Gold; ***M:*** Carl Davis. *PSM*

Sakura Killers 🦴 **1986** Killer Ninjas steal a valuable gene-splicing formula and are hunted down by an American colonel. **87m/C VHS, Beta.** Chuck Connors, Mike Kelly, Brian Wong, Thomas Lung; ***D:*** Richard Ward. *FOX*

Salaam Bombay! 🦴🦴🦴 **1988** A gritty film about a child street beggar in the slums of Bombay trying to raise enough money to return to his mother's house in the country. The boy experiences every variety of gutter life imaginable, from humiliation to love. Moving and searing. Filmed on location, with actual homeless children; Nair's first feature. In Hindi with subtitles. **114m/C VHS, Beta, LV.** *IN GB* Shafiq Syed, Hansa Vithal, Chanda Sharma, Nana Patekar, Aneeta Kanwar, Sarfuddin Quarassi, Raju Barnad, Raghubir Yadav; ***D:*** Mira Nair; ***W:*** Sooni Taraporevala; ***C:*** Sandi Sissel; ***M:*** L. Subramaniam. Nominations: Academy Awards '88: Best Foreign Language Film. *NO*

The Salamander 🦴½ **1982 (R)** A French detective tries to find the assassin of the leaders of a neo-fascist underground movement in Italy and follows clues that lead back to WWII. Disappointing, overwrought adaptation of a Morris West novel.

101m/C VHS, Beta. *GB* Franco Nero, Anthony Quinn, Martin Balsam, Sybil Danning, Christopher Lee, Cleavon Little, Paul Smith, Claudia Cardinale, Eli Wallach; ***D:*** Peter Zinner; ***M:*** Jerry Goldsmith. *NLC*

Salammbo 🦴🦴½ **1914** An early silent epic in the grand Italian tradition. Loosely based on Flaubert's novel about ancient Carthage. **49m/B VHS, Beta.** *IT* Ernesto Pagani; ***D:*** Giovanni Pastrone. *FCT*

Salem's Lot 🦴🦴½ *Blood Thirst* **1979 (PG)** Based on Stephen King's novel about a sleepy New England village which is infiltrated by evil. A mysterious antiques dealer takes up residence in a forbidding hilltop house—and it becomes apparent that a vampire is on the loose. Generally creepy; Mason is good, but Soul only takes up space in the lead as a novelist returning home. Also available in the original television miniseries version at 190 minutes on two cassettes. **112m/C VHS, Beta, LV.** David Soul, James Mason, Lance Kerwin, Bonnie Bedelia, Lew Ayres, Ed Flanders, Elisha Cook Jr., Reggie Nalder, Fred Willard, Kenneth McMillan, Marie Windsor; ***D:*** Tobe Hooper. *WAR*

Sallah 🦴🦴🦴 **1963** A North African Jew takes his family to Israel in 1949 in hopes of making his fortune. He finds himself in a transit camp and runs up against the local bureaucracy in a quest for permanent housing as well as the European work ethic. Amusing and enjoyable satire. In Hebrew with English subtitles. **105m/B VHS, Beta.** *IS* Chaim Topol, Geula Noni, Gila Almagor, Arik Einstein, Shraga Friedman, Esther Greenberg; ***D:*** Ephraim Kishon; ***C:*** Floyd Crosby. Golden Globe Awards '65: Best Foreign Film; Nominations: Academy Awards '64: Best Foreign Language Film. *MOV, ERG, NCJ*

Sally of the Sawdust 🦴🦴½ **1925** W. C. Fields' first silent feature; he is a carnival barker who adopts a young woman. Allows him to demonstrate his talent for juggling, conning customers, and car chasing. Interesting movie caught director Griffith on the decline and Fields on the verge of stardom. Remade as a talkie in 1936 entitled "Poppy." Includes musical score. **124m/B VHS, Beta.** W.C. Fields, Carol Dempster, Alfred Lunt; ***D:*** D.W. Griffith. *NOS, VYY, CCB*

Salmonberries 🦴½ **1991 (R)** East German Roswitha (Zech) is devastated when her lover is killed trying to scale the Berlin Wall. She manages to escape and finds herself stuck in a remote Eskimo community in Alaska where she becomes involved with Kotzebue (lang in her film debut), who poses as a man to work on the Alaskan pipeline. The title has something to do with preserved berries—don't bother, it makes about as much sense as the entire movie. English and German with English subtitles. **94m/C VHS.** *GE CA* Rosel Zech, k.d. lang, Chuck Connors; ***D:*** Percy Adlon; ***W:*** Percy Adlon, Felix Adlon. *FCT*

Salo, or the 120 Days of Sodom 🦴🦴 **1975** Extremely graphic film follows sixteen children (eight boys and eight girls) who are kidnapped by a group of men in Fascist Italy. On reaching a secluded villa in the woods, the children are told to follow strict rules and then subjected to incredible acts of sadomasochism, rape, violence, and mutilation. This last film of Pasolini's was taken from a novel by the Marquis de Sade. Viewers are strongly recommended to use their utmost discretion when watching this controversial film. In Italian with English subtitles. **117m/C VHS, LV.** *IT* Giorgio Cataldi, Umberto P. Quinavalle, Paolo Bonacelli; ***D:*** Pier Paolo Pasolini; ***C:*** Tonino Delli Colli; ***M:*** Ennio Morricone. *INJ, FCT, HHE*

Salome 🦴🦴½ **1922** Garish silent rendition of Oscar Wilde's scandalous tale. **54m/B VHS, Beta.** Alla Nazimova, Rose Dione, Mitchell Lewis, Earl Schenck; ***D:*** Charles Bryant. *GPV, FCT, VYY*

Salome 🦴🦴 **1953** An over-costumed version of Oscar Wilde's Biblical story about King Herod's lascivious stepdaughter who danced her way to stardom and tried to save the life of John the Baptist. Talented cast can't overcome hokey script. **103m/C VHS, Beta.** Rita Hayworth, Stewart Granger, Charles Laughton, Judith Anderson, Cedric Hardwicke, Basil Sydney, Maurice Schwartz; ***D:*** William Dieterle; ***C:*** Charles B(ryant) Lang; ***M:*** George Duning. *COL, CCB*

Salome 🦴½ **1985 (R)** An updated and graphic version of the Oscar Wilde historical fantasy about the temptress Salome who helped topple Herod's Biblical kingdom with her dance of the Seven Veils. Photographed by Pasqualino De Santis. Not really a remake of the 1953 film since this is set during the 1940s. **100m/C VHS, Beta.** Jo Ciampa, Tomas Milian, Pamela Salem; ***D:*** Claude D'Anna. *MGM*

Salome/Queen Elizabeth **1923** Two famous silent shorts: "Salome," (1923), an atmospheric adaptation of Oscar Wilde's tale, with sets designed after Aubrey Beardsley; and "Queen Elizabeth," (1912), Bernhardt's famous, and famously stilted, singular film appearance. **91m/B VHS, Beta, 8mm.** Alla Nazimova, Sarah Bernhardt, Lou Tellegen, Mitchell Lewis, Nigel de Brulier; ***D:*** Charles Bryant, Henri Desfontaines, Louis Mercanton. *VYY*

Salome, Where She Danced 🦴 **1945** Set during the Franco-Prussian war. A European dancer helps an American reporter in a spy scheme. She eventually relocates to America and becomes the toast of San Francisco. Somehow, De Carlo managed to spring from this ridiculous camp outing to stardom. **90m/C VHS, Beta.** Yvonne De Carlo, Rod Cameron, David Bruce, Walter Slezak; ***D:*** Charles Lamont; ***C:*** William Howard Greene, Hal Mohr. *NOS, BAR, DVT*

Salome's Last Dance 🦴🦴 **1988 (R)** A theatrical, set-surreal adaptation of the Wilde story. Typically flamboyant Russell. **113m/C VHS, Beta, LV.** Glenda Jackson, Stratford Johns, Nickolas Grace, Douglas Hodge, Imogen Millais Scott; ***D:*** Ken Russell; ***W:*** Ken Russell. *LIV, IME, VES*

Salsa 🦴🦴 **1988 (PG)** An auto repairman would rather dance in this "Dirty Dancing" clone. Rosa was formerly a member of the pop group Menudo. **97m/C VHS, Beta, LV.** Robby Rosa, Rodney Harvey, Magali Alvarado, Miranda Garrison, Moon Orona; ***D:*** Boaz Davidson; ***W:*** Boaz Davidson, Tomas Benitez. *MGM, CAN*

Salt of the Earth 🦴🦴🦴½ **1954** Finally available in this country after being suppressed for thirty years, this controversial film was made by a group of blacklisted filmmakers during the McCarthy era. It was deemed anti-American, communist propaganda. The story deals with the anti-Hispanic racial strife that occurs in a New Mexico zinc mine when union workers organize a strike. **94m/B VHS, Beta, LV, CD-I.** Rosaura Revueltas, Will Geer, David Wolfe; ***D:*** Herbert Biberman. *IHF, NOS, MPI*

Salty 🦴🦴 **1973** A lovable but mischievous sea lion manages to complicate two brothers' lives when they volunteer to help a friend renovate a Florida marina, which is threatened by a mortgage foreclosure. Straightforward and inoffensive tale. **93m/C VHS, Beta.** Clint Howard, Mark Slade, Nina Foch; ***D:*** Ricou Browning. *NO*

Salut l'Artiste 🦴🦴🦴 **1974** Two bad actors try to make it in the industry. Delightfully funny with an excellent cast, especially Mastroianni. Snide and irreverant, yet loving and comic look at the world of acting. In French with English subtitles. **96m/C VHS.** *FR* Marcello Mastroianni, Jean Rochefort, Francoise Fabian, Carla Gravina; ***D:*** Yves Robert; ***M:*** Vladimir Cosma. *FCT, INJ, CVC*

Salute John Citizen 🦴🦴🦴 **1942** The life of an average English family during the early days of WWII is depicted, focusing on the deprivation and horror of the Nazi blitzkrieg. **74m/B VHS, Beta.** Peggy Cummins, Stanley Holloway, Dinah Sheridan, Jimmy Hanley. *VYY*

Salute to the "King of the Cowboys," Roy Rogers **197?** Glimpses of Roy from song clips, home movies, trailers, outtakes, and other sources. **60m/B VHS, Beta.** Roy Rogers. *DVT*

Salvador 🦴🦴🦴½ **1986 (R)** Photo journalist Richard Boyle's unflinching and sordid adventures in war-torn El Salvador. Boyle (Woods) must face the realities of social injustice. Belushi and Woods are hard to like, but excellent. Early critical success for director Stone. **123m/C VHS, Beta, LV.** James Woods, James Belushi, John Savage, Michael Murphy, Elpidia Carrillo, Cynthia Gibb; ***D:*** Oliver Stone; ***W:*** Oliver Stone, Richard Boyle; ***C:*** Robert Richardson; ***M:*** Georges Delerue. Independent Spirit Awards '87: Best Actor (Woods); Nominations: Academy Awards '86: Best Actor (Woods), Best Original Screenplay. *LIV, IME, VES*

Salvation! 🦴🦴½ *Salvation! Have You Said Your Prayers Today?* **1987 (R)** A mean-tempered, timely satire about a money-hungry television evangelist beset by a family of fervent, equally money-hungry followers, who proceed to cheat, seduce and blackmail him. Occasionally quite funny, but sloppy and predictable. Underground director Beth B's first aboveground film. **80m/C Beta.** Stephen McHattie, Exene Cervenka, Dominique Davalos, Viggo Mortensen, Rockets Redglare, Billy Bastiani; ***D:*** Beth B; ***W:*** Beth B. *NO*

The Salzburg Connection 🦴½ **1972 (PG)** A list of Nazi collaborators is discovered in Austria. A vacationing American lawyer is caught up in the battle for its possession. Filmed on location, it's still a poor, cheesy adaptation of the Helen MacInnes novel. **94m/C VHS, Beta.** Barry Newman, Anna Karina, Klaus Maria Brandauer, Karen Jensen; ***D:*** Lee H. Katzin. *FOX*

Samantha 🦴🦴½ **1992 (PG)** Twenty-one year-old Samantha discovers she was left on her parents' doorstep in a basket and decides to find out where she came from. Good cast and high charm quotient help this film along. **101m/C VHS, Beta.** Martha Plimpton, Dermot Mulroney, Hector Elizondo, Mary Kay Place, Ione Skye; ***D:*** Steven La Rocque; ***W:*** John Golden, Steven La Rocque. *ACA*

Samar 🦴🦴½ **1962 (PG)** A liberal penal colony commandant rebels against his superiors by leading his prisoners through the Philippine jungles to freedom. Original action drama with an interesting premise. **89m/C VHS, Beta.** George Montgomery, Gilbert Roland, Joan O'Brien, Ziva Rodann; ***D:*** George Montgomery. *NOS*

Samaritan: The Mitch Snyder Story 🦴🦴🦴 **1986** Effective television drama based upon the true story of Vietnam vet Mitch Snyder (Sheen) who battles various government agencies and ultimately fasts to call national attention to his crusade against homelessness. Tyson appears as bag lady; Snyder eventually committed suicide. **90m/C VHS, Beta.** Martin Sheen, Roxanne Hart, Joe Seneca, Stan Shaw, Cicely Tyson; ***D:*** Richard T. Heffron. *FRH*

Same Time, Next Year 🦴🦴🦴 **1978** A chance meeting between an accountant and a housewife results in a sometimes tragic, always sentimental 25-year affair in which they meet only one weekend each year. Well-cast leads carry warm, touching story based on the Broadway play by Bernard Slade. **119m/C VHS, Beta, LV.** Ellen Burstyn, Alan Alda; ***D:*** Robert Mulligan; ***C:*** Robert L. Surtees; ***M:*** Marvin Hamlisch. Golden Globe Awards '79: Best Actress—Musical/Comedy (Burstyn); Nominations: Academy Awards '78: Best Actress (Burstyn), Best Adapted Screenplay, Best Cinematography, Best Song ("The Last Time I Felt Like This"). *MCA*

Sammy & Rosie Get Laid 🦴🦴🦴 **1987** An unusual social satire about a sexually liberated couple living in London whose lives are thrown into turmoil by the arrival of the man's father - a controversial politician in India. Provides a confusing look at sexual and class collisions. From the makers of "My Beautiful Launderette." **97m/C VHS, Beta, LV.** *GB* Shashi Kapoor, Frances Barber, Claire Bloom, Ayub Khan Din, Roland Gift, Wendy Gazelle, Meera Syal; ***D:*** Stephen Frears; ***W:*** Hanif Kureishi; ***M:*** Stanley Myers. *ORI, WAR*

Sammy, the Way-Out Seal 🦴🦴 **1962** Two young boys bring a mischievous seal to live in their beach house and try to keep it a secret from their parents. Disney in its early '60s phase. **89m/C VHS, Beta.** Michael McGreevey, Billy Mumy, Patricia Barry, Robert Culp; ***D:*** Norman Tokar. *DIS*

Sam's Son 🦴🦴 **1984 (PG)** Sentimental, autobiographical tale about how a young man's athletic prowess opens the door for an acting career in Hollywood. Good performance by Wallach as the boy's father. Self-indulgent, though entertaining. **107m/C VHS, Beta.** Eli Wallach, Anne Jackson, Timothy Patrick Murphy, Hallie Todd, James Karen, Allan Hayes, Joanna Lee,

Michael Landon; **D:** Michael Landon; **W:** Michael Landon. *WOV*

Samson 🦴 **1961** Samson attempts to keep wits and hair about him. **90m/C VHS.** *IT* Brad Harris, Brigitte Corey, Alan Steel, Serge Gainsbourg, Mara Berni; **D:** Gianfranco Parolini. *SNC, MRV*

Samson Against the Sheik **1962** Samson survives long enough to battle a sheik in the Middle Ages. **?m/C VHS, Beta.** *IT* Ed Fury. *SNC*

Samson and Delilah 🦴🦴🦴 **1950** The biblical story of the vindictive Delilah, who after being rejected by the mighty Samson, robbed him of his strength by shearing his curls. Delivered in signature DeMille style. Wonderfully fun and engrossing. Mature is excellent. **128m/C VHS, Beta, LV.** Victor Mature, Hedy Lamarr, Angela Lansbury, George Sanders, Henry Wilcoxon, Olive Deering, Fay Holden; **D:** Cecil B. DeMille; **C:** George Barnes. Academy Awards '50: Best Art Direction/Set Decoration (Color), Best Costume Design (Color); Nominations: Academy Awards '50: Best Color Cinematography, Best Original Score. *PAR*

Samson and Delilah 🦴🦴 **1984** A made for television version of the Biblical romance, semi-based on DeMille's 1950 version. Original Samson (Mature) plays Samson's father. Too long but inoffensive; see the DeMille version instead. **95m/C VHS, Beta.** Antony Hamilton, Belinda Bauer, Max von Sydow, Jose Ferrer, Victor Mature, Maria Schell; **D:** Lee Philips; **M:** Maurice Jarre. *PSM*

Samson and His Mighty Challenge 🦴½ **1964** In this rarely seen muscle epic, Hercules, Maciste, Samson and Ursus all take part in a battle royale. **?m/C VHS, Beta.** *IT* Alan Steel. *SNC*

Samson and the 7 Miracles of the World 🦴🦴 *Maciste Alla Corte Del Gran Khan; Maciste at the Court of the Great Khan; Goliath and the Golden City* **1962** This time the hero known as Maciste (renamed Samson for Americans) is in the 13th century battling brutal Tartar warlords. The very Earth itself shakes when our hero goes into battle! **80m/C VHS, Beta.** *FR IT* Gordon Scott, Yoko Tani, Gabriele Antonini, Leonardo Severini, Valeri Inkizhinov, Helene Chanel; **D:** Riccardo (Robert Hampton) Freda; **M:** Les Baxter. *SNC*

Samson in the Wax Museum 🦴½ *Santo en el Museo de Cera; Santo in the Wax Museum* **1963** Masked Mexican wrestling hero Santo (here called Samson) does battle with a scientist who has discovered a way to make wax monsters come to life. **92m/B VHS.** *MX* Santo, Claudio Brook, Ruben Rojo, Norma Mora, Roxana Bellini; **D:** Alfonso Corona Blake. *SNC, HHT*

Samson vs. the Vampire Women 🦴½ **1961** Santo (here called Samson) the masked hero and athlete, battles the forces of darkness as a horde of female vampires attempt to make an unsuspecting girl their next queen. **89m/B VHS, Beta.** *MX* Santo, Lorena Velasquez, Jaime Fernandez, Maria Duval; **D:** Alfonso Corona Blake. *SNC, HHT*

Samurai 🦴 **1945** Truly bad spy-exploitation film about a Japanese orphan who was raised in America, turns traitor, and helps plot the invasion of California. **?m/C VHS.** Paul Fung, Luke Chan, David Chow. *SNC, TPV*

Samurai 1: Musashi Miyamoto 🦴🦴🦴½ **1955** The first installment in the film version of Musashi Miyamoto's life, as he leaves his 17th century village as a warrior in a local civil war only to return beaten and disillusioned. Justly award-winning. In Japanese with English subtitles. **92m/C VHS, Beta, LV.** *JP* Toshiro Mifune; **D:** Hiroshi Inagaki. Academy Awards '55: Best Foreign Language Film. *NLC, SUE, INJ*

Samurai 2: Duel at Ichijoji Temple 🦴🦴🦴½ **1955** Inagaki's second film depicting the life of Musashi Miyamoto, the 17th century warrior, who wandered the disheveled landscape of feudal Japan looking for glory and love. In Japanese with English subtitles. **102m/C VHS, Beta, LV.** *JP* Toshiro Mifune; **D:** Hiroshi Inagaki. *NLC, SUE, INJ*

Samurai 3: Duel at Ganryu Island 🦴🦴🦴½ **1956** The final film of Inagaki's trilogy, in which Musashi Miyamoto confronts his lifelong enemy in a climactic battle. Depicts Miyamoto's spiritual awakening and realization that love and hatred exist in all of us. In Japanese with English subtitles. **102m/C VHS, Beta, LV.** *JP* Toshiro Mifune, Koji Tsurata; **D:** Hiroshi Inagaki. *SUE, INJ, NLC*

Samurai Cowboy 🦴🦴 **1993** Sato (Go) is a successful Japanese businessman who worships the American western ideal so he decides to give up the rat race by moving to Running Moose, Montana, and buying a cattle ranch. Talk about culture shock! Inoffensive fish-out-of-water comedy. Go is a popular singer in his native Japan. **101m/C VHS.** Hiromi Go, Catherine Mary Stewart, Robert Conrad, Conchata Ferrell, Matt McCoy; **D:** Michael Keusch; **W:** Michael Keusch; **M:** Osamu Kitajima. *MNC*

Samurai Reincarnation **1981** After the Shogunate government kills 18,000 Christian rioters in the revolt of 1638, and publicly beheads the leader Shiro Amakusa, Shiro reincarnates during a monstrous thunderstorm. Consumed with hatred, he discards the teachings of Jesus Christ and seeks revenge. In Japanese with English subtitles. **122m/C VHS.** *JP* **D:** Kinji Fukasaku. *FCT*

San Antonio 🦴🦴 **1945** A bad girl working in a dance hall turns over a new leaf on meeting the good guy. Trite plot, but good production. **105m/C VHS, Beta.** Errol Flynn, Alexis Smith, S.Z. Sakall, Victor Francen, Florence Bates, John Litel, Paul Kelly; **D:** David Butler; **M:** Max Steiner. Nominations: Academy Awards '45: Best Interior Decoration, Best Song ("Some Sunday Morning"). *MGM, FCT, MLB*

San Demetrio, London 🦴🦴½ **1947** Set in 1940, the crew of a crippled tanker endures harrowing situations to reach port. A decent anti-war movie in its time, it's now showing its age. Based on a true story, the plot sags with unbelievable scenes and holes on the plot side. **76m/B VHS.** Walter Fitzgerald, Mervyn Johns, Ralph Michael, Robert Beatty, Charles Victor, Frederick Piper; **D:** Charles Frend. *NOS*

San Fernando Valley 🦴🦴 **1944** Also called "San Fernando". Another lawman-in-evil-town epic. Rogers received his first on-screen kiss in 1944's biggest western. Fairly typical, pleasant cowboy tale. **54m/B VHS, Beta.** Roy Rogers, Dale Evans. *NOS, DVT*

San Francisco 🦴🦴🦴½ **1936** The San Francisco Earthquake of 1906 serves as the background for a romance between an opera singer and a Barbary Coast saloon owner. Somewhat overdone but gripping tale of passion and adventure in the West. Wonderful special effects. Finale consists of historic earthquake footage. Also available colorized. ♫San Francisco; A Heart That's Free; Would You?; Air des Bijoux; Sempre Libera. **116m/B VHS, Beta, LV.** Jeanette MacDonald, Clark Gable, Spencer Tracy, Jack Holt, Jessie Ralph, Al Shear; **D:** Woodbridge S. Van Dyke; **W:** Anita Loos. Academy Awards '36: Best Sound; Nominations: Academy Awards '36: Best Actor (Tracy), Best Director (Van Dyke), Best Picture, Best Story. *MGM*

Sanctuary of Fear 🦴½ *Girl in the Park* **1979** A priest in New York City helps an actress subjected to a series of terrorizing incidents. Uninspired would-be TV pilot based on Chesterton's "Father Brown" series. **98m/C VHS, Beta.** George Hearn, Barnard Hughes, Kay Lenz, Michael McGuire, Robert Schenkkan, David Rasche, Fred Gwynne, Elizabeth Wilson; **D:** John Llewellyn Moxey. *FOX*

Sand and Blood 🦴🦴½ *Blood and Sand; De Sable et de Sang* **1987** A young matador who wishes to escape poverty and a young, cultivated doctor, who despises bullfighting, meet and eventually become friends. A woman enters the picture and completes the love triangle. Widely praised by critics. Interesting and moving. In French with English subtitles. **101m/C VHS, Beta.** *FR* Sami Frey, Andre Dussollier, Clementine Celarie, Patrick Catalifo, Maria Casares, Catherine Rouvel; **D:** Jeanne Labrune; **W:** Jeanne Labrune. *NYF, FCT, INJ*

The Sand Pebbles 🦴🦴🦴½ **1966** An American expatriate engineer, transferred to a gunboat on the Yangtze River in 1926, falls in love with a missionary teacher. As he becomes aware of the political climate of American imperialism, he finds himself at odds with his command structure; the treatment of this issue can be seen as commentary on the situation in Vietnam at the time of the film's release. Considered one of McQueen's best performances, blending action and romance. **193m/C VHS, Beta, LV.** Steve McQueen, Richard Crenna, Richard Attenborough, Candice Bergen, Marayat Andriane, Gavin MacLeod, Larry Gates, Mako, Simon Oakland; **D:** Robert Wise; **W:** Robert Anderson; **M:** Jerry Goldsmith. Golden Globe Awards '67: Best Supporting Actor (Attenborough); Nominations: Academy Awards '66: Best Actor (McQueen), Best Art Direction/Set Decoration (Color), Best Color Cinematography, Best Film Editing, Best Picture, Best Sound, Best Supporting Actor (Mako), Best Original Score. *FOX, FCT*

Sandakan No. 8 🦴🦴🦴 *Brothel 8; Sandakan House 8* **1974** A Japanese woman working as a journalist befriends an old woman who was sold into prostitution in Borneo in the early 1900s. Justly acclaimed feminist story dramatizes the role of women in Japanese society. Japanese with English subtitles. **121m/C VHS, Beta.** *JP* Kinuyo Tanaka, Yoko Takakashi, Komake Kurihara, Eitaro Ozawa; **D:** Kei Kumai. Berlin International Film Festival '75: Best Actress; Nominations: Academy Awards '75: Best Foreign Language Film. *FCT*

Sanders of the River 🦴🦴🦴 *Bosambo* **1935** A British officer in colonial Africa must work with the local chief to quell a rebellion. Tale of imperialism. Dated but still interesting and of value. Robeson is very good; superb location cinematography. **80m/B VHS, Beta.** *GB* Paul Robeson, Leslie Banks, Robert Cochran; **D:** Zoltan Korda; **C:** Georges Perinal. *NOS, SUE, VYY*

Sandflow 🦴🦴½ **1937** Well-made Western with Jones playing a man whose father has cheated many ranchers. Jones is out to avenge all of his father's misdeeds and build a new life for himself in this above-average oater. **58m/B VHS.** Buck Jones, Lita Chevret, Robert F. (Bob) Kortman, Arthur Aylesworth, Robert Terry, Enrique DeRosas; **D:** Lesley Selander. *GPV*

The Sandlot 🦴🦴🦴 **1993 (PG)** Young Scotty (Guiry) moves to a new neighborhood in California in 1962 and tries to make friends despite not knowing anything about playing baseball. His scrappy teammates include the friendly Benny (Vitar), a chubby loud-mouthed catcher named Ham (Renna), and Squints (Leopardi), a would-be Lothario before his time. Action revolves around Scotty's attempt to get baseball autographed by Babe Ruth out of the clutches of giant killer junkyard dog owned by Jones before dad Leary discovers it missing. Small wonder is nostalgic without being sentimental, and tells its tale with grace and humor, supported by a period soundtrack. **101m/C VHS, LV.** Tom Guiry, Mike Vitar, Patrick Renna, Chauncey Leopardi, Marty York, Brandon Adams, Karen Allen, James Earl Jones, Maury Wills, Art LaFleur, Marlee Shelton; **Cameos:** Denis Leary, Brooke Adams; **D:** David Mickey Evans; **W:** Robert Gunter, David Mickey Evans; **M:** David Newman; **V:** Arliss Howard. *FXV*

The Sandpiper 🦴🦴 **1965** Free-spirited artist Taylor falls in love with Burton, the married headmaster of her son's boarding school. Muddled melodrama offers little besides starpower. Filmed at Big Sur, California. ♫The Shadow of Your Smile. **117m/C VHS, Beta.** Elizabeth Taylor, Richard Burton, Charles Bronson, Eva Marie Saint, Robert Webber, Morgan Mason; **D:** Vincente Minnelli; **C:** Milton Krasner. Academy Awards '65: Best Song ("The Shadow of Your Smile"). *MGM*

Sandra of a Thousand Delights 🦴🦴 *Sandra; Of a Thousand Delights; Vaghe Stelle Dell'Orsa* **1965** Haunting drama with strong women (and weak men). Sandra returns to Italy from her American home in order to attend a ceremony honoring her father—a Jewish scientist who died in a Nazi concentration camp. Back with her family, Sandra tries to deal with her past, including her mother's possible betrayal of her father and her brother's incestuous longings. Italian with subtitles. **100m/B VHS.** *IT* Claudia Cardinale, Jean Sorel, Marie Bell, Michael Craig, Renzo Ricci; **D:** Luchino Visconti; ***W:*** Luchino Visconti, Suso Cecchi D'Amico; ***M:*** Cesar Franck. *FCT*

Sands of Iwo Jima 🦴🦴🦴½ **1949** Wayne earned his first Oscar nomination as a tough Marine sergeant, in one of his best roles. He trains a squad of rebellious recruits in New Zealand in 1943. Later they are responsible for the capture of Iwo Jima from the Japanese—one of the most difficult campaigns of the Pacific Theater. Includes striking real war footage. **109m/B VHS, LV.** John Wayne, Forrest Tucker, John Agar, Richard Jaeckel; ***D:*** Allan Dwan. Nominations: Academy Awards '46: Best Sound; Academy Awards '49: Best Actor (Wayne), Best Film Editing, Best Story. *REP, TLF, RDG*

Sands of Sacrifice 🦴🦴½ *Tangled Trails* **1921** Hart, a Northwest Mountie, seeks an unscrupulous promoter who's selling worthless mining stock. **56m/B VHS.** Neal Hart, Violet Palmer, Gladys Hampton, Jules Cowles, Jean Bary, Ed Roseman; ***D:*** Charles Bartlett. *GPV*

Sanjuro 🦴🦴🦴 *Tsubaki Sanjuro* **1962** In this offbeat, satiric sequel to "Yojimbo," a talented but lazy samurai comes to the aid of a group of naive young warriors. The conventional ideas of good and evil are quickly tossed aside; much less earnest than other Kurosawa Samurai outings. In Japanese with English subtitles. **96m/B VHS, Beta, LV.** *JP* Toshiro Mifune, Tatsuya Nakadai; ***D:*** Akira Kurosawa. *NOS, SUE, HHT*

Sans Soleil 🦴🦴🦴 *Sunless* **1982** A female narrator reads and comments on the letters she receives from a friend, a freelance cameraman traveling through Japan, West Africa, and Iceland. The cameraman meditates on the cultural dislocation he feels and the meaning of his work and of life itself. Both narrator and cameraman remain unseen with the visuals being the cameraman's work in progress. **100m/C VHS.** *FR* ***D:*** Chris Marker; ***W:*** Chris Marker. *NYF, BTV*

Sanshiro Sugata 🦴🦴🦴 **1943** Kurosawa's first film. A young man learns discipline in martial arts from a patient master. Climactic fight scene is early signature Kurosawa. In Japanese with English subtitles. **82m/B VHS.** *JP* Denjiro Okochi, Yukiko Todoroki, Ranko Hanai, Ryonosuke Tsukigata, Sugisaku Aoyama, Kokuten Kodo, Susumo Fusuita, Takashi Shimura; ***D:*** Akira Kurosawa. *FCT, INJ, COL*

Sansho the Bailiff 🦴🦴🦴🦴 *The Bailiff; Sansho Dayu* **1954** A world masterpiece by Mizoguchi about feudal society in 11th century Japan. A woman and her children are sold into prostitution and slavery. As an adult, the son seeks to right the ills of his society. Powerful and tragic, and often more highly esteemed than "Ugetsu." In Japanese with English subtitles. **132m/B VHS, Beta, LV.** *JP* Kinuyo Tanaka, Yoshiaki Hanayagi, Kyoko Kagawa, Eitaro Shindo, Ichiro Sugai; ***D:*** Kenji Mizoguchi; ***W:*** Yoshikata Yoda; ***M:*** Fumio Hayasaka. *HMV, INJ*

Santa Claus *Woof!* **1959** Santa Claus teams up with Merlin the Magician to fend off an evil spirit who would ruin everyone's Christmas. Mexican camp classic. **94m/C VHS, Beta.** *MX* Jose Elias Moreno, Cesareo Quezadas; ***D:*** Rene Cardona Sr. *SNC, MLB*

Santa Claus Conquers the Martians 🦴 *Santa Claus Defeats the Aliens* **1964** A Martian spaceship comes to Earth and kidnaps Santa Claus and two children. Martian kids, it seems, are jealous that Earth tykes have Christmas. Features then-child star Pia Zadora. **80m/C VHS, Beta.** John Call, Pia Zadora, Leonard Hicks, Vincent Beck, Victor Stiles, Donna Conforti; ***D:*** Nicholas Webster. *COL, SNC, SUE*

Santa Claus Is Coming to Town **1970** Kris Kringle takes you along on his quest to give toys to the citizens of Sombertown. An animated classic. **53m/C VHS, Beta, LV.** ***D:*** Arthur Rankin Jr., Jules Bass; ***V:*** Mickey Rooney, Keenan Wynn, Paul Frees. *FHE, WTA, LME*

Santa Claus: The Movie 🦴🦴 **1985 (PG)** A big-budgeted spectacle about an elf who falls prey to an evil toy maker and almost ruins Christmas and Santa Claus. Boring, 'tis-the-season fantasy-drama meant to warm our cockles. **112m/C VHS, Beta, LV.** Dudley Moore, John Lithgow, David Huddleston, Judy Cornwell, Burgess Meredith; ***D:*** Jeannot Szwarc; ***W:*** David Newman; ***M:*** Henry Mancini. *MED*

The Santa Clause 🦴🦴½ **1994 (PG)** If you like Allen, you'll enjoy this lightweight holiday comedy about divorced workaholic dad Scott Calvin and eight-year-old son Charlie (Lloyd). Seems Santa injures himself falling off the Calvin roof and dad winds up putting on Santa's suit. But as it turns out when you put on Santa's suit, you become Santa, including a noticeable weight gain, a fluffy beard, and all those reindeer and elves to deal with (but where's Mrs. Claus). **97m/C VHS.** Tim Allen, Eric Lloyd, Judge Reinhold, Wendy Crewson, David Krumholtz, Mary Gross; ***D:*** John Pasquin; ***W:*** Leo Benvenuti, Steve Rudnick; ***M:*** Michael Convertino. Blockbuster Entertainment Awards '95: Male Newcomer, Theatrical (Allen); Nominations: MTV Movie Awards '95: Breakthrough Performance (Allen), Best Comedic Performance (Allen). *TOU*

Santa Fe 🦴🦴 **1951** Action-packed western with Scott playing a Confederate soldier who heads West to take a job with the Santa Fe Railroad. However, his brothers, with their wounded rebel pride, have different ideas for forgetting the defeat. Refusing to take money from Northern businesses, they become outlaws. Based on a story by Louis Stevens and the novel by James Marshall. **89m/C VHS.** Randolph Scott, Janis Carter, Jerome Courtland, Peter Thompson, John Archer, Warner Anderson, Roy Roberts, Billy House; ***D:*** Irving Pichel; ***W:*** Kenneth Gamet. *COL*

Santa Fe Bound 🦴🦴 **1937** Tyler must work to clear his name when he is falsely accused of having murdered a man. **58m/B VHS.** Tom Tyler, Jeanne Martel, Richard Cramer, Charles "Slim" Whitaker, Edward Cassidy, Lafe McKee, Dorothy Woods, Charles "Blackie" King; ***D:*** Harry S. Webb. *DVT, HEG, GPV*

Santa Fe Marshal 🦴🦴 **1940** The 27th Hopalong Cassidy movie, if anyone's counting. In the title job the Hopster goes undercover with a medicine show to smash a criminal gang. A litle different than usual, right up to the surprise identity of the crooked mastermind. **66m/B VHS.** William Boyd, Russell Hayden, Marjorie Rambeau, Bernadene Hayes, Earle Hodgins, Kenneth Harlan, Eddie Dean; ***D:*** Lesley Selander. *NOS*

Santa Fe Stampede 🦴🦴½ **1938** The Three Mesquiteers join an old prospector in his claim but when he is killed, one of them (Wayne) is framed. The photography makes up for the weak story line and direction. **58m/B VHS.** John Wayne, Ray Corrigan, Max Terhune, William Farnum, June Martel, Leroy Mason, Yakima Canutt, Curly Dresden; ***D:*** George Sherman. *NOS*

Santa Fe Trail 🦴🦴½ **1940** Historically inaccurate but entertaining tale about the pre-Civil War fight for "bloody Kansas." The action-adventure depicts future Civil War Generals J.E.B. Stuart (Flynn) and George Armstrong Custer (Reagan!) as they begin their military career (although Custer was really just a youth at this time). Good action scenes. Also available colorized. **110m/B VHS, Beta.** Errol Flynn, Olivia de Havilland, Ronald Reagan, Van Heflin, Raymond Massey, Alan Hale; ***D:*** Michael Curtiz; ***M:*** Max Steiner. *MGM, NOS, PSM*

Santa Fe Uprising 🦴🦴½ **1946** Red Ryder has to save Little Beaver from kidnappers. Good first entry for Lane in the "Red Ryder" series. **54m/B VHS, Beta.** Allan "Rocky" Lane, Robert (Bobby) Blake. *MED*

Santa Sangre 🦴🦴🦴 **1990 (R)** A circus in Mexico City, a temple devoted to a saint without arms, and a son who faithfully dotes upon his armless mother are just a few of the bizarre things in this wildly fantastic film. Fenix acts as his mother's arms, plays the piano for her, and carries out any wish she desires—including murder. Visually intoxicating but strange outing may prove too graphic for some viewers. Not as rigorous as other Jodorowsky outings. Also available in an NC-17 version. **123m/C VHS, LV.** *IT MX* Axel Jodorowsky, Sabrina Dennison, Guy Stockwell, Blanca Guerra, Thelma Tixou, Adan Jodorowsky, Faviola Tapia, Jesus Juarez; ***D:*** Alejandro Jodorowsky; ***W:*** Robert Leoni, Claudio Argento, Alejandro Jodorowsky; ***M:*** Simon Boswell. *REP, FCT, INJ*

Santee 🦴🦴 **1973 (PG)** A father-son relationship develops between a bounty hunter and the son of a man he killed. Good, but not great, Western. **93m/C VHS, Beta.** Glenn Ford, Dana Wynter, Jay Silverheels, John Larch; ***D:*** Gary Nelson. *PSM, HHE*

The Saphead 🦴🦴½ **1921** Keaton's first outing as the rich playboy has him playing the none-to-bright son of a Wall Street mogul. Some great moments provide a glimpse of cinematic greatness to come from the budding comedic genius. Based on the play "The New Henrietta" by Winchell Smith and Victor Mapes. Silent. **70m/B VHS.** William H. Crane, Buster Keaton, Carol Holloway, Edward Connelly, Irving Cummings; ***D:*** Herbert Blache. *NO*

Sapphire 🦴🦴🦴 **1959** Two Scotland Yard detectives seek the killer of a beautiful black woman who was passing for white. Good mystery and topical social comment; remains interesting and engrossing. Superbly acted all around. **92m/C VHS, Beta.** *GB* Nigel Patrick, Yvonne Mitchell, Michael Craig, Paul Massie, Bernard Miles; ***D:*** Basil Dearden. British Academy Awards '59: Best Film. *NO*

Saps at Sea 🦴🦴½ **1940** A doctor advises Ollie to take a rest away from his job at a horn factory. He and Stan rent a boat, which they plan to keep tied to the dock, until an escaped criminal happens by and uses the boys (and their boat) for his getaway. Cramer is a good bad guy; Stan and Ollie cause too much trouble, as always. **57m/B VHS, Beta, LV.** Stan Laurel, Oliver Hardy, James Finlayson, Ben Turpin, Richard Cramer; ***D:*** Gordon Douglas. *CCB, MED, VTR*

Sara Dane 🦴🦴 **1981** A strong young woman in the 18th century rises in the world through marriage and business acumen. Interesting but imperfect and slow. **150m/C VHS, Beta.** *AU* Harold Hopkins, Brenton Whittle, Barry Quin, Sean Scully; ***D:*** Rod Hardy, Gary Conway. *PSM*

Sarafina! 🦴🦴🦴 **1992 (PG-13)** Part coming-of-age saga, part political drama, part musical, and all emotionally powerful. Sarafina is a young girl in a township school in Soweto, South Africa in the mid-'70s, gradually coming into a political awakening amid the Soweto riots. Khumalo recreates her stage role as the glowing and defiant Sarafina with both Goldberg and Makeba good in their roles as Sarafina's outspoken and inspirational teacher and her long-suffering mother, respectively. Adapted from Ngema's stage musical. **98m/C VHS, Beta, LV.** Leleti Khumalo, Whoopi Goldberg, Miriam Makeba, John Kani, Mbongeni Ngema; ***D:*** Darrell Roodt; ***W:*** Mbongeni Ngema, William Nicholson; ***M:*** Stanley Myers. *TOU*

The Saragossa Manuscript 🦴🦴½ *Rekopis Znaleziony W Saragossie* **1965** Ambitious fantasy based on the 1813 novel "Sanatorium under the Hourglass" by Bruno Schultz. A romantic Belgian army officer, travelling to Spain, meets two beautiful princesses who send him on a fantastic journey to prove himself worthy of their affections. Polish with subtitles. **174m/B VHS.** *PL* Zbigniew Cybulski, Iga Cembrzynska, Joanna Jedryka, Slawomir Linder; ***D:*** Wojciech Has; ***W:*** Tadeusz Kwiatkowski; ***M:*** Krzysztof Penderecki. *FCT*

Sarah, Plain and Tall 🦴🦴🦴 **1991 (G)** New England school teacher (Close) travels to Kansas circa 1910 to care for the family of a widowed farmer who has advertised for a wife. Superior entertainment for the whole family. Adapted for television from Patricia MacLachlan's novel of the same name by MacLachlan and Carol Sobieski. Nominated for nine Emmy Awards. A "Hallmark Hall of Fame" presentation. **98m/C VHS, LV.** Glenn Close, Christopher Walken, Lexi Randall, Margaret Sophie Stein, Jon DeVries, Christopher Bell; ***D:*** Glenn Jordan. *REP*

Sarah's Child 🦴🦴½ **1996** Sarah LaMere is devastated to learn that she can never have children. While husband Michael tries to accept, Sarah's upbringing has lead her to believe that's her only purpose in life and she becomes increasingly unbalanced. Seemingly out of nowhere children's clothes and toys appear in their home and soon a strange young girl named Melissa appears, whom Sarah treats as her own child. When their landlady dies horribly after questioning Melissa, Michael is afraid the line between reality and fantasy has been breached but just how can he fight? **90m/C VHS.** Mary Parker Williams, Michael Berger, Ruth Hale, Bryce Chamberlain; ***D:*** Ron Beckstrom; ***W:*** Muffy Mead Thomas; ***C:*** Gregg Stouffer; ***M:*** Jim Ball, Glenn Workman. *AEL*

Saratoga ½ **1937** Gable plays a bookie and Harlow the daughter of an impoverished horse breeder in this romantic comedy centered around the race tracks. This was the final film appearance for Harlow, who died before the film's completion. Mary Dees was chosen as her stand-in and had to finish many of the scenes. "Saratoga" was released just a month after Harlow's death and became one of the biggest moneymakers of the year. **94m/B VHS.** Jean Harlow, Clark Gable, Lionel Barrymore, Walter Pidgeon, Frank Morgan, Una Merkel, Cliff Edwards, George Zucco, Hattie McDaniel, Jonathan Hale; ***D:*** Jack Conway; ***W:*** Anita Loos, Robert Hopkins. *MGM*

Saratoga Trunk ½ **1945** Lavish, if slow-moving, version of Edna Ferber's romance novel reteams Cooper and Bergman (who starred in "For Whom the Bell Tolls"). It's 1875 New Orleans and bitter Clio, the half-Creole illegitimate daughter of a local, is determined to marry rich. But first, she gets involved with Texas gambler Clint Maroon (Cooper). He's in a business deal with wealthy Van Steed (Warburton), about the Saratoga railroad line, and Clio decides to go after him. Of course, she really wants Clint and they go through lots of bother before ending up together. Filmed in 1943 but release was delayed because of WWII. **135m/B VHS.** Gary Cooper, Ingrid Bergman, John Warburton, Flora Robson, Florence Bates, Jerry Austin; ***D:*** Sam Wood; ***W:*** Casey Robinson; ***C:*** Ernest Haller; ***M:*** Max Steiner. Nominations: Academy Awards '45: Best Supporting Actress (Robson). *MGM*

Sardinia Kidnapped ½ **1975** A beautiful girl is trapped in a clash between two powerful families while on vacation in Sardinia, where the peasants' custom is to kidnap a member of a rival family and then exchange the victim for land. Former documentary maker Mingozzi creates a realistic and uncompromising look at culture and change. In Italian; dubbed. **95m/C VHS, Beta.** *IT* Charlotte Rampling, Franco Nero; ***D:*** Gianfranco Mingozzi. *AHV*

Sartana's Here...Trade Your Pistol for a Coffin **1970** A soldier of fortune searches for a missing shipment of gold in the Old West. **92m/C VHS, Beta.** George Hilton, Charles Southwood, Erika Blanc, Linda Sini. *UNI*

S.A.S. San Salvador **1984** A CIA agent tries to prevent a psychotic from running amok in El Salvador. **95m/C VHS, Beta.** Miles O'Keeffe, Dagmar Lassander, Catherine Jarrett. *LIV, VES*

Sasquatch *Woof!* **1976** Purported "documentary" about the mythical creature Bigfoot. Includes pictures of the "actual" monster. For those real stupid moods. **94m/C VHS, Beta.** George Lauris; ***D:*** Ed Ragozzini. *NO*

Satan in High Heels ½ **1962** Sordid show-biz tale of a carnival dancer (Myles) who dreams of making it big on Broadway. First she finagles her way into a position as a nightclub singer and the mistress of a convenient millionaire. But she loses it all for love when she falls for the millionaire's misbehaving son. Flamboyant performance by Hall as the lesbian nightclub owner. **90m/C VHS.** Meg Myles, Grayson Hall, Del Tenney; ***D:*** Jerald Intrator; ***W:*** John T. Chapman. *SMW, TPV*

The Satan Killer ½ **1993** A vicious serial killer is targeted by two tough police detectives. What makes it personal is Detective Stephen's fiance is one of the killer's victims and he's not going to let justice stand in the way of his revenge. **90m/C VHS.** Steve Sayre, Billy Franklin, James Westbrook, Belinda Creason, Cindy Healy; ***D:*** Stephen Calamari. *AIP*

Satan Met a Lady ½ **1936** A weak adaptation of Dashiell Hammett's "Maltese Falcon." This version has Davis employing a private detective to track down a mysterious woman. The hunted woman is herself searching for a valuable collectible. **74m/B VHS.** Bette Davis, Warren William, Alison Skipworth, Arthur Treacher, Marie Wilson, Porter Hall, Olin Howlin; ***D:*** William Dieterle. *MGM, FCT*

The Satanic Rites of Dracula *Count Dracula and His Vampire Bride* **1973** Count Dracula is the leader of a satanic cult of prominent scientists and politicians who develop a gruesome plague virus capable of destroying the human race. Preceded by "Dracula A.D. 1972" and followed by "The 7 Brothers Meet Dracula." **88m/C VHS.** *GB* Christopher Lee, Peter Cushing, Michael Coles, William Franklyn, Freddie Jones, Joanna Lumley, Richard Vernon, Patrick Barr, Barbara Yo Ling; ***D:*** Alan Gibson. *MLB*

Satanik **1969 (R)** A hideous old hag is turned into a lovely young woman by a stolen potion, but it doesn't last long and she becomes a monster. **85m/C VHS.** *IT SP* Magda Konopka, Julio Pena, Luigi Montini, Armando Calvo, Umberto Raho; ***D:*** Piero Vivarelli. *SNC*

Satan's Black Wedding **1975 (R)** The ghouls arrive at a Monterey monastery in their Sunday best to celebrate devildom's most diabolical ritual, the "Black Wedding." **61m/C VHS, Beta.** Greg Braddock, Ray Miles, Lisa Milano. *NO*

Satan's Blade *Woof!* **1984** The owner of an ancient talisman goes on a killing rampage at a remote mountain lodge. **87m/C VHS, Beta.** *PSM*

Satan's Brew *Satansbraten* **1976** Aspiring poet (Raab) murders his mistress and assumes the identity of 19th-century symbolist poet Stefan George, including his idol's homosexual tastes. Fassbinder at his most excessive. German with subtitles. **100m/C VHS.** *GE* Kurt Raab, Margit Carstensen, Volker Spengler, Ingrid Caven, Helen Vita; ***D:*** Rainer Werner Fassbinder; ***W:*** Rainer Werner Fassbinder; ***M:*** Peer Raben. *ORI*

Satan's Cheerleaders *Woof!* **1977 (R)** A demonic high school janitor traps a bevy of buxom cheerleaders at his Satanic altar for sacrificial purposes. The gals use all of their endowments to escape the clutches of the evil sheriff and his fat wife. Is it ever campy! **92m/C VHS, Beta.** John Carradine, John Ireland, Yvonne De Carlo, Kerry Sherman, Jacqulin Cole, Hilary Horan, Alisa Powell, Sherry Marks, Jack Kruschen, Sydney Chaplin; ***D:*** Greydon Clark. *VCI*

Satan's Harvest ½ **1965** American detective inherits estate in Johannesburg, only to find the place is being used by drug smugglers. Sidesteps the political climate and shows the beauty of the land. And a good thing: the story is virtually nonexistent. **88m/C VHS, Beta.** George Montgomery, Tippi Hedren; ***D:*** Ferde Grofe Jr. *NO*

Satan's Princess **1990** Satanic cult with a female leader runs amuck. Sloppy and forgettable. **90m/C VHS, Beta.** Robert Forster, Caren Kaye, Lydie Denier; ***D:*** Bert I. Gordon. *PAR*

Satan's Sadists **1969 (R)** Tamblyn and his biker gang terrorize folks in the Southern California desert, including a retired cop, a Vietnam vet and a trio of vacationing coeds. Violent film will probably be best appreciated by Adamson completists. **88m/C VHS.** Russ Tamblyn, Regina Carrol, Gary Kent, Jackie Taylor, John Cardos, Kent Taylor, Robert Dix, Scott Brady, Evelyn Frank, Greydon Clark, Bill Bonner, Bobby Clark, Yvonne Stewart, Cheryl Anne, Randee Lynn, Bambi Allen, Breck Warwick; ***D:*** Al Adamson. *NO*

Satan's School for Girls ½ **1973** When a young woman investigates the circumstances that caused her sister's suicide, it leads her to a satanic girl's academy. Dumb and puerile made for TV "horror." **74m/C VHS, Beta.** Pamela Franklin, Roy Thinnes, Kate Jackson, Lloyd Bochner, Jamie Smith-Jackson, Jo Van Fleet, Cheryl Ladd; ***D:*** David Lowell Rich. *PSM*

Satan's Touch *Woof!* **1984 (R)** A simpleton worships the Devil and gets burned for his trouble. **86m/C VHS, Beta.** James Lawless, Shirley Venard. *NO*

Satanwar *Woof!* **1979** A fictional look at various forms of Satan worship. **95m/C VHS, Beta.** Bart LaRue, Sally Schermerhorn, Jimmy Drankovitch. *NO*

Satisfaction **1988 (PG-13)** An all-girl, high school rock band play out the summer before college. The Keatons should have sent Bateman to her room for this stunt. **93m/C VHS, Beta, LV.** Justine Bateman, Trini Alvarado, Britta Phillips, Julia Roberts, Scott Coffey, Liam Neeson, Deborah Harry; ***D:*** Joan Freeman; ***W:*** Charles Purpura; ***M:*** Michel Colombier. *FOX*

Saturday Night Fever ½ **1977 (R)** Brooklyn teenager (Travolta), bored with his daytime job, becomes the nighttime king of the local disco. Based on a story published in "New York Magazine" by Nik Cohn. Acclaimed for its disco dance sequences, memorable soundtrack by the Bee Gees, and carefree yet bleak script; extremely dated, although it made its mark on society in its time. Followed by the sequel "Staying Alive." Also available in a 112-minute "PG" rated version. ♫Staying Alive; Night Fever; More Than a Woman; How Deep Is Your Love?. **118m/C VHS, Beta, LV.** John Travolta, Karen Gorney, Barry Miller, Donna Pescow; ***D:*** John Badham; ***C:*** Ralf Bode; ***M:*** David Shire. National Board of Review Awards '77: 10 Best Films of the Year, Best Actor (Travolta); Nominations: Academy Awards '77: Best Actor (Travolta). *PAR*

Saturday Night Live **197?** Premiere episode of the late night classic, SNL. Guests Steve Martin and Elliott Gould join in these "best of" skits which feature the Killer Bees, the Blues Brothers, and a parody of "Star Trek," among other bits. Additional episodes are available. **90m/C VHS, Beta.** Dan Aykroyd, John Belushi, Jane Curtin, Garrett Morris, Chevy Chase, Gilda Radner, Laraine Newman. *COL, MOV*

Saturday Night Serials **1940** A compilation of excerpts from four serials: "The Phantom Creeps," "The Phantom Empire," "Undersea Kingdom," and "Junior G-Men." **90m/B VHS, Beta.** Bela Lugosi, Gene Autry, Ray Corrigan, Lon Chaney Jr. *RHI*

Saturday Night Shockers **1950** Each volume in this series is comprised of two full-length horror flicks, featuring twisted twins, barbarous butchers and sinister snow creatures. Terror abounds. **150m/B VHS, Beta.** Daisy Hilton. *RHI*

Saturday Night Shockers, Vol. 2 **1958** Two horror film compilations, each with copious cartoons, film clips and trailers added. Volume 2 has "Human Gorilla" and "Manbeast" and some added clips and attractions. **150m/B VHS, Beta.** Tod Slaughter, Eric Portman, Richard Carlson. *RHI*

Saturday Night Shockers, Vol. 3 **1967** A double feature with "Murders in the Red Barn," and "Face at the Window," plus some added classic previews and shocking shorts. **150m/B VHS.** *RHI*

Saturday Night Shockers, Vol. 4 **1967** Features "The Monsters of Piedras Blancas" and "Mesa of Lost Women." **145m/B VHS.** *RHI*

Saturday Night Sleazies, Vol. 1 **1966** Two sleazy films. "College Girl Confidential" (1968) and "Suburban Confidential" (1966) are each directed by the man who helmed "Orgy of the Dead." Also includes sleazy short subjects. **150m/B VHS, Beta.** Marsha Jordan, Harvey Shane; ***D:*** A.C. Stephen; ***W:*** A.C. Stephen. *RHI*

Saturday Night Special ½ **1992 (R)** Country singer/songwriter Travis (played by Nashville stalwart Burnette) gets a job fronting the house band of Tennessee tavern owner T.J. (Dean). Travis also takes up with ambitious Darlene (Ford), who happens to be T.J.'s wife. But it's Darlene who has the brains in this unpleasant trio, she decides to get rid of hubby and sets Travis up to take the fall. It's all been done before (and better). **75m/C VHS.** Billy Burnette, Maria Ford, Rick Dean; ***D:*** Dan Golden; ***W:*** Jonathan Banks; ***M:*** Billy Burnette, Nicholas Rivera. *NHO*

Saturday the 14th ½ **1981 (PG)** A parody of the popular axe-wielding-maniac genre, about a family inheriting a haunted mansion. Poorly made; not funny or scary. Followed by even worse sequel: "Saturday the 14th Strikes Back". **91m/C VHS, Beta.** Richard Benjamin, Paula Prentiss, Severn Darden; ***D:*** Howard R. Cohen; ***W:*** Howard R. Cohen, Jeff Begun. *SUE*

Saturday the 14th Strikes Back ☙ **1988** Pathetic sequel to the horror film spoof of the "Friday the 13th" series. **91m/C VHS, Beta.** Ray Walston, Avery Schreiber, Patty McCormack, Julianne McNamara, Jason Presson; ***D:*** Howard R. Cohen; ***W:*** Howard R. Cohen. *MGM*

Saturn 3 ☙½ **1980 (R)** Two research scientists create a futuristic Garden of Eden in an isolated sector of our solar system, but love story turns to horror story when a killer robot arrives. Sporadically promising, but ultimately lame; dumb ending. For Farrah fans only. **88m/C VHS, Beta, LV.** *GB* Farrah Fawcett, Kirk Douglas, Harvey Keitel, Ed Bishop; ***D:*** Stanley Donen; ***W:*** Martin Amis; ***C:*** Billy Williams; ***M:*** Elmer Bernstein. *FOX*

Saul and David *Saul e David* **1968** Beautifully filmed story of David's life with King Saul, the battle with Goliath, and the tragic end of Saul. From the "Bible" series. **120m/C VHS, Beta.** Norman Wooland, Gianni "John" Garko. *VCI, MOV, KEP*

Savage! *Woof! Black Valor* **1973 (R)** A savage foreign mess with ex-baseball star Iglehart killing people with grenades and guns, abetted by an army full of murderous models. **81m/C VHS, Beta.** *MX* James Iglehart, Lada Edmund, Carol Speed, Rossana Ortiz, Sally Jordan, Aura Aurea, Vic Diaz; ***D:*** Cirio H. Santiago. *NLC*

Savage Abduction ☙ **1973 (R)** Two girls visiting Los Angeles are kidnapped by a bizarre man. **84m/C VHS, Beta.** Tom Drake, Stephen Oliver, Sean Kenney; ***D:*** John Lawrence. *GHV*

Savage Attraction ☙½ *Hostage: The Christine Maresch Story; Hostage* **1983 (R)** True story of a 16-year-old girl forced to marry an ex-Nazi, and her hellish life thereafter. Frustrating because it could have been much better. **93m/C VHS, Beta.** *AU GE* Kerry Mack, Ralph Schicha; ***D:*** Frank Shields. *VTR, SUE*

Savage Beach ☙ **1989 (R)** A pair of well-endowed female federal agents battle assorted buccaneers on a remote Pacific isle over a rediscovered cache of gold from WWII. Exploitative, pornographic, and degrading to watch. Sequel to "Picasso Trigger." **90m/C VHS, Beta, LV.** Dona Speir, Hope Marie Carlton, Bruce Penhall, Rodrigo Obregon, John Aprea, Teri Weigel, Lisa London; ***D:*** Andy Sidaris. *COL*

The Savage Bees ☙☙ **1976** A South American ship harbored at New Orleans during Mardi Gras unleashes killer bees into the celebratory crowds. Not bad, relatively exciting, TV thriller. **90m/C VHS, Beta.** Ben Johnson, Michael Parks, Paul Hecht, Horst Buchholz, Gretchen Corbett; ***D:*** Bruce Geller. *LIV*

Savage Capitalism ☙☙ *Capitalismo Salvaje* **1993** Melodramatic romance between a reporter and a mining company exec crumbles when the exec's presumed dead wife returns. Meanwhile, the reporter uncovers the truth behind the company's plans to mine in the interior of Brazil, which could cause ecological ruin. Portuguese with subtitles. **86m/C VHS.** *BR* Fernanda Torres, Jose Mayer, Marisa Orth, Marcelo Tass; ***D:*** Andre Klotzel; ***W:*** Andre Klotzel, Djalma Batista. *FCT*

Savage Dawn ☙½ **1984 (R)** In yet another desert town, yet another pair of combat-hardened vets are confronted by yet another vicious motorcycle gang. Haven't we seen this one before? **102m/C VHS, Beta.** George Kennedy, Karen Black, Richard Lynch, Lance Henriksen, William Forsythe; ***D:*** Simon Nuchtern. *MED, VTR*

Savage Drums ☙½ **1951** Sabu returns to his South Seas island to help end tribal warfare there. Dated and dumb, but fun-to-watch melodrama/action. **70m/B VHS, Beta, LV.** Sabu, Lita Baron; ***D:*** William (Lester Williams) Berke. *NO*

Savage Fury ☙ *Call of the Savage* **1933** Feature-length version of the popular movie serial. **80m/B VHS, Beta.** Noah Beery Jr., Dorothy Short. *NOS, DVT, HEG*

The Savage Girl ☙ **1932** A hunter journeys through the darkest jungle in search of prey. Instead, he stumbles across a beautiful white jungle girl, falls in love with her and attempts to take her back with him. **64m/B VHS.** Rochelle Hudson, Walter Byron, Harry Myers, Ted Adams, Adolph Milar, Floyd Schackleford; ***D:*** Harry Fraser. *SNC, NOS, DVT*

Savage Guns ☙☙½ *Tierra Bru Tal* **1968** A gunslinger goes after his brother's murderer. **85m/C VHS, Beta.** *TWE*

Savage Hearts ☙½ **1995** Terminally ill mob hitwoman Beatrice Baxter (D'Abo) has six months left to live and she wants her last days to be spent in style. So she steals $2 million from her mob employer Roger Focely (Harris)—who's determined to get the money back. **90m/C VHS.** Maryam D'Abo, Richard Harris, Miriam Cyr, Jerry Hall; ***D:*** Mark Ezra. *TRI*

Savage Hunger ☙ **1984** Ten plane crash survivors struggle to survive in the Baja desert. **90m/C VHS, Beta.** Chris Makepeace, Scott Hylands, Anne Lockhart; ***D:*** Sparky Green. *VES*

Savage Instinct ☙☙ **1991** A woman stumbles across a drug ring and becomes a target when they fear she could expose them. Only Mongo and his crew are even more surprised when she decides to fight back. **95m/C VHS.** Debra Sweaney, Brian Oldfield. *AIP, MOV*

Savage Intruder ☙ **1968 (R)** A wandering opportunist worms his way into the heart and home of a rich ex-movie star. She soon discovers that he's a sexual deviant who mutilates and murders for fun. Twisted doings with Hopkins in her final role. **90m/C VHS.** John David Garfield, Miriam Hopkins, Gale Sondergaard, Florence Lake, Joe Besser, Minta Durfee; ***D:*** Donald Wolfe. *UNI*

Savage Is Loose *Woof!* **1974 (R)** Drivel about a scientist, his wife, and their son stranded on a deserted island for 20 years. Not surprisingly, as junior matures he realizes there isn't a woman for him—or is there? Completely lacking in redeeming qualities. Absurd pseudo-Freudian claptrap produced by Scott. **114m/C VHS, Beta.** George C. Scott, Trish Van Devere, John David Carson, Lee Montgomery; ***D:*** George C. Scott. *MLB*

Savage Island ☙½ **1985 (R)** Women's prison in the tropics sets the scene for the usual exploitative goings-on. Blair is actually in the film only for a few minutes. Chopped-up, even worse version of "Escape From Hell." **74m/C VHS.** *SP IT* Nicholas Beardsley, Linda Blair, Anthony Steffen, Ajita Wilson, Christina Lai, Leon Askin; ***D:*** Edward Muller; ***W:*** Nicholas Beardsley. Golden Raspberry Awards '85: Worst Actress (Blair). *NO*

Savage Journey ☙½ **1983 (PG)** A wagon train of pioneers has difficulty on its westward journey. Simple story with no real appeal. **99m/C VHS, Beta.** Richard Moll, Maurice Grandmaison, Faith Clift; ***D:*** Tom McGowan. *PSM*

Savage Justice ☙ **1988** A young woman seeks revenge against leftist rebels (boo, hiss) in a Southeast Asian country who killed her parents and raped her. She hooks up with an ex-Green Beret, and they fight and love their way through the jungle. The usual nudity and violence; derivative and dumb. **90m/C Beta.** Julia Montgomery, Steven Memel. *VTR*

Savage Land ☙☙½ **1994 (PG)** Family western finds a young brother and sister travelling by stage to meet up with their father. The stage is robbed by some bumbling bad guys, who then pursue the kids and two other passengers across the frontier. The kids, of course, are smarter than most of the adults, and manage to get the best ᴦ the bad hombres. **91m/C VHS, LV.** Graham Greene, Corbin Bernsen, Vivian Schilling, Mercedes McNab, Corey Carrier, Brion James, Bo Svenson, Charlotte Ross. *HMD*

Savage Messiah ☙☙☙ **1972 (R)** Bio of young French sculptor Henri Gaudier and his intense, though platonic, affair with a refined Polish woman 20 years his senior. Stylized drama is spared most of director Russell's noted excesses but he manages to believably show their magnetic attraction. Gaudier was killed in WWI at the age of 24. Based on the biography by H.S. Ede. **96m/C VHS.** *GB* Scott Antony, Dorothy Tutin, Helen Mirren, Lindsay Kemp, Peter Vaughan, Michael Gough; ***D:*** Ken Russell; ***W:*** Christopher Logue. *MGM*

Savage Run ☙☙☙ *Run, Simon, Run* **1970** Reynolds is Papago Indian framed and imprisoned for his brother's murder. Sprung from the pen, he heads back to the reservation to find the real killers and to avenge his brother's death. Convincing made for televisiondrama. Stevens' last role before her suicide. **73m/C VHS.** Burt Reynolds, Inger Stevens, James Best, Rodolfo Acosta, Don Dubbins, Joyce Jameson, Barney Phillips, Eddie Little Sky; ***D:*** George McCowan. *SIM*

Savage Sam ☙☙ **1963** Intended as a sequel to "Old Yeller." Sam, the offspring of the heroic dog named Old Yeller, tracks down some children kidnapped by Indians. Fun, but not fully successful. **103m/C VHS, Beta.** Tommy Kirk, Kevin Corcoran, Brian Keith, Dewey Martin, Jeff York, Marta Kristen; ***D:*** Norman Tokar; ***C:*** Edward Colman. *DIS*

The Savage Seven ☙☙ **1968** An underground classic where everyone loses. A motorcycle gang rides into an Indian town which is at the mercy of corrupt businessmen. The gang's leader becomes involved in the Indians' problems but the businessmen and the cops cause trouble for all concerned. Less than memorable. Produced by Dick Clark. **96m/C VHS.** Larry Bishop, Joanna Frank, Adam Roarke, Robert Walker Jr.; ***D:*** Richard Rush. *NO*

Savage Streets ☙½ **1983 (R)** Blair seeks commando-style revenge on the street gang that raped her deaf sister. Extended rape scene betrays the exploitative intentions, though other bits are entertaining, in a trashy kind of way. **93m/C VHS, Beta, LV.** Linda Blair, John Vernon, Sal Landi, Robert Dryer, Debra Blee, Linnea Quigley; ***D:*** Danny Steinmann; ***M:*** John D'Andrea. Golden Raspberry Awards '85: Worst Actress (Blair). *LIV, VES*

Savage Weekend *Woof! The Killer Behind the Mask; The Upstate Murders* **1980 (R)** A killer behind a ghoulish mask stalks human prey in the boonies, of couse. Astoundingly, there is one interesting role—William Sanderson's looney. Otherwise, throw this one no bones. **88m/C VHS, Beta.** Christopher Allport. *NO*

Savage Wilderness ☙☙½ *The Last Frontier* **1955** When a trio of fur trappers lose a year's worth of skins to a band of marauding Indians, they decide to take scouting jobs at a cavalry outpost. But they find the new commander (Preston) hasn't gotten his nickname as the "Butcher of Shiloh" without reason. Adapted from the novel "The Gilded Rooster" by Richard Emery Roberts. **98m/C VHS.** Victor Mature, Robert Preston, Guy Madison, James Whitmore, Anne Bancroft, Russell Collins, Peter Whitney, Pat Hogan, Manuel Donde, Guy Williams; ***D:*** Anthony Mann; ***W:*** Philip Yordan, Russell S. Hughes; ***M:*** Leigh Harline. *COL*

The Savage Woman ☙☙ **1991** Marianna escapes from a desperate situation and is found unconscious in the woods by Elysee. He nurses her back to health, learns her terrible secret, and tries to help Marianna decides whether to turn herself into the police or keep running. In French with English subtitles. **100m/C VHS.** *CA* Patricia Tulasne, Matthias Habich; ***D:*** Lea Pool. *WBF*

Savages ☙☙ **1972** A group of savages descend on a palatial mansion, and after living there for some time, become refined ladies and gentlemen. The moral savages and "civilized" men are really the same. **106m/C VHS.** Lewis J. Stadlen, Anne Francine, Thayer David, Salome Jens, Susan Blakely, Kathleen Widdoes, Sam Waterston; ***D:*** James Ivory; ***C:*** Walter Lassally. *CVC, FCT*

Savages ☙☙½ **1975** Griffith as a demented nut-case stalking another man in the desert? That's right, Opie. "The Most Dangerous Game" remade-sort-of-for TV. **74m/C VHS, Beta.** Andy Griffith, Sam Bottoms, Noah Beery Jr.; ***D:*** Lee H. Katzin. *PSM*

Savages from Hell ☙ *Big Enough and Old Enough* **1968 (R)** Greasy biker dude beats up a young black guy because he was flirting with the biker's woman. The biker also tries to rape a migrant farmworker's daughter because he lusts after her. Trashy exploitation film. **79m/C VHS.** Bobbie Byers, Cyril Poitier, Diwaldo Myers, Viola Lloyd, William P. Kelley; ***D:*** Joseph Prieto; ***W:*** Joseph Prieto. *SNC, TPV*

Savannah Smiles 🦴🦴½ **1982 (PG)** Poor little rich girl Anderson runs away from home, into the clutches of two ham-handed crooks. She melts their hearts, and they change their ways. Decent, sentimental family drama. **104m/C VHS, Beta, LV.** Bridgette Anderson, Mark Miller, Donovan Scott, Peter Graves, Chris Robinson, Michael Parks; ***D:*** Pierre De Moro. *SUE, NLC*

Save Me 🦴🦴 **1993 (R)** Jim Stevens' (Hamlin) wife has left him and his boss is involved in some dirty deals that could cost Jim his job. So things couldn't get worse, could they? Well, of course they could—and do. Because Jim meets Ellie (Anthony), a sexual adventuress just destined to bring trouble to a lonely guy. Also available in an unrated version. **89m/C VHS, LV.** Harry Hamlin, Lysette Anthony, Michael Ironside, Olivia Hussey, Bill Nunn, Steve Railsback; ***D:*** Alan Roberts; ***W:*** Neil Ronco; ***M:*** Rick Marvin. *COL*

Save the Lady 🦴🦴 **1982** Plucky kids fight city hall to save an old ferry, the Lady Hope, from the scrap heap. Nothing offensive here—just a pleasant family flick. **76m/C VHS, Beta.** Matthew Excell, Robert Clarkson, Miranda Cartledge, Kim Clifford; ***D:*** Leon Thau. *NO*

Save the Tiger 🦴🦴🦴 **1973 (R)** A basically honest middle-aged man sees no way out of his failing business except arson. The insurance settlement will let him pay off his creditors, and save face. David, as the arsonist, and Gilford, as Lemmon's business partner, are superb. Lemmon is also excellent throughout his performance. **100m/C VHS, Beta, LV.** Jack Lemmon, Jack Gilford, Laurie Heineman, Patricia Smith, Norman Burton, Thayer David; ***D:*** John G. Avildsen; ***M:*** Marvin Hamlisch. Academy Awards '73: Best Actor (Lemmon); Writers Guild of America '73: Best Original Screenplay; Nominations: Academy Awards '73: Best Story & Screenplay, Best Supporting Actor (Gilford). *PAR, BTV*

Saving Grace 🦴🦴 **1986 (PG)** A tale of the fictional youngest Pope of modern times, Pope Leo XIV (Conti). Beset by duty, he decides to shed his robes and get in touch with the world's peasantry. Improbable, but that's okay; the mortal sin is that it's improbable and slow and boring. **112m/C VHS, Beta, LV, 8mm.** Tom Conti, Fernando Rey, Giancarlo Giannini, Erland Josephson, Donald Hewlett, Edward James Olmos; ***D:*** Robert M. Young; ***W:*** David S. Ward; ***M:*** William Goldstein. *SUE, NLC*

Sawbones 🦴 **1995 (R)** A woman tries to stop a sadistic doctor who gets his jollies murdering his patients and then performing gruesome surgeries on the bodies. **?m/C VHS.** Adam Baldwin, Barbara Carrera, Don Harvey, Nina Siemaszko. *NHO*

Sawdust & Tinsel 🦴🦴🦴 *The Naked Night; Sunset of a Clown; Gycklarnas Afton* **1953** Early Bergman film detailing the grisly, humiliating experiences of a traveling circus rolling across the barren Swedish countryside. Lonely parable of human relationships. In Swedish with English subtitles. **87m/B VHS, Beta, LV.** *SW* Harriet Andersson, Ake Gronberg; ***D:*** Ingmar Bergman; ***W:*** Ingmar Bergman. *HMV, INJ, NLC*

Sawmill/The Dome Doctor 🦴🦴½ **1922** Two silent comedies starring the inimitable klutz of the golden era, Larry Semon, whose name has been nearly forgotten today. **71m/B VHS, Beta.** Larry Semon, Dorothy Dwan. *VYY*

Say Anything 🦴🦴🦴 **1989 (PG-13)** A semi-mature, successful teen romance about an offbeat loner interested in the martial arts (Cusack, in a winning performance) who goes after the beautiful class brain of his high school. Things are complicated when her father is suspected of embezzling by the IRS. Joan Cusack, John's real-life sister, also plays his sister in the film. Works well on the romantic level without getting too sticky. **100m/C VHS, Beta, LV.** John Cusack, Ione Skye, John Mahoney, Joan Cusack, Lili Taylor, Richard Portnow, Pamela Segall, Jason Gould, Loren Dean, Bebe Neuwirth, Aimee Brooks, Eric Stoltz, Chynna Phillips, Joanna Frank; ***D:*** Cameron Crowe; ***W:*** Cameron Crowe; ***M:*** Anne Dudley, Richard Gibbs, Nancy Wilson. *FOX*

Say Goodbye, Maggie Cole 🦴🦴½ **1972** A widow goes to work as a doctor in a Chicago street clinic and becomes emotionally involved with a dying child. Hayward's final role in moving made-for-TV drama. **78m/C VHS, Beta.** Susan Hayward, Darren McGavin, Michael Constantine, Nichelle Nichols, Dane Clark; ***D:*** Jud Taylor. *VMK*

Say Hello to Yesterday 🦴½ **1971 (PG)** A May-December romance that takes place entirely in one day. An unhappy housewife meets an exciting young traveler while both are in London. Cast and director try hard but fail to get the point across to the audience. **91m/C VHS, Beta.** *GB* Jean Simmons, Leonard Whiting, Evelyn Laye; ***D:*** Alvin Rakoff. *PSM*

Say Yes! 🦴½ **1986 (PG-13)** A nutty millionaire (Winters) bets $250 million that his inept nephew cannot get married within 24 hours. Three times the length of usual wacky sitcom, alas. **87m/C VHS, Beta, LV.** Jonathan Winters, Art Hindle, Logan Ramsey, Lissa Layng; ***D:*** Larry Yust. *NO*

Sayonara 🦴🦴🦴 **1957** An Army major is assigned to a Japanese airbase during the Korean conflict at the behest of his future father-in-law. Dissatisfied with his impending marriage, he finds himself drawn to a Japanese dancer and becomes involved in the affairs of his buddy who, against official policy, marries a Japanese woman. Tragedy surrounds the themes of bigotry and interracial marriage. Based on the novel by James Michener. **147m/C VHS, Beta.** Marlon Brando, James Garner, Ricardo Montalban, Patricia Owens, Red Buttons, Miyoshi Umeki, Martha Scott; ***D:*** Joshua Logan; ***C:*** Ellsworth Fredericks. Academy Awards '57: Best Art Direction/Set Decoration, Best Sound, Best Supporting Actor (Buttons), Best Supporting Actress (Umeki); Nominations: Academy Awards '57: Best Actor (Brando), Best Adapted Screenplay, Best Cinematography, Best Director (Logan), Best Film Editing, Best Picture. *FOX, BTV*

The Scalawag Bunch 🦴 **1975** Yet another retelling of Robin Hood and his Merry Men and their adventures in Sherwood Forest. **100m/C VHS, Beta.** *IT* Mark Damon, Luis Davila, Silvia Dionisio; ***D:*** George Ferron. *MON, HHE*

Scalp Merchant 🦴 **1977** Private investigator Cliff Rowan hunts for a missing payroll. Someone would rather see him dead than successful. **108m/C VHS, Beta.** Cameron Mitchell, John Waters, Elizabeth Alexander, Margaret Nelson; ***D:*** Howard Rubie. *NO*

Scalpel 🦴🦴 *False Face* **1976 (R)** After his daughter's death, a plastic surgeon creates her image on another woman to get an inheritance. Violent and graphic, with a surprise ending. Not too bad; interesting premise. **95m/C VHS, Beta.** Robert Lansing, Judith Chapman, Arlen Dean Snyder; ***D:*** John Grissmer. *NLC*

The Scalphunters 🦴🦴½ **1968** Semi-successful, semi-funny western about an itinerant trapper (Lancaster) who is forced by Indians to trade his pelts for an educated black slave (Davis); many chases and brawls ensue. Good performances. **102m/C VHS, Beta.** Burt Lancaster, Ossie Davis, Telly Savalas, Shelley Winters, Nick Cravat, Dabney Coleman, Paul Picerni; ***D:*** Sydney Pollack; ***W:*** William W. Norton Sr.; ***M:*** Elmer Bernstein. *MGM*

Scalps 🦴🦴 **1983 (R)** Hunted Indian princess and man whose family was killed by Indians form uneasy alliance in old West. **90m/C VHS, Beta.** Karen Wood, Albert Farley, Benny Cardosa, Charlie Bravo, Vassili Garis; ***D:*** Werner Knox. *IMP, HHE*

Scam 🦴🦴½ **1993 (R)** Maggie and her partner Barry are con artists making their living scamming high rollers in Miami Beach. Then Maggie tries to pull a con on the wrong man. Jack Shanks is an ex-FBI agent with a score to settle and he blackmails Maggie into helping him. **102m/C VHS.** Christopher Walken, Lorraine Bracco, Miguel Ferrer; ***D:*** John Flynn. *FXV*

Scandal 🦴🦴 *Shuban* **1950** Handsome artist (Mifune) and beautiful concert singer (Yamaguchi) become the victims of a libelous article in a gossip magazine. The artist decides to sue but, being softhearted, chooses a questionable lawyer because the man's young daughter is dying. Then the unethical lawyer accepts a bribe to prejudice the case. Japanese with subtitles. **105m/B VHS.** *JP* Toshiro Mifune, Takashi Shimura, Yoshiko Yamaguchi; ***D:*** Akira Kurosawa; ***W:*** Riyuzo Kikushima, Akira Kurosawa; ***M:*** Fumio Hayasaka. *FCT*

Scandal 🦴🦴🦴 **1989 (R)** A dramatization of Britain's Profumo government sex scandal of the 1960s. Hurt plays a society doctor who enjoys introducing pretty girls to his wealthy friends. One of the girls, Christine Keeler, takes as lovers both a Russian government official and a British Cabinet Minister. The resulting scandal eventually overturned an entire political party, and led to disgrace, prison, and death for some of those concerned. Also available in an unedited 115-minute version which contains more controversial language and nudity. Top-notch performances make either version well worth watching. **105m/C VHS, Beta, LV.** *GB* John Hurt, Joanne Whalley, Ian McKellen, Bridget Fonda, Jeroen Krabbe, Britt Ekland, Roland Gift, Daniel Massey, Leslie Phillips; ***D:*** Michael Caton-Jones; ***W:*** Michael Thomas; ***M:*** Carl Davis. *HBO*

Scandal in a Small Town 🦴🦴 **1988** A cocktail waitress in a small town has to defend herself and her daughter from the town's critical eye and hateful actions. Self-righteous made for TV drama rehashes several earlier plots. **90m/C VHS, LV.** Raquel Welch, Christa Denton, Peter Van Norden, Ronny Cox; ***D:*** Anthony Page. *VMK*

Scandal Man 🦴🦴½ **1967** A French photographer gets in over his head when he snaps the daughter of an American KKK leader embracing a black man in a nightclub. In French with English subtitles. **86m/C VHS, Beta.** Maurice Ronet; ***D:*** Richard Balducci. *FCT, INJ*

Scandalous 🦴½ **1984 (PG)** A bumbling American television reporter becomes involved with a gang of British con artists. Starts well but peters out. Look for the scene where Gielgud attends a Bow Wow Wow concert. **93m/C VHS, Beta, LV.** Robert Hays, Pamela Stephenson, John Gielgud, Jim Dale, M. Emmet Walsh; ***D:*** Rob Cohen; ***W:*** Rob Cohen, Larry Cohen, John Byrum; ***M:*** Dave Grusin. *LIV, VES*

Scandalous 🦴 **1988** A duke and his uncle work together to find a secretary who disappeared after witnessing a murder. **90m/C VHS, Beta.** Albert Fortell, Lauren Hutton, Ursula Carven, Capucine; ***D:*** Robert W. Young. *VTR, PSM*

Scandalous John 🦴🦴 **1971 (G)** Comedy western about a last cattle drive devised by an aging cowboy (Keith) in order to save his ranch. Keith's shrewd acting as the ornery cattle man who won't sell to developers carries this one. **113m/C VHS, Beta.** Brian Keith, Alfonso Arau, Michele Carey, Rick Lenz, John Ritter, Harry (Henry) Morgan; ***D:*** Robert Butler. *DIS*

Scanner Cop 🦴½ **1994 (R)** When deranged scientist Sigmund Glock escapes from prison, he's determined to take revenge on Peter Harrigan, the cop who put him behind bars. With the aid of an evil assistant and a mind-altering drug, Glock kidnaps and programs innocent citizens into cop-killing maniacs. Harrigan's only weapon is a rookie cop with the Scanner power to read minds—and then destroy them. **94m/C VHS, LV.** Daniel Quinn, Darlanne Fluegel, Richard Lynch, Mark Rolston, Hilary Shepard, Gary Hudson, Cyndi Pass, Luca Bercovici, Brion James; ***D:*** Pierce David; ***W:*** John Bryant, George Saunders. *REP*

Scanners 🦴🦴½ **1981 (R)** "Scanners" are telepaths who can will people to explode. One scanner in particular harbors Hitlerian aspirations for his band of psychic gangsters. Gruesome but effective special effects. **102m/C VHS, Beta, LV.** *CA* Stephen Lack, Jennifer O'Neill, Patrick McGoohan, Lawrence Dane; ***D:*** David Cronenberg; ***W:*** David Cronenberg; ***M:*** Howard Shore. *COL, SUE*

Scanners 2: The New Order 🦴🦴½ **1991 (R)** This not-bad sequel to the 1981 cult classic finds a power-mad police official out to build a psychic militia of captured Scanners. More story than last time, plus more and better special effects. **104m/C VHS, Beta, LV.** *CA* David Hewlett, Deborah Raffin, Yvan Ponton, Isabelle Mejias, Valentin Trujillo, Tom Butler, Vlasta Vrana, Dorothee Berryman, Raoul Trujillo; ***D:*** Christian Duguay; ***W:*** B.J. Nelson; ***M:*** Marty Simon. *MED, IME, VTR*

Scanners 3: The Takeover 🦴½ **1992 (R)** The third sequel in which Scanner siblings battle for control of the world. Lacks the creativity and storyline of the first two films. **101m/C VHS, LV.** Steve Parrish, Liliana Komorowska, Valerie Valois; ***D:*** Christian Duguay. *REP*

Scanners: The Showdown 🦴½ **1994** **(R)** Carl Volkin (Kilpatrick), the "scanner" killer, has escaped jail and is stalking the streets of L.A. His ultimate target is Sam Staziak (Quinn), the scanner cop who sent him away. Since Volkin's powers grow with every kill, Staziak better get to Volkin in a hurry. **95m/C VHS.** Patrick Kilpatrick, Daniel Quinn, Khrystyne Haje, Stephen Mendel, Brenda Swanson, Jewel Shepard, Robert Forster; ***D:*** Steve Barnett; ***W:*** Mark Sevi. *REP*

The Scar 🦴🦴½ *Hollow Triumph* **1948** A cunning criminal robs the mob, then hides by "stealing" the identity of a lookalike psychologist. But he's overlooked one thing...or two. Farfetched film noir showcases a rare villainous role for Henreid (who also produced). Based on a novel by Murray Forbes. **83m/B VHS.** Paul Henreid, Joan Bennett, Eduard Franz, Leslie Brooks, John Qualen, Mabel Paige, Herbert Rudley; ***D:*** Steve Sekely. *REP, FCT, NOS*

Scar of Shame 🦴🦴 **1927** Explores the ill-fated romance between a successful black concert pianist and the lower-class woman he marries. Gives a look at the color caste system and divisions within the black community of the era. **90m/B VHS.** Harry Henderson, Lucia Lynn Moses, Ann Kennedy, Norman Johnstone; ***D:*** Frank Peregini. *FCT, BTV*

Scaramouche 🦴🦴🦴½ **1952** Thrilling swashbuckler about a nobleman (Granger, very well cast) searching for his family during the French Revolution. To avenge the death of a friend, he joins a theater troupe where he learns swordplay and becomes the character "Scaramouche." Features a rousing six-and-a-half-minute sword battle. **111m/C VHS, LV.** Stewart Granger, Eleanor Parker, Janet Leigh, Mel Ferrer, Henry Wilcoxon, Nina Foch, Richard Anderson, Robert Coote, Lewis Stone, Elisabeth Risdon, Howard Freeman; ***D:*** George Sidney; ***C:*** Charles Rosher. *FCT*

Scarecrow 🦴🦴½ **1973 (R)** Two homeless drifters (Hackman and Pacino) walk across America, heading toward a car wash business they never reach. An oft-neglected example of the early 70s extra-realistic subgenre initiated by "Midnight Cowboy." Engrossing until the end, when it falls flat. Filmed on location in Detroit. **112m/C VHS, Beta.** Gene Hackman, Al Pacino, Ann Wedgeworth, Eileen Brennan, Richard Lynch; ***D:*** Jerry Schatzberg; ***C:*** Vilmos Zsigmond. Cannes Film Festival '73: Best Film. *WAR*

Scared Stiff 🦴🦴🦴 **1953** Fleeing a murder charge, Martin and Lewis find gangsters and ghosts on a Caribbean island. Funny and scary, a good remake of "The Ghost Breakers," with cameos by Hope and Crosby. ♫San Domingo; Song of the Enchilada Man; Mama Yo Quiero; You Hit the Spot; I Don't Care If the Sun Don't Shine; I'm Your Pal; When Somebody Thinks You're Wonderful. **108m/B VHS.** Dean Martin, Jerry Lewis, Lizabeth Scott, Carmen Miranda, Dorothy Malone; ***Cameos:*** Bob Hope, Bing Crosby; ***D:*** George Marshall. *PAR, MLB, REP*

Scared Stiff 🦴 **1987 (R)** Three people move into a mansion once owned by a sadistic slave trader. Once there, they become unwilling victims of a voodoo curse. Bad special effects and script, not redeemed by decent but unoriginal story. **85m/C VHS, LV.** Andrew Stevens, Mary Page Keller; ***D:*** Richard S. Friedman; ***W:*** Richard S. Friedman, Mark Frost, Daniel F. Bacaner. *REP*

Scared to Death 🦴½ **1947** Begins with a woman dying of fright when shown the death mask of the man she framed. Dead woman then proceeds to narrate remainder of the story, which focuses on events leading up to her unfortunate, untimely, and fairly uninteresting demise. Memorable as Lugosi's only color film. **70m/C VHS, Beta.** Bela Lugosi, George Zucco, Douglas Fowley, Nat Pendleton, Joyce Compton; ***D:*** Christy Cabanne. *NOS, SNC, MWP*

Scared to Death 🦴 **1980 (R)** A scientific experiment goes awry as a mutation begins killing off the residents of Los Angeles. **93m/C VHS, Beta.** John Stinson, Diana Davidson, David Moses, Kermit Eller; ***D:*** William Malone; ***M:*** Tom Chase. *MED*

Scared to Death/Dick Tracy's Dilemma 🦴🦴 **1947** On one tape, two 40's programmers-Lugosi's only color film, about a psychotic magician who tortures a young girl, and a standard black-and-white Tracy entry. **125m/C VHS, Beta.** Bela Lugosi, George Zucco, Ralph Byrd, Kay Christopher, Ian Keith. *AOV*

Scarface 🦴🦴🦴 *Scarface: The Shame of a Nation* **1931** The violent rise and fall of a 1930s Chicago crime boss (based on the life of notorious gangster Al Capone). Release was held back by censors due to the amount of violence and its suggestion of incest between the title character and his sister. Producer Howard Hughes recut and filmed an alternate ending, without director Hawks' approval, to pacify the censors, and both versions of the film were released at the same time. Almost too violent and intense at the time. Remains brilliant and impressive. Remade in 1983. **93m/B VHS, Beta, LV.** Paul Muni, Ann Dvorak, Karen Morley, Osgood Perkins, George Raft, Boris Karloff; ***D:*** Howard Hawks; ***C:*** Lee Garmes. National Board of Review Awards '32: 10 Best Films of the Year. *MCA*

Scarface 🦴🦴🦴 **1983 (R)** Al Pacino is a Cuban refugee who becomes powerful in the drug trade until the life gets the better of him. A remake of the 1932 classic gangster film of the same name, although the first film has more plot. Extremely violent, often unpleasant, but not easily forgotten. **170m/C VHS, Beta, LV.** Al Pacino, Steven Bauer, Michelle Pfeiffer, Robert Loggia, F. Murray Abraham, Mary Elizabeth Mastrantonio, Harris Yulin, Paul Shenar, Oliver Stone; ***D:*** Brian DePalma; ***W:*** Oliver Stone; ***C:*** John A. Alonzo. *MCA*

Scarface Mob 🦴🦴 *Tueur de Ch Icago* **1962** This is the original television pilot film for the popular series "The Untouchables," about Eliot Ness's band of good guys battling Chicago's crime lord, Al Capone. Still strong stuff. Narrated by Walter Winchell. **120m/B VHS, Beta.** Robert Stack, Neville Brand, Barbara Nichols; ***D:*** Phil Karlson; ***W:*** Paul Monash. *PAR*

The Scarlet & the Black 🦴🦴½ **1983** A priest clandestinely works within the shield of the Vatican's diplomatic immunity to shelter allied soldiers from the Nazis in occupied Rome. His efforts put him at odds with the Pope and target him for Gestapo assassination. Swashbuckling adventure at its second-best. Made for television. Based on the nonfiction book "The Scarlet Pimpernel of the Vatican" by J.P. Gallagher. **145m/C VHS, Beta.** Gregory Peck, Christopher Plummer, John Gielgud, Raf Vallone; ***D:*** Jerry London; ***M:*** Ennio Morricone. *FOX, FCT, IGP*

The Scarlet Car 🦴🦴 **1917** Chaney is a bank cashier who discovers his boss has been embezzling funds. A fight causes Chaney to believe he has killed his employer and he hides out in a remote cabin where guilt preys on his mind. **50m/B VHS, Beta.** Lon Chaney Sr., Franklyn Farnum, Edith Johnson, Sam DeGrasse; ***D:*** Joseph DeGrasse. *SNC, GPV, FCT*

Scarlet Claw 🦴🦴🦴 *Sherlock Holmes and the Scarlet Claw* **1944** Holmes and Watson solve the bloody murder of an old lady in the creepy Canadian village of Le Mort Rouge. The best and most authentic of the Sherlock Holmes series. **74m/B VHS, Beta.** Basil Rathbone, Nigel Bruce, Miles Mander, Gerald Hamer, Kay Harding; ***D:*** Roy William Neill. *FOX*

The Scarlet Clue 🦴🦴 **1945** A better script and faster pacing improved this Monogram entry in the Chan series. Charlie investigates a series of mysterious deaths which lead to a plot to steal secret government radar plans. **65m/B VHS.** Sidney Toler, Benson Fong, Mantan Moreland, Robert E. Homans, Helen Devereaux; ***D:*** Phil Rosen. *MGM*

Scarlet Dawn 🦴🦴½ **1932** Lavish sets and costumes abound in this romantic drama starring Fairbanks as a Russian aristocrat and Carroll as his maid servant. Together they flee Russia during the Revolution, marry, and settle into the life of the common working class. Restless under his new status, Fairbanks pursues Tashman and tries his hand at swindling. A slow but interesting love story. Adapted from the novel "Revolt" by Mary McCall. **58m/B VHS.** Douglas Fairbanks Jr., Nancy Carroll, Lilyan Tashman, Sheila Terry, Guy Kibbee, Richard Alexander, Frank Reicher; ***D:*** William Dieterle; ***W:*** Douglas Fairbanks Jr., Niven Busch, Erwin Gelsey. *MGM*

Scarlet Empress 🦴🦴🦴½ **1934** One of Von Sternberg's greatest films tells the story of Catherine the Great and her rise to power. Dietrich stars as the beautiful royal wife who outwits her maniacal husband to become empress of Russia. Incredibly rich decor is a visual feast for the eye, as perfectionist von Sternberg fussed over every detail. Dietrich is excellent as Catherine, and von Sternberg's mastery of lighting and camerawork makes for a highly extravagant film. Based on the diary of Catherine the Great. **110m/B VHS.** Marlene Dietrich, John Lodge, Sam Jaffe, Louise Dresser, Maria Sieber, Sir C. Aubrey Smith, Ruthelma Stevens, Olive Tell; ***D:*** Josef von Sternberg; ***W:*** Manuel Komroff. *MCA, FCT*

The Scarlet Letter 🦴🦴 **1934** Unlikely comic relief provides only measure of redemption for this poorly rendered version of Hawthorne's classic novel about sin and Hester Prynne. **69m/B VHS, Beta.** Colleen Moore, Hardie Albright, Henry B. Walthall, Alan Hale, Cora Sue Collins, Betty Blythe; ***D:*** Robert G. Vignola. *NOS, BAR, VYY*

The Scarlet Letter 🦴🦴🦴 **1973** A studied, thoughtful, international production of the Nathaniel Hawthorne classic about a woman's adultery which incites puritanical violence and hysteria in colonial America. Fine modernization by Wenders. In German with English subtitles. **90m/C VHS, Beta.** *SP GE* Senta Berger, Lou Castel, Yella Rottlaender, William Layton, Yelena Samarina, Hans-Christian Blech; ***D:*** Wim Wenders. *FCT, GLV, INJ*

The Scarlet Letter *Woof!* **1995 (R)** Ewwwwww—ego-driven stinker of '95 ("Showgirls" not-withstanding). Feisty Hester Prynne (Moore) is condemned to wear the scarlet letter "A" of adultery by her 17-century Puritan neighbors because she bore a child out of wedlock. Oldman is the lusty Reverend Arthur Dimmesdale (her partner in illicit passion) while Duvall chews scenery as Hester's wronged hubby. This "freely adapted" version of the 1850 American classic should have set author Nathaniel Hawthorne spinning in his grave as his moral saga of sin and redemption meets 20th-century moviemaking by having the passion made explicit and a happy ending tacked on. **135m/C VHS, LV.** Demi Moore, Gary Oldman, Robert Duvall, Robert Prosky, Edward Hardwicke, Joan Plowright, Roy Dotrice, Dana Ivey, Sheldon Peters Wolfchild, Diane Salinger, Lisa Jolliff-Andoh, Amy Wright, Tim Woodward; ***D:*** Roland Joffe; ***W:*** Douglas Day Stewart; ***C:*** Alex Thomson; ***M:*** John Barry. Golden Raspberry Awards '95: Worst Remake/Sequel. *HPH*

The Scarlet Pimpernel 🦴🦴🦴½ **1934** "The Scarlet Pimpernel," supposed dandy of the English court, assumes a dual identity to outwit the French Republicans and aid innocent aristocrats during the French Revolution. Classic rendering of Baroness Orczy's novel, full of exploits, 18th century costumes, intrigue, damsels, etc. Produced by Alexander Korda, who fired the initial director, Rowland Brown. Remade for television in 1982. Available in colorized version. **95m/B VHS, Beta.** *GB* Leslie Howard, Joan Gardner, Merle Oberon, Raymond Massey, Anthony Bushell, Nigel Bruce; ***D:*** Harold Young. *CNG, NOS, PSM*

The Scarlet Pimpernel 🦴🦴🦴 **1982** Remake of the classic about a British dandy who saved French aristocrats from the Reign of Terror guillotines during the French Revolution. Made for British television version is almost as good as the original 1935 film, with beautiful costumes and sets and good performances from Seymour and Andrews. **142m/C VHS, Beta, LV.** *GB* Anthony Andrews, Jane Seymour, Ian McKellen, James Villiers, Eleanor David; ***D:*** Clive Donner; ***M:*** Nick Bicat. *LIV, VES, FUS*

Scarlet Spear *Woof!* **1954** Filmed in Nairobi National Park in Kenya. A great white hunter convinces a young African chief that the ancient practices of his people are uncivilized. Pathetically stated and culturally offensive by today's standards. **78m/C VHS, Beta.** John Bentley, Martha Hyer, Morasi; ***D:*** George Breakston. *MSP*

Scarlet Street ☙☙☙ **1945** A mild-mannered, middle-aged cashier becomes an embezzler when he gets involved with a predatory, manipulating woman. Lang remake of Jean Renoir's "La Chienne" (1931). Set apart from later attempts on the same theme by excellent direction by Lang and acting. Also available Colorized. **95m/B VHS, Beta.** Edward G. Robinson, Joan Bennett, Dan Duryea, Samuel S. Hinds; ***D:*** Fritz Lang; ***C:*** Milton Krasner. *CNG, NOS, HHT*

Scarlett ☙☙½ **1994** Well, fiddle-dee-dee. While purists may object to any tampering of "Gone With the Wind," this epic TV miniseries, from the Alexandra Ripley novel, manages to be good if overlong fun for those willing to sit back and relax. Scarlett tries to get back Tara and Rhett (they divorce but still battle continuously); explores her Irish family ties and even moves to Ireland; then gets involved with the wrong man and is accused of murder so Rhett can save her and everything can turn out okay (there's lots more). The big budget is up on-screen with lavish costumes and sets and a big cast—although why two Brits got the leads in this Southern melodrama is anyone's guess (Whalley-Kilmer and Dalton try hard). **360m/C VHS.** Joanne Whalley, Timothy Dalton, Ann-Margret, Barbara Barrie, Sean Bean, Brian Bedford, Stephen Collins, John Gielgud, Annabeth Gish, George Grizzard, Julie Harris, Tina Kellegher, Melissa Leo, Colm Meaney, Esther Rolle, Jean Smart, Elizabeth Wilson, Paul Winfield, Betsy Blair, Peter Eyre, Pippa Guard, Ronald Pickup, Gary Raymond, Dorothy Tutin; ***D:*** John Erman; ***W:*** William Hanley; ***M:*** John Morris. *CAF*

Scarred ☙½ *Street Love; Red on Red* **1984 (R)** Unwed teenage mother becomes prostitute to support baby. Predictable plot and acting pull this one down. **85m/C VHS, Beta.** Jennifer Mayo, Jackie Berryman, David Dean; ***D:*** Rosemarie Turko; ***W:*** Rosemarie Turko. *LIV, VES*

The Scars of Dracula ☙☙½ **1970 (R)** A young couple tangles with Dracula in their search for the man's missing brother. Gory, creepy, violent, sexy tale from the dark side. Don't see it late at night. Preceded by "Taste the Blood of Dracula" and followed by "Dracula A.D. 1972." Available on Laserdisc with "The Horror of Frankenstein." **96m/C VHS, Beta, LV.** *GB* Christopher Lee, Jenny Hanley, Dennis Waterman, Wendy Hamilton, Patrick Troughton, Michael Gwynn, Anouska Hempel, Michael Ripper; ***D:*** Roy Ward Baker; ***M:*** James Bernard. *REP, MLB*

Scavenger Hunt ☙ **1979 (PG)** Action begins when a deceased millionaire's will states that his 15 would-be heirs must compete in a scavenger hunt, and whoever collects all the items first wins the entire fortune. Big cast wanders about aimlessly. **117m/C VHS, Beta.** Richard Benjamin, James Coco, Ruth Buzzi, Cloris Leachman, Cleavon Little, Roddy McDowall, Scatman Crothers, Tony Randall, Robert Morley, Richard Mulligan, Dirk Benedict, Willie Aames, Vincent Price; ***D:*** Michael A. Schultz; ***M:*** Billy Goldenberg. *FOX*

Scavengers ☙ **1987 (PG-13)** A man and a woman become involved in a spy plot and wind up in all sorts of danger. Pathetic excuse for a "thriller." **94m/C VHS, Beta, LV.** Kenneth Gilman, Brenda Bakke, Ken Gampu, Norman Anstey, Crispin De Nys; ***D:*** Duncan McLachlan. *ACA*

Scenario du Film Passion ☙☙☙ **1982** A classically self-analyzing video piece by Godard, in which he recreates on tape the scenario for his film "Passion," resulting in a reflexive, experimental essay on the process of image-making and conceptualizing films, especially Godard's. In French with English subtitles. **54m/C VHS, Beta.** ***D:*** Jean-Luc Godard, Anne-Marie Mieville, Barnard Menoud. *EAI*

Scene of the Crime ☙☙½ **1985** Three short mysteries, which the audience is asked to solve: "The Newlywed Murder," "Medium Is the Murder" and "Vote for Murder." Made for television. **74m/C VHS, Beta.** Markie Post, Alan Thicke, Ben Piazza; ***D:*** Walter Grauman. *MCA*

Scene of the Crime ☙☙☙ **1987** Beautiful widow, trapped in small French town, is sexually awakened by escaped convict hiding out near her home. Acclaimed, but sometimes distracting camera technique and slow pace undermine the film. In French with English subtitles. **90m/C VHS.** *FR* Catherine Deneuve, Danielle Darrieux, Wadeck Stanczak, Victor Lanoux, Nicolas Giraudi, Jean Bousquet, Claire Nebout; ***D:*** Andre Techine; ***W:*** Olivier Assayas. *KIV, FCT*

Scenes from a Mall ☙☙ **1991 (R)** Conspicuous consumers spend sixteenth wedding anniversary waltzing in mall while marriage unravels with few laughs. Surprisingly superficial comedy given the depth of talent of Allen and Midler. **87m/C VHS, Beta, LV.** Woody Allen, Bette Midler, Bill Irwin, Daren Firestone, Rebecca Nickels; ***Cameos:*** Fabio Lanzoni; ***D:*** Paul Mazursky; ***W:*** Paul Mazursky; ***C:*** Fred Murphy. *TOU, IME*

Scenes from a Marriage ☙☙☙☙ **1973 (PG)** Originally produced in six one-hour episodes for Swedish television, this bold and sensitive film excruciatingly portrays the painful, unpleasant, disintegration of a marriage. Ullmann is superb. Realistic and disturbing. Dubbed. **168m/C VHS, Beta.** *SW* Liv Ullmann, Erland Josephson, Bibi Andersson, Jan Malmsjo, Anita Wall; ***D:*** Ingmar Bergman; ***W:*** Ingmar Bergman; ***C:*** Sven Nykvist. Golden Globe Awards '75: Best Foreign Film; National Board of Review Awards '74: 5 Best Foreign Films of the Year; New York Film Critics Awards '74: Best Actress (Ullmann), Best Screenplay; National Society of Film Critics Awards '74: Best Actress (Ullmann), Best Film, Best Screenplay, Best Supporting Actress (Andersson). *HMV*

Scenes from a Murder ☙½ **1972** A killer (Savalas) stalks a beautiful actress (Heywood). Dull excuse for a suspense flick. **91m/C VHS, Beta.** *IT* Telly Savalas, Anne Heywood, Giorgio Piazza; ***D:*** Alberto De Martino. *NO*

Scenes from the Class Struggle in Beverly Hills ☙☙½ **1989 (R)** Social satire about the wealthy, their servants, and their hangers-on in two Hollywood households. Two chauffeurs spend their spare time lusting after their lovely employers, and bet to see who can accomplish reality first. All kinds of erotic capers result. Usually funny and irreverent; occasionally misfires or takes itself too seriously. Reunites the trio from cult classic "Eating Raoul": Bartel, Woronov, and Beltran. Remake of Renoir's "The Rules of the Game." **103m/C VHS, Beta, LV.** Jacqueline Bisset, Ray Sharkey, Mary Woronov, Robert Beltran, Ed Begley Jr., Wallace Shawn, Paul Bartel, Paul Mazursky, Arnetia Walker, Rebecca Schaeffer; ***Cameos:*** Little Richard; ***D:*** Paul Bartel; ***W:*** Bruce Wagner; ***M:*** Stanley Myers. *NO*

Scenes from the Goldmine ☙½ **1987 (R)** A young woman joins a rock band and falls in love with its lead singer. Realistic but bland; music not memorable (performed mostly by the actors themselves). **99m/C VHS, Beta, LV.** Catherine Mary Stewart, Cameron Dye, Joe Pantoliano, John Ford Coley, Steve Railsback, Timothy B. Schmit, Jewel Shepard, Alex Rocco, Lee Ving, Lesley-Anne Down; ***D:*** Marc Rocco. *NLC*

The Scent of a Woman ☙☙½ *Sweet Smell of Woman; Profumo di Donna* **1975** An acclaimed dark comedy that may be an acquired taste for some. A blinded military officer and his valet take a sensual tour of Italy, the sightless man seducing beautiful women on the way. But at the end of the journey awaits a shock, and the real point of the tale, based on a novel by Giovanni Arpino. In Italian with English subtitles. Remade in 1992 as "Scent of a Woman." **103m/C VHS.** *IT* Vittorio Gassman; ***D:*** Dino Risi. Nominations: Cannes Film Festival '75: Best Film. *NO*

Scent of a Woman ☙☙☙ **1992 (R)** Pacino is a powerhouse (verging on caricature) in a story that, with anyone else in the lead, would be your run-of-the-mill, overly sentimental coming of age/redemption flick. Blind, bitter, and semi-alcoholic Pacino is a retired army colonel under the care of his married niece. He's home alone over Thanksgiving, under the watchful eye of local prep school student Charlie (O'Donnell). Pacino's abrasive (though wonderfully intuitive and romantic) colonel makes an impact on viewers that lingers like a woman's scent long after the last tango. O'Donnell is competently understated in key supporting role, while the tango lesson between Pacino and Anwar dances to the tune of "classic." Box-office winner is a remake of 1975 Italian film "Profumo di Donna." The laserdisc version is available in letterbox format. **157m/C VHS, LV.** Al Pacino, Chris O'Donnell, James Rebhorn, Gabrielle Anwar, Philip S. Hoffman, Richard Venture, Bradley Whitford, Rochelle Oliver, Margaret Eginton, Tom Riis Farrell, Frances Conroy; ***D:*** Martin Brest; ***W:*** Bo Goldman; ***C:*** Donald E. Thorin; ***M:*** Thomas Newman. Academy Awards '92: Best Actor (Pacino); Golden Globe Awards '93: Best Actor—Drama (Pacino), Best Film—Drama, Best Writing; Nominations: Academy Awards '92: Best Adapted Screenplay, Best Director (Brest), Best Picture; British Academy Awards '93: Best Adapted Screenplay. *MCA, MOV, BTV*

The Scent of Green Papaya ☙☙☙ **1993** Tranquil film, set in 1951 Vietnam, follows 10-year-old peasant girl Mui as she spends the next 10 years as a servant in a troubled family, gracefully accommodating herself to the small changes in her life. At 20, she finds a fairy-tale romance with her next employer, a young pianist. Presents a romanticized view of the stoicism of Vietnamese women but is visually beautiful. Directorial debut of Hung is based on his childhood memories of Vietnam, which he recreated on a soundstage outside Paris. In Vietnamese with English subtitles. **104m/C VHS, LV.** *VT* Tran Nu Yen-Khe, Lu Man San, Truong Thi Loc, Vuong Hoa Hoi; ***D:*** Tran Anh Hung; ***W:*** Tran Anh Hung, Patricia Petit. Nominations: Academy Awards '93: Best Foreign Language Film. *COL*

Scherzo **1939** One of McLaren's earliest films, an abstract meditation lost in 1939 and subsequently found and reconstructed in 1984. **2m/C VHS, Beta.** ***D:*** Norman McLaren. *NFB*

Schindler's List ☙☙☙☙ **1993 (R)** Spielberg's staggering evocation of the Holocaust finds its voice in Oscar Schindler (Neeson), womanizing German businessman and aspiring war profiteer, who cajoled, bribed, and bullied the Nazis into allowing him to employ Jews in his Polish factories during WWII. By doing so he saved over 1,000 lives. The atrocities are depicted matter of factly as a by-product of sheer Nazi evil. Shot in black and white and powered by splendid performances. Neeson uses his powerful physique as a protective buffer; Kingsley is watchful as his industrious Jewish accountant; and Fiennes personifies evil as Nazi Amon Goeth. Based on the novel by Thomas Keneally, which itself was based on survivor's memories. Filmed on location in Cracow, Poland; due to the sensitive nature of the story, sets of the Auschwitz concentration camp were reconstructed directly outside the camp after protests about filming on the actual site. A tour de force and labor of love for Spielberg, who finally garnered the attention and respect as a filmmaker he deserves. **195m/B VHS, LV.** Liam Neeson, Ben Kingsley, Ralph Fiennes, Embeth Davidtz, Caroline Goodall, Jonathan Sagalle, Mark Ivanir; ***D:*** Steven Spielberg; ***W:*** Steven Zaillian; ***C:*** Janusz Kaminski; ***M:*** John Williams. Academy Awards '93: Best Adapted Screenplay, Best Art Direction/Set Decoration, Best Cinematography, Best Director (Spielberg), Best Film Editing, Best Picture, Best Original Score; British Academy Awards '93: Best Adapted Screenplay, Best Director (Spielberg), Best Film, Best Supporting Actor (Fiennes); Golden Globe Awards '94: Best Director (Spielberg), Best Film—Drama, Best Screenplay; Los Angeles Film Critics Association Awards '93: Best Cinematography, Best Film; National Board of Review Awards '93: Best Film; New York Film Critics Awards '93: Best Cinematography, Best Film, Best Supporting Actor (Fiennes); Writers Guild of America '93: Best Adapted Screenplay; Nominations: Academy Awards '93: Best Actor (Neeson), Best Costume Design, Best Makeup, Best Sound, Best Supporting Actor (Fiennes); Golden Globe Awards '94: Best Actor—Drama (Neeson), Best Supporting Actor (Fiennes), Best Original Score; MTV Movie Awards '94: Best Film, Breakthrough Performance (Fiennes). *MCA*

Schizo ☙ *Amok; Blood of the Undead* **1977 (R)** Devious intentions abound as a middle-aged man is overcome by weird scenes and revelations, caused by the impending wedding of the figure skater he adores. Confusing tale of insanity, obsession, and skating. **109m/C VHS, Beta.** Lynne Frederick, John Layton; ***D:*** Pete Walker. *MED*

Schizoid ⚘ *Murder by Mail* **1980 (R)** Advice-to-the-lovelorn columnist Hill receives a series of threatening letters causing her to wonder whether psychiatrist Kinski is bumping off his own patients. Boring blood dripper that's difficult to follow. **91m/C VHS, Beta.** Klaus Kinski, Marianna Hill, Craig Wasson; ***D:*** David Paulsen. *MCA*

Schlock ⚘⚘ *The Banana Monster* **1973 (PG)** Accurately titled horror parody is first directorial effort for Landis, who does double duty as a missing link who kills people and falls in love with blind girl. Look for cameo appearance by Forrest J. Ackerman; ape-makeup by Rick Baker. **78m/C VHS.** John Landis, Saul Kahan, Joseph Piantadosi, Eliza Garrett; ***Cameos:*** Forrest J. Ackerman; ***D:*** John Landis; ***W:*** John Landis. *NO*

Schnelles Geld ⚘½ **1984** A mild-mannered guy gets involved with a prostitute, and is plunged into a world of crime and drugs. In German with English subtitles. **90m/C VHS, Beta.** *GE VCD, GLV*

School Daze ⚘⚘⚘ **1988 (R)** Director/writer/star Lee's second outing is a rambunctious comedy (with a message, of course) set at an African-American college in the South. Skimpy plot revolves around the college's homecoming weekend and conflict among frats and sororities and African-Americans who would lose their racial identity and others who assert it. Entertaining and thought provoking. A glimpse at Lee's "promise," fulfilled in "Do the Right Thing." **114m/C VHS, Beta, LV.** Spike Lee, Laurence "Larry" Fishburne, Giancarlo Esposito, Tisha Campbell, Ossie Davis, Joe Seneca, Art Evans, Ellen Holly, Branford Marsalis, Bill Nunn, Kadeem Hardison, Darryl M. Bell, Joie Lee, Tyra Ferrell, Jasmine Guy, Gregg Burge, Kasi Lemmons, Samuel L. Jackson, Phyllis Hyman; ***D:*** Spike Lee; ***W:*** Spike Lee; ***M:*** Bill Lee. *COL, FCT*

School for Scandal ⚘⚘ **1965** British television adaptation of Richard Sheridan's comedic play of the morals and manners of 18th century England. **100m/B VHS, Beta.** *GB* Joan Plowright, Felix Aylmer. *VYY*

School Spirit ⚘ **1985 (R)** A hormonally motivated college student is killed during a date. He comes back as a ghost to haunt the campus, disrupt the stuffy president's affair, and fall in love. Forgettable, lame, low-grade teen sex flick. **90m/C VHS, Beta.** Tom Nolan, Elizabeth Foxx, Larry Linville; ***D:*** Allan Holleb; ***W:*** Geoffrey Baere; ***M:*** Tom Bruner. *MED*

School Ties ⚘⚘⚘ **1992 (PG-13)** Encino man Fraser does a dramatic turn as a talented 1950's quarterback who gets a scholarship to the elite St. Matthew prep school. To conform with the closed-mindedness of the McCarthy era, both his father and coach suggest that he hide his Jewish religion. Fraser's compliance results in his big-man-on-campus status, until his rival in football and his love interest both find out that he is Jewish, creating an ugly rift in the school. What easily could have been just another teen hunk flick looks at much more than just Fraser's pretty face in successful, unflinching treatment of anti-Semitism. **110m/C VHS, Beta, LV.** Brendan Fraser, Matt Damon, Chris O'Donnell, Randall Batinkoff, Andrew Lowery, Cole Hauser, Ben Affleck, Anthony Rapp, Amy Locane, Peter Donat, Zeljko Ivanek, Kevin Tighe, Michael Higgins, Ed Lauter; ***D:*** Robert Mandel; ***W:*** Dick Wolf, Darryl Ponicsan; ***M:*** Maurice Jarre. *PAR*

Science Crazed ⚘½ **1990** A scientist creates a monster who could conceivably destroy the world. **90m/C VHS, Beta.** *CA* Cameron Klein; ***D:*** Ron Switzer. *NO*

Scissors ⚘½ **1991 (R)** Yes, this Hitchcock imitation needs trimming. An unstable young woman contends with a rapist, devious lookalikes, birds, and a prison-like apartment, not all of which are relevant to the plot. An unsharp stab at suspense from novelist/filmmaker DeFelitta. **105m/C VHS, Beta.** Sharon Stone, Steve Railsback, Michelle Phillips, Ronny Cox; ***D:*** Frank de Felitta; ***W:*** Frank de Felitta. *PAR*

Scorchers ⚘⚘ **1992 (R)** Back in the bayou, Splendid (Lloyd), a newlywed who won't sleep with her husband, and her cousin Talbot (Tilly), a preacher's daughter whose husband prefers the town whore Thais (Dunaway), find their lives intertwined because of their marital and sexual problems. A real "scorcher." **81m/C VHS, Beta, LV.** Faye Dunaway, Denholm Elliott, James Earl Jones, Emily Lloyd, Jennifer Tilly, Leland Crooke, James Wilder, Anthony Geary; ***D:*** David Beaird; ***W:*** David Beaird. *FXV, VTR*

Scorchy ⚘ **1976 (R)** Low-budget female cop action flick about a narcotics agent (Stevens) on the trail of a drug kingpin. Blood and guts, guns, and violence. Poor casting. **100m/C VHS, Beta.** Connie Stevens, William Smith, Cesare Danova, Marlene Schmidt; ***D:*** Howard (Hikmet) Avedis; ***W:*** Howard (Hikmet) Avedis. *LIV*

Scorned ⚘⚘ **1993 (R)** Seductive Patricia Langley loves her husband Truman so much that she'll do anything to help him get that promotion, including seducing another man. Too bad Alex Weston gets the promotion instead. Really too bad, since Patricia decides Alex has ruined her life and she's going to get revenge by ruining his. Also available in an unrated version. **100m/C VHS, LV.** Shannon Tweed, Andrew Stevens, Michael D. Arenz, Kim Morgan Greene, Stephen Young, Daniel McVicar; ***D:*** Andrew Stevens; ***W:*** Barry Avrich. *PSM*

Scorpio ⚘⚘½ **1973 (PG)** Okay cat-and-mouse espionage tale about a wily, veteran CIA agent (Lancaster) who may have turned traitor. He's set-up to be killed by a CIA boss but the assassin, code-name Scorpio (Delon), has some trouble fulfilling his assignment. Cross- and double-cross abound. **114m/C VHS.** Burt Lancaster, Alain Delon, Paul Scofield, John Colicos, Gayle Hunnicutt, J.D. Cannon, Joanne Linville, Melvin Stewart, James B. Sikking, Vladek Sheybal, William Smithers, Celeste Yarnall; ***D:*** Michael Winner. *MGM*

The Scorpio Factor ⚘⚘ **1990** Murder and mayhem follow microchip heist. **87m/C VHS.** Attila Bertalan, David Nerman, Wendy Dawn Wilson. *NO*

Scorpion ⚘ **1986 (R)** A karate-master and anti-terrorist expert defuses a skyjacking and infiltrates international assassination conspiracies. Ex-real life karate champ Tulleners is a ho-hum hero, and the story is warmed over. **98m/C VHS, Beta, LV.** Tonny Tulleners, Allen Williams, Don Murray; ***D:*** William Reed. *COL, HHE*

Scorpion with Two Tails ⚘ **1982** In an underworld of terror, people die grotesque deaths that a woman dreams of. **99m/C VHS.** John Saxon, Van Johnson. *NO*

The Scorpion Woman ⚘⚘ **1989** A female Viennese judge becomes entwined in an unusual case which partially parallels her own life. Her new young lover turns out to be bisexual. Not gripping. In German with English subtitles. **101m/C VHS, Beta.** *GE* Angelica Domrose, Fritz Hammel; ***D:*** Susanne Zanke. *NO*

The Scorpion's Tail ⚘ **1971** Graphic murder scenes rev up this early thriller by Martino filmed with plot twists and visual games. Dubbed in English. **90m/C VHS.** *IT SP* Evelyn Stewart, Anita Strindberg, George Hilton, Luigi Pistilli, Janine Reynaud; ***D:*** Sergio Martino; ***W:*** Sauro Scavolini, Ernesto Gastaldi; ***M:*** Bruno Nicolai. *VSM*

Scotland Yard Inspector ⚘⚘ *Lady in the Fog* **1952** An American newspaperman (Romero) in London looks for a killer. Nothing special. **73m/B VHS, Beta, LV.** *GB* Cesar Romero, Bernadette O'Farrell; ***D:*** Sam Newfield. *MLB*

Scott of the Antarctic ⚘⚘½ **1948** Drama of doomed British expedition of 1911 struggling to be the first group to reach the South Pole. Much of the stunning location filming was shot in the Swiss Alps. Story is authentic, but oddly uninvolving, as though seen from afar. **111m/C VHS, Beta.** *GB* John Mills, Christopher Lee, Kenneth More, Derek Bond; ***D:*** Charles Frend; ***C:*** Geoffrey Unsworth. *REP, DVT, NOS*

Scott Turow's The Burden of Proof ⚘⚘½ *The Burden of Proof* **1992** Attorney Alejandro "Sandy" Stern (Elizondo) struggles to discover the reasons behind his wife's baffling suicide and deal with the problems caused by the federal investigation of his brother-in-law's commodities business. The character of Stern was also featured in the film "Presumed Innocent" (played by Raul Julia). TV movie; on 2 cassettes. **184m/C VHS.** Hector Elizondo, Brian Dennehy, Mel Harris, Stefanie Powers, Victoria Principal, Adrienne Barbeau, Anne Bobby, Gail Strickland, Concetta Tomei, Jeffrey Tambor; ***D:*** Mike Robe; ***C:*** Kees Van Oostrum. *TVC*

Scoumoune ⚘⚘½ **1974** The local "fixer" and heavy gets into trouble and no one comes to help. A movie that searches for honesty. Dubbed in English. **87m/C VHS, Beta.** *FR* Jean-Paul Belmondo, Claudia Cardinale. *NO*

The Scout ⚘⚘ **1994 (PG-13)** Brooks is an about-to-be-canned scout for the New York Yankees who discovers a weird, though genuine, phenom pitcher (Fraser) on a trip to Mexico. He convinces the Yankees to take the phenom on, though he's not sure whether Fraser isn't a few innings shy of a complete game. But with a 100 mph fast ball and a bat that would have made Babe Ruth envious, who cares? Film straddles sports comedy and melodrama territories, satisfying in neither. Fraser plays variation on Encino Man. Brooks rewrote part of the script, adding much needed biting humor, but not enough. Bombastic real-life team owner Steinbrenner plays himself. **101m/C VHS.** Albert Brooks, Brendan Fraser, Dianne Wiest, Lane Smith, Michael Rapaport, Steve Garvey, Bob Costas, Roy Firestone, Anne Twomey, Tony Bennett; ***D:*** Michael Ritchie; ***W:*** Albert Brooks, Andrew Bergman, Monica Johnson; ***M:*** Bill Conti. *FXV*

Scout's Honor ⚘⚘ **1980** An orphan (Coleman) is determined to become the best Cub Scout ever when he joins a troop led by an executive who dislikes children. Harmless, enjoyable family tale includes several former child stars as Scout parents. Made for television. **96m/C VHS, Beta.** Gary Coleman, Katherine Helmond, Wilfrid Hyde-White, Pat O'Brien, Joanna Moore, Meeno Peluce, Jay North, Harry (Henry) Morgan, Angela Cartwright; ***D:*** Henry Levin. *NO*

Scrambled Feet ⚘⚘½ **1983** An uninhibited satire of the world of show business. **100m/C VHS, Beta.** Madeline Kahn. *TTC*

Scream ⚘ **1983 (R)** Vacationers on a raft trip down the Rio Grande are terrorized by a mysterious murderer. Hopelessly dull. **86m/C VHS, Beta.** Pepper Martin, Hank Worden, Alvy Moore, Woody Strode, John Ethan Wayne; ***D:*** Byron Quisenberry. *LIV, VES*

Scream and Scream Again ⚘⚘½ **1970 (PG)** Price is a sinister doctor who tries to create a super race of people devoid of emotions. Cushing is the mastermind behind the plot. Lee is the agent investigating a series of murders. Three great horror stars, a psychadelic disco, great '60s fashions; it's all here. **95m/C VHS, Beta.** *GB* Vincent Price, Christopher Lee, Peter Cushing, Judy Huxtable, Alfred Marks, Anthony Newlands, Uta Levka, Judi Bloom, Yutte Stensgaard; ***D:*** Gordon Hessler. *LIV, VES, ORI*

Scream, Baby, Scream ⚘ *Nightmare House* **1969** An unsuccessful artist switches from sculpting clay to carving young models' faces into hideous deformed creatures. **86m/C VHS, Beta.** Ross Harris, Eugenie Wingate, Chris Martell, Suzanne Stuart, Larry Swanson, Brad Grinter; ***D:*** Joseph Adler. *NO*

Scream Blacula Scream ⚘⚘ **1973 (R)** Blacula returns from his dusty undoing in the original movie to once again suck the blood out of greater Los Angeles. A voodoo priestess (Grier) is the only person with the power to stop him. A weak follow up to the great "Blacula," but worth a look for Marshall and Grier. **96m/C VHS.** William Marshall, Don Mitchell, Pam Grier, Michael Conrad, Richard Lawson, Lynne Moody, Janee Michelle, Barbara Rhoades, Bernie Hamilton; ***D:*** Bob Kelljan. *ORI, FCT*

Scream Bloody Murder *Woof!* **1972 (R)** A young boy grinds his father to death with a tractor but mangles his own hand trying to jump off. After receiving a steel claw and being released from a mental institution he continues his murderous ways in and around his home town. Inspiring. **90m/C VHS, Beta.** Fred Holbert, Leigh Mitchell, Robert Knox, Suzette Hamilton; ***D:*** Robert Emery. *VCI*

Scream Dream 𝄞 **1989 (R)** A beautiful rock star uses her supernatural powers to control her fans, turning them into revenge-seeking monsters when she wants to. Heavy on the blood and skin; heavily exploitative. **80m/C VHS.** Melissa Moore, Carole Carr, Nikki Riggins, Jesse Ray; ***D:*** Donald Farmer; ***W:*** Donald Farmer. *NO*

Scream for Help 𝄞 **1986 (R)** A young girl discovers that her cheating stepfather is plotting to murder her mother, but no one will believe her. Is she paranoid? So bad it's funny; otherwise, it's just bad, and far from suspenseful. **95m/C VHS, Beta, LV.** Rachael Kelly, David Brooks, Marie Masters; ***D:*** Michael Winner; ***W:*** Tom Holland. *ORI, WAR*

Scream of Fear 𝄞𝄞𝄞 *Taste of Fear* **1961** A wheelchair-bound young woman goes to visit her father and new stepmother only to find her father is away on business. But she believes she sees her father's corpse. Is someone trying to drive her mad? Abounds in plot twists and mistaken identities. A truly spooky film, suspenseful, and well-made. **81m/B VHS, Beta.** *GB* Susan Strasberg, Ronald Lewis, Ann Todd, Christopher Lee; ***D:*** Seth Holt; ***W:*** Jimmy Sangster. *COL, MLB*

Scream of the Demon Lover *Woof!* **1971 (R)** A young biochemist has a busy day as she works for a reclusive Baron. She fantasizes about him, tries to track down a murderer, and eventually discovers a mutant in the cellar. About as bad as they come, but short! **75m/C VHS, Beta.** Jennifer Hartley, Jeffrey Chase; ***D:*** J.L. Merino. *NLC*

Screamer 𝄞 **1974** A woman wants revenge after she is viciously attacked and raped. Now every man she sees is her attacker as she becomes more and more unbalanced. **71m/C VHS, Beta.** Pamela Franklin, Donal McCann. *NO*

Screamers 𝄞 *L'Isola Degli Uomini Pesce; Island of the Fishmen; Something Waits in the Dark* **1980 (R)** A mad scientist on a desert island gleefully turns escaped convicts into grotesque monstrosities. Gory and gratuitous. **83m/C VHS, Beta.** Richard Johnson, Joseph Cotten, Barbara Bach; ***D:*** Dan T. Miller, Sergio Martino. *SUE*

Screamers 𝄞𝄞 **1996 (R)** In the year 2078 Colonel Joe Hendricksson (Weller) and a small band of survivors fight a civil war on the radiation contaminated planet Sirius 6B. They run up against the screamers—mechanical creatures with razor-sharp claws, originally designed to protect humans. The screamers are bent on destroying all life in the universe while somehow mutating and breeding on their own. Unfortunately, director Duguay doesn't give any indication how this is taking place. Some fine stunt work and special effects redeem standard action adventure. Based on the novella "Second Variety" by Philip K. Dick ("Blade Runner"). **107m/C VHS, LV, 8mm.** Peter Weller, Jennifer Rubin, Andrew Lauer, Charles Powell, Ron White, Michael Caloz; ***D:*** Christian Duguay; ***W:*** Dan O'Bannon, Miguel Tejada-Flores; ***C:*** Rodney Gibbons; ***M:*** Normand Corbeil. *COL*

The Screaming Dead 𝄞 *Dracula vs. Frankenstein* **1972** Monsters rise from the tomb to do battle with planet Earth and each other. Not to be confused with the Al Adamson epic "Dracula vs. Frankenstein." **84m/C VHS.** *SP* Dennis Price, Howard Vernon, Alberto Dalbes, Mary Francis, Genevieve Deloir, Josianne Gibert, Fernando Bilbao; ***D:*** Jess (Jesus) Franco. *NO*

The Screaming Skull 𝄞½ **1958** Man redecorates house with skulls in attempt to drive already anxious wife insane. **68m/B VHS.** William Hudson, Peggy Webber, Toni Johnson, Russ Conway, Alex Nicol; ***D:*** Alex Nicol; ***M:*** Ernest Gold. *NOS, SNC*

Screams of a Winter Night 𝄞 **1979 (PG)** Ghostly tale of an evil monster from the lake and the terror he causes. **92m/C VHS, Beta.** Matt Borel, Gil Glasco. *NO*

Screamtime 𝄞 **1983 (R)** Two fiendish friends filch a trilogy of horror tapes for home viewing. After the show, real scary things happen. **89m/C VHS, Beta.** Jean Anderson, Robin Bailey, Dora Bryan, David Van Day; ***D:*** Al Beresford. *LIV*

Screen Test *Woof!* **1985 (R)** Oversexed silly teenagers arrange fake screen tests in order to meet girls. **84m/C VHS, Beta, LV.** Michael Allan Bloom, Robert Bundy, Paul Lueken, David Simpatico; ***D:*** Sam Auster; ***W:*** Sam Auster. *COL*

Screwball Academy 𝄞½ **1986 (R)** A beautiful female director makes a soft-core film on a secluded island, and gets trouble from thugs, evangelists, horny crew members and others. Former "SCTV" director John Blanchard understandably used a pseudonym to direct this lame effort. **90m/C VHS, Beta.** Colleen Camp, Kenneth Welsh, Christine Cattall; ***D:*** Reuben Rose. *TWE*

Screwballs 𝄞 **1983 (R)** Freewheeling group of high school boys stirs up trouble for their snooty and virginal homecoming queen. Another inept teen sex comedy with no subtlety whatsoever. Sequel: "Loose Screws." **80m/C VHS, Beta.** Peter Keleghan, Lynda Speciale; ***D:*** Rafal Zeilinski; ***W:*** Jim Wynorski. *WAR*

Scrooge 𝄞𝄞𝄞 **1935** On Christmas Eve a miser changes his ways after receiving visits from the ghosts of Christmas past, present, and future. Co-scripter Hicks gives an interesting performance as Ebeneezer Scrooge. Based on the classic novel "A Christmas Carol" by Charles Dickens. **61m/B VHS, Beta.** *GB* Seymour Hicks, Maurice Evans, Robert Cochran, Donald Calthrop, Mary Glynne, Oscar Asche; ***D:*** Henry Edwards; ***W:*** Seymour Hicks. *VYY, CCB, DVT*

Scrooge 𝄞𝄞½ **1970 (G)** Well-done musical version of Charles Dickens' classic "A Christmas Carol," about a miserly old man who is faced with ghosts on Christmas Eve. Finney is memorable in the title role. ♫The Beautiful Day; Happiness; Thank You Very Much; A Christmas Carol; Christmas Children; I Hate People; Farver Chris'mas; See the Phantoms; December the 25th. **86m/C VHS, Beta, LV.** *GB* Albert Finney, Alec Guinness, Edith Evans, Kenneth More; ***D:*** Ronald Neame; ***W:*** Leslie Bricusse; ***C:*** Oswald Morris; ***M:*** Leslie Bricusse. Golden Globe Awards '71: Best Actor—Musical/Comedy (Finney); Nominations: Academy Awards '70: Best Art Direction/Set Decoration, Best Costume Design, Best Song ("Thank You Very Much"), Best Original Score. *FOX, FUS*

Scrooged 𝄞𝄞 **1988 (PG-13)** Somewhat disjointed big-budgeted version of the hallowed classic. A callous television executive staging "A Christmas Carol" is himself visited by the three ghosts and sees the light. Kane is terrific as one of the ghosts. Film is heavy-handed, Murray too sardonic to be believable. **101m/C VHS, Beta, LV, 8mm.** Bill Murray, Carol Kane, John Forsythe, David Johansen, Bob(cat) Goldthwait, Karen Allen, Michael J. Pollard, Brian Doyle-Murray, Alfre Woodard, John Glover, Robert Mitchum, Buddy Hackett, Robert Goulet, Jamie Farr, Mary Lou Retton, Lee Majors; ***D:*** Richard Donner; ***W:*** Mitch Glazer, Michael O'Donoghue; ***C:*** Michael Chapman; ***M:*** Danny Elfman. *PAR*

Scrubbers 𝄞 **1982 (R)** Young girl is sent to reform school where she's forced to survive in a cruel and brutal environment. Low-budget "reform school" movie with no point, but lots of lesbianism. **93m/C VHS, Beta.** *GB* Amanda York, Chrissie Cotterill, Elizabeth Edmonds, Kate Ingram, Debbie Bishop, Dana Gillespie; ***D:*** Mai Zetterling. *NO*

Scruffy **1980** An orphan and his dog survive with the help of two crooks who are reformed through their love for the little boy. Animated. **72m/C VHS, Beta.** ***V:*** Alan Young, June Foray, Hans Conried, Nancy McKeon. *WOV, GKK, WTA*

Scruples 𝄞𝄞½ **1980** Set in the glamorous, jet-setting world of Beverly Hills, this top-rated miniseries follows the career of Billy Ikehorn (Wagner) as she weds a wealthy industrialist and opens a clothing boutique named "Scruples." She caters to high society's haute couture, and encounters unscrupulous individuals who threaten to dethrone her from her position of power and privilege. Based on the best-selling novel by Judith Krantz. **279m/C VHS, Beta.** Lindsay Wagner, Barry Bostwick, Kim Cattrall, Gavin MacLeod, Connie Stevens, Efrem Zimbalist Jr., Gene Tierney; ***M:*** Charles Bernstein. *WAR*

Scum 𝄞𝄞𝄞 **1979** Adapted from Roy Minton's acclaimed play, this British production looks at the struggle among three young men in a British Borstal (a prison for young convicts.) Portrays the physical, sexual, and psychological violence committed. Horrifying and powerful. **96m/C VHS, Beta.** *GB* Phil Daniels, Mick Ford, Ray Winstone; ***D:*** Alan Clarke. *PSM*

Sea Chase 𝄞𝄞½ **1955** An odd post-war sea adventure, wherein a renegade German freighter captain is pursued by British and German navies as he leaves Australia at the outbreak of WWII. A Prussian Wayne rivaled only by his infamous Genghis Khan in "The Conqueror" for strange character selection. Turner is on board as Wayne's girlfriend. **117m/C VHS, Beta, LV.** John Wayne, Lana Turner, Tab Hunter, James Arness, Lyle Bettger, David Farrar, Richard Davalos, Claude Akins, John Qualen; ***D:*** John Farrow; ***C:*** William Clothier. *WAR*

Sea Devils 𝄞 **1931** Sentenced to prison for a crime he didn't commit, a man escapes and joins a boatload of treasure hunters, but mutiny is afoot. Don't get soaked by this cheapie. **77m/B VHS.** Walter Long, Edmund Burns, Henry Otto, James Donnelly; ***D:*** Joseph Levering. *SNC, NOS*

Sea Devils 𝄞𝄞 **1937** The tale of a sea captain and his lovely daughter who have differing opinions on whom she should marry. While her father would like her to marry a tame gentlemen under his command, she has her heart set on another beau. Sound predictable? It is, but fun. **88m/B VHS.** Victor McLaglen, Preston Foster, Ida Lupino, Donald Woods, Gordon Jones; ***D:*** Ben Stoloff. *MED*

Sea Devils 𝄞𝄞 **1953** A smuggler and a beautiful spy come together during the Napoleonic Wars in this sea romance filled with intrigue and adventure. **86m/C VHS, Beta.** *GB* Rock Hudson, Yvonne De Carlo, Maxwell Reed; ***D:*** Raoul Walsh. *MED*

Sea Gypsies 𝄞𝄞 **1978 (G)** A sailing crew of five is shipwrecked off the Aleutian Islands. They must escape before winter or learn to survive. Passable family drama. **101m/C VHS, Beta.** Robert F. Logan, Mikki Jamison-Olsen, Heather Rattray, Cjon Damitri; ***D:*** Stewart Raffill; ***W:*** Stewart Raffill. *WAR*

The Sea Hawk 𝄞𝄞𝄞½ **1940** An English privateer learns the Spanish are going to invade England with their Armada. After numerous adventures, he is able to aid his queen and help save his country, finding romance along the way. One of Flynn's swashbuckling best. Available colorized. **128m/B VHS, Beta, LV.** Errol Flynn, Claude Rains, Donald Crisp, Alan Hale, Flora Robson, Brenda Marshall, Henry Daniell, Gilbert Roland, James Stephenson, Una O'Connor; ***D:*** Michael Curtiz; ***W:*** Howard Koch. Nominations: Academy Awards '40: Best Interior Decoration, Best Sound, Best Score. *MGM, TTC, FOX*

Sea Hound **1947** A 15-part series set in the late 1940s that charts the voyage of a group of pirates searching for buried treasure. Everything goes well until Crabbe emerges to wreck their hopes. **?m/B VHS.** Buster Crabbe, Jimmy Lloyd, Pamela Blake, Ralph Hodges, Bob Barron; ***D:*** Walter B. Eason, Mack V. Wright. *MLB, GPV*

Sea Lion 𝄞𝄞 **1921** A vicious sea captain, embittered by a past romance, becomes sadistic and intolerable, until the truth emerges. Lots of action, but plodding, rehashed plot. Silent. **50m/B VHS, Beta.** Hobart Bosworth. *VYY*

Sea of Dreams 𝄞 **1990** Don't expect much in the way of a script from this soft-core production. **80m/C VHS, Beta.** Jon Rodgers, Chad Scott, Jacky Peel, Renee O'Neil. *AHV, HHE*

Sea of Love ☠☠☠½ **1989 (R)** A tough, tightly wound thriller about an alcoholic cop with a mid-life crisis. While following the track of a serial killer, he begins a torrid relationship with one of his suspects. Pacino doesn't stand a chance when Barkin heats up the screen. **113m/C VHS, Beta, LV.** Al Pacino, Ellen Barkin, John Goodman, Michael Rooker, William Hickey, Richard Jenkins; ***D:*** Harold Becker; ***W:*** Richard Price; ***M:*** Trevor Jones. *MCA*

Sea of Sand ☠☠½ *Desert Patrol* **1958** Typical actioner set in WWII finds a British desert patrol's latest mission is to blow up Rommel's fuel supply before the battle of El Alamein. Lots of heroics against the Nazis and stiff upper lips. **97m/B VHS.** *GB* Richard Attenborough, John Gregson, Michael Craig, Vincent Ball, Ray McAnally; ***D:*** Guy Green; ***W:*** Robert Westerby; ***C:*** Wilkie Cooper; ***M:*** Clifton Parker. *FCT*

Sea Prince and the Fire Child ☠☠ **1982** Japanese animated film follows two young lovers who set off on an adventure to escape the disapproval of their parents. **70m/C VHS, Beta.** *JP COL*

Sea Racketeers ☠½ **1937** Soggy old tribute to the Coast Guard inadvertently makes them look like a bunch of bumblers, as they belatedly uncover a fur-smuggling racket working under their noses from a floating nightclub. **64m/B VHS, Beta.** Weldon Heyburn, Jeanne Madden, Warren Hymer, Dorothy McNulty, J. Carrol Naish, Joyce Compton, Charles Trowbridge, Syd Saylor, Lane Chandler, Benny Burt; ***D:*** Hamilton MacFadden. *SNC*

The Sea Serpent ☠½ **1985** A young sea captain and a crusty scientist unite to search out a giant sea monster awakened by atomic tests. Not one of Milland's better films. **92m/C VHS, Beta.** *SP* Timothy Bottoms, Ray Milland, Jared Martin; ***D:*** Gregory Greens. *LIV*

The Sea Shall Not Have Them ☠☠½ **1955** A British bomber crashes into the North Sea during WWII. Film tells of the survivors' rescue by the Air-Sea Rescue Unit. Decent drama/adventure. **92m/B VHS.** Michael Redgrave, Dirk Bogarde; ***D:*** Lewis Gilbert; ***M:*** Malcolm Arnold. *REP*

The Sea Wolf ☠☠☠½ **1941** Jack London's adventure novel about brutal, canny Captain Wolf Larsen (Robinson), his rebellious crew, and some unexpected passengers. Knox and Lupino are shipwreck survivors, picked up by Robinson and forced into working aboard his ship, the aptly named "Ghost." Crewman Garfield falls for Lupino and tries to rally his shipmates into resisting the meglomaniacal Robinson. Fine performances by all, especially Robinson as the personification of malevolent ego. Screen debut of Knox. Director Curtiz filmed entirely in studio tanks, sets, and pervasive fog machines. Previously filmed three times; later remade as "Barricade" and "Wolf Larsen." **90m/C VHS.** Edward G. Robinson, Alexander Knox, John Garfield, Ida Lupino, Gene Lockhart, Barry Fitzgerald, Stanley Ridges, Francis McDonald, David Bruce, Howard da Silva, Frank Lackteen, Ralf Harolde; ***D:*** Michael Curtiz; ***W:*** Robert Rossen. *MGM, MOV, BTV*

The Sea Wolf ☠☠ **1993** Yet another adaptation of Jack London's classic battle of wills tale. Captain Wolf Larsen (Bronson) commands a surly ship of seal hunters through sheer ruthlessness and ego. He rescues snobbish theater critic Van Weyden (Reeve) and pretty scam artist Flaxen (Stewart) from a capsized ferry. The self-educated captain wants to test out his theories about survival of the fittest by making the rich Van Weyden his cabin boy (Flaxen gets leered at). Lots of teeth-gnashing and bellowing in this turgid TV remake, although Revill has fun as the sniveling Cookie. See the Edward G. Robinson version instead. **120m/C VHS.** Charles Bronson, Christopher Reeve, Catherine Mary Stewart, Clive Revill; ***D:*** Michael Anderson Sr.; ***W:*** Andrew J. Fenady; ***M:*** Charles Bernstein. *TTC*

Sea Wolves ☠☠½ **1981 (PG)** True WWII story about a commando-style operation undertaken by a group of middle-aged, retired British cavalrymen in India in 1943. Decent acting, though Peck's British accent fades in and out, with Moore as Bond. **120m/C VHS, Beta.** *GB* Gregory Peck, Roger Moore, David Niven, Trevor Howard, Patrick Macnee; ***D:*** Andrew V. McLaglen; ***W:*** Reginald Rose. *FOX, WAR*

The Seagull ☠☠☠ **1971** A pensive, sensitive adaptation of the famed Chekhov play about the depressed denizens of an isolated country estate. In Russian with English subtitles. **99m/B VHS, Beta.** Alla Demidova, Lyudmila Savelyeva, Yuri Yakovlev; ***D:*** Yuri Karasik. *FCT, MRV, AUD*

Seance on a Wet Afternoon ☠☠☠½ **1964** Dark, thoughtful film about a crazed pseudo-psychic who coerces her husband into a kidnapping so she can gain recognition by divining the child's whereabouts. Directed splendidly by Forbes, and superb acting from Stanley and Attenborough, who co-produced with Forbes. **111m/B VHS, Beta.** *GB* Kim Stanley, Richard Attenborough, Margaret Lacey, Maria Kazan, Mark Eden, Patrick Magee; ***D:*** Bryan Forbes; ***M:*** John Barry. British Academy Awards '64: Best Actor (Attenborough); National Board of Review Awards '64: 10 Best Films of the Year, Best Actress (Stanley); Nominations: Academy Awards '64: Best Actress (Stanley). *HMV, BTV*

The Search ☠☠☠½ **1948** Clift, an American solider stationed in post-WWII Berlin, befriends a homeless nine-year-old amnesiac boy (Jandl) and tries to find his family. Meanwhile, his mother has been searching the Displaced Persons camps for her son. Although Clift wants to adopt the boy, he steps aside, and mother and son are finally reunited. "The Search" was shot on location in the American Occupied Zone of Germany. Jandl won a special juvenile Oscar in his first (and only) film role. This was also Clift's first screen appearance, although this movie was actually filmed after his debut in "Red River," it was released first. **105m/B VHS.** Montgomery Clift, Aline MacMahon, Ivan Jandl, Jarmila Novotna, Wendell Corey; ***D:*** Fred Zinnemann. Academy Awards '48: Best Original Screenplay; Golden Globe Awards '49: Best Screenplay; Nominations: Academy Awards '48: Best Actor (Clift), Best Director (Zinnemann), Best Screenplay. *MGM*

Search and Destroy ☠ *Striking Back* **1981 (PG)** Deadly vendetta is begun by a Vietnamese official during the war. It is continued in the U.S. as he hunts down the American soldiers he feels betrayed him. Sub-par, forgettable war/action flick. **93m/C VHS, Beta, LV.** Perry King, Don Stroud, Park Jong Soo, George Kennedy, Tisa Farrow; ***D:*** William Fruet. *VES*

Search and Destroy ☠ **1988 (R)** Sci-fi action flick about the capture of a secret biological warfare research station. Lotsa action, that's for sure - where's the plot? **87m/C VHS, Beta.** Stuart Garrison Day, Dan Kuchuck, Peggy Jacobsen; ***D:*** J. Christian Ingvordsen. *MCG*

Search and Destroy ☠☠ **1994 (R)** Complex story finds bankrupt businessman Martin Mirkheim (Dunne) trying to overcome his financial woes by making a film based on a book by self-help guru, Dr. Luther Waxling (Hopper). Of course, since Martin's broke, he first has to find someone willing to invest in his venture, and the shady duo (Walken and Turturro) he does just leave him with more problems. Tediously stagy adaptation of Howard Korders' play. Directorial debut by artist Salle at least looks great and provides some quirky moments. **91m/C VHS, LV.** Griffin Dunne, Dennis Hopper, Rosanna Arquette, Christopher Walken, John Turturro, Illeana Douglas, Ethan Hawke; ***Cameos:*** Martin Scorsese; ***D:*** David Salle; ***W:*** Michael Almereyda; ***C:*** Michael Spiller, Bobby Bukowski; ***M:*** Elmer Bernstein. *HMK*

The Search for Bridey Murphy ☠☠ **1956** Long before channelers, Ramtha and New-Age profiteers, there was a Colorado housewife who under hypnosis described a previous life as an Irish girl. Her famous claim was never proven—but that didn't stop this well-acted but dull dramatization. Neither sensationalist, nor likely to persuade skeptics. Based on the book by Morey Bernstein, hypnotist in the case. **84m/B VHS.** Teresa Wright, Louis Hayward, Nancy Gates, Kenneth Tobey, Richard Anderson; ***D:*** Noel Langley; ***W:*** Noel Langley. *PAR, FCT*

Search for Signs of Intelligent Life in the Universe ☠☠☠ **1991 (PG-13)** Tomlin's brilliant one-woman show has been expanded into a wonderful film. As Tomlin's cast of 12 female and male characters meet and interact, they show every viewer his/her own humanity. **120m/C VHS.** Lily Tomlin; ***D:*** John Bailey; ***W:*** Jane Wagner; ***M:*** Jerry Goodman. *WLF, BTV*

Search for the Gods ☠½ **1975** A dig in the Southwest turns interesting when one of the archeologists comes across an exquisite ancient medallion that could answer questions about alien visitors. Pilot for a television series that didn't make it. **100m/C VHS.** Kurt Russell, Stephen McHattie, Ralph Bellamy, Victoria Racimo, Raymond St. Jacques; ***D:*** Jud Taylor. *UNI, HHE*

The Searchers ☠☠☠☠ **1956** The classic Ford western, starring John Wayne as a hard-hearted frontiersman who spends years doggedly pursuing his niece, who was kidnapped by Indians. A simple western structure supports Ford's most moving, mysterious, complex film. Many feel this is the best western of all time. **119m/C VHS, Beta, LV.** John Wayne, Jeffrey Hunter, Vera Miles, Natalie Wood, Ward Bond, John Qualen, Harry Carey Jr., Olive Carey, Antonio Moreno, Henry Brandon, Hank Worden, Lana Wood, Dorothy Jordan, Patrick Wayne; ***D:*** John Ford; ***W:*** Frank Nugent; ***C:*** Winton C. Hoch; ***M:*** Max Steiner. *WAR, TLF*

Searching for Bobby Fischer ☠☠☠½ **1993 (PG)** 7-year-old Josh Waitzkin (Pomeranc, in his debut) shows an amazing gift for chess, stunning his parents, who must then try to strike the delicate balance of developing his abilities while also allowing him a "normal" childhood. Excellent cast features Mantegna and Allen as his parents, Kingsley as demanding chess teacher Pandolfini, and Fishburne as an adept speed-chess hustler. Pomeranc is great, and his knowledge of chess (he's a ranked player) brings authenticity to his role. Title comes from Pandolfini's belief that Josh may equal the abilities of chess whiz Bobby Fischer. Underrated little gem based on a true story and adapted from the book by Waitzkin's father. **111m/C VHS, Beta, LV.** Joe Mantegna, Max Pomeranc, Joan Allen, Ben Kingsley, Laurence "Larry" Fishburne, Robert Stephens, David Paymer, William H. Macy; ***D:*** Steven Zaillian; ***W:*** Steven Zaillian; ***C:*** Conrad Hall; ***M:*** James Horner. MTV Movie Awards '94: Best New Filmmaker Award (Zaillian); Nominations: Academy Awards '93: Best Cinematography. *PAR*

Seaside Swingers ☠½ *Every Day's a Holiday* **1965** A group of teenagers at a seaside resort work to win a talent competition on television. But where is the talent? Dumb teen romance comedy with accidental plot. ♫All I Want Is You; A Girls Needs a Boy; Second Time Around; Indubitably Me; Love Me, Please; Now, Ain't That Somethin'—Caw Blimey; Romeo Jones; What's Cookin. **94m/C VHS, Beta.** *GB* Michael Sarne, Grazina Frame, John Leyton; ***D:*** James Hill. *NLC*

Season for Assassins ☠½ **1971** Police commissioner Castroni is the only man who can stop a wave of violence enveloping Rome. **102m/C VHS, Beta.** Joe Dallesandro, Martin Balsam. *LIV*

Season of Change ☠½ **1994** Tepid coming of age saga set in rural Montana, circa 1946. Thirteen-year-old Sally Mae (Tom) notices the tensions between her Bible-bound mother (Anderson) and war vet dad (Madsen), who's worried about finding a job to support his family. Sally Mae tries to understand all these adult notions even as she herself becomes attracted to teen mechanic Bobby (Randall). Cliched script and awkward performances don't help. **93m/C VHS.** Nicholle Tom, Michael Madsen, Jo Anderson, Hoyt Axton, Ethan Randall; ***D:*** Robin Murray; ***W:*** Shirley Hillard. *MNC*

Season of Fear ☠½ **1989 (R)** A young man visits his estranged father's home. Abandoned as a child, he's embroiled in a murder scheme engineered by his father's beautiful young wife. Intriguing premise, forgettable execution. **89m/C VHS, Beta.** Michael Bowen, Clancy Brown, Clare Wren, Ray Wise, Michael J. Pollard; ***D:*** Douglas Campbell; ***W:*** Douglas Campbell. *FOX*

Season of the Witch ½ *Hungry Wives; Jack's Wife* **1973 (R)** A frustrated housewife becomes intrigued with a neighboring witch and begins to practice witchcraft herself, through murder and seduction. Meant to be suspenseful, thrilling, and topical, it is none of these. Poorly acted at best. Originally 130 minutes! **89m/C Beta.** Jan White, Ray Laine, Bill Thunhurst, Joedida McClain, Virginia Greenwald; ***D:*** George A. Romero; ***W:*** George A. Romero. *NO*

Sebastian ½ *Mr. Sebastian* **1968** Mathematics whiz is employed by the British to decipher codes. He falls in love with York, another code breaker, and becomes involved in international intrigue. A bit too fast-paced and busy, but enjoyable spy drama. Sutherland has a small role. **100m/C VHS.** *GB* Dirk Bogarde, Susannah York, Lilli Palmer, John Gielgud, Margaret Johnston, Nigel Davenport, Donald Sutherland; ***D:*** David Greene; ***M:*** Jerry Goldsmith. *MOV*

Sebastiane **1979** An audacious film version of the legend of St. Sebastian, packed with homoerotic imagery and ravishing visuals. Honest, faithful rendering of the Saint's life and refusal to obey Roman authorities. Jarman's first film, in Latin with English subtitles. **90m/C VHS, Beta.** Leonardo Treviglio, Barney James, Richard James, Neil Kennedy; ***D:*** Derek Jarman; ***M:*** Brian Eno. *CCN, FCT, INJ*

Second Best **1994 (PG-13)** Quiet, intimate drama about a lonely Welsh postmaster (Hurt) who decides to adopt a son (Miles). James, the 11-year-old boy he considers adopting, comes from a troubled background and is prone to violent outbursts. Graham, the village postmaster, is dealing with emotional demons of his own, and his problems are interwoven with those of the deprived, temperamental James. Although Hurt seems miscast as a shy, middle-aged Welshman, he turns in one of the best performances of his career. Richly acted and flawlessly directed, Menges has created a convincing and effective father-son drama. Based on David Cook's novel. **105m/C VHS, LV.** *GB* William Hurt, Chris Cleary Miles, Keith Allen, Prunella Scales, Jane Horrocks, Alan Cumming, John Hurt; ***D:*** Chris Menges; ***W:*** David Cook; ***M:*** Simon Boswell. *WAR*

Second Best Secret Agent in the Whole Wide World ½ *Licensed to Kill* **1965** A klutzy agent attempts to prevent a Swedish anti-gravity formula from falling into Russian hands. Surprisingly good early spoof of the James Bond genre. **93m/C VHS, Beta.** *GB* Tom Adams, Veronica Hurst, Peter Bull, Karel Stepanek, John Arnatt; ***D:*** Lindsay Shonteff. *NLC*

Second Chance ½ **1953** A former prizefighter (Mitchum) travels to Mexico where he protects a gangster's moll (Darnell) targeted for murder. But Palance is on their tail. Originally released theatrically on a wide screen in 3-D. Good melodrama. **82m/C VHS, Beta, LV.** Robert Mitchum, Linda Darnell, Jack Palance, Reginald Sheffield, Roy Roberts; ***D:*** Rudolph Mate. *MED*

Second Chance **1980** When a woman finds her husband is in love with another, her marital happiness is shattered. She leaves her betrayer and struggles to adapt to life as a single mother. Made for British television. **270m/C VHS.** *GB* Susannah York, Ralph Bates; ***D:*** Gerry Mill, Richard Handford. *NO*

Second Chorus ½ **1940** Rivalry of two trumpet players for a girl and a job with Artie Shaw Orchestra. Music, dance, and romance. Nothing great, but pleasant. ♫Would You Like to Be the Love of My Life?; Poor Mr. Chisholm; (I Ain't Hep to That Step) But I'll Dig It; Swing Concerto; Sweet Sue; I'm Yours. **83m/B VHS, Beta, LV.** Fred Astaire, Paulette Goddard, Burgess Meredith, Artie Shaw, Charles Butterworth; ***D:*** H.C. Potter. Nominations: Academy Awards '40: Best Song ("Love of My Life"), Best Score. *NOS, HHT, CAB*

Second Coming of Suzanne ½ **1980** Young actress encounters a hypnotic film director. Her role: to star in a crucifixion—which may be more real than she imagines. Winner of two international film festivals. **90m/C VHS, Beta.** Sondra Locke, Richard Dreyfuss, Gene Barry; ***D:*** Michael Barry. *GEM*

Second Fiddle ½ *Irving Berlin's Second Fiddle* **1939** Power is a studio flack who's hired to mount a huge talent search for a girl to star in a new film epic (very clear parallels to the Scarlet O'Hara "Gone With the Wind" hunt). He's sent to smalltown Minnesota where he meets Henie, who lives with her forbidding aunt (Oliver), who doesn't want her niece to go to wicked Hollywood. Nevertheless, Henie gets the part, becomes a success, and falls for her co-star Vallee. But it's all a publicity stunt on his part and Power is the one who really loves the girl. Henie gets to do some skating. ♫Back to Back; I'm Sorry for Myself; I Poured My Heart Into Song; An Old-Fashioned Tune is Always New; When Winter Comes; Song of the Metronome. **86m/B VHS.** Sonja Henie, Tyrone Power, Rudy Vallee, Edna May Oliver, Mary Healy, Lyle Talbot, Alan Dinehart, Minna Gombell; ***D:*** Sidney Lanfield; ***W:*** Harry Tugend; ***M:*** Irving Berlin. Nominations: Academy Awards '39: Best Song ("I Poured My Heart Into Song"). *FXV*

Second Sight **1989 (PG)** A detective (Larroquette) and a goofy psychic (Pinchot) set out to find a kidnapped priest. Flick is sidetracked along the way by such peculiarities as a pixieish nun for romantic, not religious, intrigue. Remember this one? No? That's because you blinked when it was released to theaters. Eminently missable. **84m/C VHS, Beta, LV.** John Larroquette, Bronson Pinchot, Bess Armstrong, James Tolkan, Christine Estabrook, Cornelia Guest, Stuart Pankin, William Prince, John Schuck; ***D:*** Joel Zwick; ***W:*** Patricia Resnick, Tom Schulman. *WAR*

Second Thoughts **1983 (PG)** Frustrated woman attorney divorces her stuffy husband and takes up with an aging hippie. She comes to regret her decision when it becomes obvious that her new man has his head firmly stuck in the 60s. Comedy-drama lacking real laughs or drama. **109m/C VHS, Beta.** Lucie Arnaz, Craig Wasson, Ken Howard, Joe Mantegna; ***D:*** Lawrence Turman; ***W:*** Steve Brown; ***M:*** Henry Mancini. *CNG*

Second Time Lucky **1984** The devil makes a bet with God that if the world began all over again Adam and Eve would repeat their mistake they made in the Garden of Eden. Bites off a lot, but has no teeth nor laughs. **98m/C VHS, Beta.** *AU NZ* Diane Franklin, Roger Wilson, Robert Morley, Jon Gadsby, Bill Ewens; ***D:*** Michael Anderson Sr. *ORI*

Second Victory ½ **1987 (PG)** Major Mark Hanlon has been appointed an Occupation Officer in the winter of 1945. He expects this will be his chance to work for peace but when a good friend is brutally murdered all his thoughts turn to revenge. Based on the novel by Morris West. **95m/C VHS, LV.** Anthony Andrews, Max von Sydow, Renee Soutendijk; ***D:*** Gerald Thomas. *AIP*

Second Wind **1990 (PG)** Wagner and Naughton are trying to settle into their new life together, but find they must make a variety of difficult choices. **93m/C VHS.** Lindsay Wagner, James Naughton. *NO*

Second Woman ½ *Here Lies Love; Twelve Miles Out* **1951** An architect, suffering from blackouts and depression, believes himself responsible for the death of his fiancee. Well-done psychodrama. **91m/B VHS, Beta.** Robert Young, Betsy Drake, John Sutton; ***D:*** James V. Kern. *NOS, VDM, SNC*

The Secret ½ **1993** Businessman and political candidate Mike Dunsmore (Douglas) comes to terms with his lifelong battle with dyslexia when his grandson begins to show signs of the same affliction. Set in picturesque New England fishing village. **92m/C VHS.** Kirk Douglas, Bruce Boxleitner, Brock Peters, Laura Harrington; ***D:*** Karen Arthur. *CAF*

Secret Admirer **1985 (R)** A teenager's unsigned love letter keeps falling into the wrong hands. Intends to be funny, and sometimes is; too often, though, it surrenders to obviousness and predictability. **98m/C VHS, Beta, LV.** C. Thomas Howell, Cliff DeYoung, Kelly Preston, Dee Wallace Stone, Lori Loughlin, Fred Ward, Casey Siemaszko, Corey Haim, Leigh Taylor-Young; ***D:*** David Greenwalt. *NO*

The Secret Adversary **1983** Set in 1920s London. Ace detectives Tommy and Tuppence Beresford must find a secret treaty before it falls into the wrong hands. Pilot for the "Partners in Crime" series. Based on the characters created by Agatha Christie. **120m/C VHS, Beta.** *GB* Francesca Annis, James Warwick. *TPV*

The Secret Agent **1936** Presumed dead, a British intelligence agent (Gielgud) reappears and receives a new assignment. Using his faked death to his advantage, he easily journeys to Switzerland where he is to eliminate an enemy agent. Strange Hitchcockian melange of comedy and intrigue; atypical, but worthy offering from the Master. **83m/B VHS, Beta, LV.** *GB* Madeleine Carroll, Peter Lorre, Robert Young, John Gielgud, Lilli Palmer; ***D:*** Alfred Hitchcock; ***W:*** Charles Bennett. *SNC, NOS, HHT*

Secret Agent **1964** Secret agent John Drake embarks upon dangerous and exciting assignments around the world in this mystery-adventure series, which ran during 1965 and 1966. All but two episodes are in black and white. **60m/B VHS, Beta.** Patrick McGoohan, Niall MacGinnis, Dawn Addams, Lelia Goldoni; ***D:*** Don Chaffey. *MOV*

Secret Agent 00 *Operation Kid Brother* **1967 (R)** A master criminal plans to blackmail the western world and only special Secret Agent 00 can stop him. Bad spy genre ripoff, interesting only as the screen debut of Sean Connery's brother. **97m/C VHS.** *IT* Neil Connery, Daniela Bianchi, Adolfo Celi; ***D:*** Alberto De Martino; ***M:*** Ennio Morricone. *NO*

Secret Agent 00-Soul ½ **1989** International spy decides to fulfill his dream of opening a detective agency in his old neighborhood. Release of this direct-to-video mishmash was delayed until '95. **71m/C VHS.** Billy Dee Williams, Amanda Le Flore, Marjean Holden, Tiny Lister; ***D:*** Julius Le Flore. *XVC*

Secret Agent Super Dragon *Super Dragon* **1966** The CIA calls in the agent known as "Super Dragon" when it is discovered that a Venezuelan drug czar plans to spike U.S. gum and candy with an LSD-like drug. Less than competent production offers some unintended laughter. **95m/C VHS, Beta.** *FR IT GE* Ray Danton, Marisa Mell, Margaret Lee, Jess Hahn, Carlo D'Angelo, Andriana Ambesi; ***D:*** Calvin Jackson Padget. *SNC*

Secret Beyond the Door **1948** A wealthy heiress marries a widower and soon discovers that he murdered his first wife. Understandably, she wonders what plans he might have for her. Capably done chiller, but the plot is hackneyed pseudo-Hitchcock. **99m/B VHS.** Joan Bennett, Michael Redgrave, Barbara O'Neil, Anne Revere; ***D:*** Fritz Lang; ***M:*** Miklos Rozsa. *REP*

Secret Ceremony ½ **1969** An aging prostitute and a young, aimless waif resemble each other's dead mother and dead daughter, respectively, and the relationship goes on, strangely, from there. This original big-screen version is very good Freudian psycho-drama; 101-minute TV version is unfortunately greatly diluted. **109m/C VHS, Beta.** Elizabeth Taylor, Robert Mitchum, Mia Farrow, Pamela Brown, Peggy Ashcroft; ***D:*** Joseph Losey; ***M:*** Richard Rodney Bennett. *BAR*

The Secret Cinema **1978** A woman is caught between reality and a cinematic nightmare in this bizarre first film by famed cult director Bartel. **37m/C VHS.** ***D:*** Paul Bartel. *RHI*

The Secret Code **1942** A 15-chapter serial with the Black Commando (Kelly) thwarting the Nazis' attempts at sabotage. After each chapter's cliffhanger ending a new form of secret code is explained and decoded. **315m/B VHS.** Paul Kelly, Anne Nagel, Clancy Cooper, Trevor Bardette, Gregory Gay, Ludwig Donath, Ed Parker; ***D:*** Spencer Gordon Bennet. *GPV*

The Secret Diary of Sigmund Freud **1984** Spoofy look at the early years of Sigmund Freud, the father of modern psychoanalysis. Freud (Cort) has an affair with lisping nurse Kane while tending to patient Shawn and answering to mama Baker, who's carrying on with mad doctor Kinski. Talented cast falls asleep on couch. **129m/C VHS, Beta.** Bud Cort, Carol Kane, Carroll Baker, Klaus Kinski, Marisa Berenson, Dick Shawn, Ferdinand "Ferdy" Mayne; ***D:*** Danford B. Greene. *FOX*

Secret File of Hollywood 🦴½ *Secret File: Hollywood* **1962** A down-and-out private eye gets a job taking photos for a sleazy Hollywood scandal sheet and finds himself in the midst of a blackmail plot masterminded by his editor. An often childish potboiler, perhaps inspired by the once-feared Confidential Magazine. **85m/B VHS.** Robert Clarke, Francine York, Syd Mason, Maralou Gray, John Warburton; ***D:*** Ralph Cushman. *NOS, LOO, TPV*

The Secret Four 🦴🦴 *The Four Just Men* **1940** Three young men seek to avenge the death of their friend at the hands of British traitors, and become involved in a plot to sabotage the Suez canal. Poorly adapted from the novel by Edgar Wallace. **79m/B VHS, Beta.** *GB* Hugh Sinclair, Griffith Jones, Francis L. Sullivan, Frank Lawton, Anna Lee, Alan Napier, Basil Sydney; ***D:*** Walter Forde. *SNC*

Secret Games 🦴½ **1992 (R)** An unhappily married woman (Brin) is searching for relief from her restrictive marriage. At the "Afternoon Demitasse," an exclusive brothel where women are paid for fulfilling their ultimate fantasies, she meets a man (Hewitt) who pushes her beyond her sexual limits and threatens to totally possess her. **90m/C VHS.** Martin Hewitt, Michele Brin, Delia Sheppard, Billy Drago; ***D:*** Alexander Gregory Hippolyte. *IMP*

Secret Games 2: The Escort 🦴½ **1993 (R)** A performance artist (Hewitt) learns how to seduce women from a beautiful escort (Rochelle). However, he falls for his trainer despite being a star pupil who could have anyone he wanted. Plot conveniently lends itself to lots of steamy love scenes. Also available in an unrated version. **?m/C VHS.** Martin Hewitt, Amy Rochelle, Sara Suzanne Brown, Marie Leroux; ***D:*** Alexander Gregory Hippolyte; ***W:*** Russell Lavalle; ***M:*** Ashley Irwin. *IMP*

Secret Games 3 🦴½ **1994 (R)** A bored doctor's wife gets her kicks by visiting a club catering to women's fantasies. But then she meets a criminal who wants her all to himself. An unrated version is available at 91 minutes. **82m/C VHS.** Woody Brown, Brenda Swanson, Rochelle Swanson; ***D:*** Alexander Gregory Hippolyte. *ACA*

The Secret Garden 🦴🦴🦴 **1949** The well-loved Frances Hodgson Burnett story has been remade and even revamped as a Broadway musical, but this is considered the definitive version. An orphan girl arrives at her uncle's somber Victorian estate. She starts tending a long-forgotten garden, and with its resurrection joy returns to the household. O'Brien leads an outstanding cast in one of her final juvenile roles. In black and white, with Technicolor for later garden scenes. **92m/B VHS, Beta, LV.** Margaret O'Brien, Herbert Marshall, Dean Stockwell, Gladys Cooper, Elsa Lanchester, Brian Roper; ***D:*** Fred M. Wilcox. *MGM*

The Secret Garden 🦴🦴½ **1984** Orphaned Mary Lennox is sent to live with her mysterious uncle after her parents die. Mary is willful and spoiled and her uncle's house holds a number of secrets, including a crippled cousin. When Mary discovers a mysteriously abandoned locked garden she makes it her mission to restore the garden to life. Based on the children's classic by Frances Hodsgon Burnett. Made for British television. **107m/C VHS.** *GB* Sarah Hollis Andrews, David Patterson; ***D:*** Katrina Murray. *MOV, SIG, TVC*

The Secret Garden 🦴🦴🦴 **1987 (PG)** Lonely orphan Mary Lennox is sent to live with her uncle in England after her parent's deaths. Mary, who has grown up in India, is selfish and unhappy until she discovers two secrets on her uncle's estate. Class production of the children's classic by Frances Hodgson Burnett with wonderful performances; added prologue and afterword showing Mary as an adult are unnecessary, but don't detract either. Made for television as a "Hallmark Hall of Fame" special. **100m/C VHS, LV.** Gennie James, Barret Oliver, Jadrien Steele, Michael Hordern, Derek Jacobi, Billie Whitelaw, Lucy Gutteridge, Julian Glover, Colin Firth, Alan Grint. *REP*

The Secret Garden 🦴🦴½ **1993 (G)** Rekindled interest in Frances Hodgon Burnett's classic tale has prompted a Broadway musical, two TV movies, and this latest big screen version. Mary Lennox is an orphan sent to live in her reclusive uncle's forbidding mansion filled with secrets, including a crippled cousin she didn't know she had. She discovers a secret neglected garden and becomes determined to bring it back to life. Befitting director Holland's reputation this version is beautiful but dark, with children prey to very adult anxieties. **102m/C VHS, Beta, LV.** Kate Maberly, Maggie Smith, Haydon Prowse, Andrew Knott, John Lynch; ***D:*** Agnieszka Holland; ***W:*** Caroline Thompson; ***C:*** Roger Deakins; ***M:*** Zbigniew Preisner. Los Angeles Film Critics Association Awards '93: Best Score; Nominations: British Academy Awards '93: Best Supporting Actress (Smith). *WAR, BTV*

Secret Honor 🦴🦴🦴 *Lords of Treason; Secret Honor: The Last Testament of Richard M. Nixon; Secret Honor: A Political Myth* **1985** Idiosyncratic, single-set, one-man film version adapted by Donald Freed and Arnold Stone from their stage play about Richard Nixon coping with the death of his presidency on the night he's decided to blow his brains out. Made with students at the University of Michigan, and carried by the ranting and raving of Hall as a tragic Shakespearean Nixon with plenty of darkly humorous lines. **90m/C VHS, Beta, LV.** Philip Baker Hall; ***D:*** Robert Altman; ***M:*** George Burt. *LIV, VES, CRC*

Secret Ingredient 🦴½ **1992** A legendary cognac recipe is the secret formula of the monks of St. Celare, whose monastery is located in the mountains of Yugoslavia. A wealthy American sends his flighty heiress daughter to pry the secret recipe from the monks but she runs into more than she bargains for when she falls for a handsome friar and gets caught up with a band of bumbling gypsies and the inept state police. **95m/C VHS.** Rick Rossovich, Catherine Hicks, Gary Kroeger, Jeff Corey, Brad Dexter, Sam Wanamaker; ***D:*** Slobodan Shijan. *HMD*

Secret Life of an American Wife 🦴🦴 **1968** A bored housewife (Jackson) tries to seduce a client of her husband's, with less than hilarious results. Too much dialogue, not enough genuine humor. Disappointing inversion of director Axelrod's "The Seven Year Itch." **97m/C VHS, Beta.** Walter Matthau, Anne Jackson, Patrick O'Neal, Edy Williams; ***D:*** George Axelrod; ***W:*** George Axelrod. *FOX*

The Secret Life of Walter Mitty 🦴🦴🦴 **1947** An entertaining adaptation of the James Thurber short story about a meek man (Kaye) who lives an unusual secret fantasy life. Henpecked by his fiancee and mother, oppressed at his job, he imagines himself in the midst of various heroic fantasies. While Thurber always professed to hate Kaye's characterization and the movie, it scored at the box office and today stands as a comedic romp for Kaye. Available with digitally remastered stereo and original movie trailer. **110m/C VHS, Beta, LV.** Danny Kaye, Virginia Mayo, Boris Karloff, Ann Rutherford, Fay Bainter, Florence Bates; ***D:*** Norman Z. McLeod; ***C:*** Lee Garmes. *HBO, SUE*

Secret Mission 🦴🦴½ **1942** Four British intelligence agents are sent into occupied France to assess the strength of Nazi forces. But after discovering the information, their cover is blown and it's a race to get the intelligence into the right hands before the Nazis get to them first. **94m/B VHS.** *GB* James Mason, Hugh Williams, Roland Culver, Michael Wilding, Carla Lehmann, Nancy Price, Percy Walsh, Karel Stepanek, Herbert Lom, Stewart Granger; ***D:*** Harold French; ***W:*** Anatole de Grunwald, Basil Bartlett; ***C:*** Bernard Knowles, Cyril Knowles; ***M:*** Mischa Spoliansky. *FCT*

Secret Obsession 🦴 **1988 (PG)** A love triangle among a father, his illegitimate son, and the woman they both love, set in North Africa in 1955. Sounds intriguing, but don't be fooled. Slow, dull, and poorly acted. **82m/C VHS, Beta.** Julie Christie, Ben Gazzara, Patrick Bruel, Jean Carmet; ***D:*** Henri Vart. *VMK*

The Secret of El Zorro 🦴½ **1957** Don Diego's friend, Don Ricardo, threatens to unmask Zorro's secret identity when he challenges the legendary swordsman to a duel. **75m/B VHS, Beta.** Guy Williams. *DIS*

The Secret of My Success 🦴🦴 **1987 (PG-13)** Country bumpkin Fox goes to the Big Apple to make his mark. He becomes the corporate mailboy who rises meteorically to the top of his company (by impersonating an executive) in order to win the love of an icy woman executive. He spends his days running frantically between his real job in the mailroom and his fantasy position, with various sexual shenanigans with the boss's wife thrown in to keep the viewer alert. Fox is charismatic while working with a cliche-ridden script that ties up everything very neatly at the end. **110m/C VHS, Beta, LV.** Michael J. Fox, Helen Slater, Richard Jordan, Margaret Whitton; ***D:*** Herbert Ross; ***W:*** Jim Cash, Jack Epps Jr., A.J. Carothers; ***M:*** David Foster. *MCA*

The Secret of Navajo Cave 🦴🦴 *Legend of Cougar Canyon* **1976 (G)** Fair family adventure. Two young friends explore the mysterious Navajo cave, where one can be assured that a secret awaits. **84m/C VHS.** Holger Kasper, Steven Benally Jr., Johnny Guerro; ***D:*** James T. Flocker. *XVC*

The Secret of NIMH 🦴🦴🦴 **1982 (G)** Animated tale, produced by a staff of Disney-trained artists led by "American Tail's" Bluth; concerns a newly widowed mouse who discovers a secret agency of superintelligent rats (they've escaped from a science lab) who aid her in protecting her family. As is usually the case with Bluth films, the animation is superb while the socially aware plot struggles to keep pace. That aside, it's still an interesting treat for the youngsters. Adapted from Robert C. O'Brien's "Mrs. Frisby and the Rats of N.I.M.H." **84m/C VHS, Beta, LV, 8mm.** ***D:*** Don Bluth; ***W:*** Don Bluth; ***M:*** Jerry Goldsmith; ***V:*** John Carradine, Derek Jacobi, Dom DeLuise, Elizabeth Hartman, Peter Strauss, Aldo Ray, Edie McClurg, Wil Wheaton. *MGM, WTA*

The Secret of Roan Inish 🦴🦴🦴½ **1994 (PG)** Irish myth comes to life in this fantasy about the importance of family and place, seen through the eyes of 10-year-old Fiona Coneelly (newcomer Courtney) who's sent to live with her grandparents in post-WWII County Donegal. Fiona's drawn to her grandfather's stories about the family's ancestral home on the island of Roan Inish and the loss of her baby brother Jamie, who was carried out to sea. Another family tale is about a Selkie—a beautiful seal/woman captured by a Coneelly fisherman who eventually returned to her ocean home. When Fiona visits Roan Inish she becomes convinced that Jamie is alive and being cared for by the island's seals. Director Sayles keeps a firm grip on the cuteness factor while cinematographer Wexler works his usual magic on the sea, sky, and land of Ireland. Based on the 1957 novel "Secret of the Ron Mor Skerry" by Rosalie K. Fry. **102m/C VHS, LV.** Jeni Courtney, Michael Lally, Eileen Colgan, John Lynch, Richard Sheridan, Susan Lynch, Cillian Byrne; ***D:*** John Sayles; ***W:*** John Sayles; ***C:*** Haskell Wexler; ***M:*** Mason Daring. Nominations: Independent Spirit Awards '96: Best Director (Sayles), Best Film, Best Screenplay. *COL*

Secret of the Black Trunk 🦴🦴½ **1962** Chilling Edgar Wallace story about a series of murders at a famed English hotel. Filmed in Great Britain. **96m/C VHS.** *GE* Joachim Hansen, Senta Berger, Hans Reiser, Leonard Steckel, Peter Carsten; ***D:*** Werner Klinger. *SNC*

The Secret of the Golden Eagle 🦴🦴 **1991** A boy and his new adventurer friend are on a quest to find the strange "Golden Statue" that causes people to grow old before their time. They must take it from criminals who are using it for evil purposes. A good adventure/fantasy for the entire family. **90m/C VHS.** Michael Berryman, Brandon McKay; ***D:*** Cole McKay. *WLA*

Secret of the Ice Cave 🦴 **1989 (PG-13)** A motley band of explorers, hijackers and mercenaries go after a secret treasure in the remote mountains. **106m/C VHS, Beta.** Michael Moriarty, Sally Kellerman, David Mendenhall, Virgil Frye, Gerald Anthony, Norbert Weisser; **D:** Radu Gabrea. *MOV*

The Secret of the Loch 🦴½ **1934** Scottish scientist claims to have seen Loch Ness Monster but everyone thinks his bagpipe's blown a reed. **80m/B VHS.** *GB* Seymour Hicks, Nancy O'Neil, Gibson Gowland, Frederick Peisley; **D:** Milton Rosmer. *NOS, SNC*

The Secret of the Telegian 🦴🦴½ **1961** Rare Japanese sci-fi flick about a soldier who uses a teleportation device to kill fellow soldiers who tried to kill him. He could find his victims wherever they hid. Also known as "The Telegian." **85m/C VHS.** *JP* Koji Tsurata, Yumi Shirakawa, Akihiko Hirata, Tadao Nakamura; **D:** Jun Fukuda. *SNC*

Secret of Yolanda 🦴 **1982 (R)** Steamy romance about a young deaf-mute whose guardian and riding instructor both fall for her. **90m/C VHS, Beta.** Aviva Ger, Asher Zarfati, Shraga Harpaz. *MGM*

The Secret Passion of Robert Clayton 🦴🦴 **1992 (R)** When Robert Clayton Jr. (Valentine) returns to his home town to take the position of D.A., he is forced to go head to head in a lurid murder trial with the defense attorney (Mahoney), who also happens to be his own father. **92m/C VHS.** John Mahoney, Scott Valentine, Eve Gordon, Kevin Conroy; **D:** E.W. Swackhamer; **W:** Brian Ross. *PAR*

Secret Passions 🦴½ **1978** A young couple are haunted by a dark, romance-novel-type secret. Made for television. **99m/C VHS, Beta.** John James, Susan Lucci; **D:** Michael Pressman. *NO*

Secret Places 🦴🦴½ **1985 (PG)** On the brink of WWII, a German girl in an English school finds friendship with a popular classmate. Touching and involving, but somehow unsatisfying. **98m/C VHS, Beta.** *GB* Maria Therese Relin, Tara MacGowran, Claudine Auger, Jenny Agutter; **D:** Zelda Barron; **W:** Zelda Barron. *FOX*

The Secret Policeman's Other Ball 🦴🦴🦴 **1982 (R)** Engaging live performance by most of the Monty Python troupe and guest rock artists, staged for Amnesty International. Follows 1979's "The Secret Policeman's Ball," and followed by 1987's "The Secret Policeman's Third Ball." **101m/C VHS, Beta, LV.** *GB* John Cleese, Graham Chapman, Michael Palin, Terry Jones, Pete Townshend, Sting, Billy Connolly, Bob Geldof; **D:** Julien Temple; **W:** Michael Palin. *MGM*

Secret Policeman's Private Parts 🦴🦴½ **1981** Various sketches and performances from the various Secret Policeman occasions, featuring classic Python sketches including "I'm a Lumberjack and I'm OK." Also featured are performances by Phil Collins, Pete Townshend, Donovan, and Bob Geldof. Thank you very much. **77m/C VHS, Beta, LV.** *GB* John Cleese, Michael Palin, Terry Jones, Pete Townshend, Julien Temple; **D:** Roger Graef. *MED*

The Secret Rapture 🦴🦴 **1994 (R)** Two sisters clash in this family drama, adapted by Hare from his 1988 play. The bohemian Isobel (Stevenson) and her estranged sister, the forbidding Marion (Wilton), are brought together by their father's death. While Isobel grieves, Marion seeks to gain advantage in the family business, and both must deal with their young, alcoholic, and volatile stepmother Katherine (Whalley-Kilmer). Emotional intensity with good performances but abrupt shifts in tone. **96m/C VHS, LV.** *GB* Juliet Stevenson, Penelope Wilton, Joanne Whalley, Alan Howard, Neil Pearson, Robert Stephens, Hilton McRae; **D:** Howard Davies; **W:** David Hare; **C:** Ian Wilson; **M:** Richard Hartley. *FXV*

A Secret Space 🦴🦴½ **1988** Story of a young man, born of secular parents, searching for the meaning of his Jewish roots as he nears his Bar Mitzvah. He is helped along by a group of Jews who are also searching for this meaning. **80m/C VHS, Beta.** Robert Klein, Phyllis Newman, John Matthews, Sam Schacht, Virginia Graham; **D:** Roberta Hodes. *ERG*

The Secret War of Harry Frigg 🦴½ **1968 (R)** Non-conformist WWII Private Harry Frigg is promoted to general as part of a scheme to help five Allied generals escape from the custody of the Germans. Rare Newman bomb; dismal comedy. **123m/C VHS, Beta.** Paul Newman, Sylva Koscina, John Williams, Tom Bosley, Andrew Duggan; **D:** Jack Smight; **C:** Russell Metty. *MCA*

Secret Weapon 🦴🦴 **1990** An Israeli technician flees his country with atomic secrets and a beautiful government agent is sent to induce him to return. Based on the true case of Mordecai Vanunu. Slow-paced and not very suspenseful. Made for cable. **95m/C VHS, Beta.** Griffin Dunne, Karen Allen, Stuart Wilson, Jeroen Krabbe, Brian Cox, John Rhys-Davies, Ian Mitchell; **D:** Ian Sharp. *TTC*

Secret Weapons 🦴½ *Secrets of the Red Bedroom* **1985** Sexy Russian babes are KGB-trained to get any secret from any man. Strains credibility as well as patience. Made for TV. **100m/C VHS.** Linda Hamilton, Sally Kellerman, Hunt Block, Viveca Lindfors, Christopher Atkins, Geena Davis, James Franciscus; **D:** Don Taylor; **M:** Charles Bernstein. *NO*

The Secretary 🦴½ **1994 (R)** Another bland variation of "The Temp." Career woman Ellen Bradford (Harris) has a new fast-track job and a highly efficient secretary in Deidre (Kelley). But it turns out Deidre's also lethally efficient in disposing of co-workers through a series of inexplicable accidents and "suicides." So just what's Ellen going to do to show Deidre who's boss? **94m/C VHS, LV.** Mel Harris, Sheila Kelley, Barry Bostwick, James Russo; **D:** Andrew Lane. *REP*

Secrets 🦴½ **1971 (R)** A wife, her husband, and her daughter each have a sexual experience which they must keep secret. Bisset's nude love scene is an eye-opener. Fast forward through the rest of this dull, overwrought drama. **86m/C VHS.** Jacqueline Bisset, Per Oscarsson, Shirley Knight, Robert Powell, Tarka Kings, Martin C. Thurley; **D:** Philip Saville; **M:** Michael Gibbs. *PSM*

Secrets 🦴 **1977** An unhappy young bride starts having numerous affairs when her mother dies. Made for television. Hardly worth the effort. **100m/C VHS.** Susan Blakely, Roy Thinnes, Joanne Linville, John Randolph, Anthony Eisley, Andrew Stevens; **D:** Paul Wendkos. *MGM*

Secrets 🦴🦴 **1982** British drama about the confused life of an innocent schoolgirl who's the victim of a mess of authoritative misunderstandings. One of David Puttnam's "First Love" series. **79m/C VHS, Beta.** *GB* Helen Lindsay, Anna Campbell-Jones, Daisy Cockburn; **D:** Gavin Millar. *MGM*

Secrets and Lies 🦴🦴 **1995** Too-long film focusing on family and identity. The adoptive parents of black Yuppie Londoner Hortense (Jean-Baptiste) have just died and she decides it's time to seek out her birth parents. She's warned about the emotional consequences, especially upon discovering her biological mother is white—factory worker Cynthia (Blethyn), who has another daughter, Roxanne (Rushbrook), who doesn't get along with mum. Naturally, when Hortense is introduced to the rest of Cynthia's family, including photographer brother Maurice (Spall), there's lots of dysfunction to explore. Good performances, although Hortense's character is bland, but pacing drags. **142m/C VHS.** *GB* Brenda Blethyn, Marianne Jean-Baptiste, Timothy Spall, Claire Rushbrook, Phyllis Logan, Lee Ross, Ron Cook, Leslie Manville; **Cameos:** Alison Steadman; **D:** Mike Leigh; **W:** Mike Leigh; **C:** Dick Pope; **M:** Andrew Dickson. Cannes Film Festival '96: Best Actress (Blethyn), Best Film. *NYR*

Secrets of a Married Man 🦴 **1984** A married man's philandering ways are his ruination when he falls hard for a beautiful prostitute. Shatner and Shepherd contain their laughter as they make their way through this hyper-earnest family drama. **96m/C VHS, Beta.** William Shatner, Cybill Shepherd, Michelle Phillips, Glynn Turman; **D:** William A. Graham. *LIV*

Secrets of a Soul 🦴🦴½ **1925** A visually impressive presentation of Freudian psychoanalytic theory, in which a professor, wanting a child and jealous of his wife's childhood sweetheart, moves toward madness (we did say Freudian) and is cured through dream interpretation. Great dream sequences bring out the arm-chair psychoanalyst. Silent. **94m/B VHS, Beta.** *GE* Werner Krauss, Ruth Weyher, Jack Trevor; **D:** G.W. Pabst. *FCT*

Secrets of Sweet Sixteen *Woof!* **1974 (R)** Gag-fest about budding sexuality in high school. **84m/C VHS, Beta.** Suzie Atkins. *NO*

Secrets of Three Hungry Wives 🦴 **1978** When a multi-millionaire is killed, the women with whom he was having affairs are suspected. Tacky made for television flick. **97m/C VHS.** Jessica Walter, Gretchen Corbett, Eve Plumb, Heather MacRae, James Franciscus, Craig Stevens; **D:** Gordon Hessler. *NO*

Secrets of Women 🦴🦴🦴 *Kvinnors Vantan; Waiting Women* **1952** A rare Bergman comedy about three sisters-in-law who tell about their affairs and marriages as they await their husbands at a lakeside resort. His first commercial success, though it waited nine years for release (1961). In Swedish with English subtitles. **114m/B VHS, Beta.** *SW* Anita Bjork, Karl Arne Homsten, Eva Dahlbeck, Maj-Britt Nilsson, Jarl Kulle; **D:** Ingmar Bergman; **W:** Ingmar Bergman. *HMV, NLC, SUE*

The Secrets of Wu Sin 🦴🦴 **1932** A suicidal news writer in Chinatown is given a reason to live by a news editor who gives her a job. She starts investigating a ring smuggling Chinese workers, with the trail leading to, of course, Chinatown. Low-budget crime thriller. **65m/B VHS.** Lois Wilson, Grant Withers, Dorothy Revier, Robert Warwick, Toschia Mori; **D:** Richard Thorpe. *SNC, NOS, DVT*

Seduce Me: Pamela Principle 2 🦴½ *Pamela Principle 2* **1994 (R)** Charles is a bored, married, architectural photographer who decides a change of pace is in order. So he starts shooting lingerie fashion spreads and gets seduced by model Pamela, who likes her men married. The only connection to the 1991 film is the married man/affair angle. **96m/C VHS.** Alina Thompson, Nick Rafter, India Allen; **D:** Edward Holzman. *APX*

Seduced 🦴🦴 **1985** When a rich businessman turns up dead, the ambitious politician who was involved with his wife must find the killer. Not memorable or exceptional, but not boring or offensive either. Made for television. **100m/C VHS.** Gregory Harrison, Cybill Shepherd, Jose Ferrer, Adrienne Barbeau, Michael C. Gwynne, Karmin Murcelo, Paul Stewart; **D:** Jerrold Freedman. *PSM*

Seduced and Abandoned 🦴🦴🦴 *Sedotta e Abbandonata* **1964** A lothario seduces his fiancee's young sister. When the girl becomes pregnant, he refuses to marry her. Family complications abound. A comic look at the Italian code of honor. In Italian with English subtitles. **118m/B VHS, Beta.** *IT* Saro Urzi, Stefania Sandrelli, Aldo Puglisi; **D:** Pietro Germi. Cannes Film Festival '64: Best Actor (Urzi); National Board of Review Awards '64: 5 Best Foreign Films of the Year. *NOS, HHT, HEG*

Seduced by Evil 🦴🦴 **1994** A journalist (Somers) is investigating a story in a small Southwest town when she encounters a sorcerer (Vargas) who decides he wants her for himself alone. Even if it means destroying everyone she holds dear. Adapted from the novel "Brujo" by Jann Arrington Wolcott. **88m/C VHS, Beta.** Suzanne Somers, John Vargas, Julie Carmen, James B. Sikking, Mindy Spence, Nancy Moonves; **D:** Tony Wharmby; **W:** Bill Svanoe. *PAR*

The Seducer 🦴🦴 **1982 (R)** Things get dangerous when a playboy's goals turn from love to death. **72m/C VHS.** Christopher Mathews; **D:** Donovan Winters. *NO*

The Seducers 🦴 **1970** An acid-dropping mother takes her shy, withdrawn son on a Mediterranean cruise and asks along some of her girlfriends in the hopes of stoking his libido. However, she finds it difficult to control her own impulses. The boy gets a chance when the ship runs aground on a remote island and he meets an innocent native girl. His mother, though, has designs of her own. Dubbed from Italian. **84m/C VHS.** *GE* Rosalba (Sara Bay) Neri, Edwige Fenech, Maud de Belleroche, Maurizio Bonuglia, Ruggero Miti, Ewa Thulin; **D:** Ottavio Alessi. *SMW, TPV*

Seducers *Death Game* **1977 (R)** Wealthy, middle-aged man unsuspectingly allows two young lesbians to use his telephone. A night of bizarre mayhem and brutal murder begins. They tease him, tear apart his house, and generally make him miserable. Why? Good question. **90m/C VHS, Beta.** Sondra Locke, Colleen Camp, Seymour Cassel, Beth Brickell; ***D:*** Peter S. Traynor. *GEM*

The Seduction **1982 (R)** Superstar television anchorwoman is harassed by a psychotic male admirer. Usual run of the mill exploitive "B" thriller with no brains behind the camera. **104m/C VHS, Beta.** Morgan Fairchild, Michael Sarrazin, Vince Edwards, Andrew Stevens, Colleen Camp, Kevin Brophy; ***D:*** David Schmoeller; ***W:*** David Schmoeller; ***M:*** Lalo Schifrin. *MED, VTR*

The Seduction of Joe Tynan ½ **1979 (R)** Political drama about a young senator (Alda) torn between his family, his political career, and his mistress (Streep). Alda also wrote the thin screenplay, which reportedly is loosely based on the remarkable life of Ted Kennedy. Relatively shallow treatment of the meaty themes of power, hypocrisy, sex, and corruption in our nation's capital. **107m/C VHS, Beta, LV.** Alan Alda, Meryl Streep, Melvyn Douglas, Barbara Harris, Rip Torn; ***D:*** Jerry Schatzberg; ***W:*** Alan Alda; ***M:*** Bill Conti. Los Angeles Film Critics Association Awards '79: Best Supporting Actor (Douglas), Best Supporting Actress (Streep); New York Film Critics Awards '79: Best Supporting Actress (Streep); National Society of Film Critics Awards '79: Best Supporting Actress (Streep). *MCA*

Seduction of Mimi **1972 (R)** Comic farce of politics and seduction about a Sicilian laborer's escapades with the Communists and the local Mafia. Giannini is wonderful as the stubborn immigrant to the big city who finds himself in trouble. One of the funniest love scenes on film. Basis for the later movie "Which Way is Up?" **92m/C VHS, Beta.** *IT* Giancarlo Giannini, Mariangela Melato; ***D:*** Lina Wertmuller; ***W:*** Lina Wertmuller. Nominations: Cannes Film Festival '72: Best Film. *FOX, OM*

Seduction: The Cruel Woman **1989** A curiously uninvolving look at sexual games and fantasies. Wanda is a dominatrix, who also owns a sado-masochistic gallery where her various friends and current and formers lovers act out their basest desires. Stylized, with some graphic sex. Based on the novel "Venus in Furs" by Leopold Sacher-Masoch. In German with English subtitles. **84m/C VHS.** *GE* Mechthild Grossmann, Carola Regnier, Udo Kier, Sheila McLaughlin; ***D:*** Elfi Mikesch, Monika Treut; ***W:*** Elfi Mikesch, Monika Treut. *INJ*

See How She Runs **1978** Running becomes a central and redefining experience for a 40-year-old divorced schoolteacher (Woodward). Her training culminates with a run in the Boston marathon. Her loved ones, though concerned for her health and sanity, cheer her on. Excellent made for TV drama. Screen daughter Newman is also Woodward's real-life daughter. **92m/C VHS, Beta.** Joanne Woodward, John Considine, Lissy Newman, Barbara Manning; ***D:*** Richard T. Heffron. *NO*

See No Evil *Blind Terror* **1971 (PG)** A blind girl gradually discovers the murdered bodies of her uncle's family. Trapped in the family mansion, she finds herself pursued by the killer. Chilling and well crafted. **90m/C VHS, Beta, LV.** Mia Farrow, Dorothy Allison, Robin Bailey; ***D:*** Richard Fleischer; ***W:*** Brian Clemens; ***M:*** Elmer Bernstein. *COL*

See No Evil, Hear No Evil **1989 (R)** Another teaming for Pryor and Wilder, in which they portray a blind man and a deaf man both sought as murder suspects. Pryor and Wilder deserve better. **103m/C VHS, Beta, LV, 8mm.** Gene Wilder, Richard Pryor, Joan Severance, Anthony Zerbe; ***D:*** Arthur Hiller; ***W:*** Gene Wilder, Andrew Kurtzman, Eliot Wald, Earl Barret, Arne Sultan; ***M:*** Stewart Copeland. *COL*

See You in the Morning ½ **1989 (PG-13)** Ill-conceived romantic comedy-drama about a divorced psychiatrist and a widow, both of whom had unhappy marriages, who meet and marry. They must cope with their respective children, family tragedies, and their own expectations, in order to make this second marriage work. **119m/C VHS, Beta, LV.** Jeff Bridges, Alice Krige, Farrah Fawcett, Drew Barrymore, Lukas Haas, Macaulay Culkin, David Dukes, Frances Sternhagen, Theodore Bikel, George Hearn, Linda Lavin; ***D:*** Alan J. Pakula; ***W:*** Alan J. Pakula. *WAR*

Seedpeople ½ **1992** Mindless horror flick has bloodthirsty plants inhabiting peaceful Comet Valley after their seeds fall from outer space and germinate. These "seedpeople" possess tremendous powers and soon have the rural residents transformed into zombies. Bears an uncanny resemblance to "Invasion of the Bodysnatchers," and is so bad it's almost good. Also available with Spanish subtitles. **87m/C VHS, Beta.** Sam Hennings, Andrea Roth, Dane Witherspoon, David Dunard, Holly Fields, Bernard Kates, Anne Betancourt, Sonny Carl Davis; ***D:*** Peter Manoogian; ***W:*** Jackson Barr; ***M:*** Bob Mithoff. *PAR*

Seeds of Evil *The Gardener* **1976 (R)** Warhol alumnus Dallesandro is a strange gardener who grows flowers that can kill. He can also turn himself into a tree and figures to seduce rich and bored housewife Houghton (niece of Katharine Hepburn) after he finishes tending her garden. Strange, quirky horror flick. **97m/C VHS, Beta.** Katharine Houghton, Joe Dallesandro, Rita Gam; ***D:*** James H. Kay. *UNI*

The Seekers **1979** The story of the Kent family continues, as Abraham Kent, his wife and young son are forced to leave the safety of Boston for the rugged, untamed Pacific Northwest. TV movie based on the novel by John Jakes; preceded by "The Bastard" and "The Rebels." **200m/C VHS.** Randolph Mantooth, Edie Adams, Neville Brand, Delta Burke, John Carradine, George DeLoy, Julie Gregg, Roosevelt Grier, George Hamilton, Alex Hyde-White, Brian Keith, Ross Martin, Gary Merrill, Martin Milner, Vic Morrow, Timothy Patrick Murphy, Hugh O'Brian, Robert Reed, Allen Rich, Barbara Rush, Sarah Rush, Stuart Whitman, Ed Harris, Jeremy Licht, Eric Stoltz; ***D:*** Sidney Hayers. *MCA*

Seems Like Old Times ½ **1980 (PG)** A sweet lawyer (Hawn) finds herself helping her ex-husband (Chase) when two robbers force him to hold up a bank. Grodin is the new spouse threatened by Chase's appearance and by the heavies he's trying to escape. Better-than-average script, with funny and appealing characters. **102m/C VHS, Beta, LV.** Goldie Hawn, Chevy Chase, Charles Grodin, Robert Guillaume, Harold Gould, George Grizzard, T.K. Carter; ***D:*** Jay Sandrich; ***W:*** Neil Simon; ***M:*** Marvin Hamlisch. *COL*

Seize the Day **1986** A man approaching middle age (Williams) feels that he is a failure. Brilliant performances by all, plus a number of equally fine actors in small roles. Based on the short novel by Saul Bellow. **93m/C VHS, Beta, LV.** Robin Williams, Joseph Wiseman, Jerry Stiller, Glenne Headly, Tony Roberts; ***D:*** Fielder Cook. *MON*

Seizure **1974 (PG)** Three demonic creatures from a writer's dreams come to life and terrorize him and his houseguests at a weekend party. Slick but disjointed; Stone's directorial debut. Interesting cast includes Tattoo from "Fantasy Island." **93m/C VHS, Beta.** *CA* Jonathan Frid, Herve Villechaize, Christina Pickles; ***D:*** Oliver Stone; ***W:*** Oliver Stone. *PSM*

Seizure: The Story of Kathy Morris **1982** The real-life anguish and struggle of a young music student who must have brain surgery and comes out of it unable to read or count. Workaday dramatization. **104m/C VHS, Beta.** Leonard Nimoy, Penelope Milford; ***D:*** Gerald I. Isenberg. *TLF*

Self-Defense ½ **1988 (R)** When a city's police force goes on strike, the citizens band together into vigilante troops. **85m/C VHS, Beta, LV.** Tom Nardini, Brenda Bazinet. *MED*

Sell Out ½ **1976 (PG)** A former spy living in Jerusalem is called out of retirement; his protege, who defected to the Soviets, now wants out. **102m/C VHS, Beta.** Richard Widmark, Oliver Reed, Gayle Hunnicutt, Sam Wanamaker; ***D:*** Peter Collinson. *MED*

Semi-Tough ½ **1977 (R)** Likeable, still current social satire involving a couple of pro-football buddies and their mutual interest in their team owner's daughter. Romantic comedy, satire of the sports world, zany highjinks—it's all here, though not enough of any of these. Pleasant and enjoyable. Based on the novel by Dan Jenkins. **107m/C VHS, Beta, LV.** Burt Reynolds, Kris Kristofferson, Jill Clayburgh, Lotte Lenya, Robert Preston, Bert Convy, Richard Masur, Carl Weathers, Brian Dennehy, John Matuszak, Ron Silver; ***D:*** Michael Ritchie; ***W:*** Walter Bernstein. *MGM, FOX*

The Senator was Indiscreet *Mr. Ashton was Indiscreet* **1947** A farcical comedy concerning a slightly loony senator with presidential aspirations. He thinks he can win the nomination because he keeps a diary that would prove embarrassing to numerous colleagues. The diary then falls into the hands of a journalist. Powell is wonderful as the daffy politician. Playwright Kaufman's only directorial effort. **75m/B VHS.** William Powell, Ella Raines, Hans Conried; ***D:*** George S. Kaufman; ***C:*** William Mellor. New York Film Critics Awards '47: Best Actor (Powell). *REP*

Send Me No Flowers **1964** Vintage Hudson-Day comedy. Hudson plays a hypochondriac who thinks his death is imminent. He decides to provide for his family's future by finding his wife a rich husband. She thinks he's feeling guilty for having an affair. **100m/C VHS, Beta.** Rock Hudson, Doris Day, Tony Randall, Paul Lynde; ***D:*** Norman Jewison; ***W:*** Julius J. Epstein, Philip G. Epstein; ***C:*** Daniel F. Fapp. *MCA, CCB*

The Sender **1982 (R)** An amnesiac young man is studied by a psychiatrist. She discovers that her patient is a "sender," who can transmit his nightmares to other patients at a hospital. **92m/C VHS, Beta, LV.** *GB* Kathryn Harrold, Zeljko Ivanek, Shirley Knight, Paul Freeman, Sean Hewitt; ***D:*** Roger Christian; ***W:*** Thomas Baum; ***M:*** Trevor Jones. *PAR*

Senior Trip **1981** New York City will never be the same after a bunch of rowdy Midwestern high school seniors tear up the town on their graduation trip. Made for television. **96m/C VHS, Beta.** Scott Baio, Mickey Rooney, Faye Grant, Vincent Spano, Jane Hoffman; ***D:*** Kenneth Johnson. *WOV*

Senior Week *Woof!* **1988** A batch of girl-hungry teens have a wacky time on their Florida vacation just before graduation. **97m/C VHS, Beta.** Michael St. Gerard, Devon Skye, Leesa Bryte; ***D:*** Stuart Goldman. *LIV, VES*

The Seniors **1978 (R)** A group of college students decide to open a phony sex clinic, but the joke is on them when the clinic becomes a success. Better than it sounds. Pretty good acting and much harmless goofiness. **87m/C VHS, Beta.** Dennis Quaid, Priscilla Barnes, Jeffrey Byron, Gary Imhoff; ***D:*** Rod Amateau. *VES*

Senora Tentacion **1949** Musical melodrama about a composer who fights to leave his mother, sister, and girlfriend in order to flee with Hortensia, a famous singer. In Spanish with English subtitles. **82m/B VHS, Beta.** David Silva, Susana Guizar, Ninon Sevilla. *VYY, APD, INJ*

Sensation **1994 (R)** A college co-ed agrees to participate in a professor's paranormal experiments in order to test her psychic abilities. Unfortunately what she senses is her prof involved in the unsolved sex-murder of a former student. **102m/C VHS, LV.** Kari Wuhrer, Eric Roberts, Ron Perlman, Ed Begley Jr., Paul LeMat, Claire Stansfield, Kieran Mulroney, Tracey Needham; ***D:*** Brian Grant; ***W:*** Doug Wallace; ***M:*** Arthur Kempel. *COL*

Sensations **1987 (R)** A woman and a man who aren't exceptionally fond of one another share a lottery ticket and win. Vincent is best known as a former director of porno flicks, and he manages to work in sexual overtones. **91m/C VHS, Beta.** Rebecca Lynn, Blake Bahner, Jennifer Delora, Rick Savage, Loretta Palma, Frank Stewart; ***D:*** Chuck Vincent. *ACA*

Sensations of 1945 ½ *Sensations* **1944** A press agent turns his firm over to one of his clients, a dancer with some wild promotional ideas. Brings together numerous variety and musical acts.

W. C. Fields has a cameo in his last film role. Mostly unremarkable, occasionally fun musical. **86m/B VHS, Beta.** Eleanor Powell, Dennis O'Keefe, Sir C. Aubrey Smith, Eugene Pallette, Cab Calloway, Sophie Tucker, Woody Herman, Lyle Talbot, Marie Blake; ***Cameos:*** W.C. Fields; ***D:*** Andrew L. Stone. Nominations: Academy Awards '44: Best Original Score. *VDM*

Sense & Sensibility **1985** BBC miniseries adaptation of Jane Austen's first novel concerning two sisters striving for happiness in their well-ordered lives. **174m/C VHS, Beta.** *GB* Irene Richard, Tracey Childs; ***D:*** Rodney Bennett. *FOX, TVC, HMV*

Sense and Sensibility ½ **1995 (PG)** Thanks to the machinations of greedy relatives, the impecunious Dashwood family is forced to move to a country cottage when father dies. Sensible Elinor (Thompson) looks after the household while overly-romantic Marianne (Winslet) pines for passion—ignoring the noble attentions of middle-aged neighbor Brandon (Rickman) for the far more dashing Willoughby (Wise). Elinor has her own hopes for marriage with boyishly ineffectual Edward (Grant) but all three men have secrets that could crush romantic dreams (at least temporarily). Somewhat slow-paced but witty adaptation (by Thompson) of Jane Austen's first novel, well-acted and beautifully photographed (oh, to be in the English countryside). **135m/C VHS, LV, 8mm.** *GB* Emma Thompson, Kate Winslet, Hugh Grant, Alan Rickman, Greg Wise, Robert Hardy, Elizabeth Spriggs, Emile Francois, Gemma Jones, James Fleet, Harriet Walter, Imogen Stubbs, Imelda Staunton, Hugh Laurie, Richard Lumsden; ***D:*** Ang Lee; ***W:*** Emma Thompson; ***C:*** Michael Coulter; ***M:*** Patrick Doyle. Academy Awards '95: Best Adapted Screenplay; British Academy Awards '95: Best Actress (Thompson), Best Film, Best Supporting Actress (Winslet); Los Angeles Film Critics Association Awards '95: Best Screenplay; National Board of Review Awards '95: Best Actress (Thompson), Best Director (Lee), Best Film; New York Film Critics Awards '95: Best Director (Lee); Screen Actors Guild Award '95: Best Supporting Actress (Winslet); Writers Guild of America '95: Best Adapted Screenplay; Nominations: Academy Awards '95: Best Actress (Thompson), Best Cinematography, Best Costume Design, Best Picture, Best Supporting Actress (Winslet), Best Score; British Academy Awards '95: Best Adapted Screenplay, Best Cinematography, Best Director (Lee), Best Supporting Actor (Rickman), Best Supporting Actress (Spriggs), Best Score; Directors Guild of America Awards '95: Best Director (Lee); Golden Globe Awards '96: Best Actress—Drama (Thompson), Best Director (Lee), Best Supporting Actress (Winslet), Best Score; Screen Actors Guild Award '95: Best Actress (Thompson), Cast. *COL*

A Sense of Freedom **1978 (R)** A hopeless racketeering criminal is thrust from institution to institution until the Scottish authorities decide on an innovative style of reform. Based on Jimmy Boyle's autobiographical book. Excellent and disturbing. **81m/C VHS, Beta.** *GB* David Hayman, Alex Norton, Jake D'Arcy, Sean Scanlan, Fulton Mackay; ***D:*** John MacKenzie. *NO*

Senso *The Wanton Contessa* **1954** Tragic story of romance and rebellion as Italian patriots battle the Austro-Hungarian empire for independence in 1866. An Italian noblewoman betrays her marriage, and almost her country, to be with a cynical Austrian soldier in this visually stunning piece of cinematography. In Italian with English subtitles or dubbed. **125m/C VHS.** *IT* Alida Valli, Massimo Girotti, Heinz Moog, Farley Granger; ***D:*** Luchino Visconti; ***C:*** Robert Krasker. *VCD, APD*

The Sensual Man ½ **1974 (R)** Hot-blooded Italian falls in love and gets married only to find out that his wife cannot consummate their marriage. Exploitative, misogynistic, and unfunny. **90m/C VHS, Beta.** Giancarlo Giannini, Rossana Podesta, Lionel Stander; ***D:*** Marco Vicario. *COL*

Sensual Partners *Woof!* **1987** Young actresses are lured to Tangier by a fake movie producer and sold as sex slaves. Emphasis on soft-focus, soft-core flesh. **87m/C VHS, Beta.** Gina Jansen, Eric Falk. *MED*

The Sensuous Nurse **1976 (R)** Italian comedy about a beautiful nurse hired by the greedy, treacherous relatives of a weak-hearted count in hopes that her voluptuousness will give him a heart attack. It doesn't, and she falls in love. Mindless, but fun and sexy. Dubbed in English. **79m/C VHS, Beta.** *IT* Ursula Andress, Mario Pisu, Dulio Del Prete, Jack Palance; ***D:*** Nello Rosatti. *FOX*

Sensuous Summer ½ **1993 (R)** When Bobby returns home to the town of Elk Lake he finds the family business, run by his brother Nick, is in deep trouble. It seems Alex, an unscrupulous banker, wants to foreclose. But business comes second to pleasure when Bobby is reunited with old flame Jill and Nick takes up again with ex-girlfriend Cindy. **80m/C VHS.** Tom Case, Christina Campbell, Brittany McGrea, Gina Jorand. *CEL*

The Sensuous Teenager *Woof! Libido; Forbidden Passions* **1970 (R)** Overwhelmingly erotic and uncontrollably seductive, a teenage girl aims to please by releasing all the sensuality within her. **80m/C VHS.** Sandra Jullien, Janine Reynaud, Michel Lemoine; ***D:*** Max Pecas. *SUN*

The Sentinel **1976 (R)** A model, who has moved into a New York City brownstone, encounters an aging priest and some unusual neighbors. When she investigates strange noises she finds out that the apartment building houses the doorway to hell - and that she's intended to be the next doorkeeper. Modest suspense film with a good cast and enough shock and special effects to keep the viewer interested. **92m/C VHS, Beta.** Chris Sarandon, Christina Raines, Ava Gardner, Jose Ferrer, Sylvia Miles, John Carradine, Burgess Meredith, Tom Berenger, Beverly D'Angelo, Jeff Goldblum; ***D:*** Michael Winner; ***W:*** Michael Winner. *MCA*

Separate But Equal ½ **1991 (PG)** One of TV's greatest history lessons, a powerful dramatization of the 1954 Brown vs. The Board of Education case that wrung a landmark civil rights decision from the Supreme Court. Great care is taken to humanize all the participants, from the humblest schoolchild to NAACP lawyer Thurgood Marshall (Poitier). On two cassettes. **194m/C VHS, LV.** Sidney Poitier, Burt Lancaster, Richard Kiley, Cleavon Little, John McMartin, Graham Beckel, Lynne Thigpen, Albert Hall; ***D:*** George Stevens Jr.; ***W:*** George Stevens Jr. *REP, FCT, PTB*

Separate Lives ½ **1994 (R)** Psych prof Lauren Porter (Hamilton) is in need of some counseling herself. Seems she has a sexy alter ego calling herself Lena and Lauren fears she may have killed someone in her Lena persona. So she turns to her student Tom (Belushi), who happens to be an excop, for help. Sketchy characters and a tired formula make this one a yawner. **101m/C VHS.** Linda Hamilton, James Belushi, Vera Miles, Elissabeth Moss, Drew Snyder, Mark Lindsay Chapman, Marc Poppel, Elizabeth Arlen; ***D:*** David Madden; ***W:*** Steven Pressfield; ***M:*** William Olvis. *VMK*

A Separate Peace **1973 (PG)** Two young men in a New England prep school during WWII come to grips with the war, coming of age, and a tragic accident. Cheap rendition of a not-so-great novel by John Knowles. **104m/C VHS, Beta.** John Heyl, Parker Stevenson, William Roerick; ***D:*** Larry Peerce; ***M:*** Charles Fox. *PAR, HMV*

Separate Tables ½ **1958** Adaptation of the Terence Rattigan play about a varied cast of characters living out their personal dramas in a British seaside hotel. Guests include a matriarch and her shy daughter, a divorced couple, a spinster, and a presumed war hero. Their secrets and loves are examined in grand style. Fine acting all around. **98m/B VHS, Beta.** Burt Lancaster, David Niven, Rita Hayworth, Deborah Kerr, Wendy Hiller, Rod Taylor, Gladys Cooper, Felix Aylmer, Cathleen Nesbitt; ***D:*** Delbert Mann; ***W:*** John Gay; ***C:*** Charles B(ryant) Lang. Academy Awards '58: Best Actor (Niven), Best Supporting Actress (Hiller); National Board of Review Awards '58: 10 Best Films of the Year; New York Film Critics Awards '58: Best Actor (Niven); Nominations: Academy Awards '58: Best Actress (Kerr), Best Adapted Screenplay, Best Black and White Cinematography, Best Picture, Best Original Score. *MGM, FOX, FCT*

Separate Tables ½ **1983 (PG)** A remake of the 1958 film adapted from Terence Rattigan's play. Separated into two parts, "Table by the Window" and "Table Number Seven." The lives of the lonely inhabitants of a hotel are dramatized through wonderful acting by Christie and Bates. Made for cable television. **50m/C VHS, Beta.** Julie Christie, Alan Bates, Claire Bloom, Irene Worth; ***D:*** John Schlesinger. *MGM*

Separate Vacations ½ **1986 (R)** A married man leaves his wife and kids to take a separate vacation, hoping he'll find exciting sex. Wife and kids end up at a ski resort, where romance comes her way. A lightweight, old story. **91m/C VHS, Beta.** David Naughton, Jennifer Dale, Mark Keyloun; ***D:*** Michael Anderson Sr. *LIV*

Separate Ways ½ **1982 (R)** Unhappily married couple involved in various affairs split up in order to deal with themselves and their marriage. Good cast; bad script wandering down Maudlin Lane. **92m/C VHS, Beta, LV.** Karen Black, Tony LoBianco, David Naughton, Sybil Danning; ***D:*** Howard (Hikmet) Avedis. *VES*

The Separation **1994** Emotions (and fine performances) rather than action move along this domestic drama. Anne (Huppert) and Pierre (Autueil) are living together in Paris with their toddler son when Anne suddenly announces that she's involved with another man. Anne doesn't see why this this should cause any rift in their domestic arrangements but Pierre slowly falls to pieces. Adapted from the novel by Dan Franck; French with subtitles. **85m/C VHS.** *FR* Isabelle Huppert, Daniel Auteuil, Karin Viard, Jerome Deschamps; ***D:*** Christian Vincent; ***W:*** Christian Vincent, Dan Franck; ***C:*** Denis Lenoir. Nominations: Cesar Awards '94: Best Actor (Auteuil), Best Actress (Huppert). *NYR*

Sepia Cinderella **1947** A songwriter, who finds himself with a hit, abandons his current life and love to try high society. He finds out it's not what he wants after all. **67m/B VHS, Beta.** Sheila Guyse, Rubel Blakely, Freddie Bartholomew, Sid Catlett, Deke Wilson. *NOS, DVT, FCT*

September ½ **1988 (PG-13)** Woody does Bergman again with a shuttered, claustrophobic drama about six unhappy people trying to verbalize their feelings in a dark summer house in Vermont. Well-acted throughout and interesting at first, but the whining and angst attacks eventually give way to boredom. Of course, the Woodman went on to "Crimes and Misdemeanors," blending his dark and comedic sides masterfully, so the best way to look at this is as a training film. **82m/C VHS, Beta, LV.** Mia Farrow, Dianne Wiest, Denholm Elliott, Sam Waterston, Elaine Stritch, Jack Warden; ***D:*** Woody Allen; ***W:*** Woody Allen; ***C:*** Carlo DiPalma; ***M:*** Art Tatum. *ORI*

September Affair ½ **1950** A married engineer and a classical pianist miss their plane from Naples. When the plane crashes, they're presumed dead, and they find themselves free to continue their illicit love affair. They find they cannot hide forever and must make peace with their pasts. Features the hit "September Song," recorded by Walter Huston. **104m/B VHS, LV.** Joseph Cotten, Joan Fontaine, Francoise Rosay, Jessica Tandy, Robert Arthur; ***D:*** William Dieterle; ***C:*** Charles B(ryant) Lang. Golden Globe Awards '52: Best Score. *PAR*

September Gun ½ **1983** A nun hires an aging gunfighter to escort her and a group of Apache children to a church school two hundred miles away. Preston is excellent as the ornery varmint in this enjoyable, pleasant western comedy. Made for television. **94m/C VHS, Beta.** Robert Preston, Patty Duke, Christopher Lloyd, Geoffrey Lewis, Sally Kellerman; ***D:*** Don Taylor. *WOV*

September 30, 1955 ½ **1977 (PG)** A college undergrad (Thomas) in a small Arkansas town is devastated when he learns of the death of his idol, James Dean. (The title refers to the day Dean died.) Jimmy gathers a group of friends together for a vigil which turns into a drinking-binge, resulting in police chases and, finally, tragedy. Film debut of

Quaid. Also known as "9/30/55." **107m/C VHS.** Richard Thomas, Lisa Blount, Deborah Benson, Tom Hulce, Dennis Christopher, Dennis Quaid, Susan Tyrrell; ***D:*** James Bridges; ***W:*** James Bridges. *MCA*

Sgt. Bilko 🦴½ **1995 (PG)** Popular 50's sitcom doesn't march so much as limp to the big screen with Martin leading the troops as the wise-cracking title character, crafted so brilliantly by Phil Silvers on the small screen. Martin flims and flams with frenetic energy as he tries to save his base from Washington cutbacks and the film from utter disaster. Enter Major Thorn (Hartman), Bilko's old adversary, who's plotting revenge on the con artist sergeant. Aykroyd's Bilko's naive boss, Col. Hall, but has little to do. Director Lynn finds his usual comic flair on leave this time around—too few laughs, spread too thin. Sentimental stroke has Catherine Silvers, Phil's daughter, playing Lt. Monday. **92m/C VHS.** Steve Martin, Dan Aykroyd, Phil Hartman, Glenne Headly, Daryl Mitchell, Max Casella, Brian Leckner, Pamela Segall, Eric Edwards, Dan Ferro, John Marshall Jones, Brian Ortiz; ***D:*** Jonathan Lynn; ***W:*** Andy Breckman; ***C:*** Peter Sova; ***M:*** Alan Silvestri. *MCA*

Sergeant Matlovich vs. the U.S. Air Force 🦴🦴½ **1978** A serviceman fights to remain in the Air Force after admitting his homosexuality. Compelling theme (from a true story) and good lead performance from Dourif are not enough to carry a rather flat made for TV script. **100m/C VHS.** Brad Dourif, Marc Singer, Frank Converse, William Daniels, Stephen Elliott, David Spielberg, Rue McClanahan, Mitchell Ryan, David Ogden Stiers; ***D:*** Paul Leaf. *LIV*

Sgt. Pepper's Lonely Hearts Club Band 🦴½ **1978 (PG)** "Rip-off" would be putting it kindly. A classic album by one of the greatest rock bands of all time deserves the respect of not having a star-studded extravaganza "filmization" made of it. Gratuitous, weird casting, bad acting give it a surreal feel. And the Bee Gees? Please. A nadir of seventies popular entertainment. ♫Sgt. Pepper's Lonely Hearts Club Band; With a Little Help From My Friends; Fixing a Hole; Getting Better; Here Comes the Sun; I Want You (She's So Heavy); Good Morning, Good Morning; Nowhere Man; Polythene Pam. **113m/C VHS, Beta, LV.** Peter Frampton, The Bee Gees, Steve Martin, George Burns, Donald Pleasence; ***D:*** Michael A. Schultz. *MCA*

Sergeant Rutledge 🦴🦴🦴 **1960** The story of a court-martial, told in flashback, about a black cavalry officer on trial for rape and murder. A detailed look at overt and covert racism handled by master director Ford. It is always apparent Strode (as Rutledge) is a heroic, yet human, figure who refuses to be beaten down by circumstances. The courtroom setting is deliberately oppressive but does make the film somewhat static. Based on the novel "Captain Buffalo" by James Warner Bellah. **112m/C VHS.** Woody Strode, Jeffrey Hunter, Constance Towers, Billie Burke, Juano Hernandez, Carleton Young, Charles Seel, Jan Styne, Mae Marsh; ***D:*** John Ford; ***W:*** Willis Goldbeck, James Warner Bellah; ***M:*** Howard Jackson. *WAR*

Sergeant Ryker 🦴🦴½ **1968** Confident lead acting from Marvin as a U.S. serviceman accused of treason during the Korean War carries this otherwise blah army/courtroom drama. Remake of 1963 TV film "The Case Against Sergeant Ryker." Dillman is good as Marvin's energetic lawyer. **85m/C VHS.** Lee Marvin, Bradford Dillman, Vera Miles, Peter Graves, Lloyd Nolan, Murray Hamilton; ***D:*** Buzz Kulik; ***M:*** John Williams. *NO*

Sergeant York 🦴🦴🦴🦴 **1941** Timely and enduring war movie based on the true story of Alvin York, the country boy from Tennessee drafted during WWI. At first a pacifist, Sergeant York (Cooper, well cast in an Oscar-winning role) finds justification for fighting and becomes one of the war's greatest heros. Gentle scenes of rural life contrast with horrific battlegrounds. York served as a consultant. **134m/B VHS, Beta.** Gary Cooper, Joan Leslie, Walter Brennan, Dickie Moore, Ward Bond, George Tobias, Noah Beery Jr., June Lockhart, Stanley Ridges, Margaret Wycherly; ***D:*** Howard Hawks; ***W:*** Abem Finkel, Harry Chandlee, Howard Koch, John Huston; ***M:*** Max Steiner. Academy Awards '41: Best Actor (Cooper), Best Film Editing; New York Film Critics Awards '41: Best Actor (Cooper); Nominations: Academy Awards '41: Best Black and White Cinematography, Best Director (Hawks), Best Interior Decoration, Best Original Screenplay, Best Picture, Best Sound, Best Supporting Actor (Brennan), Best Supporting Actress (Wycherly), Best Original Score. *MGM, FOX, BTV*

Serial 🦴🦴🦴 **1980 (R)** Fun spoof of hyper-trendiness—open marriage, health foods, fad religions, navel-gazing—in Marin County, the really cool place to live across the Golden Gate from San Francisco. Mull in his first lead is the oddly normal guy surrounded by fruits and nuts. Based on Cyra McFadden's novel. **90m/C VHS, Beta, LV.** Martin Mull, Sally Kellerman, Tuesday Weld, Tom Smothers, Bill Macy, Peter Bonerz, Barbara Rhoades, Christopher Lee; ***D:*** Bill Persky; ***W:*** Rich Eustis, Michael Elias. *PAR*

Serial Killer 🦴🦴 **1995 (R)** Selby Younger (Delaney) is able to think like a killer in order to catch them. That's how the beautiful cop captured the serial killer (Bell) who has now escaped—Selby's his ultimate target but first he wants revenge. So he uses her friends as bait and leaves the bodies for Selby to discover. **94m/C VHS.** Kim Delaney, Gary Hudson, Tobin Bell, Pam Grier, Marco Rodriguez, Lyman Ward, Cyndi Pass, Andrew Prine; ***D:*** Pierce David. *REP*

Serial Mom 🦴🦴🦴 **1994 (R)** June Cleaver-like housewife Turner is nearly perfect, except when someone disrupts her orderly life. Didn't rewind your videotape? Chose the white shoes after Labor Day? Uh oh. Stardom reigns after she's caught and the murderer-as-celebrity phenomenon is exploited to the fullest. Darkly funny Waters satire tends toward the mainstream and isn't as perverse as earlier efforts, but still maintains a shocking edge (vital organs are good for an appearance or two). Turner's chameleonic performance as the perfect mom/crazed killer is right on target, recalling "The War of the Roses." Waterston, Lake, and Lillard are terrific as her generic suburban family. **93m/C VHS, LV.** Kathleen Turner, Ricki Lake, Sam Waterston, Matthew Lillard, Mink Stole, Traci Lords; ***Cameos:*** Suzanne Somers, Joan Rivers, Patty Hearst; ***D:*** John Waters; ***W:*** John Waters; ***M:*** Basil Poledouris. *HBO*

The Serpent and the Rainbow *Woof!* **1987 (R)** A good, interesting book (by Harvard ethnobotanist Wade Davis) offering serious speculation on the possible existence and origin of zombies in Haiti was hacked and slashed into a cheap Wes Cravenized screen semblance of itself. And a shame it is: the result is racist, disrespectful, exploitative, and superficial. From the director of "Nightmare on Elm Street." **98m/C VHS, Beta, LV.** Bill Pullman, Cathy Tyson, Zakes Mokae, Paul Winfield, Conrad Roberts, Badja Djola, Theresa Merritt; ***D:*** Wes Craven; ***W:*** Richard Maxwell; ***M:*** Brad Fiedel. *MCA*

Serpent Island 🦴½ **1954** Two seamen fight over a Caribbean woman amid voodoo rituals, sea monsters and buried treasure. **63m/C VHS, Beta.** Sonny Tufts. *MED*

The Serpent of Death 🦴🦴 **1990 (R)** An archaeologist uncovers a statue and a curse which changes his life. Horror and adventure rolled into one. **90m/C VHS, Beta, LV.** *PAR*

The Serpent's Egg 🦴½ *Das Schlangenei* **1978 (R)** Big disappointment from the great Bergman in his second film in English. Ullmann is not sultry and Carradine is horrible. Big budget matched by big Bergman ego, making a big, bad parody of himself. The plot concerns a pair of Jewish trapeze artists surviving in Berlin during Hitler's rise by working in a grisly and mysterious medical clinic. **119m/C VHS, Beta.** *GE* David Carradine, Liv Ullmann, Gert Frobe, James Whitmore; ***D:*** Ingmar Bergman; ***W:*** Ingmar Bergman; ***C:*** Sven Nykvist. *LIV, INJ*

Serpico 🦴🦴🦴 **1973 (R)** Based on Peter Maas's book about the true-life exploits of Frank Serpico, a New York undercover policeman who exposed corruption in the police department. Known as much for his nonconformism as for his honesty, the real Serpico eventually retired from the force and moved to Europe. South Bronx-raised Pacino gives the character reality and strength. Excellent New York location photography. **130m/C VHS, Beta, LV.** Al Pacino, John Randolph, Jack Kehoe, Barbara Eda-Young, Cornelia Sharpe, F. Murray Abraham, Tony Roberts; ***D:*** Sidney Lumet. Golden Globe Awards '74: Best Actor—Drama (Pacino); National Board of Review Awards '73: Best Actor (Pacino); Writers Guild of America '73: Best Adapted Screenplay; Nominations: Academy Awards '73: Best Actor (Pacino), Best Adapted Screenplay. *PAR*

The Servant 🦴🦴🦴½ **1963** A dark, intriguing examination of British class hypocrisy and the master-servant relationship. A rich, bored playboy is ruined by his socially inferior but crafty and ambitious manservant. Playwright Harold Pinter wrote the adaptation of Robin Maugham's novel in his first collaboration with director Losey. The best kind of British societal navel-gazing. **112m/B VHS, Beta.** *GB* Dirk Bogarde, James Fox, Sarah Miles, Wendy Craig; ***D:*** Joseph Losey; ***W:*** Harold Pinter. British Academy Awards '63: Best Actor (Bogarde); New York Film Critics Awards '64: Best Screenplay. *NO*

Servants of Twilight 🦴🦴 **1991 (R)** Religious zealots target a small boy for assassination because their cult leader says he's the anti-Christ. Adaptation of the Dean R. Koontz novel. Packed with action, its spell on the viewer hinges on a cruel shock ending that undercuts what came before. Made for cable television. **95m/C VHS.** Bruce Greenwood, Belinda Bauer, Grace Zabriskie, Richard Bradford, Jarrett Lennon, Carel Struycken, Jack Kehoe, Kelli Maroney; ***D:*** Jeffrey Obrow; ***W:*** Stephen Carpenter. *VMK*

Sesame Street Presents: Follow That Bird *Follow That Bird* **1985 (G)** Television's Big Bird suffers an identity crisis, and leaves Sesame Street to join a family of real birds. He soon misses his home, and returns, in a danger-filled journey. **92m/C VHS, Beta, LV.** Sandra Bernhard, John Candy, Chevy Chase, Joe Flaherty, Dave Thomas, Waylon Jennings, Jim Henson's Muppets; ***D:*** Ken Kwapis; ***M:*** Lennie Niehaus. *WAR*

A Session with the Committee **1969** Collection of skits performed by a Los Angeles comedy troupe. **90m/C VHS.** Peter Bonerz, Barbara Bosson, Garry Goodrow, Carl Gottlieb, Jessica Myerson, Christopher Ross, Melvin Stewart, Melvin Sturdy; ***D:*** Jack Del. *NO*

Sessions 🦴🦴 **1983** Mentally exhausted by her roles as sister, single parent, lover, exercise enthusiast, and high-priced prostitute, Leigh Churchill (Hamel) seeks professional counselling. Hamel's first role after "Hill Street Blues" is only average in this made for TV drama. **96m/C VHS, Beta.** Veronica Hamel, Jeffrey DeMunn, Jill Eikenberry, David Marshall Grant, George Coe, Henderson Forsythe, Deborah Hedwall; ***D:*** Richard Pearce. *NO*

The Set-Up 🦴🦴🦴½ **1949** Excellent, original if somewhat overwrought morality tale about integrity set in the world of boxing. Filmed as a continuous narrative covering only 72 minutes in the life of an aging fighter (Ryan). Told to throw a fight, he must battle gangsters when he refuses. Powerful, with fine performances, especially from Ryan in the lead. Inspired by Joseph Moncure March's narrative poem. **72m/B VHS, Beta, LV.** Robert Ryan, Audrey Totter, George Tobias, Alan Baxter, James Edwards, Wallace Ford; ***D:*** Robert Wise; ***C:*** Milton Krasner. *CCB, MED*

The Set Up 🦴🦴½ **1995 (R)** Electronic engineer-turned-cat burglar Charlie Thorpe (Zane) is now apparently reformed after a prison stint and works designing and installing security systems. His latest job is for Chairman Jeremiah Cole (Coburn) at Charter Trust bank where he begins romancing the beautiful Gina (Sara). But she becomes the hostage of Charlie's ex-prison buddy Kliff (Russo), who wants Charlie's help in breaking into the bank. However, there's a doublecross (or maybe even a triplecross) that has Charlie scrambling to save his life. Based on the book "My Laugh Comes Last" by James Hadley Chase. **103m/C VHS.** Billy Zane, Mia Sara, James Coburn, James Russo; ***D:*** Strathford Hamilton; ***W:*** Michael Thoma; ***C:*** David Lewis; ***M:*** Conrad Pope. *MGM*

Seven 🦴🦴½ **1979 (R)** Freelance desperado Smith takes $7 million of your tax dollars at work from the feds to get rid of Hawaiian gangsters. Might be tongue in cheek, though sometimes it's hard to tell. Fun action pic unfortunately characterized by bad camera work and over-earnest direction. Features the original of a gag made famous in "Raiders of the Lost Ark." **100m/C VHS, Beta.** William Smith, Barbara Leigh, Guich Koock, Art Metrano, Martin Kove, Richard Le Pore, Susan Kiger; ***D:*** Andy Sidaris. *LIV*

Seven 🦴🦴🦴 **1995 (R)** If this grim thriller can't make you jump, you're dead, and you won't be the only one. Arrogant, ignorant detective David Mills (Pitt) is newly partnered with erudite old-timer William Somerset (Freeman) and they're stuck with the bizarre case of a morbidly obese man who was forced to eat himself to death. The weary Somerset is certain it's just the beginning and he's right—the non-buddy duo are on the trail of a serial killer who uses the seven deadly sins (gluttony, greed, sloth, pride, lust, envy, and wrath) as his modus operandi. Since most of the film is shot in dark, grimy, and unrelentingly rainy circumstances, much of the grotesqueness of the murders is left to the viewer's imagination—which will be in overdrive. **127m/C VHS, LV.** Brad Pitt, Morgan Freeman, Gwyneth Paltrow, Kevin Spacey, R. Lee Ermey, Richard Roundtree, John C. McGinley, Julie Araskog, Reg E. Cathey, Peter Crombie; ***D:*** David Fincher; ***W:*** Andrew Kevin Walker; ***C:*** Darius Khondji; ***M:*** Howard Shore. MTV Movie Awards '96: Best Film, Most Desirable Male (Pitt), Best Villain (Spacey); New York Film Critics Awards '95: Best Supporting Actor (Spacey); Nominations: Academy Awards '95: Best Film Editing; British Academy Awards '95: Best Original Screenplay; MTV Movie Awards '96: Best On-Screen Duo (Brad Pitt/Morgan Freeman). *NLC*

Seven Alone 🦴🦴½ *House Without Windows* **1975 (G)** Family adventure tale (based on Monroe Morrow's book "On to Oregon," based in turn on a true story) about seven siblings who undertake a treacherous 2000-mile journey from Missouri to Oregon, after their parents die along the way. Inspiring and all that; good family movie. **85m/C VHS, Beta.** Dewey Martin, Aldo Ray, Anne Collins, Dean Smith, Stewart Peterson; ***D:*** Earl Bellamy. *NO*

Seven Beauties 🦴🦴🦴🦴 *Pasqualino Settebellezze; Pasqualino: Seven Beauties* **1976** Very dark war comedy about a small-time Italian crook in Naples with seven ugly sisters to support. He survives a German prison camp and much else; unforgettably, he seduces the ugly commandant of his camp to save his own life. Good acting and tight direction. **116m/C VHS, Beta, LV.** *IT* Giancarlo Giannini, Fernando Rey, Shirley Stoler, Elena Fiore, Enzo Vitale; ***D:*** Lina Wertmuller; ***W:*** Lina Wertmuller; ***C:*** Tonino Delli Colli. Nominations: Academy Awards '76: Best Actor (Giannini), Best Director (Wertmuller), Best Foreign Language Film, Best Original Screenplay. *COL, APD*

Seven Blows of the Dragon 🦴🦴½ **1973 (R)** The Chinese novel, "All Men Are Brothers," is the basis for this spectacular martial arts epic. **81m/C VHS, Beta.** David Chiang. *WAR*

Seven Brides for Seven Brothers 🦴🦴🦴½ **1954** The eldest of seven fur-trapping brothers in the Oregon Territory brings home a wife. She begins to civilize the other six, who realize the merits of women and begin to look for romances of their own. Thrilling choreography by Michael Kidd - don't miss "The Barn Raising." Charming performances by Powell and Keel, both in lovely voice. Based on Stephen Vincent Benet's story. Thrills, chills, singin', dancin'—a classic Hollywood good time. ♫When You're In Love; Spring, Spring, Spring; Sobbin' Women; Bless Your Beautiful Hide; Goin' Co'tin; Wonderful, Wonderful Day; June Bride; Lonesome Polecat Lament. **103m/C VHS, Beta, LV, 8mm.** Howard Keel, Jane Powell, Russ Tamblyn, Julie Newmar, Jeff Richards, Tommy Rall, Virginia Gibson; ***D:*** Stanley Donen. Academy Awards '54: Best Score; National Board of Review Awards '54: 10 Best Films of the Year; Nominations: Academy Awards '54: Best Color Cinematography, Best Film Editing, Best Picture, Best Screenplay. *MGM, HMV*

The 7 Brothers Meet Dracula 🦴½ *Legend of the Seven Golden Vampires* **1973** Seven siblings meet guy with dental anomaly. **110m/C VHS.** *GB* Peter Cushing, David Chang, Robin Stewart, Julie Ege; ***D:*** Roy Ward Baker; ***M:*** James Bernard. *NO*

Seven Chances 🦴🦴🦴½ **1925** Silent classic that Keaton almost didn't make, believing instead that it should go to Harold Lloyd. Lawyer Keaton finds that he can inherit $7 million if he marries by 7:00 p.m. After his girlfriend turns down his botched proposal, chaos breaks loose when he advertises for someone—anyone—to marry him and make him rich. Suddenly he finds what seems to be hundreds of women willing to make the sacrifice, setting up one of the great film pursuits. Memorable boulder sequence was added after preview audience indicated climax was lacking that certain something. **60m/B VHS.** Buster Keaton, T. Roy Barnes, Snitz Edwards, Ruth Dwyer, Frankie Raymond; ***D:*** Buster Keaton. *NO*

Seven Cities of Gold 🦴🦴 **1955** An expedition of Spanish conquistadors and missionaries descend on 18th-century California, looking for secret Indian caches of gold. Semi-lavish costume epic. **103m/C VHS, Beta.** Anthony Quinn, Michael Rennie, Richard Egan, Rita Moreno, Jeffrey Hunter, Eduardo Noriega, John Doucette; ***D:*** Robert D. Webb. *FOX*

Seven Days Ashore/Hurry, Charlie, Hurry **1944** A comedy double feature. In "Seven Days Ashore," three merchant marines on leave in San Francisco become romantically involved with three women. In "Hurry, Charlie, Hurry," a hen-pecked husband finds himself in a lot of trouble. **141m/B VHS, Beta.** Gordon Oliver, Virginia Mayo, Dooley Wilson, Margaret Dumont, Leon Errol, Mildred Coles. *TTC*

Seven Days in May 🦴🦴🦴½ **1964** Topical but still gripping Cold War nuclear-peril thriller. An American general plans a military takeover because he considers the president's pacifism traitorous. Highly suspenseful, with a breathtaking climax. Houseman's film debut in a small role. **117m/B VHS, Beta, LV.** Burt Lancaster, Kirk Douglas, Edmond O'Brien, Fredric March, Ava Gardner, John Houseman; ***D:*** John Frankenheimer; ***W:*** Rod Serling; ***M:*** Jerry Goldsmith. Golden Globe Awards '65: Best Supporting Actor (O'Brien); Nominations: Academy Awards '64: Best Art Direction/Set Decoration (B & W), Best Supporting Actor (O'Brien). *WAR*

Seven Days' Leave 🦴🦴 **1942** Radio star-crammed musical comedy about a soldier who must marry a certain already betrothed gal (Ball) within a week so he can inherit a fortune. Songs include "Can't Get Out of this Mood," "A Touch of Texas," and "Baby, You Speak My Language." Following the completion of the film, Mature joined the Coast Guard. Lively but not memorable. **87m/B VHS, Beta.** Victor Mature, Lucille Ball, Harold Peary, Mary Cortes, Ginny Simms, Marcy McGuire, Peter Lind Hayes, Walter Reed, Wallace Ford, Arnold Stang, Buddy Clark, Charles Victor; ***D:*** Tim Whelan. *TTC*

Seven Deadly Sins 🦴🦴🦴 **1953** A collection of tales concerning destructive emotions and the downfalls they cause. Contains shorts from some of Europe's finest directors (five French and two Italian). Stories and their directors are "Avarice and Anger" (de Filippo), "Sloth" (Dreville), "Lust" (Allegret), "Envy" (Rossellini), "Gluttony" (Rim), "Pride" (Autant-Lara) and "The Eighth Sin" (Lacombe). **127m/B VHS.** *FR IT* Eduardo de Filippo, Isa Miranda, Jacqueline Plessis, Louis de Funes, Paolo Stoppa, Frank Villard, Jean Richard, Francoise Rosay, Jean Debucourt, Louis Seigner; ***D:*** Eduardo de Filippo, Jean Dreville, Yves Allegret, Roberto Rossellini, Carlo Rim, Claude Autant-Lara, Georges Lacombe. *IVY*

Seven Deaths in the Cat's Eye 🦴🦴 **1972** A ravenous beast slaughters people in a small Scottish village. This flick reveals a little-known fact about felines. **90m/C VHS, Beta.** *IT* Anton Diffring, Jane Birkin; ***D:*** Anthony (Antonio Margheriti) Dawson. *PSM*

Seven Doors of Death 🦴🦴 *The Beyond* **1982 (R)** A young woman inherits a possessed hotel. Meanwhile, hellish zombies try to check out. Chilling Italian horror flick. **80m/C VHS, Beta.** *IT* Katherine MacColl, David Warbeck, Farah Keller, Tony St. John; ***D:*** Louis Fuller. *LIV*

Seven Doors to Death 🦴 **1944** Young architect tries to solve a crime to avoid being placed under suspicion. The suspects are six shop owners in this low-budget attempt at a murder mystery. **70m/B VHS, Beta.** Chick Chandler, June Clyde, George Meeker, Gregory Gay, Edgar Dearing; ***D:*** Elmer Clifton. *VCI, MRV, SNC*

7 Faces of Dr. Lao 🦴🦴🦴 **1963** Dr. Lao is the proprietor of a magical circus that changes the lives of the residents of a small western town. Marvelous special effects and makeup (Randall plays seven characters) highlight this charming family film in the Pal tradition. Charles Finney adapted from his novel. **101m/C VHS, Beta, LV.** Tony Randall, Barbara Eden, Arthur O'Connell, Lee Patrick, Noah Beery Jr., John Qualen, John Ericson; ***D:*** George Pal. *MGM*

The Seven Hills of Rome 🦴🦴½ **1958** Quiet story of a television star (Lanza) who follows his girlfriend (Castle) to Rome after a lovers' quarrel, and there falls in love with Allasio. Fantastic music makes up for a weak plot. Based on a story by Giuseppi Amato. ♫Arrivederci Roma; Seven Hills of Rome; Never Till Now; Earthbound; Come Dance With Me; Lolita; There's Gonna Be a Party Tonight; Italian Calypso; Questa o Quella. **107m/C VHS.** Mario Lanza, Peggy Castle, Renato Rascel, Marisa Allasio, Clelia Matania, Rosella Como; ***D:*** Roy Rowland; ***W:*** Giorgio Prosperi, Art Cohn; ***M:*** Georgie Stoll. *MGM*

Seven Hours to Judgment 🦴🦴 **1988 (R)** When the punks who murdered his wife go free, a psychotic man (Leibman) decides to take justice into his own hands. He kidnaps the wife of the judge in charge (Bridges, who also directed) and leads him on a wild goose chase. Leibman steals the film as the psycho. Ex-Springsteen spouse Phillips plays the judge's wife. Ambitious but credulity-stretching revenge/crime drama. Screenplay written by de Souza under the pseudonym Elliot Stephens. **90m/C VHS, Beta, LV.** Beau Bridges, Ron Leibman, Julianne Phillips, Al Freeman Jr., Reggie Johnson; ***D:*** Beau Bridges; ***W:*** Steven E. de Souza, Walter Halsey Davis; ***M:*** John Debney. *MED, VTR*

Seven Keys to Baldplate **1917** Early version of the famous stage play by George M. Cohen in which George Washington Magee accepts a challenge that he can finish a novel in 24 hours while staying at the deserted Baldplate Inn. **66m/B VHS.** Hugh Ford, Anna Q. Nilsson, George M. Cohan, Elda Furry, Corene Uzzell, Joseph Smiley, Armand Cortes, C. Warren Cook; ***D:*** Mae Gaston. *GPV*

Seven Keys to Baldplate **1929** Early talkie version of the film which was based on the famous stage play of the same name by George M. Cohan which follows an author into a deserted Baldplate Inn on a bet that he can't finish a novel in 24 hours while in the Inn. **70m/B VHS.** Richard Dix, Miriam Seegar, Crauford Kent, Margaret Livingston, Lucien Littlefield; ***D:*** Reginald Barker. *GPV*

The Seven Little Foys 🦴🦴🦴 **1955** Enjoyable musical biography of Eddie Foy (played ebulliantly by Hope) and his famed vaudevillian troupe. Cagney's appearance as George M. Cohan is brief, but long enough for a memorable dance duet with Hope. ♫Mary's a Grand Old Name; I'm a Yankee Doodle Dandy; I'm the Greatest Father of Them All; Nobody; Comedy Ballet; I'm Tired; Chinatown, My Chinatown. **95m/C VHS, Beta.** Bob Hope, Milly Vitale, George Tobias, Angela Clark, James Cagney; ***D:*** Melville Shavelson; ***W:*** Jack Rose, Melville Shavelson. Nominations: Academy Awards '55: Best Story & Screenplay. *COL*

Seven Magnificent Gladiators 🦴 **1984 (PG)** Seven gladiators team up to save a peaceful Roman village from total annihilation. Dismal effort at a remake of "The Seven Samaurai"—see the original instead, please. Ferrigno was "The Incredible Hulk" on TV. **86m/C VHS, Beta.** Lou Ferrigno, Sybil Danning, Brad Harris, Dan Vadis, Carla Ferrigno; ***D:*** Bruno Mattei. *MGM*

Seven Miles from Alcatraz/Flight from Glory **1943** Dramatic double feature: Two escaped convicts discover a hideout for Nazi spies in "Seven Miles From Alcatraz," and an evil man tries to recruit pilots to fly planes over the Andes Mountains in "Flight From Glory." **127m/B VHS, Beta.** James Craig, Bonita Granville, Chester Morris, Van Heflin, Onslow Stevens; ***D:*** Edward Dmytryk. *TTC*

Seven Minutes in Heaven **1986 (PG)** Sensitive love story about a 15-year-old girl who invites her platonic male friend to live in her house, and finds it disturbs her boyfriend, as these things will. Ever so tasteful (unlike most other teen comedies), with gentle comedy—but forgettable. **90m/C VHS, Beta.** Jennifer Connelly, Byron Thames, Maddie Corman, Lauren Holly; ***D:*** Linda Feferman; ***W:*** Jane Bernstein. *WAR*

The Seven-Per-Cent Solution **1976 (PG)** Dr. Watson persuades Sherlock Holmes to meet with Sigmund Freud to cure his cocaine addiction. Holmes and Freud then find themselves teaming up to solve a supposed kidnapping. Adapted by Nicholas Meyer from his own novel. One of the most charming Holmes films; well-cast, intriguing blend of mystery, drama, and fun. **113m/C VHS, Beta, LV.** Alan Arkin, Nicol Williamson, Laurence Olivier, Robert Duvall, Vanessa Redgrave, Joel Grey, Samantha Eggar, Jeremy Kemp, Charles Gray, Regine; ***D:*** Herbert Ross; ***W:*** Nicholas Meyer; ***C:*** Oswald Morris; ***M:*** John Addison. National Board of Review Awards '76: 10 Best Films of the Year; Nominations: Academy Awards '76: Best Adapted Screenplay, Best Costume Design. *MCA*

Seven Samurai *Shichinin No Samurai; The Magnificent Seven* **1954** Kurosawa's masterpiece, set in 16th-century Japan. A small farming village, beset by marauding bandits, hires seven professional soldiers to rid itself of the scourge. Wanna watch a samurai movie? This is the one. Sweeping, complex human drama with all the ingredients: action, suspense, comedy. Available in several versions of varying length, all long—and all too short. Splendid acting. In Japanese with English subtitles. **204m/B VHS, Beta, LV.** *JP* Toshiro Mifune, Takashi Shimura, Yoshio Inaba, Kuninori Kodo, Ko Kimura, Seiji Miyaguchi, Minoru Chiaki; ***D:*** Akira Kurosawa; ***W:*** Akira Kurosawa; ***M:*** Fumio Hayasaka. Venice Film Festival '54: Silver Prize; Nominations: Academy Awards '56: Best Art Direction/Set Decoration (B & W), Best Costume Design (B & W). *HMV, SUE, HHT*

Seven Sinners *Cafe of the Seven Sinners* **1940** A South Seas cabaret singer (Dietrich) attracts sailors like flies, resulting in bar brawls, romance, and intrigue. Manly sailor Wayne falls for her. A good-natured, standard Hollywood adventure. Well cast; performed and directed with gusto. **83m/B VHS, Beta, LV.** Marlene Dietrich, John Wayne, Albert Dekker, Broderick Crawford, Mischa Auer, Billy Gilbert, Oscar Homolka; ***D:*** Tay Garnett. *MCA, NOS, BAR*

Seven Sixgunners **1987** A western classic from the book by Nelson Nye. **60m/C VHS.** ***D:*** George Potter; ***W:*** Nelson Nye. *NO*

Seven Thieves **1960** Charming performances and nice direction make this tale of the perfect crime especially watchable. Robinson, getting on in years, wants one last big heist. With the help of Collins and Steiger, he gets his chance. From the Max Catto novel "Lions at the Kill." Surprisingly witty and light-hearted for this subject matter, and good still comes out ahead of evil. **102m/C VHS.** Joan Collins, Edward G. Robinson, Eli Wallach, Rod Steiger; ***D:*** Henry Hathaway; ***C:*** Sam Leavitt. Nominations: Academy Awards '60: Best Costume Design (B & W). *FOX, FCT*

The Seven-Ups ½ **1973 (PG)** An elite group of New York City detectives seeks to avenge the killing of a colleague and to bust crooks whose felonies are punishable by jail terms of seven years or more. Unoriginal premise portends ill; plotless cop action flick full of car chases. Scheider tries hard. Directed by the producer of "The French Connection." **109m/C VHS, Beta, LV.** Roy Scheider, Tony LoBianco, Larry Haines, Jerry Leon; ***D:*** Phil D'Antoni. *FOX*

The Seven Year Itch **1955** Classic, sexy Monroe comedy. Stunning blonde model (who else?) moves upstairs just as happily married guy Ewell's wife leaves for a long vacation. Understandably, he gets itchy. Monroe's famous blown skirt scene is here, as well as funny situations and appealing performances. **105m/C VHS, Beta, LV.** Marilyn Monroe, Tom Ewell, Evelyn Keyes, Sonny Tufts, Victor Moore, Doro Merande, Robert Strauss, Oscar Homolka, Carolyn Jones; ***D:*** Billy Wilder; ***W:*** George Axelrod, Billy Wilder; ***C:*** Milton Krasner. Golden Globe Awards '56: Best Actor—Musical/Comedy (Ewell). *FOX, FUS, GVV*

Seven Years Bad Luck **1920** French comic Linder has the proverbial seven years' bad luck all in one day (!) after he breaks a mirror. Original and quite funny; full of fetching sophisticated sight gags. Silent with music score. **67m/B VHS, Beta.** Max Linder. *GPV, VYY*

1776 **1972 (G)** A musical comedy about America's first Continental Congress. The delegates battle the English and each other trying to establish a set of laws and the Declaration of Independence. Adapted from the Broadway hit with many members of the original cast. Available in widescreen format on laserdisc. ♫The Lees of Old Virginia; He Plays the Violin; But, Mr. Adams; Sit Down John; Till Then; Piddle, Twiddle and Resolve; Yours, Yours, Yours; Mama, Look Sharp; The Egg. **141m/C VHS, Beta, LV.** William Daniels, Howard da Silva, Ken Howard, Donald Madden, Blythe Danner, Ronald Holgate, Virginia Vestoff, Stephen Nathan, Ralston Hill; ***D:*** Peter H. Hunt; ***C:*** Harry Stradling Jr. National Board of Review Awards '72: 10 Best Films of the Year; Nominations: Academy Awards '72: Best Cinematography. *COL, FCT*

The Seventeenth Bride **1984** Set in a Czechoslovakian town; a strong-willed young woman is slowly destroyed by the insanity of war and racism. **92m/C VHS.** Lisa Hartman Black, Rosemary Leach; ***D:*** Israeli Nadav Levitan. *NO*

Seventh Cavalry ½ **1956** A somewhat different look at Custer's defeat at the Little Big Horn. A soldier who was branded a coward for not taking part in the festivities tries to assuage his guilt by heading up the burial detail. The muddled ending tries to tell us that the Indians were afraid of Custer's horse. **75m/C VHS.** Randolph Scott, Barbara Hale, Jay C. Flippen, Jeanette Nolan, Frank Faylen, Leo Gordon, Denver Pyle, Harry Carey Jr., Michael Pate, Donald Curtis, Frank Wilcox, Pat Hogan, Russell Hicks; ***D:*** Joseph H. Lewis; ***C:*** Ray Rennahan. *NOS*

The Seventh Coin ½ **1992 (PG-13)** The legendary King Herod minted seven coins bearing his image which have become coin collector Emil Saber's (O'Toole) obsession. (He's a homicidal lunatic who thinks he's the reincarnation of Herod anyway.) Saber has found six of the coins but the seventh has fallen into the unsuspecting hands of Salim (Chowdhry), a pickpocket who has actually snatched it from the equally unsuspecting Ronnie (Powers), an American teenager visiting Jerusalem (good local color). The two become allies when Saber comes after them. They're an appealing couple; O'Toole camps it up shamelessly; and the movie is easygoing escapism. **92m/C VHS, LV.** Alexandra Powers, Navin Chowdhry, Peter O'Toole, John Rhys-Davies, Ally Walker; ***D:*** Dror Soref; ***W:*** Michael Lewis, Dror Soref; ***C:*** Avi Karpik. *HMD*

The 7th Commandment ½ **1961** Unlikely melodrama about a man afflicted with amnesia following an auto accident. He becomes a successful evangelist only to be blackmailed by an old girlfriend. Don't you just hate when that happens? **82m/B VHS.** Jonathan Kidd, Lynn Statten; ***D:*** Irvin Berwick. *NOS, LOO*

The Seventh Cross **1944** Tracy stars as one of seven men who escape from a German concentration camp. When it is discovered they're gone, the commandant nails seven crosses to seven trees, intending them for the seven escapees. Watch for Tandy ("Driving Miss Daisy") in her first screen appearance. Effective war-time drama. From the novel by Anna Seghers. **110m/B VHS.** Spencer Tracy, Signe Hasso, Hume Cronyn, Jessica Tandy, Agnes Moorehead, Herbert Rudley, Felix Bressart, Ray Collins, Alexander Granach, George Macready, Steve Geray, Karen Verne, George Zucco; ***D:*** Fred Zinnemann; ***C:*** Karl Freund. Nominations: Academy Awards '44: Best Supporting Actor (Cronyn). *MGM*

The Seventh Floor ½ **1993 (R)** Kate's computer-controlled apartment becomes her prison when a psycho takes charge of the system. **99m/C VHS.** Brooke Shields, Masaya Kato, Craig Pearce, Linda Cropper; ***D:*** Ian Barry. *APX*

The Seventh Seal *Det Sjunde Inseglet* **1956** As the plague sweeps through Europe a weary knight convinces "death" to play one game of chess with him. If the knight wins, he and his wife will be spared. The game leads to a discussion of religion and the existence of God. Considered by some Bergman's masterpiece. Von Sydow is stunning as the knight. In Swedish with English subtitles. Also available on laserdisc with a filmography of Bergman's work and commentary by film historian Peter Cowie. **96m/B VHS, Beta, LV, 8mm.** *SW* Gunnar Bjornstrand, Max von Sydow, Bibi Andersson, Bengt Ekerot, Nils Poppe, Gunnel Lindblom; ***D:*** Ingmar Bergman; ***W:*** Ingmar Bergman; ***M:*** Erik Nordgren. Cannes Film Festival '57: Grand Jury Prize. *VDM, SUE, CRC*

The Seventh Sign **1988 (R)** A pregnant woman realizes that the mysterious stranger boarding in her house and the bizarre events that accompany him are connected to Biblical prophesy and her unborn child. Tries hard, but it's difficult to get involved in the supernatural goings-on. **105m/C VHS, Beta, LV.** Demi Moore, Juergen Prochnow, Michael Biehn, John Heard, Peter Friedman, Manny Jacobs, John Taylor, Lee Garlington, Akosua Busia; ***D:*** Carl Schultz; ***M:*** Jack Nitzsche. *COL*

The Seventh Veil ½ **1946** A concert pianist loses the use of her hands in a fire, and with it her desire to live. Through the help of her friends and a hypnotizing doctor, she regains her love for life. Superb, dark psycho-drama. Todd as the pianist and Mason as her guardian are both unforgettable. Wonderful music and staging. **91m/B VHS, Beta.** *GB* James Mason, Ann Todd, Herbert Lom, Hugh McDermott, Albert Lieven; ***D:*** Compton Bennett. Academy Awards '46: Best Original Screenplay. *NO*

The Seventh Victim **1943** Another Val Lewton-produced low-budget exercise in shadowy suggestion, dealing with a woman searching for her lost sister, who'd gotten involved with Satanists. The Hays Office's squeamishness regarding subject matter makes the film's action a bit cloudy but it remains truly eerie. **71m/B VHS, Beta, LV.** Kim Hunter, Tom Conway, Jean Brooks, Hugh Beaumont, Erford Gage, Isabel Jewell, Evelyn Brent; ***D:*** Mark Robson. *TTC*

The Seventh Voyage of Sinbad **1958 (G)** Sinbad seeks to restore his fiancee from the midget size to which an evil magician (Thatcher) has reduced her. Ray Harryhausen works his animation magic around a well-developed plot and engaging performances by the real actors. Great score and fun, fast-moving plot. **94m/C VHS, Beta, LV.** Kerwin Mathews, Kathryn Grant, Torin Thatcher, Richard Eyer; ***D:*** Nathan (Hertz) Juran; ***W:*** Kenneth Kolb; ***M:*** Bernard Herrmann. *COL, MLB, CCB*

Severance **1988** An ex-pilot attempts to save his daughter from the world of drugs and violence. **93m/C VHS, Beta.** Lou Liotta, Lisa Nicole Wolpe, Linda Christian-Jones; ***D:*** David Max Steinberg. *NO*

The Severed Arm *Woof!* **1973 (R)** Trapped in a cave, five men are compelled to cut off the arm of a companion in order to ward off starvation. Then as luck would have it, they're rescued. Years later, one-by-one they meet a bloody demise. Is it the one-armed man? **89m/C VHS, Beta.** Deborah Walley, Marvin Kaplan, Paul Carr, John Crawford, David Cannon; ***D:*** Thomas Alderman. *CNG, MRV, GEM*

Severed Ties ½ **1992 (R)** Brilliant genetic scientist experiments with human limb regeneration in order to re-grow his accidentally severed arm. His strange mixture of lizard and serial-killer genes results in a repulsive repitilian limb with a nasty habit of slithering out of his shoulder. His mother discovers his experiments and tries to sell his discovery to the Nazis but her son escapes into a bizarre subterranean society and vows revenge. So bad it's just bad. **95m/C VHS.** Billy Morrissette, Elke Sommer, Oliver Reed, Garrett Morris; ***D:*** Damon Santostefano. *COL*

Sex ✂✂½ **1920** Interesting dated relic. Morality play about a Broadway star who uses her charms to destroy a marriage only to dump her lover for richer prospects. The businessman she lands then shamelessly betrays her. What a title, especially for its time! **87m/B VHS, Beta.** Adrienne Renault, Louise Glaum, Irving Cummings, Peggy Pearce, Myrtle Stedman; ***D:*** Fred Niblo. *CCB, GPV, GVV*

Sex Adventures of the Three Musketeers *Woof!* **198?** Soft-core spoof of the Dumas classic. Dubbed. **79m/C VHS, Beta.** Inga Steeger, Achim Hammer, Peter Graf, Jurg Coray. *MED*

Sex and Buttered Popcorn **1991 (R)** Stylish and entertaining documentary of the Hollywood sexploitation moguls, and their films, from the 1920s through the 1950s. These films shamelessly catered to audience's prurient interests, but typically delivered saccharin-coated morality messages and stock footage of routine baby births or the horrible effects of sexually transmitted diseases. Hosted by Ned Beatty, and featuring clips from the actual films, plus an interview with the widow of Kroger Babb, the most notorious of the exploiteers. A real hoot. **70m/C VHS.** David Friedman; ***D:*** Sam Harrison. *CPM, FCT*

Sex and the College Girl ✂ **1964** Folks talk about their relationship problems while vacationing in Puerto Rico. Tame talkfest providing Grodin with his first role. Included as part of Joe Bob Brigg's "Sleaziest Movies in the History of the World" series, probably just for the title. **?m/C VHS.** Charles Grodin, Richard Arlen, Luana Anders; ***D:*** Joseph Adler. *VTR*

Sex and the Single Girl ✂✂½ **1964** Curtis is a reporter for a trashy magazine who intends to write an expose on "The International Institute of Advanced Marital and Pre-Marital Studies," an organization run by Wood. Curtis poses as a man having marital trouble, using his neighbor's name and marital problems, in order to get close to Wood. Things get sticky when Wood wants to meet Curtis' wife and three women show up claiming to be her. This confusing but amusing tale twists and turns until it reaches a happy ending. Loosely based on the book by Helen Gurley Brown. **114m/C VHS, LV.** Tony Curtis, Natalie Wood, Henry Fonda, Lauren Bacall, Mel Ferrer, Fran Jeffries, Leslie Parrish, Edward Everett Horton, Larry Storch, Count Basie; ***D:*** Richard Quine; ***C:*** Charles B(ryant) Lang; ***M:*** Neal Hefti. *WAR*

Sex and the Single Parent ✂½ **1982** St. James and Farrell, both divorced, both with kids, have a relationship. Complications set in—just how does one be a single parent and have a fulfilling sex life in this day and age? Some of these made for TV efforts are so formulaic! **98m/C VHS, Beta.** Susan St. James, Mike Farrell, Dori Brenner, Warren Berlinger, Julie Sommars, Barbara Rhoades; ***D:*** Jackie Cooper. *TLF*

Sex Crimes ✂✂ **1992** A tough female judge is brutally raped and she keeps the attack a secret. However, she does ask a friendly police detective to teach her how to use a gun. He's suspicious of her reasons and decides to trail her as she sets out for revenge on her attacker. Predictable actioner. **90m/C VHS.** Jeffery Osterhage, Maria Richwine, Fernando Garzon, Craig Alan, Grace Morley; ***D:*** David Garcia. *ATV*

Sex, Drugs, and Rock-n-Roll *Woof!* **1984** Several girls frequent a rock club looking for all the action they can get their hands on. **90m/C VHS, Beta.** Jeanne Silver, Sharon Kane, Tish Ambrose, Josey Duval. *NO*

Sex, Drugs, Rock & Roll: Eric Bogosian **1991 (R)** Bogosian's 1990 concert performance, taped live at the Wilur Theate in Boston, exhibits the electricity and finely nuanced characters for which he is justly famous. The characters share a depressingly negative side, however, which keeps this film from being strictly belly-laugh territory. **96m/C VHS.** Eric Bogosian; ***D:*** John McNaughton; ***W:*** Eric Bogosian. *MPI*

Sex Is Crazy ✂ **1979** A melange from Italian horror director Franco containing some epic, some horror, some sex, some sitcom, and some documentary. Little green aliens touch down and impregnate earth women in one skit. In another, a gambler's girlfriend demands two thugs ravage her for the sheer sexual thrill. And in a third, a severed hand commands a heroine to martyr herself to the great god Cucufat. Spanish with English subtitles. **81m/C VHS.** *SP* Lina Romay, Anthony Mayans, Tony Skios; ***D:*** Jess (Jesus) Franco. *VSM*

sex, lies and videotape ✂✂✂ **1989 (R)** Acclaimed, popular independent film by first-timer Soderbergh, detailing the complex relations among a childless married couple, the wife's adulterous sister, and a mysterious college friend of the husband's obsessed with videotaping women as they talk about their sex lives. Heavily awarded, including first prize at Cannes. Confidently uses much (too much?) dialogue and slow (too slow?) pace. Available on laserdisc with a deleted scene and interviews with the director; also includes two theatrical trailers and a short film by Soderbergh. **101m/C VHS, Beta, LV, 8mm.** James Spader, Andie MacDowell, Peter Gallagher, Laura San Giacomo, Ron Vawter, Steven Brill; ***D:*** Steven Soderbergh; ***W:*** Steven Soderbergh; ***C:*** Walt Lloyd; ***M:*** Cliff Martinez. Cannes Film Festival '89: Best Actor (Spader), Best Film; Independent Spirit Awards '90: Best Actress (MacDowell), Best Director (Soderbergh), Best Film, Best Supporting Actress (San Giacomo); Sundance Film Festival '89: Audience Award; Nominations: Academy Awards '89: Best Original Screenplay. *COL*

Sex, Love and Cold Hard Cash ✂✂½ **1993 (PG-13)** Sarah (Williams) is a high-priced hooker whose life savings ($20 million in stocks and bonds) have just been stolen. She hires an ex-con (Denison) to help recover the money and the two partners find themselves on the wrong side of some Mob trouble as well. Enough twists to keep a viewer interested as well as the prerequisite amount of shootings and chase scenes. **86m/C VHS.** JoBeth Williams, Anthony John Denison; ***D:*** Harry S. Longstreet; ***W:*** Harry S. Longstreet. *MCA*

The Sex Machine *Woof!* **1976 (R)** In the year 2037, a scientist finds two of the world's greatest lovers and unites them so he can transform their reciprocating motion into electricity. It worked on paper. **80m/C VHS, Beta.** Agostina Belli. *MED*

Sex on the Run *Woof! Cassanova and Co.; Some Like It Cool* **1978 (R)** Love-starved wife of an oil-rich sheik, stimulated by the idea of having Casanova for her lover, teases her master into delivering him, but Casanova finds peace in the arms of three convent lovelies. Disgusting, amateurish, and offensive. **88m/C VHS, Beta, LV.** Tony Curtis, Marisa Berenson, Britt Ekland; ***D:*** Francosis Legrand. *VES, MON*

Sex Through a Window ✂ *Extreme Close-Up* **1972 (R)** TV reporter becomes an obsessive voyeur after filing a report on high tech surveillance equipment. Flimsy premise is a yucky, lame excuse to show skin. **81m/C VHS, Beta.** James McMullan, James A. Watson Jr., Kate Woodville, Bara Byrnes, Al Checco, Anthony Carbone; ***D:*** Jeannot Szwarc; ***W:*** Michael Crichton. *LIV, VES*

Sex with a Smile ✂ **1976 (R)** Five slapstick episodes by five different directors with lots of sexual satire pointed at religion and politics in Italy. Don't know much about Italy? Then you'll be left out of the joke here. And really, only one episode is funny anyway (the one with Feldman of "Young Frankenstein" fame). **100m/C VHS, Beta.** *IT* Marty Feldman, Edwige Fenech, Alex Marino, Enrico Monterrano, Giovanna Ralli; ***D:*** Sergio Martino. *GEM*

Sexpot ✂ **1988 (R)** A voluptuous woman's rich husbands mysteriously keep dying, but not before they leave their fortunes to her. **95m/C VHS, Beta.** Ruth Collins, Troy Donahue, Joyce Lyons, Gregory Patrick, Frank Stewart, Jack Carter; ***D:*** Chuck Vincent. *ACA*

Sextette *Woof!* **1978 (PG)** Lavish film about an elderly star who is constantly interrupted by former spouses and well-wishers while on a honeymoon with her sixth husband. West unwisely came out of retirement for this last film role, based on her own play. Exquisitely embarrassing to watch. Interesting cast. **91m/C VHS, Beta.** Mae West, Timothy Dalton, Ringo Starr, George Hamilton, Dom DeLuise, Tony Curtis, Alice Cooper, Keith Moon, George Raft, Rona Barrett, Walter Pidgeon; ***D:*** Ken Hughes; ***M:*** Artie Butler. *MED, MLB*

Sexton Blake and the Hooded Terror ✂✂ **1938** Sexton Blake a British private detective a la Holmes, is after "The Snake," a master criminal, and his gang The Hooded Terror. One of a series of melodramatic adventures interesting chiefly for Slaughter's performance as the gangleader. **70m/B VHS, Beta.** *GB* Tod Slaughter, Greta Gynt, George Curzon; ***D:*** George King. *VYY, SNC, MRV*

Sexual Intent ✂✂ **1994 (R)** Based on the true story of pathological liar John Walsome, known as "the Sweetheart Scammer," who seduced and robbed more than 40 women. This con artist transformed himself into whatever kind of Mr. Right his victim needed—until he picked on the wrong woman. **88m/C VHS.** Gary Hudson, Michele Brin, Sarah Hill; ***D:*** Kurt MacCarley; ***W:*** Kurt MacCarley. *COL*

Sexual Malice ✂✂ **1993 (R)** Another erotic thriller finds a bored wife involved in an obsessive affair with a mystery man who has murder on his mind. Also available in an unrated version. **96m/C VHS.** Diana Barton, John Laughlin, Chad McQueen, Edward Albert, Don Swayze, Kathy Shower, Samantha Phillips; ***D:*** Jag Mundhra; ***W:*** Carl Austin. *APX*

Sexual Response ✂✂ **1992 (R)** Eve, a radio talk show "sexologist," is ironically unhappy in her marriage but scoffs at her producer's suggestion of an affair. That is until she meets a brash sculptor and they begin a torrid, and increasingly obsessive, romance. Her lover suggests that her husband have an "accident" with his hunting rifle, but Eve refuses and throws him out. The sculptor, however, breaks into the husband's loft to steal the rifle and finds some news clippings about the man's past that could ruin the lives of many. Little more than an excuse for torrid love scenes. Also available in an unrated version. **87m/C VHS, LV.** Shannon Tweed, Catherine Oxenberg, Vernon Wells, Emile Levisetti; ***D:*** Yaky Yosha. *COL*

S.F.W. ✂✂ **1994 (R)** Get out your cliche-o-meter for another look at Generation X. Suburban teen Cliff Spab (Dorff) unwillingly becomes a media sensation during a terrorist hostage crisis at a convenience store. The phrasemaking teen's apathetic words are adopted by his peers just as he realizes that there is something he actually cares about—fellow hostage Wendy Pfister (Witherspoon), a cheerleader who wouldn't have given him the time of day before. A somewhat heavy-handed commentary on fame in our tabloid-intensive society. Title acronym stands for "So F***ing What." Many reviewers had a similar reaction. Based on the novel by Andrew Wellman. **92m/C VHS.** Stephen Dorff, Reese Witherspoon, Jake Busey, Joey Adams, Pamela Gidley, David Barry Gray, Jack Noseworthy, Richard Portnow; ***D:*** Jefery Levy; ***W:*** Jefery Levy, James Foley. *PGV*

Shack Out on 101 ✂✂✂ **1955** A waitress (Moore) in an isolated cafe on a busy highway notices suspicious doings among her customers. What could they be up to? Communist subversion, of course. Of-its-era anti-pinko propoganda, but with a twist: Moore uncovers commie plots, pleases her customers, and fends off unwelcome lecherous advances all in 80 minutes, on a single set! **80m/B VHS.** Lee Marvin, Terry Moore, Keenan Wynn, Frank Lovejoy, Whit Bissell; ***D:*** Edward Dein. *REP*

Shadey ✂✂½ **1987 (PG-13)** The premise for this oddball comedy came to someone in the wee hours: I've got it! Mild-mannered mechanic can film people's thoughts; wants to use his gift only for good, but needs money for a sex-change operation. Assorted bad guys want to use him for evil purposes.

Strange, but not bad; Helmond's character is memorable. **90m/C VHS, Beta.** *GB* Anthony Sher, Billie Whitelaw, Patrick Macnee, Katherine Helmond, Leslie Ash, Larry Lamb, Bernard Hepton; ***D:*** Philip Saville; ***W:*** Snoo Wilson; ***M:*** Colin Towns. *FOX*

The Shadow ½ **1936** Scotland Yard pulls out all the stops to track down a murderous extortionist, enlisting the aid of a novelist in their efforts. Long on talk and short on action. **63m/B VHS, Beta.** *GB* Henry Kendall, Elizabeth Allan, Jeanne Stuart, Felix Aylmer, Cyril Raymond; ***D:*** George Cooper. *NOS, SNC*

The Shadow ½ **1994 (PG-13)** Who knows what evil lurks in the hearts of men? Why "The Shadow" of course, as is shown in this highly-stylized big screen version of the '30s radio show that once starred Orson Welles. Billionaire playboy Lamont Cranston (Baldwin) is a master of illusion and defender of justice thanks to his alter ego. Aided by companion Margo Lane (Miller), da Shadow battles super-criminal Shiwan Khan (Lone), the deadliest descendant of Ghenghis Khan. Numerous and elaborate special effects provide icing on the cake for those in the mood for a journey back to the radio past or a quick superhero fix. **112m/C VHS, LV.** Alec Baldwin, John Lone, Penelope Ann Miller, Peter Boyle, Ian McKellen, Tim Curry, Jonathan Winters; ***D:*** Russell Mulcahy; ***W:*** David Koepp; ***C:*** Stephen Burum. *MCA*

The Shadow Box **1980** Three terminally ill people at a California hospice confront their destinies. Pulitzer Prize-winning play by Michael Cristofer is actually improved by director Newman and a superb, well-chosen cast. Powerful. **96m/C VHS, Beta.** Joanne Woodward, Christopher Plummer, Robert Urich, Valerie Harper, Sylvia Sidney, Melinda Dillon, Ben Masters, John Considine, James Broderick; ***D:*** Paul Newman; ***M:*** Henry Mancini. *KAR*

Shadow Dancing **1988 (PG)** The proprietor of the auspicious Beaumont Theater of Dance is haunted by one of his former dancers who died unexpectedly during a performance of "Medusa." Now, over fifty years later, Jessica, the pick for the lead in a new production, begins to take on her predecessor's mannerisms and spirit as she faces her impending doom. Surprisingly believable and suspenseful—and scary! **100m/C VHS, Beta.** Nadine Van Der Velde, James Kee, John Colicos, Shirley Douglas, Christopher Plummer; ***D:*** John Furey; ***M:*** Jay Gruska. *NO*

Shadow Force ½ **1992** Homicide detective Rick Kelly is investigating the murders of a district attorney and a police sergeant. With the help of Mary, the usual beautiful female journalist, he uncovers a plot to assassinate key law enforcement officers. **?m/C VHS, LV.** Dirk Benedict, Lance LeGault, Lise Cutter, Jack Elam, Glenn Corbett, Bob Hastings; ***D:*** Darrell Davenport. *IMP*

Shadow Killers ½ **1980** There's no time to fear your own shadow, for there is a far more terrifying darkness stalking the city. **90m/C VHS, Beta.** Chen Ching, Chang Wu Lang, Chen Chiang. *NO*

The Shadow Man *Street of Shadows* **1953** A casino operator in London (Romero) is accused of killing a former girlfriend and works to clear himself. Family conventional action mystery: nothing to write home about. **76m/B VHS, Beta, LV.** *GB* Cesar Romero, Simone Silva, Kay Kendall, John Penrose, Edward Underdown; ***D:*** Richard Vernon. *NO*

Shadow Man **1975 (PG)** A mysterious thief, a master of disguise, sets out to steal the Treasure of the Knights Templar and nothing will stand in his way. **89m/C VHS, Beta.** Josephine Chaplin, Gert Frobe, Gayle Hunnicutt. *MED*

Shadow of a Doubt ½ **1943** Uncle Charlie has come to visit his relatives in Santa Rosa. Although he is handsome and charming, his young niece slowly comes to realize he is a wanted mass murderer - and he comes to recognize her suspicions. Hitchcock's personal favorite movie; a quietly creepy venture into Middle American menace. Good performances, especially by Cronyn. From the story by Gordon McConnell. **108m/B VHS, Beta, LV.** Teresa Wright, Joseph Cotten, Hume Cronyn, MacDonald Carey, Henry Travers, Wallace Ford; ***D:*** Alfred Hitchcock; ***W:*** Thorton Wilder, Sally Benson, Alma Reville; ***C:*** Joseph Valentine; ***M:*** Dimitri Tiomkin. Nominations: Academy Awards '43: Best Story. *MCA*

Shadow of Angels **1976** Beautiful prostitute Lily Brest's latest client, a wealthy real estate investor, just wants to talk and Lily's a good listener. So good, that more and more of her clients tell her all their darkest secrets and fears, leaving Lily herself falling into such a deep depression that she wonders if she can go on. German with subtitles. **103m/C VHS.** *GE* ***D:*** Daniel Schmid; ***W:*** Rainer Werner Fassbinder, Daniel Schmid. *WBF*

Shadow of Chikara *Thunder Mountain; The Curse of Demon Mountain* **1977 (PG)** A Confederate Army Captain and an orphan girl encounter unexpected adventures as they search for a fortune in diamonds hidden in a river in northern Arkansas. **96m/C VHS, Beta, LV.** Joe Don Baker, Sondra Locke, Ted Neeley, Slim Pickens. *VTR, NWV*

Shadow of China **1991 (PG-13)** A young man struggles for power and love in Hong Kong, while an English beauty and an Oriental activist hold the keys to his future and a past which could destroy him. Excellent acting, stunning location photography. Exotic and intense. Based on the Japanese best-seller "Snakehead." **100m/C VHS, LV.** John Lone, Sammi Davis, Vivian Wu; ***D:*** Mitsuo Yanagimachi; ***W:*** Mitsuo Yanagimachi, Richard Maxwell. *COL, NLC*

Shadow of Chinatown ½ **1936** Mad scientist creates wave of murder and terror in Chinatown. Edited version of a 15-chapter serial. **70m/B VHS, Beta.** Bela Lugosi, Bruce (Herman Brix) Bennett, Joan Barclay. *NOS, SNC, VCN*

Shadow of the Eagle **1932** Former wartime flying ace Wayne is accused of being a criminal known as "The Eagle." He's using his flying skills (which include skywriting) to threaten a corporation which has stolen plans for a new invention. But can Wayne really be our villain? 12-chapter serial. **226m/B VHS.** John Wayne, Dorothy Gulliver, Walter Miller; ***D:*** Ford Beebe. *GPV, VYY, VCN*

Shadow of the Thin Man **1941** In the fourth "Thin Man" film, following "Another Thin Man," Nick and Nora stumble onto a murder at the racetrack. The rapport between Powell and Loy is still going strong, providing us with some wonderful entertainment. Followed by "The Thin Man Goes Home." **97m/B VHS, Beta.** William Powell, Myrna Loy, Barry Nelson, Donna Reed, Sam Levene, Alan Baxter, Dickie Hall, Loring Smith, Joseph Anthony, Henry O'Neill; ***D:*** Woodbridge S. Van Dyke. *MGM*

Shadow of the Wolf *Agaguk: Shadow of the Wolf* **1992 (PG-13)** Phillips is Agaguk, the son of the village leader, in this epic saga of survival set against the wilderness of the Arctic. Agaguk decides he cannot accept the white man's intrusion, so he sets out on his own. His father believes his departure to be the ultimate betrayal and casts upon him the "curse of the white wolf." Now Agaguk and his companion (Tilly) must face the harsh tundra alone and struggle to stay alive in the Great White North. Based on the novel "Agaguk" by Yves Theriault. **108m/C VHS, LV.** *CA* Lou Diamond Phillips, Donald Sutherland, Jennifer Tilly, Toshiro Mifune; ***D:*** Jacques Dorfman; ***W:*** Rudy Wurlitzer, Evan Jones. Genie Awards '93: Best Art Direction/Set Decoration, Best Costume Design. *COL*

Shadow on the Sun ½ **1988** The life of Beryl Markham, pioneer female aviator and adventurer of the 1930s. Way too long and boring made for TV answer to "Out of Africa." On two cassettes. **192m/C VHS.** Stefanie Powers, Claire Bloom, Frederic Forrest, James Fox, John Rubinstein, Jack Thompson; ***D:*** Tony Richardson. *VTR, NWV*

Shadow Play ½ **1986 (R)** A successful female playwright is haunted by visions of a past lover. Her life slowly falls apart, but not before this film does. **98m/C VHS, Beta.** Dee Wallace Stone, Cloris Leachman; ***D:*** Susan Shadburne; ***W:*** Susan Shadburne. *VTR, NWV*

The Shadow Riders *Louis L'Amour's "The Shadow Riders"* **1982 (PG)** Two brothers who fought on opposite sides during the Civil War return home to find their brother's fiancee kidnapped by a renegade Confederate officer who plans to use her as ransom in a prisoner exchange, and they set out to rescue the woman. Preceded by "The Sacketts" and based on the works of Louis L'Amour. Made for television. **96m/C VHS.** Tom Selleck, Sam Elliott, Ben Johnson, Katharine Ross, Jeffery Osterhage, Gene Evans, R.G. Armstrong, Marshall Teague, Dominique Dunne, Jeanetta Arnetta; ***D:*** Andrew V. McLaglen. *VMK*

The Shadow Strikes ½ **1937** Adaptation of the radio serial. The sleuth pursues a killer and a gangster. Meanwhile, the police try to pin a robbery on the "Shadow." Who did it? The Shadow knows! **61m/B VHS, Beta.** Rod La Rocque, Lynn Anders. *GPV, NOS, CAB*

Shadowhunter **1993 (R)** Glenn stars as a burned-out big city detective who is sent to a Navajo reservation in Arizona to bring a murder suspect back to Los Angeles. When the alleged killer escapes custody Glenn must track him across forbidding desert territory and face his suspect's unusual mystical powers. **98m/C VHS, LV.** Scott Glenn; ***D:*** J.S. Cardone; ***W:*** J.S. Cardone. *REP*

Shadowlands *C.S. Lewis Through the Shadowlands* **1985** A look at the later life of bachelor-scholar C.S. Lewis (also the author of the "Chronicles of Narnia"). A devout proponent of Christianity, the middle-aged Lewis fell in love and married Joy Gresham, a divorced American poet with two young sons. Joy was diagnosed with cancer and her illness provided Lewis with the clearest test of his faith. Wonderful performances by both Ackland and Bloom. **90m/C VHS.** *GB* Joss Ackland, Claire Bloom, Rupert Baderman; ***D:*** Norman Stone. *FRV, KAR, GFV*

Shadowlands **1993 (PG)** Touching, tragic story of the late-in-life romance between celebrated author and Christian theologian C.S. Lewis (Hopkins) and brash New York divorcee Joy Gresham (Winger). Attenborough's direction is rather stately and sweeping and Winger is really too young for her role but Hopkins is excellent as (another) repressed man who finds more emotions than he can handle. Critically acclaimed adaptation of Nicholson's play will require lots of kleenex. **130m/C VHS, LV.** *GB* Anthony Hopkins, Debra Winger, Edward Hardwicke, Joseph Mazzello, Michael Denison, John Wood, Peter Firth, Peter Howell; ***D:*** Richard Attenborough; ***W:*** William Nicholson; ***M:*** George Fenton. British Academy Awards '93: Best Film; Los Angeles Film Critics Association Awards '93: Best Actor (Hopkins); National Board of Review Awards '93: Best Actor (Hopkins); Nominations: Academy Awards '93: Best Actress (Winger), Best Adapted Screenplay; British Academy Awards '94: Best Actor (Hopkins), Best Actress (Winger), Best Adapted Screenplay, Best Director (Attenborough). *HBO*

Shadows **1922** A Chinese laundryman (Chaney) lives with a group of his countrymen in a New England seacoast village. All is peaceful until the local minister decides to convert the "heathen" Chinese. Ludicrous but worth seeing for Chaney's fun performance. Silent with music score. **70m/B VHS.** Lon Chaney Sr., Harrison Ford; ***D:*** Tom Forman. *KIV, NOS, CCB*

Shadows **1960** Director Cassavettes' first indie feature finds jazz player Hugh (Hurd) forced to play dives to support his brother Ben (Carruthers) and sister Lelia (Goldoni). Light-skinned enough to pass for white, Lelia takes on the uptown New York art crowd and gets involved with the white Tony (Ray), who leaves when he finds out her true heritage. Meanwhile, Ben drifts along with his friends who abandon him when trouble finds them. Script was improvised by cast. **87m/B VHS.** Hugh Hurd, Lelia Goldoni, Ben Carruthers, Anthony Ray, Rupert Crosse, Tom Allen; ***D:*** John Cassavetes; ***C:*** Erich Kollmar; ***M:*** Charles Mingus, Shifi Hadi. *FXL*

Shadows and Fog **1992 (PG-13)** Offbeat, unpredictable Allen film that is little more than an exercise in expressionistic visual stylings. The action centers around a haunted, alienated clerk (Allen) who is awakened in the middle of the night to join a vigilante group searching the streets for a killer. Although reminiscent of a silent film, Carlo Di Palma's black and white cinematography is stunning. Several stars appear briefly throughout this extremely unfocused comedy. **85m/B VHS, LV.** Woody Allen, Kathy Bates, John Cusack, Mia Farrow, Jodie Foster, Fred Gwynne, Julie Kavner, Madonna, John Malkovich, Kenneth Mars, Kate Nelligan, Donald Pleasence, Lily Tomlin, Philip Bosco, Robert Joy, Wallace Shawn, Kurtwood Smith, Josef Sommer, David Ogden Stiers, Michael Kirby, Anne Lange; ***D:*** Woody Allen; ***W:*** Woody Allen; ***C:*** Carlo DiPalma. *ORI*

Shadows in the Storm 𝄞𝄞 **1988 (R)** A librarian/poet retreats to a secluded forest after losing his job. There he meets an exotically beautiful young woman who becomes his lover. With her love, she brings blackmail, murder, and mystery. **90m/C VHS, LV.** Ned Beatty, Mia Sara, Michael Madsen; ***D:*** Terrell Tannen. *VMK*

Shadows of Death 𝄞½ **1945** Crabbe is the hero who must track down a gang of outlaws who kill to grab the land along the path of a new railroad. One of the "Billy Carson" series. **60m/B VHS, Beta.** Buster Crabbe, Al "Fuzzy" St. John. *VCN, VCI*

Shadows of Forgotten Ancestors 𝄞𝄞𝄞 *Tini Zabutykh Predkiv; Shadows of Our Ancestors; Shadows of Our Forgotten Ancestors; Wild Horses of Fire* **1964** Set in rural Russia in the early 20th century. Brings to expressive life the story of a man whose entire life has been overtaken by tragedy. Folk drama about a peasant who falls in with the daughter of his father's killer, then marries another woman. Strange, resonant and powerful with distinctive camera work. In Ukrainian with English subtitles. **99m/C VHS, Beta.** *RU* Ivan Micholaichuk, Larisa Kadochnikova; ***D:*** Sergei Paradjanov. *CVC, INJ, AUD*

Shadows of the Orient **1937** Two detectives are out to smash a Chinese smuggling ring. **70m/B VHS.** Regis Toomey, Esther Ralston. *SNC, NOS, DVT*

Shadows on the Stairs 𝄞𝄞 **1941** A creepy boarding house is the scene of a number of mystery-drenched murders. A bizarre assortment of suspects make things even crazier. **63m/B VHS, Beta.** Frieda Inescort, Paul Cavanagh, Heather Angel, Bruce Lester, Miles Mander, Lumsden Hare, Turhan Bey; ***D:*** David Ross Lederman. *SNC*

Shadows Over Shanghai 𝄞½ **1938** This adventure relic was set during the Japanese invasion of China prior to WWII and uses much newsreel footage of that infamy. As for the plot, it's a groaner about good guys and bad skulking around the eponymous port in search of a treasure. **66m/B VHS.** James Dunn, Ralph Morgan, Robert Barrat, Paul Sutton, Edward Woods; ***D:*** Charles Lamont. *NOS, LOO*

Shadows Run Black 𝄞½ **1984** A police detective must save a college coed from the clutches of a maniac wielding a meat cleaver. Ordinary slash-em-up. Bet Costner's embarrassed now about this early role - like Stallone's porno role in "The Italian Stallion." **89m/C VHS, Beta.** William J. Kulzer, Elizabeth Trosper, Kevin Costner; ***D:*** Howard Heard. *NO*

Shadowzone 𝄞𝄞 **1989 (R)** As a result of NASA experiments in dream travel, an interdimensional monster invades our world in search of victims. Begins well, with slightly interesting premise, but degenerates into typical monster flick. Good special effects. **88m/C VHS, Beta, LV.** Louise Fletcher, David Beecroft, James Hong, Shawn Weatherly, Lu Leonard; ***D:*** J.S. Cardone; ***W:*** J.S. Cardone. *PAR*

Shaft 𝄞𝄞𝄞 **1971 (R)** A black private eye is hired to find a Harlem gangster's kidnapped daughter. Lotsa sex and violence; suspenseful and well directed. Great ending. Academy Award winning theme song by Isaac Hayes, the first music award from the Academy to an African American. Adapted from the novel by Ernest Tidyman. Followed by "Shaft's Big Score" and "Shaft in Africa." ♫Theme From Shaft. **98m/C VHS, Beta.** Richard Roundtree, Moses Gunn, Charles Cioffi; ***D:*** Gordon Parks; ***W:*** John D.F. Black. Academy Awards '71: Best Song ("Theme from Shaft"); Golden Globe Awards '72: Best Score; Nominations: Academy Awards '71: Best Original Score. *MGM*

Shaft in Africa 𝄞𝄞½ **1973 (R)** Violent actioner finds detective Shaft forced into helping an African nation stop some modern-day slave trading. Second sequel, following "Shaft's Big Score." **112m/C VHS.** Richard Roundtree, Frank Finlay, Vonetta McGee, Neda Arneric, Jacques Marin; ***D:*** John Guillermin; ***W:*** Stirling Silliphant. *MGM*

Shaft's Big Score 𝄞𝄞½ **1972 (R)** This first sequel to the extremely sucessful "Shaft" has Roundtree's detective trying to mediate between several mobsters while investigating a friend's murder. Lots of action and an exciting Brooklyn chase scene involving cars, helicopters, and boats but still routine when compared to the original. Followed by "Shaft in Africa." **105m/C VHS.** Richard Roundtree, Moses Gunn, Joseph Macoio, Drew Bundi Brown, Wally Taylor, Kathy Imrie, Julius W. Harris, Rosalind Miles, Joe Santos; ***D:*** Gordon Parks; ***W:*** Ernest Tidyman; ***M:*** Gordon Parks. *MGM*

Shag: The Movie 𝄞𝄞𝄞 **1989 (PG)** The time is 1963, the setting Myrtle Beach, South Carolina, the latest craze shaggin' when four friends hit the beach for one last weekend together. Carson (Cates) is getting ready to marry staid Harley (Power); Melaina (Fonda) wants to be discovered in Hollywood; and Pudge (Gish) and Luanne (Hannah) are off to college. They encounter lots of music, boys, and dancing in this delightful film. Not to be confused with other "teen" movies, this one boasts a good script and an above average cast. **96m/C VHS, Beta, LV.** Phoebe Cates, Annabeth Gish, Bridget Fonda, Page Hannah, Scott Coffey, Robert Rusler, Tyrone Power Jr., Jeff Yagher, Carrie Hamilton, Shirley Anne Field, Leilani Sarelle Ferrer; ***D:*** Zelda Barron; ***W:*** Robin Swicord, Lanier Laney, Terry Sweeney. *HBO*

The Shaggy D.A. 𝄞𝄞 **1976 (G)** Wilby Daniels is getting a little worried about his canine alter ego as he is about to run for District Attorney. Fun sequel to "The Shaggy Dog." **90m/C VHS, Beta.** Dean Jones, Tim Conway, Suzanne Pleshette, Keenan Wynn; ***D:*** Robert Stevenson; ***M:*** Buddy Baker. *DIS, OM*

The Shaggy Dog 𝄞𝄞½ **1959 (G)** When young Wilby Daniels utters some magical words from the inscription of an ancient ring he turns into a shaggy dog, causing havoc for family and neighbors. Disney slapstick is on target at times, though it drags in places. Followed by "The Shaggy D.A." and "Return of the Shaggy Dog." **101m/B VHS, Beta, LV.** Fred MacMurray, Jean Hagen, Tommy Kirk, Annette Funicello, Tim Considine, Kevin Corcoran; ***D:*** Charles T. Barton; ***C:*** Edward Colman. *DIS, BTV*

Shaka Zulu 𝄞𝄞𝄞 **1983** British miniseries depicting the career of Shaka, king of the Zulus (Cele). Set in the early 19th century during British ascendency in Africa. Good, absorbing cross-cultural action drama would have been better with more inspired directing by Faure. **300m/C VHS, Beta.** *GB* Edward Fox, Robert Powell, Trevor Howard, Christopher Lee, Fiona Fullerton, Henry Cele; ***D:*** William C. Faure. *PSM, FCT*

Shake Hands with Murder 𝄞𝄞 **1944** Three people spend their time bailing criminals out of jail for profit. One is murdered, and the other two become implicated in comedy. **63m/B VHS, Beta.** Iris Adrian, Frank Jenks, Douglas Fowley, Jack Raymond, Claire Rochelle, Herbert Rawlinson, Forrest Taylor; ***D:*** Al(bert) Herman. *SNC*

Shake Hands with the Devil 𝄞𝄞𝄞 **1959** It's the Irish Republican Army against the British Black and Tans as Ireland fights for independence in 1921. Cagney is a teaching surgeon who is secretly a militant, obsessed with the idea of gaining Irish freedom. He urges his students to join with him, which Irish-American Murray does. When Murray learns that Cagney is out to sabotage a peace treaty, he must decide whether to betray Cagney in order to stop further violence. Cagney is excellent as the hard-bitten revolutionary who can't see beyond his own ideals. Filmed on location in Dublin, which further heightens the film's tension. **110m/B VHS.** James Cagney, Don Murray, Dana Wynter, Glynis Johns, Michael Redgrave, Sybil Thorndike, Harry Brogan, Robert Brown; ***D:*** Michael Anderson Sr.; ***W:*** Ivan Goff. *MGM, FCT*

Shake, Rattle and Rock 𝄞𝄞½ **1957** A deejay wants to open a teen music club playing rock 'n' roll, which has all the conservative parents up in arms. A court case follows (which the kids win). Incidental plot to the great music by Fats Domino, Joe Turner, Annita Ray, and Tommy Charles. Songs include "Ain't It a Shame," "Honey Chile," "I'm in Love Again," "Feelin' Happy," and "Sweet Love on My Mind." **76m/C VHS.** Mike Connors, Lisa Gaye, Sterling Holloway, Margaret Dumont, Raymond Hatton, Douglass Dumbrille; ***D:*** Edward L. Cahn; ***W:*** Lou Rusoff. *COL, MOV, MVD*

Shakedown 𝄞𝄞½ **1988 (R)** Power-packed action film. An overworked attorney and an undercover cop work together to stop corruption in the N.Y.P.D. Although lacking greatly in logic or plot, the sensational stunts make this an otherwise entertaining action flick. **96m/C VHS, Beta, LV.** Sam Elliott, Peter Weller, Patricia Charbonneau, Antonio Fargas, Blanche Baker, Richard Brooks, Jude Ciccolella, George Loros, Tom Waits, Shirley Stoler, Rockets Redglare, Kathryn Rossetter; ***D:*** James Glickenhaus; ***W:*** James Glickenhaus; ***M:*** Jonathan Elias. *MCA*

Shaker Run 𝄞½ **1985** A stunt car driver and his mechanic transport a mysterious package. They don't know what to do—they're carrying a deadly virus that every terrorist wants! Car chases galore, and not much else. However, if you like chase scenes... **91m/C VHS, Beta, LV.** *NZ* Leif Garrett, Cliff Robertson, Lisa Harrow; ***D:*** Bruce Morrison. *SUE, NLC*

Shakes the Clown 𝄞 **1992 (R)** Chronicles the rise and fall of Shakes, an alcoholic clown wandering through the all-clown town of Palukaville. Framed for the murder of his boss by his archrival, Binky, Shakes takes it on the lam in order to prove his innocence, aided by his waitress girlfriend Judy, who dreams of becoming a professional bowler. Meant as a satire of substance-abuse recovery programs and the supposed tragedies of a performer's life, the film is sometimes zany, but more often merely unpleasant and unamusing. Williams has an uncredited role as a mime. **83m/C VHS, LV.** Bob(cat) Goldthwait, Julie Brown, Blake Clark, Adam Sandler, Tom Kenny, Sydney Lassick, Paul Dooley, Tim Kazurinsky, Florence Henderson, LaWanda Page; ***Cameos:*** Robin Williams; ***D:*** Bob(cat) Goldthwait; ***W:*** Bob(cat) Goldthwait. *COL*

Shakespeare Wallah 𝄞𝄞𝄞½ **1965** Tender, plausible drama of romance and postcolonial relations in India. A troupe of traveling Shakespeareans quixotically tours India trying to make enough money to return to England. Wonderfully acted and exquisitely and sensitively directed by Ivory. **120m/B VHS, Beta.** Laura Liddell, Geoffrey Kendal, Felicity Kendal, Shashi Kapoor, Madhur Jaffrey; ***D:*** James Ivory; ***W:*** Ruth Prawer Jhabvala, James Ivory. *SUE, INJ, NLC*

The Shakiest Gun in the West 𝄞𝄞½ **1968** Don Knotts isn't Bob Hope, but he's pretty funny in the same bumbling way. Remake of Hope's "Paleface" has Philadelphia dentist Knotts unwittingly taking on bad guys and sultry Rhoades. **101m/C VHS, LV.** Don Knotts, Barbara Rhoades, Jackie Coogan, Donald (Don "Red") Barry, Ruth McDevitt; ***D:*** Alan Rafkin. *MCA*

Shaking the Tree 𝄞𝄞½ **1992 (PG-13)** Group of four high school buddies are still in quest of self-fulfillment ten years after high school as they grapple with problems in the real world of adulthood, seeking distraction in adventure, romance, friendship, and sex. **97m/C VHS.** Arye Gross, Gale Hansen, Doug Savant, Steven Wilde, Courteney Cox, Christina Haag, Michael Arabian, Nathan Davis; ***D:*** Duane Clark; ***W:*** Duane Clark; ***M:*** David E. Russo. *ACA*

Shakma 𝄞½ **1989** A group of medical researchers involved with experiments on animal and human tendencies toward aggression take a night off to play a quiet game of "Dungeons and Dragons." The horror begins when their main experimental subject comes along and turns things nasty! **101m/C VHS.**

Roddy McDowall, Christopher Atkins, Amanda Wyss, Ari Meyers; ***D:*** Hugh Parks. *HHE*

Shalako ✂✂ **1968** Connery/Bardot pairing promises something special, but fails to deliver. European aristocrats on a hunting trip in New Mexico, circa 1880, are menaced by Apaches. U.S. Army scout tries to save captured countess Bardot. Strange British attempt at a Euro-western. Poorly directed and pointless. Based on a Louis L'Amour story. **113m/C VHS, Beta.** Brigitte Bardot, Sean Connery, Stephen Boyd, Honor Blackman, Woody Strode, Alexander Knox; ***D:*** Edward Dmytryk; ***C:*** Ted Moore. *FOX*

Shall We Dance ✂✂✂ **1937** And shall we ever! Seventh Astaire-Rogers pairing has a famous ballet dancer and a musical-comedy star embark on a promotional romance and marriage, to boost their careers, only to find themselves truly falling in love. Score by the Gershwins includes memorable songs. Thin, lame plot—but that's okay. For fans of good singing and dancing, and especially of this immortal pair. ♫Slap That Bass; Beginner's Luck; Let's Call the Whole Thing Off; Walking the Dog; They All Laughed; They Can't Take That Away From Me; Shall We Dance. **116m/B VHS, Beta, LV.** Fred Astaire, Ginger Rogers, Edward Everett Horton, Eric Blore; ***D:*** Mark Sandrich; ***M:*** George Gershwin, Ira Gershwin. Nominations: Academy Awards '37: Best Song ("They Can't Take That Away From Me"). *TTC, CCB, MED*

Shallow Grave ✂½ **1987 (R)** Four coeds en route to Florida witness a murder in rural Georgia and then are pursued relentlessly by the killer, a local sheriff. Decent premise and talented cast could have offered something better, given a meatier script. **90m/C VHS, Beta.** Tony March, Lisa Stahl, Tom Law, Carol Cadby; ***D:*** Richard Styles. *PSM, PAR*

Shallow Grave ✂✂½ **1994 (R)** Juliet (Fox), David (Eccleston), and Alex (McGregor), three completely unlikable housemates, face a moral dilemma when their new roomie, Hugo (Allen), turns up dead of a drug overdose, leaving behind a suitcase stuffed with cash. Their decision to chop up the body, bury the bits, and keep the loot leads to a well-deserved descent into paranoia, betrayal, and dementia. Interesting character study in which the veneer of civility is totally destroyed at the first hint of temptation. Style wins out over substance as the characters are never humanized before they're demonized. **91m/C VHS.** *GB* Kerry Fox, Christopher Eccleston, Ewan McGregor, Keith Allen, Ken Stott, Colin McCredie, John Hodge; ***D:*** Danny Boyle; ***W:*** John Hodge; ***M:*** Simon Boswell. *PGV*

The Shaman ✂½ **1987 (R)** Members of a family succumb to the hypnotic spell of the Shaman as he searches for the perfect one to inherit his powers. **88m/C VHS, Beta.** Michael Conforti, Elvind Harum, James Farkas, Lynn Weaver; ***D:*** Michael Yakub. *IMP*

Shame ✂✂✂½ *The Intruder; I Hate Your Guts; The Stranger* **1961** Strangely unsuccessful low-budget Corman effort, starring pre-"Star Trek" Shatner as a free-lance bigot who travels around Missouri stirring up opposition to desegregation. Moralistic and topical but still powerful. Adapted from the equally excellent novel by Charles Beaumont. Uses location filming superbly to render a sense of everydayness and authenticity. **84m/B VHS, Beta, LV.** William Shatner, Frank Maxwell, Jeanne Cooper, Robert Emhardt, Leo Gordon; ***D:*** Roger Corman. *NOS, DVT, FCT*

The Shame ✂✂✂½ **1968 (R)** A Bergman masterpiece focusing on the struggle for dignity in the midst of war. Married concert musicians Ullmann and von Sydow flee a bloody civil war for a small island off their country's coast. Inevitably, the carnage reaches them and their lives become a struggle to endure and retain a small measure of civilized behavior as chaos overtakes them. Deeply despairing and brilliantly acted. In Swedish with English subtitles. **103m/C VHS.** *SW* Max von Sydow, Liv Ullmann, Gunnar Bjornstrand, Sigge Furst, Brigitta Valberg, Hans Alfredson, Ingvar Kjellson; ***D:*** Ingmar Bergman; ***W:*** Ingmar Bergman; ***C:*** Sven Nykvist. National Society of Film Critics Awards '68: Best Actress (Ullmann), Best Director (Bergman), Best Film. *MGM, BTV*

Shame ✂✂ **1987 (R)** Strange Australian revenge drama about a female lawyer/biker who rides into a small town and finds herself avenging the rape of a 16-year-old girl. Is it a genuinely feminist movie about justice and a strong woman taking charge? Or is it exploitative trash using a politically correct theme and "message" as a peg for much - very much - gratuitous violence? Hard to tell. Cultish for sure; made on a B budget. **95m/C VHS, LV.** *AU* Deborra-Lee Furness, Tony Barry, Simone Buchanan, Gillian Jones; ***D:*** Steve Jodrell; ***W:*** Beverly Blakenship, Michael Brindley. *REP*

Shame ✂✂ **1992** In a small logging town a group of violent high school thugs get away with rape because the women are too terrified to go to the cops. Then lawyer Diana Cadell (Donohoe) gets stuck in town when her motorcycle breaks down. When she finds out what's been happening, she urges one victim (Balk) to speak out and suddenly they become the targets of both the vicious attackers and a town which would like to hush the entire mess up. Very strong performances by Donohoe and Balk. Made for cable U.S. version of the same-titled 1987 Australian movie. **91m/C VHS.** Amanda Donohoe, Fairuza Balk, Dean Stockwell, Dan Gauthier; ***D:*** Dan Lerner; ***W:*** Rebecca Soladay. *PSM*

Shame of the Jungle **1990 (R)** Animated spoof on Tarzan featuring the voices of John Belushi, Bill Murray, and Johnny Weissmuller, Jr. **73m/C VHS.** ***D:*** Boris Szulzinger, Picha; ***V:*** Johnny Weissmuller Jr., John Belushi, Bill Murray, Brian Doyle-Murray, Christopher Guest, Andrew Duncan. *JEF*

Shame, Shame on the Bixby Boys ✂½ **1982** Somewhere in the Old West, outside a small town, lives a band of misfits who persist in rustling cattle. The Bixby Boys and their Pa have made a bad habit into a family tradition. **90m/C VHS, Beta.** Monte Markham, Sammy Jackson; ***D:*** Anthony Bowers. *TLF*

The Shaming ✂½ *The Sin; Good Luck, Miss Wyckoff* **1971 (R)** Puritanical schoolteacher is raped by a janitor, then develops a voracious sexual appetite. Horrible script, offensive premise can't be saved by good cast. Based on a novel by William Inge. **90m/C VHS, Beta.** Anne Heywood, Donald Pleasence, Robert Vaughn, Carolyn Jones; ***D:*** Marvin J. Chomsky. *NO*

Shampoo ✂✂½ **1975 (R)** A satire of morals (and lack thereof) set in Southern California, concerning a successful hairdresser (Beatty) and the many women in his life. A notable scene with Julie Christie is set at a 1968 presidential election-night gathering. Fisher's screen debut, only one year before "Star Wars" made her famous. Has a healthy glow in places and a perky bounce, but too many split ends. **112m/C VHS, Beta, LV.** Warren Beatty, Julie Christie, Goldie Hawn, Jack Warden, Lee Grant, Tony Bill, Carrie Fisher, William Castle, Howard Hesseman; ***D:*** Hal Ashby; ***W:*** Warren Beatty, Robert Towne; ***M:*** John Barry. Academy Awards '75: Best Supporting Actress (Grant); National Society of Film Critics Awards '75: Best Screenplay; Writers Guild of America '75: Best Original Screenplay; Nominations: Academy Awards '75: Best Art Direction/Set Decoration, Best Original Screenplay, Best Supporting Actor (Warden). *COL, CRC*

Shamus ✂✂ **1973 (PG)** Private dick Reynolds investigates a smuggling ring, beds a sultry woman, gets in lotsa fights. Classic Burt vehicle meant as a send-up. Unoriginal but fun. **91m/C VHS, Beta, LV.** Burt Reynolds, Dyan Cannon, John P. Ryan; ***D:*** Buzz Kulik; ***W:*** Barry Beckerman; ***M:*** Jerry Goldsmith. *GKK*

Shane ✂✂✂✂ **1953** A retired gunfighter, now a drifter, comes to the aid of a homestead family threatened by a land baron and his hired gun. Ladd is the mystery man who becomes the idol of the family's young son. Classic, flawless western. Pulitzer prize-winning western novelist A.B. Guthrie, Jr. adapted from the novel by Jack Schaefer. Long and stately; worth savoring. **117m/C VHS, Beta, LV.** Alan Ladd, Jean Arthur, Van Heflin, Brandon de Wilde, Jack Palance, Ben Johnson, Elisha Cook Jr., Edgar Buchanan, Emile Meyer; ***D:*** George Stevens; ***W:*** Jack Sher; ***C:*** Loyal Griggs; ***M:*** Victor Young. Academy Awards '53: Best Color Cinematography; National Board of Review Awards '53: 10 Best Films of the Year, Best Director (Stevens); Nominations: Academy Awards '53: Best Director (Stevens), Best Picture, Best Screenplay, Best Supporting Actor (de Wilde, Palance). *PAR, TLF*

The Shanghai Cobra ✂½ **1945** Below-average mystery has Chan hired by the government to investigate several supposed cobra bite murders. All motives lead to stealing a supply of radium. **64m/B VHS.** Sidney Toler, Benson Fong, Mantan Moreland, Walter Fenner, James B. Cardwell, Joan Barclay, James Flavin; ***D:*** Phil Karlson. *MGM*

Shanghai Express ✂✂✂½ **1932** Dietrich is at her most alluring in this mystical and exotic story that made legends out of both star and director. Dietrich plays Shanghai Lily, a woman of objectionable reputation, who has a reunion of sorts with ex-lover Brooks aboard a slow-moving train through China. Remade as "Peking Express." Based on a story by Harry Hervey. **80m/B VHS.** Marlene Dietrich, Clive Brook, Anna May Wong, Warner Oland, Eugene Pallette, Lawrence Grant, Louise Closser Hale; ***D:*** Josef von Sternberg; ***W:*** Jules Furthman; ***C:*** Lee Garmes. Academy Awards '32: Best Cinematography (Garmes). *MCA, FCT*

The Shanghai Gesture ✂✂½ **1942** A wildly baroque, subversive melodrama. An English financier tries to close a gambling den, only to be blackmailed by the female proprietor—who tells him not only is the man's daughter heavily indebted to her, but that she is the wife he abandoned long ago. Based on a notorious Broadway play. Von Sternberg had to make numerous changes to the script in order to get it past the Hays censors; the director's final Hollywood work, and worthy of his oeuvre, but oddly unsatisfying. **97m/B VHS, Beta, LV.** Walter Huston, Gene Tierney, Victor Mature, Ona Munson, Albert Basserman, Eric Blore, Maria Ouspenskaya, Phyllis Brooks, Mike Mazurki; ***D:*** Josef von Sternberg. Nominations: Academy Awards '42: Best Interior Decoration. *MFV*

Shanghai Surprise ✂½ **1986 (PG-13)** Tie salesman Penn and missionary Madonna (yeah, right) are better than you'd think, and the story (of opium smuggling in China in the '30s) is intrepid and wildly fun, but indifferently directed and unsure of itself. Executive producer George Harrison wrote the songs and has a cameo. **90m/C VHS, Beta, LV.** Sean Penn, Madonna, Paul Freeman, Richard Griffiths; ***Cameos:*** George Harrison; ***D:*** Jim Goddard; ***W:*** Robert Bentley; ***M:*** George Harrison, Michael Kamen. Golden Raspberry Awards '86: Worst Actress (Madonna). *LIV, VES*

Shanghai Triad ✂✂✂½ **1995 (R)** Seventh collaboration of director Yimou and star Li takes place in violent crime dynasty of 1930s Shanghai. Here, eight days are seen through the eyes of a young boy (Cuihua) initiated into the Triad to be the lackey of the mob boss's arrogant mistress (Li). The trio and some trusty associates flee to the country after things heat up with a rival mob. Yimou subtly distinguishes the dichotomy between the jaded criminals and the naive youth with the move from the city to the country and his use of color and tone while avoiding cliche. Plot twists are fresh and technical aspects impeccable. Chinese with subtitles. **108m/C VHS, LV.** *FR CH* Gong Li, Li Bao-Tian, Li Xuejian, Shun Chun Shusheng, Wang Xiaoxiao Cuihua, Jiang Baoying; ***D:*** Zhang Yimou; ***W:*** Bi Feiyu; ***C:*** Lu Yue; ***M:*** Zhang Guangtain. Nominations: Academy Awards '95: Best Cinematography; Golden Globe Awards '96: Best Foreign Language Film. *COL*

Shanty Tramp ✂ **1967** Small-town tramp puts the moves on an evangelist, a motorcycle gang, and a young black man, who risks his life trying to save her from her loose morals. Another cheesy flick made for the drive-in crowd. **72m/B VHS.** Lee Holland, Bill Rogers, Lawrence Tobin; ***D:*** Joseph Prieto. *SNC, TPV*

Shao Lin Popeye ✂✂ **1994** A poor, but optimistic school boy has a crush on the principal's daughter. The girl's rich and rowdy boyfriend naturally begins to harass the lovesick lad. Much kicking, punching, and yelling ensues. **m/C VHS.** *CH* Ge-Ying Lin, Shao-Wen Haw, Shiao-Long She. *TPV*

Shaolin Ex-Monk 🦴 **1982** Renegade Shaolin Monk is pursued by a Kung Fu master and his disciple. **94m/C VHS, Beta.** John Liu, Ko Shou Liang, Huang Hsing Shaw. *WVE*

Shaolin Executioner 🦴 **198?** Several generations of Shaolin defend the Shaolin Temple against all high-kicking odds. **104m/C Beta.** Chen Kuan-Tai, Lo Lieh; ***D:*** Lu Chia-Liang. *NO*

Shaolin Kids 🦴 **1977** Shaolin warriors discover a conspiracy and kick it to death. **91m/C VHS, Beta.** *UNI*

Shaolin Kung Fu Mystagogue 🦴 **1984** In this action-packed chop-fest, the mysterious "Floating in Blood" weapon enlivens the battle between the Ching Dynasty and Ming rebels. **90m/C VHS, Beta.** ***D:*** Chang Peng-I. *NO*

Shaolin Temple Strikes Back 🦴 **1972** The protective inhabitants of the Shaolin temple defend themselves against invading Manchu Barbarians. **90m/C VHS, Beta.** Chen Chien Chang, Sho Kosugi, Chang Shan, Lung Fei; ***D:*** Joseph Kuo. *TWE*

Shaolin Traitor 🦴½ **1982 (R)** Exotic weapons and dazzling martial-arts action are featured in this exciting tale of intrigue and mystery. **99m/C VHS, Beta.** Carter Wong, Shangkuan Ling-Feng, Lung Chun-Eng, Chang Yi, Lung Fei. *GEM*

Shaolin Vengence 🦴½ **1982** Framed for murder and deceived into accepting guilt for the crime, a man does penance in a Shaolin temple. When he learns of the deception, he uses his newly learned Shaolin boxing skills to relentlessly pound the creeps who set him up. **?m/C VHS.** Chen Sing. *MGI*

Shark! 🦴½ *Man-Eater; Un Arma de Dos Filos* **1968 (PG)** American gun smuggler Reynolds, stranded in a tiny seaport in Africa, joins the crew of a marine biologist's boat. He soon discovers the boat's owner and his wife are trying to retrieve gold bullion that lies deep in shark-infested waters. Typical Reynoldsian action-infested dumbness. Like "Twilight Zone: The Movie", earned notoriety because of on-location tragedy: a stunt diver really was killed by a shark. Edited without the consent of Fuller, who disowned it. **92m/C VHS, Beta.** Burt Reynolds, Barry Sullivan, Arthur Kennedy; ***D:*** Samuel Fuller; ***W:*** Samuel Fuller. *REP, MRV*

Shark Hunter 🦴 **1984 (PG)** Shark hunter gets ensnared in the mob's net off the Mexican coast as they race for a cache of sunken millions. The usual garden-variety B-grade adventure. **95m/C VHS, Beta.** Franco Nero, Jorge Luke, Mike Forrest. *PSM, MRV*

Shark River 🦴½ **1953** A man attempts to get his brother, a Civil War veteran accused of murder, through the Everglades and send him to safety in Cuba. Good photography of the great swamp; disappointing story. **80m/C VHS, Beta.** Steve Cochran, Carole Mathews, Warren Stevens; ***D:*** John Rawlins. *NO*

Shark's Paradise 🦴 **1986** A madman threatens to set sharks loose on a popular Australian surf coast if his demands are not met. **93m/C VHS, Beta.** *WOV*

Sharks' Treasure 🦴½ **1975 (PG)** A band of escaped convicts commandeer a boat filled with gold. Old fashioned sunken-treasure tale unexceptional except as a virtual one man show by writer/actor/director/producer/fitness nut Wilde. **96m/C VHS, Beta.** Cornel Wilde, Yaphet Kotto, John Nellson, Cliff Osmond, David Canary, David Gilliam; ***D:*** Cornel Wilde. *MGM*

Sharky's Machine 🦴🦴½ **1981 (R)** A tough undercover cop (Reynolds) is hot on the trail of a crooked crime czar. Meanwhile he falls for a high-priced hooker. Well done but overdone action, with much violence. Based on the William Diehl novel. **119m/C VHS, Beta, LV.** Burt Reynolds, Rachel Ward, Vittorio Gassman, Brian Keith, Charles Durning, Bernie Casey, Richard Libertini, Henry Silva, John Fiedler, Earl Holliman; ***D:*** Burt Reynolds. *WAR*

Sharma & Beyond 🦴 **1984** A teenage would-be science fiction writer falls in love with the daughter of a famous sci-fi author. **85m/C VHS, Beta.** Suzanne Burden, Robert Urquhart, Michael Maloney; ***D:*** Brian Gilbert; ***M:*** Rachel Portman. *MGM*

Sharon's Secret 🦴🦴½ **1995 (R)** When the mutilated bodies of wealthy Richard Harly and his wife are discovered, investigating detective Thomas McGregor (Henry) looks to place the blame on their traumatized 16-year-old daughter Sharon (Cameron), who'll inherit a fortune. Psychiatrist Laurel O'Connor (Harris) is assigned to help Sharon recover and she's defended by family attorney Frank Bowdin (McArthur) but it seems everyone has something to hide. Made for cable. **91m/C VHS.** Candace Cameron, Mel Harris, Greg Henry, Alex McArthur, Paul Regina, Elaine Kagan, James Pickens Jr.; ***D:*** Michael Scott; ***W:*** Mark Homer. *MCA*

Sharpe's Battle 🦴🦴½ **1994** Sharpe (Bean) must prepare the Royal Irish company, led by Lord Kiely (Durr) and used to only ceremonial duties, for their first battle. Meanwhile, Kiely's wife (Byrne) goes to Sharpe for help with a personal matter and there's more trouble with the French. Based on the novel by Bernard Cornwell; made for British TV. **100m/C VHS.** *GB* Sean Bean, Daragh O'Malley, Hugh Fraser, Jason Durr, Allie Byrne; ***D:*** Tom Clegg; ***W:*** Russell Lewis. *VCO*

Sharpe's Company 🦴🦴½ **1994** Sharpe (Bean) sets out to rescue Spanish lover Teresa (Serna) and his infant daughter, trapped in the French-held city of Badajoz, which is about to be stormed by British troops. To make matters worse, Sharpe must also deal with the machinations of underhanded madman Sergeant Obadiah Hakeswill (Postlethwaite), an old enemy with a grudge to settle. Based on the novel by Bernard Cornwell; made for British TV. **100m/C VHS.** *GB* Sean Bean, Assumpta Serna, Daragh O'Malley, Pete Postlethwaite, Hugh Fraser, Clive Francis, Louise Germaine; ***D:*** Tom Clegg; ***W:*** Charles Wood. *VCO*

Sharpe's Eagle 🦴🦴½ **1993** Sharpe (Bean) and his chosen band of sharpshooters are once again in the thick of battle against Napoleon's troops but this time they have the misfortune to be led by the imbecilic Sir Henry Simmerson (Cochrane). Thanks to Simmerson's cowardice, the regimental colors are captured and a heroic officer Sharpe admires is killed. Setting out for revenge, Sharpe is determined to capture the French mascot, a carved golden eagle carried into battle, and settle some personal scores. Based on the novel by Bernard Cornwell; made for British TV. **100m/C VHS.** *GB* Sean Bean, Assumpta Serna, Brian Cox, David Troughton, Daragh O'Malley, Michael Cochrane, Katia Caballero; ***D:*** Tom Clegg; ***W:*** Eoghan Harris. *VCO*

Sharpe's Enemy 🦴🦴½ **1994** Sharpe (Bean) is sent to a mountain stronghold, held by a band of deserters, to ransom Isabella (Hurley), the bride of English colonel, Sir Augustus Farthingdale (Child). But the evil Hakeswill (Postlethwaite) is leading the criminals and he refuses to make things easy for our hero—nor will the French troops leave the English soldiers in peace. Based on the novel by Bernard Cornwell; made for British TV. **100m/C VHS.** *GB* Sean Bean, Assumpta Serna, Pete Postlethwaite, Daragh O'Malley, Hugh Fraser, Elizabeth Hurley, Michael Byrne, Jeremy Child, Nicholas Rowe; ***D:*** Tom Clegg; ***W:*** Eoghan Harris. *VCO*

Sharpe's Gold 🦴🦴½ **1994** Circa 1813 and Richard Sharpe (Bean) has now been promoted to Major—still leading his band of renegade sharpshooters. This time they're assigned to trade rifles for deserters held by the partisans and search for hidden Aztec gold, as Wellington (Fraser) prepares to push on into France. Sharpe must also protect Wellington's cousin Bess (Linehan) and her daughter Ellie (Ashbourne) as they search for Bess' missing husband. Based on the novel by Bernard Cornwell; made for British TV. **100m/C VHS.** *GB* Sean Bean, Daragh O'Malley, Hugh Fraser, Rosaleen Linehan, Jayne Ashbourne, Abel Folk, Peter Eyre; ***D:*** Tom Clegg; ***W:*** Nigel Kneale. *VCO*

Sharpe's Honour 🦴🦴½ **1994** Sharpe (Bean) becomes a pawn of French spy Pierre Ducos when he's forced to cross enemy lines, disguised as a Spanish rebel, in order to defend himself against allegations of dishonor. Sharpe's also unable to resist the attractions of the Marquesa Dorada (Krige), who's also part of Ducos' plan. Based on the novel by Bernard Cornwell; made for British TV. **100m/C VHS.** *GB* Sean Bean, Daragh O'Malley, Alice Krige, Hugh Fraser, Michael Byrne, Ron Cook; ***D:*** Tom Clegg; ***W:*** Colin MacDonald. *VCO*

Sharpe's Rifles 🦴🦴½ **1993** Swashbuckling heroics dominate as the Duke of Wellington's British soldiers battle Napoleon's French forces in the 1809 Penisular War (fought in Spain and Portugal). Common soldier Richard Sharpe (Bean) has just be promoted and given the unenviable task of leading a group of malcontent sharpshooters on a secret mission to aid Britain's Spanish allies. But it's not all hard times for Sharpe since the Spanish commander happens to be a very lovely woman. Adapted from the novel by Bernard Cornwall; made for British TV. **100m/C VHS.** *GB* Sean Bean, Assumpta Serna, Brian Cox, David Troughton, Daragh O'Malley, Julian Fellowes, Timothy Bentinck, Simon Andreu, Michael Mears, John Tams, Jason Salkey, Paul Trussell; ***D:*** Tom Clegg; ***W:*** Eoghan Harris. *VCO*

Sharpe's Sword 🦴🦴½ **1994** Sharpe's (Bean) sent to protect Wellington's top spy, El Mirador, and finds himself up against Napoleon's top swordsman Colonel Leroux (Fierry). When Sharpe's wounded, it's up to Lass (Mortimer), a young mute convent girl, to save our hero's life. Based on the novel by Bernard Cornwell; made for British TV. **100m/C VHS.** *GB* Sean Bean, Daragh O'Malley, Patrick Fierry, Emily Mortimer, John Kavanagh; ***D:*** Tom Clegg; ***W:*** Eoghan Harris. *VCO*

Shattered 🦴🦴🦴 *Scherben* **1921** Key film in Germany's kammerspiel (chamber play) movement, which emphasized naturalism with a minimum number of characters. A railway worker's daughter is seduced by her father's supervisor. When the man abandons her, the girl's father takes revenge. **62m/B VHS.** *GE* Werner Krauss, Edith Posca, Paul Otto; ***D:*** Lupu Pick; ***W:*** Carl Mayer. *FCT*

Shattered 🦴½ *Something to Hide* **1972 (R)** Finch plays Harry, a man blamed for a failed marriage, held hostage in his home by his own paranoia, and driven to bouts of drinking. Slowly his tenuous grip on sanity slips and at any moment his fragile and crumbling life may be shattered. Tired, overwrought domestic drama. **100m/C VHS, Beta.** *GB* Peter Finch, Shelley Winters, Colin Blakely; ***D:*** Alastair Reid. *MED*

Shattered 🦴🦴 **1991 (R)** An architect recovering from a serious automobile accident tries to regain the memory that he has lost. As he begins to put together the pieces of his life, some parts of the puzzle don't quite fit. For example, he recalls his now loving wife's affair as well as his own. He remembers that he hired a private detective to follow his wife and shockingly, he remembers that he once believed his wife had planned to kill him. Are these memories the real thing, or are they all part of some mad, recuperative nightmare? Who knows. **98m/C VHS, Beta, LV, 8mm.** Tom Berenger, Bob Hoskins, Greta Scacchi, Joanne Whalley, Corbin Bernsen, Theodore Bikel; ***D:*** Wolfgang Petersen; ***W:*** Wolfgang Petersen. *MGM*

Shattered Dreams 🦴🦴½ **1994** TV movie about domestic violence finds Wagner as the battered wife of a prominent, high-profile government official. Based on a true story. **94m/C VHS.** Lindsay Wagner, Michael Nouri. *LIV*

Shattered Image 🦴🦴½ **1993 (R)** Confusing thriller about the FBI's involvement in the kidnapping of the owner of a model agency, as well as plastic surgery, and a big money scam. Made for cable TV. **100m/C VHS, LV.** Bo Derek, Jack Scalia, John Savage, Dorian Harewood, Ramon Franco, Carol Lawrence, Michael Harris, David McCallum; ***D:*** Fritz Kiersch. *VMK*

Shattered Silence 🦴½ *When Michael Calls* **1971** A woman is tormented by phone calls that seem to be coming from her dead son as her life is torn apart by divorce. Leaves unanswered the question: Will there be any suspense? Made for TV. Worthless and dumb. **73m/C VHS.** Elizabeth Ashley, Ben Gazzara, Michael Douglas, Karen Pearson; ***D:*** Philip Leacock. *CCB*

Shattered Spirits 🦴½ **1991 (PG-13)** Quiet family man cracks and goes on a rampage through his normally peaceful surburban neighborhood. Been done before and better. **93m/C VHS.** Martin Sheen, Melinda Dillon, Matthew Laborteaux, Roxana Zal, Lukas Haas. *VMK*

Shattered Vows 🦴🦴 **1984** A young nun struggles with her love for a priest and her desire for a child. Bertinelli is convincing as the confused teen in otherwise ordinary TV drama. Adapted from the true story of Dr. Mary Gilligan Wong as told in her book, "Nun: A Memoir." **95m/C VHS, Beta.** Valerie Bertinelli, David Morse, Caroline McWilliams, Patricia Neal, Millie Perkins, Leslie Ackerman, Lisa Jane Persky; ***D:*** Jack Bender. *FRH*

The Shawshank Redemption 🦴🦴🦴½ **1994 (R)** Bank veep Andy (Robbins) is convicted of the murder of his wife and her lover and sentenced to the "toughest prison in the Northeast." While there he forms a friendship with lifer Red (Freeman), experiences the brutality of prison life, adapts, offers financial advice to the guards, and helps the warden (Gunton) cook the prison books...all in a short 19 years. In his debut, director Darabont avoids belaboring most prison movie cliches while Robbins' talent for playing ambiguous characters is put to good use, and Freeman brings his usual grace to what could have been a thankless role. Adapted from the novella "Rita Hayworth and the Shawshank Redemption" by Stephen King. **142m/C VHS, LV.** Tim Robbins, Morgan Freeman, Bob Gunton, William Sadler, Clancy Brown, Mark Rolston, Gil Bellows, James Whitmore; ***D:*** Frank Darabont; ***W:*** Frank Darabont; ***C:*** Roger Deakins. Nominations: Academy Awards '94: Best Actor (Freeman), Best Adapted Screenplay, Best Cinematography, Best Film Editing, Best Picture, Best Sound, Best Original Score; Directors Guild of America Awards '94: Best Director (Darabont); Golden Globe Awards '95: Best Actor—Drama (Freeman), Best Screenplay; Screen Actors Guild Award '94: Best Actor (Freeman), Best Actor (Robbins). *COL*

She 🦴🦴½ **1921** H. Rider Haggard's famous story about the ageless Queen Ayesha, (Blythe), who renews her life force periodically by walking through a pillar of cold flame. Story and titles by Haggard. Blythe is a stirringly mean queen, and the story remains fresh and fun. Silent film with music score. **69m/B VHS, Beta.** Betty Blythe, Carlyle Blackwell, Mary Odette. *NOS, VYY, DVT*

She 🦴🦴½ **1935** First sound version of H. Rider Haggard's popular 1887 adventure tale, although the film's location was changed from Africa to the frozen Arctic. Explorers Scott and Bruce are searching for a fire that preserves rather than destroys life. They are captured by a mysterious tribe and discover a living goddess—She-Who-Must-Be-Obeyed (Gahagan)—who bathed in the Flame of Life and is now eternal. She falls for Scott, who doesn't return her love, and there's trouble. Fantastic Art Deco sets and special effects. **95m/B VHS.** Helen Gahagan, Randolph Scott, Nigel Bruce, Helen Mack, Gustav von Seyffertitz; ***D:*** Irving Pichel, Lansing C. Holden; ***W:*** Dudley Nichols, Ruth Rose; ***C:*** J. Roy Hunt; ***M:*** Max Steiner. *KIV*

S*H*E 🦴🦴 **1979** A flashy made for TV spy thriller. The female agent S*H*E (Securities Hazards Expert) must save the world's oil; good locations, nifty plot and looker Sharpe as the she-Bond add up to a reasonably fun time. Scripted by "Bond"-writer Maibaum. **100m/C VHS, Beta.** Cornelia Sharpe, Robert Lansing, William Taylor, Isabella Rye, Anita Ekberg; ***Cameos:*** Omar Sharif; ***D:*** Robert Lewis; ***W:*** Richard Maibaum; ***M:*** Michael Kamen. *PSM*

She 🦴 **1983** A beautiful female warrior rules over the men in a post-holocaust world. She is kidnapped by a wealthy merchant who uses her to fight evil mutants. Utter rubbish vaguely based on the Haggard novel. **90m/C VHS, Beta.** Sandahl Bergman, Harrison Muller, Quin Kessler, David Goss; ***D:*** Avi Nesher. *LIV*

She and He 🦴🦴½ **1963** Hani's look at the oppression of women, marital and spiritual discontent, and class divisions. Naoko is a bored housewife, living in a sterile high-rise apartment with her equally dissatisfied husband, and yearning for something to express her inner feelings. She accidentally meets an old classmate of her husband's who has become a poor ragpicker and tries to aid him. But all her efforts only lead to further tragedies. In Japanese with English subtitles. **110m/C VHS.** *JP* Sachiko Hidari, Eiji Okada, Kikuji Yamashita; ***D:*** Susumu Hani. *FCT*

The She-Beast 🦴½ *Il Lago di Satana; The Revenge of the Blood Beast* **1965** Burned at the stake in 18th-century Transylvania, a witch returns in the body of a beautiful young English woman on her honeymoon (in Transylvania?!), and once again wreaks death and destruction. Caution, Barbara Steele fans: she appears for all of fifteen minutes. Sporadically funny. **74m/C VHS, Beta.** *IT YU* Barbara Steele, Ian Ogilvy, Mel Welles, Lucretia Love; ***D:*** Michael Reeves. *SNC, MPI*

She Came on the Bus *Woof!* **1969** Young thugs break into a well-kept suburban home and terrorize the housewife through rape and torture. Then they kidnap a bus and pose as the drivers until they can find more victims. Contains scenes of graphic violence which would be considered offensive even by today's standards. **58m/C VHS.** ***D:*** Harry Vincent. *SMW, TPV*

She Came to the Valley 🦴 *Texas in Flames* **1977 (PG)** A tough pioneer woman becomes embroiled in political intrigue during the Spanish-American War. Based on Cleo Dawson's book. **90m/C VHS, Beta.** Ronee Blakley, Dean Stockwell, Scott Glenn, Freddy Fender. *MED*

She Couldn't Say No 🦴🦴 *Beautiful But Dangerous* **1952** A wealthy oil heiress (Simmons) with good intentions plans to give her money away to those friends who had helped her when she was struggling. Things don't go quite as planned; her philanthropy leads to unexpected mayhem in her Arkansas hometown. Passable, but not memorable comedy. Mitchum as a small-town doctor? **88m/B VHS, Beta.** Robert Mitchum, Jean Simmons, Arthur Hunnicutt, Edgar Buchanan, Wallace Ford; ***D:*** Lloyd Bacon. *CCB*

She Demons *Woof!* **1958** Pleasure craft loaded with babes crashes into a remote island controlled by a mad ex-Nazi scientist who transforms pretty girls into rubber-faced Frankensteins. Incomprehensible, to say the least. **68m/B VHS, Beta.** Irish McCalla, Tod Griffin, Victor Sen Yung; ***D:*** Richard Cunha. *RHI, SNC, MWP*

She-Devil 🦴🦴½ **1989 (PG-13)** A comic book version of the acidic Fay Weldon novel "The Life and Loves of a She-Devil"; a fat, dowdy suburban wife (Arnold) becomes a vengeful beast when a smarmy romance novelist steals her husband. Uneven comedic reworking of a distinctly unforgiving feminist fiction. Arnold is given too much to handle (her role requires an actual range of emotions); Streep's role is too slight, though she does great things with it. **100m/C VHS, Beta, LV.** Meryl Streep, Roseanne, Ed Begley Jr., Linda Hunt, Elizabeth Peters, Bryan Larkin, A. Martinez, Sylvia Miles; ***D:*** Susan Seidelman; ***W:*** Mark Burns, Barry Strugatz; ***M:*** Howard Shore. *ORI*

She Devils in Chains 🦴🦴 **19?? (R)** A group of traveling female athletes are kidnapped by a groups of sadists who torture and beat them. In the end, however, the girls get their revenge, and it's bloody. **82m/C VHS.** Colleen Camp, Rosanne Katon, Sylvia Anderson, Ken Washington, Leo Martinez; ***D:*** Cirio H. Santiago. *SIM*

She-Devils on Wheels *Woof!* **1968** Havoc erupts as an outlaw female motorcycle gang, known as "Maneaters on Motorbikes," terrorizes a town—especially the men. Really, really bad biker flick finely honed by Lewis. **83m/C VHS, Beta.** Betty Connell, Christie Wagner, Pat Poston, Nancy Lee Noble, Ruby Tuesday; ***D:*** Herschell Gordon Lewis. *VTR*

She Done Him Wrong 🦴🦴🦴 **1933** West stars as Lil, an 1890s saloon singer in the screen version of her Broadway hit "Diamond Lily," and imparts on the negligible plot her usual share of double entendres and racy comments. Grant is likeable as the hapless sap she beds. ♫Silver Threads Among the Gold; Masie, My Pretty Daisy; Easy Rider; I Like a Guy What Takes His Time; Frankie and Johnny. **65m/B VHS, Beta, LV.** Mae West, Cary Grant, Owen Moore, Noah Beery Sr., Gilbert Roland, Louise Beavers; ***D:*** Lowell Sherman; ***C:*** Charles B(ryant) Lang. National Board of Review Awards '33: 10 Best Films of the Year; Nominations: Academy Awards '33: Best Picture. *MCA, MLB, BTV*

She-Freak 🦴 *Alley of Nightmares* **1967** Remake of Tod Brownings' "Freaks." A cynical waitress burns everyone in a circus and gets mauled by the resident freaks. Pales beside its unacknowledged, classic original. **87m/C VHS, Beta.** Claire Brennan, Lynn Courtney, Bill McKinney, Lee Raymond, Madame Lee; ***D:*** Byron Mabe. *NO*

She Gods of Shark Reef 🦴 *Shark Reef* **1956** Typical no-budget Corman exploitation tale of two brothers shipwrecked on an island inhabited by beautiful pearl-diving women. Filmed in Hawaii. **63m/C VHS.** Bill Cord, Don Durant, Lisa Montell, Carol Lindsay, Jeanne Gerson; ***D:*** Roger Corman. *SNC, MRV, HEG*

She Goes to War 🦴🦴 **1929** King's first part-sound effort that takes place in the milieu of WWI. Boardman plays a spoiled rich girl who grows up fast when confronted with the horrors of the front-line while working in a canteen. **50m/B VHS, Beta, 8mm.** Eleanor Boardman, Alma Rubens, Al "Fuzzy" St. John; ***D:*** Henry King. *NOS, GVV, DVT*

She Likes You, Charlie Brown **1986** Romantic travails for Charlie Brown and the gang. Animated. **41m/C VHS, Beta.** *BAR, WTA*

She Must Be Seeing Things 🦴🦴 **1987** Filmmaker Jo (Weaver) is making a picture about a 17th-century woman who lived her life as a man. Jo's lover Agatha (Dabney) becomes disturbed when she reads Jo's diary, learns she's been having affairs with men, and begins to fantasize about Jo's unfaithfulness with the men in her film crew. Agatha's insecurities finally lead her to disguising herself as a man in order to spy on Jo—mirroring what's happening in Jo's film. **95m/C VHS.** Sheila Dabney, Lois Weaver, Kyle DiCamp, John Erdman; ***D:*** Sheila McLaughlin; ***W:*** Sheila McLaughlin. *TVC*

She Shall Have Music 🦴½ **1936** A magnate hires a dance band to broadcast from a cruise ship. Features music by Jack Hylton and his band, one of Britain's most popular orchestras of the 1930s. **76m/B VHS, Beta.** *GB* Jack Hylton, June Clyde, Claude Dampier, Bryan Lawrence, Gwen Farrar. *MWP*

She Waits 🦴🦴 **1971** When a newlywed couple moves into an old house, the bride becomes possessed by the spirit of her husband's first wife. Unoriginal and mediocre horror. Made for television. **74m/C VHS, Beta.** Dorothy McGuire, Patty Duke, David McCallum; ***D:*** Delbert Mann. *PSM*

She Wore a Yellow Ribbon 🦴🦴🦴½ **1949** An undermanned cavalry outpost makes a desperate attempt to repel invading Indians. Wayne shines as an officer who shuns retirement in order to help his comrades. Still fun and compelling. The second chapter in director Ford's noted cavalry trilogy, preceded by "Fort Apache" and followed by "Rio Grande." **93m/C VHS, Beta, LV.** John Wayne, Joanne Dru, John Agar, Ben Johnson, Harry Carey Jr., Victor McLaglen, Mildred Natwick, George O'Brien; ***D:*** John Ford; ***C:*** Winton C. Hoch. Academy Awards '49: Best Color Cinematography. *TTC, TLF*

Sheba, Baby 🦴🦴 **1975 (PG)** A female dick (Grier) heads to Louisville where someone is trying to threaten her rich father and his loan company. Oddly non-violent for action-flick vet Grier; poorly written and directed. **90m/C VHS, Beta.** Pam Grier, Rudy Challenger, Austin Stoker, D'Urville Martin, Charles Kissinger; ***D:*** William Girdler. *ORI, FCT*

Sheena *Woof!* **1984 (PG)** Television sportscaster aids a jungle queen in defending her kingdom from being overthrown by an evil prince. Horrid bubblegum "action" fantasy. **117m/C VHS, Beta, LV.** Tanya Roberts, Ted Wass, Donovan Scott, Elizabeth Toro; ***D:*** John Guillermin; ***W:*** David Newman. *GKK*

The Sheep Has Five Legs 🦴🦴½ **1954** Quintuplet brothers return from around the world for a reunion in their small French village. Fernandel plays the father and all five sons; otherwise, comedy is only average-to-good. In French with English subtitles. **96m/B VHS, Beta, 8mm.** *FR* Fernandel, Edouard Delmont, Louis de Funes, Paulette Dubost; ***D:*** Henri Verneuil. Nominations: Academy Awards '55: Best Story. *NOS, DVT, VYY*

Sheer Madness 🦴🦴🦴 **1984** Focuses on the intense friendship between a college professor and a troubled artist, both women. Engrossing and subtle exposition of a relationship. Ambiguous ending underscores film's general excellence. Subtitled. **105m/C VHS, Beta.** *GE FR* Hanna Schygulla, Angela Winkler; ***D:*** Margarethe von Trotta; ***W:*** Margarethe von Trotta; ***C:*** Michael Ballhaus. *MGM*

The Sheik 🦴🦴🦴 **1921** High camp Valentino has English woman fall hopelessly under the romantic spell of Arab sheik who flares his nostrils. Followed by "Son of the Sheik." **80m/B VHS, Beta.** Agnes Ayres, Rudolph Valentino, Adolphe Menjou, Walter Long, Lucien Littlefield, George Waggner, Patsy Ruth Miller; ***D:*** George Melford. *PAR, GPV*

She'll Be Wearing Pink Pajamas 🦴🦴 **1984** Eight women volunteer for a rugged survival course to test their mettle. The intense shared experience gives them all food for thought. Well acted from a pretty thin story. **90m/C VHS, Beta.** Julie Walters, Anthony Higgins; ***D:*** John Goldschmidt; ***M:*** John Du Prez. *ORI*

The Shell Seekers 🦴🦴½ **1989 (PG)** The widowed Penelope Keeling (Lansbury) is recovering from a heart attack and her three grown children want her to take things easy. But the scare has convinced Penelope to revisit her past and the happiness she once knew. So she returns to her childhood home in Cornwall to see what she can discover. Fine cast in a heart-tugger (with some lovely scenery from Cornwall, England and the island of Ibiza). Adapted from the novel by Rosamunde Pilcher. A Hallmark Hall of Fame presentation. **94m/C VHS.** *GB* Angela Lansbury, Sam Wanamaker, Anna Carteret, Michael Gough, Christopher Bowen, Patricia Hodge, Denis Quilley, Sophie Ward, Irene Worth; ***D:*** Waris Hussein; ***W:*** John Pielmeier. *REP*

Shell Shock 🦴½ **198?** Four GI's fight off the Germans and the longings for home during WWII. **90m/C VHS, Beta.** ***D:*** John Hayes. *NO*

Shelley Duvall's Bedtime Stories **1992** A series of stories based on popular children's books, narrated by celebrities. Each tape is available individually and contains at least two stories. Nominated for cable's ACE award and an Emmy award. Originally produced for cable television. **25m/C VHS, LV.** *MCA*

The Sheltering Sky 🦴🦴🦴 **1990 (R)** American couple Winger and Malkovich flee the plasticity of their native land for a trip to the Sahara desert where they hope to renew their spirits and rekindle love. Accompanied by socialite acquaintance Scott with whom Winger soon has an affair, their personalities and belief systems deteriorate as they move through the grave poverty of North Africa in breathtaking heat. Based on the existential novel by American expatriate Paul Bowles who narrates and appears briefly in a bar scene. Overlong but visually stunning, with cinematography by Vittorio Storaro. **139m/C VHS, Beta, LV.** Debra Winger, John Malkovich, Campbell Scott, Jill Bennett, Timothy Spall, Eric Vu-An, Sotigui Koyate, Amina Annabi, Paul Bowles; ***D:*** Bernardo Bertolucci; ***W:*** Mark Peploe, Bernardo Bertolucci; ***C:*** Vittorio Storaro; ***M:*** Ryuichi Sakamoto, Richard Horowitz. Golden Globe Awards '91: Best Score; New York Film Critics Awards '90: Best Cinematography. *WAR, FCT, CCB*

Shenandoah 🦴🦴🦴 **1965** A Virginia farmer (Stewart, in a top-notch performance) who has raised six sons and a daughter, tries to remain neutral during the Civil War. War takes its toll as the daughter marries a Confederate soldier and his sons become involved in the fighting. Screen debut for Ross. **105m/C VHS, Beta, LV.** James Stewart, Doug McClure, Glenn Corbett, Patrick Wayne, Rosemary Forsyth, Katharine Ross, George Kennedy; ***D:*** Andrew V. McLaglen; ***C:*** William Clothier. Nominations: Academy Awards '65: Best Sound. *MCA*

Shep Comes Home 🦴 **1949** Shep the wonder canine accompanies an orphan through the Midwest where he nabs a band of bankrobbers. Sequel to "My Dog Shep." **62m/B VHS, Beta, LV.** Robert Lowery, Sheldon Leonard. *NO*

Sheriff of Tombstone 🦴½ **1941** Trouble begins when a "judge" takes a sharpshooter in a poker game. **60m/B VHS, Beta.** Roy Rogers. *NOS, DVT, RXM*

Sherlock Holmes and the Deadly Necklace 🦴🦴½ *Sherlock Holmes Und Das Halsband des Todes; Valley of Fear* **1962** Once again, Holmes and Watson are up against their old nemesis Moriarty. This time, Moriarty wants to get his hands on a necklace stolen from Cleopatra's tomb. Not only does Scotland Yard not consider him a suspect, they seek his advice. Enter Holmes and Watson, and the game's afoot. The offbeat casting and direction help make this one of the odder versions of Conan Doyle's work. **84m/B VHS.** *GE* Christopher Lee, Senta Berger, Hans Sohnker, Hans Nielsen, Ivan Desny, Leon Askin, Thorley Walters; ***D:*** Terence Fisher. *NOS, SNC*

Sherlock Holmes and the Incident at Victoria Falls 🦴½ *Incident at Victoria Falls* **1991** A substandard Holmes excursion brings the Baker Street sleuth out of retirement to transport the world's largest diamond from Africa to London. The resulting mystery involves Teddy Roosevelt, the inventor of radio, and poor plotting. **120m/C VHS.** *GB* Christopher Lee, Patrick Macnee, Jenny Seagrove; ***D:*** Bill Corcoran. *VES*

Sherlock Holmes and the Secret Weapon 🦴🦴🦴 *Secret Weapon* **1942** Based on "The Dancing Men" by Sir Arthur Conan Doyle. Holmes battles the evil Moriarty in an effort to save the British war effort. Good Holmes mystery with gripping wartime setting. Hoey is fun as bumbling Inspector Lestrade. Available colorized. **68m/B VHS, LV.** Basil Rathbone, Nigel Bruce, Karen Verne, William Post Jr., Dennis Hoey, Holmes Herbert, Mary Gordon, Henry Victor, Philip Van Zandt, George Eldridge, Leslie Denison, James Craven, Paul Fix, Hugh Herbert, Lionel Atwill; ***D:*** Roy William Neill. *REP, MED, AOV*

Sherlock Holmes Faces Death 🦴🦴🦴 **1943** Dead bodies are accumulating in a mansion where the detecting duo are staying. Underground tunnels, life-size dress boards, and unanswered mysteries... Top-notch Holmes. Peter Lawford appears briefly as a sailor. Also available with "Hound of the Baskervilles" on Laser Disc. **68m/B VHS, Beta, LV.** Basil Rathbone, Nigel Bruce, Hillary Brooke, Milburn Stone, Halliwell Hobbes, Arthur Margetson, Gavin Muir; ***D:*** Roy William Neill. *FOX*

Sherlock Holmes in Washington 🦴🦴½ **1943** A top-secret agent is murdered; seems it's those blasted Nazis again! Holmes and Watson rush off to Washington, D.C. to solve the crime and to save some vitally important microfilm. Heavily flag-waving Rathbone-Bruce episode. Dr. Watson is dumbfounded by bubble gum. **71m/B VHS, Beta.** Basil Rathbone, Nigel Bruce, Henry Daniell, George Zucco, Marjorie Lord, John Archer; ***D:*** Roy William Neill. *FOX*

Sherlock Holmes: The Master Blackmailer **1992** Brett returns as the super-sleuth, along with sidekick Dr. Watson, in a tale which has the detective working against the evil scheming of London's most cunning and ruthless blackmailer. When Holmes disguises himself to enter the blackmailer's lair he even finds himself attracting the romantic attentions of a young lady. Based on the story "The Adventure of Charles Augustus Milverton" by Arthur Conan Doyle. Made for television. **120m/C VHS.** *GB* Jeremy Brett, Edward Hardwicke, Robert Hardy. *MPI, SIG*

Sherlock Holmes: The Sign of Four 🦴🦴 **1984** Sherlock Holmes must find the man who murdered Bartholomew Sholto with a poison dart in the neck. **48m/C VHS, Beta.** ***V:*** Peter O'Toole. *WTA, PMS, PAR*

Sherlock Holmes: The Silver Blaze 🦴½ **1941** Sherlock Holmes mystery about the theft of a racehorse known as "The Silver Blaze." Remade in 1977. **70m/B VHS, Beta.** Arthur Wontner, Ian Fleming, Lyn Harding. *NOS, BAR, MWP*

Sherlock Holmes: The Voice of Terror 🦴🦴½ **1942** Holmes and Watson try to decode German radio messages during WWII. First Rathbone-as-Holmes effort for Universal, and first in which we are asked to believe the Victorian sleuth and his hairdo could have lived in this century. Patriotic and all that—and lots of fun. **65m/B VHS, Beta, LV.** Basil Rathbone, Nigel Bruce, Hillary Brooke, Reginald Denny, Evelyn Ankers, Montagu Love; ***D:*** John Rawlins. *FOX*

Sherlock Hound: Tales of Mystery **1990** Sherlock, Watson and Moriarty are all dogs in this animated children's adaptation of the popular Arthur Conan Doyle stories. Well worth a howl. **115m/C VHS, Beta.** *JFK*

Sherlock: Undercover Dog 🦴🦴½ **1994 (PG)** Billy (Eroen) arrives on Catalina island to spend the summer with his father, an eccentric inventor. He makes a human friend in Emma (Cameron) and a canine companion in Sherlock, a police dog who's able to talk but naturally only to the two kids. Seems Sherlock's policeman master has been kidnapped by bumbling smugglers and its up to the trio to come to the rescue. **80m/C VHS.** Benjamin Eroen, Brynne Cameron, Anthony Simmons, Margy Moore, Barry Philips; ***D:*** Richard Harding Gardner; ***W:*** Richard Harding Gardner; ***M:*** Lou Forestieri. *COL*

Sherlock's Rivals & Where's My Wife 🦴½ **1927** Double feature includes a detective movie in which two used car dealers become amateur sleuths and a comedy in which a man has a hard time enjoying his weekend at a seashore resort. **53m/B VHS, Beta.** Milburn Morante, Monty Banks. *VYY*

Sherman's March: An Improbable Search for Love **1986** McElwee's "epic" which was originally planned as a historical documentary about General Sherman's catastrophic march through the South, ends up being about the filmmaker himself, and his disastrous quest for love. When his girlfriend dumps him, he puts Sherman's story aside and films his own battle for romance, which includes help from his meddling family. The melodramatic women he meets and the neurotic energy of McElwee make this a very funny, uncensored film. **155m/C VHS.** ***D:*** Ross McElwee; ***W:*** Ross McElwee. *ICA, FRV, INJ*

She's a Good Skate, Charlie Brown **1980** Snoopy becomes Peppermint Patty's ice-skating coach, and he helps her train for the local competition. **30m/C VHS, Beta.** ***D:*** Phil Roman. *VTR, HSE, WTA*

She's Back 🦴½ **1988 (R)** Murderee Fisher pesters hubby Joy from beyond the grave to avenge her death at the hands of a motorcycle gang. Uneven, but occasionally funny. **89m/C VHS, Beta, LV.** Carrie Fisher, Robert Joy; ***D:*** Tim Kincaid. *VES, LIV*

She's Dressed to Kill 🦴🦴 *Someone's Killing the World's Greatest Models* **1979** Beautiful models are turning up dead during a famous designer's comeback attempt at a mountain retreat. Who could be behind these grisly deeds? Suspenseful in a made for TV kind of way, but not memorable. **100m/C VHS.** Eleanor Parker, Jessica Walter, John Rubinstein, Connie Sellecca; ***D:*** Gus Trikonis. *LIV*

She's Gotta Have It 🦴🦴🦴 **1986 (R)** Lee wrote, directed, edited, produced and starred in this romantic comedy about an independent-minded black girl in Brooklyn and the three men and one woman who compete for her attention. Full of rough edges, but vigorous, confident, and hip. Filmed entirely in black and white except for one memorable scene. Put Lee on the film-making map. **84m/B VHS,**

Beta, LV. Spike Lee, Tommy Redmond Hicks, Raye Dowell; ***D:*** Spike Lee. *FOX, FCT*

She's Having a Baby 🦴🦴½ **1988 (PG-13)** Newlyweds Bacon and McGovern tread the marital waters with some difficulty, when news of an impending baby further complicates their lives. Told from Bacon's viewpoint as the tortured young writer/ husband, who wonders if the yuppie life they lead is trapping him. Hughes' first venture into the adult world isn't as satisfying as his teen angst flicks, although the charming leads help. Major drawbacks are the arguably sexist premise and dull resolution. Great soundtrack; observant viewers will notice the beemer's license plate is the title's acronym: "SHAB." **106m/C VHS, Beta, LV, 8mm.** Kevin Bacon, Elizabeth McGovern, William Windom, Paul Gleason, Alec Baldwin, Cathryn Damon, Holland Taylor, James Ray, Isabel Lorca, Dennis Dugan, Edie McClurg, John Ashton; ***D:*** John Hughes; ***W:*** John Hughes; ***M:*** Stewart Copeland. *PAR*

She's in the Army Now 🦴 **1981** Farce about military life. Two bubble-headed females undergo basic training. Made for TV "Private Benjamin" ripoff was meant as a series pilot. **97m/C VHS, Beta.** Jamie Lee Curtis, Kathleen Quinlan, Melanie Griffith, Susan Blanchard, Julie Carmen, Janet MacLachlan; ***D:*** Hy Averback; ***M:*** Artie Butler. *SUE, NLC*

She's Out of Control 🦴½ **1989** Dad Danza goes nuts when teen daughter Dolenz (real-life daughter of Monkee Mickey Dolenz) takes the advice of Dad's girlfriend on how to attract boys. Formulaic plot could almost be an episode of "Who's the Boss?" Danza is appealing, but not enough to keep this one afloat. **95m/C VHS, Beta, LV, 8mm.** Tony Danza, Catherine Hicks, Wallace Shawn, Dick O'Neill; ***D:*** Stan Dragoti; ***M:*** Alan Silvestri. *COL*

Shifting Sands **1918** Compelling film tells the tale of a young girl looking to be a successful artist. Her landlord makes constant overtures towards her. She refuses, so he has her thrown in jail for prostitution as an act of revenge. She fears her past may prevent her from obtaining true love. **52m/B VHS, Beta, 8mm.** Gloria Swanson, Joe King, Lillian Langdon. *GPV, VYY, GVV*

Shin Heike Monogatari 🦴🦴🦴🦴 **1955** Mizoguchi's second to last film, in which a deposed Japanese emperor in 1137 endeavors to win back the throne from the current despot, who cannot handle the feudal lawlessness. Acclaimed; his second film in color. In Japanese with English subtitles. Also called "New Tales of the Taira Clan." **106m/C VHS, Beta.** *JP* Raizo Ichikawa, Ichijiro Oya, Michiyo Kogure, Eijiro Yanagi, Tatsuya Ishiguro, Yoshiko Kuga; ***D:*** Kenji Mizoguchi. *FCT*

Shinbone Alley **1970 (G)** Animated musical about Archy, a free-verse poet reincarnated as a cockroach, and Mehitabel, the alley cat with a zest for life. Based on the short stories by Don Marquis. **83m/C VHS, Beta.** ***D:*** John D. Wilson; ***V:*** Carol Channing, Eddie Bracken, John Carradine, Alan Reed. *GEM, KAR, HHE*

Shine on, Harvest Moon 🦴🦴 **1938** Rogers brings a band of outlaws to justice and clears an old man suspected of being their accomplice. Title bears no relation to storyline. **60m/B VHS, Beta.** Roy Rogers, Lynn (Mary Hart) Roberts, Stanley Andrews; ***D:*** Joseph Kane. *NOS, VYY, VDM*

The Shining 🦴🦴½ **1980 (R)** Very loose adaptation of the Stephen King horror novel about a writer and his family, snowbound in a huge hotel, who experience various hauntings caused by either the hotel itself or the writer's dementia. Technically stunning, and pretty dang scary, but too long, pretentious and implausible. Nicholson is excellent as the failed writer gone off the deep end. **143m/C VHS, Beta, LV.** Jack Nicholson, Shelley Duvall, Scatman Crothers, Danny Lloyd, Joe Turkel, Barry Nelson; ***D:*** Stanley Kubrick. *WAR*

The Shining Hour 🦴🦴½ **1938** A compelling melodrama in which Crawford portrays a New York night club dancer who is pursued by the rather conservative Douglas. His brother tries to persuade him from marrying Crawford, but then he soon finds himself attracted to her. A devastating fire wipes out all problems of family dissension in this intelligent soap opera. **76m/B VHS.** Joan Crawford, Margaret Sullavan, Melvyn Douglas, Robert Young, Fay Bainter, Allyn Joslyn; ***D:*** Frank Borzage; ***W:*** Ogden Nash, Jane Murfin. *MGM*

A Shining Season 🦴🦴🦴 **1979** Tearjerker about a potential-packed long-distance runner, John Baker, stricken with cancer. He spends his last year training a girls' track team to a championship. Earnest, well-performed and involving. Based on a true story. Made for TV. **100m/C VHS, Beta.** Timothy Bottoms, Rip Torn, Allyn Ann McLerie, Ed Begley Jr., Benjamin Bottoms, Mason Adams, Constance Forslund, Ellen Geer; ***D:*** Stuart Margolin; ***M:*** Richard Bellis. *BTV*

Shining Star 🦴½ *That's the Way of the World* **1975 (PG)** A recording company is run by the mob. Potentially interesting film is hampered by quality of sound and photography and general lack of purpose or direction. **100m/C VHS.** Harvey Keitel, Ed Nelson, Cynthia Bostick, Bert Parks; ***D:*** Sig Shore. *LIV*

Shining Through 🦴🦴½ **1992 (R)** Baby-voiced Griffith as a spy sent behind enemy lines without training? Douglas as a spy sent behind enemy lines without speaking German? Old-fashioned blend of romance, espionage, and derring-do where noble hero saves spunky heroine from nasty Nazis in WWII Germany works despite thin plot. Series of flash-forwards to an aged Griffith is annoying and tends to stop action cold, but everyone tries hard and period flavor is authentic. Adapted from best-selling Susan Isaacs novel, but bears little resemblance to book. **133m/C VHS.** Michael Douglas, Melanie Griffith, Liam Neeson, Joely Richardson, John Gielgud, Francis Guinan, Patrick Winczewski, Sylvia Syms; ***D:*** David Seltzer; ***W:*** David Seltzer; ***M:*** Michael Kamen. Golden Raspberry Awards '92: Worst Picture, Worst Actress (Griffith), Worst Director (Seltzer). *FXV*

Shinobi Ninja 🦴 **1984** Last-surviving member of Koga ninja clan returns to Japan from U.S. to save his homeland from enemy ninja clan. Mediocre pseudo ninja antics. Badly dubbed. **103m/C VHS, Beta.** *JP* Tadashi Yamashita, Eric Lee, Karen Lee Sheperd. *AHV*

Shiokari Pass 🦴🦴 **1977** A man has a divine revelation at the pass. In Japanese with English subtitles. **60m/C VHS.** *JP* ***D:*** Novuru Nakamuru. *REP, VBL*

Ship Ahoy 🦴🦴½ **1942** Songs, comedy, a spy spoof, and some patriotism thrown in for good measure. Powell plays a dancer who works with Tommy Dorsey and his orchestra. They're on their way to Puerto Rico, via ocean liner, along with her pulp fiction writer boyfriend (Skelton). Emery, posing as an FBI man, convinces Powell to smuggle a package for him but he's really a spy and the whole thing's a con which turns out to be based on one of Skelton's potboiler plots. An uncredited Frank Sinatra is the singer with the Dorsey band, along with drummer Buddy Rich and trumpeter Ziggy Elman who provide some great musical solos. ♫Last Call For Love; Poor You; On Moonlight Bay; Tampico; I'll Take Tallulah; Cape Dance; Ship Ahoy. **95m/B VHS.** Eleanor Powell, Red Skelton, Bert Lahr, Virginia O'Brien, John Emery, William Post Jr.; ***D:*** Edward Buzzell; ***W:*** Harry Kurnitz, Harry Clork, Irving Brecher. *MGM*

Ship of Fools 🦴🦴🦴 **1965** A group of passengers sailing to Germany in the '30s find mutual needs and concerns, struggle with early evidence of Nazi racism, and discover love on their voyage. Twisted story and fine acting maintain interest. Appropriate tunes written by Ernest Gold. Based on the Katherine Ann Porter novel. Leigh's last film role; she died two years later. Kramer grapples with civil rights issues in much of his work. **149m/B VHS, Beta, LV.** Vivien Leigh, Simone Signoret, Jose Ferrer, Lee Marvin, Oskar Werner, Michael Dunn, Elizabeth Ashley, George Segal, Jose Greco, Charles Korvin, Heinz Ruehmann; ***D:*** Stanley Kramer; ***W:*** Abby Mann; ***C:*** Ernest Laszlo; ***M:*** Ernest Gold. Academy Awards '65: Best Art Direction/Set Decoration (B & W), Best Black and White Cinematography; National Board of Review Awards '65: 10 Best Films of the Year, Best Actor (Marvin); Nominations: Academy Awards '65: Best Actor (Werner), Best Actress (Signoret), Best Adapted Screenplay, Best Costume Design (B & W), Best Picture, Best Supporting Actor (Dunn). *COL, SWC*

Ships in the Night 🦴🦴 **1928** Logan is the plucky heroine who is searching for her missing brother who has been captured by pirates. She is aided in her search by handsome hero Mower. **86m/B VHS, Beta.** Frank Moran, Jacqueline Logan, Jack Mower, Andy Clyde. *GVV, FCT, GPV*

Shipwreck Island 🦴🦴 **1961** Eight boys are shipwrecked on a deserted island, then make their way to another island where they must survive against wild animals and the elements for two years. **93m/C VHS.** *HTV, FCT*

Shipwrecked 🦴🦴½ *Haakon Haakonsen* **1990 (PG)** Kiddie swashbuckler based on the 1873 popular novel "Haakon Haakonsen." A cabin boy is marooned on an island where he defends the hidden pirate treasure he finds by boobytrapping the island. **93m/C VHS, LV.** *NO* Gabriel Byrne, Stian Smestad, Louisa Haigh, Trond Munch, Bjorn Sundquist, Eva Von Hanno, Kjell Stormoen; ***D:*** Nils Gaup; ***W:*** Nick Thiel, Nils Gaup; ***M:*** Patrick Doyle. *TOU*

Shirley Temple Festival **1933** A collection of four Shirley Temple short subjects from the 30s: "Dora's Dunkin Doughnuts," "Pardon My Pups," "War Babies" and "Kid N' Africa." **55m/B VHS, Beta.** Shirley Temple, Andy Clyde. *MRV*

Shirley Valentine 🦴🦴🦴 **1989** A lively middle-aged English housewife gets a new lease on life when she travels to Greece without her husband. Collins reprises her London and Broadway stage triumph. The character frequently addresses the audience directly to explain her thoughts and feelings; her energy and spunk carry the day. Good script by Russell from his play. From the people who brought us "Educating Rita." **108m/C VHS, LV, 8mm.** *GB* Pauline Collins, Tom Conti, Alison Steadman, Julia McKenzie, Joanna Lumley, Bernard Hill, Sylvia Syms; ***D:*** Lewis Gilbert; ***W:*** George Hadjinassios, Willy Russell; ***M:*** Willy Russell. British Academy Awards '89: Best Actress (Collins); Nominations: Academy Awards '89: Best Actress (Collins), Best Song ("The Girl Who Used to Be Me"). *PAR, TVC, HMV*

The Shock 🦴🦴½ **1923** Crippled low-life Chaney becomes restored spiritually by a small-town girl and rebels against his Chinese boss. This causes an unfortunate string of melodramatic tragedies, including the San Francisco earthquake of 1906. Silent. Odd, desultory tale with bad special effects is worth seeing for Chaney's good acting. **96m/B VHS, Beta.** Lon Chaney Sr., Virginia Valli; ***D:*** Lambert Hillyer. *SNC, NOS, HEG*

Shock! 🦴🦴 **1946** A psychiatrist is called on to treat a woman on the edge of a nervous breakdown. He then discovers she saw him murder his wife, and tries to keep her from remembering it. Interesting premise handled in trite B style. Price's first starring role. **70m/B VHS, Beta.** Vincent Price, Lynn Bari, Frank Latimore, Anabel Shaw; ***D:*** Alfred Werker. *SNC, NOS, BAR*

Shock Corridor 🦴🦴🦴 **1963** A reporter, dreaming of a Pulitzer Prize, fakes mental illness and gets admitted to an asylum, where he hopes to investigate a murder. He is subjected to disturbing experiences, including shock therapy, but does manage to solve the murder. However, he suffers a mental breakdown in the process and is admitted for real. Disturbing and lurid. **101m/B VHS, LV.** Peter Breck, Constance Towers, Gene Evans, Hari Rhodes, James Best, Philip Ahn; ***D:*** Samuel Fuller; ***W:*** Samuel Fuller. *HMV, CRC*

Shock 'Em Dead 🦴🦴 **1990 (R)** A devil worshipper trades his life to Lucifer for a chance at rock and roll fame and beautiful Miss Lords. Sexy thriller, with a good share of violence and tension. Ironically, ex porn great Lords is one of the few starlets who doesn't disrobe in the film. **94m/C VHS, LV.** Traci Lords, Aldo Ray, Troy Donahue, Stephen Quadros; ***D:*** Mark Freed; ***W:*** Andrew Cross. *ACA*

Shock! Shock! Shock! 🦴 **1987** Another low-budget slasher flick, with a homicidal lunatic wielding a butcher knife. Space alien jewel thieves add an element, for what it's worth. Makes one ponder the cosmic question: What's the diff between a bad slasher flick and a spoof of a bad slasher flick? Whichever this one is, it's really bad! **60m/B VHS, Beta.**

Brad Issac, Cyndy McCrossen, Allen Rickman, Brian Fuorry; ***D:*** Todd Rutt, Arn McConnell. *RHI, MWF*

A Shock to the System 🦴🦴🦴 **1990 (R)** Business exec. Caine is passed over for a long-deserved promotion in favor of a younger man. When he accidentally pushes a panhandler in front of a subway in a fit of rage, he realizes how easy murder is and thinks it may be the answer to all his problems. Tries to be a satire take on corporate greed, etc., but somehow loses steam. Excellent cast makes the difference; Caine adds class. Based on the novel by Simon Brett. **88m/C VHS, Beta, LV.** Michael Caine, Elizabeth McGovern, Peter Riegert, Swoosie Kurtz, Will Patton, Jenny Wright, John McMartin, Barbara Baxley; ***D:*** Jan Egleson; ***W:*** Andrew Klavan; ***M:*** Gary Chang. *HBO*

Shock Treatment 🦴½ *Traitement de Choc* **1981 (PG)** Seldom-seen mediocre semi-sequel to the cult classic, "The Rocky Horror Picture Show" (1975). Brad and Janet, now married and portrayed by different leads, find themselves trapped on a TV gameshow full of weirdos. Same writers, same director, and several original cast members do make an appearance. **94m/C VHS, Beta.** Richard O'Brien, Jessica Harper, Cliff DeYoung, Patricia Quinn, Charles Gray, Ruby Wax; ***D:*** Jim Sharman. *FOX*

Shock Waves 🦴🦴 *Death Corps; Almost Human* **1977 (PG)** Group of mutant-underwater-zombie-Nazi-soldiers terrorizes stranded tourists staying at a deserted motel on a small island. Cushing is the mad scientist intent on recreating the Nazi glory days with the seaweed-attired zombies. Odd B-grade, more or less standard horror flick somehow rises (slightly) above badness. Halpin's name was erroneously listed as Halprin—even on the original movie poster! **90m/C VHS, Beta.** Peter Cushing, Brooke Adams, John Carradine, Luke Halpin; ***D:*** Ken Wiederhorn; ***M:*** Richard Einhorn. *PSM*

Shocker 🦴🦴½ **1989 (R)** Another Craven gore-fest. A condemned serial killer is transformed into a menacing electrical force after being fried in the chair. Practically a remake of Craven's original "Nightmare on Elm Street." Great special effects, a few enjoyable weird and sick moments. What's Dr. Timothy Leary doing here? **111m/C VHS, Beta, LV.** Michael Murphy, Peter Berg, Cami Cooper, Mitch Pileggi, Richard Price, Timothy Leary, Heather Langenkamp, Theodore (Ted) Raimi, Richard Brooks, Sam Scarber; ***D:*** Wes Craven; ***W:*** Wes Craven; ***M:*** William Goldstein. *MCA*

Shocking Asia 🦴½ **1975** For the eye-covering delight of Western audiences, Mr. Fox compiles gruesome Asian oddities. **94m/C VHS, Beta.** *GE* ***D:*** Emerson Fox. *HHE*

The Shoes of the Fisherman 🦴½ **1968 (G)** Morris West's interesting, speculative best seller about Russian Pope brought to the big screen at much expense, but with little care or thought. Siberian prison-camp vet Quinn, elected Pope, tries to arrest nuclear war. Director Anderson wasted the prodigious talents of Olivier, Gielgud, et al. Sloppy use of good cast and promising plot. **160m/C VHS, Beta, LV.** Anthony Quinn, Leo McKern, Laurence Olivier, John Gielgud, Vittorio De Sica, Oskar Werner, David Janssen; ***D:*** Michael Anderson Sr.; ***M:*** Alex North. Golden Globe Awards '69: Best Score; National Board of Review Awards '68: Best Supporting Actor (McKern); Nominations: Academy Awards '68: Best Art Direction/Set Decoration, Best Original Score. *MGM, FCT*

Shoeshine 🦴🦴🦴🦴 **1947** Two shoeshine boys struggling to survive in post-war Italy become involved in the black market and are eventually caught and imprisoned. Prison scenes detail the sense of abandonment and tragedy that destroys their friendship. A rich, sad achievement in neo-realistic drama. In Italian with English subtitles. **90m/B VHS, Beta.** *IT* Franco Interlenghi, Rinaldo Smordoni, Annielo Mele, Bruno Ortensi, Pacifico Astrologo; ***D:*** Vittorio De Sica; ***W:*** Cesare Zavattini, Sergio Amidei, Adolfo Franci, C.G. Viola. National Board of Review Awards '47: 10 Best Films of the Year; Nominations: Academy Awards '47: Best Original Screenplay. *FCT*

Shogun 🦴🦴🦴½ *James Clavell's Shogun* **1980** Television miniseries chronicling the saga of a ship-wrecked English navigator who becomes the first Shogun, or Samurai warrior chief, from the Western world. Colorfully adapted from the James Clavell bestseller. Also released in a two-hour version, but this full-length version is infinitely better. **550m/C VHS, Beta, LV.** Richard Chamberlain, Toshiro Mifune, Yoko Shimada, John Rhys-Davies, Damien Thomas; ***D:*** Jerry London; ***M:*** Maurice Jarre. *INJ, PAR*

Shogun Assassin 🦴🦴½ **1980 (R)** Story of a proud samurai named Lone Wolf who served his Shogun master well as the Official Decapitator, until the fateful day when the aging Shogun turned against him. Extremely violent, with record-breaking body counts. Edited from two other movies in a Japanese series called "Sword of Vengeance"; a tour de force of the cutting room. The samurai pushes his son's stroller through much of the film-sets it aside to hack and slash. **89m/C VHS, Beta, LV.** *JP* Tomisaburo Wakayama; ***D:*** Kenji Misumi, Robert Houston. *MCA, OM*

Shogun's Ninja 🦴½ **1983** In 16th-century Japan, an age-old rivalry between two ninja clans sparks a search for a dagger which will lead to one clan's hidden gold. Martial arts performed and directed by Sonny Chiba. In Japanese with usual poor English dubbing. **115m/C VHS, Beta.** Henry Sanada, Sue Shiomi, Sonny Chiba; ***D:*** Noribumi Suzuki. *MED*

Shoot 🦴 **1985 (R)** Five hunting buddies fall prey to a group of crazed killers after one man is shot by accident. What's the message: Anti-gun? Anti-hunting? Silly, unbelievable, irresponsibly moralistic, and gratuitously violent. **98m/C VHS, Beta.** *CA* Ernest Borgnine, Cliff Robertson, Henry Silva, Helen Shaver; ***D:*** Harvey Hart. *SUE*

Shoot 🦴🦴 **1992 (R)** Photographer Katie Tracy goes undercover to expose an illegal gambling ring fronted by an exotic nightclub. The latest gambling stakes involve the Emperor's pearls, offered in a private auction which could turn deadly, especially when Katie gets involved with the group's handsome ringleader. **90m/C VHS.** Dedee Pfeiffer, Miles O'Keeffe, Christopher Atkins; ***D:*** Hugh Parks. *TRI, TPV*

Shoot It Black, Shoot It Blue 🦴½ **1974** Rogue cop shoots a black purse snatcher and thinks he has gotten away with it. Unknown to him, a witness has filmed the incident and turns the evidence over to a lawyer. **93m/C VHS, Beta.** Michael Moriarty. *NO*

Shoot Loud, Louder, I Don't Understand! 🦴½ *Spara Forte, Piu Forte...Non Capisco* **1966** A sculptor who has a hard time separating reality from dreams thinks he witnessed a murder. Shenanigans follow. Meant to be a black comedy, but when not dull, it is confusing. Welch looks good, as usual, but doesn't show acting talent here. In Italian with English subtitles. **101m/C VHS, Beta.** *IT* Marcello Mastroianni, Raquel Welch; ***D:*** Eduardo de Filippo; ***M:*** Nino Rota. *NLC*

Shoot the Living, Pray for the Dead 🦴🦴 **1973** While travelling through Mexico, the leader of a band of killers promises his guide half of a share in stolen gold if he can lead them to it. **90m/C VHS, Beta.** Klaus Kinski. *CNG*

Shoot the Moon 🦴🦴½ **1982 (R)** A successful writer, married and with four children, finds his life unrewarding and leaves his family to take up with a younger woman. The wife must learn to deal with her resentment, the fears of her children, and her own attempt at a new love. Fine acting but a worn-out story. **124m/C VHS, Beta, LV.** Diane Keaton, Albert Finney, Karen Allen, Peter Weller, Dana Hill, Viveka Davis, Tracey Gold, Tina Yothers; ***D:*** Alan Parker; ***W:*** Bo Goldman. Nominations: Cannes Film Festival '82: Best Film. *MGM*

Shoot the Piano Player 🦴🦴🦴🦴 *Tirez sur le Pianiste; Shoot the Pianist* **1962** Former concert pianist (Aznavour, spendidly cast) changes his name and plays piano at a low-class Paris cafe. A convoluted plot ensues; he becomes involved with gangsters, though his girlfriend wants him to try a comeback. Lots of atmosphere, character development, humor, and romance. A Truffaut masterpiece based on a pulp novel by David Goodis. In French with English subtitles. **92m/B VHS, Beta, LV.** *FR* Charles Aznavour, Marie DuBois, Nicole Berger, Michele Mercier, Albert Remy; ***D:*** Francois Truffaut; ***W:*** Marcel Moussey, Francois Truffaut; ***M:*** Georges Delerue. *HMV, HHT, WFV*

Shoot the Sun Down 🦴½ **1981 (PG)** Four offbeat characters united in a search for gold turn against each other. "Gilligan's Island"-style assortment of characters (Indian; gunfighter; girl; sea captain) are cast away in a pointless plot from which they never escape. Too bad: talented cast could have done better. **102m/C VHS, Beta.** Christopher Walken, Margot Kidder, Geoffrey Lewis, Bo Brundin, Sacheen Littlefeather; ***D:*** David Leeds. *NO*

Shoot to Kill 🦴🦴½ **1947** B-grade noir-esque mystery about a crooked D.A. and a gangster who bite the dust. Suspenseful, dark, street-level crime drama uncovered by ambitious journalist Ward. **64m/B VHS, Beta, LV.** Russell Wade, Susan Walters, Nestor Paiva, Edmund MacDonald, Vince Barnett; ***D:*** William (Lester Williams) Berke. *SNC, VYY*

Shoot to Kill 🦴🦴🦴 **1988 (R)** A city cop (Poitier, better than ever after 10 years off the screen) and a mountain guide (Berenger) reluctantly join forces to capture a killer who is part of a hunting party traversing the Pacific Northwest and which is being led by the guide's unsuspecting girlfriend (Alley). Poitier may be a bit old for the role, but he carries the implausible plot on the strength of his performance. Good action. **110m/C VHS.** Sidney Poitier, Tom Berenger, Kirstie Alley, Clancy Brown, Richard Masur, Andrew (Andy) Robinson, Frederick Coffin, Andrew (Andy) Robinson, Kevin Scannell; ***D:*** Roger Spottiswoode; ***W:*** Michael Burton, Harv Zimmel, Dan Petrie Jr.; ***C:*** Michael Chapman; ***M:*** John Scott. *TOU*

Shoot to Kill 🦴🦴 *Disparen a Matar* **1990** An innocent young man is murdered during a police round-up while his mother watches helplessly. The police try a whitewash—proclaiming the victim a criminal—but she launches a long campaign for justice. Spanish with subtitles. **90m/C VHS.** *VZ* ***D:*** Carlos Azpurua. *FCT*

The Shooter 🦴 **1994 (R)** French hit woman Simone (Detmers) supposedly shoots the Cuban ambassador to the U.N. and escapes back to her home base in Prague, followed by Czech-born U.S. Marshal Mickey Dane (Lundgren). Mickey starts to doubt that Simone is the killer (she claims she's long retired and is being set up) and the duo try to find the truth amid lots of double-crosses. Doesn't make much sense in any case. **102m/C VHS.** Dolph Lundgren, Maruschka Detmers, Assumpta Serna, Gavan O'Herlihy, John Ashton, Simon Andreu; ***D:*** Ted Kotcheff; ***W:*** Meg Thayer, Billy Ray, Yves Andre Martin; ***C:*** Fernando Arguelles; ***M:*** Stefano Mainetti. *TOU*

Shooters 🦴½ **1989** A wacky platoon of misfits is paired off against a group of vicious killers in a "war game" training session. Not completely unfunny or worthless. **84m/C VHS, Beta.** Ben Schick, Robin Sims, Aldo Ray. *AIP*

Shootfighter: Fight to the Death 🦴½ **1993 (R)** Two boys become experts in the martial arts and constant rivals. Now grown-up they take their rivalry to a deadly level in a "shoot-fight," a game which has no rules and is so brutal it's banned as a sport. Not that this stops them. An unrated version is also available. **94m/C VHS, LV.** Bolo Yeung, Martin Kove, William Zabka, Michael Bernardo, Maryam D'Abo, Edward Albert; ***D:*** Patrick Allen; ***W:*** Judd B. Lynn, Larry Feliz Jr., Peter Shaner. *COL*

The Shooting 🦴🦴🦴 **1966** A mysterious woman, bent on revenge, persuades a former bounty hunter and his partner to escort her across the desert, with tragic results. Offbeat, small film filled strong by performances of Nicholson and Oates. Filmed concurrently with "Ride in the Whirlwind," with the same cast and director. Bang-up surprise ending. **82m/C VHS, Beta, LV.** Warren Oates, Millie Perkins, Jack Nicholson, Will Hutchins; ***D:*** Monte Hellman. *MED, DVT, HHT*

Shooting 1982 Three boys run away when they think they have killed a man in a hunting accident. **60m/C VHS, Beta.** Lynn Redgrave, Lance Kerwin, Barry Primus. *NO*

Shooting Elizabeth ½ **1992 (PG-13)** A fed-up husband decides to shut his loudmouthed wife up—permanently. Only before he can kill her, she disappears. The police don't buy it and want to charge him with murder. Can he find his wife before things really get serious? **96m/C VHS, LV.** Jeff Goldblum, Mimi Rogers; ***D:*** Baz Taylor. *LIV*

The Shooting Party ½ **1977** Told in flashbacks, a story of a crime of passion, an innocent man, and guilty secrets. A magistrate cannot admit his love for a woodsman's daughter so she falls into a loveless marriage and a decadent affair. In a fit of passion, the magistrate kills her and then decides to prosecute her innocent husband for the crime. Based on a story by Chekhov. In Russian with English subtitles. **105m/C VHS.** *RU* Oleg Yankovsky, Galina Belyayeva; ***D:*** Emil Loteanu. *CVC, FCT*

The Shooting Party ½ **1985** A group of English aristocrats assemble at a nobleman's house for a bird shoot on the eve of WWI. Splendid cast crowned Mason, in his last role. Fascinating crucible class anxieties, rich with social scheming, personality conflicts, and things left unsaid. Adapted from Isabel Colegate's novel. **97m/C VHS, Beta.** *GB* James Mason, Dorothy Tutin, Edward Fox, John Gielgud, Robert Hardy, Cheryl Campbell, Judi Bowker; ***D:*** Alan Bridges; ***W:*** Julian Bond. Los Angeles Film Critics Association Awards '85: Best Supporting Actor (Gielgud); National Society of Film Critics Awards '85: Best Supporting Actor (Gielgud). *NO*

Shooting Stars **1985** Two actors who play private eyes on television are pushed out of their jobs by a jealous co-star. They take to the streets as "real" crime-fighting dicks. Interesting premise goes nowhere. Made for TV. **96m/C VHS, Beta.** Billy Dee Williams, Parker Stevenson, Efrem Zimbalist Jr., Edie Adams; ***D:*** Richard Lang. *AHV*

The Shootist ½ **1976 (PG)** Wayne, in a supporting last role, plays a legendary gunslinger afflicted with cancer who seeks peace and solace in his final days. Town bad guys Boone and O'Brian aren't about to let him rest and are determined to gun him down to avenge past deeds. One of Wayne's best and most dignified performances about living up to a personal code of honor. Stewart and Bacall head excellent supporting cast. Based on Glendon Swarthout's novel. **100m/C VHS, Beta, LV.** John Wayne, Lauren Bacall, Ron Howard, James Stewart, Richard Boone, Hugh O'Brian, Bill McKinney, Harry (Henry) Morgan, John Carradine, Sheree North, Scatman Crothers; ***D:*** Donald Siegel; ***C:*** Bruce Surtees; ***M:*** Elmer Bernstein. National Board of Review Awards '76: 10 Best Films of the Year; Nominations: Academy Awards '76: Best Art Direction/Set Decoration. *PAR, TLF*

Shop Angel **1932** A department store dress designer encounters romance and scandal in this low-budget drama of intrigue and romance. She falls in love with the fiance of her boss's daughter, and schemes to blackmail him (the boss). Competently rendered if unexceptional tale. **66m/B VHS, Beta, 8mm.** Marion Shilling, Holmes Herbert, Creighton Hale; ***D:*** E. Mason Hopper. *VYY*

The Shop Around the Corner ½ **1940** A low-key romantic classic in which Stewart and Sullavan are feuding clerks in a small Budapest shop, who unknowingly fall in love via a lonely hearts club. Charming portrayal of ordinary people in ordinary situations. Adapted from the Nikolaus Laszlo's play "Parfumerie." Later made into a musical called "In the Good Old Summertime" and, on Broadway, "She Loves Me." **99m/B VHS, LV.** Margaret Sullavan, James Stewart, Frank Morgan, Joseph Schildkraut, Sara Haden, Felix Bressart, Charles Halton; ***D:*** Ernst Lubitsch; ***C:*** William H. Daniels. *MGM*

The Shop on Main Street *The Shop on High Street; Obch Od Na Korze* **1965** During WWII, a Slovak takes a job as an "Aryan comptroller" for a Jewish-owned button shop. The owner is an old deaf woman; they slowly build a friendship. Tragedy ensues when all of the town's Jews are to be deported. Sensitive and subtle. Surely among the most gut-wrenching portrayals of human tragedy ever on screen. Exquisite plotting and direction. In Czechoslovakian with English subtitles. **111m/B VHS, Beta, LV.** *CZ* Ida Kaminska, Josef Kroner, Hana Slivkoua, Frantisek Holly, Martin Gregor; ***D:*** Jan Kadar, Elmar Klos. Academy Awards '65: Best Foreign Language Film; New York Film Critics Awards '66: Best Foreign Film; Nominations: Academy Awards '65: Best Actress (Kaminska). *COL, INJ, SWC*

Shopworn Angel **1938** Weepy melodrama about a sophisticated actress who leads on a naive Texas soldier who's in New York prior to being shipped out for WWI duty. Later, just before she goes on stage, she learns he's been killed at the front. She rallys to sing "Pack Up your Troubles in Your Old Kit Bag and Smile, Smile, Smile." Lots of tears. Adapted from the story "Private Pettigrew's Girl" by Dana Burnet. This remake of the same-titled 1929 film considerably softened the characters. Remade again in 1959 as "That Kind of Woman." **85m/B VHS.** Margaret Sullavan, James Stewart, Walter Pidgeon, Nat Pendleton, Alan Curtis, Sam Levene, Hattie McDaniel, Charley Grapewin, Charles D. Brown; ***D:*** H.C. Potter; ***W:*** Waldo Salt; ***C:*** Joseph Ruttenberg. *MGM, MOV*

Shore Leave **1925** Dressmaker Mackaill isn't getting any younger. Tough-guy sailor Bilge Smith (Barthelmess, in top form) meets her on shore leave; little does he realize her plans for him! She owns a dry-docked ship, you see, and it (and she) will be ready for him when he comes ashore next. Lovely, fun (if rather plodding) romantic comedy. Later made into musicals twice, as "Hit the Deck" and "Follow the Fleet." **74m/B VHS.** Richard Barthelmess, Dorothy Mackaill; ***D:*** John S. Robertson. *GPV, GVV, VYY*

Short Circuit **1986 (PG)** A newly-developed robot designed for the military is hit by lightning and begins to think it's alive. Sheedy and Guttenberg help it hide from the mean people at the weapons lab who want to take it home. Followed two years later, save Sheedy and Guttenberg, by the lame "Short Circuit 2." **98m/C VHS, Beta, LV.** Steve Guttenberg, Ally Sheedy, Austin Pendleton, Fisher Stevens, Brian McNamara; ***D:*** John Badham; ***W:*** S.S. Wilson, Brent Maddock; ***M:*** David Shire. *FOX*

Short Circuit 2 ½ **1988 (PG)** A sequel to the first adorable-robot-outwits-bad-guys tale. The robot, Number Five, makes his way through numerous plot turns without much human assistance or much purpose. Harmless (unless you have to spend time watching it), but pointless and juvenile. Very occasional genuinely funny moments. **95m/C VHS, Beta, LV.** Fisher Stevens, Cynthia Gibb, Michael McKean, Jack Weston, David Hemblen; ***D:*** Kenneth Johnson; ***W:*** S.S. Wilson, Brent Maddock; ***M:*** Charles Fox. *COL*

Short Cuts ½ **1993 (R)** Multi-storied, fish-eyed look at American culture with some 22 characters intersecting—profoundly or fleetingly—through each other's lives. Running the emotional gamut from disturbing to humorous, Altman's portrait of the contemporary human condition is nevertheless fascinating. Based on nine stories and a prose poem by Raymond Carver. Available on laser disc in a movie-only edition or a special edition. **189m/C VHS, LV.** Annie Ross, Lori Singer, Jennifer Jason Leigh, Tim Robbins, Madeleine Stowe, Frances McDormand, Peter Gallagher, Lily Tomlin, Tom Waits, Bruce Davison, Andie MacDowell, Jack Lemmon, Lyle Lovett, Fred Ward, Buck Henry, Huey Lewis, Matthew Modine, Anne Archer, Julianne Moore, Lili Taylor, Christopher Penn, Robert Downey Jr., Jarrett Lennon, Zane Cassidy; ***D:*** Robert Altman; ***W:*** Frank Barhydt, Robert Altman; ***C:*** Walt Lloyd; ***M:*** Mark Isham. Independent Spirit Awards '94: Best Director (Altman), Best Film, Best Screenplay; National Society of Film Critics Awards '93: Best Supporting Actress (Stowe); Venice Film Festival '93: Best Film; Nominations: Academy Awards '93: Best Director (Altman); Golden Globe Awards '94: Best Screenplay; Independent Spirit Awards '94: Best Supporting Actress (Moore). *COL*

Short Eyes ½ *The Slammer* **1979 (R)** When a child molester (Davison) enters prison, the inmates act out their own form of revenge against him. Filmed on location at New York City's Men's House of Detention, nicknamed "The Tombs." Script by Manuel Pinero from his excellent play; he also acts in the film. Top-notch performances and respectful direction from Young bring unsparingly realistic prison drama to the screen. Title is prison jargon for child molester. **100m/C VHS, Beta.** Bruce Davison, Miguel Pinero, Nathan George, Donald Blakely, Curtis Mayfield, Jose Perez, Shawn Elliott; ***D:*** Robert M. Young. *LIV*

Short Fuse ½ *Good to Go* **1988 (R)** A Washington, D.C. reporter uncovers the truth behind the rape and murder of a nurse. Interesting "go-go" music from the Washington D.C. ghetto aids an otherwise uninteresting film. **91m/C VHS, Beta.** Art Garfunkel, Robert DoQui, Harris Yulin, Richard Brooks, Reginald Daughtry; ***D:*** Blaine Novak. *VMK*

Short Time **1990 (PG-13)** Somewhere between "Tango & Cash" and "Airplane" is where you'll find "Short Time." Non-stop action/comedy stars Dabney Coleman and Teri Garr as partners in crime and humor. Coleman is a cop days from retirement; wrongly told he is dying, he tries hard to get killed so his family will be provided for. Coleman is wonderful. Garr, no longer the long-suffering wife of "Oh, God" and "Close Encounters," is appealing here as the indulgent sidekick. **100m/C VHS, LV.** Dabney Coleman, Teri Garr, Matt Frewer, Barry Corbin, Joe Pantoliano, Xander Berkeley, Rob Roy, Jak-Erik Eriksen; ***D:*** Gregg Champion; ***W:*** John Blumenthal, Michael Berry; ***M:*** Ira Newborn. *IME, LIV*

A Shot in the Dark ½ **1933** A minister suspects murder when a despised miser is thought to have committed suicide. He takes it on himself to investigate in this routine mystery. **53m/B VHS, Beta.** *GB* Dorothy Boyd, O.B. Clarence, Jack Hawkins, Russell Thorndike, Michael Shepley; ***D:*** George Pearson. *SNC*

A Shot in the Dark **1935** When his son is murdered at a New England college, a distraught dad takes it on himself to investigate. Movie cowboy Starrett plays the sleuthing pop in this undistinguished mystery. **69m/B VHS, Beta.** Charles Starrett, Robert Warwick, Edward Van Sloan, Marion Shilling, Doris Lloyd, Helen Jerome Eddy, James Bush; ***D:*** Charles Lamont. *NOS, SNC*

A Shot in the Dark ½ **1964** Second and possibly the best in the classic "Inspector Clouseau-Pink Panther" series of comedies. The bumbling Inspector Clouseau (Sellers, of course) investigates the case of a parlor maid (Sommer) accused of murdering her lover. Clouseau's libido convinces him she's innocent,even though all the clues point to her. Classic gags, wonderful music. After this film, Sellers as Clouseau disappears until 1975's "Return of the Pink Panther" (Alan Arkin played him in "Inspector Clouseau," made in 1968 by different folks). **101m/C VHS, Beta, LV.** Peter Sellers, Elke Sommer, Herbert Lom, George Sanders, Bryan Forbes; ***D:*** Blake Edwards; ***W:*** William Peter Blatty, Blake Edwards; ***M:*** Henry Mancini. *FOX, FCT*

Shotgun ½ **1955** A sheriff on the trail of a killer is accompanied by a girl he's saved from Indians. Average western cowritten by western actor Rory Calhoun, who had hoped to star in the film, but was turned down by the studio. **81m/C VHS.** Sterling Hayden, Zachary Scott, Yvonne De Carlo; ***D:*** Lesley Selander; ***C:*** Ellsworth Fredericks. *PAR*

The Shout **1978 (R)** From a strange Robert Graves story, an even stranger film. A lunatic befriends a young couple, moves in with them, and gradually takes over their lives. The movie's title refers to the man's ability to kill by shouting, a power he learned from his Australian aboriginal past. **88m/C VHS, Beta.** *GB* Alan Bates, Susannah York, John Hurt, Tim Curry; ***D:*** Jerzy Skolimowski; ***W:*** Michael Austin; ***M:*** Tony Banks. Cannes Film Festival '78: Grand Jury Prize; Nominations: Cannes Film Festival '78: Best Film. *COL*

Shout 🦴🦴 **1991 (PG-13)** Romance and rebellion set in a sleepy Texas town during the 1950s. Jesse Tucker's (Walters) rebellious ways land him in the Benedict Home for Boys and he seems lost until Jack Cabe (Travolta) enters town. Jack introduces Jesse and the gang to the exciting new sounds of rock 'n' roll. Been done before and better. **93m/C VHS, Beta, LV.** John Travolta, James Walters, Heather Graham, Richard Jordan, Linda Fiorentino, Scott Coffey; ***D:*** Jeffrey Hornaday; ***M:*** Randy Edelman. *MCA*

Shout at the Devil 🦴½ **1976 (PG)** English officer Moore and Irish-American adventurer Marvin seek to blow up a German battleship out for repairs in East Africa before the outbreak of WWI. There's also some intrigue about ivory smuggling. From the novel by Wilbur Smith and based on an actual incident, but that doesn't make the comedy adventure any more palatable. Marvin's hamming is ludicrous, Moore is unusually wooden, and the big budget permits any number of fairly pointless action-oriented excursions and explosions. **128m/C VHS, Beta, LV.** *GB* Lee Marvin, Roger Moore, Barbara Parkins, Ian Holm; ***D:*** Peter Hunt; ***M:*** Maurice Jarre. *LIV, VES*

The Show 🦴🦴 **1995 (R)** Choppy and incoherent behind-the-scenes look at the attitude and people who make up the explosive hip-hop and rap scene. Mixes black and white concert footage and interviews with Russell Simmons, LL Cool J and Snoop Doggy Dogg, who discuss their music and fans. Will be a disappointment for those looking for a more in-depth study of the music, as this exercise merely scratches the surface. Includes an abundance of cameos from today's top hip hop artists such as Notorious B.I.G., Naughty by Nature and Wu-Tang Clan. **90m/B VHS, LV.** Craig Mack, Dr. Dre, Run DMC, Slick Rick, Warren G, Kurtis Blow; ***D:*** Brian Robbins; ***C:*** Larry Banks, Steven Consentino, Ericson Core, John Demps, Todd A Dos Reis. *COL*

Show Boat 🦴🦴🦴🦴 **1936** The second of three film versions of the Jerome Kern/Oscar Hammerstein musical (based on the Edna Ferber novel), filmed previously in 1929, about a Mississippi showboat and the life and loves of its denizens. Wonderful romance, unforgettable music. Director Whale also brought the world "Frankenstein." The laser edition includes a historical audio essay by Miles Kreuger, excerpts from the 1929 version, Ziegfeld's 1932 stage revival, "Life Aboard a Real Showboat" (a vintage short), radio broadcasts, and a 300-photo essay tracing the history of showboats. Remade 15 years later. ♫Ol' Man River; Ah Still Suits Me; Bill; Can't Help Lovin' Dat Man; Only Make Believe; I Have the Room Above Her; You Are Love; Gallivantin' Around; Cotton Blossom. **110m/B VHS, Beta, LV.** Irene Dunne, Allan Jones, Paul Robeson, Helen Morgan, Hattie McDaniel, Charles Winninger, Donald Cook, Bobs Watson; ***D:*** James Whale; ***W:*** Oscar Hammerstein; ***M:*** Oscar Hammerstein, Jerome Kern. *MGM, CRC, MLB*

Show Boat 🦴🦴½ **1951** Third movie version of the 1927 musical about the life and loves of a Mississippi riverboat theater troupe. Terrific musical numbers, with fun dance routines from Champion, who went on to great fame as a choreographer. Grayson is somewhat vapid, but lovely to look at and hear. Gardner didn't want to do the part of Julie, although she eventually received fabulous reviews—her singing was dubbed by Annette Warren. The 171-foot "Cotton Blossom" boat was built on the Tarzan lake on the MGM back lot at an astounding cost of $126,468.00. Warfield's film debut—his "Ole Man River"—was recorded in one take. Laserdisc version features the original motion picture trailer, excerpts from "Broadway," "Silent Film," and radio Version of "Show Boat," a documentary featuring life on a real show boat, and a commentary on the performers, the film, and the history of show boats. ♫Make Believe; Can't Help Lovin' Dat Man; I Might Fall Back On You; Ol' Man River; You Are Love; Why Do I Love You?; Bill; Life Upon the Wicked Stage; After the Ball. **115m/C VHS, Beta, LV.** Kathryn Grayson, Howard Keel, Ava Gardner, William Warfield, Joe E. Brown, Agnes Moorehead, Gower Champion; ***D:*** George Sidney; ***C:*** Charles Rosher; ***M:*** Jerome Kern, Oscar Hammerstein. Nominations: Academy Awards '51: Best Color Cinematography, Best Original Score. *MGM, TLF, CRC*

Show Business 🦴🦴🦴 **1944** Historically valuable film record of classic vaudeville acts, especially Cantor and Davis. A number of vaudevillians recreate their old acts for director Marin—unforgettable slapstick and songs. All this pegged on a plot that follows Cantor's rise to fame with the Ziegfeld Follies. ♫Alabamy Bound; I Want a Girl (Just Like the Girl Who Married Dear Old Dad); It Had to Be You; Makin' Whoopee; Why Am I Blue; They're Wearing 'Em Higher in Hawaii; The Curse of an Aching Heart; While Strolling in the Park One Day; You May Not Remember. **92m/B VHS, Beta, LV.** Eddie Cantor, Joan Davis, George Murphy; ***D:*** Edwin L. Marin. *CCB, TTC*

A Show of Force 🦴🦴 **1990 (R)** Reporter Irving investigates the coverup of a murder with political ramifications. Brazilian director Barreto cast (surprise!) his girlfriend in the lead; she doesn't exactly carry the day. Phillips is good, but you'll end up feeling cheated if you expect to see much of highly-billed Duvall or Garcia. Based on a real incident of 1978, but hardly believable as political realism or even moralism. **93m/C VHS, Beta, LV.** Erik Estrada, Amy Irving, Andy Garcia, Robert Duvall, Lou Diamond Phillips; ***D:*** Bruno Barreto; ***W:*** Evan Jones; ***M:*** Georges Delerue. *PAR*

The Show-Off 🦴½ **1946** Aubrey Piper (Skelton) has big dreams which far out weigh his modest talents. He tells outlandish tales to impress girlfriend Amy (Maxwell) and schemes to make them come true. Dated material which even gifted comedian Skelton can't rescue. Adapted from a play by George Kelly and previously filmed in 1926, 1929, and 1934. **83m/B VHS, Beta.** Red Skelton, Marilyn Maxwell, Marjorie Main, Virginia O'Brien, Eddie Anderson, George Cleveland, Leon Ames, Marshall Thompson, Jacqueline White, Lila Leeds, Emory Parnell; ***D:*** Harry Beaumont; ***W:*** George Wells. *MGM, FCT*

Show People 🦴🦴🦴 **1928** A pretty girl from the boonies tries to make it big in Tinseltown. But as a slapstick star?! She wanted to be a leading lady! Enjoyable, fun silent comedy shows Davies's true talents. Interesting star cameos, including director Vidor at the end. **82m/B VHS.** Marion Davies, William Haines, Dell Henderson, Paul Ralli, William S. Hart, Rod La Rocque; ***Cameos:*** King Vidor; ***D:*** King Vidor. *MGM*

Show Them No Mercy 🦴🦴🦴 *Tainted Money* **1935** A couple and their baby out for a drive unwittingly stumble into a kidnapping that doesn't go as planned. Tense gangster drama reincarnated as the Western "Rawhide." **76m/B VHS.** Rochelle Hudson, Cesar Romero, Bruce Cabot, Edward Norris, Edward Brophy, Warren Hymer, Herbert Rawlinson; ***D:*** George Marshall. *FOX, FCT*

The Showdown 🦴🦴 **1940** The title actually refers to a tricky poker game, the highlight of yet another Hopalong Cassidy versus hoss thieves quickie epic. Kermit Maynard is the brother of cowboy hero Ken Maynard. **65m/B VHS.** William Boyd, Russell Hayden, Britt Wood, Morris Ankrum, Jan Clayton, Roy Barcroft, Kermit Maynard; ***D:*** Howard Bretherton. *NOS*

The Showdown 🦴🦴½ **1950** Elliott plays trail boss Shad Jones who knows one of his fellow cowhands has murdered his brother. Jones is determined to find out who it is and even the score. Brennan is cast against type as a greedy cattle baron. Elliott's last film for Republic. **86m/B VHS.** Wild Bill Elliott, Walter Brennan, Marie Windsor, Harry (Henry) Morgan, Rhys Williams, Jim Davis, Leif Erickson, Yakima Canutt; ***D:*** Stuart E. McGowan, Dorrell McGowan; ***W:*** Stuart E. McGowan, Dorrell McGowan. *REP*

Showdown 🦴🦴½ **1973 (PG)** Billy Massey (Martin) and Chuck Garvis (Hudson) had been friends since childhood, until they fell out over the attentions of the pretty Kate (Clark), whom Chuck married. Chuck became the honest town sheriff while Billy took to train robbing. Now it's up to Chuck to bring Billy to justice. Director Seaton's final film. **99m/C VHS.** Dean Martin, Rock Hudson, Susan Clark, Donald Moffat, John McLiam, Ed Begley Jr.; ***D:*** George Seaton; ***W:*** Theodore Taylor; ***C:*** Ernest Laszlo; ***M:*** David Shire. *MCA, FCT*

Showdown 🦴½ **1993 (R)** A small southern town is taken over by a motorcycle gang whose leader, Kincade, decides to set up his fencing and drug operations there. But the local law enforcement has other ideas, calling in a martial arts expert who wants revenge against Kincade for the death of his partner. **92m/C VHS.** Leo Fong, Werner Hoetzinger, Richard Lynch, Michelle McCormick, Frank Marth, Tom MacDowell, Troy Donahue; ***D:*** Leo Fong; ***W:*** Leo Fong. *AIP*

Showdown 🦴½ **1993 (R)** Ken, the new kid in a particularly nasty high school, gets picked on by the martial-arts expert school bully. After getting beaten up a lot Ken finds out the school janitor can help turn him into a high-kicking fighter. Lots of fast-paced fight scenes which is all the genre demands. An edited PG-13 version is also available. **90m/C VHS, LV.** Ken Scott, Billy Blanks, Patrick Kilpatrick, Kenneth McLeod; ***D:*** Robert Radler. *IMP*

Showdown at Boot Hill 🦴🦴 **1958** A U.S. Marshal (Bronson) kills a wanted murderer but cannot collect the reward because the townspeople will not identify the victim. **76m/B VHS.** Charles Bronson, Robert Hutton, John Carradine; ***D:*** Gene Fowler Jr. *REP*

Showdown at the Equator 🦴 **1983 (R)** Chinese cops are trained to kill criminals with their feet, and they do. **95m/C VHS, Beta.** Lo Lieh, Bruce Liang, Nora Miao, Lee Kan Kwun. *GEM*

Showdown at Williams Creek 🦴🦴½ *Kootenai Brown* **1991 (R)** A graphic Canadian Western set in the old Montana territory, where an outcast settler goes on trial for killing an old man. Testimony recounts a shocking history of greed and betrayal. The dark side of the Gold Rush, generally well-acted. Inspired by an actual incident. **97m/C VHS.** *CA* Tom Burlinson, Donnelly Rhodes, Raymond Burr, Michael Thrush, John Pyper-Ferguson, Alex Bruhanski; ***D:*** Allen Kroeker; ***W:*** John Gray; ***M:*** Michael Conway Baker. *REP*

Showdown in Little Tokyo 🦴🦴 **1991 (R)** Lundgren stars as a martial arts master/L.A. cop who was raised in Japan, and has all the respect in the world for his "ancestors" and heritage. Brandon Lee (son of Bruce) is Lundgren's partner, and he's a bona fide American-made, pop-culture, mall junkie. Together, they go after a crack-smuggling gang of "yakuza" (Japanese thugs). Lots of high-kicking action and the unique angle on stereotypes make this a fun martial arts film. **78m/C VHS, Beta, LV, 8mm.** Dolph Lundgren, Brandon Lee, Tia Carrere, Cary-Hiroyuki Tagawa; ***D:*** Mark L. Lester; ***W:*** Caliope Brattlestreet. *WAR*

Showgirls *Woof!* **1995 (NC-17)** Long on ridiculous dialogue and bad acting and short on costumes, coming-of-age tale follows one young woman as she nakedly climbs the ladder of success as a Vegas showgirl. Oh, the things she must do to be headliner. Berkley makes the jump from television's "Saved by the Bell" to portray Nomi, the young lap dancer with the gift of pelvic thrust and the will to succeed. Whether cavorting clothed or nude, Berkley is uniformly wooden, a mass of lip gloss and mascara struggling to emote. Gershon, as her sly nemesis, brings some wit and splash to her role as the jaded headliner. Eszterhas script descends below its maker's usual standards, which are not particularly high. Titanic amount of female flesh on display fails to give film even a faint hint of sexuality, proof that there is a hell. Rent it, and be prepared to fast forward (to what, we're not sure, though there is a certain camp element that might have been amusing if not imprisoned here). Also available in "R" and unrated versions. **131m/C VHS.** Elizabeth Berkley, Gina Gershon, Kyle MacLachlan, Glenn Plummer, Alan Rachins, Robert Davi, Gina Ravera; ***D:*** Paul Verhoeven; ***W:*** Joe Eszterhas; ***C:*** Jost Vacano; ***M:*** David A. Stewart. Golden Raspberry Awards '95: Worst Picture, Worst Actress (Berkley), Worst Director (Verhoeven), Worst Screenplay, Worst Song ("Walk into the Wind"), Worst New Star (Berkley); Nominations: Golden Raspberry Awards '95: Worst Actor (MacLachlan), Worst Supporting Actor (Davi), Worst Supporting Actress (Gershon). *MGM*

Shredder Orpheus **1989** Rock star Orpheus skateboards through hell to stop deadly television transmissions and rescue his wife. **93m/C VHS, Beta.** Jesse Bernstein, Robert McGinley, Vera McCaughan, Megan Murphy, Carlo Scandiuzzi; ***D:*** Robert McGinley. *AIP*

Shriek in the Night ½ **1933** Two rival reporters (Rogers and Talbot, previously paired in "The Thirteenth Guest") turn detective to solve a string of apartment murders. Made on a proverbial shoestring, but not bad. **66m/B VHS, Beta.** Ginger Rogers, Lyle Talbot, Harvey Clark; ***D:*** Albert Ray. *SNC, NOS, BAR*

Shriek of the Mutilated *Woof!* **1974 (R)** An anthropological expedition on a deserted island turns into a night of horror as a savage beast kills the members of the group one by one. **85m/C VHS, Beta.** Alan Brock, Jennifer Stock, Michael Harris; ***D:*** Michael Findlay. *LIV, SNC*

The Shrieking *Hex* **1973 (PG)** Black magic women hang out with biker types in Nebraska in 1919. **93m/C VHS, Beta, LV.** Keith Carradine, Christina Raines, Gary Busey, Robert Walker Jr., Dan Haggerty, John Carradine, Scott Glenn; ***D:*** Leo Garen; ***M:*** Charles Bernstein. *PSM, IME*

The Shrimp on the Barbie ½ **1990 (R)** When daddy refuses to bless her marriage to dim bulb boyfriend, Australian Samms hires L.A. low life Marin to pose as new beau. Another pseudonymous Smithee effort. **86m/C VHS, Beta, LV.** Richard "Cheech" Marin, Emma Samms, Vernon Wells, Bruce Spence, Carole Davis; ***D:*** Alan Smithee. *MED, VTR*

Shrunken Heads ½ **1994 (R)** Inspired by their comic book heroes three boys try to take on neighborhood thugs only to be gunned down. But along comes Mr. Sumatra, a retired voodoo specialist, who revives the three (in a somewhat smaller form) so they can fight the good fight once again. Title theme music by director Richard's brother, Danny Elfman. **86m/C VHS, Beta, LV.** Aeryk Egan, Meg Foster, Julius W. Harris, Becky Herbst, A.J. Damato, Bo Sharon, Darris Love, Leigh-Allyn Baker, Troy Fromin; ***D:*** Richard Elfman; ***W:*** Matthew Bright; ***M:*** Richard Band. *PAR*

Shy People **1987 (R)** An urbanized New York journalist and her spoiled daughter journey to the Louisiana bayou to visit long-lost relatives in order to produce an article for "Cosmopolitan." They find ignorance, madness, and ancestral secrets and are forced to examine their motives, their relationships and issues brought to light in the watery, murky, fantastic land of the bayous. Well-acted melodrama with an outstanding performance by Hershey as the cajun matriarch. Music by Tangerine Dream; cinematography by Chris Menges. **119m/C VHS, Beta, LV.** Jill Clayburgh, Barbara Hershey, Martha Plimpton, Mare Winningham, Merritt Butrick, John Philbin, Don Swayze, Pruitt Taylor Vince; ***D:*** Andrei Konchalovsky; ***W:*** Gerard Brach, Marjorie David; ***C:*** Chris Menges; ***M:*** Tangerine Dream. Cannes Film Festival '87: Best Actress (Hershey). *WAR*

Siberiade **1979** Depicts life in a Siberian village from 1909 to 1969 for a wealthy family and a peasant clan and how Soviet society affects them. Rambling narrative with strong characters. In Russian with subtitles. **190m/C VHS.** *RU* Vladimir Samoilov, Vitaly Solomin, Nikita Mikhalkov, Ludmila Gurchenko, Nathalia Andretchenko; ***D:*** Andrei Konchalovsky; ***W:*** Valentin Yezhov, Andrei Konchalovsky; ***M:*** Eduard Artemyev. Cannes Film Festival '79: Grand Jury Prize. *KIV*

The Sibling *Psycho Sisters; So Evil, My Sister* **1972 (PG)** Two sisters become involved in the accidental murder of a man who was a husband to one woman and lover to the other. Of course, one sister has just been released from the mental rehabilitation clinic. **85m/C VHS, Beta.** Susan Strasberg, Faith Domergue, Sydney Chaplin, Steve Mitchell; ***D:*** Reginald LeBorg. *PSM, HHE*

Sibling Rivalry **1990 (PG-13)** Repressed doctor's wife (redundant) Alley rolls in hay with soon to be stiff stranger upon advice of footloose sister. Stranger expires from heart attack in hay and Alley discovers that the corpse is her long-lost brother-in-law. Slapstick cover-up ensues. **88m/C VHS, Beta, LV, 8mm.** Kirstie Alley, Bill Pullman, Carrie Fisher, Sam Elliott, Jami Gertz, Ed O'Neill, Scott Bakula, Frances Sternhagen, Bill Macy; ***D:*** Carl Reiner. *COL, SUE, NLC*

The Sicilian ½ **1987** Adapted from the Mario Puzo novel and based on the life of Salvatore Giuliano. Chronicles the exploits of the men who took on the government, the Catholic Church, and the Mafia in an effort to make Sicily secede from Italy and become its own nation in the 1940s. Pretentious, overdone, and confused. This long, uncut version was unseen in America, but hailed by European critics; the 115-minute, R-rated American release is also available, but isn't as good. See "Salvatore Giuliano" (Francesco Rosi, 1962) instead of either version. **146m/C VHS, Beta, LV.** Christopher Lambert, John Turturro, Terence Stamp, Joss Ackland, Barbara Sukowa; ***D:*** Michael Cimino. *LIV, VES*

Sicilian Connection ½ **1974** A narcotics agent poses as a nightclub manager to bust a drug-smuggling organization. **100m/C VHS, Beta.** *IT* Ben Gazzara, Silvia Monti, Fausto Tozzi. *VCD*

The Sicilian Connection *The Pizza Connection* **1985 (R)** Two brothers in the mob serve out vendettas and generally create havoc wherever they go. **117m/C VHS, Beta.** Michele Placido, Mark Switzer, Simona Cavallari. *MGM*

Sid & Nancy ½ **1986 (R)** The tragic, brutal, true love story of The Sex Pistols' Sid Vicious and American groupie Nancy Spungen, from the director of "Repo Man." Remarkable lead performances in a very dark story that manages to be funny at times. Depressing but engrossing; no appreciation of punk music or sympathy for the self-destructive way of life is required. Oldman and Webb are superb. Music by Joe Strummer, the Pogues, and Pray for Rain. **111m/C VHS, Beta, LV.** Gary Oldman, Chloe Webb, Debbie Bishop, David Hayman; ***D:*** Alex Cox; ***W:*** Alex Cox. National Society of Film Critics Awards '86: Best Actress (Webb). *MVD, SUE, NLC*

Side By Side **1988** In the same vein as "Cocoon," three senior citizens who aren't ready to retire decide to start their own business and launch a sportswear company designed for seniors. A witty portrayal of graceful aging that is uneven at times. **100m/C VHS, Beta.** Milton Berle, Sid Caesar, Danny Thomas; ***D:*** Jack Bender. *TRI*

Side Out ½ **1990 (PG-13)** The first major film about volleyball!? What a claim! What a bore. Midwestern college guy spends summer in Southern Cal. working for slumlord uncle; instead enters "the ultimate" beach volleyball touring. Bogus. Don't see it, dude. **100m/C VHS, Beta, LV.** C. Thomas Howell, Peter Horton, Kathy Ireland, Sinjin Smith, Randy Stoklos, Courtney Thorne-Smith, Harley Jane Kozak, Christopher Rydell; ***D:*** Peter Israelson. *COL*

Side Show **1984** A runaway teen joins the circus, witnesses a murder, and must use his wits to stay out of reach of the killer. Forced "suspense" and "drama" of the bad made for TV ilk. **98m/C VHS, Beta.** Lance Kerwin, Red Buttons, Anthony (Tony) Franciosa, Connie Stevens; ***D:*** William Conrad; ***M:*** Ralph Burns. *TWE*

Sideburns **1991** The Pushkin Club, a group of reactionaries who try to remove the western influence from Russia, attack first a rock band, then innocent civilians as they act as a social cleaning service. Uses humor to try and warn people against the rising fascism in Russia because of the battle between conservative and reformist forces. In Russian with English subtitles. **110m/C VHS.** *RU* ***D:*** Yuri Mamin. *FCT*

Sidekicks **1993 (PG)** Cutesy ego vehicle for executive producer Norris. (Brandis) is bullied by the kids at school and doesn't find much support at home from his well-meaning but ineffectual dad. He has a severe case of hero-worship for Norris, who appears as himself in a series of daydream karate sequences, saving the good guy and maiming the bad. Director Norris is actor Norris' brother. Predictable and sappy. **100m/C VHS, LV, 8mm.** Chuck Norris, Jonathan Brandis, Beau Bridges, Mako, Julia Nickson-Soul, Danica McKellar, Richard Moll, Joe Piscopo; ***D:*** Aaron Norris; ***W:*** Donald W. Thompson, Lou Illar; ***M:*** Alan Silvestri, David Shire. *COL*

Sidewalks of London *St. Martin's Lane* **1940** Laughton's a sidewalk entertainer who takes in homeless waif Leigh and puts her in his act and in his heart. Harrison steals her away and before long she's a star in the music halls. Meanwhile, Laughton has fallen on hard times. Memorable performances. **86m/B VHS, Beta.** *GB* Charles Laughton, Vivien Leigh, Rex Harrison; ***D:*** Tim Whelan. *NOS, HHT, CAB*

Sidewalks of New York ½ **1931** A hapless New York millionaire (Keaton) falls for tenement gal Page and tries to win her heart by saving her street urchin brother from joining the local gang of toughs. Keaton was a silent screen classic as a comedian but his talkie career was disappointing as he lost creative control and battled alcohol problems. **74m/B VHS, Beta.** Buster Keaton, Anita Page, Cliff Edwards, Frank LaRue, Frank Rowan, Norman Phillips Jr.; ***D:*** Jules White, Zion Myers. *MGM, FCT*

Sidewinder One **1977 (PG)** Motocross racing is the setting for a romance between a racer and an heiress. Good racing footage, but where's the plot? If you like cars a whole lot . . . **97m/C VHS, Beta.** Michael Parks, Marjoe Gortner, Susan Howard, Alex Cord, Charlotte Rae; ***D:*** Earl Bellamy; ***W:*** Nancy Voyles Crawford. *NLC*

Sidney Sheldon's Bloodline *Woof!* *Bloodline* **1979 (R)** Wealthy businesswoman Hepburn finds she is marked for death by persons unknown. Exquisitely bad trash from another Sheldon bestseller. **116m/C VHS, Beta.** Audrey Hepburn, Ben Gazzara, James Mason, Michelle Phillips, Omar Sharif, Irene Papas, Romy Schneider, Gert Frobe, Maurice Ronet, Beatrice Straight; ***D:*** Terence Young; ***C:*** Frederick A. (Freddie) Young; ***M:*** Ennio Morricone. *PAR*

The Siege of Firebase Gloria ½ **1989** Story of the Marines who risked their lives defending an outpost against overwhelming odds during the 1968 Tet offensive in Vietnam. Purportedly patriotic war drama made by an Australian director; lead Hauser is a disgusting sadist, and plot is hopelessly hackneyed. **95m/C VHS, Beta, LV.** Wings Hauser, R. Lee Ermey; ***D:*** Brian Trenchard-Smith. *FRH*

Siegfried *Siegfrieds Tod; Siegfried's Death* **1924** Half of Lang's epic masterpiece "Der Niebelungen," based on German mythology. Title hero bathes in the blood of a dragon he has slain. He marries a princess, but wicked Queen Brumhilde has him killed. Part two, in which Siegfried's widow marries Attila the Hun, is titled "Kriemheld's Revenge." These dark, brooding, archetypal tours de force were patriotic tributes, and were loved by Hitler. Silent with music score. **100m/B VHS, LV.** *GE* Paul Richter, Margareta Schoen; ***D:*** Fritz Lang. *SNC, NOS, GPV*

Siesta ½ **1987 (R)** Barkin is a professional stunt woman who leaves her current lover/manager, played by Sheen, and returns to visit her former lover and trainer, Byrne, on the eve of his marriage to another woman. Her trip, marked by flashbacks and flights of seemingly paranoid fantasy, leads to the discovery of murder, but she cannot remember who, when, why, or where. The film distorts time, reality, and perception in a sometimes fascinating, sometimes frustrating psychological mystery. Attractively filmed by video director Lambert. Barkin and Byrne were married in real life a year after the film's release. **97m/C VHS, Beta, LV.** Ellen Barkin, Gabriel Byrne, Jodie Foster, Julian Sands, Isabella Rossellini, Martin Sheen, Grace Jones, Alexei Sayle; ***D:*** Mary Lambert; ***W:*** Patricia Louisianna Knop; ***M:*** Miles Davis, Marcus Miller. *ORI, WAR*

Sifted Evidence **1983** Woman archeologist who becomes involved with a man promises to show him an obscure archeological site in Mexico. **42m/C** *NO*

The Sign of Four ½ **1983** Sherlock Holmes and the ever-faithful Watson are hired by a young woman who has been anonymously sent an enormous diamond. An inept production which looks good but that's all. **97m/C VHS, Beta.** *GB* Ian Richardson,

David Healy, Thorley Walters, Cherie Lunghi; ***D:*** Desmond Davis. *PAR*

The Sign of the Cross ½ **1932** Depraved Emperor Nero (Laughton) decides he wants a new city so he burns down Rome—blaming the fire on the Christians he also wants to get rid of (preferably by the lions in the arena). Meanwhile, Marcus (March), the Roman Prefect, has fallen for the virginal Christian Mercia (Landi) and risks his life to save her. Besides Laughton's overwhelmingly hammy performance, Colbert slinks seductively as the emperor's vixenish wife, Poppaea. Again, lots of crowd scenes (DeMille's specialty). Based on the play by Wilson Barrett. **125m/B VHS.** Fredric March, Elissa Landi, Charles Laughton, Claudette Colbert, Ian Keith, Harry Beresford, Arthur Hohl, Nat Pendleton; ***D:*** Cecil B. DeMille; ***W:*** Waldemar Young, Sidney Buchman; ***M:*** Rudolph Kopp. *MCA*

The Sign of Zorro **1960** Adventures of the masked swordsman as he champions the cause of the oppressed in early California. Full-length version of the popular late-50s Disney television series. **89m/C VHS, Beta.** Guy Williams, Henry Calvin, Gene Sheldon, Romney Brent, Britt Lomond, George Lewis, Lisa Gaye; ***D:*** Norman Foster, Lewis R. Foster. *DIS*

Signal 7 **1983** An improvised, neo-verite document of a night in the lives of two San Francisco taxi drivers. Nilsson's first major release and a notable example of his unique scriptless, tape-to-film narrative technique. **89m/C VHS, Beta.** Bill Ackridge, Dan Leegant; ***D:*** Rob Nilsson; ***W:*** Rob Nilsson. *WAR*

Signals Through the Flames **1983** A film by Sheldon Rochlin and Maxine Harris outlining the tumultuous history of the famous experimental group, The Living Theatre. **97m/C VHS, Beta.** Julian Beck, Judith Malina, Maxine Harris; ***D:*** Sheldon Rochlin. *MFV, TPV*

Signs of Life *Lebenszeichen* **1968** German soldier Stroszek (Brogle), injured during the occupation of Crete, is sent to recuperate on the remote island of Kos. With his Greek wife Nora, Stroszek has nothing to do but guard a deserted fortress and a store of abandoned ammunition. But soon the suspicious natives and the isolation begin to drive Stroszek to madness and he decides to blow up the ammunition dump (and the island along with it). German with subtitles. **90m/B VHS.** *GE* Peter Brogle, Wolfgang Reichmann, Athina Zacharopoulous, Wolfgang Stumpf; ***D:*** Werner Herzog; ***W:*** Werner Herzog; ***C:*** Thomas Mauch; ***M:*** Stavros Xarchakos. *NYF*

Signs of Life ½ *One for Sorrow, Two for Joy* **1989 (PG-13)** A boat-building company in Maine closes its doors after centuries in business; the employees and families whose lives have been defined by it for generations learn to cope. Wonderful performances compensate only partly for a week script. An episode on PBS's "American Playhouse." **95m/C VHS, Beta, LV.** Beau Bridges, Arthur Kennedy, Vincent D'Onofrio, Kevin J. O'Connor, Will Patton, Kate Reid, Michael Lewis, Kathy Bates, Mary-Louise Parker, Georgia Engel; ***D:*** John David Coles; ***W:*** Mark Malone; ***M:*** Howard Shore. *LIV*

Silas Marner **1985** Superb made for British television adaptation of the 1861 George Eliot classic about an itinerant weaver subjected to criminal accusation, poverty, and exile. Wonderful detail and splendid acting. Shot on location in the Cotswold district of England. **92m/C VHS, Beta.** *GB* Ben Kingsley, Jenny Agutter, Patrick Ryecart, Patsy Kensit; ***D:*** Giles Foster; ***M:*** Carl Davis. *VCO, FOX, TVC*

The Silence *Tystnaden* **1963** A brutal, enigmatic allegory about two sisters, one a nymphomaniac, the other a violently frustrated lesbian, traveling with the former's young son to an unnamed country beset by war. Fascinating and memorable but frustrating and unsatisfying: What is it about? What is it an allegory of? Where is the narrative? The third in Bergman's crisis-of-faith trilogy following "Through a Glass Darkly" and "Winter Light." In Swedish with English subtitles or dubbed. **95m/B VHS, Beta, LV.** *SW* Ingrid Thulin, Gunnel Lindstrom, Birger Malmsten; ***D:*** Ingmar Bergman; ***W:*** Ingmar Bergman; ***C:*** Sven Nykvist. *HMV, INJ, NLC*

Silence *Crazy Jack and the Boy* **1973 (G)** An autistic boy gets lost in the wilderness and faces an array of difficulties while his foster parents search for him. **82m/C VHS, Beta.** Will Geer, Ellen Geer, Richard Kelton, Ian Geer Flanders, Craig Kelly; ***D:*** John Korty. *NO*

Silence Like Glass ½ **1990 (R)** Diagnosed with life-threatening illness, two young women struggle to overcome their anger at their fate. They find friendship and together, search for reasons to live. Fine performances, with pacing that keeps the melodrama to a minimum. **102m/C VHS, Beta, LV.** Jami Gertz, Martha Plimpton, George Peppard, Rip Torn, James Remar; ***D:*** Carl Schenkel; ***M:*** Anne Dudley. *MED, VTR*

Silence of the Hams ½ **1993 (R)** Very feeble parody of "The Silence of the Lambs" and others in the thriller/horror genre. Director/writer Greggio also stars as the murder victim, stabbed in the shower, who narrates the story in flashback. There's an eager FBI recruit, a femme fatale, assorted cameo turns, and DeLuise, chewing more scenery than even Anthony Hopkins could swallow, as nutcase Dr. Animal Cannibal Pizza. **85m/C VHS.** Ezio Greggio, Dom DeLuise, Billy Zane, Joanna Pacula, Charlene Tilton, Martin Balsam; ***Cameos:*** Stuart Pankin, John Astin, Phyllis Diller, Bubba Smith, Larry Storch, Rip Taylor, Shelley Winters, Mel Brooks, John Landis, John Carpenter, Joe Dante; ***D:*** Ezio Greggio; ***W:*** Ezio Greggio; ***C:*** Jacques Haitkin. *CAF*

Silence of the Heart **1984** Mother copes with aftermath of suicide of teenage son following her recent divorce. Hartley is captivating in this gripping drama. **100m/C VHS.** Mariette Hartley, Dana Hill, Howard Hesseman, Chad Lowe, Charlie Sheen; ***D:*** Richard Michaels; ***W:*** Phil Penningroth; ***M:*** Georges Delerue. *PMH, HHE, VTR*

The Silence of the Lambs ½ **1991 (R)** Foster is FBI cadet Clarice Starling, a woman with ambition, a cum laude degree in psychology, and a traumatic childhood. When a serial killer begins his ugly rounds, the FBI wants psychological profiles from other serial killers and she's sent to collect a profile from one who's exceptionally clever—psychiatrist Hannibal Lector, a vicious killer prone to dining on his victims. Brilliant performances from Foster and Hopkins, finely detailed supporting characterizations, and elegant pacing from Demme. Some brutal visual effects. Excellent portrayals of women who refuse to be victims. Based on the Thomas Harris novel. **118m/C VHS, Beta, LV.** Jodie Foster, Anthony Hopkins, Scott Glenn, Ted Levine, Brooke Smith, Charles Napier, Roger Corman, Anthony Heald, Diane Baker, Chris Isaak; ***D:*** Jonathan Demme; ***W:*** Ted Tally; ***C:*** Tak Fujimoto; ***M:*** Howard Shore. Academy Awards '91: Best Actor (Hopkins), Best Actress (Foster), Best Adapted Screenplay, Best Director (Demme), Best Picture; British Academy Awards '91: Best Actor (Hopkins), Best Actress (Foster); Directors Guild of America Awards '91: Best Director (Demme); Golden Globe Awards '92: Best Actress—Drama (Foster); National Board of Review Awards '91: Best Director (Demme), Best Film, Best Supporting Actor (Hopkins); People's Choice Awards '92: Best Film—Drama; Writers Guild of America '91: Best Adapted Screenplay; Nominations: Academy Awards '91: Best Film Editing, Best Sound. *ORI, FCT, IME*

Silence of the North ½ **1981 (PG)** A widow (Burstyn) with three children struggles to survive under rugged pioneer conditions on the Canadian frontier. The scenery is, not surprisingly, stunning. Based on a true but generic story. **94m/C VHS, Beta.** *CA* Ellen Burstyn, Tom Skerritt; ***D:*** Allan Winton King; ***M:*** Michael Conway Baker. *MCA*

The Silencer **1992 (R)** Walden stars as Harley-riding Angel who is out to stop a slavery and prostitution ring that abuses young runaways. Video-arcades hold the clues, and Angel must learn to kill without a conscience. Every time she kills, Angel seeks comfort in the arms of anonymous lovers. However, what she doesn't know is that her demented ex-boyfriend is watching. **85m/C VHS.** Lynette Walden, Chris Mulkey, Paul Ganus, Morton Downey Jr.; ***D:*** Amy Goldstein; ***W:*** Amy Goldstein, Scott Kraft. *ACA*

The Silencers ½ **1995 (R)** Secret Service agent Chuck Rafferty (Scalia) discovers that his latest enemies, known as the Men In Black, are actually human-appearing aliens seeking to conquer Earth. Now Rafferty's only hope is to team up with inter-galactic peace officer Condor (Christopher) to defeat this evil. **103m/C VHS.** Jack Scalia, Dennis Christopher, Clarence Williams III, Carlos Lauchu, Lucinda Weist; ***D:*** Richard Pepin. *PMH*

Silent Assassins **1988** Fists and bullets fly when a scientist is kidnapped in order to gain secrets to biological warfare. Chong and Rhee, real-life owners of a martial arts studio, produced and choreographed the film. Blair is here, but doesn't figure much. A notch up from most similar martial arts pics. **92m/C VHS.** Sam Jones, Linda Blair, Jun Chong, Phillip Rhee; ***D:*** Scott Thomas, Lee Doo-yong. *MCG, VTR*

Silent Code **1935** A Mountie is framed for the murder of a young miner. **55m/B VHS, Beta.** Tom Tyler. *NO*

The Silent Enemy ½ **1958** The true-life exploits of British frogmen battling Italian foes during WWII. Suspenseful and engrossing; good performances and good rendering of underwater action. Video release snips twenty minutes from the original and adds color. **91m/C VHS, Beta.** *GB* Laurence Harvey, John Clements, Michael Craig, Dawn Addams, Sidney James, Alec McCowen, Nigel Stock; ***D:*** William Fairchild. *NO*

Silent Fall ½ **1994 (R)** Grisly double murder of his parents is witnessed by autistic 9-year-old, Tim Warden (Faulkner), and his traumatized over-protective teenaged sister Sylvie (Tyler). Retired psychiatrist Jake Rainier (Dreyfuss) is reluctant to get involved, ever since an autistic child in his care died, but when authoritarian rival Dr. Harlinger (Lithgow) is called instead, Jake changes his mind. Second half of film takes a lurid turn as Jake probes Tim's damaged psyche to discover the killer. Trite, clueless whodunnit that generally wastes the talent involved; Tyler and Faulkner make their film debuts. **101m/C VHS, LV.** Richard Dreyfuss, Ben Faulkner, John Lithgow, Liv Tyler, Linda Hamilton, J.T. Walsh; ***D:*** Bruce Beresford; ***W:*** Akiva Goldsman; ***M:*** Stewart Copeland. *WAR*

Silent Hunter ½ **1994 (R)** Undercover cop Jim Paradine (O'Keeffe) retreats to a remote mountains cabin when his family is killed by a gang of bank robbers. Naturally, the thugs just happen to crash land on Paradine's mountain top with their stolen loot and he goes off to hunt them down. **97m/C VHS, LV.** Miles O'Keeffe, Fred Williamson, Lynne Adams, Peter Colvey, Jason Cavalier, Sabine Karsenti; ***D:*** Fred Williamson. *TTC, NLC*

Silent Killers ½ **19??** A scientist is responsible for the deaths of many people because of his research in germ warfare. He's haunted by the ghosts of his victims. Is he losing his mind or is it a sinister plot? **90m/C VHS.** Stephen Soul, Daniel Garfield. *MOV*

Silent Laugh Makers, No. 1 **1915** Four hilarious short movies from the silent era: "Looking for Sally," about an immigrant in search of his best girlfriend; "Lucky Dog," with the young Laurel and Hardy; "His Night Out," about a wild evening with Charlie Chaplin and Ben Turpin; and "Hop-a-Long." Non-stop side-splitting fun. **50m/B VHS, Beta.** Charley Chase, Stan Laurel, Oliver Hardy, Charlie Chaplin, Ben Turpin, Arthur Lake. *VYY*

Silent Laugh Makers, No. 2 **1917** Several short funny films of the silent picture era: "Fluttering Hearts," "Long Live the King," about a king who just can't get along with his nobles, starring Chase and Hardy; and "A Sea Dog Tale." All are unremittingly hilarious. **50m/B VHS, Beta.** Charley Chase, Oliver Hardy, Billy Bevan. *VYY*

Silent Laugh Makers, No. 3 **1919** Four comedy shorts: "Picking Peaches" (1924), directed by Frank Capra, Langdon's first for Mack Sennett; "All Tied Up" (1925), featuring "A Ton of Fun"-four rotund comedians; "Don't Shove" (1919), featuring Harold Lloyd wooing Bebe Daniels; and "Some

Baby" (1922), with Snub Pollard. **55m/B VHS, Beta.** Harry Langdon, Harold Lloyd, Bebe Daniels, Snub Pollard. *VYY*

Silent Madness **1984 (R)** A psychiatrist must stop a deranged killer, escaped from an asylum, from slaughtering helpless college coeds in a sorority house. Meanwhile, hospital execs send orderlies to kill the patient, to conceal their mistake. Ludicrous. **93m/C VHS, Beta.** Belinda J. Montgomery, Viveca Lindfors, Sydney Lassick; ***D:*** Simon Nuchtern. *MED*

The Silent Mr. Sherlock Holmes **1912** These two silent shorts are a rare treat for Holmes fans. "The Copper Beeches" was produced with the "personal supervision of Arthur Conan Doyle." In "The Man with the Twisted Lip," Holmes is hired to find out whether a banker was murdered. **68m/B VHS.** *GB* Ellie Norwood. *VYY*

Silent Motive ½ **1991** Laura is a Hollywood screenwriter who's shocked to discover that a killer is using her recent script as an outline for a series of film-industry murders. She's even more unnerved when a detective makes Laura his number one suspect. **90m/C VHS.** Patricia Wettig, Mike Farrell, Ed Asner, Rick Springfield, David Packer; ***D:*** Lee Philips; ***W:*** William Bekkala. *WOV*

Silent Movie ½ **1976 (PG)** A has-been movie director (Brooks) is determined to make a comeback and save his studio from being taken over by a conglomerate. Hilarious at times but uneven. An original idea; not as successful as it could have been. Has music and sound effects, but only one word of spoken dialogue by famous mime Marceau. **88m/C VHS, Beta, LV.** Mel Brooks, Marty Feldman, Dom DeLuise, Burt Reynolds, Anne Bancroft, James Caan, Liza Minnelli, Paul Newman, Sid Caesar, Bernadette Peters, Harry Ritz, Marcel Marceau; ***D:*** Mel Brooks; ***W:*** Mel Brooks, Ron Clark, Rudy DeLuca, Barry Levinson. National Board of Review Awards '76: 10 Best Films of the Year. *FOX*

Silent Movies...Just For the Fun of It! **1926** Three short silent films: "The Iron Mule" (1925), "For Sadie's Sake" (1926), and "Hazel from Hollywood" (1918). **56m/B VHS, Beta, 8mm.** Jimmie Adams, Dorothy Devore, Al "Fuzzy" St. John. *VYY*

Silent Night, Bloody Night *Night of the Dark Full Moon; Death House* **1973 (R)** An escaped lunatic terrorizes a small New England town, particularly a mansion that was once an insane asylum. Not great, but well done by director Gershuny, with some nail-biting suspense and slick scene changes. **83m/C VHS.** Patrick O'Neal, John Carradine, Walter Abel, Mary Woronov, Astrid Heeren, Candy Darling; ***D:*** Theodore Gershuny. *NO*

Silent Night, Deadly Night **1984 (R)** A psycho ax-murders people while dressed as jolly old St. Nick. Violent and disturbing, to say the least. Caused quite a controversy when it was released to theaters. Santa gimmick sold some tickets at the time, but resist the urge to rent it: it's completely devoid of worth, whatever the killer's outfit. As if one were not enough, we've been blessed with four sequels. **92m/C VHS, Beta, LV.** Lilyan Chauvin, Gilmer McCormick, Toni Nero; ***D:*** Charles E. Sellier; ***M:*** Perry Botkin. *LIV, IME*

Silent Night, Deadly Night 2 **1987 (R)** The psychotic little brother of the psychotic, Santa Claus-dressed killer from the first film exacts revenge, covering the same bloody ground as before. Almost half tl.is sequel consists of scenes lifted whole from the original. **88m/C VHS, Beta, LV.** Eric Freeman, James Newman, Elizabeth Cayton, Jean Miller; ***D:*** Lee Harry; ***M:*** Michael Armstrong. *LIV*

Silent Night, Deadly Night 3: Better Watch Out! ½ **1989 (R)** The now grown-up psycho goes up against a young blind woman. Santa is no longer the bad guy, thank goodness. The least bad of the lot, with black humor—though not enough to make it worth seeing. **90m/C VHS, Beta, LV.** Richard Beymer, Bill Moseley, Samantha Scully, Eric Da Re, Laura Herring, Robert Culp; ***D:*** Monte Hellman. *LIV*

Silent Night, Deadly Night 4: Initiation **1990 (R)** A secret L.A. cult of she-demons use the slasher Ricky for their own ends—making for more mayhem and horror. Has virtually nothing to do with its three "sequels"—which is not to say it's very good. **90m/C VHS, LV.** Maud Adams, Allyce Beasley, Clint Howard, Reggie Bannister; ***D:*** Brian Yuzna. *MOV*

Silent Night, Deadly Night 5: The Toymaker **1991 (R)** A young boy's Christmas is overrun by murderous Santas and viscious stuffed animals. Definitely for fans of the genre only. **90m/C VHS.** Mickey Rooney, William Thorne, Jane Higginson. *LIV*

Silent Night, Lonely Night **1969** Two lonely middle-aged people (Bridges and Jones) begin an affair at Christmas to stem the pain of their separately disintegrating marriages. Poignant but not successfully credible. Based on the play by Robert Anderson. Made for television. **98m/C VHS, Beta.** Lloyd Bridges, Shirley Jones, Jeff Bridges, Cloris Leachman, Carrie Snodgress, Lynn Carlin; ***D:*** Daniel Petrie; ***M:*** Billy Goldenberg. *MCA*

The Silent One ½ **1986** Featuring underwater photography by Ron and Valerie Taylor, this is the odd story of a mysterious Polynesian boy who has a nautical relationship with a sea turtle. **96m/C VHS, Beta.** *NZ* Telo Malese, George Henare; ***D:*** Yvonne Mackay. *NO*

The Silent Partner **1978** A bank teller (Gould) foils a robbery, but manages to take some money for himself. The unbalanced robber (Plummer) knows it and wants the money. Good script and well directed, with emphasis on suspense and detail. Unexpectedly violent at times. Early, non-comedic role for big guy Candy. **103m/C VHS, Beta, LV.** *CA* Elliott Gould, Christopher Plummer, Susannah York, John Candy; ***D:*** Daryl Duke; ***W:*** Curtis Hanson; ***C:*** Billy Williams. *VES*

The Silent Passenger ½ **1935** Amateur sleuth Lord Peter Wimsey makes cinematic debut investigating murder and blackmail on the British railway. Dorothy Sayer's character later inspired BBC mystery series. **75m/B VHS, Beta.** *GB* John Loder, Peter Haddon, Mary Newland, Austin Trevor, Donald Wolfit, Leslie Perrins, Aubrey Mather, Ralph Truman; ***D:*** Reginald Denham. *NOS, SNC*

Silent Rage **1982 (R)** Sheriff Norris of a small Texas town must destroy killer Libby who has been made indestructible through genetic engineering. Chuck Norris meets Frankenstein, sort of. Nice try, but still thoroughly stupid and boring. **100m/C VHS, Beta, LV, 8mm.** Chuck Norris, Ron Silver, Steven Keats, Toni Kalem, Brian Libby; ***D:*** Michael Miller; ***M:*** Peter Bernstein. *COL*

Silent Raiders **1954** A commando unit is sent to France in 1943 to knock out a Nazi communications center. **72m/B VHS, Beta.** Richard Bartlett, Earle Lyon, Jeanette Bordeau; ***M:*** Elmer Bernstein. *NO*

Silent Rebellion ½ **1982** A Greek immigrant (Savalas) and his son return to Greece, where they reunite with mother and brother and re-discover their heritage and each other. Cross-cultural misunderstandings abound; could have been interesting, but the story is just too generic and uninspired. **90m/C VHS, Beta.** Telly Savalas, Keith Gordon, Michael Constantine, Yula Gavala. *NO*

Silent Running **1971 (G)** Members of a space station orbiting Saturn care for the last vegetation of a nuclear-devastated earth. When orders come to destroy the vegetation, Dern takes matters into his own hands. Speculative sci-fi at its best. Trumbull's directorial debut; he created special effects for "2001" and "Close Encounters." Strange music enhances the alien atmosphere. **90m/C VHS, Beta, LV.** Bruce Dern, Cliff Potts, Ron Rifkin; ***D:*** Douglas Trumbull; ***W:*** Michael Cimino, Deric Washburn, Steven Bochco; ***M:*** Prof. Peter Schickele. *MCA*

Silent Scream ½ **1980 (R)** College kids take up residence with the owners of an eerie mansion complete with obligatory murders. Obvious to the point of being gratuitous—and just plain uninteresting. **87m/C VHS, Beta.** Rebecca Balding, Cameron Mitchell, Avery Schreiber, Barbara Steele, Steve Doubet, Brad Reardon, Yvonne De Carlo; ***D:*** Denny Harris; ***W:*** Wallace C. Bennett, Jim Wheat, Ken Wheat. *MED*

Silent Scream **1984** A former Nazi concentration camp commandant collects unusual animals and humans as a hobby. **60m/C VHS, Beta.** *GB* Peter Cushing, Brian Cox, Elaine Donnelly; ***D:*** Alan Gibson. *LIV*

Silent Tongue **1992 (PG-13)** Weird western finds the crazed Talbot Roe (Phoenix) alone in the wilderness, guarding the tree that is the burial place of his half-breed wife Awbonnie (Tousey). Roe's father (Harris) bought his son's bride from her greedy and abusive father McCree (Bates). In an effort to return Talbot to some semblance of normality, Roe offers to buy McCree's other daughter (Arredondo) for his son. But Talbot is haunted by his wife's angry ghost, who wants her spirit set free by ritual burning, and McCree himself fears the vengeance of his one-time Indian wife Silent Tongue (Cardinal). Messy, over-the-top plot with some poignant performances, especially Phoenix's. **101m/C VHS, LV.** River Phoenix, Sheila Tousey, Richard Harris, Alan Bates, Jeri Arrendondo, Dermot Mulroney, Tantoo Cardinal; ***Cameos:*** Bill Irwin, David Shiner; ***D:*** Sam Shepard; ***W:*** Sam Shepard; ***M:*** Patrick O'Hearn. *VMK*

The Silent Touch ½ **1994 (PG-13)** Irascible, aged composer Henry Kesdi (Von Sydow), living in Denmark with his long-suffering wife Helena (Miles), hasn't written a note in 40 years. Music student Stefan (Blutheau) dreams of a composition he believes Henry started but never completed. So Stefan naturally sets out to help Henry finish his symphony by mystically healing his composer's block. Yes, it does sound hokey but the fluff is saved by Von Sydow's boyantly funny performance. **92m/C VHS.** *PL DK GB* Max von Sydow, Lothaire Bluteau, Sarah Miles, Sofie Graboel, Aleksander Bardini, Peter Hesse Overgaard; ***D:*** Krzysztof Zanussi; ***W:*** Peter Morgan, Mark Wadlow; ***M:*** Wojciech Kilar. *ACA, FCT*

Silent Valley **1935** Adventure of the Old West with American cowboy star Tom Tyler. **60m/B VHS, Beta.** Tom Tyler. *NOS, VCN, DVT*

Silent Victim ½ **1992 (R)** Greene stars as Bonnie Jackson, a Georgia housewife whose marriage has not only gone wrong but turned violent. She takes a drug overdose in a suicide attempt but it results only in a miscarriage. Her furious husband sues her for the murder of their unborn child while an ambitious district attorney petitions the state to charge Bonnie with committing an illegal abortion. Bonnie's torment soon becomes a media circus as she goes on trial. Based on a true story. **116m/C VHS.** Michelle Greene, Kyle Secor, Ely Pouget, Alex Hyde-White, Dori Brenner, Leann Hunley; ***D:*** Menahem Golan; ***W:*** Nelly Adnil, Jonathan Platnick; ***M:*** William T. Stromberg. *COL*

Silent Victory: The Kitty O'Neil Story **1979** Genuinely stirring real-life-overcoming-adversity story of the deaf woman who became a top stunt woman in Hollywood and holder of the land speed record for women. Channing is very good as O'Neil. Made for television. **96m/C Beta.** Stockard Channing, Brian Dennehy, Colleen Dewhurst, Edward Albert, James Farentino; ***D:*** Lou Antonio. *NO*

Silent Witness **1985 (R)** A woman (Bertinelli) witnesses her brother-in-law and his friend rape a young woman. She must decide whether to testify against them or keep the family secret. Exploitative and weakly plotted. Rip-off of the much-discussed Massachusetts barroom rape case. Made for television. **97m/C VHS, Beta.** Valerie Bertinelli, John Savage, Chris Nash, Melissa Leo, Pat Corley, Steven Williams, Jacqueline Brookes, Alex McArthur, Katie McCombs; ***D:*** Michael Miller. *ACA*

Silhouette **1991 (R)** Detained in a small Texas town, a woman witnesses the murder of a local girl—but in silhouette, so the killer's identity takes a feature-length running time to resolve. A fair but contrived made for cable TV thriller that the leading lady co-produced. **89m/C VHS.** Faye Dunaway, David

Rasche, John Terry, Carlos Gomez, Ron Campbell, Margaret Blye, Talisa Soto, Ritch Brinkley; **D:** Carl Schenkel; **W:** Victor Buell. *MCA*

Silk 🦴 **1986 (R)** A beautiful and bloodthirsty detective cuts a swath through local heroin rings. **84m/C VHS, Beta.** Cec Verrell, Bill McLaughlin, Fred Bailey; **D:** Cirio H. Santiago. *MGM*

Silk 2 🦴 **1989 (R)** A foreign-made sequel, in which a beautiful cop stops crime in Honolulu. Ludicrous plot, bad acting, lots of skin and violence—what more could you want? Dreadful. **85m/C VHS, Beta.** Monique Gabrielle, Peter Nelson, Jan Merlin, Maria Clair; **D:** Cirio H. Santiago. *MGM*

Silk Degrees 🦴½ **1994 (R)** Actress witnesses a murder and is targeted for elimination by the killer. She's supposed to be protected by a couple of federal agents but it seems there's a traitor around. **81m/C VHS, LV.** Deborah Shelton, Marc Singer, Mark Hamill, Michael Des Barres, Charles Napier, Gilbert Gottfried, Adrienne Barbeau; **D:** Armand Garabidian; **W:** Stuart Gibbs, Douglas J. Sloan, Robert Gottlieb; **M:** Larry Wolff. *IMP*

Silk n' Sabotage 🦴½ **1994** Serious-minded Jamie comes up with a program for a new computer game. When it's stolen by a con artist, Jamie and her frivolous roommates team up to retrieve it. Since the roomies operate a lingerie business there's lots of pulchritude on display. Also available unrated. **70m/C VHS, Beta, LV.** Cherilyn Shea, Stephanie Champlin, Julie Skiru; **D:** Joe Cauley. *ACA*

The Silk Road 🦴🦴½ **1992 (PG-13)** In 11th-century China the ancient trading route leads to Dun Huang, a desert city that is the last Chinese outpost on the road. Zhao, a young scholar, travels in a caravan which is attacked by Chinese mercenaries. His life is spared and when his new home is attacked by a neighboring nation, he hides the city's treasures in nearby caves. Adapted from the novel by Yashushi Inoue, which was based on the Thousand Buddha Caves, where a treasure of Buddhist icons and scrolls were discovered in 1900. Billed as an epic, there's lots of pageantry and some impressive battle scenes but is too stately and overdone to be more than merely interesting. In Japanese with English subtitles. **99m/C VHS, LV.** *CH JP* Koichi Sato, Toshiyuki Nishida, Anna Nakagawa, Tsunehiko Watase, Daijiro Harada, Takahiro Tamura; **D:** Junya Sato; **M:** Masaru Sato. *VMK, INJ*

Silk Stockings 🦴🦴🦴 **1957** Splendid musical comedy adaptation of "Ninotchka," with Astaire as a charming American movie man, and Charisse as the cold Soviet official whose commie heart he melts. Music and lyrics by Cole Porter highlight this film adapted from George S. Kaufman's hit Broadway play. Director Mamoulian's last film. ♫Too Bad; Paris Loves Lovers; Fated to Be Mated; The Ritz Roll 'n Rock; Silk Stockings; Red Blues; All of You; Stereophonic Sound; Josephine. **117m/C VHS, Beta, LV.** Fred Astaire, Cyd Charisse, Janis Paige, Peter Lorre, George Tobias; **D:** Rouben Mamoulian; **M:** Andre Previn. *MGM, TTC*

Silkwood 🦴🦴🦴 **1983 (R)** The story of Karen Silkwood, who died in a 1974 car crash under suspicious circumstances. She was a nuclear plant worker and activist who was investigating shoddy practices at the plant. Streep acts up a storm, disappearing completely into her character. Cher surprises with her fine portrayal of a lesbian co-worker, and Russell is also good. Nichols has a tough time since we already know the ending, but he brings top-notch performances from his excellent cast. **131m/C VHS, Beta, LV.** Meryl Streep, Kurt Russell, Cher, Diana Scarwid, Bruce McGill, Fred Ward, David Strathairn, Ron Silver, Josef Sommer, Craig T. Nelson; **D:** Mike Nichols; **W:** Nora Ephron, Alice Arlen; **M:** Georges Delerue. Golden Globe Awards '84: Best Supporting Actress (Cher); Nominations: Academy Awards '83: Best Actress (Streep), Best Director (Nichols), Best Film Editing, Best Original Screenplay, Best Supporting Actress (Cher). *PAR*

Silver Bandit 🦴 **1947** A bookkeeper is sent to investigate a mine theft. Along the way he sings country and western songs. **54m/B VHS, Beta, LV.** Spade Cooley. *NOS*

Silver Bears 🦴🦴 **1978 (PG)** Caine is an unlikely mobster in this comedy. He's sent to Switzerland to buy a bank for laundering purposes and ends up being swindled himself. So-so entry adapted from the novel by Paul Erdman. **114m/C VHS, Beta.** Michael Caine, Cybill Shepherd, Louis Jourdan, Stephane Audran, David Warner, Tom Smothers, Martin Balsam, Jay Leno, Charles Gray, Joss Ackland; **D:** Ivan Passer; **M:** Claude Bolling. *NO*

The Silver Bullet **1934** Follows the adventures of Tom, the sheriff of a small gold mining town. **55m/C VHS.** Tom Tyler, Jayne Regan, Lafe McKee, Charles King, George Chesebro, Charles "Slim" Whitaker, Lew Meehan, Franklyn Farnum, Walt Williams; **D:** Bernard B. Ray. *GPV*

Silver Bullet 🦴🦴 *Stephen King's Silver Bullet* **1985 (R)** Adapted from Stephen King's "Cycle of the Werewolf," about a town whose inhabitants are being brutally murdered. It finally dawns on them the culprit is a werewolf. Action moves along at a good clip and the film has its share of suspense. **95m/C VHS, LV.** Corey Haim, Gary Busey, Megan Follows, Everett McGill; **D:** Daniel Attias; **W:** Stephen King. *PAR*

The Silver Chalice 🦴 **1954** Newman's career somehow survived his movie debut in this bloated, turgid Biblical epic about the momentous events that befall a young Greek sculptor who fashions the cup that will be used at the Last Supper. Newman later took out an ad in Variety to apologize for the film, in which Greene also made his debut. Based on the novel by Thomas Costain. **135m/C VHS, Beta.** Paul Newman, Virginia Mayo, Pier Angeli, Jack Palance, Natalie Wood, Joseph Wiseman, Lorne Greene, E.G. Marshall; **D:** Victor Saville; **M:** Franz Waxman. Nominations: Academy Awards '54: Best Color Cinematography, Best Original Score. *WAR*

Silver City 🦴🦴 **1984 (PG)** A saga depicting the plight of Polish refugees in Australia in 1949. A pair of lovers find each other in a crowded refugee camp. He's married to her friend. Too-complex, slow but earnest effort. **110m/C VHS, Beta.** *AU* Gosia Dobrowolska, Ivar Kants; **D:** Sophia Turkiewicz. *ORI*

Silver City Bonanza 🦴🦴½ **1951** Lots of action in this outrageous oater that includes a haunted ranch and an undersea battle as plot devices. Singing cowboy Allen and sidekick Ebsen use a seeing-eye dog to track down the killer of a blind man. Since Roy Rogers and Republic parted company the year of this film's release, singing star Allen was groomed to become the new "King of the Cowboys." However, by this time, the singing-cowboy craze was almost old hat. **67m/B VHS.** Rex Allen, Buddy Ebsen, Mary Ellen Kay, Billy Kimbley, Alix Ebsen, Bill Kennedy, Gregg Barton, Clem Bevans; **D:** George Blair; **W:** Bob Williams. *MOV*

Silver City Kid 🦴 **1945** A foreman for a silver mine exposes a corrupt local banker as a thief. **56m/B VHS, Beta.** Allan "Rocky" Lane. *DVT*

Silver Dream Racer 🦴½ **1983 (PG)** An English grease monkey wants to win the World Motorcycle Championship title away from an American biker. He's also after someone else's girlfriend. Boring, stilted, unoriginal "Big Race" flick. **103m/C VHS, Beta.** Beau Bridges, David Essex, Christina Raines, Diane Keen, Harry H. Corbett; **D:** David Wickes; **M:** David Essex. *LIV, VES*

The Silver Horde 🦴🦴½ **1930** Alaskan salmon fishery owner McCrea battles villainous competitor Gordon for both his livelihood and his lady-friend—dancehall dame Brent. Arthur's the society gal who briefly catches McCrea's eye. Silent screen star Sweet ended her career with a brief role. Based on a novel by Rex Beach. **80m/B VHS.** Joel McCrea, Evelyn Brent, Jean Arthur, Gavin Gordon, Louis Wolheim, Raymond Hatton, Blanche Sweet; **D:** George Archainbaud. *FCT*

Silver Lode 🦴🦴½ **1954** A man accused of murder on his wedding day attempts to clear his name while the law launches an intensive manhunt for him. Ordinary story improved by good, energetic cast. **92m/C VHS, Beta.** John Payne, Dan Duryea, Lizabeth Scott, Stuart Whitman; **D:** Allan Dwan. *NO*

Silver Queen 🦴🦴 **1942** A woman finds out her father has gambled away a silver mine and left her with debts. She opens a saloon, only to have her fiance use the money to hunt for more silver. **81m/B VHS, Beta.** Priscilla Lane, George Brent, Bruce Cabot, Eugene Pallette; **D:** Lloyd Bacon. Nominations: Academy Awards '42: Best Interior Decoration, Best Original Score. *NO*

Silver River 🦴½ **1948** Average western that marked the final collaboration between director Walsh and star Flynn. It never even comes close to their previous works. Flynn plays a no-good, power-hungry cad who will stop at nothing to get what he wants. He happens to want Sheridan, who is married to Bennett, so Flynn schemes to get rid of him. Overall, Flynn acts as though he really isn't interested in the material and had to make a pact with Walsh that he would stay sober until five in the afternoon while filming. Based on an unpublished novel by Stephen Longstreet. **108m/B VHS.** Errol Flynn, Ann Sheridan, Thomas Mitchell, Bruce (Herman Brix) Bennett, Tom D'Andrea, Barton MacLane, Monte Blue, Jonathan Hale; **D:** Raoul Walsh; **W:** Stephen Longstreet, Harriet Frank Jr.; **M:** Max Steiner. *MGM*

Silver Spurs 🦴½ **1943** Villain tries to get some oil-rich property by murdering the ranch's owner. Ranch foreman Rogers saves the day. **60m/B VHS, Beta.** Roy Rogers, Jerome Cowan, John Carradine, Phyllis Brooks, Smiley Burnette, Joyce Compton; **D:** Joseph Kane. *NOS, VCN, DVT*

Silver Stallion 🦴½ **1941** Thunder the Wonder Horse plays the title character, who fights rattlesnakes, wild dogs and hoss thieves. Too bad he doesn't give acting lessons to the humans in the this frail family western with nice scenery and action scenes. **59m/C VHS, Beta.** David Sharpe, Carol Hughes, Leroy Mason, Walter Long; **D:** Edward Finney. *VYY, GPV*

The Silver Stallion: King of the Wild Brumbies 🦴🦴½ *The Silver Brumby* **1993 (G)** The adolescent Indi is enthralled as her writer-mother relates each new chapter in the saga of Thara, the amazing silver stallion. And she images each adventure as the horse triumphs over evil men, other horses, and the elements to become leader of the herd. Based on the Australian children's novel "The Silver Brumby" by Elyne Mitchell. **93m/C VHS, Beta.** *AU* Caroline Goodall, Ami Daemion, Russell Crowe; **D:** John Tatoulis; **W:** John Tatoulis, Jon Stephens; **M:** Tassos Ioannides. *PAR*

Silver Star 🦴🦴 **1955** Man elected sheriff of a western town turns down the job because he is a pacifist. He changes his mind when his defeated opponent hires a trio of killers to come after him. **73m/B VHS, Beta.** Jimmy Wakely, Edgar Buchanan, Marie Windsor. *NO*

Silver Strand 🦴🦴½ **1995 (R)** Hunky Brian Del Piso (Bellows), a navel cadet in the S.E.A.L. training school, makes the big mistake of falling for sexy Michelle (Sheridan), who just happens to be an officer's wife. As if he didn't have enough challenges, should their affair be exposed Brian might just as well kiss his career goodbye. **104m/C VHS.** Gil Bellows, Nicolette Sheridan; **D:** George Miller; **W:** Douglas Day Stewart; **C:** David Connell; **M:** Joseph Conlan. *MGM*

The Silver Streak 🦴🦴 **1934** The sickly son of a diesel train designer needs an iron lung—pronto. A rival's super-fast locomotive is the only hope for the boy. Murders, runaway engines, and a crew that would rather walk enliven this race against time. **72m/B VHS, Beta.** Sally Blane, Charles Starrett, Arthur Lake, Edgar Kennedy, William Farnum; **D:** Thomas Atkins. *CCB*

Silver Streak 🦴🦴🦴 **1976 (PG)** Pooped exec Wilder rides a train from L.A. to Chicago, planning to enjoy a leisurely, relaxing trip. Instead he becomes involved with murder, intrigue, and a beautiful woman. Energetic Hitchcock parody features successful first pairing of Wilder and Pryor. **113m/C VHS, Beta, LV.** Gene Wilder, Richard Pryor, Jill Clayburgh, Patrick McGoohan, Ned Beatty, Ray Walston, Richard Kiel, Scatman Crothers; **D:** Arthur Hiller; **W:** Colin Higgins; **M:** Henry Mancini. Nominations: Academy Awards '76: Best Sound. *FOX*

Silverado 🦴🦴🦴 **1985 (PG-13)** Affectionate pastiche of western cliches has everything a viewer could ask for—except Indians. Straightforward plot has four virtuous cowboys rise up against a crooked lawman in a blaze of six guns. No subtlety from the first big Western in quite a while, but plenty of fun and laughs. Laserdisc edition features a wide screen film-to-tape transfer monitored by the photography director, set photos, release trailers, and other publicity hoohah as well as a special time-lapse sequence of the set construction, and interviews with the stars and director Kasdan. Letterboxed laserdisc version is available with dolby surround sound. **132m/C VHS, Beta, LV.** Kevin Kline, Scott Glenn, Kevin Costner, Danny Glover, Brian Dennehy, Linda Hunt, John Cleese, Jeff Goldblum, Rosanna Arquette, Jeff Fahey; ***D:*** Lawrence Kasdan; ***W:*** Lawrence Kasdan; ***C:*** John Bailey; ***M:*** Bruce Broughton. Nominations: Academy Awards '85: Best Sound, Best Original Score. *COL, CRC*

Simba 🦴🦴🦴 **1955** A young Englishman arrives at his brother's Kenyan farm to find him murdered in a local skirmish between the Mau Maus and white settlers. Well made, thoughtful look at colonialism, racial animosity, and violence. **98m/C VHS, Beta, LV.** *GB* Dirk Bogarde, Donald Sinden, Virginia McKenna, Orlando Martins; ***D:*** Brian Desmond Hurst; ***C:*** Geoffrey Unsworth. *NO*

Simon 🦴🦴½ **1980 (PG)** A group of bored demented scientists brainwash a college professor into believing he is an alien from a distant galaxy, whereupon he begins trying to correct the evil in America. Screwball comedy, or semi-serious satire of some kind? Hard to tell. Some terrific set pieces but the movie as a whole doesn't quite hold together. Directorial debut of Brickman, who previously worked as a scriptwriter with Woody Allen ("Sleeper," etc.). **97m/C VHS, Beta.** Alan Arkin, Madeline Kahn, Fred Gwynne, Adolph Green, Wallace Shawn, Austin Pendleton; ***D:*** Marshall Brickman; ***W:*** Marshall Brickman, Thomas Baum. *WAR*

Simon Bolivar 🦴🦴½ **1969** The title character leads the Venezuelan revolution in 1817. **110m/C VHS, Beta.** Maximilian Schell, Rosanna Schiaffino. *UNI*

Simon, King of the Witches 🦴🦴½ **1971 (R)** An L.A. warlock who lives in a sewer drain finds himself the center of attention when his spells actually work. This interesting hippie/witchcraft entry bogs down now and then but Prine's performance is droll and lively. **90m/C VHS, Beta.** Andrew Prine, Brenda Scott, George Paulsin, Norman Burton, Ultra Violet; ***D:*** Bruce Kessler. *UNI*

Simon of the Desert 🦴🦴🦴½ **1966** Not Bunuel's very best, but worthy of the master satirist. An ascetic stands on a pillar in the desert for several decades—closer to God, farther from temptation. Pinal is a gorgeous devil that tempts Simon. Hilarious, irreverent, sophisticated. What's with the weird ending, though? In Spanish with English subtitles. **46m/B VHS, Beta.** Claudio Brook, Silvia Pinal; ***D:*** Luis Bunuel; ***W:*** Luis Bunuel. *HTV, HHT, DVT*

Simple Justice 🦴½ **1989 (R)** Mindless, justice-in-own-hands anti-liberal hogwash. Overwrought, smug, and violent story of a young couple beaten by robbers who remain at large. **91m/C VHS.** Cesar Romero, John Spencer, Doris Roberts, Candy McClain; ***D:*** Deborah Del Prete. *JTC*

Simple Men 🦴🦴🦴 **1992 (R)** Odd-ball brothers Bill (a petty criminal) and Dennis (a shy college student) decide to track down their missing father in this fractured comedy. Dad, a former big-league baseball player who bombed the Pentagon in the '60s, is a long-time fugitive hiding out somewhere in the wilds of Long Island. Their search leads them to two equally opposite women, the wary Kate, whom Bill immediately falls for, and the sexy Elina, who turns out to know dear old dad quite well. Deliberately deadpan and cliched, Hartley's quirky style can either irritate or illuminate via the weird turnings of his characters' lives. **105m/C VHS, LV.** Robert Burke, William Sage, Karen Sillas, Elina Lowensohn, Martin Donovan, Mark Bailey, John MacKay; ***D:*** Hal Hartley; ***W:*** Hal Hartley; ***M:*** Hal Hartley. Nominations: Cannes Film Festival '92: Best Film. *COL, IME, NLC*

A Simple Story 🦴🦴🦴 *Une Histoire Simple* **1979** A woman faces her 40th birthday with increasing uneasiness, though her life seems perfect from the outside. She evaluates her chances at love, childbearing, and friendship, after having an abortion and breaking up with her lover. Schneider's performance is brilliant in this gentle, quiet drama. In French with English subtitles. **110m/C VHS, Beta.** *FR* Romy Schneider, Bruno Cremer, Claude Brasseur; ***D:*** Claude Sautet. Nominations: Academy Awards '79: Best Foreign Language Film; Cesar Awards '79: Best Actress (Schneider). *COL, INJ*

The Simple Truth *Woof!* **1985** A woman's romance novel is dramatized, dealing with a receptionist who has a fling with the company president. **90m/C Beta.** *PSM*

A Simple Twist of Fate 🦴🦴½ **1994 (PG-13)** Comedy drama gives Martin chance to flex serious muscles with this update of George Eliot's "Silas Marner." Adoptive father Michael McMann wants to keep his daughter Mathilda (played by the prerequisite adorable twins) in the face of demands from her biological father (Byrne), who happens to be a local politician. Then revelations brought out at the custody hearing threaten the politician's career. Cuddly dad is hardly Martin's image (in spite of "Parenthood"), though strong cast limits the sugar. **106m/C VHS, LV.** Steve Martin, Gabriel Byrne, Catherine O'Hara, Stephen Baldwin, Alana Austin, Alyssa Austin, Laura Linney, Anne Heche, Michael Des Barres, Byron Jennings; ***D:*** Gilles Mackinnon; ***W:*** Steve Martin; ***M:*** Cliff Eidelman. *TOU*

Sin of Adam & Eve 🦴½ **1972 (R)** The story of Adam and Eve in the Garden of Eden and their fall from grace. Voice-over narrator is only sound in this strange dialogue-less story of the Adam and Eve, how they got kicked out of the Garden of Eden, and how they lose and then find each other outside. Ancient plot, to say the least. **72m/C VHS, Beta.** Candy Wilson, Jorge Rivero; ***D:*** Michael Zachary. *VDM*

The Sin of Harold Diddlebock 🦴🦴½ *Mad Wednesday* **1947** A man gets fired from his job, stumbles around drunk, and wins a fortune gambling. He then buys a circus and uses a lion to frighten investors into backing him. Inventive comedy, but missing the spark and timing of "The Freshman" (1925), of which it is a sequel. The final feature film for Lloyd (who did all his own stunts), made at the urging of director Sturges. **89m/B VHS, Beta.** Harold Lloyd, Margaret Hamilton, Frances Ramsden, Edgar Kennedy, Lionel Stander, Rudy Vallee, Franklin Pangborn; ***D:*** Preston Sturges. *NOS, BAR, AOV*

The Sin of Madelon Claudet 🦴🦴🦴 *The Lullaby* **1931** Hayes plays common thief who works her way into upper crust of Parisian society only to tumble back into the street, all in the name of making a better life for her illegitimate son. Very sudsy stuff, with an outstanding performance by Hayes. **74m/B VHS.** Helen Hayes, Lewis Stone, Neil Hamilton, Robert Young, Cliff Edwards, Jean Hersholt, Marie Prevost, Karen Morley, Charles Winninger, Alan Hale; ***D:*** Edgar Selwyn. Academy Awards '32: Best Actress (Hayes). *MGM, FCT*

Sin Takes a Holiday 🦴🦴½ **1930** A woman marries her boss to save him from his girl friend. On a trip to Paris, she is wooed by a refined European gentleman, but finds that she really does love her husband. By today's standards, it doesn't sound like much, but in the '30s, it was pretty sophisticated stuff. **81m/B VHS.** Constance Bennett, Kenneth MacKenna, Basil Rathbone, Rita La Roy, ZaSu Pitts, Fred Walton, Richard Carle, Helen Johnson; ***D:*** Paul Stein. *NOS, HEG*

Sin You Sinners 🦴 **1963** Aging stripper gets ahold of an amulet that allows her to look youthful and manipulate the lives of others. When she loses the amulet, however, bad things happen. Twisted ending. **73m/B VHS.** June Colbourne, Dian Lloyd, Derek Murcott, Beverly Nazarow, Charles Clements; ***D:*** Anthony Farrar. *SNC*

Sinai Commandos 🦴🦴½ *Sinai Commandos: The Story of the Six Day War; Ha'Matarah Tiran* **1968** The story of a group of commandos in the Israeli Six-Day War in 1967 who are assigned to destroy important Arab radar installations. Includes actual combat footage. **99m/C VHS.** Robert Fuller; ***D:*** Raphael Nussbaum. *ATL, FCT*

Sinatra 🦴🦴½ **1992** Made for television biopic chronicles the stormy life of crooner Frank Sinatra. Begins with his childhood in Hoboken, New Jersey and works its way through his big band tours, bobby soxer days, career skids, and triumphant comeback with his Oscar-winning performance in "From Here to Eternity," as well as his three marriages, "Rat Pack" friends, and mob connections. Executive Producer Tina Sinatra, Frank's daughter, doesn't gloss over her father's less savory character points and Casnoff does well with his leading role. Songs are lip-synched to classic Sinatra tunes with a few early recordings redone by actor Tom Burlinson and Frank Sinatra, Jr. **245m/C VHS, Beta, LV.** Philip Casnoff, Olympia Dukakis, Joe Santos, Gina Gershon, Nina Siemaszko, Marcia Gay Harden, Rod Steiger, Bob Gunton, David Raynr, James F. Kelly, Matthew Posey, Jay Robinson, Robin Gammell, Todd Waring, Joris Stuyck, Danny Gans, Jeff Corey; ***D:*** James Sadwith; ***W:*** William Mastrosimone; ***C:*** Reynaldo Villalobos. *WAR*

Sinbad 🦴🦴 **1971** A sardonic portrait of an aging hedonist as he tries to hold onto the pleasures of drink, sex and gluttony. In Magyar (Hungarian), with English subtitles. **98m/C VHS, Beta.** *HU* ***D:*** Zoltan Huszarik. *KIV, FCT*

Sinbad and the Eye of the Tiger 🦴🦴 **1977 (G)** The swashbuckling adventures of Sinbad the Sailor as he encounters the creations of Ray Harryhausen's special effects magic. Don't see this one for the plot, which almost doesn't exist. Otherwise, mildly fun. **113m/C VHS, Beta, LV.** *GB* Patrick Wayne, Jane Seymour, Taryn Power, Margaret Whiting; ***D:*** Sam Wanamaker; ***W:*** Beverley Cross; ***C:*** Ted Moore. *COL, CCB*

Sinbad of the Seven Seas 🦴½ **1989** Italian muscle epic based on the ancient legends. Ferrigno isn't green, but he's still a hulk, and he still can't act. It's poorly dubbed, which makes little difference; it would be stupid regardless. **90m/C VHS, Beta, LV.** *IT* Lou Ferrigno, John Steiner, Leo Gullotta, Teagan Clive; ***D:*** Enzo G. Castellari. *WAR, OM*

Sinbad, the Sailor 🦴🦴🦴 **1947** Fairbanks fits well in his luminent father's swashbuckling shoes, as he searches for the treasure of Alexander the Great. Self-mocking but hamhanded, and confusing if you seek the hidden plot. Still, it's all in fun, and it is fun. **117m/C VHS, Beta, LV.** Douglas Fairbanks Jr., Maureen O'Hara, Anthony Quinn, Walter Slezak, George Tobias, Jane Greer, Mike Mazurki, Sheldon Leonard; ***D:*** Richard Wallace; ***C:*** George Barnes. *MED, TTC*

Since You Went Away 🦴🦴🦴½ **1944** An American family copes with the tragedy, heartache and shortages of wartime in classic mega-tribute to the home front. Be warned: very long and bring your hankies. Colbert is superb, as is the photography. John Derek unobtrusively made his film debut, as an extra. **172m/B VHS, Beta, LV.** Claudette Colbert, Jennifer Jones, Shirley Temple, Joseph Cotten, Agnes Moorehead, Monty Woolley, Guy Madison, Lionel Barrymore, Robert Walker, Hattie McDaniel, Keenan Wynn, Craig Stevens, Albert Basserman, Alla Nazimova, Lloyd Corrigan, Terry Moore, Florence Bates, Ruth Roman, Andrew V. McLaglen, Dorothy Dandridge, Rhonda Fleming; ***D:*** John Cromwell; ***W:*** David O. Selznick; ***M:*** Max Steiner. Academy Awards '44: Best Score; Nominations: Academy Awards '43: Best Supporting Actress (Jones); Academy Awards '44: Best Actress (Colbert), Best Black and White Cinematography, Best Film Editing, Best Interior Decoration, Best Picture, Best Supporting Actor (Woolley). *FOX*

Sincerely Charlotte 🦴🦴🦴 *Signe Charlotte* **1986** Huppert directs her sister in this film about a beautiful singer framed for her boyfriend's murder. She enlists an old lover to help her flee across the countryside. Love story/thriller is pleasingly odd and absorbing. In French with English subtitles. **92m/C VHS, Beta, LV.** *FR* Isabelle Huppert, Niels Arestrup, Christine Pascal; ***D:*** Caroline Huppert. *COL, INJ*

Sincerely Yours *Woof!* **1956** Liberace wisely stayed away from acting after inauspiciously debuting in this horrible, maudlin remake of "The Man Who Played God." He plays a pianist who loses his hearing and decides to become a philanthropist to help those less fortunate than himself. Laughably cheesy. Thirty-one musical numbers, including Liberace's inimitable arrangement of "Chopsticks." **116m/C VHS, Beta, LV.** Liberace, Joanne Dru, Dorothy Malone, William Demarest; ***D:*** Gordon Douglas; ***W:*** Irving Wallace. *WAR*

A Sinful Life **1989 (R)** A strained, offbeat, B-grade comedy about an odd, infantile mother fighting to keep her unusual child from being taken away. Definitely not a must-see; can be irritating and obnoxious, depending on viewer and mood. Morris is at her oddball comedic best as the mother and former show dancer. Adult Tefkin plays her little girl. Based on the play "Just Like the Pom Pom Girls." **112m/C VHS, Beta, LV.** Anita Morris, Rick Overton, Dennis Christopher, Blair Tefkin, Mark Rolston, Cynthia Szigeti; ***D:*** William Schreiner. *COL*

Sing ½ **1989 (PG-13)** The students in the real-life Brooklyn public school "Sing" program endure the trials of adolescence while putting together a musical revue. Hurtles over the edge into cheesiness from the start, with way too much (cheesy) music. From the creator of "Fame" and "Footloose." **111m/C VHS, Beta, LV.** Lorraine Bracco, Peter Dobson, Jessica Steen, Louise Lasser, George DiCenzo, Patti LaBelle; ***D:*** Richard Baskin; ***M:*** Jay Gruska. *COL*

Sing, Cowboy, Sing **1937** Decent adventure story about a wagon train heading west that runs into a band of outlaws doing outlaw stuff and must somehow get through. **60m/B VHS, Beta.** Tex Ritter. *NOS, DVT*

Sing Sing Nights ½ *Reprieved* **1935** A world-famous journalist is killed with three bullets. Three men have confessed, but only one could have actually done it. A professor sets out to solve the case. **60m/B VHS.** Conway Tearle, Mary Doran, Hardie Albright, Patricia "Boots" Mallory, Ferdinand Gottschalk, Berton Churchill, Jameson Thomas; ***D:*** Lewis D. Collins. *SNC*

Sing Your Worries Away **1942** Songwriter Ebsen inherits 3 million dollars and finds the money causes him nothing but trouble. Band of crooks cause the requisite wacky complications. Fun, harmless musical comedy. ♫It Just Happened to Happen; Sally, My Dear Sally; Sing Your Worries Away; Cindy Lou McWilliams; How Do You Fall in Love. **71m/B VHS, Beta.** Buddy Ebsen, Bert Lahr, June Havoc, Patsy Kelly, Margaret Dumont; ***D:*** Edward Sutherland. *CCB*

Singapore ½ **1947** Rather boring romantic drama finds pearl smuggler Matt Gordon (MacMurray) returning to Singapore to resume his illegal trade at the end of WWII. He spots Linda (Gardner), the love of his life, but discovers she's suffering from amnesia and has married another man. Gangsters want Matt's hidden supply of pearls and kidnap Linda to get his cooperation. Remade with equal dullness in 1956 as "Istanbul." **80m/B VHS.** Fred MacMurray, Ava Gardner, Roland Culver, Richard Haydn, Thomas Gomez, Spring Byington, Porter Hall; ***D:*** John Brahm; ***W:*** Seton I. Miller, Robert Thoeren; ***C:*** Maury Gertsman; ***M:*** Daniele Amfitheatrof. *MCA*

Singin' in the Rain **1952** One of the all-time great movie musicals—an affectionate spoof of the turmoil that afflicted the motion picture industry in the late 1920s during the changeover from silent films to sound. Co-director Kelly and Hagen lead a glorious cast. Music and lyrics by Arthur Freed and Nacio Herb Brown. Served as basis of story by Betty Comden and Adolph Green. Also available on laserdisc with the original trailer, outtakes, behind the scenes footage, and commentary by film historian Ronald Haver. Later a Broadway musical. ♫All I Do is Dream of You; Should I?; Singin' in the Rain; Wedding of the Painted Doll; Broadway Melody; Would You; I've Got a Feelin' You're Foolin'; You Are My Lucky Star; Broadway Rhythm. **103m/C VHS, Beta, LV.** Gene Kelly, Donald O'Connor, Jean Hagen, Debbie Reynolds, Rita Moreno, King Donovan, Millard Mitchell, Cyd Charisse, Douglas Fowley, Madge Blake, Joi Lansing; ***D:*** Gene Kelly, Stanley Donen; ***W:*** Adolph Green, Betty Comden. Golden Globe Awards '53: Best Actor—Musical/Comedy (O'Connor); National Board of Review Awards '52: 10 Best Films of the Year; Nominations: Academy Awards '52: Best Supporting Actress (Hagen), Best Original Score. *MGM, TLF, CRC*

The Singing Blacksmith ½ **1938** A relic of American Yiddish cinema, adapting popular 1909 play by David Pinski. A married blacksmith is wooed by another woman and falls victim to alcoholism. Overlong, but Oysher and his rich baritone voice still shine. In Yiddish with English subtitles. **95m/B VHS.** *PL* Miriam Riselle, Florence Weiss, Moishe Oysher; ***D:*** Edgar G. Ulmer. *ERG, INJ*

Singing Buckaroo **1937** Dastardly bandits try to pilfer money from pretty blonde damsel and have to battle with yodelin' cowboy. B-level western good guy Scott belts out a few numbers and saves the day. Innocuously pleasant. **58m/B VHS, Beta.** Fred Scott, Victoria Vinton, Cliff Nazarro; ***D:*** Tom Gibson. *NOS, VYY*

Singing Cowboys, Vol. 2 **193?** Three films starring brave and talented singing cowboys. Rogers saves a young ranch heir from a couple of con artists in "Sunset Serenade." Tex Ritter plays a deputy sheriff trying to catch a gang of claim jumpers in his first singing western, "Song of the Gringo." Autry stars in "Public Cowboy No. 1," which has old fashioned cattle rustlers using airplanes, radios, and trucks to further their thieving ways. **175m/B VHS.** Gene Autry, Tex Ritter, Roy Rogers. *BPG*

The Singing Cowgirl **1939** Band of outlaws murder a ranch owner to get to a gold mine. Heroine Page rides in to save the day but gets shot down by western stereotypes. **60m/B VHS.** Dorothy Page, Dave O'Brien, Vince Barnett, Stanley Price; ***D:*** Samuel Diege; ***W:*** Arthur Hoerl. *MOV*

The Singing Nun **1966** The true story of a Belgian nun who takes a liking to a motherless little boy. She writes a song for him, and a kind-hearted priest talks to a record producer to see about getting the song to go somewhere. The song soon becomes an international hit, and the nun ends up on the "Ed Sullivan Show." Sentimental and sugary sweet, but a big box-office hit. **98m/C VHS.** Debbie Reynolds, Ricardo Montalban, Greer Garson, Agnes Moorehead, Chad Everett, Katharine Ross, Juanita Moore, Ricky Cordell, Michael Pate, Tom Drake; ***D:*** Henry Koster; ***C:*** Milton Krasner. Nominations: Academy Awards '66: Best Original Score. *MGM*

Singing the Blues in Red **1987** Dark, pessimistic character study of a protest singer/songwriter who leaves his native East Germany to escape repression and finds his loyalties divided. A moving personal story, as well as insightful, subtle social commentary. In English and German with subtitles. Cinematography by Chris Menges. **110m/C VHS, Beta.** *GE* Gerulf Pannach, Fabienne Babe, Cristine Rose, Trevor Griffiths; ***D:*** Ken Loach; ***W:*** Trevor Griffiths. *NO*

Single Bars, Single Women ½ **1984** Utterly formulaic made for TV comedy-drama based on Dolly Parton's song is not entirely without merit. Lonely people gather in a local pickup joint and share their miseries and hopes. **96m/C VHS, Beta.** Shelley Hack, Christine Lahti, Tony Danza, Mare Winningham, Keith Gordon, Paul Michael Glaser; ***D:*** Harry Winer; ***M:*** Basil Poledouris. *PSM, PAR, VTR*

Single Room Furnished ½ **1968** The fall of a buxom blonde from uncorrupted innocence through pregnancies to desperate prostitution. Fails to demonstrate any range of talent in Mansfield, who died before it was completed. Exploitative and pathetic. **93m/C VHS, Beta.** Jayne Mansfield, Dorothy Keller; ***D:*** Matt Cimber, Matteo Ottaviano. *VCI, HEG*

The Single Standard **1929** San Francisco deb Garbo flings with artsy Asther and finds out the Hayes Code is just around the corner. **93m/B VHS.** Greta Garbo, Nils Asther, Johnny Mack Brown, Dorothy Sebastian, Lane Chandler, Zeffie Tilbury; ***D:*** John S. Robertson. *MGM, FCT*

Single White Female ½ **1992 (R)** Psycho thriller casts Fonda as chic Manhattan computer consultant Allison Jones, who advertises for a roommate after a falling out with her boyfriend. Leigh is the frumpy, shy, bookstore clerk Hedra who answers the ad and moves into Allie's great Upper West Side apartment. They hit it off, that is until Allie notices Hedra's beginning to look and sound very familiar. Hmm... Derivative, though bonus points for creative murder implements and interesting performances throughout, including Friedman as Allie's gay upstairs neighbor. Based on the novel "SWF Seeks Same" by John Lutz. **107m/C VHS, Beta, LV, 8mm.** Bridget Fonda, Jennifer Jason Leigh, Steven Weber, Peter Friedman, Stephen Tobolowsky, Francis Bay, Renee Estevez, Kenneth Tobey; ***D:*** Barbet Schroeder; ***W:*** Don Roos; ***M:*** Howard Shore. MTV Movie Awards '93: Best Villain (Leigh). *COL, BTV*

Singles **1992 (PG-13)** Seattle's music scene is the background for this lighthearted look at single twentysomethings in the '90s. Hits dead on thanks to Crowe's tight script and a talented cast, and speaks straight to its intended audience—the "Generation X" crowd. Real life band Pearl Jam plays alternative band Citizen Dick and sets the tone for a great soundtrack featuring the hot Seattle sounds of Alice in Chains, Soundgarden, and Mudhoney. The video contains six extra minutes of footage after the credits that was thankfully edited out of the final cut. Look for Horton, Stoltz (as a mime), Skerritt, and Burton in cameos. **100m/C VHS, Beta, LV.** Matt Dillon, Bridget Fonda, Campbell Scott, Kyra Sedgwick, Sheila Kelley, Jim True, Bill Pullman, James LeGros, Ally Walker, Devon Raymond, Camillo Gallardo, Jeremy Piven; ***Cameos:*** Tom Skerritt, Peter Horton, Eric Stoltz, Tim Burton; ***D:*** Cameron Crowe; ***W:*** Cameron Crowe; ***M:*** Paul Westerberg. *WAR, PMS*

Singleton's Pluck *Laughterhouse* **1984** Touching British comedy about a determined farmer who must walk his 500 geese 100 miles to market because of a strike. He becomes a celebrity when the TV stations start covering his odyssey. **89m/C VHS, Beta.** *GB* Ian Holm, Penelope Wilton, Bill Owen, Richard Hope; ***D:*** Richard Eyre. *VTR, NWV*

The Sinister Invasion *Alien Terror; The Incredible Invasion* **1968** A turn-of-the-century scientist (Karloff) discovers a death ray. Aliens, who would like a closer peek at what makes it work, use a sex-fiend's body to do so. One of Karloff's last four films, made simultaneously in Mexico. The great horror master's final offering. Excruciating. **95m/C VHS, Beta.** *MX* Boris Karloff, Enrique Guzman, Jack Hill; ***D:*** Juan Ibanez. *SNC*

The Sinister Urge *Woof! The Young and the Immortal; Hellborn* **1960** Vice cops Duncan and Moore search for the murderer of three women. Seems the disturbed slayer is unbalanced because he's been looking at pictures of naked ladies. Was this meant to be taken seriously at the time? The last film by camp director Wood, maker of the infamous "Plan 9 From Outer Space." A must see for Wood fans. **82m/B VHS, Beta.** Kenne Duncan, Duke Moore, Jean Fontaine; ***D:*** Edward D. Wood Jr. *AOV, SNC*

Sink the Bismarck **1960** British navy sets out to locate and sink infamous German battleship during WWII. Good special effects with battle sequences in this drama based on real incidents. One of the better of the plethora of WWII movies, with stirring naval battles and stylish documentary-style direction. **97m/B VHS, Beta.** Kenneth More, Dana Wynter, Karel Stepanek, Carl Mohner, Laurence Naismith, Geoffrey Keen, Michael Hordern, Maurice Denham, Esmond Knight; ***D:*** Lewis Gilbert. *FOX, HMV*

Sinners **1989** Outrageous portrait of an Italian family in the Big Apple trying to come to terms with the violence that surrounds their neighborhood. **90m/C VHS, Beta.** Joey Travolta, Robert Gallo, Joe Palese, Lou Calvelli, Angie Daglas, Sabrina Ferrand; ***D:*** Charles Kanganis. *PMH*

Sinner's Blood *Woof!* **1970 (R)** Bikers terrorize and torture a small town. **81m/C VHS, Beta.** Stephen Jacques, Crusty Beal, Nancy Sheldon, Parker Herriott, Julie Connors; ***D:*** Neil Douglas. *GHV*

Sinners in Paradise 🦴🦴 **1938** An assortment of trouble-plagued characters alternately hide and face up to their mysterious pasts when their plane crashes on a deserted island. Interesting "crucible" premise runs out of steam, but plucky, resourceful cast and competent direction keep it going. **64m/B VHS, Beta.** Madge Evans, John Boles, Bruce Cabot, Marion Martin, Gene Lockhart, Dwight Frye, Charlotte Wynters, Nana Bryant, Milburn Stone, Donald (Don "Red") Barry, Morgan Conway; ***D:*** James Whale. *SNC, MLB*

Sins **1985** On her way up the ladder of success in the fashion industry, Helene has stepped on a few toes. Those rivals and her ever-increasing acquisition of power and money make this film an exciting drama. **336m/C VHS, Beta.** Joan Collins, Timothy Dalton, Catherine Mary Stewart, Gene Kelly, James Farentino; ***D:*** Douglas Hickox. *VTR, NWV, HHE*

Sins of Desire 🦴🦴 **1992** Highly erotic thriller with Roberts going undercover as a nurse in a sex therapy clinic. It seems her sister was a former patient at the clinic and has since died a mysterious death. Linking up with private eye Cassavetes, Roberts sets out to investigate the doctors who treated her sister, searching for clues to her untimely death. **90m/C VHS.** Tanya Roberts, Jay Richardson, Delia Sheppard, Nick Cassavetes, Jan-Michael Vincent; ***D:*** Jim Wynorski; ***W:*** Mark Thomas McGee, Peter Paul Liapis. *COL, VMK, PMS*

The Sins of Dorian Gray 🦴 **1982 (PG)** A modernized adaptation of "The Portrait of Dorian Grey" by Oscar Wilde, with Dorian as a beautiful woman who remains young for 30 years, while a video screen test ages, like the original character's mirror image. Might have been intriguing and stylish; instead, only disappointing and incompetent. Made for television. **95m/C VHS, Beta.** Belinda Bauer, Joseph Bottoms, Anthony Perkins; ***D:*** Tony Maylam. *FOX*

Sins of Jezebel 🦴 **1954** Biblical epic about Jezebel, who worships an evil god. She marries the king of Israel and brings the kingdom nothing but trouble. **74m/C VHS, Beta, LV.** Paulette Goddard, George Nader, John Hoyt, Eduard Franz; ***D:*** Reginald LeBorg. *NO*

Sins of Rome 🦴🦴 **1954** Spartacus risks it all in a bold attempt to free his fellow slaves. Not nearly the equal of Kirk Douglas's "Spartacus," but much better than later Italian adventure epics. **75m/B VHS.** *IT* Ludmila Tcherina, Massimo Girotti, Gianna Maria Canale, Yves Vincent; ***D:*** Riccardo (Robert Hampton) Freda. *SNC*

Sins of the Night 🦴 **1993 (R)** An ex-con insurance investigator is hired to find a sultry exotic dancer. Also available in an unrated version. **82m/C VHS.** Nick Cassavetes, Deborah Shelton. *ACA*

Sinthia: The Devil's Doll 🦴🦴 **1970** A little girl is thought to be possessed by a demon after she has horrible dreams about killing her father. **?m/C VHS.** Shula Roan, Diane Webber; ***D:*** Ray Dennis Steckler. *SNC, TPV*

Sioux City 🦴🦴½ **1994 (PG-13)** Jesse Rainfeather Goldman (Phillips) is a Lakota Sioux adopted away from the reservation of his birth and raised in Beverly Hills by a Jewish family. Jesse's curious when his birth mother suddenly contacts him, but when he arrives at the Sioux City reservation, he discovers she's suddenly died under mysterious circumstances. So Jesse sticks around to find out what's going on and discovers his heritage along the way. Well-meaning but dull. **102m/C VHS.** Lou Diamond Phillips, Salli Richardson, Melinda Dillon, Ralph Waite, Adam Roarke, Bill Allen, Gary Farmer; ***D:*** Lou Diamond Phillips; ***W:*** L. Virginia Browne; ***M:*** Christopher Lindsey. *CAF*

Sioux City Sue 🦴🦴 **1946** Talent scouts looking to cast a western musical find Autry, then trick him into being the voice of a singing donkey in an animated production. But, the yodelin' cowboy belts out a number or two, and the poobahs give him the lead. Singin' and fancy ridin' abound in Autry's first post-WWII role. **69m/B VHS, Beta.** Gene Autry, Lynn (Mary Hart) Roberts, Sterling Holloway. *NO*

Sirens 🦴🦴½ **1994 (R)** Staid minister takes Australian artist Norman Lindsay to task for submitting scandalous works to public exhibitions. Noted by one reviewer as "Enchanted April with nipples," comedy of manners is witty but lacks plot and looks remarkably like a centerfold layout. Ample displays of nudity as the models (including supermodel MacPherson in her acting debut) frolic in the buff. Grant is terrific as the seemingly enlightened but easily shocked minister, but Neill's Lindsay is thinly written and too often takes a back seat to the vamping models. Fictionalized account of a true incident from the 1930s; Lindsay's home and some of his artworks were used. Check out writer/director Duigan as a pompous village minister. **96m/C VHS, LV.** *AU GB* Hugh Grant, Tara Fitzgerald, Sam Neill, Elle Macpherson, Kate Fischer, Portia de Rossi, Pamela Rabe, Ben Mendelsohn, John Polson, Mark Gerber, Julia Stone, Ellie MacCarthy, Vincent Ball; ***Cameos:*** John Duigan; ***D:*** John Duigan; ***W:*** John Duigan; ***M:*** Rachel Portman. Chicago Film Critics Awards '94: Most Promising Actor (Grant). *MAX*

Siringo 🦴🦴½ **1994** U.S. Deputy Marshal Charlie Siringo (Johnson) is out to capture escaped convict Wade Lewis (Macht). The two antagonists share a nasty history as Siringo, along with a young deputy, heads out to the ranch of former prostitute Kaitlin (Bernard) for a final showdown. **90m/C VHS.** Brad Johnson, Stephen Macht, Chad Lowe, Crystal Bernard; ***D:*** Kevin G. Cremin. *AVE*

Sirocco 🦴🦴½ **1951** An American gun-runner (Bogart) stuck in Syria in 1925 matches wits with a French intelligence officer amid civil war and intrigue. About the underbelly of human affairs. **111m/B VHS, Beta, LV.** Humphrey Bogart, Lee J. Cobb, Zero Mostel, Everett Sloane, Gerald Mohr; ***D:*** Curtis Bernhardt; ***C:*** Burnett Guffey. *COL*

Sister Act 🦴🦴½ **1992 (PG)** Surprising box office hit casts Goldberg as a Reno lounge singer and inadvertent witness to a mob murder who hides out in a convent—where she's as comfortable in a habit as a fish is out of water. Much to the dismay of poker-faced Mother Superior Smith, she takes over the ragtag choir and molds them into a swinging, religious version of a '60s girls group. Stock characters and situations are deflected by some genuinely funny moments and good performances, especially by Najimy and Makkena. Coached by the very clever Shaiman, Whoopie handles her singing bits with gusto, highlight of which is "My God," sung to the tune of "My Guy." **100m/C VHS, Beta, LV.** Whoopi Goldberg, Maggie Smith, Harvey Keitel, Bill Nunn, Kathy Najimy, Wendy Makkena, Mary Wickes, Robert Miranda, Richard Portnow, Joseph Maher; ***D:*** Emile Ardolino; ***W:*** Joseph Howard; ***M:*** Marc Shaiman. People's Choice Awards '93: Best Film—Musical/Comedy; NAACP Image Awards '33: Best Actress (Goldberg); NAACP Image Awards '93: Best Film. *TOU, PMS*

Sister Act 2: Back in the Habit 🦴🦴 **1993 (PG)** Mediocre retread finds Goldberg once again donning her nun's habit and getting a choir rocking. Deloris has established her singing career in Vegas, but she's persuaded by her nun friends to whip the incorrigible music students at a troubled inner-city high school into shape for an all-state choral competition. The musical numbers and singing are catchy and well-done but Goldberg seems to have phoned her work in; given her reported 7 million bucks salary a little more life is expected. She's still sharp with the one-liners but it's all familiar ground. Geared directly towards young viewers. **107m/C VHS, LV.** Whoopi Goldberg, Kathy Najimy, James Coburn, Maggie Smith, Wendy Makkena, Barnard Hughes, Mary Wickes, Sheryl Lee Ralph, Michael Jeter, Robert Pastorelli, Thomas Gottschalk, Lauryn Hill, Brad Sullivan; ***D:*** Bill Duke; ***W:*** James Orr, Jim Cruickshank, Judi Ann Mason; ***M:*** Miles Goodman. Blockbuster Entertainment Awards '95: Comedy Actress, Video (Goldberg); Nominations: MTV Movie Awards '94: Best Comedic Performance (Goldberg). *TOU*

Sister Dora 🦴🦴½ **1977** An idealistic young woman joins a nursing sisterhood in 19th century England but she questions her vocation when she falls in love. Adapted from a popular romance novel. **147m/C VHS.** *GB* Dorothy Tutin, James Grout, Peter Cellier; ***D:*** Mark Miller. *NO*

The Sister-in-Law 🦴🦴 **1974 (R)** Shady dealings, seduction, and adultery run rampant. Savage (who also wrote and sings the folk score) reluctantly agrees to deliver a package across the Canadian border for his brother. Intriguing. **80m/C VHS, Beta.** John Savage, Anne Saxon, W.G. McMillan, Meredith Baer; ***D:*** Joseph Rubin. *PSM*

The Sister-in-Law 🦴🦴½ **1995 (PG-13)** Chilling cable suspenser finds the beautiful and evil Sarah Preston (Vernon) assuming the identity of the woman she's just killed—the widow of wealthy George Richards' (McCarthy) estranged son. George is dying and pathetically eager to accept Sarah at face value as is his vulnerable daughter Madlyn (Reed). But Sarah has not chosen the Richards family at random—she has a longtime grudge and plans to take her revenge slowly—so be prepared for a few more bodies to turn up. **95m/C VHS, Beta.** Kate Vernon, Kevin McCarthy, Shanna Reed, Craig Wasson; ***D:*** Noel Nosseck; ***W:*** David Callaway, Megan Marks. *PAR*

Sister Kenny 🦴🦴🦴 **1946** Follows the story of a legendary Australian nurse crusading for the treatment of infantile paralysis. Stirring, well-made screen biography. Based on Elizabeth Kenny's memoir, "And They Shall Walk." **116m/B VHS, Beta, LV.** Rosalind Russell, Dean Jagger, Alexander Knox, Philip Merivale, Beulah Bondi, Charles Halton; ***D:*** Dudley Nichols; ***C:*** George Barnes. Golden Globe Awards '47: Best Actress—Drama (Russell); Nominations: Academy Awards '46: Best Actress (Russell). *NOS, CCB, TTC*

Sister My Sister 🦴🦴 **1994 (R)** True crime story that served as the inspiration for Jean Genet's play "The Maids." In a French provincial town lives the authoritarian Madame Danzard (Walters), who stifles daughter Isabelle (Thursfield), and subjects her two maids, sisters Christine (Richardson) and Lea (May), to an equally harsh discipline. The tension between the four women reaches a highstrung crescendo, leading to violence. Claustrophobic character study. **89m/C VHS.** *GB* Julie Walters, Joely Richardson, Jodhi May, Sophie Thursfield; ***D:*** Nancy Meckler; ***W:*** Wendy Kellelman; ***C:*** Ashley Ropwe; ***M:*** Stephen Warbeck. *APX*

Sister, Sister 🦴🦴 **1987 (R)** A Congressional aide on vacation in Louisiana takes a room in an old mansion. He gradually discovers the secret of the house and its resident sisters. Dark Southern gothicism, full of plot surprises, with a twisted ending. **91m/C VHS, Beta, LV.** Eric Stoltz, Judith Ivey, Jennifer Jason Leigh, Dennis Lipscomb, Anne Pitoniak, Natalija Nogulich; ***D:*** Bill Condon; ***W:*** Bill Condon, Joel Cohen, Ginny Cerrella; ***M:*** Richard Einhorn. *VTR, NWV*

Sister Street Fighter 🦴 **1976** Action star Sonny Chiba takes a rest from his "Street Fighter" series in favor of protege Long, who's determined to deliver her own brand of deadly justice in this martial arts fest. **81m/C VHS.** Tina Long; ***D:*** Kazuhiko Yamaguchi. *NLC*

The Sisterhood 🦴 **1988 (R)** A pair of amazons fight for women's rights in a post-nuclear future. Cheap feminist theme laid over warmed-over sci-fi plot. **75m/C VHS, Beta, LV.** Rebecca Holden, Chuck Wagner, Lynn-Holly Johnson, Barbara Hooper; ***D:*** Cirio H. Santiago. *MED*

The Sisters 🦴🦴🦴 **1938** Lavish film of three sisters and their marital problems in turn of the century San Francisco. Davis gives a great performance as the oldest sister with the most trouble—notably in the form of unreliable sports reporter Flynn. Look for Susan Hayward in a bit role, as well as Bogart's wife, Mayo Methot. Based on the bestselling novel by Myron Brinig. **98m/B VHS.** Bette Davis, Errol Flynn, Anita Louise, Jane Bryan, Ian Hunter, Henry Travers, Beulah Bondi, Donald Crisp, Dick Foran, Patric Knowles; ***D:*** Anatole Litvak; ***M:*** Max Steiner. *MGM*

Sisters 🦴🦴🦴 **1973 (R)** Siamese twins are separated surgically, but one doesn't survive the operation. The remaining sister is scarred physically and mentally with her personality split into bad and good. The bad side commits a murder, witnessed (or was it?) by an investigative reporter. And then things really get crazy. DePalma's first ode to Hitchcock, with great music by Hitchcock's favorite composer, Bernard Herrmann. Scary and suspenseful. **93m/C VHS, Beta.** Margot Kidder, Charles Durning, Barnard Hughes; ***D:*** Brian DePalma; ***W:*** Brian DePalma; ***M:*** Bernard Herrmann. *WAR, OM*

Sisters of Death 🦴🦴 **1976 (PG)** Five members of a sorority gather together for a reunion in a remote California town. Little do they know, a psychopath is stalking them, one by one. Could it have something to do with the terrible secret they each keep? Good, cheap thrills and some Bicentennial fashions to boot. **87m/C VHS, Beta.** Arthur Franz, Claudia Jennings, Cheri Howell, Sherry Boucher, Paul Carr; ***D:*** Joseph Mazzuca. *VCI*

Sisters of Gion 🦴🦴🦴½ **1936** Mizoguchi's most famous and arguably best pre-war film. Two geisha sisters in Tokyo's red-light district reflect the tension in Japanese culture by waging a quiet battle of tradition vs. progressiveness. Highly acclaimed. In Japanese with English subtitles. **69m/B VHS, Beta.** *JP* Isuzu Yamada, Yoko Umemura; ***D:*** Kenji Mizoguchi. *FCT*

Sisters of Satan 🦴🦴½ **1975 (R)** The nuns of the infamous convent St. Archangelo choose to survive by trading God for the devil. **91m/C VHS, Beta.** *MX* Claudio Brook, David Silva, Tina Romero, Susana Kamini; ***D:*** Juan Lopez Moctezuma. *ACA, MPI*

Sitting Ducks 🦴🦴🦴 **1980 (R)** Mild-mannered accountant and lecherous pal rip off and then attempt to outrun the mob—all while swapping songs and confessions. Emil and Norman make it up as they go along; their hilarious repartee is largely improvised. They pick up a gorgeous lady (Townsend) and go about their way. **88m/C VHS, Beta.** Michael Emil, Zack Norman, Patrice Townsend, Richard Romanus, Irene Forrest, Henry Jaglom; ***D:*** Henry Jaglom; ***W:*** Henry Jaglom. *MED*

Six Degrees of Separation 🦴🦴½ **1993 (R)** Some believe that any two people, anywhere in the world, are connected by links to only six other people, hence the six degrees of separation. For the upper crust New Yorker Kittredges, Ouisa (Channing) and Flan (Sutherland), this becomes an issue when they encounter a charming young man (Smith) who claims to be Sidney Poitier's son and a friend of their children. The story unfolds as they realize they've been hustled—and don't understand why. Guare adapted his hit play, but what worked well there is almost too talky here. Channing, reprising her stage role, is very good as the stuffy Ouisa, with Sutherland delivering another interesting performance. Incredibly, the play was based on a true story. **112m/C VHS, LV.** Stockard Channing, Will Smith, Donald Sutherland, Mary Beth Hurt, Bruce Davison, Ian McKellen, Richard Masur, Anthony Michael Hall, Heather Graham, Eric Thal, Anthony Rapp, Osgood Perkins, Kitty Carlisle Hart, Catherine Kellner; ***D:*** Fred Schepisi; ***W:*** John Guare; ***C:*** Ian Baker; ***M:*** Jerry Goldsmith. Nominations: Academy Awards '94: Best Actress (Channing); Golden Globe Awards '94: Best Actress—Musical/Comedy (Channing). *MGM*

Six Fois Deux/Sur et Sous la Communication 🦴🦴🦴 **1976** A six-part experimental series made for French television, in which Godard and Mieville analyze modern culture and socioeconomics via a free-form essay format, combining interviews, screened text, self-referential devices and news footage. In French with English voice-over. **100m/C VHS, Beta.** *FR* ***D:*** Jean-Luc Godard, Anne-Marie Mieville. *EAI*

Six Gun Gospel 🦴🦴 **1943** Hatton masquerades as a preacher to investigate some shady dealings. Laughs come when the women of the congregation prevail upon him to sing, and he croons a ballad about Jesse James! **59m/B VHS.** Johnny Mack Brown, Raymond Hatton, Inna Gest, Eddie Dew, Roy Barcroft, Kenneth MacDonald, Bud Osborne; ***D:*** Lambert Hillyer. *DVT, HEG*

Six Gun Rhythm 🦴½ **1939** Novelty western plot has football player traveling to Texas to avenge his father's murder. **59m/B VHS, Beta.** Tex Fletcher. *NOS, VDM, HEG*

633 Squadron 🦴🦴½ **1964** A skilled R.A.F. pilot attempts to lead his squadron on a mission deep into the fjords of Norway in search of a Nazi fuel plant. Robertson tries hard, as always, but is really not British officer material. Well-made war flick, based on a true story. **102m/C VHS, Beta.** Cliff Robertson, George Chakiris, Maria Perschy, Harry Andrews; ***D:*** Walter Grauman; ***W:*** James Clavell. *MGM*

Six in Paris 🦴🦴½ *Paris vu Par* **1968** Six short films by acclaimed French New Wave directors, each depicting a different Parisian neighborhood. "Saint-Germain-des-Pres" finds an American girl disillusioned by two French boys. "Gare du Nord" has a woman meeting a handsome stranger who announces he's going to kill himself. A shy dishwasher brings a prostitute to his room in the "Rue Saint-Denis." When a salesman is accosted by a derelict in the "Place de l'Etoile" he hits him with his umbrella and then thinks he's killed the man. "Montparnasse-Levallois" has a woman thinking she's mixed-up her meetings with her two lovers. "La Muette" finds a small boy buying earplugs to shut out the noise of his parents constant arguing. In French with English subtitles. **93m/C VHS.** *FR* Barbara Wilkin, Jean-Francois Chappey, Jean-Pierre Andreani, Nadine Ballot, Barbet Schroeder, Gilles Queant, Micheline Dax, Claude Melki, Jean-Michel Rouziere, Marcel Gallon, Joanna Shimkus, Philippe Hiquilly, Serge Davri, Stephane Audran, Gilles Chusseau, Dinah Saril, Claude Chabrol; ***D:*** Jean Douchet, Jean Rouch, Jean-Daniel Pollet, Eric Rohmer, Jean-Luc Godard, Claude Chabrol; ***W:*** Jean Douchet, George Keller, Jean Rouch, Jean-Daniel Pollet, Eric Rohmer, Jean-Luc Godard, Claude Chabrol; ***C:*** Nestor Almendros. *NYF, FCT*

Six Pack 🦴½ **1982 (PG)** The Gambler goes auto racing. Rogers, in his theatrical debut, stars as Brewster Baker, a former stock car driver. He returns to the racing circuit with the help of six larcenous orphans (the six-pack, get it?) adept at stripping cars. Kinda cute if you're in the mood for sugar-powered race car story. **108m/C VHS, Beta.** Kenny Rogers, Diane Lane, Erin Gray, Barry Corbin, Anthony Michael Hall; ***D:*** Daniel Petrie; ***M:*** Charles Fox. *FOX*

Six Shootin' Sheriff 🦴🦴 **1938** A cowboy framed for bank robbery is released and seeks to rid his town of all evil. And he gets the girl! **59m/B VHS, Beta.** Ken Maynard, Marjorie Reynolds, Walter Long; ***D:*** Harry Fraser. *VYY, VCI, VCN*

Six Weeks 🦴🦴 **1982 (PG)** A young girl dying of leukemia brings together her work-driven mother and an aspiring married politician. Manipulative hanky-wringer has good acting from both Moores but oddly little substance. **107m/C VHS, Beta, LV.** Dudley Moore, Mary Tyler Moore, Katherine Healy; ***D:*** Tony Bill; ***M:*** Dudley Moore. *COL*

Six Wives of Henry VIII 🦴🦴🦴 **197?** Michell has been called the definitive Henry VIII, and this BBC Classic Television Series (shown as part of "Masterpiece Theatre" on PBS) was perhaps the most praised series on British TV. Henry's wives were: Catherine of Aragon, Anne Boleyn, Jane Seymour, Anne of Cleves, Catherine Howard, and Catherine Parr. Each episode tells of their, sometimes tragic, fates as pawns in Henry's quest for an heir, and his changes from an eager young man to aged, bitter monarch. The 90-minute videos are available individually or as a boxed set. **540m/C VHS.** *GB* Keith Michell, Annette Crosbie, Dorothy Tutin, Anne Stallybrass, Elvi Hale, Angela Pleasence, Rosalie Crutchley. *PAP, FCT, VCO*

Sixteen 🦴🦴 *Like a Crow on a June Bug* **1972 (R)** A naive country lass is attracted to the glitter and hum of the outside world. Her determination and optimism help her triumph. **84m/C VHS, Beta.** Mercedes McCambridge, Parley Baer, Ford Rainey, Beverly Powers, John Lozier, Simone Griffeth, Maidie Norman; ***D:*** Lawrence Dobkin. *NWV*

Sixteen Candles 🦴🦴🦴 **1984 (PG)** Over a decade after hitting the theaters, "Sixteen Candles" is still popular — reaching near cult status among generation X-ers. Hilarious comedy of errors features the pouty Ringwald as an awkard teen who's been dreaming of her sixteenth birthday. But the rush of her sister's wedding causes everyone to forget, turning her birthday into her worst nightmare. Hughes may not be critically acclaimed, but his movies are so popular they nearly take on a life of their own. Ringwald and Hall are especially charming as the angst ridden teens, encountering one trauma after another. Great soundtrack includes the title song by The Stray Cats. **93m/C VHS, Beta, LV.** Molly Ringwald, Justin Henry, Michael Schoeffling, Haviland Morris, Gedde Watanabe, Anthony Michael Hall, Paul Dooley, Carlin Glynn, Blanche Baker, Edward Andrews, Carole Cook, Max Casey Adams Showalter, Liane Curtis, John Cusack, Joan Cusack, Brian Doyle-Murray, Jami Gertz, Cinnamon Idles, Zelda Rubinstein; ***D:*** John Hughes; ***W:*** John Hughes; ***M:*** Ira Newborn. *MCA*

Sixteen Fathoms Deep 🦴🦴 **1934** A sponge fisherman risks it all, including his love, when a mean businessman threatens his operation. Good underwater photography, but otherwise undistinguished. **57m/B VHS.** Lon Chaney Jr., Sally O'Neil, George Regas, Maurice Black, Russell Simpson; ***D:*** Armand Schaefer. *VYY, NOS, DVT*

'68 🦴 **1987 (R)** A Hungarian family struggles with the generation gap in 1968 America. **99m/C VHS, Beta, LV.** Eric Larson, Terra Vandergaw, Neil Young; ***D:*** Steven Kovacks. *VTR, NWV*

Sizzle 🦴🦴 **1981** When her boyfriend is murdered by the mob, nightclub singer Anderson, newly arrived from Hicksville in Roaring '20s Chicago, stops at nothing to get revenge. Bad-guy gangster Forsythe falls for her charms. Fun but unsophisticated. Made for TV. **100m/C VHS, Beta.** Loni Anderson, John Forsythe, Leslie Uggams, Roy Thinnes, Richard Lynch, Michael Goodwin; ***D:*** Don Medford; ***M:*** Artie Butler. *PSM*

Skag 🦴🦴🦴 **1979** Disabled following a stroke, a Pittsburgh steel worker confronts a change in family roles and long-ignored family problems during his convalescence. Malden is exceptional and believable as a Joe Lunchbucket in this well-written, well-cast TV outing, pilot for the NBC series. **145m/C VHS, Beta.** Karl Malden, Piper Laurie, Craig Wasson, Leslie Ackerman, Peter Gallagher, Kathryn Holcomb, Powers Boothe; ***D:*** Frank Perry. *NO*

Skateboard 🦴 **1977 (PG)** A down-and-out Hollywood agent creates a pro skateboarding team and enters them in a race worth $20,000. Quickie premise executed lamely. **97m/C VHS, Beta.** Allen (Goorwitz) Garfield, Kathleen Lloyd, Chad McQueen, Leif Garrett, Richard Van Der Wyk, Tony Alva, Antony Carbone; ***W:*** Dick Wolf. *NO*

The Skateboard Kid 🦴½ **1993 (PG)** When an outsider finds a magical talking skateboard, he suddenly becomes the envy of the in-group of skateboarding thrashers. **90m/C VHS.** Bess Armstrong, Timothy Busfield; ***D:*** Larry Swerdlove; ***W:*** Roger Corman; ***V:*** Dom DeLuise. *NHO*

Skeeter 🦴½ **1993 (R)** Yes, it's the attack of the killer mosquito! Not just any mosquito of course, but a new gigantic species bred on toxic waste. They're invading the quiet desert town of Mesquite—and they're out for blood! **95m/C VHS, LV.** Tracy Griffith, Jim Youngs, Charles Napier, Michael J. Pollard; ***D:*** Clark Brandon; ***W:*** Clark Brandon, Lanny Horn; ***M:*** David Lawrence. *COL*

Skeezer 🦴🦴½ **1982** A dog becomes a key factor in a sympathetic doctor's efforts to communicate with emotionally unstable children. Based on reality, and a good cast makes it believable and moving. Quality family fare. **100m/C VHS.** Karen Valentine, Dee Wallace Stone, Tom Atkins, Mariclare Costello, Leighton Greer, Justine Lord; ***D:*** Peter H. Hunt. *LIV*

Skeleton Coast 🦴 **1989 (R)** Borgnine plays a retired U.S. Marine colonel who organizes a Magnificent Seven-like group of tough mercenaries to go into eastern Africa to save hostages held by Angolan terrorists. Cliches abound, including a token large-breasted woman, Mulford, getting her t-shirt ripped open. No plot and a bad script. Also called "Fair Trade." **94m/C VHS, LV.** Ernest Borgnine, Robert Vaughn, Oliver Reed, Herbert Lom, Daniel Greene, Nancy Mulford, Leon Isaac Kennedy; ***D:*** John Cardos. *SUE, NLC*

Sketch Artist 🦴🦴 **1992 (R)** Jack Whitfield (Fahey) is a police sketch artist whose latest rendering of a murder suspect looks suspiciously like his wife. Jack decides to keep this information to himself while he does some quiet investigating but he may not have any time. The police have a new murder suspect in mind—Jack! Made for cable television. **89m/C VHS, Beta, LV.** Jeff Fahey, Sean Young, Drew Barrymore, Frank McRae, Tcheky Karyo, James Tolkan, Charlotte Lewis; ***D:*** Phedon Papamichael; ***W:*** Michael Angeli. *FXV, VTR*

Sketch Artist 2: Hands That See 🦴🦴½ **1994** Fahey returns as police artist Jack Whitfield, who's asked to draw a sketch of a serial rapist/murderer. Near-victim Emmy (Cox) just happens to be blind but describes to Jack how the rapist looked as she felt his face. Emmy's hubby Glenn (Silverman) is concerned, especially when the creep warns Emmy about her trip to the cops. Solid characters build to good courtroom climax. **95m/C VHS, LV.** Jeff Fahey, Courteney Cox, Jonathan Silverman, Michael Beach, Brion James, James Tolkan, Leilani Sarelle Ferrer, Michael Nicolosi, Scott Burkholder; ***D:*** Jack Sholder; ***W:*** Michael Angeli; ***M:*** Tim Truman. *MGM*

Sketches of a Strangler 🦴½ **1978** A psychotic art student sketches, then murders prostitutes. Interesting lead character but hardly chilling—just horrible to watch. Made for TV. **91m/C VHS, Beta.** Allen (Goorwitz) Garfield, Meredith MacRae; ***D:*** Paul Leder. *MED*

Ski Bum 🦴 **1975 (R)** A ski bum discovers corruption and violence at a Colorado Rockies resort. Eminently forgettable trash. Scantily based on a novel by Romain Gary. **94m/C VHS, Beta.** Charlotte Rampling, Zalman King, Dimitra Arliss, Anna Karina; ***D:*** Bruce Clark. *NLC*

Ski Patrol 🦴🦴 **1989 (PG)** Wacky ski groupies try to stop an evil developer. Good ski action in a surprisingly plotful effort from the crazy crew that brought the world "Police Academy." **85m/C VHS, Beta, LV.** Roger Rose, Yvette Nipar, T.K. Carter, Leslie Jordan, Ray Walston, Martin Mull; ***D:*** Richard Correll. *COL*

Ski School 🦴 **1991 (R)** Rival ski instructors compete for jobs and babes. Brow lowering. **89m/C VHS, LV.** Ava Fabian, Dean Cameron, Tom Breznahan, Stuart Fratkin; ***D:*** Damian Lee. *HBO*

Ski School 2 🦴½ **1994 (R)** Former ski instructor Dave finds that both his job and his ex-gal have been acquired by a jerk. So Dave decides to get them both back. **92m/C VHS.** Dean Cameron, Wendy Hamilton, Heather Campbell, Brent Sheppard, Bill Dwyer; ***D:*** David Mitchell; ***W:*** Jay Naples. *MNC*

Ski Troop Attack 🦴🦴 **1960** During WWII, an American ski patrol is sent behind Nazi lines to blow up a German railway bridge. Unexceptional low-budget Corman outing; not among the greatest of war movies. **61m/B VHS, Beta.** Michael Forest, Frank Wolff, Sheila Carol. *SNC, NOS, DVT*

Skier's Dream **1988** This spectacular action-packed film focuses on a young executive in search of the ultimate run. Shot on the most exotic ski locations in the world; covers freestyle skiing, powder skiing, snowboarding, extreme skiing, cliff jumping, paragliding, and wave riding. **75m/C VHS.** John Eaves, Ian Boyd; ***M:*** Jimi Hendrix, Tom Cochrane. *COL, RAP*

Skin 🦴½ *Howard Beach: Making the Case for Murder* **1989 (PG-13)** Prosecutor seeks the truth after a black man is chased into highway traffic by a gang of white teenaged thugs from Queens. Based on the true story of the death of a young black man in Howards Beach, Queens. Made for TV. **95m/C VHS.** Daniel J. Travanti, Joe Morton, Dan Lauria, William Daniels. *NHO*

Skin Art 🦴½ **1993 (R)** Very offbeat character study focusing on Will, a tormented tattoo artist who specializes in decorating the backs of the young Asian prostitutes who work in a nearby brothel. Haunted by his memories as a Vietnam POW, Will decides to exorcise some demons on his latest female canvas. **90m/C VHS, LV.** Kirk Baltz, Jake Weber, Nora Ariffin; ***D:*** W. Blake Herron; ***W:*** W. Blake Herron. *FXV*

Skin Deep 🦴½ **1989 (R)** A boyish Don Juan tries everything to win back his ex-wife. Ritter whines about his mid-life crisis and seduces women; this substitutes for plot. A few funny slapstick scenes still don't make this worth watching. **102m/C VHS, Beta, LV.** John Ritter, Vincent Gardenia, Julianne Phillips, Alyson Reed, Nina Foch, Chelsea Field, Denise Crosby; ***D:*** Blake Edwards; ***W:*** Blake Edwards; ***M:*** Henry Mancini. *CCB, MED, VTR*

Skin Game 🦴½ **1931** Two British families feud over land rights. Not thrilling; not characteristic of working with Hitchcock. Way too much talking in excruciating, drawn-out scenes. Adapted from the play of the same name. **87m/B VHS, Beta.** *GB* Phyllis Konstam, Edmund Gwenn, Frank Lawton, C.V. France, Jill Esmond, Helen Haye; ***D:*** Alfred Hitchcock; ***W:*** Alfred Hitchcock. *REP, NOS, MLB*

Skin Game 🦴🦴🦴 **1971 (PG)** A fast talking con-artist (Garner) and his black partner (Gossett) travel throughout the antebellum South setting up scams—Gossett is sold to a new owner by Garner, who helps him escape. Garner and Gossett make a splendid comedy team in this different kind of buddy flick. All is well until Asner turns the tables on them. Finely acted comedy-drama. **102m/C VHS, Beta.** James Garner, Louis Gossett Jr., Susan Clark, Ed Asner, Andrew Duggan; ***D:*** Paul Bogart; ***M:*** David Shire. *WAR*

Skinheads: The Second Coming of Hate 🦴 **1988 (R)** Neo-fascists run rampant. Exploitative effort from schlock-doyen Clark. **93m/C VHS.** Chuck Connors, Barbara Bain, Brian Brophy, Jason Culp, Elizabeth Sagal; ***D:*** Greydon Clark; ***W:*** Greydon Clark. *NO*

Skinned Alive *Woof!* **1989** A woman and her children travel cross-country to sell leather goods. When a detective discovers where the leather comes from he's hot on their trail. **90m/C VHS, Beta.** Mary Jackson, Scott Spiegel; ***D:*** Jon Killough; ***W:*** Jon Killough. *NO*

Skinner 🦴 **1993 (R)** Psychopath Dennis Skinner (Raimi) more than lives up to his grisly name with his penchant for stalking hookers with carving knives and cleavers. Now he's going after his innocent landlady (Lake) and it's up to Heidi (Lords), a victim who managed to get away, to find him before he can kill again. Lords in lingerie (and nasty scars) and some really disgusting skinning scenes. **89m/C VHS, LV.** Theodore (Ted) Raimi, Traci Lords, Ricki Lake; ***D:*** Ivan Nagy. *APX*

Skinner's Dress Suit 🦴🦴½ **1926** Meek, hen-pecked office clerk tells domineering wife he got a raise so she'll get off his back. She quickly insinuates them into upper crusty social circle, where the fib pays off big. Remake of the 1917 version based on Henry Irving Dodge's novel. **79m/B VHS, Beta.** Reginald Denny, Laura La Plante, Arthur Lake, Hedda Hopper; ***D:*** William A. Seiter. *GPV*

Skirts Ahoy! 🦴🦴 **1952** Williams, Evans, and Blaine are three WAVES who have their eyes set on three handsome men. To get them, of course, they must sing and dance a lot, and Williams must perform one of her famous water ballets. ♫Oh By Jingo; Hold Me Close to You; What Makes a WAVE?; What Good is a Gal Without a Guy?; Skirts Ahoy!; Glad to Have You Aboard; The Navy Waltz; I Get a Funny Feeling; We Will Fight. **109m/C VHS.** Esther Williams, Joan Evans, Vivian Blaine, Barry Sullivan, Keefe Brasselle, Billy Eckstine, Debbie Reynolds; ***D:*** Sidney Lanfield. *MGM*

The Skull 🦴🦴 **1965** Horror abounds when Cushing gets his hands on the skull of the Marquis de Sade that has mysterious, murderous powers. Based on a story by Robert Bloch. **83m/C VHS.** Peter Cushing, Patrick Wymark, Christopher Lee, Nigel Green, Jill Bennett, Michael Gough, George Coulouris, Patrick Magee; ***D:*** Freddie Francis. *PAR*

Skull: A Night of Terror 🦴🦴 **1988 (R)** A cop vows not to use guns after a tragic accident, then single-handed and unarmed, takes on terrorists who kidnap his family. **80m/C VHS, Beta.** Nadia Capone, Robert Bideman, Robbie Fox, Paul Sanders; ***D:*** Robert Bergman; ***W:*** Robert Bergman, Gerard Ciccoritti. *ACA*

Skull & Crown 🦴🦴 **1935** Rin Tin Tin, Jr. helps the hero break up a group of smugglers. A favorite of Tin fans everywhere. **58m/B VHS, Beta.** Regis Toomey, Jack Mulhall, James Murray. *VYY, DVT, HEG*

Skullduggery 🦴½ **1970 (PG)** When a peaceful race of blond ape-people are discovered in New Guinea, a courtroom battle ensues to prevent their slaughter at the hands of developers. Interesting premise sadly flops. **105m/C VHS, Beta.** Burt Reynolds, Susan Clark, Roger C. Carmel, Chips Rafferty, Edward Fox, Wilfrid Hyde-White, Rhys Williams; ***D:*** Gordon Douglas. *MED*

Skullduggery *Woof! Warlock* **1979 (PG)** Costume-store minion Haverstock carries a curse that makes him kill and mutilate. The usual unspeakable horror ensues for a group of medieval-game players. **95m/C VHS, Beta.** Thom Haverstock, Wendy Crewson, David Calderisi; ***D:*** Ota Richter. *MED*

The Sky Above, the Mud Below *Le Ciel et le Boue* **1961** An acclaimed documentary following a band of explorers transversing New Guinea in 1959, and their confrontations with native rituals, heretofore unknown cannibal tribes and physical calamities. In HiFi. **90m/C VHS, Beta.** ***D:*** Pierre-Dominique Gaisseau. Academy Awards '61: Best Feature Documentary. *ORI, WAR, FCT*

Sky Bandits 🦴½ **1940** Mounties uncover the mystery of a disappearing plane carrying gold from a Yukon mine. Last of the "Renfrew of the Mounties" pictures. **56m/B VHS, Beta, 8mm.** James Newill, Dave O'Brien, Louise Stanley. *NOS, SNC, VCN*

Sky Hei$t 🦴🦴 **1975** Criminals plan robbery of police helicopter carrying fortune in gold bullion. Made for television. **96m/C VHS.** Stefanie Powers, Joseph Campanella, Don Meredith, Larry Wilcox, Frank Gorshin, Shelley Fabares, Ken Swofford, Ray Vitte, Nancy Belle Fuller, Suzanne Somers; ***D:*** Lee H. Katzin. *UNI*

Sky High 🦴🦴½ **1922** Mix is an immigration agent after a gang smuggling Chinese laborers across the Mexican border. Thrills involve an airplane and mountaintop battles as well as some terrific location footage from the Grand Canyon. **58m/B VHS.** Tom Mix, Eva Novak, J. Farrell MacDonald, Sid Jordan; ***D:*** Lynn F. Reynolds; ***W:*** Lynn F. Reynolds. *GPV, GVV*

Sky High 🦴 **1951** A spy at an Air Force base is trying to get hold of the plans to a secret plane. A GI is recruited to catch him. **60m/B VHS, Beta, LV.** Sid Melton, Mara Lynn, Douglas Evans. *NO*

Sky High 🦴 **1984** Three college students become immersed in international intrigue when the C.I.A. and the K.G.B. pursue them through Greece looking for a secret Soviet tape. **103m/C VHS, Beta.** Daniel Hirsch, Clayton Norcross, Frank Schultz, Lauren Taylor; ***D:*** Nico Mastorakis. *LIV*

Sky Liner 🦴 **1949** An FBI agent is trailing a spy who has taken secret documents aboard a westbound flight. **62m/B VHS, Beta, LV.** Richard Travis, Pamela Blake. *NO*

The Sky Pilot 🦴🦴½ **1921** Young clergyman sets up a parish on North Pacific coast and finds he must prove himself to the cowboys. He saves young woman from stampede, but her father blames him for her maimed legs and sets the preacher's church on fire, providing girl with excuse to overcome handicap. **63m/B VHS, Beta.** John Bowers, Colleen Moore, David Butler, Donald Ian Macdonald; ***D:*** King Vidor. *GPV, FCT, GVV*

Sky Pirates *Woof!* **1987** Space epic deals about pieces of ancient stone left by prehistoric extraterrestrials, now lost in a time warp. Bad stunts, bad script and notably bad acting make it a woofer in any era. **88m/C VHS, Beta.** *AU* John Hargreaves, Max Phipps, Meredith Phillips; ***D:*** Colin Eggleston. *FOX*

Sky Riders 🦴🦴½ **1976 (PG)** Hang-gliders risk it all to take on a group of political kidnappers. Fine hang-gliding footage and glorious Greek locations make up for garden-variety plot. **93m/C VHS.** James Coburn, Susannah York, Robert Culp, Charles Aznavour, Harry Andrews, John Beck; *D:* Douglas Hickox; *W:* Jack DeWitt, Garry Michael White; *M:* Lalo Schifrin. *FOX*

Skylark ☆☆½ **1993 (G)** In a sequel to Hallmark Hall of Fame's hugely successful "Sarah, Plain and Tall," the whole Kansas crew shows up for more of their little-farm-on-the-prairie life. After two years in America's squarest state, mail-order bride Sarah (Close) loves Jacob (Walken), but not the scenery and still yearns for the lush greenery of Maine. When drought and fire threaten the farm, Jacob fears for the family's health and safety, and sends them back East for a visit. Close's "tough Yankee" expression grows a bit tiresome in a plot that is a tad predictable, yet the simplistic charm and nostalgia are unresistable and work to propel this quality Hallmark production. **98m/C VHS.** Glenn Close, Christopher Walken, Lexi Randall, Christopher Bell, Tresa Hughes, Lois Smith, Lee Richardson, Elizabeth Wilson, Margaret Sophie Stein, Jon DeVries, James Rebhorn, Woody Watson; *D:* Joseph Sargent; *W:* Patricia MacLachlan. *REP, BTV*

Skyline ☆☆☆ *La Linea Del Cielo* **1984 (R)** A Spanish photographer comes to New York City to work for a magazine and tries to adjust to his cultural dislocation. Quietly funny, with a startling ending. Partly in Spanish with English subtitles. **84m/C VHS, Beta, LV.** *SP* Antonio Resines, Beatriz Perez-Porro, Jaime Nos, Roy Hoffman; *D:* Fernando Colombo. *KIV, FCT, TPV*

The Sky's the Limit ☆☆½ **1943** Astaire spends his leave in Manhattan and falls in love with fetching journalist Leslie. He's in civvies, so little does she know he's a war hero. Nothing-special semi-musical, with Fred-Ginger spark missing. ♫One For My Baby; My Shining Hour; I've Got a Lot in Common With You. **89m/B VHS, Beta.** Fred Astaire, Joan Leslie, Robert Benchley, Robert Ryan, Elizabeth Patterson; *D:* Edward H. Griffith. Nominations: Academy Awards '43: Best Song ("My Shining Hour"), Best Original Score. *TTC, VYY, MED*

Skyscraper ☆ **1996 (R)** Gun-wielding helicopter pilot/heroine Carrie Wink (Smith) must battle villianous mercenaries holding hostages in an LA skyscraper. But she stills manages to find time for lots of steamy showers (to best display the only assets the film has). **96m/C VHS.** Anna Nicole Smith. *PMH*

Skyscraper Souls ☆☆☆ **1932** William stars as David Dwight, a ruthless businessman who manipulates stock prices and double-crosses lovers in order to have complete control of a 100-story office building. He sacrifices everything and everyone in this story of big business. Based on the novel "Skyscraper" by Faith Baldwin. **98m/B VHS.** Warren William, Maureen O'Sullivan, Gregory Ratoff, Anita Page, Verree Teasdale, Norman Foster, Jean Hersholt, Wallace Ford; *D:* Edgar Selwyn. *MGM*

Slacker ☆☆☆ **1991 (R)** Defines a new generation: Overwhelmed by the world and it's demands, "Slackers" react by retreating into lives of minimal expectations. Filmed as a series of improvisational stories about people living on the fringes of the working world and their reactions (or lack thereof) to the life swirling around them. First feature for writer/director Linklater on a budget of $23,000; filmed on location in Austin, Texas with a cast of primarily non-professional actors. **97m/C VHS.** Richard Linklater; *D:* Richard Linklater; *W:* Richard Linklater. *INJ, ORI*

Slam Dunk Ernest ☆½ **1995 (PG-13)** Ernest (Varney) becomes a basketball star in a city league exhibition game when the Basketball Angel (Abdul-Jabbar) loans him his magic shoes. **93m/C VHS, LV.** Jim Varney, Kareem Abdul-Jabbar, Joy Brazeau; *D:* John R. Cherry III; *W:* Daniel Butler, John R. Cherry III; *M:* Mark Adler. *TOU*

Slamdance ☆½ **1987 (R)** A struggling cartoonist is framed for the murder of a beautiful young woman while being victimized by the real killer. A complicated murder mystery with a punk beat and visual flash. But the tale is unoriginal - and where's the slamdancing? **99m/C VHS, Beta, LV.** Tom Hulce, Virginia Madsen, Mary Elizabeth Mastrantonio, Harry Dean Stanton, Adam Ant, John Doe; *D:* Wayne Wang. *FOX*

Slammer Girls ☆ **1987 (R)** In this sex-drenched, unfunny spoof on women's prison films, the inmates of Loch Ness Penitentiary try to break out using their sexual wiles. The actresses are pseudonymous porn stars. **82m/C VHS, Beta, LV.** Tally Brittany, Jane Hamilton, Jeff Eagle, Devon Jenkin; *D:* Chuck Vincent. *LIV*

The Slap *La Gifle* **1976 (PG)** French teens learn about love the French way. **103m/C VHS.** *FR* Isabelle Adjani, Lino Ventura; *D:* Claude Pinoteau; *M:* Georges Delerue. *SUE*

Slap Shot ☆☆☆ **1977 (R)** A profane satire of the world of professional hockey. Over-the-hill player-coach Newman gathers an odd-ball mixture of has-beens and young players and reluctantly initiates them, using violence on the ice to make his team win. The strip-tease on ice needs to be seen to be believed. Charming in its own bone-crunching way. **123m/C VHS, Beta, LV.** Paul Newman, Michael Ontkean, Jennifer Warren, Lindsay Crouse, Jerry Houser, Melinda Dillon, Strother Martin; *D:* George Roy Hill; *M:* Elmer Bernstein. *MCA*

Slapstick **193?** An anthology of great moments from Mack Sennett comedy shorts, featuring many great stars in some of their earliest film appearances. **76m/B VHS, Beta.** Charlie Chaplin, Harold Lloyd, Charley Chase, Buster Keaton, Ben Turpin, Stan Laurel. *REP*

Slapstick of Another Kind ☆½ **1984 (PG)** Lewis and Kahn play dual roles as an alien brother and sister and their adoptive Earth parents, who are being pursued by U.S. agents. Rather miserable rendition of a Kurt Vonnegut novel. **85m/C VHS, Beta, LV.** Jerry Lewis, Madeline Kahn, Marty Feldman, Jim Backus, Noriyuki "Pat" Morita, Samuel Fuller, Orson Welles; *D:* Steven Paul. *LIV, VES*

Slash ☆½ **1987** Each of four people caught in a political takeover harbors a secret that could harm one of the others. Extremely violent. **90m/C VHS, Beta.** Romano Kristoff, Michael Monty, Gwen Hung; *D:* John Gale. *NO*

Slashdance *Woof!* **1989** A really pathetic thriller follows a lady cop undercover in a chorus line to find out who's been murdering the dancers. The acting is on the level of pro wrestling. Don't be fooled by the naked babes on the cassette box - there's no nudity. **83m/C VHS, Beta.** Cindy Maranne, James Carroll Jordan, Queen Kong, Joel von Ornsteiner, Jay Richardson; *D:* James Shyman; *W:* James Shyman. *NO*

Slashed Dreams ☆☆ *Sunburst* **1974 (R)** Hippie couple travels to California wilderness in search of a friend. A pair of woodsmen assault them and rape the woman, which really messes with their heads. Retitled and packaged as slasher movie. **74m/C VHS.** Peter Hooten, Katherine Baumann, Ric Carrott, Anne Lockhart, Robert Englund, Rudy Vallee, James Keach, David Pritchard, Peter Brown; *D:* James Polakof; *W:* James Keach, David Pritchard. *ACA*

The Slasher *Woof!* **1974** A policeman must find the madman who has been killing off unfaithful married women. Miserably gory, pointless slasher (hence the title) interesting only as an early example of its kind. **88m/C VHS, Beta.** Farley Granger, Sylva Koscina, Susan Scott. *NO*

Slate, Wyn & Me ☆ **1987 (R)** Two bank-robbing, kidnapping brothers flee cross-country from the law, and fall in love with the girl they've snatched. Pointless, and pointlessly violent and vulgar. **90m/C VHS, Beta.** Sigrid Thornton, Simon Burke, Martin Sacks; *D:* Don McLennan. *SUE, NLC*

Slaughter ☆ **1972 (R)** After his parents are murdered, a former Green Beret goes after their killers. Plenty of brutality. Followed by "Slaughter's Big Rip-off." **92m/C VHS, Beta, LV.** Jim Brown, Stella Stevens, Rip Torn, Cameron Mitchell, Don Gordon, Marlene Clark; *D:* Jack Starrett. *FOX*

Slaughter High ☆ **1986 (R)** A high school nerd is accidentally disfigured by a back-firing prank. Five years later, he returns to exact bloody revenge. Available in an unrated version. **90m/C VHS, Beta.** Caroline Munro, Simon Scuddamore, Kelly Baker; *D:* George Dugdale. *LIV, VES*

Slaughter Hotel ☆ *Asylum Erotica; La Bestia Uccide a Sangue Freddo* **1971 (R)** An asylum already inhabited by extremely bizarre characters is plagued by a series of gruesome murders. Lots of skin and lots of blood; Neri shines as a nymphomaniacal lesbian nurse. **72m/C VHS, Beta.** Klaus Kinski, Rosalba (Sara Bay) Neri, Margaret Lee, John Ely; *D:* Fernando Di Leo. *MPI, GRG*

Slaughter in San Francisco ☆ *Chuck Norris vs. the Karate Cop; Yellow Faced Tiger; Karate Cop* **1981 (R)** A Chinese-American cop leads a one-man fight against corruption in the department in Daly City, near San Francisco. Norris is the bad guy; made in 1973 but not released until he had an established following (and he still has only some 18 minutes of film footage). Plenty of kicking and karate chops. **92m/C VHS, Beta.** *CH* Chuck Norris, Don Wong; *D:* William Lowe. *SUE, RHI*

Slaughter of the Innocents ☆☆ **1993 (R)** FBI agent Broderick (Glenn) is sent to Salt Lake City to investigate the murders of two children which are found to be connected to a series of bizarre killings that have occurred around Monument Valley. Unbeknownst to his associates, Broderick often uses his 11-year-old whiz-kid son Jesse's (Cameron-Glickenhaus) computer skills to aid his research. Only this time, his inquisitive son gets too close to a serial killer and unless Dad can figure things out on his own, Jesse will be the next victim. **104m/C VHS, LV.** Scott Glenn, Jesse Cameron-Glickenhaus, Sheila Tousey, Darlanne Fluegel, Zitto Kazann; *D:* James Glickenhaus; *W:* James Glickenhaus. *MCA*

The Slaughter of the Vampires *Woof!* *Curse of the Blood-Ghouls; Curses of the Ghouls* **1962** Newlyweds meet a bloodthirty vampire in a Viennese chalet. Real, real bad horror flick, poorly dubbed. **81m/C VHS, Beta.** *IT* Walter Brandi, Dieter Eppler, Graziella Granta; *D:* Robert Mauri; *W:* Robert Mauri. *SNC*

Slaughter Trail ☆☆ **1951** Rancher-turned-stage robber Young shoots two Indians and cavalry colonel Donlevy has to deal with the fallout. Peace returns when Young dies. Ordinary western with balladeer device helping the plot along, or trying to. **78m/C VHS, Beta.** Brian Donlevy, Gig Young, Virginia Grey, Andy Devine, Robert Hutton; *D:* Irving Allen. *TTC*

Slaughterday ☆½ **1977 (R)** An innocent woman is caught in the middle of an ex-con's elaborate scheme to commit the largest heist of his life. **87m/C VHS, Beta.** Rita Tushingham, William Berger, Frederick Jaeger, Michael Hauserman, Gordon Mitchell; *D:* Peter Patzak. *GHV*

Slaughterhouse *Woof!* **1987 (R)** A rotund, pig-loving country boy kills, maims, and eats numerous victims. Features the requisite dumb teens and plenty of blood. **87m/C VHS, Beta.** Joe Barton, Sherry Bendorf, Don Barrett; *D:* Rick Roessler. *NLC*

Slaughterhouse Five ☆☆ **1972 (R)** A suburban optometrist becomes "unstuck" in time and flits randomly through the experiences of his life, from the Dresden bombing to an extraterrestrial zoo. Noticed at Cannes but not at theatres; ambitious failure to adapt Kurt Vonnegut's odd novel. **104m/C VHS, Beta, LV.** Michael Sacks, Valerie Perrine, Ron Leibman, Eugene Roche, Perry King; *D:* George Roy Hill. Cannes Film Festival '72: Special Jury Prize; Nominations: Cannes Film Festival '72: Best Film. *MCA*

Slaughterhouse Rock *Woof!* **1988 (R)** The ghost of a sexy rock star draws a young man into a confrontation with a sadistic spirit that rules a deserted prison. There's also some cannibalism involved. Music group Devo did the score for this flick. **90m/C VHS, Beta.** Nicholas Celozzi, Donna Denton, Toni Basil, Hope Marie Carlton; *D:* Dimitri Logothetis. *NO*

Slaughter's Big Ripoff ☆½ **1973 (R)** Slaughter is back battling the Mob with guns, planes and martial arts. This undistinguished sequel features McMahon as a mob boss. **92m/C VHS, Beta.** Jim Brown, Brock Peters, Don Stroud, Ed McMahon, Art Metrano, Gloria Hendry; *D:* Gordon Douglas. *FOX*

Slave Girls from Beyond Infinity **1987 (R)** In this B-movie spoof, two beautiful intergalactic slave girls escape their penal colony, land on a mysterious planet, and meet a cannibalistic despot. Fun spoof of '50s "B" sci-fi movies. **80m/C VHS, Beta, LV.** Elizabeth Cayton, Cindy Beal, Brinke Stevens; ***D:*** Ken Dixon. *AFE*

A Slave of Love **1978** Poignant love story set in the Crimea as the Bolshevik Revolution rages around a film crew attempting to complete a project. Interesting as ideological cinema but also enjoyable romantic drama. In Russian with English subtitles. **94m/C VHS, Beta.** *RU* Elena Solovei, Rodion Nakhapetov, Alexander Kalyagin; ***D:*** Nikita Mikhalkov; ***M:*** Eduard Artemyev. National Board of Review Awards '78: 5 Best Foreign Films of the Year. *COL, AUD, INJ*

Slave of the Cannibal God *Woof! Il Montagna di Dio Cannibale; Mountain of Cannibal Gods* **1979 (R)** Beautiful Andress is captured by "native" cannibals; Keach must save her. **86m/C VHS, Beta.** *IT* Stacy Keach, Ursula Andress, Claudio Cassinelli; ***D:*** Sergio Martino. *VES*

Slave Trade in the World Today **1964** Slavery practices in the modern world are shown, including actual scenes of a sheik's harem, slave auctions, and the kidnapping and selling of young women. **87m/C VHS, Beta.** ***D:*** Roberto Malenotti. *VDC, TPV*

Slavers **1977 (R)** Detailed depiction of the 19th century African slave trade with a little romance thrown in. **102m/C VHS, Beta.** *GE* Trevor Howard, Britt Ekland, Ron Ely, Cameron Mitchell, Ray Milland; ***D:*** Jurgen Goslar. *VCD*

Slaves in Bondage **1937** Young, country girls are lured into the big city and initiated into a life of ill repute in this exploitation classic. A must for camp fans of the 30's. **?m/C VHS.** Lona Andre, Wheeler Oakman. *SNC*

Slaves of New York ½ **1989 (R)** Greenwich Village artists worry about life and love in the '80s and being artistic enough for New York. Adapted from the stories of Tama Janowitz, who also wrote the screenplay and appears as Abby. Disastrous adaptation of a popular novel. **115m/C VHS, Beta, LV.** Bernadette Peters, Chris Sarandon, Mary Beth Hurt, Madeleine Potter, Adam Coleman Howard, Nick Corri, Mercedes Ruehl, Joe Leeway, Charles McCaughan, John Harkins, Anna Katarina, Tama Janowitz; ***D:*** James Ivory; ***W:*** Tama Janowitz. *COL*

The Slayer *Woof! Nightmare Island* **1982 (R)** It's movies like this that give getting back to nature a bad name. That horrible monster is after those nice young people again! This time it's on an island off the coast of Georgia. **95m/C VHS, Beta.** ***D:*** J.S. Cardone; ***W:*** J.S. Cardone; ***M:*** Robert Folk. *NO*

The Slayer/The Scalps **1982 (R)** Double feature. "Scalps" is a slasher set in a Native American burial ground. "The Slayer" is about vacationing couples who run into more than they bargained for on their island retreat. **150m/C VHS, Beta.** ***D:*** J.S. Cardone. *NO*

Slayground ½ **1984 (R)** Man, distraught at the accidental death of his daughter, hires a hitman to exact revenge. Excruciating adaptation of the novel by Richard Stark (Donald E. Westlake). **85m/C VHS, Beta.** *GB* Peter Coyote, Mel Smith, Billie Whitelaw, Philip Sayer, Kelli Maroney; ***D:*** Terry Bedford; ***M:*** Colin Towns. *REP*

Sleazemania **1985** Compilation of trailers 'n' bits reviews some of the sleazier, sicker, and sexier selections of celluloid from the past 50 years. **60m/C VHS, Beta.** *RHI*

Sleazemania III: The Good, the Bad & the Sleazy **1986** Another compilation of the cheapest, funniest and scurviest moments, from grade-Z horror films, including "Mondo Psycho" and "Smut Peddler Meets Emmanuel." **90m/B VHS, Beta.** *RHI*

The Sleazy Uncle *Lo Zio Indegno* **1989** A successful but bored businessman is energized by an encounter with his vice-ridden uncle, a mooching, womanizing beatnik poet who knows how to enjoy life. An energetic but rather formulaic comedy. In Italian with English subtitles. **104m/C VHS, Beta.** *IT* Giancarlo Giannini, Vittorio Gassman, Andrea Ferreol, Stefania Sandrelli; ***D:*** Franco Brusati. *INJ, TRI*

Sledgehammer *Woof!* **1983** A madman is wreaking havoc on a small town, annihilating young women with a sledgehammer. **87m/C VHS, Beta.** Ted Prior, Doug Matley, Steven Wright. *NO*

Sleep of Death ½ **1979** Young Englishman's pursuit of a blue-blooded woman seems to set off a series of bizarre and mysterious murders. A gothic thriller based on Sheridan Le Fanu's short story. **90m/C VHS, Beta.** Brendan Price, Marilu Tolo, Patrick Magee, Curt Jurgens, Per Oscarsson; ***D:*** Calvin Floyd. *PSM*

Sleep with Me ½ **1994 (R)** What happens when love comes between friendship? Sarah (Tilly), Joseph (Stoltz), and Frank (Sheffer) are soon to find out. Sarah and Joseph are about to get married when their best friend Frank realizes he's in love with Sarah. So he sets out to seduce her and when Joseph realizes what's going on, he not only questions Frank's friendship but wonders just what signals Sarah's been giving off (although Joseph's hardly blameless). Six writers each wrote one of the social scenes detailing their triangular troubles, including a party where Tarantino does a hilarious riff on the homoerotic subtext in "Top Gun." Kelly's directorial debut. **117m/C VHS, LV.** Craig Sheffer, Eric Stoltz, Meg Tilly, Todd Field, Adrienne Shelly, Lewis Arquette, Susan Traylor, Tegan West, Parker Posey, Dean Cameron, Thomas Gibson, June Lockhart, Quentin Tarantino; ***D:*** Rory Kelly; ***W:*** Roger Hedden, Neal Jimenez, Michael Steinberg, Duane Dell'Amico, Joe Keenan, Rory Kelly; ***M:*** David Lawrence. *MGM*

Sleepaway Camp **1983 (R)** Crazed killer hacks away at the inhabitants of a peaceful summer camp in this run-of-the-mill slasher. **88m/C VHS, Beta.** Mike Kellin, Jonathan Tiersten, Felissa Rose, Christopher Collet. *MED*

Sleepaway Camp 2: Unhappy Campers ½ **1988 (R)** A beautiful camp counselor is actually a blood-thirsty, murdering madwoman. Sequel to the 1983 slasher, "Sleepaway Camp." **82m/C VHS, Beta.** Pamela Springsteen, Renee Estevez, Walter Gotell, Brian Patrick Clark; ***D:*** Michael A. Simpson. *SUE, NLC*

Sleepaway Camp 3: Teenage Wasteland *Woof!* **1989 (R)** This second sequel is as bad as the first two movies. Another disturbed camper hacks up another bevy of teenagers. Better luck at the Motel Six. **80m/C VHS, Beta, LV.** Pamela Springsteen, Tracy Griffith, Michael J. Pollard; ***D:*** Michael A. Simpson. *SUE, NLC*

Sleeper ½ **1973 (PG)** Hapless nerd Allen is revived two hundred years after an operation gone bad. Keaton portrays Allen's love interest in a futuristic land of robots and giant vegetables. He learns of the hitherto unknown health benefits of hot fudge sundaes; discovers the truth about the nation's dictator, known as The Leader; and gets involved with revolutionaries seeking to overthrow the government. Hilarious, fast-moving comedy, full of slapstick and satire. Don't miss the "orgasmatron." **88m/C VHS, Beta, LV.** Woody Allen, Diane Keaton, John Beck, Howard Cosell; ***D:*** Woody Allen; ***W:*** Woody Allen, Marshall Brickman; ***M:*** Woody Allen. *MGM, FOX, FUS*

Sleeping Beauty **1959 (G)** Classic Walt Disney version of the famous fairy tale is set to the music of Tchaikovsky's ballet. Lavishly produced. With the voices of Mary Costa, Bill Shirley, and Vera Vague. **75m/C VHS, Beta, LV.** ***D:*** Clyde Geronomi, Eric Larson, Wolfgang Reitherman, Les Clark; ***M:*** George Bruns; ***V:*** Mary Costa, Bill Shirley, Barbara Luddy, Taylor Holmes, Verna Felton, Barbara Jo Allen, Pinto Colvig, Marvin Miller. Nominations: Academy Awards '59: Best Original Score. *DIS, OM*

Sleeping Beauty **1983** Peters is the princess put to sleep by the evil queen. Handsome prince Reeve comes to the rescue in this classy retelling of the Sleeping Beauty legend. Combines live action and animation. From Shelley Duvall's "Faerie Tale Theatre." **60m/C VHS, Beta, LV.** Christopher Reeve, Bernadette Peters, Beverly D'Angelo. *FOX, FCT, WKV*

Sleeping Beauty ½ **1989** Live action version of the beloved fairy tale, with Welch in the title role. **92m/C VHS.** Tahnee Welch, Morgan Fairchild, Nicholas Clay, Sylvia Miles, Kenny Baker. *MGM, PSM, CVC*

The Sleeping Car **1990** A vindictive ghost haunts a group of people living in an old railway car. Fairly fun, fairly competent horror. **87m/C VHS, LV.** David Naughton, Judie Aronson, Kevin McCarthy, Jeff Conaway, Dani Minnick, John Carl Buechler; ***D:*** Douglas Curtis. *VMK*

Sleeping Car to Trieste **1945** Conspirators in the theft of a diplomat's diary ride the Orient Express, as a wily detective on board tries to piece together murder clues. Based on the story "Rome Express" by Clifford Grey. **95m/B VHS, Beta.** Jean Kent, Albert Lieven, David Tomlinson, Finlay Currie; ***D:*** John Paddy Carstairs. *LCA*

Sleeping Dogs ½ **1982** A man in near-future New Zealand finds it hard to remain neutral when he is caught between a repressive government and a violent resistance movement. The first New Zealand film ever to open in the U.S., and a fine debut for director Donaldson. **107m/C VHS, Beta.** *NZ* Sam Neill, Ian Mune, Nevan Rowe, Dona Akersten, Warren Oates; ***D:*** Roger Donaldson. *NO*

The Sleeping Tiger ½ **1954** A thief breaks into the home of a psychiatrist, who captures him. In exchange for his freedom, the thief agrees to become a guinea pig for the doctor's rehabilitation theories with ultimately tragic results. Director Losey was originally compelled to release the film under a pseudonym, "Victor Hanbury," because he had been blacklisted by Hollywood during the 1950s red scare. First pairing of Losey and Bogarde, who collaborated on several later films, including "Modesty Blaise" (1966) and "Accident" (1967). **89m/B VHS.** Alexis Smith, Alexander Knox, Dirk Bogarde, Hugh Griffith; ***D:*** Joseph Losey; ***M:*** Malcolm Arnold. *NOS, SNC*

Sleeping with Strangers ½ **1994 (R)** Two hoteliers in a small British Columbia town find their rivalry increasing as one hotel gets a boost when a drunken rock star and his Hollywood starlet arrive with their entourage in tow. Of course, the media follows and so does the comedic hysteria. **103m/C VHS.** Adrienne Shelly, Neil Duncan, Shawn Thompson, Kymberley Huffman, Scott McNeil; ***D:*** William T. Bolson; ***W:*** Joan Carr-Wiggin. *PAR*

Sleeping with the Enemy ½ **1991 (R)** Roberts escapes from abusive husband by faking death, flees to Iowa, falls for drama professor, and, gasp, is found by psycho husband. Occasionally chilling but oft predictable thriller based on novel by Nancy Price. **99m/C VHS, Beta, LV.** Julia Roberts, Kevin Anderson, Patrick Bergin, Elizabeth Lawrence, Kyle Secor, Claudette Nevins; ***D:*** Joseph Ruben; ***W:*** Ronald Bass; ***M:*** Jerry Goldsmith. *FXV, IME, FCT*

Sleepless in Seattle ½ **1993 (PG)** Witty, sweet romantic comedy explores the differences between men and women when it comes to love and romance. When widower Hanks talks about his wife on a national talk show, recently engaged Ryan responds. Writer/director Ephron's humorous screenplay is brought to life by a perfectly cast ensemble; it also breathed new life into the classic weepie "An Affair to Remember," comparing it to "The Dirty Dozen" in an unforgettable scene. A movie full of fine detail, from Sven Nykvist's camera work to the graphic layout of the opening credits to the great score. Captured millions at the box office, coming in as the fourth highest grossing movie of 1993. **105m/C VHS, LV, 8mm.** Tom Hanks, Meg Ryan, Bill Pullman, Ross Malinger, Rosie O'Donnell, Gaby Hoffman, Victor Garber, Rita Wilson, Barbara Garrick, Carey Lowell, Rob Reiner, Sarah Trigger; ***D:*** Nora Ephron; ***W:*** Jeffrey Arch, Larry Atlas, David S. Ward, Nora Ephron; ***C:*** Sven Nykvist; ***M:*** Marc Shaiman. Nominations: Academy Awards '93: Best Original Screenplay, Best Song ("A Wink and a Smile"); Golden Globe Awards '94: Best Actor—Musical/Comedy (Hanks), Best Actress—Musical/Comedy (Ryan), Best Film—Musical/

Comedy; MTV Movie Awards '94: Best Actress (Ryan), Breakthrough Performance (Malinger), Best On-Screen Duo (Tom Hanks/Meg Ryan), Best Song ("When I Fall in Love"). *COL, BTV, FCT*

Sleepstalker: The Sandman's Last Rites 🦴🦴 **1994 (R)** A serial killer known as the Sandman (Harris) is executed but returns as a shape-shifting horror who can strip the flesh off his victims with whirling sand. He haunts the nightmares of a reporter (Underwood), the only survivor of one of the killer's massacres, who teams up with a photographer (Morris) to learn the creature's origins and defeat him. Good special effects. **101m/C VHS.** Jay Underwood, Michael Harris, Kathryn Morris; ***D:*** Turi Meyer. *PSM*

Sleepwalk 🦴🦴 **1988 (R)** Odd independent effort about a bored New York desk worker who is given an ancient text of Chinese fairy tales to translate, and finds they're manifesting themselves in dangerous ways in real life. Cinematography by Jim Jarmusch and Franz Prinzi. **78m/C VHS, Beta, LV.** Suzanne Fletcher, Ann Magnuson; ***D:*** Sara Driver. *SUE, NLC, ICA*

Sleepwalkers 🦴½ *Stephen King's Sleepwalkers* **1992 (R)** When Mary and her son Charles arrive in the small town of Travis, Indiana, ugly things begin to happen. And no wonder, it seems the deadly duo are sleepwalkers—fiendish, cat-like vampire creatures who can only survive by sucking the life force out of unsuspecting virgins. Gory but not without some humor, particularly in Krige's portrayal of the sexy and too-loving mother. Not nearly as good as some of King's other horror classics. **91m/C VHS, LV.** Brian Krause, Madchen Amick, Alice Krige, Jim Haynie, Cindy Pickett, Lyman Ward, Ron Perlman; ***Cameos:*** Dan Martin, Glenn Shadix, Joe Dante, John Landis, Clive Barker, Tobe Hooper, Stephen King, Mark Hamill; ***D:*** Mick Garris; ***W:*** Stephen King. *COL*

The Slender Thread 🦴🦴🦴 **1965** Based on a true story, Poitier plays a college student who volunteers at a crisis center and must keep would-be suicide Bancroft on the phone until the police can find her. Filmed on location in Seattle. First film for director Pollack. **98m/C VHS.** Sidney Poitier, Anne Bancroft, Telly Savalas, Steven Hill; ***D:*** Sydney Pollack; ***W:*** Stirling Silliphant; ***C:*** Loyal Griggs; ***M:*** Quincy Jones. Nominations: Academy Awards '65: Best Art Direction/Set Decoration (B & W), Best Costume Design (B & W). *PAR*

Sleuth 🦴🦴🦴½ **1972 (PG)** A mystery novelist and his wife's lover face off in ever shifting, elaborate, and diabolical plots against each other, complete with red herrings, traps, and tricks. Playful, cerebral mystery thriller from top director Mankiewicz. Shaffer also scripted "Frenzy" for Hitchcock, from his play. **138m/C VHS, Beta, LV.** Laurence Olivier, Michael Caine; ***D:*** Joseph L. Mankiewicz; ***W:*** Anthony Shaffer; ***C:*** Oswald Morris; ***M:*** John Addison. Edgar Allan Poe Awards '72: Best Screenplay; New York Film Critics Awards '72: Best Actor (Olivier); Nominations: Academy Awards '72: Best Actor (Caine), Best Actor (Olivier), Best Director (Mankiewicz), Best Original Score. *MED, HMV, VTR*

Slightly Honorable 🦴🦴½ **1940** A lawyer gets involved in political scandals and becomes a murder suspect. Snappy comedy-drama with good performances but too many subplots. Based on the novel "Send Another Coffin" by F. G. Presnell. **75m/B VHS, Beta.** Pat O'Brien, Broderick Crawford, Edward Arnold, Eve Arden, Evelyn Keyes, Phyllis Brooks; ***D:*** Tay Garnett. *NOS, VYY, BAR*

A Slightly Pregnant Man 🦴🦴 **1979 (PG)** Comic complications abound as a construction worker becomes the world's first pregnant man. Surprise ending saves this simple and not very exciting film. **92m/C VHS, Beta.** Catherine Deneuve, Marcello Mastroianni; ***D:*** Jacques Demy. *NO*

Slightly Scarlet 🦴🦴½ **1956** Small-time hood Payne carries out an assignment from boss DeCorsia to smear a law-and-order politico running for mayor. He falls in love with the candidate's secretary, tries to go straight, and ends up running the mob when DeCorsia flees town. A spiffy, low-budget noir crime drama based on the James M. Cain novel "Love's Lovely Counterfeit." **99m/C VHS, Beta.** Rhonda Fleming, Arlene Dahl, John Payne, Kent Taylor, Ted de Corsia; ***D:*** Allan Dwan; ***W:*** Robert Blees. *NO*

Slime City 🦴 **1989** The widow of an alchemist poisons her tenants so they will join her husband in the hereafter. Very low-budget; occasionally funny. **90m/C VHS, Beta.** Robert C. Sabin, Mary Huner, T.J. Merrick, Dick Biel; ***D:*** Gregory Lamberson. *NO*

The Slime People *Woof!* **1963** Huge prehistoric monsters are awakened from long hibernation by atomic testing in Los Angeles. They take over the city, creating the fog they need to live. Thank goodness for scientist Burton, who saves the day. Filmed in a butcher shop in Los Angeles. **76m/B VHS, Beta.** Robert Hutton, Robert Burton, Susan Hart, William Boyce, Les Tremayne; ***D:*** Robert Hutton. *NOS, GEM, RHI*

The Slingshot 🦴🦴🦴 **1993 (R)** Quirky coming-of-age tale, set in 1920s Stockholm, finds 12-year-old Roland (Salen) trying to survive childhood dilemmas. His mother (Frydman) is a Russian Jew (who sells condoms illegally) and his father (Skarsgard) is a zealous socialist, so Roland is subjected to unceasing bullying and prejudice. But the resourceful Roland doesn't let society get him down—he uses the contraband condoms in an inventive slingshot design that brings him an unwarranted amount of attention. Based on the novel by Roland Schutt. Swedish with subtitles. **102m/C VHS, LV.** *SW* Jesper Salen, Stellan Skarsgard, Basia Frydman, Niclas Olund, Ernst-Hugo Jaregard, Jacob Leygraf; ***D:*** Ake Sandgren; ***W:*** Bjorn Isfalt, Ake Sandgren. *COL*

Slipping into Darkness 🦴½ **1988 (R)** Three spoiled, rich college girls are held responsible for a retarded local boy's death. Honest and overwrought. **86m/C VHS, Beta, LV.** Belle Mitchell, Laslo Papas, Rigg Kennedy, Beverly Ross, T.J. McFadden, Michelle Johnson, John DiAquino; ***D:*** Eleanor Gaver. *GHV, HHE*

Slipstream 🦴🦴 **1972** "Turgid" and "gloomy" are the words for this romantic drama set in remote Alberta. The minor plot concerns a young woman who teaches a lonely disc jockey a lesson about life and love. This film feels like a long Canadian winter. **93m/C VHS, Beta.** *CA* Julie Askew, Patti Oatman, Eli Rill. *TWE*

Slipstream 🦴🦴 **1989 (PG-13)** A sci-fi adventure set on a damaged Earthscape where people seek to escape a giant jetstream. While tracking down a bounty hunter gone bad, a futuristic cop follows his quarry into the dangerous river of wind. Ambitious "Blade Runner" clone with big names (Hamill is good) was never released theatrically in the US. **92m/C VHS, Beta, LV.** *GB* Mark Hamill, Bill Paxton, Bob Peck, Eleanor David, Kitty Aldridge, Robbie Coltrane, Ben Kingsley, F. Murray Abraham; ***D:*** Steven Lisberger; ***W:*** Tony Kayden; ***M:*** Elmer Bernstein. *VTR*

Slither 🦴🦴🦴 **1973 (PG)** Caan and Boyle become wrapped up in a scheme to recover $300,000 in cash, stolen seven years previously. Along the way they pick up speed freak Kellerman, who assists them in a variety of loony ways. Frantic chase scenes are the highlight. **97m/C VHS, Beta.** James Caan, Peter Boyle, Sally Kellerman, Louise Lasser, Allen (Goorwitz) Garfield, Richard B. Shull, Alex Rocco; ***D:*** Howard Zieff; ***W:*** W.D. Richter. *MGM*

Slithis *Woof!* **1978 (PG)** Slithis, the nuclear-waste creature, is the menace of Venice, California. Keep your pets (and yourself) indoors! **86m/C VHS, Beta.** Alan Blanchard, Judy Motulsky; ***D:*** Stephen Traxler; ***W:*** Stephen Traxler. *MED*

Sliver 🦴½ **1993 (R)** Another voyeuristic thriller starring Stone. She's Carly Norris, a lonely book editor who moves into one of Manhattan's toothpick thin buildings (the "sliver" of the title). She meets pulp novelist Jack (Berenger), whose libido is as overheated as his prose, but gets involved in a steamy affair with handsome neighbor Zeke (Baldwin), a computer whiz who also owns the building. Oh, by the way, he's installed video cameras in every unit that reveal many intimate secrets. Lots of sex and murders. Murky and underdeveloped and the ending, which was reshot, still leaves much to be desired. Lots of hype, little to recommend. **106m/C VHS, Beta, LV, CD-I.** Sharon Stone, William Baldwin, Tom Berenger, Martin Landau, Polly Walker, Colleen Camp, CCH Pounder, Nina Foch, Keene Curtis; ***D:*** Phillip Noyce; ***W:*** Joe Eszterhas; ***C:*** Vilmos Zsigmond; ***M:*** Howard Shore. MTV Movie Awards '94: Most Desirable Male (Baldwin); Nominations: MTV Movie Awards '94: Most Desirable Female (Stone), Best Song ("I Can't Help Falling in Love"). *PAR*

Sloane *Woof!* **1984** Typical sleazy sex and violence flick. For the record: organized crime baddies kidnap good guy Resnick's girlfriend and he seeks revenge. **95m/C VHS, Beta.** Robert Resnick, Debra Blee, Paul Aragon; ***D:*** Dan Rosenthal. *LIV, VES*

Slow Burn 🦴🦴 **1986** An ex-reporter tries some detective work in the seamy side of Palm Springs, and becomes embroiled in the standard drug, kidnapping, murder routine. Based on the novel "Castles Burning" by Arthur Lyons. Made for cable television. **92m/C VHS, Beta.** Eric Roberts, Beverly D'Angelo, Dan Hedaya, Dennis Lipscomb; ***D:*** Matthew Chapman; ***W:*** Matthew Chapman; ***M:*** Loek Dikker. *MCA*

Slow Burn 🦴 **1990 (R)** The Mafia and Chinese Triads are having troubles and a tired cop attempts to reach a peaceful solution. **90m/C VHS.** William Smith, Anthony James, Ivan Rogers. *XVC, DMP*

Slow Moves 🦴½ **1984** Slow story of slow people who meet slowly, have sluggish affair, and find tragedy eventually. **93m/C VHS, Beta.** Roxanne Rogers; ***D:*** Jon Jost. *FCT*

The Slugger's Wife 🦴½ *Neil Simon's The Slugger's Wife* **1985 (PG-13)** The marriage between an Atlanta Braves outfielder and a rock singer suddenly turns sour when their individual careers force them to make some tough choices. **105m/C VHS, Beta, LV.** Michael O'Keefe, Rebecca DeMornay, Martin Ritt, Randy Quaid, Loudon Wainwright III, Cleavant Derricks, Lynn Whitfield; ***D:*** Hal Ashby; ***W:*** Neil Simon; ***C:*** Caleb Deschanel. *COL*

Slugs *Woof!* **1987 (R)** A health inspector discovers that spilled toxic waste is being helpfully cleaned up by the slug population, saving Uncle Sam countless dollars. But wait! The slugs are mutating into bloodthirsty man-eaters. Is this the answer to military cutbacks? **90m/C VHS, Beta, LV.** Michael Garfield, Kim Terry, Philip Machale; ***D:*** J. Piquer Simon. *VTR, NWV*

Slumber Party '57 🦴½ **1976 (R)** At a slumber party, six girls get together and exchange stories of how they lost their virginity. Lots of great music by the Platters, Big Bopper, Jerry Lee Lewis, the Crewcuts, and Paul and Paula but complete schlock otherwise. **89m/C VHS, Beta, LV.** Noelle North, Bridget Hollman, Debra Winger, Mary Ann Appleseth, Cheryl "Rainbeaux" Smith, Janet Wood, R.L. Armstrong, Rafael Campos, Larry Gelman, Will Hutchins, Joyce Jillson, Victor Rogers, Joe E. Ross, Bill Thurman; ***D:*** William A. Levey; ***M:*** Miles Goodman. *MGM, VES*

The Slumber Party Massacre 🦴½ **1982 (R)** A psychotic killer with a power drill terrorizes a high school girls' slumber party. Contrived and forced, but not always unfunny. **84m/C VHS, Beta.** Michele Michaels, Robin Stille, Andre Honore, Michael Villela, Debra Deliso, Gina Mari, Brinke Stevens; ***D:*** Amy Holden Jones, Aaron Lipstadt; ***W:*** Rita Mae Brown. *SUE*

Slumber Party Massacre 2 *Woof!* **1987** Drowsy babes in lingerie are drilled to death by a perverse madman. Another disappointing sequel. **75m/C VHS, Beta, LV.** Crystal Bernard, Kimberly McArthur, Juliette Cummins, Patrick Lowe; ***D:*** Deborah Brock; ***W:*** Deborah Brock. *SUE, NLC*

Slumber Party Massacre 3 *Woof!* **1990 (R)** Parents: Don't let your daughters have any slumber parties! Yes, it's a drill—for the third time. **76m/C VHS, Beta.** Keely Christian, Brittain Frye, M.K. Harris, David Greenle, Hope Marie Carlton, Maria Ford; ***D:*** Sally Mattison; ***W:*** Catherine Cyran. *MGM*

The Small Back Room 🦴🦴🦴 *Hour of Glory* **1949** A crippled WWII munitions expert leads a tormented existence and laments government bureaucracy. Powerfully presented adult storyline. **106m/B VHS.** David Farrar, Jack Hawkins, Cyril Cusack, Kathleen Byron, Anthony Bushell, Michael Gough, Robert Morley; ***D:*** Michael Powell, Emeric Pressburger. *VYY, LOO, FCT*

Small Change 𝒮𝒮𝒮𝒮 **1976 (PG)** Pudgy, timid Desmouceaux and scruffy, neglected Goldman lead a whole pack of heartwarming tykes. A realistically and tenderly portrayed testament to the great director's belief in childhood as a "state of grace." Criticized for sentimentality, "Small Change" followed Truffaut's gloomy "The Story of Adele H." Steven Spielberg suggested the English translation of "L'Argent de Poche." In French with English subtitles. **104m/C VHS, Beta, LV.** *FR* Geory Desmouceaux, Philippe Goldman, Jean-Francois Stevenin, Chantal Mercier, Claudio Deluca, Frank Deluca, Richard Golfier, Laurent Devlaeminck, Francis Devlaeminck; ***D:*** Francois Truffaut; ***W:*** Suzanne Schiffman. National Board of Review Awards '76: 5 Best Foreign Films of the Year. *MGM, FCT, INJ*

A Small Circle of Friends 𝒮½ **1980 (R)** Three Harvard students struggle through their shifting relationships during their college years in the 1960s. **112m/C VHS, Beta.** Brad Davis, Jameson Parker, Karen Allen, Shelley Long; ***D:*** Rob Cohen. *FOX*

Small Hotel 𝒮𝒮 **1957** After discovering that he is to be replaced as headwaiter by a young woman, Harker plots to save his job through espionage, blackmail and cajolery. Average comedy, adapted from a popular British stage play as a star vehicle for Harker. **59m/B VHS.** Gordon Harker, Marie Lohr, John Loder, Irene Handl, Janet Munro, Billie Whitelaw, Francis Matthews, Dora Bryan; ***D:*** David MacDonald. *NOS*

Small Kill 𝒮½ **1993 (R)** Burghoff leaves his lovable MASH character far behind, testing his acting skills as a psycho who disguises himself as a female fortune teller to rob his victims of their life savings so he can become head druglord of his town (what a goal). Two cops try to stop him/her. **86m/C VHS.** Gary Burghoff, Rebecca Ferratti, Donnie Kehr, Jason Miller, Fred Carpenter; ***D:*** Robert M. Fresco; ***W:*** Fred Carpenter, James McTernan. *VCI*

A Small Killing 𝒮𝒮 **1981** An undercover cop and a college professor pose as a wino and a bag lady, when trying to put the tabs on a druglord. Made for TV mystery/romance based on "The Rag Bag Clan" by Richard Barth. **100m/C VHS, Beta.** Ed Asner, Jean Simmons, Sylvia Sidney, Andrew Prine, J. Pat O'Malley, Anne Ramsey; ***D:*** Steven Hilliard Stern. *LIV*

Small Sacrifices 𝒮𝒮½ **1989** The true story of Diane Downs, an Oregon woman who may have murdered her own three children in 1983. Fine performance from Fawcett, who seems to like made for TV tales of true-life domestic violence as an antidote to her earlier ditzy persona as a Charlie's Angel. Gripping, with a superb script. **159m/C VHS, Beta, LV.** Farrah Fawcett, Ryan O'Neal, John Shea, Emily Perkins, Gordon Clapp; ***D:*** David Greene; ***W:*** Joyce Eliason. *FRH*

Small Time 𝒮𝒮 **1991** Chronicles the downfall of a young, small-time Harlem thief. Vince knows nothing but the streets and peer pressure, indifference, and police abuse lead him inexorably to a fatal crime. Near documentary style only heightens the tensions. **88m/B VHS.** Richard Barboza, Carolyn Hinebrew, Keith Allen, Scott Ferguson, Jane Williams; ***D:*** Norman Loftis; ***W:*** Norman Loftis; ***M:*** Arnold Bieber. *XVC*

Small Town Boy 𝒮𝒮 **1937** The cast does what they can with the brief, hackneyed story of a guy whose personality changes for the worse when he finds a "fortune" (one thousand pre-inflationary dollars). **61m/B VHS.** Stuart Erwin, Joyce Compton, Jed Prouty, Clara Blandick, James "Doc" Blakely; ***D:*** Glenn Tryon; ***W:*** Glenn Tryon. *NOS, LOO, VYY*

Small Town Girl 𝒮𝒮½ *One Horse Town* **1953** Typical romantic musical of the era, as a city slicker picked up for speeding in a hick town is pursued by the sheriff's daughter. Several Busby Berkeley blockbuster musical numbers are shoehorned incongruously into the rural doings. ♫Take Me To Broadway; I've Got To Hear That Beat; My Flaming Heart; Fine, Fine, Fine; The Fellow I'd Follow; Lullaby of the Lord; Small Towns Are Smile Towns; My Gaucho. **93m/C VHS, Beta.** Jane Powell, Farley Granger, Bobby Van, Ann Miller, Billie Burke, Robert Keith, S.Z. Sakall, Fay Wray, Nat King Cole, Chill Wills; ***D:*** Leslie Kardos; ***M:*** Andre Previn. Nominations: Academy Awards '53: Best Song ("My Flaming Heart"). *MGM*

A Small Town in Texas 𝒮𝒮 **1976 (PG)** An ex-con returns home looking for the sheriff who framed him on a drug charge, and who has stolen his woman. Not-too-violent, predictable revenge flick. **96m/C VHS, Beta.** Timothy Bottoms, Susan George, Bo Hopkins; ***D:*** Jack Starrett; ***W:*** William W. Norton Sr.; ***M:*** Charles Bernstein. *VES, LIV*

The Smallest Show on Earth 𝒮𝒮𝒮 *Big Time Operators* **1957** A couple inherit not only an old movie house, but the three people who work there as well. Very funny and charming, with a wonderful cast. Sellers is delightful as the soused projectionist. **80m/B VHS.** *GB* Bill Travers, Virginia McKenna, Margaret Rutherford, Peter Sellers, Bernard Miles, Leslie Phillips; ***D:*** Basil Dearden. *NOS, FCT, VEC*

Smart-Aleck Kill **1985** An episode of the cable television-produced Phillip Marlowe series involving the drug-related murder of a Hollywood actor in the 20s. **53m/C VHS, Beta.** Powers Boothe, Michael J. Shannon, Liza Ross; ***D:*** Peter Hunt. *FOX*

Smart Alecks 𝒮½ **1942** The Bowery Boys get involved with gangsters when Jordan helps capture a crook. The usual wise-cracking from Hall and Gorcey helps keep things moving. **88m/B VHS.** Leo Gorcey, Huntz Hall, Gabriel Dell, Gale Storm, Roger Pryor Jr., Walter Woolf King, Herbert Rawlinson, Joe Kirk, Marie Windsor; ***D:*** Wallace Fox. *NOS*

Smart Money 𝒮𝒮½ **1988** A wrongly-jailed man enlists the help of his oddball pals to get revenge on the real thief who committed the computer fraud that put him behind bars. They get even while padding their pockets. **88m/C VHS.** Spencer Leigh, Alexandra Pigg, Ken Campbell. *NO*

Smash Palace 𝒮𝒮½ **1982** A compelling drama of a marriage jeopardized by his obsession with building a race car and her need for love and affection. Melodramatic, but worth watching. Robson as their young daughter is wonderful. **100m/C VHS, Beta, LV.** *NZ* Bruno Lawrence, Anna Jemison, Greer Robson, Keith Aberdein; ***D:*** Roger Donaldson; ***W:*** Bruno Lawrence. *LIV, VES*

Smash-Up: The Story of a Woman 𝒮𝒮𝒮 *A Woman Destroyed* **1947** A famous nightclub singer gives up her career for marriage and a family, only to become depressed when her husband's career soars. She turns to alcohol and her life falls apart. When her husband sues for divorce and custody of their child, she fights to recover from alcoholism. Hayward's first major role. **103m/B VHS, Beta.** Susan Hayward, Lee Bowman, Marsha Hunt, Eddie Albert; ***D:*** Stuart Heisler; ***W:*** John Howard Lawson. Nominations: Academy Awards '47: Best Actress (Hayward), Best Story. *NOS, PSM, DVT*

Smile 𝒮𝒮𝒮 **1975 (PG)** Barbed, merciless send-up of small-town America focusing on a group of naive California girls who compete for the "Young American Miss" crown amid rampant commercialism, exploitation and pure middle-class idiocy. Hilarious neglected '70s-style satire. Early role for Griffith. **113m/C VHS, Beta, LV.** Bruce Dern, Barbara Feldon, Michael Kidd, Nicholas Pryor, Geoffrey Lewis, Colleen Camp, Joan Prather, Annette O'Toole, Melanie Griffith, Denise Nickerson; ***D:*** Michael Ritchie; ***W:*** Jerry Belson; ***C:*** Conrad Hall. *MGM*

Smile, Jenny, You're Dead 𝒮𝒮 **1974** Janssen discovers that close friend's son-in-law has been murdered, and falls in love with the daughter, the main suspect. Pilot for Janssen's "Harry-O" detective series. **100m/C VHS.** David Janssen, John Anderson, Howard da Silva, Martin Gabel, Clu Gulager, Zalman King, Jodie Foster, Barbara Leigh; ***D:*** Jerry Thorpe. *UNI*

Smiles of a Summer Night 𝒮𝒮𝒮½ *Sommarnattens Leende* **1955** The best known of Bergman's rare comedies; sharp satire about eight Swedish aristocrats who become romantically and comically intertwined over a single weekend. Inspired Sondheim's successful Broadway musical "A Little Night Music," and Woody Allen's "A Midsummer Night's Sex Comedy." In Swedish with English subtitles. **110m/B VHS, Beta, LV.** *SW* Gunnar Bjornstrand, Harriet Andersson, Ulla Jacobsson, Eva Dahlbeck, Jarl Kulle, Margit Carlquist; ***D:*** Ingmar Bergman; ***W:*** Ingmar Bergman. *HMV, DVT, CRC*

Smilin' Through 𝒮𝒮𝒮 **1932** First sound version of this melodrama/romance which Franklin had directed as a silent in 1922. Shearer is set to marry Howard when jealous rival March shows up armed at the wedding and accidentally kills the bride. March escapes and Howard spends his years as a recluse until his young niece, the image of his dead fiance (naturally, since she's also played by Shearer) arrives to live with him. She meets a young man who turns out to be March's son (played again by March) and they fall in love. Pure sentiment done with high gloss. Remade in 1941. **97m/B VHS.** Norma Shearer, Fredric March, Leslie Howard, O.P. Heggie, Ralph Forbes, Beryl Mercer, Margaret Seddon; ***D:*** Sidney Franklin; ***C:*** Lee Garmes. *FCT*

Smilin' Through 𝒮𝒮½ **1941** Third filming, second with sound, first in color, of a popular melodrama. An embittered man whose wife was murdered on their wedding day raises an orphaned niece, only to have her fall in love with the son of her aunt's murderer. Made MacDonald into a singing star. Songs include title tune and "A Little Love, a Little Kiss." **101m/C VHS, Beta.** Jeanette MacDonald, Brian Aherne, Gene Raymond, Ian Hunter, Frances Robinson; ***D:*** Frank Borzage. *MGM*

Smiling Madame Beudet/The Seashell and the Clergyman 𝒮𝒮𝒮½ **1928** Two famous shorts by Dulac; the second scripted by Artaud. Both are pioneering examples of surrealistic film. Silent. **62m/B VHS, Beta.** *FR* Alix Allin; ***D:*** Germaine Dulac; ***W:*** Antonin Artaud. *FCT*

Smith! 𝒮𝒮½ **1969 (G)** Naive but well intentioned look at present-day treatment of Native Americans. Rancher Ford becomes embroiled in the trial of murder suspect Ramirez. Based on Paul St. Pierre's novel "Breaking Smith's Quarter Horse." **101m/C VHS, Beta.** Glenn Ford, Frank Ramirez, Keenan Wynn; ***D:*** Michael O'Herlihy; ***M:*** Robert F. Brunner. *DIS*

Smithereens 𝒮𝒮½ **1982 (R)** Working-class girl leaves home for New York's music scene. Rugged, hip character study. Director Seidleman's first feature. **90m/C VHS, Beta, LV.** Susan Berman, Brad Rinn, Richard Hell, Christopher Noth; ***D:*** Susan Seidelman; ***W:*** Ron Nyswaner, Peter Askin. Nominations: Cannes Film Festival '82: Best Film. *ICA, TPV, FCT*

Smoke 𝒮𝒮½ **1970** A young boy nurses a lost German sheperd back to health with the help of his new stepfather, whom he learns to trust. Then he runs away with the dog when the original owners show up. Made for television Disney fare starring Opie/Richie (and later successful director) Howard. **89m/C VHS, Beta.** Earl Holliman, Ron Howard, Andy Devine; ***D:*** Vincent McEveety; ***W:*** Paul Auster. *DIS*

Smoke 𝒮𝒮 **1993** Three days in the life of Michael, as he travels between fantasy and reality, past and present, searching for love with the perfect older man. **90m/C VHS.** ***D:*** Mark D'Aruia; ***M:*** Arnold Bieber. *WBF*

Smoke 𝒮𝒮 **1995 (R)** Brooklyn slice of life centers around the local cigar store run by Auggie Wren (Keitel). An ensemble piece, divided into five chapters, which includes such characters as down-on-his luck novelist Paul (Hurt), troubled black teenager Rashid (Perrineau Jr.), Augie's ex-wife Ruby (Channing) and supposed daughter (Judd), and many more (some of whom get lost in the shuffle). Wonderfully acted but the stories tend to disappear in a wisp of smoke. Based on a story by Auster. Wang and Auster also made an impromptu companion film "Blue in the Face." **112m/C VHS, LV.** Harvey Keitel, William Hurt, Stockard Channing, Forest Whitaker, Harold Perrineau Jr., Ashley Judd, Mary Ward, Victor Argo, Jared Harris, Giancarlo Esposito, Mel Gorham; ***D:*** Wayne Wang; ***W:*** Paul Auster; ***C:*** Adam Holender; ***M:*** Rachel Portman. Nominations: Independent Spirit Awards '96: Best Supporting Actor (Perrineau); Screen Actors Guild Award '95: Best Supporting Actress (Channing). *TOU*

Smoke in the Wind 🦴½ **1975 (PG)** Sub-par western about men accused of complicity with the Union in postbellum Arkansas. Minor role for Brennan was his last; also director Kane's last film. **93m/C VHS, Beta.** John Ashley, Walter Brennan, John Russell, Myron Healey; ***D:*** Joseph Kane. *PSM*

Smokescreen 🦴🦴½ **1990 (R)** A young ad exec meets the girl of his dreams, and finds himself working for her gangster boyfriend. Competently made and acted, but phoney ending wrecks it. **91m/C VHS, LV.** Kim Cattrall, Dean Stockwell, Matt Craven, Kim Coates, Brian George, Michael Hogan; ***D:*** Martin Lavut. *COL*

Smokey and the Bandit 🦴🦴½ **1977 (PG)** If you don't know how to end a movie, you call for a car chase. The first and best of the horrible series about bootlegger Reynolds is one long car chase. Reynolds makes a wager that he can have a truck load of Coors beer—once unavailable east of Texas—delivered to Atlanta from Texas in 28 hours. Gleason is the "smokey" who tries to stop him. Field is the hitchhiker Reynolds picks up along the way. Great stunts; director Needham was a top stunt man. **96m/C VHS, Beta, LV.** Burt Reynolds, Sally Field, Jackie Gleason, Jerry Reed, Mike Henry, Paul Williams, Pat McCormick; ***D:*** Hal Needham; ***W:*** Charles Shyer. Nominations: Academy Awards '77: Best Film Editing. *MCA*

Smokey and the Bandit, Part 2 🦴 *Smokey and the Bandit Ride Again* **1980 (PG)** Pathetic sequel to "Smokey and the Bandit" proved a box-office winner, grossing $40 million. The Bandit is hired to transport a pregnant elephant from Miami to the Republican convention in Dallas. Sheriff Buford T. Justice and family are in hot pursuit. **101m/C VHS, Beta, LV.** Burt Reynolds, Sally Field, Jackie Gleason, Jerry Reed, Mike Henry, Dom DeLuise, Pat McCormick, Paul Williams; ***D:*** Hal Needham; ***W:*** Jerry Belson, Michael Kane. *MCA*

Smokey and the Bandit, Part 3 🦴 **1983 (PG)** You thought the second one was bad? Another mega car chase, this time sans Reynolds and director Needham. **88m/C VHS, Beta, LV.** Jackie Gleason, Jerry Reed, Paul Williams, Pat McCormick, Mike Henry, Colleen Camp; ***Cameos:*** Burt Reynolds; ***D:*** Dick Lowry; ***W:*** Stuart Birnbaum, David Dashev. *MCA*

Smokey & the Hotwire Gang 🦴½ **1979** A convoy of truckers try to track down a beautiful woman driving a stolen car. **85m/C VHS, Beta.** James Keach, Stanley Livingston, Tony Lorea, Alvy Moore, George Barris. *NO*

Smokey & the Judge 🦴 **1980 (PG)** Police officer has his hands full with a trio of lovely ladies. **90m/C VHS.** Gene Price, Wayde Preston, Juanita Curiel. *SUN*

Smokey Bites the Dust 🦴 **1981 (PG)** Car-smashing gag-fest about a sheriff's daughter kidnapped by her smitten beau. Near-plotless and literally unoriginal: lifted footage from several other Corman-produced flicks, a technique that can aptly be called garbage picking. **87m/C VHS, Beta.** Janet Julian, Jimmy McNichol, Patrick Campbell, Kari Lizer, John Blythe Barrymore Jr.; ***D:*** Charles B. Griffith; ***W:*** Max Apple. *NLC*

Smokey Smith 🦴½ **1936** Ubiquitous Hayes and steely Steele hunt down the slayers of an elderly couple. Ordinary oater directed by Steele's father, Bradbury. **59m/B VHS, Beta.** Bob Steele, George "Gabby" Hayes; ***D:*** Robert North Bradbury. *VCN*

Smoking/No Smoking 🦴🦴 **1994** Two linked films director Resnais adapted from writer Alan Ayckbourn's eight-play cycle "Intimate Exchanges" (although the screenwriters have only used six stories). Azema and Arditti plays nine characters in various tableaus on marriage and affairs set at a Yorkshire school. The opening sequence of each episode provides the title tie-in, as faculty wife Celia goes onto the terrace, finds a pack of cigarettes, and decides whether or not to light up. A studio set provides all the frankly fake backdrops. Very slight and very long. French with subtitles. **285m/C VHS.** *FR* Sabine Azema, Pierre Arditti; ***D:*** Alain Resnais; ***W:*** Jean-Pierre Bacri, Agnes Jaoui. Cesar Awards '94: Best Actor (Arditti), Best Art Direction/Set Decoration, Best Director (Resnais), Best Film, Best Screenplay.

A Smoky Mountain Christmas 🦴🦴 **1986** Dolly gets away from it all in a secluded cabin that has been appropriated by a gang of orphans, and sings a half dozen songs. Innocuous seasonal country fun. Winkler's TV directing debut. **94m/C VHS, Beta.** Dolly Parton, Bo Hopkins, Dan Hedaya, Gennie James, David Ackroyd, Rene Auberjonois, John Ritter, Anita Morris, Lee Majors; ***D:*** Henry Winkler; ***W:*** Dolly Parton. *FOX*

Smooth Talk 🦴🦴🦴 **1985 (PG-13)** An innocent, flirtatious teenager catches the eye of a shady character, played by Williams. Disturbing and thought-provoking film that caused some controversy when it opened. Dern gives a brilliant performance as the shy, sheltered girl. Based on the Joyce Carol Oates story of the same name. Made for PBS' "American Playhouse" series. **92m/C VHS, Beta, LV.** Laura Dern, Treat Williams, Mary Kay Place, Levon Helm; ***D:*** Joyce Chopra; ***W:*** Tom Cole. Sundance Film Festival '86: Grand Jury Prize. *LIV, VES*

Smooth Talker *Woof!* **1990 (R)** A serial killer stalks the women of a 976 party line. Bad acting, bad dialog, not a scare to be found. **89m/C VHS.** Joe Guzaldo, Peter Crombie, Stuart Whitman, Burt Ward, Sydney Lassick, Blair Weickgenant; ***D:*** Tom Milo. *ACA*

Smouldering Fires 🦴🦴½ **1925** A tough businesswoman falls in love with an ambitious young employee, who is fifteen years her junior. After they marry, problems arise in the form of the wife's attractive younger sister. Surprisingly subtle melodrama, if that's not an oxymoron. **100m/B VHS, Beta.** Pauline Frederick, Laura La Plante, Tully Marshall, Malcolm McGregor, Wanda Hawley, Helen Lynch, George Cooper, Bert Roach; ***D:*** Clarence Brown. *VYY, GPV*

Smugglers 🦴 *Lover of the Great Bear* **1975** Opportunistic smugglers take advantage of the Russian Revolution to sack the land and make a bundle. **110m/C VHS, Beta.** *IT* Senta Berger, Giuliano Gemma; ***D:*** Valintino Orsini. *VCD*

Smugglers' Cove 🦴🦴🦴 **1948** Gorcey wrongly believes he has inherited a mansion. He and the Bowery Boys move in, only to stumble across a smuggling ring. Plenty of slapsticks; the boys at their best. **66m/B VHS.** Leo Gorcey, Huntz Hall, Gabriel Dell; ***D:*** William Beaudine. *NO*

Smuggler's Cove 🦴½ **1983** A young boy doggedly pursues a mysterious trawler captain despite warnings from his parents. **75m/C VHS, Beta.** *AU NO*

The Snake Hunter Strangler 🦴 **1966** A young girl is rescued after fifteen years from an evil cult of snake people. **65m/C VHS, Beta.** Guy Madison, Ivan Desny; ***D:*** Luigi Capuano. *NO*

Snake in the Eagle's Shadow 2 🦴 **1983** Three champions of self-defense mount a major offensive and win battle after battle. **89m/C VHS, Beta.** Wang Tao, Chen Shing, Lung Fei; ***D:*** Chang Shinn I. *TWE*

The Snake People 🦴 *Isle of the Snake People; Cult of the Dead; La Muerte Viviente; Isle of the Living Dead* **1968** A police captain investigates a small island littered with LSD-experimenting scientists, snake-worshippers, and voodoo. One of the infamous quartet of Karloff's final films, all made in Mexico. **90m/C VHS, Beta.** *MX* Boris Karloff, Julissa, Carlos East; ***D:*** Enrique Vergara. *SNC, MPI, HEG*

The Snake Pit 🦴🦴🦴½ **1948** One of the first films to compassionately explore mental illness and its treatment. Following an emotional collapse de Havilland is placed in a mental institution by her husband. The severity of her depression causes her sympathetic doctor to try such treatments as electric shock, hydrotherapy, and drugs, along with the psychoanalysis which gradually allows her to accept her fears and make her recovery. Tour-de-force performance by de Havilland. Based on the novel by Mary Jane Ward. **108m/B VHS.** Olivia de Havilland, Mark Stevens, Leo Genn, Celeste Holm, Glenn Langan, Helen Craig, Leif Erickson, Beulah Bondi; ***D:*** Anatole Litvak; ***W:*** Frank Partos, Millen Brand; ***M:*** Alfred Newman. Academy Awards '48: Best Sound; New York Film Critics Awards '48: Best Actress (de Havilland); Nominations: Academy Awards '47: Best Actress (de Havilland), Best Picture; Academy Awards '48: Best Director (Litvak), Best Screenplay, Best Original Score. *FXV, MOV, BTV*

The Snake Woman 🦴 **1961** A herpetologist working in a small English village during the 1890s is conducting strange experiments to try to cure his wife's madness. He tries injecting his pregnant wife with snake venom and she gives birth to a cold-blooded daughter, who, when she grows up, has the ability to change herself into a deadly snake. She promptly begins killing the local male populace until Scotland Yard is called in to investigate. The curvy Travers is appropriately snakey but this movie is dull. **68m/C VHS.** *GB* John P. McCarthy, Susan Travers, Arnold Marle; ***D:*** Sidney J. Furie. *CNM*

SnakeEater 🦴 **1989 (R)** Loner cop tracks down swine who killed his parents and kidnapped his sister. "Rambo" rip-off with little plot, but lots of action. Followed by two sequels. **89m/C VHS, Beta.** Lorenzo Lamas, Larry Csonka, Ron Palillo; ***D:*** George Erschbamer. *MED, VTR*

SnakeEater 2: The Drug Buster 🦴 **1989 (R)** A cop goes nuts and kills four drug dealers. As a result he is committed to an institution. Iron bars don't make a prison for this guy though, and he's soon back on the streets fighting crime with his pal "Speedboat." Silly sequel is quite bad; followed by yet another. **93m/C VHS, Beta.** Lorenzo Lamas, Larry B. Scott, Michelle Scarabelli, Harvey Atkin, Jack Blum, Kathleen Kinmont; ***D:*** George Erschbamer. *PAR*

SnakeEater 3: His Law 🦴 **1992 (R)** Tough cop Jack Kelly (Lamas), aka SnakeEater, is out to avenge a woman's beating by a gang of thug bikers. Lots of action and violence, not much plot; based on W. Glenn Duncan's novel "Rafferty's Rules." **109m/C VHS, Beta.** Lorenzo Lamas, Minor Mustain, Tracy Cook, Holly Chester, Scott "Bam Bam" Bigelow; ***D:*** George Erschbamer; ***W:*** John Dunning. *PAR*

Snapdragon 🦴🦴 **1993 (R)** Police psychologist is led astray by his libido while investigating a luscious amnesiac. His sensible vice cop girlfriend then discovers the sexpot is actually a psycho serial killer calling herself the Snapdragon but will her boyfriend even care? **96m/C VHS, Beta.** Steven Bauer, Pamela Anderson Lee, Chelsea Field; ***D:*** Worth Keeter; ***W:*** Gene Church. *PSM*

The Snapper 🦴🦴🦴½ **1993 (R)** Originally made for BBC television, Frears creates a small comic gem based on the second novel of Doyle's Barrytown trilogy. Set in Dublin, 20-year-old Sharon Curley (Kellegher) finds herself unexpectedly pregnant and refuses to name the father. Family and friends are understanding—until they discover the man's identity. Affecting performances, particularly from Meaney as Sharon's dad who takes a much greater interest in the birth of his grandchild than he ever did with his own children. Cheerful semi-sequel to "The Commitments" serves up domestic upheavals graced with humor and a strong sense of family loyalty. **95m/C VHS, LV.** *IR* Tina Kellegher, Colm Meaney, Ruth McCabe, Colm O'Byrne, Pat Laffan, Eanna MacLiam, Ciara Duffy; ***D:*** Stephen Frears; ***W:*** Roddy Doyle. Nominations: Golden Globe Awards '94: Best Actor—Musical/Comedy (Meaney). *TOU*

Snapshot 🦴 **1977 (R)** Typical grade Z sex comedy; a free-lance photographer ogles lots of variously dishabilled young women through his lens. **84m/C VHS, Beta.** Jim Henshaw, Susan Petrie. *NO*

Snatched 🦴🦴 **1972** The wives of three wealthy men are held for ransom, but one man doesn't want to pay, while one of the victims needs insulin. Standard made for television fare. **73m/C VHS.** Howard Duff, Leslie Nielsen, Sheree North, Barbara Parkins, Robert Reed, John Saxon, Tisha Sterling; ***D:*** Sutton Roley; ***M:*** Randy Edelman. *REP*

Sneakers 🦴🦴½ **1992 (PG-13)** Competent thriller about five computer hackers with questionable pasts and an equally questionable government job. Of course, nothing is as it seems. Rather slow-going considering the talents and suspense involved but includes enough turns to keep a viewer's interest. **125m/C VHS, Beta, LV.** Robert Redford, Sidney Poitier, River Phoenix, Dan Aykroyd, Ben Kingsley, David Strathairn, Mary McDonnell, Timothy Busfield, George Hearn, Eddie Jones, James Earl Jones, Stephen Tobolowsky; **D:** Phil Alden Robinson; **W:** Lawrence Lasker, Walter F. Parkes, Phil Alden Robinson; **C:** John Lindley; **M:** James Horner, Branford Marsalis. *MCA, PMS*

Sniper 🦴🦴🦴 *The Deadly Tower* **1975** Suspenseful television drama based on true story of Charles Whitman, who shot at University of Texas students from Texas Tower on a summer day in 1966. Disney alumunus Russell breaks type as mass killer, with fine support by Yniguez as a police officer on the scene and Beatty as the passerby who lends a hand. Finely crafted recreation of disturbing, true event. **85m/C VHS.** Kurt Russell, Richard Yniguez, John Forsythe, Ned Beatty, Pernell Roberts, Clifton James, Paul Carr, Alan Vint, Pepe Serna; **D:** Jerry Jameson. *XVC*

The Sniper 🦴½ **1987** A law-abiding citizen becomes a vigilante killer after witnessing a violent crime. **90m/C VHS, Beta.** Claudia Cardinale. *NO*

Sniper 🦴½ **1992 (R)** Less than compelling shoot-'em-up set in Panama. Lead characters include Sgt. Beckett (Berenger), a seasoned assassin who gets a rush from killing. Also assigned to the case is Richard Miller (Zane), a newcomer who knows his guns but not his jungles. Together they go in search of their target, a politician planning a coup with the help of a druglord. Action is poorly choreographed and plot is cursory at best. The laserdisc version is available letterboxed. **99m/C VHS, LV, 8mm.** Tom Berenger, Billy Zane, J.T. Walsh, Aden Young, Ken Radley, Reinaldo Arenas, Carlos Alvarez, Roy Edmonds; **D:** Luis Llosa; **W:** Michael Frost Beckner, Crash Leyland; **M:** Gary Chang. *COL*

Sno-Line 🦴 **1985 (R)** A New York gangster moves to Texas and begins to wipe out the competition on his way to building his drug and gambling dynasty. Bo-ring excuse for entertainment. No hope, no redemption, no titillation: just ultra-"realistic" depiction of organized crime, poorly acted. **89m/C VHS, Beta.** Vince Edwards, Paul Smith, June Wilkinson; **D:** Douglas F. Oneans. *LIV*

Snoopy, Come Home 🦴🦴🦴 **1972 (G)** Snoopy leaves Charlie Brown to visit his former owner Lila in the hospital and returns with her to her apartment house. From Charles Schultz's popular comic strip "Peanuts." **80m/C VHS, Beta, LV. D:** Bill Melendez; **W:** Charles M. Schulz. *FXV*

Snoopy's Getting Married, Charlie Brown **1985** An animated Peanuts adventure wherein Snoopy prepares to get married. **30m/C VHS, Beta.** *BAR*

Snow Country 🦴🦴½ **1957** Romantic drama of an unsuccessful, married artist from Tokyo who travels to a mountain resort to find himself. He requests a Geisha for the evening and, when none are available, the beautiful adopted daughter of the local music teacher is sent to him instead. Based on the novel by Nobel Prize winner Yasunari Kawabata. In Japanese with English subtitles. Remade in 1965. **104m/B VHS, Beta.** *JP* Ryo Ikebe, Keiko Kishi, Akira Kubo, Kaoru Yachigusa, Hisaya Morishige, Mineko Yorozuyo, Etsuko Ichihara, Noriko Sengoku, Kumeko Urabe, Eiko Miyoshi, Akira Tan, Chieko Naniwa, Daisuke Kato, Haruo Tanaka; **D:** Shiro Toyoda. *CVC, INJ*

The Snow Creature *Woof!* **1954** Stupid troop of explorers bring back a snow creature from the Himalayas. Critter escapes in L.A. and terrorizes all in its path before blending in with club crowd. Very bad monster epic (the first about a snow monster) that strains credibility frame by frame. Occasionally, depending upon camera angle, light, and viewer mood, monster appears to be something other than guy in bad suit sweating. Directed by Billy Wilder's brother and another argument against genetic consistency. **72m/B VHS, Beta.** Paul Langton, Leslie Denison; **D:** W. Lee Wilder. *NOS, SNC*

Snow Kill 🦴½ **1990** Five city-dwellers travel into the mountains for a fun survival training weekend, but the fun turns deadly when they accidentally come across a murderous drug gang. Pseudo - '30s suspense adventure fails to thrill or surprise. Made for cable. **90m/C VHS, Beta.** Terence Knox, Patti D'Arbanville, David Dukes; **D:** Thomas J. Wright; **W:** Harv Zimmel. *PAR, TTC*

The Snow Queen **1983** From "Fairie Tale Theatre" comes this adaptation of the Hans Christian Andersen tale. A boy and girl who grow up together are separated by evil when the boy is held captive in the icy palace of the Snow Queen. The girl sets out to rescue him. **60m/C VHS, Beta.** Lauren Hutton, Linda Manz, David Hemmings, Melissa Gilbert, Lee Remick, Lance Kerwin; **D:** Peter Medak. *FOX, FCT*

Snow: The Movie 🦴 **1983** Rates creative zero for title, though there is snow, as well as skiing, growing up, romance, and good times among the young people involved. Filmed in Australia. **83m/C VHS, Beta.** David Argue, Lance Curtis; **D:** Robert Gibson. *VCD*

Snow Treasure 🦴 **1967 (G)** With the help of an underground agent, Norwegian children smuggle gold out of the country right under the noses of the Nazis. Based on the novel by Marie McSwigan. **96m/C VHS, Beta.** James Franciscus, Paul Anstad; **D:** Irving Jacoby. *LIV*

Snow White 🦴🦴 **1989** The incomparable Rigg stars in this witty retelling of the beautiful girl and her seven little friends. **85m/C VHS.** Diana Rigg, Sarah Patterson, Billy Barty; **D:** Michael Berz. *WAR*

Snow White and the Seven Dwarfs 🦴🦴🦴🦴 **1937 (G)** Classic adaptation of the Grimm Brothers fairy tale about the fairest of them all. Beautiful animation, memorable characters, and wonderful songs mark this as the definitive "Snow White." Set the stage for other animated features after Walt Disney took an unprecedented gamble by attempting the first animated feature-length film, a project which took over two years to create and $1.5 million to make, and made believers out of those who laughed at the concept. Lifelike animation was based on real stars; Margery Belcher (later Champion) posed for Snow, Louis Hightower was the Prince, and Lucille LaVerne gave the Queen her nasty look. ♫Some Day My Prince Will Come; One Song; With a Smile and a Song; Whistle While You Work; Bluddle-Uddle-Um-Dum; The Dwarfs' Yodel Song; Heigh Ho; I'm Wishing; Isn't This a Silly Song?. **83m/C VHS, LV. D:** David Hand; **W:** Ted Sears, Otto Englander, Earl Hurd, Dorothy Blank, Richard Creedon, Dick Richard, Merrill De Maris, Webb Smith; **M:** Frank Churchill, Paul Smith, Larry Morey, Leigh Harline; **V:** Adriana Caseloti, Harry Stockwell, Lucille LaVerne, Moroni Olsen, Billy Gilbert, Pinto Colvig, Otis Harlan, Scotty Matraw, Roy Atwell, Stuart Buchanan, Marion Darlington, Jim Macdonald. *DIS, OM*

Snow White and the Seven Dwarfs **1983** From cable television's "Faerie Tale Theatre" comes the story of a princess who befriends seven little men to protect her from the jealous evil queen. **60m/C VHS, Beta, LV.** Elizabeth McGovern, Rex Smith, Vincent Price, Vanessa Redgrave; **D:** Peter Medak. *FOX, FCT, HMV*

Snow White and the Three Stooges 🦴 *Snow White and the Three Clowns* **1961** The Stooges fill in for the Seven Dwarfs when they go off prospecting in King Solomon's mines. Alas, see any Stooge movie but this one. **107m/C VHS, Beta.** Moe Howard, Curly Howard, Larry Fine, Carol Heiss, Patricia Medina; **D:** Walter Lang. *FOX, FCT*

Snowball Express 🦴🦴 **1972 (G)** When a New York City accountant inherits a hotel in the Rocky Mountains, he decides to move his family west to attempt to make a go of the defunct ski resort, only to find that the place is falling apart. Run-of-the-mill Disney comedy, based on the novel "Chateau Bon Vivant" by Frankie and John O'Rear. **120m/C VHS, Beta.** Dean Jones, Nancy Olson, Harry (Henry) Morgan, Keenan Wynn; **D:** Norman Tokar; **M:** Robert F. Brunner. *DIS*

Snowballin' 🦴 **1985** A ski instructor gives private lessons to a bunch of snow bunnies. **90m/C VHS, Beta.** Seline Lomez, Daniel Pilon. *JEF*

Snowballing 🦴 **1985 (PG)** Part of the polluted wave of teen-sex flicks of the 1980s, this is very mild for the genre but still no prize. Lusty high schoolers at a skiing competition look for action on and off the slopes, end up exposing a resort fraud. **96m/C VHS, Beta.** Mary McDonough, Bob Hastings. *PSM*

Snowbeast 🦴½ **1977** The residents of a ski resort are being terrorized by a half-human, half-animal beast leaving a path of dead bodies in its wake. "Jaws" hits the slopes. Not scary or even funny. Made for TV. **96m/C VHS, Beta.** Bo Svenson, Yvette Mimieux, Sylvia Sidney, Clint Walker, Robert F. Logan; **D:** Herb Wallerstein. *WOV*

Snowblind 🦴🦴 *Ski Lift to Death* **1978** Two ski gondolas derail, placing the passengers in jeopardy. Among the passengers is a mobster being pursued by an assassin. **98m/C VHS.** Deborah Raffin, Charles Frank, Howard Duff, Don Galloway, Gail Strickland, Don Johnson, Veronica Hamel, Clu Gulager, Lisa Reeves, Suzy Chaffee; **D:** William Wiard. *NO*

The Snows of Kilimanjaro 🦴🦴🦴 **1952** Called by Hemingway "The Snows of Zanuck," in reference to the great producer, this film is actually an artful pastiche of several Hemingway short stories and novels. The main story, "The Snows of Kilimanjaro," acts as a framing device, in which the life of a successful writer is seen through his fevered flashbacks as he and his rich wife, while on safari, await a doctor to save his gangrenous leg. **117m/C Beta.** Gregory Peck, Susan Hayward, Ava Gardner, Hildegarde Neff, Leo G. Carroll, Torin Thatcher, Ava Norring, Helene Stanley, Marcel Dalio, Vincente Gomez, Richard Allen, Leonard Carey; **D:** Henry King; **W:** Casey Robinson; **C:** Leon Shamroy. Nominations: Academy Awards '52: Best Art Direction/Set Decoration (Color), Best Color Cinematography. *NOS, GKK, SNC*

Snowy River, the MacGregor Saga: The Race **1993** A continuation of the "The Man from Snowy River" set in late 1800s Australia. Matt MacGregor (Clarke) is running a successful cattle ranch with his two grown sons and a teenage daughter. Naturally, there's some family strife as well as a horse race. Edited episodes from the TV series. **87m/C VHS.** *AU* Andrew Clarke. *FHE*

Snuff-Bottle Connection 🦴 **1982** Russian envoy is spying for the government while delivering a gift to a Ching dynasty emperor. **96m/C VHS, Beta.** Hwang Jang Lee, John Liu, Roy Horan. *WVE*

Snuffy Smith, Yard Bird 🦴½ *Private Snuffy Smith; Snuffy Smith* **1942** The pint-sized moonshiner finds himself in the Army, clashing with his sergeant. Followed by "Hillbilly Blitzkrieg" later the same year. Duncan is perfect for the part, and Kennedy is right on as his foil. **67m/B VHS.** Bud Duncan, Edgar Kennedy, Sarah Padden, Doris Linden, J. Farrell MacDonald, Frank Austin, Jimmie Dodd; **D:** Eddie Cline. *NOS, VYY*

So Dear to My Heart 🦴🦴🦴½ **1949** A farm boy and his misfit black sheep wreak havoc at the county fair. Several sequences combine live action with animation. Heartwarming and charming; straightforward and likeable but never sentimental. Wonderful, vintage Disney. ♫Sourwood Mountain; Billy Boy; So Dear To My Heart; County Fair; Stick-To-It-Ivity; Ol' Dan Patch; It's Whatcha Do With Watcha Got; Lavender Blue (Dilly Dilly). **82m/C VHS, Beta, LV.** Bobby Driscoll, Burl Ives, Beulah Bondi, Harry Carey Sr., Luana Patten; **D:** Harold Schuster. Nominations: Academy Awards '49: Best Song ("Lavender Blue"). *DIS, WTA*

So Ends Our Night 🦴🦴🦴 **1941** German scorns Nazi ideology, flees Austria, and meets young Jewish couple seeking asylum. Fine adaptation of Erich Maria Remarque's novel "Flotsam," with splendid performances from Sullavan (on loan from Universal) and young Ford. **117m/B VHS.** Fredric March, Margaret Sullavan, Frances Dee, Glenn Ford, Anna Sten, Erich von Stroheim; **D:** John Cromwell; **C:** William H. Daniels. Nominations: Academy Awards '41: Best Original Score. *IVY*

So Fine 🦴🦴½ **1981 (R)** Absent-minded English professor O'Neal tries to rescue his father's clothing business from going bottom-up. He accidentally invents peek-a-boo bottomed jeans, which become an immediate hit and make him rich. Comedy smorgasbord, setting outing from sometime novelist Bergman, hits and misses. O'Neal is memorable, as is the ubiquitous Warden and his sidekick. **91m/C VHS, Beta.** Ryan O'Neal, Jack Warden, Mariangela Melato, Richard Kiel; ***D:*** Andrew Bergman; ***W:*** Andrew Bergman; ***M:*** Ennio Morricone. *WAR*

So I Married an Axe Murderer ½ **1993 (PG-13)** Combination comedy/romance/thriller. Charlie is a hip bookstore owner with a commitment problem. When he finally falls in love with a butcher, he comes to suspect she's a serial killer and he's in line as her next victim. "Saturday Night Live" star Myers has a dual role: as Charlie and as Scottish dad Stuart, allowing him to be fanatically Scottish as Stuart and somewhat more restrained as the angst-ridden Charlie. One-gag movie counted on Myers' "Wayne's World" popularity, which didn't pan out at the box office. Best appreciated by Myers' fans, this one is better on the small screen. **92m/C VHS, LV, 8mm.** Mike Myers, Nancy Travis, Anthony LaPaglia, Amanda Plummer, Brenda Fricker, Matt Doherty, Charles Grodin; ***Cameos:*** Phil Hartman, Steven Wright, Alan Arkin; ***D:*** Thomas Schlamme; ***W:*** Mike Myers, Robbie Fox; ***M:*** Bruce Broughton. *COL*

So Proudly We Hail **1943** True story of the lives of three war-front nurses and their heroism under fire during WWII. Colbert is Lt. Davidson in charge of nine Red Cross Army nurses serving in the Pacific. Lake and Goddard play the other leads. With the popularity of its stars and the patriotic spirit of the film, the picture hit box office gold. Critics praised its authenticity, as the film never fell victim to the usual standards of Hollywood glamour. Fans of Lake beware: she has short hair in this film because the government requested that she not appear as a servicewoman with her famous peek-a-boo hair style because female factory workers were getting their long Lake-inspired hair caught in the machinery. **126m/B VHS.** Claudette Colbert, Paulette Goddard, Veronica Lake, George Reeves, Barbara Britton, Walter Abel, Sonny Tufts; ***D:*** Mark Sandrich; ***W:*** Allan Scott; ***M:*** Miklos Rozsa. Nominations: Academy Awards '43: Best Cinematography, Best Original Screenplay (Scott), Best Special Effects, Best Supporting Actress (Goddard). *MCA*

So This is Paris **1926** Roguish pre-Hayes Code dancing duo seeks spice through alternative lovemates. Classic sophisticated Lubitsch, with outstanding camerawork and a bit of jazz. **68m/B VHS, Beta.** Monte Blue, Patsy Ruth Miller, Lilyan Tashman, Andre de Beranger, Myrna Loy; ***D:*** Ernst Lubitsch. *GPV, FCT*

So This is Washington ½ **1943** The comedy team go to Washington with wacky inventions to help the war effort. Turns out there's too entirely too much nonsense going around, and the boys give 'em a piece of their mind. Fun, featherweight wartime comedy. **70m/B VHS, Beta.** Lum & Abner, Alan Mowbray. Nominations: Academy Awards '43: Best Sound. *NOS, DVT*

Soapdish **1991 (PG-13)** The back stage lives of a daytime soap opera, "The Sun Also Sets," and its cast. When the soap's ratings fall, a character written out of series via decapitation is brought back to give things a lift. While the writer struggles to make the reincarnation believable, the cast juggles old and new romances, and professional jealousies abound. Some genuinely funny moments as film actors spoof the genre that gave many of them a start. **97m/C VHS, Beta, LV, 8mm.** Sally Field, Kevin Kline, Robert Downey Jr., Cathy Moriarty, Whoopi Goldberg, Elisabeth Shue, Carrie Fisher, Garry Marshall, Teri Hatcher, Paul Johansson, Costas Mandylor, Stephen Nichols, Kathy Najimy, Sheila Kelley; ***Cameos:*** Leeza Gibbons, John Tesh, Finola Hughes; ***D:*** Michael Hoffman; ***W:*** Andrew Bergman, Robert Harling; ***M:*** Alan Silvestri. *PAR*

S.O.B. ½ **1981 (R)** Blake Edwards' bitter farce about Hollywood and the film industry wheelers and dealers who inhabit it. When a multi-million dollar picture bombs at the box office, the director turns suicidal, until he envisions re-shooting it with a steamy, X-rated scene starring his wife, a star with a goody-two-shoes image. Edwards used his real-life wife, Julie ("Mary Poppins") Andrews, for the scene in which she bared her breasts. Oft-inspired, but oft-terrible. Zestfully vengeful. William Holden's last film. **121m/C VHS, Beta, LV.** William Holden, Robert Preston, Richard Mulligan, Julie Andrews, Robert Webber, Shelley Winters, Robert Vaughn, Larry Hagman, Stuart Margolin, Loretta Swit, Craig Stevens, Larry Storch, Jennifer Edwards, Robert Loggia, Rosanna Arquette, Marisa Berenson; ***D:*** Blake Edwards; ***W:*** Blake Edwards; ***C:*** Harry Stradling Jr.; ***M:*** Henry Mancini. National Society of Film Critics Awards '81: Best Supporting Actor (Preston). *FOX, WAR*

Social Error **1935** An heiress mistakes her guards for a group of kidnappers. **60m/B VHS, Beta, LV.** Gertrude Messinger, David Sharpe. *NOS, HEG*

The Social Secretary ½ **1916** Driven from the rat race by lecherous men, Talmadge gets new job as rich woman's secretary, where she downdresses to avoid further lewd encounters. She falls for her boss's son, but isn't considered marriage material until she proves herself. **56m/B VHS, Beta.** Norma Talmadge, Kate Lester, Helen Weir, Gladden James, Herbert Frank; ***D:*** John Emerson. *GPV, FCT*

Society **1992 (R)** A teenager wonders if his visions are real or hallucinations when he believes his family, and everyone else around him, are flesh-eating predators. The puzzle isn't much but wait for the special-effects ladened ending to get your fill of gore. **99m/C VHS.** Billy Warlock, Devin Devasquez, Evan Richards; ***D:*** Brian Yuzna. *REP*

Sodbusters ½ **1994 (PG-13)** Western spoof about homesteaders versus a greedy cattle baron and the railroad in 1875 Colorado. A lascivious farmer's wife and a mysterious gunslinger—as well as a couple of gay cowboys—are included for additional fun. **97m/C VHS.** Kris Kristofferson, John Vernon, Fred Willard, Wendel Meldrum, Max Gail, Steve Landesburg, Don Lake, James Pickens Jr., John Hemphill; ***D:*** Eugene Levy; ***W:*** John Hemphill, Eugene Levy. *REP*

Sodom and Gomorrah *Sodome et Gomorrhe; The Last Days of Sodom and Gomorrah* **1962** The Italian-made, internationally produced epic about Lot, the Hebrews and the destruction of the two sinful biblical cities. Moderately entertaining—but ponderous, to say the least, and very long. **154m/C VHS, Beta, LV.** *IT* Stewart Granger, Stanley Baker, Pier Angeli, Anouk Aimee, Rossana Podesta; ***D:*** Robert Aldrich; ***M:*** Miklos Rozsa. *FOX, IME*

Sofie ½ **1992** Sweet family melodrama about a late 19th Jewish family in Denmark. Sofie (Mynster) is the unmarried 28-year-old daughter of loving, protective parents. She has fallen in love with a gentile artist (Christensen) but gives him up to marry within her faith. Unsuited, Sofie and Jonas (Zeller) lead melancholy lives, which Sofie redeems through her joy in her son. Self-effacing drama is Ullmann's directorial debut. Adapted from the novel "Mendel Philipsen & Son" by Henri Nathansen. In Swedish with English subtitles. **145m/C VHS.** *SW* Karen-Lise Mynster, Ghita Norby, Erland Josephson, Jesper Christensen, Henning Moritzen, Torben Zeller, Stig Hoffmeyer, Kirsten Rolffes, Lotte Herman; ***D:*** Liv Ullmann; ***W:*** Liv Ullmann, Peter Poulsen. *FCT, ING*

Soft and Hard ½ **1985** Made for English television, this video by Godard and Mieville intends to address the role of media and television in everyday life via a seemingly informal look at the couple's daily existence and the propensity for image production in it. In French with English subtitles. **48m/C VHS, Beta.** *FR* ***D:*** Anne-Marie Mieville, Jean-Luc Godard. *EAI*

Soft Deceit ½ **1994 (R)** Master criminal Trent (Bergin) gets caught in the heist of $6 million in mob money. Then Anne (Vernon) shashays into prison offering Trent a deal—half the cash in exchange for breaking him out. She succeeds but maybe a doublecross is next on the agenda. **95m/C VHS, LV.** Patrick Bergin, Kate Vernon, John Wesley Shipp, Gwynyth Walsh, Nigel Bennett, Damir Andrei; ***D:*** Jorge Montesi; ***W:*** Jorge Montesi. *TTC*

The Soft Kill **1994 (R)** LA private eye Jack Ramsey (Bernsen) becomes the prime murder suspect when his girlfriend is strangled. Can he prove his innocence before more bodies pile up and the cops catch him? **95m/C VHS.** Corbin Bernsen, Brion James, Matt McCoy, Michael Harris, Kim Morgan Greene, Carrie-Anne Moss; ***D:*** Eli Cohen. *TRI*

The Soft Skin *Le Peau Douce; Silken Skin* **1964** A classic portrayal of marital infidelity by the master director. A writer and lecturer has an affair with a stewardess. After the affair ends, his wife confronts him, with tragic results. Cliche plot is forgivable; acted and directed to perfection. Frequent Truffaut star Jean-Pierre Leaud served here as an apprentice director. In French with English subtitles. **120m/B VHS, Beta, LV.** *FR* Jean Desailly, Nelly Benedetti, Francoise Dorleac; ***D:*** Francois Truffaut; ***M:*** Georges Delerue. *HMV, FOX*

Soggy Bottom U.S.A. **1984 (PG)** A sheriff has his hands full trying to keep the law enforced in a small Southern town. Quite-good cast keeps the plot from disappearing altogether. **90m/C VHS, Beta.** Don Johnson, Ben Johnson, Dub Taylor, Ann Wedgeworth, Lois Nettleton, Anthony Zerbe; ***D:*** Theodore J. Flicker. *PSM, HHE*

Sois Belle et Tais-Toi ½ **1958** A police detective tracks jewel thieves and falls in love with a young waif. Several interesting and later famous actors have small parts. Light-hearted adventure. Subtitled in English. **110m/B VHS, Beta.** *FR* Henri Vidal, Mylene Demongeot, Jean-Paul Belmondo, Alain Delon; ***D:*** Marc Allegret. *BAR*

Solar Crisis ½ **1992 (PG-13)** Eye-popping special effects highlight this Earth-on-the-edge-of-destruction sci-fier. In 2050 the sun has gone on self-destruct and begins throwing off giant solar flares which turn the Earth extra-crispy. A space team is sent to divert the flares but the mission may become a victim of sabotage. Director Sarafian actually forgoes credit for the standard Smithee pseudonym. **111m/C VHS, LV.** Tim Matheson, Charlton Heston, Peter Boyle, Annabel Schofield, Jack Palance, Corin "Corky" Nemec; ***D:*** Richard Sarafian; ***C:*** Russell Carpenter; ***M:*** Maurice Jarre. *VMK*

Solar Force **1994 (R)** Cop (Pare), stationed on the moon, is sent to earth to find a stolen chemical that is capable of restoring a destroyed environment. But there are secrets behind the assignment which could cost him his life. **91m/C VHS, LV.** Michael Pare, Billy Drago, Walker Brandt; ***D:*** Boaz Davidson; ***W:*** Terrence Pare; ***C:*** Avi Karpik; ***M:*** Don Peake. *HMK*

Solarbabies **1986 (PG-13)** Rollerskating youths in a drought-stricken future vie for a mysterious power that will replenish the Earth's water. Shades of every sci-fi movie you've ever seen, from "Mad Max" to "Ice Pirates." Pathetic. **95m/C VHS, Beta, LV.** Richard Jordan, Sarah Douglas, Charles Durning, Lukas Haas, Jami Gertz, Jason Patric; ***D:*** Alan Johnson; ***W:*** Walon Green; ***M:*** Maurice Jarre. *MGM*

Solaris **1972** With this the USSR tried to eclipse "2001: A Space Odyssey" in terms of cerebral science-fiction. Some critics thought they succeeded. You may disagree now that the lumbering effort is available on tape. Adapted from a Stanislaw Lem novel, it depicts a dilapidated space lab orbiting the planet Solaris, whose ocean, a vast fluid "brain," materializes the stir-crazy cosmonauts' obsessions—usually morose ex-girlfriends. Talk, talk, talk, minimal special effects. In Russian with English subtitles. In a two-cassette package, with a letterbox format preserving Tarkovsky's widescreen compositions. **167m/C VHS, LV.** *RU* Donatas Banionis, Natalya Bondarchuk; ***D:*** Andrei Tarkovsky; ***M:*** Eduard Artemyev. Cannes Film Festival '72: Grand Jury Prize; Nominations: Cannes Film Festival '72: Best Film. *FXL, FCT, INJ*

Soldat Duroc...Ca Va Etre Ta Fete! *Soldier Duroc* **196?** Days after the 1944 liberation of Paris, a French soldier crosses back over the French lines to see his lover, and is caught as a German sympathizer by American troops. **105m/C**

VHS, Beta. *FR* Pierre Tornade, Robert Webber, Michel Galabru, Roger Carel. *NO*

The Soldier 🦴 *Codename: The Soldier* **1982 (R)** The Russians are holding the world at ransom with a pile of stolen plutonium, and a soldier finds himself in the position to carry out an unauthorized and dangerous plan to preserve the balance of world power. Wildly implausible, gratuitously violent spy trash. **90m/C VHS, Beta.** Ken Wahl, Klaus Kinski; ***D:*** James Glickenhaus. *COL, SUE*

Soldier Blue 🦴🦴 **1970 (R)** Two survivors of an Indian attack make their way back to an army outpost. The cavalry then seeks revenge on the Cheyenne tribe accused of the attack. Gratuitously violent Vietnam-era western hits hard on racial themes. Based on the novel "Arrow in the Sun" by Theodore V. Olsen on the Sand Creek Indian massacre. **109m/C VHS, Beta.** Candice Bergen, Peter Strauss, Donald Pleasence, Dana Elcar, Jorge Rivero; ***D:*** Ralph Nelson; ***W:*** John Gay; ***C:*** Robert B. Hauser. *COL, SUE*

Soldier Boyz 🦴½ **1995 (R)** Ex-Marine Major Howard Tolliver (Dudikoff), who now runs a high-security prison for youthful offenders, is called on to rescue a United Nations worker who's being held hostage by a group of revolutionaries in Vietnam. For help, he takes along six of his toughest prisoners. A variation of "The Dirty Dozen." **91m/C VHS.** Michael Dudikoff, Cary-Hiroyuki Tagawa, Tyrin Turner, David Barry Gray, Channon Roe, Cedrick Terrell, Demetrius Navarro, Jacqueline Obradors; ***D:*** Louis Morneau; ***W:*** Darryl Quarles. *HBO*

Soldier in Love 🦴🦴 **1967** Teleplay from "George Schaefer's Showcase Theatre" is based on the life of John Churchill, first Duke of Marlborough, and his wife Sarah. The ambitious young couple held the favor of Queen Anne for a time, until political intrigue brought about their downfall. **76m/C VHS, Beta.** Jean Simmons, Claire Bloom, Keith Michell; ***D:*** George Schaefer. *FHS*

Soldier in the Rain 🦴🦴½ **1963** An unusual friendship develops between career sergeant Gleason and wheeler-dealer McQueen. Gleason is in good form, but McQueen is listless, and the story (set in a Southern army camp) is unsatisfying. Weld is the comely teen who makes for an intriguing love triangle. From the novel by William Goldman. **88m/B VHS, Beta.** Steve McQueen, Jackie Gleason, Tuesday Weld, Tony Bill, Tom Poston, Ed Nelson; ***D:*** Ralph Nelson; ***W:*** Blake Edwards; ***M:*** Henry Mancini. *FOX*

Soldier of Fortune 🦴🦴½ **1955** A woman (Hayward) enlists mercenaries to help find her lost husband in Red China. Late Gable vehicle with the formula beginning to feel the post-war strain and the star looking a trifle long in the tooth. Still, a fun adventure from a top star. Hayward had been among the myriad starlets vying for the Scarlett O'Hara roles nearly two decades earlier. **96m/C VHS, Beta.** Clark Gable, Susan Hayward, Gene Barry, Alexander D'Arcy, Michael Rennie, Tom Tully, Anna Sten, Russell Collins, Leo Gordon, Jack Kruschen, Robert Quarry; ***D:*** Edward Dmytryk. *FOX*

Soldier of Orange 🦴🦴🦴 **1978** The lives of six Dutch students are forever changed by the WWII invasion of Holland by the Nazis. Based on the true-life exploits of Dutch resistance leader Erik Hazelhoff. Exciting and suspenseful; cerebral; carefully made and well acted. Made Rutger Hauer an international star. **144m/C VHS, Beta, LV.** *NL* Rutger Hauer, Jeroen Krabbe, Edward Fox, Susan Penhaligon; ***D:*** Paul Verhoeven; ***W:*** Paul Verhoeven; ***C:*** Jan De Bont. Los Angeles Film Critics Association Awards '79: Best Foreign Film. *MED*

Soldier of the Night 🦴½ **1984** Toy-store worker by day, vigilante killer by night. Israeli thriller set in Tel Aviv lacks vim and is badly dubbed. **89m/C VHS, Beta.** ***D:*** Dan Wolman. *MGM*

Soldier's Fortune 🦴½ **1991 (R)** A traveling gun for hire leaves the combat of Central America for the jungles of Los Angeles, only to find out that his daughter had been taken hostage. That's the last thing these kidnappers will ever do when they are found by this tough guy looking for his child. **96m/C VHS.** Gil Gerard, Charles Napier, Dan Haggerty, P.J. Soles, Barbara Bingham, Janus Blythe; ***D:*** Arthur N. Mele. *REP*

Soldier's Revenge 🦴🦴 **197?** A Vietnam vet has a hard time adjusting to life at home. **92m/C VHS, Beta.** John Savage. *TWE*

A Soldier's Story 🦴🦴🦴 **1984 (PG)** A black army attorney is sent to a Southern base to investigate the murder of an unpopular sergeant. Features WWII, Louisiana, jazz and blues, and racism in and outside the corps. From the Pulitzer-prize winning play by Charles Fuller, with most of the Broadway cast. Fine performances from Washington and Caesar. **101m/C VHS, Beta, LV.** Howard E. Rollins Jr., Adolph Caesar, Denzel Washington, Patti LaBelle, Robert Townsend, Scott Paulin, Wings Hauser, Art Evans, Larry Riley, David Alan Grier; ***D:*** Norman Jewison; ***M:*** Herbie Hancock. Edgar Allan Poe Awards '84: Best Screenplay; Los Angeles Film Critics Association Awards '84: Best Supporting Actor (Caesar); Nominations: Academy Awards '84: Best Adapted Screenplay, Best Picture, Best Supporting Actor (Caesar). *COL, FCT*

A Soldier's Tale 🦴🦴 **1991 (R)** During WWII, a menage-a-trois develops that can only lead to tragedy, yet the participants find themselves unable to resist. **96m/C VHS.** Gabriel Byrne, Marianne Basler, Judge Reinhold, Paul Wyatt; ***D:*** Larry Parr; ***M:*** John Charles. *REP*

Sole Survivor 🦴½ **1984 (R)** A group of zombies are searching for a beautiful advertising executive who was the sole survivor of a plane crash. **85m/C VHS, Beta.** Anita Skinner, Kurt Johnson, Caren Larkey; ***D:*** Thom Eberhardt. *LIV, VES*

Solid Gold Cadillac 🦴🦴🦴 **1956** Holliday is a winning lead as Laura Patridge, an idealistic, small-time stockholder who discovers that the corporate board of directors are crooked. She makes waves at a stockholders meeting, gets noticed by the press, finds romance with former CEO Edward McKeever (Douglas), and works to oust the scalawags from power. The title comes from Laura's fervent desire to own a—you guessed it—solid gold cadillac. Based on the Broadway play by George S. Kaufman and Howard Teichmann. **99m/B VHS.** Judy Holliday, Paul Douglas, Fred Clark, Neva Patterson, Arthur O'Connell, Ray Collins; ***D:*** Richard Quine; ***W:*** Abe Burrows; ***C:*** Charles B(ryant) Lang; ***M:*** Cyril Mockridge. Academy Awards '56: Best Costume Design (B & W). *COL*

The Solitary Man 🦴🦴 **1982** Glum look at a family breakup, from the husband's point of view. Holliman is good, but the exercise at large is regularly blues-inducing, and not especially inspiring or artful. Made for TV. **96m/C VHS, Beta.** Earl Holliman, Carrie Snodgress, Lara Parker, Lane Smith, Nicolas Coster, Michelle Pfeiffer; ***D:*** John Llewellyn Moxey. *TLF*

Solo 🦴🦴 **1977 (PG)** Young hitchhiker Peers enters the lives of fire patrol pilot Gil and his teenage son. A plotless friendship develops, headed nowhere—like this movie. Great New Zealand scenery might be worth the price of rental. **90m/C VHS, Beta.** Vincent Gil, Perry Armstrong, Martyn Sanderson, Lisa Peers; ***D:*** Tony Williams. *BPG, VES, HHE*

Solo 🦴🦴 **19??** A man bonds with his children as they search for his wife, their mother, after her plane disappears while making a solo flight in a rugged mountain region. Based on a true story. **96m/C VHS.** *BPG*

Solo Voyage: The Revenge 🦴🦴 **1990** A Russian "Rambo" goes on a murderous rampage, the likes of which humanity has not yet seen. **91m/C VHS.** *RU* Mikhail Nojkine, Alexandre Fatiouchine; ***D:*** Mikhail Toumanichulli. *NO*

Solomon and Sheba 🦴🦴 **1959** King Solomon's brother and the Egyptian Pharaoh send the Queen of Sheba to Israel to seduce King Solomon so they may gain his throne. Tyrone Power had filmed most of the lead role in this silly, overwrought epic when he died of a heart attack. The role was reshot, with Brynner (with a full head of hair) replacing him. Director Vidor's unfortunate last film. Shot on location in Spain. **139m/C VHS, Beta, LV.** Yul Brynner, Gina Lollobrigida, Marisa Pavan, George Sanders, Alejandro Rey; ***D:*** King Vidor; ***C:*** Frederick A. (Freddie) Young; ***M:*** Malcolm Arnold. *MGM, FOX*

The Sombrero Kid 🦴🦴 **1942** The Kid unwittingly gets involved in a murder and is nearly hanged before his friends help him discover the real culprits. Plenty of action in this straight forward, fun western. **54m/B VHS, Beta.** Donald (Don "Red") Barry, Lynn Merrick, Rand Brooks; ***D:*** George Sherman. *VDM*

Some Call It Loving 🦴 **1973 (R)** Bad, pretentious modern version of Sleeping Beauty, set in L.A. King buys the sleeping girl (Farrow) from a carnival show, but she doesn't live up to his ideal. **103m/C VHS.** Zalman King, Carol White, Tisa Farrow, Richard Pryor, Pat Priest; ***D:*** James B. Harris. *NO*

Some Came Running 🦴🦴🦴 **1958** James Jones's follow-up novel to "From Here to Eternity" does not translate nearly as well to the screen. Overlong and with little plot, the action centers around a would-be writer, his floozy girl friend, and the holier-than-thou characters which populate the town in which he grew up and to which he has now returned. Strong performances by all. **136m/C VHS, Beta, LV.** Frank Sinatra, Dean Martin, Shirley MacLaine, Martha Hyer, Arthur Kennedy, Nancy Gates; ***D:*** Vincente Minnelli; ***C:*** William H. Daniels; ***M:*** Elmer Bernstein. Nominations: Academy Awards '58: Best Actress (MacLaine), Best Costume Design, Best Song ("To Love and Be Loved"), Best Supporting Actor (Kennedy), Best Supporting Actress (Hyer). *MGM*

Some Girls 🦴🦴½ *Sisters* **1988 (R)** A man goes to Quebec to see his college girlfriend who informs him that she is not in love with him anymore. But she has two sisters ready to comfort him! Strange black comedy; Gregory as the girl's father elevates so-so story. **104m/C VHS, Beta.** Patrick Dempsey, Andre Gregory, Lila Kedrova, Florinda Bolkan, Jennifer Connelly, Sheila Kelly; ***D:*** Michael Hoffman; ***M:*** James Newton Howard. *MGM*

Some Kind of Hero 🦴🦴 **1982 (R)** A Vietnam prisoner of war returns home to a changed world. Pryor tries hard, but can't get above this poorly written, unevenly directed film. **97m/C VHS, Beta, LV.** Richard Pryor, Margot Kidder, Ray Sharkey, Ronny Cox, Lynne Moody, Olivia Cole; ***D:*** Michael Pressman; ***W:*** Robert Boris. *PAR*

Some Kind of Wonderful 🦴🦴 **1987 (PG-13)** A high-school tomboy has a crush on a guy who also happens to be her best friend. Her feelings go unrequited as he falls for a rich girl with snobbish friends. In the end, true love wins out. Deutch also directed (and John Hughes also produced) the teen flick "Pretty in Pink," which had much the same plot, with the rich/outcast characters reversed by gender. OK, but completely predictable. **93m/C VHS, LV.** Eric Stoltz, Lea Thompson, Mary Stuart Masterson, Craig Sheffer, John Ashton, Elias Koteas, Molly Hagan; ***D:*** Howard Deutch; ***W:*** John Hughes. *PAR*

Some Like It Hot 🦴🦴🦴🦴 **1959** Two unemployed musicians witness the St. Valentine's Day massacre in Chicago. They disguise themselves as women and join an all-girl band headed for Miami to escape the gangsters' retaliation. Flawless cast includes a fetching Monroe at her best; hilarious script. Curtis does his Cary Grant impression. Classic scenes between Lemmon in drag and Joe E. Brown as a smitten suitor. Brown also has the film's famous closing punchline. Monroe sings "I Wanna Be Loved By You," "Running Wild," and "I'm Through With Love." One of the very funniest movies of all time. **120m/B VHS, Beta, LV.** Marilyn Monroe, Tony Curtis, Jack Lemmon, George Raft, Pat O'Brien, Nehemiah Persoff, Joe E. Brown, Joan Shawlee, Mike Mazurki; ***D:*** Billy Wilder; ***W:*** Billy Wilder; ***C:*** Charles B(ryant) Lang; ***M:*** Adolph Deutsch. Academy Awards '59: Best Costume Design (B & W); British Academy Awards '59: Best Actor (Lemmon); Golden Globe Awards '60: Best Actor—Musical/Comedy (Lemmon), Best Actress—Musical/Comedy (Monroe), Best Film—Musical/Comedy; National Board of Review Awards '59: 10 Best Films of the Year; Nominations: Academy Awards '59: Best Actor (Lemmon), Best Adapted Screenplay, Best Art Direction/Set Decoration (B & W), Best Black and White Cinematography, Best Director (Wilder). *MGM, FOX*

Somebody Has to Shoot the Picture 🦴🦴🦴 **1990 (R)** Photographer Scheider is hired by a convicted man to take a picture of his execution. Hours before the event, Scheider uncovers evidence that leads him to believe the man is innocent. He then embarks in a race against time to save him. Adapted by Doug Magee from his book "Slow Coming Dark." Unpretentious, tough drama. Made for cable. **104m/C VHS, Beta, LV.** Roy Scheider, Bonnie Bedelia, Robert Carradine, Andre Braugher, Arliss Howard; ***D:*** Frank Pierson; ***W:*** Doug Magee. *MCA*

Somebody Up There Likes Me 🦴🦴🦴 **1956** Story of Rocky Graziano's gritty battle from his poor, street-wise childhood to his prison term and his eventual success as the middleweight boxing champion of the world. Adapted from Graziano's autobiography. Superior performance by Newman (in his third screen role, after the miserable "The Silver Chalice" and forgettable "The Rack"); screen debuts for McQueen and Loggia. **113m/B VHS, Beta.** Paul Newman, Pier Angeli, Everett Sloane, Eileen Heckart, Sal Mineo, Robert Loggia, Steve McQueen; ***D:*** Robert Wise; ***W:*** Ernest Lehman; ***C:*** Joseph Ruttenberg. Academy Awards '56: Best Art Direction/Set Decoration (B & W), Best Black and White Cinematography; Nominations: Academy Awards '56: Best Film Editing. *MGM*

Someday You'll Find Her, Charlie Brown **1981** Charlie Brown tries to find a beautiful girl he saw on tv. **24m/C VHS.** *WTA*

Someone at the Door 🦴🦴 **1950** Reporter Medwin arranges to be suspected of killing his sister, thus providing him with a good story and advancing his career. His plan almost backfires, when he is almost executed. Remake of a 1936 film of the same name. **65m/B VHS, Beta.** *GB* Michael Medwin, Garry Marsh, Yvonne Owen, Hugh Latimer; ***D:*** Francis Searle. *SNC*

Someone Behind the Door 🦴½ *Two Minds for Murder; Quelqu' Un Derriere la Porte* **1971 (PG)** Evil brain surgeon Perkins implants murderous suggestions into psychopathic amnesia victim Bronson's mind, then instructs him to kill his (the surgeon's) wife and her lover. **97m/C VHS, Beta, LV.** Charles Bronson, Anthony Perkins, Jill Ireland, Henri Garcin; ***D:*** Nicolas Gessner. *UNI, VTR*

Someone I Touched 🦴½ **1975** Way-overdone melodrama starring Leachman as a finally-pregnant woman who learns her husband and a teenager he slept with have venereal disease. **74m/C VHS, Beta.** Cloris Leachman, James Olson, Glynnis O'Connor, Andrew (Andy) Robinson, Allyn Ann McLerie; ***D:*** Lou Antonio. *WOV*

Someone to Die For 🦴🦴 **1995 (R)** Accused murderer (and cop) Bernsen is out to prove his innocence but learns that the real killer may be very close to home. **98m/C VHS.** Corbin Bernsen, Ally Walker, Robert Stewart; ***D:*** Clay Borris. *AVE*

Someone to Love 🦴🦴 **1987 (R)** Rootless filmmaker gathers all his single friends together and interviews them about their failed love lives. Welles's last film as an actor. Wildly uneven, interesting experiment. **110m/C VHS, Beta, LV.** Henry Jaglom, Orson Welles, Sally Kellerman, Andrea Marcovicci, Michael Emil, Oja Kodar, Stephen Bishop, Ronee Blakley, Kathryn Harrold, Monte Hellman; ***D:*** Henry Jaglom; ***W:*** Henry Jaglom. *PAR*

Someone to Watch Over Me 🦴🦴🦴 **1987 (R)** After witnessing the murder of a close friend, a beautiful and very wealthy woman must be protected from the killer. The working-class New York detective assigned the duty is more than taken with her, despite the fact that he has both a wife and son at home. A highly watchable, stylish romantic crime thriller. **106m/C VHS, Beta, LV.** Tom Berenger, Mimi Rogers, Lorraine Bracco, Jerry Orbach, Andreas Katsulas, Tony DiBenedetto, James Moriarty, John Rubinstein; ***D:*** Ridley Scott; ***W:*** Howard Franklin; ***C:*** Steven Poster; ***M:*** Michael Kamen. *COL*

Something for Everyone 🦴🦴½ *The Rook; Black Flowers for the Bride* **1970 (R)** A corrupt footman uses sex and murder in an attempt to take over the estate of an aristocratic Bavarian family in post-WWII Germany. He nearly succeeds in marrying the countess (Lansbury), but someone has been keeping tabs on him. Funny, ambitious black comedy. From the novel "The Code" by Harry Kressing. **112m/C VHS, Beta.** Angela Lansbury, Michael York, Anthony Corlan, Heidelinde Weis; ***D:*** Harold Prince; ***C:*** Walter Lassally. *FOX*

Something in Common 🦴🦴½ **1986** A woman discovers her 22-year-old son is having an affair with a woman her own age. Nicely done comedy; Burstyn and Weld both make good use of a solid script. Made for TV. **94m/C VHS, Beta.** Ellen Burstyn, Tuesday Weld, Don Murray, Patrick Cassidy, Eli Wallach; ***D:*** Glenn Jordan; ***W:*** Susan Rice; ***M:*** John Addison. *VTR, NWV*

Something of Value 🦴🦴🦴 **1957** Good ensemble performances in a serious colonial story about the Mau Mau rebellion in Kenya. Hudson and Poitier are torn between their friendship and their opposing loyalties. Drama solidly grounded in fact from the book by Robert Ruark. **113m/B VHS, Beta.** Rock Hudson, Sidney Poitier, Wendy Hiller, Dana Wynter, Juano Hernandez; ***D:*** Richard Brooks; ***W:*** Richard Brooks; ***M:*** Miklos Rozsa. *MGM*

Something Short of Paradise 🦴½ **1979 (PG)** The owner of a Manhattan movie theater has an on again/off again romance with a magazine writer. Would-be Allenesque romantic comedy is too talky and pretentious. **87m/C VHS, Beta.** David Steinberg, Susan Sarandon, Jean-Pierre Aumont, Marilyn Sokol; ***D:*** David Helpern; ***W:*** Fred Barron. *LIV, VES*

Something Special 🦴🦴½ *Willy Milly; I Was a Teenage Boy* **1986 (PG-13)** A fourteen-year-old girl has her wish come true when she is turned into a boy. Charming, original fantasy-comedy is fun for young and old. **93m/C VHS, LV.** Pamela Segall, Patty Duke, Eric Gurry, John Glover, Seth Green; ***D:*** Paul Schneider; ***W:*** Walter Carbone. *NO*

Something to Sing About 🦴🦴 *Battling Hoofer* **1936** Musical melodrama about a New York bandleader's attempt to make it big in Hollywood. Allows Cagney the opportunity to demonstrate his dancing talents; he also sings. Rereleased in 1947. Also available colorized. Frawley was Fred on "I Love Lucy." ♫Any Old Love; Right or Wrong; Loving You; Out of the Blue; Something to Sing About. **84m/B VHS, Beta, LV.** James Cagney, William Frawley, Evelyn Daw, Gene Lockhart; ***D:*** Victor Schertzinger. Nominations: Academy Awards '37: Best Original Score. *NOS, VHE, CAB*

Something to Talk About 🦴🦴½ *Grace Under Pressure* **1995 (R)** Romantic comedy/drama finds Grace (Roberts) running her overbearing father Wyly's (Duvall) horsebreeding operation and learning that her husband Eddie (the ever-charming Quaid) is tomcatting around. So Grace tosses him out and makes a temporary move with daughter Caroline (Aull) back home. Tart-tongued sister Emma Rae (Sedgwick) is sympathetic but long-suffering mama Georgia (Rowlands) thinks Grace should make the best of things (the way she's done). Naturally, Eddie wants his family back but the frazzled Grace is just coming to terms with what she wants out of life. Star appeal from both leads lends this familiar plot some spark. **106m/C VHS, LV.** Julia Roberts, Dennis Quaid, Robert Duvall, Gena Rowlands, Kyra Sedgwick, Brett Cullen, Haley Aull, Muse Watson, Anne Shropshire; ***D:*** Lasse Hallstrom; ***W:*** Callie Khouri; ***C:*** Sven Nykvist; ***M:*** Hans Zimmer. Nominations: Golden Globe Awards '96: Best Supporting Actress (Sedgwick). *WAR*

Something Weird *Woof!* **1968** McCabe is disfigured horribly in an electrical accident. A seemingly beautiful witch fixes his face, on condition that he be her lover. The accident also gave him ESP—and it gets cheesier from there. **80m/C VHS, Beta.** Tony McCabe, Elizabeth Lee; ***D:*** Herschell Gordon Lewis. *VMK, VDM, TWE*

Something Wicked This Way Comes 🦴🦴 **1983 (PG)** Two young boys discover the evil secret of a mysterious traveling carnival that visits their town. Bradbury wrote the screenplay for this much-anticipated, expensive adaptation of his own novel. Good special effects, but disappointing. **94m/C VHS, Beta, LV.** Jason Robards Jr., Jonathan Pryce, Diane Ladd, Pam Grier, Richard Davalos, James Stacy; ***D:*** Jack Clayton; ***W:*** Ray Bradbury; ***C:*** Stephen Burum; ***M:*** James Horner. *DIS*

Something Wild 🦴🦴½ **1986 (R)** Mild-mannered business exec Daniels is picked up by an impossibly free-living vamp with a Louise Brooks hair-do, and taken for the ride of his up-till-then staid life, eventually leading to explosive violence. A sharp-edged comedy with numerous changes of pace. Too-happy ending wrecks it, but it's great until then. Look for cameos from filmmakers John Waters and John Sayles. **113m/C VHS, Beta, LV.** Jeff Daniels, Melanie Griffith, Ray Liotta, Margaret Colin, Tracey Walter, Dana Peru, Jack Gilpin, Su Tissue, Kenneth Utt, Sister Carol East; ***Cameos:*** John Sayles, John Waters; ***D:*** Jonathan Demme; ***W:*** E. Max Frye; ***C:*** Tak Fujimoto; ***M:*** Laurie Anderson, Rosemary Paul, John Cale. Edgar Allan Poe Awards '86: Best Screenplay. *HBO*

Sometimes a Great Notion 🦴🦴🦴 *Never Give an Inch* **1971 (PG)** Trouble erupts in a small Oregon town when a family of loggers decide to honor a contract when the other loggers go on strike. Newman's second stint in the director's chair; Fonda's first role as an old man. Based on the novel by Ken Kesey. **115m/C VHS, Beta.** Paul Newman, Henry Fonda, Lee Remick, Richard Jaeckel, Michael Sarrazin; ***D:*** Paul Newman; ***W:*** John Gay; ***M:*** Henry Mancini. Nominations: Academy Awards '71: Best Song ("All His Children"), Best Supporting Actor (Jaeckel). *MCA*

Sometimes Aunt Martha Does Dreadful Things 🦴 **1988** Another deranged-slasher movie, this one featuring a female psychopath. **95m/C VHS, Beta.** *NO*

Sometimes It Works, Sometimes It Doesn't 🦴🦴½ **1983** A film in two parts, the first being interviews with Merce Cunningham and John Case about their work together, the second being the filmdance "Channels/Inserts," in its entirety. **63m/C VHS, Beta.** *NO*

Sometimes They Come Back 🦴🦴 **1991 (R)** Another Stephen King tale of terror. Matheson plays a man haunted by the tragedy in his past. A witness to his brother's death, he also witnesses the fiery crash of his brother's killers. Only now the killers have returned from the dead, to take their revenge on him. Made for television. **97m/C VHS, LV.** Tim Matheson, Brooke Adams, Robert Rusler. *VMK*

Somewhere I'll Find You 🦴🦴🦴 **1942** Clark and Turner heat up the screen as correspondents running all over the war-torn world in their second film together. ("Honky Tonk" was their first.) Notable mainly because Gable's beloved wife, Carole Lombard, was killed in a plane crash only three days into production. Gable forced himself to finish the film and it became one of the studio's biggest hits. Although critics applauded his determination to complete the film, many felt his performance was subdued and strained. Film debut of Wynn. Based on a story by Charles Hoffman. **108m/B VHS.** Clark Gable, Lana Turner, Robert Sterling, Reginald Owen, Lee Patrick, Charles Dingle, Tamara Shayne, Leonid Kinskey, Diana Lewis, Molly Lamont, Patricia Dane, Sara Haden, Keenan Wynn; ***D:*** Wesley Ruggles; ***W:*** Walter Reisch, Marguerite Roberts. *MGM*

Somewhere in Sonora 🦴🦴 **1933** Early Wayne Western set in Old Mexico. Wayne plays a rodeo performer who joins an outlaw gang to save a friend and a silver mine. Like most of the other films of the series, this was a remake of a Ken Maynard silent. Based on a story and the novel "Somewhere South in Sonora" by Will Levington Comfort. **59m/B VHS.** John Wayne, Henry B. Walthall, Shirley Palmer, J.P. McGowan, Frank Rice, Billy Franey, Paul Fix, Ralph Lewis; ***D:*** Mack V. Wright; ***W:*** Joe Roach. *MGM*

Somewhere in Time 🦴🦴½ **1980 (PG)** Playwright Reeve (in his first post-Clark Kent role) falls in love with a beautiful woman in an old portrait. Through self-hypnosis he goes back in time to 1912 to discover what their relationship might have been. The film made a star of the Grand Hotel, located on Mackinac Island in Michigan, where it was shot. Drippy rip-off of the brilliant novel "Time and Again" by Jack Finney. Reeve is horrible; Seymour is underused. All in all, rather wretched. **103m/C VHS, Beta, LV.** Christopher Reeve, Jane Seymour, Christopher Plummer, Teresa Wright; ***D:*** Jeannot Szwarc; ***W:*** Richard Matheson; ***M:*** John Barry. Nominations: Academy Awards '80: Best Costume Design. *MCA*

Somewhere Tomorrow 🦴🦴½ **1985 (PG)** A lonely, fatherless teenage girl is befriended by the ghost of a young man killed in a plane crash. Charming and moving, if not perfect. **91m/C VHS, Beta.** Sarah Jessica Parker, Nancy Addison, Tom Shea; ***D:*** Robert Wiemer. *MED*

Sommersby 🦴🦴½ **1993 (PG-13)** A too-good-to-be-true period romance based on the film "The Return of Martin Guerre." A Civil War veteran (Gere) returns to his wife's (Foster) less-than-open arms. She soon warms up to his kind, sensitive and caring manner, but can't quite believe the change that the war has wrought. Neither can the neighbors, especially the one (Pullman) who had his own eye on Laurel Sommersby. So is he really Jack Sommersby or an all too clever imposter? Lots of hankies needed for the tender-hearted. Strong performance by Foster. Filmed in Virginia (passing for the state of Tennessee.) The laserdisc version is available in letterbox format. **114m/C VHS, Beta, LV, 8mm.** Richard Gere, Jodie Foster, Bill Pullman, James Earl Jones, William Windom, Brett Kelley, Richard Hamilton, Maury Chaykin, Lanny Flaherty, Frankie Faison, Wendell Wellman, Clarice Taylor, R. Lee Ermey; ***D:*** Jon Amiel; ***W:*** Nicholas Meyer, Sarah Kernochan; ***M:*** Danny Elfman. *WAR, FCT*

Son-in-Law 🦴½ **1993 (PG-13)** Surfer-dude comic Shore's a laconic fish out of water as a city-boy rock 'n' roller who falls in love with a country beauty, marries her, and visits the family farm to meet the new in-laws. Once there, he weirds out family and neighbors before showing everyone how to live, Pauly style. Silly entertainment best appreciated by Shore fans. **95m/C VHS, Beta, LV.** Pauly Shore, Carla Gugino, Lane Smith, Cindy Pickett, Mason Adams, Patrick Renna, Dennis Burkley, Dan Gauthier, Tiffani-Amber Thiessen; ***D:*** Steve Rash; ***W:*** Shawn Schepps, Fax Bahr, Adam Small; ***M:*** Richard Gibbs. Nominations: MTV Movie Awards '94: Best Comedic Performance (Shore). *HPH*

Son of a Gun 🦴½ **1919** A loveable but ornery cowboy gets banished from the county for disturbing the peace. However, he wins the favor of the townspeople when he stands up to a gang of gambling swindlers. Silent. **68m/B VHS, Beta.** "Broncho" Billy Anderson. *NOS, DVT, RXM*

Son of Ali Baba 🦴🦴 **1952** Kashma Baba, son of Ali Baba, enters the military academy to learn to withstand adversity. He has other ideas however, until he must suddenly fill his father's shoes and fight the evil Caliph. He fights bravely with the help of his childhood friend, a beautiful princess, in this swashbuckler. **85m/C VHS.** Tony Curtis, Piper Laurie, Susan Cabot, Victor Jory, Hugh O'Brian, William Reynolds, Gerald Mohr; ***D:*** Ross Hunter. *MCA, FCT*

Son of Blob 🦴🦴 *Beware! The Blob* **1972 (PG)** A scientist brings home a piece of frozen blob from the North Pole; his wife accidentally revives the dormant gray mass. It begins a rampage of terror by digesting nearly everyone within its reach. A host of recognizable faces make for fun viewing. Post-Jeannie, pre-Dallas Hagman directed this exercise in zaniness. **87m/C VHS, Beta.** Robert Walker Jr., Godfrey Cambridge, Carol Lynley, Shelley Berman, Larry Hagman, Burgess Meredith, Gerrit Graham, Dick Van Patten; ***D:*** Larry Hagman. *GEM*

Son of Captain Blood 🦴½ *Il Figlio del Capitano Blood* **1962 (G)** The son of the famous pirate meets up with his father's enemies on the high seas. The son of the famous actor Errol Flynn—Sean—plays the son of the character the elder Flynn played in "Captain Blood." Let's just say the gimmick didn't work. **90m/C VHS, Beta.** *IT SP* Sean Flynn, Ann Todd; ***D:*** Tulio Demicheli. *PSM, MLB*

Son of Dracula 🦴🦴🦴 *Young Dracula* **1943** In this late-coming sequel to the Universal classic, a stranger named Alucard is invited to America by a Southern belle obsessed with eternal life. It is actually Dracula himself, not his son, who wreaks havoc in this spine-tingling chiller. **80m/B VHS, Beta, LV.** Lon Chaney Jr., Evelyn Ankers, Frank Craven, Robert Paige, Louise Allbritton, J. Edward Bromberg, Samuel S. Hinds; ***D:*** Robert Siodmak. *MCA*

Son of Flubber 🦴🦴½ **1963** Sequel to "The Absent Minded Professor" finds Fred MacMurray still toying with his prodigious invention, Flubber, now in the form of Flubbergas, which causes those who inhale it to float away. Disney's first-ever sequel is high family wackiness. **96m/C VHS, Beta.** Fred MacMurray, Nancy Olson, Tommy Kirk, Leon Ames, Joanna Moore, Keenan Wynn, Charlie Ruggles, Paul Lynde; ***D:*** Robert Stevenson; ***C:*** Edward Colman; ***M:*** George Bruns. *DIS*

Son of Frankenstein 🦴🦴🦴 **1939** The second sequel (after "The Bride of Frankenstein") to the 1931 version of the horror classic. The good doctor's skeptical son returns to the family manse and becomes obsessed with his father's work and with reviving the creature. Full of memorable characters and brooding ambience. Karloff's last appearance as the monster. **99m/C VHS, Beta, LV.** Basil Rathbone, Bela Lugosi, Boris Karloff, Lionel Atwill, Josephine Hutchinson, Donnie Dunagan, Emma Dunn, Edgar Norton, Lawrence Grant; ***D:*** Rowland V. Lee. *MCA*

Son of Fury 🦴🦴🦴 **1942** Dashing Ben Blake (Power) is left penniless when his sinister uncle (Sanders) wrongfully takes the family fortune. Ben escapes to sea and then to an island paradise—all the while plotting his revenge. But he still finds time to fall for the beautous Tierney. Fine 18th-century costumer done in grand style. Based on the novel "Benjamin Blake" by Edison Marshall. **98m/C VHS.** Tyrone Power, Gene Tierney, George Sanders, Frances Farmer, Roddy McDowall, John Carradine, Elsa Lanchester, Harry Davenport, Kay Johnson, Dudley Digges, Halliwell Hobbes, Marten Lamont, Arthur Hohl, Pedro de Cordoba, Dennis Hoey, Heather Thatcher; ***D:*** John Cromwell; ***W:*** Philip Dunne; ***M:*** Alfred Newman. *FXV*

Son of God's Country 🦴½ **1948** Utterly hackneyed, near-comic attempt at a western. Good-guy U.S. Marshal poses as a crook to get the low-down on the varmints. **60m/B VHS, Beta.** Monte Hale, Pamela Blake, Adrian Booth. *DVT*

Son of Godzilla 🦴🦴 *Gojira no Musuko* **1966** Dad and junior protect beauty Maeda from giant spiders on a remote island ruled by a mad scientist. Fun monster flick with decent special effects. **86m/C VHS, Beta.** *JP* Tadao Takashima, Akira Kubo; ***D:*** Jun Fukuda. *PSM, HHT, DVT*

Son of Ingagi 🦴½ **1940** Lonely ape-man kidnaps woman in search of romance. Early all-black horror film stars Williams of "Amos 'n' Andy." **70m/B VHS.** Zack Williams, Laura Bowman, Alfred Grant, Spencer Williams Jr.; ***D:*** Richard C. Kahn; ***W:*** Spencer Williams Jr. *NOS, SNC, MLB*

Son of Kong 🦴🦴½ **1933** King Kong's descendant is discovered on an island amid prehistoric creatures in this often humorous sequel to RKO's immensely popular "King Kong." Hoping to capitalize on the enormous success of its predecessor, director Schoedsack quickly threw this together. As a result, its success at the box office did not match the original's, and didn't deserve to, but it's fun. Nifty special effects from Willie O'Brien, the man who brought them to us the first time! **70m/B VHS, Beta, LV.** Robert Armstrong, Helen Mack; ***D:*** Ernest B. Schoedsack; ***M:*** Max Steiner. *NOS, MED, FCT*

Son of Lassie 🦴🦴½ **1945 (G)** It seems that Lassie's son Laddie just isn't quite as smart as his mother. After the dog sneaks onto his master's plane during WWII, the plane gets shot down, and Lawford parachutes out with Laddie in his arms. The dog goes to get help because Lawford is hurt, but he brings back two Nazis! A sequel to "Lassie Come Home." **102m/C VHS.** Peter Lawford, Donald Crisp, June Lockhart, Nigel Bruce, William Severn, Leon Ames, Donald Curtis, Nils Asther, Robert Lewis; ***D:*** Sylvan Simon. *MGM*

The Son of Monte Cristo 🦴🦴½ **1941** Illegitimate offspring of the great swashbuckler with Robert Donat proves they made pathetic, pointless sequels even back then. **102m/B VHS, Beta, LV.** Louis Hayward, Joan Bennett, George Sanders, Florence Bates, Montagu Love, Ralph Byrd, Clayton Moore; ***D:*** Rowland V. Lee. Nominations: Academy Awards '41: Best Interior Decoration. *DVT, BAR, CAB*

Son of Paleface 🦴🦴🦴½ **1952** Hilarious sequel to the original Hope gag-fest, with the Harvard-educated son of the original character (again played by Hope) heading west to claim an inheritance. Hope runs away with every cowboy cliche and even manages to wind up with the girl. Songs include "Buttons and Bows" (reprised from the original), "There's a Cloud in My Valley of Sunshine," and "Four-legged Friend." **95m/C VHS, Beta, LV.** Bob Hope, Jane Russell, Roy Rogers, Douglass Dumbrille, Iron Eyes Cody, Bill Williams, Harry von Zell; ***D:*** Frank Tashlin. Nominations: Academy Awards '52: Best Song ("Am I in Love"). *COL*

Son of Rusty 🦴🦴½ **1947** Danny and his friends are warned to stay away from the farm of suspicious Jed Barlow. But Rusty keeps running away to see Jed's dog Barb and Danny gets to know Jed. Then Danny must stand by his new friend when word of Jed's past turns folks against him. (Rusty and Barb have puppies too.) **70m/B VHS.** Ted Donaldson. *COL*

Son of Samson 🦴½ *Le Geant de la Vallee Das Rois* **1962** Man with large pectoral muscles puts an end to the evil Queen of Egypt's reign of terror **89m/C VHS.** *FR IT YU* Mark Forest, Chelo Alonso, Angelo Zanolli, Vira Silenti, Frederica Ranchi; ***D:*** Carlo Campogalliani. *SNC*

Son of Sinbad 🦴🦴 *Nights in a Harem* **1955** Sinbad, captured by the Khalif of Baghdad, must bring him the secret of Greek fire to gain his freedom and free the city from the forces of mighty Tamerlane. About three dozen nubile young women wear very little and gambol with our hero herein; much-anticipated skinfest caused a scandal, nurtured by Howard Hughes for profit. **88m/C VHS, Beta.** Dale Robertson, Sally Forrest, Vincent Price, Lili St. Cyr, Mari Blanchard, Joi Lansing; ***D:*** Ted Tetzlaff. *NO*

Son of the Morning Star 🦴🦴🦴 **1991 (PG-13)** Lavish made for TV retelling of Custer's famed-butt kicking. Complex characterizations and unusual points of view, based on the book by Evan S. Connell. **186m/C VHS, LV.** Gary Cole, Rosanna Arquette, Dean Stockwell, Rodney Grant, Terry O'Quinn, David Strathairn, Stanley Anderson, George American Horse; ***D:*** Mike Robe. *REP, FCT*

Son of the Pink Panther 🦴½ *Blake Edwards' Son of the Pink Panther* **1993 (PG)** Lame leftover from the formerly popular comedy series. Director Edwards has chosen not to resurrect Inspector Clouseau, instead opting for his son (Benigni), who turns out to be just as much of a bumbling idiot as his father. Commissioner Dreyfus (Lom), the twitching, mouth-foaming former supervisor of the original Clouseau is looking for a kidnapped princess (Farentino) along with Clouseau, Jr., who himself does not know he is the illegitimate son of his partner's dead nemesis. Many of the sketches have been recycled from previous series entrants. Rather than being funny, they seem used and shopworn like a threadbare rug. **115m/C VHS, LV.** Roberto Benigni, Herbert Lom, Robert Davi, Debrah Farentino, Claudia Cardinale, Burt Kwouk, Shabana Azmi; ***D:*** Blake Edwards; ***W:*** Blake Edwards; ***M:*** Henry Mancini. *MGM*

The Son of the Shark 🦴🦴 *Le Fils du Requin* **1993** Simon (Da Silva) and Martin Vanderhoes (Vandendaele) have been abandoned by their mother and prefer to live as homeless delinquents rather than with their drunken father. The boys commit petty crimes and vandalism to survive (always escaping from foster homes and institutions) while Martin dreams of running away to his true home in the ocean—proclaiming himself to be "the son of a female shark." Depressing and casually cruel; based on a true story. French with subtitles. **88m/C VHS.** *FR* Ludovic Vandendaele, Erick Da Silva, Sandrine Blancke, Maxime LeRoux; ***D:*** Agnes Merlet; ***W:*** Agnes Merlet; ***C:*** Gerard Simon; ***M:*** Bruno Coulais. *FXL*

Son of the Sheik 🦴🦴🦴 **1926** A desert sheik abducts an unfaithful dancing girl. Valentino's well-done, slightly self-mocking last film. Silent. Sequel to "The Sheik" (1921). **62m/B VHS, Beta, LV.** Rudolph Valentino, Vilma Banky, Agnes Ayres; ***D:*** George Fitzmaurice; ***C:*** George Barnes. *NOS, CCB, VCN*

Son of Zorro **1947** Zorro takes the law into his own hands to protect ranchers from bandits. A serial in thirteen chapters. **164m/B VHS.** George Turner, Peggy Stewart, Roy Barcroft, Edward Cassidy. *REP, VCN, MLB*

A Song is Born 🦴🦴🦴 **1948** A group of music professors try to trace the history of music. Kaye is in charge of a U.S. music foundation whose research has led him up to ragtime. He is soon, however, thrust into the sometimes seedy world of jazz joints and night spots, all in the name of research. Enter love interest Mayo, a woman on the run from her gangster boyfriend who hides out at the foundation. Not one of Kaye's funniest or best, but if you enjoy big band music, you'll love this. Includes music by Louis Armstrong and his orchestra, Tommy Dorsey and his orchestra, and Charlie Barnet and his orchestra. This was Kaye's last film for Goldwyn. ♫A Song is Born; Bach Boogie; Anitra's Dance; I'm Getting Sentimental Over You; Blind Barnabas; Mockin' Bird; Redskin Rhumba; The Goldwyn Stomp; Daddy-O. **113m/B VHS.** Danny Kaye, Virginia Mayo, Benny Goodman, Hugh Herbert, Steve Cochran, J. Edward Bromberg, Felix Bressart; ***D:*** Howard Hawks; ***C:*** Gregg Toland. *GVV*

Song O' My Heart 🦴🦴🦴 **1929** An early musical starring popular Irish tenor McCormack as a singer forced to abandon his career when he marries a woman he does not love. A tour de force for the lead in his movie debut. ♫Little Boy Blue; Paddy Me Lad; I Hear You Calling Me; A Fair Story by the Fireside; Just For a Day; Kitty My Love; The Rose of Tralee; A Pair of Blue Eyes; I Feel You Near Me. **91m/B VHS, Beta.** John McCormack, Maureen O'Sullivan, John Garrick, J.M. Kerrigan, Tommy Clifford, Alice Joyce; ***D:*** Frank Borzage. *VAI, FCT, TVC*

Song of Arizona 🦴🦴 **1946** Rogers and the Sons of the Pioneers arrive to aid their pal Hayes against a gang of bank robbers in this modern-day oater. Eight songs perpetually punctuate the perfunctory plot, particularly "Will Ya Be My Darling," "Half-a-Chance Ranch," and the title tune. **54m/B VHS, Beta.** Roy Rogers, Dale Evans, George "Gabby" Hayes, Lyle Talbot, Bob Nolan, The Pioneers; ***D:*** Frank McDonald. *NOS, VCN, HEG*

The Song of Bernadette 🦴🦴🦴 **1943** Depicts the true story of a peasant girl who sees a vision of the Virgin Mary in a grotto at Lourdes in 1858. The girl is directed to dig at the grotto for water that will heal those who believe in its powers, much to the astonishment and concern of the townspeople. Based on Franz Werfel's novel. Directed with tenderness and carefully cast, and appealing to religious and sentimental susceptibilities, it was a box-office smash. **156m/B VHS, Beta, LV.** Charles Bickford, Lee J. Cobb, Jennifer Jones, Vincent Price, Anne Revere, Gladys Cooper; ***D:*** Henry King; ***C:*** Arthur C. Miller; ***M:*** Alfred Newman. Academy Awards '43: Best Actress (Jones), Best Black and White Cinematography, Best Interior Decoration, Best Score; Golden Globe Awards '44: Best Actress—Drama (Jones), Best Director (King), Best Film—Drama; Nominations: Academy Awards '43: Best Director (King), Best Film Editing, Best Picture, Best Screenplay, Best Sound, Best Supporting Actor (Bickford), Best Supporting Actress (Cooper). *FXV, KEP, IGP*

Song of Freedom 🦴🦴½ **1938** The story of a black dockworker whose gift of voice is discovered by an opera impresario. After realizing a career as a concert performer, Robeson ventures to Africa to investigate his ancestry and finds he has royal roots. Robeson turns in a fine performance in what is otherwise an average film. **70m/B VHS, Beta.** *GB* Paul Robeson, Elizabeth Welch, George Mozart; ***D:*** J. Elder Wills. *VYY, HHT, NOS*

Song of Nevada 🦴🦴½ **1944** Rogers woos the high-society daughter (Evans, of course) of a rancher (Hall). Quintenssential Roy-n-Dale. ♫It's Love, Love, Love; New Moon Over Nevada; Hi Ho Little Dogies; The Harum Scarum Baron of the Harmonium; What Are We Going to Do?; A Cowboy Has to Yodel in the Morning. **60m/B VHS, Beta.** Roy Rogers, Dale Evans, Thurston Hall; ***D:*** Joseph Kane. *NOS, HHT, DVT*

Song of Norway 🦴🦴 **1970 (G)** A dramatization of the early life of the beloved Norwegian Romantic composer Edvard Grieg. Filmed against the beautiful mountains, waterfalls, and forests of Norway and based on the popular '40s stage production. The scenery is the best thing because Grieg's life was dull—even with cinematic liberties taken. ♫Strange Music; The Song of Norway; The Little House; Be a Boy Again; Three There Were; A Rhyme and a Reason; Wrong to Dream; I Love You; The Solitary Wanderer. **143m/C VHS, Beta.** Toralv Maurstad, Florence Henderson, Edward G. Robinson, Christina Schollin, Frank Porretta, Oscar Homolka, Robert Morley, Harry Secombe; ***D:*** Andrew L. Stone. *FOX*

Song of Old Wyoming 🦴½ **1945** Three of those songs are presented in the course of an ordinary western about a spunky widow driving badmen out of Wyoming territory. La Rue plays the villainous Cheyanne Kid; this was before he got his own series as the heroic "Lash" La Rue. **65m/C VHS.** Eddie Dean, Sarah Padden, Lash LaRue, Jennifer Holt, Emmett Lynn, John Carpenter, Ian Keith, Bob Barron; ***D:*** Robert Emmett Tansey. *NOS, HEG*

Song of Texas 🦴½ **1943** When a young woman journeys west to visit her father at "his" ranch, Roy and his pals must keep the father's secret that he is just another hired hand. Whenever possible, everyone breaks into song. **54m/B VHS, Beta.** Roy Rogers, Harry Shannon, Pat Brady, Barton MacLane, Arline Judge; ***D:*** Joseph Kane. *NOS, VYY, VCN*

Song of the Exile 🦴🦴½ **1990** A Chinese/Japanese student living in London in the early 1970s faces racial discrimination and decides to return to her native Hong Kong. But on the home front, she and her family clash emotionally until daughter and mother come to a gradual understanding of how the past affects the present. In Cantonese and Japanese with with English subtitles. **100m/C VHS.** *CH* Maggie Cheung, Shwu-Fen Chang; ***D:*** Ann Hui. *KIV, FCT, INJ*

Song of the Gringo 🦴🦴 *The Old Corral* **1936** Tex Ritter stars in his first singing western as a sheriff going after a gang of claim jumpers. **57m/B VHS, Beta.** Tex Ritter, Monte Blue, Joan Woodbury, Fuzzy Knight, Richard Adams, Warner Richmond; ***D:*** John P. McCarthy. *NOS, VCI, VCN*

Song of the Islands 🦴🦴½ **1942** Landing families in Hawaii feud over a beach, while the son of one (Mature) and the daughter of the other (Grable) fall in love. Plenty of songs, and dancing to display Grable's legs. Of course happiness and concord reign at the end. Songs include "O'Brien Has Gone Hawaiian," "Sing Me a Song of the Islands," and "What's Buzzin', Cousin?" **75m/C VHS, Beta, LV.** Betty Grable, Victor Mature, Jack Oakie, Thomas Mitchell, Billy Gilbert; ***D:*** Walter Lang. *FOX, MLB*

Song of the Thin Man 🦴🦴½ **1947** The sixth and final "Thin Man" mystery. This time Nick and Nora Charles (Powell and Loy) investigate the murder of a bandleader. Somewhat more sophisticated than its predecessor, due in part to its setting in the jazz music world. Sequel to "The Thin Man Goes Home." **86m/B VHS, Beta.** William Powell, Myrna Loy, Keenan Wynn, Dean Stockwell, Philip Reed, Patricia Morison, Gloria Grahame, Jayne Meadows, Don Taylor, Leon Ames, Ralph Morgan, Warner Anderson; ***D:*** Edward Buzzell; ***C:*** Charles Rosher. *MGM*

Song of the Trail 🦴½ **1936** Our hero saves an old man hornswoggled at cards. **65m/B VHS, Beta.** Kermit Maynard, George "Gabby" Hayes, Fuzzy Knight, Wheeler Oakman, Evelyn Brent, Andrea Leeds; ***D:*** Russell Hopton. *NOS, VDM, VCN*

Song Spinner 🦴🦴½ **1995 (G)** In a mysterious land, a stranger gives a young girl the power of music, which she hopes to share with the king. But first she must get past the kingdom's noise police. **95m/C VHS.** Meredith Henderson, Patti LuPone, John Neville; ***D:*** Randy Bradshaw. *HMK*

A Song to Remember 🦴🦴🦴 **1945** With music performed by Jose Iturbi, this film depicts the last years of the great pianist and composer Frederic Chopin, including his affair with famous author George Sand, the most renowned French woman of her day. Typically mangled film biography. ♫Valse in D Flat (Minute Waltz); Mazurka In B Flat, Opus 7, No. 1; Fantasie Impromptu, Opus 66; Etude In A Flat, Opus 25, No. 1 (partial); Polonaise In A Flat, Opus 53 (partial); Scherzo In B Flat Minor; Etude In C Minor, Opus 10, No. 12; Nocturne In C Minor, Opus 48, No. 1; Nocturn In E Flat, Opus 9, No. 2. **112m/C VHS, Beta, LV.** Cornel Wilde, Paul Muni, Merle Oberon, Nina Foch, George Coulouris; ***D:*** Charles Vidor; ***C:*** Gaetano Antonio "Tony" Gaudio; ***M:*** Miklos Rozsa. Nominations: Academy Awards '45: Best Actor (Wilde), Best Film Editing, Best Story. *COL, RDG, TVC*

Song Without End 🦴🦴½ **1960** This musical biography of 19th century Hungarian pianist/composer Franz Lizst is given the Hollywood treatment. The lavish production emphasizes Liszt's scandalous exploits with married women and his life among the royal courts of Europe rather than his musical talents. Features music from several composers including Handel, Beethoven, Bach and Schumann. This film marked the debut of Capucine. Director Vidor died during filming and Cukor stepped in, so there is a noticeable change in style. Although there is much to criticize in the story, the music is beautiful. ♫Mephisto Waltz; Spozalizio; Sonata In B Minor; Un Sospiro; Fantasy on Themes From "Rigoletto"; Consolation in D Flat; Liebestraum; Les Preludes; Piano Concerto No. 1. **130m/C VHS, LV.** Dirk Bogarde, Capucine, Genevieve Page, Patricia Morison, Ivan Desny, Martita Hunt, Lou Jacobi; ***D:*** Charles Vidor, George Cukor; ***C:*** James Wong Howe; ***M:*** Morris Stoloff, Harry Sukman. Academy Awards '60: Best Score; Golden Globe Awards '61: Best Film—Musical/Comedy. *COL, TVC*

Songs and Bullets 🦴½ **1938** Simple zen-like title sums it up. The songs total five in number, the bullets somewhat more as hero cowboys battle rustlers in routine fashion. One of a handful of films (westerns and comedies) produced by funnyman Stan Laurel. **57m/B VHS.** Fred Scott, Al "Fuzzy" St. John, Alice Ardell, Charles "Blackie" King, Karl Hackett, Frank LaRue, Budd Buster; ***D:*** Sam Newfield. *NOS, HEG*

Songwriter 🦴🦴½ **1984 (R)** A high-falutin' look at the lives and music of two popular country singers with, aptly, plenty of country tunes written and performed by the stars. Singer-businessman Nelson needs Kristofferson's help keeping a greedy investor at bay. Never mind the plot; plenty of good music. ♫How Do You Feel About Foolin' Around?; Songwriter; Who'll Buy My Memories; Write Your Own Songs; Nobody Said It Was Going To Be Easy; Good Times; Eye of the Storm; Crossing the Border; Down to Her Socks. **94m/C VHS, Beta, LV.** Willie Nelson, Kris Kristofferson, Rip Torn, Melinda Dillon, Lesley Ann Warren; ***D:*** Alan Rudolph. Nominations: Academy Awards '84: Best Original Score. *COL*

Sonny and Jed 🦴 *La Banda J.&S. Cronaca Criminale del Far West* **1973 (R)** An escaped convict and a free-spirited woman travel across Mexico pillaging freely, followed determinedly by shiny-headed lawman Savalas. Lame rip-off of the Bonnie and Clyde legend. **85m/C VHS, Beta.** *IT* Tomas Milian, Telly Savalas, Susan George, Rosanna Janni, Laura Betti; ***D:*** Sergio Corbucci; ***M:*** Ennio Morricone. *NO*

Sonny Boy *Woof!* **1987 (R)** A transvestite and a psychopath adopt a young boy, training him to do their bidding, which includes murder. **96m/C VHS, Beta, LV.** *IT* David Carradine, Paul Smith, Brad Dourif, Conrad Janis, Sydney Lassick, Savina Gersak, Alexandra Powers, Steve Carlisle, Michael Griffin; ***D:*** Robert Martin Carroll; ***W:*** Graeme Whifler. *TWE, MED*

Sonora Stagecoach ☠☠ **1944** Okay sagebrush saga with an interesting lineup; two cowboys, a heroic Indian and a tough gal pilot escort a murder suspect in the title conveyance and manage to clear him when the real bad guys attack. **61m/B VHS.** Hoot Gibson, Bob Steele, Chief Thundercloud, Rocky Camron, Betty Miles, Glenn Strange, George Eldridge, Karl Hackett; ***D:*** Robert Emmett Tansey. *NOS, HEG*

Sons ☠☠ **1991** A Vietnam veteran's son joins the military, causing strains within the family. **?m/C VHS.** ***D:*** Alexandre Rockwell; ***W:*** Alexandre Rockwell, Brandon Cole. *LRP*

Sons of Hercules in the Land of Darkness ☠ **1955** Hercules' sons kill dragons, fight titans, and generally flex up a storm. **74m/B VHS, Beta.** Dan Vadis. *VYY*

Sons of Katie Elder ☠☠☠ **1965** After their mother's death, four brothers are reunited. Wayne is a gunman; Anderson is a college graduate; silent Holliman is a killer; and Martin is a gambler. When they learn that her death might have been murder, they come together to devise a way to seek revenge on the killer. The town bullies complicate matters; the sheriff tells them to lay off. Especially strong screen presence by Wayne, in his first role following cancer surgery. One of the Duke's most popular movies of the '60s. **122m/C VHS, Beta, LV.** John Wayne, Dean Martin, Earl Holliman, Michael Anderson Jr., Martha Hyer, Dennis Hopper, Paul Fix, James Gregory; ***D:*** Henry Hathaway; ***M:*** Elmer Bernstein. *PAR, TLF*

Sons of Steel ☠☠ **1935** Two brothers, owners of a steel mill, lead vastly different lives. They raise their sons in their own images, causing problems. **65m/B VHS.** Charles Starrett, Polly Ann Young, William "Billy" Bakewell, Walter Walker, Aileen Pringle, Holmes Herbert, Florence Roberts, Adolf Millar, Lloyd Ingraham; ***D:*** Charles Lamont. *NOS*

Sons of the Desert ☠☠☠ *Sons of the Legion; Convention City; Fraternally Yours* **1933** Laurel and Hardy in their best-written film. The boys try to fool their wives by pretending to go to Hawaii to cure Ollie of a bad cold when in fact, they are attending their lodge convention in Chicago. Also includes a 1935 Thelma Todd/Patsy Kelly short, "Top Flat." **73m/B VHS, Beta.** Stan Laurel, Oliver Hardy, Mae Busch, Charley Chase, Dorothy Christy; ***D:*** William A. Seiter. *MED, MLB, FAF*

Sons of the Pioneers ☠☠ **1942** Small town sheriff Hayes hires cowboy Roy to rid town of outlaws. **61m/B VHS.** Roy Rogers, George "Gabby" Hayes, Maris Wrixon, Forrest Taylor; ***D:*** Joseph Kane. *REP*

Sooner or Later ☠½ **1978** 13-year-old girl passes herself off as 16 with a local rock idol and must decide whether to go all the way. **100m/C VHS, Beta.** Rex Smith, Judd Hirsch, Denise Miller, Morey Amsterdam, Lynn Redgrave; ***D:*** Bruce Hart. *NWV*

Sophia Loren: Her Own Story ☠☠ **1980** Bio of Sophia Loren, watching her grow from a spindly child in working-class Naples to a world-renowned movie star, beauty queen, and mother. Loren plays herself and her mother in this tedious account. Based on the biography by A.E. Hotchner. Made for TV. **150m/C VHS, Beta.** Sophia Loren, Armand Assante, Ed Flanders, John Gavin; ***D:*** Mel Stuart; ***W:*** Joanna Crawford. *NO*

Sophie's Choice ☠☠☠½ **1982 (R)** A haunting modern tragedy about Sophie Zawistowska, a beautiful Polish Auschwitz survivor settled in Brooklyn after WWII. She has intense relationships with a schizophrenic genius and an aspiring Southern writer. An artful, immaculately performed and resonant drama, with an astonishing, commanding performance by the versatile Streep; a chilling portrayal of the banality of evil. From the best-selling, autobiographical novel by William Styron. **157m/C VHS, Beta, LV.** Meryl Streep, Kevin Kline, Peter MacNicol, Rita Karin, Stephen D. Newman, Josh Mostel; ***D:*** Alan J. Pakula; ***W:*** Alan J. Pakula; ***C:*** Nestor Almendros; ***M:*** Marvin Hamlisch. Academy Awards '82: Best Actress (Streep); Golden Globe Awards '83: Best Actress—Drama (Streep); Los Angeles Film Critics Association Awards '82: Best Actress (Streep); National Board of Review Awards '82: Best Actress (Streep); New York Film Critics Awards '82: Best Actress (Streep), Best Cinematography; National Society of Film Critics Awards '82: Best Actress (Streep); Nominations: Academy Awards '82: Best Adapted Screenplay, Best Cinematography, Best Costume Design, Best Original Score. *FOX, SWC*

Sophisticated Gents ☠☠☠ **1981** Nine boyhood friends, members of a black athletic club, reunite after 25 years to honor their old coach and see how each of their lives has been affected by being black men in American society. Based on the novel "The Junior Bachelor Society" by John A. Williams. Originally made for television. **200m/C VHS.** Paul Winfield, Roosevelt Grier, Bernie Casey, Raymond St. Jacques, Thalmus Rasulala, Dick Anthony Williams, Ron O'Neal, Rosalind Cash, Denise Nicholas, Alfre Woodard, Melvin Van Peebles; ***D:*** Harry Falk; ***W:*** Melvin Van Peebles. *XVC*

Sorcerer ☠☠½ *Wages of Fear* **1977 (PG)** To put out an oil fire, four men on the run in South America agree to try to buy their freedom by driving trucks loaded with nitroglycerin over dangerous terrain—with many natural and man-made obstacles to get in their way. Remake of "The Wages of Fear" is nowhere as good as the classic original, but has exciting moments. Puzzlingly retitled, which may have contributed to the box-office failure, and the near demise of Friedkin's directing career. **121m/C VHS, LV.** Roy Scheider, Bruno Cremer, Francesco Rabal, Soudad Amidou, Ramon Bieri; ***D:*** William Friedkin; ***W:*** Walon Green; ***M:*** Tangerine Dream. Nominations: Academy Awards '77: Best Sound. *MCA, FCT*

Sorceress *Woof!* **1982 (R)** The Harris girls are sisters who use their powers of sorcery and fighting skills to battle demons, dragons, and evil. Yeah, sure. Really, they're just a pair of babes parading for the camera. **83m/C VHS, Beta.** Leigh Anne Harris, Lynette Harris, Bob Nelson, David Milbern, Bruno Rey, Anna De Sade; ***D:*** Brian Stuart; ***W:*** Jim Wynorski. *NO*

Sorceress ☠☠☠ **1988** A friar in medieval Europe feels insecure in his religious beliefs after encountering a woman who heals through ancient practices. Historically authentic and interestingly moody. Written, produced, and directed by two women: an art history professor and a collaborator of Francois Truffaut's. In French with English subtitles or dubbed. **98m/C VHS.** Tcheky Karyo, Christine Boisson, Jean Carmet; ***D:*** Suzanne Schiffman; ***W:*** Pamela Berger, Suzanne Schiffman. *MFV, INJ*

Sorceress ☠½ **1994 (R)** Larry Barnes (Poindexter) is on his way to a partnership at his law firm, especially since his wife Erica (Strain) eliminates his competition—permanently. But Erica goes after the wrong guy when she comes up against Howard Reynolds (Albert). Seems Howard's loving spouse Amelia (Blair) happens to be a witch and she has her own evil spells to cast. **93m/C VHS.** Julie Strain, Larry Poindexter, Linda Blair, Edward Albert; ***D:*** Jim Wynorski. *TRI*

Sorority Babes in the Slimeball Bowl-A-Rama ☠☠ **1987 (R)** An ancient gremlin-type creature is released from a bowling alley, and the great-looking sorority babes have to battle it at the mall, with the help of a wacky crew of nerds. Horrible horror spoof shows plenty of skin. **80m/C Beta, LV.** Linnea Quigley, Brinke Stevens, Andras Jones, John Wildman; ***D:*** David DeCoteau; ***M:*** Guy Moon. *AFE*

Sorority Girl ☠½ **1957** Camp classic in which beautiful co-ed Cabot is presented as a malicious rich kid involved in everything from petty fights to blackmail. Cheap production from the Corman factory. **60m/B VHS.** Susan Cabot, Dick Miller, Barbara Crane, June Kennedy, Fay Baker, Jeane Wood; ***D:*** Roger Corman. *NLC*

Sorority House Massacre *Woof!* **1986 (R)** A knife-wielding maniac stalks a sorority girl while her more elite sisters are away for the weekend. Yawn—haven't we seen this one before? Unfortunately for us we'll see it again because this one's followed by a sequel. **74m/C VHS, Beta.** Angela O'Neill, Wendy Martel, Pamela Ross, Nicole Rio; ***D:*** Carol Frank. *WAR*

Sorority House Massacre 2: Nighty Nightmare *Woof!* **1992** Another no-brainer with a different cast and director. This time around three lingerie-clad lovelies are subjected to the terrors of a killer their first night in their new sorority house. College just keeps getting tougher all the time. **80m/C VHS.** Melissa Moore, Robin Harris, Stacia Zhivago, Dana Bentley; ***D:*** Jim Wynorski. *NHO*

Sorority House Party ☠ **1992 (R)** A famous rock guitarist is held against his will at the sexiest sorority house on campus. He definitely has mixed feelings about the experience considering the inhabitants saunter around in bikinis and "force" him to party with them. Anders and Attila are transplants from the modeling circuit. **95m/C VHS.** Attila, April Lerman, Kim Little, Avalon Anders, Joe Mundi, Rachel Latt, Mark Stulce, Michael Xavier; ***D:*** David Michael Latt; ***W:*** John Murdy, Steve Taylor. *APX*

Sorrento Beach ☠☠ *Hotel Sorrento* **1995 (R)** A beachside community outside Melbourne, Australia, Sorrento is home to the Moynihans. The three Moynihan sisters—Meg (Goodall), Hillary (Gillmer), and Pippa (Morice)—are reunited after 10 years by their father's sudden death. Lots of tensions, rivalries, and jealousies come to the surface as well as old secrets regarding a family tragedy. Talky film hasn't quite cast off its stage origins (it's adapted from a play by Hannie Rayson) but the performances are noteworthy. **112m/C VHS.** *AU* Caroline Goodall, Caroline Gillmer, Tara Morice, Joan Plowright, John Hargreaves, Ray Barrett, Ben Thomas; ***D:*** Richard Franklin; ***W:*** Richard Franklin, Peter Fitzpatrick; ***C:*** Geoff Burton; ***M:*** Nevida Tyson-Chew. Australian Film Institute '95: Best Adapted Screenplay, Best Supporting Actor (Barrett); Nominations: Australian Film Institute '95: Best Actress (Gillmer), Best Actress (Goodall), Best Director (Franklin), Best Film. *VMK*

The Sorrow and the Pity ☠☠☠½ **1971** A classic documentary depicting the life of a small French town and its resistance during the Nazi occupation. Lengthy, but totally compelling. A great documentary that brings home the atrocities of war. In French with English narration. **265m/B VHS, Beta.** *FR* ***D:*** Marcel Ophuls. National Board of Review Awards '72: 5 Best Foreign Films of the Year. *COL, OM*

Sorrowful Jones ☠☠ **1949** A "Little Miss Marker" remake, in which bookie Hope inherits a little girl as collateral for an unpaid bet. Good for a few yuks, but the original is much better. **88m/B VHS, Beta.** Bob Hope, Lucille Ball, William Demarest, Bruce Cabot, Thomas Gomez, Mary Jane Saunders; ***D:*** Sidney Lanfield; ***W:*** Jack Rose, Melville Shavelson; ***C:*** Daniel F. Fapp. *MCA*

Sorrows of Gin ☠☠½ **1979** Eight-year-old girl searches for a sense of family amid her parents' lives. Her efforts to deal with alienation and emotional isolation lead her to run away from home. From a short story by John Cheever. **60m/C VHS, Beta.** Edward Herrmann, Sigourney Weaver, Mara Hobel, Eileen Heckart, Rachel Roberts. *FLI*

The Sorrows of Satan ☠☠☠ **1926** Dempster and Cortez star as writers in love with each other, but Cortez can't take his poverty and the rejection of publishers. As he is about to end it all, the devil appears to him in disguise and makes an offer he can hardly refuse. He is introduced to London society and winds up marrying a fortune hunter. When he discovers this he goes back to Dempster, who still loves him, and vows to give up everything for her. Menjou then reveals himself to be the devil but Dempster's faith is so strong that the evil is vanquished. **111m/B VHS, Beta.** Adolphe Menjou, Carol Dempster, Ricardo Cortez, Lya de Putti; ***D:*** D.W. Griffith. *GPV*

Sorry, Wrong Number ☠☠☠½ **1948** A wealthy, bedridden wife overhears two men plotting a murder on a crossed telephone line, and begins to suspect that one of the voices is her husband's. A classic tale of paranoia and suspense. Based on a radio drama by Louise Fletcher, who also wrote the screenplay. Remade for television in 1989. **89m/B VHS, Beta, LV.** Barbara Stanwyck, Burt Lancaster, Ann Richards, Wendell Corey, Harold Vermilyea, Ed Begley Sr.; ***D:***

Anatole Litvak. Nominations: Academy Awards '48: Best Actress (Stanwyck). *PAR*

Sorry, Wrong Number 🦴½ **1989** Cable remake of the 1948 Barbara Stanwyck thriller about a bed-ridden woman trying to get help after she realizes she's being stalked by a killer. Offers a new twist (drug dealing), but doesn't even approach the Stanwyck original. From the story by Lucille Fletcher. **90m/C VHS, Beta, LV.** Loni Anderson, Hal Holbrook, Patrick Macnee, Miguel Fernandez, Carl Weintraub; ***D:*** Tony Wharmby; ***W:*** Ann Louise Bardach; ***M:*** Bruce Broughton. *PAR*

S.O.S. Coast Guard 🦴🦴½ **1937** A fiendish scientist creates a disintegrating gas and the U.S. Coast Guard must stop him from turning it over to unfriendly foreigners. Loads of action in this 12-part serial. **224m/B VHS, LV.** Ralph Byrd, Bela Lugosi, Maxine Doyle. *NOS, SNC, REP*

S.O.S. Pacific 🦴🦴 **1960** A seaplane crashes on a nuclear-test island and the survivors find that they have only five hours before they get nuked. Even though there is plenty of the usual action one would expect from such a film, the story really revolves around the characters. The British and U.S. versions have different endings. **91m/B VHS.** *GB* Eddie Constantine, Pier Angeli, Richard Attenborough, John Gregson, Eva Bartok; ***D:*** Guy Green. *NOS*

S.O.S. Titanic 🦴🦴½ **1979** The story of the Titanic disaster, recounted in flashback, in docu-drama style. James Costigan's teleplay of the familiar story focuses on the courage that accompanied the horror and tragedy. Thoroughly professional, absorbing made-for-TV drama. **98m/C VHS, Beta.** David Janssen, Cloris Leachman, Susan St. James, David Warner, Ian Holm, Helen Mirren, Harry Andrews; ***D:*** Billy Hale; ***M:*** Howard Blake. *NO*

Sotto, Sotto 🦴🦴½ **1985 (R)** A minor Wertmuller comedy about an Italian businessman who is constantly suspicious of his wife's fidelity. As it happens, she's attracted to another woman (de Santis). Massimo Wertmuller is Lina's nephew. Entertaining. In Italian with English subtitles. **104m/C VHS, Beta.** *IT* Enrico Montesano, Veronica Lario, Massimo Wertmuller, Luisa de Santis; ***D:*** Lina Wertmuller; ***W:*** Lina Wertmuller. *COL, APD, INJ*

Soul-Fire 🦴🦴 **1925** South Pacific high seas induce Cupid's arrow. Silent. **100m/B VHS, Beta.** Richard Barthelmess, Bessie Love, Walter Long, Arthur Metcalfe; ***D:*** John S. Robertson. *GPV, FCT, GVV*

Soul Hustler *Woof!* **1976 (PG)** A con man becomes rich and famous as a tent-show evangelist. Pathetic drivel. **81m/C VHS, Beta.** Fabian, Casey Kasem, Larry Bishop, Nai Bonet; ***D:*** Burt Topper. *LIV*

Soul Man 🦴🦴 **1986 (PG-13)** Denied the funds he expected for his Harvard tuition, a young white student (Howell) masquerades as a black in order to get a minority scholarship. As a black student at Harvard, Howell learns about racism and bigotry. Pleasant lightweight comedy with romance thrown in (Chong is the black girl he falls for), and with pretensions to social satire that it never achieves. **101m/C VHS, Beta, LV.** C. Thomas Howell, Rae Dawn Chong, James Earl Jones, Leslie Nielsen, Arye Gross; ***D:*** Steve Miner; ***W:*** Carol Black. *NWV, VTR*

Soul of the Beast 🦴½ **1923** An elephant repeatedly saves Bellamy from the villainous Beery. Silent with original organ score. **77m/B VHS, Beta, 8mm.** Madge Bellamy, Cullen Landis, Noah Beery Sr. *GPV, VYY*

Soul Patrol 🦴 **1980 (R)** Black newspaper reporter clashes with the all-white police department in a racist city. **90m/C VHS, Beta.** Nigel Davenport, Ken Gampu, Peter Dyneley; ***D:*** Christopher Rowley. *SUN*

Soul Vengeance 🦴 *Welcome Home Brother Charles* **1975** Black man is jailed and brutalized for crime he didn't commit and wants revenge when he's released. Many afros and platform shoes. Vintage blaxploitation. **91m/C VHS.** Marlo Monte, Reatha Grey, Stan Kamber, Tiffany Peters, Ven Bigelow, Jake Carter; ***D:*** Jamaa Fanaka; ***W:*** Jamaa Fanaka. *XVC*

Soultaker 🦴½ **1990 (R)** The title spirit is after a young couple's souls, and they have just an hour to reunite with their bodies after a car crash. Meanwhile, they're in limbo (literally) between heaven and earth. The ending's OK, if you can make it that far. **94m/C VHS, LV.** Joe Estevez, Vivian Schilling, Gregg Thomsen, David Shark, Jean Reiner, Chuck Williams, Robert Z'Dar; ***D:*** Michael Rissi; ***W:*** Vivian Schilling. *AIP*

The Sound and the Silence 🦴🦴½ **1993** Bio of inventor Alexander Graham Bell (Bach). The Scottish Bell's father was a speech specialist and his beloved mother Eliza (Fricker) was severely hearing impaired. Bell himself trained to work with the deaf in Boston and experimented with transmitting speech electronically—a project which only grew when Bell married the deaf Mable Hubbard (Quinn). Bell's lifelong devotion lead to his development of the telephone as well as numerous other inventions (and his founding of "National Geographic" magazine). Bell was hardly a lively character but this made for television drama is lavishly done. In two parts. **93m/C VHS.** John Bach, Elizabeth Quinn, Brenda Fricker, Ian Bannen; ***D:*** John Kent Harrison; ***W:*** Tony Foster, William Schmidt, John Kent Harrison; ***M:*** John Charles. *TTC*

Sound of Horror 🦴½ *El Sonido de la Muerte; Sound From a Million Years Ago; The Prehistoric Sound* **1964** The Hound usually admires creative efforts to keep budgets down, but this is too much (or too little). A dinosaur egg hatches, and out lashes an invisible predator. Yes, you'll have to use your imagination as archaeologists are slashed to bits by the no-show terror. **85m/B VHS.** *SP* James Philbrook, Arturo Fernandez, Soledad Miranda, Ingrid Pitt; ***D:*** Jose Antonio Nieves-Conde. *NOS, LOO*

Sound of Love 🦴 **1977** The mutual attraction between a deaf female hustler and a deaf race car driver leads to a deep relationship where they both learn about their own fears and desires. **74m/C VHS, Beta.** Celia de Burgh, John Jarratt. *SUE*

Sound of Murder **1982** A successful children's book writer wants to exact revenge on his adulterous wife, but is himself murdered before he can "execute" his plan. **114m/C VHS, Beta.** Michael Moriarty, Joanna Miles. *LIV*

The Sound of Music 🦴🦴🦴🦴 **1965** The classic film version of the Rodgers and Hammerstein musical based on the true story of the singing von Trapp family of Austria and their escape from the Nazis just before WWII. Beautiful Salzburg, Austria location photography and an excellent cast. Andrews, fresh from her Oscar for "Mary Poppins," is effervescent, in beautiful voice, but occasionally too good to be true. Not Rodgers & Hammerstein's most innovative score, but lovely to hear and see. Plummer's singing was dubbed by Bill Lee. Marni Nixon, behind-the-scenes songstress for "West Side Story" and "My Fair Lady," makes her on-screen debut as one of the nuns. ♫I Have Confidence In Me; Something Good; The Sound of Music; Preludium; Morning Hymn; Alleluia; How Do You Solve A Problem Like Maria?; Sixteen, Going on Seventeen; My Favorite Things. **174m/C VHS, Beta, LV.** Julie Andrews, Christopher Plummer, Eleanor Parker, Peggy Wood, Charmian Carr, Heather Menzies, Marni Nixon, Richard Haydn, Anna Lee, Norma Varden, Nicholas Hammond, Angela Cartwright, Portia Nelson, Duane Chase, Debbie Turner, Kym Karath; ***D:*** Robert Wise; ***W:*** Ernest Lehman; ***M:*** Richard Rodgers, Oscar Hammerstein. Academy Awards '65: Best Adapted Score, Best Director (Wise), Best Film Editing, Best Picture, Best Sound; Directors Guild of America Awards '65: Best Director (Wise); Golden Globe Awards '66: Best Actress—Musical/Comedy (Andrews), Best Film—Musical/Comedy; National Board of Review Awards '65: 10 Best Films of the Year; Nominations: Academy Awards '65: Best Actress (Andrews), Best Art Direction/Set Decoration (Color), Best Color Cinematography, Best Costume Design (Color), Best Supporting Actress (Wood). *FOX, BTV, RDG*

Sounder 🦴🦴🦴🦴 **1972 (G)** The struggles of a family of black sharecroppers in rural Louisiana during the Depression. When the father is sentenced to jail for stealing in order to feed his family, they must pull together even more, and one son finds education to be his way out of poverty. Tyson brings strength and style to her role, with fine help from Winfield. Moving and well made, with little sentimentality and superb acting from a great cast. Adapted from the novel by William Armstrong. **105m/C VHS, Beta, LV.** Paul Winfield, Cicely Tyson, Kevin Hooks, Taj Mahal, Carmen Mathews, James Best, Janet MacLachlan; ***D:*** Martin Ritt; ***W:*** Lonne Elder III; ***C:*** John A. Alonzo; ***M:*** Taj Mahal. National Board of Review Awards '72: 10 Best Films of the Year, Best Actress (Tyson); Nominations: Academy Awards '72: Best Actor (Winfield), Best Actress (Tyson), Best Adapted Screenplay, Best Picture. *KUI, PAR, PTB*

Sounds of Silence 🦴🦴 **1991** A young deaf boy fears that a killer arsonist may be at large—but can he prove it? One of a number of obscure oddities featuring former youth idol Donahue. **108m/C VHS, Beta.** Troy Donahue, Peter Nelson. *NO*

Soup for One 🦴🦴½ **1982 (R)** Writer-director Kaufer's first film is a solid entry in the Woody Allen-esque Manhattanite's angst genre. Young Jewish guy Rubinek pines for the woman of his dreams, finds her, is rejected, persists, gets her, wonders if she's what he wants after all. If you like Woody Allen, this is worth seeing. **84m/C VHS, Beta.** Saul Rubinek, Marcia Strassman, Gerrit Graham, Richard Libertini, Andrea Martin; ***D:*** Jonathan Kaufer. *WAR*

Sourdough 🦴🦴 **1977** Fur trapper Perry escapes the hustle and bustle of modern life by fleeing to the Alaskan wilderness. Near-plotless travelog depends heavily on scenery—and there's plenty of that, for sure. **94m/C VHS, Beta, LV.** Gil Perry, Charles Brock, Slim Carlson, Carl Clark; ***D:*** Martin J. Spinelli. *IMP*

South Beach 🦴🦴 **1992 (R)** Two ex-football players turned private eyes are living the good life and partying it up in Miami Beach. However, their leisurely lifestyles are soon disrupted when they accept a mysterious challenge from the beautiful Vanity. **93m/C VHS.** Fred Williamson, Gary Busey, Vanity, Peter Fonda; ***D:*** Fred Williamson; ***W:*** Mark Montgomery; ***M:*** Joe Renzetti. *PSM*

South Bronx Heroes 🦴½ *The Runaways; Revenge of the Innocents* **1985 (R)** A police officer helps two children when they discover their foster home is the headquarters for a pornography ring. **105m/C VHS, Beta.** Brendan Ward, Mario Van Peebles, Megan Van Peebles, Melissa Esposito, Martin Zurla, Jordan Abeles; ***D:*** William Szarka. *NO*

South Central 🦴🦴 **1992 (R)** A low-budget urban drama set in a gang-infested L.A. neighborhood. Bobby is a young black man, and former gang leader, who has spent ten years in prison for murder. His wife has become a drug addict and his young son Jimmie has begun running with his dad's old gang. Now paroled, Bobby hopes to re-establish the bond with his son—enough to protect him from following in his nowhere-to-go-but-down footsteps. Worthy effort with an emotional ending. Feature debut of director Anderson. Based on the novel "Crips" by Donald Bakeer. **99m/C VHS, Beta, LV.** Glenn Plummer, Carl Lumbly, Christian Coleman, LaRita Shelby, Byron Keith Minns; ***D:*** Steve Anderson; ***W:*** Steve Anderson. *WAR, PMS*

South of Hell Mountain 🦴½ **1970 (R)** On the run from a gold mine robbery where they left 20 dead, the McHenry brothers meet a mother-daughter team that slows them down. **87m/C VHS, Beta.** Ann Stewart, Sam Hall, Nicol Britton; ***D:*** William Sachs, Louis Leahman. *MGM*

South of Monterey 🦴½ **1947** Western adventure with the Cisco kid. **63m/B VHS, Beta.** Gilbert Roland, Martin Garralaga, Frank Yaconelli, Marjorie Riordan; ***D:*** William Nigh. *VCN*

South of Pago Pago 🦴🦴½ **1940** The unsuspecting natives of a tropical isle are exploited by a gang of pirates searching for a seabed of rare pearls. A notch up from most similar adventure outings, with great violent action and excellent cinematography. Leading lady Farmer was thought to be a rising star, but retired at 29 in 1942 because of alcoholism and spent some time in mental institutions. "Frances" (1982), with Jessica Lange, is based on her life. **98m/B VHS, Beta.** Victor McLaglen, Jon Hall, Frances Farmer, Gene Lockhart; ***D:*** Alfred E. Green. *NO*

South of Reno ♪♪½ **1987 (R)** A man living a secluded life in the desert dreams of moving to Reno and learns his wife is cheating on him. Odd, minimal plot. Impressive first feature for Polish diretor Rezyka, who cut his teeth on music videos. **98m/C VHS, LV.** Jeffery Osterhage, Lisa Blount, Joe Phelan, Lewis Van Bergen, Julia Montgomery, Brandis Kemp, Danitza Kingsley, Mary Grace Canfield, Bert Remsen; ***D:*** Mark Rezyka; ***M:*** Nigel Holton. *REP*

South of St. Louis ♪♪½ **1948** A peaceful cattle rancher turns renegade gunrunner during the Civil War when his stock is destroyed by Union guerrillas. Overplotted but exciting and action-packed western, with Smith dazzling in a plethora of costumes. **88m/C VHS.** Joel McCrea, Zachary Scott, Victor Jory, Douglas Kennedy, Alexis Smith, Alan Hale, Dorothy Malone; ***D:*** Ray Enright; ***C:*** Karl Freund; ***M:*** Max Steiner. *REP*

South of Santa Fe ♪♪ **1932** Mexican rebels give the hero a hard time in this standard Western. **60m/B VHS.** Bob Steele, Janis Elliott, Chris-Pin Martin, Jack Clifford, Eddie Dunn, Robert Burns, Hank Bell, Allan Garcia; ***D:*** Bert Glennon. *NOS*

South of Santa Fe ♪♪ **1942** Rogers and friends take on the mob—yes, the mob, armed with machine guns and airplanes—after they are falsely implicated in a crime. In lulls between the rootin' tootin' gunfights, Rogers belts out "We're Headin' for the Home Corral," "Down the Trail," and "Open Range Ahead." **60m/B VHS, Beta.** Roy Rogers, George "Gabby" Hayes, Linda Hayes, Paul Fix, Judy Clark; ***D:*** Joseph Kane. *NOS, DVT, CAB*

South of the Border ♪♪ **1939** Autry and Burnette are government agents sent to Mexico to investigate a possible revolution instigated by foreign agents. Propaganda-heavy singing western appeared just before the U.S. entered WWII; did well at the box office and boosted Autry's career. **70m/B VHS, Beta.** Gene Autry, Smiley Burnette. *CCB, VCN*

South of the Rio Grande ♪½ **1945** The Cisco Kid rides again as he comes to the aid of a rancher whose horses were stolen. Garden-variety law-and-order western. **60m/B VHS, Beta.** Duncan Renaldo; ***D:*** Lambert Hillyer. *NO*

South Pacific ♪♪♪½ **1958** A young American Navy nurse and a Frenchman fall in love during WWII. Expensive production included much location shooting in Hawaii. Based on Rodgers and Hammerstein's musical; not as good as the play, but pretty darn good still. The play in turn was based on James Michener's novel "Tales of the South Pacific." ♫My Girl Back Home; Dites-Moi; Bali Ha'i; Happy Talk; A Cockeyed Optimist; Soliloquies; Some Enchanted Evening; Bloody Mary; I'm Gonna Wash That Man Right Out of My Hair. **167m/C VHS, Beta, LV.** Mitzi Gaynor, Rossano Brazzi, Ray Walston, France Nuyen, John Kerr, Juanita Hall, Tom Laughlin; ***D:*** Joshua Logan; ***C:*** Leon Shamroy; ***M:*** Richard Rodgers, Oscar Hammerstein; ***V:*** Giorgio Tozzi. Academy Awards '58: Best Sound; Nominations: Academy Awards '56: Best Color Cinematography; Academy Awards '58: Best Original Score. *FOX, RDG, HMV*

South Seas Massacre *Woof!* **19??** A cop and a prisoner, shackled together, try to survive modern-day pirates, natives, and each other. They may make it through, but viewers may wish they didn't. **60m/C VHS, Beta.** Troy Donahue; ***D:*** Pablo Santiago. *PSM*

Southern Comfort ♪♪♪ **1981 (R)** A group of National Guardsmen are on weekend maneuvers in the swamps of Louisiana. They run afoul of some of the local Cajuns, and are marked for death in this exciting and disturbing thriller. Boothe is excellent in a rare exploration of a little-understood way of life. Lots of blood. If you belong to the National Guard, this could make you queasy. **106m/C VHS, Beta, LV.** Powers Boothe, Keith Carradine, Fred Ward, Franklyn Seales, Brion James, T.K. Carter, Peter Coyote; ***D:*** Walter Hill; ***W:*** Walter Hill, David Giler, Michael Kane; ***M:*** Ry Cooder. *SUE, HHE*

A Southern Yankee ♪♪½ *My Hero* **1948** Skelton plays a bumbling bellboy who ends up as a Union spy during the Civil War. Enjoyable comedy, thanks largely to the off-screen input of Buster Keaton. **90m/B VHS, Beta.** Red Skelton, Brian Donlevy, Arlene Dahl, George Coulouris, Lloyd Gough, John Ireland, Minor Watson, Charles Dingle, Art Baker, Reed Hadley, Arthur Space, Addison Richards, Joyce Compton, Paul Harvey, Jeff Corey; ***D:*** Edward Sedgwick. *MGM*

The Southerner ♪♪♪♪ **1945** A man used to working for others is given some land by an uncle and decides to pack up his family and try farming for himself. They find hardships as they struggle to support themselves. A superb, naturalistic celebration of a family's fight to survive amid all the elements. From the story "Hold Autumn in Your Hand," by George Sessions Perry. Novelist Faulkner had an uncredited hand in the script. He thought Renoir the best contemporary director, and later said "The Southerner" gave him more pleasure than any of his other Hollywood work (though this is faint praise; Faulkner is said to have hated Hollywood). **91m/B VHS, Beta, 8mm.** Zachary Scott, Betty Field, Beulah Bondi, Norman Lloyd, Bunny Sunshine, Jay Gilpin, Estelle Taylor, Blanche Yurka, Percy Kilbride, J. Carrol Naish; ***D:*** Jean Renoir; ***W:*** Hugo Butler, William Faulkner, Jean Renoir. National Board of Review Awards '45: Best Director (Renoir); Venice Film Festival '46: Best Film; Nominations: Academy Awards '45: Best Director (Renoir), Best Sound, Best Original Score. *NOS, PSM, VYY*

Southward Ho! ♪♪ **1939** In the first western to team Rogers with sidekick Gabby Hayes, they portray ranchers investigating bloodshed in their valley, Roy meanwhile yodelin' four tunes. Fun outing. **56m/B VHS, Beta.** Roy Rogers, George "Gabby" Hayes. *NOS, VCN, CAB*

Souvenir ♪♪ **1988 (R)** A German soldier returns to France after WWII to find the woman he left behind and the daughter he never saw. Might have been good, but too melodramatic and overwrought, with lukewarm acting. **93m/C VHS, Beta, LV.** Christopher Plummer, Catherine Hicks, Christopher Cazenove, Michael Lonsdale; ***D:*** Geoffrey Reeve. *PAR*

Soviet Spy ♪♪ **1961** A French docu-drama written by Hans Otto Meissner, Chief of Protocol at the German Embassy in Tokyo during WWII, about the journalist Richard Sorge, a German hanged in 1944 for supplying information to the Soviets. In French with subtitles. **130m/B VHS, Beta.** *FR FCT*

Soylent Green ♪♪½ **1973 (PG)** In the 21st Century, hard-boiled police detective Heston investigates a murder and discovers what soylent green—the people's principal food—is made of. Robinson's final film is a disappointing end to a great career. Its view of the future and of human nature is relentlessly dark. Don't watch it with kids. **95m/C VHS, Beta, LV.** Charlton Heston, Leigh Taylor-Young, Chuck Connors, Joseph Cotten, Edward G. Robinson, Brock Peters; ***D:*** Richard Fleischer. *MGM*

Space Monster *Woof! First Woman Into Space; Voyage Beyond the Sun* **1964** Really bad, low-budget flick with a rubber monster and a climactic crash into a "sea of monsters" which is really a fish tank full of crabs. Ultra cheap production with handed down cast and props. **?m/B VHS.** *SMW*

Space Mutiny ♪ **1988 (PG)** Spaceship falls under the attack of the mutinous Kalgan. To keep everyone from being sold into slavery, a small band of loyal passengers strike back. Will they be successful in thwarting the attack? Who cares? **93m/C VHS, Beta.** Reb Brown, James Ryan, John Phillip Law, Cameron Mitchell; ***D:*** David Winters; ***W:*** Maria Dante. *AIP*

Space: 1999 **1975** Landau and Bain star as the leaders of Moonbase Alpha, a scientific outpost which is hurled out of orbit by a nuclear explosion. In "Voyager's Return" the crew of Moonbase Alpha discover the original Voyager probe and excitedly prepare to extract its vast knowledge of the universe. To their horror, they discover that it has somehow been transformed into a planet-destroying monster. Bitter aliens are coming to exact their revenge on the machine and the crew is caught in the middle! Additional episodes available. **52m/C VHS, LV.** *GB* Martin Landau, Barbara Bain, Barry Morse, Nick Tate, Jeremy Kemp, Barry Stokes, Alex Scott, Lawrence Trimble; ***D:*** Bob Kellett. *MOV*

Space: 1999—Alien Attack ♪♪♪ **1979** After an explosion on the moon, Moonbase Alpha loses contact with Earth forever. Pilot episode of the popular British sci-fi series. **109m/C VHS, Beta.** *GB* Martin Landau, Barbara Bain, Barry Morse, Nick Tate, Roy Dotrice, Philip Madoc, Lou Satton, Eric Carte; ***D:*** Lee H. Katzin. *LIV*

Space Ninja: Sword of the Space Ark ♪½ **1981** A young fighter pilot returns home to find his planet under siege and his family dead. He vows to seek revenge and sets out to destroy the evil emperor who is wreaking such havoc. **75m/C VHS, Beta.** ***D:*** Bunker Jenkins. *LIV*

Space Patrol **1950** Buzz Corey, Commander-in-Chief of the Space Patrol, tries to maintain interplanetary peace and protect the people of Earth's neighboring planets. These episodes television series include previews of coming attractions from classic science fiction films. Additional episodes are available. **120m/B VHS, Beta.** Edward Kemmer, Lyn Osborn. *MED, MOV*

Space Rage ♪ *Trackers* **1986 (R)** A criminal sentenced to life on a prison planet leads a revolt of the inmates. Lame, formula western set in outer space. **78m/C VHS, Beta.** Michael Pare, Richard Farnsworth, John Laughlin, Lee Purcell; ***D:*** Conrad Palmisano. *LIV*

Space Raiders ♪♪ *Star Child* **1983 (PG)** A plucky 10-year-old blasts off into a futuristic world of intergalactic desperados, crafty alien mercenaries, starship battles and cliff-hanging dangers. Recycled special effects (from producer Corman's movie factory) and plot (lifted near-whole from "Star Wars"). **84m/C VHS, Beta.** Vince Edwards, David Mendenhall; ***D:*** Howard R. Cohen; ***W:*** Howard R. Cohen. *WAR*

Space Riders *Woof!* **1983 (PG)** Action-adventure about the world's championship motorcycle race, with a rock soundtrack featuring Duran Duran, Simple Minds and Melba Moore. **93m/C VHS, Beta.** Barry Sheene, Gavan O'Herlihy, Toshiya Ito, Stephanie McLean, Sayo Inaba; ***D:*** Joe Massot. *NO*

Space Soldiers Conquer the Universe ♪♪ **1940** Edited version of the Flash Gordon serial "Flash Gordon Conquers the Universe." The evil Emperor Ming introduces a horrible plague from outer space called "The Purple Death." Dr. Zarkov, Dale, and Flash Gordon travel from the frozen wastes of Frigia to the palaces of Mongo and must take risk after risk. Twelve chapters at 20 minutes each. **240m/B VHS, Beta.** Buster Crabbe, Charles Middleton, Carol Hughes. *NOS, CAB*

Spaceballs ♪♪½ **1987 (PG)** A humorous Brooks parody of recent science fiction pictures, mostly notably "Star Wars," with references to "Alien," the "Star Trek series," and "The Planet of the Apes." Disappointingly tame and tentative, but chuckle-laden enough for Brooks fans. The great man himself appears in two roles, including puny wise man/wise guy Yogurt. **96m/C VHS, Beta, LV.** Mel Brooks, Rick Moranis, John Candy, Bill Pullman, Daphne Zuniga, Dick Van Patten, John Hurt, George Wyner, Joan Rivers, Lorene Yarnell, Sal Viscuso, Stephen Tobolowsky, Dom DeLuise, Michael Winslow; ***D:*** Mel Brooks; ***W:*** Mel Brooks, Ronny Graham, Thomas Meehan; ***M:*** John Morris. *MGM*

Spaced Invaders ♪½ **1990 (PG)** Five ultra-cool aliens crash-land in a small midwestern town at Halloween. Local denizens mistake them for trick-or-treaters. Poorly made and a waste of time. **102m/C VHS, Beta, LV.** Douglas Barr, Royal Dano, Ariana Richards, Kevin Thompson, Jimmy Briscoe, Tony Cox, Debbie Lee Carrington, Tommy Madden; ***D:*** Patrick Read Johnson; ***W:*** Scott Lawrence Alexander. *TOU*

Spaced Out *Woof! Outer Reach* **1980 (R)** Naughty sci-fi sex comedy that parodies everything from "Star Wars" to "2001," though not very well. The sultry female aliens are visually pleasing, though.

Watch this one with the sound turned off. **85m/C VHS, Beta.** Barry Stokes, Glory Annen; ***D:*** Norman J. Warren. *NO*

Spacehunter: Adventures in the Forbidden Zone ☾½ **1983 (PG)** Galactic bounty hunter agrees to rescue three damsels held captive by a cyborg. Strauss ain't no Harrison Ford. Filmed in 3-D, but who cares? **90m/C VHS, Beta, LV.** *CA* Peter Strauss, Molly Ringwald, Michael Ironside, Ernie Hudson, Andrea Marcovicci; ***D:*** Lamont Johnson; ***W:*** Len Blum; ***M:*** Elmer Bernstein. *COL*

Spaceship ☾½ *The Creature Wasn't Nice; Naked Space* **1981 (PG)** Misguided attempt to spoof creature-features. Mad scientist tries to protect kindly monster from crazed crew. Not very funny, with the exception of the song-and-dance routine by the monster. **88m/C VHS.** Cindy Williams, Bruce Kimmel, Leslie Nielsen, Gerrit Graham, Patrick Macnee, Ron Kurowski; ***D:*** Bruce Kimmel. *LIV*

Spaceways ☾½ **1953** Scientist Duff is beset by all sorts of troubles: his experimental rockets explode, his wife has an affair with an ambitious scientist, and when they disappear together, he's accused of killing them and placing their bodies in the exploded rocket. All in all, a pretty bad (and long) day for our hero. Why should we suffer through it with him? **76m/B VHS, Beta, LV.** Howard Duff, Eva Bartok, Ceclie Cheyreau, Andrew Osborn; ***D:*** Terence Fisher. *MLB*

Spaghetti House ☾½ **1982** A handful of waiters are held hostage by ruthless killers in this innocuous but worthless Italian comedy. Dubbed. **103m/C VHS, Beta.** *IT* Nino Manfredi, Rita Tushingham; ***D:*** Giullo Paradisi. *INJ*

Spaghetti Western ☾½ **1969** A farmer and a publisher take on the vile oil baron who is taking over the town. A parody-or is it?—of Eastwoodian B-grade spaghetti westerns. No director credited. **90m/C VHS, Beta.** Franco Nero, Martin Balsam, Sterling Hayden. *VDC*

Spalding Gray: Terrors of Pleasure **1988** The ultra-cool Gray tells the story of one man's dream to own land in his own inimitable way. HBO comedy special. **60m/C VHS, Beta.** Spalding Gray; ***D:*** Thomas Schlamme. *HBO*

Spangles ☾ **1926** Silent circus drama. **58m/B VHS, Beta.** Marion Nixon, Hobart Bosworth, Pat O'Malley, Gladys Brockwell; ***D:*** Frank O'Connor. *GPV*

The Spaniard's Curse ☾☾½ **1958** When a man is convicted for a murder he did not commit, he puts a curse on the judge and jury responsible. Mysteriously, the marked people begin dying. Is he responsible? Then he dies and the mystery thickens. Intriguing but sloppy murder mystery. **80m/B VHS, Beta.** *GB* Tony Wright, Lee Patterson, Michael Hordern, Ralph Truman, Henry Oscar; ***D:*** Ralph Kemplen. *SNC*

The Spanish Gardener ☾☾☾ **1957** A boy in a prominent family spends more time with the gentle gardner than with the domineering father, so dad arranges for his rival to be framed and sent to prison. An affecting British adaptation of the A.J. Cronin novel, turned into a showcase for Bogarde in the title role. **95m/C VHS.** Dirk Bogarde, Jon Whiteley, Michael Hordern, Cyril Cusack, Maureen Swanson, Lyndon Brook, Josephine Griffin, Bernard Lee; ***D:*** Philip Leacock. *NOS, VEC*

The Spanish Main ☾☾½ **1945** Typical, gusto-laden swashbuckler, RKO's first in Technicolor. Evil Spanish governor Slezak captures Dutch crew led by Henreid. They escape and kidnap his fiancee (O'Hara) off a ship coming from Mexico. Henreid forces her to marry him, but his crew uses the might of the armada and returns O'Hara to Slezak behind Henreid's back. Wow! **100m/C LV.** Paul Henreid, Maureen O'Hara, Walter Slezak, Binnie Barnes, John Emery, Barton MacLane; ***D:*** Frank Borzage; ***C:*** George Barnes. Nominations: Academy Awards '45: Best Color Cinematography. *IME*

Spanking the Monkey ☾☾☾ **1994 (R)** "What'd ya do on your summer vacation?" Ray Aibelli (Davies) has an interesting answer in this dark comedy about family dysfunction, sexual politics, incest and masturbation, topics which guarantee it a special place on the video shelf. Returning from his freshman year at M.I.T., Ray learns he must give up a prestigious internship to care for his bedridden mother (Watson) while Dad goes on an extended "business" trip. Much sexual and emotional confusion follows. Mom, it seems, is rather attractive, controlling, and in need of hands-on assistance. Black comedy is understated and sensitive, focusing attention on the story and characters rather than the delicate subject matter, but you'll be aware of the delicate subject matter, nonetheless. Sharp directorial debut by Russell features fine performances by mostly unknown cast, elevating low-budget feel. See it with a relative. **99m/C VHS, LV.** Jeremy Davies, Alberta Watson, Benjamin Hendrickson, Carla Gallo, Matthew Puckett; ***D:*** David O. Russell; ***W:*** David O. Russell. Independent Spirit Awards '95: Best First Feature; Sundance Film Festival '94: Audience Award; Nominations: Independent Spirit Awards '95: Best Supporting Actress (Gallo), Debut Performance (Davies). *NLC, IME*

Spare Parts *Woof!* **1985** Guests at a remote hotel discover that it is run by black marketeers who kill guests and sell the body parts. Of course, they don't bother signing out. **108m/C VHS, Beta.** Judith Speidel, Wolf Roth. *VMK*

Sparkle ☾☾½ **1976 (PG)** The saga of three singing sisters struggling to rise to the top of the charts in the 1950s. Sound familiar? Well done but cliched fictional version of the Supremes' career. McKee shines. Alcohol, drugs, and mobsters get in the way. Excellent musical score. **98m/C VHS, Beta.** Irene Cara, Lonette McKee, Dwan Smith, Philip Michael Thomas, Mary Alice, Dorian Harewood, Tony King; ***D:*** Sam O'Steen; ***W:*** Joel Schumacher; ***M:*** Curtis Mayfield. *WAR*

Sparrows ☾☾☾ **1926** A woman cares for nine orphan children on an impoverished farm, warding off starvation and kidnappers. Silent melodrama features notable performance by Pickford, and a musical score. **81m/B VHS, Beta, LV.** Mary Pickford, Roy Stewart, Gustav von Seyffertitz; ***D:*** William Beaudine; ***C:*** Charles Rosher; ***M:*** William Perry. *NOS, CCB, DVT*

Spartacus ☾☾☾☾ **1960 (PG-13)** The true story of a gladiator who leads other slaves in a rebellion against the power of Rome in 73 B.C. The rebellion is put down and the rebels are crucified. Douglas, whose political leanings are amply on display herein, also served as executive producer, surrounding himself with the best talent available. Magnificent climactic battle scene features 8,000 real, live Spanish soldiers to stunning effect. A version featuring Kubrick's "director's cut" is also available, featuring a restored, controversial homoerotic bath scene with Olivier and Curtis. Anthony Mann is uncredited as co-director. A box-office triumph that gave Kubrick much-desired financial independence. **196m/C VHS, Beta, LV.** Kirk Douglas, Laurence Olivier, Jean Simmons, Tony Curtis, Charles Laughton, Herbert Lom, Nina Foch, Woody Strode, Peter Ustinov, John Gavin, John Ireland, Charles McGraw, Joanna Barnes; ***D:*** Stanley Kubrick; ***W:*** Dalton Trumbo; ***C:*** Russell Metty; ***M:*** Alex North. Academy Awards '60: Best Art Direction/Set Decoration (Color), Best Color Cinematography, Best Costume Design (Color), Best Supporting Actor (Ustinov); Nominations: Academy Awards '60: Best Film Editing. *MCA, APD, BTV*

Spasms *Woof! Death Bite* **1982 (R)** Reed is the unfortunate big game hunter who encounters The Demon Serpent, known as N'Gana Simbu, the deadliest snake in the world. Lame-brained horror fantasy; the producers should have released the nifty Tangerine Dream soundtrack and chucked the movie. **92m/C VHS, Beta.** *CA* Peter Fonda, Oliver Reed; ***D:*** William Fruet. *NO*

The Spawning ☾ **1982 (R)** The sequel to "Piranha." At Club Elysium the main course is the vacationers themselves. **88m/C VHS, Beta, LV.** Steve Marachuk; ***D:*** James Cameron. *NO*

Speak Easily ☾☾½ **1932** Keaton is bored with his dull life as a college professor. Durante tries to spice things up with a phony inheritance letter, and Keaton decides to spend his supposed money backing a stage show. Keaton is the star, but Durante steals the show. Great supporting cast. **82m/B VHS.** Buster Keaton, Jimmy Durante, Ruth Selwyn, Thelma Todd, Hedda Hopper, Sidney Toler, Lawrence Grant, Henry Armetta, Edward Brophy; ***D:*** Edward Sedgwick. *MGM, GPV, NOS*

Speak of the Devil ☾ **1990** A New Orleans evangelist who seduces his followers moves to Los Angeles and strikes a bargain with Satan. Exploitative, unthinking spoof of Swaggart/Bakker scandals of recent years. **99m/C VHS.** Robert Elarton, Jean Miller, Bernice Tamara Goor, Louise Sherill, Walter Kay, Shawn Patrick Greenfield. *AIP*

Speaking Parts ☾☾☾ **1989** VCR-obsessed laundry worker and another woman battle for the attention of bit-part actor McManus who works in ritzy hotel. A telling picture of the inextricable nature of modern technology. **92m/C VHS, LV.** *CA* Michael McManus, Arsinee Khanjian, David Hemblen, Gabrielle Rose, Tony Nardi, Patricia Collins, Gerard Parkes; ***D:*** Atom Egoyan; ***W:*** Atom Egoyan; ***M:*** Mychael Danna. *FXL, FCT, INJ*

Special Bulletin ☾☾☾ **1983** A pacifistic terrorist threatens to blow up Charleston, South Carolina with a nuclear warhead. Done quite well in docu-drama style as a TV news bulletin. Interesting examination of the media's treatment of dramatic events. Top-notch made-for-TV fare. **105m/C VHS, Beta.** Ed Flanders, Christopher Allport, Kathryn Walker, Roxanne Hart; ***D:*** Edward Zwick; ***W:*** Marshall Herskovitz, Edward Zwick. *BAR, ORI, WAR*

A Special Day ☾☾☾ *Una Giornata Speciale; The Great Day* **1977** The day of a huge rally celebrating Hitler's visit to Rome in 1939 serves as the backdrop for an affair between weary housewife Loren and lonely, unhappy homosexual radio announcer Mastroianni. Good performances from two thorough pros make a depressing film well worth watching. In Italian with English subtitles or dubbed. **105m/C VHS, Beta, LV.** *IT* Sophia Loren, Marcello Mastroianni; ***D:*** Ettore Scola; ***W:*** Ettore Scola; ***C:*** Pasqualino de Santis. Golden Globe Awards '78: Best Foreign Film; National Board of Review Awards '77: 5 Best Foreign Films of the Year; Nominations: Academy Awards '77: Best Actor (Mastroianni), Best Foreign Language Film. *COL, APD, INJ*

Special Delivery ☾☾½ **1976 (PG)** Three unemployed Vietnam veterans decide to rob a bank but their getaway plans go awry. Svenson, the only robber who escapes, stashes the cash in a mailbox only to have it discovered by nutty artist, Shepherd, and crooked barkeep Gwynne. **99m/C VHS, Beta.** Bo Svenson, Cybill Shepherd, Vic Tayback, Michael C. Gwynne, Tom Atkins, Sorrell Booke, Deidre Hall, Gerrit Graham, Jeff Goldblum; ***D:*** Paul Wendkos; ***C:*** Harry Stradling Jr.; ***M:*** Lalo Schifrin. *LIV, VES*

Special Effects ☾☾ **1985 (R)** A desperate movie director murders a young actress, then makes a movie about her death. Solid, creepy premise sinks in the mire of flawed execution; a good film about Hollywood ego trips and obsession is lurking inside overdone script. **103m/C VHS, Beta.** Zoe Tamerlis, Eric Bogosian, Brad Rijn, Bill Oland, Richard Greene; ***D:*** Larry Cohen; ***W:*** Larry Cohen. *SUE, NLC*

Special Forces ☾ *Hell in Normandy* **1968** Eight specially trained soldiers drop behind enemy lines to rescue prisoners of war in WWII. **90m/C VHS, Beta.** Peter Lee Lawrence, Guy Madison, Erika Blanc, Tony Norton. *NO*

Special Investigator ☾☾½ **1936** Dix is a criminal attorney who specializes in getting his mob clients freed. Then his FBI brother gets killed by the same criminals he's been defending. So Dix becomes a special agent and sets out to get the mob boss responsible for his brother's murder. Climax is the big shootout at the gang's hideaway. Based on the novel by Earle Stanley Gardner. **60m/B VHS.** Richard Dix, J. Carrol Naish, Margaret Callahan, Erik Rhodes, Owen Davis Jr., Ray Mayer, Joseph Sawyer; ***D:*** Louis King. *GPV*

Special Olympics **1978** A father attempts to care for his three sons, one of whom is mentally retarded, following the death of his wife. Made for television. **104m/C VHS, Beta.** Charles Durning, Philip Brown, George Parry, Irene Tedrow, Mare Winningham, Herb Edelman, Debra Winger, Constance McCashin; ***D:*** Lee Philips. *GEM*

Special Police 🦴🦴½ **1985** Police inspector protecting old friend's murder-witnessing sister learns that important politicians are involved with a seedy underground political movement. French thriller also available dubbed. **92m/C VHS.** *FR* Richard Berry, Carole Bouquet, Fanny Cottencon; ***D:*** Michael Vianey; ***W:*** Michael Vianey. *FRA, FCT.*

The Specialist 🦴½ **1975 (R)** Lawyer West thinks he has seduced stunning Capri, but she has lured him into her clutches—she's been hired to kill him. Campy crud. It's old home week for '60s TV alums: West was Batman; bailiff Moore was Mr. Kimbell on Green Acres. **93m/C VHS, Beta.** Adam West, John Anderson, Ahna Capri, Alvy Moore; ***D:*** Howard (Hikmet) Avedis. *NO*

The Specialist 🦴½ **1994 (R)** Buffed bods do not a movie make—at least not in this mechanical actioner featuring Stone as the revenge-minded May Munro. Seems May's parents were killed by Cuban gangsters, led by father/son thugs Joe (Steiger) and Tomas Leon (Roberts), and she decides ex-CIA bomb specialist Ray Quick (Stallone) is just the man she needs to settle the score. But Quick has his own reasons for accepting—his ex-partner is nutball Ned Trent (Woods), who's now working for the Leons. Things blow up a lot, the two leads show off their toned flesh (but not much acting), and Woods gets to steal the movie with his amusing scenery chewing. **110m/C VHS, LV.** Sylvester Stallone, Sharon Stone, James Woods, Eric Roberts, Rod Steiger; ***D:*** Luis Llosa; ***W:*** Alexandra Seros; ***M:*** John Barry. Golden Raspberry Awards '94: Worst Actress (Stone); Nominations: MTV Movie Awards '95: Most Desirable Female (Stone); Golden Raspberry Awards '94: Worst Picture. *WAR*

Species 🦴🦴½ **1995 (R)** A "friendly" galactic message containing a recipe on how to combine extraterrestrial DNA with human DNA is sent to scientists on Earth. The scientists, led by Fitch (Kingsley), whip up a batch of genetic material resulting in a sexy half alien, half human procreating/killing machine named Sil (model Henstridge's film debut). Naturally, Sil escapes from the lab, leaving the scientists with the unenviable task of catching her/it. All-star special effects team, including "Alien" designer H. R. Giger, create over-the-top, stomach-churning thrills. Dips liberally into the tricks of many sci-fi classics. For avid gore-meisters only. **108m/C VHS, LV.** Ben Kingsley, Michael Madsen, Alfred Molina, Forest Whitaker, Marg Helgenberger, Natasha Henstridge; ***D:*** Roger Donaldson; ***W:*** Dennis Feldman; ***C:*** Andrzej Bartkowiak; ***M:*** Christopher Young. MTV Movie Awards '96: Best Kiss (Natasha Henstridge/Anthony Guidera); Nominations: MTV Movie Awards '96: Breakthrough Performance (Henstridge). *MGM*

The Speckled Band 🦴🦴🦴 **1931** Set in 1930, this early talkie is a Sherlock Holmes adventure wherein the great detective must solve the mysterious death of a young woman. Massey makes his screen debut as Holmes, making the sleuth cynical, unhappy and pessimistic. Interesting prototypical Holmes case, faithful to the like-titled Conan Doyle story. **84m/B VHS, Beta, 8mm.** Raymond Massey, Lyn Harding, Athole Stewart, Angela Baddeley, Nancy Price; ***D:*** Jack Raymond; ***C:*** Frederick A. (Freddie) Young. *SNC, NOS, VYY*

Specters 🦴 *Spettri* **1987** Archaeologists excavating the Roman catacombs break open the gates of hell. Hellishly confused plot is unoriginal, to boot; decent production values hardly compensate. **95m/C VHS, Beta.** Donald Pleasence, John Pepper, Erna Schurer; ***D:*** Marcello Avallone. *IMP*

The Spectre of Edgar Allen Poe 🦴½ **1973** The horridly fictionalized writer of horror fiction visits the asylum where his love Lenore is being held, and discovers murder and torture. Based very loosely on Poe's own torments. Dorky, rip-off horror. **87m/C VHS, Beta.** Cesar Romero, Robert Walker Jr., Tom Drake; ***D:*** Mohy Quandour. *UNI*

Spectre of the Rose 🦴🦴½ **1946** Strange film set in the world of ballet. An impressario contends with an over-the-hill ballerina and a young male dancer with a deadly affinity for knives. **90m/B VHS, LV.** Judith Anderson, Michael Chekhov, Ivan Kirov, Viola Essen, Lionel Stander; ***D:*** Ben Hecht; ***W:*** Ben Hecht. *REP*

Speechless 🦴🦴½ **1994 (PG-13)** Cute romantic comedy about sparring speechwriters who fall in love, and then briefly turn enemies when they discover they're working at professional odds. Davis is the idealistic liberal working for senatorial candidate Wannamaker, while Keaton is a TV sitcom writer doing a one-shot deal for a millionaire businessman, Republican Garvin. Both stars do a likable job; the supporting cast fares better with Reeve as an egotistical TV reporter, as well as Davis's fiance, and Bedelia as Keaton's ex-wife/campaign press secretary. Although the film parallels the real-life romance of rival Bush-Clinton spin doctors Mary Matalin and James Carville, it was written prior to the last presidential race. **99m/C VHS, LV.** Michael Keaton, Geena Davis, Christopher Reeve, Bonnie Bedelia, Ernie Hudson, Charles Martin Smith, Gailard Sartain, Ray Baker, Mitchell Ryan; ***D:*** Ron Underwood; ***W:*** Robert King; ***M:*** Marc Shaiman. Nominations: Golden Globe Awards '95: Best Actress—Musical/Comedy (Davis). *MGM*

Speed 🦴🦴🦴½ **1994 (R)** Excellent dude Reeves has grown up (and bulked up) as Los Angeles SWAT cop Jack Traven, up against bomb expert Howard Payne (Hopper, more maniacal than usual), who's after major ransom money. First it's a rigged elevator in a very tall building. Then it's a rigged bus—if it slows, it will blow, bad enough any day, but a nightmare in LA traffic. And that's still not the end. Terrific directorial debut for cinematographer De Bont, who certainly knows how to keep the adrenaline pumping. Fine support work by Daniels, Bullock, and Morton and enough wit in Yost's script to keep you chuckling. Great nonstop actioner from the "Die Hard" school. **115m/C VHS, LV.** Keanu Reeves, Dennis Hopper, Sandra Bullock, Joe Morton, Jeff Daniels, Alan Ruck, Glenn Plummer, Richard Lineback, Beth Grant, Hawthorne James, David Kriegel, Carlos Carrasco, Natsuko Ohama, Daniel Villarreal; ***D:*** Jan De Bont; ***W:*** Graham Yost; ***M:*** Mark Mancina. Academy Awards '94: Best Sound; MTV Movie Awards '95: Best Female Performance (Bullock), Most Desirable Female (Bullock), Best On-Screen Duo (Keanu Reeves/Sandra Bullock), Best Villain (Hopper), Best Action Sequence; Blockbuster Entertainment Awards '95: Movie, Video, Action Actress, Video (Bullock), Action Actress, Theatrical (Bullock); Nominations: Academy Awards '94: Best Film Editing; MTV Movie Awards '95: Best Film, Best Male Performance (Reeves), Most Desirable Male (Reeves), Best Kiss (Keanu Reeves/Sandra Bullock). *FXV*

The Speed Lovers 🦴 **1968** Stock car driver Lorenzen plays himself as an inspiration to a young man to join the auto racing circuit. More of a pat on the industry's back than a serious drama. Features footage from a number of race tracks around the country although shot principally in Atlanta. ♫Speed Lovers. **102m/C VHS.** Fred Lorenzen, William F. McGaha, Peggy O'Hara, David Marcus, Carol Street, Glenda Brunson; ***D:*** William F. McGaha; ***W:*** William F. McGaha, Elaine Wilkerson, Fred Tuch. *SMW, TPV*

Speed Reporter 🦴 **1936** Talmadge is the intrepid reporter investigating a phony reform movement that's really a front for a gang of criminals. Mediocre drama with Talmadge's thick German accent a hindrance. **56m/B VHS.** Richard Talmadge, Luana Walters, Richard Cramer; ***D:*** Bernard B. Ray. *GPV*

The Speed Spook 🦴 **1924** Silent ghost races car and steals documents. **85m/B VHS, Beta.** Johnny Hines, Warner Richmond; ***D:*** Charles Hines. *GPV*

Speed Zone 🦴 **1988 (PG)** Comic celebrities take over a high speed auto race when a redneck cop locks up the real drivers. Unfunny sequel to "Cannonball Run." **96m/C VHS, Beta, LV.** Melody Anderson, Peter Boyle, Tim Matheson, Donna Dixon, John Candy, Eugene Levy, Joe Flaherty, Matt Frewer, Shari Belafonte, Tom Smothers, Dick Smothers, Brooke Shields, Lee Van Cleef, Jamie Farr, John Schneider, Michael Spinks; ***D:*** Jim Drake. Golden Raspberry Awards '89: Worst Supporting Actress (Shields). *MED, VTR*

Speeding Up Time 🦴 **1971 (R)** An angry man wants to ice the dudes who torched his mother's tenement. **90m/C VHS, Beta.** Winston Thrash, Pamela Donegan. *NO*

Speedtrap 🦴🦴 **1978 (PG)** Typical chase scenes and cross-gender sparring characterize this tale of a private detective and a police officer pursuing car thieves. Good cast and fun chemistry between the leads; weak, typical script. **101m/C VHS, Beta.** Joe Don Baker, Tyne Daly, Richard Jaeckel, Robert Loggia, Morgan Woodward, Timothy Carey; ***D:*** Earl Bellamy. *MED*

Speedway 🦴🦴 **1968 (G)** Elvis the stock car driver finds himself being chased by Nancy the IRS agent during an important race. Will Sinatra keep to the business at hand? Or will the King melt her heart? Some cameos by real-life auto racers. Watch for a young Garr. Movie number 27 for Elvis. ♫Speedway; He's Your Uncle, Not Your Dad; There Ain't Nothing Like a Song. **90m/C VHS, Beta.** Elvis Presley, Nancy Sinatra, Bill Bixby, Gale Gordon, William Schallert, Carl Ballantine, Ross Hagen; ***Cameos:*** Richard Petty, Cale Yarborough, Teri Garr; ***D:*** Norman Taurog; ***C:*** Joseph Ruttenberg. *MGM*

Speedy 🦴🦴🦴 **1928** Lloyd comes to the rescue when the last horse car in New York City, operated by his fiance's grandfather, is stolen by a gang. Thoroughly phoney, fun pursuit/action comedy shot on location. Look for a brief appearance by Babe Ruth. **72m/B VHS, Beta.** Harold Lloyd, Bert Woodruff, Ann Christy; ***D:*** Ted Wilde. Nominations: Academy Awards '28: Best Director (Wilde). *TLF*

The Spell 🦴🦴 **1977** An obese fifteen-year-old girl has the power to inflict illness and death on the people she hates. Necessarily mean-spirited, if we're being asked to sympathize with the main character. Therein lies the rub. Made for TV. **86m/C VHS, Beta.** Lee Grant, James Olson, Susan Myers, Barbara Bostock, Lelia Goldoni, Helen Hunt; ***D:*** Lee Philips. *GKK, WOV*

The Spellbinder 🦴½ **1988 (R)** L.A. lawyer Daly falls in love with a woman he saves from an attacker, then discovers she's a fugitive from a satanic cult that wants her back. Unoriginal, but slickly made. **96m/C VHS, Beta.** Timothy Daly, Kelly Preston, Rick Rossovich, Audra Lindley; ***D:*** Janet Greek; ***W:*** Tracy Torme; ***M:*** Basil Poledouris. *FOX*

Spellbound 🦴🦴 *The Spell of Amy Nugent* **1941** Broken-hearted over dead girlfriend, young college student attempts to contact her through spiritualism, succeeds, and suffers nervous breakdown. **75m/B VHS.** *GB* Derek Farr, Vera Lindsay, Frederick Leister, Hay Petrie, Felix Aylmer; ***D:*** John Harlow. *SNC*

Spellbound 🦴🦴🦴½ **1945** Peck plays an amnesia victim accused of murder. Bergman plays the psychiatrist who uncovers his past through Freudian analysis and ends up falling in love with him. One of Hitchcock's finest films of the 1940s, with a riveting dream sequence designed by Salvador Dali. Full of classic Hitchcock plot twists and Freudian imagery. Based on Francis Beeding's novel "The House of Dr. Edwardes." **111m/B VHS, Beta, LV.** Ingrid Bergman, Gregory Peck, Leo G. Carroll, Michael Chekhov, Wallace Ford, Rhonda Fleming, Regis Toomey; ***D:*** Alfred Hitchcock; ***C:*** George Barnes; ***M:*** Miklos Rozsa. Academy Awards '45: Best Score; New York Film Critics Awards '45: Best Actress (Bergman); Nominations: Academy Awards '45: Best Actor (Chekhov), Best Black and White Cinematography, Best Director (Hitchcock), Best Picture. *FOX, IME, TLF*

Spellcaster 🦴 **1991 (R)** An evil wizard invites a DJ and a band of rock 'n roll fanatics to his thousand-year-old Italian castle for an evil and bloodcurdling treasure hunt. **83m/C VHS, LV.** Richard Blade, Gail O'Grady, Harold Pruett, Bunty Bailey, Rafal Zeilinski, Adam Ant; ***D:*** Rafal Zeilinski. *COL*

Spencer's Mountain 🦴🦴½ **1963** Fonda plays the larger-then-life patriarch of 9 (with O'Hara as his wife), who's inherited the Wyoming mountain land claimed by his father. Fonda's dream is to build a new house large enough to contain his brood but something always gets in his way. This time it's eldest son MacArthur's dream of a college education.

Sentimental family fare based on a novel by Earl Hamner, Jr., which also became the basis for the television series "The Waltons." **118m/C VHS.** Henry Fonda, Maureen O'Hara, James MacArthur, Donald Crisp, Wally Cox, Mimsy Farmer, Virginia Gregg, Lillian Bronson, Whit Bissell, Hayden Rorke, Dub Taylor, Victor French, Veronica Cartwright; ***D:*** Delmer Daves; ***W:*** Delmer Daves; ***M:*** Max Steiner. *WAR*

Spenser: Ceremony ♂♂½ **1993** Urich resumes his role as Robert B. Parker's Boston PI, which he played in the TV series "Spenser: For Hire." This time around Spenser is searching for a troubled runaway who's gotten involved in prostitution. But her suburban dad, who has political aspirations, seems reluctant to have her found. Brooks returns as Spenser's menacing associate Hawk. Toronto stands-in for Boston. Made for cable TV; based on Parker's novel "Ceremony." **?m/C VHS.** Robert Urich, Avery Brooks, Barbara Williams, Tanya Allen, David Nichols, Lynne Cormack; ***D:*** Paul Lynch; ***W:*** Joan H. Parker, Robert B. Parker. *PAR*

Spenser: Pale Kings & Princes ♂♂½ **1994** Spenser's (Urich) new case involves the murder of a reporter who was investigating a drug-ridden small New England town. But was the journalist killed for what he found out about a Colombian cocaine connection or did his womanizing have deadly consequences? Adapted from Robert B. Parker's novel; made for cable TV. **?m/C VHS.** Robert Urich, Avery Brooks, Barbara Williams. *PAR*

Spetters ♂♂½ **1980 (R)** Four Dutch teenagers follow the motorcycle racing circuit and motocross champ Hauer. Misdirected youth film with a spicy performance from Soutendijk. Plenty of violence, sex, and gripping photography. Verhoeven went on to direct "Robocop" and "Total Recall." **108m/C VHS, Beta, LV.** *NL* Rutger Hauer, Renee Soutendijk; ***D:*** Paul Verhoeven; ***C:*** Jan De Bont. *SUE*

The Sphinx **1933** Features Lionell Atwell in a duel role as a murderer and his deaf-mute twin. **63m/C VHS.** Lionel Atwill, Sheila Terry, Theodore Newton, Paul Hurst; ***D:*** Phil Rosen. *GPV*

The Sphinx ♂♂½ **1933** A murderer causes havoc for his deaf-mute twin (Atwill, good in a dual role) when he frames him for his own crimes. Remade as "The Phantom Killer." **63m/B VHS.** Lionel Atwill, Theodore Newton, Sheila Terry, Paul Hurst, Luis Alberni, George "Gabby" Hayes; ***D:*** Phil Rosen. *SNC, VYY*

Sphinx *Woof!* **1981 (PG)** Woman archaeologist searches for hidden riches in the tomb of an Egyptian king. The scenery is impressive, but otherwise, don't bother. Based on the novel by Robin Cook. **117m/C VHS, Beta.** Lesley-Anne Down, Frank Langella, John Gielgud, Maurice Ronet, John Rhys-Davies; ***D:*** Franklin J. Schaffner; ***W:*** John Byrum. *WAR*

Spices ♂♂♂ **1986** Poor woman Sonbai revolts against the sexist mores of rural colonial India in the 1940s. Features actress Patil in her final role. In Hindi with English subtitles. **98m/C VHS.** *IN* Smita Patil; ***D:*** Ketan Mehta. *MFV, FCT, INJ*

The Spider and the Fly ♂♂½ **1994 (PG-13)** Mystery writer Dianna Taylor (Harris) and her friends like to play a murder mystery charade known as "The Game." Their latest unsuspecting patsy is crime writer Michael Moore (Shackelford)—who falls for Dianna bigtime. Then their publisher is killed—in the same sort of murder scenario one of them devised. Made for cable television. **87m/C VHS, Beta.** Mel Harris, Ted Shackleford, Kim Coates, Colm Feore, Frankie Faison, Cynthia Belliveau, Kenneth Welsh, Peggy Lipton; ***D:*** Michael Katleman; ***W:*** Robert Pucci, Alanna Hamill; ***M:*** Richard Bellis. *PAR*

Spider Baby ♂ *The Liver Eaters; Spider Baby, or the Maddest Story Ever Told; Cannibal Orgy, or the Maddest Story Ever Told* **1964** A tasteless horror-comedy about a chauffeur who takes care of a psychotic family. Theme song sung by Lon Chaney. **86m/B VHS, Beta.** Lon Chaney Jr., Mantan Moreland, Carol Ohmart, Sid Haig; ***D:*** Jack Hill. *SNC, AOV, MLB*

Spider Woman ♂♂♂ *Sherlock Holmes and the Spider Woman* **1944** A modernized Holmes and Watson adventure as the duo track down a woman responsible for a series of murders. His adversary uses poisonous spiders to do her work. Zestful, superior Holmes. **62m/B VHS, Beta.** Basil Rathbone, Nigel Bruce, Gale Sondergaard, Dennis Hoey; ***D:*** Roy William Neill. *FOX*

Spiderman: The Deadly Dust **1978** A live-action episode of Spiderman, from the TV seies, as he attempts to prevent a city-destroying plutonium accident. **93m/C VHS, Beta.** Nicholas Hammond, Robert F. Simon, Chip Fields; ***D:*** Ron Satlof. *FOX*

Spiders ♂♂♂ **1918** One of the earliest surviving films by director Lang, and predates Indiana Jones by almost 60 years. In these first two chapters ("The Golden Lake" and "The Diamond Ship") of an unfinished 4-part thriller, Carl deVogt battles with the evil Spider cult for a mystically powerful Incan diamond. Restored version has original color-tinted scenes. Silent with organ score. **137m/B VHS, Beta, LV.** *GE* Lil Dagover; ***D:*** Fritz Lang; ***M:*** Gaylord Carter. *KIV, IME, GLV*

The Spider's Stratagem ♂♂♂ **1970** Thirty years after his father's murder by the facists, a young man returns to a small Italian town to learn why his father was killed. The locals resist his efforts, and he is trapped in a mysterious web where history and lies exert a stranglehold on the truth. Intriguing, high literate thriller; outrageously lovely color photography. Based on a short story by Jorge Luis Borges. In Italian with English subtitles. **97m/C VHS.** *IT* Giulio Brogi, Alida Valli; ***D:*** Bernardo Bertolucci; ***W:*** Bernardo Bertolucci. *NYF, FCT, APD*

Spies ♂♂♂½ *Spione* **1928** A sly criminal poses as a famous banker to steal government information and create chaos in the world in this silent Lang masterpiece. Excellent entertainment, tight plotting and pacing, fine performances. Absolutely relentless intrigue and tension. **88m/B VHS, Beta, LV.** *GE* Rudolf Klein-Rogge, Lupu Pick, Fritz Rasp, Gerda Maurus, Willy Fritsch; ***D:*** Fritz Lang. *GPV, NOS, VYY*

Spies, Lies and Naked Thighs ♂½ **1991** A pair of crackpot CIA agents find themselves in a whirlpool of comedic madness when they are assigned to track down a deadly assassin. The problem? The assassin happens to be the ex-wife of one of the guys. Can he go another round with her and this time come out on top? Who cares? **90m/C VHS, LV.** Harry Anderson, Ed Begley Jr., Rachel Ticotin, Linda Purl, Wendy Crewson; ***D:*** James Frawley. *NLC*

Spies Like Us ♂♂½ **1985 (PG)** Chase and Aykroyd meet while taking the CIA entry exam. Caught cheating on the test, they seem the perfect pair for a special mission. Pursued by the Soviet government, they nearly start WWIII. Silly, fun homage to the Bing Crosby-Bob Hope "Road" movies that doesn't capture those classics' quota of guffaws, but comes moderately close. Look for several cameos by film directors. **103m/C VHS, Beta, LV.** Chevy Chase, Dan Aykroyd, Steve Forrest, Bruce Davison, William Prince, Bernie Casey, Tom Hatton, Donna Dixon, Frank Oz; ***Cameos:*** Michael Apted, Constantin Costa-Gavras, Terry Gilliam, Ray Harryhausen, Joel Coen, Martin Brest, Bob Swaim; ***D:*** John Landis; ***W:*** Dan Aykroyd, Lowell Ganz, Babaloo Mandel; ***M:*** Elmer Bernstein. *WAR*

Spike of Bensonhurst ♂♂½ **1988 (R)** A Brooklyn street kid dreams of becoming a championship boxer. He tries to gain the mob's help by courting the local Don's daughter. Hip-but-stereotyped Morrissey effort is helped by great cast. **101m/C VHS, Beta, LV.** Sasha Mitchell, Ernest Borgnine, Maria Pitillo, Talisa Soto, Sylvia Miles, Anne DeSalvo, Geraldine Smith, Rick Aviles, Antonia Rey; ***D:*** Paul Morrissey; ***W:*** Alan Bowne, Paul Morrissey; ***M:*** Coati Mundi. *NO*

Spinout ♂♂ *California Holiday* **1966** A pouty traveling singer decides to drive an experimental race car in a rally. Usual Elvis fare with the King being pursued by an assortment of beauties. ♫Adam and Eve; Stop, Look, Listen; All That I Am; Am I Ready; Smorgasbord; Never Say Yes; Beach Shack; I'll Be Back; Spinout. **93m/C VHS, Beta.** Elvis Presley, Shelley Fabares, Carl Betz, Diane McBain, Cecil Kellaway, Jack Mullaney, Deborah Walley, Una Merkel, Warren Berlinger, Will Hutchins, Dodie Marshall; ***D:*** Norman Taurog. *MGM*

The Spiral Staircase ♂♂♂ **1946** A mute servant, working in a creepy Gothic mansion, may be the next victim of a murderer preying on women afflicted with deformities, especially when the next murder occurs in the mansion itself. Great performance by McGuire as the terrified victim. Remade for television in 1975. **83m/B VHS, LV.** Dorothy McGuire, George Brent, Ethel Barrymore, Kent Smith, Rhonda Fleming, Gordon Oliver, Elsa Lanchester, Sara Allgood; ***D:*** Robert Siodmak. Nominations: Academy Awards '46: Best Supporting Actress (Barrymore). *FOX*

Spiral Staircase ♂½ **1975** Mild TV remake of the 1946 classic about a mute servant who is menaced by a psychopathic killer. Why didn't they just show the original? **99m/C VHS, Beta.** *GB* Jacqueline Bisset, Christopher Plummer, John Phillip Law, Mildred Dunnock, Sam Wanamaker, Gayle Hunnicutt; ***D:*** Peter Collinson; ***W:*** Allan Scott, Chris Bryant. *WAR*

Spirit of St. Louis ♂♂♂ **1957** A lavish Hollywood biography of famous aviator Charles Lindbergh and his historic transatlantic flight from New York to Paris in 1927, based on his autobiography. Intelligent; Stewart shines as the intrepid airman. Inexplicably, it flopped at the box office. **137m/C VHS, Beta.** James Stewart, Patricia Smith, Murray Hamilton, Marc Connelly; ***D:*** Billy Wilder; ***W:*** Billy Wilder, Wendell Mayes; ***M:*** Franz Waxman. National Board of Review Awards '57: 10 Best Films of the Year. *WAR, HMV*

Spirit of '76 ♂½ **1991 (PG-13)** In the 22nd century, the Earth faces certain disaster as a magnetic storm wipes out all of American culture. Now time travellers must return to 1776 to reacquire the Constitution to fix things up. But when their computer goes on the blink, the do-gooders land, not in 1776, but in 1976 at the beginning of disco fever! **82m/C VHS, LV.** David Cassidy, Olivia D'Abo, Leif Garrett, Geoff Hoyle, Jeff McDonald, Steve McDonald, Liam O'Brien, Barbara Bain, Julie Brown, Thomas Chong, Iron Eyes Cody, Don Novello, Carl Reiner, Rob Reiner, Moon Zappa; ***D:*** Lucas Reiner; ***W:*** Lucas Reiner. *NO*

Spirit of the Beehive ♂♂♂ *El Espiritu de la Colmena* **1973** An acclaimed and haunting film about a young Spanish girl enthralled by the 1931 "Frankenstein," embarking on a journey to find the creature in the Spanish countryside. One of the best films about children's inner life; in Spanish with subtitles. **95m/C VHS, Beta, LV.** *SP* Fernando Gomez, Teresa Gimpera, Ana Torrent; ***D:*** Victor Erice. *HMV, INJ, CVC*

Spirit of the Eagle ♂♂ **1990 (PG)** Man and young son wander in mountains and make friends with feathered creature. Then boy is kidnapped, creating problems for dad. Somnolent family fare. **93m/C VHS, LV.** Dan Haggerty, Bill Smith, Don Shanks, Jeri Arrendondo, Trever Yarrish; ***D:*** Boon Collins; ***W:*** Boon Collins. *SGE, IME*

Spirit of the West ♂½ **1932** Rodeo star Gibson and his ranch foreman brother work together to save a fair damsel's land from a gang of rustlers. Routine western of its era. **61m/B VHS, Beta.** Hoot Gibson, Hooper Atchley; ***D:*** Otto Brower. *NOS, DVT, VCI*

The Spirit of West Point ♂½ **1947** The true story of West Point's two All-American football greats, Doc Blanchard and Glenn Davis (who play themselves), while on leave after graduation from the title school. **77m/B VHS, Beta, LV.** Felix "Doc" Blanchard, Glenn Davis, Tom Harmon, Alan Hale Jr., Anne Nagel, Robert Shayne; ***D:*** Ralph Murphy. *NWV*

The Spirit of Youth ♂♂ **1937** Joe Louis supports his family with menial jobs until he shows his knack as a fighter. When he's knocked down, his gal appears at ringside to inspire him, and does. **70m/B VHS, Beta.** Joe Louis, Mantan Moreland. *VYY, NOS, VCN*

Spirit Rider ♂♂♂ **1993** Jesse Threebears is a sullen 16-year-old Ojibway who has been shuttled from foster homes since the age of six. Repatriated to his family's Canadian reservation, he's left in the care of his grandfather, Joe Moon. The entire community works to make Jesse's return successful but there are Jesse's resentments and some family tragedies to be overcome first. Based on the novel "Winners" by Mary-Ellen Lang Collura. **120m/C VHS.** *CA* Herbie Barnes, Adam Beach, Graham Greene, Tantoo Cardinal, Gordon Tootoosis, Tom Jackson, Michelle St. John. *PME, BTV*

Spiritism 🦴🦴 *Espiritismo* **1961** Mother uses one of her three wishes to bring back her dead son. Adapted from the "Monkey's Paw." **85m/B VHS.** *MX* Nora Veyran, Jose Luis Jimenez, Jorge Mondragon, Rene Cardona Jr.; ***D:*** Benito Alazraki. *SNC*

Spirits 🦴½ **1990 (R)** A priest tormented by his lust-filled dreams breaks his vows of chastity with a woman who turns out to be a murderer. Bad luck. **88m/C VHS.** Erik Estrada, Carol Lynley, Robert Quarry, Brinke Stevens, Oliver Darrow, Kathrin Lautner; ***D:*** Fred Olen Ray. *VMK*

Spirits of the Dead 🦴🦴🦴 *Histoires Extraordinaires* **1968 (R)** Three Edgar Allan Poe stories adapted for the screen and directed by three of Europe's finest. "Metzengerstein," directed by Roger Vadim stars the Fonda siblings in a tale of incestuous lust. "William Wilson" finds Louis Malle directing Delon and Bardot in the story of a vicious Austrian army officer haunted by a murder victim. Finally, Fellini directs "Never Bet the Devil Your Head" or "Toby Dammit" in which Stamp plays a drunken British film star who has a gruesome date with destiny. Although Fellini's segment is generally considered the best (and was released on its own) all three provide an interesting, atmospheric vision of Poe. **117m/C VHS.** *IT FR* Jane Fonda, Peter Fonda, Carla Marlier, Francoise Prevost, James Robertson Justice, Brigitte Bardot, Alain Delon, Katia Christine, Terence Stamp, Salvo Randone; ***D:*** Roger Vadim, Louis Malle, Federico Fellini; ***M:*** Nino Rota. *WBF, MLB, FRG*

Spite Marriage 🦴🦴🦴 **1929** When Sebastian's lover dumps her like yesterday's garbage, she marries Keaton out of spite. Much postnuptual levity follows. Keaton's final silent. **82m/B VHS, Beta, LV.** Buster Keaton, Dorothy Sebastian, Edward Earle, Leila Hyams, William Bechtel, Hank Mann; ***D:*** Edward Sedgwick. *MGM, FCT*

Spitfire 🦴🦴🦴 **1934** Sentimental comedy drama starring Hepburn as a hillbilly faith healer from the Ozarks who falls into a love triangle. One in a string of early box-office flops for Hepburn. She wanted to play a role other than patrician Eastern Seaboard, and did, but audiences didn't buy it. **90m/B VHS, Beta, 8mm.** Katharine Hepburn, Robert Young, Ralph Bellamy, Sidney Toler; ***D:*** John Cromwell; ***M:*** Max Steiner. *NO*

Spitfire 🦴🦴🦴 *The First of the Few* **1942** True story of Reginald J. Mitchell, who designed "The Spitfire" fighter plane, which greatly assisted the Allies during WWII. Howard's last film. Heavily propagandist but enjoyable and uncomplicated biography, with a splendid score. **88m/B VHS, Beta.** *GB* Leslie Howard, David Niven, Rosamund John, Roland Culver, David Horne, J.H. Roberts, Patricia Medina; ***D:*** Leslie Howard; ***C:*** Georges Perinal; ***M:*** William Walton. *CNG, NOS, HHT*

Spitfire 🦴½ **1994 (R)** Drug cartel has kidnapped the secret agent father of a feisty gymnast, who sets out to rescue him aided by her half brothers and sisters who also happen to be spies. **95m/C VHS.** Lance Henriksen, Tim Thomerson, Sarah Douglas; ***D:*** Albert Pyun. *VMK*

The Spitfire Grill 🦴🦴½ *Care of the Spitfire Grill* **1995 (PG-13)** Newly released from prison, Perry Talbott (Elliott) moves to smalltown Gilead, Maine and gets a waitressing job at the Spitfire Grill, run by the cranky Hannah (Burstyn). Perry's upfront about her jail time, which doesn't endear her to the suspicious locals. Particularly censorious is businessman Nahum Goddard (Patton), who sends his downtrodden wife Shelby (Harden) to keep an eye on Perry. There are a number of personal dilemmas that take their toll in this familiar setting—redeemed by strong performances. **117m/C VHS.** Alison Elliott, Ellen Burstyn, Marcia Gay Harden, Will Patton, Kieran Mulroney, Gailard Sartain, Louise De Cormier; ***D:*** Lee David Zlotoff; ***W:*** Lee David Zlotoff; ***C:*** Rob Draper. Sundance Film Festival '96: Audience Award. *NYR*

Spittin' Image 🦴 **1983** After falling from her mean-spirited father's wagon, a young girl befriends a kind mountain man. She learns the ways of the wilderness and tobacco spitting. **92m/C VHS, Beta.** Sunshine Parker, Trudi Cooper, Sharon Barr, Karen Barr; ***D:*** Russell Kern. *PSM*

Splash 🦴🦴½ **1984 (PG)** A beautiful mermaid ventures into New York City in search of a man she's rescued twice when he's fallen overboard. Now it's her turn to fall—in love. Charming performances by Hanks and Hannah. Well-paced direction from Howard, with just enough slapstick. Don't miss the lobster scene. **109m/C VHS, Beta, LV, 8mm.** Tom Hanks, Daryl Hannah, Eugene Levy, John Candy, Dody Goodman, Shecky Greene, Richard B. Shull, Bobby DiCicco, Howard Morris; ***D:*** Ron Howard; ***W:*** Babaloo Mandel, Lowell Ganz. National Society of Film Critics Awards '84: Best Screenplay; Nominations: Academy Awards '84: Best Original Screenplay. *TOU*

Splatter University *Woof!* **1984** A deranged killer escapes from an asylum and begins to slaughter and mutilate comely coeds at a local college. Abysmally motiveless killing and gratuitous sex. Also available in a 78-minute "R" rated version. **79m/C VHS, Beta.** Francine Forbes, Dick Biel, Cathy Lacommaro, Ric Randing, Dan Eaton; ***D:*** Richard W. Haines; ***M:*** Chris Burke. *LIV, VES*

Splendor in the Grass 🦴🦴🦴 **1961** A drama set in rural Kansas in 1925, concerning a teenage couple who try to keep their love on a strictly intellectual plane and the sexual and family pressures that tear them apart. After suffering a mental breakdown and being institutionalized, the girl returns years later in order to settle her life. Film debuts of Beatty, Dennis, and Diller. Inge wrote the screenplay specifically with Beatty in mind, after the actor appeared in one of Inge's stage plays. Filmed not in Kansas, but on Staten Island and in upstate New York. **124m/C VHS, Beta, LV.** Natalie Wood, Warren Beatty, Audrey Christie, Barbara Loden, Zohra Lampert, Phyllis Diller, Sandy Dennis; ***D:*** Elia Kazan; ***W:*** William Inge; ***C:*** Charles Durnham; ***M:*** David Amram. Academy Awards '61: Best Story & Screenplay; Nominations: Academy Awards '61: Best Actress (Wood). *WAR*

Split 🦴 **1990** Humanoids from another dimension manipulate earth activity. **85m/C VHS.** John Flynn, Timothy Dwight, Chris Shaw, Joan Bechtel; ***D:*** Chris Shaw. *AIP*

Split Decisions 🦴🦴 **1988 (R)** An Irish family of boxers, dad and his two sons, slug it out emotionally and physically, as they come to terms with career choices and each other. Good scenes in the ring but the drama leans toward melodrama. Decent family drama, but somewhat of a "Rocky" rip-off. **95m/C VHS, LV, 8mm.** Gene Hackman, Craig Sheffer, Jeff Fahey, Jennifer Beals, John McLiam, Eddie Velez, Carmine Caridi, James Tolkan; ***D:*** David Drury; ***W:*** David Fallon; ***M:*** Basil Poledouris. *WAR*

Split Image 🦴🦴🦴 **1982 (R)** An all-American boy comes under the spell of a cult. His parents then hire a deprogrammer to bring the boy back to reality. Exceptional performances by Dennehy and Woods. This is a worthwhile film that spent far too little time in theatres. **113m/C VHS, Beta.** Michael O'Keefe, Karen Allen, Peter Fonda, Brian Dennehy, James Woods; ***D:*** Ted Kotcheff; ***W:*** Robert Mark Kamen; ***M:*** Bill Conti. *SUE*

Split Second 🦴🦴½ **1953** An escaped prisoner holds hostages in a Nevada atomic bomb testing area. McNally's excellent performance as the kidnapper, in addition to strong supporting performances, enhance a solid plot. Powell's directorial debut. **85m/B VHS, Beta.** Paul Kelly, Richard Egan, Jan Sterling, Alexis Smith, Stephen McNally; ***D:*** Dick Powell; ***W:*** William Bowers, Irving Wallace. *TTC*

Split Second 🦴½ **1992 (R)** Hauer is a futuristic cop tracking down a vicious alien serial killer in London in the year 2008. The monster rips out the hearts of his victims and then eats them in what appears to be a satanic ritual in this blood-soaked thriller wanna-be. Hauer gives a listless performance and overall, the action is quite dull. The music soundtrack also manages to annoy with the Moody Blues song "Nights in White Satin" playing at the most inappropriate times. A British/American co-production. **91m/C VHS.** *GB* Rutger Hauer, Kim Cattrall, Neil Duncan, Michael J. Pollard, Alun Armstrong, Pete Postlethwaite, Ian Dury, Roberta Eaton; ***D:*** Tony Maylam. *HBO*

Splitting Heirs 🦴🦴½ **1993 (PG-13)** Idle stars as the offspring of titled parents who is accidentally abandoned in a restaurant as an infant and raised by poor Pakistanis. (His mother winds up claiming the wrong abandoned baby.) When he discovers he's actually the 15th Duke of Bournemouth he plots, ineffectually, to kill off the present unknowing imposter, a nitwit American (Moranis). Cleese pops in as a shabby lawyer hired by Idle to help him claim the title with Hershey as Idle's real mother, the addle-brained and sex-starved Duchess. Convoluted plot, bland comedy. **87m/C VHS, LV.** Eric Idle, Rick Moranis, Barbara Hershey, John Cleese, Catherine Zeta Jones, Sadie Frost, Stratford Johns, Brenda Bruce, William Franklyn, Jeremy Clyde; ***D:*** Robert M. Young; ***W:*** Eric Idle; ***M:*** Michael Kamen. Nominations: Cannes Film Festival '93: Best Film. *MCA*

Splitz *Woof!* **1984 (PG-13)** An all-girl rock band agrees to help out a sorority house by participating in a series of sporting events. **89m/C VHS, Beta.** Robin Johnson, Patti Lee, Shirley Stoler, Raymond Serra; ***D:*** Domonic Paris. *LIV, VES*

Spoiled Children 🦴🦴½ *Des Enfants Gates* **1977** A famous film director (Piccoli) tries to work on his new script at home but is too distracted by his family life. So he rents a high-rise apartment for peace and quiet but winds up involved in a tenant/landlord dispute and with a girl half his age. In French with English subtitles. **113m/B VHS.** *FR* Michel Piccoli, Christine Pascal, Michel Aumont, Gerard Jugnot, Arlette Bonnard; ***D:*** Bertrand Tavernier; ***W:*** Christine Pascal, Charlotte Dubreuil, Bertrand Tavernier; ***M:*** Philippe Sarde. *FCT, CVC*

The Spoilers 🦴🦴½ **1914** Virtually unstaged account of gold hunting in the Alaskan wilderness enhanced by gritty film quality. Was a gold mine when released. **110m/B VHS, Beta.** William Farnum, Thomas Santschi, Kathlyn Williams, Bessie Eyton, Frank Clark, Wheeler Oakman; ***D:*** Colin Campbell. *GPV*

The Spoilers 🦴🦴🦴 **1942** Two adventurers in the Yukon are swindled out of their gold mine and set out to even the score. A trademark scene of all versions of the movie (and there are many) is the climactic fistfight, in this case between hero Wayne and bad-guy Scott. One of the better films adapted from the novel by Rex Beach. William Farnum, who starred in both the 1914 and the 1930 versions, has a small part. **88m/B VHS, Beta, LV.** John Wayne, Randolph Scott, Marlene Dietrich, Margaret Lindsay, Harry Carey Sr., Richard Barthelmess, Charles Halton; ***D:*** Ray Enright; ***C:*** Milton Krasner. Nominations: Academy Awards '42: Best Interior Decoration. *MCA, MLB, FCT*

Spontaneous Combustion 🦴🦴 **1989 (R)** A grisly horror film detailing the travails of a hapless guy who has the power to inflict the title phenomenon on other people. **97m/C VHS, Beta, LV.** Brad Dourif, Jon Cypher, Melinda Dillon, Cynthia Bain, William Prince; ***D:*** Tobe Hooper; ***M:*** Graeme Revell. *LIV, VTR*

Spook Busters 🦴🦴½ **1948** The Bowery Boys take jobs as exterminators, only to find themselves assigned the unenviable task of ridding a haunted house of ghosts. To make matters worse, the resident mad scientist wants to transplant Sach's brain into a gorilla. Essential viewing for anyone who thought "Ghostbusters" was an original story. **68m/B VHS.** Leo Gorcey, Huntz Hall, Douglass Dumbrille, Bobby Jordan, Gabriel Dell, Billy Benedict, David Gorcey, Bernard Gorcey, Tanis Chandler, Maurice Cass, Charles Middleton; ***D:*** William Beaudine. *WAR, GPV*

The Spook Who Sat By the Door 🦴½ **1973 (PG)** A black CIA agent organizes an army of inner-city youths and launches a revolution. Based on the novel by Sam Greenlee. **95m/C VHS, Beta.** Lawrence Cook, Paula Kelly, J.A. Preston; ***D:*** Ivan Dixon; ***M:*** Herbie Hancock. *VCD*

Spookies *Woof!* **1985 (R)** An old master sorcerer who lives in a run-down haunted house sacrifices humans to give eternal life to his unconscious bride. He needs only a few more victims when a group of teenagers come along to explore the house. **85m/C VHS, Beta, LV.** Felix Ward, Dan Scott, Maria Pechukas, Brendan Faulkner, Eugine Joseph; ***D:*** Thomas Doran. *NO*

Spooks Run Wild 🦴🦴½ **1941** The East Side Kids seek refuge in a spooky mansion owned by the eerie Lugosi. A fun horror-comedy with the Kids' antics playing off Lugosi's scariness quite well. Co-scripter Carl Foreman later co-wrote "High-Noon," "The Bridge on the River Kwai," and "The Guns of Navarone." Not the same movie as "Ghosts on the Loose" which followed in '43 and also featured Lugosi and the Kids. **64m/B VHS, Beta.** Huntz Hall, Leo Gorcey, Bobby Jordan, Sammy Morrison, Dave O'Brien, Dennis Moore, Bela Lugosi; ***D:*** Phil Rosen; ***W:*** Carl Foreman. *NOS, SNC, VYY*

The Sporting Club *Woof!* **1972 (R)** A semi-gothic melodrama about a strict all men's club which, during a 100th anniversary party, reverts to savagery and primitive rites. **104m/C VHS, Beta.** Robert Fields, Margaret Blye, Nicolas Coster, Ralph Waite, Jack Warden, Linda Blair; ***D:*** Larry Peerce. *NLC*

Spotlight Scandals 🦴🦴 **1943** A barber and a vaudevillian team up and endure the ups and downs of showbiz life in this low-budget musical from prolific B-movie director Beaudine. ♫The Restless Age; Goodnight Now; The Lilac Tree; Tempo of the Trail; Oh Johnny. **79m/B VHS.** Billy Gilbert, Frank Fay, Bonnie Baker; ***D:*** William Beaudine. *NOS, LOO*

Spraggue 🦴🦴 **1984** A Boston professor and his eccentric aunt put the moves on a doctor who may have committed murder. Served as a TV pilot for a series that never materialized. **78m/C VHS.** Michael Nouri, Glynis Johns, James Cromwell, Mark Herrier, Patrick O'Neal, Andrea Marcovicci; ***D:*** Larry Elikann. *LIV*

The Spring 🦴½ **1989** Two archaeologists search Florida for the fountain of youth after they find new clues to its whereabouts. However, a greedy industrialist and an evil priest are both on their trail, fighting to keep the secret for themselves at any cost. **110m/C VHS.** Dack Rambo, Gedde Watanabe, Shari Shattuck, Steven Keats; ***D:*** John D. Patterson. *NO*

Spring Break 🦴 **1983 (R)** Four college students go to Fort Lauderdale on their spring vacation and have a wilder time that they bargained for, though viewer is deprived of excitement. **101m/C VHS, Beta, LV.** Perry Lang, David Knell, Steve Bassett, Paul Land, Jayne Modean, Corinne Alphen; ***D:*** Sean S. Cunningham. *COL*

Spring Fever 🦴½ **1981** Heartaches of the junior tennis circuit are brought to the screen in this sports comedy. Previews promised a lot more than this film could ever hope to deliver. Even tennis fans will be disappointed. **93m/C VHS, Beta.** *CA* Susan Anton; ***D:*** Joseph L. Scanlan. *LIV, VES*

Spring Symphony 🦴🦴½ *Fruhlingssinfonie* **1986 (PG-13)** A moody, fairy-tale biography of composer Robert Schumann, concentrating on his rhapsodic love affair with pianist Clara Weick. Kinski is very good as the rebellious daughter, while the music is even better. Reasonably accurate in terms of history; dubbed. **102m/C VHS, Beta.** *GE* Nastassia Kinski, Rolf Hoppe, Herbert Gronemeyer; ***D:*** Peter Schamoni. *LIV*

Springfield Rifle 🦴🦴½ **1952** Based on the real-life story of Major Les Kearney, who joined forces with outlaws to catch the thief stealing government weapons. Average. **93m/C VHS.** Gary Cooper, Phyllis Thaxter, David Brian, Lon Chaney Jr., Paul Kelly, Phil Carey, Guinn "Big Boy" Williams; ***D:*** Andre de Toth; ***M:*** Max Steiner. *WAR*

Springhill 🦴½ **197?** The true story of a mining disaster in which seven miners fought to survive the elements while buried 13,000 feet underground. **90m/C VHS, Beta.** *TWE*

Springtime in the Rockies 🦴🦴 **1937** Autry is a cattle-ranch foreman whose employer decides to try raising sheep. This doesn't set well with the other ranchers, but Autry manages to save the day and sing a little too. **60m/B VHS, Beta.** Gene Autry, Polly Rowles, Smiley Burnette; ***D:*** Joseph Kane. *NOS, VCN, DVT*

Springtime in the Rockies 🦴🦴½ **1942** A Broadway duo just can't get along despite being in love with each other. Top-notch musical, with a touch of romantic tension and comedy. Beautifully filmed in the Canadian Rockies. ♫I Had the Craziest Dream; Run Little Rainrop Run; A Poem Set to Music; Pan American Jubilee; I Like to Be Love by You; Chattanooga Choo Choo; Tic Tac Do Meu Coracao. **91m/C VHS, LV.** Betty Grable, John Payne, Carmen Miranda, Cesar Romero, Charlotte Greenwood, Edward Everett Horton, Jackie Gleason; ***D:*** Irving Cummings; ***C:*** Ernest Palmer. *FOX, MLB*

Springtime in the Sierras 🦴🦴½ *Song of the Sierra* **1947** Rogers and Devine band together to fight a gang of poachers who prey on the wildlife of a game preserve. Features a number of songs by Rogers and The Sons of the Pioneers. **54m/B VHS, Beta.** Roy Rogers, Andy Devine, Jane Frazee, Stephanie Bachelor; ***D:*** William Witney. *NOS, CAB, DVT*

The Sprinter 🦴🦴½ **1984** A young homosexual, while trying to submerge his confusion in professional track and field, gets to know a homely shot-putter and is seduced by her. In German with English subtitles. **90m/C VHS, Beta.** *VCD, GLV*

Spurs 🦴🦴 **1930** A rodeo star takes on a whole gang of rustlers and their imposing machine gun. This transitional western was made both with and without sound. **60m/B VHS.** Hoot Gibson, Robert E. Homans; ***D:*** B. Reeves Eason. *NOS, DVT, HEG*

Sputnik 🦴🦴 *A Dog, a Mouse, and a Sputnik* **1961** A Frenchman, amnesiac after a car crash, comes up against Russian scientists, space-bound dogs, and weightlessness. Pleasant and charming family fun though clearly dated. Another fine performance from Auer. Dubbed. **80m/B VHS, Beta.** *FR* Noelia Noel, Mischa Auer, Denise Grey; ***D:*** Jean Dreville. *INJ*

Spy 🦴🦴 **1989** A former spy who knows too much becomes the target of a renegade agency. Made for television. **88m/C VHS, Beta, LV.** Ned Beatty, Tim Choate, Bruce Greenwood, Catherine Hicks, Jameson Parker, Michael Tucker; ***D:*** Philip Frank Messina. *PAR*

Spy Hard 🦴 **1996 (PG-13)** Nielsen does yet another genre spoof—this time a combo of "Die Hard" meets James Bond. Agent Dick Steele aka WD40 (Nielsen) is brought out of retirement to thwart the plans of crazed General Rancor (Griffith) for world domination. Not much else plotwise, which ropes Nielsen along in domino fashion through the myriad of unimaginative spoofs on such films as "Speed" and "Pulp Fiction." Minus the charm and pace of parody pioneers Zucker/Abrahams/Zucker, this latest entry should retire the whole genre. Directorial debut of Friedberg. **80m/C VHS.** Leslie Nielsen, Nicolette Sheridan, Andy Griffith, Charles Durning, Marcia Gay Harden, Barry Bostwick; ***D:*** Rick Friedberg; ***W:*** Rick Friedberg, Dick Chudnow, Jason Friedberg, Aaron Seltzer; ***C:*** John R. Leonetti; ***M:*** Bill Conti. *NYR*

Spy in Black 🦴🦴🦴 **1939** A German submarine captain returns from duty at sea during WWI and is assigned to infiltrate one of the Orkney Islands and obtain confidential British information. Known in the U.S. as "U-Boat 29," this film is based on a J. Storer Clouston novel. This was the first teaming of director Powell and writer Pressburger, who followed with "Contraband" in 1940 . **82m/B VHS, Beta, LV.** *GB* Conrad Veidt, Valerie Hobson, Sebastian Shaw, Marius Goring, June Duprez, Helen Haye, Cyril Raymond, Hay Petrie; ***D:*** Michael Powell; ***M:*** Miklos Rozsa. *NOS, VYY, DVT*

Spy of Napoleon 🦴🦴 **1936** A French aristocrat agrees to marry the illegitimate daughter of Emperor Napoleon III and finds himself working to uncover traitors to the throne. Based on Baroness Orczy's novel. **77m/B VHS, Beta.** *GB* Richard Barthelmess, Dolly Haas, Francis L. Sullivan. *VYY*

Spy Smasher **1942** A war reporter uses his supposed death (and a covenient twin brother) to go underground and fight Nazi counterfeiters trying to wreck the economy. 12-episode serial. "Spy Smasher Returns" is actually a condensed-version not a sequel. **185m/B VHS.** Kane Richmond, Marguerite Chapman, Sam Flint, Hans Schumm, Tristram Coffin; ***D:*** William Witney. *REP*

Spy Smasher Returns **1942** The exciting 12-part serial "Spy Smasher" was cut and edited into feature length and released under this title. The masked marvel and his twin brother battle enemy agents during WWII. This new version is just as exciting as the original cliffhanger. **185m/B VHS.** Kane Richmond, Marguerite Chapman, Sam Flint, Hans Schumm, Tristram Coffin; ***D:*** William Witney. *REP, MLB*

Spy Story 🦴🦴 **1986** A Cold War conflict, counter-intelligence, conspiracy, and a nuclear sub chase highlight this tale by Len Deighton. **105m/C VHS, Beta.** *VCD, MOV*

Spy Trap 🦴🦴½ **1992** Four junior-high school friends concoct bogus military plans using futuristic toys for blueprints. The "secret" plans get sold to the Russians and the kids find themselves chased by the unhappy KGB and the CIA. Family adventure. **96m/C VHS.** Elya Baskin, Danielle Du Clos, Jason Kristofer, Cameron Johann, Devin Ratray, Kimble Joyner; ***D:*** Arthur Sherman. *HMD*

The Spy Who Came in from the Cold 🦴🦴🦴½ **1965** The acclaimed adaptation of the John Le Carre novel about an aging British spy who attempts to infiltrate the East German agency. Prototypical Cold War thriller, with emphasis on deglamorizing espionage. Gritty and superbly realistic with a documentary style which hampered it at the box office. **110m/B VHS, Beta, LV.** Richard Burton, Oskar Werner, Claire Bloom, Sam Wanamaker, Peter Van Eyck, Cyril Cusack, Rupert Davies, Michael Hordern; ***D:*** Martin Ritt; ***C:*** Oswald Morris. British Academy Awards '66: Best Film; Edgar Allan Poe Awards '65: Best Screenplay; Golden Globe Awards '66: Best Supporting Actor (Werner); Nominations: Academy Awards '65: Best Actor (Burton). *PAR*

The Spy Who Loved Me 🦴🦴 **1977 (PG)** James Bond teams up with female Russian Agent XXX to squash a villain's plan to use captured American and Russian atomic submarines in a plot to destroy the world. The villain's henchman, 7'2" Kiel, is the steel-toothed Jaws. Carly Simon sings the memorable, Marvin Hamlisch theme song, "Nobody Does It Better." **136m/C VHS, Beta, LV.** *GB* Roger Moore, Barbara Bach, Curt Jurgens, Richard Kiel, Caroline Munro, Walter Gotell, Geoffrey Keen, Valerie Leon, Bernard Lee, Lois Maxwell, Desmond Llewelyn; ***D:*** Lewis Gilbert; ***M:*** Marvin Hamlisch, Paul Buckmaster. Nominations: Academy Awards '77: Best Art Direction/Set Decoration, Best Song ("Nobody Does It Better"), Best Original Score. *MGM, FOX, TLF*

Spy with a Cold Nose 🦴🦴 **1966** A sporadically funny spy spoof about a bugged dog passed between British and Soviet intelligence. Hard-working cast keeps it from collapsing. **93m/C VHS, Beta.** *GB* Laurence Harvey, Daliah Lavi, Lionel Jeffries; ***D:*** Daniel Petrie. *NLC*

The Spy Within 🦴🦴 **1994 (R)** Spy Alex (Russell) is working undercover as a call girl and Will (Glenn) is an explosives expert on the run from his past. The two share more than a mutual attraction since a covert organization wants them both dead. Confusing plot but fast-paced action. Railsback's directorial debut. **92m/C VHS.** Theresa Russell, Scott Glenn, Lane Smith, Terence Knox, Katherine Helmond, Alex Rocco, Joe Pantoliano, Rudy Ramos; ***D:*** Steve Railsback; ***W:*** Lewis Green. *NHO*

Spymaker: The Secret Life of Ian Fleming 🦴🦴½ *Spymaker* **1990** Fictionalized account of the creator of the ultimate spy, James Bond, and his early days in the British Secret Service. Fans of the Bond movies will appreciate the numerous inside jokes. Connery is the son of Sean. Made for British television. **96m/C VHS.** *GB* Jason Connery, Kristin Scott Thomas, Joss Ackland, Patricia Hodge, David Warner, Fiona Fullerton, Richard Johnson; ***D:*** Ferdinand Fairfax. *TTC*

S*P*Y*S 🦴 **1974 (PG)** An attempt to cash in on the success of "M*A*S*H," this unfunny spy spoof details the adventures of two bumbling CIA men who botch a Russian defection, and get both sides after them. Usually competent director Kershner had a bad day. **87m/C VHS, Beta.** Donald Sutherland, Elliott Gould, Joss Ackland, Zouzou, Shane Rimmer, Vladek Sheybal, Nigel Hawthorne; ***D:*** Irvin Kershner; ***W:*** Malcolm Marmorstein, Lawrence J. Cohen; ***M:*** Jerry Goldsmith. *FOX*

Squanto: A Warrior's Tale 🦴🦴🦴 **1994 (PG)** Family adventure fare about 17th-century Massachusetts brave Squanto (Beach), who's captured by English traders and taken to Plymouth, England for display as a "savage." He manages to escape, eventually hiding aboard a trading vessel bound for America, and on returning home even brings about a peace between fearful Pilgrims and a neighboring tribe (which culminates in the first Thanksgiving feast). It may be history lite but it's also a thoughtful, adventurous saga with good performances, and fine location filming in Nova Scotia and Cape Breton, Canada. **101m/C VHS, LV.** Adam Beach, Mandy Patinkin, Michael Gambon, Nathaniel Parker, Eric Schweig, Donal Donnelly, Stuart Pankin, Alex Norton, Irene Bedard; ***D:*** Xavier Koller; ***W:*** Darlene Craviotto; ***M:*** Joel McNeely. *DIS*

Square Dance 🦴🦴½ *Home is Where the Heart Is* **1987 (PG-13)** A Texas teenager leaves the farm where she's been raised by her grandfather to live in the city with her promiscuous mother (Alexander, cast against type) where she befriends a retarded young man (yes, it's Lowe, also cast against type). Too slow, but helped by good acting. **118m/C VHS, Beta, LV.** Jane Alexander, Jason Robards Jr., Rob Lowe, Winona Ryder, Deborah Richter, Guich Koock, Elbert Lewis; ***D:*** Daniel Petrie; ***W:*** Alan Hines; ***M:*** Bruce Broughton. *NO*

Square Dance Jubilee 🦴½ **1951** Television scouts hit Prairie City in search of cowboy stars, and stumble onto cattle rustlers. Twenty-one C & W tunes support a near-invisible plot, suitable for fridge runs. **78m/B VHS, Beta, LV.** Mary Beth Hughes, Donald (Don "Red") Barry, Wally Vernon, John Eldridge; ***D:*** Paul Landres. *NO*

Square Shoulders 🦴½ **1929** Adventures of young military school student with geometric anatomy (Coghlan). **58m/B VHS, Beta.** Frank "Junior" Coghlan, Louis Wolheim, Anita Louise, Montague Shaw; ***D:*** E. Mason Hopper. *GPV, FCT*

The Squeaker 🦴🦴½ *Murder on Diamond Row* **1937** Good Edgar Wallace mystery about a disgraced inspector trying to clear his name. **?m/C VHS.** Edmund Lowe, Sebastian Shaw; ***M:*** Miklos Rozsa. *SNC*

The Squeaker 🦴🦴½ **1965** Complicated but interesting thriller about the underworld goings-on after a big-time diamond heist. German remake of an early (1930) British talkie, also done in 1937, based on the Edgar Wallace novel. **95m/B VHS.** *GE* Heinz Drache, Eddi Arent, Klaus Kinski, Barbara Rutting; ***D:*** Alfred Vohrer. *SNC*

The Squeeze 🦴🦴 **1977 (R)** Scotland Yard detective Keach, fired for drunkeness, gets a chance to reinstate himself when his ex-wife is caught up in a brutal kidnapping scheme. Slim script gives good cast uphill work. Ordinary thriller. Available with Spanish subtitles. **106m/C VHS, Beta, LV.** Stacy Keach, Carol White, David Hemmings, Edward Fox, Stephen Boyd; ***D:*** Michael Apted. *WAR*

The Squeeze 🦴½ **1980** An aging safecracker is hired for a final job, but learns that his cohorts plan to kill him when the heist is finished. Blah revenge thriller. **93m/C VHS, Beta.** *IT* Lee Van Cleef, Karen Black, Edward Albert, Lionel Stander, Robert Alda; ***D:*** Anthony (Antonio Margheriti) Dawson. *NO*

The Squeeze *Woof!* **1987 (PG-13)** Keaton is wasted in this attempt at a comedy about a small-time con artist who discovers a Mafia plan to fix a lottery electromagnetically. **101m/C VHS, Beta, LV.** Michael Keaton, Rae Dawn Chong, John Davidson, Ric Abernathy, Bobby Bass, Joe Pantoliano, Meat Loaf, Paul Herman; ***D:*** Roger Young; ***M:*** Miles Goodman. *HBO*

Squeeze Play *Woof!* **1979** Group of young women start a softball team and challenge the boyfriends to a game. Standard battle of the sexes takes places, with a wet T-shirt contest thrown in for good measure. Cheap, plotless, offensive trash from Troma. **92m/C VHS, Beta, LV.** Al Corley, Jenni Hetrick, Jim Metzler; ***D:*** Lloyd (Samuel Weil) Kaufman. *NO*

Squirm 🦴🦴 **1976 (R)** Storm disrupts a highly charged power cable, electrifying a host of garden-variety worms. The worms then turn themselves into giant monsters that terrorize a small town in Georgia. The opening credits claim it's based on an actual 1975 incident. Yeah, right. Okay entry in the giant worm genre. **92m/C VHS, Beta, LV.** Don Scardino, Patricia Pearcy, Jean Sullivan; ***D:*** Jeff Lieberman; ***W:*** Jeff Lieberman. *LIV, VES*

Squizzy Taylor 🦴🦴 **1984** The rise and fall of real-life Australian mob boss Squizzy Taylor in the 1920s. Colorful period gangster drama loses steam about halfway through. **82m/C VHS, Beta.** *AU* Jacki Weaver, Alan Cassell, David Atkins; ***D:*** Kevin Dobson. *NO*

S.S. Experiment Camp 2 🦴 **1986** Hitler's elite corps of sadists get their kicks torturing and maiming prisoners during the dark days of WWII. **90m/C VHS, Beta.** John Braun, Macha Magal. *NO*

SS Girls *Woof!* **1978** After the assassination attempt of July 1944, Hitler does not trust the Wehrmacht and extends the power of the SS over Germany. General Berger entrusts Hans Schillemberg to recruit a specially chosen group of prostitutes who must test the fighting spirit and loyalty of the generals. Seedy exploitation. **82m/C VHS, Beta.** Gabriele Carrara, Marina Daunia, Vassilli Karis, Macha Magal, Thomas Rudy, Lucic Bogoljub Benny, Ivano Staccioli. *MED*

S.S. Love Camp No. 27 **197?** A beautiful young girl's life is torn to shreds when she is imprisoned in a Nazi brothel. **90m/C VHS, Beta.** *VCD*

Stacey 🦴½ *Stacey and Her Gangbusters* **1973 (R)** Ex-Playmate Randall stars as Stacey Hansen, a beautiful, implausibly talented private detective. Hyper-convoluted plot, too much sex and violence detract from a potentially not-wretched whodunit. **87m/C VHS, Beta.** Anne Randall, Marjorie Bennett, Anitra Ford, Alan Landers, James Westmoreland, Christina Raines; ***D:*** Andy Sidaris. *GEM*

Stacking 🦴🦴 *Season of Dreams* **1987 (PG)** In the 1950s, a Montana family is threatened with losing their farm. Typical, boring '80s farmland tragedy with coming of age tale. **111m/C VHS, Beta, LV.** Christine Lahti, Megan Follows, Frederic Forrest, Peter Coyote, Jason Gedrick; ***D:*** Martin Rosen; ***M:*** Patrick Gleeson. *NLC*

Stacy's Knights 🦴🦴 *Double Down* **1983 (PG)** A seemingly shy girl happens to have an uncanny knack for blackjack. With the odds against her and an unlikely group of "knights" to aid her, she sets up an implausible "sting" operation. Blah TV fodder for the big screen. **95m/C VHS, Beta.** Kevin Costner, Andra Millian; ***D:*** Jim Wilson; ***W:*** Michael Blake. *LIV, VES*

Stage Door 🦴🦴🦴½ **1937** An energetic ensemble peek at the women of the theater. A boarding house for potential actresses houses a wide variety of talents and dreams. Patrician Hepburn and wise-cracking Rogers make a good team in a talent-packed ensemble. Realistic look at the sub-world of Broadway aspirations includes dialogue taken from idle chat among the actresses between takes. Based on the play by Edna Ferber and George S. Kaufman, who suggested in jest a title change to "Screen Door," since so much had been changed. Watch for young stars-to-be like Ball, Arden and Miller. **92m/B VHS, Beta.** Katharine Hepburn, Ginger Rogers, Lucille Ball, Eve Arden, Andrea Leeds, Jack Carson, Adolphe Menjou, Gail Patrick; ***D:*** Gregory La Cava. National Board of Review Awards '37: 10 Best Films of the Year; New York Film Critics Awards '37: Best Director (La Cava); Nominations: Academy Awards '37: Best Director (La Cava), Best Picture, Best Screenplay, Best Supporting Actress (Leeds). *TTC, CCB, MED*

Stage Door Canteen 🦴🦴½ **1943** The Stage Door Canteens were operated by the American Theatre Wing during WWII for servicemen on leave. They were staffed by some of the biggest stars of the day, 65 of whom are featured here. The slight, hokey plot concerns three soldiers who fall for canteen workers while on furlough in New York City. Many musical numbers, cameos, and walk-ons by a plethora of stars. ♫We Mustn't Say Goodbye; Bombshell From Brooklyn; The Machine Gun Song; Sleep, Baby, Sleep in Your Jeep; Quick Sands; You're Pretty Terrific Yourself; Don't Worry Island; We Meet in the Funniest Places; A Rookie and His Rhythm. **135m/B VHS, Beta, LV.** Cheryl Walker, William Terry, Marjorie Riordan, Lon McCallister, Sunset Carson, Tallulah Bankhead, Merle Oberon, Katharine Hepburn, Paul Muni, Ethel Waters, Judith Anderson, Ray Bolger; ***Cameos:*** Helen Hayes, Harpo Marx, Gertrude Lawrence, Ethel Merman, Edgar Bergen, George Raft, Benny Goodman, Peggy Lee, Count Basie, Kay Kyser, Guy Lombardo, Xavier Cugat, Johnny Weissmuller; ***D:*** Frank Borzage. Nominations: Academy Awards '26: Best Song ("We Mustn't Say Goodbye"); Academy Awards '43: Best Original Score. *CNG, NOS, PSM*

Stage Fright 🦴🦴🦴 **1950** Wyman will stop at nothing to clear her old boyfriend, who has been accused of murdering the husband of his mistress, an actress (Dietrich). Disguised as a maid, she falls in love with the investigating detective, and discovers her friend's guilt. Dietrich sings "The Laziest Gal in Town." The Master's last film made in England until "Frenzy" (1971). **110m/B VHS, Beta, LV.** *GB* Jane Wyman, Marlene Dietrich, Alastair Sim, Sybil Thorndike, Michael Wilding, Kay Walsh; ***D:*** Alfred Hitchcock. National Board of Review Awards '50: 10 Best Films of the Year. *WAR, MLB*

Stage Fright 🦴 **1983** Bashful actress is transformed into a homicidal killer after a latent psychosis in her becomes active. **82m/C VHS, Beta, LV.** Jenny Neumann, Gary Sweet. *NO*

Stage Struck 🦴🦴½ **1957** Strasberg reprises the role made famous by Katharine Hepburn as a determined, would-be actress in this mediocre remake of "Morning Glory" (1933). Christopher Plummer's screen debut shows little of his later talent. **95m/B VHS, Beta, LV.** Henry Fonda, Susan Strasberg, Christopher Plummer, Herbert Marshall, Joan Greenwood; ***D:*** Sidney Lumet; ***M:*** Alex North. *IME*

Stage to Mesa City 🦴🦴 **1948** Marshal LaRue must find out who is behind the pesky attacks on the stage line to Mesa City. Chesebro, as usual, is a good bad guy. A few chuckles between fist fights and shoot-em-ups. **52m/B VHS, Beta.** Lash LaRue, Al "Fuzzy" St. John, George Chesebro, Jennifer Holt, Russell Arms; ***D:*** Ray Taylor. *COL, GPV*

Stagecoach 🦴🦴🦴🦴 **1939** Varied group of characters with nothing in common are stuck together inside a coach besieged by bandits and Indians. Considered structurally perfect, with excellent direction by Ford, it's the film that made Wayne a star as the Ringo Kid, an outlaw looking to avenge the murder of his brother and father. The first pairing of Ford and Wayne changed the course of the modern western. Stunning photography by Bert Glennon and Ray Binger captured the mythical air of Monument Valley, a site that Ford was often to revisit. Based on the story "Stage to Lordsburg" by Ernest Haycox. Remade miserably with in 1966 and again—why?—as a TV movie in 1986. **100m/B VHS, Beta, LV.** John Wayne, Claire Trevor, Thomas Mitchell, George Bancroft, John Carradine, Andy Devine, Donald Meek, Louise Platt, Berton Churchill, Tim Holt, Tom Tyler, Chris-Pin Martin, Francis Ford, Jack Pennick; ***D:*** John Ford. Academy Awards '39: Best Supporting Actor (Mitchell), Best Score; National Board of Review Awards '39: 10 Best Films of the Year; New York Film Critics Awards '39: Best Director (Ford); Nominations: Academy Awards '39: Best Black and White Cinematography, Best Director (Ford), Best Film Editing, Best Interior Decoration, Best Picture. *WAR, VES, TLF*

Stagecoach 🦴 **1986** A forgettable made-for-television remake of the classic 1939 western about a motley crew of characters in a cross-country coach beset by thieves and Indians. **95m/C VHS, Beta.** Willie Nelson, Waylon Jennings, Johnny Cash, Kris Kristofferson,

John Schneider, Elizabeth Ashley, Mary Crosby, Anthony Newley, Anthony (Tony) Franciosa; *D:* Ted Post; *M:* Willie Nelson. *VMK*

Stagecoach to Denver ☠☠ **1946** Lane as Red Ryder investigates a stagecoach wreck and uncovers a land-grabbing plot led by-who else?—the pillar of the community (Barcroft). Well-directed "Red Ryder" episode. **53m/B VHS, Beta.** Allan "Rocky" Lane, Roy Barcroft, Robert (Bobby) Blake, Peggy Stewart, Martha Wentworth; *D:* R.G. Springsteen. *NOS, CAB, VCN*

Stagefright ☠ **1987** A maniacal serial killer tries to cover his trail by joining the cast of a play about mass murder. The other actors soon have more to worry about than remembering their lines. Typical low-grade horror. **95m/C VHS, Beta.** David Brandon, Barbara Cupisti, Robert Gligorov; *D:* Michele (Michael) Soavi. *IMP*

Stakeout ☠☠ **1962** An ex-con tries to start life anew, but every time he finds a good job, his past catches up with him. A return to the life of crime looks tempting. Predictable and familiar plot, but performances are sincere. **81m/B VHS.** Bing Russell, Billy Hughes, Bill Hale, Jack Harris; *D:* James Landis; *W:* James Landis. *SNC*

Stakeout ☠☠½ **1987 (R)** A sometimes violent comedy-thriller about a pair of detectives who stake out a beautiful woman's apartment, hoping for a clue to the whereabouts of her psycho boyfriend who has broken out of prison. One of them (Dreyfuss) then begins to fall in love with her. Natural charm among Estevez, Dreyfuss, and Stowe that adds to the proceedings, which are palpably implausible and silly. Slapstick sequel "Another Stakeout" followed in 1993. **117m/C VHS, Beta, LV, 8mm.** Richard Dreyfuss, Emilio Estevez, Madeleine Stowe, Aidan Quinn, Forest Whitaker, Dan Lauria, Earl Billings; *D:* John Badham; *W:* Jim Kouf; *M:* Arthur B. Rubinstein. Edgar Allan Poe Awards '87: Best Screenplay. *TOU*

Stalag 17 ☠☠☠☠ **1953** A group of American G.I.s in a German POW camp during WWII suspects the opportunistic Holden of being the spy in their midst. One of the very best American movies of the 1950's, adapted from the play by Donald Bevan and Edmund Trzcinski. Wilder, so good at comedy, proved himself equally adept at drama, and brought a top-drawer performance out of Holden. Features superb photography from Ernest Laszlo, and a wonderful score. **120m/B VHS, Beta, LV.** William Holden, Don Taylor, Peter Graves, Otto Preminger, Harvey Lembeck, Robert Strauss, Sig Rumann, Richard Erdman, Neville Brand; *D:* Billy Wilder; *W:* Billy Wilder, Edwin Blum; *C:* Ernest Laszlo; *M:* Franz Waxman. Academy Awards '53: Best Actor (Holden); National Board of Review Awards '53: 10 Best Films of the Year; Nominations: Academy Awards '53: Best Director (Wilder), Best Supporting Actor (Strauss). *PAR, TLF, BTV*

Stalag Luft **19??** Senior British officer James Forrester (Fry) is regarded by fellow POWs as a first-class idiot, since he has a record 23 escapes and recaptures. But he's determined to break all 327 prisoners out of their Nazi camp while the nervous German Kommandant keeps one eye on the advancing Allied army and the other on his prisoners. **103m/C VHS.** *GB* Stephen Fry, Geoffrey Palmer, Nicholas Lyndhurst. *VCO*

Stalin ☠☠½ **1992** The story of the leader of the Soviet Union who ruled with an iron fist from 1924-1953. One of the most feared men of the 20th century, he wrenched the largest country in the world singlehandedly from a backward, pastoral farmland to an industrial landscape. He was also responsible for the feared purges of the late 1930s where more than a million people were executed. Also explored is the dictator's relationships with his family, including how marriage to a cunning, sadistic, paranoid tyrant affected his wife. Filmed at actual historical locations in Russia. Made for cable television. **173m/C VHS, LV.** Robert Duvall, Julia Ormond, Jeroen Krabbe, Joan Plowright, Maximilian Schell, Frank Finlay, Roshan Seth, Daniel Massey, Miriam Margolyes, Jim Carter, Joanna Roth, Andras Balint; *D:* Ivan Passer; *W:* Paul Monash; *C:* Vilmos Zsigmond. *MGM, BTV*

Stalk the Wild Child ☠½ **1976** Well-intentioned but unconvincing American remake of Truffaut's "The Wild Child," about a child psychologist's efforts to rehabilitate a boy raised by wolves. TV pilot inspired "Lucan," a short-lived series. **78m/C VHS.** David Janssen, Trish Van Devere, Benjamin Bottoms, Joseph Bottoms; *D:* William Hale. *WOV*

Stalked ☠½ **1994 (R)** Daryl Gleeson (Underwood) saves the life of the widowed Brooke's (D'Abo) young son (Fennell). Naturally, she's grateful—only Daryl takes her gratitude for something more intimate and becomes fixated on her every move. **95m/C VHS, LV.** Maryam D'Abo, Jay Underwood, Tod Fennell, Lisa Blount, Alex Karzis, Karen Robinson, Vivian Reis; *D:* Douglas Jackson. *REP*

Stalker ☠☠☠ **1979** A meteorite, crashing to Earth, has caused a wasteland area known as the Zone. The Zone is forbidden to anyone except special guides called Stalkers. Three Stalkers enter the region searching for its center, which contains a room that supposedly reveals fantasies. From the Soviet team that made "Solaris." Filmed with both color and black-and-white sequences. Suspenseful atmosphere due to the director's use of long takes, movement, and color. In Russian with English subtitles. **160m/C VHS.** *RU* Alexander Kaidanovsky, Nikolai Grinko, Anatoli Solonitzin, Alice Freindlikh; *D:* Andrei Tarkovsky; *M:* Eduard Artemyev. *FXL, FCT*

Stalking Danger ☠½ *C.A.T. Squad* **1986 (PG)** A secret government group must terminate an assassination plot by a terrorist organization. **97m/C VHS, Beta, LV.** Joe Cortese, Steve James, Patricia Charbonneau, Jack Youngblood; *D:* William Friedkin; *M:* Ennio Morricone. *VMK*

Stalking Laura ☠½ *I Can Make You Love Me: The Stalking of Laura Black* **1993** Laura Black (Shields) has just landed her first job at a California engineering firm where she meets co-worker Richard Farley (Thomas). He asks her out—she turns him down—he starts harassing her. Laura reports it to the company, who eventually fire Farley, and obtains a restraining order. He goes on a murderous rampage. Fact-based TV movie with Thomas effective as the dangerous obsessive. **90m/C VHS.** Brooke Shields, Richard Thomas, Viveka Davis, William Allen Young, Richard Yniguez, Scott Bryce. *AEL*

The Stalking Moon ☠½ **1969 (G)** Indian scout Peck, ready to retire, meets a woman and her half-breed son who have been captives of the Apaches for 10 years. He agrees to help them escape but learns that the woman's Indian husband is hunting them down. Skeletal plot with little meat on it; great scenery but you wouldn't know it. **109m/C VHS.** Gregory Peck, Eva Marie Saint, Robert Forster, Noland Clay; *D:* Robert Mulligan; *W:* Alvin Sargent. *ACE, WAR*

Stamp Day for Superman ☠☠ **1953** Based on the "Superman" television series, this program was made to promote defense savings stamps for kids. A "Superman" cartoon is also included. **25m/B VHS, Beta.** George Reeves, Jack Larson, Robert Shayne. *VDM*

Stamp of a Killer ☠ **1987 (PG)** A tough cop tries to decipher the pattern of a rampaging serial killer. Made for television. **95m/C VHS.** Jimmy Smits, Judith Light, Audra Lindley, Michael Parks, Rhea Perlman; *D:* Larry Elikann. *VTR, NWV*

Stan Without Ollie, Vol. 1 **1923** Three silent comedy shorts featuring Laurel on his own, years before teaming with Ollie: "Kill or Cure," "Oranges & Lemons," and "The Noon Whistle." **53m/B VHS, Beta.** Stan Laurel. *VYY*

Stan Without Ollie, Vol. 2 **1923** Three silent shorts from Laurel before he met the big guy. **55m/B VHS, Beta.** Stan Laurel. *VYY*

Stan Without Ollie, Vol. 3 **1923** Three early Laurel shorts: "White Wings," "Man About Town," and "Smithy." **51m/B VHS, Beta.** Stan Laurel, James Finlayson. *VYY*

Stan Without Ollie, Vol. 4 **1925** Three classic pre-Hardy shorts featuring Laurel: "Half a Man," "Yes, Yes, Nanette," and "Save the Ship." **64m/B VHS, Beta, 8mm.** Stan Laurel, Blanche Payson, James Finlayson. *VYY*

Stand Alone ☠☠ **1985 (R)** WWII vet Durning battles local dope dealers in his New York neighborhood. Self-serious anti-drug flick miscasts Durning (overweight and looking silly in fight scenes) and Grier. **94m/C VHS, Beta.** Charles Durning, Pam Grier, James Keach; *D:* Alan Beattie; *W:* Roy Carlson. *NWV, VTR*

Stand and Deliver ☠☠ **1928** War vet joins Greek ranks for the smell of gunpowder in the morning and meets woman of his dreams. Kidnapped by infamous outlaws, he pledges allegiance to them before turning them over to the authorities, and he's free to live happily ever after with heartthrob. **57m/B VHS, Beta.** Rod La Rocque, Lupe Velez, Warner Oland, James Dime, Frank Lanning, Donald Crisp; *D:* Donald Crisp. *GPV*

Stand and Deliver ☠☠☠ **1988 (PG)** A tough teacher inspires students in an East L.A. barrio to take the Advanced Placement Test in calculus. A superb, inspirational true story, with a wonderful performance from Olmos. **105m/C VHS, LV, 8mm.** Edward James Olmos, Lou Diamond Phillips, Rosana De Soto, Andy Garcia, Will Gotay, Ingrid Oliu, Virginia Paris, Mark Eliot; *D:* Ramon Menendez; *W:* Tom Musca, Ramon Menendez; *M:* Craig Safan. Independent Spirit Awards '89: Best Actor (Olmos), Best Director (Menendez), Best Film, Best Screenplay, Best Supporting Actor (Phillips), Best Supporting Actress (De Soto); Nominations: Academy Awards '88: Best Actor (Olmos). *WAR, HMV*

Stand By Me ☠☠☠ **1986 (R)** A sentimental, observant adaptation of the Stephen King novella "The Body." Four 12-year-olds trek into the Oregon wilderness to find the body of a missing boy, learning about death and personal courage. Told as a reminiscence by narrator "author" Dreyfuss with solid performances from all four child actors. Too much gratuitous obscenity, but a very good, gratifying film from can't-miss director Reiner. Based on the novella "The Body" by Stephen King. **87m/C VHS, Beta, LV, 8mm.** River Phoenix, Wil Wheaton, Jerry O'Connell, Corey Feldman, Kiefer Sutherland, Richard Dreyfuss, Casey Siemaszko, John Cusack; *D:* Rob Reiner; *W:* Raynold Gideon; *M:* Jack Nitzsche. Nominations: Academy Awards '86: Best Adapted Screenplay. *COL*

Stand-In ☠☠☠ **1937** When a Hollywood studio is threatened with bankruptcy, the bank sends in timid efficiency expert Howard to save it. Satire of studio executives and big-budget movie making. Bogart is interestingly cast and effective in his first comedy role, playing a drunken producer in love with star Shelton. **91m/B VHS, Beta.** Humphrey Bogart, Joan Blondell, Leslie Howard, Alan Mowbray, Marla Shelton, Jack Carson; *D:* Tay Garnett. *NO*

Stand-In ☠ **1985** A strange comedy-action film that takes a behind-the-scenes look at sleaze films and organized crime. **87m/C VHS, Beta.** Danny Glover; *D:* Robert Zagone. *NO*

Stand Off ☠½ **1989** Two young hoodlums with guns take eighteen girls hostage in a dormitory. In Hungarian with English subtitles. **97m/C VHS.** *HU* Ary Beri, Gabor Svidrony, Zbigniew Zapassiewicz, Istvan Szabo; *D:* Gyula Gazdag. *EVD, FCT, INJ*

Stand Up and Cheer ☠☠½ **1934 (PG)** The new federal Secretary of Entertainment organizes a huge show to raise the country's depressed spirits. Near-invisible plot, fantastic premise are an excuse for lots of imagery, dancing, and comedy, including four-year-old Temple singing "Baby Take a Bow." Also available colorized. ♫I'm Laughing; We're Out of the Red; Broadway's Gone Hillbilly; Baby Take a Bow; This Is Our Last Night Together; She's Way Up Thar; Stand Up and Cheer. **80m/B VHS, Beta.** Shirley Temple, Warner Baxter, Madge Evans, Nigel Bruce, Stepin Fetchit, Frank Melton, Lila Lee, James Dunn, John Boles, Scotty Beckett; *D:* Hamilton MacFadden; *W:* Will Rogers, Ralph Spence; *C:* Ernest Palmer. *FOX*

Standing Tall 🦴🦴 **1978** A small-time cattle rancher takes on a high-class land baron in this average, made-for-TV western set during the Depression. Playing a "half-breed," Forster carries an otherwise mediocre effort. **100m/C VHS.** Robert Forster, Linda Evans, Will Sampson, L.Q. Jones; ***D:*** Harvey Hart. *WOV*

Stanley 🦴½ **1972 (PG)** Seminole Vietnam veteran Robinson uses rattlesnakes as his personal weapon of revenge against most of mankind. Thoroughly wretched effort in the gross-pets vein of "Willard" and "Ben." **108m/C VHS, Beta.** Chris Robinson, Alex Rocco, Susan Carroll; ***D:*** William Grefe. *NO*

Stanley and Iris 🦴🦴½ **1990 (PG-13)** Blue collar recent widow Fonda meets co-worker De Niro, whose illiteracy she helps remedy. Romance follows, inevitably but excruciatingly. Leads' strong presence helps along a very slow, underdeveloped plot. **107m/C VHS, Beta, LV.** Jane Fonda, Robert De Niro, Swoosie Kurtz, Martha Plimpton, Harley Cross, Jamey Sheridan, Feodor Chaliapin Jr, Zohra Lampert, Loretta Devine, Julie Garfield; ***D:*** Martin Ritt; ***W:*** Harriet Frank Jr., Irving Ravetch; ***M:*** John Williams. *MGM, FCT*

Stanley and Livingstone 🦴🦴🦴 **1939** The classic Hollywood kitsch version of the Victorian legend-based-on-fact. American journalist Tracy sets out into darkest Africa to locate a long lost Brisith explorer. Lavish, dramatically solid fictionalized history. (The real Stanley did not become a missionary—but hey, this is the movies). Tracy is excellent, as usual, and low-key. **101m/B VHS, Beta.** Spencer Tracy, Cedric Hardwicke, Nancy Kelly, Walter Brennan, Richard Greene, Charles Coburn, Henry Hull, Henry Travers, Miles Mander, Holmes Herbert, Paul Stanton, Brandon Hurst, Joseph Crehan, Russell Hicks; ***D:*** Henry King; ***C:*** George Barnes; ***M:*** Alfred Newman. *FOX*

Star! 🦴🦴 *Those Were the Happy Times* **1968** Campy showbiz extravaganza based on the life of famed musical comedy performer Gertrude Lawrence (Andrews), star of the London and Broadway stage. Film follows Lawrence's adventures from the British music halls to her fateful meeting with Noel Coward (Massey), who would not only become her dearest friend but perform with and write for her as well. A tumultuous private life is also on display. 17 lavishly staged musical numbers helped boost the cost of the film to $14 million—big bucks in '68. Movie was a colossal flop on opening and was recut, deleting 50 minutes, but still didn't recoup its losses. Has gained a cult following. ♫Down at the Old Bull and Bush; Piccadilly; Star!; Oh, It's a Lovely War; In My Garden of Joy; Forbidden Fruit; Parisian Pierrot; Someday I'll Find You; Has Anybody Seen Our Ship?. **172m/C VHS, LV.** Julie Andrews, Daniel Massey, Richard Crenna, Michael Craig, Robert Reed, Bruce Forsyth, Beryl Reid, John Collin, Alan Oppenheimer, Anthony Eisley, Jenny Agutter, J. Pat O'Malley, Richard Karlan, Lynley Laurence, Harvey Jason, Elizabeth St. Clair; ***D:*** Robert Wise; ***W:*** William Fairchild; ***C:*** Ernest Laszlo. Nominations: Academy Awards '68: Best Art Direction/Set Decoration, Best Cinematography, Best Costume Design, Best Song ("Star!"), Best Sound, Best Supporting Actor (Massey), Best Original Score. *FXV, BTV, FCT*

The Star Chamber 🦴🦴 **1983 (R)** A conscientious judge (Douglas) sees criminals freed on legal technicalities and wonders if he should take justice into his own hands. He finds a secret society that administers justice extra-legally. Implausible yet predictable. **109m/C VHS, Beta, LV.** Michael Douglas, Hal Holbrook, Yaphet Kotto, Sharon Gless, James B. Sikking; ***D:*** Peter Hyams; ***W:*** Peter Hyams, Roderick Taylor. *FOX*

Star Crash 🦴🦴½ *Stella Star* **1978 (PG)** Trio of adventurers (woman, man, and robot) sent by emperor Plummer square off against interstellar evil (Spinell) by using their wits and technological wizardry. Semi-funny and cheesy sci-fi, done with style beyond its limited budget. **92m/C VHS, Beta, LV.** *IT* Caroline Munro, Marjoe Gortner, Christopher Plummer, David Hasselhoff, Robert Tessier, Joe Spinell, Nadia Cassini, Judd Hamilton; ***D:*** Lewis (Luigi Cozzi) Coates; ***W:*** Lewis (Luigi Cozzi) Coates; ***M:*** John Barry. *NLC*

Star Crystal 🦴 **1985 (R)** Aboard a spaceship, an indestructible alien hunts down the human crew. Cheap imitation of "Alien." **93m/C VHS, Beta.** C. Jutson Campbell, Faye Bolt, John W. Smith; ***D:*** Lance Lindsay. *NWV, VTR, HHE*

Star 80 🦴🦴½ **1983 (R)** Based on the true-life tragedy of Playmate of the Year Dorothy Stratten and her manager-husband Paul Snider as they battle for control of her body, her mind, and her money, with gruesome results. Roberts is overpowering as the vile Snider, but the movie is generally unpleasant. Fosse's last film. **104m/C VHS, Beta, LV.** Mariel Hemingway, Eric Roberts, Cliff Robertson, David Clennon, Josh Mostel, Roger Rees, Carroll Baker; ***D:*** Bob Fosse; ***C:*** Sven Nykvist; ***M:*** Ralph Burns. *WAR*

A Star is Born 🦴🦴🦴½ **1937** A movie star declining in popularity marries a shy girl and helps her become a star. Her fame eclipses his and tragic consequences follow. Shows Hollywood-behind-the-scenes machinations. Stunning ending is based on the real-life tragedy of silent film star Wallace Reid, who died of a morphine overdose in 1923 at age 31. Remade twice, in 1954 and 1976. **111m/C VHS, Beta, LV.** Janet Gaynor, Fredric March, Adolphe Menjou, May Robson, Andy Devine, Lionel Stander, Franklin Pangborn; ***D:*** William A. Wellman; ***W:*** William A. Wellman, David O. Selznick, Dorothy Parker; ***C:*** William Howard Greene; ***M:*** Max Steiner. Academy Awards '37: Best Story; National Board of Review Awards '37: 10 Best Films of the Year; Nominations: Academy Awards '37: Best Actor (March), Best Actress (Gaynor), Best Director (Wellman), Best Picture, Best Screenplay. *CNG, NOS, VYY*

A Star is Born 🦴🦴🦴½ **1954 (PG)** Aging actor helps a young actress to fame. She becomes his wife, but alcoholism and failure are too much for him. She honors his memory. Remake of the 1937 classic was Garland's triumph, a superb and varied performance. Newly restored version reinstates over 20 minutes of long-missing footage, including three Garland musical numbers. ♫I'll Get By; You Took Advantage of me; Black Bottom; Peanut Vendor; My Melancholy Baby; Swanee; It's A New World; Gotta Have Me Go With You; Somewhere There's Someone. **175m/C VHS, Beta, LV.** Judy Garland, James Mason, Jack Carson, Tommy Noonan, Charles Bickford, Emerson Treacy, Charles Halton; ***D:*** George Cukor; ***C:*** Sam Leavitt. Golden Globe Awards '55: Best Actor—Musical/Comedy (Mason), Best Actress—Musical/Comedy (Garland); Nominations: Academy Awards '54: Best Actor (Mason), Best Actress (Garland), Best Art Direction/Set Decoration (Color), Best Costume Design (Color), Best Song ("The Man That Got Away"), Best Original Score. *WAR*

A Star is Born 🦴🦴 **1976 (R)** Miserable update of the 1937 and 1954 classics permitting Ms. Streisand to showcase her hit song "Evergreen." The tragic story of one rock star (the relentlessly unhip Streisand) on her way to the top and another (good old boy Kristofferson) whose career is in decline. Kristofferson is miscast, Streisand eventually numbing, but film may interest those looking into big-budget, big-star misfires. ♫Watch Closely Now; Spanish Lies; Hellacious Acres; With One More Look At You; Woman in the Moon; Queen Bee; Everything; Crippled Cow; I Believe in Love. **140m/C VHS, Beta.** Barbra Streisand, Kris Kristofferson, Paul Mazursky, Gary Busey, Sally Kirkland, Oliver Clark, Marta Heflin, Robert Englund; ***D:*** Frank Pierson; ***W:*** Frank Pierson, Joan Didion, John Gregory Dunne; ***C:*** Robert L. Surtees; ***M:*** Paul Williams. Academy Awards '76: Best Song ("Evergreen"); Golden Globe Awards '77: Best Actor—Musical/Comedy (Kristofferson), Best Actress—Musical/Comedy (Streisand), Best Film—Musical/Comedy, Best Song ("Evergreen"), Best Score; Nominations: Academy Awards '76: Best Cinematography, Best Sound, Best Original Score. *WAR*

The Star Maker 🦴🦴 *The Star Man; L'Uomo delle Stelle* **1995 (R)** Con man Joe Morelli (Castellitto) travels through the villages of 1950s Sicily claiming to be a movie talent scout. For a fee, he offers the locals a chance to shoot a screen test, which reveals various bits and pieces of their lives. There's a brief romance and Joe's scam eventually comes to light but the story's more nostalgia than narrative. Italian with subtitles. **113m/C VHS.** *IT* Sergio Castellitto, Tiziana Lodato; ***D:*** Giuseppe Tornatore; ***W:*** Giuseppe Tornatore, Fabio Rinaudo; ***C:*** Dante Spinotti; ***M:*** Ennio Morricone. Nominations: Academy Awards '95: Best Foreign Language Film. *NYR*

Star of Midnight 🦴🦴 **1935** A lawyer/detective becomes involved in the disappearance of the leading lady in a Broadway show and the murder of a columnist. Powell and Rogers take on characters similar to Nick and Nora Charles, but the pizazz of the "Thin Man" series is missing. **90m/B VHS, Beta, LV.** Ginger Rogers, William Powell, Paul Kelly; ***D:*** Stephen Roberts. *TTC*

The Star Packer 🦴🦴 **1934** Wayne puts on a marshal's badge, straightens out a gang of crooks, and still finds time for romance. Implausible and kind of dull early Wayne vehicle. **53m/B VHS, Beta.** John Wayne, George "Gabby" Hayes, Earl Dwire, Yakima Canutt; ***D:*** Robert North Bradbury. *COL, REP, NOS*

Star Quest 🦴 *Beyond the Rising Moon; Space 2074* **1989** A genetically engineered woman fights for freedom from her corporate creators. Mediocre effects and some pointless action; done much better by Ridley Scott in "Blade Runner." **90m/C VHS, Beta, LV.** Tracy Davis, Hans Bachman, Michael Mack; ***D:*** Phillip Cook. *NO*

Star Quest 🦴🦴½ **1994 (R)** Eight astronauts, suspended in a cryogenic sleep for nearly 100 years, awaken to find the human race has been destroyed by a nuclear holocaust. **95m/C VHS, LV.** Steven Bauer, Emma Samms, Alan Rachins, Brenda Bakke, Ming-Na Wen, Gregory McKinney, Cliff DeYoung; ***D:*** Rick Jacobson. *NHO*

Star Reporter 🦴½ **1939** A son takes over his father's newspaper when dad is killed by gangsters. The son uses the paper in an attempt to destroy the underworld, but stumbles on some startling personal information that could drastically backfire on him. Generally interesting plot, but has some implausibility and too-broad characterization. **62m/B VHS, Beta.** Warren Hull, Marsha Hunt, Morgan Wallace, Clay Clement, Wallis Clark, Virginia Howell, Paul Fix, Joseph Crehan; ***D:*** Howard Bretherton. *SNC*

Star Slammer 🦴½ **1987 (R)** A beautiful woman is unjustly sentenced to a brutal intergalactic prison ship. She leads the convicts to escape amid zany situations. Unevenly funny sci-fi comedy. **85m/C VHS, Beta, LV.** Ross Hagen, John Carradine, Sandy Brooke, Aldo Ray; ***D:*** Fred Olen Ray. *VMK*

Star Spangled Girl 🦴½ **1971 (G)** One of Neil Simon's lesser plays, one of his least movies. A pert, patriotic young lady captures the hearts of two left-wing alternative-newspaperguys next door; their political conflicts never rise above bland sitcom level. **94m/C VHS.** Sandy Duncan, Tony Roberts, Todd Susman, Elizabeth Allen; ***D:*** Jerry Paris; ***W:*** Neil Simon; ***C:*** Sam Leavitt; ***M:*** Charles Fox. *PAR*

Star Spangled Rhythm 🦴🦴🦴 **1942** Movie studio guard (Moore) has told his son (Bracken), a sailor, that he's actually the head of the studio in this WW2 musical/comedy. When he learns his son and his pals are coming for a visit, he enlists the aid of a friendly studio switchboard operator (Hutton) to pull a fast one. (Luckily, the real studio boss is out of town). Plot doesn't matter anyway since its just an excuse for a lot of studio stars to show up and perform. ♫A Sweater, a Sarong and a Peek-a-Boo Bang; That Old Black Magic; Hit the Road to Dreamland; Old Glory; On the Swing Shift; Doing It for Defense; Sharp as a Tack; He Loved Me Till the All-Clear Came. **99m/B VHS.** Betty Hutton, Eddie Bracken, Victor Moore, Bing Crosby, Ray Milland, Bob Hope, Veronica Lake, Dorothy Lamour, Susan Hayward, Dick Powell, Mary Martin, Alan Ladd, Paulette Goddard, Cecil B. DeMille, Arthur Treacher, Preston Sturges, Eddie Anderson, William Bendix; ***D:*** George Marshall. *MCA*

Star Time 🦴½ **1992** Henry is a mentally ill loser who wants to be as happy and famous as his favorite TV stars. Deciding to kill himself, Henry is stopped by the mysterious Sam Bones, who offers him TV stardom—at a steep price. Henry achieves his 15 minutes of fame as a serial killer and his only link to reality is a female social worker. **85m/C VHS.**

Michael St. Gerard, John P. Ryan, Maureen Teefy; ***D:*** Alexander Cassini; ***W:*** Alexander Cassini. *MNC*

Star Trek: The Motion Picture ☊☊½ **1980 (G)** The Enterprise fights a strange alien force that threatens Earth in this first film adaptation of the famous television series. Very slow moving; followed by numerous sequels. Twelve additional minutes of previously unseen footage have been added to this home video version of the theatrical feature. The laserdisc edition offers the film in widescreen format. **143m/C VHS, Beta, LV.** William Shatner, Leonard Nimoy, DeForest Kelley, James Doohan, Stephen Collins, Persis Khambatta, Nichelle Nichols, Walter Koenig, George Takei; ***D:*** Robert Wise; ***M:*** Jerry Goldsmith. Nominations: Academy Awards '79: Best Art Direction/Set Decoration, Best Original Score. *PAR*

Star Trek 2: The Wrath of Khan ☊☊☊ **1982 (PG)** Picking up from the 1967 Star Trek episode "Space Seed," Admiral James T. Kirk and the crew of the Enterprise must battle Khan, an old foe out for revenge. Warm and comradly in the nostalgic mode of its successors. Introduced Kirk's former lover and unknown son to the series plot, as well as Mr. Spock's "death," which led to the next sequel (1984's "The Search for Spock"). Can be seen in widescreen format on laserdisc. **113m/C VHS, Beta, LV, 8mm.** William Shatner, Leonard Nimoy, Ricardo Montalban, DeForest Kelley, Nichelle Nichols, James Doohan, George Takei, Walter Koenig, Kirstie Alley, Merritt Butrick, Paul Winfield; ***D:*** Nicholas Meyer; ***M:*** James Horner. *PAR*

Star Trek 3: The Search for Spock ☊☊½ **1984 (PG)** Captain Kirk hijacks the USS Enterprise and commands the aging crew to go on a mission to the Genesis Planet to discover whether Mr. Spock still lives (supposedly he died in the last movie). Klingons threaten, as usual. Somewhat slow and humorless, but intriguing. Third in the series of six (so far) Star Trek movies. The laserdisc edition carries the film in widescreen format. **105m/C VHS, Beta, LV, 8mm.** William Shatner, Leonard Nimoy, DeForest Kelley, James Doohan, George Takei, Walter Koenig, Mark Lenard, Robin Curtis, Merritt Butrick, Christopher Lloyd, Judith Anderson, John Larroquette, James B. Sikking, Nichelle Nichols, Cathie Shirriff, Miguel Ferrer, Grace Lee Whitney; ***D:*** Leonard Nimoy; ***W:*** Harve Bennett; ***M:*** James Horner. *PAR*

Star Trek 4: The Voyage Home ☊☊☊ **1986 (PG)** Kirk and the gang go back in time (to the 1980s, conveniently) to save the Earth of the future from destruction. Filled with hilarious moments and exhilarating action; great special effects enhance the timely conservation theme. Watch for the stunning going-back-in-time sequence. Spock is particularly funny as he tries to fit in and learn the 80s lingo! Can be seen in widescreen format on laserdisc. Also available as part of Paramount's "director's series," in which Nimoy discusses various special effects aspects in the making of the film. The best in the six-part (so far) series. **119m/C VHS, Beta, LV, 8mm.** William Shatner, DeForest Kelley, Catherine Hicks, James Doohan, Nichelle Nichols, George Takei, Walter Koenig, Mark Lenard, Leonard Nimoy; ***D:*** Leonard Nimoy; ***W:*** Nicholas Meyer, Harve Bennett. Nominations: Academy Awards '86: Best Cinematography, Best Sound, Best Original Score. *PAR*

Star Trek 5: The Final Frontier ☊½ **1989 (PG)** A renegade Vulcan kidnaps the Enterprise and takes it on a journey to the mythic center of the universe. Shatner's big-action directorial debut (he also co-wrote the script) is a poor follow-up to the Nimoy-directed fourth entry in the series. Heavy-handed and pretentiously pseudo-theological. Available in widescreen format on laserdisc. **107m/C VHS, Beta, LV, 8mm.** William Shatner, Leonard Nimoy, DeForest Kelley, James Doohan, Laurence Luckinbill, Walter Koenig, George Takei, Nichelle Nichols, David Warner; ***D:*** William Shatner; ***W:*** William Shatner; ***M:*** Jerry Goldsmith. Golden Raspberry Awards '89: Worst Picture, Worst Actor (Shatner), Worst Director (Shatner). *PAR*

Star Trek 6: The Undiscovered Country ☊☊½ **1991 (PG)** The final chapter in the long running Star Trek series is finally here. The Federation and the Klingon Empire are preparing a much-needed peace summit but Captain Kirk has his doubts about the true intentions of the Federation's longtime enemies. When a Klingon ship is attacked, Kirk and the crew of the Enterprise, who are accused of the misdeed, must try to find the real perpetrator. Has an exciting, climactic ending. As is typical of the series, the film highlights current events—glasnost—in its plotlines. Meyer also directed Star Trek movie 2 ("The Wrath of Khan") and wrote the screenplay for 4 ("The Voyage Home"). **110m/C VHS, Beta, CD-I.** William Shatner, Leonard Nimoy, DeForest Kelley, James Doohan, George Takei, Walter Koenig, Nichelle Nichols, Christopher Plummer, Kim Cattrall, Iman, David Warner, Mark Lenard, Grace Lee Whitney, Brock Peters, Kurtwood Smith, Rosana De Soto, John Schuck, Michael Dorn; ***D:*** Nicholas Meyer; ***W:*** Nicholas Meyer, Denny Martin Flinn; ***M:*** Cliff Eidelman. Nominations: Academy Awards '91: Best Makeup. *PAR*

Star Trek Bloopers **1969** The television cast of "Star Trek" appears in these flubs and goofs that were edited out of the actual episodes. The blooper reels from all three seasons are included on this tape. **25m/C VHS, Beta.** William Shatner, Leonard Nimoy, DeForest Kelley, Nichelle Nichols, James Doohan, George Takei, Walter Koenig, Frank Gorshin. *MOV*

Star Trek Deep Space Nine: Emissary **1993** The second "Star Trek" spinoff, following "The Next Generation," finds Federation Commander Benjamin Sisko (Brooks) arriving at the space station, which orbits the planet Bajor. Bajor has just undergone a war of independence against the Cardassians, who have left both the planet and the station in a devastated condition. Sisko, naturally, must find a way to deal with a variety of unpleasant situations, crew, and station residents. The TV pilot is available as part of a boxed set; additional episodes are also available. **92m/C VHS, Beta.** Avery Brooks, Colm Meaney, Rene Auberjonois, Nana Visitor, Terry Farrell, Alexander Siddig, Armin Shimerman, Cirroc Lofton. *PAR*

Star Trek Generations ☊☊☊ **1994 (PG)** The sci-fi phenomena continues with the first film spun off from the recently departed "Star Trek: The Next Generation" TV series and the seventh following the adventures of the Enterprise crew. Captain Kirk is propelled into the future thanks to an explosion and manages to hook up with current starship captain, Picard. Of course, just in time to save the galaxy from the latest space loon, the villainous Dr. Soren (McDowell), renegade Klingons, and your basic mysterious space entity. For comic relief, android Data gets an emotion chip. Terrific special effects (courtesy of Industrial Light and Magic) and yes, the heroic Kirk receives his mandatory grandiose death scene. Other original characters making a brief appearance are Scotty and Chekov. An entertaining romp through time and space. **117m/C VHS, Beta.** William Shatner, Patrick Stewart, Malcolm McDowell, Whoopi Goldberg, Jonathon Frakes, Brent Spiner, LeVar Burton, Michael Dorn, Gates McFadden, Marina Sirtis, James Doohan, Walter Koenig, Alan Ruck; ***D:*** David Carson; ***W:*** Ronald D. Moore, Brannon Braga; ***M:*** Dennis McCarthy. *PAR*

Star Trek: The Cage **1965** This cult series only ran from 1966-1969 but it's impact has been lasting. Join Captain Kirk and the crew of the starship Enterprise on its voyages of discovery. Additional episodes available. In this original pilot episode for the series Captain Chris Pike of the Enterprise faces the challenge of his life when he is captured by the telepathic aliens of Talos IV. Never telecast in its original form and later edited to form the flashback sequences of the two-part episode "Menagerie." Some portions are in black and white. Version was long believed to be lost, but was reconstituted from original color footage. **73m/C VHS, Beta, LV.** Jeffrey Hunter, Leonard Nimoy, Susan Oliver, Majel Barrett, Meg Wyllie, John Hoyt, Gene Roddenberry; ***D:*** Robert Butler. *PAR, MOV*

Star Trek the Next Generation: Encounter at Farpoint **1987** Roddenberry, the creator of the original "Star Trek" television series, spearheaded this episodic reincarnation for network syndication. Set 80 or so years beyond the original, with an entirely new crew and a modernized vessel, it places less emphasis on violent solutions to conflicts than the original TV series. In this first installment, a powerful life force named "Q" threatens the lives of Captain Picard and his crew as they attempt to figure out what's going on at Farpoint Station. Look for a cameo by Kelley, "Bones" from the original series, as a very old man waxing nostalgic about the old U.S.S. Enterprise. Excellent production values, including fine special effects. Additional episodes available. **96m/C VHS, LV.** Patrick Stewart, Michael Dorn, Jonathon Frakes, Gates McFadden, Marina Sirtis, Denise Crosby, Brent Spiner, Wil Wheaton, LeVar Burton; ***Cameos:*** DeForest Kelley; ***W:*** Gene Roddenberry. *PAR, MOV*

Star Trek the Next Generation, the Final Episode: All Good Things... **1994** Since Q (de Lancie) was there to cause trouble in the first series episode, it seems only fitting that he's up to his usual tricks in the finale. A spatial anomaly has Picard time-traveling between past, present, and future with the very fate of humanity resting on his shoulders—and Q around to tell him that everyone's doomed. **92m/C VHS, Beta.** Patrick Stewart, LeVar Burton, Brent Spiner, Marina Sirtis, Jonathon Frakes, Gates McFadden, Michael Dorn, John de Lancie, Denise Crosby, Colm Meaney, Andreas Katsulas; ***D:*** Winrich Kolbe; ***W:*** Ronald D. Moore, Brannon Braga. *PAR*

Star Trek 25th Anniversary Special **1991** Shatner and Nimoy are joined by other members of the original series as well as cast from "Star Trek: The Next Generation" in this tribute to the enduring popularity of the television/film series. Includes commentary by "Star Trek" creator Gene Roddenberry, highlights from the films and both television series, bloopers, and a behind-the-scenes look at "Star Trek VI: The Undiscovered Country." **100m/C VHS, Beta.** Gene Roddenberry. *PAR*

Star Trek Voyager: Caretaker **1995** The third TV spinoff from the franchise sci-fi series features the 24th century adventures of Captain Kathryn Janeway (Mulgrew) and the USS Voyager. In the pilot episode, the crew is searching for Maquis rebels in an area of space known as the Badlands when the ship is mysteriously tossed 70,000 lightyears across the galaxy. The Voyager does find the Maquis ship, as well as an alien named Nelix (Phillips) and a planet run by a force called the Caretaker, whose inhabitants all live underground. This episode is currently available only as part of "The Captains Collection," a four-tape set. **92m/C VHS.** Kate Mulgrew, Robert Beltran, Robert Picardo, Ethan Phillips, Roxann Biggs-Dawson, Robert Duncan McNeill, Tim Russ, Jennifer Lien, Garrett Wang; ***D:*** Winrich Kolbe. *PAR*

Star Wars ☊☊☊☊ **1977 (PG)** First entry Lucas's "Star Wars" trilogy proved to be one of the biggest box-office hits of all time. A young hero, a captured princess, a hot-shot pilot, cute robots, a vile villain, and a heroic and mysterious Jedi knight blend together with marvelous special effects in a fantasy tale about rebel forces engaged in a life or death struggle with the tyrant leaders of the Galactic Empire. Set a new cinematic standard for realistic special effects, making many pre-"Star Wars" effects seem almost laughable in retrospect. Followed by "The Empire Strikes Back" (1980) and "Return of the Jedi" (1983). **121m/C VHS, Beta, LV.** Mark Hamill, Carrie Fisher, Harrison Ford, Alec Guinness, Peter Cushing, Kenny Baker, James Earl Jones, David Prowse, Anthony Daniels; ***D:*** George Lucas; ***W:*** George Lucas; ***M:*** John Williams. Academy Awards '77: Best Art Direction/Set Decoration, Best Costume Design, Best Film Editing, Best Sound, Best Visual Effects, Best Original Score; Golden Globe Awards '78: Best Score; Los Angeles Film Critics Association Awards '77: Best Film; National Board of Review Awards '77: 10 Best Films of the Year; People's Choice Awards '78: Best Film; Nominations: Academy Awards '77: Best Director (Lucas), Best Original Screenplay, Best Picture, Best Supporting Actor (Guinness). *FOX, RDG, HMV*

Starbird and Sweet William ꝏꝏ **1973 (G)** On a solo plane flight, a young Native American crashes in the wilderness. He must fight for survival in the harsh woods with his only friend, a bear cub. Good family fare. **95m/C VHS.** A. Martinez, Louise Fitch, Dan Haggerty, Skip Homeier; ***D:*** Jack B. Hively. *NO*

Starchaser: The Legend of Orin ꝏꝏ½ **1985 (PG)** Animated fantasy about a boy who must save the world of the future from malevolent hordes. **107m/C VHS, Beta, LV.** ***D:*** Steven Hahn; ***M:*** Andrew Belling. *PAR*

Stardust Memories ꝏꝏ½ **1980 (PG)** Allen's "8 1/2." A comic filmmaker is plagued with creative blocks, relationships, modern fears and fanatical fans. The last film in Allen's varying self-analysis, with explicit references to Fellini and Antonioni. **88m/B VHS, Beta, LV.** Woody Allen, Charlotte Rampling, Jessica Harper, Marie-Christine Barrault, Tony Roberts, Helen Hanft, Cynthia Gibb, Amy Wright, Daniel Stern; ***D:*** Woody Allen; ***W:*** Woody Allen; ***C:*** Gordon Willis. *MGM, FOX*

The Starfighters ꝏ½ **1963** Air Force Lieutenant Dornan must prove his courage to his disapproving war hero Congressman father. Dornan flies his F-104 through a dangerous storm, thereby earning his father's respect, which leads them to form a bond. **84m/C VHS, Beta.** Robert Dornan, Richard Jordahl, Shirley Olmstead. *NO*

Starflight One ꝏꝏ **1983** A space shuttle is called on to save the world's first hypersonic airliner trapped in an orbit above earth. Also called "Starflight: The Plane That Couldn't Land." The film features good special effects, but also a predictable "rescue-mission" plot. **155m/C VHS, Beta.** Ray Milland, Lee Majors, Hal Linden, Lauren Hutton, Robert Webber, Terry Kiser; ***D:*** Jerry Jameson. *LIV, VES*

Stargate ꝏꝏ **1994 (PG-13)** U.S. military probe of a ring-shaped ancient Egyptian artifact (your tax dollars at work) sends he-man colonel Russell and geeky Egyptologist Spader into a parallel universe. There they meet the builders of the pyramids who are enslaved by an evil despot (Davidson) posing as a sun god. Ambitious premise zapped from prepubescent imaginations gets an A for effort, but a silly plot that jumbles biblical epic panoramas and space odyssey special effects with otherworldly mysticism and needless emotional hang-ups trade shlock for style. Spader's shaggy scholar is neurotically fun, Russell's jarhead a bore, and Davidson's vampy villain an unintended hoot. **119m/C VHS, LV.** Kurt Russell, James Spader, Jaye Davidson, Viveca Lindfors, Alexis Cruz, Leon Rippy, John Diehl, Erik Avari, Mili Avital; ***D:*** Roland Emmerich; ***W:*** Dean Devlin, Roland Emmerich; ***C:*** Jeff Okun. *LIV*

Starhops ꝏ½ **1978 (R)** A trio of buxom young women attract business to their drive-in restaurant by wearing skimpy outfits. Surprisingly inoffensive for an "R" rating. **92m/C VHS.** Dorothy Buhrman, Sterling Frazier, Jillian Kesner, Peter Paul Liapis, Paul Ryan, Anthony Mannino, Dick Miller; ***D:*** Barbara Peeters; ***W:*** Stephanie Rothman. *NO*

Stark ꝏ½ **1985** Wichita detective journeys to Las Vegas in an effort to locate his missing sister. During his search, he finds himself taking on the mob. A television pilot for a series that never happened, and Tidyman's last screenplay. A sequel "Stark: Mirror Image," was made in 1986. **94m/C VHS, Beta.** Nicolas Surovy, Dennis Hopper, Marilu Henner, Seth Jaffe; ***D:*** Rod Holcomb; ***W:*** Ernest Tidyman. *FOX*

Starlight Hotel ꝏꝏ½ **1990 (PG)** An unhappy teenage girl sets off to find her father, with the help of a shellshocked veteran wrongly accused of a crime. Set in New Zealand during the Depression. Lovely scenery and good acting highlight nice story of odd friendship. **90m/C VHS, LV.** *NZ* Greer Robson, Peter Phelps, Marshall Napier, Pat Smythe, Alice Fraser; ***D:*** Sam Pillsbury. *REP*

Starman ꝏꝏꝏ **1984 (PG)** An alien from an advanced civilization lands in Wisconsin. He hides beneath the guise of a grieving young widow's recently deceased husband. He then makes her drive him across country to rendezvous with his spacecraft so he can return home. Well-acted, interesting twist on the "Stranger in a Strange Land" theme. Bridges is fun as the likeable starman; Allen is lovely and earthy in her worthy follow-up to "Raiders of the Lost Ark." Available in widescreen format on laserdisc. **115m/C VHS, Beta, LV.** Jeff Bridges, Karen Allen, Charles Martin Smith, Richard Jaeckel; ***D:*** John Carpenter; ***W:*** Bruce A. Evans, Raynold Gideon; ***C:*** Donald M. Morgan; ***M:*** Jack Nitzsche. Nominations: Academy Awards '84: Best Actor (Bridges). *COL*

Starring Bugs Bunny! **1948** Bug Bunny teams up with Yosemite Sam and others in some of these great hits. Friz Freleng's "Buccaneer Bunny" and "Hare Force," as well as Chuck Jones' "Hare Tonic." **54m/C VHS.** ***D:*** Isadore "Friz" Freleng, Chuck Jones, Robert McKimson. *MGM, WTA*

Stars and Bars ꝏꝏ **1988 (R)** O'Connor misfire strands Day-Lewis in the midst of hillbillies. A stuffy English art expert travels from New York to Georgia to price a Renoir, and happens on a bizarre backwoods family marginally run by Stanton. Stereotypical pursuit of humor teeters precariously on the edge of black comedy without actually being funny. Stinky script dooms fine cast to just acting weird in a "Deliverance" sort of way. Based on the novel by William Boyd. **95m/C VHS, Beta, LV.** Daniel Day-Lewis, Harry Dean Stanton, John Cusack, Joan Cusack, Spalding Gray, Will Patton, Martha Plimpton, Glenne Headly, Laurie Metcalf, Maury Chaykin; ***D:*** Pat O'Connor; ***W:*** William Boyd. *COL*

Stars and Stripes Forever ꝏꝏꝏ *Marching Along* **1952** Sumptious, Hollywoodized bio of composer John Phillip Sousa, based on his memoir "Marching Along," but more concerned with the romantic endeavors of young protege Wagner. Accuracy aside, it's solid entertainment even if you're not mad about march music. ♫Stars and Stripes Forever; El Capitan; Washington Post; King Cotton; The Battle Hymn of the Republic; Dixie; Light Cavalry; Turkey in the Straw; Hail to the Chief. **89m/C VHS.** Clifton Webb, Debra Paget, Robert Wagner, Ruth Hussey, Finlay Currie; ***D:*** Henry Koster. *FXV, FCT*

The Stars Fell on Henrietta ꝏꝏ½ **1994 (PG)** Down-on-his-luck wildcatter Mr. Cox (Duvall) searches for oil and redemption. He's looking for it on the failing farm of couple Don and Cora Day (Quinn and Fisher) in the middle of the 1930's Texas dustbowl with the reluctant backing of more successful oil man (Dennehy). Quiet character study of an obsessed wheeler-dealer playing with his last poker chip verges on the romantic in its quest for black gold, true to its message about never giving up hope. Directorial debut for Keach is led by typically excellent portrayals by Duvall and Dennehy, but Quinn and Fisher are given little to work with. Marks the first movie Clint Eastwood's Malpaso company has produced in which he didn't star or direct since "Ratboy." **110m/C VHS.** Robert Duvall, Aidan Quinn, Frances Fisher, Brian Dennehy, Lexi Randall, Kaytlyn Knowles, Francesca Ruth Eastwood; ***D:*** James Keach; ***W:*** Philip Railsback; ***C:*** Bruce Surtees; ***M:*** David Benoit. *WAR*

Stars in My Crown ꝏꝏꝏ **1950** McCrea provides a moving performance as the pistol-wielding preacher who helps the residents of a 19th-century small town battle a typhoid epidemic and KKK terrorism. Adapted from the novel by Joe David Brown. **89m/B VHS.** Joel McCrea, Ellen Drew, Dean Stockwell, Alan Hale, Lewis Stone, Amanda Blake, Juano Hernandez, Charles Kemper, Connie Gilchrist, Ed Begley Sr., James Arness, Jack Lambert, Arthur Hunnicutt; ***D:*** Jacques Tourneur; ***W:*** Margaret Fitts; ***M:*** Adolph Deutsch. *MGM*

The Stars Look Down ꝏꝏꝏ **1939** A mine owner forces miners to work in unsafe conditions in a Welsh town and disaster strikes. Redgrave is a miner's son running for office, hoping to improve conditions, and to escape the hard life. Forceful, well-directed effort suffered at the box office, in competition with John Ford's similar classic "How Green Was My Valley." From the novel by A.J. Cronin. **96m/B VHS, Beta.** *GB* Michael Redgrave, Margaret Lockwood, Emlyn Williams, Cecil Parker; ***D:*** Carol Reed. National Board of Review Awards '41: 10 Best Films of the Year. *NOS, HHT, CAB*

Starship ꝏ *Lorca and the Outlaws* **1987 (PG)** British sci-fi seems to be an oxymoron. To wit, this lame "Star Wars" ripoff is about human slaves on a planet run by evil robots. **91m/C VHS, Beta.** *GB* John Tarrant, Cassandra Webb, Donough Rees, Deep Roy, Ralph Cotterill; ***D:*** Roger Christian. *HHE*

Starship Invasions ꝏ **1977 (PG)** Lee leads a group of bad aliens seeking to take over the Earth. He's thwarted by UFO expert Vaughn, who is aided by a group of good aliens. Cheesy special effects have this one looking like a bad sci-fi serial from the '40s. **89m/C VHS.** *CA* Christopher Lee, Robert Vaughn, Daniel Pilon, Helen Shaver, Henry Ramer, Victoria (Vicki) Johnson; ***D:*** Edward Hunt; ***W:*** Edward Hunt. *WAR*

Starstruck ꝏꝏ½ **1982 (PG)** Fun-loving folly about a teen who tries to help his talented cousin make it as a singer. Playfully tweeks Hollywood musicals. Enjoyable and fun. **95m/C VHS.** *AU* Jo Kennedy, Ross O'Donovan, Pat Evison; ***D:*** Gillian Armstrong. *FXL*

Start the Revolution Without Me ꝏꝏꝏ **1970 (PG)** Hilarious, Moliere-esque farce about two sets of identical twins (Wilder and Sutherland) separated at birth, who meet 30 years later, just before the French Revolution. About as hammy as they come; Wilder is unforgettable. Neglected when released, but now deservedly a cult favorite. **91m/C VHS, Beta.** Gene Wilder, Donald Sutherland, Orson Welles, Hugh Griffith, Jack MacGowran, Billie Whitelaw, Victor Spinetti, Ewa Aulin; ***D:*** Bud Yorkin; ***W:*** Lawrence J. Cohen; ***M:*** John Addison. *WAR*

Starting Over ꝏꝏꝏ **1979 (R)** His life racked by divorce, Phil Potter learns what it's like to be single, self-sufficient, and lonely once again. When a blind date grows into a serious affair, the romance is temporarily halted by his hang-up for his ex-wife. Enjoyable love-triangle comedy loses direction after a while, but Reynolds is subtle and charming, and Bergen good as his ex, a very bad songwriter. Based on a novel by Dan Wakefield. **106m/C VHS, Beta, LV.** Burt Reynolds, Jill Clayburgh, Candice Bergen, Frances Sternhagen, Austin Pendleton, Mary Kay Place, Kevin Bacon, Daniel Stern; ***D:*** Alan J. Pakula; ***W:*** James L. Brooks; ***C:*** Sven Nykvist; ***M:*** Marvin Hamlisch. Nominations: Academy Awards '79: Best Actress (Clayburgh), Best Supporting Actress (Bergen). *PAR*

Starvengers **1982** Animated adventures with action and excitement meeting futuristic technology, resulting in the high-powered super-intelligence of the robot Starvenger. **105m/C VHS, Beta.** *JP FUS, WTA, FHE*

State Department File 649 ꝏ½ **1949** Insipid spy drama set in northern China. Mongolian rebels hold U.S. agent Lundigan captive; he hopes to capture a Chinese warlord. **87m/C VHS, Beta.** Virginia Bruce, William Lundigan; ***D:*** Sam Newfield. *SNC, NOS, DVT*

State Fair ꝏꝏꝏ *It Happened One Summer* **1945** The second version of the glossy slice of Americana about a family at the Iowa State Fair, featuring plenty of great songs by Rodgers and Hammerstein. Adapted from the 1933 screen version of Phil Stong's novel. Remade again in 1962. ♫It Might as Well Be Spring; It's a Grand Night for Singing; That's For Me; Isn't It Kinda Fun?; All I Owe Iowa; Our State Fair. **100m/C VHS, Beta.** Charles Winninger, Jeanne Crain, Dana Andrews, Vivian Blaine, Dick Haymes, Fay Bainter, Frank McHugh, Percy Kilbride, Donald Meek, William Marshall, Harry (Henry) Morgan; ***D:*** Walter Lang; ***W:*** Oscar Hammerstein; ***C:*** Leon Shamroy; ***M:*** Richard Rodgers, Oscar Hammerstein. Academy Awards '45: Best Song ("It Might as Well Be Spring"); Nominations: Academy Awards '45: Best Original Score. *FOX*

State Fair ꝏꝏ **1962** The third film version of the story of a farm family who travel to their yearly state fair and experience life. The original songs are still there, but otherwise this is a letdown. Texas setting required dropping the song "All I Owe Iowa." ♫Our State Fair; It's a Grand Night for Singing; That's for Me; It Might as Well Be Spring; Isn't It Kinda Fun?; More Than Just a Friend; It's the Little Things in Texas; Willing and Eager; This Isn't Heaven. **118m/C**

VHS, Beta. Pat Boone, Ann-Margret, Bobby Darin, Tom Ewell, Alice Faye, Pamela Tiffin, Wally Cox; ***D:*** Jose Ferrer; ***C:*** William Mellor. *FOX*

State of Emergency 🦴🦴½ **1994 (R)** John Novelli (Mantegna) is a cynical, overworked emergency-room doctor for an over-crowded, under-equipped big-city hospital. His latest casualty is a head trauma case the hospital is ill-prepared to handle and as the patient's condition worsens both doctor and hospital are put at risk. Made for television. **97m/C VHS, LV.** Joe Mantegna, Lynn Whitfield, Paul Dooley; ***D:*** Lesli Linka Glatter; ***W:*** Susan Black, Dr. Lance Gentile. *HBO*

State of Grace 🦴🦴🦴 **1990 (R)** Irish hood Penn returns to old NYC neighborhood as undercover cop and becomes involved with an Irish Westies mob in a fight for survival as urban renewal encroaches on their Hell's Kitchen turf. Shrinking client base for shakedown schemes and protection rackets forces them to become contract killers for the Italian mafia. Fine performances, with Penn tense but restrained, gang honcho Harris intense, and Oldman chewing up gritty urban scenery as psycho brother of Harris, but the story is long and meandering. Well-choreographed violence. **134m/C VHS, LV.** Sean Penn, Ed Harris, Gary Oldman, Robin Wright, John Turturro, Burgess Meredith, John C. Reilly; ***D:*** Phil Joanou; ***W:*** Dennis McIntyre; ***M:*** Ennio Morricone. *ORI*

State of Siege 🦴🦴🦴 *Etat de Siege* **1973** Third pairing of Montand and Costa-Gavras, about the real-life death of USAID employee Daniel Mitrione, suspected to be involved in torture and murder in Uruguay in the '60s. Quietly suspenseful, with snazzy editing; conspiracy-theory premise is similar to Stone's "JFK," and similarly disturbing, whether you believe it or not. Dubbed. **119m/C VHS, Beta, LV.** *FR* Yves Montand, Renato Salvatori, O.E. Hasse, Jacques Perrin; ***D:*** Constantin Costa-Gavras. *COL, INJ*

State of the Union 🦴🦴🦴½ *The World and His Wife* **1948** Liberal multimillionaire Tracy is seeking the Republican presidential nomination. His estranged wife (Hepburn) is asked to return so they can masquerade as a loving couple for the sake of his political career. Hepburn tries to help Tracy, as the backstage political machinations erode his personal convictions. Adapted from a highly successful, topical Broadway play; the writers changed dialogue constantly to reflect the news. Capra and his partners at Liberty Pictures originally hoped to cast Gary Cooper and Claudette Colbert. Hepburn and Menjou were at odds politically (over communist witch hunts in Hollywood) but are fine together onscreen. **124m/B VHS, Beta, LV.** Spencer Tracy, Katharine Hepburn, Angela Lansbury, Van Johnson, Adolphe Menjou, Lewis Stone, Howard Smith; ***D:*** Frank Capra. *MCA*

State of Things 🦴🦴🦴 **1982** Ostensibly a mystery involving a film crew trying to remake a B-movie, "The Most Dangerous Man On Earth," but also an in-depth look at the process of filmmaking, a scathing look at nuclear warfare and an homage to Roger Corman and Hollywood at large. An enigmatic, complex film from Wenders prior to his American years. In German with English subtitles; some dialogue in English. **120m/B VHS, Beta, LV.** *GE* Patrick Bauchau, Allen (Goorwitz) Garfield, Isabelle Weingarten, Viva, Samuel Fuller, Paul Getty III, Roger Corman; ***D:*** Wim Wenders. Venice Film Festival '82: Best Film. *GLV, INJ*

Stateline Motel 🦴½ *Last Chance For a Born Loser* **1975 (R)** Cheap Italian ripoff of "The Postman Always Rings Twice," with a surprise ending but little of great interest. **86m/C VHS, Beta.** *IT* Eli Wallach, Ursula Andress, Fabio Testi, Barbara Bach; ***D:*** Maurizio Lucidi. *NO*

State's Attorney 🦴🦴½ *Cardigan's Last Case* **1931** A burned-out attorney finds himself falling in love with the least likely person, a prostitute he is defending. Contrived, improbable story succumbs to star-quality lead acting from Barrymore. Remade in 1937 with Lee Tracy as "Criminal Lawyer." **79m/B VHS, Beta.** John Barrymore, Jill Esmond, William "Stage" Boyd, Helen Twelvetrees; ***D:*** George Archainbaud; ***M:*** Max Steiner. *TTC*

Static 🦴🦴½ **1987 (PG-13)** A strange, disquieting independent film about an eccentric youth who claims to have built a machine through which one can see heaven. Uneven, with some dull stretches. **89m/C VHS, Beta, LV.** Keith Gordon, Amanda Plummer, Bob Gunton, Jane Hoffman, Barton Heyman, Lily Knight; ***D:*** Mark Romanek; ***W:*** Keith Gordon, Mark Romanek. *MCG*

Station 🦴🦴½ **1981** A Japanese detective's love affair is corrupted by his ruthless search for a bloodthirsty cop killer. With English subtitles. **130m/C VHS, Beta.** *JP* Ken Takakura, Chieko Baisho; ***D:*** Yasuo Furuhata. *NO*

The Station 🦴🦴 **1992** A sophisticated woman, who has just abandoned her fiancee, waits in a tiny station for an early train. The only person around is the young and ordinary stationmaster. Gradually the two are drawn together in a number of charming and comic romantic fantasies. In Italian with English subtitles. **92m/C VHS.** *IT* Margherita Buy, Ennio Fantastichini; ***D:*** Sergio Rubini; ***W:*** Sergio Rubini. *FXL*

Station West 🦴🦴🦴 **1948** A disguised Army officer is sent to uncover a mystery of hijackers and murderers. Along the way, he meets up with and falls for a beautiful woman who may be involved in the treachery. Good, solid western with a fine cast and plenty of fun action shot against the requisite beautiful western landscapes. Based on the Luke Short story. Also available colorized. **92m/B VHS, Beta.** Dick Powell, Jane Greer, Agnes Moorehead, Burl Ives, Tom Powers, Raymond Burr; ***D:*** Sidney Lanfield. *CCB, TTC*

The Stationmaster's Wife 🦴🦴½ **1977** In Germay's Weimar Republic a provincial stationmaster's wife expresses her boredom with her pleasant ineffectual husband by having numerous meaningless affairs. Meant to invoke postwar German dread and the fake bourgeois morality which covered political and social resentments. Originally shown as a 200-minute miniseries for German television. In German with English subtitles. **111m/C VHS.** *GE* Elisabeth Trissenaar, Kurt Raab, Gustal Bayrhammer, Bernard Helfrich, Udo Kier, Volker Spengler; ***D:*** Rainer Werner Fassbinder; ***W:*** Rainer Werner Fassbinder; ***C:*** Michael Ballhaus; ***M:*** Peer Raben. *NYF, FCT*

The Statue 🦴 **1971 (R)** Famed sculptress unveils a nude rendering of her Nobel Prize-winning husband. Much hilarity in the British vein is meant to ensue, but doesn't. Niven is OK, but this empty, plotless farce should have been much shorter. **84m/C VHS, Beta.** *GB* David Niven, Virna Lisi, Robert Vaughn, Ann Bell, John Cleese; ***D:*** Rod Amateau. *PSM*

Stavisky 🦴🦴🦴 **1974** Sumptuously lensed story of Serge Stavisky, a con-artist and bon-vivant whose machinations almost brought down the French government when his corruption was exposed in 1934. Belmondo makes as charismatic an antihero as you could find. Excellent score complements the visuals. In French with English subtitles. **117m/C VHS.** Jean-Paul Belmondo, Anny Duperey, Charles Boyer, Francois Perier, Gerard Depardieu; ***D:*** Alain Resnais; ***M:*** Stephen Sondheim. New York Film Critics Awards '74: Best Supporting Actor (Boyer); Nominations: Cannes Film Festival '74: Best Film. *INJ, INT*

Stay As You Are 🦴½ **1978** Aging French architect Mastroianni has designs on a teenager who may be his illegitimate daughter from an earlier affair. **95m/C VHS, Beta.** *FR* Marcello Mastroianni, Nastassia Kinski, Francesco Rabal; ***D:*** Alberto Lattuada. *WAR, OM*

Stay Awake 🦴 **1987 (R)** A demon stalks, haunts and tortures eight young girls sleeping together at a secluded Catholic school. Title might be addressed to the viewer, who will be tempted to snooze. **90m/C VHS, Beta, LV.** *SA* Shirley Jane Harris, Tanya Gordon, Jayne Hutton, Heath Porter; ***D:*** John Bernard. *SUE, NLC*

Stay Away, Joe 🦴 **1968 (PG)** The King is a singing half-breed rodeo star who returns to his reservation where he finds love and trouble. Utterly cliche, embarrassing, and stupid even by Elvis-movie standards. **98m/C VHS, Beta.** Elvis Presley, Burgess Meredith, Joan Blondell, Thomas Gomez, L.Q. Jones, Katy Jurado, Henry Jones; ***D:*** Peter Tewkesbury. *MGM*

Stay Hungry 🦴🦴🦴 **1976 (R)** A wealthy southerner (Bridges) is involved in a real estate deal which depends on the sale of a gym where a number of body builders hang out. He becomes immersed in their world and finds himself in love with the working-class Field. Big Arnold's first speaking role in his own inimitable accent (his first role in "Hercules in New York" was dubbed.) Offbeat and occasionally uneven comedy-drama based on a novel by Charles Gaines is a sleeper. **102m/C VHS, Beta, LV.** Jeff Bridges, Sally Field, Arnold Schwarzenegger, Robert Englund, Scatman Crothers; ***D:*** Bob Rafelson; ***W:*** Bob Rafelson. *MGM, FOX*

Stay Tuned 🦴 **1992 (PG-13)** Suburban yuppie couple buys a large-screen TV and satellite dish from Hellvision salesman, are sucked into their dish, and wind up starring in hellish TV shows such as "Wayne's Underworld," "Northern Overexposure," "Sadistic Home Videos," and "My Three Sons of Bitches." If they can survive for 24 hours, they'll be able to return to their normal lives. Clever idea for a film is wasted as this one never really gets off the ground; viewers may not want to stay tuned to the low comedy and frantic yucks. **90m/C VHS, LV.** John Ritter, Pam Dawber, Jeffrey Jones, Eugene Levy, David Tom, Heather McComb; ***D:*** Peter Hyams; ***W:*** Tom S. Parker; ***M:*** Bruce Broughton. *WAR*

Stay Tuned for Murder 🦴½ **1988** A sexy news reporter gets caught in a web of financial wrongdoings and corruption. The financiers, lawyers, and other sinister types she's investigating decide to give her a story she will never forget—if she ever gets the chance to tell it! **92m/C VHS, Beta.** Terry Reeves Wolf, Christopher Ginnaven; ***D:*** Gary Jones. *IME*

Staying Alive 🦴½ **1983 (PG)** "Saturday Night Fever" was the ultimate cheesy 70's musical, hence likeable in a dorky way. This pathetic sequel (directed by Stallone from a Rocky-esque script about beating the odds, etc.) is utterly predictable and forgettable. Music mostly by Frank Stallone, the great heir to Rodgers and Hammerstein. ♫The Woman In You; I Love You Too Much; Breakout; Someone Belonging to Someone; Life Goes On; Far From Over; Devils and Seducers; (We Dance) So Close to the Fire; Hope We Never Change. **96m/C VHS, Beta, LV.** John Travolta, Cynthia Rhodes, Finola Hughes, Norma Donaldson; ***D:*** Sylvester Stallone; ***W:*** Sylvester Stallone; ***M:*** Frank Stallone. *PAR*

Staying On 🦴🦴½ **1980** Based on the Paul Scott novel, this English drama follows the life of a post-colonial British colonel and his wife who chose to remain in India. **87m/C VHS, Beta.** *GB* Trevor Howard, Celia Johnson; ***D:*** Irene Shubik. *MTI*

Staying Together 🦴½ **1989 (R)** Three midwestern brothers go into a panic when their father decides to sell the restaurant they've worked at all their adult lives. Somehow they manage the transition and learn about life. Sloppy comedy-drama with way too many unresolved subplots. **91m/C VHS, Beta, LV.** Dermot Mulroney, Tim Quill, Sean Astin, Stockard Channing, Melinda Dillon, Daphne Zuniga; ***D:*** Lee Grant; ***W:*** Monte Merrick; ***M:*** Miles Goodman. *HBO*

The Steagle 🦴 **1971 (R)** The threat of the Cuban missile crisis lets a fantasizing professor loose to enact his wildest dreams. Odd Mitty-esque fantasy comedy might have worked, but ends up confusing and frustrating. **101m/C VHS, Beta.** Richard Benjamin, Cloris Leachman; ***D:*** Paul Sylbert. *NLC*

Steal Big, Steal Little 🦴🦴 **1995 (PG-13)** Twins Robby and Reuben Martinez (Garcia) battle over the California ranch land left to Reuben by their mother. Evil, manipulative Robby, all fancy suits and slicked-back hair, wants to build condos while gentle, less-fashionable Reuben must fight to fulfill his dream of building a home for the migrant workers he employs. Yawn. Writer/director Davis' flashy action movie technique doesn't fit into the dramatic social commentary—it's too fast and forced to work. Garcia's radical character changes are impressive though. Arkin provides comic relief as the good-hearted used-car dealer who tries to save the day, if not the film. **130m/C VHS, LV.** Andy Garcia, Alan Arkin, Rachel Ticotin,

Joe Pantoliano, David Ogden Stiers, Charles Rocket, Holland Taylor; *D:* Andy Davis; *W:* Lee Blessing, Jeanne Blake, Terry Kahn, Andy Davis; *C:* Frank Tidy; *M:* William Olvis. *HBO*

Steal the Sky ☠☠ **1988** Israeli agent Hemingway seduces Iraqi pilot Cross and persuades him to steal a Soviet MIG jet and defect to Israel. Unlikely plot but swell flying scenes. Hemingway is poorly cast, as she often is. Made for cable television. **110m/C VHS, Beta, LV.** Mariel Hemingway, Ben Cross, Etta Ankri; *D:* John Hancock. *HBO*

Stealing Beauty ☠☠½ **1996 (R)** The film's main asset, besides the beautiful Tuscan scenery, is the coltish charm of Tyler, who stars as virginal teenager Lucy Harmon. An innocent abroad, she's spending the summer with family friends after her mother's suicide. Ostensibly artist Ian Grayson (McCann) is doing her portrait but Lucy's more interested in finding romance with neighbor lad Niccolo (Zibetti), who bestowed her first kiss on a previous visit. Lucy's sunny appeal doesn't go unnoticed by the villa's other inhabitants, including dying playwright Alex (Irons), but it seems Lucy's growing up won't be easy on anyone (not even herself). **118m/C VHS.** *IT GB FR* Liv Tyler, Jeremy Irons, Donal McCann, Sinead Cusack, Jean Marais, D.W. Moffett, Stefania Sandrelli, Carlo Cecchi, Roberto Zibetti, Joseph Fiennes, Jason Flemyng, Leonardo Treviglio; *D:* Bernardo Bertolucci; *W:* Susan Minot, Bernardo Bertolucci; *C:* Darius Khondji; *M:* Richard Hartley. *NYR*

Stealing Heaven ☠☠½ **1988 (R)** Based on the lives of Abelard and Heloise. In 12th-century Paris, a theologian and teacher falls in love with a beautiful young woman, and the two must defend their bond from all comers, including her righteous uncle. Steamy; trimmed to 108 minutes after threatened X rating. Attractive and cerebral. Available in a 115 minute-uncut, unrated version. **108m/C VHS, Beta, LV.** *GB YU* Derek De Lint, Kim Thomson, Denholm Elliott, Mark Jax, Bernard Hepton, Kenneth Cranham, Angela Pleasence, Rachel Kempson; *D:* Clive Donner; *W:* Chris Bryant; *M:* Nick Bicat. *NO*

Stealing Home ☠☠½ **1988 (PG-13)** A washed-up baseball player learns his former babysitter (who was also his first love and inspiration), has committed suicide. Their bittersweet relationship is told through flashbacks. Foster's superb performance steals the show in this quiet sleeper. **98m/C VHS, LV.** Mark Harmon, Jodie Foster, William McNamara, Blair Brown, Harold Ramis, Jonathan Silverman, John Shea, Helen Hunt, Richard Jenkins, Ted Ross, Thatcher Goodwin, Yvette Croskey; *D:* Steven Kampmann, Will Aldis; *W:* Steven Kampmann, Will Aldis; *M:* David Foster. *WAR*

Steamboat Bill, Jr. ☠☠☠½ **1928** City-educated student returns to his small home-town and his father's Mississippi river boat, where he's an embarrassment to dad. But bond they do, to ward off the owner of a rival riverboat, whose daughter Keaton falls for. Engaging look at small-town life and the usual wonderful Keaton antics, including braving the big tornado. **75m/B VHS, Beta, LV.** Buster Keaton, Ernest Torrence, Marion Byron, Tom Lewis; *D:* Charles Riesner. *NOS, CCB, DVT*

Steaming ☠☠ **1986 (R)** Six women get together in a London bathhouse and review their various troubles with men. Unfortunate adaptation of the good play by Nell Dunn. Where are the laughs—and what happened to the dramatic tension? The last film of Dors and director Losey. **102m/C VHS, Beta.** *GB* Vanessa Redgrave, Sarah Miles, Diana Dors; *D:* Joseph Losey. *VTR, NWV*

Steel ☠☠ *Look Down and Die; Men of Steel* **1980 (R)** Construction workers on a mammoth skyscraper face insurmountable odds and strong opposition. Will they finish their building? Worth watching, if you don't have anything else to do. **100m/C VHS, Beta, LV.** Lee Majors, Jennifer O'Neill, Art Carney, George Kennedy, Harris Yulin, Terry Kiser, Richard Lynch, Roger E. Mosley, Albert Salmi, R.G. Armstrong; *D:* Steve Carver; *W:* Leigh Chapman; *M:* Michel Colombier. *VES*

Steel and Lace ☠½ **1990 (R)** Davison is the scientist brother of a classical pianist who commits suicide after being raped. He revives her as a cyborg, which promptly sets out to enact its revenge. Depressing, morbid sci-fi. **92m/C VHS, Beta, LV.** Bruce Davison, Clare Wren, Stacy Haiduk, David Naughton, David Lander; *D:* Ernest Farino; *W:* Joseph Dougherty, Dave Edison. *FRH*

Steel Arena ☠ **1972 (PG)** Several real life stunt-car drivers appear in this action-packed film, crammed with spins, jumps, explosions and world-record-breaking, life risking stunts. **99m/C VHS, Beta.** Dusty Russell, Gene Drew, Buddy Love; *D:* Mark L. Lester. *LIV, VES*

The Steel Claw ☠☠ **1961** One-handed ex-Marine Montgomery organizes guerilla forces against the Japanese in the Philippines in WWII. Good location shooting and plenty of action. **95m/C VHS, Beta.** George Montgomery, Charito Luna, Mario Barri; *D:* George Montgomery. *NO*

Steel Cowboy ☠☠ **1978** With his marriage, sanity, and livelihood on the line, an independent trucker agrees to haul a hot herd of stolen steers. Passable made-for-TV macho adventure. **100m/C VHS, Beta.** James Brolin, Rip Torn, Jennifer Warren, Strother Martin, Melanie Griffith, Lou Frizzell; *D:* Harvey Laidman; *M:* Charles Bernstein. *NO*

Steel Dawn ☠½ **1987 (R)** Another "Mad Max" clone: A leather-clad warrior wields his sword over lots of presumably post-apocalyptic desert terrain. Swayze stars with his real-life wife Niemi in unfortunate follow-up to "Dirty Dancing." **90m/C VHS, Beta, LV.** Patrick Swayze, Lisa Niemi, Christopher Neame, Brett Hool, Brion James, Anthony Zerbe; *D:* Lance Hool. *LIV, VES*

Steel Fisted Dragon ☠ **1982 (R)** Son seeks revenge on the gang who murdered his mother and burned her house to the ground. **85m/C VHS, Beta.** Stephen Lee, Johnny Kong Kong, Peter Chan. *NO*

Steel Frontier ☠½ **1994 (R)** Post-apocalypse actioner finds a group of survivors trying to make a new life in a town they call New Hope. But then a group of bandit soldiers take over—until a lone hero comes along to save the day. **94m/C VHS, LV.** Joe Lara, Brion James, Bo Svenson, Stacie Foster; *D:* Paul G. Volk, Jacobsen Hart; *W:* Jacobsen Hart. *PMH*

The Steel Helmet ☠☠☠½ **1951** Hurriedly made Korean War drama stands as a top-notch war film. Brooding and dark, GIs don't save the world for democracy or rescue POWs; they simply do their best to survive a horrifying situation. Pointless death, confused loyalties and cynicism abound in writer-director Fuller's scathing comment on the madness of war. **84m/B VHS, Beta, LV.** Gene Evans, Robert Hutton, Steve Brodie, William Chun, James Edwards, Richard Loo, Sid Melton; *D:* Samuel Fuller; *W:* Samuel Fuller. *RXM*

Steel Magnolias ☠☠☠ **1989 (PG)** Julia Roberts plays a young woman stricken with severe diabetes who chooses to live her life to the fullest despite her bad health. Much of the action centers around a Louisiana beauty shop where the women get together to discuss the goings-on of their lives. Screenplay by R. Harling, based on his partially autobiographical play. Sweet, poignant, and often hilarious, yet just as often overwrought. MacLaine is funny as a bitter divorcee; Parton is sexy and fun as the hairdresser. But Field and Roberts go off the deep end and make it all entirely too weepy. **118m/C VHS, Beta, LV, 8mm.** Sally Field, Dolly Parton, Shirley MacLaine, Daryl Hannah, Olympia Dukakis, Julia Roberts, Tom Skerritt, Sam Shepard, Dylan McDermott, Kevin J. O'Connor, Bill McCutcheon, Ann Wedgeworth, Janine Turner; *D:* Herbert Ross; *W:* Robert Harling; *C:* John A. Alonzo; *M:* Georges Delerue. Golden Globe Awards '90: Best Supporting Actress (Roberts); People's Choice Awards '90: Best Film—Drama; Nominations: Academy Awards '89: Best Supporting Actress (Roberts). *COL*

Steele Justice ☠ **1987 (R)** A tough 'Nam vet takes on the whole Vietnamese Mafia in Southern California after his friend is murdered. One of those head-scratchers: Should I laugh, or be offended? **96m/C VHS, Beta, LV.** Martin Kove, Sela Ward, Ronny Cox, Bernie Casey, Joseph Campanella, Sarah Douglas; *D:* Robert Boris; *W:* Robert Boris. *PAR*

Steele's Law ☠☠ **1991 (R)** A loner cop is forced to take the law into his own hands in order to track down an insane international assassin. **90m/C VHS, LV.** Fred Williamson, Bo Svenson, Doran Inghram, Phyllis Cicero; *D:* Fred Williamson. *ACA*

Steelyard Blues ☠☠½ *The Final Crash* **1973 (PG)** A motley-crew comedy about a wacky gang that tries to steal an abandoned WW II airplane. Zany pranks abound. Technically flawed direction from Myerson mars a potentially hilarious story. **93m/C VHS, Beta.** Jane Fonda, Donald Sutherland, Peter Boyle, Howard Hesseman, John Savage, Garry Goodrow; *D:* Alan Myerson; *W:* David S. Ward; *M:* David Shire. *WAR*

Stella ☠☠½ **1955** Mercouri's film debut has her as a free-spirited bar singer who gets involved in a tragic romantic triangle with a middle-class writer and a local football hero. Melodramatic but Mercouri's earthy joie de vivre is already apparent. In Greek with English subtitles. **94m/B VHS.** *GR* Melina Mercouri, Yiorgo Fountas, Aiekos Alexandrikis, Sophia Vembo; *D:* Michael Cacoyannis; *M:* Manos Hadjidakis. *FCT*

Stella ☠½ **1989 (PG-13)** Anachronistic remake update of "Stella Dallas" casts Midler as a single mother who sacrifices everything to give her daughter a better life. Barbara Stanwyck did it much better in 1937. Based on Olive Higgins Prouty's novel. **109m/C VHS, Beta, LV.** Bette Midler, John Goodman, Stephen Collins, Eileen Brennan, Ben Stiller, Trini Alvarado, Marsha Mason; *D:* John Erman; *W:* Robert Getchell; *C:* Billy Williams. *TOU*

Stella Dallas ☠☠☠ **1937** An uneducated woman lets go of the daughter she loves when she realizes her ex-husband can give the girl more advantages. What could be sentimental turns out believable and worthwhile under Vidor's steady hand. Stanwyck never makes a wrong step. From a novel by Olive Higgins Prouty. Remade in 1989 as "Stella," starring Bette Midler. **106m/B VHS, Beta, LV.** Barbara Stanwyck, Anne Shirley, John Boles, Alan Hale, Marjorie Main; *D:* King Vidor. Nominations: Academy Awards '37: Best Actress (Stanwyck), Best Supporting Actress (Shirley). *SUE*

Stella Maris ☠☠☠ **1918** Pickford plays tattered waif who's a slave to an alcoholic who's married to the man she loves. But he's in love with Pickford playing a sheltered rich invalid. Brimming with the tragic consequences of love. **70m/B VHS, Beta.** Mary Pickford, Conway Tearle, Camille Ankewich, Ida Waterman; *D:* Marshall Neilan. *GPV, FCT*

Step Lively ☠☠½ **1944** A young playwright tries to recover the money he lent to a fast-talking Broadway producer and is forced to take the leading role in his play. Lively musical remake of "Room Service" (1938) was Sinatra's first starring role. Look for Dorothy Malone as a brunette switchboard operator. ♫Some Other Time; As Long As There's Music; Where Does Love Begin?; Come Out, Come Out, Wherever You Are; Why Must There Be an Opening Song?; And Then You Kissed Me; Ask the Madame. **88m/B VHS, Beta, LV.** Frank Sinatra, Gloria De Haven, George Murphy, Walter Slezak, Adolphe Menjou, Anne Jeffreys; *D:* Tim Whelan. Nominations: Academy Awards '44: Best Interior Decoration. *CCB*

The Stepfather ☠☠☠ **1987 (R)** Creepy thriller about a seemingly ordinary stepfather who is actually a homicidal maniac searching for the "perfect family." An independently produced sleeper tightly directed and well written. Followed by two inferior sequels. **89m/C VHS, Beta, LV.** Terry O'Quinn, Shelley Hack, Jill Schoelen, Stephen Shellan, Charles Lanyer; *D:* Joseph Ruben; *W:* Donald E. Westlake; *M:* Patrick Moraz. *COL, SUE*

Stepfather 2: Make Room for Daddy ☠½ **1989 (R)** A poor sequel to the suspenseful sleeper, wherein the psychotic family man escapes from an asylum and woos another suburban family, murdering anyone who may suspect his true identity. Followed by yet another sequel. **93m/C VHS,**

Beta, LV. Terry O'Quinn, Meg Foster, Caroline Williams, Jonathan Brandis; ***D:*** Jeff Burr; ***W:*** John P. Auerbach. *NO*

Stepfather 3: Father's Day **1992 (R)** The father from Hell is back! Escaping from the loony bin with a surgically altered face, the stepfather settles in a small town and gets a job at a nursery (the plant kind, not the children kind). His favorite gardening tool fast becomes the mulch machine, and soon locals are fertilizing the garden. Well below the original, but it may please fans of this genre. **110m/C VHS, LV.** Robert Wightman, Priscilla Barnes, Season Hubley; ***D:*** Guy Magar. *VMK*

Stephano Quantestorie **1993** Walter Mitty-ish story about daydreaming cop Stephano (Nichetti) who falls for the prime suspect in a robbery he's investigating. He escapes his conflicting feelings by imagining himself living other lives—as a math professor, airline pilot, saxophone player, and thief, but soon all these alter ego are intruding into his work. Italian with subtitles. **90m/C VHS.** *IT* Maurizio Nichetti; ***D:*** Maurizio Nichetti; ***W:*** Maurizio Nichetti. *KIV*

Stephen King's Golden Years ½ **1991** Stephen King creates a chilling vision of scientific progress gone awry in this shocking techno-thriller. After being accidentally exposed to exotic chemicals in a lab explosion, an aging janitor undergoes an extraordinary transformation and the government will sacrifice anything to learn more about it. Originally a made-for-television miniseries. **232m/C VHS, LV.** Keith Szarabajka, Frances Sternhagen, Ed Lauter, R.D. Call. *WOV*

Stephen King's It ½ **1990** A group of small town children, who were terrorized by an evil force in their youth, are traumatized again some thirty years later, when they learn a new series of child murders occurred in their Eastern home town. The adults, who now all have successful and diverse careers, must come to terms with the terrible secret they share, as "IT" has returned to wreak havoc in their New England home town. Based on horror master King's bestselling novel of the same name. **193m/C VHS, Beta, LV.** Tim Reid, Richard Thomas, John Ritter, Annette O'Toole, Richard Masur, Dennis Christopher, Harry Anderson, Olivia Hussey, Tim Curry, Jonathan Brandis; ***D:*** Tommy Lee Wallace; ***W:*** Stephen King; ***M:*** Richard Bellis. *WAR*

Stephen King's The Langoliers ½ *The Langoliers* **1995 (PG-13)** Bloated variation of "Ten Little Indians" finds 10 airline passengers dozing off on their L.A.-to-Boston flight and awakening to find their fellow passengers and the crew have vanished. Of course, one passenger (Morse) is a pilot and he gets them to Bangor, Maine (where the miniseries was filmed), only to discover the airport is deserted and very weird things are going on. Oh yeah, the "langoliers" look like flying cannonballs with piranha teeth and have something to do with neurotic Pinchot's character. Not that you'll care much. **180m/C VHS, LV.** David Morse, Bronson Pinchot, Patricia Wettig, Dean Stockwell, Kate Maberly, Christopher Collet, Kimber Riddle, Mark Lindsay Chapman, Frankie Faison, Baxter Harris; ***Cameos:*** Stephen King, Tom Holland; ***D:*** Tom Holland; ***W:*** Tom Holland; ***C:*** Paul Maibaum; ***M:*** Vladimir Horunzhy. *REP*

Stephen King's The Stand ½ *The Stand* **1994** Ghoulish made for TV adaptation of the King novel about a superflu/plague that decimates the U.S. population. The few survivors are soon divided into two camps—those dreaming of a godly old black woman known as Mother Abigail and others of the satanic Randall Flagg, the Walkin' Dude. Boulder, Colorado (where King was living when he wrote the novel) serves as headquarters for Abigail's brood while Las Vegas (where else) is Flagg territory. It all comes down to a battle of good vs. evil, with the future of mankind at stake. Religious allegory can get tedious but it's a varied cast with some scenes not for those with queasy stomachs. On four cassettes. **360m/C VHS, LV.** Jamey Sheridan, Ruby Dee, Gary Sinise, Molly Ringwald, Miguel Ferrer, Laura San Giacomo, Rob Lowe, Adam Storke, Matt Frewer, Corin "Corky" Nemec, Ray Walston, Bill Fagerbakke, Ossie Davis, Shawnee Smith, Rick Aviles; ***Cameos:*** Ed Harris, Kathy Bates, Kareem Abdul-Jabbar, Stephen King; ***D:*** Mick Garris; ***W:*** Stephen King; ***C:*** Eddie Pei. *REP*

Stephen King's The Tommyknockers ½ *The Tommyknockers* **1993 (R)** Another of King's creepy tales, adapted for TV. Bobbi (Helgenberger) and Gard (Smits) live in the small town of Haven, Maine (actually filmed on New Zealand's North Island). She's an aspiring writer; he's a fading poet with a drinking problem and a metal plate in his head (this is important). Walking in the woods, Bobbi stumbles over a long-buried spaceship which begins to take possession of the townspeople—their eyes shine green, their teeth fall out, and they act out their (often violent) fantasies—all but Gard. The whole thing's more silly than scary. The title comes from an old children's rhyme. **120m/C VHS, LV.** Jimmy Smits, Marg Helgenberger, Joanna Cassidy, E.G. Marshall, Traci Lords, John Ashton, Allyce Beasley, Cliff DeYoung, Robert Carradine, Leon Woods, Paul McIver; ***D:*** John Power; ***W:*** Lawrence D. Cohen. *VMK*

Stepmonster ½ **1992 (PG-13)** A boy tries to convince his father that his new stepmother is a monster—literally. Doesn't work any better than "My Stepmother Is an Alien." **?m/C VHS.** Alan Thicke, Robin Riker, Corey Feldman, John Astin, Ami Dolenz, George Gaynes. *NHO*

The Stepmother ½ **1971** Yet another Hitchcock ripoff story involving an evil stepmother. Rey is passable, but there's not much else to recommend this dredge. **100m/C VHS.** Alejandro Rey, John Anderson, Katherine Justice, John David Garfield, Marlene Schmidt, Claudia Jennings, Larry Linville; ***D:*** Howard (Hikmet) Avedis. Nominations: Academy Awards '72: Best Song ("Strange Are the Ways of Love"). *ACA*

Steppenwolf ½ **1974 (PG)** Static, enigmatic film version of the famous Herman Hesse novel about a brooding writer searching for meaning and self-worth. Interesting to watch, but the offbeat novel doesn't translate to the screen; leaves you flat. **105m/C VHS, Beta, LV.** Max von Sydow, Dominique Sanda; ***D:*** Fred Haines. *VMK, GLV*

Stepping Out **1991 (PG)** Minnelli stars as a would-be Broadway dancer who gives tap dancing lessons in an old church to an assortment of offbeat and interesting characters. When the troupe is asked to perform for a local charity, they make the most of their opportunity. A warm and touching ensemble piece that avoids over-sentimentalizing and utilizes its cast to best advantage. **113m/C VHS, Beta, LV.** Liza Minnelli, Shelley Winters, Bill Irwin, Ellen Greene, Julie Walters, Robyn Stevan, Jane Krakowski, Sheila McCarthy, Andrea Martin, Carol Woods, Nora Dunn; ***D:*** Lewis Gilbert; ***W:*** Richard Harris; ***M:*** Peter Matz. *PAR*

Steps from Hell **1992** Vald Tempest is an evil immortal in control of a cult of zombie women. He's stolen a sacred map that will lead to a gateway which, when opened, will unleash a supreme evil on the world. Unless the heroic John Clark can find a way to prevent it, of course. **90m/C VHS.** Bernardo Rosa, Rocky Tucker, Ron Odell, Philip Cable, Liz Stoeckel, Steve Quimby, Lisa Lund; ***D:*** James Tucker; ***W:*** James Tucker. *CTD*

Stepsisters *Woof!* **1985** Murderous double-crosses occur among a pilot, his wife, and her sister. **75m/C VHS, Beta.** Hal Fletcher, Sharyn Talbert, Bond Gideon. *NO*

The Sterile Cuckoo *Pookie* **1969 (PG)** An aggressive co-ed pursues a shy freshman who seems to embody her romantic ideal. Minnelli's performance is outstanding; Burton as the naive young man is also fine. Pakula's splendid first directing job. **108m/C VHS, Beta, LV.** Liza Minnelli, Wendell Burton, Tim McIntire; ***D:*** Alan J. Pakula; ***W:*** Alvin Sargent; ***C:*** Milton Krasner. Nominations: Academy Awards '69: Best Actor (Minnelli), Best Song ("Come Saturday Morning"). *PAR*

Steve Martin Live ½ **1985** Martin shows veteran comedians his famous Universal Amphitheatre performance and his short "The Absent-Minded Waiter." **58m/C VHS, Beta, LV.** Steve Martin, Teri Garr, Buck Henry, David Letterman, Paul Simon. *LIV, VES*

Stevie **1978** Jackson brings her flawless skill to the role of British poet Stevie Smith. Excellent performance from Washbourne as Stevie's spinster aunt. Wooden, lifeless screen rendition for the Hugh Whitemore stage play is helped greatly by good performances, but is too talky and, frankly, rather dull and self-absorbed. **102m/C VHS.** *GB* Glenda Jackson, Mona Washbourne, Alec McCowen, Trevor Howard; ***D:*** Robert Enders; ***C:*** Frederick A. (Freddie) Young. Los Angeles Film Critics Association Awards '78: Best Supporting Actress (Washbourne); Montreal World Film Festival '78: Best Actress (Jackson); New York Film Critics Awards '78: Best Supporting Actress (Washbourne). *UAV, SUE*

Stewardess School *Woof!* **1986 (R)** Airline spoof aims at wackiness, but misses the runway. Generic title betrays probable badness which turns out to be all too real. An utter woofer. **84m/C VHS, Beta, LV.** Sandahl Bergman, Wendie Jo Sperber, Judy Landers, Julia Montgomery, Corinne Bohrer; ***D:*** Ken Blancato; ***W:*** Ken Blancato; ***M:*** Robert Folk. *NO*

Stick ½ **1985 (R)** Ex-con Stick (Reynolds, directing himself) wants to start a new life for himself in Miami. Lots of drug dealers and guns don't help the interest level in this dull underworld tale. Based upon the Elmore Leonard novel. **109m/C VHS, Beta, LV.** Burt Reynolds, Candice Bergen, George Segal, Charles Durning, Dar Robinson; ***D:*** Burt Reynolds; ***W:*** Elmore Leonard; ***M:*** Stephen Dorff. *MCA*

The Stick-Up *Mud* **1977** In 1935, a young American traveling in Great Britain is introduced to some rather illegal fun. Rather sorry attempt at romance/comedy/adventure. **101m/C VHS, Beta.** David Soul, Pamela McMyler; ***D:*** Jeffrey Bloom; ***W:*** Jeffrey Bloom. *HHE*

Stickfighter **1989 (PG)** The oppressive reign of an evil Spanish ruler of the Philippines is challenged by the world's best stickfighter. **102m/C VHS.** *PH* Dean Stockwell, Nancy Kwan, Alejandro Rey, Roland Dantes; ***D:*** Luis Nepomuceno. *PSM*

Sticky Fingers **1988 (PG-13)** Two female musicians, asked to watch nearly a million bucks in drug money, go on a mega shopping spree. Completely incredible, unlikeable and mean-spirited attempt at zany comedy. **89m/C VHS, Beta, LV.** Melanie Mayron, Helen Slater, Eileen Brennan, Carol Kane, Christopher Guest, Danitra Vance, Gwen Welles, Stephen McHattie; ***D:*** Catlin Adams; ***W:*** Melanie Mayron, Catlin Adams; ***M:*** Gary Chang. *MED*

Stigma ½ **1973** "Miami Vice" star Thomas (then 23; later to restore his middle name, Michael) is a young doctor who treats a syphilis epidemic in a small town. He's indistinguishable, but better than anything else here. Ever seen close-ups of advanced syphilis? Here's your chance—but it's not pretty. **93m/C Beta.** Philip Michael Thomas, Harlan Cary Poe; ***D:*** David E. Durston. *NO*

Stiletto ½ **1969 (R)** Good cast is wasted in this mediocre depiction of the trouble encountered by a contract Mafia assassin when he decides to change careers. Based on the usual pulp cheese by Harold Robbins. **101m/C VHS, Beta.** Alex Cord, Britt Ekland, Patrick O'Neal, Joseph Wiseman, Barbara McNair, Roy Scheider, M. Emmet Walsh; ***Cameos:*** Raul Julia; ***D:*** Bernard L. Kowalski; ***C:*** Jack Priestley. *SUE*

Still Life **1992 (PG-13)** The press has dubbed him "the Art Killer," a serial murderer who makes sculptures out of his victims. He's a sensation—and not ready to stop. This sicko's next "Still Life" may just be a struggling young musician. **83m/C VHS.** Jason Gedrick, Jessica Steen, Stephen Shellan; ***D:*** Graeme Campbell; ***M:*** Mychael Danna. *PSM*

Still Not Quite Human **1992** Teenage android Chip must do battle with unscrupulous industrialists and their robot weapon Spartacus to rescue his inventor father from their deadly clutches. **84m/C VHS, Beta.** Alan Thicke, Christopher Neame, Betsy Palmer, Adam Philipson, Rosa Nevin, Ken Pogue, Jay Underwood; ***D:*** Eric Luke; ***W:*** Eric Luke. *DIS*

Still of the Night 🦴🦴 **1982 (PG)** A Hitchcock-style thriller about a psychiatrist infatuated with a mysterious woman who may or may not be a killer. **91m/C VHS, Beta, LV.** Meryl Streep, Roy Scheider, Jessica Tandy, Joe Grifasi, Sara Botsford, Josef Sommer; ***D:*** Robert Benton; ***W:*** Robert Benton, David Newman. *MGM*

The Stilts 🦴🦴🦴 **1984** From modern Spanish cinema's preeminent director, this is a study of sexual dynamics revolving around a doomed love triangle. Aging professor Gomez wants young Del Sol to commit to him, but she won't; she has another, younger lover. Overwrought at times, but well acted. In Spanish with English subtitles. **95m/C VHS, Beta.** *SP* Laura Del Sol, Francesco Rabal, Fernando Gomez; ***D:*** Carlos Saura. *XVC, MED, INJ*

The Sting 🦴🦴🦴½ **1973 (PG)** Newman and Redford together again in this sparkling story of a pair of con artists in 1930s Chicago. They set out to fleece a big-time racketeer, pitting brain against brawn and pistol. Very inventive, excellent acting, Scott Joplin's wonderful ragtime music adapted by Marvin Hamlisch. The same directorial and acting team from "Butch Cassidy and the Sundance Kid" triumphs again. **129m/C VHS, Beta, LV.** Paul Newman, Robert Redford, Robert Shaw, Charles Durning, Eileen Brennan, Harold Gould, Ray Walston; ***D:*** George Roy Hill; ***W:*** David S. Ward; ***C:*** Robert L. Surtees; ***M:*** Marvin Hamlisch. Academy Awards '73: Best Adapted Score, Best Art Direction/Set Decoration, Best Costume Design, Best Director (Hill), Best Film Editing, Best Picture, Best Story & Screenplay; Directors Guild of America Awards '73: Best Director (Hill); People's Choice Awards '75: Best Film; Nominations: Academy Awards '73: Best Actor (Redford), Best Cinematography, Best Sound. *MCA, BTV*

The Sting 2 🦴½ **1983 (PG)** Complicated comic plot concludes with the final con game, involving a fixed boxing match where the stakes top a million dollars and the payoff could be murder. Lame sequel to "The Sting" (1973). **102m/C VHS, Beta, LV.** Jackie Gleason, Mac Davis, Teri Garr, Karl Malden, Oliver Reed; ***D:*** Jeremy Paul Kagan; ***W:*** David S. Ward; ***M:*** Lalo Schifrin. Nominations: Academy Awards '83: Best Original Score. *MCA*

Sting of the Dragon Masters 🦴 **1974 (R)** Martial arts adventure featuring Bruce Lee's female Kung-Fu counterpart, Angela Mao. **96m/C VHS, Beta.** Angela Mao, Thoon Rhee, Carter Huang; ***D:*** Huang Feng. *VCI*

Sting of the West 🦴 **1976 (PG)** Journeyman con artist swindles his way across the Wild West. **90m/C VHS, Beta.** Jack Palance, Timothy Brent, Lionel Stander. *MPI*

Stingray 🦴½ **1978 (PG)** Two guys buy a Corvette, not knowing it's loaded with stolen heroin. Gangsters with an interest in the dope come after them, and the chase is on. Very violent and not all that funny. **105m/C VHS, Beta.** Chris Mitchum, Sherry Jackson, Les Lannom; ***D:*** Richard Taylor. *COL, SUE*

Stir Crazy 🦴🦴½ **1980 (R)** Two down-on-their luck losers find themselves convicted of a robbery they didn't commit and sentenced to 120 years behind bars with a mean assortment of inmates. **111m/C VHS, Beta, LV.** Richard Pryor, Gene Wilder, Nicolas Coster, Lee Purcell, Craig T. Nelson, JoBeth Williams; ***D:*** Sidney Poitier. *COL*

Stitches 🦴 **1985 (R)** Adolescent comedy about med students playing practical jokes on the dean using laboratory specimens. So bad the director (actually Rod Holcomb) allegedly did not want his name associated with it. **92m/C VHS, Beta.** Eddie Albert, Parker Stevenson, Geoffrey Lewis, Brian Tochi; ***D:*** Alan Smithee; ***W:*** Michael Choquette. *MED*

Stocks and Blondes *Woof!* **1985 (R)** The world of industrial finance is used as a background for some raunchy sex humor. **79m/C VHS, Beta.** *LIV, VES*

The Stolen Children 🦴🦴🦴½ *Il Ladro di Bambini* **1992** Highly acclaimed Italian neo-realist film that tells the story of a shy carabiniere and two children who have been placed in his care. They are an emotionally battered 11-year-old girl who was forced into prostitution by her mother and her sullen 9-year-old brother. As they journey from Milan to Sicily and gradually get to know each other, all three of the characters undergo a slight transformation. Gracefully executed, this haunting masterpiece explores the overriding themes of guilt and innocence and keeps you thinking about them long after the movie's over. Italian with subtitles. **108m/C VHS.** *IT* Enrico Lo Verso, Valentina Scalici, Giuseppe Ieracitano, Florence Darel, Marina Golovine, Fabio Alessandrini; ***D:*** Gianni Amelio; ***W:*** Gianni Amelio, Sandro Petraglia, Stefano Rulli; ***M:*** Franco Piersanti. Cannes Film Festival '92: Grand Jury Prize; Nominations: Cannes Film Festival '92: Best Film. *NYR*

A Stolen Face 🦴🦴 **1952** Creepy, implausible drama of a plastic surgeon, spurned by a beautiful concert pianist, who transforms a female convict to look just like her. The convict runs away, but perhaps there's hope in the future with the pianist. **71m/B VHS, Beta, LV.** *GB* Paul Henreid, Lizabeth Scott, Andre Morell, Susan Stephen; ***D:*** Terence Fisher; ***M:*** Malcolm Arnold. *MLB*

Stolen Hours 🦴🦴½ **1963** Inferior remake of Bette Davis' "Dark Victory" casts Hayward as an oil-rich heiress who learns she has a fatal illness. Bring the tissues for this tearjerker. Based on the play "Dark Victory" by George Emerson Brewer, Jr. and Bertram Block. **100m/C VHS.** Susan Hayward, Michael Craig, Diane Baker, Edward Judd, Paul Rogers; ***D:*** Daniel Petrie; ***W:*** Jessamyn West, Joseph Hayes. *MGM, FCT*

Stolen Identity 🦴½ **1953** A Viennese cabbie sees his American dream dashed for lack of the proper papers. When an American businessman is murdered in his cab he is quick to seize the moment...and the dead man's identity. In no time at all he finds himself involved with the widow, entangled with the murderer and under suspicion for the killing. Predictable and sluggish, the story inches its way to the foregone conclusion. **81m/B VHS, Beta.** Francis Lederer, Donald Buka, Joan Camden, Adrienne Gessner; ***D:*** Gunther Fritsch. *SNC*

Stolen Kisses 🦴🦴🦴½ *Baisers Voles* **1968** Sequel to "The 400 Blows," the story of Antoine Doinel: his unsuccessful career prospects as a detective in Paris, and his initially awkward but finally successful adventures with women. Made during Truffaut's involvement in a political crisis involving the sack of Cinematique Francais director Henri Langlois. Truffaut dedicated the film to Langlois and the Cinematique, but it is a thoroughly apolitical, small-scale, charming (some say too charming) romantic comedy, Truffaut-style. Followed by "Bed and Board." **90m/C VHS, Beta.** *FR* Jean-Pierre Leaud, Delphine Seyrig; ***D:*** Francois Truffaut; ***M:*** Antoine Duhamel. National Board of Review Awards '69: 5 Best Foreign Films of the Year; National Society of Film Critics Awards '69: Best Director (Truffaut); Nominations: Academy Awards '68: Best Foreign Language Film. *COL*

A Stolen Life 🦴🦴 **1946** Remake of 1939 film of the same title starring Elizabeth Bergner. Oddly, Davis chose this as her first and last producing effort. Implausible tale of an evil twin (Davis) who takes her sister's (Davis) place so she can have the man they both love. Davis pulls it off as both twins; Ford is good as the hapless hubby. **107m/B VHS, Beta.** Bette Davis, Glenn Ford, Dane Clark, Walter Brennan, Charlie Ruggles, Bruce (Herman Brix) Bennett, Esther Dale, Peggy Knudsen; ***D:*** Curtis Bernhardt; ***M:*** Max Steiner. *MGM*

Stolen Painting 🦴½ **1979** A man's wife is kidnapped by an evil gang while having her portrait painted. Her husband rescues her, and they, in turn, are chased by the kidnappers. **11m/C VHS, Beta.** *BFA*

The Stone Boy 🦴🦴🦴½ **1984 (PG)** A boy accidentally kills his older brother on their family's Montana farm. The family is torn apart by sadness and guilt. Sensitive look at variety of reactions during a crisis, with an excellent cast led by Duvall's crystal-clear performance. **93m/C VHS, Beta.** Glenn Close, Robert Duvall, Jason Presson, Frederic Forrest, Wilford Brimley, Linda Hamilton; ***D:*** Christopher Cain; ***W:*** Gina Berriault; ***C:*** Juan Ruiz-Anchia; ***M:*** James Horner, John Beal. *FOX*

Stone Cold *Woof!* **1991 (R)** Flamboyant footballer Bosworth made his acting debut in this sensitive human document, playing the usual musclebound, one-punk-army terminator cop, out to infiltrate a sadistic band of fascist biker barbarians engaged in drug running and priest shooting. Profane, lewd, gory, self-deifying; a crash course (accent on crashes) in everything despicable about modern action pics. **91m/C VHS, Beta, LV, 8mm.** Brian Bosworth, Lance Henriksen, William Forsythe, Arabella Holzbog, Sam McMurray; ***D:*** Craig R. Baxley. *COL*

Stone Cold Dead 🦴½ **1980 (R)** Rugged cop Crenna battles crime lord Williams (Paul Williams? Yeah, sure) over a prostitution ring. Meanwhile, a sniper starts killing hookers. Unoriginal and thoroughly dull would-be thriller. **100m/C VHS, Beta.** Richard Crenna, Paul Williams, Linda Sorensen, Belinda J. Montgomery; ***D:*** George Mendeluk; ***W:*** George Mendeluk. *MED*

Stone Fox 🦴🦴 **1987** Heartwarming family drama in which a young man must win a dogsled race to save the family farm. Based on John Reynolds Gardiner's popular children's book. **96m/C VHS.** Buddy Ebsen, Joey Cramer, Belinda J. Montgomery, Gordon Tootoosis; ***D:*** Harvey Hart. *WOV*

The Stone Killer 🦴🦴½ **1973 (R)** Bronson stars as a tough plainclothes cop in this action-packed drama about a Mafia plot to use Vietnam vets in a mass killing. Violent but tense and action-packed revenge adventure set in the underworlds of New York and Los Angeles. **95m/C VHS, Beta, LV.** Charles Bronson, Martin Balsam, Norman Fell, Ralph Waite, John Ritter; ***D:*** Michael Winner. *COL*

The Stoned Age 🦴 **1994 (R)** Buddies look to get wasted and find some chicks. Set in the '70s. **90m/C VHS.** Michael Kopelow, China Kantner, Renee Griffen; ***D:*** James Melkonian. *VMK*

Stones of Death 🦴 **1988 (R)** An aboriginal curse is invoked when a subdivision is built too close to an ancient burial site. Teenagers begin having all-too-real nightmares about death. **90m/C VHS, Beta.** Tom Jennings, Natalie McCurry, Zoe Carides, Eric Oldfield; ***D:*** James Bagle. *NO*

The Stooge 🦴🦴½ **1951** Singer Bill Miller (Martin) asks the antic Ted Rogers (Lewis) to join him in his vaudeville act, where Rogers' clowning has them on the road to success. But then Miller decides he wants to go solo. Sounds more than a little autobiographical. ♫A Girl Named Mary and a Boy Named Bill; Who's Your Little Whozis?; Just One More Chance; With My Eyes Wide Open I'm Dreaming; Louise; I'm Yours. **100m/B VHS.** Dean Martin, Jerry Lewis, Polly Bergen, Marion Marshall, Eddie Mayehoff, Richard Erdman, Frances Bavier; ***D:*** Norman Taurog; ***W:*** Martin Rackin, Fred Finklehoffe, Elwood Ullman; ***C:*** Daniel F. Fapp. *PAR*

Stoogemania 🦴 **1985** A nerd becomes so obsessed with the Three Stooges that they begin to take over his life and ruin it. Harmless except as a waste of time. Includes actual Stooge footage including some colorized—but see an old Stooges movie instead. **95m/C VHS, Beta.** Josh Mostel, Melanie Chartoff, Sid Caesar; ***D:*** Chuck Workman; ***M:*** Hummie Mann. *PAR*

The Stoogephile Trivia Movie **1986** A program of trivia points, quizzes and clips about Larry, Moe, Curly and Shemp for Stooges fanatics. **55m/C VHS, Beta.** *MPI*

Stooges Shorts Festival **194?** This collection of shorts includes "Disorder in the Court" (1936), "Sing a Song of Six Pants" (1947), and "Malice in the Palace" (1949). **55m/B VHS, Beta.** *HHT*

The Stooges Story 🦴🦴🦴 **1990** "The Stooges Anthology" presents a history of the comedy team, from their vaudevillian beginnings to their television resurgence in the 60s. "Disorder in the Court" finds the trio making a mockery of the United States justice system, and in "Brideless Groom," Shemp must find a bride within forty-eight hours in order to collect an inheritance. **90m/B VHS.** Moe Howard, Larry Fine, Curly Howard, Shemp Howard. *SIM*

Stop! Look! and Laugh! 🦴🦴½ **1960** Paul Winchell and his dummy Jerry Mahoney host a look at some of the Stooges funniest moments. Features the Marquis Chimps' interpretation of Cinderella for some reason. **78m/B VHS.** Moe Howard, Curly Howard, Shemp Howard, Larry Fine; ***D:*** Jules White. *COL*

Stop Making Sense 🦴🦴🦴½ **1984** The Talking Heads perform eighteen of their best songs in this concert filmed in Los Angeles. Considered by many to be the best concert movie ever made. The band plays with incredible energy and imagination, and Demme's direction and camera work is appropriately frenzied and original. Features such Talking Heads songs as "Burning Down the House," "Psycho Killer," and "Once in a Lifetime." Band member Tina Weymouth's Tom Tom Club also performs for the audience. **99m/C VHS, Beta, LV.** ***D:*** Jonathan Demme; ***Performed by:*** David Byrne, Tina Weymouth, Chris Franz, Jerry Harrison. *MVD, COL*

Stop! or My Mom Will Shoot 🦴 **1992 (PG-13)** Getty is an overbearing mother paying a visit to her cop son (Stallone) in Los Angeles. When mom witnesses a crime she has to stay in town longer than intended, which gives her time to meddle in her son's work and romantic lives. If Stallone wants to change his image this so-called comedy isn't the way to do it—because the joke is only on him. Viewers who rent this may find the joke is on them. **87m/C VHS, Beta, LV.** Sylvester Stallone, Estelle Getty, JoBeth Williams, Roger Rees, Martin Ferrero, Gailard Sartain, Dennis Burkley; ***D:*** Roger Spottiswoode; ***W:*** William Osborne, William Davies, Blake Snyder; ***M:*** Alan Silvestri. Golden Raspberry Awards '92: Worst Actor (Stallone), Worst Supporting Actress (Getty), Worst Screenplay. *MCA*

Stop That Cab 🦴½ **1951** Sloppy crooks accidentally leave precious jewels in the back seat of a taxi, and pursue and torture the cabby who found and hid them. Rather mean-spirited, uninteresting comedy. **56m/B VHS, Beta, LV.** Sid Melton, Iris Adrian, Tom Neal. *NO*

Stopover Tokyo 🦴🦴 **1957** An American intelligence agent uncovers a plot to assassinate the American ambassador while on leave in Japan. Nice location shooting and scenery; limp story and characters. Based on a novel by John P. Marquand. **100m/C VHS, Beta.** Robert Wagner, Joan Collins, Edmond O'Brien, Ken Scott; ***D:*** Richard L. Breen. *FOX*

The Stork Club 🦴🦴 **1945** A little song, a little dance, will Betty Hutton find romance? The actors manage to rise above the script in this silly, overdone fable. Hutton stars as the poor but spunky hat-check girl who unwittingly saves the life of a cynical billionaire. His expressions of gratitude are less than appreciated by her G.I. beau. Done mainly as a vehicle for Hutton's promotion, so Betty's die-hard fans may find it to their liking. ♫Doctor, Lawyer, Indian Chief; Baltimore Oriole; I'm a Square in the Social Circle; If I Had a Dozen Hearts; Love Me; China Boy; In the Shade of the Old Apple Tree. **98m/B VHS.** Betty Hutton, Barry Fitzgerald, Don DeFore, Robert Benchley, Bill Goodwin, Iris Adrian, Noel Neill, Andy Russell; ***D:*** Hal Walker. *NOS*

Storm 🦴½ **1987 (PG-13)** Uneven thriller finds college students on a camping trip who must fight for their lives when they are confronted by killer thieves. Somewhat contrived, but interesting ending to this low-budget outing. **99m/C VHS.** *CA* David Palfy, Stan Kane, Harry Freedman, Lawrence Elion, Tom Schioler; ***D:*** David Winning; ***M:*** Amin Bhatia. *WAR*

Storm and Sorrow 🦴🦴 **1990** Molly Higgins is known as the "Spiderwoman of the Rockies" for her legendary mountain climbing abilities. Then she joins a team looking to scale the 24,000-foot peaks of Russia's Pamir Mountains. The group meets deadly hazards—both natural and those caused by the ego-driven rivalries of the group's members. A fact-based drama based on the novel by Richard Craig. **96m/C VHS.** Lori Singer, Todd Allen, Steve Anderson, Jay Baker; ***W:*** Leigh Chapman. *WOV*

Storm in a Teacup 🦴🦴½ **1937** A reporter starts a campaign to save a sheepdog that the town magistrate has ordered killed because the owner, an old woman, is unable to pay the license tax. As the dog's fate hangs in the balance, this often humorous film provides an interesting look at British society of the 1930s. **80m/B VHS, Beta.** *GB* Vivien Leigh, Rex Harrison, Cecil Parker, Sara Allgood; ***D:*** Victor Saville. *NOS, BAR, DVT*

Storm Over Asia 🦴🦴🦴🦴 *The Heir to Genghis Khan* **1928** A Mongolian trapper is discovered to be descended from Genghis Khan and is made puppet emperor of a Soviet province. Beautiful and evocative. Silent masterpiece. **70m/B VHS, Beta.** *RU* I. Inkizhinov, Valeri Inkizhinov, A. Christiakov, A. Dedinstev, V. Tzoppi, Paulina Belinskaya; ***D:*** Vsevolod Pudovkin. National Board of Review Awards '30: 5 Best Foreign Films of the Year. *IHF, FST, INJ*

Storm Over Wyoming 🦴🦴 **1950** The old sheep-and-cattle battle again; Holt and Martin find themselves haplessly embroiled in a Wyoming range war. Action-packed but thin, ordinary western. **60m/B VHS, Beta.** Tim Holt, Richard Martin. *NO*

Storm Rider 🦴🦴 **1957** A gunman hired to protect a group of ranchers from a powerful rancher falls in love with a local widow. After his job is done, however, he leaves her behind. Typical western fare. **70m/B VHS.** Scott Brady, Mala Powers, Bill Williams, Olin Howlin, William "Bill" Fawcett, John Goddard; ***D:*** Edward L. Bernds; ***W:*** Edward L. Bernds; ***M:*** Les Baxter. *NO*

The Storm Within 🦴🦴🦴½ *Les Parents Terribles* **1948** Based on Cocteau's play, many consider this domestic drama of a troubled family's tortured existence to be his finest work. De Bray plays the domineering mother, Marais plays the son, and Day is the woman he (and his father) love in this complex story of sexuality, parental rivalry and jealousy. With the film set in only two locations, Cocteau creates a claustrophobic intimacy within the walls of de Bray's family apartment and Day's apartment. An inferior remake, "Intimate Relations" was released in Britain in 1953. In French with English subtitles. **98m/B VHS.** *FR* Jean Marais, Yvonne de Bray, Gabrielle Dorziat, Marcel Andre, Josette Day; ***D:*** Jean Cocteau; ***W:*** Jean Cocteau. *WBF*

Stormquest *Woof!* **1987** Deep in the jungle, a band of women warriors live without men. When it is discovered that one of the group has a male lover, she is sentenced to death. Her man tries to rescue her, and it turns into a war of the sexes—literally. In Spanish with subtitles. **90m/C VHS.** *SP* Kai Baker, Brent Huff; ***D:*** Alex Sessa. *MED*

Stormswept 🦴½ **1995** Actress Brianna (Hughes) rents a haunted Louisiana mansion housing the spirit of a slave master. When a storm strands Brianna and friends, the spirit causes everyone to get up to all sorts of sexual escapades. **94m/C VHS.** Julie Hughes, Melissa Moore, Kathleen Kinmont; ***D:*** David Marsh. *MTH*

Stormy Monday 🦴🦴½ **1988 (R)** An American developer conspires to strike it rich in Newcastle, England real estate by resorting to violence and political manipulations. Sting plays the jazz club owner who opposes him. Slow plot, but acted and directed well; interesting photography. **108m/C VHS, Beta, LV, 8mm.** *GB* Melanie Griffith, Tommy Lee Jones, Sting, Sean Bean, James Cosmo, Mark Long, Brian Lewis; ***D:*** Mike Figgis; ***W:*** Mike Figgis; ***M:*** Mike Figgis. *PAR, OM*

Stormy Trails 🦴🦴 **1936** Bell battles bellicose bad guys who are after his property. At least all the gunfights should keep a viewer awake! **59m/B VHS, Beta.** Rex Bell. *VCN*

Stormy Waters 🦴🦴½ *Remorques* **1941** A romantic French drama about a sea captain falling in love with a woman he rescues from a storm. He goes back to his wife, however, when she becomes critically ill. Director Gremillon insisted on realistic footage of storms at sea; production was delayed because of the difficulties of the German occupation. Dubbed. **75m/B VHS, Beta.** *FR* Jean Gabin, Michele Morgan, Madeleine Renaud; ***D:*** Jean Gremillon. *VYY, INJ*

Stormy Weather 🦴🦴½ **1943** In this cavalcade of black entertainment the plot takes a back seat to the nearly non-stop array of musical numbers, showcasing this stellar cast at their performing peak. ♫There's No Two Ways About Love; Stormy Weather; Ain't Misbehavin'; Rhythm Cocktail; Rang Tang Tang; Dat, Dot, Dah; That Ain't Right; I Can't Give You Anything But Love, Baby; Digga Digga Doo. **77m/B VHS, Beta, LV.** Lena Horne, Bill Robinson, Fats Waller, Dooley Wilson, Cab Calloway, Nicholas Brothers; ***D:*** Andrew L. Stone; ***C:*** Leon Shamroy. *FOX, PTB, FCT*

The Story Lady 🦴🦴½ **1993 (G)** A retiree uses her story-telling abilities as a hostess on a public-access children's program. She becomes so popular that two network execs want to exploit her as a spokesperson for a toy company. Only a young girl can help her find a way to resist going commercial. **93m/C VHS.** Jessica Tandy, Lisa Jakub, Ed Begley Jr., Charles Durning, Stephanie Zimbalist; ***D:*** Larry Elikann. *UNT*

The Story of a Cheat 🦴🦴🦴 **1936** The hero of the film discovers at an early age that dishonesty is probably the best policy and he sets out to put his theory into use. Director/writer Guitry also turns in a great performance as the central character. Guitry was a major influence on such different directors as Welles, Resnais and Truffaut. Based on Guitry's novel "Memoires d'Un Tricheur." In French with English subtitles. **83m/B VHS.** *FR* Sacha Guitry; ***D:*** Sacha Guitry; ***W:*** Sacha Guitry. *INT, FCT*

Story of a Cowboy Angel 🦴 **1981** On the Christmas Mountain Ranch, a cowboy angel descends to Earth to bestow various beneficences. **90m/C VHS, Beta.** Slim Pickens. *LIV, VES*

The Story of a Love Story 🦴🦴½ *Impossible Object* **1973** Bates plays a writer whose imagination gets the better of him when he attempts an extra-marital affair. Was he with her or not? Unusual concept doesn't stand up in the long run. Fine cast is under-utilized. **110m/C VHS.** *FR* Alan Bates, Dominique Sanda, Evans Evans, Lea Massari, Michel Auclair, Laurence De Monaghan; ***D:*** John Frankenheimer; ***W:*** Alan Bates. *NO*

The Story of a Three Day Pass 🦴🦴½ *La Permission* **1968** A black American GI falls in love with a French girl he meets in peacetime Paris. With English subtitles. Made on a low budget and flawed, but poignant and impressive. **87m/B VHS, Beta.** Harry Baird, Nicole Berger, Pierre Doris; ***D:*** Melvin Van Peebles; ***W:*** Melvin Van Peebles. *DVT, FCT, HEG*

Story of Adele H. 🦴🦴🦴 *L'Histoire d'Adele H* **1975 (PG)** The story of Adele Hugo, daughter of Victor Hugo, whose love for an English soldier leads to obsession and finally to madness after he rejects her. Sensitive and gentle unfolding of characters and story. Beautiful photography. In French with English subtitles. **97m/C VHS, Beta, LV.** *FR* Isabelle Adjani, Bruce Robinson; ***D:*** Francois Truffaut; ***W:*** Suzanne Schiffman, Jean Gruault; ***C:*** Nestor Almendros. National Board of Review Awards '75: 5 Best Foreign Films of the Year, Best Actress (Adjani); National Society of Film Critics Awards '75: Best Actress (Adjani); Nominations: Academy Awards '75: Best Actress (Adjani). *MGM, FCT, INJ*

The Story of Alexander Graham Bell 🦴🦴🦴 **1939** Lavish Fox biography on the inventor of the telephone provided Ameche with his most popular role. He's a serious Scot who comes to Boston to teach speech to the deaf and falls in love with the rich, beautiful and hearing impaired Young (whose three sisters, Georgianna, Polly Ann, and Sally are also in the film). Thanks to Young's rich daddy (Coburn), Bell gets the money to work on his invention, aided by enthusiastic assistant Watson (Fonda). No, it's not an entirely accurate retelling but it's well-done. **97m/B VHS.** Don Ameche, Loretta Young, Henry Fonda, Charles Coburn, Spring Byington, Gene Lockhart, Sally Blane, Polly Ann Young, Georgianna Young, Bobs Watson, Jonathan Hale, Harry Davenport; ***D:*** Irving Cummings; ***W:*** Lamar Trotti; ***C:*** Leon Shamroy. *FXV*

The Story of Boys & Girls *Storia de Ragazzi e di Ragazze* **1991** Two very different families come together for the wedding feast of their children, during which family secrets are revealed and we come to know and care for everyone present. A twenty-course meal rivals the food scenes in "Babette's Feast" and is guaranteed to make your mouth water. Fine ensemble of actors, well directed, with a vivid evocation of 1930s Italy. In Italian with English subtitles. **92m/C VHS, LV.** *IT* Lucrezia Lante della Rovere, Massimo Bonetti, Davide Bechini, Enrica Maria Modugno, Valeria Bruni Tadeschi, Lina Bernardi, Anna Bonaiuto, Alessandro Haber; ***D:*** Pupi Avati; ***W:*** Pupi Avati; ***M:*** Riz Ortolani. *FXL, INJ*

The Story of David **1976 (PG)** Well-done Old Testament Bible drama about the shepherd boy who slew Goliath, overcame the Philistines, and united Israel. Then, as King David, he winds up involved in an illicit love affair with Bathsheba that threatens to destroy his kingdom. Fine acting and a literate script highlight this made for television production. On two cassettes. **192m/C VHS.** Timothy Bottoms, Anthony Quayle, Jane Seymour, Keith Michell, Susan Hampshire; ***D:*** Alex Segal; ***W:*** Ernest Kinoy. *COL*

The Story of Dr. Wassell ½ **1944** Courageous true story of Corydon M. Wassell (Cooper), who won the Navy Cross for humanitarianism in WWII. Stationed in Java when the Japanese overrun the island, Wassell's placed in charge of evacuating the wounded. When he learns that stretcher cases must be left behind, he disobeys orders to rescue some badly wounded soldiers and get them to safety. (Naturally, there has to be some romance, so Cooper's paired with Day as a Red Cross nurse). Based on the book by James Hilton. **137m/C VHS.** Gary Cooper, Laraine Day, Signe Hasso, Dennis O'Keefe, Carol Thurston, Carl Esmond, Stanley Ridges, Paul Kelly, Elliott Reid, Philip Ahn, Barbara Britton; ***D:*** Cecil B. DeMille; ***W:*** Charles Bennett, Alan LeMay; ***C:*** Victor Milner; ***M:*** Victor Young. *MCA*

The Story of Fausta ½ *Romance da Empregada* **1988 (R)** An unhappily married cleaning woman in the slums of Rio entices all the money and gifts she can out of an elderly widower. Decidely grim comedy-drama, well-done but unsparing in its depiction of overwhelming greed. In Portuguese with English subtitles. **90m/C VHS.** *BR* Betty Faria, Daniel Filho, Brandao Filho; ***D:*** Bruno Barreto; ***M:*** Ruben Blades. *FXL, INJ, FCT*

The Story of Jacob & Joseph **1974 (R)** Fine Biblical drama finds brothers Jacob and Esau fighting over their birthright, tearing apart their family for twenty years. When the brothers finally reconcile it's only to cast an envious eye on youngest brother Joseph, whom they sell into slavery. Taken to Egypt Joseph uses his talents to become the Pharaoh's chief advisor but he can never forget his family or what was done to him. All-around good acting, directing and writing. Made for television. **96m/C VHS.** Keith Michell, Tony LoBianco, Julian Glover, Colleen Dewhurst, Herschel Bernardi, Harry Andrews; ***D:*** Michael Cacoyannis; ***W:*** Ernest Kinoy. *COL*

The Story of Louis Pasteur **1936** Formulaic Hollywood biopic raised a notch or two by Muni's superb portrayal of the famous scientist and his career leading up to his most famous discoveries. Acclaimed in its time; excellent despite low budget. **85m/B VHS, Beta.** Paul Muni, Josephine Hutchinson, Anita Louise, Fritz Leiber, Donald Woods, Porter Hall, Akim Tamiroff, Walter Kingsford; ***D:*** William Dieterle; ***C:*** Gaetano Antonio "Tony" Gaudio. Academy Awards '36: Best Actor (Muni), Best Story & Screenplay; National Board of Review Awards '36: 10 Best Films of the Year; Nominations: Academy Awards '36: Best Picture. *MGM, BTV*

The Story of O **1975** A young woman's love for one man moves her to surrender herself to many men, in order to please him. Soft-core porn with bondage and S&M beautified by camera work. Based on the classic Freudian-erotic novel by Pauline Reage. **97m/C VHS, Beta, LV.** Corinne Clery, Anthony Steel; ***D:*** Just Jaeckin. *HHE*

The Story of O, Part 2 **1987** A sort-of sequel to the erotic classic, in which the somewhat soiled vixen takes over an American conglomerate by seducing everyone in it. **107m/C Beta, LV.** Sandra Wey, Carole James. *LIV, VES, HHE*

The Story of Qui Ju **1991 (PG)** A simple story, beautifully directed and acted, about a peasant woman's search for justice. The pregnant Qui Ju's husband is assaulted and injured by the head of their village. Outraged, Qui Ju slowly climbs the Chinese administrative ladder from official to higher official as she insistently seeks redress. Presents a close observance of daily life and customs with a strong female lead. Adapted from the novel "The Wan Family's Lawsuit" by Chen Yuan Bin. In Mandarin Chinese with English subtitles. **100m/C VHS, LV.** *CH* Gong Li, Lei Lao Sheng, Liu Pei Qu, Ge Zhi Jun, Ye Jun, Yang Liu Xia; ***D:*** Zhang Yimou; ***W:*** Liu Heng. National Society of Film Critics Awards '93: Best Foreign Film; Venice Film Festival '92: Best Actress (Li), Best Film; Nominations: Independent Spirit Awards '94: Best Foreign Film. *COL*

The Story of Robin Hood & His Merrie Men *The Story of Robin Hood* **1952** Well-made swashbuckler based on the English legend was Disney's second live action feature. Almost, but not quite, as memorable as the 1938 Michael Curtiz "Adventures of Robin Hood." Curtiz's version had Errol Flynn, after all. **83m/C VHS, Beta.** Richard Todd, Joan Rice, Peter Finch, Martita Hunt; ***D:*** Ken Annakin. *DIS*

The Story of Ruth **1960** Biblical saga of adventures of Ruth as she denounces her pagan gods and flees to Israel. Typically "epic" with overwrought performances. Alternately not too bad to downright boring. **132m/C VHS, Beta.** Elana Eden, Viveca Lindfors, Peggy Wood, Tom Tryon, Stuart Whitman, Jeff Morrow, Thayer David, Eduard Franz; ***D:*** Henry Koster. *FOX, IGP*

The Story of Seabiscuit ½ *Pride of Kentucky* **1949** The famous racing winner Seabiscuit is featured in a fluffy story of a racetrack romance. Temple is in love with a jockey (McCallister) but wants him to give up racing. Her uncle (Fitzgerald), who is Seabiscuit's trainer, has other things in mind. **93m/C VHS.** Shirley Temple, Barry Fitzgerald, Lon McCallister, Rosemary DeCamp; ***D:*** David Butler. *MGM, BTV*

Story of the Dragon **1982** How Bruce Lee developed the martial arts technique of Jeet Kune Do. **93m/C VHS, Beta.** Bruce Li, Hwang Jang Lee, Carter Wong, Roy Horan. *WVE*

The Story of the Late Chrysanthemum ½ **1939** Classic drama about the son of a Kabuki actor who falls in love with a servant girl against his father's wishes. Their doomed affair is the center of the plot. Acclaimed and sensitive drama, in Japanese with English subtitles. **115m/B VHS, Beta.** *JP* Shotaro Hanayagi, Kakuo Mori, Kokichi Takada, Gonjuro Kawarazaki, Yoko Umemura; ***D:*** Kenji Mizoguchi. *FCT*

The Story of Vernon and Irene Castle **1939** In this, their last film together for RKO, Astaire and Rogers portray the internationally successful ballroom dancers who achieved popularity in the early 1900s. Irene Castle served as technical advisor for the film and exasperated everyone on the set by insisting that Rogers be a brunette. Still fun, vintage Fred and Ginger. ♫Only When You're In My Arms; Missouri Waltz; Oh, You Beautiful Doll; Nights of Gladness; By the Beautiful Sea; Glow, Little Glow Worm; Destiny Waltz; Row, Row, Row; The Yama Yama Man. **93m/B VHS, Beta, LV.** Fred Astaire, Ginger Rogers, Edna May Oliver, Lew Fields, Jack Perrin, Walter Brennan; ***D:*** H.C. Potter. *TTC, MED*

Story of William S. Hart/Sad Clowns **192?** Features William S. Hart as a cowboy in "Hell's Hinges" and "Tumbleweeds" (1925). From "The History of the Motion Picture" series. **50m/B VHS, Beta.** William S. Hart, Buster Keaton, Harry Langdon. *CCB*

The Story of Women *Une Affaire de Femmes* **1988** Riveting factual account of a woman (Huppert) who was guillotined for performing abortions in Nazi-occupied France. In French with English subtitles. **110m/C VHS.** *FR* Isabelle Huppert, Francois Cluzet, Marie Trintignant, Nils Tavernier, Louis Ducreux; ***D:*** Claude Chabrol; ***W:*** Claude Chabrol, Colo Tavernier O'Hagan; ***M:*** Matthieu Chabrol. Los Angeles Film Critics Association Awards '89: Best Foreign Film; New York Film Critics Awards '89: Best Foreign Film; Venice Film Festival '88: Best Actress (Huppert). *NYF, INJ*

Storybook ½ **1995 (G)** Eight-year-old Brandon finds a magic storybook and enters into a realm of fantasy. He discovers the only way to return home from Storyland is to save the kingdom from the rule of Queen Evilia and along with Woody the Woodsman, Pouch the Boxing Kangaroo, and Hoot the Wise Owl, Brandon just may succeed. **88m/C VHS.** Sean Fitzgerald, William McNamara, Swoosie Kurtz, Robert Costanzo, James Doohan, Brenda Epperson, Gary Morgan, Richard Moll, Jack Scalia, Milton Berle; ***D:*** Lorenzo Doumani; ***W:*** Lorenzo Doumani, Susan Bowen. *REP*

Storytime Classics **1983** A collection of popular fairy tales narrated by Katharine Hepburn. **78m/C VHS, Beta.** *VES*

Storyville ½ **1974 (PG)** Love and music overcome prostitution and poverty in this turn-of-the-century New Orleans jazz drama, but tragedy prevails. **96m/C VHS, Beta.** Tim Rooney, Jeannie Wilson, Butch Benit, Wayne Mack, Bond Gideon, Oley Sassone; ***D:*** Jack Weis. *NO*

Storyville **1992 (R)** Southern Gothic tale set in New Orleans about a feckless young lawyer running for a local congressional seat. Neither Cray nor his family are strong candidates for the family values vote. Cray is separated from his wife and willingly indulges in an affair with a beautiful and mysterious young woman. This leads to a blackmail plot when he finds out his lover has been videotaping their antics. There's also a murder investigation and a host of family skeletons rattling around. Robards is fine as the crafty uncle but Spader's low-key attitude works against the story. Directorial debut of Frost. **112m/C VHS, LV.** James Spader, Joanne Whalley, Jason Robards Jr., Charlotte Lewis, Michael Warren, Piper Laurie, Michael Parks, Chuck McCann, Woody Strode, Charles Haid; ***D:*** Mark Frost; ***W:*** Mark Frost, Lee Reynolds; ***M:*** Carter Burwell. *COL*

Stowaway **1936 (G)** After her missionary parents are killed in a Chinese revolution, Shirley stows away on a San Francisco-bound liner and plays cupid to a bickering couple who adopt her. ♫Good Night, My Love; One Never Knows, Does One; You Gotta S-M-I-L-E to Be H-A-P-P-Y; I Wanna Go To the Zoo; That's What I Want For Christmas. **86m/B VHS, Beta.** Shirley Temple, Robert Young, Alice Faye, Eugene Pallette, Helen Westley, Arthur Treacher, Astrid Allwyn; ***D:*** William A. Seiter; ***C:*** Arthur C. Miller. *FOX*

Straight for the Heart *A Corps Perdu* **1988** Photojournalist Pierre returns to Montreal after a harrowing assignment in Nicaragua. His homecoming is less than happy when he discovers both his lovers, David and Sarah, have deserted him. Pierre takes to wandering the Montreal streets, taking pictures, hoping they will help him make some sense of his life and help him re-establish a connection with beauty and humanity. In French with English subtitles. **92m/C VHS.** *CA* Matthias Habich, Johanne-Marie Tremblay; ***D:*** Lea Pool. *WBF*

Straight Line **1988** T.S. Turner is a private investigator who goes after street gangs in order to prevent further violence in this action-packed story. **95m/C VHS.** Mr. T, Sean Roberge, Ron Ryan. *CAF, MOV*

Straight Out of Brooklyn **1991 (R)** A bleak, nearly hopeless look at a struggling black family in a Brooklyn housing project. The son seeks escape through crime, his father in booze. An up-close and raw look at part of society seldom shown in mainstream film, its undeniable power is sapped by ragged production values and a loose narrative prone to melodrama. Rich (seen in a supporting role) was only 19 years old when he completed this, funded partly by PBS-TV's "American Playhouse." **91m/C VHS.** George T. Odis, Ann D. Sanders, Lawrence Gilliard, Mark Malone Jr., Reana E. Drummond, Barbara Sanon; ***D:*** Matty Rich; ***W:*** Matty Rich. Independent Spirit Awards '92: Best First Feature; Sundance Film Festival '91: Special Jury Prize. *HBO, FCT, WAR*

Straight Shooter ☙ **1940** An early sagebrush programmer. **60m/B VHS, Beta.** Tim McCoy. *NOS, DVT*

Straight Shootin' ☙☙½ **1917** Ford's first major effort launched both Carey and Gibson to national fame. Prototypical western; great action, great scenery. Silent. **53m/B VHS, Beta.** Harry Carey Sr., Hoot Gibson, Mollie Malone; ***D:*** John Ford. *GPV, VCN, DVT*

Straight Talk ☙☙½ **1992 (PG)** Shirlee (Parton), a down-home gal from Arkansas, heads for Chicago to start life anew. She finds a job as a receptionist at WNDY radio, but is mistaken for the new radio psychologist. Her homespun advice ("Get off the cross. Somebody needs the wood.") becomes hugely popular and soon "Dr." Shirlee is the toast of the town. Parton's advice is the funniest part of this flimsy movie, but she is helped immensely by Dunne and Orbach. Woods, however, is not in his element in a romantic comedy, and holds the movie down. **91m/C VHS, Beta.** Dolly Parton, James Woods, Griffin Dunne, Michael Madsen, Deidre O'Connell, John Sayles, Teri Hatcher, Spalding Gray, Jerry Orbach, Philip Bosco, Charles Fleischer, Jay Thomas; ***D:*** Barnet Kellman; ***W:*** Craig Bolotin, Patricia Resnick; ***M:*** Brad Fiedel. *HPH*

Straight Time ☙☙☙ **1978 (R)** Ex-con Hoffman hits the streets for the first time in six years and finds himself again falling into a life of crime. Well-told, sobering story flopped at the box office and has never received the recognition it deserved. Convincing, realistic portrayal of a criminal. Hoffman was the original director, but gave the reins to Grosbard. Based on the novel "No Beast So Fierce" by Edward Bunker. **114m/C VHS, Beta.** Dustin Hoffman, Harry Dean Stanton, Gary Busey, Theresa Russell, M. Emmet Walsh, Kathy Bates; ***D:*** Ulu Grosbard; ***W:*** Jeffrey Boam, Alvin Sargent, Edward Bunker; ***C:*** Owen Roizman; ***M:*** David Shire. *WAR*

Straight to Hell ☙½ **1987 (R)** A wildly senseless, anachronistic western spoof about a motley, inept gang of frontier thieves. An overplayed, indiscriminating punk spaghetti oat-opera. **86m/C VHS, Beta.** Dennis Hopper, Joe Strummer, Elvis Costello, Grace Jones, Jim Jarmusch, Dick Rude, Courtney Love, Sy Richardson; ***D:*** Alex Cox; ***W:*** Alex Cox. *FOX, OM*

Straight Up ☙½ **1990** A musical f/x-ridden attempts to warn MTV-era children about drugs, but visual gimmicks often overwhelm the message. Gossett sings nicely as a cosmic sage of abstinence, who cautions a boy against substance abuse. The smartest segment lambasts cigarette and alcohol ads. **75m/C VHS, Beta.** Chad Allen, Louis Gossett Jr. *RHI*

Strait-Jacket ☙☙½ **1964** After Crawford is released from an insane asylum where she was sent 20 years for axing her husband and his mistress, mysterious axe murders begin to occur in the neighborhood. Coincidence? Aging axist Crawford is the prime suspect, and even she cannot say for sure who's doing it. Daughter Baker is there to help her adjust. Moderately creepy grade B+ slasher is lifted somewhat by Crawford. Written by Robert Bloch ("Psycho"). Never one to miss a gimmick, director Castle arranged for the distribution of cardboard "bloody axes" to all theater patrons attending the movie. **89m/B VHS, Beta.** Joan Crawford, Leif Erickson, Diane Baker, George Kennedy; ***D:*** William Castle; ***W:*** Robert Bloch; ***M:*** Van Alexander. *COL*

Stranded ☙☙ **1987 (PG-13)** A group of aliens escaping interplanetary persecution land on Earth and enlist the aid of an Earth family. Solid characters make it more than sci-fi; sort of a parable of intolerance, human (and alien) goodness, etc. **80m/C VHS, Beta, LV.** Maureen O'Sullivan, Ione Skye, Cameron Dye; ***D:*** Tex Fuller; ***W:*** Alan Castle. *COL*

The Strange Affair of Uncle Harry ☙☙½ *Uncle Harry* **1945** Small-town gothic with fine acting by Sanders, an aging bachelor who plots murder when his romance is threatened by a jealous sister. A title card asks you not to reveal the 'surprise' ending—a hackneyed twist that appeased the censors but made producer Joan Harrison resign in protest. Based on a play by Robert Job. Tape suffers from poor film-video transfer. **80m/B VHS, LV.** George Sanders, Geraldine Fitzgerald, Ella Raines, Sara Allgood, Moyna MacGill, Samuel S. Hinds, Harry von Zell; ***D:*** Robert Siodmak. *REP, FCT*

A Strange and Deadly Occurence ☙½ **1974** Strange things start to happen to a family when they move to a house in a remote area. Made-for-television. **74m/C VHS, Beta.** Robert Stack, Vera Miles, L.Q. Jones, Herb Edelman; ***D:*** John Llewellyn Moxey. *WOV*

Strange Awakening ☙ **1958** Traveling in France while recuperating from amnesia, Barker is trapped in a plot of fraud and theft. Confused and contrived. **75m/B VHS.** *GB* Lex Barker, Carole Mathews, Nora Swinburne, Richard Molinos, Peter Dyneley; ***D:*** Montgomery Tully. *SNC*

Strange Bedfellows ☙☙½ **1965** Within 24 hours of Carter Hudson (Hudson) arriving to work in London, he's met and married eccentric Italian Toni Vincenti (Lollobrigida). Complete opposites, the marriage is soon over and Carter returns to the States. Seven years later, he's back in London, ready to officially divorce Toni but learns from company PR whiz Dick Bramwell (Young) that his big promotion is contingent on his happy marriage. Carter courts Toni again, and tries to support her liberal causes and friends, but it turns out her latest stunt is aimed at his firm. Supposedly a check of the closing credits shows the film was shot on a Universal back lot and not on location. **104m/C VHS.** Rock Hudson, Gina Lollobrigida, Gig Young, Edward Judd, Howard St. John, Nancy Kulp, Bernard Fox, Terry-Thomas; ***D:*** Melvin Frank; ***W:*** Melvin Frank, Michael Pertwee; ***C:*** Leo Tover; ***M:*** Leigh Harline. *MCA*

Strange Behavior ☙☙ *Dead Kids; Small Town Massacre* **1981 (R)** In a small Midwestern town, the police chief follows the clues from a series of murders to the experimental lab of the local college. Seems there's a mad scientist involved... Grisly and creepy, but unduly ballyhooed when it appeared. Shot on location in New Zealand. **105m/C Beta.** Michael Murphy, Louise Fletcher, Dan Shor, Fiona Lewis, Arthur Dignam, Marc McClure, Scott Brady; ***D:*** Michael Laughlin; ***W:*** Bill Condon. *COL, RHI*

Strange Brew ☙☙½ **1983 (PG)** The screen debut of the SCTV alumni's characters Doug & Bob MacKenzie, the Great White North duo. They do battle with a powerful, megalomaniacal brew master over - what else? - a case of beer. Dumb, but what did you expect? Watch it, or be a hoser. **91m/C VHS, Beta, LV.** Rick Moranis, Dave Thomas, Max von Sydow, Paul Dooley; ***D:*** Rick Moranis, Dave Thomas; ***W:*** Rick Moranis, Dave Thomas, Steve DeJarnatt; ***M:*** Charles Fox. *MGM*

Strange Cargo ☙☙½ **1940** Convicts escaping from Devil's Island are mystically entranced by a Christ-like fugitive en route to freedom. An odd, pretentious Hollywood fable waiting for a cult following. Gable and Crawford's eighth and final pairing. Adapted by Anita Loos from the book "Not Too Narrow...Not Too Deep" by Richard Sale. **105m/B VHS, Beta.** Clark Gable, Joan Crawford, Ian Hunter, Peter Lorre, Paul Lukas, Albert Dekker, J. Edward Bromberg, Eduardo Ciannelli, Frederick Worlock; ***D:*** Frank Borzage. *MGM*

Strange Case of Dr. Jekyll & Mr. Hyde ☙☙ **1968** An adaptation of the classic Robert Louis Stevenson book about a scientist who conducts experiments on himself to separate good from evil. Palance is oddly but appealingly cast; Jarrott's bad direction wrecks it. Made for TV. **128m/C VHS, Beta.** Jack Palance, Leo Genn, Oscar Homolka, Billie Whitelaw, Denholm Elliott; ***D:*** Charles Jarrott. *LIV, MPI*

Strange Case of Dr. Jekyll & Mr. Hyde ☙☙½ **1989** The Robert Louis Stevenson classic, with Hyde portrayed as an icy, well-dressed sociopath. In Shelley Duvall's "Nightmare Classics" series. More psychological than special effect-y. Made for cable. **60m/C VHS, Beta.** Anthony Andrews, Laura Dern, George Murdock, Nicholas Guest; ***D:*** Michael Lindsay-Hogg. *WAR, OM*

The Strange Case of the End of Civilization as We Know It ☙☙½ **1993** Cleese stars as the detective grandson of Sherlock Holmes, who also has a reputation for making a mockery of police investigations. Nevertheless, the police commissioner summons him to capture that diabolical criminal Professor Moriarty. **55m/C VHS.** *GB* John Cleese, Stratford Johns, Connie Booth, Arthur Lowe. *KUL, FCT, SIG*

Strange Confession **1945** Contains one of the truly rare Inner Sanctum Mysteries from Universal. **62m/C VHS.** Lon Chaney Jr., Brenda Joyce, J. Carrol Naish, Milburn Stone, Lloyd Bridges; ***D:*** Jon Hoffman. *GPV*

The Strange Countess ☙☙ **1961** A girl is almost murdered and no apparent motive can be found until a 20-year old murder is uncovered in this Edgar Wallace story. **96m/C VHS.** *GE* Joachim Fuchsberger, Lil Dagover, Marianne Hoppe, Brigitte Grothum; ***D:*** Josef von Baky. *SNC*

Strange Days ☙☙☙ **1995 (R)** It's 1999 in volatile L.A. and vice cop-turned-street-hustler Lenny Nero (Fiennes) is plying his SQUID trade—discs that offer the wearer the chance to experience any vice. The seedily likeable Lenny draws the line at peddling snuff clips until one capturing the murder of his friend, hooker Iris (Bako), shows up. Lenny's in way over his head and turns to self-sufficient security agent Mace (Bassett) to save him. The phenomenal Bassett heats up the screen (and kicks major butt) while the generally cerebral Fiennes shows why someone could care about his desperate lowlife. Bigelow's an action expert and struts on the film's dark visuals while offering some emotional impact with her society-on-the-eve-of-destruction saga. **145m/C VHS.** Ralph Fiennes, Angela Bassett, Juliette Lewis, Tom Sizemore, Michael Wincott, Brigitte Bako, Vincent D'Onofrio, William Fichtner, Richard Edson, Glenn Plummer, Josef Sommer; ***D:*** Kathryn Bigelow; ***W:*** James Cameron, Jay Cocks; ***C:*** Matthew F. Leonetti; ***M:*** Graeme Revell. *FXV*

Strange Fruit ☙☙ **1979** Based on Lillian Smith's novel, this program tells the story of a black painter in Georgia, 1948, who faces racism. At first avoiding voter registration, he becomes involved and is killed. His death serves as an inspiration to his community. **33m/C VHS, Beta.** *LCA*

Strange Illusion ☙☙½ *Out of the Night* **1945** Unbalanced teen Lydon believes his mother, about to remarry, was responsible for his father's death. He feigns insanity in a plan to catch her, but is sent to an asylum, where he nearly goes insane for real. Slow and implausible, but creepy enough to hold your interest. **87m/B VHS, Beta.** Jimmy Lydon, Warren William, Sally Eilers, Regis Toomey, Charles Arnt, George Reed; ***D:*** Edgar G. Ulmer. *SNC*

Strange Interlude ☙☙☙ *Strange Interval* **1932** Shearer is at her best in screen adaptation of talky Eugene O'Neill play in which she portrays a young wife who wants a child, but discovers that insanity runs in her husband's family. Doing the only sensible thing, she decides to have a child by another man (Gable). Interesting because the characters' thoughts are revealed to the audience through voice-overs. **110m/B VHS.** Norma Shearer, Clark Gable, May Robson, Ralph Morgan, Robert Young, Mary Alden, Maureen O'Sullivan, Henry B. Walthall; ***D:*** Robert Z. Leonard; ***C:*** Lee Garmes. *MGM*

Strange Interlude ☙☙½ **1990** Slow PBS production of Eugene O'Neill's famous drama covering two decades of the lives and loves of an upper-class family. Excellent performances help to make up for talkiness. On two cassettes. **190m/C VHS.** Glenda Jackson, Jose Ferrer, David Dukes, Ken Howard, Edward Petherbridge; ***D:*** Herbert Wise. *FRH, TVC*

Strange Invaders 1983 (PG) Body-snatchers-from-space sci-fi with an attitude—fun spoof of '50s alien flicks. Space folks had taken over a midwestern town in the '50s, assuming the locals' appearance and attire before returning to their ship. Seems one of them married an earthling—but divorced and moved with her half-breed daughter to New York City. So the hicksters from space arrive in Gotham wearing overalls... **94m/C VHS, Beta, LV.** Paul LeMat, Nancy Allen, Diana Scarwid, Michael Lerner, Louise Fletcher, Wallace Shawn, Fiona Lewis, Kenneth Tobey, June Lockhart, Charles Lane, Dey Young, Mark Goddard; ***D:*** Michael Laughlin; ***W:*** Bill Condon. *VES*

The Strange Love of Martha Ivers 1946 Douglas is good in his screen debut as the wimpy spouse of unscrupulous Stanwyck. Stanwyck shines as the woman who must stay with Douglas because of a crime she committed long ago... Tough, dark melodrama; classic film noir. **117m/B VHS, Beta, LV.** Barbara Stanwyck, Van Heflin, Kirk Douglas, Lizabeth Scott, Judith Anderson; ***D:*** Lewis Milestone; ***C:*** Victor Milner; ***M:*** Miklos Rozsa. Nominations: Academy Awards '46: Best Story. *NOS, BAR, DVT*

The Strange Love of Molly Louvain ½ *Molly Louvain* **1932** Unwed mother Dvorak finds herself in hiding after her criminal beau fatally shoots a police officer. She falls in love with the unsuspecting newsman (Tracy) hot on her trail. Good performance from Dvorak but the film in general lacks sparkle. Adapted from the play "Tinsel Girl" by Maurine Watkins. **70m/B VHS.** Ann Dvorak, Lee Tracy, Richard Cromwell, Guy Kibbee, Leslie Fenton, Frank McHugh, Evalyn Knapp, Charles Middleton, Mary Doran, C. Henry Gordon; ***D:*** Michael Curtiz; ***W:*** Erwin Gelsey, Brown Holmes. *MGM*

Strange New World ½ 1975 Three astronauts awake from 188 years in the fridge to find cloning has arrived. Made for TV as a pilot for a hoped-for series that might have been even worse. **100m/C VHS.** John Saxon, Kathleen Miller, Keene Curtis, Martine Beswick, James Olson, Catherine Bach, Richard Farnsworth, Ford Rainey; ***D:*** Robert Butler. *UNI*

Strange Shadows in an Empty Room *Blazing Magnums; Shadows in an Empty Room* **1976 (R)** Sleuth Whitman wants answers about the murder of his kid sis. He beats lots of people up, and the viewer leaves the empty living room to look at the inside of the fridge, which is more interesting. **97m/C VHS, Beta.** Stuart Whitman, John Saxon, Martin Landau, Tisa Farrow, Carole Laure, Gayle Hunnicutt; ***D:*** Martin Herbert. *VES*

Strange Tales 198? A collection of fantasy shorts, including "Twilight Journey," "The Crystal Quest" and "The Visitant." **60m/C VHS, Beta.** *VDC*

Strange Tales/Ray Bradbury Theatre ½ 1986 (R) An anthology of thrillers based on Bradbury stories: "Banshee," "The Screaming Woman," and "The Town Where No One Got Off." **86m/C VHS, Beta.** Jeff Goldblum, Peter O'Toole, Drew Barrymore, Charles Martin Smith. *CNG*

The Strange Woman 1946 Uneventful Hollywood costume drama. Lamarr stalks man after man, but never creates much excitement in spite of Ulmer's fancy camera work and intense pace. **100m/B VHS.** Hedy Lamarr, George Sanders, Louis Hayward, Gene Lockhart, Hillary Brooke, June Storey; ***D:*** Edgar G. Ulmer. *NOS, FCT*

Strange World of Coffin Joe 1968 A collection of three shocking horror episodes about a truly disgusting dollmaker who becomes tempted by his human-like creations, a balloon seller's repulsive necrophiliac impulses, and a doctor (the disguised Coffin Joe) with a sadistic gift for excruciating torture. In Spanish with English subtitles. **?m/C VHS.** *BR* Jose Mojica Marins; ***D:*** Jose Mojica Marins. *SMW, FCT, TPV*

The Strangeness *Woof!* **1985** Miners in search of gold release a "strange" creature from far beneath the earth—eek! Made on a negative budget. **90m/C VHS, Beta.** Dan Lunham, Terri Berland; ***D:*** David Michael Hillman. *TWE*

The Stranger ½ 1946 Notably conventional for Welles, but swell entertainment nonetheless. War crimes tribunal sets Nazi thug Shayne free hoping he'll lead them to his superior, Welles. Robinson trails Shayne through Europe and South America to a small town in Connecticut. Tight suspense made on a tight budget saved Welles's directorial career. **95m/B VHS, Beta.** Edward G. Robinson, Loretta Young, Martha Wentworth, Konstantin Shayne, Richard Long, Orson Welles; ***D:*** Orson Welles; ***C:*** Russell Metty. Nominations: Academy Awards '46: Best Story. *CNG, NOS, PSM*

The Stranger ½ 1973 Corbett crash-lands on a planet an awful lot like Earth - and must stay on the run. Uneven fugitive thriller in sci-fi drag. Made for TV. **100m/C VHS.** Cameron Mitchell, Glenn Corbett, Sharon Acker, Lew Ayres, George Coulouris, Dean Jagger; ***D:*** Lee H. Katzin. *NO*

The Stranger 1987 (R) Amnesiac car-wreck victim Bedelia begins regaining her memory, and realizes she witnessed several grisly murders. Is her shrink (Riegert) helping her remember, or keeping something from her? Good, neglected thriller. **93m/C VHS, Beta, 8mm.** *AR* Bonnie Bedelia, Peter Riegert, Barry Primus, David Spielberg, Julio de Grazia, Cecilia Roth, Marcus Woinski; ***D:*** Adolfo Aristarain; ***W:*** Dan Gurskis; ***M:*** Craig Safan. *COL*

The Stranger 1995 (R) Mystery woman (Long) rides into small town and rids it of a vicious motorcycle gang. Femme version of the lone hero saga. **98m/C VHS.** Kathy Long, Andrew Divoff, Eric Pierpont, Robin Lynn Heath; ***D:*** Fritz Kiersch; ***W:*** Gregory Poirier. *COL*

A Stranger Among Us 1992 (PG-13) A missing jeweler turns up dead and more than $1 million in diamonds has disappeared. NYPD Detective Emily Eden (Griffith) is called in to solve the case, and she decides she must go undercover in a community of Hasidic Jews to find the perpetrator. She not only finds the criminal, but she also falls in love with one of the group's most devout residents. Griffith is out of her element as a tough cop with her baby voice and cutesy style, but other actors, including Thal (in his movie debut) and Sara, perform splendidly, even though they are held back by a cumbersome script that is similar in many respects to "Witness." **109m/C VHS, Beta, LV.** Melanie Griffith, Eric Thal, John Pankow, Tracy Pollan, Lee Richardson, Mia Sara, Jamey Sheridan; ***D:*** Sidney Lumet; ***W:*** Robert J. Avrech; ***M:*** Jerry Bock. Golden Raspberry Awards '92: Worst Actress (Griffith). *HPH*

The Stranger and the Gunfighter 1976 The baddest spaghetti western of all time - or is it a kung fu movie? Alcoholic cowpoke Van Cleef and kung fu master Lieh pair up to find hidden treasure. There is a map, but parts are printed on the assorted fannies of various women. **106m/C VHS, Beta, LV.** Patty Shepard, Lee Van Cleef, Lo Lieh; ***D:*** Anthony (Antonio Margheriti) Dawson. *COL*

Stranger by Night 1994 (R) Detective Bobby Corcoran and his partner are hunting a mutilating serial killer. Since Corcoran suffers from blackouts and fits of rage the evidence begins pointing very close to home. **96m/C VHS.** Steven Bauer, William Katt, Jennifer Rubin, Michael Parks, Michelle Greene, J.J. Johnston; ***D:*** Gregory Brown; ***W:*** Daryl Haney; ***M:*** Ashley Irwin. *APX*

The Stranger from Pecos 1945 Brown fights a cheater who swindles people at poker and then uses the money to buy their mortgages. Meanwhile, his pal Hatton finds a novel way to help a robbery victim buy back his property. **55m/B VHS.** Johnny Mack Brown, Raymond Hatton, Kirby Grant, Christine McIntyre, Steve Clark, Kermit Maynard; ***D:*** Lambert Hillyer. *DVT, HEG*

The Stranger from Venus *Woof! Immediate Disaster; The Venusian* **1954** "The Day the Earth Stood Still" warmed over. Venusian Dantine tells earth lady Neal he's worried about the future of her planet. Real low budget. Includes previews of coming attractions from classic sci-fi. **78m/C VHS, Beta.** Patricia Neal, Helmut Dantine, Derek Bond. *MED, MLB*

Stranger in Paso Bravo 1973 A distraught drifter returns to a strange Italian town to avenge the murders of his wife and daughter years before. Dubbed. **92m/C VHS, Beta.** *IT* Anthony Steffen, Giulia Rubini, Eduardo Fajardo, Andriana Ambesi. *UNI*

Stranger in Town 1957 A young journalist looks into the murder of an American composer in a sleepy English village. He discovers blackmail and intrigue. So-so thriller. Based on the novel "The Uninvited" by Frank Chittenden. **73m/B VHS, Beta.** *GB* Alex Nicol, Ann Page, Mary Laura Wood, Mona Washbourne, Charles Lloyd Pack; ***D:*** George Pollock. *SNC*

A Stranger is Watching ½ 1982 (R) Rapist-murderer Torn holds his victim's 10-year-old daughter hostage, along with a New York television anchorwoman. Complicated and distasteful. Made for TV. **92m/C VHS, Beta.** Rip Torn, Kate Mulgrew, James Naughton; ***D:*** Sean S. Cunningham. *MGM*

Stranger on the Third Floor 1940 Reporter McGuire's testimony helped convict cabbie Cook of murder, but he begins to have doubts. Odd, shadowy psycho-thriller considered by some the first film noir. The reporter comes to be suspected of the crime...and his fiancee pounds the pavement to prove him innocent. Average acting, but great camera work gives the whole a deliciously menacing feel. **64m/B VHS, Beta, LV.** Peter Lorre, John McGuire, Elisha Cook Jr., Margaret Tallichet, Charles Halton; ***D:*** Boris Ingster. *CCB, MED*

Stranger than Paradise 1984 (R) Regular guy, nerdy sidekick and Hungarian girl cousin traipse around America being bored and having fun and adventure. New York, then - on to Cleveland! The thinking person's mindless flick. Inventive, independent comedy made on quite a low budget was acclaimed at Cannes. **90m/B VHS, Beta, LV.** *GE* Richard Edson, Eszter Balint, John Lurie; ***D:*** Jim Jarmusch; ***W:*** Jim Jarmusch; ***M:*** John Lurie. National Society of Film Critics Awards '84: Best Film. *FOX*

The Stranger Who Looks Like Me 1974 Adoptees Baxter and Bridges set out to find their real parents. Not-bad TV fare. Blake is Baxter's real-life mom. Look for a young Patrick Duffy. **74m/C VHS, Beta.** Meredith Baxter, Beau Bridges, Whitney Blake; ***D:*** Larry Peerce. *WOV*

The Stranger Within ½ 1974 Made-for-TV "Rosemary's Baby" rip-off. Eden is in a family way, though hubby Grizzard is impotent. The stranger within begins commanding her to do its bidding, just as if she were a genie. **74m/C VHS, Beta.** Barbara Eden, George Grizzard, Joyce Van Patten, Nehemiah Persoff; ***D:*** Lee Philips; ***M:*** Charles Fox. *LIV*

The Stranger Wore a Gun 1953 Hoping to remove a black mark against his name, Jeff Travis (Scott) goes to Arizona and ends up foiling a stagecoach robbery. Features a great action sequence in a burning saloon. Originally shot in 3-D, this is based on the novel "Yankee Gold" by John M. Cunningham. **83m/C VHS.** Randolph Scott, Claire Trevor, Joan Weldon, George Macready, Alfonso Bedoya, Lee Marvin, Ernest Borgnine, Pierre Watkin, Joseph Vitale; ***D:*** Andre de Toth. *COL*

Strangers 1990 Australian horror film revolves around a man in a troubled marriage who fools around with another woman, only to realize she is dead set on mating for life. When he hesitates, she vows to murder his wife. Very similar to the smash hit "Fatal Attraction." **83m/C VHS.** *AU* James Healey, Anne Looby; ***D:*** Craig Lahiff. *NO*

Strangers 1991 (R) Features three provocative vignettes that take place far from home. Fiorentino, Chen, and Hutton each star in an erotic story played out in a foreign land. **85m/C VHS, LV.** Linda Fiorentino, Joan Chen, Timothy Hutton; ***D:*** Joan Tewkesbury. *PSM*

Stranger's Gold 1971 A mysterious gunslinger eliminates corruption in a western mining town. **90m/C VHS, Beta.** Gianni "John" Garko, Antonio Vilar, Daniela Giordano. *GEM*

Strangers in Good Company ☠☠☠ *The Company of Strangers* **1991 (PG)** A loving metaphor to growing older. Director Scott uses non-actors for every role in this quiet little film about a bus-load of elderly women lost in the Canadian wilderness. They wait for rescue without hystrionics, using the opportunity instead to get to know each other and nature. Beautifully made, intelligent, uncommon and worthwhile. **101m/C VHS, Beta.** *CA* Alice Diabo, Mary Meigs, Cissy Meddings, Beth Webber, Winifred Holden, Constance Garneau, Catherine Roche, Michelle Sweeney; ***D:*** Cynthia Scott; ***W:*** Cynthia Scott, David Wilson, Gloria Demers, Sally Bochner; ***M:*** Marie Bernard. *TOU*

Strangers in Paradise ☠½ **1986** A scientist who had cryogenically frozen himself to escape the Nazis is thawed out in the present, and his powers are used by a delinquent-obsessed sociopath. **81m/C VHS, Beta.** ***D:*** Ulli Lommel; ***W:*** Ulli Lommel. *LIV, VES*

Strangers in the City ☠☠ **1962** Puerto Ricans newly arrived in New York try to make their way. Serious but slightly overwrought immigrant-family melodrama. **80m/B VHS, Beta.** Robert Gentile, Camilo Delgado, Rosita De Triana; ***D:*** Rick Carrier. *NLC*

Strangers Kiss ☠☠½ **1983 (R)** Circa 1955: Hollywood director encourages his two leads to have an off-screen romance to bring reality to his film. Conflict arises when the leading lady's boyfriend, the film's financier, gets wind of the scheme. Intriguing, fun, slightly off-center. Based on Stanley Kubrick's film "Killer Kiss." **93m/C VHS, Beta.** Peter Coyote, Victoria Tennant, Blaine Novak, Dan Shor, Richard Romanus, Linda Kerridge, Carlos Palomino; ***D:*** Matthew Chapman; ***W:*** Blaine Novak, Matthew Chapman; ***M:*** Gato Barbieri. *CNG*

Strangers of the Evening ☠☠ **1932** In its day this dark comedy/mystery caught flak for its gruesomeness. There's been a mixup at the undertaker's, and the wrong body was buried— possibly alive. Good photography and acting make the humor work, intentionally or not. Based on the novel "The Illustrious Corpse," by Tiffany Thayer. **70m/B VHS.** ZaSu Pitts, Eugene Pallette, Lucien Littlefield, Tully Marshall, Miriam Seegar, Theodore von Eltz; ***D:*** H. Bruce Humberstone. *SNC, NOS*

Strangers on a Train ☠☠☠☠ **1951** Long before there was "Throw Momma from the Train," there was this Hitchcock super-thriller about two passengers who accidentally meet and plan to "trade" murders. Amoral Walker wants the exchange and the money he'll inherit by his father's death; Granger would love to end his stifling marriage and wed Roman, a senator's daughter, but finds the idea ultimately sickening. What happens is pure Hitchcock. Screenplay co-written by murder-mystery great Raymond Chandler. Patricia Hitchcock, the director's only child, plays Roman's sister. The concluding "carousel" scene is a masterpiece. From the novel by Patricia Highsmith. **101m/B VHS, Beta, LV.** Farley Granger, Robert Walker, Ruth Roman, Leo G. Carroll, Patricia Hitchcock, Marion Lorne; ***D:*** Alfred Hitchcock; ***W:*** Raymond Chandler; ***C:*** Robert Burks; ***M:*** Dimitri Tiomkin. National Board of Review Awards '51: 10 Best Films of the Year; Nominations: Academy Awards '51: Best Black and White Cinematography. *WAR, MLB*

Strangers: The Story of a Mother and Daughter ☠☠☠ **1979** Rowlands is the long-estranged daughter of Davis, who won an Emmy for her portrayal of the embittered widow. The great actress truly is at her recent best in this made-for-TV tearjerker, and Rowlands keeps pace. **88m/C VHS, Beta.** Bette Davis, Gena Rowlands, Ford Rainey, Donald Moffat; ***D:*** Milton Katselas. *TLF*

Strangers When We Meet ☠☠½ **1960** A married architect and his equally married neighbor begin an affair. Their lives become a series of deceptions. Lavish but uninvolving soaper. Written by Evan Hunter and based on his novel. **117m/B VHS, Beta.** Kirk Douglas, Kim Novak, Ernie Kovacs, Walter Matthau, Barbara Rush, Virginia Bruce, Kent Smith; ***D:*** Richard Quine; ***C:*** Charles B(ryant) Lang. *COL*

Stranglehold ☠½ **1994 (R)** Cooper (Trimble) is the executive assistant of Congresswoman Fillmore (McWhirter), who becomes the hostage of a nerve gas holding nutcase (Wells). Cooper manages to evade the nutcase's thugs while using his martial arts prowess to rescue his boss. **73m/C VHS.** *AU* Jerry Trimble, Jillian McWhirter, Vernon Wells; ***D:*** Cirio H. Santiago. *NHO*

The Strangler ☠½ **1964** A confused, mother-fixated psychopath strangles young women. Made at the time the Boston Strangler was terrorizing Beantown. The film slayer strangles ten lasses before his love of dolls gives him away. **89m/B VHS, Beta.** Victor Buono, David McLean, Diane Sayer, Ellen Corby, Jeanne Bates, James B. Sikking; ***D:*** Burt Topper. *FXV, FOX, FCT*

Strangler of Blackmoor Castle ☠☠ **1963** Someone is murdering people at an old English castle and Scotland Yard sends an investigator to track down the killer. **?m/C VHS.** *GE* Karin Dor, Ingmar Zeisberg. *SNC*

Strangler of the Swamp ☠½ **1946** The ghost of an innocent man wrongly hanged for murder returns to terrorize the village where he was lynched. Decidedly B-grade horror features an out-of-focus ghost and Edwards—on the other side of the camera—as one of his would-be victims. **60m/B VHS, Beta.** Rosemary La Planche, Blake Edwards, Charles Middleton, Robert Barrat; ***D:*** Frank Wisbar. *COL*

Strangler of the Tower **1964** Edgar Wallace thriller made in Germany. **?m/C VHS.** *GE NO*

Strapless ☠☠½ **1990 (R)** Just-turned-40 American doctor Brown lives and works in London. She has just ended a long-term romance, and takes up with suave foreigner Ganz. Her young sister Fonda, arrives for a visit. Good, interesting if sometimes plodding story of adult relationships. **99m/C VHS, Beta, LV.** Blair Brown, Bridget Fonda, Bruno Ganz, Alan Howard, Michael Gough, Hugh Laurie, Suzanne Burden, Camille Coduri, Alexandra Pigg, Billy Roch, Gary O'Brien; ***D:*** David Hare; ***W:*** David Hare; ***M:*** Nick Bicat. *COL*

Strapped ☠☠½ **1993** Earnest urban drama about a young man who needs quick cash and turns to selling guns to get it. ("Strapped" in street lingo means both carrying a gun and needing money.) Diquan's (Woodbine) pregnant girlfriend is in jail for selling crack and he doesn't have the bail money. So he and a partner begin selling guns but it turns out Diquan has also cut a deal with the cops and the deal doesn't stay a secret for long. Whitaker's directorial debut. Made for cable television. **102m/C VHS, LV.** Bokeem Woodbine, Kia Joy Goodwin, Fred "Fredro" Scruggs, Michael Biehn, Craig Wasson; ***D:*** Forest Whitaker; ***W:*** Dena Kleiman. *HBO*

Strategic Air Command ☠☠½ **1955** A classic post-WWII chunk of Air Force patriotism. Veteran third baseman Stewart is recalled to flight duty at the hint of a nuclear war. He's already put in his time in the Big One and thinks he's being singled out now, but he answers his Uncle Sam's call. Allyson plays Stewart's wife for the third time. **114m/C VHS, Beta, LV.** James Stewart, June Allyson, Frank Lovejoy, Barry Sullivan; ***D:*** Anthony Mann; ***C:*** William H. Daniels. Nominations: Academy Awards '55: Best Story. *PAR*

The Stratton Story ☠☠☠ **1949** Stewart and Allyson teamed up for the first of the three pictures they'd make together in this true story of Monty Stratton, the Chicago White Sox pitcher. A baseball phenom, Stratton suffers a devastating hunting accident which leads to the amputation of one leg. Learning to walk with an artificial limb, Stratton also struggles to resume his baseball career. Stewart's fine as always, with Allyson lending noble support as the loving wife. Chisox manager Jimmy Dykes played himself as did pitcher Gene Bearden, lending further authenticity to an excellent production. **106m/B VHS, Beta.** James Stewart, June Allyson, Frank Morgan, Agnes Moorehead, Bill Williams, Bruce Cowling; ***D:*** Sam Wood; ***W:*** Guy Trosper, Douglas S. Morrow. Academy Awards '49: Best Story. *MGM, FCT, BTV*

Straw Dogs ☠☠☠ **1972 (R)** An American mathematician, disturbed by the predominance of violence in American society, moves with his wife to an isolated Cornish village. He finds that primitive savagery exists beneath the most peaceful surface. After his wife is raped, Hoffman's character seeks revenge. Hoffman is good, a little too wimpy at times. A violent, frightening film reaction to the violence of the 1960s. **118m/C VHS, Beta, LV.** *GB* Dustin Hoffman, Susan George, Peter Vaughan, T.P. McKenna, David Warner; ***D:*** Sam Peckinpah; ***W:*** David Zelag Goodman. Nominations: Academy Awards '71: Best Original Score. *FOX*

Strawberry and Chocolate ☠☠☠ *Fresa y Chocolate* **1993 (R)** Sex, politics, and friendship set in 1979 Havana. University student David (Cruz) is sitting morosely in a cafe eating chocolate ice cream when he's spotted by older, educated, gay, strawberry-eating Diego (Perugorria), who manages to persuade David to visit him at his apartment. Resolutely hetero (and communist), David is appalled not only by Diego's sexuality but by his subversive politics. But gradually David's seduced by Diego's ideas and friendship into questioning the regime's harsh policies (and homophobia). Satiric and sympathetic—not only to the characters but to Cuba itself. Ill with cancer, Gutierrez Alea finished the film with the aid of Tabio. From the short story "The Wolf, the Forest and the New Man" by sceenwriter Paz. Spanish with subtitles. **110m/C VHS.** *CU* Jorge Perugorria, Vladimir Cruz, Mirta Ibarra, Francisco Gattorno, Jorge Angelino, Marilyn Solaya; ***D:*** Thomas Gutierrez Alea, Juan Carlos Tabio; ***W:*** Thomas Gutierrez Alea, Senel Paz; ***C:*** Mario Garcia Joya; ***M:*** Jose Maria Vitier. Nominations: Academy Awards '94: Best Foreign Language Film. *TOU*

Strawberry Blonde ☠☠☠ **1941** A romantic comedy set in the 1890s, with Cagney as a would-be dentist infatuated with money-grubbing Hayworth (the strawberry blonde of the title), who wonders years later whether he married the right woman (chestnut brunette de Havilland). Attractive period piece remade from 1933's "One Sunday Afternoon," and revived yet again in 1948 by Raoul Walsh. **100m/B VHS, Beta.** James Cagney, Olivia de Havilland, Rita Hayworth, Alan Hale, George Tobias, Jack Carson, Una O'Connor, George Reeves; ***D:*** Raoul Walsh; ***W:*** Julius J. Epstein, Philip C. Epstein; ***C:*** James Wong Howe. Nominations: Academy Awards '41: Best Original Score. *MGM*

Strawberry Roan ☠☠ **1933** Maynard plays a stubborn rodeo cowboy, out to prove he ain't whipped yet. One of Maynard's most popular films. Gene Autry bought the story to help him out in later years; the 1948 Autry "remake" uses only the title. **59m/B VHS.** Ken Maynard, Ruth Hall; ***D:*** Ken Maynard. *NOS, DVT, HEG*

The Strawberry Statement ☠☠ **1970 (R)** Dated message film about a campus radical who persuades a college student to take part in the student strikes on campus during the '60s. Ambitious anti-violence message is lost in too many subplots. Soundtrack features songs by Crosby, Stills, Nash and Young and John Lennon. **109m/C VHS, Beta.** Kim Darby, Bruce Davison, Bud Cort, James Coco, Kristina Holland, Bob Balaban, David Dukes, Jeannie Berlin; ***D:*** Stuart Hagmann; ***W:*** Israel Horovitz. Cannes Film Festival '70: Special Jury Prize; Nominations: Cannes Film Festival '70: Best Film. *MGM*

Stray Dog ☠☠☠ **1949** A tense, early genre piece by Kurosawa, about a police detective who has his revolver picked from his pocket on a bus, and realizes soon after it's being used in a series of murders. Technically somewhat flawed, but tense and intense. Mifune's pursuit of the criminal with his gun becomes metaphorically compelling. In Japanese with English subtitles. **122m/B VHS, Beta.** *JP* Toshiro Mifune, Takashi Shimura, Isao Kimura; ***D:*** Akira Kurosawa. *INJ, COL*

Strays ☠☠ **1991 (R)** Here kitty kitty! A young couple move into their dream home, convinced it is the perfect place to raise their daughter. What they don't know is that the area is populated by a pack of wild cats. Before they can get rid of the kitties, one has marked their bedroom as his territory and they find themselves battling a swarm of mean kitties during a bad storm. **83m/C VHS, LV.** Kathleen Quinlan, Timothy Busfield, Claudia Christian; ***D:*** John McPherson; ***W:*** Shaun Cassidy. *MCA*

Streamers 🦴🦴 **1983 (R)** Six young soldiers in a claustrophobic army barracks tensely await the orders that will send them to Vietnam. Written by Rabe from his play. Well acted but downbeat and drawn out. **118m/C VHS, Beta, LV.** Matthew Modine, Michael Wright, Mitchell Lichtenstein, George Dzundza; ***D:*** Robert Altman; ***W:*** David Rabe. *MED, IME, FCT*

The Street 🦴🦴½ **1923** A dark classic of German Kammerspiel film, notable for its expressionist treatment of Paris street life. A middle-aged man decides to abandon his wife and job to see what excitement he can find. He is duped by a prostitute, accused of murder, imprisoned, and nearly commits suicide before being rescued. Silent. **87m/B VHS, Beta.** *GE* ***D:*** Karl Grune; ***W:*** Karl Grune. *VYY, INJ*

Street Asylum 🦴 **1990 (R)** Real-life Watergate spook Liddy is pathetically bad as an evil genius who cooks up a scheme to rid the streets of deadbeats and scumbags by implanting cops with a gizmo that makes them kill. Also available in a 94-minute unrated version. **94m/C VHS, Beta, LV.** Wings Hauser, Alex Cord, Roberta Vasquez, G. Gordon Liddy, Marie Chambers, Sy Richardson, Jesse Doran, Jesse Aragon, Brion James; ***D:*** Gregory Brown. *NO*

Street Crimes 🦴🦴 **1992 (R)** A street-wise cop convinces gang members to put down their weapons and settle their grudges in the boxing ring. But when a gang leader starts shooting down the police and civilians, the cop and his young partner must work together to keep the neighborhood safe. **?m/C VHS, LV.** Dennis Farina, Max Gail, Mike Worth; ***D:*** Stephen Smoke; ***W:*** Stephen Smoke; ***M:*** John Gonzalez. *PMH*

The Street Fighter 🦴½ **1975** Fast-paced martial arts action finds freelance fighter Terry Tsuguri (Chiba) hired to spring a convicted killer from prison. But after he succeeds, his employers renege on their payment. Big mistake. Dubbed from Japanese. Three sequels: "Return of the Street Fighter," "The Street Fighter's Last Revenge," and "Sister Street Fighter." **91m/C VHS, LV.** Sonny Chiba; ***D:*** Sakae Ozawa. *NLC*

Street Fighter 🦴½ **1994 (PG-13)** Yes, it's a movie based on a popular video game (guess no one worried about the colossal flop of "Super Mario Bros"). Van Damme is action-minded Colonel Guile who is assigned to defeat crazed dictator General Bison (Julia in one of his last roles) in order to rescue kidnapped relief workers. Yes, there's lots of cartoon action but the game's more exciting (and even makes more sense). Shot on location in Australia and Bangkok. **101m/C VHS, LV.** Jean-Claude Van Damme, Raul Julia, Wes Studi, Ming-Na Wen, Damian Chapa, Simon Callow, Roshan Seth, Kylie Minogue, Byrun Mann; ***D:*** Steven E. de Souza; ***W:*** Steven E. de Souza; ***M:*** Graeme Revell. *MCA*

The Street Fighter's Last Revenge 🦴 **1979** Third in the martial arts series finds Terry Tsuguri (Chiba) hired by a mob boss to do some dirty work and then getting double-crossed—resulting in the death of Terry's girl. So, Terry hunts the miscreants down one by one. Lots of action, not much acting. Followed by "Sister Street Fighter." **80m/C VHS.** Sonny Chiba, Sue Shiomi; ***D:*** Sakae Ozawa. *NLC*

Street Girls 🦴 **1975 (R)** A father enters the world of urban drugs and prostitution to find his runaway daughter. **77m/C VHS, Beta.** Carol Case, Christine Souder, Paul Pompian; ***D:*** Michael Miller. *NLC*

Street Hawk 🦴 **1984** A government agent operates an experimental, crime-fighting motorcycle in battling against a high-powered drug smuggling ring. **60m/C VHS, Beta.** Rex Smith, Jayne Modean, Richard Venture, Christopher Lloyd. *MCA*

Street Hero *Woof!* **1984** A young thug is torn between familial common sense and Mafia connections. **102m/C VHS, Beta.** Vince Colosimo, Sigrid Thornton, Sandy Gore. *LIV, VES*

Street Hitz 🦴½ **1992** Two brothers in the South Bronx find their family loyalties tested. Joey wants to finish college and get away from the violence in the streets while his brother Junior turns to the gangs to survive. **92m/C VHS.** Angelo Lopez, Melvin Muza, Lyota Ramirez; ***D:*** Joseph B. Vasquez. *AIP*

Street Hunter *Woof!* **1990 (R)** Former cop turned freelance fighter quit the force when his integrity was questioned, but he still helps out now and then. Scumbag drug dealers line up a thug to waste him; epic kung fu battle ensues. **120m/C VHS, LV.** Steve James, Rob Brown, John Leguizamo, Valarie Pettiford, Frank Vincent, Richie Havens; ***D:*** John A. Gallagher; ***C:*** Phil Parmet. *COL*

Street Justice 🦴½ **1989 (R)** Over-complex tale of a CIA agent on the lam. Returning from years of Russian imprisonment, Ontkean finds his wife remarried, his daughter grown and both battling the corrupt town government. Good performances can't help the confusion of too many characters too flatly developed. **94m/C VHS, Beta.** Michael Ontkean, Joanna Kerns, Catherine Bach, J.D. Cannon, Jeanette Nolan, Richard Cox, William Windom; ***D:*** Richard Sarafian. *WAR*

Street Knight 🦴🦴 **1993 (R)** Gang warfare in L.A. in a routine actioner. Jake is an ex-cop who gets drawn into a battle between two rival gangs when their truce is broken by mysterious murders on both sides. Seems there's an unsuspected third party involved—a para-military band of professional killers that want the gang violence to divert police interest from their own nefarious operations. **88m/C VHS, Beta, LV.** Jeff Speakman, Christopher Neame, Lewis Van Bergen, Bernie Casey, Jennifer Gatti, Richard Coca; ***D:*** Albert Magnoli. *WAR, CAN*

Street Law 🦴 **1979 (R)** Vivid and violent study of one man's frustrated war on crime. **77m/C VHS, Beta.** Franco Nero, Barbara Bach, Reno Palmer. *NO*

Street Law 🦴🦴 **1995 (R)** John Ryan (Wincott) is a down-on-his-luck trial lawyer whose childhood buddy Luis Calderone (Prieto) is willing to lend a helping hand. Too bad Luis is an ex-con who hasn't left his dangerous street ways behind him and now John is caught up in some unsavory action. **98m/C VHS.** Jeff Wincott, Paco Christian Prieto, Christina Cox. *TRI*

Street Music 🦴🦴½ **1981** The elderly people living in an old hotel join forces with a young couple to organize a protest that may save their building. Well-directed urban comedy-drama; good location shooting in San Francisco's Tenderloin. **88m/C VHS, Beta.** Larry Breeding, Elizabeth Daily, Ned Glass; ***D:*** Jenny Bowen. Sundance Film Festival '82: Grand Jury Prize. *LIV, VES*

Street of Forgotten Women 🦴 **1925** Hollywood, in one of its periodic morality binges, came up with this purported expose on prostitution. An innocent girl is seduced and brutalized by a theatrical agent and eventually finds herself walking the pavement for less than moral purposes. Lots of shots of scantily clad showgirls and our heroine in her undies. **55m/B VHS.** *SNC, VYY*

Street of Shame 🦴🦴🦴½ **1956** A portrayal of the abused lives of six Tokyo prostitutes. Typically sensitive to the roles and needs of women and critical of the society that exploits them, Mizoguchi creates a quiet, inclusive coda to his life's work in world cinema. Kyo is splendid as a hardened hooker and has a memorable scene with her father. Kogure is also good. The great director's last finished work was instrumental in the outlawing of prostitution in Japan. In Japanese with English subtitles. **88m/B VHS, Beta.** *JP* Machiko Kyo, Aiko Mimasu, Michiyo Kogure; ***D:*** Kenji Mizoguchi. *SUE, INJ, NLC*

Street People *Woof!* **1976 (R)** Gratuitous car chases and violence do not a movie make, as in this case in point. Utter woofer has Brit Moore cast as a mafiosa. Yeah, right. **92m/C VHS, Beta.** Roger Moore, Stacy Keach, Ivo Garrani, Ettore Manni; ***D:*** Maurizio Lucidi. *LIV, VES*

Street Scene 🦴🦴🦴 **1931** Life in a grimy New York tenement district, circa 1930. Audiences nationwide ate it up when Elmer Rice adapted his own Pulitzer Prize-winning play and top helmsman Vidor gave it direction. **80m/B VHS, Beta, 8mm.** Sylvia Sidney, William Collier Jr., Estelle Taylor, Beulah Bondi, David Landau; ***D:*** King Vidor; ***C:*** George Barnes; ***M:*** Alfred Newman. *NOS, HHT, CAB*

Street Smart 🦴🦴½ **1987 (R)** Reeve was blah as Superman (let's be frank), and he's blah here as a desperate New York freelance writer who fakes a dramatic story about prostitution. When his deception returns to haunt him, he's in trouble with pimps and murderers, as well as the D.A. Freeman and Baker are both superb. Based on screenwriter David Freeman's own experience with "New York" magazine. **97m/C VHS, Beta, LV.** Christopher Reeve, Morgan Freeman, Kathy Baker, Mimi Rogers, Andre Gregory, Jay Patterson, Anna Maria Horsford; ***D:*** Jerry Schatzberg; ***W:*** David Freeman; ***C:*** Adam Holender; ***M:*** Miles Davis. Independent Spirit Awards '88: Best Supporting Actor (Freeman); Los Angeles Film Critics Association Awards '87: Best Supporting Actor (Freeman); New York Film Critics Awards '87: Best Supporting Actor (Freeman); National Society of Film Critics Awards '87: Best Supporting Actor (Freeman), Best Supporting Actress (Baker); Nominations: Academy Awards '87: Best Supporting Actor (Freeman). *MED, IME*

Street Soldiers 🦴½ **1991 (R)** Martial artists are out to take back the streets from the punks and scum who now rule them. **98m/C VHS, Beta, LV.** Jun Chong, Jeff Rector, David Homb, Jonathan Gorman, Joon Kim, Katherine Armstrong, Joel Weiss; ***D:*** Lee Harry. *ACA*

Street Trash *Woof!* **1987** In Brooklyn, a strange poisonous liquor is being sold cheap to bums, making them melt and explode. A gross, cheap, tongue-in-cheek shocker from the makers of "The Toxic Avenger." **91m/C VHS, Beta.** R.L. Ryan, Vic Noto, Miriam Zucker, Bill Chepil, Mike Lackey; ***D:*** Jim Muro. *LIV*

Street War 🦴 **197?** A cop pursues the Mob in the name of revenge as well as duty. **90m/C VHS, Beta.** James Mason, Cyril Cusack, Raymond Pellegrin. *NO*

Street Warriors *Woof!* **1987** Ostensibly "serious" look at juvenile crime. Actually miserable, exploitative, offensive junk. **105m/C VHS, Beta.** Christa Leem, Nadia Windell, Victor Petit, Francisco (Frank) Brana; ***D:*** Jose Antonio De La Loma. *NO*

Street Warriors, Part 2 *Woof!* **1987** Even worse than its predecessor, and that's saying something. Horrible dubbing from Spanish would be laughable, if the rapes weren't so graphic. **105m/C VHS, Beta.** Angel Fernandez, Paul Ramirez, Teresa Giminez, Veronica Miriel, Conrad Tortosa; ***D:*** Jose Antonio De La Loma. *NO*

Street Wars 🦴½ **1991 (R)** Violent low-budgeter about 17-year-old Sugarpop, who takes over older brother Frank's Los Angeles drug operation, after Frank is murdered, and finds himself battling a rival gang. **90m/C VHS, LV.** Alan Joseph, Bryan O'Dell, Clifford Shegog, Jean Pace, Vaughn Cromwell, Cardella Demilo; ***D:*** Jamaa Fanaka; ***W:*** Jamaa Fanaka; ***M:*** Michael Dunlap, Yves Chicha. *TRI*

The Street with No Name 🦴🦴🦴 **1948** In follow-up to "Kiss of Death," Widmark confirms rep as one disturbed guy playing psychotic career criminal whose life is grisly trail of murder and brutality. **93m/B VHS.** Mark Stevens, Richard Widmark, Lloyd Nolan, Barbara Lawrence, Ed Begley Sr., Donald Buka, Joseph Pevney; ***D:*** William Keighley. *FOX, FCT*

A Streetcar Named Desire 🦴🦴🦴🦴 **1951 (PG)** Powerful film version of Tennessee Williams' play about a neurotic southern belle with a hidden past who comes to visit her sister and is abused and driven mad by her brutal brother-in-law. Grim New Orleans setting for terrific performances by all, with Malden, Leigh, and Hunter winning Oscars, and Brando making highest impact on audiences. Brando disliked the role, despite the great impact it had on his career. Remade for television in 1984.

122m/B VHS, Beta, LV. Vivien Leigh, Marlon Brando, Kim Hunter, Karl Malden; ***D:*** Elia Kazan; ***W:*** Tennessee Williams; ***C:*** Harry Stradling; ***M:*** Alex North. Academy Awards '51: Best Actress (Leigh), Best Art Direction/Set Decoration (B & W), Best Supporting Actor (Malden), Best Supporting Actress (Hunter); Golden Globe Awards '52: Best Supporting Actress (Hunter); National Board of Review Awards '51: 10 Best Films of the Year; New York Film Critics Awards '51: Best Actress (Leigh), Best Director (Kazan), Best Film; Nominations: Academy Awards '50: Best Actor (Brando), Best Director (Kazan), Best Picture; Academy Awards '51: Best Black and White Cinematography, Best Costume Design (B & W), Best Screenplay, Best Sound, Best Original Score. *FOX, WAR, BTV*

A Streetcar Named Desire 🦴🦴🦴 **1984** Excellent made for television adaptation of the Tennessee Williams drama about fading southern belle Blanche du Bois (Ann-Margret in a terrific performance). D'Angelo is her plain sister Stella who lives with brutish husband Stanley (Williams) in the seamy French Quarter of New Orleans. Can't surpass the original but this version does have the advantage of not having to soft-pedal the drama for the fifties censors. **94m/C VHS.** Ann-Margret, Beverly D'Angelo, Treat Williams, Randy Quaid, Rafael Campos, Erica Yohn; ***D:*** John Erman; ***M:*** Marvin Hamlisch. *FCT*

A Streetcar Named Desire 🦴🦴 ½ **1995** Baldwin and Lange recreate their 1992 stage roles of brutal Stanley Kowalski and fragile Southern belle Blanche DuBois from the Broadway revival of Tennessee Williams 1947 Pulitzer Prize-winning play. This TV version is truer to the dialogue and situations of the original production than the censored '51 film. **156m/C VHS.** Jessica Lange, Alec Baldwin, Diane Lane, John Goodman, Frederick Coffin; ***D:*** Glenn Jordan; ***C:*** Ralf Bode; ***M:*** David Mansfield. *TCF*

Streetfight 🦴 ½ *Coonskin* **1975 (R)** Semi-animated racist exploitation from the creator of "Fritz the Cat." Features some superb animation. **89m/C VHS, Beta.** Philip Michael Thomas, Scatman Crothers; ***D:*** Ralph Bakshi; ***W:*** Ralph Bakshi. *ACA, WTA*

Streets 🦴🦴 **1990 (R)** Applegate (of Fox TV's "Married...With Children") is believable as an illiterate runaway teen. Good drama set in Venice, California about life on the streets is flawed by near-gratuitous pairing with story of a crazy prostitute-killing cop. **90m/C VHS, Beta.** Christina Applegate, David Mendenhall, Eb Lottimer; ***D:*** Katt Shea Ruben, Andy Ruben; ***W:*** Andy Ruben. *MGM*

Streets of Fire 🦴🦴 ½ **1984** A soldier of fortune rescues his ex-girlfriend, now a famous rock singer, after she's been kidnapped by a malicious motorcycle gang. Violently energetic in its insistent barrage of imagery. Director Hill's never-never land establishes a retro-futuristic feel and is beautifully photographed, however vacuous the ending may be. **93m/C VHS, Beta, LV.** Michael Pare, Diane Lane, Rick Moranis, Amy Madigan, Willem Dafoe, Deborah Van Valkenburgh, Richard Lawson, Rick Rossovich, Bill Paxton, Lee Ving, Stoney Jackson, Robert Townsend, Grand Bush, Mykelti Williamson, Elizabeth Daily, Lynne Thigpen, Marine Jahan, Ed Begley Jr., John Dennis Johnston, Olivia Brown; ***D:*** Walter Hill; ***W:*** Walter Hill, Larry Gross; ***M:*** Ry Cooder. *MCA*

Streets of Gold 🦴🦴 ½ **1986 (R)** Brandauer is good as a Soviet boxer who defected and now washes dishes in Brooklyn. He trains a pair of street youngsters in the hope of beating his old coach in the Olympics. "Rocky"-like in the boxing, and in the rags-to-riches optimism. **94m/C VHS, Beta, LV.** Klaus Maria Brandauer, Adrian Pasdar, Wesley Snipes; ***D:*** Joe Roth; ***W:*** Richard Price, Heywood Gould, Tom Cole; ***M:*** Jack Nitzsche. *LIV, VES*

The Streets of L.A. 🦴🦴 ½ **1979** A frustrated middle-aged woman teaches some punks from an L.A. barrio a thing or two about pride and motivation when she demands reimbursement for the tires they slashed. Without thoroughly professional Woodward to carry it, there would not be much of a movie. Woodward's character is resourceful, and so is the actress. Made for TV. **94m/C VHS, Beta.** Joanne Woodward, Robert Webber, Michael C. Gwynne; ***D:*** Jerrold Freedman. *NO*

The Streets of San Francisco 🦴🦴🦴 **1972** The pilot that spawned the popular TV series. A streetwise old cop and his young college-boy partner (who else but Malden and Douglas as Stone and Keller) investigate the murder of a young woman. Adapted from "Poor, Poor Ophelia" by Carolyn Weston. **120m/C VHS, Beta.** Karl Malden, Robert Wagner, Michael Douglas, Andrew Duggan, Tom Bosley, Kim Darby, Mako; ***D:*** Walter Grauman. *GKK*

Streets of Sin 🦴🦴 ½ *Not Wanted* **1949** Written and produced by movie star Lupino, this morality play tells the story of a naive girl's tribulations when she becomes infatuated with a musician and allows herself to become pregnant by him. Shunned by the musician, she enters a home for unwed mothers to sort out her life and feelings for a crippled veteran who wants to marry her. **91m/B VHS.** Sally Forrest, Keefe Brasselle, Leonard Penn, Dorothy Adams, Rita Lupino; ***D:*** Elmer Clifton; ***W:*** Ida Lupino. *NOS*

Streetwalkin' 🦴 **1985 (R)** Life in the Big Apple isn't always rosy for a brother and sister who must contend with prostitutes, drug dealers, and tough cops. She turns to prostitution to get by. Miserable, exploitative trash. **86m/C VHS, Beta, LV.** Melissa Leo, Dale Midkiff, Leon Robinson, Julie Newmar, Randall Batinkoff, Annie Golden, Antonio Fargas; ***D:*** Joan Freeman; ***W:*** Joan Freeman, Robert Alden. *LIV, VES*

Streetwise 🦴🦴🦴 ½ **1985** Eye-opening and candid documentary inspired by a "Life" magazine article. Frank and honest look at homeless children making a living on the streets. Seattle provides the backdrop to the story as the filmmakers hang around with the kids, earning their trust, and receive the truth from them. Cruel, funny, enraging, but always sobering look into a population of homeless in America. A deservedly acclaimed, terrifying vision of urban America. **92m/C VHS, Beta, LV.** ***D:*** Martin Bell; ***M:*** Tom Waits. *ORI, NWV*

Strictly Ballroom 🦴🦴🦴 ½ **1992 (PG)** Offbeat, cheerfully tacky dance/romance amusingly turns every movie cliche slightly askew. Scott (Mercurio) has been in training for the Pan-Pacific ballroom championships since the age of six. While talented, he also refuses to follow convention and scandalizes the stuffy dance establishment with his new steps. When his longtime partner leaves him, Scott takes up with a love-struck beginner (Morice), with some surprises of her own. Ballet dancer Mercurio (in his film debut) is appropriately arrogant yet vulnerable, with Morice as the plain Jane turned steel butterfly. Wonderful supporting cast; great debut for director Luhrmann. **94m/C VHS, LV.** *AU* Paul Mercurio, Tara Morice, Bill Hunter, Pat Thomsen, Barry Otto, Gia Carides, Peter Whitford, John Hannan, Sonia Kruger-Tayler, Kris McQuade, Pip Mushin, Leonie Page, Antonio Vargas, Armonia Benedito; ***D:*** Baz Luhrmann; ***W:*** Craig Pearce, Baz Luhrmann; ***M:*** David Hirshfelder. Australian Film Institute '92: Best Costume Design, Best Director (Luhrmann), Best Film, Best Film Editing, Best Supporting Actor (Otto), Best Supporting Actress (Thomsen), Best Writing; Nominations: Golden Globe Awards '94: Best Film—Musical/Comedy. *MAX, TOU, BTV*

Strictly Business 🦴 ½ **1991 (PG-13)** An upwardly mobile black broker has his career aspirations in order until he meets a beautiful club promoter who finds him square and boring. Wanting to impress her he asks the advice of a young man who works in the mail room for the proper way to dress and talk. A low-rent Pygmalion story. **83m/C VHS.** Halle Berry, Tommy Davidson, Joseph C. Phillips; ***D:*** Kevin Hooks; ***M:*** Michel Colombier. *WAR, FCT*

Strictly G.I. 1944 A collection of war-time patriotic shorts, including "All Star Bond Rally." The support and perception of WWII is historically intriguing. **45m/B VHS, Beta.** Bing Crosby, Frank Sinatra, Betty Grable, Judy Garland, Harpo Marx, Harry James, Bob Hope, Jerry Colonna. *NOS, DVT, HEG*

Strike 🦴🦴🦴 ½ **1924** Eisenstein's debut, and a silent classic. Stirring look at a 1912 clash between striking factory workers and Czarist troops. **78m/B VHS, Beta.** *RU* ***D:*** Sergei Eisenstein. *NOS, KIV, IHF*

Strike a Pose 🦴 ½ **1993 (R)** Erotic thriller finds international model-turned-fashion photographer Miranda Cross, her boyfriend LAPD detective Nick Carter, and Miranda's model friends stalked by a revenge-minded killer. Also available in an unrated version. **?m/C VHS, LV.** Margie Peterson, Robert Eastwick, Michelle LaMothe; ***D:*** Dean Hamilton. *PMH*

Strike Back 🦴🦴 **1980** A convict escapes from prison to find the girl he loves, and is hounded by the police and the mob. **89m/C VHS, Beta.** Dave Balko, Brigette Wollner; ***D:*** Carl Schenkel. *LIV, VES*

Strike Commando *Woof!* **1987 (R)** Cheap, exploitative ripoff of the expensive, exploitative mega-action thriller "Rambo." Sleepwalking actors; horrible, overwrought script. **92m/C VHS, Beta.** Reb Brown, Christopher Connelly, Locs Kamme; ***D:*** Vincent Dawn. *NO*

Strike Force 🦴 *Crack* **1975** A New York City cop, a Federal agent and a state trooper work together to battle a large drug ring. Failed made-for-TV pilot. Early Gere appearance; not related to later Robert Stack film with the same title. **74m/C VHS, Beta.** Cliff Gorman, Richard Gere, Donald Blakely; ***D:*** Barry Shear. *VMK*

Strike Force 🦴🦴 **1981** The jurors on an embezzlement case turn up bloody and headless around town, so a special criminal strike force is brought in to solve the murders. Why do the murders happen only on Tuesdays? Made for TV. **90m/C VHS, Beta.** Robert Stack, Dorian Harewood, Herb Edelman; ***D:*** Richard Lang. *AHV*

Strike It Rich 🦴 ½ *Loser Take All* **1990 (PG)** A honeymooning couple find themselves resorting to the Monte Carlo gambling tables in order to raise money for the ride home. Lightweight fluff unfortunately adapted from Graham Greene's short novel "Loser Takes All." Only for hard-core Gielgudites. **86m/C VHS, Beta, LV.** Molly Ringwald, Robert Lindsay, John Gielgud, Max Wall, Simon de la Brosse; ***D:*** James Scott; ***M:*** Cliff Eidelman. *HBO*

Strike Up the Band 🦴🦴 ½ **1940** A high school band turns to hot swing music and enters a national radio contest. Rooney and Garland display their usual charm in this high-energy stroll down memory lane. ♫Over the Waves; The Light Cavalry Overture; Walkin Down Broadway; Five Foot Two, Eyes of Blue; After the Ball; Nobody; Strike Up the Band. **120m/B VHS, Beta, LV.** Judy Garland, Mickey Rooney, Paul Whiteman, William Tracy, June Preisser; ***D:*** Busby Berkeley. Academy Awards '40: Best Sound; Nominations: Academy Awards '40: Best Song ("Our Love Affair"), Best Score. *MGM*

Strikeback 🦴🦴 **1984** A young boy comes painfully of age in West Berlin. **88m/C VHS, Beta.** *VES*

Striker 🦴🦴 **1988 (R)** Mercenary John "Striker" Slade is sent to Nicaragua to free a captured American journalist, not knowing his superiors have betrayed him to the Contras and the Sandinistas. He battles it out with both groups while seeking revenge on the businessmen who set him up. **90m/C VHS, Beta.** Frank Zagarino, Melanie Rogers, Paul Werner; ***D:*** Stephen M. Andrews. *AIP*

Striker's Mountain 🦴 ½ **1987** Story of a sports enthusiast who creates heliskiing and builds it into a business. Great ski scenes, but skip the rest. **99m/C VHS.** Bruce Greenwood, Mimi Kuzyk, Leslie Nielsen, August Schellenberg; ***D:*** Allen Simmonds. *VTR*

Striking Distance 🦴🦴 ½ **1993 (R)** Tom Hardy (Willis) is a hard-nosed fifth-generation Pittsburgh homicide cop whose police detective father (Mahoney) is killed, apparently by a serial killer. Hardy insists the perp was really a fellow cop and winds up on the River Rescue squad (at least his partner is the fetching Parker). When the serial killer starts striking at women with some connection to Hardy, he finds scant support from his fellow cops. High action quotient but the killer's identity won't be any surprise. **101m/C VHS, LV, 8mm.** Bruce Willis, Sarah Jessica Parker, Dennis Farina, Tom Sizemore, Brion James, Robert Pastorelli, Timothy Busfield, John Mahoney, Andre Braugher; ***D:*** Rowdy Herrington; ***W:*** Marty Kaplan, Rowdy Herrington; ***M:*** Brad Fiedel. *COL*

Striking Point 🦴½ **1994 (R)** Police detectives are determined to stop ex-KGB commandoes from smuggling high-tech weapons into the country. **96m/C VHS.** Chris Mitchum, Tracy Spaulding. *CAF*

Stripes 🦴🦴½ **1981 (R)** Feeling like losers and looking to straighten out their lives, two friends enlist in the Army under the mistaken impression that military life is something like a summer camp for grown-ups. A box-office success (despite a poorly written and directed script) due in large part to Murray's charm and his verbal and sometimes physical sparring with Oates, who is good as the gruff-tempered platoon sergeant. Features humorous stints from various "Second City" players, including Candy, whom Murray turns into a "lean, mean fighting machine." **105m/C VHS, Beta, LV.** Bill Murray, Harold Ramis, P.J. Soles, Warren Oates, John Candy, John Larroquette, Judge Reinhold, Sean Young, Dave Thomas, Joe Flaherty; ***D:*** Ivan Reitman; ***W:*** Len Blum, Harold Ramis; ***M:*** Elmer Bernstein. *COL*

Stripped to Kill 🦴🦴 **1987 (R)** A female cop goes undercover to lure a psycho killing strippers. Not-bad entry from Corman and cohorts. Followed by—you guessed it—"Stripped to Kill II." **88m/C VHS, Beta.** Kay Lenz, Greg Evigan, Norman Fell; ***D:*** Katt Shea Ruben; ***W:*** Katt Shea Ruben, Andy Ruben. *MGM*

Stripped to Kill II: Live Girls 🦴 **1989** A young woman with extra-sensory powers dreams of murders which she discovers are all too real. A weak sequel, despite the interesting premise. **83m/C VHS, Beta.** Maria Ford, Eb Lottimer, Karen Mayo Chandler, Marjean Holden, Birke Tan, Debra Lamb; ***D:*** Katt Shea Ruben; ***W:*** Katt Shea Ruben. *MGM*

The Stripper 🦴🦴½ *Woman of Summer* **1963** A middle-aged stripper in a traveling show returns to the small Kansas town of her youth. Left stranded, she moves in with an old friend whose teenage son promptly falls in love with her. Based on the play "A Loss of Roses" by William Inge. **95m/B VHS, Beta.** Joanne Woodward, Richard Beymer, Claire Trevor, Carol Lynley, Robert Webber, Gypsy Rose Lee; ***D:*** Franklin J. Schaffner; ***M:*** Jerry Goldsmith. Nominations: Academy Awards '63: Best Black and White Cinematography. *FOX*

Stripper 🦴🦴½ **1986 (R)** A good under-the-covers glimpse of the life and work of several real-life strippers, culminating in the First Annual Stripper's Convention in 1984. **90m/C VHS, Beta.** Janette Boyd, Sara Costa, Kimberly Holcomb; ***D:*** Jerome Gary; ***M:*** Jack Nitzsche. *FOX*

Stripshow 🦴 **1995 (R)** Veteran Vegas stripper shows the ropes to newcomer and then must vie with the upstart for her boyfriend's interest. **?m/C VHS.** Monique Parent, Tane McClure, Steven Tietsort; ***D:*** Gary Orona; ***W:*** Gary Orona. *MTH*

Striptease 🦴 **198?** A slew of slowly-declothing women do their thing. **60m/C VHS, Beta.** *JEF*

Striptease 🦴🦴½ **1996 (R)** Single mom (Moore) loses custody of her daughter (Moore's real-life offspring, Rumer) to her lowlife ex. In order to raise the money for an appeal, she dances at a Miami strip club, where she runs across a politician (Reynolds) with unusual tastes. Unlike "Showgirls," this one's intentionally funny and features some fine script work and performances. Moore set a lead actress record with her $12 million paycheck, 4 mil of which reportedly was for agreeing to dance nude. Based on the novel by Carl Hiaasen. **?m/C VHS.** Demi Moore, Armand Assante, Ving Rhames, Robert Patrick, Burt Reynolds, Rumer Willis; ***D:*** Andrew Bergman; ***W:*** Andrew Bergman.

Stripteaser 🦴½ **1995 (R)** Sicko psycho Dean holds dancers and patrons hostage in an L.A. strip joint where he provides various humiliations for his captives. Ford's the beautiful ecdysiast whose been the object of the fellow's secret obsessions. Also available unrated. **82m/C VHS.** Rick Dean, Maria Ford, Lance August; ***D:*** Dan Golden. *NHO*

Stroke of Midnight 🦴½ **1990 (PG)** Souped-up Cinderella with Lowe as egotistic high fashion designer, Grey as struggling shoe designer and a pumpkin-colored VW Bug. **102m/C VHS, Beta, LV.** Rob Lowe, Jennifer Grey, Andrea Ferreol; ***D:*** Tom Clegg. *MED, VTR*

Stroker Ace *Woof!* **1983 (PG)** Flamboyant stock car driver tries to break an iron-clad promotional contract signed with a greedy fried-chicken magnate. Off duty, he ogles blondes as dopey as he is. One of the worst from Reynolds—and that's saying something. **96m/C VHS, Beta.** Burt Reynolds, Ned Beatty, Jim Nabors, Parker Stevenson, Loni Anderson, Bubba Smith; ***D:*** Hal Needham; ***W:*** Hal Needham, Hugh Wilson. Golden Raspberry Awards '83: Worst Supporting Actor (Nabors). *WAR*

Stromboli 🦴🦴½ **1950** Bergman is a Czech refugee who marries an Italian fisherman in order to escape from her displaced persons camp. He brings her to his home island of Stromboli where she finds the life bleak and isolated and her marriage a trial. In Italian with English subtitles. The melodrama was even greater off-screen than on; this is the movie which introduced Bergman and Rossellini and began their (then) scandalous affair. **81m/B VHS, Beta.** *IT* Ingrid Bergman, Mario Vitale, Renzo Cesana; ***D:*** Roberto Rossellini. *INJ*

Strong Man 🦴🦴🦴 **1926** A WWI veteran, passing himself off as an unlikely circus strongman, searches an American city for the girl whose letters gave him hope during the war. Perhaps Langdon's best full-length film. **78m/B VHS, Beta, LV.** Harry Langdon, Gertrude Astor, Tay Garnett; ***D:*** Frank Capra. *HBO, IME*

Strong Medicine 🦴🦴½ **1984** Strange, avant-garde film about a strange, off-written young woman. Cleverly directed experiment that's not for everyone. **84m/C VHS, Beta.** Carol Kane, Raul Julia, Wallace Shawn, Kate Manheim, David Warrilow; ***D:*** Guy Green. *NO*

Stroszek 🦴🦴🦴 **1977** Three German misfits—a singer, a prostitute and an old man—tour the U.S. in search of their dreams. Touching, hilarious comedy-drama with a difference and an attitude. One of Herzog's easiest and also best films. In English and German with English subtitles. **108m/C VHS.** *GE* Eva Mattes, Bruno S, Clemens Scheitz; ***D:*** Werner Herzog; ***M:*** Chet Atkins. *NYF, FCT, INJ*

The Structure of Crystals 🦴🦴½ *Struktura Krysztalu* **1969** A member of the scientific elite meets with an old friend who has moved to a remote meteorological station and tries to persuade him to return to the city and resume his work. Zanussi's cerebral first feature was also the first of a series of films to explore the scientific community. In Polish with English subtitles. **76m/B VHS.** *PL* Andrzej Zarnecki, Jan Myslowicz, Barbara Wrzesinska, Wladyslaw Jarema, Daniel Olbrychski; ***D:*** Krzysztof Zanussi; ***W:*** Edward Zebrowski, Krzysztof Zanussi. *FCT*

Stryker *Woof!* **1983 (R)** The ever-lovin' nuclear holocaust has occurred, and good guys and bad guys battle it out for scarce water. If you liked "Mad Max," go see it again; don't watch this miserable effort. **86m/C VHS, Beta.** *PH* Steve Sandor, Andria Fabio; ***D:*** Cirio H. Santiago; ***W:*** Howard R. Cohen. *SUE, VTR*

Stuart Saves His Family 🦴🦴 **1994 (PG-13)** Fired from his self-help television show on a Chicago public-access station, New-age advice guru and Smalley (Franken) returns home to help his pathetically dysfunctional family sort out their problems and an inheritance, a nonplot that gives Smalley a chance to do his 12-step shtick. And that's...O.K. A tolerable installment in the endless parade of mediocre "Saturday Night Live" sketches stretched for the big screen that takes a few surprisingly maudlin turns. Based on Franken's book of Smalley's "daily affirmations," "I'm Good Enough, I'm Smart Enough, and Doggone It, People Like Me!" **97m/C VHS, Beta.** Al Franken, Laura San Giacomo, Vincent D'Onofrio, Shirley Knight, Harris Yulin; ***D:*** Harold Ramis; ***W:*** Al Franken; ***M:*** Marc Shaiman. *PAR*

Stuck on You 🦴 **1984 (R)** Couple engaged in a palimony suit takes their case to a judge to work out their differences. Wing-clipped angel Gabriel (Corey) comes to earth to help them patch it up. Never mind. **90m/C VHS, Beta.** Prof. Irwin Corey, Virginia Penta, Mark Mikulski; ***D:*** Lloyd (Samuel Weil) Kaufman, Michael Herz. *SUE*

Stuckey's Last Stand 🦴 **1978 (PG)** A group of camp counselors prepare to take 22 children on a nature hike they will never forget. Mindless teen fodder. **95m/C VHS, Beta.** Whit Reichert, Tom Murray, Rich Casentino. *NO*

The Stud *Woof!* **1978 (R)** Owner of a fashionable "after hours" dance spot hires a young, handsome stud to manage the club and attend to her personal needs. Low-budget look and seemingly scriptless. Faithfully adapted by sister Jackie Collins from her novel. **90m/C VHS, Beta.** *GB* Joan Collins, Oliver Tobias; ***D:*** Quentin Masters; ***W:*** Jackie Collins. *NO*

Student Affairs *Woof!* **1988 (R)** A bunch of highschool misfits vie for roles in a movie about a bunch of high school misfits. **92m/C VHS, Beta.** Louie Bonanno, Jim Abele, Alan Fisler, Deborah Blaisdell; ***D:*** Chuck Vincent. *LIV, VES*

Student Bodies *Woof!* **1981 (R)** A "Halloween"-style spoof of high-school horror films, except it's not funny. And what's so funny about bloody murder anyway? When the on-the-set problems and strife arose (which they did), why didn't everyone just cut their losses and go home? **86m/C VHS, Beta, LV.** Kristen Riter, Matthew Goldsby, Richard Brando, Joe Flood; ***D:*** Mickey Rose. *PAR*

Student Confidential 🦴 **1987 (R)** A Troma-produced spoof of seedy high school youth movies, new and old, involving four students who are led into the world of adult vices by a mysterious millionaire. Badly made and dull. Douglas and Jackson both have brothers named Michael. **99m/C VHS, Beta.** Eric Douglas, Marlon Jackson, Susan Scott, Ronee Blakley, Elizabeth Singer; ***D:*** Richard Horian. *MED*

The Student Nurses 🦴🦴 **1970 (R)** The adventures, amourous and otherwise, of four last-year nursing students. Followed by four sequels: "Private Duty Nurses," "Night Call Nurses," "The Young Nurses," and "Candy Stripe Nurses." Better than average exploitation fare. First release from Roger Corman's New World studios; it goes down hill from there. **89m/C VHS, Beta.** Elaine Giftos, Karen Carlson, Brioni Farrell, Barbara Leigh, Reni Santoni, Richard Rust, Lawrence Casey, Darrell Larson, Paul Camen, Richard Stahl, Scottie MacGregor, Pepe Serna; ***D:*** Stephanie Rothman. *NLC*

Student of Prague 🦴🦴🦴 **1913** Early silent classic based on the German Faust legend: a student makes a pact with the devil to win a beautiful woman. Poor fellow. With either German or English title cards. Music track. **60m/B VHS, Beta.** *GE* Lothar Koemer, Grete Berger, Paul Wegener; ***D:*** Paul Wegener, Stellan Rye. *DVT, GLV, GVV*

The Student Prince 🦴🦴 **1954** Delightful rendition of Sigmund Romberg's famous operetta in which Purdom stars as the Prince of Heidelberg who falls for barmaid Blyth. Lanza recorded the soundtrack, but could not star in this film because of his weight problem. Previously filmed in 1919 and 1927 without music. ♫Golden Days; Serenade; Deep in My Heart; To the Inn We're Marching; Drink, Drink, Drink; Come Boys, Let's All Be Gay, Boys; Summertime in Heidelberg; Beloved; I Walk With God. **107m/C VHS.** Ann Blyth, Edmund Purdom, John Ericson, Louis Calhern, Edmund Gwenn, S.Z. Sakall, Betta St. John; ***D:*** Richard Thorpe; ***C:*** Paul Vogel. *MGM*

The Student Prince in Old Heidelberg 🦴🦴½ *Old Heidelberg* **1927** Prince Karl Heinrich silently falls in love with lowly barmaid. **102m/B VHS.** Ramon Novarro, Norma Shearer; ***D:*** Ernst Lubitsch. *MGM, FCT*

The Student Teachers 🦴½ **1973** Yet another soft-core Corman product. Three student teachers sleep around, on screen. **79m/C VHS, Beta.** Susan Damante Shaw, Brooke Mills, Bob Harris, John Cramer, Chuck Norris; ***D:*** Jonathan Kaplan. *SUE*

Studs Lonigan 🦴🦴 **1960** Drifting, too artsy rendering a James T. Farrell's trilogy about an Irish drifter growing up in Chicago in the twenties. Good period detail, but oddly off-kilter and implausible as history. **96m/B VHS, Beta.** Christopher Knight, Frank Gorshin, Jack Nicholson; ***D:*** Irving Lerner; ***W:*** Philip Yordan; ***M:*** Jerry Goldsmith. *MGM*

A Study in Scarlet **1933** Owen played Watson the previous year in "Sherlock Holmes;" here he's miscast as Holmes, and the plot differs from the Doyle story of the same title. **77m/B VHS, Beta.** Reginald Owen, Alan Mowbray, Anna May Wong, June Clyde, Alan Dinehart; ***D:*** Edwin L. Marin; ***W:*** Reginald Owen. *SNC, NOS, CAB*

A Study in Terror *Sherlock Holmes Grosster Fall; Fog* **1966** A well-appointed Sherlock Holmes thriller. The second Holmes film in color. Premise has a young, athletic Holmes in pursuit of a well-educated Jack the Ripper in the atmosphere of London in the 1880s. **94m/C VHS, Beta, LV.** *GE GB* John Neville, Donald Houston, Judi Dench, Anthony Quayle, Robert Morley, Frank Finlay, Cecil Parker; ***D:*** James Hill. *COL*

The Stuff ½ **1985 (R)** Surreal horror semi-spoof about an ice cream mogul and a hamburger king who discover that the new, fast-selling confection in town zombifies its partakers. Forced, lame satire from producer/director/writer Cohen. **93m/C VHS, Beta.** Michael Moriarty, Andrea Marcovicci, Garrett Morris, Paul Sorvino, Danny Aiello, Brooke Adams; ***D:*** Larry Cohen; ***W:*** Larry Cohen. *NWV, VTR*

Stuff Stephanie in the Incinerator **1989 (PG-13)** A Troma gagfest about wealthy cretins who torture and kill young women. "Funny" title betrays utter, exploitive mindlessness. **97m/C VHS, Beta, LV.** Catherine Dee, William Dame, M.R. Murphy, Dennis Cunningham; ***D:*** Don Nardo. *LIV*

The Stunt Man **1980 (R)** A marvelous and unique exercise in meta-cinematic manipulation. O'Toole, in one of his very best roles, is a power-crazed movie director; Railsback is a fugitive sheltered by him from sherrif Rocco. When a stunt man is killed in an accident, O'Toole prevails on Railsback to replace him, leading Railsback to wonder if O'Toole wants him dead. A labor of love for director-producer Rush, who spent nine years working on it, and waited two years to see it released, by Fox. Based on the novel by Paul Brodeur. **129m/C VHS, Beta, LV.** Peter O'Toole, Steve Railsback, Barbara Hershey, Chuck Bail, Alex Rocco, Allen (Goorwitz) Garfield, Adam Roarke, Sharon Farrell, Philip Bruns; ***D:*** Richard Rush; ***W:*** Lawrence B. Marcus, Richard Rush; ***M:*** Dominic Frontiere. Golden Globe Awards '81: Best Score; Montreal World Film Festival '80: Best Film; National Board of Review Awards '80: 10 Best Films of the Year; National Society of Film Critics Awards '80: Best Actor (O'Toole); Nominations: Academy Awards '80: Best Actor (O'Toole), Best Adapted Screenplay, Best Director (Rush). *FOX*

Stunt Pilot **1939** A young man takes a job at a film studio as a stunt pilot and finds mayhem and romance on and off the ground. One in the "Tailspin Tommy" series. Well-paced and fun to watch. **61m/C VHS.** John Trent, Marjorie Reynolds, Milburn Stone, Jason Robards Sr., Pat O'Malley; ***D:*** George Waggner. *NOS, MOV*

Stunt Rock **1980 (PG)** A feature film combining rock music, magic, and some of the most incredible stunts ever attempted. **90m/C VHS, Beta.** *NO*

Stunts *Who Is Killing the Stuntman* **1977 (PG)** See "The Stunt Man" instead. OK script hides near-invisible plot; stunt man engages in derring-do. **90m/C VHS, Beta.** Robert Forster, Fiona Lewis, Joanna Cassidy, Darrell Fetty, Bruce Glover, James Luisi; ***D:*** Mark L. Lester; ***M:*** Michael Kamen. *NO*

Stuntwoman ½ **1981** Welch plays a stunt-woman whose death-defying job interferes with her love life. What ever shall she do? **95m/C VHS.** Raquel Welch, Jean-Paul Belmondo; ***D:*** Claude Zidi. *NO*

The Stupids ½ **1995 (PG)** In the tradition of "Dumb and Dumber," the aptly-named Stupids—dad Stanley, mom Joan, brother Buster, and sis Petunia—blunder unwittingly into and out of dangerous adventures. Landing Arnold for the lead seems like the casting coup of the decade. Based on the children's best-selling books. Keep a lookout for Captain Kangaroo. **?m/C VHS.** Tom Arnold, Jessica Lundy, Bug Hall, Alex McKenna; ***D:*** John Landis; ***W:*** Brent Forrester. *NYR*

Submarine Seahawk **1959** When a group of Japanese warships mysteriously disappear, allied intelligence suspect a big battle is brewing. An inexperienced commander who has been tracking the movement of the Japanese ships is put in charge of the submarine Seahawk, even though the crew lacks faith in his command abilities. His own men may prove a bigger obstacle than any of the Japanese. Lots of action and stock WWII footage. **83m/B VHS.** John Bentley, Brett Halsey, Wayne Heffley, Steve Mitchell, Henry McCann, Frank Gerstle; ***D:*** Spencer Gordon Bennet. *COL*

Submission ½ **1977 (R)** A pharmacist's sensuality is reawakened when she has a provocative affair with a clerk in her shop. **107m/C VHS, Beta.** *IT* Franco Nero, Lisa Gastoni; ***D:*** Salvatore Samperi. *PSM*

Subspecies ½ **1990 (R)** New improved vampire demons descend on earth. The first full-length feature film shot on location in Transylvania. For horror buffs only. **90m/C VHS, LV, 8mm.** Laura Tate, Michael Watson, Anders Hove, Michelle McBride, Irina Movila, Angus Scrimm; ***D:*** Ted Nicolaou. *PAR, BTV*

The Substitute **1993 (R)** Donohue plays a sexy high-school substitute teacher who turns out to have homicidal tendencies, which she decides to take out on her students. Film debut for rapper/underwear model Mark. **86m/C VHS, Beta.** Amanda Donohoe, Dalton James, Natasha Gregson Wagner, Eugene Glazer, Mark Wahlberg; ***D:*** Martin Donovan; ***W:*** Cynthia Verlaine; ***M:*** Gerald Gouriet. *PAR*

The Substitute **1996 (R)** Berenger plays a Vietnam vet mercenary who poses as a substitute teacher to uncover a drug ring after his girlfriend (Venora) is roughed up by the gang. At one point, he displays his unique teaching style by throwing some unruly students out of the second floor window. Hmm...wonder if that was on the test. Being a concerned teacher, he decides to uncover the kingpin of the unruly drug gang. Being an unruly drug gang, they decide to shoot at him...a lot. Unless you're a fan of heavy weaponry, banal one liners or yelling at the screen in frustration, substitute another movie for this one. **114m/C VHS, LV.** Tom Berenger, Ernie Hudson, Diane Venora, Mark Anthony, Glenn Plummer, Cliff DeYoung, William Forsythe, Raymond Cruz, Sharron Corley, Richard Brooks, Rodney Grant, Luis Guzman; ***D:*** Robert Mandel; ***W:*** Roy Frumkes, Rocco Simonelli, Alan Ormsby; ***C:*** Bruce Surtees; ***M:*** Gary Chang. *LIV*

The Substitute Wife ½ **1994 (PG-13)** A dying Nebraska frontier woman (Thompson) decides to find her husband (Weller) a new wife to help on the farm and look after their four children. But women are so scarce (and the farm is so isolated) that the only one willing to give it a try is a prostitute (Fawcett) fed up with her profession. Amusing relationships develop between the two women and the bewildered husband. Made for TV. **?m/C VHS.** Farrah Fawcett, Lea Thompson, Peter Weller; ***D:*** Peter Werner; ***W:*** Stan Daniels; ***M:*** Mark Snow. *VMK*

Subterfuge **1968** When a special American security agent goes to England for a "vacation," his presence causes speculation and poses several serious questions for both British Intelligence and the underworld. Nothing special, with the occasional suspenseful moment. **89m/C VHS, Beta.** *GB* Joan Collins, Gene Barry, Richard Todd; ***D:*** Peter Graham Scott. *REP*

Suburban Commando **1991 (PG)** A goofy, muscular alien mistakenly lands on Earth while on vacation. He does his best to remain inconspicuous, resulting in numerous hilarious situations. Eventually he is forced to confront his arch, interstellar nemesis in order to defend the family who befriended him. A harmless, sometimes cute vehicle for wrestler Hogan, which will certainly entertain his younger fans. **88m/C VHS, LV.** Hulk Hogan, Christopher Lloyd, Shelley Duvall, Larry Miller, William Ball, JoAnn Dearing, Jack Elam, Roy Dotrice, Christopher Neame, Tony Longo; ***D:*** Burt Kennedy; ***W:*** Frank Cappello. *COL, NLC*

Suburban Roulette **1967** "Adults only" feature from splattermaster Lewis caters to the prurient. Groovy themes like wife swapping and other very daring subjects. Totally sixties. Presented as part of Joe Bob Brigg's "Sleaziest Movies in the History of the World" series. **91m/C VHS.** ***D:*** Herschell Gordon Lewis. *VTR*

Suburbia *The Wild Side* **1983 (R)** When a group of punk rockers move into a condemned suburban development, they become the targets of a vigilante group. Low budget, needless violent remake of any-one of many '50s rebellion flicks that tries to have a "message." **99m/C VHS, Beta, LV.** Chris Pederson, Bill Coyne, Jennifer Clay, Timothy Eric O'Brien, Andrew Pece, Don Allen; ***D:*** Penelope Spheeris. *LIV, VES*

Subway ½ **1985 (R)** Surreal, MTV-esque vision of French fringe life from the director of "Le Dernier Combat." A spike-haired renegade escapes the law by plunging into the Parisian subway system. Once there, he encounters a bizarre subculture living under the city. Plenty of angry-youth attitude, but where's the point? And frankly, too much bad New Wave music. **103m/C VHS, Beta, LV.** *FR* Christopher Lambert, Isabelle Adjani, Jean-Hugues Anglade, Jean Reno; ***D:*** Luc Besson; ***W:*** Luc Besson. Cesar Awards '86: Best Actor (Lambert), Best Art Direction/Set Decoration, Best Sound; Nominations: Cesar Awards '86: Best Supporting Actor (Anglade). *FOX*

Subway to the Stars ½ *Un Trem Para as Estrelas* **1987** Young saxophonist Fontes searches the back streets of Rio for his missing girlfriend. Realistic and sometimes depressing, if aimless at times. Overall, an intriguing "underworld" flick from Brazil. Portuguese with subtitles. **103m/C VHS.** *BR* Guilherme Fontes, Milton Goncalves, Taumaturgo Ferreira, Ze Trindade, Ana Beatriz Wiltgen; ***D:*** Carlos Diegues. *FCT, NWV*

Success is the Best Revenge ½ **1984** A Polish film director living in London struggles with his rebellious teenage son. Both struggle with questions of exile and identity. Uneven but worthwhile and based on Skolimowski's own experiences. His better earlier film is "Moonlighting." **95m/C VHS, LV.** *GB* Michael York, Michel Piccoli, Anouk Aimee, John Hurt, Jane Asher, Joanna Szerbic, Michael Lyndon, George Skolimowski; ***D:*** Jerzy Skolimowski; ***M:*** Hans Zimmer. Nominations: Cannes Film Festival '84: Best Film. *IME*

The Sucker *Le Corniauds* **1965** Antoine Marecchal (Bouvril) is on his way to an Italian vacation when his car is wrecked in an accident. The businessman who smashed his car offers Antoine a Cadillac to drive but this turns him into a smuggler. However, Antoine isn't as dumb as he may appear and he makes the most of his unusual situation. French with subtitles. **90m/C VHS.** *FR* Bourvil, Louis de Funes; ***D:*** Gerard Oury. *FCT*

Sucker Money ½ *Victims of the Beyond* **1934** Newspaper reporter works to expose phony spiritualist. Good title; little else. Boring. **59m/B VHS, Beta, LV.** Mischa Auer, Phyliss Barrington, Earl McCarthy, Ralph Lewis, Mae Busch; ***D:*** Dorothy Davenport Reid. *NOS, SNC, VYY*

Sudden Death **1950** Shamrock and Lucky are back as cowboys posing as hired gunmen in order to foil a wealthy, homesteader-hating land baron. **55m/B VHS, Beta, LV.** James Ellison, Russell Hayden, Stanley Price, Raymond Hatton, Julie Adams. *NO*

Sudden Death **1977 (R)** Two professional violence merchants put themselves up for hire. **84m/C VHS, Beta.** Robert Conrad, Felton Perry, Don Stroud, Bill Raymond, Ron Vawter, Harry Roskolenko; ***D:*** Richard Foreman. *MED*

Sudden Death **1985 (R)** A beautiful businesswoman decides to kill every rapist she can find after she herself has been attacked. Exploitative in its own fashion; fueled and felled by rage. **95m/C VHS, Beta.** Denise Coward, Frank Runyeon, Jamie Tirelli; ***D:*** Sig Shore. *LIV, VES*

Sudden Death **1995 (R)** Terrorists invade a hockey arena where the Vice President and 17,000 fans, including Fire Marshal Jean-Claude and his kids, are watching the seventh game of the Stanley Cup Finals. The latest in the "Die Hard in a..." genre covers the territory with the now-standard lack of characterization, family member in peril, and ever-increasing body count. Boothe (playing Alan Rickman playing a bad guy) does most of the talking while Van Damme kicks people in the head and plays goalie. Producer Howard Baldwin owns the Pittsburgh Penguins, coincidentally one of the teams on the ice for the second pairing of "Timecop" vets Hyams and Van Damme. **110m/C VHS, LV.** Jean-Claude Van Damme, Powers Boothe, Ross Malinger, Whittni Wright, Raymond J. Barry, Dorian Harewood, Kate McNeil, Audra Lindley; ***D:*** Peter Hyams; ***W:*** Gene Quintano; ***C:*** Peter Hyams; ***M:*** John Debney. *MCA*

Sudden Fear **1952** Successful playwright/heiress Myra Hudson (Crawford) has a whirlwind romance, leading to marriage, with oh-so-charming actor Lester Blaine (Palance). But Les is more interested in Myra's money and gets together with former flame Irene (always the bad girl Grahame) to get rid of his new bride and inherit her fortune. But Myra finds out about the plot and puts her writing talent to work in coming up with a new scenario. Good suspenser with fine performances. Adapted from the book by Edna Sherry. **111m/B VHS.** Joan Crawford, Jack Palance, Gloria Grahame, Bruce (Herman Brix) Bennett, Virginia Huston, Mike Connors; ***D:*** David Miller; ***W:*** Lenore Coffee, Robert Smith; ***C:*** Charles B(ryant) Lang; ***M:*** Elmer Bernstein. Nominations: Academy Awards '52: Best Actress (Crawford). *KIV*

Sudden Impact ½ **1983 (R)** Eastwood directs himself in this formula thriller, the fourth "Dirty Harry" entry. This time "Dirty Harry" Callahan tracks down a revenge-obsessed murderess and finds he has more in common with her than he expected. Meanwhile, local mobsters come gunning for him. This is the one where he says, "Go ahead. Make my day." Followed by "The Dead Pool." **117m/C VHS, Beta, LV, 8mm.** Clint Eastwood, Sondra Locke, Pat Hingle, Bradford Dillman; ***D:*** Clint Eastwood; ***W:*** Charles B. Pierce; ***C:*** Bruce Surtees; ***M:*** Lalo Schifrin. *WAR, TLF*

Sudden Terror *Eyewitness* **1970 (PG)** The murder of an African dignitary is witnessed by a young boy who has trouble convincing his parents and the police about the incident. Suspenseful but less than original. Shot on location in Malta. **95m/C VHS, Beta.** *GB* Mark Lester, Lionel Jeffries, Susan George, Tony Bonner; ***D:*** John Hough. *FOX*

Suddenly ½ **1954** Crazed gunman Sinatra holds a family hostage in the hick town of Suddenly, California, as part of a plot to kill the president, who's passing through town. Tense thriller is a good display for Sinatra's acting talent. Unfortunately hard to find because Sinatra forced United Artists to take it out of distribution after hearing that Kennedy assassin Lee Harvey Oswald had watched "Suddenly" only days before November 22, 1963. Really, Ol' Blue Eyes should have stuck with making top-notch thrillers like this one, instead of degenerating into the world's greatest lounge singer. **75m/B VHS, Beta.** Frank Sinatra, Sterling Hayden, James Gleason, Nancy Gates, Paul Frees; ***D:*** Lewis Allen. *SNC, NOS, VEC*

Suddenly, Last Summer ½ **1959** Brain surgeon is summoned to the mansion of a rich New Orleans matron who wishes him to perform a lobotomy on her niece, supposedly suffering from a mental breakdown. Based on the play by Tennessee Williams. Softened for the censors, though the themes of homosexuality, insanity, and murder, characterizations of evil, and unusual settings presage many movies of the next two decades. Extremely fine performances from Hepburn and Taylor. Clift never completely recovered from his auto accident two years before and does not come across with the strength of purpose really necessary in his character. Still, fine viewing. **114m/B VHS, Beta, LV.** Elizabeth Taylor, Katharine Hepburn, Montgomery Clift, Mercedes McCambridge, Albert Dekker; ***D:*** Joseph L. Mankiewicz; ***W:*** Gore Vidal; ***C:*** Jack Hildyard; ***M:*** Malcolm Arnold. Golden Globe Awards '60: Best Actress—Drama (Taylor); National Board of Review Awards '59: 10 Best Films of the Year; Nominations: Academy Awards '59: Best Actress (Hepburn), Best Actress (Taylor), Best Art Direction/Set Decoration (B & W). *COL*

Sudie & Simpson **1990** Heart-tugging tale of friendship set in rural 1940s Georgia. Twelve-year-old white Sudie's forbidden friendship with the adult black Simpson provides a lot of talk in their small town. Racial barriers finally cause Simpson to be accused of child molestation and the odds of his survival, despite his innocence, don't seem great. Based on Sara Flanigan Carter's autobiographical novel. Made for cable television. **95m/C VHS.** Sara Gilbert, Louis Gossett Jr., Frances Fisher, John M. Jackson, Paige Danahy, Ken Strong; ***D:*** Joan Tewkesbury; ***W:*** Sara Flanigan Carter, Ken Koser. *WOV*

Suds ½ **1920** Pickford is tragic laundress with major crush on a guy who left his shirt at the laundry. **75m/B VHS, Beta, LV.** Mary Pickford, William Austin, Harold Goodwin, Rose Dione, Theodore Roberts; ***D:*** John Francis Dillon. *GPV*

Suffering Bastards ½ **1990** Buddy and Al have never worked a day in their lives—Mom's nightclub always gave them something to do and a regular paycheck. But when Mom's swindled out of the family business, they decide it's time to take charge. Soon they're caught between bullets, babes, and belly laughs in this action-filled comedy. **95m/C VHS.** Eric Bogosian, John C. McGinley, David Warshofsky. *AIP*

Sugar Cane Alley *Rue Cases Negres* **1983 (PG)** After the loss of his parents, an 11-year-old orphan boy goes to work with his grandmother on a sugar plantation. She realizes that her young ward's only hope is an education. Set in Martinique in the 1930s among black workers. Poignant and memorable. French with subtitles. **106m/C VHS, LV.** *FR* Garry Cadenat, Darling Legitimus, Douta Seck; ***D:*** Euzhan Palcy; ***W:*** Euzhan Palcy. *NYF, FCT*

Sugar Cookies *Woof!* **1977 (R)** Erotic horror story in which young women are the pawns as a satanic satyr and an impassioned lesbian play out a bizarre game of vengeance, love, and death. **89m/C VHS, Beta.** Mary Woronov, Lynn Lowry, Monique Van Vooren; ***D:*** Michael Herz. *NO*

Sugar Hill **1994 (R)** Two brothers (Wright & Snipes) are heroin dealers who have built their own crime empire in the Sugar Hill section of Harlem. Snipes is moved to reconsider his career options when he falls for an aspiring actress (Randle). Jarring editing sequence recaps the seminal event in the brothers' upbringing and serves to explain how the wide-eyed boys became cold-blooded pushers. Good performances by all, but formulaic plot will leave viewers asking themselves if they haven't seen it before and why it was they saw it then. Junkie dad Williams was Linc on "The Mod Squad" on television in the late 1960s and director of "Tales from the Hood." **123m/C VHS, LV.** Wesley Snipes, Michael Wright, Theresa Randle, Clarence Williams III, Abe Vigoda, Ernie Hudson, Larry Joshua, Leslie Uggams, Khandi Alexander, Raymond Serra, Joe Dallesandro, Vondie Curtis-Hall; ***D:*** Leon Ichaso; ***W:*** Barry Michael Cooper; ***M:*** Terence Blanchard. *FXV*

Sugarbaby *Zuckerbaby* **1985 (R)** An acclaimed German film about a fat mortuary attendant living in Munich who transforms herself (but doesn't lose weight) in order to seduce a young, handsome subway conductor. Touching and warm film that introduced Sagebrecht to American audiences. A bit too cutting-edge cinematographically. In German with English subtitles. Remade as "Babycakes." Sagebrecht and director Adlon team up again for "Bagdad Cafe" and "Rosalie Goes Shopping." **103m/C VHS, Beta.** *GE* Marianne Sagebrecht, Eisi Gulp, Toni Berger, Will Spendler, Manuela Denz; ***D:*** Percy Adlon; ***W:*** Percy Adlon. *ORI, GLV, APD*

The Sugarland Express **1974 (PG)** To save her son from adoption, a young woman helps her husband break out of prison. In their flight to freedom, they hijack a police car, holding the policeman hostage. Spielberg's first feature film is a moving portrait of a couple's desperation. Based on a true story, adapted by Hal Barwood and Matthew Robbins. **109m/C VHS, Beta, LV.** Goldie Hawn, Ben Johnson, Michael Sacks, William Atherton; ***D:*** Steven Spielberg; ***W:*** Steven Spielberg, Matthew Robbins, Hal Barwood; ***C:*** Vilmos Zsigmond; ***M:*** John Williams. Nominations: Cannes Film Festival '74: Best Film. *MCA*

Sugartime ½ **1995 (R)** Based on the true-life romance of '60s Chicago mobster Sam Giacana (Turturro) and song bird Phyllis Maguire (Parker), one of the wholesome Maguire Sisters. Naturally, getting involved with a crime boss did little for her image and Maguire's career hit the skids while Giacana's volatile jealousy brought unwanted attention from both fellow gangsters and the feds. (He was murdered in 1975 but had broken off with Phyllis before that). The real Maguire denounced the inaccuracy of the TV production. Suggested by William F. Roemer, Jr.'s book "Roemer: Man Against the Mob." **108m/C VHS.** John Turturro, Mary-Louise Parker, Elias Koteas, Maury Chaykin, Louis Del Grande, Christopher Barry, Richard Blackburn; ***D:*** John N. Smith; ***W:*** Martyn Burke; ***C:*** Pierre Letarte. *HBO*

Suicide Battalion/Hell Squad **1958** A war movie double feature. In "Suicide Battalion," American troops must sneak through enemy territory to destroy a captured American command outpost in the Philippines during WWII. Five American soldiers are lost in the North African desert in "Hell Squad." After a series of fights with various enemies, one soldier survives, only to nearly be doublecrossed by a Nazi he meets in the desert. **150m/B VHS.** Mike Connors, John Ashley, Russ Bender, Jewell Lain, Bing Russell, Wally Campo, Brandon Carroll, Frederic Galvin; ***D:*** Edward L. Cahn, Burt Topper; ***W:*** Burt Topper. *COL*

The Suicide Club ½ **1988 (R)** A wealthy, depressed young woman joins a club filled with affluent people who play mysterious games. She finds that winning their games means more than she bargained for. Hemingway looks great in her off-kilter way, but really, there's no point, and the on-screen decadence gets tiresome. **92m/C VHS, Beta, LV.** Mariel Hemingway, Robert Joy, Lenny Henry, Madeleine Potter, Michael O'Donoghue, Anne Carlisle; ***D:*** James Bruce. *ACA*

Suicide Cult *Woof!* **1977** A CIA employee predicts the second coming of Christ, and a battle ensues between the forces of good and evil for possession of the child. **82m/C VHS, Beta.** *NO*

Suicide Patrol **197?** A small band of saboteurs patrols a German-controlled Mediterranean island during WWII. **90m/C VHS, Beta.** Gordon Mitchell, Pierre Richard, Max Dean. *UNI, MOV*

Suite 16 **1994** A penthouse suite in a French Riviera hotel is occupied by rich, manipulative, wheelchair-bound Glover (Postlethwaite). Young gigolo/thief Chris (Kamerling), who believes he's killed his latest victim, is given refuge by Glover in exchange for allowing the aging voyeur to watch Chris (via camera) perform with a succession of prostitutes. Finally, Chris wants to leave but Glover offers him a huge amount of money for one final vicarious thrill—this time he wants Chris, while wearing a microphone, to randomly find a young woman and kill her while Glover listens. Eurotrash, with corny dialogue, but Postlethwaite's chillingly creepy. **109m/C VHS.** *BE GB* Pete Postlethwaite, Antoine Kamerling, Geraldine Pailhas, Tom Jansen; ***D:*** Dominique Deruddere; ***W:*** Charles Higson, Lise Mayer; ***C:*** Jean-Francois Robin; ***M:*** Walter Hus. *APX*

The Suitors **1988** When a group of Iranians decide to sacrifice a lamb in their apartment, the New York police send in SWAT team assuming they're terrorists. First time effort by Ebrahimian, in Farsi with English subtitles. **106m/C VHS.** ***D:*** Ghasem Ebrahimian. *FCT, INJ*

Sullivan's Travels **1941** Sturges' masterpiece is a sardonic, whip-quick romp about a Hollywood director tired of making comedies who decides to make a serious, socially responsible film and hits the road masquerading as a hobo in order to know hardship and poverty. Beautifully sustained, inspired satire that mercilessly mocked the ambitions of Depression-era social cinema. Gets a little overdark near the end before the happy ending; Sturges insisted on 20-year-old Lake as The Girl; her pregnancy forced him to rewrite scenes and design new costumes for her. As ever, she is stunning. **90m/B VHS, Beta, LV.** Joel McCrea, Veronica Lake, William Demarest, Robert Warwick, Franklin Pangborn, Porter Hall, Eric Blore, Byron Foulger, Robert Greig, Torben Meyer, Jimmy Conlin, Margaret Hayes, Chester Conklin, Alan Bridge; ***D:*** Preston Sturges; ***W:*** Preston Sturges. National Board of Review Awards '42: 10 Best Films of the Year. *MCA*

The Sum of Us **1994 (R)** Sweet and faithful adaptation of David Stevens' stage play about a father and his gay son. Widowed Harry Mitchell (Thompson) shares his house with son Jeff (Crowe), who's never made a secret of his sexual orientation. Affable Harry only wants what's best for his boy, including his over-enthusiastic welcome to Jeff's potential new boyfriend (Polson). Too bad Harry's not so lucky in love—his new woman friend Joyce (Kennedy) has problems with Jeff's sexuality. Well, she just has to adjust. Pervasive feel-good message may leave less well-adjusted viewer addled. Sensitive performances, though the film's antecedents as a play are highlighted by having the main characters talk directly to the camera. Aussie slang provides a challenge. **99m/C VHS.** *AU* Jack Thompson, Russell Crowe, John Polson, Deborah Kennedy, Mitch Mathews, Julie Herbert, Joss Moroney, Rebekah Elmaloglou; ***D:*** Kevin Dowling, Geoff Burton; ***W:*** David Stevens; ***M:*** Dave Faulkner. Australian Film Institute '94: Best Adapted Screenplay; Montreal World Film Festival '94: Best Screenplay; Nominations: Australian Film Institute '94: Best Film, Best Supporting Actor (Polson), Best Supporting Actress (Kennedy). *HMK*

Summer ½ *Le Rayon Vert; The Green Ray* **1986 (R)** The fifth and among the best of Rohmer's "Comedies and Proverbs" series. A romantic but glum young French girl finds herself stuck in Paris during the tourist season searching for true romantic love. Takes time and patience to seize the viewer; moving ending makes it all worthwile. In French with English subtitles. **90m/C VHS, Beta, LV.** *FR* Marie Riviere, Lisa Heredia, Beatrice Romand, Eric Hamm, Rosette, Isabelle Riviere; ***D:*** Eric Rohmer; ***W:*** Eric Rohmer. *FCT, INJ, TPV*

Summer Affair ½ **1979** Two young lovers run away from their bickering parents and get shipwrecked on a desert island. **90m/C VHS, Beta.** *IT* Ornella Muti, Les Rannow; ***D:*** George S. Casorati. *NO*

Summer and Smoke ½ **1961** Repressed, unhappy Page falls for handsome doctor Harvey. A tour de force for Page, but that's all; adapted clumsily from the overwrought Tennessee Williams play. **118m/C VHS, Beta, LV.** Laurence Harvey, Geraldine Page, Rita Moreno, Una Merkel, John McIntire, Thomas Gomez, Pamela Tiffin, Lee Patrick, Max Casey Adams Showalter, Earl Holliman, Harry Shannon, Pattee Chapman; ***D:*** Peter Glenville; ***C:*** Charles B(ryant) Lang; ***M:*** Elmer Bernstein. Golden Globe Awards '62: Best Actress—Drama (Page); National Board of Review Awards '61: Best Actress (Page); Nominations: Academy Awards '61: Best Actress (Page), Best Art Direction/Set Decoration (Color), Best Supporting Actress (Merkel), Best Original Score. *PAR, FCT*

Summer Camp Nightmare ½ *The Butterfly Revolution* **1986 (PG-13)** See "Lord of the Flies" instead. A young fascist incites children at two summer camps to overthrow and imprison the adults. Barbarism rears its ugly head. Self-serious and anticlimatic. Based on the novel "The Butterfly Revolution" by William Butler. **89m/C VHS, Beta, LV.** Chuck Connors, Charles Stratton, Harold Pruett, Tom Fridley, Adam Carl; ***D:*** Bert L. Dragin. *SUE, NLC*

Summer City ½ *Coast of Terror* **1977** Fun-and-sun surfing movie complete with romance, hot rods, murder and great shots of the sea features Gibson in his debut. Ever wonder what Australian surf bums do on weekends? The same as their California counterparts—except they talk funny. **83m/C VHS, Beta.** *AU* Mel Gibson, Phillip Avalon, John Jarratt, Christopher Fraser. *VCD*

Summer Fantasy **1984** Mindless TV surf saga about a curvy teen who would rather watch the beach hunks then go to medical school. **96m/C VHS, Beta.** Julianne Phillips, Ted Shackleford, Michael Gross, Dorothy Lyman; ***D:*** Noel Nosseck; ***M:*** Peter Bernstein. *NO*

Summer Heat ½ **1987 (R)** In rural, mid-Depression North Carolina, a young, lonely wife and mother is seduced by a drifter and together they plot murder. Her husband neglects her, and you should neglect to see this utter yawner. Based on a Louise Shivers novel. **80m/C VHS, Beta, LV.** Lori Singer, Anthony Edwards, Bruce Abbott, Kathy Bates; ***D:*** Michie Gleason. *PAR*

Summer Holiday ½ **1948** Rooney comes of age with a vengeance during summer vacation in musical rendition of "Ah, Wilderness." Undistinguished musical numbers, inferior to the original, but jazzy Technicolor cinematography. Ended up in the red by over $1.5 million, lotsa money back then. ♫It's Our Home Town; Afraid to Fall in Love; All Hail, Danville High; The Stanley Steamer; It's Independence Day; I Think You're the Sweetest Kid I've Ever Known; Weary Blues. **92m/C VHS.** Mickey Rooney, Gloria De Haven, Walter Huston, Frank Morgan, Jackie "Butch" Jenkins, Marilyn Maxwell, Agnes Moorehead, Selena Royle, Anne Francis; ***D:*** Rouben Mamoulian. *MGM, TTC, FCT*

The Summer House ½ **1994** Comedy of manners set in 1959 England about the manipulations of three middle-aged women (Moreau, Plowright, Walters) over the impending marriage of one's dreamy young daughter (Headey) to a dolt (Threlfall). Moreau stirs things up as the spirited and skeptical friend of Walters, the deluded bride's mother whom she must interrupt from her busy nuptial preparations and somehow communicate the obvious. Plowright is perfectly cast as the gimlet-eyed groom's mother, well aware of her son's flaws, who achieves an odd alliance with polar opposite Moreau. Strong performances from all the veterans carry the day. Based on the novel by Alice Thomas Ellis. **85m/C VHS.** *GB* Jeanne Moreau, Joan Plowright, Julie Walters, Lena Headey, David Threlfall, Padraig Casey, Britta Smith, John Wood; ***D:*** Waris Hussein; ***W:*** Martin Sherman; ***M:*** Stanley Myers. *HMK*

Summer Interlude ½ *Illicit Interlude; Summerplay; Sommarlek* **1950** A ballerina recalls a romantic summer spent with an innocent boy, who was later tragically killed. Contains many earmarks and visual ideas of later Bergman masterpieces. In Swedish with English subtitles. **95m/B VHS, Beta.** *SW* Maj-Britt Nilsson, Birger Malmsten, Alf Kjellin; ***D:*** Ingmar Bergman; ***W:*** Ingmar Bergman. *HMV, INJ, NLC*

Summer Lovers **1982 (R)** Summer vacation finds young couple traveling to the exotic Greek island of Santorini. They meet up with a fun-loving woman and discover three-way sexual tension, but little in the way of plot, dialogue, or acting. From the director of "Grease" and "Blue Lagoon" and best watched late at night while half conscious. **98m/C VHS, Beta, LV.** Peter Gallagher, Daryl Hannah, Valerie Quennessen; ***D:*** Randal Kleiser; ***M:*** Basil Poledouris. *COL, SUE*

Summer Magic **1963** An impecunious recent widow is forced to leave Boston and settle her family in a small town in Maine. Typical, forgettable Disney drama; early Mills vehicle. A remake of "Mother Carey's Chickens." **116m/C VHS, Beta.** Hayley Mills, Burl Ives, Dorothy McGuire, Deborah Walley, Una Merkel, Eddie Hodges; ***D:*** James Neilson; ***M:*** Buddy Baker. *DIS*

Summer Night **1987 (R)** A female tycoon who is concerned for the environment decides to strike out at the terrorists who are destroying it. This caper turns into one big comedy. In Italian with English subtitles. **94m/C VHS, Beta.** *IT* Mariangela Melato, Michele Placido, Roberto Herlitzka, Massimo Wertmuller; ***D:*** Lina Wertmuller. *LIV*

Summer Night with Greek Profile, Almond Eyes & Scent of Basil **1987 (R)** A wealthy woman tycoon hires an ex-CIA man to kidnap a high-priced, professional terrorist and hold him for ransom. An ironic battle of the sexes follows. In Italian with English subtitles. **94m/C VHS, Beta.** *IT* Mariangela Melato, Michele Placido, Roberto Herlitzka; ***D:*** Lina Wertmuller; ***W:*** Lina Wertmuller. *TPV, INJ*

Summer of Fear *Stranger in Our House* **1978** A happy young woman must overcome evil forces when her cousin comes to live with her family. Based on a novel by Lois Duncan. Pretty scary if ordinary, dumb made-for-TV horror from later-famous Craven. **94m/C VHS, Beta.** Linda Blair; ***D:*** Wes Craven. *NO*

Summer of '42 **1971 (R)** Touching if sentimental story about a 15-year-old boy's sexual coming of age during his summer vacation on an island off New England. While his friends are fumbling with girls their own age, he falls in love with a beautiful 22-year-old woman whose husband is off fighting in the war. **102m/C VHS, Beta, LV.** Jennifer O'Neill, Gary Grimes, Jerry Houser, Oliver Conant; ***D:*** Robert Mulligan; ***C:*** Robert L. Surtees. Academy Awards '71: Best Original Score; Nominations: Academy Awards '71: Best Cinematography, Best Film Editing, Best Story & Screenplay. *WAR*

The Summer of Miss Forbes *El Verano de la Senora Forbes* **1988** A governess rules over two young boys with an iron hand by day and cavorts nude and drunk by night. The boys fantasize about her murder, but fate has different plans. In Spanish with English subtitles. **85m/C VHS, LV.** *SP* Hanna Schygulla, Alexis Castanares, Victor Cesar Villalobos, Guadalupe Sandoval, Fernando Balzaretti, Yuriria Munguia; ***D:*** Jaime Humberto Hermosillo. *FXL, FCT, INJ*

The Summer of My German Soldier **1978** A young Jewish girl befriends an escaped German prisoner of war in a small town in Georgia during WWII. Occasionally sentimental but more often genuinely moving made for TV drama. Rolle won a deserved Emmy as the housekeeper. Adapted from Bette Green's novel. **98m/C VHS, Beta.** Kristy McNichol, Esther Rolle, Bruce Davison; ***D:*** Michael Tuchner. *MTI*

Summer of Secrets **1976 (PG)** Young couple get more than they bargained for when they make love in a demented doctor's beach house. **100m/C VHS, Beta.** *AU NO*

A Summer Place **1959** Melodrama about summer liaisons amid the young and middle-aged rich on an island off the coast of Maine. Too slick; romantic drama is little more than skin-deep, and dialogue is excruciating. Donahue's first starring role. Based on the novel by Sloan Wilson. Featuring "Theme from a Summer Place," which was a number-one hit in 1959. **130m/C VHS, Beta, LV.** Troy Donahue, Richard Egan, Sandra Dee, Dorothy McGuire, Arthur Kennedy, Constance Ford, Beulah Bondi; ***D:*** Delmer Daves; ***C:*** Harry Stradling; ***M:*** Max Steiner. *WAR*

Summer Rental **1985 (PG)** That John Candy just can't win, can he? Here, as a hopeless, harried air traffic controller, he tries to have a few days to relax in sunny Florida. Enter mean rich guy Crenna. Candy can add something hefty to the limpest of plots, and does so here. Watch the first hour for yuks, then rewind. **87m/C VHS, Beta, LV, 8mm.** John Candy, Rip Torn, Richard Crenna, Karen Austin, Kerri Green, John Larroquette, Pierrino Mascarino; ***D:*** Carl Reiner; ***M:*** Alan Silvestri. *PAR*

Summer School **1977 (R)** A teenaged boy's girlfriend will stop at nothing to prevent him from going out with the pretty new girl in town. **80m/C VHS, Beta.** John McLaughlin, Steve Rose, Phoebe Schmidt. *AHV*

Summer School ½ **1987 (PG-13)** A high-school teacher's vacation plans are ruined when he gets stuck teaching remedial English in summer school. It seems all these students are interested in is re-enacting scenes from "The Texas Chainsaw Massacre." Actually, one of the better films of this genre. **98m/C VHS, Beta, LV.** Mark Harmon, Kirstie Alley, Nels Van Patten, Courtney Thorne-Smith, Lucy Lee Flippin, Shawnee Smith, Robin Thomas, Dean Cameron; ***D:*** Carl Reiner; ***W:*** Jeff Franklin; ***M:*** Danny Elfman. *PAR*

Summer School Teachers *Woof!* **1975 (R)** Three sultry femmes bounce about Los Angeles high school and make the collective student body happy. Typical Corman doings; sequel to "The Students Teachers." **87m/C VHS, Beta.** Candice Rialson, Pat

Anderson, Rhonda Leigh Hopkins, Christopher Wales; ***D:*** Barbara Peeters. *NLC*

Summer Snow *Nuiyan, Seisap; Woman, Forty* **1994** Broad comedy mixed (not always successfully) with family drama. May (Siao) is forced to take in her father-in-law Sun (Chiao) after his wife dies. The old man immediately causes chaos with his habit of wandering off and bizarre behavior, which is finally diagnosed as being Alzheimer's disease. Working mother May tries to find a practical way to deal with her dilemmas but the strains are beginning to crack the family apart. Cantonese with subtitles. **106m/C VHS.** *HK* Josephine Siao, Roy Chiao, Law Kar-ying, Allen Ting; ***D:*** Ann Hui; ***W:*** Chan Man-keung; ***C:*** Lee Ping-bing; ***M:*** Yoshihide Otomo. Berlin International Film Festival '94: Best Actress (Siao). *NYR*

Summer Solstice ½ **1981** Fonda and Loy are splendid as a couple married half a century who revisit the beach where they first met. Fonda especially shines, as a crusty old artist. Yes, it is an awful lot like "On Golden Pond." Made for TV. **75m/C VHS, Beta.** Henry Fonda, Myrna Loy, Lindsay Crouse, Stephen Collins; ***D:*** Ralph Rosenblum. *MTT*

Summer Stock *If You Feel Like Singing* **1950** Garland plays a farm owner whose sister arrives with a summer stock troupe, led by Kelly, to rehearse a show in the family barn. Garland agrees, if the troupe will help her with the farm's harvest. When her sister decamps for New York, leaving the leading lady role open, guess who steps into the breach. Slim plot papered over with many fun song-and-dance numbers. Also features Garland's first MGM short, "Every Sunday," made in 1936 with Deanna Durbin. ♫Friendly Star; Mem'ry Island; Dig-Dig-Dig For Your Dinner; If You Feel Like Singing, Sing; Howdy Neighbor; Blue Jean Polka; Portland Fancy; You, Wonderful You; Get Happy. **109m/C VHS, Beta, LV.** Judy Garland, Gene Kelly, Gloria De Haven, Carleton Carpenter, Eddie Bracken, Phil Silvers, Hans Conried, Marjorie Main, Ray Collins, Deanna Durbin; ***D:*** Charles Walters. *MGM, TTC*

A Summer Story **1988 (PG-13)** Superbly acted, typically British period drama about beautiful farm girl Stubbs and city lawyer Wilby, who fall in love. But can they overcome difference of social class? From the story "The Apple Tree" by John Galsworthy. **97m/C VHS, Beta.** *GB* James Wilby, Imogen Stubbs, Susannah York, Sophie Ward, Kenneth Colley, Jerome Flynn; ***D:*** Piers Haggard; ***W:*** Penelope Mortimer; ***M:*** Georges Delerue. *MED*

A Summer to Remember *Seryozha* **1961** A five-year-old boy spends a summer with his stepfather on a Soviet collective farm. The two become deeply attached. Scenes of collective life will be of more interest to Westerners than the near-sentimental story. Star Bondarchuk later directed the epic, award-winning "War and Peace." **80m/B VHS, Beta.** *RU* Borya Barkhazov, Sergei Bondarchuk, Irana Skobtseva. National Board of Review Awards '61: 5 Best Foreign Films of the Year. *NO*

A Summer to Remember ½ **1984 (PG)** A deaf boy (played by Gerlis, himself deaf since birth) develops a friendship with an orangutan through sign language. Bad guys abduct the friendly ape - but all is right in the end. Nice, innocuous family viewing. Based on a story by Scott Swanton and Robert Lloyd Lewis. **93m/C VHS, Beta.** Tess Harper, James Farentino, Burt Young, Louise Fletcher, Sean Gerlis, Bridgette Anderson; ***D:*** Robert Lewis; ***M:*** Charles Fox. *MCA*

Summer Vacation: 1999 *1999—Nen No Natsu Yasumi* **1988** Four boys are left behind at boarding school during their summer vacation. They experience all the early pangs of adolescence from love to jealousy. Their summer is then disturbed by the arrival of another boy who appears to be the reincarnation of a dead friend. Romantic look at youth caught between innocence and awareness. In Japanese with English subtitles. **90m/C VHS, Beta.** *JP* Eri Miyagima, Miyuki Nakano, Tomoko Otakra, Rie Mizuhara; ***D:*** Shusuke Kaneko. *NYF, FCT, INJ*

Summer Wishes, Winter Dreams **1973 (PG)** Woodward and Balsam are a materially prosperous middle-aged couple with little but tedium in their lives—a tedium accurately replicated, in what feels like real life, in this slow, dull film. The two leads and Sidney—in her first screen role in 17 years—are all excellent, but the story of regret and present unhappiness wears the viewer down. **95m/C VHS, Beta.** Joanne Woodward, Martin Balsam, Sylvia Sidney, Dori Brenner, Ron Richards; ***D:*** Gilbert Cates; ***W:*** Stewart Stern. British Academy Awards '74: Best Actress (Woodward); National Board of Review Awards '73: Best Supporting Actress (Sidney); New York Film Critics Awards '73: Best Actress (Woodward); Nominations: Academy Awards '73: Best Actress (Woodward), Best Supporting Actress (Sidney). *COL*

Summerdog **1978 (G)** Harmless family tale about vacationers who rescue a cheerful, lovable mutt named Hobo. And a good thing they found him: He saves them from many perils. Thanks, Hobo! **90m/C VHS, Beta.** James Congdon, Elizabeth Eisenman, Oliver Zabriskie, Tavia Zabriskie; ***D:*** John Clayton. *GEM*

Summer's Children **1984** Man who suffers from amnesia as a result of a car crash becomes the target of a mysterious killer. Forget about it. **90m/C VHS, Beta.** Tom Haoff, Paully Jardine, Kate Lynch. *TWE*

Summer's Games ½ **1987** Buxom girls cavort on the beach, competing in various games designed specifically to expose as much flesh as possible—mud wrestling, bikini boxing, wet T-shirting and more. **60m/C VHS, Beta, LV.** *CEL*

Summertime ½ *Summer Madness* **1955** Spinster Hepburn vacations in Venice and falls in love with Brazzi. She is hurt when inadvertently she learns he is married, but her life has been so bleak she is not about to end her one great romance. Moving, funny, richly photographed in a beautiful Old World city. From Arthur Laurents' play "The Time of the Cuckoo." **98m/C VHS, Beta, LV.** Katharine Hepburn, Rossano Brazzi; ***D:*** David Lean; ***C:*** Jack Hildyard. National Board of Review Awards '55: 10 Best Films of the Year; New York Film Critics Awards '55: Best Director (Lean); Nominations: Academy Awards '55: Best Actress (Hepburn), Best Director (Lean). *SUE, CRC, NLC*

Summertree **1971 (PG)** Douglas stars as a young musician in the 1960s trying to avoid the draft and the wrath of his parents. Contrived and heavy-handed. Produced by Douglas pere, Kirk. Adapted from the play by Ron Cower. **88m/C VHS, Beta.** Michael Douglas, Jack Warden, Brenda Vaccaro, Barbara Bel Geddes, Kirk Calloway, Bill Vint; ***D:*** Anthony Newley; ***M:*** David Shire. *WAR, OM*

The Sun Comes Up **1949** MacDonald, in her last screen appearance, plays a bitter widow whose life is changed by an orphan's love for a collie. Songbird MacDonald manages to sing a number of songs, some of them backed by a chorus of "orphans." Based on short stories by Marjorie Kinnan Rawlings. **93m/C VHS.** Jeanette MacDonald, Lloyd Nolan, Claude Jarman Jr., Lewis Stone, Dwayne Hickman; ***D:*** Richard Thorpe; ***W:*** William Ludwig; ***M:*** Andre Previn. *MGM, FCT*

Sun Ra & His Intergalactic Solar Arkestra: Space is the Place **1974** Space age flick starring most appropriately Sun Ra, space-age prophet/jazz musician. Sun Ra returns from a space odyssey and embarks on saving black youth from the world's oppressive control by bringing them back into space with him. The shaman's philosophy on film. ♫Watusi; Outer Spaceways Inc.; The Satellites are Spinning. **63m/C VHS.** ***D:*** John Coney; ***W:*** Joshua Smith. *RHP*

The Sun Shines Bright **1953** Heavily stereotyped, contrived tale of a Southern judge with a heart of gold who does so many good deeds (defending a black man accused of rape; helping a desperate prostitute) that he jeopardizes his re-election. Set during Reconstruction. An unfortunate remake of Ford's own 1934 "Judge Priest," starring Will Rogers. **92m/B VHS.** Charles Winninger, Arleen Whelan, John Russell, Stepin Fetchit, Milburn Stone, Russell Simpson; ***D:*** John Ford; ***C:*** Archie Stout. *REP*

Sun Valley Serenade ½ **1941** Wartime musical fluff about a band that adopts a Norwegian refugee waif as a publicity stunt. She turns out to be a full-grown man-chaser who stirs up things at a ski resort. Fun, but it ends abruptly—because, they say, Henie fell during the huge skating finale, and Darryl Zanuck wouldn't greenlight a reshoot. One of only two feature appearances by Glenn Miller and his Orchestra (the other was "Orchestra Wives"), on video with a soundtrack restored from original dual-track recordings. ♫Chattanooga Choo Choo; I Know Why and So Do You; It Happened In Sun Valley; The Kiss Polka; In the Mood. **86m/C VHS.** Sonja Henie, John Payne, Glenn Miller, Milton Berle, Lynn Bari, Joan Davis, Dorothy Dandridge; ***D:*** H. Bruce Humberstone. Nominations: Academy Awards '41: Best Black and White Cinematography, Best Song ("Chattanooga Choo Choo"), Best Original Score. *FXV, FCT, MLB*

Sunburn ½ **1979 (PG)** Insurance investigator Grodin hires model Fawcett to pretend to be his wife to get the scoop on a suicide/murder case of a rich guy in Acapulco. Made-for-TV drivel. **110m/C VHS, Beta.** Farrah Fawcett, Charles Grodin, Joan Collins, Art Carney, William Daniels; ***D:*** Richard Sarafian; ***W:*** James Booth. *PAR*

Sundance **1972** Surf dudes get together on the beaches of Hawaii and California for some romance and, of course, plenty of wave riding. **87m/C VHS, Beta.** *NO*

Sundance and the Kid **1976 (PG)** Two brothers try to collect an inheritance against all odds. Originally known as "Sundance Cassidy and Butch the Kid." **84m/C VHS, Beta.** John Wade, Karen Blake; ***D:*** Arthur Pitt. *NO*

Sunday, Bloody Sunday **1971 (R)** Adult drama centers around the intertwined love affairs of the homosexual Finch, the heterosexual Jackson, and self-centered bisexual artist Head, desired by both. Fully-drawn characters brought to life by excellent acting make this difficult story well worth watching—though Head's central character is sadly rather dull. Day-Lewis makes his first (brief) screen appearance as a car vandalizing teenager. Powerful, sincere and sensitive. **110m/C VHS, LV.** *GB GB* Glenda Jackson, Peter Finch, Murray Head, Daniel Day-Lewis; ***D:*** John Schlesinger. British Academy Awards '71: Best Actor (Finch), Best Actress (Jackson), Best Director (Schlesinger), Best Film; Golden Globe Awards '72: Best Foreign Film; New York Film Critics Awards '71: Best Screenplay; National Society of Film Critics Awards '71: Best Actor (Finch), Best Screenplay; Writers Guild of America '71: Best Original Screenplay; Nominations: Academy Awards '71: Best Actor (Finch), Best Actress (Jackson), Best Director (Schlesinger), Best Story & Screenplay. *FOX*

Sunday Daughters **1980** A teenage girl kept in a detention home constantly tries to escape and find some kind of familial love. Stronger performances mix with keen direction. In Hungarian with English subtitles. **100m/C VHS, Beta.** *HU* Julianna Nyako; ***D:*** Janosz Rozsa. *FCT*

A Sunday in the Country ½ *Un Dimanche a la Campagne* **1984 (G)** A lush, distinctively French affirmation of nature and family life. This character study with a minimal plot takes place during a single summer day in 1910 France. An elderly impressionist painter-patriarch is visited at his country home by his family. Highly acclaimed, though the pace may be too slow for some. Beautiful location photography. In French with English subtitles. **94m/C VHS, Beta.** *FR* Louis Ducreux, Sabine Azema, Michel Aumont; ***D:*** Bertrand Tavernier; ***W:*** Bertrand Tavernier, Colo Tavernier O'Hagan. Cannes Film Festival '84: Best Director (Tavernier); Cesar Awards '85: Best Actress (Azema), Best Cinematography, Best Writing; National Board of Review Awards '84: Best Supporting Actress (Azema); New York Film Critics Awards '84: Best Foreign Film. *MGM*

Sunday in the Park with George **1986** Taped theatrical performance of the Tony, Grammy, and Pulitzer Prize-winning musical play, which is based upon impressionist Georges Seurat's painting "A Sunday Afternoon on the Island of Grande Jatte." Features a celebrated music score by Sondheim. **120m/C VHS, Beta, LV.** Mandy Patinkin, Bernadette Peters, Barbara Byrne, Charles Kimbrough; ***D:*** James Lapine; ***M:*** Stephen Sondheim. *ORI, WAR*

Sunday Too Far Away 🦴🦴🦴 **1974** The rivalries between Australian sheep shearers and graziers leads to an ugly strike at a remote outback area in 1955. An uncomplicated story and a joy to watch. **100m/C VHS, Beta.** *AU* Jack Thompson; ***D:*** Ken Hannam. Australian Film Institute '74: Best Actor (Thompson), Best Film. *SUE*

Sundays & Cybele 🦴🦴🦴½ *Les Dimanches de Ville d'Arvay; Cybele* **1962** A ragged war veteran and an orphaned girl develop a strong emotional relationship, which is frowned upon by the townspeople. Warm and touching. In French with English subtitles. Also available in a letterboxed edition. **110m/B VHS, Beta.** *FR* Hardy Kruger, Nicole Courcel; ***D:*** Serge Bourguignon; ***M:*** Maurice Jarre. Academy Awards '62: Best Foreign Language Film; National Board of Review Awards '62: 5 Best Foreign Films of the Year. *NOS, HHT, DVT*

Sunday's Children 🦴🦴🦴½ **1994** Lyrical exploration of childhood continues trilogy that includes "Fanny and Alexander" and "Best Intentions." Wistful childhood memoir takes up the story of Ingmar Bergman's family eight years after the director was born. Many of the same familial issues surface, but story soon narrows its focus to the relationship between little Ingmar, whom everyone calls Pu, and his stern father Henrik. Deeply emotional and intense, film represents the steps toward forgiveness that the elder Bergman is finally able to take regarding the painful relationship he had with his own father. Father-son theme made more poignant with Ingmar's son Daniel making his feature debut as director. **118m/C VHS.** *SW* Thommy Berggren, Lena Endre, Henrik Linnros, Jacob Leygraf, Maria Bolme, Bjorje Ahistedt, Per Myrberg; ***D:*** Daniel Bergman; ***W:*** Ingmar Bergman. *ICA*

Sundown 🦴🦴½ **1941** In Africa at the beginning of WWII, a local girl aids the British against a German plot to run guns to the natives and start a rebellion. Engaging performances and efficient direction keep it above the usual cliches. Also available in a colorized version. **91m/B VHS, Beta.** Gene Tierney, Bruce Cabot, George Sanders, Harry Carey Sr., Cedric Hardwicke, Joseph Calleia, Dorothy Dandridge, Reginald Gardiner; ***D:*** Henry Hathaway; ***C:*** Charles B(ryant) Lang; ***M:*** Miklos Rozsa. Nominations: Academy Awards '41: Best Black and White Cinematography, Best Interior Decoration, Best Original Score. *NOS, VYY, DVT*

Sundown 🦴½ **1991 (R)** An ambitious shot at a vampire western fails because it drains almost all vampire lore and winds up resembling a standard oater. Carradine plays a reformed vampire king (guess who) running a desert clinic that weans bloodsuckers away from preying on humans. But undead renegades attack using sixguns and wooden bullets. The climax may outrage horror purists. **104m/C VHS.** David Carradine, Bruce Campbell, Deborah Foreman, Maxwell Caulfield, Morgan Brittany; ***D:*** Anthony Hickox. *VES*

Sundown Fury 🦴 **1942** Young cowboy fights against a group of bandits to hold a telegraph office. **56m/B VHS, Beta.** Donald (Don "Red") Barry. *VCN*

Sundown Kid 🦴½ **1943** A Pinkerton agent goes undercover to break up a counterfeiting operation. Routine western. **55m/B VHS, Beta.** Donald (Don "Red") Barry. *DVT*

Sundown Riders 🦴 **1948** Cowhands are victimized by noose-happy outlaws. Filmed in just over a week on a $30,000 budget and originally shot on 16mm to make it accessible to hospitals and schools with basic viewing equipment. The lesson here: it takes time and money to make a good western. **56m/B VHS, Beta, LV.** Russell Wade, Andy Clyde, Jay Kirby; ***D:*** Lambert Hillyer. *NO*

Sundown Saunders 🦴 **1936** A standard oater about a cowboy whose prize for winning a horse race is a ranch. Trouble is, an outlaw wants the homestead as well. **64m/B VHS, Beta.** Bob Steele; ***D:*** Robert North Bradbury. *NOS, VYY, HEG*

The Sundowners 🦴🦴🦴½ **1960** Slow, beautiful, and often moving epic drama about a family of Irish sheepherders in Australia during the 1920s who must continually uproot themselves and migrate. They struggle to save enough money to buy their own farm and wind up training a horse they hope will be a money-winner in racing. Well-acted by all, with Johns and Ustinov providing some humorous moments. Adapted from the novel by Jon Cleary. Filmed in Australia and London studios. **133m/C VHS, Beta, LV.** Deborah Kerr, Robert Mitchum, Peter Ustinov, Glynis Johns, Dina Merrill, Chips Rafferty, Michael Anderson Jr., Lola Brooks, Wylie Watson; ***D:*** Fred Zinnemann; ***C:*** Jack Hildyard; ***M:*** Dimitri Tiomkin. National Board of Review Awards '60: 10 Best Films of the Year, Best Actor (Mitchum); Nominations: Academy Awards '60: Best Actress (Kerr), Best Adapted Screenplay, Best Director (Zinnemann), Best Picture, Best Supporting Actress (Johns). *WAR, VTR, CCB*

Sunny 🦴🦴 **1941** Another glossed-over, love-conquers-all musical with Neagle as a circus star who falls for a wealthy car maker's son. Dad and crew disapprove, putting a damper on the romance. In spite of the weak storyline and flat direction, Kerns' music and Bolger's dancing make it enjoyable. ♫Who?; D'ya Love Me?; Sunny; Two Little Bluebirds. **98m/B VHS.** Anna Neagle, Ray Bolger, John Carroll, Edward Everett Horton, Frieda Inescort, Helen Westley, Benny Rubin, Richard Lane, Martha Tilton; ***D:*** Herbert Wilcox. Nominations: Academy Awards '41: Best Original Score. *NOS*

Sunny Side Up 🦴🦴½ **1928** As stress of pickle factory work takes toll on woman's friend, she makes heroic effort to help her to the country to recover. **66m/B VHS, Beta.** Vera Reynolds, ZaSu Pitts, Edmund Burns, Sally Rand; ***D:*** Donald Crisp. *GPV*

Sunny Skies 🦴 **1930** Bargain-basement retread has Lease donating a pint of blood. ♫Sunny Days; I Must Have You; Wanna Find a Boy; Must Be Love. **75m/B VHS.** Benny Rubin, Marceline Day, Rex Lease, Marjorie Kane, Wesley Barry; ***D:*** Norman Taurog. *NOS*

Sunnyside *Woof!* **1979 (R)** Travolta plays a street kid trying to bring an end to the local gang warfare so he can move to Manhattan. Features a host of pop tunes in an attempt to ride the coattails of brother John's successful "Saturday Night Fever." Laughably bad. **100m/C VHS.** Joey Travolta, John Lansing, Stacey Pickren, Andrew Rubin, Michael Tucci, Talia Balsam, Joan Darling; ***D:*** Timothy Galfas. *AIP, FOX*

Sunrise 🦴🦴🦴🦴 *Sunrise—A Song of Two Humans* **1927** Magnificent silent story of a simple country boy who, prodded by an alluring city woman, tries to murder his wife. Production values wear their age well. Gaynor won an Oscar for her stunning performance. Remade in Germany as "The Journey to Tilsit." Based on a story by Hermann Suderman. **110m/B VHS.** George O'Brien, Janet Gaynor, Bodil Rosing, Margaret Livingston, J. Farrell MacDonald, Carl Mayer; ***D:*** F.W. Murnau; ***C:*** Charles Rosher, Karl Struss. Academy Awards '28: Best Actress (Gaynor), Best Cinematography; Nominations: Academy Awards '28: Best Interior Decoration. *GPV*

Sunrise at Campobello 🦴🦴🦴 **1960** A successful adaptation (with Bellamy and Donehue repeating their roles) of the Tony award-winning play that chronicles Franklin D. Roosevelt's battle to conquer polio and ultimately receive the Democratic presidential nomination in 1924. Garson gives an excellent performance as Eleanor Roosevelt. Screenplay by Schary, who adapted his own play, and also produced. **143m/C VHS, Beta.** Ralph Bellamy, Greer Garson, Hume Cronyn, Jean Hagen, Jack Perrin, Lyle Talbot; ***D:*** Vincent J. Donehue; ***W:*** Dore Schary. Golden Globe Awards '61: Best Actress—Drama (Garson); National Board of Review Awards '60: 10 Best Films of the Year, Best Actress (Garson); Nominations: Academy Awards '60: Best Actress (Garson), Best Art Direction/Set Decoration (Color), Best Costume Design (Color), Best Sound. *WAR*

Sunrise Trail 🦴🦴½ **1931** Lots of action with Steele working undercover for the sheriff, trying to stop a rustler. He also finds the time to fall for barmaid Mehaffey. **65m/B VHS.** Bob Steele, Blanche Mehaffey, Jack Clifford, Eddie Dunn; ***D:*** John P. McCarthy. *GPV*

The Sun's Burial 🦴🦴🦴 **1960** Oshima's stylized and violent drama depicts life in Osaka's worst slum—a teeming underworld populated by teen gangs, prostitutes, and criminals. All want control of the area's most profitable business, an illegal blood-selling operation. In Japanese with English subtitles. **87m/C VHS.** *JP* Kayoko Honoo, Koji Nakahara, Masahiko Tsugawa, Fumio Watanabe; ***D:*** Nagisa Oshima. *NYF*

Sunset 🦴🦴 **1988 (R)** Edwards wanders the range in this soft-centered farce about a couple of Western legends out to solve a mystery. On the backlots of Hollywood, silent screen star Tom Mix (Willis) meets aging marshal Wyatt Earp (Garner) and participates in a time-warp western circa 1927. They encounter a series of misadventures while trying to finger a murderer. Garner ambles enjoyably, lifting him a level above the rest of the cast. **101m/C VHS, Beta, LV.** Bruce Willis, James Garner, Mariel Hemingway, Darren McGavin, Jennifer Edwards, Malcolm McDowell, Kathleen Quinlan, M. Emmet Walsh, Patricia Hodge, Richard Bradford, Joe Dallesandro, Dermot Mulroney; ***D:*** Blake Edwards; ***W:*** Blake Edwards, Rod Amateau; ***M:*** Henry Mancini. Golden Raspberry Awards '88: Worst Director (Edwards); Nominations: Academy Awards '88: Best Costume Design. *COL*

Sunset Boulevard 🦴🦴🦴½ **1950** Famed tale of Norma Desmond (Swanson), aging silent film queen, who refuses to accept that stardom has ended for her and hires a young down-on-his-luck screenwriter (Holden) to help engineer her movie comeback. The screenwriter, who becomes the actress' kept man, assumes he can manipulate her, but finds out otherwise. Reality was almost too close for comfort, as Swanson, von Stroheim (as her major domo), and others very nearly play themselves. A darkly humorous look at the legacy and loss of fame with witty dialog, stellar performances, and some now-classic scenes. Based on the story "A Can of Beans" by Brackett and Wilder. **100m/B VHS, Beta, LV.** Gloria Swanson, William Holden, Erich von Stroheim, Nancy Olson, Buster Keaton, Jack Webb, Cecil B. DeMille, Fred Clark; ***D:*** Billy Wilder; ***W:*** Billy Wilder, Charles Brackett, D.M. Marshman Jr. Academy Awards '50: Best Art Direction/Set Decoration (B & W), Best Story & Screenplay, Best Score; Golden Globe Awards '51: Best Actress—Drama (Swanson), Best Director (Wilder), Best Film—Drama, Best Score; Nominations: Academy Awards '50: Best Actor (Holden), Best Actress (Swanson), Best Black and White Cinematography, Best Director (Wilder), Best Film Editing, Best Picture, Best Supporting Actor (von Stroheim), Best Supporting Actress (Olson). *PAR, HMV*

Sunset Grill 🦴🦴 **1992 (R)** While investigating his wife's murder, detective Ryder Hart (Weller) discovers a pattern of grisly killings. Sexy singer Loren Duquesne (Singer) leads him south of the border to her boss and his bloody money-making scheme. Unrated version also available. **103m/C VHS.** Peter Weller, Lori Singer, Alexandra Paul, John Rhys-Davies, Michael Anderson Jr., Stacy Keach; ***D:*** Kevin Connor. *NLC, PMS*

Sunset Heat 🦴🦴 *Midnight Heat* **1992 (R)** Former drug dealer (Pare) returns to his home in Los Angeles with a legit job as a photojournalist. He stays with an old friend who turns out to be involved with the obsessed drug czar that Pare used to work for. Trouble comes along when the drug lord is robbed and blames Pare for the crime. Action-packed, with some good plot twists. An unrated version contains two additional minutes of footage. **94m/C VHS.** Michael Pare, Dennis Hopper, Adam Ant, Daphne Ashbrook, Charlie Schlatter; ***D:*** John Nicolella. *NLC*

Sunset in El Dorado 🦴½ **1945** Roy and Dale thwart a villainous scheme to defraud farmers of their land. **56m/B VHS, Beta.** Roy Rogers, Dale Evans, George "Gabby" Hayes, Hardie Albright, Roy Barcroft, Tom London, Edmund Cobb; ***D:*** Frank McDonald. *GPV, VCN*

Sunset Limousine 🦴🦴½ **1983** An out-of-work stand-up comic gets thrown out by his girlfriend, then takes a job as a chauffeur. Standard vehicle with occasional bursts of speed. **92m/C VHS, Beta.** John Ritter, Martin Short, Susan Dey, Paul Reiser, Audrie Neehan, Lainie Kazan; ***D:*** Terry Hughes. *LIV*

Sunset on the Desert ½ **1942** Rogers gets to wear a white hat and a black hat as both the leader of a gang of outlaws and the hero who brings them to justice. A poor man's Western omelette. **53m/B VHS, Beta.** Roy Rogers, George "Gabby" Hayes, Lynne Carver, Frank M. Thomas Sr., Bob Nolan, Beryl Wallace, Glenn Strange, Douglas Fowley, Roy Barcroft, Pat Brady; ***D:*** Joseph Kane. *VYY*

Sunset Park **1996 (R)** Brooklyn phys ed teacher Phyllis Saroka (Perlman) becomes the coach of a high school basketball team that, despite her total lack of knowledge about the game, makes it to the city championships. The cast's excellent performances hold interest, even though the predictable storyline gives away all of its moves before it gets near the hoop. Starr (of the rap group Onyx) is outstanding as the most talented (and most troubled) member of the team. **100m/C VHS.** Rhea Perlman, Carol Kane, Terrence DaShon Howard, Camille Saviola, Fredro Starr, James Harris, Antwon Tanner, Shawn Michael Howard, De'Aundre Bonds; ***D:*** Steve Gomer; ***W:*** Seth Zvi Rosenfeld, Kathleen McGhee-Anderson; ***C:*** Robbie Greenberg; ***M:*** Kay Gee, Miles Goodman. *NYR*

Sunset Range ½ **1935** The "World's All-Around Champion Cowboy" of 1912 stars in this chaps-slappin', bit-chompin', dust-raisin' saga of the plains. **59m/B VHS, Beta.** Hoot Gibson. *NOS, VCN, VCI*

Sunset Serenade **1942** Roy and Gabby outwit murderous duo who plan to eliminate the new heir to a ranch. **60m/B VHS, Beta.** Roy Rogers, George "Gabby" Hayes, Helen Parrish; ***D:*** Joseph Kane. *NOS, MED, HEG*

Sunset Strip **1985** A photographer investigates a friend's murder, and enters the seamy world of drugs and rock and roll in L.A. **83m/C VHS, Beta.** Tom Elpin, Cheri Cameron Newell, John Mayall. *LIV, VES*

Sunset Strip *Woof!* **1991 (R)** A young dancer finds a job in a strip club and competes against the other women there to find the man of her dreams. The women take their jobs very seriously—even attending ballet classes to improve their performances. However, the viewer probably won't take this movie very seriously since it is just another excuse to show women in as little clothing as possible. **95m/C VHS, LV.** Jeff Conaway, Michelle Foreman, Shelley Michelle; ***D:*** Paul G. Volk; ***M:*** John Gonzalez. *PMH*

Sunset Trail **1932** Routine Maynard sagebrush saga with the hero protecting a woman rancher from outlaws. **60m/B VHS, Beta.** Ken Maynard. *NOS, VCI, DVT*

The Sunshine Boys **1975 (PG)** Two veteran vaudeville partners, who have shared a love-hate relationship for decades, reunite for a television special. Adapted by Neil Simon from his play. Matthau was a replacement for Jack Benny, who died before the start of filming. Burns, for his first starring role since "Honolulu" in 1939, won an Oscar. **111m/C VHS, Beta, LV.** George Burns, Walter Matthau, Richard Benjamin, Lee Meredith, F. Murray Abraham, Carol Arthur, Howard Hesseman; ***D:*** Herbert Ross; ***W:*** Neil Simon. Academy Awards '75: Best Supporting Actor (Burns); Golden Globe Awards '76: Best Actor—Musical/Comedy (Matthau), Best Film—Musical/Comedy, Best Supporting Actor (Benjamin); Nominations: Academy Awards '75: Best Actor (Matthau), Best Adapted Screenplay, Best Art Direction/Set Decoration. *MGM, BTV*

Sunshine Run ½ **1979 (PG)** Two escaped slaves and a young widow search for Spanish treasure in the Everglades. Also on video as "Black Rage." **102m/C VHS, Beta.** Chris Robinson, Ted Cassidy, David Legge, Phyllis Robinson; ***D:*** Chris Robinson. *NO*

Sunstroke **1992 (R)** Seymour plays a desperate mother searching for her kidnapped child through the Arizona desert. Framed for murder, she cannot contact the police but must track the kidnappers herself, until she meets a drifter with secrets of his own. **91m/C VHS, Beta.** Jane Seymour, Stephen Meadows, Steve Railsback, Ray Wise, Don Ameche; ***D:*** James Keach; ***W:*** Duane Poole. *PAR*

The Super ½ **1991 (R)** Pesci stars as a slumlord who faces a prison sentence thanks to his terminal neglect. The option given to him is to live in his own rat hole until he provides reasonable living conditions. This he does, and predictably learns a thing or two about his own greed and the people who suffer as a result of it. Pesci as always gives an animated performance but poor scripting laden with stereotypes and cliches successfully restricts effort. **86m/C VHS.** Joe Pesci, Vincent Gardenia, Madolyn Smith, Ruben Blades; ***D:*** Rod Daniel; ***C:*** Bruce Surtees. *FXV, CCB*

Super Bitch ½ *Mafia Junction* **1989** Nasty, cold, and uncaring woman uses men to keep up her expensive habits, then ruthlessly tosses them aside when she is done. She purposely entangles them in her drug trade and thinks nothing of their deaths. Proving once again that you get what you pay for. **90m/C VHS.** Stephanie Beacham, Patricia Hayes, Gareth Thomas; ***D:*** Massimo Dallamano. *ATL*

Super Brother **1990 (R)** The feared and respected leader of an oppressed people is imprisoned, much to everyone's regret. **90m/C VHS, Beta.** Woody Strode. *ELE*

Super Force **1990** When astronaut Zach Stone (Olandt) returns from an assignment on Mars he finds his policeman brother has been murdered. He quits NASA and joins the force to get revenge, battling evil crime boss Tao Satori (Liddy). Stone also moonlights as a vigilante, complete with motorcycle and high-tech armoured suit. It's dumb but there's lots of action. **92m/C VHS, LV.** Ken Olandt, G. Gordon Liddy, Larry B. Scott, Lisa Niemi, Marshall Teague; ***Cameos:*** Patrick Macnee; ***D:*** Richard Compton. *MCA*

Super Fuzz ½ *Supersnooper* **1981 (PG)** Rookie policeman develops super powers after being accidentally exposed to radiation. Somewhat ineptly, he uses his abilities to combat crime. Somewhat ineptly acted, written, and directed as well. **97m/C VHS, Beta.** Terence Hill, Joanne Dru, Ernest Borgnine; ***D:*** Sergio Corbucci; ***W:*** Sergio Corbucci. *SUE*

Super Mario Bros. ½ **1993 (PG)** $42 million adventure fantasy based on the popular Nintendo video game. The brothers are in hot pursuit of the Princess Daisy who's been kidnapped by evil slimebucket Hopper and taken to Dinohattan, a fungi-infested, garbage-strewn, rat-hole version of Manhattan. Hopper will amuse the adults, doing a gleeful reptilian version of Frank Booth from "Blue Velvet." Hoskins and Leguizamo act gamely in broad Nintendo style, enthusiastically partaking in high-tech wizardry and the many gags. Hits bullseye of target audience—elementary and junior high kids—with frenetic pace, gaudy special effects, oversized sets, and animatronic monsters. **104m/C VHS, Beta, LV.** Bob Hoskins, John Leguizamo, Samantha Mathis, Fisher Stevens, Richard Edson, Dana Kaminsky, Dennis Hopper, Fiona Shaw, Mojo Nixon, Lance Henriksen; ***D:*** Rocky Morton, Annabel Jankel; ***W:*** Edward Solomon, Parker Bennett, Terry Runte; ***M:*** Alan Silvestri. *HPH, BTV, TOU*

Super Ninjas **198?** A ninja battles evil hordes of like-trained ninja warriors, and wins over and over again. **104m/C VHS, Beta.** Cheng Tien Chi, Lung Tien Hsiang, Chen Pei Hsi. *NO*

Super Seal **1977 (G)** An injured seal pup disrupts a family's normal existence after the young daughter adopts him. **95m/C VHS, Beta.** Foster Brooks, Sterling Holloway, Sarah Brown; ***D:*** Michael Dugan. *VCI*

Super Soul Brother **198?** A lazy no-goodnik accidentally ingests a strange potion which turns him into a master thief. **80m/C VHS.** Wildman Steve. *XVC*

Superargo *Il Re Dei Criminali; Superargo the Giant; The King of Criminals* **1967** A wrestler becomes a super-hero with psychic powers and a bulletproof leotard. He fights against a madman who is turning athletes into robots. Successful Italian hero who wouldn't last two minutes in the ring with Batman. **95m/C VHS, Beta.** *IT SP* Guy Madison, Ken Wood, Liz Barrett, Diana Loris; ***D:*** Paul Maxwell. *SNC, MAD*

Superbug Super Agent ½ **1976** Dodo, the wonder car puts the brakes on crime in this silly action-adventure tale. A lemon in a lot full of Herbies. **90m/C VHS, Beta.** Robert Mark, Heidi Hansen, George Goodman. *JEF*

Superchick *Woof!* **1971 (R)** Mild-mannered stewardess by day, sexy blonde with karate black-belt by night. In addition to stopping a skyjacking she regularly makes love to men around the world. A superbomb that never gets off the ground. **94m/C VHS, Beta.** Joyce Jillson, Louis Quinn, Thomas Reardon; ***D:*** Ed Forsyth. *PSM*

Superdad **1973 (G)** A middle-aged parent is determined to bridge the generation gap by trying his hand at various teenage activities. Disney family fare that's about as complicated as a television commercial. The adolescents are two-dimensional throwbacks to the fun-loving fifties. **94m/C VHS, Beta.** Bob Crane, Kurt Russell, Joe Flynn, Barbara Rush, Kathleen Cody, Dick Van Patten; ***D:*** Vincent McEveety; ***M:*** Buddy Baker. *DIS*

Superfly ½ **1972 (R)** Controversial upon release, pioneering blaxploitation has Harlem dope dealer finding trouble with gangs and police as he attempts to establish retirement fund from one last deal. Excellent period tunes by Curtis Mayfield. Two lesser sequels. **98m/C VHS, Beta.** Ron O'Neal, Carl Lee, Sheila Frazier, Julius W. Harris; ***D:*** Gordon Parks Jr.; ***M:*** Curtis Mayfield. *WAR*

Superfly T.N.T. *Woof! Super Fly T.N.T* **1973 (R)** This confusing sequel to "Superfly" finds O'Neal returning as Youngblood Priest. The now ex-drug dealer has retired with his girlfriend to Rome where he is approached by an African gun-runner (Browne) for help in a revolution against an oppressive government. Cheap exploitation. **87m/C VHS.** Ron O'Neal, Roscoe Lee Browne, Sheila Frazier, Robert Guillaume, Jacques Sernas, William Berger; ***D:*** Ron O'Neal; ***W:*** Alex Haley. *PAR*

Supergirl ½ **1984 (PG)** Big-budget bomb in which Slater made her debut and nearly killed her career, with the help of Kryptonite. Unexciting and unsophisticated story of a young woman, cousin to Superman, with super powers, based on the comic book series. She's in pursuit of a magic paperweight, but an evil sorceress wants it too. Dunaway is a terrifically vile villainess with awesome black magic powers. Slater is great to look at, but is much better in almost any other film. **114m/C VHS, Beta, LV.** *GB* Faye Dunaway, Helen Slater, Peter O'Toole, Mia Farrow, Brenda Vaccaro, Marc McClure, Simon Ward, Hart Bochner, Maureen Teefy, David Healy, Matt Frewer; ***D:*** Jeannot Szwarc; ***M:*** Jerry Goldsmith. *LIV*

Supergrass **1987 (R)** A low-brow British farce about a nebbish who poses as a drug smuggler to impress his girlfriend, and is then mistaken for a real one by the authorities. **105m/C VHS, Beta.** *GB* Adrian Edmondson, Peter Richardson, Nigel Planer, Jennifer Saunders, Ronald Allen, Dawn French; ***D:*** Peter Richardson. *NLC*

Superman: The Movie ½ **1978 (PG)** The DC Comics legend comes alive in this wonderfully entertaining saga of Superman's life from a baby on the doomed planet Krypton to Earth's own Man of Steel. Hackman and Beatty pair marvelously as super criminal Lex Luthor and his bumbling sidekick. Award-winning special effects and a script that doesn't take itself too seriously make this great fun. Followed by three sequels. **144m/C VHS, Beta, LV.** Christopher Reeve, Margot Kidder, Marlon Brando, Gene Hackman, Glenn Ford, Susannah York, Ned Beatty, Valerie Perrine, Jackie Cooper, Marc McClure, Trevor Howard, Sarah Douglas, Terence Stamp, Jack O'Halloran, Phyllis Thaxter; ***D:*** Richard Donner; ***W:*** Mario Puzo, Robert Benton, David Newman; ***C:*** Geoffrey Unsworth; ***M:*** John Williams. Academy Awards '78: Best Visual Effects; National Board of Review Awards '78: 10 Best Films of the Year; Nominations: Academy Awards '78: Best Film Editing, Best Sound, Best Original Score. *WAR*

Superman 2 𝔅𝔅𝔅 **1980 (PG)** The sequel to "the movie" about the Man of Steel. This time, he has his hands full with three super-powered villains from his home planet of Krypton. The romance between reporter Lois Lane and our superhero is made believable and the storyline has more pace to it than the original. A sequel that often equals the first film—leave it to Superman to pull off the impossible. **127m/C VHS, Beta, LV.** Christopher Reeve, Margot Kidder, Gene Hackman, Ned Beatty, Jackie Cooper, Sarah Douglas, Jack O'Halloran, Susannah York, Marc McClure, Terence Stamp, Valerie Perrine, E.G. Marshall; ***D:*** Richard Lester; ***W:*** Mario Puzo, David Newman; ***M:*** John Williams. *WAR*

Superman 3 𝔅𝔅 **1983 (PG)** Villainous businessman Vaughn tries to conquer Superman via the expertise of bumbling computer expert Pryor and the judicious use of an artifical form of Kryptonite. Superman explores his darker side after undergoing transformation into sleaze ball. Promising satiric start ultimately defeated by uneven story and direction and boring physical comedy. Notable is the absence of Lois Lane as a main character. Followed by "Superman 4." **123m/C VHS, Beta, LV.** Christopher Reeve, Richard Pryor, Annette O'Toole, Jackie Cooper, Margot Kidder, Marc McClure, Annie Ross, Robert Vaughn; ***D:*** Richard Lester; ***W:*** David Newman; ***M:*** John Williams. *WAR*

Superman 4: The Quest for Peace 𝔅𝔅 **1987 (PG)** The third sequel, in which the Man of Steel endeavors to rid the world of nuclear weapons, thereby pitting himself against nuclear-entrepreneur Lex Luthor and his superpowered creation, Nuclear Man. Special effects are dime-store quality and it appears that someone may have walked off with parts of the plot. Reeve deserves credit for remaining true to character through four films. **90m/C VHS, Beta, LV.** Christopher Reeve, Gene Hackman, Jon Cryer, Marc McClure, Margot Kidder, Mariel Hemingway, Sam Wanamaker; ***D:*** Sidney J. Furie; ***W:*** Mark Rosenthal; ***M:*** John Williams; ***V:*** Susannah York. *WAR, APD*

Superman & the Mole Men 𝔅𝔅½ *Superman and the Strange People* **1951** The cast of the popular 1950s' television show made this rarely seen feature as a "pilot" for the series. Superman faces the danger threatened by the invasion of radioactive mole-men who make their way to the surface world from the bowels of the earth through an oil-well shaft. Simple fun. **58m/C VHS, Beta.** George Reeves, Phyllis Coates, Jeff Corey; ***D:*** Lee Sholem. *WAR*

Superman: The Serial, Vol. 1 **1948** Superman was first seen in live action in this 15-part theatrical serial that has been rarely shown since its original release. **248m/B VHS, Beta.** Kirk Alyn, Noel Neill, Pierre Watkin, Tommy "Butch" Bond, Thomas Carr; ***D:*** Spencer Gordon Bennet. *WAR*

Supernatural 𝔅𝔅½ **1933** Roma (Lombard) falls prey to a phony medium (Dinehart) who promises to call up the spirit of her recently murdered twin brother. At the same moment of the seance a murderess dies in the electric chair and her body is used in Dr. Houston's (Warner) life-after-death experiment. Too bad Roma becomes possessed by the woman's evil spirit. Now the doctor and Roma's fiance (Scott) must undo the curse. A hokey B-grade movie disliked by Lombard. **78m/B VHS.** Carole Lombard, Randolph Scott, H.B. Warner, Alan Dinehart, Vivienne Osborne, Beryl Mercer, William Farnum, Willard Robertson; ***D:*** Victor Halperin; ***W:*** Harvey Thew, Brian Marlow; ***C:*** Arthur Martinelli. *MCA*

The Supernaturals 𝔅½ **1986 (R)** Confederate Civil War-era ghosts, bent on avenging their deaths, haunt a wooded area in which modern Yankee army maneuvers are practiced. Antebellum boredom. **85m/C VHS, Beta.** Maxwell Caulfield, LeVar Burton, Nichelle Nichols; ***D:*** Armand Mastroianni. *SUE, NLC*

Supersonic Man *Woof!* **1978 (PG)** Incoherent shoestring-budget Superman spoof with a masked hero fighting to save the world from the evil intentions of a mad scientist. **85m/C VHS, Beta.** *SP* Michael Coby, Cameron Mitchell, Diana Polakov; ***D:*** J. Piquer Simon. *VCI*

Superstar: The Life and Times of Andy Warhol 𝔅𝔅𝔅 **1990** Even if you didn't grok Andy's 'pop' artwork and self-created celebrity persona, this ironic, kinetic, oft-rollicking documentary paints a vivid picture of the wild era he inspired and exploited. Interviewees range from Warhol cohorts like Dennis Hopper to proud executives at the Campbell Soup plant. One highlight: a Warhol guest shot on "The Love Boat." **87m/C VHS.** Tom Wolfe, Sylvia Miles, David Hockney, Taylor Mead, Dennis Hopper; ***D:*** Chuck Workman. *VES*

Superstition 𝔅½ *The Witch* **1982** A reverend and his family move into a vacant house despite warnings about a curse from the townsfolk. Some people never learn. **85m/C VHS, Beta.** James Houghton, Albert Salmi, Lynn Carlin; ***D:*** James Robertson. *LIV*

Supervixens 𝔅𝔅 **1975** True to Meyer's low-rent exploitation film canon, this wild tale is filled with characteristic Amazons, sex and violence. A gas station attendant is framed for the grisly murder of his girlfriend and hustles out of town, meeting a succession of well-endowed women during his travels. As if it needed further problems, it's hampered by a tasteless storyline and incoherent writing. **105m/C VHS.** Shari Eubank, Charles Napier; ***D:*** Russ Meyer; ***W:*** Russ Meyer. *RMF*

Support Your Local Gunfighter 𝔅𝔅𝔅 **1971 (G)** Garner plays a western con man with his tongue firmly in his cheek. He comes to the small town of Purgatory and is thought to be a notorious gunfighter. He decides to go with the mistaken identity and use it to his profitable advantage. Elam is his bumbling sidekick and Pleshette the love interest. A delightful, deliberately cliche-filled western. A follow-up, not a sequel, to "Support Your Local Sheriff" (1969). **92m/C VHS.** James Garner, Jack Elam, Suzanne Pleshette, Harry (Henry) Morgan, Dub Taylor, John Dehner, Joan Blondell, Ellen Corby, Henry Jones; ***D:*** Burt Kennedy. *MGM*

Support Your Local Sheriff 𝔅𝔅𝔅½ **1969 (G)** Amiable, irreverent western spoof with more than its fair share of laughs. When a stranger stumbles into a gold rush town, he winds up becoming sheriff. Garner is perfect as the deadpan sheriff, particularly in the scene where he convinces Dern to remain in jail, in spite of the lack of bars. Neatly subverts every western cliche it encounters, yet keeps respect for formula western. Followed by "Support Your Local Gunfighter." **92m/C VHS, Beta, LV.** James Garner, Joan Hackett, Walter Brennan, Bruce Dern, Jack Elam, Harry (Henry) Morgan; ***D:*** Burt Kennedy; ***W:*** William Bowers; ***C:*** Harry Stradling Jr. National Board of Review Awards '69: 10 Best Films of the Year. *FOX, MGM*

Suppose They Gave a War and Nobody Came? 𝔅𝔅½ *War Games* **1970 (G)** A small Southern town battles with a local army base in this entertaining but wandering satire. The different acting styles used as the producers wavered on making this a comedy or drama were more at war with one another than the characters involved. **113m/C VHS, LV.** Tony Curtis, Brian Keith, Ernest Borgnine, Suzanne Pleshette, Ivan Dixon, Bradford Dillman, Don Ameche; ***D:*** Hy Averback; ***W:*** Don McGuire. *FOX*

Surabaya Conspiracy 𝔅½ **1975** Mystery and intrigue surround a quest for gold in Africa. **90m/C VHS, Beta.** Michael Rennie, Richard Jaeckel, Barbara Bouchet, Mike Preston; ***D:*** Roy Davis. *NO*

Sure Fire 𝔅𝔅 **1990** Wes (Blair) is a mercurial entrepreneur who thinks he has found the financial ticket to paradise with his vacation home scheme. Much to the chagrin of his wife Ellen (Dezina), he refuses to let anything stand in the way of his sure-fire fortune, even his family. Wes develops a little self-control as he realizes he's beginning to flake out, but it may be too late. Director Jost has put together a surprisingly unpretentious film with a virtually no-name cast, its plot speaking volumes on the American condition while unfolding in the bleak Utah desert. **86m/C VHS.** Tom Blair, Kristi Hager, Robert Ernst, Kate Dezina, Phillip R. Brown; ***D:*** Jon Jost; ***W:*** Jon Jost. *WAC*

The Sure Thing 𝔅𝔅𝔅 **1985 (PG-13)** College students who don't like each other end up travelling to California together, and of course, falling in love. Charming performances make up for predictability. Can't-miss director (and ex-Meathead) Reiner's second direct hit at the box office. **94m/C VHS, Beta, LV, 8mm.** John Cusack, Daphne Zuniga, Anthony Edwards, Boyd Gaines, Lisa Jane Persky, Viveca Lindfors, Nicolette Sheridan, Tim Robbins; ***D:*** Rob Reiner; ***W:*** Jonathan Roberts, Steven L. Bloom. *COL, SUE*

Surf Nazis Must Die 𝔅 **1987** A piece of deliberate camp in the Troma mold, about a group of psychotic neo-Nazi surfers taking over the beaches of California in the wake of a devastating earthquake. Tongue-in-cheek, tasteless and cheap, but intentionally so. **83m/C VHS, Beta.** Barry Brenner, Gail Neely, Michael Sonye, Dawn Wildsmith, Tom Shell, Bobbie Bresee; ***D:*** Peter George; ***W:*** John Ayre. *MED, VTR*

Surf Ninjas 𝔅𝔅½ *Surf Warriors* **1993 (PG)** Action comedy for the kiddies finds two young surfer dudes who are actually the long-lost crown princes of the obscure nation of Patu San. The country's incompetent (what a surprise, it's Nielsen) warlord wants the boys to stay lost. Lame jokes and tame martial arts sequences. **87m/C VHS, LV.** Ernie Reyes Jr., Nick Cowen, Rob Schneider, Leslie Nielsen, Tone Loc, John Karlen, Ernie Reyes Sr.; ***D:*** Neal Israel; ***W:*** Dan Gordon; ***M:*** David Kitay. *COL, NLC, IME*

Surf Party 𝔅½ **1964** Romance among the sands of Malibu with Vinton as the owner of a surf shop. Risque in 1964; utterly campy today. ♫If I Were an Artist; That's What Love Is; Pearly Shells. **68m/C VHS.** Bobby Vinton, Jackie De Shannon, Patricia Morrow, Kenny Miller; ***D:*** Maury Dexter. *MOV*

Surf 2 *Woof!* *Surf 2: The End of the Trilogy* **1984 (R)** A most excellent group of surfers get sick from drinking tainted Buzz Cola concocted by demented chemist Deezen in most heinous effort to obliterate surfer population from Southern California. Bogus, dude. No, you didn't miss "Surf 1" (there's not one), the title is the sort of in-joke this exercise in mental meltdown perpetuates as comedy. Ha. **91m/C VHS, Beta.** Morgan Paull, Cleavon Little, Lyle Waggoner, Ruth Buzzi, Linda Kerridge, Carol Wayne, Eddie Deezen, Eric Stoltz, Brandis Kemp, Terry Kiser; ***D:*** Randall Badat; ***W:*** Randall Badat; ***M:*** Peter Bernstein. *MVD, MED*

Surfacing *Woof!* **1984** A girl braves the hostile northern wilderness to search for her missing father. This pseudo-psychological, sex-driven suspense flick makes little sense. **90m/C VHS, Beta.** Joseph Bottoms, Kathleen Beller, R.H. Thomson, Margaret Dragu; ***D:*** Claude Jutra. *NO*

The Surgeon 𝔅 *Exquisite Tenderness* **1994** Routine hospital horror finds Dr. Theresa McCann (Glasser) caught up in murder when patients and doctors become poison victims. Aided by toxicologist Benjamin Hendricks (Remar), McCann finds a lollipop left behind and realizes the killer is ex-boyfriend/doctor Julian Matar (Haberle), whose unlawful experiments in tissue regeneration got him suspended. Now he's hiding out in the hospital and killing to get the pituitary glands necessary for his miracle serum. Film's original title "Exquisite Tenderness" is a term for the point when pain becomes so extreme it turns to pleasure—the film merely turns grisly. **100m/C VHS.** *GE* Isabel Glasser, James Remar, Sean Haberle, Charles Dance, Peter Boyle, Malcolm McDowell, Charles Bailey-Gates, Gregory West, Mother Love; ***D:*** Carl Schenkel; ***W:*** Patrick Cirillo; ***C:*** Thomas Burstyn; ***M:*** Christopher Franke. *APX*

Surprise Attack 𝔅 **197?** The Spanish Civil War forms the backdrop for this action opus. **124m/C VHS, Beta.** Simon Andrew, Danny Martin, Patty Shepard; ***D:*** Joseph Loman. *NO*

Surrender 𝔅½ **1987 (PG)** A struggling woman artist and a divorced author fall in love but won't admit it for fear of being hurt again. Jumbled plot, unfortunate casting. Available in a Spanish-subtitled version. **95m/C VHS, Beta, LV.** Michael Caine, Sally Field, Steve Guttenberg, Peter Boyle, Jackie Cooper, Julie Kavner, Louise Lasser, Iman; ***D:*** Jerry Belson; ***W:*** Jerry Belson; ***C:*** Juan Ruiz-Anchia; ***M:*** Michel Colombier. *WAR, GVV*

Surrogate **1988** A young couple fights to keep their marriage afloat by turning to a sex surrogate. Strong cast helps carry odd, confusing script, with plenty of (you guessed it) sex, and a mystery to solve. **100m/C VHS, Beta.** *CA* Art Hindle, Shannon Tweed, Carole Laure, Michael Ironside, Marilyn Lightstone; ***D:*** Don Carmody. *MED*

Survival Earth **19??** After civilization collapses, humans begin reverting back to a primitive way of life. A young couple and a soldier of fortune fight against it, hoping for a better existence. **90m/C VHS.** *NO*

Survival Game **1987** A young combat expert (Chuck Norris's son) gets involved with some ex-hippies in search of a $2 million cache. High-kickin' action. **91m/C VHS, Beta.** Mike Norris, Deborah Goodrich, Seymour Cassel; ***D:*** Herb Freed. *MED*

Survival of a Dragon **197?** A medieval Chinese warrior is transported into the future, where he goes on a kicking rampage. **88m/C VHS, Beta.** Squall Hung, Jaguar Lee. *NO*

Survival of Spaceship Earth **1990** Man, his world and the protection of its ecology are discussed in this beautiful and fascinating film. Winner of numerous international awards due to the strength of its production values and writing. Nominated for 10 Emmy awards, winner of 2 Emmys. **63m/C VHS.** Rue McClanahan; ***D:*** Dirk Summers; ***W:*** Dirk Summers. *CPM, FCT, CRY*

Survival Quest ½ **1989 (R)** Students in a Rocky Mountain survival course cross paths with a band of bloodthirsty mercenaries-in-training. A battle to the death ensues; you'll wish they'd all put each other out of their misery a lot sooner. **90m/C VHS, Beta.** Lance Henriksen, Dermot Mulroney, Mark Rolston, Steve Antin, Paul Provenza, Ben Hammer, Traci Lind, Catherine Keener, Reggie Bannister; ***D:*** Don A. Coscarelli; ***W:*** Don A. Coscarelli. *FOX*

Survival Run **1980 (R)** Six California teenagers become stranded in the Mexican desert, where they witness Graves and Milland making a shady deal. The chase is on, the story is lame, the gory parts aren't gory—so why bother? **90m/C VHS, Beta.** Peter Graves, Ray Milland, Vincent Van Patten; ***D:*** Larry Spiegel; ***W:*** Gerard M. Cahill. *MED*

Survival Zone *Woof!* **1984 (R)** Nuclear holocaust survivors battle a violent band of marauding motorcyclists on the barren ranches of the 21st century. Advice to director Rubens and cohorts: Next time, find a plot that's not growing mold. **90m/C VHS, Beta.** Gary Lockwood, Morgan Stevens, Camilla Sparv; ***D:*** Percival Rubens. *PSM*

The Survivalist **1987 (R)** An arms-ready survivalist nut defends his family and supplies against a panicked society awaiting nuclear war. Poorly acted, little tension, and ineffective plotting make boredom seem a more critical issue than survival. **96m/C VHS, Beta, LV.** Steve Railsback, Susan Blakely, Marjoe Gortner, David Wayne, Cliff DeYoung; ***D:*** Sig Shore; ***W:*** Robert Dillon. *VES*

Surviving Desire **1991** Donovan plays Jude, a neurotic, romantic English professor who falls madly in love with an independently-minded student, Sophie. Unfortunately, Sophie is more interested in how the seduction will advance her writing than how it will affect her life. The lovers explore their brief affair by analyzing every emotion and motive in a series of quirky conversations. Intelligent, amusing, and stylized film from director Hartley. The tape also includes two Hartley shorts: "Theory of Achievement" and "Ambition." **86m/C VHS.** Martin Donovan, Mary B. Ward, Matt Malloy, Rebecca Nelson; ***D:*** Hal Hartley. *FXL, INJ*

Surviving the Game **1994 (R)** Poorly made hunt-the-human story. Homeless Ice-T is hired by a group of men to assist them on their annual hunt. But wait, he's the prey. Unbelievable premise pits the streetwise, down and out Ice-T against the savvy and weapons rich group—and he beats them at their own game. Few high-impact action sequences. The violence, although there isn't as much as might be expected, is graphic. **94m/C VHS, LV.** Rutger Hauer, Ice-T, F. Murray Abraham, Gary Busey, Charles S. Dutton, John C. McGinley, William McNamara, Jeff Corey; ***D:*** Ernest R. Dickerson; ***W:*** Eric Bernt; ***M:*** Stewart Copeland. *NLC*

Survivor **1980** A jetliner crashes, leaving but one survivor, the pilot, who is then plagued by visions, tragedies, and ghosts of dead passengers. Viewers also suffer. **91m/C VHS, Beta.** *AU* Robert Powell, Jenny Agutter, Joseph Cotten, Angela Punch McGregor; ***D:*** David Hemmings; ***W:*** David Ambrose. *ORI, WAR*

Survivor **1987** A lone warrior on a post-nuclear holocaust wasteland battles a megalomaniac ruler. Moll as the evil villian is watchable, but overall the film is a wasteland, too. **92m/C VHS, Beta, LV.** Chip Mayer, Richard Moll, Sue Kiel; ***D:*** Michael Shackleton. *LIV, VES*

Survivors **1983 (R)** Two unemployed men find themselves the target of hit man, whom they have identified in a robbery attempt. One of the men goes gun-crazy protecting himself. Uneven comedy with wild Williams and laid-back Matthau. **102m/C VHS, Beta, LV.** Robin Williams, Walter Matthau, Jerry Reed, John Goodman; ***D:*** Michael Ritchie; ***W:*** Michael Leeson; ***C:*** Billy Williams. *COL*

Susan and God *The Gay Mrs. Trexel* **1940** A selfish socialite returns from Europe and starts practicing a new religion, much to the dismay of her friends and family. Despite her preaching, her own domestic life is falling apart and she realizes that her preoccupation and selfish ways have caused a strain on her marriage and her relationship with her daughter. An excellent script and a fine performance from Crawford make this a highly satisfying film. **115m/B VHS.** Joan Crawford, Fredric March, Ruth Hussey, John Carroll, Rita Hayworth, Nigel Bruce, Bruce Cabot, Rose Hobart, Rita Quigley, Marjorie Main, Gloria De Haven; ***D:*** George Cukor; ***W:*** Anita Loos. *MGM*

Susan Lenox: Her Fall and Rise ½ *The Rise of Helga; Rising to Fame* **1931** Garbo, the daughter of an abusive farmer, falls into the arms of the handsome Gable to escape an arranged marriage. Both stars are miscast, but the well-paced direction keeps the melodrama moving. **84m/B VHS, Beta.** Greta Garbo, Clark Gable, Jean Hersholt, John Miljan, Alan Hale, Hale Hamilton; ***D:*** Robert Z. Leonard; ***C:*** William H. Daniels. *MGM, FCT*

Susan Slept Here ½ **1954** While researching a movie on juvenile delinquents, a Hollywood script writer (Powell) is given custody of a spunky 18-year-old delinquent girl (Reynolds) during the Christmas holidays. Cute sex comedy. Based on the play "Susan," by Alex Gottlieb and Steve Fisher. **98m/C VHS, Beta, LV.** Dick Powell, Debbie Reynolds, Anne Francis; ***D:*** Frank Tashlin. Nominations: Academy Awards '54: Best Song ("Hold My Hand"), Best Sound. *NO*

Susana **1951** Minor though still interesting Bunuel, in which a sexy delinquent young girl is rescued from vagrancy by a Spanish family, and how she subsequently undermines the family's structure through sexual allurement and intimidation. In Spanish with English subtitles. **87m/B VHS, Beta.** *MX* Rosita Quintana, Fernando Soler, Victor Manuel Mendoza, Matilde Palou; ***D:*** Luis Bunuel. *XVC, INJ, APD*

Susanna Pass **1949** Oil deposits underneath a fish hatchery lake attract bad guys. They set off explosions to destroy the fishery, but game warden Rogers investigates. Minor outing for Roy. **67m/C VHS.** Roy Rogers, Dale Evans, Estelita Rodriguez, Martin Garralaga, Robert Emmett Keane, Lucien Littlefield, Douglas Fowley; ***D:*** William Witney. *REP*

Susannah of the Mounties ½ **1939 (PG)** An adorable young girl is left orphaned after a wagon train massacre and is adopted by a Mountie. An Indian squabble gives Shirley a chance to play little peacemaker and teach Scott how to tap dance, too. Could she be any cuter? Available colorized. **78m/B VHS, Beta.** Shirley Temple, Randolph Scott, Margaret Lockwood, J. Farrell MacDonald, Moroni Olsen, Victor Jory; ***D:*** William A. Seiter; ***C:*** Arthur C. Miller. *FXV*

Suspect ½ **1987 (R)** An overworked Washington, DC, public defender (Cher) is assigned to a controversial murder case in which her client is a deaf-mute, skid-row bum. A cynical lobbyist on the jury illegally researches the case himself. They work together to uncover a far-reaching conspiracy. Unrealistic plot, helped along by good performances and tight direction. **101m/C VHS, Beta, LV, 8mm.** Dennis Quaid, Cher, Liam Neeson, E. Katherine Kerr, Joe Mantegna, John Mahoney, Philip Bosco; ***D:*** Peter Yates; ***W:*** Eric Roth; ***C:*** Billy Williams; ***M:*** Michael Kamen. *COL*

Suspect Device ½ *Roger Corman Presents: Suspect Device* **1995 (R)** Nonsensical cable thriller finds government computer researcher Dan (Howell) mistakenly accessing a secret file and becoming an immediate assassination target. Then Dan discovers he isn't even human—he's really a genetically engineered cross between a robot and a nuclear bomb! Part "Terminator," part "Three Days of the Condor," and all silliness. **90m/C VHS.** C. Thomas Howell, Stacy Travis, Jed Allan, John Beck, Marcus Aurelius, Jonathan Fuller; ***D:*** Rick Jacobson; ***W:*** Alex Simon; ***C:*** John Aronson; ***M:*** Christopher Lennertz. *NHO*

Suspended Alibi ½ *Suspected Alibi* **1956** British crime-drama about an adulterous man unjustly accused when his alibi is murdered. Overlook the convenient coincidence. **64m/B VHS.** *GB* Patrick Holt, Honor Blackman, Andrew Keir, Valentine Dyall; ***D:*** Alfred Shaughnessy. *NOS, SNC*

Suspicion ½ **1941** Alfred Hitchcock's suspense thriller about a woman who gradually realizes she is married to a killer and may be next on his list. An excellent production unravels at the end due to RKO's insistence that Grant retain his "attractive" image. This forced the writers to leave his guilt or innocence undetermined. Available colorized. **99m/B VHS, Beta, LV.** Cary Grant, Joan Fontaine, Cedric Hardwicke, Nigel Bruce, May Whitty, Leo G. Carroll, Heather Angel; ***D:*** Alfred Hitchcock; ***C:*** Harry Stradling. Academy Awards '41: Best Actress (Fontaine); New York Film Critics Awards '41: Best Actress (Fontaine); Nominations: Academy Awards '41: Best Picture. *MED, MLB, BTV*

Suspicion **1987** Remake of the chilling Hitchcock tale. Newlywed bride is consumed with fears about her wealthy new husband. The suspense builds as she comes to suspect that she is married to a cold-blooded killer. Curtin in way over her head. **97m/C VHS, Beta.** Jane Curtin, Anthony Andrews; ***D:*** Andrew Grieve. *MED*

Suspicious Agenda ½ **1994 (R)** Cop with a past is assigned to a task force that's hunting down a sadistic vigilante. **97m/C VHS.** Richard Grieco, Nick Mancuso, Jim Byrnes; ***D:*** Clay Borris; ***W:*** Kevin Rock. *AVE*

Suspiria **1977 (R)** An American dancer enters a weird European ballet academy and finds they teach more than movement as bodies begin piling up. Sometimes weak plot is aided by great-but-gory special effects, fine photography, good music, and a chilling opening sequence. Also available in unrated version. **92m/C VHS, Beta, LV.** *IT* Jessica Harper, Joan Bennett, Alida Valli, Udo Kier; ***D:*** Dario Argento; ***W:*** Dario Argento. *HHE, QVD*

Suture **1993** Quirky thriller is a homage to late '50s melodramas with its strange tale of mistaken identity. Vincent wants to hide his unsavory past by assuming the identity of his estranged half-brother, Clay, which should be difficult since Vincent is white and Clay is black but the movie's premise is that everyone confuses the two. Vincent tries to kill Clay in an explosion but he survives—with amnesia and with everyone in the hospital assuming he's Vincent. Shifting points of view as he struggles to piece together his memory offer disorientation not just for Clay but the viewer as well. Feature film debut for the directors. **96m/B VHS.** Dennis Haysbert, Sab Shimono, Mel Harris, Michael Harris, Dina Merrill, David Graf, Fran Ryan; ***D:*** Scott McGehee, David Siegel; ***W:*** Scott McGehee, David Siegel; ***C:*** Greg Gardiner; ***M:*** Cary Berger. Sundance Film Festival '94: Best Cinematography; Nominations: Independent Spirit Awards '95: Best Cinematography, Best First Feature. *HMK*

Suzanne 🦴½ **1980 (R)** Set in 1950s Quebec, the story of a good woman whose criminal boyfriend leaves her pregnant when he is sent to prison. Ten years later, he returns, threatening her happy marriage. Confused script can't be saved by valiant cast. **90m/C VHS, Beta.** Sondra Locke, Richard Dreyfuss, Gene Barry. *VES*

Suzy 🦴🦴½ **1936** Harlow's fourth film and her only one with Grant is a mixture of romance, action, and comedy set during WWI. Grant plays a French flier who falls in love with Harlow, although she is married to Tone. Excellent air footage and some good funny scenes keep this film moving right along. Even has Grant singing hit song, "Did I Remember?" **99m/B VHS.** Jean Harlow, Franchot Tone, Cary Grant, Benita Hume, Lewis Stone, Inez Courtney; ***D:*** George Fitzmaurice. *MGM*

Svengali 🦴🦴🦴 **1931** A music teacher uses his hypnotic abilities to manipulate one of his singing students and make her a star. Soon the young woman is singing for sell-out crowds, but only if her teacher is present. Barrymore in a hypnotic performance. Adapted from "Trilby" by George Du Maurier. Remade in 1955 and 1983. **76m/B VHS, Beta.** John Barrymore, Marian Marsh, Donald Crisp; ***D:*** Archie Mayo. Nominations: Academy Awards '31: Best Cinematography, Best Interior Decoration. *NOS, GPV, SNC*

Svengali 🦴🦴½ **1955** Limp remake of the 1931 film about Trilby, an artist's model, falling under the mesmerizing spell of the title character, who is determined to make her into a famous singer. Chiefly notable for its visuals which were based on the illustrations from the original novel "Trilby" by George du Maurier. **82m/C VHS.** *GB* Hildegarde Neff, Donald Wolfit, Terence Morgan, Derek Bond, Paul Rogers, David Kossoff; ***D:*** Noel Langley; ***W:*** Noel Langley. *NO*

Svengali 🦴🦴½ **1983** Flamboyant but faded music star O'Toole mentors Foster, a young pop singer looking for stardom. Boring, made for television remake of the Barrymore classic. **96m/C VHS.** Peter O'Toole, Jodie Foster, Elizabeth Ashley, Larry Joshua, Pamela Blair, Barbara Byrne, Holly Hunter; ***D:*** Anthony Harvey; ***M:*** John Barry. *NO*

Swamp Fire 🦴½ **1946** Mississippi river-boat captain Weissmuller, wrestles alligators and battles with Crabbe for the woman he loves in this turgid drama. Look for Janssen in an early screen performance. **69m/B VHS, Beta.** Johnny Weissmuller, Virginia Grey, Buster Crabbe, Carol Thurston, Edwin Maxwell, Pedro de Cordoba, Pierre Watkin, David Janssen; ***D:*** William H. Pine. *NOS, SNC*

Swamp of the Lost Monster 🦴 **1965** An incredible Mexican horror/western/musical that features a mouse-like monster that'll scare the cheese out of you. **88m/B VHS, Beta.** *MX* Gaston Santos, Sarah Cabrera, Manuel Donde; ***D:*** Rafael Baledon. *NOS, SNC, GHV*

Swamp Thing 🦴🦴½ **1982 (PG)** Overlooked camp drama about scientist accidentally turned into tragic half-vegetable, half-man swamp creature, with government agent Barbeau caught in the middle, occasionally while topless. A vegetarian nightmare or ecology propaganda? You be the judge. Adapted from the comic book by Craven. **91m/C VHS, Beta, LV.** Adrienne Barbeau, Louis Jourdan, Ray Wise, Dick Durock; ***D:*** Wes Craven; ***W:*** Wes Craven. *COL, SUE*

Swamp Women 🦴 *Swamp Diamonds; Cruel Swamp* **1955** Four escaped women convicts, known as the "Nardo Gang," chase after a stash of diamonds in this super cheap, super bad action adventure from cult director Corman. **73m/C VHS.** Mike Connors, Marie Windsor, Beverly Garland, Carole Mathews, Susan Cummings; ***D:*** Roger Corman. *SNC*

The Swan 🦴🦴½ **1925** Princess' arranged marriage with a prince is complicated by a poor man also in love with her. Classic romantic comedy of the silent era. Remade in 1956. Based on a play by Ferenc Molnar. **50m/B VHS, Beta.** Adolphe Menjou, Ricardo Cortez, Frances Howard; ***D:*** Dimitri Buchowetzki. *NOS, DVT*

The Swan 🦴🦴🦴 **1956** A twist on the Cinderella story with Kelly (in her last film before her marriage) as the charming beauty waiting for her prince. Both Guinness, as the crown prince, and Jourdan, as her poor tutor, want her hand (and the rest of her). Attractive cast, but story gets slow from time to time. Remake of a 1925 silent film. The laser disc version also includes "Wedding in Monaco," the news short showing Kelly's wedding to Prince Rainier. **112m/C VHS, LV.** Grace Kelly, Louis Jourdan, Alec Guinness, Jessie Royce Landis, Brian Aherne, Estelle Winwood; ***D:*** Charles Vidor; ***C:*** Joseph Ruttenberg, Robert L. Surtees. *MGM*

The Swan Princess 🦴🦴½ **1994 (G)** Formulaic prince-and-princess love story based loosely on "Swan Lake" takes a modern twist: Princess Odette, offended by the emphasis her intended, Prince Derek, places on her beauty, flees the kingdom. She's kidnapped by the evil Rothbart, an enchanter who turns her into a swan able to take human form only when touched by moonlight. A snappy trio of animal characters eventually helps Odette reunite with her newly P.C. love, with lots of zesty musical numbers and various Disney-inspired plot points along the way. Adults may yawn, but kiddies will be charmed just the same. **90m/C VHS.** ***D:*** Richard Rich; ***W:*** Richard Rich, Brian Nissen; ***M:*** Lex de Azevedo; ***V:*** Jack Palance, Michelle Nicastro, Howard McGillin, Liz Callaway, John Cleese, Steven Wright, Steve Vinovich, Dakin Matthews, Sandy Duncan, Mark Harelik, James Arrington, Davis Gaines, Joel McKinnon Miller. Nominations: Golden Globe Awards '95: Best Song ("Far Longer than Forever"). *TTC*

Swann in Love 🦴🦴½ *Un Amour De Swann* **1984 (R)** A handsome, wealthy French aristocrat makes a fool of himself over a beautiful courtesan who cares nothing for him. Elegant production lacks spark. Based upon a section of Marcel Proust's "Remembrance of Things Past." In French with English subtitles or an English language version. **110m/C VHS, Beta.** *FR GE* Jeremy Irons, Ornella Muti, Alain Delon, Fanny Ardant, Marie-Christine Barrault; ***D:*** Volker Schlondorff; ***W:*** Peter Brook, Jean-Claude Carriere; ***C:*** Sven Nykvist. Cesar Awards '85: Best Art Direction/Set Decoration, Best Costume Design. *XVC, MED, INJ*

The Swap 🦴½ **1971 (R)** Ex-con searches for his brother's killer. Muddled story uses clips from early De Niro film "Sam's Song." **120m/C VHS.** Robert De Niro, Jered Mickey, Jennifer Warren, Terrayne Crawford, Martin Kelley; ***D:*** Jordan Leondopoulos. *MGM, CAN*

Swap Meet 🦴 **1979 (R)** Wacky teen sex comedy about shenanigans at a small town swap meet. Strictly bargain basement. **86m/C VHS.** Ruth Cox, Deborah Richter, Danny Goldman, Cheryl Rixon, Jonathan Gries; ***D:*** Brice Mack. *NO*

The Swarm 🦴 **1978 (PG)** Low-brow insect contest as scientist Caine fends off a swarm of killer bees when they attack metro Houston. The bees are really just black spots painted on the film. And the acting is terrible. "B" movie on bees, but it's still better than "The Bees." **116m/C VHS, Beta.** Michael Caine, Katharine Ross, Richard Widmark, Lee Grant, Richard Chamberlain, Olivia de Havilland, Henry Fonda, Fred MacMurray, Patty Duke, Ben Johnson, Jose Ferrer, Slim Pickens, Bradford Dillman, Cameron Mitchell; ***D:*** Irwin Allen; ***W:*** Stirling Silliphant; ***C:*** Fred W. Koenekamp; ***M:*** Jerry Goldsmith, John Williams. Nominations: Academy Awards '78: Best Costume Design. *WAR*

Swashbuckler 🦴 *Scarlet Buccaneer* **1976 (PG)** Jaunty pirate returns from sea to find his friends held captive by dastardly dictator for their political views. He rescues them, and helps them overthrow the erstwhile despot. **101m/C VHS, LV.** Robert Shaw, James Earl Jones, Peter Boyle, Genevieve Bujold, Beau Bridges, Geoffrey Holder; ***D:*** James Goldstone; ***W:*** Jeffrey Bloom; ***M:*** John Addison. *MCA*

Swashbuckler 🦴½ *The Scarlet Buccaneer* **1984** Eighteenth-century pirate fracas that can't compete with Errol Flynn. **100m/C VHS.** *FR* Jean-Paul Belmondo, Marlene Jobert, Laura Antonelli, Michel Auclair, Julien Guiomar; ***D:*** Jean-Paul Rappeneau. *MCA*

Sweater Girls *Woof!* **1978 (R)** Sex comedy about two girls starting their own club called the "Sweater Girls." Terrible teen exploitaiton film. **90m/C VHS, Beta.** Charlene Tilton, Harry Moses, Meegan King, Noelle North, Kate Sarchet, Carol Seflinger, Tamara Barkley, Julie Parsons; ***D:*** Donald M. Jones. *NO*

Swedenhielms 🦴🦴½ **1935** A poor Swedish scientist struggles to support his family while hoping to win a Nobel prize, while his two sons get involved in a moneylending scandal. Bergman is the rich fiance of one son, to whom poverty is a puzzlement. Fine performances by Ekman and the 20-year-old Bergman (in her third film). In Swedish with English subtitles. **92m/B VHS, Beta, LV.** *SW* Gosta Ekman, Karin Swanstrom, Bjorn Berglund, Hakan Westergren, Tutta Rolf, Ingrid Bergman, Sigurd Wallen; ***D:*** Gustaf Molander. *WAC, LUM, INJ*

Sweeney Todd: The Demon Barber of Fleet Street **1984** A filmed performance of Sondheim's Tony-winning Broadway musical. Creepy thriller about a demon barber, his razor, and his wife's meatpies. **139m/C VHS, Beta, LV.** *GB* Angela Lansbury, George Hearn; ***D:*** Harold Prince; ***M:*** Stephen Sondheim. *MVD, STS, TTC*

The Sweeper 🦴🦴½ **1995 (R)** LA cop Mark Goddard (Howell) has a problem—his suspects have a bad habit of dying in his custody. Then he's recruited by a secret police organization whose aim is to dispense their own brand of deadly justice and Mark discovers a key to his troubled past and the murder of his cop father (Fahey). **101m/C VHS.** C. Thomas Howell, Ed Lauter, Cynda Williams, Jeff Fahey; ***D:*** Joseph Merhi. *PMH*

Sweet Adeline 🦴🦴 **1926** Smalltime hayseed makes it big in the music business while brother steals his girl back home. Not easily put off, young songster perseveres. **60m/B VHS, Beta.** Charles Ray, Gertrude Olmsted, Jack Clifford, Ida Lewis; ***D:*** Jerome Storm. *GPV, FCT*

Sweet Adeline 🦴🦴½ **1935** Dunne attracts all the men in her father's Hoboken beer garden but Woods plays the songwriter with whom she finds real love. Wonderful score. ♫Play Us a Polka, Dot; Here Am I; We Were So Young; Why Was I Born?; Mollie O'Donahue; Lonely Feet; 'Twas Not So Long Ago; Don't Ever Leave Me. **87m/B VHS.** Irene Dunne, Donald Woods, Hugh Herbert, Ned Sparks, Joseph Cawthorn, Louis Calhern; ***D:*** Mervyn LeRoy; ***M:*** Jerome Kern, Oscar Hammerstein. *MGM*

Sweet Beat 🦴 *The Amorous Sex* **1962** A young woman gets a chance to become a singer when she reaches the finals of a British beauty contest. Pedestrian story enlivened by music from popular British bands of the time. **66m/B VHS, Beta.** Julie Amber, Sheldon Lawrence, Irv Bauer, Billy Myles. *NOS, INC, TPV*

Sweet Bird of Youth 🦴🦴🦴 **1962** An acclaimed adaptation of the Tennessee Williams play about Chance Wayne, a handsome drifter who travels with an aging movie queen to his small Florida hometown, hoping she'll get him started in a movie career. However, coming home turns into a big mistake, as the town boss wants revenge on Chance for seducing his daughter, Heavenly. Williams' original stage ending was cleaned up, providing a conventional "happy" movie ending for the censors. Remade for television in 1989 with Elizabeth Taylor and Mark Harmon in the lead roles. **120m/C VHS, Beta, LV.** Paul Newman, Geraldine Page, Ed Begley Sr., Mildred Dunnock, Rip Torn, Shirley Knight, Madeline Sherwood; ***D:*** Richard Brooks; ***W:*** Richard Brooks; ***C:*** Milton Krasner. Academy Awards '62: Best Supporting Actor (Begley); Golden Globe Awards '63: Best Actress—Drama (Page); Nominations: Academy Awards '62: Best Actress (Page), Best Supporting Actress (Knight). *MGM, BTV, TRI*

Sweet Bird of Youth 🦴🦴 **1989 (R)** Made for television remake of the Tennessee Williams' play, which was filmed for the big screen in 1962, with Harmon and Taylor having the unenviable task of following in the roles played by Paul Newman and Geraldine Page. She is an egotistical, has-been movie star and he is her ambitious gigolo who wants a movie career of his own. Unfortunately, the trouble that drove him from his Florida hometown is still there when he reappears, actress in tow. Things don't bode well. The television production uses Williams' original ending, which was cleaned up for a "happier" version in the '62 film. **95m/C VHS.** Elizabeth Taylor, Mark Harmon, Rip Torn, Valerie Perrine, Ruta Lee, Seymour Cassel, Kevin Geer, Michael Wilding Jr.; ***D:*** Nicolas Roeg; ***W:*** Gavin Lambert; ***M:*** Ralph Burns. *TRI*

Sweet Charity ✗✗✗ **1969** An ever-optimistic dime-a-dance girl has a hard time finding a classy guy to marry. MacLaine is appealing in this big-budget version of the popular Broadway musical by Neil Simon (derived from Fellini's "Notti di Cabiria"). Fosse's debut as film director. Watch for Cort as a flower child. ♫My Personal Property; It's a Nice Face; Hey, Big Spender; Rich Man's Frug; If My Friends Could See Me Now; There's Gotta Be Something Better Than This; Rhythm of Life; Sweet Charity; I'm a Brass Band. **148m/C VHS, Beta, LV.** Shirley MacLaine, Chita Rivera, John McMartin, Paula Kelly, Sammy Davis Jr., Ricardo Montalban, Bud Cort; ***D:*** Bob Fosse; ***C:*** Robert L. Surtees; ***M:*** Cy Coleman. Nominations: Academy Awards '69: Best Art Direction/Set Decoration, Best Costume Design, Best Original Score. *MCA*

Sweet Country ✗½ **1987 (R)** During the overthrow of the Allende government in Chile, the lives of a Chilean family and an American couple intertwine. Heavy-going propaganda is a cross between tragedy and unintentional comedy. Made by the director of "Zorba the Greek." **147m/C VHS, Beta, LV.** Jane Alexander, John Cullum, Carole Laure, Franco Nero, Joanna Pettet, Randy Quaid, Irene Papas, Jean-Pierre Aumont, Pierre Vaneck, Katia Dandoulaki; ***D:*** Michael Cacoyannis. *NO*

Sweet Country Road ✗½ **1981** A rock singer journeys to Nashville to try to cross over into country music. **95m/C VHS, Beta.** Buddy Knox, Kary Lynn, Gordy Trapp, Johnny Paycheck, Jeanne Pruett. *NWV*

Sweet Creek County War ✗ **1982** Retired sheriff must leave his quiet ranch to battle a greedy businessman. **90m/C VHS, Beta.** Richard Egan, Albert Salmi, Nita Talbot, Slim Pickens. *NO*

Sweet Dreams ✗✗½ **1985 (PG-13)** Biography of country singer Patsy Cline, focusing mostly on her turbulent marriage. Her quick rise to stardom ended in an early death. Fine performances throughout. Cline's original recordings are used. ♫Walking After Midnight; Crazy; Sweet Dreams; San Antonio Rose; Blue Moon of Kentucky; Lovesick Blues; Seven Lonely Days; Foolin' Around; Your Cheatin' Heart. **115m/C VHS, Beta, LV.** Jessica Lange, Ed Harris, Ann Wedgeworth, David Clennon; ***D:*** Karel Reisz; ***W:*** Robert Getchell; ***C:*** Robbie Greenberg. Nominations: Academy Awards '85: Best Actress (Lange). *NO*

Sweet Ecstasy ✗½ *Douce Violence; Sweet Violence* **1962** Wealthy shenanigans on the French Riviera. Pezy is the upright young man who can't sleep with anyone unless he's in love, much to Sommer's dismay. **75m/B VHS.** *FR* Elke Sommer, Pierre Brice, Christian Pezy, Claire Maurier; ***D:*** Max Pecas. *NO*

Sweet 15 **1990** A young Hispanic girl learns that there is more to growing up than parties when she learns her father is an illegal alien. Originally aired on PBS as part of the "Wonderworks" family movie series. **120m/C VHS.** Karla Montanà, Panchito Gomez, Tony Plana, Jenny Gago, Susan Ruttan; ***D:*** Victoria Hochberg. *PME, HMV, FCT*

Sweet Georgia ✗ **1972** Soft-core star Jordan is a lusty wife whose husband is an alcoholic, so she has a roll in the hay with almost every other cast member. Lots of action, too, including a pitchfork fight. Ride 'em cowboy. **80m/C VHS.** Marsha Jordan. *VDM*

Sweet Hearts Dance ✗✗ **1988 (R)** Parallel love stories follow two long-time friends, one just falling in love, the other struggling to keep his marriage together. Charming performances from all, but a slow pace undermines the film. **95m/C VHS, Beta, LV.** Don Johnson, Jeff Daniels, Susan Sarandon, Elizabeth Perkins, Justin Henry, Holly Marie Combs; ***D:*** Robert Greenwald; ***W:*** Ernest Thompson; ***M:*** Richard Gibbs. *COL*

Sweet Hostage ✗✗½ **1975** Escaped mental patient kidnaps uneducated farm girl and holds her captive in a remote cabin. Blair and Sheen turn in good performances. Adaptation of Nathaniel Benchley's "Welcome to Xanadu." Made-for-television. **93m/C VHS.** Linda Blair, Martin Sheen, Jeanne Cooper, Lee DeBroux, Dehl Berti, Bert Remsen; ***D:*** Lee Philips. *IMP*

Sweet Justice ✗½ **1992 (R)** This time its the women who get to be commandos, have all the adventures, and get revenge on various scum. The nominal plotline has Sunny Justice (Carter) and her group of gal-warriors avenging the sadistic murder of a friend. Martial arts, weapons, and action galore. **92m/C VHS.** Finn Carter, Kathleen Kinmont, Marc Singer, Frank Gorshin; ***Cameos:*** Mickey Rooney; ***D:*** Allen Plone; ***W:*** Allen Plone, Jim Tabilio. *TRI*

Sweet Killing ✗✗ **1993 (R)** A banker murders his shrewish wife to be with another woman. He thinks he has the perfect alibi, but then his fictitious excuse comes to life when a mysterious stranger begins stalking him. Based on the novel "Qualthrough" by Agnes Hall. **87m/C VHS, Beta.** Anthony Higgins, F. Murray Abraham, Leslie Hope, Michael Ironside, Andrea Ferreol; ***D:*** Eddy Matalon; ***W:*** Eddy Matalon. *PAR*

Sweet Liberty ✗✗ **1986 (PG)** Alda's hometown is overwhelmed by Hollywood chaos during the filming of a movie version of his novel about the American Revolution. Pleasant but predictable. **107m/C VHS, Beta, LV.** Alan Alda, Michael Caine, Michelle Pfeiffer, Bob Hoskins, Lillian Gish; ***D:*** Alan Alda; ***W:*** Alan Alda; ***M:*** Bruce Broughton. *MCA*

Sweet Lies ✗½ **1988 (R)** An insurance investigator tracking a scam artist in Paris is preyed upon by a group of single women betting one another that any man can be seduced. Slow comedy. **86m/C VHS, Beta.** Treat Williams, Joanna Pacula, Julianne Phillips, Laura Manszky, Norbert Weisser, Marilyn Dodd-Frank; ***D:*** Nathalie Delon; ***M:*** Trevor Jones. *FOX*

Sweet Light in a Dark Room ✗✗✗ *Romeo, Julia a Tma; Romeo, Juliet and Darkness* **1960** A student in Prague during the Nazi Occupation hides a Jewish girl. He falls in love with her but becomes the suspect in the murder of a Nazi officer. Directed by the great Czech filmmaker Weiss who was himself forced to leave his country during Nazi occupation. In Czech with English subtitles. **93m/B VHS.** *CZ* Ivan Mistrik, Dana Smutna; ***D:*** Jiri Weiss. *FCT, DVT, HEG*

Sweet Lorraine ✗✗✗ **1987 (PG-13)** A bittersweet, nostalgic comedy about the staff and clientele of a deteriorating Catskills hotel on the eve of its closing. **91m/C VHS, Beta.** Maureen Stapleton, Lee Richardson, Trini Alvarado, Freddie Roman, John Bedford Lloyd, Giancarlo Esposito, Edie Falco, Todd Graff, Evan Handler; ***D:*** Steve Gomer; ***W:*** Michael Zettler, Shelly Altman; ***M:*** Richard Robbins. *PAR*

Sweet Love, Bitter ✗✗½ *It Won't Rub Off, Baby; Black Love, White Love* **1967** The downfall of a black jazz saxophonist in the 1950's. The character is loosely based on the life of legendary musician Charlie "Bird" Parker. Alto sax man Charles McPherson dubs Gregory's solos. Adapted from the novel "Night Song" by John A. Williams. **92m/C VHS.** Dick Gregory, Don Murray, Diane Varsi, Robert Hooks; ***D:*** Herbert Danska; ***W:*** Lewis Jacobs, Herbert Danska; ***M:*** Mal Waldron. *RHP, MVD, FCT*

Sweet Movie ✗✗ **1975** A provocative cult classic concerning a South African tycoon who purchases a virgin bride and then exploits her sexually. In English and French with subtitles. **120m/C VHS, Beta.** *YU* Carole Laure, Pierre Clementi, Sami Frey; ***D:*** Dusan Makavejev; ***W:*** Dusan Makavejev; ***M:*** Manos Hadjidakis. *FCT, MOV*

Sweet Murder *Woof!* **1993 (R)** "Single White Female" rip-off features Udy allowing Davidtz to share her apartment—with nasty consequences. **101m/C VHS.** Helene Udy, Embeth Davidtz, Russell Todd; ***D:*** Percival Rubens. *VMK*

Sweet Perfection ✗✗ **1990 (R)** Jackson plans a big promotion for her beauty contest. Who will be voted the "Perfect Woman?" Tired premise, but it has its moments. **90m/C VHS.** Stoney Jackson, Anthony Norman McKay, Catero Colbert, Liza Crusat, Reggie Theus, Tatiana Tumbtzen. *XVC, HHE*

Sweet Poison ✗✗ **1991 (R)** Bobby Stiles is a ruthless criminal who has just broken out of prison. He wants to get home and settle the score with his brother, who actually committed the crime Bobby was imprisoned for. Henry and Charlene Odell are traveling cross-country when Bobby crosses their path and forces them to drive him home. Bobby's not too busy eluding the police to notice that his captives' marriage is a little shaky—and that Charlene is attractive and sexy. As Bobby and Charlene get closer husband Henry just becomes another problem. **101m/C VHS.** Steven Bauer, Patricia Healy, Edward Herrmann; ***D:*** Brian Grant. *MCA*

Sweet Revenge ✗✗ **1987 (R)** TV journalist kidnapped by a white slavery ring in the Asian jungles. After escaping, she returns for vegeance. Meek drama. **79m/C VHS, Beta.** Ted Shackleford, Nancy Allen, Martin Landau; ***D:*** Mark Sobel. *MED*

Sweet Revenge ✗✗ **1990** When a judge tells a divorced couple that the woman must pay the man alimony, she hires an actress to marry her ex. The tables are turned in this way-out marriage flick, reminiscent of the screwball comedies of the 1940s. **89m/C VHS, Beta.** Rosanna Arquette, Carrie Fisher, John Sessions; ***D:*** Charlotte Brandstrom; ***W:*** Janet Brownell; ***M:*** Hubert Bougis. *TTC*

Sweet Rosie O'Grady ✗✗½ **1943** Musical-comedy star Grable has returned to New York after success in England, where she caught the eye of nobleman Gardiner. Ex-boyfriend Young is a tabloid reporter who's expected by editor Menjou to get the scoop on her past. Seems she used to perform in Bowery saloons although that's not what Grable's been telling everyone. Slight story, charming performers, and lots of songs. Remade in 1948 as "That Wonderful Urge." ♫My Heart Tells Me; My Sam; Oh Where is the Groom?; The Wishing Waltz; Going to the Country Fair; Get Your Police Gazette; Battle Cry; Sweet Rosie O'Grady; Two Little Girls in Blue. **74m/C VHS.** Betty Grable, Robert Young, Adolphe Menjou, Reginald Gardiner, Virginia Grey, Phil Regan, Sig Rumann, Alan Dinehart; ***D:*** Irving Cummings; ***C:*** Ernest Palmer. *RXM*

Sweet 16 ✗✗ **1981 (R)** Serial killings in Texas town begin to set off muffled alarms in big head of sheriff Hopkins. Sixteen-year-old Melissa has recently moved into town. She's beautiful, mysterious, and promiscuous, and she has a big problem—all her boyfriends end up dead. No real puzzle. **90m/C VHS, Beta.** Susan Strasberg, Bo Hopkins, Don Stroud, Dana Kimmell, Patrick Macnee, Larry Storch; ***D:*** Jim Sotos. *VES*

Sweet Smell of Success ✗✗✗½ **1957** Evil New York City gossip columnist J.J. Hunsecker (Lancaster) and sleazy press agent (Curtis) cook up smear campaign to ruin career of jazz musician in love with J.J.'s sister. Engrossing performances, great dialogue. **96m/C VHS, LV.** Burt Lancaster, Tony Curtis, Martin Milner, Barbara Nichols, Sam Levene; ***D:*** Alexander MacKendrick; ***W:*** Ernest Lehman, Clifford Odets; ***C:*** James Wong Howe; ***M:*** Elmer Bernstein. *MGM*

Sweet Spirits *Woof!* **198?** Soft-sell European fluff about a modern mannequin having a raucous affair with an artist. **87m/C VHS, Beta.** Erika Blanc, Farley Granger. *MED*

Sweet Sugar ✗½ *Chaingang Girls; Captive Women 3: Sweet Sugar* **1972 (R)** Slave girls try to escape from a Costa Rican sugar cane plantation and its cruel owner. Needless to say, vulgar exploitation runs hither and yon in this film. **90m/C VHS.** Phyllis E. Davis, Ella Edwards, Pamela Collins, Cliff Osmond, Timothy Brown; ***D:*** Michel Levesque. *NO*

Sweet Sweetback's Baadasssss Song ✗✗✗ **1971** A black pimp kills two policemen who beat up a black militant. He uses his streetwise survival skills to elude his pursuers and escape to Mexico. A thriller, but racist, sexist, and violent.

97m/C VHS, Beta. Melvin Van Peebles, Simon Chuckster, John Amos; ***D:*** Melvin Van Peebles; ***W:*** Melvin Van Peebles. *SUN*

Sweet Talker 🦴🦴½ **1991 (PG)** Following his release from prison, a charming con man shows up in a small coastal village, thinking the townsfolk will be ripe for the picking. What he doesn't know is they can do some sweet talking of their own, and he soon finds himself caring for a pretty widow and her son. Enjoyable light comedy works thanks to likable leads. **91m/C VHS, LV.** *AU* Bryan Brown, Karen Allen, Chris Haywood, Bill Kerr, Bruce Spence, Bruce Myles, Paul Chubb, Peter Hehir, Justin Rosniak; ***D:*** Michael Jenkins; ***W:*** Tony Morphett; ***M:*** Richard Thompson, Peter Filleul. *LIV*

Sweet Trash *Woof!* **1989 (R)** A vice cop, having an affair with a 17-year-old prostitute, is blackmailed by an underworld figure. Lives up to its name. **80m/C VHS.** Sebastian Gregory, Sharon Matt, Luke Perry, Bonnie Clark, Gene Blackey; ***D:*** John Hayes. *NO*

Sweet William 🦴🦴🦴 **1979 (R)** A philandering and seemingly irresistible young man finds that one sensitive woman hasn't the patience or time for his escapades. Adult comedy concerned with sex without displaying any on the screen. **88m/C VHS, Beta.** *GB* Sam Waterston, Jenny Agutter, Anna Massey, Arthur Lowe; ***D:*** Claude Whatham; ***W:*** Beryl Bainbridge. *PSM*

Sweet Young Thing **19??** Young students at a French girls' school receive all sorts of attention from the male staff. **83m/C VHS, Beta.** Jean Tolzac, Bernard Musson. *MED*

Sweetheart of the Navy 🦴½ **1937** Sailors help a cafe singer out of a jam, with one of them almost giving up his career for her. Standard fare, but Parker is well worth listening to. **63m/B VHS.** Eric Linden, Cecilia Parker, Roger Imhof, Bernadene Hayes, Jason Robards Sr., Don Barclay; ***D:*** Duncan Mansfield. *NOS*

Sweethearts 🦴🦴🦴 **1938** MacDonald and Eddy star as married stage actors trying to get some time off from their hectic schedule in this show-within-a-show. Trouble ensues when their conniving producer begs, pleads and tricks them into staying. Lots of well-staged musical numbers. ♫Wooden Shoes; Every Lover Must Meet His Fate; Sweethearts; Pretty as a Picture; Summer Serenade; On Parade. **114m/C VHS, LV.** Jeanette MacDonald, Nelson Eddy, Frank Morgan, Florence Rice, Ray Bolger, Mischa Auer; ***D:*** Woodbridge S. Van Dyke. Nominations: Academy Awards '38: Best Sound, Best Score. *MGM*

Sweetie 🦴🦴🦴 **1989 (R)** Bizarre, expressive Australian tragicomedy about a pair of sisters—one a withdrawn, paranoid Plain Jane, the other a dangerously extroverted, overweight sociopath who re-enters her family's life and turns it upside down. Campion's first feature. **97m/C VHS, Beta, LV.** *AU* Genevieve Lemon, Karen Colston, Tom Lycos, Jon Darling, Dorothy Barry, Michael Lake, Andre Pataczek; ***D:*** Jane Campion; ***W:*** Gerard Lee, Jane Campion; ***M:*** Martin Armiger. Nominations: Academy Awards '91: Best Foreign Language Film. *LIV*

Sweetwater 🦴🦴 **1984** An independent woman and a feisty young orphan find each other amid society's rejections. **30m/C VHS, Beta.** *LCA*

Swept Away... 🦴🦴🦴 *Swept Away...By an Unusual Destiny in the Blue Sea of August* **1975 (R)** A rich and beautiful Milanese woman is shipwrecked on a desolate island with a swarthy Sicilian deck hand, who also happens to be a dedicated communist. Isolated, the two switch roles, with the wealthy woman dominated by the crude proletarian. Sexy and provocative. **116m/C VHS, Beta, LV.** *IT* Giancarlo Giannini, Mariangela Melato; ***D:*** Lina Wertmuller; ***W:*** Lina Wertmuller. National Board of Review Awards '75: 5 Best Foreign Films of the Year. *COL, APD*

Swift Justice 🦴🦴 **1988** Mayor of a small town thinks he's gotten away with murder after leaving a young girl for dead in a junk yard. However, the mayor and his violent pals are soon hunted by an ex-Green Beret with a penchant for justice. **90m/C VHS, Beta.** Jon Greene, Sindi Rome, Cameron Mitchell, Aldo Ray, Chuck "Porky" Mitchell, Wilson Dunster, Ted Leplat; ***D:*** Harry Hope. *TWE*

Swifty 🦴½ **1936** A cowpoke is accused of murder but escapes to track down the real culprit and win the hand of the girl he loves. **60m/B VHS, Beta.** Hoot Gibson. *VCN*

Swim Team 🦴 **1979** New coach for a terminally inept school swimming team whips them into shape. Doesn't hold much water. **81m/C VHS, Beta.** Stephen Furst, James Daughton, Jenny Neumann, Kim Day, Buster Crabbe; ***D:*** James Polakof. *PSM*

The Swimmer 🦴🦴🦴½ **1968 (PG)** A lonely suburbanite swims an existential swath through the pools of his neighborhood landscape in an effort at self-discovery. A surreal, strangely compelling work based on a story by John Cheever. **94m/C VHS, Beta, LV.** Burt Lancaster, Janice Rule, Janet Landgard, Marge Champion, Kim Hunter, Rose Gregorio, John David Garfield; ***D:*** Frank Perry; ***M:*** Marvin Hamlisch. *GKK*

Swimming Pool 🦴🦴½ **1970 (PG)** Two men and two women spend a weekend in a villa on the French Riviera, manipulating each other, playing sexual games, and changing partners. Their escapades end in murder. Romantic melodrama is sensuous if slow-moving. French film dubbed in English. **85m/C VHS, Beta.** *FR* Romy Schneider, Alain Delon, Maurice Ronet, Jane Birkin; ***D:*** Jacques Deray. *NLC*

Swimming to Cambodia 🦴🦴🦴 **1987** Gray tells the story of his bit part in "The Killing Fields," filmed in Cambodia, and makes ironic observations about modern life. It works. **87m/C VHS, Beta, LV.** Spalding Gray; ***D:*** Jonathan Demme; ***C:*** John Bailey; ***M:*** Laurie Anderson. *ORI, WAR*

Swimming with Sharks 🦴🦴🦴 *The Buddy Factor* **1994 (R)** Budding screenwriter Guy (Whaley) goes to work for notoriously insulting movie producer Buddy (Spacey). Soon, Guy grows tired of his boss's demeaning treatment and cruel means of communication and devises a scheme which would even the score. Hollywood satire has more bite than "The Player," and a devious cilmax, but it's mostly an opportunity for Spacey to hang his hams, which he does with glee. Debut for director Huang, who based his script on his experience as a production assistant. See it with your boss. **93m/C VHS, LV.** Kevin Spacey, Frank Whaley, Michele Forbes, Benicio Del Toro; ***D:*** George Huang; ***W:*** George Huang; ***C:*** Steven Firestone. New York Film Critics Awards '95: Best Supporting Actor (Spacey); Nominations: Independent Spirit Awards '96: Best Actor (Spacey). *VMK*

Swimsuit: The Movie 🦴½ **1989** A young ad executive decides to revitalize a swimsuit company's failing business by sponsoring a contest for the perfect swimsuit model. Made-for-television fluff. **100m/C VHS.** William Katt, Catherine Oxenberg, Cyd Charisse, Nia Peeples, Tom Villard, Cheryl Pollak, Billy Warlock, Jack Wagner; ***D:*** Chris Thomson; ***W:*** Robert Schiff; ***M:*** John D'Andrea. *AIP*

The Swindle 🦴🦴 *Il Bidone* **1955** Three Italian conmen pull capers in Rome trying to make a better life for themselves. Dark overtones permeate one of Fellini's lesser efforts. Good cast can't bring up the level of this film. In Italian with English subtitles. **92m/C VHS, LV.** *IT* Broderick Crawford, Giulietta Masina, Richard Basehart, Franco Fabrizi; ***D:*** Federico Fellini; ***W:*** Federico Fellini, Tullio Pinelli, Ennio Flaiano; ***M:*** Nino Rota. *INJ, IME, CVC*

Swindle 🦴 **1992** Two life-long friends set up scam after scam in their quest for sex and money. Their latest con involves a phony marriage broker business, which provides the opportunity to meet a lot of lovely ladies. Only it turns out the hustlers may be the ones getting hustled. **85m/C VHS.** Robby West, Britt Houston, Elaina Dunn, Samantha Fong, Bobby Tess, Donna Thomas; ***D:*** Jason Holt. *CEL*

Swing **1947** An all-black musical revue. **80m/B VHS, Beta.** *NOS, DVT*

Swing High, Swing Low 🦴🦴½ **1937** A trumpet player fights the bottle and the dice to become a hit in the jazz world and marry the woman he loves. Solid drama. From the stage play "Burlesque." Made first as "The Dance of Life," then as "When My Baby Smiles At Me." **95m/B VHS, Beta.** Carole Lombard, Fred MacMurray, Charles Butterworth, Dorothy Lamour; ***D:*** Mitchell Leisen. *NOS, HHT, DVT*

Swing It, Professor 🦴🦴½ *Swing it Buddy* **1937** A stodgy music professor refuses to recognize jazz as a valid musical form and subsequently loses his job. During his unemployment, he wanders into a nightclub and discovers jazz isn't so bad after all. Nice camera work. ♫I'm Sorta Kinda Glad I Met You; An Old-Fashioned Melody; Richer Than A Millionaire. **62m/B VHS.** Pinky Tomlin, Paula Stone, Mary Kornman, Milburn Stone, Pat Gleason; ***D:*** Marshall Neilan. *NOS, DVT, HEG*

Swing It, Sailor! 🦴🦴 **1937** Two footloose sailors go after the same woman while on shore leave. Decent screwball comedy. **61m/B VHS, Beta.** Wallace Ford, Ray Mayer, Isabel Jewell, Mary Treen; ***D:*** Raymond Cannon. *VYY, NOS*

Swing Kids 🦴🦴 **1993 (PG-13)** In 1939 in Germany, big band or "swing" music is the instrument used by a group of young people to rebel against the conformity demanded by Hitler. Highlights the politics of the era, but concentrates mainly on three teenagers and the strains that Nazi power put on their friendship. Although the premise is based in historic fact, there is still something disturbingly silly about the entire production. Dance sequences are lively and well-choreographed. Branagh (in an uncredited role) plays a smooth-talking Gestapo chief. Filmed on location in Prague, Czechoslovakia (as a substitute for Hamburg, Germany). **114m/C VHS, Beta, LV.** Robert Sean Leonard, Christian Bale, Frank Whaley, Barbara Hershey, Tushka Bergen, David Tom, Kenneth Branagh; ***D:*** Thomas Carter; ***W:*** Jonathan Marc Feldman; ***M:*** James Horner. *HPH*

Swing Parade of 1946 🦴½ **1946** One of the multitude of 1940s musicals. Young songwriter falls in love with club owner. Highlights include an appearance by the Three Stooges. ♫Stormy Weather; Just a Little Fond Affection; Don't Worry About the Mule; A Tender Word Will Mend It All; On the Sunny Side of the Street; Oh, Brother; After All This Time; Caledonia. **74m/B VHS.** Gale Storm, Phil Regan, Moe Howard, Edward Brophy, Connee Boswell; ***D:*** Phil Karlson. *NO*

Swing Shift 🦴🦴½ **1984 (PG)** When Hawn takes a job at an aircraft plant after her husband goes off to war, she learns more than riveting. Lahti steals the film as her friend and co-worker. A detailed reminiscence of the American home front during WWII that never seems to gel. Produced by Hawn. **100m/C VHS, Beta, LV.** Goldie Hawn, Kurt Russell, Ed Harris, Christine Lahti, Holly Hunter, Chris Lemmon, Belinda Carlisle, Fred Ward, Roger Corman, Lisa Pelikan; ***D:*** Jonathan Demme; ***W:*** Ron Nyswaner, Bo Goldman; ***C:*** Tak Fujimoto. New York Film Critics Awards '84: Best Supporting Actress (Lahti); Nominations: Academy Awards '84: Best Supporting Actress (Lahti). *WAR*

Swing Time 🦴🦴🦴 **1936** Astaire, a dancer who can't resist gambling, is engaged to marry another woman, until he meets Ginger. One of the team's best efforts. Laserdisc version includes: production photos and stills, commentary on Fred Astaire and musical films, and excerpts from "Hooray for Love" featuring Bill "Bojangles" Robinson and Fats Waller. ♫The Way You Look Tonight; Waltz in Swing Time; Never Gonna Dance; Pick Yourself Up; A Fine Romance; Bojangles of Harlem. **103m/B VHS, Beta, LV.** Fred Astaire, Ginger Rogers, Helen Broderick, Betty Furness, Eric Blore, Victor Moore; ***D:*** George Stevens; ***M:*** Jerome Kern, Dorothy Fields. Academy Awards '36: Best Song ("The Way You Look Tonight"). *TTC, MED, CRC*

A Swingin' Summer 🦴½ **1965** A bunch of groovy guys and gals go-go to the beach for a vacation of fun and sun and end up starting a rock 'n' roll concert series. Everybody gets part of the action...even the bespectacled Welch, who gets a chance to sing. Performances from the Righteous Brothers and rock semi-legends Donnie Brooks, Gary Lewis and the Playboys, and the Rip Chords. ♫Red Hot Roadster; Justine; Penny the Poo; Out to Lunch; Nitro; Ready to Groove. **81m/C VHS.** James Stacy, William Wellman Jr., Quinn O'Hara, Martin West, Mary Mitchell, Allan Jones, Raquel Welch; ***D:*** Robert Sparr; ***W:*** Leigh Chapman. *NO*

The Swinging Cheerleaders **1974 (PG)** A group of amorous cheerleaders turn on the entire campus in this typical sexploiter. **90m/C VHS, Beta.** Cheryl "Rainbeaux" Smith, Colleen Camp, Jo Johnston; ***D:*** Jack Hill. *MON*

Swinging Wives **1979 (R)** Ribald humor for the discriminating viewer. **84m/C VHS, Beta.** Gale Mayberrie, Ron James. *NO*

Swiss Conspiracy 🦴🦴 **1977 (PG)** Against the opulent background of the world's richest financial capital and playground of the wealthy, one man battles to stop a daring and sophisticated blackmailer preying on the secret bank account set. Fast-paced, if sometimes confusing. **92m/C VHS, Beta.** *GE* David Janssen, Senta Berger; ***D:*** Jack Arnold. *NO*

The Swiss Family Robinson 🦴🦴🦴 **1960** A family, seeking to escape Napoleon's war in Europe, sets sail for New Guinea, but shipwrecks on a deserted tropical island. There they build an idyllic life, only to be confronted by a band of pirates. Lots of adventure for family viewing. Filmed on location on the island of Tobago. Based on the novel by Johann Wyss. **126m/C VHS, Beta, LV.** John Mills, Dorothy McGuire, James MacArthur, Tommy Kirk, Janet Munro, Sessue Hayakawa; ***D:*** Ken Annakin. *DIS, IGP*

Swiss Miss 🦴🦴½ **1938** Stan and Ollie are mousetrap salesmen on the job in Switzerland. Highlights include Stan's tuba serenade and the gorilla-on-the-bridge episode. Also included on this tape is a 1935 Thelma Todd/Patsy Kelly short, "Hot Money." **97m/B VHS, Beta.** Stan Laurel, Oliver Hardy, Della Lind, Walter Woolf King, Eric Blore, Thelma Todd, Patsy Kelly; ***D:*** John Blystone. *CCB, MED, FCT*

The Switch 🦴🦴 **1989 (R)** An escaped convict takes the place of a talented conman and chaos ensues. **?m/C VHS.** Anthony Quinn, Adriano Celentano, Capucine, Corinne Clery. *NO*

Switch 🦴🦴🦴 **1991 (R)** A chauvinist louse, slain by the girlfriends he misused, is sent back to Earth as an alluring female to learn the other side's point of view. The plot may lack urgency, but this is a sparkling adult comedy that scores as it pursues the gimmicky concept to a logical, outrageous and touching conclusion. Barkin's act as swaggering male stuck in a woman's body is a masterwork of physical humor. **104m/C VHS, LV.** Ellen Barkin, Jimmy Smits, JoBeth Williams, Lorraine Bracco, Perry King, Bruce Martyn Payne, Tony Roberts; ***D:*** Blake Edwards; ***W:*** Blake Edwards; ***M:*** Henry Mancini. *HBO, WAR*

Switchblade Sisters *Woof! The Jezebels; Playgirl Gang* **1975** Crime gang of female ex-cons wreaks pseudo-feminist havoc. Bruce is Lenny Bruce's daughter. **90m/C VHS, Beta.** Robbie Lee, Joanne Nail, Monica Gayle, Kitty Bruce; ***D:*** Jack Hill; ***M:*** Les Baxter. *HHE*

Switched at Birth 🦴🦴½ **1991 (PG)** A fact-based made for television drama about two girls, switched in a hospital nursery at birth. Only when one girl dies, a decade later, do her parents discover that she could not have been their biological child. Their search for their daughter leads to an emotional conflict between the girl, the man that raised her, and the biological parents who seek to claim her. Beware of the sappy Hollywood ending, five years later the story of Kimberly Mays is still going through the U.S. judicial system. **200m/C VHS.** Bonnie Bedelia, Brian Kerwin, Ed Asner, Caroline McWilliams, John M. Jackson, Lois Smith, Eve Gordon, Judith Hoag, Ariana Richards; ***D:*** Waris Hussein. *COL, PMS*

Switching Channels 🦴🦴½ **1988 (PG)** A modernized remake of "His Girl Friday," and therefore the fourth version of "The Front Page." Beautiful television anchorwoman (Turner) wants to marry handsome tycoon (Reeve), but her scheming ex-husband (Reynolds) gets in the way. Weak performances from everyone but Beatty and lackluster direction render this off-told story less funny than usual. **108m/C VHS, Beta, LV.** Burt Reynolds, Kathleen Turner, Christopher Reeve, Ned Beatty, Henry Gibson, George Newbern, Al Waxman, Ken James, Joe Silver, Charles Kimbrough, Tony Rosato; ***D:*** Ted Kotcheff; ***W:*** Jonathan Reynolds; ***M:*** Michel Legrand. *COL*

Swoon 🦴🦴🦴 **1991** Kalin's directorial debut is a stylish rendering of the sensational 1924 kidnapping and murder of Bobby Franks by Richard Loeb and Nathan Leopold Jr. and their subsequent trial and imprisonment. Core elements of the case remain but Kalin imposes contemporary styles and morals on the past, particularly his protest against the homophobic attitudes influencing the trial while acknowledging the jaded and dispassionate behavior of the two young men. Previous cinematic versions of the murder case include "Rope" and "Compulsion" but Kalin graphically portrays the characters homosexuality, which was only hinted at in the earlier films. **95m/B VHS, LV.** Daniel Schlachet, Craig Chester, Ron Vawter, Michael Kirby, Michael Stumm, Valda Z. Drabla, Natalie Stanford; ***D:*** Tom Kalin; ***W:*** Tom Kalin; ***M:*** James Bennett. Sundance Film Festival '92: Best Cinematography. *NLC, IME*

The Sword and the Cross 🦴½ **1958** A grade-B adventure about the life of Mary Magdelene. **93m/B VHS, Beta.** Yvonne De Carlo, George Mistral; ***D:*** Carlo L. Bragaglia. *NO*

Sword & the Dragon 🦴🦴 *Ilya Mourometz* **1956** A young warrior must battle any number of giant mythical creatures. **81m/C VHS, Beta.** *RU* Boris Andreyer, Andrei Abrikosov; ***D:*** Alexander Ptushko. *VCI, SNC*

The Sword & the Rose 🦴🦴½ *When Knighthood Was in Flower* **1953** Mary Tudor, sister of King Henry VIII, shuns the advances of a nobleman for the love of a commoner. Johns is an obstinate princess; Justice, a fine king. Based on the book "When Knighthood Was in Flower." **91m/C VHS, Beta, LV.** Richard Todd, Glynis Johns, Michael Gough, Jane Barrett, James Robertson Justice; ***D:*** Ken Annakin; ***C:*** Geoffrey Unsworth. *DIS, HHE, BTV*

Sword & the Sorcerer 🦴½ **1982 (R)** Young prince strives to regain control of his kingdom, now ruled by an evil knight and a powerful magician. Mediocre script and acting is enhanced by decent special effects. **100m/C VHS, Beta, LV.** Lee Horsley, Kathleen Beller, George Maharis, Simon MacCorkindale, Richard Lynch, Richard Moll, Robert Tessier, Nina Van Pallandt, Anna Bjorn, Jeff Corey; ***D:*** Albert Pyun; ***W:*** Albert Pyun. *MCA*

The Sword in the Stone 🦴🦴🦴 **1963 (G)** The Disney version of the first volume of T.H. White's "The Once and Future King" wherein King Arthur, as a boy, is instructed in the ways of the world by Merlin and Archimedes the owl. Although not in the Disney masterpiece fold, boasts the usual superior animation and a gripping mythological tale. **79m/C VHS, Beta, LV.** ***D:*** Wolfgang Reitherman; ***M:*** George Bruns; ***V:*** Ricky Sorenson, Sebastian Cabot, Karl Swenson, Junius Matthews, Alan Napier, Norman Alden, Martha Wentworth, Barbara Jo Allen. Nominations: Academy Awards '63: Best Original Score. *DIS, KUI, HMV*

Sword of Doom 🦴🦴🦴 *Daibosatsu Toge* **1967** A rousing samurai epic detailing the training of an impulsive, bloodlusting warrior by an elder expert. In Japanese with English subtitles. **120m/B VHS, Beta.** *JP* Tatsuya Nakadai, Toshiro Mifune; ***D:*** Kihachi Okamoto. *SUE, INJ, NLC*

The Sword of El Cid 🦴½ *La Spada del Cid* **1962** Not much dash and very little daring-do in this poorly plotted, overly dramatic saga of good vs. evil, Spanish style. Rightful heir to the crown threatens, challenges and enevitably crosses swords with the pretender to his throne. Costume mavens may find something to hold their interest. **86m/C VHS, Beta.** *SP IT* Roland Carey, Sandro Moretti, Chantal Deberg, Iliana Grimaldi, Jose Luis Pellicena, Daniela Bianchi; ***D:*** Miguel Iglesias. *SNC*

Sword of Fury II 🦴½ **1973** The sequel. Two samurai fight to the death to determine who will become the premier swordsman of all Japan. With English subtitles. **77m/C VHS, Beta.** *JP* Hideki Takahashi, Jiro Tamiya. *NO*

Sword of Gideon 🦴🦴½ **1986** An action packed and suspenseful made for television film about an elite commando group who set out to avenge the Munich Olympic killings of 1972. Adapted from "Vengeance" by George Jonas. **148m/C VHS.** Steven Bauer, Michael York, Rod Steiger, Colleen Dewhurst, Robert Joy, Laurent Malet, Lino Ventura, Leslie Hope; ***D:*** Michael Anderson Sr.; ***W:*** Chris Bryant; ***M:*** Georges Delerue. *NO*

Sword of Honor 🦴½ **1994 (R)** Undercover cop and martial arts expert Johnny Lee (Leigh) investigates his partner's mysterious death amidst the tawdry glamor of Vegas. **?m/C VHS, LV.** Steven Leigh, Sophia Crawford, Angelo Tiffe, Jerry Tiffe, Jeff Pruitt, Debbie Scofield; ***D:*** Robert Tiffe; ***W:*** Robert Tiffe, Clay Ayers; ***M:*** David Rubinstein. *PMH*

Sword of Lancelot 🦴🦴½ *Lancelot and Guinevere* **1963** A costume version of the Arthur-Lancelot-Guinevere triangle, with plenty of swordplay and a sincere respect for the old legend. **115m/C VHS, Beta.** *GB* Cornel Wilde, Jean Wallace, Brian Aherne, George Baker; ***D:*** Cornel Wilde. *MCA*

Sword of Monte Cristo 🦴½ **1951** Masked female avenger, seeking the liberty of the French people, discovers a valuable sword that holds the key to a vast fortune. But the sword is also desired by an evil government minister. **80m/C VHS, Beta.** George Montgomery, Rita (Paula) Corday; ***D:*** Maurice Geraghty. *VHE*

Sword of Sherwood Forest 🦴🦴½ **1960** The Earl of Newark plots the murder of the Archbishop of Canterbury in yet another rendition of the Robin Hood legend. Cushing is truly evil as the villain. **80m/C VHS.** *GB* Richard Greene, Peter Cushing, Niall MacGinnis, Richard Pasco, Jack Gwillim, Sarah Branch, Nigel Green, Oliver Reed; ***D:*** Terence Fisher. *COL, MLB*

Sword of the Valiant 🦴🦴 **1983 (PG)** The Green Knight arrives in Camelot to challenge Gawain. Remake of "Gawain And The Green Knight." Connery adds zest to a minor epic. **102m/C VHS, Beta.** *GB* Sean Connery, Miles O'Keeffe, Cyrielle Claire, Leigh Lawson, Trevor Howard, Peter Cushing, Wilfrid Brambell, Lila Kedrova, John Rhys-Davies; ***D:*** Stephen Weeks; ***W:*** Philip M. Breen; ***C:*** Frederick A. (Freddie) Young. *MGM*

Sword of Venus 🦴 *Island of Monte Cristo* **1953** Uninspired production finds the son of the Count of Monte Cristo the victim in a scheme to deprive him of his wealth. **73m/B VHS.** Robert Clarke, Catherine McLeod, Dan O'Herlihy, William Schallert; ***D:*** Harold Daniels. *FCT*

Swords of Death 🦴🦴 **1971** Final film by Uchida, released posthumously, deals with the adventurous period exploits of the irrepressible Miyamoto Musashi. With English subtitles. **76m/C VHS, Beta.** *JP* Kinnosuke Nakamura, Rentaro Mikuni; ***D:*** Tomu Uchida. *VDA*

The Swordsman 🦴🦴½ **1992 (R)** The quest to return the stolen sword of the legendary Alexander the Great to a museum is muscular detective Lamas' assignment. Turns out the detective and his evil millionaire antagonist have been chasing each other through time in their endless quest for revenge and power. **98m/C VHS, LV.** Lorenzo Lamas, Claire Stansfield, Michael Champion; ***D:*** Michael Kennedy; ***W:*** Michael Kennedy. *REP*

Sybil 🦴🦴🦴 **1976** Fact-based story of a woman who developed 16 distinct personalities, and the supportive psychiatrist who helped her put the pieces of her ego together. Excellent made-for-television production with Field's Emmy-winning performance. **122m/C VHS, Beta.** Sally Field, Joanne Woodward, Brad Davis, Martine Bartlett, Jane Hoffman; ***D:*** Daniel Petrie. *FOX*

Sylvester 🦴🦴 **1985 (PG)** A 16-year-old girl and a cranky stockyard boss team up to train a battered horse named Sylvester for the National Equestrian trials. Nice riding sequences and good performances can't overcome familiar plot, but the kids will enjoy this one. **104m/C VHS, Beta, LV.** Melissa Gilbert, Richard Farnsworth, Michael Schoeffling, Constance Towers; ***D:*** Tim Hunter. *COL*

Sylvia ♂♂½ **1986 (PG)** Biography of author/educator Sylvia Ashton-Warner, and her efforts to teach Maori children in New Zealand to read via unorthodox methods. David is a marvel. Based on Ashton-Warner's books "Teacher" and "I Passed This Way." **99m/C VHS, Beta.** *NZ* Eleanor David, Tom Wilkinson, Nigel Terry, Mary Regan; ***D:*** Michael Firth. *FOX*

Sylvia and the Phantom ♂♂♂ *Sylvia and the Ghost* **1945** A charming French comedy about a lonely young girl who is befriended by the ghost of a man killed decades earlier in a duel over the girl's grandmother. Based on the play by Alfred Adam. In French with English subtitles. **88m/B VHS, Beta.** *FR* Odette Joyeux, Jacques Tati, Francois Perier; ***D:*** Claude Autant-Lara. *HMV, INJ, NLC*

Sylvia Scarlett ♂♂½ **1935** An odd British comedy about a woman who masquerades as a boy while on the run with her father, who causes all kinds of instinctive confusion in the men she meets. **94m/B VHS, Beta, LV.** Katharine Hepburn, Cary Grant, Brian Aherne, Edmund Gwenn, Natalie Paley, Dennie Moore, Lennox Pawle, Daisy Belmore, Nola Luxford; ***D:*** George Cukor; ***C:*** Russell Metty. *FCT, TTC*

Sympathy for the Devil ♂♂ *One Plus One* **1970** Rolling Stones provide music for confused, revolutionary documentary. Episodic jumble is odd, sometimes fascinating. **110m/C VHS, Beta.** *FR* Mick Jagger, Rolling Stones; ***D:*** Jean-Luc Godard. *FOX, OM*

Symphony in the Mountains ♂♂½ **1935** An early German sound romance, where an Austrian singing teacher falls in love with the sister of one of his student's. Featuring choral work by the Vienna Boys' Choir. In German with English subtitles. **75m/B VHS, Beta.** *GE FCT, IHF, GLV*

Symphony of Living ♂½ **1935** Intended heartwarmer about a man's bitter betrayal by his family and the hardship and tragedy he experiences. **73m/B VHS, Beta.** *VYY*

Synapse ♂♂ **1995 (R)** Black-marketeer Andre (Makepeace) is doublecrossed by a partner and arrested by Life Corp., which runs this futuristic civilization. As an experimental punishment, his mind is implanted into the body of Celeste (Duffy), who manages to escape and join up with a band of revolutionaries determined to destroy the evil corporation. Fast-paced story and good special effects. **89m/C VHS.** Karen Duffy, Saul Rubinek, Matt McCoy, Chris Makepeace; ***D:*** Allan Goldstein. *AVE*

Syngenor ♂½ **1990 (R)** Syngenor stands for Synthesized Genetic Organism, to differentiate it from all other organisms. Created by science, it escapes, and a crack team of scientists and gung-ho military types are mobilized to track it down. **98m/C VHS.** Starr Andreeff, Michael Laurence, David Gale, Charles Lucia, Riva Spier, Jeff Doucette, Bill Gratton, Lewis Arquette, Jon Korkes, Melanie Shatner; ***D:*** George Elanjian Jr.; ***M:*** Tom Chase, Steve Rucker. *HMD*

T-Bird Gang ♂½ **1959** A high school student goes undercover to infiltrate a teen gang. When his cover is blown, things get hairy. Laughable sleazebag production. **75m/B VHS.** Ed Nelson, John Brinkley, Pat George, Beach Dickerson, Tony Miller; ***D:*** Richard Harbinger; ***M:*** Shelley Manne. *SNC*

T Bone N Weasel ♂♂ **1992 (PG-13)** Hines and Lloyd play not-so-ex-cons who steal a car and try to lead a life of ease. Crime doesn't pay. Made for cable television. **94m/C VHS, LV.** Gregory Hines, Christopher Lloyd. *TTC*

T-Force ♂♂½ **1994 (R)** T-Force is a successful cybernetic law enforcement team set up in the year 2007. But when innocent people get caught in the T-Force crossfire, a team shutdown is ordered, causing the members to turn renegade and fight for their survival instead. The plot rarely gets in the way of the hard-hitting action. **101m/C VHS, LV.** Jack Scalia, Erin Gray, Evan Lurie, Daron McBee; ***D:*** Richard Pepin. *PMH*

T-Men ♂♂♂ **1947** Two agents of the Treasury Department infiltrate a counterfeiting gang. Filmed in semi-documentary style, exciting tale serves also as an effective commentary on the similarities between the agents and those they pursue. Mann and cinematographer John Alton do especially fine work here. **96m/B VHS, Beta, LV.** Alfred Ryder, Dennis O'Keefe, June Lockhart, Mary Meade, Wallace Ford, Charles McGraw; ***D:*** Anthony Mann; ***C:*** John Alton. Nominations: Academy Awards '47: Best Sound. *MED*

Table for Five ♂♂½ **1983 (PG)** A divorced father takes his children on a Mediterranean cruise and while sailing, he learns that his ex-wife has died. The father and his ex-wife's husband struggle over who should raise the children. Sentimental and well-acted. **120m/C VHS, Beta, LV.** Jon Voight, Millie Perkins, Richard Crenna, Robbie Kiger, Roxana Zal, Son Hoang Bui, Marie-Christine Barrault, Kevin Costner; ***D:*** Robert Liebmann; ***W:*** David Seltzer; ***M:*** Miles Goodman. *FOX*

Table Settings ♂♂ **1984** A taped performance of James Lapines' comedy about the lives of three generations of a Jewish family. **90m/C VHS, Beta.** Robert Klein, Stockard Channing, Dinah Manoff, Eileen Heckart. *NO*

Tabloid! ♂½ **1988** Unorthodox woman prints and sells racy trash for enquiring minds. **99m/C VHS.** Scott Davis, Glen Coburn; ***D:*** Bret McCormick, Matt Shaffen. *HHE*

Tabu: A Story of the South Seas ♂♂♂½ **1931** Fascinating docudrama about a young pearl diver's ill-fated romance. The gods have declared the young woman he desires "taboo" to all men. Filmed on location in Tahiti. Authored and produced by Murnau and Flaherty. Flaherty left in mid-production due to artistic differences with Murnau, who was later killed in an auto accident one week before the premiere of film. Oscar-winning cinematography by Floyd Crosby. **81m/B VHS, Beta.** ***D:*** Robert Flaherty, F.W. Murnau; ***C:*** Floyd Crosby. Academy Awards '31: Best Cinematography; National Board of Review Awards '31: 10 Best Films of the Year. *MIL, GVV, LUM*

Taffin ♂½ **1988 (R)** An Irish bill collector battles a group of corrupt businessmen who want to replace the local soccer field with a hazardous chemical plant. Pretty dull fare, overall, with Brosnan much less charismatic than usual. **96m/C VHS, Beta, LV.** *GB* Pierce Brosnan, Ray McAnally, Alison Doody, Patrick Bergin; ***D:*** Francis Megahy; ***W:*** David Ambrose. *MGM*

Tag: The Assassination Game ♂½ **1982 (PG)** An exciting new game has been discovered by a group of university students. Players act as spies and assassins, "killing" each other to make points. But a school newspaper sportswriter finds the game has become more real than make-believe. Timely topic in the early '80s when Dungeons and Dragons and other "war" games were popular on college campuses across the nation. **92m/C VHS, Beta.** Robert Carradine, Linda Hamilton, Michael Winslow, Kristine DeBell, Perry Lang; ***D:*** Nick Castle; ***W:*** Nick Castle. *SUE*

Tagget ♂ **1990 (PG-13)** A former CIA operative who has erased his nightmarish stint in Vietnam gradually begins to recall his past. When pieces of the puzzle begin to come together, he remembers a few things that the government would prefer he forget. Soon, CIA men are on his trail and their mission is to see that he forgets his past—permanently. Made for cable television. **89m/C VHS.** Daniel J. Travanti, William Sadler, Roxanne Hart, Stephen Tobolowsky, Peter Michael Goetz, Sarah Douglas, Noel Harrison; ***D:*** Richard T. Heffron. *MCA*

Tai-Pan ♂½ **1986 (R)** A 19th century Scottish trader and his beautiful Chinese mistress are the main characters in this confusing attempt to dramatize the story of Hong Kong's development into a thriving trading port. Too many subplots and characters are introduced in a short time to do justice to James Clavell's novel of the same name, the basis for the movie. The first American production completely filmed in China. **130m/C VHS, Beta, LV.** Bryan Brown, Joan Chen, John Stanton, Kyra Sedgwick, Tim Guinee, Russell Wong, Bert Remsen; ***D:*** Daryl Duke; ***W:*** John Briley; ***C:*** Jack Cardiff; ***M:*** Maurice Jarre. *VES*

Tails You Live, Heads You're Dead ♂♂ **1995 (R)** Cable thriller features Bernsen as a psycho who kills at random—and tells a stranger, McGinley, whom he met at a bar that the man is his next victim. After several unsuccessful attempts on his life, McGinley turns to detective Matheson for help. Based on the short story "Liar's Dice" by Bill Pronzini. **91m/C VHS, Beta.** Corbin Bernsen, Ted McGinley, Tim Matheson; ***D:*** Tim Matheson; ***W:*** Miguel Tejada-Flores. *PAR*

Tailspin: Behind the Korean Airline Tragedy ♂♂ **1989** Made-for-TV docudrama on the 1983 downing of Korean Aire flight 007 in Soviet airspace. Purports to show the U.S. government's reaction to what became a major international incident. **82m/C VHS, Beta, LV.** Michael Moriarty, Michael Murphy, Chris Sarandon, Harris Yulin, Gavan O'Herlihy, Ed O'Ross; ***D:*** David Darlow; ***M:*** David Ferguson. *PSM, PAR*

Tailspin Tommy **1934** Features twelve chapters of the great action serial. **?m/B VHS.** Maurice Murphy, Noah Beery Jr., Walter Miller, Patricia Farr, Grant Withers, John Davidson, William Desmond, Charles A. Browne; ***D:*** Lew (Louis Friedlander) Landers. *GPV*

Tainted ♂½ **1988** Small-town woman tries to endure after being raped. Both her husband and the attacker are killed, and she is forced to conceal their deaths. Poorly scripted. **90m/C VHS, Beta.** Shari Shattuck, Park Overall, Gene Tootle, Magilla Schaus, Blaque Fowler; ***D:*** Orestes Matacena. *HMD*

Tainted Blood ♂♂ **1993 (R)** Welch stars as an investigative reporter whose latest story has her attempting to find the teenage twin of a psychotic killer. **86m/C VHS, Beta.** Raquel Welch, Alley Mills, Kerri Green, Natasha Gregson Wagner, Joan Van Ark; ***D:*** Matthew Patrick; ***W:*** Kathleen Rowell, Ginny Cerrella. *PAR*

Tainted Image ♂♂ **1991** Artist woman starts to lose sanity with help of boyfriend, psycho neighbor and rash of bizarre deaths. She turns to canvas for solace and decides she needs secret ingredient that can't be found in art supply store to complete masterpiece. **95m/C VHS.** Tom Saunders, Sandra Frances, Annetta Arpin, Ken La Mothe, Heidi Emerich, Steve Kornacki. *HHT, DMP*

The Take ♂♂ **1990 (R)** Recovering alcoholic cop faces wrath of drug lord and marriage on the rocks. **91m/C VHS.** Ray Sharkey, R. Lee Ermey, Lisa Hartman Black, Larry Manetti, Joe Lala; ***D:*** Leon Ichaso; ***W:*** Edward Anhalt, Handel Glassberg; ***M:*** David Beal. *MCA*

Take a Hard Ride ♂½ **1975 (R)** Dull spaghetti western about a cowboy transporting money to Mexico, evading bandits and bounty hunters. **103m/C VHS, Beta.** Jim Brown, Lee Van Cleef, Fred Williamson, Jim Kelly, Barry Sullivan; ***D:*** Anthony (Antonio Margheriti) Dawson; ***M:*** Jerry Goldsmith. *FOX*

Take Down ♂♂ **1979 (PG)** Hermann is charming as a high school English teacher turned reluctant wrestling coach. **96m/C VHS, Beta.** Lorenzo Lamas, Kathleen Lloyd, Maureen McCormick, Edward Herrmann; ***D:*** Keith Merrill. *UNI*

Take It Big ♂½ **1944** Uninspired B-musical starring the Tin Man from the "Wizard of Oz." Haley is an impoverished actor who inherits a ranch and saves it by—surprise—putting on a show. ♫Sunday, Monday, and Always; Love and Learn; Life Can Be Beautiful; Take It Big; I'm a Big Success with You. **75m/B VHS, Beta.** Jack Haley, Harriet Hilliard Nelson, Mary Beth Hughes, Arline Judge, Nils T. Granlund, Fuzzy Knight, Ozzie Nelson; ***D:*** Frank McDonald. *NOS, VYY, DVT*

Take Me Back to Oklahoma ♂ **1940** Musical western with comedy. **64m/B VHS, Beta.** Tex Ritter, Terry Walker, Karl Hackett, George Eldridge; ***D:*** Al(bert) Herman. *NOS, VCN, VYY*

Take Me Out to the Ball Game ♂♂½ *Everybody's Cheering* **1949** Williams manages a baseball team, locks horns with players Sinatra and Kelly, and wins them over with song. Naturally, there's a water ballet scene. Contrived and forced, but enjoyable. ♫Take Me Out to the Ball Game; The Hat My Father Wore on St. Patrick's Day; O'Brien to Ryan to Goldberg; The Right Girl for Me;

It's Fate, Baby, It's Fate; Yes, Indeedy; Strictly U.S.A. **93m/C VHS, Beta, LV.** Frank Sinatra, Gene Kelly, Esther Williams, Jules Munshin, Betty Garrett, Edward Arnold, Tom Dugan, Richard Lane; ***D:*** Busby Berkeley. *MGM*

Take the Money and Run 🦴🦴🦴 **1969 (PG)** Allen's directing debut; he also co-wrote and starred. "Documentary" follows a timid, would-be bank robber who can't get his career off the ground and keeps landing in jail. Little plot, but who cares? Nonstop one-liners and slapstick. **85m/C VHS, Beta, LV.** Woody Allen, Janet Margolin, Marcel Hillaire, Louise Lasser; ***D:*** Woody Allen; ***W:*** Woody Allen; ***M:*** Marvin Hamlisch. *FOX*

Take This Job & Shove It 🦴🦴 **1981 (PG)** The Johnny Paycheck song inspired this story of a hot-shot efficiency expert who returns to his hometown to streamline the local brewery. Encounters with old pals inspire self-questioning. Alternately inspired and hackneyed. Cameos by Paycheck and other country stars. **100m/C VHS, Beta.** Robert Hays, Art Carney, Barbara Hershey, David Keith, Martin Mull, Eddie Albert, Penelope Milford; ***Cameos:*** Johnny Paycheck, David Allen Coe, Charlie Rich, Lacy J. Dalton; ***D:*** Gus Trikonis; ***W:*** Barry Schneider. *COL, SUE*

Take Two 🦴 **1987 (R)** A woman has an affair with her husband's twin brother. Interesting metaphysically: Are you my husband or my lover? But is an adultery/murder drama with Frank Stallone worth 101 minutes of your time? **101m/C VHS, Beta, LV.** Grant Goodeve, Robin Mattson, Frank Stallone, Warren Berlinger, Darwyn Swalve, Nita Talbot; ***D:*** Peter Rowe. *ACA*

Take Your Best Shot 🦴½ **1982** Standard TV fare about an out-of-work actor struggling with his low self-esteem and his failing marriage. Made-for-television comedy. **96m/C VHS, Beta.** Robert Urich, Meredith Baxter, Jeffrey Tambor, Jack Bannon, Claudette Nevins; ***D:*** David Greene. *LIV*

Taken Away 🦴🦴½ **1989** Struggling young divorcee Stephanie Monroe waits tables during the day and studies to be a computer tech at night in order to provide her 8-year-old daughter Abby with a better life. Unable to afford child care, Stephanie leaves Abby alone in the afternoon until she can get home from work. But when the welfare system finds out Stephanie is accused of child neglect and must fight a bureaucratic nightmare in order to get her child back. Made for television. **94m/C VHS, LV.** Valerie Bertinelli, Kevin Dunn, Joshua Maurer, Anna Maria Horsford, Juliet Sorcey, Nada Despotovich, Matthew Faison, James Arone; ***D:*** John D. Patterson; ***W:*** Robert Freedman, Selma Thomson. *MCA*

The Takeover 🦴🦴 **1994 (R)** East coast crime boss Danny Stein (Drago) decides to take over the L.A. operations of rival Tony Valachi (Mancuso). Lots of mayhem ensues. **91m/C VHS, LV.** Billy Drago, Nick Mancuso, John Savage, Eric Da Re, Cali Timmins, David Amos, Gene Mitchell; ***D:*** Troy Cook; ***W:*** Gene Mitchell; ***M:*** Jimmy Lifton. *LIV*

Takin' It All Off **1987** In this sequel to "Takin' It Off," Kitten does it again with unbelievable bumps and grinds. **90m/C VHS.** Francesca "Kitten" Natividad; ***D:*** Ed Hansen. *LIV, VES*

Taking Care of Business 🦴½ *Filofax* **1990 (R)** Too familiar tale of switched identity has crazed Cubs fan Belushi find Grodin's Filofax, allowing him to pose as businessman. Old jokes and a story full of holes. **108m/C VHS, Beta, LV.** James Belushi, Charles Grodin, Anne DeSalvo, Loryn Locklin, Veronica Hamel, Hector Elizondo, Mako, Gates McFadden, Stephen Elliott; ***D:*** Arthur Hiller; ***W:*** Jeffrey Abrams. *HPH*

Taking My Turn **1984** A taped performance of the off Broadway musical revue about growing old gracefully. **87m/C VHS, Beta.** *NO*

The Taking of Beverly Hills 🦴½ **1991 (R)** Deranged billionaire Bat Masterson designs a bogus toxic spill that leaves the wealth of Beverly Hills his for the taking. Football hero Boomer Hayes teams up with renegade cop Ed Kelvin to try and stop Masterson and save the city of Beverly Hills. **96m/C VHS, LV.** Ken Wahl, Matt Frewer, Robert Davi, Harley Jane Kozak, Lee James, Branscombe Richmond, Lyman Ward, Michael Bowen, William Prince, Ken Swofford, George Wyner; ***D:*** Sidney J. Furie; ***W:*** Sidney J. Furie, David Burke. *COL, NLC*

The Taking of Flight 847: The Uli Derickson Story 🦴🦴🦴 *The Flight* **1988** Wagner plays the stewardess who acted as a go-between for the passengers during a 1985 terrorist hijacking, saving all but one life. True-story drama is suspenseful and entertaining, nominated for several Emmys. Made-for-television drama. **100m/C VHS, LV.** Laurie Walters, Sandy McPeak, Ray Wise, Leslie Easterbrook, Lindsay Wagner, Eli Danker, Joseph Naser; ***D:*** Paul Wendkos; ***W:*** Norman Merrill. *IME*

The Taking of Pelham One Two Three 🦴🦴🦴 **1974 (R)** A hijack team, lead by the ruthless Shaw, seizes a New York City subway car and holds the 17 passengers for one million dollars ransom. Fine pacing keeps things on the edge. New cinematic techniques used by cameraman Owen Roizman defines shadowy areas like never before. **105m/C VHS, Beta.** Robert Shaw, Walter Matthau, Martin Balsam, Hector Elizondo, James Broderick, Earl Hindman, Dick O'Neill, Jerry Stiller, Tony Roberts, Doris Roberts, Kenneth McMillan, Julius W. Harris, Sal Viscuso; ***D:*** Joseph Sargent; ***C:*** Owen Roizman; ***M:*** David Shire. *MGM, FOX*

Taking the Heat 🦴🦴½ **1993 (R)** When mobster Arkin kills a sporting-goods dealer with a golf club the murder is witnessed by yuppie Goldwyn. Whitfield is the ambitious cop who wants Goldwyn to testify against the gangster—if she can keep him alive long enough to get him to court. One long chase scene. Made for cable television. **91m/C VHS.** Lynn Whitfield, Tony Goldwyn, Alan Arkin, George Segal, Peter Boyle; ***D:*** Tom Mankiewicz; ***W:*** Dan Gordon. *FXV*

Tale of a Vampire 🦴🦴½ **1992 (R)** In present day London, ageless vampire Alex (Sands) still mourns his long-lost vampiric love, Virginia, when he meets Anne (Hamilton) (who resembles Virginia). Alex doesn't know he's being stalked by Virginia's husband, Edgar (Cranham), also a vampire. Edgar decides to use Anne (with whom Alex has fallen in love) as bait, in a revenge plot. A tiny budget and slow pacing mar the film's fine visual style and good work by the two male leads. Film debut for director Sato. **93m/C VHS.** *GB* Julian Sands, Kenneth Cranham, Suzanna Hamilton; ***D:*** Shimako Sato; ***W:*** Jane Corbett, Shimako Sato; ***M:*** Julian Joseph. *VMK*

The Tale of Ruby Rose 🦴🦴🦴 **1987 (PG)** Living in the mountains of Tasmania, Ruby Rose, her husband Henry, and their adopted son Gem, struggle to survive the '30s depression by hunting and trapping. Having spent all her life in the mountains, Ruby Rose has a very superstitious view of life and a terror of nightfall. But after an argument with her husband, Ruby Rose sets out on a cross-country journey to find her grandmother and discover the secrets of her past. **101m/C VHS.** *AU* Melita Jurisic, Chris Haywood; ***D:*** Roger Sholes; ***W:*** Roger Sholes; ***M:*** Paul Schutze. *NO*

A Tale of Springtime 🦴🦴½ **1992 (PG)** Comedy-romance is the first film in Rohmer's planned new series, the "Tales of the Four Seasons," not to be confused with his "Six Moral Tales" or his "Comedies and Proverbs." Centers around Jeanne, a high school philosophy teacher; Natacha, a young student; and Igor, Natacha's father. As characteristic of Rohmer films, texture and character largely overshadow linear plots and social messages. However, the efficiency and directness of his camerawork make it a pleasure to watch. **107m/C VHS.** *FR* Anne Teyssedre, Hugues Quester, Florence Darel, Eloise Bennett, Sophie Robin; ***D:*** Eric Rohmer; ***W:*** Eric Rohmer. *ORI*

The Tale of the Frog Prince 🦴🦴🦴½ **1983** Superb edition of Shelley Duvall's "Faerie Tale Theatre" finds Williams the victim of an angry fairy godmother's spell. Garr to the rescue as the self-centered princess who saves him with a kiss. Directed and written by Idle of Monty Python fame. **60m/C VHS, Beta, LV.** Robin Williams, Teri Garr; ***D:*** Eric Idle; ***W:*** Eric Idle. *FOX*

A Tale of Two Cities 🦴🦴🦴🦴 **1935** Lavish production of the Dickens' classic set during the French Revolution, about two men who bear a remarkable resemblance to each other, both in love with the same girl. Carefree lawyer Sydney Carton (Colman) roused to responsibility, makes the ultimate sacrifice. A memorable Madame DeFarge from stage star Yurka in her film debut, with assistance from other Dickens' film stars Rathbone, Oliver and Walthall. **128m/B VHS, Beta.** Ronald Colman, Elizabeth Allan, Edna May Oliver, Reginald Owen, Isabel Jewell, Walter Catlett, H.B. Warner, Donald Woods, Basil Rathbone, Blanche Yurka, Henry B. Walthall; ***D:*** Jack Conway; ***W:*** W.P. Lipscomb, S.N. Behrman; ***M:*** Herbert Stothart. Nominations: Academy Awards '36: Best Film Editing, Best Picture. *MGM, KUI, IGP*

A Tale of Two Cities 🦴🦴🦴 **1958** A well-done British version of the Dickens' classic about a lawyer who sacrifices himself to save another man from the guillotine during the French Reign of Terror. The sixth remake of the tale. **117m/B VHS, Beta.** *GB* Dirk Bogarde, Dorothy Tutin, Christopher Lee, Donald Pleasence, Ian Bannen, Cecil Parker; ***D:*** Ralph Thomas. *SUE, LCA, FHS*

A Tale of Two Cities 🦴🦴½ **1980** Impressive looking but bloodless adaptation of the Dickens novel set in the French Revolution. Saradon takes on the dual role of sacrificing English lawyer Carton and French nobleman Darnay, with Krige as the lovely woman caught between the two. Made for television. **156m/C VHS.** Chris Sarandon, Alice Krige, Peter Cushing, Kenneth More, Barry Morse, Flora Robson, Billie Whitelaw; ***D:*** Jim Goddard; ***W:*** John Gay. *LIV, FUS*

A Tale of Two Cities 🦴🦴🦴 **1991** Masterpiece Theatre production of the classic Dickens tale. The French revolution was a time of revenge and brutality, but also provided the proving ground for a love greater than life. Terrific cast and perfectly detailed production. On two cassettes. **240m/C VHS.** James Wilby, Serena Gordon, John Mills, Jean-Pierre Aumont, Anna Massey. *PBS, TVC*

Tale of Two Cities/In the Switch Tower 🦴½ **1915** A package of two medium-length silent films, the latter featuring a rare acting appearance by director Borzage. **70m/B VHS, Beta, 8mm.** Walter Edwards, Maurice Costello, Florence Turner, Frank Borzage, Norma Talmadge, Leo Delaney. *VYY*

Tale of Two Sisters 🦴🦴½ **1989** Sheen narrates sensual drama about two beautiful, ambitious sisters. **90m/C VHS.** Valerie Breiman, Claudia Christian, Sydney Lassick, Jeff Conaway. *NO*

A Tale of Winter 🦴🦴½ *Conte D'Hiver* **1992** Portrays the romantic trials of a young French woman who cannot choose between her two smitten lovers and her one true love, the long disappeared father of her child. Felicie (Very) hopelessly loves Charles (Van Den Driessche), whom she met five years before, but mistakenly gave the wrong address. Rohmer's trademark conversation-filled scenes find her brooding over her predicament, running from one lover and back again, until a revelation during a viewing of Shakespeare's "The Winter's Tale." A charming cast carries the story to a surprise twist of an ending. Second in the series "Tales of the Four Seasons." In French with English subtitles. **114m/C VHS.** *FR* Charlotte Very, Frederic Van Dren Driessche, Michel Voletti, Herve Furic, Ava Loraschi, Jean-Luc Revol, Haydee Caillot, Jean-Claude Biette, Rosette, Marie Riviere; ***D:*** Eric Rohmer; ***W:*** Eric Rohmer; ***C:*** Luc Pages; ***M:*** Sebastien Erms. *NYF*

Talent for the Game 🦴🦴½ **1991 (PG)** A slight but handsomely produced baseball pleasantry about a talent scout who recruits a phenomenonal young pitcher, then sees the kid exploited by the team owner. More like an anecdote than a story, with an ending that aims a little too hard to please. Good for sports fans and family audiences. **91m/C VHS, Beta, LV.** Edward James Olmos, Lorraine Bracco, Jeff Corbett, Jamey Sheridan, Terry Kinney; ***D:*** Robert M. Young; ***W:*** David Himmelstein, Tom Donnelly, Larry Ferguson; ***M:*** David Newman. *PAR*

Tales from Avonlea, Vol. 1: The Journey Begins *Road to Avonlea; Avonlea* **1990** From the producer of the popular "Anne of Green Gables" movie and its sequel comes this weekly TV series, a collaboration of the Disney channel and CBC Television. In "The Journey Begins," Sara meets her stuffy Aunt Hetty and her cousins Felix and Felicity. Unhappy with her life, she decides whether to stay or run away. "The Proof of the Pudding" finds the grownups away and Felicity in charge of her siblings and Sara for the weekend. The same attention to detail, particularly in scenic views of lovely Prince Edward Island and the costumes, is shown in the series. Based on the writings of Lucy Maud Montgomery. **106m/C VHS, Beta.** *CA* Sarah Polley, Jackie Burroughs, Gema Zamprogna. *DIS, BTV*

Tales from the Crypt 🦴🦴🦴 **1972 (PG)** A collection of five scary stories from the classic EC comics that bear the movie's title. Richardson tells the future to each of five people gathered in a cave, each tale involving misfortune and, of course, gore. **92m/C VHS, Beta.** *GB* Ralph Richardson, Joan Collins, Peter Cushing, Richard Greene, Ian Hendry; ***D:*** Freddie Francis. *PSM*

Tales from the Crypt **1989** Three contemporary tales of the macabre, "The Man Who Was Death," "'Twas the Night Before," and "Dig That Cat...He's Real Gone," linked together by a special-effects host. Ry Cooder provides the musical score for the second episode. Based on stories published by William M. Gaines in EC Comics; made-for-cable-television. **81m/C VHS, Beta, LV.** William Sadler, Mary Ellen Trainor, Larry Drake, Joe Pantoliano, Robert Wuhl, Gustav Vintas; ***D:*** Walter Hill, Robert Zemeckis, Richard Donner; ***M:*** Ry Cooder, Alan Silvestri. *HBO*

Tales from the Crypt Presents Bordello of Blood 🦴🦴½ *Bordello of Blood* **1996 (R)** Detective Rafe Guttman (Miller) is on the case of a Bible thumper's (Eleniak) missing brother (Feldman). The trail leads him to a unique establishment, a brothel presided over by vampire queen Lilith (Everhart), whose clients all wind up dead (but probably with smiles on their faces), and the strange Reverend Current (Sarandon, who made a fine vampire himself in "Fright Night"). Crypt Keeper's second big screen outing showcases Miller's slant on the leading man gig and serves up campy fun with the blood. **?m/C VHS.** Dennis Miller, Angie Everhart, Chris Sarandon, Corey Feldman, Erika Eleniak; ***D:*** Gilbert Adler; ***W:*** Gilbert Adler, A.L. Katz. *NYR*

Tales from the Crypt Presents Demon Knight 🦴🦴 *Demon Knight; Demon Keeper* **1994 (R)** Gruesomely garish big-screen version of the TV series that was inspired by the lurid 1950s E.C. comics. Horrormeister Crypt Keeper offers his usual pun-filled introduction to a tale set in a seedy boarding-house. Brayker (Sadler) is the guardian of an ancient key that keeps the forces of darkness from overwhelming mankind, a key desired by the charismatic Collector (Zane), who unleashes a disgusting mix of demons against the house's inhabitants. Curious hybrid of spoof/splatter pic that doesn't quite work in either genre. **93m/C VHS, LV.** Billy Zane, William Sadler, Jada Pinkett, Brenda Bakke, CCH Pounder, Dick Miller, Thomas Haden Church, John Schuck, Gary Farmer, Charles Fleischer; ***D:*** Ernest R. Dickerson; ***W:*** Ethan Reiff, Cyrus Voris, Mark Bishop; ***M:*** Ed Shearmur; ***V:*** John Kassir. *MCA, NHO*

Tales from the Crypt, Vol. 3 **1990** Three more tales of terror from the made-for-cable-television series. "Dead Right" has Moore as a gold-digger who takes a fortuneteller's advice and marries a penniless slob. "Cutting Cards" has Tighe and Hendricksen involved in a very high stakes game. "The Switch" features Hickey as a wealthy old man bartering for a new body to woo the beautiful Preston. **80m/C VHS, Beta.** Demi Moore, William Hickey, Kelly Preston, Jeffrey Tambor, Rick Rossovich, Lance Henriksen, Kevin Tighe; ***D:*** Arnold Schwarzenegger, Walter Hill, Howard Deutch. *WAR, MOV*

Tales from the Darkside **1985** Each episode of this series features several short Twilight Zone-esque stories of fantasy and suspense. Additional tapes available. **70m/C VHS, Beta, LV.** *LIV, MOV*

Tales from the Darkside: The Movie **1990 (R)** Three short stories in the tradition of the ghoulish TV show are brought to the big screen, with mixed results. The plot centers around a boy who is being held captive by a cannibal. In order to prolong his life, he tells her horror stories. The tales were written by Sir Arthur Conan Doyle, Stephen King, and Michael McDowell. **93m/C VHS, Beta, LV.** Deborah Harry, Christian Slater, David Johansen, William Hickey, James Remar, Rae Dawn Chong, Julianne Moore, Robert Klein; ***D:*** John Harrison; ***W:*** Stephen King, Michael McDowell, Sir Arthur Conan Doyle. *PAR*

Tales from the Gimli Hospital 🦴🦴 **1988** A smallpox outbreak at the turn of the century finds Einar and Gunnar sharing a hospital room. They begin telling each other increasingly bizarre personal secrets and develop a serious rivalry. Sharp dialogue with some equally grotesque imagery. Director Maddin first feature film. **72m/B VHS.** Kyle McCulloch, Michael Gottli; ***D:*** Guy Maddin. *KIV, FCT*

Tales from the Hood 🦴🦴 **1995 (R)** Horror anthology with that urban twist. Three young thugs search for lost drugs inside a funeral parlor run by creepy Mr. Simms (Williams III) and instead walk into a world of four chilling and funny stories of fright dealing with racism and black on black crime. Tales aren't very original and are often too preachy for true enjoyment, but its nice to see someone attempt to breath life into an old and familiar genre. Williams III, with his pop-eyed stares and Don King coif, is fitting as the eerie storyteller. **97m/C VHS.** Clarence Williams III, Corbin Bernsen, David Alan Grier, Wings Hauser, Rosalind Cash, Rusty Cundieff, Joe Torry, Anthony Griffith; ***D:*** Rusty Cundieff; ***W:*** Rusty Cundieff, Darin Scott; ***C:*** Anthony Richmond; ***M:*** Christopher Young. *HBO*

Tales from the Snow Zone **1991** "Tales from the Snow Zone" is the latest feature length ski film from RAP producers Jon Long and James Angrove. Filmed entirely in the 1991 ski season, this film captures the essence of the sport and lifestyle. "Tales" covers true extreme skiing, radical free skiing, moguls, downhill ski racing, telemarking, snowboarding, and monoskiing. Filmed in Europe and North America, "Tales" features skiers from the United States, Canada, France, Sweden, and Australia. **70m/C VHS.** *RAP*

Tales of Beatrix Potter 🦴🦴🦴½ *Peter Rabbit and Tales of Beatrix Potter* **1971 (G)** The Royal Ballet Company of England performs in this adaptation of the adventures of Beatrix Potter's colorful and memorable creatures. Beautifully done. **90m/C VHS.** *GB* ***D:*** Reginald Mills. *REP, HMV*

The Tales of Hoffmann 🦴🦴½ **1951** A ballet-opera consisting of three stories by Jacques Offenbach covering romance, magic and mystery arising out of a poet's misadventures in love. Lavishly designed and highly stylized. **138m/C VHS, LV.** Robert Rounseville, Robert Helpmann, Moira Shearer; ***D:*** Michael Powell, Emeric Pressburger. Nominations: Academy Awards '51: Best Art Direction/Set Decoration (Color), Best Costume Design (Color). *HMV, PME*

Tales of Manhattan 🦴🦴🦴 **1942** Star-studded anthology about a tailor who curses a tailcoat that then travels, with varying degrees of good and bad fortune, from owner to owner. There's a love triangle, a love match, a concert appearance, a down-on-his-luck lawyer, a swanky party, a crook, and a windfall for some sharecroppers. Fields' party episode (he wears the coat to give a lecture and winds up wrecking havoc) was cut out of the original theatrical release. **118m/C VHS.** Charles Boyer, Rita Hayworth, Thomas Mitchell, Ginger Rogers, Henry Fonda, Cesar Romero, Elsa Lanchester, Charles Laughton, Edward G. Robinson, George Sanders, Jackie Gleason, J. Carrol Naish, Paul Robeson, Ethel Waters, Eddie Anderson, W.C. Fields, Margaret Dumont; ***D:*** Julien Duvivier; ***W:*** Ben Hecht, Donald Ogden Stewart, Samuel Hoffenstein, Ferenc Molnar, Alan Campbell; ***C:*** Joseph Walker; ***M:*** Sol Kaplan. *TCF*

Tales of Ordinary Madness 🦴 **1983** Gazzara as a poet who drinks and sleeps with assorted women. Based on the stories of Charles Bukowski. Pretentious and dull. **107m/C VHS, Beta.** Ben Gazzara, Ornella Muti, Susan Tyrrell, Tanya Lopert, Roy Brocksmith, Katya Berger; ***D:*** Marco Ferreri; ***C:*** Tonino Delli Colli. *LIV, VES*

Tales of Robin Hood 🦴½ **1952** A low-budget depiction of the Robin Hood legend. **59m/B VHS, Beta, LV.** Robert Clarke, Mary Hatcher; ***D:*** James Tinling. *NO*

Tales of Terror 🦴🦴 *Poe's Tales of Terror* **1962** Three tales of terror based on stories by Edgar Allan Poe: "Morella," "The Black Cat," and the "The Case of M. Valdemar." Price stars in all three segments and is excellent as the bitter and resentful husband in "Morella." **90m/C VHS, Beta.** Vincent Price, Peter Lorre, Basil Rathbone, Debra Paget, Joyce Jameson; ***D:*** Roger Corman; ***W:*** Richard Matheson; ***C:*** Floyd Crosby; ***M:*** Les Baxter. *MLB, ORI*

Tales of the Klondike: In a Far Country 🦴🦴 **1987** An adaptation of Jack London's story exploring the fears, dangers, and joys experienced by prospectors in the harsh wilderness of northwest Canadian gold country. **60m/C VHS, Beta.** Robert Carradine, Scott Hylands; ***D:*** Janine Manatis. *AHV*

Tales of the Klondike: Race for Number One 🦴🦴 **1987** Two men compete in a highly contested dog-sled race—the goal of which is to be the first to reach a tract of gold-laden land. Adapted from a story by Jack London. **60m/C VHS, Beta.** David Ferry, John Ireland; ***D:*** David Cobham. *AHV*

Tales of the Klondike: The Scorn of Women 🦴🦴 **1987** An available man is enthusiastically courted by every single woman in Dawson City, Alaska. From a story by Jack London. **60m/C VHS, Beta.** Tom Butler, Eva Gabor; ***D:*** Claude Fournier. *AHV*

Tales of the Klondike: The Unexpected 🦴🦴 **1987** Five gold prospectors grow rich, but lose all that is most valuable through overwhelming greed. Adapted from a story by Jack London. **60m/C VHS, Beta.** John Candy, Cherie Lunghi; ***D:*** Peter Pearson. *AHV*

Tales of the Unexpected 🦴🦴½ **1991** Four tales designed to startle the senses and provoke the imagination. Episodes include "People Don't Do Such Things," about a marriage gone awry, "Youth from Vienna," about a weird fountain of youth, "Skeleton in the Cupboard," which tells of a man desperately trying to hide some strange secret and finally, "Bird of Prey," in which a pet parrot leaves its owners an enormous egg before dying. **101m/C VHS, Beta, LV.** Arthur Hill, Samantha Eggar, Don Johnson, Dick Smothers, Sharon Gless, James Carroll Jordan, Charles Dance, Zoe Wanamaker, Sondra Locke, Frank Converse; ***D:*** Gordon Hessler, Norman Lloyd, Paul Annett, Ray Danton. *PSM, IME*

Tales That Witness Madness 🦴🦴½ **1973 (R)** An asylum is the setting for four tales of horror, as a doctor tells a visitor how four patients ended up in his clinic. Stories are "Mr. Tiger," "Penny Farthing," "Mel" and "Luau." At the time this was Novak's first film appearance in four years. **90m/C VHS.** *GB* Jack Hawkins, Donald Pleasence, Suzy Kendall, Joan Collins, Kim Novak, Mary Tamm, Georgia Brown, Donald Houston, David Wood, Peter McEnery; ***D:*** Freddie Francis. *PAR*

Talion 🦴🦴 *An Eye for an Eye* **1966 (PG)** A western revenge movie that features two disabled men, a rancher and a bounty hunter, who team up to find the gang that slaughtered the rancher's family. **92m/C VHS, Beta.** Robert Lansing, Slim Pickens, Patrick Wayne; ***D:*** Michael Moore. *COL, NLC*

Talk 🦴🦴 **1994** Sharp conversation between two thirtysomething women as they wander around the streets of Sydney. Stephanie (Milliken) and Julia (Longley) are collaborators on graphic novels—Stephanie's single and adventurous while Julia is seemingly settled in the country with her lover and child. As they talk, the women learn that both their lives have conflicts. Fantasy sequences, which slow the story down, find the women stepping into their own comic-book adventures. **86m/C VHS.** *AU* Victoria Longley, Angie Milliken, Richard Roxburgh, Jacqueline McKenzie, John Jarratt; ***D:*** Susan Lambert; ***W:*** Jan Cornall; ***C:*** Ron Hagen; ***M:*** John Clifford White. *NYR*

Talk of the Town ♪♪♪ **1942** A brilliantly cast, strange mixture of screwball comedy and lynch-mob melodramatics. An accused arsonist, a Supreme Court judge and the girl they both love try to clear the former's name and evade the cops. **118m/B VHS, Beta, LV.** Ronald Colman, Cary Grant, Jean Arthur, Edgar Buchanan, Glenda Farrell, Rex Ingram, Emma Dunn; ***D:*** George Stevens. Nominations: Academy Awards '42: Best Black and White Cinematography, Best Film Editing, Best Interior Decoration, Best Picture, Best Screenplay, Best Story, Best Original Score. *COL*

Talk Radio ♪♪♪ **1988 (R)** Riveting Stone adaptation of Bogosian's one-man play. An acidic talk radio host confronts America's evil side and his own past over the airwaves. The main character is loosely based on the life of Alan Berg, a Denver talk show host who was murdered by white supremacists. **110m/C VHS, Beta, LV.** Eric Bogosian, Alec Baldwin, Ellen Greene, John Pankow, John C. McGinley, Michael Wincott, Leslie Hope; ***D:*** Oliver Stone; ***W:*** Eric Bogosian, Oliver Stone; ***C:*** Robert Richardson; ***M:*** Stewart Copeland. *MCA*

Talk to Me ♪½ **1982** A successful New York accountant checks into the Hollins Communication Institute to cure his stuttering. While there, he meets and falls in love with a squirrel-hunting stuttering woman from Arkansas. **90m/C VHS, Beta.** Austin Pendleton, Michael Murphy, Louise Fletcher, Brian Backer, Clifton James. *FOX*

Talkin' Dirty After Dark ♪♪ **1991 (R)** Sexy comedy starring Lawrence as a suave comedian who will do anything to get a late-night spot at Dukie's comedy club. **89m/C VHS.** Martin Lawrence, Jedda Jones, Phyllis Stickney, Darryl Sivad; ***D:*** Topper Carew; ***W:*** Topper Carew. *NLC, FCT*

Talking About Sex ♪♪½ **1994** Publishing party for a shrink's self-help manual sparks many conversations about sex and romance among a group of fashionable Los Angelenos. The breezy party chatter is broken up by B&W pseudo-documentary interludes of women exchanging confidences. **83m/C VHS.** Kim Wayans, Marcy Walker, Daniel Beer, Randy Powell, Kerry Ruff, Joe Richards, Daria Lynn; ***D:*** Aaron Speiser; ***W:*** Aaron Speiser, Carl Nelson; ***M:*** Tim Landers. *LEO*

Talking Walls ♪½ *Motel Vacancy* **1985** A college sociology student uses high-tech surveillance equipment to spy on the clients of a seedy motel, in order to complete his thesis on human sexuality. **85m/C VHS, Beta.** Stephen Shellan, Marie Laurin, Barry Primus, Sally Kirkland; ***D:*** Stephen Verona. *VTR, NWV*

The Tall Blond Man with One Black Shoe ♪♪♪ *Le Grand Blond Avec Une Chassure Noire* **1972 (PG)** A violinist is completely unaware that rival spies mistakenly think he is also a spy, and that he is the center of a plot to booby-trap an overly ambitious agent at the French Secret Service. A sequel followed called "Return of the Tall Blond Man with One Black Shoe" which was followed by a disappointing American remake, "The Man with One Red Shoe." In French with English subtitles or dubbed. **90m/C VHS, Beta, 8mm.** *FR* Pierre Richard, Bernard Blier, Jean Rochefort, Mireille Darc, Jean Carmet; ***D:*** Yves Robert; ***W:*** Francis Veber; ***M:*** Vladimir Cosma. *CVC, COL, VYY*

Tall, Dark and Deadly ♪♪½ **1995 (R)** TV cable movie finds Roy (Scalia) romancing Maggie (Delaney), a young woman he's met in a bar. The viewer's already clued in that Roy's a bad 'un (seein' as how he's killed one woman) and when he chains Maggie to a sink, she picks up on the idea that he's a wacko. Basic damsel-in-distress with a cast that manages to keep straight faces in the most preposterous of circumstances. **88m/C VHS.** Jack Scalia, Kim Delaney, Todd Allen, Gina Mastrogiacomo, Ely Pouget; ***D:*** Kenneth Fink; ***W:*** MaryAnne Kasica, Michael Scheff; ***M:*** Joseph Vitarelli. *PAR*

The Tall Guy ♪♪♪ **1989 (R)** Goldblum is a too-tall actor who tries the scene in London and lands the lead in a musical version of 'The Elephant Man,' becoming an overnight success. Not consistently funny, but good British comedy, including an interesting sex scene. **92m/C VHS, LV.** Jeff Goldblum, Emma Thompson, Rowan Atkinson, Geraldine James, Kim Thomson, Anna Massey; ***D:*** Mel Smith; ***W:*** Richard Curtis; ***M:*** Peter Brewis. *COL, FCT*

Tall in the Saddle ♪♪½ **1944** A misogynist foreman (Wayne) finds himself accused of murder. Meanwhile, he falls in love with his female boss's niece. An inoffensive and memorable western. **79m/B VHS, Beta, LV.** John Wayne, Ella Raines, George "Gabby" Hayes, Ward Bond; ***D:*** Edwin L. Marin. *MED, TTC*

Tall Lie ♪♪ *For Men Only* **1953** A student quits a fraternity hazing exercise. He's pursued by a psychotic bunch of his fraternity brothers and is killed in a smash-up. A local doctor goes onto an anti-hazing campaign in the aftermath. **93m/B VHS, Beta, LV.** Paul Henreid, Robert Sherman; ***D:*** Paul Henreid. *NO*

The Tall Men ♪♪ **1955** Standard western features frontier hands on a rough cattle drive confronting Indians, outlaws, and the wilderness while vying with each other for the love of Russell. **122m/C VHS, Beta.** Clark Gable, Jane Russell, Robert Ryan, Cameron Mitchell, Mae Marsh; ***D:*** Raoul Walsh. *FOX*

Tall Story ♪♪ **1960** Perkins is a star basketball player who must pass a crucial test in order to continue to play the game. In addition to the pressure of the exam, he is being pressured by gamblers to throw a game against the Russians. Fonda makes her screen debut as a cheerleader who is so awestruck by Perkins that she takes the same classes just to be close to him. Based on the play by Howard Lindsay and Russel Crouse, and the novel "The Homecoming Game" by Howard Nemerov. **91m/C VHS, LV.** Anthony Perkins, Jane Fonda, Ray Walston, Marc Connelly, Anne Jackson, Tom Laughlin; ***D:*** Joshua Logan; ***W:*** Julius J. Epstein, Philip C. Epstein; ***C:*** Ellsworth Fredericks. *WEA*

The Tall T **1957** A veteran rancher (Pat) stumbles onto big trouble when by chance he catches a stage coach that is eventually overrun by an evil band of cut-throats. After killing everyone on the coach except Pat and the daughter of a wealthy copper mine owner (Doretta), the renegades decide to leave the scene with the unfortunate two as hostages. Pat and Doretta, although in dire straits, find time to fall in love and devise an intricate plan for their escape. Regarded in certain western-lover circles as a cult classic. **77m/B VHS.** Randolph Scott, Richard Boone, Maureen O'Sullivan, Arthur Hunnicutt, Skip Homeier, Henry Silva, Robert Burton, Robert Anderson; ***D:*** Budd Boetticher; ***W:*** Burt Kennedy. *GKK*

Tall Tale: The Unbelievable Adventures of Pecos Bill ♪ **1995 (PG)** Having trouble with greedy land ownners out for his pa's land, Daniel Hackett (Stahl) summons the help of three Old West legends: Pecos Bill (Swayze), John Henry (Brown), and Paul Bunyan (Platt) to face off with the evil industrialist J.P. Stiles (Glenn). Disney's variation on the "Wizard of Oz" is riddled with cartoonish characters and sleep-inducing dialogue. It would truly be a tall tale if it were said that this movie was any good. **98m/C VHS, LV.** Patrick Swayze, Oliver Platt, Roger Brown, Nick Stahl, Scott Glenn, Stephen Lang, Jared Harris, Catherine O'Hara; ***D:*** Jeremiah S. Chechik; ***W:*** Steven L. Bloom, Robert Rodat; ***C:*** Janusz Kaminski. *DIS*

Tall, Tan and Terrific **1946** Things really go crazy when the owner of a nightclub in Harlem is accused of murder. **40m/C VHS, Beta.** Mantan Moreland, Monte Hawley, Francine Everett, Dots Johnson; ***D:*** Bud Pollard. *NOS*

Tall Texan ♪♪½ **1953** A motley crew seeks gold in an Indian burial ground in the desert. Flawed but interesting and suspenseful. Greed, lust, Indians and desert heat. **82m/B VHS, Beta, LV.** Lloyd Bridges, Lee J. Cobb, Marie Windsor, George Steele; ***D:*** Elmo Williams; ***C:*** Joseph Biroc. *RXM*

Talons of the Eagle ♪♪ **1992 (R)** Martial arts adventure centers around three undercover agents who go up against crimelord Mr. Li (Hong). To impress Li, martial arts champion Tyler Wilson (Blanks) and vice detective Michael Reeds (Merhi) enter a deadly martial arts tournament. They later hook up with beautiful agent Cassandra Hubbard (Barnes), who has already investigated Li's drug, gambling, and prostitution rings. Features the most advanced fighting techniques ever filmed. **96m/C VHS, LV.** Billy Blanks, Jalal Merhi, James Hong, Priscilla Barnes, Matthias Hues; ***D:*** Michael Kennedy; ***W:*** J. Stephen Maunder. *MCA, SGE*

Tamango ♪♪ **1959** A confusing drama set on a slave ship travelling from Africa to Cuba in 1830. Jurgens is the ship's captain who takes the black Dandridge as his mistress. Meanwhile, the slaves are plotting a revolt, with Dandridge as a conspirator. Will Jurgens quell the rebellion and still keep his mistress? The interracial romance does takes a secondary role to the racial conflicts. The title refers to the leader of the slave revolt, played by Cressan. Filmed in both English- and French-language versions. **98m/C VHS.** *FR* Curt Jurgens, Dorothy Dandridge, Jean Servais, Alex Cressan; ***D:*** John Berry. *IVY*

The Tamarind Seed ♪½ **1974** Andrews and Sharif are star-crossed lovers kept apart by Cold War espionage. Dated, dull and desultory. **123m/C VHS, Beta.** Julie Andrews, Omar Sharif, Anthony Quayle, Dan O'Herlihy, Sylvia Syms; ***D:*** Blake Edwards; ***W:*** Blake Edwards; ***C:*** Frederick A. (Freddie) Young; ***M:*** John Barry. *SUE*

The Taming of the Shrew ♪♪½ **1929** Historically interesting early talkie featuring sole (if perhaps unfortunate) pairing of Pickford and Fairbanks. Features the legendary credit line "By William Shakespeare, with additional dialogue by Sam Taylor." Re-edited in 1966; 1967 Zeffirelli remake featured Taylor and Burton. **66m/B VHS, Beta, LV.** Mary Pickford, Douglas Fairbanks Sr., Edwin Maxwell, Joseph Cawthorn; ***D:*** Sam Taylor; ***C:*** Karl Struss. *NOS, CCB*

The Taming of the Shrew ♪♪♪½ **1967** A lavish screen version of the classic Shakespearean comedy. Burton and Taylor are violently physical and perfectly cast as the battling Katherine and Petruchio. At the time the film was made, Burton and Taylor were having their own marital problems, which not only added an inner fire to their performances, but sent the interested moviegoers to the theatres in droves. **122m/C VHS, Beta, LV.** *IT* Elizabeth Taylor, Richard Burton, Michael York, Michael Hordern, Cyril Cusack; ***D:*** Franco Zeffirelli; ***W:*** Franco Zeffirelli; ***C:*** Oswald Morris; ***M:*** Nino Rota. National Board of Review Awards '67: 10 Best Films of the Year; Nominations: Academy Awards '67: Best Art Direction/Set Decoration, Best Costume Design. *COL, TVC, PBS*

The Taming of the Shrew ♪♪ **1981** The classic Shakespearean comedy about the battle of the sexes where Petruchio attempts to tame his fiery, free-spirited wife, Kate. **152m/C VHS, Beta.** ***D:*** Peter Dews. *SUE*

Tammy and the Bachelor ♪♪½ **1957** A backwoods Southern girl becomes involved with a romantic pilot and his snobbish family. They don't quite know what to make of her but she wins them over with her down-home philosophy. Features the hit tune, "Tammy." Charming performance by Reynolds. **89m/C VHS, Beta.** Debbie Reynolds, Leslie Nielsen, Walter Brennan, Fay Wray, Sidney Blackmer, Mildred Natwick, Louise Beavers; ***D:*** Joseph Pevney; ***W:*** Oscar Brodney. Nominations: Academy Awards '57: Best Song ("Tammy"). *MCA*

Tammy and the Doctor ⅋⅋ **1963** Sandra Dee reprises Debbie Reynolds's backwoods gal ("Tammy and the Bachelor"). Dee becomes a nurse's aide and is wooed by doctor Fonda, in his film debut. **88m/C VHS, Beta.** Sandra Dee, Peter Fonda, MacDonald Carey; ***D:*** Harry Keller; ***W:*** Oscar Brodney. *MCA*

Tammy and the T-Rex ⅋⅋½ **1994 (PG-13)** All Michael (Walker) wanted was a date with the lovely Denise (Richards)—he didn't expect to almost die for her. Nor did he expect a mad scientist to transplant his brain into a mechanical three-ton dinosaur. Part teen angst—part camp horror—all good-natured hooey. **82m/C VHS, LV.** Paul Walker, Denise Richards, Terry Kiser, John Franklin; ***D:*** Stewart Raffill. *IMP*

Tampopo ⅋⅋⅋ **1986** A hilarious, episodic Japanese comedy. A widowed noodle shop owner is coached by a ten-gallon-hatted stranger in how to make the perfect noodle. Popular, free-form hit that established Itami in the West. In Japanese with English subtitles. **114m/C VHS, LV.** *JP* Ken Watanabe, Tsutomu Yamazaki, Nobuko Miyamoto, Koji Yakusho, Rikiya Yasuoka, Kinzo Sakura, Shoji Otake; ***D:*** Juzo Itami. *REP, INJ*

Tangiers ⅋ **1983** The disappearance of a British intelligence agent in Gibraltar sets off a chain-reaction of violent incidents. **82m/C VHS.** Ronny Cox. *WAR*

Tangled Destinies ⅋⅋½ **1932** Old dark house thriller involving a deserted mansion, murder, and faux diamonds. Good acting and a decent storyline make it one of the few successful independently made films of its time. **64m/B VHS.** Lloyd Whitlock, Glenn Tryon, Vera Reynolds, Doris Hill, Sidney Bracy; ***D:*** Frank Strayer; ***W:*** Edward T. Lowe. *SNC*

Tango ⅋½ **1936** An early melodrama follows the ups and down of a chorus girl and the guy who sticks with her through thick and thin and poorly-filmed dance routines. Based on a novel by Vida Hurst. **66m/B VHS.** Marion Nixon, Chick Chandler, Matty Kemp, Marie Prevost, Warren Hymer, Herman Bing, Franklin Pangborn, George Meeker; ***D:*** Phil Rosen. *NOS, LOO*

Tango and Cash ⅋⅋ **1989 (R)** Stallone and Russell are L.A. cops with something in common: they both think they are the best in the city. Forced to work together to beat drug lord Palance, they flex their muscles a lot. Directing completed by Albert Magnoli, after Andrei Konchalovsky left in a huff. **104m/C VHS, Beta, LV, 8mm.** Sylvester Stallone, Kurt Russell, Jack Palance, Brion James, Teri Hatcher, Michael J. Pollard, James Hong, Marc Alaimo, Robert Z'Dar; ***D:*** Andrei Konchalovsky; ***W:*** Randy Feldman; ***M:*** Harold Faltermeyer. *WAR*

Tango Bar ⅋⅋½ **1988** A romantic triangle between a tango dancer who leaves Argentina during a time of political unrest, his former partner, and his wife, who both stay behind. They are reunited after years of separation. Gives the viewer a detailed vision of the historical and cultural significance of the tango. Charming, interesting and very watchable. In Spanish with English subtitles. **90m/C VHS, Beta.** *AR* Raul Julia, Valeria Lynch, Ruben Juarez; ***D:*** Marcos Zurinaga. *WAR, INJ*

Tank ⅋½ **1983 (PG)** Retired Army officer Garner's son is thrown into jail on a trumped-up charge by a small town sheriff. Dad comes to the rescue with his restored Sherman tank. Trite and unrealistic portrayal of good versus bad made palatable by Garner's performance. **113m/C VHS, Beta, LV.** James Garner, Shirley Jones, C. Thomas Howell, Mark Herrier, Sandy Ward, Jenilee Harrison, Dorian Harewood, G.D. Spradlin; ***D:*** Marvin J. Chomsky; ***M:*** Lalo Schifrin. *MCA*

Tank Commando ⅋½ **1959** Mediocre WWII actioner, set in Italy, about a demolition squad of battle-hardened Americans trying to locate a secret German crossing point. It turns out to be an underwater bridge and an Italian orphan is the only one, besides the Germans, to know its location. Can the Americans persuade the kid to talk? **79m/B VHS.** Bob Barron, Wally Campo, Maggie Lawrence, Donato Farretta, Leo V. Metranga, Jack Sowards, Anthony Rich, Larry Hudson; ***D:*** Burt Topper; ***W:*** Burt Topper. *COL*

Tank Girl ⅋½ **1994 (R)** Big-budget adaption of the underground British comic book about a brash punker chick (Petty), her mutant friends, and the evil establishment in the post-apocalyptic future. The heavily-armed pixie battles the tyrannical Department of Water and Power, run by evil Dr. Kesslee (McDowell), for control of the world's water supply in the year 2033. Straying a bit too far from the source comic, the plot (such as it is) is crammed into a rigid action-movie structure that lacks excitement. Plays like a cheap Gen-X marketing ploy with its bizarre mixture of pop culture references and a hipper-than-thou soundtrack coordinated by Courtney Love. **104m/C VHS, LV.** Lori Petty, Malcolm McDowell, Ice-T, Naomi Watts, Jeff Kober, Reg E. Cathey, Scott Coffey, Ann Cusack, Don Harvey, Brian Wimmer, Staci Linn Ramsower; ***Cameos:*** Iggy Pop, Ann Magnuson; ***D:*** Rachel Talalay; ***W:*** Tedi Sarafian; ***M:*** Graeme Revell. *MGM*

Tanks a Million ⅋⅋ **1941** Despite the title, tanks aren't even mentioned in this. Tracy stars as a wacky genius who gets drafted. His excellent memory keeps getting him into one predicament after another. Though he gets promoted quickly, he shows himself no leader. Lots of time-worn gags, but they still work. **50m/B VHS.** William Tracy, James Gleason, Noah Beery Jr., Joseph Sawyer, Elyse Knox, Douglas Fowley, Frank Faylen, Dick Wessel, Frank Melton, Harold Goodwin, William Gould, Norman Kerry; ***D:*** Fred Guiol. Nominations: Academy Awards '41: Best Original Score. *NOS*

Tanner '88 *Tanner: A Political Fable* **1988** Murphy is excellent as a longshot politician on the trail of the Democratic presidential nomination. Story by Gary Trudeau of Doonesbury fame. A precise political satire made for cable. **120m/C VHS, LV.** Michael Murphy, Pamela Reed, Cynthia Nixon; ***D:*** Robert Altman. *INJ, PBS, BTV*

Tanya's Island ⅋⅋½ **1981 (R)** Abused girlfriend fantasizes about life on deserted island and romance with an ape. Vanity billed as D.D. Winters. **100m/C VHS, Beta.** Vanity, Dick Sargent, Mariette Levesque, Don McCleod; ***D:*** Alfred Sole. *NO*

Tap ⅋⅋½ **1989 (PG-13)** The son of a famous tap dancer, a dancer himself, decides to try to get away from his former life of crime by helping an aging hoofer revitalize the art of tap dancing. Fun to watch for the wonderful dancing scenes. Davis' last big screen appearance. Hines is sincere in this old-fashioned story, and dances up a storm. Captures some never-before filmed old hoofers. **106m/C VHS, Beta, LV.** Gregory Hines, Sammy Davis Jr., Suzanne Douglas, Joe Morton, Terrance McNally, Steve Condos, Jimmy Slyde, Harold Nicholas, Etta James, Savion Glover, Dick Anthony Williams, Sandman Sims, Bunny Briggs, Pat Rico, Arthur Duncan; ***D:*** Nick Castle; ***W:*** Nick Castle; ***M:*** James Newton Howard. *COL, MVD*

Tapeheads ⅋⅋½ **1989 (R)** Silly, sophomonic, sexy comedy starring Cusack and Robbins as young wannabe rock-video producers who strike it big. Many big-name cameos; good soundtrack; laughs. **93m/C VHS, Beta, LV.** John Cusack, Tim Robbins, Mary Crosby, Connie Stevens, Susan Tyrrell, Lyle Alzado, Don Cornelius, Katy Boyer, Doug McClure, Clu Gulager, Jessica Walter; ***Cameos:*** Stiv Bators, Sam Moore, Junior Walker, Martha Quinn, Ted Nugent, Weird Al Yankovic; ***D:*** Bill Fishman. *NO*

Taps ⅋⅋½ **1981 (PG)** Military academy students led by Hutton are so true to their school they lay siege to it to keep it from being closed. An antiwar morality play about excesses of zeal and patriotism. Predictable but impressive. **126m/C VHS, Beta.** Timothy Hutton, George C. Scott, Ronny Cox, Sean Penn, Tom Cruise; ***D:*** Harold Becker; ***W:*** Darryl Ponicsan, Robert Mark Kamen; ***M:*** Maurice Jarre. *FOX*

Tarantula ⅋⅋⅋ **1955** If you're into gigantic killer insect movies this is one of the best with nifty special effects and some good action. Carroll plays a scientist working on a growth formula which he's testing on a spider when it accidentally gets loose. This eight-legged horror grows to 100 feet high and causes havoc in the Arizona desert until the Air Force napalms the sucker. Look for Eastwood in the final sequence as an Air Force pilot. **81m/B VHS.** Leo G. Carroll, John Agar, Mara Corday, Nestor Paiva, Ross Elliott, Clint Eastwood; ***D:*** Jack Arnold; ***W:*** Robert M. Fresco, Martin Berkeley. *MCA*

Tarantulas: The Deadly Cargo ⅋ **1977** Eek! Hairy spiders terrizing our sleepy town and destroying our orange crop! Made-for-TV cheapie not creepy; will make you sleepy. **100m/C VHS.** Claude Akins, Charles Frank, Deborah Winters, Pat Hingle, Sandy McPeak, Bert Remsen, Howard Hesseman, Tom Atkins, Charles Siebert; ***D:*** Stuart Hagmann. *LIV*

Taras Bulba ⅋⅋½ **1962** Well-photographed costume epic on the 16th century Polish revolution. Brynner as the fabled Cossack; Curtis plays his vengeful son. Good score. Shot on location in Argentina. Based on the novel by Nikolai Gogol. **122m/C VHS, LV.** Tony Curtis, Yul Brynner, Christine Kaufmann, Sam Wanamaker, George Macready, Vladimir Sokoloff, Perry Lopez; ***D:*** J. Lee Thompson. Nominations: Academy Awards '62: Best Original Score. *MGM*

Target ⅋⅋ **1985 (R)** Normal dad/hubby Hackman slips into a figurative phone booth and emerges as former CIA when his better half is kidnapped in Paris. Good action scenes, but poorly scripted and too long. **117m/C VHS, Beta, LV.** Gene Hackman, Matt Dillon, Gayle Hunnicutt, Josef Sommer; ***D:*** Arthur Penn; ***W:*** Howard Berk. *FOX*

Target Eagle ⅋⅋ **1984** Spanish police chief von Sydow hires mercenary Rivero to infiltrate drug ring. Good performances; ho-hum story. **99m/C VHS, Beta.** *SP MX* Max von Sydow, George Peppard, Maud Adams, Chuck Connors, George Rivero, Susana Dosamantes; ***D:*** J. Anthony Loma. *NO*

Target: Favorite Son ⅋⅋ **1987 (R)** An attractive, ammunition-laden woman sharp-shoots her way to power in this made-for-TV movie. **115m/C VHS.** Linda Kozlowski, Harry Hamlin, Robert Loggia, Ronny Cox, James Whitmore. *VMK*

Target for Killing ⅋⅋ **1966** Mediocre thriller about a secret agent who must protect a young heiress from a Lebanese syndicate that's out to kill her. **93m/C VHS.** Stewart Granger, Curt Jurgens, Molly Peters, Adolfo Celi, Klaus Kinski, Rupert Davies; ***D:*** Manfred Kohler. *SNC*

Targets ⅋⅋⅋ **1968 (PG)** Bogdanovich's suspenseful directorial debut. An aging horror film star plans his retirement, convinced that real life is too scary for his films to have an audience. A mad sniper at a drive-in movie seems to prove he's right. Some prints still have anti-gun prologue, which was added after Robert Kennedy's assassination. **90m/C VHS, Beta.** Boris Karloff, James Brown, Tim O'Kelly; ***D:*** Peter Bogdanovich; ***W:*** Peter Bogdanovich. *PAR*

Tarka the Otter **198?** The story of Tarka the Otter who encounters many dangers as he pursues his favorite eel meals. **91m/C VHS, Beta.** *TWE*

Tarnished Angels ⅋⅋⅋ **1957** Reporter Burke Devlin (Hudson) is writing a story for the local New Orleans paper about a tormented trio of air circus barmstormers. A former WWI ace, Roger Shumann (Stack) cares more about flying than he does his sizzling wife Laverne (Malone), who's loved-from-afar by loyal mechanic Jiggs (Carson). When Roger's plane cracks up, he uses his wife to obtain use of an experimental aircraft in order to win a race—and brings disaster crashing around them all. Good action, fine cast. Based on William Faulkner's 1930 novel "Pylon." **91m/B VHS.** Rock Hudson, Robert Stack, Dorothy Malone, Jack Carson, Robert Middleton, Troy Donahue, Alan Reed, Robert J. Wilke, William Schallert; ***D:*** Douglas Sirk; ***W:*** George Zuckerman; ***C:*** Irving Glassberg; ***M:*** Frank Skinner. *MCA*

Tartuffe ⅋⅋½ **1984** Popular French leading man Depardieu makes directorial debut with Moliere classic about religious hypocrisy and an imposter taking advantage of a wealthy merchant and his family. In French with English subtitles. **140m/C VHS, LV.** *FR* Gerard Depardieu, Francois Perier, Elisabeth Depardieu; ***D:*** Gerard Depardieu. *CVC, FCT, APD*

Tartuffe 🦴🦴½ **1990** Moliere's famous comedy has Tartuffe posing as a holy man who has attracted the incredulous merchant Orgon. Orgon is willing to give Tartuffe anything—money, social position, even his daughter—and Tartuffe is more than happy to accept. **110m/C VHS, Beta.** Anthony Sher, Nigel Hawthorne, Alison Steadman; ***D:*** Bill Alexander. *TTC, INJ*

Tarzan and His Mate 🦴🦴🦴 **1934** Second entry in the lavishly produced MGM Tarzan series. Weissmuller and O'Sullivan cohabit in unmarried bliss before the Hays Code moved them to a tree house with twin beds. Many angry elephants, nasty white hunters, and hungry lions. Laserdisc includes the original trailer. **93m/B VHS, LV.** Johnny Weissmuller, Maureen O'Sullivan, Neil Hamilton, Paul Cavanagh; ***D:*** Jack Conway; ***C:*** Clyde De Vinna. *MGM, FCT*

Tarzan and the Green Goddess 🦴½ *New Adventures of Tarzan* **1938** Tarzan searches for a statue that could prove dangerous if in the wrong hands. **72m/B VHS, Beta.** Bruce (Herman Brix) Bennett, Ula Holt, Frank Baker; ***D:*** Edward Kull. *HHT, SNC, VYY*

Tarzan and the Trappers 🦴½ **1958** Bad-guy trappers and would-be treasure-seekers wish they hadn't messed with the ape man. **74m/B VHS, Beta.** Gordon Scott, Eve Brent, Ricky Sorenson, Maurice Marsac; ***D:*** H. Bruce Humberstone. *SNC, NOS, VYY*

Tarzan Escapes 🦴🦴🦴 **1936** Jane is tricked by evil hunters into abandoning her fairy tale life with Tarzan, so the Ape Man sets out to reunite with his one true love. The third entry in MGM's Weissmuller/O'Sullivan series is still among the better Tarzan movies thanks to the leads, but the Hays Office made sure Jane was wearing a lot more clothes this time around. **95m/B VHS.** Johnny Weissmuller, Maureen O'Sullivan, John Buckler, Benita Hume, William Henry; ***D:*** Richard Thorpe. *FOX, FCT*

Tarzan Finds a Son 🦴🦴🦴 **1939** Weissmuller and O'Sullivan returned to their roles after three years with the addition of the five-year-old Sheffield as Boy. He's an orphan whose awful relatives hope he stays lost so they can collect an inheritance. Jane and Tarzan fight to adopt the tyke and when the new family are captured by a wicked tribe only an elephant stampede can save them! **90m/B VHS.** Johnny Weissmuller, Maureen O'Sullivan, Johnny Sheffield, Ian Hunter, Henry Stephenson, Frieda Inescort, Henry Wilcoxon; ***D:*** Richard Thorpe. *MGM*

Tarzan of the Apes 🦴🦴 **1917** Brawny Lincoln is the original screen Tarzan. Silent film well done and more faithful to the book than later versions. **63m/B VHS, Beta.** Elmo Lincoln, Enid Markey; ***D:*** Scott Sidney. *GPV, VYY, WFV*

Tarzan, the Ape Man 🦴🦴🦴 **1932** The definitive Tarzan movie; the first Tarzan talkie; the original of the long series starring Weissmuller. Dubiously faithful to the Edgar Rice Burroughs story, but recent attempts to remake, update or improve it (notably the pretentious 1984 Greystoke) have failed to near the original's entertainment value or even its technical quality. O'Sullivan as Jane and Weissmuller bring style and wit to their classic roles. **99m/B VHS, Beta, LV.** Johnny Weissmuller, Maureen O'Sullivan, Neil Hamilton; ***D:*** Woodbridge S. Van Dyke; ***C:*** Clyde De Vinna. *MGM, FCT*

Tarzan, the Ape Man *Woof!* **1981 (R)** Plodding, perverted excuse to see Derek cavort nude in jungle. So bad not even hard-core Tarzan fans should bother. **112m/C VHS, Beta, LV.** Bo Derek, Richard Harris, John Phillip Law, Miles O'Keeffe; ***D:*** John Derek; ***M:*** Perry Botkin. Golden Raspberry Awards '81: Worst Actress (Derek). *MGM*

Tarzan the Fearless 🦴½ **1933** Tarzan (Crabbe) helps a young girl find her missing father. **84m/B VHS, Beta.** Buster Crabbe, Jacqueline Wells, E. Alyn Warren, Edward Woods, Philo McCullough, Matthew Betz; ***D:*** Robert F. "Bob" Hill. *SNC, NOS, CAB*

Tarzan the Tiger **1929** Series of 15 chapters is loosely based on the Edgar Rice Burroughs novel entitled "Tarzan and the Jewels of Opar." These chapters were filmed as silent pieces, and were later released with a musical score and synchronized sound effects. Here Merrill is the first to sound the cry of the bull ape, Tarzan's trademark. **?m/B VHS.** Frank Merrill, Natalie Kingston, Lilian Worth, Al Ferguson; ***D:*** Henry MacRae. *NOS, FCT, MOV*

Tarzana, the Wild Girl 🦴 **1972** Jungle cheapie about an expedition that finds a beautiful, scantily clad girl living wildly in the jungle. **87m/C VHS.** Kenneth Clark, Franca Polesello, Frank Ressel, Andrew Ray, James Reed; ***W:*** Philip Shaw. *SNC*

Tarzan's New York Adventure 🦴🦴½ **1942** O'Sullivan's final appearance as Jane is a so-so adventure with some humorous moments when Tarzan meets the big city. When Boy is kidnapped by an evil circus owner, Tarzan, Jane, and Cheta head out to rescue him. Tarzan shows off his jungle prowess by climbing skyscrapers and diving off the Brooklyn Bridge into the Hudson River. Lincoln, the screen's first Tarzan, has a cameo. **70m/B VHS.** Johnny Weissmuller, Maureen O'Sullivan, Johnny Sheffield, Virginia Grey, Charles Bickford, Paul Kelly, Chill Wills, Russell Hicks, Cy Kendall; ***Cameos:*** Elmo Lincoln; ***D:*** Richard Thorpe. *MGM*

Tarzan's Revenge 🦴 **1938** Morris is a better Olympic runner than actor; Holm is horrible. Only for serious Tarzan fans. **70m/B VHS, Beta.** Glenn Morris, Eleanor Holm, Hedda Hopper; ***D:*** David Ross Lederman. *SNC, NOS, VYY*

Tarzan's Secret Treasure 🦴🦴½ **1941** Tarzan saves an expedition from a savage tribe only to be repaid by having the greedy hunters hold Jane and Boy hostage. They want Tarzan's help in finding a secret cache of gold. But Tarzan doesn't take kindly to threats to his family and teaches those evil-doers a lesson! **81m/B VHS.** Johnny Weissmuller, Maureen O'Sullivan, Johnny Sheffield, Reginald Owen, Barry Fitzgerald, Tom Conway, Philip Dorn; ***D:*** Richard Thorpe. *MGM*

Task Force 🦴🦴½ **1949** History of naval aviation and the development of the aircraft carrier highlighted by actual WWII combat footage (in color). Cooper and his naval buddies try to convince the brass that planes can be landed on the decks of ships. Slowly the Navy goes ahead and when Pearl Harbor is attacked, Cooper is given command of his own aircraft carrier. The use of the carriers proved very effective in Pacific battles and Cooper is finally vindicated. **116m/B VHS, Beta.** Gary Cooper, Jane Wyatt, Wayne Morris, Walter Brennan, Julie London, Bruce (Herman Brix) Bennett, Jack Holt, Stanley Ridges, John Ridgely, Richard Rober, Art Baker, Moroni Olsen; ***D:*** Delmer Daves; ***W:*** Delmer Daves. *MGM, FCT*

A Taste for Flesh and Blood **1990 (R)** A monster from outer space comes to earth and is delighted with the easy pickings for his insatiable appetite. A brave boy and girl, and a NASA commander must join forces to take the alien out. This one is billed as a campy salute to '50s B movies. **84m/C VHS.** Rubin Santiago, Lori Karz, Tim Ferrante. *NO*

A Taste for Killing 🦴🦴 **1992 (R)** Two boys, both from well-to-do families, decide to take summer jobs on an offshore Texas oil rig. The best friends think a summer of adventure awaits them; however, their lives are made miserable by their blue-collar boss, who is resentful of their high society background. Then they meet Bo Landry, who befriends them and helps them survive. Unfortunately, Bo turns out to be anything but a friend as he reveals himself as a deadly con-artist in this intense psychological thriller. **87m/C VHS, LV.** Jason Bateman, Henry Thomas, Michael Biehn, Blue Deckert, Helen Cates; ***D:*** Lou Antonio; ***W:*** Dan Bronson. *MCA*

Taste of Death 🦴 **1977** A youth discovers his courage within when he stands up to the bandits invading his village. **90m/C VHS, Beta.** John Ireland. *NO*

A Taste of Hell 🦴 **1973 (PG)** Two American soldiers fight a guerilla outfit in the Pacific during WWII. A low-budget film with few redeeming characteristics. **90m/C VHS, Beta.** William Smith, John Garwood. *NWV, VTR*

A Taste of Honey 🦴🦴🦴 **1961** A plain working-class girl falls in love with a black sailor. When she becomes pregnant, a homosexual friend helps her out. A moving film with strong, powerful performances. Based on the London and Broadway hit play by Shelagh Delaney. **100m/B VHS.** *GB* Rita Tushingham, Robert Stephens, Dora Bryan, Murray Melvin, Paul Danquah; ***D:*** Tony Richardson; ***W:*** Tony Richardson, Shelagh Delaney; ***C:*** Walter Lassally; ***M:*** John Addison. British Academy Awards '61: Best Film, Best Supporting Actress (Bryan); Cannes Film Festival '62: Best Actor (Melvin), Best Actress (Tushingham). *NO*

Taste the Blood of Dracula 🦴🦴½ **1970 (PG)** Lee's Dracula only makes a brief appearance in this Hammer horror film which has three children taking over from the bloodsucker. Three Victorian dandies have killed the wizard who revived Dracula and he seeks their deaths by using their own children as the means of his revenge. Not enough Lee but still creepy. Preceded by "Dracula Has Risen from the Grave" and followed by "Scars of Dracula." **91m/C VHS.** *GB* Christopher Lee, Ralph Bates, Geoffrey Keen, Gwen Watford, Linda Hayden, John Carson, Peter Sallis, Isla Blair, Martin Jarvis, Roy Kinnear; ***D:*** Peter Sasdy; ***M:*** James Bernard. *WAR*

Tatie Danielle 🦴🦴🦴 **1991** Pitch-black comedy from the director of "Life Is a Long Quiet River" sees a bitter, elderly widow moving in with her young nephew and making his life a hell. In French with yellow English subtitles. **114m/C VHS, LV.** *FR* Tsilla Chelton, Catherine Jacob, Isabelle Nanty, Neige Dolsky, Eric Prat, Laurence Fevrier; ***D:*** Etienne Chatiliez; ***W:*** Etienne Chatiliez. *LIV, INJ*

The Tattered Web 🦴🦴 **1971** A police sergeant confronts and accidently kills the woman with whom his son-in-law has been cheating. He's then assigned the case. When he tries to frame a wino for the murder, things get more and more messy. Fine performances aid this made-for-television story. **74m/C VHS, Beta.** Lloyd Bridges, Frank Converse, Broderick Crawford, Murray Hamilton, Sallie Shockley; ***D:*** Paul Wendkos. *ORI*

Tattle Tale 🦴½ **1992 (PG)** Vindictive ex-wife writes book accusing her actor ex of abusing her and he loses out on his career-breaking role. So he decides to disguise himself and seduce her into telling the truth. Even dumber than it sounds. **96m/C VHS, LV.** C. Thomas Howell, Ally Sheedy; ***D:*** Baz Taylor. *LIV*

Tattoo 🦴🦴 **1981 (R)** A model becomes the object of obsession for a crazy tattoo artist. He relentlessly pursues her, leaving behind all his other more illustrated clients. Starts out fine, but deteriorates rapidly. Controversial love scene between Dern and Adams. **103m/C VHS, Beta.** Bruce Dern, Maud Adams, Leonard Frey, Rikke Borge, John Getz; ***D:*** Bob Brooks; ***W:*** Joyce Bunuel. *FOX*

Tattoo Connection 🦴 **1978 (R)** A gang of lethal Oriental diamond thieves is pursued with whip-snapping flamboyance by a taciturn kung-fu investigator. **95m/C VHS, Beta.** Jim Kelly; ***D:*** Luk Pak Sang. *SUE, ORI*

Tattooed Hit Man 🦴 **1976** Japanese gangster violence in a revenge-doesn't-pay action story. **81m/C VHS, Beta.** *JP* Mayumi Nagisa, Bunta Sugawara, Tsunehiko Watase. *MED*

Tax Season 🦴🦴 **1990 (PG-13)** A small-time businessman buys a Hollywood tax service sight-unseen, and finds it employing a hooker, a bookie and a variety of other unconventional types. **93m/C VHS, Beta.** Fritz Bronner, James Hong, Jana Grant, Toru Tanaka, Dorie Krum, Kathryn Knotts, Arte Johnson, Rob Slyker; ***D:*** Tom Law. *PAR*

Taxi Blues 🦴🦴🦴½ **1990** A political allegory with the two protagonists representing the new and old Soviet Union. A hard-working, narrow-minded cabdriver keeps the saxophone of a westernized, Jewish, jazz-loving musician who doesn't have his fare. The two strike up a wary friendship as each tries to explain his view of life to the other. Good look at the street life of Moscow populated by drunks, punks, and black marketeers. Directorial debut of

Lounguine. In Russian with English subtitles. **110m/C VHS.** *RU* Piotr Mamonov, Piotr Zaitchenko, Natalia Koliakanova, Vladimir Kachpour; ***D:*** Pavel Lounguine; ***W:*** Pavel Lounguine. Cannes Film Festival '90: Best Director (Lounguine). *NYF, INJ*

Taxi Dancers ½ **1993** Smalltown Billie arrives in Hollywood with dreams of becoming an actress. Naturally, her dreams turn to despair and she resorts to "dancing" at the Shark Club where she becomes involved with a gambler who owes money to the wrong people. **97m/C VHS, LV.** Sonny Landham, Robert Miano, Brittany McCrena, Tina Fite, Mirage Micheaux, Michele Hess, Randall Irwin; ***D:*** Norman Thaddeus Vane; ***W:*** Norman Thaddeus Vane; ***M:*** Larry Blank. *AIP*

Taxi Driver **1976 (R)** A psychotic New York City taxi driver tries to save a child prostitute and becomes infatuated with an educated political campaigner. He goes on a violent rampage when his dreams don't work out. Repellant, frightening vision of alienation and urban catharsis. On-target performances from Foster and De Niro. The laserdisc version is slightly longer, with commentary by Scorsese and screenwriter Paul Schrader, storyboards, complete screenplay, and Scorsese's production photos. **112m/C VHS, Beta, LV, 8mm.** Robert De Niro, Jodie Foster, Harvey Keitel, Cybill Shepherd, Peter Boyle, Albert Brooks; ***D:*** Martin Scorsese; ***W:*** Paul Schrader; ***C:*** Michael Chapman. British Academy Awards '76: Best Supporting Actress (Foster); Cannes Film Festival '76: Best Film; Los Angeles Film Critics Association Awards '76: Best Actor (De Niro); New York Film Critics Awards '76: Best Actor (De Niro); National Society of Film Critics Awards '76: Best Actor (De Niro), Best Director (Scorsese), Best Supporting Actress (Foster); Nominations: Academy Awards '76: Best Actor (De Niro), Best Picture, Best Supporting Actress (Foster), Best Original Score. *COL*

The Taxi Mystery **1926** Guy saves Broadway starlet from band of ne'er-do-wells thanks to deserted taxi, then tries to figure out who she is, unaware that her sinister understudy plans to do her in. **50m/B VHS, Beta.** Edith Roberts, Robert Agnew, Virginia Pearson, Phillips Smalley; ***D:*** Fred Windermere. *GPV*

Taxi zum Klo **1981** An autobiographical semi-documentary about the filmmaker's aimless existence and attempts at homosexual affairs after being fired from his job as a teacher. Explicit. In German with English subtitles. Sordid sexual situations. **98m/C VHS, Beta.** *GE* Bernd Broaderup, Frank Ripploh; ***D:*** Frank Ripploh. *FCT, GLV, CCN*

A Taxing Woman ½ *Marusa No Onna* **1987** Satiric Japanese comedy about a woman tax collector in pursuit of a crafty millionaire tax cheater. Followed by the equally hilarious "A Taxing Woman's Return." In Japanese with English subtitles. **127m/C VHS, Beta, LV.** *JP* Nobuko Miyamoto, Tsutomu Yamazaki; ***D:*** Juzo Itami; ***W:*** Juzo Itami. *FXL, INJ, LUM*

A Taxing Woman's Return *Marusa No Onna II* **1988** Funny, sophisticated, action-packed. Miyamoto returns as the dedicated tax investigator to fight industrialists, politicians, and other big swindlers, who have contrived to inflate Tokyo's real estate values. Sequel to "A Taxing Woman." In Japanese with English subtitles. **127m/C VHS, LV.** *JP* Nobuko Miyamoto, Rentaro Mikuni, Masahiko Tsugawa, Tetsuro Tamba, Toru Masuoka, Takeya Nakamura, Hosei Komatsu, Mihoko Shibata; ***D:*** Juzo Itami; ***W:*** Juzo Itami. *NYF, INJ*

TC 2000 ½ **1993 (R)** Jason Storm and Zoey Kinsella are cops working for The Controller, who has the unenviable task of protecting the community from roving gangs of vicious punks. When Zoey is killed, The Controller converts her into a super-cybernetic killing machine unleashed on the gangs. Meanwhile Jason is considered a liability and must battle the gangs, The Controller, and cyber-Zoey to save himself. Oh, there's also something about saving the Earth's atmosphere from nuclear destruction. Lots of action. **92m/C VHS, LV.** Billy Blanks, Bobbie Philips, Jalal Merhi, Bolo Yeung, Matthias Hues; ***D:*** T.J. Scott; ***W:*** T.J. Scott. *MCA, SGE*

Tchaikovsky ½ **1971** The glorious music is all that saves this pedestrian biography of the 19th century Russian composer, which ignores his homosexuality and glosses over the dissolution of his marriage. Lead performance by Smoktunovsky does manage to rise above the moribund script. Originally released at 191 minutes. In Russian with English subtitles. **153m/C VHS.** *RU* Innokenti Smoktunovsky, Antonina Shuranova, Yevgeny Leonov, Maya Plisetskaya, Vladislav Strzeltchik, Alla Demidova, Kirill Lavrov; ***D:*** Igor Talankin. Nominations: Academy Awards '71: Best Foreign Language Film. *KIV, FCT*

Tchao Pantin **1984** An acclaimed French film noir about an ex-cop being drawn into drug smuggling underground via a young Arab. English subtitles. Finely drawn characters skillfully portrayed make this a winner. **100m/C VHS, Beta.** *FR* Coluche, Richard Anconina, Agnes Soral; ***D:*** Claude Berri. Cesar Awards '84: Best Actor (Coluche), Best Cinematography, Best Sound, Best Supporting Actor (Anconina). *SUE*

Tea and Sympathy **1956** A young prep school student, confused about his sexuality, has an affair with an older woman, his teacher's wife. The three leads recreate their Broadway roles in this tame adaption of the Robert Anderson play which dealt more openly with the story's homosexual elements. **122m/C VHS, LV.** Deborah Kerr, John Kerr, Leif Erickson, Edward Andrews, Darryl Hickman, Norma Crane, Dean Jones; ***D:*** Vincente Minnelli; ***W:*** Robert Anderson; ***C:*** John Alton. *MGM, FCT*

Tea For Three **1984 (R)** Sexual trio develops and seeks therapy after a fledgling doctor has been having sexual relationships with two women, and the females finally meet. **89m/C VHS, Beta.** Iris Berben, Mascha Gonska, Heinz Marecek; ***D:*** Gerhard Janda. *MED*

Tea for Two **1950** This take-off on the Broadway play "No, No, Nanette" features Day as an actress who takes a bet that she can answer "no" to every question for twenty-four hours (life was less complex back then). If she can, she gets to finance and star in her own Broadway musical. ♫I Know That You Know; Crazy Rhythm; Charleston; I Only Have Eyes For You; Tea For Two; I Want to be Happy; Oh Me, Oh My; The Call of the Sea; Do Do Do. **98m/C VHS.** Doris Day, Gordon MacRae, Gene Nelson, Patrice Wymore, Eve Arden, Billy DeWolfe, S.Z. Sakall, Bill Goodwin, Virginia Gibson, Crauford Kent, Harry Harvey; ***D:*** David Butler. *WAR, CCB, MVD*

The Teacher *The Seductress* **1974 (R)** TV's "Dennis the Menace" (North) has an affair with his high school teacher; the pair is menaced by a deranged killer. Cheap but enjoyable. **97m/C VHS, Beta, LV.** Angel Tompkins, Jay North, Anthony James; ***D:*** Howard (Hikmet) Avedis. *NO*

Teachers **1984 (R)** A lawsuit is brought against a high school for awarding a diploma to an illiterate student. Comedy-drama starts slowly and seems to condemn the school system, never picking up strength or resolving any issues, though Nolte is fairly intense. Shot in Columbus, Ohio. **106m/C VHS, Beta, LV.** Nick Nolte, JoBeth Williams, Lee Grant, Judd Hirsch, Ralph Macchio, Richard Mulligan, Royal Dano, Morgan Freeman, Laura Dern, Crispin Glover, Madeline Sherwood, Zohra Lampert; ***D:*** Arthur Hiller. *MGM, FOX*

Teacher's Pet **1958** This charming comedy features a cynical newspaper editor who enrolls in a night college journalism course, believing that it won't teach anything of substance. He later becomes enamored of his instructor. Well written script and superb performance by Young as Gable's rival for Day. **120m/B VHS, Beta.** Clark Gable, Doris Day, Mamie Van Doren, Gig Young, Nick Adams; ***D:*** George Seaton; ***W:*** Fay Kanin, Michael Kanin. Nominations: Academy Awards '58: Best Story & Screenplay, Best Supporting Actor (Young). *PAR, BAR*

The Teahouse of the August Moon ½ **1956** An adaptation of the John Patrick play. Post-war American troops are assigned to bring civilization to a small village in Okinawa and instead fall for Okinawan culture and romance. Lively cast keeps it generally working, but assessments of Brando's comedic performance vary widely. **123m/C VHS, Beta, LV.** Glenn Ford, Marlon Brando, Eddie Albert, Paul Ford, Machiko Kyo, Harry (Henry) Morgan; ***D:*** Daniel Mann; ***C:*** John Alton. *MGM*

Teamster Boss: The Jackie Presser Story **1992 (R)** A well-done made-for-cable-television movie powered by a riveting performance by Dennehy. Presser followed Jimmy Hoffa as president of the Teamsters and was equally caught between the mob and the government as he tried to do what he considered best for the union. **111m/C VHS, LV.** Brian Dennehy, Jeff Daniels, Maria Conchita Alonso, Eli Wallach, Robert Prosky, Donald Moffat, Tony LoBianco, Kate Reid, Henderson Forsythe, Al Waxman; ***D:*** Alastair Reid. *HBO, PMS*

Tearaway ½ **1987 (R)** Australian story of a street punk with an alcoholic father. Story has potential, but ends up going nowhere. **100m/C VHS, Beta.** *NZ AU* Matthew Hunter, Mark Pilisi, Peter Bland, Kim Willoughby, Rebecca Saunders; ***D:*** Bruce Morrison. *ORI, WAR*

Tears in the Rain **1988** Casey Cantrell (Stone) travels to London to deliver a deathbed letter from her mother to Lord Richard Bredon. While in England, she is pursued by two men, an heir to the Bredon fortune, and his wealthy friend. After she finds a love which is forbidden, she makes a bizarre discovery that changes her life forever. Made for British television. **100m/C VHS.** *GB* Sharon Stone, Christopher Cazenove, Leigh Lawson, Paul Daneman; ***D:*** Don Sharp. *VCO*

Tecumseh: The Last Warrior ½ **1995** Oh-so-noble TV biography of the Shawnee leader (1768-1813) and his refusal to give up the battle against white settlement of the Indiana Territory. North Carolina substitutes for Ohio and Indiana. Based on the book "Panther in the Sky" by James Alexander Thom. **90m/C VHS.** Jesse Borrego, David Clennon, Tantoo Cardinal, David Morse, Holt McCallany, August Schellenberg, Jimmie F. Skaggs, Jeri Arrendondo; ***D:*** Larry Elikann; ***W:*** Paul F. Edwards; ***M:*** David Shire. *TTC*

Ted & Venus ½ **1993 (R)** Cort plays Ted, an oddball cult poet in love with Linda, a beach beauty who finds him repulsive. The more she rejects him, the more obsessed about her Ted gets, especially when his equally oddball friends offer him romantic advice. **100m/C VHS.** Bud Cort, Kim Adams, Rhea Perlman, James Brolin, Carol Kane; ***Cameos:*** Gena Rowlands, Martin Mull, Woody Harrelson, Andrea Martin, Timothy Leary, Cassandra Peterson; ***D:*** Bud Cort; ***W:*** Bud Cort, Paul Ciotti. *COL*

Teddy at the Throttle **1916** Teddy, the Great Dane, must rescue Gloria Swanson from a villain who has tied up her boyfriend. Silent. **20m/B VHS, Beta.** Bobby Vernon, Gloria Swanson, Wallace Beery; ***D:*** Clarence Badger. *CCB*

Teddy at the Throttle/Speeding Along **1917** A silent comedy about stealing fortunes from innocent heroines and another about racing cars in a farm area. **54m/B VHS, Beta.** Gloria Swanson, Wallace Beery, Bobby Vernon. *VYY*

Teen Alien *The Varrow Mission* **1988 (PG)** On Halloween, a young boy and his friends run into a hostile alien. It could happen. **88m/C VHS, Beta.** Vern Adix; ***D:*** Peter Senelka. *PSM*

Teen Mothers *Seed of Innocence* **1980 (R)** Bittersweet story of two unwed teenagers forced to take their child and leave home for the tenements of New York. **91m/C VHS, Beta.** *NO*

Teen Vamp **1988** Dorky high schooler is bitten by a prostitute; becomes a cool vampire. Mindless "comedy." **87m/C VHS, Beta.** Clu Gulager, Karen Carlson, Angela Brown; ***D:*** Samuel Bradford. *VTR, NWV*

Teen Witch **1989 (PG-13)** A demure high schooler uses black magic to woo the most popular guy in school. **94m/C VHS, Beta.** Robin Lively, Zelda Rubinstein, Dan Gauthier, Joshua Miller, Dick Sargent; ***D:*** Dorian Walker; ***W:*** Robin Menken. *MED, VTR*

Teen Wolf 🦴🦴½ **1985 (PG)** A nice, average teenage basketball player begins to show werewolf tendencies which suddenly make him popular at school when he leads the team to victory. The underlying message is to be yourself, regardless of how much hair you have on your body. Lighthearted comedy carried by the Fox charm; followed by subpar "Teen Wolf Too." **92m/C VHS, Beta, LV, 8mm.** Michael J. Fox, James Hampton, Scott Paulin, Susan Ursitti; ***D:*** Rod Daniel; ***M:*** Miles Goodman. *PAR*

Teen Wolf Too 🦴🦴 **1987 (PG)** The sequel to "Teen Wolf" in which the Teen Wolf's cousin goes to college on a boxing scholarship. More evidence that the sequel is rarely as good as the original. **95m/C VHS, Beta.** Jason Bateman, Kim Darby, John Astin, Paul Sand; ***D:*** Christopher Leitch. *PAR*

Teenage 🦴 **1944** Low budget juvenile schlock film that tries to figure out what's wrong with modern youth. Pure camp. **?m/C VHS.** Herbert Heyes, Wheeler Oakman. *SNC*

Teenage Bad Girl 🦴🦴½ *Bad Girl; My Teenage Daughter* **1959** A woman who edits a magazine for teenagers can't control her own daughter. The kid does time in the pen after staying out all night and generally running around with the wrong crowd. Syms first lead performance is memorable in an otherwise routine teensploitation flick. **100m/B VHS, Beta.** Anna Neagle, Sylvia Syms, Norman Wooland, Wilfrid Hyde-White, Kenneth Haigh, Julia Lockwood; ***D:*** Herbert Wilcox. *SNC, DVT*

Teenage Bonnie & Klepto Clyde 🦴½ **1993 (R)** Like their 30s namesakes Clyde Barrow and Bonnie Parker are just two high-spirited kids who let their need for excitement get in the way of their better judgement (ha!). Bonnie and Clyde meet in a fast-food joint, become shoplifting buddies, fall in love, graduate to armed robbery, try to run for the border, and die. **90m/C VHS.** Maureen Flannigan, Scott Wolf; ***Cameos:*** Don Novello. *VMK*

Teenage Caveman 🦴🦴 *Out of the Darkness; Prehistoric World* **1958** A teenage boy living in a post-apocalypse yet prehistoric world journeys across the river, even though he was warned against it, and finds an old man who owns a book about past civilizations in the 20th Century. Schlocky, and one of the better bad films around. The dinosaur shots were picked up from the film "One Million B.C." **66m/B VHS.** Robert Vaughn, Darrah Marshall, Leslie Bradley, Frank De Kova; ***D:*** Roger Corman. *COL*

Teenage Crime Wave 🦴 **1955** Route 66 provides thrills for a couple of teen punks, but things get out of hand when they blow a sheriff's head off. They scoop up a couple of babes and hightail it with the police close behind, ultimately confronting their destiny at a mountain top observatory. **77m/B VHS, Beta.** Tommy Cook, Mollie McCart, Sue England, Frank Griffin, James Bell, Kay Riehl; ***D:*** Fred F. Sears. *SNC, AOV*

Teenage Devil Dolls 🦴 **1953** A cheap exploitation teenage flick wherein an innocent girl is turned on to reefer and goofballs, and eventually ends up on the street. **70m/C VHS, Beta.** Barbara Marks, Bramlef L. Price Jr.; ***D:*** B. Lawrence Price. *RHI*

Teenage Exorcist 🦴½ **1993** Tired horror spoof finds the prim Diane (Stevens) renting a creepy house from an equally creepy real estate agent (Berryman). After she moves in, Diane begins having horrible nightmares and calls her family for help. When they arrive Diane has turned into a chainsaw-wielding seductress. The family is so distressed that they misdial the phone and wind up with a pizza delivery geek (Deezen) instead of the exorcist they need. **90m/C VHS, LV.** Brinke Stevens, Eddie Deezen, Michael Berryman, Robert Quarry, Jay Richardson, Tom Shell, Elena Sahagun; ***D:*** Grant Austin Waldman; ***W:*** Brinke Stevens. *AIP*

Teenage Frankenstein 🦴½ **1958** A descendent of Dr. Frankenstein makes his own scramble-faced monster out of a teenage boy. Lurid '50s drive-in fare (companion to "I Was a Teenage Werewolf") is campy fun in small doses only. **72m/B VHS.** Whit Bissell, Phyllis Coates, Robert Burton, Gary Conway, George Lynn, John Cliff; ***D:*** Herbert L. Strock. *COL*

Teenage Gang Debs 🦴 **1966** These chicks throw a sleazy coming out party the likes of which defy description. Simply the most important social function of 1966. **77m/B VHS.** Diana Conti, Linda Gale, Eileen Scott, Sandra Kane, Robin Nolan, Linda Cambi, Sue McManus, Geri Tyler, Joey Naudic, John Batis, Tom Yourk, Thomas Andrisano, George Winship, Doug Mitchell, Tom Eldred, Frank Spinella, Alec Primrose, Gene Marrin, Lyn Kennedy, Janet Banzet; ***D:*** Sande Johnsen; ***W:*** Hy Cahl. *SMW, TPV*

Teenage Mother *Woof!* **1967** A Swedish sex education teacher comes to town and poisons the minds of the local high school kids. Naturally one becomes pregnant and has to try to trick the father into marrying her. More awful stuff from the director of "Girl On a Chain Gang." **78m/C VHS, Beta.** Arlene Sue Farber, Frederick Riccio, Julie Ange, Howard Le May, George Peters; ***D:*** Jerry Gross. *SNC, TPV*

Teenage Mutant Ninja Turtles: The Movie 🦴🦴½ **1990 (PG)** Four sewer-dwelling turtles that have turned into warrior ninja mutants due to radiation exposure take it upon themselves to rid the city of crime and pizza. Aided by a television reporter and their ninja master, Splinter the Rat, the turtles encounter several obstacles, including the evil warlord Shredder. A most excellent live-action version of the popular comic book characters which will hold the kids' interest. Much head-kicking and rib-crunching action as Leonardo, Donatello, Raphael, and Michelangelo fight for the rights of pre-adolescents everywhere. Combines real actors with Jim Henson creatures. **95m/C VHS, Beta, LV, 8mm.** Judith Hoag, Elias Koteas; ***D:*** Steven Barron; ***W:*** Todd W. Langen; ***M:*** John Du Prez; ***V:*** Robbie Rist, Corey Feldman, Brian Tochi, Kevin Clash, David McCharen. *FHE, LIV, WTA*

Teenage Mutant Ninja Turtles 2: The Secret of the Ooze 🦴🦴 **1991 (PG)** Amphibious pizza-devouring mutants search for the toxic waste that turned them into marketable martial artist ecologically correct kid idols. Same formula as the first go-round with some new characters tossed in. Animatronic characters from the laboratory of Jim Henson, first screen appearance by rapper Vanilla Ice. Marked end of pre-teen turtle craze. **88m/C VHS, Beta.** Francois Chau, David Warner, Paige Turco, Ernie Reyes Jr., Vanilla Ice; ***D:*** Michael Pressman. *COL, NLC*

Teenage Mutant Ninja Turtles 3 🦴🦴 **1993 (PG)** Check it out dudes; the Teenage Mutant Ninja Turtles hit 17th century Japan to rescue loyal friend, reporter April O'Neil. Plenty of smoothly executed, blood-free martial arts moves keep the pace rolling, while the turtles battle an evil lord and English pirates. Seeing the TMNT's use a little more of their reptilian grey matter, and snarf a little less pizza should contribute to a relatively high adult tolerance level (considering the genre), and loads of good clean fun for the kiddies. **95m/C VHS, LV.** Elias Koteas, Paige Turco, Stuart Wilson, Sab Shimono, Vivian Wu; ***D:*** Stuart Gillard; ***W:*** Stuart Gillard; ***M:*** John Du Prez; ***V:*** Randi Mayem Singer, Matt Hill, Jim Raposa, David Fraser. *NLC, COL, IME*

Teenage Strangler *Woof!* **1964** A homicidal teen terrorizes his school. Cheap film features drag races, rumbles, dances, babes, rock 'n' roll and more. One for the "bad enough to be fun" category. **61m/C VHS, Beta.** Bill A. Bloom, Jo Canterbury, John Ensign; ***D:*** Bill Posner. *SNC, SMW*

Teenage Wolfpack 🦴½ **1957** Boring film about German juvenile delinquents, robbery, violence, and murder. **90m/C VHS.** *GE* Horst Buchholz, Karin Baal, Christian Doermer; ***D:*** Georg Tressler. *SNC*

Teenage Zombies *Woof!* **1958** Mad scientist on remote island kidnaps teenagers and uses her secret chemical formula to turn them into zombies as part of her plan to enslave the world. Not as good as it sounds. **71m/B VHS, Beta.** Don Sullivan, Katherine Victor, Chuck Niles; ***D:*** Jerry Warren; ***W:*** Jacques LeCotier. *NOS, SNC, VYY*

Teenager 🦴 **1974 (R)** Three desperate, reckless individuals, all caught up in making a low budget movie, interact and eventually self-destruct. **91m/C VHS, Beta.** Andrea Cagan, Reid Smith, Susan Bernard; ***D:*** Gerald Seth Sindell. *NWV*

Teenagers from Outer Space *Woof!* *The Gargon Terror* **1959** Low-budget sci-fi effort finds extraterrestrial youngsters visiting earth to conquer it and find food for their "monstrous pets" (they're really lobster shadows.) So cheaply made and melodramatic that it just may be good for a laugh. **86m/B VHS.** Tom Graeff, Dawn Anderson, Harvey B. Dunn, Bryant Grant, Tom Lockyear; ***D:*** Tom Graeff. *SNC*

TekWar 🦴🦴½ **1994** It's 2044 and society is plagued by "Tek," an illegal, addictive drug-like computer disk that creates powerful but destructive virtual-reality fantasies. Jake Cardigan (Evigan) is an cop framed on drug and murder charges, fresh out of prison, who's trying to both clear his name and find out what happened to his now ex-wife and son. Shatner, who wrote the Tek novels, guests as Walter Bascom, the head of a detective agency who promises to help Cardigan if Jake helps find a missing scientist. Made for TV. **92m/C VHS.** Greg Evigan, Eugene C. Clark, Torri Higginson, William Shatner; ***D:*** William Shatner. *MCA*

Telefon 🦴🦴 **1977 (PG)** Suspenseful, slick spy tale. Soviet agents battle a lunatic comrade who tries to use hypnotized Americans to commit sabotage. Daly, later of TV's "Cagney and Lacey," is memorable. **102m/C VHS, Beta.** Charles Bronson, Lee Remick, Donald Pleasence, Tyne Daly, Patrick Magee, Sheree North; ***D:*** Donald Siegel; ***W:*** Stirling Silliphant, Peter Hyams; ***M:*** Lalo Schifrin. *MGM*

Telegraph Trail 🦴½ **1933** Weak Wayne entry about an Army scout who helps some workers complete the first transcontinental wire line. Of course, Wayne ends up getting tough with some Indians. Cheaply made, with most of the action footage lifted from the 1926 silent, "The Red Raiders." **60m/B VHS.** John Wayne, Marceline Day, Frank McHugh, Otis Harlan, Yakima Canutt, Lafe McKee; ***D:*** Tenny Wright; ***W:*** Kurt Kempler. *MGM*

The Telephone *Woof!* **1987 (R)** A neurotic out-of-work actress begins a comedic chain of events via a few prank phone calls. Goldberg has managed to salvage some bad material with the strength of her comedic performances, but not so here. In fact, she sued to prevent this version from ever seeing the light of day. Too bad she didn't have a better lawyer. Torn's directorial debut. **96m/C VHS, Beta, LV.** Whoopi Goldberg, Elliott Gould, John Heard, Amy Wright; ***D:*** Rip Torn; ***W:*** Terry Southern. *VTR, NWV*

Tell It to the Judge 🦴🦴½ **1949** Russell plays the exuberant ex-wife of lawyer Cummings. They repeatedly try reconciling but ditzy blonde McDonald always manages to catch Cummings' eye. Fed up Russell takes off for a holiday in the mountains where she meets Young. When her ex-hubby follows her, she decides to try and make him jealous using Young as the bait. **87m/B VHS.** Rosalind Russell, Robert Cummings, Gig Young, Marie McDonald, Harry Davenport, Louise Beavers; ***D:*** Norman Foster. *FCT*

Tell Me a Riddle 🦴🦴½ **1980 (PG)** A dying woman attempts to reconcile with her family in this poignant drama about an elderly couple rediscovering their mutual love after 47 years of marriage. Fine acting; Grant's directorial debut. **94m/C VHS, Beta.** Melvyn Douglas, Lila Kedrova, Brooke Adams, Peter Coyote; ***D:*** Lee Grant; ***W:*** Joyce Eliason. *MED*

Tell Me That You Love Me 🦴½ **1984 (R)** A tear-jerking portrait of a disintegrating modern marriage. **88m/C VHS, Beta.** Nick Mancuso, Barbara Williams, Belinda J. Montgomery; ***D:*** Tzipi Trope. *LIV, VES*

Tell Me Where It Hurts 🦴🦴 **1974** A middle-aged housewife changes her life when she forms a women's consciousness-raising group with her friends. The script won an Emmy. Stapleton's performance is redeeming in this otherwise slow movie. **78m/C VHS, Beta.** Maureen Stapleton, Paul Sorvino; ***D:*** Paul Bogart; ***M:*** David Shire. *LCA*

The Tell-Tale Heart 🦴🦴½ *The Hidden Room of 1,000 Horrors* **1962** Daydreaming author fantasizes about falling for major babe and killing his best friend for her. Adapted Poe tale. **78m/B VHS.** *GB* Laurence Payne, Adrienne Corri, Dermot Walsh, Selma Vaz Dias, John Scott, John Martin, Annette Carell, David Lander; ***D:*** Ernest Morris; ***W:*** Brian Clemens. *NOS, SNC, LOO*

Tell Them Willie Boy Is Here 🦴🦴🦴 **1969 (PG)** Western drama set in 1909 California about a Paiute Indian named Willie Boy and his white bride. They become the objects of a manhunt (led by the reluctant local sheriff, Redford) after Willie kills his wife's father in self-defense. This was once-blacklisted Polonsky's first film in 21 years. **98m/C VHS, Beta, LV.** Robert Redford, Katharine Ross, Robert (Bobby) Blake, Susan Clark, Barry Sullivan, John Vernon, Charles McGraw; ***D:*** Abraham Polonsky; ***W:*** Abraham Polonsky; ***C:*** Conrad Hall; ***M:*** Dave Grusin. *MCA*

The Temp *Woof!* **1993 (R)** Unbelievably bad attempt at office horror. Beautiful, mysterious Kris temps for Hutton, a junior exec at the Mrs. Appleby baked goods company. She's almost too good to be true with unbelievable organizational skills and her dead serious ambition to climb the corporate ladder. Pyscho-drama has pyscho, but lacks drama, direction, plot development, intelligent dialogue, and anything resembling motive. While Hutton is tolerable, we nominate ex-Twin Peaker Boyle for the bad acting hall of shame as the conniving psycho. **99m/C VHS, Beta, LV.** Timothy Hutton, Lara Flynn Boyle, Faye Dunaway, Dwight Schultz, Oliver Platt, Steven Weber, Scott Coffey, Colleen Flynn, Dakin Matthews, Maura Tierney; ***D:*** Tom Holland; ***W:*** Kevin Falls. Golden Raspberry Awards '93: Worst Supporting Actress (Dunaway). *PAR*

The Tempest 🦴🦴🦴 **1928** A Russian peasant soldier rises through the ranks to become an officer, only to be undone by his love for the daughter of his commanding officer. Silent with musical score. **105m/B VHS, Beta.** John Barrymore, Louis Wolheim; ***D:*** Sam Taylor; ***C:*** Charles Rosher. Academy Awards '28: Best Interior Decoration; Nominations: Academy Awards '28: Best Cinematography. *NOS, CCB, VYY*

The Tempest 🦴🦴½ **1963** Shakespeare's classic tale of the fantasy world of spirits, sorcerers, maidens, monsters, and scheming noblemen is brought to life in George Schaefer's ethereal production. **76m/C VHS, Beta.** Maurice Evans, Richard Burton, Roddy McDowall, Lee Remick, Tom Poston; ***D:*** George Schaefer. *TVC, FHS*

The Tempest 🦴🦴🦴 **1982 (PG)** A New York architect, fed up with city living, chucks it all and brings his daughter to live with him on a barren Greek island. Based on Shakespeare's play of the same name. Well-written, thoughtfully acted, and beautifully filmed. **140m/C VHS, Beta, LV.** John Cassavetes, Gena Rowlands, Susan Sarandon, Vittorio Gassman, Molly Ringwald, Paul Stewart, Sam Robards, Raul Julia; ***D:*** Paul Mazursky; ***W:*** Paul Mazursky, Leon Capetanos. *COL*

The Tempest/The Eagle 🦴🦴🦴 **1927** A Russian soldier during the Revolution is betrayed and humiliated by the woman he loves in "The Tempest." In "The Eagle," an outcast guardsman becomes the Russian version of Robin Hood. **56m/B VHS, Beta.** John Barrymore, Camilla Horn, Rudolph Valentino, Louise Dresser; ***D:*** Sam Taylor, Clarence Brown. *CCB*

Temptation 🦴🦴 **1994 (R)** Ex-con Eddie (Fahey) gets hired to work on a luxury yacht, which helps him keep track of his double-crossing former partner. Too bad for Eddie that the guy's wife is such a distraction. **91m/C VHS, LV.** Jeff Fahey, Alison Doody, Philip Casnoff, David Keith, Patricia Durham, W. Paul Bodie; ***D:*** Strathford Hamilton. *LIV*

Temptation of a Monk 🦴🦴 **1994** Costume drama about China's seventh-century Tang Dynasty finds General Shi (Hsin-kuo) duped into an assassination plot against the crown prince. After a massacre, the General flees and finds sanctuary with a group of Buddhist monks at a remote temple. There's also the General's sometime lover and a mystery woman (both played by Chen). Sometimes slow-moving and confusing but with exotic visuals. Based on a novel by Lilian Lee; Mandarin with subtitles. **118m/C VHS.** *CH* Wu Hsin-kuo, Joan Chen, Zhang Fengyi, Michael Lee; ***D:*** Clara Law; ***C:*** Andrew Lesnie. *FXL*

The Tempter 🦴 *L'Anticristo; The Antichrist* **1974 (R)** Mirrors the gruesomeness of "The Exorcist," with story following an invalid's adventures with witchcraft, bestiality, and Satanism. **96m/C VHS, Beta.** *IT* Mel Ferrer, Carla Gravina, Arthur Kennedy, Alida Valli, Anita Strindberg, George Coulouris; ***D:*** Alberto De Martino; ***M:*** Ennio Morricone. *SUE*

The Temptress 🦴🦴½ **1949** A doctor attempting to find a cure for polio is coerced by an irresistible woman into murder and blackmail. Well-told story, if somewhat grim. **85m/B VHS, Beta.** *GB* Joan Maude, Arnold Bell, Don Stannard, Shirley Quentin, John Stuart, Ferdinand "Ferdy" Mayne; ***D:*** Oswald Mitchell. *SNC*

Temptress 🦴🦴 **1995 (R)** Photographer Karin Swann (Delaney) returns from a spiritual retreat in India obsessed with the deadly goddess Kali. Karin's new overtly sexual personality startles lover Matthew (Sarandon) while her work has also undergone some changes. When a friend is murdered, Matthew begins to wonder if Kali's evil powers have overtaken Karin. **93m/C VHS, Beta.** Kim Delaney, Chris Sarandon, Corbin Bernsen, Dee Wallace Stone, Jessica Walter, Ben Cross; ***D:*** Lawrence Lanoff; ***W:*** Melissa Mitchell; ***M:*** Michael Stearns. *PAR*

10 🦴🦴½ **1979 (R)** A successful songwriter who has everything finds his life is incomplete without the woman of his dreams, the 10 on his girl-watching scale. His pursuit brings surprising results. Also popularizes Ravel's "Bolero." **121m/C VHS, Beta, LV.** Dudley Moore, Julie Andrews, Bo Derek, Dee Wallace Stone, Brian Dennehy, Robert Webber; ***D:*** Blake Edwards; ***W:*** Blake Edwards; ***M:*** Henry Mancini. Nominations: Academy Awards '79: Best Song ("Song from 10 (It's Easy to Say)"), Best Original Score. *WAR, FCT*

Ten Brothers of Shao-lin 🦴 **198?** Martial arts adventure from the days of warlords and warriors, when men were fierce and strong and struggles to the death occurred several times a day. **90m/C VHS, Beta.** Chia Ling, Wang Tao, Chang Yi. *NO*

The Ten Commandments 🦴🦴½ **1923** The silent epic that established DeMille as a popular directorial force and which he remade 35 years later as an even bigger epic with sound. Follows Moses' adventures in Egypt, plus a modern story of brotherly love and corruption. Features a new musical score by Gaylord Carter. Remade in 1956. **146m/B VHS, Beta.** Theodore Roberts, Richard Dix, Rod La Rocque, Edythe Chapman, Nita Naldi; ***D:*** Cecil B. DeMille; ***C:*** Archie Stout; ***M:*** Gaylord Carter. *PAR*

The Ten Commandments 🦴🦴🦴 **1956 (G)** DeMille's remake of his 1923 silent classic (and his last film) is a lavish Biblical epic that tells the life story of Moses, who turned his back on a privileged life to lead his people to freedom outside of Egypt. Exceptional cast, with Fraser Heston (son of Charlton) as the baby Moses. Parting of Red Sea rivals any modern special effects. Available in widescreen on laserdisc. A 35th Anniversary Collector's Edition is available uncut at 245 minutes, in widescreen format and Dolby Surround stereo, and 1,000 copies of an Autographed Limited Edition that includes an engraved bronze plaque and an imprinted card written and personally signed by Charlton Heston are also available. **219m/C VHS, Beta, LV.** Charlton Heston, Yul Brynner, Anne Baxter, Yvonne De Carlo, Nina Foch, John Derek, H.B. Warner, Henry Wilcoxon, Judith Anderson, John Carradine, Douglass Dumbrille, Cedric Hardwicke, Martha Scott, Vincent Price, Debra Paget; ***D:*** Cecil B. DeMille; ***C:*** Loyal Griggs; ***M:*** Elmer Bernstein. Academy Awards '56: Best Special Effects; Nominations: Academy Awards '56: Best Art Direction/Set Decoration (Color), Best Color Cinematography, Best Costume Design (Color), Best Film Editing, Best Picture, Best Sound. *PAR, FUS, IGP*

Ten Days That Shook the World 🦴🦴🦴½ *October* **1927** Silent masterpiece based on American author John Reed's book of the same name. Eisenstein, commissioned by the Soviet government, spared no expense to chronicle the Bolshevik Revolution of 1917 (in a flattering Communist light, of course). He was later forced to cut his portrayal of Leon Trotsky, who was then an enemy of the state. Includes rare footage of the Czar's Winter Palace in Leningrad. Haunting score, combined with some of Eisenstein's most striking work. See Warren Beatty's "Reds" for a fictional look at Reed and the Russian Revolution. **104m/B VHS, Beta, LV.** *RU* Nikandrov, N. Popov, Boris Livanov; ***D:*** Grigori Alexandrov, Sergei Eisenstein; ***M:*** Dimitri Shostakovich. *VYY, IHF, WFV*

Ten Days Wonder 🦴🦴½ **1972 (PG)** Mystery/drama focuses on the patriarch of a wealthy family (Welles), his young wife, and his adopted son (Perkins), who is having an affair with his stepmother. It also turns out that Perkins is certifiable and is trying to break all of the Ten Commandments, which he succeeds in doing before killing himself (gruesomely). Based on the mystery novel by Ellery Queen. **101m/C VHS.** *FR* Orson Welles, Anthony Perkins, Marlene Jobert, Michel Piccoli, Guido Alberti; ***D:*** Claude Chabrol. *INJ, MOV, CVC*

Ten Little Indians 🦴🦴½ *And Then There Were None* **1975 (PG)** Ten people are gathered in an isolated inn under mysterious circumstances. One by one they are murdered, each according to a verse from a children's nursery rhyme. British adaptation of the novel and stage play by Agatha Christie. **98m/C VHS, Beta, LV.** *GB* Herbert Lom, Richard Attenborough, Oliver Reed, Elke Sommer, Charles Aznavour, Stephane Audran, Gert Frobe, Adolfo Celi, Orson Welles; ***D:*** Peter Collinson. *NLC*

Ten Little Indians 🦴🦴 *Agatha Christie's Ten Little Indians* **1989 (PG)** A group of prize-winning vacationers find themselves embarking on an African adventure. They all wind up at the same camp, and realize that they are being murdered one by one. Based on the work of Agatha Christie. **100m/C VHS, Beta, LV.** Donald Pleasence, Brenda Vaccaro, Frank Stallone, Herbert Lom, Sarah Maur-Thorp; ***D:*** Alan Birkinshaw. *CAN*

The Ten Million Dollar Getaway 🦴🦴 **1991 (PG-13)** True story of the 1978 Lufthansa robbery at Kennedy Airport in which the criminals were forced to leave ten of their twenty-million-dollar heist behind when a pick-up van didn't show. Standard made-for-cable fare produced to cash in on the same scenario played out in "Goodfellas." **93m/C VHS, Beta.** John Mahoney, Karen Young, Tony LoBianco, Gerry Bamman, Joseph Carberry, Terrence Mann, Kenneth John McGregor, Christopher Murney; ***D:*** James A. Contner; ***W:*** Christopher Canaan. *PAR*

Ten Nights in a Bar Room 🦴🦴 **1913** The evils of alcohol are dramatized when they ruin a man's life. One of many propaganda films about alcohol and the problems that it caused that were made during the prohibition era. Silent, with a musical score. Remade in 1931. **68m/B VHS, Beta.** Robert Lawrence, Marie Trado. *VCN*

Ten Nights in a Bar-Room 🦴🦴 **1931** A turn-of-the-century mill owner succumbs to alcoholism and ruins his life and family. Later, he sees the error of his ways and gives up drinking. This was one of many films made during this era that chronicled the evils of alcohol and fanned the flames of the prohibition debate. Remake of the 1913 silent film. **60m/B VHS, Beta.** William Farnum, Thomas Santschi, John Darrow, Robert Frazer; ***D:*** William O'Connor. *VYY, GPV*

Ten North Frederick 🦴🦴½ **1958** A shrewish wife (Fitzgerald) forces her gentle lawyer husband (Cooper) into cut-throat politics. He consoles himself in the arms of a much younger woman. Good performances, hokey script, based on the John O'Hara novel. **102m/B VHS.** Gary Cooper, Diane Varsi, Suzy Parker, Geraldine Fitzgerald, Tom Tully, Stuart Whitman; ***D:*** Philip Dunne; ***W:*** Philip Dunne. *TCF*

10 Rillington Place 🦴🦴🦴 **1971 (PG)** A grimy, upsetting British film about the famed serial killer John Christie and the man wrongly hanged for his crimes, the incident that led to the end of capital punishment in England. Impeccably acted. One of Hurt's earliest films. **111m/C VHS, Beta, LV.** *GB* Richard

Attenborough, John Hurt, Judy Geeson, Gabrielle Daye, Andre Morell; **D:** Richard Fleischer. *MOV*

Ten Speed ☠☠ **1976** Two advertising executives compete in a 400-mile bicycle race from San Francisco to Malibu. **89m/C VHS, Beta.** William Woodbridge, Patricia Hume, David Clover. *LIV*

Ten to Midnight ☠☠ **1983 (R)** Vigilante Bronson is on the prowl again, this time as a police officer after a kinky serial murderer. The psychotic killer stalks his daughter and Dad's gonna stop him at any cost. **101m/C VHS, Beta, LV.** Charles Bronson, Wilford Brimley, Lisa Eilbacher, Andrew Stevens; **D:** J. Lee Thompson; **W:** William Roberts. *MGM*

10 Violent Women *Woof!* **1979 (R)** Ten women who take part in a million dollar jewelry heist are tossed into a women's prison where brutal lesbian guards subject them to degradation and brutality. **97m/C VHS, Beta.** Sherri Vernon, Dixie Lauren, Sally Gamble; **D:** Ted V. Mikels. *NO*

Ten Wanted Men ☠ **1954** A successful cattle baron is confronted by a pistol-wielding landowner determined to ruin him. Standard fare, with better than average performances from Scott and Boone. **80m/C VHS, Beta, LV.** Randolph Scott, Jocelyn Brando, Richard Boone, Skip Homeier, Leo Gordon, Jack Perrin, Donna Martell; **D:** H. Bruce Humberstone; **W:** Harriet Frank Jr., Irving Ravetch. *COL*

Ten Who Dared ☠☠ **1960** Ten Civil War heroes brave the Colorado River in an effort to chart its course. Although it's based on an actual historic event, the film is poorly paced and lacks suspense. **92m/C VHS, Beta.** Brian Keith, John Beal, James Drury; **D:** William Beaudine. *DIS*

The Tenant ☠☠☠ ½ *Le Locataire* **1976 (R)** Disturbing story of a hapless office worker who moves into a spooky Paris apartment house. Once lodged inside its walls, he becomes obsessed with the previous occupant, who committed suicide, and the belief that his neighbors are trying to kill him. Based on a novel by Roland Topor. **126m/C VHS, Beta.** *FR* Roman Polanski, Isabelle Adjani, Melvyn Douglas, Jo Van Fleet, Bernard Fresson, Shelley Winters; **D:** Roman Polanski; **W:** Roman Polanski, Gerard Brach; **C:** Sven Nykvist. Nominations: Cannes Film Festival '76: Best Film. *PAR*

The Tender Age ☠☠ *The Little Sister* **1984** Troubled 18-year-old girl gets out of a detention home and is put on probation. She captivates her idealistic probation officer, whose interest may extend beyond professional concern. Fine idea, but under-played. **103m/C VHS, Beta.** John Savage, Tracy Pollan, Roxanne Hart, Richard Jenkins; **D:** Jan Egleson; **W:** Jan Egleson. *LIV*

Tender Comrade ☠☠ **1943** Flag-waving violin-accompanied tearjerker about five women who live together to make ends meet while their men do manly things during WWII. Intended to puff your heart up with patriotic gusto. Ironically, thanks to the girls' communal living arrangement, director Dmytryk was later accused of un-American activities. **101m/B VHS.** Ginger Rogers, Robert Ryan, Ruth Hussey, Patricia Collinge, Mady Christians, Kim Hunter, Jane Darwell, Mary Forbes, Richard Martin; **D:** Edward Dmytryk. *TTC, FCT*

Tender Is the Night ☠☠ ½ **1955** A television-special adaptation of the F. Scott Fitzgerald classic, set in the roaring '20s, in which a psychiatrist marries one of his patients and then heads down the road to ruin, driven by his marriage and the times in which he lives. An entry from the "Front Row Center" series. **60m/B VHS, Beta.** Mercedes McCambridge, James Daly. *NOS, DVT*

Tender Loving Care ☠ **1973** Three nurses dispense hefty doses of T.L.C. in their hospital, and the patients aren't the only ones on the receiving end. **72m/C VHS, Beta.** Donna Desmond, Leah Simon, Anita King; **D:** Don Edmunds. *SUE*

Tender Mercies ☠☠☠ **1983 (PG)** A down-and-out country western singer finds his life redeemed by the love of a good woman. Aided by Horton Foote's script, Duvall, Harper and Barkin keep this from being simplistic and sentimental. Duvall wrote as well as performed the songs in his Oscar-winning performance. Wonderful, life-affirming flick. **88m/C VHS, Beta, LV.** Robert Duvall, Tess Harper, Betty Buckley, Ellen Barkin, Wilford Brimley; **D:** Bruce Beresford; **W:** Horton Foote; **M:** George Dreyfus. Academy Awards '83: Best Actor (Duvall), Best Original Screenplay; Golden Globe Awards '83: Best Actor—Drama (Duvall); Los Angeles Film Critics Association Awards '83: Best Actor (Duvall); New York Film Critics Awards '83: Best Actor (Duvall); Writers Guild of America '83: Best Original Screenplay; Nominations: Academy Awards '83: Best Director (Beresford), Best Picture, Best Song ("Over You"). *REP, BTV, HMV*

The Tender Trap ☠☠ ½ **1955** Charlie Reader (Sinatra) is a bachelor not content with the many women in his life. He meets the innocent Julie Gillis (Reynolds) and falls head over heels for her. He then torments himself over a marriage proposal, unwilling to let go of his freedom. **111m/C VHS, LV.** Frank Sinatra, Debbie Reynolds, Celeste Holm, David Wayne, Carolyn Jones, Lola Albright, Tom Helmore, Howard St. John, Willard Sage, James Drury, Benny Rubin, Frank Sully, David White; **D:** Charles Walters; **W:** Julius J. Epstein; **C:** Paul Vogel. Nominations: Academy Awards '55: Best Song ("(Love Is) The Tender Trap"). *MGM, MOV*

The Tender Warrior ☠☠ **1971 (G)** A beautifully photographed animal adventure with Haggerty as the woodsman. **85m/C VHS, Beta.** Dan Haggerty, Charles Lee, Liston Elkins; **D:** Stewart Raffill. *VCD*

The Tender Years ☠☠ **1947** Sentimental drama of a minister trying to outlaw dog fighting, spurred on by his son's fondness for a particular dog. **81m/B VHS, Beta.** Joe E. Brown, Richard Lyon, Noreen Nash, Charles Drake, Josephine Hutchinson; **D:** Harold Schuster. *TCF*

Tenement ☠ *Game of Survival* **1985** Unspeakably violent story of urban low-lifes, frightened slum-dwellers, and revenge. **94m/C VHS, Beta.** *NO*

Tennessee Stallion ☠ **1978** A low-class horse-trainer breaks into the world of aristocratic thoroughbred racing. **87m/C VHS, Beta.** Audrey Landers, Judy Landers, James Van Patten. *LIV, VES*

Tennessee's Partner ☠☠ **1955** Enjoyable, unexceptional buddy Western. Reagan intervenes in an argument and becomes Payne's pal. Adapted from a story by Bret Harte. **87m/C VHS, Beta.** Ronald Reagan, Rhonda Fleming, John Payne; **D:** Allan Dwan. *NO*

Tension at Table Rock ☠☠ **1956** Accused of cowardice, a lone gunman must prove he killed in self-defense. Well-cast serious Western. **93m/C VHS, Beta.** Richard Egan, Dorothy Malone, Cameron Mitchell; **D:** Charles Marquis Warren. *NO*

Tentacles *Woof!* **1977 (PG)** Cheesy Italian version of "Jaws" lacking only the suspense and cogent storytelling. Huston slums as the investigator charged with finding the octopus gone mad, while Fonda collects check and makes a quick exit. Hopkins is in charge of the killer whales that save the day. You'll cheer when Winters is devoured by sea pest. From the director of an "Exorcist" rip-off, "Beyond the Door" (that's not a recommendation). **90m/C VHS, Beta.** *IT* John Huston, Shelley Winters, Bo Hopkins, Henry Fonda, Cesare Danova; **D:** Oliver Hellman; **W:** Steven W. Carabatsos. *LIV, VES*

Tentacles of the North ☠☠ ½ **1926** Two ships are trapped in the ice of the Arctic with the only survivor of one ship being a fearful young girl. Tinted print. **54m/B VHS.** Gaston Glass, Alice Calhoun, Al Ferguson, Joseph Girard; **D:** Louis Chaudet. *GPV*

The Tenth Man ☠☠ ½ **1988** Hopkins stars as a wealthy French lawyer, captured by the Nazis and sentenced to death. He discovers a fellow prisoner who is willing to take his place in exchange for Hopkins' wealth going to support the man's family. After his release, Hopkins returns to his old home, now occupied by the dead man's family, but doesn't reveal his true identity. When an imposter appears, claiming to be Hopkins, another twist is added. Slow-going but the usual excellent performances by Hopkins and Jacobi. Based on a novella by Graham Greene. Made for television. **99m/C VHS, LV.** Anthony Hopkins, Kristin Scott Thomas, Derek Jacobi, Cyril Cusack, Brenda Bruce, Paul Rogers; **D:** Jack Gold. *MGM*

Tenth Month ☠☠ **1979** Carol Burnett plays a divorced, middle-aged woman who becomes pregnant by a married man. She refuses help, choosing instead to live alone and keep an ever hopeful vigil for the birth of her child. Sappy but touching made-for-TV drama. **123m/C VHS, Beta.** Carol Burnett, Keith Michell, Dina Merrill; **D:** Joan Tewkesbury. *TLF*

10th Victim ☠☠☠ *La Decima Vittima; La Dixieme Victime* **1965** Sci-fi cult film set in the 21st century has Mastroianni and Andress pursuing one another in a futuristic society where legalized murder is used as the means of population control. Intriguing movie where Andress kills with a double-barreled bra, the characters hang out at the Club Masoch, and comic books are considered literature. Based on "The Seventh Victim" by Robert Sheckley. **92m/C VHS, Beta.** *IT* Ursula Andress, Marcello Mastroianni, Elsa Martinelli, Salvo Randone, Massimo Serato; **D:** Elio Petri; **W:** Tonino Guerra. *SUE, NLC*

Teorema ☠☠ **1968** Scathing condemnation of bourgeois complacency. Stamp, either a devil or a god, mysteriously appears and enters into the life of a well-to-do Milanese family and raises each member's spirituality by sleeping with them. Ultimately, the experience leads to tragedy. In Italian with English subtitles. **98m/C VHS.** *IT* Terence Stamp, Silvana Mangano, Massimo Girotti, Anna Wiazemsky, Laura Betti, Andres Jose Cruz; **D:** Pier Paolo Pasolini; **M:** Ennio Morricone. *TPV, INJ, CVC*

Tequila Sunrise ☠☠ ½ **1988 (R)** Towne's twisting film about two lifelong friends and a beautiful woman. Gibson is a (supposedly) retired drug dealer afraid of losing custody of his son to his nagging ex-wife. Russell is the cop and old friend who's trying to get the lowdown on a drug shipment coming in from Mexico. Pfeiffer runs the poshest restaurant on the coast and is actively pursued by both men. Questions cloud the plot and confuse the viewer; loaded with double-crosses, intrigue and surprises around every corner, still the photogenic leads are pleasant to watch. Steamy love scene between Pfeiffer and Gibson. **116m/C VHS, Beta, LV, 8mm.** Mel Gibson, Kurt Russell, Michelle Pfeiffer, Raul Julia, Arliss Howard, Arye Gross, J.T. Walsh, Ann Magnuson; **D:** Robert Towne; **W:** Robert Towne; **C:** Conrad Hall; **M:** Dave Grusin. Nominations: Academy Awards '88: Best Cinematography. *WAR*

Teresa Venerdi ☠☠☠ **1941** An unusual Italian comedy about a man and his financial difficulties. His mistress, his fiance and a young girl make his troubles more confusing. Unusually sweet and humorous DeSica. **90m/B VHS, Beta.** *IT* **D:** Vittorio De Sica. *CIG*

Teresa's Tattoo ☠ **1994** A bimbo (Shelly) with a Chinese dragon tattoo somehow obtains a pair of earrings containing details of the U.S. space program. She's kidnapped by inept thugs and dies in a freak accident. Now the kidnappers need a look-alike for their extortion scheme so they kidnap another girl (Shelly again) and drug and tattoo her. Naturally, when she wakes up she manages to escape. Thin farce striving too hard to be madcap and whimsical. **88m/C VHS.** Adrienne Shelly, C. Thomas Howell, Nancy McKeon, Lou Diamond Phillips, Casey Siemaszko, Jonathan Silverman; **Cameos:** Majel Barrett, Anthony Clark, Nanette Fabray, Tippi Hedren, k.d. lang, Joe Pantoliano, Mary Kay Place, Mare Winningham, Kiefer Sutherland; **D:** Julie Cypher; **W:** Georgie Huntington; **M:** Melissa Etheridge. *VMK*

Tereza ☠☠☠ **1961** In politically chaotic Czechoslovakia, a female police detective tries to solve an intricate murder mystery. In Czech with English subtitles. **91m/B VHS, Beta.** *CZ* Jirina Svorcova; **D:** Pavel Blumenfeld. *FCT, IHF*

Terminal Bliss ☠ ½ **1991 (R)** Teen heartthrob Perry stars as a spoiled rich druggie in this "Less Than Zero" knock-off. Perry and childhood pal Owen grow up sharing everything—lacrosse, girlfriends, and drugs. However, their friendship is really put to the test when a beautiful new girl (Chandler) moves to town just before graduation. Release was delayed, but obviously wants to capitalize on Perry's popularity. **94m/C VHS, LV.** Luke Perry, Timothy Owen, Estee Chandler; ***D:*** Jordan Allen; ***W:*** Jordan Allen; ***M:*** Frank Becker. *WAR, CAN*

Terminal Choice 🦴½ **1985 (R)** Staff at a hospital conduct a betting pool on patients' life expectancies. Someone decides he should win more often and uses a computer to help hedge his bets. Wasted cast on this unsuspenseful and bloody film. **98m/C VHS, Beta.** Joe Spano, Diane Venora, David McCallum, Ellen Barkin; ***D:*** Sheldon Larry; ***W:*** Neal Bell. *VES*

Terminal Entry 🦴½ **1987 (R)** Teen computer geeks accidentally find a terrorist online network, and inadvertently begin transmitting instructions to destroy U.S. targets. The premise is intriguing but poorly done. **95m/C VHS, Beta.** Edward Albert, Yaphet Kotto, Kabir Bedi; ***D:*** John Kincade. *CEL*

Terminal Exposure 🦴🦴 **1989 (R)** Predictable but likeable comedy-mystery. A pair of Venice, CA, beach denizens capture a murder on film and try to solve it. **105m/C VHS, Beta, LV.** Steve Donmyer, John Vernon, Ted Lange, Joe Phelan, Hope Marie Carlton, Mark Hennessy, Scott King; ***D:*** Nico Mastorakis. *LIV, VES*

Terminal Force 🦴 **1988 (R)** Stupid, poorly executed story of kidnapping and the mob. So bad it never saw the inside of a theater; went straight to video. **83m/C VHS, LV.** Troy Donahue, Richard Harrison, Dawn Wildsmith; ***D:*** Fred Olen Ray. *VTR, NWV*

Terminal Impact 🦴🦴 **1995 (R)** Two independent federal marshals find themselves battling indestructible, hi-tech soldiers when they investigate the disappearance of a television news reporter. **94m/C VHS, LV.** Bryan Genesse, Frank Zagarino, Jennifer Miller. *NLC*

Terminal Island 🦴½ **1973 (R)** Tough southern California penal colony is crowded with inmates from death row. When prison becomes coed, violence breaks out. Exploitative and unappealing. **88m/C VHS, Beta.** Phyllis E. Davis, Tom Selleck, Don Marshall, Ena Hartman, Marta Kristen; ***D:*** Stephanie Rothman. *NO*

The Terminal Man 🦴🦴½ **1974 (R)** A slick, visually compelling adaptation of the Michael Crichton novel. A scientist plagued by violent mental disorders has a computer-controlled regulator implanted in his brain. The computer malfunctions and he starts a murdering spree. Futuristic vision of man-machine symbiosis gone awry. Well acted, but still falls short of the novel. **107m/C VHS, Beta.** George Segal, Joan Hackett, Jill Clayburgh, Richard Dysart, James B. Sikking, Norman Burton; ***D:*** Mike Hodges; ***W:*** Mike Hodges. *WAR*

Terminal Velocity 🦴🦴 **1994 (PG-13)** Skydiving instructor Ditch Brodie (Sheen) thinks he sees student Chris Morrow (Kinski) plummet to her death, only it turns out she's not dead and certainly not a beginner. Upon further investigation, he finds the usual web of international intrigue descending upon him, and that the KGB definitely wants him to mind his own business. Still, he pushes on. Another no-brainer actioner with few surprises satisfies the guilty pleasures of action addicts only. **132m/C VHS, LV.** Charlie Sheen, Nastassia Kinski, James Gandolfini, Christopher MacDonald, Melvin Van Peebles; ***D:*** Deran Sarafian; ***W:*** David N. Twohy; ***M:*** Joel McNeely. *HPH*

The Terminator 🦴🦴🦴 **1984 (R)** Futuristic cyborg is sent to present-day Earth. His job: kill the woman who will conceive the child destined to become the great liberator and arch-enemy of the Earth's future rulers. The cyborg is also pursued by another futuristic visitor, who falls in love with the intended victim. Cameron's pacing is just right in this exhilarating, explosive thriller which displays Arnie as one cold-blooded villain who utters a now famous line: "I'll be back." Followed by "Terminator 2: Judgment Day." **108m/C VHS, Beta, LV.** Arnold Schwarzenegger, Michael Biehn, Linda Hamilton, Paul Winfield, Lance Henriksen, Bill Paxton, Rick Rossovich, Dick Miller; ***D:*** James Cameron; ***W:*** James Cameron; ***M:*** Brad Fiedel. *NO*

Terminator 2: Judgment Day 🦴🦴🦴½ **1991 (R)** He said he'd be back and he is, programmed to protect the boy who will be mankind's post-nuke resistance leader. But the T-1000, a shape-changing, ultimate killing machine, is also on the boy's trail. Twice the mayhem, five times the special effects, ten times the budget of the first, but without Arnold it'd be half the movie. The word hasn't been invented to describe the special effects, particularly THE scariest nuclear holocaust scene yet. Worldwide megahit, but the $100 million budget nearly ruined the studio; Arnold accepted his $12 million in the form of a jet. Laserdisc features include pan and scan, widescreen and a "Making of T-2" short. **139m/C VHS, LV, 8mm.** Arnold Schwarzenegger, Linda Hamilton, Edward Furlong, Robert Patrick, Earl Boen, Joe Morton; ***D:*** James Cameron; ***W:*** James Cameron; ***M:*** Brad Fiedel. Academy Awards '91: Best Makeup, Best Sound, Best Sound Effects Editing, Best Visual Effects; MTV Movie Awards '92: Best Film, Best Male Performance (Schwarzenegger), Best Female Performance (Hamilton), Breakthrough Performance (Furlong), Most Desirable Female (Hamilton), Best Action Sequence; People's Choice Awards '92: Best Film; Nominations: Academy Awards '91: Best Cinematography, Best Sound. *LIV*

Termini Station 🦴🦴½ **1989** Dewhurst gives an excellent performance as the alcoholic matriarch of a small-town Canadian family. She drinks all day and dreams of traveling to Italy, while her children work and believe there is something more to life than their mundane existence. When they finally do leave, they discover an intriguing new world. Dewhurst and Follows also appear together in "Anne of Green Gables" and "Anne of Avonlea." **105m/C VHS.** *CA* Colleen Dewhurst, Megan Follows, Gordon Clapp, Hannah Lee, Leon Pownall, Debra McGrath, Elliott Smith, Norma Dell'Agnese; ***D:*** Allen King; ***M:*** Mychael Danna. *FXL, FCT*

Terms of Endearment 🦴🦴🦴 **1983 (PG)** A weeper following the changing relationship between a young woman and her mother, over a thirty-year period. Beginning as a comedy, turning serious as the years go by, this was Brooks' debut as screenwriter and director. Superb supporting cast headed by Nicholson's slyly charming neighbor/astronaut, with stunning performances by Winger and MacLaine as the two women who often know and love each other too well. Adapted from Larry McMurtry's novel. **132m/C VHS, Beta, LV.** Shirley MacLaine, Jack Nicholson, Debra Winger, John Lithgow, Jeff Daniels, Danny DeVito; ***D:*** James L. Brooks; ***W:*** James L. Brooks; ***M:*** Michael Gore. Academy Awards '83: Best Actress (MacLaine), Best Adapted Screenplay, Best Director (Brooks), Best Picture, Best Supporting Actor (Nicholson); Golden Globe Awards '84: Best Actress—Drama (MacLaine), Best Film—Drama, Best Screenplay, Best Supporting Actor (Nicholson); National Board of Review Awards '83: Best Actress (MacLaine), Best Director (Brooks), Best Supporting Actor (Nicholson); National Society of Film Critics Awards '83: Best Actress (Winger), Best Supporting Actor (Nicholson); Nominations: Academy Awards '83: Best Actress (Winger), Best Art Direction/Set Decoration, Best Film Editing, Best Sound, Best Supporting Actor (Lithgow), Best Original Score. *PAR, BTV, HMV*

Terraces 🦴🦴½ **1977** TV series pilot about high-rise tenants whose balconies are their only common ground. Good performances. **90m/C VHS, Beta.** Lloyd Bochner, Eliza Garrett, Julie Newmar, Tim Thomerson; ***D:*** Lila Garrett. *WOV*

Terrified 🦴🦴½ **1995 (R)** Erotic thriller about a nympho being stalked by a mystery assailant. Genuinely creepy. **90m/C VHS.** Heather Graham, Lisa Zane. *APX*

The Terror 🦴🦴 **1938** A hostelry is the scene of a number of brutal murders. Remake of a 1928 film and based on a play by Edgar Wallace. Good story, but weak version of it. **63m/B VHS, Beta.** *GB* Wilfred Lawson, Bernard Lee, Arthur Wontner, Linden Travers, Henry Oscar, Alastair Sim; ***D:*** Richard Bird. *SNC*

The Terror 🦴🦴 *Lady of the Shadows* **1963** A lieutenant in Napoleon's army chases a lovely maiden and finds himself trapped in a creepy castle by a mad baron. Movie legend has it Corman directed the movie in 3 days as the sets (from his previous movie "The Raven") were being torn down around them. **81m/C VHS, Beta.** Boris Karloff, Jack Nicholson, Sandra Knight; ***D:*** Roger Corman. *NOS, SNC, PSM*

The Terror *Woof!* **1979 (R)** After 100 years, a man reveals in a film that his family killed a witch. Friends who see the film are attacked by supernatural forces. Originally double-billed with "Dracula's Dog." **86m/C VHS, Beta.** John Nolan, Carolyn Courage, James Aubrey; ***D:*** Norman J. Warren. *VCI, VCD, HHE*

Terror at London Bridge 🦴🦴 *Bridge Across Time; Arizona Ripper* **1985** London Bridge is transported brick by brick to Arizona. It carries its history with it, including the havoc-wreaking spirit of Jack the Ripper. Campy made-for-TV effort. **96m/C VHS, Beta.** David Hasselhoff, Stephanie Kramer, Adrienne Barbeau, Randolph Mantooth; ***D:*** E.W. Swackhamer. *FRH*

Terror at Red Wolf Inn 🦴🦴 *Club Dead; Terror House; The Folks at Red Wolf Inn* **1972 (R)** Young woman wins a vacation; finds she's been invited for dinner, so to speak. Not campy enough to overcome stupidity. **90m/C VHS, Beta.** Linda Gillin, Arthur Space, John Neilson, Mary Jackson, Janet Wood, Margaret Avery; ***D:*** Bud Townsend. *ACA*

Terror at Tenkiller 🦴 **1986** Two girls vacationing in the mountains are seemingly surrounded by a rash of mysterious murders. Made for video. **87m/C VHS, Beta.** Mike Wiles, Stacey Logan. *VCI*

Terror at the Opera 🦴½ **1988 (R)** A bizarre staging of Verdi's "Macbeth" is plagued by depraved gore murders. But the show must go on, as one character chirps in badly-dubbed English. Italian horrormeister Argento's ever-fluid camera achieves spectacular shots, but the lurid, ludicrous script make this one for connoisseurs only. The operatic scenes employ the voice of Maria Callas. Available in an edited "R" rated version. **107m/C VHS.** Christina Marsillach, Ian Charleson, Urbano Barberini, William McNamara, Antonella Vitale, Barbara Cupisti, Coralina Cataldi Tassoni, Daria Nicolodi; ***D:*** Dario Argento; ***W:*** Dario Argento. *FCT*

Terror Beach 🦴 **198?** A doctor and his bride move to a coastal village, only to find it enmeshed in witchcraft and devil worship. **90m/C VHS, Beta.** Victor Petit, Julie James, Mary Costi, Sandra Mozar. *NO*

Terror Beneath the Sea 🦴🦴½ *Kaitei Daisenso; Water Cyborgs* **1966** A mad scientist wants to rule the world with his cyborgs. American and Japanese scientists unite to fight him. Fine special effects, especially the transformation from human to monster. **85m/C VHS, Beta.** *JP* Sonny Chiba, Peggy Neal, Franz Gruber, Gunther Braun, Andrew Hughes, Mike Daneen; ***D:*** Hajime Sato. *DVT*

Terror by Night 🦴🦴½ **1946** Holmes and Watson attempt to solve the murder of the owner of a gigantic, beautiful jewel. Their investigation must be completed before their train arrives at its destination, where the murderer can escape. **60m/B VHS, LV.** Basil Rathbone, Nigel Bruce; ***D:*** Roy William Neill. *CNG, REP, FOX*

Terror by Night/Meeting at Midnight 🦴🦴 **1946** In "Terror by Night" (1946), Sherlock Holmes and Dr. Watson board a train to protect a fabulous diamond. In "Meeting at Midnight" (1944), Charlie Chan becomes involved in magic and murder. **122m/B VHS, Beta.** Basil Rathbone, Nigel Bruce, Sidney Toler; ***D:*** Roy William Neill. *MED*

Terror Creatures from the Grave 🦴 **1966** Husband summons medieval plague victims to rise from the grave to drop in on his unfaithful wife. Should've been better. **85m/C VHS.** *IT* Barbara Steele, Riccardo Garrone, Walter Brandi; ***D:*** Ralph Zucker. *SNC*

Terror Eyes 🦴½ **1987 (PG-13)** Spoof-thriller revolves around an "agent from Hell," sent to Earth to recruit writers for a horror film. **90m/C VHS, Beta.** Daniel Roebuck, Vivian Schilling, Dan Bell, Lance August. *AIP*

Terror in Beverly Hills *Woof!* **1990** When the President's daughter is kidnapped, it's up to an ex-marine to save her. The trouble is, the head terrorist hates the marine's guts as he blames him for the deaths of his wife and children. So incredibly bad it's campy and fun. **88m/C VHS, Beta, LV.** Frank Stallone,

Cameron Mitchell, William Smith; *D:* John Myhers; *W:* John Myhers. *AIP*

Terror in Paradise ☠½ **1990 (R)** Jason and Vickie think they're going to have a romantic holiday on a beautiful island paradise. But they've picked the wrong spot to vacation. It seems the island harbors a terrorist group and when they see more than they should the lovers become the next targets. **?m/C VHS.** Joanna Pettet, Gary Lockwood, David Anthony Smith, Leslie Ryan; *D:* Peer J. Oppenheimer. *NHO*

Terror in the Haunted House ☠☠½ **1958** Newlyweds move into an old house. The bride remembers it from her nightmares. First release featured the first use of Psychorama, a technique in which scary words or advertising messages were flashed on the screen for a fraction of a second—just long enough to cause subliminal response. The technique was banned later in the year. **90m/C VHS, Beta.** Gerald Mohr, Cathy O'Donnell, William Ching; *D:* Harold Daniels. *RHI, MLB, CCB*

Terror in the Jungle ☠ **1968 (PG)** Plane crashes in Peruvian wilds and young boy survivor meets Jivaro Indians who think he's a god. Much struggling to survive and battling with horrible script. **95m/C VHS.** Jimmy Angle, Robert Burns, Fawn Silver; *D:* Tom De Simone; *M:* Les Baxter. *ACA*

Terror in the Swamp ☠ **1985 (PG)** When not hanging out in the local murky waters, a swamp creature terrorizes the residents of a small town. **89m/C VHS, Beta, LV.** Billy Holliday; *D:* Joe Catalanotto. *NWV, VTR*

Terror in the Wax Museum *Woof!* **1973 (PG)** The owner of a wax museum is killed while mulling over the sale of the museum. The new owner has little better luck as the bodies continue to pile up. Production uses every out-of-work horror film actor of the time. The most suspenseful part of this low-budget flick is waiting to see how long the "wax dummies" can hold their breath. **94m/C VHS, Beta.** Ray Milland, Broderick Crawford, Elsa Lanchester, Louis Hayward, Maurice Evans, John Carradine; *D:* Georg Fenady; *W:* Jameson Brewer; *M:* George Duning. *LIV*

Terror in Toyland ☠½ *Christmas Evil; You Better Watch Out* **1985** Once again a knife-wielding lunatic dresses as Santa Claus to strike terror and death into the hearts of children. **90m/C VHS, Beta.** Brandon Maggart, Jeffrey DeMunn; *D:* Lewis Jackson. *ACA*

Terror Is a Man ☠☠ *Blood Creature* **1959** A mad scientist attempts to turn a panther into a man on a secluded island. Early Filipino horror attempt inspired by H.G. Wells' "The Island of Doctor Moreau." **89m/B VHS.** *PH* Francis Lederer, Greta Thyssen, Richard Derr, Oscar Keesee; *D:* Gerardo (Gerry) De Leon. *SNC*

Terror of Mechagodzilla ☠½ *Monsters from the Unknown Planet; The Escape of Megagodzilla; Mekagojira No Gyakushu* **1978 (G)** It's monster vs. machine in the heavyweight battle of the universe as a huge mechanical Godzilla built by aliens is pitted against the real thing. The last Godzilla movie made until "Godzilla 1985." **79m/C VHS, Beta.** *JP* Katsuhiko Sasakai, Tomoko Al. *PAR*

Terror of Rome Against the Son of Hercules ☠ **1964** Muscle-bound gladiators battle it out in this low-budget Italian action flick. Dubbed. **100m/C VHS, Beta.** *FR IT* Mark Forest, Marilu Tolo; *D:* Mario Ciano. *SNC, NLC*

Terror of the Bloodhunters ☠ **1962** A French author is sentenced to Devil's Island for a crime he didn't commit. The warden's daughter takes a liking to him and arranges for him and a friend to escape, but numerous perils await them in the jungle. **60m/B VHS, Beta.** Robert Clarke, Steve Conte, Dorothy Haney; *D:* Jerry Warren; *W:* Jerry Warren. *SNC*

Terror of the Steppes ☠ **1964** Yet another sword and sandal extravaganza in which a musclebound hero conquers all. **?m/C VHS, Beta.** *IT* Kirk Morris. *SNC*

Terror of Tiny Town ☠☠ **1938** Main characteristic of this musical/western is its entire midget cast, all members of Jed Buell's Midgets. Otherwise the plot is fairly average and features a bad guy and the good guy who finally teaches him a lesson. Newfield plays up the cast's short stature—they walk under saloon doors and ride Shetland ponies. **65m/B VHS, Beta.** Bill Curtis, Yvonne Moray; *D:* Sam Newfield. *SNC, NOS, DVT*

Terror on Alcatraz ☠ **1986** The only prisoner to successfully escape from Alcatraz Island returns to retrieve the safety deposit box key he needs to get his stolen loot. And anyone who gets in his way is in for trouble. **96m/C VHS.** Veronica Porsche Ali, Sandy Brooke, Aldo Ray, Scott Ryder; *D:* Philip Marcus. *TWE, HHE*

Terror on the 40th Floor ☠ **1974** Seven people make an attempt to escape from the 40th floor of an inflamed skyscraper. Poorly done re-hash of "Towering Inferno." Uninspired. **98m/C VHS, Beta.** John Forsythe, Anjanette Comer, Don Meredith, Joseph Campanella; *D:* Jerry Jameson. *PSM*

Terror on Tour *Woof!* **1983** The Clowns, a rock group on their way up, center their stage performance around sadistic, mutilating theatrics. When real murders begin, they become prime suspects. Exploitive, bloody, disgusting. **90m/C VHS, Beta.** Dave Galluzzo, Richard Styles, Rick Pemberton; *D:* Don Edmunds. *MED*

Terror Out of the Sky ☠½ **1978** A scientist must disguise himself as one of the insects to divert the attention of a horde of killing bees from a busload of elementary children. Sub-par sequel to "The Savage Bees." **95m/C VHS, Beta.** Efrem Zimbalist Jr., Dan Haggerty; *D:* Lee H. Katzin; *M:* William Goldstein. *LIV*

Terror Ship ☠☠ **1954** Three people find an abandoned yacht which they believe was used for smuggling. While searching it, they find that it was used to transport stolen uranium. Before the police can arrive, the thieves show up. Not a very good handling of what was actually an interesting idea. Released as "Dangerous Voyage" in Great Britain. **72m/B VHS.** *GB* William Lundigan, Naomi Chance, Vincent Ball, Jean Lodge, Richard Stewart; *D:* Vernon Sewell. *NOS*

Terror Squad ☠☠ **1987** An unsuspecting high school population is put under siege by Libyan terrorists. The students get a hands-on lesson in revolution and guerrilla war tactics. **95m/C VHS.** Kerry Brennan, Bill Calvert, Chuck Connors, Greer Brodie; *D:* Peter Maris. *MCG, VTR*

Terror Stalks the Class Reunion ☠☠½ **1993 (PG-13)** Kay (Nelligan) is a teacher who disappears at a class reunion. Police dismiss the case as a runaway wife, except for Virginia, a young detective (Beals) who doesn't accept that theory. And she's right—Kay is held hostage in a remote cabin by an obsessed former student (Davies). Kay needs all her wits to fend off her deranged and possibly deadly suitor while Virginia races to find her. Based on the novel by Mary Higgins Clark. **95m/C VHS.** Kate Nelligan, Jennifer Beals, Geraint Wyn Davies. *REP*

Terror Street ☠ **1954** An Air Force pilot's wife is murdered. He has 36 hours to clear his name and find the killer. **84m/B VHS, Beta, LV.** Dan Duryea, Elsy Albiin, Ann Gudrun, Eric Pohlmann. *NO*

Terror Trail ☠½ **1933** As usual, Mix uses guns and fists to bring bad guys to justice, and gets the girl in the bargain. **62m/B VHS.** Tom Mix, Naomi Judge, Arthur Rankin, Raymond Hatton, Francis McDonald, Robert F. (Bob) Kortman, John St. Polis, Lafe McKee, Buffalo Bill Jr.; *D:* Armand Schaefer. *GPV, HEG, DVT*

Terror Train ☠☠ *Train of Terror* **1980 (R)** A masquerade party is held on a chartered train. But someone has more than mask-wearing in mind as a series of dead bodies begin to appear. Copperfield provides magic, Curtis provides screams in this semi-scary slasher movie. **97m/C VHS, Beta, LV.** Jamie Lee Curtis, Ben Johnson, Hart Bochner, David Copperfield, Vanity; *D:* Roger Spottiswoode. *FOX*

The Terror Within ☠ **1988 (R)** Reptilian mutants hit the streets searching for human women to breed with. Have the Teenage Mutant Ninja Turtles grown up? **90m/C VHS, Beta.** George Kennedy, Andrew Stevens, Starr Andreeff, Terri Treas; *D:* Thierry Notz; *W:* Thomas McKelvey Cleaver; *M:* Rick Conrad. *MGM*

The Terror Within 2 ☠½ **1991 (R)** In a world destroyed by biological warfare, a warrior and the woman he rescued traverse the badlands occupied by hideous mutants. What they don't know is that the real terror comes from within. How can they possibly survive? Not without decent dialogue, that's for sure. **90m/C VHS.** Andrew Stevens, Stella Stevens, Chick Vennera, R. Lee Ermey; *D:* Andrew Stevens. *VES, LIV*

Terrorgram ☠ **1990 (R)** Not a very special delivery. An offscreen James Earl Jones introduces three lesser tales of terror. Best seg: a sleazy filmmaker gets trapped in the world of his own exploitation scripts. The other two are bloody but negligible revenge-from-the-grave yarns. All start off with the receipt of a sinister package, hence a postal motif. **88m/C VHS.** Michael Hartson, J.T. Wallace. *NO*

The Terrorists ☠½ **1974 (PG)** Just as later he was a Scottish Lithuanian sub-commander in "The Hunt for Red October" (1990), here Connery is a Scottish Norwegian security chief. Good cinematography and premise are wasted; generic title betrays sloppy execution. **89m/C VHS, Beta.** Sean Connery, Ian McShane, John Quentin; *D:* Caspar Wrede; *M:* Jerry Goldsmith. *FOX*

Terrorists ☠ **1983** An Army investigator discovers a plot to assassinate the President. It's up to him to move quickly enough to stop it. Brutal action. **61m/C VHS, Beta.** Marland Proctor, Irmgard Millard. *NO*

The Terrornauts *Woof!* **1967** When man begins space exploration, Earth is attacked by aliens. The defenders are taken to an out-dated fortress where they learn that their forebears were similarly attacked. Juvenile, lackluster, contrived, and really dumb. **77m/C VHS, Beta.** *GB* Simon Oates, Zena Marshall, Charles Hawtrey, Stanley Meadows; *D:* Montgomery Tully. *NLC*

Terrorvision *Woof!* **1986 (R)** OUR TV GAVE BIRTH TO SPACE ALIENS! It's amazing what modern technology can do: Suburban family buys a fancy satellite dish; bad black comedy and gory special effects result. **84m/C VHS, Beta.** Gerrit Graham, Mary Woronov, Diane Franklin, Bert Remsen, Alejandro Rey; *D:* Ted Nicolaou; *W:* Ted Nicolaou; *M:* Richard Band. *LIV*

The Terry Fox Story ☠☠☠ **1983** In the spring of 1980, a young man who had lost his right leg to cancer dipped his artificial limb into the Atlantic Ocean and set off on a fund-raising "Marathon of Hope" across Canada, drawing national attention. Inspiring made-for-TV true story is well-scripted and avoids corniness. Good acting from real-life amputee Fryer and, as usual, from Duvall. **96m/C VHS, Beta.** Eric Fryer, Robert Duvall, Chris Makepeace, Michael Zelniker, Rosalind Chao; *D:* Ralph L. Thomas; *M:* Bill Conti. Genie Awards '84: Best Actor (Fryer), Best Film, Best Supporting Actor (Zelniker). *VES*

Tess ☠☠☠ **1980 (PG)** Sumptuous adaptation of the Thomas Hardy novel "Tess of the D'Ubervilles." Kinski is wonderful as an innocent farm girl who is seduced by the young aristocrat she works for and then finds marriage to a man of her own class only brings more grief. Polanski's direction is faithful and artful. Nearly three hours long, but worth every minute. **170m/C VHS, Beta, LV.** *GB FR* Nastassia Kinski, Peter Firth, Leigh Lawson, John Collin; *D:* Roman Polanski; *W:* Roman Polanski, Gerard Brach; *C:* Ghislan Cloquet, Geoffrey Unsworth. Academy Awards '80: Best Art Direction/Set Decoration, Best Cinematography, Best Costume Design; Cesar Awards '80: Best Cinematography, Best Director (Polanski), Best Film; Golden Globe Awards '81: Best Foreign Film; Los Angeles Film Critics Association Awards '80: Best Cinematography, Best Director (Polanski); New York Film Critics Awards '80: Best Cinematography; Nominations: Academy Awards '80: Best Director (Polanski), Best Picture, Best Original Score. *COL*

Test of Donald Norton 🦴🦴½ **1926** Good early Western. A young man raised by Indians finds work with the Hudson's Bay Company and does well, but is haunted by suspicions that he is a half-breed. **68m/B VHS, Beta, 8mm.** George Walsh, Tyrone Power Sr., Eugenia Gilbert, Robert Graves, Virginia True Boardman; ***D:*** B. Reeves Eason. *GPV, VYY*

A Test of Love 🦴🦴 *Annie's Coming Out* **1984 (PG)** Incorrectly diagnosed as retarded, a young woman with cerebral palsy struggles to adjust to life outside an institution. Predictable but touching and well-acted. **93m/C VHS, Beta.** *AU* Angela Punch McGregor, Drew Forsythe, Tina Arhondis; ***D:*** Gil Brealey; ***W:*** Chris Borthwick. Australian Film Institute '84: Best Film. *MCA*

Test Pilot 🦴🦴🦴½ **1938** Gable and Spencer star as daring test pilot and devoted mechanic respectively. When Gable has to land his experimental craft in a Kansas cornfield, he meets and falls in love with farm girl Loy. The two marry and raise a family, all the while she worries over his dangerous profession. When the Air Force asks him to test their new B-17 bomber, she refuses to watch, thinking the test will end in tragedy. Superb aviation drama featuring excellent cast. **118m/B VHS, Beta.** Clark Gable, Myrna Loy, Spencer Tracy, Lionel Barrymore, Samuel S. Hinds; ***D:*** Victor Fleming. Nominations: Academy Awards '38: Best Film Editing, Best Picture, Best Story. *MGM, TLF, CCB*

Test Tube Babies *Woof!* **1948** A married couple's morals begin to deteriorate as they mourn the fact they can't have a child. The day is saved, however, when they learn about the new artificial insemination process. Amusing, campy propaganda in the vein of "Reefer Madness." Rereleased in 1967 as "The Pill" with extra scenes featuring Monica Davis and John Maitland. **83m/B VHS, Beta.** Dorothy Dube, Timothy Farrell, William Thompson; ***D:*** W. Merle Connell. *GVV, SNC, DVT*

Test Tube Teens from the Year 2000 🦴 *Virgin Hunters* **1993 (R)** When sex is banned in the year 2000, horny teenagers are left with no choice but to travel through time for some action. **74m/C VHS, Beta, LV.** Morgan Fairchild, Ian Abercrombie, Brian Bremer, Christopher Wolf, Michelle Matheson, Sara Suzanne Brown, Don Dowe; ***D:*** Ellen Cabot; ***W:*** Kenneth J. Hall; ***M:*** Reg Powell. *PAR*

Testament 🦴🦴🦴 **1983 (PG)** Well-made and thought-provoking story of the residents of a small California town struggling to survive after a nuclear bombing. Focuses on one family who tries to accept the reality of post-holocaust life. We see the devastation but it never sinks into sensationalism. An exceptional performance from Alexander. **90m/C VHS, Beta, LV.** Jane Alexander, William Devane, Ross Harris, Roxana Zal, Kevin Costner, Rebecca DeMornay; ***D:*** Lynne Littman; ***W:*** John Sacret Young; ***M:*** James Horner. Nominations: Academy Awards '83: Best Actress (Alexander). *PAR*

The Testament of Dr. Cordelier 🦴🦴🦴 **1959** A strange, experimental fantasy about a Jekyll and Hyde-type lunatic stalking the streets and alleys of Paris. Originally conceived as a television play, Renoir attempted to create a new mise-en-scene, using multiple cameras covering the sequences as they were performed whole. In French with English subtitles. **95m/C VHS, Beta.** *FR* Jean-Louis Barrault; ***D:*** Jean Renoir. *FCT*

Testament of Dr. Mabuse 🦴🦴½ *The Crimes of Dr. Mabuse; The Last Will of Dr. Mabuse* **1962** The director of an asylum is controlled by the evil genius, Dr. Mabuse, who hypnotizes him in this well-done remake of Lang's 1933 classic. **?m/C VHS.** Gert Frobe, Wolfgang Preiss, Senta Berger. *SNC, LSV*

The Testament of Orpheus 🦴🦴🦴½ **1959** Superb, personal surrealism; writer-director Cocteau's last film. Hallucinogenic, autobiographical dream-journey through time. Difficult to follow, but rewarding final installment in a trilogy including "The Blood of the Poet" and "Orpheus." In French with English subtitles. **80m/B VHS, Beta.** *FR* Jean Cocteau, Edouard Dermithe, Maria Casares, Francois Perier, Yul Brynner, Jean-Pierre Leaud, Daniel Gelin, Jean Marais, Pablo Picasso, Charles Aznavour; ***D:*** Jean Cocteau. *HMV, FCT, INJ*

Tetsuo: The Iron Man 🦴🦴 **1992** A weird live-action science-fiction cartoon about a white-collar Japanese worker who finds himself being gradually transformed into a walking metal collection of cables, drills, wires, and gears. The newly-formed metal creature then faces off with an equally bizarre metals fetishist (played by the director). In Japanese with English subtitles. **67m/B VHS.** *JP* Tomoroh Taguchi, Kei Fujiwara, Shinya Tsukamoto; ***D:*** Shinya Tsukamoto; ***W:*** Shinya Tsukamoto. *FXL*

Tevye 🦴🦴½ *Teyve der Milkhiker* **1939** Sholom Aleichem's story of Jewish family life, intermarriage, and turmoil in Poland. When Khave, the daughter of Tevye the dairyman, seeks to marry a Ukrainian peasant, Tevye must come to terms with his love for his daughter and his faith and loyalty to tradition. Also the basis for the musical "Fiddler on the Roof." In Yiddish with English subtitles. **96m/B VHS, Beta.** Maurice Schwartz, Miriam Riselle; ***D:*** Maurice Schwartz. *ERG, NCJ, INJ*

Tex 🦴🦴½ **1982 (PG)** Fatherless brothers in Oklahoma come of age. Dillon is excellent. Based on the novel by S.E. Hinton. **103m/C VHS, Beta, LV.** Matt Dillon, Jim Metzler, Meg Tilly, Bill McKinney, Frances Lee McCain, Ben Johnson, Emilio Estevez; ***D:*** Tim Hunter; ***M:*** Pino Donaggio. *DIS, OM*

Tex Rides with the Boy Scouts 🦴½ **1937** Scouts aid Ritter in capturing gold bandits with a little bit of singing thrown in for good measure. **60m/B VHS, Beta.** Tex Ritter. *NOS, DVT*

The Texans 🦴🦴½ **1938** Ex-Confederate soldier Kirk Jordan (Scott) struggles to make a new life for himself as a trail boss, aiming to get 10,000 head of cattle to the railroad in Abilene. But there's temptation in the form of Ivy Preston (Bennett) and a scheme to reignite the war. Remake of 1924 silent "North of '36." **93m/B VHS.** Randolph Scott, Joan Bennett, Walter Brennan, May Robson, Robert Cummings, Raymond Hatton, Robert Barrat, Harvey Stephens, Chris-Pin Martin, Francis Ford; ***D:*** James Hogan; ***W:*** Bertram Millhauser, Paul Sloane, William Haines. *MCA*

Texas 🦴🦴🦴 **1941** Two friends wander through the West after the Civil War getting into scrapes with the law and eventually drifting apart. Ford takes a job on a cattle ranch run by Trevor and discovers Holden has joined a gang of rustlers aiming to steal her herd. The two men vie for Trevor's affections. Although friends, a professional rivalry also existed between the two leading actors and they competed against each other, doing their own stunts during filming. Well-acted, funny, and enthusiastic Western. **94m/B VHS, Beta.** William Holden, Glenn Ford, Claire Trevor, Edgar Buchanan, George Bancroft; ***D:*** George Marshall. *COL*

Texas 🦴🦴½ *James A. Michener's Texas* **1994** Stephen Austin (Duffy) sets up a colony in 1821 Texas, with Mexican law requiring the settlers to become Mexican citizens. Eventually, calls for statehood begin and Austin's initial resistance is overturned by rebellion and prodding from Sam Houston (Keach) and Jim Bowie (Keith). Lots of action amidst the history, including the battle for the Alamo, but it's a routine extravaganza. Made for TV miniseries adapted from Michener's novel. Filmed on location in Del Rio, Texas. **180m/C VHS, LV.** Patrick Duffy, Stacy Keach, David Keith, Maria Conchita Alonso, Anthony Michael Hall, Rick Schroder, Benjamin Bratt, Chelsea Field, John Schneider, Grant Show, Randy Travis, Woody Watson; ***D:*** Richard Lang; ***W:*** Sean Meredith; ***M:*** Lee Holdridge. *REP, PAP*

Texas Across the River 🦴🦴½ **1966** Sam Hollis (Martin) is a wise-cracking gun runner who, along with Indian sidekick Kronk (Bishop), is recruiting men to help him ship guns through hostile Comanche territory. Don Andrea, a Spanish nobleman (played by Frenchman Delon) wrongly accused of murder, joins up and much comic misadventure ensues. **101m/C VHS, LV.** Dean Martin, Alain Delon, Joey Bishop, Rosemary Forsyth, Tina Aumont, Peter Graves, Michael Ansara, Linden Chiles, Andrew Prine, Richard Farnsworth; ***D:*** Michael Gordon; ***W:*** Ben Starr, Wells Root, Harold Greene; ***C:*** Russell Metty. *MCA, BTV, FCT*

Texas Bad Man 🦴½ **1932** Sheriff Mix goes undercover to get in with Kohler's gang of outlaws and bring them to justice. **60m/B VHS.** Tom Mix, Fred Kohler Sr., Lucille Powers, Ed LeSaint, Richard Alexander; ***D:*** Edward Laemmle. *GPV*

Texas Buddies 🦴½ **1932** Steele plays a former military pilot who uses his trusty monoplane to round up outlaws. Interesting twist on standard oater, but suffers from poor execution. **57m/B VHS.** Bob Steele, Nancy Drexel, George "Gabby" Hayes, Francis McDonald, Harry Semels; ***D:*** Robert North Bradbury; ***W:*** Robert North Bradbury. *MOV, GPV*

Texas Carnival 🦴🦴 **1951** Williams and Skelton star as carnival performers who operate the dunk tank. When Skelton is mistaken for an oil tycoon, he lives high on the hog until the mistake is discovered. Believe it or not, this musical has only one water ballet sequence. Songs include "It's Dynamite," "Whoa! Emma," and "Young Folks Should Get Married." **77m/C VHS.** Esther Williams, Red Skelton, Howard Keel, Ann Miller, Paula Raymond, Keenan Wynn, Tom Tully; ***D:*** Charles Walters. *MGM*

The Texas Chainsaw Massacre 🦴🦴½ **1974 (R)** The movie that put the "power" in power tools. An idyllic summer afternoon drive becomes a nightmare for a group of young people pursued by a chainsaw-wielding maniac. Made with tongue firmly in cheek, this is nevertheless a mesmerizing saga of gore, flesh, mayhem, and violence. **86m/C VHS, LV.** Marilyn Burns, Allen Danzinger, Paul A. Partain, William Vail, Teri McMinn, Edwin Neal, Jim Siedow, Gunnar Hansen, John Dugan, Jerry Lorenz; ***D:*** Tobe Hooper; ***W:*** Ken Henkel, Tobe Hooper; ***M:*** Wayne Bell. *MPI*

Texas Chainsaw Massacre, Part 2 *Woof!* **1986 (R)** A tasteless, magnified sequel to the notorious blood-bucket extravaganza, about a certain family in southern Texas who kill and eat passing travelers. Followed by "Leatherface: Texas Chainsaw Massacre III." **90m/C VHS, Beta, LV.** Dennis Hopper, Caroline Williams, Bill Johnson, Jim Siedow; ***D:*** Tobe Hooper; ***W:*** L.M. Kit Carson. *MED, VTR*

Texas Cyclone 🦴🦴 **1932** A stranger rides into a town that turns out to be incredibly friendly. Later he realizes the entire town thinks he is a prominent citizen who disappeared years ago. **58m/B VHS.** Tim McCoy, Wheeler Oakman, Shirley Grey, Walter Brennan, John Wayne, Wallace MacDonald, Vernon Dent, Mary Gordon; ***D:*** David Ross Lederman. *COL, DVT, NOS*

Texas Detour 🦴 **1977** On a trip across country, a trio of young Californians have their van stolen. They decide to take the law into their own hands when the redneck sheriff gives them no help. Dull, undistinguished "action" flick. **90m/C VHS, Beta.** Cameron Mitchell, Priscilla Barnes, Patrick Wayne, Mitch Vogel, Lindsay Bloom, R.G. Armstrong; ***D:*** Howard (Hikmet) Avedis. *PSM*

Texas Gunfighter 🦴🦴 **1932** Your basic western from the Maynard series, with everything a western could have. **60m/B VHS, Beta.** Ken Maynard. *NOS, VCI, DVT*

Texas Guns 🦴🦴 *Once Upon a Texas Train* **1990 (PG)** A gritty western about an old-time gunman (Nelson) and his quest for one last robbery, killing those who stand in his way and some just for fun. Also watch for Cassidy's comeback. **96m/C VHS, LV.** Willie Nelson, Richard Widmark, Shaun Cassidy, Angie Dickinson, Kevin McCarthy, Royal Dano, Chuck Connors, Ken Curtis, Dub Taylor. *VMK*

Texas Jack 🦴½ **1935** The head of a medicine show tries to trace the disappearance of his sister. **55m/B VHS.** Jack Perrin, Jayne Regan, Nelson McDowell, Budd Buster, Lew Meehan; ***D:*** Bernard B. Ray. *GPV*

Texas John Slaughter: Geronimo's Revenge 🦴🦴 **1960** An Indian-loving rancher frets and fights when Geronimo attacks innocent settlers. Compiled fom Walt Disney television episodes. **77m/C VHS, Beta.** Tom Tryon, Darryl Hickman, Betty Lynn; ***D:*** Harry Keller. *DIS*

Texas John Slaughter: Stampede at Bitter Creek ♂♂ **1962** Good guy Texas John Slaughter meets a variety of threatening obstacles when he tries to move his cattle herd into New Mexico. Originally from the "Walt Disney Presents" television series. **90m/C VHS, Beta.** Tom Tryon; ***D:*** Harry Keller. *DIS*

Texas Justice ♂½ **1942** The "Lone Rider" cavorts around in the desert, dispensing justice in the guise of a monk. **60m/B VHS, Beta.** George Houston, Al "Fuzzy" St. John, Dennis Moore, Wanda McKay, Claire Rochelle; ***D:*** Sam Newfield. *NOS, DVT*

Texas Kid ♂½ **1943** A typical western. Hero helps a vengeance-minded kid catch the robber-gang who robbed and killed his father. Yee-Haw. **53m/B VHS, Beta.** Johnny Mack Brown, Kermit Maynard, Raymond Hatton, Shirley Patterson, Edmund Cobb, Charles "Blackie" King; ***D:*** Lambert Hillyer. *VDM, GPV*

Texas Lady ♂♂ **1956** When a woman wins $50,000 gambling, she buys a Texas newspaper on the stipulation that she can edit it in this standard fare western. Good vehicle for Colbert to look beautiful, but the plot and script are average and uninspired. **86m/C VHS.** Claudette Colbert, Barry Sullivan, Gregory Walcott; ***D:*** Tim Whelan. *REP*

Texas Layover *Woof!* **1975** Impossible-to-describe western/exploitation entry from trashmeister Adamson involving multiple stewardesses and the remnants of the Ritz Brothers. **88m/C VHS.** Yvonne De Carlo, Bob Livingston, Donald (Don "Red") Barry, Connie Hoffman, Regina Carrol, Jimmy Ritz, Harry Ritz; ***D:*** Al Adamson. *NO*

Texas Legionnaires ♂♂ *Man from Music Mountain* **1943** Roy comes back to his home town and gets caught between feuding cattle and sheep herders. **71m/B VHS.** Roy Rogers, Ruth Terry, Paul Kelly, Ann Gillis, George Cleveland, Pat Brady; ***D:*** Joseph Kane. *NOS, DVT*

Texas Lightning ♂½ **1981 (R)** Innocuous B-grade touching movie about a father and son and their family woes. **93m/C VHS, Beta.** Cameron Mitchell, Channing Mitchell, Maureen McCormick, Peter Jason. *MED*

Texas Masquerade ♂♂ **1944** Standard good cowboys versus land-grabbers action filler. William Boyd plays Hopalong Cassidy. Andy Clyde plays California Carson. Jimmy Rogers plays...Jimmy Rogers. **59m/B VHS.** William Boyd, Andy Clyde, Jimmy Rogers, Mady Correll, Don Costello, Russell Simpson, Nelson Leigh, Francis McDonald, J. Farrell MacDonald; ***D:*** George Archainbaud. *NOS, RXM*

Texas Payback ♂♂ **1995 (R)** Convicted killer busts out of prison in order to get revenge on the now-retired-and-working-in-Vegas Texas Ranger who put him away. **96m/C VHS.** Sam Jones, Gary Hudson, Kathleen Kinmont, Bo Hopkins; ***D:*** Richard W. Munchkin; ***W:*** Brian Page; ***C:*** Mark Morris; ***M:*** Jim Halfpenny. *CAF*

Texas Pioneers ♂½ *The Blood Brother* **1932** A frontier scout is sent to an outpost town besieged by crooks. **54m/B VHS, Beta.** Bill Cody. *VDM*

The Texas Rangers ♂♂½ **1936** Banditos Jim Hawkins (MacMurray) and Wahoo Jones (Oakie) roam the Texas frontier until the Rangers come in, establishing order. So, they switch over to the good guys but are then told to bring in their old partner-in-crime Sam McGee (Nolan). Lots of confronting villains and battling varmints. Based on the book by Walter Prescott Webb. Followed by "The Texas Rangers Ride Again" and remade as "The Streets of Laredo" (1949). **99m/B VHS.** Fred MacMurray, Jack Oakie, Lloyd Nolan, Jean Parker, Edward Ellis, Fred Kohler Sr., George "Gabby" Hayes; ***D:*** King Vidor; ***W:*** Louis Stevens. *MCA*

The Texas Rangers ♂♂ **1951** A prisoner is given the opportunity to capture the notorious Sam Bass gang in exchange for freedom. Good B Western; lotsa shootin'. **68m/C VHS, Beta.** George Montgomery, Gale Storm, Jerome Courtland, Noah Beery Jr.; ***D:*** Phil Karlson. *GKK*

The Texas Rangers Ride Again ♂♂½ **1940** When cattle keep disappearing from the Dangerfield ranch, owner Robson secretly calls in the Texas Rangers to find out what's going on. Howard and Crawford work undercover to root out the criminals while Howard also finds the time to make goo-goo eyes at Robson's granddaughter Drew. **68m/B VHS.** John Howard, Broderick Crawford, May Robson, Ellen Drew, Anthony Quinn, Akim Tamiroff, Charley Grapewin, Harvey Stephens; ***D:*** James Hogan; ***W:*** William R. Lipman, Horace McCoy. *MCA*

Texas Terror ♂♂ **1935** Young Wayne resigns his badge when he mistakenly believes he has shot and killed his friend. He later rescues his friend's sister, learns the truth, and (naturally) finds true love. **50m/B VHS.** John Wayne, George "Gabby" Hayes, Lucille Browne. *COL, CNG, NOS*

Texas to Bataan ♂½ **1942** The Range Busters ship horses to the Philippines and encounter enemy spies. Part of the "Range Busters" series. **56m/B VHS, Beta.** John "Dusty" King, David Sharpe, Max Terhune; ***D:*** Robert Emmett Tansey. *VYY*

Texas Trouble ♂½ **193?** Standard matinee fare with cowboy Bob Steele. **0m/B VHS, Beta.** Bob Steele. *VCN*

Texas Wildcats ♂½ **1939** A cowboy helps make sure that sinister adversaries are brought to justice on the American Frontier. **60m/B VHS, Beta.** Tim McCoy. *NOS, DVT, MOV*

Texasville ♂♂½ **1990 (R)** Sequel to "The Last Picture Show" finds the characters still struggling after 30 years, with financial woes from the energy crisis, mental illness inspired by the Korean War, and various personal tragedies. Lacks the melancholy sensitivity of its predecessor, but has some of the wit and wisdom that comes with age. Based again on a Larry McMurtry novel. Not well received during its theatrical release. **120m/C VHS, LV.** Timothy Bottoms, Jeff Bridges, Annie Potts, Cloris Leachman, Eileen Brennan, Randy Quaid, Cybill Shepherd, William McNamara; ***D:*** Peter Bogdanovich; ***W:*** Peter Bogdanovich. *COL, VMK*

Thank God It's Friday ♂½ **1978 (PG)** Episodic and desultory disco-dancing vehicle which won the Best Song Oscar for Donna Summer's rendition. Life is irony. Co-produced by Motown. ♫Last Dance; After Dark; Find My Way; It's Serious; Let's Make A Deal; Romeo and Juliet; You're the Reason I Feel Like Dancing; From Here to Eternity; Dance All Night. **100m/C VHS, Beta.** Valerie Landsburg, Teri Nunn, Chick Vennera, Jeff Goldblum, Debra Winger; ***D:*** Robert Klane; ***W:*** Armyan Bernstein. Academy Awards '78: Best Song ("Last Dance"). *COL*

Thank You & Good Night **1991** Director Oxenberg gathers members of her own family around a purple armchair of grandma's to talk about life, love, and family memories, including grandma's illness and recent death. **81m/C VHS.** ***D:*** Jan Oxenberg; ***W:*** Jan Oxenberg; ***C:*** Claudia Rashke. *ORI, BTV, FXL*

Thank Your Lucky Stars ♂♂♂ **1943** A lavish, slap-dash wartime musical that emptied out the Warner's lot for an array of uncharacteristic celebrity turns. Features Shore in her movie debut. ♫They're Either Too Young or Too Old; Blues in the Night; Hotcha Cornia; Ridin' For A Fall; We're Staying Home Tonight; Goin' North; Love Isn't Born, It's Made; No You, No Me; Ice Cold Katie. **127m/B VHS, Beta, LV.** Eddie Cantor, Dinah Shore, Joan Leslie, Errol Flynn, Bette Davis, Edward Everett Horton, Humphrey Bogart, John Garfield, Alan Hale, Ann Sheridan, Ida Lupino, Jack Carson, Dennis (Stanley Morner) Morgan, Olivia de Havilland; ***D:*** David Butler; ***W:*** Norman Panama. Nominations: Academy Awards '43: Best Song ("They're Either Too Young or Too Old"). *MGM*

Tharus Son of Attila ♂ **1987** A couple of sword-wielding barbarians battle each other and an evil emperor. **89m/C VHS, Beta.** Jerome Courtland, Rik von Nutter, Lisa Gastoni; ***D:*** Robert Montero. *TWE*

That Brennan Girl ♂½ **1946** A maudlin soap opera about how a girl's upbringing by an inconsiderate mother makes her a devious little wench. Fortunately her second husband had a better mom, and redemption is at hand. **95m/B VHS.** James Dunn, Mona Freeman, William Marshall, June Duprez, Frank Jenks, Charles Arnt; ***D:*** Alfred Santell. *NOS*

That Certain Thing ♂♂½ **1928** Very early silent Capra comedy about a bachelor with a silver spoon in his mouth who loses his inheritance when he marries for love. It's got that certain Capra screwball feeling. **65m/B VHS, Beta.** Viola Dana, Ralph Graves, Burr McIntosh, Aggie Herring, Syd Crossley; ***D:*** Frank Capra. *GPV*

That Certain Woman ♂♂½ **1937** Sentimental drama with Davis portraying a gangster's widow who wants to make a new life for herself. Fonda plays the rich playboy with whom she falls in love. Because of Davis' star power, she demanded that Fonda play opposite her. It seems Davis had a real life crush on him when they were both players in a stock company several years earlier. Remake of Goulding's "The Trespasser" which starred Gloria Swanson. **91m/B VHS.** Bette Davis, Henry Fonda, Ian Hunter, Anita Louise, Donald Crisp, Katherine Alexander, Minor Watson; ***D:*** Edmund Goulding; ***W:*** Edmund Goulding; ***M:*** Max Steiner. *MGM*

That Championship Season ♂♂ **1982 (R)** Long-dormant animosities surface at the reunion of a championship basketball team. Unfortunate remake of Miller's Pulitzer-prize winning play, with none of the fire which made it a Broadway hit. **110m/C VHS, Beta.** Martin Sheen, Bruce Dern, Stacy Keach, Robert Mitchum, Paul Sorvino, Jason Miller; ***D:*** Jason Miller; ***C:*** John Bailey; ***M:*** Bill Conti. *MGM*

That Cold Day in the Park ♂♂½ **1969 (R)** Early Altman. An unhappy woman takes in a homeless young man from the park near her home. The woman (Dennis) is obsessive and odd; so is the film. Dennis is excellent. Reminiscent of "The Collector." **91m/C VHS, Beta.** Sandy Dennis, Michael Burns, Suzanne Benton, Michael Murphy, John David Garfield; ***D:*** Robert Altman. *REP, FCT*

That Darn Cat ♂♂½ **1965 (G)** Vintage Disney comedy about a Siamese cat that helps FBI Agent Jones thwart kidnappers. Could be shorter, but suspenseful and funny with characteristic Disney slapstick. Based on the book "Undercover Cat" by The Gordons. **115m/C VHS, Beta.** Hayley Mills, Dean Jones, Dorothy Provine, Neville Brand, Elsa Lanchester, Frank Gorshin, Roddy McDowall; ***D:*** Robert Stevenson; ***C:*** Edward Colman; ***M:*** Robert F. Brunner. *DIS*

That Darn Sorceress ♂ **1988** A child witch has grown up, and so has her power. To keep her disciples, she must perform increasingly horrible feats. **89m/C VHS, Beta.** Pauline Adams, Betty Page; ***D:*** Whitney Bain. *NO*

That Eye, The Sky ♂♂ **1994** Alice (Harrow) and Sam (Fairall) Flack live on a small farm with their two children and senile grandmother. Sam's in a serious car crash and is eventually returned home still in a deep coma. Alice, who's having trouble coping, is grateful when wandering evangelist Harry Warburton (Coyote) shows up on her doorstep offering his help. But is this mystery man offering a miracle or more heartache? Based on the book by Tim Winton. **105m/C VHS.** *AU* Lisa Harrow, Peter Coyote, Mark Fairall, Jamie Croft, Amanda Douge, Alethea McGrath; ***D:*** John Ruane; ***W:*** John Ruane, Jim Barton; ***C:*** Ellery Ryan; ***M:*** David Bridie. Australian Film Institute '95: Best Actress (Douge); Nominations: Australian Film Institute '95: Best Actress (Harrow), Best Director (Ruane), Best Film. *NYR*

That Forsyte Woman ♂♂ *The Forsyte Saga* **1950** Based on the novel "A Man of Property" by John Galsworthy, a married Victorian woman falls for an architect engaged to be wed. Remade later, and better for BBC-television as "The Forsythe Saga." **112m/C VHS.** Errol Flynn, Greer Garson, Walter Pidgeon, Robert Young, Janet Leigh, Harry Davenport, Stanley Logan, Lumsden Hare, Aubrey Mather, Matt Moore; ***D:*** Compton Bennett; ***C:*** Joseph Ruttenberg. Nominations: Academy Awards '50: Best Costume Design (Color). *MGM, CCB*

That Gang of Mine 🦴🦴 **1940** "East Side Kids" episode about gang member Mugg's ambition to be a jockey. Good racing scenes. **62m/B VHS, Beta.** Bobby Jordan, Leo Gorcey, Clarence Muse, Dave O'Brien; ***D:*** Joseph H. Lewis. *NOS, DVT, HEG*

That Girl from Paris 🦴🦴½ **1936** An opera singer from Paris stows away on an ocean liner to be near the swing bandleader she has fallen in love with. An entertaining film with many songs; remade as "Four Jacks and a Jill." ♫Una Voce Poco Fa; The Blue Danube; Love and Learn; The Call to Arms; Seal It With A Kiss; My Nephew From Nice; Moon Face; Tarantella. **105m/B VHS, Beta.** Lily Pons, Gene Raymond, Jack Oakie, Herman Bing, Lucille Ball, Mischa Auer, Frank Jenks; ***D:*** Leigh Jason. Nominations: Academy Awards '36: Best Sound. *TTC*

That Hamilton Woman 🦴🦴🦴 *Lady Hamilton* **1941** Screen biography of the tragic 18th-century love affair between British naval hero Lord Nelson and Lady Hamilton. Korda exaggerated the film's historical distortions in order to pass the censor's production code about adultery. Winston Churchill's favorite film which paralleled Britain's heroic struggles in WWII. **125m/B VHS, Beta, LV.** Laurence Olivier, Vivien Leigh, Gladys Cooper, Alan Mowbray, Sara Allgood, Henry Wilcoxon; ***D:*** Alexander Korda; ***M:*** Miklos Rozsa. Academy Awards '41: Best Sound; Nominations: Academy Awards '41: Best Black and White Cinematography, Best Interior Decoration. *HBO, SUE*

That Long Night in '43 🦴🦴½ **1960** A gripping story of fascist terror during WWII. **110m/B VHS, Beta.** ***D:*** Florestano Vancini. *CIG*

That Lucky Touch 🦴🦴 **1975** York is a reporter covering NATO games; Moore is Bond warmed over as an arms dealer. Sexual and professional tension becomes unlikely romance. Slight and dull. Cobb's last film. **92m/C VHS, Beta.** Roger Moore, Susannah York, Shelley Winters, Lee J. Cobb, Jean-Pierre Cassel, Raf Vallone, Sydne Rome; ***D:*** Christopher Miles; ***W:*** John Briley. *TWE*

That Man from Rio 🦴🦴½ *L'Homme de Rio; L'Uomo di Rio* **1964** Engaging adventure spoof with Belmondo as a pilot whose girlfriend (Dorleac) has just been kidnapped. Her father led an expedition to South America in search of an Amazon treasure and the kidnappers think she knows how to find it. So of course Belmondo does some international adventuring in order to rescue her. In French with English subtitles. **114m/C VHS.** *FR IT* Jean-Paul Belmondo, Francoise Dorleac, Jean Servais, Simone Renant; ***D:*** Philippe de Broca; ***W:*** Philippe de Broca, Jean-Paul Rappeneau; ***M:*** Georges Delerue. New York Film Critics Awards '64: Best Foreign Film. *MGM*

That Man Is Pregnant 🦴 **1980 (PG)** NYPD detective gets the incredible news that he is pregnant. Viewers can't believe it, either. **80m/C VHS, Beta.** *NO*

That Midnight Kiss 🦴🦴½ **1949** Glossy production of a musical romance featuring Lanza in his film debut. Thin plot has Lanza starring as a singing truck driver who is discovered by opera diva Grayson. ♫They Didn't Believe Me; I Know, I Know, I Know; Three O'Clock in the Morning; Santa Lucia; Down Among the Sheltering Palms; Revolutionary Etude; Cara Nome; Celeste Aida; Una Furtiva Lacrima. **96m/C VHS.** Kathryn Grayson, Jose Iturbi, Ethel Barrymore, Mario Lanza, Keenan Wynn, J. Carrol Naish, Jules Munshin; ***D:*** Norman Taurog; ***C:*** Robert L. Surtees. *MGM*

That Naughty Girl 🦴🦴 **1958** The bored daughter of a nightclub owner decides to experience all life has to offer. **77m/C VHS, Beta.** *FR* Brigitte Bardot, Jean Bretonniere, Francoise Fabian; ***D:*** Michel Boisrond. *JEF*

That Night 🦴🦴½ **1993 (PG-13)** A view of romance through the eyes of a young girl, circa 1961. Ten-year-old Alice (Dushku) is the confidant of rebellious 17-year-old neighbor Cheryl (Lewis), who enlists the young girl's aid as a go-between with her wrong-side-of-the tracks boyfriend Rick (Howell). 21 soundtrack oldies are featured. Directorial debut for screenwriter Bolotin. Based on a novel by Alice McDermott. **89m/C VHS, Beta, LV.** C. Thomas Howell, Juliette Lewis, Eliza Dushku, Helen Shaver, John Dossett; ***D:*** Craig Bolotin; ***W:*** Craig Bolotin. *WAR*

That Obscure Object of Desire 🦴🦴🦴½ *Cet Obscur Objet Du Desir* **1977 (R)** Bunuel's last film, a comic nightmare of sexual frustration. A rich Spaniard obtains a beautiful girlfriend who, while changing physical identities, refuses to sleep with him. Based on a novel by Pierre Louys, which has been used as the premise for several other films, including "The Devil is a Woman," "La Femme et le Pantin," and "The Female." Available with subtitles or dubbed. **100m/C VHS, Beta, LV.** *SP* Fernando Rey, Carole Bouquet, Angela Molina; ***D:*** Luis Bunuel; ***W:*** Luis Bunuel, Jean-Claude Carriere. Los Angeles Film Critics Association Awards '77: Best Foreign Film; National Board of Review Awards '77: 5 Best Foreign Films of the Year, Best Director (Bunuel); Nominations: Academy Awards '77: Best Adapted Screenplay, Best Foreign Language Film. *COL, APD, SUE*

That Sinking Feeling 🦴🦴🦴 **1979 (PG)** A group of bored Scot teenagers decide to steal 90 sinks from a plumber's warehouse. Well received early film from Forsyth is genuinely funny as the boys try to get rid of the sinks and turn a profit. **82m/C VHS, Beta, LV.** *GB* Robert Buchanan, John Hughes, Billy Greenlees, Alan Love; ***D:*** Bill Forsyth; ***W:*** Bill Forsyth. *SUE*

That Summer of White Roses 🦴🦴½ **1990 (R)** Compelling action drama about a lifeguard working at a resort in Nazi-occupied Yugoslavia and his love for a woman resistance fighter and her child. **98m/C VHS, Beta, LV.** Tom Conti, Susan George, Rod Steiger; ***D:*** Rajko Grlic. *MED, IME, VTR*

That Touch of Mink 🦴🦴½ **1962** In New York City, an unemployed secretary finds herself involved with a business tycoon. On a trip to Bermuda, both parties get an education as they play their game of "cat and mouse." Enjoyable romantic comedy. **99m/C VHS, LV.** Cary Grant, Doris Day, Gig Young, Audrey Meadows, John Astin, Dick Sargent; ***D:*** Delbert Mann; ***C:*** Russell Metty. Golden Globe Awards '63: Best Film—Musical/Comedy; Nominations: Academy Awards '62: Best Art Direction/Set Decoration (Color), Best Sound, Best Story & Screenplay. *REP, MLB*

That Uncertain Feeling 🦴🦴½ **1941** Light comedy about a couple's marital problems increasing when she develops the hiccups and a friendship with a flaky piano player. A remake of the earlier Lubitsch silent film, "Kiss Me Again." Available colorized. **86m/B VHS, Beta.** Merle Oberon, Melvyn Douglas, Burgess Meredith, Alan Mowbray, Eve Arden, Sig Rumann, Harry Davenport; ***D:*** Ernst Lubitsch; ***C:*** George Barnes. Nominations: Academy Awards '41: Best Original Score. *NOS, VYY, DVT*

That Was Then...This Is Now 🦴🦴 **1985 (R)** Lame adaptation of S.E. Hinton teen novel about a surly kid who is attached to his adoptive brother and becomes jealous when the brother gets a girlfriend. **102m/C VHS, Beta, LV.** Emilio Estevez, Craig Sheffer, Kim Delaney, Jill Schoelen, Barbara Babcock, Frank Howard, Larry B. Scott, Morgan Freeman; ***D:*** Christopher Cain; ***W:*** Emilio Estevez. *PAR*

That'll Be the Day 🦴🦴½ **1973 (PG)** The early rock 'n' roll of the 1950s is the only outlet for a frustrated young working-class Brit. Prequel to "Stardust." Good, meticulous realism; engrossing story. **86m/C VHS, Beta, LV.** Ringo Starr, Keith Moon, David Essex, Rosemary Leach; ***D:*** Claude Whatham; ***W:*** Ray Connelly. *REP, TVC, CNG*

That's Adequate 🦴🦴 **1990 (R)** Mock documentary about a fictional film studio. Lampoons just about every movie made in the last 60 years. Premise might have been adequate for a sketch, but hardly for a feature-length film. Zaniness gets old quickly. **82m/C VHS.** Tony Randall, Robert Downey, Rocky Aoki, Bruce Willis, Robert Townsend, James Coco, Jerry Stiller, Peter Riegert, Susan Dey, Richard Lewis, Robert Vaughn, Renee Taylor, Stuart Pankin, Brother Theodore, Anne Bloom, Chuck McCann, Anne Meara; ***D:*** Harry Hurwitz; ***W:*** Harry Hurwitz. *HMD*

That's Dancing! **1985 (G)** This anthology features some of film's finest moments in dance from classical ballet to break-dancing. **104m/C VHS, Beta, LV.** Fred Astaire, Ginger Rogers, Ruby Keeler, Cyd Charisse, Gene Kelly, Shirley MacLaine, Liza Minnelli, Sammy Davis Jr., Mikhail Baryshnikov, Ray Bolger, Jennifer Beals, Dean Martin; ***D:*** Jack Haley Jr.; ***M:*** Henry Mancini. *MGM*

That's Entertainment **1974 (G)** A compilation of scenes from the classic MGM musicals beginning with "The Broadway Melody" (1929) and ending with "Gigi" (1958). Great fun, especially for movie buffs. **132m/C VHS, Beta, LV.** Judy Garland, Fred Astaire, Frank Sinatra, Gene Kelly, Esther Williams, Bing Crosby; ***D:*** Jack Haley Jr.; ***M:*** Henry Mancini. *MGM*

That's Entertainment, Part 2 **1976 (G)** A cavalcade of great musical and comedy sequences from MGM movies of the past. Also stars Jeanette MacDonald, Nelson Eddy, the Marx Brothers, Laurel and Hardy, Jack Buchanan, Ann Miller, Mickey Rooney, Louis Armstrong, Oscar Levant, Cyd Charisse, Elizabeth Taylor, Maurice Chavalier, Bing Crosby, Jimmy Durante, Clark Gable, and the Barrymores. Not as unified as its predecessor, but priceless nonetheless. **129m/C VHS, Beta, LV.** Fred Astaire, Gene Kelly. *MGM*

That's Entertainment, Part 3 **1993 (G)** Third volume contains 62 MGM musical numbers from over 100 films, hosted by nine of the original stars, and is based on outtakes and unfinished numbers from studio archives. One new technique used here is a split-screen showing both the actual film with a behind-the-scenes shot that includes cameramen, set designers, and dancers scurrying around. Although it has its moments, TE3 doesn't generate the same reverence for Hollywood's Golden Age that its predecessors managed to do. That 18-year gap between sequels may say something about what the studio execs thought of their film vault's remainders. **113m/C VHS, Beta, LV.** ***D:*** Bud Friedgen, Michael J. Sheridan; ***W:*** Bud Friedgen, Michael J. Sheridan; ***M:*** Marc Shaiman. *MGM*

That's Life! 🦴🦴 **1986 (PG-13)** A lackluster semi-home movie starring Edwards' family and friends. A single weekend in the lives of a writer who's turning sixty, his singer wife who has been diagnosed with cancer, and their family. **102m/C VHS, Beta, LV.** Jack Lemmon, Julie Andrews, Sally Kellerman, Chris Lemmon, Emma Walton, Rob Knepper, Robert Loggia, Jennifer Edwards; ***D:*** Blake Edwards; ***W:*** Blake Edwards; ***M:*** Henry Mancini. Nominations: Academy Awards '86: Best Song ("Life in a Looking Glass"). *CCB, LIV, VES*

That's My Baby! 🦴 **1988 (PG-13)** A man wants his girlfriend to have their baby, but the only thing she wants is a career. War between the sexes poorly done. **97m/C VHS, Beta.** Sonja Smits, Timothy Webber; ***D:*** Edie Yolles, John Bradshaw. *TWE*

That's Singing: The Best of Broadway **1984** A tribute to the American musical theatre featuring performances of memorable songs from twenty Broadway shows. **111m/C VHS, Beta, LV.** *ORI, WAR*

Theatre of Blood 🦴🦴🦴 **1973 (R)** Critics are unkind to Shakespearian ham Price, and he eliminates them by various Bard-inspired methods with the assistance of his lovely daughter. Top drawer comedy noir. **104m/C VHS, LV.** *GB* Vincent Price, Diana Rigg, Ian Hendry, Robert Morley, Dennis Price, Diana Dors, Milo O'Shea; ***D:*** Douglas Hickox. *MGM*

Theatre of Death 🦴🦴½ *Blood Fiend* **1967** Horror master Lee is back, this time as a theatre director in Paris. Meanwhile, police are baffled by a series of mysterious murders, each bearing a trace of vampirism. Well-plotted suspense. A racy voodoo dance sequence, often cut, is available on some video versions. **90m/C VHS, Beta.** Christopher Lee, Lelia Goldoni, Julian Glover, Evelyn Laye, Jenny Till, Ivor Dean; ***D:*** Samuel Gallu. *REP, SNC*

Thelma & Louise 🦴🦴🦴 **1991 (R)** Hailed as the first "feminist-buddy" movie, Sarandon and Davis bust out as best friends who head directly into one of the better movies of the year. Davis is the ditzy Thelma, a housewife rebelling against her dominating, unfaithful, abusive husband (who, rather than being disturbing, provides some of the best comic relief in the film). Sarandon is Louise, a hardened and world-weary waitress in the midst of an unsatisfactory relationship. They hit the road for a respite from their mundane lives, only to find violence and a part of themselves they never knew existed. Outstanding performances from Davis and especially Sarandon, with Pitt notable as the stud who gets Davis' motor revved. Director Scott has a fine eye for set details. **130m/C VHS, Beta, LV, 8mm.** Susan Sarandon, Geena Davis, Harvey Keitel, Christopher McDonald, Michael Madsen, Brad Pitt, Timothy Carhart, Stephen Tobolowsky, Lucinda Jenney; ***D:*** Ridley Scott; ***W:*** Callie Khouri; ***M:*** Hans Zimmer. Academy Awards '91: Best Original Screenplay; National Board of Review Awards '91: 10 Best Films of the Year, Best Actress (Sarandon, Davis); Writers Guild of America '91: Best Original Screenplay; Nominations: Academy Awards '91: Best Actress (Davis), Best Actress (Sarandon), Best Cinematography, Best Director (Scott), Best Film Editing. *MGM, OM*

Them! **1954** A group of mutated giant ants wreak havoc on a southwestern town. The first of the big-bug movies, and far surpassing the rest, this is a classic fun flick. See how many names you can spot among the supporting cast. **93m/B VHS, Beta, LV.** James Whitmore, Edmund Gwenn, Fess Parker, James Arness, Onslow Stevens, Jack Perrin; ***D:*** Gordon Douglas. *WAR*

The Theme *Tema* **1979** Esenin is a mediocre middle-aged playwright who knows his success comes from kow-towing to the party line. Trying to find inspiration he visits his native village where he meets the young Sasa, an artist who has refused to compromise. Although Esenin falls for her, Sasa has only contempt for his lack of principles and stays with her poet/lover, who is reduced to digging graves and has decided to emigrate to Israel. The film went unreleased for 8 years because of its themes of artistic freedom and emigration. In Russian with English subtitles. **100m/C VHS.** *RU* Mikhail Ulyanov, Inna Churikova, Stanislav Lyubshin, Evgeny Vesnik, Sergei Nikonenko, Natalya Selezneva; ***D:*** Gleb Panfilov. Berlin International Film Festival '79: Golden Berlin Bear. *KIV, FCT*

Theodora Goes Wild **1936** Tiny, priggish Lynnfield, Connecticut is shocked to discover that a scandalous best seller about smalltown life has been written pseudonymously by their very own Theodora Lynn (Dunne). When Theodora gets a chance to meet sophisticated New Yorker Michael Grant (Douglas), who did the illustrations for her book, she falls for him. But both must throw aside their own (and everyone else's) expectations and limitations for them to be happy. Dunne's first comedic lead role. **94m/B VHS.** Irene Dunne, Melvyn Douglas, Thomas Mitchell, Thurston Hall, Rosalind Keith, Spring Byington, Elisabeth Risdon, Margaret McWade; ***D:*** Richard Boleslawski; ***W:*** Sidney Buchman; ***C:*** Joseph Walker; ***M:*** Morris Stoloff. Nominations: Academy Awards '36: Best Actress (Dunne). *COL*

Theodore Rex ½ **1995 (PG)** Futuristic comedy finds cynical, seasoned cop Katie Coltrane (Goldberg) furious at being teamed with Teddy, who just happens to be an eight-foot-tall, three-ton, returned-from-extinction Tyrannosaurus Rex (who has a taste for cookies). And Teddy's not exactly the brightest dinosaur on the block, which makes Katie's job all the harder when they stumble across a major crime caper. **92m/C VHS, LV.** Whoopi Goldberg, Armin Mueller-Stahl, Richard Roundtree, Juliet Landau; ***D:*** Jonathan Betuel; ***W:*** Jonathan Betuel; ***C:*** David Tattersall; ***M:*** Robert Folk. *NLC*

There Goes Barder **1964** Constantine plays a con-man who's hired by a crooked ship owner to be a security agent. **?m/C VHS.** *FR* Eddie Constantine, May Britt. *SNC, VYY*

There Goes Kelly ½ **1945** Moran and Miller are page boys at a radio station who try to get the station receptionist a singing job. When the vocalist on a popular show is murdered, the duo not only get their protege a break but get themselves a mystery to solve as well. **62m/B VHS.** Jackie Moran, Sidney Miller, Wanda McKay, Ralph Sanford, Jan Wiley, Anthony Warde; ***D:*** Phil Karlson. *GPV*

There Goes My Baby ½ **1992 (R)** Eight California high school grads confront their futures on two nights in '65 (as the Watts riots ignite). There are Vietnam protests, flower children, would-be rock stars, friendships, and romantic complications. Yes, it sounds a lot like "American Graffiti" but the cast are winning and there's a good deal of affection without sinking to mawkishness. **99m/C VHS, LV.** Dermot Mulroney, Rick Schroder, Kelli Williams, Jill Schoelen, Noah Wyle, Kristin Minter, Lucy Deakins, Kenny Ransom, Seymour Cassel, Paul Gleason, Frederick Coffin, Andrew (Andy) Robinson, Shon Greenblatt, J.E. Freeman; ***D:*** Floyd Mutrux; ***W:*** Floyd Mutrux. *ORI*

There Goes the Neighborhood ½ **1992 (PG-13)** A dying convict tells prison psychiatrist Daniels where he has buried 8.5 million dollars—under the home of neighbor O'Hara. Daniels and O'Hara try to discreetly dig up the fortune but when the neighborhood finds out everyone wants a chance at the cash. **88m/C VHS, Beta.** Jeff Daniels, Catherine O'Hara, Dabney Coleman, Hector Elizondo, Judith Ivey, Rhea Perlman, Harris Yulin, Jonathan Banks, Chazz Palminteri, Mary Gross; ***D:*** Bill Phillips; ***M:*** David Bell. *PAR*

There was a Crooked Man ½ **1970 (R)** An Arizona town gets some new ideas about law and order when an incorruptible and innovative warden takes over the town's prison. The warden finds he's got his hands full with one inmate determined to escape. Offbeat western black comedy supported by an excellent and entertaining production, with fine acting all around. **123m/C VHS, Beta.** Kirk Douglas, Henry Fonda, Warren Oates, Hume Cronyn, Burgess Meredith, John Randolph, Arthur O'Connell, Alan Hale Jr., Lee Grant; ***D:*** Joseph L. Mankiewicz; ***W:*** Robert Benton, David Newman; ***C:*** Harry Stradling Jr. *WAR*

Theremin: An Electronic Odyssey **1995 (PG)** Profiles the life of Russian scientist Leon Theremin (who died in 1993), founder of electronic music, and his revolutionary musical invention, the Theremin. Martin located the 95-year old Thermin in Moscow in 1991, interviewed him on camera, then brought him back to the U.S. to film reunions with friends and colleages he hadn't seen in 50 years. Martin's focus is on the impact of the Theremin on Hollywood movie scores heard in 50s sci-fi and thriller classics ("The Day the Earth Stood Still") and in popular music (The Beach Boys' "Good Vibrations" is commented on by Brian Wilson). Theremin's life proves as curious as his instrument, with his controversial interracial marriage to a ballet star, abduction by Russian agents, and imprisonment in a Soviet mental hospital. "Theremin" provides a fascinating and heartfelt tribute to the man's work and life. **84m/C VHS, LV.** ***D:*** Steven M. Martin; ***W:*** Steven M. Martin; ***C:*** Robert Stone, Edward Lachman, Chris Lombardi; ***M:*** Hal Wilner. *ORI*

There's a Girl in My Soup **1970 (R)** Sellers is a gourmet who moonlights as a self-styled Casanova. Early post "Laugh-In" Hawn is the young girl who takes refuge at his London love nest when her boyfriend dumps her. Lust ensues. Has its funny parts, but not a highlight of anyone's career. Based on the hit play. **95m/C VHS, Beta.** *GB* Peter Sellers, Goldie Hawn, Diana Dors; ***D:*** Roy Boulting. *GKK*

There's No Business Like Show Business **1954** A top husband and wife vaudevillian act make it a family affair. Filmed in CinemaScope, allowing for full and lavish musical numbers. Good performances and Berlin's music make this an enjoyable film. ♫When the Midnight Choo-Choo Leaves for Alabam; Let's Have Another Cup of Coffee; Play a Simple Melody; After You Get What You Want You Don't Want It; You'd Be Surprised; A Sailor's Not a Sailor; A Pretty Girl is Like a Melody; If You Believe Me; A Man Chases a Girl Until She Catches Him. **117m/C VHS, Beta, LV.** Ethel Merman, Donald O'Connor, Marilyn Monroe, Dan Dailey, Johnny Ray, Mitzi Gaynor, Frank McHugh, Hugh O'Brian; ***D:*** Walter Lang. Nominations: Academy Awards '54: Best Costume Design (Color), Best Story, Best Original Score. *FOX, FCT*

There's No Time for Love, Charlie Brown **1987** An animated adventure with the Peanuts gang as they travel to a museum on a class trip. **30m/C VHS, Beta.** *BAR*

There's Nothing Out There **1990** A group of seven teenagers spends Spring Break at a secluded mountain cabin. It sounds wonderful, but one of the boys (who claims to have seen every horror movie on video) knows the signs of a horror movie just waiting to happen. **91m/C VHS, Beta, LV.** Craig Peck, Wendy Bednarz, Mark Collver, Bonnie Bowers, John Carhart III, Claudia Flores, Jeff Dachis; ***D:*** Rolfe Kanefsky; ***W:*** Rolfe Kanefsky. *PSM*

Therese **1986** Stylish biography of a young French nun and her devotion to Christ bordering on romantic love. Explores convent life. Real-life Therese died of TB and was made a saint. A directorial tour de force for Cavalier. In French with English subtitles. **90m/C VHS, Beta.** *FR* Catherine Mouchet, Aurore Prieto, Sylvie Habault, Ghislaine Mona; ***D:*** Alain Cavalier; ***W:*** Alain Cavalier. Cannes Film Festival '86: Special Jury Prize; Cesar Awards '87: Best Cinematography, Best Director (Cavalier), Best Film, Best Writing. *INJ, APD, MED*

Therese & Isabelle ½ *Therese Und Isabell* **1968** Story of growing love and physical attraction between two French schoolgirls. On holiday together, they confront their mutual desires. Richly photographed soft porn. Not vulgar, but certainly for adults. **102m/C VHS, Beta.** *GE* Essy Persson, Anna Gael, Barbara Laage, Anne Vernon; ***D:*** Radley Metzger. *NO*

These Girls Won't Talk **192?** Three female stars of early silent pictures are featured separately in: "Her Bridal Nightmare," "Campus Carmen," and "As Luck Would Have It." **50m/B VHS, Beta.** Colleen Moore, Carole Lombard, Betty Compson. *VYY*

These Three ½ **1936** A teenaged girl ruins the lives of two teachers by telling a malicious lie. Excellent cast. Script by Lillian Hellman, based on her play "The Children's Hour." Remade by the same director as "The Children's Hour" in 1961. **92m/B VHS, Beta, LV.** Miriam Hopkins, Merle Oberon, Joel McCrea, Bonita Granville, Marcia Mae Jones, Walter Brennan, Margaret Hamilton; ***D:*** William Wyler; ***C:*** Gregg Toland. Nominations: Academy Awards '36: Best Supporting Actress (Granville). *SUE*

They *Invasion from Inner Earth; Hell Fire* **1977** Beings from beneath the earth's crust take their first trip to the surface. **88m/C VHS, Beta.** Paul Dentzer, Debbie Pick, Nick Holt; ***D:*** Ito Rebane. *NO*

They All Laughed **1981 (PG)** Three detectives become romantically involved with the women they were hired to investigate. Essentially lighthearted fluff with little or no script. Further undermined by the real-life murder of Stratten before the film's release. **115m/C VHS, Beta, LV.** Ben Gazzara, John Ritter, Audrey Hepburn, Colleen Camp, Patti Hansen, Dorothy Stratten, Elizabeth Pena; ***D:*** Peter Bogdanovich; ***W:*** Peter Bogdanovich. *VES*

They Bite *Woof!* **1995 (R)** A pornographic filmmaker's latest epic about lustful gill-men is filming at the same Florida beach where a zoologist is investigating reports of man-like fish monsters killing swimmers. Just a coincidence? Ultra- (and deliberately) cheesy; an unrated version is also available. **96m/C VHS.** Donna Frotscher, Nick Baldasare, Charlie Barnett; ***D:*** Bret Piper. *MTH*

They Call It Sin *The Way of Life* **1932** Often told story of a young country girl heading to the Big Apple in search of her big break and "Mr. Right." Young is a chorus line girl romantically involved with her married producer (Calhern) while faithful admirer Brent waits nearby. Predictable plot adapted from the novel by Alberta Stedman Eagan. **68m/B VHS.** Loretta Young, George Brent, David Manners, Louis Calhern, Una Merkel, Joseph Cawthorn, Helen Vinson; ***D:*** Thornton Freeland; ***W:*** Lillie Hayward, Howard J. Green. *MGM*

They Call Me Bruce? ✂✂ *A Fist Full of Chopsticks* **1982 (PG)** A bumbling Bruce Lee look-alike meets a karate-chopping Mafia moll in this farce. Silly premise creates lots of laughs. Followed by a sequel, "They Still Call Me Bruce." **88m/C VHS, Beta.** Johnny Yune, Margaux Hemingway; ***D:*** Elliot Hong; ***W:*** Tim Clawson. *VES*

They Call Me Mr. Tibbs! ✂✂ **1970 (R)** Lieutenant Virgil Tibbs (Poitier) investigates the murder of a prostitute. The prime suspect is his friend, the Reverend Logan Sharpe (Landau). He is torn between his duty as a policeman, his concern for the reverend, and the turmoil of his domestic life. Less tense, less compelling sequel to "In the Heat of the Night." **108m/C VHS, Beta.** Sidney Poitier, Barbara McNair, Martin Landau, Juano Hernandez, Anthony Zerbe, Ed Asner, Norma Crane, Jeff Corey; ***D:*** Gordon Douglas; ***W:*** Alan R. Trustman; ***M:*** Quincy Jones. *MGM, FOX*

They Call Me Trinity ✂✂½ *Lo Chiamavano Trinita* **1972 (G)** Lazy drifter-gunslinger and his outlaw brother join forces with Mormon farmers to rout bullying outlaws. Spoofs every western cliche with relentless comedy, parodying "The Magnificent Seven" and gibing the spaghetti western. Followed by "Trinity is Still My Name." Dubbed. **110m/C VHS, Beta.** *IT* Terence Hill, Bud Spencer, Farley Granger, Steffen Zacharias; ***D:*** E.B. Clucher. *CCB, SUE, HHE*

They Came from Beyond Space ✂ **1967** Aliens invade the earth and possess the brains of humans. They only want a few slaves to help them repair their ship which crashed on the moon. The only person able to stop them is a scientist with a steel plate in his head. Silly and forgettable. **86m/C VHS, Beta.** *GB* Robert Hutton, Michael Gough; ***D:*** Freddie Francis. *SUE*

They Came from Within ✂✂½ *Shivers; The Parasite Murders* **1975 (R)** The occupants of a high-rise building go on a sex and violence spree when stricken by an aphrodisiac parasite. Queasy, sleazy and weird. First major film by Cronenberg. **87m/C VHS, Beta.** *CA* Paul Hampton, Joe Silver, Lynn Lowry, Barbara Steele; ***D:*** David Cronenberg; ***W:*** David Cronenberg. *LIV, VES*

They Came to Cordura ✂✂½ **1959** Mexico, 1916: a woman and six American soldiers—five heroes and one who has been branded a coward—begin a journey to the military headquarters in Cordura. Slow journey brings out personalities. Look for "Bewitched" hubby Dick York. Based on Glendon Swarthout's best-seller. **123m/C VHS, Beta, LV.** Gary Cooper, Rita Hayworth, Van Heflin, Tab Hunter, Dick York, Richard Conte; ***D:*** Robert Rossen. *COL*

They Died with Their Boots On ✂✂✂ **1941** The Battle of Little Big Horn is recreated Hollywood style. Takes liberties with historical fact, but still an exciting portrayal of General Custer's last stand. The movie also marks the last time de Havilland worked with Flynn. Also available colorized. **141m/B VHS, Beta.** Errol Flynn, Sydney Greenstreet, Anthony Quinn, Hattie McDaniel, Arthur Kennedy, Gene Lockhart, Regis Toomey, Olivia de Havilland, Charley Grapewin; ***D:*** Raoul Walsh; ***M:*** Max Steiner. *MGM, MLB, FOX*

They Drive by Night ✂✂✂½ *The Road to Frisco* **1940** Two truck-driving brothers break away from a large company and begin independent operations. After an accident to Bogart, Raft is forced to go back to the company where Lupino, the boss's wife, becomes obsessed with him and kills her husband to gain the company and win Raft. When he rejects her, she accuses him of the murder. Well-plotted film with great dialogue. Excellent cast gives it their all. **97m/B VHS, Beta.** Humphrey Bogart, Ann Sheridan, George Raft, Ida Lupino, Alan Hale, Gale Page, Roscoe Karns, Charles Halton; ***D:*** Raoul Walsh. *FOX, FCT*

They Got Me Covered ✂✂ **1943** Two WWII-era journalists get involved in a comic web of murder, kidnapping and romance. Hope is very funny and carries the rest of the cast. Look for Doris Day in a bit part and listen for Bing Crosby singing whenever Hope opens his cigarette case. **95m/B VHS, Beta, LV.** Bob Hope, Dorothy Lamour, Otto Preminger, Eduardo Ciannelli, Donald Meek, Walter Catlett; ***D:*** David Butler. *SUE*

They Knew What They Wanted ✂✂✂ **1940** A lonely San Francisco waitress begins a correspondence romance with a grape grower and agrees to marry him after he sends her a photo which shows him as being young and handsome. She arrives to discover Laughton had sent her a picture of another man. An accident, an affair, and a pregnancy provide further complications before a satisfactory ending is suggested. Flawed adaptation of Sidney Howard's play still has strong performances from Lombard and Laughton. **96m/B VHS, Beta.** Charles Laughton, Carole Lombard, Harry Carey Sr., Karl Malden, William Gargan; ***D:*** Garson Kanin; ***C:*** Harry Stradling. Nominations: Academy Awards '40: Best Supporting Actor (Gargan). *NO*

They Live ✂✂½ **1988 (R)** A semi-serious science-fiction spoof about a drifter who discovers an alien conspiracy. They're taking over the country under the guise of Reaganism, capitalism and yuppiedom. Screenplay written by Carpenter under a pseudonym. Starts out fun, deteriorates into cliches and bad special effects makeup. **88m/C VHS, Beta, LV.** Roddy Piper, Keith David, Meg Foster, George Flower, Peter Jason, Raymond St. Jacques, John Lawrence, Sy Richardson, Jason Robards III, Larry Franco; ***D:*** John Carpenter; ***W:*** John Carpenter; ***M:*** Alan Howarth, John Carpenter. *MCA*

They Live by Night ✂✂✂½ *The Twisted Road; Your Red Wagon* **1949** A young fugitive sinks deeper into a life of crime thanks to his association with two hardened criminals. Classic film noir was Ray's first attempt at directing. Based on Edward Anderson's novel "Thieves Like Us," under which title it was remade in 1974. Compelling and suspenseful. **95m/B VHS, Beta, LV.** Cathy O'Donnell, Farley Granger, Howard da Silva, Jay C. Flippen, Helen Craig; ***D:*** Nicholas Ray. *HHT*

They Made Me a Criminal ✂✂½ *I Became a Criminal; They Made Me a Fugitive* **1939** A champion prizefighter, believing he murdered a man in a drunken brawl, runs away. He finds refuge in the West with the Dead End Kids. Remake of "The Life of Jimmy Dolan." Berkeley was best-known for directing and choreographing musicals and surprisingly did very well with this movie. **92m/B VHS, Beta, LV.** John Garfield, Ann Sheridan, Claude Rains, Leo Gorcey; ***D:*** Busby Berkeley; ***C:*** James Wong Howe; ***M:*** Max Steiner. *NOS, PSM, VHE*

They Meet Again ✂✂ **1941** The final segment of the Dr. Christian series. The country doctor sets out to prove the innocence of a man who has been wrongly accused of stealing money. Slow moving and not particularly exciting. **68m/B VHS, Beta, 8mm.** Jean Hersholt, Dorothy Lovett; ***D:*** Erle C. Kenton. *NOS, VYY, VYY*

They Met in Bombay ✂✂½ **1941** Two jewel thieves team up in this romantic action-comedy, complete with exotic locations and two big box-office stars. A Japanese invasion makes Russell reconsider her life of crime and gives Gable a chance to play hero. Look for Alan Ladd in a bit part in his pre-"This Gun for Hire" days. Based on a story by John Kafka. **86m/B VHS.** Clark Gable, Rosalind Russell, Peter Lorre, Jessie Ralph, Reginald Owen, Eduardo Ciannelli, Alan Ladd; ***D:*** Clarence Brown; ***W:*** Anita Loos, Edwin Justus Mayer, Leon Gordon. *MGM*

They Might Be Giants ✂✂✂ **1971 (G)** Woodward is a woman shrink named Watson who treats retired judge Scott for delusions that he is Sherlock Holmes. Scott's brother wants him committed so the family loot will come to him. Very funny in places; Woodward and Scott highlight a solid cast. **98m/C VHS, Beta.** George C. Scott, Joanne Woodward, Jack Gilford, Eugene Roche, Kitty Winn, F. Murray Abraham, M. Emmet Walsh; ***D:*** Anthony Harvey; ***M:*** John Barry. *MCA*

They Never Come Back ✂½ **1932** A boxer is thrown in jail and then stages a comeback. **62m/B VHS, Beta, LV.** Regis Toomey, Dorothy Sebastian. *SNC*

They Only Kill Their Masters ✂✂½ **1972 (PG)** Garner plays a California police chief investigating the death of a wild beach town resident, supposedly killed by her doberman pinscher. He discovers the woman was actually drowned and there are any number of secrets to uncover. Mild whodunit. **98m/C VHS.** James Garner, Katharine Ross, June Allyson, Hal Holbrook, Harry Guardino, Christopher Connelly, Tom Ewell, Peter Lawford, Edmond O'Brien, Arthur O'Connell, Ann Rutherford, Art Metrano; ***D:*** James Goldstone; ***M:*** Perry Botkin. *MGM*

They Paid with Bullets: Chicago 1929 ✂½ **197?** The story of one man's rise to power, and eventual downfall as a Mafia consigliatore. **88m/C VHS, Beta.** Peter Lee Lawrence, Ingrid Schoeller. *CNG*

They Saved Hitler's Brain *Woof! Madmen of Mandoras; The Return of Mr. H* **1964** Fanatical survivors of the Nazi holocaust gave eternal life to the brain of their leader in the last hours of the war. Now it's on a Caribbean island giving orders again. One of the truly great "bad" movies. Shot in pieces in the U.S., the Philippines, and elsewhere, with chunks of other films stuck in to hold the "story" together. **91m/B VHS, Beta, 8mm.** Walter Stocker, Audrey Caire; ***D:*** David Bradley. *VYY*

They Shall Have Music ✂✂ *Melody of Youth; Ragged Angels* **1939** A poverty-stricken child hears a concert by violinist Heifetz and decides to become a musician. He joins Brennan's nearly bankrupt music school and persuades Heifetz to play at a benefit concert. Hokey but enjoyable Goldwyn effort to bring classical music to the big screen. ♫Rondo Capriccioso; Hora Staccato; Estrellita; Melody; Concerto in E Minor for Violin and Orchestra; Waltz in D Flat, Opus 64, No. 1; Cara Nome; Casta Diva. **101m/B VHS, Beta.** Walter Brennan, Joel McCrea, Gene Reynolds, Jascha Heifetz, Marjorie Main, Porter Hall, Andrea Leeds, Terence Kilburn; ***D:*** Archie Mayo. Nominations: Academy Awards '39: Best Score. *SUE, HBO*

They Shoot Horses, Don't They? ✂✂✂½ **1969 (R)** Powerful period piece depicting the desperation of the Depression Era. Contestants enter a dance marathon in the hopes of winning a cash prize, not realizing that they will be driven to exhaustion. Fascinating and tragic. **121m/C VHS, LV.** Jane Fonda, Michael Sarrazin, Susannah York, Gig Young, Red Buttons, Bonnie Bedelia, Bruce Dern, Allyn Ann McLerie, Chaing I; ***D:*** Sydney Pollack. Academy Awards '69: Best Supporting Actor (Young); British Academy Awards '70: Best Supporting Actress (York); Golden Globe Awards '70: Best Supporting Actor (Young); New York Film Critics Awards '69: Best Actress (Fonda); Nominations: Academy Awards '69: Best Actress (Fonda), Best Adapted Screenplay, Best Art Direction/Set Decoration, Best Costume Design, Best Director (Pollack), Best Film Editing, Best Supporting Actress (York), Best Original Score. *ABC, TCF, FOX*

They Still Call Me Bruce ✂ **1986 (PG)** A Korean searches for the American who saved his life when he was young and instead becomes big brother to an orphan. Supposedly a sequel to "They Call Me Bruce," but has little in common with it. Poorly done and not particularly entertaining. **91m/C VHS, Beta.** Johnny Yune, Robert Guillaume, Pat Paulsen; ***D:*** Johnny Yune. *NWV, VTR*

They Watch ✂✂½ *They* **1993 (PG-13)** Workaholic Bergin neglects his family and suffers the consequences when his young daughter dies in an auto accident. In fact, he's so distressed that he relies on blind psychic Redgrave to get in touch with his little girl's spirit. Based on the story "They" by Rudyard Kipling. Made for television. **100m/C VHS.** Patrick Bergin, Vanessa Redgrave, Valerie Mahaffey; ***D:*** John Korty; ***W:*** Edithe Swensen; ***M:*** Gerald Gouriet. *COL*

They Went That-a-Way & That-a-Way *Woof!* **1978 (PG)** Two bumbling deputies pose as convicts in this madcap prison caper. Terrible re-hash of Laurel-and-Hardy has nothing going for it. **96m/C VHS, Beta.** Tim Conway, Richard Kiel, Chuck McCann; ***D:*** Edward Montagne; ***W:*** Tim Conway. *SUE*

They Were Expendable ☙☙☙½ **1945** Two American captains pit their PT boats against the Japanese fleet. Based on the true story of a PT boat squadron based in the Philippines during the early days of WWII. One of the best (and most underrated) WWII films. Also available in a colorized version. **135m/B VHS, Beta.** Robert Montgomery, John Wayne, Donna Reed, Jack Holt, Ward Bond, Cameron Mitchell, Leon Ames, Marshall Thompson; ***D:*** John Ford. Nominations: Academy Awards '45: Best Sound. *MGM*

They Were So Young ☙☙½ **1955** European models become the pawns of wealthy Brazilian magnates when they are sent to South America. They are threatened with death if they do not cooperate. The scenes were shot in Italy and Berlin. Well acted and believable, although rather grim story. **78m/B VHS, Beta, LV.** *GE* Scott Brady, Johanna Matz, Raymond Burr; ***D:*** Kurt Neumann. *NO*

They Were Ten ☙☙½ **1961** Ten Soviet Jews make Palestine their home in the 1800s despite Arab and Turkish persecution and pressures among themselves. In Hebrew with English subtitles. **105m/B VHS, Beta.** *IS* Ninette, Oded Teomi, Leo Filer, Yosef Safra; ***D:*** Baruch Dienar. *ERG, FCT, INJ*

They Won't Believe Me ☙☙☙ **1947** A man plots to kill his wife, but before he does, she commits suicide. He ends up on trial for her "murder." Interesting acting by Young and Hayward against type. Surprising, ironic ending. **95m/B VHS, Beta, LV.** Robert Young, Susan Hayward, Rita Johnson, Jane Greer; ***D:*** Irving Pichel. *MED, TTC*

They Won't Forget ☙☙☙½ **1937** When a young girl is murdered in a southern town, personal interests take precedence over justice. Turner is excellent in her first billed role, as are the other actors. Superb script, and expert direction by LeRoy pulls it all together. Based on Ward Greene's "Death in the Deep South." **95m/B VHS.** Claude Rains, Otto Kruger, Lana Turner, Allyn Joslyn, Elisha Cook Jr., Edward Norris; ***D:*** Mervyn LeRoy; ***W:*** Robert Rossen, Aben Kandel. *WAR, OM*

They're Playing with Fire *Woof!* **1984 (R)** An English teacher seduces a student and gets him involved in a murder plot to gain an inheritance. Turns out someone else is beating them to the punch. Sleazy semi-pornographic slasher. **96m/C VHS, Beta.** Sybil Danning, Eric Brown, Andrew Prine, Paul Clemens, K.T. Stevens, Alvy Moore; ***D:*** Howard (Hikmet) Avedis; ***W:*** Howard (Hikmet) Avedis. *VTR*

Thicker Than Water ☙☙ **1993** Eerie psychological thriller exploring the relationship between identical twins. Sam Crawford (Pryce) is a successful doctor, happily married to Jo (Russell), whose sister Debbie (Russell again) is completely different in temperament. The two share a strong psychic bond, however, and when Jo dies in a suspicious hit-and-run accident Debbie feels compelled to make Sam her own. Based on the novel by Dylan Jones. **150m/C VHS.** *GB* Theresa Russell, Jonathan Pryce, Robert Pugh; ***D:*** Marc Evans; ***W:*** Trevor Preston. *TVC*

The Thief ☙☙ **1952** An American commits treason and is overcome by guilt. Novel because there is not one word of dialogue, though the gimmmick can't sustain the ordinary story. A product of the Communist scare of the 1950s, it tends to be pretentious and melodramatic. **84m/C VHS, Beta, LV.** Ray Milland, Rita Gam, Martin Gabel, Harry Bronson, John McKutcheon; ***D:*** Russel Rouse; ***C:*** Sam Leavitt. Nominations: Academy Awards '52: Best Original Score. *VCI*

Thief **1971** A successful businessman (Crenna) attempts to put his criminal past behind him. He's trapped when looking for a quick way to get some money to pay off a gambling debt. Made for television drama that's well-written and directed with tepid acting. **74m/C VHS, Beta.** Richard Crenna, Angie Dickinson, Cameron Mitchell, Hurd Hatfield, Robert Webber; ***D:*** William A. Graham. *ORI*

Thief ☙☙☙ *Violent Streets* **1981 (R)** A big-time professional thief likes working solo, but decides to sign up with the mob in order to make one more big score and retire. He finds out it's not that easy. Taut and atmospheric thriller is director Mann's feature film debut. **126m/C VHS, Beta, LV.** James Caan, Tuesday Weld, Willie Nelson, James Belushi, Elizabeth Pena, Robert Prosky; ***D:*** Michael Mann; ***W:*** Michael Mann; ***C:*** Donald E. Thorin. Nominations: Cannes Film Festival '81: Best Film. *MGM, FOX*

The Thief of Bagdad ☙☙☙½ **1940** A wily young thief enlists the aid of a powerful genie to outwit the Grand Vizier of Baghdad. An Arabian Nights spectacular with lush photography, fine special effects, and striking score. Outstanding performance by Ingram as the genie. **106m/C VHS, Beta, LV.** Sabu, Conrad Veidt, June Duprez, Rex Ingram; ***D:*** Tim Whelan, Michael Powell, Ludwig Berger; ***C:*** Georges Perinal; ***M:*** Miklos Rozsa. Nominations: Academy Awards '40: Best Color Cinematography, Best Original Score. *SUE, MLB, FUS*

The Thief of Baghdad ☙☙☙ **1924** The classic silent crowd-pleaser, about a roguish thief who uses a genie's magic to outwit Baghdad's evil Caliph. With famous special effects in a newly struck print, and a new score by Davis based on Rimsky-Korsakov's "Scheherezade." Remade many times. **153m/B VHS, Beta, LV.** Douglas Fairbanks Sr., Snitz Edwards, Charles Belcher, Anna May Wong, Etta Lee, Brandon Hurst, Sojin, Julanne Johnston; ***D:*** Raoul Walsh; ***M:*** Carl Davis. *SNC, NOS, CCB*

Thief of Baghdad ☙☙ *Il Ladro Di Bagdad; Le Voleur De Bagdad* **1961** An Arabian Nights fantasy about a thief in love with a Sultan's daughter who has been poisoned. He seeks out the magical blue rose which is the antidote. Not as lavish as the previous two productions by this title, nor as much fun. **89m/C VHS, Beta.** *IT* Georgia Moll, Steve Reeves; ***D:*** Arthur Lubin. *SUE*

The Thief of Baghdad ☙☙½ **1978 (G)** A fantasy-adventure about a genie, a prince, beautiful maidens, a happy-go-lucky thief, and magic. Easy to take, but not an extraordinary version of this oft-told tale. Ustinov is fun as he tries to marry off his daughter. Made for television. **101m/C VHS, Beta.** Peter Ustinov, Roddy McDowall, Terence Stamp, Frank Finlay, Ian Holm; ***D:*** Clive Donner. *GEM*

Thief of Hearts ☙☙ **1984 (R)** A thief steals a woman's diary when he's ransacking her house. He then pursues the woman, using his secret knowledge. Slick, but too creepy. Re-edited with soft porn scenes in some video versions. Stewart's first film. **101m/C VHS, Beta, LV.** Steven Bauer, Barbara Williams, John Getz, Christine Ebersole, George Wendt; ***D:*** Douglas Day Stewart; ***M:*** Harold Faltermeyer. *PAR*

The Thief Who Came to Dinner ☙☙ **1973 (PG)** A computer analyst and a wealthy socialite team up to become jewel thieves and turn the tables on Houston's high society set. Comedy plot gets complex, though O'Neal and Bisset are likeable. Early Clayburgh role as O'Neal's ex. Based on a novel by Terence Lore Smith. **103m/C VHS, Beta.** Ryan O'Neal, Jacqueline Bisset, Warren Oates, Jill Clayburgh, Ned Beatty, Gregory Sierra, Michael Murphy, Austin Pendleton, John Hillerman, Charles Cioffi; ***D:*** Bud Yorkin; ***W:*** Walter Hill; ***M:*** Henry Mancini. *WAR*

Thieves Like Us ☙☙☙½ **1974 (R)** Story of doomed lovers during the Depression is thoughtfully told by Altman. Older criminals Remsen and Schuck escape from jail with young killer Carradine. They only know one way to make a living—robbing banks—and it isn't long before they're once more working at their trade. They get a lot of press but they have a distinct problem. They're not really very good at what they do. Cops on their trail, the gang tries, unsuccessfully, to survive. Fletcher's film debut as Remsen's sister-in-law. Good period atmosphere and strong characters. Based on the novel by Edward Anderson and previously filmed as "They Live by Night." **123m/C VHS.** Keith Carradine, Shelley Duvall, Bert Remsen, John Schuck, Louise Fletcher, Anne Latham, Tom Skerritt; ***D:*** Robert Altman; ***W:*** Joan Tewkesbury, Calder Willingham, Robert Altman. *MGM*

Thieves of Fortune *Woof!* **1989 (R)** Former Miss Universe stars as a contestant in a high stakes fortune hunt that spans half the globe. She meets with more than her share of action-packed encounters among the ruffians who compete for the $28 million purse. Implausible; horrible script; cliched. **100m/C VHS, Beta, LV.** Michael Nouri, Lee Van Cleef, Shawn Weatherly. *ACA*

The Thin Blue Line ☙☙☙½ **1988** The acclaimed docudrama about the 1977 shooting of a cop in Dallas County, and the incorrect conviction of Randall Adams for the crime. A riveting, spellbinding experience. Due to the film's impact and continued lobbying by Morris, Adams is now free. **101m/C VHS, Beta, LV.** ***D:*** Errol Morris; ***M:*** Philip Glass. Edgar Allan Poe Awards '88: Best Screenplay. *HBO, CCB*

Thin Ice ☙☙☙ **1937** Successful musical romance featuring European prince Power falling for commoner Henie. A fine score, solid script, and Henie's excellent ice skating routines make this her best film. Based on the play "Der Komet" by Attila Obok. ♫I'm Olga from the Volga; My Swiss Hillbilly; My Secret Love Affair; Over Night. **78m/B VHS.** Sonja Henie, Tyrone Power, Arthur Treacher, Raymond Walburn, Joan Davis, Alan Hale, Sig Rumann, Melville Cooper, Maurice Cass, George Givot, Torben Meyer; ***D:*** Sidney Lanfield; ***W:*** Boris Ingster, Milton Sperling. *FXV*

A Thin Line Between Love and Hate ☙ **1996 (R)** Writer/director/star Lawrence shows that there's no line between a crude, foul-mouthed ego trip and an unfunny, unsuspenseful film. Darnell Wright is a smooth talker constantly on the lookout for women to conquer and discard. Eventually, he meets the wrong lady (Whitfield), a classic movie psycho who turns his life upside down. Drawing heavily from "Fatal Attraction," this halfhearted effort offers bad pacing, a weak script, and totally unsympathetic characters, which could almost be overlooked if it was at all funny. Whitfield holds the flick's only redeeming value as the femme fatale. **108m/C VHS.** Martin Lawrence, Lynn Whitfield, Regina King, Bobby Brown, Della Reese, Roger E. Mosley, Malinda Williams, Daryl Mitchell, Simbi Khali; ***D:*** Martin Lawrence; ***W:*** Martin Lawrence, Bentley Kyle Evans, Kenny Buford, Kim Bass; ***C:*** Francis Kenny; ***M:*** Roger Troutman. *NYR*

The Thin Man ☙☙☙½ **1934** Married sleuths Nick and Nora Charles investigate the mysterious disappearance of a wealthy inventor. Charming and sophisticated, this was the model for all husband-and-wife detective teams that followed. Don't miss Asta, their wire-hair terrier. Based on the novel by Dashiell Hammett. Its enormous popularity triggered five sequels, starting with "After the Thin Man." **90m/B VHS, Beta, LV.** William Powell, Myrna Loy, Maureen O'Sullivan, Cesar Romero, Porter Hall, Nat Pendleton, Minna Gombell, Natalie Moorhead, Edward Ellis; ***D:*** Woodbridge S. Van Dyke; ***C:*** James Wong Howe. Nominations: Academy Awards '34: Best Actor (Powell), Best Adapted Screenplay, Best Director (Van Dyke), Best Picture. *MGM, HMV*

The Thin Man Goes Home ☙☙½ **1944** Married sleuths Nick and Nora Charles solve a mystery with Nick's disapproving parents looking on in the fifth film from the "Thin Man" series. Despite a three-year gap and slightly less chemistry between Powell and Loy, audiences welcomed the skinny guy. Sequel to "Shadow of the Thin Man;" followed by "Song of the Thin Man." **100m/B VHS, Beta.** William Powell, Myrna Loy, Lucile Watson, Gloria De Haven, Anne Revere, Harry Davenport, Helen Vinson, Lloyd Corrigan, Donald Meek, Edward Brophy, Charles Halton; ***D:*** Richard Thorpe. *MGM*

The Thing ☙☙☙½ *The Thing From Another World* **1951** One of the best of the Cold War allegories and a potent lesson to those who won't eat their vegetables. Sci fi classic about an alien craft and creature (Arness in monster drag), discovered by an Arctic research team. The critter is accidentally thawed and then wreaks havoc, sucking the blood from sled dog and scientist alike. It's a giant seed-dispersing vegetable run amuck, unaffected by missing body parts, bullets, or cold. In other words, Big Trouble. Excellent direction, assisted substantially by producer Hawks, and supported by strong performances. Available colorized; remade in 1982. Loosely based on "Who Goes There?" by John Campbell. **87m/B VHS, Beta, LV.** James Arness, Kenneth Tobey, Margaret Sheridan, Dewey Martin; ***D:*** Christian Nyby, Howard Hawks; ***W:*** Charles Lederer; ***M:*** Dimitri Tiomkin. *MED, TTC, MLB*

The Thing ½ **1982 (R)** A team of scientists at a remote Antarctic outpost discover a buried spaceship with an unwelcome alien survivor still alive. Bombastic special effects overwhelm the suspense and the solid cast. Less a remake of the 1951 science fiction classic than a more faithful version of John Campbell's short story "Who Goes There?," since the seeds/spores take on human shapes. **127m/C VHS, Beta, LV.** Kurt Russell, Wilford Brimley, T.K. Carter, Richard Masur, Keith David, Richard Dysart, David Clennon, Donald Moffat, Thomas G. Waites, Charles Hallahan; ***D:*** John Carpenter; ***C:*** Dean Cundey; ***M:*** Ennio Morricone. *MCA*

The Thing Called Love ½ **1993 (PG-13)** Take last year's surprise hit "Singles" and replace grunge rock and Seattle with Country/Western and Nashville for this unsentimental tale of four twentysomething singles trying to make their mark in the world of country music. The idea for the plot comes from the real-life Bluebird Cafe—the place where all aspiring singers and songwriters want to perform. Phoenix, Mathis, Mulroney, and Bullock did their own singing; look for Oslin as the Cafe owner. Phoenix's last completed film role. **116m/C VHS, Beta, LV.** River Phoenix, Samantha Mathis, Sandra Bullock, Dermot Mulroney, K.T. Oslin, Anthony Clark, Webb Wilder; ***Cameos:*** Trisha Yearwood; ***D:*** Peter Bogdanovich; ***W:*** Allan Moyle, Carol Heikkinen. *PAR*

Things **198?** A man creates a monster during his freakish experiments with artificial insemination. The monster returns to his house seeking revenge, and the man's visiting brother and a friend disappear, probably a clever move given their lackluster circumstances. **90m/C VHS, Beta.** Barry Gillis, Amber Lynn, Doug Bunston, Bruce Roach; ***D:*** Andrew Jordan. *NO*

Things ½ **1993** Two horror tales told by a jilted wife who's holding her husband's mistress hostage. "The Box" finds evil Mayor Black (Delama) incensed about a newly-opened brothel in his hick Nevada town. So he decides to teach the hookers a lesson with the help of a bizarre, boxed creature that's with him at all times. "Thing in a Jar" finds an abusive husband and his mistress plotting to kill his mousy wife. Only the murder victim comes back to haunt the deadly duo—at least parts of her do. Nicely grotesque special effects courtesy of Mike Tristano. **90m/C VHS.** Neil Delama, Trey Howard, Debra Stevens, Courtney Lercara, Kinder Hunt; ***Cameos:*** Jeff Burr; ***D:*** Dennis Devine, Jay Woelfel; ***W:*** Dennis Devine, Steve Jarvis, Mike Bowler. *VSE*

Things Change **1988 (PG)** An old Italian shoeshine guy agrees, for a fee, to be a fall guy for the Mafia. A lower-echelon mob hood, assigned to watch over him, decides to give the old guy a weekend of fun in Vegas before going to jail. Director Mamet co-wrote the screenplay with Silverstein, best-known for his children's books ("Where the Sidewalk Ends," "The Giving Tree"). Combines charm and menace with terrific performances, especially from Ameche and Mantegna. **114m/C VHS, Beta, LV.** Joe Mantegna, Don Ameche, Robert Prosky, J.J. Johnston, Ricky Jay, Mike Nussbaum, Jack Wallace, Dan Conway, J.T. Walsh; ***D:*** David Mamet; ***W:*** Shel Silverstein, David Mamet; ***M:*** Alaric Jans. Venice Film Festival '80: Best Actor (Ameche); Venice Film Festival '88: Best Actor (Mantegna). *COL*

Things Happen at Night **1948** Scientist and insurance investigator determine that friendly ghost has possessed a family's youngest daughter. Not much happens. **79m/B VHS, Beta.** *GB* Gordon Harker, Alfred Drayton, Robertson Hare, Olga Lindo, Wylie Watson; ***D:*** Francis Searle. *NOS, SNC*

Things in Their Season ½ **1974** Made for TV melodrama about the imminent death of the mother of a Wisconsin farm family who makes those around her realize the value of happiness. Neal is excellent, rest of cast better than average in a well-told and sincere film. **79m/C VHS, Beta.** Patricia Neal, Ed Flanders, Marc Singer, Meg Foster; ***D:*** James Goldstone. *LCA*

The Things of Life *Les Choses De La Vie* **1970** A car crash makes a man re-evaluate his life, goals, and loves. In the end he must choose the course of his future and decide between his wife and mistress. In French with English subtitles. **90m/C VHS, Beta, LV.** *FR* Romy Schneider, Michel Piccoli, Lea Massari; ***D:*** Claude Sautet. Nominations: Cannes Film Festival '70: Best Film. *CVC, INJ*

Things to Come ½ **1936** Using technology, scientists aim to rebuild the world after a lengthy war, followed by a plague and other unfortunate events. Massey and Scott each play two roles, in different generations. Startling picture of the world to come, with fine sets and good acting. Based on an H.G. Wells story, "The Shape of Things to Come." **92m/B VHS, Beta.** *GB* Raymond Massey, Margaretta Scott, Ralph Richardson, Cedric Hardwicke, Derrick DeMarney; ***D:*** William Cameron Menzies; ***C:*** Georges Perinal. *NOS, PSM, SNC*

Things to Do In Denver When You're Dead **1995 (R)** Jimmy the Saint (Garcia) is an ex-mobster gone straight who is called upon by his former boss, the Man With the Plan (Walken), to do one last easy-money job. Jimmy agrees and rounds up his old gang, a colorfully off-color group which includes Pieces (Lloyd), a porn movie projectionist and Critical Bill (Williams), a hair-trigger psycho who works in a funeral parlor. The job goes awry and the group becomes a target of hitman Mr. Shhh (Buscemi). Hipster dialogue, crime-gone-wrong formula, and the presence of Buscemi instantly scream Tarantino rip-off, but the performances make it a worthwhile genre entry. **114m/C VHS.** Andy Garcia, Christopher Lloyd, William Forsythe, Bill Nunn, Treat Williams, Jack Warden, Steve Buscemi, Fairuza Balk, Gabrielle Anwar, Christopher Walken; ***D:*** Gary Fleder; ***W:*** Scott Rosenberg; ***C:*** Elliot Davis; ***M:*** Michael Convertino. *TOU*

Think Big ½ **1990 (PG-13)** Former professional wrestlers, the Pauls are truck drivers in this silly, enjoyable comedy. They pick up a brilliant teenager running from bad guys. Mayhem ensues. **86m/C VHS, Beta, LV.** Peter Paul, David Paul, Martin Mull, Ari Meyers, Richard Kiel, David Carradine, Richard Moll, Peter Lupus; ***W:*** Jim Wynorski, R.J. Robertson. *LIV, VTR*

Think Dirty *Every Home Should Have One* **1970 (R)** Lascivious comedy about advertising executive Feldman's attempt to develop a series of sexy commercials to sell cereal. At the same time his wife forms a "clean up television" group. Not very interesting or funny. **93m/C VHS, Beta.** *GB* Marty Feldman, Judy Cornwell, Shelley Berman; ***D:*** Jim Clark. *COL*

Thinkin' Big **1987 (R)** Guys and gals cavort on the Texas coast, except for one lonely fat guy who tries to increase his sexual prowess. The usual teen sex frenzy. **96m/C VHS, Beta.** Bruce Anderson, Kenny Sargent, Randy Jandt, Nancy Buechler, Darla Ralston; ***D:*** S.F. Brownrigg. *VTR, PSM*

Third Degree Burn **1989** A made-for-cable-television mystery about a small-time detective hired by a businessman to follow a woman, only to become a suspect when the woman's real husband is killed. **97m/C VHS, Beta, LV.** Treat Williams, Virginia Madsen, Richard Masur; ***D:*** Roger Spottiswoode. *PAR*

The Third Key ½ *The Long Arm* **1957** A solid British crime drama follows a dogged detective as he probes serial safe-crackings, with a climax set at London's Festival Hall. Based on the book by Robert Barr, who co-scripted. **96m/B VHS.** Jack Hawkins, Dorothy Allison, Geoffrey Keen, Richard Leech, Ian Bannen; ***D:*** Charles Frend. *NOS*

The Third Man **1949** An American writer of pulp westerns (Cotten) arrives in post-war Vienna to take a job with an old friend, but discovers he has been murdered. Or has he? Based on Graham Greene's mystery, this classic film noir thriller plays on national loyalties during the Cold War. Welles is top-notch as the manipulative Harry Lime, blackmarket drugdealer extraordinare. The underground sewer sequence is not to be missed. With a haunting (sometimes irritating) theme by Anton Karas on unaccompanied zither. Special edition features trailer. **104m/B VHS, Beta, LV, 8mm.** Joseph Cotten, Orson Welles, Alida Valli, Trevor Howard, Bernard Lee, Wilfrid Hyde-White; ***D:*** Carol Reed; ***W:*** Graham Greene; ***C:*** Robert Krasker. Academy Awards '50: Best Black and White Cinematography; British Academy Awards '49: Best Film; Cannes Film Festival '49: Best Film; Directors Guild of America Awards '49: Best Director (Reed); National Board of Review Awards '50: 5 Best Foreign Films of the Year; Nominations: Academy Awards '50: Best Director (Reed), Best Film Editing. *SNC, REP, MED*

Third Man on the Mountain ½ *Banner in the Sky* **1959 (G)** A family epic about mountain climbing, shot in Switzerland and based on James Ramsey Ullman's "Banner in the Sky." A young man is determined to climb the "Citadel" as his ancestors have. He finds there's more to climbing than he imagined. Look for Helen Hayes (MacArthur's mother) in a cameo. Standard Disney adventure drama. **106m/C VHS, Beta.** James MacArthur, Michael Rennie, Janet Munro, James Donald, Herbert Lom, Laurence Naismith; ***Cameos:*** Helen Hayes; ***D:*** Ken Annakin. *DIS*

The Third Sex **1959** One of the first films to deal with homosexuality in which parents try to "straighten out" their gay son. **?m/C VHS.** Paul Dahlke, Paula Wesley. *SNC*

Third Solution *Russicum* **1989 (R)** An Italian-made film about the discovery of a secret pact made between the Kremlin and the Vatican that may start WWIII. Well-cast, but poorly conceived spook drama, with music by Vangelis. **93m/C VHS, Beta, LV.** *IT* Treat Williams, F. Murray Abraham, Danny Aiello, Nigel Court, Rita Rusic, Rossano Brazzi; ***D:*** Pasquale Squitieri; ***M:*** Vangelis. *COL*

Third Walker **1979** A desperate woman sacrifices her marriage to immerse herself in efforts to reunite her twin sons, who were inadvertently separated at birth. An original and intriguing directorial debut by McLuhan. **85m/C VHS, Beta.** William Shatner, Colleen Dewhurst; ***D:*** Marshall McLuhan. *NO*

Thirst **1987 (R)** A girl is abducted by a secret society that wants her to become their new leader. There is just one catch: she has to learn to like the taste of human blood. Chilling but weakly plotted. **96m/C VHS, Beta.** David Hemmings, Henry Silva, Chantal Contouri; ***D:*** Rod Hardy. *MED*

The Thirsty Dead *Woof! The Blood Cult of Shangri-La* **1974 (PG)** Maybe they could learn to like Gatorade. An eternally young jungle king is looking for a wife. She can be young forever too, if she's not above vampirism and sacrificing virgins. In spite of the jungle vampire slant, this Filipino-made movie is a woofer. Also released on video, as "Blood Hunt." **90m/C VHS, Beta.** *PH* John Considine, Jennifer Billingsley, Judith McConnell, Fredricka Meyers, Tani Phelps Guthrie; ***D:*** Terry Becker. *NO*

13 Ghosts ½ **1960** A dozen ghosts need another member to round out their ranks. They have four likely candidates to choose from when a family moves into the house inhabited by the ghoulish group. Originally viewed with "Illusion-O," a technology much like 3-D, which allowed the viewing of the ghosts only through a special pair of glasses. **88m/C VHS, Beta.** Charles Herbert, Jo Morrow, Martin Milner, Rosemary DeCamp, Donald Woods, Margaret Hamilton; ***D:*** William Castle. *GKK*

13 Rue Madeleine **1946** Cagney plays a WWII spy who infiltrates Gestapo headquarters in Paris in order to find the location of a German missile site. Actual OSS footage is used in this fast-paced early postwar espionage propaganda piece. Rex Harrison rejected the part taken by Cagney. **95m/B VHS, Beta.** James Cagney, Annabella, Richard Conte, Frank Latimore, Walter Abel, Sam Jaffe, Melville Cooper, E.G. Marshall, Karl Malden, Red Buttons; ***D:*** Henry Hathaway. *FOX, FCT*

Thirteenth Day of Christmas **1985** A made-for-British-television yarn about a psychotic boy left alone by his parents on Christmas night. **60m/C VHS, Beta.** *GB* Patrick Allen, Elizabeth Spiggs. *PSM*

The 13th Floor 🦴½ **1988 (R)** A young girl fuses with the spirit of a young boy her father ruthlessly killed years before, and together they wreak havoc. **86m/C VHS, Beta.** Lisa Hensley, Tim McKenzie, Miranda Otto; ***D:*** Chris Roach. *PAR*

13th Guest 🦴🦴 *Lady Beware* **1932** Two people try to solve a murder that occurred at a dinner party. An incredibly creaky early talkie melodrama that created some of the cliches of the genre. **70m/B VHS, Beta.** Ginger Rogers, Lyle Talbot, J. Farrell MacDonald, Paul Hurst; ***D:*** Albert Ray. *SNC, NOS, VYY*

The Thirteenth Man 🦴🦴½ **1937** When a journalist investigating the murder of a district attorney is also killed, the paper's gossip columnist takes the case. Entertaining, fast-paced mystery. **70m/B VHS, Beta.** Weldon Heyburn, Inez Courtney, Selmer Jackson, Milburn Stone, Matty Fain; ***D:*** William Nigh. *NOS, SNC, MLB*

The 13th Mission 🦴½ **1991** A low-budget overseas combat adventure, no better than the first twelve. **95m/C VHS.** Robert Marius, Jeff Griffith, Michael Monty, David Morisson, Paul Home, John Falch, Albert Bronski, Chantal Manz; ***D:*** Antonio Perez. *VTR*

Thirteenth Reunion 🦴 **1981** A newspaperwoman uncovers a bizarre secret society when she does a routine story on a health spa. **60m/C VHS, Beta.** Julia Foster, Dinah Sheridan, Richard Pearson; ***D:*** Peter Sasdy. *LIV*

The 30-Foot Bride of Candy Rock 🦴 **1959** A junk dealer invents a robot, catapults into space and causes his girlfriend to grow to 30 feet in height. Lightweight, whimsical fantasy was Costello's only solo starring film, and his last before his untimely death. **73m/B VHS, Beta.** Lou Costello, Dorothy Provine, Gale Gordon; ***D:*** Sidney Miller. *GKK*

30 Is a Dangerous Age, Cynthia 🦴🦴½ **1968** Dudley Moore stars as a nightclub pianist who spends a lot of his time daydreaming about being rich, famous and married to a beautiful woman. Moore determines to attain all these dreams before his thirtieth birthday, which is only six weeks away. **85m/C VHS, Beta.** *GB* Dudley Moore, Suzy Kendall, Eddie Foy Jr.; ***D:*** Joseph McGrath; ***W:*** Dudley Moore; ***M:*** Dudley Moore. *NO*

The Thirty-Nine Steps 🦴🦴½ **1979** Hitchcock remake is a visually interesting, but mostly uninvolving, mystery. Powell is the man suspected of stealing plans to begin WWI. Above average, but not by much. **98m/C VHS, Beta.** *GB* Robert Powell, David Warner, Eric Porter, Karen Dotrice, John Mills, Andrew Keir; ***D:*** Don Sharp. *MED, VYY, CNG*

Thirty Seconds Over Tokyo 🦴🦴🦴 **1944** Dated but still interesting classic wartime flag-waver details the conception and execution of the first bombing raids on Tokyo by Lt. Col. James Doolittle and his men. Look for Blake Edwards, as well as Steve Brodie in his first screen appearance. Based on a true story. **138m/B VHS, Beta.** Spencer Tracy, Van Johnson, Robert Walker, Robert Mitchum, Phyllis Thaxter, Scott McKay, Stephen McNally, Louis Jean Heydt, Leon Ames, Paul Langton; ***D:*** Mervyn LeRoy; ***W:*** Dalton Trumbo; ***C:*** Robert L. Surtees. Academy Awards '44: Best Special Effects; Nominations: Academy Awards '44: Best Black and White Cinematography. *MGM, FCT, TLF*

32 Short Films about Glenn Gould 🦴🦴🦴 **1993** Perceptive docudrama about the iconoclastic Canadian classical pianist who secluded himself in the studio, forsaking live performances for much of his career. A combination of dramatic recreation, archival material, and interviews depict the biographical details of the driven artist who died at the age of 50. Feore is memorable in the title role, especially since he's never actually shown playing the piano. Title and film structure refer to Bach's "Goldberg" Variations, a recording which made Gould's reputation. **94m/C VHS, LV.** *CA* Colm Feore, Gale Garnett, David Hughes; ***D:*** Francois Girard; ***W:*** Don McKellar, Francois Girard. Genie Awards '93: Best Cinematography, Best Director (Girard), Best Film, Best Film Editing; Nominations: Independent Spirit Awards '95: Best Foreign Language Film. *COL*

36 Fillete 🦴🦴🦴 **1988** Lili, an intellectually precocious 14-year old French girl who's literally bursting out of her children's dress size 36 fillete, discovers her sexuality. So while on vacation with her family she becomes determined to see if she can seduce a middle-aged playboy. In French with English subtitles. **88m/C VHS.** *FR* Delphine Zentout, Etienne Chicot, Olivier Parniere, Jean-Pierre Leaud; ***D:*** Catherine Breillat. *FXL, INJ*

Thirty-Six Hours of Hell 🦴½ **1977** A troop of Marines battle Japanese forces in the South Pacific during WWII. Dubbed. **95m/C VHS, Beta.** Richard Harrison, Pamela Tudor; ***D:*** Roberto Marrtero. *UNI*

'38: Vienna Before the Fall 🦴🦴½ **1988** Wartime Vienna explodes with love and politics. Academy Award Nominee for best foreign language film. In German with English subtitles. **97m/C VHS, LV.** *GE* Tobias Engel, Sunnyi Melles; ***D:*** Wolfgang Gluck. *LUM*

The 39 Steps 🦴🦴🦴🦴 **1935** The classic Hitchcock mistaken-man-caught-in-intrigue thriller, featuring some of his most often copied set-pieces and the surest visual flair of his pre-war British period. The laserdisc version includes a twenty-minute documentary tracing the director's British period. Remade twice, in 1959 and 1979. **81m/B VHS, Beta, LV, 8mm.** *GB* Robert Donat, Madeleine Carroll, Godfrey Tearle, Lucie Mannheim, Peggy Ashcroft, John Laurie, Wylie Watson; ***D:*** Alfred Hitchcock; ***W:*** Charles Bennett, Alma Reville; ***M:*** Louis Levy. *CNG, NOS, SUE*

This Boy's Life 🦴🦴🦴 **1993 (R)** Carolyn and her teenage son are in search of a new life, far from her abusive ex-boyfriend. In the town of Concrete, just outside Seattle, she meets ex-military man Dwight (De Niro), a slick but none too suave mechanic who might be the answer to her dreams, but then again, he might not. Nicely crafted performances from all, but keep your eye on DiCaprio (great in his first major role) as the confused and abused teen divided between dreams of prep school and the allure of the going-nowhere crowd. Based on the memoirs of Tobias Wolff; director Caton-Jones sensitively illustrates the skewed understanding of masculinity in the 1950s. Vintage soundtrack takes you back. **115m/C VHS, Beta, LV.** Robert De Niro, Ellen Barkin, Leonardo DiCaprio, Jonah Blechman, Eliza Dushku, Chris Cooper, Carla Gugino, Zachary Ansley, Tracey Ellis, Kathy Kinney, Gerrit Graham; ***D:*** Michael Caton-Jones; ***W:*** Robert Getchell; ***C:*** David Watkin; ***M:*** Carter Burwell. *WAR, FCT, BTV*

This Could Be the Night 🦴🦴½ **1957** Rocco and Tony are two small-fry gangsters who run a nightclub. Anne is a prim schoolteacher who takes a part-time job as their secretary. She falls for the handsome Tony much to the dismay of Rocco who knows his partner's less-than-sterling character. Sweet but minor comedy. Franciosa's first film. ♫This Could Be The Night; Hustlin' News Gal; I Got It Bad; I'm Gonna Live Till I Die; Taking a Chance on Love; Trumpet Boogie; Mamba Combo; Blue Moon; Dream Dancing. **105m/B VHS, LV.** Jean Simmons, Paul Douglas, Anthony (Tony) Franciosa, Joan Blondell, Julie Wilson, Neile Adams, J. Carrol Naish, Rafael Campos, ZaSu Pitts, Tom Helmore; ***D:*** Robert Wise. *MGM, MOV*

This England 🦴½ **1942** Patriotic morale booster is a rather dull jog through Britain's fight for freedom as an American journalist, visiting England, learns a village's history from a country squire, including surviving the Norman conquest, Spanish Armada, Napoleonic Wars, WWI, and the 1940 air attacks. **84m/B VHS.** *GB* Emlyn Williams, John Clements, Constance Cummings; ***D:*** David MacDonald. *FCT*

This Gun for Hire 🦴🦴🦴½ **1942** In his first major film role, Ladd plays a hired gun seeking retribution from a client who betrays him. Preston is the cop pursuing him and hostage Lake. Ladd's performance as the cold-blooded killer with a soft spot for cats is stunning; his train-yard scene is an emotional powerhouse. Based on Graham Greene's novel "A Gun for Sale." Remade as "Short Cut to Hell." The first of several films using the Ladd-Lake team, but the only one in which Ladd played a villain. **81m/B VHS, Beta, LV.** Alan Ladd, Veronica Lake, Robert Preston, Laird Cregar; ***D:*** Frank Tuttle; ***W:*** Albert Maltz, W.R. Burnett. *MCA, FCT*

This Gun for Hire 🦴🦴 **1990 (R)** A professional assassin finds that he has been duped into killing a powerful political figure, whom he was told was a New Orleans mobster. Now on the run, he takes a nightclub performer hostage, unaware that she is the fiance of the FBI agent who is after him. All odds are against him, but the special relationship he forms with the woman may just be his ticket out. Adapted from novel by Graham Greene. **89m/C VHS.** Robert Wagner, Nancy Everhard, Frederic Lehne, John Harkins; ***D:*** Lou Antonio. *MCA*

This Happy Breed 🦴🦴🦴½ **1947** A celebrated film version of Noel Coward's classic play depicts the changing fortunes of a large family in England between the world wars. Happiness, hardships, triumph and tragedy mix a series of memorable episodes, including some of the most cherished moments in popular British cinema, though its appeal is universal. Narrated by Laurence Olivier. **114m/C VHS.** *GB* Robert Newton, Celia Johnson, John Mills, Kay Walsh, Stanley Holloway; ***D:*** David Lean; ***W:*** David Lean. *HMV, FCT*

This Happy Feeling 🦴🦴½ **1958** Reynolds is a young woman who is romantically attracted to both Jurgens, a sophisticated retired actor, and Saxon, a younger suitor who is Jurgens' neighbor. Good acting all around. Charming telling of old tale. **83m/C VHS, Beta.** Curt Jurgens, Debbie Reynolds, John Saxon, Alexis Smith, Mary Astor, Estelle Winwood; ***D:*** Blake Edwards; ***W:*** Blake Edwards. *BAR, FCT*

This Is a Hijack 🦴 **1975 (PG)** Gambler hijacks the plane carrying his wealthy boss to help pay his debts. What it lacks in suspense, it lacks in performance and direction as well. **90m/C VHS, Beta.** Adam Roarke, Neville Brand, Jay Robinson, Lynn Borden, Dub Taylor. *NO*

This Is Elvis 🦴🦴 **1981 (PG)** The life of Elvis, combining documentary footage with dramatizations of events in his life. Includes more than three dozen songs. Generally seen as an attempt to cash in on the myth, but was well-received by his fans. **144m/C VHS, Beta.** Elvis Presley; ***D:*** Malcolm Leo, Andrew Solt; ***W:*** Malcolm Leo, Andrew Solt. *MVD, WAR*

This Is My Life 🦴🦴 **1992 (PG-13)** The story of a working mother torn between her skyrocketing career as a stand-up comic and her two daughters. Kavner plays the divorced mom who is determined to chuck her cosmetic sales job for comic success. Her career starts to really take off; she hires an agent and makes appearances on talk shows. As offers pour in, she eventually realizes that her girls are suffering as a result of her success. Good performances highlight an otherwise average drama. **105m/C VHS.** Julie Kavner, Samantha Mathis, Carrie Fisher, Dan Aykroyd, Gaby Hoffman; ***D:*** Nora Ephron; ***W:*** Nora Ephron, Delia Ephron. *FXV*

This Is Not a Test 🦴🦴 **1962** When news comes of an impending nuclear attack, a state trooper at a roadblock offers sanctuary to passing travellers. The effectiveness of the film's social commentary is hindered by its small budget. **72m/B VHS, Beta.** Seamon Glass, Mary Morlass, Thayer Roberts, Aubrey Martin; ***D:*** Frederic Gadette. *SNC*

This Is Spinal Tap 🦴🦴🦴½ *Spinal Tap* **1984 (R)** Pseudo-rockumentary about heavy-metal band Spinal Tap, profiling their career from "England's loudest band" to an entry in the "where are they now file." Hilarious satire, featuring music performed by Guest, McKean, Shearer, and others. Included are Spinal Tap's music video "Hell Hole," and an ad for their greatest hits album, "Heavy Metal Memories." Features great cameos, particularly David Letterman's Paul Schaefer as a record promoter and Billy Crystal as a surly mime. First feature for Reiner (Meathead on "All in the Family"). Followed by "The Return of Spinal Tap." **82m/C VHS, Beta, LV, 8mm.** Michael McKean, Christopher Guest, Harry Shearer, Tony Hendra, Bruno Kirby, Rob Reiner, June Chadwick, Howard Hesseman, Dana Carvey, Ed Begley Jr., Patrick Macnee, Fran Drescher; ***Cameos:*** Billy Crystal, Paul Shaffer, Anjelica Huston; ***D:*** Rob Reiner; ***W:*** Christopher Guest. *MVD, SUE, NLC*

This Is the Army ½ **1943** A robust tribute to the American soldier of WWII based on the hit play by Irving Berlin. Murphy, who later was a senator from California, played Reagan's father. ♫Your Country and My Country; My Sweetie; Poor Little Me, I'm on K.P.; We're On Our Way to France; What Does He Look Like?; This is the Army, Mr. Jones; I'm Gettin' Tired So I Can Sleep; Mandy; Ladies of the Chorus. **105m/C VHS, Beta.** George Murphy, Joan Leslie, Ronald Reagan, Alan Hale, Kate Smith, George Tobias, Irving Berlin, Joe Louis; ***D:*** Michael Curtiz; ***M:*** Max Steiner. Academy Awards '43: Best Score; Nominations: Academy Awards '43: Best Interior Decoration, Best Sound. *NOS, DVT, CAB*

This Island Earth ½ **1955** The planet Metaluna is in desperate need of uranium to power its defense against enemy invaders. A nuclear scientist and a nuclear fission expert from Earth are kidnapped to help out. The first serious movie about interplanetary escapades. Bud Westmore created pulsating cranium special effects make-up. **86m/C VHS, Beta, LV.** Jeff Morrow, Faith Domergue, Rex Reason, Russell Johnson; ***D:*** Joseph M. Newman; ***M:*** Herman Stein. *MCA, MLB*

This Land is Mine **1943** A timid French schoolteacher gathers enough courage to defy the Nazis when they attempt to occupy his town. Laughton's characterization is effective as the meek fellow who discovers the hero within himself in this patriotic wartime flick. **103m/B VHS, Beta, LV.** Charles Laughton, Maureen O'Hara, George Sanders, Walter Slezak, George Coulouris, Una O'Connor; ***D:*** Jean Renoir. Academy Awards '43: Best Sound. *TTC*

This Lightning Always Strikes Twice **1985** An elegant murder mystery made for British television. **60m/C VHS, Beta.** *GB* Claire Bloom, Trevor Howard, Charles Dance. *PSM*

This Man Must Die ½ *Que La Bete Meure; Uccidero Un Uomo* **1970 (PG)** A man searches relentlessly for the driver who killed his young son in a hit-and-run. When found, the driver engages him in a complex cat-and-mouse chase. Another stunning crime and punishment tale from Chabrol. **112m/C VHS, Beta.** *FR* Michael Duchaussoy, Caroline Cellier, Jean Yanne; ***D:*** Claude Chabrol. National Board of Review Awards '70: 5 Best Foreign Films of the Year. *FOX*

This Property is Condemned **1966** It's a hot time down south once again in this adaptation of the Tennessee Williams play. Wood is the overly-flirtatious southern charmer who takes a shine to the latest tenant of her loathsome mama's boardinghouse. And since it's Redford, who can blame her. Things steam up when he returns her interest but there's trouble a'brewin'. Both leads are lovely but the film itself is overly southern-fried. Williams was reportedly unhappy with the script and wanted his name removed from the film. **109m/C VHS, Beta, LV.** Robert Redford, Natalie Wood, Charles Bronson, Kate Reid, Mary Badham, Jon Provost, Robert (Bobby) Blake, John Harding; ***D:*** Sydney Pollack; ***W:*** Francis Ford Coppola, Edith Sommer, Fred Coe. *PAR*

This Special Friendship ½ *Les Amities Particulieres* **1967** Powerful, if overdone French drama about an emotionally sensitive young man at a Catholic boarding school. His sexual relationship with another boy leads to tragedy. Based on the novel by Roger Peyrefitte. **99m/B VHS, Beta.** *FR* Francis Lacombrade, Didier Haudepin, Lucien Nat, Louis Seigner, Michel Bouquet, Francois Leccia; ***D:*** Jean Delannoy. *FCT*

This Sporting Life **1963** A gritty, depressing portrait of a former coal miner who breaks into the violent world of professional rugby, and whose inability to handle social differences causes problems. He begins an affair with the widow from whom he rents a room but finds they are capable of only a physical attachment. One of the best of the British early '60s working-class angry young man melodramas. **134m/B VHS, Beta.** *GB* Richard Harris, Rachel Roberts, Alan Badel, William Hartnell, Colin Blakely, Vanda Godsell, Arthur Lowe; ***D:*** Lindsay Anderson; ***W:*** David Storey. British Academy Awards '63: Best Actress (Roberts); Cannes Film Festival '63: Best Actor (Harris); National Board of Review Awards '63: 10 Best Films of the Year; Nominations: Academy Awards '63: Best Actor (Harris), Best Actress (Roberts). *PAR*

This Stuff'll Kill Ya! *Woof!* **1971 (PG)** A backwoods preacher who believes in free love and moonshining runs into trouble with the locals when a series of gruesome religious murders are committed. Southern drive-in material from one of the genre's masters. Holt's last film. **100m/C VHS.** Jeffrey Allen, Tim Holt, Gloria King, Ray Sager, Eric Bradly, Terence McCarthy; ***D:*** Herschell Gordon Lewis; ***W:*** Herschell Gordon Lewis. *TWE, FRG, TPV*

This Sweet Sickness ½ *Dites-Lui Que Je L'Aime* **1977** Destructive passion and sexual delusion is explored in this adaptation of the Patricia Highsmith novel. David seems to be a hardworking loner who is loved by the sweet Juliette. Rejected by him, Juliette then discovers that David has built a remote mountain chalet for the woman he does love, Lise, who's married and unaware of David's obsessional devotions. Extravagant emotions lead to tragedy. In French with English subtitles. **107m/C VHS.** *FR* Gerard Depardieu, Miou-Miou, Dominique Laffin, Claude Pieplu, Christian Clavier; ***D:*** Claude Miller; ***W:*** Luc Beraud, Claude Miller. *WAC, FCT*

This Time I'll Make You Rich **1975 (PG)** Two American hoodlums work out a drug-ring heist in the Far East. **97m/C VHS, Beta.** Tony Sabato, Robin McDavid; ***D:*** Frank Kramer. *NLC*

The Thomas Crown Affair *Thomas Crown and Company; The Crown Caper* **1968 (R)** A multi-millionaire (McQueen) decides to plot and execute the perfect theft, a daring daylight robbery of a bank. Dunaway is the gorgeous and efficient insurance investigator determined to nab him. One of the best visual scenes is the chess match between the two as they begin to fall in love. Strong production with Oscar-winning theme "The Windmills of Your Mind." ♫The Windmills of Your Mind. **102m/C VHS, Beta.** Steve McQueen, Faye Dunaway, Jack Weston, Yaphet Kotto; ***D:*** Norman Jewison; ***W:*** Alan R. Trustman; ***C:*** Haskell Wexler. Academy Awards '68: Best Song ("The Windmills of Your Mind"); Golden Globe Awards '69: Best Song ("The Windmills of Your Mind"). *MGM, FCT, FOX*

Thomas Graal's Best Film **1917** The famous comical adventures of a film scriptwriter wooing his secretary, followed by "Thomas Graal's First Child." Silent. **70m/B VHS, Beta.** *SW* Victor Sjostrom, Karin Molander; ***D:*** Mauritz Stiller. *FCT, GPV*

Thomas Graal's First Child **1918** The sequel to "Thomas Graal's Best Film." The comical screenwriter and actress couple attempt to raise a baby. Silent. **70m/B VHS, Beta.** Victor Sjostrom, Karin Molander; ***D:*** Mauritz Stiller. *FCT*

Thompson's Last Run ½ **1990** Boyhood friends grow up on either side of the law. They come face-to-face, though, when one is assigned to transport the other to prison. Made for television. **95m/C VHS, Beta, LV.** Robert Mitchum, Wilford Brimley, Kathleen York, Susan Tyrrell; ***D:*** Jerrold Freedman; ***M:*** Miles Goodman. *NO*

Thor and the Amazon Women **1960** The mighty Thor leads his enslaved men on an attack against the evil Queen Nera and her female-dominated Amazon society. **85m/C VHS.** Joe Robinson, Susy Anderson. *AIP*

The Thorn ½ **1973 (R)** The Virgin Mary and Joseph try to raise Jesus Christ in the modern world. **90m/C VHS, Beta.** Bette Midler, John Bassberger. *NO*

The Thorn Birds **1983** Pioneers find danger and romance in the Australian outback as they struggle to begin a dynasty. Charismatic priest sometimes hurts, sometimes helps them. One of Stanwyck's last performances; Ward's American television debut. Originally a ten-hour television epic based on Colleen McCullough novel. Emmy nominations for Actor Chamberlain, Supporting Actor(s) Brown and Plummer, Supporting Actress Laurie, direction, photography, music, costume design, and editing. On four cassettes. **486m/C VHS, Beta.** Rachel Ward, Richard Chamberlain, Jean Simmons, Ken Howard, Mare Winningham, Richard Kiley, Piper Laurie, Bryan Brown, Christopher Plummer, Barbara Stanwyck; ***D:*** Daryl Duke; ***M:*** Henry Mancini. *WAR, MOV, TVC*

Thoroughbreds Don't Cry ½ **1937** Rooney plays a jockey who throws a race so his no-good father can win enough money to pay for his supposed medical problems. The owner of the horse then drops dead from a heart attack. Rooney feels guilty, so he asks his father to loan the owner's grandson $1,000 to run in another race. His father says no, so Rooney steals the money from him, and when the father finds out he tells the track officials that Rooney threw the race. Garland is Rooney's best friend and moral support, and she sings a few songs too! A fairly good horse racing story. **80m/B VHS.** Judy Garland, Mickey Rooney, Sophie Tucker, Sir C. Aubrey Smith, Ronald Sinclair, Forrester Harvey; ***D:*** Alfred E. Green. *MGM, MVD*

Thoroughly Modern Millie ½ **1967 (G)** Andrews is a young woman who comes to New York in the early 1920s where she meets another newcomer, the innocent Moore. Andrews decides to upgrade her image to that of a "modern" woman, a flapper, and sets out to realize her ambition, to become a stenographer and marry the boss. Meanwhile, Moore has become an object of interest to Lillie, who just happens to run a white-slavery ring. Lots of frantic moments and big production numbers in this campy film. Channing and Lillie are exceptional fun. ♫Thoroughly Modern Millie; The Tapioca; Jimmy; The Jewish Wedding Song; Baby Face; Do It Again; Poor Butterfly; Rose of Washington Square; I Can't Believe That You're In Love With Me. **138m/C VHS, Beta, LV.** Julie Andrews, Carol Channing, Mary Tyler Moore, John Gavin, Beatrice Lillie, James Fox, Noriyuki "Pat" Morita; ***D:*** George Roy Hill; ***W:*** Richard Morris; ***C:*** Russell Metty; ***M:*** Elmer Bernstein. Academy Awards '67: Best Original Score; Golden Globe Awards '68: Best Supporting Actress (Channing); Nominations: Academy Awards '67: Best Art Direction/Set Decoration, Best Costume Design, Best Song ("Thoroughly Modern Millie"), Best Supporting Actress (Channing), Best Original Score. *MCA*

Those Calloways ½ **1965 (PG)** A small town family attempts to establish a sanctuary for the flocks of wild geese who fly over the woods of Swiftwater, Maine. Fine Disney family fare, with good cast. Based on Paul Annixter's novel "Swiftwater." **131m/C VHS, Beta.** Brian Keith, Vera Miles, Brandon de Wilde, Walter Brennan, Ed Wynn, John Qualen, Linda Evans; ***D:*** Norman Tokar; ***C:*** Edward Colman; ***M:*** Max Steiner. *DIS*

Those Daring Young Men in Their Jaunty Jalopies *Monte Carlo or Bust; Quei Temerari Sulle Loro Pazze, Scatenate, Scalcinate Carriole* **1969 (G)** Daring young men in noisy slow cars trek 1500 miles across country in the 1920s and call it a race. **125m/C VHS, LV.** *GB* Tony Curtis, Susan Hampshire, Terry-Thomas, Eric Sykes, Gert Frobe, Peter Cook, Dudley Moore, Jack Hawkins; ***D:*** Ken Annakin; ***W:*** Ken Annakin, Jack Davies. *PAR, FCT*

Those Endearing Young Charms **1945** Romance develops between a young Air Corps mechanic and a salesgirl. Complications arise when another man enters the scene. Light romantic comedy. Based on the play by Edward Chodorov. **82m/B VHS, Beta.** Robert Young, Laraine Day, Anne Jeffreys, Lawrence Tierney; ***D:*** Lewis Allen. *CCB*

Those Fantastic Flying Fools ½ *Blast-Off; Jules Verne's Rocket to the Moon* **1967** A mad race to be the first on the moon brings hilarious results. Loosely based on a Jules Verne story. **95m/C VHS.** *GB* Burl Ives, Troy Donahue, Gert Frobe, Terry-Thomas, Hermione Gingold, Daliah Lavi, Lionel Jeffries; ***D:*** Don Sharp. *NO*

Those Glory, Glory Days ½ **1983** An English woman, secure in her position as an outstanding sports journalist, reminisces about the days when she and her friends idolized the boys on the soccer team. Nothing extraordinary, but nicely made.

92m/C VHS, Beta. *GB* Zoe Nathenson, Liz Campion, Cathy Murphy; ***D:*** Philip Saville; ***M:*** Trevor Jones. *MGM*

Those Lips, Those Eyes ☆☆½ **1980 (R)** A pre-med student takes a job as a prop boy in a summer stock company and winds up falling in love with the company's lead dancer. Sub-plot about aging actor is more interesting, better played by Langella. O'Connor is appropriately lovely. Nicely made, charming sleeper of a film. **106m/C VHS, Beta.** Frank Langella, Tom Hulce, Glynnis O'Connor, Jerry Stiller, Kevin McCarthy; ***D:*** Michael Pressman. *MGM*

Those Magnificent Men in Their Flying Machines ☆☆☆ **1965** In 1910, a wealthy British newspaper publisher is persuaded to sponsor an air race from London to Paris. Contestants come from all over the world and shenanigans, hijinks, double-crosses, and romance are found along the route. Skelton has fun in prologue, while Terry-Thomas is great as the villain. Fun from start to finish. **138m/C VHS, Beta, LV.** *GB* Stuart Whitman, Sarah Miles, Robert Morley, Alberto Sordi, James Fox, Gert Frobe, Jean-Pierre Cassel, Flora Robson, Sam Wanamaker, Terry-Thomas, Irina Demick, Benny Hill, Gordon Jackson, Millicent Martin, Red Skelton; ***D:*** Ken Annakin; ***W:*** Ken Annakin, Jack Davies. Nominations: Academy Awards '65: Best Story & Screenplay. *FOX*

Thou Shalt Not Kill...Except ☆ **1987** A Vietnam vet seeks revenge on the violent cult who kidnapped his girlfriend. **84m/C VHS, Beta.** Brian Schulz, Robert Rickman, John Manfredi, Tim Quill, Cheryl Hansen, Sam Raimi. *PSM*

Thoughts are Free ☆☆☆½ **1984 (PG)** A young soldier, wounded in WWII, escapes from the train that is transporting him and his comrades to a Soviet labor camp and rejoins his family. Under the repressive communist regime, he plots his family's escape to the West but his plans are thwarted when the Berlin Wall is erected, leaving him in the West and his wife and daughter in the East. As the years go by, they can get together only by outwitting the bureaucrats. The film's title is taken from an old German folk song "Die Gedanken sind frei." **93m/C VHS, Beta.** Herbert Ludwig, Kathrin Kratzer; ***D:*** Josef Sommer. *NO*

A Thousand and One Nights ☆☆½ **1945** Handsome Aladdin (Wilde) falls in love with beautiful Princess Armina (Jergens) but fate steps in and Aladdin and sidekick Abdullah (Silvers) are off in search of a magic lamp. This time around the genie is a beautiful woman (Keyes), who falls for Aladdin herself and tries to thwart his would-be romance. Clever fun. **92m/C VHS.** Cornel Wilde, Evelyn Keyes, Adele Jergens, Phil Silvers, Rex Ingram, Dennis Hoey, Philip Van Zandt, Gus Schilling; ***D:*** Alfred E. Green; ***W:*** Jack Henley, Richard English; ***C:*** Ray Rennahan; ***M:*** Marlin Skiles. *COL*

A Thousand Clowns ☆☆☆ **1965** A non-conformist has resigned from his job as chief writer for an obnoxious kiddie show in order to enjoy life. But his independence comes under fire when he becomes guardian for his young nephew and social workers take a dim view of his lifestyle. Balsam won an Oscar for his role as Robard's agent brother. Adapted from Herb Gardner's Broadway comedy. **118m/B VHS, Beta.** Jason Robards Jr., Barry Gordon, William Daniels, Barbara Harris, Gene Saks, Martin Balsam; ***D:*** Fred Coe; ***W:*** Herb Gardner. Academy Awards '65: Best Supporting Actor (Balsam); National Board of Review Awards '65: 10 Best Films of the Year; Nominations: Academy Awards '65: Best Adapted Screenplay, Best Picture, Best Original Score. *MGM, FOX, BTV*

The Thousand Eyes of Dr. Mabuse ☆☆½ *The Secret of Dr. Mabuse; The Diabolical Dr. Mabuse; The Shadow Versus the Thousand Eyes of Dr. Mabuse* **1960** Lang's last film is a return to his pre-war German character, the evil Dr. Mabuse. A series of strange murders occur in a Berlin hotel and police believe the killer thinks he's a reincarnation of the doctor. Disorienting chiller. **103m/B VHS.** *GE* Dawn Addams, Peter Van Eyck, Gert Frobe, Wolfgang Preiss; ***D:*** Fritz Lang. *FCT, GPV*

A Thousand Heroes ☆☆½ **1994 (PG)** Based on the true story of United Airlines Flight 232 which took off on a flight from Denver to Chicago and then suffered engine explosions over Iowa. The jumbo jet crashed in a fiery explosion but some 200 people survived. **95m/C VHS, LV.** Richard Thomas, Charlton Heston, James Coburn. *NHO*

Thousand Pieces of Gold ☆☆☆ **1991 (PG-13)** A young Chinese woman is sold by her father to a marriage broker, but instead of a respectable marriage she is shipped to America and expected to work as a prostitute in an Idaho mining town. Instead she works taking in laundry as she tries to make her way in a man's world, finding a sweet romance of opposites along the way. Based on a true story. Excellent performances by Chao and Cooper. **105m/C VHS, LV.** Rosalind Chao, Dennis Dun, Michael Paul Chan, Chris Cooper, Jimmie F. Skaggs, William Oldham, David Hayward, Beth Broderick; ***D:*** Nancy Kelly; ***W:*** Anne Makepeace; ***M:*** Gary Remal Malkin. *HMD, INJ*

Thousands Cheer ☆☆½ **1943** A flag-waving wartime musical about a tap-dancing Army private who falls in love with the colonel's daughter, culminating with an all-star (MGM) USO show. Songs include "Honeysuckle Rose," sung by Horne, and "The Joint Is Really Jumping Down at Carnegie Hall," sung by Garland. **126m/C VHS, Beta, LV.** Gene Kelly, Kathryn Grayson, Judy Garland, Mickey Rooney, Mary Astor, John Boles, Lucille Ball, Eleanor Powell, Virginia O'Brien, Margaret O'Brien, Red Skelton, Lionel Barrymore, June Allyson, Frank Morgan, Kay Kyser, Bob Crosby, Lena Horne, Donna Reed; ***D:*** George Sidney. Nominations: Academy Awards '43: Best Color Cinematography, Best Interior Decoration, Best Original Score. *MGM*

Thrashin' ☆ **1986 (PG-13)** A new-to-L.A. teen must prove himself to a tough gang on skateboards by skateboarding a certain treacherous race. For skateboarding fans only. **93m/C VHS, Beta.** Josh Brolin, Pamela Gidley, Robert Rusler, Chuck McCann; ***D:*** David Winters; ***W:*** Paul Brown; ***M:*** Barry Goldberg. *NO*

Threads ☆☆☆ **1985** The famed dramatic recreation of the effects of nuclear war on a British city and two of its families. A disturbing, uncompromising, and somewhat plausible drama. Made for British television. **110m/C VHS, Beta.** *GB* Karen Meagher, Rita May, David Brierly, Reece Dinsdale, Harry Beety; ***D:*** Mick Jackson. *NO*

Threat ☆☆½ **1949** A killer escapes from jail and returns to settle the score with those who convicted him. Tense, fast-moving thriller. **66m/B VHS, Beta.** Michael O'Shea, Virginia Grey, Charles McGraw; ***D:*** Felix Feist. *NO*

Three Ages ☆☆☆ **1923** A parody of D.W. Griffith's 1916 film "Intolerance." Keaton's first feature film casts him in prehistoric days, ancient Rome, and in modern times. Silent with musical score. **59m/B VHS, Beta.** Wallace Beery, Oliver Hardy, Buster Keaton; ***D:*** Buster Keaton, Eddie Cline. *NOS, VDM, DVT*

Three Amigos ☆☆ **1986 (PG)** Three out-of-work silent screen stars are asked to defend a Mexican town from bandits; they think it's a public appearance stint. Spoof of Three Stooges and Mexican bandito movies that at times falls short, given the enormous amount of comedic talent involved. Generally enjoyable with some very funny scenes. Co-written by former "Saturday Night Live" producer Michaels. Short's first major film appearance. **105m/C VHS, Beta, LV.** Chevy Chase, Steve Martin, Martin Short, Joe Mantegna, Patrice Martinez, Jon Lovitz, Alfonso Arau, Randy Newman; ***D:*** John Landis; ***W:*** Steve Martin, Randy Newman, Lorne Michaels; ***M:*** Elmer Bernstein. *HBO*

The Three Avengers ☆☆½ **1980 (R)** Hung Tack (Lee) is the master of a kung fu school in a town plagued by two evil businessmen, who force Hung to take on the local gangs. During a fight, he's spotted by a talent scout and starts a career in the movies but is around to rescue a friend who's gotten into trouble. Hey, the fighting's the important part anyway. **93m/C VHS.** Bruce Lee. *FCT*

Three Broadway Girls ☆☆☆ *The Greeks Had a Word for Them* **1932** Three gold-diggers go husband-hunting. Well-paced, very funny telling of this old story. Remade many times, including "How to Marry a Millionaire," "Three Blind Mice," "Moon Over Miami," and "Three Little Girls in Blue." **78m/B VHS, Beta.** Joan Blondell, Ina Claire, Madge Evans, David Manners, Lowell Sherman; ***D:*** Lowell Sherman. *NOS, CAB, BAR*

Three Brothers ☆☆☆ **1980 (PG)** An acclaimed Italian film by veteran Rosi about three brothers summoned to their small Italian village by a telegram saying their mother is dead. Sensitive and compassionate. In Italian with English subtitles. Adapted from Platonov's story "The Third Son." **113m/C VHS, Beta.** *IT* Philippe Noiret, Charles Vanel, Michele Placido, Vittorio Mezzogiorno, Andrea Ferreol; ***D:*** Francesco Rosi; ***W:*** Francesco Rosi; ***C:*** Pasqualino de Santis. Nominations: Academy Awards '81: Best Foreign Language Film. *SUE, APD*

Three Bullets for a Long Gun ☆½ **1973 (PG)** Two prairie renegades battle bandits as they search for an inherited gold mine. **89m/C VHS, Beta.** Keith Van Der Wat, Beau Brummel, Patrick Munhardt; ***D:*** Peter Henkel; ***W:*** Keith Van Der Wat. *COL, NLC, SIM*

Three by Hitchcock ☆☆ **1928** Condensed versions of three of Hitchcock's early films (1927-28). Consists of "The Ring," "Champagne," and "The Manxman," his last silent film. **90m/B VHS, Beta.** ***D:*** Alfred Hitchcock. *GVV*

The Three Caballeros ☆☆½ **1945** Donald Duck stars in this journey through Latin America. Full of music, variety, and live-action/animation segments. Stories include "Pablo the Penguin," "Little Gauchito," and adventures with Joe Carioca, who was first introduced in Disney's "Saludos Amigos." Today this film stands as one of the very best pieces of animation ever created. Great family fare. "Saludos Amgios" is available on the laserdisc version. ♫The Three Caballeros; Baia. **71m/C VHS, Beta, LV.** ***D:*** Norman Ferguson; ***V:*** Sterling Holloway, Aurora Miranda. Nominations: Academy Awards '45: Best Sound, Best Original Score. *DIS, APD, WTA*

Three Came Home ☆☆☆ **1950** Colbert is an American married to a British administrator in the Far East during WWII. Conquering Japanese throw the whole family into a brutal POW concentration camp, and their confinement is recounted in harrowing and unsparing detail. Superior drama, also laudable for a fairly even-handed portrayal of the enemy captors. Based on an autobiographical book by Agnes Newton-Keith. **106m/B VHS.** Claudette Colbert, Patric Knowles, Sessue Hayakawa; ***D:*** Jean Negulesco. *NOS, HEG*

Three Cases of Murder ☆☆☆ **1955** Three fast-paced tales of mayhem. "In the Picture" features a deranged taxidermist, a creepy house, and a hapless museum guide. From a story by Roderick Wilkinson. Two friends are in love with the same girl in "You Killed Elizabeth" and when she turns up dead it's clear one of them is guilty. From a story by Brett Halliday. The best features Welles as "Lord Mountdrago," who destroys the career of a fellow Parliament Member and is haunted by fears of retaliation. Based on a story by W. Somerset Maugham. **99m/B VHS.** *GB* Alan Badel, John Gregson, Orson Welles, Elizabeth Sellars, Hugh Pryse, Jack Lambert; ***D:*** Wendy Toye, David Eady, George More O'Ferrell; ***W:*** Donald Wilson, Sidney Carroll, Ian Dalrymple; ***C:*** Georges Perinal; ***M:*** Doreen Carwithen. *HMV*

Three Charlies and One Phoney! **1918** Three of Charlie Chaplin's best comedy shorts, plus one featuring his best-known imitator—Billy West. Included are "Recreation" ("Fun is Fun") ("Spring Fever"), "His Musical Career" ("The Piano Movers") ("Musical Tramps"), "The Bond" (featuring Charlie in a Liberty Bond appeal) and "His Day Out" with Billy West imitating Chaplin. All but "His Day Out" were written and directed by Chaplin. **69m/B VHS, Beta, 8mm.** Charlie Chaplin, Mack Swain, Charley Chase, Edna Purviance, Sydney Chaplin, Albert Austin; ***D:*** Charlie Chaplin; ***W:*** Charlie Chaplin. *VYY*

Three Coins in the Fountain 🦴🦴½
1954 Three women throw money into fountain and get romantically involved with Italian men. Outstanding CinemaScope photography captures beauty of Italian setting. Sammy Cahn theme song sung by Frank Sinatra. ♫Three Coins in the Fountain. **102m/C VHS, Beta.** Clifton Webb, Dorothy McGuire, Jean Peters, Louis Jourdan, Maggie McNamara, Rossano Brazzi; ***D:*** Jean Negulesco; ***C:*** Milton Krasner. Academy Awards '54: Best Color Cinematography, Best Song ("Three Coins in the Fountain"). *FOX*

Three Comrades 🦴🦴🦴 **1938** Taylor, Tone, and Young are three friends, reunited in bleak, post-WWI Germany, who meet and befriend Sullavan, a tubercular beauty. Reluctant to marry because of her health, she's finally persuaded to wed Taylor, amidst the country's increasing unrest. Tragedy strikes Sullavan and the politicized Young and the two remaining comrades face an uncertain future. Bleak but forceful and passionate drama. Sullavan's performance is superb. Based on the novel by Erich Maria Remarque. Fitzgerald's script was heavily re-written because both Sullavan and producer Mankiewicz found his approach too literary with unspeakable dialogue. **99m/B VHS.** Robert Taylor, Margaret Sullavan, Robert Young, Franchot Tone, Lionel Atwill, Guy Kibbee, Henry Hull, George Zucco, Monty Woolley, Charley Grapewin, Spencer Charters, Sarah Padden; ***D:*** Frank Borzage; ***W:*** F. Scott Fitzgerald, Edward Paramore; ***C:*** Joseph Ruttenberg; ***M:*** Franz Waxman. New York Film Critics Awards '38: Best Actress (Sullavan); Nominations: Academy Awards '38: Best Actress (Sullavan). *MGM, MOV, BTV*

Three Daring Daughters 🦴🦴½ **1948** When her husband leaves her and she almost misses her daughter's graduation due to a fainting spell, MacDonald takes hiatus on a cruise ship where she meets and marries pianist Iturbi. Unknowing, the three daughters at home conspire to get Dad back in the family. Enraged when Mom returns with new-found hubby, the threesome do all in their power to make the newlyweds as miserable as possible. Happily-ended musical-comedy is chock full of memorable tunes. Based on the play "The Bees and the Flowers" by Kohner and Albert Manning. ♫Route 66; The Dickey Bird Song; Alma Mater; Fleurette; Passepied; Where There's Love; Ritual Fire Dance; You Made Me Love You; Happy Birthday. **115m/C VHS.** Jeanette MacDonald, Jose Iturbi, Jane Powell, Edward Arnold, Harry Davenport, Moyna MacGill, Elinor Donahue, Ann Todd; ***D:*** Fred M. Wilcox; ***W:*** Sonya Levien, John Meehan, Albert Mannheimer, Frederick Kohner. *MGM*

Three Days in Beirut 🦴 **1983 (PG)** A soldier of fortune and a beautiful interpreter join forces against a backdrop of Middle Eastern politics, espionage, and violence. **94m/C VHS, Beta.** Diana Sands, Calvin Lockhart; ***D:*** Michael A. Schultz. *PSM*

Three Days of the Condor 🦴🦴🦴
1975 (R) CIA researcher Redford finds himself on the run from unknown killers when he is left the only survivor of the mass murder of his office staff. Good performance by Dunaway as the photographer who shelters him. Excellent suspense tale. Based on "Six Days of the Condor" by James Grady. **118m/C VHS, Beta, LV.** Robert Redford, Faye Dunaway, Cliff Robertson, Max von Sydow, John Houseman; ***D:*** Sydney Pollack; ***W:*** David Rayfiel; ***C:*** Owen Roizman; ***M:*** Dave Grusin. Edgar Allan Poe Awards '75: Best Screenplay; Nominations: Academy Awards '75: Best Film Editing. *PAR*

Three Days to a Kill 🦴🦴 **1991 (R)** Calvin Sims is a mercenary hired to rescue a kidnapped ambassador—by any means necessary. **90m/C VHS, LV.** Fred Williamson, Bo Svenson, Henry Silva, Chuck Connors, Van Johnson, Sonny Landham; ***D:*** Fred Williamson. *HBO*

Three Desperate Men 🦴🦴 **1950** Three brothers accused of murder become outlaws. Not innovative, but satisfactory tale of the Old West. **71m/B VHS, Beta.** Preston Foster, Virginia Grey, Jim Davis; ***D:*** Sam Newfield. *NO*

The Three Faces of Eve 🦴🦴🦴½
1957 An emotionally disturbed woman seeks the help of a psychiatrist, who discovers she has three distinct personalities. Powerful performances highlight this fascinating study based on a true story. **91m/B VHS, LV.** Joanne Woodward, David Wayne, Lee J. Cobb, Nancy Kulp, Vince Edwards; ***D:*** Nunnally Johnson. Academy Awards '57: Best Actress (Woodward); Golden Globe Awards '58: Best Actress—Drama (Woodward). *FXV, BTV*

Three Faces West 🦴🦴 *The Refugee* **1940** A dust bowl community is helped by a Viennese doctor who left Europe to avoid Nazi capture. He's aided by the Duke in this odd combination of Western frontier saga and anti-Nazi propaganda. Works only part of the time. **79m/B VHS.** John Wayne, Charles Coburn, Sigrid Gurie, Sonny Bupp, Russell Simpson; ***D:*** Bernard Vorhaus. *REP*

3:15—The Moment of Truth 🦴🦴 **1986 (R)** A vicious high school gang is confronted by an angry ex-member in this so-so teen delinquent film. **86m/C VHS, Beta.** Adam Baldwin, Deborah Foreman, Rene Auberjonois, Danny De La Paz; ***D:*** Larry Gross; ***W:*** Sam Bernard; ***M:*** Gary Chang. *MED*

Three for Bedroom C 🦴🦴 **1952** A movie star and a scientist make romance on a train bound for Los Angeles. Swanson's follow-up to "Sunset Boulevard." **74m/C VHS, Beta.** Gloria Swanson, Fred Clark, Steve Brodie, Hans Conried, Margaret Dumont; ***D:*** Milton Bren. *LIV*

Three for the Road 🦴🦴 **1987 (PG)** A young aspiring political aide and his roommate must escort a Senator's ill-mannered and spoiled daughter to a reform institution. On the road, they run into more than a few obstacles. Good performances elevate a bland script. Sheen made this movie before his riveting performance as a young GI in "Platoon." **98m/C Beta, LV.** Charlie Sheen, Kerri Green, Alan Ruck, Sally Kellerman; ***D:*** Bill W.L. Norton; ***W:*** Tim Metcalfe; ***M:*** Barry Goldberg. *NO*

Three Fugitives 🦴🦴 **1989 (PG-13)** An ex-con holdup man determined to go straight is taken hostage by a bungling first-time bank robber, who is only attempting the holdup in order to support his withdrawn young daughter. Ex-con Nolte winds up on the lam with the would-be robber and his daughter. The comedy is fun, the sentimental moments too sweet and slow. Remake of French "Les Fugitifs." **96m/C VHS, Beta, LV.** Nick Nolte, Martin Short, James Earl Jones, Kenneth McMillan, Sarah Rowland Doroff, Alan Ruck; ***D:*** Francis Veber; ***W:*** Francis Veber; ***C:*** Haskell Wexler. *TOU*

Three Godfathers 🦴🦴🦴 **1948** A sweet and sentimental western has three half-hearted outlaws on the run, taking with them an infant they find in the desert. Dedicated to western star and Ford alumni Harry Carey, Sr. (whose son is one of the outlaws in the film), who died of cancer the year before. Ford had first filmed the tale with Carey Sr. as "Marked Men" in 1919. **82m/C VHS, Beta.** John Wayne, Pedro Armendariz Sr., Harry Carey Jr., Ward Bond, Mae Marsh, Jane Darwell, Ben Johnson, Mildred Natwick, Guy Kibbee; ***D:*** John Ford; ***C:*** Winton C. Hoch. *MGM*

Three Guys Named Mike 🦴🦴 **1951** Wyman plays an overly enthusiastic airline stewardess who finds herself the object of affection from three guys named Mike, including an airline pilot, an advertising man, and a scientist. A cute comedy. **89m/B VHS.** Jane Wyman, Van Johnson, Barry Sullivan, Howard Keel, Phyllis Kirk, Jeff Donnell; ***D:*** Charles Walters; ***W:*** Sidney Sheldon. *VDM*

The 317th Platoon 🦴🦴🦴 **1965** An emotionally gripping war drama of the French-Vietnemese War in which the 317th Platoon of the French Army, consisting of 4 French commanders and 41 Laotians, is ordered to retreat to camp Dien Bien Phu. The men begin their march and slowly succomb to the elements and ambushes. Days later, when what is left of the platoon finally reaches Dien Bien Phu, the camp is in enemy hands and the remnants of the 317th Platoon are killed in cold blood. Director Shoendoerffer portrays this struggle, conflict, and the quiet haunting tension of war with great skill. In French with English subtitles. **100m/B VHS, LV.** *FR* Jacques Perrin, Bruno Cremer, Pierre Fabre, Manuel Zarzo; ***D:*** Pierre Schoendoerffer; ***W:*** Pierre Schoendoerffer. *INT, IME, FCT*

357 Magnum 🦴 **1977** Jonathan Hightower, the CIA's special investigator in the Far East, speaks softly and carries a very big gun. **71m/C VHS, Beta.** Marland T. Stewart, James Whitworth, Kathryn Hayes. *NO*

Three Husbands 🦴🦴½ **1950** A deceased playboy leaves letters for the title characters incriminating their wives in extramarital affairs. The men's reactions are pure farce—even though this same concept was played straight with a sex change in the earlier "A Letter to Three Wives." **79m/B VHS.** Eve Arden, Ruth Warrick, Vanessa Brown, Howard da Silva, Sheperd Strudwick, Jane Darwell; ***D:*** Irving Reis. *NOS, VDM*

Three in the Attic 🦴½ **1968 (R)** A college student juggles three girlfriends at the same time. When the girls find out they are being two-timed, they lock their boyfriend in an attic and exhaust him with forced sexual escapades. Then they talk. Limited trashy and foolish appeal. **92m/C VHS, Beta.** Christopher Jones, Yvette Mimieux, John Beck; ***D:*** Richard Wilson. *SUE, MLB*

Three in the Cellar 🦴🦴 *Up in the Cellar* **1970 (R)** A disgruntled college student seeks revenge on the school president by seducing his wife, daughter and mistress. Good screenplay helps carry it off. **92m/C VHS.** Wes Stern, Joan Collins, Larry Hagman, Judy Pace; ***D:*** Theodore J. Flicker. *HBO*

Three in the Saddle 🦴½ **1945** Ritter and the Texas Rangers fight for law and order. **61m/B VHS, Beta.** Tex Ritter, Dave O'Brien, Charles "Blackie" King; ***D:*** Harry Fraser. *NOS, VCN*

Three Kinds of Heat 🦴 **1987 (R)** Three Interpol agents track down a warring Oriental crime lord. Alternately tongue-in-cheek and silly. Never released in theaters, it found a home on video. Stevens created "The Outer Limits" for television. **88m/C VHS, Beta.** Robert Ginty, Victoria Barrett, Shakti; ***D:*** Leslie Stevens. *WAR*

Three Legionnaires 🦴🦴½ *Three Crazy Legionnaires* **1937** Three soldiers cavort in a post-WWI Siberian tank town. **67m/B VHS, Beta, LV.** Robert Armstrong, Lyle Talbot, Fifi d'Orsay, Anne Nagel, Donald Meek. *VYY*

The Three Little Pigs **1984** From "Faerie Tale Theatre" comes the story of three little pigs, the houses they lived in and the wolf that tried to do them in. **60m/C VHS, Beta.** Billy Crystal, Jeff Goldblum, Valerie Perrine; ***D:*** Howard Storm. *KUI, FOX, FCT*

Three Little Words 🦴🦴½ **1950** A musical biography of songwriting team Harry Ruby and Bert Kalmar, filled with Kalmar-Ruby numbers. Helen Kane (famous for her boop-boop-de-boops) dubbed "I Wanna Be Loved By You" for Reynolds. A musical in the best MGM tradition. ♫I Wanna Be Loved By You; Who's Sorry Now?; Three Little Words; I Love You So Much; She's Mine, All Mine; So-Long, Oo-Long; Hooray for Captain Spaulding; Up In the Clouds; All Alone Monday. **102m/C VHS, Beta.** Fred Astaire, Red Skelton, Vera-Ellen, Arlene Dahl, Keenan Wynn, Gloria De Haven, Debbie Reynolds, Gale Robbins; ***D:*** Richard Thorpe; ***M:*** Andre Previn. Golden Globe Awards '51: Best Actor—Musical/Comedy (Astaire); Nominations: Academy Awards '50: Best Original Score. *MGM*

The Three Lives of Thomasina 🦴🦴🦴 **1963 (PG)** In turn-of-the-century Scotland, a veterinarian orders his daughter's beloved cat destroyed when the pet is diagnosed with tetanus. After the cat's death (with scenes of kitty heaven), a beautiful and mysterious healer from the woods is able to bring the animal back to life and restore the animal to the little girl. Lovely Disney fairy tale with good performances by all. **95m/C VHS, Beta.** Patrick McGoohan, Susan Hampshire, Karen Dotrice, Matthew Garber; ***D:*** Don Chaffey. *DIS, TVC*

Three Men and a Baby 1987 (PG) The arrival of a young baby forever changes the lives of three sworn bachelors living in New York. Well-paced, charming and fun, with good acting from all. A remake of the French movie "Three Men and a Cradle." **102m/C VHS, Beta, LV, 8mm.** Tom Selleck, Steve Guttenberg, Ted Danson, Margaret Colin, Nancy Travis, Philip Bosco, Celeste Holm, Derek De Lint, Cynthia Harris, Lisa Blair, Michelle Blair; ***D:*** Leonard Nimoy; ***W:*** James Orr, Jim Cruickshank; ***M:*** Marvin Hamlisch. People's Choice Awards '88: Best Film—Musical/Comedy. *TOU*

Three Men and a Cradle ½ *Trois Hommes et un Couffin* **1985 (PG-13)** Remade in the U.S. in 1987 as "Three Men and a Baby," this French film is about three bachelors living together who suddenly find themselves the guardians of a baby girl. After the initial shock of learning how to take care of a child, they fall in love with her and won't let her go. Fans of the American version may find themselves liking the original even more. In French with English subtitles. **100m/C VHS, LV.** *FR* Roland Giraud, Michel Boujenah, Andre Dussollier; ***D:*** Coline Serreau; ***W:*** Coline Serreau. Cesar Awards '86: Best Film, Best Supporting Actor (Boujenah), Best Writing; Nominations: Academy Awards '85: Best Foreign Language Film. *LIV, MGM, INJ*

Three Men and a Little Lady ½ **1990 (PG)** In this sequel to "Three Men and a Baby," the mother of the once abandoned infant decides that her child needs a father. Although she wants Selleck, he doesn't get the message and so she chooses a snooty British director. The rest of the movie features various semi-comic attempts to rectify the situation. **100m/C VHS, Beta, LV.** Tom Selleck, Steve Guttenberg, Ted Danson, Nancy Travis, Robin Weisman, Christopher Cazenove, Fiona Shaw, Sheila Hancock, John Boswall, Jonathan Lynn, Sydney Walsh; ***D:*** Emile Ardolino; ***W:*** Charlie Peters, Sara Parriott, Josann McGibbon; ***M:*** James Newton Howard. *TOU*

Three Men on a Horse **1936** Comedy classic about mild-mannered McHugh's ability to predict horse races and the bettors that try to take advantage of him. Blondell is great as the Brooklynese girlfriend of one of the bettors. Lots of laughs, but don't watch for the horse-racing scenes, because there aren't many. **88m/B VHS.** Frank McHugh, Joan Blondell, Carol Hughes, Allen Jenkins, Guy Kibbee, Sam Levene; ***D:*** Mervyn LeRoy. *MGM*

The Three Musketeers *D'Artagnan* **1916** One of the many movie adaptation of Alexandre Dumas' adventure, but this one comes from the hand of famed movie pioneer Ince. D'Artagnan joins the title characters in saving France's Queen Anne from a nefarious plot. Silent with the original organ score. **74m/B VHS, Beta, 8mm.** Orin Johnson, Dorothy Dalton, Louise Glaum, Walt Whitman; ***D:*** Charles Swickard. *VYY, GPV, DVT*

The Three Musketeers ½ **1921** D'Artagnan swashbuckles silently amid stylish sets, scores of extras and exquisite costumes. Relatively faithful adaptation of Alexandre Dumas novel, slightly altered in favor of D'Artagnan's lover. Classic Fairbanks, who also produced. **120m/B VHS, Beta, LV.** Douglas Fairbanks Sr., Leon Barry, George Siegmann, Eugene Pallette, Boyd Irwin, Thomas Holding, Sidney Franklin, Charles Stevens, Nigel de Brulier, Willis Robards; ***D:*** Fred Niblo. *GPV, FCT*

The Three Musketeers **1933** Modern adaptation of the classic tale by Alexander Dumas depicts the three friends as members of the Foreign Legion. Weakest of Wayne serials, in 12 parts. **215m/B VHS, Beta.** John Wayne, Raymond Hatton, Lon Chaney Jr. *NOS, VCN, VDM*

The Three Musketeers **1935** Three swordsmen, loyal to each other, must battle the corrupt Cardinal Richelieu. Generally regarded as the least exciting adaptation of Alexander Dumas' classic tale. The first talking version. **95m/B VHS, Beta, LV.** Walter Abel, Paul Lukas, Moroni Olsen, Ian Keith, Margot Grahame, Heather Angel, Onslow Stevens, Miles Mander; ***D:*** Rowland V. Lee; ***M:*** Max Steiner. *IME, TTC*

The Three Musketeers ½ *The Singing Musketeer* **1939** Musical-comedy version of the famed Alexandre Dumas swashbuckling saga. Ameche is a singing D'Artagnan and the three Ritz brothers are the inept and cowardly Musketeers (who turn out to be phonies, after all). Silly fun. ♫My Lady; Song of the Musketeers; Voila; Chicken Soup. **73m/B VHS.** Don Ameche, The Ritz Brothers, Binnie Barnes, Lionel Atwill, Miles Mander, Gloria Stuart, Pauline Moore, Joseph Schildkraut, John Carradine, Douglass Dumbrille; ***D:*** Allan Dwan; ***W:*** M.M. Musselman, William A. Drake, Sam Hellman. *FXV*

The Three Musketeers ½ **1948** The three musketeers who are "all for one and one for all" join forces with D'Artagnan to battle the evil Cardinal Richelieu in this rambunctious adaptation of the classic tale by Alexander Dumas. Good performances by the cast, who combined drama and comedy well. Turner's first color film. **126m/C VHS, Beta, LV.** Lana Turner, Gene Kelly, June Allyson, Gig Young, Angela Lansbury, Van Heflin, Keenan Wynn, Robert Coote, Reginald Owen, Frank Morgan, Vincent Price, Patricia Medina; ***D:*** George Sidney. Nominations: Academy Awards '46: Best Color Cinematography. *MGM, CCB*

The Three Musketeers ½ **1974 (PG)** Extravagant and funny version of the Dumas classic. Three swashbucklers and their country cohort, who wishes to join the Musketeers, set out to save the honor of the French Queen. To do so they must oppose the evil cardinal who has his eyes on the power behind the throne. A strong cast leads this winning combination of slapstick and high adventure. Followed by "The Four Musketeers" and "The Return of the Musketeers." **105m/C VHS, Beta.** Richard Chamberlain, Oliver Reed, Michael York, Raquel Welch, Frank Finlay, Christopher Lee, Faye Dunaway, Charlton Heston, Geraldine Chaplin, Simon Ward, Jean-Pierre Cassel; ***D:*** Richard Lester; ***C:*** David Watkin. Golden Globe Awards '75: Best Actress—Musical/Comedy (Welch). *COL*

The Three Musketeers ½ **1993 (PG)** Yet another version of the classic swashbuckler with Porthos, Athos, Aramis, and the innocent D'Artanan banding together against the evil Cardinal Richelieu and the tempting Milady DeWinter to save France. Cute stars, a little swordplay, a few jokes, and cartoon bad guys. Okay for the younger crowd. **105m/C VHS, LV.** Kiefer Sutherland, Charlie Sheen, Chris O'Donnell, Oliver Platt, Rebecca DeMornay, Tim Curry, Gabrielle Anwar, Julie Delpy, Michael Wincott; ***D:*** Stephen Herek; ***W:*** David Loughery; ***M:*** Michael Kamen. Nominations: MTV Movie Awards '94: Best Song ("All for Love"). *DIS*

3 Ninjas ½ **1992 (PG)** Lively kid's actioner about three brothers who are trained as ninjas by their grandpa. When a group of bad guys tries to kidnap the boys, they're in for trouble. Sort of a cross between "The Karate Kid" and "Home Alone" that is suitable for family viewing. Followed by "3 Ninjas Kick Back." **84m/C VHS, Beta, LV.** Victor Wong, Michael Treanor, Max Elliott Slade, Chad Power, Rand Kingsley, Alan McRae, Margarita Franco, Toru Tanaka, Patrick Laborteaux; ***D:*** Jon Turteltaub; ***W:*** Edward Emanuel; ***M:*** Rick Marvin. *TOU, PMS*

3 Ninjas Kick Back ½ **1994 (PG)** Sequel to the popular "3 Ninjas." Three brothers help their grandfather protect a ceremonial knife won in a ninja tournament in Japan 50 years earlier. Gramps' ancient adversary in that tournament, now an evil tycoon, wants the sword back and he's willing to enlist the aid of his three American grandchildren, members of garage band Teenage Vomit, to get it. The showdown eventually heads to Japan, where "Kick Back," unlike predecessors, dispenses with the Japan-bashing. High-spirited action fare that kids will enjoy. **95m/C VHS, LV.** Victor Wong, Max Elliott Slade, Sean Fox, Evan Bonifant, Sab Shimono, Dustin Nguyen, Jason Schombing, Caroline Junko King, Angelo Tiffe; ***D:*** Charles Kanganis; ***W:*** Mark Saltzman; ***M:*** Rick Marvin. *COL*

3 Ninjas Knuckle Up ½ **1992 (PG-13)** Brothers Rocky (Treanor), Tum Tum (Power), and Colt (Slade) spend their summer vacation with everwise Grandpa Mori (Wong) and get to practice their martial arts skills on a variety of villains. Seems a waste management company has been illegally dumping toxins onto the nearby Indian reservation where the boys' friend Jo (Lightning) lives and have even kidnapped her dad (Shanks) to keep him silent. So it's our pint-sized heroes to the rescue. Filmed in '92 but released after "3 Ninjas Kick Back," which explains why Treanor and Power are missing from the second film. **94m/C VHS, LV.** Victor Wong, Michael Treanor, Chad Power, Max Elliott Slade, Crystle Lightning, Patrick Kilpatrick, Don Shanks, Charles Napier, Nick Ramus, Vincent Schiavelli; ***D:*** Simon S. Sheen; ***W:*** Alex S. Kim; ***C:*** Eugene Shlugleit; ***M:*** Gary Stevan Scott. *COL*

Three Nuts in Search of a Bolt ½ **1964 (R)** Three neurotics send a surrogate to a comely psychiatrist for help, but the shrink thinks the surrogate's a three-way multiple personality. Raunchy monkey-shines ensue. Includes Van Doren's infamous beer bath scene. **78m/C VHS, Beta.** Mamie Van Doren, Tommy Noonan, Paul Gilbert, Alvy Moore; ***D:*** Tommy Noonan. *NO*

301, 302 **1994** Confusing horror story told in flashbacks focuses on two women in neighboring high-rise apartments. A young policeman is investigating the disappearance of the woman from apartment 302 (Hwang). He questions the tenant across the hall in 301 (Pang), an obsessive cook who tries to share her culinary results with Hwang, who happens to be an anorexic writer. Both have dark secrets in their pasts, which they share, leading to a grotesque resolution of their friendship. **99m/C VHS.** Eun-Jin Pang, Sin-Hye Hwang; ***D:*** Chul-Soo Park; ***W:*** Suh-Goon Lee. *NYR*

Three O'Clock High ½ **1987 (PG)** A nerdy high school journalist is assigned a profile of the new kid in school, who turns out to be the biggest bully, too. He approaches his task with great unease. Silly teen-age farce is given souped-up direction by Spielberg protege Joanou. Features decent work by the young cast. **97m/C VHS, Beta, LV.** Casey Siemaszko, Anne Ryan, Stacey Glick, Jonathan Wise, Richard Tyson, Jeffrey Tambor, Philip Baker Hall, John P. Ryan; ***D:*** Phil Joanou; ***W:*** Richard Christian Matheson, Thomas Szollosi; ***M:*** Tangerine Dream. *MCA*

Three of Hearts ½ **1993 (R)** Slick look at love in contemporary downtown New York. The triangle consists of Connie (Lynch), just dumped by bisexual girlfriend Ellen (Fenn), who is in turn seduced by hired escort Joe (Baldwin), who will break her heart, causing her to turn back to the sympathetic Connie. But guess what happens. Hiply superficial plot is transparent although the three leads are likeable, especially Lynch as the lanky lovelorn Connie. Don't read further if you don't want to know what happens since the film was shot with two endings. The U.S. release pairs Joe and Ellen for a typically American happy ending; the European release doesn't. **102m/C VHS, LV.** Kelly Lynch, William Baldwin, Sherilyn Fenn, Joe Pantoliano, Gail Strickland, Cec Verrell, Claire Callaway, Tony Amendola; ***D:*** Yurek Bogayevicz; ***W:*** Philip C. Epstein, Adam Greenman; ***M:*** Richard Gibbs. *COL, IME, FCT*

Three on a Match **1932** An actress, a stenographer and a society woman get together for a tenth year reunion. They become embroiled in a world of crime when Blondell's gangster boyfriend takes a liking to Dvorak. She leaves her husband and takes up with the crook. The results are tragic. Bogart's first gangster role. **64m/B VHS, Beta.** Joan Blondell, Warren William, Ann Dvorak, Bette Davis, Lyle Talbot, Humphrey Bogart, Patricia Ellis, Grant Mitchell; ***D:*** Mervyn LeRoy. *MGM, FCT*

Three on a Meathook *Woof!* **1972** When a young man and his father living on an isolated farm receive female visitors, bloodshed is quick to follow. Essentially a remake of "Psycho," and very loosely based on the crimes of Ed Gein. Filmed in Louisville, Kentucky. **85m/C VHS, Beta.** Charles Kissinger, James Pickett, Sherry Steiner, Carolyn Thompson; ***D:*** William Girdler; ***W:*** William Girdler. *NO*

The Three Penny Opera 🦴🦴🦴 *Die Dreigroschenoper* **1962** Mack the Knife presides over an exciting world of thieves, murderers, beggars, prostitutes and corrupt officials in a seedy section of London. Based on the opera by Kurt Weill and Bertold Brecht, which was based on "The Beggar's Opera" by John Gay. Remake of "The Threepenny Opera" (1931). **124m/C VHS, Beta, LV.** *GE* Curt Jurgens, Hildegarde Neff, Gert Frobe, June Ritchie, Lino Ventura, Sammy Davis Jr. *MVD, FCT*

Three Secrets 🦴🦴½ **1950** A plane crashes and the only survivor is a five-year-old boy. Three women, each with a secret, seek to claim him as the child each gave up for adoption five years before. Tearjerker with good cast. **98m/B VHS.** Eleanor Parker, Patricia Neal, Ruth Roman, Frank Lovejoy, Leif Erickson; ***D:*** Robert Wise. *REP*

Three Smart Girls 🦴🦴🦴½ **1936** Fast-moving musical features three high-spirited sisters who attempt to bring their divorced parents back together. Their plan is thwarted when they learn of their father's plan to marry a gold digger. 15-year-old singing sensation Durbin made her debut in this film. Based on a story by Commandini. Followed by "Three Smart Girls Grow Up." ♫My Heart is Singing; Someone to Care for Me. **84m/B VHS.** Deanna Durbin, Binnie Barnes, Alice Brady, Ray Milland, Charles Winninger, Mischa Auer, Nan Grey, Barbara Read; ***D:*** Henry Koster; ***W:*** Adele Commandini, Austin Parker; ***C:*** Joseph Valentine. *MCA*

Three Smart Girls Grow Up 🦴🦴🦴 **1939** Durbin once again plays matchmaker, this time for her two older sisters and their fellas. A delightful mix of comedy and song, this lighthearted sequel turned out to be one of the top-grossing films of the year. Durbin sings "Because," which became one of her biggest hits. **88m/B VHS.** Deanna Durbin, Charles Winninger, Nan Grey, Helen Parrish, Robert Cummings, William Lundigan, Ernest Cossart; ***D:*** Henry Koster; ***W:*** Felix Jackson, Bruce Manning. *MCA*

Three Sovereigns for Sarah 🦴🦴½ **1985** Witch-hunters tortured and toasted Sarah's two sisters for practicing witchcraft in the past. Now, accused of witchery herself, she struggles to prove the family's innocence. Excellent, made-for-PBS. Fine performances from all, especially Redgrave. **152m/C VHS, Beta.** Vanessa Redgrave, Phyllis Thaxter, Patrick McGoohan; ***D:*** Philip Leacock. *PSM, PBS*

Three Stooges Comedy Capers: Vol. 1 **194?** Compilation includes: "Disorder in the Court" (1936), "Malice in the Palace" (1949), "Sing a Song of Six Pants" (1947), and "The Brideless Groom" (1947). **80m/B VHS, Beta.** Moe Howard, Larry Fine, Curly Howard, Shemp Howard. *NOS, MED*

Three Stooges Comedy Classics **1949** The antics of the Stooges are featured in this collection of five original shorts, along with an early Ted Healy comedy that features all four Stooges: "Hollywood on Parade," "Disorder in the Court," "Malice in the Palace," "Brideless Groom," and "Sing a Song of Six Pants." **79m/B VHS.** Moe Howard, Larry Fine, Curly Howard, Shemp Howard, Ted Healy. *REP*

Three Stooges: Cookoo Cavaliers and Other Nyuks **1940** The boys star in "Cookoo Cavaliers," "Busy Buddies," and "Booby Dupes." **55m/B VHS.** Moe Howard, Curly Howard, Larry Fine. *COL*

Three Stooges Festival **1949** Three original shorts by the comedy trio, including: "Disorder in the Court" (1936-Curly), "Sing a Song of Six Pants" (1949-Shemp) and "Malice in the Palace" (1949-Shemp). **60m/B VHS, Beta.** Moe Howard, Larry Fine, Shemp Howard, Curly Howard. *AOV, VYY*

Three Stooges: From Nurse to Worse and Other Nyuks **1945** The irrepressible Stooges star in "From Nurse to Worse," "Crash Goes the Hash," and "G.I. Wanna Go Home." **55m/B VHS.** Moe Howard, Larry Fine, Curly Howard. *COL*

The Three Stooges: Half-Wit's Holiday and Other Nyuks **1935** Includes, "Half-Wit's Holiday," "Horse Collars," and "How High Is Up?" **55m/B VHS.** Moe Howard, Curly Howard, Larry Fine. *COL*

The Three Stooges: Idiots Deluxe and Other Nyuks **1940** Curly, Larry and Moe star in, "Idiots Deluxe," "I Can Hardly Wait," and "Idle Roomers." **55m/B VHS.** Moe Howard, Curly Howard, Larry Fine. *COL*

Three Stooges in Orbit 🦴🦴½ **1962** Three television performers (you know who) looking for a schtick and a place to live, encounter a crazy scientist with a rocket-like invention. In a shocking plot twist, the boys accidently launch the rocket and must battle Martians to save the world and their TV career. **87m/B VHS.** Moe Howard, Larry Fine, Joe DeRita, Emil Sitka, Carol Christensen, Edson Stroll; ***D:*** Edward L. Bernds. *COL*

The Three Stooges Meet Hercules 🦴🦴½ **1961** The Three Stooges are transported back to ancient Ithaca by a time machine with a young scientist and his girlfriend. When the girl is captured, they enlist the help of Hercules to rescue her. **80m/B VHS, Beta.** Moe Howard, Larry Fine, Joe DeRita, Vicki Trickett, Quinn Redeker; ***D:*** Edward L. Bernds. *GKK, COL*

The Three Stooges: Nutty but Nice and Other Nyuks **1936** The boys star in "Nutty but Nice," "The Sitter-Downers," and "Slippery Silks." **55m/B VHS.** Moe Howard, Curly Howard, Larry Fine. *COL*

The Three Stooges: They Stooge to Conga and Other Nyuks **1940** WWII madness from the Stooges in "They Stooge to Conga," "You Natzy Spy!" and "I'll Never Heil Again." **55m/B VHS.** Moe Howard, Curly Howard, Larry Fine. *COL*

Three Stops to Murder 🦴 **1953** An FBI agent investigates the murder of a beautiful model in this early, unspectacular Hammer production. **76m/B VHS, Beta.** *GB* Tom Conway, Mila Parely, Naomi Chance, Eric Pohlmann, Andrew Osborn, Richard Wattis, Eileen Way, Delphi Lawrence; ***D:*** Terence Fisher. *SNC, MLB*

Three Strange Loves 🦴🦴🦴 *Thirst* **1949** Men and women struggle with loneliness, old age, and sterility. Sometimes disjointed, but for the most part, well-made. Finely acted. In Swedish with English subtitles. **88m/B VHS, Beta.** *SW* Eva Henning, Brigit Tengroth, Birger Malmsten; ***D:*** Ingmar Bergman. *NOS, HHT, SUE*

3:10 to Yuma 🦴🦴🦴½ **1957** In order to collect $200 he desperately needs, a poor farmer has to hold a dangerous killer at bay while waiting to turn the outlaw over to the authorities arriving on the 3:10 train to Yuma. Stuck in a hotel room with the outlaw's gang gathering outside, the question arises as to who is the prisoner. Farmer Heflin is continually worked on by the outlaw Ford, in a movie with more than its share of great dialogue. Suspenseful, well-made action western adapted from an Elmore Leonard story. **92m/B VHS, Beta, LV.** Glenn Ford, Van Heflin, Felicia Farr, Richard Jaeckel; ***D:*** Delmer Daves; ***M:*** George Duning. *GKK*

Three Texas Steers 🦴½ *Danger Rides the Range* **1939** A circus owner inherits some land that the government wants for a water project and her manager tries to get it for himself. Enter the terrific trio to set things right. Last of the series for Terhune. The scenes of the circus fire were taken from "Circus Girl" (1937). **59m/B VHS.** John Wayne, Ray Corrigan, Max Terhune, Carole Landis, Ralph Graves, Roscoe Ates; ***D:*** George Sherman. *NOS*

Three the Hard Way 🦴🦴½ **1974 (R)** An insane white supremacist has a plan to eliminate blacks by contaminating water supplies. A big blaxploitation money maker and the first to team Brown, Williamson, and Kelly, who would go on to make several more pictures together. **93m/C VHS.** Jim Brown, Fred Williamson, Jim Kelly, Sheila Frazier, Jay Robinson, Alex Rocco; ***D:*** Gordon Parks. *XVC*

Three Violent People 🦴🦴 **1957** Family feud set in post-Civil War Old West features Heston and Baxter impulsively marrying and returning to run the family ranch. Heston's brother (Tryon) wants to sell the ranch in order to get his share of the inheritance and then Heston finds out Baxter was once a prostitute. In this case family squabbles don't make for an exciting film. **100m/C VHS.** Charlton Heston, Anne Baxter, Gilbert Roland, Tom Tryon, Forrest Tucker, Elaine Stritch, Bruce (Herman Brix) Bennett, Barton MacLane; ***D:*** Rudolph Mate; ***W:*** James Edward Grant; ***C:*** Loyal Griggs; ***M:*** Walter Scharf. *PAR*

Three Warriors 🦴½ **1977** Young Native American boy is forced to leave the city and return to the reservation, where his contempt for the traditions of his ancestors slowly turns to appreciation and love. **100m/C VHS, Beta.** Charles White Eagle, Lois Red Elk, McKee "Kiko" Red Wing, Christopher Lloyd, Randy Quaid. *NO*

Three Way Weekend 🦴 **1981 (R)** Two young girls set off on a back-packing trip through the mountains of Southern California to enjoy camping and romance. **78m/C VHS, Beta.** Dan Diego, Jody Lee Olhava, Richard Blye, Blake Parrish; ***D:*** Emmett Alston. *ACA*

The Three Weird Sisters 🦴🦴 **1948** The three weird sisters from "Macbeth" strive to maintain their life of luxury by plotting to kill their half-brother for the inheritance. Not a bad effort for Birt's first time out as director; script co-written by his wife, Louise and poet Thomas. **82m/B VHS.** *GB* Nancy Price, Mary Clare; ***D:*** Daniel Birt; ***W:*** Dylan Thomas, Louise Birt. *VDM, SNC, VMK*

Three Wishes 🦴🦴 **1995 (PG)** Mysterious—and perhaps mystical—stranger Jack (Swayze) moves into the lives of a 1950s suburban widow (Mastrantonio) and her kids (Mazzello and Mumy) after she hits him with her car. Jack proceeds to use Zen philosophy, stories of a genie disguised as a dog, and nude sunbathing to help the kids' Little League team, make a boy fly, and scandalize the neighborhood. Adults will recognize the beatnik, Kerouac-influenced philosophy of nonconformity. They'll also recognize the sellout of that ideal with the sickeningly sappy ending. Mumy is the son of former "Lost in Space" child star Billy Mumy. **115m/C VHS, LV.** Patrick Swayze, Mary Elizabeth Mastrantonio, Joseph Mazzello, David Marshall Grant, Michael O'Keefe, John Diehl, Jay O. Sanders, Diane Venora, Seth Mumy; ***D:*** Martha Coolidge; ***W:*** Elizabeth Anderson; ***C:*** Johnny E. Jensen; ***M:*** Cynthia Millar. *HBO*

Three Word Brand 🦴🦴 **1921** Hart plays three roles in this film, a homesteader who is killed by Indians and his twin sons, who are separated after their father's death and reunited many years later. Silent with musical score. **75m/B VHS, Beta.** William S. Hart, Jane Novak, S.J. Bingham; ***D:*** Lambert Hillyer. *GPV, VYY*

The Three Worlds of Gulliver 🦴🦴½ *The Worlds of Gulliver* **1959** A colorful family version of the Jonathan Swift classic about an Englishman who discovers a fantasy land of small and giant people. Visual effects by Ray Harryhausen. **100m/C VHS, Beta, LV.** Kerwin Mathews, Jo Morrow, Basil Sydney, Mary Ellis; ***D:*** Jack Sher; ***W:*** Arthur Ross, Jack Sher; ***M:*** Bernard Herrmann. *COL, MLB, CCB*

The Threepenny Opera 🦴🦴 *Die Dreigroschenoper; L'Opera De Quat'Sous; Beggars' Opera* **1931** A musical about the exploits of gangster Mack the Knife. Adapted from Bertolt Brecht's play and John Gay's "The Beggar's Opera." In German with English subtitles. **107m/B VHS.** Rudolph Forster, Lotte Lenya, Carola Neher, Reinhold Schunzel, Fritz Rasp, Valeska Gert; ***D:*** G.W. Pabst. *VDM, AUD, INJ*

Three's Trouble 🦴🦴 **1985** A middle-class family erupts when a young male babysitter enters to care for its three mischievous sons. **93m/C VHS, Beta.** *AU* John Waters, Jacki Weaver, Steven Vidler; ***D:*** Chris Thomson. *NWV*

Threesome *Woof!* **1994 (R)** Another Generation X movie that tries hard to be hip, but fails miserably. Due to a college administrative error, Alex (Boyle) winds up sharing a suite with two male roommates, Eddy (Charles) and Stuart (Baldwin). Despite having completely different personalities, they soon become best friends and form one cozy little group, with cozy being the key word. Sexual tension abounds—Alex wants Eddy who wants Stuart who wants Alex. Filled with pathetic dialogue (most of it relating to bodily functions and body parts) and shallow, obnoxious characters, this menage a trois film is a flop. **93m/C VHS, LV, 8mm.** Lara Flynn Boyle, Stephen Baldwin, Josh Charles, Alexis Arquette, Mark Arnold, Martha Gehman, Michelle Matheson; ***D:*** Andrew Fleming; ***W:*** Andrew Fleming; ***M:*** Thomas Newman. *COL*

Threshold 🦴🦴½ **1983 (PG)** An internationally-acclaimed research biologist is frustrated by his inability to save a dying 20-year-old woman born with a defective heart. She becomes the recipient of the first artificial heart. Solid performances. **97m/C VHS, Beta.** *CA* Donald Sutherland, Jeff Goldblum, John Marley, Mare Winningham; ***D:*** Richard Pearce. Genie Awards '83: Best Actor (Sutherland). *FOX*

The Thrill Killers *Woof! The Monsters Are Loose; The Maniacs Are Loose* **1965** Young murderous thugs rampage through Los Angeles suburbs, killing indiscriminately. Pretentious and exploitative. Sometimes shown with Hallucinogenic Hypo-Vision—a prologue announcing the special effect would be shown before the film, and on cue, hooded ushers would run through the theatre with cardboard axes. Weird. **82m/C VHS, Beta.** Cash Flagg, Liz Renay, Brick Bardo, Carolyn Brandt, Atlas King; ***D:*** Ray Dennis Steckler. *NO*

Thrill of a Romance 🦴🦴 **1945** Johnson, an Army hero, meets Williams, a swimming instructor of all things, at a resort in the Sierra Nevadas. The only problem is that she's married. Typical swim-romance vehicle. ♫Please Don't Say No, Say Maybe; I Should Care; Lonely Night; Vive L'Amour; Schubert's Serenade; The Thrill of a Romance. **105m/C VHS.** Esther Williams, Van Johnson, Frances Gifford, Henry Travers, Spring Byington, Lauritz Melchior; ***D:*** Richard Thorpe. *MGM*

The Thrill of It All! 🦴🦴½ **1963** An average housewife becomes a star of television commercials, to the dismay of her chauvinist husband, a gynecologist. Fast and funny, with numerous acidic jokes about television sponsors and programs. **108m/C VHS, Beta.** James Garner, Doris Day, Arlene Francis, Edward Andrews, Carl Reiner, Elliott Reid, Reginald Owen, ZaSu Pitts; ***D:*** Norman Jewison; ***W:*** Carl Reiner; ***C:*** Russell Metty. *MCA*

Thrilled to Death 🦴½ **1988 (R)** An utterly naive husband and wife get caught in the middle of a lethal game when they befriend a scheming couple. **90m/C VHS.** Blake Bahner, Rebecca Lynn, Richard Maris, Christine Moore; ***D:*** Chuck Vincent. *REP*

Thrillkill 🦴 **1984** A young girl is enmeshed in a multi-million-dollar burglary scheme after her computer-whiz/embezzler sister disappears. **88m/C VHS, Beta.** Robin Ward, Gina Massey, Anthony Kramroither; ***D:*** Anthony D'Andrea. *MED*

Throne of Blood 🦴🦴🦴🦴 *Kumonosujo, Kumonosu-djo; Cobweb Castle; The Castle of the Spider's Web* **1957** Kurosawa's masterful adaptation of "Macbeth" transports the story to medieval Japan and the world of the samurai. Mifune and Chiaki are warriors who have put down a rebellion and are to be rewarded by their overlord. On their way to his castle they meet a mysterious old woman who prophesizes that Mifune will soon rule—but his reign will be short. She is dismissed as crazy but her prophesies come to pass. So steeped in Japanese style that it bears little resemblance to the Shakespearean original, this film is an incredibly detailed vision in its own right. In Japanese with English subtitles. **105m/B VHS, Beta, LV.** *JP* Toshiro Mifune, Isuzu Yamada, Takashi Shimura, Minoru Chiaki, Akira Kubo; ***D:*** Akira Kurosawa; ***W:*** Hideo Oguni, Shinobu Hashimoto, Riyuzo Kikushima, Akira Kurosawa; ***M:*** Masaru Sato. *HMV, INJ, CRC*

Throne of Fire *Woof!* **1982** A mighty hero battles the forces of evil to gain control of the powerful Throne of Fire. Dubbed. **91m/C VHS, Beta.** *IT* Peter McCoy, Sabrina Siani; ***D:*** Franco Prosperi. *MGM*

Through a Glass Darkly 🦴🦴🦴 **1961** Oppressive interactions within a family sharing a holiday on a secluded island: a woman recovering from schizophrenia, her husband, younger brother, and her psychologist father. One of Bergman's most mysterious, upsetting and powerful films. In Swedish with English subtitles. Part of Bergman's Silence-of-God trilogy followed by "Winter Light" and "The Silence." **91m/B VHS, Beta.** *SW* Harriet Andersson, Max von Sydow, Gunnar Bjornstrand, Lars Passgard; ***D:*** Ingmar Bergman; ***W:*** Ingmar Bergman; ***C:*** Sven Nykvist. Academy Awards '61: Best Foreign Language Film; National Board of Review Awards '62: 5 Best Foreign Films of the Year; Nominations: Academy Awards '62: Best Story & Screenplay. *NOS, SUE, INJ*

Through Naked Eyes 🦴🦴½ **1987** Made-for-television thriller about two people who spy on each other. They witness a murder and realize that someone else is watching them. What a coincidence. **91m/C VHS, Beta.** David Soul, Pam Dawber; ***D:*** John Llewellyn Moxey. *MED*

Through the Breakers 🦴½ **1928** Heartbroken woman suffers silently on South Pacific isle. **55m/B VHS, Beta.** Margaret Livingston, Holmes Herbert, Clyde Cook, Natalie Joyce. *GPV, FCT*

Through the Eyes of a Killer 🦴🦴½ **1992 (R)** Laurie Fisher (Helgenberger) has dumped cheating boyfriend Jerry (Pantoliano) and has declared her independence by finding a spacious but crummy New York apartment in desperate need of renovation. Enter handsome handyman Ray Bellano (Anderson), who's happy to work on the apartment—and Laurie as well. But where Laurie sees a fling, Ray sees true love, and since brooding Ray's got the prerequisite mystery past, you know Laurie's in for the shock of her life. Long-time nice guy Anderson does a credible turn as an obsessive psycho. Based on the short story "The Master Builder" by Christopher Fowler; made for TV. **94m/C VHS, Beta.** Richard Dean Anderson, Marg Helgenberger, Joe Pantoliano, David Marshall Grant, Melinda Culea, Tippi Hedren; ***D:*** Peter Markle; ***W:*** John Pielmeier; ***M:*** George S. Clinton. *PAR*

Through the Olive Trees 🦴🦴🦴 *Under the Olive Trees* **1994 (G)** Film-within-a-film is the last of a trilogy concerned with Persian village life, following "Where Is My Friend's House?" and "And Life Goes On." Director, filming in an earthquake-ravaged village, discovers that the young bricklayer playing the bridegroom in his film is actually in love with the local girl who's playing the bride. However, she's turned down his real-life marriage proposal, feeling that the uneducated man is beneath her. Farsi with subtitles. It may be rated G but considering the subject matter and the fact that the film is subtitled, don't consider this one for the kiddies. **104m/C VHS.** Hossein Rezai, Mohamad Ali Keshavarz, Taherek Ladania; ***D:*** Abbas Kiarostami; ***W:*** Abbas Kiarostami; ***C:*** Hossein Jafarian, Farhad Saba. Nominations: Independent Spirit Awards '96: Best Foreign Language Film. *NYR*

Throw Momma from the Train 🦴🦴🦴 **1987 (PG-13)** DeVito plays a man, henpecked by his horrific mother, who tries to persuade his writing professor (Crystal) to exchange murders. DeVito will kill Crystal's ex-wife and Crystal will kill DeVito's mother. Only mama isn't going to be that easy to get rid of. Fast-paced and entertaining black comedy. Ramsey steals the film. Inspired by Hitchcock's "Strangers on a Train." **88m/C VHS, Beta, LV.** Danny DeVito, Billy Crystal, Anne Ramsey, Kate Mulgrew, Kim Greist, Branford Marsalis, Rob Reiner, Bruce Kirby; ***D:*** Danny DeVito; ***W:*** Stu Silver; ***M:*** David Newman. Nominations: Academy Awards '87: Best Supporting Actress (Ramsey). *ORI*

The Throwback 🦴½ **1935** When Jones was a lad the townspeople accused his father of cattle rustling. When he returns as an adult he sets out to clear his father's name. **61m/B VHS.** Buck Jones, Muriel Evans, Eddie Phillips, George "Gabby" Hayes, Bryant Washburn, Paul Fix, Frank LaRue; ***D:*** Ray Taylor. *GPV*

Thumb Tripping 🦴🦴 **1972 (R)** A dated sixties/hippie film. Two flower children hitchhike and encounter all kinds of other strange people in their travels on the far-out roads. **94m/C VHS, Beta.** Meg Foster, Michael Burns, Bruce Dern, Marianna Hill, Michael Conrad, Joyce Van Patten; ***D:*** Quentin Masters. *NLC*

Thumbelina **1982** From "Faerie Tale Theatre" comes the story of a tiny girl who gets kidnapped by a toad and a mole, but meets the man of her dreams in the nick of time. Adapted from the classic tale by Hans Christian Andersen. Made for television. **60m/C VHS, Beta, LV.** Carrie Fisher, William Katt, Burgess Meredith; ***D:*** Michael Lindsay-Hogg. *KUI, FOX, FCT*

Thumbelina 🦴🦴½ *Hans Christian Andersen's Thumbelina* **1994 (G)** Ornery little girl named Mia gets magically sucked into the pages of the "Thumbelina" storybook she's reading and finds all sorts of adventures. Loose adaptation of Hans Christian Andersen fairy tale from Bluth is lackluster, with acceptable songs. Not up to the level of recent Disney animated features, but pleasant enough for the kids. **86m/C VHS, Beta, LV.** ***D:*** Don Bluth, Gary Goldman; ***W:*** Don Bluth; ***M:*** William Ross, Barry Manilow, Barry Manilow, Jack Feldman, Bruce Sussman; ***V:*** Jodi Benson, Gary Imhoff, Charo, Gilbert Gottfried, Carol Channing, John Hurt, Will Ryan, June Foray, Kenneth Mars. Golden Raspberry Awards '94: Worst Song ("Marry the Mole"). *WAR*

Thunder Alley 🦴½ **1985** In middle America, two friends and their rock group struggle for success. One of the friends dies after an accidental overdose and the other's grief propels him to stardom. ♫Can't Look Back; Just Another Pretty Boy; Sometimes in the Night; Heart to Heart; Can You Feel My Heart Beat; Do You Feel Alright?; Danger, Danger; Surrender; Gimme Back My Heart. **102m/C VHS, Beta.** Roger Wilson, Leif Garrett, Jill Schoelen; ***D:*** J.S. Cardone; ***W:*** J.S. Cardone. *MGM*

Thunder and Lightning 🦴🦴 **1977 (PG)** A mismatched young couple chase a truckload of poisoned moonshine. Action-packed chases ensue. Nice chemistry between Carradine and Jackson. **94m/C VHS, Beta.** David Carradine, Kate Jackson, Roger C. Carmel, Sterling Holloway, Eddie Barth; ***D:*** Corey Allen. *FOX*

Thunder & Mud **1989** Female mud wrestlers battle over their favorite rock band. Hahn's attempt to cash in on her notoriety after the Bakker scandal. **90m/C VHS, Beta, LV.** Jessica Hahn; ***D:*** Penelope Spheeris. *COL*

Thunder Bay 🦴🦴🦴 **1953** Stewart and Duryea are a pair of Louisiana wildcat oil drillers who believe there is oil at the bottom of the Gulf of Mexico off the coast of the town of Port Felicity. They decide to construct an oil platform which the shrimp fisherman of the town believe will interfere with their livelihoods. Tensions rise between the two groups and violence seems likely. Action packed, with timely storyline as modern oil drillers fight to drill in waters that have historically been off-limits. **82m/C VHS, Beta.** James Stewart, Joanne Dru, Dan Duryea, Gilbert Roland, Marcia Henderson; ***D:*** Anthony Mann; ***W:*** John Michael Hayes; ***C:*** William H. Daniels. *MCA*

Thunder County 🦴½ **1974** Federal agents and drug runners are after a group of four convicts who have just escaped from prison. **78m/C VHS, Beta.** Mickey Rooney, Ted Cassidy, Chris Robinson. *PSM*

Thunder in God's Country 🦴 **1951** A dishonest gambler eyes a peaceful western town as the next Vegas-like gambling capital. Before this occurs he is exposed as a cheat. **67m/B VHS, Beta.** Rex Allen, Mary Ellen Kay. *DVT*

Thunder in Paradise 🦴🦴½ **1993 (PG-13)** R.J. Hurricane Spencer (Hogan) is a soldier of fortune who heads into Cuba to help a woman and child escape political imprisonment, using his high-tech, weapon-filled speedboat. He has to fight off a small army and manages to find a buried treasure as well. Simple-minded TV pilot. **104m/C VHS, LV.** Hulk Hogan, Robin Weisman, Chris Lemmon, Carol Alt, Patrick Macnee, Sam Jones, Charlotte Rae; ***D:*** Douglas Schwartz. *VMK*

Thunder in Paradise 2 🦴½ **1994 (PG)** Damsel sends up a distress signal and it's the Hulkster and his pal to the rescue. Unfortunately, their commando raid fails and now they need an escape plan. From the syndicated TV series. **90m/C VHS.** Hulk Hogan, Chris Lemmon, Carol Alt, Patrick Macnee; ***D:*** Douglas Schwartz. *VMK*

Thunder in Paradise 3 🦴½ **1994 (PG-13)** Hogan is on a top secret mission to capture a drug lord who's holding his daughter hostage. **88m/C VHS.** Hulk Hogan. *VMK*

Thunder in the City 🦴🦴🦴 **1937** Robinson is an intense American promoter in the sales game who is sent to London by his employers to learn a more subdued way of doing business. Instead, he meets a pair of down-on-their-luck artistocrats whose only asset is an apparently worthless Rhodesian mine. Robinson, however, comes up with a way to promote the mine and get enough capital together to make it profitable. Good satire with Robinson well cast. Robinson wasn't taken with the script in its original form and persuaded his friend, playwright Robert Sherwood, to re-write it. **85m/B VHS, Beta.** *GB* Edward G. Robinson, Nigel Bruce, Ralph Richardson, Constance Collier; ***D:*** Marion Gering; ***M:*** Miklos Rozsa. *NOS, DVT, BAR*

Thunder in the Desert 🦴 **1938** A cowhand joins an outlaw gang in order to catch his uncle's killer. **56m/C VHS, Beta.** Bob Steele, Louise Stanley, Don Barclay, Charles "Blackie" King, Lew Meehan, Budd Buster; ***D:*** Sam Newfield. *NOS, DVT, GPV*

Thunder in the Pines 🦴 **1949** Two lumberjack buddies send for the same French girl to marry, unbeknownst to each other. When she arrives, the dismayed men agree to a contest to see who will marry her. Meanwhile the French girl falls for the local saloon owner and his jilted girlfriend vows to get even. She does, with the help of the lumberjacks. **61m/B VHS, Beta, LV.** Denise Darcel, George Reeves, Ralph Byrd, Lyle Talbot, Michael Whalen, Roscoe Ates, Vince Barnett; ***D:*** Robert Edwards. *NO*

Thunder Mountain 🦴½ **1935** Zane Grey's novel about two prospectors who are bushwhacked on their way to file a claim comes to life on the screen. **56m/B VHS, Beta.** George O'Brien. *DVT, HHE, MLB*

Thunder Over Texas 🦴 **1934** The cowboy hero gets embroiled in a railroad scandal that involves a kidnapping. Directed by Edgar G. Ulmer, who used the alias John Warner because he was moonlighting. His first western; previously he was best known for "The Black Cat." **52m/B VHS, Beta.** Marion Shilling, Helen Westcott, Victor Potel, Tiny Skelton; ***D:*** Edgar G. Ulmer. *VDM*

Thunder Pass 🦴🦴 **1937** Gold and greed are the motives for murder as two young brothers become separated when their wagon train is attacked and their family is slaughtered. One brother searches for the other and finds him several years later. Based on the novel "Arizona Ames" by Zane Grey. Also released as "Thunder Trail." **58m/B VHS.** Charles Bickford, Marsha Hunt, Gilbert Roland, Monte Blue; ***D:*** Charles T. Barton. *NOS, VDM, DVT*

Thunder Pass 🦴🦴 **1954** Routine story about a wagon train threatened by hostile Indians and the Army officer who leads them to safety. Based on a story by George Van Marter. **76m/B VHS.** Dane Clark, Dorothy Patrick, Andy Devine, Raymond Burr, John Carradine, Mary Ellen Kay; ***D:*** Frank McDonald; ***W:*** Tom Hubbard, Fred Eggers. *MOV*

Thunder River Feud 🦴🦴 **1942** The Rangebusters help two ranchers avoid a range war. Part of "The Rangebusters" series. **58m/B VHS, Beta.** Ray Corrigan, John "Dusty" King, Max Terhune. *NOS, VCN, DVT*

Thunder Road 🦴🦴🦴 **1958 (PG)** Mitchum comes home to Tennessee from Korea and takes over the family moonshine business, fighting both mobsters and federal agents. An exciting chase between Mitchum and the feds ends the movie with the appropriate bang. Robert Mitchum not only produced, wrote and starred in this best of the moonshine-running films, but also wrote the theme song "Whippoorwill" (which later became a radio hit). Mitchum's son, James, made his film debut, and later starred in a similar movie "Moonrunners." A cult favorite, still shown in many drive-ins around the country. **92m/B VHS, Beta.** Robert Mitchum, Jacques Aubuchon, Gene Barry, Keely Smith, Trevor Bardette, Sandra Knight, Jim Mitchum, Betsy Holt, Frances Koon; ***D:*** Arthur Ripley; ***W:*** Robert Mitchum. *MGM*

Thunder Run 🦴 **1986 (PG-13)** When a load of uranium needs to be transferred across Nevada, a retired trucker takes on the job. The trip is made more difficult since terrorists are trying to hijack the shipment to use for a bomb. **84m/C VHS, Beta.** Forrest Tucker, John Ireland, John Shepherd, Jill Whitlow, Wally Ward, Cheryl Lynn; ***D:*** Gary Hudson; ***W:*** Charles Davis. *MED*

Thunder Trail **1937** Set of twins, separated by a wagon trail massacre, meet up years later on opposite sides of the law. **58m/C VHS.** Gilbert Roland, Charles Bickford, Marsha Hunt, J. Carrol Naish, James Craig, Monte Blue; ***D:*** Charles T. Barton. *GPV*

Thunder Warrior 🦴 *Thunder* **1985 (R)** A young Indian turns into a one-man army determined to punish the local authorities who are abusing his fellow tribe members. **84m/C VHS, Beta.** Raymond Harmstorf, Bo Svenson, Mark Gregory; ***D:*** Larry Ludman. *TWE*

Thunder Warrior 2 🦴 **1985 (PG-13)** A tough Native American is provoked to violence by small-town prejudice. **114m/C VHS, Beta.** *IT* Mark Gregory, Karen Reel, Bo Svenson; ***D:*** Larry Ludman. *TWE*

Thunder Warrior 3 🦴 **1988** The Indian Thunder has vowed to live in peace, but forswears the oath when his wife is kidnapped and family is terrorized. Revenge is the top priority as he torments the bad guys. **90m/C VHS.** Mark Gregory, John Phillip Law, Ingrid Lawrence, Werner Pochat, Horts Schon; ***D:*** Larry Ludman. *IMP*

Thunderball 🦴🦴½ **1965 (PG)** The fourth installment in Ian Fleming's James Bond series finds 007 on a mission to thwart SPECTRE, which has threatened to blow up Miami by atomic bomb if 100 million pounds in ransom is not paid. One of the more tedious Bond entries but a big box-office success. Tom Jones sang the title song. Remade as "Never Say Never Again" in 1983 with Connery reprising his role as Bond after a 12-year absence. **125m/C VHS, Beta, LV.** *GB* Sean Connery, Claudine Auger, Adolfo Celi, Luciana Paluzzi, Rik von Nutter, Martine Beswick, Molly Peters, Guy Doleman, Bernard Lee, Lois Maxwell, Desmond Llewelyn; ***D:*** Terence Young; ***W:*** John Hopkins, Richard Maibaum; ***C:*** Ted Moore; ***M:*** John Barry. Academy Awards '65: Best Visual Effects. *MGM, TLF*

Thunderbolt & Lightfoot 🦴🦴🦴 **1974 (R)** Eastwood is an ex-thief on the run from his former partners (Kennedy and Lewis) who believe he's made off with the loot from their last job, the robbery of a government vault. He joins up with drifter Bridges, who helps him to escape. Later, Eastwood manages to convince Kennedy he doesn't know where the money is. Bridges then persuades the men that they should plan the same heist and rob the same government vault all over again, which they do. But their getaway doesn't go exactly as planned. All-around fine acting; notable is Bridges' scene dressed in drag. First film for director Cimino. **115m/C VHS, Beta, LV.** Clint Eastwood, Jeff Bridges, George Kennedy, Geoffrey Lewis, Gary Busey; ***D:*** Michael Cimino; ***W:*** Michael Cimino; ***M:*** Dee Barton. Nominations: Academy Awards '74: Best Supporting Actor (Bridges). *MGM*

Thunderground 🦴 **1989 (R)** A beautiful con artist teams with a fighter and together they travel to New Orleans to arrange a bout with the king of bare-knuckled fighting. **92m/C VHS, LV.** Paul Coufos, Margaret Langrick, Jesse Ventura, M. Emmet Walsh; ***D:*** David Mitchell. *IME*

Thunderheart 🦴🦴🦴 **1992 (R)** Young FBI agent Kilmer is sent to an Oglala Sioux reservation to investigate a murder. He is himself part Sioux, but resents being chosen for the assignment because of it. Aided by a veteran partner (Shepard), Ray learns, professionally and personally, from a shrewd tribal police officer (well played by Greene). Set in the late 70's the film is loosely based on actual events plaguing the violence-torn Native American community at that time. Great cinematography by Roger Deakins. Filmed on the Pine Ridge Reservation in South Dakota. Director Apted deals with the actual incidents this film is based on in his documentary about Leonard Peltier, "Incident at Oglala." **118m/C VHS, LV.** Val Kilmer, Sam Shepard, Graham Greene, Fred Ward, Fred Dalton Thompson, Sheila Tousey, Chief Ted Thin Elk, John Trudell, Dennis Banks, David Crosby; ***D:*** Michael Apted; ***W:*** John Fusco; ***C:*** Roger Deakins; ***M:*** James Horner. *COL, FCT, BTV*

Thundering Forest 🦴🦴 **1941** Australian actioneer pitting loggers against saboteurs. **?m/C VHS.** *AU* Frank Leighton. *LOO*

Thundering Gunslingers 🦴 **1940** A group of gunmen terrorizing townspeople finally meet their match in this Western. **61m/B VHS, Beta.** Buster Crabbe. *NOS, DVT*

Thundering Ninja 🦴½ **198?** Three secret agents fight off an army of ninjas. Plenty of heel-to-head antics. **89m/C VHS, Beta.** Bernard Geurts, Joe Redner, Klaus Mutter, Ken Kerr, Jimmy Wang Yu; ***D:*** Joseph Kong. *TWE*

Thundering Trail 🦴 *Thunder on the Trail* **1951** Two cowboys encounter plenty of trouble before they take the President's newly appointed territorial governor to his office. **55m/B VHS, Beta.** Lash LaRue, Al "Fuzzy" St. John, Sally Anglim, Archie Twitchell, Ray Bennett. *NOS, DVT*

Thundersquad 🦴 **1985** Mercenaries help a South American rebel leader rescue his kidnapped son. **90m/C VHS, Beta.** Sal Borgese, Julia Fursich, Antonio Sabato. *NO*

Thursday's Child 🦴🦴 **1943** A child's success in films causes trouble for her family. Melodramatic and sappy, but Howes, as the kid, is excellent. One of Granger's early supporting roles. **95m/B VHS, Beta.** *GB* Stewart Granger, Sally Ann Howes; ***D:*** Rodney Ackland. *NOS, DVT, HEG*

Thursday's Game 🦴🦴🦴 **1974 (PG)** Two crisis-besieged businessmen meet every Thursday, using poker as a ruse to work on their business and marital problems. Wonderful cast; intelligently written. Made for television. **99m/C VHS, Beta, LV.** Gene Wilder, Ellen Burstyn, Bob Newhart, Cloris Leachman, Nancy Walker, Valerie Harper, Rob Reiner; ***D:*** James L. Brooks; ***W:*** James L. Brooks. *VMK*

THX 1138 🦴🦴🦴 **1971 (PG)** In the dehumanized world of the future, people live in underground cities run by computer, are force-fed drugs to keep them passive, and no longer have names—just letter/number combinations (Duvall is THX 1138). Emotion is also outlawed and when the computer-matched couple THX 1138 and LUH 3417 discover love, they must battle the computer system to escape. George Lucas' first film, which was inspired by a student film he did at USC. The laserdisc format carries the film in widescreen. **88m/C VHS, Beta, LV.** Robert Duvall, Donald Pleasence, Maggie McOmie; ***D:*** George Lucas; ***W:*** George Lucas; ***M:*** Lalo Schifrin. *WAR, FUS*

Tiara Tahiti 🦴🦴 **1962** Intrigue, double-cross, romance, and violence ensue when two old army acquaintances clash in Tahiti. Very fine performances from the two leading men. **100m/C VHS, Beta.** James Mason, John Mills, Claude Dauphin, Rosenda Monteros, Herbert Lom; ***D:*** Ted Kotcheff. *SUE*

Ticket of Leave Man 🦴🦴 **1937** London's most dangerous killer fronts a charitable organization designed to help reform criminals. It actually steers them into a crime syndicate that cheats philanthropists out of their fortunes. **71m/B VHS, Beta.** *GB* Tod Slaughter, John Warwick, Marjorie Taylor. *VYY, SNC*

Ticket to Heaven 🦴🦴🦴 **1981 (PG)** A young man, trying to deal with the painful breakup of a love affair, falls under the spell of a quasi-religious order. His friends and family, worried about the cult's influence, have him kidnapped in order for him to be de-programmed. Mancuso is excellent, as are his supporting players Rubinek and Thomson. **109m/C VHS, Beta.** Nick Mancuso, Meg Foster, Kim Cattrall, Saul Rubinek, R.H. Thomson; ***D:*** Ralph L. Thomas; ***W:*** Anne Cameron. Genie Awards '82: Best Actor (Mancuso), Best Film, Best Supporting Actor (Rubinek). *MGM*

Ticket to Tomahawk ½ **1950** A gunslinger is hired by a stagecoach company to sabotage a railroad. Look for Marilyn Monroe as a chorus girl in a musical number. **90m/C VHS.** Anne Baxter, Rory Calhoun, Walter Brennan, Charles Kemper, Connie Gilchrist, Arthur Hunnicutt, Victor Sen Yung; ***D:*** Richard Sale. *TCF*

Tickle Me ½ **1965** An unemployed rodeo star finds work at an all-girl health spa and dude ranch. He falls in love with a young lady who has a treasure map and keeps her safe from the evil men who want her fortune. For die-hard Elvis fans only. ♫(It's a) Long, Lonely Highway; Night Rider; It Feels So Right; Dirty, Dirty Feeling; (Such an) Easy Question; Put the Blame on Me; I'm Yours; I Feel That I've Known You Forever; Slowly but Surely. **90m/C VHS, Beta.** Elvis Presley, Julie Adams, Jack Mullaney; ***D:*** Norman Taurog. *FOX, MVD*

Ticks ½ *Infested* **1993 (R)** Mammoth mutant killer insects terrorize a Northern California campground! The predatory woodticks are the victims of steroids dumped in the water supply and a group of unwary teen campers fall prey to their deadly venom! And if that's not bad enough, a forest fire breaks out, trapping the teens! **85m/C VHS, LV.** Ami Dolenz, Rosalind Allen, Alfonso Ribeiro, Peter Scolari; ***D:*** Tony Randel. *REP*

Tidal Wave ½ *Nippon Chiubotsu; The Submersion of Japan; Japan Sinks* **1975 (PG)** Scientists discover that Japan is slowly sinking and order the island to be evacuated. Originally a popular Japanese production, the American version is a poorly dubbed, re-edited mess. **82m/C VHS.** *JP* Lorne Greene, Keiju Kobayashi, Rhonda Leigh Hopkins, Hiroshi Fujioka, Shiro Moriana; ***D:*** Andrew Meyer. *NWV*

Tides of War **1990** In the twilight of the second world war, a German officer begins to question his role in a proposed missile attack on Washington in light of the S.S. brutality he witnesses. **90m/C VHS.** Yvette Heyden, Rodrigo Obregon, David Soul, Bo Svenson; ***D:*** Neil Rossati. *NO*

Tidy Endings ½ **1988** A man who died from AIDS leaves behind his male lover and his ex-wife. The two form a friendship as they both try to cope with the man's death. Based on the play by Fierstein. **54m/C VHS, Beta.** Harvey Fierstein, Stockard Channing; ***D:*** Gavin Millar; ***W:*** Harvey Fierstein. *PSM*

Tie Me Up! Tie Me Down! ½ **1990 (NC-17)** A young psychiatric patient kidnaps a former porno actress he has always had a crush on, and holds her captive, certain that he can convince her to love him. Black comedy features a fine cast and is well directed. At least one fairly explicit sex scene and the bondage theme caused the film to be X-rated, although it was originally released unrated by the distributor. In Spanish with English subtitles. **105m/C VHS, LV.** *SP* Victoria Abril, Antonio Banderas, Loles Leon, Francesco Rabal, Julieta Serrano, Maria Barranco, Rossy de Palma; ***D:*** Pedro Almodovar; ***W:*** Pedro Almodovar; ***M:*** Ennio Morricone. *COL, INJ*

The Tie That Binds **1995 (R)** Insipid thriller is a cheap imitation of its cousin, "The Hand that Rocks the Cradle" (made by the same producers), but what the former movie did to the nanny business, this flick does to a whole genre. Leanne and John Netherwood (Hannah and Carradine) are psycho parents out to reclaim their daughter from the lame-brain yuppie couple (Spano and Kelly) who adopted her. Out of all the children there, they choose the one who likes to sleep with a butcher knife under her pillow. Duh! Every "family in danger from psychotic" cliche is employed in a vain attempt to build suspense for the silly conclusion. Dismal directorial debut of screenwriter Strick. **98m/C VHS, LV.** Daryl Hannah, Keith Carradine, Moira Kelly, Vincent Spano, Julia Devin, Ray Reinhardt, Cynda Williams; ***D:*** Wesley Strick; ***W:*** Michael Auerbach; ***C:*** Bobby Bukowski; ***M:*** Graeme Revell. *MAX*

Tiefland ½ **1944** Melodrama based on the libretto for D'Albert's opera about a gypsy dancer and her loves. Unreleased until 1954, this film is the last of Riefenstahl's career; she subsequently turned to still photography. In German with English subtitles. **98m/B VHS, Beta.** *GE* Leni Riefenstahl, Franz Eichberger, Bernard Minetti, Maria Koppenhofer, Luise Rainer; ***D:*** Leni Riefenstahl. *NOS, FCT, GLV*

Tiffany Jones **1975 (R)** Tiffany Jones is a secret agent who has information that presidents and revolutionaries are willing to kill for. **90m/C VHS, Beta.** Anouska Hempel, Ray Brooks, Eric Pohlmann, Martin Benson, Susan Sneers; ***D:*** Pete Walker. *MON*

Tiger and the Pussycat ½ *Il Tigre* **1967 (R)** A successful Italian businessman's infatuation with an attractive American art student leads him to marital and financial woes. **110m/C VHS, Beta.** Ann-Margret, Vittorio Gassman, Eleanor Parker; ***D:*** Dino Risi. *SUE, HHE*

Tiger Bay **1959** A young Polish sailor, on leave in Cardiff, murders his unfaithful girlfriend. Lonely ten-year-old Gillie sees the crime and takes the murder weapon, thinking it will make her more popular with her peers. Confronted by a police detective, she convincingly lies but eventually the sailor finds Gillie and kidnaps her, hoping to keep her quiet until he can get aboard his ship. A delicate relationship evolves between the child and the killer as she tries to help him escape and the police close in. Marks Hayley Mills' first major role and one of her finest performances. **107m/B VHS, Beta.** *GB* John Mills, Horst Buchholz, Hayley Mills, Yvonne Mitchell; ***D:*** J. Lee Thompson. *PAR*

Tiger Claws ½ **1991 (R)** The pretty, petite Rothrock has been called the female Bruce Lee. Perhaps, but at least he got a good script every once in a while. This time Rothrock's a kung-fu cop investigating the strange ritual-murders of martial-arts champions. **93m/C VHS, Beta, LV.** Cynthia Rothrock, Bolo Yeung, Jalal Merhi; ***D:*** Kelly Markin. *MCA*

Tiger Fangs ½ **1943** When Nazis threaten the Far East rubber production with man-eating tigers, real-life big game hunter Frank Buck comes to the rescue. **57m/B VHS.** Frank Buck, June Duprez, Duncan Renaldo; ***D:*** Sam Newfield. *SNC, NOS, DVT*

Tiger Heart ½ **1996 (PG-13)** Teenaged karate champ Eric Chase (Roberts) is looking forward to a lazy summer with girlfriend Stephanie (Lyons) before heading off to college. But when his neighborhood comes under attack from an unscrupulous developer and Stephanie runs afoul of his goons, Eric decides to take action. **90m/C VHS.** Ted Jan Roberts, Jennifer Lyons, Robert LaSardo, Carol Potter, Timothy Williams; ***D:*** Dominique Roulet. *PMH*

Tiger Joe **1985** There's trouble in Southeast Asia, and the U.S. military confuses things even more. **96m/C VHS.** Alan Collins, David Warbeck; ***D:*** Anthony (Antonio Margheriti) Dawson. *LIV*

Tiger of the Seven Seas **1962** A female pirate takes over her father's command and embarks on adventures on the high seas. Generous portions of action, intrigue, and romance. Sequel to "Queen of the Pirates." **90m/C VHS.** *IT FR* Gianna Maria Canale, Anthony Steel, Grazia Maria Spina, Ernesto Calindri; ***D:*** Luigi Capuano. *NO*

Tiger Town ½ **1983 (G)** A baseball player, ending an illustrious career with the Detroit Tigers, sees his chance of winning a pennant slipping away. A young fan, however, proves helpful in chasing that elusive championship. Made for the Disney cable station. **76m/C VHS, Beta.** Roy Scheider, Justin Henry, Ron McLarty, Bethany Carpenter, Noah Moazezi; ***D:*** Alan Shapiro. *DIS*

A Tiger Walks ½ **1964** A savage tiger escapes from a circus and local children start a nationwide campaign to save its life. Notable for its unflattering portrayal of America's heartland and small town dynamics. Radical departure from most Disney films of the period. **88m/C VHS, Beta.** Sabu, Pamela Franklin, Brian Keith, Vera Miles, Kevin Corcoran, Peter Brown, Una Merkel, Frank McHugh, Edward Andrews; ***D:*** Norman Tokar; ***M:*** Buddy Baker. *DIS*

Tiger Warsaw ½ *The Tiger* **1987 (R)** A young man returns to the town where he once lived, before he shot his father. He hopes to sort out his life and repair family problems. Muddled and sappy. **92m/C VHS, Beta, LV.** Patrick Swayze, Barbara Williams, Piper Laurie, Bobby DiCicco, Kaye Ballard, Lee Richardson, Mary McDonnell; ***D:*** Amin Q. Chaudhri. *COL*

Tigers in Lipstick ½ *Wild Beds* **1980 (R)** Seven short vignettes featuring the beautiful actresses as aggressive women and the men that they influence. **88m/C VHS, Beta.** *IT* Laura Antonelli, Monica Vitti, Ursula Andress, Sylvia Kristel; ***D:*** Luigi Zampa. *MON*

A Tiger's Tale ½ **1987 (R)** A middle-aged divorced nurse begins an affair with her daughters's ex-boyfriend. **97m/C VHS, Beta, LV.** Ann-Margret, C. Thomas Howell, Charles Durning, Kelly Preston, Ann Wedgeworth, Tim Thomerson, Steven Kampmann, Traci Lind, Angel Tompkins; ***D:*** Peter Douglas; ***C:*** Tony Pierce-Roberts. *NO*

Tigershark **1987 (R)** A martial arts expert goes to Southeast Asia to rescue his girlfriend, who has been kidnapped by communist forces and held captive for arms and ammunition. Strictly for fans of the martial arts. **97m/C VHS, Beta.** Mike Stone, John Quade, Pamela Bryant; ***D:*** Emmett Alston; ***W:*** Ivan Rogers. *NO*

Tightrope **1984 (R)** Police inspector Wes Block pursues a killer of prostitutes in New Orleans' French Quarter. The film is notable both as a thriller and as a fascinating vehicle for Eastwood, who experiments with a disturbing portrait of a cop with some peculiarities of his own. **115m/C VHS, Beta, LV.** Clint Eastwood, Genevieve Bujold, Dan Hedaya, Jennifer Beck, Alison Eastwood, Randi Brooks, Regina Richardson, Jamie Rose; ***D:*** Richard Tuggle; ***C:*** Bruce Surtees; ***M:*** Lennie Niehaus. *WAR, TLF*

The Tigress ½ **1993 (R)** In 1920s Berlin two con artists set out to scam a rich American using sex as a lure. Things don't go as planned. Also available in an unrated version. **89m/C VHS, LV.** Valentina Vargas, James Remar, George Peppard. *VMK*

Tilai *The Law* **1990** When Saga returns to his African village after a long absence, it's to discover that his young fiancee, Nogma, has been forced into marriage with his own father. According to his tribe's code of honor Saga can do nothing but love won't be denied and they begin an affair, which is deemed incestuous by the village. So Saga and Nogma flee, hoping to live out of the reach of tribal law. **81m/C VHS.** ***D:*** Idrissa Ouedraogo. Cannes Film Festival '90: Grand Jury Prize. *NYF*

Till Death Do Us Part ½ **1972 (PG)** Three married couples spend a weekend at a counseling retreat, unaware that the proprietor is a murderous maniac. **77m/C VHS, Beta.** James Keach, Claude Jutra, Matt Craven; ***D:*** Timothy Brand. *VES*

Till Death Do Us Part **1992 (R)** An ex-cop turns into an evil killer who seduces unsuspecting women and murders them for their insurance money. Contains footage not seen in the TV movie. Based on a true story and the book by Vincent Bugliosi. **93m/C VHS, Beta.** Treat Williams, Arliss Howard, Rebecca Jenkins; ***D:*** Yves Simoneau. *TRI*

Till Marriage Do Us Part ½ *Dio Mio, Come Sono Caduta in Basso; How Long Can You Fall?* **1974 (R)** An innocent couple discovers on their wedding night that they are really brother and sister. Since they can't in good conscience get a divorce or consummate their marriage, they must seek sexual gratification elsewhere. Antonelli is deliciously tantalizing in this silly satire. In Italian with English subtitles. **97m/C VHS, Beta, LV.** *IT* Laura Antonelli, Alberto Lionello, Jean Rochefort, Michele Placido, Karin Schubert; ***D:*** Luigi Comencini. *VES, INJ*

Till Murder Do Us Part 🦴🦴½ *A Woman Scorned: The Betty Broderick Story* **1992 (PG-13)** Based on the true story of Betty Broderick, an obsessively devoted wife and mother whose husband leaves her for another woman. Even after a bitter divorce, Betty refuses to let go. Until she commits murder. Made for television. **95m/C VHS.** Meredith Baxter, Stephen Collins, Michelle Johnson, Kelli Williams, Stephen Root; ***D:*** Dick Lowry. *NHO*

Till the Clouds Roll By 🦴🦴½ **1946** An all-star, high-gloss musical biography of songwriter Jerome Kern, that, in typical Hollywood fashion, bears little resemblance to the composer's life. Filled with wonderful songs from his Broadway hit. ♫Showboat Medley; Till the Clouds Roll By; Howja Like to Spoon with Me?; The Last Time I Saw Paris; They Didn't Believe Me; I Won't Dance; Why Was I Born?; Who?; Sunny. **137m/C VHS, Beta, LV.** Robert Walker, Van Heflin, Judy Garland, Frank Sinatra, Lucille Bremer, Kathryn Grayson, June Allyson, Dinah Shore, Lena Horne, Virginia O'Brien, Tony Martin; ***D:*** Richard Whorf; ***C:*** Harry Stradling. *CNG, NOS, MGM*

Till the Clouds Roll By/A Star Is Born 🦴🦴🦴 **1946** Ostensibly concerns the life and career of songwriter Jerome Kern. Highlighted by stellar performances from a number of musical stars of the day. Maudlin and unconcerned with factual accuracy, the film nonetheless is an exuberant celebration of Kern's talent. **249m/C VHS, Beta.** Judy Garland, Frank Sinatra, Robert Walker, Fredric March, Janet Gaynor, Andy Devine, Lionel Stander, Franklin Pangborn, Van Heflin, Lucille Bremer, Kathryn Grayson, Lena Horne, Tony Martin, Angela Lansbury, Dinah Shore, Virginia O'Brien, Cyd Charisse, Adolphe Menjou; ***D:*** William A. Wellman, Richard Whorf. *DVT*

Till the End of the Night 🦴½ **1994 (R)** D'arcy (Enos) is an ex-con who will do anything to get back his ex-wife Diana Davenport (Lang) and it doesn't matter that she has a new husband, John (Valentine) and two kids. D'arcy manages to kidnap Diana and it's up to John to save his wife. **90m/C VHS.** John Enos, Katherine Kelly Lang, Scott Valentine, David Keith; ***D:*** Larry Brand; ***W:*** Larry Brand. *COL*

Till the End of Time 🦴🦴½ **1946** Three GIs have trouble adjusting to civilian life in their home town after WWII. Fine performances and excellent pacing. Popular title song. Adapted from "They Dream of Home" by Niven Busch. **105m/C VHS, Beta, LV.** Robert Mitchum, Guy Madison, Bill Williams, Dorothy McGuire, William Gargan, Tom Tully; ***D:*** Edward Dmytryk. *TTC*

Till There was You 🦴 **1991 (PG-13)** A struggling musician travels to a faraway tropical isle to solve the mystery of his brother's death. **94m/C VHS.** Mark Harmon, Deborah Unger, Jeroen Krabbe, Shane Briant; ***D:*** John Seale; ***M:*** Graeme Revell. *MCA*

Tillie Wakes Up 🦴🦴½ **1917** Third in the Tillie series, following "Tillie's Punctured Romance" and "Tillie's Tomato Surprise." Tillie (Dressler) decides she needs a little fun in her life so she asks her hen-pecked nieghbor Mr. Pipkin (Hines) to spend the day with her on Coney Island. **48m/B VHS.** Marie Dressler, Johnny Hines, Frank Beamish, Ruby de Remer; ***D:*** Harry Davenport; ***W:*** Frances Marion. *GPV*

Tillie's Punctured Romance 🦴🦴 **1914** The silent comedy which established Chaplin and Dressler as comedians. Chaplin, out of his Tramp character, is the city slicker trying to put one over on farm girl Dressler, who pursues revenge. First feature length comedy film. Followed by "Tillie's Tomato Surprise" and "Tillie Wakes Up," which starred Dressler but not Chaplin. **73m/B VHS, Beta, LV.** Charlie Chaplin, Marie Dressler, Mabel Normand, Mack Swain, Chester Conklin; ***D:*** Mack Sennett. *NOS, CCB, HHT*

Tilt 🦴 **1978 (PG)** Flimsy storyline concerns a young runaway's adventures with an aspiring rock star. Shields' pinball expertise eventually leads her to a match against pinball champ Durning. **111m/C VHS.** Charles Durning, Ken Marshall, Brooke Shields, Geoffrey Lewis; ***D:*** Rudy Durand; ***W:*** Rudy Durand, Donald Cammell. *NO*

Tim 🦴🦴½ **1979** Follows the relationship between a handsome, mentally retarded young man and an attractive older businesswoman. Sappy storyline is redeemed by Gibson's fine debut performance. Based on Colleen McCullough's first novel. **94m/C VHS, Beta.** *AU* Mel Gibson, Piper Laurie, Peter Gwynne, Alwyn Kurts, Pat Evison; ***D:*** Michael Pate. Australian Film Institute '79: Best Actor (Gibson). *MED, OM*

Tim Tyler's Luck **1937** Lost but not forgotten serial in its twelve-chapter entirety. The fearless Tim Tyler uses whatever he can to do battle with the sinister Spider Web gang. **235m/B VHS.** Frankie Thomas Jr., Frances Robinson, Al Shear, Norman Willis, Earl Douglas, Jack Mulhall, Frank Mayo, Pat O'Brien; ***D:*** Ford Beebe, Wyndham Gittens. *NOS, GPV, FCT*

Timber Queen 🦴🦴 **1944** A WWII flier comes home and aids his best friend's widow, who must make a quota of timber or lose her sawmill to gangsters. Old-fashioned. **66m/B VHS.** Richard Arlen, Mary Beth Hughes, June Havoc, Sheldon Leonard, George E. Stone, Dick Purcell; ***D:*** Frank McDonald. *NOS, LOO*

Timber Terrors 🦴 *Morton of the Mounted* **1935** A Mountie investigates his partner's murder. **50m/B VHS, Beta.** *NO*

Time After Time 🦴🦴🦴 **1979 (PG)** In Victorian London, circa 1893, H.G. Wells is experimenting with his time machine. He discovers the machine has been used by an associate, who turns out to be Jack the Ripper, to travel to San Francisco in 1979. Wells follows to stop any further murders and the ensuing battle of wits is both entertaining and imaginative. McDowell is charming as Wells and Steenburgen is equally fine as Well's modern American love interest. **112m/C VHS, Beta, LV.** Malcolm McDowell, David Warner, Mary Steenburgen, Patti D'Arbanville, Charles Cioffi; ***D:*** Nicholas Meyer; ***W:*** Nicholas Meyer; ***M:*** Miklos Rozsa. National Board of Review Awards '79: 10 Best Films of the Year. *WAR*

Time Bandits 🦴🦴½ **1981 (PG)** A group of dwarves help a young boy to travel through time and space with the likes of Robin Hood, Napoleon, Agamemnon, and other time-warp playmates. Epic fantasy from Monty Python alumni. **110m/C VHS, Beta, LV.** *GB* John Cleese, Sean Connery, Shelley Duvall, Katherine Helmond, Ian Holm, Michael Palin, Ralph Richardson, Kenny Baker, Peter Vaughan, David Warner; ***D:*** Terry Gilliam; ***W:*** Michael Palin, Terry Gilliam. *PAR*

Time Burst: The Final Alliance **1989** A man fights for his soul to protect the secret of immortality at any cost. **93m/C VHS, Beta.** *AIP*

Time Chasers 🦴🦴 **1995** Nick Miller (Burch) invents a device that permits his airplane to travel through time. But, after selling his invention, he soon discovers that it has turned the future into a desolate wasteland. Now Nick must try to regain control and put things back to normal. **90m/C VHS.** Matthew Burch, Bonnie Pritchard, Peter Harrington; ***D:*** David Giancola. *SDE*

Time Fighters 🦴½ **1985** A time machine has the ability to travel at the speed of light from prehistoric times to the distant future. This is a great help to the Time fighters. **60m/C VHS, Beta.** *SUE*

Time Flies When You're Alive **1989** A made-for-cable-television presentation of actor Linke's performance monologue detailing the traumas and experiences he and his family underwent as his wife Francesca slowly died of cancer. **79m/C VHS, Beta.** Paul Linke; ***D:*** Roger Spottiswoode. *HBO*

A Time for Miracles 🦴½ **1980** Dramatic biography of the first native-born American saint, Elizabeth Bayley Seton, who was canonized in 1975. Made for television. **97m/C VHS, Beta.** Kate Mulgrew, Lorne Greene, Rossano Brazzi, John Forsythe, Jean-Pierre Aumont, Milo O'Shea; ***D:*** Michael O'Herlihy. *NLC*

Time for Murder **198?** A series of British dramatizations of famous murder mystery stories. Made for television. **60m/C Beta.** *GB PSM*

Time for Revenge 🦴🦴½ **1982** A demolitions worker attempts to blackmail his corrupt employer by claiming a workplace explosion made him speechless. He finds himself in a contest of silence and wits. In Spanish with English subtitles. **112m/C VHS, Beta.** *AR* Federico Luppi, Haydee Padilla, Julio de Grazia, Ulises Dumont; ***D:*** Adolfo Aristarain. Montreal World Film Festival '82: Best Film. *XVC, MED, AUD*

The Time Guardian 🦴½ **1987 (PG)** Time-travelers of the future arrive in the Australian desert in 1988, intent on warning the local populace of the impending arrival of killer cyborgs from the 40th century. Muddled and confusing. **89m/C VHS, Beta, LV, 8mm.** Tom Burlinson, Carrie Fisher, Dean Stockwell, Nikki Coghill; ***D:*** Brian Hannant; ***W:*** Brian Hannant, John Baxter. *COL, SUE, NLC*

Time Indefinite 🦴🦴 **1993** Cinema verite effort once again follows filmmaker McElwee who returns to his Southern roots to confront personal tragedy by recording every moment on film. It is an emotional journey in which he discovers that his camera may not be enough to protect him from his own feelings. Moving, with occasional lapses into self-absorption. Companion film to McElwee's "Sherman's March." **117m/C VHS.** ***D:*** Ross McElwee; ***W:*** Ross McElwee. *ICA*

Time is Running Out 🦴🦴 **1952** A man races against the clock in this taut thriller. **?m/C VHS.** Dave Clark, Mike Smith, Lenny Davidson. *SNC*

Time Lock 🦴🦴 **1957** An expert safecracker races against time to save a child who is trapped inside a bank's pre-set time-locked vault. Canada is the setting, although the film was actually made in England. Based on a play by Arthur Hailey. **73m/B VHS, Beta.** *GB* Sean Connery, Robert Beatty, Lee Patterson, Betty McDowall, Vincent Winter; ***D:*** Gerald Thomas. *NO*

The Time Machine 🦴🦴🦴 **1960** English scientist living near the end of the 19th century invents time travel machine and uses it to travel into various periods of the future. Rollicking version of H.G. Wells' classic cautionary tale boasts Oscar-winning special effects. Remade in 1978. **103m/C VHS, Beta, LV.** Rod Taylor, Yvette Mimieux, Whit Bissell, Sebastian Cabot, Alan Young; ***D:*** George Pal; ***C:*** Paul Vogel. Academy Awards '60: Best Special Effects. *MGM, MLB*

Time Machine 🦴½ **1978 (G)** Yet another adaptation of H.G. Wells' classic novel about a scientist who invents a machine that enables him to travel through time. Inferior remake of the 1960 version. **99m/C VHS, Beta.** John Beck, Priscilla Barnes, Andrew Duggan; ***D:*** Henning Schellerup. *NO*

A Time of Destiny 🦴🦴 **1988 (PG-13)** During WWII, an American soldier vows to kill his brother-in-law, who he believes caused his father's death. Meanwhile, the two men have become good friends in the army, never realizing their connection. A strange, overblown family saga from the director of "El Norte." Beautiful photography, terrific editing. **118m/C VHS, Beta, LV, 8mm.** William Hurt, Timothy Hutton, Melissa Leo, Stockard Channing, Megan Follows, Francesco Rabal; ***D:*** Gregory Nava; ***W:*** Gregory Nava, Anna Thomas; ***M:*** Ennio Morricone. *COL, SUE*

Time of Indifference 🦴🦴 *Gli Indifferenti; Les Deux Rivales* **1964** Based on the novel by Alberto Moravia. Tale of the disintegration of values in 1920s Italy is unable to take full advantage of its fine cast or potentially thought-provoking themes. **84m/B VHS.** *IT* Rod Steiger, Shelley Winters, Claudia Cardinale, Paulette Goddard, Tomas Milian; ***D:*** Francesco Maselli. *GKK*

Time of Tears 🦴½ **1987 (PG)** A young boy, grieving after his grandfather's death, meets a lonely old man and they fill each other's emotional needs. **95m/C VHS, Beta.** *VTR, NWV*

Time of the Apes 🦴 **1987** A Japanese-made horror film about a woman and two kids thrust into an underground world ruled by intelligent gorillas. **98m/C VHS, Beta.** *JP CEL*

Time of the Gypsies 🦴🦴🦴 *Dom Za Vesanje* **1990 (R)** Acclaimed Yugoslavian saga about a homely, unlucky Gypsy boy who sets out to steal his way to a dowry large enough to marry the girl of his dreams. Beautifully filmed, magical, and very long. In the Gypsy language, Romany, it's the first feature film made in the Gypsy tongue. **136m/C VHS, Beta, LV.** *YU* Davor Dujmovic, Sinolicka Trpkova, Ljubica Adzovic, Hunsija Hasimovic, Bora Todorovic; ***D:*** Emir Kusturica. Cannes Film Festival '89: Best Director (Kusturica). *COL, INJ*

The Time of Their Lives 🦴🦴½ *The Ghost Steps Out* **1946** A pair of Revolutionary War-era ghosts haunt a modern country estate. One of the best A & C comedies. **82m/B VHS, Beta.** Bud Abbott, Lou Costello, Marjorie Reynolds, Binnie Barnes, Gale Sondergaard, John Shelton; ***D:*** Charles T. Barton. *MCA*

The Time of Your Life 🦴🦴🦴½ **1948** The only Cagney film that ever lost money. A simple but engaging story of people trying to live their dreams. Cagney is delightful as a barroom philosopher who controls the world around him from his seat in the tavern. Although it was not very popular with audiences at the time, the critics hailed it as an artistic achievement. Based on William Saroyan's play. **109m/B VHS.** James Cagney, William Bendix, Jeanne Cagney, Broderick Crawford, Ward Bond, James Barton, Paul Draper, Natalie Schafer; ***D:*** H.C. Potter. *NOS, VEC, HEG*

Time Out for Love 🦴🦴½ *Les Grandes Personnes; The Five Day Lover* **1961** An American girl travels to Paris in search of romance, but discovers more than she bargained for. In French with English subtitles. **91m/B VHS.** *IT FR* Jean Seberg, Micheline Presle, Maurice Ronet, Francoise Prevost, Annabelle Ninchi, Fernando Bruno; ***D:*** Jean Valere; ***M:*** Georges Delerue. *DVT, HEG*

Time Runner 🦴🦴 **1992 (R)** It's 2022 and the Earth is being used as target practice by alien invaders. Space captain Hamill manages to find a hole in time and slip back to 1992 where he can battle the first of the alien infiltrators and maybe change Earth's destiny. The time-travel theme (including Hamill watching his own birth) is fun and the special effects are well done. **90m/C VHS, LV.** Mark Hamill, Brion James, Rae Dawn Chong; ***D:*** Michael Mazo. *NLC, COL*

Time Stands Still 🦴🦴🦴 **1982** Two brothers experience troubled youth in Budapest. Artful, somberly executed, with American pop soundtrack. Subtitled in English. **99m/C VHS, Beta.** *HU* Istvan Znamenak, Henrik Pauer, Aniko Ivan, Sander Soth, Peter Galfy; ***D:*** Peter Gothar. New York Film Critics Awards '82: Best Foreign Film. *COL*

Time to Die 🦴½ *Seven Graves for Rogan* **1983 (R)** WWII victim of heinous war crimes, obsessed with revenge, stalks his prey for a final confrontation, while eluding U.S. intelligence. Disappointing despite good cast working with Mario Puzo story. **89m/C VHS, Beta.** Edward Albert, Rex Harrison, Rod Taylor, Raf Vallone; ***D:*** Matt Cimber; ***M:*** Ennio Morricone. *MED*

A Time to Die 🦴½ **1991 (R)** Lords plays a police photographer who, well, photographs the police. But her camera catches one in the act of murder. Routine crime thriller. **93m/C VHS, LV.** Traci Lords, Jeff Conaway, Richard Roundtree, Bradford Bancroft, Nitchie Barrett; ***D:*** Charles Kanganis; ***W:*** Charles Kanganis; ***M:*** Ennio Morricone. *PMH*

Time to Kill *Tempo di Uccidere* **1989 (R)** A young soldier in Africa wanders away from his camp and meets a woman whom he rapes and kills. But when he returns to his outfit he finds he can't escape his tormenting conscience. **110m/C VHS, LV.** Nicolas Cage, Giancarlo Giannini, Robert Liensol; ***D:*** Guiliano Montaldo; ***W:*** Furio Scarpelli; ***M:*** Ennio Morricone. *REP*

A Time to Kill 🦴🦴🦴 **1996 (R)** John Grisham had a lot of clout when he finally sold his first and favorite novel to the movies, including veto power over the leading man—director Schumacher was for Woody Harrelson, Grisham was opposed but both finally agreed on newcomer McConaughey. He's idealistic southern lawyer Jake Brigance, called to defend Mississippi factory worker Carl Lee Hailey (Jackson), who's accused of killing the rednecks who raped his young daughter. Jake's assisted by former mentor Lucien Wilbanks (Sutherland) and ambitious law student Ellen Roark (Bullock) but ruthless prosecutor Rufus Buckley (Spacey) won't make things easy. Grisham's done well on screen and with McConaughey rising to the challenge and Schumacher (who also did "The Client") at the helm, this is one tension-filled trip. **?m/C VHS.** Matthew McConaughey, Samuel L. Jackson, Sandra Bullock, Kevin Spacey, Donald Sutherland, Brenda Fricker, Oliver Platt, Charles S. Dutton, Ashley Judd, Patrick McGoohan; ***D:*** Joel Schumacher; ***W:*** Akiva Goldsman; ***C:*** Peter Menzies Jr.; ***M:*** Elliot Goldenthal. *NYR*

A Time to Live 🦴½ **1985** Made-for-television adaptation of Mary Lou Weisman's "Intensive Care" about a family's adjustment to a young boy's fight with Muscular Dystrophy. Minnelli's first appearance in a television movie. **97m/C Beta.** Liza Minnelli, Jeffrey DeMunn, Swoosie Kurtz, Corey Haim, Scott Schwartz; ***D:*** Rick Wallace; ***M:*** Georges Delerue. *NO*

A Time to Live and a Time to Die 🦴🦴 *Tong Nien Wang Shi* **1985** Family from southern mainland China emigrate to Taiwan in the '40s to escape from hardship and are unable to return after the communist takeover. They find themselves cut off from their cultural heritage, and though the years pass, everyone still thinks of the mainland as home. Taiwanese with subtitles. **137m/C VHS.** *CH* ***D:*** Hou Hsaio-hsien. *FCT*

A Time to Love & a Time to Die 🦴🦴½ **1958** Lush adaptation of Erich Maria Remarque novel about WWII German soldier who falls in love with a young girl during furlough. The two are married, only to be separated when he is forced to return to the Russian front. Sympathetic treatment of Germans opposed to Hitler's policies. Hutton's first film, credited to his real name, Dana J. Hutton. **133m/C VHS, Beta.** John Gavin, Lilo (Liselotte) Pulver, Jock Mahoney, Keenan Wynn, Klaus Kinski, Jim Hutton; ***D:*** Douglas Sirk; ***M:*** Miklos Rozsa. Nominations: Academy Awards '58: Best Sound. *BAR*

A Time to Remember 🦴½ **1990** Sticky with sentiment, this family film tells of a boy with a gift for singing, encouraged by a priest, discouraged by his father. At one point the kid loses his voice—he probably choked on the pathos. **90m/C VHS.** Donald O'Connor, Morgana King. *IGP*

Time Trackers 🦴🦴 **1988 (PG)** A Roger Corman cheapie about a race through time, from present-day New York to medieval England, to recover a time machine before it alters the course of history. **87m/C VHS, Beta.** Kathleen Beller, Ned Beatty, Will Shriner; ***D:*** Howard R. Cohen. *MGM*

The Time Travelers 🦴🦴 *Time Trap* **1964** Scientists discover and pass through a porthole leading to earth's post-armageddon future where they encounter unfriendly mutants. Frightened, they make a serious effort to return to the past. Remade as "Journey to the Center of Time." **82m/C VHS, Beta.** Preston Foster, Phil Carey, Merry Anders, John Hoyt, Joan Woodbury, Dolores Wells, Dennis Patrick; ***D:*** Ib Melchior. *NO*

Time Troopers 🦴 *Morgen Grauen; Morning Terror* **1989 (R)** In another post-nuke society, special police must execute anyone who has misused their allotted "energy clips" for illicit behavior. Dime-store budget sci-fi. **90m/C VHS, Beta.** *AT* Albert Fortell, Hannelore Elsner; ***D:*** L.E. Neiman. *PSM*

Time Walker 🦴 **1982 (PG)** An archaeologist unearths King Tut's coffin in California. An alien living inside is unleashed and terrorizes the public. **86m/C VHS, Beta.** Ben Murphy; ***D:*** Tom Kennedy; ***M:*** Richard Band. *NLC*

Time Without Pity 🦴🦴½ **1957** Anti-capital punishment plea finds desperate alcoholic David Graham (Redgrave) discovering that his son Alec (McCowen) is about to be executed for murder. But David doesn't believe in the boy's guilt and has 24 hours to find the real killer. The audience knows Alec is innocent from the get-go, making for a certain suspense. Based on the play "Someone Waiting" by Emlyn Williams. **88m/B VHS.** *GB* Michael Redgrave, Alec McCowen, Ann Todd, Leo McKern, Peter Cushing, Renee Houston, Paul Daneman, Lois Maxwell, Richard Wordsworth, George Devine, Joan Plowright; ***D:*** Joseph Losey; ***W:*** Ben Barzman; ***C:*** Freddie Francis; ***M:*** Tristram Cary. *HMV, TVC*

Timebomb 🦴🦴½ **1991 (R)** When someone attempts to kill Biehn, he turns to a beautiful psychiatrist for help. She triggers flashbacks that send her hunted patient on a dangerous, perhaps deadly, journey into his past. **96m/C VHS, Beta, LV.** Michael Biehn, Patsy Kensit, Tracy Scoggins, Robert Culp, Richard Jordan, Raymond St. Jacques, Jim Maniaci, Billy Blanks, Ray "Boom Boom" Mancini, Steven J. Oliver; ***D:*** Avi Nesher; ***W:*** Avi Nesher; ***M:*** Patrick Leonard. *MGM*

Timecop 🦴🦴½ **1994 (R)** "Terminator" rip-off is fodder for Van Damme followers with lots of action and special effects (you weren't expecting acting too). 2004 policeman Max Walker (Van Damme) must travel back in time to prevent corrupt politician Aaron McComb (Silver) from altering history for personal gain. It's also Walker's chance to alter his personal history since his wife Melissa (Sara) was killed in an explosion he can now prevent. Futuristic thriller based on a Dark Horse comic. **98m/C VHS, LV.** Jean-Claude Van Damme, Ron Silver, Mia Sara, Bruce McGill, Scott Lawrence, Kenneth Welsh, Gabrielle Rose, Duncan Fraser, Ian Tracey, Gloria Reuben, Scott Bellis, Jason Schombing, Kevin McNulty, Sean O'Byrne, Malcolm Stewart, Alfonso Quijada, Glen Roald, Theodore Thomas; ***D:*** Peter Hyams; ***W:*** Mark Verheiden, Gary De Vore. *MCA*

Timemaster 🦴🦴½ **1995 (PG-13)** The orphaned 12-year-old Jesse (Cameron-Glickenhaus) dreams his parents are alive in another time, so he asks inventor Isaiah (Morita) for help. The duo discover Jesse's parents are being held hostage by a galactic dictator (Dorn), who's using them in sinister virtual-reality games and Jesse must time-travel to rescue them. **100m/C VHS, LV.** Jesse Cameron-Glickenhaus, Noriyuki "Pat" Morita, Joanna Pacula, Michael Dorn, Duncan Regehr, Michelle Williams; ***D:*** James Glickenhaus; ***W:*** James Glickenhaus. *MCA*

Timepiece 🦴🦴 **1965** This tape features one of Jim Henson's earlier films about an overworked, young executive. **10m/C VHS, Beta.** Jim Henson. *FLL*

Timerider 🦴½ *The Adventure of Lyle Swan* **1983 (PG)** Motorcyclist riding through the California desert is accidentally thrown back in time to 1877, the result of a scientific experiment that went awry. There he finds no gas stations and lots of cowboys. Co-written and co-produced by Michael Nesmith, best known for his days with the rock group "The Monkees." **93m/C VHS, Beta, LV.** Fred Ward, Belinda Bauer, Peter Coyote, Richard Masur, Ed Lauter, L.Q. Jones, Tracey Walter; ***D:*** William Dear; ***W:*** William Dear. *NO*

Times of Harvey Milk **1983** A powerful and moving documentary about the life and career of San Francisco supervisor and gay activist Harvey Milk. The film documents the assassination of Milk and Mayor George Moscone by Milk's fellow supervisor, Dan White. Highly acclaimed by both critics and audiences, the film gives an honest and direct look at the murder and people's reactions. News footage of the murders and White's trial is included. **90m/C VHS, Beta, LV.** ***D:*** Robert Epstein. Academy Awards '83: Best Feature Documentary. *TPV*

Times Square **1980 (R)** A 13-year-old girl learns about life on her own when she teams up with a defiant, anti-social child of the streets. Unappealing and unrealistic, the film features a New Wave music score. **111m/C VHS, Beta.** Tim Curry, Trini Alvarado, Robin Johnson, Peter Coffield, Elizabeth Pena, Anna Maria Horsford; ***D:*** Allan Moyle; ***W:*** Jacob Brackman. *NO*

Times to Come 🦴🦴🦴 *Lo Que Vendra* **1981** Taut thriller reminiscent of bleak futuristic movies like "Clockwork Orange." Three people try to survive in a desolate, aggressive, and unstable future. In Spanish with English subtitles. **98m/C VHS.** *AR* Hugo Soto, Juan Leyrado, Charly Garcia; ***D:*** Gustavo Mosquera. *CCN, FCT, INJ*

Timestalkers 🦴🦴½ **1987** A college professor's infatuation with a young woman is complicated by their pursuit of a criminal from the 26th century into the past. Mildly entertaining adventure. Tucker's last film. Made for television. **100m/C VHS.** William Devane, Lauren Hutton, Klaus Kinski, John Ratzenberger, Forrest Tucker, Gail Youngs; ***D:*** Michael A. Schultz. *FRH*

Timothy and the Angel 🦴½ **1979** A young man with a deep desire to be a ranger must pass up the rival temptations of a baseball scholarship and a life of speed and drugs offered by a motorcyclist. **29m/C VHS, Beta.** *LCA*

Tin Cup **1996 (R)** You've got your romantic triangle, you got your sports, you've got Costner reteamed with Shelton—"Bull Durham" on a golf course? Can lightening strike twice? Ron "Tin Cup" McAvoy (Costner) is a West Texas golf hustler who had the ability but not the steadiness to be on the pro tour. When McAvoy decides on a last-ditch effort to qualify for the U.S. Open, he turns to psychologist Dr. Molly Griswold (Russo) to get his game together. And the fact that Molly is the girlfriend of McAvoy's longtime rival—and successful PGA player—Don Simms (Johnson), well Tin Cup isn't adverse to playing for the lady's affections either. The U.S. Open scenes were filmed at Houston's Kingwood Country Club and the actors do hit their own shots. **?m/C VHS.** Kevin Costner, Don Johnson, Rene Russo, Richard "Cheech" Marin, Linda Hart; ***D:*** Ron Shelton; ***W:*** Ron Shelton. *NYR*

The Tin Drum *Die Blechtrommel* **1979 (R)** German child in the 1920s wills himself to stop growing in response to the increasing Nazi presence in Germany. He communicates his anger and fear by pounding on a tin drum. Memorable scenes, excellent cast. In German with English subtitles. Adapted from the novel by Gunter Grass. **141m/C VHS, Beta.** *GE* David Bennent, Mario Adorf, Angela Winkler, Daniel Olbrychski, Katharina Thalbach, Heinz Bennent, Andrea Ferreol, Charles Aznavour; ***D:*** Rainer Werner Fassbinder, Volker Schlondorff; ***W:*** Jean-Claude Carriere, Volker Schlondorff; ***M:*** Maurice Jarre. Academy Awards '79: Best Foreign Language Film; Cannes Film Festival '79: Best Film; Los Angeles Film Critics Association Awards '80: Best Foreign Film; National Board of Review Awards '80: 5 Best Foreign Films of the Year. *WAR, APD, GLV*

Tin Man ½ **1983** Garage mechanic born totally deaf designs and builds a computer that can both hear and speak for him. His world is complicated, however, when a young speech therapist introduces him to new and wonderful sounds and unscrupulous and exploitative computer salesmen. Interesting premise and nice performances. **95m/C VHS, Beta.** Timothy Bottoms, Deana Jurgens, Troy Donahue; ***D:*** John G. Thomas. *MED*

Tin Men ½ **1987 (R)** Set in Baltimore in the 1960s, this bitter comedy begins with two aluminum-siding salesmen colliding in a minor car accident. They play increasingly savage pranks on each other until one seduces the wife of the other, ruining his marriage. Like "Diner," the movie is full of Levinson's idiosyncratic local Baltimore color. **112m/C VHS, Beta, LV.** Richard Dreyfuss, Danny DeVito, Barbara Hershey, John Mahoney, Jackie Gayle, Stan Brock, Seymour Cassel, Bruno Kirby, J.T. Walsh, Michael Tucker; ***D:*** Barry Levinson; ***W:*** Barry Levinson; ***C:*** Peter Sova; ***M:*** David Steele. *TOU*

Tin Pan Alley ½ **1940** Tin Pan Alley songwriters Oakie and Payne meet singing sisters Faye and Grable, who agree to plug their material. At first their music business thrives but when the women head off to sing in a hit London show, the business goes downhill. Since WWI has been declared, the boys enlist and wind up in England, where they get a second chance to see their gals. The first teaming of Faye and Payne, who would star together in three more films. Remade as "I'll Get By." ♫The Sheik of Araby; You Say the Sweetest Things, Baby; America I Love You; Goodbye Broadway, Hello France; K-K-K-Katy; Moonlight Bay; Honeysuckle Rose; Moonlight and Roses. **92m/B VHS.** Alice Faye, John Payne, Betty Grable, Jack Oakie, Allen Jenkins, Esther Ralston, John Loder, Elisha Cook Jr., Fred Keating, Billy Gilbert; ***D:*** Walter Lang; ***W:*** Robert Ellis, Helen Logan; ***C:*** Leon Shamroy; ***M:*** Alfred Newman. Academy Awards '40: Best Original Score. *FXV*

The Tin Soldier ½ **1995 (PG)** Updated version of the Hans Christian Andersen story finds 12-year-old Billy (Knight) moving with his widowed mom (Sheedy) to a tough L.A. neighborhood. He's intimidated by the school bully to join a gang and smitten by a pretty girl who doesn't like his new friends. What's a guy to do? Why meet a mysterious toy shop owner (DeLuise), who gives Billy a tin soldier that magically transforms into a very real medieval knight named Yarik (Voight). Good intentions—no subtlety. Voight's directorial debut; made for cable TV. **99m/C VHS.** Trenton Knight, Ally Sheedy, Dom DeLuise, Jon Voight; ***D:*** Jon Voight. *REP*

The Tin Star **1957** Perkins is the young sheriff who persuades veteran bounty hunter Fonda to help him rid the town of outlaws. Excellent Mann western balances humor and suspense. **93m/B VHS, Beta.** Henry Fonda, Anthony Perkins, Betsy Palmer, Neville Brand, Lee Van Cleef, John McIntire, Michel Ray; ***D:*** Anthony Mann; ***C:*** Loyal Griggs; ***M:*** Elmer Bernstein. Nominations: Academy Awards '57: Best Story & Screenplay. *PAR, BAR*

Tintorera...Tiger Shark *Woof! Tintorera; Tintorera...Bloody Waters* **1978 (R)** Three shark hunters attempt to discover why buxom swimmers are disappearing. Phony takeoff of "Jaws." **91m/C VHS, Beta.** *GB MX* Susan George, Fiona Lewis, Jennifer Ashley; ***D:*** Rene Cardona Jr. *MED*

Tiny Toon Adventures: How I Spent My Vacation **1991** How the tiny toons of Acme Acres spend their summer vacation in this animated adventure that spoofs several popular films and amusements. Plucky Duck and Hampton Pig journey to "Happy World Land" (a takeoff on Walt Disney World), Babs and Buster Bunny's water adventure parodies "Deliverance," there's a spoof of "The Little Mermaid," and the Road Runner even makes a cameo appearance. Parents will be equally entertained by the level of humor and the fast-paced action. Based on the Steven Spielberg TV cartoon series, this is the first made-for-home-video animated feature ever released in the United States. **80m/C VHS, Beta, LV, 8mm.** *WAR*

The Tioga Kid ½ **1948** Dean takes on two roles here, that of a Texas Ranger and an outlaw who goes by the name of "The Tioga Kid." Andy Parker and the Plainsmen provide the cowboy tunes. **54m/B VHS.** Eddie Dean, Roscoe Ates, Jennifer Holt, Dennis Moore, William "Bill" Fawcett; ***D:*** Ray Taylor; ***W:*** Ed Earl Repp. *MOV*

The Tip-Off ½ **1931** Lovable boxer (Armstrong) and vivacious girlfriend (Rogers) save less-than-bright friend from getting involved with mean mobster's girlfriend. Major chemistry between Rogers and Armstrong. **75m/B VHS.** Eddie Quillan, Robert Armstrong, Ginger Rogers, Joan Peers, Ernie Adams; ***D:*** Albert Rogell. *TTC, FCT*

'Tis a Pity She's a Whore ½ *Addio, Fratello, Crudele* **1973 (R)** A brother and sister engage in an incestuous affair. She becomes pregnant and is married off. Her husband, however, becomes infuriated when he learns of his wife's pregnancy. Photography is by Vittorio Storaro in this highly stylized drama set in Renaissance Italy. **102m/C VHS, Beta.** *IT* Charlotte Rampling, Oliver Tobias, Fabio Testi, Antonio Falsi, Rick Battaglia, Angela Luce, Rino Imperio; ***D:*** Giuseppe Patroni Griffi; ***M:*** Ennio Morricone. *ACA*

Titanic **1953** Hollywoodized version of the 1912 sinking of the famous luxury liner sets the scene for the personal drama of a mother (Stanwyck) who wants to flee her husband (Webb) for a new life in America. Story gets a little too melodramatic, but it's not a bad retelling of the sea tragedy. Film is quite effective in conveying the panic and the calm of the actual sinking. A 20-foot-long model of the ship was built for the re-creation of that fateful moment when the "Titanic" hit the inevitable iceberg. **98m/B VHS.** Clifton Webb, Barbara Stanwyck, Robert Wagner, Richard Basehart, Audrey Dalton, Thelma Ritter, Brian Aherne; ***D:*** Jean Negulesco; ***W:*** Charles Brackett, Walter Reisch, Richard L. Breen. Academy Awards '53: Best Screenplay, Best Story; Nominations: Academy Awards '53: Best Screenplay, Best Story. *FXV*

Title Shot **1981 (R)** A crafty manager convinces a millionaire to bet heavily on the guaranteed loss of his heavyweight contender in an upcoming fight. He doesn't realize the boxer is too stupid to throw the fight. **88m/C VHS, Beta.** Tony Curtis, Richard Gabourie, Susan Hogan, Robert Delbert; ***D:*** Les Rose. *LIV*

Tito and Me **1992** Ten-year-old Zoran lives in 1954 Belgrade and is fascinated by Yugoslavian leader Marshall Tito. Crowded into a flat with his extended family, Zoran learns about volatility first-hand. Then there's romance—he has a crush on a classmate who breaks up with him when she is chosen as one of Tito's Young Pioneers, which means a two-week trip to the country. Political indoctrination means nothing but love—ahh. Debut role for the young Vojnov, who carries the weight of the movie with perfect aplomb. In Serbo-Croation with English subtitles. **104m/C VHS.** *YU* Dimitrie Vojnov, Lazar Ristovski, Anica Dobra, Predrag Manojlovic, Olivera Markovic; ***D:*** Goran Markovic; ***W:*** Goran Markovic. *FXL, FCT*

TNT Jackson *Woof!* **1975 (R)** A kung fu mama searches for her brother while everyone in Hong Kong tries to kick her out of town. **73m/C VHS, Beta.** Jeanne Bell; ***D:*** Cirio H. Santiago. *NLC*

To All a Goodnight *Woof!* **1980 (R)** Five young girls and their boyfriends are planning an exciting Christmas holiday until a mad Santa Claus puts a damper on things. Total gorefest, with few, if any, redeeming virtues. **90m/C VHS, Beta.** Jennifer Runyon, Forrest Swanson, Linda Gentile, William Lover; ***D:*** David Hess. *MED*

To All My Friends on Shore **1971** A made-for-television story about a father dealing with his young son's sickle cell anemia. Fine performances, realistic script make this an excellent outing. **74m/C VHS, Beta.** Bill Cosby, Gloria Foster, Dennis Hines; ***D:*** Gilbert Cates. *NO*

To Be or Not to Be ½ **1942** Sophisticated black comedy set in wartime Poland. Lombard and Benny are Maria and Josef Tura, the Barrymores of the Polish stage, who use the talents of their acting troupe against the invading Nazis. The opening sequence is regarded as a cinema classic. One of Benny's finest film performances, the movie marks Lombard's final screen appearance. Classic Lubitsch. Remade in 1983. **102m/B VHS, Beta.** Carole Lombard, Jack Benny, Robert Stack, Sig Rumann, Lionel Atwill, Felix Bressart, Helmut Dantine, Tom Dugan, Charles Halton; ***D:*** Ernst Lubitsch. Nominations: Academy Awards '42: Best Original Score. *VES, WAR*

To Be or Not to Be ½ **1983 (PG)** In this remake of the 1942 film, Bancroft and Brooks are actors in Poland during WWII. They accidently become involved with the Polish Resistance and work to thwart the Nazis. Lots of laughs, although at times there's a little too much slapstick. **108m/C VHS, Beta, LV.** Mel Brooks, Anne Bancroft, Charles Durning, Jose Ferrer, Tim Matheson, Christopher Lloyd; ***D:*** Alan Johnson; ***W:*** Ronny Graham. Nominations: Academy Awards '83: Best Supporting Actor (Durning). *FOX*

To Be the Best ½ **1993 (R)** Eric, a member of the U.S. Kickboxing Team, lets his love for the beautiful Cheryl and his hot temper get the best of him. When a ruthless gambler threatens to kill Cheryl if Eric doesn't throw his big match, he joins with his family, fellow teammates, and most feared opponent, to set things right. **99m/C VHS.** Mike Worth, Martin Kove, Phillip Troy, Brittney Powell, Alex Cord, Steven Leigh; ***D:*** Joseph Merhi; ***W:*** Michael January. *PMH*

To Catch a Killer **1992** A chilling performance by Dennehy highlights this true-crime tale of a detective's relentless pursuit of serial killer John Wayne Gacy, who preyed on young men and hid the bodies in his home. Made for television. **95m/C VHS, LV.** Brian Dennehy, Michael Riley, Margot Kidder, Meg Foster; ***D:*** Eric Till. *WOV*

To Catch a King **1984** Garr is a singer working in Wagner's nightclub in 1940s' Lisbon. The pair becomes involved in trying to foil the Nazi plot to kidnap the vacationing Duke and Duchess of Windsor. Average made-for-cable fare. **120m/C VHS, Beta.** Robert Wagner, Teri Garr, Horst Janson, Barbara Parkins, John Standing; ***D:*** Clive Donner; ***M:*** Nick Bicat. *PSM*

To Catch a Thief **1955** On the French Riviera, a reformed jewel thief falls for a wealthy American woman, who suspects he's up to his old tricks when a rash of jewel thefts occur. Oscar-winning photography by Robert Burks, a notable fireworks scene, and snappy dialogue. A change of pace for Hitchcock, this charming comedy-thriller proved to be as popular as his other efforts. Kelly met future husband Prince Rainier during shooting in Monaco. Based on the novel by David Dodge. **103m/C VHS, Beta, LV.** Cary Grant, Grace Kelly, Jessie Royce Landis, John Williams, Charles Vanel, Brigitte Auber; ***D:*** Alfred Hitchcock; ***W:*** John Michael Hayes; ***C:*** Robert Burks. Academy Awards '55: Best Color Cinematography; Nominations: Academy Awards '55: Best Art Direction/Set Decoration (Color), Best Costume Design (Color). *PAR, MLB, HMV*

To Cross the Rubicon ☠☠½ **1995** Romantic comedy finds Kendall (Royce) getting dumped by David (Souther), her boyfriend of eight years, who then reconciles with former flame, Claire (Devon). Meanwhile, Kendall involves herself with James (Burke), a young musician, and becomes new best friends with—you guessed it—Claire. But will David and Kendall's previous relationship cause friction? **120m/C VHS.** Patricia Royce, J.D. Souther, Lorraine Devon, Billy Burke; ***D:*** Barry Caillier. *MTH*

To Dance with the White Dog ☠☠☠ **1993 (PG)** Robert Samuel Peek (Cronyn) is a pecan-tree grower from rural Georgia who has been married to Cora (Tandy) for 57 years. Then she dies and their fussing daughters (Baranski and Wright) wonder how their father will survive. But Sam's increasing loneliness is checked when he befriends a stray white dog that it seems no one else can see. Based on the novel by Terry Kay. Made for television. **98m/C VHS.** Hume Cronyn, Jessica Tandy, Christine Baranski, Amy Wright, Esther Rolle, Harley Cross, Frank Whaley, Terry Beaver, Dan Albright, David Dwyer; ***D:*** Glenn Jordan; ***W:*** Susan Cooper; ***C:*** Neil Roach. *REP, PAP*

To Die for ☠½ **1989 (R)** A vampire stalks, woos, and snacks on a young real estate woman. **99m/C VHS, Beta, LV.** Brendan Hughes, Scott Jacoby, Duane Jones, Steve Bond, Sydney Walsh, Amanda Wyss, Ava Fabian; ***D:*** Deran Sarafian; ***M:*** Cliff Eidelman. *ACA*

To Die For ☠☠☠ **1995 (R)** Beauteous, manipulative Suzanne Stone (Kidman) wants to be somebody—preferably a big TV personality—and nothing will stop her. She recruits a scruffy threesome to help her ice sweet-but-dim hubby, Larry (Dillon), even if it does means seducing aimless teenager Jimmy (Phoenix). Black comedy, loosely based on the Pamela Smart murder case and adapted from the novel by Joyce Maynard, takes on the media-obsessed culture with a wicked grin. Van Sant retains his fresh and hip storytelling in his first film for a major studio. Backed by Henry's zesty script, all the actors shine—with standout performances from Kidman as the monstrous Suzanne and Phoenix (River's younger brother) as the lost/horny Jimmy. Shot entirely in Canada. **103m/C VHS, LV, 8mm.** Nicole Kidman, Matt Dillon, Joaquin Rafael (Leaf) Phoenix, Casey Affleck, Alison Folland, Illeana Douglas, Dan Hedaya, Wayne Knight, Kurtwood Smith, Holland Taylor, Maria Tucci, Susan Traylor; ***Cameos:*** George Segal, Buck Henry; ***D:*** Gus Van Sant; ***W:*** Buck Henry, Johnny Burne; ***C:*** Eric Alan Edwards; ***M:*** Danny Elfman. Golden Globe Awards '96: Best Actress—Musical/Comedy (Kidman); Nominations: British Academy Awards '95: Best Actress (Kidman); MTV Movie Awards '96: Most Desirable Female (Kidman). *COL*

To Die for 2: Son of Darkness ☠½ **1991 (R)** This far outclasses part one in terms of acting and production values, but the plot still isn't back from the grave. Strange, because all the vampires are; despite their fiery deaths last time they flock around the adoptive mother of a baby secretly sired by a bloodsucker. **95m/C VHS.** Rosalind Allen, Steve Bond, Scott Jacoby, Michael Praed, Jay Underwood, Amanda Wyss, Remy O'Neill; ***D:*** David F. Price. *VMK*

To Die Standing ☠½ **1991 (R)** Two mavericks team up to do what the D.E.A. and cops simply cannot... capture a dangerous international drug lord. High action. **87m/C VHS, LV.** Cliff DeYoung, Robert Beltran, Jamie Rose, Gerald Anthony, Orlando Sacha, Michael Ford; ***D:*** Louis Morneau; ***W:*** Ross Bell, Daryl Haney. *COL*

To Forget Venice ☠☠½ **1979** Portrays the sensitive relationships among four homosexuals, and their shared fears of growing older. Dubbed in English. **90m/C VHS, Beta.** *IT* Erland Josephson, Mariangela Melato, David Pontremoli, Elenora Giorgi; ***D:*** Franco Brusati. Nominations: Academy Awards '79: Best Foreign Language Film. *COL*

To Grandmother's House We Go ☠☠½ **1994** The Olsen twins want to give mom a restful Christmas vacation so they decide to visit Grandma (on their own) and wind up in the hands of a pair of bumbling kidnappers. Made for TV movie. **89m/C VHS.** Ashley Olsen, Mary-Kate Olsen, Cynthia Geary, Rhea Perlman, J. Eddie Peck, Stuart Margolin; ***Cameos:*** Bob Saget, Lori Loughlin; ***D:*** Jeff Franklin; ***W:*** Jeff Franklin. *WAR*

To Have & Have Not ☠☠☠½ **1944** Martinique charter boat operator gets mixed up with beautiful woman and French resistance fighters during WWII. Top-notch production in every respect. Classic dialogue and fiery romantic bouts between Bogart and Bacall. Bacall's first film. Based on a story by Ernest Hemingway. Remade in 1950 as "The Breaking Point" and in 1958 as "The Gun Runners." **100m/B VHS, Beta, LV.** Humphrey Bogart, Lauren Bacall, Walter Brennan, Hoagy Carmichael, Marcel Dalio, Dolores Moran, Sheldon Leonard, Dan Seymour; ***D:*** Howard Hawks. *MGM*

To Heal a Nation ☠☠½ **1988** The story of veteran Jan Scruggs, who spearheaded the movement to build the Vietnam Veterans memorial. The then little-known Ross Perot provided major financial support for Scruggs' dream. Made for television. **100m/C VHS.** Eric Roberts, Conrad Bachmann, Glynnis O'Connor, Marshall Colt, Scott Paulin, Lee Purcell, Laurence Luckinbill, Linden Chiles, Brock Peters; ***D:*** Michael Pressman; ***W:*** Lionel Chetwynd. *TTC*

To Hell and Back ☠☠½ **1955** Adaptation of Audie Murphy's autobiography. Murphy plays himself, from his upbringing to WWII, where he was the most-decorated American soldier. Features realistic battle sequences punctuated with grand heroics. **106m/C VHS, Beta.** Audie Murphy, Marshall Thompson, Jack Kelly; ***D:*** Jesse Hibbs. *MCA, TLF*

To Joy ☠☠☠ **1950** The rocky marriage of a violinist and his wife illuminate the problems of the young in Swedish society. Early Bergman. In Swedish with English subtitles or dubbed. **90m/B VHS, Beta, LV.** *SW* ***D:*** Ingmar Bergman. *SUE, INJ*

To Kill a Clown ☠☠ **1972 (R)** Painter and his wife working to save their marriage are trapped on an isolated island and terrorized by a crazed Vietnam veteran. This helps pull them together. Some holes in the plot, but generally effective. **82m/C VHS, Beta.** Alan Alda, Blythe Danner, Heath Lamberts; ***D:*** George Bloomfield. *MED*

To Kill a Mockingbird ☠☠☠☠ **1962** Faithful adaptation of powerful Harper Lee novel, both an evocative portrayal of childhood innocence and a denunciation of bigotry. Peck's performance as southern lawyer defending a black man accused of raping a white woman is flawless. Duvall debuted as the dim-witted Boo Radley. Lee based her characterization of "Dill" on Truman Capote, a childhood friend. **129m/B VHS, Beta, LV.** Gregory Peck, Brock Peters, Phillip Alford, Mary Badham, Robert Duvall, Rosemary Murphy, William Windom, Alice Ghostley, John Megna, Frank Overton, Paul Fix, Collin Wilcox; ***D:*** Robert Mulligan; ***W:*** Horton Foote; ***M:*** Elmer Bernstein. Academy Awards '62: Best Actor (Peck), Best Adapted Screenplay, Best Art Direction/Set Decoration (B & W); Golden Globe Awards '63: Best Actor—Drama (Peck), Best Score; Nominations: Academy Awards '62: Best Black and White Cinematography, Best Director (Mulligan), Best Picture, Best Supporting Actress (Badham), Best Original Score. *KUI, MCA, BTV*

To Kill a Priest ☠☠ **1989 (R)** Based on the true story of Father Jerzy Popieluszko, a young priest in 1984 Poland who defies his church and speaks out publicly on Solidarity. He is killed by the government as a result. Harris is good as the menacing police official. **110m/C VHS, Beta, LV.** Christopher Lambert, Ed Harris, David Suchet, Tim Roth, Joanne Whalley, Pete Postlethwaite, Cherie Lunghi, Joss Ackland; ***D:*** Agnieszka Holland; ***W:*** Agnieszka Holland; ***C:*** Adam Holender; ***M:*** Georges Delerue. *COL*

To Kill a Stranger ☠☠ **1984** A beautiful pop singer is stranded in a storm, and then victimized by a mad rapist/murderer. **100m/C VHS, Beta.** Donald Pleasence, Dean Stockwell, Angelica Maria, Aldo Ray, Sergio Aragones. *NO*

To Live ☠☠☠☠ *Huozhe* **1994** Superb drama follows the lives of one family—weak but adaptable Fugui (You), his strong-willed wife Jiazhen (Li), and their young daughter and son—from prerevolutionary China in the 1940s through the '60s Cultural Revolution. Fugui loses the family fortune in the gambling houses, actually a blessing when the Communists come to power, and the family must struggle to survive financial and increasingly difficult political changes, where fate can change on a whim. Subtle saga about ordinary human lives reacting to terrifying conditions boasts extraordinary performances and evocative imagery. Adapted from the novel "Lifetimes" by Yu Hua. Chinese with subtitles. **130m/C VHS, LV.** *CH* Ge You, Gong Li, Niu Ben, Guo Tao, Jiang Wu; ***D:*** Zhang Yimou; ***W:*** Lu Wei, Yu Hua; ***M:*** Zhao Jiping. British Academy Awards '94: Best Foreign Film; Cannes Film Festival '94: Best Actor (You), Grand Jury Prize; Nominations: Golden Globe Awards '95: Best Foreign Language Film. *HMK, IME*

To Live and Die in Hong Kong ☠½ **1989** Two sailors arrive in Hong Kong for a little R & R, until they are mistaken for spies by both the Hong Kong police and the Chinese mob. Action-packed tale. **98m/C VHS.** Rowena Cortes, Lawrence Jan, Mike Kelly, Laurens C. Postma; ***D:*** Lau Shing Hon. *ELV*

To Live & Die in L.A. ☠☠ **1985 (R)** Fast-paced, morally ambivalent tale of cops and counterfeiters in L.A. After his partner is killed shortly before his retirement, a secret service agent sets out to track down his ruthless killer. Lots of violence; some nudity. Notable both for a riveting car chase and its dearth of sympathetic characters. **114m/C VHS, Beta, LV.** William L. Petersen, Willem Dafoe, John Pankow, Dean Stockwell, Debra Feuer, John Turturro, Darlanne Fluegel, Robert Downey; ***D:*** William Friedkin; ***W:*** William Friedkin. *LIV, VES*

To Love Again ☠½ **1980** A middle-aged love story about a reclusive college professor and the campus handyman. **96m/C VHS, Beta.** Lynn Redgrave, Brian Dennehy, Conchata Ferrell; ***D:*** Joseph Hardy. *NLC*

To Paris with Love ☠☠½ **1955** A British man and his son fall in love with a shop girl and her boss while on vacation in Paris. Charming and humorous, with a witty performance from Guinness. **75m/C VHS, Beta.** Alec Guinness, Odile Versois, Vernon Gray; ***D:*** Robert Hamer; ***M:*** Edwin Astley. *NO*

To Play or To Die ☠☠ **1991** The introverted Kees attends an all-boy school where powerful bullies and sadomasochistic games are the rule. Kees is fascinated by the handsome Charel, the bullies leader. He invites Charel to his home, intending to turn the tables on his tormentor, but nothing goes as planned. Intense and controversial look at gay teens. Directorial debut of Krom. In Dutch with English subtitles. **150m/C VHS.** *NL* Geert Hunaerts, Tjebbo Gerritsma; ***D:*** Frank Krom; ***W:*** Anne Van De Putte, Frank Krom. *WBF*

To Play the King ☠☠☠ **1993** Sequel to "The House of Cards" finds Francis Urquhart (Richardson), having murdered his way to the Prime Ministery, now bored with his political situation. But things may be changing—the Queen has been succeeded by her liberal son (Kitchen) and Francis, goaded by his equally vicious wife (Fletcher), plots treachery to bring down the monarchy. Followed by "The Final Cut;" adapted from the novel by Michael Dobbs. **212m/C VHS.** *GB* Ian Richardson, Michael Kitchen, Diane Fletcher, Kitty Aldridge, Bernice Stegers, Colin Jeavons, Rowena King, Erika Hoffman, Nicholas Farrell; ***D:*** Paul Seed; ***W:*** Andrew Davies. *FOX, TVC*

To Please a Lady 🦴🦴½ *Red Hot Wheels* **1950** Romantic comedy-drama about race car driver Gable and reporter Stanwyck. Although leads do their best with the script, they're unable to generate any sparks. However, race track scenes are excellent. Filmed at the Indianapolis Speedway, the spectacular racing footage makes up for overall average film. **91m/B VHS.** Clark Gable, Barbara Stanwyck, Adolphe Menjou, Will Geer, Roland Winters; ***D:*** Clarence Brown; ***W:*** Barre Lyndon, Marge Decker. *MGM*

To Protect and Serve 🦴🦴 **1992 (R)** When crooked cops start getting killed, two young cops are assigned to investigate. Suspicion points to a rookie (Howell), who just may have decided to clean things up his own way. **93m/C VHS.** C. Thomas Howell, Leslie Deane, Richard Romanus, Joe Cortese; ***D:*** Eric Weston. *LIV*

To Race the Wind 🦴🦴 **1980** Blind man wants to be treated like a normal person as he struggles through Harvard Law School. Based upon Harold Krents' autobiography "Butterflies Are Free." Made for television. **97m/C VHS, Beta.** Steve Guttenberg, Lisa Eilbacher, Randy Quaid, Barbara Barrie; ***D:*** Walter Grauman. *UNI*

To See Such Fun **1981** Hilarious excerpts from 80 years of the greatest British movie comedies. **90m/C VHS, Beta.** *GB* Peter Sellers, Marty Feldman, Benny Hill, Eric Idle, Alec Guinness, Margaret Rutherford, Dirk Bogarde, Spike Milligan. *NO*

To Sir, with Love 🦴🦴½ **1967** Teacher in London's tough East End tosses books in the wastebasket and proceeds to teach his class about life. Skillful and warm performance by Poitier as idealistic teacher; supporting cast also performs nicely. Based on the novel by E.R. Braithwaite. LuLu's title song was a big hit in 1967-68. **105m/C VHS, Beta.** *GB* Sidney Poitier, Lulu, Judy Geeson, Christian Roberts, Suzy Kendall, Faith Brook; ***D:*** James Clavell; ***W:*** James Clavell. *COL*

To Sleep with a Vampire 🦴🦴 **1992 (R)** A Los Angeles bloodsucker is tired of his violent existence and craves the one thing he can't have—daylight. As he stalks his latest victim, a stripper, he decides to take her home and have her tell him about living in daytime. When she realizes what's going on, the intended victim decides to fight for her life. Action and eroticism raises this one above the norm. Remake of "Dance of the Damned." **90m/C VHS.** Scott Valentine, Charlie Spradling, Richard Zobel, Ingrid Vold, Stephanie Hardy; ***D:*** Adam Friedman. *NHO*

To Sleep with Anger 🦴🦴🦴½ **1990 (PG)** At first a comic, introspective look at a black middle-class family going about their business in the heart of Los Angeles. Sly charmer Glover shows up and enthralls the entire family with his slightly sinister storytelling and a gnawing doom gradually permeates the household. Insightful look into the conflicting values of Black America. Glover's best performance. **105m/C VHS, Beta.** Danny Glover, Mary Alice, Paul Butler, Richard Brooks, Carl Lumbly, Vonetta McGee, Sheryl Lee Ralph; ***D:*** Charles Burnett; ***W:*** Charles Burnett; ***C:*** Walt Lloyd. Independent Spirit Awards '91: Best Actor (Glover), Best Director (Burnett), Best Screenplay, Best Supporting Actress (Ralph); Sundance Film Festival '90: Special Jury Prize. *COL, FCT, IME*

To the Camp & Back 🦴½ **1985** A romantic novel transposed to tape, with equal amounts of unfettered sentiment, fantasy, and style. **60m/C Beta.** Jan Niklas. *PSM*

To the Death 🦴½ **1993 (R)** A kickboxer wants to retire from the boxing tournaments but the corrupt promoters refuse to let him go unless he manages to kill his rivals in the ring. **90m/C VHS, LV.** John Barrett, Michael Quissi; ***D:*** Darrell Roodt. *CAN*

To the Devil, A Daughter 🦴🦴 *Child of Satan* **1976 (R)** A nun is put under a spell by a priest who has been possessed by Satan. She is to bear his child. A writer on the occult intervenes. Based on the novel by Dennis Wheatley. One of Kinski's early films. **93m/C VHS, Beta.** Richard Widmark, Christopher Lee, Nastassia Kinski, Honor Blackman, Denholm Elliott, Michael Goodliffe; ***D:*** Peter Sykes; ***C:*** David Watkin. *REP, MLB*

To the Last Man 🦴 **1933** An early Scott sagebrush epic, about two feuding families. Temple is seen in a small role. Based on Zane Grey's novel of the same name. **70m/B VHS, Beta.** Randolph Scott, Esther Ralston, Jack LaRue, Noah Beery Sr., Buster Crabbe, Gail Patrick, Barton MacLane, Fuzzy Knight, John Carradine, Jay Ward, Shirley Temple; ***D:*** Henry Hathaway. *NOS, DVT, MLB*

To the Lighthouse 🦴🦴 **1983** A proper British holiday turns into a summer of disillusionment in this adaptation of the Virginia Woolf novel. **115m/C VHS, Beta.** Rosemary Harris, Michael Clough, Suzanne Bertish, Lynsey Baxter. *NO*

To the Limit 🦴 **1995 (R)** Actioner finds the pulchritudinous Colette (Smith) revealing to mobster Frank (Travolta) that she's a CIA agent (and if you believe that I have a bridge in Brooklyn to sell you) and that they are the targets of a rogue agent (Richmond). No, Smith can't act but since she takes lots of showers and is supported by some professionals who can, this gets by on trash value alone. **96m/C VHS.** Anna Nicole Smith, Joey Travolta, Michael Nouri, Branscombe Richmond, John Aprea, Kathy Shower, Rebecca Ferratti, David Proval; ***D:*** Raymond Martino; ***W:*** Joey Travolta, Raymond Martino; ***M:*** Jim Halfpenny. *PMH*

To the Shores of Hell 🦴🦴 **1965** Leaving his sweetheart behind, Major Greg Donahue attacks Da Nang and plots to rescue his brother from the Viet Cong. **82m/C VHS, Beta.** Marshall Thompson, Kiva Lawrence, Richard Jordahl. *NO*

To the Shores of Tripoli 🦴🦴 **1942** Wartime propaganda in the guise of drama, in which a smarmy playboy is transformed into a Marine in boot camp. **82m/C VHS, Beta.** John Payne, Maureen O'Hara, Randolph Scott, Nancy Kelly, Harry (Henry) Morgan, Maxie "Slapsie" Rosenbloom, William Tracy, Minor Watson, Alan Hale Jr., Hugh Beaumont, Hillary Brooke; ***D:*** H. Bruce Humberstone. Nominations: Academy Awards '42: Best Color Cinematography. *FOX, MLB*

To Wong Foo, Thanks for Everything, Julie Newmar 🦴🦴½ **1995 (PG-13)** Hot on the high heels of "The Adventures of Priscilla, Queen of the Desert," comes the sanitized for your protection Yankee version. And its all about hanging on to your dreams and how we're all the same inside, with politically correct gay drag queens doing the sermonizing. Yes, this is the feel-good drag road movie for the 90s. Den mother Vida (Swayze), tough beauty queen Noxeema (Snipes), and hot-blooded Chi Chi (Leguizamo doing his best Rosie Perez) head to Hollywood in a 1967 Cadillac convertible that inconveniently breaks down in a tiny Nebraska town. The "girls" work their magic, and presumably the people of this uncultured, anachronistic backwater will never be the same. One-dimensional characters, flat direction, and inconsistent script undercut exceptional efforts by Swayze and Leguizamo. **108m/C VHS, LV.** Wesley Snipes, Patrick Swayze, John Leguizamo, Stockard Channing, Blythe Danner, Melinda Dillon, Arliss Howard, Jason London, Christopher Penn; ***Cameos:*** Julie Newmar, Robin Williams; ***D:*** Beeban Kidron; ***W:*** Douglas Carter Beane; ***M:*** Rachel Portman. Nominations: Golden Globe Awards '96: Best Actor—Musical/Comedy (Swayze), Best Supporting Actor (Leguizamo). *MCA*

The Toast of New Orleans 🦴🦴½ **1950** A poor fisherman rises to stardom as an opera singer. Likable, though fluffy production features a plethora of musical numbers. ♫Be My Love; Tina Lina; I'll Never Love You; The Toast of New Orleans; Song of the Bayou; Boom Biddy Boom Boom. **97m/C VHS, Beta.** Kathryn Grayson, Mario Lanza, David Niven, Rita Moreno, J. Carrol Naish; ***D:*** Norman Taurog. Nominations: Academy Awards '50: Best Song ("Be My Love"). *MGM*

Toast of New York 🦴🦴🦴 **1937** Arnold plays Jim Fisk, a New England peddler who rises to become one of the first Wall Street giants of industry. Atypical Grant performance. **109m/B VHS, Beta, LV.** Edward Arnold, Cary Grant, Frances Farmer, Jack Oakie, Donald Meek, Billy Gilbert; ***D:*** Rowland V. Lee. *TTC*

Tobor the Great 🦴½ **1954** Sentimental and poorly executed, this film tells the tale of a boy, his grandfather, and Tobor the robot. Villainous communists attempt to make evil use of Tobor, only to be thwarted in the end. **77m/B VHS, LV.** Charles Drake, Billy Chapin, Karin Booth, Taylor Holmes, Joan Gerber, Steve Geray; ***D:*** Lee Sholem. *REP*

Tobruk 🦴🦴 **1966** American GI's endeavor to knock out the guns of Tobruk, to clear the way for a bombing attack on German fuel supply depots of North Africa in this WWII actioner. **110m/C VHS, Beta.** Rock Hudson, George Peppard, Guy Stockwell, Nigel Green; ***D:*** Arthur Hiller. *MCA*

Toby McTeague 🦴🦴 **1987 (PG)** A story about an Alaskan family that breeds Siberian Huskies. When his father is injured, the youngest son tries to replace him in the regional dog-sled race. **94m/C VHS, Beta, LV.** Winston Rekert, Wannick Bisson, Timothy Webber; ***D:*** Jean-Claude Lord; ***W:*** Djordje Milicevic, Jamie Brown. *COL, NLC*

Toby Tyler 🦴🦴🦴 **1959 (G)** A boy runs off to join the circus, and teams up with a chimpanzee. A timeless and enjoyable Disney film that still appeals to youngsters. Good family-fare. **93m/C VHS, Beta.** Kevin Corcoran, Henry Calvin, Gene Sheldon, Bob Sweeney; ***D:*** Charles T. Barton. *DIS*

Today I Hang 🦴🦴 **1942** A man is framed for murder and sentenced to hang. His buddies on the outside do their best to prove his innocence. Meanwhile, in prison, the accused encounters any number of interesting characters. **67m/B VHS, Beta.** Walter Woolf King, Mona Barrie, William Farnum, Harry Woods, James Craven; ***D:*** Oliver Drake. *SNC*

Today We Kill, Tomorrow We Die 🦴 **1971 (PG)** A rancher is unjustly sent to prison; when his sentence is over he hires a gang to relentlessly track down the culprit who framed him. **95m/C VHS, Beta.** Montgomery Ford, Bud Spencer, William Berger, Tatsuya Nakadai, Wayde Preston; ***D:*** Tonino Cervi. *PSM*

Today We Live 🦴🦴½ **1933** Triangle love story set in WWI. Crawford is a hedonistic Brit having a fling with her naval brother's (Tone) friend (Young). When American flyer Cooper appears she sets her sights on him but soon he's off to combat in France where he's reported killed. Crawford returns to Young but, naturally, reports of Cooper's death have been greatly exaggerated and the two eventually reunite. Faulkner co-scripted from his story "Turn About" which had no female character and concerned the rivalry between naval officers and fly boys. **113m/B VHS, Beta.** Gary Cooper, Joan Crawford, Franchot Tone, Robert Young, Roscoe Karns, Louise Closser Hale; ***D:*** Howard Hawks; ***W:*** Dwight Taylor, William Faulkner, Edith Fitzgerald. *MGM, FCT*

The Todd Killings 🦴½ *A Dangerous Friend; Skipper* **1971 (R)** A psychotic young man commits a series of murders involving young women. Sleazy, forgettable picture wastes a talented cast. **93m/C VHS.** Robert F. Lyons, Richard Thomas, Barbara Bel Geddes, Ed Asner, Sherry Miles, Gloria Grahame, Belinda J. Montgomery; ***D:*** Barry Shear; ***W:*** Joel Oliansky. *WAR*

Toga Party 🦴 **1979 (R)** Fraternity house throws a wild toga party in this raunchy low-rent depiction of college life. **82m/C VHS, Beta.** Bobby H. Charles, Mary Mitchell. *NO*

Together? 🦴½ **1979 (R)** Divorced woman and a male chauvinist test the limits of their sexual liberation as well as viewer patience. **91m/C VHS, Beta.** *IT* Maximilian Schell, Jacqueline Bisset, Terence Stamp, Monica Guerritore; ***D:*** Armenia Balducci; ***M:*** Burt Bacharach. *SUE*

Togetherness 🦴½ **1970** Two wealthy, good-for-nothing playboys chase after the same blonde, a Communist, in Greece. **101m/C VHS, Beta, LV.** George Hamilton, Peter Lawford, Olinka Berova, John Banner, Jesse White; ***D:*** Arthur Marks. *NO*

Tokyo Decadence 🦴½ **1991 (NC-17)** Ai is a high-paid prostitute working in Tokyo for an agency that specializes in sado-masochism. Film follows her various sexual escapades in humiliating detail as well as her drug-addled search for a client Ai thinks she's in love with. Since Ai remains a cipher, the film also remains unfocused except for its creepy and explicit sex scenes. Adaptation of director Murakami's novel "Topaz." In Japanese with English subtitles or dubbed. **92m/C VHS, LV.** *JP* Miho Nikaidoh, Tenmei Kano, Yayoi Kusama, Sayoko Amano; ***D:*** Ryu Murakami; ***W:*** Ryu Murakami; ***M:*** Ryuichi Sakamoto. *TRI, FCT*

Tokyo-Ga ½ **1985** Impelled by his love for the films of Yasujiro Ozu, Wenders traveled to Tokyo and fashioned a caring document of both the city and of Ozu's career, using images that recall and comment on Ozu's visual motifs. **92m/C VHS, Beta.** ***D:*** Wim Wenders; ***W:*** Wim Wenders. *INJ, TPV*

Tokyo Joe ½ **1949** A war hero/nightclub owner returns to Tokyo and becomes ensnared in blackmail and smuggling while searching for his missing wife and child. Slow-moving tale has never been considered one of Bogart's better movies. **88m/B VHS, Beta, LV.** Humphrey Bogart, Florence Marly, Alexander Knox, Sessue Hayakawa, Jerome Courtland, Lore Lee Michel; ***D:*** Stuart Heisler. *COL*

Tokyo Olympiad **1966** A monumental sports documentary about the 1964 Olympic Games in its entirety. Never before available for home viewing. Letterboxed with digital sound. In Japanese with English subtitles. **170m/C VHS, Beta, LV.** *JP* ***D:*** Kon Ichikawa. *TPV, WFV, CRC*

Tokyo Pop ½ **1988 (R)** A punk rocker travels to Japan to find stardom and experiences a series of misadventures. Enjoyable in its own lightweight way. Hamilton is the daughter of Carol Burnett. **99m/C VHS, LV.** Carrie Hamilton, Yutaka Tadokoro, Tetsuro Tamba, Taiji Tonoyama, Masumi Harukawa; ***D:*** Fran Rubel Kazui; ***W:*** Lynn Grossman, Fran Rubel Kazui; ***M:*** Alan Brewer. *WAR*

Tokyo Story **1953** Poignant story of elderly couple's journey to Tokyo where they receive little time and less respect from their grown children. Masterful cinematography, and sensitive treatment of universally appealing story. In Japanese with English subtitles. **134m/B VHS.** *JP* Chishu Ryu, Chieko Higashiyama, So Yamamura, Haruko Sugimura, Setsuko Hara; ***D:*** Yasujiro Ozu; ***W:*** Yasujiro Ozu. *NYF, FCT, INJ*

Tol'able David **1921** A simple tale of mountain folk, done in the tradition of Mark Twain stories. A family of hillbillies is embroiled in a feud with a clan of outlaws. When the community's mail is stolen by the troublesome ruffians, the family's youngest member, who harbors dreams of becoming a mail driver, comes to the rescue. Silent film. **79m/B VHS, Beta.** Richard Barthelmess, Gladys Hulette, Ernest Torrence; ***D:*** Henry King. *NOS, VYY, CCB*

Toll Gate ½ **1920** Quick on the draw outlaw Hart risks capture to rescue drowning child, and consequently gets involved with the boy's mother. Silent classic. **55m/B VHS, Beta.** William S. Hart, Anna Q. Nilsson, Jack Richardson, Joseph Singleton; ***D:*** Lambert Hillyer. *GPV, VCN*

Toll of the Desert **1935** A lawman learns that his father is a ruthless, back-stabbing renegade. Now he must try and catch him. **58m/B VHS, Beta, LV.** Roger Williams, Ted Adams, Edward Cassidy, Tom London, John Elliott, Earl Dwire, Betty Mack, Fred Kohler Jr.; ***D:*** William (Lester Williams) Berke. *NOS, DVT*

Tollbooth **1994 (R)** Romantic dreamer Jack (Von Dohlen) mans a tollbooth on a stretch of Florida Keys highway while his equally longing honey Doris (Balk) works at a nearby gas station and has a thing going on the side with bait salesman Dash (Patton). The return of Doris' long-gone daddy Leon (Cassel) causes some family problems while Jack's new associate Vic (Wilder) has a scam that's drawing interest from the state police. Thin plot but lots of charm from the two leads helps hold interest in Breziner's first film. **108m/C VHS, LV.** Fairuza Balk, Lenny Von Dohlen, Will Patton, Seymour Cassel, James Wilder, Louise Fletcher, William Katt; ***D:*** Salome Breziner; ***W:*** Salome Breziner; ***C:*** Henry Vargas; ***M:*** Adam Gorgoni. *NLC*

Tom and Huck **1995 (PG)** Tom Sawyer and pal Huck Finn are the only witnesses to a murder. Tom's friend Muff is framed for the crime and the boys are being tracked by the real killer, Injun Joe. They must decide to come forward, expose the true fiend, and risk their own hides or run away and let an innocent man hang. True to the Twain story, Thomas plays a mischievious Tom to Renfro's troublemaking Huck. Film was shot in Mooresville, Alabama, population 69, just down the road a piece from the Hannibal, Missouri of Twain fame. **91m/C VHS.** Jonathan Taylor Thomas, Brad Renfro, Eric Schweig, Charles Rocket, Amy Wright, Micheal McShane, Marian Seldes, Rachel Leigh Cook, Lanny Flaherty, Courtland Mead, Peter M. MacKenzie, Heath Lamberts; ***D:*** Pete Hewitt; ***W:*** Stephen Sommers, David Loughery; ***C:*** Bobby Bukowski; ***M:*** Stephen Endelman. *TOU*

Tom and Jerry: The Movie **1993 (G)** Everybody's favorite animated cat/mouse duo (who began life in a 1940 MGM short "Puss Gets the Boot") hit the big screen, this time talking (unlike their animated shorts). Rather than cartoon mayhem our two protagonists are goody-two-shoes (with songs yet!) but still retain their charm. Kids will like it, but true "Tom and Jerry" fans should probably stick to the original cartoons. **84m/C VHS.** ***D:*** Phil Roman; ***W:*** Dennis Marks; ***M:*** Henry Mancini, Leslie Bricusse; ***V:*** Richard Kind, Dana Hill, Charlotte Rae, Henry Gibson, Rip Taylor, Howard Morris, Edmund Gilbert, David Lander. *FHE, WTA*

Tom & Viv **1994 (PG-13)** American T.S. Eliot (Dafoe) is an Oxford student in 1914 when he meets the moody, monied Vivien Haigh-Wood (Richardson). After a whirlwind courtship, they marry—disastrously. Eliot begins to establish himself as a poet, while Vivien serves as muse/typist and unsuccessfully battles her misdiagnosed illnesses with too much drinking and drugs, as well as embarrassing public scenes. As Eliot gains success, he increasingly distances himself from the unhappy Viv, until finally committing her to an asylum. Dafoe is fine as the chilly, withdrawn poet but Richardson steals the film as his flamboyant, lost wife. Based on the play by Michael Hastings, who co-wrote the screenplay. **115m/C VHS, LV.** *GB* Willem Dafoe, Miranda Richardson, Rosemary Harris, Tim Dutton, Nickolas Grace, Philip Locke, Clare Holman, Joanna McCallum; ***D:*** Brian Gilbert; ***W:*** Michael Hastings, Adrian Hodges; ***M:*** Debbie Wiseman. National Board of Review Awards '94: Best Actress (Richardson), Best Supporting Actress (Harris); Nominations: Academy Awards '94: Best Actress (Richardson), Best Supporting Actress (Harris); Golden Globe Awards '95: Best Actress—Drama (Richardson). *TOU*

Tom Brown's School Days ½ *Adventures at Rugby* **1940** Depicts life among the boys in an English school during the Victorian era. Based on the classic novel by Thomas Hughes. Remade in 1951. **86m/B VHS, Beta.** *GB* Cedric Hardwicke, Jimmy Lydon, Freddie Bartholomew; ***D:*** Robert Stevenson. *NOS, HHT, PSM*

Tom Brown's School Days **1951** Tom enrolls at Rugby and is beset by bullies in classic tale of English school life. British remake of the 1940 version. Based on the novel by Thomas Hughes. **93m/B VHS, Beta.** *GB* Robert Newton, John Howard Davies, James Hayter; ***D:*** Gordon Parry. *VCI*

Tom, Dick, and Harry ½ **1941** Dreamy girl is engaged to three men and unable to decide which to marry. It all depends on a kiss. Remade as "The Girl Most Likely." **86m/B VHS, Beta, LV.** Ginger Rogers, George Murphy, Burgess Meredith, Alan Marshal, Phil Silvers; ***D:*** Garson Kanin. National Board of Review Awards '41: 10 Best Films of the Year; Nominations: Academy Awards '41: Best Story. *CCB, TTC, FCT*

Tom Horn **1980 (R)** The final days of one of the Old West's legends. Gunman Tom Horn, hired by Wyoming ranchers to stop cattle rustlers, goes about his job with a zeal that soon proves embarrassing to his employers. Beautifully photographed and authentic in its attention to details of the period, the film nonetheless takes liberties with the facts of Horn's life and is lacking in other aspects of production. **98m/C VHS, Beta.** Steve McQueen, Linda Evans, Richard Farnsworth, Billy Green Bush, Slim Pickens; ***D:*** William Wiard; ***W:*** Thomas McGuane; ***C:*** John A. Alonzo; ***M:*** Ernest Gold. *WAR*

Tom Jones **1963** Bawdy comedy based on Henry Fielding's novel about a rustic playboy's wild life in 18th century England. Hilarious and clever with a grand performance by Finney. One of the sexiest eating scenes ever. Redgrave's debut. Theatrically released at 129 minutes, the film was recut by the director, who decided it needed tightening before its 1992 re-release on video. **121m/C VHS, Beta, LV.** *GB* Albert Finney, Susannah York, Hugh Griffith, Edith Evans, Joan Greenwood, Diane Cilento, George Devine, David Tomlinson, Joyce Redman, Lynn Redgrave, Julian Glover, Peter Bull, David Warner; ***D:*** Tony Richardson; ***W:*** John Osborne; ***C:*** Walter Lassally; ***M:*** John Addison. Academy Awards '63: Best Adapted Screenplay, Best Director (Richardson), Best Picture, Best Original Score; British Academy Awards '63: Best Film, Best Screenplay; Directors Guild of America Awards '63: Best Director (Richardson); Golden Globe Awards '64: Best Film—Musical/Comedy, Best Foreign Film; National Board of Review Awards '63: Best Director (Richardson); New York Film Critics Awards '63: Best Actor (Finney), Best Director (Richardson), Best Film; Nominations: Academy Awards '63: Best Actor (Finney), Best Art Direction/Set Decoration (Color), Best Supporting Actor (Griffith), Best Supporting Actress (Cilento, Evans, Redman). *HBO, FOX, BTV*

Tom Mix Compilation 1 **1916** This compilation of six "Great American Cowboy" films from Tom Mix's early period includes: "Jimmy Hayes and Muriel," "The Stagecoach Driver and the Girl," "Sagebrush Tom," "An Arizona Wooing," "Roping a Bride" and "Local Color." **60m/B VHS, Beta.** Tom Mix. *GVV*

Tom Mix Compilation 2 **1916** Five films from Tom Mix's early period include "Never Again," "An Angelic Attitude," "A Western Masquerade," "A $5,000 Elopement," and "Local Color." **60m/B VHS, Beta.** Tom Mix. *GVV*

Tom Sawyer **1930** Winning adaptation of Mark Twain's oft told tale of boyhood in Hannibal, Missouri. Cast reprised their roles the following year in "Huckleberry Finn." **86m/B VHS, Beta.** Jackie Coogan, Mitzie Green, Lucien Littlefield, Tully Marshall; ***D:*** John Cromwell; ***C:*** Charles B(ryant) Lang. *MGM*

Tom Sawyer ½ **1973 (G)** Musical version of the Mark Twain tale of the boisterous Tom, his friend Becky Thatcher, and various adventures, including the fence whitewashing. Amusing kid fare shot on location in Missouri. ♫River Song; Gratification; Tom Sawyer; Freebootin'; Aunt Polly's Soliloquy; If'n I Was God; A Man's Gotta Be What He's Born To Be; How Come?; Hannibal, Mo. **104m/C VHS, LV.** Johnny Whitaker, Jodie Foster, Celeste Holm, Warren Oates, Jeff East; ***D:*** Don Taylor; ***M:*** John Williams. *MGM*

Tom Thumb **1958** Diminutive boy saves village treasury from bad guys. Adapted from classic Grimm fairy tale. Special effects combine live actors, animation, and puppets. **92m/C VHS, Beta, LV.** *GB* Russ Tamblyn, Peter Sellers, Terry-Thomas; ***D:*** George Pal; ***C:*** Georges Perinal. Academy Awards '58: Best Special Effects. *MGM*

Tomb **1986** Fortune seekers disturb the slumber of a magical, sadistic princess much to their everlasting regret. Adapted from a Bram Stoker novel. **106m/C VHS, Beta.** Cameron Mitchell, John Carradine, Sybil Danning, Richard Hench, Michelle (McClellan) Bauer; ***D:*** Fred Olen Ray. *TWE*

Tomb of Ligeia *Tomb of the Cat* **1964** The ghost of a man's first wife expresses her displeasure when groom and new little missus return to manor. One of the better Corman adaptations of Poe. Also available with "The Conqueror Worm" on Laser Disc. **82m/C VHS, Beta, LV.** *GB* Vincent Price, Elizabeth Shepherd, John Westbrook, Oliver Johnston, Richard Johnson; ***D:*** Roger Corman; ***W:*** Robert Towne. *MLB*

Tomb of the Undead ½ **1972** The sadistic guards of a prison camp are rudely awakened by the prisoners they tortured to death when they return as flesh-eating zombies looking to settle the score. **60m/C VHS, Beta.** *GB* Duncan McLeod, Lee Frost, John Dennis; ***D:*** John Hayes. *NOS, INC*

Tomb of Torture *Woof! Metempsycose* **1965** Murdered countess is reincarnated in the body of a newspaperman's mistress. Together they investigate monster reports in a murder-ridden castle. The butler may have something to do with it. Filmed in Sepiatone and dubbed. **88m/B VHS, Beta.** Annie Albert, Thony Maky, Mark Marian; ***D:*** William Grace. *MSP*

The Tomboy ☠½ **1924** A young woman behaves boyishly in Colonial America. **64m/B VHS, Beta.** Dorothy Devore, Lotta Williams, Herbert Rawlinson, Harry Gribbon, Lee Moran; ***D:*** David Kirkland. *GPV, FCT*

Tomboy ☠ **1940** Shy country boy and a not-so-shy city girl meet, fall in love, and overcome obstacles that stand in their path. **70m/B VHS, Beta.** Jackie Moran, Marcia Mae Jones. *VYY*

Tomboy *Woof!* **1985 (R)** A pretty auto mechanic is determined to win not only the race but the love and respect of a superstar auto racer. **91m/C VHS, Beta.** Betsy Russell, Eric Douglas, Jerry Dinome, Kristi Somers, Richard Erdman, Toby Iland; ***D:*** Herb Freed. *LIV, VES*

Tomboy & the Champ ☠☠ **1958** Despite many obstacles, a music-loving calf becomes a prize winner with the help of its loving owner. Kids will love it, but adults will find this one a little sugary. **82m/C VHS, Beta.** Candy Moore, Ben Johnson, Jesse White; ***D:*** Francis D. Lyon. *VCI*

Tombs of the Blind Dead ☠☠½ *The Blind Dead; La Noche dell Terror Ciego* **1972 (PG)** Blinded by crows for using human sacrifice in the thirteenth century, zombies rise from the grave to wreak havoc upon 20th-century Spaniards. Atmospheric chiller was extremely popular in Europe and spawned three sequels. Originally titled "The Blind Dead." The sequels, also on video, are "Return of the Evil Dead" and "Horror of the Zombies." **86m/C VHS, Beta.** *SP PT* Caesar Burner, Lone Fleming, Helen Harp; ***D:*** Armando de Ossorio. *NO*

Tombstone ☠☠☠ **1993 (R)** Saga of Wyatt Earp and his band of law-abiding large moustaches beat the Kasdan/Costner vehicle to the big screen by several months. Legendary lawman Wyatt (Russell) moves to Tombstone, AZ aiming to start a new life with his brothers, but alas, that's not to be. The infamous gunfight at the OK Corral is here, and so is best buddy Doc Holliday, gunslinger and philosopher, a role designed for scenery chewing (Kilmer excels). Romance is supplied by actress Josephine, though Delany lacks the necessary romantic spark. Russell spends a lot of time looking troubled by the violence while adding to the body count. Too self-conscious, suffers from '90s western revisionism, but blessed with a high energy level thanks to despicable villains Lang, Biehn, and Boothe. **130m/C VHS, LV.** Kurt Russell, Val Kilmer, Michael Biehn, Sam Elliott, Dana Delany, Bill Paxton, Powers Boothe, Stephen Lang, Jason Priestley, Dana Wheeler-Nicholson, Billy Zane, Thomas Haden Church, Joanna Pacula, Michael Rooker, Harry Carey Jr., Billy Bob Thornton, Charlton Heston, Robert Burke, John Corbett, Buck Taylor, Terry O'Quinn, Pedro Armendariz Jr., Chris Mitchum, Jon Tenney; ***D:*** George P. Cosmatos; ***W:*** Kevin Jarre; ***M:*** Bruce Broughton. Nominations: MTV Movie Awards '94: Best Actor (Kilmer), Most Desirable Male (Kilmer). *HPH*

Tombstone Canyon ☠½ **1935** Death rides the range until Maynard and his horse Tarzan put a halt to it. **60m/B VHS, Beta.** Ken Maynard, Sheldon Lewis, Cecilia Parker. *SNC, NOS, RXM*

Tombstone Terror ☠ **1934** A cowboy is beleaguered by a case of mistaken identity. **55m/B VHS, Beta.** Bob Steele. *NO*

Tomcat: Dangerous Desires ☠☠ **1993 (R)** Tom (Grieco) suffers from a rare degenerative condition and agrees to become a guinea pig in a secret, genetic imprinting experiment that has him injected with feline RNA. Tom's health is restored but the side effects give him the predatory instincts of a cat and the need to kill to stay alive. **96m/C VHS, LV.** Richard Grieco, Maryam D'Abo, Natalie Radford. *REP*

Tommy ☠☠ **1975 (PG)** Peter Townsend's rock opera as visualized in the usual hyper-Russell style about the deaf, dumb, and blind boy who becomes a celebrity due to his amazing skill at the pinball machines. A parade of rock musicians perform throughout the affair, with varying degrees of success. Despite some good moments, the film ultimately falls prey to ill-conceived production concepts and miscasting. ♫Underture; Captain Walker Didn't Come Home; It's A Boy; '51 is Going to Be A Good Year; What About the Boy?; The Amazing Journey; Christmas; See Me, Feel Me; Eyesight to the Blind. **108m/C VHS, Beta, LV.** Ann-Margret, Elton John, Oliver Reed, Tina Turner, Roger Daltrey, Eric Clapton, Keith Moon, Pete Townshend, Jack Nicholson, Robert Powell; ***D:*** Ken Russell; ***W:*** Ken Russell. Golden Globe Awards '76: Best Actress—Musical/Comedy (Ann-Margret); Nominations: Academy Awards '75: Best Actress (Ann-Margret), Best Original Score. *COL, MVD, WME*

Tommy Boy ☠☠ **1995 (PG-13)** Not-too-bright rich kid Tommy (Farley) teams up with snide, officious accountant Richard (Spade) to save the family auto parts business after dad (Dennehy) buys the farm. Tommy and Richard must deal with a conniving stepmom and stepbrother (Derek and Lowe), a ruthless rival (Aykroyd), and a road trip from hell to drum up some new business. Not as bad as it sounds, but suffers from connection with the currently unfunny "Saturday Night Live." Inconsistent direction and too-familiar characters offset the amusing chemistry between Farley and Spade, who show promise as a possible "Abbott and Costello"-type comedy team for the 90's. **98m/C VHS, Beta.** Chris Farley, David Spade, Brian Dennehy, Bo Derek, Dan Aykroyd, Julie Warner, Rob Lowe; ***D:*** Peter Segal; ***W:*** Bonnie Turner, Terry Turner; ***M:*** David Newman. MTV Movie Awards '96: Best On-Screen Duo (Chris Farley/David Spade); Nominations: MTV Movie Awards '96: Best Comedic Performance (Farley). *PAR*

Tomorrow ☠☠☠ **1972 (PG)** Powerful tale of the love of two lonely people. Outstanding performance by Duvall as lumber mill worker who falls for a pregnant woman. Based on the neglected Faulkner story. **102m/B VHS, Beta.** Robert Duvall, Olga Bellin, Sudie Bond; ***D:*** Joseph Anthony; ***W:*** Horton Foote. *MON*

Tomorrow at Seven ☠☠½ **1933** A mystery writer is determined to discover the identity of the Ace of Spades, a killer who always warns his intended victim, then leaves an ace of spades on the corpse as his calling card. **62m/B VHS, Beta.** Chester Morris, Vivienne Osborne, Frank McHugh, Allen Jenkins, Henry Stephenson; ***D:*** Ray Enright. *SNC, NOS, VYY*

Tomorrow Is Forever ☠☠½ **1946** Welles and Colbert marry shortly before he goes off to fight in WWI. Badly wounded and disfigured, he decides to stay in Europe while Colbert, believing Welles dead, eventually marries Brent. Fast forward to WWII when Brent, a chemical manufacturer, hires a new scientist to work for him in the war effort (guess who). This slow-moving melodrama wastes a good cast. Six-year-old Wood debuts as Colbert's daughter. **105m/B VHS.** Claudette Colbert, Orson Welles, George Brent, Lucile Watson, Richard Long, Natalie Wood; ***D:*** Irving Pichel; ***C:*** Joseph Valentine; ***M:*** Max Steiner. *MGM*

Tomorrow Never Comes ☠½ **1977** When he discovers his girlfriend has been unfaithful, a guy goes berserk and eventually finds himself in a stand-off with the police. Violent. **109m/C VHS, Beta.** Oliver Reed, Susan George, Raymond Burr, John Ireland, Stephen McHattie, Donald Pleasence; ***D:*** Peter Collinson. *UNI, HHE*

Tomorrow's Child ☠☠ **1982** Made-for-television drama about in vitro fertilization (test-tube babies) and surrogate motherhood. **100m/C VHS, Beta.** Stephanie Zimbalist, William Atherton, Bruce Davison, Ed Flanders, Salome Jens, James Shigeta, Susan Oliver, Arthur Hill; ***D:*** Joseph Sargent. *FOX*

Tomorrow's Children ☠ **1934** An alarmist melodrama warning against the threat of government-induced female sterilization asks the question: if a woman's family is weird, should her tubes be tied? **55m/B VHS, Beta.** Sterling Holloway, Diana Sinclair, Sarah Padden, Don Douglas; ***D:*** Crane Wilbur. *SNC, NOS, VYY*

The Tong Man ☠☠½ **1919** Robbins owes the tong money and Hayakawa, as the tong's executioner, is sent to kill him when he won't pay up. Only it turns out Hayakawa is in love with Eddy, Robbins daughter, and refuses. Then the tong decide to kill him for disobeying their orders. **58m/B VHS.** Sessue Hayakawa, Helen Jerome Eddy, Marc Robbins, Toyo Fujita; ***D:*** William Worthington. *GPV*

Tongs: An American Nightmare ☠ **1988 (R)** Chinese-American street gangs in Chinatown battle over turf and drug shipments. **80m/C VHS, Beta.** Ian Anthony Leung, Christopher O'Conner, Simon Yam; ***D:*** Philip Chan. *ACA*

Toni ☠☠☠½ **1934** An Italian worker falls for his landlady and they make plans to marry. A grim turn of events, however, brings tragic consequences. Based on the lives of several townsfolk in the village of Les Martiques, the film was shot in the town and members of the local populace were used as characters. In French with English subtitles. **90m/B VHS, Beta.** *FR* Charles Blavette, Jenny Helia, Edouard Delmont, Celia Montalvan; ***D:*** Jean Renoir. *DVT*

Tonight and Every Night ☠☠½ **1945** Cabaret singer and RAF pilot fall in love during WWII. Her music hall post puts her in the midst of Nazi bombing, and her dedication to her song and dance career puts a strain on the romance. Imaginative production numbers outweigh pedestrian storyline. ♫Cry and You Cry Alone; What Does an English Girl Think of a Yank; Anywhere; The Boy I Left Behind; You Excite Me; Tonight and Every Night. **92m/C VHS, Beta.** Rita Hayworth, Lee Bowman, Janet Blair, Marc Platt, Leslie Brooks; ***D:*** Victor Saville. Nominations: Academy Awards '45: Best Song ("Anywhere"), Best Original Score. *COL*

Tonight for Sure ☠½ **1961** Coppola made this nudie, his first film, as a student at UCLA. Two men, one who spies on women and the other who imagines nude women everywhere, plan an escapade. **66m/B VHS, Beta.** ***D:*** Francis Ford Coppola; ***W:*** Francis Ford Coppola; ***M:*** Carmine Coppola. *VYY, TPV*

Tonio Kroger ☠☠ **1965** A young writer travels through Europe in search of intellectual and sensual relationships and a home that will suit him. He must balance freedom and responsibility. Works best if one is familiar with the Thomas Mann novel on which film is based. In German with English subtitles. **92m/B VHS, Beta.** *GE* Jean-Claude Brialy, Nadja Tiller, Gert Frobe; ***D:*** Rolf Thiele. *VYY, APD, GLV*

Tonka ☠☠½ *A Horse Named Comanche* **1958** A children's story about a wild horse tamed by a young Indian, only to have it recruited for the Battle of Little Bighorn. Mineo is fine as the Indian brave determined to be reunited with his steed. The film also makes a laudable effort to portray the Indians as a dignified race. The movie, however, stumbles at its conclusion and is contrived throughout. **97m/C VHS, Beta.** Sal Mineo, Phil Carey, Jerome Courtland; ***D:*** Lewis R. Foster. *DIS*

Tonto Basin Outlaws ☠☠ **1941** The Range Busters team up with Teddy Roosevelt's Rough Riders in order to stop a gang of cattle rustlers. Standard oater material. Based on the story by Earle Snell. **60m/B VHS.** Ray Corrigan, John "Dusty" King, Max Terhune, Jan Wiley, Tristram Coffin, Edmund Cobb; ***D:*** S. Roy Luby; ***W:*** John Vlahos. *MOV*

The Tonto Kid ☠ **1935** Action-packed western featuring Rex Bell. **56m/B VHS, Beta.** Rex Bell, Ruth Mix, Buzz Barton, Joseph Girard, Jack Rockwell, Murdock McQuarrie; ***D:*** Harry Fraser. *NOS, DVT, VDM*

Tony Draws a Horse ☠☠½ **1951** An eight-year old draws an anatomically correct horse on the door of his father's office, leading to a rift between the parents as they argue how to handle the heartbreak of precociousness. Somewhat uneven but engaging comedy, based on a play by Lesley Storm. **90m/B VHS.** Cecil Parker, Anne Crawford, Derek Bond, Barbara Murray, Mervyn Johns, Barbara Everest, David Hurst; ***D:*** John Paddy Carstairs. *NOS*

Tony Rome ½ **1967** The Marvin H. Albert private eye agency investigates a millionaire's daughter's disappearance and her involvement in organized crime. Entertaining and complex plot, although the cast is a numbingly large one. **110m/C VHS, Beta.** Frank Sinatra, Jill St. John, Simon Oakland, Gena Rowlands, Richard Conte, Lloyd Bochner, Jeffrey Lynn, Sue Lyon; ***D:*** Gordon Douglas. *FOX*

Too Beautiful for You *Trop Belle Pour Toi* **1988 (R)** A successful car salesman, married for years to an extraordinarily beautiful woman, finds himself head over heels for his frumpy secretary. Depardieu plays the regular guy who finds he's never believed in the love and fidelity of a woman he thinks is too beautiful for him. In French with English subtitles. **91m/C VHS.** *FR* Gerard Depardieu, Josiane Balasko, Carole Bouquet, Roland Blanche; ***D:*** Bertrand Blier; ***W:*** Bertrand Blier. Cannes Film Festival '89: Grand Jury Prize; Cesar Awards '90: Best Actress (Bouquet), Best Director (Blier), Best Film, Best Writing. *ORI, FXL, FCT*

Too Far to Go **1979** Terrific TV adaptation of a series of John Updike stories focusing on the rocky longtime marriage of not-so-proper New Englanders Danner and Moriarty. **98m/C VHS.** Blythe Danner, Michael Moriarty, Glenn Close, Ken Kercheval; ***W:*** William Hanley. *MON*

Too Hot to Handle **1938** Two rival photographers searching for a beautiful lady-pilot's missing brother wind up in Brazil, where they encounter a dangerous tribe of voodoo types. Amusing, if exaggerated, picture of the lengths to which reporters will go to for a story. Classic Gable. **105m/B VHS.** Clark Gable, Myrna Loy, Walter Pidgeon, Walter Connolly, Leo Carrillo, Virginia Weidler; ***D:*** Jack Conway. *MGM, FCT*

Too Hot to Handle **1976** Voluptuous lady contract killer fights against the mob with all the weapons at her disposal. Filmed on location in Manila. **88m/C VHS, Beta.** Cheri Caffaro, Aharon Ipale, Vic Diaz, Corinne Calvet; ***D:*** Don Schain. *WAR*

Too Late for Tears *Killer Bait* **1949** An honest husband and his not so honest wife stumble on a load of mob-stolen cash and become entangled in a web of deceit and murder as the wife resorts to increasingly desperate measures to keep her newfound fortune. Atmospheric and entertaining film noir albeit sometimes confusing. **99m/B VHS, Beta.** Lizabeth Scott, Don DeFore, Dan Duryea, Arthur Kennedy, Kristine Miller, Barry Kelley, Denver Pyle; ***D:*** Byron Haskin. *SNC, VDM, NOS*

Too Late the Hero *Suicide Run* **1970 (PG)** Unlikely band of allied soldiers battle Japanese force entrenched in the Pacific during WWII. Rousing adventure, fine cast. **133m/C VHS, Beta.** Michael Caine, Cliff Robertson, Henry Fonda, Ian Bannen, Harry Andrews, Denholm Elliott; ***D:*** Robert Aldrich; ***C:*** Joseph Biroc. *FOX*

Too Many Crooks **1959** A British spoof of crime syndicate films. Crooks try to extort, but bungle the job. Terry-Thomas is fun, as always. **85m/B VHS, Beta.** *GB* Terry-Thomas, Brenda de Banzie, George Cole; ***D:*** Mario Zampi. *NO*

Too Many Girls ½ **1940** Beautiful heiress goes to a small New Mexico college to escape from a cadre of gold-digging suitors. Passable adaptation of the successful Rodgers and Hart Broadway show, with many original cast members and the original stage director. Lucy and Desi met while making this film, and married shortly after. ♫Spic and Spanish; Heroes in the Fall; Pottawatomie; 'Cause We All Got Cake; Love Never Went to College; Look Out; I Didn't Know What Time It Was; The Conga; You're Nearer. **85m/B VHS, Beta, LV.** Lucille Ball, Richard Carlson, Eddie Bracken, Ann Miller, Desi Arnaz Sr., Hal LeRoy, Libby Bennett, Frances Langford, Van Johnson; ***D:*** George Abbott; ***M:*** George Bassman, Richard Rodgers, Lorenz Hart. *TTC*

Too Much Sun ½ **1990 (R)** A dying man can prevent his fortune from falling into the hands of a corrupt priest simply by having one of his two children produce an heir. The problem is, they're both gay! **97m/C VHS, LV.** Robert Downey Jr., Ralph Macchio, Eric Idle, Andrea Martin, Laura Ernst, Jim Haynie; ***D:*** Robert Downey. *COL*

Too Pretty to Be Honest *Trop Jolie pour Etre Honette* **1972** Four women sharing an apartment witness a robbery and begin to suspect that their neighbor is the culprit. So they decide to steal the money from him. In French with subtitles. **95m/C VHS, Beta.** *FR* Jane Birkin, Bernadette LaFont, Serge Gainsbourg; ***D:*** Richard Balducci; ***M:*** Serge Gainsbourg. *FCT*

Too Scared to Scream ½ **1985 (R)** Policeman and an undercover agent team up to solve a bizarre series of murders at a Manhattan apartment house. **104m/C VHS, Beta.** Mike Connors, Anne Archer, Leon Isaac Kennedy, John Heard, Ian McShane, Maureen O'Sullivan, Murray Hamilton; ***D:*** Tony Lo-Bianco; ***W:*** Neal Barbera. *LIV, VES*

Too Shy to Try **1982 (PG)** A incredibly shy man meets his dream girl, and enrolls in a psychology course to overcome his ineptitude. A ribald, slapstick French comedy. **89m/C VHS, Beta.** *FR* Pierre Richard, Aldo Maccione; ***D:*** Pierre Richard. *SUE*

Too Wise Wives **1921** A story of would-be marital infidelity and misunderstandings. Silent. **90m/C VHS, Beta.** Louis Calhern, Claire Windsor; ***D:*** Lois Weber. *GVV*

Too Young to Die **1990 (R)** Teenager Amanda (Lewis) and her street-smart boyfriend (Pitt) are in the live fast, die young category. Now Amanda's on trial for murder. Fact-based TV movie. **92m/C VHS.** Juliette Lewis, Brad Pitt, Michael Tucker, Alan Fudge, Emily Longstreth, Michael O'Keefe; ***D:*** Robert Markowitz; ***M:*** Charles Bernstein. *REP*

The Toolbox Murders **1978 (R)** Unknown psychotic murderer brutally claims victims one at a time, leaving police mystified and townsfolk terrified. Sick and exploitative, with predictably poor production values. **93m/C VHS, Beta.** Cameron Mitchell, Pamelyn Ferdin, Wesley Eure, Nicholas Beauvy, Aneta Corsaut, Tim Donnelly, Evelyn Guerrero; ***D:*** Dennis Donnelly. *VCI, VTR*

Tootsie **1982 (PG)** A stubborn, unemployed actor disguises himself as a woman to secure a part on a soap opera. As his popularity on television mounts, his love life becomes increasingly soap operatic. Hoffman is delightful, as is the rest of the stellar cast. Debut of Davis; Murray's performance unbilled. Laserdisc version features audio commentary by director Sidney Pollack, behind the scenes footage and photographs, and complete coverage of Tootsie's production. **110m/C VHS, Beta, LV.** Dustin Hoffman, Jessica Lange, Teri Garr, Dabney Coleman, Bill Murray, Charles Durning, Geena Davis, George Gaynes, Estelle Getty, Christine Ebersole, Sydney Pollack; ***D:*** Sydney Pollack; ***W:*** Larry Gelbart, Murray Schisgal, Don McGuire; ***C:*** Owen Roizman; ***M:*** Dave Grusin. Academy Awards '82: Best Supporting Actress (Lange); British Academy Awards '83: Best Actor (Hoffman); Golden Globe Awards '83: Best Actor—Musical/Comedy (Hoffman), Best Film—Musical/Comedy, Best Supporting Actress (Lange); New York Film Critics Awards '82: Best Director (Pollack), Best Screenplay, Best Supporting Actress (Lange); Writers Guild of America '82: Best Original Screenplay; Nominations: Academy Awards '82: Best Actor (Hoffman), Best Cinematography, Best Director (Pollack), Best Film Editing, Best Original Screenplay, Best Picture, Best Song ("It Might Be You"), Best Sound, Best Supporting Actress (Garr). *COL, CRC, BTV*

Top Dog ½ **1995 (PG-13)** Another cop-and-dog-team-up-to-get-the-bad-guys flick. This one, however, is meant to appeal to the kids who liked "Sidekicks." That raises a problem with the unfortunately topical right-wing-hate group-bombing plot. Jake Wilder (Norris), a beer-swillin' karate-choppin' loner cop, teams up with canine Reno, whose ex-partner was killed by the neo-Nazi terrorists. Weak script and erratic storyline can't find a comfortable balance between the too-cute pooch scenes and the (admittedly toned-down) violence. Reno steals every scene he's in, and provides the flick's few redeeming moments. **93m/C VHS, LV.** Chuck Norris, Clyde Kusatsu, Michele Lamar Richards, Carmine Caridi, Peter Savard Moore, Erik von Detten, Herta Ware, Kai Wulff, Francesco Quinn, Timothy Bottoms; ***D:*** Aaron Norris; ***W:*** Ron Swanson; ***C:*** Joao Fernandes. *LIV*

Top Gun ½ **1986 (PG)** Young Navy pilots compete against one another on the ground and in the air at the elite Fighter Weapons School. Cruise isn't bad as a maverick who comes of age in Ray Bans, but Edwards shines as his buddy. Awesome aerial photography and high-cal beefcake divert from the contrived plot and stock characters. The Navy subsequently noticed an increased interest in fighter pilots. Features Berlin's Oscar-winning song "Take My Breath Away." ♫Take My Breath Away; Danger Zone; Destination Unknown; Heaven in Your Eyes; Hot Summer Nights; Mighty Wings; Playing with the Boys; Through the Fire; Top Gun Anthem. **109m/C VHS, Beta, LV, 8mm, CD-I.** Tom Cruise, Kelly McGillis, Val Kilmer, Tom Skerritt, Anthony Edwards, Meg Ryan, Rick Rossovich, Michael Ironside, Barry Tubb, Whip Hubley, John Stockwell, Tim Robbins, Adrian Pasdar; ***D:*** Tony Scott; ***W:*** Jim Cash, Jack Epps Jr.; ***M:*** Harold Faltermeyer. Academy Awards '86: Best Song ("Take My Breath Away"); Golden Globe Awards '87: Best Song ("Take My Breath Away"); People's Choice Awards '87: Best Film; Nominations: Academy Awards '86: Best Film Editing, Best Sound. *PAR*

Top Hat **1935** Ginger isn't impressed by Fred's amorous attentions since she's mistaken him for a friend's other half. Many believe it to be the duo's best film together. Choreography by Astaire and score by Berlin makes this one a classic Hollywood musical. Look for a young Lucille Ball as a clerk in a flower shop. ♫Cheek to Cheek; Top Hat, White Tie and Tails; Isn't This A Lovely Day; The Piccolino; No Strings. **97m/B VHS, Beta, LV, 8mm.** Fred Astaire, Ginger Rogers, Erik Rhodes, Helen Broderick, Edward Everett Horton, Eric Blore, Lucille Ball; ***D:*** Mark Sandrich; ***W:*** Dwight Taylor, Allan Scott; ***M:*** Irving Berlin, Max Steiner. Nominations: Academy Awards '35: Best Interior Decoration, Best Picture, Best Song ("Cheek to Cheek"). *TTC, HMV*

Top of the Heap **1972 (R)** A cop is denied a promotion and gets angry. Deciding to chuck the laws of due process, he goes on a criminal-killing rampage. **91m/C VHS, Beta.** Christopher St. John, Paula Kelly, Patrick McVey; ***D:*** Christopher St. John. *NO*

Top Secret! **1984 (PG)** Unlikely musical farce parodies spy movies and Elvis Presley films. Young American rock star Nick Rivers goes to Europe on goodwill tour and becomes involved with Nazis, the French Resistance, an American refugee, and more. Sophisticated it isn't. From the creators of "Airplane!" **90m/C VHS, Beta, LV.** Val Kilmer, Lucy Gutteridge, Christopher Villiers, Omar Sharif, Peter Cushing, Jeremy Kemp, Michael Gough; ***D:*** Jim Abrahams, Jerry Zucker, David Zucker; ***W:*** Jim Abrahams, Jerry Zucker, David Zucker, Martyn Burke; ***M:*** Maurice Jarre. *PAR*

Topaz **1969 (PG)** American CIA agent and French intelligence agent combine forces to find information about Russian espionage in Cuba. Cerebral and intriguing, but not classic Hitchcock. Based on the novel by Leon Uris. Laser disc video release includes two alternate endings. **126m/C VHS, Beta, LV.** John Forsythe, Frederick Stafford, Philippe Noiret, Karin Dor, Michel Piccoli; ***D:*** Alfred Hitchcock; ***C:*** Jack Hildyard; ***M:*** Maurice Jarre. National Board of Review Awards '69: 10 Best Films of the Year, Best Director (Hitchcock), Best Supporting Actor (Noiret). *MCA*

Topaze **1933** American adaptation of the Marcel Pagnol play, about an innocent, doltish schoolmaster who becomes the unknowing front for a baron's illegal business scam. Remade in two French versions, in 1933, and in 1951 by Pagnol. **127m/B VHS, Beta, LV.** John Barrymore, Myrna Loy, Jobyna Howland, Jackie Searl; ***D:*** Harry D'Abbadie D'Arrast. *FOX*

Topaze **1933** A shy, depressed teacher is fired from his job at a private school and takes a new job, unaware that his boss is using him in a business scam. From the French play by Marcel Pagnol. An American version was also filmed in 1933; Pagnol produced his own version in '51. In French with English subtitles. **92m/B VHS, Beta.** *FR* Louis Jouvet, Edwige Feuillere, Marcel Vallee; ***D:*** Louis Gasnier; ***W:*** Marcel Pagnol; ***M:*** Max Steiner. *INT, FOX, INJ*

Topaze ☙☙☙½ **1951** After losing his job, a pathetic school teacher gets involved with the mob and winds up a powerful businessman. Remake of two earlier versions, one French and one American. Based on the play by director Pagnol. In French with English subtitles. **95m/B VHS.** *FR* Fernandel, Helen Perdriere, Pierre Larquey; ***D:*** Marcel Pagnol. *DVT, APD, INJ*

The Topeka Terror ☙☙ **1945** Lane stars as a federal agent who joins forces with a frontier lawyer to stop greedy land-grabber Barcroft from ripping off a group of homesteaders. Based on a story by Patricia Harper. **55m/B VHS.** Allan "Rocky" Lane, Linda Stirling, Roy Barcroft, Earle Hodgins, Bud Geary; ***D:*** Howard Bretherton; ***W:*** Patricia Harper, Norman S. Hall. *MOV*

Topkapi ☙☙☙ **1964** An international bevy of thieves can't resist the treasures of the famed Topkapi Palace Museum, an impregnable fortress filled with wealth and splendor. Comic thriller based on Erie Ambler's "The Light of Day." **122m/C VHS, Beta.** Melina Mercouri, Maximilian Schell, Peter Ustinov, Robert Morley, Akim Tamiroff; ***D:*** Jules Dassin; ***M:*** Manos Hadjidakis. Academy Awards '64: Best Supporting Actor (Ustinov); National Board of Review Awards '64: 10 Best Films of the Year. *FOX*

Topper ☙☙☙½ **1937** George and Marion Kerby return as ghosts after a fatal car accident, determined to assist their pal Cosmo Topper. Immensely popular at the box office, followed by "Topper Takes a Trip" and "Topper Returns." The series uses trick photography and special effects to complement the comedic scripts. Inspired a television series and remade in 1979 as television movie. Also available colorized. **97m/B VHS, Beta.** Cary Grant, Roland Young, Constance Bennett, Billie Burke, Eugene Pallette, Hoagy Carmichael; ***D:*** Norman Z. McLeod. Nominations: Academy Awards '37: Best Sound, Best Sound, Best Supporting Actor (Young). *MED, CCB, VTR*

Topper Returns ☙☙☙ **1941** Cosmo Topper helps ghost find the man who mistakenly murdered her and warns her friend, the intended victim. Humorous conclusion to the trilogy preceded by "Topper" and "Topper Takes a Trip." Followed by a television series. Also available colorized. **87m/B VHS, Beta, LV.** Roland Young, Joan Blondell, Dennis O'Keefe, Carole Landis, Eddie Anderson, H.B. Warner, Billie Burke; ***D:*** Roy Del Ruth. Nominations: Academy Awards '41: Best Sound. *SNC, NOS, CAB*

Topper Takes a Trip ☙☙☙ **1939** Cosmo Topper and his wife have falling out and ghosts Kerby help them get back together. The special effects sequences are especially funny. Followed by "Topper Returns." Also available colorized. **85m/B VHS, Beta.** Constance Bennett, Roland Young, Billie Burke, Franklin Pangborn, Alan Mowbray; ***D:*** Norman Z. McLeod. Nominations: Academy Awards '39: Best Special Effects. *MED, VTR*

Topsy Turvy ☙½ **1984 (R)** A comedy about reckless romance and not much else. **90m/C VHS, Beta.** Lisbet Dahl, Ebbe Rode; ***D:*** Edward Fleming. *LIV, VES*

Tor ☙½ **1964** Medieval barbarian endeavors to free an enslaved village from a band of murderous hoodlums. **94m/C VHS, Beta.** Joe Robinson, Bella Cortez, Harry Baird; ***D:*** Antonio Leonuiola. *TWE*

Tora! Tora! Tora! ☙☙ **1970 (G)** The story of events leading up to December 7, 1941, is retold by three directors from both Japanese and American viewpoints in this tense, large-scale production. Well-documented and realistic treatment of the Japanese attack on Pearl Harbor that brought the US into WWII; notable for its good photography but lacks a storyline equal to its epic intentions. **144m/C VHS, Beta, LV.** Martin Balsam, Soh Yomamura, Joseph Cotten, E.G. Marshall, Tatsuya Mihashi, Wesley Addy, Jason Robards Jr., James Whitmore, Leon Ames, George Macready; ***D:*** Richard Fleischer, Toshio Masuda, Kinji Fukasaku; ***M:*** Jerry Goldsmith. Academy Awards '70: Best Visual Effects; National Board of Review Awards '70: 10 Best Films of the Year; Nominations: Academy Awards '70: Best Art Direction/Set Decoration, Best Cinematography, Best Film Editing. *FOX, TLF, HMV*

The Torch ☙☙½ **1950** Mexican revolutionary restores law and order when he captures a small town but then finds himself in turmoil as he falls for an aristocratic young woman. **90m/C VHS.** *MX* Gilbert Roland, Paulette Goddard, Pedro Armendariz Sr., Walter Reed; ***D:*** Emilio Fernandez. *FCT*

Torch Song ☙☙ **1953** In this muddled melodrama, a tough, demanding Broadway actress meets her match when she is offered true love by a blind pianist. Contains a couple of notoriously inept musical numbers. Made to show off Crawford's figure at age 50. Crawford's singing in the movie is dubbed. **90m/C VHS, LV.** Joan Crawford, Michael Wilding, Marjorie Rambeau, Gig Young, Harry (Henry) Morgan, Dorothy Patrick, Benny Rubin, Nancy Gates; ***D:*** Charles Walters. Nominations: Academy Awards '53: Best Supporting Actress (Rambeau). *MGM*

Torch Song Trilogy ☙☙½ **1988 (R)** Adapted from Fierstein's hit Broadway play about a gay man who "just wants to be loved." Still effective, but the rewritten material loses something in the translation to the screen. Bancroft heads a strong cast with a finely shaded performance as Fierstein's mother. **126m/C VHS, Beta, LV.** Anne Bancroft, Matthew Broderick, Harvey Fierstein, Brian Kerwin, Karen Young, Charles Pierce; ***D:*** Paul Bogart; ***W:*** Harvey Fierstein; ***C:*** Mikael Salomon; ***M:*** Peter Matz. *COL*

Torchlight ☙ **1985 (R)** A young couple's life begins to crumble when a wealthy art dealer teaches them how to free base cocaine. Heavy-handed treatment of a subject that's been tackled with more skill elsewhere. **90m/C VHS, Beta, LV.** Pamela Sue Martin, Steve Railsback, Ian McShane, Al Corley, Rita Taggart; ***D:*** Thomas J. Wright. *SUE*

Torero ☙ *Bullfighter* **1956** A young man becomes a bullfighter to overcome his fear of bulls. **89m/B VHS, Beta.** *MX* Luis Procuna, Manolete, Dolores Del Rio, Carlos Arruza; ***D:*** Carlos Velo. *MAD*

Torment ☙☙☙ *Hets; Frenzy* **1944** Tragic triangle has young woman in love with fellow student and murdered by sadistic teacher. Atmospheric tale hailed by many as Sjoberg's finest film. Ingmar Bergman's first filmed script. In Swedish with English subtitles. **90m/B VHS, Beta.** *SW* ***D:*** Alf Sjoberg; ***W:*** Ingmar Bergman. *SUE, INJ, NLC*

Torment ☙ **1985 (R)** A mild-mannered fellow is secretly a mass murderer specializing in young lovers. He struggles to hide his secret as his daughter approaches dating age and a relentless detective gets closer to the truth. A low-budget slasher. **85m/C VHS, Beta.** Taylor Gilbert, William Witt, Eve Brenner; ***D:*** Samson Aslanian, John Hopkins; ***W:*** Samson Aslanian, John Hopkins. *VTR, NWV*

Tormented ☙½ **1960** Man pushes his mistress out of a lighthouse, killing her. Her ethereal body parts return to haunt him. **75m/B VHS.** Richard Carlson, Susan Gordon, Juli Reding; ***D:*** Bert I. Gordon. *SNC*

The Tormentors *Woof!* **198? (R)** Vaguely neo-Nazi gangs rape and murder a man's family, and he kills them all in revenge. **78m/C VHS, Beta.** James Craig, Anthony Eisley, Chris Nole; ***D:*** Boris Eagle. *NO*

Torn Allegiance ☙ **1984** An Australian anti-war epic set in the Boer War about the effects of war on one family and their fight for survival on the veldt. **102m/C VHS, Beta.** *AU PSM, FCT*

Torn Apart ☙☙ **1989 (R)** Traditional Middle East hatreds undermine the love affair between two young people. Excellent performances from the principals highlight this drama. Adapted from the Chayin Zeldis novel "A Forbidden Love." **95m/C VHS, Beta.** Adrian Pasdar, Cecilia Peck, Machram Huri, Arnon Zadok, Barry Primus; ***D:*** Jack Fisher; ***M:*** Peter Arnow. *WAR, BTV*

Torn Between Two Lovers ☙☙ **1979** A beautiful married woman has an affair with an architect while on a trip. Remick is enjoyable to watch, but it's a fairly predictable yarn. Made for television. **100m/C VHS.** Lee Remick, Joseph Bologna, George Peppard, Giorgio Tozzi; ***D:*** Delbert Mann. *LIV*

Torn Curtain ☙☙½ **1966** American scientist poses as a defector to East Germany in order to uncover details of the Soviet missile program. He and his fiancee, who follows him behind the Iron Curtain, attempt to escape to freedom. Derivative and uninvolving. **125m/C VHS, Beta, LV.** Paul Newman, Julie Andrews, Lila Kedrova, David Opatoshu; ***D:*** Alfred Hitchcock; ***W:*** Brian Moore; ***M:*** John Addison. *MCA*

Tornado ☙ **1983** An army sergeant revolts against his superiors and the enemy when his captain leaves him stranded in Vietnam. **90m/C VHS, Beta.** Timothy Brent, Tony Marsina, Alan Collins; ***D:*** Anthony (Antonio Margheriti) Dawson. *LIV*

Tornado! ☙½ **1996 (PG)** TV movie with cheesy special effects chronicles a week with tornado chaser Campbell, meteorologist Hudson, and government accountant Sturges who wants to stop funding for Hudson's new storm-warning device. **90m/C VHS.** Bruce Campbell, Ernie Hudson, Shannon Sturges, L.Q. Jones, Bo Eason. *HMK*

Torpedo Alley ☙☙ **1953** A guilt-ridden WWII Navy pilot feels responsible for the deaths of his crew. After the war, he joins a submarine crew and gradually learns to deal with his guilt. Average drama with plenty of submarine footage. **84m/B VHS.** Dorothy Malone, Mark Stevens, Charles Winninger, Bill Williams; ***D:*** Lew (Louis Friedlander) Landers. *REP*

Torpedo Attack ☙ **1972** Greek sailors, in an outdated submarine, bravely but hopelessly attack Mussolini's Italy during WWII. **88m/C VHS, Beta.** *GR* John Ferris, Sidney Kazan; ***D:*** George Law. *LIV*

Torpedo Run ☙☙ **1958** Standard submarine melodramatics, about a U.S. sub that must torpedo a Japanese aircraft carrier which holds some of the crew's family members. Sometimes slow, generally worthwhile. **98m/C VHS, Beta.** Glenn Ford, Ernest Borgnine, Dean Jones, Diane Brewster, L.Q. Jones; ***D:*** Joseph Pevney. *MGM*

Torrents of Spring ☙☙ **1990 (PG-13)** Based on an Ivan Turgenev story, this lavishly filmed and costumed drama concerns a young Russian aristocrat circa 1840 who is torn between two women. Predictably, one is a good-hearted innocent, the other a scheming seductress. **102m/C VHS, Beta, LV.** Timothy Hutton, Nastassia Kinski, Valeria Golino, William Forsythe, Urbano Barberini, Francesca De Sapio, Jacques Herlin; ***D:*** Jerzy Skolimowski. *NO*

Torso *Woof! I Corpi Presentano Tracce Di Violenza Carnale* **1973 (R)** Crazed psychosexual killer stalks beautiful women and dismembers them. Fairly bloodless and uninteresting, in spite of lovely Kendall. Italian title translates: The Bodies Showed Signs of Carnal Violence—quite an understatement for people missing arms and legs. **91m/C VHS, Beta.** *IT* Suzy Kendall, Tina Aumont, John Richardson; ***D:*** Sergio Martino; ***W:*** Ernesto Gastaldi, Sergio Martino. *PSM*

Tortilla Flat ☙☙☙ **1942** Based on the John Steinbeck novel of the same name, two buddies, Tracy and Garfield, struggle to make their way on the wrong side of the tracks in California. Garfield gets a break by inheriting a couple of houses, Tracy schemes to rip-off a rich, but eccentric, dog owner. In the meantime, both fall for the same girl, Lamarr, in perhaps the finest role of her career. Great performances from all, especially Morgan. **105m/B VHS.** Spencer Tracy, Hedy Lamarr, John Garfield, Frank Morgan, Akim Tamiroff, Sheldon Leonard, John Qualen, Donald Meek, Connie Gilchrist; ***D:*** Victor Fleming; ***C:*** Karl Freund. Nominations: Academy Awards '42: Best Supporting Actor (Morgan). *MGM, CCB*

Torture Chamber of Baron Blood ☙☙½ *Baron Blood* **1972 (PG)** Baron with gorgeous thirst for the red stuff is reanimated and lots of innocent bystanders meet a grisly fate in this spaghetti gorefest. Familiar story has that certain Bava feel. **90m/C VHS, Beta.** *IT* Joseph Cotten, Elke Sommer, Massimo Girotti, Rada Rassimov; ***D:*** Mario Bava; ***M:*** Les Baxter. *NO*

The Torture Chamber of Dr. Sadism ☙☙½ *Blood Demon; Castle of the Walking Dead; Die Schlangengrube und das Pendel* **1969** Decapitated and drawn and quartered for sacrificing twelve virgins, the evil Count Regula is pieced together forty years later to continue his wicked ways. Great fun, terrific art direction. Very loosely based on Poe's "The Pit and the Pendulum." Beware of the heavily edited video version. **120m/C VHS, Beta.** *GE* Christopher

Lee, Karin Dor, Lex Barker, Carl Lange, Vladimir Medar, Christiane Rucker, Dieter Eppler; ***D:*** Harald Reinl. *NO*

Torture Dungeon 🦴 **1970 (R)** Director Milligan tortures audience with more mindless medieval pain infliction from Staten Island. **80m/C VHS.** Jeremy Brooks, Susan Cassidy; ***D:*** Andy Milligan. *NO*

Torture Garden 🦴🦴 **1967** A sinister man presides over an unusual sideshow where people can see what is in store if they allow the evil side of their personalities to take over. Written by Bloch ("Psycho") and based on four of his short stories. **93m/C VHS, Beta, LV.** *GB* Jack Palance, Burgess Meredith, Peter Cushing, Beverly Adams; ***D:*** Freddie Francis; ***W:*** Robert Bloch; ***M:*** Don Banks, James Bernard. *COL*

The Torture of Silence 🦴🦴½ *Master Dolorosa* **1917** A simple little drama about a doctor's neglected wife seeking out the doctor's best friend for love, remade by Gance again in 1932; both originally titled "Mater Dolorosa." Silent. **55m/B VHS, Beta.** ***D:*** Abel Gance. *FCT*

Torture Ship 🦴½ **1939** Director Halperin, who earlier made the minor horror classic "White Zombie," was all at sea in this becalmed thriller about a mad doctor who uses convicts for glandular experiment in his shipboard laboratory. Based on the short story "A Thousand Deaths" by Jack London. **57m/B VHS.** Lyle Talbot, Irving Pichel, Jacqueline Wells, Sheila Bromley; ***D:*** Victor Halperin. *NOS, LOO*

Torture Train 🦴½ **1983 (R)** Mayhem, murder and knife-wielding psychosis occurs on board a train. **78m/C VHS, Beta.** Patty Edwards, Kay Beal. *JEF*

Total Eclipse 🦴 **1995 (R)** Unfortunate look at the mutually destructive relationship between 19th-century French poets Arthur Rimbaud (DiCaprio) and Paul Verlaine (Thewlis). Rimbaud was a 16-year-old Parisian sensation for his iconoclastic work but what's presented is an obnoxious showoff, while the older, married Verlaine is a drunken lout who abuses his teenaged wife Mathilde (Bohringer). There's lots of dissolute, violent behavior and absolutely no insight into their work (which is the only reason to care). Ugly film wastes a lot of talent. **111m/C VHS.** Leonardo DiCaprio, David Thewlis, Romane Bohringer, Dominique Blanc; ***D:*** Agnieszka Holland; ***W:*** Christopher Hampton; ***C:*** Yorgos Arvanitis. *NLC*

Total Exposure 🦴 **1991 (R)** Total idiocy involving unclad babes and hormonally imbalanced men in blackmail and murder. 1990 Playboy Playmate Deborah Driggs proves there is life of sorts after playmatedom. **96m/C VHS, LV.** Michael Nouri, Season Hubley, Christian Bocher, Robert Prentiss, Deborah Driggs, Jeff Conaway; ***D:*** John Quinn. *REP*

Total Recall 🦴🦴🦴 **1990 (R)** Mind-bending sci-fi movie set in the 21st century. Construction worker Quaid (Schwarzenegger) dreams every night about the colonization of Mars, so he decides to visit a travel service that specializes in implanting vacation memories into its clients' brains and buy a memory trip to the planet. Only during the implant, Quaid discovers his memories have been artificially altered and he must find out just what's real and what's not. Intriguing plot and spectacular special effects. Laced with graphic violence. Based on Phillip K. Dick's "We Can Remember It For You Wholesale." **113m/C VHS, Beta, LV, 8mm.** Arnold Schwarzenegger, Rachel Ticotin, Sharon Stone, Michael Ironside, Ronny Cox, Roy Brocksmith, Marshall Bell, Mel Johnson Jr.; ***D:*** Paul Verhoeven; ***W:*** Gary Goldman, Dan O'Bannon; ***C:*** Jan De Bont; ***M:*** Jerry Goldsmith. Academy Awards '90: Best Visual Effects; Nominations: Academy Awards '90: Best Sound. *IME, FUS, LIV*

Totally F*ed Up** 🦴🦴 **1994** The first of director Araki's teen trilogy, followed by "The Doom Generation" and "Nowhere," concerns itself with the teen angst experienced by a loose group of friends—four gays and a lesbian couple. In short chapters, they meet, talk, and wander through a soulless L.A. as one of their group, film school student Steven (Luna), makes a video documentary about their situation (footage of which in intercut throughout the film). **80m/C VHS.** James Duval, Gilbert Luna, Lance May, Roko Belic, Susan Behshid, Jenee Gill, Alan Boyce; ***D:*** Gregg Araki; ***W:*** Gregg Araki; ***C:*** Gregg Araki. *NYR*

Toto le Heros 🦴🦴🦴 *Toto the Hero* **1991 (PG-13)** Bitter old man, who as a child fantasized that he was a secret agent named Toto, harbors deep resentment over not living the life he's convinced he should have had. He maintains a childhood fantasy that he and his rich neighbor were switched at birth in the confusion of a fire at the hospital. Series of flashbacks and fast forwards show glimpses of his life, not necessarily as it was, but how he perceived it. Sounds complex, but it's actually very clear and fluid. Mix of comedy and tragedy, with lots of ironic twists, and precise visuals. In French with English subtitles. **90m/C VHS, Beta, LV.** *FR* Michel Bouquet, Jo De Backer, Thomas Godet, Mireille Perrier, Sandrine Blancke, Didier Ferney, Hugo Harold Harrisson, Gisela Uhlen, Peter Bohlke; ***D:*** Jaco Van Dormael; ***W:*** Jaco Van Dormael. Cesar Awards '91: Best Foreign Film. *PAR, BTV*

The Touch 🦴½ *Be Roringen* **1971 (R)** Straightforward story of a woman who is satisfied with her husband until the arrival of a stranger. The stranger soon has her yearning for a life she has never known. Bergman's first English film lacks the sophistication of his earlier work. **112m/C VHS, Beta.** *SW* Bibi Andersson, Elliott Gould, Max von Sydow; ***D:*** Ingmar Bergman; ***W:*** Ingmar Bergman; ***C:*** Sven Nykvist. *FOX*

Touch & Go 🦴🦴 **1980 (PG)** Three beautiful women commit grand larceny in order to raise funds for underprivileged children. **92m/C VHS, Beta.** *AU* Wendy Hughes; ***D:*** Peter Maxwell; ***W:*** Alan Ormsby. *NO*

Touch and Go 🦴½ **1986 (R)** Sentimental drama about a self-interested hockey pro who learns about love and giving through a young delinquent and his attractive mother. **101m/C VHS, Beta, LV.** Michael Keaton, Maria Conchita Alonso, Ajay Naidu, Maria Tucci, Max Wright, John C. Reilly; ***D:*** Robert Mandel; ***W:*** Harry Colomby. *NO*

Touch Me Not 🦴🦴 *The Hunted* **1974 (PG)** A neurotic secretary is used by an industrial spy to gain information on her boss. Weak thriller. **84m/C VHS.** *GB* Lee Remick, Michael Hinz, Ivan Desny, Ingrid Garbo; ***D:*** Douglas Fifthian. *NO*

A Touch of Class 🦴🦴🦴 **1973 (PG)** Married American insurance adjustor working in London plans quick and uncommitted affair but finds his heart doesn't obey the rules. Jackson and Segal create sparkling record of a growing relationship. **105m/C VHS, Beta.** George Segal, Glenda Jackson, Paul Sorvino, Hildegarde Neil, K. Callan, Mary Barclay, Cec Linder; ***D:*** Melvin Frank; ***W:*** Jack Rose. Academy Awards '73: Best Actress (Jackson); Golden Globe Awards '74: Best Actor—Musical/Comedy (Segal), Best Actress—Musical/Comedy (Jackson); Nominations: Academy Awards '73: Best Picture, Best Song ("All That Love Went to Waste"), Best Story & Screenplay, Best Original Score. *MED*

Touch of Evil 🦴🦴🦴🦴 **1958** Stark, perverse story of murder, kidnapping and police corruption in Mexican border town. Welles portrays a police chief who invents evidence to convict the guilty. Filled with innovative photography reminiscent of "Citizen Kane," as filmed by Russell Metty. **108m/B VHS, Beta, LV.** Charlton Heston, Orson Welles, Janet Leigh, Joseph Calleia, Akim Tamiroff, Marlene Dietrich, Valentin de Vargas, Dennis Weaver, Zsa Zsa Gabor, Mort Mills, Victor Milian, Joanna Moore, Joi Lansing; ***Cameos:*** Ray Collins, Mercedes McCambridge, Joseph Cotten; ***D:*** Orson Welles; ***W:*** Orson Welles; ***C:*** Russell Metty; ***M:*** Henry Mancini. *MCA*

The Touch of Satan 🦴 *The Touch of Melissa; Night of the Demon; Curse of Melissa* **1970 (PG)** Lost on the road, a young man meets a lovely young woman and is persuaded to stay at her nearby farmhouse. Things there are not as they seem, including the young woman—who turns out to be a very old witch. **90m/C VHS, Beta.** Michael Berry, Emby Mallay, Lee Amber, Yvonne Wilson, Jeanne Gerson; ***D:*** Don Henderson. *NO*

Touched 🦴🦴 **1982 (R)** Two young people struggle with the outside world after their escape from a mental institution. Although melodramatic and poorly scripted, the film is saved by fine performances by Hays and Beller. **89m/C VHS, Beta.** Robert Hays, Kathleen Beller, Ned Beatty, Gilbert Lewis; ***D:*** John Flynn. *MED*

Touched by Love 🦴🦴½ *To Elvis, With Love* **1980 (PG)** The true story of a handicapped child who begins to communicate when her teacher suggests she write to Elvis Presley. Sincere and well performed. **95m/C VHS, Beta.** Deborah Raffin, Diane Lane, Christina Raines, Clu Gulager, John Amos; ***D:*** Gus Trikonis; ***W:*** Hesper Anderson; ***M:*** John Barry. *COL*

Tough and Deadly 🦴½ **1994 (R)** CIA agent teams up with bounty hunter to stop a drug ring. **92m/C VHS.** Billy Blanks, Roddy Piper. *MCA*

Tough Assignment 🦴 **1949** A reporter in the West discovers and infiltrates a gang of organized rustlers who are forcing butchers to buy inferior meat. **64m/B VHS, Beta, LV.** Donald (Don "Red") Barry, Marjorie Steele, Steve Brodie. *NO*

Tough Enough 🦴🦴 **1983 (PG)** A country-western singer and songwriter decides to finance his fledgling singing career by entering amateur boxing matches. Insipid and predictable, with fine cast wasted. **107m/C VHS, Beta.** Dennis Quaid, Charlene Watkins, Warren Oates, Pam Grier, Stan Shaw, Bruce McGill, Wilford Brimley, Bob Watson; ***D:*** Richard Fleischer. *FOX*

Tough Guy 🦴 **1953** Based on the play by Bruce Walker, a London hood carouses, mugs, breaks hearts and personifies his generation's anxiety. **73m/B VHS, Beta.** *GB* James Kenney, Hermione Gingold, Joan Collins; ***D:*** Lewis Gilbert. *UNI*

Tough Guy 🦴 **197?** Two undercover policemen battle local gangsters in a bid to smash their crime ring. **90m/C VHS, Beta.** Chen Ying, Charlie Chiang; ***D:*** Chieng Hung. *NO*

Tough Guys 🦴🦴½ **1986 (PG)** Two aging ex-cons, who staged America's last train robbery in 1961, try to come to terms with modern life after many years in prison. Amazed and hurt by the treatment of the elderly in the 1980s, frustrated with their inability to find something worthwhile to do, they begin to plan one last heist. Tailor-made for Lancaster and Douglas, who are wonderful. Script becomes cliched at end. **103m/C VHS, Beta, LV.** Burt Lancaster, Kirk Douglas, Charles Durning, Eli Wallach, Lyle Alzado, Dana Carvey, Alexis Smith, Darlanne Fluegel, Billy Barty, Monty Ash; ***D:*** Jeff Kanew; ***W:*** James Orr, Jim Cruickshank; ***M:*** James Newton Howard. *TOU*

Tough Guys Don't Dance 🦴🦴½ **1987 (R)** Mailer directed this self-satiric mystery thriller from his own novel. A writer may have committed murder—but he can't remember. So he searches for the truth among various friends, enemies, lovers, and cohorts. **110m/C VHS, Beta, LV.** Ryan O'Neal, Isabella Rossellini, Wings Hauser, Debra Sandlund, John Bedford Lloyd, Lawrence Tierney, Clarence Williams III, Penn Jillette, Frances Fisher; ***D:*** Norman Mailer; ***W:*** Norman Mailer; ***M:*** Angelo Badalamenti. Golden Raspberry Awards '87: Worst Director (Mailer). *MED, CDV, VTR*

Tough Kid 🦴 **1939** A bad kid with gang connections attempts to shield his boxer brother from corruption at the hands of the same gang. Poor production all around. **61m/B VHS, Beta.** Frankie Darro, Dick Purcell, Judith Allen, Lillian Elliot; ***D:*** Howard Bretherton. *SNC*

Tough to Handle 🦴½ **1937** ...And no picnic to watch, either. A reporter cracks a criminal racket that rips off lottery sweepstakes winners. A laughably inept production. **58m/B VHS.** Frankie Darro, Kane Richmond, Phyllis Fraser, Harry Worth; ***D:*** S. Roy Luby. *NOS, LOO*

Tougher than Leather 🦴 **1988 (R)** The rap triumvirate battles criminals, vigilante-style, in their home neighborhood. Poorly executed and exploitative fare. **92m/C VHS, Beta.** Run DMC, The Beastie Boys, Slick Rick, Richard Edson, Jenny Lumet; ***D:*** Rick Rubin. *COL*

Toughlove 🦴🦴 **1985** The parents of a juvenile delinquent organize a tough parental philosophy and a support group for other parents having a difficult time with their teens. Made for television. **100m/C VHS, Beta.** Lee Remick, Bruce Dern, Piper Laurie, Louise Latham, Dana Elcar, Jason Patric, Eric Schiff, Dedee Pfeiffer; ***D:*** Glenn Jordan. *FRH*

Touki Bouki 🦴🦴 *Journey of the Hyena* **1973** Feeling alienated from their African society, Mory and Anta see freedom in the flashy consumerism of European culture and embark on a quest to meet happiness in Paris. A Bonnie & Clyde-like story symbolizing Africa's advancement toward a technological civilization. In Wolof with English subtitles. **85m/C VHS.** ***D:*** Djibril Diop Mambety. *KIV*

Tour of Duty 🦴🦴½ **1987** Follows the trials that the members of an American platoon face daily during the Vietnam war. The pilot movie for a television series. **93m/C VHS, Beta, LV.** Terence Knox, Stephen Caffrey, Joshua Maurer, Ramon Franco; ***D:*** Bill W.L. Norton. *NWV, HHE*

Tourist Trap 🦴 **1979 (PG)** While traveling through the desert, a couple's car has a flat. A woman's voice lures the man into an abandoned gas station, where he discovers that the voice belongs to a mannequin. Or is it? Not very interesting or suspenseful. **90m/C VHS, Beta, LV.** Tanya Roberts, Chuck Connors, Robin Sherwood, Jocelyn Jones; ***D:*** David Schmoeller; ***W:*** David Schmoeller; ***M:*** Pino Donaggio. *PAR*

Tournament 🦴🦴½ **1929** Renoir's second-to-last silent film, in which Protestants and Catholics joust out their differences in era of Catherine de Medici. French title: "Le Tournoi dans la Cite." **90m/B VHS, Beta.** *FR* Aldo Nadi; ***D:*** Jean Renoir. *FCT*

Tous les Matins du Monde 🦴🦴🦴 *All the Mornings of the World* **1992** Haunting tale of two 17th century French baroque composers and their relationship with each other and their music. Gerard Depardieu plays Marin Marais who eventually becomes a court composer at Versailles. As a young man, he studies under Sainte Colombe, a private and soulful musician, about whom little is known even today. Depardieu's son Guillaume (in his film debut) plays the young Marais, who startles the quiet Sainte Colombe home and has an affair with one of his daughters (Brochet). Filmmaker Corneau lends a quiet austere tone which parallels the life and music of Sainte Colombe. In French with English subtitles. **114m/C VHS, LV.** *FR* Gerard Depardieu, Guillaume Depardieu, Jean-Pierre Marielle, Anne Brochet, Caroline Sihol, Carole Richert, Violaine Lacroix, Nadege Teron, Miriam Boyer, Michel Bouquet; ***D:*** Alain Corneau; ***W:*** Pascal Quignard, Alain Corneau; ***C:*** Yves Angelo; ***M:*** Jordi Savall. Cesar Awards '92: Best Cinematography, Best Director (Corneau), Best Film, Best Supporting Actress (Brochet), Best Score. *TOU*

Toute Une Nuit 🦴🦴🦴 *All Night Long* **1982** Assorted people stumble melodramatically in and out of one another's lives on steamy summer night in Brussels. Fine combination of avant-garde technique and narrative. In French with English subtitles. **90m/C VHS.** *BE FR* Aurore Clement, Tcheky Karyo, Veronique Silver, Angelo Abazoglou, Natalia Ackerman; ***D:*** Chantal Akerman; ***W:*** Andra Akers. *WAC, FCT, INJ*

Toward the Terra 🦴🦴 **1980** In the distant future mankind is forced to evacuate Earth and settles on the planet Atarakusha. Society ruthlessly suppresses anything which could destabalize it in an effort to prevent the mistakes which destroyed the Earth. The most destablizing presence is the MU, a new race with incredible mental powers, who are ruthlessly hunted and eliminated. But the leader of the MU reaches out to a human with his own inexplicable powers to aid in establishing a new world. In Japanese with subtitles. **112m/C VHS.** *JP CPM*

Tower of Evil *Woof! Horror on Snape Island; Beyond the Fog* **1972 (R)** Anthropologists and treasure hunters unite in search of Phoenician hoard on Snape Island. Suddenly, inanimate bodies materialize. Seems the island's single inhabitant liked it quiet. Cult favorite despite uneven performances. So bad it's not bad. **86m/C VHS, Beta.** *GB* Bryant Halliday, Jill Haworth, Jack Watson, Mark Edwards, George Coulouris; ***D:*** James O'Connolly. *NO*

The Tower of London 🦴🦴½ **1939** Tells the story of Richard III (Rathbone), the English monarch who brutally executed the people who tried to get in his way to the throne. This melodrama was considered extremely graphic for its time, and some of the torture scenes had to be cut before it was released. **93m/B VHS.** Basil Rathbone, Boris Karloff, Barbara O'Neil, Ian Hunter, Vincent Price, Nan Grey, John Sutton, Leo G. Carroll, Miles Mander; ***D:*** Rowland V. Lee. *MCA*

Tower of London 🦴🦴 **1962** A deranged lord (Price) murdering his way to the throne of England is eventually crowned Richard III. Sophisticated and well-made Poe-like thriller. More interesting as historic melodrama than as horror film. A remake of the 1939 version starring Basil Rathbone, in which Price played a supporting role. **79m/B VHS, Beta.** Vincent Price, Michael Pate, Joan Freeman, Robert Brown; ***D:*** Roger Corman. *MGM, FCT*

Tower of Screaming Virgins 🦴 **1968** The Queen of France maintains a tower in which she has her lovers killed—after she makes love to them. An extremely loose adaptation of a Dumas novel; with English subtitles. **89m/C VHS, Beta, 8mm.** *GE* Terry Torday, Jean Piat. *VYY, VDM, SNC*

Tower of Terror 🦴½ **1942 (NC-17)** Woman escapes from a German concentration camp and takes refuge in a lighthouse. The proprietor sees in her an uncanny resemblance to his late wife, whom he killed, and soon plots to do away with her. Story hampered by poor acting. **62m/B VHS, Beta.** *GB* Wilfred Lawson, Movita, Michael Rennie, Morland Graham, John Longden, George Woodbridge; ***D:*** Lawrence Huntington. *NOS, SNC*

The Towering Inferno 🦴🦴 **1974 (PG)** Raging blaze engulfs the world's tallest skyscraper on the night of its glamorous dedication ceremonies. Allen had invented the disaster du jour genre two years earlier with "The Poseidon Adventure." Features a new but equally noteworthy cast. ♫We May Never Love Like This Again. **165m/C VHS, Beta, LV.** Steve McQueen, Paul Newman, William Holden, Faye Dunaway, Fred Astaire, Jennifer Jones, Richard Chamberlain, Susan Blakely, O.J. Simpson, Robert Vaughn, Robert Wagner; ***D:*** John Guillermin, Irwin Allen; ***W:*** Stirling Silliphant; ***C:*** Joseph Biroc, Fred W. Koenekamp; ***M:*** John Williams. Academy Awards '74: Best Cinematography, Best Film Editing, Best Song ("We May Never Love Like This Again"); Golden Globe Awards '75: Best Supporting Actor (Astaire); Nominations: Academy Awards '74: Best Art Direction/Set Decoration, Best Picture, Best Sound, Best Supporting Actor (Astaire), Best Original Score. *FOX*

A Town Called Hell 🦴 *A Town Called Bastard* **1972 (R)** Two men hold an entire town hostage while looking for "Aguila," the Mexican revolutionary. Greed, evil, and violence take over. Shot in Spain. Whatever you call it, just stay out of it. **95m/C VHS, Beta.** *GB SP* Robert Shaw, Stella Stevens, Martin Landau, Telly Savalas, Fernando Rey; ***D:*** Robert Parrish. *GEM*

A Town Like Alice 🦴🦴½ **1985** An Australian miniseries based on a novel by Nevil Shute. The story follows women prisoners of war during WWII. Jean Paget is a British prisoner in the camps of Malaya when she meets and falls in love with a fellow prisoner, the rugged Australian, Joe. Separated by their captors, they reunite years later and try to see if their love has survived. Remake of a 1951 film of the same name that is also known as "Rape of Malaya." **301m/C VHS, Beta.** *AU* Bryan Brown, Helen Morse, Gordon Jackson; ***D:*** David Stevens. *SIG, NWV, IME*

Town that Dreaded Sundown 🦴🦴½ **1976 (R)** A mad killer is on the loose in a small Arkansas town. Based on a true story, this famous 1946 murder spree remains an unsolved mystery. **90m/C VHS, Beta.** Ben Johnson, Andrew Prine, Dawn Wells; ***D:*** Charles B. Pierce. *WAR, OM*

The Toxic Avenger 🦴½ **1986 (R)** Tongue-in-cheek, cult fave has 98-pound weakling fall into barrel of toxic waste to emerge as a lumbering, bloodthirsty hulk of sludge and mire. He falls for a blind babe and sets out to do good (and get revenge). Billed as "The first Super-Hero from New Jersey." Two sequels followed: "Toxic Avenger Part II" and "Toxic Avenger Part III: The Last Temptation of Toxie." **90m/C VHS, Beta, LV.** Mitchell Cohen, Andree Maranda, Jennifer Baptist, Robert Prichard, Cindy Manion; ***D:*** Michael Herz, Lloyd (Samuel Weil) Kaufman; ***W:*** Joe Ritter. *VES, LIV*

The Toxic Avenger, Part 2 🦴½ **1989 (R)** Sequel to "Toxic Avenger." Hulky slimer targets Japanese corporations that built toxic chemical dump in Tromaville. Followed by "Toxic Avenger Part III: The Last Temptation of Toxie." **90m/C VHS, Beta, LV.** Ron Fazio, Phoebe Legere, Rick Collins, John Altamura; ***D:*** Michael Herz, Lloyd (Samuel Weil) Kaufman; ***W:*** Lloyd (Samuel Weil) Kaufman, Gay Partington Terry. *WAR*

The Toxic Avenger, Part 3: The Last Temptation of Toxie 🦴½ **1989 (R)** Unemployed superhero is tempted to sell out to greedy capitalists when his cutie Claire needs an eye operation. Also available in an unrated version. **102m/C VHS.** Ron Fazio, Phoebe Legere, John Altamura, Rick Collins, Lisa Gaye, Jessica Dublin; ***D:*** Michael Herz, Lloyd (Samuel Weil) Kaufman; ***W:*** Lloyd (Samuel Weil) Kaufman, Gay Partington Terry. *VES, LIV*

Toxic Zombies 🦴 **1989** Pot farmers become crazy cannibals when the marijuana is sprayed with an untested chemical. **90m/C VHS, Beta.** *NO*

The Toy 🦴½ **1982 (PG)** Penniless reporter finds himself the new "toy" of the spoiled son of a multimillionaire oil man. Unfortunate casting of Pryor as the toy owned by Gleason, with heavy-handed lecturing about earning friends. Slow and terrible remake of the Pierre Richard comedy "Le Jouet." **99m/C VHS, Beta, LV, 8mm.** Richard Pryor, Jackie Gleason, Ned Beatty, Wilfrid Hyde-White; ***D:*** Richard Donner. *COL*

Toy Soldiers 🦴½ **1984 (R)** A group of college students are held for ransom in a war-torn Central American country. When they escape, they join forces with a seasoned mercenary who leads them as a vigilante force. **85m/C VHS, Beta, LV.** Cleavon Little, Jason Miller, Tim Robbins, Tracy Scoggins; ***D:*** David Fisher. *NWV, VTR*

Toy Soldiers 🦴🦴 **1991 (R)** This unlikely action tale stops short of being laughable but still has a fair share of silliness. South American narco-terrorists seize an exclusive boys' school. The mischievous students turn their talent for practical jokes to resistance-fighting. Orbach has an uncredited cameo. Based on a novel by William P. Kennedy. **104m/C VHS, Beta, LV, 8mm.** Sean Astin, Wil Wheaton, Keith Coogan, Andrew Divoff, Denholm Elliott, Louis Gossett Jr.; ***Cameos:*** Jerry Orbach; ***D:*** Dan Petrie Jr.; ***W:*** Dan Petrie Jr.; ***M:*** Robert Folk. *COL*

Toy Story 🦴🦴🦴🦴 **1995 (G)** First feature length, wholly computer animated film confirms what we suspected all along—toys do have lives of their own when we're not around. Pull-string cowboy Woody (Hanks), as favorite toy, presides over his fellow playthings in Andy's room. Enter new toy on the block, Buzz Lightyear (Allen), a space ranger action figure who thinks he's real. Jealous Woody and his delusional, high-tech companion soon find themselves in the outside world, where they must join forces to survive. Funny, intelligent script and voice characterizations that rival many live-action movies in depth and emotion. All this, and Don Rickles berating an actual hockey puck. **80m/C VHS.** ***D:*** John Lasseter; ***W:*** Joss Whedon, Joel Cohen, Alec Sokolow; ***M:*** Randy Newman; ***V:*** Tom Hanks, Tim Allen, Annie Potts, John Ratzenberger, Wallace Shawn, Jim Varney, Don Rickles, John Morris, R. Lee Ermey, Laurie Metcalf, Erik von Detten. Nominations: Academy Awards '95: Best Screenplay, Best Song ("You've Got a Friend"), Best Score; Golden Globe Awards '96: Best Film—Musical/Comedy, Best Song ("You Got a Friend in Me"). *TOU*

Toys 🦴½ **1992 (PG-13)** Diappointingly earnest comedy about Leslie (Williams), the whimsical son of a toy manufacturer who must fight to keep the playful spirit of the factory alive after it passes into the hands of his deranged uncle (Gambon). This uncle is a general who attempts to transform the factory into an armaments plant. Leslie receives assistance in this battle from his sister Alsatia (Cusack) and his cousin Patrick (L.L. Cool J). Flat characters; generally falls short by trying too hard to send a message to viewers about the folly of war. Does have extremely vivid and intriguing visuals and special effects. **121m/C VHS.** Robin Williams, Joan Cusack, Michael Gambon, L.L. Cool J., Robin Wright; ***Cameos:*** Donald O'Connor; ***D:*** Barry

Levinson; **W:** Valerie Curtin, Barry Levinson. Nominations: Academy Awards '92: Best Art Direction/Set Decoration, Best Costume Design. *FXV*

Toys in the Attic ☠☠½ **1963** A man returns to his home in New Orleans with his child bride, where they will live with his two impoverished, spinster sisters. Toned-down version of the Lillian Hellman play. **88m/B VHS.** Dean Martin, Geraldine Page, Yvette Mimieux, Wendy Hiller, Gene Tierney, Nan Martin, Larry Gates, Frank Silvera; **D:** George Roy Hill; **W:** James Poe; **C:** Joseph Biroc. Nominations: Academy Awards '63: Best Costume Design (B & W). *MGM*

Traces of Red ☠☠ **1992 (R)** Set in affluent Palm Beach, and filled with dead bodies, colorful suspects, and red herrings. The complex plot, often so serious it's funny, leads viewers through a convoluted series of events. Cop Jack Dobson (Belushi) is found dead in the opening scene; in homage to "Sunset Boulevard," his corpse acts as the narrator, a vehicle which unfortunately doesn't work as well here. He promises to recount the events leading up to his death which circle around a series of murders, and the people in his life who are possible suspects. Although Belushi's performance is average, Goldwyn, as Dobson's partner, shows off the talent he displayed in "Ghost." **105m/C VHS, LV.** James Belushi, Lorraine Bracco, Tony Goldwyn, William Russ, Michelle Joyner, Joe Lisi, Jim Piddock; **D:** Andy Wolk; **M:** Graeme Revell. *HBO*

Track of the Moonbeast ☠☠ **1976** An American Indian uses mythology to capture the Moonbeast, a lizard-like creature that is roaming the deserts of New Mexico. **90m/C VHS, Beta.** Chase Cordell, Donna Leigh Drake; **D:** Richard Ashe. *PSM*

Track of the Vampire ☠½ *Blood Bath* **1966** Half an hour of leftover footage from a Yugoslavian vampire movie stuck into the story of a California painter who kills his models. Gripping and atmospheric, but disjointed. **80m/B VHS.** *YU* William Campbell, Jonathan Haze, Sid Haig, Marissa Mathes, Lori Saunders, Sandra Knight; **D:** Stephanie Rothman, Jack Hill. *SNC, GNS*

Track 29 ☠½ **1988 (R)** A confusing black comedy about a lonely woman, her husband who has a model train fetish, and a stranger who claims to be her son. Filmed in North Carolina. **90m/C VHS.** Theresa Russell, Gary Oldman, Christopher Lloyd, Colleen Camp, Sandra Bernhard, Seymour Cassel, Leon Rippy, Vance Colvig; **D:** Nicolas Roeg; **W:** Dennis Potter. *MGM, CAN*

The Tracker ☠☠½ *Dead or Alive* **1988** HBO western about a retired gunman/tracker who must again take up arms. His college-educated son joins him as he searches for a murdering religious fanatic. Fairly decent for the genre. Made for cable television. **102m/C VHS, Beta.** Kris Kristofferson, Scott Wilson, Mark Moses, David Huddleston, John Quade, Don Swayze, Brynn Thayer; **D:** John Guillermin. *HBO, WAR*

The Trackers ☠½ **1971** A frontier man searches for the people who kidnapped his daughter and killed his son. He is joined by a cocky black tracker. Borgnine brings strength to his character as the rancher seeking revenge. Made for television. **73m/C VHS, Beta.** Sammy Davis Jr., Ernest Borgnine, Julie Adams, Connie Kreski, Jim Davis; **D:** Earl Bellamy. *FOX*

Tracks ☠½ **1976 (R)** Vietnam veteran accompanies the body of a buddy on a long train ride home. He starts suffering flashbacks from the war and begins to think some of the passengers are out to get him. **90m/C VHS, Beta.** Dennis Hopper, Dean Stockwell, Taryn Power; **D:** Henry Jaglom; **W:** Henry Jaglom. *PAR*

Tracks of a Killer ☠☠ **1995 (R)** David and Clair Hawker are vacationing at an isolated winter retreat that's invaded by a killer. **100m/C VHS, LV.** Kelly Le Brock, James Brolin, Wolf Larson, Courtney Taylor, George Touliatos; **D:** Harvey Frost; **W:** Michael Cooney; **C:** Bruce Worrall; **M:** Barron Abramovitch. *LIV*

Trade Off ☠☠ **1995 (R)** Beautiful, unhappily married Jackie (Russell) seduces equally miserable married businessman Thomas (Baldwin) and jokes about getting rid of their respective spouses. Then Thomas' wife is killed in a car crash and Thomas learns Jackie caused the "accident." He should have watched "Strangers on a Train" to see where trading murders can get you. **92m/C VHS, LV.** Theresa Russell, Adam Baldwin, Megan Gallagher, Barry Primus, Pat Skipper; **D:** Andrew Lane. *REP*

Trade Secrets ☠☠ **199?** Special investigator Jerry Morrison is assigned to probe the mysterious death of an heiress to a wine fortune. His investigation leads to the secrets and private fantasies of the woman's family and friends. **91m/C VHS.** Sam Waterston, Marisa Berenson, Lauren Hutton, Arielle Dombasle; **D:** Claude Feraldo; **W:** Claude Feraldo. *TRI*

Trader Horn ☠☠½ **1931** Early talkie was the first Hollywood picture to be filmed in Africa. Carey and Renaldo are traders who tangle with a native tribe while searching for the long-lost daughter of a missionary, who turns out to be a tribal goddess. Based on a novel by Alfred Aloysius Horn and Ethelreda Lewis. Boring remake in 1973. **105m/B VHS.** Harry Carey Sr., Duncan Renaldo, Edwina Booth, Sir C. Aubrey Smith, Mutia Omoolu, Olive Golden Carey; **D:** Woodbridge S. Van Dyke; **W:** Cyril Hume, Richard Schayer, Dale Van Every, John Thomas Neville; **C:** Clyde De Vinna. Nominations: Academy Awards '31: Best Picture. *MGM*

Trader Tom of the China Seas **1954** A young island trader and a shipwrecked beauty get involved in espionage while helping the UN to safeguard the Asian corridor. A 12-part serial on two cassettes. **167m/B VHS.** Harry Lauter, Aline Towne, Lyle Talbot, Fred Graham. *REP*

Trading Hearts ☠☠ **1987 (PG)** Over-the-hill baseball player falls for an unsuccessful singer and single mom at a Florida training camp set in the 1950s. **88m/C VHS, Beta, LV.** Beverly D'Angelo, Raul Julia, Jerry Lewis, Parris Buckner, Robert Gwaltney; **D:** Neil Leifer; **W:** Frank Deford. *LIV*

Trading Mom ☠☠½ **1994 (PG)** Harried single parent Spacek is erased from the lives of her three kids, who decide they want a parent who's more fun. So, thanks to some magic, they head off to the Mommy Mart to try out a trio of bizarre choices. This gives Spacek a chance at three more roles before the kids come to their senses. Based on "The Mommy Market" by Nancy Brelis; directorial debut for daughter Tia. **82m/C VHS, LV.** Sissy Spacek, Anna Chlumsky, Aaron Michael Metchik, Asher Metchik, Maureen Stapleton; **D:** Tia Brelis; **W:** Tia Brelis; **M:** David Kitay. *VMK*

Trading Places ☠☠½ **1983 (R)** Two elderly businessmen wager that environment is more important than heredity in creating a successful life, using a rich nephew and an unemployed street hustler as guinea pigs. Curtis is winning as a hooker-with-a-heart-of-gold who helps the hapless Aykroyd. Oft-told tale succeeds thanks to strong cast. Murphy's second screen appearance. **118m/C VHS, Beta, LV, 8mm.** Eddie Murphy, Dan Aykroyd, Jamie Lee Curtis, Ralph Bellamy, Don Ameche, Denholm Elliott, Paul Gleason, James Belushi; **D:** John Landis; **W:** Herschel Weingrod, Timothy Harris; **M:** Elmer Bernstein. British Academy Awards '83: Best Supporting Actor (Elliott), Best Supporting Actress (Curtis); Nominations: Academy Awards '83: Best Original Score. *PAR*

Traenen in Florenz ☠ *Tears in Florence* **1984** A woman involved in a car accident winds up falling in love with the man who injured her, only to discover later that they are actually brother and sister, long separated. In German with English subtitles. **90m/C VHS, Beta.** *GE* **D:** Marianne Schafer. *VCD, APD, GLV*

Traffic ☠☠½ **1971** Eccentric auto designer Monsieur Hulot tries to transport his latest contraption from Paris to Amsterdam for an international auto show. As usual, everything goes wrong. Tati's last feature film and his fifth to feature Hulot. French with subtitles. **89m/C VHS.** *FR* Jacques Tati, Maria Kimberly, Marcel Fraval; **D:** Jacques Tati. *HMV*

Traffic in Souls ☠☠☠ **1913** A silent melodrama dealing with white slavery. Immigrants and gullible country girls are lured into brothels where they are trapped with no hope of escape until, in a hail of bullets, the police raid the dens of vice and rescue them. **74m/B VHS, Beta.** Matt Moore, Jane Gail, William Welsh; **D:** George Tucker. *GPV, KIV*

Traffic Jam ☠☠½ *Jutai* **1991** A light comedy about a Japanese family's attempt to travel on a holiday weekend. Tokyo couple and their two young children decide to visit the husband's family who happen to live on a distant island. Naturally, traffic's horrendous, they have very little time, and things continuously go wrong. Japanese with subtitles. **108m/C VHS.** *JP* Kenichi Hagiwara, Hitomi Kuroki, Ayako Takarada, Shingo Yazawa, Eiji Okada; **D:** Mitsuo Kurotsuchi. *WBF*

Traffik ☠☠☠ **1990** A tense, unnerving look at the international world of heroin smuggling. The British drama follows the lives of three men involved in the drug trade: a farmer in the poppy fields of Pakistan, a drug smuggler in Hamburg, and a Tory cabinet minister who heads his government's anti-drug cabinet and then comes to realize his own daughter is an addict. On three cassettes. Made for British television. **360m/C VHS.** *GB* Lindsay Duncan, Bill Paterson, Jamal Shah, Talat Hussain, Fritz Muller-Scherz, Julia Ormond; **D:** Alastair Reid. *SIG, TVC, PBS*

The Tragedy of a Ridiculous Man ☠☠ *La Tragedia di un Uomo Ridicolo* **1981 (PG)** The missing son of an Italian cheese manufacturer may or may not have been kidnapped by terrorists. Lesser Bertolucci effort may or may not have a point. In Italian with English subtitles. **116m/C VHS.** *IT* Ugo Tognazzi, Anouk Aimee, Victor Cavallo, Ricardo Tognazzi, Laura Morante; **D:** Bernardo Bertolucci; **W:** Bernardo Bertolucci; **C:** Carlo DiPalma; **M:** Ennio Morricone. Cannes Film Festival '81: Best Actor (Tognazzi); Nominations: Cannes Film Festival '81: Best Film. *WAR, FCT, INJ*

Tragedy of Flight 103: The Inside Story ☠☠☠ **1991 (PG)** Dramatization of the events surrounding the destruction of Pan Am flight 103 over Lockerbie, Scotland, due to a terrorist-planted bomb. **89m/C VHS.** Ned Beatty, Peter Boyle, Vincent Gardenia, Timothy West, Michael Wincott, Harry Ditson, Aharon Ipale, John Shrapnel; **D:** Leslie Woodhead. *MGM*

Trahir ☠☠☠ *Betrayal* **1993** In 1948 Romania journalist George Vlaicu (Leysen) writes a controversial article on the death of democracy in his country and is imprisoned for 11 years. In 1959 he's offered a deal, go free as long as he talks weekly to a police inspector (Repan). He begins a new career as a poet and marries his former typist, Laura (Perrier), but after a tragedy learns that his meetings with the inspector aren't as innocuous as they've seemed. Excellent performances and a cold look at how a police state is able to control its artists and writers. Filmed primarily in Romania. Director Mihaileanu's first feature film. French with subtitles. **104m/C VHS.** *FR SI SP RO* Johan Leysen, Mireille Perrier, Alexandru Repan, Razvan Vasilescu, Maia Morgenstern, Radu Beligan; **D:** Radu Mihaileanu; **W:** Laurent Moussard, Radu Mihaileanu; **M:** Temistocle Popa. Montreal World Film Festival '93: Best Actor (Leysen), Best Film. *NYR*

Trail Beyond ☠½ **1934** A cowboy and his sidekick go on the trek to the northwest to find a girl and a gold mine. **57m/B VHS.** John Wayne, Noah Beery Sr., Verna Hillie; **D:** Robert North Bradbury. *COL, REP, NOS*

Trail Drive ☠ **1935** Adventures of a cowboy during a big cattle drive. **63m/B VHS, Beta.** Ken Maynard. *NOS, VCN, CAB*

Trail of Robin Hood ☠☠½ **1950** Rogers sees to it that poor families get Christmas trees, in spite of the fact that a big business wants to raise the prices. Features a number of western stars, including Holt playing himself. **67m/C VHS.** Roy Rogers, Penny Edwards, Gordon Jones, Jack Holt, Emory Parnell, Rex Allen, Allan "Rocky" Lane, Clifton Young, Monte Hale, Kermit Maynard, Tom Keene, Ray Corrigan, William Farnum; **D:** William Witney. *REP*

Trail of Terror ☠ **1935** G-Man poses as an escaped convict to get the goods on a gang. **60m/B VHS, Beta, LV.** Bob Steele, Beth Marion, Forrest Taylor, Charles "Blackie" King, Lloyd Ingraham, Charles French; **D:** Robert North Bradbury. *GPV*

Trail of the Hawk ☠ **1937** Saga of frontier justice and love on the plains. **50m/B VHS, Beta.** Yancey Lane, Betty Jordan, Dick Jones; **D:** Edward Dmytryk. *NOS, DVT, RXM*

Trail of the Mounties 🦴 **1947** A Mountie gallops smack into a murdering slew of fur thieves. **41m/B VHS, Beta, LV.** Donald (Don "Red") Barry, Robert Lowery, Tom Neal, Russell Hayden. *NO*

Trail of the Pink Panther 🦴🦴 **1982 (PG)** The sixth in Sellers' "Pink Panther" series. Inspector Clouseau disappears while he is searching for the diamond known as the Pink Panther. Notable because it was released after Sellers' death, using clips from previous movies to fill in gaps. Followed by "Curse of the Pink Panther." **97m/C VHS, Beta, LV.** Peter Sellers, David Niven, Herbert Lom, Capucine, Burt Kwouk, Robert Wagner, Robert Loggia; ***D:*** Blake Edwards; ***W:*** Blake Edwards, Frank Waldman; ***M:*** Henry Mancini. *MGM*

Trail of the Silver Spurs 🦴½ **1941** A lone man remaining in a ghost town discovers gold and becomes rich. Part of the "Range Busters" series. **57m/B VHS.** Ray Corrigan, John "Dusty" King, Max Terhune, I. Stanford Jolley, Dorothy Short; ***D:*** S. Roy Luby. *NOS, DVT*

Trail Riders 🦴½ **1942** The Range Busters set a trap to capture a gang of outlaws who killed the son of the town marshal during a bank robbery. Part of the "Range Busters" series. **55m/B VHS, Beta.** John "Dusty" King, David Sharpe, Max Terhune, Evelyn Finley, Forrest Taylor, Charles "Blackie" King. *NOS, VYY, DVT*

Trail Street 🦴½ **1947** Scott is Bat Masterson, the western hero. He aids the struggle of Kansans as they conquer the land and local ranchers. **84m/B VHS, Beta.** Randolph Scott, Robert Ryan, Anne Jeffreys, George "Gabby" Hayes, Madge Meredith, Jason Robards Sr.; ***D:*** Ray Enright. *CCB, MED*

Trailin' 🦴🦴½ **1921** Mix stars as a cowboy in search of his parentage. Based on the Max Brand story. **58m/B VHS.** Tom Mix, Eva Novak, James Gordon; ***D:*** Lynn F. Reynolds. *GPV*

Trailing Double Trouble 🦴½ **1940** A corrupt attorney murders a rancher to pursue a business scheme. Three ranch hands kidnap the rancher's orphaned baby to keep her safe from the attorney. The second entry in the "Range Busters" series. **56m/B VHS, Beta.** Ray Corrigan, John "Dusty" King, Max Terhune. *NOS, VDM, VYY*

Trailing Trouble 🦴½ **1930** Gibson is a cowpoke who gets robbed of the money he received for a cattle sale. When he rescues a Chinese girl from danger she helps him recover the money. He also has to battle a rival for his girlfriend's affections. He should have battled for a better script. **58m/B VHS.** Hoot Gibson, Margaret Quimby, Peter Morrison, Olive Young, William McCall; ***D:*** Arthur Rosson. *GPV, VYY, DVT*

Trails West 🦴 **194?** Western adventure starring Steele. **?m/B VHS, Beta.** Bob Steele. *VCN*

The Train 🦴🦴🦴🦴 *Le Train; Il Treno* **1965** During the German occupation of Paris in 1944, a German colonel (Scofield) is ordered to ransack the city of its art treasures and put them on a train bound for Germany. Word gets to the French Resistance who then persuade the train inspector (Lancaster) to sabotage the train. A battle of wills ensues between Scofield and Lancaster as each becomes increasingly obsessed in outwitting the other—though the cost to all turns out to be as irreplaceable as the art itself. Filmed on location in France. Frankenheimer used real locomotives, rather than models, throughout the film, even in the spectacular crash sequences. **133m/C VHS, LV.** Burt Lancaster, Paul Scofield, Jeanne Moreau, Michel Simon, Suzanne Flon, Wolfgang Preiss, Albert Remy; ***D:*** John Frankenheimer; ***W:*** Frank Davis, Walter Bernstein; ***M:*** Maurice Jarre. Nominations: Academy Awards '65: Best Story & Screenplay. *MGM*

The Train Killer 🦴 **1983** A mad Hungarian is bent on destroying the Orient Express. **90m/C VHS, Beta.** Michael Sarrazin; ***D:*** Sandor Simo. *VES*

Train of Events 🦴🦴½ **1949** An interesting look at lives affected by a train wreck just outside London, taking the form of four short episodes. Three are frankly somber, depressing tales of the ill-fated train driver, a murderer and an escaped prisoner-of-war. The fourth segment is a refreshingly lighthearted piece about romantic jealousies in a traveling orchestra. A precursor to the later swarm of crass disaster movies, except here emphasis is on character over special effects. **89m/B VHS.** Jack Warner, Gladys Henson, Susan Shaw, Patric Doonan, Miles Malleson, Leslie Phillips, Joan Dowling, Laurence Payne, Valerie Hobson, John Clements, Peter Finch, Mary Morris, Laurence Naismith, Michael Hordern; ***D:*** Sidney Cole, Basil Dearden, Charles Crichton. *NOS, FCT*

Train Robbers 🦴🦴 **1973 (PG)** A widow employs the services of three cowboys to help her recover some stolen gold in order to clear her late husband's name. At least that's what she says. **92m/C VHS, Beta, LV.** John Wayne, Ann-Margret, Rod Taylor, Ben Johnson, Christopher George, Ricardo Montalban, Bobby Vinton, Jerry Gatlin; ***D:*** Burt Kennedy; ***W:*** Burt Kennedy; ***C:*** William Clothier. *WAR*

Train Station Pickups 🦴 **197?** Trashy film about young girls who hook at a local train depot, until something goes wrong. **96m/C VHS.** Marco Knoger, Katja Carrol, Ingeborg Steinbach, Benjamin Carwath; ***D:*** Walter Boos. *ACN*

Train to Hollywood 🦴🦴🦴 **1986** Marilyn Monroe-obsessed young Polish girl daydreams incessantly as she works on dining car. Funny and surreal. Polish dialogue with English subtitles. **96m/C VHS.** *PL* ***D:*** Radoslaw Piwowarski. *FCT*

Train to Tombstone 🦴 **1950** A train running from Albuquerque to Tombstone carries a motley mob of the usual characters. **60m/B VHS, Beta, LV.** Donald (Don "Red") Barry, Judith Allen, Robert Lowery, Tom Neal; ***D:*** Charles F. Reisner. *NO*

Trained to Kill 🦴½ **1988** Two brothers seek revenge on the mean streets of L.A. **94m/C VHS, LV.** Frank Zagarino, Glen Eaton, Lisa Aliff, Marshall Teague, Robert Z'Dar, Henry Silva, Arlene Golonka, Ron O'Neal, Harold Diamond, Chuck Connors; ***D:*** H. Kaye Dyal; ***W:*** H. Kaye Dyal, Arthur Webb. *PSM*

Trained to Kill, U.S.A. 🦴½ **1983 (R)** Vietnam veteran relives his war experiences when a gang of terrorists threaten his hometown. **88m/C VHS, Beta.** Stephen Sander, Heidi Vaughn, Rockne Tarkington. *NO*

Trainspotting 🦴🦴🦴 **1995 (R)** From the same team who offered the violently comedic "Shallow Grave," comes an equally destructive look at a group of Edinburgh junkies and losers. Heroin-user Mark Renton (McGregor) once again decides to get off junk but to do so he has to get away from his friends: knife-wielding psycho Begbie (Carlyle), Sick Boy (Miller), Spud (Bremner), and Tommy (McKidd). He heads for a semi-respectable life in London but Begbie and Spud wind up involving him in a serious money drug deal that spells trouble. Strong fantasy visuals depict drug highs and lows while heavy Scottish accents (and humor) may prove difficult. Based on the 1993 cult novel by Irvine Welsh. **94m/C VHS.** *GB* Ewan McGregor, Ewen Bremmer, Jonny Lee Miller, Robert Carlyle, Kevin McKidd, Kelly Macdonald, Shirley Henderson, Pauline Lynch; ***D:*** Danny Boyle; ***W:*** John Hodge; ***C:*** Brian Tufano. British Academy Awards '95: Best Adapted Screenplay; Nominations: British Academy Awards '95: Best Film. *NYR*

The Traitor 🦴½ **1936** Undercover man joins a gang of bandits. **57m/B VHS, Beta.** Tim McCoy; ***D:*** Sam Newfield. *NOS, VCI, VCN*

Tramp & a Woman 🦴🦴 **1915** Two shorts made for the Essanay Company in 1915 which offer the Little Tramp wooing Purviance in typical Chaplin fashion. Silent with musical score. **45m/B VHS, Beta.** Charlie Chaplin, Edna Purviance. *VYY*

Tramp at the Door 🦴🦴½ **1987** Delightful drama about a wandering, magical man who enters the lives of an embittered family. He helps them sort the skeletons in their closets, and works wonders on their relationships. **81m/C VHS, Beta.** Ed McNamara, August Schellenberg, Monique Mercure, Eric Peterson; ***D:*** Allen Kroeker. *NO*

Tramplers 🦴 **1966** A rebel father and son split over the hanging of a Yankee during the Civil War. Italian made spaghetti western without much plot and lots of gratuitous gunplay. **103m/C VHS, Beta.** *IT* Joseph Cotten, Gordon Scott; ***D:*** Albert Band, Mario Sequi. *COL, SUE, HHE*

Trancers 🦴🦴 *Future Cop* **1984 (PG-13)** A time-traveling cult from the future goes back in time to 1985 to meddle with fate. Only Jack Deth, defender of justice, can save mankind. Low-budget "Blade Runner." Followed by two sequels. **76m/C VHS, Beta, LV.** Tim Thomerson, Michael Stefoni, Helen Hunt, Art LaFleur, Telma Hopkins; ***D:*** Charles Band; ***W:*** Danny Bilson. *LIV, VES*

Trancers 2: The Return of Jack Deth 🦴 **1990 (R)** Retro cop is back from the future again, but seems to have lost his wit and nerve in between sequels. Ward is miscast and the pacing undermines whatever suspense that might have been. **85m/C VHS, Beta, LV.** Tim Thomerson, Helen Hunt, Megan Ward, Biff Manard, Martine Beswick, Jeffrey Combs, Barbara Crampton, Richard Lynch; ***D:*** Charles Band. *PAR*

Trancers 3: Deth Lives 🦴½ **1992 (R)** In the third film of the "Trancers" series, time-traveling cop Jack Deth fights the deadliest form of government-sponsored Trancer yet—it has a brain. **83m/C VHS, Beta, LV.** Tim Thomerson, Melanie Smith, Andrew (Andy) Robinson, Tony Pierce, Dawn Ann Billings, Helen Hunt, Megan Ward, Stephen Macht, Telma Hopkins; ***D:*** C. Courtney Joyner; ***W:*** C. Courtney Joyner; ***M:*** Richard Band. *PAR*

Trancers 4: Jack of Swords 🦴🦴½ **1993 (R)** Time-traveling cop Jack Deth finds himself in a mystical new dimension where the blooksucking Trancers have enslaved the local population as feeders. If Jack expects to conquer he'll first need to survive an ancient wizard's prophecy of death. Filmed on location in Romania. **74m/C VHS, Beta.** Tim Thomerson, Stacie Randall, Ty Miller, Terri Ivens, Mark Arnold, Clare Hartley, Alan Oppenheimer, Stephen Macht, David Nutter; ***W:*** Peter David; ***M:*** Gary Fry. *PAR*

Trancers 5: Sudden Deth 🦴🦴½ **1994 (R)** Irreverant time-travelling cop Jack Deth (Thomerson) returns to help the Tunnel Rats occupy the castle of Caliban. But the evil Lord Caliban is resurrected and his only desire is to destroy Jack. This is supposedly the final chapter of Deth's saga. **73m/C VHS, Beta.** Tim Thomerson, Stacie Randall, Ty Miller, Terri Ivens, Mark Arnold, Clare Hartley, Alan Oppenheimer, Jeff Moldovan, Lochlyn Munro, Stephen Macht; ***D:*** David Nutter; ***W:*** Peter David; ***M:*** Gary Fry. *PAR*

Transatlantic Merry-Go-Round 🦴🦴 **1934** An early semi-musical mystery about an eclectic assortment of passengers aboard a luxury liner. ♫It Was Sweet of You; Rock and Roll; Moon Over Monte Carlo; Oh Leo, It's Love; If I Had a Million Dollars. **90m/B VHS, Beta.** Jack Benny, Gene Raymond, Nancy Carroll, Boswell Sisters, Ralph Morgan, Sidney Blackmer; ***D:*** Ben Stoloff. *NO*

Transatlantic Tunnel 🦴🦴½ *The Tunnel* **1935** An undersea tunnel from England to America is attempted, despite financial trickery and undersea disasters. Made with futuristic sets which were advanced for their time. **94m/B VHS, Beta.** *GB* Richard Dix, Leslie Banks, Madge Evans, Helen Vinson, Sir C. Aubrey Smith, George Arliss, Walter Huston; ***D:*** Maurice Elvey. *VYY, SNC, HHT*

Transformations 🦴½ **1988 (R)** An interplanetary pilot battles a deadly virus that threatens life throughout the universe. Obscure space jetsam. **84m/C VHS, LV.** Rex Smith, Patrick Macnee, Lisa Langlois, Christopher Neame; ***D:*** Jay Kamen. *VTR*

Transformers: The Movie 🦴 **1986 (G)** A full-length animated film featuring the universe-defending robots fighting the powers of evil. These robots began life as real toys, so there's some marketing going on. **85m/C VHS, Beta.** ***D:*** Nelson Shin; ***V:*** Orson Welles, Eric Idle, Judd Nelson, Leonard Nimoy, Robert Stack. *FHE*

Transmutations 🦴 *Underworld* **1985 (R)** Mad scientist Elliott develops a mind-altering drug which is tested by a group of young people. They find out too late that the drug causes horrible facial disfigurement, as well as leaving them hopelessly addicted, and they hide out underground, plotting their revenge. Cowper, a young hooker in the group, turns out to be immune to the side effects and works with her ex-mobster boss to get help. Confusing. Barker co-scripted from one of his stories but later disowned the film. **103m/C VHS, Beta, LV.** *GB* Denholm Elliott, Steven Berkoff, Miranda Richardson, Nicola Cowper, Larry Lamb, Art Malik, Ingrid Pitt, Irina Brook, Paul Brown; ***D:*** George Pavlou; ***W:*** James Caplin, Clive Barker. *LIV, VES*

Transport from Paradise 🦴🦴½ *Transport Z Raje* **1965** Follows the story of Jewish life in the Terezin ghetto before the inhabitants are imprisoned and shipped off to Auschwitz as part of Hitler's final solution. Based on a novel by Arnold Lustig. In Czech with English subtitles. **93m/B VHS, Beta.** *CZ* ***D:*** Zbynek Brynych. *FCT*

Transylvania 6-5000 🦴 **1985 (PG)** Agreeably stupid horror spoof about two klutzy reporters who stumble into modern-day Transylvania and encounter an array of comedic creatures. Shot in Yugoslavia. **93m/C VHS, Beta, LV.** Jeff Goldblum, Joseph Bologna, Ed Begley Jr., Carol Kane, John Byner, Geena Davis, Jeffrey Jones, Norman Fell; ***D:*** Rudy DeLuca; ***W:*** Rudy DeLuca. *VTR, NWV*

Transylvania Twist 🦴½ **1989 (PG-13)** Moronic comedy about vampires, teenage vampire hunters and half-naked babes. **90m/C VHS, Beta.** Robert Vaughn, Teri Copley, Steve Altman, Ace Mask, Angus Scrimm, Jay Robinson, Brinke Stevens; ***D:*** Jim Wynorski; ***W:*** R.J. Robertson. *MGM*

The Trap 🦴🦴 **1922** Chaney kidnaps the son of a man he's sent to prison on false charges. Rather than give up the kid when the man is released, he plans a trap. **?m/C VHS.** Lon Chaney Sr., Alan Hale, Irene Rich. *SNC, GVV*

The Trap 🦴🦴½ *The Baited Trap* **1959** In trying to escape justice, a ruthless crime syndicate boss holds a small desert town in a grip of fear. **84m/C VHS, Beta.** Richard Widmark, Tina Louise, Lee J. Cobb, Earl Holliman, Lorne Greene, Carl Benton Reid; ***D:*** Norman Panama; ***W:*** Norman Panama. *BAR*

Trap 🦴🦴 *L'Aventure Sauvage* **1966** A trapper buys a mute girl as his wife. Together they try to make a life for themselves in the Canadian wilderness. Fine telling of interesting western tale. Unusual and realistic. **106m/C VHS, Beta.** *GB CA* Rita Tushingham, Oliver Reed, Rex Sevenoaks; ***D:*** Sidney Hayers; ***C:*** Robert Krasker. *NO*

Trap on Cougar Mountain 🦴 **1972 (G)** A young boy begins a crusade to save his animal friends from the traps and bullets of hunters. **97m/C VHS, Beta, LV.** Erik Larsen, Keith Larsen, Karen Steele; ***D:*** Keith Larsen. *NWV, VTR*

Trap Them & Kill Them 🦴 **1984** American group traveling through the Amazon jungle encounter a terrifying aborigine tribe. Point of trip undergoes considerable reexamination. **90m/C VHS, Beta.** Gabriele Tinti, Susan Scott, Donald O'Brien. *TWE*

Trapeze 🦴🦴🦴 **1956** Lancaster is a former trapeze artist, now lame from a triple somersault accident. Curtis, the son of an old friend, wants Lancaster to teach him the routine. Lollobrigida, an aerial acrobat, is interested in both men. Exquisite European locations, fine camera work. The actors perform their own stunts. **105m/C VHS, Beta, LV.** Burt Lancaster, Tony Curtis, Gina Lollobrigida, Katy Jurado, Thomas Gomez; ***D:*** Carol Reed; ***C:*** Robert Krasker; ***M:*** Malcolm Arnold. *MGM, FOX*

Trapped 🦴🦴½ **1949** Semi-documentary crime drama shows in semi-documentary style how the feds hunt down a gang of counterfeiters by springing one of their comrades from prison. Well-paced, suspenseful and believable. **78m/B VHS.** Lloyd Bridges, Barbara Payton, John Hoyt, James Todd; ***D:*** Richard Fleischer. *NOS, DVT, HEG*

Trapped 🦴½ **1989 (R)** A woman working late in her high-rise office is stalked by a killer and must rely on her ingenuity to outwit him. Made-for-cable-television thriller. **93m/C VHS, Beta.** Kathleen Quinlan, Bruce Abbott, Katy Boyer, Ben Loggins; ***D:*** Fred Walton; ***W:*** Fred Walton. *MCA*

Trapped Alive 🦴½ **1993** Robin and Monica are abducted by three escaped convicts who want their car as a getaway vehicle. Trying to avoid a police roadblock the car crashes through the cover of a long-abandoned mine. When the group try to find their way out of the maze of tunnels they realize they're not down there alone. **92m/C VHS.** Alex Kubik, Elizabeth Kent, Michael Nash, Randolph Powell, Mark Witsken, Sullivan Hester, Laura Kallison, Cameron Mitchell; ***D:*** Leszek Burzynski; ***W:*** Leszek Burzynski. *AIP*

Trapped by the Mormons 🦴🦴 *The Mormon Peril* **1922** Mormons seduce innocent young girls to add to their harems. An interesting piece of paranoid propaganda. Silent with original organ music. **97m/B VHS, Beta, 8mm.** Evelyn Brent, Lewis Willoughby. *GPV, VYY, NOS*

Trapped In Paradise 🦴½ **1994 (PG-13)** Three bungling brothers make off with a bundle of cash from the Paradise—the town not the afterlife—bank on Christmas Eve. The locals, naive refugees from a Rockwell painting, don't recognize the buffoons as criminals, and reward their crime with hospitality that would make Frank Capra proud. Chase scenes and subplots abound as the boys spend what seems an eternity trying to make their getaway. Routine, humdrum comedy is hampered by an obvious plot. Watchable only because of Carvey, Lovitz, and Cage. **111m/C VHS, LV.** Nicolas Cage, Jon Lovitz, Dana Carvey, John Ashton, Madchen Amick, Donald Moffat, Richard Jenkins, Florence Stanley, Angela Paton, Vic Manni, Frank Pesce, Sean McCann, Paul Lazar, Richard B. Shull; ***D:*** George Gallo; ***W:*** George Gallo; ***M:*** Robert Folk. *FXV*

Trapped in Silence 🦴🦴 **1986** Young Sutherland, abused since childhood, stops speaking to protect himself mentally and physically. Psychologist Mason is determined to break down the walls to help him confront his pain. Interesting cameo by Silver as a gay counselor forced out of his job when his sexual preference is discovered. Mildly melodramatic made-for-TV message drama. **94m/C VHS.** Marsha Mason, Kiefer Sutherland, John Mahoney, Amy Wright; ***Cameos:*** Ron Silver; ***D:*** Michael Tuchner. *TTC*

Trapped in Space 🦴🦴½ **1994 (PG-13)** On a mission to Venus a space shuttle is damaged by a meteor strike, leaving only enough oxygen for one person. So, what's everyone else suppose to do? Based on a short story by Arthur C. Clarke. **87m/C VHS, Beta.** Jack Wagner, Jack Coleman, Craig Wasson, Sigrid Thornton, Kay Lenz; ***D:*** Arthur Seidelman; ***W:*** John Vincent Curtis, Melinda M. Snodgrass; ***M:*** Jay Gruska. *PAR*

Trapper County War 🦴 **1989 (R)** A city boy and a Vietnam vet band together to rescue a young woman held captive by a backwoods clan. **98m/C VHS, LV.** Robert Estes, Bo Hopkins, Ernie Hudson, Betsy Russell, Don Swayze; ***D:*** Worth Keeter. *REP*

Traps 🦴🦴½ **1993 (R)** Australian journalist Michael Duffield (Reynolds) and his English photographer wife Louise (Reeves) arrive for an assignment in 1950 French Indochina. Michael is to write about life on a French-owned rubber plantation, managed by Daniel (Frey), who lives with his rather peculiar daughter Viola (McKenzie). The plantation is troubled by the increasingly militant Viet-Minh rebels and it becomes clear that the four characters all have their own emotional difficulties to deal with, as well. Loosely adapted from the novel "Dreamhouse" by Kate Grenville. Feature film directing debut for Chan. **95m/C VHS.** *AU* Saskia Reeves, Robert Reynolds, Sami Frei, Jacqueline McKenzie; ***D:*** Pauline Chan; ***W:*** Pauline Chan, Robert Carter; ***C:*** Kevin Hayward; ***M:*** Douglas Stephen Rae. *NYR*

Trash 🦴🦴 **1970** Andy Warhol's profile of a depraved couple (Warhol-veteran Dallesandro and female impersonater Woodlawn) living in a lower east side basement and scouting the streets for food and drugs. Not for those easily offended by nymphomaniacs, junkies, lice, and the like; a must for fans of underground film and the cinema verite style. **110m/C VHS, Beta.** Joe Dallesandro, Holly Woodlawn, Jane Forth, Micael Sklar, Geri Miller, Bruce Pecheur; ***D:*** Paul Morrissey. *PAR*

Trauma 🦴½ **1962** A girl suffers amnesia after the trauma of witnessing her aunt's murder. She returns to the mansion years later to piece together what happened. A sometimes tedious psychological thriller. **93m/C VHS, Beta.** John Conte, Lynn Bari, Lorrie Richards, David Garner, Warren Kemmerling, William Bissell, Bond Blackman, William Justine; ***D:*** Robert M. Young. *VES*

Traveling Man 🦴🦴 **1989** A made-for-cable-television drama about a veteran traveling salesman who's assigned an eager young apprentice when his sales go down. Lithgow gives a great performance as the burnt-out traveling salesman. **105m/C VHS, Beta.** John Lithgow, Jonathan Silverman, Margaret Colin, John Glover; ***D:*** Irvin Kershner; ***M:*** Miles Goodman. *HBO*

Travelling North 🦴🦴 **1987 (PG-13)** A belligerent retiree falls in love with a divorcee and they move together to a rustic retreat. They have an idyllic existence until the man discovers he has a serious heart condition. Adaptation of David Williamson's play has fine performances. **97m/C VHS, Beta.** *AU* Leo McKern, Julia Blake; ***D:*** Carl Schultz; ***W:*** David Williamson. Australian Film Institute '87: Best Actor (McKern); Montreal World Film Festival '87: Best Actor (McKern). *NO*

Travels with My Aunt 🦴🦴½ **1972 (PG)** A banker leading a mundane life is taken on a wild, whirlwind tour of Europe by an eccentric woman claiming to be his aunt. Based on Graham Greene's best-selling novel. **109m/C LV.** Maggie Smith, Alec McCowen, Louis Gossett Jr., Robert Stephens, Cindy Williams; ***D:*** George Cukor; ***W:*** Jay Presson Allen. Academy Awards '72: Best Costume Design; Nominations: Academy Awards '72: Best Actress (Smith), Best Art Direction/Set Decoration, Best Cinematography. *MGM*

Traxx 🦴 **1987 (R)** Satire about an ex-cop soldier of fortune. Not surprisingly, Stevens doesn't do much with this lame script. **84m/C VHS, Beta.** Shadoe Stevens, Priscilla Barnes, William E. Pugh, John Hancock, Robert Davi, Rick Overton; ***D:*** Jerome Gary; ***W:*** Gary De Vore; ***M:*** Jay Gruska. *HBO*

Treacherous Crossing 🦴🦴 **1992 (PG)** When her husband disappears on their honeymoon cruise heiress Wagner tries to get the ship's crew to help her. They think she's crazy, but aided by new friend Dickinson, Wagner intends to find out just what's going on. Based on the radio play "Cabin B-13" by John Dickson Carr. **88m/C VHS, Beta.** Lindsay Wagner, Angie Dickinson, Grant Show, Joseph Bottoms, Karen Medak, Charles Napier, Jeffrey DeMunn; ***D:*** Tony Wharmby; ***W:*** Elisa Bell. *PAR, PMS*

Treasure Island 🦴🦴🦴½ **1934** Fleming's adaptation of Robert Louis Stevenson's eighteenth century English pirate tale of Long John Silver is a classic. Beery is great as the pirate; Cooper has trouble playing the boy. Also available colorized. Multitudinous remakes. **102m/B VHS, Beta, LV.** Wallace Beery, Jackie Cooper, Lionel Barrymore, Lewis Stone, Otto Kruger, Douglass Dumbrille, Chic Sale, Nigel Bruce; ***D:*** Victor Fleming; ***C:*** Clyde De Vinna. *MGM, TLF, HMV*

Treasure Island 🦴🦴🦴½ **1950 (PG)** Spine-tingling Robert Louis Stevenson tale of pirates and buried treasure, in which young cabin boy Jim Hawkins matches wits with Long John Silver. Some editions excise extra violence. Stevenson's ending is revised. Full Disney treatment, excellent casting. **96m/C VHS, Beta, LV.** Bobby Driscoll, Robert Newton, Basil Sydney, Walter Fitzgerald, Denis O'Dea, Ralph Truman, Finlay Currie; ***D:*** Byron Haskin; ***C:*** Frederick A. (Freddie) Young. *DIS, IGP*

Treasure Island 🦴🦴 *La Isla Del Tersoro* **1972 (G)** Unexceptional British reheat of familiar pirate tale. Welles' interpretation of Long John Silver may be truer to Stevenson, but it's one heckuva blustering binge. **94m/C VHS.** *GB* Orson Welles, Kim Burfield, Walter Slezak, Lionel Stander; ***D:*** John Hough; ***W:*** Orson Welles. *BTV*

Treasure Island ½ **1989** Excellent made for cable version of the classic Robert Louis Stevenson pirate tale with Heston as Long John Silver. Written, produced and directed by Fraser Heston, son of Charlton. **131m/C VHS.** Charlton Heston, Christian Bale, Julian Glover, Richard Johnson, Oliver Reed, Christopher Lee, Clive Wood, Nicholas Amer, Michael Halsey; ***D:*** Fraser Heston; ***W:*** Fraser Heston. *TTC*

Treasure of Arne ½ **1919** A 16th century Scottish mercenary kills and loots the estate of rich, well-to-do property owner Sir Arne. Famous early Swedish silent that established Stiller as a director. **78m/B VHS, Beta.** *SW* ***D:*** Mauritz Stiller. *FCT*

The Treasure of Bengal ½ **1953** Sabu attempts to stop his chief from trading the village's precious gem (the largest ruby in the world) for firearms. **72m/C VHS.** Sabu. *NO*

Treasure of Fear ½ *Scared Stiff* **1945** A bungling newspaper reporter gets involved with four jade chessmen once owned by Kubla Khan. A few laughs in this contrived haunted house story. **66m/B VHS, Beta.** Jack Haley, Barton MacLane, Ann Savage, Veda Ann Borg; ***D:*** Frank McDonald. *SNC, NOS, FCT*

The Treasure of Jamaica Reef ½ **1974 (PG)** Adventurers battle sharks and other nasty fish as they seek a sunken Spanish galleon and its cache of golden treasure. **96m/C VHS, Beta.** Cheryl Ladd, Stephen Boyd, Roosevelt Grier, David Ladd, Darby Hinton; ***D:*** Virginia Lively Stone. *NO*

The Treasure of Matecumbe **1976 (G)** A motley crew of adventurers led by a young boy search for buried treasure as they are pursued by Indians and other foes. Filmed in the Florida Key Islands. **107m/C VHS, Beta.** Billy Attmore, Robert Foxworth, Joan Hackett, Peter Ustinov, Vic Morrow; ***D:*** Vincent McEveety; ***M:*** Buddy Baker. *DIS*

Treasure of Monte Cristo **1950** A woman marries a seaman said to be an ancestor of the Count for his inheritance. Instead, she finds love and mystery. **78m/B VHS, Beta, LV.** *GB* Adele Jergens, Steve Brodie, Glenn Langan; ***D:*** William (Lester Williams) Berke. *NO*

Treasure of Pancho Villa ½ **1955** An American adventurer plots a gold heist to help Villa's revolution. He encounters every obstacle in the West while on his way to help the Mexican rebel. **96m/C VHS, Beta.** Rory Calhoun, Shelley Winters, Gilbert Roland; ***D:*** George Sherman. *NO*

The Treasure of the Amazon ½ *El Tesoro del Amazones* **1984** Three fortune hunters embark on a perilous search for wealth in the South American jungles. Silly and unnecessarily violent. **105m/C VHS, Beta.** *MX* Stuart Whitman, Donald Pleasence, Ann Sydney, Bradford Dillman, John Ireland; ***D:*** Rene Cardona Jr. *LIV, VES*

Treasure of the Four Crowns **1982 (PG)** Aging history professor hires a team of tough commandos to recover four legendary crowns containing the source of mystical powers. The crowns are being held under heavy guard by a crazed cult leader. **97m/C VHS, Beta.** *SP* Tony Anthony, Anna Obregon, Gene Quintano; ***D:*** Ferdinando Baldi; ***W:*** Lloyd Battista, James Bryce; ***M:*** Ennio Morricone. *MGM*

Treasure of the Golden Condor ½ **1953** A swashbuckler heads to the jungles of 18th-century Guatemala in search of ancient treasure. Contains interesting footage of Mayan ruins, but otherwise ordinary. A remake of "Son of Fury." **93m/C VHS.** Cornel Wilde, Connie Smith, Fay Wray, Anne Bancroft, Leo G. Carroll, Robert (Bobby) Blake; ***D:*** Delmer Daves. *TCF*

Treasure of the Lost Desert ½ **1983** A Green Beret crushes a terrorist operation in the Middle East. **93m/C VHS, Beta.** Bruce Miller, Susan West, Larry Finch; ***D:*** Tony Zarindast. *LIV*

Treasure of the Moon Goddess *Woof!* **1988 (R)** A dizzy nightclub singer is mistaken by Central American pirates and natives for the earthly manifestation of their Moon Goddess. **90m/C VHS, Beta.** Don Calfa, Joann Ayres, Asher Brauner; ***D:*** Joseph Louis Agraz. *VMK*

Treasure of the Sierra Madre **1948** Three prospectors in search of gold in Mexico find suspicion, treachery and greed. Bogart is superbly believable as the paranoid, and ultimately homicidal, Fred C. Dobbs. Huston directed his father and wrote the screenplay, based on a B. Traven story. **126m/B VHS, Beta, LV.** Humphrey Bogart, Walter Huston, Tim Holt, Bruce (Herman Brix) Bennett, Barton MacLane, Robert (Bobby) Blake, Alfonso Bedoya; ***D:*** John Huston; ***W:*** John Huston; ***M:*** Max Steiner. Academy Awards '48: Best Director (Huston), Best Screenplay, Best Supporting Actor (Huston); National Board of Review Awards '48: 10 Best Films of the Year, Best Actor (Huston); Nominations: Academy Awards '48: Best Picture. *MGM, FOX, TLF*

Treasure of the Yankee Zephyr *Race for the Yankee Zephyr* **1983 (PG)** Trio joins in the quest for a plane that has been missing for 40 years...with a cargo of $50 million. They have competition in the form of Peppard and cronies. Decent cast muddles through the predictable plotting. **108m/C VHS, Beta.** *AU NZ* Ken Wahl, George Peppard, Donald Pleasence, Lesley Ann Warren, Bruno Lawrence, Grant Tilly; ***D:*** David Hemmings. *LIV, VES*

The Treasure Seekers **1979** Four rival divers set off on a perilous Caribbean expedition in search of the legendary treasure of Morgan the Pirate. **88m/C VHS, Beta.** Rod Taylor, Stuart Whitman, Elke Sommer, Keenan Wynn, Jeremy Kemp. *MGM*

A Tree Grows in Brooklyn ½ **1945 (PG)** Sensitive young Irish lass growing up in turn-of-the-century Brooklyn tries to rise above her tenement existence. Based on the novel by Betty Smith. Kazan's directorial debut. **128m/B VHS, Beta, LV.** Peggy Ann Garner, James Dunn, Dorothy McGuire, Joan Blondell, Lloyd Nolan, Ted Donaldson, James Gleason, John Alexander, Charles Halton; ***D:*** Elia Kazan; ***C:*** Leon Shamroy; ***M:*** Alfred Newman. Academy Awards '45: Best Supporting Actor (Dunn); National Board of Review Awards '45: 10 Best Films of the Year; Nominations: Academy Awards '45: Best Screenplay. *FXV, BTV, HMV*

The Tree of Wooden Clogs ½ *L'Albero Degli Zoccoli* **1978** Epic view of the lives of four peasant families working on an estate in turn of the century Northern Italy. The title comes from the shoes the peasants wear. When a young boy breaks a shoe, his father risks punishment by cutting down one of his landlord's trees to make a new pair of clogs. Slow moving and beautiful, from former industrial filmmaker Olmi. In Italian with English subtitles. **185m/C VHS, Beta, LV.** *IT* Luigi Ornaghi, Francesca Moriggi, Omar Brignoll, Antonio Ferrari; ***D:*** Ermanno Olmi; ***W:*** Ermanno Olmi. Cannes Film Festival '78: Best Film; New York Film Critics Awards '79: Best Foreign Film. *FXL, APD, INJ*

Tremors ½ **1989 (PG-13)** A tiny desert town is attacked by giant man-eating worm-creatures. Bacon and Ward are the handymen trying to save the town. Amusing, with good special effects. **96m/C VHS, Beta, LV.** Kevin Bacon, Fred Ward, Finn Carter, Michael Gross, Reba McEntire, Bibi Besch, Bobby Jacoby, Charlotte Stewart, Victor Wong, Tony Genaros; ***D:*** Ron Underwood; ***W:*** S.S. Wilson, Brent Maddock; ***M:*** Ernest Troost. *MCA*

Tremors 2: Aftershocks ½ **1996 (PG-13)** They're baaaaack! The Graboids have resurfaced to eat their way through Mexican oil fields and it's up to tough guys Earl Bassett (Ward) and Burt Gummer (Gross) to get rid of the toothy worms once and for all. Same mix of tongue-in-cheek humor and special effects as the first film. **100m/C VHS, LV.** Fred Ward, Michael Gross, Helen Shaver, Christopher Gartin, Marcelo Tubert; ***D:*** S.S. Wilson; ***W:*** S.S. Wilson, Brent Maddock. *MCA*

Trenchcoat ½ **1983** Aspiring mystery writer travels to Malta to research her new novel and is drawn into a real-life conspiracy. Silly and contrived spoof of the detective genre. **95m/C VHS, Beta.** Margot Kidder, Robert Hays; ***D:*** Michael Tuchner; ***W:*** Jeffrey Price, Peter S. Seaman; ***M:*** Charles Fox. *DIS, OM*

Trespass *Looters* **1992 (R)** Violent crime tale set in East St. Louis, Illinois. Two redneck firemen learn about stolen gold artifacts supposedly hidden in an abandoned building and go on a treasure hunt. When they witness a murder they also get involved in a battle between two crime lords—who want these interlopers dead. What follows is a deadly game of cat-and-mouse. Lots of action but it's all fairly routine. Original release date of summer 1992 was delayed until the winter because of unfortunate similarities to the L.A. riots. **104m/C VHS, Beta, LV.** Ice Cube, Ice-T, William Sadler, Bill Paxton, Art Evans; ***D:*** Walter Hill; ***W:*** Robert Zemeckis, Bob Gale; ***C:*** Lloyd Ahern; ***M:*** Ry Cooder. *MCA*

Trespasser **1985** A painter has an affair with a young woman. He comes to regret destroying his family and their life together. Based on a D.H. Lawrence novel. **90m/C VHS, Beta.** Alan Bates, Dinah Stabb, Pauline Morgan, Margaret Whiting. *NO*

Trespasses **1986 (R)** A rape victim and a cattleman get involved and become the target of her husband's revenge. Murder and lust in a small Texas town in this tedious film. **90m/C VHS, Beta.** Lou Diamond Phillips, Robert Kuhn, Ben Johnson, Adam Roarke, Mary Pillot, Van Brooks; ***D:*** Lauren Bivens. *ACA, MTX, VTR*

The Trial *Le Proces; Der Prozess; Il Processo* **1963** Expressionistic Welles adaptation of classic Kafka novella about an innocent man accused, tried, and convicted of an unknown crime in an unnnamed exaggeratedly bureaucratic country. Another Welles project that met with constant disaster in production, with many lapses in continuity. **118m/B VHS, Beta.** *FR* Anthony Perkins, Jeanne Moreau, Orson Welles, Romy Schneider, Akim Tamiroff, Elsa Martinelli; ***D:*** Orson Welles. *CVC, NOS, HHT*

The Trial **1993** Spare adaptation of Franz Kafka's novel finds Prague bank clerk Joseph K (MacLachlan) arrested on unknown charges. His increasing guilt and paranoia fit well into a world where the most illogical things happen in the most matter of fact way. Good visuals. **120m/C VHS, LV.** Kyle MacLachlan, Anthony Hopkins, Jason Robards Jr., Polly Walker, Juliet Stevenson, Alfred Molina; ***D:*** David Jones; ***W:*** Harold Pinter. *ORI*

Trial and Error ½ **1992** Peter Hudson (Matheson) is an overly-zealous prosecutor who successfully convicts a small time criminal of murder, sending him to death row. This launches Hudson's political career and five years later he's about to be nominated for Lieutenant Governor, just as the felon's execution draws near. Suddenly, new evidence points to the man's innocence, but if Hudson investigates it could ruin his political future. But he's got a bigger problem—the real killer decides to make Hudson's wife his next victim. **91m/C VHS, Beta.** Tim Matheson, Helen Shaver, Sean McCann, Eugene C. Clark; ***D:*** Mark Sobel. *MCA*

Trial by Jury ½ **1994 (R)** Strong cast, lame script. Idealistic single mother Valerie Alston (Whalley-Kilmer) winds up on the jury trying notorious mobster Rusty Pirone (Assante). Rusty's henchman, Tommy Vesey (Hurt), lets Valerie know that her son is in mortal danger if she doesn't find his boss innocent. Of course DA Daniel Graham (Byrne) is equally adamant about a conviction and is willing to use Valerie any way he has to. **107m/C VHS, LV.** Joanne Whalley, William Hurt, Gabriel Byrne, Armand Assante, Kathleen Quinlan, Stuart Whitman, Margaret Whitton, Ed Lauter, Joe Santos, Richard Portnow; ***D:*** Heywood Gould; ***W:*** Heywood Gould; ***M:*** Terence Blanchard. *WAR*

The Trial of Billy Jack *Woof!* **1974 (PG)** Billy Jack takes on the feds and beats the hell out of a lot of people to prove that the world can live in peace. Awful, pretentious film. **175m/C VHS.** Tom Laughlin, Delores Taylor, Victor Izay, Teresa Laughlin, William Wellman Jr.; ***D:*** Frank Laughlin; ***M:*** Elmer Bernstein. *NO*

The Trial of Lee Harvey Oswald **1977** What would've happened if Jack Ruby had not shot Oswald. Oswald's trial and its likely results are painstakingly created. In 2 volumes. Made for television. **192m/C VHS, Beta.** Ben Gazzara, Lorne Greene, John Pleshette, Lawrence Pressman; ***D:*** Gordon Davidson. *WOV*

Trial of the Catonsville Nine ½ **1972 (PG)** Riveting political drama that focuses on the trial of nine anti-war activists, including Father Daniel Berrigan, during the Vietnam War days of the late 1960s. Imperfect, but involving. **85m/C VHS, Beta.** Ed Flanders, Douglas Watson, William Schallert, Peter Strauss, Richard Jordan; ***D:*** Gordon Davidson. *COL*

The Trial of the Incredible Hulk **1989** The Hulk returns to battle organized crime and is aided by his blind superhero/lawyer friend Daredevil. Followed by "The Death of the Incredible Hulk." Made for television. **96m/C VHS.** Bill Bixby, Lou Ferrigno, Rex Smith, John Rhys-Davies, Marta DuBois, Nancy Everhard, Nicholas Hormann; ***D:*** Bill Bixby. *VTR*

The Trials of Oscar Wilde *The Man with the Green Carnation; The Green Carnation* **1960** Finch is the highlight as playwright/wit Wilde, who ill-advisedly sues the Marquis of Queensbury (Jeffries) for libel when the peer accuses him of being a sodomite. Wilde is, in fact, having an affair with the Marquis' son, Lord Alfred Douglas (Fraser), which eventually leads to Wilde's imprisonment and the destruction of his life. Based on the play "The Stringed Lute" by John Furnell and the book "The Trials of Oscar Wilde" by Montgomery Hyde. **123m/C VHS.** *GB* Peter Finch, John Fraser, Lionel Jeffries, Nigel Patrick, James Mason, Yvonne Mitchell, Maxine Audley, James Booth, Paul Rogers, Ian Fleming, Laurence Naismith; ***D:*** Ken Hughes; ***W:*** Ken Hughes; ***C:*** Ted Moore; ***M:*** Ron Goodwin. *FCT*

The Triangle Factory Fire Scandal **1979** Based on the true-life Triangle factory fire at the turn of the century. The fire killed 145 garment workers and drastically changed industrial fire and safety codes. Made for television. **100m/C VHS.** Tom Bosley, David Dukes, Tovah Feldshuh, Janet Margolin, Stephanie Zimbalist, Lauren Front, Stacey Nelkin, Ted Wass, Charlotte Rae, Milton Selzer, Valerie Landsburg; ***D:*** Mel Stuart. *LIV*

Tribes ½ *The Soldier Who Declared Peace* **1970** A made-for-television movie about a hippie drafted into the Marines. Despite the furious efforts of his drill sergeant, he refuses to conform to military life. Soon his boot-camp mates are trying his methods of defiance and survival. Well-made mix of comedy and social commentary. **90m/C VHS, Beta.** Jan-Michael Vincent, Darren McGavin, Earl Holliman; ***D:*** Joseph Sargent. *MGM, FOX*

Tribute **1980 (PG)** A dying man is determined to achieve a reconciliation with his estranged son. Adapted by Bernard Slade from his play. **125m/C VHS, Beta, LV.** *CA* Jack Lemmon, Robby Benson, Lee Remick, Kim Cattrall; ***D:*** Bob (Benjamin) Clark. Nominations: Academy Awards '80: Best Actor (Lemmon). *VES, FCT*

Tribute to a Bad Man **1956** Hard-nosed rancher Cagney will stop at nothing to retain his worldly possessions in this 1870's Colorado territory western. His ruthless behavior drives girlfriend Papas into the arms of hired hand Dubbins. Spencer Tracy and Grace Kelly were originally cast for the roles of Jeremy Rodock and Jocasta Constantine, but Kelly backed out and Tracy was fired due to differences with director Wise. Based on the short story by Jack Schaefer. **95m/C VHS.** James Cagney, Don Dubbins, Stephen McNally, Irene Papas, Vic Morrow, Royal Dano, Lee Van Cleef, James Griffith, Onslow Stevens, James Bell, Jeanette Nolan, Bud Osborne, Tom London, Dennis Moore, Buddy Roosevelt, Carl Pitti; ***D:*** Robert Wise; ***W:*** Michael Blankfort; ***M:*** Miklos Rozsa. *MGM*

A Tribute to the Boys **1992** An all-star salute to the comedy of Laurel & Hardy featuring clips from more than 30 of their comedies, including scenes from their silent film days. Guests include Johnny Carson, Steve Allen, Walter Matthau, Rich Little, Henny Youngman, Robert Klein, Bronson Pinchot, and The Smothers Brothers. **85m/C VHS.** *CAF*

Tricheurs *Cheaters* **1984** Scam artists hit largest casino in the world and look forward to golden years of retirement. From the director of "Reversal of Fortune." In French with English subtitles. **95m/C VHS, Beta.** *FR* Jacques Dutronc, Bulle Ogier, Kurt Raab, Virgilio Teixeira, Steve Baes; ***D:*** Barbet Schroeder. *WAR, BTV, FCT*

Trick or Treat ½ **1986 (R)** A high school student is helped to exact violent revenge against his bullying contemporaries. His helper is the spirit of a violent heavy metal rock star who he raises from the dead. Sometimes clever, not terribly scary. **97m/C VHS, Beta.** Tony Fields, Marc Price, Ozzy Osbourne, Gene Simmons; ***D:*** Charles Martin Smith. *ORI, WAR*

Trick or Treats *Woof!* **1982 (R)** Young boy's pranks on his terrified babysitter backfire on Halloween night. His deranged father, escaped from an asylum, shows up to help him "scare" her. Giroux doesn't look very frightened in this extremely tedious film from Welles' best camera man. **90m/C VHS, Beta.** Carrie Snodgress, David Carradine, Jackie Giroux, Steve Railsback; ***D:*** Gary Graver. *LIV, VES*

Tricks of the Trade **1988 (R)** Goody-two-shoe housewife and hooker accomplice search for husband's murderer. Racy made-for-television fodder. **100m/C VHS, LV.** Cindy Williams, Markie Post, Chris Mulkey, James Whitmore Jr., Scott Paulin, John Ritter, Apollonia; ***D:*** Jack Bender. *ACA*

Trident Force **1988** International counter-terrorism team is ordered to destroy the Palestinian Revolutionary Legion by any means possible. **90m/C VHS, Beta.** Anthony Alonzo, Mark Gil, Nanna Anderson, Steve Rogers, Eddie M. Gaerlan; ***D:*** Richard Smith. *NO*

Trifles ½ **1979** Five people enter a farmhouse kitchen in the bleak Midwest plains where a man was murdered upstairs. Whodunit? The solution lies in piecing together certain "trifles" that seem even more trivial later. **21m/C VHS, Beta.** *BFA*

The Trigger Effect ½ **1996 (R)** Nightmare in yuppiedom when a suspicious electromagnetic pulse knocks out all electrical power, telephone, and broadcast signals for hundreds of miles around a tranquil southern California community, which becomes increasingly unsettled. Matt (MacLachlan), wife Annie (Shue), and friend Joe (Mulroney) hang out together during the mystery power outage with lots of mounting tension both within and without. Film, however dread-producing, doesn't really make that much sense. **98m/C VHS.** Kyle MacLachlan, Elisabeth Shue, Dermot Mulroney, Michael Rooker, Richard T. Jones, Bill Smitrovich, William Lucking, Molly Morgan, Richard Schiff; ***D:*** David Koepp; ***W:*** David Koepp; ***C:*** Newton Thomas Sigel; ***M:*** James Newton Howard. *NYR*

Trigger, Jr. ½ **1950** Rogers and his Western Show find themselves in the middle of a dispute between intimidated ranchers and an evil local range patrol office. When Trigger is injured by a killer stallion, Roy turns to two unlikely allies—a 10-year-old boy who's scared of horses and frisky Trigger, Jr. **67m/B VHS.** Roy Rogers, Dale Evans, Grant Withers, Pat Brady, Gordon Jones, Peter Miles, George Cleveland; ***D:*** William Witney; ***W:*** Gerald Geraghty. *REP*

Trigger Men ½ *Billy the Kid's Fighting Pals* **1941** Steele, Young, and St. John find a dying U.S. marshal who has been ambushed by the villainous Peil. Seems Peil and his gang have taken over a small border town in order to set up a smuggling operation with Mexico. So the trio avenge the marshal by putting a stop to the nefarious doings. Newfield directed under the pseudonym Sherman Scott. **59m/B VHS.** Bob Steele, Al "Fuzzy" St. John, Carleton Young, Edward Peil Sr., Phyllis Adair, Charles "Blackie" King, Curly Dresden, Hal Price, George Chesebro, Forrest Taylor, Budd Buster; ***D:*** Sam Newfield. *GPV, DVT*

Trigger Pals ½ **1939** Jarrett stars in this basic oater about bringing a gang of rustlers to justice. Besides the usual gunplay, he also attempts to sing a few songs. **58m/B VHS.** Art Jarrett, Lee Powell, Al "Fuzzy" St. John, Dorothy Fay, Charles "Blackie" King, Frank LaRue; ***D:*** Sam Newfield. *GPV, VCN, DVT*

Trigger Tricks ½ **1930** Gibson's brother becomes the victim of a vicious cattleman and Hoot is out for revenge. **60m/B VHS.** Hoot Gibson, Sally Eilers, Neal Hart, Monte Montague, Peter Morrison, Robert E. Homans, Jack Richardson; ***D:*** B. Reeves Eason. *GPV, DVT*

The Trigger Trio ½ **1937** Rancher with diseased cattle kills a ranch inspector. The Three Mesquiteers are called in to crack the case. **54m/B VHS, Beta.** Ray Corrigan, Max Terhune, Ralph Byrd, Robert Warwick, Cornelius Keefe, Wally Wales; ***D:*** William Witney. *VCN, DVT, GPV*

Trilby **1917** Original screen production of Du Maurier's classic tale of Svengali. **59m/B VHS, Beta.** Clara Kimball Young, Wilton Lackaye, Chester Barnett; ***D:*** Maurice Tourneur. *GPV, FCT*

Trilogy of Terror ½ **1975** Black shows her versatility as she plays a tempting seductress, a mousy schoolteacher and the terrified victim of an African Zuni fetish doll in three horror shorts. Made for television. **78m/C VHS, Beta.** Karen Black, Robert Burton, John Karlen, Gregory Harrison; ***D:*** Dan Curtis; ***W:*** Richard Matheson. *NO*

Trinity is Still My Name ½ *Continuavamo A Chiamarlo Trinita* **1975 (G)** Sequel to "They Call Me Trinity." Insouciant bumbling brothers Trinity and Bambino, oblivious to danger and hopeless odds, endure mishaps and adventures as they try to right wrongs. A funny parody of Western cliches that never becomes stale. **117m/C VHS, Beta, LV.** *IT* Bud Spencer, Terence Hill, Harry Carey Jr.; ***D:*** E.B. Clucher. *CCB, SUE, HHE*

Trio **1950** Sequel to "Quartet," featuring the W. Somerset Maugham stories "The Verger," "Mr. Knowall" and "Sanatorium Acclaimed." Cinematography by Geoffrey Unsworth and Reg Wyer. **88m/B VHS, Beta.** Jean Simmons, Michael Rennie, Bill Travers, James Hayter, Kathleen Harrison, Felix Aylmer, Nigel Patrick, Finlay Currie, John Laurie; ***D:*** Ken Annakin, Harold French. Nominations: Academy Awards '50: Best Sound. *NO*

The Trip **1967** A psychedelic journey to the world of inner consciousness, via drugs. A television director, unsure where his life is going, decides to try a "trip" to expand his understanding. Hopper is the drug salesman, Dern, the tour guide for Fonda's trip through sex, witches, torture chambers and more. Great period music. **85m/C VHS, Beta.** Peter Fonda, Dennis Hopper, Susan Strasberg, Dick Miller, Peter Bogdanovich, Bruce Dern; ***D:*** Roger Corman; ***W:*** Jack Nicholson; ***M:*** Barry Goldberg. *LIV, VES*

The Trip to Bountiful **1985 (PG)** An elderly widow, unhappy living in her son's fancy modern home, makes a pilgrimage back to her childhood home in Bountiful, Texas. Based on the Horton Foote play. Fine acting with Oscar-winning performance from Page. **102m/C VHS, Beta, LV, 8mm.** Geraldine Page, Rebecca DeMornay, John Heard, Carlin Glynn, Richard Bradford; ***D:*** Peter Masterson; ***W:*** Horton Foote; ***C:*** Fred Murphy. Academy Awards '85: Best Actress (Page); Independent Spirit Awards '86: Best Actress (Page), Best Screenplay; National Media Owl Awards '87: First Prize; Nominations: Academy Awards '85: Best Adapted Screenplay. *COL, BTV, SUE*

Triple Cross **1967** Plummer is a British safecracker imprisoned on the channel islands at the outbreak of WWII. When the Germans move in, he offers to work for them if they set him free. The Germans buy his story and send him to England, but once there he offers his services to the British as a double agent. Based on the exploits of Eddie Chapman, adapted from his book, "The Eddie Chapman Story." **91m/C VHS, Beta.** *FR GB* Christopher Plummer, Romy Schneider, Trevor Howard, Gert Frobe, Yul Brynner, Claudine Auger, Georges Lycan, Jess Hahn, Howard Vernon; ***D:*** Terence Young. *ACE, MOV, HHE*

Triple Echo ½ *Soldier in Skirts* **1977 (R)** A young woman falls for an army deserter who is hiding from the military police by dressing as a woman. Mistrust and deception get the best of some of the involved parties. **90m/C VHS, Beta.** *GB* Glenda Jackson, Oliver Reed, Brian Deacon; ***D:*** Michael Apted; ***W:*** Robin Chapman. *NO*

Triple Impact **1992** Hall, Cook, and Riley are three martial-arts experts who join forces against illegal gambling syndicates who are staging full-contact bloodmatches. Their alliance leads them to Asia where the prize is death—or a fortune in gold. **97m/C**

VHS, LV. Dale "Apollo" Cook, Ron Hall, Bridgett "Baby Doll" Riley, Robert Marius, Steve Rogers, Nick Nicholson, Ned Hourani, Mike "Cobra" Cole; ***D:*** David Hunt; ***W:*** Steve Rogers. *AIP*

Triple Trouble/Easy Street **1918** Two of Chaplin's classic two-reel silent comedy shorts are shown on video. **60m/B VHS, Beta, 8mm.** Charlie Chaplin, Edna Purviance, Eric Campbell. *VYY*

TripleCross 🦴½ **1985** Three former cops strike it rich and although they love the money, they miss the game, so they get involved in a murder case. These wealthy detectives encounter high-level gangsters, a baseball scandal, and a hit man in their race to solve the perfect crime. **97m/C VHS, Beta.** Ted Wass, Markie Post, Gary Swanson; ***D:*** David Greene. *PSM*

Triplecross 🦴🦴½ **1995 (R)** Jewel thief Jimmy Ray (Bergin) is after a fortune in diamonds and obsessive FBI agent Oscar (Williams) is looking to bring him down. Oscar decides to use Jimmy Ray's ex-cell mate Teddy (Pare) but Teddy gets involved with J.R.'s girlfriend Julia (Laurence) instead of tending to business. Wooden crime caper made for cable TV. **95m/C VHS.** Patrick Bergin, Billy Dee Williams, Michael Pare, Ashley Laurence; ***D:*** Jeno Hodl. *HMK*

Tripods: The White Mountains 🦴½ **1984** Sci-fi thriller about the takeover of earth by alien tripods. The conquerors start controlling human minds, but not until after they are sixteen years old. Two boys seek to end the terror. **150m/C VHS, Beta, LV.** John Shackley, Jim Baker, Cari Seel; ***D:*** Graham Theakston. *IME*

Tripwire 🦴½ **1989 (R)** A vengeance-crazed government agent tracks down the terrorist who murdered his wife. **120m/C VHS, Beta, LV.** Terence Knox, David Warner, Charlotte Lewis, Isabella Hoffman, Yaphet Kotto, Thomas Chong, Meg Foster; ***D:*** James Lemmo. *COL*

Tristana 🦴🦴🦴🦴 **1970 (PG)** Allegorical tale of a beautiful girl (Deneuve) who moves in with a hypocritical benefactor following the death of her mother. She is quickly exploited and seduced by the one who would protect her, but runs away with an artist in pursuit of love. Searing in its commentary on Catholicism, death, lust, and the woebegone place of humanity in the world, the movie is also widely seen as a depiction of fascist Spain's attempt to find its place in the twentieth century. Based on the novel by Benito Perez Galdos. In Spanish with English subtitles. **98m/C VHS.** *SP IT FR* Catherine Deneuve, Fernando Rey, Franco Nero, Lola Gaos, Antonio Casas, Jesus Fernandez, Vincent Solder; ***D:*** Luis Bunuel; ***W:*** Luis Bunuel. *HTV, INJ*

The Triumph of Sherlock Holmes 🦴🦴½ **1935** Wontner and Fleming teamed for an early series of Holmesian romps. In one of their best outings, Sherlock Holmes comes out of retirement as a series of bizarre murders of Pennsylvania coal miners lure him back into action. From "The Valley of Fear" by Sir Arthur Conan Doyle. **84m/B VHS, Beta.** *GB* Arthur Wontner, Ian Fleming; ***D:*** Leslie Hiscott. *SNC, NOS, CAB*

Triumph of the Son of Hercules **1963** All other victories pale when compared to this, the Son of Hercules' greatest! **?m/C VHS, Beta.** *IT* Kirk Morris, Cathia Caro. *SNC*

Triumph of the Spirit 🦴🦴🦴 **1989 (R)** Gritty account of boxer Salamo Arouch's experiences in Auschwitz. The boxer became champion in matches between prisoners conducted for the amusement of Nazi officers. Filmed on location in Auschwitz. **115m/C VHS, Beta, LV.** Willem Dafoe, Robert Loggia, Edward James Olmos, Wendy Gazelle, Kelly Wolf, Costas Mandylor, Kario Salem; ***D:*** Robert M. Young; ***W:*** Andrzej Krakowski, Laurence Heath, Arthur Coburn, Millard Lampell, Robert M. Young, Shimon Arama; ***M:*** Cliff Eidelman. *COL*

Triumph of the Will **1934** Director Riefenstahl's formidable, stunning film, documenting Hitler and the Sixth Nazi Party Congress in 1934 in Nuernberg, Germany. The greatest and most artful propaganda piece ever produced. German dialogue. Includes English translation of the speeches. **115m/B VHS, Beta.** *GE* ***D:*** Leni Riefenstahl. *NOS, SUE, VYY*

Triumphs of a Man Called Horse 🦴🦴 **1983 (R)** An Indian must save his people from prospectors in order to keep his title as Peace, Chief of the Yellow Hand Sioux. Inadequate sequel to two previous films: "A Man Called Horse" and "The Return of a Man Called Horse." **91m/C VHS, Beta.** *MX* Richard Harris; ***D:*** John Hough; ***W:*** Carlos Aured, Jack DeWitt, Kenneth G. Blackwell. *NO*

Trois Couleurs: Blanc 🦴🦴🦴 *White; Three Colors: White* **1994 (R)** Bittersweet comedic rags-to-riches tale spiced with revenge and lasting love. "White" focuses on equality and begins when a bewildered Polish hairdresser is divorced by his disdainful French wife, who takes him for everything he has. Returning to his family in Poland, Karol doggedly works his way into wealth. Then he decides to fake his death and leave his fortune to the ex he still loves—or does he? In Polish and French with English subtitles. Part 2 of Kieslowski's trilogy, following "Trois Couleurs: Bleu" and followed by "Trois Couleurs: Rouge." **92m/C VHS.** *FR SI PL* Zbigniew Zamachowski, Julie Delpy, Janusz Gajos, Jerzy Stuhr; ***Cameos:*** Juliette Binoche, Florence Pernel; ***D:*** Krzysztof Kieslowski; ***W:*** Krzysztof Piesiewicz. Berlin International Film Festival '94: Best Director (Kieslowski). *MAX*

Trois Couleurs: Bleu 🦴🦴🦴 *Three Colors: Blue; Blue* **1993 (R)** First installment of director Kieslowski's trilogy inspired by the French tricolor flag. "Blue" stands for liberty—here freedom is based on tragedy as Julie (Binoche) reshapes her life after surviving an accident which killed her famous composer husband and their young daughter. Excellent performance by Binoche, which relies on the internalized grief and bitter emotion which flits across her face rather than overwhelming displays for expression. In French with English subtitles. **98m/C VHS, LV.** *FR* Juliette Binoche, Benoit Regent, Florence Pernel, Charlotte Very; ***Cameos:*** Emmanuelle Riva; ***D:*** Krzysztof Kieslowski; ***W:*** Krzysztof Piesiewicz, Krzysztof Kieslowski; ***C:*** Slawomir Idziak. Cesar Awards '94: Best Actress (Binoche), Best Film Editing, Best Sound; Los Angeles Film Critics Association Awards '93: Best Score; Venice Film Festival '93: Best Actress (Binoche), Best Film; Nominations: Golden Globe Awards '94: Best Actress—Drama (Binoche), Best Foreign Language Film, Best Original Score. *TOU*

Trois Couleurs: Rouge 🦴🦴🦴½ *Three Colors: Red; Red* **1994 (R)** "Red" is for fraternity in the French tricolor flag and, in director Kieslowski's last film in his trilogy, emotional connections are made between unlikely couples. There's law student Auguste and his girlfriend Karin, young fashion model Valentine, and a nameless retired judge, brought together by circumstance and destined to change each other's lives. Subtle details make for careful viewing but it's a rewarding watch and a visual treat (keep an eye on cinematographer Sobocinski's use of the color red). Binoche and Delpy, who starred in the earlier films, also make an appearance, as Kieslowski uses the finale to tie up loose ends. In French with English subtitles. **99m/C VHS, LV.** *FR PL SI* Irene Jacob, Jean-Louis Trintignant, Frederique Feder, Jean-Pierre Lorit; ***Cameos:*** Juliette Binoche, Julie Delpy, Benoit Regent, Zbigniew Zamachowski; ***D:*** Krzysztof Kieslowski; ***W:*** Krzysztof Kieslowski, Krzysztof Piesiewicz; ***C:*** Piotr Sobocinski; ***M:*** Zbigniew Preisner. Cesar Awards '94: Best Score; Independent Spirit Awards '95: Best Foreign Film; Los Angeles Film Critics Association Awards '94: Best Foreign Film; New York Film Critics Awards '94: Best Foreign Film; National Society of Film Critics Awards '94: Best Foreign Film; Nominations: Academy Awards '94: Best Cinematography, Best Director (Kieslowski), Best Original Screenplay; Cesar Awards '94: Best Actor (Trintignant), Best Actress (Jacob), Best Director (Kieslowski), Best Film; Golden Globe Awards '95: Best Foreign Language Film. *MAX*

Trojan Women 🦴🦴 **1971 (G)** Euripides' tragedy on the fate of the women of Troy after the Greeks storm the famous city. The play does not translate well to the screen, in spite of tour-de-force acting. **105m/C VHS, Beta.** Katharine Hepburn, Vanessa Redgrave, Irene Papas, Genevieve Bujold, Brian Blessed, Patrick Magee; ***D:*** Michael Cacoyannis. National Board of Review Awards '71: Best Actress (Papas). *FHS*

Troll 🦴½ **1986 (PG-13)** A malevolent troll haunts an apartment building and possesses a young girl in hopes of turning all humans into trolls. Sometimes imaginative, sometimes embarrassing. Followed by a sequel. **86m/C VHS, Beta, LV.** Noah Hathaway, Gary Sandy, Anne Lockhart, Sonny Bono, Shelley Hack, June Lockhart, Michael Moriarty; ***D:*** John Carl Buechler; ***M:*** Richard Band. *LIV, VES*

Troll 2 🦴½ **1992 (PG-13)** A young boy can only rely on his faith in himself when no one believes his warnings about an evil coming to destroy his family. Entering into a nightmare world, Joshua must battle witches' spells and the evil trolls who carry out their bidding. **95m/C VHS.** Michael Stephenson, Connie McFarland; ***D:*** Drago Floyd; ***W:*** Clyde Anderson. *COL*

A Troll in Central Park 🦴🦴½ **1994 (G)** Animated fantasy about Stanley the troll, who is cast out of his kingdom (because he's a good guy) and winds up in New York's Central Park. There, Stanley brings happiness to a little girl and her skeptical brother, all the while battling the evil troll queen. Strictly average family fare. **76m/C VHS, LV.** ***D:*** Don Bluth, Gary Goldman; ***W:*** Stu Krieger; ***M:*** Robert Folk; ***V:*** Dom DeLuise, Cloris Leachman, Jonathan Pryce, Hayley Mills, Charles Nelson Reilly, Phillip Glasser, Robert Morley, Sy Goraleb, Tawney Sunshine Glover, Jordan Metzner. *WAR*

Troma's War *Woof!* **1988 (R)** The survivors of an air crash find themselves amid a tropical terrorist-run civil war. Also available in a 105-minute, unrated version. Devotees of trash films shouldn't miss this one. **90m/C VHS.** Ara Romanoff, Michael Ryder, Carolyn Beauchamp, Sean Bowen; ***D:*** Michael Herz, Lloyd (Samuel Weil) Kaufman. *TTV*

Tromba, the Tiger Man 🦴½ *Tromba* **1952** A circus tiger tamer uses a special drug that hypnotizes the critters into obeying his every whim. When he tries the same drug on women, things get out of hand. **62m/B VHS, Beta.** *GE* Rene Deltgen, Angelika Hauff, Gustav Knuth, Hilde Weissner, Grethe Weiser, Gardy Granass, Adrian Hoven; ***D:*** Helmut Weiss. *SNC*

Tron 🦴🦴 **1982 (PG)** A video game designer enters into his computer, where he battles the computer games he created and seeks revenge on other designers who have stolen his creations. Sounds better than it plays. Terrific special effects, with lots of computer-created graphics. **96m/C VHS, Beta, LV.** Jeff Bridges, Bruce Boxleitner, David Warner, Cindy Morgan, Barnard Hughes, Dan Shor; ***D:*** Steven Lisberger. Nominations: Academy Awards '82: Best Costume Design, Best Sound. *DIS*

Troop Beverly Hills 🦴 **1989 (PG)** Spoiled housewife Long isn't really spoiled, just misunderstood. She takes over leadership of her daughter's Wilderness Girls troop and finds the opportunity to redeem herself by offering her own unique survival tips to the uncooperative little brats who make up the troop. Everyone learns meaningful life lessons, Long is finally understood, and everyone lives happily ever after in posh Beverly Hills. Sheer silliness makes this one almost painful to watch, a shame since it boasts a good cast whose talent is totally wasted. **105m/C VHS, Beta, LV, 8mm.** Shelley Long, Craig T. Nelson, Betty Thomas, Mary Gross, Stephanie Beacham, Audra Lindley, Edd Byrnes, Ami Foster, Jenny Lewis, Kellie Martin; ***D:*** Jeff Kanew; ***W:*** Pamela Norris, Margaret Grieco Oberman; ***M:*** Randy Edelman. *COL*

Tropic of Cancer 🦴🦴🦴 **1970 (NC-17)** Based on Henry Miller's once-banned, now classic novel, this film portrays the sexual escapades of the expatriate author living in 1920's Paris. Torn stars as the carefree, loose-living writer and Burstyn plays his disgusted wife. **87m/C VHS.** Rip Torn, James Callahan, Ellen Burstyn, David Bauer, Phil Brown; ***D:*** Joseph Strick. *PAR, FCT*

Tropical Heat 🦴🦴 **1993 (R)** When the Maharajah is killed on safari, his grieving widow (D'Abo) files a five-million-dollar insurance claim before returning to India. She's followed by an investigator (Rossovich) who becomes infatuated with the lovely D'Abo. Through palaces, primitive villages, and ancient jungle temples, they are drawn into a mystery involving blackmail and murder. Based on a story by Jag Mundhra, Michael W. Potts, and Simon Levy. **86m/C VHS.** Rick Rossovich, Maryam D'Abo, Lee Anne Beaman, Asha Siewkumar; ***D:*** Jag Mundhra; ***W:*** Michael W. Potts; ***M:*** Del Casher. *PSM*

Tropical Snow ☆ **1988 (R)** A pair of lovers living poorly in Colombia decide to enter the drug trade in exchange for passage to the U.S. offered to them by drug kingpin Carradine. Unfortunately, they get more than they bargained for. Shot on location. **87m/C VHS, Beta, LV.** David Carradine, Madeleine Stowe, Nick Corri, Argermiro Catiblanco; ***D:*** Ciro Duran. *PAR*

Trouble Along the Way ☆☆½ **1953** Wayne is a once big-time college football coach who takes a coaching job at a small, financially strapped Catholic college in an effort to retain custody of his young daughter. His underhanded recruiting methods result in his firing—and the probable loss of his daughter. Unusual and sentimental role for Wayne proves he can handle comedy as well as action. **110m/B VHS.** John Wayne, Donna Reed, Charles Coburn, Tom Tully, Sherry Jackson, Marie Windsor, Tom Helmore, Dabbs Greer, Leif Erickson, Douglas Spencer; ***D:*** Michael Curtiz; ***W:*** Jack Rose, Melville Shavelson; ***M:*** Max Steiner. *WAR*

Trouble Bound ☆☆ **1992 (R)** Madsen is Harry, a guy just out of prison, on his way to Nevada with trouble dogging him every step. He's got a dead body in the car trunk, drug dealers after him, and when he offers a lift to a pretty cocktail waitress (Arquette) his luck only gets worse. She plans to kill a Mob boss and it's no secret. Chases and violence. **90m/C VHS, LV.** Michael Madsen, Patricia Arquette, Florence Stanley, Seymour Cassel, Sal Jenco; ***D:*** Jeff Reiner; ***W:*** Darrell Fetty, Francis Delia; ***M:*** Vinnie Golia. *FXV*

Trouble Busters ☆ **1933** Troubled locals worry about who to call when oil is discovered in their town, bringing evil profiteers with it. The Trouble Busters come into town to set things straight. **51m/B VHS, Beta.** Jack Hoxie, Lane Chandler; ***D:*** Lewis D. Collins. *NOS, DVT*

Trouble in Mind ☆☆☆ **1986 (R)** Stylized romance is set in the near future in a rundown diner. Kristofferson is an ex-cop who gets involved in the lives of a young couple looking for a better life. Look for Divine in one of her/his rare appearances outside of John Waters' works. **111m/C VHS, Beta, LV, 8mm.** Kris Kristofferson, Keith Carradine, Genevieve Bujold, Lori Singer, Divine, Joe Morton, George Kirby, John Considine; ***D:*** Alan Rudolph; ***W:*** Alan Rudolph. Independent Spirit Awards '86: Best Cinematography. *COL, NLC*

Trouble in Paradise ☆☆ **1988** Welch stars as a widow stranded in a tropical island paradise with an Australian sailor. The two must struggle as they are stalked by a gang of drug smugglers, hence the title. Made for television. **92m/C VHS.** Raquel Welch, Jack Thompson, Nicholas Hammond, John Gregg; ***D:*** Di Drew. *CAF*

Trouble in Store ☆☆½ **1953** A bumbling department store employee stumbles on a gangster's plot. Fun gags and a good cast. **85m/B VHS.** *GB* Margaret Rutherford, Norman Wisdom, Moira Lister, Megs Jenkins; ***D:*** John Paddy Carstairs. *REP*

Trouble in Texas ☆☆ **1937** Outlaws go to a rodeo and try to steal the prize money. Tex wants to find out who killed his brother and in his spare time, sings and tries to stop the crooks. Notable because it is the last film Hayworth made under her original stage name (Rita Cansino). **65m/B VHS, Beta.** Tex Ritter, Rita Hayworth, Earl Dwire, Yakima Canutt; ***D:*** Robert North Bradbury. *NOS, DVT, VCI*

Trouble in the Glen ☆☆½ **1954** A Scottish-American soldier returns to his ancestral home and becomes involved in a dispute between the town residents and a lord over a closed road. Uneven script undermines comic idea. **91m/C VHS.** *GB* Orson Welles, Victor McLaglen, Forrest Tucker, Margaret Lockwood; ***D:*** Herbert Wilcox. *REP*

The Trouble with Angels ☆☆½ **1966 (PG)** Two young girls turn a convent upside down with their endless practical jokes. Russell is everything a Mother Superior should be: understanding, wise, and beautiful. **112m/C VHS, Beta, LV.** Hayley Mills, June Harding, Rosalind Russell, Gypsy Rose Lee, Binnie Barnes; ***D:*** Ida Lupino; ***C:*** Lionel Lindon; ***M:*** Jerry Goldsmith. *COL*

The Trouble with Dick ☆ **1988 (R)** An ambitious young science fiction writer's personal troubles begin to appear in his writing. Although the box cover displays a "Festival Winner" announcement, don't be fooled! Story becomes tedious after first five minutes. **86m/C VHS, Beta.** Tom Villard, Susan Dey; ***D:*** Gary Walkow; ***M:*** Roger Bourland. Sundance Film Festival '87: Grand Jury Prize. *ACA*

The Trouble with Father *The Stu Erwin Show* **1950** Erwin starred in the classic comedy series about a bumbling father which aired from 1950-1955. Two episodes per tape. On this tape: "Yvette," a 1954 episode in which Stu tries to surprise June with a lifelike female mannequin as an aniversary gift and the 1952 episode "What Paper Do you Read" when June enrolls in Stu's evening government classes. **50m/B VHS, Beta.** Stuart Erwin, June Collyer Erwin, Sheila James, Ann Todd, Martin Milner, Willie Best. *NOS, MOV, DVT*

The Trouble with Girls (and How To Get Into It) ☆☆☆ *The Chautauqua* **1969 (G)** A 1920s traveling show manager tries to solve a local murder. Not as much singing as his earlier films, but good attention is paid to details. This is definitely one of the better Elvis vehicles. ♫Almost; Clean Up Your Own Back Yard. **99m/C VHS, Beta.** Elvis Presley, Marlyn Mason, Nicole Jaffe, Sheree North, Edward Andrews, John Carradine, Vincent Price, Joyce Van Patten, Dabney Coleman, John Rubinstein, Anthony Teague; ***D:*** Peter Tewkesbury. *MGM*

The Trouble with Harry ☆☆☆ **1955 (PG)** When a little boy finds a dead body in a Vermont town, it causes all kinds of problems for the community. No one is sure who killed Harry and what to do with the body. MacLaine's film debut and Herrmann's first musical score for Hitchcock. **90m/C VHS, Beta, LV.** John Forsythe, Shirley MacLaine, Edmund Gwenn, Jerry Mathers, Mildred Dunnock, Mildred Natwick, Royal Dano; ***D:*** Alfred Hitchcock; ***W:*** John Michael Hayes; ***C:*** Robert Burks; ***M:*** Bernard Herrmann. *MCA, HMV*

The Trouble with Spies ☆ **1987 (PG-13)** A bumbling British spy goes to Ibizia to locate a Russian agent, makes a million mistakes and wins anyway. A loser of a film, wasted a fine cast. Made in 1984; no one bothered to release it for 3 years. **91m/C VHS, Beta.** Donald Sutherland, Malcolm Morley, Lucy Gutteridge, Ruth Gordon, Ned Beatty, Michael Hordern, Robert Morley; ***D:*** Burt Kennedy; ***W:*** Burt Kennedy. *HBO*

Troublemakers ☆½ **1994 (PG)** Travis (Hill) is the fastest gun in the west—too bad his brother Moses (Spencer) is the country's meanest bounty hunter. But their mother loves them, and wants both her boys home for Christmas. So she leaves it up to Travis to lure Moses back to the homestead. **98m/C VHS.** Terence Hill, Bud Spencer. *TRI*

Truck Stop ☆ **19??** This truck stop has all a trucker needs—including the owner, voluptuous Pamela. **80m/C VHS.** Nikki Gentile, Elizabeth Turner; ***D:*** Jean Marie Pallardy. *MED*

Truck Stop Women ☆☆ **1974 (R)** Female truckers become involved in smuggling and prostitution at a truck stop. The mob wants a cut of the business and will do anything to get their way. Better than it sounds. **88m/C VHS, Beta.** Claudia Jennings, Lieux Dressler, John Martino, Dennis Fimple, Dolores Dorn, Gene Drew, Paul Carr, Jennifer Burton; ***D:*** Mark L. Lester. *VES*

Truck Turner ☆½ **1974 (R)** He's a bounty hunter, he's black and he's up against a threadbare plot. Hayes methodically eliminates everyone involved with his partner's murder while providing groovy soundtrack. Quintessential blaxploitation. **91m/C VHS.** Isaac Hayes, Yaphet Kotto, Annazette Chase, Nichelle Nichols, Scatman Crothers, Dick Miller; ***D:*** Jonathan Kaplan; ***W:*** Leigh Chapman; ***M:*** Isaac Hayes. *ORI, FCT*

Trucker's Woman ☆ **1983 (R)** Man takes a job driving an 18-wheel truck in order to find the murderers of his father. **90m/C VHS, Beta.** Michael Hawkins, Mary Cannon; ***D:*** Will Zens. *NO*

True Believer ☆☆½ **1989 (R)** Cynical lawyer, once a '60s radical, now defends rich drug dealers. Spurred on by a young protege, he takes on the hopeless case of imprisoned Asian-American accused of gang-slaying. Tense thriller with good cast. **103m/C VHS, Beta, LV.** James Woods, Robert Downey Jr., Yuji Okumoto, Margaret Colin, Kurtwood Smith, Tom Bower, Miguel Fernandez, Charles Hallahan; ***D:*** Joseph Ruben; ***W:*** Wesley Strick; ***M:*** Brad Fiedel. *COL*

True Blood ☆☆ **1989 (R)** A man returns to his home turf to save his brother from the same ruthless gang who set him up for a cop's murder. **100m/C VHS, Beta, LV.** Chad Lowe, Jeff Fahey, Sherilyn Fenn; ***D:*** Peter Maris. *FRH, IME*

True Colors ☆☆½ **1987 (PG-13)** A woman fights for her homeland of France in order to save the country from being taken over by Hitler. **160m/C VHS, Beta.** Noni Hazlehurst, John Waters, Patrick Ryecart, Shane Briant, Alan Andrews; ***D:*** Pino Amenta. *ACA*

True Colors ☆☆ **1991 (R)** Law school buddies take divergent paths in post grad real world. Straight and narrow Spader works for Justice Department while dropout Cusack manipulates friends and acquaintances to further his position as Senator's aid. Typecast, predictable and, moralizing. **111m/C VHS, Beta, LV.** John Cusack, James Spader, Imogen Stubbs, Mandy Patinkin, Richard Widmark; ***D:*** Herbert Ross. *PAR*

True Confessions ☆☆☆ **1981 (R)** Tale of corruption pits two brothers, one a priest and the other a detective, against each other. Nice 1940s period look, with excellent performances from De Niro and Duvall. Based on a true case from the Gregory Dunne novel. **110m/C VHS, Beta, LV.** Robert De Niro, Robert Duvall, Kenneth McMillan, Charles Durning, Cyril Cusack, Ed Flanders, Burgess Meredith, Louisa Moritz; ***D:*** Ulu Grosbard; ***W:*** John Gregory Dunne, Joan Didion; ***C:*** Owen Roizman; ***M:*** Georges Delerue. *MGM*

True Crime ☆☆½ *Dangerous Kiss* **1995 (R)** High school student turns detective when a classmate is killed, hooks up with a police cadet, and finds herself on the trail of a serial killer. **94m/C VHS.** Alicia Silverstone, Kevin Dillon; ***D:*** Pat Verducci. *VMK*

The True Game of Death **197?** A story of the circumstances behind the death of superstar Bruce Lee. **90m/C VHS, Beta.** Shou Lung. *NO*

True Grit ☆☆☆ **1969 (G)** Hard-drinking U.S. Marshal Rooster Cogburn (Wayne) is hired by a young girl (Darby) to find her father's killer. Won Wayne his only Oscar. Based on the Charles Portis novel. Prompted sequel, "Rooster Cogburn." **128m/C VHS, Beta, LV.** John Wayne, Glen Campbell, Kim Darby, Robert Duvall; ***D:*** Henry Hathaway; ***M:*** Elmer Bernstein. Academy Awards '69: Best Actor (Wayne); Golden Globe Awards '70: Best Actor—Drama (Wayne); National Board of Review Awards '69: 10 Best Films of the Year; Nominations: Academy Awards '69: Best Song ("True Grit"). *PAR, HHE, TLF*

True Heart Susie ☆☆½ **1919** A simple, moving story about a girl who is in love with a man who marries another girl from the city. Silent. **87m/B VHS, Beta.** Lillian Gish, Robert "Bobbie" Harron; ***D:*** D.W. Griffith. *NOS, VYY, DVT*

True Identity ☆☆ **1991 (R)** Henry, a comic superstar in England, stars as an innocent black man marked for death by the Mafia. He hides by disguising himself as white and gets a taste of life on the other side of the color line. The interesting premise was based on a classic Eddie Murphy sketch on "Saturday Night Live," but isn't treated with sufficient imagination or humor here. **94m/C VHS, Beta.** Lenny Henry, Frank Langella, Anne-Marie Johnson, Charles Lane; ***D:*** Charles Lane; ***W:*** Andy Breckman. *TOU, FCT*

True Lies ☆☆½ **1994 (R)** Brain candy with a bang offers eye popping special effects and a large dose of unbelievability. Sort of like a big screen "Scarecrow and Mrs. King" as supposed computer salesman Ah-nuld keeps his spy work secret from mousy, neglected wife Curtis, who has a few secrets of her own and inadvertantly ends up right in the thick of things. Raunchy and extremely sexist, but not without charm; the stupidity is part of the fun. Perfectly cast sidekick Arnold holds his own as a pig, but Heston is wasted as the head honcho. Tons of special effects culiminate in a smashing finish. Very loosely adapted from the 1991 French comedy "La Total." **114m/C VHS, LV.** Arnold Schwarzenegger, Jamie Lee Curtis, Tom Arnold, Bill Paxton, Tia Carrere, Art Malik, Eliza Dushku, Charlton Heston, Grant Heslov; ***D:*** James Cameron; ***W:*** James Cameron; ***C:*** Russell Carpenter. Golden Globe Awards '95: Best Actress—Musical/Comedy (Curtis); Blockbuster Entertainment Awards '96: Action Actress, Video (Curtis); Nominations: Academy Awards '94: Best Visual Effects; MTV Movie Awards '95: Best Female Performance (Curtis), Best Comedic Performance (Arnold), Best Kiss (Arnold Schwarzenegger/Jamie Lee Curtis), Best Action Sequence, Best Dance Sequence (Arnold Schwarzenegger/Tia Carrere). *FXV*

True Love 𝒮𝒮𝒮 **1989 (R)** Low-budget, savagely observed comedy follows the family and community events leading up to a Bronx Italian wedding. Authentic slice-of-life about two young people with very different ideas about what marriage and commitment mean. Acclaimed script and performances. **104m/C VHS, Beta, LV.** Annabella Sciorra, Ron Eldard, Aida Turturro, Roger Rignack, Michael J. Wolfe, Star Jasper, Kelly Cinnante, Rick Shapiro, Suzanne Costallos, Vinny Pastore; ***D:*** Nancy Savoca; ***W:*** Nancy Savoca, Richard Guay. Sundance Film Festival '89: Grand Jury Prize. *MGM*

True Romance 𝒮𝒮½ **1993 (R)** Geeky Clarence (Slater) and wide-eyed whore Alabama (Arquette) meet and fall instantly in love (and marriage). The inept duo skips town after an accidental murder and hit the road to L.A. with the mob in pursuit. Gem performances in small roles include Walken's debonair mafioso who's not adverse to torture; Clarence's dad (Hopper), an ex-cop who runs afoul of Walken; Pitt's space-case druggie; and the ghost of Elvis (Kilmer), whom Clarence talks to in times of stress. Horrific violence mixed with very black humor (courtesy of a script by pre "Reservoir Dogs" Tarantino and "Last Boy Scout" director Scott). An unrated version is also available. **116m/C VHS, Beta, LV.** Christian Slater, Patricia Arquette, Gary Oldman, Brad Pitt, Val Kilmer, Dennis Hopper, Christopher Walken, Samuel L. Jackson, Christopher Penn, Bronson Pinchot, Michael Rapaport, Saul Rubinek, Conchata Ferrell, James Gandolfini, Tom Sizemore, Ed Lauter; ***D:*** Tony Scott; ***W:*** Quentin Tarantino; ***M:*** Hans Zimmer. Nominations: MTV Movie Awards '94: Best Kiss (Christian Slater/Patricia Arquette). *WAR, BTV*

True Stories 𝒮𝒮𝒮½ **1986 (PG)** Quirky, amusing look at the eccentric denizens of a fictional, off-center Texas town celebrating its 150th anniversary. Notable are Kurtz as the Laziest Woman in America and Goodman as a blushing suitor. Directorial debut of Byrne. Worth a look. **89m/C VHS, Beta, LV.** David Byrne, John Goodman, Swoosie Kurtz, Spalding Gray, Annie McEnroe, Pops Staples, Tito Larriva; ***D:*** David Byrne; ***W:*** David Byrne, Beth Henley, Stephen Tobolowsky; ***M:*** David Byrne. *MVD, WAR*

True West 𝒮𝒮𝒮 **1986** Filmed performance of the acclaimed Sam Shepard play about two mismatched brothers. Made for Television. **110m/C VHS, Beta.** John Malkovich, Gary Sinise; ***D:*** Allan Goldstein. *ACA*

Truly, Madly, Deeply 𝒮𝒮𝒮 **1991 (PG)** The recent death of her lover drives a young woman into despair and anger, until he turns up at her apartment one day. Tender and well written tale of love and the supernatural, with believable characters and plot-line. Playwright Minghella's directorial debut. **107m/C VHS.** Juliet Stevenson, Alan Rickman, Bill Paterson, Michael Maloney, Christopher Rozycki, Keith Bartlett, David Ryall, Stella Maris; ***D:*** Anthony Minghella; ***W:*** Anthony Minghella. Australian Film Institute '92: Best Foreign Film; British Academy Awards '91: Best Original Screenplay. *TOU*

Truman 𝒮𝒮½ **1995 (PG)** Cable bio follows "Give 'em Hell" Harry (Sinise) from 1917 to 1968. The 33rd U.S. President, derided as a political hack, was determined to prove himself against the odds and by making the tough decisions, including authorizing use of the A-bomb on Japan. Sinise gives the appropriate no-nonsense performance, matched by Scarwid as ever-loyal wife Bess. Based on David McCullough's Pulitzer Prize-winning book. **?m/C VHS.** Gary Sinise, Diana Scarwid, Colm Feore, Richard Dysart, James Gammon, Tony Goldwyn, Pat Hingle, Harris Yulin, Leo Burmester, Zeljko Ivanek, David Lansbury, Marian Seldes, Lois Smith, Richard Venture, Daniel von Bargen; ***D:*** Frank Pierson; ***W:*** Tom Rickman; ***C:*** Paul Elliott; ***M:*** David Mansfield. *HBO*

Trumps 𝒮𝒮 *Enormous Changes at the Last Minute* **1983 (R)** Three dramas about women and contemporary relationships in New York City. Based on three stories—"Faith's Story," "Virginia's Story," and "Alexandra's Story"—by Grace Paley. **90m/C VHS.** Ellen Barkin, Kevin Bacon, Maria Tucci, Ron McLarty, Zvee Scooler, David Strathairn, Jeffrey DeMunn, Sudie Bond; ***D:*** Mirra Bank, Ellen Hovde; ***W:*** John Sayles, Susan Rice. *HHE*

Trust 𝒮𝒮 **1991 (R)** An obnoxious girl, tossed out by her family after becoming pregnant, forms a loving bond with a strange, possibly deranged guy from an abusive household. Similar in style and theme to Hartley's "The Unbelievable Truth" - a peculiar sardonic comedy/drama not for every taste. **107m/C VHS, LV.** Adrienne Shelly, Martin Donovan, Merritt Nelson, Edie Falco, John MacKay; ***D:*** Hal Hartley; ***W:*** Hal Hartley. Sundance Film Festival '91: Best Screenplay. *REP*

Trust Me 𝒮𝒮 **1989 (R)** A cynical L.A. art dealer decides to promote a young artist's work and then kill him off to increase the value of his paintings. Satirical view of the Los Angeles art crowd. **94m/C VHS, Beta, LV.** Adam Ant, Talia Balsam, David Packer, Barbara Bain, Joyce Van Patten, William DeAcutis; ***D:*** Bobby Houston. *NO*

Trusting Beatrice 𝒮½ **1992 (PG)** Lame comedy finds feckless landscaper Claude (Jacobs) the bewildered caretaker of Beatrice (Jacob), a Frenchwoman stranded in America without a green card and with a young Cambodian refugee girl. So Claude decides to take Beatrice home to his determinedly eccentric family. Tries for quirky but fails miserably. **86m/C VHS.** Irene Jacob, Mark Evan Jacobs, Leonardo Cimino, Charlotte Moore, Steve Buscemi, Pat McNamara; ***D:*** Cindy Lou Johnson; ***W:*** Cindy Lou Johnson. *ICA*

The Truth About Cats and Dogs 𝒮𝒮𝒮 **1996 (PG-13)** Funny, intelligent Abby (Garofalo) hosts a popular radio call-in show for pet lovers. When a handsome Brit photographer (Chaplin) phones in with a Great Dane problem, he becomes intrigued by her voice, and asks for a date. Insecure about her looks, Abby asks her beautiful-but-dim girlfriend Noelle (Thurman) to fill in. Naturally, both women fall for the shy Englishman. Charming, updated version of "Cyrano de Bergerac" theme works because of strong lead performances, especially Garofalo, who steals the show with her dry, self-effacing wit. Entertaining romantic comedy features some nice scenes of Santa Monica too. **97m/C VHS.** Janeane Garofalo, Uma Thurman, Ben Chaplin, Jamie Foxx, Richard Coca, Stanley DeSantis; ***D:*** Michael Lehmann. *NYR*

Truth About Women 𝒮𝒮 **1958** An old aristocrat recounts his youthful adventures to his son-in-law. A pale British comedy of manners. **107m/C VHS, Beta.** *GB* Laurence Harvey, Julie Harris, Mai Zetterling, Eva Gabor, Wilfrid Hyde-White, Derek Farr; ***D:*** Muriel Box. *NOS*

Truth or Dare? 𝒮 **1986** The childhood game of truth or dare turns deadly in this violent thriller. **87m/C VHS, Beta.** John Brace, Mary Fanaro, Geoffrey Lewis Miller; ***D:*** Yale Wilson. *HHE*

Truth or Dare 𝒮𝒮½ *In Bed with Madonna; Madonna Truth or Dare* **1991 (R)** A quasi-concert-documentary—here is music superstar Madonna tarted up in fact, fiction, and fantasy—exhibitionism to the nth power. Tacky, self-conscious and ultimately, if you are a Madonna fan, moving. On camera Madonna stings ex-boyfriend Warren Beatty, disses admirer Kevin Costner, quarrels with her father, reminisces, and does sexy things with a bottle. Oh yes, she occasionally sings and dances. Both those who worship and dislike the Material Girl will find much to pick apart here. Available in Widescreen format on laserdisc. **118m/C VHS, LV.** Madonna; ***D:*** Alek Keshishian. *LIV, FCT*

Truth or Die 𝒮𝒮 *Doing Life* **1986 (PG-13)** This trite, cliched TV movie chronicles the life of convict Jerry Rosenberg, the first prisoner to earn a law degree from his cell. Still, an uncharacteristic role for sitcom guy Danza. Based on Rosenberg's book "Doing Life." **96m/C VHS, LV.** Tony Danza, Jon DeVries, Lisa Langlois, Rocco Sisto; ***D:*** Gene Reynolds. *VMK*

Try and Get Me 𝒮𝒮 *Sound of Fury* **1950** A small town is incited into a manhunt for kidnappers who murdered their victim. Suspenseful melodrama analyzes mob rule and the criminal mind. **91m/B VHS.** Lloyd Bridges, Kathleen Ryan, Richard Carlson, Frank Lovejoy, Katherine Locke; ***D:*** Cy Endfield. *REP*

Tryst 𝒮½ **1994 (R)** Julia plots to kill her husband with the help of a detective, but when her housekeeper's son arrives, Julia decides another pawn is just what her deceitful plan needs. **101m/C VHS.** Barbara Carrera, Louise Fletcher, David Warner, Steve Bond, Andy Romano, Johnny LaSpada; ***D:*** Peter Foldy; ***W:*** Peter Foldy; ***M:*** Tom Howard. *PAR*

The Tsar's Bride 𝒮𝒮𝒮 *Tsarskaya Nevesta* **1966** A lovely young woman is chosen to be the bride of the horrible Tsar Glebov but when the Tsar's bodyguard falls for her, romantic difficulties ensue. A hybrid of the 1899 Rimsky-Korsakov opera and an 1849 play. **95m/B VHS.** *RU* Raisa Nedashkovskaya, Natalya Rudnaya, Otar Koberidze; ***D:*** Vladimir Gorikker. *KUL, MVD, PME*

Tucker: The Man and His Dream 𝒮𝒮𝒮 **1988 (PG)** Portrait of Preston Tucker, entrepreneur and industrial idealist, who in 1946 tried to build the car of the future and was effectively run out of business by the powers-that-were. Ravishing, ultra-nostalgic lullaby to the American Dream. Watch for Jeff's dad, Lloyd, in a bit role. **111m/C VHS, Beta, LV, 8mm.** Jeff Bridges, Martin Landau, Dean Stockwell, Frederic Forrest, Mako, Joan Allen, Christian Slater, Lloyd Bridges, Elias Koteas, Nina Siemaszko, Corin "Corky" Nemec, Marshall Bell, Don Novello, Peter Donat, Dean Goodman, Patti Austin; ***D:*** Francis Ford Coppola; ***W:*** Arnold Schulman, David Seidler; ***M:*** Joe Jackson, Carmine Coppola. Golden Globe Awards '89: Best Supporting Actor (Landau); New York Film Critics Awards '88: Best Supporting Actor (Stockwell); Nominations: Academy Awards '88: Best Art Direction/Set Decoration, Best Costume Design, Best Supporting Actor (Landau). *PAR*

Tuff Turf 𝒮𝒮 **1985 (R)** The new kid in town must adjust to a different social lifestyle and a new set of rules when his family is forced to move to a low-class section of Los Angeles. He makes enemies immediately when he courts the girlfriend of one of the local toughs. Fast-paced with a bright young cast. Music by Jim Carroll, Lene Lovich, and Southside Johnny. **113m/C VHS, Beta, LV.** James Spader, Kim Richards, Paul Mones, Matt Clark, Olivia Barash, Robert Downey Jr., Catya Sassoon; ***D:*** Fritz Kiersch; ***M:*** Jonathan Elias. *NWV, VTR*

Tulips 𝒮½ **1981 (PG)** Would-be suicide takes a contract out on himself, and then meets a woman who makes life worth living again. Together they attempt to evade the gangland hit man. Limp comedy. **91m/C VHS, Beta.** *CA* Gabe Kaplan, Bernadette Peters, Henry Gibson; ***D:*** Stan Ferris. *SUE*

Tulsa 𝒮𝒮𝒮 **1949** High-spirited rancher's daughter begins crusade to save her father's oil empire when he's killed. Having become ruthless and determined to succeed at any cost, she eventually sees the error of her ways. Classic Hayward. **96m/C VHS, Beta.** Susan Hayward, Robert Preston, Chill Wills, Ed Begley Sr., Pedro Armendariz Sr.; ***D:*** Stuart Heisler; ***C:*** Winton C. Hoch. *NOS, BPG, MED*

Tumbledown Ranch in Arizona 𝒮 **1941** After a rodeo accident, an unconscious college student dreams of adventure out west. Part of the "Range Busters" series. **60m/B VHS.** Ray Corrigan, John "Dusty" King, Max Terhune, Sheila Darcy, Marian Kerby; ***D:*** S. Roy Luby. *NOS, DVT*

Tumbleweed Trail ½ **1942** Action-packed thundering western. **57m/B VHS, Beta.** William Boyd, Art Davis, Lee Powell, Jack Rockwell; ***D:*** Sam Newfield. *VCN*

Tumbleweeds **1925** William S. Hart's last western. Portrays the last great land rush in America, the opening of the Cherokee Strip in the Oklahoma Territory to homesteaders. Preceded by a sound prologue, made in 1939, in which Hart speaks for the only time on screen, to introduce the story. Silent, with musical score. **114m/B VHS, Beta, LV.** William S. Hart, Lucien Littlefield, Barbara Bedford; ***D:*** King Baggot. *GPV, CCB, VYY*

Tundra ½ *The Mighty Thunder* **1936** Quasi adventure-drama/documentary set in the Alaskan tundra. A young man, known only as the "Flying Doctor," tends to the sick in small villages throughout the wilderness. But his own survival is at stake when his small plane crashes. Filmed on location. **72m/B VHS.** Del Cambre; ***D:*** Norman Dawn. *VYY*

The Tune **1992** 30,000 ink and watercolor drawings make up this animated gem which tells the story of Del (Neiden), a failed songwriter who gets a fresh start when he makes a wrong turn on the freeway and winds up in Flooby Nooby. The strange inhabitants of this town teach Del to throw out his rhyming dictionary and write about his experiences. Plympton's first full-length animated feature. Also includes "The Making of The Tune" and the animated short "Draw." **80m/C VHS.** ***D:*** Bill Plympton; ***W:*** Maureen McElheron, Bill Plympton; ***V:*** Daniel Neiden, Maureen McElheron, Marty Nelson, Emily Bindiger, Chris Hoffman. *TRI, WTA*

Tune in Tomorrow **1990 (PG-13)** Lovesick young Martin (Reeves) wants to woo divorced older babe aunt-by-marriage Julia (Hershey) and is romantically counseled by wacky soap opera writer Pedro (Falk). Seems even soap operas draw on real life, and Martin's story is immortalized on the airwaves, circa 1951 New Orleans. The story-within-a-story also features Pedro's radio characters coming to hammy life. Sometimes funny, sometimes not (the Albanian jokes are tiresome). Adapted from the novel "Aunt Julia and the Scriptwriter" by Mario Vargas Llosa. **90m/C VHS, LV.** Barbara Hershey, Keanu Reeves, Peter Falk, Bill McCutcheon, Patricia Clarkson, Peter Gallagher, Dan Hedaya, Buck Henry, Hope Lange, John Larroquette, Elizabeth McGovern, Robert Sedgwick, Henry Gibson; ***D:*** Jon Amiel; ***W:*** William Boyd; ***M:*** Wynton Marsalis. *HBO*

Tunes of Glory ½ **1960** Guinness and Mills are wonderful in this well made film about a brutal, sometimes lazy colonel and a disciplined and educated man moving up through the ranks of the British military. York's film debut. From the novel by James Kennaway, who adapted it for the screen. Laserdisc version contains interview with director Neame. **107m/C VHS, Beta, LV.** *GB* Alec Guinness, John Mills, Dennis Price, Kay Walsh, Susannah York; ***D:*** Ronald Neame; ***M:*** Malcolm Arnold. Nominations: Academy Awards '60: Best Adapted Screenplay. *TVC, SUE, NLC*

Tunes of Glory/Horse's Mouth **1960** Guinness double feature. First, "Tunes of Glory" looks at the relationship between good and bad soldiers vying for the same rank. "Horse's Mouth" takes a much lighter tone. Guinness plays a truly obsessed painter who creates his work on public property. Wildly humorous. **305m/C VHS, Beta.** Alec Guinness, Kay Walsh, Renee Houston, John Mills, Robert Coote; ***D:*** James Kennaway, Ronald Neame. *CRC*

The Tunnel ½ **1989 (R)** Obsessive romance film with a trace of suspense. Artist sees the woman of his dreams at a showing of his work. Her marriage, and her trepidation, don't keep his obsession from consuming him. **99m/C VHS, Beta, LV.** Jane Seymour, Peter Weller, Fernando Rey; ***D:*** Antonio Drove. *VES, IME*

The Tunnel of Love ½ **1958** Day and Widmark are a married couple who find themselves over their heads in red tape when they try to adopt a baby. A beautiful, disapproving adoption investigator also causes more problems for the couple when she believes Widmark is less than ideal father material. Widmark is not in his element at comedy but Day and Young (as their next-door neighbor) are fine in this lightweight adaptation of the Joseph Fields-Peter DeVries play. **98m/B VHS, LV.** Doris Day, Richard Widmark, Gig Young, Gia Scala, Elisabeth Fraser, Elizabeth Wilson; ***D:*** Gene Kelly. *MGM, MOV*

Tunnel Vision ½ **1995 (R)** Detective Kelly Wheatstone (Kensit) and her partner Frank Yanovitch (Reynolds) are after a serial killer whose victims are all beautiful women killed in a ritualistic fashion. But all the clues begin to point to Yanovitch as the one committing the crimes. **100m/C VHS.** *AU* Patsy Kensit, Robert Reynolds, Rebecca Rigg; ***D:*** Clive Fleury. *TRI*

Tunnelvision ½ **1976 (R)** A spoof of television comprised of irreverent sketches. Fun to watch because of the appearances of several now-popular stars. **70m/C VHS, Beta.** Chevy Chase, John Candy, Laraine Newman, Joe Flaherty, Howard Hesseman, Gerrit Graham, Al Franken, Tom Davis, Ron Silver; ***D:*** Neal Israel. *NO*

Turf Boy *Mr. Celebrity* **1942** Desperate for cash, a boy and his uncle try to get an old horse into prime condition for racing. A minor equine melodrama, just the right length for an old-time matinee double-feature. **68m/B VHS.** Robert "Buzzy" Henry, James Seay, Doris Day, William Halligan, Gavin Gordon; ***D:*** William Beaudine. *NOS, LOO*

Turk 182! ½ **1985 (PG-13)** The angry brother of a disabled fireman takes on City Hall in order to win back the pension that he deserves. He attacks through his graffiti art. Hutton is too heavy for the over-all comic feel of this mostly silly film. **96m/C VHS, Beta.** Timothy Hutton, Robert Culp, Robert Urich, Kim Cattrall, Peter Boyle, Darren McGavin, Paul Sorvino; ***D:*** Bob (Benjamin) Clark. *FOX*

Turkish Delights ½ **1973** Free spirit sculptor falls in love with free spirit gal from bourgeois family and artsy soft porn ensues. That is until a brain tumor puts an end to their fun, and he's left to wallow in flashbacks and more artsy soft porn. Dubbed. Verhoeven later became big box office in the U.S. with "Total Recall." **100m/C VHS.** *NL* Monique Van De Ven, Rutger Hauer, Tonny Huurdeman, Wim Van Den Brink; ***D:*** Paul Verhoeven; ***C:*** Jan De Bont. Nominations: Academy Awards '73: Best Foreign Language Film. *NO*

The Turn of the Screw **1974** Supernatural powers vie with a young governess for control of the souls of the two children in her charge. Redgrave does well in this chilling film adapted from the Henry James story. Remade in 1989. **120m/C VHS, Beta, LV.** Lynn Redgrave, Jasper Jacobs, Eva Griffith; ***D:*** Dan Curtis. *LIV*

The Turn of the Screw **1989 (R)** The young charges of an English nanny are sought for their souls by a dark, unimaginable evil in the mansion. Another version of the Henry James classic. **60m/C VHS, Beta, LV.** Amy Irving, David Hemmings; ***D:*** Graeme Clifford. *CAN*

The Turn of the Screw **1992 (R)** Yet another version of the Henry James classic as a young governess struggles with sexual obsession and the two children in her care who are possessed by evil. **95m/C VHS, LV.** Julian Sands, Patsy Kensit, Stephane Audran, Marianne Faithfull; ***D:*** Rusty Lemorande; ***M:*** Simon Boswell. *LIV*

Turnaround **1987 (R)** Unusual action/suspense film set in a small town. Relentless gang rampages the citizens. Finally, a man decides he's had enough, and turns on the heathens with his knowledge of magic. **97m/C VHS, Beta.** Doug McKeon, Tim Maier, Eddie Albert, Gayle Hunnicutt; ***D:*** Ola Solum. *NO*

Turner and Hooch **1989 (PG)** A dog witnesses a murder, and a fussy cop is partnered with the drooling mutt and a weak script in his search for the culprit. Drool as a joke will only go so far, but Hanks is his usual entertaining self. **99m/C VHS, Beta, LV.** Tom Hanks, Mare Winningham, Craig T. Nelson, Scott Paulin, J.C. Quinn; ***D:*** Roger Spottiswoode; ***W:*** Jim Cash, Jack Epps Jr., Michael Blodgett. *TOU*

The Turning Point ½ **1977 (PG)** A woman who gave up ballet for motherhood must come to terms as her daughter launches a ballet career and falls for the lead male dancer. The mother finds herself threatened by her daughter's affection toward an old friend who sacrificed a family life for the life of a ballerina. Baryshnikov's film debut. Melodramatic ending and problems due to ballet sequences. **119m/C VHS, Beta.** Shirley MacLaine, Anne Bancroft, Tom Skerritt, Leslie Browne, Martha Scott, Marshall Thompson, Mikhail Baryshnikov; ***D:*** Herbert Ross; ***W:*** Arthur Laurents; ***C:*** Robert L. Surtees. Golden Globe Awards '78: Best Director (Ross), Best Film—Drama; Los Angeles Film Critics Association Awards '77: Best Director (Ross); National Board of Review Awards '77: 10 Best Films of the Year, Best Actress (Bancroft), Best Supporting Actor (Skerritt); Nominations: Academy Awards '77: Best Actress (Bancroft), Best Actress (MacLaine), Best Art Direction/Set Decoration, Best Cinematography, Best Director (Ross), Best Film Editing, Best Original Screenplay, Best Picture, Best Sound, Best Supporting Actor (Baryshnikov), Best Supporting Actress (Browne). *FOX*

Turtle Diary **1986 (PG)** Two lonely Londoners collaborate to free giant turtles from the city aquarium with the aid of a zoo-keeper, and the turtles' freedom somehow frees them as well. Jackson and Kingsley are stunning. Adapted by Harold Pinter from the Russell Hoban book. **90m/C VHS, Beta, LV.** *GB* Ben Kingsley, Glenda Jackson, Richard Johnson, Michael Gambon, Rosemary Leach, Jeroen Krabbe, Eleanor Bron; ***D:*** John Irvin; ***W:*** Harold Pinter; ***M:*** Geoffrey Burgon. *LIV, VES*

Turumba **1984** A quiet satire about a family of papier-mache animal makers in a Philippine village who get a gargantuan order in time for the Turumba holiday, and desperately try to fill it. In Tagalog with English subtitles. **94m/C VHS, Beta.** *PH* ***D:*** Kidlat Tahimik. *FFM, FCT*

The Tuskegee Airmen **1995 (PG-13)** Cable drama based on the formation and WWII achievements of the U.S. Army Air Corps' first squadron of black combat fighter pilots, the "Fighting 99th" of the 332nd Fighter Group. They were nicknamed after the segregated military outpost where they trained in Tuskegee, Alabama and distinguished themselves in combat, never losing a single bomber, and receiving more than 800 medals. Cast all do a fine job in what turns out to essentially be a standard action/war movie. Based on a story by former Tuskegee airman, Robert W. Williams. **107m/C VHS.** Laurence "Larry" Fishburne, Cuba Gooding Jr., Allen Payne, Malcolm Jamal Warner, Courtney B. Vance, Andre Braugher, John Lithgow, Rosemary Murphy, Christopher McDonald; ***D:*** Robert Markowitz; ***W:*** Paris Qualles, Ron Hutchinson, Trey Ellis; ***C:*** Ronald Orieux; ***M:*** Lee Holdridge. *HBO*

Tusks ½ *Fire in Eden* **1989 (R)** A ruthless hunter tries to kill elephants. **99m/C VHS, Beta, LV.** Andrew Stevens, John Rhys-Davies, Lucy Gutteridge, Julian Glover; ***D:*** Tara Hawkins Moore. *NO*

Tut & Tuttle ½ **1982** Young dabbler in magic is transported to ancient Egypt where he is able to demonstrate courage and wits against the evil Horemheb, who has kidnapped Prince Tut. **97m/C VHS, Beta.** Christopher Barnes, Eric Greene, Hans Conried, Vic Tayback. *NO*

The Tuttles of Tahiti **1942** The Tuttles lead a life of leisure in the South Seas. Laughton's child becomes enamoured of his rival's offspring, causing problems between the two families. More interesting than it sounds. **91m/C VHS, Beta, LV.** Charles Laughton, Jon Hall, Peggy Drake, Victor Francen, Gene Reynolds, Florence Bates, Mala, Alma Ross, Curt Bois; ***D:*** Charles Vidor. *HHT*

Tuxedo Warrior ½ **1982** Set in South Africa, this film involves the adventures of a well-dressed mercenary who is caught between the police, diamond thieves, and an old girlfriend's bank robbing. **93m/C VHS, Beta.** John Wyman, Carol Royle, Holly Palance; ***D:*** Andrew Sinclair. *VTR, NWV*

TV's Best Adventures of Superman **1951** This first package of episodes from the original television series, which ran from 1951-1957, contains "Superman on Earth," the black & white series pilot about the Man of Steel's childhood on Krypton and Earth, and "All That Glitters," the series' final episode, wherein Lois Lane and Jimmy Olsen acquire super powers. Also includes the 1941 animated cartoon "Superman," the first-ever screen appearance of the superhero. Additional episodes available. **62m/C VHS, Beta.** George Reeves, Phyllis Coates, Noel Neill, Jack Larson, John Hamilton, Robert Shayne. *WAR, MOV*

Twelve Angry Men **1957** Fonda sounds the voice of reason as a jury inclines toward a quick-and-dirty verdict against a boy on trial. Excellent ensemble work. Lumet's feature film debut, based on a television play by Reginald Rose. **95m/B VHS, Beta, LV.** Henry Fonda, Martin Balsam, Lee J. Cobb, E.G. Marshall, Jack Klugman, Robert Webber, Ed Begley Sr., John Fiedler, Jack Warden, George Voskovec, Edward Binns, Joseph Sweeney; ***D:*** Sidney Lumet; ***W:*** Reginald Rose; ***C:*** Boris Kaufman. Berlin International Film Festival '57: Golden Berlin Bear; British Academy Awards '57: Best Actor (Fonda); Edgar Allan Poe Awards '57: Best Screenplay; National Board of Review Awards '57: 10 Best Films of the Year; Nominations: Academy Awards '57: Best Adapted Screenplay, Best Director (Lumet), Best Picture. *MGM, FOX*

Twelve Chairs **1970 (PG)** Take-off on Russian folktale first filmed in Yugoslavia in 1927. A rich matron admits on her deathbed that she has hidden her jewels in the upholstery of one of twelve chairs that are no longer in her home. A Brooksian treasure hunt ensues. **94m/C VHS, Beta, LV.** Mel Brooks, Dom DeLuise, Frank Langella, Ron Moody, Bridget Brice; ***D:*** Mel Brooks; ***W:*** Mel Brooks. *MED*

12 Monkeys **1995 (R)** Forty years after a plague wipes out 99 percent of the human population and sends the survivors underground, scientists send prisoner James Cole (Willis) to the 1990s to investigate the connection between the virus and seriously deranged fanatic Jeffrey Goines (Pitt), whose father happens to be a renowned virologist. Director Gilliam's demented vision is a bit tougher and less capricious than usual, and the convoluted plot and accumulated detail require a keen attention span, but as each piece of the puzzle falls into place the story becomes a fascinating sci-fi spectacle. Pitt drops the pretty-boy image with a nutzoid performance that'll make revelers stop swooning in a heartbeat. Inspired by the 1962 French short "La Jetee." **131m/C VHS, LV.** Bruce Willis, Madeleine Stowe, Brad Pitt, Christopher Plummer, David Morse, Frank Gorshin, John Seda; ***D:*** Terry Gilliam; ***W:*** David Peoples, Janet Peoples; ***M:*** Paul Buckmaster. Golden Globe Awards '96: Best Supporting Actor (Pitt); Nominations: Academy Awards '95: Best Costume Design, Best Supporting Actor (Pitt). *MCA*

Twelve O'Clock High ½ **1949** Epic drama about the heroic 8th Air Force, with Peck as bomber-group commander sent to shape up a hard-luck group, forced to drive himself and his men to the breaking point. Compelling dramatization of the strain of military command. Includes impressive footage of actual WWII battles. Best-ever flying fortress movie. **132m/B VHS, Beta, LV.** Gregory Peck, Hugh Marlowe, Gary Merrill, Millard Mitchell, Dean Jagger, Paul Stewart; ***D:*** Henry King; ***C:*** Leon Shamroy. Academy Awards '49: Best Sound, Best Supporting Actor (Jagger); Nominations: Academy Awards '49: Best Actor (Peck), Best Picture; New York Film Critics Awards '50: Best Actor (Peck). *FXV, FCT, BTV*

12:01 ½ **1993 (PG-13)** It's the "Groundhog Day" premise played for thrills. Barry Thompson (Silverman) is an employee at a scientific research firm who finds himself reliving the same twenty-four hour period over and over again. And what a day it is—he discovers a secret project is causing the mysterious time warp, falls in love with beauteous scientist Lisa (Slater) and watches as she gets murdered. Can Barry figure out how to stop what's going on and change things enough to save her? Adaptation of the short story "12:01" by Richard Lupoff, which was previously made into a short film. Made for television. **92m/C VHS, LV.** Jonathan Silverman, Helen Slater, Martin Landau, Nicolas Surovy, Jeremy Piven; ***D:*** Jack Sholder. *NLC, IME*

12 Plus 1 *The Thirteen Chairs* **1970 (R)** A man sells 13 chairs left to him by his aunt, only to find that one of them contained a hidden fortune. He chases across Europe in search of each of them. Some good cameos help move this re-make of a Russian folk-tale along, but it remains lightweight. Tate's last movie, before her death at the hands of Manson and his "family." **94m/C VHS, Beta.** *FR IT* Sharon Tate, Orson Welles, Vittorio Gassman, Mylene Demongeot, Terry-Thomas, Tim Brooke; ***Cameos:*** Vittorio De Sica; ***D:*** Nicolas Gessner. *NO*

Twentieth Century **1934** Maniacal Broadway director Barrymore transforms shop girl Lombard into a smashing success adored by public and press. Tired of Barrymore's manic-excessive ways, she heads for the Hollywood hills, pursued by the Profile in fine form. **91m/B Beta.** Carole Lombard, John Barrymore, Walter Connolly, Roscoe Karns, Edgar Kennedy, Ralph Forbes, Charles Lane, Etienne Girardot, Snow Flake; ***D:*** Howard Hawks; ***W:*** Charles MacArthur, Ben Hecht. *COL*

Twenty Bucks **1993 (R)** Whimsical film follows a $20 dollar bill from its "birth" at a cash machine to its "death" as it is returned to the bank, tattered and torn, for shredding. The bill is passed from owner to owner, sometimes simply and briefly, sometimes altering fate. The original screenplay is nearly 60 years old: Endre Bohem originally drafted it in 1935, and his son revised and updated it. Clever transitions allow the various stories and characters to blend almost seamlessly. The strongest character is Shue's, a young waitress and aspiring writer. Rosenfeld's directorial debut is worth a look. Filmed in Minneapolis. **91m/C VHS.** Linda Hunt, David Rasche, George Morfogen, Brendan Fraser, Gladys Knight, Elisabeth Shue, Steve Buscemi, Christopher Lloyd, Sam Jenkins, Kamal Holloway, Melora Walters, William H. Macy, Diane Baker, Spalding Gray, Matt Frewer; ***D:*** Keva Rosenfeld; ***W:*** Leslie Bohem, Endre Bohem; ***M:*** David Robbins. Independent Spirit Awards '94: Best Supporting Actor (Lloyd). *COL*

Twenty Dollar Star ½ **1991 (R)** Steamy thriller about an prominent actress who leads a double life as a cheap hooker, and consequent occupational hazards. The title may as well refer to the budget. **92m/C VHS.** Rebecca Holden, Bernie White, Eddie Barth, Marilyn Hassett, Dick Sargent; ***D:*** Paul Leder. *PAR*

20 Million Miles to Earth ½ **1957** A spaceship returning from an expedition to Venus crashes on Earth, releasing a fast-growing reptilian beast that rampages throughout Athens. Another entertaining example of stop-motion animation master Ray Harryhausen's work, offering a classic battle between the monster and an elephant. **82m/B LV.** William Hopper, Joan Taylor, Frank Puglia, John Zaremba; ***D:*** Nathan (Hertz) Juran. *COL*

20,000 Leagues Under the Sea **1916** Outstanding silent adaptation of Jules Verne's "20,000 Leagues Under the Sea" and "The Mysterious Island" filmed with a then revolutionary underwater camera. Much octopus fighting. Look for newly mastered edition. **105m/B VHS, Beta.** Matt Moore, Allen Holubar, June Gail, William Welsh, Chris Benton, Dan Hamlon; ***D:*** Stuart Paton; ***W:*** Stuart Paton. *KIV, GPV, DVT*

20,000 Leagues Under the Sea ½ **1954** From a futuristic submarine, Captain Nemo wages war on the surface world. A shipwrecked scientist and sailor do their best to thwart Nemo's dastardly schemes. Buoyant Disney version of the Jules Verne fantasy. **127m/C VHS, Beta, LV.** Kirk Douglas, James Mason, Peter Lorre, Paul Lukas, Robert J. Wilke, Carleton Young; ***D:*** Richard Fleischer. Academy Awards '54: Best Art Direction/Set Decoration (Color), Best Special Effects; National Board of Review Awards '54: 10 Best Films of the Year; Nominations: Academy Awards '54: Best Film Editing. *DIS*

Twenty-One ½ **1991 (R)** Modern morality tale of a young English woman who moves to the U.S. to make a new start, but falls into the same old habits. Kensit is frank and charming, in spite of difficulties with her drug addict boyfriend and the illegal alien she marries. Director Boyd leaves it to the viewer to decide between right and wrong and where Kensit fits. **92m/C VHS, LV.** Patsy Kensit, Jack Shepherd, Patrick Ryecart, Maynard Eziashi, Rufus Sewell, Sophie Thompson, Susan Wooldridge, Julia Goodman; ***D:*** Don Boyd; ***W:*** Don Boyd; ***M:*** Michael Berkeley. *NO*

21 Days ½ *Twenty-One Days Together; The First and the Last* **1937** Dull film somewhat redeemed by its stars. Leigh is a married woman carrying on with Olivier. When her husband confronts them, Olivier accidentally kills him in a fight. They keep quiet but then a mentally deranged man is taken into custody for the crime. Since he will be held 21 days before coming to trial, the lovers decide to spend the time together before Olivier confesses. Based on the play "The First and the Last" by John Galsworthy. **75m/C VHS.** *GB* Vivien Leigh, Laurence Olivier, Leslie Banks, Francis L. Sullivan, Hay Petrie, Esme Percy, Robert Newton; ***D:*** Basil Dean; ***W:*** Graham Greene, Basil Dean. *FCT*

21 Hours at Munich **1976** Made-for-TV treatment of the massacre of Israeli athletes by Arab terrorists at the 1972 Olympics. Well-done. The film was produced using the actual Munich locations. **100m/C VHS.** William Holden, Shirley Knight, Franco Nero, Anthony Quayle, Noel Willman; ***D:*** William A. Graham. *MOV*

23 1/2 Hours Leave **1937** Amusing WWI service comedy as a barracks wiseacre bets that by the following morning he'll be breakfasting with a general. It's a song-filled remake of a 1919 film, whose star Douglas MacLean later produced this. **73m/B VHS.** James Ellison, Terry Walker, Morgan Hill, Arthur Lake, Paul Harvey; ***D:*** John Blystone. *NOS, LOO*

Twenty-Four Eyes *Nijushi No Hitomi* **1954** Miss Oishi (Takamine), a teacher on a remote Japanese island in the 1920's, attempts to transmit peaceful values to her 12 pupils amidst the clamor of a nation gearing up for war. As she watches them grow up, many of them doomed to an early death, she remains a pillar of quiet strength. In Japanese with English subtitles. **158m/B VHS, Beta.** *JP* Hideko Takamine, Chishu Ryu, Toshiko Kobayashi; ***D:*** Keisuke Kinoshita. *INJ*

24 Hours in a Woman's Life **1961** A girl in love with an irresponsible guy hears a cautionary tale from grandma Bergman, who once had a whirlwind romance with a young gambler and naively thought she could reform him. A static TV adaptation of an oft-filmed Stefan Zweig novel, unusually lavish for its time but on the dull side. **90m/C VHS.** Ingrid Bergman, Rip Torn, John Williams, Lili Darvas, Jerry Orbach; ***D:*** Silvio Narizzano; ***W:*** John Mortimer. *FCT*

24 Hours to Midnight ½ **1992** A widow uses her ninja skills to wipe out the crime bosses and henchmen who killed her husband. **91m/C VHS.** Cynthia Rothrock, Stack Pierce; ***D:*** Leo Fong. *AIP*

25 Fireman's Street **1973** An evocative drama about the residents of an old house in Hungary which is about to be torn down, and their evening of remembrances of life before, during and after WWII. In Hungarian with English subtitles. **97m/C VHS, Beta.** Rita Bekes, Peter Muller, Lucyna Winnicka; ***D:*** Istvan Szabo. *KIV, INJ*

29th Street ½ **1991 (R)** Compelling comedy-drama based on the true story of Frank Pesce, a New York actor who won six million dollars in that state's first lottery. Great performance from Aiello, as usual, but the direction falters in the dramatic sequences. Based on the book by Frank Pesce and James Franciscus. **101m/C VHS.** Danny Aiello, Anthony LaPaglia, Lainie Kazan, Frank Pesce, Donna Magnani, Rick Aiello, Vic Manni, Ron Karabatsos, Robert Forster, Joe Franklin, Pete Antico; ***D:*** George Gallo; ***W:*** George Gallo; ***M:*** William Olvis. *FXV, CCB*

The 27 Day ½ **1957** Temperate cold war allegory has aliens deliver five mysterious capsules to five Earthlings from different countries. Each capsule, if opened, is capable of decimating the population of the entire planet, but is rendered ineffective after 27 days or upon the death of the holder. Wild ending. Based on John Mantley novel. **75m/B VHS.** Gene Barry, Valerie French, George Voskovec, Arnold Moss,

Stefan Schnabel, Ralph Clanton, Friedrich Ledebur, Mari Tsien. *MOV, MLB*

Twice a Judas 🦴 **196?** An amnesiac is swindled and has his family killed by a ruthless renegade. He wants to get even, even though he can't remember who anyone is. **90m/C VHS, Beta.** Klaus Kinski. *UNI, MOV*

Twice a Woman 🦴 **1979** Man and woman divorce, and then both fall in love with the same provocative young woman. It's complicated. **90m/C VHS, Beta.** Bibi Andersson, Anthony Perkins, Sandra Dumas. *PSM*

Twice Dead *Woof!* **1988** A family moves into a ramshackle mansion haunted by a stage actor's angry ghost. The ghost helps them battle some attacking delinquent boys. Uninteresting story, poorly done. Never released in theaters. **94m/C VHS, Beta, LV.** Tom Breznahan, Jill Whitlow, Sam Melville, Brooke Bundy, Todd Bridges, Jonathan Chapin, Christopher Burgard; ***D:*** Bert L. Dragin; ***M:*** David Bergeaud. *SUE, NLC*

Twice in a Lifetime 🦴🦴🦴 **1985 (R)** Middle-aged man takes stock of his life when he's attracted to Ann-Margret. Realizing he's married in name only, he moves in with his new love while his former wife and children struggle with shock, disbelief, and anger. Well-acted, realistic, and unsentimental. **117m/C VHS, Beta, LV.** Gene Hackman, Ellen Burstyn, Amy Madigan, Ann-Margret, Brian Dennehy, Ally Sheedy; ***D:*** Bud Yorkin; ***W:*** Colin Welland. *LIV, VES*

Twice-Told Tales 🦴🦴🦴 *Nathaniel Hawthorne's "Twice Told Tales"* **1963** Horror trilogy based loosely on three Nathaniel Hawthorne tales, "Dr. Heidegger's Experiment," "Rappaccini's Daughter," and "The House of Seven Gables." Price is great in all three of these well-told tales. **120m/C VHS, Beta.** Vincent Price, Sebastian Cabot, Brett Halsey; ***D:*** Sidney Salkow. *MGM, MLB*

Twilight in the Sierras 🦴🦴½ **1950** Lots of heroics and music in this action-packed western. An ex-outlaw gone straight is kidnapped for his notorious criminal finesse. Rogers must come to rescue. **67m/C VHS.** Roy Rogers, Dale Evans, Estelita Rodriguez, Pat Brady, Russ Vincent, George Meeker; ***D:*** William Witney. *REP*

Twilight of the Cockroaches 🦴½ *Gokiburi* **1990** Mr. Saito is a slovenly bachelor who winds up leaving the remains of his meals for the anthropomorphic cockroaches that infest his apartment. The cockroaches have had it so good for so long that they don't know about insecticides and fearing humans. That is, until Mr. Saito's fastidious new girlfriend makes her appearance and declares war on the vermin. A lifelessly animated tale too dumb for both children and adults and with decidedly unpleasant subject matter, despite the singing, dancing insects. In Japanese with English subtitles. **105m/C VHS, LV.** *JP* ***D:*** Hiroaki Yoshida; ***V:*** Kaoru Kobayashi, Setsuko Karamsumarau. *FCT, STP, LUM*

Twilight on the Rio Grande 🦴 **1941** Autry runs into a female knife thrower and some jewel smugglers in this far-fetched western. **54m/B VHS, Beta.** Gene Autry, Sterling Holloway, Adele Mara, Bob Steele; ***D:*** Frank McDonald. *VCN*

Twilight on the Trail 🦴🦴 **1941** Cattle rustlers disappear and Hopalong Cassidy and his sidekicks become "dude" detectives to solve the crime. **54m/B VHS, Beta.** William Boyd, Brad King, Andy Clyde, Jack Rockwell, Wanda McKay, Howard Bretherton. *GVV*

Twilight People *Woof!* *Beasts* **1972 (PG)** When a mad scientist's creations turn on him for revenge, he runs for his life. Boring, gory, with bad make-up and even poorer acting. This one should fade away into the night. **84m/C VHS, Beta.** *PH* John Ashley, Pat Woodell, Jan Merlin, Pam Grier; ***D:*** Eddie Romero. *VCI*

The Twilight Zone **1961** Travel through another dimension in Rod Serling's classic science fiction series. Two episodes per tape. On this tape: "The Invaders," written by Richard Matheson, sees a farm house inhabited by a mute woman become the destination of strange, miniature space travellers. In "Nothing in the Dark," written by George Clayton Johnson, an elderly woman is given an interesting lesson regarding her fear of death. **50m/B VHS, Beta, LV.** Agnes Moorehead, Douglas Heyes, Gladys Cooper, Robert Redford, R.G. Armstrong; ***D:*** Lamont Johnson; ***W:*** Richard Matheson, George Clayton Johnson. *FXV, FOX, MOV*

Twilight Zone: The Movie 🦴🦴½ **1983 (PG)** Four short horrific tales are anthologized in this film as a tribute to Rod Sterling and his popular television series. Three of the episodes, "Kick the Can," "It's a Good Life" and "Nightmare at 20,000 Feet," are based on original "Twilight Zone" scripts. Morrow was killed in a helicopter crash during filming. **101m/C VHS, Beta, LV.** Dan Aykroyd, Albert Brooks, Vic Morrow, Kathleen Quinlan, John Lithgow, Billy Mumy, Scatman Crothers, Kevin McCarthy, Bill Quinn, Selma Diamond, Abbe Lane, John Larroquette, Jeremy Licht, Patricia Barry, William Schallert, Burgess Meredith, Cherie Currie; ***D:*** John Landis, Steven Spielberg, George Miller, Joe Dante; ***W:*** John Landis; ***M:*** Jerry Goldsmith. *WAR*

Twilight's Last Gleaming 🦴🦴½ **1977 (R)** A maverick general takes a SAC missile base hostage, threatening to start WWIII if the U.S. government doesn't confess to its Vietnam policies and crimes. Gripping film, with good performances. Based on a novel by Walter Wager, "Viper Three." **144m/C VHS, Beta, LV.** Burt Lancaster, Charles Durning, Richard Widmark, Melvyn Douglas, Joseph Cotten, Paul Winfield, Burt Young, Roscoe Lee Browne, Richard Jaeckel, William Marshall, Vera Miles, Leif Erickson, Charles McGraw, William Smith, John Ratzenberger; ***D:*** Robert Aldrich; ***W:*** Ronald M. Cohen; ***C:*** Robert B. Hauser; ***M:*** Jerry Goldsmith. *FOX*

Twin Peaks 🦴🦴 **1990** Sketchy home video distillation of the eccentric TV series. It preserves much of the setup episode (the murder of teen-queen Laura Palmer and nest of small-town weirdness it reveals), then rushes piecemeal through the rest of the season. There's an altered quasi-solution to the enigma and a bizarre backward sequence not broadcast in the US. In this compressed form it's best for initiates of the TP cult; others won't be converted. **113m/C VHS, LV.** Kyle MacLachlan, Michael Ontkean, Sherilyn Fenn, Lara Flynn Boyle, Joan Chen, Peggy Lipton, Piper Laurie, Michael Horse, Russ Tamblyn, Richard Beymer, Madchen Amick, Catherine Coulson, Warren Frost, Everett McGill, Jack Nance, Ray Wise, Eric Da Re, Harry Goaz, Sheryl Lee; ***D:*** David Lynch; ***M:*** Angelo Badalamenti. *WAR, FCT*

Twin Peaks **1990** Premiere episode of David Lynch's bizarre TV drama. In this episode, Agent Cooper and Sheriff Truman begin the investigation into the death of prom queen, Laura Palmer. All seven episodes are available in a boxed set. **50m/C VHS.** Michael Ontkean, Kyle MacLachlan, Joan Chen, Piper Laurie, Sherilyn Fenn, Peggy Lipton, Madchen Amick, Lara Flynn Boyle, Michael Horse, Russ Tamblyn, Richard Beymer, Dana Ashbrook, Warren Frost, Everett McGill, Jack Nance, Ray Wise, Eric Da Re, Catherine Coulson, Harry Goaz, Sheryl Lee; ***D:*** David Lynch; ***M:*** Angelo Badalamenti. *WOV, MOV*

Twin Peaks: Fire Walk with Me 🦴🦴 **1992 (R)** Prequel to the cult TV series is weird and frustrating, chronicling the week before Laura Palmer's death. Suspense is lacking since we know the outcome, but Lynch manages to intrigue with dream-like sequences and interestingly offbeat characters. On the other hand, it's exploitative and violent enough to alienate series fans. Includes extremely brief and baffling cameos by Bowie as an FBI agent and Stanton as the manager of a trailer park. Several of the show's regulars are missing, and others appear and disappear very quickly. On the plus side are the strains of Badalamenti's famous theme music and Isaak as an FBI agent with amazingly acute powers of observation. **135m/C VHS, LV.** Kyle MacLachlan, Sheryl Lee, Moira Kelly, Chris Isaak, Ray Wise, Kiefer Sutherland, Peggy Lipton, Dana Ashbrook, James Marshall, David Lynch; ***Cameos:*** David Bowie, Harry Dean Stanton; ***D:*** David Lynch; ***W:*** David Lynch; ***M:*** Angelo Badalamenti. Nominations: Cannes Film Festival '92: Best Film. *NLC*

Twins 🦴🦴½ **1988 (PG)** A genetics experiment gone awry produces twins rather than a single child. One is a genetically-engineered superman, the other a short, lecherous petty criminal. Schwarzenegger learns he has a brother, and becomes determined to find him, despite their having been raised separately. The two meet and are immediately involved in a contraband scandal. Amusing pairing of Schwarzenegger and DeVito. **107m/C VHS, Beta, LV.** Arnold Schwarzenegger, Danny DeVito, Kelly Preston, Hugh O'Brian, Chloe Webb, Bonnie Bartlett, Marshall Bell, Trey Wilson, Nehemiah Persoff; ***D:*** Ivan Reitman; ***W:*** William Davies, William Osborne, Timothy Harris, Herschel Weingrod; ***M:*** Georges Delerue, Randy Edelman. People's Choice Awards '89: Best Film—Musical/Comedy. *MCA*

Twins of Evil 🦴½ **1971** Beautiful female twins fall victim to the local vampire, and their God-fearing uncle is out to save/destroy them. Hammer sex and blood-sucking epic starring the Collinsons, who were featured in the October 1970 issue of Playboy as the first twin Playmates. **86m/C VHS, Beta.** *GB* Madeleine Collinson, Mary Collinson, Peter Cushing, Kathleen Byron, Dennis Price, Damien Thomas, David Warbeck, Katya Wyeth, Maggie Wright, Luan Peters, Kristen Lindholm, Judy Matheson; ***D:*** John Hough. *MLB*

Twinsanity 🦴 *Goodbye Gemini* **1970 (R)** Evil twins are charged with the murder of a man who attempted to blackmail them. **91m/C VHS, Beta.** *GB* Judy Geeson, Martin Potter, Alexis Kanner, Michael Redgrave, Freddie Jones, Peter Jeffrey; ***D:*** Alan Gibson; ***W:*** Edmund Ward; ***M:*** Christopher Gunning. *PSM*

Twinsitters 🦴🦴½ **1995 (PG-13)** Twins Peter and David Falcone (Peter and David Paul) find themselves unexpectedly saving the life of corrupt businessman Frank Hillhurst (Martin). Hillhurst is turning state's evidence on his crooked operations and his disturbed partners have threatened both his life and the lives of his twin 10-year-old nephews. So Hillhurst hires the Falcones to protect his hellacious pint-sized relatives—who manage to get themselves kidnapped. **93m/C VHS.** Peter Paul, David Paul, Christian Cousins, Joseph Cousins, Jared Martin, George Lazenby, Rena Sofa, Mother Love; ***D:*** John Paragon; ***W:*** John Paragon. *COL*

Twirl 🦴🦴 **1981** Satirical look at the cutthroat world of baton twirling. Parents apply relentless pressure on their daughters to win a contest. Decent made-for-TV movie. **100m/C VHS, Beta.** Stella Stevens, Charles Haid, Lisa Whelchel, Erin Moran, Edd Byrnes, Sharon Spelman, Matthew Tobin, Donna McKechnie, Rosalind Chao, Heather Locklear, Deborah Richter, Jamie Rose, Tracy Scoggins; ***D:*** Gus Trikonis. *LIV*

Twist 🦴½ *Folies Bourgeoises* **1976** A tepid French drama chronicling the infidelities of various wealthy aristocrats. The aristocrats are boring, as is the film. In French with English subtitles or dubbed. **105m/C VHS, Beta.** *FR* Bruce Dern, Stephane Audran, Ann-Margret, Sydne Rome, Jean-Pierre Cassel, Curt Jurgens, Maria Schell, Charles Aznavour; ***D:*** Claude Chabrol; ***M:*** Manuel De Sica. *LIV*

Twist & Shout 🦴🦴🦴 *Hab Og Karlighed* **1984 (R)** Sequel to the popular Danish import "Zappa," in which two teenage lovers discover sex and rock and roll. Transcends the teens discovering sex genre. Danish with English subtitles. Profanity, nudity, and sex. **107m/C VHS, Beta.** *DK* Lars Simonsen, Adam Tonsberg, Ulrikke Juul Bondo, Camilla Soeberg; ***D:*** Bille August; ***W:*** Bille August. *NO*

Twisted 🦴🦴 **1986 (R)** This curio from Slater's early career came out on tape to take advantage of his rising stardom. He's properly creepy as a brilliant but evil teen using electronics, psychology, and swordplay to terrorize victims. The suspense isn't too bad when direction doesn't go overboard, which unfortunately is half the time. Based on the play "Children! Children!" by Jack Horrigan **87m/C VHS.** Lois Smith, Christian Slater, Tandy Cronyn, Brooke Tracy, Dina Merrill, Dan Ziskie, Karl Taylor, Noelle Parker, John Cunningham, J.C. Quinn; ***D:*** Adam Holender. *NO*

Twisted Brain ☠ *Horror High* **1974 (R)** An honor student develops a serum that makes him half man and half beast. Now he can exact revenge on all the jocks and cheerleaders who have humiliated him in the past. Cardi is okay, the rest of the cast is awful. Silly, horrific teen monster epic. **89m/C VHS, Beta.** Pat Cardi, Austin Stoker, Rosie Holotik, John Niland, Joyce Hash, Jeff Alexander, Joe "Mean Joe" Greene; ***D:*** Larry N. Stouffer. *NO*

Twisted Justice ☠½ **1989** Set in 2020, Heavener is a cop determined to stop a ruthless killer. Matters become complicated, however, when his gun is taken away. Now he's forced to rely on his cunning to outwit his sadistic opponent. **90m/C VHS.** David Heavener, Erik Estrada, Jim Brown, Shannon Tweed, James Van Patten, Don Stroud, Karen Black, Lori Warren; ***D:*** David Heavener; ***W:*** David Heavener. *NO*

Twisted Love ☠½ **1995 (R)** Wallflower becomes obsessed with the most popular guy in school. He has a motorcycle accident-that-was-no-accident and winds up in her tender care. Sounds like "Misery" to me. **80m/C VHS.** Lisa Dean Ryan, Mark Paul Gosselaar, Soleil Moon Frye; ***D:*** Eb Lottimer. *NHO*

Twisted Nightmare ☠ **1987 (R)** The people responsible for a young retarded boy's death are hunted by a strange figure lurking in the shadows. **95m/C Beta.** Rhonda Gray, Cleve Hall, Brad Bartrum, Robert Padilla; ***D:*** Paul Hunt. *TWE*

Twisted Obsession ☠☠ **1990 (R)** A man becomes passionately obsessed with a woman, and it leads to murder. **109m/C VHS, Beta, LV.** Jeff Goldblum, Miranda Richardson, Anemone, Dexter Fletcher, Daniel Ceccaldi, Liza Walker, Jerome Natali, Arielle Dombasle; ***D:*** Fernando Trueba; ***M:*** Antoine Duhamel. *LIV*

Twister ☠☠ **1989 (PG-13)** An intriguing independent feature about a bizarre midwestern family, its feverish eccentricities and eventual collapse. Awaiting a cult following. **93m/C VHS, Beta, LV.** Dylan McDermott, Crispin Glover, Harry Dean Stanton, Suzy Amis, Jenny Wright, Lindsay Christman, Lois Chiles; ***D:*** Michael Almereyda; ***W:*** Michael Almereyda; ***M:*** Hans Zimmer. *LIV, VES*

Twister ☠☠½ **1996 (PG-13)** Director De Bont's sophomore directorial effort is another non-stop adrenline drive, but instead of a mad bomber, nature is the bad guy. Hunt leads a collegiate team of storm chasing scientists thourgh Oklahoma in hopes of placing a robotic mechanism inside a tornado which, in turn, will help them predict and prepare for future funnel forces. There's also the matter of Hunt's soon-to-be ex-husband Paxton, and a competitor (Elwes) who's in charge of a slick group of rival scientists. There's a lot of things flying around, including trucks, houses, cows and the plausibility of the plot. But a contrived plot didn't keep from making $100 million dollars in its first two weeks of release. Some nice chemistry between Hunt and Paxton, apparently the only people who can still look attractive in high winds and blowing debris. **105m/C VHS.** Bill Paxton, Helen Hunt, Cary Elwes, Jami Gertz, Alan Ruck, Lois Smith, Sean Whalen, Gregory Sporleder, Abraham Benrubi, Jake Busey; ***D:*** Jan De Bont; ***W:*** Michael Crichton, Anne-Marie Martin; ***C:*** Jack N. Green; ***M:*** Mark Mancina. *WAR*

Twister Kicker ☠ **1985** When the woman he loves is in jeopardy, an invincible man battles the best of fighters from three continents. Despite all this action, it's pretty ho-hum. **93m/C VHS.** Wang Hoi, Yeung Oi Wa, Po Pei. *NO*

Twitch of the Death Nerve ☠☠ *Bay of Blood; Last House on the Left, Part 2; Carnage* **1971 (R)** Four vacationers are relentlessly pursued by a homicidal maniac armed with a sickle, bent on decapitation. Supposedly the inspiration for the "Friday the 13th" series. **87m/C VHS, Beta.** *IT* Claudine Auger, Chris Avran, Isa Miranda, Claudio Volonte, Luigi Pistilli; ***D:*** Mario Bava. *NO*

Two Assassins in the Dark ☠ **198?** Martial arts adventure about a pair of kung-fu killers who fight in the dark. **90m/C VHS, Beta.** Wang Tao, Chang Yi, Lung Chun-Eng. *NO*

Two Bits ☠☠½ *A Day to Remember* **1996 (PG-13)** Depression-era drama tells the story of a 12-year old boy and his emotional coming of age. Title refers to a quarter Gennaro (Barone, in his film debut) seeks in order to attend the grand opening of a glamorous, air-conditioned movie palace. A heavily made-up Pacino (looking suspiciously like Marlon Brando in the garden scene of the "Godfather"), co-stars as the boy's grandfather, who leaves him his last quarter. Gramps promises that he can collect later that day, when, he says, he will die. Fine performances all around and some powerful scenes go a long way toward masking the fact that the material is a bit too thin to stretch over an entire feature film. **85m/C VHS.** Al Pacino, Gerlando Barone, Mary Elizabeth Mastrantonio, Joe Grifasi, Joanna Merlin, Andy Romano, Ron McLarty, Donna Mitchell, Patrick Borriello, Mary Lou Rosato, Rosemary DeAngelis; ***D:*** James Foley; ***W:*** Joseph Stefano; ***C:*** Juan Ruiz-Anchia; ***M:*** Jane Musky; ***V:*** Alec Baldwin. *TOU*

Two Bits & Pepper ☠☠½ **1995 (PG)** Bumbling criminals (both played by Piscopo) still manage to kidnap a a young girl and her friend and it's up to the title characters, a pet horse and a pony, to attempt a daring rescue. **90m/C VHS.** Joe Piscopo, Lauren Eckstrom, Rachel Crane, Perry Stephens, Kathrin Lautner, Dennis Weaver; ***D:*** Corey Michael Eubanks; ***W:*** Corey Michael Eubanks; ***C:*** Jacques Haitkin; ***M:*** Louis Febre. *REP*

Two by Forsyth ☠☠ **1986** Two short films based on stories by Frederick Forsyth, one dealing with a dying millionaire's clever efforts to prevent his fortune from being inherited by greedy relatives, the other about a mild-mannered stamp dealer who avenges himself on a nasty gossip columnist. **60m/C VHS, Beta.** Dan O'Herlihy, Cyril Cusack, Milo O'Shea, Shirley Anne Field. *PSM*

Two Daughters ☠☠☠ *Teen Kanya* **1961** Director Ray wrote the scripts for two stories based on the writings of Nobel Prize winner Rabindranath Tagore, one about the relationship between an orphan and a postman, the other about a young man who declines to marry the girl arranged to be his intended. In Hindi with English subtitles. **114m/B VHS, Beta.** *IN* ***D:*** Satyajit Ray; ***W:*** Satyajit Ray. *SUE, INJ, NLC*

Two English Girls ☠☠☠½ *Les Deux Anglaises et le Continent* **1972 (R)** A pre-WWI French lad, with a possessive mother, loves two English sisters, one an impassioned, reckless artist, the other a repressed spinster. Tenderly delineates the triangle's interrelating love and friendship over seven years. Based on the novel "Les Deux Anglaises et le Continent" by Henri-Pierre Roche. In French with English subtitles. **108m/C VHS, Beta, LV.** *FR* Jean-Pierre Leaud, Kika Markham, Stacey Tendeter, Sylvia Marriott, Marie Mansert, Philippe Leotard; ***D:*** Francois Truffaut; ***C:*** Nestor Almendros; ***M:*** Georges Delerue. *HMV, FOX, APD*

Two Evil Eyes ☠☠ *Due Occhi Diabolici* **1990 (R)** Horror kings Romero and Argento each direct an Edgar Allan Poe tale in this release, hence the title. Barbeau, the scheming younger wife of a millionaire, hypnotizes her husband with the help of her lover in "The Facts in the Case of M. Valdemar." When hubby dies too soon to validate changes made in his will, the lovers decide to freeze him for two weeks in order that death can be recorded at the correct time. In "Black Cat" a crime photographer used to photographing gore adopts a feline friend and starts getting sick on the job. **121m/C VHS, Beta, LV.** *IT* Adrienne Barbeau, Ramy Zada, Harvey Keitel, Madeleine Potter; ***D:*** George A. Romero, Dario Argento; ***W:*** Dario Argento; ***M:*** Pino Donaggio. *FXV, VTR*

Two-Faced Woman ☠☠☠ **1941** Garbo, in her last film, attempts a ruse when she finds her husband may be interested in an old flame. Pretending to be her twin sister in an attempt to lure Douglas away from the other woman, she's fooled a little herself. Romantic comedy unfortunately miscasts Garbo as an Americanized ski bunny. **90m/B VHS, Beta.** Greta Garbo, Melvyn Douglas, Constance Bennett, Roland Young, Ruth Gordon, Robert Sterling, George Cleveland, Frances Carson; ***D:*** George Cukor; ***C:*** Joseph Ruttenberg. *MGM*

The Two Faces of Dr. Jekyll ☠☠½ *House of Fright; Jekyll's Inferno* **1960** Henry Jekyll's (Massie) experiments lead to the release of his suave alter ego Edward Hyde. When Hyde discovers that Jekyll's long-suffering wife has taken up with his best friend, Hyde pits everyone against each other, while Jekyll struggles to retain control over his invidious other half. **87m/C VHS.** *GB* Paul Massie, Dawn Addams, Christopher Lee, David Kossoff; ***D:*** Terence Fisher. *COL*

The Two Faces of Evil ☠ **1982** A family's vacation turns into a night of unbearable terror when they pick up a sinister hitchhiker. **60m/C VHS, Beta.** Anna Calder-Marshall, Gary Raymond, Denholm Elliott, Pauline Delany, Philip Latham; ***D:*** Peter Sasdy, Alan Gibson. *LIV*

Two Fathers' Justice **1985** Two dads, one tough and one a wimp, seek revenge on the men who killed their kids. Made for television. **100m/C VHS.** Robert Conrad, George Hamilton, Brooke Bundy, Catherine Corkill, Whitney Kershaw, Greg Terrell; ***D:*** Rod Holcomb. *MCG*

Two Fisted Justice ☠ **1931** A cowboy protects a town against a daring and deadly Indian attack. **45m/B VHS, Beta.** Tom Tyler. *VDM*

Two-Fisted Justice ☠ **1943** The Range Busters do their part to maintain law and order in the old West. **55m/B VHS, Beta.** John "Dusty" King, David Sharpe, Max Terhune. *NOS, DVT*

Two-Fisted Law ☠½ **1932** McCoy plays a rancher who borrows big bucks from the corrupt Oakman, who's actually a land grabber. McCoy then teams up with a posse to bring the evildoer to justice. Early (and small) screen roles for Wayne and Brennan. **58m/B VHS.** Tim McCoy, Tully Marshall, Wheeler Oakman, Alice Day, Wallace MacDonald, John Wayne, Walter Brennan; ***D:*** David Ross Lederman. *COL*

Two for the Road ☠☠☠½ **1967** After over a decade of marriage, Finney and Hepburn look back and find only fragments of their relationship. Mancini score adds poignancy to the couple's reflections on their stormy life. Touching and well-acted. **112m/C VHS, LV.** Audrey Hepburn, Albert Finney, Eleanor Bron, William Daniels, Claude Dauphin, Nadia Gray, Jacqueline Bisset; ***D:*** Stanley Donen; ***W:*** Frederic Raphael; ***M:*** Henry Mancini. Nominations: Academy Awards '67: Best Story & Screenplay. *FXV, BTV, FUS*

Two for the Seesaw ☠☠☠ **1962** Mitchum stars as a Nebraska attorney who comes to New York and gets involved with MacLaine. Humorous and touching comedy-drama worked better on stage, because the large screen magnified the talkiness of Gibson's play. Unusual casting of Mitchum as a Midwest lawyer and MacLaine as a New York Jewish bohemian. **119m/B VHS, LV.** Robert Mitchum, Shirley MacLaine, Edmon Ryan, Elisabeth Fraser, Eddie Firestone, Billy Gray, Vic Lundin; ***D:*** Robert Wise; ***W:*** Isobel Lennart; ***M:*** Andre Previn. Nominations: Academy Awards '62: Best Black and White Cinematography, Best Song ("Song fromm Two for the Seesaw (Second Chance)"). *MGM*

Two Girls and a Sailor ☠☠☠ **1944** Wartime musical revue loosely structured around a love triangle involving a sailor on leave. Vintage hokum with lots of songs. ♫Paper Doll; The Young Man with a Horn; Concerto for Index Finger; Take it Easy; Ritual Fire Dance; Inka Dinka Doo; My Mother Told Me; A Love Like Ours; In A Moment of Madness. **124m/B VHS, Beta, LV.** June Allyson, Gloria De Haven, Van Johnson, Xavier Cugat, Jimmy Durante, Tom Drake, Lena Horne, Harry James, Gracie Allen, Virginia O'Brien, Jose Iturbi, Carlos Ramirez, Donald Meek, Ben Blue; ***Cameos:*** Buster Keaton; ***D:*** Richard Thorpe; ***C:*** Robert L. Surtees. Nominations: Academy Awards '44: Best Original Screenplay. *MGM*

Two Graves to Kung-Fu ☠ **1982 (R)** Young kung-fu student is framed for murder. When the real murderers kill his teacher, he escapes from prison to seek revenge. **95m/C VHS, Beta.** Liu Chia-Yung, Shek Kin, Chen Hung-Lieh. *GEM*

The Two Great Cavaliers 🦴 **1973** A Ming warrior has a hard time with the Manchurian army, fending it off as he must with only his bare instep, heel, and wrist. **95m/C VHS, Beta.** Chen Shing, Mao Ying; ***D:*** Yeung Ching Chen. *UNI*

Two Gun Man 🦴½ **1931** America's first singing cowboy, Ken Maynard, performs hair-raising stunts in this old oater. One of the first "talkies!" **60m/B VHS, Beta.** Ken Maynard, Lafe McKee, Charles "Blackie" King, Tom London, Lucille Powers; ***D:*** Phil Rosen. *GPV, VCN, DVT*

Two-Gun Man from Harlem **1938** Big city guy travels to the wild West in search of a little truth. **60m/B VHS.** Herbert Jeffries, Marguerite Whitten, Mantan Moreland, Matthew "Stymie" Beard; ***D:*** Richard C. Kahn. *NOS, TPV*

Two-Gun Troubador 🦴 *The Lone Troubador* **1937** A masked singing cowboy struggles to uncovers his father's murderer. **59m/B VHS, Beta.** Fred Scott, Claire Rochelle, John Merton. *NOS, BAR, HEG*

200 Motels 🦴½ **1971 (R)** Rambling, non-narrative self-indulgent video album by and about Frank Zappa and the Mothers of Invention, as they document a long and especially grueling road tour. For fans only. **99m/C VHS, Beta.** Frank Zappa, Ringo Starr; ***D:*** Frank Zappa. *MVD, MGM*

Two If by Sea 🦴½ *Stolen Hearts* **1995 (R)** Small-time hood Frank (Leary) and his girlfriend Roz (Bullock) hole up in a New England mansion after Frank steals a valuable Matisse painting. Between verbal sparring matches, the two try to mingle with the upper crusty residents with predictable results. Pursuing the pair are the FBI, led by the deluded O'Malley (Kotto), and Frank's bonehead cousin Beano (Robson) and his trio of dim henchmen. Tries to be a caper/romantic comedy but fails to deliver on all fronts. The usually caustic Leary takes some of the edge off of his trademark bitter humor, and the alleged witty repartee is just plain annoying as a result. Nova Scotia turns in a fine performance as New England. **96m/C VHS, LV.** Sandra Bullock, Denis Leary, Stephen Dillane, Yaphet Kotto, Wayne Robson, Jonathan Tucker, Mike Starr, Michael Badalucco, Lenny Clarke, John Friesen; ***D:*** Bill Bennett; ***W:*** Denis Leary, Michael Armstrong; ***C:*** Andrew Lesnie. *WAR*

The Two Jakes 🦴🦴 **1990 (R)** Ten years have passed and Jake Gittes is still a private investigator in this sequel to 1974's "Chinatown." When a murder occurs while he's digging up dirt on an affair between the wife of a real estate executive and the executive's partner, Jake must return to Chinatown to uncover the killer and face the painful memories buried there. Despite solid dialogue and effective performances, it's unreasonably difficult to follow if you haven't seen "Chinatown." Outstanding photography by Vilmos Zsigmond. **137m/C VHS, Beta, LV.** Jack Nicholson, Harvey Keitel, Meg Tilly, Madeleine Stowe, Eli Wallach, Ruben Blades, Frederic Forrest, David Keith, Richard Farnsworth, Tracey Walter; ***D:*** Jack Nicholson; ***W:*** Robert Towne; ***C:*** Vilmos Zsigmond; ***M:*** Van Dyke Parks. *PAR, FCT*

Two Kinds of Love 🦴🦴 **1985** Adapted from Peggy Mann's novel "There Are Two Kinds of Terrible" this is the story of a young boy who learns to love his distant, workaholic father after his protective mother suddenly dies. Made for television. **94m/C VHS, Beta.** Rick Schroder, Lindsay Wagner, Peter Weller; ***D:*** Jack Bender. *FOX*

Two Lost Worlds *Woof!* **1950** A young hero battles monstrous dinosaurs, pirates, and more in this cheapy when he and his shipmates are shipwrecked on an uncharted island. Don't miss the footage from "Captain Fury," "One Billion B.C. ," and "Captain Caution" and Arness long before his Sheriff Dillon fame, and his "big" role in "The Thing." **63m/B VHS, Beta.** James Arness, Laura Elliott, Bill Kennedy; ***D:*** Norman Dawn. *NO*

Two Men & a Wardrobe **1958** Polanski's project while a student at the Polish Film Institute. Consideration of modern man's lack of privacy and made without dialogue. Two men emerge from the sea carrying nothing but a large piece of furniture. Absurd and funny. **19m/B VHS, Beta.** ***D:*** Roman Polanski. *IHF, GVV*

Two Minute Warning 🦴 **1976 (R)** A sniper plans to take out the president of the United States at an NFL playoff game in this boring, pointless, disaster film that goes on forever. Features all the ready-made characters inherent in the genre, but, until its too late, precious little of the mayhem. To get caught watching the TV version, which features more characters and an additional subplot, would be truly disastrous. **116m/C VHS, LV.** Charlton Heston, John Cassavetes, Martin Balsam, Beau Bridges, Marilyn Hassett, David Janssen, Jack Klugman, Walter Pidgeon, Gena Rowlands; ***D:*** Larry Peerce; ***M:*** Charles Fox. Nominations: Academy Awards '76: Best Film Editing. *MCA*

The Two Mrs. Carrolls 🦴🦴½ **1947** Bogart is a psycho-killer/artist who paints portraits of his wives as the Angel of Death—and then kills them. The married Bogart falls for Stanwyck, poisons his current wife, and the two marry. After a few years, Bogart falls for Smith and decides to rid himself of Stanwyck in the same manner as his first killing. Stanwyck, however, becomes increasingly suspicious and calls on an old beau for help. Melodrama cast Bogart against type (not always successfully). Filmed in 1945, but was unreleased until 1947. **99m/B VHS.** Humphrey Bogart, Barbara Stanwyck, Alexis Smith, Nigel Bruce, Pat O'Moore, Ann Carter; ***D:*** Peter Godfrey. *MGM*

Two Moon Junction 🦴½ **1988 (R)** A soon-to-be-wed Southern debutante enters into a wild love affair with a rough-edged carnival worker. Poorly acted, wildly directed, with many unintentional laughs. **104m/C VHS, Beta, LV.** Sherilyn Fenn, Richard Tyson, Louise Fletcher, Burl Ives, Kristy McNichol, Millie Perkins, Don Galloway, Herve Villechaize, Dabbs Greer, Jay Hawkins; ***D:*** Zalman King; ***W:*** Zalman King; ***M:*** Jonathan Elias. Golden Raspberry Awards '88: Worst Supporting Actress (McNichol). *COL*

Two Much 🦴½ **1996 (PG-13)** Banderas does double duty as a con man pretending to be twins in order to romance two sisters (Griffith and Hannah). Embarrassingly light comedy suffers from a complicated plot (which still manages to leave holes), weak or non-existent characterization, and a general lack of humor. About the only thing it has going for it is Cusack as a wisecracking secretary. It was on the set of this film that Banderas and Griffith started their real-life romance. While that may have helped the box office and gossip columns in Banderas's homeland, the fireworks didn't find their way to the screen. **115m/C VHS.** Melanie Griffith, Antonio Banderas, Daryl Hannah, Joan Cusack, Danny Aiello, Eli Wallach, Vincent Schiavelli; ***D:*** Fernando Trueba; ***W:*** Fernando Trueba, David Trueba; ***C:*** Jose Luis Alcaine; ***M:*** Michel Camilo. *NYR*

Two Mules for Sister Sara 🦴🦴🦴 **1970 (PG)** American mercenary in 19th century Mexico gets mixed up with a cigar-smoking nun and the two make plans to capture a French garrison. MacLaine and Eastwood are great together. Based on a Boetticher story. **105m/C VHS, Beta.** Clint Eastwood, Shirley MacLaine; ***D:*** Donald Siegel; ***W:*** Albert Maltz; ***M:*** Ennio Morricone. *MCA*

Two Nights with Cleopatra 🦴½ *Due Notti Con Cleopatra* **1954** A piece of Italian pizza involving Cleopatra's double (also played by Loren) falling in love with one of the guards. Notable only for the 19-year-old Sophia's brief nudity. **77m/C VHS, Beta.** *IT* Sophia Loren, Ettore Manni, Alberto Sordi, Paul Muller, Alberto Talegalli, Rolf Tasna, Gianni Cavalieri, Fernando Bruno, Riccardo Garrone, Carlo Dale; ***D:*** Mario Mattoli; ***W:*** Nino Maccari, Ettore Scola. *VDM*

Two of a Kind 🦴🦴½ **1982** In his television movie debut, Burns plays an elderly man whose mentally handicapped grandson helps him put the starch back in his shirt. Sensitively produced and performed. **102m/C VHS, Beta.** George Burns, Robby Benson, Cliff Robertson, Barbara Barrie, Frances Lee McCain, Geri Jewell, Ronny Cox; ***D:*** Roger Young. *FOX*

Two of a Kind 🦴 **1983 (PG)** Angels make a bet with God—two selfish people will redeem themselves or God can blow up the Earth. Bad acting, awful direction, and the script needs divine intervention. **88m/C VHS, Beta, LV.** John Travolta, Olivia Newton-John, Charles Durning, Beatrice Straight, Scatman Crothers, Oliver Reed; ***D:*** John Herzfeld; ***C:*** Fred W. Koenekamp. *FOX*

The Two of Us 🦴🦴🦴½ *Le Vieil Homme Et L'Enfant; Claude; The Old Man and the Boy* **1968** Young Jewish boy flees Nazi-occupied Paris to live in the country with an irritable, bigoted guardian. Sensitive, eloquent movie about racial prejudice and anti-Semitism. In French with English subtitles. **86m/B VHS.** *FR* Michel Simon, Alain Cohen, Luce Fabiole, Roger Carel, Paul Preboist, Charles Denner; ***D:*** Claude Berri; ***M:*** Georges Delerue. *NO*

Two Rode Together 🦴🦴½ **1961** A Texas marshal and an army lieutenant negotiate with the Comanches for the return of captives, but complications ensue. **109m/C VHS, Beta, LV.** James Stewart, Richard Widmark, Shirley Jones, Linda Cristal, Andy Devine, John McIntire; ***D:*** John Ford. *COL*

The Two Sisters **1937** Goldstein, in her only film role, plays an older sister who sacrifices everything for the younger. The younger thanks her by stealing her fiance. In Yiddish with English subtitles. **70m/B VHS.** Jenney Goldstein, Michael Rosenberg. *ALD*

Two Small Bodies 🦴🦴 **1993** Police detective Brann investigates the disappearance of two young children, suspecting their mother Eileen may have murdered them. Two character study set in Eileen's home with both verbally recreating versions of the possible crime. Based on the play by Neal Bell. **85m/C VHS.** Fred Ward, Suzy Amis; ***D:*** Beth B; ***W:*** Beth B, Neal Bell. *ORI*

2000 Maniacs 🦴🦴½ **1964** One of cult director Lewis' most enjoyably watchable films. A literal Civil War "ghost town" takes its revenge 100 years after being slaughtered by renegade Union soldiers by luring unwitting "yankee" tourists to their centennial festival. The hapless Notherners are then chopped, crushed, ripped apart etc. while the ghostly rebels party. Quite fun in a cartoonishly gruesome sort of way. Filmed in St. Cloud, FL. **75m/C VHS, Beta.** Thomas Wood, Connie Mason, Jeffrey Allen, Ben Moore, Gary Bakeman, Jerome Eden, Shelby Livingston, Michael Korb, Yvonne Gilbert, Mark Douglas, Linda Cochran, Vincent Santo, Andy Wilson; ***D:*** Herschell Gordon Lewis; ***W:*** Herschell Gordon Lewis. *NO*

2001: A Space Odyssey 🦴🦴🦴🦴 **1968** Space voyage to Jupiter turns chaotic when a computer, HAL 9000, takes over. Seen by some as a mirror of man's historical use of machinery and by others as a grim vision of the future, the special effects and music are still stunning. Critically acclaimed and well accepted by some, simply confusing to others. Martin Balsam originally recorded the voice of HAL, but was replaced by Rain. From Arthur C. Clarke's novel "The Sentinel." Followed by a sequel "2010: The Year We Make Contact." Laserdisc edition is presented in letterbox format and features a special supplementary section on the making of "2001," a montage of images from the film, production documents, memos and photos. Also included on the disc is a NASA film entitled "Art and Reality," which offers footage from the Voyager I and II flybys of Jupiter. **139m/C VHS, Beta, LV.** *GB* Keir Dullea, Gary Lockwood, William Sylvester, Dan Richter; ***D:*** Stanley Kubrick; ***W:*** Arthur C. Clarke, Stanley Kubrick; ***C:*** Geoffrey Unsworth; ***V:*** Douglas Raines. Academy Awards '68: Best Visual Effects; National Board of Review Awards '68: 10 Best Films of the Year; Nominations: Academy Awards '68: Best Art Direction/Set Decoration, Best Director (Kubrick), Best Story & Screenplay. *MGM, CRC, FCT*

2010: The Year We Make Contact 🦴🦴🦴 **1984 (PG)** The film version of Arthur C. Clarke's novel "The Sentinel" continues in this sequel to "2001: A Space Odyssey." Americans and Russians unite to investigate the abandoned starship Discovery's decaying orbit around Jupiter and try to determine why the HAL 9000 computer sabotaged its mission years before, while signs of cosmic change are detected on and around the giant planet. **116m/C VHS, Beta, LV.** Roy Scheider, John Lithgow, Helen Mirren, Bob Balaban, Keir Dullea, Madolyn Smith, Mary Jo Deschanel; ***D:*** Peter Hyams; ***W:*** Peter Hyams; ***M:*** David Shire; ***V:*** Douglas Raines. Nominations: Academy Awards '84: Best Art Direction/Set Decoration, Best Makeup, Best Sound. *MGM*

2020 Texas Gladiators *Woof!* **1985 (R)** In the post-nuclear holocaust world, two groups, one good, one evil, battle for supremacy. **91m/C VHS, Beta.** *IT* Harrison Muller, Al Cliver, Daniel Stephen, Peter Hooten, Al Yamanouchi, Sabrina Santi; ***D:*** Kevin Mancuso. *MED*

2069: A Sex Odyssey 🦴½ **1978 (R)** Team of beautiful, sensuous astronauts are sent to Earth to obtain male sperm which they must bring back to Venus. Tongue-in-cheek soft core sci-fi spoof. **73m/C VHS, Beta.** Alena Penz, Nina Fredric, Gerti Sneider, Raul Retzer, Catherine Conti, Heidi Hammer, Michael Mein, Herb Heesel; ***D:*** George Keil. *ACA, HHE*

Two Tickets to Broadway 🦴🦴½ **1951** A small-town singer and a crooner arrange a hoax to get themselves on Bob Crosby's television show. Appealing but lightweight. ♫Let the Worry Bird Worry For You; Pagliacci; There's No Tomorrow; Manhattan; Big Chief Hole in the Ground; The Closer You Are; Baby, You'll Never Be Sorry; Pelican Falls High; It Began In Yucatan. **106m/C VHS, Beta.** Tony Martin, Janet Leigh, Gloria De Haven, Joi Lansing; ***D:*** James V. Kern; ***M:*** Leo Robin, Jule Styne; ***Performed by:*** Smith & Dale. Nominations: Academy Awards '51: Best Sound. *TTC*

Two to Tango 🦴½ **1988 (R)** A hired assassin goes to Buenos Aires to kill a crime boss, and falls in love with his tango-dancing mistress. Based on the novel by J.P. Feinman. **87m/C VHS, Beta.** *AR* Don Stroud, Adrienne Sachs; ***D:*** Hector Olivera. *NO*

Two-Way Stretch 🦴🦴½ **1960** Three prison inmates in a progressive jail plan to break out, pull a diamond heist, and break back in, all in the same night. Fast-paced slapstick farce. **84m/B VHS, Beta.** *GB* Peter Sellers, Wilfrid Hyde-White, Liz Fraser, David Lodge; ***D:*** Robert Day. *NO*

Two Weeks in Another Town 🦴🦴 **1962** Douglas and Robinson are a couple of Hollywood has-beens who set out to make a comeback picture but meet with adversity at every turn. Extremely sappy melodrama is based on Irwin Shaw's trashy novel and represents one of director Minnelli's poorer efforts. Laserdisc features a letterboxed screen and the original movie trailer. **107m/C VHS, LV.** Kirk Douglas, Edward G. Robinson, Cyd Charisse, George Hamilton, Daliah Lavi, Claire Trevor, James Gregory, Rosanna Schiaffino, George Macready, Stefan Schnabel, Vito Scotti, Leslie Uggams; ***D:*** Vincente Minnelli; ***C:*** Milton Krasner. *MGM*

Two Weeks to Live 🦴½ **1943** The comedy team inherits a railroad line, only to find it's a pile of junk. **60m/B VHS, Beta.** Lum & Abner, Franklin Pangborn. *NOS, DVT*

Two Weeks with Love 🦴🦴 **1950** Reynolds and family wear funny bathing suits in the Catskills in the early 1900s while the Debster sings songs and blushes into young adulthood. ♫Aba Daba Honeymoon; The Oceana Roll; A Heart That's Free; By the Light of the Silvery Moon; My Hero; Row, Row, Row; That's How I Need You; Beautiful Lady. **92m/C VHS.** Debbie Reynolds, Jane Powell, Ricardo Montalban, Louis Calhern, Ann Harding, Phyllis Kirk, Carleton Carpenter, Clinton Sundberg, Gary Gray; ***D:*** Roy Rowland. *MGM, FCT*

Two Women 🦴🦴🦴🦴 *La Ciociara* **1961** A mother and her 13-year-old daughter travel war-torn Italy during WWII and must survive lack of food, crazed monks and brutal soldiers. Tragic, moving, well-directed. Loren received well-deserved Oscar. In Italian with English subtitles or dubbed. **99m/B VHS, Beta.** *IT* Sophia Loren, Raf Vallone, Eleonora Brown, Jean-Paul Belmondo; ***D:*** Vittorio De Sica; ***W:*** Cesare Zavattini, Vittorio De Sica; ***M:*** Armando Trovajoli. Academy Awards '61: Best Actress (Loren); British Academy Awards '61: Best Actress (Loren); Cannes Film Festival '61: Best Actress (Loren); Golden Globe Awards '62: Best Foreign Film; National Board of Review Awards '61: 5 Best Foreign Films of the Year; New York Film Critics Awards '61: Best Actress (Loren). *COL, APD, BTV*

Two Wondrous Tigers 🦴 **1979** Awesome Kung-fu gang terrorizes a small town until a local dares to out-chop the bullies. **87m/C VHS, Beta.** John Chang; ***D:*** Wilson Tong. *TWE*

The Two Worlds of Jenny Logan 🦴🦴½ **1979** A woman travels back and forth in time whenever she dons a 19th century dress she finds in her old house. She is also able to fall in love twice, in different centuries. Made for television and adapted from "Second Sight," a novel by David Williams. Stylish and well made. **97m/C VHS, Beta.** Lindsay Wagner, Marc Singer, Alan Feinstein, Linda Gray, Constance McCashin, Henry Wilcoxon, Irene Tedrow, Joan Darling, Allen Williams, Pat Corley, Gloria Stuart; ***D:*** Frank de Felitta. *FRH, LIV*

Two Wrongs Make a Right 🦴 **1989** A quiet nightclub owner beats and clubs his way through his tough neighborhood to protect himself and his woman. **85m/C VHS, Beta.** Ivan Rogers, Ron Blackstone, Rich Komenich; ***D:*** Robert Brown. *UNI*

Twogether 🦴🦴½ **1994 (R)** Struggling artist John (Cassavettes) and environmentalist Allison (Bakke) have this lust thing going on. It leads to a drunken Las Vegas wedding and a quickie divorce but they still don't keep their hands off of each other (or any other body parts) and Allison gets pregnant. They decide to become partners in raising the baby but first they'll have to do some growing up of their own. Also available unrated. **108m/C VHS.** Brenda Bakke, Nick Cassavetes, Jeremy Piven, Jim Beaver; ***D:*** Andrew Chiaramonte; ***W:*** Andrew Chiaramonte; ***C:*** Eugene Shlugleit; ***M:*** Nigel Holton. *COL*

Tycoon 🦴🦴½ **1947** Wayne goes to Latin America to build a road for an American industrialist. When the industrialist insists on a shorter but more dangerous route, Wayne must satisfy his own sense of honor. Meanwhile, he's found romance with the industrialist's half-Spanish daughter. Long, but well-acted. **129m/C VHS, Beta, LV.** John Wayne, Laraine Day, Cedric Hardwicke, Judith Anderson, James Gleason, Anthony Quinn; ***D:*** Richard Wallace. *CCB, TTC*

Typhoon Treasure 🦴 **1939** Whilst recovering his sunken treasure, the hero battles bad guys, savage natives and a crocodile, all of whom could probably have made a more sophisticated film. **68m/B VHS.** *AU* Campbell Copelin, Gwen Munro, Joe Valli, Douglas Herald; ***D:*** Noel Monkman. *NOS, LOO*

Tyrant of Lydia Against the Son of Hercules **1963** Hercules' son takes on a wicked king in this startling adventure. **?m/C VHS, Beta.** *IT* Gordon Scott, Massimo Serato. *SNC*

Tyson 🦴🦴 **1995** Based on the life of former World Heavyweight Champion, Mike Tyson (White) who rose from the streets of Brownsville to a million dollar lifestyle and a spectacular fall to a rape conviction and a prison term (which are handled in voice-over). Story begins with trainer Cus D'Amato (Scott) finding unpolished and troubled young Tyson and training him for the Junior Olympics. When promoter Don King (Winfield) enters the picture, Tyson's career really takes off. Pulls no punches about Tyson's short fuse and brutal abilities. Based on the book "Fire and Fear: The Inside Story of Mike Tyson" by Jose Torres. **90m/C VHS.** Michael Jai White, Paul Winfield, George C. Scott, Malcolm Jamal Warner, Tony LoBianco, James B. Sikking, Clark Gregg, Kristen Wilson, Sheila Wills, Holt McCallany, Lilyan Chauvin, Georg Stanford Brown, Joe Santos, Charles Napier; ***D:*** Uli Edel; ***W:*** Robert Johnson; ***M:*** Stewart Copeland. *HBO*

U-Boat Prisoner 🦴 **1944** Bennett is an American sailor who's captured by a Nazi U-boat. He promptly defeats the crew, leaving the U-boat to the mercy of a U.S. destroyer. Silly, silly, silly. **65m/B VHS.** Bruce (Herman Brix) Bennett, John Abbott, John Wood, Kenneth MacDonald, Erik Rolf, John Wengraf; ***D:*** Lew (Louis Friedlander) Landers. *GPV*

UFO: Target Earth 🦴 **1974 (G)** Scientist attempts to fish flying saucer out of lake and costs studio $70,000. **80m/C VHS.** Nick Plakias, Cynthia Cline, Phil Erickson; ***D:*** Michael de Gaetano. *MOV*

Uforia 🦴🦴 **1981** Two rival evangelists meet up with a UFO-infatuated girl. Under her guidance, they wait for UFO encounters they intend to use to milk their revivalist audiences. Sometimes clumsy, but more often fun. **92m/C VHS, Beta.** Cindy Williams, Harry Dean Stanton, Fred Ward; ***D:*** John Binder; ***W:*** John Binder; ***M:*** Richard Baskin. *MCA*

Ugetsu 🦴🦴🦴½ *Ugetsu Monogatari* **1953** The classic film that established Mizoguchi's reputation outside of Japan. Two 16th century Japanese peasants venture from their homes in pursuit of dreams, and encounter little more than their own hapless folly and a bit of the supernatural. A wonderful mix of comedy and action with nifty camera movement. Based on the stories of Akinara Ueda. In Japanese with English subtitles. **96m/B VHS, Beta, LV, 8mm.** *JP* Machiko Kyo, Masayuki Mori, Kinuyo Tanaka, Sakae Ozawa; ***D:*** Kenji Mizoguchi. Venice Film Festival '53: Silver Prize; Nominations: Academy Awards '55: Best Costume Design (B & W). *HMV, SUE, WFV*

The Ugly American 🦴🦴½ **1963** A naive American ambassador to a small, civil-war-torn Asian country fights a miniature Cold War against northern communist influence. Too preachy, and the "Red Menace" aspects are now very dated, but Brando's performance is worth watching. Based on the William J. Lederer novel. **120m/C VHS, Beta.** Marlon Brando, Sandra Church, Eiji Okada, Pat Hingle, Arthur Hill; ***D:*** George Englund; ***W:*** Stewart Stern. *MCA*

The Ugly Dachshund 🦴🦴½ **1965** Jones and Pleshette are married dog lovers who raise Dachshunds. When Ruggles convinces them to take a Great Dane puppy, the fun begins! The Great Dane thinks he is a Dachshund because he has been raised with them—just imagine what happens when such a large dog acts as if he is small! Kids will love this wacky Disney film. **93m/C VHS, Beta.** Dean Jones, Suzanne Pleshette, Charlie Ruggles, Kelly Thordsen, Parley Baer; ***D:*** Norman Tokar; ***C:*** Edward Colman. *DIS, OM*

UHF 🦴🦴 **1989 (PG-13)** A loser is appointed manager of a bargain-basement UHF television station. He turns it around via bizarre programming ideas. Some fun parodies of TV enhance this minimal story. Developed solely as a vehicle for Yankovic. **97m/C VHS, Beta, LV.** Weird Al Yankovic, Kevin McCarthy, Victoria Jackson, Michael Richards, David Bowie, Anthony Geary; ***D:*** Jay Levey; ***M:*** John Du Prez. *ORI*

Ulterior Motives 🦴½ **1992 (R)** P.I. Jack Blaylock agrees to protect a pretty reporter from Japanese gangsters. He finds himself caught up in deception and betrayal and uses all his considerable, and violent, skills to make certain he does his job. **90m/C VHS.** Thomas Ian Griffith, Mary Page Keller, Joe Yamanaka, Ellen Crawford, Ken Howard, Tyra Ferrell; ***D:*** James Becket. *IMP*

Ultimate Desires 🦴🦴 **1991 (R)** When a high class hooker is brutally killed, beautiful Scoggins puts on what there is of the victim's clothes in order to solve the mystery. But trouble lies in wait as she actually begins to enjoy her funky new double life. Can she solve the crime before becoming lost in her own hot fantasy world? **93m/C VHS, Beta.** Tracy Scoggins, Brion James, Marc Singer, Marc Baur, Marc Bennett, Suzy Joachim, Jason Scott, John Wood; ***D:*** Lloyd A. Simanol. *PSM*

The Ultimate Imposter 🦴 **1979** A secret agent acquires voluminous knowledge through a computer brain linkup, but can only retain the knowledge for 72 hours. In that timespan he has to rescue a defecting Russian from hordes of assassins. Made for television. **97m/C VHS, Beta.** Keith Andes, Erin Gray, Joseph Hacker, Macon McCalman; ***D:*** Paul Stanley. *MCA*

The Ultimate Thrill 🦴½ *The Ultimate Chase* **1974 (PG)** Businessman's paranoia about his wife's affairs leads him to follow her to Colorado on a ski holiday and stalk her lovers. Well-filmed skiing scenes and not much else. Also known as "The Ultimate Chase." **84m/C VHS, Beta.** Britt Ekland, Barry Brown, Michael Blodgett, John Davis Chandler, Eric (Hans Gudegast) Braeden; ***D:*** Robert Butler. *GEM, CNG*

The Ultimate Warrior 🦴🦴½ **1975 (R)** Yul Brynner must defend the plants and seeds of a pioneer scientist to help replenish the world's food supply in this thriller set in 2012. **92m/C VHS, Beta.** Yul Brynner, Max von Sydow, Joanna Miles, Richard Kelton, Lane Bradbury, William Smith; ***D:*** Robert Clouse; ***W:*** Robert Clouse. *WAR*

Ultra Flash **1983** A fantasy that is performed to some of today's hottest dance music. In stereo **60m/C VHS, Beta.** *LIV, VES*

Ultra Warrior 🦴½ *Welcome to Oblivion* **1992 (R)** A basic post-apocalyptic adventure tale of a radioactive earth, mutants, and various battles by the good guys to save the planet. **80m/C VHS.** Dack Rambo, Meshach Taylor, Clare Beresford. *NHO*

Ulysses 🦴🦴½ *Ulisse* **1955** An Italian made version of the epic poem by Homer, as the warrior returns to his homeland and the ever-faithful Penelope after the Trojan war. Ambitious effort provides for the ultimate mixed review. Douglas is good in the role and his stops along the ten-year way are well visualized. Sometimes sluggish with poor dubbing. Seven writers helped bring Homer to the big screen. **104m/C VHS, Beta.** *IT* Kirk Douglas, Silvana Mangano, Anthony Quinn, Rossana Podesta; ***D:*** Mario Camerini. *WAR, OM*

Ulysses 🦴🦴½ **1967** James Joyce's probably unfilmable novel was given a noble effort in this flawed film covering a day in the life of Leopold Bloom as he wanders through Dublin. Shot in Ireland with a primarily Irish cast. **140m/B VHS, LV.** Milo O'Shea, Maurice Roeves, T.P. McKenna, Martin Dempsey, Sheila O'Sullivan, Barbara Jefford; ***D:*** Joseph Strick. Nominations: Academy Awards '67: Best Adapted Screenplay. *MFV*

Ulysses' Gaze 🦴🦴 *The Look of Ulysses; To Vlemma Tou Odyssea; The Gaze of Ulysses* **1995** Nameless Greek-American filmmaker (Keitel) journeys across the Balkans from Athens to Sarajevo while making a documentary on pioneer filmmakers, the Manakia brothers, who ignored national and ethnic strife in order to record the lives of ordinary people. Keitel has heard that some undeveloped film shot by the brothers has turned up in Sarajevo and he's determined to see it despite the turmoil in Bosnia. Moving and pessimistic depiction of the Balkan conflict seen through a filmmaker's eyes. English and Balkan dialogue. **177m/C VHS.** *GR FR IT* Harvey Keitel, Maia Morgenstern, Erland Josephson, Thanassis Vengos, Yorgos Michalokopoulos, Dora Volonaki; ***D:*** Theo Angelopoulos; ***W:*** Theo Angelopoulos, Tonino Guerra, Petros Markaris; ***C:*** Yorgos Arvanitis; ***M:*** Eleni Karaindrou. Cannes Film Festival '95: Grand Jury Prize. *NYR*

Ulzana's Raid 🦴🦴🦴 **1972 (R)** An aging scout and an idealistic Cavalry lieutenant lock horns on their way to battling a vicious Apache chieftain. A violent, gritty western that enjoyed critical re-evaluation years after its first release. **103m/C VHS, Beta, LV.** Burt Lancaster, Bruce Davison, Richard Jaeckel, Lloyd Bochner, Jorge Luke; ***D:*** Robert Aldrich; ***C:*** Joseph Biroc. *MCA*

Umberto D 🦴🦴🦴🦴 **1955** A government pensioner, living alone with his beloved dog, struggles to keep up a semblance of dignity on his inadequate pension. De Sica considered this his masterpiece. A sincere, tender treatment of the struggles involved with the inevitability of aging. In Italian with English subtitles. Laser edition features letterboxed print. **89m/B VHS, Beta, LV, 8mm.** *IT* Carlo Battista, Maria Pia Casilio, Lina Gennari; ***D:*** Vittorio De Sica; ***W:*** Cesare Zavattini, Vittorio De Sica. New York Film Critics Awards '55: Best Foreign Film; Nominations: Academy Awards '56: Best Story. *HMV, SUE, HHT*

Umbrellas of Cherbourg 🦴🦴🦴½ *Les Parapluies De Cherbourg; Die Regenschirme Von Cherbourg* **1964** A bittersweet film operetta with no spoken dialog. Deneuve is the teenaged daughter of a widow who owns an umbrella shop. She and her equally young boyfriend are separated by his military duty in Algeria. Finding she is pregnant, the girl marries a wealthy man, and when her former lover returns, he too marries someone else. But when they meet once again will their love be rekindled? Lovely photography and an evocative score enhance the story. In French with subtitles; also available dubbed in English (not with the same effectiveness). Oscar nominee for cinematography and story. **90m/C VHS, Beta.** *FR* Catherine Deneuve, Nino Castelnuovo, Anne Vernon, Ellen Farner, Marc Michel, Mireille Perrey, Jean Champion, Alfred Wolff, Dorothee Blanck; ***D:*** Jacques Demy; ***W:*** Jacques Demy; ***M:*** Michel Legrand. Cannes Film Festival '64: Best Film; Nominations: Academy Awards '65: Best Foreign Language Film, Best Song ("I Will Wait for You"), Best Story & Screenplay, Best Original Score. *LIV, APD*

Un Chien Andalou 🦴🦴🦴🦴 **1928** Masterful surrealist short features a host of classic sequences, including a razor across an eye, a severed hand lying in the street, ants crawling from a hole in a man's hand, priests, dead horses, and a piano dragged across a room. A classic. Score features both Wagner and tango. **20m/B VHS, Beta.** *FR* Pierre Batcheff, Simone Marevil, Jaime Miravilles; ***D:*** Luis Bunuel, Salvador Dali. *HHT, GVV, APD*

Un Coeur en Hiver 🦴🦴½ *A Heart in Winter* **1993** An anti-romance romantic drama where passion is frozen and real emotion is reserved for the inanimate. Serious Stephane (Auteuil) is a master craftsman at repairing violins; his partner Maxime (Dussollier) runs the business side and deals with the musicians, including beautiful violinist Camille (Beart) with whom he has fallen in love. Camille is single-mindedly fixated on her career and she recognizes a kindred spirit in Stephane but their calculated emotional seduction causes problems for all. Can be frustrating since the smooth surface of the characters is rarely cracked. In French with English titles. **100m/C VHS, LV.** *FR* Emmanuelle Beart, Daniel Auteuil, Andre Dussollier, Elisabeth Bourgine, Brigitte Catillon, Maurice Garrel, Miriam Boyer; ***D:*** Claude Sautet; ***W:*** Yves Ulmann, Jacques Fieschi, Jerome Tonnerre. Cesar Awards '93: Best Director (Sautet), Best Supporting Actor (Dussollier); Nominations: British Academy Awards '93: Best Foreign Language Film. *REP*

Un Singe en Hiver 🦴🦴½ *A Monkey in Winter; It's Hot in Hell* **1962** A young wanderer (Belmondo) befriends a crusty old alcoholic (Gabin) who has kept his vow to abstain since his village survived the German bombing of WWII. Moving tale of regret and the passage of time. In French with English subtitles. **105m/B VHS, Beta.** Jean-Paul Belmondo, Jean Gabin, Suzanne Flon, Paul Frankeur; ***D:*** Henri Verneuil. *BAR, INJ*

The Unapproachable 🦴🦴½ **1982** A rendition of the Polish director's two one-act plays concerning a reclusive aging stage star being manipulated by her hangers-on. **92m/C VHS, Beta.** *PL* Leslie Caron, Daniel Webb, Leslie Malton; ***D:*** Krzysztof Zanussi. *MGM*

The Unbearable Lightness of Being 🦴🦴🦴½ **1988 (R)** Tomas (Day Lewis), a young Czech doctor in the late 1960s, leads a sexually and emotionally carefree existence with a number of women, including provocative artist Olin. When he meets the fragile Binoche, he may be falling in love for the first time. On the eve of the 1968 Russian invasion of Czechoslovakia the two flee to Switzerland, but Binoche can't reconcile herself to exile and returns, followed by the reluctant Tomas who has lost his position because of his new-found political idealism. They lead an increasingly simple life, drawn ever closer together. The haunting ending caps off superb performances. Based on the novel by Milan Kundera. **172m/C VHS, Beta, LV.** Daniel Day-Lewis, Juliette Binoche, Lena Olin, Derek De Lint, Erland Josephson, Pavel Landovsky, Donald Moffat, Daniel Olbrychski, Stellan Skarsgard; ***D:*** Philip Kaufman; ***W:*** Jean-Claude Carriere, Philip Kaufman; ***C:*** Sven Nykvist. British Academy Awards '88: Best Adapted Screenplay; Independent Spirit Awards '89: Best Cinematography; National Society of Film Critics Awards '88: Best Director (Kaufman), Best Film; Nominations: Academy Awards '88: Best Adapted Screenplay, Best Cinematography. *ORI, INJ*

The Unbeaten 28 🦴 **198?** A group of kung fu masters is forced to fight for their lives against evil criminals. **90m/C VHS, Beta.** Lisa Chang, Meng Fei, Lung Sikar; ***D:*** Joseph Kuo. *MPI*

The Unbelievable Truth 🦴🦴½ **1990 (R)** Ex-con Robocop-to-be Burke meets armageddon-obsessed model and sparks fly until bizarre murder occurs. Quirky black comedy shot in less than two weeks. **100m/C VHS, LV.** Adrienne Shelly, Robert Burke, Christopher Cooke, Julia Mueller, Julia McNeal, Mark Bailey, Gary Sauer, Kathrine Mayfield; ***D:*** Hal Hartley; ***W:*** Hal Hartley; ***M:*** Jim Coleman. *VMK*

The Unborn 🦴½ **1991 (R)** An infertile wife gets inseminated at unorthodox clinic. But once pregnant she suspects that her unborn baby is a monstrous being. Tasteless B-movie with an A-performance from Adams; if the rest had been up to her standard this could have been another "Stepford Wives." Instead it cops out with cheap gore. **85m/C VHS, LV.** Brooke Adams, Jeff Hayenga, James Karen, K. Callan, Jane Cameron; ***D:*** Rodman Flender. *COL*

The Unborn 2 🦴 **1994 (R)** Greene's blood-craving baby thinks nothing of feasting off the babysitter until a gun-wielding avenger comes to the rescue. Some notably gross scenes. **84m/C VHS, LV.** Michelle Greene, Scott Valentine, Robin Curtis; ***D:*** Rick Jacobson. *NHO*

The Unbreakable Alibi 🦴🦴 **1983** A wealthy young man asks Tommy and Tuppence Beresford to help him prove that one of two alibis an Australian journalist created is false. Based on the mysteries by Agatha Christie. Made for television. **51m/C VHS, Beta.** *GB* Francesca Annis, James Warwick. *TPV*

Uncaged 🦴 *Angel in Red* **1991 (R)** Five beautiful young prostitutes hit Sunset Strip, each of them dreaming of a better life. When a crazy pimp brutally murders one of their friends, they set out to avenge that girl, and her broken dreams. **78m/C VHS, LV.** Leslie Bega, Jeffrey Dean Morgan, Pamella O'Pella, Gregory Millar, Henry Brown, Jason Oliver, Elena Sahagun; ***D:*** William Duprey; ***W:*** Robert Alden, Joan Freeman, Catherine Cyran. *COL*

The Uncanny *Woof!* **1978** Horror anthology of three tales concerned with feline attempts to control the world. Waste of good cast and cats on silly stories. Not released in the U.S. **85m/C VHS, Beta.** *GB* Peter Cushing, Ray Milland, Samantha Eggar, Donald Pleasence; ***D:*** Denis Heroux. *MED*

Uncensored 🦴½ **1985** This fast-paced comedy special features dozens of hilarious skits and sketches. **60m/C VHS, Beta.** Murray Langston, Cassandra Peterson, John Paragon, Ben Powers. *NO*

Uncertain Glory 🦴🦴 **1944** Errol plays a French thief who's willing to pretend to be a saboteur and die for his country. Based on a story by Joe May and Laszlo Vadnay. **102m/B VHS.** Errol Flynn, Paul Lukas, Jean Sullivan, Lucile Watson, Faye Emerson, James Flavin, Douglass Dumbrille, Dennis Hoey, Sheldon Leonard; ***D:*** Raoul Walsh; ***W:*** Laszlo Vadnay, Max Brand. *MGM*

The Unchastened Woman 🦴🦴 **1925** A married couple is torn apart by infidelity despite their impending parenthood, and wife Bara heads overseas to run wild and have the baby. She returns with a foreign flame, whom she dumps when erstwhile husband finds fatherly feelings in his heart. One of Bara's last films. **52m/B VHS, Beta.** Theda Bara, Wyndham Standing, Dale Fuller, John Miljan; ***D:*** James Young. *GPV, FCT*

Uncivilized 🦴🦴 **1994** Young couple, on a vacation in the mountains, run into a gang of drug runners who don't want their whereabouts revealed. So, the duo have to play a deadly game of hide-and-seek to survive. **90m/C VHS.** Martin Kove, Rick Aiello. *SWI*

Uncle Buck 🦴🦴🦴 **1989 (PG)** When Mom and Dad have to go away suddenly, the only babysitter they can find is good ol' Uncle Buck, a lovable lout who spends much of his time smoking cigars, trying to make up with his girlfriend, and enforcing the teenage daughter's chastity. More intelligent than the average slob/teen comedy with a heart, due in large part to Candy's dandy performance. Memorable pancake scene. **100m/C VHS, Beta, LV.** John Candy, Amy Madigan, Jean Kelly, Macaulay Culkin, Jay Underwood, Gaby Hoffman, Laurie Metcalf, Elaine Bromka, Garrett M. Brown; ***D:***

John Hughes; ***W:*** John Hughes; ***C:*** Ralf Bode; ***M:*** Ira Newborn. *MCA*

Uncle Moses 🦴🦴½ **1932** The clash of old-world values and new-world culture in a story of East European Jewish immigrants transplanted to turn of the century New York's Lower East Side. Patriarch Uncle Moses struggles to keep traditional family values as romantic difficulties and labor union struggles intrude. Based on the novel by Sholem Asch. In Yiddish with English subtitles. **87m/B VHS.** Maurice Schwartz, Rubin Goldberg, Judith Abarbanel, Zvee Scooler; ***D:*** Sidney Goldin, Aubrey Scotto. *ERG, NCJ*

Uncle Tom's Cabin 🦴🦴 **1914** Satisfying version of Harriet Beecher Stowe's tale from the view of a founder of the underground railroad. Lucas was the first black actor to garner a lead role. **54m/C VHS, Beta.** Mary Eline, Irving Cummings, Sam Lucas; ***D:*** William Robert Daly. *GPV, FCT, DVT*

Uncle Tom's Cabin 🦴½ *Onkel Toms Hutte; La Case de L'Oncle Tom; Cento Dollari D'Odio; Cica Tomina Koliba* **1969 (G)** Ambitious adaptation of Harriet Beecher Stowe's stirring book about the Southern slavery and the famous underground railroad devised to aid those most determined to reach freedom. The film has the habit of drifting away from the facts. Though set in Kentucky, the picture was filmed in Yugoslavia with an international cast. **120m/C VHS, Beta.** *FR IT YU GE* Herbert Lom, John Kitzmiller, O.W. Fischer, Eleanora Rossi-Drago, Mylene Demongeot, Juliette Greco; ***D:*** Geza von Radvanyi; ***V:*** Ella Fitzgerald. *XVC, AFR*

Uncle Tom's Cabin 🦴🦴½ **1987** The first American sound version of this film. Excellent cast and interestingly adapted script are perfect for a message that is still socially relevant today. Based on the novel by Harriet Beecher Stowe. Made for television. **110m/C VHS.** Avery Brooks, Kate Burton, Bruce Dern, Paula Kelly, Phylicia Rashad, Kathryn Walker, Edward Woodward, Frank Converse, George Coe, Albert Hall; ***D:*** Stan Lathan. *FCT, WOV*

Uncle Was a Vampire 🦴🦴 **1959** Lee stars as Count Dracula in this vampire story. **?m/C VHS.** Christopher Lee, Kay Fisher. *SNC*

Uncommon Valor 🦴🦴½ **1983 (R)** After useless appeals to the government for information on his son listed as "missing in action" in Vietnam, Colonel Rhodes takes matters into his own hands. Hackman is solid and believable as always, surrounded with good cast in generally well-paced film. **105m/C VHS, Beta, LV, 8mm.** Gene Hackman, Fred Ward, Reb Brown, Randall "Tex" Cobb, Robert Stack, Patrick Swayze, Harold Sylvester, Tim Thomerson; ***D:*** Ted Kotcheff; ***C:*** Stephen Burum; ***M:*** James Horner. *PAR*

Unconquered 🦴🦴½ **1947** Silly epic about America finds indentured servant Abby (Goddard), meeting Virignia militia man Christopher Holden (Cooper). He nobly buys her contract and frees her but scurvy trader Martin Garth (da Silva) manages to get Abby working in his saloon. Garth also illegally sells guns to the local Seneca Indian tribe and persuades their chief, Guyasuta (Karloff), to attack the colonists. Cooper has to keep rescuing Goodard throughout the movie, as well as battling da Silva and helping the settlers fight Indians. Based on the novel "The Judas Tree" by Neil H. Swanson. **147m/C VHS.** Gary Cooper, Paulette Goddard, Howard da Silva, Boris Karloff, Cecil Kellaway, Ward Bond, Katherine DeMille, Henry Wilcoxon, Sir C. Aubrey Smith, Victor Varconi, Virginia Grey, Mike Mazurki, Porter Hall; ***D:*** Cecil B. DeMille; ***W:*** Charles Bennett, Jesse Lasky Jr., Frederic M. Frank; ***C:*** Ray Rennahan; ***M:*** Victor Young. *MCA*

The Undead 🦴🦴🦴 **1957** A prostitute is accidentally sent back to the Middle Ages as the result of a scientific experiment and finds herself condemned to die for witchcraft. Early Corman script filled with violence and heaving bosoms. **75m/B VHS.** Pamela Duncan, Richard Garland, Allison Hayes, Mel Welles; ***D:*** Roger Corman. *NOS, AIP, MLB*

Undeclared War 🦴🦴 **1991 (R)** Suspenseful espionage thriller that takes you behind the scenes of an international terrorist plot, which has been cleverly disguised as a bloody global revolution. Intense action heightened by conflicts between worldwide intelligence networks, the news media and terrorist organizations. **103m/C VHS, LV.** Vernon Wells, David Hedison, Olivia Hussey, Peter Lapis; ***D:*** Ringo Lam. *IMP*

Undefeatable 🦴½ **1994 (R)** Rothrock is out to avenge the murder of her sister at the hands of a serial killer who, coincidentally, happens to be a martial arts expert. You watch for Cynthia to kick butt not for plot anyway. **88m/C VHS.** Cynthia Rothrock, Don Niam, John Miller, Donna Jason; ***D:*** Godfrey Hall. *FXV*

The Undefeated 🦴🦴 **1969 (G)** A Confederate and Yankee find they must team up on the Rio Grande. They attempt to build new lives in the Spanish held Mexico territory, but are caught in the battle for Mexican independence. Standard fare made palatable only by Wayne and Hudson. **119m/C VHS, Beta, LV.** John Wayne, Rock Hudson, Lee Meriwether, Merlin Olsen, Bruce Cabot, Ben Johnson, Jan-Michael Vincent, Harry Carey Jr., Antonio Aguilar, Roman Gabriel; ***D:*** Andrew V. McLaglen; ***C:*** William Clothier. *FOX*

Under California Stars 🦴🦴 *Under California Skies* **1948** Shady gang making a living rounding up wild horses decides they can make more money by capturing Rogers' horse, Trigger. **71m/C VHS, Beta.** Roy Rogers, Andy Devine, Jane Frazee, The Pioneers; ***D:*** William Witney. *NOS, VYY, DVT*

Under Capricorn 🦴🦴½ **1949** Bergman is an Irish lass who follows her convict husband Cotten out to 1830s Australia where he makes a fortune. She turns to drink, perhaps because of his neglect, and has her position usurped by a housekeeper with designs on her husband. When Bergman's cousin (Wilding) arrives, Cotten may have cause for his violent jealousy. There's a plot twist involving old family skeletons, but this is definitely lesser Hitchcock. Adapted from the Helen Simpson novel. Remade in 1982. **117m/C VHS, Beta, LV.** *GB* Ingrid Bergman, Joseph Cotten, Michael Wilding, Margaret Leighton, Jack Watling, Cecil Parker, Denis O'Dea; ***D:*** Alfred Hitchcock. *VES*

Under Capricorn 🦴🦴 **1982** An Australian remake of the 1949 Hitchcock film about family secrets, an unhappy marriage, and violence set in 1830's Australia. **120m/C VHS, Beta.** *AU* Lisa Harrow, John Hallam, Peter Cousens, Julia Blake, Catherine Lynch; ***D:*** Rod Hardy. *PSM*

Under Fire 🦴🦴🦴½ **1983 (R)** Three foreign correspondents, old friends from the past working together, find themselves in Managua, witnessing the 1979 Nicaraguan revolution. In a job requiring objectivity, but a situation requiring taking sides, they battle with their ethics to do the job right. Fine performances, including Camp as a mercenary. Interesting view of American media and its political necessities. **128m/C VHS, Beta, LV.** Gene Hackman, Nick Nolte, Joanna Cassidy, Ed Harris, Richard Masur, Hamilton Camp, Jean-Louis Trintignant; ***D:*** Roger Spottiswoode; ***W:*** Ron Shelton, Clayton Frohman; ***M:*** Jerry Goldsmith. Nominations: Academy Awards '83: Best Original Score. *VES*

Under Investigation 🦴🦴½ **1993 (R)** Burned out cop Hamlin is after a crazed killer. His cool lover Pacula turns out to be the prime suspect. Who's deceiving who? **94m/C VHS.** Harry Hamlin, Joana Pacula, Ed Lauter, Richard Beymer, Lydie Denier; ***D:*** Kevin Meyer; ***W:*** Kevin Meyer. *NLC*

Under Milk Wood 🦴🦴½ **1973 (PG)** An adaptation of the Dylan Thomas play about the lives of the residents of a village in Wales. Burton and O'Toole are wonderful in this uneven, but sometimes engrossing film. **90m/C VHS, Beta.** *GB* Richard Burton, Elizabeth Taylor, Peter O'Toole, Glynis Johns, Vivien Merchant; ***D:*** Andrew Sinclair. *FOX*

Under Montana Skies 🦴½ **1930** An early talkie western features music and comedy in abundance, relegating the action to second place. A singing cowboy protects a travelling burlesque show from evildoers. **55m/B VHS, Beta.** Kenneth Harlan, Dorothy Gulliver, Lafe McKee, Ethel Wales, Slim Summerville; ***D:*** Richard Thorpe. *GPV*

Under Nevada Skies 🦴🦴½ **1946** Fairly good matinee-era western centers on a missing map to a uranium deposit, climaxing with Rogers heading a posse of Indian allies to the rescue. The Sons of the Pioneers contribute songs. **69m/B VHS.** Roy Rogers, George "Gabby" Hayes, Dale Evans, Douglass Dumbrille, Tristram Coffin, Rudolph Anders, Iron Eyes Cody; ***D:*** Frank McDonald. *NOS, HEG*

Under Satan's Sun 🦴🦴🦴 *Under the Sun of Satan; Sous le Soleil de Satan* **1987** A rural priest is tortured by what he sees as his sins and failings to his parishioners. He is further tempted from the straight path by a beautiful murderess, a worldly priest, and, perhaps by Satan in disguise. Stylized film is not easily accessible, but Depardieu's performance is worth the effort. Based on the Georges Bernanos book "Diary of a Country Priest." In French with English subtitles. **97m/C VHS.** *FR* Gerard Depardieu, Sandrine Bonnaire, Yann Dedet, Alain Artur, Maurice Pialat; ***D:*** Maurice Pialat; ***W:*** Maurice Pialat. Cannes Film Festival '87: Best Film. *INJ, FCT, CVC*

Under Siege 🦴🦴 **1992 (R)** The USS Missouri becomes the battleground for good-guy-with-a-secret-past Seagal. He's up against the deranged Jones, as an ex-Special Forces leader, and Busey, a corrupt naval officer looking to steal the battleship's nuclear arsenal. May be predictable (especially the graphic violence) but the action is fast, the villains swaggering, and Seagal efficient at dispatching the enemy. Work for "Die Hard 3" was reportedly scrapped after Warner announced this film because DH's John McClane was supposed to save the passengers of a boat from terrorists. Sound familiar? **100m/C VHS, Beta, LV, 8mm.** Steven Seagal, Tommy Lee Jones, Gary Busey, Patrick O'Neal, Erika Eleniak; ***D:*** Andrew Davis; ***W:*** J.F. Lawton; ***M:*** Gary Chang. Nominations: Academy Awards '92: Best Sound, Best Sound Effects Editing. *WAR*

Under Siege 2: Dark Territory 🦴🦴 **1995 (R)** Kicking terrorists' butts and slinging hash have worn out ex-Navy SEAL and gourmet chef Casey Ryback (Seagal), so he takes a little vacation to the Rocky Mountains. By coincidence, the train he boards is command central for psychotic computer expert Dane's (Bogosian) scheme to control the world's deadliest satellite. Pretty familiar territory for Seagal, who's acting technique consists of "look mad and hurt poeple." Bigger budget means bigger, and more frequent, explosions. Bogosian takes over the Jones/Busey role of evil villain-talented actor. **100m/C VHS, LV.** Steven Seagal, Eric Bogosian, Katherine Heigl, Morris Chestnut, Everett McGill, Andy Romano, Nick Mancuso, Brenda Bakke; ***D:*** Geoff Murphy; ***W:*** Richard Hatem; ***C:*** Robbie Greenberg; ***M:*** Basil Poledouris. *WAR*

Under Suspicion 🦴🦴½ **1992 (R)** Christmas 1959 in Brighton finds seedy private eye Tony Aaron and his wife faking adultery cases for those desperate to get around England's strict divorce laws. Sordid tale takes a turn when Tony bursts in to snap incriminating photos and finds both his wife and their client, a famous artist, murdered. Dark who-dunnit has some interesting twists that could have made it exceptional rather than the conventional melodrama it turned out to be. Neeson is very good as the charmingly sleazy Tony but nobody else stands out, except the unfortunately miscast San Giacomo. Theatrical feature debut for director Moore. **99m/C VHS, LV.** *GB* Liam Neeson, Laura San Giacomo, Alphonsia Emmanuel, Kenneth Cranham, Maggie O'Neill, Martin Grace, Stephen Moore; ***D:*** Simon Moore; ***W:*** Simon Moore; ***M:*** Christopher Gunning. *COL*

Under the Biltmore Clock 🦴🦴 **1985** F. Scott Fitzgerald's story, "Myra Meets His Family," is the basis for this American Playhouse installment for PBS television. It is outwit or be outwitted in this tale of a fortune-hunting '20s flapper who is outsmarted by the man she has set her sights on when he hires actors to play his eccentric "family." **70m/C VHS, Beta, LV, 8mm.** Sean Young, Lenny Von Dohlen, Barnard Hughes; ***D:*** Neal Miller. *SUE, NLC*

Under the Boardwalk 🦴½ **1989 (R)** A pair of star-crossed teenage lovers struggle through familial and societal differences in 1980s California. This is, like, bogus, ya know. **102m/C VHS, Beta, LV.** Keith Coogan, Danielle von Zerneck, Richard Joseph Paul, Hunter von Leer, Tracey Walter, Roxana Zal, Dick Miller, Sonny Bono, Corky Carroll; ***D:*** Fritz Kiersch. *VTR, NWV*

Under the Cherry Moon 🦴½ **1986 (PG-13)** Prince portrays a fictional musician of the 1940s who travels to the French Riviera, seeking love and money. Songs include "Under the Cherry Moon," "Kiss," "Anotherloverholeinyohead," "Sometimes It Snows in April," and "Mountains." A vanity flick down to its being filmed in black and white. **100m/B VHS, Beta, LV.** Prince, Jerome Benton, Francesca Annis, Kristin Scott Thomas; ***D:*** Prince. Golden Raspberry Awards '86: Worst Picture, Worst Actor (Prince), Worst Supporting Actor (Benton), Worst Director (Prince), Worst Song ("Love or Money"). *MVD, WAR, FCT*

Under the Earth 🦴🦴🦴 *Debajo del Mundo* **1986 (R)** An Argentine-Czech co-production, depicting the plight of a family of Polish Jews forced to live underground for two years to avoid the Nazis. Harrowing and critically well-received. In Spanish with subtitles. **100m/C VHS, Beta, LV.** *SP* Victor Laplace; ***D:*** Beda Ocampo Feijoo, Juan Bautista Stagnaro. *NWV, SWC*

Under the Gun 🦴🦴 **1988 (R)** A cop recruits a lawyer to help him find the man who murdered his brother. Action drives this formulaic plot along. **89m/C VHS, LV.** Sam Jones, Vanessa Williams, John Russell, Michael Halsey; ***D:*** James Sbardellati; ***W:*** James Sbardellati, Almer John Davis. *IME*

Under the Gun 🦴½ **1995 (R)** Debt-ridden club owner Frank Torrance (Norton) is in trouble with everyone he knows. But he can't clear his debts just by quitting the business, so he decides to fight back. **90m/C VHS, LV.** Richard Norton, Kathy Long; ***D:*** Matthew George. *TRI*

Under the Hula Moon 🦴🦴½ **1995 (R)** Buzzard (Baldwin) and Betty (Lloyd) Wall are living unhappily in the charmless desert town of Cactus Gulch. Their trailer home is festooned in faux-Hawaiian finery and the duo dream of the day they can actually move to their island paradise. Buzz's invented an ultraprotective sunscreen that may be their ticket out, if his prison-escapee, trigger-happy half-brother Turk (Penn), who's also kidnapped Betty, doesn't get them all killed first. Charming lead performances—very lightweight story. **94m/C VHS.** Stephen Baldwin, Emily Lloyd, Christopher Penn, Musetta Vander, Edie McClurg, Pruitt Taylor Vince, Bill Campbell, Carel Struycken; ***D:*** Jeff Celentano; ***W:*** Jeff Celentano; ***C:*** Phil Parmet. *TTC*

Under the Rainbow *Woof!* **1981 (PG)** Comic situations encountered by a talent scout and a secret service agent in a hotel filled with Munchkins during filming of "The Wizard of Oz." Features midgets, spies, and a prevailing lack of taste. International intrigue adds to the strange attempt at humor. **97m/C VHS, Beta.** Chevy Chase, Carrie Fisher, Eve Arden, Joseph Maher, Robert Donner, Mako, Pat McCormick, Billy Barty, Zelda Rubinstein; ***D:*** Steve Rash; ***W:*** Pat McCormick, Martin Smith, Harry Hurwitz, Fred Bauer, Pat Bradley. *WAR*

Under the Red Robe 🦴🦴½ **1936** A French soldier of fortune is trapped into aiding Cardinal Richelieu in his persecution of the Huguenots and winds up falling in love with the sister of his intended victim. Good costume adventure-drama. Sjostrom's last film as a director. **82m/B VHS, Beta.** *GB* Raymond Massey, Conrad Veidt, Annabella, Romney Brent; ***D:*** Victor Sjostrom; ***C:*** James Wong Howe. *NOS, HHT, WFV*

Under the Roofs of Paris 🦴🦴🦴½ *Sous les Toits de Paris* **1929** An early French sound film about the lives of young Parisian lovers. A gentle, highly acclaimed melodrama. In French with English subtitles. **95m/B VHS, Beta.** *FR* Albert Prejean, Pola Illery, Gaston Modot; ***D:*** Rene Clair; ***C:*** Georges Perinal. National Board of Review Awards '31: 5 Best Foreign Films of the Year. *VYY, NOS, CAB*

Under the Volcano 🦴🦴🦴 **1984** An alcoholic British ex-consul finds his life further deteriorating during the Mexican Day of the Dead in 1939. His half-brother and ex-wife try to save him from himself, but their affair sends him ever-deeper into his personal hell. Finney's performance is pathetic and haunting. Adapted from the novel by Malcolm Lowry. **112m/C VHS, Beta, LV.** Albert Finney, Jacqueline Bisset, Anthony Andrews, Katy Jurado; ***D:*** John Huston; ***M:*** John Beal, Alex North. Los Angeles Film Critics Association Awards '84: Best Actor (Finney); Nominations: Academy Awards '84: Best Actor (Finney), Best Original Score; Cannes Film Festival '84: Best Film. *MCA*

Under Western Stars 🦴 **1945** Roy's first starring vehicle. A newly elected congressman goes to Washington and fights battles for his constituents, caught in the middle of the Dust Bowl and drought. **83m/B VHS, Beta.** Roy Rogers, Smiley Burnette; ***D:*** Jean Yarbrough. *NOS, DVT, VCN*

The Underachievers 🦴 **1988 (R)** A night school is the scene for typical libido-oriented gags, but this time instead of teenagers it's adult education providing the plot. Only a few real laughs in this one. **90m/C VHS, Beta.** Barbara Carrera, Edward Albert, Michael Pataki, Vic Tayback, Garrett Morris, Susan Tyrrell; ***D:*** Jackie Kong. *LIV, VES*

Undercover 🦴½ **1987 (R)** Routine cop action film in which an eastern detective finds himself undercover in a southern high school in search of a cop-murdering drug ring. Plagued with cliches. Director Stockwell is appropriately better known for his role as "Cougar" in "Top Gun." **92m/C VHS.** David Neidorf, Jennifer Jason Leigh, Barry Corbin, David Harris, Kathleen Wilhoite; ***D:*** John Stockwell; ***M:*** Bruce Smeaton. *WAR*

Undercover 🦴½ **1994 (R)** Police detective (and hot babe) Cindy Hanen (Massey) gets an undercover assignment to capture a murderer who's targeted an upscale brothel. It's an excuse for interesting undies (or less). **93m/C VHS.** Athena Massey, Tom Tayback, Anthony Guidera, Rena Riffel, Jeffrey Dean Morgan, Meg Foster; ***D:*** Alexander Gregory Hippolyte; ***W:*** Lalo Wolf, Oola Bloome. *APX*

Undercover Blues 🦴🦴½ **1993 (PG-13)** Comedy-thriller starring Turner and Quaid as married spies Jane and Jeff Blue, on parental leave from the espionage biz, who are on vacation with their 11-month-old daughter in New Orleans. But the holiday is interrupted when they're recruited by their boss to stop an old adversary from selling stolen weapons. The leads play cute together and the baby is adorable but this is strictly routine escapism. Stick with "The Thin Man" instead. **90m/C VHS, LV.** Kathleen Turner, Dennis Quaid, Fiona Shaw, Stanley Tucci, Larry Miller, Obba Babatunde, Park Overall, Tom Arnold, Saul Rubinek, Michelle Schuelke; ***D:*** Herbert Ross; ***W:*** Ian Abrams; ***M:*** David Newman. *MGM*

Undercover Cop 🦴🦴 **1994** True story of Sergeant George Aguilar and the high-speed chase that left one dead and the police dealing their revenge on all the offenders. **90m/C VHS.** Danny Trejo, Kevin Anthony Cole; ***D:*** Martin Greene; ***W:*** Glenn A. Bruce; ***M:*** Randall Kent Heddon. *AIP*

Undercover Man 🦴½ **1936** A Wells Fargo agent goes undercover to expose a crooked sheriff. **57m/B VHS.** Johnny Mack Brown, Suzanne Kaaren, Ted Adams, Lloyd Ingraham, Horace Murphy; ***D:*** Albert Ray. *NOS, DVT, RXM*

The Underdog 🦴½ **1943** After the bank forecloses, a farm family must move to the city. The family's young son has only his loyal dog to turn to for friendship, but the gallant animal proves his mettle by rounding up a gang of spies plotting some WWII sabotage. Believe it if you dare. **65m/B VHS, Beta, 8mm.** Barton MacLane, Bobby Larson, Jan Wiley; ***D:*** William Nigh. *VYY*

Undergrads 🦴🦴🦴 **1985** A bright generational Disney comedy with Carney, estranged from his stick-in-the-mud son, deciding to attend college with his free-thinking grandson. Made for television. **102m/C VHS, Beta.** Art Carney, Chris Makepeace, Jackie Burroughs, Len Birman; ***D:*** Steven Hilliard Stern. *DIS*

Underground 🦴🦴🦴 *Once Upon a Time There Was a Country* **1995** Exhausting black comedy, set in Yugoslavia from 1941 to 1992, follows the adventures of Marko (Manojlovic) and his best friend Blacky (Ristovski). They run a black-market operation and lead Communist Party meetings while trying to avoid the Gestapo in WWII Belgrade. Hiding out in a cellar, where refugees have put together a munitions factory, the treacherous Marko manages to convince everyone that the war is still going on—20 years later in fact—until the truth unexpectedly comes out (thanks to a pet monkey). The final section sees Marko unscrupulously dealing arms and drugs amidst the breakup of Yugoslavia in a civil war and the violence on all sides. **192m/C VHS.** *FR GE HU* Miki Manojlovic, Lazar Ristovski, Mirjana Jokovic, Slavko Stimac, Ernst Stotzner, Srdan Todorovic, Mirjana Karanovic; ***Cameos:*** Emir Kusturica; ***D:*** Emir Kusturica; ***W:*** Emir Kusturica, Dusan Kovacevic; ***C:*** Vilko Filac; ***M:*** Goran Bregovic. Cannes Film Festival '95: Best Film. *NYR*

Underground Aces *Woof!* **1980 (PG)** A group of parking lot attendants transforms a sheik into an attendant in order to help him meet the girl of his dreams. A bad "Car Wash" spinoff. **93m/C VHS, Beta.** Dirk Benedict, Melanie Griffith, Frank Gorshin, Jerry Orbach, Robert Hegyes, Audrey Landers; ***D:*** Robert Butler; ***W:*** Jim Carabatsos. *LIV, VES*

Underground Rustlers 🦴 **1941** The Range Busters are commissioned by the government to stop unscrupulous gold-marketeers. **58m/B VHS, Beta.** Ray Corrigan, Max Terhune, John "Dusty" King; ***D:*** S. Roy Luby. *VDM*

Underground Terror 🦴 **1988** A gang of murderers, organized by a psychopath, rampages through the New York City subway system. One cop enthusiastically tries to snuff out each one. **91m/C VHS.** Doc Dougherty, Lenny Y. Loftin; ***D:*** James McCalmont. *NO*

Underground U.S.A. 🦴 **1984** Street hustler picks up a has-been underground movie star at the chic New York new wave disco, The Mudd Club. **85m/C VHS, Beta.** Patti Astor, Eric Mitchell; ***D:*** Eric Mitchell. *NO*

The Underneath 🦴🦴🦴 **1995 (R)** Recovering gambling addict Michael Chambers (Peter Gallagher) returns home after skipping out on his debts and his wife Rachel (sultry newcomer Elliot) several years before. Old passions ignite in more ways than one, and Michael's lust for his ex, now married to a hot-tempered hoodlum, leads him to risk it all for a final big score. Moody and tense study of the complexities of emotion is capped by smart lead performances but style wins out over substance and the finale definitely leaves more questions than answers. Remake of the 1949 film noir classic "Criss Cross," based on Don Tracy's novel of the same name. **99m/C VHS.** Peter Gallagher, Alison Elliott, William Fichtner, Elisabeth Shue, Adam Trese, Paul Dooley; ***D:*** Steven Soderbergh; ***W:*** Sam Lowry, Daniel Fuchs; ***C:*** Elliot Davis; ***M:*** Cliff Martinez. Nominations: Independent Spirit Awards '96: Best Cinematography. *MCA*

Undersea Kingdom **1936** Adventure beneath the ocean floor. In twelve chapters of thirteen minutes each; the first chapter runs twenty minutes. Later re-edited into one film, "Sharad of Atlantis." **226m/B VHS, LV.** Ray Corrigan, Lon Chaney Jr.; ***D:*** B. Reeves Eason. *NOS, SNC, VCN*

Understudy: The Graveyard Shift 2 🦴½ **1988 (R)** Vampire survives poorly directed cliche-riddled original to be cast as a vampire cast as a vampire in a horror movie within a horrible sequel. **88m/C VHS, Beta, LV.** Wendy Gazelle, Mark Soper, Silvio Oliviero; ***D:*** Gerard Ciccoritti. *NO*

The Undertaker and His Pals 🦴🦴 **1967** Undertaker teams up with diner owners in murder scheme to improve mortician's business and expand restaurateurs' menu. Pretty violent stuff, with some good laughs and a campy flare, but not for every one's palate. **70m/C VHS.** Ray Dannis, Brad Fulton, Larrene Ott, Robert Lowery, Sally Frei; ***D:*** David C. Graham. *MTH*

Undertow 🦴🦴 **1995 (R)** Drifter gets stranded in a cabin with a terrified woman and her crazy husband. Cable thriller. **90m/C VHS.** Lou Diamond Phillips, Mia Sara, Charles Dance; ***D:*** Eric Red; ***W:*** Kathryn Bigelow, Eric Red; ***M:*** John Frizzell. *REP*

Underwater! 🦴🦴 **1955** A team of skin divers faces danger when they try to retrieve treasure from a Spanish galleon. The second film after "The Outlaw" masterminded by Howard Hughes, primarily to show off Russell's figure. **99m/C VHS, Beta, LV.** Jane Russell, Richard Egan, Gilbert Roland, Jayne Mansfield; ***D:*** John Sturges. *MED, TTC*

Underworld 🦴🦴🦴 **1927** Inspired gangster saga finds bank robber Bull Weed (Bancroft) befriending a genteel bum, known as Rolls Royce (Brook), and taking him into his gang. The bum has brains and soon makes Weed king of the underworld but there's jealousy when Weed's moll Feathers (Brent) falls for Royce. Climactic shootout set a standard for the genre. **85m/B VHS.** George Bancroft, Clive Brook, Evelyn Brent, Larry Semon, Fred Kohler Sr.; ***D:*** Josef von Sternberg. *GPV*

Underworld Scandal 🦴🦴 **1947** An editor attempts to break up a ring of basketball game fixers. **?m/C VHS.** Philip Reed, Hillary Brooke. *SNC*

The Underworld Story 🦴🦴½ **1950** Big city journalist at large moves to smalltown New England after losing job for unethical reporting and uncovers scheme to frame innocent man for murder. Solid performances. **90m/B VHS.** Dan Duryea, Herbert Marshall, Gale Storm, Howard da Silva, Michael O'Shea, Mary Anderson, Gar Moore, Melville Cooper, Frieda Inescort, Art Baker, Harry Shannon, Alan Hale Jr., Steve Dunne, Roland Winters; ***D:*** Cy Endfield. *FOX, FCT*

Underworld, U.S.A. 🦴🦴🦴 **1960** A man infiltrates a tough crime syndicate to avenge his father's murder, which winds up with him caught between the mob and the feds. A well-acted and directed look at the criminal underworld. **99m/B VHS, Beta.** Cliff Robertson, Dolores Dorn, Beatrice Kay, Robert Emhardt, Larry Gates, Paul Dubov; ***D:*** Samuel Fuller; ***W:*** Samuel Fuller; ***C:*** Hal Mohr. *COL*

The Undying Monster 🦴🦴½ *The Hammond Mystery* **1942** Upper crusty Brit is werewolf with insatiable appetite. Familiar story with lots of atmosphere and style. Photography by Lucien Ballard. **63m/B VHS.** James Ellison, Heather Angel, John Howard, Bramwell Fletcher, Heather Thatcher, Aubrey Mather, Halliwell Hobbes, Heather Wilde; ***D:*** John Brahm. *MOV*

Une Jeunesse 🦴🦴🦴 **1983** A middle-aged French couple reminisce about their meeting and courtship. In French with English subtitles. **100m/C VHS, Beta.** *FR FCT*

The Unearthing 🦴 **1993 (R)** An unwated pregnancy seems to find a happy solution when a woman decides to marry the heir to a wealthy estate and pass off her child as his. Only the family has some very strange tastes, including a taste for the blood of the unborn. Based on a Filipino vampire legend (!) **83m/C VHS, LV.** Norman Moses, Tina Ona Paukstelis; ***D:*** Wyre Martin, Barry Poltermann; ***W:*** Wyre Martin, Barry Poltermann. *PSM*

The Unearthly 🦴½ **1957** A mad scientist is trying to achieve immortality through his strange experiments, but all he winds up with is a basement full of mutants. When his two latest about-to-be victims fall in love, the doctor's mutant assistant decides enough is enough and things come to an unpleasant end. Carradine is typecast. Absurd, but fun. **76m/B VHS, Beta.** John Carradine, Tor Johnson, Allison Hayes, Myron Healey; ***D:*** Brooke L. Peters. *SNC, DVT, MLB*

The Unearthly Stranger 🦴🦴½ **1964** Earth scientist marries woman and decides she's from another planet. Not a nineties style gender drama; seems she's part of an invading alien force, but really does love her earth man. Surprisingly good low-budget sci-fi. **75m/B VHS.** *GB* John Neville, Gabriella Licudi, Philip Stone, Patrick Newell, Jean Marsh, Warren Mitchell; ***D:*** John Krish. *MOV*

Uneasy Terms 🦴 **1948** Rennie is a detective investigating the murder of one of his own clients. Evidence points to stepchildren and inheritance money but things may not be as they seem. Written for the screen by Peter Cheyney, adapted from his own novel. **91m/B VHS, Beta.** *GB* Michael Rennie, Moira Lister, Faith Brook, Joy Shelton, Patricia Goddard, Barry Jones; ***D:*** Vernon Sewell. *SNC*

Unexplained Laughter 🦴🦴 **1989** A cynical journalist vacations in Wales with her timid vegetarian friend and stumbles across a mystery in this darkly comic British TV-movie. **85m/C VHS.** *GB* Diana Rigg, Elaine Page, Jon Finch. *FCT, VCO*

Unfaithfully Yours 🦴🦴🦴½ **1948** A conductor suspects his wife is cheating on him and considers his course of action. He imagines punishment scenarios while directing three classical works. Well-acted by all, but particularly by Harrison as the egotistical and jealous husband. Another of Sturges' comedic gems. Remade in 1984. **105m/B VHS, Beta, LV.** Rex Harrison, Linda Darnell, Kurt Kreuger, Rudy Vallee, Lionel Stander, Edgar Kennedy; ***D:*** Preston Sturges; ***C:*** Victor Milner. *FOX*

Unfaithfully Yours 🦴🦴 **1984 (PG)** A symphony conductor suspects his wife of fooling around with a musician; in retaliation, he plots an elaborate scheme to murder her with comic results. No match for the 1948 Preston Sturges film it's based on. **96m/C VHS, Beta, LV.** Dudley Moore, Nastassia Kinski, Armand Assante, Albert Brooks, Cassie Yates, Richard Libertini, Richard B. Shull; ***D:*** Howard Zieff; ***W:*** Valerie Curtin, Barry Levinson, Robert Klane; ***M:*** Bill Conti. *FOX*

Unfinished Business 🦴🦴½ **1989** A 17 year-old girl leads a troubled adolescent life with her divorced parents. She decides running away will ease her problems—not a smart move. Sequel to "Nobody Waved Goodbye." **88m/C VHS, Beta.** *CA* Isabelle Mejias, Peter Kastner, Leslie Toth, Peter Spence, Chuck Shamata, Julie Biggs; ***D:*** Don Owen. *JEF*

An Unfinished Piece for a Player Piano 🦴🦴🦴½ **1977** A general's widow invites family and friends to a weekend house party in 1910 Russia. Romantic and familial entanglements begin to intrude in a lyrical adaptation of Chekov's play "Platonov." In Russian with English subtitles. **100m/C VHS, Beta.** *RU* Alexander Kalyagin, Elena Solovei, Antonina Shuranova, Oleg Tabakov, Yuri Bogatyrev, Nikita Mikhalkov; ***D:*** Nikita Mikhalkov. *FCT, INJ, CVC*

Unforgettable 🦴🦴½ **1996 (R)** Unfortunately, the film doesn't live up to its title. On-the-edge medical examiner David Krane (Liotta) has barely escaped conviction for his wife's brutal murder. Living under a cloud of suspicion, he turns to university researcher Martha Briggs (Fiorentino, wasted as a nerdy scientist), whose experiments in memory transference lead David to believe he can uncover the killer. But, like a Chinese puzzle box, one discovery only leads to a further complication. Too many, in fact, for the story to stay focused (and the ending is less than satisfying). **116m/C VHS, LV.** Ray Liotta, Linda Fiorentino, Peter Coyote, Christopher McDonald, Kim Cattrall, David Paymer, Kim Coates, Duncan Fraser, Garwin Sanford; ***D:*** John Dahl; ***W:*** Bill Geddie; ***C:*** Jeffrey Jur; ***M:*** Christopher Young. *MGM*

An Unforgettable Summer 🦴🦴½ **1994** The elegant Marie-Therese Dumitriu (Scott Thomas) has married Army officer Petre (Bleont) and tried to focus on maintaining a serene life, following the Communist takeover of Romania. When Petre is transferred to an isolated border town, he and his family are caught between what the Army demands and what is just. The local Bulgarian peasants are accused of attrocities against the soldiers and Petre is ordered to execute a group of them as an example—guilty or not. Set in 1925 and based on the short story "La Salade" by Petru Dumitriu. English, French, and Romanian with subtitles. **82m/C VHS.** *RO* Kristin Scott Thomas, Claudiu Bleont, Olga Tudorache, George Constantin; ***D:*** Lucian Pintilie; ***W:*** Lucian Pintilie; ***C:*** Calin Ghibu; ***M:*** Anton Suteu. *NYF*

The Unforgiven 🦴🦴🦴 **1960** A western family is torn asunder when it is suspected that the eldest daughter is of Indian birth. Film takes place in 1850s' Texas. One of Huston's weakest ventures, but viewed in terms of 1950s' prejudices it has more resonance. Fine acting from all the cast, especially Gish. Watch for the stunning Indian attack scene. **123m/C VHS, Beta, LV.** Burt Lancaster, Audrey Hepburn, Lillian Gish, Audie Murphy, John Saxon, Charles Bickford, Doug McClure, Joseph Wiseman, Albert Salmi; ***D:*** John Huston. *MGM, BTV*

Unforgiven 🦴🦴🦴½ **1992 (R)** Will Munny (Eastwood) lives a quiet life with his stepchildren on his failing pig farm, but his desperado past catches up with him when the Schofield Kid invites him to a bounty hunt. Munny reluctantly agrees, mistakenly believing that once the killing is through he can take up his peaceful ways again. Enter sadistic sheriff Little Bill Daggett (Hackman), who doesn't want any gunmen messing up his town. Eastwood uses his own status as a screen legend to full advantage as the aging gunman who realizes too late that his past can never be forgotten. Director Eastwood is also in top form with his well-seasoned cast and myth-defying Old West realism. Surprising critical and box office hit. The laserdisc version is available in letterbox format. **131m/C VHS, Beta, LV, 8mm.** Clint Eastwood, Gene Hackman, Morgan Freeman, Richard Harris, Jaimz Woolvett, Saul Rubinek, Frances Fisher, Anna Thomson, David Mucci, Rob Campbell, Anthony James; ***D:*** Clint Eastwood; ***W:*** David Peoples; ***C:*** Jack N. Green; ***M:*** Lennie Niehaus. Academy Awards '92: Best Director (Eastwood), Best Film Editing, Best Picture, Best Supporting Actor (Hackman); Directors Guild of America Awards '92: Best Director (Eastwood); Golden Globe Awards '93: Best Director (Eastwood), Best Supporting Actor (Hackman); New York Film Critics Awards '92: Best Supporting Actor (Hackman); National Society of Film Critics Awards '92: Best Director (Eastwood), Best Film, Best Screenplay, Best Supporting Actor (Hackman); Nominations: Academy Awards '92: Best Actor (Eastwood), Best Art Direction/Set Decoration, Best Cinematography, Best Original Screenplay, Best Sound. *WAR, MOV, BTV*

The Unholy 🦴½ **1988 (R)** A New Orleans priest battles a demon that's killing innocent parishioners. Confusing and heavy-handed. **100m/C VHS, Beta, LV.** Ben Cross, Hal Holbrook, Trevor Howard, Ned Beatty, William Russ, Jim Carroll; ***D:*** Camilo Vila; ***W:*** Philip Yordan; ***M:*** Roger Bellon. *LIV, VES, HHE*

Unholy Four 🦴½ **1954** An amnesiac returns home after three years to attempt to find out which of his three fishing buddies left him for dead. Confusing at times, but has some suspenseful moments. British title was "A Stranger Came Home." **80m/B VHS, Beta, LV.** *GB* Paulette Goddard, Paul Carpenter, William Sylvester, Patrick Holt, Russell Napier; ***D:*** Terence Fisher; ***W:*** Michael Carreras. *NO*

Unholy Rollers 🦴 *Leader of the Pack* **1972 (R)** Jennings stars as a factory worker who makes it big as a tough, violent roller derby star. Typical "Babes-on-Wheels" film that promises nothing and delivers even less. **88m/C VHS.** Claudia Jennings, Louis Quinn, Betty A. Rees, Roberta Collins, Alan Vint, Candice Roman; ***D:*** Vernon Zimmerman. *HBO*

The Unholy Three 🦴🦴🦴½ **1925** Ventriloquist Chaney, working with other carnival cohorts, uses his talent to gain entrance to homes which he later robs. Things go awry when two of the gang strike out on their own and the victim is killed. When the wrong man is accused, his girl, one of Chaney's gang, begs Chaney to get him free, which he does by using his vocal talents. Chaney decides being a criminal is just too hard and goes back to his ventriloquism. **70m/B VHS.** Lon Chaney Sr., Harry Earles, Victor McLaglen, Mae Busch, Matt Moore, Matthew Betz, William Humphreys; ***D:*** Tod Browning. *NO*

The Unholy Three 🦴🦴🦴 **1930** Chaney remade his silent hit of 1925 for his first and only talking picture (he died before the film was released). The story is essentially the same. Chaney is a ventriloquist who, with his circus friends, work as scam artists and thieves. When an innocent man is accused of their crimes Chaney tries his ventriloquist tricks to come to his aid, only in this version Chaney is exposed as a fraud and is sent to prison. Rumors that Chaney was a mute had him agreeing to appear in a "talkie" and he actually used five different voices for his various roles. **75m/B VHS, LV.** Lon Chaney Sr., Lila Lee, Elliott Nugent, Harry Earles, John Miljan; ***D:*** Jack Conway. *FCT*

Unholy Wife ☠½ **1957** A young woman plans to murder her wealthy husband, but her plan goes awry when she accidentally kills someone else. Muddled and heavy-handed, with Steiger chewing scenery. **94m/C VHS, Beta.** Rod Steiger, Diana Dors, Tom Tryon, Marie Windsor, Beulah Bondi; ***D:*** John Farrow. *HHE*

Unicorn ☠☠ **1983** A small boy hears the legend that if one rubs the horn of a Unicorn his wishes will come true. Mistakenly he buys a one-horned goat and sets out to fulfill his dreams. **29m/C VHS, Beta.** *GB* Diana Dors, David Kossoff, Celia Johnson; ***D:*** Carol Reed. *SUE, NLC*

Unidentified Flying Oddball ☠☠½ **1979 (G)** An astronaut and his robotic buddy find their spaceship turning into a time machine that throws them back into Arthurian times and at the mercy of Merlin the magician. Futuristic version of Twain's "A Connecticut Yankee at King Arthur's Court." **92m/C VHS, Beta.** Dennis Dugan, Jim Dale, Ron Moody, Kenneth More, Rodney Bewes; ***D:*** Russ Mayberry. *DIS*

The Uninvited ☠☠☠ **1944** A brother and sister buy a house in England, only to find it is haunted. Doors open and close by themselves, strange scents fill the air, and they hear sobbing during the night. Soon they are visited by a woman with an odd link to the house—her mother is the spirit who haunts the house. Chilling and unforgettable, this is one of the first films to deal seriously with ghosts. **99m/B VHS, LV.** Ray Milland, Ruth Hussey, Donald Crisp, Cornelia Otis Skinner, Gail Russell; ***D:*** Lewis Allen; ***C:*** Charles B(ryant) Lang. Nominations: Academy Awards '44: Best Black and White Cinematography. *MCA*

The Uninvited *Woof!* **1988** A mutant cat goes berserk onboard a luxury yacht, killing the passengers one by one with big, nasty, pointy teeth. **89m/C VHS, Beta, LV.** George Kennedy, Alex Cord, Clu Gulager, Toni Hudson, Eric Larson, Shari Shattuck, Austin Stoker; ***D:*** Greydon Clark. *NO*

Uninvited ☠☠½ **1993 (R)** Grady is a mysterious old man who leads eight misfits to the top of a sacred mountain with the promise of finding gold. But the fortune hunters have trespassed in a sacred Indian burial ground and find their nightmares becoming a violent reality. **?m/C VHS, LV.** Jack Elam, Christopher Boyer, Erin Noble, Bari Buckner, Jerry Rector, Zane Paolo, Dennis Gibbs, Ted Haler, Eno Brutto; ***D:*** Michael Derek Bohusz; ***W:*** Michael Derek Bohusz. *IMP, IME*

Union City ☠☠ **1981 (R)** Deborah "Blondie" Harry's husband gets a little edgy when someone steals the milk. Murder ensues, and they're on the run from the law. Intended as a film noir spoof, and not without some good moments. **82m/C VHS, Beta, LV.** Deborah Harry, Everett McGill, Dennis Lipscomb, Pat Benatar; ***D:*** Mark Reichart. *COL*

Union Pacific ☠☠☠ **1939** Full DeMille treatment highlights this saga about the building of America's first transcontinental railroad. Jeff Butler (McCrea) is the construction overseer who must battle saboteurs and Indians (although the U.S. Cavalry does arrive to save the day). He also gets to fall for self-sufficient postmistress Mollie Monahan (Stanwyck). DeMille borrowed the actual golden spike used to drive in the last rail in 1869 for his reenactment of the completion celebration. Based on the book "Trouble Shooters" by Ernest Haycox. **136m/B VHS.** Joel McCrea, Barbara Stanwyck, Robert Preston, Brian Donlevy, Akim Tamiroff, Lynne Overman, Robert Barrat, Anthony Quinn, Stanley Ridges, Henry Kolker, Evelyn Keyes, Regis Toomey; ***D:*** Cecil B. DeMille; ***W:*** Walter DeLeon, Jesse Lasky Jr., C. Gardner Sullivan; ***C:*** Victor Milner. *MCA*

Union Station ☠☠ **1950** Holden plays the chief of the railway police for Chicago's Union Station. He learns the station is to be used as a ransom drop in a kidnapping; but for all his security, the main thug gets away with the money, and the hunt is on. Good acting raises this film above the ordinary. **80m/B VHS, Beta.** William Holden, Barry Fitzgerald, Nancy Olson, Jan Sterling, Lee Marvin, Allene Roberts, Lyle Bettger; ***D:*** Rudolph Mate; ***C:*** Daniel F. Fapp. *BAR*

Universal Soldier ☠☠ **1992 (R)** A reporter discovers a secret government project to design perfect robo-soldiers by using the bodies of dead GIs, including tough guys Lundgren and Van Damme who were killed in Vietnam. But the knowledge is going to get her killed until Van Damme has flashbacks of his past (the soldier's memories have supposedly been erased) and agrees to help her. Lundgren doesn't have the same compassion and goes after them both. Big-budget thriller with some good action sequences and a lot of violence. **98m/C VHS, LV.** Jean-Claude Van Damme, Dolph Lundgren, Ally Walker, Ed O'Ross, Jerry Orbach; ***D:*** Roland Emmerich. *LIV*

The Unkissed Bride ☠ *Mother Goose A Go-Go* **1966 (PG)** A young newlywed couple are driven to distraction by the husband's inexplicable fainting spells and his strange obsession with Mother Goose. **82m/C VHS, Beta.** Tommy Kirk, Anne Helm, Danica D'Hondt, Henny Youngman; ***D:*** Jack H. Harris. *NWV*

The Unknown ☠☠☠½ **1927** Typically morbid Chaney fare has him working as a circus freak while trying to win the heart of his assistant. After drastic romancing he's still rejected by her, so he plots to kill the object of her intentions. Ghoulish as it is, the picture is really top-notch. **60m/B VHS.** Lon Chaney Sr., Norman Kerry, Joan Crawford, Nick De Ruiz, Frank Lanning, John St. Polis; ***D:*** Tod Browning. *FCT*

Unknown Island ☠½ **1948** Scientists travel to a legendary island where dinosaurs supposedly still exist. Bogus dinosaurs and cliche script. **76m/C VHS.** Virginia Grey, Philip Reed, Richard Denning, Barton MacLane; ***D:*** Jack Bernhard. *NOS, MOV, HEG*

Unknown Powers *Woof!* **1980 (PG)** Science and drama are combined to examine ESP and magic. Are they gifts or curses, and how are peoples' lives affected by them? Members of the cast introduce various sections of this totally inept film. **97m/C VHS, Beta.** Samantha Eggar, Jack Palance, Will Geer, Roscoe Lee Browne; ***D:*** Don Como. *GEM*

The Unknown Ranger ☠½ **1936** Allen's first cowboy role has him foiling a gang of rustlers. The real highlight turns out to be the battle between his horse and a wild stallion. Eat your heart out, Trigger! **57m/B VHS.** Robert Allen, Harry Woods, Martha Tibbetts, Hal Taliaferro, Robert "Buzzy" Henry; ***D:*** Spencer Gordon Bennet. *GPV*

Unknown World ☠ **1951** A group of scientists tunnel to the center of the Earth to find a refuge from the dangers of the atomic world. Big start winds down fast. Director Terry Morse sometimes credited as Terrell O. Morse. **73m/B VHS, Beta.** Bruce Kellogg, Marilyn Nash, Victor Kilian, Jim Bannon; ***D:*** Terry Morse; ***M:*** Ernest Gold. *NOS, PSM, SNC*

Unlawful Entry ☠☠ **1992 (R)** After a break-in, Karen and Michael Carr naturally call the cops. Handsome, polite policeman Pete Davis responds to the call and agrees to help burglar-proof their home. But Pete has some definite quirks—he falls for the beauteous Karen and begins stalking the couple, deciding to get rid of Michael in order to have his wife. A lurid combination of the worst moments of "Internal Affairs" and "Fatal Attraction" undermines this usually-talented cast. **107m/C VHS, LV.** Kurt Russell, Ray Liotta, Madeleine Stowe, Roger E. Mosley, Ken Lerner, Deborah Offner, Carmen Argenziano, Andy Romano, Barry W. Blaustein, Dick Miller; ***D:*** Jonathan Kaplan; ***W:*** Lewis Colick; ***M:*** James Horner. *FXV*

Unlawful Passage **1994 (R)** Vacation turns into a nightmare when a man's wife is kidnapped. **?m/C VHS.** Lee Horsley.

Unmarried Mothers ☠ **1955** A number of young ladies engage in sex before marriage and must suffer the consequences. **?m/C VHS.** *SW SNC*

An Unmarried Woman ☠☠☠ **1978 (R)** Suddenly divorced by her husband of 17 years, a woman deals with change. She enters the singles scene, copes with her daughter's growing sexuality, and encounters a new self-awareness. Mazursky puts real people on screen from start to finish. **124m/C VHS, Beta.** Jill Clayburgh, Alan Bates, Cliff Gorman, Michael Murphy; ***D:*** Paul Mazursky; ***W:*** Paul Mazursky; ***M:*** Bill Conti. Cannes Film Festival '78: Best Actress (Clayburgh); Los Angeles Film Critics Association Awards '78: Best Screenplay; National Board of Review Awards '78: 10 Best Films of the Year; New York Film Critics Awards '78: Best Screenplay; National Society of Film Critics Awards '78: Best Screenplay; Nominations: Academy Awards '78: Best Actress (Clayburgh), Best Original Screenplay, Best Picture; Cannes Film Festival '78: Best Film. *FOX*

Unmasked Part 25 ☠½ **1988** A second-generation serial killer takes up where dad left off. This one is intended to be a parody of slasher films, but it's still very bloody. **85m/C VHS, Beta.** *GB* Gregory Cox, Fiona Evans, Edward Brayshaw, Debbie Lee London; ***D:*** Anders Palm. *ACA*

Unmasking the Idol ☠ **1986** A suave hero with tongue firmly in check battles Ninja warlords. Sequel to "Order of the Black Eagle." **90m/C VHS, Beta.** *GB* Ian Hunter, William T. Hicks, Charles K. Bibby; ***D:*** Worth Keeter. *CEL*

The Unnamable ☠ **1988** The adaptation of the H.P. Lovecraft story about a particular New England ancestral home haunted by a typically Lovecraftian bloodthirsty demon borne of a woman hundreds of years before. College students, between trysts, investigate the myths about it. Uncut version, unseen in theaters, available only on video good for a few giggles and thrills. **87m/C VHS, Beta, LV.** Mark Kinsey Stephenson, Alexandra Durrell; ***D:*** Jean-Paul Ouellette. *VTR, VMK*

The Unnamable 2: The Statement of Randolph Carter ☠½ **1992 (R)** Randolph Carter is investigating a series of murders at Miskatonic University. Evidence leads Carter back to a 17th-century warlock who had the misfortune to summon an evil creature known as Alyda. The half-demon, half-woman now wants to permanently return to the mortal plane and every new victim just helps her evil purpose along. Based on a story by H.P. Lovecraft. **104m/C VHS, LV.** Mark Kinsey Stephenson, John Rhys-Davies, David Warner, Julie Strain, Maria Ford; ***D:*** Jean-Paul Ouellette. *PSM*

Unnatural ☠☠½ **1952** A mad scientist creates a souless child from the genes of a murderer and a prostitute. The child grows up to be the beautiful Neff, who makes a habit of seducing and destroying men. Dark, arresting film from a very popular German story. **90m/B VHS.** Hildegarde Neff, Erich von Stroheim, Karl-Heinz Boehm, Harry Meyen, Harry Helm, Denise Vernac, Julia Koschka; ***D:*** Arthur Maria Rabenalt. *SNC*

Unnatural Causes ☠☠☠ **1986** A dying Vietnam vet believes that his illness is the result of exposure to Agent Orange. With the help of a VA counselor, they lobby for national programs to assist other veterans who have been exposed to the chemical and together bring publicity to the issue. A made-for-television drama that is exceptionally well-acted. **96m/C VHS, Beta, LV.** John Ritter, Patti LaBelle, Alfre Woodard, John Sayles, Sean McCann, John Vargas, Gwen E. Davis; ***D:*** Lamont Johnson; ***W:*** John Sayles; ***M:*** Charles Fox. *NO*

Unnatural Pursuits ☠☠ **1991** Playwright Simon Gray's black comic look at a British playwright's sojourn from London to L.A., Dallas, and New York and the Broadway debut of his new work. Alcoholic Hamish Partt (Bates), in the throes of a midlife crisis, is plagued by ego, indignities, and hostile actors, audiences, and critics as he tries desperately to work. Made for British TV. **60m/C VHS.** *GB* Alan Bates, Keith Szarabajka, Deborah Rush, John Mahoney, Tom Hickey, Richard Wilson, David Healy, Jack Gilpin, Paul Zimet, Bob Balaban; **W:** Simon Gray. *TVC*

An Unremarkable Life ₰₰ **1989 (PG)** Two aging sisters live symbiotically together, until one views the other's romantic attachment to a charming widower as destructive to her own life. **97m/C VHS, Beta.** Shelley Winters, Patricia Neal, Mako, Rochelle Oliver, Charles S. Dutton, Lily Knight; **D:** Amin Q. Chaudhri. *IME, COL*

Unsane ₰₰½ *Tenebrae* **1982** A mystery novelist realizes that a series of bizarre murders strangely resembles the plot of his latest book. Bloody fun from Argento. **91m/C VHS.** *IT* Anthony (Tony) Franciosa, John Saxon, Daria Nicolodi, Giuliano Gemma, Christian Borromeo, Mirella D'Angelo, Veronica Lario; **D:** Dario Argento; **W:** Dario Argento. *MED*

The Unseen ₰½ **1980** Three young women from a television station are covering a story in a remote area of California. Before nightfall, two are horribly killed, leaving the third to come face to face with the terror. **91m/C VHS, Beta.** Barbara Bach, Sydney Lassick, Stephen Furst; **D:** Peter Foleg. *NO*

Unsettled Land ₰₰ **1988 (PG)** Young Israeli settlers try to survive the elements and Bedouin attackers in Palestine during the 1920s. **109m/C VHS, Beta, LV, 8mm.** *IS* Kelly McGillis, John Shea, Arnon Zadok, Christine Boisson; **D:** Uri Barbash. *SUE, NLC*

The Unsinkable Molly Brown ₰₰₰ **1964** A spunky backwoods girl is determined to break into the upper crust of Denver's high society and along the way survives the sinking of the Titanic. This energetic version of the Broadway musical contains many Meredith Willson ("Music Man") songs and lots of hokey, good-natured fun. ♫Colorado Is My Home; Leadville Johnny Brown (Soliloquy); I Ain't Down Yet; Belly Up to the Bar, Boys; He's My Friend; I've Already Started; The Beautiful People of Denver; I May Never Fall in Love with You; Up Where the People Are. **128m/C VHS, Beta, LV.** Debbie Reynolds, Harve Presnell, Ed Begley Sr., Martita Hunt, Hermione Baddeley; **D:** Charles Walters; **C:** Daniel F. Fapp; **M:** Meredith Willson. Nominations: Academy Awards '64: Best Actress (Reynolds), Best Art Direction/Set Decoration (Color), Best Color Cinematography, Best Costume Design (Color), Best Sound, Best Original Score. *MGM*

The Unstoppable Man ₰½ **1959** The son of an American businessman is kidnapped while they are in London. No pushover he, dad develops his own plan to destroy the criminals, eventually pursuing them with a flame thrower. **68m/B VHS, Beta.** *GB* Cameron Mitchell, Marius Goring, Harry H. Corbett, Lois Maxwell, Denis Gilmore; **D:** Terry Bishop. *NOS, SNC*

Unstrung Heroes ₰₰½ **1995 (PG)** Semi-autobiographical tale of Steven Lidz (Watt), growing up in 1960s California with a mother who is dying of cancer (MacDowell) and a nutty professor-type father (Turturro) who refuses to accept her illness. A desperate Steven goes to live with his two oddball uncles (Richards and Chaykin) who provide understanding and insight for the youngster, as well as a new name, Franz. Moving and quirky without being sappy, Keaton's feature debut avoids what would've been easy stereotypes. Based on the autobiography by Franz Lidz. **93m/C VHS, LV.** Andie MacDowell, John Turturro, Michael Richards, Maury Chaykin, Nathan Watt, Kendra Krull; **D:** Diane Keaton; **W:** Richard LaGravenese; **C:** Phedon Papamichael; **M:** Thomas Newman. Nominations: Academy Awards '95: Best Score. *HPH*

Unsuitable Job for a Woman ₰₰½ **1982** Independent Cordelia Gray, following the death of her boss, takes over his detective agency and gets involved with murder. Based on the novel by P.D. James. **94m/C VHS, Beta.** *GB* Pippa Guard, Paul Freeman, Billie Whitelaw; **D:** Christopher Petit. *NO*

The Untamable ₰₰ **1923** Unusual silent about volatile woman suffering from schizophrenia. **65m/B VHS, Beta.** Gladys Walton, Malcolm McGregor, John St. Polis, Etta Lee; **D:** Herbert Blache. *GPV, FCT*

Untamed Heart ₰₰½ **1993 (PG-13)** Adam (Slater), the painfully shy busboy with a heart condition, loves Caroline (Tomei), the bubbly waitress, from afar. She doesn't notice him until he saves her from some would-be rapists and their love blooms in the coffee shop where they both work. Tomei and Slater are both strong in the leads and Perez, as Caroline's best buddy Cindy, hurls comic barbs with ease. Charmingly familiar surroundings help set this formulaic romance apart. Filmed on location in Minneapolis. Laserdisc version is in letterbox format. **102m/C VHS, Beta, LV.** Christian Slater, Marisa Tomei, Rosie Perez, Kyle Secor, Willie Garson; **D:** Tony Bill; **W:** Tom Sierchio; **M:** Cliff Eidelman. MTV Movie Awards '93: Most Desirable Male (Slater), Best Kiss (Christian Slater/Marisa Tomei). *MGM*

Until September ₰₰ **1984 (R)** An American tourist becomes stranded in Paris. She meets and falls in love with a married banker while she is stuck in her hotel. Routine romance. **96m/C VHS, Beta.** Karen Allen, Thierry Lhermitte, Christopher Cazenove, Johanna Pavlis; **D:** Richard Marquand; **M:** John Barry. *MGM*

Until The End of The World ₰₰₰½ **1991 (R)** Convoluted road movie set in 1999 follows the travails of Sam Farber (Hurt) through 15 cities in 8 countries on 4 continents as he is chased by Dommartin, her lover (Neill), a bounty hunter, a private detective, and bank robbers, until all wind up in the Australian outback. And this is only the first half of the movie. For true cinematic satisfaction, don't expect logic—just go with the flow. Visually stunning, unexpectedly humorous, with excellent performances from an international cast. Footage created with high definition (HDTV) video technology is a technological first. The soundtrack features Lou Reed, David Byrne, U2, and others. **158m/C VHS, Beta, LV.** William Hurt, Solveig Dommartin, Sam Neill, Max von Sydow, Ruediger Vogler, Ernie Dingo, Jeanne Moreau; **D:** Wim Wenders; **W:** Wim Wenders, Peter Carey; **M:** Graeme Revell. *WAR*

Until They Get Me ₰½ **1918** Northern Mountie rides horse in silence as he tracks criminal to the edge of the earth. **58m/B VHS, Beta.** Pauline Starke, Joe King. *GPV, FCT*

Until They Sail ₰₰½ **1957** Soap opera set in New Zealand during WWII. Plot centers around the lives of four sisters involved in love and murder. Dee's film debut. Based on a story by James Michener. **95m/B VHS.** Jean Simmons, Joan Fontaine, Paul Newman, Piper Laurie, Charles Drake, Sandra Dee, Wally Cassell, Alan Napier; **D:** Robert Wise; **W:** Robert Anderson. *MGM*

The Untouchables ₰₰₰½ **1987 (R)** Big-budget, fast-paced and exciting re-evaluation of the popular TV series about the real-life battle between Treasury officer Eliot Ness and crime boss Al Capone in 1920s' Chicago. History sometimes takes a back seat to Hollywood's imagination in the screenplay, but it doesn't really matter since there are splendid performances by De Niro as Capone and Connery as Ness' mentor to help it look realistic. Costner does a fine job showing the change in Ness from naive idealism to steely conviction. Beautifully filmed with excellent special effects. **119m/C VHS, Beta, LV, 8mm.** Kevin Costner, Sean Connery, Robert De Niro, Andy Garcia, Charles Martin Smith, Billy Drago, Richard Bradford, Jack Kehoe; **D:** Brian DePalma; **W:** David Mamet; **C:** Stephen Burum; **M:** Ennio Morricone. Academy Awards '87: Best Supporting Actor (Connery); Golden Globe Awards '88: Best Supporting Actor (Connery); National Board of Review Awards '87: 10 Best Films of the Year, Best Supporting Actor (Connery); Nominations: Academy Awards '87: Best Art Direction/Set Decoration, Best Costume Design, Best Original Score. *PAR, BTV*

Unveiled ₰₰½ **1994 (R)** Stephanie Montgomery's (Zane) friend falls victim to a killer in Marrakesh. So Steph sets out to trap the killer, with the help of government offficial Peter (Hubley). **103m/C VHS, LV.** Lisa Zane, Whip Hubley, Nicholas Chinlund, Martha Gehman; **D:** William Cole; **W:** Michael Diamond, Roger Kumble; **M:** Christopher Tyng. *FXV*

Unzipped ₰₰₰ **1994 (R)** Witty, behind-the-scenes look at whiz-kid fashion designer Isaac Mizrahi as he prepares for the showing of his 1994 collection. Alternately filmed in black-and-white and color in a variety of film stocks, Keeve (Mizrahi's former lover) captures Mizrahi's varying moods, from his creative struggles to his unique sense of humor and gift for mimicry. Highlights include scenes with Mizrahi's doting mother. Fashionphiles will love every minute, and strictly off-the-rack viewers can enjoy the supermodels on parade. **76m/C VHS, LV. D:** Douglas Keeve. Sundance Film Festival '95: Audience Award. *WAR*

Up Against the Wall ₰₰ **1991 (PG-13)** A black kid from the Chicago projects attends school in the affluent suburbs, but there too he must resist temptation, crime and violence. A well-intentioned but didactic cautionary drama, adapted from the book by African-American author/commentator Dr. Jawanza Kunjufu. **103m/C VHS.** Marla Gibbs, Stoney Jackson, Catero Colbert, Ron O'Neal, Salli Richardson; **D:** Ron O'Neal. *BMG*

Up Close and Personal ₰₰₰ **1996 (PG-13)** Ambitious Reno card dealer Tally Atwater (Pfeiffer) wants to get into broadcasting and finds her chance at a Miami TV station where she's mentored by successful veteran-reporter-turned-producer Warren Justice (Redford). They fall in love but find their careers clashing as Tally climbs the media success ladder. Originally inspired by the tragic life of NBC reporter Jessica Savitch, whose problems with drugs and abusive relationships lead to a sad ending, film turned into a star-powered romance with media trappings and another variation of "A Star is Born." It's now "suggested" by Alanna Nash's book "Golden Girl." **124m/C VHS.** Michelle Pfeiffer, Robert Redford, Kate Nelligan, Stockard Channing, Joe Mantegna, Glenn Plummer, James Rebhorn, Noble Willingham, Scott Bryce, Raymond Cruz, Dedee Pfeiffer, Miguel Sandoval, James Karen; **D:** Jon Avnet; **W:** Joan Didion, John Gregory Dunne; **C:** Karl Walter Lindenlaub; **M:** Thomas Newman. *NYR*

Up from the Depths ₰½ **1979 (R)** Something from beneath the ocean is turning the paradise of Hawaii into a nightmare. Prehistoric fish are returning to the surface with one thing on their minds—lunch. "Jaws" rip-off played for humor. **85m/C VHS, Beta.** Sam Bottoms, Suzanne Reed, Virgil Frye; **D:** Charles B. Griffith; **W:** Alfred Sweeney; **M:** James Horner. *LIV, VES*

Up in Arms ₰₰ **1944** Danny Kaye's first film presents a typical Kaye scenario: he plays a twitching hypochondriac who is drafted into the Army and sneaks his girlfriend aboard the troopship bound for the Pacific. Features an appearance by the Goldwyn Girls. Remake of the film "The Nervous Wreck." ♫Theatre Lobby Number; Now I Know; All Out for Freedom; Tess's Torch Song; Melody in 4-F. **105m/C VHS, Beta, LV.** Danny Kaye, Dinah Shore, Constance Dowling, Dana Andrews, Margaret Dumont, Goldwyn Girls, Lyle Talbot, Louis Calhern, Charles Halton; **D:** Elliott Nugent; **C:** Ray Rennahan. Nominations: Academy Awards '44: Best Song ("Now I Know"), Best Original Score. *SUE*

Up in the Air ₰₰ **1940** Darro and Moreland have ambitions as radio comedians, and their friend Reynolds wants to be a singer. Their break comes when other performers are murdered on the air. First, though, they must solve the killings. **62m/B VHS.** Frankie Darro, Marjorie Reynolds, Mantan Moreland, Gordon Jones, Tristram Coffin, John Holland, Carleton Young; **D:** Howard Bretherton. *NOS*

Up Periscope ₰₰½ **1959** Garner is a demolitions expert unwillingly assigned to a submarine commanded by O'Brien. His mission: to sneak onto a Japanese-held island and steal a top-secret code book. Trouble is, O'Brien may not wait for Garner to complete his mission before taking the sub back underwater. A routine submarine film. **111m/C VHS, LV.** James Garner, Edmond O'Brien, Andra Martin, Alan Hale Jr., Carleton Carpenter, Frank Gifford, Richard Bakalayan; **D:** Gordon Douglas. *WAR*

Up River **1979** Wealthy land baron rapes and murders the wife of a simple pioneer, who is beaten and whose homestead is burned by the baron as well. The pioneer lives to seek terrible vengeance. **90m/C VHS.** Jeff Corey, Morgan Stevens, Debbie AuLuce; ***D:*** Carl Kitt. *NO*

Up the Academy *Mad Magazine's Up the Academy; The Brave Young Men of Weinberg* **1980 (R)** Four teenaged delinquents are sent to an academy for wayward boys where they encounter a sadistic headmaster and a gay dance instructor. Sometimes inventive, often tasteless fare from "Mad" magazine. **88m/C VHS, Beta.** Ron Leibman, Ralph Macchio, Barbara Bach, Tom Poston, Stacey Nelkin, Wendell Brown, Tom Citera; ***D:*** Robert Downey. *WAR*

Up the Creek **1958** Crazy antics abound in this tale of an old British destroyer, a black-market scheme run by the crew, and the new skipper whose hobby is rocket building. Followed by "Further Up the River." **83m/B VHS, Beta.** *GB* David Tomlinson, Wilfrid Hyde-White, Peter Sellers, Vera Day, Michael Goodliffe, Lionel Jeffries; ***D:*** Val Guest. *MON*

Up the Creek ½ **1984 (R)** Four college losers enter a whitewater raft race to gain some respect for their school. The soundtrack features songs by Heart, Cheap Trick and The Beach Boys. Routine. **95m/C VHS, Beta, LV.** Tim Matheson, Jennifer Runyon, Stephen Furst, John Hillerman, James B. Sikking, Julia Montgomery, Jeana Tomasina; ***D:*** Robert Butler; ***M:*** William Goldstein. *LIV, VES*

Up the Down Staircase **1967** A naive, newly trained New York public school teacher is determined to teach the finer points of English literature to a group of poor students. She almost gives up until one student actually begins to learn. Good production and acting. Based on Bel Kaufman's novel. **124m/C VHS.** Sandy Dennis, Patrick Bedford, Eileen Heckart, Ruth White, Jean Stapleton, Sorrell Booke; ***D:*** Robert Mulligan. *WAR, OM*

Up the Sandbox **1972 (R)** A bored housewife fantasizes about her life in order to avoid facing her mundane existence. Fine acting from Streisand, with real problems of young mothers accurately shown. **98m/C VHS, Beta.** Barbra Streisand, David Selby, Jane Hoffman, Barbara Rhoades; ***D:*** Irvin Kershner; ***C:*** Gordon Willis; ***M:*** Billy Goldenberg. *WAR*

Up to a Certain Point *Up to a Point; Hasta Clerto Punto* **1983** Writer Oscar believes he has a liberal attitude (to go along with Cuban political ideology) but his belief is shaken when he interviews workers on the Havana docks about their notions of machismo. Seems when Oscar falls for a sexy dockworker his ideas of maleness and a woman's place are more traditional than he imagines. Spanish with subtitles. **70m/C VHS.** *CU* Oscar Alvarez, Mirta Ibarra, Omar Valdes, Coralia Veloz, Rogelio Blain, Ana Vina; ***D:*** Thomas Gutierrez Alea; ***W:*** Thomas Gutierrez Alea; ***M:*** Leo Brower. *NYF*

Up Your Alley **1989 (R)** A female reporter, pursuing a story on homelessness, and a skidrow bum find romance. Langston, who produced and cowrote the film, is better known as "The Unknown Comic." **90m/C VHS, Beta, LV.** Linda Blair, Murray Langston, Ruth Buzzi, Johnny Dark, Bob Zany, Yakov Smirnoff; ***D:*** Bob Logan. *LIV*

Uphill All the Way **1985** A couple of card-cheatin' good old boys are pursued by posses and cavalry alike, and end up killing real outlaws. Made for television. **91m/C VHS, Beta.** Roy Clark, Mel Tillis, Glen Campbell, Trish Van Devere, Burl Ives, Burt Reynolds; ***D:*** Frank Q. Dobbs. *NWV, VTR*

Upper Crust ½ **1988** Boring tale of corruption and greed that takes place at the highest levels of American business and government. **95m/C VHS, Beta.** Frank Gorshin, Broderick Crawford, Nigel Davenport. *NO*

The Uprising **1981** A Nicaraguan drama filmed just months after the 1979 Sandinista revolution, wherein a young guard of Somoza retains his job for the money, while his father is active in the revolutionary forces. In Spanish with English subtitles. **96m/C VHS, Beta.** *SP* ***D:*** Peter Lilienthal. *KIV, INJ*

Uptown Angel **1990 (R)** A young woman is determined to work her way out of her home on the wrong side of town. Black cast brings new life to old premise. **90m/C VHS.** Caron Tate, Cliff McMullen, Gloria Davis Hill, Tracy Hill; ***D:*** Joy Shannon; ***W:*** Joy Shannon. *XVC*

Uptown New York **1932** A young man pressured by his family marries a rich girl instead of the woman he loves, who in turn marries a man she does not love. Routine melodrama. **81m/B VHS, Beta.** Jack Oakie, Shirley Green, Leon Ames, Shirley Grey, George Cooper, Raymond Hatton; ***D:*** Victor Schertzinger. *NOS, FCT, DVT*

Uptown Saturday Night ½ **1974 (PG)** Two working men attempt to recover a stolen lottery ticket from the black underworld after being ripped off at an illegal gambling place. Good fun, with nice performances from both leads and from Belafonte doing a black "Godfather" parody of Brando. Followed by "Let's Do It Again." **104m/C VHS, Beta.** Sidney Poitier, Bill Cosby, Harry Belafonte, Flip Wilson, Richard Pryor, Calvin Lockhart; ***D:*** Sidney Poitier; ***W:*** Richard Wesley; ***C:*** Fred W. Koenekamp. *WAR*

The Uranium Conspiracy ½ **1978 (PG)** A secret agent and a mercenary soldier try to stop a shipment of uranium out of Zaire from falling into enemy hands. It won't be easy. **100m/C VHS, Beta.** Fabio Testi, Janet Agren, Assaf Dayan. *NO*

Uranus **1991 (R)** After WWII a French provincial town has been liberated from Nazi invaders—but not its own suspicions, as citizens try to rebuild knowing some of them collaborated with the enemy. An important subject is heavily talked over in static fashion, with a robust Depardieu either a standout or a ham as the earthy saloon-keeper. Based on a novel by Marcel Ayme, himself accused of pro-Vichy leanings during the era. In French with English subtitles. **100m/C VHS, LV.** *FR* Gerard Depardieu, Michel Blanc, Jean-Pierre Marielle, Philippe Noiret, Gerard Desarthe, Michel Galabru, Fabrice Luchini, Daniel Prevost; ***D:*** Claude Berri; ***W:*** Claude Berri; ***M:*** Jean-Claude Petit. *INJ*

Urban Cowboy ½ **1980 (PG)** A young Texas farmer comes to Houston to work in a refinery. After work he hangs out at Gilley's, a roadhouse bar. Here he and his friends, dressed in their cowboy gear, drink, fight, and prove their manhood by riding a mechanical bull. Film made Winger a star, was an up in Travolta's roller coaster career, and began the craze for country western apparel and dance and them there mechanical bulls. Ride 'em, cowboy! **135m/C VHS, Beta, LV.** John Travolta, Debra Winger, Scott Glenn, Madolyn Smith, Barry Corbin; ***D:*** James Bridges; ***W:*** James Bridges, Aaron Latham; ***C:*** Reynaldo Villalobos; ***M:*** Ralph Burns. *PAR*

Urban Crossfire ½ **1994 (PG-13)** Two veteran white Brooklyn detectives investigating gang violence are aided by a young black patrolman whose partner was killed by a gang leader. Solid cast, fast paced action. **95m/C VHS, LV.** Mario Van Peebles, Ray Sharkey, Peter Boyle, Michael Boatman; ***D:*** Dick Lowry. *NHO*

Urban Warriors **1975** Savage barbarians roam and pillage a post-nuclear war Earth, but one invincible warrior ushers them out. **90m/C VHS, Beta.** Karl Landgren, Alex Vitale, Deborah Keith; ***D:*** Joseph Warren. *CAN*

Urge to Kill **1984 (PG)** A man returning from a mental hospital after pleading temporary insanity to the murder of his girlfriend returns to her town and tries to uncover the truth, with the help of her younger sister. Made for television. **96m/C VHS, Beta.** Karl Malden, Holly Hunter, William Devane, Alex McArthur; ***D:*** Mike Robe. *FOX, VTR*

Urotsukidoj 1: Legend of the Overfiend *The Wandering Kid* **1993 (NC-17)** Legend has it that the world is made up of Humans, Man-Beasts, and Monster-Demons. Every 3000 years superfiend Chojin is supposed to unite the three into a single Land of Eternity. However, the heroic Amano discovers this land will be a nightmare world and unless he can successfully battle Chojin humanity may not survive. Ultra-violent and sexually explicit. Animated; dubbed into English. **108m/C VHS.** *JP CPM, MOV*

Urotsukidoj 2: Legend of the Demon Womb **1993** The fiendish Dr. Munhihausen's life work has been to render the dimensional boundaries between the World of Man-Beasts and the World of Monster Demons and to conjure the dreaded Overfiend. Years later, his son seeks to find a way to conquer the Overfiend and his cohorts from Hell and assume its powers for himself. Munhihausen's efforts may soon be rewarded when his hapless cousin, who accidentally received the demon's blood, begins developing monstrous powers. Animated; dubbed from Japanese. **88m/C VHS.** *JP CPM, MOV*

Ursus in the Valley of the Lions ½ *The Mighty Ursus; Ursus* **1962** Ursus attempts to rescue his love from druids but is dismayed to find that she has taken up homicide in her free time. **92m/C VHS.** *IT SP* Ed Fury, Luis Prendes, Moira Orfei, Cristina Gajoni, Maria Luisa Merlo; ***D:*** Carlo Campogalliani. *SNC*

Urusei Yatsura Movie 1: Only You **198?** Lum is a Princess of the Oni, an alien race who have come to repossess Earth. The planet's one chance is for an earthling to beat Lum in the Oni's national sport—tag. When unlucky teenager Ataru Moroboshi is chosen he actually beats Lum. Which means he has to marry her. In Japanese with English subtitles. **100m/C VHS.** *JP ANI*

Urusei Yatsura Movie 2: Beautiful Dreamer **1992** Unlucky teenager Ataru Moroboshi and his classmates at Tomobiki High School find themselves reliving the day before the School Festival over and over again. Funny and dreamlike. In Japanese with English subtitles. **90m/C VHS, LV.** *JP* ***D:*** Oshii Mamoru. *CPM, INJ, ANI*

Urusei Yatsura Movie 3: Remember My Love **1985** A magician family friend of Princess Lum put a curse on her at birth when she wasn't invited to Lum's christening (shades of "Sleeping Beauty")—that Lum would never be happy with her true love. But Ataru is the real victim. When the magician happens upon him in the new amusement park she turns him into a pink hippotamus to spite Lum. In Japanese with English subtitles. **93m/C VHS, LV.** *JP ANI*

Urusei Yatsura Movie 4: Lum the Forever **1986** When a great cherry tree is cut down near where Lum and friends are making a movie she mysteriously loses her horns, and with them her powers. In Japanese with English subtitles. **94m/C VHS, LV.** *JP ANI, WTA, ING*

Urusei Yatsura Movie 5: The Final Chapter **19??** Boy meets girl with Japanimation twist. Lum's fiance, Lupa, is introduced and the fate of the Earth is in Ataru's hands. Japanese with English subtitles. **90m/C VHS, LV.** *JP WTA*

Urusei Yatsura Movie 6: Always My Darling **1991** Space princess Lupica abducts Aturu in order to get the greatest love potion in the galaxy. Lum wants him back. In Japanese with English subtitles. **77m/C VHS.** *JP ANI, ING*

Used Cars **1980 (R)** A car dealer is desperate to put his jalopy shop competitors out of business. The owners go to great lengths to stay afloat. Sometimes too obnoxious, but often funny. **113m/C VHS, Beta, LV, 8mm.** Kurt Russell, Jack Warden, Deborah Harmon, Gerrit Graham, Joe Flaherty, Michael McKean; ***D:*** Robert Zemeckis; ***W:*** Robert Zemeckis. *COL*

Used People ½ **1992 (PG-13)** A study in ethnicity and characterization, three Oscar-winning actresses lead a talented cast playing a Jewish family living in Queens in 1969. When the father dies, Joe (Mastroianni), an old friend with an old torch for the widow, Pearl (MacLaine), shows up at the funeral and manages to charm her into a date for coffee. Pearl's new relationship with her Italian suitor affects each of the somewhat off-balance family members and washes the whole clan with a sense of hope and renewal. Adpated from screenwriter Graff's play "The Grandma Plays" that was based on memories of his grandmother. Director Kidron's American debut. **116m/C VHS, LV.** Shirley MacLaine, Marcello Mastroianni, Kathy Bates, Marcia Gay Harden, Jessica Tandy, Sylvia Sidney, Bob Dishy, Joe Pantoliano, Matthew Branton, Louis Guff, Charles Cioffi, Doris Roberts, Helen Hanft; ***D:*** Beeban Kidron; ***W:*** Todd Graff; ***M:*** Rachel Portman. *FXV*

Users ☙☙ **1978** Small-town girl who worked as a prostitute meets a faded film star and becomes involved in the movie business. Ode to decadent Hollywood. Based on the Joyce Haber novel. Made for television. **125m/C VHS, Beta.** Jaclyn Smith, Tony Curtis, John Forsythe, Red Buttons, George Hamilton; ***D:*** Joseph Hardy; ***M:*** Maurice Jarre. *PSM*

The Usual Suspects ☙☙☙½ **1995 (R)** Twisted noir-thriller about some crooks, a $91 million heist, and mysterious crime lord Keyser Soze. Customs agent Kujan (Palminteri) tries to get a straight story out of small-time con man "Verbal" Kint (Spacey) about a burning tanker in the San Pedro harbor, 27 dead bodies, and the other four tempermental criminals involved: ex-cop-turned thief Keaton (Byrne), explosives expert Hockney (Pollak), and hot-headed partners McManus (Baldwin) and Fenster (Del Toro). Nothing is as it seems, and the ending keeps everyone guessing, right up to the final credits. Terrific performances from all complement the intelligent, humorous script. And yes, the title does come from the famous line in "Casablanca." **105m/C VHS, LV.** Kevin Spacey, Gabriel Byrne, Chazz Palminteri, Kevin Pollak, Stephen Baldwin, Benicio Del Toro, Giancarlo Esposito, Pete Postlethwaite, Dan Hedaya, Suzy Amis, Paul Bartel; ***D:*** Bryan Singer; ***W:*** Christopher McQuarrie; ***C:*** Newton Thomas Sigel; ***M:*** John Ottman. Academy Awards '95: Best Original Screenplay, Best Supporting Actor (Spacey); Independent Spirit Awards '96: Best Screenplay, Best Supporting Actor (Del Toro); New York Film Critics Awards '95: Best Supporting Actor (Spacey); Nominations: Academy Awards '95: Best Screenplay; British Academy Awards '95: Best Film; Golden Globe Awards '96: Best Supporting Actor (Spacey); Independent Spirit Awards '96: Best Cinematography; Screen Actors Guild Award '95: Best Supporting Actor (Spacey). *PGV*

Utah ☙☙ **1945** A musical comedy star who inherits a ranch wishes to sell it to finance one of her shows. She is persuaded not to by Rogers, the ranch foreman. **54m/B VHS, Beta.** Roy Rogers, Dale Evans, George "Gabby" Hayes; ***D:*** John English. *NOS, VDM, VCN*

Utah Trail ☙ **1938** Lawman Ritter is hired to stop a gang of cattle rustlers. Cheapie oater made for Grand National, which went bankrupt soon after. **57m/B VHS, Beta.** Tex Ritter; ***D:*** Al(bert) Herman. *NOS, VCN, DVT*

Utamaro and His Five Women ☙☙½ *Five Women Around Utamaro; Utamaro O Meguru Gonin No Onna* **1946** Utamaro is a legendary 19th-century Edo artist who gained inspiration from Tokyo's "floating world," of courtesans, brothels, drinking parties, and violent passions. His gorgeous portraits worship women but he dislikes the complications that flesh-and-blood females bring. Heavily stylized look at the artistic impulse. In Japanese with English subtitles. **89m/B VHS.** *JP* Minnosuke Bando, Kinuyo Tanaka, Kotaro Bando, Hisato Osawa, Tamezo Mochizuki, Hiroko Kawasaki; ***D:*** Kenji Mizoguchi; ***W:*** Yoshikata Yoda. *NYF, FCT*

Utilities ☙½ *Getting Even* **1983 (PG)** A frustrated social worker enlists the help of his friends in his efforts to impress an attractive policewoman by taking on a large corporate utility. **94m/C VHS, Beta, LV.** *CA* Robert Hays, Brooke Adams, John Marley, Ben Gordon, Helen Burns; ***D:*** Harvey Hart. *LIV, VES*

Utopia ☙☙ *Atoll K; Robinson Crusoeland; Escapade* **1951** Laurel and Hardy inherit a paradisaical island, but their peace is disturbed when uranium is discovered. Final screen appearance of the team is diminished by poor direction and script. **82m/B VHS, Beta.** *FR* Stan Laurel, Oliver Hardy, Suzy Delair, Max Elloy; ***D:*** Leo Joannon. *CNG, MRV, VYY*

Utu ☙☙☙ **1983 (R)** A Maori tribesman serving with the colonizing British army in 1870 explodes into ritual revenge when his home village is slaughtered. Filmed in New Zealand. **104m/C VHS, Beta.** *NZ* Anzac Wallace, Kelly Johnson, Tim Elliot, Bruno Lawrence; ***D:*** Geoff Murphy; ***M:*** John Charles. *FOX*

Utz ☙☙½ **1993** The Baron von Utz (Mueller-Stahl) collects both women and priceless porcelain figures. When his friend, art dealer Marius Fischer (Riegert), travels to Prague for a visit he finds that both Utz's housekeeper (Fricker), who has suffered from unrequited love, and the porcelain have disappeared. So Marius teams up with the Baron's old friend Dr. Orlick (Scofield) to find out what's going on. Based on the novel by Bruce Chatwin. **95m/C VHS.** *GB GE IT* Armin Mueller-Stahl, Peter Riegert, Brenda Fricker, Paul Scofield; ***D:*** George Sluizer. *FRV, BTV, FCT*

V ☙☙☙ **1983** Very creepy sci-fi miniseries that spawned a short-lived TV show. Advanced aliens, known as the Visitors, come to Earth on a seemingly friendly quest. But their human-like appearance is a facade—as is their mission. Fake skin masks a repitilian hide and what they want is complete planetary control. Naturally, some earthlings don't fall for their smooth talk and a resistance movement is born. Followed by miniseries conclusion "V: The Final Battle." **190m/C VHS.** Marc Singer, Jane Badler, Faye Grant, Robert Englund, Michael Durrell, Peter Nelson, Neva Patterson, Andrew Prine, Richard Herd, Rafael Campos; ***D:*** Kenneth Johnson; ***W:*** Kenneth Johnson. *WAR, MOV*

V: The Final Battle ☙☙½ **1984** It's four-months since the Visitors appeared on earth, proclaiming their false friendship. But a resistance movement knows these reptiles, who hide behind a human appearance, are only interested in harvesting earth's inhabitants as a new food source. Continuation of the TV miniseries "V." **285m/C VHS.** Marc Singer, Robert Englund, Michael Ironside; ***D:*** Richard T. Heffron. *WAR*

The Vagabond **1916** The Little Tramp is a pathetic fiddler making a scanty living who rescues a damsel in distress. Silent with musical soundtrack added. **20m/B VHS, Beta.** Charlie Chaplin, Edna Purviance, Eric Campbell, Albert Austin; ***D:*** Charlie Chaplin. *CAB, GVV, VYY*

Vagabond ☙☙☙½ *Sans Toit Ni Loi* **1985** Bleak, emotionally shattering, powerful and compelling, this film traces the peripatetic life of an amoral and selfish young French woman who has no regard for social rules and tremendous fear of responsibility in her drifting yet inexorable journey into death. Told via flashbacks from the moment when she is found dead, alone, and unaccounted for by the roadside, this film will not leave you unscathed. Written by New Wave director Varda. In French with English subtitles. **105m/C VHS, Beta, LV.** *FR* Sandrine Bonnaire, Macha Meril, Stephane Freiss, Elaine Cortadellas, Marthe Jarnias, Yolanda Moreau; ***D:*** Agnes Varda; ***W:*** Agnes Varda. Cesar Awards '86: Best Actress (Bonnaire); Los Angeles Film Critics Association Awards '86: Best Actress (Bonnaire), Best Foreign Film. *INJ, TPV*

Vagabond Lover ☙☙½ **1929** The amusing tale of the loves, hopes, and dreams of an aspiring saxophone player. Rudy croons through his megaphone in his movie debut. Appealing, with Dressler sparkling in the role of the wealthy aunt. ♫If You Were the Only Girl in the World; A Little Kiss Each Morning; Heigh Ho Everybody; Piccolo Pete; I Love You; I'll Be Reminded of You; I'm Just a Vagabond Lover. **66m/B VHS, Beta.** Rudy Vallee, Sally Blane, Marie Dressler; ***D:*** Marshall Neilan. *VYY, RXM, DVT*

The Vagrant ☙ **1992 (R)** Run-of-the-mill creeper with a mind-game playing derelict inhabiting the home of a young exec. A series of murders has this wimp yuppie wondering how to get rid of his unwelcome intruder. **91m/C VHS.** Bill Paxton, Michael Ironside, Marshall Bell, Stuart Pankin; ***D:*** Chris Walas. *MGM*

Valdez is Coming ☙☙½ **1971 (PG)** Though not a world-class western, this filmed-in-Spain saga does feature a probing script (based on an Elmore Leonard novel) on the nature of race relations. Fine performance by Lancaster as a Mexican-American who ignites the passions of a town, and ultimately confronts the local land baron. **90m/C VHS.** Burt Lancaster, Susan Clark, Jon Cypher, Barton Heyman, Richard Jordan, Frank Silvera, Hector Elizondo; ***D:*** Edwin Sherin; ***W:*** David Rayfiel. *MGM*

Valentino ☙☙ **1977 (R)** Another one of director Russell's flamboyantly excessive screen biographies, this time of silent screen idol Rudolph Valentino (Nureyev). The details hardly matter but the movie is told in flashback from Valentino's funeral to his beginnings as a dance instructor and his eventual success as a screen lover. Nureyev is noticeably stiff in his screen debut but at least he possesses some charisma. **127m/C VHS.** *GB* Rudolf Nureyev, Leslie Caron, Michelle Phillips, Carol Kane, Felicity Kendal, Seymour Cassel, Peter Vaughan, William Hootkins, Huntz Hall, David DeKeyser, Alfred Marks, Anton Diffring; ***D:*** Ken Russell; ***W:*** Mardik Martin, Ken Russell, John Byrum. *MGM*

Valentino Returns ☙☙ **1988 (R)** A kid in 1955 California buys a pink Cadillac he nicknames "Valentino Returns," thinking it will help him meet girls, as his parents undergo a stormy divorce. Weak script fades fast from fine premise, good start. Nice period feel. **97m/C VHS, Beta, LV.** Frederic Forrest, Veronica Cartwright, Jenny Wright, Barry Tubb; ***D:*** Peter Hoffman. *VMK*

Valley Girl ☙☙½ *Bad Boyz* **1983 (R)** Slight but surprisingly likeable teen romantic-comedy inspired by Frank Zappa novelty tune. Title stereotype falls for a leather-jacketed rebel. Really. It may look like a music video, but the story is straight from "Romeo and Juliet" via Southern California. Helped launch Cage's career. Music by Men at Work, Culture Club, and others. **95m/C VHS, Beta, LV.** Nicolas Cage, Deborah Foreman, Colleen Camp, Frederic Forrest; ***D:*** Martha Coolidge; ***W:*** Wayne Crawford. *VES*

The Valley Obscured by the Clouds ☙☙ **1972** A group of dropouts and seekers search for the valley of the gods in the wilds of New Guinea, and experience a sexual and spiritual metamorphosis. In French with English subtitles. **106m/C VHS.** *FR* ***D:*** Barbet Schroeder; ***M:*** Pink Floyd. *FCT, WAR, BTV*

The Valley of Decision ☙☙☙ **1945** Entertaining poor-girl-meets-rich-boy story with Peck as a wealthy mill owner who falls in love with beautiful housemaid Garson (the Queen of MGM at the time). Set in 1870 Pittsburgh; based on Marcia Davenport's novel. **111m/B VHS.** Gregory Peck, Greer Garson, Donald Crisp, Lionel Barrymore, Preston Foster, Gladys Cooper, Marsha Hunt, Reginald Owen, Dan Duryea, Jessica Tandy, Barbara Everest; ***D:*** Tay Garnett; ***W:*** John Meehan, Sonya Levien; ***C:*** Joseph Ruttenberg. *MGM*

Valley of Fire ☙☙ **1951** Autry is the mayor of a boom town that suffers from a lack of women. He decides to import a caravan of brides for the men in town but villains attempt to kidnap the women. **63m/B VHS, Beta.** Gene Autry, Gail Davis, Pat Buttram; ***D:*** John English. *CCB*

The Valley of Gwangi ☙☙☙ **1969 (G)** One of the best prehistoric-monster-westerns out there. Cowboys discover a lost valley of dinosaurs and try to capture a vicious, carnivorous allosaurus. Bad move, kemosabe! The creatures move via the stop-motion model animation by f/x maestro Ray Harryhausen, here at his finest. **95m/C VHS, Beta, LV.** James Franciscus, Gila Golan, Richard Carlson, Laurence Naismith, Freda Jackson; ***D:*** James O'Connolly; ***W:*** William Bast. *WAR*

Valley of Terror ☙½ **1938** Maynard is framed for cattle rustling. Can he prove his innocence? **59m/B VHS, Beta.** Kermit Maynard, Harley Wood, John Merton, Jack Ingram, Dick Curtis, Roger Williams; ***D:*** Al(bert) Herman. *NOS, CCB, DVT*

Valley of the Dolls ☙☙ **1967 (PG)** Camp/trash classic was rated as a bomb by many critics but is really of the so-bad-it's-good variety. Three beauties, Tate, Duke, and Parkins, dream of Hollywood stardom but fall victim to Hollywood excess, including drug dependency (the "dolls" of the title). There's unhappy love affairs, porno parts, health risks, and hysterics of various kinds—all designed to have you dropping your jaw in disbelief. The bathroom scene between Duke and Hayward involving a wig is not to be missed. Based on the novel by Jacqueline Susann who has a bit part as a reporter. Remade for television as "Jacqueline Susann's Valley of the Dolls" in 1981. **123m/C VHS.** Barbara Parkins, Patty Duke, Sharon Tate, Paul Burke, Tony Scotti, Martin Milner, Susan Hayward, Charles Drake, Lee Grant, Alex Davion, Robert Harris, Robert Viharo, Joey Bishop, George Jessel; ***Cameos:*** Jacqueline Susann; ***D:*** Mark Robson; ***W:*** Dorothy Kingsley, Helen Deutsch; ***C:*** William H. Daniels; ***M:*** John Williams. Nominations: Academy Awards '67: Best Original Score. *FXV, BTV*

Valley of the Eagles ½ **1951** When his wife and partner take off into the Lapland wilderness with his new invention, a scientist leads the police across the tundra in pursuit. Setting is at least a plus. **83m/B VHS, Beta.** *GB* Jack Warner, Nadia Gray, John McCallum, Martin Boddey, Christopher Lee; ***D:*** Terence Young; ***M:*** Nino Rota. *MSP*

Valley of the Lawless **1936** A cowboy rides into trouble aplenty while out searching for treasure. A routine western for Brown fans only. **59m/B VHS, Beta, LV.** Johnny Mack Brown; ***D:*** Robert North Bradbury; ***W:*** Robert North Bradbury. *NO*

Valley of the Sun **1942** A government agent tracks a crooked Indian liaison to prevent an Indian uprising in Arizona. Ball, well before her "Lucy" days, plays the restaurant owner both men romance. Better than average, with good cast, some laughs, and lots of excitement. **84m/B VHS, Beta.** Lucille Ball, James Craig, Cedric Hardwicke, Dean Jagger, Peter Whitney, Billy Gilbert, Tom Tyler, Antonio Moreno, George Cleveland, Hank Bell; ***D:*** George Marshall. *TTC*

Valley of Wanted Men ½ **1935** Three cons escape during a jailbreak and one uses his wits and nerve to prove another was framed. **56m/B VHS, Beta, 8mm.** Frankie Darro. *VYY*

Valmont **1989 (R)** Another adaptation of the Choderlos de Laclos novel "Les Liaisons Dangereuses." Various members of the French aristocracy in 1782 mercilessly play each other for fools in a complex game of lust and deception. Firth and Bening are at first playfully sensual, then the stakes get too high. They share an interesting bathtub scene. Well-acted, the 1988 Frears version, "Dangerous Liaisons," is edgier. Seeing the two films together makes for interesting comparisons of characters and styles. **137m/C VHS, Beta, LV.** Colin Firth, Meg Tilly, Annette Bening, Fairuza Balk, Sian Phillips, Jeffrey Jones, Fabia Drake, Henry Thomas, Vincent Schiavelli, T.P. McKenna, Ian McNeice; ***D:*** Milos Forman; ***W:*** Jean-Claude Carriere; ***M:*** Christopher Palmer. Cesar Awards '90: Best Art Direction/Set Decoration, Best Costume Design; Nominations: Academy Awards '89: Best Costume Design. *ORI, INJ*

The Vals ½ **1985 (R)** The glibly hip lethargy which is characteristic of four southern California teenaged girls turns to socially conscious resolve when a local orphanage is threatened. Like, for sure. **100m/C VHS, Beta.** Jill Carroll, Elana Stratheros, Gina Calabrese, Michelle Laurita, Chuck Connors, Sonny Bono, John Carradine, Michael Leon; ***D:*** James Polakof. *LIV, VES*

Vamp ½ **1986 (R)** Two college freshmen encounter a slew of weird, semi-vampiric people in a seamy red-light district nightclub. Starts cute but goes kinky. Jones is great as the stripping vampire. **93m/C VHS, Beta, LV.** Grace Jones, Chris Makepeace, Robert Rusler, Gedde Watanabe; ***D:*** Richard Wenk; ***M:*** Jonathan Elias. *NWV, VTR*

Vamping ½ **1984 (PG)** Struggling musician plans to burglarize a wealthy widow's home. Once inside, he finds himself attracted to his proposed victim. Tedious going. **110m/C VHS, Beta.** Patrick Duffy, Catherine Hyland, Rod Arrants, Fred A. Keller; ***D:*** Frederick King Keller. *FOX*

The Vampire *Mark of the Vampire* **1957** Pale man with big teeth attempts to swindle a beautiful babe out of fortune. Followed by "The Vampire's Coffin." **95m/B VHS.** *MX* Abel Salazar, Ariadne Welter, German Robles, Carmen Montejo, Jose Luis Jimenez; ***D:*** Fernando Mendez. *SNC*

Vampire at Midnight ½ **1988** Fairly stupid homicide detective stalks a rampaging vampire in Los Angeles. Occasional moments of gratuitous sex thrown in for good measure. **93m/C VHS, Beta.** Jason Williams, Gustav Vintas, Jeanie Moore, Christina Whitaker, Leslie Milne; ***D:*** Gregory McClatchy. *FOX*

The Vampire Bat ½ **1932** A mad scientist and a vampire bat and its supernatural demands set the stage for murders in a small town. Sets and actors borrowed from Universal Studios in this low-budget flick that looks and plays better than it should. Weird and very exploitative for 1932, now seems dated. **69m/B VHS, Beta.** Lionel Atwill, Fay Wray, Melvyn Douglas, Dwight Frye, Maude Eburne, George E. Stone; ***D:*** Frank Strayer. *VYY, SNC, WFV*

Vampire Circus ½ **1971 (R)** A circus appears in an isolated Serbian village in the 19th century but instead of bringing joy and happiness, this circus brings only death, mutilation and misery. It seems all the members are vampires who have the unique ability to transform themselves into animals. They intend to take revenge on the small town, whose inhabitants killed their evil ancestor 100 years previously. Excellent Hammer production. **84m/C VHS.** *GB* Adrienne Corri, Laurence Payne, Thorley Walters, John Moulder-Brown, Lynne Frederick, Elizabeth Seal, Anthony Corlan, Richard Owens, Domini Blythe, David Prowse; ***D:*** Robert W. Young. *FRG, MLB*

Vampire Cop ½ **1990 (R)** A vampire cop (not to be confused with zombie, maniac, midnight, psycho, future or Robo) teams up with a beautiful reporter to 'collar' a drug kingpin. **89m/C VHS.** Melissa Moore, Ed Cannon, Terence Jenkins. *ATL*

The Vampire Happening ½ **1971 (R)** An actress discovers to her chagrin that her ancestors were vampires and so is she. **90m/C VHS, Beta.** *GE* Ferdinand "Ferdy" Mayne; ***D:*** Freddie Francis. *NO*

The Vampire Hookers *Cemetary Girls; Sensuous Vampires; Night of the Bloodsuckers; Twice Bitten* **1978 (R)** Man in makeup recruits bevy of beautiful bloodsuckers to lure warm blooded victims to his castle. High ham performance by Carradine. Alternate titles: "Cemetery Girls," "Sensuous Vampires," "Night of the Bloodsuckers." **82m/C VHS, Beta.** *PH* John Carradine, Bruce Fairbairn, Trey Wilson, Karen Stride, Lenka Novak, Katie Dolan, Lex Winter; ***D:*** Cirio H. Santiago. *NO*

Vampire in Brooklyn **1995 (R)** Murphy switches gears to play a Carribean vampire traveling to New York in search of his vampiric lady love—who turns out to be half-vamp-half-cop Bassett. As in "Coming to America," Murphy plays multiple characters, but that's three times the disappointment. Stale humor and cheap horror effects do little to break the zombie curse plaguing Murphy's career. Three days into filming, a stunt double for Bassett was killed after doing a routine jump on the set, providing a bad omen Murphy should have heeded. **103m/C VHS.** Eddie Murphy, Angela Bassett, Kadeem Hardison, Allen Payne, Zakes Mokae, John Witherspoon; ***D:*** Wes Craven; ***W:*** Charles Murphy, Christopher Parker, Michael Lucker; ***C:*** Mark Irwin; ***M:*** J. Peter Robinson. *PAR*

The Vampire Lovers ½ **1970 (R)** An angry father goes after a lesbian vampire who has ravished his daughter and other young girls in a peaceful European village. Innovative story was soon used in countless other vampire vehicles. Hammer Studio's first horror film with nudity, another addition to the genre which spread rapidly. Based on the story "Carmilla" by Sheridan Le Fanu. Followed by, "Lust for a Vampire." **91m/C VHS, Beta.** *GB* Ingrid Pitt, Pippa Steele, Madeleine Smith, Peter Cushing, George Cole, Dawn Addams, Kate O'Mara, Ferdinand "Ferdy" Mayne; ***D:*** Roy Ward Baker. *ORI, MLB, SUE*

The Vampire People ½ *The Blood Drinkers* **1966 (PG)** A dwarf-assisted vampire attempts to save the life of his true love by transplanting her sister's heart. Typical Filipino vampire movie. In color and sepia-tone. **79m/C VHS, Beta.** *PH* Ronald Remy, Amalia Fuentes, Eddie Fernandez, Eva Montez; ***D:*** Gerardo (Gerry) De Leon. *SNC*

Vampire Raiders—Ninja Queen *Woof!* **1989** The white ninjas versus the black ninjas. The evil black ninjas are plotting to infiltrate the hotel industry. The white ninjas come to the rescue. **90m/C VHS.** Agnes Chan, Chris Petersen; ***D:*** Bruce Lambert. *TWE*

Vampire Vixens from Venus **1994** Three hideous drug smuggling aliens transform themselves into bodacious babes on earth so they can get what they came for. Seems their drug fix is derived from the life essence of men and they plan to drain every last drop they can. **90m/C VHS.** Michelle (McClellan) Bauer, Charlie Callas. *SHR*

The Vampire's Coffin ½ *El Ataud Del Vampiro; El Ataud Del Coffin* **1958** Count Lavud is relieved when faithful servant removes stake implanted in his heart. **86m/B VHS.** *MX* Abel Salazar, Ariadne Welter, German Robles; ***D:*** Fernando Mendez. *SNC*

The Vampire's Ghost **1945** A 400-hundred-year-old vampire/zombie, doomed to walk the earth forever, heads the African underworld. He can't be killed and can even go out during the day if he wears sunglasses. His future's so bright he's just gotta wear shades. **59m/B VHS.** John Abbott, Peggy Stewart; ***D:*** Lesley Selander. *NOS, DVT, HEG*

Vampire's Kiss **1988 (R)** Cage makes this one worthwhile; his twisted transformation from pretentious post-val dude to psychotic yuppie from hell is inspired. If his demented torment of his secretary (Alonso) doesn't give you the creeps, his scene with the cockroach will. Cage fans will enjoy his facial aerobics; Beals fans will appreciate her extensive sucking scenes (she's the vamp of his dreams). More for psych majors than horror buffs. **103m/C VHS, Beta, LV.** Nicolas Cage, Elizabeth Ashley, Jennifer Beals, Maria Conchita Alonso, Kasi Lemmons, Bob Lujan, Jennifer Lundy; ***D:*** Robert Bierman; ***M:*** Colin Towns. *HBO*

Vampyr *Vampyr, Ou L'Etrang e Aventure De David Gray; Vampyr, Der Traum Des David Gray; Not Against the Flesh; Castle of Doom; The Strange Adventure of David Gray; The Vampire* **1931** Dreyer's classic portrays a hazy, dreamlike world full of chilling visions from the point of view of a young man who believes himself surrounded by vampires and who dreams of his own burial in a most disturbing way. Evil lurks around every corner as camera angles, light and shadow sometimes overwhelm plot. A high point in horror films based on a collection of horror stories by Sheridan le Fanu. In German with English subtitles. **75m/B VHS, Beta.** *GE* Julien West, Sybille Schmitz, Harriet Gerard, Maurice Schutz; ***D:*** Carl Theodor Dreyer; ***W:*** Carl Theodor Dreyer; ***M:*** Wolfgang Zeller. *VYY, NOS, SNC*

The Vampyr **1992** Uncut version of the BBC musical production about a lustful vampire. Text sets present-day lyrics to the 1827 opera by Heinrich Marschner. Vampire Ripley (Ebrahim) has just been set free in London after having been trapped in an underground tomb for 200 years. Unless he puts the bite on three lovely ladies within three days he will be condemned to eternal damnation. Everyone gets to sing in the nude. Surreally amusing. **115m/C VHS.** *GB* Omar Ebrahim, Willemijn Van Gent, Fiona O'Neill, Sally-Ann Shepherdson. *FOX*

Vampyres ½ *Vampyres, Daughters of Dracula; Blood Hunger; Satan's Daughters* **1974 (R)** Alluring female vampires coerce unsuspecting motorists to their castle for a good time, which ends in death. Anulka was the centerfold girl in Playboy's May 1973 issue. Originally titled "Vampyres, Daughters of Dracula." **90m/C VHS, Beta.** *GB* Marianne Morris, Anulka, Murray Brown, Brian Deacon, Sally Faulkner; ***D:*** Joseph Larraz. *NO*

The Van *Chevy Van* **1977 (R)** A recent high school graduate passes on the college scene so he can spend more time picking up girls in his van. A lame sex (and sexist) comedy. **92m/C VHS, Beta.** Stuart Getz, Deborah White, Danny DeVito, Harry Moses, Maurice Barkin; ***D:*** Sam Grossman. *NO*

The Van 🦴🦴🦴 **1995 (R)** The last of writer Roddy Doyle's Barrytown trilogy (following "The Commitments" and "The Snapper") is set in 1989-90, in Dublin, where baker Bimbo (O'Kelly) has just lost his job. Tired of sitting around the pub, he takes his redundancy money and buys a filthy, dilapidated fish 'n' chips van, which he decides to run with best friend Larry (Meany), with their families helping out. The months pass quickly and their venture turns out to be a big success but the close quarters puts a strain on the mens' friendship until Bimbo has another idea. **105m/C VHS.** *GB* Donal O'Kelly, Colm Meaney, Ger Ryan, Caroline Rotwell, Neili Conroy, Ruaidhri Conroy; ***D:*** Stephen Frears; ***W:*** Roddy Doyle; ***C:*** Oliver Stapleton; ***M:*** Eric Clapton, Richard Hartley. *NYR*

Van Gogh 🦴🦴🦴 **1992 (R)** "One doesn't produce 100 masterpieces in a state of depression—Van Gogh died from having had a glimpse of happiness." This is the way director Pialat sums up his approach to the last 67 days in the life of Vincent Van Gogh. Dutronc is skillful in portraying Van Gogh as a man with no excuses, and even a sense of humor. Not a psychological portrait and offers no answers—it's simply one artist's view of another. In French with English subtitles. **155m/C VHS.** *FR* Jacques Dutronc, Alexandra London, Gerard Sety, Bernard LeCoq, Corinne Bourdon; ***D:*** Maurice Pialat; ***W:*** Maurice Pialat; ***M:*** Edith Vesperini. Cesar Awards '92: Best Actor (Dutronc). *COL, FCT*

Van Nuys Blvd. 🦴½ **1979 (R)** The popular boulevard is the scene where the cool southern California guys converge for cruising and girl watching, so naturally it's where a country hick comes to test his drag racing skills and check out the action. **93m/C VHS, Beta.** Bill Adler, Cynthia Wood, Dennis Bowen, Melissa Prophet; ***D:*** William Sachs. *NO*

Vanina Vanini 🦴🦴🦴½ **1961** An acclaimed Rossellini historical drama about the daughter of an Italian aristocrat in 1824 who nurses and falls in love with a wounded patriot hiding in her house. Based on a Stendhal short story. In Italian with English subtitles. **113m/B VHS, Beta.** *IT* Sandra Milo, Laurent Terzieff; ***D:*** Roberto Rossellini. *FCT, INJ*

The Vanishing 🦴🦴🦴 *Spoorloos* **1988** When his wife suddenly disappears, a young husband finds himself becoming increasingly obsessed with finding her. Three years down the road, his world has become one big, mad nightmare. Then, just as suddenly, the answer confronts him, but the reality of it may be too horrible to face. Well-made dark thriller based on "The Golden Egg" by Tim Krabbe. In French and Dutch with English subtitles. Remade by Sluizer in 1992. **107m/C VHS.** *NL FR* Barnard Pierre Donnadieu, Johanna Ter Steege, Gene Bervoets; ***D:*** George Sluizer. *FXL, INJ*

The Vanishing 🦴🦴½ **1993 (R)** Director Sluizer remakes his own 1988 Dutch film "Spoorloos" to lesser effect. Tense thriller about the disappearance of a woman (Bullock) at a highway rest stop. Her boyfriend (Sutherland) becomes obsessed with locating her, searching for some three years as he is haunted by her memory. Unlike the Dutch original, the remake resorts to a clumsy ending designed for feel-good appeal. Based on the novel "The Golden Egg" by Tim Krabbe. **110m/C VHS.** Jeff Bridges, Kiefer Sutherland, Nancy Travis, Sandra Bullock, Park Overall, Lisa Eichhorn, George Hearn, Maggie Linderman, Lynn Hamilton; ***D:*** George Sluizer; ***W:*** Todd Graff; ***M:*** Jerry Goldsmith. *FXV*

Vanishing Act 🦴🦴½ **1988 (PG)** While on his honeymoon, Harry Kenyon reports his wife missing to the local police. Within a short period of time his wife is found, but Harry says the woman is an impostor. This thriller follows Harry's desperate attempt to get to the truth. Made for television. **94m/C VHS, Beta.** Mike Farrell, Margot Kidder, Elliott Gould, Fred Gwynne, Graham Jarvis; ***D:*** David Greene; ***W:*** Richard Levinson, William Link. *VMK*

Vanishing American 🦴🦴 **1926** The mistreatment of the American Indian is depicted in this sweeping Western epic. Musical score. **114m/B VHS, Beta.** Richard Dix, Noah Beery Sr.; ***D:*** George B. Seitz. *GPV, VYY*

Vanishing Legion **1931** Western serial with outdoor action and gunplay. Twelve chapters, 13 minutes each. **156m/B VHS, Beta.** Frankie Darro, Harry Carey Sr.; ***D:*** B. Reeves Eason. *GPV, NOS, VCN*

Vanishing Point 🦴🦴 **1971 (PG)** An ex-racer makes a bet to deliver a souped-up car from Denver to San Francisco in 15 hours. Taking pep pills along the way, he eludes police, meets up with a number of characters, and finally crashes into a roadblock. Rock score helps attract this film's cult following. **98m/C VHS, Beta, LV.** Barry Newman, Cleavon Little, Gilda Texler, Dean Jagger, Paul Koslo, Robert Donner, Severn Darden, Victoria Medlin; ***D:*** Richard Sarafian; ***C:*** John A. Alonzo. *FOX*

Vanishing Prairie 🦴🦴🦴 **1954** This documentary examines the wonders of nature that abound in the American prairie. From the "True-Life Adventures" series. **60m/C VHS, Beta.** ***D:*** James Algar. Academy Awards '54: Best Feature Documentary. *DIS*

The Vanishing Westerner 🦴🦴 **1950** A cowboy, falsely accused of murder, works to vindicate himself and uncovers a series of robberies. This one has enough plot twists to take it out of the routine. **60m/B VHS, Beta.** Monte Hale, Arthur Space, Aline Towne, Paul Hurst, Roy Barcroft, Richard Anderson, William Phipps, Rand Brooks; ***D:*** Philip Ford. *DVT*

Vanishing Wilderness 🦴🦴 **1973 (G)** This documentary looks at the wild animals roaming across North America. **90m/C VHS, Beta.** ***D:*** Arthur Dubs. *MED, VTR*

Vanity Fair 🦴🦴 **1932** Loy stars in this tale of a wily and manipulative woman looking for the perfect marriage. This was the 58th film for the 27-year-old Loy, but even she couldn't save it. Of course, none of the three films based on the story by Thackeray have done it justice. **67m/B VHS.** Myrna Loy, Conway Tearle, Barbara Kent, Walter Byron, Anthony Bushell, Billy Bevan, Montagu Love, Mary Forbes; ***D:*** Chester M. Franklin. *NOS, HEG*

Vanya on 42nd Street 🦴🦴🦴½ **1994 (PG)** Group of actors in street clothes rehearse a workshop production of Chekhov's play, "Uncle Vanya" in New York's dilapidated New Amsterdam Theater. Theatrical director Gregory first gets his group together in 1989, with Mamet's contemporary adaptation, and they continue to work in private until Malle films their production some four years later before a small, select audience. Shawn, best known for "My Dinner with Andre" portrays Vanya with depth and complexity. The other actors shine as well, often against type, in this complex Russian drama of desperation. **119m/C VHS, LV.** Wallace Shawn, Julianne Moore, Brooke Smith, Larry Pine, George Gaynes, Lynn Cohen, Madhur Jaffrey, Phoebe Brand, Jerry Mayer, Andre Gregory; ***D:*** Louis Malle; ***W:*** David Mamet; ***C:*** Declan Quinn; ***M:*** Joshua Redman. Nominations: Independent Spirit Awards '95: Best Supporting Actor (Pine), Best Supporting Actress (Smith). *COL*

Varan the Unbelievable 🦴 *Daikaiju Baran; The Monster Baran* **1961** A chemical experiment near a small island in the Japanese archipelago disturbs a prehistoric monster beneath the water. The awakened monster spreads terror on the island. Most difficult part of this movie is deciding what the rubber monster model is supposed to represent. **70m/B VHS, Beta.** *JP* Myron Healey, Tsuruko Kobayashi; ***D:*** Inoshiro Honda. *NOS, VCI*

Varieties on Parade 🦴 **1952** A vaudeville show on film, featuring an array of second-rate comics and musical personalities. Sad to watch its demise. **55m/B VHS, Beta, LV.** Jackie Coogan, Eddie Garr, Tom Neal, Iris Adrian. *NO*

Variety 🦴🦴🦴🦴 **1925** Simple and tragic tale of a scheming young girl and the two men of whom she takes advantage. The European circus in all its beautiful sadness is the setting. Extraordinary cast and superb cinematography. Silent. **104m/B VHS, Beta.** *GE* Emil Jannings, Lya de Putti, Warwick Ward, Werner Krauss; ***D:*** E.A. Dupont. *VYY, NOS, DVT*

Variety 🦴🦴½ **1983** A girl takes a job selling tickets in a Times Square porn theater. Her initial loathing for the genre gives way to a fascination with its clients, one of whom is a gangster, and she becomes drawn to the seamy world inside. An independently made feature. **101m/C VHS, Beta.** Sandy McLeod, Will Patton, Richard Davidson; ***D:*** Bette Gordon. *MED*

Variety Lights 🦴🦴🦴½ *Luci Del Varieta; Lights of Variety* **1951** Fellini's first (albeit joint) directorial effort, wherein a young girl runs away with a travelling vaudeville troupe and soon becomes its main attraction as a dancer. Filled with Fellini's now-familiar delight in the bizarre and sawdust/tinsel entertainment. In Italian with English subtitles. **93m/B VHS, Beta.** *IT* Giulietta Masina, Peppino de Filippo, Carla Del Poggio, Folco Lulli; ***D:*** Federico Fellini, Alberto Lattuada; ***W:*** Federico Fellini, Tullio Pinelli, Ennio Flaiano, Alberto Lattuada. *HMV, INJ, APD*

Vasectomy: A Delicate Matter *Woof!* *Vasectomy* **1986 (PG-13)** A mother of eight issues a final decree to her husband about their sex life. He must get a vasectomy or there won't be any. As good as it sounds. **92m/C VHS, Beta.** Paul Sorvino, Abe Vigoda, Cassandra Edwards, Lorne Greene, Ina Balin, June Wilkinson, William Marshall; ***D:*** Robert Burge; ***W:*** Robert Burge. *WOV*

Vatican Conspiracy 🦴½ **1981** The members of the Vatican's College of Cardinals do everything in their power to discredit a newly-appointed radical pontiff. **90m/C VHS, Beta.** Terence Stamp; ***D:*** Marcello Aliprandi. *NO*

Vault of Horror 🦴🦴½ *Tales from the Crypt II* **1973 (R)** A collection of five terrifying tales based on original stories from the E.C. comic books of the 1950s. Stories include, "Midnight Mess," "Bargain in Death," "This Trick'll Kill You," "The Neat Job" and "Drawn and Quartered." **86m/C VHS, Beta.** *GB* Terry-Thomas, Curt Jurgens, Glynis Johns, Dawn Addams, Daniel Massey, Tom Baker, Michael Craig, Anna Massey, Denholm Elliott; ***D:*** Roy Ward Baker; ***W:*** Milton Subotsky. *MED*

Vegas 🦴 **1978** A private detective, with Las Vegas beauties as assistants and pursuers, solves the murder of a teenage runaway girl. Pilot for television series. Scriptwriter Mann went on to do "Miami Vice." **74m/C VHS, Beta.** Robert Urich, June Allyson, Tony Curtis, Will Sampson, Greg Morris; ***D:*** Richard Lang; ***W:*** Michael Mann. *PSM*

Vegas in Space *Woof!* **1994** Four male astronauts take a secret mission to the planet Clitoris, the all-female pleasure plant where men are forbidden to trod. To capture a heinous villainous, they swallow gender-reversal pills in order to infiltrate the resort as show-girls. Typical Troma trash. Boasts an all-transvestite cast. **85m/C VHS.** ***D:*** Phillip R. Ford; ***W:*** Phillip R. Ford. *TTV*

The Vegas Strip Wars 🦴🦴 *Las Vegas Strip War* **1984** Rival casino owners battle it out in the land of lady luck. Unmemorable except for Jones's Don King impersonation and the fact that it was Hudson's last TV movie. **100m/C VHS, Beta.** Rock Hudson, James Earl Jones, Noriyuki "Pat" Morita, Sharon Stone, Robert Costanzo; ***D:*** George Englund. *LIV*

Velnio Nuotaka 🦴🦴½ *The Devil's Bride* **1975** A popular Lithuanian musical based on the play "Baltargio Malunas" by K. Boruta. English subtitles. **78m/C VHS, Beta.** *LI IHF*

Velvet Smooth 🦴 **1976 (R)** A protection agency's sultry boss, Velvet Smooth, gets involved solving the problems of a numbers racket. **89m/C VHS.** Johnnie Hill; ***D:*** Janace Fink. *NO*

Velvet Touch 🦴🦴🦴 **1948** Well-engineered thriller about an actress who craftily murders her producer. A theater-loving police detective winds up accusing the wrong woman—sending the overwrought murderess into a moral tailspin. Things don't work out as you may expect. Fine acting. **97m/B VHS, Beta.** Rosalind Russell, Leo Genn, Claire Trevor, Sydney Greenstreet, Leon Ames, Frank McHugh, Walter Kingsford, Dan

Tobin, Lex Barker, Nydia Westman; **D:** John Gage; **W:** Leo Rosten. *TTC*

The Velvet Vampire ☙☙ *Cemetary Girls; Through the Looking Glass* **1971 (R)** Yarnall is a sexy, sun-loving, dune buggy-riding vampiress who seduces a young, sexy, swinging, Southern California couple in her desert home. Lots of atmosphere to go along with the blood and nudity. **82m/C VHS, Beta, LV.** Michael Blodgett, Sherry Miles, Celeste Yarnall, Gene Shane, Jerry Daniels, Sandy Ward, Paul Prokop, Chris Woodley, Robert Tessier; **D:** Stephanie Rothman. *SUE*

Vendetta ☙½ **1985** A woman gets herself arrested and sent to the penitentiary in order to exact revenge there for her sister's death. Acting and pacing make this better than the average sexploitation flick. **89m/C VHS, Beta.** Karen Chase, Sandy Martin, Durga McBroom, Kin Shriner; **D:** Bruce Logan; **M:** David Newman. *LIV, VES*

Vendetta for the Saint ☙ **1968** A feature-length episode of the television series "The Saint," in which Simon Templar pursues a Sicilian mobster on a personal vendetta. **98m/C VHS, Beta.** *GB* Roger Moore; **D:** James O'Connolly. *FOX*

Vengeance ☙☙ **1937** A police officer resigns in shame after failing to thwart a holdup. He attempts to redeem himself by working on his own to infiltrate the same gang. **61m/B VHS.** Lyle Talbot, Wendy Barrie, Wally Albright, Marc Lawrence; **D:** Del Lord. *VYY, MOV*

Vengeance ☙ **1980** Four burglars take hostages after their robbery is bungled, but they won't get away—especially after the hostages die. **92m/C VHS, Beta.** Sally Lockett, Nicholas Jacquez, Bob Elliott; **D:** Bob Blizz. *NO*

Vengeance ☙ **1986** A low-budget film about rebels fighting off an authoritarian government. **114m/C VHS, Beta.** Jason Miller, Lea Massari; **D:** Antonio Isasi. *TWE*

Vengeance ☙☙ *Vengeance: The Story of Tony Cimo* **1989 (R)** A bereaved young man strikes out against the injustice of his parents' murder. His revenge against the killers takes him several steps beyond the law, and he's not so sure it was the right idea. Made for television. **90m/C VHS, LV.** Brad Davis, Roxanne Hart, Brad Dourif, William Conrad; **D:** Marc Daniels. *IME*

Vengeance Is Mine ☙☙☙ **1979** Told in flashbacks, the film focuses on the life of a habitual criminal whose life of deprivation leads to murder. Contains violence and nudity. Based on a true story. In Japanese with English subtitles. **129m/C VHS, LV.** *JP* Ken Ogata; **D:** Shohei Imamura. *FCT, INJ*

Vengeance Is Mine *Woof!* **1984 (R)** A demented farmer captures three criminals and tortures them in horrifyingly sadistic ways. Gratuitously grisly. **90m/C VHS, Beta, LV.** Ernest Borgnine, Michael J. Pollard, Hollis McLaren; **D:** John Trent. *VTR, GEM*

Vengeance of the Snowmaid ☙½ **197?** Some Kung Fu creepies raped her mom. Now nobody can get a sword in edgewise on the Snow Maid as she seeks revenge. **82m/C VHS, Beta.** Mo Ka Kei, Chen Chen. *NO*

Vengeance of the Zombies ☙½ **1972** A madman seeks revenge by setting an army of walking corpses to stalk the streets of London. **90m/C VHS, Beta.** *SP* Paul Naschy; **D:** Leon Klimovsky. *SNC*

Vengeance Valley ☙☙ **1951** Lancaster and Walker are foster brothers with Walker being an envious weasel who always expects Lancaster to get him out of scrapes. Lancaster is even accused of a crime committed by Walker and must work to clear himself. Good cast is let down by uneven direction. **83m/C VHS, Beta.** Burt Lancaster, Joanne Dru, Robert Walker, Sally Forrest, John Ireland, Hugh O'Brian; **D:** Richard Thorpe. *NOS, DVT, CAB*

Venom *Woof!* **1982 (R)** Deadly black mamba is loose in an elegant townhouse, terrorizing big-name cast. The snake continually terrorizes an evil kidnapper, his accomplices and his kidnapped victim. Participants walk through tired cliches with that far-away look in their eyes—like they wish they were anywhere else. Original director Tobe Hooper was replaced. **92m/C VHS, Beta.** *GB* Sterling Hayden, Klaus Kinski, Sarah Miles, Nicol Williamson, Cornelia Sharpe, Susan George, Michael Gough, Oliver Reed; **D:** Piers Haggard; **W:** Robert B. Carrington; **M:** Michael Kamen. *VES*

Venus Against the Son of Hercules **1962** Our hero must use all his genetically procured musculature in his battle against the lovely but deadly Venus. **?m/C VHS, Beta.** *IT* Roger Brown, Jackie Lane. *SNC*

Venus in Furs ☙½ *Paroxismus; Puo Una Morta Rivivere Per Amore?; Venus in Peltz* **1970 (R)** Jazz musician working in Rio de Janeiro becomes obsessed with a mysterious woman; she resembles a murder victim whose body he discovered months earlier. Weird mix of horror, sadism, black magic, and soft porn. **90m/C VHS, Beta.** *GB* James Darren, Klaus Kinski, Barbara McNair, Dennis Price, Maria Rohm; **D:** Jess (Jesus) Franco. *REP, TPV*

Venus Rising ☙☙ **1995 (R)** In the year 2000, Eve and August manage to escape from the island prison on which they were raised. They discover that the mainland world features emotions that are controlled by drugs and love is only a game on the virtual reality network. Hunted, the fugitives try to fit in and figure out what's real and what's fantasy. Be forewarned—Fairchild's role is very small. **91m/C VHS.** Audie England, Costas Mandylor, Billy Wirth, Morgan Fairchild; **D:** Leora Barish; **W:** Leora Barish. *COL*

Venus the Ninja ☙ **198?** A comely female Ninja battles an evil warlord. **90m/C VHS, Beta.** Pearl Cheung, Meng Fei; **D:** Sze Ma Peng. *TWE*

Vera Cruz ☙☙½ **1953** Two soldiers of fortune become involved in the Mexican Revolution of 1866, a stolen shipment of gold, divided loyalties, and gun battles. Less than innovative plot is made into an exciting action flick. **94m/C VHS, Beta, LV.** Gary Cooper, Burt Lancaster, Denise Darcel, Cesar Romero, George Macready, Ernest Borgnine, Charles Bronson, Jack Elam; **D:** Robert Aldrich; **C:** Ernest Laszlo. *MGM, FOX, FCT*

Verboten! ☙☙½ **1959** In post-war occupied Berlin, an American G.I. falls in love with a German girl. Good direction maintains a steady pace. **93m/B VHS.** James Best, Susan Cummings, Tom Pittman, Paul Dubov; **D:** Samuel Fuller. *IME*

Verdi ☙☙ **1953** The story of the Italian operatic composer and the loves of his life. Dubbed in English. **80m/C VHS.** *IT* Pierre Cressoy. *FCT*

The Verdict ☙☙☙ **1982 (R)** Newman plays an alcoholic failed attorney reduced to ambulance chasing. A friend gives him a supposedly easy malpractice case which turns out to be a last chance at redeeming himself and his career. Adapted from the novel by Barry Reed. One of Newman's finest performances. **122m/C VHS, Beta, LV.** Paul Newman, James Mason, Charlotte Rampling, Jack Warden, Milo O'Shea, Lindsay Crouse; **D:** Sidney Lumet; **W:** David Mamet. National Board of Review Awards '82: Best Director (Lumet); Nominations: Academy Awards '82: Best Actor (Newman), Best Adapted Screenplay, Best Director (Lumet), Best Picture, Best Supporting Actor (Mason). *FOX*

Vermont Is for Lovers ☙½ **1992** Pre-wedding jitters consume stressed-out Manhattanites Marya (Cohn) and George (Thrush) when they travel to bucolic Tunbridge, Vermont to get married on Marya's Aunt Ann's farm. After continuously arguing, they decide to spend the day before the wedding apart and George wanders around the community asking marriage advice from various old-timers. The Yuppie leads aren't terribly compelling and neither is the improvised dialogue. **86m/C VHS.** George Thrush, Marya Cohn, Ann O'Brien; **D:** John O'Brien; **C:** John O'Brien; **M:** Tony Silbert. *FCT, KIV*

Verne Miller ☙☙ **1988 (R)** A film of the true story of Verne Miller, Al Capone's hit man. After rescuing a friend from the Feds, Miller is hunted down by both the cops and the mob. **95m/C VHS, Beta, LV.** Scott Glenn, Barbara Stock, Thomas G. Waites, Lucinda Jenney, Sonny Carl Davis; **D:** Rod Hewitt. *SUE, NLC*

The Vernonia Incident ☙½ **1989** Urban guerillas invade a small town, killing the police chief. The townspeople gather up their shotguns and fight back. That's entertainment. **95m/C VHS, Beta.** David Jackson, Shawn Stevens, Floyd Ragner, Ed Justice, Robert Louis Jakson; **D:** Ray Etheridge; **W:** Ray Etheridge. *NO*

Veronico Cruz ☙☙½ *La Dueda Interna; The Debt* **1987** Despite its sincerity, Pereira's feature debut offers muddled response to the human waste incurred by the Falklands War. Set in a tiny remote village in the Argentinean mountains, the film's narrative is derived from the growing friendship between a shepherd boy and a teacher from the city. Well-meaning anti-war movie. In Spanish with English subtitles. **96m/C VHS.** *AR GB* Juan Jose Camero, Gonzalo Morales, Rene Olaguivel, Guillermo Delgado; **D:** Miguel Pereira. *CCN, TPV*

Veronika Voss ☙☙☙ *Die Sehns Ucht Der Veronika Voss* **1982 (R)** Highlights the real life of fallen film star Sybille Schmitz who finally took her own life out of despair. Played by Zech, Voss is exploited by her physician to turn over all of her personal belongings for morphine. A lover discovers the corruption and reveals it to the authorities. This causes great upheaval resulting in Voss' suicide. Highly metaphoric and experimental in its treatment of its subject. In German with English subtitles. **105m/C VHS.** *GE* Rosel Zech, Hilmar Thate, Conny Froboess, Anna Marie Duringer, Volker Spengler; **D:** Rainer Werner Fassbinder; **M:** Peer Raben. *APD, FCT, INJ*

Vertigo ☙☙☙☙ **1958 (PG)** Hitchcock's romantic story of obsession, manipulation and fear. Stewart plays a detective forced to retire after his fear of heights causes the death of a fellow policeman and, perhaps, the death of a woman he'd been hired to follow. The appearance of her double (Novak), whom he compulsively transforms into the dead girl's image, leads to a mesmerizing cycle of madness and lies. Features Herrmann's haunting music. **126m/C VHS, Beta, LV.** James Stewart, Kim Novak, Barbara Bel Geddes, Tom Helmore, Ellen Corby, Henry Jones, Raymond Bailey, Lee Patrick; **D:** Alfred Hitchcock; **W:** Sam Taylor; **C:** Robert Burks; **M:** Bernard Herrmann. Nominations: Academy Awards '58: Best Art Direction/Set Decoration, Best Sound. *MCA, TLF*

A Very Brady Christmas ☙☙ **1988** Many of the original Bradys returned for this yuletide special. After Mike and Carol's vacation plans go awry, they decide to invite the whole bunch home for a family reunion. This was the highest rated television movie in 1989. Spawned yet another unsuccessful "Brady" series sequel. **94m/C VHS.** Florence Henderson, Robert Reed, Ann B. Davis, Maureen McCormick, Eve Plumb, Jennifer Runyon, Barry Williams, Christopher Knight, Michael Lookinland, Jerry Houser, Caryn Richman; **D:** Peter Baldwin. *PAR*

A Very Brady Sequel ☙☙½ **1996 (PG-13)** They're back! The cast from the surprise hit "The Brady Bunch Movie" returns and Brady mom Carol is shocked when her presumed dead first husband (Matheson) suddenly appears on their doorstep. The Bradys must travel to Hawaii to attempt to save the family (based on a three-part episode from the original TV series). The stuck-in-the-'70s gang is still too far-out for the '90s, but in Hawaii it's always a sunshine day. **?m/C VHS.** Shelley Long, Gary Cole, Tim Matheson, Christopher Daniel Barnes, Christine Taylor, Paul Sutera, Jennifer Elise Cox, Henriette Mantel, Olivia Hack, Jesse Lee; **D:** Arlene Sanford; **W:** Harry Elfont, Deborah Kaplan, Stan Zimmerman, James Berg. *NYR*

A Very British Coup ☙☙☙ **199?** McAnally plays Harry Perkins, a former steelworker who gets involved in British politics. Although a left-wing radical, the charismatic Perkins is actually elected Prime Minister. However, his radical policies cause the entrenched government officials to conspire to bring him down. And you thought American politics were dirty! Made for British television. **180m/C VHS.** *GB* Ray McAnally. *SIG, TVC, FUS*

Very Close Quarters 🦴 **1984** Thirty people face many trials and tribulations as they share an apartment in Moscow. Interesting cast is wasted in this mostly un-funny flick. **97m/C VHS, Beta.** Shelley Winters, Paul Sorvino, Theodore Bikel, Farley Granger; ***D:*** Vladmir Rif. *LIV, VES*

A Very Curious Girl 🦴🦴½ *La Fiancee du Pirate; Dirty Mary; Pirate's Fiancee* **1969 (R)** A peasant girl realizes she is being used by the male population of her village, and decides to charge them for sex, creating havoc. In French with English subtitles. **105m/C VHS, Beta.** *FR* Bernadette LaFont, Georges Geret; ***D:*** Nelly Kaplan. *SUE, OM*

The Very Edge 🦴🦴½ **1963** A pregnant woman suffers a miscarriage after being brutally attacked. The repercussions nearly destroy her marriage until her attacker is caught. A disturbing psycho-drama. **90m/C VHS, Beta.** *GB* Anne Heywood, Richard Todd, Jeremy Brett; ***D:*** Cyril Frankel. *NO*

A Very Natural Thing 🦴🦴 **1973** Twenty-six-year-old Jason leaves the priesthood to pursue a gay lifestyle in New York. He becomes a teacher, meets ad exec David, and finds love. Considered to be the first film to explore homosexuality in a realistic manner, made by a gay director, and given national, commercial distribution. **85m/C VHS.** Robert Joel, Curt Gareth, Bo White; ***D:*** Christopher Larkin; ***W:*** Christopher Larkin, Joseph Coencas. *WBF*

A Very Old Man with Enormous Wings 🦴🦴 *Un Senor Muy Viejo Con Unas Alas Enormes* **1988** An angel, battered during a hurricane, seeks refuge on a tiny Caribbean island. There, two men keep him and charge an increasingly curious world admission to view the creature. A colorful, musical expose of human failings based on a story by Gabriel Garcia Marquez. In Spanish with English subtitles. **90m/C VHS, LV.** *SP IT* Daisy Granados, Asdrubal Melendez, Luis Alberto Ramirez, Fernando Birri; ***D:*** Fernando Birri. *FXL, FCT, INJ*

A Very Private Affair 🦴🦴½ *La Vie Privee; Vita Privata* **1962** A movie star finds that she has no privacy from the hordes of fans and paparazzi who flock to her side. The glare of publicity helps to destroy her relationship with a married director, and to fuel her desire for privacy, a desire that ends tragically. An appealing, better-than-average Bardot vehicle, it is nonetheless below-average (early) Malle. In French with English subtitles. **95m/C VHS, Beta.** *FR* Marcello Mastroianni, Brigitte Bardot; ***D:*** Louis Malle. *MGM*

V.I. Warshawski 🦴🦴 **1991 (R)** The filmmakers seem to think they can slum with the oldest cliches in detective shows just as long as the tough gumshoe is a woman. They're wrong. Turner is terrific as the leggy shamus of the title (from a popular series of books by Sara Paretsky), but the plot is nothing special, featuring stock characters in the killing of a pro athlete and a real-estate deal. **89m/C VHS, Beta, LV.** Kathleen Turner, Jay O. Sanders, Angela Goethals, Charles Durning; ***D:*** Jeff Kanew; ***W:*** Nick Thiel, David Aaron Cohen; ***M:*** Randy Edelman. *HPH*

Via Appia 🦴🦴 **1992** Fictional documentary about Frank, a German airline steward who brings a film crew with him when travels back to Rio de Janeiro in search of the street hustler who gave him AIDS. Grim guided tour of the city's gay subculture along the "Via Appia," the Rio district where the male prostitutes hang out. Film is firmly unapologetic for its sexual explicitness and lack of moralizing. In German and Portuguese with English subtitles. **90m/C VHS.** *GE BR* Peter Senner, Guilherme de Padua, Yves Jansen, Margarita Schmidt, Luiz Kleber; ***D:*** Jochen Hick; ***W:*** Jochen Hick. *MOV, FCT*

Vibes 🦴 **1988 (PG)** Two screwball psychics are sent on a wild goose chase through the Ecuadorean Andes in search of cosmic power and, of course, fall in love. Flat offering from the usually successful team of writers, Lowell Ganz and Babaloo Mandel ("Splash" and "Night Shift"). Lauper's first starring role (and so far, her last). **99m/C VHS, Beta.** Jeff Goldblum, Cyndi Lauper, Julian Sands, Googy Gress, Peter Falk, Elizabeth Pena; ***D:*** Ken Kwapis; ***W:*** Babaloo Mandel, Lowell Ganz; ***C:*** John Bailey; ***M:*** James Horner. *COL*

Vibrations 🦴🦴½ **1994 (R)** Anamika (Applegate), a dance club manager, befriends TJ (Marshall), a homeless, alcoholic, once-promising musician who lost his hands in a brutal attack. The duo find romance as Anamika encourages TJ to try again. **104m/C VHS, LV.** James Marshall, Christina Applegate, Faye Grant, Paige Turco, Bruce Altman, David Burke, Scott Cohen, Shane Butterworth; ***D:*** Michael Paseornek; ***W:*** Michael Paseornek; ***M:*** Bob Christianson. *TOU*

Vice Academy 🦴½ **1988 (R)** Two females join the Hollywood vice squad. Allen was a former porn queen. **90m/C VHS, Beta, LV.** Linnea Quigley, Ginger Lynn Allen, Karen Russell, Jayne Hamil, Ken Abraham, Stephen Steward, Jeannie Carol; ***D:*** Rick Sloane. *PSM*

Vice Academy 2 🦴 **1990 (R)** Two vice cop babes try to stop a female crime boss from dumping aphrodesiacs in the city's water supply. **90m/C VHS, Beta.** Linnea Quigley, Ginger Lynn Allen, Jayne Hamil, Scott Layne, Jay Richardson, Joe Brewer, Marina Benvenga, Teagan Clive; ***D:*** Rick Sloane. *PSM*

Vice Academy 3 *Woof!* **1991 (R)** The worst of the series, and not just because cult actress Linnea Quigley is absent. Wit, pacing and even sets are nonexistent as the girls battle a toxic villainess called Malathion. **88m/C VHS, Beta.** Ginger Lynn Allen, Elizabeth Kaitan, Julia Parton, Jay Richardson, Johanna Grika, Steve Mateo; ***D:*** Rick Sloane; ***W:*** Rick Sloane. *PSM*

Vice Squad 🦴🦴 **1931** Lukas is forced to turn police informer to save his own neck, which almost ruins him. Just when he thinks he's free of the cops they come back threatening the woman he loves unless he plays stoolie again. Rather flat, but the different cop/criminal angle makes for some unusual twists. **80m/B VHS, Beta, LV.** Paul Lukas, Kay Francis, Helen Johnson, William B. Davidson, Esther Howard; ***D:*** John Cromwell; ***C:*** Charles B(ryant) Lang. *SUE*

Vice Squad *Woof!* **1982 (R)** Violent and twisted killer-pimp goes on a murderous rampage, and a hooker helps a vice squad plainclothesman trap him. Sleazy and disturbing, with little to recommend it. **97m/C VHS, Beta, LV.** Wings Hauser, Season Hubley, Gary Swanson, Cheryl "Rainbeaux" Smith; ***D:*** Gary Sherman; ***W:*** Robert Vincent O'Neil. *SUE, NLC*

Vice Versa 🦴🦴🦴 **1988 (PG)** Another 80s comedy about a workaholic father and his 11-year-old son who switch bodies, with predictable slapstick results. Reinhold and Savage carry this, appearing to have a great time in spite of over-done story. **97m/C VHS, Beta, LV.** Judge Reinhold, Fred Savage, Swoosie Kurtz, David Proval, Corinne Bohrer, Jane Kaczmarek, William Prince, Gloria Gifford; ***D:*** Brian Gilbert; ***W:*** Dick Clement, Ian LaFrenais; ***M:*** David Shire. *COL*

Vicious 🦴 **1988** A bored young woman falls in with people your mother warned you about and soon their high school hi-jinks turn into murder. Graphic violence. **88m/C VHS.** Tamblyn Lord, Craig Pearce, Tiffany Dowe; ***D:*** Karl Zwicky. *NO*

The Vicious Circle 🦴🦴½ *The Circle* **1957** A prominent London physician becomes involved in murder and an international crime ring when he agrees to perform an errand for a friend. Good performances and tight pacing. **84m/B VHS, Beta.** *GB* John Mills, Wilfrid Hyde-White, Rene Ray, Lionel Jeffries, Noelle Middleton; ***D:*** Gerald Thomas. *NO*

Victim 🦴🦴🦴½ **1962** A successful married English barrister (Bogarde) with a hidden history of homosexuality is threatened by blackmail after the death of his ex-lover. When the blackmailers, who are responsible for his lover's suicide, are caught, Bogarde decides to prosecute them himself, even though it means revealing his hidden past. One of the first films to deal straightforwardly with homosexuality. Fine performances. **100m/C VHS, Beta.** *GB* Dirk Bogarde, Sylvia Syms, Dennis Price, Peter McEnery; ***D:*** Basil Dearden. *SUE*

Victim of Beauty 🦴🦴 **1991** A small-town girl comes to the big city and becomes a successful model. However, she then becomes the victim of a fatal attraction killer as all her would-be suitors get killed off one by one. Made for cable television. **90m/C VHS.** Jennifer Rubin, Sally Kellerman, Stephen Shellan, Peter Outerbridge; ***Cameos:*** Michael Ironside; ***D:*** Paul Lynch. *WOV, PMS*

Victim of Desire 🦴½ **1994 (R)** Mysterious death of an embezzler is investigated, only the investigator falls for the sexy widow and begins to doubt her innocence. Also available in an unrated version. **85m/C VHS.** Shannon Tweed, Julie Strain. *NHO*

Victim of Love 🦴🦴 **1991 (PG-13)** A therapist doesn't know whom to believe when she finds out she and one of her more neurotic patients are sharing the same boyfriend. Only the patient claims the man murdered his wife to be with his lover. Who will be the next victim? Made for television. **92m/C VHS, Beta, LV.** Pierce Brosnan, JoBeth Williams, Virginia Madsen, Georgia Brown; ***D:*** Jerry London. *ACA*

Victimless Crimes **1990 (R)** The seemingly victimless crime of robbing art galleries turns deadly when betrayal and murder enter the picture. **85m/C VHS.** Debra Sandlund, Craig Bierko, Larry Brandenburg, Peggy Dunne, Richard Redlin, Cheryl Lynn Bruce; ***D:*** Peter Hawley. *NO*

Victor/Victoria 🦴🦴🦴 **1982 (PG)** An unsuccessful actress in Depression-era Paris impersonates a man impersonating a woman and becomes a star. Luscious music and sets. Warren as femme fatale and Preston as Andrews' gay mentor are right on target; Garner is charming as the gangster who falls for the woman he thinks she is. ♫You and Me; The Shady Dame from Seville; Le Jazz Hot; Crazy World; Chicago Illinois; Gay Peree. **133m/C VHS, Beta, LV.** Julie Andrews, James Garner, Robert Preston, Lesley Ann Warren, Alex Karras, John Rhys-Davies; ***D:*** Blake Edwards; ***W:*** Blake Edwards; ***M:*** Henry Mancini. Academy Awards '82: Best Score; Cesar Awards '83: Best Foreign Film; Golden Globe Awards '83: Best Actress—Musical/Comedy (Andrews); National Board of Review Awards '82: Best Supporting Actor (Preston); Writers Guild of America '82: Best Adapted Screenplay; Nominations: Academy Awards '82: Best Actress (Andrews), Best Adapted Screenplay, Best Art Direction/Set Decoration, Best Costume Design, Best Supporting Actor (Preston), Best Supporting Actress (Warren). *MGM*

Victoria Regina 🦴🦴 **1961** In a succession of vignettes, the life of Queen Victoria is viewed, from her ascension to the throne of England in 1837 through the celebration of her Diamond Jubilee. A presentation from "George Schaefer's Showcase Theatre." Made for television. **76m/C VHS, Beta.** Julie Harris, James Donald, Felix Aylmer, Pamela Brown, Basil Rathbone; ***D:*** George Schaefer. *FHS*

Victory 🦴🦴½ **1981 (PG)** Soccer match between WWII American prisoners of war and a German team is set up so that the players can escape through the sewer tunnels of Paris. Of course they want to finish the game first. Not particularly believable as either a soccer flick (even with Pele and other soccer stars) or a great escape, but watchable. **116m/C VHS, Beta.** Sylvester Stallone, Michael Caine, Max von Sydow, Pele, Carole Laure, Bobby Moore, Daniel Massey; ***D:*** John Huston; ***W:*** Jeff Maguire, Djordje Milicevic; ***M:*** Bill Conti. *FOX, WAR*

The Victory 🦴🦴 **1988 (PG)** In 1967 Montreal, an American college exchange student falls in love with a French-Canadian co-ed. Can love survive their different cultures? **95m/C VHS, Beta.** Vincent Van Patten, Cloris Leachman, Eddie Albert, Claire Pimpare, Nicholas Campbell, Jack Wetherall, Jacques Godin, Marthe Mercure; ***D:*** Larry Kent. *PSM*

Video Americana **1985** A collection of seven video shorts by various avant-garde artists depicting the absurdities of modern life. **60m/C VHS, Beta.** *NO*

Video Baby 🦴 **1989** The joys and frustrations of parenting a video child can be yours without the mess, expense or longterm responsibility. Watch baby laugh, cry and sleep on command. **13m/C VHS, Beta.** *LIV*

The Video Dead *Woof!* **1987 (R)** Gore-farce in which murderous zombies emerge from a possessed television and wreak havoc. **90m/C VHS, Beta.** Roxanna Augesen, Rocky Duvall, Michael St. Michaels; ***D:*** Robert Scott. *SUE, NLC*

Video Murders **1987** A police detective tracks down a rapist/murderer who tapes all his own crimes. **90m/C VHS, Beta.** Eric Brown, Virginia Loridans, John Ferita. *TWE*

Video Violence **1987** A gory spoof about a video store owner who discovers that his customers have grown bored with the usual Hollywood horror movies and decide to shoot some flicks of their own. Followed by a sequel. **90m/C VHS, Beta.** Art Neill, Jackie Neill, William Toddie, Bart Sumner; ***D:*** Gary P. Cohen. *NO*

Video Violence Part 2...The Exploitation! **1987** Two sickos named Howard and Eli run a cable television network where talk show guests are spindled and mutilated. **90m/C VHS, Beta.** Uke, Bart Sumner, Lee Miller; ***D:*** Gary P. Cohen. *NO*

Video Wars *Woof!* **1984** Video games explode randomly. A wicked computer whiz is behind it all in a blackmail scheme. **90m/C VHS.** George Diamond. *BFV*

Videodrome **1983** Woods is a cable TV programmer with a secret yen for sex and violence, which he satisfies by watching a pirated TV show. "Videodrome" appears to show actual torture and murder, and also seems to control the thoughts of its viewers—turning them into human VCRs. Cronenberg's usual sick fantasies are definitely love 'em or leave 'em. Special effects by Rick Baker. **87m/C VHS, Beta, LV.** *CA* James Woods, Deborah Harry, Sonja Smits, Peter Dvorsky; ***D:*** David Cronenberg; ***W:*** David Cronenberg; ***M:*** Howard Shore. Genie Awards '84: Best Director (Cronenberg). *MCA*

Vietnam: Chronicle of a War **1981** Drawing upon the resources of the CBS News archives, this CBS News Collectors Series program presents a retrospective portrait of American military involvement as witnessed by on-the-scene correspondents and camera crews. Some portions are in black-and-white. **88m/C VHS, Beta.** *FOX, KUI*

Vietnam, Texas **1990 (R)** Vietnam vet leaves his past to become a priest. But he returns to violence when he discovers his Vietnamese daughter is in the hands of Houston's most relentless gangster. **101m/C VHS, Beta, LV.** Robert Ginty, Haing S. Ngor, Tamlyn Tomita, Tim Thomerson; ***D:*** Robert Ginty; ***W:*** C. Courtney Joyner, Tom Badal. *COL*

Vietnam War Story 1 **1988** Three hard-hitting Vietnam War stories on tape. "The Mine," "Home," and "The Pass." Each is an intimate account straight from the men who lived them. Poignant and action-packed. Made for television. **87m/C VHS.** Eriq La Salle, Nicholas Cascone, David Harris, Tom Fridley. *NO*

Vietnam War Story 2 **1988** Three short, made-for-television war stories set in Vietnam: "An Old Ghost Walks the Earth," "R & R," and "The Fragging." **90m/C VHS, Beta.** Tim Guinee, Tate Donovan, Cynthia Bain, Wesley Snipes, David Niedorf. *NO*

Vietnam War Story 3 **1989** Three episodes of the television series: "Separated," "Dusk to Dawn" and "The Promise." **90m/C VHS, Beta.** Tom Hodges, Todd Graff, Gregory Cooke, Francois Chau, Stacy Edwards, Laura Harrington, Raymond Cruz. *NO*

A View to a Kill **1985 (PG)** This James Bond mission takes him to the United States, where he must stop the evil Max Zorin from destroying California's Silicon Valley. Feeble and unexciting plot with unscary villain. Duran Duran performs the catchy title tune. Moore's last appearance as 007. **131m/C VHS, Beta, LV.** *GB* Roger Moore, Christopher Walken, Tanya Roberts, Grace Jones, Patrick Macnee, Lois Maxwell, Dolph Lundgren, Desmond Llewelyn; ***D:*** John Glen; ***W:*** Michael G. Wilson; ***M:*** John Barry. *FOX, TLF*

Vigil **1984** A stark, dreamy parable about a young girl, living on a primitive farm in a remote New Zealand valley, who watches her family collapse after a stranger enters their territory. Visually ravishing and grim; Ward's first American import. Predecessor to "The Navigator." **90m/C VHS, Beta.** *NZ* Penelope Stewart, Bill Kerr, Fiona Kay, Gordon Shields, Frank Whitten; ***D:*** Vincent Ward; ***W:*** Vincent Ward. Nominations: Cannes Film Festival '84: Best Film. *PSM*

Vigilante *Woof! Street Gang* **1983 (R)** Frustrated ex-cop, tired of seeing criminals returned to the street, joins a vigilante squad dedicated to law and order. Often ridiculous and heavy handed. **91m/C VHS, Beta.** Carol Lynley, Robert Forster, Rutanya Alda; ***D:*** William Lustig. *LIV, VES*

The Vigilantes are Coming **1936** "The Eagle" sets out to avenge his family and upsets a would-be dictator's plot to establish an empire in California. In twelve chapters; the first is 32 minutes, and additional chapters are 18 minutes each. **230m/B VHS, Beta.** Bob Livingston, Kay Hughes, Guinn "Big Boy" Williams, Raymond Hatton, William Farnum; ***D:*** Mack V. Wright, Ray Taylor. *NOS, VCN, MED*

Vigilantes of Boom Town ½ **1946** A championship prize fight is the cover for a bank robbery which must be foiled by Red Ryder. **54m/B VHS, Beta.** Allan "Rocky" Lane, Robert (Bobby) Blake, Peggy Stewart, Martha Wentworth, Roscoe Karns, Roy Barcroft, George Turner, John Dehner; ***D:*** R.G. Springsteen. *NOS, VCN, MED*

Viking Massacre ½ *Knives of the Avenger; I Coltelli Del Vendicatore* **1965** Brutal ax-bearing Vikings ruin the days of hundreds in this primitive story of courage and desperation. John Hold is the pseudonym for director Mario Bava. **90m/C VHS, Beta.** *IT* Cameron Mitchell; ***D:*** John Hold. *NO*

The Vikings ½ **1958** A Viking king and his son kidnap a Welsh princess and hold her for ransom. Depicts the Vikings' invasion of England. Great location footage of both Norway and Brittany. Basic costume epic with good action scenes. Narrated by Welles. **116m/C VHS, Beta, LV.** Kirk Douglas, Ernest Borgnine, Janet Leigh, Tony Curtis, James Donald, Alexander Knox; ***D:*** Richard Fleischer; ***W:*** Calder Willingham; ***C:*** Jack Cardiff. *MGM*

Villa Rides **1968** A flying gun-runner aids Francisco "Pancho" Villa's revolutionary Mexican campaign. Considering the talent involved, this one is a disappointment. Check out Brynner's hair. **125m/C VHS, Beta.** Yul Brynner, Robert Mitchum, Charles Bronson, Herbert Lom, Jill Ireland, Robert Towne; ***D:*** Buzz Kulik; ***W:*** Robert Towne, Sam Peckinpah; ***C:*** Jack Hildyard; ***M:*** Maurice Jarre. *BAR*

Village of the Damned **1960** A group of unusual children are born in a small English village. They avoid their fathers and other men, except for the one who is their teacher. He discovers they are the vanguard of an alien invasion and leads the counter-attack. Exciting and bone-chilling low-budget thriller. From the novel, "The Midwich Cuckoos," by John Wyndham. The sequel, "The Children of the Damned" (1964) is even better. **78m/B VHS, Beta, LV.** *GB* George Sanders, Barbara Shelley, Martin Stephens, Laurence Naismith, Michael C. Goetz; ***D:*** Wolf Rilla; ***W:*** Stirling Silliphant. *MGM, MLB*

Village of the Damned ½ **1995 (R)** The quiet town of Midwich, California has been enveloped by a strange force that seems to have impregnated the local women. The albino children born of this incident have disturbing telepathic powers that they display through their bright orange and red eyes— supposedly precipitating a plot to take control. A pale remake of the 1960 British horror classic, which was based on John Wyndham's novel "The Midwich Cuckoos." Fails to capture the eeriness of it's predecessor and is bogged down with awkward casting, absurd dialogue and a brood of children with glowing eyes that make them less like a threat and more like Nintendo addicts. **98m/C VHS, LV.** Christopher Reeve, Kirstie Alley, Linda Kozlowski, Mark Hamill, Meredith Salenger, Michael Pare, Peter Jason, Constance Forslund; ***D:*** John Carpenter; ***W:*** John Carpenter, David Himmelstein; ***C:*** Gary B. Kibbe; ***M:*** John Carpenter, Dave Davies. *MCA*

Village of the Giants **1965** A group of beer-guzzling teenagers become giants after eating a mysterious substance invented by a twelve-year-old genius. Fun to pick out all the soon-to-be stars. Totally silly premise with bad special effects and minimal plot follow-through. Based on an H.G. Wells story. **82m/C VHS, Beta.** Ron Howard, Johnny Crawford, Tommy Kirk, Beau Bridges, Freddy Cannon, Beau Brummel; ***D:*** Bert I. Gordon; ***M:*** Jack Nitzsche. *NLC, MLB, SUE*

The Villain ½ *Cactus Jack* **1979 (PG)** An unfunny spoof of "B" westerns that is almost like a live-action "Roadrunner" cartoon. Douglas plays Cactus Jack, a highwayman who keeps trying to kidnap fair damsel Ann-Margret. Hero Schwarzenegger keeps rescuing her. Lynde is amusing as the uptight Indian chief Nervous Elk. **93m/C VHS.** Kirk Douglas, Ann-Margret, Arnold Schwarzenegger, Paul Lynde, Foster Brooks, Ruth Buzzi, Jack Elam, Strother Martin, Robert Tessier, Mel Tillis; ***D:*** Hal Needham. *COL*

The Villain Still Pursued Her **1941** A poor hero and rich villain vie for the sweet heroine in this satire of old-fashioned temperance melodrama. Keaton manages to shine as the hero's sidekick. **67m/B VHS, Beta.** Anita Louise, Alan Mowbray, Buster Keaton, Hugh Herbert; ***D:*** Eddie Cline. *NOS, VYY, DVT*

Vincent & Theo ½ **1990 (PG-13)** The story of Impressionist painter Vincent van Gogh, and his brother Theo, a gallery owner who loved his brother's work, yet could not get the public to buy it. Increasing despair and mental illness traps both men, as each struggles to create beauty in a world where it has no value. Altman has created a stunning portrait of "the artist" and his needs. The exquisite cinematography will make you feel as if you stepped into van Gogh's work. **138m/C VHS, Beta, LV.** Tim Roth, Paul Rhys, Johanna Ter Steege, Wladimir Yordanoff; ***D:*** Robert Altman. *INJ, TVC*

Vincent, Francois, Paul and the Others **1976** Three middle-aged Frenchmen rely on their friendships to endure a host of mid-life crises. In French with English subtitles. **113m/C VHS, Beta, LV.** *FR* Yves Montand, Gerard Depardieu, Michel Piccoli, Stephane Audran; ***D:*** Claude Sautet. *FCT, INJ, CVC*

Vincent: The Life and Death of Vincent van Gogh **1987** Van Gogh's work and creativity is examined in a documentary manner through his life and his letters. Thoughtful and intriguing production. Narrated by John Hurt as van Gogh. **99m/C VHS, LV.** *AU* ***D:*** Paul Cox; ***W:*** Paul Cox; ***M:*** Norman Kaye; ***V:*** John Hurt. *FCT, CRY, SIG*

The Vindicator *Frankenstein '88* **1985 (R)** A scientist killed in a lab accident is transformed into a cyborg who runs amok and murders indiscriminately. A modernized Frankenstein, with interesting special effects and well drawn characters. **92m/C VHS, Beta.** *CA* Terri Austin, Richard Cox, David McIlwraith, Pam Grier; ***D:*** Jean-Claude Lord. *FOX*

The Vineyard **1989 (R)** Hapless victims are lured to a Japanese madman's island, where he drinks their blood and maintains a questionable immortality. **95m/C VHS, Beta, LV.** James Hong, Karen Witter, Michael Wong; ***D:*** James Hong, Bill Rice. *VTR, NWV*

Violated **1953** Pathetic production about New York police attempting to track down a sex-maniac murderer who slays his victims and then gives them a haircut. Unbelievably bad. **78m/B VHS.** Wim Holland, Lili Dawn, Mitchell Kowal, Vicki Carlson, William Martel; ***D:*** Walter Strate. *SNC*

Violated *Woof!* **1984** A detective endeavors to implicate a local businessman in the rapes of two beautiful women. Exploitative and dreary. **88m/C VHS, Beta.** John Heard, J.C. Quinn, April Daisy White, Samantha Fox; ***D:*** Richard Cannistraro. *LIV, VES*

Violence at Noon ꝗꝗꝗ **1966** Highly disturbing film in which two women protect a brutal sex murderer from the law. Living among a quiet community of intellectuals, this conspiracy ends in a shocking finale in Oshima's stylized masterpiece. In Japanese with English subtitles. **99m/B VHS.** *JP* Saeda Kawaguchi, Akiko Koyama; ***D:*** Nagisa Oshima. *KIV, INJ*

Violent Breed ꝗ **1983** A CIA operative is sent on a mission to put a black marketeer out of business. **91m/C VHS, Beta.** *IT* Henry Silva, Harrison Muller, Woody Strode; ***D:*** Fernando Di Leo. *MGM*

The Violent Men ꝗꝗ½ *Rough Company* **1955** Big-time land baron Robinson is trying to push out all other landowners in the valley, including Ford. At first Ford refuses to fight back, but after one of Robinson's henchmen kills one of his hired hands, he starts an all-out war against Robinson to save his land. Stanwyck as Robinson's wife and Keith as his brother are wicked as the two urging him on and having an affair behind his back. Based on the novel "Rough Company" by Donald Hamilton. **95m/C VHS, LV.** Glenn Ford, Barbara Stanwyck, Edward G. Robinson, Dianne Foster, Brian Keith, May Wynn; ***D:*** Rudolph Mate; ***C:*** Burnett Guffey. *COL*

Violent Ones *Woof!* **1968** Three men who are suspected of raping a young girl are threatened with lynching by an angry mob of townspeople. Badly acted, poorly directed, uneven and feeble. **96m/C VHS, Beta.** Fernando Lamas, David Carradine; ***D:*** Fernando Lamas. *REP*

Violent Professionals ꝗ½ *La Polizia vuole Giustizia* **1973** Suspended cop runs into resistance inside and outside the force when he infiltrates the mob to get the goods on a crime boss. **100m/C VHS, Beta.** *IT* Richard Conte, Luc Merenda; ***D:*** Sergio Martino. *NO*

Violent Women ꝗ **1959** Five female convicts escape and embark on a bloody journey through the countryside, pursued by the authorities. Shows women can be just as brutal as any man. **61m/C VHS, Beta.** Jennifer Slater, Jo Ann Kelly, Sandy Lyn, Eleanor Blair, Pati Magee; ***D:*** Barry Mahon. *VMK*

The Violent Years *Woof!* *Female* **1956** Spoiled high-school debutantes form a vicious all-girl gang and embark on a spree that includes murder, robbery, and male rape. Justice wins out in the end. Exploitive trash written by Wood, who directed the infamous "Plan 9 from Outer Space." **60m/B VHS, Beta.** Jean Moorehead, Barbara Weeks, Glenn Corbett; ***D:*** Edward D. Wood Jr., Franz Eichhorn; ***W:*** Edward D. Wood Jr. *SNC, RHI, AOV*

Violent Zone ꝗ **1989** Mercenaries go on a supposed rescue mission in the wilderness. **92m/C VHS.** John Douglas, Chad Hayward, Christopher Weeks; ***D:*** John Garwood; ***W:*** David Pritchard, John Bushelman. *HMD*

Violets Are Blue ꝗꝗ½ **1986 (PG-13)** Two high-school sweethearts are reunited in their hometown years later and try to rekindle their romance—even though the man is married. **86m/C VHS, Beta, LV.** Kevin Kline, Sissy Spacek, Bonnie Bedelia, John Kellogg, Augusta Dabney, Jim Standford; ***D:*** Jack Fisk; ***W:*** Naomi Foner; ***C:*** Ralf Bode; ***M:*** Patrick Williams. *COL*

Violette ꝗꝗꝗ *Violette Noziere* **1978 (R)** Fascinating true-life account of a nineteen-year-old French girl in the 1930s who, bored with her life and wanting to be with her lover, decides to poison her parents so she can receive her inheritance. Her mother survives but her father dies, and the girl is sent to prison for murder. Extraordinary performance by Huppert and the film is visually stunning. **122m/C VHS.** *FR* Isabelle Huppert, Stephane Audran, Jean Carmet, Jean Francoise, Bernadette LaFont; ***D:*** Claude Chabrol. Cannes Film Festival '78: Best Actress (Huppert); Cesar Awards '79: Best Supporting Actress (Audran); Nominations: Cannes Film Festival '78: Best Film. *NYF*

VIP, My Brother Superman **1990** The Vips are modern-day descendants of superbeings about to become legends in their own times. SuperVip is broad of chest and pure in spirit while his brother MiniVip possesses only limited powers. From the creator of "Allegro Non Troppo" comes this enticing, amusing piece of animation. **90m/C VHS.** ***D:*** Bruno Bozzetto. *EXP, TPV*

Viper ꝗ **1988** A woman battles a cryptic anti-terrorist band to avenge the murder of her husband. **96m/C VHS.** Linda Purl, Chris Robinson, James Tolkan; ***D:*** Peter Maris. *FRH*

The V.I.P.'s ꝗꝗꝗ **1963** Slick, sophisticated drama set in the V.I.P. lounge of a British airport. Trapped by fog, several of the passengers get acquainted and are forced to face their problems as they spend the night in the airport lounge. Taylor stars as Frances Andros, a wealthy young woman leaving her husband (Burton) for life in the U.S. with her lover, Jourdan. A movie tycoon, an Australian entrepreneur, his secretary, and a duchess are among the other passengers grounded by the fog. Both Rutherford and Smith give excellent performances and it was a tossup as to which actress would be nominated for the Oscar. **119m/C VHS.** *GB* Elizabeth Taylor, Richard Burton, Louis Jourdan, Elsa Martinelli, Margaret Rutherford, Maggie Smith, Rod Taylor, Orson Welles, Linda Christian, Dennis Price; ***D:*** Anthony Asquith; ***W:*** Terence Rattigan; ***C:*** Jack Hildyard; ***M:*** Miklos Rozsa. Academy Awards '63: Best Supporting Actress (Rutherford); Golden Globe Awards '64: Best Supporting Actress (Rutherford); National Board of Review Awards '63: Best Supporting Actress (Rutherford). *MGM*

Virgin Among the Living Dead ꝗ **1971 (R)** Young woman travels to remote castle when she hears of relative's death. Once there, she finds the residents a tad weird and has bad dreams in which zombies chase her. Bizarre even for Franco, who seems to have been going through a "Pasolini" phase while making this one. **90m/C VHS, Beta.** *SP* Christina von Blanc, Britt Nichols, Howard Vernon, Anne Libert, Rose Kiekens, Paul Muller; ***D:*** Jess (Jesus) Franco. *NO*

The Virgin and the Gypsy ꝗꝗ½ **1970 (R)** An English girl brought up in a repressive household in 1920s England falls in love with a gypsy. Based on the novel by D.H. Lawrence. Directorial debut of Miles. **92m/C VHS.** *GB* Joanna Shimkus, Franco Nero, Honor Blackman, Mark Burns; ***D:*** Christopher Miles; ***W:*** Alan Plater. *NO*

Virgin High ꝗ **1990 (R)** Three young men sneak into an all-girls Catholic boarding school with hilarious consequences. Ward (TV's Robin, from "Batman") makes a special appearance in bondage in this sex farce. **90m/C VHS, LV.** Burt Ward, Linnea Quigley, Tracy Dali, Richard Gabai, Catherine McGuiness, Chris Dempsey; ***D:*** Richard Gabai; ***W:*** Richard Gabai, Jeff Neal. *COL*

The Virgin of Nuremberg ꝗ½ *Horror Castle; Terror Castle; Castle of Terror; La Vergine de Norimberga* **1965** A young woman enters her new husband's ancestral castle and is stalked by the specter of a legendary sadist. **82m/C VHS, Beta.** *IT* Rossana Podesta, George Riviere, Christopher Lee, Jim Dolen; ***D:*** Anthony (Antonio Margheriti) Dawson. *MOV*

The Virgin Queen ꝗꝗꝗ **1955** Davis stars in this historical drama, which focuses on the stormy relationship between the aging Queen and Sir Walter Raleigh. Collins is the lady-in-waiting who is the secret object of Raleigh's true affections. Previously, Davis played Queen Elizabeth I in "Elizabeth and Essex." Davis holds things together. **92m/C VHS, Beta.** Bette Davis, Richard Todd, Joan Collins, Herbert Marshall, Dan O'Herlihy, Jay Robinson, Romney Brent; ***D:*** Henry Koster. Nominations: Academy Awards '55: Best Costume Design (Color). *FOX*

Virgin Queen of St. Francis High ꝗ **1988 (PG)** Two high school foes make a bet that one of them can take the "virgin" title away from gorgeous Christensen by summer's end. She has to fight off their advances, but grows to like Straface. **89m/C VHS, Beta, LV.** *CA* Joseph R. Straface, Stacy Christensen, J.T. Wotton; ***D:*** Francesco Lucente. *MED*

Virgin Sacrifice ꝗ **1959** A great white hunter looking for zoo-bound jaguars confronts the virgin-sacrificing, Tiger God-revering natives of Guatemala. **67m/C VHS, Beta, LV.** David Dalie, Antonio Gutierrez, Angelica Morales, Fernando Wagner; ***D:*** Fernando Wagner. *NO*

The Virgin Soldiers ꝗꝗ½ **1969 (R)** A British comedy about greenhorn military recruits stationed in Singapore, innocent of women as well as battle, and their struggles to overcome both situations. A good cast raises this above the usual low-brow sex farce. Based on the novel by Leslie Thomas. Followed by "Stand Up Virgin Soldiers." **96m/C VHS, Beta.** *GB* Hywel Bennett, Nigel Davenport, Lynn Redgrave, Nigel Patrick, Rachel Kempson, Jack Shepherd, Tsai Chin; ***D:*** John Dexter; ***W:*** John Hopkins. *COL*

The Virgin Spring ꝗꝗꝗ½ *Jungfrukallan* **1959** Based on a medieval ballad and set in 14th-century Sweden. The rape and murder of a young innocent spurs her father to vengeance and he kills her attackers. Over the girl's dead body, the father questions how God could have let any of it happen, but he comes to find solace and forgiveness. Stunning Bergman compositions. In Swedish with English subtitles; also available in dubbed version. **88m/B VHS, Beta.** *SW* Max von Sydow, Brigitta Valberg, Gunnel Lindblom, Brigitta Pattersson, Axel Duborg; ***D:*** Ingmar Bergman; ***C:*** Sven Nykvist. Academy Awards '60: Best Foreign Language Film; Golden Globe Awards '61: Best Foreign Film; Nominations: Academy Awards '60: Best Costume Design (B & W). *HMV, INJ*

The Virgin Witch ꝗ½ *Lesbian Twins* **1970 (R)** Two beautiful sisters are sent to the British countryside, ostensibly for a modeling job. They soon find themselves in the midst of a witches' coven however, and discover one of them is to be sacrificed. The Michelles were "Playboy" magazine's first sister centerfolds. **89m/C VHS, Beta.** *GB* Anne Michelle, Vicki Michelle, Patricia Haines, Keith Buckley, James Chase, Neil Hallett; ***D:*** Ray Austin. *PSM*

Virginia City ꝗꝗꝗ **1940** Action-packed western drama set during the Civil War. Flynn is a Union soldier who escapes from a Confederate prison run by Scott, after learning of a gold shipment being sent by Southern sympathizers to aid the Confederacy. He ends up in Virginia City (where the gold-laden wagon train is to leave from) and falls for a dance-hall girl (Hopkins) who turns out to be a Southern spy working for Scott but who falls for Flynn anyway. Bogart is miscast as a half-breed outlaw who aids Scott but wants the gold for himself. Considered a follow-up to "Dodge City." **121m/C VHS.** Errol Flynn, Miriam Hopkins, Randolph Scott, Humphrey Bogart, Frank McHugh, Alan Hale, Guinn "Big Boy" Williams, Douglass Dumbrille, Charles Halton; ***D:*** Michael Curtiz; ***M:*** Max Steiner. *MGM*

The Virginia Hill Story ꝗꝗ **1976** Fictionalized biography of mobster Bugsy Siegel's girlfriend who, in the mid-fifties, was subpoenaed to appear before the Kefauver investigation on crime in the U.S. As the examining lawyer presents questions regarding her background and connections with the underworld, we see the story of her life. Made for television. **90m/C VHS, Beta.** Dyan Cannon, Harvey Keitel, Robby Benson, Allen (Goorwitz) Garfield, John Vernon; ***D:*** Joel Schumacher. *NO*

The Virginian ꝗꝗ½ **1923** The second silent version of Owen Wister's classic western novel, inferior to both the 1914 Cecil B. DeMille silent and the 1929 Victor Fleming talkie. Harlan plays the title role as the cowpoke who leads a posse against cattle rustlers and falls in love with a schoolteacher. **79m/B VHS.** Kenneth Harlan, Florence Vidor, Russell Simpson, Pat O'Malley, Raymond Hatton; ***D:*** Tom Forman. *GPV*

The Virginian ꝗꝗꝗ **1929** A classic early-talkie western about a ranch-hand defeating the local bad guys. One line of dialogue has become, with modification, a standard western cliche: "If you want to call me that, smile." Based on the novel by Owen Wister. With this starring role, Cooper broke away from the juvenile lovers he had been playing to the laconic, rugged male leads he would be known for. Huston is perfectly cast as the outlaw leader. **95m/B VHS, Beta.** Gary Cooper, Walter Huston, Richard Arlen, Chester Conklin, Eugene Pallette; ***D:*** Victor Fleming. *BAR*

The Virginian 𝒳𝒳½ **1946** Cowboy good guy, known as the Virginian (McCrea), and his best pal Steve (Tufts) both fall for Molly (Britton), the Eastern-bred schoolmarm who's come to their Wyoming town. Steve wants to make some quick money and joins up with leader Trampas' (Donlevy) cattle rustling gang. So the Virginian is forced to chose between friendship and the code of the west and Molly wonders if she can accepts the country's harsh ways. Based on Owen Wister's 1902 novel. **87m/C VHS.** Joel McCrea, Sonny Tufts, Barbara Britton, Brian Donlevy, Fay Bainter, Tom Tully, Henry O'Neill, William Frawley; ***D:*** Stuart Gilmore; ***W:*** Frances Goodrich, Albert Hackett; ***C:*** Harry Hallenberger; ***M:*** Daniele Amfitheatrof. *MCA*

Viridiana 𝒳𝒳𝒳𝒳 **1961** Innocent girl, with strong ideas about goodness, visits her worldly uncle's home before she takes her vows as a nun. He has developed a sick obsession for her, but after drugging the girl he finds he cannot violate her purity. He tells her, however, she is no longer chaste so she will not join the church. After her uncle's suicide, Viridiana learns she and his illegitimate son Jorge have inherited her uncle's rundown estate. Viridiana opens the house to all sorts of beggars, who take shameless advantage, while Jorge works slowly to restore the estate and improve the lives of those around him. Considered to be one of Bunuel's masterpieces and a bitter allegory of Spanish idealism versus pragmatism and the state of the world. In Spanish with English subtitles. **90m/B VHS, Beta.** *SP MX* Silvia Pinal, Francesco Rabal, Fernando Rey, Margarita Lozano, Victoria Zinny; ***D:*** Luis Bunuel; ***W:*** Luis Bunuel. Cannes Film Festival '61: Best Film. *NOS, HHT, DVT*

Virtual Assassin 𝒳𝒳 *Cyberjack* **1995 (R)** 21st century sci-fi actioner finds the crooked Zef (James) leading his band of thugs into a research lab to steal a powerful computer virus. Naturally, the janitor (Dudikoff) just happens to be an ex-cop with a score to settle with Zef. Predictable but with decent special effects. **99m/C VHS, LV.** *CA JP* Michael Dudikoff, Brion James, Jon Cuthbert, Suki Kaiser, James Thom; ***D:*** Robert Lee; ***W:*** Eric Poppen. *TTC*

Virtual Combat 𝒳𝒳 **1995 (R)** Ex-cop Quarry (Wilson) teams up with some cyber-girls to stop a madman who's able to manipulate virtual reality programs into living beings and releases a killer who wants to lead a destructive virtual army. **97m/C VHS.** Don "The Dragon" Wilson, Athena Massey, Loren Avedon, Kenneth McLeod, Turhan Bey, Stella Stevens; ***D:*** Andrew Stevens. *APX*

Virtual Desire 𝒳½ **1995 (R)** Brad Collins is bored with his marriage and finds some excitement via sexual games on the Internet. But someone is taking a very close interest in Brad's virtual amours and when his wife is murdered, Brad becomes the prime suspect. **92m/C VHS, LV.** Michael Meyer, Julie Strain, Gail Harris. *TRI*

Virtue's Revolt 𝒳½ **1924** A small-town girl is corrupted by the sleazy world of showbiz. Silent. **51m/B VHS, Beta.** Edith Thornton, Crauford Kent. *NO*

Virtuosity 𝒳½ **1995 (R)** Ex-cop-with-a-tragic-past Parker Barnes (Washington) is sprung from prison to help capture computer-generated killer Sid 6.7 (Crowe), who escapes from cyberspace and goes on a rampage in 1997 Los Angeles. Seems this virtual reality bad guy has a personality composed of some 200 serial killers and criminal minds so Parker's got his work cut out for him. But criminal-behavior psychologist Madison Carter (Lynch) is around to lend her expert advice. Both the charismatically evil Crowe and the sufferingly noble Washington are wasted in this effects-laden thriller that sacrifices character for flash. **105m/C VHS, Beta.** Denzel Washington, Russell Crowe, Kelly Lynch, Stephen Spinella, William Forsythe, Louise Fletcher, William Fichtner, Costas Mandylor, Kevin J. O'Connor; ***D:*** Brett Leonard; ***W:*** Eric Bernt; ***C:*** Gale Tattersall; ***M:*** Christopher Young. *PAR*

Virus 𝒳𝒳 *Fukkatsu no Hi* **1982 (PG)** After nuclear war and plague destroy civilization, a small group of people gather in Antarctica and struggle with determination to carry on life. A look at man's genius for self-destruction and his endless hope. **102m/C VHS, Beta.** *JP* George Kennedy, Sonny Chiba, Glenn Ford, Robert Vaughn, Stuart Gillard, Stephanie Faulkner, Ken Ogata, Bo Svenson, Olivia Hussey, Chuck Connors, Edward James Olmos; ***D:*** Kinji Fukasaku. *VTR, MED*

The Vision 𝒳𝒳 **1987** Suspenseful British production about televangelists who attempt to control their viewers' minds through worldwide satellite broadcasting. **103m/C VHS, Beta.** *GB* Lee Remick, Dirk Bogarde, Helena Bonham Carter, Eileen Atkins; ***D:*** Norman Stone. *NO*

Vision Quest 𝒳𝒳½ *Crazy for You* **1985 (R)** A high school student wants to win the Washington State wrestling championship and the affections of a beautiful older artist. He gives it his all as he trains for the meet and goes after his "visionquest." A winning performance by Modine raises this above the usual teen coming-of-age movie. Madonna sings "Crazy for You" in a nightclub. Based on novel by Terry Davis. **107m/C VHS, Beta, LV.** Matthew Modine, Linda Fiorentino, Ronny Cox, Roberts Blossom, Daphne Zuniga, Charles Hallahan, Michael Schoeffling; ***D:*** Harold Becker; ***W:*** Darryl Ponicsan; ***Performed by:*** Madonna. *WAR*

Visions 𝒳½ **1990** A man's ability to "see" murders before they happen leads police to suspect him of committing them, and he must clear himself. **90m/C VHS.** Joe Balogh, Alice Villarreal, Tom Taylor, A.R. Newman, J.R. Pella; ***D:*** Stephen E. Miller. *NO*

Visions of Evil 𝒳 **1973** A young woman, recently released from a mental institution, is plagued by a series of terrifying visions when she moves into a house where a brutal axe murder took place. **85m/C VHS, Beta.** Lori Sanders, Dean Jagger. *PSM*

Visions of Light: The Art of Cinematography 𝒳𝒳𝒳 **1993** Excellent documentary on the way films look and how the art of photographing movies can contribute as much, if not more, than cast, director, and script. Scenes from 125 films, from "Birth of a Nation" to "GoodFellas" are shown, with commentary from a number of cinematographers, including Gordon Willis, William A. Fraker, Conrad Hall, Ernest Dickerson, Vilmos Zsigmond, and Michael Chapman, on how they achieved certain effects and their collaborations with the director of the film. **95m/C VHS, LV.** ***D:*** Arnold Glassman, Stuart Samuels, Todd McCarthy; ***W:*** Todd McCarthy. New York Film Critics Awards '93: Best Feature Documentary; National Society of Film Critics Awards '93: Best Feature Documentary. *FXV*

Visitants 𝒳 **1987** Aliens descend irreverently on a small town in the 1950s, with unexpected comedic results. **93m/C VHS, Beta.** Marcus Vaughter, Johanna Grika, Joel Hile, Nicole Rio; ***D:*** Rick Sloane. *TWE*

Visiting Hours 𝒳 *The Fright; Get Well Soon* **1982 (R)** Psycho-killer slashes his female victims and photographs his handiwork. Grant is one of his victims who doesn't die, so the killer decides to visit the hospital and finish the job. Fairly graphic and generally unpleasant. **101m/C VHS, Beta.** *CA* Lee Grant, William Shatner, Linda Purl, Michael Ironside; ***D:*** Jean-Claude Lord; ***W:*** Brian Taggert. *FOX*

The Visitor 𝒳½ **1980 (R)** Affluent handsome doctor and mate conspire with grisly devil worshippers to conceive devil child. **90m/C VHS.** Mel Ferrer, Glenn Ford, Lance Henriksen, John Huston, Shelley Winters, Joanne Nail, Sam Peckinpah; ***D:*** Giullo Paradisi. *UAV, HHE*

Visitor from the Grave 𝒳 **1981** When an American heiress and her boyfriend dispose of a dead man's body, his spirit comes back to haunt them. This annoys them. **60m/C VHS, Beta.** Simon MacCorkindale, Kathryn Leigh Scott, Gareth Thomas, Mia Nadasi. *LIV*

The Visitors 𝒳½ **1989 (R)** Ghosts come to stay at a young family's dream house in Sweden. Not exactly a novel treatment or a novel premise. **102m/C VHS, Beta, LV.** *SW* Keith Berkeley, Lena Endre, John Force, John Olsen, Joanna Berg, Brent Landiss, Patrick Ersgard; ***D:*** Joakim Ersgard. *VMK*

Vital Signs 𝒳 **1990 (R)** Hackneyed drama about six medical students enduring the tribulations of their profession. **102m/C VHS, Beta, LV.** Adrian Pasdar, Diane Lane, Jack Gwaltney, Laura San Giacomo, Jane Adams, Tim Ransom, Bradley Whitford, Lisa Jane Persky, William Devane, Norma Aleandro, Jimmy Smits, James Karen, Telma Hopkins; ***D:*** Marisa Silver; ***W:*** Jeb Stuart; ***M:*** Miles Goodman. *FOX*

Viva Knievel *Woof! Seconds to Live* **1977 (PG)** Crooks plan to sabotage Knievel's daredevil jump in Mexico and then smuggle cocaine back into the States in his coffin. Unintentionally campy. **106m/C VHS, Beta.** Evel Knievel, Gene Kelly, Lauren Hutton, Red Buttons, Leslie Nielsen, Cameron Mitchell, Marjoe Gortner, Albert Salmi, Dabney Coleman; ***D:*** Gordon Douglas; ***M:*** Charles Bernstein. *WAR*

Viva Las Vegas 𝒳𝒳½ *Love in Las Vegas* **1963** Race care driver Elvis needs money to compete against rival Danova in the upcoming Las Vegas Grand Prix. He takes a job in a casino and romances fellow employee Ann-Margret, who turns out to be his rival for the grand prize in the local talent competition. Good pairing between the two leads, and the King does particularly well with the title song. ♫The Lady Loves Me; Viva Las Vegas; What'd I Say; I Need Somebody to Lean On; Come On, Everybody; Today, Tomorrow and Forever; If You Think I Don't Need You; Appreciation; My Rival. **85m/C VHS, Beta, LV.** Elvis Presley, Ann-Margret, William Demarest, Jack Carter, Cesare Danova, Nicky Blair, Larry Kent; ***D:*** George Sidney; ***C:*** Joseph Biroc. *MGM*

Viva Maria! 𝒳𝒳½ **1965 (R)** Tongue-in-cheek comedy with Bardot and Moreau as two dancers (both named Maria) in a show traveling through Mexico. The two become incensed by the poverty of the peasants and decide to turn revolutionary (especially after Moreau has an affair with revolutionary leader Hamilton, who promptly gets killed). The two French sex symbols are a fine match. **119m/C VHS.** *FR IT* Jeanne Moreau, Brigitte Bardot, George Hamilton, Paulette Dubost, Claudio Brook; ***D:*** Louis Malle; ***W:*** Louis Malle, Jean-Claude Carriere; ***M:*** Georges Delerue. *MGM*

Viva Max 𝒳𝒳½ **1969** A blundering modern-day Mexican general and his men recapture the Alamo, and an equally inept American force, headed by Winters, is sent to rout them out. Mostly works, with some very funny scenes. Ustinov is great. **93m/C VHS.** Peter Ustinov, Jonathan Winters, John Astin, Pamela Tiffin, Keenan Wynn; ***D:*** Jerry Paris. *REP*

Viva Villa! 𝒳𝒳𝒳 **1934** Exciting action biography of Mexican revolutionary Pancho Villa, well-portrayed by the exuberant Beery. The film follows the early Robin Hood-like exploits of Villa and his men who soon join Walthall and his peasant army in overthrowing the government. But Villa's bandito instincts and ego cause problems and a power struggle ensues. Director Howard Hawks went uncredited for his work on the film, being fired by the studio after an incident while on location in Mexico. **115m/B VHS, LV.** Wallace Beery, Fay Wray, Stuart Erwin, Leo Carrillo, Donald Cook, George E. Stone, Joseph Schildkraut, Henry B. Walthall, Katherine DeMille, David Durand, Frank Puglia; ***D:*** Jack Conway; ***W:*** Ben Hecht. Nominations: Academy Awards '34: Best Adapted Screenplay, Best Picture, Best Sound. *MGM, MOV, BTV*

Viva Zapata! 𝒳𝒳𝒳𝒳 **1952** Chronicles the life of Mexican revolutionary Emiliano Zapata. Brando is powerful as he leads the peasant revolt in the early 1900s, only to be corrupted by power and greed. Quinn well deserved his Best Supporting Actor Oscar for his performance as Zapata's brother. Based on the novel "Zapata the Unconquered" by Edgcumb Pinchon. **112m/B VHS, Beta, LV.** Marlon Brando, Anthony Quinn, Jean Peters, Margo, Arnold Moss, Joseph Wiseman, Mildred Dunnock; ***D:*** Elia Kazan; ***W:*** John Steinbeck; ***M:*** Alex North. Academy Awards '52: Best Supporting Actor (Quinn); British Academy Awards '52: Best Actor (Brando); Cannes Film Festival '52: Best Actor (Brando); Nominations: Academy Awards '52: Best Actor (Brando), Best Art Direction/Set Decoration (B & W), Best Story & Screenplay, Best Original Score. *FOX, BTV*

Vivacious Lady 🦴🦴🦴 **1938** Romantic comedy about a mild-mannered college professor who marries a chorus girl. Problems arise when he must let his conservative family and his former fiancee in on the marriage news. Good performances. Appealing. **90m/B VHS, Beta.** Ginger Rogers, James Stewart, James Ellison, Beulah Bondi, Charles Coburn, Jack Carson, Franklin Pangborn; ***D:*** George Stevens. Nominations: Academy Awards '38: Best Cinematography, Best Sound. *CCB, MED*

Vogues of 1938 🦴🦴 *All This and Glamour Too; Vogues* **1937** As a lark, a rich girl takes a job as a fashion model and incurs the displeasure of Baxter, the owner of the chic fashion house where she works. An early Technicolor fashion extravaganza. ♫That Old Feeling; Lovely One; Turn On the Red Hot Heat (Burn the Blues Away); King of Jam. **110m/C VHS, Beta.** Joan Bennett, Warner Baxter, Helen Vinson, Mischa Auer, Hedda Hopper, Penny Singleton, Alan Mowbray; ***D:*** Irving Cummings. Nominations: Academy Awards '37: Best Interior Decoration, Best Song ("That Old Feeling"). *NO*

Voice of Hollywood 🦴½ **1929** Some of Hollywood's great stars are caught off guard in this collection of short subjects. **60m/B VHS, Beta.** Buster Keaton, Ken Maynard, Johnny Mack Brown. *VDM, DVT, GVV*

Volere Volare 🦴🦴½ **1992 (R)** Shy sound engineer Nichetti shares a studio with his brother. The brother employs a bevy of beauties to dub sound effects onto soft-core porn films while Nichetti works on dubbing classic cartoons. He becomes so involved in his work he actually turns into a cartoon figure, which does nothing for his love life. Then he meets Martina, who's strangely attracted to this cartoon figure. Quirky comedy mixes animation and live action with too many gimmicks and not enough heart. In Italian with English subtitles. **92m/C VHS, LV.** *IT* Maurizio Nichetti, Angela Finocchiaro, Mariella Valentini, Patrizio Roversi, Remo Remotti, Renato Scarpa; ***D:*** Maurizio Nichetti, Guido Manuli; ***W:*** Maurizio Nichetti, Guido Manuli. Montreal World Film Festival '92: Best Director (Nichetti). *COL, WTA, FCT*

Volpone 🦴🦴🦴 **1939** A classic adaptation of Ben Jonson's famous tale. A greedy merchant pretends he is dying, leaving a fortune behind, in order see what his family will do to become his heir. In French with English subtitles. **95m/B VHS, Beta.** *FR* Harry Baur, Louis Jouvet, Fernand Ledoux; ***D:*** Maurice Tourneur. *NOS, HHT, APD*

Volunteers 🦴🦴 **1985 (R)** Ivy League playboy joins the newly formed Peace Corps to escape gambling debts and finds himself on a bridge-building mission in Thailand. Has its comedic moments, especially with Candy. **107m/C VHS, Beta, LV.** Tom Hanks, John Candy, Rita Wilson, Tim Thomerson, Gedde Watanabe, George Plimpton, Ernest Harada; ***D:*** Nicholas Meyer; ***M:*** James Horner. *NO*

Von Ryan's Express 🦴🦴🦴 **1965** An American Air Force colonel leads a group of prisoners-of-war in taking control of a freight train in order to make their exciting escape from a WWII P.O.W. camp in Italy. Strong cast. **117m/C VHS, Beta, LV.** Frank Sinatra, Trevor Howard, Brad Dexter, Raffaella Carra, Sergio Fantoni, John Leyton, Vito Scotti, Edward Mulhare, Adolfo Celi, James Brolin, James B. Sikking; ***D:*** Mark Robson; ***W:*** Wendell Mayes; ***C:*** William H. Daniels; ***M:*** Jerry Goldsmith. *FOX, FCT*

Voodoo 🦴🦴 **1995 (R)** College student Andy (Feldman) must battle a fraternity, lead by an evil voodoo priest, when they decide to make his girlfriend their next human sacrifice. **91m/C VHS, LV.** Corey Feldman, Sarah Douglas, Jack Nance; ***D:*** Rene Eram; ***W:*** Brian DiMuccio, Dino Vindeni; ***M:*** Keith Bilderbeck. *APX*

Voodoo Black Exorcist 🦴 **1989** Some 3000 years ago, a black prince was buried alive for messin' with another man's woman. Now he's back...and he's mad—real mad. He's prepared to kill just about everyone. Can he be stopped before all in the modern world are dead?? **?m/C VHS.** Aldo Sambrel, Tenyeka Stadle, Fernando Sancho. *HHE*

Voodoo Dawn 🦴🦴 **1989 (R)** Two New Yorkers travel to the Deep South to visit a friend who, it turns out, is the latest victim in a series of really gross voodoo murders. A beautiful girl is written into the plot, and the New York guys have an excuse to stay in voodooville, even though bimbolina's southern accent comes and goes for no discernable reason. Filmed near Charleston, South Carolina and co-written by Russo of "Night of the Living Dead" fame. **83m/C VHS.** Raymond St. Jacques, Theresa Merritt, Gina Gershon, Kirk Baily, Billy "Sly" Williams, J. Grant Albrecht, Tony Todd; ***D:*** Steven Fierberg; ***W:*** John Russo, Jeffrey Delman. *ACA*

Voodoo Woman 🦴 **1957** An innocent girl is lured into the jungle by an evil scientist who is trying to create the perfect woman to commit murders. He turns the girl into an ugly monster in an attempt to get her to obey his telepathic commands. A campy classic that's as bad as it sounds. **77m/B VHS.** Marla English, Tom Conway, Mike Connors, Lance Fuller; ***D:*** Edward L. Cahn. *COL, PAR*

Vortex 🦴½ **1981** Punk/film noir style in which a female private eye becomes immersed in corporate paranoia and political corruption. **87m/C VHS.** Lydia Lunch, James Russo, Bill Rice; ***D:*** Scott B, Beth B; ***W:*** Scott B, Beth B. *ICA*

Voulez-Vous Danser Avec Moi? 🦴🦴 *Come Dance with Me; Do You Want to Dance with Me?* **1959** A young bride endeavors to clear her husband of murder charges and find the real killer. In French with English subtitles. **90m/C VHS, Beta.** *FR* Brigitte Bardot, Henri Vidal; ***D:*** Michel Boisrond. *BAR, INJ*

A Vow to Kill 🦴🦴½ **1994 (PG-13)** Predictable made for cable thriller finds the wealthy Phillips marrying the charming Grieco after a whirlwind courtship. Then, on their honeymoon, she accidentally learns that her new husband has contacted her family and is masquerading as a kidnapper—demanding a large ransom for her safe release. But maybe it's not such a masquerade after all. **91m/C VHS, Beta.** Julianne Phillips, Richard Grieco, Gordon Pinsent, Peter MacNeill, Tom Cavanagh, Nicole Oliver; ***D:*** Harry S. Longstreet; ***W:*** Harry S. Longstreet, Sean Silas. *PAR*

Voyage 🦴½ **1993 (R)** Boring rip-off of "Dead Calm" and other couple-in-peril-from-psycho-on-boat films. Hauer and Allen are having marital problems and decide to sail away from their troubles with new-found friends Roberts and Nielson. Only their guests are sociopaths. Hauer takes a breather from his psycho roles for a turn as the good guy while Roberts could do his patented crazy act in his sleep. Made for cable television. **?m/C VHS.** Rutger Hauer, Karen Allen, Eric Roberts, Connie Nielson; ***D:*** John MacKenzie. *ITC*

Voyage en Balloon 🦴🦴½ **1959** This is the delightful story of a young boy (played by the star of "The Red Balloon") who stows away on his grandfather's hot air balloon for an adventurous trip across France. **82m/C VHS, Beta.** *FR* Pascal Lamorisse, Andre Gille, Maurice Baquet; ***D:*** Albert Lamorisse; ***W:*** Albert Lamorisse. *COL, INJ, SUE*

Voyage en Douce 🦴🦴 **1981** Helene and Lucie have been friends since childhood. Helene wants to rent a summer house, and Lucie, fed up with her marriage, agrees to join her on a leisurely journey through the south of France. Thoughtful look at friendship among women. French with subtitles. **95m/C VHS.** *FR* Dominique Sanda, Geraldine Chaplin; ***D:*** Michel DeVille. *NYF*

The Voyage of Tanai 🦴🦴 **1975 (G)** A young Polynesian battles nature's snarls on his quest to save his village. **90m/C VHS, Beta.** ***D:*** John Latos. *NO*

Voyage of Terror: The Achille Lauro Affair 🦴🦴½ **1990** Recounting of the 1985 Italian cruise-ship hijacking by four Palestinians. Lancaster is the wheelchair-bound Leon Klinghoffer and Saint is wife Marilyn. Shot on the actual ship and route where the tragedy occurred. Originally a made-for-television miniseries. **120m/C VHS.** Burt Lancaster, Eva Marie Saint, Robert Culp, Brian Bloom, Dominique Sanda, Rebecca Schaeffer, Joseph Nasser, Gabriele Ferzetti, Renzo Nontagnani; ***D:*** Alberto Negrin. *PSM*

Voyage of the Damned 🦴🦴🦴 **1976 (G)** The story of one of the most tragic incidents of WWII. In 1939, 1,937 German-Jewish refugees fleeing Nazi Germany are bound for Cuba aboard the Hamburg-America liner S.S. St. Louis. They are refused permission to land in Cuba (and everywhere else) and must sail back to Germany and certain death. Based on the novel by Gordon Thomas and Max Morgan-Witts. **134m/C VHS, Beta.** Faye Dunaway, Max von Sydow, Oskar Werner, Malcolm McDowell, Orson Welles, James Mason, Lee Grant, Katharine Ross, Ben Gazzara, Lynne Frederick, Wendy Hiller, Jose Ferrer, Luther Adler, Sam Wanamaker, Denholm Elliott, Nehemiah Persoff, Julie Harris, Maria Schell, Janet Suzman; ***D:*** Stuart Rosenberg; ***C:*** Billy Williams; ***M:*** Lalo Schifrin. Golden Globe Awards '77: Best Supporting Actress (Ross); Nominations: Academy Awards '76: Best Adapted Screenplay, Best Supporting Actress (Grant), Best Original Score. *FOX*

Voyage of the Heart 🦴🦴 **1990** An aging fisherman meets up with a sexy college girl and the passion begins. **88m/C VHS.** Bill Aldrij, Dunja Djordjenic. *AIP*

Voyage of the Rock Aliens 🦴 **1987** A quasi-satiric space farce about competing alien rock stars. **97m/C VHS, Beta.** Pia Zadora, Tom Nolan, Craig Sheffer, Rhema, Ruth Gordon, Michael Berryman, Jermaine Jackson; ***D:*** James Fargo. *PSM*

The Voyage of the Yes 🦴🦴 **1972 (PG)** Two teenagers, one white and one black, in a small sailboat hit rough weather and battle the elements while learning about themselves. Average made-for-television movie. **100m/C VHS.** Desi Arnaz Jr., Mike Evans, Beverly Garland, Skip Homeier, Della Reese, Scoey Mitchell; ***D:*** Lee H. Katzin. *NO*

A Voyage' Round My Father 🦴🦴🦴 **1989** John Mortimer's adaptation of his semi-autobiographical stage play. Olivier is the eccentric, opinionated blind barrister-father and Bates the exasperated son as both try to come to terms with their stormy family relationship. Well-acted and directed. Made for television. **85m/C VHS, Beta.** *GB* Laurence Olivier, Alan Bates, Jane Asher, Elizabeth Sellars; ***D:*** Alvin Rakoff. *HBO*

Voyage-Suprise 🦴🦴🦴 **1946** A slapstick comedy about a crazy old man who runs a mystery tour from a dilapidated bus as he takes an unknowing mob of tourists on a cross-country escapade through a brothel, a wedding, criminals, police, terrorists and the Haute-Provence. In French with English subtitles. **108m/B VHS, Beta.** *FR* Martine Carol, Sioel; ***D:*** Pierre Prevert; ***C:*** Jean Bourgoin. *FCT, FST*

Voyage to Italy 🦴🦴½ **1953** An unhappy couple, on the verge of divorce, inherit a house in Italy and make a trip to see it. In Italy, they dally with other people but realize their attachment to each other demands they attempt to salvage their marriage. Not the best of the Rossellini-Bergman collaborations. Poor editing and directing undermine weak script. Sanders and Bergman do their best. **87m/B VHS, Beta.** Ingrid Bergman, George Sanders; ***D:*** Roberto Rossellini. *NOS, FCT*

Voyage to the Bottom of the Sea 🦴🦴🦴 **1961** The crew of an atomic submarine must destroy a deadly radiation belt which has set the polar ice cap ablaze. Fun stuff, with good special effects and photography. Later became a television show. **106m/C VHS, Beta, LV.** Walter Pidgeon, Joan Fontaine, Barbara Eden, Peter Lorre, Robert Sterling, Michael Ansara, Frankie Avalon; ***D:*** Irwin Allen; ***W:*** Irwin Allen, Charles Bennett; ***C:*** Winton C. Hoch. *FOX, FCT*

Voyage to the Planet of Prehistoric Women *Woof! Gill Woman; Gill Women of Venus* **1968** Astronauts journey to Venus, where they discover a race of gorgeous, sea-shell clad women led by Van Doren, as well as a few monsters. Incomprehensible but fun. The third film incorporating the Russian "Planeta Burg" footage. Directed (and narrated) by Bogdanovich under the pseudonym Derek Thomas. **78m/C VHS.** Mamie Van Doren, Mary Mark, Paige Lee; ***D:*** Peter Bogdanovich. *SNC*

Voyage to the Prehistoric Planet 🦴½ *Voyage to a Prehistoric Planet* **1965** In the year 2020, an expedition to Venus is forced to deal with dinosaurs and other perils. In the making of this movie, Roger Corman edited in special effects and additional footage from a recently acquired Russian film, "Planeta Burg," and his own "Queen of Blood." **80m/C VHS.** Basil Rathbone, Faith Domergue, Marc Shannon, Christopher Brand; ***D:*** Curtis Harrington. *NOS, SNC*

Voyager 🦴🦴🦴 **1991 (PG-13)** Restless, middle-aged engineer Walter Faber (Shepherd) tells his life story in a series of flashbacks. Twenty years before (the film starts in 1957) he abandons his pregnant girlfriend who promises to get an abortion. He laters hears she married, had a child, and divorced. While sailing to New York from France Walter falls in love with a young student and accompanies her to Greece to visit her mother. Only then does he realize her true identity, leading to a tragic conclusion. Shepherd's is a glum, repressed performance (in keeping with the character) while Delpy personifies youthful sweetness. Based on the novel "Homo Faber" by Max Frisch. **110m/C VHS, LV.** *FR GE* Sam Shepard, Julie Delpy, Barbara Sukowa, Dieter Kirchlechner, Traci Lind, Deborra-Lee Furness, August Zirner, Thomas Heinze; ***D:*** Volker Schlondorff; ***W:*** Volker Schlondorff, Rudy Wurlitzer. *ACA, INJ*

The Voyeur 🦴 **1994** After ten years of marriage, a couple tries to ignite those sexual fires by spending a weekend in Napa Valley and indulging in erotic sexual games. Based on Lonnie Barbach's book "Erotic Edge." **80m/C VHS.** Al Sapienza, Kim Dawson; ***D:*** Deborah Shames; ***W:*** Udana Power. *TPV*

Vulcan God of Fire *Woof! Vulcan, Son of Jupiter* **1962** Flash is a muscle-bound Vulcan fighting off cheesy monsters in an effort to win the hand of Venus. **76m/C VHS, Beta.** *IT* Rob Flash, Gordon Mitchell, Bella Cortez; ***D:*** Emmimo Salvi. *TWE*

Vulture 🦴 **1967** In an attempt to carry out a curse on the descendants of the man who killed his forefather, a scientist tries an atomic transmutation experiment and winds up combining himself with a bird. **91m/C VHS, Beta.** Robert Hutton, Akim Tamiroff, Broderick Crawford, Diane Clare, Philip Friend, Patrick Holt, Annette Carell; ***D:*** Lawrence Huntington. *NO*

Vultures 🦴 **1984** A dying patriarch summons his predatory family to his home in order to straighten out the distribution of inheritance. One by one, they fall victim to a mysterious murderer. **101m/C VHS, Beta.** Yvonne De Carlo, Stuart Whitman, Jim Bailey, Meredith MacRae, Aldo Ray; ***D:*** Paul Leder. *PSM*

W 🦴½ *I Want Her Dead* **1974 (PG)** A woman and her husband are terrorized and must find out why. A single letter "W" is found at the scene of the crimes. Notable only as model Twiggy's first film. **95m/C VHS, Beta.** Twiggy, Dirk Benedict, John Vernon, Eugene Roche; ***D:*** Richard Quine. *LIV, VES*

Wackiest Ship in the Army 🦴🦴½ **1961** A completely undisciplined warship crew must smuggle an Australian spy through Japanese waters during WWII. Odd, enjoyable mixture of action and laughs. Became a TV series. In the middle of the war effort, Nelson straps on a guitar and sings "Do You Know What It Means to Miss New Orleans." **99m/C VHS, Beta, LV.** Jack Lemmon, Ricky Nelson, Chips Rafferty, John Lund, Mike Kellin, Patricia Driscoll; ***D:*** Richard Murphy. *COL*

Wackiest Wagon Train in the West 🦴 **1977 (G)** Hapless wagon master is saddled with a dummy assistant as they guide a party of five characters across the West. Based on the minor TV sitcom "Dusty's Trail." Produced by the same folks who delivered the similarly premised TV series "Gilligan's Island" and "The Brady Bunch." **86m/C VHS, Beta.** Bob Denver, Forrest Tucker, Jeannine Riley. *MED*

Wacko *Woof!* **1983 (PG)** Group of nymphettes and tough guys get caught up in a wild Halloween-pumpkin-lawnmower murder. This spoof of the "Halloween" series works too hard for as few laughs as it gets. **84m/C VHS, Beta, LV.** Stella Stevens, George Kennedy, Joe Don Baker, Andrew Dice Clay; ***D:*** Greydon Clark. *VES*

The Wacky World of Wills & Burke 🦴🦴 **1985** Comedy based on the adventures of Wills and Burke, the two 19th-century explorers who led the first unsuccessful expedition across the outback—the Lewis and Clark of Australia, if you will. In real life they died during the adventure, a less than wacky finale. "Burke and Wills," out the same year, was a serious treatment of the same story. **102m/C VHS, Beta.** *AU* Garry McDonald, Kim Gyngell, Peter Collingwood, Jonathon Hardy, Mark Little; ***D:*** Bob Weis. *NO*

Wager of Love 🦴🦴 **1990** While vacationing on their annual pleasure cruise, four women bet on their individual power of seduction. They find themselves competing for passion as each woman's erotic adventure unravels in this exciting and sensual tale. **75m/C VHS.** Steve Landers, Shelly Johnson, Elliot Silverman, Lisa Cook; ***D:*** Jason Holt. *CEL*

Wages of Fear 🦴🦴🦴🦴 *Le Salaire De La Peur* **1955** American oil company controls a desolate Central American town whose citizens desperately want out—so desperately that four are willing to try a suicide mission to deliver nitroglycerine to put out a well-fire raging 300 miles away. The company's cynical head has offered $2,000 to each man, enough to finance escape from the hell-hole they live in. Complex, multi-dimensional drama concentrates on character development for the first half—crucial to the film's greatness. This is the restored version. Remade by William Friedkin as "Sorcerer" in 1977. Based on a novel by Georges Arnaud. In French with English subtitles. **138m/B VHS, Beta, LV.** *FR* Yves Montand, Charles Vanel, Peter Van Eyck, Vera Clouzot, Folco Lulli, William Tubbs; ***D:*** Henri-Georges Clouzot; ***W:*** Henri-Georges Clouzot; ***M:*** Georges Auric. British Academy Awards '54: Best Film; Cannes Film Festival '53: Best Actor (Vanel), Best Film. *HHT, SNC, VYY*

Wagner: The Complete Epic 🦴🦴 **1985** The unedited version of the epic made-for-television miniseries dramatizing the life of German composer Richard Wagner. The excellent photography does justice to the elaborate production, shot on some 200 different locations. The actors cringe in the presence of the subject's grandeur; Burton, a shell of his former cinematic self, is painful to watch in his last released film. Frankly, this is way too long. **540m/C VHS, Beta.** *GB HU* Richard Burton, Vanessa Redgrave, Ralph Richardson, John Gielgud, Laurence Olivier; ***D:*** Tony Palmer. *MVD, KUL*

Wagner: The Movie 🦴½ **1985** Slightly half it's original length, the world's biggest biopic is still huge, sweeping, and long. Incoherent and overacted. Wagner's music is conducted by Sir Georg Solti. Made for television. **300m/C VHS, Beta.** *GB HU* Richard Burton, Vanessa Redgrave, John Gielgud, Franco Nero, Laurence Olivier; ***D:*** Tony Palmer. *MVD, SUE, GLV*

Wagon Master 🦴🦴🦴 **1950** Two cowboys are persuaded to guide a group of Mormons, led by Bond, in their trek across the western frontier. They run into a variety of troubles, including a band of killers who joins the wagon train to escape a posse. Sensitively directed, realistic and worthwhile. Inspired the TV series "Wagon Train." Also available colorized. **85m/B VHS, Beta, LV.** Ben Johnson, Joanne Dru, Harry Carey Jr., Ward Bond, Jane Darwell, James Arness; ***D:*** John Ford. *MED, TTC*

Wagon Tracks 🦴🦴½ **1919** Hart searches for the man responsible for his brother's death. **64m/B VHS.** William S. Hart, Jane Novak, Robert McKim, Lloyd Bacon; ***D:*** Lambert Hillyer. *GPV*

Wagon Trail 🦴🦴½ **1935** The sheriff's son is blackmailed into helping a gang of robbers, with terrible consequences for himself and his father (Carey), who is fired from his job after the son breaks jail. The new sheriff is secretly chief of the outlaw band. Carey rides back into town and eventually virtue triumphs. Good, tense—but not too tense—western. **59m/B VHS, Beta.** Harry Carey Sr.; ***D:*** Harry Fraser. *VCN*

Wagon Wheels 🦴🦴 *Caravans West* **1934** Recycling was in vogue in '34, when unused footage from "Fighting Caravans" (1931) with Gary Cooper was used to remake the very same plot. The result is biodegradable. Settlers heading to Oregon are ambushed by bad guy Blue, employed by fur traders. Blue sics Injuns on them too, but don't worry, they make it. Adapted from Zane Grey's novel "Fighting Caravans." **54m/B VHS, Beta.** Randolph Scott, Monte Blue, Gail Patrick, Billy Lee; ***D:*** Charles T. Barton. *NOS, DVT*

Wagons East 🦴 **1994 (PG-13)** Fed up with prairie hardships, pioneers decide to hitch up to a wagon train and head east. Candy (who died during filming) plays the drunken former wagonmaster hired to get them back home, with Lewis (out of his depth) as a neurotic ex-doctor, and McGinley stuck in the role of a gay bookseller that reeks of stereotypical mannerisms. Script is desperate for humor, which it never finds, and it's hard to watch Candy's performance knowing this mess was his last role. **100m/C VHS, LV.** John Candy, Richard Lewis, Ellen Greene, John C. McGinley, Robert Picardo, William Sanderson, Thomas F. Duffy, Russell Means, Rodney Grant, Michael Horse, Gailard Sartain, Lochlyn Munro, Stuart Proud Eagle Grant; ***D:*** Peter Markle; ***W:*** Matthew Carlson, Jerry Abrahamson. *LIV*

Wagon's Westward 🦴½ **1940** Good government agent Morris assumes identity of bad twin brother, who's in jail, in order to catch some outlaws. **53m/B VHS.** Chester Morris, Buck Jones, Guinn "Big Boy" Williams, Douglas Fowley, George "Gabby" Hayes, Anita Louise, Ona Munson; ***D:*** Lew (Louis Friedlander) Landers. *GPV*

Waikiki 🦴½ **1980** Two private eyes set out to prove that their friend is not the "cane field murderer" who is terrorizing the Hawaiian island of Oahu. Harmless but pointless TV pilot. **96m/C VHS, Beta.** Dack Rambo, Steve Marachuk, Donna Mills, Cal Bellini, Darren McGavin; ***D:*** Ron Satlof. *ORI*

Waikiki Wedding 🦴🦴🦴 **1937** Enjoyable musical about a scheming pineapple promoter (Crosby) who meets the woman of his dreams in a contest he concocted. Contest winner Ross dislikes Hawaii and wants to go home and Crosby must keep her from going...first for business reasons and later, for love. Supporting cast includes Hawaiian Prince Leilani and a pig. Lots of song and dance and Hawaiian sunsets, along with Burns and Raye, the other couple destined for love on the islands, keep the story moving. ♫Sweet Leilani; Sweet Is the Word for You; In a Little Hula Heaven; Blue Hawaii; Okolehao; Nani Ona Pua. **89m/B VHS.** Bing Crosby, Bob Burns, Martha Raye, Shirley Ross, George Barbier, Leif Erickson, Grady Sutton, Granville Bates, Anthony Quinn; ***D:*** Frank Tuttle; ***W:*** Frank Butler, Don Hartman, Walter DeLeon, Francis Martin; ***C:*** Karl Struss; ***M:*** Leo Robin, Ralph Rainger. Academy Awards '37: Best Song ("Sweet Leilani"). *MCA*

Wait Till Your Mother Gets Home 🦴🦴 **1983** "Mr. Mom"-like zaniness abounds as a football coach cares for the kids and does chores while his wife takes her first job in 15 years. Almost too darn cute, but well written. Made for television. **97m/C VHS, Beta.** Paul Michael Glaser, Dee Wallace Stone, Peggy McKay, David Doyle, Raymond Buktenica, James Gregory, Joey Lawrence, Lynne Moody; ***D:*** Bill Persky. *PSM*

Wait Until Dark 🦴🦴🦴 **1967** A photographer unwittingly smuggles a drug-filled doll into New York, and his blind wife, alone in their apartment, is terrorized by murderous crooks in search of it. A compelling thriller based on the Broadway hit by Frederick Knott, who also wrote "Dial M for Murder." The individual actors' performances were universally acclaimed in this spinetingler. **105m/C VHS, Beta, LV.** Audrey Hepburn, Alan Arkin, Richard Crenna, Efrem Zimbalist Jr., Jack Weston; ***D:*** Terence Young; ***W:*** Robert B. Carrington; ***C:*** Charles B(ryant) Lang; ***M:*** Henry Mancini. Nominations: Academy Awards '67: Best Actress (Hepburn). *WAR*

Wait Until Spring, Bandini 🦴🦴½ **1990 (PG-13)** A flavorful immigrant tale about a transplanted Italian family weathering the winter in 1925 Colorado, as seen through the eyes of a young son.

Alternately funny and moving, with one of Dunaway's scenery-chewing performances as a local temptation for the father. Based on the autobiographical novel by John Fante, co-produced by Francis Ford Coppola. **104m/C VHS.** Joe Mantegna, Faye Dunaway, Burt Young, Ornella Muti, Alex Vincent, Renata Vanni, Michael Bacall, Daniel Wilson; ***D:*** Dominique Deruddere; ***M:*** Angelo Badalamenti. *WAR*

Waiting for the Light ☠☠½ **1990 (PG)** When a woman takes over a small-town diner, she gets the surprise of her life. Seems an angel has made his home there and now the townsfolk are flocking to see him. MacLaine is wonderful and Garr is fetching and likeable. Set during the Cuban missile crisis. Enjoyable, tame comedy. **94m/C VHS, LV, 8mm.** Shirley MacLaine, Teri Garr, Vincent Schiavelli, John Bedford Lloyd; ***D:*** Christopher Monger; ***W:*** Christopher Monger. *COL*

Waiting for the Moon ☠½ **1987 (PG)** Hunt as Alice B. Toklas is a relative treat in this ponderous, frustrating biopic about Toklas and Gertrude Stein, her lover. Made for "American Playhouse" on PBS. **88m/C VHS, Beta.** Linda Hunt, Linda Bassett, Andrew McCarthy; ***D:*** Jill Godmilow. Sundance Film Festival '87: Grand Jury Prize. *FOX*

Waiting to Exhale ☠☠☠ **1995 (R)** Adaptation of Terry McMillan's novel about four African-American women hoping to reach the point in their love lives when they can relax and stop waiting for the right man. After the string of dogs and users they choose, you want to tell them not to hold their breath. The women are supposed to be close friends, but all of their stories are broken up into vignettes. This erodes the ensemble feeling of the movie, but performances are strong all around. Retaining the book's feel of just-between-friends girl talk, it may be a little harsh for those who are, shall we say, estrogen-challenged. A lush R&B soundtrack is the perfect backdrop for the ladies' soulful yearning for real love. **120m/C VHS.** Whitney Houston, Angela Bassett, Loretta Devine, Lela Rochon, Gregory Hines, Dennis Haysbert, Mykelti Williamson, Michael Beach, Leon, Wendell Pierce, Donald A. Faison, Jeffrey D. Sams, Toyomichi Kurita; ***Cameos:*** Wesley Snipes; ***D:*** Forest Whitaker; ***W:*** Ronald Bass; ***M:*** Babyface. MTV Movie Awards '96: Best Song ("Sittin' Up in My Room"); Nominations: MTV Movie Awards '96: Breakthrough Performance (Rochon), Best Song ("Exhale (Shoop Shoop)"). *TCF*

Waitress *Woof! Soup to Nuts* **1981 (R)** Three beautiful girls are waitresses in a crazy restaurant where the chef gets drunk, the kitchen explodes, and the customers riot. Awful premise, worse production. **85m/C VHS, Beta.** Jim Harris, Carol Drake, Carol Bever; ***D:*** Lloyd (Samuel Weil) Kaufman. *NO*

Wake Island ☠☠☠ **1942** After Pearl Harbor, a small group of Marines face the onslaught of the Japanese fleet on a small Pacific Island. Although doomed, they hold their ground for 16 days. Exciting, realistic, and moving. The first film to capitalize on early "last stands" of WWII; also among the most popular war movies. Shown to soldiers in training camps with great morale-raising success. **88m/B VHS, Beta.** Robert Preston, Brian Donlevy, William Bendix, MacDonald Carey, Albert Dekker, Walter Abel, Rod Cameron, Barbara Britton; ***D:*** John Farrow. New York Film Critics Awards '42: Best Director (Farrow); Nominations: Academy Awards '42: Best Director (Farrow), Best Original Screenplay, Best Picture, Best Supporting Actor (Bendix). *MCA, TLF*

Wake of the Red Witch ☠☠½ **1949** Wayne captains the ship of the title and battles shipping tycoon Adler for a fortune in pearls and the love of a beautiful woman (Russell). Wayne shows impressive range in a non-gun-totin' role. **106m/B VHS, Beta.** John Wayne, Gail Russell, Gig Young, Luther Adler, Henry Daniell; ***D:*** Edward Ludwig. *REP*

Walk, Don't Run ☠☠½ **1966** Romantic comedy involving a British businessman (Grant) unable to find a hotel room in Tokyo due to the crowds staying for the 1964 summer Olympic Games. He winds up renting a room from an Embassy secretary (Eggar) and then meets and invites Hutton, a member of the U.S. Olympic walking team, also without a place to stay, to share it with him. Grant then proceeds to play matchmaker, despite the fact that Eggar has a fiance. Grant's last film. Innocuous, unnecessary remake of "The More the Merrier." **114m/C VHS, Beta.** Cary Grant, Samantha Eggar, Jim Hutton, John Standing, Miiko Taka; ***D:*** Charles Walters; ***M:*** Quincy Jones. *COL*

A Walk in the Clouds ☠☠½ **1995 (PG-13)** Gorgeously photographed, if sappy, romantic fantasy finds WWII vet Paul Sutton (Reeves), returning to his unhappy marriage and salesman job. So when the good-hearted Paul meets beautiful Victoria (Sanchez-Gijon), the pregnant and unmarried daughter of a possessive Napa vineyard owner (Giannini), he's more than happy to help by posing as her husband. Naturally, dad is livid at their "marriage" and Paul falls in love with his sham bride. Quinn gets to do his part as wise family patriarch and yes, there's even a grape harvest (and some grape stomping) to put everyone in the proper romantic mood. Based on the 1942 Italian film "Four Steps in the Clouds." **103m/C VHS.** Keanu Reeves, Aitana Sanchez-Gijon, Giancarlo Giannini, Anthony Quinn, Angelica Aragon, Evangelina Elizondo, Freddy Rodriguez, Debra Messing; ***D:*** Alfonso Arau; ***W:*** Robert Mark Kamen; ***C:*** Emmanuel Lubezki; ***M:*** Leo Brower. Golden Globe Awards '96: Best Score; Nominations: MTV Movie Awards '96: Most Desirable Male (Reeves), Best Kiss (Keanu Reeves/Aitana Sanchez-Gijon). *FXV*

Walk in the Spring Rain ☠☠½ **1970 (PG)** The bored wife of a college professor follows him to rural Tennessee when he goes on sabbatical, where she meets the married Quinn and the two begin an affair. When Quinn's disturbed son learns of the affair, he attacks the woman, with tragic results. Fine cast should have had better effect on low-key script. **98m/C VHS, Beta.** Ingrid Bergman, Anthony Quinn, Fritz Weaver, Katherine Crawford, Tom Fielding, Virginia Gregg; ***D:*** Guy Green; ***W:*** Stirling Silliphant; ***C:*** Charles B(ryant) Lang; ***M:*** Elmer Bernstein. *NO*

A Walk in the Sun ☠☠☠½ *Salerno Beachhead* **1946** The trials of a group of infantrymen in WWII from the time they land in Italy to the time they capture their objective, a farmhouse occupied by the Germans. Excellent ensemble acting shows well the variety of civilians who make up any fighting force and explores their fears, motivations, and weaknesses. Producer and director Milestone also made "All Quiet on the Western Front" and the Korean War masterpiece "Pork Chop Hill." Released in the final days of the war, almost concurrently with two other WWII films of the first echelon, "The Story of G.I. Joe" and "They Were Expendable." **117m/B VHS, Beta, LV, 8mm.** Dana Andrews, Richard Conte, John Ireland, Lloyd Bridges, Sterling Holloway; ***D:*** Lewis Milestone; ***W:*** Robert Rossen. *LUM, NOS, DVT*

Walk into Hell ☠☠ **1957** A mining engineer and his assistant searching for oil meet the primitive natives of New Guinea. Tedious at times and dated, but pleasant enough. **91m/C VHS, Beta.** *AU* Chips Rafferty, Francoise Christophe, Reg Lye; ***D:*** Lee Robinson. *VYY, NLC*

Walk Like a Man ☠½ **1987 (PG)** In a take-off of Tarzan movies, Mandel plays a man raised by wolves. Comic problems arise when he is found by his mother and the family attempts to civilize him. Juvenile script wastes fine cast. **86m/C VHS, Beta.** Howie Mandel, Christopher Lloyd, Cloris Leachman, Colleen Camp, Amy Steel, George DiCenzo; ***D:*** Melvin Frank. *MGM*

Walk on the Wild Side ☠☠ **1962** In 1930s New Orleans, a man searches for his long-lost love, finds her working in a whorehouse and fights to save her from the lesbian madame Stanwyck. Melodrama, based only loosely on the Nelson Algren novel and adapted by cult novelist John Fante, with Edmund Morris. Much-troubled on the set, and it shows. **114m/B VHS, Beta.** Jane Fonda, Laurence Harvey, Barbara Stanwyck, Capucine, Anne Baxter; ***D:*** Edward Dmytryk; ***M:*** Elmer Bernstein. Nominations: Academy Awards '62: Best Song ("Walk on the Wild Side"). *COL*

Walk Softly, Stranger ☠☠ **1950** Two-bit crook is reformed by the love of an innocent peasant girl. If you can stand the cliche masquerading as a plot, the performances are good. **81m/B VHS, Beta.** Alida Valli, Joseph Cotten, Spring Byington, Paul Stewart, Jack Paar, Jeff Donnell, John McIntire; ***D:*** Robert Stevenson. *TTC*

Walker ☠☠ **1987 (R)** Slapdash, tongue-in-cheek historical pastiche about the real-life American William Walker (played previously in "Burn!" by Marlon Brando), and how he led a revolution in Nicaragua in 1855 and became its self-declared president. A bitter, revisionist farce never for a moment attempting to be accurate. Matlin's unfortunate, though fortunately brief, follow-up to her Oscar-winning performance. **95m/C VHS, Beta.** Ed Harris, Richard Masur, Peter Boyle, Rene Auberjonois, Marlee Matlin, Miguel Sandoval; ***D:*** Alex Cox; ***W:*** Rudy Wurlitzer; ***M:*** Joe Strummer. *MCA*

Walker: Texas Ranger: Deadly Reunion ☠☠½ **1994** Feature-length version of the TV series finds Walker (Norris) trying to protect a senator, with presidential leanings and big enemies, who's been targeted by a killer posing as a cop. In addition to the usual good guys, Walker is assisted by veteran ex-Ranger Laredo (Whitman), who has his own reasons for going after the bad guy. **92m/C VHS.** Chuck Norris, Clarence Gilyard Jr., Sheree J. Wilson, Noble Willingham, Stuart Whitman, Jonathan Banks. *WAR*

Walker: Texas Ranger: One Riot, One Ranger ☠☠½ **1993 (PG-13)** Norris sticks with the action-adventure mode with this tv pilot movie about Cordell Walker, a good guy with a code and some martial arts skills, who teams up with an ex-gridiron star and a female district attorney to go after lawbreakers. This time its bank robbers and three hoods after a teenaged girl. **96m/C VHS, LV.** Chuck Norris, Sheree J. Wilson, Clarence Gilyard Jr., Gailard Sartain, Floyd "Red Crow" Westerman, James Drury; ***D:*** Virgil W. Vogel; ***W:*** Louise McCarn. *CAN, MOV*

Walking Back ☠☠ **1926** Troubled teens go for joyride and bash mirthmobile to smithereens. The body shop agrees to give them a different car, but they find themselves in the middle of a heist at a plant belonging to the father of one of the boys. **53m/B VHS, Beta.** Sue Carol, Richard Walling, Ivan Lebedeff, Robert Edeson, Florence Turner, Arthur Rankin; ***D:*** Rupert Julian. *GPV, FCT*

The Walking Dead ☠☠ **1994 (R)** Depicts the Vietnam War from the perspectives of four black and one white Marine assigned to rescue POWs from a North Vietnam camp in 1972. Fairly routine story with stock characters (by-the-book sergeant, family man, naive youngster, cynical hustler) and flashbacks to depict their back home struggles. Cast tries but is defeated by a one-dimensional script. **89m/C VHS.** Joe Morton, Eddie Griffin, Allen Payne, Vonte Sweet, Roger Floyd; ***D:*** Preston A. Whitmore II; ***W:*** Preston A. Whitmore II; ***C:*** John L. Demps Jr.; ***M:*** Gary Chang. *HBO*

Walking on Air **1987** Ray Bradbury's story comes to life as a handicapped boy dreams of completing a real space walk. Originally aired on PBS as part of the "Wonderworks" series. **60m/C VHS.** Lynn Redgrave, Jordan Marder, James Treuer, Katheryn Trainor; ***D:*** Ed Kaplan. *PME, FCT, BTV*

Walking Tall ☠☠½ **1973 (R)** A Tennessee sheriff takes a stand against syndicate-run gambling and his wife is murdered in response. Ultra-violent crime saga wowed the movie going public and spawned several sequels and a TV series. Based on the true story of folk-hero Buford Pusser, admirably rendered by Baker. **126m/C VHS, Beta, LV.** Joe Don Baker, Elizabeth Hartman, Noah Beery Jr., Gene Evans, Rosemary Murphy, Felton Perry; ***D:*** Phil Karlson; ***W:*** Mort Briskin. *LIV*

Walking Tall: Part 2 ☠☠ **1975 (PG)** Club-wielding Tennessee sheriff Buford Pusser, this time played less memorably by Svenson, attempts to find the man who killed his wife. Even more violent than the original. **109m/C VHS, Beta, LV.** Bo Svenson, Noah Beery Jr., Angel Tompkins, Richard Jaeckel; ***D:*** Earl Bellamy. *LIV, VES*

Walking Tall: The Final Chapter 🦴½ **1977 (PG)** The final months in the life of Tennessee sheriff Buford Pusser and the mystery surrounding his death. It wasn't the final chapter. Still to come: a TV flick and series. **112m/C VHS, Beta, LV.** Bo Svenson, Forrest Tucker, Leif Garrett, Morgan Woodward; ***D:*** Jack Starrett; ***C:*** Robert B. Hauser. *LIV*

Walking the Edge 🦴½ **1983 (R)** A widow hires a taxi driver to help her seek vengeance against the men who killed her husband and her son. Forster does what he can with the lousy story and script. **94m/C VHS, Beta.** Robert Forster, Nancy Kwan, Joe Spinell, Aarika Wells; ***D:*** Norbert Meisel; ***W:*** Curt Allen. *LIV*

Walking Through the Fire 🦴🦴½ **1980** A young woman's real-life struggle with Hodgkin's disease. Her fight for her own and her unborn baby's survival is a stirring testament to the power of faith. Absorbing made-for-television drama. **143m/C VHS, Beta.** Bess Armstrong, Tom Mason, Bonnie Bedelia, Richard Masur, Swoosie Kurtz, J.D. Cannon, June Lockhart; ***D:*** Robert Day. *TLF*

The Wall 🦴🦴🦴½ *Guney's The Wall; Le Mur; Duvar* **1983** The last film by Guney, author of "Yol," about orphaned boys in prison in the Turkish capitol of Ankara trying to escape and/or rebel after ceaseless rapings, beatings and injustice. An acclaimed, disturbing film made from Guney's own experience. He died in 1984, three years after escaping from prison. Brutal and horrifying. In Turkish with English subtitles. **117m/C VHS, Beta.** *TU* Ayse Emel Mesci, Saban, Sisko; ***D:*** Yilmaz Guney; ***W:*** Yilmaz Guney. Nominations: Cannes Film Festival '83: Best Film. *INJ*

Wall Street 🦴🦴🦴 **1987 (R)** Stone's energetic, high-minded big business treatise in which naive, neophyte stockbroker Sheen is seduced into insider trading by sleek entrepreneur Douglas, much to his blue-collar father's chagrin. A fast-moving drama of 80's-style materialism with a mesmerizing, award-winning performance by Douglas as greed personified. Expert direction by Stone, who co-wrote the not-very-subtle script. His father, to whom this film is dedicated, was a broker. Look for Stone in a cameo. **126m/C VHS, Beta, LV.** Michael Douglas, Charlie Sheen, Martin Sheen, Daryl Hannah, Sean Young, James Spader, Hal Holbrook, Terence Stamp, Richard Dysart, John C. McGinley, Saul Rubinek, James Karen, Josh Mostel, Millie Perkins, Cecilia Peck, Grant Shaud, Franklin Cover; ***Cameos:*** Oliver Stone; ***D:*** Oliver Stone; ***W:*** Oliver Stone, Stanley Weiser; ***C:*** Robert Richardson; ***M:*** Stewart Copeland. Academy Awards '87: Best Actor (Douglas); Golden Globe Awards '88: Best Actor—Drama (Douglas); National Board of Review Awards '87: Best Actor (Douglas); Golden Raspberry Awards '87: Worst Supporting Actress (Hannah). *FOX, BTV*

Wall Street Cowboy 🦴 **1939** When his land is threatened, a cowboy fights big business in the big city. **54m/B VHS, Beta.** Roy Rogers. *NOS, DVT, TIM*

Wallaby Jim of the Islands 🦴🦴 **1937** The singing captain of a pearl fishing boat must protect his treasure from marauding pirates. Pleasant enough musical adventure. **61m/B VHS.** George Houston, Douglas Walton; ***D:*** Charles Lamont. *NOS, DVT, HEG*

The Walloping Kid 🦴½ **1926** A B-western with photography done in Monument Valley. Silent with original organ music. **67m/B VHS, Beta, 8mm.** Kit Carson, Pauline Curley; ***D:*** Robert J. Horner. *VYY*

Walls of Glass 🦴🦴½ **1985 (R)** An aging New York cabby tries to make it as an actor. Effective performances by all override the thin plot. Slow and uneven, but involving. Also called "Flanagan." **85m/C VHS, Beta.** Geraldine Page, Philip Bosco, William Hickey, Olympia Dukakis, Brian Bloom, Linda Thorson; ***D:*** Scott Goldstein. *MED*

The Walls of Malapaga 🦴🦴 *Au-Dela des Grilles; Le Mura di Malapaga* **1949** Frenchman Gabin, who's killed his mistress, stows away aboard a ship to Italy. He arrives in Genoa only to have all his money and papers stolen. Gabin then meets Miranda, a lonely waitress with a young daughter, and the two fall in love. But it's only temporary as the authorities come closing in. French with subtitles. **91m/C VHS.** *FR IT* Jean Gabin, Isa Miranda, Vera Talchi, Andrea Checchi, Robert Dalban; ***D:*** Rene Clement; ***W:*** Jean Aurenche, Pierre Bost; ***M:*** Roman Vlad. *FCT*

Walpurgis Night 🦴🦴🦴 *Valborgmassoafton* **1941** Soapy Swedish drama about abortion was racy for its time. Office gal Bergman secretly loves her boss (Hanson). His wife refuses to have children and goes through an abortion. An unscrupulous fellow blackmails her with this knowledge. Bergman bides her time. Stay tuned... Interesting document on the mores of another time. In Swedish with English subtitles. **82m/B VHS, Beta.** *SW* Lars Hanson, Karin Carlsson, Victor Sjostrom, Ingrid Bergman, Erik Berglund, Sture Lagerwall, Georg Rydeberg, Georg Blickingberg; ***D:*** Gustaf Edgren. *WAC, INJ*

The Waltons: A Thanksgiving Story **1973** As the Walton family anticipates the Thanksgiving holiday, John-Boy prepares for college entrance exams and Jenny Pendleton's visit. John-Boy suffers a head injury and is faced with a risky operation that may either help him or leave him permanently disabled. A holiday special from the television series. **100m/C VHS.** Richard Thomas, Ralph Waite, Michael Learned, Will Geer, Ellen Corby, Judy Norton-Taylor, Kami Cotler, Jon Walmsley, Mary McDonough, Eric Scott, David W. Harper; ***D:*** Philip Leacock. *IGP*

The Waltons: The Christmas Carol 🦴🦴 **1980** The winter solstice brings no special joy to Walton's mountain; WWII has taken many men, with short wave reports indicating the Nazi terror spreading across Europe. But huddled in the glow of Walton's barn, the children rediscover the true meaning of Christmas. **94m/C VHS, Beta.** Judy Norton-Taylor, Jon Walmsley, Mary McDonough, Eric Scott, Kami Cotler, Joe Conley, Ronnie Clare, Leslie Winston, Peggy Rea; ***D:*** Lawrence Dobkin. *ORI*

Waltz Across Texas 🦴🦴½ **1983** Young oil man Jastrow and good-lookin' rock scientist Archer at first don't take to each other, but there's something in the air, and romance blossoms. Jastrow and Archer cowrote and coproduced, and cohabitated as spouses in real-life. **100m/C VHS, Beta.** Terry Jastrow, Anne Archer, Mary Kay Place, Richard Farnsworth; ***D:*** Ernest Day; ***M:*** Stephen Dorff. *VES*

Waltz King 🦴🦴 **1963** Typically hokey Disney biography of the young composer Johann Strauss during his Old Viennese heyday. Fine music, pretty German locations. Well-made family fare. **94m/C VHS, Beta.** Kerwin Mathews, Senta Berger, Brian Aherne; ***D:*** Steve Previn. *DIS*

Waltz of the Toreadors 🦴🦴🦴 *The Amorous General* **1962** Retired general Sellers doesn't care for his wealthy, shrewish wife and tries to re-kindle a 17-year-old romance with a French woman. It doesn't work out (seems his illegitimate son also has a soft spot for the lady), but the general decides to keep his eyes open for other possibilities. Interestingly cast adaptation of Jean Anouilh's play. Sellers is hilarious, as usual. **105m/C VHS, Beta.** *GB* Peter Sellers, Dany Robin, Margaret Leighton, Cyril Cusack; ***D:*** John Guillermin. *NO*

A Waltz Through the Hills **1988** Two orphans head into the Australian outback and experience many adventures en route to the coast where they can set sail for England and their grandparents. Aired on PBS as part of the "Wonderworks" series. **116m/C VHS.** Tina Kemp, Andre Jansen, Ernie Dingo, Dan O'Herlihy; ***D:*** Frank Arnold. *PME, HMV, FCT*

Wanda Nevada 🦴½ **1979 (PG)** Gambler Fonda wins nubile young Shields in a poker game, so he drags her with him to the Grand Canyon to look for gold. Director/star Fonda sure picked a lemon for his only screen appearance with dad Henry (a grizzled old varmint appearing briefly). Shields is in her usual form—stellar for a shampoo commercial. **105m/C VHS, Beta.** Peter Fonda, Brooke Shields, Henry Fonda, Fiona Lewis, Luke Askew, Ted Markland, Severn Darden, Paul Fix; ***D:*** Peter Fonda. *NO*

Wanda, The Sadistic Hypnotist 🦴 **1967** A comely vixen hypnotizes an innocent pedestrian, ties him up and whips him to indulge her whims. Despite the "victim's" protests, she unleashes a gang of sexually playful women on him, and he is subjected to a multitude of "tortures." **70m/C VHS.** Katharine Shubeck, Janice Sweet, Dick Dangerfield, Daryl Cobinot; ***D:*** Gregory Corarito. *SMW, TPV*

The Wanderer 🦴🦴 *Le Grand Meaulnes* **1967** Two friends fall in love—Frantz with Valentine and his friend Augustin with Frantz's sister, Yvonne. When the two women disappear on Frantz's wedding day, the two men begin a search to find both the women and the reasons for their disappearance. In French with English subtitles. **108m/C VHS.** *FR* Brigitte Fossey, Jean Blaise, Alain Noury, Juliette Villard; ***D:*** Jean-Gabriel Albicocco. *INJ, CVC*

Wanderers 🦴🦴🦴½ **1979 (R)** Richard Price's acclaimed novel about youth gangs coming of age in the Bronx in 1963. The "Wanderers," named after the Dion song, are a gang of Italian-American teenagers about to graduate high school, who prowl the Bronx with the feeling that something is slipping away from them. Fascinating, funny and touching. Manz is unforgettable as a scrappy gal. A wonderful 60s soundtrack (Dion, the Four Seasons) colors this "coming of age the hard way" film. **113m/C VHS, Beta.** Ken Wahl, John Friedrich, Karen Allen, Linda Manz; ***Cameos:*** Richard Price; ***D:*** Philip Kaufman; ***W:*** Philip Kaufman; ***C:*** Michael Chapman. *WAR*

Wandering Jew 🦴🦴½ **1920** An excellent print of the rare Austrian film version of the classic legend, one of at least three silent versions. A Jew is condemned to wander the earth for eternity. **65m/B VHS, Beta.** *AT* Rudolf Schildkraut, Joseph Schildkraut. *GVV*

The Wannsee Conference 🦴🦴🦴½ *Wannseekonferenz* **1984** A startling, important film depicting, in real time, the conference held at the Wannsee on January 20, 1942, during which 14 members of the Nazi hierarchy decided in 85 minutes the means and logistics of effecting the Final Solution. Recreated from the original secretary's notes. Horrifying and chilling. Along with "Shoah," a must-see for understanding the Holocaust and the psychology of genocide. In German with English subtitles. **87m/C VHS, Beta, LV.** *GE* Dietrich Mattausch, Gerd Brockmann, Friedrich Beckhaus; ***D:*** Heinz Schirk. *HMV, APD, GLV*

Wanted: Babysitter *Woof!* **1975** A young student accidentally becomes involved by her roommate in a plot to kidnap the child she is babysitting. Schneider is truly awful; Italian comic Pazzetto is at sea in a bad role as her boyfriend. Also released as "The Babysitter." **90m/C VHS, Beta.** Robert Vaughn, Vic Morrow, Maria Schneider, Renato Pozzetto, Nadja Tiller, Carl Mohner, Sydne Rome; ***D:*** Rene Clement. *AHV*

Wanted: Dead or Alive **1959** This western series, which ran from 1958-1961, launched the career of McQueen who starred as bounty hunter Josh Randall. In this episode, "Reunion for Revenge," Randall must protect the man in his custody from escaped criminals with vengeance on their mind. Also available colorized. Additional episodes available. **22m/B VHS, Beta.** Steve McQueen, Wright King, Jane Burns, James Coburn, Cloris Leachman, John Baer, Ralph Meeker; ***D:*** Thomas Carr, Richard Donner. *MOV*

Wanted Dead or Alive 🦴½ **1986 (R)** Ex-CIA agent Hauer is now a high-tech bounty hunter assigned to bring in an international terrorist. When the terrorist kills Hauer's friend and girlfriend, he forgets the $50,000 bonus for bringing him in alive. Official "sequel" to the Steve McQueen television series with Hauer as the McQueen character's great-grandson. The link is meaningless, and the plot is a thin excuse for much violence and anti-terrorist flag-waving. **104m/C VHS, Beta, LV.** Rutger Hauer, Gene Simmons, Robert Guillaume, William Russ, Jerry Hardin, Mel Harris; ***D:*** Gary Sherman; ***W:*** Brian Taggert. *NWV, VTR*

Wanted: The Perfect Guy 🦴🦴½ **1990** Danny and Melanie try to find Mister Right for their divorced Mom (Kahn). An Emmy Award winner about single parents and their children. **45m/C VHS.** Madeline Kahn, Melanie Mayron. *AIM*

The War ☠☠½ **1994 (PG-13)** Post-Vietnam war drama, set in 1970 Mississippi, centers on a children's battle over a treehouse but becomes a sermon on love, death, family values, pacifism, and the physical and spiritual wounds of war. After helping son Stu (Wood) and daughter Lidia (Randall) build their treehouse, troubled Vietnam vet Stephen Simmons (Costner) tries to coax Stu to make peace with the bullies trying to take it over. However cliched, director Avnet allows a talented cast of kids to thoughtfully express a child's view of the world but gosh-darn-it the preachy tone can get down-right annoying. **126m/C VHS, LV.** Elijah Wood, Kevin Costner, Lexi Randall, Mare Winningham, Christine Baranski, Bruce A. Young, Gary Basaraba, Raynor Scheine, Nick Searcy; ***D:*** Jon Avnet; ***W:*** Kathy McWorter. *MCA*

War & Love ☠☠ **1984 (PG-13)** Two Jewish teenagers in Warsaw are torn apart by WWII and Nazi persecution. After the war they search for each other. Sincere, but not adequately developed, drama based on the book "The Survivors" by film's producer Jack Eisner. **112m/C VHS, Beta.** Sebastian Keneas, Kyra Sedgwick; ***D:*** Moshe Mizrahi. *MGM, SWC*

War and Peace ☠☠½ **1956** Lengthy adaptation of Tolstoy's great (and likewise lengthy) novel about three families caught up in Russia's Napoleonic Wars from 1805 to 1812; filmed in Rome. Bad casting and confused script (by six writers) are somewhat overcome by awesome battle scenes and Hepburn. Remade in 1968. **208m/C VHS, Beta, LV.** Audrey Hepburn, Mel Ferrer, Henry Fonda, Anita Ekberg, Vittorio Gassman, John Mills, Oscar Homolka, Herbert Lom, Helmut Dantine; ***D:*** King Vidor; ***M:*** Nino Rota. Golden Globe Awards '57: Best Foreign Film; National Board of Review Awards '56: 5 Best Foreign Films of the Year; Nominations: Academy Awards '56: Best Color Cinematography, Best Costume Design (Color), Best Director (Vidor). *PAR*

War and Peace ☠☠☠ **1968** The massive Russian production of Leo Tolstoy's masterpiece, adapting the classic tome practically scene by scene. All of the production took place in the Soviet Union. So painstaking that it took more than five years to finish, no other adaptation can touch it. Hugely expensive ($100 million, claimed the Russians), wildly uneven production. Great scenes of battle and aristocratic life. Though this version is far from perfect, one asks: Is it humanly possible to do screen justice to such a novel? In Russian with English subtitles. On four tapes. (Beware the two-part, poorly dubbed version that was also released.) **373m/C VHS, Beta, LV.** *RU* Lyudmila Savelyeva, Sergei Bondarchuk, Vyacheslav Tihonor, Hira Ivanov-Golarko, Irina Gubanova, Antonina Shuranova; ***D:*** Sergei Bondarchuk. Academy Awards '68: Best Foreign Language Film; Golden Globe Awards '69: Best Foreign Film; National Board of Review Awards '68: 5 Best Foreign Films of the Year; New York Film Critics Awards '68: Best Foreign Film; Nominations: Academy Awards '68: Best Art Direction/Set Decoration. *KUL, INJ, TVC*

War & Remembrance, Part 1 ☠½ **1988** Tedious sequel to the epic television mini-series "The Winds of War," based on the novel by Herman Wouk. Historical fiction is created around the events of WWII, including Nazi persecution and naval battles in the Pacific. Seven cassette series. Followed by "War and Remembrance: The Final Chapter." **120m/C VHS, Beta.** Robert Mitchum, Jane Seymour, Hart Bochner, Victoria Tennant, Barry Bostwick, Polly Bergen, David Dukes, Michael Woods, Sharon Stone, Robert Morley, Sami Frey, Chaim Topol, John Rhys-Davies, Ian McShane, William Schallert, Jeremy Kemp, Steven Berkoff, Robert Hardy, Ralph Bellamy, John Gielgud; ***D:*** Dan Curtis. *MPI, MOV*

War & Remembrance, Part 2 ☠½ **1989** The final installments of the excruciatingly boring and long mini-series. Herman Wouk's historical fiction concerning the last years of WWII. Six cassettes, in Hi-Fi stereo. **120m/C VHS, Beta.** Robert Mitchum, Jane Seymour, Hart Bochner, Ralph Bellamy, Victoria Tennant, Barry Bostwick, John Gielgud, Polly Bergen, David Dukes, Michael Woods; ***D:*** Dan Curtis. *MPI*

War & Remembrance, Part 3 **1988** A brief glimmer of hope appears in this volume involving the lovers' reunion in Hawaii and the military power's changing of hands due to command of the Americans following the infamous Midway battle. **120m/C VHS, Beta.** Robert Mitchum, Jane Seymour, Hart Bochner, Victoria Tennant, Polly Bergen, David Dukes, Michael Woods; ***D:*** Dan Curtis. *MPI*

War & Remembrance, Part 4 **1988** The middle part of 1942 sees its way through the American infilration of Guadacanal, the treacherous stranglehold of Nazi Germany on Europe and other parts of the world, and the defiance toward defeat of the Russian Army. **120m/C VHS, Beta.** Robert Mitchum, Jane Seymour, Hart Bochner, Victoria Tennant, Polly Bergen, David Dukes, Michael Woods; ***D:*** Dan Curtis. *MPI*

War & Remembrance, Part 5 **1988** As 1942 draws to a close, Wouk's well-known character, Pug, finds himself heading for a new assignment. North Africa welcomes the Allies in lieu of the Nazis. Stalingrad is mortified by an ever-strong Nazi invasion. **120m/C VHS, Beta.** Robert Mitchum, Jane Seymour, Hart Bochner, Victoria Tennant, Polly Bergen, David Dukes, Michael Woods; ***D:*** Dan Curtis. *MPI*

War & Remembrance, Part 6 **1988** After leaving his dear cruiser behind, Pug says hello to Russia. The Ally leaders meet with much to discuss. Hitler is getting stronger and shrewder. **120m/C VHS, Beta.** Robert Mitchum, Jane Seymour, Hart Bochner, Victoria Tennant, Polly Bergen, David Dukes, Michael Woods; ***D:*** Dan Curtis. *MPI*

War & Remembrance, Part 7 **1988** The Sicilian win by Patton brings about the devestation of Mussolini. Hitler's henchman are getting nervous and tired of battle. Germany succumbs to Allied troops in North Africa. **120m/C VHS, Beta.** Robert Mitchum, Jane Seymour, Hart Bochner, Victoria Tennant, Polly Bergen, David Dukes, Michael Woods; ***D:*** Dan Curtis. *MPI*

War & Remembrance: The Final Chapter, Part 8 **1989** The final episodes of Herman Wouk's sweeping saga, following "The Winds of War" and "War and Remembrance," deal with the struggle of a Jewish family in war-torn Europe. Natalie and her son, Louis, are trapped in a ghetto under the reign of a vicious Nazi, who considers a bribe for the sake of the mother and son. On 5 cassettes. **120m/C VHS, Beta.** Robert Mitchum, Jane Seymour, Hart Bochner, Victoria Tennant, Polly Bergen, David Dukes, Michael Woods, Sharon Stone, Robert Morley, Sami Frey, Chaim Topol, John Rhys-Davies, Ian McShane, William Schallert, Jeremy Kemp, Steven Berkoff, Robert Hardy, Ralph Bellamy, John Gielgud; ***D:*** Dan Curtis. *MPI, MOV*

War & Remembrance: The Final Chapter, Part 9 **1989** Both D-Day and an assasination of Hitler are in the works. Natalie and Louis are still in a desperate situation with the tyrannical Nazi endangering them constantly. **120m/C VHS, Beta.** Robert Mitchum, Jane Seymour, Hart Bochner, Victoria Tennant, Polly Bergen, David Dukes, Michael Woods; ***D:*** Dan Curtis. *MPI*

War & Remembrance: The Final Chapter, Part 10 **1989** Though Louis becomes gravely ill, Natalie and Aaron are shipped to Auschwitz. Hitler lives in spite of the botched assasination threat, but the allies are closing in rapidly. **120m/C VHS, Beta.** Robert Mitchum, Jane Seymour, Hart Bochner, Victoria Tennant, Polly Bergen, David Dukes, Michael Woods; ***D:*** Dan Curtis. *MPI*

War & Remembrance: The Final Chapter, Part 11 **1989** The infamous Battle of the Bulge takes place. Louis is taken away in the Nazi retreat. Natalie and Aaron continue to defy death in Auschwitz. **120m/C VHS, Beta.** Robert Mitchum, Jane Seymour, Hart Bochner, Victoria Tennant, Polly Bergen, David Dukes, Michael Woods; ***D:*** Dan Curtis. *MPI*

War & Remembrance: The Final Chapter, Part 12 **1989** The climax culminates into the death of both FDR and Hitler, whose suicide shocked and relieved an entire world. The Nazi reign of terror crumbles, and the allies are victorious. But this series ends on the note of displacement and the effort of rebuilding what has so quickly and deftly been destroyed. **120m/C VHS, Beta.** Robert Mitchum, Jane Seymour, Hart Bochner, Victoria Tennant, Polly Bergen, David Dukes, Michael Woods; ***D:*** Dan Curtis. *MPI*

War Arrow ☠☠ **1953** Army Major Howell Brady (Chandler) is sent by Washington to end the Kiowa uprisings in Texas in this cavalry vs. Indians western. Along the way, he tries to win the heart of O'Hara. **79m/C VHS.** Maureen O'Hara, Jeff Chandler, Suzan Ball, John McIntire, Noah Beery Jr., Henry Brandon, Dennis Weaver, Jay Silverheels; ***D:*** George Sherman; ***W:*** John Michael Hayes. *MCA*

War Between the Tates ☠☠ **1976** A college professor's affair with a female student is the basis for a tension filled stand-off with his wife. Mediocre made for television adaptation of the Allison Lurie novel, somewhat redeemed by Ashley's performance. **90m/C VHS, Beta.** Richard Crenna, Elizabeth Ashley, Granville Van Dusen; ***D:*** Lee Philips; ***M:*** John Barry. *TLF*

The War Boy ☠☠½ **1985 (R)** Difficulties encountered by a young Canadian boy as he grows up in Central Europe during WWII. Not to be compared with "Empire of the Sun" or "Hope and Glory," both of which were released later; successful in its modest ambitions. Beautiful performance from 12-year-old star Hopely. **86m/C VHS.** *CA* Helen Shaver, Kenneth Welsh, Jason Hopely; ***D:*** Allan Eastman. *HHE*

War Brides ☠ **198?** Civil War brides confront life after the war. Low-budget drama. **100m/C VHS, Beta.** Elizabeth Richardson, Sharry Fleet, Sonja Smits. *TWE*

War Bus Commando ☠ **1989** A fully loaded bus is the only way out when soldiers are caught behind enemy lines in Afghanistan. A case of the spoof coming first: The plot is almost exactly the same as "Stripes"—only this one isn't funny. In Hi-Fi. **90m/C VHS.** *IT* Savina Gersak, Mark Gregory, John Vernon; ***D:*** Frank Valenti. *NO*

War in Space ☠ **1977** Powerful U.N. Space Bureau Starships and UFOs band together to battle alien invaders among the volcanoes and deserts of Venus. **91m/C VHS, Beta.** *JP* Kensaku Marita, Yuko Asano, Ryo Ikebe. *VDA*

War in the Sky ☠☠☠ **1982** Director William Wyler's documentary account of the Army Air Corps in action. Extraordinary footage of the Thunderbolt, the P47 Fighter, and the B17 Bomber. **90m/C VHS, Beta.** ***D:*** William Wyler. *GEM*

The War Lord ☠☠☠ **1965** Set in the 11th century, Heston stars as Chrysagon, a Norman knight and war lord who commands a peasant village. While battling his enemies, he becomes enamored of a peasant girl named Bronwyn (Forsyth), who is unfortunately engaged to someone else. Pulling rank, Chrysagon uses an ancient law that allows noblemen the first night with a bride and the two fall in love. The two vow to never part, but that sets the stage for even more bloody battles. Fine acting and great production values make this a well-adapted version of the play "The Lovers" by Leslie Stevens. **121m/C VHS, Beta, LV.** Charlton Heston, Richard Boone, Rosemary Forsyth, Guy Stockwell, Niall MacGinnis, Henry Wilcoxon, James Farentino, Maurice Evans, Michael Conrad; ***D:*** Franklin J. Schaffner; ***W:*** John Collier, Millard Kaufman; ***C:*** Russell Metty. *MCA*

War Lover ☠☠½ **1962** An American daredevil flying captain and his co-pilot find themselves vying for the affections of a woman during WWII in England. Seeks human frailty beneath surface heroism. McQueen is impressive, no thanks to mediocre script. Excellent aerial photography, and featuring one of only a very few serviceable WWII B-17s then remaining. Based on John Hersey's novel. **105m/B VHS, Beta, LV.** *GB* Steve McQueen, Robert Wagner, Shirley Anne Field, Bill Edwards, Gary Cockrell; ***D:*** Philip Leacock; ***W:*** Howard Koch. *GKK*

War of the Buttons ☠☠½ **1995 (PG)** Two sleepy Irish fishing villages provide childish battle grounds for two groups of local lads. The Ballys (Ballydowse village), lead by Fergus (Fitzgerald), and the Carricks (Carrickdowse), with leader Geronimo (Coffey), have an intense rivalry and capture by the other gang leads to the removal of every clothing button for the unfortunate captive. When Fergus becomes a Carrick victim, he organizes a retaliatory strike, and emotions threaten to overwhelm all concerned. Based on the French novel "La Guerre des Boutons" by Louis Pergaud. Filmed on location in West Cork, Ireland. **94m/C VHS.** Gregg Fitzgerald, John Coffey, Liam Cunningham, Paul Batt, Eveanna Ryan, Colm Meaney, Johnny Murphy; ***D:*** John Roberts; ***W:*** Colin Welland; ***C:*** Bruno de Keyzer; ***M:*** Rachel Portman. *WAR*

The War of the Colossal Beast &½ *The Terror Strikes* **1958** This sequel to "The Amazing Colossal Man" finds the seventy-foot Colonel Manning even angrier at the attempts to kill him than he was in the first film. So he wreaks more havoc until scolded by his sister into committing suicide for being such a troublemaker. Cheesy special effects but good for a laugh. **68m/B VHS.** Dean Parkin, Sally Fraser, Russ Bender, Roger Pace, Charles Stewart; ***D:*** Bert I. Gordon. *COL*

War of the Gargantuas & *Furankenshutain No Kaijusanda Tai Gailah; Sanda Tai Gailah; Duel of the Gargantuas* **1970 (G)** Tokyo is once again the boxing ring for giant monsters. This time it's a good gargantua (half human, half monster) against a bad gargantua. This is a strange one. **92m/C VHS, LV.** *JP* Russ Tamblyn, Kumi Mizuno, Kipp Hamilton, Yu Fujiki. *PAR*

War of the Robots & **1978** A dying alien civilization kidnaps two brilliant Earth scientists in the hope that they'll help it survive. **99m/C VHS, Beta, LV.** Antonio Sabato, Melissa Long, James R. Stuart. *VCI*

The War of the Roses &&& **1989 (R)** Acidic black comedy about a well-to-do suburban couple who can't agree on a property settlement in their divorce so they wage unreserved and ever-escalating combat on each other, using their palatial home as a battleground. Expertly and lovingly (if that's the word) directed by DeVito, who plays the lawyer. Turner and Douglas are splendid. Adapted from the novel by Warren Adler. Laserdisc version includes previously deleted scenes and commentary from DeVito. **116m/C VHS, Beta, LV.** Michael Douglas, Kathleen Turner, Danny DeVito, Marianne Sagebrecht, Sean Astin, G.D. Spradlin, Peter Donat, Heather Fairfield, Dan Castellaneta, Danitra Vance; ***D:*** Danny DeVito; ***W:*** Michael Leeson; ***C:*** Stephen Burum; ***M:*** David Newman. *FOX, IME*

War of the Wildcats &&½ *In Old Oklahoma* **1943** Fast-moving western with Wayne as a tough cowboy battling a powerful land baron. They fight over land, oil and a woman. Unusual because Wayne's character acts on behalf of the Indians to drill and transport oil. **102m/B VHS.** John Wayne, Martha Scott, Albert Dekker, George "Gabby" Hayes, Sidney Blackmer; ***D:*** Albert Rogell. Nominations: Academy Awards '43: Best Sound. *REP*

War of the Wizards &½ *The Phoenix* **1981 (PG)** Low-budget sci-fi thriller about an alien woman with supernatural powers who comes to take over the Earth. But, lucky for all earthlings, she's challenged by a hero-type just in the nick of time. **90m/C VHS, Beta.** Richard Kiel; ***D:*** Richard Caan. *NO*

The War of the Worlds &&&½ **1953** H.G. Wells's classic novel of the invasion of Earth by Martians, updated to 1950s California, with spectacular special effects of destruction caused by the Martian war machines. Pretty scary and tense; based more on Orson Welles's radio broadcast than on the book. Still very popular; hit the top 20 in sales when released on video. Classic thriller later made into a TV series. Produced by George Pal, who brought the world much sci-fi, including "The Time Machine," "Destination Moon," and "When Worlds Collide," and who appears here as a street person. **85m/C VHS, Beta, LV.** Gene Barry, Ann Robinson, Les Tremayne, Lewis Martin, Robert Cornthwaite, Sandro Giglio; ***D:*** Byron Haskin; ***C:*** George Barnes. Academy Awards '53: Best Special Effects; Nominations: Academy Awards '53: Best Film Editing, Best Sound. *PAR*

War Party && **1989 (R)** During a 100-year commemoration of an Indian massacre in the Midwest, a murder occurs and a lynch mob chases a pack of young Blackfeet into the mountains before the inevitable showdown. A feeble attempt at portraying the unfair treatment of Native Americans. Un-subtle, Hollywood style, this time in favor of the Indians, and therefore un-serious. Too bad; the premise had potential. **99m/C VHS, Beta, LV.** Kevin Dillon, Billy Wirth, Tim Sampson, M. Emmet Walsh; ***D:*** Franc Roddam. *HBO*

The War Room &&& **1993 (PG)** Eye opening, sometimes disturbing documentary presents a behind the scenes peek at what really goes on during a Presidential campaign. When filming began in June '92 Bill Clinton was an unknown political quantity and advisors George Stephanopoulous and James Carville were masterminding his campaign. The "War Room" refers to the building in Little Rock where they struggled to organize a small army of volunteers into a winning team. Highlights include the Democratic National Convention, the North Carolina leg of Clinton's campaign bus tour, three Presidential debates, and the week leading up to election night. **93m/C VHS, LV.** ***D:*** Chris Hegedus, D.A. Pennebaker. National Board of Review Awards '93: Best Feature Documentary; Nominations: Academy Awards '93: Best Feature Documentary. *VMK*

War Victims &½ **1985** Drama about Japanese POW prisons in WWII. **90m/C VHS, Beta.** *IT VCD*

The War Wagon &&& **1967** The Duke plans revenge on Cabot, the greedy mine owner who stole his gold claim and framed him for murder for which he spent years in prison. He assembles a gang to aid him, including a wise-cracking Indian (Keel) and the man sent by Cabot to kill him (Douglas). Wayne's plan is to steal the gold being shipped in Cabot's armor-plated stagecoach, the "war wagon." Well-written, good performances, lots of action. Based on the book "Badman" by Clair Huffaker. The laserdisc version is available in letterbox format. **101m/C VHS, Beta, LV.** John Wayne, Kirk Douglas, Howard Keel, Robert Walker Jr., Keenan Wynn, Bruce Dern, Bruce Cabot, Joanna Barnes; ***D:*** Burt Kennedy; ***C:*** William Clothier. *MCA*

Warbirds && **1988 (R)** American pilots are off to quell a revolution in a Middle East country. Too little action fails to support mediocre plot and characters. **88m/C VHS, Beta.** Jim Eldert, Cully Holland, Bill Brinsfield; ***D:*** Ulli Lommel; ***W:*** Ulli Lommel. *VTR, VMK*

Warbus && **1985 (R)** Marines lead a school bus load of Americans through war-torn Vietnam to safety. Decent action and surprisingly enjoyable characters. Otherwise mediocre. **90m/C VHS, Beta.** Daniel Stephen, Romano Kristoff, Urs Althaus; ***D:*** Ted Kaplan. *SUE, NLC*

WarCat & *Angel of Vengeance* **1988** The daughter of a green beret fights for her life against a bloodthirsty gang. **78m/C VHS.** Macka Foley, Jannina Poynter, David O'Hara, Carl Erwin; ***D:*** Ted V. Mikels. *TWE*

Ward Six && **19??** An insane asylum is the setting for various analogies regarding the perception of reality as defined by societal values. When it is felt that the residing physician is no more sane than his patients, he is placed among them, in Ward Six. Adapted from a story by Anton Chekhov. In Serbian with English subtitles. **93m/C VHS, Beta.** *YU* ***D:*** Lucian Pintilie. *FCT*

Wardogs &½ *The Assassination Team* **1987** A man tries to rescue his brother from becoming one of an elite, brainwashed group of ex-Vietnam vets trained by the government as professional assassins. Might not have been quite so bad; promising inversion of many 'Nam cliches wrecked by unnecessary violence and bad acting. **95m/C Beta.** *SW* Tim Earle, Bill Redvers, Daniel Hubenbecker; ***D:*** Daniel Hubenbecker. *NO*

WarGames &&½ **1983 (PG)** A young computer whiz, thinking that he's sneaking an advance look at a new line of video games, breaks into the country's NORAD missile-defense system and challenges it to a game of Global Thermonuclear Warfare. The game might just turn out to be the real thing. Slick look at the possibilities of an accidental start to WWIII. Entertaining and engrossing, but with a B-grade ending. **110m/C VHS, Beta, LV.** Matthew Broderick, Dabney Coleman, John Wood, Ally Sheedy; ***D:*** John Badham; ***W:*** Walter F. Parkes, Lawrence Lasker. Nominations: Academy Awards '83: Best Cinematography, Best Original Screenplay, Best Sound. *FOX*

Warkill &&½ **1965** WWII action set in the jungles of the Philippines. Journalist who idolizes violent, hard-edged colonel, loses his illusions, but gains a more genuine respect for his men. Not-bad war flick. **99m/C VHS, Beta.** George Montgomery, Tom Drake, Eddie Infante; ***D:*** Ferde Grofe Jr.; ***W:*** Ferde Grofe Jr. *AHV*

Warlock &&& **1959** Claustrophic, resonant town-bound tale of a marshal (Fonda) and his adoring sidekick (Quinn) who clean up a town which then turns against him. Unusual story, fine performances carry this well beyond the run-of-the-mill cow flick. Fonda re-established himself at the box office as a western star, after "Stage Struck" and "Twelve Angry Men." From the novel by Oakley Hall. Look for "Bones" McCoy from "Star Trek" in a bit part. **122m/C VHS, Beta.** Henry Fonda, Anthony Quinn, Richard Widmark, Dorothy Malone, Wallace Ford, Richard Arlen, Regis Toomey, DeForest Kelley; ***D:*** Edward Dmytryk; ***W:*** Robert Alan Aurthur. *VTR, FOX*

Warlock &&½ **1991 (R)** It's 1691 and the most powerful warlock (Sands) in the New World is only hours away from execution. Luckily, his pal, Satan, whisks him (and witchhunter Grant, by mistake) three hundred years in the future to present-day Los Angeles, where he crash-lands in Singer's house. Surprisingly witty dialogue and neat plot twists outshine occasionally cheesy special effects. **103m/C VHS.** Richard E. Grant, Julian Sands, Lori Singer, Mary Woronov, Richard Kuss, Kevin O'Brien, Anna Levine, Allan Miller, David Carpenter; ***D:*** Steve Miner; ***W:*** David N. Twohy; ***M:*** Jerry Goldsmith. *VMK*

Warlock Moon &½ **1973** Young woman is lured to a secluded spa and falls prey to a coven of witches. **75m/C VHS, Beta.** *MX* Laurie Walters, Joe Spano; ***D:*** Bill Herbert. *UNI*

Warlock: The Armageddon &&½ **1993 (R)** Sequel finds Sands back again as the sinister Warlock. This time he's out to gather six Druidic rune stones which have the power to summon Satan's emissary (in the wrong hands) or to stop his nefarious activities (in the right ones). A sect in a small California town serves as the keeper of the stones, only their designated champions are two unprepared teenagers. Sands has all the fun, gleefully dispatching his would-be opponents with some good special effects. **93m/C VHS.** Julian Sands, Chris Young, Paula Marshall, Steve Kahan, Charles Hallahan, R.G. Armstrong, Bruce Glover, Zach Galligan, Dawn Ann Billings, Joanna Pacula; ***D:*** Anthony Hickox; ***W:*** Kevin Rock, Sam Bernard. *VMK*

Warlords &½ **1988 (R)** Lone soldier Carradine battles mutant hordes in a post-apocalyptic desert. Amateurish futuristic drivel. **87m/C VHS, Beta, LV.** David Carradine, Sid Haig, Ross Hagen, Fox Harris, Robert Quarry, Victoria Sellers, Brinke Stevens, Dawn Wildsmith; ***D:*** Fred Olen Ray. *VMK*

Warlords from Hell *Woof!* **1987 (R)** Two young men motorcycling through Mexico are captured by a bloodthirsty gang and forced to do hard labor in the marijuana fields. We can only hope that they just learn to say no. **76m/C VHS, Beta.** Brad Henson, Jeffrey Rice; ***D:*** Clark Henderson. *WAR*

Warlords of the 21st Century &½ *Battletruck* **1982** Bandit gang speed around the galaxy in an indestructible battle cruiser. Then the boys are challenged by a space lawman. Gratuitously violent action pic lacking real action. Filmed on planet New Zealand. **91m/C VHS, Beta.** Michael Beck, Annie McEnroe, James Wainwright; ***D:*** Harley Cokliss; ***W:*** Harley Cokliss, Irving Austin, John Beech; ***C:*** Chris Menges. *SUE*

Warlords 3000 🦴½ **1993 (R)** In the future, Earth is a barren wasteland ravaged by raging electrical storms. Deadly cancers are rampant and the few people who have survived take their comfort in a hallucinogenic drug that provides a temporary pleasure and a permanent madness. Drug lords control the planet but one man is out to eliminate the scum and save the future. **92m/C VHS.** Jay Roberts Jr., Denise Marie Duff, Steve Blanchard, Wayne Duvall; ***D:*** Faruque Ahmed; ***W:*** Ron Herbst, Faruque Ahmed. *COL*

Warm Nights on a Slow-Moving Train 🦴🦴 **1987 (R)** A hot-blooded schoolteacher turns tricks for cash to support her brother on the Sunday-night train to Melbourne, until she meets a stranger who has a deadly masquerade of his own. Interestingly different; much sex, as you can imagine. Australian-made. **90m/C VHS, Beta, LV.** *AU* Wendy Hughes, Colin Friels, Norman Kaye, John Clayton, Peter Whitford; ***D:*** Bob Ellis; ***W:*** Bob Ellis, Denny Lawrence. *PSM, PAR*

Warm Summer Rain 🦴½ **1989 (R)** A young couple meet under unusual circumstances and develop a relationship in a desert cabin as they reflect on their unfulfilled pasts. Lust, self-doubt and longing for something to hold onto draw them together as the days pass. Thoroughly self-indulgent romantic comedy that's oddly self-pitying and poorly directed. **85m/C VHS, Beta, LV.** Kelly Lynch, Barry Tubb; ***D:*** Joe Gayton. *COL*

The Warning 🦴 **1980** A pair of proverbial honest cops investigate ties between the mob and the police department. Hard to follow. **101m/C VHS, Beta.** *IT* Martin Balsam, Giuliano Gemma, Giancarlo Zanetti; ***D:*** Damiano Damiani. *MED*

Warning from Space 🦴½ *The Mysterious Satellite; The Cosmic Man Appears in Tokyo; Space Men Appear in Tokyo; Unknown Satellite Over Tokyo; Uchujin Tokyo Ni Arawaru* **1956** Aliens visit Earth to warn of impending cosmic doom. When it becomes apparent that the one-eyed starfish look is off-putting, they assume human form. Japanese sci fi. **87m/B VHS.** *JP* Toyomi Karita, Keizo Kawasaki, Isao Yamagata, Shozo Nanbu, Buntaro Miake, Mieko Nagai, Kiyoko Hirai; ***D:*** Koji Shima. *NOS, SMW, SNC*

Warning Shadows 🦴🦴🦴 **1923** Classic example of interior German Expressionism. Brilliantly portrays a jealous husband's emotions and obsessions through shadows. Innocent events seem to reek of sin. A seldom-seen study of the oft-precarious distinction between love and obsession; directly influenced by the classic "The Cabinet of Dr. Caligari." Silent with German and English titles. **93m/B VHS, Beta, 8mm.** *GE* Fritz Kortner; ***D:*** Arthur Robison. *GPV, FCT, GLV*

Warning Sign 🦴½ **1985 (R)** A high-tech thriller in which a small town is terrorized by the accidental release of an experimental virus at a research facility. Shades of "The Andromeda Strain" and "The China Syndrome," though less originality and quality. **99m/C VHS, Beta.** Sam Waterston, Kathleen Quinlan, Yaphet Kotto, Richard Dysart, Rick Rossovich; ***D:*** Hal Barwood; ***W:*** Hal Barwood, Matthew Robbins. *FOX*

The Warrior & the Sorceress 🦴½ **1984 (R)** Mercenary Carradine offers his services to rival factions fighting for control of a water well in an impoverished desert village located on a planet with two suns. He attempts to aggravate the conflicts between the factions, playing the shifty go-between. The sorceress is topless throughout. "A Fistful of Dollars" goes to outer space. Inoffensive, except that better judgment is expected of Carradine. **81m/C VHS, Beta, LV.** David Carradine, Luke Askew, Maria Socas, Harry Townes; ***D:*** John Broderick; ***W:*** John Broderick. *LIV, VES*

Warrior of the Lost World *Woof!* **1984** A warrior must destroy the evil Omega Force who tyrannically rules the world in the distant future, etcetera, etcetera. One-size-fits-all premise; horrible special effects; miserably directed. Only for really hardcore Pleasence fans. **90m/C VHS, Beta.** Robert Ginty, Persis Khambatta, Donald Pleasence; ***D:*** David Worth. *NO*

Warrior Queen 🦴 **1987 (R)** Long ago in ancient Rome, overly histrionic mayor Pleasence married porn queen with a wandering eye Fox, and much gratuitous sex and erupting volcanoes resulted. Even the score blows. Also available in an "Unrated" version. Brit pop star Fox is billed as Stasia Micula. **69m/C VHS, LV.** Sybil Danning, Donald Pleasence, Richard Hill, Josephine Jacqueline Jones, Tally Chanel, Samantha Fox. *LIV, VES*

Warrior Spirit 🦴🦴½ **1994 (PG-13)** After getting kicked out of their prep school, two boys decide to head for the Yukon and search for gold. **94m/C VHS.** Lukas Haas, Jimmy Herman, Allan Musy; ***D:*** Rene Manzor. *VMK*

Warrior Within 🦴 **1980** Eight Kung Fu greats pay tribute to the memory of Bruce Lee by kicking and jumping about. **85m/C VHS, Beta.** Chuck Norris, Dan Inosanto, Mike Stone, Fumio Demura, Ron Taganashi. *VTR*

The Warriors 🦴🦴½ *The Dark Avenger* **1955** Swashbuckling adventure about Prince Edward's valiant rescue of Lady Joan and her children from the clutches of the evil Count De Ville. Flynn looks old and pudgy, but buckles his way gallantly through intrepid adventure. Also the last Flynn to see: fun, but more or less completely derivative and familiar. Filmed in England. **85m/C VHS, Beta.** *GB* Errol Flynn, Peter Finch, Joanne Dru, Yvonne Furneaux, Noel Willman, Michael Hordern; ***D:*** Henry Levin. *FOX, MLB*

The Warriors 🦴🦴½ **1979 (R)** Action story about a turf battle between New York City street gangs that rages from Coney Island to the Bronx. Silly plot works because of fine performances and direction, excellent use of action and color, and nonstop pace. Fight scenes are very carefully, even obviously, choreographed. **94m/C VHS, Beta, LV.** Michael Beck, James Remar, Deborah Van Valkenburgh, Thomas G. Waites, David Patrick Kelly; ***D:*** Walter Hill; ***W:*** Walter Hill. *PAR*

Warriors 🦴🦴 **1994 (R)** Col. Frank Vail (Busey) is the leader of a top secret government anti-terrorist hit squad, considered so deadly that its members are confined behind the walls of a military prison. But when Vail escapes, it's up to his lethal protege Colin Newl (Pare) to hunt him down. **100m/C VHS, LV.** Gary Busey, Michael Pare; ***D:*** Shimon Dotan. *REP*

Warriors from Hell 🦴½ **1990 (R)** Western forces in a small African country battle rebel fighters who threaten the hapless native villagers. **90m/C VHS.** Deon Stewardson, Shayne Leith, Adrienne Pierce, Glen Gabela, Hector Manthanda, Ivan Dean, Connie Chume; ***D:*** Ronnie Isaacs; ***W:*** Ronnie Isaacs. *COL*

Warriors of the Apocalypse *Woof! Searchers of the Voodoo Mountain; Time Raiders* **1985 (R)** After a nuclear holocaust, heavily sworded and loin-clothed men search for the secret of eternal life and instead find an Amazon realm in the jungle. A terrible waste of post-apocalyptic scenery. **96m/C VHS, Beta.** Michael James, Debrah Moore, Ken Metcalfe, Franco Guerrero; ***D:*** Bobby Suarez. *LIV*

Warriors of the Wasteland *Woof! The New Barbarians; I Nuovi Barbari* **1983 (R)** It's the year 2019, and the world has been devastated by a nuclear war. The few survivors try to reach a distant land which emits radio signals indicating the presence of human life. They are hindered by attacks from the fierce homosexual Templars, led by a self-proclaimed priest called One. Mindless rip-off of "Road Warrior" and obviously made on the proverbial shoestring budget. Dubbed. **92m/C VHS, Beta.** *IT* Fred Williamson, Timothy Brent, Anna Kanakis; ***D:*** Enzo G. Castellari. *NO*

The Wash 🦴🦴🦴 **1988** Quiet domestic drama about a couple who drift apart after 40 years of marriage. Set interestingly among Japanese-Americans in California; treats social and cultural factors with intelligence. Superb cast takes it a notch higher. **94m/C VHS, Beta, LV.** Mako, Nobu McCarthy, Sab Shimono; ***D:*** Michael Toshiyuki Uno; ***C:*** Walt Lloyd. *ACA*

Washington Affair 🦴🦴 **1977 (PG)** A tale of intrigue in the nation's capital. Sullivan is a businessman who uses women and blackmail to capture government contracts. Selleck is the hapless bureaucrat he preys on. Remake of Stoloff's own "Intimacy" was not released until "Magnum P.I." became a hit. **90m/C VHS, Beta.** Tom Selleck, Carol Lynley, Barry Sullivan; ***D:*** Victor Stoloff. *SUE*

Washington Mistress 🦴½ **1981** Emminently ordinary made-for-TV grist about Capitol Hill aide Arnaz, politician Jordan, and their affair. Listless performances. **96m/C VHS.** Lucie Arnaz, Richard Jordan, Tony Bill; ***D:*** Peter Levin. *NO*

The Wasp Woman 🦴½ **1959** In her quest for eternal beauty, a woman uses a potion made from wasp enzymes. Naturally, she turns into a wasp monster at night. Good fun, courtesy of Corman. **84m/B VHS.** Susan Cabot, Anthony Eisley, Barboura Morris, Michael Marks, William Roerick, Frank Gerstle, Bruno Ve Sota, Frank Wolff; ***D:*** Roger Corman. *NOS, RHI, SNC*

Watch It 🦴🦴🦴 **1993 (R)** Four self-absorbed twenty-something guys share a house in Chicago for the summer. They pursue a post-adolescent game, consisting of increasingly complicated practical jokes, where the unsuspecting victim is set up for a "watch it" gag. The rivalry escalates, and turns increasingly unpleasant, when cousins John and Michael vie for the affections of Anne, who's wary of involvement because of male selfishness. A first-rate cast with recognizable situations and emotions. **102m/C VHS.** Jon Tenney, Peter Gallagher, Suzy Amis, John C. McGinley, Tom Sizemore, Lili Taylor, Cynthia Stevenson, Terri Hawkes, Jordanna Capra; ***D:*** Tom Flynn; ***W:*** Tom Flynn; ***M:*** Stanley Clarke. *PAR*

Watch Me When I Kill 🦴 **1981 (R)** We'd rather not. A young nightclub dancer stops by a drugstore seconds after the owner was killed. She doesn't see the killer's face, but his rasping voice remains to torment her and the viewer. Dubbed. **95m/C VHS, Beta.** *IT* Richard Stewart, Sylvia Kramer, Anthony Bido. *NO*

Watch on the Rhine 🦴🦴🦴½ **1943** Couple involved with the anti-Nazi underground has escaped the country, but is pursued and harassed by Nazi agents. Adapted by Hammett and Hellman from her play. Performed on stage before the U.S. entered the war, it was the first American play and movie to portray the ugliness of fascism as an ideology, as opposed to the more devious evil of its practical side. The Production Code at the time required that a killer always be punished; the murderer (whose screen motives had been noble) refused to film the offending scene, which explains the tacked-on ending. Superb drama from a pair of highly gifted writers and a great cast. Shumlin also directed the play. **114m/B VHS, Beta.** Bette Davis, Paul Lukas, Donald Woods, Beulah Bondi, Geraldine Fitzgerald, George Coulouris, Henry Daniell, Helmut Dantine; ***D:*** Herman Shumlin; ***W:*** Lillian Hellman, Dashiell Hammett; ***C:*** Hal Mohr; ***M:*** Max Steiner. Academy Awards '43: Best Actor (Lukas); Golden Globe Awards '44: Best Actor—Drama (Lukas); National Board of Review Awards '43: 10 Best Films of the Year; New York Film Critics Awards '43: Best Actor (Lukas), Best Film; Nominations: Academy Awards '43: Best Picture, Best Screenplay, Best Supporting Actress (Watson). *FOX, MGM, FCT*

Watch the Birdie 🦴🦴½ **1950** It's Skelton three times over as cameraman, father, and grandfather! First, he accidentally films a scam that would send the lovely Miss Dahl filing for bankruptcy. Later a crazy chase scene unfolds, that will have viewers rolling, as Skelton the cameraman nabs the bad guys and turns them over to the cops. Light fun that will charm Skelton fans. **70m/B VHS, Beta.** Red Skelton, Arlene Dahl, Ann Miller, Leon Ames; ***D:*** Jack Donohue. *MGM*

Watched 🦴🦴 **1973** A former U.S. attorney, gone underground, has a nervous breakdown and kills the narcotics agent who has him under surveillance. Self-important, too serious social/political conspiracy drama of the Watergate era. Keach and Yulin are good, but not good enough to save it. **95m/C VHS, Beta.** Stacy Keach, Harris Yulin, Bridgit Polk; ***D:*** John Parsons. *LIV, VES*

The Watcher in the Woods 1981 (PG) When an American family rents an English country house, the children are haunted by the spirit of a long-missing young girl. A very bland attempt at a ghost story. **83m/C VHS, Beta.** Bette Davis, Carroll Baker, David McCallum, Ian Bannen, Lynn-Holly Johnson; ***D:*** John Hough; ***W:*** Brian Clemens. *DIS*

Watchers 1988 (R) From the suspense novel by Dean R. Koontz, a secret experiment goes wrong, creating half-human monsters. A boy and his extremely intelligent dog are soon pursued. Low-budget, Corman-influenced production is tacky but effective. **99m/C VHS, Beta, LV.** Barbara Williams, Michael Ironside, Corey Haim; ***D:*** Jon Hess; ***M:*** Joel Goldsmith. *LIV*

Watchers 2 1990 (R) Sequel to "Watchers" follows the further adventures of a super-intelligent golden retriever who leads a Marine to an animal psychologist and then attempts to warn them both of a mutant killer. The dog says woof, but this movie doesn't quite. Fun for lovers of hounds or horror flicks. **101m/C VHS, Beta, LV.** Marc Singer, Tracy Scoggins; ***D:*** Thierry Notz; ***M:*** Rick Conrad. *LIV*

Watchers 3 ½ 1994 (R) A secret military outpost in the South American jungles is attacked by a carnivorous predator. Ex-military convicts are sent to rescue the remaining survivors and to make certain the government experiment that started the terror never comes to light. **95m/C VHS.** Wings Hauser, Gregory Scott Cummins, Daryl Roach, John K. Linton, Lolita Ronalds, Frank Novak; ***D:*** Jeremy Stanford. *NHO*

Water 1985 (PG-13) The resident governor of a Caribbean British colony juggles various predatory interests when a valuable mineral water resource is found. The good cast is wasted in this all-too-silly effort. **89m/C VHS, Beta.** *GB* Michael Caine, Brenda Vaccaro, Leonard Rossiter, Valerie Perrine, Jimmie Walker; ***Cameos:*** Eric Clapton, George Harrison, Fred Gwynne, Ringo Starr; ***D:*** Dick Clement; ***W:*** Dick Clement, Ian LaFrenais, Bill Persky. *PAR*

Water Babies *Slip Slide Adventures* 1979 (G) When a chimney sweep's 12-year-old apprentice is wrongly accused of stealing silver, the boy and his dog fall into a pond and eventually rescue some of the characters they find there. Combination of live-action and animated fairy-tale story set in nineteenth-century London. Boring, unless you're a young child with equivalent standards. Based on the book by Charles Kingsley. **93m/C VHS, Beta.** *GB* James Mason, Billie Whitelaw, David Tomlinson, Paul Luty, Sammantha Coates; ***D:*** Lionel Jeffries. *SUE*

The Water Engine ½ 1992 Charles Lang (Macy) is a luckless machinist struggling to survive in Depression-era Chicago. Lang invents a remarkable engine, that runs on water, and holds the promise of limitless, cheap power. To protect his invention he finds a seedy patent attorney (Mahoney), which leads to the sinister Oberman (Mantegna), a mysterious and powerful figure who wants Lang's invention—at any cost. Based on the play by David Mamet; made for cable TV. **110m/C VHS.** Charles Durning, Patti LuPone, William H. Macy, John Mahoney, Joe Mantegna, Joanna Miles, Mike Nussbaum, Treat Williams, Andrea Marcovicci, Peter Michael Goetz, David Mamet; ***D:*** Steven Schachter; ***W:*** David Mamet. *TTC*

Water Rustlers ½ 1939 Unscrupulous land baron builds a dam on his side of the creek with the intention of drying out the cattle pastures. Heroine Page, whose pop has been rubbed out by varmints, and good guy/lover O'Brien save her property and avenge her father. Second of three Page westerns. **55m/B VHS, Beta.** Dorothy Page, Dave O'Brien; ***D:*** Samuel Diege. *VCN, VDM*

The Waterdance 1991 (R) Autobiographical film based on the experiences of writer/co-director Jimenez. When writer Joel Garcia (Stoltz) is paralyzed in a hiking accident he finds himself dealing with not only the rehab process itself but his feelings, the feelings of his married lover, and those of his fellow patients. Deals unsentimentally with all the physical adjustments, including the sexual ones. Resolutions may be predictable but the performances rise above any script weaknesses. The title refers to Hill's dream of dancing on water—and the fear of drowning if he stops. **106m/C VHS, LV.** Eric Stoltz, Wesley Snipes, William Forsythe, Helen Hunt, Elizabeth Pena, Grace Zabriskie; ***D:*** Neal Jimenez, Michael Steinberg; ***W:*** Neal Jimenez; ***M:*** Michael Convertino. Independent Spirit Awards '93: Best First Feature, Best Screenplay; Sundance Film Festival '92: Best Screenplay, Audience Award. *COL, PMS, BTV*

Waterfront ½ 1939 Dreary dockside melodrama, with drinking and brawling longshoreman Jim (Morgan) avenging his brother's death. Based on the play "Blindspot" by Kenyon Nicholson. **59m/B VHS.** Dennis (Stanley Morner) Morgan, Gloria Dickson, Marie Wilson, Larry Williams, Sheila Bromley, Ward Bond, Frank Faylen; ***D:*** Terry Morse; ***W:*** Arthur Ripley, Lee Katz. *GPV*

Waterfront 1944 Nazis coerce German-Americans into helping them in WWII-era San Francisco. Credulity defying spy doings, but that's okay. Fairly entertaining wartime drama about paranoia on the home front. **68m/B VHS, Beta.** John Carradine, J. Carrol Naish, Terry Frost, Maris Wrixon, Edwin Maxwell; ***D:*** Steve Sekely. *SNC, VCI*

Waterfront ½ 1983 Effective romantic drama set in Melbourne, Australia. Australian workers strike after taking forced pay cuts. As a result, Italian immigrants are hired as scabs to keep the docks going. Despite the tension, an Italian woman and an Australian man fall deeply in love, only to find that they must struggle to keep that love alive. **294m/C VHS, Beta.** *AU* Jack Thompson, Greta Scacchi, Frank Gallacher, Tony Rickards, Mark Little, Jay Mannering, Ray Barrett, Chris Haywood, Warren Mitchell, Noni Hazlehurst, John Karlsen, Elin Jenkins; ***D:*** Chris Thomson. *PSM, PAR*

Waterhole #3 ½ 1967 (PG) Three Confederate army buddies steal a fortune in gold bullion from the Union Army and hide it in a waterhole in the desert. One of the funnier entries in the Western comedy genre. **95m/C VHS.** James Coburn, Carroll O'Connor, Margaret Blye, Claude Akins, Bruce Dern, Joan Blondell, James Whitmore; ***D:*** William A. Graham; ***C:*** Robert Burks; ***M:*** Dave Grusin. *PAR*

Waterland 1992 (R) Meandering drama about a history teacher who tries to solve a personal crisis by using his class as a sounding board to describe his troubled past in England. Dark secrets abound, including incest, madness, murder, and the terrifying love between the teacher and his childhood bride. Melancholy, overwrought but partially redeemed by the lead performances of Irons and his (real-life and cinematic) wife, Cusack. The film's setting has been unfortunately moved from London to Pittsburgh, destroying story links. Based on the novel by Graham Swift. **95m/C VHS, LV.** Jeremy Irons, Ethan Hawke, Sinead Cusack, John Heard, Grant Warnock, Lena Headey, Pete Postlethwaite, Cara Buono; ***D:*** Stephen Gyllenhaal; ***W:*** Peter Prince; ***M:*** Carter Burwell. *NLC, COL*

Waterloo 1971 (G) Massive chronicle of Napoleon's European conquests and eventual defeat at the hands of Wellington. Filmed on location in Italy and the Ukraine, it bombed due largely to Steiger's bizarre rendition of Napoleon. **122m/C VHS.** *IT RU* Rod Steiger, Orson Welles, Virginia McKenna, Michael Wilding, Donal Donnelly, Christopher Plummer, Jack Hawkins, Dan O'Herlihy, Terence Alexander, Rupert Davies, Ivo Garrani, Gianni "John" Garko; ***D:*** Sergei Bondarchuk; ***W:*** H.A.L. Craig, Sergei Bondarchuk; ***M:*** Nino Rota. *PAR, FCT, FUS*

Waterloo Bridge 1940 In London during WWI, a soldier from an aristocratic family and a ballet dancer begin a tragic romance when they meet by chance on the foggy Waterloo Bridge. When he's listed as dead, her despair turns her to prostitution. But then he returns from POW camp, they once again meet by accident on Waterloo Bridge, and their romance resumes. Four-hanky drama with fine performances by Leigh (her first after "Gone with the Wind") and Taylor. **109m/B VHS, Beta, LV.** Vivien Leigh, Robert Taylor, Lucile Watson, Sir C. Aubrey Smith, Maria Ouspenskaya, Virginia Field; ***D:*** Mervyn LeRoy; ***C:*** Joseph Ruttenberg. Nominations: Academy Awards '40: Best Black and White Cinematography, Best Original Score. *MGM*

Watermelon Man 1970 (R) The tables are turned for a bigoted white guy when he wakes up one morning to discover he has become a black man. Broad comedy with not much place to go is still engaging. Cambridge takes on both roles, appearing in unconvincing white makeup. **97m/C VHS, Beta, LV.** Godfrey Cambridge, Erin Moran, Estelle Parsons, Howard Caine; ***D:*** Melvin Van Peebles. *COL, FCT*

Watership Down ½ 1978 (PG) Wonderfully animated story based on Richard Adams's allegorical novel about how a group of rabbits escape fear and overcome oppression while searching for a new and better home. It's really an adult theme with sufficient violence to the poor wittle wabbits to scare the kiddies. **92m/C VHS, Beta, LV, 8mm.** *GB* ***D:*** Martin Rosen; ***W:*** Martin Rosen; ***V:*** Ralph Richardson, Zero Mostel, John Hurt, Denholm Elliott, Harry Andrews, Michael Hordern, Joss Ackland. *WAR, TVC, WTA*

Waterworld ½ 1995 (PG-13) "The Man From Atlantis" meets "Mad Max." Industry knives sharpened with glee before release, with some insiders calling this luck-impaired project "Fishtar" and "Kevin's Gate." With an estimated $150 million budget, the film must look to overseas sales and secondary markets to make any money. Most of said budget seems to have ended up on screen, which makes for a visually striking, and at times daunting, film. Costner, who did just about everything but cater the meals, stars as Mariner, a mutant man-fish who reluctantly helps human survivors search for the mythical Dryland since the polar ice caps melted, flooding the earth. The bad guys are the Smokers, led by the evil Hopper, who can play these roles in his sleep. Entertaining, but not riveting, as the budget and PR hype leads one to expect. The floating set was anchored (not very well, apparently) off the Hawaiian coast and was lost once during a tropical storm. Costner bet the boat on this one and stands to lose more than just money. With rumors of internal production battles, out of control budgets, and his other recent box office disappointments, his star power is in question. **135m/C VHS, LV.** Kevin Costner, Dennis Hopper, Jeanne Tripplehorn, Tina Majorino, Michael Jeter, R.D. Call, Robert Joy; ***D:*** Kevin Reynolds; ***W:*** Peter Rader, Marc Norman, David N. Twohy; ***C:*** Dean Semler; ***M:*** James Newton Howard. Golden Raspberry Awards '95: Worst Supporting Actor (Hopper); Nominations: Academy Awards '95: Best Sound; Golden Raspberry Awards '95: Worst Picture, Worst Actor (Costner). *MCA*

Wavelength ½ 1983 (PG) A rock star living in the Hollywood Hills with his girlfriend stumbles on an ultra-secret government project involving friendly aliens from outer space recovered from a recent UFO crash site. Fun, enthusiastically unoriginal cheap sci-fi. Soundtrack by Tangerine Dream. **87m/C VHS, Beta, LV.** Robert Carradine, Cherie Currie, Keenan Wynn; ***D:*** Mike Gray; ***W:*** Mike Gray; ***M:*** Tangerine Dream. *SUE, VTR*

Wavelength ½ 1996 (R) Physicist and Oxford professor Paul Higgins (Piven) has a few problems—a wife, Claire (Williams), a girlfriend, Lucy (Walker), Lucy's father who just happens to be the head of the physics department, and a mysterious presence (Attenborough) who's trying to help Paul with his research on nuclear fission. **94m/C VHS.** Jeremy Piven, Kelli Williams, Liza Walker, James Villiers, James Faulkner, Richard Attenborough, Byrne Piven, Nicholas Marco, Dominic West; ***D:*** Benjamin Fry; ***W:*** Benjamin Fry; ***C:*** Chris Middleton; ***M:*** Michael Storey. *PAR*

Wax, or the Discovery of Television Among the Bees 1993 Intricate and eccentric fable dealing with alternate realities and perceptions. Jacob Maker (Blair) keeps a hive of very unusual bees, a family legacy passed down from his grandfather. Jacob begins experiencing a eerie communication with his bees and suffering mysterious blackouts, which cause him to perceive the world through blurred bee vision. New Mexico desert setting provides a surreal and desolate landscape. **85m/C VHS.** David Blair, Meg Savlov, Florence Ormezzano, William S. Burroughs; ***D:*** David Blair; ***W:*** David Blair; ***M:*** Beo Morales, Brooks Williams. *ICA*

Waxwork 🦴½ **1988 (R)** A wax museum opens up, and it is soon evident that the dummies are not what they seem. Garbled nonthriller. Available in a 100-minute unrated version. **97m/C VHS, Beta, LV.** Zach Galligan, Deborah Foreman, Michelle Johnson, Dana Ashbrook, Miles O'Keeffe, Patrick Macnee, David Warner; ***D:*** Anthony Hickox; ***M:*** Roger Bellon. *LIV, VES*

Waxwork 2: Lost in Time 🦴🦴½ **1991 (R)** A young couple (Galligan and Schnarre) barely escape with their lives when the infamous waxworks museum burns down. A severed hand also gets loose and follows Schnarre home and murders her stepfather, leaving her to take the blame. In order to prove her innocence, the couple must travel through a bizarre time machine. Extraordinary special effects, strange plot twists, and recreations of scenes from past horror movies make this a highly entertaining sequel. **104m/C VHS.** Zach Galligan, Alexander Godunov, Bruce Campbell, Michael Des Barres, Monika Schnarre; ***D:*** Anthony Hickox. *LIV*

Waxworks 🦴🦴🦴 **1924** A major achievement in German Expressionism, in which a poet imagines scenarios in a wax museum fairground that involve Jack the Ripper, Ivan the Terrible and Haroun al-Rashid. Influential and considered ahead of its time. Silent. **63m/B VHS, Beta.** *GE* William Dieterle, Emil Jannings, Conrad Veidt, Werner Krauss, John Gottowt, Olga Belajeff; ***D:*** Paul Leni; ***W:*** Henrik Galeen. *SNC, NOS, LIV*

Way Back Home 🦴🦴 *Old Greatheart; Other People's Business* **1932** Man wants to adopt a boy to release him from the clutches of his cruel guardian. Minor role for the then unknown Davis. **81m/B VHS, Beta.** Phillips Lord, Frank Albertson, Bette Davis; ***D:*** William A. Seiter; ***M:*** Max Steiner. *TTC, FCT*

Way Down East 🦴🦴🦴 **1920** Melodramatic silent drama of a country girl who is tricked into a fake marriage by a scheming playboy. The famous final scene of Gish adrift on the ice floes is in color. One of Griffith's last critical and popular successes. This tape includes the original Griffith-approved musical score. Remade in 1935 with Henry Fonda. **107m/B VHS, Beta, LV.** Lillian Gish, Richard Barthelmess, Lowell Sherman, Creighton Hale; ***D:*** D.W. Griffith. *NOS, BAR, VYY*

Way Down South 🦴½ **1939** The orphan son of a plantation owner tries to take over his father's estate, only to find out that the place has been run into the ground by a corrupt lawyer and a cruel slave driver. Black poet Hughes and actor Muse collaborated on the screenplay. German-born director Vorhaus was in his second year in Hollywood, after making his mark in Britain directing talkies. ♫Good Ground; Louisiana; Nobody Know De Trouble I See; Sometimes I Feel Like a Motherless Child; Lord I You Can't Come Send One Angel Down. **62m/B VHS.** Bobby Breen, Alan Mowbray, Ralph Morgan, Clarence Muse, Steffi Duna, Sally Blane, Edwin Maxwell; ***D:*** Bernard Vorhaus; ***W:*** Clarence Muse, Langston Hughes. Nominations: Academy Awards '39: Best Score. *NOS*

Way He Was 🦴🦴 **1976 (R)** A satirical reenactment of the events that led up to the Watergate burglary and the coverup that followed. **87m/C VHS, Beta.** Steve Friedman, Al Lewis, Merrie Lynn Ross, Doodles Weaver. *VCI*

Way of the Black Dragon 🦴 **1981** When slave-trading drug traffickers threaten the moral fiber of our nation, two commandoes join forces to halt their operation. **88m/C VHS, Beta.** Ron Van Cliff, Carter Wang, Charles Bonet; ***D:*** Chan Wui Ngai. *TWE*

Way of the West 🦴½ **1935** Them durn pesky sheepherders are up to it again! Okay, so the cow/sheep thing is a classic western plot, but here it's offered perfunctorily. **52m/B VHS, Beta.** Wally Wales, William Desmond, Art Mix, Jim Sheridan, Bobby Nelson; ***D:*** Robert Emmett Tansey. *NOS, DVT, RXM*

The Way Out 🦴🦴 *Dial 999* **1956** Average crime drama starring Nelson as a fugitive accused of killing a bookie. **90m/C VHS.** *GB* Gene Nelson, Mona Freeman, John Bentley, Michael Goodliffe, Sydney Tafler; ***D:*** Montgomery Tully. *SNC*

Way Out West 🦴🦴🦴 **1937** The classic twosome journey way out west to deliver the deed to a gold mine to the daughter of their late prospector pal. The obligatory romance is missing, but you'll be laughing so hard you won't notice. One of Stan and Ollie's best. Score includes the song "Trail of the Lonesome Pine." Also included on this tape is a 1932 Todd and Pitts short, "Red Noses." Available colorized. **86m/B VHS, Beta.** Stan Laurel, Oliver Hardy, Rosina Lawrence, James Finlayson, Sharon Lynne, ZaSu Pitts, Thelma Todd, William Haines; ***D:*** James W. Horne. Nominations: Academy Awards '37: Best Original Score. *CCB, MED, MLB*

The Way We Were 🦴🦴🦴 **1973 (PG)** Big box-office hit follows a love story between opposites from the 1930s to the 1950s. Streisand is a Jewish political radical who meets the handsome WASP Redford at college. They're immediately attracted to one another, but it takes years before they act on it and eventually marry. They move to Hollywood where Redford is a screenwriter and left-wing Streisand becomes involved in the Red scare and the blacklist, much to Redford's dismay. Though always in love, their differences are too great to keep them together. An old-fashioned and sweet romance, with much gloss. Hit title song sung by Streisand. Adapted by Arthur Laurents from his novel. ♫The Way We Were. **118m/C VHS, Beta, LV, 8mm.** Barbra Streisand, Robert Redford, Bradford Dillman, Viveca Lindfors, Herb Edelman, Murray Hamilton, Patrick O'Neal, James Woods, Sally Kirkland; ***D:*** Sydney Pollack; ***W:*** Arthur Laurents; ***C:*** Harry Stradling Jr.; ***M:*** Marvin Hamlisch. Academy Awards '73: Best Song ("The Way We Were"), Best Original Score; Golden Globe Awards '74: Best Song ("The Way We Were"); National Board of Review Awards '73: 10 Best Films of the Year; Nominations: Academy Awards '73: Best Actress (Streisand), Best Art Direction/Set Decoration, Best Cinematography; Academy Awards '76: Best Costume Design. *COL*

The Way West 🦴½ **1967** A wagon train heads to Oregon. A poor and muddled attempt at recreating the style of a John Ford western. What really galls is that it's based on the Pulitzer-winning novel by A.B. Guthrie, Jr. Boy, is the book better than the movie. Field's first film. **122m/C VHS.** Kirk Douglas, Robert Mitchum, Richard Widmark, Lola Albright, Michael Witney, Stubby Kaye, Sally Field, Jack Elam; ***D:*** Andrew V. McLaglen; ***C:*** William Clothier. *MGM*

Wayne Murder Case 🦴🦴🦴 *Strange Adventure* **1938** A fast-moving, cleverly constructed murder mystery. A rich old man dies just as he is about to sign a new will. Though no one was standing near him, a knife is found stuck in his back. **61m/B VHS, Beta.** June Clyde, Regis Toomey, Jason Robards Sr. *SNC, VYY*

Wayne's World 🦴🦴🦴 **1992 (PG-13)** Destined to become one of the top movies of all time—Not! This "Saturday Night Live" skit proved to be so popular that it got its own movie, not unlike the plot, which has slimy producer Lowe take the public access "Wayne's World" into the world of commercial television. The zany duo of Wayne and Garth are as much fun on the big screen as they are on SNL and there are many funny moments, several of which are destined to become comedy classics. A huge box office hit that spawned a sequel. **93m/C VHS, LV.** Mike Myers, Dana Carvey, Rob Lowe, Tia Carrere, Brian Doyle-Murray, Lara Flynn Boyle, Kurt Fuller, Colleen Camp, Donna Dixon, Ed O'Neill; ***Cameos:*** Alice Cooper, Meat Loaf; ***D:*** Penelope Spheeris; ***W:*** Mike Myers, Bonnie Turner, Terry Turner; ***M:*** J. Peter Robinson. MTV Movie Awards '92: Best On-Screen Duo (Mike Myers/Dana Carvey). *PAR, FCT*

Wayne's World 2 🦴🦴 **1993 (PG-13)** Good-natured rerun of the original has plenty of sophomoric gags, but feels tired. Wayne and Garth are on their own, planning a major concert, Waynestock. "If you book them they will come," Jim Morrison says in a dream. Meanwhile, Wayne's girlfriend (Carrere) is falling for slimeball record promoter Walken. Offers a few brilliantly funny segments. If you liked the "Bohemian Rhapsody" spot in the original, get ready for the Village People here. Heston has a funny cameo, and Walken and Basinger push the limits without going over the top. Feature film debut for director Surjik. **94m/C VHS, Beta, LV.** Mike Myers, Dana Carvey, Tia Carrere, Christopher Walken, Ralph Brown, Kim Basinger, James Hong, Chris Farley, Ed O'Neill, Olivia D'Abo, Kevin Pollak, Drew Barrymore; ***Cameos:*** Charlton Heston, Rip Taylor; ***D:*** Stephen Surjik; ***W:*** Mike Myers, Bonnie Turner, Terry Turner; ***M:*** Carter Burwell. Nominations: MTV Movie Awards '94: Best On-Screen Duo (Mike Myers/Dana Carvey), Best Kiss (Dana Carvey/Kim Basinger). *PAR*

The Wayward Wife 🦴🦴 *La Provinciale* **1952** Young woman, married to a university professor, is blackmailed over her less-than-respectable past. Based on the novel by Alberto Moravia. Italian with subtitles. **92m/B VHS.** *IT* Gina Lollobrigida, Gabriele Ferzetti, Franco Interlenghi, Renalto Baldini; ***D:*** Mario Soldati. *FCT*

W.C. Fields Comedy Bag **1933** Compilation of three classic Fields shorts: "The Golf Specialist" (1930), "The Dentist" (1932) and "The Fatal Glass of Beer" (1933). **56m/B VHS, Beta.** W.C. Fields, Babe Kane, Dorothy Granger, George Chandler. *BAR*

W.C. Fields: Flask of Fields **1930** Three classic Fields shorts: "The Golf Specialist" (1930), in which J. Effington Bellweather finds himself teaching a lovely young lady how to play the game; "The Fatal Glass of Beer" (1933); and "The Dentist" (1932), in which Fields tackles a room filled with patients. **61m/B VHS, Beta, 8mm.** W.C. Fields, Babe Kane, Elise Cavanna, Bud Jamison, Rosemary Theby. *VYY*

We All Loved Each Other So Much 🦴🦴🦴½ **1977** Sensitive comedy follows three friends over 30 years, beginning at the end of WWII. All three have loved the same woman, an actress. Homage to friendship and to postwar Italian cinema. Includes a full-scale recreation of the fountain scene in "La Dolce Vita." In Italian with English subtitles. **124m/C VHS, Beta, LV.** *IT* Vittorio Gassman, Nino Manfredi, Stefano Satta Flores, Stefania Sandrelli, Marcello Mastroianni, Federico Fellini; ***D:*** Ettore Scola. *COL, APD, INJ*

We are the Children 🦴🦴 **1987** Cynical reporter covering the famine in Ethiopia meets an idealistic nurse who's been living there for years. Romance blossoms among the starving in made-for-TV drama co-produced by Danson. **92m/C VHS, Beta.** Ally Sheedy, Ted Danson, Judith Ivey, Zia Mohyeddin; ***D:*** Robert M. Young. *PSM*

We Dive at Dawn 🦴🦴🦴 **1943** Interesting, tense British submarine drama. The "Sea Tiger" attempts to sink the German battleship "Brandenburg" off Denmark. Good cast. Mills prepared for the role by riding an actual submarine, turning "a pale shade of pea-green" when it crash-dived. **98m/B VHS, Beta.** *GB* Eric Portman, John Mills; ***D:*** Anthony Asquith. *NOS, DVT, MED*

We of the Never Never 🦴🦴🦴 **1982 (G)** In turn-of-the-century Australia a city-bred woman marries a cattle rancher and moves from civilized Melbourne to the barren outback of the Northern Territory. Based on the autobiographical story written by Jeannie Gunn, the first white woman to travel in the aboriginal wilderness. She finds herself fighting for her own rights as well as for those of the aborigines in this sincere, well-done film. **136m/C VHS, Beta.** *AU* Angela Punch McGregor, Arthur Dignam, Tony Barry; ***D:*** Igor Auzins. *COL*

We the Living 🦴🦴½ **1942** The torpid long-lost and restored Italian version of Ayn Rand's unique political tome. Deals with a young Soviet woman in revolutionary Petrograd who is slowly ruined by the system and her affair with a romantic counter-revolutionary. Made under the Fascists' nose during WWII. A fascinating dialectic between utopian melodrama and Rand dogma. In Italian with subtitles. **174m/B VHS, Beta, LV.** *IT* Alida Valli, Rossano Brazzi, Fosco Giachetti; ***D:*** Goffredo Alessandrini. *LUM*

We Think the World of You 🦴🦴🦴 **1988 (PG)** When bisexual Oldman goes to prison, his lover Bates, whose feelings are unresolved and complex, finds friendship with Oldman's dog. Odd, oft-bitter comedy-drama of love and loyalty characterized by excellent acting and respectful, gentle direction. From the novel by Joseph R. Ackerly. **94m/C VHS, Beta, LV.** *GB* Alan Bates, Gary Oldman, Frances Barber, Liz Smith, Max Wall, Kerry Wise; ***D:*** Colin Gregg. *SUE, NLC*

We Will Not Enter the Forest ☆☆☆ **1979** Moral dilemmas afflict a group of French Resistance fighters during WWII when they must decide what to do with four German deserters they've captured. In French with subtitles. **88m/C VHS, Beta.** *FR* Marie-France Pisier; ***D:*** Georges Dumoulin. *FCT*

The Weaker Sex ☆☆½ **1949** Typical patriotic British weepie finds a British widow and her daughters trying to hold on to hope as D-Day approaches. **89m/B VHS.** *GB* Ursula Jeans, Cecil Parker, Joan Hopkins, Derek Bond, Lana Morris; ***D:*** Roy Ward Baker. *FCT*

Weapons of Death ☆ **1983** Kung Fu expert Lee splatters his enemies all over San Francisco's Chinatown. **90m/C VHS, Beta.** Eric Lee, Bob Ramos, Ralph Catellanos. *NO*

Weather in the Streets ☆½ **1984 (PG)** A young woman enters into an ill-fated love affair after spending a few moments with an aristocratic married man. Cliched drama set in England between the two world wars. **108m/C VHS, Beta.** Michael York, Joanna Lumley, Lisa Eichhorn, Isabel Dean, Norman Pitt; ***M:*** Carl Davis. *NO*

Web of Deceit ☆☆½ **1990 (PG-13)** Defense lawyer Purl returns to her Southern hometown to defend an unjustly accused teenager. She falls in love with the prosecutor, but could he be the killer? Shades of "Jagged Edge." Good, suspenseful made-for-TV movie. **93m/C VHS, Beta.** Linda Purl, James Read, Paul DeSouza, Larry Black, Len Birman, Barbara Rush; ***D:*** Sandor Stern; ***W:*** Sandor Stern. *PAR*

Web of Deception ☆ **1971 (R)** A jewel thief disappears with five million dollars worth of jewels. When the case turns to murder, a private detective becomes the prime suspect. **90m/C VHS, Beta.** *SP* Thomas Hunter, Aelina Nathaniel, Gabriele Tinti, Marilia Branco. *NO*

Web of the Spider ☆☆ *Nella Stretta M Orsa Del Ragno; In the Grip of the Spider; Dracula in the Castle of Blood; And Comes the Dawn...But Colored Red* **1970** Kinski as Poe is really the only good thing about this run-of-the-mill horror outing. A man stays the night in a spooky house to prove it's not haunted. Remake of "Castle of Blood." **94m/C VHS.** *GE FR IT* Anthony (Tony) Franciosa, Klaus Kinski, Michele Mercier, Peter Carsten, Karin Field; ***D:*** Anthony (Antonio Margheriti) Dawson. *SNC*

A Wedding ☆½ **1978 (PG)** The occasion of a wedding leads to complications galore for the relatives and guests on the happy day. Silent film legend Gish's 100th screen role. Miserable, self-indulgent outing for Altman, who went through quite a dry spell after "Nashville." **125m/C VHS, Beta.** Mia Farrow, Carol Burnett, Lillian Gish, Lauren Hutton, Viveca Lindfors, Geraldine Chaplin, Paul Dooley, Howard Duff, Dennis Christopher, Peggy Ann Garner, John Considine, Nina Van Pallandt, Dina Merrill, Pat McCormick, Vittorio Gassman, Desi Arnaz Jr.; ***D:*** Robert Altman; ***W:*** John Considine, Allan Nicholls, Patricia Resnick, Robert Altman. *FOX*

Wedding Band ☆☆ **1989** Episodic comedy about a rock 'n roll band that plays all sorts of weddings. Thin and lame but inoffensive. **95m/C VHS, Beta, LV.** William Katt, Joyce Hyser, Tino Insana, Fran Drescher, David Rasche, Joe Flaherty, Tim Kazurinsky, James Belushi; ***D:*** Daniel Raskov. *COL*

The Wedding Banquet ☆☆☆ *Xiyan* **1993 (R)** Charming story about a clash of customs and secrets. Naturalized American Wai Tung (Chao, in his debut) lives comfortably with his lover Simon (Lichtenstein) while hiding the fact that he's gay from his Chinese parents. To appease his parents and get his "wife" a green card, he marries for convenience and watches as the deception snowballs. Comedy of errors was shot on a small budget ($750,000) and examines small details with as much care as the larger ones. A fine effort from director Lee that's solidly humorous, but also poignant. In English and Chinese with English subtitles. **111m/C VHS, LV.** *TW* Winston Chao, May Chin, Mitchell Lichtenstein, Sihung Lung, Ah-Leh Gua; ***D:*** Ang Lee; ***W:*** Ang Lee, Neil Peng, James Schamus. Nominations: Academy Awards '93: Best Foreign Language Film; Golden Globe Awards '94: Best Foreign Language Film; Independent Spirit Awards '94: Best Actor (Lichtenstein), Best Actress (Chin), Best Director (Lee), Best Film, Best Screenplay, Best Supporting Actress (Gua). *FXV*

The Wedding Gift ☆☆☆ *Wide-Eyed and Legless* **1993 (PG-13)** Offbeat charm and humor go a long way to overcome the inherent tragedy in this true story made for British TV. Longtime happily marrieds Diana (Walters) and Deric (Broadbent) Longden are struggling to ccpe with Diana's mysterious and increasingly debilitating illness, which causes blackouts, pain, and the inability to use her limbs. Diana comes to accept the fact that she's going to die and decides to find her hubby a new wife, aided by Deric's friendship with a blind novelist (Thomas). Terrific performances keep the mawkishness at bay. Based on Deric Longden's books "Diana's Story" and "Lost for Words." **87m/C VHS, LV.** *GB* Julie Walters, Jim Broadbent, Sian Thomas, Thora Hird, Andrew Lancel, Anastasia Mulrooney; ***D:*** Richard Loncraine; ***W:*** Jack Rosenthal. *MAX*

Wedding in Blood ☆☆☆ **1974 (PG)** Two French lovers plot to kill their respective spouses, and proceed to do so amid calamity and much table-turning. Sharp social satire and suspenseful mystery. Based on a true story. In French with English subtitles. **98m/C VHS, Beta.** *FR IT* Claude Pieplu, Stephane Audran, Michel Piccoli; ***D:*** Claude Chabrol. *COL*

A Wedding in Galilee ☆☆☆ *Noce In Galilee* **1987** The elder of a Palestinian village is given permission to have a traditional wedding ceremony for his son if Israeli military officers can attend as the guests of honor. As the event approaches, conflicts arise among the villagers, the family, and the Israelis. Long but fascinating treatment of traditional culture in the modern world amidst political tension. In Arabic and Hebrew, with English subtitles. **113m/C VHS, LV.** *BE FR* Ali M. El Aleili, Nazih Akleh, Anna Achdian; ***D:*** Michel Khleifi. *KIV, INJ*

Wedding in White ☆☆ **1972 (R)** A rape and out-of-wedlock pregnancy trouble a poor British clan living in Canada during WWII. Sad, glum way to spend an evening. Kane is good in a non-comic role. Her screen father cares more for her honor than he does for her. **103m/C VHS, Beta.** *CA* Donald Pleasence, Carol Kane, Leo Phillips; ***D:*** William Fruet. *SUE*

The Wedding March ☆☆☆☆ **1928** Von Stroheim's famous silent film about romantic couplings in pre-WWI Vienna. The director also stars as a prince preparing to marry for money, who falls in love with a beautiful, but poor woman. Romance and irony, with a memorable finale. Like many of his other great films, it was taken from him and re-edited. Initially the first of two halves; the second, "The Honeymoon," has been lost. Next to "Greed," his most successful film. **113m/B VHS, Beta.** Erich von Stroheim, Fay Wray, ZaSu Pitts, George Fawcett, Maude George, Matthew Betz, George Nicholls, Cesare Gravina; ***D:*** Erich von Stroheim; ***C:*** Hal Mohr; ***M:*** Gaylord Carter. *PAR*

The Wedding Party ☆½ **1969** Apprehensive groom is overwhelmed by his too-eager bride and her inquisitive relatives at a prenuptial celebration. Hokey, dull, would-be comedy. First screen appearances of both Clayburgh and De Niro (spelled DeNero in the credits). **90m/C VHS, Beta.** Jill Clayburgh, Robert De Niro, William Finley; ***D:*** Brian DePalma, Cynthia Munroe, Wilford Leach; ***W:*** Brian DePalma. *NO*

Wedding Rehearsal ☆☆½ **1932** A young nobleman thwarts his grandmother's plans to marry him off by finding suitors for all the young ladies offered to him until he finally succumbs to the charms of his mother's secretary. Enjoyable, fun comedy. First featured roles for actresses Oberon, Barrie, and Gardner. **84m/B VHS, Beta, LV.** Merle Oberon, Roland Young, John Loder, Wendy Barrie, Maurice Evans, Joan Gardner; ***D:*** Alexander Korda. *SUE*

Wee Willie Winkie ☆☆☆ **1937 (PG)** A precocious little girl is taken in by a British regiment in India. Sugar-coated. If you're a cinematic diabetic, be warned. If you're a Temple fan, you've probably already seen it. If not, you're in for a treat. Inspired by the Rudyard Kipling story. **99m/B VHS, Beta.** Shirley Temple, Victor McLaglen, Sir C. Aubrey Smith, June Lang, Michael Whalen, Cesar Romero, Constance Collier; ***D:*** John Ford; ***C:*** Arthur C. Miller. Nominations: Academy Awards '37: Best Interior Decoration. *FOX*

Weeds ☆☆☆ **1987 (R)** A highly fictionalized account of the career of Rick Cluchey, who, as a lifer in San Quentin federal prison, wrote a play. He was eventually paroled and went on to form a theater group made up of ex-cons. Original and often enjoyable with a tight ensemble performance. Filmed on location at Stateville Correctional Center in Illinois, with inmates serving as extras. **115m/C VHS, Beta, LV.** Nick Nolte, Rita Taggart, William Forsythe, Lane Smith, Joe Mantegna, Ernie Hudson, John Toles-Bey, Mark Rolston, Anne Ramsey, Charlie Rich; ***D:*** John Hancock; ***W:*** John Hancock, Dorothy Tristan; ***M:*** Angelo Badalamenti. *HBO*

Week-End In Havana ☆☆½ **1941** Set in pre-revolution Cuba, this frothy musical finds salesgirl Faye on a long-awaited cruise when her ship gets stranded in Havana. She's escorted around town by shipping-official Payne and catches the eye of gambler-lothario Romero, who has a jealous girlfriend in Miranda. Fun fluff. ♫Romance and Rhumba; Tropical Magic; The Nango; A Weekend in Havana; When I Love, I Love; Maria Inez; Rebola a Bola. **80m/C VHS.** Alice Faye, John Payne, Cesar Romero, Carmen Miranda, Cobina Wright Jr., George Barbier, Sheldon Leonard, Billy Gilbert; ***D:*** Walter Lang; ***W:*** Karl Tunberg; ***M:*** Alfred Newman. *FXV*

Weekend ☆☆☆ **1967** A Parisian couple embark on a drive to the country. On the way they witness and are involved in horrifying highway wrecks. Leaving the road they find a different, equally grotesque kind of carnage. Godard's brilliant, surreal, hyper-paranoiac view of modern life was greatly influenced by the fact that his mother was killed in an auto accident in 1954 (he himself suffered a serious motorcycle mishap in 1975). In French with English subtitles. **105m/C VHS.** *FR IT* Mireille Darc, Jean Yanne, Jean-Pierre Kalfon, Valerie Lagrange, Jean-Pierre Leaud, Yves Beneyton; ***D:*** Jean-Luc Godard; ***W:*** Jean-Luc Godard; ***M:*** Antoine Duhamel. *NYF, FCT, INJ*

Weekend at Bernie's ☆☆½ *Hot and Cold* **1989 (PG-13)** Two computer nerds discover embezzlement at their workplace after being invited to their boss's beach house for a weekend party. They find their host murdered. They endeavor to keep up appearances by (you guessed it) dressing and strategically posing the corpse during the party. Kiser as the dead man is memorable, and the two losers gamely keep the silliness flowing. Lots of fun. **101m/C VHS, VHS, Beta.** Andrew McCarthy, Jonathan Silverman, Catherine Mary Stewart, Terry Kiser, Don Calfa, Louis Giambalvo; ***D:*** Ted Kotcheff; ***W:*** Robert Klane; ***M:*** Andy Summers. *LIV*

Weekend at Bernie's 2 ☆½ **1993 (PG)** Unlikely but routine sequel to the original's cavorting cadaver slapstick, except now McCarthy and Silverman are frantically hunting for Bernie's (Kiser) cash stash, a quest that takes them and poor dead Bernie to the Caribbean. See Bernie get stuffed in a suitcase, see Bernie hang glide, see Bernie tango, see Bernie attract the opposite sex. Thin script with one-joke premise done to death but fun for those in the mood for the postmortem antics of a comedic stiff. Plenty of well-executed gags involving the well-preserved corpse (particularly one that's been dead for two films now) should lure back fans of the 1989 original. **89m/C VHS, LV.** Andrew McCarthy, Jonathan Silverman, Terry Kiser, Tom Wright, Steve James, Troy Beyer, Barry Bostwick; ***D:*** Robert Klane; ***W:*** Robert Klane; ***M:*** Peter Wolf. *COL*

Weekend at the Waldorf ☆☆☆ **1945** Glossy, americanized remake of "Grand Hotel" set at the famous Park Avenue hotel, the Waldorf-Astoria, in New York City. Turner and Rogers star in the roles originated by Joan Crawford and Greta Garbo.

Johnson and Pidgeon play their love interests. Combining drawing room comedy with slapstick and a touch of romance proved to be a hit, as this film was one of the top grossers of 1945 and was just what war-weary moviegoers wanted to see. Based on the play "Grand Hotel" by Vicki Baum. **130m/B VHS.** Ginger Rogers, Walter Pidgeon, Van Johnson, Lana Turner, Robert Benchley, Edward Arnold, Leon Ames, Warner Anderson, Phyllis Thaxter, Keenan Wynn, Porter Hall, Samuel S. Hinds; ***D:*** Robert Z. Leonard; ***W:*** Samuel Spewack, Bella Spewack, Guy Bolton. *MGM*

Weekend of Shadows 𝄞𝄞𝄞 **1977** Confident, moralistic murder drama about a posse after an innocent immigrant they believe has killed a woman. Police sergeant Roberts is interested only in his reputation, not in justice. Posse member Waters begins to sympathize with the hunted man and defends his innocence. Intelligent, well-conceived, and professionally directed. **94m/C VHS, Beta.** John Waters, Melissa Jaffer, Graeme Blundell, Wyn Roberts, Barbara West, Graham Rouse; ***D:*** Tom Jeffrey. *SUE*

Weekend Pass 𝄞 **1984 (R)** Moronic rookie sailors who have just completed basic training are out on a weekend pass, determined to forget everything they have learned. They find this surprisingly easy to do. **92m/C VHS, Beta, LV.** D.W. Brown, Peter Ellenstein, Phil Hartman, Patrick Hauser, Chip McAllister; ***D:*** Lawrence Bassoff; ***W:*** Lawrence Bassoff. *LIV, VES*

Weekend War 𝄞𝄞½ **1988 (PG-13)** A group of National Guardsmen are sent to the Honduras for their annual tour of duty. But when a guerilla war between Honduras and Nicaragua breaks out, the Guardsmen are forced to fight for their lives. The "Bridge on the River Kwai" finale features the dilemma over a bridge linking the two countries. Made for television. **96m/C VHS.** Daniel Stern, Stephen Collins, Charles Haid, Evan Mirand, Michael Beach, Scott Paulin, James Tolkan; ***D:*** Steven Hilliard Stern; ***M:*** Brad Fiedel. *COL*

Weekend Warriors 𝄞½ **1986 (R)** Young film-studio employees evade the draft in 1961 by enlisting for National Guard weekend duty. Grade "C" dumb comedy from professional celebrity and first-time director Convy. **88m/C VHS, Beta.** Chris Lemmon, Lloyd Bridges, Daniel Greene, Tom Villard, Vic Tayback; ***D:*** Bert Convy; ***W:*** Bruce Belland; ***M:*** Perry Botkin. *LIV*

Weekend with the Babysitter *Woof! Weekend Babysitter* **1970 (R)** Sordid teen drama about a weekend babysitter who goes to a film director's house and babysits everyone but the kids, running into a heroin-smuggling ring along the way. Casting-couch story with a twist. **93m/C VHS, Beta.** Susan Roman, George E. Carey, James Almanzar, Luanne Roberts; ***D:*** Don Henderson. *PSM*

Weep No More My Lady 𝄞𝄞 **1993 (PG-13)** Suspense-filled whodunit about a wealthy businessman who comes between two sisters and a sibling rivalry that turns into a deadly game of murder. Based on the best-selling book by Mary Higgins Clark. **92m/C VHS.** Daniel J. Travanti, Shelley Winters, Kristin Scott Thomas. *REP*

Weird Science 𝄞𝄞 **1985 (PG-13)** Hall is appealing, and Hughes can write dialogue for teens with the best of them. However, many of the jokes are in poor taste, and the movie seems to go on forever. Hall and his nerdy cohort Mitchell-Smith use a very special kind of software to create the ideal woman who wreaks zany havoc in their lives from the outset. **94m/C VHS, Beta, LV.** Kelly Le Brock, Anthony Michael Hall, Ilan Mitchell-Smith, Robert Downey Jr., Bill Paxton; ***D:*** John Hughes; ***W:*** John Hughes; ***C:*** Matthew F. Leonetti; ***M:*** Ira Newborn. *MCA*

Weird World of LSD 𝄞½ **1967** Cheap exploitation film featuring the evil effects of LSD. **?m/C VHS.** Terry Tessem, Ann Lindsay, Yolanda Morino. *SNC, TPV*

The Weirdo 𝄞 **1989** "The Jerk" meets Freddie Krueger. This film is absolutely wretched, even by horror movie standards. **91m/C VHS, Beta.** Steve Burlington, Jessica Straus; ***D:*** Andy Milligan. *NO*

Welcome Back Mr. Fox **1983** An award-winning science fiction short wherein an obnoxious movie producer cheats death by being cryogenically frozen, and then wakes up years later no wiser for the experience. Suitably, he receives his comeuppance. **21m/C VHS, Beta.** E.D. Phillips, Gustav Vintas; ***D:*** Walter W. Pitt III. *NO*

Welcome Home 𝄞𝄞 **1989 (R)** A missing-in-action Vietnam vet (Kristofferson) leaves his wife and children in Cambodia to return to America more than 15 years after he was reported dead. He finds his first wife remarried and discovers a teen-aged son he unknowingly fathered. This plotless, sporadically-moving film was Schaffner's last. Made for cable television. **92m/C VHS, Beta, LV.** Kris Kristofferson, JoBeth Williams, Sam Waterston, Brian Keith, Trey Wilson, Thomas Wilson Brown; ***D:*** Franklin J. Schaffner; ***C:*** Fred W. Koenekamp; ***M:*** Henry Mancini. *VES, LIV*

Welcome Home, Roxy Carmichael 𝄞𝄞 **1990 (PG-13)** Ryder, as a young misfit, is the bright spot in this deadpan, would-be satire. Hollywood star Roxy Charmichael returns to her small Ohio hometown and begins fantasizing that she is really her mother. It is obvious why this deadpan, hard-to-follow movie was a box-office flop. **98m/C VHS, Beta, LV, 8mm.** Winona Ryder, Jeff Daniels, Laila Robins, Dinah Manoff, Ava Fabian, Robbie Kiger, Sachi Parker; ***D:*** Jim Abrahams. *PAR*

Welcome Stranger 𝄞𝄞½ **1947** New doctor's ideas clash with the old doctor's ways in a small town until the younger saves the live of the elder. Crosby and Fitzgerald star as the two clashing medics in this reunion of the cast of "Going My Way." He wins the heart of the town and the heart of local teacher Caulfield in the meantime. Sheekman's script calls for Marx Brothers'-like comedy and director Nugent appears in a cameo as another doctor. **107m/B VHS.** Bing Crosby, Barry Fitzgerald, Joan Caulfield, Wanda Hendrix, Frank Faylen, Elizabeth Patterson, Robert Shayne, Don Beddoe, Percy Kilbride, Larry Young; ***Cameos:*** Elliott Nugent; ***D:*** Elliott Nugent; ***W:*** Arthur Sheekman; ***C:*** Lionel Lindon; ***M:*** Johnny Burke, James Van Heusen. *MCA*

Welcome to Blood City 𝄞½ **1977** An anonymous totalitarian organization kidnaps a man and transports him electronically to a fantasy western town where the person who murders the most people becomes the town's "kill master." Amateurish and low-budget. **96m/C VHS, Beta.** Jack Palance, Keir Dullea, Samantha Eggar, Barry Morse. *LIV*

Welcome to 18 𝄞 **1987 (PG-13)** Three girls, just out of high school, take summer jobs at a dude ranch, work a local casino, flirt, tease and get in trouble. The movie isn't funny in the least, and is filled with utter nonsense. Hargitay is the daughter of actress Jayne Mansfield. **91m/C VHS, Beta.** Courtney Thorne-Smith, Mariska Hargitay, Jo Ann Willette, Christine Kaufmann; ***D:*** Terry Carr. *LIV*

Welcome to L.A. 𝄞𝄞𝄞 **1977 (R)** Rudolph's ambitious directorial debut focuses on the sexual escapades of a group of Southern Californians. Based on the music suite "City of the One Night Stands" by Baskin, which also (unfortunately) serves as the soundtrack. Rudolph improved greatly after this initial effort. **106m/C VHS, Beta.** Sissy Spacek, Sally Kellerman, Keith Carradine, Geraldine Chaplin, Lauren Hutton, Viveca Lindfors, Harvey Keitel, John Considine; ***D:*** Alan Rudolph; ***W:*** Alan Rudolph; ***M:*** Richard Baskin. *FOX*

Welcome to Spring Break 𝄞½ **1988 (R)** College co-eds are stalked by a killer on the beaches of Florida. **92m/C VHS, Beta, LV.** John Saxon, Michael Parks. *NO*

Welcome to the Dollhouse 𝄞𝄞½ **1995 (R)** Eleven-year-old, glasses-wearing Dawn Wiener (Matarazzo) is the middle child of a middle-class family in an average New Jersey town. It's her first year in junior high and Dawn's bewildered—by school, by family, by life in general and where she fits in. Puberty sucks. **87m/C VHS.** Heather Matarazzo, Brendan Sexton Jr., Daria Kalinina, Matthew Faber, Angela Pietropinto, Eric Mabius; ***D:*** Todd Solondz; ***W:*** Todd Solondz; ***C:*** Randy Drummond; ***M:*** Jill Wisoff. Sundance Film Festival '96: Grand Jury Prize. *NYR*

The Well 𝄞𝄞𝄞 **1951** A young black girl disappears and a white man (Morgan) is accused of kidnapping her. When it is discovered that the girl is trapped in a deep well, Morgan's expertise is needed to help free her. **85m/B VHS, Beta.** Richard Rober, Harry (Henry) Morgan, Barry Kelley, Christine Larson; ***D:*** Leo Popkin, Russel Rouse; ***C:*** Ernest Laszlo. Nominations: Academy Awards '51: Best Film Editing, Best Story & Screenplay. *VCI*

Well-Digger's Daughter 𝄞𝄞𝄞 *La Fille Du Puisatier* **1946** As her lover goes off to war, a well-digger's daughter discovers that she is pregnant causing both sets of parents to feud over who's to blame. This is the first film made in France after the end of WWII and marks the return of the French film industry. In French with English subtitles. **142m/B VHS, Beta.** *FR* Raimu, Josette Day, Fernandel, Charpin; ***D:*** Marcel Pagnol. *NOS, DVT, APD*

Wend Kuuni 𝄞𝄞 *God's Gift* **1982** A fable for modern times set in Burkina Faso before the coming of Islam or Christianity. A mute, memoryless child is found by a peddler and adopted by the peddler's village. One day the boy finds a body hanging from a tree, shocked he recovers his speech and tells the story of his tragic past, when he and his mother were cast out of their own village. When his mother dies, the boy is bereft of family and tradition and without these ties to his history he loses both speech and memory. In More with English subtitles. **70m/C VHS.** ***D:*** Gaston Kabore. *KIV*

We're Back! A Dinosaur's Story 𝄞𝄞½ **1993 (G)** Animated adventures of a pack of revived dinosaurs who return to their old stomping grounds—which are now modern-day New York City. Smart-mouth human boy Louie and his girlfriend Cecilia take the dinos under their wing (so to speak), wise them up to modern life, and try to prevent their capture by the evil Professor Screweyes. Slow-moving with some violence. Adapted from the book by Hudson Talbott. **78m/C VHS, LV.** ***D:*** Dick Zondag, Ralph Zondag, Phil Nibbelink, Simon Wells; ***W:*** John Patrick Shanley; ***V:*** John Goodman, Felicity Kendal, Walter Cronkite, Joey Shea, Jay Leno, Julia Child, Kenneth Mars, Martin Short, Rhea Perlman, Rene LeVant, Blaze Berdahl, Charles Fleischer, Yeardley Smith. *MCA*

We're in the Legion Now 𝄞½ **1937** Denny and Barnett star as a couple of American gangsters who join the French Foreign Legion to escape rival hoods from back home. **56m/B VHS, Beta, 8mm.** Reginald Denny, Vince Barnett, Esther Ralston. *VYY*

We're in the Navy Now **1927** The famed comedy duo is back again with another armed forces farce. A mild successor to "Behind the Front." **60m/B VHS, Beta.** Wallace Beery, Raymond Hatton. *GPV, FCT*

We're No Angels 𝄞𝄞½ **1955** Three escapees from Devil's Island hide out with the family of a kindly French storekeeper. One of Bogart's few comedies. From the French stage play of the same name. Claustrophobic and talky. Later remade with De Niro and Penn. **103m/C VHS, Beta.** Humphrey Bogart, Aldo Ray, Joan Bennett, Peter Ustinov, Basil Rathbone, Leo G. Carroll; ***D:*** Michael Curtiz; ***C:*** Loyal Griggs. *PAR*

We're No Angels 𝄞𝄞½ **1989 (R)** Two escaped cons disguise themselves as priests and get in the appropriate series of jams. De Niro and Penn play off each other well, turning in fine comic performances. Distantly related to the 1955 film of the same name and the David Mamet play. **110m/C VHS, Beta, LV.** Robert De Niro, Sean Penn, Demi Moore, Hoyt Axton, Bruno Kirby, James Russo, John C. Reilly, Ray McAnally, Wallace Shawn; ***D:*** Neil Jordan; ***W:*** David Mamet; ***C:*** Philippe Rousselot; ***M:*** George Fenton. *PAR*

We're Not Dressing 𝄞𝄞𝄞 **1934** Loose musical adaptation of J.M. Barrie's "The Admirable Crichton" with the butler transformed into singing sailor Crosby. Fabulously wealthy heiress Lombard invites her pals for a South Seas yachting adventure. Only the ship gets wrecked and everyone winds up on a small island where the practical Crosby whips everyone into shape (and romances Lombard).

Burns and Allen supply additional comedy as a pair of botanists who just happen to be studying the local fauna. ♫Good Night Lovely Little Lady; I'll Sing About the Birds and the Bees; It's Just a New Spanish Custom; Let's Play House; Love Thy Neighbor; May I?; Once in a Blue Moon; She Reminds Me of You. **74m/B VHS, LV.** Bing Crosby, Carole Lombard, George Burns, Gracie Allen, Ethel Merman, Leon Errol, Ray Milland; ***D:*** Norman Taurog; ***W:*** Horace Jackson, Francis Martin; ***M:*** Harry Revel, Mack Gordon. *MCA*

We're Not Married ♂♂♂ **1952** Five couples learn that they are not legally married when a judge realizes his license expired before he performed the ceremonies. The story revolves around this quintet of couples who now must cope with whether or not they really do want to be married. Although the episodes vary in quality, the Allen-Rogers sequence is excellent. Overall, the cast performs well in this lightweight comedy. **85m/B VHS.** Ginger Rogers, Fred Allen, Victor Moore, Marilyn Monroe, Paul Douglas, David Wayne, Eve Arden, Louis Calhern, Zsa Zsa Gabor, James Gleason, Jane Darwell, Eddie Bracken, Mitzi Gaynor; ***D:*** Edmund Goulding; ***W:*** Nunnally Johnson, Dwight Taylor. *FXV*

We're Talkin' Serious Money ♂♂½ **1992 (PG-13)** Sal and Charlie are a couple of loser scam-artists always after the elusive big score. They borrow $10,000 from the mob for another get-rich-quick scheme and wind up over their heads with both the mob and the FBI out to get them. **92m/C VHS, LV.** Dennis Farina, Leo Rossi, Fran Drescher, John Lamotta; ***D:*** James Lemmo; ***W:*** Leo Rossi, James Lemmo; ***M:*** Scott Grusin. *COL*

Werewolf in a Girl's Dormitory ♂ *Lycanthropus; The Ghoul in School* **1961** Girls' school headmaster undergoes dental transformation at night. Atrocious dubbing, with equally atrocious theme song "The Ghoul in School." **82m/B VHS.** *IT* Barbara Lass, Carl Schell, Curt Lowens, Maurice Marsac; ***D:*** Richard Benson. *SMW, SNC*

Werewolf of London ♂♂½ **1935** A scientist searching for a rare Tibetan flower is attacked by a werewolf. He scoffs at the legend, but once he's back in London, he goes on a murderous rampage every time the moon is full. Dated but worth watching as the first werewolf movie made. **75m/B VHS.** Henry Hull, Warner Oland, Valerie Hobson, Lester Matthews, Spring Byington; ***D:*** Stuart Walker. *MCA*

Werewolf of Washington ♂♂ **1973 (PG)** Stockwell is a White House press secretary with a problem—he turns into a werewolf. And bites the President, among others. Sub-plot involves a short mad scientist who operates a secret monster-making lab in a White House bathroom. Occasionally engaging horror spoof and political satire made during Watergate era. **90m/C VHS, Beta.** Dean Stockwell, Biff Maguire, Clifton James; ***D:*** Milton Moses Ginsberg. *NO*

The Werewolf vs. the Vampire Woman ♂½ *Blood Moon* **1970 (R)** Hirsute Spanish wolfman teams with two female students in search of witch's tomb. One is possessed by the witch, and eponymous title results. **82m/C VHS.** *SP GE* Paul Naschy, Gaby Fuchs, Barbara Capell, Patty Shepard, Valerie Samarine, Julio Pena, Andres Resino; ***D:*** Leon Klimovsky. *SNC, HEG*

Werewolves on Wheels *Woof!* **1971 (R)** A group of bikers are turned into werewolves due to a Satanic spell. A serious attempt at a biker/werewolf movie, however, too violent and grim, not at all funny, and painful to sit through. McGuire had a hit with "Eve of Destruction." **85m/C VHS, Beta.** Stephen Oliver, Severn Darden, Donna Anderson, Duece Barry, Billy Gray, Barry McGuire; ***D:*** Michel Levesque. *UNI*

Wes Craven Presents Mind Ripper ♂♂ *Mind Ripper* **1995 (R)** A top secret government experiment, intended to produce a superhuman, goes wrong and traps the scientists in a remote desert outpost with their deadly, pissed-off creation. **90m/C VHS.** Lance Henriksen, John Diehl, Natasha Gregson Wagner, Dan Blom, Claire Stansfield; ***D:*** Joe Gayton; ***W:*** Jonathan Craven, Phil Mittleman; ***C:*** Fernando Arguelles; ***M:*** J. Peter Robinson. *AVE*

Wes Craven's New Nightmare ♂♂♂ **1994 (R)** Seems the six previous conjurings of Freddy's tortured but fictional soul have inadvertently created a real supernatural force bent on tormenting the lives of retired scream queen Langenkamp, her son (Hughes), writer-director Craven, and surprisingly mild alter-ego Englund. Craven's solution is to write a script that reunites series principals for a final showdown with the slashmaster in Hell. Clever and original in a genre known for neither trait, this movie-in-a-movie-about-a-movie is equal parts playful gimmick and inspired terror that will give even the most seasoned Kruegerphile the heebie-jeebies. **112m/C VHS, LV.** Robert Englund, Heather Langenkamp, Miko Hughes, David Newsom, Tracy Middendorf, Fran Bennett, John Saxon, Wes Craven, Robert Shaye, Sara Risher, Marianne Maddalena; ***D:*** Wes Craven; ***W:*** Wes Craven; ***M:*** J. Peter Robinson. Nominations: Independent Spirit Awards '95: Best Film. *NLC*

West-Bound Limited ♂♂½ **1923** A Romantic adventurer rescues a girl from certain death as a train is about to hit her, and the two fall in love. Lucky for him, she happens to be the boss' daughter. This film is a good example of classic silent melodrama with music score. **70m/B VHS, Beta.** John Harron, Ella Hall, Claire McDowell. *VYY*

West of Nevada ♂♂ **1936** A rare film, featuring the former Lieutenant Governor of Nevada (and Clara Bow's husband) in a fast-moving adventure about a band of Indians who must protect their gold from thieves. Bell is the good guy who aids the Indians. **59m/B VHS, Beta.** Rex Bell, Joan Barclay, Al "Fuzzy" St. John, Steve Clark. *GVV*

West of Pinto Basin ♂♂ **1940** The Range Busters are riding around checking the territory for badmen in this tale of the old west. The music score includes "That Little Prairie Gal of Mine," "Rhythm of the Saddle," and "Ridin' the Trail Tonight." **60m/B VHS, Beta.** Ray Corrigan, Max Terhune, John "Dusty" King, Jack Perrin. *NOS, DVT*

West of the Divide ♂♂½ **1934** A young cowboy (Wayne) impersonates an outlaw in order to hunt down his father's killer and find his missing younger brother. He saves a proud rancher and his feisty daughter along the way. A remake of "Partners of the Trail," and a solid early Wayne oater. **53m/B VHS, Beta.** John Wayne, George "Gabby" Hayes, Lloyd Whitlock, Yakima Canutt; ***D:*** Robert North Bradbury. *COL, REP, NOS*

West of the Law ♂♂ **1942** A group of ranchers turn to lawmen for protection from a band of outlaws. Part of the Rough Riders series. **60m/B VHS, Beta.** Buck Jones, Tim McCoy, Raymond Hatton; ***D:*** Howard Bretherton. *NOS, VCN, DVT*

West of the Pecos ♂♂½ **1945** Rill (Hale) is a society gal on her way to the family ranch in Texas. She's disguised as a boy for safety, which turns out to be a smart idea when outlaws attack the stagecoach. Fortunately, Pecos Smith (Mitchum) is also around to lend a hand. Based on the novel by Zane Grey; first filmed in 1935. **66m/B VHS.** Robert Mitchum, Barbara Hale, Richard Martin, Thurston Hall, Rita (Paula) Corday, Russell Hopton, Harry Woods; ***D:*** Edward Killy; ***C:*** Russell Metty. *GPV*

West of Zanzibar ♂♂½ **1928** Chaney plays an ivory trader, ruling a jungle kingdom, who lives for revenge on the man who left him a cripple. He decides to ruin the man's daughter and turn her into a prostitute but his plan backfires. Chaney and director Browning offer a steamy atmosphere amidst a number of script flaws. **63m/B VHS, LV.** Lon Chaney Sr., Lionel Barrymore, Warner Baxter, Mary Nolan; ***D:*** Tod Browning. *FCT*

The West Point Story ♂♂½ *Fine and Dandy* **1950** Cagney stars as an on-the-skids Broadway director offered a job staging a show at West Point. Seems cadet MacRae has written a musical and his uncle happens to be a producer. Cagney, with girlfriend Mayo, finds all the rules and regulations getting the better of his temper, so much so that he's told unless he can conform to academy standards the show won't go on! Day is the showgirl MacRae falls for. Cagney's energy and charm carry the too-long film but it's not one of his better musical efforts. ♫Ten Thousand Sheep; You Love Me; By the Kissing Rock; Long Before I Knew You; Brooklyn; It Could Only Happen in Brooklyn; Military Polka. **107m/B VHS.** James Cagney, Virginia Mayo, Gordon MacRae, Doris Day, Roland Winters, Gene Nelson, Alan Hale Jr., Wilton Graff, Jerome Cowan; ***D:*** Roy Del Ruth; ***W:*** John Monks Jr., Charles Hoffman, Irving Wallace; ***M:*** Sammy Cahn, Jule Styne. Nominations: Academy Awards '50: Best Original Score. *WAR, MVD*

West Side Story ♂♂♂½ **1961** Gang rivalry and ethnic tension on New York's West Side erupts in a ground-breaking musical. Loosely based on Shakespeare's "Romeo and Juliet," the story follows the Jets and the Sharks as they fight for their turf while Tony and Maria fight for love. Features frenetic and brilliant choreography by co-director Robbins, who also directed the original Broadway show, and a high-caliber score by Bernstein and Sondheim. Wood's voice was dubbed by Marni Nixon and Jimmy Bryant dubbed Beymer's. The laserdisc version includes the complete storyboards, production sketches, re-issue trailer, and an interview with Wise in a letterbox format with digital stereo surround sound. ♫Prologue; Jet Song; Something's Coming; Dance at the Gym; Maria; America; Tonight; One Hand, One Heart; Gee, Officer Krupke. **151m/C VHS, Beta, LV.** Natalie Wood, Richard Beymer, Russ Tamblyn, Rita Moreno, George Chakiris, Simon Oakland, Ned Glass; ***D:*** Robert Wise, Jerome Robbins; ***W:*** Ernest Lehman; ***C:*** Daniel F. Fapp; ***M:*** Leonard Bernstein, Stephen Sondheim. Academy Awards '61: Best Art Direction/Set Decoration (Color), Best Color Cinematography, Best Costume Design (Color), Best Director (Wise), Best Film Editing, Best Picture, Best Sound, Best Supporting Actor (Chakiris), Best Supporting Actress (Moreno), Best Score; Directors Guild of America Awards '61: Best Director (Wise), Best Director (Robbins); New York Film Critics Awards '61: Best Film; Nominations: Academy Awards '61: Best Adapted Screenplay. *MGM, OM*

West to Glory ♂½ **1947** Glory isn't necessarily exciting, as the hero helps a Mexican rancher save his gold and jewels from evildoers in this slow-paced oater. **61m/B VHS.** Eddie Dean, Roscoe Ates, Dolores Castle, Gregg Barton, Alex Montoya, Harry Vejar; ***D:*** Ray Taylor. *NOS*

Western Double Feature 1 **1938** In "Utah" (1945, 55 minutes), Rogers foils a land swindle and helps a lady ranch owner; in "Man from Music Mountain" (1938, 60 minutes), Autry foils a worthless gold mining stock swindle. **115m/B VHS, Beta.** Roy Rogers, Dale Evans, George "Gabby" Hayes, Gene Autry, Smiley Burnette; ***D:*** Joseph Kane. *HHT*

Western Double Feature 1: Wild Bill & Sunset Carson **194?** Double feature: in "Calling Wild Bill Elliott" (1943), Wild Bill comes to the aid of homesteaders; in "Santa Fe Saddlemates" (1945), Carson breaks up a diamond smuggling ring. **120m/B VHS, Beta.** Wild Bill Elliott, Sunset Carson; ***D:*** Spencer Gordon Bennet. *MED*

Western Double Feature 2 **1933** Wayne and Hayes are teamed together in two hour-long B-westerns: "Star Packer" (1934) and "West of the Divide" (1933). **120m/B VHS, Beta.** John Wayne, George "Gabby" Hayes; ***D:*** Robert North Bradbury. *HHT*

Western Double Feature 2: Wayne & Hale *Nightriders; Home on the Range* **198?** Double feature; in "Night Riders" (1939), Wayne battles injustice; in "Home on the Range" (1946, color), Hale protects a wild animal refuge. **120m/B VHS, Beta.** John Wayne, Monte Hale; ***D:*** George Sherman. *MED*

Western Double Feature 3 **1936** Two Wayne westerns are on this tape: "Helltown" (1938, 59 minutes), in which Wayne catches a cattle rustler; and "Winds of the Wasteland" (1936, 54 minutes), where he plays an out-of-work Pony Express rider. **113m/B VHS, Beta.** John Wayne, Johnny Mack Brown, Marsha Hunt, Phyllis Fraser; ***D:*** Charles T. Barton, Mack V. Wright. *HHT*

Western Double Feature 3: Rogers & Allen **1950** Double feature. In "Twilight in the Sierras" (1950), Rogers catches a gang of crooks; in "Under Mexicali Stars" (1950), Allen is a cowboy who uncovers a counterfeiting ring. **134m/C VHS, Beta.** Roy Rogers, Dale Evans, Rex Allen; ***D:*** William Witney. *MED*

Western Double Feature 4 **1937** Rogers plays a dual role in a case of mistaken identity in "Billy the Kid Returns" (1938, 56 minutes); in "Round Up Time in Texas" (1937, 56 minutes), Autry is framed on a charge of diamond smuggling. **112m/B VHS, Beta.** Roy Rogers, Gene Autry, Smiley Burnette; ***D:*** Joseph Kane. *HHT*

Western Double Feature 4: Rogers & Evans *Don't Fence Me In; Sheriff of Wichita* **194?** In "Don't Fence Me In" (1945), Rogers helps out a woman reporter; in "Sheriff of Wichita" (1948), a frontier investigator solves a crime. **120m/B VHS, Beta.** Roy Rogers, Dale Evans, George "Gabby" Hayes, Allan "Rocky" Lane. *MED*

Western Double Feature 5 **1935** Wayne stars in both halves of this double feature: in "Desert Trail" (1935, 54 minutes), he plays a rodeo star; in "Man from Utah" (1934, 55 minutes), he brings a gang of murderers to justice. **109m/B VHS, Beta.** John Wayne, Polly Ann Young; ***D:*** Robert North Bradbury. *HHT*

Western Double Feature 5: Rogers & Autry **1937** "The Big Show" (1937) features songs, action, and horses; in "Home in Oklahoma" (1946), Roger tracks down a murderer. **108m/B VHS, Beta.** Gene Autry, Roy Rogers, Smiley Burnette; ***D:*** Mack V. Wright, William Witney. *MED*

Western Double Feature 6: Rogers & Trigger *Trigger, Jr.; Gangs of Sonora* **1950** "Trigger Jr." (1950) is the story of Trigger's colt; "Gangs of Sonora" (1941, black and white) deals with a fight to save a small frontier newspaper. **120m/C VHS, Beta.** Roy Rogers, Dale Evans, Bob Livingston, Bob Steele; ***D:*** William Witney. *MED*

Western Double Feature 7: Wild Bill & Crabbe *Phantom of the Plains; Prairie Rustlers* **1945** "Phantom of the Plains" deals with a plan to save a woman from a gigolo; "Prairie Rustlers" tells of the problems of a man who is the identical double of Billy the Kid. **120m/B VHS, Beta.** Wild Bill Elliott, Buster Crabbe. *MED*

Western Double Feature 8: Hale & Carradine **194?** In "Silver Spurs" (1943), ranchers wanting to get the right-of-way through oil land run into an ambitious resort owner; in "Out California Way" (1946), Hale is a young cowboy looking for work in Hollywood. **121m/B VHS, Beta.** Roy Rogers, Monte Hale, John Carradine. *MED*

Western Double Feature 9: LaRue & Beery **194?** In "Cheyenne Takes Over" (1947), LaRue battles outlaws; in "Tulsa Kid" (1940), a young man must face a gunfighter. **120m/B VHS, Beta.** Lash LaRue, Donald (Don "Red") Barry, Noah Beery Sr. *MED*

Western Double Feature 10: Roy, Dale, & Trigger **198?** In "Bells of Coronado" (1950), Rogers must solve a murder and uranium ore theft; in "King of the Cowboys" (1943, black and white), Roy investigates a band of saboteurs. **120m/C VHS, Beta.** Roy Rogers, Dale Evans; ***D:*** William Witney. *MED*

Western Double Feature 11 **1950** Roy and Trigger act as modern day Robin Hoods to end crooked dealing in the West; Roy hides behind a smile and a song to capture murderers of a deputy and a ranch owner. **121m/B VHS, Beta.** Roy Rogers, Penny Edwards, Gordon Jones, George "Gabby" Hayes. *MED*

Western Double Feature 12 **1944** Red Ryder learns of a plot to scare ranchers into selling out before an oil strike is discovered; the Three Musketeers are sent to the Caribbean as U.S. envoys to sell Army horses. **108m/B VHS, Beta.** Bob Livingston, Wild Bill Elliott, Duncan Renaldo, Robert (Bobby) Blake. *MED*

Western Double Feature 13 **194?** Red Ryder foils outlaws trying to swindle the Duchess' stage line in a small isolated town in "Wagon Wheels Westward" (1945). "Rocky Mountain Rangers" (1940), features the Three Mesquiteers pursuing the deadly Barton Gang. **108m/B VHS, Beta.** Red Ryder, Bob Livingston, Robert (Bobby) Blake. *MED*

Western Double Feature 14 **1952** Outlaws, good guys, and romance on the old frontier. Amateur Robin Hoods steal back money wrongfully taken. **123m/B VHS, Beta.** Tim Holt, Jack Holt, Nan Leslie, Noreen Nash. *MED*

Western Double Feature 15 **1950** Rogers breaks up a cattle rustling ring; the good guys try to bring law and order to a vast Wyoming territory plagued by a crooked political boss. **122m/B VHS, Beta.** Roy Rogers, Penny Edwards, Donald (Don "Red") Barry, Lynn Merrick. *MED*

Western Double Feature 16 **1946** Autry is sent to quell a revolution in Mexico; Rogers's horse Lady and Hayes's horse Golden Sovereign are the focal points of the second part of this double feature. **108m/B VHS, Beta.** Gene Autry, Smiley Burnette, Roy Rogers, George "Gabby" Hayes. *MED*

Western Double Feature 17 **194?** Rogers stars in "The Golden Stallion" (1949). Roy battles diamond smugglers who use wild horses to transport the goods. "The Cherokee Flash" (1945), starring Carson, deals with a respectable citizen's outlaw past catching up to him. **121m/C VHS, Beta.** Roy Rogers, Sunset Carson; ***D:*** William Witney. *MED*

Western Double Feature 18 **194?** A Rogers double feature: in "Eyes of Texas" (1948), a westerner turns his ranch into a camp for war-orphaned boys; in "Helldorado" (1946), Roy travels to Las Vegas. **108m/B VHS, Beta.** Roy Rogers, Andy Devine, Dale Evans; ***D:*** William Witney. *MED*

Western Double Feature 19 **1945** Rogers helps a young woman foil a plot by crooks to swindle her inheritance. Roy appears in his first starring role (1938) and fights an outlaw gang. **108m/B VHS, Beta.** Roy Rogers, Dale Evans, Pat Brady. *MED*

Western Double Feature 21 **194?** Roy battles crooks in "Susanna Pass" (1949). In "Sheriff of Las Vegas" (1944), Red must find the murderer of Judge Blackwell. **121m/C VHS, Beta.** Roy Rogers, Red Ryder, Dale Evans, Robert (Bobby) Blake; ***D:*** William Witney. *MED*

Western Double Feature 22 **194?** A Rogers double feature: "Under California Stars" (1948), Roy rounds up a gang of wild horse rustlers; "San Fernando Valley" (1944), Roy brings law and order to the valley. **108m/B VHS, Beta.** Roy Rogers; ***D:*** William Witney. *MED*

Western Double Feature 24 **194?** In "Cowboy and the Senorita" (1944), Roy solves the mystery of a missing girl. "Colorado Serenade" (1946) is a musical western in Cinecolor starring Dean. **122m/C VHS, Beta.** Roy Rogers, Dale Evans, Eddie Dean. *MED*

Western Frontier 🦴🦴 **1935** Ordinary cowpoke Maynard is called on to lead the fight against a band of outlaws led by the Indian-raised sister he never knew he had. Action-packed, fast, and fun. Maynard's first outing for Columbia. **56m/B VHS, Beta.** Ken Maynard, Lucille Browne, Nora Lane, Robert "Buzzy" Henry, Frank Yaconelli; ***D:*** Al(bert) Herman. *NOS, DVT*

Western Gold **1937** Western set during the Civil War in which the character played by Smith Ballew is sent west to stop thieves who are stealing gold from the Union. **57m/C VHS.** Smith Ballew, Heather Angel, Leroy Mason, Howard Hickman, Ben Alexander, Frank McGlynn, Otis Harlan, Tom London, Bud Osborne; ***D:*** Howard Bretherton. *GPV*

Western Justice 🦴🦴 **1935** Good Guy Steele brings western-style justice to a lawless town. Ordinary oater with horses, etc., and a few chuckles on the side. **56m/B VHS, Beta.** Bob Steele; ***D:*** Robert North Bradbury. *VTR, NOS*

Western Mail 🦴🦴 **1942** Yet another western in which the hero goes undercover so he can bring the bad guys to justice. Yaconelli plays a guitar tune, accompanied by his monkey. **54m/B VHS.** Tom Keene, Frank Yaconelli, Leroy Mason, Jean Trent, Fred Kohler Jr.; ***D:*** Robert Emmett Tansey. *NOS, DVT, HEG*

Western Pacific Agent 🦴🦴 **1951** A Western Pacific agent chases an outlaw who has committed robbery and murder. The agent falls in love with the victim's sister and, of course, prevails. Rather violent. **62m/B VHS, Beta, LV.** Kent Taylor, Sheila Ryan, Mickey Knox, Robert Lowery; ***D:*** Sam Newfield. *NO*

Western Trails 🦴 **1938** Forgettable western about the clean-up of a Wild West town terrorized by outlaws. Thin script, bad acting, and a little singin' and funnin' around. **59m/B VHS, Beta.** Bob Baker, Marjorie Reynolds, Robert Burns; ***D:*** George Waggner. *NOS, DVT, HEG*

Western Union 🦴🦴🦴½ **1941** A lavish, vintage epic romantically detailing the political machinations, Indian warfare and frontier adventure that accompanied the construction of the Western Union telegraph line from Omaha, Nebraska, to Salt Lake City, Utah, during the Civil War. A thoroughly entertaining film in rich Technicolor. This was Lang's second western, following his personal favorite, "The Return of Frank James." Writer Carson utilized the title, but not the storyline, of a Zane Grey book. The German Lang showed himself a master of the most American of genres, yet made only one more western, "Rancho Notorious" (1952), another masterpiece. **94m/C VHS, Beta.** Randolph Scott, Robert Young, Dean Jagger, Slim Summerville, Virginia Gilmore, John Carradine, Chill Wills, Barton MacLane, Minor Watson, Charles Middleton, Irving Bacon; ***D:*** Fritz Lang. *FOX, MLB*

The Westerner 🦴🦴🦴½ **1940** A sly, soft-spoken drifter champions Texas border homesteaders in a land war with the legendary Judge Roy Bean. "The Law West of the Pecos" sentences drifter Cooper to hang, but Cooper breaks out of jail. He falls for damsel Davenport and stays in the area, advocating the rights of homesteaders to Brennan. Brennan's Bean is unforgettable and steals the show from Cooper. Film debuts of actors Tucker and Andrews. Amazing cinematography; Brennan's Oscar was his third, making him the first performer to pull a hat trick. **100m/B VHS, Beta, LV.** Gary Cooper, Walter Brennan, Doris Davenport, Dana Andrews, Forrest Tucker, Charles Halton; ***D:*** William Wyler; ***C:*** Gregg Toland. Academy Awards '40: Best Supporting Actor (Brennan); Nominations: Academy Awards '40: Best Interior Decoration, Best Story. *HBO, SUE, BTV*

Westfront 1918 🦴🦴🦴 **1930** A dogmatic anti-war film by the German master (his first talkie), about German and French soldiers on the fields of WWI, dying together without victory. Stunning in its portrayal of war's futility, with excellent photography that achieves a palpable realism. In German with English subtitles. **90m/B VHS, Beta.** *GE* Gustav Diesl, Fritz Kampers, Claus Clausen, Hans Joachim Moebis; ***D:*** G.W. Pabst. *SUE, GLV, INJ*

Westward Ho 🦴½ **1935** Wayne is determined to bring to justice his parents' slayer. Haven't we seen this one before? Seems the bad guys have corrupted his brother. Wayne's group of vigilantes is called "The Singing Riders," so naturally he sings—or is made to appear to. He looks and sounds ridiculous. **55m/B VHS.** John Wayne, Sheila Mannors; ***D:*** Robert North Bradbury. *REP, VCN, NOS*

Westward Ho, the Wagons! 🦴½ **1956** The promised land lies in the west, but to get there these pioneers must pass unfriendly savages, thieves, villains, and scoundrels galore. Suitable for family viewing, but why bother? Well, the cast does include four Mouseketeers. **94m/B VHS, Beta.** Fess Parker, Kathleen Crowley, Jeff York, Sebastian Cabot, George Reeves; ***D:*** William Beaudine; ***M:*** George Bruns. *DIS*

Westward the Women 🦴🦴🦴 **1951** Taylor is Buck Wyatt, a scout hired to wagon-train 150 mail-order brides from Chicago to California. When his lustful hired hands turn out to be all hands, Taylor and the ladies must fight off attacking Indians on their own. Notable film allowing women to be as tough as men is not your typical western. Based on the Frank Capra story. **116m/C VHS.** Robert Taylor, Denise Darcel, Hope Emerson, John McIntire, Beverly Dennis, Lenore Lonergan, Marilyn Erskine, Julie Bishop, Renata Vanni, Frankie Darro, George Chandler; ***D:*** William A. Wellman; ***W:*** Charles Schnee; ***C:*** William Mellor; ***M:*** Jeff Alexander. *MGM*

Westworld **1973 (PG)** Crichton wrote and directed this story of an adult vacation resort of the future which offers the opportunity to live in various fantasy worlds serviced by lifelike robots. Brolin and Benjamin are businessmen who choose a western fantasy world. When an electrical malfunction occurs, the robots begin to go berserk. Brynner is perfect as a western gunslinging robot whose skills are all too real. **90m/C VHS, Beta, LV.** Yul Brynner, Richard Benjamin, James Brolin, Dick Van Patten, Majel Barrett; ***D:*** Michael Crichton; ***W:*** Michael Crichton. *MGM*

Wet and Wild Summer *Woof!* **1992 (R)** Topless beach resort is the playground for stud lifeguards and sexy resort owners. **95m/C VHS, LV.** Christopher Atkins, Elliott Gould, Julian McMahon, Rebecca Cross; ***D:*** Maurice Murphy. *VMK*

Wet Gold **1984** A beautiful young woman and three men journey to retrieve a sunken treasure. Nice scenery. Proves that it is possible to make "The Treasure of the Sierra Madre" without making a classic. John Huston, where are you? Made for television. **90m/C VHS, Beta.** Brooke Shields, Brian Kerwin, Burgess Meredith, Tom Byrd; ***D:*** Dick Lowry. *NO*

Wetherby **1985 (R)** Playwright David Hare's first directorial effort, which he also wrote, about a Yorkshire schoolteacher whose life is shattered when a young, brooding stranger comes uninvited to a dinner party, and then shoots himself in her living room. Compelling but oh, so dark. Richardson, who plays a young Redgrave, is actually Redgrave's daughter. **97m/C VHS, Beta.** *GB* Vanessa Redgrave, Ian Holm, Judi Dench, Joely Richardson, Tim McInnery, Suzanna Hamilton; ***D:*** David Hare; ***W:*** David Hare; ***M:*** Nick Bicat. Berlin International Film Festival '85: Golden Berlin Bear; National Society of Film Critics Awards '85: Best Actress (Redgrave). *MGM*

Whale for the Killing ½ **1981** An ecologist stranded in a remote Alaskan fishing village battles to save a beached humpbacked whale from a malicious Russian fisherman. Platitudinous and self-congratulatory, if well-meaning. Made for television from a book by Farley Mowat. **145m/C VHS, Beta.** Richard Widmark, Peter Strauss, Dee Wallace Stone, Bruce McGill, Kathryn Walker; ***D:*** Richard T. Heffron; ***M:*** Basil Poledouris. *FOX*

Whale Music **1994** Off-beat saga of a burned-out rock star and the runaway who invades his life. Desmond Howl (Chaykin) has retreated to a tumbledown estate in the Pacific Northwest, tired of the music grind, and wanting to devote himself to his masterwork—a symphony for whales. Runaway Claire (Preston) provides a surprisingly welcome presence in contrast to Howl's other visitors—ex-wife Fay (Dale), who wants him to sell the estate, rapacious recording exec Kenneth (Welsh), and Howl's brother, singer Daniel (Gross), who happens to be dead and haunting his sibling. Haphazard direction helps dissipate powerful lead performances. Adapted from the novel by Paul Quarrington. **100m/C VHS.** *CA* Maury Chaykin, Cyndy Preston, Jennifer Dale, Kenneth Welsh, Paul Gross; ***D:*** Richard J. Lewis; ***W:*** Paul Quarrington, Richard J. Lewis; ***C:*** Vic Sarin; ***M:*** George Blondheim. Genie Awards '94: Best Actor (Chaykin), Best Song ("Claire"), Best Sound; Nominations: Genie Awards '94: Best Director (Lewis), Best Film. *NYR*

Whale of a Tale **1976 (G)** A young boy trains a killer whale to appear in the big show in the main tank at "Marineland." **90m/C VHS, Beta.** William Shatner, Marty Allen, Abby Dalton, Andy Devine, Nancy O'Conner; ***D:*** Ewing Miles Brown. *VCI, WTA*

The Whales of August ½ **1987** Based on the David Berry play, the story of two elderly sisters—one caring, the other cantankerous, blind, and possibly senile—who decide during a summer in Maine whether or not they should give up their ancestral house and enter a nursing home. Gish and Davis are exquisite to watch, and the all-star supporting cast is superb—especially Price as a suave Russian. Lovingly directed by Anderson in his first US outing. **91m/C VHS, Beta, LV, 8mm.** Lillian Gish, Bette Davis, Vincent Price, Ann Sothern, Mary Steenburgen, Harry Carey Jr.; ***D:*** Lindsay Anderson; ***W:*** David Berry. National Board of Review Awards '87: Best Actress (Gish); National Media Owl Awards '88: First Prize; Nominations: Academy Awards '87: Best Supporting Actress (Sothern). *SUE, NLC*

The Wharf Rat **1995 (R)** Waterfront con man Petey Martin (Phillips) teams up with a journalist (Ticotin) to avenge the murder of his policeman brother by a group of corrupt cops lead by the crazy Doc (Reinhold). Made for cable. **88m/C VHS.** Lou Diamond Phillips, Rachel Ticotin, Judge Reinhold, Rita Moreno, Scott Cohen; ***D:*** Jimmy Huston; ***W:*** Jimmy Huston; ***C:*** Levie Isaacks; ***M:*** Mervyn Warren. *PAR*

What a Carve-Up! *No Place Like Homicide* **1962** A group of relatives gather in an old, spooky mansion to hear the reading of a will. Tries too hard. Remake of "The Ghoul." **87m/B VHS.** *GB* Kenneth Connor, Sidney James, Shirley Eaton, Donald Pleasence, Dennis Price, Michael Gough; ***D:*** Pat Jackson. *SNC*

What a Way to Die ½ **1970 (R)** An evil assassin plots dispatching with a difference. **87m/C VHS, Beta.** William Berger, Anthony Baker, Helga Anders, Georgia Moll; ***D:*** Helmut Foernbacher. *NO*

What About Bob? **1991 (PG)** Bob, a ridiculously neurotic patient, follows his psychiatrist on vacation, turning his life upside down. The psychiatrist's family find Bob entertaining and endearing. Murray is at his comedic best; Dreyfuss's overly excitable characterization occasionally wears thin. **99m/C VHS, Beta, LV.** Richard Dreyfuss, Bill Murray, Julie Hagerty, Charlie Korsmo, Tom Aldredge, Roger Bowen, Fran Brill, Kathryn Erbe, Doris Belack, Susan Willis; ***D:*** Frank Oz; ***W:*** Tom Schulman, Alvin Sargent; ***C:*** Michael Ballhaus; ***M:*** Miles Goodman. *TOU*

What Comes Around **1985 (PG)** A good-ole-boy drama about a doped-up country singer who is kidnapped by his brother for his own good. The singer's evil manager sends his stooges out to find him. Might have been funny, but isn't. But is it meant to be? Good Reed songs; mildly interesting plot. **92m/C VHS, Beta, LV.** Jerry Reed, Bo Hopkins, Arte Johnson, Barry Corbin; ***D:*** Jerry Reed. *NLC*

What Did You Do in the War, Daddy? ½ **1966** Unfunny comedy set in WWII about a group of weary American soldiers trying to get a small town in Sicily to surrender. Things don't go smoothly thanks to a combination soccer game/wine festival, not to mention the Germans deciding to attack. Director Edwards comedic verve deserted him. **119m/C VHS.** Dick Shawn, James Coburn, Sergio Fantoni, Giovanna Ralli, Aldo Ray, Harry (Henry) Morgan, Carroll O'Connor, Jay Novello, Vito Scotti; ***D:*** Blake Edwards; ***W:*** William Peter Blatty, Blake Edwards; ***M:*** Henry Mancini. *MGM*

What Do You Say to a Naked Lady? ½ **1970** Funt takes his Candid Camera to the streets to find out how people react when confronted by nude members of the opposite sex. Sporadically hilarious. **92m/C VHS, Beta.** ***D:*** Allen Funt. *FOX*

What Ever Happened To... ½ **1993** Sisters play sisters as the Redgraves (in their first film together) tackle this remake of "What Ever Happened to Baby Jane?" in all its demented glory. Former actress Blanche (Vanessa) and former child star "Baby Jane" (Lynn) are living in a decaying mansion, which Blanche, confined to a wheelchair, is talking about selling. "Baby" snaps (not that she was ever very stable) and proceeds to torment her sis (more than usual). **94m/C VHS.** Vanessa Redgrave, Lynn Redgrave, Bruce A. Young, Amy Steel, John Scott Clough, John Glover; ***D:*** David Greene; ***W:*** Brian Taggert. *AEL, FCT*

What Ever Happened to Baby Jane? ½ **1962** Davis and Crawford portray aging sisters and former child stars living together in a decaying mansion. When the demented Jane (Davis) learns of her now-crippled sister's (Crawford) plan to institutionalize her, she tortures the wheelchair-bound sis. Davis plays her part to the hilt, unafraid of Aldrich's unsympathetic camera, and the viciousness of her character. She received her tenth Oscar nomination for the role. **132m/B VHS, Beta, LV.** Bette Davis, Joan Crawford, Victor Buono, Anna Lee, B.D. Merrill; ***D:*** Robert Aldrich. Nominations: Academy Awards '62: Best Actress (Davis), Best Black and White Cinematography, Best Sound, Best Supporting Actor (Buono). *WAR*

What Happened to Rosa? **1921** This early Goldwyn release, a whimsical Cinderella story, casts Normand as an endearing shop girl duped by a gypsy's bogus predictions. Believing herself to be the reincarnation of a Castillian noblewoman she dons a fancy gown, attends a fancy shipboard ball and captures the heart of the fancy doctor of her dreams. But fearing his rejection of her true identity she slips away during the chaos of a brawl, leading the good doctor to believe that she is dead. A comedy of errors unfolds before they meet again and live happily ever after. No doubt it jerked a few tears in its day. **42m/B VHS.** Mabel Normand, Hugh Thompson, Doris Pawn, Tully Marshall, Eugenie Besserer, Buster Trow; ***D:*** Victor Schertzinger. *NOS, FHV*

What Happened Was... **1994 (R)** Two-character study about a weirdly nightmarish first date. Law secretary Jackie (Sillas) has been eyeing bookish paralegal Michael (Noonan) and finally invites him for dinner at her loft. The two struggle to relax and make small talk that turns into some unexpected soul baring. Emotionally distant Michael is unexpectedly hostile about his job and claims to be writing an expose of their law firm while overly-friendly Jackie is writing a children's book, which turns out to be jarringly violent and apparently autobiographical. Provides an idiosyncratic, if limited, appeal thanks to a compelling performance by Sillas. **92m/C VHS.** Tom Noonan, Karen Sillas; ***D:*** Tom Noonan; ***W:*** Tom Noonan; ***C:*** Joe DeSalvo; ***M:*** Lodovico Sorret. Sundance Film Festival '94: Best Screenplay, Grand Jury Prize; Nominations: Independent Spirit Awards '95: Best Actress (Sillas), First Screenplay. *HMK*

What Have I Done to Deserve This? *Que He Hecho Yo Para Merecer Esto!?* **1985** A savage parody on Spanish mores, about a speed-addicted housewife who ends up selling her son and killing her husband with a ham bone. Black, black comedy, perverse and funny as only Almodovar can be. In Spanish with subtitles. Nudity and profanity. **100m/C VHS, Beta, LV.** Carmen Maura, Chus Lampreave; ***D:*** Pedro Almodovar; ***W:*** Pedro Almodovar. *INJ, CCN, TPV*

What! No Beer? **1933** Two dim-bulb friends decide to put their money into a defunct brewery hoping for the end of Prohibition. They start up operations too soon and wind up attracting the unwelcome attentions of gangster bootleggers and the cops. Mediocre comedy and Keaton's last starring role as his own problems with alcohol affected his work. **66m/B VHS.** Buster Keaton, Jimmy Durante, Phyllis Barry, Roscoe Ates, John Miljan, Henry Armetta, Edward Brophy; ***D:*** Edward Sedgwick. *MGM*

What Price Glory? **1952** Remake of the 1926 silent classic about a pair of comradely rivals for the affections of women in WWI France. Strange to have Ford directing an offbeat comedy, but it works: masterful direction, good acting. Demarest broke both legs in a motorcycle accident during shooting. **111m/C VHS, Beta.** James Cagney, Dan Dailey, Corinne Calvet, William Demarest, James Gleason, Robert Wagner, Max Casey Adams Showalter, Craig Hill, Marisa Pavan; ***D:*** John Ford. *FOX, FCT*

What Price Hollywood? 🦴🦴🦴 **1932** Aspiring young starlet decides to crash film world by using an alcoholic director as her stepping stone. Bennett is lovely; Sherman is superb as an aging, dissolute man who watches his potential slip away. From a story by Adela Rogers St. Johns. Remade three times as "A Star is Born." **88m/B VHS, Beta, LV.** Constance Bennett, Lowell Sherman, Neil Hamilton; ***D:*** George Cukor; ***C:*** Charles Rosher; ***M:*** Max Steiner. Nominations: Academy Awards '32: Best Original Screenplay. *CCB, TTC, FCT*

What the Moon Saw 🦴🦴½ **1990** When a young boy is confronted by a less than friendly theater owner, he uses favorite scenes from "Sinbad" to deal with the aggressor. **86m/C VHS.** Pat Evison; ***D:*** Pino Amenta. *FHE, BTV*

What the Peeper Saw 🦴🦴 *Night Hair Child; Child of the Night* **1972** The wife of a wealthy author finds her comfortable life turning into a terrifying nightmare when her young stepson starts acting funny. Juicy and terrifying. **97m/C VHS, Beta.** Britt Ekland, Mark Lester, Hardy Kruger, Lilli Palmer. *VCI*

What Waits Below 🦴½ **1983 (PG)** A scientific expedition encounters a lost race living in caves in South America. Good cast, bad acting, and lousy script. Might have been much better. **88m/C VHS, Beta.** Timothy Bottoms, Robert Powell, Lisa Blount; ***D:*** Don Sharp. *LIV*

Whatever Happened to Aunt Alice? 🦴🦴🦴 **1969 (PG)** After murdering her husband to inherit his estate, a poor, eccentric widow develops an awful habit: she hires maids, only to murder them and steal their savings. The only evidence is a growing number of trees by the drive. Sleuth Ruth Gordon (of "Harold and Maude" fame, acting here just as odd) takes the job in hopes of solving the mystery. Thoroughly amusing. **101m/C VHS, Beta.** Geraldine Page, Ruth Gordon, Rosemary Forsyth, Robert Fuller, Mildred Dunnock; ***D:*** Lee H. Katzin; ***C:*** Joseph Biroc. *FOX, MLB*

Whatever Happened to Susan Jane? 🦴½ **1984** A bored housewife searches for an off-beat college friend, and enters into the seamy, strange world of San Francisco's lunatic fringe. Music by Tuxedo Moon, Indoor Life and other punk groups. **90m/C VHS, Beta.** *NO*

What's Eating Gilbert Grape 🦴🦴🦴 *Gilbert Grape* **1993 (PG-13)** Offbeat is mildly descriptive. Depp stars as Gilbert Grape, the titular head of a very dysfunctional family living in a big house in a small Iowa town. His Momma (Cates) weighs more than 500 pounds and hasn't left the house in 7 years, he has two squabbling teenage sisters, and 17-year-old brother Arnie (DiCaprio) is mentally retarded and requires constant supervision. What's a good-hearted grocery clerk to do? Well, when free-spirited Becky (Lewis) is momentarily marooned in town, Gilbert may have found a true soulmate. Performances, especially DiCaprio's, save this from the oddball/cute factor although flick would have benefitted from streamlining, particularly the scenes involving Depp and bad-haircut Lewis. Based on the novel by Hedges. **118m/C VHS, Beta, LV.** Johnny Depp, Leonardo DiCaprio, Juliette Lewis, Mary Steenburgen, Darlene Cates, Laura Harrington, Mary Kate Schellhardt, Kevin Tighe, John C. Reilly, Crispin Glover, Penelope Branning; ***D:*** Lasse Hallstrom; ***W:*** Peter Hedges; ***M:*** Alan Parker, Bjorn Isfalt. National Board of Review Awards '93: Best Supporting Actor (DiCaprio); Nominations: Academy Awards '93: Best Supporting Actor (DiCaprio); Golden Globe Awards '94: Best Supporting Actor (DiCaprio). *PAR*

What's Good for the Goose 🦴🦴½ **1969** Stuffy, married financial institution executive's lifestyle receives a major overhaul when he attends a banking conference and meets a beautiful and free-spirited young woman whom he takes as a lover. Unfortunately, he perpetually finds her in bed with other men, and then his wife gets in on the act, too. Classic British humor. **104m/C VHS.** *GB* Norman Wisdom, Sally Geeson, Sarah Atkinson, Sally Bazely; ***D:*** Menahem Golan; ***W:*** Norman Wisdom, Menahem Golan; ***M:*** Reg Tilsley. *NMD*

What's Love Got to Do with It? 🦴🦴½ **1993 (R)** Energetic biopic of powerhouse songstress Tina Turner. Short sequences cover her early life before moving into her abusive relationship with Ike and solo comeback success. Bassett may not look like Tina, but her exceptionally strong performance leaves no question as to who she's supposed to be, even during on-stage Tina sequences. Some credibility is lost when Turner is shown in the final concert sequence—Gibson would have been wise to let Bassett finish what she started. Fishburne is a sympathetic but still chilling Ike, rising to the challenge of showing both Ike's initial charm and longtime cruelty. Based on "I, Tina" by Turner and Kurt Loder. **118m/C VHS, LV.** Angela Bassett, Laurence "Larry" Fishburne, Vanessa Bell Calloway, Jenifer Lewis, Phyllis Stickney, Khandi Alexander, Pamela Tyson, Penny Johnson, Rae'ven Kelly, Robert Miranda, Chi; ***D:*** Brian Gibson; ***W:*** Kate Lanier; ***M:*** Stanley Clarke. Golden Globe Awards '94: Best Actress—Musical/Comedy (Bassett); Blockbuster Entertainment Awards '95: Female Newcomer, Video (Bassett); Nominations: Academy Awards '93: Best Actor (Fishburne), Best Actress (Bassett). *TOU*

What's New Pussycat? 🦴🦴🦴 *Quoi De Neuf, Pussycat?* **1965** A young engaged man, reluctant to give up the girls who love him, seeks the aid of a married psychiatrist who turns out to have problems of his own. Allen's first feature as both actor and screenwriter. Oscar-nominated title song sung by Tom Jones. **108m/C VHS, Beta, LV.** Peter Sellers, Peter O'Toole, Romy Schneider, Paula Prentiss, Woody Allen, Ursula Andress, Capucine; ***D:*** Clive Donner; ***W:*** Woody Allen; ***M:*** Burt Bacharach, Hal David. Nominations: Academy Awards '65: Best Song ("What's New Pussycat?"). *FOX, FCT*

What's the Matter with Helen? 🦴🦴½ **1971 (PG)** Two women, the mothers of murderous sons, move to Hollywood to escape their past and start a new life. They open a school for talented children, and seem to be adjusting to their new lives until strange things start happening. It is soon revealed that one of the mothers is a psychotic killer, and the other mother becomes part of an eerie finale. A fine starring vehicle for two aging actresses. Great score. **101m/C VHS.** Debbie Reynolds, Shelley Winters, Dennis Weaver, Agnes Moorehead, Michael MacLiammoir; ***D:*** Curtis Harrington. Nominations: Academy Awards '71: Best Costume Design. *MGM*

What's Up, Doc? 🦴🦴🦴 **1972 (G)** A shy musicologist from Iowa (Ryan) travels to San Francisco with his fiance (Kahn) for a convention. He meets the eccentric Streisand at his hotel and becomes involved in a chase to recover four identical flight bags containing top secret documents, a wealthy woman's jewels, the professor's musical rocks, and Streisand's clothing. Bogdanovich's homage to the screwball comedies of the '30s. Kahn's feature film debut. **94m/C VHS, Beta.** Barbra Streisand, Ryan O'Neal, Kenneth Mars, Austin Pendleton, Randy Quaid, Madeline Kahn; ***D:*** Peter Bogdanovich; ***W:*** David Newman, Buck Henry, Robert Benton; ***M:*** Artie Butler. Writers Guild of America '72: Best Original Screenplay. *WAR*

What's Up Front 🦴½ *The Fall Guy; A Fourth for Marriage* **1963** Occasionally funny '60s gag-fest about an ogle-eyed bra salesman who decides to sell door-to-door in order to save a failing brassiere company. Filmed in "Girl-O-Rama" by the young Vilmos Zsigmond. Dated and weird, with camp value. No nudity. Costumes were done by Frederick's of Hollywood. **90m/C VHS, Beta.** Tommy Holden, Marilyn Manning, Carolyn Walker, William Watters; ***D:*** Bob Wehling. *RHI*

What's Up, Tiger Lily? 🦴🦴🦴 **1966** This legitimate Japanese spy movie—"Kagi No Kag" (Key of Keys), a 1964 Bond imitation—was re-edited by Woody Allen, who added a new dialogue track, with hysterical results. Characters Terri and Suki Yaki are involved in an international plot to secure egg salad recipe; Allen's brand of Hollywood parody and clever wit sustain the joke. Music by the Lovin' Spoonful, who make a brief appearance. **90m/C VHS, Beta, LV.** *JP* Woody Allen, Tatsuya Mihashi, Mie Hama, Akiko Wakabayashi; ***D:*** Woody Allen, Senkichi Taniguhi; ***M:*** Jack Lewis. *VES*

Wheel of Fortune 🦴🦴 *A Man Betrayed; Citadel of Crime* **1941** A shrewd small-town lawyer, working on a case in the big city, is forced to expose his girlfriend's father as a crooked politician. Strange to see the Duke here in the lead, but what the hey. Not great, but interesting. **83m/B VHS.** John Wayne, Frances Dee, Edward Ellis, Ward Bond, Wallace Ford; ***D:*** John H. Auer. *REP*

The Wheeler Dealers 🦴🦴🦴 *Separate Beds* **1963** Garner plays a supposedly penniless investor (actually a Texas millionaire) who comes to New York stock analyst Remick for investment advice. Her shyster boss (Backus) tells her to sell the aw-shucks cowboy worthless stock which turns out to be worth a fortune. Zany spoof of Wall Street ethics. **100m/C VHS.** James Garner, Lee Remick, Jim Backus, Phil Harris, Shelley Berman, Chill Wills, John Astin, Louis Nye; ***D:*** Arthur Hiller. *MGM*

Wheels of Fire 🦴 *Vindicator* **1984 (R)** The earth is a wasteland controlled by sadistic highway hoodlums. When they kidnap the hero's sister, he fights back in a flame-throwing car. Horrible "Road Warrior" rip-off. **81m/C VHS, Beta, LV.** Gary Watkins, Lynda Wiesmeier; ***D:*** Cirio H. Santiago. *LIV, VES*

Wheels of Terror 🦴 **1990 (R)** Possessed black car stalks children in isolated village. Bus driver Cassidy gets behind the wheel of V-8 super-charged school bus to initiate most interminable chase scene in screen history. **86m/C VHS, Beta.** Joanna Cassidy, Marcie Leeds, Carlos Cervantes, Arlen Dean Snyder; ***D:*** Christopher Cain; ***M:*** Jay Gruska. *PAR*

When a Man Loves a Woman 🦴🦴½ *To Have and to Hold; Significant Other* **1994 (R)** Time to get suspicious when song titles become film titles. Alice Green (Ryan) is the mother in a perfect little family, with a loving husband (Garcia), two little girls, and a satisfying career. She's also a closet alcoholic. Less about her alcoholism than the effect on her family and her hubby in particular, shown as a '90s sort of guy who allows Alice to keep her secret. Ryan's detox treatments and struggle back to sobriety are fertile ground for psycho-babble and 12-step cliches, but solid performances save this picture from drying out. **126m/C VHS, LV.** Meg Ryan, Andy Garcia, Lauren Tom, Philip S. Hoffman, Tina Majorino, Mae Whitman, Ellen Burstyn, Eugene Roche, Latanya Richardson; ***D:*** Luis Mandoki; ***W:*** Ronald Bass, Al Franken; ***M:*** Zbigniew Preisner. Blockbuster Entertainment Awards '95: Drama Actress, Video (Ryan); Nominations: MTV Movie Awards '95: Best Female Performance (Ryan), Most Desirable Male (Garcia). *TOU*

When a Man Rides Alone 🦴🦴 **1933** Tyler relieves trains of their gold shipments in order to reimburse swindled investors. Lovely Lacey frowns on his initiative, so he kidnaps her to keep her quiet. The two fall in love, and the man who rides alone works beside his beloved. **60m/B VHS.** Tom Tyler, Adele Lacey, Alan Bridge, Robert Burns, Frank Ball, Alma Chester, Bud Osborne; ***D:*** J.P. McGowan. *NOS, GPV*

When a Man Sees Red 🦴½ **1934** Jones is a ranch foreman whose new boss is Campbell (she inherited the property). The two argue constantly but then come to realize all the fighting is just hiding true love. **60m/B VHS.** Buck Jones, Peggy Campbell, Dorothy Revier, Syd Saylor, Leroy Mason, Charles French, Robert F. (Bob) Kortman; ***D:*** Alan James. *GPV*

When a Stranger Calls 🦴½ **1979 (R)** Babysitter is terrorized by threatening phone calls and soon realizes that the calls are coming from within the house. Story was expanded from director Walton's short film "The Sitter." Distasteful and unlikely, though the first half or so is tight and terrifying. **97m/C VHS, Beta, LV.** Carol Kane, Charles Durning, Colleen Dewhurst, Rachel Roberts; ***D:*** Fred Walton. *COL*

When a Stranger Calls Back 🦴🦴½ **1993 (R)** Sequel to "When a Stranger Calls" finds college student Julia Jenz (Schoelen) still trying to put her life together five years after a terrifying ordeal with a stalker. She turns to her advisor Jill (Kane), who went through a similar fate, but once Jill becomes involved she again becomes the pawn of a psychopath. It's up to retired detective John Clifford (Durning), who saved Jill before, to do his heroics once again. Scary opening sequence but suspense peters out toward the end. Made for cable television. **94m/C VHS, LV.** Carol Kane, Charles Durning, Jill Schoelen, Gene Lythgow, Karen Austin; ***D:*** Fred Walton; ***W:*** Fred Walton. *MCA*

When a Woman Ascends the Stairs ℒℒ *Onna Ga Kaidan O Agaru Toki* **1960** A young widow with an elderly mother and a useless brother supports them all by working as a Ginza bar hostess. As she approaches the perilous professional age of 30, Keiko must decide whether to open her own bar or marry once again. In Japanese with English subtitles. **110m/B VHS.** *JP* Hideko Takamine, Tatsuya Nakadai, Masayuki Mori; ***D:*** Mikio Naruse. *WAC, INJ*

When Angels Fly ℒ **1982** In this emotional tale of love and murder, a young woman sets out to find the exact circumstances surrounding the mysterious death of her sister. **96m/C VHS, Beta.** Jennifer Dale, Robin Ward. *UNI, MOV*

When Comedy was King **1959** A compilation of the greatest silent screen comedians, including Keaton, Chaplin, Langdon, and Turpin. **81m/C VHS, Beta, LV.** Buster Keaton, Charlie Chaplin, Harry Langdon, Ben Turpin; ***D:*** Robert Youngson. *NO*

When Dinosaurs Ruled the Earth ℒℒ **1970 (G)** When "One Million Years B.C." ruled the box office the Brits cranked out a few more lively prehistoric fantasies. A sexy cavegirl, exiled because of her blond hair, acquires a cave-beau and a dinosaur guardian. Stop-motion animation from Jim Danforth, story by J.G. Ballard. Under the name Angela Dorian, Vetri was Playmate of the Year in 1968 (A.D.). **96m/C VHS, Beta, LV.** *GB* Victoria Vetri, Robin Hawdon, Patrick Allen, Drewe Henley, Sean Caffrey, Magda Konopka, Imogen Hassall, Patrick Holt, Jan Rossini; ***D:*** Val Guest; ***W:*** Val Guest. *WAR, FCT, MLB*

When Every Day was the Fourth of July ℒℒ½ **1978** A nine-year-old girl asks her father, a lawyer, to defend a mute handyman accused of murder, knowing this will bring on him the contempt of the community. Well handled, but see "To Kill a Mockingbird" first. Based on producer/director Curtis's childhood. Sequel: "The Long Days of Summer." Made for television. **100m/C VHS, Beta.** Katy Kurtzman, Dean Jones, Louise Sorel, Harris Yulin, Chris Petersen, Geoffrey Lewis, Scott Brady, Henry Wilcoxon, Michael Pataki; ***D:*** Dan Curtis. *LIV*

When Father was Away on Business ℒℒℒ½ **1985 (R)** Set in 1950s Yugoslavia. A family must take care of itself when the father is sent to jail for philandering with a woman desired by a Communist Party offical. The moving story of the family's day-to-day survival is seen largely through the eyes of the father's six-year-old son, who believes dad is "away on business." In Yugoslavian with English subtitles. **144m/C VHS.** *YU* Moreno D'E Bartolli, Miki Manojlovic, Mirjana Karanovic; ***D:*** Emir Kusturica. Cannes Film Festival '85: Best Film; Nominations: Academy Awards '85: Best Foreign Language Film. *FXL, INJ*

When Gangland Strikes ℒℒ **1956** A country lawyer, blackmailed by the mob, tries to protect his family without caving in. Unexceptional remake of "Main Street Lawyer." **70m/B VHS.** Raymond Greenleaf, Marjie Millar, Anthony Caruso, Jack Perrin, John Hudson; ***D:*** R.G. Springsteen; ***M:*** Van Alexander. *REP*

When Harry Met Sally... ℒℒℒ **1989 (R)** Romantic comedy follows the long relationship between two adults who try throughout the changes in their lives (and their mates) to remain platonic friends—and what happens when they don't. Wry and enjoyable script is enhanced by wonderful performances. Another directional direct hit for "Meathead" Reiner, and a tour de force of comic screenwriting for Ephron, with improvisational help from Crystal. Great songs by Sinatra sound-alike Connick. **96m/C VHS, Beta, LV, 8mm.** Billy Crystal, Meg Ryan, Carrie Fisher, Bruno Kirby, Steven Ford, Lisa Jane Persky, Michelle Nicastro, Harley Jane Kozak; ***D:*** Rob Reiner; ***W:*** Nora Ephron; ***M:*** Harry Connick Jr., Marc Shaiman. British Academy Awards '89: Best Original Screenplay; Nominations: Academy Awards '89: Best Original Screenplay. *NLC, SUE*

When Hell Broke Loose ℒ½ **1958** Routine WWII actioner about a small-time crook (Bronson) who joins the Army, changes his ways because of the love of a good woman, and gets a chance to be a hero when he stumbles upon a Nazi assassination plot against General Eisenhower. **78m/B VHS.** Charles Bronson, Violet Rensing, Richard Jaeckel, Arvid Nelson, Robert Easton; ***D:*** Kenneth Crane; ***W:*** Oscar Brodney. *PAR*

When Hell Was in Session ℒℒℒ **1982** In more than seven years as a prisoner of the Viet Cong, Holbrook is subjected to torture, starvation, and psychological warfare to break his will. Based on the true story of Navy Commander Jeremiah Denton. Painful and violent. Made for TV. **98m/C VHS, Beta.** Hal Holbrook, Eva Marie Saint, Ronny Cox; ***D:*** Paul Krasny. *TLF*

When He's Not a Stranger ℒℒℒ **1989** Date rape is the subject of this made-for-television drama. Lyn is a college freshman who goes to a campus party hosted by the football team. When Ron, the star quarterback, invites Lyn to his dorm room, the situation gets out of hand. Only Lyn calls it rape and Ron calls her a liar. Intense performances are a highlight of this well-done story. **100m/C VHS.** Annabeth Gish, John Terlesky, Kevin Dillon, Paul Dooley, Kim Meyers; ***D:*** John Gray. *TRI*

When Knights were Bold ℒℒ½ **1936** An English nobleman living in India inherits a castle in his native land. Returning home, he is knocked unconscious by a falling suit of armor while trying to impress a young lady and dreams himself back to medieval days. Enjoyable comedy about that ubiquitous British class hierarchy. **55m/B VHS, Beta.** Fay Wray, Jack Buchanan, Martita Hunt; ***C:*** Frederick A. (Freddie) Young. *VYY*

When Ladies Meet ℒℒ½ **1941** Entertaining story of a love quadrangle that features several of MGM's top stars of the '40s. In this remake of the 1933 film, Crawford plays a novelist and an early proponent of the women's liberation movement. She falls in love with her publisher (Marshall), who just happens to be married to Garson. Meanwhile, Taylor, who is in love with Crawford, attempts to show her that he isa more suitable match for her than Marshall, but Crawford has yet to catch on.The lengthy dialogue on women's rights is badly dated, but the real-life rivalry between Crawford and Garson adds a certain bite to their witty exchanges. Also known as "Strange Skirts." **105m/B VHS.** Joan Crawford, Robert Taylor, Greer Garson, Herbert Marshall, Spring Byington; ***D:*** Robert Z. Leonard; ***W:*** Anita Loos, S.K. Lauren. Nominations: Academy Awards '41: Best Interior Decoration. *MGM*

When Lightning Strikes *Woof!* **1934** Lightning the Wonder Dog prevents the owner of a rival lumber company from stealing his master's land. He gets to use his talents of running, swimming, barking, and smoking cigars. Proves that real woofers were made way back when, even though in 1934 they didn't feature scantily clad babes. Part of Video Yesteryear's Golden Turkey series. **51m/B VHS, Beta.** Francis X. Bushman. *VYY*

When Nature Calls *Woof!* **1985 (R)** A city family "gets back to nature" in this collection of mostly ineffective gags and poor satirical ideas. Probably your first and last chance to see Liddy and Mays on screen together. **76m/C VHS, Beta, LV.** Davie Orange, Barbara Marineau, Nicky Beim, Tina Marie Staiano, Willie Mays, G. Gordon Liddy; ***D:*** Charles Kaufman. *MED*

When Night is Falling ℒℒℒ **1995 (R)** Camille (Bussieres) is a professor of mythology at a Calvinist college in Toronto and engaged to theologian Martin (Czerny). Vaguely unsatisfied, Camille meets Petra (Crawford), a trapeze artist in a traveling circus, gets drawn into her world, falls in love, and must decide what she wants from her life. Lots of yearning, romance, and fantasy. Lesbian lovemaking scenes caused a ratings problem (the MPAA originally deemed them worthy of NC-17). **96m/C VHS.** *CA* Pascale Bussieres, Rachael Crawford, Henry Czerny, David Fox, Don McKellar, Tracy Wright; ***D:*** Patricia Rozema; ***W:*** Patricia Rozema; ***C:*** Douglas Koch; ***M:*** Lesley Barber. *NYR*

When Taekwondo Strikes ℒ **1983 (R)** One brave Taekwondo master leads the Korean freedom fighters against the occupying army of WWII Japan. **95m/C VHS, Beta.** Jhoon Rhee, Ann Winton, Angela Mao, Huang Ing Sik; ***D:*** Raymond Chow. *SUE*

When the Bough Breaks ℒℒ **1986** A psychologist helps the police with the case of a murder-suicide witnessed by a child. He finds one sick secret society at work in this unkinder, ungentler TV thriller, based on the novel by Jonathan Kellerman. Danson co-produced. **100m/C VHS.** Ted Danson, Richard Masur, Rachel Ticotin, David Huddleston, James Noble, Kim Miyori, Merritt Butrick; ***D:*** Waris Hussein. *WOV*

When the Bough Breaks ℒℒ **1993 (R)** A Texas police chief (Sheen) discovers seven severed hands and turns to a forensic expert (Walker) for help. But then the specialist discovers a psychic link between a mentally disturbed child and the serial killer. **103m/C VHS.** Ally Walker, Martin Sheen, Ron Perlman; ***D:*** Michael Cohn; ***W:*** Michael Cohn. *TTC*

When the Clouds Roll By ℒℒℒ½ **1919** Psycho-satire pits demented doctor against Fairbanks in experiment to make him suicidal basket case. Fairbanks seems to contract ferocious nightmares, passionate superstitions, a spurning lover, and a warrant for his arrest, none of which suppresses his penchant for acrobatics. **77m/B VHS, Beta.** Douglas Fairbanks Sr., Herbert Grimwood, Kathleen Clifford, Frank Campeau, Ralph Lewis, Daisy Robinson, Albert MacQuarrie; ***D:*** Victor Fleming. *GPV, FCT*

When the Dark Man Calls ℒℒ½ **1995 (R)** Shock ending and a strong lead performance by Van Ark enhance this cable TV mystery. Call-in radio shrink Julianne Kaiser (Van Ark) is stalked by ex-con Parmenter (Lewis). Twenty-five years ago she testified that he murdered her parents although the bitter man's always proclaimed his innocence. Now Kaiser is having grisly flashbacks to her childhood but can she figure out the truth before Parmenter kills her? Based on a novel by Stuart M. Kaminsky. **89m/C VHS.** Joan Van Ark, Geoffrey Lewis, Chris Sarandon, James Read, Frances Hyland, Janet-Laine Green; ***D:*** Nathaniel Gutman; ***W:*** Pablo F. Fenjves. *PAR*

When the Greeks ℒℒ *Ton Kero Ton Hellinon* **1981** At the turn of the century, a rich young landowner is kidnapped by a group of nationalist bandits who demand a hefty ransom. But soon the young man realizes he's seeing his true Greek heritage for the first time and begins to identify with his captors. Greek with subtitles. **100m/C VHS.** *GR* Alexis Damianos, Kostas Arzoglou, George Sampanis, Stavros Mermighis; ***D:*** Lakis Papastathis; ***W:*** Lakis Papastathis; ***M:*** George Papadakis. *FCT*

When the Legends Die ℒℒℒ **1972 (PG)** A Ute Indian strives to preserve his heritage in an often harsh modern world. Recorded in hi-fi. **105m/C VHS, Beta.** Richard Widmark, Frederic Forrest; ***D:*** Stuart Millar. *FOX*

When the Line Goes Through ℒ **1971** A drifter arrives in a small West Virginia town and changes the lives of two pretty sisters. **90m/C VHS, Beta.** Martin Sheen, Davey Davidson, Beverly Washburn. *NO*

When the North Wind Blows ℒℒ **1974 (G)** An old, lone trapper hunts for and later befriends the majestic snow tiger of Siberia in the Alaskan wilderness. A good family film. **113m/C VHS, Beta.** Henry Brandon, Herbert Nelson, Dan Haggerty; ***D:*** Stewart Raffill. *VCI*

When the Party's Over ℒℒ½ **1991 (R)** Twenty-somethings share a southern California house and a hip—but ultimately empty— lifestyle. **114m/C VHS.** Rae Dawn Chong, Fisher Stevens, Elizabeth Berridge, Sandra Bullock, Kris Kramm; ***D:*** Matthew Irmas. *LIV*

When the Screaming Stops ☾ **1973** **(R)** A hunter is hired to find out who has been cutting the hearts out of young women who reside in a small village near the Rhine River. Turns out it's a she-monster who rules a kingdom beneath the river. Bad effects; gory gore; outlandish plot. All the ingredients, in other words, of a classic dog. **86m/C VHS, Beta.** *SP* Tony Kendall, Helga Line, Sylvia Tortosa; ***D:*** Armando de Ossorio. *LIV*

When the Time Comes ☾☾ **1991** **(PG-13)** A woman dying of cancer wants to take her own life, but when her husband refuses, she seeks the help of a male friend. Excellent acting doesn't provide the needed depth. Less a disease-of-the-week TV movie, more of an ethical-dilemma-of-the-week, and just as trivial. **94m/C VHS.** Bonnie Bedelia, Brad Davis, Terry O'Quinn, Karen Austin, Donald Moffat, Wendy Schaal; ***D:*** John Erman; ***M:*** Marvin Hamlisch. *REP*

When the West Was Young ☾½ **1932** An outdoor adventure about rounding up horses in the Old West. Based on a novel by Zane Grey; also titled "Wild Horse Mesa." **58m/B VHS, Beta.** Randolph Scott, Sally Blane, Guinn "Big Boy" Williams; ***D:*** Henry Hathaway. *NOS, DVT, VYY*

When the Whales Came ☾☾½ **1989** **(PG)** A conservationist fable about two children and a grizzled old codger living on a remote British isle during WWI. They try to avert disaster as mysterious narwhal whales descend on the island. Moralistic and uninvolving; poorly acted; slumber-inducing. Adapted from the novel by Morpugo. **100m/C VHS, Beta, LV.** *GB* Paul Scofield, Helen Mirren, David Threlfall, David Suchet, Jeremy Kemp, Max Rennie, Helen Pearce, Barbara Jefford; ***D:*** Clive Rees; ***W:*** Michael Morpugo; ***M:*** Christopher Gunning, Ruth Rennie. *FOX*

When the Wind Blows ☾☾☾ **1986** An animated feature about a retired British couple when their peaceful—and naive—life in the country is destroyed by nuclear war. Poignant, sad, and thought-provoking, and just a little scary. Features the voices of Ashcroft and Mills; Roger Waters, David Bowie, Squeeze, Genesis, Hugh Cornell, and Paul Hardcastle all contribute to the soundtrack. Based on the novel by Raymond Briggs. **80m/C VHS, Beta, LV.** *GB* ***D:*** Jimmy T. Murakami; ***V:*** Peggy Ashcroft, John Mills. *LIV*

When Thief Meets Thief ☾½ **1937** A cat burglar finds his world turned upside down when he begins to fall in love with one of his victims. Not much happening except a few nice stunts by Fairbanks. **85m/B VHS, Beta.** *GB* Douglas Fairbanks Jr., Valerie Hobson, Alan Hale, Jack Melford, Leo Genn, Ian Fleming; ***D:*** Raoul Walsh. *NOS, SNC*

When Time Ran Out ☾ **1980** **(PG)** A volcano erupts on a remote Polynesian island covered with expensive hotels and tourists with no way to escape. Contains scenes not seen in the theatrically released print of the film. A very good cast is wasted in this compilation of disaster film cliches. **144m/C VHS, Beta.** Paul Newman, Jacqueline Bisset, William Holden, Ernest Borgnine, Edward Albert, Barbara Carrera, Valentina Cortese, Burgess Meredith, Noriyuki "Pat" Morita, Red Buttons; ***D:*** James Goldstone; ***W:*** Stirling Silliphant; ***C:*** Fred W. Koenekamp; ***M:*** Lalo Schifrin. Nominations: Academy Awards '80: Best Costume Design. *WAR*

When Wolves Cry ☾½ *The Christmas Tree* **1969** **(G)** Tearjerker about an estranged father and young son reunited on a Corsican vacation. Their newfound joy sours when the lad is diagnosed with a fatal illness. Hardly one of Holden's best films. **108m/C VHS, Beta.** William Holden, Virna Lisi, Brook Fuller, Andre Bourvil; ***D:*** Terence Young. *GEM, VCI*

When Women Had Tails ☾½ *Quando De Donne Avevando La Coda* **1970** **(R)** A primitive comedy about prehistoric man's discovery of sex. And boy, did they ever discover it. Harmless (more or less), though not exactly cerebral. Followed by "When Women Lost Their Tails." **99m/C VHS, Beta.** *IT* Senta Berger, Frank Wolff; ***D:*** Pasquale Festa Campanile; ***M:*** Ennio Morricone. *SNC*

When Women Lost Their Tails ☾ **1975** **(R)** Ostensible sequel to "When Women Had Tails" about prehistoric cavemen and their sexual habits. **94m/C VHS, Beta.** *IT* Senta Berger; ***D:*** Pasquale Festa Campanile; ***M:*** Ennio Morricone. *NO*

When Worlds Collide ☾☾½ **1951** **(G)** Another planet is found to be rushing inevitably towards earth, but a select group of people attempt to escape in a spaceship; others try to maneuver their way on board. Oscar-quality special effects and plot make up for cheesy acting and bad writing. **81m/C VHS, Beta, LV.** Richard Derr, Barbara Rush, Larry Keating, Peter Hanson; ***D:*** Rudolph Mate; ***C:*** William Howard Greene. Academy Awards '51: Best Special Effects; Nominations: Academy Awards '51: Best Color Cinematography. *PAR*

When Your Lover Leaves ☾ **1983** Alleged comedy about a woman, dumped by her married boyfriend, who gets involved in a short-lived relationship with a neighbor. When that also doesn't work out, she decides she must first do something to please herself. Here endeth the lesson. Produced by Fonzie and Richie of "Happy Days." Made for television. **100m/C VHS.** Valerie Perrine, Betty Thomas, David Ackroyd, Ed O'Neill, Dwight Schultz, Shannon Wilcox; ***D:*** Jeff Bleckner; ***M:*** Randy Edelman. *NWV, VTR*

When's Your Birthday? ☾☾½ **1937** Brown stars in this comedy about a prize-fighter who is working his way through astrology school with his fighting skills. The stars, in turn, tell him when to fight. Lame zaniness (what other kind is there?) meant as a vehicle for Brown, though Kennedy is funnier. The opening sequence, an animated cartoon showing the influence of the moon over the planets, was filmed in Technicolor. **77m/B VHS, Beta.** Joe E. Brown, Marian Marsh, Edgar Kennedy; ***D:*** Harry Beaumont. *NOS, VYY, JEF*

Where ☾☾ **1994** Young man living in Budapest begins a psycho-sexual relationship with a young woman that explores the nature of domination and submission. After moving to Los Angeles, he subjects himself to the whims of a student. In English and Hungarian with subtitles. **?m/C VHS.** *HU* ***D:*** Gabor Zabo. *WAC*

Where Angels Fear to Tread ☾☾☾ **1991** **(PG)** Another turn-of-the-century tale of the English in Italy from the pen of E.M. Forster. Widowed, fortyish Lilia (Mirren) is urged by her stuffy in-laws to spend some time in Italy. Much to everyone's dismay she impulsively marries a 21-year-old Italian—with disastrous consequences. Based on Forster's first novel, the characters are more stereotypical and the story less defined than his later works and the movies made from them. Impressive performances and beautiful settings make up for a somewhat lackluster direction that isn't up to the standards set by the team of Merchant Ivory, responsible for the Forster films "A Room with a View" and "Howard's End." **112m/C VHS, LV.** *GB* Rupert Graves, Helena Bonham Carter, Judy Davis, Helen Mirren, Giovanni Guidelli, Barbara Jefford, Thomas Wheatley, Sophie Kullman; ***D:*** Charles Sturridge; ***M:*** Rachel Portman. *NLC, INJ*

Where Angels Go, Trouble Follows ☾☾½ **1968** Follow-up to "The Trouble with Angels," with Russell reprising her role as the wise Mother Superior challenged by her mischief loving students. Younger, modern nun Stevens tries to convince Russell to update her old-fashioned ways and persuades her to take the convent students on a bus trip to a California peace rally. A very young Saint James is one of the convent's irrepressible troublemakers. Very dated but still mildly amusing. **94m/C VHS.** Rosalind Russell, Stella Stevens, Binnie Barnes, Mary Wickes, Susan St. James, Dolores Sutton, Alice Rawlings; ***Cameos:*** Milton Berle, Arthur Godfrey, Van Johnson, Robert Taylor; ***D:*** James Neilson; ***W:*** Blanche Hanalis. *COL*

Where Are the Children? ☾½ **1985** **(R)** Based on Mary Higgins Clark's bestseller. A woman who was cleared of murdering the children from her first marriage remarries. Then the children from her second marriage are kidnapped. Sustains suspense completely, until it falls apart. **92m/C VHS, Beta.** Jill Clayburgh, Max Gail, Barnard Hughes, Clifton James, Harley Cross, Elisabeth Harnois, Elizabeth Wilson, Frederic Forrest; ***D:*** Bruce Malmuth. *COL*

Where Eagles Dare ☾☾☾ **1968** **(PG)** During WWII, a small group of Allied commandos must rescue an American general held by the Nazis in a castle in the Bavarian Alps. Relentless plot twists and action keep you breathless. Well-made suspense/adventure. Alistair MacLean adapted his original screenplay into a successful novel. **158m/C VHS, Beta, LV.** Clint Eastwood, Richard Burton, Mary Ure, Michael Hordern, Anton Diffring, Ingrid Pitt, Patrick Wymark, Robert Beatty; ***D:*** Brian G. Hutton. *MGM, TLF*

Where East Is East ☾☾½ **1929** In Indochina a badly scarred trapper (Chaney) lives with his daughter (Velez) and sells wild animals to circuses. Velez falls in love with a circus owner's son but finds out her own mother, seeking revenge on her ex-husband, trying to seduce the young man. A gorilla figures in the plot as well. Chaney's makeup, which contributed to his "Man of a Thousand Faces" nickname, highlights a contrived movie. **140m/B VHS.** Lon Chaney Sr., Lupe Velez, Estelle Taylor, Lloyd Hughes. *FCT*

Where Have All the People Gone? ☾ **1974** Solar explosion turns most of Earth's inhabitants to dust while the Anders family vacations in a cave. The family tries to return home amid the devastation. Bad timing, bad acting, bad script. Made for television. **74m/C VHS, Beta.** Peter Graves, Kathleen Quinlan, Michael-James Wixted, George O'Hanlon Jr., Verna Bloom; ***D:*** John Llewellyn Moxey. *ORI*

Where Is My Child? ☾☾½ **1937** Immigration to the New World brings only misfortune and betrayal in this tale of Jews in Eastern Europe between 1911 and 1937, as many experience the loss of family ties and religion. In Yiddish with English subtitles. **92m/B VHS.** Celia Adler, Anna Lillian, Morris Strassberg; ***D:*** Abraham Leff, Harry Lynn. *NCJ*

Where Love Has Gone ☾☾½ **1964** A soaper about a teenage daughter who kills her nympho mother's current boyfriend. Her divorced parents end up dragging the ordeal out in a murder trial/custody battle and a lot of family skeletons come out of their closets. Davis is the manipulative grand dame grandmother. Based on the novel by Harold Robbins. **114m/C VHS.** Bette Davis, Susan Hayward, Joey Heatherton, Jane Greer, George Macready; ***D:*** Edward Dmytryk; ***W:*** John Michael Hayes. Nominations: Academy Awards '64: Best Song ("Where Love Has Gone"). *PAR, FCT*

Where Sleeping Dogs Lie ☾☾ **1991** **(R)** A struggling writer moves into an abandoned California home five years after a wealthy family was murdered there. While doing research for his novel on their brutal killings, he revives their ghosts as well as the very real presence of their killer. **92m/C VHS.** Dylan McDermott, Tom Sizemore, Sharon Stone; ***D:*** Charles Finch. *COL*

Where the Boys Are ☾☾½ **1960** Four college girls go to Fort Lauderdale to have fun and meet boys during their Easter vacation. Features the film debuts of Francis, who had a hit single with the film's title song, and Prentiss. Head and shoulders above the ludicrous '84 remake. **99m/C VHS, Beta, LV.** George Hamilton, Jim Hutton, Yvette Mimieux, Connie Francis, Paula Prentiss, Dolores Hart; ***D:*** Henry Levin. *MGM*

Where the Boys Are '84 *Woof!* **1984** **(R)** Horrible remake of the 1960 comedy still features girls searching for boys during spring break in Fort Lauderdale. Telling about its era: charm gives way to prurience. **95m/C VHS, Beta.** Lisa Hartman Black, Wendy Schaal, Lorna Luft, Lynn-Holly Johnson; ***D:*** Hy Averback; ***W:*** Jeff Burkhart. Golden Raspberry Awards '84: Worst Supporting Actress (Johnson). *FOX*

Where the Buffalo Roam ☾½ **1980** **(R)** Early starring role for Murray as the legendary "gonzo" journalist Hunter S. Thompson. Meandering satire based on Thompson's books "Fear and Loathing in Las Vegas" and "Fear and Loathing on the Campaign Trail '72." Either confusing or offensively sloppy, depending on whether you've read Thompson. Music by Neil Young, thank goodness, or this might be a woof. **98m/C VHS, Beta.** Bill Murray, Peter Boyle, Susan Kellerman; ***D:*** Art Linson; ***M:*** Neil Young. *MCA*

Where the Bullets Fly ☠☠ **1966** Fast-paced Bond spoof. A British spy takes on the intelligence forces of several governments in his search for a new fuel elixir. Fun, if not scintillating. **88m/C VHS.** *GB* Tom Adams, Dawn Addams, Michael Ripper, Tim Barrett; ***D:*** John Gilling. *FOX*

Where the Day Takes You ☠☠½ **1992 (R)** Runaways on Hollywood Boulevard are depicted in an unfortunately heavy-handed drama. King (Mulroney) is the slightly older leader of a group of street kids who tries to discourage his friends from getting involved in the violence and drugs they see all around them. He falls in love with new runaway Heather (Boyle) but their love is blighted by the relentless bleakness of their lives. Among the other members of King's "family" are Astin, as a young druggie in thrall to his older dealer (MacLachlan) and Getty, as a young hustler drawn to violence. The story's predictability undercuts some convincing acting. **105m/C VHS, LV.** Dermot Mulroney, Lara Flynn Boyle, Balthazar Getty, Sean Astin, James LeGros, Ricki Lake, Kyle MacLachlan, Rob Knepper, Peter Dobson, Stephen Tobolowsky, Will Smith, Adam Baldwin, Christian Slater, Nancy McKeon, Alyssa Milano, David Arquette, Leo Rossi, Rachel Ticotin; ***D:*** Marc Rocco; ***W:*** Michael Hitchcock, Kurt Voss, Marc Rocco; ***M:*** Mark Morgan; ***V:*** Laura San Giacomo. *COL*

Where the Eagle Flies ☠☠ *Pickup on 101* **1972 (PG)** Ersatz sixties rock'n'roll road movie shuffles together free spirited college coed, hobo with heart of gold, and rock and roller who's making a lane change out of the fast track. **93m/C VHS.** Jack Albertson, Lesley Ann Warren, Martin Sheen, Michael Ontkean; ***D:*** John Florea. *NO*

Where the Green Ants Dream ☠☠½ *Wo Die Grunen Ameisen Traumen* **1984** A mining excavation in the Outback is halted by Aborigines who declare ownership of the sacred place where the mythical green ants are buried. A minor entry in the Herzog vision of modern-versus-primal civilization. Too obvious and somehow unsure of itself artistically. **99m/C VHS, Beta.** *GE* Bruce Spence, Wandjuk Marika, Roy Marika, Ray Barrett, Norman Kaye, Colleen Clifford; ***D:*** Werner Herzog. Nominations: Cannes Film Festival '84: Best Film. *XVC, MED, INJ*

Where the Heart Is ☠☠ **1990 (R)** Wealthy dad Coleman kicks his spoiled kids out on the streets to teach them the value of money. Meant as farce with a message. Flops in a big way; one senses it should have been much better. **111m/C VHS, LV.** Dabney Coleman, Uma Thurman, Joanna Cassidy, Suzy Amis, Crispin Glover, Christopher Plummer; ***D:*** John Boorman; ***W:*** John Boorman, Telsche Boorman. National Society of Film Critics Awards '90: Best Cinematography. *TOU*

Where the Hot Wind Blows ☠☠ *La Legge; La Loi; The Law* **1959** The sexual scene in Sicily is sadly not succinctly summarized in this so-so cinematic soap. Cross-generational and cross-class couplings are constant. Think of it as "The Last Picture Show" in a similarly sorry setting, except boring. **120m/C VHS, Beta.** *FR IT* Gina Lollobrigida, Marcello Mastroianni, Yves Montand, Melina Mercouri, Paolo Stoppa; ***D:*** Jules Dassin; ***W:*** Jules Dassin. *VYY, NOS, FCT*

Where the Lilies Bloom ☠☠☠ **1974 (G)** The touching story of four backwoods children who are left orphans when their father dies. They don't report his death to authorities, because they are afraid the family will be separated and sent to an orphanage. Stanton is great as the crusty landlord the children gradually accept as a friend. Based on the book by Vera and Bill Cleaver. **96m/C VHS.** Julie Gholson, Jan Smithers, Matthew Burrill, Helen Harmon, Harry Dean Stanton, Rance Howard, Sudie Bond, Tom Spratley, Helen Bragdon, Alice Beardsley; ***D:*** William A. Graham. *MGM*

Where the North Begins ☠ **1947** A Mountie ransacks the Canadian countryside in search of crime. **41m/B VHS, Beta, LV.** Russell Hayden, Jennifer Holt. *NO*

Where the Red Fern Grows ☠☠½ **1974 (G)** A young boy in Dust Bowl-era Oklahoma learns maturity from his love and responsibility for two Redbone hounds. Well produced, but tends to be hokey; good family fare. Followed by a sequel nearly twenty years later. **97m/C VHS, Beta.** James Whitmore, Beverly Garland, Jack Ging, Lonny Chapman, Stewart Peterson; ***D:*** Norman Tokar; ***C:*** Dean Cundey. *FHE, VES, HHE*

Where the Red Fern Grows: Part 2 ☠☠½ **1992 (G)** Sequel to one of the most popular family movies of all time starring Brimley as Grandpa Coleman. Set deep in the Louisiana woods, this magical coming of age tale will touch the hearts of young and old viewers alike. **105m/C VHS.** Wilford Brimley, Doug McKeon, Lisa Whelchel, Chad McQueen; ***D:*** Jim McCullough. *VCI*

Where the River Runs Black ☠☠ **1986 (PG)** An orphaned Indian child is raised in the Brazilian jungles by river dolphins. He is eventually befriended by a kindly priest who brings him into the modern world of violence and corruption. Slow pace is okay until the boy arrives at the orphanage, at which point the dolphin premise sadly falls by the wayside. **96m/C VHS, Beta.** Charles Durning, Peter Horton, Ajay Naidu, Conchata Ferrell, Alessandro Rabelo, Castulo Guerra; ***D:*** Christopher Cain; ***C:*** Juan Ruiz-Anchia; ***M:*** James Horner. *FOX*

Where the Rivers Flow North ☠☠½ **1994 (PG-13)** Vermont logger Noel Lord (Torn) has lived on the land all his life and doesn't want to sell out to the power company. His blunt-talking Indian housekeeper/lover Bangor (Cardinal) knows it's best to take the money and move on. Set in 1927 and adapted from the novella by Howard Frank Mosher. Flat storytelling with a good performance by Cardinal. **104m/C VHS.** Rip Torn, Tantoo Cardinal, Bill Raymond, Mark Margolis, John Griesemer, Amy Wright, Dennis Mientka, Jusef Bulos; ***Cameos:*** Michael J. Fox, Treat Williams; ***D:*** Jay Craven; ***W:*** Jay Craven, Don Bredos. *APX*

Where the Sky Begins **1984** From the director of "Black Orpheus," this is a seven-part recreated history of turn-of-the-century aviation. **420m/C VHS, Beta.** *FR* ***D:*** Marcel Camus. *VCD*

Where the Spirit Lives ☠☠½ **1989 (PG)** Native children kidnapped by Canadian government agents are forced to live in dreadful boarding schools where they are abused emotionally and physically. St. John is a new arrival who refuses to put up with it and tries to escape. Engrossing and moving. **97m/C VHS.** *CA* Michelle St. John; ***D:*** Bruce Pittman. *BTV, HHE, UWA*

Where There's Life ☠☠½ **1947** Wisecracking Hope is a New York DJ about to be married to Marshe when he discovers he's the heir to the kingdom of Borovia (whose last king was assassinated). Hasso works her feminine wiles as the general who's guarding Hope when the assassins come after him. Oh, and Marshe and her cop brother Bendix are tracking him down to go through with the wedding ceremony. Frantic antics. **75m/B VHS.** Bob Hope, Signe Hasso, William Bendix, Vera Marshe, George Coulouris, George Zucco, Dennis Hoey, John Alexander; ***D:*** Sidney Lanfield; ***W:*** Melville Shavelson, Allen Boretz. *MCA*

Where Time Began ☠☠ **1977 (G)** The discovery of a strange manuscript of a scientist's journey to the center of the earth leads to the decision to recreate the dangerous mission. Based on Jules Verne's classic novel "Journey to the Center of the Earth," but not anywhere near as fun or stirring. **87m/C VHS, Beta.** Kenneth More, Pep Munne, Jack Taylor; ***D:*** J. Piquer Simon. *SUE*

Where Trails Divide ☠½ **1937** Keene is a U.S. Marshal who poses as a lawyer to bring a gang of thieves to justice. Lacks action. **54m/B VHS.** Tom Keene, Eleanor Stewart, Warner Richmond, David Sharpe, Charles French, Hal Price, Bud Osborne; ***D:*** Robert North Bradbury. *GPV*

Where Trails End ☠☠ **1942** Novel sci-fi western set during WWII with just about everything, including phosphorescent-clothed good guys, Nazis, scoundrels, literate horses, and Gallic sidekicks. Interestingly different. **54m/B VHS, Beta.** Tom Keene, Joan Curtis, Charles "Blackie" King; ***D:*** Robert Emmett Tansey. *VDM, VYY*

Where Were You When the Lights Went Out? ☠½ **1968 (PG)** A complicated, unsuccessful farce about a retiring Broadway actress, her jealous, possibly philandering husband, her greedy agent, an embezzler, and a citywide blackout. Film was actually not based on the 1965 New York City blackout but on a French play, "Monsieur Masure" by Claude Magnier, which was written nine years before. **94m/C VHS.** Doris Day, Patrick O'Neal, Robert Morse, Terry-Thomas, Lola Albright, Steve Allen, Jim Backus, Ben Blue, Pat Paulsen; ***D:*** Hy Averback. *MGM, MOV*

Where's Piccone ☠☠☠ **1984** A woman attempts, with the assistance of a two-bit hustler, to locate her missing husband, only to discover that he has led a double life in the Neapolitan underworld. Giannini as the sleazy hubby is perfectly cast. On-target social and political satire. In Italian with English subtitles. **110m/C VHS, Beta.** *IT* Giancarlo Giannini, Lina Sastri, Aldo Guiffre, Clelia Rondinelli; ***D:*** Nanni Loy. *INJ, FCT, WBF*

Where's Poppa? ☠☠☠ *Going Ape* **1970** A Jewish lawyer's senile mother constantly ruins his love life, and he considers various means of getting rid of her, including dressing up as an ape to scare her to death. Filled with outlandish and often tasteless humor, befitting its reign as a black comedy cult classic. Adapted by Robert Klane from his novel. **84m/C VHS, Beta, LV.** George Segal, Ruth Gordon, Ron Leibman, Vincent Gardenia, Rob Reiner, Trish Van Devere; ***D:*** Carl Reiner; ***C:*** Jack Priestley. *FOX*

Where's Willie? **1977 (G)** Willie is a very bright boy; perhaps a little too bright. When he reveals his latest invention to the folks in his small town, everyone is out to get him. **91m/C VHS, Beta.** Guy Madison, Henry Darrow, Kate Woodville, Marc Gilpin; ***D:*** John Florea. *NO*

Which Way Home ☠☠ **1990** A Red Cross nurse attempts to flee Cambodia with four young orphans. An Australian smuggler befriends and helps her. Way too long and wandering, though like many a TV movie, it means well. **141m/C VHS, Beta.** Cybill Shepherd, John Waters, Peta Toppano, John Ewart, Ruben Santiago-Hudson, Marc Gray; ***D:*** Carl Schultz; ***W:*** Michael Laurence. *TTC*

Which Way Is Up? ☠☠½ **1977 (R)** Pryor plays three roles in this story of an orange picker who accidentally becomes a union hero. He leaves his wife and family at home while he seeks work in Los Angeles. There he finds himself a new woman, starts a new family, and sells out to the capitalists. American version of the Italian comedy "The Seduction of Mimi" tries with mixed success for laughs. Pryor as a dirty old man is the high point. **94m/C VHS, Beta.** Richard Pryor, Lonette McKee, Margaret Avery, Morgan Woodward, Marilyn Coleman; ***D:*** Michael A. Schultz; ***W:*** Carl Gottlieb. *MCA*

Which Way to the Front? ☠½ **1970 (G)** Assorted Army rejects form a guerilla band and wage their own small-scale war during WWII. **96m/C VHS, Beta.** Jerry Lewis, Jan Murray, George L. Baxt, Steve Franken; ***D:*** Jerry Lewis; ***W:*** Dee Caruso. *WAR*

Whiffs ☠ **1975 (PG)** A gullible man plays guinea pig in an Army experiment on germ warfare which leaves him with the intellect of a chimpanzee. Naturally, he then devises a plan to use the volatile gas in a chain of bank robberies. The title is appropriate—this movie is a stinker. **91m/C VHS.** Elliott Gould, Eddie Albert, Harry Guardino, Godfrey Cambridge, Jennifer O'Neill, Alan Manson; ***D:*** Ted Post; ***W:*** Malcolm Marmorstein. Nominations: Academy Awards '75: Best Song ("Now That We're in Love"). *MED*

While I Live ✂½ **1947** Woman meets female pianist with uncanny resemblance to sister who's been dead 25 years and rethinks her position on reincarnation. **85m/B VHS, Beta.** *GB* Tom Walls, Clifford Evans, Carole Raye, Patricia Burke, Sonia Dresdel, John Warwick; ***D:*** John Harlow; ***C:*** Frederick A. (Freddie) Young. *SNC*

While the City Sleeps ✂✂✂ **1956** Three newspaper reporters vie to crack the case of a sex murderer known as "The Lipstick Killer" with the editorship of their paper the prize. Good thriller-plus with the emphasis on the reporters' ruthless methods of gaining information rather than on the killer's motivations. Lang's last big success. Based on "The Bloody Spur" by Charles Einstein. **100m/B VHS, Beta, LV.** Dana Andrews, Rhonda Fleming, George Sanders, Howard Duff, Thomas Mitchell, Ida Lupino, Vincent Price, Mae Marsh; ***D:*** Fritz Lang; ***C:*** Ernest Laszlo. *VCI*

While You Were Sleeping ✂✂✂ **1995 (PG)** Feel-good romantic comedy finds lonely Lucy Moderatz (Bullock) collecting tokens for the Chicago train system and admiring Yuppie lawyer Peter Callaghan (Gallagher) as he commutes to and fro. Fate conspires to throw them together when Lucy rescues Peter after a mugging. Trouble is, he's not conscious so Lucy goes to the hospital with him, where she's mistaken for his fiancee. She continues the charade and is warmly welcomed by the Callaghan family, with the exception of Peter's brother, Jack (Pullman), who smells a rat even as he falls under the token collector's spell. Meanwhile, Peter remains in a coma, allowing Jack and Lucy to supply romantic comedy. Gallagher brings a serenity to his role as the unconscious Peter, while Bullock and Pullman take the predictable plot and deliver performances that earn them another notch on the climb to stardom. **103m/C VHS, LV.** Sandra Bullock, Bill Pullman, Peter Gallagher, Jack Warden, Peter Boyle, Glynis Johns, Micole Mercurio, Jason Bernard, Michael Rispoli, Ally Walker, Monica Keena; ***D:*** Jon Turteltaub; ***W:*** Fred Lebow, Daniel G. Sullivan; ***C:*** Phedon Papamichael; ***M:*** Randy Edelman. Blockbuster Entertainment Awards '96: Comedy Actress, Video (Bullock), Comedy Actress, Theatrical (Bullock); Nominations: Golden Globe Awards '96: Best Actress—Musical/Comedy (Bullock); MTV Movie Awards '96: Best Female Performance (Bullock), Most Desirable Female (Bullock). *TOU*

Whirlwind Horseman ✂ **1938** Substandard horse opera. Maynard's search for a gold prospector friend leads him to a rancher and his pretty daughter. He beats up some bad guys, etcetera. **60m/B VHS, Beta.** Ken Maynard, Joan Barclay, Bill Griffith; ***D:*** Robert F. "Bob" Hill. *NOS, DVT, VCN*

Whiskey Galore ✂✂✂½ *Tight Little Island* **1948** During WWII, a whiskey-less Scottish island gets a lift when a ship, carrying 50,000 cases of spirits, wrecks off the coast. A full-scale rescue operation and the evasion of both local and British government authorities ensue. The classic Ealing studio comedy is based on the actual wreck of a cargo ship off the Isle of Eriskay in 1941. **81m/B VHS, Beta.** *GB* Basil Radford, Joan Greenwood, Gordon Jackson, James Robertson Justice; ***D:*** Alexander MacKendrick. *HMV*

Whiskey Mountain ✂ **1977 (PG)** Two couples go on a treasure hunt to Whiskey Mountain but instead find terror. **95m/C VHS, Beta.** Christopher George, Preston Pierce, Linda Borgeson, Roberta Collins, Robert Leslie; ***D:*** William Grefe. *BFV*

A Whisper to a Scream ✂✂ **1988 (R)** An actress, in researching a film part, takes a job at a telephone sex service, creating different personas as she talks to keep herself interested. Soon, women resembling the personas are being murdered. Great premise fails to deliver fully, though there is some suspense. **96m/C VHS, Beta, LV.** *CA* Nadia Capone, Yaphet Kotto, Lawrence Bayne, Silvio Oliviero; ***D:*** Robert Bergman; ***W:*** Robert Bergman, Gerard Ciccoritti. *NO*

The Whispering ✂✂ **1994 (R)** Scary little low-budget tale about an insurance investigator who's checking out several suicides and meets up with the Grim Reaper (who just happens to be female). **88m/C VHS.** Leif Garrett, Leslie Danon, Tom Patton, Maxwell Rutherford, Mette Holt; ***D:*** Gregory Gieras; ***W:*** Leslie Danon. *APX*

Whispering City ✂✂✂ **1947** A female reporter receives an inside tip incriminating a prominent attorney in a murder committed several years earlier. She tries to get the evidence she needs before she becomes his latest victim. Highly suspenseful, thanks to competent scripting and directing. **89m/B VHS, Beta.** *CA* Helmut Dantine, Mary Anderson, Paul Lukas; ***D:*** Fedor Ozep. *NOS, SNC*

Whispering Shadow **1933** Serial starring the master criminal known as the "faceless whisperer." Twelve chapters, 13 minutes each. **156m/B VHS, Beta.** Bela Lugosi, Robert Warwick; ***D:*** Al(bert) Herman, Colbert Clark. *NOS, SNC, VCN*

Whispers ✂✂ **1989 (R)** Psycho Le Clerc repeatedly bothers writer Tennant even though she seems to have killed him. This dismays police guy Sarandon. Based on the novel by Dean R. Koontz. **96m/C VHS, LV.** Victoria Tennant, Chris Sarandon, Jean LeClerc; ***D:*** Douglas Jackson; ***W:*** Anita Doohan, Don Carmody. *LIV*

Whispers in the Dark ✂✂ **1992 (R)** A psychiatrist counsels two odd patients—one is an ex-con turned painter with a violent streak, the other is a woman who reveals her kinky sexual experiences with a mystery man. Things get interesting when the doctor finds out her new lover is her patient's mystery man, and the patient turns up murdered. Confusing thriller seems forced but the experienced cast is worth watching. **103m/C VHS, Beta, LV.** Annabella Sciorra, Jamey Sheridan, Anthony LaPaglia, Jill Clayburgh, John Leguizamo, Deborah Unger, Alan Alda, Anthony Heald; ***D:*** Christopher Crowe; ***W:*** Christopher Crowe; ***M:*** Thomas Newman. *PAR, PMS*

Whispers of White ✂½ **1993 (R)** Bridgetown's mayor has been trying for years to put a stop to the drug dealing going on in his fair community. Finally, his new Chief of Police decides to deploy a special task force to clean-up the streets—using whatever methods are necessary (and they're all violent). **98m/C VHS.** Nicholette Goulet, Anthony De Sardo, Tony Craig, April Bransome, Ron Gorton Sr.; ***D:*** Ron Gorton Sr.; ***W:*** Ron Gorton Sr. *AIP*

The Whistle Blower ✂✂✂ **1987** A young government worker in England with a high-security position mysteriously dies. His father, a former intelligence agent, begins investigating his son's death and discovers sinister Soviet-related conspiracies. A lucid, complex British espionage thriller. Adapted from the John Hale novel by Julian Bond. **98m/C VHS, Beta, LV.** *GB* Michael Caine, Nigel Havers, John Gielgud, James Fox, Felicity Dean, Gordon Jackson, Barry Foster; ***D:*** Simon Langton; ***W:*** Julian Bond; ***M:*** John Scott. *SUE, NLC*

Whistle Down the Wind ✂✂✂½ **1962** Three children of strict religious upbringing find a murderer hiding in their family's barn and believe him to be Jesus Christ. A well done and hardly grim or dull allegory of childhood innocence based on a novel by Mills's mother, Mary Hayley Bell. For a film relying heavily on child characters, it's important to portray childhood well and realistically. That is done here, as in "To Kill a Mockingbird." Mills is perfect. The film is Forbes's directorial debut and Richard Attenborough's second production. **98m/B VHS, Beta.** *GB* Hayley Mills, Bernard Lee, Alan Bates; ***D:*** Bryan Forbes; ***M:*** Malcolm Arnold. National Board of Review Awards '62: 10 Best Films of the Year. *SUE, NLC*

Whistle Stop ✂✂ **1946** A small-town girl divides her attentions between low-life gambler Raft, and villainous nightclub owner McLaglen, who plans a robbery-murder to get rid of any rivals. A forgettable gangster drama. **85m/B VHS, Beta.** George Raft, Ava Gardner, Victor McLaglen; ***D:*** Leonide Moguy; ***W:*** Philip Yordan. *NOS, DVT, FCT*

Whistlin' Dan ✂✂ **1932** Yet another lead cowpoke sets out to avenge the murder of a close relative. Maynard whistles while he walks (and rides) woodenly through this one. **60m/B VHS, Beta.** Ken Maynard, Joyzelle Joyner, Lew Meehan, Georges Renevant, Dan Terry, Harlan E. Knight, Bud McClure, Hank Bell, Iron Eyes Cody, Frank Ellis; ***D:*** Phil Rosen. *NOS, VCI, GPV*

Whistling Bullets ✂✂½ **1936** Action galore in the story of an undercover Texas Ranger infiltrating a gang of thieves. The low budget doesn't detract from an exciting script and tight direction. **58m/B VHS, Beta.** Kermit Maynard, Jack Ingram; ***D:*** John English. *NOS, DVT, RXM*

Whistling in Brooklyn ✂✂½ **1943** Skelton again plays radio crime-solver Wally Benton in this third and last entry following "Whistling in the Dark" and "Whistling in Dixie." A cop-killer and the Brooklyn Dodgers baseball team figure in the mystery, which finds Skelton a suspect in the crimes. **87m/B VHS.** Red Skelton, Ann Rutherford, Jean Rogers, Rags Ragland, Ray Collins, Henry O'Neill, William Frawley, Sam Levene; ***D:*** Sylvan Simon; ***M:*** George Bassman. *MGM*

Whistling in Dixie ✂✂½ **1942** The second appearance of Skelton as radio sleuth Wally "The Fox" Benton (following "Whistling in the Dark") finds him traveling to Georgia with girlfriend Carol (Rutherford). She's worried about an ex-sorority sister who knows the secret of a hidden Civil War treasure. When Wally gets involved, humorous trouble follows. Followed by "Whistling in Brooklyn." **73m/B VHS, Beta.** Red Skelton, Ann Rutherford, George Bancroft, Guy Kibbee, Diana Lewis, Peter Whitney, Rags Ragland; ***D:*** Sylvan Simon; ***W:*** Nat Perrin. *MGM, FCT*

Whistling in the Dark ✂✂✂ **1941** Skelton plays Wally Benton, a radio sleuth nicknamed "The Fox," in the first of a three-film series. Veidt (an always excellent villain) is the leader of a phony religious cult, after the money of one of his followers. He decides to kidnap Skelton and have him come up with a plan for the perfect murder but of course there are all sorts of comic complications. Skelton's first starring role is a clever comic mystery and a remake of the 1933 film. Followed by "Whistling in Dixie" and "Whistling in Brooklyn." **78m/B VHS.** Red Skelton, Ann Rutherford, Conrad Veidt, Virginia Grey, Rags Ragland, Eve Arden, Don Douglas, Don Costello, Paul Stanton, William Tannen, Reed Hadley; ***D:*** Sylvan Simon. *MGM*

Whitcomb's War ✂½ **1987** Small town becomes a battleground among a host of comic characters who are unaware who really is in charge. **67m/C VHS.** Patrick Pankhurst, Leon Charles, Bill Morey, Robert Denison, Garnett Smith; ***D:*** Russell S. Doughten Jr.

White Apache ✂✂ **1988** Emotionally charged saga of a man barred from both Indian and white societies, focusing on the impact of prejudice toward a white man raised by Apaches. **90m/C VHS, Beta.** *IMP*

The White Balloon ✂✂✂½ *Badkonake Sefid* **1995** Beautifully told story from the viewpoint of determined 7-year-old Tehranian Razieh (Mohammadkhani), who wants to properly celebrate the Islamic New Year by buying a particularly plump goldfish (a symbol of harmony) from the pet shop. She manages to beg the money from her mother and sets off but, distracted by the street sights, Reziah loses the banknote, which falls into a street grate. Various characters seek to help her out but it's Reziah's resourceful brother Ali (Kafili) who gets a balloon seller to finally retrieve the money. Farsi with subtitles. **85m/C VHS.** Aida Mohammadkhani, Mohsen Kalifi, Fereshteh Sadr Ofrani, Anna Bourkowska, Mohammad Shahani, Mohammad Bahktiari; ***D:*** Jafar Panahi; ***W:*** Abbas Kiarostami; ***C:*** Farzad Jowdat. *NYR*

The White Buffalo ✂✂ *Hunt to Kill* **1977 (PG)** A strange, semi-surreal western parable about the last days of Wild Bill Hickok (Bronson) and his obsession with a mythical white buffalo that represents his fear of mortality. Something of a "Moby Dick" theme set in the Wild West. Clumsy but intriguing. **97m/C VHS, Beta.** Charles Bronson, Jack Warden, Will Sampson, Kim Novak, Clint Walker, Stuart Whitman, John Carradine, Slim Pickens, Cara Williams, Douglas Fowley; ***D:*** J. Lee Thompson; ***M:*** John Barry. *MGM*

White Cannibal Queen *Woof!* **1974** A young girl is captured by cannibals in the Amazon jungle, and her father spends years tracking her down. **90m/C VHS, Beta.** *VCD*

White Cargo 🦴🦴½ **1942** Lamarr holds the corny story together with one of her best-known roles as sultry native girl Tondelayo. Pidgeon is a cynical African rubber planter who advises new assistant Carlson against Lamarr's sarong-clad charms. But hormones speak louder than warnings and Pidgeon has to take some strong action to save Carlson from this femme fatale. Based on the novel "Hell's Playground" by Ida Vera Simonton and adapted for both stage and screen by Gordon. **90m/B VHS.** Hedy Lamarr, Walter Pidgeon, Richard Carlson, Frank Morgan, Reginald Owen, Bramwell Fletcher, Henry O'Neill, Clyde Cook, Richard Ainley; ***D:*** Richard Thorpe; ***W:*** Leon Gordon; ***M:*** Bronislau Kaper. *MGM*

White Christmas 🦴🦴🦴 **1954** Two ex-army buddies become a popular comedy team and play at a financially unstable Vermont inn at Christmas for charity's sake. Many swell Irving Berlin songs rendered with zest. Paramount's first Vista Vision film. Presented in widescreen on laserdisc. ♫The Best Things Happen While You're Dancing; Love, You Didn't Do Right By Me; Choreography; Count Your Blessings Instead of Sheep; What Can You Do With a General; Mandy; The Minstrel Show; Sisters; Heat Wave. **120m/C VHS, Beta, LV, 8mm, CD-I.** Bing Crosby, Danny Kaye, Rosemary Clooney, Vera-Ellen, Dean Jagger; ***D:*** Michael Curtiz; ***W:*** Norman Panama; ***C:*** Loyal Griggs. Nominations: Academy Awards '54: Best Song ("Count Your Blessings Instead of Sheep"). *PAR, FUS*

The White Cliffs of Dover 🦴🦴🦴 **1944** Prime example of a successful 40s "women's weepie." American Dunne goes to England in 1914, falls in love, and marries the British Marshal. He joins the WWI troops and is killed, without knowing he had a son. Dunne raises the boy in England as a new threat looms with the rise of Hitler. Now grown, he goes off to do his duty and she joins the Red Cross, where she sees him again among the wounded, another victim of the ravages of war. Dunne is fine in her noble, sacrificing role. McDowall is the young son with Taylor (with whom he'd already worked in "Lassie Come Home") as a childhood friend. Based on the poem by Alice Duer Miller. Bring the hankies. **126m/B VHS.** Irene Dunne, Alan Marshal, Frank Morgan, Peter Lawford, Gladys Cooper, May Whitty, Sir C. Aubrey Smith, Roddy McDowall, Van Johnson, Elizabeth Taylor, June Lockhart, John Warburton, Jill Esmond, Norma Varden, Tom Drake, Arthur Shields; ***D:*** Clarence Brown. Nominations: Academy Awards '44: Best Black and White Cinematography. *MGM, MOV*

White Comanche 🦴½ **1967** Half-breed twins battle themselves and each other to a rugged climax. **90m/C VHS, Beta.** William Shatner, Joseph Cotten, Perla Cristal, Rossana Yanni; ***D:*** Gilbert Kay. *NOS, VCI, VTR*

The White Dawn 🦴🦴½ **1975 (PG)** Three whalers are stranded in the Arctic in the 1890s and are taken in by an Eskimo vilage. They teach the villagers about booze, gambling, and other modern amenities. Resentment grows until a clash ensues. All three leads are excellent, especally Oates. Much of the dialogue is in an Eskimo language, subtitled in English, as in "Dances with Wolves." **110m/C VHS, Beta, LV.** Warren Oates, Timothy Bottoms, Louis Gossett Jr., Simonie Kopapik, Joanasie Salomonie; ***D:*** Philip Kaufman; ***C:*** Michael Chapman; ***M:*** Henry Mancini. *PAR*

White Dwarf 🦴½ **1995** Confusing sci-fi adventure finds edgy Manhattan internist Driscoll Rampart (McDonough) serving his residency on Rusta, a war-torn planet located in a white-dwarf star system. The planet is divided into two hemispheres, one in perpetual darkness and the other in constant light. Rampart learns the ropes from mystical doc Akada (Winfield), who's also involved in a peace accord between Rusta's warring leaders. Visually striking but overly-ambiguous—probably because it was intended as the pilot for a weekly series. **91m/C VHS.** Paul Winfield, Neal McDonough, CCH Pounder, Ele Keats, Michael McGrady, Katy Boyer; ***D:*** Peter Markle; ***W:*** Bruce Wagner; ***M:*** Stewart Copeland. *CAF*

White Eagle 🦴🦴 **1932** A white man who believes himself to be an Indian gets a job as a Pony Express rider and gets mixed up with horse rustlers. When he finds out who he really is, he is free to marry the white woman he's had his eye on. Interesting plot twist caused by the narrow-mindedness of the Hays Office. **64m/B VHS.** Buck Jones, Barbara Weeks, Robert Ellis, Jason Robards Sr., Robert Elliott, Jim Thorpe, Ward Bond; ***D:*** Lambert Hillyer. *DVT, HEG*

White Fang 🦴🦴🦴 **1991 (PG)** Boy befriends canine with big teeth and both struggle to survive in third celluloid rendition of Alaska during the Gold Rush. Beautiful cinematography. Fun for the entire family based on Jack London's book. Followed by "White Fang 2: The Myth of the White Wolf." **109m/C VHS, LV.** Klaus Maria Brandauer, Ethan Hawke, Seymour Cassel, James Remar, Susan Hogan; ***D:*** Randal Kleiser; ***W:*** Jeanne Rosenberg, Nick Thiel, David Fallon; ***C:*** Tony Pierce-Roberts; ***M:*** Basil Poledouris. *TOU, DIS, TVC*

White Fang 2: The Myth of the White Wolf 🦴🦴 **1994 (PG)** White boy and his wolf-dog lead starving Native American tribe to caribou during the Alaskan Gold Rush. Simplistic story with obvious heroes and villains, yes, but this is also wholesome (and politically correct) family fare compliments of Disney. Focuses less on the wolf, a flaw, and more on Bairstow and his love interest Craig, a Haida Indian princess, while exploring Native American mythology and dreams in sequences that tend to stop the action cold. Still, kids will love it, and there are plenty of puppies to achieve required awwww factor. Beautiful scenery filmed on location in Colorado and British Columbia. **106m/C VHS, LV.** Scott Bairstow, Alfred Molina, Geoffrey Lewis, Charmaine Craig, Victoria Racimo, Paul Coeur, Anthony Michael Ruivivar, Al Harrington; ***Cameos:*** Ethan Hawke; ***D:*** Ken Olin; ***W:*** David Fallon; ***M:*** John Debney. *TOU*

White Fang and the Hunter 🦴🦴 **1985 (G)** The adventures of a boy and his dog who survive an attack from wild wolves and then help to solve a murder mystery. Loosely based on the novel by Jack London. **87m/C VHS, Beta.** Pedro Sanchez, Robert Wood; ***D:*** Alfonso Brescia. *VTR, HHE*

White Fire 🦴🦴 *Three Steps to the Gallows* **1953** Brady, in search of his lost brother, gets involved in a smuggling ring. Seems the brother is falsely accused of murder and about to hang. Brady and bar singer Castle solve the case. Good photography; bad script. **82m/C VHS, Beta.** *GB* Scott Brady, Mary Castle, Ferdinand "Ferdy" Mayne; ***D:*** John Gilling. *NOS, SNC, VYY*

White Fire 🦴 **1983** Two jewel thieves will stop at nothing to own White Fire, a two hundred-carat diamond. **90m/C VHS, Beta.** Robert Ginty, Fred Williamson. *TWE*

White Fury **1990** Couples on a campout are victimized by sleazy hoodlums during a snowstorm. **89m/C VHS.** Deke Anderson, Sean Holton, Douglas Hartier, Christine Shinn, Chastity Hammons; ***D:*** David A. Prior. *AIP*

White Ghost 🦴 **1988 (R)** An Intelligence Officer who disappeared in the jungles of Asia 18 years ago is ready to come back to the United States, but not everyone wants to see him again. **90m/C VHS, Beta.** William Katt, Rosalind Chao, Martin Hewitt, Wayne Crawford, Reb Brown; ***D:*** B.J. Davis. *TWE*

White Gold 🦴🦴🦴 **1928** Shepherd's son weds Mexican woman and his disgruntled father contrives apparent rendezvous between the wife and a ranchhand, who's found dead in her bedroom. Seems no one believes the wife's story. Unprecedented, dark, silent drama. **73m/B VHS, Beta.** Jetta Goudal, Kenneth Thomson, George Bancroft, George Nicholls Jr., Clyde Cook; ***D:*** William K. Howard. *GPV*

White Gorilla *Woof!* **1947** A great white hunter sets out to kill a gigantic white gorilla that is terrorizing the black natives. Imperialist trash. On any informed person's list of all-time worst movies. **62m/B VHS, Beta, LV.** Ray Corrigan, Lorraine Miller. *NO*

White Heat 🦴🦴🦴½ **1949** A classic gangster film with one of Cagney's best roles as a psychopathic robber/killer with a mother complex. The famous finale—perhaps Cagney's best-known scene—has Cagney trapped on top of a burning oil tank shouting "Made it, Ma! Top of the world!" before the tank explodes. Cagney's character is allegedly based on Arthur "Doc" Barker and his "Ma," and his portrayal is breathtaking. Also available colorized. **114m/B VHS, Beta, LV.** James Cagney, Virginia Mayo, Edmond O'Brien, Margaret Wycherly, Steve Cochran; ***D:*** Raoul Walsh; ***M:*** Max Steiner. Nominations: Academy Awards '49: Best Story. *MGM, FOX*

White Hot 🦴½ **1988 (R)** A young businessman loses his prestigious Wall Street job, and in order to live the good life, he resorts to selling drugs. Benson stars and directs. **95m/C VHS, Beta, LV.** Robby Benson, Tawny Kitaen, Danny Aiello, Sally Kirkland, Judy Tenuta; ***D:*** Robby Benson. *ACA*

White Hot: The Mysterious Murder of Thelma Todd 🦴🦴 **1991** Thelma Todd was a Hollywood starlet found dead under strange circumstances in 1935. Buffs have sought a solution to the maybe-murder ever since; this treatment (based on the book "Hot Toddy" by Andy Edmunds) leaves too many loose ends for purists and isn't sufficiently gripping for the uninitiated. **95m/C VHS.** Loni Anderson, Robert Davi, Paul Dooley, Lawrence Pressman; ***D:*** Paul Wendkos. *NO*

White Hunter, Black Heart 🦴🦴🦴 **1990 (PG)** Eastwood casts himself against type as Hustonesque director who is more interested in hunting large tusked creatures than shooting the film he came to Africa to produce. Based on Peter Viertel's 1953 account of his experiences working on James Agee's script for Huston's "African Queen." Eastwood's Huston impression is a highlight, though the story occasionally wanders off with the elephants. **112m/C VHS, Beta, LV, 8mm.** Clint Eastwood, Marisa Berenson, George Dzundza, Jeff Fahey, Timothy Spall, Charlotte Cornwell, Mel Martin, Alun Armstrong, Richard Vanstone; ***D:*** Clint Eastwood; ***W:*** Peter Viertel, James Bridges, Burt Kennedy; ***C:*** Jack N. Green; ***M:*** Lennie Niehaus. *MGM, FCT, WAR*

White Huntress 🦴½ *Golden Ivory* **1957** Two brothers venturing into the jungle encounter a beautiful young woman, the daughter of a settlement leader. Meanwhile, a killer is on the loose. **86m/C VHS, Beta.** *GB* Robert Urquhart, John Bentley, Susan Stephen; ***D:*** George Breakston. *SNC*

The White Legion 🦴½ **1936** Workers and engineers push their way through steaming jungles and reeking swamps while building the Panama Canal. Many fall victim to yellow fever. Physician Keith does some medical sleuthing and saves the day. Plodding, predictable drama. **81m/B VHS, Beta.** Ian Keith, Tala Birell, Snub Pollard; ***D:*** Karl Brown. *VYY*

White Lie 🦴🦴½ **1991 (PG-13)** Len Madison, Jr. (Hines), a press secretary for the mayor of New York, receives an old photo of a lynched black man who he learns is his father, hung for raping a white woman. Madison returns to his Southern hometown to find out the truth behind his father's death, assisted by a white doctor (O'Toole) whose mother was a rape victim. They fall in love, adding to an already complicated situation, and incur the wrath of locals who are trying to keep the truth hidden. Based on the novel "Louisiana Black" by Samuel Charters. **93m/C VHS.** Gregory Hines, Annette O'Toole, Bill Nunn; ***D:*** Bill Condon. *MCA*

White Light 🦴🦴 **1990 (R)** "Flatliners" with a flatfoot; after a near-death experience a cop returns with memories of a beautiful woman. He tries to find out who she is/was in plodding fashion. The voyage to the afterlife is represented by a jog through a storm sewer. **96m/C VHS, LV.** Martin Kove, Allison Hossack, Martha Henry, Heidi von Palleske, James Purcell, Bruce Boa; ***D:*** Al Waxman. *ACA*

White Lightning 🦴🦴½ *McKlusky* **1973 (PG)** Good ol' boy Reynolds plays a moonshiner going after the crooked sheriff who murdered his brother. Good stunt-driving chases enliven the formula. The inferior sequel is "Gator." **101m/C VHS, Beta.** Burt Reynolds, Ned Beatty, Bo Hopkins, Jennifer Billingsley, Louise Latham; ***D:*** Joseph Sargent; ***W:*** William W. Norton Sr.; ***M:*** Charles Bernstein. *MGM*

White Line Fever ♂♂½ **1975 (PG)** A young trucker's search for a happy life with his childhood sweetheart is complicated by a corrupt group in control of the long-haul trucking business. Well-done action film of good triumphing over evil. **89m/C VHS, Beta, LV.** Jan-Michael Vincent, Kay Lenz, Slim Pickens, L.Q. Jones, John David Garfield; ***D:*** Jonathan Kaplan; ***W:*** Jonathan Kaplan, Ken Friedman; ***C:*** Fred W. Koenekamp. *COL*

White Mama ♂♂♂ **1980** A poor widow (Davis, in a splendid role) takes in a street-wise black kid (Harden) in return for protection from the neighborhood's dangers, and they discover friendship. Poignant drama, capably directed by Cooper, featuring sterling performances all around Made-for-TV drama at its best. **96m/C VHS, Beta.** Bette Davis, Ernest Harden, Eileen Heckart, Virginia Capers, Lurene Tuttle, Anne Ramsey; ***D:*** Jackie Cooper. *LIV*

White Mane ♂♂♂ **1952** The poignant, poetic story of a proud and fierce white stallion that continually eludes attempts by ranchers to capture it. In French with English subtitles. **38m/B VHS, Beta, LV.** Alain Emery, Frank Silvera; ***D:*** Albert Lamorisse. Cannes Film Festival '52: Best Film. *NLC, SUE, HMV*

White Man's Burden ♂♂ **1995 (R)** In a world where blacks have all the wealth and power, and whites comprise the struggling underclasses, Caucasian factory worker Louis Pinnock (John Travolta) is fired by his bigoted black CEO (Belafonte) due to a misunderstanding. Driven by poverty-level financial strain, Louis kidnaps his wealthy boss to show him how the other half lives. Gimmicky premise is full of reversed stereotypes, such as black cops beating a white guy, and skinheads taking over as inner-city gangsters. Treads too lightly, and rehashes too many familiar stories, to make any real impact. Travolta had to be talked into this role by "Pulp Fiction" producer Lawrence Bender. **89m/C VHS.** John Travolta, Harry Belafonte, Kelly Lynch, Margaret Avery, Tom Bower, Carrie Snodgress, Sheryl Lee Ralph; ***D:*** Desmond Nakano; ***W:*** Desmond Nakano; ***C:*** Willy Kurant; ***M:*** Howard Shore. *HBO*

White Men Can't Jump ♂♂ **1992 (R)** Sometimes they can't act either. Small-time con man Harrelson stands around looking like a big nerd until someone dares him to play basketball and he proves to be more adept than he looks. After he beats Snipes, they become friends and start hustling together. Harrelson lays to rest the rumor that he can't act; here, he proves it. Fast-paced, obscenity-laced dialogue does not cover up for the fact that the story line hovers between dull and dismal, redeemed only by the surreal "Jeopardy" game show sequence and the convincing b-ball action. Snipes manages to rise above the material as well as the rim, while Perez, as wooden Woody's spitfire Hispanic girlfriend, is appropriately energetic. **115m/C VHS.** Wesley Snipes, Woody Harrelson, Rosie Perez, Tyra Ferrell, Cylk Cozart, Kadeem Hardison, Ernest Harden, John Jones; ***D:*** Ron Shelton; ***W:*** Ron Shelton. *FXV*

White Mile ♂♂½ **1994 (R)** Abusive L.A. advertising exec Dan Cutler (Alda) invites his top execs and important clients on a white-water rafting expedition along the Chilko River in the Canadian Rockies (filmed at Northern California's Russian River). But competition and arrogance causes the deaths of several participants and the widow of one sues the agency for damages. Alda excels in arrogant, self-serving nastiness. Fact-based TV movie based on court transcripts. **97m/C VHS, LV.** Alan Alda, Peter Gallagher, Robert Loggia, Fionnula Flanagan, Dakin Matthews, Bruce Altman, Robert Picardo, Max Wright, Jack Gilpin, Ken Jenkins; ***D:*** Robert Butler; ***W:*** Michael Butler. *HBO*

White Mischief ♂♂♂ **1988 (R)** An alternately ghastly and hilarious indictment of the English upper class between the World Wars, and the decadence the British colonists perpetrated in Kenya, which came to world attention with the murder of the philandering Earl of Errol in 1941. Exquisitely directed and photographed. Acclaimed and grandly acted, especially by Scacchi; Howard's last appearance. **108m/C VHS, Beta, LV, 8mm.** Greta Scacchi, Charles Dance, Joss Ackland, Sarah Miles, John Hurt, Hugh Grant, Geraldine Chaplin, Trevor Howard, Murray Head, Susan Fleetwood, Alan Dobie, Jacqueline Pearce; ***D:*** Michael Radford; ***C:*** Roger Deakins; ***M:*** George Fenton. *SUE, NLC*

White Nights ♂♂♂ **1957** Based on a love story by Dostoyevski. A young woman pines for the return of her sailor while a mild-mannered clerk is smitten by her. Both of their romantic fantasies are explored the dance-hall cadence is mixed with dreamy, fantastic flashbacks. In Italian with English subtitles. Equally good Soviet version made in 1959. **107m/C VHS.** *IT* Maria Schell, Jean Marais, Marcello Mastroianni; ***D:*** Luchino Visconti; ***M:*** Nino Rota. *FCT, INJ*

White Nights ♂♂½ **1985 (PG-13)** A Russian ballet dancer who defected to the U.S. (Baryshnikov) is a passenger on a jet that crashes in the Soviet Union. With the aid of a disillusioned expatriate tap dancer (Hines), he plots to escape again. The excellent dance sequences elevate the rather lame story. ♫Say You, Say Me. **135m/C VHS, Beta, LV.** Mikhail Baryshnikov, Gregory Hines, Isabella Rossellini, Helen Mirren, Jerzy Skolimowski, Geraldine Page; ***D:*** Taylor Hackford; ***C:*** David Watkin; ***M:*** Michel Colombier. Academy Awards '85: Best Song ("Say You, Say Me"); Golden Globe Awards '86: Best Song ("Say You, Say Me"); Nominations: Academy Awards '85: Best Song ("Separate Lives (Love Theme from White Nights)"). *COL, MOV*

White of the Eye ♂♂♂ **1988 (R)** A murdering lunatic is on the loose in Arizona, and an innocent man must find him to acquit himself of the murders. A tense, effective thriller; dazzling technique recalls the experimental films of the 1960s. **111m/C VHS, Beta.** David Keith, Cathy Moriarty, Art Evans, Alan Rosenberg, Michael Greene, Alberta Watson, Marc Hayashi; ***D:*** Donald Cammell; ***W:*** China Cammell, Donald Cammell; ***M:*** Nick Mason, Rick Fenn, George Fenton. *PAR*

The White Orchid ♂♂ **1954** Romantic triangle ventures into the wilds of Mexico in search of Toltec ruins. Exceptional sets. **81m/C VHS, Beta.** William Lundigan, Peggy Castle, Armando Silvestre, Rosenda Monteros; ***D:*** Reginald LeBorg. *SNC, DVT, HEG*

White Palace ♂♂½ **1990 (R)** Successful widowed Jewish lawyer Spader is attracted to older, less educated hamburger waitress Sarandon, and ethnic/cultural strife ensues, as does hot sex. Adapted from the Glenn Savan novel, it starts out with promise but fizzles toward the end. **103m/C VHS, LV.** Susan Sarandon, James Spader, Jason Alexander, Eileen Brennan, Griffin Dunne, Kathy Bates, Steven Hill, Rachel Levin, Corey Parker, Spiros Focas, Renee Taylor, Kim Myers; ***D:*** Luis Mandoki; ***W:*** Alvin Sargent, Ted Tally; ***C:*** Lajos Koltai; ***M:*** George Fenton. *MCA, FCT, CCB*

White Phantom: Enemy of Darkness ♂ **1987** Ninja warriors in modern day society battling against other evil ninjas. **89m/C VHS, Beta.** Page Leong, Jay Roberts Jr., Bo Svenson; ***D:*** Dusty Nelson; ***W:*** David Hamilton, Chris Gallagher. *VMK*

White Pongo *Woof!* **1945** A policeman goes undercover with a group of British biologists to capture a mythic white gorilla believed to be the missing link. A camp jungle classic with silly, cheap special effects. **73m/B VHS, Beta.** Richard Fraser, Maris Wrixon, Lionel Royce; ***D:*** Sam Newfield. *SNC, NOS, HHT*

The White Rose ♂♂♂ **1923** An aspiring minister travels to see the world he intends to save, and winds up falling from grace. Complicated menage a trois is finally sorted out at the end. Silent. **120m/B VHS, Beta.** Mae Marsh, Carol Dempster, Ivor Novello, Neil Hamilton, Lucille LaVerne; ***D:*** D.W. Griffith. *GPV*

The White Rose ♂♂♂ **1983** The true story of a group of dissident students in Munich in 1942, who put their lives in danger by distributing leaflets telling the truth of what was going on in the concentration camps. Hans Scholl was an Army officer who discovered the truth and told the others. In the end, most of the students were captured by the Gestapo and executed. "The White Rose" was the name of the group, but none survived to tell where the name came from. Verhoeven's film telling is engrossing and compelling, with excellent acting from the young cast. In German with English subtitles. **108m/C VHS, Beta.** *GE* Lena Stolze, Wulf Kessler, Oliver Siebert, Ulrich Tucker; ***D:*** Michael Verhoeven. *MGM, GLV, SWC*

White Sands ♂♂½ **1992 (R)** When a dead man's body is found at a remote Indian reservation clutching a gun and a briefcase filled with $500,000, the local sheriff (Dafoe) takes his identity to see where the money leads. Using a phone number found on a piece of paper in the dead man's stomach, the sheriff follows clues until he finds himself mixed up with a rich woman (Mastrantonio) who sells black market weapons and uses the money to support "worthy" causes, and an FBI man (Jackson) who uses him as bait to lure a CIA turncoat/arms dealer (Rourke). Sound confusing? It is, and despite the strong cast and vivid scenery of the southwest United States, this film just doesn't cut it. **101m/C VHS, Beta, LV.** Willem Dafoe, Mary Elizabeth Mastrantonio, Mickey Rourke, Mimi Rogers, Samuel L. Jackson, M. Emmet Walsh, James Rebhorn, Maura Tierney, Beth Grant, Miguel Sandoval, John Lafayette; ***Cameos:*** Fred Dalton Thompson, John P. Ryan; ***D:*** Roger Donaldson; ***W:*** Daniel Pyne; ***M:*** Patrick O'Hearn. *WAR, FCT*

The White Shadow, Vol. 1 **1978** After an injury curtails his career with the Chicago Bulls, Ken Reeves (Howard) becomes the basketball coach at Carver High School in Los Angeles, an inner-city school with a team of wisecracking players. The pilot episode finds Reeves trying to adjust to his new life and help his students. **60m/C VHS.** Ken Howard, Ed Bernard, Kevin Hooks, Byron Stewart, Thomas Carter, Timothy Van Patten, Ira Angustain, Joan Pringle, Eric Kilpatrick, Nathan Cook, Ken Michelman. *MOV, MTM*

White Shadows in the South Seas ♂♂½ **1928** Alcohol, drugs, and prostitution take their toll on the native population of Tahiti in this early talkie. Blue plays a western doctor who marries the daughter of a native chief. However, he finds greed for the island's pearl treasures drawing other unscrupulous westerners to destroy the unspoiled paradise. **88m/B VHS.** Monte Blue, Robert Anderson, Raquel Torres; ***D:*** Woodbridge S. Van Dyke; ***C:*** Clyde De Vinna. *FCT*

The White Sheik ♂♂♂ *Lo Sceicco Bianco* **1952** Fellini's first solo effort. A newly wed bride meets her idol from the comic pages (made with photos, not cartoons; called fumetti) and runs off with him. She soon finds he's as ordinary as her husband. Brilliant satire in charming garb. Remade as "The World's Greatest Lover." Woody Allen's "The Purple Rose of Caine" is in a similar spirit. In Italian with subtitles. **86m/B VHS.** *JP* Alberto Sordi, Giulietta Masina, Brunella Bova, Leopoldo Trieste; ***D:*** Federico Fellini; ***W:*** Federico Fellini, Tullio Pinelli, Ennio Flaiano; ***M:*** Nino Rota. *HMV, INJ, APD*

The White Sin ♂♂ **1924** An innocent country girl hires on as maid of a rich woman and is seduced and abandoned by the woman's profligate son, but everything turns out all right by the end of the third handkerchief. Silent with original organ music. **93m/B VHS, Beta, 8mm.** Madge Bellamy, John Bowers, Billy Bevan; ***D:*** William A. Seiter. *VYY*

The White Sister ♂♂♂½ **1923** Gish is an Italian aristocrat driven from her home by a conniving sister. When her true love (Colman) is reported killed she decides to become a nun and enters a convent. When her lover does return he tricks her into leaving the convent but before he can persuade her to renounce her vows Vesuvius erupts and he goes off to warn the villagers, dying for his efforts. Gish then rededicates herself to her faith. Colman's first leading role, which made him a romantic star. Filmed on location in Italy. **108m/B VHS, Beta.** Lillian Gish, Ronald Colman, Gail Kane, J. Barney Sherry, Charles Lane; ***D:*** Henry King. *DVT, HEG*

White Slave *Amazonia: The Catherine Miles Story* **1986 (R)** An Englishwoman is captured by bloodthirsty cannibals and, rather than being eaten, is tormented and made a slave. **90m/C VHS, Beta.** Elvive Avoray, Will Gonzales, Andrew Louis Coppola; ***D:*** Roy Garrett. *NO*

White Squall ½ **1996 (PG-13)** Based on the 1960 true story of 13 young men who become students at Ocean Academy, a year-long adventure spent aboard the brigantine Albatross. Bridges plays the ship's captain and surrogate dad. The boys agonize over their various crises, making the first half of the movie into a veritable "Dead Poets Yachting Society." However, a sudden storm overtakes the ship in the Caribbean and several crew members are killed. There's a shift to a "Caine Mutiny" type trial in which Bridges must prove the tragedy was not his fault while the survivors rally to his defense. Director Scott excels at showing the fury of nature in the prolonged storm scene, but takes his time getting there. **128m/C VHS.** Jeff Bridges, Scott Wolf, Caroline Goodall, Balthazar Getty, John Savage, Jeremy Sisto, Jason Marsden, David Selby, Zeljko Ivanek, Ryan Phillippe, David Lascher, Eric Michael Cole, Julio Mechoso, Ethan Embry; ***D:*** Ridley Scott; ***W:*** Todd Robinson; ***C:*** Hugh Johnson; ***M:*** Jeff Rona. *TOU*

White Tiger ½ **1923** Three crooks pull off a major heist and hide out in a mountain cabin where their mistrust of each other grows. **81m/C VHS.** Priscilla Dean, Matt Moore, Raymond Griffith, Wallace Beery; ***D:*** Tod Browning. *GPV, FCT*

White Tiger ½ **1995 (R)** DEA agent decides to take the law into his own fists when his partner is murdered by a Chinese gang leader. **93m/C VHS.** Gary Daniels, Matt Craven, Cary-Hiroyuki Tagawa, Julia Nickson-Soul; ***D:*** Richard Martin; ***W:*** Gordon Melbourne; ***M:*** Graeme Coleman. *HMK*

The White Tower **1950** Five men and a woman set out to scale the infamous White Tower in the Alps. Each person's true nature is revealed as he or she scales the peak, which has defied all previous attempts. Slightly overwrought, but exciting. Filmed in Technicolor on location in the Swiss Alps. **98m/C VHS, Beta.** Glenn Ford, Claude Rains, Cedric Hardwicke, Oscar Homolka, Lloyd Bridges; ***D:*** Ted Tetzlaff. *HHT, TTC*

White Water Summer ½ *Rites of Summer* **1987 (PG)** A group of young adventurers trek into the Sierras, and find themselves struggling against nature and each other to survive. Bacon is the rugged outdoorsman (yeah, sure) who shows them what's what. Chances are it was never at a theater near you, and with good reason. **90m/C VHS, Beta, LV.** Kevin Bacon, Sean Astin, Jonathan Ward, Matt Adler; ***D:*** Jeff Bleckner; ***M:*** Michael Boddicker. *COL*

White Wolves 2: Legend of the Wild ½ **1994 (PG)** Troubled teens are on a school assignment involving a conservation foundation's rescue of a pair of young wolves. They must overcome lots of obstacles, including the fact that they can't stand each other. Average teens-in-the-woods adventure. **95m/C VHS.** Corin "Corky" Nemec, Justin Whalin, Jeremy London, Elizabeth Berkley, Ernie Reyes Jr., Ele Keats; ***D:*** Terence H. Winkless. *NHO*

The White Zombie **1932** Lugosi followed his success in "Dracula" with the title role in this low-budget horror classic about the leader of a band of zombies who wants to steal a beautiful young woman from her new husband. Set in Haiti; the first zombie movie. Rich and dark, though ludicrous. Based on the novel "The Magic Island" by William Seabrook. **73m/B VHS, Beta.** Bela Lugosi, Madge Bellamy, John Harron; ***D:*** Victor Halperin; ***M:*** Xavier Cugat. *NOS, PSM, CAB*

WhiteForce **1988 (R)** A secret agent tracks an enemy. His government tracks him. He runs around with a big machine gun and a couple of hand grenades. He fires the gun and throws the grenades. **90m/C Beta.** Sam Jones, Kimberly Pistone; ***D:*** Eddie Romero. *NO*

Whitewater Sam ½ **1978 (G)** Whitewater Sam and his Siberian Husky, Sybar, embark on an exciting trip through the uncharted wilds of the Great Northwest. The likeable, intelligent hound steals the show. Good family adventure. **87m/C VHS, Beta.** Keith Larsen; ***D:*** Keith Larsen; ***W:*** Keith Larsen. *MON*

Who Am I This Time? **1982** Two shy people can express their love for each other only through their roles in a local theater production of "A Streetcar Named Desire." Good cast responds well to competent direction from Demme; poignant, touching and memorable. Based on a story by Kurt Vonnegut, Jr. Made for television. **60m/C VHS, Beta, LV.** Susan Sarandon, Christopher Walken, Robert Ridgely; ***D:*** Jonathan Demme. *MON, BTV*

Who Done It? **1942** Average Abbott and Costello comedy about two would-be radio mystery writers, working as soda-jerks, who play detective after the radio station's president is murdered. **77m/B VHS, Beta.** Bud Abbott, Lou Costello, William Gargan, Patric Knowles, Louise Allbritton, Don Porter, Jerome Cowan, William Bendix, Mary Wickes; ***D:*** Erle C. Kenton. *MCA*

Who Framed Roger Rabbit ½ **1988 (PG)** Technically marvelous, cinematically hilarious, eye-popping combination of cartoon and live action create a Hollywood of the 1940s where cartoon characters are real and a repressed minority working in films. A 'toon-hating detective is hired to uncover the unfaithful wife of 2-D star Roger, and instead uncovers a conspiracy to wipe out all 'toons. Special appearances by many cartoon characters from the past. Coproduced by Touchstone (Disney) and Amblin (Spielberg). Adapted from "Who Censored Roger Rabbit?" by Gary K. Wold. **104m/C VHS, Beta, LV.** Bob Hoskins, Christopher Lloyd, Joanna Cassidy, Alan Tilvern, Stubby Kaye; ***D:*** Robert Zemeckis; ***W:*** Jeffrey Price, Peter S. Seaman; ***C:*** Dean Cundey; ***M:*** Alan Silvestri; ***V:*** Charles Fleischer, Mae Questel, Kathleen Turner, Amy Irving, Mel Blanc, June Foray, Frank Sinatra. Academy Awards '88: Best Film Editing, Best Visual Effects; National Board of Review Awards '88: 10 Best Films of the Year; Nominations: Academy Awards '88: Best Art Direction/Set Decoration, Best Cinematography, Best Sound. *TOU, WTA*

Who Has Seen the Wind? **1977** Two boys grow up in Saskatchewan during the Depression. So-so family viewing drama. Ferrer as a bootlegger steals the otherwise small-paced show. **102m/C VHS, Beta.** Jose Ferrer, Brian Painchaud, Charmion King, Helen Shaver. *SUE*

Who Is Killing the Great Chefs of Europe? *Too Many Chefs; Someone is Killing the Great Chefs of Europe* **1978 (PG)** A fast-paced, lightly handled black comedy. When a gourmand, well-played by Morley, learns he must lose weight to live, a number of Europe's best chefs are murdered according to their cooking specialty. A witty, crisp, international mystery based on Ivan and Nan Lyon's novel. **112m/C VHS.** George Segal, Jacqueline Bisset, Robert Morley, Jean-Pierre Cassel, Philippe Noiret, Jean Rochefort, Joss Ackland, Nigel Havers; ***D:*** Ted Kotcheff; ***M:*** Henry Mancini. Los Angeles Film Critics Association Awards '78: Best Supporting Actor (Morley). *WAR*

Who Is the Black Dahlia? **1975** In L.A. in 1947, a detective tries to find out who murdered a star-struck 22-year-old woman nicknamed "The Black Dahlia" (Arnaz). Based on a famous unsolved murder case which was later the basis for "True Confessions." Made for TV. **96m/C VHS, Beta.** Efrem Zimbalist Jr., Lucie Arnaz, Ronny Cox, MacDonald Carey, Linden Chiles; ***D:*** Joseph Pevney; ***W:*** Robert W. Lenski. *WOV*

Who Killed Baby Azaria? **1983** Parents are arrested for infanticide after they claim their baby was stolen by a wild dog while vacationing on a supposedly haunted Australian mountain, or was it an aboriginal spirit that absconded with the tyke? Less compelling than the American remake, "A Cry in the Dark." Made for Australian TV. **96m/C VHS, Beta.** *AU* Elaine Hudson, John Hamblin, Peter Carroll; ***D:*** Judy Rymer. *PSM*

Who Killed Doc Robbin? *Sinister House; Curley and His Gang in the Haunted Mansion* **1948** A group of youngsters try to clear their friend, Dan, the town handyman, when the sinister Dr. Robbin is murdered. The follow-up to "The Adventures of Curly and His Gang;" intended as part of a Roach kid-comedy series in the manner of "Our Gang." Fast pace and lots of slapstick give a first impression of spirited juvenile hijinks, but not much is genuinely funny. And the names of the two black kids—"Dis" and "Dat"—aren't funny either. **50m/C VHS, Beta.** Larry Olsen, Don Castle, Bernard Carr, Virginia Grey. *SNC, NOS, HHT*

Who Killed Mary What's 'Er Name? *Death of a Hooker* **1971 (PG)** A diabetic ex-fighter tracks a prostitute's killer through Greenwich Village. Illogical, incredible and disjointed attempt at comedy/mystery. Odd, unsatisfying ending, with the boxer going into a coma. Good supporting cast. **90m/C VHS, Beta.** Red Buttons, Sylvia Miles, Conrad Bain, Ron Carey, David Doyle, Sam Waterston; ***D:*** Ernie Pintoff. *GEM, PSM*

Who Shot Pat? ½ *Who Shot Patakango?* **1992 (R)** Funny, nostalgic, coming of age story set in fifties Brooklyn. Knight stars as Bic Bickham, the leader of a clean-living "gang" of seniors at a Brooklyn vocational school. Memorable vintage soundtrack features hits by legendary artists Chuck Berry and Bo Diddly. **102m/C VHS.** David Knight, Sandra Bullock, Kevin Otto, Aaron Ingram, Brad Randall; ***D:*** Robert Brooks; ***W:*** Halle Brooks, Robert Brooks. *WAR*

Who Slew Auntie Roo? ½ *Whoever Slew Auntie Roo?; Gingerbread House* **1971 (PG)** An updated twist on the Hansel and Gretel fairy tale. Features Winters as an odd, reclusive widow mistaken for the fairy tale's children-eating witch by one of the orphans at her annual Christmas party—with dire consequences. **90m/C VHS, Beta.** Shelley Winters, Ralph Richardson, Mark Lester, Lionel Jeffries, Hugh Griffith; ***D:*** Curtis Harrington; ***W:*** Robert Blees. *VES*

Whodunit **1982 (R)** The bad horror flicks always seem to have (usually young) characters murdered one at a time, often on a remote island. This loser is no exception. **82m/C VHS, Beta.** Rick Bean, Gary Phillips; ***D:*** Bill Naud; ***W:*** Anthony Shaffer. *LIV, VES*

The Whole Shootin' Match **1979** Two thirty something Texas nobodies chase the American Dream via a sure-fire invention called the Kitchen Wizard, after failing in the small-animal biz and polyurethane. Offbeat, very low-budget independent feature shot interestingly in sepia tones. Sympathetic and human. **108m/C VHS.** Matthew L. Perry, Sonny Carl Davis, Doris Hargrave; ***D:*** Eagle Pennell. *NO*

Who'll Save Our Children? **1982** Two children are abandoned and left on the doorstep of a middle-aged, childless couple. Years later the natural parents, now reformed, attempt to reclaim their children. Well cast and topical. Made for TV. **96m/C VHS, Beta.** Shirley Jones, Len Cariou, Conchata Ferrell, Frances Sternhagen, Cassie Yates, David Hayward; ***D:*** George Schaefer. *TLF*

Who'll Stop the Rain? ½ *Dog Soldiers* **1978 (R)** A temperamental Vietnam vet (Nolte) is enlisted in a smuggling scheme to transport a large amount of heroin into California. An excellent blend of drama, comedy, action, suspense, and tragedy. Based on Robert Stone's novel "Dog Soldiers." Outstanding period soundtrack by Creedence Clearwater Revival, including title song. Violent and compelling tale of late-'60s disillusionment. **126m/C VHS, Beta, LV.** Nick Nolte, Tuesday Weld, Michael Moriarty, Anthony Zerbe, Richard Masur, Ray Sharkey, David Opatoshu, Charles Haid, Gail Strickland; ***D:*** Karel Reisz; ***W:*** Judith Rascoe. Nominations: Cannes Film Festival '78: Best Film. *MGM*

Wholly Moses! *Woof!* **1980 (PG)** Set in biblical times, this alleged comedy concerns a phony religious prophet who begins to believe that his mission is to lead the chosen. Horrible ripoff of "Life of Brian," released the previous year. What a cast—what a waste! **125m/C VHS, Beta, LV.** Dudley Moore, Laraine Newman, James Coco, Paul Sand, Dom DeLuise, Jack Gilford, John Houseman, Madeline Kahn, Richard Pryor, John Ritter; ***D:*** Gary Weis. *COL*

Whoopee! 🦴🦴 **1930** Cantor stars in his first sound picture as a rich hypochondriac sent out west for his health, where he encounters rugged cowboys and Indians. Filmed in two-color Technicolor and based on Ziegfeld's 1928 Broadway production with the same cast. Dances supervised by Busby Berkeley. ♫The Song of the Setting Sun; Mission Number; Makin' Whoopee; A Girlfriend of a Boyfriend of Mine; My Baby Just Cares for Me; I'll Still Belong to You; Stetson. **93m/C VHS, Beta.** Eddie Cantor, Ethel Shutta, Paul Gregory, Eleanor Hunt, Betty Grable; ***D:*** Thornton Freeland. Nominations: Academy Awards '31: Best Interior Decoration. *SUE, HBO*

The Whoopee Boys 🦴 **1986 (R)** A New York lowlife in Palm Beach tries to reform himself by saving a school for needy children so his rich girlfriend will marry him. Full of unfunny jokes and very bad taste, with no redeeming qualities whatever. **89m/C VHS, Beta, LV.** Michael O'Keefe, Paul Rodriguez; ***D:*** John Byrum; ***W:*** Jeff Bukai; ***M:*** Jack Nitzsche. *PAR*

Whoops Apocalypse 🦴🦴½ **1983** Satiric account of events leading up to WWIII. Invasion in South America leads British prime minister to suggest nuclear retaliation. Uneven, lacking in the Strangelovian element, but funny in spots. Based on the British hit television series and scripted by series writers Marshall and Renwick. **137m/C VHS, Beta.** *GB* John Cleese, John Barron, Richard Griffiths, Peter Jones, Bruce Montague, Barry Morse, Rik Mayall, Ian Richardson, Alexei Sayle, Herbert Lom, Joanne Pearce; ***D:*** Tom Bussmann; ***W:*** Andrew Marshall, David Renwick. *NO*

Whoops Apocalypse 🦴🦴 **1988 (R)** America's first female president Swit, recently ensconced after the untimely death of the ex-circus clown previous president, is forced to contend with hotheaded superpowers who want to kick off WWIII with a bang. Uneven black comedic satire of holocaust genre. Based on the BBC TV series. **93m/C VHS, Beta.** Loretta Swit, Peter Cook, Michael Richards. *MGM*

Whore 🦴🦴 *If You Can't Say It, Just See It* **1991 (R)** Ken Russell's gritty night in the life of cynical prostitute Theresa Russell is strong medicine, a powerful antidote to sappy Hollywood films that glorify streetwalking. Also available in the 92-minute original uncut version, an 85-minute NC-17 version, and an alternate R-Rated version. **80m/C VHS.** Theresa Russell, Antonio Vargas; ***D:*** Ken Russell; ***W:*** Ken Russell, Deborah Dalton. *VMK*

Whore 2 🦴½ *Bad Girls* **1994 (R)** Jack is a middle-aged writer who moves into Hell's Kitchen in order to do research for a book about prostitutes. Then Jack gets involved with two of the girls—the tough, jealous Lori and childlike Mary Lou. **85m/C VHS, LV.** Amos Kollek, Marla Sucharetza, Mari Nelson; ***D:*** Amos Kollek; ***W:*** Amos Kollek. *VMK*

Who's Afraid of Virginia Woolf? 🦴🦴🦴🦴 **1966** Nichols debuts as a director in this biting Edward Albee play. A teacher and his wife (Segal and Dennis) are invited to the home of a burned-out professor and his foul-mouthed, bitter, yet seductive wife (Burton and Taylor). The guests get more than dinner, as the evening deteriorates into brutal verbal battles between the hosts. Taylor and Dennis won Oscars; Burton's Oscar-nominated portrait of the tortured husband is magnificent. Richard and Liz's best film together. **127m/B VHS, Beta, LV.** Richard Burton, Elizabeth Taylor, George Segal, Sandy Dennis; ***D:*** Mike Nichols; ***W:*** Ernest Lehman; ***M:*** Alex North. Academy Awards '66: Best Actress (Taylor), Best Art Direction/Set Decoration (B & W), Best Black and White Cinematography, Best Costume Design (B & W), Best Supporting Actress (Dennis); National Board of Review Awards '66: 10 Best Films of the Year, Best Actress (Taylor); Nominations: Academy Awards '66: Best Actor (Burton), Best Adapted Screenplay, Best Director (Nichols), Best Film Editing, Best Picture, Best Sound, Best Supporting Actor (Segal), Best Original Score. *WAR, BTV*

Who's Got the Action? 🦴½ **1963** Martin and Turner are a husband and wife divided by his love of playing the ponies. In order to keep his gambling under control Turner schemes to become his new bookie. But when Martin suddenly goes on a winning streak, the new bookie is in trouble with her former competition, who just happen to be the Mob. Strained, flat comedy with Turner especially miscast. **93m/C VHS.** Lana Turner, Dean Martin, Walter Matthau, Eddie Albert, Nita Talbot, Margo, Paul Ford, John McGiver, Jack Albertson; ***D:*** Daniel Mann; ***W:*** Jack Rose. *PAR*

Who's Harry Crumb? 🦴½ **1989 (PG-13)** Bumbling detective Candy can't even investigate a routine kidnapping! His incompetence is catching: the viewer can't detect a single genuinely funny moment. Candy is the only likeable thing in this all-around bad, mindless farce. **95m/C VHS, Beta, LV.** John Candy, Jeffrey Jones, Annie Potts, Tim Thomerson, Barry Corbin, Shawnee Smith, Valri Bromfield, Renee Coleman, Joe Flaherty, Lyle Alzado, James Belushi, Stephen Young; ***D:*** Paul Flaherty; ***W:*** Robert Conte; ***M:*** Michel Colombier. *COL*

Who's Minding the Mint? 🦴🦴🦴 **1967** A money checker at the U.S. Mint must replace $50,000 he accidentally destroyed. He enlists a retired money printer and an inept gang to infiltrate the mint and replace the lost cash, with predictable chaos resulting. Non-stop zaniness in this wonderful comedy that never got its due when released. Thieves who befriend Hutton include Denver of "Gilligan's Island" and Farr, later of "M*A*S*H." **97m/C VHS, Beta.** Jim Hutton, Dorothy Provine, Milton Berle, Joey Bishop, Bob Denver, Walter Brennan, Jamie Farr; ***D:*** Howard Morris; ***C:*** Joseph Biroc. *GKK*

Who's That Girl? 🦴 **1987 (PG)** A flighty, wrongly-convicted parolee kidnaps her uptight lawyer and they have wacky adventures as she goes in search of the crumb that landed her in the pokey. Plenty of Madonna tunes, if that's what you like; they briefly keep you from wondering why you're not laughing. Kind of a remake (a bad one) of "Bringing Up Baby" (1938). **94m/C VHS, Beta, LV, 8mm.** Madonna, Griffin Dunne, John Mills, Haviland Morris; ***D:*** James Foley. Golden Raspberry Awards '87: Worst Actress (Madonna). *WAR*

Who's That Knocking at My Door? 🦴🦴🦴 *J.R.; I Call First* **1968** Interesting debut for Scorsese, in which he exercises many of the themes and techniques that he polished for later films. An autobiographical drama about an Italian-American youth growing up in New York City, focusing on street life, Catholicism and adolescent bonding. Begun as a student film called "I Call First"; later developed into a feature. Keitel's film debut. **90m/B VHS, Beta.** Harvey Keitel, Zena Bethune; ***D:*** Martin Scorsese. *FCT, WAR*

Who's the Man? 🦴🦴 **1993 (R)** Two clowning companions who work in a barbershop in Harlem get recruited onto the police force to investigate a murder. Doctor Dre and Ed Lover (themselves) make use of their hip-hop music connections and full-throttle slapstick humor to enliven the search. Salt of "Salt 'n' Pepa," is the female lead and Ice-T plays a gangster. First-time director Demme works his star duo for both foolish and vulgar humor. Filming done mostly on location in Harlem. Includes a lengthy list of cameo appearances by several hip-hop performers. For fans; based on a story by Dre, Lover, and Seth Greenland. **124m/C VHS.** Ed Lover, Cheryl "Salt" James, Ice-T, Jim Moody, Colin Quinn, Kim Chan, Rozwill Young, Badja Djola, Richard Bright, Denis Leary, Andre B. Blake, Bill Bellamy; ***D:*** Ted Demme; ***W:*** Seth Greenland; ***M:*** Michael Wolff. *NLC, IME, COL*

Who's Who 🦴🦴 **1978** In a satire on climbing the British social ladder, workers in a London brokerage firm struggle with class issues and find the higher you climb, the more you find greed, pettiness, and stupidity. Made for British television. **75m/C VHS.** *GB* Bridget Kane, Simon Chandler, Adam Norton, Philip Davis, Joolia Cappleman; ***D:*** Mike Leigh; ***W:*** Mike Leigh. *WBF, BTV, FCT*

Whose Child Am I? 🦴 **1975 (R)** A woman so desperately wants a child of her own that she doesn't mind who the father is. Ludicrous and vulgar. **90m/C VHS.** Kate O'Mara, Paul Freeman, Edward Judd, Felicity Devonshire; ***D:*** Lawrence Britten. *ATL*

Whose Life Is It Anyway? 🦴🦴🦴½ **1981 (R)** Black humor abounds. Sculptor Dreyfuss is paralyzed from the neck down in an auto accident. What follows is his struggle to persuade the hospital authorities to let him die. Excellent cast headed impressively by Dreyfuss; Lahti as his doctor and hospital head Cassavetes also are superb. From Brian Clark's successful Broadway play. **118m/C VHS, Beta.** Richard Dreyfuss, John Cassavetes, Christine Lahti, Bob Balaban, Kenneth McMillan, Kaki Hunter, Thomas Carter; ***D:*** John Badham; ***W:*** Reginald Rose, Brian Clark. *MGM*

Why Change Your Wife? 🦴🦴½ **1920** A rare, recently re-discovered silent comedy. Swanson and Meighan play married couple Beth and Robert who find themselves drifting apart after ten years of marriage. Robert becomes involved with someone else and Beth demands a divorce. After Robert remarries, Beth decides she wants him back and the real fun begins as she tries every trick in the book to regain her ex-husband. Piano scored. **100m/B VHS, Beta.** Gloria Swanson, Thomas Meighan, Bebe Daniels; ***D:*** Cecil B. DeMille. *GPV*

Why Does Herr R. Run Amok? 🦴🦴 *Warum Lauft Herr R Amok?* **1969** Notorious Fassbinder black comedy about a middle-class man, unable to cope with the increasing problems of modern life, who suddenly murders his family. The characters are called by the actors' names to heighten the sense of reality. Film is based on a case history. In German with English subtitles. **88m/C VHS.** *GE* Kurt Raab, Lilith Ungerer, Amadeus Fengler, Hanna Schygulla, Franz Maron; ***D:*** Rainer Werner Fassbinder, Michael Fengler; ***W:*** Rainer Werner Fassbinder, Michael Fengler. *NYF, FCT, ING*

Why Has Bodhi-Darma Left for the East 🦴🦴 **1989** Set in a remote monastery in the Korean mountains, film follows an old master, close to death, who must lead his disciples in their search for spiritual freedom. The film's title is a Zen koan—an unanswerable riddle that serves as an aid on the path to enlightenment. Korean with subtitles. **135m/C VHS.** ***D:*** Bae Young-kyun; ***W:*** Bae Young-kyun; ***C:*** Bae Young-kyun. *MIL*

Why Me? 🦴🦴 **1990 (R)** Two jewel thieves unknowingly steal an enormously valuable ruby ring and are in over their heads trying to evade the cops and everyone else. In the same vein as the much-funnier "Nuns on the Run," this caper is done in by bad acting and too much ill-conceived slapstick. Adapted by Donald E. Westlake from his own novel. **96m/C VHS, LV.** Christopher Lambert, Christopher Lloyd, Kim Greist, J.T. Walsh, Michael J. Pollard, Tony Plana, John Hancock, Lawrence Tierney; ***D:*** Gene Quintano; ***W:*** Donald E. Westlake. *COL*

Why Shoot the Teacher 🦴🦴🦴 **1979** A young teacher sent to a one-room schoolhouse in a small prairie town in Saskatchewan during the Depression gets a cold reception on the cold prairie. One of the more popular films at the Canadian box office. Cort was Harold in "Harold and Maude." Based on the novel by Max Braithwaite. **101m/C VHS, Beta.** *CA* Bud Cort, Samantha Eggar, Chris Wiggins; ***D:*** Silvio Narizzano; ***W:*** James DeFelice. *SUE*

The Wicked 🦴 **1989** Though packaged as serious horror, this is a cheap, tacky spoof with folks stranded at the country residence of a vampire family. Sole point of interest: these Transylvanian cliches take place in the Australian outback. Kids might actually like this (gore isn't severe), if they can surmount the thick Down Under accents. **87m/C VHS.** Brett Cumo, Richard Morgan, Angela Kennedy, Maggie Blinco, John Doyle; ***D:*** Colin Eggleston. *HMD*

Wicked City 🦴🦴 **1992** Humans are uneasily coexisting with Reptoids (creatures that can assume human shape) in this sci-fi tale based on a Japanese comic strip. Then Hong Kong police discover a plot by the Reptoids to destroy mankind and rule the world (what else is new). Nifty special effects. Available dubbed or in Cantonese with subtitles. **88m/C VHS.** *HK* Jacky Cheung, Leon Lai, Michelle Li; ***D:*** Peter Mak. *FXL*

The Wicked Lady ꝏ **1945** Posh but lame costume drama about a bored 17th century noblewoman who takes to highway robbery to spice up her life. Credulity-stretcher extraordinaire. Based on "The Life and Death of Wicked Lady Skelton" by Magdalen King-Hall. Mason is cheeky as a fellow highwayman. Remade in 1983 with Faye Dunaway. **103m/B VHS, Beta.** *GB* James Mason, Margaret Lockwood, Patricia Roc, Michael Rennie, Felix Aylmer, Enid Stamp-Taylor, Griffith Jones; ***D:*** Leslie Arliss. *NO*

The Wicked Lady ꝏ½ **1983 (R)** Remake of the 1945 costumer about a 17th-century noblewoman trying her hand at highway robbery. More noted for its low-cut costumes and racy humor than any talent involved. **99m/C VHS, Beta.** *GB* Faye Dunaway, John Gielgud, Denholm Elliott, Alan Bates, Glynis Barber, Oliver Tobias, Prunella Scales; ***D:*** Michael Winner; ***W:*** Michael Winner; ***C:*** Jack Cardiff; ***M:*** Tony Banks. *MGM*

Wicked Stepmother ꝏ **1989 (PG-13)** A family discovers that an aged stepmother is actually a witch. Davis walked off the film shortly before she died, and was replaced by Carrera. Davis's move was wise; the result is dismal, and would have been had she stayed. As it is the viewer wonders: How come the stepmother isn't Davis anymore? Davis's unfortunate last role. **90m/C VHS, Beta.** Bette Davis, Barbara Carrera, Colleen Camp, Lionel Stander, David Rasche, Tom Bosley, Seymour Cassel, Evelyn Keyes, Richard Moll, Laurene Landon; ***D:*** Larry Cohen; ***W:*** Larry Cohen; ***M:*** Robert Folk. *MGM*

The Wicker Man ꝏꝏꝏ½ **1975** The disappearance of a young girl leads a devoutly religious Scottish policeman to an island whose denizens practice bizarre pagan sexual rituals. An example of occult horror that achieves its mounting terror without gratuitous gore. The first original screenplay by playwright Shaffer. Beware shortened versions that may still lurk out there; the 103-minute restored director's cut is definitive. **103m/C VHS, Beta.** Edward Woodward, Christopher Lee, Britt Ekland, Diane Cilento, Ingrid Pitt; ***D:*** Robin Hardy; ***W:*** Anthony Shaffer. *REP*

Wide Open Faces ꝏꝏ **1938** Every crook in town is looking for some missing stolen loot. Soda jerk Brown outwits them all in his own inimitable way. The story may be predictable, but Brown's physical humor keeps things interesting. **67m/B VHS.** Joe E. Brown, Jane Wyman, Alison Skipworth, Alan Baxter, Lucien Littlefield, Sidney Toler, Berton Churchill, Barbara Pepper, Stanley Fields, Horace Murphy; ***D:*** Kurt Neumann; ***C:*** Paul Vogel. *NOS*

Wide Sargasso Sea ꝏꝏ **1992 (NC-17)** Jamaica in the 1840's is a seething, mysterious paradise—a former British slave colony with a mix of powerful voodoo culture, beauty, and eroticism providing a very potent brew, a perfect setting for this soaper. Based on the novel by Jean Rhys, which is something of a prequel to Charlotte Bronte's "Jane Eyre." Properly English Edward Rochester meets and marries the tragic Antoinette—the same mad wife locked in the attic in the Bronte novel. Explicit nudity and sex earn the NC-17, but the film is tragic without being sensationalized. Also available in an edited R-rated and unrated versions. **98m/C VHS, LV.** *AU* Karina Lombard, Nathaniel Parker, Rachel Ward, Michael York, Martine Beswick, Claudia Robinson, Rowena King, Huw Christie Williams; ***D:*** John Duigan; ***W:*** Jan Sharp, Carole Angier, John Duigan; ***M:*** Stewart Copeland. *NLC, IME, BTV*

The Widow ꝏꝏ **1976** A story about a woman slowly learning to deal with her own grief, her children's traumas and monetary worries after the death of her husband. Straightforward, passable made for TV domestic drama based on Lynn Caine's best-selling novel. **99m/C VHS, Beta.** Michael Learned, Farley Granger, Bradford Dillman, Robert Lansing; ***D:*** J. Lee Thompson. *TLF*

Widow Couderc ꝏꝏꝏ **1974** A provincial widow unknowingly includes an escaped murderer among her liaisons. Based on a novel by Georges Simenon. In French with English subtitles. **92m/C VHS, Beta.** *FR* Simone Signoret, Alain Delon; ***D:*** Pierre Granier-Deferre. *FCT*

Widow's Kiss ꝏꝏ **1996 (R)** Young man is suspicious when his dad dies in the arms of his sexy, younger bride and he hires a detective who learns that the widow has left a number of dead husbands behind. So, the grieving son decides to get close to his new stepmommy to find out what's going on. **103m/C VHS.** Beverly D'Angelo, Bruce Davison, MacKenzie Astin, Dennis Haysbert; ***D:*** Peter Foldy. *HBO*

Widow's Nest ꝏꝏ **1977** Three widowed sisters live in a bizarre fantasy world when they lock themselves in a dingy mansion in Cuba of the 1930s. Filmed in Spain. **90m/C VHS, Beta.** Patricia Neal, Susan Oliver, Lila Kedrova, Valentina Cortese; ***D:*** Tony Navarro. *NO*

Widow's Peak ꝏꝏ½ **1994 (PG)** 1920's Irish community is run by a dictatorship of well-to-do widows with Mrs. Doyle-Counihan (Plowright) at the helm. Troubles begin for the town non-widow (Farrow) upon the arrival of recently widowed Broome (Richardson), who attracts Dunbar, the nitwit son of Plowright. Entertaining performances (Farrow shows that success is possible after the Wood-man) and beautiful scenery help boost a script that seems torn between whimsical comedy and dark drama. **98m/C VHS, LV.** Mia Farrow, Joan Plowright, Natasha Richardson, Adrian Dunbar, Jim Broadbent, John Kavanagh, Gerard McSorley, Anne Kent, Rynagh O'Grady, Michael James Ford, Garrett Keogh; ***D:*** John Irvin; ***W:*** Hugh Leonard; ***M:*** Carl Davis. *NLC*

Wife Versus Secretary ꝏꝏꝏ½ **1936** Excellent acting against type creates a near-perfect picture of romantic relationships. Harlow and Gable play a secretary and her boss who have a wonderful professional relationship, but Loy worries something else is afoot. Could have been a heavy-handed soap opera, but the witty dialogue and Brown's fine pacing make it much more. Stewart later claimed that he purposely messed up his romantic scenes with Harlow in order to spend more time in her arms. **89m/B VHS.** Clark Gable, Jean Harlow, Myrna Loy, May Robson, Hobart Cavanaugh, James Stewart, George Barbier, Gilbert Emery; ***D:*** Clarence Brown. *MGM*

Wifemistress ꝏꝏ½ *Mogliamante; Lover, Wife* **1979 (R)** In the early 1900s, an invalid wife resents her neglectful husband. When he goes into hiding because of a murder he didn't commit, she begins to drift into a world of sexual fantasies. Fine performances. Italian dialogue with English subtitles. **101m/C VHS, Beta.** *IT* Marcello Mastroianni, Laura Antonelli; ***D:*** Marco Vicario. *COL*

Wigstock: The Movie ꝏꝏ½ **1995 (R)** Documentary of the eponymous annual Labor Day event in Manhattan, billed as the Superbowl of drag. Shils intercuts stage numbers with interviews from a variety of the talented, witty festival performers, such as Lypsinka, Mistress Formika, and RuPaul. One of the best numbers is performed by the Dueling Bankheads (as in Tallulah) singing "Born to Be Wild." Like the event itself, documentary is more a celebration than a probing, psychological look at drag. Won't appeal to everyone, but a lot of fun for those who can appreciate high hair and high fashion. **92m/C VHS.** ***D:*** Barry Shils. *HMK*

The Wilby Conspiracy ꝏꝏꝏ **1975 (PG)** A political activist and an Englishman on the wrong side of the law team up to escape the clutches of a prejudiced cop in apartheid Africa. The focus of the film is on the chase, not the political uprising taking place around it. Well-done chase film with fine performances throughout. **101m/C VHS.** Sidney Poitier, Michael Caine, Nicol Williamson, Prunella Gee, Persis Khambatta, Saeed Jaffrey, Rutger Hauer, Helmut Dantine; ***D:*** Ralph Nelson; ***W:*** Rod Amateau. *MGM, FCT*

The Wild Aces ꝏ½ **1985** A relentless action flick with real documentary footage of the aerial war above Vietnam. **58m/C VHS, Beta.** *BMV, FGF*

The Wild and the Free ꝏꝏ **1980** Lighthearted comedy about research chimps. The lab-raised bunch become the instruments for radioactive experimenting. Scheming scientists return the chimps to their home to save them from their demise. Made for TV. **100m/C VHS, Beta.** Granville Van Dusen, Linda Gray, Bill Gribble; ***D:*** James Hill. *LIV*

Wild & Wooly ꝏ½ **1978** In 1903, a tough cowgirl and her friends must prevent the assassination of the President. Made for television. **120m/C VHS, Beta.** Chris DeLisle, Susan Bigelow, Elyssa Davalos, Jessica Walter, Doug McClure, David Doyle, Ross Martin, Vic Morrow, Charles Seibert, Sherry Bain, Paul Burke; ***D:*** Philip Leacock; ***M:*** Charles Bernstein. *PSM*

The Wild Angels ꝏꝏ½ **1966 (PG)** Excessively violent film but B-movie classic about an outlaw biker gang and the local townspeople. Typical Corman fodder was one of AIP's most successful productions. **124m/C VHS.** Peter Fonda, Nancy Sinatra, Bruce Dern, Diane Ladd, Michael J. Pollard, Gayle Hunnicutt; ***D:*** Roger Corman; ***W:*** Charles B. Griffith, Peter Bogdanovich. *ORI*

Wild at Heart ꝏꝏꝏ½ **1990 (R)** Dern and Cage are on the lam, going across country to escape her mother, his parole officer, and life. Humorous and frightening, sensual and evocative as only Lynch can be. Sweet love story of Sailor and Lula is juxtaposed with the violent and bizarre, obsessive brand of love of the people they encounter. Unmistakable Wizard of Oz imagery sprinkled throughout, as are some scenes of graphic violence. Ladd is unnerving as Dern's on-screen mother (she also has the role off-screen). **125m/C VHS, Beta, LV.** Nicolas Cage, Laura Dern, Diane Ladd, Willem Dafoe, Isabella Rossellini, Harry Dean Stanton, Crispin Glover, Grace Zabriskie, J.E. Freeman, Freddie Jones, Sherilyn Fenn, Sheryl Lee; ***D:*** David Lynch; ***W:*** David Lynch; ***M:*** Angelo Badalamenti. Cannes Film Festival '90: Best Film; Independent Spirit Awards '91: Best Cinematography; Nominations: Academy Awards '90: Best Supporting Actress (Ladd). *CCB, MED, IME*

The Wild Beasts *Woof! Savage Beasts* **1985** Children and animals clash violently after drinking water tainted with PCP. Disgusting premise; unredeemably violent. **92m/C VHS, Beta.** John Aldrich, Lorraine De Selle; ***D:*** Franco Prosperi. *LIV*

Wild Bill ꝏꝏ½ **1995 (R)** Realistic, un-heroic portrait of Wild Bill Hickok (Bridges), seen mostly in flashback. From trapper and lawman to his last days in Deadwood, South Dakota, focus is on the events haunting the glaucoma-stricken, opium-addicted legend in his later years, such as twice deserting his true love (Lane). Action packed first twenty minutes mellows along with the aging Hickok and the rest gets a bit talky for a Western, albeit an arty one. Bridges's Hickok is brilliant, but Barkin is given a somewhat tedious Calamity Jane. Based on the novel "Deadwood" by Pete Dexter and the play "Fathers and Sons" by Thomas Babe. **97m/C VHS, LV.** Jeff Bridges, Ellen Barkin, John Hurt, Diane Lane, Keith Carradine, Christina Applegate, Bruce Dern, James Gammon, David Arquette, Marjoe Gortner; ***D:*** Walter Hill; ***W:*** Walter Hill; ***C:*** Lloyd Ahern; ***M:*** Van Dyke Parks. *MGM*

The Wild Bunch ꝏꝏꝏꝏ **1969 (R)** Acclaimed western about a group of aging outlaws on their final rampage, realizing time is passing them by. Highly influential in dialogue, editing style, and lyrical slow-motion photography of violence; Peckinpah's main claim to posterity. Holden and Ryan create especially memorable characters. Arguably the greatest western and one of the greatest American films of all times. Beware of shortened versions; after a pre-release showing to the East Coast critics, producer Feldman cut key scenes without Peckinpah's knowledge or consent. **145m/C VHS, Beta, LV.** William Holden, Ernest Borgnine, Robert Ryan, Warren Oates, Strother Martin, L.Q. Jones, Albert Dekker, Bo Hopkins, Edmond O'Brien, Ben Johnson, Jaime Sanchez, Emilio Fernandez, Dub Taylor; ***D:*** Sam Peckinpah; ***W:*** Walon Green, Sam Peckinpah; ***C:*** Lucien Ballard. National Society of Film Critics Awards '69: Best Cinematography; Nominations: Academy Awards '69: Best Story & Screenplay, Best Original Score. *WAR*

Wild Cactus ♪♪ **1992 (R)** Philip and Alexandria Marcus decide to take a romantic vacation at a desert resort where they meet up with a homicidal ex-con and his seductive girlfriend. The two couples find themselves entangled in some violent and kinky games. An unrated version is also available. **92m/C VHS.** David Naughton, India Allen, Gary Hudson, Michelle Moffett, Kathy Shower, Robert Z'Dar, Paul Gleason, Anna Karin, David Wells; ***D:*** Jag Mundhra; ***W:*** Carl Austin. *IMP*

The Wild Child ♪♪♪½ *L'Enfant Sauvage* **1970 (G)** The brilliant film based on the journal of a 19th century physician who attempts to educate and civilize a young boy who has been found living in the wilderness, without any comprehension of human life. Tenderly told coming of age tale, with surprising sensitivity for its subject. In French with English subtitles. **85m/B VHS.** *FR* ***D:*** Francois Truffaut; ***W:*** Jean Gruault; ***C:*** Nestor Almendros; ***M:*** Antoine Duhamel. National Board of Review Awards '70: Best Director (Truffaut); National Society of Film Critics Awards '70: Best Cinematography. *MGM, INJ, FCT*

Wild Country ♪½ **1947** Tame western. A U.S. Marshal races to stop the bad guy from killing the late sheriff's daughter and snatching her ranch. **57m/B VHS.** Eddie Dean, Roscoe Ates, Peggy Wynn, Douglas Fowley, I. Stanford Jolley, William "Bill" Fawcett; ***D:*** Ray Taylor. *NOS, HEG*

The Wild Country ♪♪½ *The Newcomers* **1971 (G)** Children's fare detailing the trials and tribulations of a Pittsburgh family moving into an inhospitable Wyoming ranch in the 1880s. Based on the novel "Little Britches" by Ralph Moody. **92m/C VHS, Beta.** Steve Forrest, Ron Howard, Clint Howard, Rance Howard; ***D:*** Robert Totten; ***M:*** Robert F. Brunner. *DIS*

The Wild Duck ♪½ **1984 (PG)** A father discovers that his beloved daughter is illegitimate and turns against her. To regain his love, she plans to sacrifice her most prized possession. Irons overacts; Ullmann almost disappears into the woodwork. Child star Jones is insufferable, and the whole family squeaks with "literary" pomposity. A horrid adaptation of the classic Ibsen play. **96m/C VHS, Beta.** *AU* Jeremy Irons, Liv Ullmann, Lucinda Jones, Arthur Dignam; ***D:*** Henri Safran. *LIV, VES*

Wild Engine/Mistaken Orders ♪♪ **1923** The early screen daredevil Holmes stars in two railroad-and-betrayal epics. **48m/B VHS, Beta.** Helen Holmes, Jack Hoxie, Hoot Gibson. *CCB*

Wild Frontier ♪♪½ **1948** A rugged old lawman and his sons team up to rid a town of outlaws. Lane, playing a character with his own name for first time, takes over from his murdered father and roots out the evildoer (Holt). Decent, enjoyable, good-guys-win western. **59m/B VHS, Beta.** Allan "Rocky" Lane, Jack Holt. *DVT*

Wild Geese ♪♪ **1978 (R)** The adventure begins when a veteran band of mercenaries land deep inside Africa to rescue the imprisoned leader of an emerging African nation, in the interest of protecting British commercial interest. Their mission meets an unexpected turn when they are betrayed by their financial backers. Too much training in the early part; too long; too much dialogue. Where's the action? **132m/C VHS, Beta, LV.** *GB* Richard Burton, Roger Moore, Richard Harris, Hardy Kruger, Stewart Granger, Frank Finlay, Jeff Corey; ***D:*** Andrew V. McLaglen; ***W:*** Reginald Rose. *FOX*

Wild Geese 2 ♪½ **1985 (R)** Lame sequel to the flamed and overlong "Wild Geese," which depended on its name stars. More of the same, this time sans Burton, Harris and Moore. Sure, it's got Olivier, but it still stinks. **124m/C VHS, Beta.** *GB* Laurence Olivier, Edward Fox, Scott Glenn, Barbara Carrera, Robert Webber; ***D:*** Peter Hunt; ***W:*** Reginald Rose. *MGM*

Wild Guitar *Woof!* **1962** A swinging youth cycles into Hollywood and, improbably, becomes an instant teenidol. Considered a top contender for "Worst Picture of All Time" honors. **92m/B VHS, Beta.** Arch Hall Jr.; ***D:*** Ray Dennis Steckler. *RHI*

Wild Gypsies ♪ **1969** A band of gypsies seek revenge against a renegade member who returned to rape and pillage. Without merit except for the good photography of Steven Burum, who has become respected doing cinematographically intriguing films like "Rumblefish." **85m/C VHS, Beta, LV.** Todd Grange, Gayle Clark, Laurel Welcome. *NWV*

Wild Hearts Can't Be Broken ♪♪♪ **1991 (G)** Depicts the true-life story of Sonora Webster, a small town Georgia girl who runs away from a foster home to join a carnival in the early 1930s, hoping to become a stunt rider. She becomes a horse-diver (a Depression-era sideshow phenomena) and is blinded in a diving accident, but returns to find romance and ride again. Storyline has little screen tension, but it doesn't detract from this fresh family film with a feisty heroine, a sweet romance, and horses. Nice U.S. screen debut for British actress Anwar. **89m/C VHS, Beta.** Gabrielle Anwar, Cliff Robertson, Dylan Kussman, Michael Schoeffling, Kathleen York, Frank Renzulli; ***D:*** Steve Miner; ***W:*** Oley Sassone; ***M:*** Mason Daring. *DIS*

Wild Horse ♪½ *Silver Devil* **1931** Gibson is the lead (in his favorite talking role), but his magnificent mount Mut commands most of the attention. Interesting historically as an example of stars' (Gibson's in this case) difficulty adjusting to talking pictures. **68m/B VHS, Beta.** Hoot Gibson, Stepin Fetchit, Edmund Cobb, Alberta Vaughn; ***D:*** Richard Thorpe, Sidney Algier. *NOS, GPV, VYY*

Wild Horse Canyon ♪♪ **1925** Yakima Canutt, the man credited with creating the profession of stunt man, stars in this tale about a lady rancher who requires saving from her evil foreman. The climactic stampede scene gives Yakima a chance to demonstrate a high dive off a cliff and a somersault onto his horse. Silent, with musical score. **68m/B VHS, Beta.** Yakima Canutt, Edward Cecil, Helene Rosson, Jay Talbet. *NOS, GPV, VYY*

Wild Horse Canyon ♪½ **1939** One of those westerns designed to run as half of a double-feature, this one's shorter than most, but hardly notable. The hero goes after a rustler who shot his brother. **57m/B VHS.** Jack Randall, Dorothy Short, Frank Yaconelli, Dennis Moore, Warner Richmond, Charles "Blackie" King, Sherry Tansey; ***D:*** Robert F. "Bob" Hill. *NOS, GPV*

Wild Horse Hank ♪♪ **1979** A young woman risks everything to save a herd of wild mustangs from being slaughtered for use as dog food. Creena is good; otherwise, it's sentimental family fare. Based on the novel "The Wild Horse Killers" by Mel Ellis. **94m/C VHS, Beta.** *CA* Linda Blair, Richard Crenna, Michael Wincott, Al Waxman; ***D:*** Eric Till. *LIV, VES*

Wild Horse Phantom ♪♪ **1944** A Wild West banker plans to fake a robbery in a diabolical deception to part honest ranchers from their lands. Surely this man's not a member of the F.D.I.C. Okay sagebrush saga. **56m/B VHS, Beta.** Buster Crabbe, Al "Fuzzy" St. John, Charles "Blackie" King, John Merton, Lane Chandler, Edward Cassidy, Bud Osborne; ***D:*** Sam Newfield. *GPV*

Wild Horse Rodeo ♪½ **1937** When a gunman appears at a rodeo, trouble starts. Part of "The Three Mesquiteers" series. Ordinary action-packed western, the good guys win. Actor Dick Weston, who sings, later gained fame as singing cowboy Roy Rogers. **53m/B VHS, Beta.** Ray Corrigan. *NOS, DVT*

Wild Horses ♪♪ **1982** A man attempts to make a living by capturing and selling wild horses. Adventure fans will love this film which deals with the common theme of man against nature. **88m/C VHS, Beta.** *NZ* Keith Aberdein, John Bach, Robyn Gibbes; ***D:*** Derek Morton. *VES*

Wild Horses ♪♪ **1984** Ex-rodeo champ Rogers is hankering to escape his dull life. He joins a roundup of wild horses and with Dawber's help exposes a bureaucrat's scheme for them. Rogers is likable and sings, but the supporting cast carries this one. Made for TV. **90m/C VHS, Beta.** Kenny Rogers, Pam Dawber, Ben Johnson, Richard Masur, David Andrews, Karen Carlson; ***D:*** Dick Lowry. *NO*

Wild in the Country ♪♪½ **1961** Backwoods delinquent Presley is aided in his literary aspirations by woman psychiatrist Lange. Okay, so that's fairly novel. Strange plot lines but in general Elvis is going to college and reading and writing and singing and playing his guitar. Meanwhile Weld wanders around seductively to provide that hint of Tennessee Williams ambience as interpreted by Odet but hey, who cares? Interesting if convoluted Elvis dramatic turn. ♫Wild in the Country; In My Way; I Slipped, I Stumbled, I Fell; Lonely Man. **114m/C VHS, Beta.** Elvis Presley, Hope Lange, Tuesday Weld, Millie Perkins, John Ireland, Gary Lockwood, Alan Napier; ***D:*** Philip Dunne; ***W:*** Clifford Odets; ***C:*** William Mellor. *FOX, MVD*

Wild in the Streets ♪♪½ **1968** Satire set in the future, where a malcontent rock star becomes president after the voting age is lowered to 14. Adults over 30 are imprisoned and fed a daily dose of LSD. The president gets his comeuppance when challenged by even younger youths. Very groovy, very political in its own way, very funny. **97m/C VHS, Beta, LV.** Shelley Winters, Christopher Jones, Hal Holbrook, Richard Pryor, Diane Varsi, Millie Perkins, Ed Begley Sr.; ***D:*** Barry Shear; ***M:*** Les Baxter. Nominations: Academy Awards '68: Best Film Editing. *HBO*

The Wild Life ♪ **1984 (R)** A recent high school graduate takes on a wild and crazy wrestler as his roommate in a swinging singles apartment complex. The same writer and producer as "Fast Times at Ridgemont High" but lacks that film's commercial success. Just as adolescent, though. **96m/C VHS, Beta, LV.** Christopher Penn, Randy Quaid, Rick Moranis, Hart Bochner, Eric Stoltz, Jenny Wright, Lea Thompson, Sherilyn Fenn, Lee Ving, Ashley St. John, Francesca "Kitten" Natividad; ***D:*** Art Linson; ***W:*** Cameron Crowe. *MCA*

Wild Man ♪ **1989** A Las Vegas gambling magnate with supernatural powers decides to avenge the murder of his friend and sets out on an adventure to find the killer. Crummy acting in yet another "ex-agent called back for one more mission" yarn. **106m/C VHS, Beta.** Ginger Lynn Allen, Michelle (McClellan) Bauer, Don Scribner, Kathleen Middleton; ***D:*** Fred J. Lincoln. *CEL*

Wild Mustang ♪♪½ **1935** Sheriff's son (Gordon) joins some outlaws to help father (Carey) spring a trap. The plan is sidetracked, and Gordon is captured and nearly branded by the baddies. Don't worry, though; everything turns out all right. Good western. **62m/B VHS, Beta.** Harry Carey Sr., Del Gordon; ***D:*** Harry Fraser. *NOS, VCN, DVT*

The Wild One ♪♪♪½ **1954** The original biker flick: two motorcycle gangs descend upon a quiet midwestern town and each other. Brando is the leader of one, struggling against social prejudices and his own gang's lawlessness to find love and a normal life. The classic tribute to 1950s rebelliousness. Based vaguely on a real incident in California. Quaint after nearly 40 years, but still the touchstone for much that has come since, and still a central role in Brando's now-long career. Brando himself believes it failed to explore Motivations for youth gangs and violence, only depicting them. Banked in Britain until 1967. **79m/B VHS, Beta, LV.** Marlon Brando, Lee Marvin, Mary Murphy, Robert Keith, Jerry Paris, Alvy Moore, Jay C. Flippen; ***D:*** Laslo Benedek; ***C:*** Hal Mohr. *COL*

Wild Ones on Wheels *Woof! Drivers to Hell* **1962** A gang of teenage hot-rod punks meet an ex-con in the Mojave desert who is searching for the half-a-million bucks he buried there years earlier. Before they find out where the money is, they kill him. In an attempt to find the stash, they kidnap the dead con's wife, hoping she'll sing like a bird. Plenty of unintended laughter. **92m/B VHS, Beta.** Francine York, Edmund Tontini, Robert Blair; ***D:*** Rudolph Cusumano. *SNC*

Wild Orchid ♪ **1990 (R)** One of the most controversial theatrical releases of 1990. Rourke is a mystery millionaire involved with two beautiful women in lovely Rio de Janeiro. Bisset is strange as an international real estate developer with unusual sexual mores. Very explicit sex scenes, but otherwise mostly boring and unbelievable. Rourke allegedly took his method-acting technique to the limit in the last love scene with Otis. Available in an unrated version as well. From the producers of "9 1/2 Weeks." Followed by an unrelated sequel. **107m/C VHS, Beta, LV.** Mickey Rourke, Jacqueline Bisset, Carre Otis, Assumpta Serna, Bruce Greenwood; ***D:*** Zalman King; ***W:*** Zalman King. *COL, FCT*

Wild Orchid 2: Two Shades of Blue *Woof!* **1992 (R)** Blue's jazz-musician, heroin-addict dad dies after a bad fix and she's sold into prostitution, until she runs away to find her true love and live a "normal" life. Effort from soft-core expert King has nothing to do with the first "Wild Orchid" and is almost laughably bad. Siemaszko is whiny, the plot is unbelievable, and the dialogue is unintentionally funny. Yes, you get sex, lots of it, but rather than passionate, it merely looks staged. Also available in an unrated version at 111 minutes. **105m/C VHS.** Nina Siemaszko, Wendy Hughes, Brent Fraser, Robert Davi, Tom Skerritt, Joe Dallesandro, Christopher McDonald, Liane Curtis; ***D:*** Zalman King; ***W:*** Zalman King. *COL*

Wild Orchids ☙☙½ **1928** A husband suspects his wife of infidelity while they take a business cruise to Java. One of Garbo's earliest silent films. Garbo is lushly surrounded with great scenery, costumes and sets, making the best of her as she makes the best of a cheery tale. **119m/B VHS, Beta.** Greta Garbo, Lewis Stone, Nils Asther; ***D:*** Sidney Franklin; ***C:*** William H. Daniels. *MGM, FCT*

The Wild Pair ☙½ *Hollow Point; Devil's Odds* **1987 (R)** Two cops track down a cocaine smuggling ring and uncover a private army planning to conquer the United States. Lloyd Bridges is memorable as a rabid right-winger, and the wild pairing of Bubba and Beau inspires head-scratching. Otherwise, what we have here is a typical action pic, complete with car chases. Beau Bridges' inauspicious feature directing debut. **89m/C VHS, Beta, LV.** Beau Bridges, Bubba Smith, Lloyd Bridges, Gary Lockwood, Raymond St. Jacques; ***D:*** Beau Bridges; ***M:*** John Debney. *MED, VTR*

Wild Palms ☙☙ **1993** In 2007 Los Angeles, Harry (Belushi) takes a job at a TV station that offers virtual reality programming to viewers, only this isn't benign technology. Delany is stuck in a thankless role as his wife, Cattrall is his former lover, but Dickinson has the most fun as Harry's power-mad mother-in-law who's also a sadistic co-conspirator of a nasty senator (Loggia). Lesson in weird style over substance really doesn't make much sense, but unlike "Twin Peaks" (to which this TV miniseries was heavily compared) it at least has an ending. Executive producer Stone has a cameo which concerns the JFK conspiracy. Based on the comic strip by Wagner. In two parts. **300m/C VHS.** James Belushi, Robert Loggia, Dana Delany, Kim Cattrall, Angie Dickinson, Ernie Hudson, Bebe Neuwirth, Nick Mancuso, Charles Hallahan, Robert Morse, David Warner, Ben Savage, Bob Gunton, Brad Dourif, Charles Rocket; ***Cameos:*** Oliver Stone; ***D:*** Phil Joanou, Kathryn Bigelow, Keith Gordon, Pete Hewitt; ***W:*** Bruce Wagner; ***C:*** Phedon Papamichael; ***M:*** Ryuichi Sakamoto. *ABC, FCT*

Wild Party ☙☙½ **1974 (R)** It's 1929, a year of much frivolity in Hollywood. Drinking, dancing, maneuvering and almost every sort of romance are the rule of the night at silent film comic Jolly Grimm's sumptuous, star-studded party that climaxes with, among other things, a murder. Well performed but somehow hollow; ambitious Ivory effort unfortunately falls short. Based on Joseph Moncure March's poem, and loosely on the Fatty Arbuckle scandal. **90m/C VHS, Beta.** Raquel Welch, James Coco, Perry King, David Dukes, Royal Dano, Tiffany Bolling; ***D:*** James Ivory; ***C:*** Walter Lassally. *SUE*

Wild Pony ☙ **1983** A young boy spurns his new stepfather, preferring to live with his pony instead. Reversal of the evil-stepmother-and-girl-loves-horse theme. **87m/C VHS, Beta.** Marilyn Lightstone, Art Hindle, Josh Byrne; ***D:*** Kevin Sullivan; ***M:*** Hagood Hardy. *FHE, VES, LIV*

Wild Rapture ☙ **1950** The hunting and dissecting of an elephant and gorilla, a look at a tribe that practices lip-splitting, and other gruesome events abound in this shock-fest. Banned for 18 years. **68m/B VHS, Beta.** *NOS, HEG*

Wild Rebels ☙ **1971 (R)** A two-faced member of a ruthless motorcycle gang informs the police of the gang's plans to rob a bank. Lots of bullet-flying action. Dumb, ordinary biker flick; star Pastrano was a former boxing champ in real life. **90m/C VHS, Beta.** Steve Alaimo, Willie Pastrano, John Vella, Bobbie Byers; ***D:*** William Grefe. *ACA*

Wild Reeds ☙☙☙ *Les Roseaux Sauvages* **1994** Emotional coming of age tale set in 1962 (at the end of the French war in Algeria) and focusing on three classmates at a French boarding school. Sensitive Francois (Morel) is just coming to the realization that he likes boys, particularly working-class Serge (Rideau) who's attracted to Francois's confidante Maite (Bouchez). The provocateur is Algerian-born Henri (Gorny), a bitter political militant who enjoys his battles with classmates and teachers alike. Politics and youthful passions are forced into crises. French historical/political context may prove a barrier. French with subtitles. **110m/C VHS.** *FR* Gael Morel, Stephane Rideau, Elodie Bouchez, Frederic Gorny, Michele Moretti; ***D:*** Andre Techine; ***W:*** Gilles Taurand, Olivier Massart, Andre Techine; ***C:*** Jeanne Lapoirie. Cesar Awards '95: Best Director (Techine), Best Film, Best Screenplay; Los Angeles Film Critics Association Awards '95: Best Foreign Film; National Society of Film Critics Awards '95: Best Foreign Film. *NYR*

The Wild Ride ☙☙ **1960** Nicholson, in an early starring role, portrays a rebellious punk of the Beat generation who hotrods his way into trouble and tragedy. He kidnaps now-straight ex-buddy Bean's squeeze (Carter); kills a few cops; then is killed. Interesting only if you're interested in Nicholson. **59m/B VHS, Beta.** Jack Nicholson, Georgianna Carter, Robert Bean; ***D:*** Harvey Berman. *SNC, NOS, VYY*

Wild Riders *Woof! Angels for Kicks* **1971 (R)** Two ruthless, amoral bikers molest, kidnap, rape, and beat two beautiful, naive young society ladies. Despicable story, with deplorable acting, but the ending, in which a husband slays a biker with a cello, surely is unique. **91m/C VHS, Beta.** Alex Rocco, Elizabeth Knowles, Sherry Bain, Arell Blanton; ***D:*** Richard Kanter. *ACA*

Wild Rovers ☙☙ **1971 (PG)** An aging cowboy and his younger colleague turn to bank robbing and are pursued by a posse in a wacky comedy-adventure from director Edwards. Uneven script and too much referential baggage (faint shades of "Butch Cassidy") doom this valiant effort, with the two stars hanging right in there all the way. **138m/C VHS, Beta, LV.** William Holden, Ryan O'Neal, Karl Malden, Lynn Carlin, Tom Skerritt, Joe Don Baker, Rachel Roberts, Moses Gunn; ***D:*** Blake Edwards; ***W:*** Blake Edwards; ***M:*** Jerry Goldsmith. *MGM*

Wild Side ☙☙ **1995 (R)** Bank employee Alex (Heche) moonlights as a hooker and gets caught in a federal sting operation. Forced to inform on one of her clients, Bruno (Walken), who's involved in a money-laundering scheme, Alex complicates matters by falling in love with Bruno's mistress, Victoria (Chen). The unrated version is 96 minutes. **90m/C VHS.** Anne Heche, Christopher Walken, Joan Chen, Steven Bauer; ***D:*** Franklyn Brauner. *HMK*

Wild Strawberries ☙☙☙☙ *Smultron-Stallet* **1957** Bergman's landmark film of fantasy, dreams and nightmares. An aging professor, on the road to accept an award, must come to terms with his anxieties and guilt. Brilliant performance by Sjostrom, Sweden's first film director and star. Excellent use of flashbacks and film editing. An intellectual and emotional masterpiece. In Swedish with English subtitles. **90m/B VHS, Beta, LV, 8mm.** *SW* Victor Sjostrom, Bibi Andersson, Max von Sydow, Ingrid Thulin, Gunnar Bjornstrand, Folke Sundquist, Bjorn Bjelvenstam; ***D:*** Ingmar Bergman; ***W:*** Ingmar Bergman. Golden Globe Awards '60: Best Foreign Film; National Board of Review Awards '59: 5 Best Foreign Films of the Year; Nominations: Academy Awards '59: Best Story & Screenplay. *VYY, HMV, FOX*

Wild Style ☙☙ **1983** Zoro, a mild-mannered Bronx teenager, spends his evenings spray-painting subway cars. Intended as a depiction of urban street life, including graffiti, breakdancing and rap music. Mildly interesting social comment, but unconvincing as cinema. Too "realistic," with too little vision. **82m/C VHS, Beta.** Lee George Quinones, Fredrick Braithwaite, Dondi White; ***D:*** Charlie Ahearn; ***M:*** Fred Brathwaite. *FCT*

Wild Thing ☙½ **1987 (PG-13)** A modern variation on the Wild Child/Tarzan myth, as a feral kid stalks a crime-ridden ghetto. Sayles, a usually imaginative writer and director, really takes a dive here. And of course, the Troggs' overplayed title hit is abused as the theme. **92m/C VHS, Beta, LV.** Kathleen Quinlan, Rob Knepper, Robert Davi, Betty Buckley, Maury Chaykin; ***D:*** Max Reid, Ken Cameron; ***W:*** John Sayles; ***M:*** George S. Clinton, Guy Moon. *NO*

Wild Times ☙☙ **1979** Too long but pleasant rendition of the life of High Candill, early Wild West showman. Based on the novel by Brian Garfield. Made for TV, originally in two parts. **200m/C VHS, Beta.** Sam Elliott, Trish Stewart, Ben Johnson, Dennis Hopper, Pat Hingle; ***D:*** Richard Compton. *PSM*

Wild Weed ☙ *The Devil's Weed; She Shoulda Said No; Marijuana the Devil's Weed* **1949** Funny smelling cigarettes ruin the lives of all who inhale. Viewers' advice: just say no. Leed's actual drug bust with Robert Mitchum got her the lead. **70m/B VHS.** Lila Leeds, Alan Baxter, Lyle Talbot, Jack Elam, David Gorcey; ***D:*** Sam Newfield. *SNC, AOV, TPV*

Wild West ☙☙ *Prairie Outlaws* **1946** The hero and loyal companions (with names like Skinny, Stormy and Soapy) tackle desperadoes trying to stop telegraph line construction. More mild than wild, it was later trimmed and released under its alternate title, but here you're getting the original. **73m/C VHS.** Eddie Dean, Roscoe Ates, Lash LaRue, Robert "Buzzy" Henry, Sarah Padden, Louise Currie, Warner Richmond, Chief Yowlachie, Bud Osborne; ***D:*** Robert Emmett Tansey. *NOS, HEG*

Wild West **1987** A compilation of scenes from dozens of western films. **90m/C VHS, Beta.** John Wayne, Clint Eastwood, Steve McQueen, Charles Bronson. *NO*

Wild West ☙☙ **1993** Three Pakistani brothers, living in London, decide to form an American-style country and western band they call the Honky Tonk Cowboys and dream of making it big in Nashville. A little romance, lots of energy, but too many gags leave the film unfocused. **83m/C VHS.** *GB* Naveen Andrews, Sarita Choudhury, Ronny Jhutti, Ravi Kapoor; ***D:*** David Attwood; ***W:*** Harwant Bains. *VMK*

Wild Wheels *Woof!* **1975 (PG)** A group of dune-buggy enthusiasts seek revenge against a gang of motorcyclists who have ravaged a small California beach town. **81m/C VHS, Beta.** Casey Kasem, Dovie Beams, Terry Stafford, Robert Dix. *GEM*

Wild, Wild Planet ☙½ **1965** Alien beings from a distant planet are miniaturizing Earth's leaders in a bid to destroy our planet, and a dubbed, wooden hero comes to the rescue. A rarely seen Italian SF entry, great fun for genre fans. A must for "robot girls in skin tight leather outfits" completists. **93m/C VHS.** *IT* Tony Russell, Lisa Gastoni, Massimo Serato, Franco Nero; ***D:*** Anthony (Antonio Margheriti) Dawson. *SMW*

Wild, Wild West Revisited ☙☙½ **1979** A feature-length reprise of the tongue-in-cheek western series. Irreverent and fun, in the spirit of its admirable predecessor-though it's probably just as well the proposed new series didn't see fruition. Made for television. **95m/C VHS, Beta.** Robert Conrad, Ross Martin, Harry (Henry) Morgan, Rene Auberjonois; ***D:*** Burt Kennedy. *FOX*

Wild, Wild World of Jayne Mansfield ☙☙ **1968** The life and times of Mansfield are explored in this unique documentary, which was unfinished at the time of her death. Jayne takes the viewer on a worldwide examination of sexual mores, from prostitution, nudist colonies, and the racy strip clubs of Europe, to the transvestite and topless bars of America. Perverse (but did you expect otherwise?), footage of her fatal car crash was included. **89m/C VHS, Beta.** Jayne Mansfield. *VDM, DVT, TPV*

Wild Women 🦴 **1953** Extremely hilarious schlocker about a safari of white men captured by a savage tribe of jungle women. Total camp. **?m/C VHS.** Lewis Wilson, Frances Dubay, Dana Wilson. *SNC, HEG*

Wild Women 🦴½ **1970** Five female convicts are released during the Texas/Mexico dispute to help smuggle arms to American forces. Innocuous western, original in a made-for-TV kind of way. **90m/C VHS, Beta.** Hugh O'Brian, Anne Francis, Marilyn Maxwell, Marie Windsor; ***D:*** Don Taylor. *FOX*

Wild Women of Wongo 🦴½ **1959** The denizens of a primitive isle, essentially beautiful women and ugly men, meet the natives of a neighboring island, handsome men and ugly women. Not quite bad enough to be true camp fun, but stupidly silly in a low-budget way. **73m/C VHS, Beta.** Pat Crowley, Ed Fury, Adrienne Bourbeau, Jean Hawkshaw, Johnny Walsh; ***D:*** James L. Wolcott. *DVT, MED, HEG*

The Wild World of Batwoman 🦴🦴 **1966** A campy cult film in which Batwoman and a bevy of Bat Girls are pitted against an evil doctor in order to find the prototype of an atomic hearing aid/nuclear bomb. Also released theatrically as "She Was a Hippy Vampire." **70m/C VHS, Beta.** Katherine Victor, George Andre, Steve Brodie, Lloyd Nelson; ***D:*** Jerry Warren. *RHI, SNC, DVT*

Wild Zone 🦴 **1989 (R)** An American ex-soldier combats mercenaries in Africa in order to rescue his kidnapped father. **100m/C VHS, Beta, LV.** Edward Albert, Philip Brown, Carla Herd; ***D:*** Percival Rubens. *COL*

Wildcard 🦴½ **1992 (PG-13)** When a veteran pilot is killed in a helicopter crash, a friend suspects foul play. He calls in Preacher, a special forces veteran, to investigate and what he discovers is murder, greed, and corruption. **86m/C VHS, LV.** Powers Boothe, Cindy Pickett, Rene Auberjonois, Terry O'Quinn, M. Emmet Walsh, John Lacy; ***D:*** Mel Damski; ***W:*** Scobie Richardson. *MCA*

Wildcat 🦴🦴 **1942** Crabbe, famous as the serials' Flash Gordon, is a villain in this petrochemical adventure. The hero overextends his credit when he buys an oil well and must produce a gusher or else. **73m/B VHS.** Richard Arlen, Arline Judge, Buster Crabbe, William Frawley, Arthur Hunnicutt, Elisha Cook Jr., Billy Benedict; ***D:*** Frank McDonald. *NOS*

Wildcats 🦴🦴 **1986 (R)** A naive female phys-ed teacher (Hawn) is saddled with the job of coach for a completely undisciplined, inner city, high school football team. Formulaic, connect-the-dots comedy; moderately funny, and of course Hawn triumphs in adversity, but at nearly two hours a very long sitcom episode. **106m/C VHS, Beta, LV.** Goldie Hawn, James Keach, Swoosie Kurtz, Bruce McGill, M. Emmet Walsh, Woody Harrelson, Wesley Snipes, Tab Thacker; ***D:*** Michael Ritchie; ***M:*** James Newton Howard. *WAR*

Wilder Napalm 🦴½ **1993 (PG-13)** Lame comedy about two at-odds brothers, the woman they both love, and their dangerous pyrokinetic abilities. Wilder (Howard) and Wallace (Quaid) Foudroyant have been feuding for years—and not just over the fact that Wallace is in love with Wilder's wife Vida (Winger). Wallace wants to use their family "gift" to become rich and famous but Wilder doesn't want them to exploit their fiery powers. They finally decide on an incendiary showdown to settle the score once and for all. Good actors lost in witless characters and a incoherent plot. **109m/C VHS, LV.** Dennis Quaid, Arliss Howard, Debra Winger, M. Emmet Walsh, Jim Varney, Mimi Lieber, Marvin J. McIntyre; ***D:*** Glenn Gordon Caron; ***W:*** Vince Gilligan; ***M:*** Michael Kamen. *COL*

Wildest Dreams 🦴½ *Bikini Genie* **1990 (R)** Released from its bottle by a lovely nebbish, a genie puts a love spell on one beautiful girl after another in order to find him the right one, resulting in a bevy of women clamoring for our hero's attention. **84m/C VHS, Beta, LV.** James Davies, Heidi Paine, Deborah Blaisdell, Ruth Collins, Jane Hamilton, Jill Johnson; ***D:*** Chuck Vincent. *LIV, VES*

The Wildest Office Party *Woof!* **1987** A sex-filled tape for and about wild, rowdy office parties. **60m/C VHS, Beta.** *LIV, VES*

Wildfire 🦴½ **1945** Two horse traders come to the aid of ranchers beset by horse thieves. Early color outing for Steele. Harmless, ordinary oater. **60m/C VHS, Beta, LV.** Bob Steele, Sterling Holloway, John Miljan, William Farnum, Eddie Dean, Sarah Padden, Frank Ellis; ***D:*** Robert Emmett Tansey. *NOS, VDM, HEG*

Wildfire 🦴🦴 **1988 (PG)** As teenagers, Frank and Kay run away to get married but Frank is sent to prison for robbing a bank and Kay winds up making a new life for herself. Released from prison after eight years, Frank discovers Kay is married with two children and doesn't want anything further to do with him. But when Frank violates his parole, Kay discovers she can't leave him again and the two go on the run together. **98m/C VHS, LV.** Steven Bauer, Linda Fiorentino, Will Patton, Marshall Bell; ***D:*** Zalman King; ***W:*** Zalman King, Matthew Bright; ***M:*** Maurice Jarre. *MCA*

Wildflower 🦴🦴🦴 **1991** Set in the Depression-era South, Alice is a 17 year-old partially deaf girl who also suffers from epilepsy. Her stepfather believes she's possessed and confines her to a shed. Growing up ignorant and abused Alice is befriended by a neighboring brother and sister who decide to rescue her. A three-hankie family picture with moving performances and inspirational themes. Based on the novel "Alice" by Sara Flanigan. Made for cable television. **94m/C VHS.** Patricia Arquette, Beau Bridges, Susan Blakely, William McNamara, Reese Witherspoon, Collin Wilcox Paxton; ***D:*** Diane Keaton. National Academy of Cable Programming ACE Awards '93: Best Actress (Arquette). *WOV*

Wilding 🦴½ **1990** A pair of cops are on the trail of a gang of kids who go "wilding," which involves sprees of killing, raping and looting. Exploitive fare based on horrible, recent events in New York. The filmmakers skirt controversy by making the criminals rich suburban kids. **92m/C VHS, Beta.** Wings Hauser, Joey Travolta, Karen Russell, Steven Cooke; ***D:*** Eric Louzil. *AIP*

Wildrose 🦴🦴🦴 **1985** Eichhorn is memorable as a recent divorcee who must assert herself among her otherwise all-male co-workers at a Minnesota strip mine. She finds a new love, and tries to put her life back together. Filmed on location. **96m/C VHS, Beta.** Lisa Eichhorn, Tom Bower, James Cada; ***D:*** John Hanson; ***W:*** John Hanson, Eugene Corr. *LIV*

Will: G. Gordon Liddy 🦴🦴½ **1982** The life of the Watergate conspirator, based on his autobiography. Made for TV. Producer/star Conrad reportedly objected strongly to cuts from the original three-hour length, apparently with cause: the first half is superficial pap. The portrayal of Liddy's time in prison, though, is fascinating, and Conrad is excellent. **100m/C VHS.** Robert Conrad, Kathy Cannon, Gary Bayer, Peter Ratray, James Rebhorn, Red West, Maurice Woods, Danny Lloyd; ***D:*** Robert Liebmann. *LIV*

Will Penny 🦴🦴🦴½ **1967** Just back from a cattle drive, a range-wandering loner looks for work in the wrong place and offends a family of outlaws who come after him. His escape from them leads to another kind of trap—one set by a love-hungry woman (Hackett, in a strong performance). Heston considers this film his personal best, and he's probably right. Superbly directed western, with excellent cinematography and professional, realistic portrayals, flopped in theaters, moviegoers preferring simultaneous Heston outing "Planet of the Apes." Photography by Lucien Ballard. **109m/C VHS, Beta, LV.** Charlton Heston, Joan Hackett, Donald Pleasence, Lee Majors, Bruce Dern, Anthony Zerbe, Ben Johnson, Clifton James; ***D:*** Tom Gries; ***M:*** Elmer Bernstein. *PAR*

Will Success Spoil Rock Hunter? 🦴🦴½ **1957** Dated advertising satire finds ad man Hunter (Randall) hoping to get the key to the executive washroom but he may instead find himself on the unemployment line unless he can convince the profitable Stay-Put lipstick account not to change agencies. One day Rock see movie star Rita Marlowe (Mansfield), and her kissable lips, on TV and tries to convince her to endorse the product but she'll only agree if he'll pose as her new boyfriend to make ex-beau Bobo (Mansfield's real-life hubby Hargitay) jealous. Naturally, the lipstick ads take off bigtime but success does indeed spoil Rock (at least temporarily). Very slightly based on the play by George Axelrod. **94m/C VHS.** Tony Randall, Jayne Mansfield, Betsy Drake, Mickey Hargitay, John Williams, Henry Jones, Joan Blondell; ***Cameos:*** Groucho Marx; ***D:*** Frank Tashlin; ***W:*** Frank Tashlin; ***C:*** Joe MacDonald; ***M:*** Cyril Mockridge. *FXV*

Willa 🦴🦴 **1979** Raffin, a hash-joint waitress with two kids and one in the pipeline, is deserted by her husband and determines to get ahead by becoming a trucker. Okay made-for-TV drama. **95m/C VHS, Beta.** Cloris Leachman, Deborah Raffin, Clu Gulager, John Amos, Diane Ladd; ***D:*** Claudio Guzman, Joan Darling; ***M:*** John Barry. *PSM*

Willard 🦴🦴 **1971 (PG)** Willard is a lonely, psychotic youngster who trains a group of rats, his only friends, to attack his enemies. Not as disgusting as it might have been (rated PG), but pretty weird and not redeemed by any sense of style or humor. Popular at the box office; followed by inferior "Ben." Based on by Stephen Gilbert's novel "Ratman's Notebooks." **95m/C VHS, Beta, LV.** Bruce Davison, Ernest Borgnine, Elsa Lanchester, Sondra Locke; ***D:*** Daniel Mann; ***C:*** Robert B. Hauser; ***M:*** Alex North. *PSM, PAR*

Willie & Phil 🦴🦴½ **1980 (R)** At the start of the '70s, two buddies (Ontkean and Sharkey) fall for the same girl (Kidder). They become a threesome and are entangled in each other's lives for the rest of the decade. Insightful comedy-drama. **111m/C VHS, LV.** Michael Ontkean, Margot Kidder, Ray Sharkey, Jan Miner, Julie Bovasso, Natalie Wood, Laurence "Larry" Fishburne, Louis Guss, Kaki Hunter, Kristine DeBell; ***D:*** Paul Mazursky; ***W:*** Paul Mazursky; ***C:*** Sven Nykvist; ***M:*** Claude Bolling. *FXV*

The Willies 🦴🦴 **1990 (PG-13)** Three youngsters gross each other out with juvenile tales of horror and scariness while camping out in the backyard. Pointless but not without a few yuks (in both senses of the term). **120m/C VHS, LV.** James Karen, Sean Astin, Kathleen Freeman, Jeremy Miller; ***D:*** Brian Peck. *PSM*

Willow 🦴🦴½ **1988 (PG)** Blockbuster fantasy epic combines the story of Moses with "Snow White," dwarves and all. Willow is the little Nelwyn who finds the lost baby Daikini and is assigned the task of returning her safely to her people. Willow discovers that the girl is actually a sacred infant who is destined to overthrow the evil queen Bavmorda and rule the land. As you might expect from executive producer George Lucas, there is much action and plenty of clever, high-quality special effects. But the "Star Wars"-esque story (by Lucas) is strangely predictable, and a bit too action-packed. Not really for children. **118m/C VHS, Beta, LV, 8mm.** Warwick Davis, Val Kilmer, Jean Marsh, Joanne Whalley, Billy Barty, Pat Roach, Ruth Greenfield, Patricia Hayes, Gavan O'Herlihy, Kevin Pollak; ***D:*** Ron Howard; ***W:*** Bob Dolman; ***M:*** James Horner. *COL*

Willy Wonka & the Chocolate Factory 🦴🦴🦴½ **1971 (G)** When the last of five coveted "golden tickets" falls into the hands of sweet but very poor Charlie, he and his Grandpa Joe get a tour of the most wonderfully strange chocolate factory in the world. The owner is the most curious hermit ever to hit the big screen. He leads the five young "winners" on a thrilling and often dangerous tour of his fabulous factory. Adapted from Roald Dahl's "Charlie and the Chocolate Factory." Without a doubt one of the best "kid's" movies ever made; a family classic worth watching again and again. ♫ Willy Wonka, the Candy Man; Cheer Up, Charlie; I've Got a Golden Ticket; Oompa-Loompa-Doompa-Dee-Doo; Pure Imagination. **100m/C VHS, Beta, LV.** Gene Wilder, Jack Albertson, Denise Nickerson, Peter Ostrum, Roy Kinnear, Aubrey Woods, Michael Bollner, Ursula Reit, Leonard Stone, Dodo Denney; ***D:*** Mel Stuart; ***M:*** Leslie Bricusse. Nominations: Academy Awards '71: Best Original Score. *WAR, APD, HMV*

Wilma ☆☆ **1977** Based on the true story of Wilma Rudolph, a young black woman who overcame childhood illness to win three gold medals at the 1960 Olympics. Plodding made-for-TV biography suffers from sub-par script and acting. **100m/C VHS, Beta.** Joe Seneca, Cicely Tyson, Shirley Jo Finney; ***D:*** Bud Greenspan; ***M:*** Irwin Bazelon. *COL, FCT*

Wilson ☆☆☆ **1944** Biography of Woodrow Wilson from his days as the head of Princeton University, to the governorship of New York, and as U.S. President during WWI. After the war, Wilson conceives of the League of Nations but is unable to sell it to a U.S. still bent on isolationism. This lavish film won critical plaudits but was a major money-loser. **154m/C VHS.** Alexander Knox, Charles Coburn, Geraldine Fitzgerald, Thomas Mitchell, Ruth Nelson, Cedric Hardwicke, Vincent Price, William Eythe, Mary Anderson, Sidney Blackmer, Stanley Ridges, Eddie Foy Jr., Charles Halton; ***D:*** Henry King; ***W:*** Lamar Trotti; ***C:*** Leon Shamroy; ***M:*** Alfred Newman. Academy Awards '44: Best Color Cinematography, Best Film Editing, Best Interior Decoration, Best Original Screenplay, Best Sound; Golden Globe Awards '45: Best Actor—Drama (Knox); Nominations: Academy Awards '44: Best Actor (Knox), Best Director (King), Best Picture, Best Original Score. *FXV, MOV, BTV*

Wimps ☆ **1987 (R)** A collegiate wimp is subjected to a brutal fraternity initiation, but eventually gets the girl. Cheap ripoff of Cyrano de Bergerac, turned into a teen sex flick. **94m/C VHS, Beta.** Louie Bonanno, Jim Abele, Deborah Blaisdell; ***D:*** Chuck Vincent. *LIV*

Win, Place, or Steal ☆½ *The Big Payoff; Three For the Money; Just Another Day at the Races* **1972 (PG)** Lame comedy set at the racetrack about three grown men and their adolescent schemes to win big. Better you should scratch. **88m/C VHS, Beta.** McLean Stevenson, Alex Karras, Dean Stockwell; ***D:*** Richard Bailey. *LIV, VES*

Winchester '73 ☆☆☆½ **1950** Superb acting and photography characterize this classic, landmark western. Simple plot—cowboy Stewart pursues his stolen state-of-the-art rifle as it changes hands—speeds along and carries the viewer with it, ending with an engrossing and unforgettable shoot-out. Almost singlehandedly breathed new life into the whole genre. Laser videodisc version contains a special narration track provided by Stewart. Mann's and Stewart's first teaming. **82m/C VHS, Beta, LV.** James Stewart, Shelley Winters, Stephen McNally, Dan Duryea, Millard Mitchell, John McIntire, Will Geer, Jay C. Flippen, Rock Hudson, Tony Curtis, Charles Drake; ***D:*** Anthony Mann; ***C:*** William H. Daniels. *MCA*

The Wind ☆☆☆☆ **1928** One of the last great silents still stands as a magnificent entertainment. Gish, in possibly her best role, is an innocent Easterner who finds herself married to a rough cowpoke and raped by a married man in a bleak frontier town. Director Sjostrom has a splendid feel for landscape, and the drama—climaxing with a tumultuous desert storm—is intense yet fully believable. Based on the novel by Dorothy Scarborough. **74m/B VHS, Beta.** Lillian Gish, Lars Hanson, Montagu Love, Dorothy Cumming, Edward Earle, William Orlamond; ***D:*** Victor Sjostrom; ***W:*** Frances Marion. *MGM*

The Wind ☆ **1987** Foster is terrorized by Hauser while attempting to write her next thriller in Greece. Let's hope her book is more exciting than this movie. Shot on location in Greece. **92m/C VHS, Beta.** Meg Foster, Wings Hauser, Steve Railsback, David McCallum, Robert Morley; ***D:*** Nico Mastorakis. *LIV*

Wind ☆☆½ **1992 (PG-13)** Sailor Will Parker (Modine) chooses the opportunity to be on the America's Cup team over girlfriend Grey and then has the dubious honor of making a technical error that causes their loss. Undaunted, he locates Grey and her new engineer boyfriend (Skarsgard) and convinces them to design the ultimate boat for the next set of races. ESPN carried extensive coverage of the America's Cup races for the first time in the summer of '92 and viewers discovered that a little goes a long way. The same holds true for "Wind" which has stunning race footage, but little else. The script lacks substance and was written as filming progressed, and it shows. **123m/C VHS, LV, 8mm.** Matthew Modine, Jennifer Grey, Cliff Robertson, Jack Thompson, Stellan Skarsgard, Rebecca Miller, Ned Vaughn; ***D:*** Carroll Ballard; ***W:*** Rudy Wurlitzer, Mac Gudgeon; ***C:*** John Toll; ***M:*** Basil Poledouris. *COL*

The Wind and the Lion ☆☆☆ **1975 (PG)** In turn-of-the-century Morocco, a sheik (Connery) kidnaps a feisty American woman (Bergen) and her children and holds her as a political hostage. President Teddy Roosevelt (Keith) sends in the Marines to free the captives, who are eventually released by their captor. Directed with venue and style by Milius. Highly entertaining, if heavily fictionalized. Based very loosely on a historical incident. **120m/C VHS, Beta, LV.** Sean Connery, Candice Bergen, Brian Keith, John Huston, Geoffrey Lewis; ***D:*** John Milius; ***W:*** John Milius; ***C:*** Billy Williams; ***M:*** Jerry Goldsmith. Nominations: Academy Awards '75: Best Sound, Best Original Score. *MGM*

A Wind Named Amnesia **1993** A strange amnesia wind sweeps away all of mankind's knowledge and human civilization vanishes. Then a mysterious young man is miraculously re-educated and searches for those who destroyed man's memories. In Japanese with English subtitles. **80m/C VHS.** *JP* ***D:*** Kazuo Yakmazaki; ***W:*** Hideyuki Kikuchi. *CPM*

The Wind That Walks **1985** Two girls trek into the New Jersey wilds after an unknown animal called by the Indians "the wind that walks." **30m/C Beta.** *NJN*

Windjammer ☆☆ **1937** Western star O'Brien took a break from the lone prairie to make this seafaring rescue drama. He is a deputy state's attorney who signs up for a yacht race in order to serve a subpoena. Bad guys arrive on the scene, and the initially moody yacht denizens rely on our trusty hero to save them. Decent adventure. **75m/B VHS.** George O'Brien, Constance Worth; ***D:*** Sam Newfield. *NOS, DVT, HEG*

Windmills of the Gods ☆☆½ *Sidney Sheldon's Windmills of the Gods* **1988** Glamor, romance, intrigue, and politics all mixed together in eastern Europe. Smith is named ambassador to Romania, finds the suave Wagner in residence, and becomes the target of assassins. Based on the novel by Sidney Sheldon. Made for television. **95m/C VHS.** Jaclyn Smith, Robert Wagner, Franco Nero, Christopher Cazenove, David Ackroyd, Jean-Pierre Aumont, Ruby Dee, Jeffrey DeMunn, Michael Moriarty, Ian McKellen, Susan Tyrrell; ***D:*** Lee Philips; ***W:*** John Gay; ***M:*** Perry Botkin. *LIV*

Windom's Way ☆☆☆ **1957** Finch, in a strong role in this intriguing political drama, is an idealistic doctor in a remote village in Malaysia. He juggles a failing marriage and a budding romance, then finds himself caught in a local labor dispute. He works for a peaceful solution, but is captured by an insurgent army. Disillusioned, he plans to leave the country, but his wife persuades him to stay and tend the wounded. Based on a novel by James Ramsey Ullman. **90m/B VHS, Beta.** *GB* Peter Finch, Mary Ure; ***D:*** Ronald Neame. *NO*

The Window ☆☆☆½ **1949** A little boy (Disney star Driscoll, intriguingly cast by director, Tetzlaff) has a reputation for telling lies, so no one believes him when he says he witnessed a murder...except the killers. Almost unbearably tense, claustrophobic thriller about the helplessness of childhood. Tetzlaff clearly learned more than a thing or two from the master, Hitchcock, for whom he photographed "Notorious." Based on the novella "The Boy Who Cried Murder" by Cornell Woolrich. Driscoll was awarded a special miniature Oscar as Outstanding Juvenile for his performance. **73m/B VHS, Beta, LV.** Bobby Driscoll, Barbara Hale, Arthur Kennedy, Ruth Roman; ***D:*** Ted Tetzlaff. Edgar Allan Poe Awards '49: Best Screenplay; Nominations: Academy Awards '49: Best Film Editing. *MED*

Window Shopping ☆☆½ **1986** Multiple, confusing romances occur at the "Toison d' Or" shopping mall in Paris. A modern, French homage to the classic Hollywood musical. In French with English subtitles. **96m/C VHS.** *FR* Delphine Seyrig, Charles Denner, Fanny Cottencon, Miriam Boyer, Lio, Pascale Salkin, Jean-Francois Balmer; ***D:*** Chantal Akerman; ***W:*** Chantal Akerman. *WAC, FCT, INJ*

Window to Paris ☆☆ **1995 (PG-13)** East and West meet unexpectedly when a young music teacher (Dontsov) rents a room in St. Petersburg with a secret window that opens onto a Paris rooftop. Loony adventures ensue as Dontsov and his friends escape their dreary existence to exploit the bounties of Western capitalism in this sharp satire of Russian social ills. Relentless humor based on cross-cultural stereotypes wears thin (the Russians are cantankerous drunks; the Parisians, self-important snobs), but it keeps a sunny cast upon what could have been a scathing commentary. Russian and French with subtitles. **92m/C VHS, LV.** *RU FR* Serguej Dontsov, Agnes Soral, Viktor Michailov, Nina Oussatova; ***D:*** Yuri Mamin; ***W:*** Arkadi Tigai, Yuri Mamin; ***M:*** Aleksei Zalivalov, Yuri Mamin. *COL*

Windows ☆ **1980 (R)** A lonely lesbian (Ashley) becomes obsessed with her quiet neighbor (Shire) and concocts a plot to get close to her. Director Willis is known for his unbeatable cinematography, most notably for Woody Allen in "Manhattan." His debut in the chair is a miserable, offensive flop. **93m/C VHS.** Talia Shire, Joe Cortese, Elizabeth Ashley, Kay Medford, Linda Gillin; ***D:*** Gordon Willis; ***C:*** Gordon Willis; ***M:*** Ennio Morricone. *NO*

Windrider ☆½ **1986** Simple love story made in Australia. A wind surfer and a rock star become lovers. Self-indulgent overwrought garbage with rare moments of promise. **83m/C VHS.** *AU* Tom Burlinson, Nicole Kidman, Charles Tingwell, Jill Perryman, Simon Chilvers; ***D:*** Vincent Monton. *MGM*

Windrunner ☆☆½ **1994 (PG)** Angry at his football-star dad and rejected by the local high school team, Greg Cima (Wiles) finds an unlikely ally in the spirit of Native American Olympic hero Jim Thorpe (Means). Seems Thorpe needs some aid to return to the spirit world and, by coaching Cima, he'll also get the help he needs. Believable performances and an exploration of the power of Native American mysticism help the unlikely premise along. **110m/C VHS.** Russell Means, Jason Wiles, Amanda Peterson, Margot Kidder, Jake Busey, Max Casella, Bruce Weitz; ***D:*** William Clark; ***W:*** Mitch Davis; ***M:*** Arthur Kempel. *AVE*

The Winds of Jarrah ☆½ **1983** English woman runs from broken heart to Australia to become nanny for misogynist, and Harlequin code prevails. Based on a Harlequin romance novel. **78m/C VHS, Beta.** *AU* Terence Donovan, Susan Lyons; ***D:*** Mark Egerton; ***M:*** Bruce Smeaton. *NO*

The Winds of Kitty Hawk ☆☆ **1978** Visually interesting but talky account of the Wright brothers attempt to beat their rival Glenn Curtiss and his backer, phone man Alexander Graham Bell. Rule of thumb: Fast-forward through the parts when they are on the ground, or see Stacy Keach's public-TV version instead. **96m/C VHS, Beta.** Michael Moriarty, David Huffman, Kathryn Walker, Eugene Roche, John Randolph, Scott Hylands; ***D:*** E.W. Swackhamer; ***M:*** Charles Bernstein. *FRH*

Winds of the Wasteland ☆☆½ **1936** Would-be Pony Express contractors, Wayne and Chandler, race rivals to land government work. Competent western that put Wayne on the Hollywood map. **54m/B VHS.** John Wayne, Phyllis Fraser, Lane Chandler, Yakima Canutt; ***D:*** Mack V. Wright. *REP, NOS, VCN*

The Winds of War ☆☆ **1983** On seven tapes, the excruciatingly long and dull television miniseries based on Herman Wouk's bestseller about WWII. The book was much better; Mitchum appears to be fighting sleep unsuccessfully for much of the show. Two follow-ups were produced: "War and Remembrance" and "War and Remembrance: The Final Chapter." **900m/C VHS, Beta.** Robert Mitchum, Ali MacGraw, Ralph Bellamy, Polly Bergen, Jan-Michael Vincent, David Dukes, John Houseman, Victoria Tennant, Peter Graves, Chaim Topol, Ben Murphy, Jeremy Kemp, Anton Diffring, Lawrence Pressman, Andrew Duggan, Barbara Steele; ***D:*** Dan Curtis. *PAR, MOV*

Windwalker **1981** Howard, the only cast member who is not a Native American, is an aged chief who shares the memories of his life with his grandchildren. Filmed in the Crow and Cheyenne Indian languages and subtitled in English throughout. A beautifully photographed, intelligent independent project. **108m/C VHS, Beta.** Trevor Howard, James Remar, Dusty Iron Wing McCrea; ***D:*** Keith Merrill. *FOX*

Windy City **1984 (R)** A group of seven childhood friends must come to terms with the harsh realities of their failed ambitions when they meet for a weekend in Chicago. Told from the point of view of one of the group, recounting the sorts of memories we all prefer to forget. Typical and overwrought '80s yuppie reunion/regret drama. Aren't these people too young to be unhappy? **103m/C VHS, Beta, LV.** John Shea, Kate Capshaw, Josh Mostel, Jeffrey DeMunn, Lewis J. Stadlen, James Sutorius; ***D:*** Armyan Bernstein; ***W:*** Armyan Bernstein; ***M:*** Jack Nitzsche. *FOX*

A Wing and a Prayer **1944** Better-than-average WWII Air Force action flick. Battles rage throughout the Pacific theater and the men aboard the aircraft carrier struggle to do their part to save the world for freedom. Fine cast receives Hathaway's excellent unsentimental direction. **97m/B VHS.** Don Ameche, Dana Andrews, William Eythe, Charles Bickford, Cedric Hardwicke, Kevin O'Shea, Richard Jaeckel, Harry (Henry) Morgan; ***D:*** Henry Hathaway. Nominations: Academy Awards '44: Best Original Screenplay. *FXV*

Wing Chun **1994** Wing Chun (Yeoh) battles horse stealing bandits and the male chauvinists around her that don't think a woman can be strong and independent (as well as a fighting expert). Chinese with subtitles or dubbed. **93m/C VHS, LV.** *HK* Michelle Yeoh, Donnie Yan, Waise Lee; ***D:*** Yuen Woo Ping. *TAI*

Wings ½ **1927** The silent classic about friends, Rogers and Arlen, their adventures in the Air Corps during WWI, and their rivalry for the hand of a woman. Contains actual footage of combat flying from the Great War. Won the very first Best Picture Oscar. Too-thin plot hangs on (barely) to the stirring, intrepid dogfight scenes. **139m/B VHS, Beta, LV.** Clara Bow, Charles "Buddy" Rogers, Richard Arlen, Gary Cooper; ***D:*** William A. Wellman. Academy Awards '27: Best Picture. *BTV, PAR*

Wings of Danger *Dead on Course* **1952** A pilot tries to save his friend from blackmailing gold smugglers. **72m/B VHS, Beta, LV.** *GB* Zachary Scott, Kay Kendall, Robert Beatty, Naomi Chance; ***M:*** Malcolm Arnold. *MLB, RXM*

Wings of Desire ½ *Der Himmel Uber Berlin* **1988 (PG-13)** An ethereal, haunting modern fable about one of many angels observing human life in and above the broken existence of Berlin, and how he begins to long to experience life as humans do. A moving, unequivocable masterpiece, with as many beautiful things to say about spiritual need as about the schizophrenic emptiness of contemporary Germany; Wenders' magnum opus. In German with English subtitles, and with black-and-white sequences. Magnificent cinematography by Henri Alekan. **130m/C VHS, Beta, LV.** *GE* Bruno Ganz, Peter Falk, Solveig Dommartin, Otto Sander, Curt Bois; ***D:*** Wim Wenders; ***W:*** Wim Wenders, Peter Handke. Independent Spirit Awards '89: Best Foreign Film; Los Angeles Film Critics Association Awards '88: Best Cinematography, Best Foreign Film; New York Film Critics Awards '88: Best Cinematography; National Society of Film Critics Awards '88: Best Cinematography. *ORI, GLV, INJ*

Wings of Eagles ½ **1957** Hollywood biography of Frank 'Spig' Wead, a famous WWI aviation pioneer turned screenwriter. Veers wildly from comedy to stolid drama, though Bond's lampoon of Ford as "John Dodge" is justly famous. **110m/C VHS, Beta.** John Wayne, Ward Bond, Maureen O'Hara, Dan Dailey, Edmund Lowe, Ken Curtis, Kenneth Tobey, Sig Rumann, Veda Ann Borg; ***D:*** John Ford; ***C:*** Paul Vogel. *MGM*

Wings of Fame ½ **1993 (R)** Comic afterlife fantasy skewering celebrity status. Recently departed celebs check into a posh hotel, but as their fame on earth declines so do their afterlife accomodations, until they reach the state of oblivion. The latest hotel arrivals are a renowned, arrogant actor (O'Toole) and the frustrated writer (Firth) whose claim to fame has come from murdering him. **109m/C VHS, Beta.** Peter O'Toole, Colin Firth; ***D:*** Otakar Votocek; ***W:*** Herman Koch, Otakar Votocek. *PAR*

Wings Over the Pacific ½ **1943** Love and his daughter Cooper are living quietly on a Pacific island when a pair of pilots, American Norris and the Nazi Guttman, crash-land after a dogfight. The island is strategic because of its oil supply but Norris manages to prevent the Nazis from taking control and wins Cooper's love in the process. Veteran actor Love died shortly before the film's release. **60m/B VHS.** Montagu Love, Inez Cooper, Edward Norris, Henry Guttman, Robert Armstrong, Ernie Adams; ***D:*** Phil Rosen; ***W:*** George Wallace Sayre. *GPV*

A Winner Never Quits ½ **1986 (PG)** A true story based on the life of 1940s baseball player Pete Gray. As a boy Gray lost his right arm above the elbow in an accident. He's determined to prove himself as a baseball player and during WWII is given a tryout, although his teammates consider him a sideshow freak. A Memphis sportswriter takes an interest in Pete's career and Gray's success on the field leads to a career with the St. Louis Browns. Along the way he becomes the inspiration to a young fan, who's also lost an arm. Made for television. **96m/C VHS.** Keith Carradine, Mare Winningham, Huckleberry Fox, Dennis Weaver, Dana Delany, G.W. Bailey, Charles Hallahan, Fionnula Flanagan, Jack Kehoe; ***D:*** Mel Damski; ***W:*** Burt Prelutsky. *COL*

Winner Takes All **1986 (R)** A young college student during the Vietnam War comes to grips with maturity and growing pains. **94m/C VHS, Beta.** *GB* Jason Connery, Diane Cilento. *ACA*

Winners of the West **1940** A landowner schemes to prevent a railroad from running through his property. The railroad's chief engineer leads the good guys in an attempt to prevent sabotage. A fun serial in thirteen chapters, full of shooting, blown-up bridges, locomotives afire, etc.; and of course, the requisite damsel in distress. **250m/B VHS.** Anne Nagel, Dick Foran, James Craig, Harry Woods; ***D:*** Ray Taylor, Ford Beebe. *GPV, VCN, NOS*

Winners Take All **1987 (PG-13)** A handful of friends compete in Supercross races. Spirited but thoroughly cliche sports flick. **103m/C VHS, Beta, LV.** Don Michael Paul, Kathleen York, Robert Krantz; ***D:*** Fritz Kiersch. *SUE, NLC*

Winning **1969 (PG)** A race car driver (Newman) will let nothing, including his new wife (Woodward), keep him from winning the Indianapolis 500. Newman does his own driving. Thomas' film debut. **123m/C VHS, Beta, LV.** Paul Newman, Joanne Woodward, Robert Wagner, Richard Thomas, Clu Gulager; ***D:*** James Goldstone; ***M:*** Dave Grusin. *MCA*

Winning of the West **1953** Yodelin' ranger Autry vows to protect a crusading publisher from unscrupulous crooks, including his own doggone brothers. The brothers see the light, and the two corral the varmints. Autry tunes include "Cowboy Blues," "Cowpoke Poking Along," and "Find Me My 45." **57m/B VHS, Beta.** Gene Autry, Smiley Burnette, Gail Davis, Richard Crane; ***D:*** George Archainbaud. *CCB*

The Winning Team ½ **1952** Reagan stars in this biography of baseball legend Grover Cleveland Alexander and Day plays his dedicated wife. Some controversial issues were glossed over in the film, such as Alexander's real-life drinking problem and the fact that he had epilepsy. Although this was one of Reagan's favorite roles, he was upset by the studio's avoidance of all-too-human problems. Nonetheless, it's an entertaining enough movie about a very talented ballplayer. **98m/B VHS, LV.** Doris Day, Ronald Reagan, Frank Lovejoy, Eve Miller, James Millican, Russ Tamblyn; ***D:*** Lewis Seiler. *WAR*

The Winslow Boy ½ **1948** A cadet at the Royal Naval College is wrongly accused of theft and expelled. Donat as the boy's lawyer leads a splendid cast. Despite consequences for his family, the boy's father (Hardwicke) sues the government and fights his son's battle, as the case makes the papers and he approaches bankruptcy. Plot would seem far-fetched if it weren't based on fact. Absorbing. Based on a play by Rattigan, who co-wrote the script. **112m/B VHS, Beta.** *GB* Robert Donat, Cedric Hardwicke, Margaret Leighton, Frank Lawton, Kathleen Harrison, Basil Radford; ***D:*** Anthony Asquith; ***W:*** Terence Rattigan; ***C:*** Frederick A. (Freddie) Young. *HEG*

Winter Flight **1984** A small, gentle British drama about an RAF recruit and a barmaid who quickly become lovers, and then are confronted with her pregnancy. **105m/C VHS, Beta.** *GB* Reece Dinsdale, Nicola Cowper, Gary Olsen; ***D:*** Roy Battersby. *MGM*

Winter Kills **1979 (R)** Distinctive political black comedy suffers a hilariously paranoid version of American public life. Bridges, the younger brother of a U.S. president assassinated 15 years earlier, uncovers the plot. Huston is delightful as Bridges' horny old father. Uneven, but well worth seeing; flopped at the box office, but was re-released in 1983. Taylor was not billed. **97m/C VHS, Beta, LV.** Jeff Bridges, John Huston, Anthony Perkins, Richard Boone, Sterling Hayden, Eli Wallach, Ralph Meeker, Belinda Bauer, Dorothy Malone, Toshiro Mifune, Elizabeth Taylor, Donald Moffat, Tisa Farrow, Brad Dexter, Joe Spinell; ***D:*** William Richert; ***M:*** Maurice Jarre. *COL, SUE*

The Winter Light ½ *Nattvardsgaesterna* **1962** The second film in Bergman's famous trilogy on the silence of God, preceded by "Through a Glass Darkly" and followed by "The Silence." Bleak and disturbing view of a tortured priest who searches for the faith and guidance he is unable to give his congregation. Hard to swallow for neophyte Bergmanites, but challenging, deeply serious and rewarding for those accustomed to the Swede's angst. Polished and personal. In Swedish with English subtitles. **80m/B VHS, Beta, LV.** *SW* Gunnar Bjornstrand, Ingrid Thulin, Max von Sydow; ***D:*** Ingmar Bergman; ***W:*** Ingmar Bergman; ***C:*** Sven Nykvist. National Board of Review Awards '63: 5 Best Foreign Films of the Year. *SUE, INJ, NLC*

Winter Meeting **1948** Overwrought drama with Bette Davis starring as a spinster poetess who falls in love with a war hero who wants to be a priest. Very talky script, of interest only as the sole romantic lead for James Davis, whose claim to fame was westerns and the TV series "Dallas." **104m/B VHS.** Bette Davis, Janis Paige, James Davis, John Hoyt, Florence Bates, Walter Baldwin, Ransom Sherman; ***D:*** Bretaigne Windust; ***M:*** Max Steiner. *MGM*

The Winter of Our Dreams ½ **1982** Down Under slice of seamy life as a heroin-addicted prostitute becomes involved with an unhappy bookshop owner. Davis shines in otherwise slow and confusing drama. **89m/C VHS, Beta.** *AU* Judy Davis, Bryan Brown, Cathy Downes, Baz Luhrmann, Peter Mochrie, Mervyn Drak, Margie McCrae, Marcie Deane-Johns; ***D:*** John Duigan. Australian Film Institute '81: Best Actress (Davis). *LIV*

Winter People ½ **1989 (PG-13)** A clock-making widower and a woman living alone with her illegitimate son experience tough times together with feuding families in a Depression-era Appalachian community. Silly, rehashed premise doesn't deter McGillis, who gamely gives a fine performance. Based on the novel by John Ehle. **109m/C VHS, Beta, LV, 8mm.** Kurt Russell, Kelly McGillis, Lloyd Bridges, Mitchell Ryan, Jeffrey Meek, Eileen Ryan, Amelia Burnette; ***D:*** Ted Kotcheff; ***W:*** Carol Sobieski; ***M:*** John Scott. *SUE, NLC*

Winterbeast **1992** Winter resort community dwellers begin mysteriously disappearing until somebody remembers that the resort was built over a sacred Indian burial ground. Sgt. Bill Whitman, the valiant park ranger and his Barney Fife-like assistant Stillman, question the town's wise old sage, Sheldon, who's sitting on a secret that could threaten the entire community. **77m/C VHS.** Tim R. Morgan, Mike Magri. *TEM, MOV*

Winterset ½ **1936** A son seeks to clear his father's name of a falsely accused crime 15 years after his electrocution. Powerful at the time, though time has lessened its impact. Loosely based on the trial of Sacco and Vanzetti and adapted from Maxwell Anderson's Broadway play, with stars in the same roles. Meredith's film debut. **85m/B VHS, Beta.** Burgess Meredith, Margo, John Carradine; ***D:*** Alfred Santell. Nominations: Academy Awards '36: Best Interior Decoration, Best Original Score. *NOS, HHT, CAB*

Wintertime ♪½ **1943** Forgettable and mindless Henie musical. Plot revolves around Henie travelling in Canada with her wealthy uncle, and saving an old, run-down hotel. An appearance by Woody Herman and his Orchestra give the film a much-needed boost. Based on a story by Arthur Kober. **82m/B VHS.** Sonja Henie, Jack Oakie, Cesar Romero, Carole Landis, S.Z. Sakall, Cornel Wilde, Woody Herman; ***D:*** John Brahm; ***W:*** E. Edwin Moran, Jack Jevne, Lynn Starling. *FXV*

Wired ♪ **1989 (R)** A justly lambasted, unintentionally hilarious biography of comic genius and overdose victim John Belushi, very loosely based on Bob Woodward's bestselling muckraking book. The chronicle of addiction and tragedy is tried here as a weird sort of comedy; was it meant as a tribute to its offkilter subject? If so, it misses by a mile. And, we're sorry, but Chiklis doesn't cut it as Belushi—who would?! **112m/C VHS, Beta, LV.** Michael Chiklis, Ray Sharkey, Patti D'Arbanville, J.T. Walsh, Gary Groomes, Lucinda Jenney, Alex Rocco, Jere Burns, Billy Preston; ***D:*** Larry Peerce; ***M:*** Basil Poledouris. *LIV*

Wired to Kill *Woof!* **1986 (R)** In a futuristic world, two teenagers seek justice for their parents' murder by building a remote-controlled erector set programmed for revenge. Laughably porous plot drops any pretence of credibility. Dizzyingly bad. **96m/C VHS, Beta.** Merritt Butrick, Emily Longstreth, Devin Hoelscher, Frank Collison; ***D:*** Francis Schaeffer. *LIV*

Wisdom ♪½ **1987 (R)** Unemployed young guy (Estevez) becomes a bank robber with Robin Hood aspirations, coming to the aid of American farmers by destroying mortgage records. Estevez became the youngest person to star in, write, and direct a major motion picture. And, my goodness, it shows. **109m/C VHS, Beta, LV.** Emilio Estevez, Demi Moore, Tom Skerritt, Veronica Cartwright; ***D:*** Emilio Estevez; ***M:*** Danny Elfman. *WAR*

Wise Blood ♪♪♪½ **1979 (PG)** Gothic drama about a drifter who searches for sin and becomes a preacher for a new religion, The Church Without Christ. Excellent cast in achingly realistic portrayal of ersatz religion, southern style. Many laughs are more painful than funny. Superb, very dark comedy from Huston. Adapted from the Flannery O'Connor novel. **106m/C VHS, Beta.** Brad Dourif, John Huston, Ned Beatty, Amy Wright, Harry Dean Stanton; ***D:*** John Huston; ***M:*** Alex North. *MCA*

Wise Guys ♪½ **1986 (R)** Two small-time hoods decide to rip off the mob. When their boss figures out their plan he decides to set them up instead. Lame black comedy that has too few moments. **100m/C VHS, Beta.** Joe Piscopo, Danny DeVito, Ray Sharkey, Captain Lou Albano, Dan Hedaya, Julie Bovasso, Patti LuPone; ***D:*** Brian DePalma; ***M:*** Ira Newborn. *FOX, FCT*

Wisecracks ♪♪♪ **1993** Women comics perform and talk about their work in this documentary directed by Gail Singer. The comics featured have, in some cases, little more in common than their work, but all share interesting perspectives on what they do. Interesting mix of performance clips and interviews sometimes includes banal comments about the nature of comedy, but is more often insightful, especially remarks by seasoned vet Phyllis Diller. Although there exists here the potential for an angry feminist diatribe on gender-based humor, the focus is more towards talented women who are just plain funny. **93m/C VHS.** ***D:*** Gail Singer; ***Performed by:*** Whoopi Goldberg, Paula Poundstone, Ellen DeGeneres, Kim Wayans, Pam Stone, Joy Behar, Maxine Lapidus, Phyllis Diller, Jenny Jones. *MNC*

Wish Me Luck ♪½ **1995** A babe genie (Avalon) has a dilemma—unless she can make a man of a geek college student (Gesner) in 48 hours, she'll become the property of an evil sorcerer for a thousand years. She gets three equally bodacious college cheerleaders to help her out. Also available in an edited version that cuts six minutes worth of fleshy fantasies. **91m/C VHS.** Avalon Anders, Zen Gesner; ***D:*** Philip Jones. *SDE*

Wish You Were Here ♪♪♪ **1987** Poignant yet funny slice of British postwar life roughly based on the childhood memoirs of famous madame, Cynthia Payne. A troubled and freedom-loving teenager expresses her rebellion in sexual experimentation. Mum is dead and Dad just doesn't understand, so what's a girl to do, but get the boys excited? Lloyd, in her first film, plays the main character with exceptional strength and feistiness. Payne's later life was dramatized in the Leland-scripted "Personal Services." **92m/C VHS, Beta, LV.** *GB* Emily Lloyd, Tom Bell, Clare Clifford, Barbara Durkin, Geoffrey Hutchings, Charlotte Barker, Chloe Leland, Trudy Cavanagh, Jesse Birdsall, Geoffrey Durham, Pat Heywood; ***D:*** David Leland; ***W:*** David Leland; ***M:*** Stanley Myers. British Academy Awards '87: Best Original Screenplay; National Society of Film Critics Awards '87: Best Actress (Lloyd). *FRH, TVC*

Wishful Thinking ♪♪ **1992** A lovelorn screenwriter rescues a peculiar man from mysterious assassins and receives a magical writing pad for his efforts. It seems that whatever Michael writes on the paper will come true, so he decides to write himself into the life of the luscious Diane. **94m/C VHS.** Murray Langston, Michelle Johnson, Ruth Buzzi, Billy Barty, Johnny Dark, Ray "Boom Boom" Mancini, Vic Dunlop, Kip Addotta; ***D:*** Murray Langston. *HMD*

The Wishing Ring ♪♪♪ **1914** Light and charming romance, beautifully filmed by Tourneur, based on Owen Davis' play. The son of an earl in Old England is expelled from college and told by his father he must earn half a crown on his own before the family will take him back. With the help of a minister's daughter, he sets things right. **50m/B VHS, Beta.** Vivian Martin, Alec B. Francis, Chester Barnett, Simeon Wiltsie, Walter Morton; ***D:*** Maurice Tourneur; ***W:*** Maurice Tourneur. *GPV*

The Wishmaker **1985** A young man squanders the three wishes granted to him for helping a strange old woman and her timid daughter. **54m/C VHS, Beta.** *GEM*

Wishman ♪♪½ **1993** Hollywood hustler Basie Banks (Le Mat) meets Hitch (Lewis), a two million year old genie whose magic bottle has been stolen. In exchange for Banks' help in recovering his home, Hitch agrees to help Banks get the girl of his dreams. **89m/C VHS.** Paul LeMat, Geoffrey Lewis, Paul Gleason, Quin Kessler, Nancy Parsons, Gailard Sartain, Brion James; ***D:*** Mike Marvin; ***W:*** Mike Marvin. *MNC*

The Wistful Widow of Wagon Gap ♪♪ *The Wistful Widow* **1947** Lou, a traveling salesman, accidentally kills a man, and according to the law of the west he has to take care of the dead man's widow and children—all seven of them. Because the family is so unsavory, Lou knows that no other man will kill him, so he allows himself to be appointed sheriff and clears the town of lowlifes. Usual Abbott & Costello fare is highlighted with their zany antics. **78m/B VHS.** Bud Abbott, Lou Costello, Marjorie Main, George Cleveland, Gordon Jones, William Ching, Peter Thompson, Glenn Strange, Olin Howlin; ***D:*** Charles T. Barton. *MCA*

The Witch ♪½ *La Strega in Amore; Aura* **1966** Historian hired by family to assemble the late father's works falls in love with beautiful daughter. Seems she's no angel. **103m/B VHS.** *IT* Rosanna Schiaffino, Richard Johnson, Sarah Ferrati, Gian Marie Volonte, Margherita Guzzinati; ***D:*** Damiano Damiani. *SNC*

Witch Hunt ♪♪½ **1994 (R)** Mock fantasy/mystery set in 1953 Hollywood. Private eye H. Phillip Lovecraft (Hopper) is hired by actress Kim Hudson (Miller) to shadow her philandering studio hubby Gottlieb (Rosenberg), who dies in an untimely fashion. The kicker is that witchcraft is commonplace, with the studio hiring witches and warlocks to cast spells. Also, a blowhard senator (Bogosian) is heading a McCarthy-like campaign to ban magic and Lovecraft fears his sorceress friend (Ralph) is going to be the scapegoat for Gottlieb's murder. Great special effects; fuzzy plot. **101m/C VHS.** Dennis Hopper, Penelope Ann Miller, Eric Bogosian, Sheryl Lee Ralph, Julian Sands, Alan Rosenberg, Valerie Mahaffey, Debi Mazar; ***D:*** Paul Schrader; ***W:*** Joseph Dougherty; ***M:*** Angelo Badalamenti. *HBO*

Witch Who Came from the Sea ♪½ **1976 (R)** Witch terrorizes all the ships at sea, but doesn't exactly haunt the viewer. **98m/C VHS, Beta.** Millie Perkins, Lonny Chapman, Vanessa Brown, Peggy Feury, Rick Jason; ***D:*** Matt Cimber. *UNI*

A Witch Without a Broom ♪½ *Una Bruja Sin Escoba* **1968** Shoestring time travel fantasy. When an American professor catches the eye of a 15th century apprentice witch, the trip begins. Since the witch is only learning the ropes, they end up visiting a number of periods other than their own before the professor gets home. **78m/C VHS.** *SP* Jeffrey Hunter, Maria Perschy, Perla Cristal, Gustavo Rojo; ***D:*** Joe Lacy. *NO*

Witchboard ♪♪½ **1987 (R)** During a college party, a group of friends bring out the Ouija board and play with it for laughs. One of the girls discovers she can use the board to communicate with a small boy who died years before. In her effort to talk with him she unwittingly releases the evil spirit of an ax murderer who haunts and murders members of the group. An entertaining, relatively inoffensive member of its genre that displays some attention to characterization and plot. **98m/C VHS, Beta, LV.** Todd Allen, Tawny Kitaen, Stephen Nichols, Kathleen Wilhoite, Burke Byrnes, Rose Marie, James W. Quinn, Judy Tatum, Gloria Hayes, J.P. Luebsen, Susan Nickerson; ***D:*** Kevin S. Tenney; ***W:*** Kevin S. Tenney; ***C:*** Roy Wagner; ***M:*** Dennis Michael Tenney. *HHE*

Witchboard 2: The Devil's Doorway ♪♪½ **1993 (R)** There seem to be a lot of doorways to hell because someone is always finding a new one (and making a movie about it). This time it's the innocent Paige Benedict (Dolenz), who moves into an artist's loft and finds an old Ouija board in a closet. Through the board, Paige is contacted by a former tenant who claims to be a murder victim. Soon her fellow tenants are dying in violent and mysterious ways and Paige's dreams are haunted by evil. What hath she wrought—and can she get it back in the closet where it belongs. **98m/C VHS, LV.** Ami Dolenz, Laraine Newman, Timothy Gibbs, John Gatins; ***D:*** Kevin S. Tenney; ***W:*** Kevin S. Tenney; ***M:*** Dennis Michael Tenney. *REP*

Witchboard 3: The Possession ♪♪½ **1995 (R)** A Ouija board opens the gates to hell (yet again or we wouldn't have a movie) and the board's spirit steals Brian's soul and takes control of his body—much to the bewilderment of his girlfriend Julie. **93m/C VHS.** David Nerman, Locky Lambert, Cedric Smith, Donna Sarrasin; ***D:*** Peter Svatek; ***W:*** Kevin S. Tenney, Jon Ezrine; ***C:*** Barry Gravelle. *REP*

Witchcraft *Woof!* **1988 (R)** A young mother meets a couple killed three centuries ago for performing witchcraft. They want her baby, of course, to be the son of the devil. "Rosemary's Baby" rip-off, that is thoroughly predictable. **90m/C VHS, Beta, LV.** Anat "Topol" Barzilai, Gary Sloan, Lee Kisman, Deborah Scott; ***D:*** Robert Spera. *ACA*

Witchcraft 2: The Temptress ♪ **1990 (R)** A sensuous woman seduces an innocent young man into the rituals of witchcraft and the occult. Sequel to "Witchcraft" does not succeed where original failed, but does have a fair share of sex and violence. **88m/C VHS, Beta, LV.** Charles Solomon, Mia Ruiz, Delia Sheppard; ***D:*** Mark Woods. *ACA*

Witchcraft 3: The Kiss of Death ♪♪ **1990 (R)** Once a master of the occult, William Spanner now seeks only to live a normal life. His plans are changed, however, when a sensual creature from Hell is sent to seduce him. More sex and violence, with an emphasis on sex. The best of the "Witchcraft" trio, for those trying to plan a festive evening. **85m/C VHS.** Charles Solomon, Lisa Toothman, William L. Baker, Lena Hall; ***D:*** R.L. Tillmanns. *ACA*

Witchcraft 4: Virgin Heart ☠ **1992 (R)** Supernatural horror continues as attorney Will Spanner sinks even deeper into his enemy's satanic trap in this shocking sequel to the popular series. His only hope is to use his own black magic powers and to enlist the help of a seductive stripper (Penthouse Pet Strain). **92m/C VHS, LV.** Charles Solomon, Julie Strain, Clive Pearson, Jason O'Gulihar, Lisa Jay Harrington, Barbara Dow; ***D:*** James Merendino. *ACA*

Witchcraft 5: Dance with the Devil ☠ **1992 (R)** This undistinguished horror series continues with several successful people finding the unpleasant loopholes in their satanic contracts. A demon named Cain is behind all the trouble. The horror special effects are cheap but there are several soft-core sex scenes (pointless to the plot) which provide a minimal interest. An unrated version is also available. **94m/C VHS.** Marklen Kennedy, Carolyn Taye-Loren, Nicole Sassaman, Aysha Hauer; ***D:*** Talun Hsu. *ACA*

Witchcraft 6: The Devil's Mistress ☠ **1994 (R)** Police detectives Lutz and Garner's new case involves young women turning up naked and dead. Turns out satanic disciple Savanti is expected to impress the boss with a virgin sacrifice before an impending eclipse. But since virgins are scarce, he's having a real tough time. Practically no gore but lots of skin, along with hit-or-miss humor. **86m/C VHS.** Kurt Alan, John E. Holiday, Bryan Nutter, Jerry Spicer, Shannon Lead; ***D:*** Julie Davis; ***W:*** Julie Davis. *NO*

Witchcraft 7: Judgement Hour ☠ **1995 (R)** Modern-day warlock must sacrifice his earthly existence to kill an evil vampire. **91m/C VHS.** David Byrnes, April Breneman, Alisa Christensen, John Cragen, Loren Schmalle; ***D:*** Michael Paul Girard; ***W:*** Peter Fleming; ***C:*** Denis Maloney; ***M:*** Miriam Cutler. *APX*

Witchcraft Through the Ages ☠☠☠ *Haxan* **1922** The demonic Swedish masterpiece in which witches and victims suffer against various historical backgrounds. Nightmarish and profane, especially the appearance of the Devil as played under much make-up by Christiansen himself. Silent. **74m/B VHS, Beta.** *SW* Maren Pedersen, Clara Pontoppidan; ***D:*** Benjamin Christiansen. *GPV, MPI, WFV*

Witchery ☠ **1988** A photographer and his girlfriend vacation at a New England hotel where they discover a horrifying, satanic secret. One by one (as always, in this kind of bad flick, in the interest of "suspense"), people are killed off. Seems it's a witch, bent on revenge. Forget room service and bar the door. **96m/C VHS, Beta.** David Hasselhoff, Linda Blair, Catherine Hickland, Hildegarde Knef, Leslie Cumming, Bob Champagne, Richard Farnsworth, Michael Manches; ***D:*** Fabrizio Laurenti. *VMK*

The Witches ☠☠☠½ **1990 (PG)** Nine-year-old boy on vacation finds himself in the midst of a witch convention, and grand high witch Huston plans to turn all children into furry little creatures. The boy, with the help of his good witch grandmother, attempts to prevent the mass transmutation of children into mice. Top-notch fantasy probably too spooky for the training wheel set. Wonderful special effects; the final project of executive producer Jim Henson. Based on Roald Dahl's story. **92m/C VHS, Beta, LV, 8mm.** Anjelica Huston, Mai Zetterling, Jasen Fisher, Rowan Atkinson, Charlie Potter, Bill Paterson, Brenda Blethyn, Jane Horrocks; ***D:*** Nicolas Roeg; ***W:*** Allan Scott; ***M:*** Stanley Myers. Los Angeles Film Critics Association Awards '90: Best Actress (Huston); National Society of Film Critics Awards '90: Best Actress (Huston). *WAR, FCT, ORI*

Witches' Brew ☠☠ **1979 (PG)** Three young women try to use their undeveloped skills in witchcraft and black magic to help Garr's husband get a prestigious position at a university, with calamitous results. Oft-funny spoof is silly and oft-predictable. Turner's role is small as an older, experienced witch. **98m/C VHS, Beta.** Teri Garr, Richard Benjamin, Lana Turner, Kathryn Leigh Scott; ***D:*** Richard Shorr, Herbert L. Strock. *SUE*

Witches' Mountain ☠ **1971** A troubled couple is captured by a coven of witches in the Pyrenees. Dull and pointless. **98m/C VHS, Beta.** *MX* Patty Shepard, John Caffari, Monica Randall; ***D:*** Raul Artigot. *UNI, HEG*

The Witches of Eastwick ☠☠½ **1987 (R)** "Mad Max" director Miller meets Hollywood in this unrestrained, vomit-filled treatment of John Updike's novel about three lonely small-town New England women and their sexual liberation. A strange, rich, overweight and balding, but nonetheless charming man knows their deepest desires and makes them come true with decadent excess. Raunchy fun, with Nicholson over-acting wildly as the Mephisto. Miller lends a bombastic violent edge to the effort, sometimes at the expense of the story. Filmed on location in Cohasset, Massachusetts. **118m/C VHS, Beta, LV, 8mm.** Jack Nicholson, Cher, Susan Sarandon, Michelle Pfeiffer, Veronica Cartwright, Richard Jenkins, Keith Joakum, Carel Struycken; ***D:*** George Miller; ***W:*** Michael Cristofer; ***C:*** Vilmos Zsigmond; ***M:*** John Williams. Los Angeles Film Critics Association Awards '87: Best Actor (Nicholson); New York Film Critics Awards '87: Best Actor (Nicholson); Nominations: Academy Awards '87: Best Sound, Best Original Score. *WAR*

Witchfire ☠ **1986 (R)** After their pyschiatrist dies in an automobile accident, three maniacal women escape from an asylum and hide out in the woods. Winters then holds seances to contact the dead doctor, but instead captures a young, very much alive hunter. For dedicated fans of Winters. **92m/C VHS, Beta.** Shelley Winters, Gary Swanson, David Mendenhall, Corinne Chateau; ***D:*** Vincent J. Privitera; ***W:*** Vincent J. Privitera. *LIV*

The Witching *Woof! Necromancy* **1972** Poorly made story of man's continuing quest for supernatural power. Welles slums as the high priest out to get victim Franklin. **90m/C VHS, Beta.** Orson Welles, Pamela Franklin, Michael Ontkean, Lee Purcell; ***D:*** Bert I. Gordon; ***C:*** Winton C. Hoch. *NO*

The Witching of Ben Wagner ☠☠½ **1995 (G)** Strange occurrences have Ben believing his friend Regina and her grandmother may be witches. But, if so, they're friendly ones as they help Ben adjust to a new home and neighborhood. **96m/C VHS.** Justin Gocke, Harriet Hall, Sam Bottoms; ***D:*** Paul Annett. *AVE*

Witching Time ☠½ **1984** Elvira presents this film, in which a young composer is visited by a horny 17th-century witch while his wife is away from home. When the wife returns, both women fight to possess him. **60m/C VHS, Beta.** Jon Finch, Prunella Gee, Patricia Quinn, Ian McCulloch; ***D:*** Don Leaver. *LIV*

The Witchmaker ☠ *Legend of Witch Hollow; Witchkill* **1969** Remote, crocodile-infested bayou in Louisiana is the scene of witchcraft and the occult as young girls are murdered in order for a group of witches to become youthful again. **101m/C VHS, Beta.** John Lodge, Alvy Moore, Thordis Brandt, Anthony Eisley, Shelby Grant, Robyn Millan; ***D:*** William O. Brown; ***W:*** William O. Brown. *NO*

The Witch's Mirror ☠☠ **1960** A sorceress plots to destroy the murderer of her god- daughter. The murderer, a surgeon, begins a project to restore the disfigured face and hands of his burned second wife, and he doesn't care how he gets the materials. For true fans of good bad horror flicks. Badly dubbed (which adds to the charm); dark (of course); and offbeat (naturally). **75m/B VHS, Beta.** *MX* Rosita Arenas, Armando Calvo, Isabela Corona, Dina De Marco; ***D:*** Chano Urueto. *SNC, HHT*

WitchTrap ☠ **1989 (R)** Lame sequel to "Witchboard." A mansion's new owner hires psychics to exorcise the disturbed ghost of his predecessor. **87m/C VHS, Beta, LV.** James W. Quinn, Kathleen Bailey, Linnea Quigley; ***D:*** Kevin S. Tenney. *IME*

With Honors ☠☠½ **1994 (PG-13)** Pesci is a bum who finds desperate Harvard student Fraser's Honors thesis, and, like any quick-witted bum with a yen for literature, holds it for ransom. Desperate to salvage his future gold card, Fraser and his roommates agree to fix Joe's homeless state. Self-involved students learn something about love and life while Madonna drones in the background. Fraser is believable as the ambitious student about to endure Pesci's enlightenment. Pesci is Pesci, doing his best to overcome numerous script difficulties. **100m/C VHS, LV.** Joe Pesci, Brendan Fraser, Moira Kelly, Patrick Dempsey, Josh Hamilton, Gore Vidal; ***D:*** Alek Keshishian; ***W:*** William Mastrosimone; ***M:*** Patrick Leonard. Nominations: Golden Globe Awards '95: Best Song ("I'll Remember"); MTV Movie Awards '95: Best Song ("I'll Remember"). *WAR*

With Kit Carson Over the Great Divide ☠☠½ **1925** A large-scale silent western about a doctor's family gone asunder and then reunited during the Fremont expeditions out of St. Louis in the 1840s. Snow's final screen appearance. Recently refound. Fun cinematic history (in two senses of the phrase). Beautiful landscape. **72m/B VHS, Beta, 8mm.** Roy Stewart, Henry B. Walthall, Marguerite Snow, Sheldon Lewis, Earl Metcalfe; ***D:*** Frank S. Mattison. *VYY*

With Six You Get Eggroll ☠☠ *A Man in Mommy's Bed* **1968 (G)** A widow with three sons and a widower with a daughter elope and then must deal with the antagonism of their children and even their dogs. Brady Bunch-esque family comedy means well, but doesn't cut it. Hershey's debut. Jamie Farr, William Christopher, and Vic Tayback have small parts. To date, Day's last big-screen appearance. **95m/C VHS, Beta.** Doris Day, Brian Keith, Pat Carroll, Alice Ghostley, Vic Tayback, Jamie Farr, William Christopher, Barbara Hershey; ***D:*** Howard Morris; ***C:*** Harry Stradling Jr. *FOX*

Withnail and I ☠☠☠½ **1987 (R)** A biting and original black comedy about a pair of unemployed, nearly starving English actors during the late 1960s. They decide to retreat to a country house owned by Withnail's uncle, for a vacation and are beset by comic misadventures, particularly when the uncle, who is gay, starts to hit on his nephew's friend. Robinson, who scripted "The Killing Fields," makes his successful directorial debut, in addition to drafting the screenplay from his own novel. Co-produced by George Harrison and Richard Starkey (Ringo Starr). **108m/C VHS, Beta, LV.** *GB* Richard E. Grant, Paul McGann, Richard Griffiths; ***D:*** Bruce Robinson; ***W:*** Bruce Robinson; ***M:*** David Dundas. *MED*

Without a Clue ☠☠½ **1988 (PG)** Spoof of the Sherlock Holmes legend, in which Holmes is actually portrayed by a bumbling, skirt-chasing actor, and Watson is the sole crime-solving mastermind, hiring the actor to impersonate the character made famous by the doctor's published exploits. The leads have some fun and so do we; but laughs are widely spaced. **107m/C VHS, Beta, LV.** *GB* Michael Caine, Ben Kingsley, Jeffrey Jones, Lysette Anthony, Paul Freeman, Nigel Davenport, Peter Cook, Pat Keen; ***D:*** Thom Eberhardt; ***W:*** Gary Murphy, Larry Strawther; ***M:*** Henry Mancini. *ORI*

Without a Trace ☠☠ **1983 (PG)** One morning, a six-year-old boy is sent off to school by his loving mother, never to return. The story of the mother's relentless search for her son. Cardboard characters, wildly unrealistic ending that is different from the real-life incident on which it's based. Scripted by Gutcheon from her book "Still Missing." Jaffe's directorial debut. **119m/C VHS, Beta.** Kate Nelligan, Judd Hirsch, Stockard Channing, David Dukes; ***D:*** Stanley R. Jaffe; ***C:*** John Bailey; ***M:*** Jack Nitzsche. *FOX*

Without Anesthesia ☠☠ *Rough Treatment; Bez Znieczulenia* **1978** Journalist Jerzy returns from a trip abroad to discover his wife has left him for an obnoxious young writer. Against advice, Jerzy fights the divorce and searches for an explanation. Meanwhile, he has mysteriously fallen out of political favor and finds his career falling apart as well. Polish with English subtitles. **111m/C VHS.** *PL* Zbigniew Zapassiewicz, Ewa Dalkowska, Krystyna Janda, Andrzej Seweryn; ***D:*** Andrzej Wajda; ***W:*** Agnieszka Holland, Andrzej Wajda. *NYF*

Without Honors ☠☠ **1932** A man seeks to restore the reputation of his dead brother, accused of murder and theft. He joins the Texas Rangers and brings the real criminals to justice. Excellent location shooting lifts ordinary early western. **62m/B VHS, Beta,**

LV. Harry Carey Sr., Mae Busch, Gibson Gowland, George "Gabby" Hayes; ***D:*** William Nigh. *NO*

Without Love 🦴🦴½ **1945** Tracy is a scientist, Hepburn, a woman with an empty basement for his laboratory. Since the neighbors would be scandalized by the idea of unmarried people living together, however platonically, they decide to get married, although each has sworn off romance. Snappy dialogue, expertly rendered by the Tracy/Hepburn team. Terrific supporting cast keeps this minimally plotted outing afloat. Adapted from the play of the same name by Philip Barry. **113m/B VHS, Beta.** Spencer Tracy, Katharine Hepburn, Lucille Ball, Keenan Wynn, Carl Esmond, Patricia Morison, Felix Bressart; ***D:*** Harold Bucquet; ***W:*** Donald Ogden Stewart; ***C:*** Karl Freund. *MGM*

Without Love 🦴🦴 **1980** Ambitious young journalist experiences resentment from her peers because of her aggressive methods, and they decide to teach her a lesson by drawing her into a situation destined for disaster. In Polish with English subtitles. **104m/C VHS.** *PL* ***D:*** Barbara Sass. *FCT*

Without Mercy 🦴½ **1995 (R)** Marine platoon is shafted by the government when they're left to die while on a U.N. peacekeeping mission in Africa. Survivor Zagarino then winds up in a deadly martial arts contest, only to find himself set up by corrupt promoters. **88m/C VHS, LV.** Frank Zagarino, Martin Kove, Ayu Azhari, Frans Tumbuan; ***D:*** Robert Anthony; ***W:*** Robert Anthony; ***C:*** Gerry Lively. *LIV*

Without Reservations 🦴🦴½ **1946** Hollywood-bound novelist Colbert encounters Marine flyer Wayne and his pal (DeFore) aboard a train. She decides he would be perfect for her newest movie. They both dislike her famous book and don't realize they're traveling with the renowned author. Misadventures and misunderstandings abound as this trio make their way to Tinseltown. Of course, Colbert and Wayne fall in love. Box-office success with a tired script and too few real laughs. The Duke is interesting but miscast. Based on the novel "Thanks, God, I'll Take It From Here" by Jane Allen. **101m/B VHS, Beta, LV.** Claudette Colbert, John Wayne, Don DeFore, Phil Brown, Frank Puglia; ***Cameos:*** Louella Parsons, Cary Grant, Jack Benny; ***D:*** Mervyn LeRoy; ***C:*** Milton Krasner. *VCI, VCN, TTC*

Without Warning 🦴🦴½ *The Story Without A Name* **1952** Inexperienced director and actors pull out a minor success in this fairly ordinary murder mystery, about a serial killer of beautiful blondes. **75m/C VHS.** *FR* Maurice Ronet, Adam Williams, Gloria Franklin, Edward Binns; ***D:*** Arnold Laven. *NO*

Without Warning: The James Brady Story 🦴🦴🦴 **1991 (R)** White House Press Secretary Brady took a bullet in the brain during the 1981 shooting of President Reagan, and made a slow, grueling recovery. This fine made for cable TV film spares none of it, concentrating on the stricken man and his family, and opting out of disease-of-the-week cliches (though the pic's politics won't please the gun-adorers). Based on Mollie Dickinson's biography "Thumbs Up." **120m/C VHS.** Beau Bridges, Joan Allen, David Strathairn, Christopher Bell, Gary Grubbs, Bryan Clark, Steve Flynn, Christine Healy, Susan Brown; ***D:*** Michael Toshiyuki Uno; ***W:*** Robert Bolt. *HBO*

Witness 🦴🦴🦴½ **1985 (R)** A young Amish boy traveling from his father's funeral witnesses a murder in a Philadelphia bus station. The investigating detective (Ford, in one of his best roles) soon discovers the killing is part of a conspiracy involving corruption in his department. He follows the child and his young widowed mother to their home in the country. A thriller with a difference, about the encounter of alien worlds, with a poignant love story. McGillis, in her first major role, is luminous as the Amish mother, while Ford is believable as both a cop and a sensitive man. An artfully crafted drama, richly focusing on the often misunderstood Amish lifestyle. **112m/C VHS, Beta, LV, 8mm.** Harrison Ford, Kelly McGillis, Alexander Godunov, Lukas Haas, Josef Sommer, Danny Glover, Patti LuPone; ***D:*** Peter Weir; ***C:*** John Seale; ***M:*** Maurice Jarre. Academy Awards '85: Best Film Editing, Best Original Screenplay; Edgar Allan Poe Awards '85: Best Screenplay; Writers Guild of America '85: Best Original Screenplay; Nominations: Academy Awards '85: Best Actor (Ford), Best Art Direction/Set Decoration, Best Cinematography, Best Director (Weir), Best Picture, Best Original Score. *PAR, HMV*

Witness for the Prosecution 🦴🦴🦴½ **1957** An unemployed man is accused of murdering a wealthy widow whom he befriended. Ailing defense attorney Laughton can't resist taking an intriguing murder case, and a straitforward court case becomes increasingly complicated in this energetic adaptation of an Agatha Christie story and stage play. Outstanding performances by Laughton, with excellent support by real life wife, Lanchester, as his patient nurse. Power, as the alleged killer, and Dietrich as a tragic woman are top-notch (see if you can detect Dietrich in an unbilled second role). **116m/B VHS, Beta, LV.** Charles Laughton, Tyrone Power, Marlene Dietrich, Elsa Lanchester, John Williams, Henry Daniell, Una O'Connor; ***D:*** Billy Wilder; ***W:*** Harry Kurnitz, Billy Wilder. Golden Globe Awards '58: Best Supporting Actress (Lanchester); Nominations: Academy Awards '57: Best Actor (Laughton), Best Director (Wilder), Best Film Editing, Best Picture, Best Sound, Best Supporting Actress (Lanchester). *MGM, FOX, MLB*

Witness to the Execution 🦴🦴 **1994 (PG-13)** It's 1999 and Tycom Entertainment, a pay-per-view network, is looking for some hot entertainment. Top exec Jessica (Young) decides to televise the electric chair execution of convicted criminal Dennis Casterline (Daly). But Casterline claims to be innocent and as the execution date nears Jessica is unsettled by new evidence that may supports his claim. The cutthroat TV execs provide amusement but this TV movie fare quickly becomes muddled. **92m/C VHS.** Sean Young, Timothy Daly, Len Cariou, George Newbern; ***D:*** Tommy Lee Wallace; ***W:*** Thomas Baum. *VMK*

Wittgenstein 🦴🦴 **1993** Complicated, experimental portrait of Viennese-born philosopher Ludwig Wittgenstein (Johnson), executed as a series of blackout sketches (that feature a green Martian dwarf and such friends as Bertrand Russell and Ottoline Morrell). Assumes a familiarity with the eccentric Wittgenstein's ideas but does manage to convey some emotion and wit. **75m/C VHS.** *GB* Karl Johnson, Michael Gough, Tilda Swinton, John Quentin, Nabil Shaban; ***D:*** Derek Jarman; ***W:*** Derek Jarman, Terry Eagleton, Ken Butler. *KIV*

Wives Under Suspicion 🦴🦴½ **1938** While prosecuting a man who murdered his wife out of jealousy, a district attorney finds his own home life filled with similar tension. Director Whale's unnecessary remake of his own earlier film, "The Kiss Before the Mirror." He is best known for "Frankenstein." **75m/B VHS, Beta.** Warren William, Gail Patrick, Constance Moore, William Lundigan; ***D:*** James Whale. *NOS, DVT, HEG*

The Wiz 🦴🦴 **1978 (G)** Black version of the long-time favorite "The Wizard of Oz," based on the Broadway musical. Ross plays a Harlem schoolteacher who is whisked away to a fantasy version of New York City in a search for her identity. Some good character performances and musical numbers, but generally an overblown and garish effort with Ross too old for her role. Pryor is poorly cast, but Jackson is memorable as the Scarecrow. High-budget ($24 million) production with a ton of name stars, lost $11 million, and cooled studios on black films. Horne's number as the good witch is the best reason to sit through this one. ♫The Feeling That We Have; Can I Go On Not Knowing; Glinda's Theme; He's the Wizard; Soon as I Get Home; You Can't Win; Ease on Down the Road; What Would I Do If I Could Feel?; Slide Some Oil to Me. **133m/C VHS, Beta, LV.** Diana Ross, Michael Jackson, Nipsey Russell, Ted Ross, Mabel King, Thelma Carpenter, Richard Pryor, Lena Horne; ***D:*** Sidney Lumet; ***W:*** Joel Schumacher; ***C:*** Oswald Morris; ***M:*** Quincy Jones. Nominations: Academy Awards '78: Best Art Direction/Set Decoration, Best Cinematography, Best Costume Design. *MCA, FCT*

The Wizard 🦴½ **1989 (PG)** Facing the dissolution of his dysfunctional family, a youngster decides to take his autistic, video game-playing little brother across the country to a national video competition. Way too much plot in pretentious, blatantly commercial feature-length Nintendo ad, featuring the kid from "The Wonder Years." For teen video addicts only. **99m/C VHS, Beta, LV.** Fred Savage, Beau Bridges, Christian Slater, Luke Edwards, Jenny Lewis; ***D:*** Todd Holland; ***W:*** David Chisholm. *MCA*

The Wizard of Gore 🦴 **1970 (R)** The prototypical Lewis splatter party, about a magician whose on-stage mutilations turn out to be messily real. High camp and barrels of bright movie blood. **96m/C VHS, Beta.** Ray Sager, Judy Cler, Wayne Ratay, Phil Lauenson, Jim Rau, Don Alexander, Monika Blackwell, Corinne Kirkin; ***D:*** Herschell Gordon Lewis. *NO*

The Wizard of Loneliness 🦴🦴½ **1988 (PG-13)** A disturbed young boy goes to live with his grandparents during WWII, and slowly discovers family secrets centering on his aunt. Excellent performances barely save an aimless plot with an overdone denouement. Based on the novel by John Nichols. **110m/C VHS, Beta, LV.** Lukas Haas, Lea Thompson, John Randolph, Lance Guest, Anne Pitoniak, Jeremiah Warner, Dylan Baker; ***D:*** Jenny Bowen; ***W:*** Nancy Larson; ***M:*** Michel Colombier. *NO*

The Wizard of Oz 🦴🦴½ **1925** An early silent version of the L. Frank Baum fantasy, with notable plot departures from the book and later 1939 adaptation, starring long-forgotten comedian Semon as the Scarecrow, supported by a pre-Laurel Hardy as the Tin Woodman. With music score. **93m/B VHS, Beta, 8mm.** Larry Semon, Dorothy Dwan, Bryant Washburn, Charles Murray, Oliver Hardy, Josef Swickard, Virginia Pearson; ***D:*** Larry Semon. *NOS, VYY, MLB*

The Wizard of Oz 🦴🦴🦴🦴 **1939** From the book by L. Frank Baum. Fantasy about a Kansas farm girl (Garland, in her immortal role) who rides a tornado to a brightly colored world over the rainbow, full of talking scarecrows, munchkins and a wizard who bears a strange resemblance to a Kansas fortune-teller. She must outwit the Wicked Witch if she is ever to go home. Delightful performances from Lahr, Bolger, and Hamilton; King Vidor is uncredited as co-director. Director Fleming originally wanted Deanna Durbin or Shirley Temple for the role of Dorothy, but settled for Garland who made the song "Over the Rainbow" her own. She received a special Academy Award for her performance. For the 50th anniversary of its release, "The Wizard of Oz" was restored and includes rare film clips of Bolger's "Scarecrow Dance" and the cut "Jitterbug" number, and shots by Buddy Ebsen as the Tin Man before he became ill and left the production. Laserdisc edition includes digital sound, commentary by film historian Ronald Haver, and test footage, trailers and stills, as well as Jerry Maren talking about his experiences as a Munchkin. Yet another special release of the film, "The Ultimate Oz," contains a documentary on the making of the film, a reproduction of the original script, still photos, and liner notes. ♫Munchkinland; Ding Dong the Witch is Dead; Follow the Yellow Brick Road; If I Only Had a Brain/a Heart/the Nerve; If I Were the King of the Forest; The Merry Old Land of Oz; Threatening Witch; Into the Forest of the Wild Beast; The City Gates are Open. **101m/C VHS, Beta, LV.** Judy Garland, Margaret Hamilton, Ray Bolger, Jack Haley, Bert Lahr, Frank Morgan, Charley Grapewin, Clara Blandick, Mitchell Lewis, Billie Burke; ***D:*** Victor Fleming; ***W:*** Noel Langley; ***M:*** Herbert Stothart. Academy Awards '39: Best Song ("Over the Rainbow"), Best Original Score; Nominations: Academy Awards '39: Best Color Cinematography, Best Interior Decoration, Best Picture, Best Special Effects. *MGM, APD, TLF*

The Wizard of Speed and Time 🦴🦴½ **1988 (PG)** A special-effects wizard gets the break of his life when he's hired by a movie studio, but there's more to this particular studio than he realizes. Jittlov, a real special-effects expert, plays himself in this personally financed production. Although brimming with inside jokes and references, this self-indulgence succeeds with its enthusiasm and ambition, despite being rather obviously self-produced. Unique special effects make it memorable. **95m/C VHS, LV.** Mike Jittlov, Richard Kaye, Page Moore,

David Conrad, Steve Brodie, John Massari, Frank Laloggia, Philip Michael Thomas, Angelique Pettyjohn, Arnetia Walker, Paulette Breen; **D:** Mike Jittlov; **W:** Mike Jittlov, Richard Kaye, Deven Chierighino; **M:** John Massari. *WTA*

Wizards ℒℒ½ **1977 (PG)** A good, bumbling sorcerer battles for the sake of a magic kingdom and its princess against his evil brother who uses Nazi propaganda films to inspire his army of mutants. Profane, crude, & typically Bakshian fantasy with great graphics. Animated. **81m/C VHS, Beta, LV.** **D:** Ralph Bakshi; **W:** Ralph Bakshi; **M:** Andrew Belling; **V:** Bob Holt, Jesse Wells, Richard Romanus, David Proval. *FOX, WTA*

Wizards of the Lost Kingdom ℒ½ **1985 (PG)** A boy magician, aided by various ogres and swordster Svenson battles an all-powerful wizard for control of his kingdom. Family fare a bit too clean and harmless. **76m/C VHS, Beta.** Bo Svenson, Vidal Peterson, Thom Christopher; **D:** Hector Olivera. *MED*

Wizards of the Lost Kingdom 2 ℒ **1989 (PG)** A boy wizard is charged with vanquishing the evil tyrants from three kingdoms. Barely a sequel; no plot continuation or cast from earlier kiddie sword epic. **80m/C VHS, Beta.** David Carradine, Bobby Jacoby, Lana Clarkson, Mel Welles, Susan Lee Hoffman, Sid Haig; **D:** Charles B. Griffith. *MED*

WKRP in Cincinnati, Vol. 1 **1978** In the pilot episode for the TV sitcom, WKRP is a failing radio station with the cautious Arthur Carlson as the station manager (the station is owned by his mother). Andy Travis is hired as the new program director to turn things around and promptly turns WKRP towards rock and roll. Other regulars included newsman Les Nesman, sales manager Herb Tarlek, DJs Dr. Johnny Fever and Venus Flytrap, as well as ever-efficient secretary Jennifer Marlowe. **50m/C VHS.** Gary Sandy, Gordon Jump, Loni Anderson, Richard Sanders, Frank Bonner, Jan Smithers, Howard Hesseman, Tim Reid. *MTM*

Wolf ℒ **1986** To everyone's lasting regret, an ex-Vietnam POW strives to rescue an American ambassador kidnapped by Central American rebels. **95m/C VHS, Beta.** J. Antonio Carreon, Ron Marchini; **D:** Charlie Ordonez. *TWE*

Wolf ℒℒ½ **1994 (R)** Harrison's original script is massaged by Nichols into an upscale new age men's movement horror spectacle lacking a suitable climax. Stressed out Manhattan book editor Will Randall's (Nicholson) car hits a wolf on a country road and he's bitten when he tries to help the animal. Normally a wishy-washy guy, he notices some distinctly hairy changes to both his body and personality, leading him to make some drastic changes at work by knocking off his firm's greedy honchos and taking over. Talk about being ruthless in business. Boss' daughter Pfeiffer takes a shine to Randall's new animal magnetism, but is just visual candy. Walks a fine line between black comedy, camp, romance, and horror, though Jack baying at the moon seems sort of campy. **125m/C VHS, Beta, LV, 8mm.** Jack Nicholson, Michelle Pfeiffer, James Spader, Kate Nelligan, Christopher Plummer, Richard Jenkins, Om Puri, Eileen Atkins, David Hyde Pierce, Ron Rifkin, Prunella Scales; **D:** Mike Nichols; **W:** Wesley Strick, Jim Harrison; **C:** Giuseppe Rotunno; **M:** Ennio Morricone. *COL*

The Wolf at the Door ℒℒ½ **1987 (R)** A well-appointed, sincere biography of impressionist Paul Gauguin in the middle period of life, during his transition from the petty demands of his Parisian life to the freedom of Tahiti. Not definitive or compelling, but serves the purpose of a biography—arousing interest in the subject's life and art. **90m/C VHS, Beta.** *DK FR* Donald Sutherland, Jean Yanne, Sofie Graboel, Ghita Norby, Max von Sydow, Merete Voldstedlund, Fanny Bastien, Valerie Morea; **D:** Henning Carlsen; **W:** Christopher Hampton; **M:** Roger Bourland. *FOX, INJ*

Wolf Blood ℒℒ½ **1925** When Dick (Chesebro) is hurt in an accident, Dr. Horton uses wolf's blood for a transfusion. Soon there are unexplained deaths and Dick fears he's becoming a man-beast. Early precursor to the wolfman films. **68m/B VHS.** George Chesebro, Marguerite Clayton, Ray Hanford, Roy Watson, Milburn Morante; **D:** George Chesebro, George Mitchell. *GPV*

Wolf Call ℒ½ **1939** Carroll plays the son of a miner who travels with his devoted hound to see his father's old mine and start it working again. Gangsters and a beautiful Indian maiden get in his way. Master and pooch both find romance, and both sing. From the Jack London novel. **62m/B VHS, Beta, 8mm.** John Carroll, Movita, Wheeler Oakman, Peter George Lynn; **D:** George Waggner. *VYY, FCT*

Wolf Dog **1933** A boy and his dog. Outdoor action and adventure. Twelve chapters, 13 minutes each. **156m/B VHS, Beta.** Frankie Darro, Patricia "Boots" Mallory; **D:** Harry Fraser, Colbert Clark. *SNC, VCN, MLB*

Wolf Lake ℒ½ **1979** WWII veteran, whose son was killed in Vietnam, and a Vietnam army deserter clash with tragic consequences during their stay at a Canadian hunting lodge. Steiger gives it a go, but overwrought revenge pic resists quality upgrade. **90m/C VHS, Beta.** Rod Steiger, David Hoffman, Robin Mattson, Jerry Hardin, Richard Herd, Paul Mantu; **D:** Burt Kennedy. *PSM*

The Wolf Man ℒℒℒ½ **1941** Fun, absorbing classic horror with Chaney as a man bitten by werewolf Lugosi. His dad thinks he's gone nuts, his screaming gal pal just doesn't understand, and plants on the Universal lot have no roots. Ouspenskaya's finest hour as the prophetic gypsy woman. Owooo! Chilling and thrilling. **70m/B VHS, Beta, LV.** Lon Chaney Jr., Claude Rains, Maria Ouspenskaya, Ralph Bellamy, Bela Lugosi, Warren William, Patric Knowles, Evelyn Ankers; **D:** George Waggner; **C:** Joseph Valentine. *MCA*

Wolfen ℒℒℒ **1981 (R)** Surrealistic menace darkens this original and underrated tale of super-intelligent wolf creatures terrorizing New York City. Police detective Finney tries to track down the beasts before they kill again. Notable special effects in this thriller, which covers environmental and Native American concerns while maintaining the tension. Feature film debuts of Hines and Venora. Based on the novel by Whitley Strieber. Available in widescreen on laserdisc. **115m/C VHS, Beta, LV.** Albert Finney, Gregory Hines, Tom Noonan, Diane Venora, Edward James Olmos; **D:** Michael Wadleigh; **M:** James Horner. *WAR*

Wolfen Ninja ℒ **198?** A girl is raised by wolves and is taught by them the secrets of Ninja fighting. **92m/C VHS, Beta.** *TWE*

Wolfheart's Revenge **1925** An honest cowboy, helped by Wolfheart the Wonder Dog, steps in when a sheep rancher is murdered. Silent film with original organ score. **64m/B VHS, Beta, 8mm.** Guinn "Big Boy" Williams. *VYY, GPV*

The Wolfman ℒ **1982** In 1910, a young man learns that his family is heir to the curse of the Werewolf. Same old stuff. **91m/C VHS, Beta.** Earl Owensby, Kristina Reynolds; **D:** Worth Keeter. *NO*

The Wolves ℒℒℒ **1982** Gosha shows the world of the yakuza (gangster) during the 1920s. Reminiscent of the samurai, the movie combines ancient Japanese culture with the rapidly changing world of 20th Century Japan. In Japanese with English subtitles. **131m/C VHS, LV.** *JP* Tatsuya Nakadai; **D:** Hideo Gosha. *INJ*

A Woman and a Woman ℒℒ **1980** Covers a ten-year period in the friendship of Barbara and Irena and how it survives their professional and personal conflicts. In Polish with English subtitles. **99m/C VHS.** *PL* Halina Labonarska, Anna Romantowska; **D:** Richard Bugajski. *FCT*

A Woman at Her Window ℒℒ½ *Une Femme a sa Fentre* **1977** Aristocratic, jaded Margot (Schneider), the wife of dissolute nobleman Rico (Orsini), is pursued by capitalistic businessman Raoul (Noiret). But Margot herself is taken by idealistic Michel (Lanoux), a communist evading the secret police in 1936 Greece, and has a daughter from their brief and ultimately tragic union. Years later, Margot's now-grown daughter returns to Greece to learn more about her parents. Adapted from the novel by Pierre Drieu La Rochelle. French with subtitles. **110m/C VHS.** *FR* Romy Schneider, Philippe Noiret, Victor Lanoux, Umberto Orsini, Delia Boccardo, Gastone Moschin, Carl Mohner; **D:** Pierre Granier-Deferre; **W:** Pierre Granier-Deferre, Jorge Semprun. *FCT*

A Woman at War ℒℒ½ **1994 (PG-13)** True-story of a young woman's heroic fight against the Nazis. Nineteen-year-old Helene Moskiewicz (Plimpton) has had her parents arrested by the Gestapo in occupied Brussels, Belgium. She joins the resistance and falls for Franz Boehler (Stoltz), a young businessman who is not above lining his pockets with Nazi profits. When persecution of the Jews intensifies, Helene risks infiltrating Gestapo headquarters in order to save lives. **115m/C VHS.** Martha Plimpton, Eric Stoltz; **D:** Edward Bennett. *REP*

A Woman Called Golda ℒℒℒ **1982** Political drama following the life and career of Golda Meir, the Israeli Prime Minister and one of the most powerful political figures of the 20th century. Davis portrays the young Golda, Bergman taking over as she ages. Superior made-for-television bio-epic. **192m/C VHS, Beta.** Ingrid Bergman, Leonard Nimoy, Anne Jackson, Ned Beatty, Robert Loggia, Judy Davis; **D:** Alan Gibson; **W:** Steven Gethers, Howard Gast. *PAR*

A Woman Called Moses ℒℒ½ **1978** The story of Harriet Ross Tubman, who bought her freedom from slavery, founded the underground railroad, and helped lead hundreds of slaves to freedom before the Civil War. Wonderful performance by Tyson but the made-for-television film is bogged down by a so-so script. Based on the novel by Marcy Heldish. **200m/C VHS.** Cicely Tyson, Dick Anthony Williams, Will Geer, Robert Hooks, Hari Rhodes, James Wainwright; **D:** Paul Wendkos; **W:** Lonne Elder III. *XVC, FCT, CCP*

Woman Condemned ℒ½ **1933** A reporter tries to clear a woman's name of murder. **58m/B VHS, Beta, LV.** Mischa Auer, Lola Lane, Claudia Dell, Richard Hemingway. *NO*

The Woman He Loved ℒℒ½ **1988** The infamous romance of Edward VIII, who gave up the throne of England for American divorcee, Wallis Warfield Simpson. Seymour and Andrews are fine in their roles but the made-for-television drama is slow-going. **100m/C VHS.** Anthony Andrews, Jane Seymour, Olivia de Havilland, Lucy Gutteridge, Julie Harris, Robert Hardy, Phyllis Calvert; **D:** Charles Jarrott. *VTR*

A Woman, Her Men and Her Futon ℒℒ **1992 (R)** A beautiful woman tries to find her identity by having a number of lovers but none can satisfy her every need. **90m/C VHS.** Jennifer Rubin, Lance Edwards, Grant Show, Michael Ceveris, Delaune Michel, Robert Lipton; **D:** Mussef Sibay; **W:** Mussef Sibay; **M:** Joel Goldsmith. *REP*

Woman Hunt *Woof! The Highest Bidder* **1972 (R)** Men kidnap women, then hunt them in the jungle for fun. So deeply offensive, we would give it negative bones if we could. "Hee Haw" bimbo Todd plays a sadistic lesbian. **81m/C VHS, Beta.** John Ashley, Lisa Todd, Eddie Garcia, Laurie Rose; **D:** Eddie Romero. *NLC*

The Woman Hunter ℒ½ **1972** A wealthy woman recovering from a traffic accident in Mexico believes someone is after her for her jewels and possibly her life. Eden dressed well, if nothing else; suspense builds ploddingly to a "Yeah, sure" climax. Made for television. **73m/C VHS, Beta.** Barbara Eden, Robert Vaughn, Stuart Whitman, Sydney Chaplin, Larry Storch, Enrique Lucero; **D:** Bernard L. Kowalski. *NO*

Woman in Black ℒℒ½ **1989** Chilling ghost story set in 1925 and adapted from the novel by Susan Hill. Soliciter Arthur Kidd is sent to a remote house to settle the estate of a client. He's haunted by the mysterious figure of a woman in black, who according to the locals, has put a curse on the village. Arthur's driven close to the edge of sanity by the ghostly figure and the tragedy that haunts the past. Made for television. **100m/C VHS.** *GB* Adrian Rawlins; **D:** Herbert Wise. *VCO, FCT, TVC*

Woman in Brown ℒℒ½ *The Vicious Circle; The Circle* **1948** It's Hungary, 1882, and five Jewish men are on trial for the murder of a man who actually committed suicide. Despite the prejudice and hatred from the locals, their lawyer believes in and fights for their innocence. **77m/B VHS, Beta.** Conrad Nagel, Fritz Kortner, Reinhold Schunzel, Philip Van Zandt, Eddie LeRoy, Edwin Maxwell; ***D:*** W. Lee Wilder. *SNC*

A Woman in Flames 🦴🦴🦴 *Die Flambierte Frau* **1984 (R)** A bored middle-class housewife leaves her overbearing husband and becomes a high-priced prostitute. She has a passionless affair with an aging bisexual gigolo. Dark and dreary tale of human relationships and the role of sex in people's lives. Interesting but depressing. **106m/C VHS, Beta.** *GE* Gudrun Landgrebe, Robert Van Ackeren, Matthieu Carriere, Gabriele Lafari, Hanns Zischler; ***D:*** Robert Van Ackeren. *GLV*

The Woman in Green 🦴🦴 *Sherlock Holmes and the Woman in Green* **1945** Murder victims are found with missing index fingers, and it's up to Holmes and Watson to try to solve this apparently motiveless crime. Available colorized. **68m/B VHS, LV.** Basil Rathbone, Nigel Bruce, Hillary Brooke, Henry Daniell, Paul Cavanagh, Frederick Worlock, Mary Gordon, Billy Bevan; ***D:*** Roy William Neill. *SNC, REP, VYY*

Woman in Grey 🦴🦴 **1919** A man and a woman battle wits when they attempt to locate and unravel the Army Code while staying one step ahead of J. Haviland Hunter, a suave villain after the same fortune. Silent. **205m/B VHS, Beta.** Arline Pretty, Henry Sell. *NOS, CCB, MLB*

The Woman in Red 🦴🦴½ **1984 (PG-13)** Executive Wilder's life unravels when he falls hard for stunning Le Brock. Inferior Hollywood-ized remake of the ebulliant "Pardon Mon Affaire." Somehow the French seem to do the sexual force thing with more verve, but this one has its moments, and Wilder is likeable. Music by Stevie Wonder. ♫I Just Called to Say I Love You; Don't Drive Drunk; It's More Than You; It's You; Love Light in Flight; Moments Aren't Moments; Weakness; Woman in Red. **87m/C VHS, Beta, LV.** Gene Wilder, Charles Grodin, Kelly Le Brock, Gilda Radner, Judith Ivey, Joseph Bologna; ***D:*** Gene Wilder; ***W:*** Gene Wilder; ***M:*** John Morris. Academy Awards '84: Best Song ("I Just Called to Say I Love You"); Golden Globe Awards '85: Best Song ("I Just Called to Say I Love You"). *LIV, VES*

Woman in the Dunes 🦴🦴🦴🦴 *Suna No Onna; Woman of the Dunes* **1964** Splendid, resonant allegorical drama. A scientist studying insects in the Japanese sand dunes finds himself trapped with a woman in a hut at the bottom of a pit. Superbly directed and photographed (by Hiroshi Segawa). Scripted by Kobo Abe from his acclaimed novel. In Japanese with English subtitles. **123m/B VHS, Beta.** *JP* Eiji Okada, Kyoko Kishida, Koji Mitsui, Hiroko Ito, Sen Yano; ***D:*** Hiroshi Teshigahara; ***M:*** Toru Takemitsu. Cannes Film Festival '64: Grand Jury Prize; Nominations: Academy Awards '64: Best Director (Teshigahara), Best Foreign Language Film. *CVC, NOS, VDM*

Woman in the Moon 🦴🦴½ *By Rocket to the Moon; Girl in the Moon* **1929** Assorted people embark on a trip to the moon and discover water, and an atmosphere, as well as gold. Lang's last silent outing is nothing next to "Metropolis," with a rather lame plot (greedy trip bashers seek gold), but interesting as a vision of the future. Lang's predictions about space travel often hit the mark. Silent with music. **115m/B VHS, Beta.** *GE* Klaus Pohl, Willy Fritsch, Gustav von Wagenheim, Gerda Maurus; ***D:*** Fritz Lang. *VYY, IHF, LSV*

Woman in the Shadows 🦴🦴 **1934** A ex-con retreats to the woods for serenity and peace, but is assaulted by mysterious women, jealous lovers, and gun-slinging drunks, until he explodes. A man can only take so much. From a Dashiell Hammett story. **70m/B VHS, Beta.** Fay Wray, Ralph Bellamy, Melvyn Douglas, Roscoe Ates, Joe King. *VYY*

Woman In the Window 🦴🦴🦴 **1944** Psycho-melodrama finds staid college professor Richard Wanley straying off the straight and narrow into a world of trouble—thanks to beautiful model Alice (Bennett). She invites him over but when her jealous boyfriend Claude (Loft) arrives unexpectedly, he attacks them both and Richard kills Claude in self-defense. Thinking no one will believe them, and afraid of scandal, the inept duo bury the body in the woods. Too bad Richard's best friend Frank (Massey) is the D.A. and there's a blackmailer around. Or is there? Surprise ending. Based on the novel "Once Off Guard" by J.H. Wallis. **99m/B VHS.** Edward G. Robinson, Joan Bennett, Raymond Massey, Arthur Loft, Dan Duryea, Edmund Breon, Dorothy Peterson, Robert (Bobby) Blake; ***D:*** Fritz Lang; ***W:*** Nunnally Johnson; ***C:*** Milton Krasner; ***M:*** Arthur Lange. *MGM*

The Woman Inside 🦴½ **1983 (R)** Low-budget gender-bender depicts the troubled life of a Vietnam veteran who decides on a sex-change operation to satisfy his inner yearnings. Blondell's unfortunate last role as his/her aunt. Cheesy like Limburger; almost too weird and boring even for camp buffs. **94m/C VHS, Beta.** *CA* Gloria Manon, Dave Clark, Joan Blondell; ***D:*** Joseph Van Winkle. *NO*

A Woman is a Woman 🦴🦴🦴 *Une Femme Est Une Femme; La Donna E Donna* **1960** Godard's affectionate sendup of Hollywood musicals is a hilarious comedy about a nightclub dancer (Karina) who desperately wants a baby. When boyfriend Belmondo balks, she asks his best friend Brialy. Much ado is had, with the three leads all splendid. Godard's first film shot in color and cinemascope, with great music. In French with English subtitles. **88m/C VHS.** *FR* Jean-Claude Brialy, Jean-Paul Belmondo, Anna Karina, Marie Dubois; ***D:*** Jean-Luc Godard; ***M:*** Michel Legrand. *INT, INJ*

A Woman Named Jackie 🦴🦴½ **1991 (PG)** Three-part TV miniseries covering the life of Jacqueline Bouvier Kennedy Onassis. Downey offers a pretty picture as the enigmatic and beleagured heroine but this version is simplistic at best. Based on the book by C. David Heymann. On three cassettes. **246m/C VHS, LV.** Roma Downey, Stephen Collins, William Devane, Joss Ackland, Rosemary Murphy, Wendy Hughes, Josef Sommer; ***D:*** Larry Peerce; ***W:*** Roger O. Hirson. *NHO, IME*

The Woman Next Door 🦴🦴🦴 *La Femme d'a Cote* **1981 (R)** One of Truffaut's last films before his sudden death in 1984. The domestic drama involves a suburban husband who resumes an affair with a tempestuous now-married woman after she moves next door, with domestic complications all around. An insightful, humanistic paean to passion and fidelity by the great artist, though one of his lesser works. Supported by strong outings from the two leads. In French with English subtitles. **106m/C VHS, Beta, LV.** *FR* Gerard Depardieu, Fanny Ardant, Michele Baumgartner, Veronique Silver, Roger Van Hool; ***D:*** Francois Truffaut; ***W:*** Suzanne Schiffman; ***M:*** Georges Delerue. *HMV, FOX*

A Woman Obsessed 🦴 **1988 (R)** Pathetic, over-cooked drama about a woman obsessed with her long-lost son. "Ruth Raymond" is really porn-flick vet Georgina Spelvin. Soon-to-be camp classic takes itself with utter seriousness. **105m/C VHS, VHS, Beta.** Ruth Raymond, Gregory Patrick, Troy Donahue, Linda Blair; ***D:*** Chuck Vincent. *ACA*

A Woman of Affairs 🦴🦴 **1928** Garbo, who can't have the guy she really loves (Gilbert), marries scoundrel. When she finds out husband's true profession, he kills himself and Gilbert comes back. In order to preclude happy ending, she decides the affair wasn't meant to be and expires. Tragically. Silent. **90m/B VHS.** Greta Garbo, John Gilbert, Lewis Stone, Johnny Mack Brown, Douglas Fairbanks Jr., Hobart Bosworth, Dorothy Sebastian; ***D:*** Clarence Brown. *MGM, FCT*

Woman of Desire 🦴 **1993 (R)** Christina Ford (Derek) is a femme fatale who is yachting with rich boyfriend Ted when there is a terrible storm. Christina, Ted, and yacht captain Jack are washed overboard and Jack is found washed ashore with no memory. When Christina turns up she claims Jack killed Ted. So Jack gets a lawyer, Walter J. Hill (played by the redoubtable Mitchum) but is he wily enough to discredit the deceitful Christina? Bo's body is once again on display. Also available in an unrated version. **97m/C VHS, LV.** Bo Derek, Jeff Fahey, Steven Bauer, Robert Mitchum. *VMK*

A Woman of Distinction 🦴🦴🦴 **1950** Slapstick comedy with potential to be ordinary is taken over the top by a good, vivacious cast. Russell, the stuffy Dean of a women's college, is driven to distraction by a reporter linking her romantically to Milland, a visiting professor. **85m/C VHS, Beta, LV.** Ray Milland, Rosalind Russell, Edmund Gwenn, Francis Lederer; ***Cameos:*** Lucille Ball; ***D:*** Edward Buzzell. *COL*

Woman of Paris/Sunnyside 🦴🦴🦴½ **1923** This double feature highlights the talents of Charlie Chaplin. "A Woman of Paris" is the tragic story of a French country girl who winds up a kept woman. Chaplin's only dramatic directional outing; he makes only a cameo appearance. Straightforward but hip story of sex and society. In "Sunnyside," an example of high Chaplin highjinks, the comic plays a hotel handyman who can't win. **111m/B VHS, Beta.** Adolphe Menjou, Edna Purviance, Carl Miller, Lydia Knott; ***Cameos:*** Charlie Chaplin; ***D:*** Charlie Chaplin. *FOX*

A Woman of Rome 🦴🦴 *La Romana* **1956** Standard Italian star vehicle, with Lollobrigida portraying a successful prostitute in Rome who decides to change her life. Dubbed. **93m/B VHS, Beta.** *IT* Gina Lollobrigida, Daniel Gelin, Franco Fabrizi, Raymond Pellegrin; ***D:*** Luigi Zampa. *NOS, FCT*

A Woman of Substance, Episode 1: Nest of Vipers 🦴🦴½ **1984** The woman of the title, Emma Harte, rises from poverty to wealth and power through self-discipline. First episode of three. Made for TV saga has our heroine working as a servant for the snooty Fairley family. **100m/C VHS, Beta.** Jenny Seagrove, Barry Bostwick, Deborah Kerr; ***D:*** Don Sharp. *LIV*

A Woman of Substance, Episode 2: The Secret is Revealed 🦴🦴½ **1984** Emma Harte struggles to rise from a life of poverty to wealth and social acceptance. Second miniseries episode has Emma fighting to get by in the big city. Fun TV drama. **100m/C VHS, Beta.** Jenny Seagrove, Barry Bostwick, Deborah Kerr; ***D:*** Don Sharp. *LIV*

A Woman of Substance, Episode 3: Fighting for the Dream 🦴🦴½ **1984** Third installment is pretty good romantic TV saga. Rags-to-riches Emma finds love and happiness—at last! **100m/C VHS, Beta.** Jenny Seagrove, Barry Bostwick, Deborah Kerr; ***D:*** Don Sharp. *LIV*

The Woman of the Town 🦴🦴½ **1944** Frontier marshal and newspaperman Bat Masterson is portrayed convincingly by Dekker as a very human hero who seeks justice when the woman he loves, a dance hall girl who works in the town for social causes, is killed by an unscrupulous rancher. Fictionalized but realistic western shows "heroes" as good, ordinary people. **90m/B VHS, Beta.** Claire Trevor, Albert Dekker, Barry Sullivan, Henry Hull, Porter Hall, Percy Kilbride; ***D:*** George Archainbaud; ***M:*** Miklos Rozsa. Nominations: Academy Awards '44: Best Original Score. *NOS, HEG, FCT*

Woman of the Year 🦴🦴🦴🦴 **1942** First classic Tracy/Hepburn pairing concerns the rocky marriage of a renowned political columnist and a lowly sportswriter. Baseball scene with Hepburn at her first game is delightful. Hilarious, rich entertainment that tries to answer the question "What really matters in life?" Tracy and Hepburn began a close friendship that paralleled their quarter-century celluloid partnership. Hepburn shepherded Kamin and Lardner's Oscar-winning script past studio chief Louis B. Mayer, wearing four-inch heels to press her demands. Mayer caved in, Tracy was freed from making "The Yearling," and the rest is history. **114m/B VHS, Beta, LV.** Spencer Tracy, Katharine Hepburn, Fay Bainter, Dan Tobin, Reginald Owen, Roscoe Karns, William Bendix, Minor Watson; ***D:*** George Stevens; ***W:*** Ring Lardner Jr., Michael Kanin; ***C:*** Joseph Ruttenberg; ***M:*** Franz Waxman. Academy Awards '42: Best Original Screenplay; Nominations: Academy Awards '42: Best Actress (Hepburn). *MGM*

A Woman Rebels 🦴🦴½ **1936** A young Victorian woman challenges Victorian society by fighting for women's rights. Excellent performance from Hepburn lifts what might have been a forgettable drama. Screen debut of Van Heflin. Based on

Netta Syrett's "Portrait of a Rebel." **88m/B VHS, Beta.** Katharine Hepburn, Herbert Marshall, Elizabeth Allan, Donald Crisp, Van Heflin; ***D:*** Mark Sandrich. *CCB*

Woman Times Seven 🦴🦴½ *Sept Fois Femme; Sette Volte Donna* **1967 (PG)** Italian sexual comedy: seven sketches, each starring MacLaine with a different leading man. Stellar cast and good director should have delivered more, but what they have provided has its comedic moments. **99m/C VHS, Beta.** *IT FR* Shirley MacLaine, Peter Sellers, Rossano Brazzi, Vittorio Gassman, Lex Barker, Elsa Martinelli, Robert Morley, Alan Arkin, Michael Caine, Patrick Wymark, Anita Ekberg, Philippe Noiret; ***D:*** Vittorio De Sica. *COL, SUE, NLC*

A Woman Under the Influence 🦴🦴🦴 **1974 (R)** Strong performances highlight this overlong drama about a family's disintegration. Rowlands is the lonely, middle-aged housewife who's having a breakdown and Falk is her blue-collar husband who can't handle what's going on. **147m/C VHS, Beta.** Gena Rowlands, Peter Falk, Matthew Cassel, Matthew Laborteaux, Christina Grisanti; ***D:*** John Cassavetes; ***W:*** John Cassavetes. Golden Globe Awards '75: Best Actress—Drama (Rowlands); National Board of Review Awards '74: Best Actress (Rowlands); Nominations: Academy Awards '74: Best Actress (Rowlands), Best Director (Cassavetes). *TOU, FCT*

Woman Undone 🦴🦴½ **1995 (R)** Husband Allen Hansen (Quaid) and wife Terri (McDonnell) are involved in a car crash on a lonely stretch of desert highway. He dies, she's thrown clear, but an autopsy reveals he was actually shot in the head before the accident. Then attorney Ross Bishop (Elliott) gets involved and in a California courtroom Terri must prove that her unhappy marriage wasn't ended by murder. **91m/C VHS, LV.** Mary McDonnell, Randy Quaid, Sam Elliott, Benjamin Bratt; ***D:*** Evelyn Purcell; ***W:*** William Mickelberry; ***C:*** Toyomichi Kurita; ***M:*** Daniel Licht. *REP*

The Woman Who Came Back 🦴🦴 **1945** A young woman who believes she suffers from a witch's curse returns to her small hometown with unhappy results. Good cast; bad script. Indifference inducing. **69m/B VHS, Beta.** Nancy Kelly, Otto Kruger, John Loder, Ruth Ford, Jeanne Gail; ***D:*** Walter Colmes. *COL*

The Woman Who Willed a Miracle 🦴🦴 **1983** Made-for-television drama has a devoted mother encouraging her mentally retarded son to pursue his interest in the piano. **72m/C VHS, Beta.** Cloris Leachman, James Noble; ***D:*** Sharron Miller. *NO*

Woman With a Past 🦴🦴½ **1992 (PG-13)** Reed gets out of an abusive marriage only to have her ex kidnap their kids. Since the law's no help she hires a bounty hunter to find them—committing armed robbery to pay the fees. Caught and imprisoned, Reed escapes, changes her identity, remarries, and even is reunited with her sons. Then she's suddenly arrested when her fugitive status comes to light 10 years later. Based on a true story; made for TV melodrama. **95m/C VHS.** Pamela Reed, Dwight Schultz, Paul LeMat, Carrie Snodgress, Richard Lineback; ***D:*** Mimi Leder. *NHO*

A Woman Without Love 🦴🦴🦴 **1951** A rarely seen film from Bunuel's Mexican period based on a classic Guy de Maupassant tale about a forbidden romance. Family tragedy results later when the husband "misbequeaths" his fortune. Minor but fascinating bug-the-bourgeoisie Bunuel. In Spanish with English subtitles. **91m/C VHS, Beta.** *MX* Rosario Granados, Julio Villareal, Tito Junco; ***D:*** Luis Bunuel. *XVC, MED, INJ*

A Woman's Face 🦴🦴🦴 *En Kvinnas Ansikte* **1938** An unpleasant, bitter woman with a hideous scar on her face blackmails illicit lovers as a form of revenge for a happiness she doesn't know. She even plots to murder a child for his inheritance. But after plastic surgery, she becomes a nicer person and doubts her plan. Lean, tight suspense with a bang-up finale. In Swedish with English subtitles. Remade in Hollywood in 1941. **100m/B VHS, Beta.** *SW* Ingrid Bergman, Anders Henrikson, Karin Carlsson, Georg Rydeberg, Goran Bernhard, Tore Svennberg; ***D:*** Gustaf Molander. *WAC, INJ*

A Woman's Face 🦴🦴🦴 **1941** A physically and emotionally scarred woman becomes part of a blackmail ring. Plastic surgery restores her looks and her attitude. Begins with a murder trial and told in flashbacks; tight, suspenseful remake of the 1938 Swedish Ingrid Bergman vehicle. Climax will knock you out of your chair. **107m/B VHS, Beta.** Joan Crawford, Conrad Veidt, Melvyn Douglas, Osa Massen, Reginald Owen, Albert Basserman, Marjorie Main, Donald Meek, Charles Quigley, Henry Daniell, George Zucco, Robert Warwick; ***D:*** George Cukor. *MGM*

A Woman's Guide to Adultery 🦴🦴½ **1993** Four female friends, living and working in London, find their lives turned upside down by their passions for unavailable men. Political advisor Jo (Donohoe) is involved with married politician Martin (McElhinney) while art tutor Jennifer (Gillies) wants her student David (Morrissey), despite his having a live-in girlfriend. Ad execs Helen (Lacey) and Michael (Dunbar) find their marriage in tatters when Helen admits to an affair with their boss and photographer Rose (Russell) breaks her own rule about adultery by getting involved with married university instructor Paul (Bean). Based on the novel by Carol Clewlow. Made for TV. **145m/C VHS.** *GB* Theresa Russell, Amanda Donohoe, Sean Bean, Adrian Dunbar, Ingrid Lacey, Fiona Gillies, Neil Morrissey, Danny Webb, Ian McElhinney, Julie Peasgood, Caroline Lee-Johnson; ***D:*** David Hayman; ***W:*** Frank Cottrell Boyce; ***C:*** Graham Frake; ***M:*** Daemion Barry. *VCO*

A Woman's Secret 🦴🦴 **1949** O'Hara admits to murder she didn't commit. Why? It's as indiscernible as why the plot should be muddled by flashbacks. RKO lost big bucks on this one. **85m/B VHS, Beta.** Maureen O'Hara, Melvyn Douglas, Gloria Grahame, Bill Williams, Victor Jory, Jay C. Flippen; ***D:*** Nicholas Ray; ***W:*** Herman J. Mankiewicz. *TTC, FCT*

A Woman's Tale 🦴🦴🦴 **1992 (PG-13)** The superlative performance of Florence highlights this look at aging and death. Martha, 78, has been diagnosed with terminal lung cancer. She is looked after by a much-younger nurse and in turn looks after the older friends who share her apartment house. This gentle story quietly depicts the feisty, joyous Martha's last days and the simple pleasures she derives from her remaining time. Florence herself died from cancer not long after completing the film. **94m/C VHS, LV.** *AU* Sheila Florence, Gosia Dobrowolska, Norman Kaye, Chris Haywood, Myrtle Woods, Ernest Gray, Monica Maughan, Bruce Myles, Alex Menglet; ***D:*** Paul Cox; ***W:*** Paul Cox. Australian Film Institute '91: Best Actress (Florence). *ORI, BTV*

A Woman's World 🦴🦴🦴 **1954** Slick, sophisticated look at big business in the '50s, with Webb as the boss who chooses his next general manager based on the suitability of the executive's wives. Beautiful costumes, witty dialogue, and good acting make this worthwhile viewing. Plus, film offers a nostalgic look at New York in the '50s, with several shots of Fifth Avenue, Macy's, Park Avenue, and the long-gone Stork Club. Based on a story by Mona Williams. **94m/C VHS.** Clifton Webb, June Allyson, Van Heflin, Lauren Bacall, Fred MacMurray, Arlene Dahl, Cornel Wilde, Elliott Reid, Margalo Gillmore, Alan Reed, David Hoffman, George Melford; ***D:*** Jean Negulesco; ***W:*** Claude Binyon, Richard Sale, Mary Loos, Howard Lindsay, Russel Crouse. *FXV*

Wombling Free 🦴🦴 **1977** An English girl makes friends with a race of tiny, litter-hating furry creatures called Wombles. The creatures are visible only to the little girl because she is the only one who believes. Together they try to clean up a dirty world. British society is less cutting-edge about social roles, etc. than our enlightened one; be prepared for retrograde characterizations. Fun scene with Kelly/Astaire-style dance number. **86m/C VHS, Beta.** *GB* Bonnie Langford, David Tomlinson; ***D:*** Lionel Jeffries; ***M:*** George Bassman. *COL*

The Women 🦴🦴🦴½ **1939** A brilliant adaptation of the Clare Boothe Luce stage comedy about a group of women who destroy their best friends' reputations at various social gatherings. Crawford's portrayal of the nasty husband-stealer is classic, and the fashion-show scene in Technicolor is one not to miss. Hilarious bitchiness all around. Remade semi-musically as "The Opposite Sex." Another in that long list of stellar 1939 pics. **133m/B VHS, Beta, LV.** Norma Shearer, Joan Crawford, Rosalind Russell, Joan Fontaine, Mary Boland, Lucile Watson, Margaret Dumont, Paulette Goddard, Ruth Hussey, Marjorie Main; ***D:*** George Cukor; ***W:*** Anita Loos; ***C:*** Joseph Ruttenberg. *MGM*

Women & Men: In Love There Are No Rules 🦴🦴½ **1991 (R)** Made for cable extravaganza chronicling the relationships of three couples, each adapted from the short story of a renowned author. Irwin Shaw's "Return to Kansas City" tells of a young boxer who is prematurely pushed into a match by his ambitious wife. In Carson McCullers' "A Domestic Dilemma," a marriage begins to crumble thanks to an alcoholic wife. Finally, Henry Miller's "Mara" has an aging man and a young Parisian prostitute spending a revealing evening together. **90m/C VHS, LV.** Matt Dillon, Kyra Sedgwick, Ray Liotta, Andie MacDowell, Scott Glenn, Juliette Binoche, Jerry Stiller; ***D:*** Kristi Zea, Walter Bernstein, Mike Figgis. *HBO*

Women & Men: Stories of Seduction 🦴🦴½ **1990** Three famous short stories are brought to the screen in this made for TV collection. Mary McCarthy's "The Man in the Brooks Brothers Shirt," Dorothy Parker's "Dusk Before Fireworks," and Hemingway's "Hills Like White Elephants" between them cover every aspect of male-female relationships. Since there are three casts and three directors, there is little to join the stories in style, calling attention to some flaws in pacing and acting ability; still, worth watching. **90m/C VHS, LV.** James Woods, Melanie Griffith, Peter Weller, Elizabeth McGovern, Beau Bridges, Molly Ringwald; ***D:*** Ken Russell, Tony Richardson, Frederic Raphael. *HBO, FCT*

Women From the Lake of Scented Souls 🦴🦴 **1994** Mournful film, set in a rural Chinese village, focuses on matriarchal businesswoman Xiang (Gaowa), who runs the local sesame oil making factory that has just attracted the attention of Japanese investors. Seems the water of the nearby lotus-covered lake, scene of local tragedies, is Xiang's special ingredient. With her new-found wealth, Xiang is able to purchase a very reluctant bride, Huanhuan (Yujuan), for her mentally-retarded son—a disaster in the making. Rich detail and nuanced performances; Chinese with subtitles. **105m/C VHS.** *CH* Siqin Gaowa, Wu Yujuan, Lei Luosheng, Chen Baoguo; ***D:*** Xie Fei; ***W:*** Xie Fei; ***C:*** Bao Xianran; ***M:*** Wang Liping. *AVI*

Women in Cell Block 7 *Woof! Diario Segreto Di Un Carcere Femminele* **1977 (R)** Exploitative skinfest about women in prison suffering abuse from their jailers and each other. Seems that one of the prisoners knows the location of massive heroin stash. Badly dubbed. **100m/C VHS, Beta.** *IT* Anita Strindberg, Eve Czemeys, Olga Bisera, Jane Avril, Valeria Fabrizi, Jenny Tamburi; ***D:*** Rino Di Silvestro. *NO*

Women in Fury *Woof!* **1984** A woman is sentenced to imprisonment in a mostly lesbian Brazilian jail, and subsequently leads a breakout. **94m/C VHS, Beta.** *BR* Suzanne Carvalno, Gloria Cristal, Zeni Pereira, Leonardo Jose. *LIV*

Women in Love 🦴🦴🦴 **1970 (R)** Drama of two steamy affairs, based on D.H. Lawrence's classic novel. Deservedly Oscar-winning performance by Jackson; controversial nude wrestling scene with Bates and Reed is hard to forget. Plot is dumped on in favor of atmosphere. Followed nearly two decades later (1989) by a "prequel": "The Rainbow," also from Lawrence, also directed by Russell and starring Jackson. **129m/C VHS, Beta, LV.** *GB* Glenda Jackson, Jennie Linden, Alan Bates, Oliver Reed, Michael Gough, Eleanor Bron; ***D:*** Ken Russell; ***C:*** Billy Williams; ***M:*** Georges Delerue. Academy Awards '70: Best Actress (Jackson); Golden Globe Awards '71: Best Foreign Film; National Board of Review Awards '70: 10 Best Films of the Year, Best Actress (Jackson); National Society of Film Critics Awards '70: Best Actress (Jackson); Nominations: Academy Awards '70: Best Adapted Screenplay, Best Cinematography, Best Director (Russell). *MGM, FOX, BTV*

Women in Prison 🦴🦴 *Women without Names* **1949** A pseudo-documentary style expose of the hardships endured by women in Italian detention camps following WWII. Controversial for its examination of such themes as human rights, abortion, lesbianism, and sexuality. English, French, Italian, with English subtitles. **94m/C VHS.** *IT* Simone Simon; ***D:*** Geza Radvanyi; ***W:*** Geza Radvanyi. *FCT*

The Women of Brewster Place 🦴🦴🦴 **1989** Seven black women living in a tenement fight to gain control of their lives. (Men in general don't come out too well.) Excellent, complex script gives each actress in a fine ensemble headed by Winfrey (in her TV dramatic debut) time in the limelight. Pilot for the series "Brewster Place." Based on the novel by Gloria Naylor. Winfrey was executive producer. **180m/C VHS, Beta.** Oprah Winfrey, Mary Alice, Olivia Cole, Robin Givens, Moses Gunn, Jackee, Paula Kelly, Lonette McKee, Paul Winfield, Cicely Tyson; ***D:*** Donna Deitch; ***W:*** Karen Hall; ***M:*** David Shire. *JTC, FCT*

Women of the Prehistoric Planet *Woof!* **1966** On a strange planet, the members of a space rescue mission face deadly perils. Typical bad sci-fi of its era, with horrid special effects, including "giant" lizards. Get this: there's one woman, and she's not of the planet in question. See if you can last long enough to catch the amazing plot twist at the end. **87m/C VHS, Beta.** Wendell Corey, Irene Tsu, Robert Ito, Stuart Margolin, Lyle Waggoner, Adam Roarke, Merry Anders; ***D:*** Arthur C. Pierce. *NO*

Women of Valor 🦴½ **1986** During WWII, a band of American nurses stationed in the Philippines are captured by the Japanese and struggle to survive in a brutal POW camp. TV feature was made 40 years too late, adding up to a surreal experience. **95m/C VHS, Beta.** Susan Sarandon, Kristy McNichol, Alberta Watson, Valerie Mahaffey, Suzanne Lederer, Pat Bishop, Terry O'Quinn, Neva Patterson; ***D:*** Buzz Kulik; ***M:*** Georges Delerue. *VTR, PSM*

Women on the Verge of a Nervous Breakdown 🦴🦴🦴½ *Mujeres al Borde de un Ataque de Nervios* **1988 (R)** Surreal and hilarious romp through the lives of film dubber Maura, her ex-lover, his crazed ex-mistress, his new lover, his son, and his son's girlfriend. There's also Maura's friend Barranco, who inadvertantly lent her apartment to Shiite terrorists and now believes the police are after her as an accomplice in an airline hijacking. They meet in a comedy of errors, missed phone calls, and rental notices, while discovering the truth and necessity of love. Fast-paced and full of black humor, with loaded gazpacho serving as a key element. Introduced Almodovar to American audiences. In Spanish with English subtitles. **88m/C VHS, Beta, LV.** *SP* Carmen Maura, Fernando Guillen, Julieta Serrano, Maria Barranco, Rossy de Palma, Antonio Banderas; ***D:*** Pedro Almodovar; ***W:*** Pedro Almodovar; ***M:*** Bernardo Bonazzi. National Board of Review Awards '88: 5 Best Foreign Films of the Year; New York Film Critics Awards '88: Best Foreign Film; Nominations: Academy Awards '88: Best Foreign Language Film. *ORI, INJ*

Women Unchained *Woof!* **197? (R)** Five women escape from a maximum security prison and make a run for the Mexican border, shunning civilized behavior along the way. Much less-than-honorable entry in desperate women genre. **82m/C VHS, Beta.** Carolyn Judd, Teri Guzman, Darlene Mattingly, Angel Colbert, Bonita Kalem; ***D:*** Kent Osborne; ***W:*** Kent Osborne. *GEM*

Women's Club 🦴½ **1987 (R)** Table-turning sex comedy about a wealthy matron who patronizes a talented (?) young movie writer, but really wants—you know what. She begins lending his services to friends—and does he ever get worn out! This excuse may be intended to be uproarious, but it's hard to tell. And all that sex gets very perfunctory after awhile. **89m/C VHS, Beta.** Michael Pare, Maud Adams, Eddie Velez; ***D:*** Sandra Weintraub; ***M:*** Paul Antonelli. *LIV, VES*

Women's Prison Escape 🦴½ *Cell Block Girls* **19??** Four tough broads blow the pen and are forced to high-tail it through the Everglades. They can't decide which is worse, the snakes and 'gators, or the corrupt and sleazy life they left behind. Only cinematic pairing of Rooney and Lurch. **90m/C VHS.** Ted Cassidy, Chris Robinson, Mickey Rooney; ***D:*** Chris Robinson. *QVD*

Women's Prison Massacre *Woof!* **1985** Four male convicts temporarily detained at a woman's prison (why?) violently take hostages and generally make trouble for the authorities and the women. Horribly dubbed. **89m/C VHS, Beta.** *IT* Laura Gemser, Lorraine De Selle, Francoise Perrot, Ursula Flores, Gabriele Truti; ***D:*** Gilbert Roussel. *LIV, VES*

Wonder Man 🦴🦴½ **1945** When a brash nightclub entertainer (Kaye) is killed by gangsters, his mild-mannered twin brother (Kaye) takes his place to smoke out the killers. One of Kaye's better early films. The film debuts of Vera-Ellen and Cochran. Look for Mrs. Howell of "Gilligan's Island." ♫So In Love; Bali Boogie; Ortchi Chornya; Opera Number. **98m/C VHS, Beta, LV.** Danny Kaye, Virginia Mayo, Vera-Ellen, Steve Cochran, S.Z. Sakall, Otto Kruger; ***D:*** H. Bruce Humberstone; ***C:*** Victor Milner. Academy Awards '45: Best Special Effects; Nominations: Academy Awards '45: Best Song ("So in Love"), Best Sound, Best Original Score. *SUE*

The Wonderful, Horrible Life of Leni Riefenstahl **1993** Documentary portrait of Hitler's favorite filmmaker. At 91, Riefenstahl tells of her start as an actress, her first directorial effort "The Blue Light" (1932), and the two infamous propaganda films, "Triumph of the Will" (1935) and "Olympia" (1938), which still provoke. She discusses her relationship with Hitler and Joseph Goebbels and the accusations that have continued to haunt her life. Still active, Riefenstahl's current work documents the Nuba tribes of Africa and underwater filming of rare aquatic life in the Seychelles Islands. German with English subtitles. **180m/C VHS.** *GE* ***D:*** Ray Muller. *KIV*

The Wonderful World of the Brothers Grimm 🦴🦴½ **1962** Big-budget fantasy based very loosely on the Grimm Brothers' lives and three of their stories: "The Dancing Princesses," "The Cobbler and the Elves," and "The Singing Bone." Good, fun Puppetoon scenes, but leaves much else to be desired. A megawatt cast and the ubiquitous hand of producer-director Pal are not enough to cover the flaws. The biographical parts are hokey, and the tales used are the wrong ones. Disappointing but historically interesting. The second-ever story film done in Cinerama. ♫The Theme From the Wonderful World of the Brothers Grimm; Gypsy Rhapsody; Christmas Land; Ah-Oom; Above the Stars; Dee-Are-A-Gee-O-En (Dragon). **134m/C VHS, Beta, LV.** Laurence Harvey, Karl-Heinz Boehm, Claire Bloom, Buddy Hackett, Terry-Thomas, Russ Tamblyn, Yvette Mimieux, Oscar Homolka, Walter Slezak, Beulah Bondi, Martita Hunt, Otto Kruger, Barbara Eden, Jim Backus, Arnold Stang; ***D:*** Henry Levin, George Pal; ***W:*** William Roberts; ***C:*** Paul Vogel. Academy Awards '62: Best Costume Design (Color); Nominations: Academy Awards '62: Best Art Direction/Set Decoration (Color), Best Color Cinematography, Best Original Score. *MGM*

Wonderland 🦴🦴🦴 *The Fruit Machine* **1988** Campy thriller follows two young gay boys in England, inadvertent witnesses to a murder, who find themselves on the run. Fast paced, dreamy atmosphere makes up for the sometimes confusing plot. Often overlooked British import. **103m/C VHS, LV.** *GB* Emile Charles, Tony Forsyth, Robert Stephens, Clare Higgins, Bruce Payne, Robbie Coltrane; ***D:*** Philip Saville; ***W:*** Frank Clarke; ***M:*** Hans Zimmer. *LIV, VES*

Wonderland Cove 🦴 **1975** Seafaring adventurer adopts five orphan children and embarks on journeys to exotic locales. **78m/C Beta.** Clu Gulager, Sean Marshall, Randi Kiger, Lori Walsh; ***D:*** Jerry Thorpe. *PSM*

The Wonders of Aladdin 🦴½ *Les Mille Et Une Nuits; Le Meraviglie Di Aladino* **1961** Slapstick comedy based on the ancient rubbed-lamp-and-genie chestnut. Kids'll love it; adults will yawn. **93m/C VHS, Beta.** *IT FR* Donald O'Connor, Vittorio De Sica; ***D:*** Henry Levin, Mario Bava. *NLC*

Wonderwall: The Movie 🦴½ **1969** Bizarre characters trip over themselves in love while groovy music plays in background. **82m/C VHS, Beta.** *GB* Jack MacGowran, Jane Birkin, Irene Handl; ***D:*** Joe Massot; ***M:*** George Harrison, Eric Clapton, Ravi Shankar. *FCT, MVD*

Wonsan Operation 🦴 **1978** U.N. soldiers plunge into the muddy depths of enemy territory in search of secret information that would end the Korean War. Dubbed. **100m/C VHS, Beta.** Lew Montania, Frederick Hill; ***D:*** Terrence Sul. *VDA*

Woodchipper Massacre *Woof!* **1989** Aunt Tess is frozen in the freezer, waiting to be turned into whatever the fleshy equivalent of woodchips is by her three unloving relations, and her totally evil son has just broken out of prison looking to retrieve his inheritance. You think you have problems? You'll have one less if you leave this one on the shelf. **90m/C VHS, Beta.** Jon McBride, Patricia McBride; ***D:*** Jon McBride. *DMP*

The Wooden Gun 🦴🦴½ **1979** Conflicts arise between two teenage factions in 1950's Tel Aviv: native Israelis, and the children of Jews arrived from Europe since WWII. In Hebrew with English subtitles. **91m/C VHS, Beta.** *IS* ***D:*** Han Moshenson. *ERG, FCT, INJ*

Wooden Horse 🦴🦴🦴 **1950** Lean thriller of British POWs escaping a Nazi camp through a tunnel beneath their exercise horse. Based on a true incident in 1943 and on "The Tunnel Escape" by Eric Williams; set the tone for all British prison-camp movies to follow: stiff upper lip and all that, and adolescent-style trickery reminiscent of English boarding schools. **98m/C VHS, Beta.** Anthony Steel, Leo Genn, David Tomlinson, Bryan Forbes, Peter Finch; ***D:*** Jack Lee. *NO*

The Wooden Man's Bride 🦴🦴 **1994** The inhabitants of this austere 1920s, northwest Chinese community live in stone fortresses, fearful of being attacked by roving armed bandits. Which is what happens to the bridal party of Young Mistress (Lan), who's kidnapped by bandit leader Tang (Mingjun). She's released unharmed when her servant Kui (Shih) impresses Tang with his bravery but her bridegroom has been killed in a freak accident and formidable Madame Liu (Yu-mei), who runs the fortress, forces her to marry a wooden likeness of the deceased. Despairing Young Mistress begins an affair with Kui, which can only end badly. Mandarin with subtitles. **114m/C VHS.** *CH* Wang Lan, Chang Shih, Wang Yu-mei, Kao Mingjun; ***D:*** Huang Jianxin; ***W:*** Yang Zhengguang; ***C:*** Zhang Xiaoguang; ***M:*** Zhang Dalong. *HMK*

Woodstock 🦴🦴🦴🦴 **1970 (R)** Step into the way-back machine and return to the times of luv, peace, and understanding. Powerful chronicle of the great 1969 Woodstock rock concert celebrates the music and lifestyle of the late '60s. More than 400,000 spectators withstood lack of privacy, bathrooms, parking, and food while wallowing in the mud for four days to catch classic performances by a number of popular performers and groups. Martin Scorcese helped edit the documentary, trail-blazing in its use of split-screen montage. A director's cut is available at 225 minutes. **180m/C VHS, Beta, LV.** ***D:*** Michael Wadleigh. Academy Awards '70: Best Feature Documentary; Nominations: Academy Awards '70: Best Film Editing, Best Sound. *MVD, WAR, PAP*

Woodstock '94 **1994** The 25th anniversary of the original festival was celebrated with a three-day music explosion (complete with mud). Includes backstage footage and interviews with some of the 30 acts, including Aerosmith, Peter Gabriel, Blind Melon, Metallica, and the Red Hot Chili Peppers. **165m/C VHS.** *PGV, MVD*

Woof! 🦴🦴½ **1990** Follows the misadventures of a boy who metamorphosed into a dog. **82m/C VHS.** ***D:*** David Cobham. *FHE, UND, BTV*

The Word 🦴🦴½ **1978** Intriguing premise has an archeologist finding a perviously unknown text purporting to be written by the younger brother of Jesus. If authentic and publicized, it would wreak theological havoc. Janssen is off to Italy to check up; he finds murder and skullduggery. Well-acted, interesting story. **300m/C VHS, Beta, LV.** David Janssen, James Whitmore, Florinda Bolkan, Eddie Albert, Geraldine Chaplin, Hurd Hatfield, John Huston, Kate Mulgrew, Janice Rule, Nicol Williamson; ***D:*** Richard Lang; ***M:*** Alex North. *FRH*

Words and Music ♂♂½ **1948** Plot based on the careers of Rodgers and Hart is little more than a peg on which to hang lots of classic songs, sung by a parade of MGM stars. Also includes Kelly's dance recreation of "Slaughter on Tenth Avenue." Good advice: if no one's singing or dancing, fast forward. **122m/C VHS, Beta.** Mickey Rooney, Tom Drake, Judy Garland, Gene Kelly, Lena Horne, Mel Torme, Cyd Charisse, Marshall Thompson, Janet Leigh, Betty Garrett, June Allyson, Perry Como, Vera-Ellen, Ann Sothern; ***D:*** Norman Taurog; ***M:*** Richard Rodgers, Lorenz Hart. *MGM*

Words by Heart **1984** An African American family in turn of the century Missouri faces issues of discrimination and prejudice. Twelve-year-old Lena wins a speech contest and begins to question their place in the community and their aspirations for a better life. Based on a book by Ouida Sebestyen. Aired by PBS as part of the "Wonderworks" family movie series. **116m/C VHS.** Charlotte Rae, Robert Hooks, Alfre Woodard; ***D:*** Robert Thompson. *PME, FCT, HMV*

Work/Police ♂♂♂½ **1916** Two Chaplin two-reelers. In "Work (The Paper Hanger)" (1915), a family hires Charlie and cohorts Armstrong and Purviance to re-paper a house. Little did they know! In "Police" (1916), Charlie plays an ex-con released into the cruel world. Unremittingly hilarious. Silent with music score. **54m/B VHS, Beta.** Charlie Chaplin, Billy Armstrong, Charles Insley, Marta Golden, Edna Purviance; ***D:*** Charlie Chaplin. *VYY*

Workin' for Peanuts **1985** A young man who sells beer at a baseball stadium falls in love with the stadium owner's daughter. **52m/C VHS, Beta.** Carl Marotte, Jessica Steer. *NO*

Working Girl ♂♂♂ **1988 (R)** Romantic comedy set in the Big Apple has secretary Griffith working her way to the top in spite of her manipulative boss (Weaver in a powerful parody). Griffith gets her chance to shine when Weaver breaks a leg. She meets Ford for business that turns to romance. A 1980s Cinderella story that's sexy, funny, and sharply written and directed. Nice work by Ford, but this is definitely Griffith's movie. And keep an eye on gal pal Cusack. ♫Let the River Run. **115m/C VHS, Beta, LV.** Melanie Griffith, Harrison Ford, Sigourney Weaver, Joan Cusack, Alec Baldwin, Philip Bosco, Ricki Lake, Nora Dunn, Olympia Dukakis, Oliver Platt, James Lally, Kevin Spacey, Robert Easton; ***D:*** Mike Nichols; ***W:*** Kevin Wade; ***C:*** Michael Ballhaus; ***M:*** Carly Simon, Rob Mounsey. Academy Awards '88: Best Song ("Let the River Run"); Golden Globe Awards '89: Best Actress—Musical/Comedy (Griffith), Best Film—Musical/Comedy, Best Song ("Let the River Run"), Best Supporting Actress (Weaver); Nominations: Academy Awards '88: Best Actress (Griffith), Best Director (Nichols), Best Picture, Best Supporting Actress (Cusack, Weaver). *FOX*

Working Girls ♂ **1975 (R)** Three girls who share an apartment in Los Angeles are willing to do anything for money. And they do. For lack of anything else to recommend, watch for the striptease by Peterson, better known as Elvira on TV. **80m/C VHS, Beta.** Sarah Kennedy, Laurie Rose, Mark Thomas, Cassandra Peterson; ***D:*** Stephanie Rothman. *VCI*

Working Girls ♂♂♂ **1987** An acclaimed, controversial look by independent filmmaker Borden into lives of modern brothel prostitutes over the period of one day. The sex is realistically candid and perfunctory; the docudrama centers on a prostitute who is a Yale graduate and aspiring photographer living with a female lover. Compelling, touching, and lasting, with sexually candid language and scenery. **93m/C VHS, Beta.** Amanda Goodwin, Louise Smith, Ellen McElduff, Maurisia Zach, Janne Peters, Helen Nicholas; ***D:*** Lizzie Borden; ***W:*** Lizzie Borden, Sandra Kay; ***M:*** David Van Tiegham. *COL, NLC, HHE*

Working Winnie/Oh So Simple **1922** Two rare, second-echelon short silent comedies. **61m/B VHS, Beta, 8mm.** Ethlyn Gibson, Bobby Ray. *VYY*

The World According to Garp ♂♂♂ **1982 (R)** Comedy turns to tragedy in this relatively faithful version of John Irving's popular (and highly symbolic) novel, adapted by Steve Tesich. Chronicles the life of T.S. Garp, a struggling everyman beset by the destructive forces of modern society. Nevertheless, Garp maintains his optimism even as his life unravels around him. At the core of the film is a subplot involving a group of extreme feminists inspired in part by Garp's mother, the author of "A Sexual Suspect." Close and Lithgow (as a giant transsexual) are spectacular, while Williams is low-key and tender as the beleagured Garp. Ultimately pointless, perhaps, but effectively and intelligently so. **136m/C VHS, Beta, LV.** Robin Williams, Mary Beth Hurt, John Lithgow, Glenn Close, Hume Cronyn, Jessica Tandy, Swoosie Kurtz, Amanda Plummer, Warren Berlinger, Brandon Maggart; ***Cameos:*** George Roy Hill; ***D:*** George Roy Hill; ***W:*** Steve Tesich; ***M:*** David Shire. Los Angeles Film Critics Association Awards '82: Best Supporting Actor (Lithgow), Best Supporting Actress (Close); New York Film Critics Awards '82: Best Supporting Actor (Lithgow); Nominations: Academy Awards '82: Best Supporting Actor (Lithgow), Best Supporting Actress (Close). *WAR*

The World Accuses ♂½ **1935** A woman takes a job in a nursery, unaware that one child is her own, put up for adoption after her wealthy husband died. Then, her ex-lover shows up in her attic after escaping from prison and takes her hostage. Whew! Everything works out, except that the viewer is left confused and incredulous. **62m/B VHS.** Vivian Tobin, Dickie Moore, Russell Hopton, Cora Sue Collins, Mary Carr; ***D:*** Charles Lamont. *NOS, DVT*

A World Apart ♂♂♂½ **1988 (PG)** Cinematographer Menges' first directoral effort is a blistering, insightful drama told from the point of view of a 13-year-old white girl living in South Africa, oblivious to apartheid until her crusading journalist mother is arrested under the 90-Day Detention Act, under which she might remain in prison permanently. Political morality tale is also a look at the family-vs-cause choices activists must make. Heavily lauded, with good reason; the autobiographical script is based on Slovo's parents, persecuted South African journalists Joe Slovo and Ruth First. **114m/C VHS, Beta, LV.** *GB* Barbara Hershey, Jodhi May, Linda Mvusi, David Suchet, Jeroen Krabbe, Paul Freeman, Tim Roth; ***D:*** Chris Menges; ***W:*** Shawn Slovo; ***M:*** Hans Zimmer. British Academy Awards '88: Best Original Screenplay; Cannes Film Festival '88: Best Actress (Hershey), Best Actress (May, Mvusi), Grand Jury Prize; New York Film Critics Awards '88: Best Director (Menges). *MED*

The World Gone Mad ♂♂½ *The Public Be Hanged; Public Be Damned* **1933** During Prohibition, a tough reporter discovers the district attorney is the intended victim of a murder plot involving crooked Wall Street types. Full circle: this interesting drama of white-collar crime is again topical, though dialogue heavy and desultory. **70m/B VHS, Beta.** Pat O'Brien, Louis Calhern, J. Carrol Naish; ***D:*** Christy Cabanne. *NOS, CAB, DVT*

World Gone Wild ♂½ **1988 (R)** Action yarn about a post-apocalyptic world of the future where an evil cult leader brainwashes his disciples. Together they battle a small band of eccentrics for the world's last water source. Stale rehash (with ineffective satiric elements) of the Mad Max genre, served with Ant for campy appeal. **95m/C VHS, Beta, LV.** Bruce Dern, Michael Pare, Adam Ant, Catherine Mary Stewart, Rick Podell; ***D:*** Lee H. Katzin. *MED, VTR*

The World is Full of Married Men *Woof!* **1980 (R)** A philandering ad exec gets involved with a reckless model, inspiring his fed-up wife also to look for extramarital sex. Promiscuously raunchy melodrama was written by the queen of sleaze, Jackie Collins, based on her novel. **106m/C VHS, Beta.** *GB* Anthony (Tony) Franciosa, Carroll Baker, Sherrie Croon, Gareth Hunt, Paul Nicholas; ***D:*** Robert W. Young; ***W:*** Jackie Collins. *FOX*

The World of Abbott & Costello **1964** Compilation of the duo's most famous routines from their 18 films, including the frog in the soup sketch from "The Wistful Widow of Wagon Gap," the cobra skit from "Abbott & Costello Meet the Mummy," and their legendary baseball routine "Who's on First?" from "The Naughty Nineties." **75m/B VHS.** Bud Abbott, Lou Costello. *MCA*

The World of Apu ♂♂♂♂ *Apu Sansat; Apur Sansar* **1959** Finale of director Ray's acclaimed Apu trilogy (following "Pather Panchali" and "Aparajito"). Aspiring writer Apu drops out of the university for want of money and takes up with an old chum. An odd circumstance leads him to marry his friend's cousin, whom he comes to love. She dies in childbirth (though her baby boy lives); Apu is deeply distraught, destroys the novel he was working on, and becomes a wanderer. His friend finds him five years later and helps him begin again with his young son. Wonderfully human, hopeful story told by a world-class director. From the novel "Aparajito" by B. Bandopadhaya. In Bengali with English subtitles. **103m/B VHS, Beta.** *IN* Soumitra Chatterjee, Sharmila Tagore, Alok Charkravarty, Swapan Makerji; ***D:*** Satyajit Ray; ***W:*** Satyajit Ray; ***M:*** Ravi Shankar. National Board of Review Awards '60: 5 Best Foreign Films of the Year. *HHT, VYY, DVT*

The World of Henry Orient ♂♂♂½ **1964** Charming, eccentric comedy about two 15-year-old girls who, madly in love with an egotistical concert pianist, pursue him all around New York City. Sellers is hilarious, Walker and Spaeth are adorable as his teen groupies; Bosley and Lansbury are great as Walker's indulgent parents. For anyone who has ever been uncontrollably infatuated. Screenplay by the father/daughter team, Nora and Nunnally Johnson, based on Nora Johnson's novel. **106m/C VHS, Beta, LV.** Peter Sellers, Tippy Walker, Merrie Spaeth, Tom Bosley, Angela Lansbury, Paula Prentiss; ***D:*** George Roy Hill; ***W:*** Nunnally Johnson, Nora Johnson; ***C:*** Boris Kaufman; ***M:*** Elmer Bernstein. National Board of Review Awards '64: 10 Best Films of the Year. *MGM, FCT*

A World of Strangers ♂♂♂ **1962** A harsh look at apartheid through the eyes of an Englishman who has traveled to South Africa to manage a publishing house. Filmed in strict secrecy in Johannesburg due to the film's aggressive condemnation of the practice. Based on a novel by Nadine Gordimer. **89m/B VHS.** *DK* Ivan Jackson, Zakes Mokae; ***D:*** Henning Carlsen. *CVC, INJ*

The World of Suzie Wong ♂♂ **1960** Asian prostitute Kwan plays cat-and-mouse with American painter Holden. She lies to him about her profession, her family, and herself. His association with her ruins relationships in his life. Why, then, does he not get a clue? Good question, not answered by this soap opera that would be a serious drama. Offensively sanitized picture of the world of prostitution in an Asian metropolis. On the other hand, it's all nicely shot, much of it on location in Hong Kong. Based on Paul Osborn's play which was taken from Richard Mason's novel. **129m/C VHS, Beta, LV.** *GB* William Holden, Nancy Kwan, Sylvia Syms, Michael Wilding, Laurence Naismith, Jacqueline "Jackie" Chan; ***D:*** Richard Quine; ***C:*** Geoffrey Unsworth. *PAR*

World of the Depraved ♂ **1967** Tango (Storm) runs an exercise club for young lovelies that are systematically being stalked by the mysterious full moon sex killer. Enter police detectives Riley and Hamilton (Decker, Reed), joking types who peep on their charges through keyholes, etc. When the plot finally gets around to the issue of the killer, the point of the movie has already been made clear. Silly, trivial, sophomoric humor lacking a trace of sincerity. Volume 6 of Frank Henenlotter's Sexy Shockers series. **73m/C VHS.** Tempest Storm, Johnnie Decker, Larry Reed; ***D:*** Herbert Jeffries; ***W:*** Herbert Jeffries. *SMW*

The World Owes Me a Living ♂♂ **1947** Melodrama about pilot Farrar losing his memory in a plane crash and Campbell trying to spark his recollection of the past. **91m/B VHS.** *GB* David Farrar,

Judy Campbell, Jack Livesey, John Laurie; **D:** Vernon Sewell; **W:** Vernon Sewell. *LOO*

World War II: When Lions Roared 🦴🦴½ **1994** The "Lions" are Franklin Delano Roosevelt, Winston Churchill, and Joseph Stalin. The three Allied leaders formed an uneasy alliance to crush Hitler and Mussolini, all against much internal treachery. Uses lots of WWII newsreel footage. Made for television; on two cassettes. **186m/C VHS.** John Lithgow, Bob Hoskins, Michael Caine, Ed Begley Jr., Jan Tiska; **D:** Joseph Sargent; **W:** David W. Rintels; **C:** John A. Alonzo. *MPI, PAP*

World War III 🦴🦴½ **1986** How's that for a title? A Russian plot is afoot to seize and destroy the Alaskan pipeline. When the plot is discovered, negotiation is needed to prevent world war. Executive branch showdown ensues between U.S. prez Hudson and Soviet chief Keith. Director Boris Sagal was killed on location, whereupon Greene took over, and shooting was moved indoors with dramatic tension lost in the transition. Made for TV. **186m/C VHS, Beta.** Brian Keith, David Soul, Rock Hudson, Cathy Lee Crosby, Katherine Helmond, Robert Prosky, James Hampton, Richard Yniguez, Herbert Jefferson Jr.; **D:** David Greene; **W:** Robert L. Joseph. *FOX*

The Worldly Madonna 🦴🦴½ **1922** Young plays two roles as Janet, a convent novitiate, and her cabaret dancer sister, Lucy. Lucy thinks she's killed a man and Janet agrees to change places with her. **47m/B VHS.** Clara Kimball Young, Richard Tucker, George Hackathorne, William P. Carleton, Jean De Limur, William Marion, Milla Davenport; **D:** Harry Garson. *GPV, FCT*

The World's Greatest Athlete 🦴🦴 **1973 (G)** Lame Disney comedy about a Tarzan-like jungle-man (Vincent) recruited by an unsuccessful American college coach (Amos) and his bumbling assistant (Conway). Fun special effects, weak script add up to mediocre family fare. Cameo by Howard Cosell as—who else?—himself. **89m/C VHS, Beta.** Jan-Michael Vincent, Tim Conway, John Amos, Roscoe Lee Browne, Dayle Haddon; **Cameos:** Howard Cosell; **D:** Robert Scheerer; **W:** Dee Caruso; **M:** Marvin Hamlisch. *DIS, OM*

World's Greatest Lover 🦴🦴½ **1977 (PG)** Milwaukee baker Rudi Valentine, played oft-hilariously by Wilder, tries to make it big in 1920s Hollywood. He has a screen test as a Hollywood movie sheik, but his wife (Kane) leaves him for the real McCoy. Episodic and uneven, it's alternately uproarious, touching and downright raunchy. **89m/C VHS, LV.** Gene Wilder, Carol Kane, Dom DeLuise, Fritz Feld, Carl Ballantine, Michael Huddleston, Matt Collins, Ronny Graham; **D:** Gene Wilder; **W:** Gene Wilder. *FOX*

The World's Oldest Living Bridesmaid 🦴🦴½ **1992** Hokey romantic comedy about a successful woman attorney who just can't find Mr. Right. Brenda feels even worse when she attends yet another friend's wedding. However, when she hires a younger, male secretary (former model Wimmer) the romantic sparks fly. An appealing and attractive cast helps this made-for-television fare. **100m/C VHS.** Donna Mills, Brian Wimmer, Beverly Garland, Winston Reckert, Art Hindle, Laura Press; **D:** Joseph L. Scanlan. *AIP*

The Worm Eaters *Woof!* **1977 (PG)** Mean developers want to take over a reclusive worm farmer's land. He unleashes his livestock on them. The bad guys turn into—eeck!—"worm people." A truck runs over our hero nearly 75 minutes too late to save the viewer. **75m/C VHS, Beta.** Herb Robins, Barry Hostetler, Lindsay Armstrong Black; **D:** Herb Robins; **W:** Herb Robins. *NO*

The Worst of Faces of Death *Woof!* **1990** Grisly deaths recorded on film by sick Dr. Fllelis. Absolutely gruesome. **60m/C VHS, Beta.** *GRG*

The Worst of Hollywood: Vol. 1 **1990** Two really bad movies for your viewing displeasure. "Maniac" is a mad-scientist fest and "Protect Your Daughter" warns of the perils of the Flapper era. **115m/B VHS, Beta.** Bill Woods, Horace Carpenter, Phyllis Diller; **D:** Dwain Esper. *INC*

The Worst of Hollywood: Vol. 2 **1990** A von Stroheim-fest of mediocrity. In "Fugitive Road" Erich plays an Austrian officer of the First World War. "The Crime of Dr. Crespi" has him portray a mad scientist. **131m/B VHS, Beta.** Erich von Stroheim, Dwight Frye; **D:** Erich von Stroheim. *INC*

The Worst of Hollywood: Vol. 3 **1990** Two more awful, exploitive docudramas. "Nation Aflame" features many silent screen stars who teach the virtues of living in racial harmony. "Probation" boasts the first screen appearance of Grable, as a promiscuous woman who ends up in prison. **140m/B VHS, Beta.** Betty Grable. *INC*

The Worst Witch 🦴🦴½ **1986 (G)** Fantasy about a school for young witches where the educational lessons never go quite as planned. Adapted from the children's book "The Worst Witch" by Jill Murphy. **70m/C VHS, Beta, LV.** Diana Rigg, Charlotte Rae, Tim Curry, Fairuza Balk; **D:** Robert M. Young. *PSM, IME*

Worth Winning 🦴½ **1989 (PG-13)** A notoriously eligible Philadelphia bachelor takes a bet to become engaged to three women within three months, and finds himself in hot water. A critically dead-in-the-water chucklefest. **103m/C VHS, Beta, LV.** Mark Harmon, Lesley Ann Warren, Madeleine Stowe, Maria Holvoe, Mark Blum, Andrea Martin, Alan Blumenfeld, Brad Hall, Tony Longo; **D:** Will MacKenzie; **W:** Sara Parriott, Josann McGibbon. *FOX*

The Would-Be Gentleman 🦴🦴½ **1958** The Comedie Francaise troupe performs Moliere's famous farce-comedy. Valuable as a record of the famous troupe on stage. When they're long gone, our grandkids can enjoy this. We can too (if we can't afford the trip to France), though it's less a film than a filming of a play. In French with English subtitles. **93m/C VHS, Beta.** *FR* Louis Seigner, Jean Meyer, Jean Piat. *DVT, INJ*

Woyzeck 🦴🦴🦴 **1978** Chilling portrayal of a man plunging into insanity. Mired in the ranks of the German Army, Woyzeck is harassed by his superiors and tortured in scientific experiments, gradually devolving into homicidal maniac. Based on Georg Buchner play. In German with English subtitles. **82m/C VHS.** *GE* Klaus Kinski, Eva Mattes, Wolfgang Reichmann, Josef Bierbichler; **D:** Werner Herzog; **W:** Werner Herzog. Nominations: Cannes Film Festival '79: Best Film. *NYF, INJ*

WR: Mysteries of the Organism 🦴🦴🦴 **1971** Makavejev's breakthrough film, a surreal, essayist exploration of the conflict/union between sexuality and politics—namely, Wilheim Reich and Stalin. A raunchy, bitterly satiric non-narrative that established the rule-breaking Yugoslav internationally. In Serbian with English subtitles. **84m/C VHS, Beta.** Milena Dravic, Jagoda Kaloper, Tuli Kupferberg, Jackie Curtis; **D:** Dusan Makavejev; **W:** Dusan Makavejev. *FCT*

The Wraith 🦴½ **1987 (PG-13)** Drag-racing Arizona teens find themselves challenged by a mysterious, otherworldly stranger. Hot cars; cool music; little else to recommend it. Lousy script; ludicrous excuse for a premise. Most of the stars herein are related to somebody famous. **92m/C VHS, Beta, LV.** Charlie Sheen, Nick Cassavetes, Sherilyn Fenn, Randy Quaid, Matthew Barry, Clint Howard, Griffin O'Neal; **D:** Mike Marvin. *LIV*

Wrangler 🦴🦴½ **1988** When an Australian rancher dies his daughter tries to hang on to the family ranch from a ruthless creditor. She also has to deal with the attentions of two men—one a businessman and the other a cattleman, both equally dashing and handsome. Beautiful scenery of the Australian Outback as well as romance and adventure. **93m/C VHS, LV.** Jeff Fahey, Tushka Bergen, Steven Vidler, Richard Moir, Shane Briant, Drew Forsythe, Cornelia Frances, Sandy Gore, Frederick Parslow; **D:** Ian Barry; **W:** John Sexton; **M:** Mario Millo. *NO*

The Wreck of the Mary Deare 🦴🦴½ **1959** Slow-moving adventure drama focusing on the wreck of the freighter called the Mary Deare. Heston plays a ship salvager who comes upon a seemingly empty ship one night and Cooper is the only crew member on board. Special effects are the main attraction in this interesting sea drama. Film originally was to be directed by Hitchcock, but he turned down the offer to do "North by Northwest." **105m/C VHS, LV.** *GB* Gary Cooper, Charlton Heston, Michael Redgrave, Emlyn Williams, Cecil Parker, Alexander Knox, Virginia McKenna, Richard Harris; **D:** Michael Anderson Sr. *MGM*

The Wrestler 🦴 **1973** All-star wrestling, which is fictional anyway, gets said treatment in the appropriate way. Honest promoter (yeah, sure) bumps heads with bad-guy crooks who want in on the action. Made-for-TV opportunity for Asner to slum. **103m/C VHS, Beta.** Ed Asner, Elaine Giftos, Verne Gagne, Harold Sakata. *NWV*

Wrestling Ernest Hemingway 🦴🦴 **1993 (PG-13)** A shy barber and a rollicking sea captain, both 75 and retired, form an unlikely companionship in a Florida retirement mecca. Duvall is the persnickety introvert who quietly follows routine and Harris is the would-be ladies' man whose endless tall tales include having tangled with Papa Hemingway in his youth. They share walks in the park, little league baseball from the bleachers, and coffee klatches that reveal the emptiness of their lives. Director Haines' focus on the principals' emotional baggage considerably dampens the proceedings. Depression in the elderly may be a topic that is not quite ready to come out of Hollywood's closet. **123m/C VHS, LV.** Robert Duvall, Richard Harris, Piper Laurie, Shirley MacLaine, Sandra Bullock; **D:** Randa Haines; **W:** Steve Conrad; **C:** Lajos Koltai; **M:** Michael Convertino. *WAR*

Wrestling Racket Girls *Woof!* **1939** An alleged white slavery expose, replete with seamy material that is only slightly laughable by modern terms, reducing overall camp appeal and increasing rating on boredom meter. **72m/B VHS, Beta.** *TPV*

Wrestling Women vs. the Aztec Ape *Woof! Doctor of Doom* **1962** An unclassifiable epic wherein female wrestlers battle a mad doctor and his Aztec robot gorilla. Dubbed badly, of course. Much anticipated follow-up to "Wrestling Women vs. the Aztec Mummy." **75m/C VHS, Beta.** *MX* Elizabeth Campbell, Lorena Velasquez, Armando Silvestre, Roberto Canedo; **D:** Rene Cardona Sr. *RHI, HHT, SNC*

Wrestling Women vs. the Aztec Mummy *Woof!* **1959** Women, broad of shoulder, wrestle an ancient Aztec wrestler who comes to life. Furnished with a new rock soundtrack. **88m/C VHS, Beta.** *MX* Lorena Velasquez, Armando Silvestre; **D:** Rene Cardona Sr. *SNC, RHI, HHT*

Write to Kill 🦴½ **1991 (R)** A young mystery writer seeks revenge when his brother is murdered by a ring of counterfeiters. **120m/C VHS, LV.** Scott Valentine, Chris Mulkey, Joan Severance, G.W. Bailey, Ray Wise; **D:** Ruben Preuss. *COL*

Writer's Block 🦴🦴 **1991 (R)** Fairchild is a successful thriller writer whose latest books feature a serial killer. She decides to kill the character off and is soon stalked by a psycho who is using her plots for some copy-cat killings. Tepid made for cable television movie with San Diego locations the only highlight. **90m/C VHS, Beta.** Morgan Fairchild, Joe Regalbuto, Michael Praed, Cheryl Anderson, Mary Ann Pascal, Douglas Rowe, Ned Bellamy; **D:** Charles Correll; **W:** Elisa Bell. *PAR*

Written on the Wind 🦴🦴🦴½ **1956** Sirk's frenzied, melodrama-as-high-art dissection of both the American Dream and American movies follows a Texas oil family's self-destruction through wealth, greed and unbridled lust. Exaggerated depiction of and comment on American ambition and pretension, adapted from Robert Wilder's novel. **99m/C VHS, Beta.** Lauren Bacall, Rock Hudson, Dorothy Malone, Robert Stack, Robert Keith, Grant Williams, Edward Platt, Harry Shannon; **D:** Douglas Sirk; **W:** George Zuckerman; **C:** Russell Metty. Academy Awards '56: Best Supporting Actress (Malone); Nominations: Academy Awards '56: Best Song ("Written on the Wind"), Best Supporting Actor (Stack). *MCA, BTV*

The Wrong Arm of the Law ☆☆☆ **1963** Loopy gangster yarn about a trio of Aussie gangsters who arrive in London and upset the local crime balance when they dress up as cops and confiscate loot from apprehended robbers. General confusion erupts among the police, the local crooks, and the imposters. Riotous and hilarious, with Sellers leading a host of familiar faces. **94m/B VHS, Beta.** *GB* Peter Sellers, Lionel Jeffries, Nanette Newman, Bernard Cribbins, Dennis Price; ***D:*** Cliff Owen; ***M:*** Richard Rodney Bennett. *MON*

The Wrong Box ☆☆☆ **1966** Two elderly Victorian brothers try to kill each other so that one of them may collect the large inheritance left to them. Based on a Robert Louis Stevenson novel. Well-cast black comedy replete with sight gags, many of which flop. **105m/C VHS, Beta.** *GB* Peter Sellers, Dudley Moore, Peter Cook, Michael Caine, Ralph Richardson, John Mills; ***D:*** Bryan Forbes; ***W:*** Larry Gelbart; ***M:*** John Barry. *COL*

The Wrong Guys ☆ **1988 (PG)** Five giants of stand-up comedy star as a group of men who reunite their old boy scout pack and go camping. A crazed convict mistakes them for FBI agents. It's supposed to get zany after that, but succeeds only in being clumsy and embarassing. **86m/C VHS, Beta, LV.** Richard Lewis, Richard Belzer, Louie Anderson, Tim Thomerson, Franklin Ajaye, John Goodman, Ernie Hudson, Timothy Van Patten; ***D:*** Danny Bilson; ***W:*** Danny Bilson, Paul DeMeo. *VTR, NWV*

Wrong is Right ☆☆ *The Man With The Deadly Lens* **1982 (R)** A black action comedy about international terrorism, news reporting and the CIA. Connery is terrific, as usual, as a TV reporter in a head-scratching attempt at satire of our TV-influenced society. **117m/C VHS, Beta, LV.** Sean Connery, Katharine Ross, Robert Conrad, George Grizzard, Henry Silva, G.D. Spradlin, John Saxon, Leslie Nielsen, Robert Webber, Rosalind Cash, Hardy Kruger, Dean Stockwell, Ron Moody, Jennifer Jason Leigh; ***D:*** Richard Brooks; ***W:*** Richard Brooks; ***C:*** Fred W. Koenekamp. *COL*

The Wrong Man ☆☆☆½ **1956** Nightclub musician Fonda is falsely accused of a robbery and his life is destroyed. Taken almost entirely from the real-life case of mild-mannered bass player "Manny" Balestrero; probes his anguish at being wrongly accused; and showcases Miles (later to appear in "Psycho") and her character's agony. Harrowing, especially following more lighthearted Hitchcock fare such as "The Trouble with Harry." Part of the "A Night at the Movies" series, this tape simulates a 1956 movie evening with a color Bugs Bunny cartoon, "A Star Is Bored," a newsreel and coming attractions for "Toward the Unknown." **126m/B VHS, Beta, LV.** Henry Fonda, Vera Miles, Anthony Quayle, Nehemiah Persoff; ***D:*** Alfred Hitchcock; ***C:*** Robert Burks. *WAR, MLB*

The Wrong Man ☆☆½ **1993 (R)** American sailor Alex Walker (Anderson) is framed for the murder of a Mexican smuggler. He eludes the police and winds up hitching a ride from wacko couple Phillip (Lithgow) and Missy Mills (Arquette). Missy does topless table dancing and is very interested in their fugitive passenger. Alex may be better off with the police. Made for cable television. **98m/C VHS, LV.** Kevin Anderson, John Lithgow, Rosanna Arquette, Robert Harper; ***D:*** Jim McBride. *REP*

The Wrong Move ☆☆½ **1978** A loose adaptation of Goethe's "Sorrows of Young Werther" by screenwriter Peter Handke. Justly acclaimed and engrossing, though slow. Kinski's first film. A young poet, searching for life's meaning, wanders aimlessly through Germany. In German with English subtitles. **103m/C VHS, Beta.** *GE* Nastassia Kinski, Hanna Schygulla, Ruediger Vogler, Hans-Christian Blech; ***D:*** Wim Wenders. *FCT, GLV, INJ*

The Wrong Road ☆½ **1937** A young couple embark on a robbery spree, and subsequently end up in prison. On their release, they search for the loot they had previously hidden, but find the man who was holding it for them has died. Will they ever recover their ill-gotten stash? **62m/B VHS, Beta.** Richard Cromwell, Helen Mack, Lionel Atwill, Horace McMahon, Russ Powell, Billy Bevan, Marjorie Main, Rex Evans; ***D:*** James Cruze. *SNC*

The Wrong Woman ☆☆½ **1995 (PG-13)** When Melanie Brooke's (McKeon) boss is murdered, she's framed to take by rap by the company's sleazy comptroller (Field). Melanie begins a desperate hunt for the real culprit with the killer and the cops both after her. **90m/C VHS.** Nancy McKeon, Chelsea Field. *REP*

Wuthering Heights ☆☆☆☆ **1939** The first screen adaptation of Emily Bronte's romantic novel about the doomed love between Heathcliff and Cathy on the Yorkshire moors. This film dynamically captures the madness and ferocity of the classic novel, remaining possibly the greatest romance ever filmed. Excellent performances from Wyler's sure direction, particularly Olivier's, which made him a star, and Oberon in her finest hour as the exquisite but selfish Cathy. Remade twice, in 1953 (by Luis Bunuel) and in 1970. **104m/B VHS, Beta, LV.** Laurence Olivier, Merle Oberon, David Niven, Geraldine Fitzgerald, Flora Robson, Donald Crisp, Cecil Kellaway, Leo G. Carroll, Miles Mander, Hugh Williams; ***D:*** William Wyler; ***W:*** Ben Hecht, Charles MacArthur; ***C:*** Gregg Toland; ***M:*** Alfred Newman. Academy Awards '39: Best Black and White Cinematography; National Board of Review Awards '39: 10 Best Films of the Year; New York Film Critics Awards '39: Best Film; Nominations: Academy Awards '39: Best Actor (Olivier), Best Director (Wyler), Best Interior Decoration, Best Picture, Best Screenplay, Best Supporting Actress (Fitzgerald), Best Original Score. *HBO, SUE, HMV*

Wuthering Heights ☆☆½ *Abismos de Pasion* **1953** Bunuel tackles the Bronte classic during his Mexican period, and comes up with a film containing little passion, but much of the customary Bunuel manic cynicism. The 1939 version is far superior, but fans of Bunuel will probably enjoy this one. Loosely adapted; in Spanish with English subtitles. Remade in another English-language version in 1970. **90m/B VHS, Beta.** *MX* Irasema Dilian, Jorge Mistral, Lilia Prado, Ernesto Alonso; ***D:*** Luis Bunuel. *XVC, MED, APD*

Wuthering Heights ☆☆½ **1970 (G)** The third screening of the classic Emily Bronte romance about two doomed lovers. Fuest's version features excellent photography, and Calder-Marshall's and Dalton's performances are effective, but fail even to approach the intensity and pathos of the 1939 film original (or of the book). Filmed on location in Yorkshire, England. **105m/C VHS, Beta.** *GB* Anna Calder-Marshall, Timothy Dalton, Harry Andrews, Pamela Brown, Judy Cornwell, James Cossins, Rosalie Crutchley, Hilary Dwyer, Hugh Griffith, Ian Ogilvy; ***D:*** Robert Fuest. *CNG, KAR, TVC*

Wyatt Earp ☆☆½ **1994 (PG-13)** Revisionist epic suffers from bad timing as it follows "Tombstone" in telling the story of tarnished badge Earp (Costner), his brothers, and tubercular friend Doc Holliday (Quaid). Costner is barely believable as a twentysomething lad, but fares better as he ages. 40 pounds lighter and likely delusional from lack of food, Quaid is unrecognizable but terrific, hacking his way to supporting Oscar territory. 'Course, Val Kilmer got there first. Huge cast finds screen time precious, even though film is some 40 minutes too long, due to prolonged intro to early Wyatt life. Originally envisioned as a TV miniseries till sheriff Costner took a hankering to bring tall tale to the big screen. Filmed on location in Sante Fe, New Mexico. For the full Earp effect, see it with "Tombstone" and relive the legend. **191m/C VHS, LV.** Kevin Costner, Dennis Quaid, Gene Hackman, Jeff Fahey, Mark Harmon, Michael Madsen, Catherine O'Hara, Bill Pullman, Isabella Rossellini, Tom Sizemore, JoBeth Williams, Mare Winningham, Betty Buckley, Adam Baldwin, Rex Linn, Todd Allen, David Andrews, Linden Ashby, Annabeth Gish, Joanna Going, Martin Kove, Tea Leoni, James Caviezel, Karen Grassle; ***D:*** Lawrence Kasdan; ***W:*** Dan Gordon, Lawrence Kasdan; ***C:*** Owen Roizman; ***M:*** James Newton Howard. Golden Raspberry Awards '94: Worst Remake/Sequel, Worst Actor (Costner); Nominations: Academy Awards '94: Best Cinematography; Golden Raspberry Awards '94: Worst Picture. *WAR*

Wyatt Earp: Return to Tombstone ☆☆½ **1994** O'Brian, who starred in TV's "The Life and Legend of Wyatt Earp" from 1955 to 1961, returns to Tombstone in 1914. Colorized clips from the series are used for flashbacks. Filmed on location in Tombstone, Arizona. **94m/C VHS, LV.** Hugh O'Brian, Bruce Boxleitner, Paul Brinegar, Harry Carey Jr., Bo Hopkins, Martin Kove, Don Meredith, Alex Hyde-White, Jay Underwood. *ORI*

Wyoming Outlaw ☆☆ **1939** Based on an actual incident, the story revolves around a small-town man who kills an outlaw. Barry, in the role that made him a western star, is forced into crime after a corrupt politician extorts money from him in exchange for a job. Lincoln, the screen's first Tarzan, appears in a supporting role. **62m/B VHS.** John Wayne, Ray Corrigan, Raymond Hatton, Donald (Don "Red") Barry, Adele Pearce, Leroy Mason, Charles Middleton, Elmo Lincoln, Jack Ingram, Yakima Canutt, Curly Dresden; ***D:*** George Sherman. *NOS, MLB*

The X-Files: Pilot Episode/Deep Throat **1993** By-the-book FBI agent Dana Scully (Anderson) is first paired with maverick Fox Mulder (Duchovny), who's devoted to the study of unexplained phenomena and works only on cases outside the mainstream. In the pilot episode they investigate the mysterious deaths of Oregon high school students. "Deep Throat" finds Mulder investigating the disappearance of a test pilot—the sixth at the same air force base. Mulder's given encouragement and information from a government contact known only by his code name. Additional episodes available. **90m/C VHS.** David Duchovny, Gillian Anderson, Charles Cioffi, Cliff DeYoung, Zachary Ansley, Jerry Hardin; ***D:*** Robert Mandel, Daniel Sackheim; ***W:*** Chris Carter. *FXV, MOV*

X from Outer Space ☆ **1967 (PG)** A space voyage to Mars brings back a giant rampaging creature. Badly dubbed. **85m/C VHS, Beta.** *JP* Eiji Okada, Peggy Neal, Toshiya Wazaki, Itoko Harada, Shinichi Yanagisawa, Franz Gruber, Keisuke Sonoi, Mike Daning, Torahiko Hamada; ***D:*** Nazui Nihonmatsu. *ORI*

X Marks the Spot ☆☆ **1942** When a police sergeant is killed, his detective son investigates his murder. He's drawn into a crime ring which smuggles rubber (a scarce commodity during WWII). Quick pacing enlivens standard cliches. **55m/B VHS, Beta.** Damian O'Flynn, Helen Parrish, Dick Purcell, Jack LaRue, Neil Hamilton, Robert E. Homans, Anne Jeffreys, Dick Wessel, Vince Barnett; ***D:*** George Sherman. *SNC*

X: The Man with X-Ray Eyes ☆☆☆ *The Man With the X-Ray Eyes; X* **1963** First-rate Corman has Milland gain power to see through solid materials. Predates Little Caesars campaign. **79m/C VHS, Beta, LV.** Ray Milland, Diana Van Der Vlis, Harold J. Stone, John Hoyt, Don Rickles, Dick Miller, Jonathan Haze; ***D:*** Roger Corman; ***W:*** Ray Russell, Robert Dillon; ***C:*** Floyd Crosby; ***M:*** Les Baxter. *WAR*

X, Y & Zee ☆½ *Zee & Co* **1972 (R)** A brassy, harsh version of the menage a trois theme, wherein the vicious wife (Taylor) of a philanderer (Caine) decides to avenge herself by seducing his mistress. An embarrassment for everyone involved. **110m/C VHS, Beta.** Michael Caine, Elizabeth Taylor, Susannah York, Margaret Leighton; ***D:*** Brian G. Hutton; ***W:*** Edna O'Brien; ***C:*** Billy Williams. *COL*

Xanadu *Woof!* **1980 (PG)** Dorky star-vehicle remake (of 1947's "Down to Earth") eminently of its era, which is now better forgotten. Newton-John is a muse who descends to Earth to help two friends open a roller disco. In the process she proves that as an actor, she's a singer. Kelly attempts to soft shoe some grace into the proceedings, though he seems mystified as anyone as to why he's in the movie. Don Bluth adds an animated sequence. ♫I'm Alive; The Fall; Don't Walk Away; All Over the World; Xanadu; Magic; Suddenly; Dancing; Suspended in Time. **96m/C VHS, Beta, LV.** Olivia Newton-John, Michael Beck, Gene Kelly, Sandahl Bergman; ***D:*** Robert Greenwald; ***W:*** Richard Danus. Golden Raspberry Awards '80: Best Director (Greenwald). *MCA*

Xica **1976** A diamond rush in 18th century Brazil transformed that country's interior into a place of undreamed wealth and excess. Black slave Xica uses her sexual allure to rise out of poverty and capture the attentions of Joao, the governor of the diamond-mining town. She gleefully wields her increasing wealth and power, becoming the unofficial Empress of Brazil. Reportedly based on a real-life character. In Portuguese with English subtitles. **109m/C VHS.** *BR* Zeze Motta, Walmor Chagas, Altair Lima, Jose Wilker, Marcus Vinicius, Elke Maravilha; ***D:*** Carlos Diegues; ***W:*** Joao Felicio. *NYF, BTV, FCT*

Xtro *Woof!* **1983 (R)** An Englishman, abducted by aliens three years before, returns to his family with a deadly, transforming disease. Slime-bucket splatter flick notable for the scene where a woman gives birth to a full-grown man, and various sex slashings. **80m/C VHS, Beta, LV.** *GB* Philip Sayer, Bernice Stegers, Danny Brainin, Simon Nash, Maryam D'Abo, David Cardy, Anna Wing, Peter Mandell, Robert Fyfe; ***D:*** Harry Bromley Davenport. *NLC*

Xtro 2: The Second Encounter **1991 (R)** Research facility conducts an experiment to transfer people to a parallel dimension. Out of the three researchers sent to the other side, only one returns, unconscious. Turns out that he is playing host to a biohazardous creature brought over from the other dimension who escapes into the air shafts and threatens to kill everyone in the building. One more problem: if the creature isn't killed, the computer system will fill the building with radiation. Sound familiar? It should, because this is a low-budget remake of "Alien." Good photography, adequate acting, but Vincent just isn't credible as a brilliant scientist. A sequel to "Xtro" in name only. **92m/C VHS, LV.** *CA* Jan-Michael Vincent, Paul Koslo, Tara Buckman, Jano Frandsen, Nicholas Lea, W.F. Wadden, Rolf Reynolds, Nic Amoroso, Tracy Westerholm; ***D:*** Harry Bromley Davenport. *NLC*

Xtro 3: Watch the Skies **1995 (R)** Military unit arrives at a remote island where the government has covered up a UFO landing. However, the island is now inhabited by a pissed-off alien whose mate has been killed. **90m/C VHS, LV.** Sal Landi, Jim Hanks, Robert Culp, Andrew Divoff, Karen Moncrieff; ***D:*** Harry Bromley Davenport. *TRI*

The Yakuza ½ *Brotherhood of the Yakuza* **1975 (R)** An ex G.I. (Mitchum) returns to Japan to help an old army buddy find his kidnapped daughter. He learns the daughter has been kidnapped by the Japanese version of the Mafia (the Yakuza) and he must call on old acquaintances to help free her. A westernized oriental gangster drama with a nice blend of buddy moments, action, ancient ritual, and modern Japanese locations. **112m/C VHS, Beta, LV.** Robert Mitchum, Richard Jordan, Ken Takakura, Brian Keith, Herb Edelman; ***D:*** Sydney Pollack; ***W:*** Paul Schrader, Leonard Schrader, Robert Towne; ***M:*** Dave Grusin. *WAR*

Yanco **1964** A young Mexican boy makes visits to an island where he plays his homemade violin. Unfortunately, no one can understand or tolerate his love for music, save for an elderly violinist, who gives him lessons on an instrument known as "Yanco." No dialogue. Not exactly riveting, but sensitively played. **95m/B VHS, Beta.** *MX* Ricardo Ancona, Jesus Medina, Maria Bustamante. *WFV, DVT, INJ*

A Yank in Australia **1943** Australian farce/war mystery/romance/documentary tells the story of two WWII newspaper reporters whose ship gets torpedoed, stranding them in the Australian outback, where they manage to foil a Japanese invasion. **56m/B VHS, Beta, 8mm.** *AU VYY*

Yank in Libya ½ **1942** No, not the American bombing raid of Khadafy, rather a low-budget WWII adventure pitting an American man and an English girl against Libyan Arabs and Nazis. **65m/B VHS, Beta.** Walter Woolf King, Joan Woodbury, H.B. Warner, Parkyakarkus. *VCI*

A Yank in the R.A.F. ½ **1941** Power's enthusiastic performance as a brash American pilot boosts this dated WWII adventure. He and his British allies seem more concerned over who gets showgirl Betty Grable than in the Nazis, but climactic air attacks retain excitement. Produced by Darryl F. Zanuck to drum up American support for embattled Britain and France. **98m/B VHS, Beta.** Tyrone Power, Betty Grable, John Sutton, Reginald Gardiner; ***D:*** Henry King. *FOX, FCT*

Yankee Clipper ½ **1927** Deceit, treachery, and romance are combined in this depiction of a fierce race from China to New England between the American ship Yankee Clipper, and the English ship Lord of the Isles. Silent. **68m/B VHS, Beta.** William Boyd, Elinor Fair, Frank "Junior" Coghlan, John Miljan, Walter Long; ***D:*** Rupert Julian. *GPV, VYY, CCB*

Yankee Doodle Dandy **1942** Nostalgic view of the Golden Era of show business and the man who made it glitter—George M. Cohan. His early days, triumphs, songs, musicals and romances are brought to life by the inexhaustible Cagney in a rare and wonderful song-and-dance performance. Told in flashback, covering the Irishman's struggling days as a young song writer and performer to his salad days as the toast of Broadway. Cagney, never more charismatic, dances up a storm, reportedly inventing most of the steps on the spot. ♫Give My Regards to Broadway; Yankee Doodle Dandy; You're a Grand Old Flag; Over There; I Was Born in Virginia; Off the Record; You're a Wonderful Girl; Blue Skies, Grey Skies; Oh You Wonderful Girl. **126m/B VHS, Beta, LV.** James Cagney, Joan Leslie, Walter Huston, Richard Whorf, Irene Manning, Rosemary DeCamp, Jeanne Cagney, S.Z. Sakall, Walter Catlett, Frances Langford, Eddie Foy Jr., George Tobias, Michael Curtiz; ***D:*** Michael Curtiz; ***W:*** Robert Buckner; ***C:*** James Wong Howe. Academy Awards '42: Best Actor (Cagney), Best Sound, Best Score; New York Film Critics Awards '42: Best Actor (Cagney); Nominations: Academy Awards '42: Best Director (Curtiz), Best Picture, Best Story, Best Supporting Actor (Huston). *MGM, FOX, FCT*

Yankee Doodle in Berlin ½ **1919** A spoof of WWI dramas, with the hero dressing up as a woman and seducing the Kaiser into giving up his war plans. Typical Sennett slapstick with a music and effects score added to the silent film. **60m/B VHS, Beta.** Ford Sterling, Ben Turpin, Marie Prevost, Bothwell Browne. *GPV, CCB*

Yankee Zulu **1995 (PG)** A young black boy, Zulu, and a young white boy, Rhino, begin a friendship in their South African homeland that is torn apart by apartheid. Twenty-five years later, they are reunited by chance and forced into race-reversal roles that lead to a number of comedic disasters and a renewal of their boyhood friendship. **89m/C VHS.** *SA* Leon Schuster, John Matshikiza, Wilson Dunster, Terri Treas; ***D:*** Gray Hofmeyr; ***W:*** Leon Schuster, Gray Hofmeyr. *COL*

Yanks **1979** An epic-scale but uneventful drama depicts the legions of American soldiers billeted in England during WWII, and their impact—mostly sexual—on the staid Britons. No big story, no big deal, despite a meticulous recreation of the era. **139m/C VHS, LV.** Richard Gere, Vanessa Redgrave, William Devane, Lisa Eichhorn, Rachel Roberts, Chick Vennera, Arlen Dean Snyder, Annie Ross; ***D:*** John Schlesinger; ***W:*** Colin Welland, Walter Bernstein; ***M:*** Richard Rodney Bennett. British Academy Awards '79: Best Supporting Actress (Roberts); National Board of Review Awards '79: Best Director (Schlesinger). *MCA*

A Year in Provence **1989** Retired London executive Peter Mayle and his wife Annie decide to leave England to live in the south of France. They buy a 200-year-old farmhouse and experience all the trials and amusements of forging a new life in a different country, complete with different language and customs. They hoped for tranquility and what they got were eccentric neighbors, endless renovations, lots of company, and a taste for good food and drink. Based on Mayle's autobiographical novels "A Year in Provence" and "Tonjours Provence" and filmed on location. Made for British television. On four cassettes, each depicting one season of the year. **360m/C VHS.** *GB* John Thaw, Lindsay Duncan, Bernard Spiegel, Jean-Pierre Delage, Maryse Kuster, Louis Lyonnet; ***D:*** David Tucker; ***W:*** Michael Sadler. *AAE, SIG, BTV*

The Year My Voice Broke **1987 (PG-13)** Above average adolescent drama: a girl breaks a boy's heart by getting pregnant by a tougher, older boy; then leaves town. Blues-inducing, explicit, and not pleasant; but good acting from newcomers carries the day. Followed by "Flirting." **103m/C VHS, Beta, LV.** *AU* Noah Taylor, Leone Carmen, Ben Mendelsohn, Graeme Blundell, Lynette Curran, Malcolm Robertson, Judi Farr; ***D:*** John Duigan; ***W:*** John Duigan; ***M:*** Christine Woodruff. Australian Film Institute '87: Best Film. *LIV*

The Year of Living Dangerously ½ **1982 (PG)** Political thriller features Gibson as an Australian journalist covering a political story in Indonesia, circa 1965. During the coup against President Sukarno, he becomes involved with a British attache (Weaver) at the height of the bloody fighting and rioting in Jakarta. Hunt is excellent as male photographer Billy Swan, central to the action as the moral center. Rumored to be based on the activities of CNN's Peter Arnett, although the original source is a novel by C.J. Koch, who reportedly collaborated/battled with Weir on the screenplay. Fascinating, suspenseful film, set up brilliantly by Weir. Shot on location in the Philippines (then moved to Sydney after cast and crew were threatened). First Australian movie financed by a U.S. studio. **114m/C VHS, Beta, LV.** *AU* Mel Gibson, Sigourney Weaver, Linda Hunt, Michael Murphy; ***D:*** Peter Weir; ***W:*** Peter Weir, David Williamson; ***C:*** John Seale; ***M:*** Maurice Jarre. Academy Awards '83: Best Supporting Actress (Hunt); Los Angeles Film Critics Association Awards '83: Best Supporting Actress (Hunt); National Board of Review Awards '83: Best Supporting Actress (Hunt); New York Film Critics Awards '83: Best Supporting Actress (Hunt); Nominations: Cannes Film Festival '83: Best Film. *MGM, BTV*

Year of the Comet **1992 (PG-13)** Amusing adventure/romantic comedy throws straightlaced Maggie (Miller) together with carefree Oliver (Daly) in a quest for a rare bottle of wine. Fine wine is Maggie's passion, and snagging this particular bottle will boost her status in the family business. Oliver is a pretzels and beer kind of guy, but his boss wants this bottle and will pay a lot to get it. Wants to be another "Romancing the Stone," but plot and characters are too thin. Nice chemistry between Miller and Daly sort of saves this one despite a disappointing script. Beautiful location shots of Scotland. **135m/C VHS, LV.** Penelope Ann Miller, Timothy Daly, Louis Jourdan, Art Malik, Ian Richardson, Ian McNeice, Timothy Bentinck, Julia McCarthy, Jacques Mathou; ***D:*** Peter Yates; ***W:*** William Goldman; ***M:*** Hummie Mann. *NLC*

Year of the Dragon ½ **1985 (R)** Polish police Captain Stanley White of the NYPD vows to neutralize the crime lords running New York's Chinatown. Brilliant cinematography, well-done action scenes with maximum violence, a racist hero you don't want to root for, murky script, and semi-effective direction are the highlights of this tour through the black market's underbelly and hierarchy. Based on Robert Daley's novel. **136m/C VHS, Beta, LV.** Mickey Rourke, John Lone, Ariane, Leonard Termo, Raymond J. Barry; ***D:*** Michael Cimino; ***W:*** Oliver Stone, Michael Cimino. *MGM*

Year of the Gun ½ **1991 (R)** McCarthy is an American journalist in Rome who begins a novel based on the political instability around him, using the names of real people in his first draft. Soon, ambitious photojournalist Stone wants to collaborate with him, and the Red Brigade terrorist group wants to "remove" anyone associated with the book. Although failing on occassion to balance the thin line it establishes between reality and perception, "Gun" aspires to powerful drama, offering a realistic look at the lives and priorities of political terrorists. Love scenes between Stone and McCarthy are torrid. **111m/C VHS, LV, 8mm.** Andrew McCarthy, Sharon Stone, Valeria Golino, John Pankow, Mattia Sbragia, George Murcell; ***D:*** John Frankenheimer; ***W:*** David Ambrose, Jay Presson Allen; ***M:*** Bill Conti. *COL*

Year of the Quiet Sun ♪♪♪½ **1984 (PG)** A poignant, acclaimed love story about a Polish widow and an American soldier who find each other in the war-torn landscape of 1946 Europe. Beautifully rendered, with a confident sense of time and place, making this much more than a simple love story. In Polish with English subtitles. **106m/C VHS, Beta, LV.** *PL GE* Scott Wilson, Maja Komorowska; ***D:*** Krzysztof Zanussi. Venice Film Festival '84: Best Film. *BAR, WAR, INJ*

The Yearling ♪♪♪½ **1946** This family classic is a tear-jerking adaptation of the Marjorie Kinnan Rawlings novel about a young boy's love for a yearling fawn during the post civil-war era. His father's encouragement and his mother's bitterness play against the story of unqualified love amid poverty and the boy's coming of age. Wonderful footage of Florida. Jarman was awarded a special Oscar as outstanding child actor. **128m/C VHS, Beta, LV.** Gregory Peck, Jane Wyman, Claude Jarman Jr., Chill Wills, Henry Travers, Jeff York, Forrest Tucker, June Lockhart, Margaret Wycherly; ***D:*** Clarence Brown; ***C:*** Charles Rosher. Academy Awards '46: Best Color Cinematography, Best Interior Decoration; Golden Globe Awards '47: Best Actor—Drama (Peck); Nominations: Academy Awards '46: Best Actor (Peck), Best Actress (Wyman), Best Director (Brown), Best Film Editing, Best Picture. *KUI, MGM, TLF*

The Yearling ♪♪½ **1994** TV remake of the classic Marjorie Kinnan Rawlings novel about a boy and his orphaned fawn. The Baxters are struggling in '30s Florida: Pa Penny (Strauss) is a hardscrabble farmer and severe Ma Ora (Smart) has lost three of her four children. Surviving son, 12-year-old Jody (Horneff), gets more than his share of life's hard lessons—with even his adored pet causing problems. On the cloying side, the 1946 big-screen version is still the one to watch. Filmed in South Carolina. **98m/C VHS.** Peter Strauss, Jean Smart, Wil Horneff, Brad Greenquist, Jarred Blanchard, Philip S. Hoffman, Nancy Moore Atchison; ***D:*** Rod Hardy; ***W:*** Joe Wiesenfeld; ***M:*** Lee Holdridge. *CAF*

The Yellow Cab Man ♪♪½ **1950** Skelton plays a cab driver who is also an inventor of safety gadgets. When he invents unbreakable elastic glass he finds various crooks after him for the formula. Skelton's wacky inventions are amusing and the movie culminates in a breakneck chase through a home show exposition. **85m/B VHS.** Red Skelton, Gloria De Haven, Walter Slezak, Edward Arnold, James Gleason, Jay C. Flippen, Paul Harvey; ***D:*** Jack Donohue. *MGM*

Yellow Cargo ♪♪ **1936** Ingenious "B" movie about a pair of undercover agents who blow the lid off a smuggling scam. It seems that the smugglers have been masquerading as a movie crew, and use disguised Chinese "extras" to transport their goods. The agents pose as actors to infiltrate the gang. **70m/B VHS, Beta.** Conrad Nagel, Eleanor Hunt, Vince Barnett, Jack LaRue, Claudia Dell; ***D:*** Crane Wilbur; ***W:*** Crane Wilbur. *SNC, DVT*

Yellow Dust ♪½ **1936** Dull story of a gold miner (Dix) who hits a big strike but before he can make good on it he's accused of a series of stagecoach robberies. So he goes undercover to clear his name. Based on the play "Mother Lode" by Dan Totheroh and George O'Neil. **68m/B VHS.** Richard Dix, Leila Hyams, Andy Clyde, Onslow Stevens, Moroni Olsen, Jessie Ralph; ***D:*** Wallace Fox. *GPV*

Yellow Earth ♪♪½ *Huang Tudi* **1989** In 1939 a soldier arrives in a small Chinese village to research folk songs. He becomes involved in the lives of a local peasant family, including a 14-year-old girl who wishes to escape from a pre-arranged marriage. Mixture of poetry, dance, music, and drama set against the barren landscape of the title. In Mandarin Chinese with English subtitles. **89m/C VHS.** *CH* Xue Bai, Wang Xueqi, Tan Tuo, Liu Qiang; ***D:*** Chen Kaige; ***W:*** Zhang Ziliang. *FXL, FCT, BTV*

Yellow Hair & the Fortress of Gold ♪½ *Yellow Hair and the Pecos Kid* **1984 (R)** Princess who's part Indian and her sidekick fight bad guys and seek gold. Well-meaning, self-conscious parody. **102m/C VHS, Beta.** *SP* Laurene Landon, Ken Robertson; ***D:*** Matt Cimber; ***W:*** Matt Cimber. *LIV*

The Yellow Rose of Texas ♪♪ **1944** Rogers works as an undercover insurance agent (he's singing on a river boat) to clear the name of an old man falsely accused of a stagecoach robbery. The usual melodious Rogers lead. **55m/B VHS, Beta.** Roy Rogers, Dale Evans, Grant Withers, Harry Shannon; ***D:*** Joseph Kane. *NOS, VCN, CAB*

Yellow Submarine ♪♪♪½ **1968 (G)** The acclaimed animated fantasy based on a plethora of mid-career Beatles songs, sees the Fab Four battle the Blue Meanies for the sake of Sgt. Pepper, the Nowhere Man, Strawberry Fields, and Pepperland. The first full-length British animated feature in 14 years features a host of talented cartoonists. Fascinating LSD-esque animation and imagery. Speaking voices provided by John Clive (John), Geoff Hughes (Paul), Peter Batten (George), and Paul Angelis (Ringo). The Beatles themselves do appear in a short scene at the end of the film. Martin fills in as music director, and Segal of "Love Story" fame co-scripts. ♫Yellow Submarine; All You Need is Love; Hey, Bulldog; When I'm Sixty Four; Nowhere Man; Lucy in the Sky With Diamonds; Sgt. Pepper's Lonely Hearts Club Band; A Day in the Life; All Together Now. **87m/C VHS, Beta, LV.** *GB* ***D:*** George Duning, Dick Emery; ***W:*** Erich Segal; ***M:*** George Martin. *MVD, MGM, WTA*

Yellowbeard ♪♪ **1983 (PG)** An alleged comedy with a great cast who wander about with little direction. Follows the efforts of an infamous pirate (Chapman) to locate a buried treasure using the map tattooed on the back of his son's head. Final role for Feldman, who died during production. **97m/C VHS, Beta, LV.** Graham Chapman, Peter Boyle, Richard "Cheech" Marin, Thomas Chong, Peter Cook, Marty Feldman, Martin Hewitt, Michael Hordern, Eric Idle, Madeline Kahn, James Mason, John Cleese, Susannah York, David Bowie; ***D:*** Mel Damski; ***W:*** Graham Chapman, Peter Cook, Bernard McKenna. *VES*

Yellowneck ♪♪ **1955** A handful of Confederate Army soldiers desert, hoping to cross the Florida Everglades and eventually reach Cuba. The swamp takes its toll, however, and one by one the men fall by the wayside. A sole survivor reaches the coast. Will the escape boat be waiting for him? **83m/C VHS.** Lin McCarthy, Stephen Courtleigh, Berry Kroeger, Harold Gordon, Bill Mason; ***D:*** R. John Hugh. *FCT*

Yellowstone ♪♪ **1936** An ex-con is murdered at Yellowstone National Park, at the site of a hidden cache of money, of which assorted folks are in search. Uncomplicated, well-meaning mystery. **65m/B VHS, Beta, 8mm.** Andy Devine, Ralph Morgan, Judith Barrett; ***D:*** Arthur Lubin. *NOS, DVT, VYY*

Yentl ♪♪½ **1983 (PG)** The famous Barbra adaptation of Isaac Bashevis Singer's story set in 1900s Eastern Europe about a Jewish girl who masquerades as a boy in order to study the Talmud, and who becomes enmeshed in romantic miscues. Lushly photographed, with a repetitive score that nevertheless won an Oscar. Singer was reportedly appalled by the results of Streisand's hyper-controlled project. ♫A Piece of Sky; No Matter What Happens; This Is One of Those Moments; Tomorrow Night; Where Is It Written; No Wonder; The Way He Makes Me Feel; Papa, Can You Hear Me; Will Someone Ever Look at Me That Way?. **134m/C VHS, Beta, LV.** Barbra Streisand, Mandy Patinkin, Amy Irving, Nehemiah Persoff, Steven Hill, Allan Corduner, Ruth Goring, David DeKeyser, Bernard Spear; ***D:*** Barbra Streisand; ***C:*** David Watkin; ***M:*** Michel Legrand, Alan Bergman, Marilyn Bergman. Academy Awards '83: Best Original Score; Golden Globe Awards '84: Best Director (Streisand), Best Film—Musical/Comedy; Nominations: Academy Awards '83: Best Art Direction/Set Decoration, Best Song ("Papa, Can You Hear Me?", "The Way He Makes Me Feel"), Best Supporting Actress (Irving). *MGM, IME*

Yes, Giorgio ♪♪ **1982 (PG)** Opera singer Pavarotti in his big-screen debut. He has an advantage over other non-actors trapped in similar situations (e.g., Hulk Hogan): He can sing (but of course, not wrestle). Lame plot (famous opera star falls for lady doctor) is the merest excuse for the maestro to belt out "If We Were in Love," "I Left My Heart in San Francisco," and arias by Verdi, Donizetti, and Puccini. **111m/C VHS, Beta, LV.** Luciano Pavarotti, Kathryn Harrold, Eddie Albert, James Hong; ***D:*** Franklin J. Schaffner; ***W:*** Norman Steinberg; ***M:*** John Williams. Nominations: Academy Awards '82: Best Song ("If We Were in Love"). *MGM*

Yes, Sir, Mr. Bones ♪½ **1951** Entertaining but dated musical about a boy who wanders into a rest home and inspires the old folks there to reminisce about their days as riverboat minstrels. ♫I Want to Be a Minstrel Man; Stay Out of the Kitchen; Is Your Rent Paid Up in Heaven?; Flying Saucers; Memphis Bill; Southland. **60m/B VHS, Beta.** Pete Daily, Jimmy O'Brien, Sally Anglim, Cotton Watts, Chick Watts, Chet Davis, F.E. Miller, Scatman Crothers; ***D:*** Ron Ormond; ***W:*** Ron Ormond. *NO*

The Yesterday Machine *Woof!* **1963** Camp sci-fi: A mad doctor tries to bring back Hitler. Don't worry, though: the good guys win. Predictable, dumb drivel. **85m/B VHS, Beta.** Tim Holt, James Britton, Jack Herman; ***D:*** Russ Marker. *SNC, VCD*

Yesterday, Today and Tomorrow ♪♪♪½ *Ieri, Oggi E Domani; She Got What She Asked For* **1964** Trilogy of comic sexual vignettes featuring Loren and her many charms. She plays a black marketeer, a wealthy matron, and a prostitute. Funny, and still rather racy. Loren at her best, in all senses; includes her famous striptease for Mastroianni. **119m/C VHS.** *IT FR* Sophia Loren, Marcello Mastroianni, Tony Pica, Giovanni Ridolfi; ***D:*** Vittorio De Sica. Academy Awards '64: Best Foreign Language Film; British Academy Awards '64: Best Actor (Mastroianni). *JEF, HHE, INJ*

Yesterday's Hero ♪½ **1979** A fading soccer star finds his career and love-life on the upswing. Poor production with equally lame pop music score. **95m/C VHS, Beta.** *GB* Ian McShane, Suzanne Somers, Adam Faith, Paul Nicholas, Glynis Barber, Sandy Ratcliff; ***D:*** Neil Leifer; ***W:*** Jackie Collins. *HHE*

Yidl Mitn Fidl ♪♪ *Yiddle with a Fiddle; Castle in the Sky* **1936** Disguised as a man, a young woman travels about the countryside with a group of musicians, revealing her female identity only after falling for a man. One of Picon's finest roles and Green's biggest successes. Vaudevillian fare in Yiddish with English subtitles. ♫Yiddle With His Fiddle; Arye With His Bass. **92m/B VHS, Beta.** *PL* Molly Picon, Simche Fostel, Max Bozyk, Leon Liebgold; ***D:*** Joseph Green. *ERG, DVT, INJ*

Yin & Yang of Mr. Go ♪ **1971 (R)** A CIA operative must retrieve the stolen plans of an awesome weapons system. Set in Hong Kong, features a strong cast in a tangled tale of no particular merit. Unworthy spoof of Oriental intrigue flicks. **89m/C VHS, Beta.** Jeff Bridges, James Mason, Broderick Crawford, Burgess Meredith; ***D:*** Burgess Meredith; ***W:*** Burgess Meredith. *NO*

Yodelin' Kid From Pine Ridge ♪½ *The Hero of Pine Ridge* **1937** Autry tries to stop a war between cattlemen and woodsmen in Georgia. Standard horse opera notable for its location. **59m/B VHS, Beta.** Gene Autry, Smiley Burnette, Betty Bronson, Charles Middleton, Art Mix; ***D:*** Joseph Kane. *NOS, VCN, DVT*

Yog, Monster from Space ♪ *The Space Amoeba* **1971 (G)** When a spaceship crashes somewhere near Japan, the aliens in it create monsters out of ordinary critters in order to destroy all the cities. A promoter gets a gleam in his eye and sees the potential for a vacation spot featuring the viscious creatures. Standard Japanese monster flick utilizing the usual out-of-synch dub machine. Dubbed. **105m/C VHS, Beta.** *JP* Akira Kubo, Yoshio Tsuchiya; ***D:*** Inoshiro Honda. *SNC*

Yojimbo ♪♪♪♪ **1961** Two clans vying for political power bid on the services of a samurai (Mifune) who comes to town. The samurai sells his services to both parties, with devastating results for all. In Japanese with English subtitles or dubbed. Re-made by Sergio Leone as the western "A Fist Full of Dollars." **110m/B VHS, Beta, LV, 8mm.** *JP* Toshiro Mifune, Eijiro Tono, Suuzu Yamda, Seizaburo Kawazu, Isuzu Yamada; ***D:***

Akira Kurosawa; *W:* Hideo Oguni, Shinobu Hashimoto, Akira Kurosawa; *M:* Masaru Sato. Nominations: Academy Awards '61: Best Costume Design (B & W). *VYY, SUE, HHT*

Yol ♂♂♂½ **1982 (PG)** Five Turkish prisoners are granted temporary leave to visit their families. An acclaimed, heartfelt film, written by Guney while he himself was in prison. A potent protest against totalitarianism. In Turkish with English subtitles. **126m/C VHS, Beta.** *TU* Tarik Akan, Serif Sezer; *D:* Serif Goren; *W:* Yilmaz Guney; *M:* Sebastian Argol. Cannes Film Festival '82: Best Film. *COL, AUD, INJ*

Yolanda and the Thief ♂♂½ **1945** A charming, forgotten effort from the Arthur Freed unit about a con man who convinces a virginal South American heiress that he is her guardian angel. Songs include a lengthy Dali-esque ballet built around "Will You Marry Me?" ♫This is the Day for Love; Angel; Yolanda; Coffee Time; Will You Marry Me. **109m/C VHS, Beta.** Fred Astaire, Lucille Bremer, Leon Ames, Mildred Natwick; *D:* Vincente Minnelli; *C:* Charles Rosher; *M:* Arthur Freed, Harry Warren. *MGM*

Yongkari Monster of the Deep ♂ *Dai Koesu Yongkari; Monster Yongkari; Great Monster Yongkari* **1967 (PG)** A giant burrowing creature is causing earthquakes and generally ruining scores of Japanese models. Dubbed. **79m/C VHS, Beta.** Oh Young Il, Nam Chung-Im; *D:* Kim Ki-dak. *ORI*

Yor, the Hunter from the Future ♂ *Mondo Di Yor; The World of Yor* **1983 (PG)** Lost in a time warp where the past and the future mysteriously collide, Yor sets out on a search for his real identity, with his only clue a golden medallion around his neck. **88m/C VHS, Beta, LV.** *IT* Reb Brown, Corinne Clery, John Steiner; *D:* Anthony (Antonio Margheriti) Dawson; *W:* Anthony (Antonio Margheriti) Dawson, Robert Bailey. *COL*

You Are Not Alone ♂♂ **1982** Boys in a small parochial school grow up and try to draw a defining line between friendship and love. In Danish with English subtitles. **90m/C VHS, Beta.** *DK FCT*

You Are Not I **1984** After a multi-car accident a young woman escapes from psychiatric confinement and goes to her sister's house. **50m/B VHS, Beta.** *NO*

You Can't Cheat an Honest Man ♂♂♂ **1939** The owner of a misfit circus suffers a variety of headaches including the wisecracks of Charlie McCarthy. Contains Field's classic ping-pong battle and some of his other best work. **79m/B VHS, Beta.** W.C. Fields, Edgar Bergen, Constance Moore, Eddie Anderson, Mary Forbes, Thurston Hall; *D:* George Marshall; *C:* Milton Krasner. *BAR*

You Can't Fool Your Wife ♂♂ **1940** Ball in two roles gives zip to this otherwise ordinary marital comedy. Previously blah hubby has a fling; previously blah better half wins him back with glamour. **69m/C VHS, Beta.** Lucille Ball, James Ellison, Robert Coote, Emma Dunn, Nita Naldi; *D:* Ray McCarey. *TTC*

You Can't Hurry Love ♂ **1988 (R)** A jilted-at-the-altar Ohio bachelor moves to Los Angeles and flounders in the city's fast-moving fast lane. A dull film with Fonda, daughter of "Easy Rider" Peter, playing a minor role. **92m/C VHS, Beta, LV.** David Leisure, Scott McGinnis, Sally Kellerman, Kristy McNichol, Charles Grodin, Anthony Geary, Bridget Fonda, David Packer, Frank Bonner; *D:* Richard Martini. *LIV, VES*

You Can't Take It with You ♂♂♂½ **1938** The Capra version of the Kaufman-Hart play about an eccentric New York family and their nonconformist houseguests. Alice Sycamore (Arthur), the stable family member of an offbeat clan of free spirits, falls for Tony Kirby (Stewart), the down-to-earth son of a snooty, wealthy and not always quite honest family. Amidst the confusion over this love affair, the two families rediscover the simple joys of life. **127m/B VHS, Beta, LV.** James Stewart, Jean Arthur, Lionel Barrymore, Spring Byington, Edward Arnold, Mischa Auer, Donald Meek, Samuel S. Hinds, Ann Miller, H.B. Warner, Halliwell Hobbes, Dub Taylor, Mary Forbes, Eddie Anderson, Harry Davenport, Lillian Yarbo; *D:* Frank Capra; *W:* Robert Riskin. Academy Awards '38: Best Director (Capra), Best Picture; Nominations: Academy Awards '38: Best Cinematography, Best Film Editing, Best Screenplay, Best Sound, Best Supporting Actress (Byington). *COL, BTV*

You Can't Take It with You ♂♂♂ **1984** Taped performance of the Kaufman and Hart comedy about the strange pastimes of the Sycamore family who must behave themselves to impress their daughter's boyfriend's stuffy family. **116m/C VHS, Beta, LV.** Colleen Dewhurst, James Coco, Jason Robards Jr., Elizabeth Wilson, George Rose; *D:* Ellis Raab. *COL, VES, LIV*

You Light Up My Life *Woof!* **1977 (PG)** Sappy sentimental story of a young singer trying to break into the music business. Premise of the movie was loosely taken from Debbie Boone's title song, which was a radio smash that drove many people over the edge. ♫You Light Up My Life. **91m/C VHS, Beta.** Didi Conn, Michael Zaslow, Melanie Mayron; *D:* Joseph Brooks; *W:* Joseph Brooks; *M:* Joseph Brooks. Academy Awards '77: Best Song ("You Light Up My Life"); Golden Globe Awards '78: Best Song ("You Light Up My Life"). *COL*

You Must Remember This **199?** When Uncle Buddy (Guillaume) receives a mysterious trunk, Ella's curiosity gets the best of her. She opens the trunk to discover a number of old movies made by W.B. Jackson—Uncle Buddy. Ella takes the films to a movie archive to find out about her uncle's past as an independent black filmmaker. After researching the history of black cinema, Ella convinces her uncle to be proud of his contribution to the film world. Includes a viewers' guide. Part of the "Wonderworks" series. **110m/C VHS.** Robert Guillaume, Tim Reid, Daphne Maxwell Reid, Vonetta McGee. *PME, HMV, BTV*

You Only Live Once ♂♂½ **1937** Ex-con Fonda wants to mend his ways and tries to cross into Canada with his girlfriend in tow. Impressively scripted, but a glum and dated Depression-era tale. **86m/B VHS, Beta.** Henry Fonda, Sylvia Sidney, Ward Bond, William Gargan, Barton MacLane, Margaret Hamilton; *D:* Fritz Lang. *NO*

You Only Live Twice ♂♂½ **1967 (PG)** 007 travels to Japan to take on arch-nemesis Blofeld, who has been capturing Russian and American spacecraft in an attempt to start WWIII. Great location photography; theme sung by Nancy Sinatra. Implausible plot, however, is a handicap, even though this is Bond. **125m/C VHS, Beta, LV.** *GB* Sean Connery, Mie Hama, Akiko Wakabayashi, Tetsuro Tamba, Karin Dor, Charles Gray, Donald Pleasence, Tsai Chin, Bernard Lee, Lois Maxwell, Desmond Llewelyn; *D:* Lewis Gilbert; *C:* Frederick A. (Freddie) Young; *M:* John Barry. *MGM, TLF*

You So Crazy ♂½ *Martin Lawrence You So Crazy* **1994** Scandalous star of television show "Martin" and host of HBO's "Def Comedy Jam" follows in the footsteps of raunchy humorists Richard Pryor and Eddie Murphy. Threatened with an NC-17 rating, Lawrence refused to edit and Miramax, the original distributor, dropped it. It was picked up by Samuel Goldwyn, who released the original version, uncut and unrated. Filmed live at the Brooklyn Academy of Music, Lawrence displays too little of his considerable talent, and too much vulgarity and poor taste. **85m/C VHS.** Martin Lawrence; *D:* Thomas Schlamme. *HBO*

You Talkin' to Me? ♂ **1987 (R)** Fledgling actor who idolizes De Niro moves to the West Coast for his big break. He fails, so he dyes his hair blond and digs the California lifestyle. Embarrassingly bad. **97m/C VHS, Beta.** Chris Winkler, Jim Youngs, Faith Ford; *D:* Charles Winkler; *W:* Charles Winkler. *MGM*

You Were Never Lovelier ♂♂♂½ **1942** Charming tale of a father who creates a phony Romeo to try to interest his daughter in marriage. Astaire appears and woos Hayworth in the flesh. The dancing, of course, is superb, and Hayworth is stunning. ♫Dearly Beloved; I'm Old Fashioned; Shorty George; Wedding in the Spring; You Were Never Lovelier. **98m/B VHS, Beta, LV.** Fred Astaire, Rita Hayworth, Leslie Brooks, Xavier Cugat, Adolphe Menjou, Larry Parks; *D:* William A. Seiter; *M:* Jerome Kern, Johnny Mercer. Nominations: Academy Awards '42: Best Song ("Dearly Beloved"), Best Sound, Best Original Score. *COL*

You'll Find Out ♂♂ **1940** A comic mix of music and mystery as Kay Kyser and his Band, along with a debutante in distress, are terrorized by Lugosi, Karloff, and Lorre. ♫The Bad Humor; I'd Know You Anywhere; You've Got Me This Way; Like the Fella Once Said; I've Got a One-Track Mind; Don't Think it Ain't Been Charming. **97m/B VHS, Beta.** Peter Lorre, Kay Kyser, Boris Karloff, Bela Lugosi, Dennis O'Keefe, Helen Parrish; *D:* David Butler. Nominations: Academy Awards '40: Best Song ("I'd Know You Anywhere"). *HHT, MLB*

You'll Never Get Rich ♂♂♂ **1941** A Broadway dance director is drafted into the Army, where his romantic troubles cause him to wind up in the guardhouse more than once. He of course gets the girl. Exquisitely funny. ♫Since I Kissed My Baby Goodbye; The A-stairable Rag; Shootin' the Works for Uncle Sam; Wedding Cake Walk; Dream Dancing; Boogie Barcarolle; So Near and Yet So Far. **88m/B VHS, Beta, LV.** Fred Astaire, Rita Hayworth, Robert Benchley; *D:* Sidney Lanfield. Nominations: Academy Awards '41: Best Song ("Since I Kissed My Baby Goodbye"), Best Original Score, Best Original Score. *COL*

The Young Americans ♂♂ **1993 (R)** Tough New York cop John Harris (Keitel) is sent to London to aid the police with their investigations into a series of killings related to a drug smuggling operation working out of the club scene. Harris wants to tie everything to the sleazeball gangster Carl Frazer (Mortensen) that he's been trailing. Slick formula with hard-working cast. Debut for 25-year-old director Cannon. **108m/C VHS, LV.** *GB* Harvey Keitel, Viggo Mortensen, Iain Glen, John Wood, Keith Allen, Craig Kelly, Thandie Newton, Terence Rigby; *D:* Danny Cannon; *W:* Danny Cannon, David Hilton; *M:* David Arnold. *LIV*

Young & Free ♂½ **1978** Following the death of his parents, a young man must learn to face the perils of an unchartered wilderness alone. Ultimately he must choose between returning to civilization, or remain with his beloved wife and life in the wild. **87m/C VHS, Beta.** Erik Larsen; *D:* Keith Larsen. *MON*

Young and Innocent ♂♂♂ *The Girl Was Young* **1937** Somewhat uneven thriller about a police constable's daughter who helps a fugitive prove he didn't strangle a film star. **80m/B VHS, Beta, LV.** *GB* Derrick DeMarney, Nova Pilbeam, Percy Marmont; *D:* Alfred Hitchcock. *SNC, NOS, VDM*

The Young and the Guilty ♂♂ **1958** Two star-crossed teenagers are frustrated in their romance when their parents find one of their love letters and hit the ceiling. Told not to see each other again, the two take to sneaking around, which adds an edge to their relationship. Moving performances by the two young leads. **65m/B VHS.** Phyllis Calvert, Andrew Ray, Edward Chapman, Janet Munro, Campbell Singer; *D:* Peter Cotes. *NOS*

Young & Willing ♂♂½ **1942** A group of struggling actors gets hold of a terrific play and tries various schemes to get it produced. Based on the Broadway Play "Out of the Frying Pan" by Francis Swann. Unexceptional but enjoyable comedy. **83m/B VHS, Beta.** William Holden, Susan Hayward, Eddie Bracken, Robert Benchley, Martha O'Driscoll, Barbara Britton; *D:* Edward H. Griffith; *W:* Virginia Van Upp. *NO*

Young Aphrodites ♂♂½ *Mikres Aphrodites* **1963** Two young teenagers of a primitive Greek tribe discover sexuality. An acclaimed film retelling the myth of Daphnis and Chloe. Narrated in English. **87m/B VHS, Beta.** *GR* *D:* Nikos Koundouros. Berlin International Film Festival '63: Best Director (Koundouros). *SUE, NLC*

Young at Heart ♂♂½ **1954** Fanny Hurst's lighthearted tale of a cynical hard-luck musician who finds happiness when he falls for a small town girl. A remake of the 1938 "Four Daughters." ♫Young at Heart; Someone to Watch Over Me; One for My Baby; Hold Me in Your Arms; Ready, Willing and Able; Till My Love Comes Back to Me; There's a Rising Moon For Every Falling Star; You, My Love. **117m/C VHS.** Frank Sinatra, Doris Day, Gig Young, Ethel Barrymore, Dorothy Malone, Robert Keith, Elisabeth Fraser, Alan Hale Jr.; *D:* Gordon Douglas; *W:* Julius J. Epstein, Liam O'Brien. *REP*

Young Bess 🦴🦴🦴½ **1953** Simmons and real-life husband Granger star in this splashy costume drama about 16th century England's young Queen. Features outstanding performances by Simmons as Elizabeth I and Laughton (repeating his most famous role) as Henry VIII. Based on the novel by Margaret Irwin. **112m/C VHS.** Jean Simmons, Stewart Granger, Deborah Kerr, Charles Laughton, Kay Walsh, Guy Rolfe, Kathleen Byron, Cecil Kellaway, Rex Thompson; ***D:*** George Sidney; ***W:*** Jan Lustig, Arthur Wimperis; ***C:*** Charles Rosher; ***M:*** Miklos Rozsa. *MGM*

Young Bill Hickok 🦴🦴 **1940** A Rogers vehicle in the form of a very fictionalized biography of the famous gunfighter. **54m/B VHS, Beta.** Roy Rogers, George "Gabby" Hayes. *NOS, DVT, TIM*

Young Blood 🦴🦴 **1933** A cowboy robs from the rich to help the poor. He's also interested in a foreign actress having trouble bonding with the townfolk. Lots of old fashioned western violence. **61m/B VHS, Beta.** Bob Steele, Charles "Blackie" King, Helen Foster; ***D:*** Phil Rosen. *NOS, DVT*

The Young Bruce Lee **19??** Bruce learns and uses the deadly skills that made him famous while only knee-high to a grasshopper. **90m/C VHS, Beta.** Han Kwok Choi. *MGI*

Young Buffalo Bill 🦴🦴 **1940** Buffalo Bill battles the Spanish land-grant patrons. **54m/B VHS, Beta.** Roy Rogers, George "Gabby" Hayes, Pauline Moore; ***D:*** Joseph Kane. *NOS, DVT*

Young Caruso 🦴🦴 **1951** Dramatic biography of legendary tenor Enrico Caruso, following his life from childhood poverty in Naples to the beginning of his rise to fame. Dubbed in English. **78m/B VHS, Beta.** Gina Lollobrigida, Ermanno Randi, Mario del Monaco. *VYY, NOS, MVD*

Young Catherine 🦴🦴🦴 **1991** Made-for-TV account of Russia's strongest female ruler, the girl who would be Catherine the Great. Star-studded cast and excellent production values. Script and strong cast make Ormond look like a lightweight. Filmed in Leningrad. Also available in 186-minute version. **150m/C VHS, Beta.** Vanessa Redgrave, Christopher Plummer, Marthe Keller, Franco Nero, Julia Ormond, Maximilian Schell, Reece Dinsdale, Mark Frankel; ***D:*** Michael Anderson Sr.; ***W:*** Chris Bryant. *TTC*

Young Charlie Chaplin 🦴🦴 **1988** A British-made TV biography of the legendary silent screen comic. **160m/C VHS, Beta.** Ian McShane, Twiggy; ***M:*** Rachel Portman. *NO*

The Young Detectives on Wheels 🦴🦴½ **1987** Brother and sister team find a $3 million stolen treasure in their backyard, which authorities believe was planted there by the duo's father. The siblings solve the crime and clear their father's name. **107m/C VHS.** *VMK, FHE, BTV*

Young Doctors in Love 🦴🦴 **1982 (R)** Spoof of medical soap operas features a chaotic scenario at City Hospital, where the young men and women on the staff have better things to do than attend to their patients. Good cast keeps this one alive, though many laughs are forced. Includes cameos by real soap star, including then-General Hospital star Moore. **95m/C VHS, Beta, LV.** Dabney Coleman, Sean Young, Michael McKean, Harry Dean Stanton, Hector Elizondo, Patrick Macnee, Pamela Reed, Saul Rubinek; ***Cameos:*** Demi Moore, Janine Turner; ***D:*** Garry Marshall; ***W:*** Michael Elias, Rich Eustis; ***M:*** Maurice Jarre. *PAR, VES*

Young Dragon 🦴½ **1977 (R)** The Young Dragon's girlfriend is kidnapped by the underworld society, and he sets out to rescue her single-handedly. **90m/C VHS.** Yang Sze, Lo Lai, Yuen Man Chi, Wong Ching, Nora Miao. *SUN*

Young Eagles **1934** Serial with 12 chapters, 13 minutes each. **156m/B VHS, Beta.** Bobby Cox, Jim Vance, Carter Dixon. *VYY, VCN, MLB*

Young Einstein 🦴🦴 **1989 (PG)** A goofy, irreverent Australian farce starring, directed, co-scripted and co-produced by Serious, depicting Einstein as a young Outback clod who splits beer atoms and invents rock and roll. Winner of several Aussie awards. Fun for the kids. **91m/C VHS, Beta, LV.** *AU* Yahoo Serious, Odile Le Clezio, John Howard, Pee Wee Wilson, Su Cruickshank; ***D:*** Yahoo Serious; ***W:*** Yahoo Serious; ***M:*** Martin Armiger. *WAR*

Young Frankenstein 🦴🦴🦴🦴 **1974 (PG)** Young Dr. Frankenstein (Wilder), a brain surgeon, inherits the family castle back in Transylvania. He's skittish about the family business, but when he learns his grandfather's secrets, he becomes obsessed with making his own monster. Wilder and monster Boyle make a memorable song-and-dance team to Irving Berlin's "Puttin' on the Ritz," and Hackman's cameo as a blind man is inspired. Garr ("What knockers!" "Oh, sank you!") is adorable as a fraulein, and Leachman ("He's vass my—boyfriend!") is wonderfully scary. Wilder saves the creature with a switcheroo, in which the doctor ends up with a certain monster-sized body part. Hilarious parody. **108m/B VHS, Beta, LV.** Peter Boyle, Gene Wilder, Marty Feldman, Madeline Kahn, Cloris Leachman, Teri Garr, Kenneth Mars, Richard Haydn; ***Cameos:*** Gene Hackman; ***D:*** Mel Brooks; ***W:*** Gene Wilder, Mel Brooks; ***M:*** John Morris. Nominations: Academy Awards '74: Best Adapted Screenplay, Best Sound. *FOX, HMV*

The Young Graduates 🦴 **1971 (PG)** Hormonally imbalanced teens come of age in spite of meandering plot. Features "Breaking Away" star Christopher in big screen debut. **99m/C VHS.** Patricia Wymer, Steven Stewart, Gary Rist, Bruce Kirby, Jennifer Ritt, Dennis Christopher; ***D:*** Robert Anderson. *ACA*

Young Guns 🦴🦴½ **1988 (R)** A sophomoric Wild Bunch look-alike that ends up resembling a western version of the Bowery Boys. Provides a portrait of Billy the Kid and his gang as they move from prairie trash to demi-legends. Features several fine performances by a popular group of today's young stars. **107m/C VHS, Beta, LV.** Emilio Estevez, Kiefer Sutherland, Lou Diamond Phillips, Charlie Sheen, Casey Siemaszko, Dermot Mulroney, Terence Stamp, Terry O'Quinn, Jack Palance, Brian Keith, Patrick Wayne, Sharon Thomas; ***D:*** Christopher Cain; ***W:*** John Fusco; ***M:*** Anthony Marinelli, Brian Backus, Brian Banks. *LIV, VES*

Young Guns 2 🦴🦴 **1990 (PG-13)** Brat Pack vehicle neo-Western sequel about Billy the Kid (Estevez) and his gang. This time they're making a run for the border with the law on their trail. **105m/C VHS, LV.** Emilio Estevez, Kiefer Sutherland, Lou Diamond Phillips, Christian Slater, William L. Petersen, Alan Ruck, R.D. Call, James Coburn, Balthazar Getty, Jack Kehoe, Rob Knepper, Jenny Wright, Tracey Walter, Ginger Lynn Allen, Jon Bon Jovi; ***D:*** Geoff Murphy; ***W:*** John Fusco; ***M:*** Alan Silvestri. Golden Globe Awards '91: Best Song ("Blaze of Glory"); Nominations: Academy Awards '90: Best Song ("Blaze of Glory"). *FXV, BTV, CCB*

The Young in Heart 🦴🦴🦴 **1938** A lonely, old woman allows a family of con-artists into her life for companionship. Impressed by her sweet nature, the parasitic brood reforms. The cute comedy was a real crowd-pleaser in its day, especially after the bittersweet ending was replaced with a happier variety. Based on the novel "The Gay Banditti" by I.A.R. Wylie. **90m/C VHS.** Janet Gaynor, Douglas Fairbanks Jr., Paulette Goddard, Roland Young, Billie Burke, Minnie Dupree, Richard Carlson, Charles Halton; ***D:*** Richard Wallace; ***W:*** Charles Bennett, Paul Osborn. Nominations: Academy Awards '38: Best Cinematography, Best Score. *NO*

Young Lady Chatterly 2 🦴½ **1985** A poor sequel to the popular MacBride film, with only the name of the Lawrence classic. Chatterly inherits the family mansion and fools around with the servants and any one else who comes along. Unrated version with 13 minutes of deleted footage is also available. **87m/C VHS, Beta, LV.** Sybil Danning, Adam West, Harlee MacBride; ***D:*** Alan Roberts. *LIV*

The Young Land 🦴½ **1959** Less-than-inspiring western does feature a good performance by Hopper as malcontent bully Hatfield Carnes. Carnes kills a respected Mexican in a barroom gunfight in 1848 California and sheriff Jim Ellison (Wayne) is quick to call territorial judge Isham (O'Herlihy) to insure a fair trial—with the rest of the Spanish-speaking town looking on in skepticism. Based on the story "Frontier Frenzy" by John Reese. **88m/C VHS.** Dennis Hopper, Patrick Wayne, Dan O'Herlihy, Yvonne Craig, Ken Curtis, Pedro Gonzalez-Gonzalez; ***D:*** Ted Tetzlaff; ***W:*** Norman S. Hall; ***C:*** Winton C. Hoch, Henry Sharp; ***M:*** Dimitri Tiomkin. *HTV*

The Young Lions 🦴🦴🦴 **1958** A cynical WWII epic following the experiences of a young American officer and a disillusioned Nazi in the war's last days. Martin does fine in his first dramatic role. As the Nazi, Brando sensitively considers the belief that Hitler would save Germany. A realistic anti-war film. **167m/B VHS, Beta, LV.** Marlon Brando, Montgomery Clift, Dean Martin, Hope Lange, Barbara Rush, Lee Van Cleef, Maximilian Schell; ***D:*** Edward Dmytryk; ***W:*** Edward Anhalt. Nominations: Academy Awards '58: Best Black and White Cinematography, Best Sound, Best Original Score. *FOX*

Young Love, First Love 🦴½ **1979** A made-for-television movie about a young woman who must decide whether to have sex with her boyfriend. Sound familiar? Pretty blah, earnest story, though well cast. **100m/C VHS, Beta.** Valerie Bertinelli, Leslie Ackerman, Timothy Hutton, Arlen Dean Snyder, Fionnula Flanagan; ***D:*** Steven Hilliard Stern. *LIV*

Young Love—Lemon Popsicle 7 🦴 **1987 (R)** Three hunks stalk the beaches in search of babes. **91m/C VHS, Beta.** Yftach Katzur, Zachi Noy, Jonathan Segall, Sonja Martin; ***D:*** Walter Bennett. *WAR*

Young Man with a Horn 🦴🦴🦴 **1950** Dorothy Baker's novel, which was loosely based on the life of jazz immortal Bix Beiderbecke, was even more loosely adapted for this film, featuring Kirk as an angst-ridden trumpeter who can't seem to hit that mystical "high note." ♫The Very Thought of You; I May be Wrong; The Man I Love; Too Marvelous for Words; With a Song in My Heart; Pretty Baby; I Only Have Eyes for You; Limehouse Blues; Melancholy Rhapsody. **112m/B VHS, Beta, LV.** Kirk Douglas, Doris Day, Lauren Bacall, Hoagy Carmichael; ***D:*** Michael Curtiz. *WAR*

Young Mr. Lincoln 🦴🦴🦴½ **1939** A classy Hollywood biography of Lincoln in his younger years from log-cabin country boy to idealistic Springfield lawyer. A splendid drama, and one endlessly explicated as an American masterpiece by the French auteur critics in "Cahiers du Cinema." **100m/B VHS, Beta, LV.** Henry Fonda, Alice Brady, Marjorie Weaver, Arleen Whelan, Eddie Collins, Ward Bond, Donald Meek, Richard Cromwell, Eddie Quillan, Charles Halton; ***D:*** John Ford; ***W:*** Lamar Trotti. National Board of Review Awards '39: 10 Best Films of the Year; Nominations: Academy Awards '39: Best Story. *FOX*

The Young Nurses 🦴🦴 *Nightingale* **1973 (R)** The fourth entry in the Roger Corman produced "nurses" series. Three sexy nurses uncover a drug ring run from their hospital, headed by none other than director Fuller. Also present is Moreland, in his last role. Preceded by "The Student Nurses," "Private Duty Nurses," "Night Call Nurses," followed by "Candy Stripe Nurses." Also on video as "Young L.A. Nurses 3." **77m/C VHS, Beta.** Jean Manson, Ashley Porter, Angela Gibbs, Zack Taylor, Dick Miller, Jack LaRue, William Joyce, Sally Kirkland, Allan Arbus, Mary Doyle, Don Keefer, Nan Martin, Mantan Moreland, Samuel Fuller; ***D:*** Clinton Kimbrough. *NLC*

Young Nurses in Love 🦴 **1989 (R)** Low-budget sex farce in which a foreign spy poses as a nurse to steal sperm from a sperm bank donated by world leaders, celebrities and geniuses. **82m/C VHS, Beta, LV.** Jeanne Marie, Alan Fisher, Barbra Robb, James Davies; ***D:*** Chuck Vincent. *LIV, VES*

The Young One 🦴🦴½ *La Joven* **1961** Traver (Hamilton) is a black jazz musician who escapes from his southern town when he's wrongly accused of raping a white woman. He hides out on a small island which is used as a private hunting ground for rich sportsmen, overseen by Miller (Scott), the game keeper. Hamilton gets work as the new handyman and becomes close to the young Evalyn (Meersman). When Miller rapes Evalyn, it's Traver who's once again accused until things can be put right. Racist elements are heavy-handed; one of Bunuel's lesser efforts. Based on the story "Travelin' Man" by Peter Matthiessen. **94m/C VHS.** *MX* Bernie Hamilton, Zachary Scott, Kay Meersman, Claudio Brook, Graham Denton; ***D:*** Luis Bunuel; ***W:*** Luis Bunuel. *CVC, FCT*

The Young Ones **1988** Three episodes from the hilarious, offbeat British television sitcom about four violently eccentric college roommates. Episodes included are "Oil," "Boring," and "Flood." **96m/C VHS, Beta.** *GB* Rik Mayall, Ade Edmondson, Nigel Planer, Christopher Ryan, Alexei Sayle; ***D:*** Geoffrey Posner. *FOX*

Young People 🦴🦴½ **1940 (G)** Temple's 12 in this lesser vehicle and almost-adolesence doesn't serve her well with this tired plot. She's an orphan adopted by showbiz team Oakie and Greenwood who've decided to retire to rural life. They even get to put on a show to prove to the small-minded small-towners what a swell trio they are. Temple's last film for 20th-Century Fox does include nostalgic clips from earlier Shirley hits, including "Stand Up and Cheer" and "Curly Top," to explain her character's background. ♫Tra-La-La; Fifth Avenue; I Wouldn't Take a Million; The Mason-Dixon Line; Young People. **78m/C VHS.** Shirley Temple, Jack Oakie, Charlotte Greenwood, Arleen Whelan, George Montgomery, Kathleen Howard; ***D:*** Allan Dwan; ***W:*** Edwin Blum, Don Ettlinger. *FXV*

The Young Philadelphians 🦴🦴🦴 *The City Jungle* **1959** Ambitious young lawyer Newman works hard at making an impression on the snobbish Philadelphia upper crust. As he schemes and scrambles, he woos debutante Rush and defends buddy Vaughn on a murder charge. Long, but worth it. Part of the "A Night at the Movies" series, this package simulates a 1959 movie evening with a Bugs Bunny cartoon, "People Are Bunny," a newsreel and coming attractions for "The Nun's Story" and "The Hanging Tree." **136m/B VHS, Beta.** Paul Newman, Barbara Rush, Alexis Smith, Billie Burke, Brian Keith, John Williams, Otto Kruger, Robert Vaughn; ***D:*** Vincent Sherman; ***C:*** Harry Stradling; ***M:*** Ernest Gold. Nominations: Academy Awards '59: Best Black and White Cinematography, Best Costume Design (B & W), Best Supporting Actor (Vaughn). *WAR*

The Young Poisoner's Handbook 🦴🦴🦴 **1994** Based on the true story of London teenager Graham (O'Conor), who's obsessed with chemistry and at odds with his stepmother. So, he poisons her chocolates and she dies. Sent to Broadmoor prison for the criminally insane, Graham comes under the care of Dr. Ziegler (Sher), who, eight years later, recommends Graham for parole. Now working in a photographic lab, Graham decides to experiment with doctoring his co-workers tea—which results in eight more deaths before Graham is caught. Locked up again, Graham spends his time writing a poisoner's handbook for Dr. Ziegler. Be warned that the sufferings of the poisoned victims are gruesome. **99m/C VHS.** *GB* Hugh O'Conor, Anthony Sher, Ruth Sheen, Charlotte Coleman, Roger Lloyd Pack, Paul Stacey, Samantha Edmonds, Charlie Creed-Miles; ***D:*** Benjamin Ross; ***W:*** Benjamin Ross, Jeff Rawle; ***C:*** Hubert Taczanowski; ***M:*** Robert Lane, Frank Strobel. *CAF*

Young Sherlock Holmes 🦴🦴 **1985 (PG-13)** Holmes and Watson meet as schoolboys. They work together on their first case, solving a series of bizarre murders gripping London. Watch through the credits for an interesting plot twist. Promising "what if" sleuth tale crashes and burns, becoming a typical high-tech Spielberg film. Second half bears too strong a resemblance to "Indiana Jones and the Temple of Doom." **109m/C VHS, Beta, LV, 8mm.** Nicholas Rowe, Alan Cox, Sophie Ward, Freddie Jones, Michael Hordern; ***D:*** Barry Levinson; ***W:*** Chris Columbus; ***M:*** Bruce Broughton. *PAR*

The Young Teacher 🦴½ **1985** A novice teacher finds out that trying to apply her college education to a real life elementary school environment isn't as easy as it sounds. **90m/C VHS, Beta.** *GEM*

Young Tiger 🦴🦴 **1980 (R)** First a ninety-minute movie never before seen in the U.S. featuring an expert in martial arts who is accused of murder. Next is a twelve-minute documentary featuring Jackie Chan, kung-fu sensation, demonstrating his skills. What an evening. **102m/C VHS, Beta.** Jackie Chan. *GEM*

Young Tom Edison 🦴🦴½ **1940** Two teenaged years in the life of Thomas Alva Edison, as he drives his family crazy with his endless experiments on his way to becoming the famed inventor. Rooney manages to be enthusiastic without being overwhelming. Followed by "Edison the Man," with Spencer Tracy in the adult role. **82m/B VHS, Beta.** Mickey Rooney, Fay Bainter, George Bancroft, Virginia Weidler, Eugene Pallette, Victor Kilian, Bobby Jordan, Lloyd Corrigan; ***D:*** Norman Taurog; ***W:*** Dore Schary, Bradbury Foote, Hugo Butler. *MGM, FCT, BTV*

Young Warlord 🦴🦴 **1975** Arthur roams western England in 500 AD, leading a band of guerrilla cavalrymen. When the Saxons invade, Arthur unites the tribe, holds off the attack and becomes king. **97m/C VHS, Beta.** Oliver Tobias, Michael Gothard, Jack Watson, Brian Blessed; ***D:*** Peter Sasdy. *NO*

Young Warriors 🦴½ **1983 (R)** Frat boys turn vigilante to avenge a street gang murder. Weird mix of teen sex comedy, insufferable self-righteous preachiness, and violence. **104m/C VHS, Beta.** Ernest Borgnine, James Van Patten, Richard Roundtree, Lynda Day George, Dick Shawn; ***D:*** Lawrence Foldes; ***W:*** Lawrence Foldes, Richard Matheson, Russell W. Colgin. *MGM*

Young Winston 🦴🦴🦴 **1972 (PG)** Based on Sir Winston Churchill's autobiography "My Early Life: A Roving Commission." Follows him through his school days, journalistic career in Africa, early military career, and his election to Parliament at the age of 26. Ward is tremendous as the prime minister-to-be. **145m/C VHS, Beta.** *GB* Simon Ward, Robert Shaw, Anne Bancroft, John Mills, Jack Hawkins, Ian Holm, Anthony Hopkins, Patrick Magee, Edward Woodward, Jane Seymour; ***D:*** Richard Attenborough. Golden Globe Awards '73: Best Foreign Film; Nominations: Academy Awards '72: Best Art Direction/Set Decoration, Best Costume Design, Best Story & Screenplay. *COL, TVC*

Youngblood 🦴🦴 **1986 (R)** An underdog beats the seemingly insurmountable odds and becomes a hockey champion. Some enjoyable hockey scenes although the success storyline is predictable. **111m/C VHS, Beta, LV.** Rob Lowe, Patrick Swayze, Cynthia Gibb, Ed Lauter, George Finn, Fionnula Flanagan, Keanu Reeves; ***D:*** Peter Markle. *MGM*

Younger & Younger 🦴🦴½ **1994 (R)** Jonathan Younger (Sutherland) is forced to run the family storage business after his long-suffering wife Penny (Davidovich) dies. The business starts to fail, even after Jonathan's son (Fraser) arrives to help out, and the widower begins having visions of the woman he mistreated. And each time he sees her she looks younger and more beautiful than ever. **97m/C VHS, LV.** Donald Sutherland, Brendan Fraser, Lolita Davidovich, Sally Kellerman, Julie Delpy, Linda Hunt; ***D:*** Percy Adlon; ***W:*** Percy Adlon, Felix Adlon; ***C:*** Bernd Heinl; ***M:*** Hans Zimmer. *PAR*

Your Place or Mine 🦴½ **1983** Self-indulgent made-for-television yuppie pap about middle-aged singles trying to find the right mate. **100m/C VHS, Beta.** Bonnie Franklin, Robert Klein, Peter Bonerz, Tyne Daly, Penny Fuller; ***D:*** Robert Day; ***M:*** Gerald Alters. *LIV*

Your Show of Shows **1950** The legendary variety program was a Saturday night fixture from 1950-1954 and featured the comedic talents of Sid Caesar, Imogene Coca, Carl Reiner, Howard Morris, and a bevy of guest stars. Additional episodes available. **30m/B VHS, Beta.** *MOV, RDG, VYY*

Your Ticket Is No Longer Valid 🦴 **1984 (R)** Prurient excuse for a serious drama. Impotent failed businessman has disturbing erotic dreams about his girlfriend. Adapted from a novel by Romain Gary. **96m/C VHS, Beta.** *CA* Richard Harris, George Peppard, Jeanne Moreau; ***D:*** George Kaczender. *VES*

Your Turn Darling 🦴🦴 *A Toi De Faire; Mignonne* **1963** French espionage thriller with Constantine once again playing Lemmy Caution, a U.S. secret agent involved with a gang of spies. **93m/C VHS.** *FR* Eddie Constantine, Gaia Germani, Elga Andersen; ***D:*** Bernard Borderie. *SNC*

You're a Big Boy Now 🦴🦴🦴 **1966** Kastner, a virginal young man working in the New York Public Library, is told by his father to move out of his house and grow up. On his own, he soon becomes involved with man-hating actress Hartman and a discotheque dancer. A wild and weird comedy. Coppola's commercial directorial debut. **96m/C VHS, Beta.** Elizabeth Hartman, Geraldine Page, Peter Kastner, Julie Harris, Rip Torn, Michael Dunn, Tony Bill, Karen Black; ***D:*** Francis Ford Coppola; ***W:*** Francis Ford Coppola. Nominations: Academy Awards '66: Best Supporting Actress (Page). *WAR*

You're a Good Man, Charlie Brown **1987** A filmed version of Charles Schulz's Broadway musical, based on his famous characters. **60m/C VHS, Beta.** *BAR, KAR, WTA*

You're in Love, Charlie Brown **1967** The animated Peanuts gang in a new adventure about Charlie Brown and the proverbial little red-haired girl. **30m/C VHS, Beta.** *BAR*

You're Jinxed, Friend, You've Met Sacramento 🦴🦴 **1970** The tongue-in-cheek adventures of a cool-headed cowboy as he passes from town to colorful town. Great title, too. **99m/C VHS, Beta.** Ty Hardin, Christian Hay, Jenny Atkins; ***D:*** George Cristallini. *UNI*

Yours, Mine & Ours 🦴🦴½ **1968** Bigger, better, big screen version of "The Brady Bunch." It's the story of a lovely lady (Ball) with eight kids who marries a a widower (Fonda) who has ten. Imagine the zany shenanigans! Family comedy manages to be both wholesome and funny. Based on a true story. **114m/C VHS, Beta, LV.** Lucille Ball, Henry Fonda, Van Johnson, Tim Matheson, Tom Bosley, Tracy Nelson; ***D:*** Melville Shavelson; ***W:*** Melville Shavelson. *MGM*

Youth Aflame *Woof! Hoodlum Girls* **1959** Trash film that tells the tale of two sisters—one good, one bad. Poor dialogue and weak performances do, however, make for some great camp. Based on a story by Helen Kiedy. **61m/B VHS.** Joy Reese, Warren Burr, Kay Morley, Michael Owen, Rod Rogers; ***D:*** Elmer Clifton; ***W:*** Elmer Clifton. *SNC*

Youth on Parole 🦴½ **1937** Same old story: Boy gets paroled. Girl gets paroled. Parolee meets parolette and romance blossoms as they beat a further rap. **60m/B VHS.** Marian Marsh, Gordon Oliver. *LOO, VYY*

You've Got to Have Heart 🦴 **1977 (R)** A young bridegroom's life gets complicated after he does not sexually satisfy his bride on their wedding night. **98m/C VHS, Beta.** Carroll Baker, Edwige French. *PSM*

You've Ruined Me, Eddie 🦴 **1958** A spoiled rich girl gets knocked up and her boyfriend will never know peace again. Meanwhile, their once quiet town is outraged. **m/B VHS.** *SMW, TPV*

Yukon Flight 🦴🦴 **1940** A Renfrew of the Mounties adventure. The hero finds illegal gold mining operations and murder in the Yukon. **57m/B VHS, Beta.** James Newill, Dave O'Brien. *NOS, VCN*

The Yum-Yum Girls 🦴½ **1978 (R)** Pair of innocent girls arrive in New York City to pursue their dreams. Gives an inside looks at the fashion industry. Not as funny or as cute as it wants to be. **89m/C VHS, Beta.** Judy Landers, Tanya Roberts, Barbara Tully, Michelle Daw; ***D:*** Barry Rosen. *MCA*

Yuma 🦴🦴 **1970** An old-style made-for-television Western about a sheriff (Walker) who rides into town, cleans it up, and saves his own reputation from a plot to discredit him. Dull in places, but action-packed ending saves the day. **73m/C VHS, Beta.** Clint Walker, Barry Sullivan, Edgar Buchanan; ***D:*** Ted Post; ***M:*** George Duning. *FOX, VTR*

Yuri Nosenko, KGB 🦴🦴½ **1986** Fact-based account of a KGB defector and the CIA agent who must determine if he's on the up-and-up. Made for British television. **85m/C VHS.** *GB* Tommy Lee Jones, Oleg Rudnik, Josef Sommer, Ed Lauter, George Morfogen, Stephen D. Newman; ***D:*** Mick Jackson. *CNG*

Z 🦴🦴🦴🦴 **1969** The assassination of a Greek nationalist in the 1960s and its aftermath are portrayed by the notorious political director as a gripping detective thriller. Excellent performances, adequate cinematic techniques, and important politics in this highly acclaimed film. **128m/C VHS, Beta, LV.** *FR* Yves Montand, Jean-Louis Trintignant, Irene Papas, Charles Denner, Georges Geret, Jacques Perrin, Francois Perier, Marcel Bozzuffi; ***D:*** Constantin Costa-Gavras; ***W:*** Constantin Costa-Gavras. Academy Awards '69: Best Film Editing, Best Foreign Language Film; Cannes Film Festival '69: Special Jury Prize, Best Actor (Trintignant); Golden Globe Awards '70: Best Foreign Film; New York Film Critics Awards '69: Best Director (Costa-Gavras), Best Film; National Society of Film Critics Awards '69: Best Film; Nominations: Academy Awards '69: Best Adapted Screenplay, Best Director (Costa-Gavras), Best Picture; Cannes Film Festival '69: Best Film. *COL*

Zabriskie Point 🦴🦴🦴 **1970 (R)** Antonioni's first U.S. feature. A desultory, surreal examination of the American way of life. Worthy but difficult. Climaxes with a stylized orgy in Death Valley. **112m/C VHS, Beta, LV.** Mark Frechette, Daria Halprin, Paul Fix, Rod Taylor, Harrison Ford, G.D. Spradlin; ***D:*** Michelangelo Antonioni; ***W:*** Michelangelo Antonioni, Sam Shepard, Fred Gardner, Tonino Guerra, Clare Peploe. *MGM, MLB*

Zachariah 🦴🦴½ **1970 (PG)** A semi-spoof '60s rock western, wherein two gunfighters given to pursuing wealth-laden bands of outlaws separate and experience quixotic journeys through the cliched landscape. Scripted by members of The Firesign Theater and featuring appearances by Country Joe and The Fish, The New York Rock Ensemble and The James Gang. **93m/C VHS, Beta.** Don Johnson, John Rubinstein, Pat Quinn, Dick Van Patten; ***D:*** George Englund. *FOX*

Zalmen or the Madness of God 🦴🦴½ **1975** Elie Wiesel's mystical story about a rabbi's struggle against religious persecution in post-Stalin Russia. **120m/C VHS, Beta.** Joseph Wiseman. *WNE*

Zandalee *Woof!* **1991 (R)** The sexual adventures of a bored sexy young woman who has a fling with her husband's friend. Bad script, graphic sex. Also available in an unrated version. **100m/C VHS, LV.** Nicolas Cage, Judge Reinhold, Erika Anderson, Viveca Lindfors, Aaron Neville, Joe Pantoliano, Ian Abercrombie, Marisa Tomei, Zach Galligan; ***D:*** Sam Pillsbury; ***W:*** Mari Kornhauser. *LIV*

Zandy's Bride 🦴½ **1974 (PG)** Basic story about a rancher who sents for a mail-order bride. She's shocked by his ill-treatment of her and stands up to his bullying, thus winning his respect and love. Beautiful scenery, courtesy of Big Sur, California, but predictable all-around and essentially a waste of an experienced cast. Based on the novel "The Stranger" by Lillian Bos Ross. **97m/C VHS.** Gene Hackman, Liv Ullmann, Eileen Heckart, Harry Dean Stanton, Joe Santos, Sam Bottoms, Susan Tyrrell, Frank Cady; ***D:*** Jan Troell; ***W:*** Marc Norman; ***M:*** Michael Franks. *WAR*

The Zany Adventures of Robin Hood 🦴 **1984** Hackneyed spoof of the Robin Hood legend. Medieval man robs from the rich to help the poor. Not nearly as funny as. Mel Brooks' TV series that spoofed "Robin Hood." **95m/C VHS, Beta.** George Segal, Morgan Fairchild, Roddy McDowall, Roy Kinnear, Janet Suzman, Tom Baker; ***D:*** Ray Austin. *MED*

Zapped! 🦴 **1982 (R)** Teen genius discovers he possesses telekinetic powers. He does the natural thing, using his talent to remove clothing from nearby females. A teen boy's dream come true. **98m/C VHS, Beta, LV.** Scott Baio, Willie Aames, Robert Mandan, Felice Schachter, Scatman Crothers, Roger Bowen, Marya Small, Greg Bradford, Hilary Beane, Sue Ane Langdon, Heather Thomas, Merritt Butrick, LaWanda Page, Rosanne Katon; ***D:*** Robert J. Rosenthal; ***M:*** Charles Fox. *SUE, NLC*

Zapped Again 🦴 **1989 (R)** The lame-brained sequel to 1982's "Zapped" about a high schooler who has telekinetic powers and lust on his mind. **93m/C VHS, Beta, LV, 8mm.** Todd Eric Andrews, Kelli Williams, Reed Rudy, Linda Blair, Karen Black, Lyle Alzado; ***D:*** Douglas Campbell. *COL, SUE*

Zardoz 🦴🦴 **1973** A surreal parable of the far future, when Earth society is broken into strict classes: a society of intellectuals, a society of savages, and an elite unit of killers who keep the order. Connery is the man who destroys the old order of things. Visually interesting but pretentious. **105m/C VHS, Beta, LV.** Sean Connery, Charlotte Rampling, John Alderton, Sara Kestelman; ***D:*** John Boorman; ***W:*** John Boorman. *FOX*

Zarkorr! The Invader 🦴🦴 **1996 (PG)** Aliens studying earth decide humans need a challenge (like we don't have enough problems of our own) so they send a 185-foot tall, laser-eyed monster to crush (American) cities and cause general terror in the population. And who's our hero? A postal worker—aided by a five-inch tall alien girl. **80m/C VHS, LV.** Rhys Pugh, Deprise Grossman, Mark Hamilton, Charles Schneider, Eileen Wesson; ***D:*** Aaron Osborne; ***W:*** Benjamin Carr; ***C:*** Joe C. Maxwell; ***M:*** Richard Band. *AFE*

Zatoichi: Master Ichi and a Chest of Gold 🦴🦴 **1964** A violent thriller about a blind gambler and former samurai who tries to clear his name after being framed for a gold robbery. Adapted from a novel by Kazuo Miyagawa. In Japanese with English subtitles. **83m/C VHS.** *JP* Shintaro Katsu; ***D:*** Kazuo Ikehiro. *FCT*

Zatoichi: The Blind Swordsman and the Chess Expert 🦴🦴 **1965** Zatoichi, the blind gambler and former samurai, befriends a master chess player and gets involved with Japanese gangsters. In Japanese with English subtitles. **87m/C VHS.** *JP* Shintaro Katsu; ***D:*** Kenji Misumi. *FCT*

Zatoichi: The Blind Swordsman and the Fugitives 🦴🦴 **1968** This time Zatoichi, the blind masseur and master swordsman, is pitted against a band of outlaws. When the local bandits brutalize the countryside Zatoichi steps in to defend the weak and faces a showdown with outlaw leader Genpachiro. In Japanese with English subtitles. **82m/C VHS.** *JP* Shintaro Katsu, Yumiko Nogawa, Kayo Mikimoto, Kyosuke Machida; ***D:*** Kimiyoshi Yasuda. *FCT*

Zatoichi: The Blind Swordsman's Vengeance 🦴🦴 **1966** Zatoichi defends a dying man against a group of gangsters who have taken over an isolated village. In Japanese with English subtitles. **83m/C VHS.** *JP* Shintaro Katsu, Shigeru Amachi, Kei Sato, Mayumi Ogawa; ***D:*** Tokuzo Tanaka. *FCT*

Zatoichi: The Life and Opinion of Masseur Ichi 🦴🦴 **1962** The first film in the action series about the Zen-like blind masseur, gambler, and swordsman. Zatoichi is drawn into a revenge match between two ruthless gangs. When one gang tries to hire him the other hires a savage killer. This sets in motion a war between the yakuza gangs and mercenary samurai. In Japanese with English subtitles. **96m/C VHS.** *JP* Shintaro Katsu, Masayo Mari, Ryuzo Shimada, Gen Mitamura, Shigeru Amachi; ***D:*** Kenji Misumi. *FCT*

Zatoichi vs. Yojimbo 🦴🦴🦴½ *Zatoichi Meets Yojimbo; Zato Ichi To Yojimbo* **1970** The legendary blind warrior-samurai, Zatoichi, wants to retire, but his village is being held captive by outlaws. He is forced to fight Yojimbo, the crude wandering samurai without a master, and the sparks really fly! This was a comic send-up of Akiro Kurosawa's "Yojimbo" with Mifune recreating his role here and playing it for laughs. Subtitled. **90m/C VHS.** *JP* Toshiro Mifune, Shintaro Katsu, Osamu Takizawa; ***D:*** Kihachi Okamoto. *VDA*

Zatoichi: Zatoichi's Flashing Sword 🦴🦴 **1964** Blind swordsman Zatoichi gets caught up in a feud between two competing yakuza bosses. When Zatoichi declares his alliegence to Tsumugi, the unhappy Yasu tries to get his revenge. In Japanese with English subtitles. **82m/C VHS.** *JP* Shintaro Katsu, Mayumi Nagisa, Naoko Kubo, Ryutaro Gami, Yutaka Nakamura; ***D:*** Kazuo Ikehiro. *FCT*

Zazie dans le Metro 🦴🦴🦴½ *Zazie in the Underground; Zazie in the Subway* **1961** One of Malle's early movies, this is one of the best of the French New Wave comedies. A young girl, wise beyond her years, visits her drag queen uncle in Paris. She wants to ride the subway, but the ensuing hilarious adventures keep her from her goal. In French with English subtitles. **92m/C VHS.** *FR* Catherine Demonget, Philippe Noiret, Carla Marlier; ***W:*** Louis Malle. *NYF, INJ*

Zebra Force 🦴 **1976 (R)** Group of army veterans embark on a personal battle against organized crime, using their military training with deadly precision. Non-distinguished substandard action-adventure. **81m/C VHS, Beta.** Mike Lane, Richard X. Slattery, Rockne Tarkington, Glenn Wilder, Anthony Caruso; ***D:*** Joe Tornatore. *MED*

Zebra in the Kitchen 🦴🦴½ **1965** A 12-year-old boy living in a small town is upset when he sees the run-down condition of the local zoo. So he decides to set all the animals free, which causes pandemonium in the town. Pleasant family fare. **92m/C VHS.** Jay North, Martin Milner, Andy Devine, Joyce Meadows, Jim Davis; ***D:*** Ivan Tors. *MGM, BTV*

Zebrahead 🦴🦴🦴 **1992 (R)** Zack and Nikki are two high schoolers in love—which would be okay except Zack's white and Nikki's black. Will their romance succumb to the pressures of society, family, and friends? Writer/director Drazan's expressive debut features one of last appearances by Sharkey as Zack's dad. Outstanding performances by the young and largely unknown cast, particularly Rapaport and Wright, and a great musical score enrich the action. Filmed on location in Detroit, with plenty of authentic Motown scenery to chew on, including Cody High School and a shootout at the eastside Skateland. Developed with assistance by the Sundance Institute. **102m/C VHS, LV, 8mm.** Michael Rapaport, N'Bushe Wright, Ray Sharkey, DeShonn Castle, Ron Johnson, Marsha Florence, Paul Butler, Abdul Hassan Sharif, Dan Ziskie, Candy Ann Brown, Helen Shaver, Luke Reilly, Martin Priest; ***D:*** Tony Drazan; ***W:*** Tony Drazan; ***M:*** Taj Mahal. Sundance Film Festival '92: Filmmakers Trophy. *COL*

A Zed & Two Noughts 🦴🦴🦴 **1988** A serio-comic essay by the acclaimed British filmmaker. Twin zoologists, after their wives are killed in an accident, explore their notions of death by, among other things, filming the decay of animal bodies absconded from the zoo. Heavily textured and experimental; Greenaway's second feature film. **115m/C VHS, Beta.** *GB* Eric Deacon, Brian Deacon, Joss Ackland, Andrea Ferreol, Frances Barber; ***D:*** Peter Greenaway; ***W:*** Peter Greenaway; ***M:*** Michael Nyman. *TPV*

Zelig 🦴🦴🦴½ **1983 (PG)** Documentary spoof stars Allen as Leonard Zelig, the famous "Chameleon Man" of the 1920s, whose personality was so vague he would assume the characteristics of those with whom he came into contact, and who had a habit of showing up among celebrities and at historic events. Filmed in black-and-white; intersperses bits of newsreel and photographs with live action. Allen-style clever filmmaking at its best. **79m/B VHS, Beta, LV, 8mm.** Woody Allen, Mia Farrow, Susan Sontag, Saul Bellow, Irving Howe; ***D:*** Woody Allen; ***W:*** Woody Allen; ***C:*** Gordon Willis. New York Film Critics Awards '83: Best Cinematography; Nominations: Academy Awards '83: Best Cinematography, Best Costume Design. *WAR*

Zelly & Me 🦴🦴🦴 *Phoebe* **1988 (PG)** A strange little drama about a young orphan living with her maniacally possessive grandmother, who forces the child into her own interior life through humiliation and isolation from anyone she cares for. Well-acted and interesting film that suffers from an overly introspective plot and confusing gaps in the narrative. Look for director Lynch on the other side of the camera. **87m/C VHS, Beta, LV.** Isabella Rossellini, Alexandra Johnes, David Lynch, Glynis Johns, Kaiulani Lee, Joe Morton; ***D:*** Tina Rathborne; ***W:*** Tina Rathborne; ***C:*** Mikael Salomon; ***M:*** Pino Donaggio. *COL*

Zentropa 🦴🦴 **1992 (R)** Clever cinematic allusions and visuals aside, this is essentially a conventional thriller. German-American pacifist Leopold travels to Germany in 1945 to help in the postwar rebuilding. He finds work as a sleeping-car conductor for a giant railway system called Zentropa and finds himself romancing the mysterious Katharina, who draws the hapless Leopold into an intrigue involving Nazi sympathizers. Director von Trier uses the voice of Von Sydow as an omniscient narrator to address the audience and move the story along. Filmed primarily in black-and-white with bursts of color denoting dramatic moments. In English and German with English subtitles. **112m/C VHS, Beta, LV.** *GE* Jean-Marc Barr, Barbara Sukowa, Udo Kier, Eddie Constantine; ***D:*** Lars von Trier; ***W:*** Niels Vorsel, Lars von Trier. *TOU*

Zeppelin ♂♂½ **1971 (G)** During WWI, the British enlist the aid of York as a double agent. His mission is to steal Germany's plans for a super-dirigible. Accompanying the Germans on the craft's maiden voyage, York discovers they are actually on a mission to steal British treasures. Although the script is poor, the battle scenes and the blimp itself are very impressive. **102m/C VHS, Beta, LV.** *GB* Michael York, Elke Sommer, Peter Carsten, Marius Goring, Anton Diffring, Andrew Keir, Rupert Davies, Alexandra Stewart; ***D:*** Etienne Perier. *WAR, FCT*

Zeram ♂♂ **1991** Zeram is a giant renegade space alien lured to earth by a female bounty hunter. How does she expect to capture it? Why with a warp machine, space bazooka, electric shield, and a computer named Bob, of course. Dubbed. **92m/C VHS.** *JP* Yuko Moriyama, Yukihiro Hotaru, Kunihiko Ida; ***D:*** Keita Amemiya; ***W:*** Hajime Matsumoto. *FXL, FCT*

Zero **1984** WWII story about the building of the zero fighter that was used to devastating effect in the invasion of Pearl Harbor. **128m/C VHS, Beta.** Yuzo Kayama, Tetsuro Tamba; ***D:*** Toshio Masuda. *NO*

Zero Boys *Woof!* **1986 (R)** Teenage survivalists in the Californian wilderness are stalked by a murderous lunatic. Exploitative and mean-spirited. **89m/C VHS, Beta.** Daniel Hirsch, Kelli Maroney, Nicole Rio, Joe Phelan; ***D:*** Nico Mastorakis. *LIV*

Zero for Conduct ♂♂♂♂ *Zero de Conduit* **1933** Vigo's classic French fantasy about an outrageous rebellion of schoolboys against bureaucratic adults. More of a visual poem than a drama, it inspired Lindsay Anderson's "If...." One of only four films created by Vigo before his early death. Banned across Europe at release. In French with English subtitles. **49m/B VHS, Beta.** *FR* Jean Daste, Robert Le Flon, Louis Lef'evre, Constantin Kelber, Gerard de Bedarieux; ***D:*** Jean Vigo; ***W:*** Jean Vigo; ***C:*** Boris Kaufman. *VYY, NOS, HHT*

Zero for Conduct/Taris/A Propos de Nice **1991** Three short films by the famed Jean Vigo. "Zero for Conduct" is a fascinating and fluid surrealist film about rebellion in a boy's prep school. "Taris" consists of underwater footage of the swimmer Jean Taris, and "A Propos de Nice" is a documentary that focuses on the great economic schism of the rich and the poor in the popular French vacation spot, Nice. **75m/B VHS.** *FR* ***D:*** Jean Renoir. *NO*

Zero Patience ♂♂ **1994** Yes, it's an audacious film musical about AIDS myths and ghosts and Victorian explorers—among other things. Infamous Patient Zero (Fauteux) is the Canadian flight attendant reputed to have carried the virus to North America. Ghostly Zero pleads for someone to tell his story and his cause is taken up by Victorian explorer Sir Richard Francis Burton (Robinson), who happens to have achieved eternal life after an encounter with the Fountain of Youth, and who is also preparing an exhibit on contagious diseases. Sharp mix of politics, humor, and fantasy. **100m/C VHS.** *CA* John Robinson, Normand Fauteux, Dianne Heatherington, Ricardo Keens-Douglas; ***D:*** John Greyson; ***W:*** John Greyson; ***M:*** Glenn Schellenberg. *CCN*

Zero Pilot *Woof!* **1984** A Japanese film about the heroic fighter pilots of WWII. **90m/C VHS, Beta.** *JP VCD*

Zero Population Growth ♂½ *Z.P.G* **1972** In the 21st century the government has decreed that no babies may be born for a 30-year span in order to control the population. But Chaplin and Reed secretly have a child and when they are discovered are sent to be executed. Can they escape? Maudlin and simplistic. **95m/C VHS.** Oliver Reed, Geraldine Chaplin, Diane Cilento, Don Gordon; ***D:*** Michael Campus; ***W:*** Frank de Felitta, Max Ehrlich. *PAR*

Zero to Sixty ♂ **1978 (PG)** Newly divorced man finds his car has been repossessed for nonpayment. Seeking out the manager of the finance company, he gets a job as a repo man with a sassy 16-year-old girl as his assistant. Repartee develops, stuff happens, and the movie ends. **96m/C VHS, Beta.** Darren McGavin, Sylvia Miles, Denise Nickerson, Joan Collins; ***D:*** Don Weis; ***M:*** John Beal. *SUE*

Zero Tolerance ♂♂½ **1993 (R)** FBI agent Jeff Douglas (Patrick) is assigned to travel to Mexico and pick up a drug-runner who works for the White Hand cartel, whose latest product is liquid heroin. When they are ambushed Douglas is forced to carry a shipment of drugs across the border—the lives of his wife and child hang in the balance. But after the dirty deed is done, Douglas finds his family has been murdered anyway. So he sets out to execute the cartel druglords. **92m/C VHS, LV.** Robert Patrick, Miles O'Keeffe, Mick Fleetwood, Titus Welliver, Jeffrey Anderson-Gunter, Gustav Nintas, Michael Gregory, Maurice Lamont; ***D:*** Joseph Merhi; ***W:*** Jacobsen Hart. *PMH, WEA*

Zertigo Diamond Caper ♂ **1982** Utilizing his heightened senses, a blind boy solves a diamond caper and proves his mother's innocence. **50m/C VHS, Beta.** Adam Rich, David Groh, Jane Elliot. *GEM*

Ziegfeld Follies ♂♂½ **1946** A lavish revue of musical numbers and comedy sketches featuring many MGM stars of the WWII era. Highlights include Astaire and Kelly's only duet and a Astaire-Bremer ballet number. ♫Bring on Those Wonderful Men; Bring on Those Beautiful Girls; The Drinking Song; La Traviata; This Heart is Mine; Love; When Television Comes; There's Beauty Everywhere; The Babbitt and the Bromide. **115m/C VHS, Beta, LV.** Fred Astaire, Judy Garland, Gene Kelly, Red Skelton, Fanny Brice, William Powell, Jimmy Durante, Edward Arnold, Lucille Bremer, Hume Cronyn, Victor Moore, Lena Horne, Lucille Ball, Esther Williams; ***D:*** Vincente Minnelli; ***C:*** Charles Rosher. *MGM, MLB*

Ziegfeld Girl ♂♂♂ **1941** Three star-struck girls are chosen for the Ziegfeld follies and move on to success and heartbreak. Lavish costumes and production numbers in the MGM style. ♫You Stepped Out of a Dream; I'm Always Chasing Rainbows; Minnie from Trinidad; Mr. Gallagher & Mr. Shean; You Never Looked So Beautiful. **131m/B VHS, Beta, LV.** James Stewart, Judy Garland, Hedy Lamarr, Lana Turner, Tony Martin, Jackie Cooper, Ian Hunter, Charles Winninger, Al Shear, Edward Everett Horton, Philip Dorn, Paul Kelly, Eve Arden, Dan Dailey, Fay Holden, Felix Bressart, Mae Busch, Reed Hadley; ***D:*** Robert Z. Leonard. *MGM*

Zipperface ♂ **1992** A Palm Beach serial killer is making mincemeat of the local prostitutes. In order to capture the scum, the prerequisite beautiful police detective goes undercover only to find herself the killer's biggest thrill. **90m/C VHS, LV.** Dona Adams, David Clover, John Dagnen; ***D:*** Mansour Pourmand. *AIP*

Zis Boom Bah ♂½ **1942** Musical-comedy star buys a cafe for her college son. He and his friends transform the place into a restaurant-theater with predictable results. ♫Annabella; It Makes No Difference When You're In the Army; Put Your Trust in the Moon; Zis Boom Bah; Good News Tomorrow; I've Learned to Smile Again. **61m/B VHS, Beta.** Peter Lind Hayes, Mary Healy, Grace Hayes, Huntz Hall, Benny Rubin. *NOS, HEG, DVT*

The Zodiac Killer ♂½ **1971 (R)** Based on a true story, this tells the violent tale of the San Francisco murders that occurred in the late 1960s. Doesn't have the suspense it should. **87m/C VHS, Beta.** Tom Pittman, Hal Reed, Bob Jones, Ray Lynch; ***D:*** Tom Hanson. *ACA*

Zoltan...Hound of Dracula ♂½ *Dracula's Dog* **1978** The vampire and his bloodthirsty dog go to Los Angeles to find the last of Count Dracula's living descendants. Campy and just original enough to make it almost worth watching. **85m/C VHS, Beta.** Michael Pataki, Reggie Nalder, Jose Ferrer; ***D:*** Albert Band; ***W:*** Frank Ray Perilli; ***M:*** Andrew Belling. *REP, VCI, FCT*

Zombie ♂ *Zombie Flesh Eaters* **1980** Italian-made white-men-in-the-Caribbean-with-flesh-eating-zombies cheapie. **91m/C VHS, Beta, LV.** *IT* Tisa Farrow, Ian McCulloch, Richard Johnson, Al Cliver, Arnette Gay, Olga Karlatos, Stefania D'Amario; ***D:*** Lucio Fulci. *VES*

The Zombie Army ♂ **1993** Tough drill sergeant tries to whip a bunch of raw female recruits up to muster for a special mission. Toward that end, the government has conveniently bought a defunct lunatic asylum as a training ground. Only problem is that a few of the former inmates have been left behind and are able to menace the troops with their penchant for psychotic weirdness. **80m/C VHS.** Eileen Saddow. *TEM, MOV*

Zombie High ♂ *The School That Ate My Brain* **1987 (R)** Students at a secluded academy are being lobotomized by the school president. Mindless, in two senses of the word. **91m/C VHS, Beta.** Virginia Madsen, Richard Cox, Kay E. Kuter, James Wilder, Sherilyn Fenn, Paul Williams, Scott Coffey; ***D:*** Ron Link. *VTR*

Zombie Island Massacre ♂ **1984 (R)** In this trying film, tourists travel to see a voodoo ritual, and then are systematically butchered by the rite-inspired zombies. Featuring former congressional wife and Playboy Magazine model Jenrette. **89m/C VHS, Beta.** Rita Jenrette, David Broadnax; ***D:*** John N. Carter. *MED*

Zombie Lake ♂ **1984** Killed in an ambush by villagers during WWII, a group of Nazi soldiers turned zombies reside in the town's lake, preying on unsuspecting swimmers, especially dog paddling nude young women. Laughable FX, almost bad enough to be good. From the team that produced "Oasis of the Zombies." **90m/C VHS.** *FR SP* Howard Vernon, Pierre Escourrou, Anouchka, Anthony Mayans, Nadine Pascale, Jean Rollin; ***D:*** J.A. Laser. *VCI*

Zombie Nightmare *Woof!* **1986 (R)** A murdered teenager is revived by a voodoo queen and slaughters his punk-teen assailants. Cheap and stupid just about sums this one up. Music by Motorhead, Death Mask, Girlschool and Thor. **89m/C VHS, Beta.** Adam West, Jon Mikl Thor, Tia Carrere, Frank Dietz, Linda Singer, Mandn E. Turbride, Hamibh McEwen; ***D:*** John Bravman. *NWV*

Zombies of Moratau *Woof!* **1957** A diver and his girlfriend seek to retrieve an undersea treasure of diamonds protected by zombies. So boring you'll want to die. **70m/B VHS, Beta.** Gregg Palmer, Allison Hayes, Jeff Clark, Autumn Russel, Joel Ashley; ***D:*** Edward L. Cahn. *COL, MLB*

Zombies of the Stratosphere *Satan's Satellites* **1952** A serial in twelve chapters in which a cosmic policeman fights Zombies attempting to blow the Earth out of orbit. Also available in a 93 minute, colorized version. **152m/B VHS, Beta, LV.** Judd Holdren, Aline Towne, Leonard Nimoy, John Crawford, Ray Boyle; ***D:*** Fred Brannon. *REP, VCN, MLB*

Zombies on Broadway ♂♂½ *Loonies On Broadway* **1944** Two press agents travel to the Caribbean in search of new talent, but find Lugosi performing experiments on people and turning them into sequel material. RKO hoped this would be equally successful follow-up to "I Walked with a Zombie." **68m/B VHS, LV.** Wally Brown, Alan Carney, Bela Lugosi, Anne Jeffreys, Sheldon Leonard, Frank Jenks, Russell Hopton, Joseph Vitale, Ian Wolfe, Louis Jean Heydt, Darby Jones, Sir Lancelot; ***D:*** Gordon Douglas. *TTC, FCT, IME*

Zombiethon ♂½ **1986** A campy compilation of clips from cheapo zombie films, such as "Space Zombies," "Zombie Lake," and "The Invisible Dead." **90m/C VHS, Beta.** Dominique Singleton, Janelle Lewis, Tracy Burton. *NO*

Zone of the Dead ♂ **1978** A mortician is using his morgue for other than embalming—and it isn't pretty! **81m/C VHS, Beta.** John Ericson, Ivor Francis, Charles Aidman, Bernard Fox. *NO*

Zone Troopers ♂½ **1984 (PG)** Five American G.I.'s in WWII-ravaged Europe stumble upon a wrecked alien spacecraft and enlist the extraterrestrial's help in fending off the Nazis. **86m/C VHS, Beta.** Timothy Van Patten, Tim Thomerson, Art LaFleur, Biff Manard; *D:* Danny Bilson; *W:* Danny Bilson, Paul DeMeo; *M:* Richard Band. *LIV*

Zontar, the Thing from Venus 🦴 **1966** Scientist is taken over by alien batlike thing from Venus, and attempts to take over the Earth. A parody of itself. **68m/C VHS.** John Agar, Anthony Huston, Susan Bjorman, Pat Delaney, Warren Hammack; *D:* Larry Buchanan; *W:* Larry Buchanan; *C:* John Alcott. *SNC, VDM*

The Zoo Gang 🦴½ **1985 (PG-13)** A group of teens want to open a nightclub. Will they bring their dream to fruition, or will the mean rival gang foil their plans? **96m/C VHS, Beta.** Jackie Earle Haley, Tiffany Helm, Ben Vereen, Jason Gedrick, Eric Gurry; *D:* John Watson, Pen Densham; *W:* John Watson, Pen Densham; *M:* Patrick Gleeson. *NWV, VTR*

Zoo Radio 🦴½ **1990 (R)** Run by a wacky assortment of characters, a zany underground radio station embarks on a battle against bureaucracy. **90m/C VHS.** *WAX*

Zooman 🦴🦴🦴 **1995 (R)** Hard-hitting message on violence and responsibility. Gang member Zooman (Kain) spots members of a rival gang in a Brooklyn neighborhood, whips out his gun, and begins firing. When the shooting stops, a little girl sitting on her stoop is dead—what's even worse for her estranged parents is the fact that obvious witnesses refuse to identify the gunman for fear of their own safety. So father Reuben (Gossett Jr.) puts up a sign about their plight, attracting lots of media attention, and neighborhood hostility. Based on Fuller's 1978 play "Zooman and the Sign." Made for cable TV. **95m/C VHS.** Louis Gossett Jr., Charles S. Dutton, Khalil Kain, Cynthia Martells, CCH Pounder, Vondie Curtis-Hall, Hill Harper; *D:* Leon Ichaso; *W:* Charles Fuller. *REP*

Zoot Suit 🦴🦴🦴 **1981 (R)** Based on Luis Valdez' play, this murder mystery/musical is rooted in the historical Sleepy Lagoon murder in the 1940s. Valdez plays a Mexican-American accused of the crime. His friends (and defense lawyers) rally around him to fight this travesty of justice. Lots o'music and dancing. **104m/C VHS, LV.** Edward James Olmos, Daniel Valdez, Tyne Daly, Charles Aidman, John Anderson; *D:* Luis Valdez; *W:* Luis Valdez. *MCA, FCT*

Zora Is My Name! 🦴🦴½ **1990** The funny, moving story of Zora Neal Hurston, a Black writer known for her stories and folklore of the rural South of the '30s and '40s. From PBS's American Playhouse. **90m/C VHS, LV.** Ruby Dee, Louis Gossett Jr. *PBS, KAR, FCT*

Zorba the Greek 🦴🦴🦴½ *Zormba* **1964** A young British writer (Bates) comes to Crete to find himself by working his father's mine. He meets Zorba, an itinerant Greek laborer (Quinn), and they take lodgings together with an aging courtesan, who Zorba soon romances. The writer, on the other hand, is attracted to a lovely young widow. When she responds to him, the townsmen jealously attack her. Zorba teaches the young man the necessary response to life and its tragedies. Based on a novel by Nikos Kazantzakis. Masterpiece performance from Quinn. Beautifully photographed, somewhat overlong. Film later written for stage production. **142m/B VHS, Beta, LV.** Anthony Quinn, Alan Bates, Irene Papas, Lila Kedrova; *D:* Michael Cacoyannis; *C:* Walter Lassally. Academy Awards '64: Best Art Direction/Set Decoration (B & W), Best Black and White Cinematography, Best Supporting Actress (Kedrova); Nominations: Academy Awards '64: Best Actor (Quinn), Best Adapted Screenplay, Best Director (Cacoyannis), Best Picture. *FXV, BTV, FUS*

Zorro Rides Again **1937** Zorro risks his life to outwit enemy agents endeavoring to secure ancestor's property. In twelve chapters, the first runs 30 minutes, the rest 17. **217m/B VHS, Beta.** John Carroll, Helen Christian, Noah Beery Sr., Duncan Renaldo; *D:* William Witney, John English. *NOS, VCN, MED*

Zorro, the Gay Blade 🦴🦴½ **1981 (PG)** Tongue-in-cheek sword play with Hamilton portraying the swashbuckling crusader and his long-lost brother, Bunny Wigglesworth, in this spoof of the Zorro legend. The fashion-conscious hero looks his best in plum. Leibman is fun to watch. **96m/C VHS, Beta.** George Hamilton, Lauren Hutton, Brenda Vaccaro, Ron Leibman; *D:* Peter Medak; *W:* Greg Alt; *C:* John A. Alonzo. *FOX*

Zorro's Black Whip **1944** A young girl dons the mask of her murdered brother (Zorro) to fight outlaws in the old West. Serial in twelve episodes. **182m/B VHS, LV.** George Lewis, Linda Stirling, Lucien Littlefield, Francis McDonald, Tom London; *D:* Spencer Gordon Bennet; *W:* Wallace Grissell. *NOS, GPV, MED*

Zorro's Fighting Legion **1939** Zorro forms a legion to help the president of Mexico fight a band of outlaws endeavoring to steal gold shipments. A serial in 12 chapters. **215m/B VHS, LV.** Reed Hadley, Sheila Darcy; *D:* William Witney, John English. *NOS, VCN, VDM*

Zotz! 🦴🦴 **1962** The holder of a magic coin can will people dead by uttering "zotz"; spies pursue the mild-mannered professor who possesses the talisman. Adapted from a Walter Karig novel. Typical William Castle fare; his gimic in the theatrical release of the movie was to distribute plastic "zotz" coins to the theatre patrons. **87m/B VHS, Beta.** Tom Poston, Julia Meade, Jim Backus, Fred Clark, Cecil Kellaway; *D:* Ray Russell; *W:* Ray Russell. *COL*

Zou Zou 🦴🦴½ **1934** Lavish backstage musical/drama of a laundress who fills in for the leading lady on opening night and becomes a hit. Baker's talking picture debut. In French with English subtitles. **92m/B VHS, LV.** *FR* Josephine Baker, Jean Gabin; *D:* Marc Allegret. *MVD, KIV, APD*

Zulu 🦴🦴½ **1964** In 1879, a small group of British soldiers try to defend their African outpost from attack by thousands of Zulu warriors. Amazingly, the British win. Dated colonial epic based on an actual incident; battle scenes are magnificent. Prequel "Zulu Dawn" (1979) depicts British mishandling of the situation that led to the battle. **139m/C VHS, Beta, LV.** Michael Caine, Jack Hawkins, Stanley Baker, Nigel Green; *D:* Cy Endfield; *M:* John Barry. *NLC*

Zulu Dawn 🦴🦴🦴 **1979 (PG)** An historical epic about British troops fighting the Zulus at Ulandi in 1878. Shows the increasing tensions between the British colonial government and the Zulus. Stunning landscapes unfortunately don't translate to the small screen. Good but unoriginal colonial-style battle drama. **117m/C VHS, Beta, LV.** Burt Lancaster, Peter O'Toole, Denholm Elliott, Nigel Davenport, John Mills, Simon Ward, Bob Hoskins, Freddie Jones; *D:* Douglas Hickox; *M:* Elmer Bernstein. *TWE*

Zvenigora 🦴🦴🦴🦴 **1928** Dovzhenko's first major film, and a lyrical revelation in the face of Soviet formality: a passionate, funny fantasy tableaux of 1,000 years of Ukrainian history, encompassing wild folk myths, poetic drama, propaganda and social satire. Silent. **73m/B VHS, Beta.** *RU* Mikola Nademsy, Alexander Podorozhny, Semyon Svashenko; *D:* Alexander Dovzhenko. *FCT, INJ*

Category List

The **Category Index** contains genre, sub-genre, thematic, or significant scene classifications, ranging from the very general (drama, comedy) to the fairly particular (phone terror, killer cars). The terms are defined (more or less) below. We've done our best to provide serious subject references while also including fun categories and lists to make your video viewing experience a little more enjoyable. No one list is all-inclusive. We are continuously reclassifying, adding, and subtracting movies. Many of the categories in this list are new and represent only a beginning. We're also trying to pare down some of the bigger categories, like **Romance**, by creating more focused subject categories, such as **Lovers on the Lam** or **Romantic Triangles.** *VideoHound* invites readers to join in this pastime by sending in suggestions for new categories and new titles for existing ones. **An asterisk (*) denotes a new category for this edition.**

ABBA-ca-da-bra: Australian films pay homage to the kitschy '70s pop icons, reviving "Dancing Queen" and "Waterloo"

Action-Adventure: Adrenaline testers for those weary of the conventions of plot— think Stallone, think Snipes, and quit thinking

Adoption & Orphans: Cute kids lacking permanent authority figures, ranging from *Annie* to *Wild Hearts Can't Be Broken*

Adventure Drama: Action with more attention to dramatic content—*Apocalypse Now* to *Robin Hood, Prince of Thieves*

Advertising: Corporate shenanigans at the agency—*How to Get Ahead in Advertising* to *The Horse in the Gray Flannel Suit*

Africa: Banana Republic franchise; *Out of Africa* to *Zulu DawnAfrican America:* Dominant African American themes

AIDS: Someone usually dies; *An Early Frost* to *Longtime Companion*

Air Disasters: Contraptions up in the sky, but not for long

Airborne: Contraptions up in the sky

Alien Beings—Benign: Friendly space visitors, including *Howard the Duck* and little buddy *E.T.*

Alien Beings—Vicious: Not-so-friendly space visitors, notably the multi-jawed *Alien* continually harassing Sigourney Weaver

American South: Theatrics amid much brow mopping and drawling; *A Streetcar Named Desire* rattling down *Flamingo Road*

America's Heartland: Generally heartwarming small-town sagas

Amnesia: Phone call for *Anastasia*

Amusement Parks: Cotton candy, ferris wheels, Coney Island, *Godzilla on Monster Island, Rollercoaster*

Angels: Benevolent winged visitors from above: *Wings of Desire*

Animated Musicals: Boys, girls, dogs, ducks, birds, mice, and monkeys croon; many of Disney vintage, including *Aladdin* and *Sleeping Beauty*

Animation & Cartoons: Antics of Daffy, Donald, Bugs, Mickey, Chip, Dale, Tom, Jerry, Fred, Wilma, Charlie, and the rest of the gang

Anthology: More than one story to a cassette

Anti-Heroes: From *Billy Jack* to *Dirty Harry* to *Thelma & Louise*

Anti-War War Movies: Recognizes that war really is hell—from *All Quiet on the Western Front* to *Glory* to *M*A*S*H*

Apartheid: Afrikaans term for racial segregation in South Africa

Art & Artists: They paint, pause, and propagate with equal passion

Asia: *China White, Red Dust, Sand Pebbles*

Asian America: Asian experience in the US—*The Joy Luck Club, Come See the Paradise*

Assassinations: Lincoln, *JFK, La Femme Nikita, Times of Harvey Milk*, and more

At the Movies: The movie within a movie or movies about watching the movies, from *The Purple Rose of Cairo* to *Last Action Hero* to *Matinee*

Avant-garde: Ahead of its time or completely bewildering to most in the audience

Babysitting: Supervision of small-fry pranksters not your own; *Uncle Buck* to *The Hand that Rocks the Cradle*

Bad Dads: Daddy-Os with unpredictable mean streak: *The Shining, Kiss Daddy Goodbye*

Ballet: On your toes—*The Turning Point*

Ballooning: Up, up and away, or *Around the World in 80 Days*

Baltimore: Take a look at the Maryland city, hometown of director Barry Levinson and favorite digs of John Waters

Baseball: Action on the diamond, ranging from *Bull Durham* to *A League of Their Own* to *Rookie of the Year*

Basketball: Roundball thrillers, including the memorable *The Fish that Saved Pittsburgh* and *White Men Can't Jump*

Bathroom Scenes: Encompassing bathtubs, hottubs, showers, sinks and toilets, including *Psycho, Fatal Attraction* and that poor fellow in *Jurassic Park*

Beach Blanket Bingo: Annette, Frankie, sand, surf, bikinis

Beauty Pageants: From the heartless to the hilarious, beauty is a big business—*Smile* girls!

Behind the Scenes: Peek behind show business curtain, from *A Chorus Line* to *Truth or Dare*

Berlin: City in Germany divided after WWII, now it's one big happy city again

Bicycling: Two wheels, no motor, much leg action and sweating

Big Battles: Big-budget (or at least illusion of such) clash of large, opposing military forces, from *Cromwell* to *Ran*

Big Budget Stinkers: Millions spent for no apparent reason

Big Daddies: Usually troublesome, with Freudian overtones

Big Digs: Anthropology and archaeology, from Indiana Jones to various mummy on-the-loose stories

Big Ideas: Philosophy, ideology and other semi-mental pursuits somehow translated to film

Big Rigs: *Smokey and the Bandit* speed down *Thieves' Highway* in a *Convoy*

Bigfoot/Yeti: Large, hairy, seldom-seen beast with really big feet

Bikers: Usually with a mean streak and traveling in leather-clad packs

Birds: Beaks, feathers, talons, bird #%!; *The Birds, Beaks: The Movie, Howard the Duck*

Bisexuality: Going both ways—*Basic Instinct, Three of Hearts*

Black Comedy: Funny in a biting or despairing sort of way, from *The Addams Family* to *The Hospital*

Black Gold: That's oil; aka *Oklahoma Crude*

***Blackmail:** I'm gonna tell, unless... *The Last Seduction, Letter to My Killer*

Blaxploitation: '70s remakes of horror classics with black casts: *Blacula, Blackenstein, Dr. Black, Mr. Hyde*

Blindness: Can't see or sight impaired; *Afraid of the Dark*

Bloody Mayhem: Expanded scenes of arterial explosions, including *Blood Bride, Blood Cult, Blood Diner, Blood Feast, Blood Lake, Blood Legacy, Blood Mania*, and *Bloodbath in Psycho Town*

Bloody Messages: Cryptic warnings to the living written in the blood of the poor slob who was just killed—Redrum

Bodyguards: Costner looks after Whitney's personal business

Books: As a major plot device: *La Lectrice* to *Crossing Delancey*

Boom!: Really big explosions, bombs, and other noisy or fiery messes popular in big budget action flicks

Boomer Reunions: thirtysomethings gather and reminisce: *The Big Chill*

***Boston:** Beantown, where everybody knows your name.

Bowling: Heavy round ball is thrown down waxed alley toward club-like pins; all fall down

Boxing: Yo, Adrian!

Bringing Up Baby: *Look Who's Talking* to *Raising Arizona* , plus infants with that little something different—*Alien 3, Enemy Mine, Basket Case 3: The Progeny*

Buddies: Butch and Sundance, Bill and Ted, Rubin and Ed, *Thelma and Louise*

Buddy Cops: Couple of police hanging together, usually practicing limited repartee at a donut shop; *Lethal Weapon, Tango and Cash*

Buses: Large truck-like passenger vehicles—*Speed, The Big Bus, The Trip to Bountiful*

Calcutta: Big, overpopulated city in India

Camelot (New): The exploits of JFK, Jackie, and various relatives and hangers-on

Camelot (Old): The exploits of King Arthur and his *Knights of the Round Table*

Campus Capers: What really goes on at college—*Assault of the Party Nerds*

Canada: Renfrew the Mounties plus lots of wilderness and the occasional hockey puck

Canine Cops: He's a cop, he's got a badge, he's a dog—*K-9, Turner & Hooch*

Cannibalism: People who eat people are the luckiest people; *Alive, Rabid Grannies, Cannibal Women in the Avocado Jungle of Death, The Cook, the Thief, His Wife & Her Lover*

Capitol Capers: Hollywood versions of hijinks in Washington, D.C.—*Dave, Mr. Smith Goes to Washington, All the President's Men*

Carnivals & Circuses: Big top, little top, domes: *Shakes the Clown* to *Rollercoaster*, plus *Big Top Pee Wee, State Fair*, and metaphoric circuses: *Brewster McCloud, La Strada*

Cats: Lesser vertebrate nonetheless much beloved by Hollywood

Cave People: From the most primitive (*The Clan of the Cave Bear*) to the fairly modernized (*The Flintstones*)

Central America: Mostly Latin warfare, with at least three sides to every conflict

Chases: Who are those guys? Someone's after someone else, usually at high-speed with transportation ranging from horses to autos to bikes to trains to trucks

Cheerleaders: Give me an A! *The Positively True Adventures of the Alleged Texas Cheerleader-Murdering Mom* meets *Revenge of the Cheerleaders*

Chicago: City in Illinois, right at the bottom of Lake Michigan

Child Abuse: Not very funny at all—*Mommie Dearest, Fallen Angel*

Childhood Visions: Stories dominated by the kid point of view, or by an adult flashbacking to childhood; *Au Revoir Les Enfants, Home Alone*

China: *The Last Emperor* to *Red Sorghum* to *The World of Suzie Wong*

Christmas: Reindeer, Santa, children make appearance amid much sentimentality

Cinderella Stories: Gal down on her luck meets fairy godmother (or father) and finds true love—*Pretty Woman, Flashdance, Cinderella*

Civil Rights: Fighting for equality—*The Autobiography of Miss Jane Pittman, Mississippi Burning*

Civil War: The Yankees against the Confederates; aka *The Blue and the Gray*

Classic Horror: Boris Karloff, Vincent Price, piercing screams

Clowns: Big red noses, huge feet, painted smiles frighten many

Cold Spots: Set in a frostbitten locale with lots of shivering; *Ice Station Zebra, Never Cry Wolf, Quest for Fire*

Comedy: Yuck fests not listed in other comedy categories—*Fletch, I Wanna Hold Your Hand, Tampopo*

Comedy Anthologies: More than one yuck fest on a cassette

Comedy Drama: Drama with a comedic touch or comedy underwired with drama—*Avalon, The Big Chill, Fried Green Tomatoes, One Flew Over the Cuckoo's Nest, Tootsie*

***Comedy Mystery:** Wacky whodunits like *Murder by Death, Clue*

***Comedy Sci-Fi:** Laughs in space! *Spaceballs*

Comic Adventure: Adventurous romps liberally laced with humor: *Romancing the Stone* to *Bird on a Wire* to *Crocodile Dundee*

Coming of Age: Hard-fought adolescent battle for adulthood, led by *American Graffiti, The Apprenticeship of Duddy Kravitz, The Karate Kid*

Computers: Bits and bytes play major role

Concert Films: Rock or comedy concerts—from *Woodstock* to *Divine Madness* to *Eddie Murphy: Raw*

Contemporary Musicals: Thematically modern and made during last 20 years; *All That Jazz*

Contemporary Noir: Dark and moody or tributes to dark and moody that pay homage to the original Film Noir genre—*Blue Velvet, 9 Weeks, sex, lies, and videotape, Wild Orchid*

Cops: Police and pseudo-police work, including *Action Jackson, Blue Steel, The Choirboys, RoboCop, Lethal Weapon, National Lampoon's Loaded Weapon 1*

Corporate Shenanigans: Big Business runs amuck—*Barbarians at the Gate, Wall Street*

Credits Chaos!: Don't rewind, 'cuz it's not over till it's over

Creepy Houses: Scary dwellings—*Amityville Horror* 1 through 33

Crime & Criminals: Bad guys and gals, including *Avenging Disco Godfather, The Grifters, In Cold Blood*

Crime Sprees: Bad guy, gal or couple goes on a crime binge and other tales of obsessional criminal activity, including *Bonnie & Clyde, The Boys Next Door*

Crimes of Passion: Love, sex, and death

Crop Dusters: Down on the farm: *Bitter Harvest, Pelle the Conqueror, Jean de Florette, The River*

Cult Items: Recognized for that something different by a relatively small group (at least initially) of boomer-type people: *Basket Case, Blood Simple, Harold and Maude, Mad Max*, and the greatest cult of them all—*The Rocky Horror Picture Show*

Cult Items—New: Revered by a relatively large group of Generation X-type people: *Bill & Ted's Excellent Adventure, Grease, Sixteen Candles, The Sure Thing*

Cults: Something like a gang but more intense and usually governed by a state of mind similar to irrationality—*Helter Skelter*

Cyberpunk: Dark, moody, futuristic flicks—*Blade Runner, Freejack, Tank Girl*

Dads: Fathers play a major role

Dance Fever: Whole lotta foot-tapping going on, including *An American in Paris, Daddy Long Legs*, and *Dirty Dancing*

Dates from Hell: Fun evening for two singles turns into a nightmare for one of them—*Bye Bye Love, Singles, Something Wild*

Deafness: Can't hear or hearing impaired; *Bridge to Silence, The Miracle Worker*

Death & The Afterlife: Could be ghosts, could be voices from the beyond, could be any number of post-dead things—*Beetlejuice, Carnival of Souls, Flatliners, Poltergeist, Weekend at Bernie's*

***Death Row:** Waitin' for a call from the Governor; *Dead Man Walking, Angels with Dirty Faces*

Dedicated Teachers: From *The Dead Poet's Society* to *The Blackboard Jungle* to *The Miracle Worker*

Deep Blue: The sea around us, including *ffolkes* and *Splash*

Demons & Wizards: Swords, sorcery and wrinkled old men with wands—*The Alchemist, The Hobbit, The Sword & the Sorcerer*

Dental Mayhem: Tooth-pickin' uproars; *Marathon Man, The Dentist*

Desert War/Foreign Legion: Big battles among the dunes

Deserts: Endless beach minus the water—*Ishtar, Lawrence of Arabia*

Detective Spoofs: Putting together clues in humorous fashion—*The Adventures of Sherlock Holmes' Smarter Brother, The Naked Gun*

Detectives: Clue happy but often grizzled and cynical—*The Drowning Pool, V.I. Warshawski*

Devils: Some may meet on *Judgment Day*

Dinosaurs: *Jurassic Park* and other less animated thundering lizards

Disaster Flicks: Natural and man-made, including 47 *Airport* sequels

Disco Musicals: '70s tackiness reigns supreme, from *Saturday Night Fever* to *Xanadu*

Disease of the Week: Bulimia, anorexia, polio, cancer, and so on

Disorganized Crime: Stupid crime, including *Amos and Andrew, Dog Day Afternoon, Home Alone, Quick Change*

Divorce: Breaking up is hard to do; *Accidental Tourist, Heartburn, Kramer vs. Kramer*

Doctors & Nurses: Men and women in scrubs concerned about health of complete strangers for profit, often to the dismay of the patient—*Autopsy, Candy Stripe Nurses, Dead Ringers*

Docudrama: *The Thin Blue Line* between documentaries and drama

Documentary: Real life manipulated on film—*A Brief History of Time, The Last Waltz, Paris Is Burning, Roger and Me*

Down Under: Australian, New Zealand settings—*The Rescuers Down Under, Gallipoli, The Man from Snowy River, The Thorn Birds*

***Dragons:** Legendary medieval lizards, usually with fiery dispositions; *Dragonheart, Pete's Dragon*

Drama: Conflict, tension, climax, resolution

Dream Girls: Product of mid-life male crisis; *Battling Amazons, Cycle Vixens, The Doll Squad, The Woman in Red*

Earthquakes: Common occurrence in California

Eco-Vengeance!: Nature wreaks havoc on man—watch out for *Alligators, Frogs* and *Piranhas*

Edibles: Something's cooking—*Babette's Feast, Like Water for Chocolate*

Elevators: Sometimes the oddest things happen in them...

Emerging Viruses: Deadly virus spreads like wildfire as frantic medical personnel search for a cure; think ebola

The Empire State Building: Used to be the tallest building in NYC, still the most famous

Erotic Thrillers: Hot sex and murder, including *Basic Instinct, Body of Evidence*

Ethics & Morals: Examination of values (or lack of)—*Crimes & Misdemeanors, Judgment at Nuremberg*

Etiquette: Usually comedy of manners: *Educating Rita, My Fair Lady* **Evil Doctors:** Don't go to these guys for a checkup—*Malice, Dead Ringers*, and *Doctor X*

Exploitation: Rigged to take advantage of viewer, including historic treats like *Reefer Madness* and more recent ventures such as *Sleazemania*

Explorers: Going boldly where no man or woman has regularly gone before

Extraordinary Pairings: Jesse James meets Frankenstein's Daughter

Eyeballs!: Unnerving scenes involving pupils, irises, lids, and occasionally, lashes

Fairs & Expositions: Short term amusement parks: *State Fair*

Family Ties: Blood runs deep—*Back to the Future, Five Easy Pieces, The Godfather, Homeward Bound, Lorenzo's Oil, The Mosquito Coast, Rocket Gibraltar*

Fantasy: Tales of the imagination, including *Alice* and her looking glass, *E.T., Ladyhawke, My Stepmother Is an Alien*

Fast Cars: *Eat My Dust;* racing in the street or on the track; *The Last American Hero*

Feds: Men and women of the Bureau, the Agency, or any national police organization with an acronym and a dress code

***Female Bonding:** Women get together, usually to the men's dismay; *Waiting to Exhale*

Femme Fatale: She done him and him and him wrong

Fencing: En garde, dude

Film & Film History: *America at the Movies;* includes movies important to film history

Film Noir: Dark and moody or tributes to dark and moody—-*Farewell, My Lovely, The Postman Always Ring Twice, The Third Man, Who Framed Roger Rabbit?*

Film Stars: Movies or bios about cinema celebs, real or make-believe—Bogie, Chaplin, Sinatra

Filmmaking: The making of a film within a film: *The Player*

Firemen: *Backdraft, Fahrenheit 451*, and other tales of brave people with hoses

Fires: *Frankenstein, Quest for Fire, Pyrates*

***Flashback:** Why I remember like it was yesterday. It all started when...*The Usual Suspects, Casablanca*

Flatulence: Embarrassing gaseous emissions

Flower Children: The sixties are still alive at *Alice's Restaurant*—reflect on *The Big Chill, The Doors*, and *Woodstock*; we all live in a *Yellow Submarine*

Folklore & Mythology: Age-old adult tales covering Atlantis, little people, Hercules, Ulysses

Football: Everything from terrorist attacks on the Superbowl (*Black Sunday*) to prison competition (*The Longest Yard*) plus *Diner*

Foreign Intrigue: Overseas mystery, with emphasis on accent and location

Frame-ups: Someone's set up to take the rap: *My Cousin Vinny* to *Consenting Adults*

France: From *Dirty Rotten Scoundrels* to *The Moderns* to *Gigi* to *The Last Metro* to *Killer Tomatoes Eat France*

Front Page: *Citizen Kane, All the President's Men, The Philadelphia Story*, and other journalistic stories

Fugitives: Running from the law; *Breathless, Nowhere to Hide, Posse*

Funerals: The final good-bye—*Four Weddings and a Funeral, Gardens of Stone, The Big Chill*

Gambling: Aces and Eights, *The Color of Money, Eight Men Out, Honeymoon in Vegas*

Game Shows: *The Running Man* and *Queen for a Day*

Gangs: Criminally enterprising teens and adults running in packs: *State of Grace, Miller's Crossing, Public Enemy, The Wanderers*

Gays: Gay themes—*Kiss of the Spider Woman, The Hunger*

Gender Bending: *The Crying Game, La Cage aux Folles, Her Life as a Man* and other instances of boys becoming girls and vice versa

Generation X: Slacking in the '90s—*Reality Bites, Singles*

Genetics: Fooling with the double helix—*The Fly*

Genies: *Aladdin* finds magic lamp filled with compressed Robin Williams

Genre Spoofs: Wacky takes on serious films, starting with the granddaddy of them all: *Airplane!*

Germany: *The Blue Angel, Wings of Desire*

Ghosts, Ghouls, & Goblins: *Ghostbusters, Topper, Poltergeist*

Giants: *The Amazing Colossal Man* visits *Village of the Giants*

Gifted Children: Kids show amazing talents that astound adults, from *Rookie of the Year* to *Little Man Tate*

Gigolos: Men try the oldest profession in the world, working around biological limitations

Go Fish: Casting a line in the river that runs through it; *Man of Aran, A Fish Called Wanda, Captains Courageous*

Going Native: Outsiders try to blend in; *Dances with Wolves, The Swiss Family Robinson*

Golf: Slow boring game best experienced on screen ("Be the ball, Danny")

Good Earth: Ecology, environment, nature, sod

Grand Hotel: Checkout time is noon; *Blame It on the Bellboy*

Great Britain: Thwarted royals (*Charles & Diana: A Palace Divided, Edward and Mrs. Simpson*), kings (*King Ralph*), queens (*The Naked Civil Servant*), class distinctions (*The Ruling Class*), vanished empires (*Cromwell, A Man for All Seasons*), criminals (*The Krays, The Long Good Friday*) plus multiple stiff upper lips, the Brontes, and Dickens

Great Death Scenes: Signing off with style or elaboration; *Buffy the Vampire Killer, Bonnie and Clyde, Breaker Morant*

Great Depression: The era, not the state of mind—*Bound for Glory, Of Mice and Men, The Grapes of Wrath, Rambling Rose*

Great Escapes: Seizing the day for freedom—*The Big Doll House, Escape from Alcatraz, Papillon*

Growing Older: *On Golden Pond, *batteries not included, Cocoon, Driving Miss Daisy, The Shootist, The Wild Bunch*

Guys in Kilts: Celtic hunks like *Rob Roy* in plaid skirts

Gymnastics: Human pretzels

Happy Hookers: Prostitution with a rosy glow; *The Happy Hooker Goes to Hollywood* and meets *Pretty Woman*

Hard Knock Life: Poverty and bad luck; *City of Joy, The Match Factory Girl*

Hearts!: Unnerving scenes involving human hearts, generally seen by the audience and almost always still pumping

***Hawaii:** The 50th state, fun in the sun, if the volcanoes are behaving.

Heaven Sent: Visits or returns from the place where good souls and all dogs go— *Field of Dreams* to *Made in Heaven* to *Oh God!*

Heists: The big lift

Hell High School: Place where adolescents gather against their will; also known as *Rock 'n' Roll High School*

Hispanic America: Dominant Hispanic American themes (*Salsa, Mi Vida Loca*)

Historical Drama: Usually at least loosely based on a real incident or personality

Hit Men: Boys and girls armed with silencers; *Prizzi's Honor, Romeo is Bleeding*

Hockey: *Slap Shot* and other icy tales of passing the puck

Holidays: Easter, Thanksgiving, New Year's, Halloween, but generally not Christmas

Holocaust: *Playing for Time, Schindler's List*

Home Alone: Kids find themselves without adult supervision—*Adventures in Babysitting* to *Young Sherlock Holmes*

Homeless: Street people with no homes

Horrible Holidays: Holidays with a ghoulish twist—*Bloody New Year, Halloween, My Bloody Valentine, Silent Night, Bloody Night*

Horror: Modern cut 'em up scare theater

Horror Anthologies: More than one scarefest on a cassette

Horror Comedy: Tongue-in-bloody cheek—*The Fearless Vampire Killers, Piranha, Sorority Babes in the Slimeball Bowl-A-Rama*

Horses: Can you say *Black Beauty?*

Hospitals & Medicine: Dysfunctional institutional health care—*Article 99, The Hospital, One Flew Over the Cuckoo's Nest, Young Doctors in Love*

Hostage!: People held against their will for bargaining purposes

***Houston:** That big city in Texas where J.R. didn't live, but Roger Clemens did.

Hunted!: Humans tracking humans for trophy purposes

Hunting: Where's dat wascally wabbit? *Caddyshack, The Bear, White Hunter, Black Heart*

Hurling: What goes down sometimes comes back up—*The Exorcist, Parenthood*

I Love Detroit: The Motor City, home of Motown, lots of cars, and—VideoHound

Identity: Who am I? Who are you? Who are we? Why do you ask so many questions?

Immigration: Melting pot stories—*Avalon, Far and Away, Living on Tokyo Time*

Incest: Implied or actual relationships among family members—*The Grifters, Spanking the Monkey*

India: On the road to *Bombay*

Interviews: When asked questions, people talk

Inventors & Inventions: Those wacky folks and their newfangled machines; *Chitty Chitty Bang Bang*

Interracial Affairs: Couple from different racial backgrounds cause trauma for family and friends —*Mississippi Masala, Jungle Fever*

Ireland: Aye, make that a pint for take away; *The Field, Cal, The Playboys*

Islam: Religious themes

Island Fare: Thin, isolated stretch of land surrounded by water notorious for encouraging natural appetites in men and women

Israel: *Cast a Giant Shadow, Exodus*

Italy: Passion, vino, lust, vino, Sophia Loren

Japan: *Land of the Rising Sun, Godzilla, Hiroshima, Mon Amour*

Japanimation: Animated cartoons from Japan with cult following

Judaism: *Fiddler on the Roof* meets *Funny Girl*

Jungle Stories: Tarzan, tribes, trees, treasure, temperature, temptresses, tigers

Justice Prevails?: The verdict's in, but is it fair? *And Justice for All, In the Name of the Father, Presumed Innocent*

Kidnapped!: Held for ransom or just for the heck of it—*A Perfect World, Raising Arizona*

Killer Apes: *King Kong* lives on *The Planet of the Apes*

Killer Appliances: Defrosted refrigerator goes on killing binge

Killer Beasts: Cloned dinosaurs run amuck in backyard, destroying patio

Killer Brains: Literally has a mind of its own, i.e., *The Brain That Wouldn't Die*

Killer Bugs: Giant and/or miserably mean spiders, ants, bees, worms, flies, slugs, tarantulas, wasps, and other creepy things

Killer Cars: You should have changed *Christine*'s oil

Killer Dogs: Fido takes a walk on the wild side—*Cujo*, baby

Killer Dreams: More like nightmares on elm street

Killer Kats: Kitties with a killer instinct

Killer Pigs: Evil swine

Killer Plants: Too much fertilizer produces killer tomatoes (stewed)

Killer Rodents: Nasty mice, rats, bats, and shrews

Killer Toys: Demented play things develop homicidal urges; why hello, Chucky

Kindness of Strangers: Baffling altruistic behavior

King of Beasts (Dogs): Need we say more?

Korean War: *M*A*S*H* and friends

L.A.: Smoggy city in California also known as Los Angeles or the City of Angels; includes Hollywood & Beverly Hills

Labor & Unions: *Hoffa* and other working stiffs

Late Bloomin' Love: Better late than not blooming at all

Law & Lawyers: Tom Cruise joins *The Firm* and other realistic legal adventures

Lesbians: Lesbian themes—*Lianna, Bar Girls*

***Libraries & Librarians:** Important things happen where you can't talk–sometimes people even read!

***Life Imitates Art:** Kids, don't try this at home. (They did.)

Lifeguards: Rescuers of the swimming-challenged

London: City in merry old England, home to many generations of the most famous royals

Loner Cops: *Dirty Harry* Syndrome

Lost Worlds: From *Brigadoon* to *The People That Time Forgot*

***Lovable Loonies:** Crazy, but not Norman Bates crazy; *Crazy People, Benny & Joon*

Lovers on the Lam: Couple commit crimes and find themselves on the run—*Badlands, Natural Born Killers, True Romance*

Macho Men: Ah-nuld, The Duke, Van Damme, Stallone, Burt, Clint, Norris, Seagal, and many more cases of excessive testosterone

Mad Scientists: *The Brain That Wouldn't Die* spends an evening with *Frankenhooker*

Magic: Hocus pocus, often with evil intent

Magic Carpet Rides: *Aladdin* joins *Sinbad the Sailor* for *The Golden Voyage of Sinbad*

Marriage: Wedding bells, honeymoons, affairs, divorce, and growing old together, as well as the occasional unfortunate marital union with a blood-sucking vampire or knife-wielding satanist

Martial Arts: Fists of Aluminum Foil; much head-kicking, rib-crunching, chop-socky action

Martyred Pop Icons: For us, they gave their all; Buddy Holly, Elvis, Marilyn, James Dean, *Stardust Memories*

Mass Media: From *Network* to *Broadcast News* to *My Favorite Year*

***May-December Romance:** Older people meet younger people and the romantic sparks fly; *Harold and Maude* visit *Atlantic City*.

The Meaning of Life: The search for the elusive answer—*My Life, The Remains of the Day, Shadowlands*

Medieval Romps: Dirty peasants, deodorized and glorified kings and queens, splendid knights in shining armor, and one for all and all for one

Meltdown: Or how I learned to stop worrying and love the bomb; also bad wiring at local nuclear plants

Men: What is man? Is he neither fish nor fowl? Or perhaps linoleum?

Men in Prison: Working on a chain gang; what we have here is a failure to communicate

Mental Retardation: *Bill, Charly*, Dominick, Lenny, Raymond (definitely)

Metamorphosis: Ch-ch-ch-changes—From *The Fly* to *Wolf*

Mexico: *South of Sante Fe* and *Against All Odds*

Miami: Extremely warm coastal city in southern Florida

Middle East: Desert fare and camel close-ups ranging from *Ishtar* to *Lawrence of Arabia* to *The Jewel of the Nile*

Military Comedy: Marching to a different drummer, including *Stripes, M*A*S*H* and *No Time for Sergeants*

Miners & Mining: Helmets with the little flashlights are nifty; *Matewan* and *McCabe & Mrs. Miller*

***Minnesota: Northern state that makes Michigan seem like the tropics. Home of theTwin cities and Prince, eh?**

Missing Persons: People who disappear for a variety of reasons, sometimes because other people have taken them away

Missionaries: On a mission from God to save native populations

Misspelled Titles: Not proper Anglish

Mistaken Identity: You mean to say you're not the King of France?

Modern Cowboys: Fun-lovin' rascals adept at riding horses through busy city streets or with a yen to experience mid-life crisis by doing a rodeo

Moms: Maternal figures have a prominent role

Monkeyshines: Critters from the jungle, sometimes cute and fluffy, often wreaking havoc—*Congo, Monkey Trouble, Outbreak*

Monster Moms: Loving on the outside, evil on the inside—-*Mommie Dearest, Serial Mom*

Monsters, General: Not killer beasts, bugs, plants, appliances, aliens, toys, giants, vampires, werewolves, or politicians

***Montreal:** Cosmopolitan city of francophones currently in Canada

Moscow: City in Russia (the country formerly known as USSR)

Motor Vehicle Dept.: *Chitty Chitty Bang Bang* at the *Car Wash*, plus *Tucker, Herbie*, and the *Repo Man*

Mountaineering: *Cliffhangers*

Movie & TV Trailers: Snippets of stuff

Mummies: Dead guys with leather-like skin, often wrapped in sheets

***Murderous Children:** *Children of the Corn* hang out on the outskirts of the *Village of the Damned*...isn't that near the 7-Eleven of Doom?

Music: *Amadeus* meets *The Fabulous Baker Boys* and *The Commitments* by way of *Mo' Better Blues* at *The Cotton Club*

Musical Comedy: Laughter, singing, and dancing

Musical Drama: Singing and dancing, less laughter, more tension

Musical Fantasy: Singing and dancing in a figment of someone's imagination

Musicals: High-energy singing and dancing, often for no particular reason

Musician Biopics: Real-life musicians get the Hollywood treatment

Mutiny: Gang of disgruntled sailors takes over the ship

Mystery & Suspense: Edge-of-the-couch thrillers and whodunits

***Nashville:** Tennessee city that country music and Robert Altman made famous

Nashville Narratives: *Honkytonk Man* elopes with the *Coal Miner's Daughter*

Native America: Dancing with the wolves on *Pow Wow Highway*

Nazis & Other Paramilitary Slugs: *The Boys from Brazil* and *The Dirty Dozen* plus SS she-wolf *Ilsa* and modern David Duke adaptations

Negative Utopia: Things seemed so perfect until...

New Black Cinema: Spike is Godfather

New York, New York: It's a hell of a town...

New Orleans: City in Louisiana that boasts the Mardi Gras and cajun cookin'

***New Year's Eve:** Stay up late, count down with Dick Clark, drink too much, greet the New Year feeling like...

Nifty '50s: *Grease, La Bamba, The Man in the Moon, Peggy Sue Got Married, School Ties* and 60 more from the Eisenhower era

Nightclubs: *Casablanca*, of course

No-Exit Motel: Sleazy motels with extremely lenient late-checkout policies

***Not-So-True Identity:** People pass themselves off as something else; *Soul Man, Gentleman's Agreement*

Nuns & Priests: Collars and habits; *Agnes of God, The Cardinal, Going My Way, Nuns on the Run, Sister Act*

***Nuns With Guns:** Sister Mary Margaret has traded up from the ol' yardstick. Better practice that penmanship.

Nursploitation!: *Night Call Nurses* offer *Tender Loving Care* in *The Hospital of Terror*

***Obsessive Love:** You like me. You really, really, *really* like me.

Occult: Witches, warlocks, devil worshippers, spell makers, spell breakers, haunted houses, and so on

Oldest Profession: It's not accounting

The Olympics: *Chariots of Fire* and other tales of athletic discipline

On the Rocks: Alcoholism, alcohol, barflies, moonshining, Prohibition—*Arthur, Days of Wine and Roses, Papa's Delicate Condition, My Favorite Year*

Only the Lonely: 50 ways to play solitaire—*The Cemetery Club, The Heart Is a Lonely Hunter, Sleepless in Seattle*

Opera: Shouting in a melodic way while in costume

Order in the Court: Courtroom tales, including *The Accused, And Justice for All, A Few Good Men, Witness for the Prosecution*

Organized Crime: Gangsters with Franklin Planners

Otherwise Engaged: Couple buys ring, sets date, and gets ready to march down the aisle, sometimes with a new fiancee—*Moonstruck, Only You, Sleepless in Seattle*

Outtakes & Bloopers: Inadvertent laugh riots

Overlooked Gems: No box office to speak of, but worth a rent

Pacific Islands: Hawaii, Tahiti, Philippines, etc.

Paperboys: Kids who toss papers everywhere but your front porch

Parades & Festivals: *Animal House* and *Ferris Bueller's Day Off*

Parallel Universes: There's a whole other world out there—*Cool World, Who Framed Roger Rabbit?*

Parenthood: Moms, dads, substitutes—*Dutch, Ma Barker's Killer Brood, Father of the Bride, Three Men and a Baby, Yours, Mine, and Ours, Raising Arizona*

Paris: Ze city in France with rude occupants and ze Eiffel Tower

Party Hell: *Psycho Girls* have fun at a sleepover until *Monsters Crash the Pajama Party* and it becomes *The Slumber Party Massacre*

Patriotism & Paranoia: Run the flag up the pole and salute it—Rambo, Patton, Norris, etc.

Peace: *Friendly Persuasion, Gandhi*

Period Piece: Costume epics or evocative of a certain time and place—*Bugsy, Cleopatra, Doctor Zhivago, The French Lieutenant's Woman, Swing Kids*

Persian Gulf War: Smart bombs away

Phobias!: Eeeeeeeeeeeeeeeek!

***Phone Sex:** Is it really the next best thing to being there?

Phone Terror: *Don't Answer the Phone*

Physical Problems: *My Left Foot, Coming Home, The Elephant Man, The Other Side of the Mountain, Untamed Heart, The Waterdance*

Pigs: Loveable swine—*Gordy, Babe the Gallant Pig*

Pill Poppin': Life with a drugstore cowboy; consumption of drugs, mostly illegal or in extra-large dosages

***Pirates:** Avast, ye scurvy dogs! *Captain Blood* drops in on *Treasure Island*

***Pittsburgh:** City in western Pennsylvania, home of sports teams fond of the colors black and yellow.

Poetry: Not exactly a booming category, but think of *Poetic Justice*

Poisons: *Arsenic and Old Lace* and *D.O.A.*

***Political Conspiracy:** *All the President's Men* present a *Clear and Present Danger* to the Constitution

Politics: *Bob Roberts, Mandela, Whoops Apocalypse*

Pool: *The Hustler*

Pornography: *Hardcore, Body Double*

Post Apocalypse: No more convenience stores

Postwar: After effects of war, generally WWI or WWII but sometimes the Civil War, the War of 1812, the Revolutionary War, and the Ohio Automobile Dealers War

POW/MIA: Captured by the enemy

Pregnant Men: Ahh-nuld fails the *Rabbit Test*

Pregnant Pauses: Humorous takes on pregnancy and birth—*Nine Months, She's Having a Baby*

Presidency: Mr. Lincoln, *JFK*, LBJ, FDR, and, of course, *Dave*

Price of Fame: What goes up...

***Production Problems:** When bad things happen to good (*The Crow*) and bad (*Vampire in Brooklyn*) movies

Propaganda: Deliberately stretching the truth in order to persuade

***Protests:** Hell no, we won't go (to bad movies)! Make popcorn, not war!

Psycho-Thriller: It's all in your mind—*Bad Influence, House of Games, The Silence of the Lambs*

Psychotics/Sociopaths: *Killer Inside Me, Reservoir Dogs, The Stepfather*

Puppets: Usually with strings, but also muppets

Pure Ego Vehicles: Big stars doing their big star thing—-*Hudson Hawk, Harlem Nights, Yes, Giorgio*

Race Against Time: Tick, tock, tick, tock—*China Syndrome, Lorenzo's Oil*

Radio: Over the airwaves—*Choose Me, The Fisher King, Radio Days, Sleepless in Seattle*

Rags to Riches: Grit, determination, and hustling (or just pure dumb luck) lead to fortune—*Trading Places, Working Girls*

Rape: Victims and often their revenge

Rebel With a Cause: Bucking the establishment for a reason

Rebel Without a Cause: Bucking the establishment just because it's the establishment

Red Scare: Cold War and Communism—*The Commies Are Coming, The Commies Are Coming, Reds*

Religion: *Witness, The Last Temptation of Christ*

Religious Epics: Charlton Heston parts the Red Sea—religion on a really big scale

Renegade Body Parts: Hands, fingers, eyes, brains with a life of their own

Repressed Men: Often British (*see* Anthony Hopkins or Hugh Grant), always with plenty of stiffness in upper lip and little elsewhere

Rescue Missions: I'll save you—*The Searcher, Free Willy*

Rescue Missions Involving Time Travel: I'll save you in another dimension—*Back to the Future*

The Resistance: WWII rebels with an anti-Nazi cause

Revenge: A key motivating factor—*Cape Fear, Death Wish, Hamlet*

Revolutionary War: Fought over tea

***Rio:** As in de Janeiro–that swingin' South American party town.

Road Trip: Escapism courtesy of two- and four-wheel vehicles—*Easy Rider, Coupe de Ville, Pee Wee's Big Adventure, Wild at Heart*

Roaring '20s: Flappers, prohibition, bobbed hair

Robots/Androids: Mechanical but fascinating; *Blade Runner* and *The Terminator*

Rock Stars on Film: But can they act? Prince (Symbol), Sting, Elvis, Lennon, The Monkees, Whitney, and so on

Rodeos: Rope tricks with steers

Role Reversal: Vice versa; empathy test—*Freaky Friday, My Fair Lady, Switch, Soul Man*

Roll Over Beethoven: Plot revolves around the music-meister, or he makes an appearance— *Bill & Ted's Excellent Adventure, Immortal Beloved*

Romantic Adventures: Love among the chases and explosions—*The African Queen, Romancing the Stone*

Romantic Comedy: Falling in love has its hilarious moments—*French Kiss, Crossing Delancey, Modern Romance, Much Ado About Nothing*

Romantic Drama: Love thing leads to tension and anxiety-—-*Cyrano de Bergerac, Far and Away, Sommersby, Tender Mercies*

Romantic Triangles: Three where there's only room for two—*The Age of Innocence, Casablanca, Three of Hearts*

Roommates from Hell: Sometimes they won't do the dishes, sometimes they're homicidal— *Single White Female*

Royalty: Emperors, kings, queens, princes, princesses, crowns, scepters

***Royalty, British:** Emperors, kings, queens, etc in Merry Olde England

***Royalty, Russian:**Emperors, czars, and czarinas who ran things in Moscow till those mean old Bolsheviks showed up

Running: Jogging, panting, collapsing

Russia: Back in what used to be the USSR

Sail Away: Vessels on the water—*Mutiny on the Bounty, Erik the Viking, Mister Roberts*

Saints: *Bernadette, Saint Joan, A Time for Miracles*

Salespeople: Have I got a deal for you...

San Francisco: Set in the Northern California city known for hills and sourdough bread

Sanity Check: Inmates running the asylum; also deviant mental states

Satanism: *Speak of the Devil*

Satire & Parody: Biting social commentary or genre spoofs, including *Being There, Airplane!, Down and Out in Beverly Hills, I'm Gonna Git You Sucka, Monty Python's The Meaning of Life, The Player*

Savants: Half-minded geniuses; *Rain Man, Forrest Gump*

Scams, Stings & Cons: The hustle—*The Billionaire Boys Club, The Color of Money, A Fish Called Wanda, The Grifters, The Sting*

School Daze: Education, school, and teachers, generally grammar school days—*Lean on Me, Dead Poet's Society, To Sir, with Love, Teachers*

Sci Fi: Imagination fueled by science and a vision of the future

Science & Scientists: *Altered States, Darkman, Them, They, Son of Flubber, The Story of Louis Pasteur*

Scotland: Lush hills, thick brogues, kilts, bagpipes, and *Whiskey Galore*

Screwball Comedy: Snappy repartee between a man and a woman dealing with an impossibly silly situation

Scuba: Wet suits, including *The Abyss, Navy SEALS*

Sea Critter Attack: Monsters from the deep (and not so deep) surface and surprise:*Jaws, Orca, Moby Dick*

Sea Disasters: We've sprung a leak—*The Poseidon Adventure*

Seattle: Showcases the city in Washington state where it rains a lot; the home of grunge rock

Serial Killers: They just won't stop—*Henry: Portrait of a Serial Killer, The Rosary Murders*

Serials: Segmented adventures; Heyday was in the 1930s—*The Adventures of Red Ryder, The Little Rascals, Flash Gordon*

Sex & Sexuality: Focus is on lust, for better or worse—*Alfie, Barbarella, Emmanuelle, Looking for Mr. Goodbar, Rambling Rose, She's Gotta Have It*

Sex on the Beach: Flashing the fish and getting sand in the darndest places; the most famous couple was in *From Here to Eternity* and *Airplane!* lost no time making fun of them

Sexploitation: Softcore epics usually lacking in plot but not skin—*The Erotic Adventures of Pinocchio*

Sexual Abuse: Victims and their stories—*Twin Peaks, Fire Walk with Me*

Sexual Harassment: When I say no, I mean it

Shipwrecked: Stranded on an island when your boat sinks

Showbiz Comedies: Laughter behind the scenes in Hollywood or on Broadway

Showbiz Dramas: Tension behind the scenes in Hollywood or on Broadway

***Showbiz Musicals:** Singing and dancing behind the scenes in Hollywood or on Broadway

Showbiz Thrillers: Screaming behind the scenes in Hollywood or on Broadway

Shrinks: Psychiatry or equivalent, with *The Prince of Tides, One Flew Over the Cuckoo's Nest*

Shutterbugs: Photographers and their pictures—*The Public Eye, The Eyes of Laura Mars, Peeping Tom*

Silent Films: No small talk/no big talk/no talk talk

Silent Horror/Fantasy Classics: Silent screams, expressions of terror

Singles: Not always swinging but still solidly single—*About Last Night, Singles, When Harry Met Sally*

Skateboarding: Teens on wheels—*Gleaming the Cube*

Skating: Roller and ice, including *The Cutting Edge, Xanadu*

Skiing: Slap on a couple of waxed boards and off you go—*Downhill Racer, Swinging Ski Girls*

***Skinheads:** Nazi wannabes wreak havoc and cause trouble

Skydiving: Jumping from a plane with a polyester slip

Slapstick Comedy: Humor of the physical sort, including Abbott and Costello, the Marx Brothers, sports comedies, Ernest, Pink Panther, Home Alone, the Three Stooges

Slavery: *Roots, Spartacus*

Slice of Life: Charming small stories of life the way it might be—*The Bicycle Thief, Fried Green Tomatoes, Marty*

Snakes: Slithering creatures who frighten many—*Raiders of the Lost Ark*

Soccer: Known as football outside of the USA—*Victory, Ladybugs*

South America: Right below North America—*Aguirre, the Wrath of God, The Mission*

Southern Belles: Southern gals ooze charm—*Blaze, Driving Miss Daisy, Steel Magnolias*

Space Operas: Going where no spam has gone before—*Alien, Star Trek, 2001: A Space Odyssey, Apollo 13*

Spaghetti Western: Clint with a squint, *A Fistful of Dollars, My Name is Nobody, Once Upon a Time in the West*

Spain: Siesta

Speculation: In search of...

Spies & Espionage: Trench coats, dark glasses, Bond, *North by Northwest*

Sports Comedies: Humorous athletic tales, generally not based on a true story

Sports Dramas: Intense athletic tales, often based on a true story

Spousal Abuse: *The Burning Bed, What's Love Got to Do With It?*

***Stagestruck:** Stories of the theatre; *Broadway Melody* sung at the *Stage Door* by *The Dolly Sisters*

***Stalked:** No, I do not want to switch to MCI

Star Gazing: Not Hollywood stars, astrology/astronomy type stars

Stepparents: New spouse hiding either alien origins or sociopathic tendencies greets existing clan

Stewardesses: *Three Guys Named Mike* go to *Stewardess School* and meet *Blazing Stewardesses*

***Stolen from Asia:** American remakes of Asian classics–usually Kurosawa's; *Seven Samurai* becomes *The Magnificent Seven*

***Stolen from Europe:** American remakes of European fare; *A Walk in the Clouds, The Vanishing, Scent of a Woman*

***Stolen From France:** Hollywood goes to its favorite remake well; *Diabolique, Cousins, Nine Months, Three Men and a Baby*

Storytelling: *Amazing Stories, Grim Prairie Tales*

Strained Suburbia: Neighborhood is not what it seems—*Dennis the Menace, Neighbors, Edward Scissorhands*

Strippers: Take it off, take it all off

Struggling Musicians: Talented, but still reaching for the top

Stupid Is...: Stupidity on purpose—*Billy Madison, Dumb and Dumber*, or dumbness as a plot device—*Being There, Forrest Gump*

Submarines: Deep sea diving; *Das Boot, Up Periscope, Run Silent, Run Deep, Hunt for Red October*

Subways: A train for shorter trips—*Speed, The Taking of Pelham One Two Three*

Suicide: Premature ends—*The Big Chill, Scent of a Woman, Romeo and Juliet*

Summer Camp: Where children go to misbehave, including *Meatballs* and *Sleepaway Camp*

Super Heroes: Men and women of extraordinary strength and abilities wearing silly looking costumes

Supernatural Comedies: *Beetlejuice* marries *She-Devil* and they take *The Ghost Train* to their *Haunted Honeymoon*

Supernatural Cop Thrillers: *Angel Heart, Maniac Cop, Wolfen*

Supernatural Horror: Forces from beyond terrorize those who are here

Supernatural Martial Arts: Kung fu *From Beyond the Grave*

Supernatural Westerns: Forces from beyond terrorize cowboys in the Old West

Surfing: Awesome wave, dude! *Mad Wax, The Surf Movie, Surf Nazis Must Die, Endless Summer*

Survival: *Alive, The Bridge over the River Kwai, Testament*

Suspended Animation: Frozen in time—*Coma, Late for Dinner*

Swashbucklers: Crossed swords and rope swinging, including *Robin Hood*, Zorro, various Musketeers, *Captain Blood, The Three Amigos*

Swimming: Ranging from *Gremlins* to *Jaws* to *The Swimmer* to *Cocoon*

Swingers: *Bob & Carol & Ted & Alice* try *Group Marriage* and Carol and Alice become *Swinging Wives*

Sword & Sandal: *See* Arnold Schwarzenegger's early career

***Tattoos:** *The Illustrated Man* visits *Cape Fear* to do battle with *Cyber Bandits*

Team Efforts: Working together pays off—*Hoosiers, Memphis Belle, Renaissance Man*

Tearjerkers: Crying fests—*Love Story, Steel Magnolias, Old Yeller*

Technology—Rampant: Machines that wreak havoc—*Metropolis, Death Ray 2000, Blade Runner*

Teen Angst: Adolescent anxieties, including *Baby It's You* and almost everything produced or directed by John Hughes

Tennis: Anyone?

Terror in Tall Buildings: From *Die Hard* to *Speed* to *The Towering Inferno*

Terrorism: Love affairs with hidden bombs

This Is Your Life: Biography and autobiography, including *The Babe Ruth Story, Amazing Howard Hughes, Amadeus, Catherine the Great, Great Balls of Fire, Raging Bull, What's Love Got to Do With It?*

3-D Flicks: Bring your special glasses

Thumbs Up: Hitchin' a ride—*Even Cowgirls Get the Blues, The Hitcher*

Time Travel: Fast forward or reverse with Bill and Ted, *Dr. Who, Back to the Future*, and *Peggy Sue Got Married*

Tokyo: Crowded city in Japan terrorized by Godzilla

***Torn in Two (or More):** *Sybil* and *Dr. Jekyll and Mr. Hyde* are *Raising Cain* leading *Separate Lives* on the *Edge of Sanity*

Torrid Love Scenes: Steamy and/or sticky—*Angel Heart, Bull Durham, From Here to Eternity, Risky Business, The Unbearable Lightness of Being*

Toys: *Babes in Toyland, The Toy, Toys*

Tragedy: The fate of humankind, magnified—*King Lear, Madame Bovary, Tess, The World According to Garp*

Trains: Rhythm of the clackity clack—*Romance on the Orient Express, Throw Momma from the Train, Running Scared, The Silver Streak*

Trapped with a Killer!: And there's no escape—*Dead Calm, Misery, The Shining*

Treasure Hunt: Looking for hidden riches—*Klondike Fever, Treasure of Sierra Madre, Romancing the Stone*

Trees & Forests: Can't see one for the other, that wilderness paradox—includes *Mr. Sycamore* and *The Wizard of Oz*

True Crime: Based on fact, including *The Boston Strangler, The Executioner's Song, Helter Skelter*

True Stories: Approximations of real-life events often significantly fictionalized for the screen, including *All The President's Men, Chariots of Fire, Cry Freedom, Heart Like a Wheel, The Killing Fields, Silkwood*

TV Movies: First shown on broadcast, cable, or foreign television (BBC, etc.)— *Adam, Autobiography of Miss Jane Pittman, Barbarians at the Gate, I, Claudius, Longtime Companion, The Day After*

TV Pilot Movies: Some became series; some did not

TV Series: Collections, anthologies, and individual episodes of memorable shows— *I Love Lucy, Star Trek, The Fugitive*

Twins: *Double Trouble, Double Vision, Mirror Images*

***Twister!:** The big wind not caused by Mexican food that picks up heavy things (houses, cows, trucks) and deposits them elsewhere

Unexplained Phenomena: No apparent reason for an event

Up All Night: Movie takes place mostly after the sun goes down and *Before Sunrise*

Urban Drama: *American Me* to *Boyz N the Hood* to *Grand Canyon* to *Zebrahead*

Vacations: From *City Slickers* to *Deliverance* to *Fraternity Vacation*

Vampire Babes: Blood sucking dames—*The Brides of Dracula*

Vampire Spoof: Comedic blood suckers, including *Buffy, Andy Warhol's Dracula, Dracula Sucks*

Vampires: More serious vein of blood sucking varmint, including *Dracula* in his many manifestations

Variety: Little bit of everything

Venice: Italian city of gondolas

Veterans: Retired fighting men (and women)—*Alamo Bay* to *Who'll Stop the Rain*

Vietnam War: *Platoon, Hamburger Hill, Apocalypse Now, Good Morning, Vietnam*

Vigilantes: Individuals take the law into their own hands—*Death Wish, The Outlaw Josie Wales*

Viva Las Vegas!: Celebrating America's tackiest city—*Honeymoon in Vegas, Sister Act*

Volcanoes: Mountain blowing off steam, including *Joe Versus the Volcano*

Volleyball: *Side Out* used to be the only one till we remembered the barechested boys from *Top Gun*

Voodoo: From *Angel Heart* to *How to Stuff a Wild Bikini* to *Weekend at Bernie's 2*

Waitresses: *Alice Doesn't Live Here Anymore*, she went to *Atlantic City* to get some *Mystic Pizza*

War Between the Sexes: Men and women battle for supremacy—*It Happened One Night, The King and I, He Said, She Said, Romancing the Stone, When Harry Met Sally, The War of the Roses, Thelma & Louise*

War, General: Generally any conflict that defies other classification—*The Alamo, Gunga Din, The Last of the Mohicans*

Wedding Bells: Memorable weddings; *Father of the Bride, Four Weddings and a Funeral, Sixteen Candles, The Wedding*

Wedding Hell: Horror-filled or anxiety-ridden weddings; *The Blood Spattered Bride, The Brides Wore Blood, The Graduate, Wedding Banquet*

Werewolves: Full moon wonders, like *Wolf*

Western Comedy: Gags and horses—*Ballad of Cable Hogue, Blazing Saddles, Rancho Deluxe, Support Your Local Sheriff*

Westerns: Cowboys, cowgirls, horses and jingle jangling spurs on the frontier

Westrogens: The Old West through women's eyes

Whitewater Rafting: Wild ride down a raging river, often in the company of a psycho

Wild Kingdom: Animals on their own and interacting with confused humans, including *The Bear, Dumbo, Born Free, Free Willy, Never Cry Wolf*

Wilderness: More trees than a forest, plus wild critters—*The Life and Times of Grizzly Adams*

Witchcraft: From *Hocus Pocus* to *Three Sovereigns for Sarah* to *The Wizard of Oz*

Women: Impressive women, less than impressive women, and issues concerning women—*Crimes of the Heart, My Brilliant Career, Passion Fish, Working Girls*

Women Cops: Female officers of the law

Women in Prison: The things that go on in the big doll house

Wonder Women: *Attack of the 50-Foot Woman, Ripley, La Femme Nikita, Supergirl*

World War I: The First Big One, including *African Queen, Gallipoli, Grand Illusion*

World War II: The Last Big One, including *A Bridge Too Far, Guadalcanal Diary, The Guns of Navarone, Hope and Glory, Memphis Belle, Tora! Tora! Tora!*

Wrestling: Choreographed sport involving men and women—*No Holds Barred, All the Marbles, Wrestling Women vs. the Aztec Ape*

***Writers:** Tortured souls who put pen to paper when they're not putting bottle to lips. Does not include the ink-stained wretches of the journalistic trade

Wrong Side of the Tracks: Often involves relationship with someone on the right side— *Cannery Row, The Flamingo Kid, Pretty in Pink, White Palace*

You Lose, You Die: Sports goes nuts—only the winner survives; *Arena, Rollerball, Tron*

Yuppie Nightmares: Young adults find best-laid plans for attaining wealth and privilege going astray—*Baby Boom, Desperately Seeking Susan, The Mighty Ducks, Pacific Heights, Something Wild, Wall Street*

Zombie Soldiers: Recently undead in the army—*They Saved Hitler's Brain*

Zombies: Recently undead everywhere—*I Walked with a Zombie, Night of the Living Dead*

Category Index

The **Category Index** includes subject terms ranging from straight genre descriptions (Drama, Comedy, etc.) to more off-the-wall themes (Nuns with Guns, Eyeballs!). These terms can help you identify unifying themes (Baseball, Heists), settings (Miami, Nifty '50s), events (The Great Depression, World War II), occupations (Clowns, Cops, Doctors & Nurses), or suddenly animate objects (Killer Appliances, Killer Cars). Category definitions and cross-references precede the index; category terms are listed alphabetically.

Bobbie Jo and the Outlaw
Body Count
The Bold Caballero
Boomerang
Border Radio
Borderline
Born American
Born Killer
Born to Be Wild
Born to Race
Born to Ride
Bounty Hunters
Boxcar Blues
Boy of Two Worlds
Braddock: Missing in Action 3
Brady's Escape
Brannigan
The Brave Bunch
Breach of Trust
Breakaway
Breaking Loose
Breakout
Breathing Fire
A Breed Apart
The Bridge at Remagen
Bridge to Hell
The Bridge to Nowhere
The Bridges at Toko-Ri▶
Bring Me the Head of Alfredo Garcia
Broken Arrow
The Brotherhood of the Rose
Brothers Lionheart
Brutal Fury
The Buccaneer
Buffalo Stampede
Bulldog Drummond
Bulldog Drummond Escapes
Bulldog Drummond's Peril
Bulldog Drummond's Secret Police
The Bulldozer Brigade
A Bullet in the Head▶
Bulletproof
Bummer
Bunco
Burn 'Em Up Barnes
The Bushbaby
The Bushwackers
The C-Man
The Cage
Caged Fear
Caged Fury
Caged Hearts
Caged Heat
Caged Heat 2: Stripped of Freedom
Caged Terror
Call Him Mr. Shatter
Call of the Wild
Camorra: The Naples Connection
Canadian Mounties vs. Atomic Invaders
Candleshoe
Cannonball
The Canon Operation
Canvas: The Fine Art of Crime
Captain America
Captain America 2: Death Too Soon
Captain Blood▶
Captain Kidd
Captain Scarlett
Captain Sinbad
Captive Rage
The Capture of Bigfoot
Captured in Chinatown
Car Crash
Carolina Skeletons
Cartel
The Cary Grant Collection
Casey Jones and Fury (Brave Stallion)
Catch Me...If You Can
Cause of Death
Ceiling Zero▶
Chain Gang Killings
Chained Heat
Chained Heat 2
Chains
The Challenge

Challenge To Be Free
Challenge to White Fang
Chameleon
Chance
Chandu on the Magic Island
Chandu the Magician
Charlie and the Great Balloon Chase
Charlie Bravo
Charlie Grant's War
Charlie, the Lonesome Cougar
The Chase
The Cheaters
Cheetah
Child of Glass
China O'Brien
China Seas▶
China White
Chinatown Connection
The Chinatown Murders: Man Against the Mob
Chinese Boxes
Chinese Web
Choke Canyon
Chrome and Hot Leather
Chrome Hearts
C.I.A.: Code Name Alexa
C.I.A. 2: Target Alexa
Circle Man
Circle of Fear
Class of Fear
The Claw
Clayton County Line
Cliffhanger▶
Cloak & Dagger
Cloud Waltzing
Cobra
Cobra Woman
Code Name: Dancer
Code Name: Zebra
Code of Silence
Codename Kyril
Codename: Terminate
Codename: Vengeance
Codename: Wildgeese
Cold Steel
Cold Steel for Tortuga
Cold Sweat
Cold War Killers
Coldfire
The Colditz Story
Cole Justice
The Colombian Connection
Colossus and the Amazon Queen
Colossus of the Arena
Combat Killers
Combat Shock
Commando▶
Commando Invasion
Commando Squad
Commandos
Commandos Strike at Dawn
Comrades in Arms
Conan the Barbarian▶
Conan the Destroyer
Confidential
Conflict of Interest
Congo
The Conqueror
Conqueror & the Empress
Conquest of the Normans
Contra Company
Contraband
Convoy
Cool As Ice
A Cop for the Killing
Cop in Blue Jeans
Corleone
Coroner Creek
The Corrupt Ones
The Corsican Brothers
Could It Happen Here?
Counter Measures
Counterforce
Cover Girl Models
Cover-Up
Covert Action
Covert Assassin
Crack House
Crackerjack
Crash Dive

Crazed Cop
Crime Killer
Crime Lords
Crime Zone
Criminal Hearts
The Criminal Mind
Crimson Pirate▶
Cross Mission
Cross of Iron
Crosscut
Crossfire
Crossing the Line
Crusoe
A Cry in the Wild▶
Cry of Battle
Cry of the Black Wolves
Cry of the Innocent▶
Crystalstone
Cuba▶
Curiosity Kills
Curse of the Crystal Eye
The Cut Throats
Cutthroat Island
Cyborg Cop
Cyborg Soldier
Cycle Vixens
Cyclone
Cyclone Cavalier
Cyclotrode "X"
The Dallas Connection
Damn the Defiant▶
Dance with Death
Danger: Diabolik
Danger Zone
Danger Zone 2
Danger Zone 3: Steel Horse War
Dangerous Charter
Dangerous Orphans
Dangerous Prey
Darby's Rangers
Daredevils of the Red Circle
Daring Dobermans
Dark Age
Dark Justice
Dark of the Sun
Dark Rider
Darkest Africa
Daughter of Don Q
DaVinci's War
Davy Crockett and the River Pirates
Davy Crockett, King of the Wild Frontier▶
Day of Atonement
Day of the Assassin
Day of the Cobra
The Day of the Dolphin
Days of Hell
Dayton's Devils
Dead Aim
Dead Badge
Dead Bang
Dead Center
Dead Easy
Dead End City
The Dead Pool
Dead to Rights
Dead Wrong
Deadline Auto Theft
Deadly Alliance
The Deadly and the Beautiful
Deadly Bet
Deadly Breed
Deadly Conspiracy
Deadly Diamonds
Deadly Encounter▶
Deadly Mission
Deadly Prey
Deadly Reactor
Deadly Revenge
Deadly Stranger
Deadly Surveillance
Deadly Thief
Deadly Vengeance
Deadly Weapon
Deadly Weapons
Death Before Dishonor
Death Chase
Death Feud
Death House
Death Hunt

Death Journey
Death of the Incredible Hulk
Death Race 2000
Death Ray
Death Ring
Death Shot
The Death Squad
Death Target
Death Wish
Death Wish 2
Death Wish 3
Death Wish 4: The Crackdown
Death Wish 5: The Face of Death
Deathstalker 4: Match of Titans
Decoy
Deep Cover
Defenders of the Law
Defiant
Delos Adventure
Delta Force
Delta Force 2: Operation Stranglehold
Delta Force 3: The Killing Game
Delta Force Commando
Delta Force Commando 2
Delta Fox
Delta Heat
Demolition
Demolition Man
The Demolitionist
Demon with a Glass Hand
Dersu Uzala▶
Desert Commandos
Desert of the Lost
The Desert of the Tartars
Desert Steel
Desperado▶
Desperate Cargo
Desperate Crimes
Desperate Journey
Desperate Target
Destroyer▶
The Destructors
Detonator
Detonator 2: Night Watch
Detroit 9000
Devastator
Devil Dogs of the Air
Devil Monster
Devil of the Desert Against the Son of Hercules
Devil Wears White
Devil's Angels
The Devil's Brigade
Devil's Crude
Diamond Fleece
Diamond Ninja Force
Diamonds Are Forever▶
Diary of a Hitman
Diary of a Rebel
Dick Tracy, Detective
Dick Tracy Double Feature #1
Dick Tracy Double Feature #2
Dick Tracy Meets Gruesome
Dick Tracy Returns
Dick Tracy: The Original Serial, Vol. 1▶
Dick Tracy: The Original Serial, Vol. 2▶
Dick Tracy: The Spider Strikes
Dick Tracy vs. Crime Inc.
Dick Tracy vs. Cueball
Dick Tracy's Dilemma
Direct Hit
The Dirty Dozen▶
The Dirty Dozen: The Deadly Mission
The Dirty Dozen: The Fatal Mission
The Dirty Dozen: The Next Mission
Dirty Games
Dirty Heroes
Dirty Mary Crazy Larry▶
Dirty Work
Disaster at Silo 7
Distant Justice
The Divine Enforcer
Divine Nymph
Dixie Dynamite
Do or Die

The Doberman Gang
Doc Savage
Dr. No▶
Dr. Syn
Dr. Syn, Alias the Scarecrow
Dog Eat Dog
The Dogfighters
The Dogs of War
The Doll Squad
Dollman
Dominion
The Don is Dead
Don Juan▶
Don Q., Son of Zorro
Don Quixote▶
Don Winslow of the Coast Guard
Don Winslow of the Navy
Don't Change My World
Door to Door Maniac
Double Revenge
The Dove
Down Twisted
Dragon Force
Dragon Princess
Dragon vs. Needles of Death
Dragonard
Dragonfight
Dragon's Claw
The Dragon's Showdown
Dreadnaught Rivals
Driven to Kill
The Driver
Driving Force
Drop Zone
Drums
Drums of Fu Manchu▶
Dual Flying Kicks
Dudes
Duel of Champions
Dune Warriors
Dynamite
Dynasty
The Eagle▶
Eagles Attack at Dawn
East L.A. Warriors
East of Kilimanjaro
Easy Kill
800 Leagues Down the Amazon
Eighteen Jade Arhats
El Barbaro
El Cid▶
El Mariachi▶
Electra Glide in Blue▶
Elephant Boy▶
Emerald of Artama
Emil and the Detectives
Emperor of the Bronx
Empire State
The Enchanted Forest
Endangered
Enemy Gold
Enemy Unseen
The Enforcer
Enforcer from Death Row
Enigma
Enter the Dragon▶
Enter the Panther
Erik
Erik, the Viking
Erotic Touch of Hot Skin
Escapade in Japan
Escape from Alcatraz▶
Escape from Cell Block 3
Escape from Death Row
Escape from DS-3
Escape from El Diablo
Escape from L.A.
Escape from New York
Escape from Safehaven
Escape from the Bronx
Escape from the KGB
Escape to Athena
Escape to Burma
Escape to the Sun
The Evil Below
The Evil That Men Do
Evolver
Ex-Cop
Excessive Force
Excessive Force 2: Force on Force

Executioner of Venice
Exiled in America
Exterminator
Exterminator 2
Extreme Prejudice
Extreme Vengeance
An Eye for an Eye
Eye of the Eagle
Eye of the Eagle 2
Eye of the Eagle 3
Eye of the Stranger
Eye of the Tiger
Eyes of a Witness
F/X 2: The Deadly Art of Illusion
Fabiola▶
Fabulous Adventures of Baron Munchausen
Fair Game
Falcon
Fall from Grace
The Family
Famous Five Get into Trouble
Far East
Fass Black
Fast Getaway 2
Fast Gun
Fast Kill
Fast Money
Faster Pussycat! Kill! Kill!
Fatal Beauty
Fatal Chase
Fatal Error
Fatal Justice
Fatal Mission
Fatal Passion
Fatal Skies
A Father's Revenge
Fear in the City
Federal Agents vs. Underworld, Inc.
Federal Operator 99
The Female Bunch
Femme Fontaine: Killer Babe for the C.I.A.
Fever
ffolkes
Field of Fire
Fight for Us
Fighting Devil Dogs
Fighting Mad
Fighting Marines
The Fighting Rookie
Fighting Seabees
The Fighting 69th▶
The Final Alliance
The Final Countdown▶
Final Justice
Final Mission
Final Round
Final Sanction
The Finest Hour
Fire Birds
Fire, Ice and Dynamite
The Fire in the Stone
Fire Monsters Against the Son of Hercules
Fireback
Firecracker
Firefall
Firefight
Firefox
Firehawk
Firehead
Firepower
Firewalker
The Firing Line
First Blood
First Yank into Tokyo
Fish Hawk
F.I.S.T.
Fist
Fist Fighter
Fist of Fear, Touch of Death
Fist of Honor
Fists of Blood
Fit to Kill
Five Came Back
Five Fingers▶
Five for Hell
Five Golden Dragons
Five Miles to Midnight
Five Weeks in a Balloon
The Fix
The Flame & the Arrow▶
Flaming Signal
Flash & Firecat
Flashpoint Africa
Flat Top
Flatbed Annie and Sweetiepie: Lady Truckers
Fled
Flesh and Blood
Fleshburn
The Flight
Flight from Glory
Flight from Singapore
Flight of Black Angel
Flight of Dragons
Flight of the Eagle
Flight of the Intruder
The Flight of the Phoenix▶
Flight to Fury
Flight to Nowhere
Flipper
Flipper's New Adventure▶
Flipper's Odyssey
The Florida Connection
Florida Straits
Flying Discman from Mars
Follow That Car
For Your Eyes Only▶
Force: Five
Force of One
Force 10 from Navarone
Forced to Kill
Forced Vengeance
The Forgotten
Fortune Dane
48 Hours to Live
Four Robbers
Foxtrap
Foxy Brown
Frame Up
Framed
The French Connection▶
French Connection 2▶
French Quarter Undercover
Friday Foster
From Hell to Borneo
From Russia with Love▶
Full Metal Ninja
Further Adventures of the Wilderness Family, Part 2
Fury
The Fury of Hercules
Fury on Wheels
Future Cop
Future Force
Future Hunters
Future Kill
Futurekick
G-Men Never Forget
G-Men vs. the Black Dragon
Gallagher's Travels
The Galloping Ghost
Galyon
The Gamble
The Gambling Samurai
Game of Death
Game of Survival
Gang Wars
Gangsters
Gator
Gator Bait
Gator Bait 2: Cajun Justice
The Gauntlet
The General Died at Dawn▶
Gentle Giant
Get Christie Love!
The Getaway
Getting Even
Ghetto Blaster
The Ghost of Fletcher Ridge
Ghostwarrior
G.I. Executioner
The Giant of Marathon
The Giant of Metropolis
The Gift Horse
Ginger
Girls Are for Loving
Girls Riot
The Gladiator
The Glass Jungle
Gloria
The Glory Boys
The Glory Stompers
The Glove
Go for Broke
Go Kill and Come Back
Go Tell the Spartans▶
God's Bloody Acre
Goetz von Berlichingen
Goin' Coconuts
Gold Diggers: The Secret of Bear Mountain
Gold Raiders
Golden Lady
The Golden Salamander
Golden Sun
The Golden Triangle
Golden Voyage of Sinbad
Goldeneye▶
Goldfinger▶
Goliath Against the Giants
Goliath and the Barbarians
Goliath and the Dragon
Goliath and the Sins of Babylon
Goliathon
Gone in 60 Seconds
Good Guys Wear Black
Goodbye Pork Pie
The Goonies
Gordon's War
Government Agents vs. Phantom Legion
Grand Canyon Trail
Grand Larceny
Grand Theft Auto
Great K & A Train Robbery
The Great Los Angeles Earthquake
Great Movie Stunts & the Making of Raiders of the Lost Ark
Great Ride
The Great Skycopter Rescue
Great Smokey Roadblock
The Great Texas Dynamite Chase
The Great Waldo Pepper▶
The Green Berets
The Green Hornet
Green Inferno
Greenstone
Ground Zero▶
Ground Zero
The Groundstar Conspiracy▶
Gung Ho!
Guns
Guns Don't Argue
The Guns of Navarone▶
The Guy from Harlem
Gypsy
Gypsy Angels
H-Bomb
Hangmen
Hard-Boiled
Hard Drivin'
Hard Hunted
Hard Justice
Hard Knocks
The Hard Ride
Hard Target
Hard Ticket to Hawaii
Hard Vice
Hardcase and Fist
Hardware
Harley Davidson and the Marlboro Man
Harry Black and the Tiger
Hatari!▶
Haunted Harbor
Hawk of the Wilderness
Hawk the Slayer
Hawkeye
Hawkeye: Premiere Episode
Heartbreak Ridge▶
Heartbreaker
Hearts & Armour
Heat
Heat of the Flame
Heat Street
Heated Vengeance
Heck's Way Home
The Heist
Hell Hounds of Alaska
Hell Hunters
Hell is for Heroes▶
Hell on the Battleground
Hell on Wheels
Hell Raiders
Hell Ship Mutiny
Hell Up in Harlem
Hellbenders
Hellbent
Hellcats
The Hellfire Club
Hellriders
Hell's Angels Forever
Hell's Angels '69
Hell's Belles
Hell's Headquarters
Hercules
Hercules 2
Hercules Against the Moon Men
Hercules in New York
Hero Bunker
Hero of Rome
Heroes in Hell
Heroes Stand Alone
Hi-Riders
The Hidden Fortress▶
High Ballin'
High Crime
High Ice
High Risk
High Rolling in a Hot Corvette
High Velocity
Highlander▶
Highlander: The Final Dimension
Highlander: The Gathering
Hired to Kill
His Majesty O'Keefe
His Majesty, the American
Hit Men
Hit Woman: The Double Edge
Hitler: Dead or Alive
The Hitman
The Hitter
Hollywood Cop
Holt of the Secret Service
Homeboy
Honeybaby
Hong Kong Nights
Hong Kong '97
Honor Among Thieves
Honor and Glory
The Hooked Generation
Hornet's Nest
The Horsemen
Hostage
The Hostage Tower
Hostile Takeover
Hot Blood
Hot Box
Hot Pursuit
Hot Rod
Hot Rod Girl
Hour of the Assassin
Hula
The Human Shield
Hundra
The Hunt for Red October▶
Hunted
The Hunted
The Hunted Lady
Hunter
The Hunter
Hunter's Blood
Hunters of the Golden Cobra
Hurricane Express
I Spit on Your Corpse
Ice
The Ice Runner
Ice Station Zebra
The Idol Dancer
If Looks Could Kill
Illegal Entry: Formula for Fear
The Immortals
In Deadly Heat
In Gold We Trust
In Hot Pursuit
In Search of the Castaways▶
In Your Face
Incident at Deception Ridge
The Incredible Hulk
The Incredible Hulk Returns
The Incredible Journey
Indiana Jones and the Last Crusade▶
Indio
Indio 2: The Revolt
Inside Edge
Inside Information
The Inside Man
Inside Out
Instant Justice
Interceptor
The Invaders
Invaders from Mars
Invasion Force
Invasion U.S.A.
Invincible Barbarian
Invincible Gladiators
The Invincible Six
The Invisible Monster
Iron Angel
The Iron Crown
Iron Eagle
Iron Eagle 2
Iron Eagle 4
Iron Horsemen
Iron Thunder
Ironheart
Ironmaster
The Island
The Island at the Top of the World
Island of the Lost
Istanbul
Jacare
Jack the Giant Killer▶
Jail Bait
Jailbait
Jailbreakin'
Jakarta
Jaws of Death
Jericho
Jericho Fever
Jessie's Girls
The Jesus Trip
Jet Attack/Paratroop Command
Jive Turkey
Johnny Handsome▶
Johnny Shiloh
Jornada de Muerte
Journey
Journey of Honor
Journey to the Lost City
Judge Dredd
Judgment Night
Jungle Assault
The Jungle Book
Jungle Bride
Jungle Drums of Africa
Jungle Heat
Jungle Hell
Jungle Holocaust
Jungle Inferno
Jungle Master
Jungle Raiders
Jungle Siren
Jungle Warriors
Jungleground
Junior G-Men
Junior G-Men of the Air
The Junkman
K-9000
Kagemusha▶
The Karate Kid▶
The Karate Kid: Part 2
The Karate Kid: Part 3
Karate Warriors
Keep Talking Baby
Kelly of the Secret Service
Kelly's Heroes
Kentucky Blue Streak
The Key to Rebecca
Kickboxer the Champion
Kicks
Kid and the Killers
The Kill
Kill Alex Kill
Kill Factor
Kill Line
Kill or Be Killed
Kill Slade
Killcrazy
Killer Commandos
Killer Force

Action

Killers
The Killer's Edge
Killing at Hell's Gate
The Killing Device
The Killing Edge
The Killing Game
Killing in the Sun
The Killing Man
Killing Streets
The Killing Zone
Killzone
Kilma, Queen of the Amazons
Kim▶
Kim
King Arthur, the Young Warlord
King Boxers
King Dinosaur
King Kong
King Kong Lives
King Kong vs. Godzilla
King of the Congo
King of the Damned
King of the Forest Rangers
King of the Kongo
King of the Mountain
King of the Rocketmen
King Solomon's Mines▶
King's Ransom
The King's Thief
Kinjite: Forbidden Subjects
Knightriders
Knock Outs
Koroshi
Kowloon Assignment
L.A. Bounty
L.A. Gangs Rising
L.A. Heat
L.A. Vice
L.A. Wars
Lady of the Lake
Lady Street Fighter
Lady Terminator
Lafayette Escadrille
Land of the Pharaohs
Laser Mission
Laserblast
Lassie, Come Home
The Last Boy Scout
The Last Contract
The Last Flight of Noah's Ark
Last Flight to Hell
The Last Hit
The Last Hour
Last Man Standing
Last Mercenary
The Last of the Mohicans▶
The Last of the Redmen
Last Plane Out
The Last Reunion
The Last Samurai
The Last Valley
The Last Warrior
Last Witness
Laughing at Danger
Law of the Jungle
Law of the Sea
Law of the Wild
The Lawless Land
Le Mans▶
The Leatherneck
The Left Hand of God▶
The Legend of Hillbilly John
Legend of the Lost
Legend of the Northwest
Legends of the North
Legion of Iron
Legion of Missing Men
Let 'Em Have It
Lethal Games
Lethal Weapon▶
Lethal Weapon 2▶
Lethal Weapon 3
Lethal Woman
Let's Get Harry
Liberty & Bash
License to Kill▶
The Lifetaker
Light at the Edge of the World
The Light in the Forest
Lightblast
Lightning Bolt
Lion Man
The Lion of Africa
The Lion's Share
Little Caesar▶
Little Laura & Big John
Little Marines
Little Ninjas
Little Treasure
The Littlest Horse Thieves
The Littlest Viking
Live and Let Die
Live Wire
Live Wire: Human Timebomb
The Lives of a Bengal Lancer▶
The Living Daylights▶
The Lone Runner
Long John Silver
Loophole
Lords of Magick
The Lost City
Lost City of the Jungle
The Lost Command
The Lost Continent
The Lost Empire
The Lost Idol/Shock Troop
The Lost Patrol▶
Lost Squadron
The Lost Tribe
The Lost World
Love and Bullets
The Loves of Hercules
The Lucifer Complex
Mad Dog
Mad Max▶
Mad Max: Beyond Thunderdome
Mad Wax: The Surf Movie
Madman
The Magic Sword
The Magic Voyage of Sinbad
Magnum Force
Malaya
Malibu Express
Malone
Mama's Dirty Girls
A Man, a Woman and a Killer
Man from Cairo
Man from Deep River
The Man from U.N.C.L.E.
The Man in the Iron Mask▶
The Man Inside
Man on a String
The Man Who Would Be King▶
Manfish
Manhunt
Manhunt in the African Jungle
Mankillers
Marauder
March or Die
Mark of the Beast
Mark of Zorro▶
The Mark of Zorro▶
Marked for Death
Marked for Murder
Marked Money
Marshal Law
Martial Law
Martial Law 2: Undercover
Mask of the Dragon
The Masked Marvel
Massive Retaliation
Master Blaster
Master Key
Master Ninja
Master of Dragonard Hill
Max is Missing
Maximum Breakout
Maximum Force
Maya
McBain▶
McQ
Mean Frank and Crazy Tony
Mean Johnny Barrows
Mean Machine
The Mechanic
Melvin Purvis: G-Man
Men of Sherwood Forest
Men of the Fighting Lady▶
Men of War
Menace on the Mountain
The Mercenaries
Mercenary Fighters
Merchants of War
Merlin
Merrill's Marauders
Messalina vs. the Son of Hercules
The Messenger
Miami Beach Cops
Miami Cops
Miami Vendetta
Midnight Murders
Midnight Ride
Midnight Warrior
Midnite Spares
Mighty Jungle
Mighty Morphin Power Rangers: The Movie
Mind Trap
Mines of Kilimanjaro
Ministry of Vengeance
Missing in Action
Missing in Action 2: The Beginning
Missing Link
Mission Batangas
Mission Corbari
Mission: Impossible▶
Mission in Morocco
Mission Inferno
Mission Manila
Mission to Kill
Mr. Majestyk
Mister Mean
Mistress of the Apes
Mob War
Model by Day
Mole Men against the Son of Hercules
Molly and Gina
Mona Lisa▶
Money to Burn
The Mongols
Mooncussers
Moonfleet
Moonraker
Moonshine County Express
Morgan the Pirate
Mortal Kombat: The Movie
Mother Lode
Motor Psycho
Mountain Charlie
Mountain Fury
Mountains of the Moon▶
Murder on Flight 502
Murder One
Mutiny
Mutiny on the Bounty▶
Mutiny on the Bounty
My Family Treasure
My New Partner
Mysterious Island of Beautiful Women
Mystery Island
Mystery of the Million Dollar Hockey Puck
Mystery Squadron
Nabonga
Nails
The Naked and the Dead
The Naked Angels
The Naked Prey▶
Naked Warriors
Namu, the Killer Whale
Napoleon and Samantha▶
Nasty Hero
Nate and Hayes
The Navigator▶
Navy SEALS
Neptune Factor
Neutron and the Black Mask
Neutron vs. the Amazing Dr. Caronte
Neutron vs. the Death Robots
Neutron vs. the Maniac
Never Let Me Go
Never Pick Up a Stranger
Never Say Die
Never Say Never Again
Never So Few
Never Too Young to Die
The New Adventures of Tarzan
Next of Kin
Nick Knight
Nick of Time
Night Ambush
Night Children
Night Flight from Moscow
Night of the Fox
Night of the Juggler
Night of the Running Man
Night of the Sharks
The Night Patrol
Night Siege Project: Shadowchaser 2
Nightforce
Nightmare at Noon
Nikki, the Wild Dog of the North
9 1/2 Ninjas
1990: The Bronx Warriors
Ninja 3: The Domination
Ninja Connection
Ninja, the Violent Sorcerer
No Contest
No Dead Heroes
No Escape
No Escape, No Return
No Holds Barred
No Man's Land
No Mercy
No Safe Haven
No Way Back
Nomad Riders
Northeast of Seoul
Northville Cemetery Massacre
Nowhere to Run
Nukie
Number 1 of the Secret Service
Nyoka and the Tigermen
Octopussy
The Odyssey of the Pacific
Off Limits
O.H.M.S.
Old Ironsides▶
Omoo Omoo, the Shark God
On Deadly Ground
On Her Majesty's Secret Service▶
On the Run
Once a Hero
One Down, Two to Go!
One-Eyed Soldiers
One Man Out
One Man's Justice
One Million Years B.C.
One Step to Hell
Operation C.I.A.
Operation Intercept
Orca
Order of the Black Eagle
Order of the Eagle
Order to Kill
Organized Crime & Triad Bureau
The Original Flash Gordon Collection
Original Gangstas
Orphans of the North
Osa
The Other Side of the Law
Out of Control
The Outfit
The Outlaw Bikers—Gang Wars
Outpost in Morocco
Overkill
Overthrow
Overture
Pacific Inferno
Panther Squad
Paper Tiger
Paradise Canyon
Pattern for Plunder
Pay or Die
Payback
Peacemaker
Pentathlon
Perfect Crime
The Perfect Weapon
The Perils of Pauline
Perils of the Darkest Jungle
The Persuaders
Phantom Express
The Phantom Flyer
Phantom of the Air
Phoenix
P.I. Private Investigations
Picasso Trigger
Pink Cadillac
Pirate Ship
Pirate Warrior
Pirates of the Coast
Pirates of the Seven Seas
Platoon the Warriors
Platypus Cove
Pocahontas: The Legend
Point Break
Point of Impact
The Polar Bear King
The Port of Missing Girls
The P.O.W. Escape
Powder Keg
Pray for Death
Prayer of the Rollerboys
The President's Plane is Missing
President's Target
Presumed Guilty
Prettykill
Prey for the Hunter
Primary Target
Prime Risk
Prince Valiant
Prison Planet
Prisoner of Zenda▶
Prisoner of Zenda
Private Life of Don Juan
Private Road: No Trespassing
Private War
Private Wars
The Professional
Professionals
Project: Eliminator
Project: Shadowchaser
Protector
Provoked
Psychopath
Pucker Up and Bark Like a Dog
Punch the Clock
The Punisher
Python Wolf
Q & A
Queen of Diamonds
Queen of the Amazons
Queen of the Jungle
Queen of the Road
The Quest
Quest for Fire▶
Quest of the Delta Knights
Quick
Quiet Cool
Quiet Fire
Quiet Thunder
Quo Vadis
The Racers
Radar Secret Service
Rage of Honor
Rage to Kill
Raid on Entebbe▶
Raid on Rommel
Raiders of Atlantis
Raiders of Ghost City
Raiders of the Sun
Rainbow Drive
The Rainbow Gang
Rambo: First Blood, Part 2
Rambo 3
Ransom Money
Ranson's Folly
Rapa Nui
The Rape of the Sabines
Rapid Fire
Raw Deal
Raw Justice
Real Bullets
The Real McCoy
Reason to Die
Rebel Storm
Red Ball Express
Red Dawn
Red Dust▶
The Red Fury
Red Heat
Red Scorpion
Red Scorpion 2
Red Signals
Red Snow
Red Tent▶
Relentless 2: Dead On
Rent-A-Cop
Repo Jake

Rescue Force
Retrievers
Return Fire
The Return of Casey Jones
Return of Chandu
The Return of Eliot Ness
The Return of Grey Wolf
Return of Superfly
Return of the Dinosaurs
Return of the Dragon
Return of the Man from U.N.C.L.E.
Return of the Tiger
Return to Africa
Return to Fantasy Island
Return to Macon County
Return to the Lost World
Revenge of the Barbarians
Revenge of the Ninja
The Revenger
Revolt of the Barbarians
Revolt of the Dragon
Revolver
Ricco
The Riddle of the Sands
Riding High
Riding the Edge
Ring of Steel
Rip-Off
The Rip Off
Rip Roarin' Buckaroo
River of Death
River of Diamonds
River of Evil
Road House
Road Kill USA
The Road Killers
The Road Warrior▶
Roadkill
Robbers of the Sacred Mountain
Robby
Robin Hood▶
Robin Hood...The Legend: Herne's Son
Robin Hood...The Legend: Robin Hood and the Sorcerer
Robin Hood...The Legend: The Swords of Wayland
Robin Hood...The Legend: The Time of the Wolf
Robinson Crusoe
Robinson Crusoe & the Tiger
Robinson Crusoe of Clipper Island
Robinson Crusoe of Mystery Island
RoboCop 2
RoboCop 3
The Rock▶
Rock House
The Rocketeer▶
Rocketship X-M
Rogue Lion
Rogue Male
Roller Blade Warriors: Taken By Force
Rollercoaster
Rolling Vengeance
The Rookie
Rosebud
R.O.T.O.R.
Rough Cut
Roughnecks
The Rousters
Royce
Ruckus
Rulers of the City
Run
Run, Angel, Run!
Run, Rebecca, Run
Runaway
The Runaway Barge
Runaway Nightmare
Running Blind
Running Cool
Running Hot
The Running Man
Running Scared
Rush
The Russian Terminator
The Rutanga Tapes

Safari 3000
Saga of the Vagabond
Sahara▶
Sahara
Saigon Commandos
Saints and Sinners
Salty
Salvador▶
Samar
Samson Against the Sheik
Samurai 1: Musashi Miyamoto▶
Samurai 2: Duel at Ichijoji Temple▶
Samurai 3: Duel at Ganryu Island▶
Sands of Sacrifice
Sanjuro▶
S.A.S. San Salvador
The Satan Killer
Satan's Sadists
Savage!
Savage Beach
Savage Dawn
Savage Drums
Savage Fury
The Savage Girl
Savage Instinct
Savage Island
Scarface▶
The Scarlet & the Black
Sea Devils
Sea Hound
Sea of Sand
Sea Prince and the Fire Child
The Sea Wolf▶
The Sea Wolf
Search and Destroy
Second Chance
Secret Agent Super Dragon
The Secret Code
Secret Mission
The Secret of El Zorro
Secret of the Ice Cave
Serpent Island
Sesame Street Presents: Follow That Bird
Seven Blows of the Dragon
Seven Magnificent Gladiators
Seven Sinners▶
The Seven-Ups
The Seventh Coin
The Seventh Voyage of Sinbad▶
Sex, Love and Cold Hard Cash
Shadow Man
Shadow of Chikara
Shadow of the Eagle
Shadow of the Wolf
Shadowhunter
Shaft in Africa
Shaft's Big Score
Shakedown
Shaker Run
Shamus
Shaolin Ex-Monk
Shaolin Vengence
Shark Hunter
Shark River
Sharks' Treasure
Sharky's Machine
Sharpe's Battle
Sharpe's Company
Sharpe's Eagle
Sharpe's Enemy
Sharpe's Gold
Sharpe's Honour
Sharpe's Rifles
Sharpe's Sword
S*H*E
She Devils in Chains
Sheba, Baby
Sheena
The Sheik▶
Shep Comes Home
Ships in the Night
Shipwrecked
Shogun's Ninja
Shoot
Shoot the Sun Down
The Shooter
Showdown at the Equator
Sidekicks

Sidewinder One
The Sign of Zorro
Silent Hunter
Silk 2
Silk Degrees
Sinbad and the Eye of the Tiger
Sinbad of the Seven Seas
Sinbad, the Sailor▶
633 Squadron
Sixteen Fathoms Deep
The Skateboard Kid
Skeleton Coast
Ski Bum
Ski Troop Attack
Skull: A Night of Terror
Skull & Crown
Sky Hei$t
Sky High
Sky Pirates
Skyscraper
Slate, Wyn & Me
Slaughter
Slaughter's Big Ripoff
Slave of the Cannibal God
Sloane
Slow Burn
Smokey & the Hotwire Gang
Smuggler's Cove
SnakeEater
SnakeEater 2: The Drug Buster
SnakeEater 3: His Law
Soldier Boyz
Soldier's Fortune
Solo Voyage: The Revenge
Son of Captain Blood
Son of Fury▶
Son of Kong
The Son of Monte Cristo
Son of Samson
Son of Sinbad
Son of Zorro
S.O.S. Coast Guard
Sourdough
South Beach
South of Pago Pago
South Seas Massacre
Southern Comfort▶
Space Mutiny
Space Raiders
Space Riders
Spacehunter: Adventures in the Forbidden Zone
The Spanish Main
Spartacus▶
Special Investigator
Speeding Up Time
Speedtrap
Spiderman: The Deadly Dust
Spiders▶
The Spirit of Youth
Spitfire
The Spoilers
Spy
Spy in Black▶
Spy Smasher
Spy Smasher Returns
The Spy Who Loved Me
Stalking Danger
Stamp Day for Superman
Stand and Deliver
Star Quest
Starbird and Sweet William
Starchaser: The Legend of Orin
Starflight One
Stargate
Steel Arena
Steel Dawn
Stone Cold
Storm and Sorrow
Stormquest
The Story of Dr. Wassell
The Story of Robin Hood & His Merrie Men▶
Straight Line
The Stranger
Street Asylum
Street Fighter
Street Hawk
Street Knight
Street Law
Street Soldiers
Street Wars

Strike Back
Strike Commando
Striking Point
Stunt Pilot
Stunt Rock
Stunts
Subway
Sudden Death
Sudden Impact
Suicide Battalion/Hell Squad
Suicide Patrol
Summerdog
Sunshine Run
Super Mario Bros.
Superargo
Superbug Super Agent
Superchick
Superfly T.N.T.
Supergirl
Superman: The Movie▶
Superman 2▶
Superman 3
Superman 4: The Quest for Peace
Superman & the Mole Men
Supersonic Man
Supervixens
Surprise Attack
Survival Quest
Surviving the Game
Suspicious Agenda
Swamp Fire
Swamp Women
Swashbuckler
The Sweeper
Sweet Justice
Sweet Revenge
Sweet Sugar
Sweet Trash
Swift Justice
The Switch
Switchblade Sisters
The Sword & the Rose
The Sword of El Cid
Sword of Gideon
Sword of Lancelot
Sword of Monte Cristo
Sword of Sherwood Forest
Sword of Venus
The Swordsman
Taffin
Tailspin Tommy
The Take
The Takeover
The Taking of Beverly Hills
Tales of Robin Hood
Tales of the Klondike: In a Far Country
Tales of the Klondike: Race for Number One
Tales of the Klondike: The Unexpected
Tangiers
Tango and Cash
Tank Commando
Tank Girl
Target Eagle
Target: Favorite Son
Target for Killing
Tarka the Otter
Tarzan and His Mate▶
Tarzan and the Green Goddess
Tarzan and the Trappers
Tarzan Finds a Son▶
Tarzan of the Apes
Tarzan, the Ape Man▶
Tarzan, the Ape Man
Tarzan the Fearless
Tarzan the Tiger
Tarzana, the Wild Girl
Tarzan's New York Adventure
Tarzan's Revenge
Tarzan's Secret Treasure
A Taste of Hell
Tattooed Hit Man
Taxi Dancers
TC 2000
Teenage Bonnie & Klepto Clyde
Ten to Midnight
10 Violent Women
Ten Who Dared
The Tender Warrior

Terminal Island
Terminal Velocity
The Terminator▶
Terminator 2: Judgment Day▶
Terror in Beverly Hills
Terror in Paradise
Terror in the Jungle
Terror of Rome Against the Son of Hercules
Terror of the Bloodhunters
Terror on Alcatraz
Terror on the 40th Floor
Terror Ship
Terror Squad
The Terrorists
Texas Detour
Texas Payback
Tharus Son of Attila
Thieves of Fortune
Third Man on the Mountain
13 Rue Madeleine▶
The 13th Mission
This Gun for Hire
This Is a Hijack
Thoughts are Free▶
Thrashin'
Three Days in Beirut
Three Days to a Kill
357 Magnum
Three Legionnaires
The Three Musketeers
Throne of Fire
Thumb Tripping
Thunder Bay▶
Thunder County
Thunder in Paradise
Thunder in Paradise 2
Thunder in Paradise 3
Thunder Road▶
Thunder Run
Thunder Warrior
Thunder Warrior 2
Thunderball
Thunderbolt & Lightfoot▶
Thundering Forest
Thundersquad
Tiara Tahiti
Tiffany Jones
Tiger Joe
Tiger of the Seven Seas
Tilt
Time Machine
Time to Die
The Time Travelers
Time Walker
Timebomb
Tintorera...Tiger Shark
To Die Standing
To Live and Die in Hong Kong
To Live & Die in L.A.
To Protect and Serve
To the Limit
To the Shores of Hell
Tobruk
Toby McTeague
Tokyo Joe
Tomorrow Never Comes
Tongs: An American Nightmare
Tonka
Top of the Heap
Tor
Tora! Tora! Tora!
Torer[illegible]
The [illegible]entors
Tornad[illegible]
Total Exposure
Touch & Go
Tough and Deadly
Tough Guy
Tougher than Leather
A Town Called Hell
Toy Soldiers
Tracks of a Killer
Trader Horn
Trader Tom of the China Seas
Trained to Kill
Trap
Trap on Cougar Mountain
Trapper County War
Treasure Island▶
Treasure Island
The Treasure of Bengal

The Treasure of Jamaica Reef
The Treasure of Matecumbe
Treasure of Monte Cristo
The Treasure of the Amazon
Treasure of the Four Crowns
Treasure of the Golden Condor
Treasure of the Sierra Madre▶
Treasure of the Yankee Zephyr
The Treasure Seekers
Trespass
The Trial of the Incredible Hulk
Trident Force
Triple Impact
Triplecross
Tripwire
Troma's War
Tropical Snow
Trouble Bound
Truck Stop Women
Truck Turner
Try and Get Me
Tundra
Tusks
Tut & Tuttle
20,000 Leagues Under the Sea▶
Twilight's Last Gleaming
Twister
2020 Texas Gladiators
Two to Tango
Two Wrongs Make a Right
Typhoon Treasure
U-Boat Prisoner
Ulterior Motives
Ultra Warrior
Ulysses
Uncivilized
Undeclared War
Under Siege
Under Siege 2: Dark Territory
Under the Gun
Under the Red Robe
Undercover
Underground Terror
Underwater!
Unholy Rollers
Universal Soldier
Unknown Island
Unlawful Passage
Unmasking the Idol
Until They Get Me
The Uranium Conspiracy
Urban Crossfire
Urban Warriors
Utu▶
Valley of the Eagles
Vengeance
Vera Cruz
The Vernonia Incident
V.I. Warshawski
Vice Squad
Vietnam, Texas
A View to a Kill
The Vigilantes are Coming
The Vikings
Violent Professionals
Violent Zone
Viper
Virgin Sacrifice
Viva Knievel
Viva Villa!▶
Voyage en Balloon
The Voyage of Tanai
The Voyage of the Yes
Wake of the Red Witch
Walk into Hell
Walker: Texas Ranger: Deadly Reunion
Walker: Texas Ranger: One Riot, One Ranger
Wanted Dead or Alive
War & Remembrance, Part 1
War & Remembrance, Part 2
War & Remembrance: The Final Chapter, Part 8
War & Remembrance: The Final Chapter, Part 9
War Bus Commando
War Party
Warbirds
Warbus
WarCat
Wardogs
Warlords from Hell
Warlords 3000
Warrior Spirit
The Warriors
Warriors
Warriors from Hell
Warriors of the Apocalypse
Warriors of the Wasteland
Waterworld
Web of Deception
Wet Gold
Wheels of Fire
When Hell Broke Loose
When Lightning Strikes
When the North Wind Blows
Where Eagles Dare▶
Where the River Runs Black
Whispers of White
White Cannibal Queen
The White Dawn
White Fang▶
White Fang 2: The Myth of the White Wolf
White Fang and the Hunter
White Ghost
White Gorilla
White Huntress
White Lightning
White Line Fever
The White Orchid
White Pongo
White Slave
White Water Summer
WhiteForce
Whitewater Sam
Who Killed Mary What's 'Er Name?
The Wild Angels
Wild Geese
Wild Gypsies
Wild Horses
Wild Man
Wild Rebels
Wild Women
The Wild World of Batwoman
Wild Zone
Wilding
Willow
The Wind That Walks
Windjammer
Wings of Danger
Wings Over the Pacific
Winners Take All
Wisdom
Wolf
Wolf Dog
Woman in Grey
Women in Fury
Women's Prison Escape
Women's Prison Massacre
Wonderland Cove
The Wreck of the Mary Deare
Write to Kill
The Yakuza
Yank in Libya
Yankee Clipper
Yellowstone
Yojimbo▶
Yor, the Hunter from the Future
You Only Live Twice
Young Eagles
Zatoichi: Master Ichi and a Chest of Gold
Zatoichi: The Blind Swordsman and the Chess Expert
Zatoichi: The Blind Swordsman and the Fugitives
Zatoichi: The Blind Swordsman's Vengeance
Zatoichi: The Life and Opinion of Masseur Ichi
Zatoichi: Zatoichi's Flashing Sword
Zebra Force
Zero
Zero Tolerance
Zipperface

Adolescence

see Coming of Age; Hell High School; Summer Camp; Teen Angst

Adoption & Orphans

see also Hard Knock Life; Only the Lonely

A la Mode
Across the Great Divide
Adoption▶
Aladdin▶
All Mine to Give
Andre
Angel in a Taxi
Anne of Green Gables▶
Annie
Babes on Broadway
Bachelor Mother▶
Battle Hymn
The Beniker Gang
Big Red
Blossoms in the Dust
Born Free▶
Born in America
The Boy with the Green Hair▶
The Children of An Lac
Christmas Lilies of the Field
City Boy▶
A Cry from the Streets
Crystalstone
Daddy Long Legs▶
Dangerous Orphans
D.A.R.Y.L.
David Copperfield▶
David Copperfield
Deadly Sanctuary
Defiant
Dick Tracy▶
Don't Cry, It's Only Thunder
Eagle's Shadow
Earthling
Escape to Witch Mountain▶
A Far Off Place
The Father Clements Story
Fighting Father Dunne
First Love
Flirting with Disaster▶
Free Willy
Goldy: The Last of the Golden Bears
Goldy 2: The Saga of the Golden Bear
Great Expectations▶
Great Expectations
Great Expectations▶
Great Expectations: The Untold Story
Heaven on Earth
Hector's Bunyip
Home at Last
A Home of Our Own
Hoodoo Ann
Immediate Family
The Jack Knife Man▶
James and the Giant Peach▶
Jane Eyre
Jane Eyre▶
The Kid▶
The Kid/Idle Class▶
The Kid Who Loved Christmas
King, Queen, Knave▶
Korczak▶
La Passante▶
Lady from Yesterday
The Lady is Willing
The Land Before Time▶
The Little Kidnappers
Little Orphan Annie
The Little Princess
A Long Way Home
Losing Isaiah▶
Love Without Fear
The Loves of Edgar Allen Poe
Mad Max: Beyond Thunderdome
The Magic Christian▶
Major Payne
Man, Woman & Child
Manny's Orphans
Mighty Aphrodite
Mighty Joe Young
Min & Bill
Moll Flanders▶
My Dog Shep
Mystery of the Million Dollar Hockey Puck
Napoleon and Samantha▶
Nice Girl Like Me
Nothing But the Night
The Odyssey of the Pacific
The Official Story▶
Oliver!▶
Oliver & Company
Oliver Twist▶
Oliver Twist
Oliver Twist▶
Oliver Twist
On the Right Track
One Good Cop
The Orphan
Orphan Train▶
Orphans▶
Orphans of the Storm▶
Paper Moon▶
Peck's Bad Boy
Penny Serenade▶
Pixote▶
A Place for Annie
Pollyanna
Pollyanna▶
The Poor Little Rich Girl
The Prince of Central Park▶
Prison for Children
Problem Child
Queen Kelly▶
The Quest
Rags to Riches
Rebecca of Sunnybrook Farm
Record of a Tenement Gentleman
Redwood Curtain
Rent-A-Kid
The Revolt of Job▶
Rikisha-Man▶
The Road Home
The Road to Life
Sally of the Sawdust
Samantha
Scout's Honor
The Sea Serpent
Second Best▶
Secrets and Lies
Shep Comes Home
Sidewalks of London▶
A Simple Twist of Fate
Sioux City
Snow White and the Seven Dwarfs▶
Sois Belle et Tais-Toi
Sparrows▶
The Stranger Who Looks Like Me
Streetwise▶
Sugar Cane Alley▶
The Sugarland Express▶
Sundays & Cybele▶
Superman: The Movie▶
Susannah of the Mounties
Sweetwater
Tarzan Finds a Son▶
They Still Call Me Bruce
Three Secrets
The Tie That Binds
The Tunnel of Love
Way Back Home
Where the River Runs Black
Which Way Home
Who'll Save Our Children?▶
Wild Hearts Can't Be Broken▶
The World Accuses
Young & Free
Young People

Adventure Drama

see also Action Adventure; Boom!; Drama

Ace of Aces
Act of Piracy
Action in the North Atlantic
The Adventures of Frontier Fremont
The Adventures of Huck Finn▶
The Adventures of Huckleberry Finn▶
The Adventures of Huckleberry Finn
The Adventures of Milo & Otis▶
The Adventures of Robin Hood▶
The Adventures of the Wilderness Family
The Adventures of Tom Sawyer▶
Air Force▶
Al Capone▶
The Alaska Wilderness Adventure
Alexander Nevsky▶
Ali Baba and the Forty Thieves
All the Rivers Run
Allan Quatermain and the Lost City of Gold
Alligator Alley
Aloha, Bobby and Rose
The Amazing Panda Adventure
Amazon
The Amazons
American Empire
American Roulette
The American Scream
American Tiger
And I Alone Survived
Angels of the City
Anzacs: The War Down Under▶
Apocalypse Now▶
Apollo 13▶
Appointment with Crime
The Arab Conspiracy
Archer's Adventure
Arctic Blue
Arizona Heat
Around the World in 80 Days▶
Around the World in 80 Days
The Ascent
Assassination
Assault on Precinct 13▶
The Association
The Aviator
Back in the USSR
Backdraft
Backlash
Barbary Coast▶
The Baron
Bataan
Battle Hell
The Battle of El Alamein
Battle of the Eagles
The Battle of the Japan Sea
Battleforce
Beach Babes from Beyond Infinity
Bear Island
Beau Geste▶
The Beloved Rogue▶
Beneath the 12-Mile Reef
Benji the Hunted
The Berlin Conspiracy
Between Heaven and Hell▶
Beyond Rangoon
Big Bad Mama
The Big Push
The Big Scam
Bigfoot: The Unforgettable Encounter
Billy Budd▶
Black Arrow▶
The Black Arrow
Black Bikers from Hell
Black Moon Rising
Black Rain
Blackout
Blood and Sand▶
Blood Debts
Blowing Wild
Blown Away
The Blue and the Gray
Blue Fin
The Blue Lamp▶
Blue Thunder
Boiling Point
Bomb at 10:10
Bombardier
Born Wild
Botany Bay

The Bounty▶
Brighty of the Grand Canyon
Brotherhood of Death
A Bullet Is Waiting
Burke & Wills
Cadence
California Gold Rush
Call of the Wild
Camel Boy
Casablanca Express
The Castilian
Casualties of War▶
The Cat
Chain Reaction
Chains of Gold
The Challenge▶
Challenge of a Lifetime
The Charge of the Light Brigade▶
Children of the Wild
Children's Island
China Gate▶
Chrome Soldiers
Clarence, the Cross-eyed Lion▶
Claws
Clear and Present Danger
The Climb
The Coast Patrol
Code Name: Emerald
Cold Heat
Cold Justice
Command Decision
Commando Attack
Con Man
Coogan's Bluff▶
The Cop & the Girl
Cop-Out
Corsair
The Count of Monte Cristo
The Count of Monte Cristo▶
The Count of Monte Cristo
Courage Mountain
Courage of Black Beauty
Courage of Rin Tin Tin
Crimebusters
Crimson Romance
Crimson Tide▶
Dam Busters▶
Dangerous Moonlight▶
Dangerous Passage
Daring Game
Dark Before Dawn
Dark Mountain
Dark Tide
The Darkside
The Dawson Patrol
The Day Will Dawn▶
Days of Thunder
Deadlock
Deadlock 2
Deadly Sanctuary
Death in the Garden
The Death Merchant
Death Stalk
The Deceivers
Deliverance▶
Desert Warrior
Destination Tokyo
Dick Tracy▶
Dick Turpin
Die Hard▶
Die Hard 2: Die Harder▶
Die Hard: With a Vengeance
Dillinger▶
Dillinger
Dinosaur Island
Diplomatic Immunity
Dive Bomber▶
Down to the Sea in Ships
Dragonfly Squadron
Dust▶
Each Dawn I Die
The Eagle Has Landed▶
East of Borneo
Edge of Honor
84 Charlie Mopic▶
The Elusive Pimpernel
The Emerald Forest▶
Enchanted Island
Enemy Below▶
The Enforcer
Eraser

Escape to Witch Mountain▶
Evel Knievel
Executive Decision
The Expendables
Eye of the Octopus
Eye of the Wolf
Fangs of the Wild
Fantastic Balloon Voyage
Fantastic Seven
Far from Home: The Adventures of Yellow Dog
A Far Off Place
Farewell to the King
Ferry to Hong Kong
55 Days at Peking▶
The Fighting Prince of Donegal
Fire Alarm
Fire in the Night
Firepower
Flame Over India▶
The Flash
The Flash 2: Revenge of the Trickster
Flight of the Grey Wolf
Flipper▶
Flying Leathernecks▶
Flying Tigers
Follow Me
For Whom the Bell Tolls▶
Fort Saganne
Fortunes of War
Forty Thousand Horsemen
The Four Feathers▶
The Four Feathers
F.P. 1
F.P. 1 Doesn't Answer
Free Grass
Free Willy 2: The Adventure Home
The Fugitive▶
Full Eclipse
Fury to Freedom: The Life Story of Raul Ries
Future Zone
Game for Vultures
God's Country
Goliath Awaits
Great Adventure
The Great Elephant Escape
The Great Escape▶
The Great Escape 2: The Untold Story
The Great Locomotive Chase
The Great Train Robbery▶
The Green Glove
Greystoke: The Legend of Tarzan, Lord of the Apes
Guadalcanal Diary
Gun Cargo
Gunblast
Gunga Din▶
The Gunrunner
Hackers
The Halls of Montezuma
Hamlet▶
Hangfire
Hard Knocks
Hard Rain-The Tet 1968
Harley
Hawk and Castile
Heat▶
Hell Commandos
Hell in the Pacific▶
Hell River
Hell Squad
Hell to Eternity
Hellcats of the Navy
Hellfighters
Hell's Angels▶
Hell's Brigade: The Final Assault
Here Come the Littles: The Movie
The Heroes of Desert Storm
Heroes Three
High Country Calling
Himatsuri▶
Hired to Kill
Hiroshima: Out of the Ashes▶
Hit!
Homeward Bound: The Incredible Journey▶
Huck and the King of Hearts

Hurricane Smith
Hustler Squad
Immortal Sergeant
Imperial Navy
In Harm's Way
In Love and War
In Search of a Golden Sky
In Which We Serve▶
Indiana Jones and the Temple of Doom▶
Inferno in Paradise
The Iron Mask
Iron Will
Island of Adventure
Island of the Blue Dolphins
Island Trader
Islands
Isle of Forgotten Sins
Istanbul
It Rained All Night the Day I Left
JAG
Jaguar
Jamaica Inn
Jaws of Justice
Jenny's War
Jet Pilot
Johnny Mnemonic
The Journey of Natty Gann▶
Journey to the Center of the Earth
Joy Ride to Nowhere
Juggernaut▶
Jungle
Jungle Goddess
Jurassic Park▶
Kamikaze
Kamikaze '89▶
Karate Polish Style
Kashmiri Run
Kavik the Wolf Dog
Keeper of the City
Keeping Track
Kid Colter
Kidnap Syndicate
Kidnapped
The Killer▶
The Killer Elite
Killer Instinct
King of New York▶
King Solomon's Mines▶
King Solomon's Mines
King Solomon's Treasure
Kingfisher Caper
Kiss and Kill
Klondike Fever
Kojiro▶
K2: The Ultimate High
Lady Avenger
Lady Cocoa
Lady Scarface/The Threat
Landslide
Lassie: Adventures of Neeka
Lassie: Well of Love
Lassiter
The Last Hunter
Last Man Standing
The Last of the Finest
The Last of the Mohicans
The Last Place on Earth
The Last Riders
The Last Season
Legend of Billie Jean
Legend of Lobo
The Legend of Sea Wolf
The Legend of the Sea Wolf
The Legend of Wolf Mountain
Lethal Pursuit
Liana, Jungle Goddess
Life & Times of Grizzly Adams
The Lion Man
Lion of the Desert▶
The Lion of Venice
The Live Wire
Loaded Guns
Lockdown
Lost
Lost Zeppelin
Macao▶
The Mad Bomber
Made for Love
Magnificent Adventurer
The Man from Beyond

The Man in the Iron Mask▶
Man of Legend
Manhunt for Claude Dallas
Massacre in Dinosaur Valley
The Master of Ballantrae
The McConnell Story
Memphis Belle▶
Men in War
Men of Steel
Merlin and the Sword
Miami Vice
Miami Vice 2: The Prodigal Son
Midnight Crossing
Midway
Milo & Otis
Ms. 45▶
Mission Phantom
Mission to Death
Mr. Kingstreet's War
Mobsters
Moby Dick▶
Money Movers
Money Train
The Moon-Spinners
Moran of the Lady Letty
Mountain Family Robinson
Moving Target
Murder without Motive
The Mutiny of the Elsinore
My Dog Shep
Naked Jungle▶
The Navy Comes Through
Night Crossing
The Night Train to Kathmandu
Nightstick
No Greater Love
No Time to Die
Noon Sunday
Norseman
The North Star▶
Northern Pursuit
Northwest Passage▶
Number One with a Bullet
Objective, Burma!▶
Obsessed
Oceans of Fire
Omega Syndrome
On Wings of Eagles
One Armed Executioner
One Man Force
One Minute to Zero
One of Our Aircraft Is Missing▶
One That Got Away▶
Operation Cross Eagles
Operation Haylift
Operation Inchon
Operation Julie
Operation 'Nam
Operation Thunderbolt
Operation War Zone
Opposing Force
Oubliette
Outbreak▶
Outlaw Blues
Outlaw Force
The Package
Paco
Palais Royale
The Palermo Connection
Papillon▶
Party Line
Passenger 57
Passion
Pathfinder▶
The Patriot
Patriot Games▶
Payoff
Penitentiary
Penitentiary 2
Penitentiary 3
The Perils of Gwendoline
Permission To Kill
The Phantom
Pharaoh
Pirates of the High Seas
Place in Hell
Platoon▶
Platoon Leader
Plunder Road
Plunge Into Darkness
Policewomen
Pork Chop Hill▶

Portrait of a Hitman
Pray for the Wildcats
The Presidio
Prime Target
Prince Brat and the Whipping Boy▶
Prisoner in the Middle
Private Investigations
PT 109
Pursuit of the Graf Spee
Radio Patrol
Raiders in Action
Raiders of the Lost Ark▶
Rainbow Warrior
Ran▶
Raw Courage
The Real Glory▶
Reap the Wild Wind
Red Barry
Red Flag: The Ultimate Game
Renegades
Report to the Commissioner▶
Requiem for a Heavyweight▶
The Rescue
Retreat, Hell!
Revenge
Riot in Cell Block 11▶
The River Pirates
The River Wild
The Roaring Twenties▶
Robbery
Robin Hood: Prince of Thieves
RoboCop▶
Rudyard Kipling's The Jungle Book
Runaway Train▶
The St. Valentine's Day Massacre
San Demetrio, London
The Sand Pebbles▶
Sands of Iwo Jima▶
Sardinia Kidnapped
Savage Hunger
Savage Justice
Savage Sam
Savage Streets
Scaramouche▶
Scarface▶
The Scarlet Car
Scarlet Spear
Scorchy
Scott of the Antarctic
Sea Chase
Sea Devils
Sea Gypsies
The Sea Hawk▶
The Sea Shall Not Have Them
Sea Wolves
Search and Destroy
Secret Weapon
Self-Defense
Sell Out
Sergeant York▶
Seven Alone
Sex Crimes
The Shadow
Shadow Force
Shame
Shark!
She
She Came to the Valley
Shell Shock
Shipwreck Island
Shogun Assassin
Shoot to Kill▶
Shooting Stars
Shout at the Devil
The Siege of Firebase Gloria
The Silent Enemy
Silent Raiders
Silk
The Silver Stallion: King of the Wild Brumbies
Sinai Commandos
The Sinister Urge
Sink the Bismarck▶
Sins of Rome
Six Pack
Sky Riders
Slow Moves
Smugglers
The Sniper

Sniper
Sno-Line
Sodom and Gomorrah
Soldier of Fortune
Sonny Boy
Sorcerer
Soul Vengeance
South of Hell Mountain
Special Forces
The Specialist
Speed▶
Spirit of the Eagle
The Spring
Squanto: A Warrior's Tale▶
Stanley and Livingstone▶
The Starfighters
State of Grace▶
The Steel Claw
The Steel Helmet▶
Steele Justice
Steele's Law
The Sting▶
The Stone Killer
Strange Days▶
Street Crimes
Street War
Streets of Fire
Strike Force
Striker
Striker's Mountain
Submarine Seahawk
The Substitute
Sudden Death
Sundown
Sunset Grill
Sunset Heat
Surabaya Conspiracy
Surfacing
Survival Run
The Swiss Family Robinson▶
The Taking of Pelham One Two Three▶
Tank
Taps
The Ten Million Dollar Getaway
Tenement
Thelma & Louise▶
They Were Expendable▶
Things to Do In Denver When You're Dead▶
Thirty-Six Hours of Hell
The Thomas Crown Affair▶
Those Calloways
The 317th Platoon▶
The Three Musketeers
The Three Musketeers▶
Three the Hard Way
Thunderground
Tides of War
Tiger Fangs
A Tiger Walks
Tim Tyler's Luck
Tom Sawyer
Top Gun
Tour of Duty
Toy Soldiers
Triple Cross▶
Trouble in Paradise
True Blood
Truth or Die
Turnaround
Twisted Justice
Unconquered
Underworld▶
The Untouchables▶
Up Periscope
Valley of Wanted Men
Viking Massacre
Violent Breed
Von Ryan's Express▶
Wake Island▶
A Walk in the Sun▶
Walking Back
A Waltz Through the Hills
War & Remembrance, Part 3
War & Remembrance, Part 4
War & Remembrance, Part 5
War & Remembrance, Part 6
War & Remembrance, Part 7
War & Remembrance: The Final Chapter, Part 10
War & Remembrance: The Final Chapter, Part 11
War & Remembrance: The Final Chapter, Part 12
The War Boy
Warkill
We Dive at Dawn▶
Weekend War
What a Way to Die
Wheel of Fortune
Where the Spirit Lives
White Fire
White Fury
White Hot
White Squall
The White Tower▶
White Wolves 2: Legend of the Wild
The Wicked Lady
The Wild Pair
Wild Riders
Wild Thing
A Wing and a Prayer▶
Winning▶
Wooden Horse▶
World War III
The Year of Living Dangerously▶
Yellowneck
Young & Free
Young Warlord
Young Warriors
Zeppelin
Zero Pilot
Zulu
Zulu Dawn▶

Advertising

see also Front Page; Mass Media

The Agency
Beauty School
Beer
Bliss▶
C.O.D.
Crazy People
DROP Squad
A Few Moments with Buster Keaton and Laurel and Hardy▶
A Fool and His Money
The Girl Can't Help It
Her Husband's Affairs
The Horse in the Gray Flannel Suit
How to Get Ahead in Advertising▶
The Hucksters▶
I Married a Woman
Image of Passion
Kramer vs. Kramer▶
Lost in America▶
Lover Come Back
The Man in the Gray Flannel Suit
Mr. Blandings Builds His Dream House▶
Mr. Write
Nothing in Common
Pray for the Wildcats
Renaissance Man
Ten Speed
Think Dirty
The Thrill of It All!
Thunder in the City▶
Transformers: The Movie
Waikiki Wedding▶
White Mile
Will Success Spoil Rock Hunter?

Africa

see also Apartheid

Abdulla the Great
Ace Ventura: When Nature Calls
The Adventurers
Africa Screams
An African Dream
African Journey
The African Queen▶
African Rage
The Air Up There
Albino
Algiers▶
Allan Quatermain and the Lost City of Gold
Amin: The Rise and Fall
The Ascent
Black Force
Black Terrorist
Black Vampire
Bopha!▶
Born Wild
The Bushbaby
Call Me Bwana
Cheetah
Chocolat▶
City of Blood
The Claw
Cleopatra
Come Back, Africa▶
Coming to America▶
Congo
Country Lovers, City Lovers
Curse 3: Blood Sacrifice
Dark of the Sun
Darkest Africa
The Desert Fox▶
Dingaka
The Dogs of War
A Dry White Season▶
East of Kilimanjaro
The Egyptian
Eyes of a Witness
Faces of Women
A Far Off Place
Firefall
Five Weeks in a Balloon
The Flame Trees of Thika▶
Fort Saganne
Friends
The Garden of Allah▶
The Gods Must Be Crazy▶
The Gods Must Be Crazy 2
The Golden Salamander
A Good Man in Africa
Gorillas in the Mist▶
The Great Elephant Escape
Greystoke: The Legend of Tarzan, Lord of the Apes
Guns at Batasi
Hatari!▶
In Desert and Wilderness
In the Army Now
In the Shadow of Kilimanjaro
It Rained All Night the Day I Left
Ivory Hunters
Jaguar
Jericho
The Jewel of the Nile
Jit
Jungle Drums of Africa
Jungle Master
The Key to Rebecca
Killers
King Kong▶
King Solomon's Mines▶
King Solomon's Mines
The Kitchen Toto▶
La Vie est Belle
The Last Safari
Les Aventuriers
The Light in the Jungle
The Lion of Africa
The Lost Patrol▶
The Lost World
Made for Love
Mandela▶
Manhattan Baby
Manhunt in the African Jungle
March or Die
The Mark of the Hawk▶
Master Harold and the Boys▶
Men of Two Worlds
Mercenary Fighters
Mighty Joe Young
Mines of Kilimanjaro
Mister Johnson▶
Mr. Kingstreet's War
Mogambo▶
Monster from Green Hell
Mountains of the Moon▶
My African Adventure
Nairobi Affair
The Naked Prey▶
Night of the Sorcerers
Notes for an African Orestes
Oddball Hall
One Step to Hell
Options
Out of Africa▶
Over Indulgence
Overseas: Three Women with Man Trouble▶
The Passenger▶
Pepe Le Moko▶
Place of Weeping
Quartier Mozart
Red Scorpion
Return to Africa
Rhodes
Rogue Lion
Sanders of the River▶
Sarafina!▶
Satan's Harvest
Secret Obsession
Shaft in Africa
Shaka Zulu▶
The Sheltering Sky▶
Simba▶
Skeleton Coast
The Snows of Kilimanjaro▶
Something of Value▶
Song of Freedom
Sundown
Tilai
Time to Kill
Tobruk
Touki Bouki
Trader Horn
The Treasure of Bengal
Tuxedo Warrior
Warriors from Hell
We are the Children
Wend Kuuni
White Cargo
White Hunter, Black Heart▶
White Mischief▶
Wild Geese
A World Apart▶
Yankee Zulu
Zulu
Zulu Dawn▶

African America

see also New Black Cinema

Above the Rim
Across 110th Street
The Affair
America's Dream▶
Ashes and Embers
Assault at West Point: The Court-Martial of Johnson Whittaker
The Autobiography of Miss Jane Pittman▶
Avenging Disco Godfather
Bebe's Kids
Beware
Bingo Long Traveling All-Stars & Motor Kings▶
Black Brigade
The Black King
Black Like Me
Black Vampire
Blood of Jesus
Boardinghouse Blues
Body and Soul
Bopha!▶
Bronze Buckaroo
Bush Mama
Charlotte Forten's Mission: Experiment in Freedom▶
Christmas Lilies of the Field
Chuck Berry: Hail! Hail! Rock 'n' Roll▶
Clockers▶
Come Back, Africa▶
Cosmic Slop
Crooklyn▶
Dead Presidents
Devil In a Blue Dress▶
The Devil's Daughter
Do the Right Thing▶
Double Deal
A Dream for Christmas▶
DROP Squad
Drums O'Voodoo
Dutchman▶
The Ernest Green Story
A Family Thing▶
Fear of a Black Hat
The Five Heartbeats▶
Fly by Night
For Us, the Living▶
Foreign Student
Fresh
Friday
Gang War
The George McKenna Story
Girl from Chicago
The Glass Shield
Glory▶
Go Down Death
Go Tell It On the Mountain
A Good Day to Die
The Great White Hope
Green Pastures▶
Guess Who's Coming to Dinner▶
Half Slave, Half Free
Hallelujah!▶
Hank Aaron: Chasing the Dream▶
Harlem on the Prairie
A Hero Ain't Nothin' But a Sandwich
Higher Learning
Hollywood Shuffle
Hoop Dreams▶
House Party▶
House Party 2: The Pajama Jam
House Party 3
How U Like Me Now?▶
I Know Why the Caged Bird Sings▶
Identity Crisis
I'm Gonna Git You Sucka▶
Imitation of Life▶
In the Heat of the Night▶
The Inkwell
The Jackie Robinson Story▶
Jason's Lyric
J.D.'s Revenge
Jericho
The Jesse Owens Story
The Joe Louis Story
Joe's Bed-Stuy Barbershop: We Cut Heads
Juice
Just Another Girl on the I.R.T.
Keep Punching
Killing Floor
King▶
La Vie est Belle
Laurel Avenue
Lily in Winter
Livin' Large
Lone Star▶
Look Out Sister▶
Losing Isaiah▶
Lost Boundaries
Love Your Mama
Lying Lips
Malcolm X▶
Mandela▶
Menace II Society▶
The Meteor Man
Miracle in Harlem
Mr. & Mrs. Loving▶
Monkey Hustle
Moon over Harlem
Murder on Lenox Avenue
New Faces of 1952
New Jack City
New Jersey Drive
No Fear, No Die
Nothing But a Man
Once Upon a Time...When We Were Colored▶
Original Gangstas
Out of Sync
Panther
Paris is Burning▶
Perfume
The Piano Lesson▶
Piece of the Action

Poetic Justice
Putney Swope▶
Quartier Mozart
Race to Freedom: The Story of the Underground Railroad
A Raisin in the Sun▶
The Respectful Prostitute
Return of Superfly
The River Niger
Rockwell: A Legend of the Wild West
Roots▶
Roots: The Gift
Roots: The Next Generation▶
Sarafina!▶
Scar of Shame
Secrets and Lies
Sergeant Rutledge▶
Shadows▶
Shaft▶
Shaft in Africa
Shaft's Big Score
Shanty Tramp
The Show
Small Time
Sophisticated Gents▶
Sounder▶
South Central
Strapped
Sugar Hill
Sun Ra & His Intergalactic Solar Arkestra: Space is the Place
Superfly
Superfly T.N.T.
Sweet Love, Bitter
Sweet Sweetback's Baadasssss Song▶
Tales from the Hood
A Time to Kill▶
Truck Turner
The Tuskegee Airmen▶
Uncle Tom's Cabin
The Walking Dead
Way Down South
Wend Kuuni
Words by Heart
A World of Strangers▶
Xica▶
You Must Remember This
You So Crazy
Zebrahead▶
Zooman▶

AIDS

***see also** Disease of the Week; Gays*

And the Band Played On▶
As Is
Blue
Boys on the Side
Common Threads: Stories from the Quilt
The Cure
An Early Frost▶
Forrest Gump▶
Heaven's a Drag
Intimate Contact▶
It's My Party
Jeffrey
Joey Breaker▶
Les Nuits Fauves▶
Longtime Companion▶
Love Without Fear
Men in Love
A Mother's Prayer
Our Sons
Parting Glances▶
Peter's Friends
Philadelphia▶
A Place for Annie
Postcards from America
Via Appia
Zero Patience

Air Disasters

***see also** Airborne; Disaster Flicks; Sea Disasters*

Airport▶
Airport '75
Airport '77
Alaska
Alive
Apollo 13▶
Broken Arrow
The Buddy Holly Story▶
The Concorde: Airport '79
The Crash of Flight 401
Die Hard 2: Die Harder▶
Executive Decision
Fearless▶
Fire and Rain
Flight to Fury
Get Shorty▶
Heaven's Prisoners
Hero▶
The Hindenburg
Jet Over the Atlantic
Madam Satan
Mercy Mission
Operation Intercept
Sole Survivor
Survivor
Tailspin: Behind the Korean Airline Tragedy
A Thousand Heroes
Tragedy of Flight 103: The Inside Story▶

Airborne

***see also** Air Disasters*

Above and Beyond▶
Ace Drummond
Ace of Aces
Aces: Iron Eagle 3
Adventures of Smilin' Jack
The Adventures of the Flying Cadets
Afterburn▶
Air America
Air Force▶
Air Hawk
Airplane!▶
Airplane 2: The Sequel
Airport▶
Airport '75
Airport '77
Always
Amelia Earhart: The Final Flight
And I Alone Survived
Angels One Five
Attack Squadron
The Aviator
Bail Out at 43,000
Battle of Britain
Battle of the Eagles
Beyond the Time Barrier
Biggles
Birds of Prey
Black Box Affair
The Blue Max
Blue Thunder
Blue Tornado
Boeing Boeing
Bombardier
Brewster McCloud▶
Bulldog Drummond at Bay
By Dawn's Early Light
Captains of the Clouds
Ceiling Zero▶
Chain Lightning
Christopher Strong
The Concorde: Airport '79
The Crash of Flight 401
Crimson Romance
Danger in the Skies
Dangerous Moonlight▶
Dawn Patrol▶
Deadly Encounter▶
Delta Force
Devil Dogs of the Air
Die Hard 2: Die Harder▶
Dive Bomber▶
The Dogfighters
The Doomsday Flight
Dragonfly Squadron
Drop Zone
Dumbo▶
Enola Gay: The Men, the Mission, the Atomic Bomb
Executive Decision
Fighter Attack
Fighting Pilot
Final Approach
Final Mission
Fire Birds
Firefox
Five Came Back
Five Weeks in a Balloon
Flaming Signal
Flat Top
Flight from Glory
Flight from Singapore
Flight of Black Angel
Flight of the Intruder
The Flight of the Phoenix▶
Flight to Fury
Flying Blind
The Flying Deuces▶
Flying Down to Rio
Flying Leathernecks▶
Flying Tigers
For the Moment
Forget Paris
French Kiss
The Great Skycopter Rescue
The Great Waldo Pepper▶
A Guy Named Joe
Gypsy Angels
Hell's Angels▶
High Road to China
Hostage
Hot Shots!▶
The Hunters
Interceptor
Into the Sun
Iron Eagle
Iron Eagle 2
Iron Eagle 4
The Island at the Top of the World
It Happened at the World's Fair
Jet Over the Atlantic
Jet Pilot
Kamikaze
Keep 'Em Flying
La Bamba▶
La Grande Vadrouille▶
Lafayette Escadrille
L'Anne Sainte
The Left Hand of God▶
The Lion Has Wings
Look Who's Talking Now
Lost Squadron
Love Affair
Malta Story
The Man with the Golden Gun
The McConnell Story
Memphis Belle▶
Memphis Belle: A Story of a Flying Fortress
Men of Steel
Men of the Fighting Lady▶
Mercy Mission
Millenium
Moon Pilot
Murder on Flight 502
Mystery Squadron
No Highway in the Sky▶
One of Our Aircraft Is Missing▶
Only Angels Have Wings▶
Operation Dumbo Drop
Out of Control
Pancho Barnes
Party Plane
Passenger 57
The Phantom
Phantom of the Air
Phone Call from a Stranger
Piece of Cake
The Pursuit of D.B. Cooper
Reach for the Sky
Red Flag: The Ultimate Game
Return to Earth
Revenge of the Red Baron
The Right Stuff▶
Robot Pilot
Sabre Jet
Savage Hunger
Seven Miles from Alcatraz/Flight from Glory
Shadow of the Eagle
Shadow on the Sun
633 Squadron
Sky Hei$t
Sky Liner
Sky Riders
Spirit of St. Louis▶
Spitfire▶
The Starfighters
Starflight One
Steal the Sky
Stephen King's The Langoliers
Strategic Air Command
Stunt Pilot
Survivor
Tailspin: Behind the Korean Airline Tragedy
The Taking of Flight 847: The Uli Derickson Story▶
Tarnished Angels▶
Task Force
Terminal Velocity
Test Pilot▶
Texas Buddies
Those Endearing Young Charms
Those Magnificent Men in Their Flying Machines▶
Today We Live
Top Gun
Tragedy of Flight 103: The Inside Story▶
The Tuskegee Airmen▶
Twelve O'Clock High▶
War in the Sky▶
War Lover
Warbirds
Where the Sky Begins
The Wild Aces
The Winds of Kitty Hawk
A Wing and a Prayer▶
Wings
Wings of Danger
Wings of Eagles
The World Owes Me a Living
Zeppelin
Zero
Zero Pilot

Airplanes

***see** Air Disasters; Airborne*

Alcoholism

***see** On the Rocks*

Alien Beings—Benign

***see also** Alien Beings—Vicious; Space Operas*

The Abyss▶
Aftershock
Alien from L.A.
Alien Nation
Alien Nation: Dark Horizon
Alien Private Eye
Alien Women
Amanda and the Alien
The Aurora Encounter
*batteries not included
Big Meat Eater
The Brother from Another Planet▶
The Cat from Outer Space
Close Encounters of the Third Kind▶
Cocoon▶
Cocoon: The Return
Communion
Coneheads
The Cosmic Eye▶
The Cosmic Man
The Day the Earth Stood Still▶
Doctor Who
Doin' Time on Planet Earth
Earth Girls Are Easy
Earth vs. the Flying Saucers
The Empire Strikes Back▶
Enemy Mine
Escape to Witch Mountain▶
E.T.: The Extra-Terrestrial▶
The Ewok Adventure
The Ewoks: Battle for Endor
Explorers
Fire in the Sky
Flight of the Navigator
Gremlins▶
Gremlins 2: The New Batch▶
The Hidden▶
Howard the Duck
Hyper-Sapien: People from Another Star
Intruders
It Came From Outer Space▶
Josh Kirby...Time Warrior: Chapter 5, Journey to the Magic Cavern
Labyrinth▶
The Last Starfighter
Mac and Me
Man Facing Southeast▶
The Man from Atlantis
The Man Who Fell to Earth▶
Martians Go Home!
Masters of Venus
Missile to the Moon
Moon Pilot
Morons from Outer Space
Munchie
My Stepmother Is an Alien
Mysterious Planet
Mysterious Two
Nukie
Official Denial
Pajama Party
Pet Shop
The Phantom Planet
Project: Genesis
Purple People Eater
Real Men
Repo Man▶
Return of the Jedi▶
Search for the Gods
Simon
Spaced Invaders
Star Trek 3: The Search for Spock
Star Trek 4: The Voyage Home▶
Star Wars▶
Stardust Memories
Starman▶
Starship Invasions
Suburban Commando
Super Mario Bros.
Supergirl
Superman: The Movie▶
Superman 2▶
Superman 3
Superman 4: The Quest for Peace
Teenage Mutant Ninja Turtles 2: The Secret of the Ooze
The Terronauts
The 27 Day
The Twilight Zone
UFO: Target Earth
Vegas in Space
Voyage of the Rock Aliens
War of the Robots
Warning from Space
Wavelength

Alien Beings—Vicious

***see also** Alien Beings—Benign; Space Operas*

The Adventures of Buckaroo Banzai Across the Eighth Dimension▶
Alien▶
Alien 3
Alien Contamination
Alien Dead
The Alien Factor
Alien Massacre
Alien Nation: Dark Horizon
Alien Predators
Alien Prey
Alien Seed
Alien Space Avenger
Alien Terminator
Alienator
Aliens▶
Aliens Are Coming
The Alpha Incident

The Ambushers
The Angry Red Planet
The Arrival
The Astounding She-Monster
The Astro-Zombies
Atomic Submarine
Backlash: Oblivion 2
Bad Channels
Bad Taste▶
Battle Beyond the Stars
Battle of the Worlds
Battlestar Galactica
Bio Hazard
The Blob
The Blob▶
Bloodsuckers from Outer Space
Blue Flame
Blue Monkey
Body Snatchers
The Borrower
The Brain
The Brain Eaters
The Brain from Planet Arous
Cat Women of the Moon
Class of Nuke 'Em High 3: The Good, the Bad and the Subhumanoid
The Cosmic Monsters
Creature
Creeping Terror
The Cremators
Critters
Critters 2: The Main Course
Critters 3
Critters 4
The Curse
D-Day on Mars
The Dark
Dark Star▶
Dark Universe
Day the World Ended
Day Time Ended
Dead Space
Dead Weekend
Deceit
Deep Red
Deep Space
Destroy All Monsters
Destroy All Planets
Devil Girl from Mars
Dr. Alien
Doctor Who
Doctor Who: An Unearthly Child
Doctor Who and the Daleks
Doctor Who: Cybermen—The Early Years
Dollman
Dracula vs. Frankenstein
Earth vs. the Flying Saucers
Eat and Run
The Empire Strikes Back▶
Encounter at Raven's Gate
End of the World
Escape from Galaxy Three
Escapes
Evils of the Night
The Eye Creatures
Eyes Behind the Stars
The Fear Chamber
First Man into Space
Flight to Mars
Flying Discman from Mars
Forbidden World
Forbidden Zone: Alien Abduction
Frankenstein Meets the Space Monster
From Beyond▶
Fugitive Alien
Galaxy Invader
Galaxy of Terror
Gamera vs. Guiron
Gamera vs. Zigra
Ghidrah the Three Headed Monster
The Giant Claw
The Giant Spider Invasion
God Told Me To
Godzilla vs. the Cosmic Monster
Grampa's Sci-Fi Hits
Grand Tour: Disaster in Time
The Green Slime
Gremlins▶
Gremlins 2: The New Batch▶
The Guyver
Guyver 2: Dark Hero
Hands of Steel
The Hidden▶
The Hidden 2
High Desert Kill
Horror of the Blood Monsters
Horror Planet
The Human Duplicators
I Come in Peace
I Married a Monster from Outer Space
Independence Day▶
Invader
The Invaders
Invaders from Mars
Invasion
Invasion Earth: The Aliens Are Here!
Invasion of the Animal People
Invasion of the Bee Girls▶
Invasion of the Body Snatchers▶
Invasion of the Body Stealers
Invasion of the Girl Snatchers
Invasion of the Saucer Men
Invasion of the Space Preachers
Invisible Adversaries
Invisible Invaders
Island of the Burning Doomed
It Came From Outer Space▶
It Conquered the World
It! The Terror from Beyond Space
J-Men Forever!▶
Killer Klowns from Outer Space
Killers from Space
Killings at Outpost Zeta
Kronos
Laboratory
Leviathan
Liquid Sky▶
Lords of the Deep
Mars Needs Women
The Martian Chronicles: Part 3
Masters of Venus
Metallica
Midnight Movie Massacre
Mindwarp
Mission Mars
Mom and Dad Save the World
Monolith
The Monolith Monsters
Monster
Monster a Go-Go!
Monster High
Moontrap
Munchies
The Mysterians
Night Beast
Night Caller from Outer Space
Night of the Blood Beast
Night of the Creeps
No Survivors, Please
Not of This Earth
Oblivion
The Outer Limits: Galaxy Being
The Outer Limits: Sandkings▶
The P.A.C.K.
Peacemaker
Pet Shop
Phantom from Space
The Phantom Planet
The Pink Chiquitas
Plan 9 from Outer Space
Plan 10 from Outer Space
Planet of Blood
Planets Against Us
Predator
Predator 2
The Puppet Masters
Quatermass 2▶
Quatermass and the Pit
The Quatermass Experiment▶
Radar Men from the Moon
Reactor
Remote Control
The Return
Return of the Aliens: The Deadly Spawn
Return of the Jedi▶
Revenge of the Teenage Vixens from Outer Space
Robot Monster
Rock 'n' Roll Nightmare
Scared to Death
The Silencers
The Sinister Invasion
Slapstick of Another Kind
Son of Blob
Species
Split
Split Second
Star Crystal
Star Trek: The Motion Picture
Star Trek 3: The Search for Spock
Star Trek: The Cage
Star Wars▶
Stargate
Starship Invasions
Stephen King's The Langoliers
Stephen King's The Tommyknockers
Strange Invaders▶
The Stranger from Venus
Super Mario Bros.
Superman 2▶
A Taste for Flesh and Blood
Teen Alien
Teenagers from Outer Space
Terror of Mechagodzilla
They
They Came from Beyond Space
They Live
The Thing▶
The Thing
This Island Earth
Time Runner
Time Walker
Tripods: The White Mountains
20 Million Miles to Earth
The Twilight Zone
The Unearthly Stranger
V▶
V: The Final Battle
Vampire Vixens from Venus
Village of the Damned▶
Village of the Damned
War in Space
War of the Wizards
The War of the Worlds▶
Wicked City
Wild, Wild Planet
Women of the Prehistoric Planet
X from Outer Space
Xtro
Xtro 2: The Second Encounter
Xtro 3: Watch the Skies
Zarkorr! The Invader
Zeram
Zombies of the Stratosphere
Zontar, the Thing from Venus

American Indians

see Native America

American South

see also Miami; Nashville Narratives; New Orleans; Southern Belles

Ain't No Way Back
Alligator Alley
Andersonville▶
Angel Baby
Angel City
Angel Heart
As Summers Die
The Autobiography of Miss Jane Pittman▶
Baby Doll▶
Bad Georgia Road
The Ballad of the Sad Cafe
The Beguiled▶
Belizaire the Cajun
Between Heaven and Hell▶
Beulah Land
The Big Easy▶
Black Like Me
Blind Vengeance
Boxcar Bertha
Bucktown
Camilla
Cape Fear▶
Cat on a Hot Tin Roof▶
Cat on a Hot Tin Roof
Chiefs
Christy
Cold Sassy Tree▶
The Color Purple▶
Dead Right
Delta Heat
Dixiana
Driving Miss Daisy▶
The Drowning Pool
Drum
A Family Thing▶
Final Cut
Fire in the Night
Flamingo Road▶
Fled
Fletch Lives
Follow That Car
Forrest Gump▶
Foxfire▶
Fried Green Tomatoes▶
The Fugitive Kind
Gettysburg▶
The Ghost of Fletcher Ridge
The Girl from Tobacco Row
The Glass Menagerie▶
God's Little Acre▶
Gone with the Wind▶
The Great Santini▶
Hard Drivin'
Home from the Hill▶
Hooch
Hootch Country Boys
Hot Spell
Hunter's Blood
Hush, Hush, Sweet Charlotte▶
I Know Why the Caged Bird Sings▶
I'd Climb the Highest Mountain▶
In a Shallow Grave
In the Heat of the Night▶
Intruder in the Dust▶
Invitation to a Gunfighter
Jezebel▶
The Journey of August King
Judge Horton and the Scottsboro Boys
Judge Priest▶
Just Cause
Kentucky Kernels
The Klansman
Lady for a Night
Lady from Louisiana
The Lash of the Penitents
Last Dance
The Life and Assassination of the Kingfish
Lily in Winter
A Lion Is in the Streets▶
The Lords of Discipline
Louisiana
Louisiana Story▶
Macon County Line
Mandingo
Miss Firecracker▶
Mississippi Burning▶
Mississippi Masala▶
Mr. & Mrs. Loving▶
Moonshine Highway
Moonshine Mountain
Morning Glory
Murder in Coweta County
The Murder of Mary Phagan▶
Murder on the Bayou▶
My Cousin Vinny▶
My Sweet Charlie
Mystery of the Riverboat
The Neon Bible
Netherworld
No Mercy
Norma Rae▶
North and South Book 1▶
North and South Book 2▶
Nothing But a Man
On the Run
On Valentine's Day
Once Upon a Time...When We Were Colored▶
One False Move▶
Orpheus Descending
Outside Chance
Paradise▶
Paris Trout
Passion Fish▶
Perfect Harmony
Poor Pretty Eddie
Poor White Trash
Poor White Trash 2
The Prince of Tides▶
Psycho from Texas
Queen Bee
Rambling Rose▶
A Real American Hero
Reflections in a Golden Eye
Return to Mayberry
Return to Two Moon Junction
Rich in Love
Riverbend
Road to Nashville
Roll of Thunder, Hear My Cry
Rooster: Spurs of Death!
Roots▶
Roots: The Next Generation▶
The Rose Tattoo▶
Ruby Gentry
Running Mates▶
Saratoga Trunk
Scarlett
Scorchers
Shag: The Movie▶
Shanty Tramp
Shy People▶
Sister, Sister
Sixteen
Smokey Bites the Dust
Snuffy Smith, Yard Bird
Something to Talk About
Sounder▶
Southern Comfort▶
The Southerner▶
Stormswept
Storyville
A Streetcar Named Desire▶
A Streetcar Named Desire
Summer and Smoke
The Supernaturals
Swamp Fire
Sweet Bird of Youth▶
Sweet Bird of Youth
Sweet Country Road
Tammy and the Bachelor
Tammy and the Doctor
Tank
Texasville
They Won't Forget▶
This Stuff'll Kill Ya!
A Tiger's Tale
A Time to Kill▶
To Kill a Mockingbird▶
The Trip to Bountiful▶
Tune in Tomorrow
2000 Maniacs
Uncle Tom's Cabin
Uphill All the Way
Voodoo Dawn
Walk in the Spring Rain
Walking Tall
Walking Tall: Part 2
Walking Tall: The Final Chapter
The War
What Comes Around
Where the Lilies Bloom▶
White Lie
The White Rose▶
Wildflower▶
Wise Blood▶
A Woman Called Moses

America's Heartland

see also Slice of Life

Arachnophobia
Blessing
Carried Away
The Crude Oasis
Doc Hollywood
Fargo▶
Field of Dreams▶
Fire in the Sky
Fried Green Tomatoes▶
Grandview U.S.A.

Grumpier Old Men
Hard Promises
Macon County Line
The Milagro Beanfield War▶
Miles from Home
Murphy's Romance▶
The Music Man▶
My Cousin Vinny▶
Normal Life
Now and Then
Oklahoma!▶
Our Town▶
Our Town
Powder
Reckless
Return to Macon County
Return to Mayberry
Steel Magnolias▶
To Wong Foo, Thanks for Everything, Julie Newmar
Tom and Huck▶
Twister

Amnesia

see also Identity

Amateur▶
Anastasia▶
Anastasia: The Mystery of Anna
As You Desire Me▶
Blackout
The Bourne Identity▶
Clean Slate
Crack-Up
Dead Again▶
Desperately Seeking Susan
Diabolically Yours
Final Approach
The Great Dictator▶
Gypsy Angels
Hellhole
I Love You Again▶
Istanbul
Jane Doe
Landslide
Lost Honeymoon
Memories of Murder
Mirage▶
Murder by Night
Overboard
Palombella Rossa
A Pure Formality
Regarding Henry▶
Return of the Soldier▶
Second Woman
The Sender
Shattered
Siesta
Singapore
Someone Behind the Door
Spellbound▶
Strange Awakening
The Stranger▶
Summer's Children
Twice a Judas
Unholy Four

Amusement Parks

see also Carnivals & Circuses; Fairs & Expositions

The Beast from 20,000 Fathoms
Bebe's Kids
Beverly Hills Cop 3
Dragonworld
Fatal Attraction▶
Funland
Godzilla on Monster Island
KISS Meets the Phantom of the Park
The Lady from Shanghai▶
Luv
My Life
National Lampoon's Vacation▶
Rollercoaster
Strangers on a Train▶
The Third Man▶

Angels

see also Heaven Sent

Always
Angels in the Outfield▶
Angels in the Outfield
The Bishop's Wife▶
Clarence
Creation of Adam
Date with an Angel
Defending Your Life▶
Faraway, So Close!
Fear No Evil
Field of Dreams▶
For Heaven's Sake
Forever Darling
Green Pastures▶
A Guy Named Joe
Heart and Souls
Heaven Can Wait▶
The Heavenly Kid
Here Comes Mr. Jordan▶
The Horn Blows at Midnight▶
I Married an Angel
It Came Upon a Midnight Clear
It's a Wonderful Life▶
The Kid with the Broken Halo
La Merveilleuse Visite
The Littlest Angel
Made in Heaven
One Magic Christmas
The Prophecy
Raging Angels
Slam Dunk Ernest
Two of a Kind
Waiting for the Light
Wings of Desire▶

Animals

see Birds; Cats; Horses; King of Beasts (Dogs); Wild Kingdom

Animated Musicals

see also Animation & Cartoons; Musicals

Aladdin▶
All Dogs Go to Heaven
All Dogs Go to Heaven 2
An American Tail
An American Tail: Fievel Goes West
Beauty and the Beast▶
Charlotte's Web
Cinderella▶
Gay Purr-ee
The Hunchback of Notre Dame▶
Jack & the Beanstalk
The Jungle Book▶
Lady and the Tramp▶
The Lion King▶
The Little Mermaid▶
The Magic Voyage
The Pebble and the Penguin
Pink Floyd: The Wall
Pinocchio▶
Pocahontas▶
The Return of Jafar
Robin Hood▶
Rock-a-Doodle
Shinbone Alley
Sleeping Beauty▶
Snow White and the Seven Dwarfs▶
The Swan Princess
Thumbelina
The Tune
Water Babies
Yellow Submarine▶
You're a Good Man, Charlie Brown

Animation & Cartoons

see also Animated Musicals

The Adventures of Ichabod and Mr. Toad▶
The Adventures of Mark Twain▶
Aladdin and the King of Thieves
Alakazam the Great!
Alice in Wonderland
Alice in Wonderland▶
Allegro Non Troppo▶
Animal Farm▶
The Aristocats▶
Babar: The Movie
Baby Snakes: The Complete Version
Balto
Bambi▶
Batman: Mask of the Phantasm
Be My Valentine, Charlie Brown
Bebe's Kids
Best of Bugs Bunny & Friends
Bon Voyage, Charlie Brown▶
A Boy Named Charlie Brown▶
The Brave Little Frog
Bugs & Daffy: The Wartime Cartoons
The Bugs Bunny/Road Runner Movie
Bugs Bunny Superstar
Butterfly Ball
The Care Bears Movie
The Care Bears Movie 2: A New Generation
The Castle of Cagliostro
A Charlie Brown Celebration
A Charlie Brown Christmas
A Charlie Brown Thanksgiving
Charlie Brown's All-Stars
The Chipmunk Adventure
Chuck Amuck: The Movie
Cool World
The Cosmic Eye▶
Daffy Duck's Movie: Fantastic Island
Daffy Duck's Quackbusters
Disney's Storybook Classics
DuckTales the Movie: Treasure of the Lost Lamp
Dumbo▶
Evil Toons
Family Dog: Complete Series
Fantasia▶
Fantastic Planet▶
Felix the Cat: The Movie
Ferngully: The Last Rain Forest
Fire and Ice
Flight of Dragons
The Flintstones
The Fox and the Hound▶
Freddie the Frog
Fritz the Cat▶
Gargoyles, The Movie: The Heroes Awaken
Good Grief, Charlie Brown
The Good, the Bad, and Huckleberry Hound
A Goofy Movie
Grave of the Fireflies▶
The Great Mouse Detective▶
Grendel, Grendel, Grendel
Gulliver's Travels
Gumby: The Movie
Happily Ever After
Happy New Year, Charlie Brown
Harmagedon
Heavy Metal▶
Heavy Traffic▶
Here Come the Littles: The Movie
He's Your Dog, Charlie Brown!
Hey Good Lookin'
Hey There, It's Yogi Bear
The Hobbit▶
Hoppity Goes to Town
How the Grinch Stole Christmas▶
Huckleberry Finn
Hugo the Hippo
Is This Goodbye, Charlie Brown?
It Was a Short Summer, Charlie Brown
It's a Mystery, Charlie Brown
It's an Adventure, Charlie Brown!
It's Arbor Day, Charlie Brown
It's Flashbeagle, Charlie Brown/She's a Good Skate, Charlie Brown
It's Magic, Charlie Brown/Charlie Brown's All Star
It's the Great Pumpkin, Charlie Brown
It's Three Strikes, Charlie Brown
It's Your First Kiss, Charlie Brown/Someday You'll Find Her, Charlie Brown
The Jetsons Meet the Flintstones
Jetsons: The Movie
Journey Back to Oz
Journey to the Center of the Earth
The Land Before Time▶
The Land Before Time 2: The Great Valley Adventure
The Land Before Time 3: The Time of the Great Giving
The Last Unicorn
The Legend of Sleepy Hollow
Lensman
Life is a Circus, Charlie Brown/You're the Greatest, Charlie Brown
Light Years
The Little Mermaid
Little Nemo: Adventures in Slumberland
Looney Looney Looney Bugs Bunny Movie▶
The Lord of the Rings
Lucky Luke: The Ballad of the Daltons
Mad Monster Party
Man from Button Willow
The Many Adventures of Winnie the Pooh
Marco Polo, Jr.
Mickey's Christmas Carol▶
Mouse and His Child
My Little Pony: The Movie
The Nightmare Before Christmas▶
Nine Lives of Fritz the Cat
The Nutcracker Prince
The Old Curiosity Shop
Oliver & Company
Once Upon a Forest
Once Upon a Time
101 Dalmatians▶
1001 Arabian Nights
Peter Pan▶
Phantom Tollbooth▶
Phantom 2040 Movie: The Ghost Who Walks
The Plague Dogs
Play It Again, Charlie Brown
Pogo for President: "I Go Pogo"
The Point
Pound Puppies and the Legend of Big Paw
The Princess and the Goblin
Project A-ko
The Puppetoon Movie
Race for Your Life, Charlie Brown
Raggedy Ann and Andy: A Musical Adventure
The Reluctant Dragon
The Rescuers▶
The Rescuers Down Under
Return of the Dinosaurs
The Return of the King
Rock & Rule
Rover Dangerfield
Rudolph & Frosty's Christmas in July
Rudolph the Red-Nosed Reindeer
Santa Claus Is Coming to Town
Scruffy
Sea Prince and the Fire Child
The Secret of NIMH▶
Shame of the Jungle
She Likes You, Charlie Brown
Shelley Duvall's Bedtime Stories
Sherlock Hound: Tales of Mystery
She's a Good Skate, Charlie Brown
Sinbad and the Eye of the Tiger
Snoopy, Come Home▶
Snoopy's Getting Married, Charlie Brown
Someday You'll Find Her, Charlie Brown
Starchaser: The Legend of Orin
Starvengers
Streetfight
The Sword in the Stone▶
There's No Time for Love, Charlie Brown
The Three Caballeros
Tiny Toon Adventures: How I Spent My Vacation▶
Tom and Jerry: The Movie
Tom Thumb▶
Toy Story▶
Transformers: The Movie
A Troll in Central Park
Twilight of the Cockroaches
Urotsukidoj 1: Legend of the Overfiend
Urotsukidoj 2: Legend of the Demon Womb
VIP, My Brother Superman
Watership Down
We're Back! A Dinosaur's Story
When the Wind Blows▶
Wizards
You're in Love, Charlie Brown

Anthology

see also Comedy Anthologies; Horror Anthologies; Serials

Actors and Sin
Akermania, Vol. 1▶
America at the Movies
American Tickler
America's Dream▶
Amore▶
Bad Girls in the Movies
The Best of Bogart▶
The Best of the Kids in the Hall
Bim/Dream of the Wild Horses
Black Sabbath▶
Boys Life
The Brighton Strangler/Before Dawn
The Busby Berkeley Disc
Camp Classics #1
Cannon Ball/Eyes Have It
The Cary Grant Collection
Cat's Eye
The Chaplin Revue
Charade
The Charlie Chan Collection
Charlie Chaplin's Keystone Comedies #5
Chasing Those Depression Blues
Cord & Dischords/Naughty Nurse
Cosmic Slop
Country Lovers, City Lovers
Dark Eyes▶
Dawn Rider/Frontier Horizon
The Deadliest Art: The Best of the Martial Arts Films
Deadtime Stories
The Decameron▶
Decameron Nights
The Devil Thumbs a Ride/Having Wonderful Crime
Dr. Terror's House of Horrors
Duke: The Films of John Wayne
Early Cinema Vol. 1
Early Russian Cinema, Vol. 1: Beginnings
Early Russian Cinema, Vol. 2: Folklore & Legend
Early Russian Cinema, Vol. 3: Starewicz's Fantasies
Early Russian Cinema, Vol. 4: Provincial Variations
Early Russian Cinema, Vol. 5: Chardynin's Pushkin
Early Russian Cinema, Vol. 6: Class Distinctions
Early Russian Cinema, Vol. 7: Evgenii Bauer
Early Russian Cinema, Vol. 8: Iakov Protazanov

Early Russian Cinema, Vol. 9: High Society
Early Russian Cinema, Vol. 10: The End of an Era
Early Sound Films
Escapes
Eyes of Turpin Are Upon You!
Fallen Angels 1▶
Fallen Angels 2▶
Film House Fever
The First Movie Cowboy
Four Rooms
Frightshow
From Beyond the Grave
Gene Autry Matinee Double Feature #1
Gene Autry Matinee Double Feature #2
Gene Autry Matinee Double Feature #3
The Great Train Robbery: Cinema Begins
Grit of the Girl Telegrapher/In the Switch Tower
Gun Smugglers/Hot Lead
Hitchcock Collection
Hotel Room
John Wayne Anthology: Star Packer/Lawless Range
Kaos▶
The Kid/Idle Class▶
Kino Pravda/Enthusiasm
Kurt Vonnegut's Monkey House
Kwaidan▶
Le Plaisir
Letters from My Windmill▶
The Little Theatre of Jean Renoir▶
Love in the City▶
Mack Sennett Comedies: Vol. 1
Mack Sennett Comedies: Vol. 2
Mania
Masque of the Red Death/ Premature Burial
Max
Mickey the Great
More American Graffiti
Mutant Video
Mystery of the Leaping Fish/ Chess Fever
Mystery Train▶
Night Gallery▶
Night on Earth▶
Nightmares
Once Upon a Midnight Scary
One Step Beyond
Paisan▶
Picture Windows
Prison Stories: Women on the Inside▶
Pulp Fiction▶
Range Rider
Red Balloon/Occurrence at Owl Creek Bridge▶
Red Shoe Diaries 3: Another Woman's Lipstick
Red Shoe Diaries 4: Auto Erotica
Red Shoe Diaries 5: Weekend Pass
Red Shoe Diaries 6: How I Met My Husband
Renegade Ranger/Scarlet River
Renoir Shorts▶
Riders of the Range/Storm Over Wyoming
RoGoPaG
Seven Deadly Sins▶
Sherlock's Rivals & Where's My Wife
Short Cuts▶
The Silent Mr. Sherlock Holmes
Six in Paris
Slacker▶
Sleazemania III: The Good, the Bad & the Sleazy
Smiling Madame Beudet/The Seashell and the Clergyman▶
Strange Tales
Strange Tales/Ray Bradbury Theatre
Strictly G.I.
Tales from the Crypt▶
Tales from the Crypt
Tales from the Darkside
Tales of Manhattan▶
Tales of the Unexpected
Tales That Witness Madness
Terrorgram
That's Dancing!
That's Entertainment
That's Entertainment, Part 2
That's Entertainment, Part 3
Three Cases of Murder▶
Time for Murder
Tom Mix Compilation 1
Tom Mix Compilation 2
Tunes of Glory/Horse's Mouth
Twice-Told Tales▶
Twilight Zone: The Movie
The Unapproachable
The Uncanny
Vanishing Legion
Video Americana
Vietnam War Story 1
Vietnam War Story 2
Vietnam War Story 3
Western Double Feature 1: Wild Bill & Sunset Carson
Western Double Feature 3
Western Double Feature 3: Rogers & Allen
Western Double Feature 4
Western Double Feature 4: Rogers & Evans
Western Double Feature 5
Western Double Feature 5: Rogers & Autry
Western Double Feature 6: Rogers & Trigger
Western Double Feature 7: Wild Bill & Crabbe
Western Double Feature 8: Hale & Carradine
Western Double Feature 9: LaRue & Beery
Western Double Feature 10: Roy, Dale, & Trigger
Western Double Feature 11
Western Double Feature 12
Western Double Feature 13
Western Double Feature 14
Western Double Feature 15
Western Double Feature 16
Western Double Feature 17
Western Double Feature 18
Western Double Feature 19
Western Double Feature 21
Western Double Feature 22
Western Double Feature 24
Woman of Paris/Sunnyside▶
Women & Men: In Love There Are No Rules
Women & Men: Stories of Seduction
Zero for Conduct/Taris/A Propos de Nice

Anti-Heroes

***see also** Rebel With a Cause*

The Adventures of Robin Hood▶
Billy Jack
Bonnie & Clyde▶
Born Losers
Butch Cassidy and the Sundance Kid▶
Casino▶
The Dead Pool
Dirty Harry▶
Easy Rider▶
The Enforcer
H
Hero▶
In a Lonely Place▶
Magnum Force
Rebel Without a Cause▶
Robin Hood: Prince of Thieves
Sudden Impact
Thelma & Louise▶
Things to Do In Denver When You're Dead▶
To Wong Foo, Thanks for Everything, Julie Newmar
The Trial of Billy Jack
12 Monkeys▶
Wisdom

Anti-War War Movies

***see also** Satire & Parody*

All Quiet on the Western Front▶
All Quiet on the Western Front
Amazing Grace & Chuck
Apocalypse Now▶
The Big Parade▶
Born on the Fourth of July▶
The Bridge
The Bridges at Toko-Ri▶
The Burmese Harp▶
Catch-22▶
Civilization▶
Come and See▶
Coming Home▶
Cup Final
Dr. Strangelove, or: How I Learned to Stop Worrying and Love the Bomb▶
Field of Honor
Fires on the Plain▶
Forbidden Games▶
The Four Horsemen of the Apocalypse▶
The Four Horsemen of the Apocalypse
Gallipoli▶
Glory▶
Grand Illusion▶
Hamburger Hill
Hell in the Pacific▶
Henry V▶
J'Accuse▶
Jud
The King of Hearts▶
Latino
Les Carabiniers▶
The Line
M*A*S*H▶
M*A*S*H: Goodbye, Farewell & Amen▶
Master of the World
Nurse Edith Cavell▶
Paths of Glory▶
Platoon▶
The Red Badge of Courage▶
Revolution
San Demetrio, London
She Goes to War
The Steel Helmet▶
A Time to Love & a Time to Die
The Tin Drum▶
Torn Allegiance
Twilight's Last Gleaming
Veronico Cruz
Wackiest Ship in the Army
Westfront 1918▶
What Price Glory?▶
The Young Lions▶

Apartheid

***see also** Africa; Civil Rights*

An African Dream
Bopha!▶
City of Blood
Come Back, Africa▶
Cry Freedom
Cry, the Beloved Country▶
A Dry White Season▶
Funeral for an Assassin
Mandela▶
Master Harold and the Boys▶
Place of Weeping
The Power of One
Sarafina!▶
The Wilby Conspiracy▶
A World Apart▶
A World of Strangers▶
Yankee Zulu

Archaeology

***see** Big Digs*

Art & Artists

The Adventures of Picasso
The Agony and the Ecstasy
All the Vermeers in New York▶
An American in Paris▶
Andrei Rublev▶
Artists and Models
Back in the USSR
Backbeat▶
The Belly of an Architect▶
Bergonzi Hand
Black Magic Woman
The Blue Light▶
Bluebeard
A Bucket of Blood▶
Camille Claudel▶
Canvas: The Fine Art of Crime
Caravaggio▶
Carrington
Cauldron of Blood
Circle of Two
Color Me Blood Red
The Color of Evening
The Competition▶
Crucible of Terror
Crumb▶
Dante's Inferno: Life of Dante Gabriel Rossetti
Dark Side of Genius
Death in Venice▶
Detonator 2: Night Watch
Dishonored Lady
Driller Killer
Ebony Tower
Echoes
Edie in Ciao! Manhattan
Edvard Munch
Empty Canvas
Entre-Nous▶
Escapade in Florence
Et La Tenoresse?...Bordel!
Femme Fatale
Fleshtone
Framed
Frida
From the Mixed-Up Files of Mrs. Basil E. Frankweiler
Gothic▶
Haunted Summer
Headless Eyes
The Hideaways
The Horse's Mouth▶
Hot Touch
Hour of the Wolf▶
House of Horrors
House of Wax▶
How to Steal a Million▶
Hullabaloo Over Georgie & Bonnie's Pictures
Hunger
The Hypothesis of the Stolen Painting
If Lucy Fell
In the Land of the Owl Turds
I've Heard the Mermaids Singing▶
A Kink in the Picasso
La Belle Noiseuse▶
La Vie de Boheme▶
The Life of Emile Zola▶
Little Noises
Lust for Life▶
Mahler▶
Men...▶
Milo Milo
Mistral's Daughter
The Moderns▶
Modigliani
Moll Flanders▶
The Moon and Sixpence▶
Morgan!
Moulin Rouge▶
Murder by Numbers
The Naked Maja
New York Stories▶
The Object of Beauty▶
Paint It Black
Picture Windows
Portrait in Terror
Portrait of Grandpa Doc
Portrait of Jennie▶
Postcards from America
Prick Up Your Ears▶
Primal Secrets
Pucker Up and Bark Like a Dog
A Question of Attribution
Rembrandt▶
Rembrandt—1669
Retribution
Salut l'Artiste▶
The Sandpiper
Savage Messiah▶
Scenario du Film Passion▶
Scream, Baby, Scream
The Seventh Veil▶
Sheer Madness▶
Shifting Sands
The Silver Chalice
Sirens
Slaves of New York
Stars and Bars
Stealing Beauty
Still Life
Strange Fruit
A Sunday in the Country▶
Sunday in the Park with George▶
Superstar: The Life and Times of Andy Warhol▶
Tainted Image
The Testament of Orpheus▶
Track of the Vampire
Trespasser
Trust Me
Tunes of Glory/Horse's Mouth
Two If by Sea
The Two Mrs. Carrolls
Two Much
Utamaro and His Five Women
Utz
Van Gogh▶
Victimless Crimes
Video Americana
Vincent & Theo▶
Vincent: The Life and Death of Vincent van Gogh▶
The Wolf at the Door
The World of Suzie Wong

Asia

***see also** China; Japan*

Beyond Rangoon
Bloodsport 2: The Next Kumite
A Bullet in the Head▶
China White
Eat Drink Man Woman▶
Emmanuelle
Emmanuelle in Bangkok
Emmanuelle, the Joys of a Woman
Escape to Burma
Far East
Flight from Singapore
Flower Drum Song
Fortunes of War
The Golden Triangle
Hong Kong '97
Inn of Temptation
Istanbul
Jakarta
The Kill
The Killing Beach
Little Buddha
Lost Horizon▶
Love Is a Many-Splendored Thing
Malaya
The Man with the Golden Gun
The Mongols
Natural Causes
The Quest
Red Dust▶
The Sand Pebbles▶
The Scent of Green Papaya▶
Shadow of China▶
Shanghai Surprise
Shocking Asia
Singapore
The 13th Mission
Tigershark

The Two Great Cavaliers
The Ugly American
White Ghost

Asian America

Chan is Missing▶
Color of a Brisk and Leaping Day
Combination Platter
Come See the Paradise▶
Dim Sum: A Little Bit of Heart▶
Double Happiness▶
Eat a Bowl of Tea▶
Golden Gate
The Joy Luck Club▶
Living on Tokyo Time
The Wedding Banquet▶

Assassinations

see also Camelot (New); Foreign Intrigue; Hit Men; Spies & Espionage

Abraham Lincoln
Ace of Hearts
Act of Vengeance
An Affair in Mind
African Rage
The American Friend▶
The American Soldier
Antonio Das Mortes
The Arab Conspiracy
Ashes and Diamonds▶
Assassination
The Assassination Bureau▶
The Assignment
Belfast Assassin
Black Sunday
Blood for Blood
Blow Out▶
Brass Target
Brother Orchid▶
The Brotherhood of the Rose
The Burning Season▶
Cal▶
Center of the Web
The Clockmaker▶
Cold Front
Coming Out Alive
The Criminal Mind
Dagger Eyes
The Dallas Connection
Dangerous Pursuit
The Day of the Dolphin
The Day of the Jackal▶
The Day That Shook the World
Deadly Exposure
Death Force
The Destructors
Diamond Run
The Dirty Dozen: The Next Mission
Disappearance
The Domino Principle
The Eagle Has Landed▶
The Eagle Has Two Heads▶
Emmanuelle, the Queen
Enigma
Equalizer 2000
The Evil That Men Do
Excessive Force 2: Force on Force
Executive Action
F/X▶
Fatal Justice
Flashpoint
Flirting with Fate▶
Foul Play▶
Friday Foster
From Russia with Love▶
Funeral for an Assassin
Godson▶
Hard Way
Harum Scarum
Hit Lady
The Hunted
I Spit on Your Corpse
In the Line of Fire▶
Invitation to a Gunfighter
JFK▶
Judgment Night
Kill Castro
The Killer Elite
Killer Likes Candy
The Killing Device
King Richard and the Crusaders
Kingfish: A Story of Huey P. Long
La Femme Nikita▶
La Passante▶
La Scorta▶
Love and Anarchy▶
Love Kills
Loves & Times of Scaramouche
Malcolm X▶
The Man Who Knew Too Much▶
The Man Who Knew Too Much
The Man with the Golden Gun
The Manchurian Candidate▶
Maniac
Mark of the Beast
The Mercenaries
Murder of a Moderate Man
Nick of Time
A Night of Love
Night of the Assassin
Ninja Death Squad
Nowhere to Hide
The Odd Job
Omar Khayyam
One Man Out
Operation C.I.A.
The Ordeal of Dr. Mudd▶
The Parallax View▶
Paris Belongs to Us
Point of No Return
Programmed to Kill
PT 109
Quicker Than the Eye
Quiet Thunder
Red King, White Knight
Red Scorpion
Revenge of the Pink Panther
Rogue Male
Ruby
Running Against Time
Russian Roulette
Scorpio
The Shooter
Stalking Danger
State of Siege▶
Steele's Law
Suddenly▶
Target: Favorite Son
The Terminator▶
This Gun for Hire
Times of Harvey Milk
Two Minute Warning
Walker: Texas Ranger: Deadly Reunion
Wardogs
What a Way to Die
When Hell Broke Loose
Where There's Life
Windmills of the Gods
Winter Kills▶
Without Warning: The James Brady Story▶
Yojimbo▶
Z▶

Astronomy & Astrology

see Star Gazing

At the Movies

see also Behind the Scenes

Anguish
Cinema Paradiso▶
Come See the Paradise▶
Dead End Drive-In
Demons
Get Shorty▶
The Inner Circle▶
Last Action Hero
The Long Day Closes▶
Matinee
Midnight Movie Massacre
The Movie House Massacre
One Summer Love
Popcorn
The Projectionist▶
The Purple Rose of Cairo▶
Rorret▶
Something Short of Paradise
Things to Do In Denver When You're Dead▶
Wes Craven's New Nightmare▶

Australia

see Down Under

Automobiles

see Fast Cars; Motor Vehicle Dept.

Avant-Garde

All Screwed Up▶
Angel City
Anita, Dances of Vice
Aria
Band of Outsiders
Baraka▶
Bell Diamond
Bim/Dream of the Wild Horses
Blonde Cobra/The Doctor's Dream
The Blood of a Poet
The Boxer and Death▶
Boy Meets Girl▶
Breathless▶
Caligari's Cure▶
Careful
Chameleon
Complex
Corrida Interdite
The Cosmic Eye▶
David Holzman's Diary▶
Death of the Rat
Diamonds of the Night▶
Dr. Caligari
Dog Star Man▶
Dreamwood▶
Entr'acte
Eraserhead▶
False Note
Fat and the Lean▶
Films by Peter Thompson
The Foreigner
France/Tour/Detour/Deux/Enfants▶
Godard/Truffaut Shorts
Hiroshima, Mon Amour▶
The Hypothesis of the Stolen Painting
Italianamerican/The Big Shave
Journeys from Berlin/1971
The Joy of Knowledge
Koyaanisqatsi▶
The Last Movie
The Last of England▶
Les Carabiniers▶
Liquid Sky▶
Lola▶
A Man, a Woman and a Killer
The Man Who Envied Women
Mixed Blood
My Neighborhood
News from Home
Notes for an African Orestes
Numero Deux
Offnight
Paul Bartel's The Secret Cinema
Peril
Periphery
Permanent Vacation
Phantom of Liberty▶
Powaqqatsi: Life in Transformation▶
Renoir Shorts▶
The Report on the Party and the Guests▶
Repulsion▶
RoGoPaG
Rome '78
Sans Soleil▶
Santa Sangre▶
Scenario du Film Passion▶
Scherzo
Seduction of Mimi▶
Sherman's March: An Improbable Search for Love
Shoot Loud, Louder, I Don't Understand!
Signals Through the Flames▶
Six Fois Deux/Sur et Sous la Communication▶
Smiling Madame Beudet/The Seashell and the Clergyman▶
Soft and Hard
Sometimes It Works, Sometimes It Doesn't
Strong Medicine
The Testament of Dr. Cordelier▶
The Testament of Orpheus▶
The Thrill Killers
Time Indefinite
Two Men & a Wardrobe
Un Chien Andalou▶
Underground U.S.A.
Veronika Voss▶
Video Americana
WR: Mysteries of the Organism▶
You Are Not I
A Zed & Two Noughts▶

Babysitting

see also Bringing Up Baby; Parenthood

Addams Family Values
Adventures in Babysitting
Are You in the House Alone?
The Baby-Sitters Club
The Babysitter
Battling for Baby
Bebe's Kids
Corrina, Corrina
The Crazysitter
Don't Bother to Knock
Fright
A Global Affair
The Guardian
The Hand that Rocks the Cradle
Laurel & Hardy: Brats
Look Who's Talking▶
Midnight's Child
Mr. Nanny
My Daughter's Keeper
Perfect Family
Three's Trouble
Uncle Buck▶
Wanted: Babysitter
Weekend with the Babysitter
When a Stranger Calls
When a Stranger Calls Back

Bad Dads

see also Dads; Monster Moms; Parenthood

The Attic
Beatrice▶
First Born
Flesh and Bone▶
The Great Santini▶
Kiss Daddy Goodbye
Kiss Daddy Goodnight
Parents▶
The Shining
The Stepfather▶
Stepfather 2: Make Room for Daddy
Stepfather 3: Father's Day

Ballet

see also Dance Fever

The Bacchantes
Black Tights
Body Beat
Brain Donors
Carmen▶
The Children of Theatre Street
The Cowboy & the Ballerina
Dance
Dancers
George Balanchine's The Nutcracker
Le Bourgeois Gentilhomme
Limelight▶
Little Ballerina
Mirrors
Never Let Me Go
Nijinsky
Nine Months
Nutcracker Sweet
Nutcracker: The Motion Picture
The Red Shoes▶
Shadow Dancing▶
Shall We Dance▶
Spectre of the Rose
Suspiria▶
Tales of Beatrix Potter▶
The Tales of Hoffmann
The Turning Point
Waterloo Bridge▶

Ballooning

Around the World in 80 Days▶
Around the World in 80 Days
The Balloonatic/One Week
Charlie and the Great Balloon Chase
Fantastic Balloon Voyage
Five Weeks in a Balloon
Flight of the Eagle
Frankenstein Island
Lost Zeppelin
Mysterious Island▶
Night Crossing
Olly Olly Oxen Free
The Red Balloon▶
Voyage en Balloon

Baltimore

The Alien Factor
And Justice for All
Avalon▶
Breathing Lessons▶
Diner▶
Hairspray▶
He Said, She Said
Sleepless in Seattle▶
Tin Men

Baseball

Amazing Grace & Chuck
Angels in the Outfield▶
Angels in the Outfield
The Babe
Babe Ruth Story
The Bad News Bears▶
The Bad News Bears Go to Japan
The Bad News Bears in Breaking Training
Bang the Drum Slowly
Bang the Drum Slowly▶
Baseball
Battling Orioles
Bingo Long Traveling All-Stars & Motor Kings▶
Blood Games
Blue Skies Again
Brewster's Millions
Bull Durham▶
The Busher
Casey at the Bat
Charlie Brown's All-Stars
Chasing Dreams
Chu Chu & the Philly Flash
Cobb▶
Comeback Kid
The Comrades of Summer
Cooperstown
Damn Yankees▶
Don't Look Back: The Story of Leroy "Satchel" Paige
Ed
Eight Men Out▶
The Fan
Fear Strikes Out▶
Field of Dreams▶
Hank Aaron: Chasing the Dream▶
Heading Home
Ironweed▶
It Happens Every Spring▶
It's Arbor Day, Charlie Brown
It's Good to Be Alive
It's My Turn
The Jackie Robinson Story▶
Jim Thorpe: All American

The Kid from Left Field
A League of Their Own▶
Little Big League
Long Gone
Love Affair: The Eleanor & Lou Gehrig Story▶
Major League
Major League 2
The Man from Left Field
Mr. Baseball
Mr. Destiny
The Natural▶
Night Game
One in a Million: The Ron LeFlore Story
Past the Bleachers
Pastime▶
Pride of St. Louis
The Pride of the Yankees▶
Rookie of the Year
The Sandlot▶
The Scout
The Slugger's Wife
Squeeze Play
Stealing Home
The Stratton Story▶
Take Me Out to the Ball Game
Taking Care of Business
Talent for the Game
Three Wishes
Tiger Town
Timothy and the Angel
Trading Hearts
Wait Until Spring, Bandini
Whistling in Brooklyn
A Winner Never Quits
The Winning Team
Woman of the Year▶
Workin' for Peanuts

Basketball

Above the Rim
The Absent-Minded Professor▶
The Air Up There
Annie O
The Basketball Diaries
Big Mo
Blue Chips
Celtic Pride
Coach
Cornbread, Earl & Me
Eddie
Fast Break
Final Shot: The Hank Gathers Story
The Fish that Saved Pittsburgh
For Heaven's Sake
Forget Paris
Heaven is a Playground
Hoop Dreams▶
Hoosiers▶
Inside Moves
One on One
Pistol: The Birth of a Legend
The St. Tammany Miracle
Slam Dunk Ernest
Sunset Park
Tall Story
Teen Wolf
That Championship Season
White Men Can't Jump
The White Shadow, Vol. 1

Bathroom Scenes

About Last Night...▶
American Gigolo
An American Werewolf in London▶
Arachnophobia
Body Double▶
Brain Damage
Breathless
Bull Durham▶
Club Paradise
Copycat
Diabolique▶
Diabolique
Dressed to Kill
An Eye for an Eye
Fatal Attraction▶
Ghostbusters 2
He Knows You're Alone
High Anxiety
Hollywood Hot Tubs
Hollywood Hot Tubs 2: Educating Crystal
Jinxed
The Legacy
Lethal Weapon 2▶
Married to the Mob▶
Midnight Express▶
Mister Roberts▶
Mixed Nuts
National Lampoon's Vacation▶
Poltergeist▶
Porky's
The Postman Always Rings Twice
Psycho▶
Psycho 2
Pulp Fiction▶
The Rain Killer
St. Elmo's Fire
Schizo
Shakes the Clown
Silkwood▶
Snow White and the Seven Dwarfs
Stripes
Tequila Sunrise
They Came from Within
Tie Me Up! Tie Me Down!
Valley Girl
Valmont▶

Beach Blanket Bingo

***see also** Lifeguards; Sex on the Beach; Surfing; Swimming*

Back to the Beach
Baywatch the Movie: Forbidden Paradise
Beach Babes from Beyond Infinity
Beach Blanket Bingo▶
Beach Girls
The Beach Girls and the Monster
Beach House
Beach Party
Bikini Beach
Bikini Summer
Body Waves
California Dreaming
Computer Beach Party
Horror of Party Beach
How to Stuff a Wild Bikini
Malibu Beach
Muscle Beach Party
Pajama Party
Ride the Wild Surf
Seaside Swingers
Shag: The Movie▶
Surf Party
A Swingin' Summer
Wet and Wild Summer
Where the Boys Are

Beauty Pageants

***see also** Dream Girls*

The Case of the Lucky Legs
The Duchess of Idaho
I Wanna Be a Beauty Queen
Miss All-American Beauty
Miss Firecracker▶
No Contest
Shag: The Movie▶
Smile▶
Waikiki Wedding▶

Behind Bars

***see** Great Escapes; Men in Prison; Women in Prison*

Behind the Scenes

***see also** At the Movies; Film History*

Actors and Sin
The Affairs of Annabel
...And God Spoke
Augustin
Bela Lugosi Scrapbook
Bellissimo: Images of the Italian Cinema
Beloved Infidel
Best Friends
Beware of a Holy Whore
The Big Knife▶
Big Show
Body Chemistry 3: Point of Seduction
The Bodyguard
Bombay Talkie
Boy Meets Girl▶
Broadway Rhythm
Bugs Bunny Superstar
Bullets Over Broadway▶
Buster Keaton Rides Again/The Railrodder
Carny▶
Casino▶
Chaplin▶
The Chaplin Revue
A Chorus Line
A Chorus of Disapproval
Chuck Berry: Hail! Hail! Rock 'n' Roll▶
The Confessional
Contempt▶
Crossover Dreams
Dames▶
Dance of Life
Dancing Lady
Dangerous Game
The Death Kiss
Delirious
Don't Let Your Meat Loaf
Double Threat
Dracula: A Cinematic Scrapbook
The Dresser▶
The Ed Wood Story: The Plan 9 Companion
Face the Music
Fangoria's Weekend of Horrors
Footlight Parade▶
Frankenstein: A Cinematic Scrapbook
Free and Easy
The Freeway Maniac
The French Lieutenant's Woman▶
Get Shorty▶
The Ghost Walks
Give a Girl a Break
Going Hollywood▶
The Goldwyn Follies
Goodbye, Norma Jean
Goodnight, Sweet Marilyn
The Grace Kelly Story
Grief
Grunt! The Wrestling Movie
The Hard Way▶
He Said, She Said
The Hearst and Davies Affair
Hearts of Darkness: A Filmmaker's Apocalypse▶
Help!▶
Hollywood Boulevard
Hollywood Man
Hollywood Mystery
Hollywood Scandals and Tragedies
Hollywood Shuffle
Hooper
The Horror of It All
In a Moment of Passion
In the Soup
Inside Daisy Clover
Into the Sun
The Jayne Mansfield Story
Joey Breaker▶
The Killing of Sister George
La Dolce Vita▶
L.A. Goddess
The Last Word
Le Schpountz
Legs
Living in Oblivion▶
The Lonely Lady
Make a Wish
A Man in Love▶
Man of a Thousand Faces▶
Matinee
Meet the Feebles
A Midwinter's Tale
Miss All-American Beauty
Mistress
The Mozart Brothers▶
The Muppets Take Manhattan▶
My Life's In Turnaround
Naked in New York
New Faces of 1952
A Night for Crime
Night of the Living Dead, 25th Anniversary Documentary
Nixon▶
Noises Off
On an Island with You
Opening Night
Pastime▶
Pick a Star
The Pickle
The Player▶
Rave Review
Ready to Wear
Rhythm on the River
Roadie
Rorret▶
Search and Destroy
Sex Is Crazy
The Show
Silent Motive
Sioux City Sue
S.O.B.
Somewhere in Time
Stage Door▶
Stand-In
The Star Maker
Star Spangled Rhythm▶
Star Trek 25th Anniversary Special
State of Things▶
Steve Martin Live
The Stunt Man▶
Stunts
Sullivan's Travels▶
Summer Stock▶
Sunset
Sunset Boulevard▶
Sweet Liberty
Sweet Perfection
Swimming with Sharks▶
Teenager
They Bite
Through the Olive Trees▶
Tootsie▶
Truth or Dare
Ulysses' Gaze
Under the Rainbow
Users
Valley of the Dolls
Velvet Touch▶
A Very Private Affair
Wes Craven's New Nightmare▶
The West Point Story
What Price Hollywood?▶
Whodunit
Witch Hunt
Zou Zou

Berlin

***see also** Germany*

Anita, Dances of Vice
The Apple
Berlin Alexanderplatz▶
The Berlin Conspiracy
Berlin Tunnel 21
The Blue Hour
The Captain from Koepenick
Chinese Boxes
Club Extinction
Cold Room
David▶
Demons
Faraway, So Close!
Fatherland
Forbidden
Funeral in Berlin▶
I Am a Camera▶
Indiana Jones and the Last Crusade▶
The Innocent
Judgment in Berlin
Kamikaze '89▶
The Looking Glass War
The Oppermann Family
Periphery
The Promise
Salmonberries
The Search▶
The Serpent's Egg
Shining Through
Strikeback
The Tigress
Verboten!
Wings of Desire▶

Bicycling

American Flyers
BMX Bandits
Breaking Away▶
Off the Mark
Pee Wee's Big Adventure▶
Quicksilver
Rad
Rush It
Ten Speed

Big Battles

***see also** Civil War; Korean War; Korean War; Persian Gulf War; Revolutionary War; Vietnam War; World War I; World War II*

The Alamo▶
Alexander Nevsky▶
Alexander the Great
Aliens▶
Anzio
Apocalypse Now▶
Arena
Back to Bataan
Barry Lyndon▶
Battle Beyond the Sun
Battle of Britain
The Battle of El Alamein
Battle of the Bulge
The Battle of the Japan Sea
Battle of the Worlds
Battleground▶
The Battleship Potemkin▶
Ben-Hur▶
The Big Parade▶
The Big Red One▶
The Birth of a Nation▶
A Bridge Too Far
Cage 2: The Arena of Death
Captain Caution
The Castilian
Cromwell
Cross of Iron
The Crusades
Das Boot▶
Diamonds Are Forever▶
Dragonheart
Dragonslayer▶
El Cid▶
The Empire Strikes Back▶
Enemy Below▶
Excalibur▶
The Fall of the Roman Empire▶
The Fighting Sullivans▶
First Knight
Gallipoli▶
Gettysburg▶
The Giant of Marathon
Giants of Rome
Gladiators 7
Glory▶
Godzilla vs. the Smog Monster
Goldfinger▶
The Guns of Navarone▶
Heaven & Earth▶
Henry V▶
Highlander▶
John Paul Jones
The King of the Kickboxers
The Last Command
The Lighthorsemen▶
The Long Riders▶
The Longest Day▶
The Man Who Would Be King▶
Memphis Belle▶

Midway
The Mongols
Monty Python and the Holy Grail▶
Moonraker
Motel Hell
Naked Warriors
A Nightmare on Elm Street
Patton▶
Raiders of the Lost Ark▶
Ran▶
Rawhide▶
Red Dawn
Return of the Jedi▶
Revolution
Ring of Fire
Robot Jox
Samson and His Mighty Challenge
The Sand Pebbles▶
Sands of Iwo Jima▶
The Siege of Firebase Gloria
The Silk Road
Son of the Morning Star▶
Star Crash
Star Wars▶
Street Hunter
Ten Days That Shook the World▶
They Died with Their Boots On▶
Thunderball
To Hell and Back
Tora! Tora! Tora!
Twelve O'Clock High▶
War and Peace
War and Peace▶
The War Lord▶
The Wild Bunch▶
Zulu
Zulu Dawn▶

Big Budget Stinkers

***see also** Pure Ego Vehicles*

The Adventurers
Alexander the Great
American Anthem
Annie
Christopher Columbus: The Discovery
Cleopatra
The Conqueror
The Cotton Club▶
Dune
Harlem Nights
Heaven's Gate
Howard the Duck
Hudson Hawk
I'll Do Anything
Ishtar
Last Action Hero
Midway
Money Train
Moon in the Gutter
1941
One from the Heart
Pirates
Rambo 3
Santa Claus: The Movie
The Scarlet Letter
The Shoes of the Fisherman
The Silver Chalice
Summer Holiday
Supergirl
Tora! Tora! Tora!
Two Minute Warning
Two of a Kind
Waterloo

Big Daddies

***see also** American South*

All the King's Men▶
The Big Country
Cat on a Hot Tin Roof▶
Cat on a Hot Tin Roof
Fire in the Night
The Great Santini▶
The Learning Tree
The Long, Hot Summer▶
Man of Evil
Other People's Money
Papa's Delicate Condition▶
The Paper Chase▶
A Piece of Pleasure▶
Running Mates▶
Smokey Bites the Dust
Sons of Hercules in the Land of Darkness
Stay As You Are
Sweet Bird of Youth▶
This Property is Condemned
Touch of Evil▶
Vultures
Where the Heart Is

Big Digs

The Curse of King Tut's Tomb
Deadly Intent
The Golden Salamander
Indiana Jones and the Last Crusade▶
Indiana Jones and the Temple of Doom▶
King of the Forest Rangers
March or Die
The Mask
The Mole People
The Mummy▶
The Mummy's Hand
Pimpernel Smith
Raiders of the Lost Ark▶
Search for the Gods
The Serpent of Death
Sound of Horror
Specters
Stargate
Tomb
The Word

Big Ideas

***see also** Ethics & Morals*

The Addiction
Barefoot in Athens
Being Human
Blaise Pascal▶
Blue
Dead Man
Faraway, So Close!
The Incredible Shrinking Man▶
I.Q.
Jonathan Livingston Seagull
Judgment at Nuremberg▶
Kicking and Screaming▶
Meetings with Remarkable Men
The Messiah▶
Metropolitan▶
Mindwalk: A Film for Passionate Thinkers▶
Mr. North
My Dinner with Andre▶
1900▶
Nostradamus
The Occult Experience
The Quarrel
The Razor's Edge▶
The Razor's Edge
Return to Eden
Samurai 3: Duel at Ganryu Island▶
Sans Soleil▶
The Seventh Seal▶
Sorceress▶
That Championship Season
Up to a Certain Point
Wittgenstein
The Wrong Move
Zabriskie Point▶

Big Rigs

***see also** Motor Vehicle Dept.; Road Trip*

Big Trouble in Little China
Breaker! Breaker!
California Straight Ahead
Citizens Band▶
Coast to Coast
Convoy
Desperate
Driving Force
Duel▶
Every Which Way But Loose
F.I.S.T.
Flatbed Annie and Sweetiepie: Lady Truckers
Great Smokey Roadblock
High Ballin'
The Long Haul
Pee Wee's Big Adventure▶
Rolling Vengeance
Smokey and the Bandit
Smokey and the Bandit, Part 2
Smokey and the Bandit, Part 3
Sorcerer
Steel Cowboy
The Sure Thing▶
They Drive by Night▶
Think Big
Wages of Fear▶
White Line Fever
Willa

Bigfoot/Yeti

Big Foot
Bigfoot: The Unforgettable Encounter
The Capture of Bigfoot
Frostbiter: Wrath of the Wendigo
Half Human
Harry and the Hendersons
Legend of Big Foot
Legend of Boggy Creek
Man Beast
Night of the Demon
Night of the Howling Beast
Return to Boggy Creek
Sasquatch
The Snow Creature
Snowbeast

Bikers

The Acid Eaters
Adventures Beyond Belief
Angel Unchained
Angels Die Hard
Angels from Hell
Angels Hard as They Come
Angels' Wild Women
Beach Party
Beyond the Law
Black Bikers from Hell
Blonde in Black Leather
Born Losers
Born to Ride
Breaking Loose
Bury Me an Angel
Chopper Chicks in Zombietown
Chrome and Hot Leather
Chrome Hearts
Chrome Soldiers
City Limits
Cleopatra Jones
Club Life
Crossing the Line
Cycle Psycho
Cycle Vixens
Cyclone
Danger Zone
Danger Zone 2
Danger Zone 3: Steel Horse War
Dark Rider
Darktown Strutters
Deadly Reactor
Devil's Angels
Dirt Bike Kid
Dirt Gang
Easy Rider▶
Easy Wheels
Eat the Peach
Electra Glide in Blue▶
Evel Knievel
Every Which Way But Loose
Eye of the Tiger
The Final Alliance
The Girl on a Motorcycle
The Glory Stompers
Go for Broke
The Great Escape▶
Great Ride
The Great Skycopter Rescue
Greedy Terror
The Hard Ride
Harley
Harley Davidson and the Marlboro Man
Hellcats
Hellriders
Hell's Angels Forever
Hell's Angels on Wheels
Hell's Angels '69
Hell's Belles
Hog Wild
Hollywood Chaos
In Your Face
Iron Horsemen
The Jesus Trip
Knightriders
Loners
The Losers
Loveless
Mad Max▶
Mask▶
The Masters of Menace
Master's Revenge
Motor Psycho
Motorcycle Gang
The Naked Angels
Nam Angels
Nomad Riders
Northville Cemetery Massacre
The Only Way Home
The Outlaw Bikers—Gang Wars
Outlaw Riders
Peacekillers
Pray for the Wildcats
Psychomania
Punk Vacation
Race for Glory
Raising Arizona▶
Raw Courage
Rebel Rousers
Return of the Rebels
Riding High
Riding the Edge
Roadside Prophets
Run, Angel, Run!
Running Cool
Satan's Sadists
Savage Dawn
The Savage Seven
Savages from Hell
Shame
She-Devils on Wheels
The Shrieking
Sidewinder One
Silver Dream Racer
Sinner's Blood
Space Riders
Spetters
Stone Cold
Street Hawk
Streets of Fire
Survival Zone
Timerider
Timothy and the Angel
Viva Knievel
Warlords from Hell
Werewolves on Wheels
The Wild Angels
Wild Guitar
The Wild One▶
Wild Rebels
Wild Riders
Wild Wheels
Winners Take All

Biography

***see** This is Your Life*

Birds

Beaks: The Movie
Bill and Coo
Birdman of Alcatraz▶
The Birds▶
The Birds 2: Land's End
Blade Master
A Breed Apart
Brewster McCloud▶
Cockfighter▶
Continental Divide
Cry of the Penguins
The Giant Claw
The Goodbye Bird
High Anxiety
Howard the Duck
Mating Season
Million Dollar Duck
No Fear, No Die
The Pebble and the Penguin
Rooster: Spurs of Death!
Sesame Street Presents: Follow That Bird
Spirit of the Eagle
Vulture

Bisexuality

***see also** Gays; Lesbians*

Basic Instinct
California Suite▶
The Crying Game▶
Dog Day Afternoon▶
Dona Herlinda & Her Son
Happily Ever After
Les Biches▶
Liquid Sky▶
Mary, Mary, Bloody Mary
The Scorpion Woman
Showgirls
Sunday, Bloody Sunday▶
Three of Hearts
Threesome
A Woman in Flames▶

Black Comedy

***see also** Comedy; Comedy Drama; Satire & Parody*

Abigail's Party
The Addams Family
Addams Family Values
The Advocate▶
After Hours▶
Age Isn't Everything
Alberto Express
Alice▶
All Over Town
Alone in the T-Shirt Zone
The Americanization of Emily▶
America's Deadliest Home Video
Angels Over Broadway▶
The Anniversary
The Applegates
Ariel▶
Army Brats
Arnold
Arrivederci, Baby!
Arsenic and Old Lace▶
The Assassination Bureau▶
Assault of the Killer Bimbos
At Home with the Webbers
The Atomic Kid
Baby Face Morgan
Baby Love
Bad Boy Bubby
Bad Charleston Charlie
Bare Hunt
Barjo
Barton Fink▶
Battle of the Bullies
Beat the Devil▶
Bizarre Bizarre▶
Bliss▶
Brazil▶
Bread and Chocolate▶
Brewster McCloud▶
Buddy Buddy
Buffet Froid▶
The Cable Guy
Canadian Bacon
Careful
The Cars That Ate Paris▶
Catch-22▶
Checking Out
Choice of Weapons
The Choirboys
Clerks▶
Coldblooded
The Comic▶
Consuming Passions
The Cook, the Thief, His Wife & Her Lover▶
Coup de Torchon▶
Crimes of the Heart

The Criminal Life of Archibaldo de la Cruz▶
The Dark Backward
A Day in the Death of Joe Egg▶
Deadly Advice
Death Becomes Her▶
Death in Brunswick
Delicatessen▶
Divine
Dr. Strangelove, or: How I Learned to Stop Worrying and Love the Bomb▶
Don's Party▶
The Doom Generation▶
Eat the Rich
Eating Raoul▶
El: This Strange Passion▶
Ellie
The End▶
Enid Is Sleeping
Entertaining Mr. Sloane
Exquisite Corpses
The Exterminating Angel▶
Fargo▶
Female Trouble
A Fine Madness▶
The Firemen's Ball▶
A Fish Called Wanda▶
Four Bags Full
Four Rooms
The 4th Man▶
Freaked
The Funeral▶
Funny Bones▶
Funny, Dirty Little War
The Garden of Delights▶
Gas-s-s-s!
The Gazebo▶
Genghis Cohn
Getting Away With Murder
Ghost Chase
The Gift
Goodbye Cruel World
Grace Quigley
The Great Madcap
Greetings▶
Guilty as Charged
Harold and Maude▶
Hawks
Headless Body in Topless Bar
Heart Condition
Heathers▶
Hexed
Hi, Mom!▶
High Heels
High Heels▶
Highway 61
Hold Me, Thrill Me, Kiss Me
Home Sweet Home
Homebodies
The Honey Pot
The Hospital▶
The Hot Rock▶
How Tasty Was My Little Frenchman
How to Get Ahead in Advertising▶
The Hudsucker Proxy▶
Husbands, Wives, Money, and Murder
I Love You to Death
I Ought to Be in Pictures
Infernal Trio
Into the Night
The Killing of Sister George
Kind Hearts and Coronets▶
King of Comedy▶
King, Queen, Knave▶
Kiss of Death
The Ladykillers▶
The Laserman
The Last Supper
Leolo
Life Is Sweet▶
Little Murders▶
Loot...Give Me Money, Honey!
The Loved One▶
Lucky Stiff
L'Udienza
Mad Dog and Glory▶
Man Bites Dog
Matador
A Matter of WHO
Max, Mon Amour
Meet the Feebles
Miracle Mile▶
Mixed Blood
Mondo Balardo
Monsieur Verdoux▶
Montenegro▶
Mortuary Academy
Mother, Jugs and Speed
Muriel's Wedding▶
Murphy's Fault
My New Gun
Mystery Train▶
The Natural History of Parking Lots
No Problem
No Surrender▶
Nuts in May
O Lucky Man!▶
The Oak
The Odd Job
Oh Dad, Poor Dad (Momma's Hung You in the Closet & I'm Feeling So Sad)
Out Cold
Pain in the A—▶
Parents▶
Passed Away
Paul Bartel's The Secret Cinema
Penn and Teller Get Killed
The Pornographers▶
Private Parts
Pulp Fiction▶
Raising Arizona▶
Reckless
Red Earth
The Red Inn
The Ref▶
Repo Man▶
Reuben, Reuben▶
Riff Raff▶
Rubin & Ed
Salvation!
The Scent of a Woman
Serial Mom▶
Seven Beauties▶
Shadey
Shakes the Clown
Shallow Grave
She-Devil
Shoot Loud, Louder, I Don't Understand!
A Sinful Life
So I Married an Axe Murderer
Some Girls
Something for Everyone
Something Wild
Spanking the Monkey▶
Stars and Bars
The Steagle
Sticky Fingers
The Story of Fausta
Sweet Movie
Swimming with Sharks▶
Tatie Danielle▶
That Obscure Object of Desire▶
There was a Crooked Man▶
Throw Momma from the Train▶
Tie Me Up! Tie Me Down!
To Be or Not to Be▶
To Die For▶
Toto le Heros▶
Trainspotting▶
Transylvania Twist
Trois Couleurs: Blanc▶
The Unbelievable Truth
Underground▶
Unexplained Laughter
Unnatural Pursuits
Vampire's Kiss▶
The War of the Roses▶
What Have I Done to Deserve This?▶
Where's Piccone▶
Where's Poppa?▶
Who Is Killing the Great Chefs of Europe?▶
Why Does Herr R. Run Amok?
Wilder Napalm
Wise Guys
The Witches of Eastwick
Withnail and I▶
Women on the Verge of a Nervous Breakdown▶
World of the Depraved
The Wrong Box▶

Black Gold

The Abyss▶
Black Gold
Blowing Wild
Boom Town
Comes a Horseman
Country Gentlemen
The Crude Oasis
Dead Ahead: The Exxon Valdez Disaster▶
Devil's Crude
The Dive
Double Deal
Fighting Texans
Five Easy Pieces▶
The Formula
Gas Pump Girls
Giant▶
The Guns and the Fury
Hellfighters
Intruder Within
Legend of Frenchie King
Lie Down with Lions
Local Hero▶
Louisiana Story▶
The Madwoman of Chaillot
Mission in Morocco
Naked Gun 2 1/2: The Smell of Fear
'Neath the Arizona Skies
Oceans of Fire
Oklahoma Crude
On Deadly Ground
Red Rock West▶
Roughnecks
The Stars Fell on Henrietta
Thunder Bay▶
Tulsa▶
Waltz Across Texas
War of the Wildcats
Wildcat
Written on the Wind▶

Blackmail

see also Corporate Shenanigans; Crime & Criminals; Disorganized Crime; Organized Crime

Captives
Hard Evidence
Letter to My Killer
Mulholland Falls
The Silent Partner▶
Victim▶

Blaxploitation

see also African America; New Black Cinema

Black Vampire
Black Werewolf
Blackenstein
Blacula
Dr. Black, Mr. Hyde
The House on Skull Mountain
No Way Back
Scream Blacula Scream

Blindness

see also Physical Problems

Afraid of the Dark
Against the Drunken Cat Paws
Alligator Eyes
Amy
Ballad in Blue
Blackout
Blind Fear
Blind Justice
Blind Man's Bluff
Blind Witness
Blink
Breaking Free
Butterflies Are Free▶
Cactus
Can You Feel Me Dancing?
City for Conquest▶
City Lights▶
Don't Look Now▶
Eight Witnesses
Eighteen Jade Arhats
Elmer
Eye on the Sparrow
The Human Monster
Ice Castles
If You Could See What I Hear
Jennifer 8
The Killer▶
La Symphonie Pastorale▶
Last Game
Life on a String
Love at First Sight
Love Leads the Way
Minnesota Clay
The Miracle Worker▶
Night Gallery▶
Night Is My Future
Octavia
On Dangerous Ground▶
Ordinary Heroes
A Patch of Blue
People Who Own the Dark
Places in the Heart▶
Proof▶
Return of the Evil Dead
The Scent of a Woman
Scent of a Woman▶
See No Evil▶
See No Evil, Hear No Evil
Sketch Artist 2: Hands That See
They Watch
To Race the Wind
Until The End of The World▶
Wait Until Dark▶
The Whales of August▶
Zertigo Diamond Caper

Bloody Mayhem

see also Bloody Messages; Horror

The Addiction
Alien▶
Alien 3
Anguish
Army of Darkness▶
Aroused
The Art of Dying▶
At Midnight, I'll Take Your Soul
The Avenger
The Awful Dr. Orlof
Baby Cart 4: Heart of a Parent...Heart of a Child
Bad Blood
Bad Dreams
Ballbuster
The Banker
Barn of the Naked Dead
Basket Case▶
Basket Case 2
Basket Case 3: The Progeny
Beast of the Yellow Night
Between God, the Devil & a Winchester
Big Meat Eater
Bits and Pieces
Black Christmas
Black Shampoo
Blade of the Ripper
Blood and Black Lace
Blood Bride
Blood Cult
Blood Diner
Blood Feast
Blood Lake
Blood Legacy
Blood Mania
Blood of Ghastly Horror
Blood Orgy of the She-Devils
Blood Screams
Blood Sisters
Blood Tide
Blood Tracks
Bloodbath in Psycho Town
Bloodshed
Bloodstalkers
Bloody Birthday
Bloody Mama
Body Count
Body Parts
The Body Shop
The Borrower
The Boys Next Door
The Brainiac
The Brides of Dracula
Bring Me the Head of Alfredo Garcia
Brothers in Arms
Burial Ground
Buried Alive
Cannibal Campout
Cardiac Arrest
Carnage
Carnival of Blood
The Carpathian Eagle
Carrie▶
Castle of the Creeping Flesh
Cataclysm
Challenge
The Channeler
Cheerleader Camp
Children of the Corn 2: The Final Sacrifice
Child's Play
Child's Play 2
Child's Play 3
Chopping Mall
C.H.U.D.
The Church▶
Circus of Horrors
City of the Walking Dead
Cocaine Wars
Color Me Blood Red
The Corpse Vanishes
Crawlspace
Craze
Crazed
The Crazies
Cujo
Curfew
Curse of the Alpha Stone
Curse of the Screaming Dead
Cutting Class
Cyborg Soldier
Dangerous Game
The Dark Half
Dawn of the Dead▶
Day of Judgment
Day of the Dead
Dead Alive
Dead Girls
The Dead Next Door
Deadly Blessing
Deadly Dreams
Deadly Neighbor
Dear Dead Delilah
Death Magic
Death Promise
Death Screams
Death Spa
Deep Red: Hatchet Murders
Delirium
Dementia 13
The Demon
Demon Possessed
Demonic Toys
Demons
Demons 2
Deranged
Desperado▶
Destroy All Monsters
Devastator
The Devil
Devil Rider
Dirty Harry▶
Doctor Butcher M.D.
Dr. Hackenstein
Dr. Jekyll's Dungeon of Death
Dogs of Hell
Dollman vs Demonic Toys
Dolls
Don't Go in the Woods
Doom Asylum
Dorm That Dripped Blood
Dracula vs. Frankenstein
Driller Killer
Drive-In Massacre
Eat and Run
Edge of the Axe
Encounter at Raven's Gate

Bloody Messages

see also Bloody Mayhem

Boating

see Sail Away

Bodyguards

Books

see also Storytelling

Boom!

see also Action Adventure; Fires

Hiroshima: Out of the Ashes▶
Lethal Weapon 3
Live Wire: Human Timebomb
The Rock▶
Sea of Sand
The Specialist
Speed▶
Sudden Death
The Terminator▶
Testament▶
Thirty Seconds Over Tokyo▶
Total Recall▶
True Lies
The Usual Suspects▶

Boomer Reunions

see also Flower Children

Beautiful Girls
The Big Chill▶
The Heidi Chronicles
Indian Summer
Parallel Lives
Peter's Friends
Return of the Secaucus 7▶

Boston

Athena
Before and After
Blown Away
The Boston Strangler
A Case of Deadly Force▶
Celtic Pride
Coma▶
Criminal Law
Fear Strikes Out▶
Fuzz
Gentleman Bandit
The Great Moment
Johnny We Hardly Knew Ye
Love Story▶
The Scarlet Letter
The Scarlet Letter▶
The Scarlet Letter
See How She Runs▶
The Seekers
Spenser: Ceremony
Spenser: Pale Kings & Princes
Spraggue

Bowling

Dreamer
Grease 2
Kingpin
Mr. Wonderful

Boxing

Abbott and Costello Meet the Invisible Man▶
Any Which Way You Can
Arena
Back Roads
Battling Bunyon
Battling Butler
Belle of the Nineties
Best of the Best
The Big Man: Crossing the Line▶
Billyboy
Blue Ribbon Babes
Body and Soul▶
Body & Soul
Bowery Blitzkrieg
Boxcar Blues
The Boxer and Death▶
Breakdown
Brutal Glory
The Cage
The Champ▶
The Champ
Champion▶
Circle Man
City for Conquest▶
Confessions of Tom Harris
Counter Punch
Dempsey
Diggstown
Dynamite Dan
Fallen Champ: The Untold Story of Mike Tyson▶
Far and Away
Fat City▶
Fight for the Title
The Fighter▶
Fighting Champ
Firepower
Fist Fighter
Gentleman Jim▶
Gladiator
Golden Boy▶
Great Guy
The Great White Hope
The Great White Hype
The Greatest
Hard Times▶
The Harder They Fall▶
Heart
Heart of a Champion: The Ray Mancini Story
Here Comes Mr. Jordan▶
The Hitter
Hollywood Stadium Mystery
Homeboy
Honeyboy
The Joe Louis Story
Keep Punching
Kelly the Second
Kid Dynamite
Kid from Brooklyn
Kid Galahad▶
Kid Galahad
Killer's Kiss
The Last Fight
Last Man Standing
Les Miserables
The Main Event
Marciano
Matilda
Meatballs 2
Milky Way
Miracle Kid
Movie, Movie
Navy Way
Night and the City▶
Off Limits
On the Waterfront▶
One-Punch O'Day
The Opponent
Palooka
Penitentiary
Penitentiary 2
Penitentiary 3
Percy & Thunder
The Power of One
Pride of the Bowery
Prison Shadows
Prize Fighter
The Prizefighter and the Lady▶
Pulp Fiction▶
The Quest
The Quiet Man▶
Raging Bull▶
Requiem for a Heavyweight▶
Ricky 1
The Ring
Ringside
Rip Roarin' Buckaroo
Roaring City
Rocky▶
Rocky 2
Rocky 3
Rocky 4
Rocky 5
The Set-Up▶
Shaolin Vengence
Somebody Up There Likes Me▶
Spike of Bensonhurst
The Spirit of Youth
Split Decisions
The Sting 2
Street Crimes
Streets of Gold
Teen Wolf Too
They Made Me a Criminal
They Never Come Back
Thunderground
Title Shot
Tough Enough
Tough Kid
Triumph of the Spirit▶
Tyson
Vigilantes of Boom Town
When's Your Birthday?

Bringing Up Baby

see also Parenthood; Pregnant Men; Pregnant Pauses

Addams Family Values
Alien 3
Almost Pregnant
Alternative
And Baby Makes Six
Angie
The Baby
The Baby and the Battleship
Baby Boom
The Baby Maker
Babyfever
Baby's Day Out
Bachelor Mother▶
Basket Case 3: The Progeny
Billy: Portrait of a Street Kid
Brand New Life
Brink of Life
The Brood
Bundle of Joy
By Design
Celia: Child Of Terror
Cheyenne Warrior
Child of Darkness, Child of Light
Cocktail
Enemy Mine
Eraserhead▶
The Evil Within
Eye on the Sparrow
A Family Thing▶
Fanny▶
Father's Little Dividend▶
For Keeps
Four Days in July
Fran
From Here to Maternity
Funny Girl▶
Generation
The Girls of Huntington House
Grave of the Vampire
The Great Lie▶
Growing Pains
Hell Comes to Frogtown
Help Wanted: Male
A Hole in the Head
I Don't Want to Be Born
Immediate Family
In Search of a Golden Sky
It's Alive▶
It's Alive 2: It Lives Again
It's Alive 3: Island of the Alive
Jack and Sarah
A Kind of Loving▶
Le Cas du Dr. Laurent▶
Let's Get Married
The Lightning Incident
Little Man Tate▶
Look Who's Talking▶
Look Who's Talking, Too
Love Child
Mamele
The Match Factory Girl▶
The Miracle▶
Mom & Dad
Monika
Nickel Mountain
Night Cries
Paternity
Penny Serenade▶
Problem Child 2
Promises! Promises!
Psycho 4: The Beginning
Raising Arizona▶
Rosemary's Baby▶
Rumpelstiltskin
The Saga of the Draculas
Scarred
The Snapper▶
Son of Godzilla
The Stranger Within
The Sugarland Express▶
Table for Five
A Taste of Honey▶
The Tender Years
Tenth Month
The Terminator▶
Test Tube Babies
That's My Baby!
The 13th Floor
Thomas Graal's First Child▶
Three Men and a Baby▶
Three Men and a Cradle▶
Tomorrow▶
Tomorrow's Child
Tomorrow's Children
The Unborn
The Unborn 2
Unnatural
The Very Edge
Video Baby
Willa
Winter Flight
A Woman is a Woman▶

Buddhism

Little Buddha
Raw Force
Temptation of a Monk
Why Has Bodhi-Darma Left for the East

Buddies

see also Buddy Cops

Abbott and Costello Meet Frankenstein▶
Adios Amigo
The Adventures of Huck Finn▶
The Adventures of Huckleberry Finn
The Adventures of Milo & Otis▶
The Adventures of Rusty
Ain't No Way Back
The Alamo▶
An American Story
Amongst Friends
Andre
Another 48 Hrs.
Another You
Anzacs: The War Down Under▶
At First Sight
The Baby-Sitters Club
Babyfever
Bachelor Party
Backbeat▶
Bad Boys
Bad Company▶
Bad Girls
The Basketball Diaries
The Battle of Blood Island
The Bear▶
Beautiful Girls
Behind Prison Walls
A Better Tomorrow
A Better Tomorrow, Part 2
Between Heaven and Hell▶
The Big Chill▶
Big Deadly Game
Big Mo
Big Shots
The Big Slice
Bigfoot: The Unforgettable Encounter
Bill & Ted's Bogus Journey
Birdy▶
Black Beauty
Black Fox: The Price of Peace
Blonde in Black Leather
Blue De Ville
The Blue Lamp▶
Blue Skies▶
Boot Hill
Boots Malone
Born to Be Wild
A Boy and His Dog
The Boy Who Could Fly▶
The Boys in the Band
The Boys Next Door
Branded Men
Breaking the Rules
Bride of Killer Nerd
Broadway Melody of 1940
The Buddy System
A Bullet in the Head▶
Bundle of Joy
Butch Cassidy and the Sundance Kid▶
The Cable Guy
The Caddy
Calendar Girl
The Campus Corpse
Campus Man
Captive Hearts
The Cat
Celtic Pride
Charlie's Ghost: The Secret of Coronado
Cheap Shots
Circle of Two
The Cisco Kid
City Heat
City Slickers▶
City Slickers 2: The Legend of Curly's Gold
Class Act
Clayton County Line
Clerks▶
Clown Murders
The Color Purple▶
Colorado Serenade
Company Business
The Concrete Cowboys
Convict Cowboy
Cops and Robbers
Corleone
Country Gentlemen
Courage of Black Beauty
The Cowboy Way
Crime Busters
Crime Lords
Cross My Heart
Crossfire
Crossing the Bridge
Cry Freedom
The Cure
Cycle Vixens
Dead Presidents
Dead Reckoning▶
Deadlock
Deadly Surveillance
December
The Deer Hunter▶
Defenseless
The Defiant Ones▶
Die Hard: With a Vengeance
Digger
Diner▶
Dogfight▶
Donovan's Reef▶
Down Under
Downtown
Dragonheart
Dragonworld
Dream a Little Dream 2
The Dresser▶
Driving Miss Daisy▶
Drop Dead Fred
Drums in the Deep South
Dumb & Dumber
Easy Rider▶
Eat the Peach
The Eighth Day
El Dorado▶
Elmer
Enemy Mine
Entre-Nous▶
Every Which Way But Loose
Extreme Prejudice
F/X 2: The Deadly Art of Illusion
The Falcon and the Snowman▶
Far from Home: The Adventures of Yellow Dog
Federal Hill
The Five Heartbeats▶
Fled
The Flintstones
For the Moment
Forsaking All Others
48 Hrs.▶
Francis in the Navy
Free Willy
Free Willy 2: The Adventure Home
Freeze-Die-Come to Life▶
The Frisco Kid
Frontier Fugitives
Galaxies are Colliding
Gallipoli▶
Getting Even
Going Back

Gold Diggers: The Secret of Bear Mountain
Goodfellas▶
Gordy
Grand Illusion▶
Grandes Amigos
Grumpier Old Men
Grumpy Old Men▶
Guarding Tess
Gunga Din▶
Gunmen
Hangin' with the Homeboys▶
Harley Davidson and the Marlboro Man
The Hasty Heart
Hate▶
Hats Off
Hawaii Calls
Heartaches▶
Heartbreakers▶
Heavenly Creatures▶
The Highest Honor
Hired Hand
Hollywood or Bust
Home Free All
Homeward Bound 2: Lost in San Francisco
Hong Kong Nights
Huck and the King of Hearts
The Hunters
If Lucy Fell
The In-Laws▶
In the Navy
Indian Summer
Inn of Temptation
Ishtar
Jimmy Hollywood
Johnny Come Lately
Joy Ride to Nowhere
Judgment Night
Juice
Jules and Jim▶
Just Between Friends
K-9000
The Kansas Terrors
The Karate Kid▶
The Karate Kid: Part 2
The Karate Kid: Part 3
The Killing Fields▶
King of the Mountain
Kingpin
Kings of the Road—In the Course of Time▶
K2: The Ultimate High
Ladies on the Rocks
Last American Virgin
The Last Boy Scout
Last Summer
Le Beau Serge▶
Le Doulos▶
Leaving Normal
The Lemon Sisters
Les Comperes▶
Let 'er Go Gallegher
Lethal Weapon▶
Lethal Weapon 2▶
Lethal Weapon 3
Let's Do It Again
Little Rascals, Book 1
Little Rascals Christmas Special
Little Rascals, Vol. 1
Little Rascals, Vol. 2
The Littlest Outlaw
The Long Voyage Home▶
Looking for Miracles
The Lords of Flatbush
Lost in the Barrens
Macaroni
Mad Dog and Glory▶
Mallrats
The Man Who Would Be King▶
Manhattan Melodrama▶
March or Die
Me and Him
Mean Frank and Crazy Tony
Meet Danny Wilson
The Men's Club
Midnight Cowboy▶
Midnight Run▶
The Mighty Quinn
Mikey & Nicky
Mina Tannenbaum
Misunderstood
Molly and Gina
Money to Burn
Moon over Miami▶
Moonlight and Valentino
Mortal Thoughts
The Mosaic Project
My Beautiful Laundrette▶
My Best Friend's Girl
My Dinner with Andre▶
My Girl
Mystic Pizza▶
Naked Youth
The Naughty Nineties
Night Beat
Nightforce
The Nightingale
The Odd Couple▶
Old Explorers
Oliver & Company
Once Upon a Time in America▶
One Crazy Summer
One Sings, the Other Doesn't
The Opposite Sex and How to Live With Them
Pals
Papillon▶
Parallel Lives
Past the Bleachers
Peck's Bad Boy with the Circus
The Penitent
Perfectly Normal
Peter's Friends
The Phantom of 42nd Street
Piece of Cake
P.K. and the Kid
Platoon▶
Playmates
A Pleasure Doing Business
Plunder Road
Portrait of a Showgirl
Psycho Cop 2
Racing with the Moon▶
Rafferty & the Gold Dust Twins
Rape
The Red Balloon▶
The Reivers▶
Reno and the Doc
Requiem for Dominic▶
The Return of Grey Wolf
The Return of the Musketeers
Return of the Secaucus 7▶
Revenge of the Nerds
Revenge of the Nerds 2: Nerds in Paradise
Rich and Famous
Ride the High Country▶
Rio Conchos▶
The Road to Hong Kong
The Road to Morocco▶
Roadside Prophets
Robby
Robert et Robert▶
Roommates
Rubin & Ed
The Run of the Country▶
Running Scared
Russkies
Rusty's Birthday
St. Elmo's Fire
The Saint of Fort Washington
Saints and Sinners
Salut l'Artiste▶
The Sandlot▶
The Seventh Veil▶
Shag: The Movie▶
Shaking the Tree
She Gods of Shark Reef
Showdown in Little Tokyo
Silence Like Glass
Snoopy's Getting Married, Charlie Brown
Snow White and the Seven Dwarfs
So This is Washington
Some Like It Hot▶
Something of Value▶
Son of Rusty
Songwriter
Sophisticated Gents▶
Spies Like Us
Spittin' Image
Spotlight Scandals
Stand By Me▶
Star Trek 4: The Voyage Home▶
Starbird and Sweet William
Stealing Home
Steaming
The Steel Helmet▶
The Stoned Age
Strawberry and Chocolate▶
Stuckey's Last Stand
Sudden Death
Summer City
Sunny Skies
The Sunshine Boys▶
Ten Who Dared
Tequila Sunrise
Terminal Bliss
That Sinking Feeling▶
Thelma & Louise▶
There's No Time for Love, Charlie Brown
Three Amigos
Three Legionnaires
Three Men and a Baby▶
Three Men and a Cradle▶
The Three Musketeers
The Three Musketeers▶
The Three Musketeers
Thunder in the Pines
Thursday's Game▶
To Forget Venice
To Wong Foo, Thanks for Everything, Julie Newmar
Tombstone▶
Top Dog
Top Gun
Tough Guys
Tour of Duty
Toy Story▶
Trainspotting▶
True Colors
The Turning Point
Two Weeks to Live
Ugetsu▶
Underworld▶
Unholy Four
The Van▶
Veronico Cruz
Vincent, Francois, Paul and the Others▶
The Virginian
Warrior Spirit
Wayne's World▶
Wayne's World 2
We're in the Legion Now
What Price Glory?▶
Whatever Happened to Susan Jane?
Where the River Runs Black
White Christmas▶
White Mama▶
White Men Can't Jump
White Nights
Who's the Man?
Why Me?
The Wild Life
Wild Rovers
Windy City
Winners Take All
Withnail and I▶
Wrestling Ernest Hemingway
The Wrong Guys
The Wrong Road
The Yakuza
Yankee Zulu
You Are Not Alone
Young Guns 2
You're in Love, Charlie Brown

Buddy Cops

see also Canine Cops; Cops; Women Cops

Another 48 Hrs.
Another Stakeout
Arizona Heat
Bad Boys
Car 54, Where Are You?
City Heat
Collision Course
Exit to Eden
48 Hrs.▶
The Hard Way▶
La Chevre▶
Lethal Weapon▶
Lethal Weapon 2▶
Lethal Weapon 3
Liberty & Bash
Money Train
Mulholland Falls
National Lampoon's Loaded Weapon 1
Night Children
Nighthawks
The Presidio
Red Heat
Renegades
The Rookie
Shakedown
Shoot to Kill▶
Speed▶
Stakeout
Tango and Cash

Buses

The Adventures of Priscilla, Queen of the Desert▶
The Big Bus
Bull Durham▶
Forrest Gump▶
The Fugitive▶
Heart and Souls
Incident at Deception Ridge
A League of Their Own▶
Magical Mystery Tour
A Man of No Importance▶
Mexican Bus Ride
National Lampoon's Senior Trip
Planes, Trains & Automobiles
The Runaway Bus
Speed▶
The Trip to Bountiful▶
Where Angels Go, Trouble Follows

Calcutta

see also India

The Adversary
Baraka▶
City of Joy
Company Limited
Days and Nights in the Forest
The Quest

Camelot (New)

see also Assassinations; Presidency

Jacqueline Bouvier Kennedy
JFK▶
The JFK Conspiracy
JFK: Reckless Youth
JFK Remembered
Kennedy
The Kennedys Don't Cry
Prince Jack
PT 109
Robert Kennedy and His Times
Ruby

Camelot (Old)

see also Medieval Romps; Swashbucklers

Camelot
A Connecticut Yankee▶
A Connecticut Yankee in King Arthur's Court
Excalibur▶
First Knight
A Kid in King Arthur's Court
King Arthur, the Young Warlord
Knights of the Round Table
Merlin and the Sword
Monty Python and the Holy Grail▶
The Sword in the Stone▶
Sword of Lancelot
Sword of the Valiant

Campus Capers

see also Hell High School; School Daze

Accident
Adventures in Spying
The Affairs of Dobie Gillis
All-American Murder
American Tiger
Animal Behavior
Assault of the Party Nerds
Attack of the Killer Refrigerator
Baby Love
Bachelor of Hearts
Back to School
Beware
Beyond Dream's Door
Black Christmas
Black Tower
Blood Cult
Blood Sisters
Blue Chips
Bride of Killer Nerd
The Campus Corpse
Campus Knights
Campus Man
Carnal Knowledge▶
Catch Me...If You Can
The Cheerleaders
A Chump at Oxford
Circle of Friends
Class
Class of '44
College▶
College Swing
Computer Beach Party
The Computer Wore Tennis Shoes
The Cousins▶
Curse of the Alpha Stone
Deadly Lessons
Deadly Obsession
Deadly Possession
Death Screams
Didn't You Hear?
Doctor in the House▶
Dorm That Dripped Blood
Ernest Rides Again
Escapade in Florence
Father Was a Fullback
Final Exam
First Affair
First Love
First Time
Foreign Student
Francis Goes to West Point
Fraternity Vacation
The Freshman▶
The Freshman
Fright Night 2
Getting Away With Murder
Getting In
Ghoulies 3: Ghoulies Go to College
Girl Crazy▶
Girls Night Out
The Gladiator▶
Good News
Gotcha!
Gross Anatomy
Gross Misconduct
Hamburger...The Motion Picture
Harmon of Michigan
Harrad Experiment
Harrad Summer
HauntedWeen
The Heart of Dixie
Hell Night
Higher Education
Higher Learning
Horse Feathers▶
H.O.T.S.
The House on Sorority Row
House Party 2: The Pajama Jam
How I Got into College
I Don't Buy Kisses Anymore
The Initiation
Initiation of Sarah
I.Q.
Is There Life Out There?
Jock Petersen
Kicking and Screaming▶
The Kid with the 200 I.Q.
A Killer in Every Corner
Killer Party
Knock Outs
Let's Go Collegiate

Life 101
Little Sister
A Little Stiff
Lucky Jim
Making the Grade
Malice
A Matter of Degrees
Mazes and Monsters
Midnight Madness
The Misadventures of Merlin Jones
Monkey's Uncle
Monster on the Campus
Mortuary Academy
Mugsy's Girls
Murder on the Campus
My Lucky Star
The Naked Witch
National Lampoon's Animal House▶
Navy Blue and Gold
A Night in the Life of Jimmy Reardon
Night of the Creeps
Nightwish
Odd Jobs
Oleanna
The Paper Chase▶
Parallel Lives
Party Animal
P.C.U.
Pieces
Pledge Night
Preppies
The Program
A Reason to Believe
Return Engagement
Revenge of the Nerds
Revenge of the Nerds 2: Nerds in Paradise
Revenge of the Nerds 3: The Next Generation
Ring of Terror
Roommate
Rosalie
R.P.M.* (*Revolutions Per Minute)
Rudy
Rush Week
Scent of a Woman▶
School Daze▶
School Spirit
The Seniors
Sensation
Shallow Grave
Silent Madness
Silent Scream
Sky High
Slipping into Darkness
A Small Circle of Friends
Sniper▶
Sorority Babes in the Slimeball Bowl-A-Rama
Sorority Girl
Sorority House Massacre
Sorority House Massacre 2: Nighty Nightmare
Sorority House Party
Soul Man
Spellbound
The Spirit of West Point
Splatter University
Splitz
Spring Break
Star Spangled Girl
Stitches
The Sure Thing▶
Surviving Desire▶
Sweet Young Thing
Tag: The Assassination Game
Talking Walls
Tall Lie
Tall Story
Teen Wolf Too
Three in the Attic
Three in the Cellar
Threesome
Toga Party
Undergrads▶
The Unnamable
Up the Creek
The Victory
Voodoo
War Between the Tates
Wavelength
When He's Not a Stranger▶
The Wild Life
Wish Me Luck
Witchboard
Witches' Brew
With Honors
Zero for Conduct▶
Zis Boom Bah

Canada

***see also* Cold Spots; Hockey**

Abducted
The Adjuster
The Agency
American Boyfriends
The Amityville Curse
And Then You Die▶
Angel Square
Angela
Anne of Avonlea▶
Anne of Green Gables▶
The Apprenticeship of Duddy Kravitz▶
Atlantic City▶
The Bay Boy
Beautiful Dreamers
The Big Crimewave
Big Meat Eater
Big Red
Black Christmas
Black Robe▶
Blades of Courage
Blood Clan
Blood of the Hunter
Blood Relations
The Bloody Brood
Boy in Blue
The Boys of St. Vincent▶
Breaking All the Rules
The Brood
Buffalo Jump▶
Bullies
Busted Up
By Design
Bye Bye Blues
Cafe Romeo
Camilla
Canada's Sweetheart: The Saga of Hal C. Banks
Canadian Bacon
Candy Mountain
The Cariboo Trail
Cathy's Curse
The Changeling
Christina
Circle of Two
City on Fire
Class of 1984
Clean, Shaven
Clearcut
Close to Home
Cold Comfort
Concrete Angels
The Confessional
Confidential
Cordelia
Covergirl
Cross Country
A Cry in the Wild▶
Curtains
Dan Candy's Law
Dance Me Outside
Dancing in the Dark
Danger Ahead
Daughter of Death
The Dawson Patrol
Dead Ringers▶
Death Ship
Death Weekend
Deathdream
The Decline of the American Empire▶
Decoy
Deranged▶
The Deserters
Dirty Tricks
Disappearance
Distant Thunder
Dog Pound Shuffle▶
The Dog Who Stopped the War
A Doll's House▶
The Double Negative
Drying Up the Streets
Eddie and the Cruisers 2: Eddie Lives!
Explosion
Fighting Mad
For the Moment
Going Home
Heaven on Earth
Heck's Way Home
Holy Matrimony
House of the Living Dead
The Incredible Journey
Intersection
Jaws of Justice
Ladies of the Lotus
Lassie's Great Adventure
The Little Kidnappers
The Lotus Eaters
Love and Human Remains▶
Magic in the Water
Margaret's Museum
Maria Chapdelaine
Men of Steel
Murder on the Yukon
My American Cousin▶
Mystery Trooper
A Name for Evil
Narrow Margin
'Neath Canadian Skies
90 Days▶
Nomads of the North
Northern Extremes
Obsessed
Phantom Patrol
Renfrew of the Royal Mounted
Renfrew on the Great White Trail
The Return of Grey Wolf
Riel
Rose Marie▶
Silent Code
Slipstream
Some Girls
Spirit Rider▶
Strangers in Good Company▶
Tales from Avonlea, Vol. 1: The Journey Begins
Tales of the Klondike: In a Far Country
Tales of the Klondike: Race for Number One
Tales of the Klondike: The Unexpected
Termini Station
Timber Terrors
Time Lock
Trail of the Mounties
Wedding in White
Where the North Begins
Who Has Seen the Wind?
Yukon Flight

Canine Cops

***see also* Cops**

K-9
Top Dog
Turner and Hooch

Cannibalism

***see also* Edibles; Horror**

Adventures of Eliza Fraser
Alien Prey
Alive
Auntie Lee's Meat Pies
Back from Eternity
Beast of the Yellow Night
Beware! Children at Play
Black Werewolf
Blood Clan
Blood Diner
Blood Hook
Blood Sisters
Blood Tracks
Bloodsucking Freaks
Bloodsucking Pharoahs of Pittsburgh
Body Count
A Boy and His Dog
The 'Burbs
Buried Alive
Cannibal Campout
Cannibal Women in the Avocado Jungle of Death
The Chilling
C.H.U.D.
C.H.U.D. 2: Bud the Chud
Consuming Passions
The Cook, the Thief, His Wife & Her Lover▶
The Corpse Grinders
Crazy Fat Ethel II
Criminally Insane
Curse of the Living Dead
Dawn of the Dead▶
Dawn of the Mummy
Delicatessen▶
Demon Barber of Fleet Street
Deranged▶
Donner Pass: The Road to Survival
Eat the Rich
Eating Raoul▶
Emerald Jungle
Enchanted Island
Fiend
Flesh Eating Mothers
The Forest
Frightmare
The Further Adventures of Tennessee Buck
Gore-Met Zombie Chef From Hell
Grim Reaper
Gruesome Twosome
The Hills Have Eyes
How Tasty Was My Little Frenchman
Human Beasts
I Drink Your Blood
I Eat Your Skin
Igor & the Lunatics
Incredible Melting Man
Invasion of the Flesh Hunters
Jungle Holocaust
Leatherface: The Texas Chainsaw Massacre 3
The Mad Butcher
A Man Called Rage
Mom
The Monster Club
Motel Hell
Murderer's Keep
Night of the Living Dead▶
Night of the Living Dead
Night of the Zombies
Nightstalker
The Offspring
Parents▶
The Perverse Countess
Porcile
Rabid Grannies
Raw Force
Redneck Zombies
The Severed Arm
The Silence of the Lambs▶
Slaughterhouse
Slaughterhouse Rock
Slave Girls from Beyond Infinity
Slave of the Cannibal God
Society
Soylent Green
Terror at Red Wolf Inn
The Texas Chainsaw Massacre
Texas Chainsaw Massacre, Part 2
Three on a Meathook
Toxic Zombies
The Undertaker and His Pals
Warlock Moon
White Cannibal Queen
Zombie
Zombie Island Massacre
Zombie Lake
Zombiethon

Capitol Capers

Abraham Lincoln
All the President's Men▶
Born Yesterday▶
Born Yesterday
Dave▶
Eraser
Image of Death
In the Line of Fire▶
J. Edgar Hoover
Mack Sennett Comedies: Vol. 2
Mr. Smith Goes to Washington▶
Nixon▶
1776▶
Three Days of the Condor▶
Washington Affair
Washington Mistress
Without Love

Carnivals & Circuses

***see also* Amusement Parks; Clowns; Fairs & Expositions**

Arizona Mahoney
At the Circus
Ava's Magical Adventure
Bad Man of Deadwood
Barnum
Bells of Rosarita
Berserk!
Betrayal from the East
Big Top Pee Wee
Billy Rose's Jumbo▶
Black Orpheus▶
Boca
Brewster McCloud▶
The Cabinet of Dr. Caligari▶
Candyman 2: Farewell to the Flesh
Captive Wild Woman
Carnival Lady
Carnival Story
Carny▶
Carousel▶
Castle of the Living Dead
The Circus▶
Circus of Fear
Circus of Horrors
Circus World
Cloud Dancer
Clowning Around
Clowning Around 2
The Clowns▶
Court Jester▶
Dixiana
Dual Alibi
Dumbo▶
Elvira Madigan▶
Encore▶
Flamingo Road▶
Fox and His Friends▶
Freaked
Freaks▶
Freakshow
The Funhouse
Glass Tomb
Goldy: The Last of the Golden Bears
The Great Wallendas
The Greatest Show on Earth▶
He Who Gets Slapped▶
Incredibly Strange Creatures Who Stopped Living and Became Mixed-Up Zombies
Julia Misbehaves▶
Killer Klowns from Outer Space
La Strada▶
Life is a Circus, Charlie Brown/You're the Greatest, Charlie Brown
Lili▶
Lola Montes▶
Luther the Geek
Make-Up
The Man Who Laughs▶
Moscow on the Hudson▶
Multiple Maniacs
One Arabian Night▶
Outrage
Parade▶
Peck's Bad Boy with the Circus
The Road to Zanzibar▶
Roustabout
The Rousters
Sally of the Sawdust
Santa Sangre▶

Sawdust & Tinsel▶
The Serpent's Egg
7 Faces of Dr. Lao▶
Shakes the Clown
She-Freak
Side Show
So Dear to My Heart▶
Something Wicked This Way Comes
Spangles
State Fair
Strong Man▶
Texas Carnival
Three Texas Steers
Tillie Wakes Up
Toby Tyler▶
Trapeze▶
Tromba, the Tiger Man
Two Moon Junction
The Unholy Three▶
The Unknown▶
Vampire Circus
Variety▶
Variety Lights▶
When Night is Falling▶
Where East Is East
Wild Hearts Can't Be Broken▶
Wilder Napalm
You Can't Cheat an Honest Man▶

Cats

see also Killer Kats

The Adventures of Milo & Otis▶
After the Revolution
The Aristocats▶
Batman Returns
The Big Cat
The Black Cat▶
The Black Cat
Black Cat
The Cat
The Cat from Outer Space
Cat Girl
Cat People
Cat's Eye
The Corpse Grinders
Felix the Cat: The Movie
Fritz the Cat▶
Gay Purr-ee
Harry and Tonto▶
Homeward Bound 2: Lost in San Francisco
Homeward Bound: The Incredible Journey▶
The Incredible Journey
The Late Show▶
Le Chat▶
Milo & Otis
Night of a Thousand Cats
Oliver & Company
Pet Sematary
Puss 'n Boots
Return of Chandu
Rubin & Ed
Seven Deaths in the Cat's Eye
The Stars Fell on Henrietta
That Darn Cat
The Three Lives of Thomasina▶
Tom and Jerry: The Movie
Two Evil Eyes
The Uncanny
The Uninvited

Cave People

Being Human
Cave Girl
Caveman
The Clan of the Cave Bear
Creatures the World Forgot
Encino Man
The Flintstones
Iceman▶
One Million B.C.
Prehistoric Women
Quest for Fire▶
Teenage Caveman
When Dinosaurs Ruled the Earth
When Women Had Tails
When Women Lost Their Tails

Censorship

The Fugitive▶
Guilty by Suspicion

Central America

see also Mexico; South America

Appointment in Honduras
Cyclone Cavalier
Delta Force Commando
Devil Wears White
El Norte▶
The Evil That Men Do
Exiled in America
The Firing Line
Last Plane Out
Latino
Marie Galante▶
The Mosquito Coast
Panama Menace
Panama Patrol
Romero
Salvador▶
Toy Soldiers
Under Fire▶
Virgin Sacrifice
Wages of Fear▶

Chases

see also Road Trip

Abbott and Costello Meet the Keystone Kops
Abroad with Two Yanks
Action U.S.A.
The Adventures of Ichabod and Mr. Toad▶
Against All Odds
Albino
Alfie▶
American Autobahn
American Graffiti▶
The Arrival
At the Circus
Baby on Board
Bad Boys
The Bank Dick▶
Beverly Hills Cop
Beverly Hills Cop 2
Beverly Hills Cop 3
Beyond Rangoon
The Big Sweat
Bird on a Wire
Black Ice
Black Rain
Blue Jeans and Dynamite
The Blue Lamp▶
The Blues Brothers
Boiling Point
Border Radio
Born to Be Wild
Breathless▶
Broken Arrow
Buck Privates Come Home▶
Bullitt▶
Butch Cassidy and the Sundance Kid▶
Chain Reaction
Charlie and the Great Balloon Chase
The Chase
Christine
Comrade X
Corvette Summer
The Cowboy Way
Criminal Hearts
Dead Easy
Deadlock
The Death Merchant
Deja Vu
Desperate
Devil & Leroy Basset
Diamonds Are Forever▶
Dick Tracy▶
Dirty Mary Crazy Larry▶
Disorderly Orderly
Dr. No▶
Dr. Terror's House of Horrors
Dog Day
The Driver
Duel▶
Dumb & Dumber
Eat My Dust
Eddie Macon's Run
Enemy Below▶
Entr'acte
E.T.: The Extra-Terrestrial▶
Every Girl Should Have One
Exiled in America
Fifty/Fifty
Follow That Car
For the Love of It
For Your Eyes Only▶
48 Hrs.▶
Foul Play▶
The Fourth Protocol▶
Freebie & the Bean
The French Connection▶
From Russia with Love▶
The Fugitive▶
Fugitive Among Us
The Fugitive: Premiere Episode
Gator
The Gauntlet
The Getaway
The Ghost and the Guest
Girl Shy▶
The Golden Child
Goldeneye▶
Goldfinger▶
Gone in 60 Seconds
Goodbye Pork Pie
Grand Theft Auto
Great Chase
The Great Escape▶
Great Smokey Roadblock
The Great Texas Dynamite Chase
Hard Bounty
The Hearse
Honeymoon in Vegas
Hootch Country Boys
Hopscotch▶
Horror of the Zombies
Hot Pursuit
The Hunt for Red October▶
Hunted
The Hunted
Indiana Jones and the Temple of Doom▶
Into the Night
The Italian Job
It's a Mad, Mad, Mad, Mad World
Jackson County Jail
Jericho Fever
The Jewel of the Nile
Judgment Night
The Junkman
Jurassic Park▶
King of the Rodeo
A Kink in the Picasso
Larry McMurtry's Streets of Laredo▶
The Lavender Hill Mob▶
Les Miserables▶
Lethal Weapon▶
Lethal Weapon 2▶
Lethal Weapon 3
License to Drive
Live and Let Die
Mackintosh Man
Mad Max▶
The Man from Snowy River
Man of the House
A Man with a Maid
The Man with the Golden Gun
Manhunt for Claude Dallas
Memoirs of an Invisible Man
Midnight Run▶
Mr. Billion
Mr. Majestyk
Money to Burn
Money Train
Monkey Trouble
The Most Dangerous Game▶
My Favorite Blonde▶
Never Give a Sucker an Even Break▶
Night of the Running Man
No Way Out▶
North by Northwest▶
No. 17▶
Nuns on the Run
Octopussy
On Her Majesty's Secret Service▶
One Down, Two to Go!
One Man Jury
Out of Bounds
Outbreak▶
Outrageous Fortune
Paris Holiday
Paths to Paradise▶
Pee Wee's Big Adventure▶
The Pelican Brief
Pentathlon
A Perfect World
The Perverse Countess
Planet Busters
Planet of the Apes▶
Point Break
The Presidio
Profile
Pursuit
Race with the Devil
Raiders of the Lost Ark▶
Raising Arizona▶
Return of the Jedi▶
Return to Macon County
The Road Warrior▶
The Rock▶
Romancing the Stone▶
Round Trip to Heaven
Run
Running Scared
Savage Land
Seven Chances▶
Sex, Love and Cold Hard Cash
Shaft's Big Score
The Shining
Silent Hunter
Slither▶
Smokey and the Bandit
Smokey and the Bandit, Part 2
Smokey and the Bandit, Part 3
Smokey & the Hotwire Gang
Smokey Bites the Dust
Son of Lassie
The Spy Who Loved Me
Stagecoach▶
Star Wars▶
Stephen King's Golden Years
The Sting▶
Stray Dog▶
The Sugarland Express▶
Sweet Sweetback's Baadasssss Song▶
Tagget
Taking the Heat
Teenage Crime Wave
Tell Them Willie Boy Is Here▶
The Terminator▶
Terror of the Bloodhunters
Thelma & Louise▶
The Third Man▶
This Man Must Die▶
Thunder and Lightning
Thunder Road▶
Thunderball
Thunderbolt & Lightfoot▶
Time After Time▶
To Live and Die in Hong Kong
To Live & Die in L.A.
Tom and Jerry: The Movie
Top Gun
Tornado!
Toy Story▶
Trapped In Paradise
Trouble Bound
True Lies
12 Plus 1▶
Until The End of The World▶
Valley of the Eagles
Vanishing Point
Virtuosity
Watch the Birdie
What's Up, Doc?▶
Where There's Life
White Lightning
Who Framed Roger Rabbit▶
Who Killed Mary What's 'Er Name?
The Wilby Conspiracy▶
Wolfen▶
Year of the Comet
You Only Live Twice

Cheerleaders

see also Campus Capers; Hell High School

Buffy the Vampire Slayer▶
Cheering Section
Cheerleader Camp
The Cheerleaders
Cheerleaders' Wild Weekend
Gimme an F
The Majorettes
National Lampoon's Animal House▶
The Positively True Adventures of the Alleged Texas Cheerleader-Murdering Mom▶
Revenge of the Cheerleaders
Satan's Cheerleaders
The Swinging Cheerleaders

Chicago

Adventures in Babysitting
Big Town
The Blues Brothers
Chain Reaction
City That Never Sleeps
A Family Thing▶
Ferris Bueller's Day Off▶
The Front Page
Mickey One
Risky Business▶
Running Scared
While You Were Sleeping▶

Child Abuse

Blind Fools
The Boys of St. Vincent▶
Close to Home
Dolores Claiborne▶
Fallen Angel
Fatal Confinement
Father Hood
Hush Little Baby, Don't You Cry
Impulse
Indictment: The McMartin Trial▶
Johnny Belinda
Judgment▶
Lamb
Mommie Dearest
The Offence▶
Postcards from America
Psychopath
A Question of Guilt
Radio Flyer
Raising Cain
Short Eyes▶
South Bronx Heroes
The Stolen Children▶
This Boy's Life▶
Where the Spirit Lives
Who Killed Baby Azaria?
Wildflower▶

Childhood Visions

see also Home Alone

Afraid of the Dark
All I Want for Christmas
Alsino and the Condor▶
American Heart▶
And Now Miguel
Andre
Angela
Angels in the Outfield
Army Brats
Au Revoir Les Enfants▶
The Baby-Sitters Club
Beethoven Lives Upstairs
The Beniker Gang
Big▶
Big Bully
Black Beauty▶
The Black Stallion▶
Blankman
Born to Run
Brighton Beach Memoirs
Broken Harvest
But Where Is Daniel Wax?

The Cable Guy
Cameron's Closet
Camp Nowhere
Captain January
Careful, He Might Hear You▶
Casey's Shadow
Casper▶
The Cat
The Cellar
Chapter in Her Life
Child in the Night
The Children Are Watching Us▶
Children of Divorce
Children's Island
Child's Play
China, My Sorrow
Chocolat▶
A Christmas Story▶
Cinema Paradiso▶
Cria▶
Crooklyn▶
David Copperfield▶
Days of Heaven▶
Demons in the Garden▶
Desert Bloom▶
Deutschland im Jahre Null▶
The Diary of Anne Frank▶
Digger
Diva▶
Emma's Shadow▶
Empire of the Sun▶
Escapade▶
E.T.: The Extra-Terrestrial▶
The Fallen Idol▶
Fanny and Alexander▶
Far Away and Long Ago
Father▶
The Flame Trees of Thika▶
Flight of the Grey Wolf
Flight of the Innocent
For a Lost Soldier
Forbidden Games▶
Fresh
Girl from Hunan▶
A Girl of the Limberlost
The Golden Seal
Grazuole
Heavyweights
Heidi
Heidi▶
Heidi
Heidi▶
Home Alone▶
Home for Christmas
Home of Angels
Hook
Hope and Glory▶
How Green Was My Valley▶
Hue and Cry▶
The Indian in the Cupboard
Into the West▶
Invaders from Mars
Jack
Jack Be Nimble
Jacquot
Josh and S.A.M.
Journey for Margaret▶
The Kid from Left Field
The Kid with the Broken Halo
King of the Hill▶
The Kitchen Toto▶
The Lady in White▶
Lassie's Great Adventure
Last Action Hero
The Last Winter
Lawnmower Man 2: Beyond Cyberspace
Lazarillo
Le Grand Chemin▶
Leolo
Les Violons du Bal
Lies My Father Told Me▶
Little Big League
Little Buddha
Little Man Tate▶
Little Monsters
The Little Princess▶
A Little Princess▶
The Little Rascals
The Littlest Horse Thieves
The Long Days of Summer
Look Who's Talking▶
Look Who's Talking, Too
Lord of the Flies▶
Lord of the Flies
Lost in Yonkers
Louisiana Story▶
Love Film
Magic in the Water
Magic of Lassie
Man of the House
Matilda
Merlin of the Crystal Cave
The Mirror▶
Misty
Mommie Dearest
Mosby's Marauders
My Childhood▶
My Friend Flicka▶
My Life as a Dog▶
My Mother's Castle▶
My Name is Ivan▶
National Velvet▶
The Neon Bible
New York Stories▶
The Night of the Shooting Stars▶
North
Now and Then
Old Swimmin' Hole
Oliver!▶
An Orphan Boy of Vienna
Orphans▶
Our Gang
Parents▶
Peck's Bad Boy
Pelle the Conqueror▶
Pixote▶
Pollyanna▶
Poltergeist▶
Poltergeist 2: The Other Side
A Poor Little Rich Girl▶
The Poor Little Rich Girl
Powder
Psycho 4: The Beginning
The Quest
Radio Flyer
The Railway Children▶
Real Genius▶
The Red Balloon▶
The Red Pony▶
The Reflecting Skin
Return from Witch Mountain
Richie Rich
Rock-a-Doodle
Roll of Thunder, Hear My Cry
Running Free
Salaam Bombay!▶
Savage Sam
Searching for Bobby Fischer▶
The Secret Garden▶
The Secret Garden
The Secret Garden▶
The Secret Garden
Sidekicks
The Silence of the Lambs▶
The Slingshot▶
Small Change▶
Sounds of Silence
Spirit of the Beehive▶
Square Shoulders
Stealing Home
Sudden Terror
Sudie & Simpson▶
A Summer to Remember▶
Sunday Daughters▶
Sunday's Children▶
Taps
Three Wishes
The Tin Drum▶
Tito and Me▶
To Kill a Mockingbird▶
Toto le Heros▶
Toy Story▶
Trading Mom
Train to Hollywood▶
Treasure Island▶
Turf Boy
12 Monkeys▶
Unicorn
Wait Until Spring, Bandini
The War
The War Boy
Welcome to the Dollhouse
What the Moon Saw
When Father was Away on Business▶
Where's Willie?
Whistle Down the Wind▶
White Fang▶
The Wild Country
The Witching of Ben Wagner
The Wizard of Loneliness
Wombling Free
A World Apart▶
The Yearling▶
Yes, Sir, Mr. Bones
Zazie dans le Metro▶
Zero for Conduct▶

Children

see Animated Musicals; Animation & Cartoons; Childhood Visions; Storytelling

China

see also Asia

Adventures of Smilin' Jack
The Amazing Panda Adventure
Battle of China
Bethune
Beyond the Next Mountain
The Bitter Tea of General Yen▶
The Blue Kite▶
China Cry
China, My Sorrow
Crows and Sparrows▶
The Day the Sun Turned Cold▶
Deadly Target
Dragon Seed
Empire of the Sun▶
Farewell My Concubine
Fight to the Death
The General Died at Dawn▶
Girl from Hunan▶
The Good Earth▶
A Great Wall▶
The Horse Thief▶
The Inn of the Sixth Happiness▶
Iron & Silk
The Joy Luck Club▶
Ju Dou▶
Kashmiri Run
The Keys of the Kingdom▶
The Killer▶
Lai Shi: China's Last Eunuch
The Last Emperor▶
The Leatherneck
M. Butterfly
The Mountain Road
Princess Yang Kwei Fei▶
Raise the Red Lantern▶
Red Firecracker, Green Firecracker
Red Sorghum▶
The Reincarnation of Golden Lotus▶
The Sand Pebbles▶
Shadows of the Orient
Shadows Over Shanghai
Shanghai Express▶
Shanghai Triad▶
The Silk Road
Soldier of Fortune
Song of the Exile
The Story of Qui Ju▶
Tai-Pan
Temptation of a Monk
To Live▶
Women From the Lake of Scented Souls
The Wooden Man's Bride
The World of Suzie Wong

Christmas

see also Holidays; Horrible Holidays

ABC Stage 67: Truman Capote's A Christmas Memory
All I Want for Christmas
An American Christmas Carol
Babes in Toyland
Batman Returns
Benji's Very Own Christmas Story
Bernard and the Genie
The Best Christmas Pageant Ever
The Bishop's Wife▶
Black Christmas
Bloodbeat
A Charlie Brown Christmas
Child's Christmas in Wales
A Christmas Carol▶
A Christmas Carol
A Christmas Carol▶
The Christmas Coal Mine Miracle
Christmas Comes to Willow Creek
Christmas in Connecticut▶
Christmas in Connecticut
Christmas in July▶
The Christmas Kid
Christmas Lilies of the Field
A Christmas Story▶
The Christmas That Almost Wasn't
A Christmas to Remember
The Christmas Wife
A Christmas Without Snow
Die Hard▶
Diner▶
Don't Open Till Christmas
Dorm That Dripped Blood
A Dream for Christmas▶
Elves
Ernest Saves Christmas
Funny Farm
The Gathering
The Gathering: Part 2
George Balanchine's The Nutcracker
The Gift of Love
Gremlins▶
Here Comes Santa Claus
Hobo's Christmas
Holiday Affair
Holiday Inn▶
Home Alone▶
Home Alone 2: Lost in New York
Home for Christmas
Home of Angels
Homecoming: A Christmas Story
A House Without a Christmas Tree
How the Grinch Stole Christmas▶
It Came Upon a Midnight Clear
It's a Bundyful Life
It's a Wonderful Life▶
The Kid Who Loved Christmas
Kramer vs. Kramer▶
Lady On a Train▶
The Lemon Drop Kid
Lethal Weapon▶
Lily in Winter
The Lion in Winter▶
The Little Drummer Girl▶
The Little Match Girl
Little Rascals Christmas Special
Little Women▶
The Man in the Santa Claus Suit
The Man Upstairs
March of the Wooden Soldiers▶
A Matter of Principle
Merry Christmas, Mr. Lawrence▶
Mickey's Christmas Carol▶
A Midnight Clear▶
A Midwinter's Tale
Miracle Down Under
Miracle in the Wilderness
Miracle on 34th Street▶
Miracle on 34th Street
Mr. Corbett's Ghost
Mixed Nuts
The Muppet Christmas Carol
The Mystery of Edwin Drood
National Lampoon's Christmas Vacation
Nativity
The Night of the Hunter▶
The Night They Saved Christmas
The Nightmare Before Christmas▶
Nutcracker, A Fantasy on Ice
The Nutcracker Prince
Nutcracker: The Motion Picture
One Magic Christmas
Prancer
The Railway Children▶
Reckless
The Ref▶
Remember the Night▶
The Robe
Roots: The Gift
Rudolph & Frosty's Christmas in July
Rudolph the Red-Nosed Reindeer
Santa Claus
Santa Claus Conquers the Martians
Santa Claus Is Coming to Town
Santa Claus: The Movie
The Santa Clause
Scrooge▶
Scrooge
Scrooged
Silent Night, Deadly Night
Silent Night, Deadly Night 2
Silent Night, Deadly Night 3: Better Watch Out!
Silent Night, Deadly Night 5: The Toymaker
Silent Night, Lonely Night
A Smoky Mountain Christmas
The Sum of Us▶
Susan Slept Here
A Tale of Winter
Terror in Toyland
Thirteenth Day of Christmas
Three Godfathers▶
A Time to Remember
To All a Goodnight
To Grandmother's House We Go
Trading Places
Trail of Robin Hood
Trapped In Paradise
Untamed Heart
A Very Brady Christmas
The Waltons: The Christmas Carol
While You Were Sleeping▶
White Christmas▶
Who Slew Auntie Roo?

CIA

see Feds; Spies & Espionage

Cinderella Stories

Angus
Arthur▶
Born Yesterday▶
Born Yesterday
Cinderella▶
First Love
Flashdance
Hero▶
The Little Mermaid▶
Milk Money
Mrs. Winterbourne
My Fair Lady▶
Once Around
Pretty Woman▶
Pygmalion▶
Splash
A Star is Born▶
Stroke of Midnight
Working Girl▶
The World of Suzie Wong

Circuses

see Carnivals & Circuses; Clowns

Cities

see Urban Drama

City Lights

see Baltimore; Berlin; Calcutta; Capitol Capers; Chicago; I Love Detroit; L.A.; London; Miami; Moscow; New Orleans; New York, New York; Paris; San Francisco; Seattle; Tokyo; Urban Drama; Venice; Viva Las Vegas!

Civil Rights

see also Apartheid; Slavery

An African Dream
And the Children Shall Lead
As Summers Die
The Autobiography of Miss Jane Pittman▶
Bucktown
The Bus Is Coming
The Color Purple▶
The Conversation▶
Crisis at Central High▶
Driving Miss Daisy▶
A Dry White Season▶
Dutchman▶
The Ernest Green Story
Final Comedown
For Us, the Living▶
Free, White, and 21
Freedom Road
The Fringe Dwellers
Game for Vultures
Half Slave, Half Free
Hank Aaron: Chasing the Dream▶
Hawmps!
The Heart of Dixie
Hidden Agenda
Home of the Brave▶
King▶
The Kitchen Toto▶
Long Shadows
The Long Walk Home▶
Malcolm X: Make It Plain
The McMasters
Mississippi Burning▶
Mr. & Mrs. Loving▶
A Nation Aflame
Panther
The Red Fury
The Ring
A Soldier's Story▶
The Two of Us▶
We of the Never Never▶

Civil War

see also American South; Southern Belles

Abraham Lincoln
Alvarez Kelly
Andersonville▶
The Andersonville Trial▶
Bad Company▶
Band of Angels
The Beguiled▶
The Birth of a Nation▶
Blood at Sundown
Bloody Trail
The Blue and the Gray
The Bushwackers
Cavalry
Cavalry Charge
Charlotte Forten's Mission: Experiment in Freedom▶
Civil War Diary
The Civil War, Episode 1: The Cause—1861▶
The Civil War, Episode 2: A Very Bloody Affair—1862▶
The Civil War, Episode 3: Forever Free—1862▶
The Civil War, Episode 4: Simply Murder—1863▶
The Civil War, Episode 5: The Universe of Battle—1863▶
The Civil War, Episode 6: Valley of the Shadow of Death—1864▶
The Civil War, Episode 7: Most Hallowed Ground—1864▶
The Civil War, Episode 8: War is All Hell—1865▶
The Civil War, Episode 9: The Better Angels of Our Nature—1865▶
Class of '61
Colorado
Copper Canyon
Dark Command▶
Drums in the Deep South
Escape from Fort Bravo
Finger on the Trigger
The Fool Killer
Friendly Persuasion▶
Frontier Pony Express
Frontier Scout
The General▶
General Spanky
Gettysburg▶
The Ghost Brigade
Glory▶
Gone with the Wind▶
The Good, the Bad and the Ugly▶
Gore Vidal's Lincoln
Great Day in the Morning
The Great Locomotive Chase
Hangman's Knot
Hellbenders
The Horse Soldiers
How the West Was Won▶
Ironclads
It Happened in New Orleans
Johnny Shiloh
Kansas Pacific
Little Women▶
Little Women
Little Women▶
The Littlest Rebel
Louisiana
Love Me Tender
Love's Savage Fury
Macho Callahan
The McMasters
Menace on the Mountain
Mosby's Marauders
Mysterious Island▶
No Drums, No Bugles
North and South Book 1▶
North and South Book 2▶
Of Human Hearts
The Old Maid▶
Oldest Confederate Widow Tells All▶
The Ordeal of Dr. Mudd▶
Pharoah's Army
The Private History of a Campaign That Failed
Raiders of Ghost City
Raintree County
Rebel Love
Rebel Vixens
The Red Badge of Courage▶
The Rose and the Jackal
Run of the Arrow
The Sacketts
Shadow of Chikara
The Shadow Riders
Shenandoah▶
Sommersby
South of St. Louis
A Southern Yankee
The Supernaturals
Tramplers
The Undefeated
Virginia City▶
War Brides
Way Down South
Western Gold
Yellowneck

Classic Horror

see also Horror; Horror Anthologies

The Abominable Dr. Phibes▶
And Now the Screaming Starts
The Ape
The Ape Man
The Appointment
Asylum
Asylum of Satan
Atom Age Vampire
Attack of the Beast Creatures
Attack of the Mayan Mummy
Attack of the Swamp Creature
Avenging Conscience
The Awakening
Barn of the Naked Dead
The Bat▶
The Bat
The Bat People
The Beast from Haunted Cave
Bedlam▶
Before I Hang▶
The Birds▶
The Black Cat▶
The Black Room▶
Black Sabbath▶
The Black Scorpion
Black Sunday▶
Black Werewolf
Blood and Roses
Blood Beast Terror
Blood Island
Blood of Dracula
Blood of Dracula's Castle
Blood of the Vampire
The Bloodsuckers
Bluebeard
The Body Snatcher▶
The Bride
The Bride of Frankenstein▶
Bride of the Gorilla
Bride of the Monster
Bring Me the Vampire
The Brute Man
Burn Witch, Burn!▶
The Cabinet of Dr. Caligari▶
Carnival of Souls▶
Castle of Blood
Castle of Evil
Castle of the Living Dead
Cat Girl
Cat in the Cage
Cat People▶
Cat People
Cauldron of Blood
Cave of the Living Dead
Chamber of Horrors
The Changeling
Circus of Fear
Condemned to Live
The Conqueror Worm▶
Corridors of Blood
Count Dracula
Count Yorga, Vampire
The Crawling Eye
Creature from the Black Lagoon▶
Creature of Destruction
Creature of the Walking Dead
The Creature Walks Among Us
Creature with the Blue Hand
The Creeper
The Creeping Flesh
Creeping Terror
Creepshow
Creepshow 2
The Crime of Dr. Crespi
Crimes at the Dark House▶
Crimes of Dr. Mabuse▶
The Crimes of Stephen Hawke
The Crimson Cult
Crucible of Horror
Cry of the Banshee
Cry of the Werewolf
Crypt of the Living Dead
The Curse of Frankenstein
Curse of the Devil
Curse of the Swamp Creature
Cyclops
Dance of the Damned
Daughters of Darkness▶
Dementia 13
Demon Barber of Fleet Street
Demons of the Mind
The Devil Bat
The Devil Bat's Daughter
Devil Doll▶
Devil Kiss
Dr. Death, Seeker of Souls
Dr. Jekyll and Mr. Hyde▶
Dr. Jekyll and Mr. Hyde
Doctor X
Dolly Dearest
Dorian Gray
Dracula▶
Dracula
Dracula/Garden of Eden
Dracula (Spanish Version)
Dracula vs. Frankenstein
Dracula's Daughter▶
Dracula's Great Love
Dracula's Last Rites
Dracula's Widow
The Evil of Frankenstein
Exorcist 3: Legion
Eye of the Demon
Eyes of Fire
Eyes of the Panther
The Fall of the House of Usher
The Fall of the House of Usher▶
The Fall of the House of Usher
Fangs of the Living Dead
The Fear Chamber
Fear No Evil
The Fog
Frankenstein▶
Frankenstein
Frankenstein and the Monster from Hell
Frankenstein '80
Frankenstein Island
Frankenstein Meets the Wolfman▶
Frankenstein Unbound▶
Frankenstein's Daughter
Fright Night
Fright Night 2
The Fury
The Fury of the Wolfman
Genie of Darkness
The Ghost of Frankenstein
The Ghoul
The Gorgon
Gothic▶
Grampa's Monster Movies
Grave of the Vampire
Graveyard Shift
The Greed of William Hart
Growing Pains
Guardian of the Abyss
Halloween Night
The Hanging Woman
The Haunted
The Haunted Strangler
Haunted Summer
The Haunting▶
Haunting Fear
The Haunting of Morella
The Head
The Horror of Dracula▶
House of Dark Shadows
House of Dracula
House of Frankenstein
House of the Black Death
The House of Usher
House of Wax▶
House on Haunted Hill
The House that Dripped Blood
How to Make a Monster
The Hunchback of Notre Dame▶
The Hunger
I Walked with a Zombie▶
I Was a Teenage Werewolf
Invasion of the Vampires
The Invisible Dr. Mabuse▶
The Invisible Man▶
The Invisible Ray
Island of Dr. Moreau
Island of Lost Souls▶
Isle of the Dead
Jaws▶
Jaws 2
Jaws 3
Jaws: The Revenge
King of the Zombies
La Chute de la Maison Usher▶
Lady Frankenstein
The Lair of the White Worm▶
The Legend of Blood Castle
Legend of the Werewolf
The Legend of the Wolf Woman
Lemora, Lady Dracula
The Living Coffin
The Mad Monster
The Man They Could Not Hang
Mark of the Vampire▶
Martin▶
Mary Shelley's Frankenstein
Masque of the Red Death▶
Masque of the Red Death
Masque of the Red Death/ Premature Burial
Miami Horror
Mirrors
The Mummy▶
Mummy & Curse of the Jackal
The Mummy's Curse
The Mummy's Ghost
The Mummy's Hand
The Mummy's Tomb
Murders in the Rue Morgue
Mystery of the Wax Museum▶
Night of Dark Shadows
Nosferatu▶
Once Upon a Midnight Scary
Pandora's Box▶
The Phantom of the Opera▶
The Phantom of the Opera
Picture of Dorian Gray▶
The Pit and the Pendulum▶
The Pit & the Pendulum
Psycho 4: The Beginning
The Raven▶
Return of the Vampire
Revenge of the Creature
Revenge of the Zombies
Scared to Death
The Snow Creature
Son of Dracula▶
Son of Frankenstein▶
Teenage Frankenstein
The Undying Monster
The Vampire
The Vampire Bat
The Vampire People
The Vampire's Coffin
The Vampire's Ghost
Vampyr▶
Werewolf of London
The Werewolf vs. the Vampire Woman
The White Zombie▶
Witchcraft Through the Ages▶
The Wolf Man▶

Clowns

see also Carnivals & Circuses

Clown House
Clown Murders
Clowning Around
Clowning Around 2
The Clowns▶
Court Jester▶
The Funhouse
Funland
He Who Gets Slapped▶
Killer Klowns from Outer Space
Make-Up
The Man Who Laughs▶
Painted Hero
Poltergeist▶
Quick Change
Shakes the Clown
To Catch a Killer▶

Cold Spots

Alaska
The Alaska Wilderness Adventure
Antarctica
Arctic Blue

Atomic Submarine
Balto
The Big Push
Bog
Call of the Wild
Challenge To Be Free
Christmas Comes to Willow Creek
Cool Runnings
Courage Mountain
Crackerjack
Cry of the Penguins
The Day the Earth Froze
Dead Ahead: The Exxon Valdez Disaster▶
Dead of Winter▶
Doctor Zhivago▶
The Eiger Sanction
Firefox
Ice Palace
The Ice Runner
Ice Station Zebra
Intruder Within
Iron Will
The Juniper Tree
Kavik the Wolf Dog
Klondike Annie
The Last Place on Earth
Lost in Alaska
Lost Zeppelin
Map of the Human Heart
Never Cry Wolf▶
North to Alaska▶
Operation Haylift
Pathfinder▶
The Pebble and the Penguin
Pipe Dreams
Quest for Fire▶
Salmonberries
Shadow of the Wolf
She
The Shining
Silent Hunter
The Spoilers▶
Tentacles of the North
The Thing▶
The Thing
Virus
The White Dawn
White Fang 2: The Myth of the White Wolf
Winter People

Cold War

see Red Scare

Comedy

see also Black Comedy; Comedy Drama; Comic Adventure; Horror Comedy; Military Comedy; Musical Comedy; Romantic Comedy; Satire & Parody; Screwball Comedy; Slapstick Comedy; Sports Comedies; Western Comedy

A la Mode
Across the Moon
The Adventures of a Gnome Named Gnorm
Afrita Hanen▶
After the Revolution
Ah, Wilderness!▶
The Air Up There
Airheads
Alfie▶
...All the Marbles
Amanda and the Alien
Amazing Grace
...And God Spoke
Andy Griffith Show
Angels in the Outfield▶
Angus
Annie: A Royal Adventure
Another You
Anything for Love
April Fool
Around the World in a Daze
Assault of the Party Nerds 2: Heavy Petting Detective
At First Sight
Attack of the 60-Foot Centerfold
Augustin
Ava's Magical Adventure
Baby Face Harry Langdon
Baby Love
Baby of the Bride
Backfield in Motion
Bank Robber
Based on an Untrue Story
Battling for Baby
Beach Girls
Beach House
Beauty School
Behave Yourself!
Behind Prison Walls
The Bellboy and the Playgirls
Belle Americaine
Belle of the Nineties
The Belles of St. Trinian's▶
Ben Turpin: An Eye for an Eye
Beneath the Valley of the Ultra-Vixens
Best Friends
Better Late Than Never
Better Off Dead
Between the Lines▶
The Beverly Hillbillies
Beverly Hills Brats
Big Bully
Big Business Girl
Big Deal on Madonna Street▶
The Big Dis
The Big Gag
The Big Green
A Big Hand for the Little Lady
Big Man on Campus
Big Shots
Big Top Pee Wee
Big Trouble
Bikini Bistro
The Bikini Car Wash Company 2
Bikini Drive-In
Bikini Summer
Bikini Summer 2
Billie
The Billion Dollar Hobo
A Billion for Boris
Billy Madison
Biloxi Blues
Bio-Dome
The Birdcage▶
Birthday Boy
The Black Maid
Black Sheep
Black Venus
The Blacksmith/The Balloonatic
The Blacksmith/The Cops
Blank Check
Blankman
Blazing Stewardesses
Blessed Event▶
Blondes Have More Guns
Blondie
Blondie Has Trouble
Blondie Hits the Jackpot
Blondie in Society
Blondie Knows Best
Blondie Takes a Vacation
Blondie's Blessed Event
Blue De Ville
Blue Money
Boarding School
The Boatniks
Bombs Away!
Bon Voyage!
Book of Love
Boom in the Moon
Born to Be Wild
The Boss' Wife
Bottle Rocket
Boudu Saved from Drowning▶
Bound and Gagged: A Love Story
Boy Meets Girl▶
Boys' Night Out▶
Boys of the City
The Brain
Brain Smasher...A Love Story
Breakfast in Hollywood
Breaking In▶
Brewster's Millions
The Bride Walks Out
Broadway Bill▶
Broadway Bound
Broadway Danny Rose▶
Broadway Limited
Broth of a Boy
Brothers in Law
Buffy the Vampire Slayer▶
Buford's Beach Bunnies
Bullets Over Broadway▶
Burlesque of Carmen
Bushwhacked
A Business Affair
Bustin' Loose▶
Buy & Cell
By Design
Bye Bye, Love
Cabin Boy
Cadillac Man
California Girls
Call Me Bwana
Camp Nowhere
Campus Man
Can I Do It...Till I Need Glasses?
Cancel My Reservation
Candy Stripe Nurses
Cannon Ball/Eyes Have It
The Canterville Ghost
Captain Nuke and the Bomber Boys
Captain Ron
The Captain's Table
Car 54, Where Are You?
Carlton Browne of the F.O.
The Case of the Lucky Legs
Casper▶
Casual Sex?
Catch as Catch Can
Catherine & Co.
Caught in the Draft▶
Cave Girl
Celtic Pride
Champagne for Breakfast
Charge of the Model T's
Charley and the Angel
Charley Chase Festival, Vol. 1
Charlie Chase and Ben Turpin
Charlie's Ghost: The Secret of Coronado
Chasing Butterflies
Chasing Those Depression Blues
Chattanooga Choo Choo
Chatterbox
Cheap Shots
Cheaper by the Dozen▶
Check Is in the Mail
Cheech and Chong's Nice Dreams
Cheering Section
The Cheerleaders
Cheerleaders' Wild Weekend
Cherry Hill High
Chesty Anderson USN
The Chicken Chronicles
C.H.O.M.P.S.
A Christmas Story▶
Ciao, Professore!
Circonstances Attenuantes
Citizens Band▶
Clarence
Class
Class Act
Clean Slate
Cleo/Leo
Clifford
Club Fed
Club Paradise
Cocoon▶
C.O.D.
Cold Comfort Farm▶
Colonel Effingham's Raid
Comfort and Joy▶
Comic Cabby
Coming Up Roses
Complex World
Computer Beach Party
Computer Wizard
The Computer Wore Tennis Shoes
Comrade X
The Comrades of Summer
Condorman
A Connecticut Yankee▶
Cookie
Cooking Up Trouble
Cool Runnings
Cop and a Half
Cops and Robbers
Cops and Robbersons
Cops/One Week
Corporate Affairs
Cotton Comes to Harlem▶
Cotton Queen
Country Gentlemen
Coupe de Ville
Crazy for Love
Crazy Mama
Crazy People
The Crazysitter
Crime & Passion
Crime Busters
Critical Condition
The Crooked Circle
Crooks & Coronets
Cry Uncle
Curley
Daddy's Boys
Daddy's Dyin'...Who's Got the Will?
Daffy Duck's Quackbusters
Dames Ahoy
Dangerous Curves
Dave▶
The Day My Parents Ran Away
Day the Bookies Wept
The Day the Women Got Even
The Daydreamer
Dazed and Confused▶
D.C. Cab
Dead Solid Perfect
Dear Wife
Deceit
Delinquent School Girls
Delirious
Delivery Boys
Delusions of Grandeur
Denise Calls Up
Dennis the Menace
Dennis the Menace: Dinosaur Hunter
Desperate Scoundrel/The Pride of Pikeville
Detective Sadie & Son
The Devil & Max Devlin
Die Laughing
Digby, the Biggest Dog in the World
Digging Up Business
Diggstown
Diner▶
Dirty Laundry
Dirty Mind of Young Sally
Dirty Tricks
Disorganized Crime
The Distinguished Gentleman
Divorce American Style
Divorce—Italian Style▶
Dixie: Changing Habits▶
Dr. Alien
Doctor at Large
Doctor Duck's Super Secret All-Purpose Sauce
Dr. Goldfoot and the Bikini Machine
Dr. Jekyll and Ms. Hyde
Doin' Time
Doin' Time on Planet Earth
Dollars▶
Donovan's Reef▶
Don't Go Near the Water
Don't Let Your Meat Loaf
Don't Tell Mom the Babysitter's Dead
Door to Door
Double Double Toil and Trouble
Double Dynamite
Double Trouble
Doughnuts & Society
Downtown
Dream a Little Dream
Dream a Little Dream 2
Dream Machine
Dreaming Out Loud
Dressmaker
Drive-In
Driving Me Crazy
Drop Dead Fred
Drop-Out Mother
Dumb Waiter
Dunston Checks In
Dutch
Dutch Girls
Dutch Treat
Early Cinema Vol. 1
Early Days
Earthworm Tractors
East Side Kids
East Side Kids/The Lost City
Echo Park
Ed
Ed Wood▶
Eddie
The Efficiency Expert
18 Again!
Elvis Stories
Empire Records
Encino Man
Ensign Pulver
Enter Laughing
Ernest Saves Christmas
Erotic Dreams
Escapade▶
Et La Tenoresse?...Bordel!
Every Day's a Holiday
Evil Toons
Ex-Mrs. Bradford▶
Exit to Eden
Experience Preferred... But Not Essential
The Experts
Explorers
Eyes of Turpin Are Upon You!
Fabulous Joe
Faces of Women
Fall and Rise of Reginald Perrin 1▶
Fall and Rise of Reginald Perrin 2▶
Falling in Love Again
Family Reunion
Fancy Pants
The Fantastic World of D.C. Collins
Fantasy Man
Far Out Man
The Farmer's Wife
Fast Food
Fast Times at Ridgemont High▶
Fat Guy Goes Nutzoid
Father and Scout
Father of the Bride▶
Father of the Bride
Father of the Bride Part II
Father Was a Fullback
Father's Little Dividend▶
Fatty and Mabel Adrift/Mabel, Fatty and the Law
Fatty Finn
Fawlty Towers
Fear, Anxiety and Depression
Feel My Pulse
Felix the Cat: The Movie
Fernandel the Dressmaker
Ferris Bueller's Day Off▶
The Fiendish Plot of Dr. Fu Manchu
Find the Lady
Firehouse
Firesign Theatre Presents Nick Danger in the Case of the Missing Yolks
The First Time
Flashback▶
Fletch
Fletch Lives
A Flight of Rainbirds
The Flintstones
Flirting with Disaster▶
Flush
The Flustered Comedy of Leon Errol
Flying Karamazov Brothers Comedy Hour
Flying Wild

Follow Me, Boys!▶
A Fool and His Money
Footsteps in the Dark
For Better and For Worse
For Pete's Sake
For Richer, For Poorer
For the Love of It
Foreign Body
Foreplay
Forever, Lulu
40 Pounds of Trouble
Fowl Play
Frasier the Sensuous Lion
Fraternity Vacation
Freaky Friday
Freebie & the Bean
French Fried Vacation
Friday
Frog
Frogs!
The Front Page▶
The Front Page
Frozen Assets
Fun with Dick and Jane
The Funny Farm
Galaxies are Colliding
Gambit
Games Girls Play
The Garbage Pail Kids Movie
Gas Pump Girls
The General▶
General Spanky
Getting Even with Dad
Getting In
Ghost Crazy
The Gift
Ginger Ale Afternoon
Girl 6
A Girl in a Million
Girl in His Pocket
Girls Just Want to Have Fun
Girls Next Door
The Gladiator▶
Glitch!
A Global Affair
Glory Years
The Go-Getter
Go West, Young Man
Goin' to Town
Going Ape!
Going in Style▶
Going Overboard
Going to Town
Going Under
Going Undercover
Gold of the Amazon Women
The Gold Rush▶
Golden Earrings
Gone are the Days
Good Girls Don't
Goodbye Love
Goon Movie
Gordy
Gotcha!
Grad Night
The Grass is Always Greener Over the Septic Tank
Greased Lightning
The Great American Sex Scandal
Great Bank Hoax
Great Bikini Off-Road Adventure
The Great Impostor
The Great Muppet Caper▶
The Great Outdoors
The Great Rupert▶
The Great St. Trinian's Train Robbery
Greedy
Green Grow the Rushes
Green Pastures▶
Grosse Fatigue▶
Group Marriage
Grumpier Old Men
Guarding Tess
The Guardsman▶
Guest Wife
A Guide for the Married Woman
Gumball Rally
The Gun in Betty Lou's Handbag
Gung Ho

Hail Caesar
Halloween with the Addams Family
Hamburger...The Motion Picture
Hanging on a Star
The Happiest Days of Your Life▶
Happy Birthday, Gemini
Happy Gilmore
The Happy Hooker
The Happy Hooker Goes Hollywood
The Happy Hooker Goes to Washington
Happy Hour
A Happy New Year!
Happy New Year
Hardbodies
Hardbodies 2
Harper Valley P.T.A.
Harry and the Hendersons
Harry & Walter Go to New York
Harry's War
Have Rocket Will Travel
Hawmps!
Head Office
Heading for Heaven
Headline Woman
Heart and Souls
Heartbreak Hotel
Heaven Help Us
The Heavenly Kid
Heavy Traffic▶
Heavyweights
Hello Again
Help Wanted: Male
Her Life as a Man
Herbie Goes Bananas
Herbie Rides Again
Hero at Large
Hi-Di-Hi
Hiding Out
High School USA
High Strung
Hijazo de Mi Vidaza
Hillbilly Blitzkrieg
His Girl Friday▶
His Picture in the Papers
Hit the Ice
The Hoboken Chicken Emergency
Hocus Pocus
Hog Wild
Hold 'Em Jail
Holiday Hotel
Holiday Rhythm
Hollywood Zap
Holy Matrimony
Home Is Where the Hart Is
Home Remedy
Homer Comes Home
Hometown Boy Makes Good
Hometown U.S.A.
Homeward Bound 2: Lost in San Francisco
Homo Eroticus/Man of the Year
Honey, I Blew Up the Kid
The Honeymoon Machine
Honky Tonk Freeway
Hooch
Hootch Country Boys
Hopscotch▶
The Horse in the Gray Flannel Suit
The Horse's Mouth▶
Hostage for a Day
Hot Millions▶
Hot Pursuit
Hot Resort
Hot Stuff
Hot Summer in Barefoot County
Hot T-Shirts
Hot Touch
Hot Under the Collar
Hot Wire
Hotel Paradiso
H.O.T.S.
House Arrest
House of Errors
House Party▶
House Party 2: The Pajama Jam
House Party 3

Houseguest
Housemaster
How Come Nobody's On Our Side?
How Funny Can Sex Be?
How I Won the War
How to Be a Perfect Person in Just Three Days
How to Beat the High Cost of Living
How to Break Up a Happy Divorce
How to Commit Marriage
How to Kill 400 Duponts
How to Make a Doll
How to Murder Your Wife▶
How to Pick Up Girls
How to Seduce a Woman
How to Succeed with Girls
Huckleberry Finn
Hullabaloo Over Georgie & Bonnie's Pictures
Hunk
I Love Lucy
I Wanna Hold Your Hand
I Was a Male War Bride▶
I Was a Teenage TV Terrorist
I Wonder Who's Killing Her Now?
Identity Crisis
If I Were Rich
If It's Tuesday, This Must Be Belgium▶
If You Don't Stop It...You'll Go Blind
Illegally Yours
I'm No Angel▶
The Immigrant▶
Immortal Bachelor
Importance of Being Earnest▶
The Imported Bridegroom
The Impossible Years
Improper Channels
The In-Laws▶
In the Army Now
In the Money
In the Spirit
Inn of Temptation
Innocent Sorcerers
The Innocents Abroad
Innocents in Paris
Inside the Law
The Inspector General▶
Intervista▶
Into the Sun
Invasion of the Space Preachers
The Invisible Kid
The Invisible Woman▶
Irish Luck
Irreconcilable Differences
Is This Goodbye, Charlie Brown?
It Could Happen to You
It Happens Every Spring▶
It Takes Two
It Was a Short Summer, Charlie Brown
The Italian Job
It's A Gift▶
It's a Great Life
It's a Joke, Son!
It's Not the Size That Counts
It's Pat: The Movie
Izzy & Moe
Jabberwalk
Jack
Jack and His Friends
The Jackpot
Jeeves & Wooster: Jeeves' Arrival
The Jerky Boys
Jimmy the Kid
Jinxed
Jocks
Joe's Apartment
Johnny Stecchino▶
Jokes My Folks Never Told Me
Jonah Who Will Be 25 in the Year 2000▶
Josh and S.A.M.
Jumpin' Jack Flash
Junior

Jury Duty
Just One of the Guys
Just William's Luck
K-9
Keaton's Cop
Kelly the Second
Kid from Brooklyn
A Kid in King Arthur's Court
Kid Sister
The Kid with the 200 I.Q.
Kidco
Kika
Kill My Wife...Please!
Killer Dill
Kingpin
A Kink in the Picasso
Kiss Me, Stupid!
Kisses for My President
Kitty and the Bagman
Klondike Annie
The Knack▶
Konrad
La Boum
La Cage aux Folles▶
La Cage aux Folles 2
La Cage aux Folles 3: The Wedding
La Grande Bouffe▶
La Grande Vadrouille▶
La Vie est Belle
Ladies Who Do
Lady Godiva Rides
Lady Killer▶
Lady of the Evening
L'Anne Sainte
Las Vegas Hillbillys
Las Vegas Weekend
Last Night at the Alamo▶
Last of the Red Hot Lovers
The Last Porno Flick
Last Resort
The Lavender Hill Mob▶
Law of Desire▶
Le Bourgeois Gentilhomme
Le Cavaleur
Le Gendarme de Saint-Tropez
Le Gentleman D'Epsom
Le Sex Shop▶
Leader of the Band
The League of Gentlemen▶
Leap Year
The Lemon Drop Kid
Leningrad Cowboys Go America
Leon the Pig Farmer
Les Aventuriers
Les Comperes▶
Les Patterson Saves the World
Lesson in Love
Let It Ride
Let's Do It Again
Let's Get Tough
License to Drive
Lie Down with Dogs
The Life & Times of the Chocolate Killer
Life Is a Long Quiet River▶
Life with Father▶
Life with Mikey
Like Father, Like Son
Li'l Abner
Listen, Darling
Little Big League
Little Darlings
Little Giants
Little Indian, Big City
Little Miss Marker▶
Little Miss Marker
Little Miss Millions
The Little Rascals
Little World of Don Camillo▶
Livin' Large
Living in Oblivion▶
Living on Tokyo Time
Lobster for Breakfast
Lonely Wives
The Longest Yard
Look Who's Laughing
Look Who's Talking Now
Lookin' to Get Out
Loose Cannons
Lost Diamond

Lost Honeymoon
Lost in America▶
The Love Boat
The Love God?
Love Nest
Lucky Jim
Luggage of the Gods
Lupo
Luv
Ma and Pa Kettle at Home
Ma and Pa Kettle on Vacation
Mabel & Fatty
Macaroni
Mack Sennett Comedies: Vol. 1
Mack Sennett Comedies: Vol. 2
Mad About You
Mad Miss Manton
The Magic Christian▶
Maid to Order
Major League
Major League 2
Major Payne
Make a Million
Make Me an Offer
Making the Grade
Malcolm
The Malibu Beach Vampires
Mallrats
The Man from Left Field
Man from Nowhere
Man in the Silk Hat
Man of Destiny
The Man on the Box
The Man with the Perfect Swing
The Mandarin Mystery
Manhandled
Manhattan Murder Mystery▶
Marriage Is Alive and Well
Married to It
Martians Go Home!
Master Minds
Matilda
A Matter of Degrees
Max
Maxie
Maybe...Maybe Not
Me and the Kid
Me and the Mob
Medicine Man
Meet the Hollowheads
Meet the Mob
Meet the Parents
Melvin and Howard▶
Men at Work
Merton of the Movies
Mexican Spitfire at Sea
Mexican Spitfire/Smartest Girl in Town
Mickey the Great
Midnight▶
A Midwinter's Tale
Mighty Aphrodite
Million Dollar Duck
Million Dollar Mystery
A Million to Juan
Milo Milo
The Misadventures of Mr. Wilt
Misbehaving Husbands
Miss Firecracker▶
Miss Grant Takes Richmond
The Missing Corpse
Mrs. Doubtfire
Mistaken Identity
Mr. Baseball
Mr. Blandings Builds His Dream House▶
Mr. Hobbs Takes a Vacation▶
Mr. Mike's Mondo Video
Mr. Nice Guy
Mr. Peek-A-Boo
Mister Roberts▶
Mr. Skitch
Mr. Walkie Talkie
Mr. Wise Guy
Mr. Wrong
Mistress
Mixed Nuts
Modern Problems
Mon Oncle▶
Mon Oncle D'Amerique▶
Monsieur Beaucaire▶
Mother Goose Rock 'n' Rhyme

The Tuttles of Tahiti▶
Twelve Chairs▶
Twentieth Century▶
Twinsitters
Two Bits & Pepper
200 Motels
The Ugly Dachshund
Uncle Buck▶
Undercover Blues
Undergrads▶
Unfaithfully Yours▶
Unfaithfully Yours
Unidentified Flying Oddball
Used Cars▶
Varieties on Parade
Vasectomy: A Delicate Matter
Vermont Is for Lovers
A Very Brady Christmas
A Very Brady Sequel
Virgin High
Visitants
Voice of Hollywood
Volere Volare
Volunteers
The Wacky World of Wills & Burke
Water
Wayne's World▶
Wayne's World 2
A Wedding
Wedding Band
Wedding Rehearsal
Weekend Warriors
Weekend with the Babysitter
Weird Science
Welcome to 18
Welcome to the Dollhouse
We're in the Legion Now
We're in the Navy Now
We're Talkin' Serious Money
Wet and Wild Summer
What About Bob?▶
What Did You Do in the War, Daddy?
What Do You Say to a Naked Lady?
What's Up Front
The Wheeler Dealers▶
When Knights were Bold
When's Your Birthday?
Where Angels Go, Trouble Follows
Where There's Life
Where's Willie?
Whiffs
Whiskey Galore▶
Who Framed Roger Rabbit▶
Wholly Moses!
Who's Got the Action?
Who's Harry Crumb?
Who's Minding the Mint?▶
Who's the Man?
The Wild Life
Wild West
Will Success Spoil Rock Hunter?
Win, Place, or Steal
Window to Paris
Wings of Fame
Wish Me Luck
Women's Club
Woof!
Working Winnie/Oh So Simple
The Wrong Guys
Yankee Zulu
You Can't Hurry Love
You So Crazy
You Talkin' to Me?
Young Einstein
Young Love—Lemon Popsicle 7
Zazie dans le Metro▶
Zebra in the Kitchen
Zero to Sixty

Comedy Anthologies

see also Comedy

The Adventures of Hairbreadth Harry
All Night Long/Smile Please
Amazon Women on the Moon
And Now for Something Completely Different▶
The Best of Chaplin
Best of Eddie Murphy
Best of Ernie Kovacs
The Best of John Candy on SCTV
The Best of the Kenny Everett Video Show
The Best of the Kids in the Hall
The Best of the Two Ronnies
Best of W.C. Fields
Boccaccio '70
Charlie Chaplin: The Early Years, Vol. 1
Charlie Chaplin: The Early Years, Vol. 2
Charlie Chaplin: The Early Years, Vol. 3
Charlie Chaplin: The Early Years, Vol. 4
Daffy Duck's Quackbusters
Desperate Scoundrel/The Pride of Pikeville
Early Cinema Vol. 1
Elvis Stories
Everything You Always Wanted to Know about Sex (But Were Afraid to Ask)▶
A Few Moments with Buster Keaton and Laurel and Hardy▶
The Flintstones
The Floorwalker/By the Sea▶
For Auld Lang Syne: The Marx Brothers
Foreplay
Going to Congress/Don't Park There
Golden Age of Comedy
Great Chase
The Groove Tube
His Prehistoric Past/The Bank
His Royal Slyness/Haunted Spooks
Hollywood Boulevard
Hollywood Clowns
Hot Foot/A Happy Married Couple
Hot Water/Safety Last
I'm on My Way/The Non-Stop Kid
Kentucky Fried Movie▶
Kid 'n' Hollywood and Polly Tix in Washington
Kid's Auto Race/Mabel's Married Life
Kings, Queens, Jokers
The Knockout/Dough and Dynamite▶
Laugh with Linder!
Laughfest
Laurel & Hardy and the Family
Laurel & Hardy: At Work
Laurel & Hardy Comedy Classics, Vol. 1
Laurel & Hardy Comedy Classics, Vol. 2
Laurel & Hardy Comedy Classics, Vol. 3
Laurel & Hardy Comedy Classics, Vol. 4
Laurel & Hardy Comedy Classics, Vol. 5
Laurel & Hardy Comedy Classics, Vol. 6
Laurel & Hardy Comedy Classics, Vol. 7
Laurel & Hardy Comedy Classics, Vol. 8
Laurel & Hardy Comedy Classics, Vol. 9
Laurel & Hardy On the Lam
Laurel & Hardy Special
Laurel & Hardy Spooktacular
Laurel & Hardy: Stan "Helps" Ollie
Little Rascals, Book 1
Little Rascals, Vol. 1
Little Rascals, Vol. 2
The Lizzies of Mack Sennett
Looney Looney Looney Bugs Bunny Movie▶
The Lost Stooges
Love Notes
Mack & Carole
The Marx Brothers in a Nutshell▶
MGM's The Big Parade of Comedy
Monty Python's Parrot Sketch Not Included
Monty Python's The Meaning of Life▶
National Lampoon Goes to the Movies
National Lampoon's Favorite Deadly Sins
Never Weaken/Why Worry?▶
New York Stories▶
Oldest Profession
Our Gang
Our Gang Comedies
Our Gang Comedy Festival
Our Gang Comedy Festival 2
Outtakes
Parade▶
Plaza Suite▶
Pop Goes the Cork
Queen for a Day
Rascal Dazzle
Really Weird Tales
The Return of Our Gang
Rink/Immigrant
Ripping Yarns
Road Lawyers and Other Briefs
Sailor-Made Man/Grandma's Boy▶
Sawmill/The Dome Doctor
Sex and Buttered Popcorn
Shirley Temple Festival
Silent Laugh Makers, No. 1▶
Silent Laugh Makers, No. 2▶
Silent Laugh Makers, No. 3
Silent Movies...Just For the Fun of It!
Slapstick
Stan Without Ollie, Vol. 1
Stooges Shorts Festival
The Stooges Story▶
Stop! Look! and Laugh!
Three Stooges Comedy Capers: Vol. 1
Three Stooges Comedy Classics
Three Stooges: Cookoo Cavaliers and Other Nyuks
Three Stooges Festival
Three Stooges: From Nurse to Worse and Other Nyuks
The Three Stooges: Half-Wit's Holiday and Other Nyuks
The Three Stooges: Idiots Deluxe and Other Nyuks
The Three Stooges: Nutty but Nice and Other Nyuks
The Three Stooges: They Stooge to Conga and Other Nyuks
Tigers in Lipstick
To See Such Fun
A Tribute to the Boys
Tunnelvision
Uncensored
When Comedy was King
Woman Times Seven
The World of Abbott & Costello
The Young Ones
Yours, Mine & Ours

Comedy Drama

see also Black Comedy; Comedy

Adventure
Alice Doesn't Live Here Anymore
Alice's Restaurant
All I Want for Christmas
All My Good Countrymen
All Screwed Up▶
An Almost Perfect Affair
Aloha Summer
Always▶
Amarcord▶
American Boyfriends
American Graffiti▶
And Baby Makes Six
Androcles and the Lion
Andy Hardy Gets Spring Fever
Andy Hardy's Double Life
Andy Hardy's Private Secretary
Angel in a Taxi
Angie
Antonia's Line
The Apprenticeship of Duddy Kravitz▶
Arabian Nights▶
Arizona Dream
Armistead Maupin's Tales of the City
Article 99
Author! Author!
Autumn Marathon
Avalon▶
Awakenings▶
Ay, Carmela!▶
Babette's Feast▶
Baby It's You▶
The Baby-Sitters Club
Baby, Take a Bow
Back Roads
Bad Behavior
Bail Jumper
The Baker's Wife▶
The Ballad of Paul Bunyan
Band of Outsiders
Barcelona▶
Bartleby
Baxter
Beautiful Girls
Being Human
Being Two Isn't Easy
The Bells of St. Mary's▶
Benji▶
The Best Way
Bhaji on the Beach
Big▶
The Big Chill▶
Big Girls Don't Cry...They Get Even
Big Night
Big Wednesday
Billy Liar▶
The Bishop's Wife▶
The Black King
Blueberry Hill
Blues Busters
Blume in Love▶
Born to Win
Borsalino▶
The Boys Next Door
The Breakfast Club▶
Breaking Away▶
Breaking the Rules
Breaking Up Is Hard to Do
The Bretts▶
Bright Eyes
Brighton Beach Memoirs
Broadcast News▶
Bud and Lou
The Buddy System
Buddy's Song
Buffalo Bill
Bulldog Drummond's Revenge
A Bunny's Tale
Bureau of Missing Persons
Butterflies Are Free▶
Caesar and Cleopatra
Cafe Express
Calendar Girl
Candy Mountain
Cannery Row
Captain Newman, M.D.
Carbon Copy
Carnal Knowledge▶
Carnival in Flanders▶
Caro Diario▶
Carried Away
The Cary Grant Collection
Casey's Shadow
Cesar▶
Cesar & Rosalie▶
The Challengers
Charles et Lucie▶
Charlie and the Great Balloon Chase
Cheaper to Keep Her
Chimes at Midnight▶
China, My Sorrow
Chips, the War Dog
Chloe in the Afternoon▶
Choose Me▶
A Chorus of Disapproval
The Christmas Wife
Chungking Express▶
City Lights▶
City of Women
Claire's Knee▶
Clara's Heart
Class Reunion
Cleo from 5 to 7▶
Clipped Wings
Clown
Coast to Coast
Cocoon: The Return
Combination Platter
Come to the Stable▶
Comment Ca Va?
Conspiracy of Terror
Cooperstown
Corvette Summer
Country Life
Coupe de Ville
The Courtship of Eddie's Father▶
Cousin, Cousine▶
Cousins▶
Crazy from the Heart▶
Crimes & Misdemeanors▶
Crooklyn▶
Danny Boy
David Holzman's Diary▶
Death of the Rat
The Decameron▶
The Decline of the American Empire▶
Der Purimshpiler
Desperate Teenage Lovedolls
Destiny Turns on the Radio
Details of a Duel: A Question of Honor
Detour to Danger
The Devil & Daniel Webster▶
Devil on Horseback
The Devil's Eye
Diary of a Chambermaid▶
Diary of a Mad Housewife▶
Diary of a Young Comic
Diary of Forbidden Dreams▶
Digger
Dim Sum: A Little Bit of Heart▶
The Dining Room
Dinner at Eight▶
Dinner at Eight
The Discovery Program
Dixie Lanes
Do the Right Thing▶
Doctor at Sea
Dr. Christian Meets the Women
Dog Eat Dog
Don Quixote▶
Don't Drink the Water
Double Happiness▶
Down by Law▶
Dream Chasers
The Dream Team
DROP Squad
Drugstore Cowboy▶
D2: The Mighty Ducks
Eat a Bowl of Tea▶
Eat Drink Man Woman▶
Eat My Dust
Eat the Peach
Eating
Educating Rita▶
El Cochecito▶
Eli Eli
Elizabeth of Ladymead▶
Emanon
End of the Line
Enemies, a Love Story▶
Enormous Changes▶
Even Cowgirls Get the Blues
Extra Girl
Eyes Right!
The Fabulous Baker Boys▶

Faithful
Family Business
Far North
Fast Talking
Fatso
The Fifth Monkey
First Name: Carmen▶
The Fisher King▶
Five Corners▶
The Five Heartbeats▶
The Flamingo Kid▶
Flesh▶
Flirting▶
Floundering
FM
Follow the Leader
For Keeps
For the Love of Benji
A Foreign Field
Forrest Gump▶
Four Adventures of Reinette and Mirabelle▶
Four Days in July
Four Deuces
Four Friends▶
The Four Musketeers▶
The Four Seasons
Fried Green Tomatoes▶
From the Hip
From the Mixed-Up Files of Mrs. Basil E. Frankweiler
Full Moon in Blue Water
Fuzz
Garbo Talks
Generation
George!
Georgy Girl▶
Get Shorty▶
Getting Over
Getting Straight
Ghost Chasers
The Gig
Gin Game▶
Ginger & Fred▶
The Girl with the Hat Box
Girlfriends▶
A Girl's Folly
The Gold of Naples▶
Gone are the Days
A Good Man in Africa
Good Morning, Vietnam▶
Good Sam
The Goodbye Bird
Goodbye Columbus▶
The Goodbye People
Goodnight, Michelangelo
The Gospel According to Vic
The Graduate▶
Grandes Amigos
Grandview U.S.A.
The Great Man Votes▶
The Great McGinty▶
The Great Moment
A Great Wall▶
The Great War
Gregory's Girl▶
Grief
Gross Anatomy
Grown Ups
Grumpy Old Men▶
Guess What We Learned in School Today?
Guess Who's Coming to Dinner▶
Half a Sixpence
Hangin' with the Homeboys▶
Hannah and Her Sisters▶
Happily Ever After
Happy Since I Met You▶
Hard-Boiled Mahoney
Hard Promises
The Hard Way▶
Harlem Nights
The Hawks & the Sparrows
Head Winds
The Heartbreak Kid▶
Heartburn▶
Here Come the Marines
Hero▶
Hero of the Year
Hey, Babu Riba
The Hideaways

His Double Life
His First Command
Hold Your Man▶
A Hole in the Head
Hollywood Heartbreak
Hollywood Vice Sqaud
Home for the Holidays
Home Free All
Homer and Eddie
Horsemasters
The Hot Line
The Hotel New Hampshire
House of Angels
Household Saints▶
The Householder
Housekeeping▶
I Live My Life
I Live with Me Dad
I Vitelloni▶
The Ice Flood
If You Could See What I Hear
Il Sorpasso
Immediate Family
Impure Thoughts
In Praise of Older Women
In the Land of the Owl Turds
In the Mood
In the Soup
Indian Summer
Inside Monkey Zetterland
Insignificance▶
It Couldn't Happen Here
It Started in Naples▶
It's a Wonderful Life▶
Jack and Sarah
Jamon, Jamon
The January Man
Jazzman▶
Jimmy Hollywood
Jo Jo Dancer, Your Life is Calling
Joe
Joe's Bed-Stuy Barbershop: We Cut Heads
Johnny Suede
The Jolly Paupers
Joshua Then and Now▶
Judge Priest▶
The Jumper
Junior High School
Just Another Pretty Face
Kicking and Screaming▶
The Kid▶
Kid Dynamite
The Kid from Left Field
The Kid/Idle Class▶
The Killing Game
A King in New York
Knights & Emeralds
Kostas
Kotch▶
La Discrete▶
La Dolce Vita▶
La Ronde▶
Lady by Choice
Lady for a Day▶
The Lady Says No
Larks on a String▶
The Last American Hero▶
The Last Days of Chez Nous
The Last Detail▶
Last Holiday▶
The Last of Mrs. Cheyney▶
Last Summer In the Hamptons▶
Law and Disorder▶
Le Beau Serge▶
Le Petit Amour▶
A League of Their Own▶
Leap of Faith
Leave 'Em Laughing
The Lemon Sisters
Les Grandes Gueules
Letter to Brezhnev▶
Letters from My Windmill▶
Letting Go
Life 101
Like Water for Chocolate▶
Lily in Love
Little Annie Rooney
Little Red Schoolhouse
A Little Sex

The Little Theatre of Jean Renoir▶
The Little Thief▶
Little Vegas
Live Nude Girls
Local Hero▶
Long Shot
Loose Connections
The Lovable Cheat
Love and Human Remains▶
Love Finds Andy Hardy▶
Love in the City▶
Lovers and Other Strangers▶
Loves of a Blonde▶
Lucas▶
Mac and Me
Madame Sousatzka▶
Made for Each Other▶
Made in USA
Magic Town
Make Room for Tomorrow
Malibu Hot Summer
Mama Turns a Hundred▶
The Man Upstairs
Manny's Orphans
Mantrap
Marathon
Maria's Child
Marius▶
The Marriage of Maria Braun▶
Marry Me, Marry Me▶
Masala
M*A*S*H▶
M*A*S*H: Goodbye, Farewell & Amen▶
Max Dugan Returns
May Fools▶
Mediterraneo▶
Memories of Me
Men at Work
Men Don't Leave
Mermaids▶
Metropolitan▶
Mexican Bus Ride
Middle Age Crazy
Midnight Auto Supply
The Mighty Ducks
The Mighty Quinn
The Milagro Beanfield War▶
Million Dollar Kid
Min & Bill
Miracle on 34th Street
Mischief
The Misfit Brigade
Miss Annie Rooney
Mrs. 'Arris Goes to Paris
Mrs. Wiggs of the Cabbage Patch
Mr. Deeds Goes to Town▶
Mr. Mom▶
Mr. North
Mr. Saturday Night
Mr. Winkle Goes to War
M'Lady's Court
Mom, the Wolfman and Me
Money for Nothing
The Moneytree
Moon over Parador
Moonlighting
More American Graffiti
Morgan Stewart's Coming Home
Moscow on the Hudson▶
The Mozart Brothers▶
Murmur of the Heart▶
My Beautiful Laundrette▶
My Bodyguard▶
My Dinner with Andre▶
My Father's Nurse
My Girl
My Life as a Dog▶
My Other Husband
My Therapist
My Twentieth Century▶
My Wonderful Life
Mystic Pizza▶
Nadine
The Nasty Girl▶
Nasty Rabbit
Nea
'Neath Brooklyn Bridge
Never Let Go

The New Age
A New Life
New Year's Day▶
Next Stop, Greenwich Village▶
Next Summer▶
Night on Earth▶
1969▶
90 Days▶
The Ninth Configuration▶
No Man of Her Own
No Small Affair
Nobody's Fool▶
Norman, Is That You?
North
North Dallas Forty▶
Nothing in Common
Nurse on Call
The Object of Beauty▶
Oblomov▶
Off Your Rocker
Oh, Alfie
Oh, What a Night
Olly Olly Oxen Free
Once Around
One Arabian Night▶
One Flew Over the Cuckoo's Nest▶
Only One Night
Only When I Laugh▶
Orphans▶
Other People's Money
Our Little Girl
Out
Outrageous!▶
Outside Chance of Maximillian Glick
Over the Brooklyn Bridge
Paddy
Padre Nuestro
Palm Springs Weekend
Palooka
The Paper▶
The Paper Chase▶
Parenthood▶
Patti Rocks▶
People Will Talk▶
Peppermint Soda▶
Perfect Timing
Perfumed Nightmare▶
Period of Adjustment▶
Pete 'n' Tillie
Peter's Friends
The Philadelphia Story▶
The Pickle
Pictures
Ping Pong
Pink Cadillac
Pink Nights
P.K. and the Kid
Playboy of the Western World
Pocketful of Miracles▶
The Pointsman
Pollyanna
Pollyanna▶
Pontiac Moon
Popi▶
Portnoy's Complaint
Postcards from the Edge▶
Power
Powwow Highway▶
Pretty in Pink
Pride of the Bowery
The Prime of Miss Jean Brodie▶
Primrose Path
The Princess & the Call Girl
Prisoner of Second Avenue
Prisoners of Inertia
The Private History of a Campaign That Failed
Prizzi's Honor▶
Problem Child
Promised Land▶
Provincial Actors
Psychedelic Fever
Punchline
Purple People Eater
Pushing Hands
Quarterback Princess
Queen of Hearts▶
The Rachel Papers▶
Racquet
Rafferty & the Gold Dust Twins

Rags to Riches
Raining Stones
The Rascals
Ratboy
The Red Light Sting
Remedy for Riches
Reno and the Doc
Return of the Secaucus 7▶
Rich and Famous
Ride the Wild Surf
Robert et Robert▶
Rocket Gibraltar▶
Romance of a Horsethief
Roommate
Roommates
The Rules of the Game▶
The Runnin' Kind
Sadie McKee▶
Saving Grace
Say Anything▶
Scenes from a Mall
Scoumoune
Second Thoughts
Secrets of Women▶
Seduced and Abandoned▶
The Seducer
The Seven-Per-Cent Solution▶
Seven Thieves▶
Shadows and Fog
Shag: The Movie▶
She Must Be Seeing Things
Shirley Valentine▶
A Shock to the System▶
Shooters
Short Cuts▶
Side Out
Signs of Life
Simon, King of the Witches
A Simple Twist of Fate
Single Bars, Single Women
Six in Paris
Six Weeks
Skin Game▶
Slap Shot▶
Slaves of New York
Slightly Honorable
The Slingshot▶
The Slugger's Wife
Smart Alecks
Smugglers' Cove▶
The Snapper▶
Snoopy, Come Home▶
Soldier in the Rain
Some Kind of Hero
Some Kind of Wonderful
Something in Common
Something Special
Something to Talk About
Song of the Thin Man
Soul Man
Spencer's Mountain
Spike of Bensonhurst
Spitfire▶
Splash
Spoiled Children
Spook Busters
The Sprinter
Stage Door▶
Star of Midnight
Star Spangled Girl
Stardust Memories
Starlight Hotel
The Stars Fell on Henrietta
Starting Over▶
Staying Together
Stealing Beauty
Steamboat Bill, Jr.▶
Stoogemania
Storm in a Teacup
The Story of Seabiscuit
Stranger than Paradise▶
Strawberry Blonde▶
Street Music
Strong Man▶
Stroszek▶
Stuck on You
Student Confidential
Sugarbaby▶
The Sugarland Express▶
Summer Fantasy
Summer Snow
The Sunshine Boys▶

Suppose They Gave a War and Nobody Came?
Swedenhielms
Sweet Adeline
Sweet Hearts Dance
Sweet Lorraine▶
Sweet William▶
Sweetie▶
Swept Away...▶
Swing Shift
Sylvia Scarlett
T Bone N Weasel
Table Settings
Take Down
Take This Job & Shove It
Take Your Best Shot
A Tale of Springtime
Tales of Manhattan▶
Talk
Talking Walls
Taxi Blues▶
A Taxing Woman▶
Teachers
Teacher's Pet▶
Teddy at the Throttle
Teddy at the Throttle/Speeding Along
10
Teresa Venerdi▶
Texasville
That's Life!
That's My Baby!
There Goes My Baby
They Might Be Giants▶
The Thin Man Goes Home
Things Change▶
This Is My Life
Those Lips, Those Eyes
A Thousand Clowns▶
Three for the Road
Three in the Attic
Three Men and a Baby▶
Three Men and a Cradle▶
Three Men and a Little Lady
Thunder in the City▶
Thursday's Child
Thursday's Game▶
A Tiger's Tale
The Time of Your Life▶
Timepiece
Tin Men
The Tip-Off
Tito and Me▶
To Please a Lady
To Sleep with Anger▶
Toby Tyler▶
Tom Brown's School Days
Tom Brown's School Days▶
Tom Sawyer▶
Tony Draws a Horse
Too Pretty to Be Honest
Tootsie▶
Topaze▶
Torch Song Trilogy
Toys
Trading Hearts
The Tragedy of a Ridiculous Man
Train to Hollywood▶
Travels with My Aunt
Trouble Along the Way
Trouble in the Glen
True Love▶
Truly, Madly, Deeply▶
Trust
Truth About Women
Tunes of Glory/Horse's Mouth
Turk 182!
Turkish Delights
Twenty Bucks▶
Twenty-One
29th Street
Twister
Two for the Road▶
Two for the Seesaw▶
Twogether
Ugetsu▶
Under the Biltmore Clock
Under the Boardwalk
An Unfinished Piece for a Player Piano▶
Up the Down Staircase▶
Up the Sandbox
Used People
The Vals
The Van▶
Very Close Quarters
The Virgin Soldiers
Volpone▶
Wait Until Spring, Bandini
Walls of Glass
We Think the World of You▶
Weekend at the Waldorf▶
Welcome Home, Roxy Carmichael
We're No Angels
Whatever Happened to Susan Jane?
When Your Lover Leaves
Where the Heart Is
Whitcomb's War
The Whole Shootin' Match▶
Who's Who
Whose Life Is It Anyway?▶
Widow's Peak
Wild in the Streets
Willie & Phil
Wings of Eagles
Winter Kills▶
Wired
Wise Blood▶
Wish You Were Here▶
With Honors
The Wizard
The Women▶
The World According to Garp▶
The World of Henry Orient▶
WR: Mysteries of the Organism▶
The Wrong Arm of the Law▶
A Yank in Australia
A Year in Provence▶
The Year My Voice Broke▶
Yesterday, Today and Tomorrow▶
You Are Not Alone
The Young in Heart▶
You're a Big Boy Now▶
A Zed & Two Noughts▶

Comedy Mystery

***see also* Black Comedy; Comedy; Comedy Drama; Genre Spoofs; Satire & Parody**

Charade▶
Clue
Curse of the Pink Panther
Deathtrap
High Anxiety
Lady On a Train▶
Murder by Death
The Pink Panther▶
The Pink Panther Strikes Again▶
The Princess Comes Across▶
Return of the Pink Panther
Revenge of the Pink Panther
A Shot in the Dark▶
Trail of the Pink Panther
Whistling in Brooklyn
Whistling in Dixie
Whistling in the Dark▶

Comedy Performance

***see* Concert Films**

Comedy Sci-fi

***see also* Comedy; Comic Adventure; Genre Spoofs; Satire & Parody; Sci Fi**

The Absent-Minded Professor▶
Coneheads
Honey, I Shrunk the Kids
Ice Pirates
Out There
Sleeper▶
Son of Flubber
Spaceballs
Theodore Rex

Comic Adventure

***see also* Action Adventure; Comedy**

Adventures Beyond Belief
Adventures in Babysitting
Adventures in Spying
Adventures of a Private Eye
Adventures of a Taxi Driver
The Adventures of Bullwhip Griffin
Air America
Alien from L.A.
All the Lovin' Kinfolk
All the Way, Boys
The Amazing Dobermans
The Ambushers
The Americano
Andy and the Airwave Rangers
Angel of H.E.A.T.
Angels Hard as They Come
Another 48 Hrs.
Another Stakeout
The Armour of God
Avenging Disco Godfather
Baby on Board
Back Roads
Back to the Future▶
Back to the Future, Part 2
Back to the Future, Part 3▶
Bad Guys
Bagdad Cafe▶
The Balloonatic/One Week
The Baltimore Bullet
Bananas Boat
Behind the Front
Beverly Hills Cop
Beverly Hills Cop 2
Beverly Hills Cop 3
The Big Slice
Big Zapper
Bingo
Bird on a Wire
Bloodstone
Blue Iguana
Body Trouble
Boris and Natasha: The Movie
Brink's Job▶
Brothers O'Toole
Burglar
Butler's Dilemma
California Straight Ahead
Campus Knights
Cannibal Women in the Avocado Jungle of Death
Cannonball Run
Cannonball Run 2
The Captain from Koepenick
Captain Swagger
Cartouche▶
Chan is Missing▶
Chasers
Chu Chu & the Philly Flash
City Heat
Club Med
Collision Course
The Concrete Cowboys
Crocodile Dundee▶
Crocodile Dundee 2
Dirt Bike Kid
Doctor Detroit
Dog Pound Shuffle▶
Dolemite 2: Human Tornado
The Double O Kid
Down to Earth▶
Every Girl Should Have One
Explosion
Fast Getaway
Feds
The Fifth Musketeer
Fifty/Fifty
The Fighting American
Flatfoot
Flipper▶
Flirting with Fate▶
Flush It
Forever Young
48 Hrs.▶
Foul Play▶
Free Ride
The Further Adventures of Tennessee Buck
Ghostbusters▶
Ghostbusters 2
Go for It
The Golden Child
The Gumshoe Kid
Gunmen
Hambone & Hillie
Harriet the Spy
Having Wonderful Time/Carnival Boat
Hawthorne of the USA
Here We Go Again!
High Road to China
High Voltage
Highpoint
Hudson Hawk
In Like Flint
In 'n Out
It's in the Bag
Jake Speed
Jane & the Lost City
The Jewel of the Nile
Just Tell Me You Love Me
Kazaam
Kindergarten Cop
King Kung Fu
Kiss My Grits
Kuffs
Landlord Blues
Last Action Hero
Leonard Part 6
A Low Down Dirty Shame
Lucky Devil
Lunch Wagon
Lust in the Dust▶
Mad About Money
Mademoiselle Striptease
Madigan's Millions
Magic Island
Magic Kid
A Man Called Sarge
The Man in the Raincoat
The Man Who Wasn't There
The Man with One Red Shoe
Master Mind
The Masters of Menace
Memoirs of an Invisible Man
Messalina, Empress of Rome
Miami Supercops
Midnight Madness
Midnight Run▶
Miracles
Mr. Billion
Mr. Nanny
Mr. Robinson Crusoe
Mr. Superinvisible
Mitchell
Mo' Money
Mob Story
Mom and Dad Save the World
The Money
Monkey Hustle
Monkey's Uncle
Muppet Treasure Island
Mutants In Paradise
My African Adventure
My Breakfast with Blassie
My Dog, the Thief
My Science Project
The Naked Sword of Zorro
No Deposit, No Return
Oddball Hall
Odds and Evens
Operation Dumbo Drop
Our Man Flint
Over the Hill
Pippi Goes on Board
Pippi in the South Seas
Pippi Longstocking
Pippi on the Run
Pirates
Prehysteria
The Prince of Thieves
Red Lion
Reggie Mixes In▶
The Reivers▶
Rescue Me
The Return of the Musketeers
Return of the Rebels
Riff-Raff
Romancing the Stone▶
Round Trip to Heaven
Royal Flash▶
Rumble in the Bronx
Running Scared
Russkies
Seven
Sherlock: Undercover Dog
Sherlock's Rivals & Where's My Wife
She's Back
Shoot
Short Time▶
Shredder Orpheus
Silver Streak▶
Ski Patrol
Sky High
Slither▶
Smokey and the Bandit
Smokey and the Bandit, Part 2
Smokey and the Bandit, Part 3
Smokey & the Judge
Smokey Bites the Dust
Spaghetti House
Special Delivery
Speed Zone
Speedy▶
Spies, Lies and Naked Thighs
Spy Trap
Spy with a Cold Nose
S*P*Y*S
The Squeeze
Stakeout
Stand-In
Steelyard Blues
Stepmonster
The Stick-Up
The Sting 2
Stingray
Stop! or My Mom Will Shoot
Stop That Cab
Stuntwoman
Suburban Commando
Suffering Bastards
The Suitors
Summer Night
Summer Night with Greek Profile, Almond Eyes & Scent of Basil
Sunburn
Super Fuzz
Super Soul Brother
Surf Nazis Must Die
Surf Ninjas
Survivors
Swashbuckler
The Tall Blond Man with One Black Shoe▶
Tall, Tan and Terrific
A Taxing Woman's Return▶
Teenage Mutant Ninja Turtles: The Movie
Teenage Mutant Ninja Turtles 2: The Secret of the Ooze
Teenage Mutant Ninja Turtles 3
Terminal Exposure
That Man from Rio
That Sinking Feeling▶
They Met in Bombay
The Thief Who Came to Dinner
Think Big
This Time I'll Make You Rich
Those Daring Young Men in Their Jaunty Jalopies
Those Fantastic Flying Fools
Those Magnificent Men in Their Flying Machines▶
Three Amigos
Three Fugitives
Three Kinds of Heat
The Three Musketeers▶
3 Ninjas
3 Ninjas Kick Back
3 Ninjas Knuckle Up
Thunder and Lightning
Thunder in the Pines
Title Shot
Toga Party
Tom and Huck▶
Too Hot to Handle▶
Top Dog
Topkapi▶
Tough Guys
Treasure of the Moon Goddess

Coming of Age

see also ***Teen Angst***

Computers

see also ***Robots & Androids; Technology-Rampant***

Prime Risk
The Scorpio Factor
Superman 3
Tin Man
Virtual Assassin
Virtual Desire
WarGames

Concert Films

see also Rock Stars on Film

Benny Hill's Crazy World
The Best of Abbott & Costello Live
The Best of the Kids in the Hall
Bloodhounds of Broadway
Clark & McCullough
Divine Madness
Eddie Murphy: Raw
An Evening with Robin Williams
Gimme Shelter
Hollywood Goes to War
Jo Jo Dancer, Your Life is Calling
John Cleese on How to Irritate People
The Last Waltz
Lenny▶
Lenny Bruce Performance Film
Mad Dog and Glory▶
Mr. Mike's Mondo Video
Monster in a Box▶
Monterey Pop▶
Monty Python Live at the Hollywood Bowl▶
National Lampoon's Class of '86
Punchline
Scrambled Feet
Search for Signs of Intelligent Life in the Universe▶
The Secret Policeman's Other Ball▶
Secret Policeman's Private Parts
A Session with the Committee
Sex, Drugs, Rock & Roll: Eric Bogosian
Spalding Gray: Terrors of Pleasure
Steve Martin Live
Stop Making Sense▶
Wisecracks▶
Woodstock▶
You Can't Take It with You▶
You So Crazy

Contemporary Musicals

see also Musicals

Absolute Beginners
All That Jazz▶
The Apple
Blame It on the Night
Body Beat
Breakin'
Breakin' 2: Electric Boogaloo
Breakin' Through
Breaking Glass
A Chorus Line
Fame▶
The Josephine Baker Story▶
One from the Heart

Contemporary Noir

see also Film Noir

After Dark, My Sweet▶
After Hours▶
Against All Odds
The American Friend▶
Angel Heart
Betty Blue▶
The Big Easy▶
Blade Runner▶
Blood Simple▶
Blue Velvet▶
Bodies, Rest & Motion
Bodily Harm
Body Double▶
Bring Me the Head of Alfredo Garcia
Cape Fear▶
Chinatown▶
Choose Me▶
The Crude Oasis
Cutter's Way
Dance with a Stranger▶
Devil In a Blue Dress▶
D.O.A.
Dressed to Kill
The Driver
Experiment in Terror▶
Eyes of Laura Mars
Fatal Attraction▶
52 Pick-Up
First Degree
The Girl in a Swing
The Grifters▶
Guncrazy
Hammett
The Horseplayer
The Hot Spot
Husbands and Lovers
The Hustle
Kill Me Again
Killing Zoe
Kiss of Death
The Last Seduction▶
The Long Goodbye▶
The Manchurian Candidate▶
Manhunter▶
Marlowe
Mirage
Mulholland Falls
The Music of Chance
Narrow Margin
Night Moves▶
9 1/2 Weeks
No Way Out▶
One False Move▶
Performance▶
Promised Land▶
The Public Eye▶
Pulp Fiction▶
Red Rock West▶
Reservoir Dogs▶
Romeo Is Bleeding
sex, lies and videotape▶
Shattered
The Silence of the Lambs▶
Something Wild
Stormy Monday
Taxi Driver▶
Tequila Sunrise
Things to Do In Denver When You're Dead▶
To Live & Die in L.A.
Track 29
Trouble in Mind▶
True Believer
True Confessions▶
Twin Peaks
The Two Jakes
Union City
The Usual Suspects▶
Who'll Stop the Rain?▶
Wild at Heart▶
Wild Orchid
Wild Orchid 2: Two Shades of Blue

Cooking

see Edibles

Cops

see also Buddy Cops; Canine Cops; Detectives; Future Cop; Loner Cops; Women Cops

Above Suspicion
Abraxas: Guardian of the Universe
Across 110th Street
Action Jackson
The Adventures of a Gnome Named Gnorm
Alien Nation
Alone in the Neon Jungle
American Cop
American Justice
The Amsterdam Kill
Animal Instincts
Arizona Heat
Armed and Dangerous
Assault on Precinct 13▶
At Gunpoint
Back in Action
Backstreet Justice
Bad Boys
B.A.D. Cats
Bad Lieutenant▶
Badge of the Assassin
Badge 373
Ballbuster
Ballistic
Band of the Hand
Before Morning
Belfast Assassin
Bellamy
Beretta's Island
Best Kept Secrets
Best Seller▶
Beverly Hills Cop
Beverly Hills Cop 2
Beverly Hills Cop 3
Beyond Forgiveness
Beyond the Law
Big Chase
Big Combo▶
The Big Easy▶
The Big Heat▶
Big Score
The Big Slice
Birds of Prey
Black Dragon
Black Eliminator
The Black Marble▶
Black Rain
Blackmail▶
Blackout
Blade
Blink
Blood for Blood
Blood on the Badge
Bloody Avenger
Blown Away
Blue Desert▶
Blue Flame
The Blue Knight
The Blue Lamp▶
Blue Steel
Blue Thunder
Bodily Harm
Bopha!▶
The Boston Strangler
Brainscan
Brannigan
Brass
Breach of Trust
Breaking Point
Broken Badge▶
Bullets or Ballots▶
Bunco
Busting
Car 54, Where Are You?
Caroline at Midnight
The Carpathian Eagle
A Case of Deadly Force▶
Champion Operation
The Chase
Chiefs
China Moon
Chinatown Connection
The Chinatown Murders: Man Against the Mob
Choice of Weapons
The Choirboys
Chungking Express▶
City Hall▶
City Heat
City That Never Sleeps
Clayton County Line
Clockers▶
Cobra
Code of Silence
Cold Front
Cold Light of Day
Cold Steel
Coldfire
Colors▶
Confessions of a Police Captain
Conflict of Interest
Coogan's Bluff▶
Cop
Cop and a Half
The Cop & the Girl
A Cop for the Killing
Cop-Out
Cops and Robbersons
Copycat
Cornbread, Earl & Me
Corrupt▶
Cotton Comes to Harlem▶
Coup de Torchon▶
Cover Me
Crime Busters
The Crow
The Custodian
Danger Ahead
The Dark
Dark Before Dawn
Dead Badge
Dead Bang
Dead Heat
Dead to Rights
Deadly Breed
Deadly Conspiracy
Deadly Diamonds
Deadly Hero▶
Deadly Sins
Deadly Surveillance
Dear Detective
Death Shot
The Death Squad
Deceptions
Deep Cover
Deep Space
The Delicate Delinquent
Delta Heat
Demolition Man
The Detective▶
Detective Story▶
Detroit 9000
Devil In a Blue Dress▶
Devil's Angels
The Devil's Undead
Devlin
Die Hard▶
Die Hard 2: Die Harder▶
Die Hard: With a Vengeance
Dirty Harry▶
Dirty Mind of Young Sally
Distant Justice
Diva▶
Do or Die
Dollman
Dollman vs Demonic Toys
Double Trouble
Dragnet
Dream Man
Drop Zone
Drying Up the Streets
Dying Game
Electra Glide in Blue▶
Ex-Cop
Exit to Eden
Extreme Justice
Extreme Prejudice
Extreme Vengeance
An Eye for an Eye
Eyewitness
Eyewitness to Murder
Fair Game
Fargo▶
Fatal Chase
Fatal Error
Fatal Instinct
The Female Jungle
Fever
Final Embrace
Final Equinox
Find the Lady
Firepower
The First Deadly Sin
First Degree
Flashfire
Flashpoint
Flatfoot
The Force
Force of One
The Formula
Fort Apache, the Bronx▶
Fortune Dane
48 Hrs.▶
Foul Play
Frame by Frame
Frame Up
Freebie & the Bean
The French Connection▶
French Connection 2▶
The French Detective▶
French Quarter Undercover
French Silk
Full Eclipse
Full Exposure: The Sex Tape Scandals
Future Cop
Future Force
Fuzz
Gambler's Choice
The Gauntlet
Get Christie Love!
The Glass Shield
The Glitter Dome
Glitz
Go for It
God Told Me To
Gone are the Days
Gone in 60 Seconds
Gorky Park▶
Hard-Boiled
Hard Justice
The Hard Truth
Hard Vice
The Hard Way▶
Hardcase and Fist
Hate▶
Hawkeye
He Walked by Night▶
Hear No Evil
Heat▶
Heaven's Heroes
Hellbound
Heroes in Blue
The Hidden▶
The Hidden 2
High & Low▶
High Crime
Hill Street Blues, Vol. 1: Hill Street Station
Hollywood Vice Sqaud
Hologram Man
Homicide▶
The Hot Rock▶
Hot Stuff
The Hunted Lady
I Take This Oath
Illegal in Blue
Impulse
In the Heat of the Night▶
In the Kingdom of the Blind the Man with One Eye is King
Indecent Behavior
The Indian Runner
Innocent Blood
Inside Information
Internal Affairs
It Could Happen to You
Jailbait
The January Man
Jennifer 8
Jigsaw
Judge Dredd
Jungleground
Just Cause
K-9
K-9000
Kamikaze '89▶
Karate Cop
Keaton's Cop
Keeper of the City
Kidnapped
The Kill Reflex
The Killer's Edge
The Killing Mind
The Killing Time
Kiss of Death▶
The Klansman
Klute▶
Knife in the Head
Kuffs
L.627▶
La Balance▶
L.A. Bounty
L.A. Heat
La Scorta▶
L.A. Vice
L.A. Wars

Lady Scarface/The Threat
Ladykiller
Laguna Heat
Laser Moon
Last Man Standing
The Last of the Finest
The Laughing Policeman
Law and Disorder▶
Legacy of Lies
Les Miserables
Lethal Obsession
Lethal Weapon▶
Lethal Weapon 2▶
Lethal Weapon 3
Lightblast
Lockdown
Lone Star▶
Lone Star Law Men
Love and Bullets
Love on the Run
Mad Dog and Glory▶
Mad Max▶
Madigan▶
Malarek
A Man in Uniform
The Man Inside
Man on a String
Manhunt
Maniac Cop
Maniac Cop 2
Maniac Cop 3: Badge of Silence
Mardi Gras for the Devil
Martial Law
Martial Law 2: Undercover
Martial Outlaw
Maximum Force
McQ
Miami Beach Cops
Miami Blues
Miami Cops
Miami Vice
Midnight Ride
Midnight Witness
Mind, Body & Soul
A Mind to Kill
Mind Twister
Mission of Justice
Mr. Inside, Mr. Outside
Mitchell
The Mod Squad
Model by Day
Money to Burn
Money Train
Monolith
Moonshine Highway
More! Police Squad
Motor Patrol
Moving Violations
Mulholland Falls
Murder without Motive
Murdered Innocence
My New Partner
Mystery Date
Nails
The Naked City▶
The Naked Gun: From the Files of Police Squad▶
Naked Gun 33 1/3: The Final Insult
Naked Gun 2 1/2: The Smell of Fear
The Narrow Margin▶
National Lampoon's Loaded Weapon 1
The New Centurions
New Jack City
New Jersey Drive
New York Cop
New York Ripper
Next of Kin
Night Children
Night Game
Night of the Cyclone
Night Partners
The Night Patrol
Night Patrol
Night Stalker
Nightstick
Ninja Vengeance
No Escape, No Return
No Man's Land
No Place to Hide
Northwest Trail
Off the Wall
The Offence▶
One Man Force
One Man Jury
The Onion Field▶
Organized Crime & Triad Bureau
Outside the Law
Pair of Aces
Past Tense
Pendulum
P.I. Private Investigations
Piece of the Action
Point of Impact
Police
Police Academy
Police Academy 2: Their First Assignment
Police Academy 3: Back in Training
Police Academy 4: Citizens on Patrol
Police Academy 5: Assignment Miami Beach
Police Academy 6: City Under Siege
Police Academy: Mission to Moscow
Police Squad! Help Wanted!
Policewoman Centerfold
Policewomen
Portraits of a Killer
Prime Suspect▶
Prime Suspect 2▶
Prime Suspect 3▶
Prime Suspect: Inner Circles
Prime Suspect: The Lost Child▶
Prime Target
Prince of the City▶
Private Investigations
Probable Cause
The Prophecy
Provoked
Prowler
Puppet on a Chain
A Pure Formality
Q & A
Question of Honor
Rage and Honor 2: Hostile Takeover
Rainbow Drive
Rapid Fire
A Real American Hero
Recruits
Red Sun Rising
Relentless
Relentless 2: Dead On
Renfrew of the Royal Mounted
Rent-A-Cop
Return to Macon County
Return to Mayberry
Ricochet▶
The Right to Remain Silent
Ring of Death
Rising Sun▶
RoboCop▶
RoboCop the Series: The Future of Law Enforcement
Rock House
Romeo Is Bleeding
The Rookie
Roots of Evil
Rush▶
The Rutherford County Line
Saints and Sinners
Sands of Sacrifice
The Satan Killer
Scanner Cop
Scanners: The Showdown
Scorchy
Season for Assassins
Self-Defense
Serial Killer
Serpico▶
Seven▶
Shadow Force
Shadowhunter
Shakedown
Sharky's Machine
Sharon's Secret
Shoot It Black, Shoot It Blue
Shoot to Kill
Short Time▶
Showdown at the Equator
Silk 2
Siringo
Sketch Artist
Sketch Artist 2: Hands That See
Skull: A Night of Terror
Slipstream
Slow Burn
Small Kill
A Small Killing
Smokey & the Judge
Snapdragon
Soggy Bottom U.S.A.
Solar Force
Son of the Pink Panther
Soul Patrol
South Seas Massacre
Speed▶
Speedtrap
Split Second
Stamp of a Killer
Station
Steele's Law
Stephano Quantestorie
The Stone Killer
Stop! or My Mom Will Shoot
Strange Days▶
A Stranger Among Us
Stranger by Night
Street Crimes
Street War
Strike Force
Striking Distance
Super Force
Super Fuzz
Supervixens
Suspicious Agenda
The Sweeper
Sweet Trash
Sword of Honor
T-Force
The Take
Taking the Heat
Ten to Midnight
Tereza▶
Terror Stalks the Class Reunion
Theodore Rex
They Call Me Mr. Tibbs!
They Only Kill Their Masters
Tightrope▶
Till Death Do Us Part
A Time to Die
Timecop
To Protect and Serve
Top Dog
Top of the Heap
Touch of Evil▶
Traces of Red
Trancers
Trancers 2: The Return of Jack Deth
Trancers 3: Deth Lives
Trancers 4: Jack of Swords
Trancers 5: Sudden Deth
True Romance
Tunnel Vision
Turner and Hooch
Twisted Justice
Two Small Bodies
Under Investigation
Undercover
Undercover Cop
Underground Terror
Unforgettable
Union Station
Unlawful Entry
Urban Crossfire
The Usual Suspects▶
Vampire Cop
Vampire in Brooklyn
Vengeance
Vice Academy
Vice Academy 2
Vice Academy 3
Virtuosity
Walker: Texas Ranger: Deadly Reunion
Walker: Texas Ranger: One Riot, One Ranger
Walking Tall: The Final Chapter
The Warning
The Wharf Rat
Whispers of White
The Wild Pair
Witchcraft 6: The Devil's Mistress
Witness▶
X Marks the Spot
Year of the Dragon
The Young Americans
Zipperface

Corporate Shenanigans

see also Advertising; Salespeople

The Abduction of Allison Tate
Acceptable Risks
All in a Night's Work
And Nothing But the Truth
Any Wednesday
The Apartment▶
April Fools
As Young As You Feel▶
Ask Any Girl
Bad Company
The Bad Sleep Well▶
Barbarians at the Gate▶
The Battle of the Sexes▶
Beggars in Ermine
Behind Office Doors
The Best of Everything▶
Big Business
Big Business Girl
Big Trees▶
The Bikini Car Wash Company
The Bikini Car Wash Company 2
Blood Red
Body Language
Boom Town
Boomerang
Buy & Cell
The Capture of Bigfoot
The Carpetbaggers
Cash McCall
Catherine & Co.
The China Syndrome▶
China White
C.H.O.M.P.S.
Circle of Power
Class of Nuke 'Em High 2: Subhumanoid Meltdown
The Coca-Cola Kid▶
The Colombian Connection
The Colony
Consuming Passions
Corporate Affairs
Crime of Honor
The Crime of Monsieur Lange▶
Cyborg 2
Dark River: A Father's Revenge
The Daydreamer
Deadly Business▶
Deadly Conspiracy
Dealers
Death Chase
Death Collector
Death Machine
The Devil & Miss Jones▶
Devil's Crude
Disclosure
Dodsworth▶
Dragonfight
Dutch Treat
Ebbtide
The Efficiency Expert
Empire Records
The Empty Beach
End of the Line
Eternity
Executive Suite▶
Fatal Confinement
Fatal Skies
Feel the Motion
The Flintstones
FM
For Love or Money
Ford: The Man & the Machine
Freaked
Frozen Assets
Gas
Gas Pump Girls
Glengarry Glen Ross▶
Good Neighbor Sam▶
Goodfellas▶
Gremlins 2: The New Batch▶
Gung Ho
Hackers
Halloween 3: Season of the Witch
Happy Hour
The Harder They Come
Head Office
Her Husband's Affairs
Herbie Rides Again
His Girl Friday▶
Home Town Story
Hot Chocolate
How the West was Fun
How to Get Ahead in Advertising▶
How to Succeed in Business without Really Trying▶
The Hucksters▶
The Hudsucker Proxy▶
I Love Trouble
If I Were Rich
Indio 2: The Revolt
Johnny Mnemonic
Journey to Spirit Island
Kids In the Hall Brain Candy
A Kiss Before Dying
La Truite▶
Ladies Who Do
Land of Promise
The Last Hour
The Lavender Hill Mob▶
Lawnmower Man 2: Beyond Cyberspace
Letter to My Killer
Life Stinks
Limit Up
Little Giant
Lloyds of London▶
Local Hero▶
Love or Money?
Ma and Pa Kettle at Waikiki
Major League
Mama, There's a Man in Your Bed▶
The Man in the Gray Flannel Suit
The Man in the White Suit▶
The Man Inside
Married to It
A Matter of WHO
Megaville
Millions
Miss Grant Takes Richmond
Mo' Money
Moon 44
Morals for Women
Naked Gun 2 1/2: The Smell of Fear
Network▶
The Night They Saved Christmas
9 to 5
No Room to Run
No Time to Die
Noble House
Nowhere to Run
One, Two, Three▶
Other People's Money
The Other Side of Midnight
Outland
Overdrawn at the Memory Bank
The Pajama Game▶
The Paper▶
Parrish
Patterns▶
Playback
The Player▶
Power
Primal Scream
Private Wars
Property
A Public Affair
Putney Swope▶
The Queen of Mean
Quicksand: No Escape
Race the Sun
The Reluctant Agent

Return Fire
Richie Rich
Rising Sun▶
RoboCop▶
RoboCop 2
RoboCop 3
RoboCop the Series: The Future of Law Enforcement
Roger & Me▶
Rollover
Sabrina
Scrooged
The Secret of My Success
The Secretary
Sensations of 1945
Shadow of China▶
The Shawshank Redemption▶
Shining Star
A Shock to the System▶
The Silver Horde
The Simple Truth
Sins
Ski Bum
Skyscraper Souls▶
Solid Gold Cadillac▶
Stand-In▶
Stocks and Blondes
Stormy Monday
The Story of O, Part 2
Strange Bedfellows
Strange Brew
Swimming with Sharks▶
Switching Channels
Synapse
Taffin
Take This Job & Shove It
A Taxing Woman▶
The Temp
They Drive by Night▶
3 Ninjas Knuckle Up
Tiger Heart
Timepiece
Tin Men
Tommy Boy
Topaze▶
The Toxic Avenger, Part 3: The Last Temptation of Toxie
Trading Places
Tucker: The Man and His Dream▶
Upper Crust
Utilities
Vortex
Wall Street▶
Wall Street Cowboy
Washington Affair
Weekend at Bernie's
Weekend at Bernie's 2
The Wheeler Dealers▶
White Mile
Who's Who
The Wildest Office Party
Wolf
A Woman's World▶
Working Girl▶
The World Gone Mad
The Wrong Woman

Courtroom Drama

see Order in the Court

Credits Chaos!

see also Genre Spoofs; Satire & Parody

The Adventures of Baron Munchausen▶
Airplane!▶
Airplane 2: The Sequel
Being There▶
The Birdcage▶
Blazing Saddles▶
Coming to America▶
Fatal Instinct
Ferris Bueller's Day Off▶
The Flintstones
Four Rooms
The Great White Hype
Grumpier Old Men
Grumpy Old Men▶
Hot Shots!▶
Hot Shots! Part Deux
Monty Python and the Holy Grail▶
Monty Python's Life of Brian▶
Monty Python's Parrot Sketch Not Included
Monty Python's The Meaning of Life▶
The Naked Gun: From the Files of Police Squad▶
Naked Gun 33 1/3: The Final Insult
Naked Gun 2 1/2: The Smell of Fear
Nightscare
Police Squad! Help Wanted!
Sneakers
Spy Hard
Strange Brew
Young Sherlock Holmes

Creepy Houses

see also Horror

Afterward
The Amityville Horror
Amityville 2: The Possession
Amityville 3: The Demon
Amityville 4
The Amityville Curse
Amityville 1992: It's About Time
The Bat Whispers
Beyond Darkness
Beyond Evil
The Black Castle
Black Cat
Blondie Has Trouble
Blood Island
Blood Legacy
Blue Blood
Burnt Offerings
Candles at Nine
Carnage
Casper▶
Castle Freak
Castle in the Desert
Castle of Blood
Castle of the Living Dead
The Cat and the Canary
Cellar Dweller
The Colony
Contagion
The Craft
Crazed
Cthulhu Mansion
Demon Wind
Die Sister, Die!
Dolls
Don't Be Afraid of the Dark
Dream Demon
Endless Night
The Evictors
The Evil
Evil Laugh
Evil Toons
Fatally Yours
Fear in the Night▶
Flowers in the Attic
Forever: A Ghost of a Love Story
Francis in the Haunted House
Fright House
Fright Night
The Ghastly Ones
The Ghost and Mr. Chicken
The Ghost Breakers▶
Girls School Screamers
Goblin
Haunted
House▶
House 2: The Second Story
House 4: Home Deadly Home
House of Mystery
The House of Secrets
House of the Dead
House of the Living Dead
House of the Long Shadows
House of the Rising Sun
House on Haunted Hill
The House on Tombstone Hill
The House that Bled to Death
The House that Dripped Blood
The House that Vanished
House Where Evil Dwells
The Innocents▶
La Chute de la Maison Usher▶
The Legend of Hell House▶
Malice
The Mephisto Waltz▶
Million Dollar Mystery
Monsters Crash the Pajama Party
Mother's Day
Murder Mansion
The Nesting
Next of Kin
Night Nurse
Night of the Demons 2
The Old Dark House▶
Paranoiac
The People Under the Stairs
The Perverse Countess
The Phantom
Psycho▶
Psycho 2
Psycho 3
Psycho 4: The Beginning
Rest In Pieces
Revenge in the House of Usher
The Rocky Horror Picture Show▶
Salem's Lot
The Screaming Skull
The Shining
Silent Scream
Sister, Sister
Spookies
Stormswept
A Strange and Deadly Occurence
Superstition
Tangled Destinies
Teenage Exorcist
Terror in the Haunted House
13 Ghosts
Three Cases of Murder▶
Treasure of Fear
The Uninvited▶
Visions of Evil
Web of the Spider
What a Carve-Up!
Who Killed Doc Robbin?

Crime & Criminals

see also Crime Sprees; Crimes of Passion; Disorganized Crime; Fugitives; Organized Crime; Serial Killers; Vigilantes

Action Jackson
Air Hawk
Al Capone▶
Algiers▶
Alias, La Gringa
Alien Nation
All Dogs Go to Heaven
Alligator Alley
Almost an Angel
Ambush Trail
American Autobahn
Amongst Friends
Amor Bandido
And Then You Die▶
Angel's Brigade
Angels Hard as They Come
Another 48 Hrs.
Apprentice to Murder
Arrest Bulldog Drummond
Assault
Assault on a Queen
At Gunpoint
The Avenging Hand
Baby, the Rain Must Fall
Back Door to Heaven▶
Backlash
Bad Blood
Bad Boys
Bad Love
Bandit Queen
Bandits
Batman▶
Batman Forever▶
Batman Returns
The Bay Boy
The Beast from Haunted Cave
Because of the Cats
Before and After
Behind the Mask
Being at Home with Claude
Bells of San Angelo
The Best of Cracker Mysteries▶
Best Seller▶
Betrayed
Beverly Hills Cop
Beverly Hills Cop 2
Beyond Desire
Big Bluff
The Big Easy▶
The Big Heat▶
Billionaire Boys Club
Black Friday
Black Hand
Black Scorpion
Black Sister's Revenge
Blackout
Blind Justice
Blindside
Blindsided
Blonde Crazy
Blood Money: The Story of Clinton and Nadine
Blood Ties
Bloodstone
Bloody Mama
Blown Away
Blue Canadian Rockies
Blue Iguana
Body Double▶
Bonnie's Kids
Boomerang▶
Borderline
Borsalino▶
Boys Town▶
Branded a Bandit
Breaking In▶
Breathless▶
Brewster McCloud▶
Bring Me the Head of Alfredo Garcia
Broken Vows
Brotherhood of Justice
Bugsy Malone
Bulldog Drummond's Revenge
Bulletproof Heart▶
Burglar
Busted Up
Buster
Buying Time
The C-Man
Cape Fear▶
Caper of the Golden Bulls
Captain Swagger
Captive
Caribe
Carlito's Way▶
Cartier Affair
Cast a Dark Shadow▶
The Cat
The Cat o' Nine Tails
Catch the Heat
Catlow
Chance
Charade▶
Charley Varrick▶
Cheech and Chong: Things Are Tough All Over
The Choirboys
C.I.A.: Code Name Alexa
Circle of Fear
Circonstances Attenuantes
The City
City Hall▶
City in Fear▶
City in Panic
Clean, Shaven
Cleopatra Jones
Cleopatra Jones & the Casino of Gold
Cliffhanger▶
Clockers▶
Clown Murders
The Coast Patrol
Cocaine Wars
Cold Feet
Cold Sweat
Color Me Dead
Colors▶
Commando Squad
Compromising Positions
Con Man
Concrete Beat
Confessions of a Hit Man
Confessions of Tom Harris
Confidentially Yours▶
The Connection
Contraband
Convicts at Large
Cop
The Cop & the Girl
Cop in Blue Jeans
Cotton Comes to Harlem▶
Couples and Robbers
The Courier
Covert Action
Crazy Mama
Crime Story: The Complete Saga
Crimes & Misdemeanors▶
Crimewave
Criminal Hearts
Criminal Law
Criss Cross▶
Crocodile Dundee 2
The Crow
The Crow 2: City of Angels▶
Cruisin' High
Cry, the Beloved Country▶
The Cursed Mountain Mystery
Daddy's Boys
Dagger Eyes
Dance Fools Dance▶
Dance or Die
Dance with Me, Henry
Dancing in the Dark
Danger Zone
The Dangerous
Dangerous Heart
Dangerous Mission
Dangerous Orphans
Dangerous Passion
Dangerous Pursuit
Dark Passage
Dark Side of Midnight
Darktown Strutters
Day of Atonement
Day of the Assassin
Dayton's Devils
Dead Bang
Dead Center
Dead Heat
Dead Heat on a Merry-Go-Round▶
Dead Man
Dead Man Walking▶
Dead Men Don't Wear Plaid
Dead Pigeon on Beethoven Street
The Dead Pool
Dead Presidents
Dead Wrong
Deadline Assault
Deadly Darling
Deadly Hero▶
Deadly Illusion
Deadly Revenge
Deadly Strangers
Deadly Sunday
Deadly Thief
Death of a Scoundrel
Death Ring
Death Wish 4: The Crackdown
Deathfight
The Defender
The Demolitionist
Desire▶
Desperate Hours▶
Desperate Hours
The Destructors
The Detective▶
Detective Sadie & Son
Detective School Dropouts
Detour to Danger
Detroit 9000
Devil & Leroy Basset
The Devil at 4 O'Clock
Devil Doll▶
Devil In a Blue Dress▶
The Devil's Brother

Crime

The Devil's Commandment
The Devil's Sleep
The Devlin Connection
Diamonds
Diamonds on Wheels
Dick Tracy
Dick Tracy▶
Dick Tracy, Detective
Dick Tracy, Detective/The Corpse Vanishes
Dick Tracy Returns
Dick Tracy: The Original Serial, Vol. 1▶
Dick Tracy: The Original Serial, Vol. 2▶
Dick Tracy vs. Crime Inc.
Dick Tracy vs. Cueball
Dick Tracy's Dilemma
Dillinger▶
Dillinger
Dirty Hands
Dirty Mary Crazy Larry▶
Dirty Work
The Disciple
Disorganized Crime
Disturbance
Diva▶
The Doberman Gang
The Doctor and the Devils
Dr. Death, Seeker of Souls
Dr. Mabuse, Parts 1 & 2▶
Dr. Mabuse vs. Scotland Yard
Dog Day
Dog Day Afternoon▶
The Doll Squad
Don Amigo/Stage to Chino
The Don is Dead
Doomed to Die
Door to Door Maniac
Double Identity
Double Indemnity▶
Down & Dirty▶
Down Twisted
Downtown
Dream No Evil
The Dream Team
Drive-In Massacre
The Driver
Dumb Waiter
East Side Kids
Echo Murders
8 Million Ways to Die
El Muerto
The Element of Crime
11 Harrowhouse▶
Emil and the Detectives
Emperor Jones/Paul Robeson: Tribute to an Artist
Emperor of the Bronx
Endangered Species
Endplay
The Enforcer
Enforcer from Death Row
The Equalizer: Memories of Manon
Escapade in Florence
Eternal Evil
Every Girl Should Have One
Everybody Wins
Evil Judgement
The Executioner
The Executioner, Part 2: Frozen Scream
Experiment in Terror▶
Experiment Perilous▶
Exquisite Corpses
Extreme Prejudice
An Eye for an Eye
Eye Witness
Eyeball
Eyewitness
The Face at the Window
The Falcon in Hollywood
Fall Time
Family Enforcer
A Family Matter
Family Plot
The Fantasist
Fantastic Seven
Fargo▶
Fast Getaway
Fast Talking
Fatal Beauty
The Fatal Hour
Fatal Vision
FBI Girl
The FBI Story▶
Fear
Fear in the Night▶
Federal Hill
Female Trouble
Fever
Fiction Makers
52 Pick-Up
Fight for Your Life
Fighting Back
Final Appeal
Final Judgement
Final Justice
Final Mission
The Finger Man
Fingers▶
The Fire in the Stone
The First Deadly Sin
First Name: Carmen▶
The First Power
A Fish Called Wanda▶
F.I.S.T.
Fists of Blood
Fit to Kill
Flame of the Islands
A Flash of Green
Flesh and Bone▶
Flight to Nowhere
Flipper's New Adventure▶
Flying Wild
Fog Island
Follow the Leader
Force of Evil▶
Fort Apache, the Bronx▶
Fortune Dane
48 Hrs.▶
Four Rooms
Foxy Brown
Frantic▶
Freebie & the Bean
French Connection 2▶
French Quarter Undercover
Frenzy▶
Fresh Kill
Friday Foster
From Dusk Till Dawn
Fun with Dick and Jane
Future Force
The Galloping Ghost
Game of Seduction
Gang Bullets
Gangs, Inc.
Gangster Wars
Gangway
Gator
The Gauntlet
The Gazebo▶
Genuine Risk
Get Shorty▶
Getting Even
Getting In
Ginger
Girl from Chicago
The Girl in Lover's Lane
Girl in the Cadillac
The Girl Said No
The Girl Who Had Everything
The Glass Key▶
Glitz
The Glove
God Told Me To
The Godfather▶
The Godfather 1902-1959: The Complete Epic▶
The Godfather, Part 2▶
Godson▶
The Golden Triangle
Gone in 60 Seconds
Gone to Ground
The Goonies
Gordon's War
Great Flamarion
The Great Lover
The Great Riviera Bank Robbery
The Great St. Louis Bank Robbery
The Great Texas Dynamite Chase
The Greed of William Hart
Green Ice
The Grey Fox▶
The Grifters▶
Grisbi
The Guardian
Guilty as Charged
A Gun in the House
Gunmen
The Gunrunner
Hallucination
Hand Gun
Happy New Year▶
The Hard Way▶
The Harder They Come
The Haunted Strangler
Having Wonderful Crime
He Walked by Night▶
Heartbeat
Heat▶
Heaven's Prisoners
Held for Murder
Hell Harbor
Hello Trouble
Henry: Portrait of a Serial Killer▶
Hide-Out
High & Low▶
High Crime
Hit Lady
The Hit List
Hollywood Vice Sqaud
Homicide▶
Honeymoon Killers▶
Honor Among Thieves
The Hooded Terror
The Hostage Tower
Hot Blood
Hot Child in the City
Hot Millions▶
Hot Pursuit
The Hot Rock▶
The Hot Spot
A House In The Hills
House of Errors
House of Mystery
How Come Nobody's On Our Side?
How to Beat the High Cost of Living
How to Kill 400 Duponts
Hudson Hawk
Hue and Cry▶
The Human Factor
The Hunt for the Night Stalker
Hunt the Man Down
The Hunted
The Hunter
Husbands, Wives, Money, and Murder
I Can't Escape
I Hate Blondes
I, Mobster
I Wake Up Screaming▶
I'd Give My Life
I'll Get You
Image of Death
The Immortals
In a Stranger's Hand
In Cold Blood▶
In Deadly Heat
In the Heat of the Night▶
In the King of Prussia
The Incident
An Innocent Man
Instant Justice
Interrupted Journey
The Invincible Six
The Invisible Man Returns▶
The Ipcress File▶
Istanbul
Jack the Ripper
Jack the Ripper▶
Jail Bait
Jamaica Inn
Jesse James▶
Jigsaw▶
Johnnie Gibson F.B.I.
Johnny Dangerously
Joyride
Kansas
Kansas City Confidential▶
Kelly of the Secret Service
The Kennel Murder Case
Kickboxer the Champion
Kid and the Killers
Kidnap Syndicate
The Killers
Killing Zoe
King Creole
King of New York▶
Kiss of Death
Knock on Any Door
L.A. Bounty
L.A. Crackdown
L.A. Crackdown 2
La Salamandre
La Scorta▶
Lady from Nowhere
Lady Ice
Lady in Red
Lady Scarface/The Threat
Lady Street Fighter
The Lady Vanishes
The Ladykillers▶
Laguna Heat
Las Vegas Serial Killer
Last Dance
Last House on the Left
The Last Ride
The Last Riders
The Last Word
Laughing at Danger
The Lavender Hill Mob▶
Law of the Underworld
Laws of Gravity▶
Le Jour Se Leve▶
Left for Dead
The Leopard Woman
Let 'Em Have It
Let Him Have It▶
Lethal Weapon▶
Lethal Weapon 2▶
Lethal Weapon 3
The Letter▶
Little Murders▶
Little Odessa
Little White Lies
Lock Up
The Lone Rider in Ghost Town
Lone Star▶
Loot...Give Me Money, Honey!
Love, Cheat & Steal
Love from a Stranger
Ma Barker's Killer Brood
Macao▶
Mad Dog
Mademoiselle Striptease
Magnificent Obsession
Malarek
Mama's Dirty Girls
Man on the Run
The Man Outside
The Manhandlers
Mania
Maniac
Mankillers
Marathon Man▶
Marked Woman▶
The Meteor Man
Miami Supercops
Miami Vice
Miami Vice 2: The Prodigal Son
Midnight Edition
Midnight Run▶
Midnight Tease
Miles from Home
Miller's Crossing▶
Mississippi Burning▶
Mr. Reeder in Room 13
Mitchell
Mixed Blood
Mob War
Mona Lisa▶
Monsieur Verdoux▶
Moon in the Gutter
Moonraker
Moonshine Mountain
More! Police Squad
Morning Glory
Motorcycle Squad
Murder at the Vanities
Murder by Phone
Mute Witness
Nadine
The Naked Gun: From the Files of Police Squad▶
Nashville Beat
National Lampoon's Class Reunion
Native Son
The Natural History of Parking Lots
Nature of the Beast
'Neath Brooklyn Bridge
Ned Kelly
The Neon Empire
Neutron vs. the Maniac
Never a Dull Moment
Never Love a Stranger
The New Centurions
New Jack City
New Jersey Drive
New Year's Evil
New York Cop
Newman's Law
Night and the City▶
Night Birds
Night Children
A Night for Crime
Night Game
The Night Patrol
Night Screams
Night Shadow
Night Time in Nevada
Nixon▶
No Deposit, No Return
No Trace
The North Avenue Irregulars
No. 17▶
Nuns on the Run
Oddball Hall
O.H.M.S.
Oliver!▶
Oliver & Company
Oliver Twist
Oliver Twist▶
On the Edge
One Man Force
One Shoe Makes It Murder
Open Secret
The Opponent
Ossessione▶
Out of Annie's Past
Out of Bounds
Out of the Darkness▶
The Outside Man
Outside the Law
Over Indulgence
Pepe Le Moko▶
A Perfect Little Murder
Perfect Strangers
A Perfect World
Petrified Forest▶
Physical Evidence
Pierrot le Fou▶
Pigs
Pink Strings and Sealing Wax
Pixote▶
Platypus Cove
Point of Impact
Police Squad! Help Wanted!
The Poppy Is Also a Flower
Port of New York
Portrait in Terror
Postal Inspector
The Postman Always Rings Twice▶
The Postman Always Rings Twice
Prayer for the Dying
Pretty Poison▶
Prime Cut
Prime Suspect: Inner Circles
The Private Files of J. Edgar Hoover
Probe
Psycho▶
Public Enemy▶
The Quest
A Question of Guilt
Quicksand
The Racket▶
Rafferty & the Gold Dust Twins
Raiders of Ghost City
Raising Arizona▶
Rashomon▶

Crime Sprees

see also Fugitives; Lovers on the Lam

Crimes of Passion

Crop Dusters

see also America's Heartland

Cult Items

see also Cult Items—New

Eating Raoul▶
Ed Wood▶
The Ed Wood Story: The Plan 9 Companion
Eraserhead▶
Evil Dead
Faster Pussycat! Kill! Kill!
The Fearless Vampire Killers▶
The Female Jungle
Female Trouble
The First Nudie Musical
Five Easy Pieces▶
Flesh Gordon 2: Flesh Gordon Meets the Cosmic Cheerleaders
The Fly▶
Frankenstein Unbound▶
Freaks▶
Fritz the Cat▶
Geek Maggot Bingo
Glen or Glenda: Confessions of Ed Wood
God Told Me To
The Gods Must Be Crazy▶
Greetings▶
A Hard Day's Night▶
Harold and Maude▶
Heavy Metal▶
Hercules Against the Moon Men
High School Confidential
Highlander▶
Honeymoon Killers▶
The Horror Chamber of Dr. Faustus▶
The Hospital▶
House of Wax▶
The Hunger
I Married a Monster from Outer Space
I Walked with a Zombie▶
I Was a Teenage Werewolf
The Incredible Two-Headed Transplant
Incredibly Strange Creatures Who Stopped Living and Became Mixed-Up Zombies
Invasion of the Body Snatchers▶
It Conquered the World
It Takes a Thief
It's A Gift▶
Jackson County Jail
Jesse James Meets Frankenstein's Daughter
Johnny Guitar▶
Kamikaze Hearts
The King of Hearts▶
Kiss Me Deadly▶
Koyaanisqatsi▶
La Cage aux Folles▶
La Cage aux Folles 2
La Cage aux Folles 3: The Wedding
Last Tango in Paris▶
Leningrad Cowboys Go America
Liquid Sky▶
Little Shop of Horrors▶
The Lost Stooges
Loveless
The Loves of Hercules
Mad Max▶
The Man Who Fell to Earth▶
Manos, the Hands of Fate
The Manster
Married Too Young
Mars Needs Women
Martin▶
Mill of the Stone Women
Ms. 45▶
Missile to the Moon
Mom & Dad
Mommie Dearest
Mondo Trasho
Monsieur Verdoux▶
Monty Python and the Holy Grail▶
Monty Python's Life of Brian▶
Motel Hell
Motor Psycho
Multiple Maniacs
The Mummy▶
The Muppet Movie▶
My Darling Clementine▶
Naked Kiss
Nasty Rabbit
Never Give a Sucker an Even Break▶
The Night of the Hunter▶
Night of the Living Dead▶
Oh Dad, Poor Dad (Momma's Hung You in the Closet & I'm Feeling So Sad)
Orgy of the Dead
Out of the Past▶
The Outlaw
Peeping Tom▶
Performance▶
Petulia▶
Phantasm
Phantom of the Paradise
Pink Flamingos
Plan 9 from Outer Space
Please Don't Eat My Mother
The Plot Against Harry▶
Private Parts
The Producers▶
The Projectionist▶
Psycho▶
Quadrophenia▶
Queen of Outer Space
The Rain People▶
Rancho Deluxe▶
Re-Animator▶
Rebel Without a Cause▶
Reefer Madness
Repo Man▶
Return of the Killer Tomatoes!
Ride the High Country▶
The Road Warrior▶
Roadkill
Robot Monster
Rock 'n' Roll High School▶
The Rocky Horror Picture Show▶
Satan's Sadists
Schlock
Sebastiane▶
The Secret Cinema
Sid & Nancy▶
The Slumber Party Massacre
Sorority Babes in the Slimeball Bowl-A-Rama
Spider Baby
Start the Revolution Without Me▶
Stoogemania
Strange Cargo
Surf Nazis Must Die
Sweet Movie
Tales from the Gimli Hospital
The Tall T
10th Victim▶
Them!▶
There's Nothing Out There
The Thing▶
Thunder Road▶
The Toxic Avenger
The Toxic Avenger, Part 2
Trash
Twin Peaks
Twin Peaks: Fire Walk with Me
Twister
2000 Maniacs
2001: A Space Odyssey▶
The Undertaker and His Pals
Vanishing Point
Vortex
Wanderers▶
The Warriors
The Wasp Woman
What Have I Done to Deserve This?▶
Where the Boys Are
Where's Poppa?▶
White Heat▶
Wild Rapture
Wild Women of Wongo
The Wild World of Batwoman
Willy Wonka & the Chocolate Factory▶
Zachariah
Zardoz
Zontar, the Thing from Venus

Cult Items—New

see also Cult Items

The Adventures of Baron Munchausen▶
Airplane!▶
Better Off Dead
Bill & Ted's Excellent Adventure
The Blues Brothers
The Brady Bunch Movie▶
The Breakfast Club▶
Caddyshack▶
Fast Times at Ridgemont High▶
Ferris Bueller's Day Off▶
A Fish Called Wanda▶
Grease▶
Heathers▶
Joe's Apartment
Mystery Science Theater 3000: The Movie
National Lampoon's Animal House▶
Pretty in Pink
St. Elmo's Fire
Saturday Night Fever
Sixteen Candles▶
The Sure Thing▶
This Is Spinal Tap▶
A Very Brady Sequel
Wayne's World▶

Cults

see also Occult; Satanism

Bad Dreams
The Believers
Beware! Children at Play
Blinded by the Light
Blood Clan
Bloodbath
Burial of the Rats
Children of the Corn 2: The Final Sacrifice
Cobra Woman
Cult of the Cobra
The Dark Secret of Harvest Home
Deadly Blessing
Death of an Angel
The Deceivers
Fatal Passion
Force: Five
Forever Evil
The Guyana Tragedy: The Story of Jim Jones
Helter Skelter
The House on Todville Road
In the Line of Duty: Ambush in Waco
The Lash of the Penitents
The Lightning Incident
Lord of Illusions
The Mephisto Waltz▶
Mind, Body & Soul
Next One
The Night God Screamed
Night of the Death Cult
Putney Swope▶
The Pyx▶
Raging Angels
The Reincarnate
Rest In Pieces
Revenge
Sabaka
Safe▶
Servants of Twilight
Shock 'Em Dead
Shocking Asia
The Snake Hunter Strangler
The Snake People
The Spellbinder
Split Image▶
Steps from Hell
Suicide Cult
Thou Shalt Not Kill...Except
Ticket to Heaven▶
Treasure of the Four Crowns
Withnail and I▶

Cyberpunk

Arcade
Blade Runner▶
The Crow
The Crow 2: City of Angels▶
Cyborg
Cyborg 2
Cyborg Cop
Cyborg Soldier
Demolition Man
Escape from L.A.
Escape from New York
Freejack
Hackers
Johnny Mnemonic
The Lawnmower Man
Lawnmower Man 2: Beyond Cyberspace
Mad Max▶
Mad Max: Beyond Thunderdome
Megaville
Nemesis
Overdrawn at the Memory Bank
The Road Warrior▶
RoboCop▶
RoboCop 2
RoboCop 3
Tank Girl
TekWar
The Terminator▶
Terminator 2: Judgment Day▶
Tetsuo: The Iron Man
Total Recall▶
Tron
Universal Soldier
Virtual Combat
Virtuosity

Dads

see also Bad Dads; Moms; Monster Moms; Parenthood

The Brady Bunch Movie▶
Eat Drink Man Woman▶
Father of the Bride▶
The Favorite Son▶
Getting Even with Dad
Ghost Dad
A Goofy Movie
Imaginary Crimes▶
Indiana Jones and the Last Crusade▶
Life with Father▶
Lone Star▶
Magic in the Water
Memories of Me
Mr. Mom▶
Mom and Dad Save the World
My Father Is Coming
My Father the Hero
National Lampoon's Christmas Vacation
National Lampoon's European Vacation
National Lampoon's Vacation▶
Nick of Time
Parenthood▶
Raising Arizona▶
The Run of the Country▶
Sleepless in Seattle▶
So I Married an Axe Murderer
The Sum of Us▶
Superdad
Three Men and a Baby▶
Three Men and a Cradle▶
Three Men and a Little Lady
A Very Brady Sequel
Wait Till Your Mother Gets Home

Dance Fever

see also Ballet; Disco Musicals

All That Jazz▶
An American in Paris▶
Anchors Aweigh▶
April In Paris
Babes in Arms
The Bacchantes
The Band Wagon▶
The Barefoot Contessa▶
The Barkleys of Broadway▶
Beat Street
The Belle of New York
Bert Rigby, You're a Fool
The Best of the Kenny Everett Video Show
Billy Rose's Jumbo▶
Black Orpheus▶
Blood Wedding▶
Body Moves
Body Rock
Born to Dance
Breakin'
Breakin' 2: Electric Boogaloo
Breakin' Through
Broadway Melody of 1940
Cabin in the Sky▶
Can-Can
Captain January
Carefree▶
Carmen▶
Charleston▶
A Chorus Line
Chu Chu & the Philly Flash
Cover Girl▶
Daddy Long Legs▶
Dames▶
Dance, Girl, Dance
Dance or Die
Dancing Lady
Danzon▶
Deadly Dancer
Delightfully Dangerous
Delivery Boys
Dirty Dancing▶
The Discovery Program
Doll Face
The Eighties
El Amor Brujo▶
Everybody's Dancin'
Faith
Fame▶
Fass Black
Fast Forward
Faster Pussycat! Kill! Kill!
Femmes de Paris
Flashdance
Flower Drum Song
Flying Down to Rio
Follies Girl
Follow the Fleet▶
Footlight Parade▶
Footloose
The Forbidden Dance
42nd Street▶
French Can-Can▶
The Gay Divorcee▶
Ginger & Fred▶
Girl in Gold Boots
Girls Just Want to Have Fun
Give a Girl a Break
The Glass Slipper
Gold Diggers of 1933▶
Gold Diggers of 1935▶
Gotta Dance, Gotta Sing
Grease▶
Grease 2
The Harvey Girls▶
Heavenly Bodies
Hit the Deck
Holiday in Havana
Idiot's Delight▶
The In Crowd
Invitation to the Dance
Isadora▶
It Started in Naples▶
Kiss Me Kate▶
Lambada
Last Dance
Le Bal▶
Legs
Les Girls
Let's Dance
Liquid Dreams
Little Ballerina
Mad Youth
Mantis in Lace
Meet Me in Las Vegas
Midnight Dancer
Minsky's Follies
Music in My Heart
Neurotic Cabaret
No Time for Romance
Nutcracker: The Motion Picture

Dates From Hell

***see also** Singles*

Deafness

***see also** Physical Problems*

Death & the Afterlife

***see also** Angels; Funerals; Ghosts, Ghouls, & Goblins; Great Death Scenes; Heaven Sent; Occult; Suicide*

Death Row

***see also** Men in Prison; Women in Prison*

Dedicated Teachers

***see also** Hell High School; School Daze*

Conrack▶
The Corn is Green▶
Dangerous Minds
Dead Poets Society▶
Educating Rita▶
Forever Mary▶
Goodbye, Mr. Chips▶
Goodbye, Mr. Chips
High School High
Homework
If Lucy Fell
Johnny Tiger
Kindergarten Cop
Lean on Me▶
Lovey: A Circle of Children 2
Madame Sousatzka▶
Matilda
The Miracle Worker▶
Mr. Holland's Opus▶
The Next Karate Kid
Night Visitor
The Paper Chase▶
Passion for Life
Powder
The Prime of Miss Jean Brodie▶
The Principal
Race the Sun
Renaissance Man
Stand and Deliver▶
The Substitute
Summer School
Sunset Park
Teachers
To Sir, with Love
Up the Down Staircase▶

Deep Blue

***see also** Go Fish; Sail Away; Shipwrecked; Submarines*

The Abyss▶
Andre
Assault on a Queen
Baywatch the Movie: Forbidden Paradise
Crimson Tide▶
ffolkes
Flipper▶
1492: Conquest of Paradise
Free Willy
Free Willy 2: The Adventure Home
Lords of the Deep
Mission of the Shark▶
Namu, the Killer Whale
Pirates
Shipwrecked
The Silent Enemy
Splash
The Spy Who Loved Me
Waterworld
Whale of a Tale
Wind

Demons & Wizards

***see also** Occult*

The Alchemist
Archer: The Fugitive from the Empire
Army of Darkness▶
Beyond Darkness
Bloodlust: Subspecies 3
Bloodstone: Subspecies 2
Blue Blood
Born of Fire
The Church▶
Conan the Barbarian▶
Conan the Destroyer
Cthulhu Mansion
Curse 4: The Ultimate Sacrifice
Deathstalker
Deathstalker 3
Deathstalker 4: Match of Titans
Demon Rage
Demon Wind
Demon Witch Child
Demonoid, Messenger of Death
The Demons
Demons
Demons of Ludlow
Demonstone
Demonwarp
The Devil
The Devil's Web
El Barbaro
Ernest Scared Stupid
Evil Dead
Evil Dead 2: Dead by Dawn
Evil Toons
Excalibur▶
Fire and Ice
Gate 2
Ghosts That Still Walk
The Giants of Thessaly
Gor
Hellraiser
Hellraiser 4: Bloodline
The Heroic Trio
The Hobbit▶
Jack-O
Krull
Ladyhawke
The Legacy
The Mephisto Waltz▶
Mirror, Mirror
Natas...The Reflection
Outlaw of Gor
Pumpkinhead
Pumpkinhead 2: Blood Wings
Quest for the Mighty Sword
The Raven▶
Rawhead Rex
Red Sonja
The Return of the King
Rock & Rule
Seizure
Silent Night, Deadly Night 4: Initiation
Sinthia: The Devil's Doll
Sorceress
Spellcaster
Stay Awake
Supergirl
Sword & the Sorcerer
The Sword in the Stone▶
Tales from the Crypt Presents Demon Knight
Terror Eyes
Trancers 4: Jack of Swords
Troll
Troll 2
The Unholy
The Unnamable 2: The Statement of Randolph Carter
Urotsukidoj 1: Legend of the Overfiend
Urotsukidoj 2: Legend of the Demon Womb
Warlock
Warlock: The Armageddon
Willow
Witchcraft 5: Dance with the Devil
The Witchmaker
Wizards of the Lost Kingdom
Wizards of the Lost Kingdom 2

Dental Mayhem

***see also** Doctors & Nurses; Evil Doctors*

Brazil▶
Captives
Chasing Those Depression Blues
Compromising Positions
The Dentist▶
Don't Raise the Bridge, Lower the River
Eversmile New Jersey
Houseguest
The In-Laws▶
Little Shop of Horrors▶
Marathon Man▶
The Paleface▶
Reuben, Reuben▶
Serial Mom▶
The Shakiest Gun in the West
Strawberry Blonde▶
12 Monkeys▶
W.C. Fields: Flask of Fields

Desert War/Foreign Legion

***see also** Deserts; Persian Gulf War*

Abbott and Costello in the Foreign Legion
Beau Geste▶
Delta Force 3: The Killing Game
The Flying Deuces▶
Follow That Camel
Gallipoli▶
Gunga Din▶
The Last Remake of Beau Geste
Man of Legend
March or Die
Morocco▶
Outpost in Morocco
Sahara▶

Deserts

***see also** Desert War/ Foreign Legion*

The Adventures of Priscilla, Queen of the Desert▶
Baja
Broken Arrow
The Desert Fox▶
Desert Gold
Desert Hearts▶
The Desert Rats▶
The Desert Song
Dune
Dune Warriors
Faster Pussycat! Kill! Kill!
Fatal Attraction▶
In the Army Now
Indiana Jones and the Last Crusade▶
Ishtar
The Jewel of the Nile
Lawrence of Arabia▶
Mad Max▶
Mad Max: Beyond Thunderdome
Morocco▶
New Eden
The Passenger▶
Patriot Games▶
The Road to Morocco▶
The Road Warrior▶
Sahara▶
Sahara
Sea of Sand
The Sheik▶
The Sheltering Sky▶
Son of the Sheik▶
Star Wars▶
Stargate
Tremors
Tremors 2: Aftershocks
White Sands
The Wind and the Lion▶

Detective Spoofs

***see also** Detectives*

Ace Ventura: Pet Detective
Ace Ventura: When Nature Calls
The Adventures of Sherlock Holmes' Smarter Brother▶
Blondes Have More Guns
Clean Slate
Clue
Cry Uncle
Curse of the Pink Panther
Dead Men Don't Wear Plaid
Dragnet
Fatal Instinct
Gumshoe
Hollywood Harry
The Hound of the Baskervilles
The Man with Bogart's Face
More! Police Squad
Murder by Death
The Naked Gun: From the Files of Police Squad▶
Naked Gun 33 1/3: The Final Insult
Naked Gun 2 1/2: The Smell of Fear
Night Patrol
Oh, Heavenly Dog!
One Body Too Many
The Pink Panther▶
The Pink Panther Strikes Again▶
Police Squad! Help Wanted!
Rentadick
Return of the Pink Panther
Revenge of the Pink Panther
Secret Agent 00-Soul
A Shot in the Dark▶
The Strange Case of the End of Civilization as We Know It
Trail of the Pink Panther

Detectives

***see also** Cops; Detective Spoofs; Feds*

Abbott and Costello Meet the Invisible Man▶
Abduction of St. Anne
Above the Law
Accomplice
Ace Crawford, Private Eye
Ace Ventura: Pet Detective
Ace Ventura: When Nature Calls
Adventures of a Private Eye
The Adventures of Sherlock Holmes
The Adventures of Sherlock Holmes: Hound of the Baskervilles
The Adventures of Sherlock Holmes' Smarter Brother▶
The Affair of the Pink Pearl
After the Thin Man▶
All-American Murder
The Alphabet Murders
Alphaville▶
Angel City
Angel Heart
Another Stakeout
Appointment with Death
Are You Lonesome Tonight
Arrest Bulldog Drummond
The Art of Crime
Assault of the Party Nerds 2: Heavy Petting Detective
Backstreet Justice
Bad Company
The Barbary Coast
Bare Hunt
Behind Locked Doors
Below the Deadline
Beretta's Island
The Big Sleep▶
The Big Sleep
Big Store
Black Bird
Blackmail▶
Blackout
Blade in Hong Kong
Bloody Avenger
The Blue Lightning
The Body in the Library
Bootleg
Bulldog Drummond
Bulldog Drummond Comes Back
Bulldog Drummond Escapes
Bulldog Drummond in Africa/ Arrest Bulldog Drummond
Bulldog Drummond's Bride
Bulldog Drummond's Peril
Bulldog Drummond's Revenge
Bulldog Drummond's Secret Police
Bulldog Jack▶
Bullitt▶
Calling Paul Temple
Carry On Dick
Carry On Screaming
Case of the Baby Sitter
The Case of the Lucky Legs
The Case of the Missing Lady
Cast a Deadly Spell▶
Castle in the Desert
Cat and Mouse▶
Cave of the Living Dead
Charlie Chan and the Curse of the Dragon Queen
Charlie Chan at the Opera▶
Charlie Chan at the Wax Museum
The Charlie Chan Collection
Charlie Chan in Paris
Charlie Chan in Rio
Charlie Chan in the Secret Service
Charlie Chan's Secret
The Cheap Detective▶
Chinatown▶
The Chinese Cat
Clean Slate
The Clergyman's Daughter
Columbo: Murder By the Book
Columbo: Prescription Murder
Conspiracy of Terror
The Crackler
Criminals Within
The Crooked Circle
The Crucifer of Blood
Cry Uncle
Curse of the Pink Panther
The Dain Curse
Dancing with Danger
Dark Corner▶
The Dark Hour
Dark Side of Midnight
Dead Again▶
Dead Connection
Dead Men Don't Wear Plaid
Dead Pigeon on Beethoven Street
Deadly Force
Deadly Illusion
Deadly Passion
Deadly Sins
Death from a Distance
Death on the Nile
Death Train
Deathmask
The Detective▶
Detective Sadie & Son
Detective School Dropouts
Detective Story▶
Devil In a Blue Dress▶
The Devil's Cargo
The Devlin Connection
Dick Barton, Special Agent
Dick Barton Strikes Back
Dick Tracy▶
Dick Tracy, Detective
Dick Tracy, Detective/The Corpse Vanishes
Dick Tracy Double Feature #1
Dick Tracy Double Feature #2
Dick Tracy Meets Gruesome
Dick Tracy Returns
Dick Tracy: The Original Serial, Vol. 1▶
Dick Tracy: The Original Serial, Vol. 2▶
Dick Tracy: The Spider Strikes
Dick Tracy vs. Crime Inc.
Dick Tracy vs. Cueball
Dick Tracy's Dilemma
Dirkham Detective Agency
Dragnet
Dressed to Kill
The Drowning Pool
Edge of Darkness
The Element of Crime
Emil and the Detectives
The Empty Beach
Endangered Species
The Enforcer
Entangled
Everybody Wins
Evil under the Sun
Ex-Mrs. Bradford▶
The Falcon in Hollywood
The Falcon in Mexico
The Falcon Takes Over/Strange Bargain
The Falcon's Adventure/ Armored Car Robbery
The Falcon's Brother
Falling Down
False Witness
Farewell, My Lovely▶
Fearless
Fiction Makers

Devils

Dinosaurs

see also *Killer Beasts*

Disaster Flicks

see also *Action Adventure; Air Disasters; Meltdown; Sea Disasters*

The Lost Missile
Meteor
A Night to Remember▶
Planet on the Prowl
The Poseidon Adventure
The Rains Came
Raise the Titanic
Red Alert
St. Helen's, Killer Volcano
Snowblind
S.O.S. Titanic
Space: 1999—Alien Attack▶
The Survivalist
Survivor
Tailspin: Behind the Korean Airline Tragedy
Terror on the 40th Floor
Tidal Wave
The Towering Inferno
Tragedy of Flight 103: The Inside Story▶
Two Minute Warning
When Time Ran Out
White Squall

Disco Musicals

see also ***Musicals***

Can't Stop the Music
Car Wash
KISS Meets the Phantom of the Park
Pirate Movie
The Rocky Horror Picture Show▶
Saturday Night Fever
Thank God It's Friday
The Wiz
Xanadu

Disease of the Week

see also ***AIDS; Emerging Viruses***

The Affair▶
The Ann Jillian Story
Bang the Drum Slowly
Beaches▶
The Best Little Girl in the World▶
Between Two Women
Bobby Deerfield
The Boy in the Plastic Bubble
Brian's Song▶
Camille▶
The Carrier
The Cassandra Crossing
Champions
Checking Out
C.H.U.D.
Cleo from 5 to 7▶
Cries and Whispers▶
Crystal Heart
The Curse
Damien: The Leper Priest
Daybreak
Dead Man Walking
Dead Space
Dick Barton, Special Agent
The Doctor
A Dream of Kings▶
Duet for One
Dying Young
An Early Frost▶
East of Kilimanjaro
The End▶
Eric▶
The First Deadly Sin
Fourth Wish
Gaby: A True Story▶
Germicide
Glory Enough for All: The Discovery of Insulin
Griffin and Phoenix: A Love Story
Incredible Melting Man
Interrupted Melody▶
Intimate Contact▶
Isle of the Dead
Jericho Fever
Killer on Board
L.A. Bad
The Last Best Year
The Last Man on Earth
Lightning Over Water
Lorenzo's Oil▶
Love Affair: The Eleanor & Lou Gehrig Story▶
Love Story▶
Mad Death
A Matter of WHO
Miles to Go
A Mother's Prayer
My Father's House
My Life
Nasty Rabbit
On Her Majesty's Secret Service▶
Panic in Echo Park
Parting Glances▶
Philadelphia▶
Pilgrim, Farewell
The Plague
The Plague Dogs
The Pride of the Yankees▶
Princes in Exile
Project: Alien
Promises in the Dark
The Proud Ones
Quarantine
Question of Faith
A Quiet Duel
Rabid
Reborn
Right of Way
The Road to Wellville
The Shadow Box▶
Shadowlands▶
A Shining Season▶
Silence Like Glass
The Silver Streak
Six Weeks
Stigma
Terms of Endearment▶
Terror Creatures from the Grave
A Time to Live
Walking Through the Fire
The Wedding Gift▶
When the Time Comes
When Wolves Cry
The White Legion
Xtro

Disorganized Crime

see also ***Crime & Criminals; Organized Crime***

Ace Crawford, Private Eye
Airheads
Amos and Andrew
The Apple Dumpling Gang
The Apple Dumpling Gang Rides Again
Armed and Dangerous
Baby on Board
Baby's Day Out
Bottle Rocket
Cop and a Half
Crackers
Dr. Otto & the Riddle of the Gloom Beam
Ernest Goes to Jail
Fargo▶
Finders Keepers
A Fine Mess
Get Shorty▶
Glitch!
The Gun in Betty Lou's Handbag
Happy New Year
Headless Body in Topless Bar
Her Alibi
Herbie Goes Bananas
Home Alone▶
Home Alone 2: Lost in New York
I Wonder Who's Killing Her Now?
Inside the Law
The Italian Job
The Jerky Boys
Killing Zoe
The League of Gentlemen▶
Leather Jackets
Lunch Wagon
Mad Dog and Glory▶
A Man, a Woman, and a Bank
Man of the House
Menage▶
Mexican Hayride
Milo Milo
Miss Grant Takes Richmond
Mixed Nuts
Mutant on the Bounty
The Night They Robbed Big Bertha's
Ocean's 11
Once Upon a Crime
Oscar
Out on a Limb
Pouvoir Intime
Quick Change
Ransom Money
Reservoir Dogs▶
Round Trip to Heaven
Ruthless People▶
St. Benny the Dip
See No Evil, Hear No Evil
Shake Hands with Murder
Silver Bears
Sister Act
Sitting Ducks▶
Stop! or My Mom Will Shoot
Stop That Cab
The Super
Super Soul Brother
Survivors
Tall, Tan and Terrific
The Thief Who Came to Dinner
Things to Do In Denver When You're Dead▶
Three Kinds of Heat
Thrilled to Death
Too Many Crooks
Trapped In Paradise
Two If by Sea
We're Talkin' Serious Money
The Wrong Arm of the Law▶
The Young in Heart▶

Divorce

see also ***Marriage; Singles***

The Accidental Tourist▶
All I Want for Christmas
Alpha Beta
The Awful Truth▶
Between Friends
A Bill of Divorcement
Breaking Up
Breaking Up Is Hard to Do
Bye Bye, Love
California Suite▶
Can She Bake a Cherry Pie?
Cheaper to Keep Her
Children of Divorce
Clara's Heart
Cold Heat
A Conspiracy of Love
Cross My Heart
Desert Hearts▶
Divorce American Style
Divorce His, Divorce Hers
Divorce—Italian Style▶
The Divorcee
Early Frost
Escapade▶
E.T.: The Extra-Terrestrial▶
Face the Music
Faces▶
Falling Down
Family Pictures▶
Father Figure
Fergie & Andrew: Behind Palace Doors
A Fight for Jenny
Found Alive
The Good Father▶
The Good Mother
Goodbye Love
Hard Promises
Heartburn▶
High Society▶
History is Made at Night▶
House Arrest
How to Break Up a Happy Divorce
How to Commit Marriage
Husbands and Wives▶
Interiors▶
Irreconcilable Differences
Kramer vs. Kramer▶
Let's Make It Legal
The Liberation of L.B. Jones
Love and Hate: A Marriage Made in Hell
Love Matters
Marie▶
Melanie
Misbehaving Husbands
The Misfits▶
Mrs. Doubtfire
Mr. Skeffington▶
Mr. Wonderful
Nadine
Naked Paradise
Necessary Parties
Never Say Goodbye
A New Life
Night Life in Reno
Nothing in Common
Now and Then
The Odd Couple▶
The Odd Job
One Cooks, the Other Doesn't
Patti Rocks▶
Peggy Sue Got Married
The Personals
Petulia▶
Pilgrim, Farewell
Play It Again, Sam▶
The Prize Pulitzer
Rich in Love
Rich Kids
Riptide▶
Scenes from a Marriage▶
Second Chance
See You in the Morning
Sex and the Single Parent
Shattered Silence
The Solitary Man
Starting Over▶
Strange Bedfellows
Sweet Revenge
Table for Five
Tattle Tale
Tell It to the Judge
Tell Me That You Love Me
Tenth Month
Till Murder Do Us Part
Twister
An Unmarried Woman▶
Valentino Returns
Wanted: The Perfect Guy
The War of the Roses▶
Without Anesthesia

Doctors & Nurses

see also ***AIDS; Dental Mayhem; Disease of the Week; Emerging Viruses; Evil Doctors; Hospitals & Medicine; Nursploitation!; Sanity Check; Shrinks***

All Creatures Great and Small▶
Alone in the Dark
And the Band Played On▶
The Android Affair
Arrowsmith
Ashanti, Land of No Mercy
The Asphyx▶
Autopsy
Awakenings▶
Baby Girl Scott
Bad Medicine
Battle Circus
Bethune
Between Wars
The Black Dragons
Black Friday
Blind Justice
Blonde Cobra/The Doctor's Dream
Blood Mania
Bloodlink
Body Parts
Botany Bay
The Bramble Bush
The Broken Mask
Calling Paul Temple
Candy Stripe Nurses
Carry On Doctor▶
Castle of the Creeping Flesh
Caught▶
Century
Children of Rage
China Beach▶
Circus of Horrors
The Citadel▶
City of Joy
The Clonus Horror
Club Havana
Coma▶
Corregidor
Corridors of Blood
Courageous Dr. Christian
Crimes & Misdemeanors▶
Crossover
Dead Ringers▶
Dead Sleep
Death Becomes Her▶
Death by Prescription
Death Nurse
The Devil's Web
Doc Hollywood
The Doctor
Dr. Alien
The Doctor and the Devils
Doctor at Large
Doctor at Sea
Dr. Bethune▶
Dr. Black, Mr. Hyde
Doctor Blood's Coffin
Doctor Butcher M.D.
Dr. Caligari
Dr. Christian Meets the Women
Dr. Cyclops
Dr. Death, Seeker of Souls
Doctor Detroit
Doctor Dolittle
Doctor Faustus
Dr. Frankenstein's Castle of Freaks
Dr. Hackenstein
Dr. Heckyl and Mr. Hype
Doctor in Distress
Doctor in the House▶
Dr. Jack/For Heaven's Sake
Dr. Jekyll and Mr. Hyde
Dr. Kildare's Strange Case
Dr. Mabuse, Parts 1 & 2▶
Dr. Mabuse vs. Scotland Yard
Dr. Petiot
Doctor Quinn, Medicine Woman
Doctor Satan's Robot
Doctor Takes a Wife▶
Dr. Tarr's Torture Dungeon
Dr. Terror's House of Horrors
Doctor Who
Doctor X
Doctors and Nurses
Doctors' Wives
Donor Unknown
Don't Cry, It's Only Thunder
Don't Look in the Basement
Drunken Angel▶
East of Borneo
The Egyptian
The Elephant Man▶
Emmanuelle in the Country
ER
False Faces
Fantastic Voyage▶
Flatliners
Flesh Feast
Foreign Body
The Fortune Cookie▶
Glory Enough for All: The Discovery of Insulin
The Great Moment
Gross Anatomy
Guest in the House
Hands Up▶
Healer
High Heels
Holy Terror
The Horrible Dr. Hichcock
The Horror Chamber of Dr. Faustus▶
Horror Hospital
The Hospital▶

Hospital of Terror
House Calls▶
I Love My...Wife
I Never Promised You a Rose Garden▶
The In-Laws▶
The Incredible Journey of Dr. Meg Laurel▶
An Indecent Obsession
Internes Can't Take Money
The Interns
Invasion
Jesse
Johnny Belinda▶
Johnny Belinda
Junior
Kidnapping of Baby John Doe
Korczak▶
The Last Angry Man▶
The Lazarus Syndrome
Le Cas du Dr. Laurent▶
Lie Down with Lions
Life Is a Long Quiet River▶
The Light in the Jungle
Love Is a Many-Splendored Thing
Mad Love▶
The Mad Monster
The Madness of King George▶
Make-Up
Malice
Mania
M*A*S*H▶
M*A*S*H: Goodbye, Farewell & Amen▶
M*A*S*H: The Collector's Edition
The Mask of Fu Manchu
A Matter of Life and Death
Meet Dr. Christian
Memories of Me
Men of Ireland
Metamorphosis: The Alien Factor
The Millionairess
Mr. North
Monty Python's The Meaning of Life▶
Murder in Texas▶
Murder Once Removed
Murder or Mercy
My Father's Nurse
Nell
Night Call Nurses
Night Monster
Night Nurse▶
Night Nurse
Nightbreaker▶
Nine Months
Nomads
Not as a Stranger
Nurse
Nurse Edith Cavell▶
Nurse on Call
Old Swimmin' Hole
One Flew Over the Cuckoo's Nest▶
The Ordeal of Dr. Mudd▶
Outbreak▶
Panic in Echo Park
Panic in the Streets▶
Paper Mask
People Will Talk▶
Persona▶
Petulia▶
A Place for Annie
The Plague
Praying Mantis
Private Duty Nurses
Promises in the Dark
Purple Hearts
A Quiet Duel
The Raven▶
Reckless Disregard
Red Beard▶
Restoration▶
Riot Squad
The Road to Wellville
Roommates
Sawbones
Say Goodbye, Maggie Cole
Scalpel
Sister Dora
Sister Kenny▶
Skeezer
Slaughter Hotel
Spraggue
State of Emergency
Stigma
Stitches
The Story of Dr. Wassell
The Student Nurses
The Surgeon
Teenage Frankenstein
Tender Loving Care
Torture Ship
Tundra
The Unbearable Lightness of Being▶
The Vicious Circle
Vital Signs
We are the Children
Welcome Stranger
White Dwarf
Women of Valor
Young Doctors in Love
The Young Nurses

Docudrama

see also Documentary

Above Us the Waves▶
Adam▶
After the Shock
Al Capone▶
All You Need Is Cash▶
The Amy Fisher Story
And the Band Played On▶
Babyfever
The Battle of Algiers▶
Blind Ambition
Bob Roberts▶
The Boston Strangler
Bound for Glory▶
Call Northside 777▶
Casualties of Love: The "Long Island Lolita" Story
Christian the Lion
Close to Home
Cocaine: One Man's Seduction
Conspiracy: The Trial of the Chicago Eight▶
Countdown
The Courtesans of Bombay▶
Cruel Sea▶
A Cry in the Dark▶
Edge of the World▶
The Flaming Teen-Age
Free, White, and 21
The General Line▶
Glen or Glenda: Confessions of Ed Wood
H
Henry: Portrait of a Serial Killer▶
Hiroshima▶
The History of White People in America
The History of White People in America: Vol. 2
Hostages▶
Immortal Battalion▶
In Cold Blood▶
Inside the Third Reich
Iron & Silk
James Dean
The Jayne Mansfield Story
JFK: Reckless Youth
Journey Through Rosebud
Kamikaze Hearts
Kids
King▶
The Last Polka▶
Lethal Lolita—Amy Fisher: My Story
The Lion Has Wings
Murder in Texas▶
The Naked City▶
Panther
Pickpocket▶
The Poppy Is Also a Flower
Prince of the City▶
Qui Etes Vous, Mr. Sorge?
Real Life▶
The Red Menace
The Rise of Louis XIV▶
Shaka Zulu▶
S.O.S. Titanic
Soviet Spy
Special Bulletin▶
The Spy Who Came in from the Cold▶
T-Men▶
Tailspin: Behind the Korean Airline Tragedy
Take the Money and Run▶
Teenage Devil Dolls
Ten Days That Shook the World▶
That's Adequate
The Thin Blue Line▶
32 Short Films about Glenn Gould▶
This Is Spinal Tap▶
Times of Harvey Milk
The Wild Aces
Women in Prison
Working Girls▶
Zelig▶

Documentary

see also Docudrama

Alive: 20 Years Later
American Fabulous
The American Gangster
Assassination of Trotsky
The Atomic Cafe▶
Baseball
Battle of China
The Battle of Russia
The Battle of San Pietro
Bob Dylan: Don't Look Back▶
Born to Boogie
A Brief History of Time▶
Brother's Keeper▶
Bruce Lee: Curse of the Dragon▶
Burden of Dreams
Campaign in Poland
Caravaggio▶
The Carnivores
The Celluloid Closet▶
A Century of Women
The Children of Theatre Street
Chuck Amuck: The Movie
Chuck Berry: Hail! Hail! Rock 'n' Roll▶
Ciao Federico! Fellini Directs Satyricon
The Civil War, Episode 1: The Cause—1861▶
The Civil War, Episode 2: A Very Bloody Affair—1862▶
The Civil War, Episode 3: Forever Free—1862▶
The Civil War, Episode 4: Simply Murder—1863▶
The Civil War, Episode 5: The Universe of Battle—1863▶
The Civil War, Episode 6: Valley of the Shadow of Death—1864▶
The Civil War, Episode 7: Most Hallowed Ground—1864▶
The Civil War, Episode 8: War is All Hell—1865▶
The Civil War, Episode 9: The Better Angels of Our Nature—1865▶
The Clowns▶
Come Back, Africa▶
Common Threads: Stories from the Quilt
Crumb▶
Dance Hall Racket
Dear America: Letters Home from Vietnam▶
December 7th: The Movie
Decline of Western Civilization 1▶
Decline of Western Civilization 2: The Metal Years
Derby▶
The Doors: Soft Parade, a Retrospective
Dracula: A Cinematic Scrapbook
Ebony Dreams
Ed Wood: Look Back in Angora
The Ed Wood Story: The Plan 9 Companion
Elvis in Hollywood▶
Emperor Jones/Paul Robeson: Tribute to an Artist
Encounter with the Unknown
The Endless Summer▶
The Endless Summer 2▶
Fallen Champ: The Untold Story of Mike Tyson▶
Fangoria's Weekend of Horrors
Flying Saucers Over Hollywood: The Plan 9 Companion
France/Tour/Detour/Deux/Enfants▶
Frank and Ollie▶
Frankenstein: A Cinematic Scrapbook
Germany in Autumn
Gotta Dance, Gotta Sing
Guilty of Treason
Hank Aaron: Chasing the Dream▶
Harlan County, U.S.A.
Hearts of Darkness: A Filmmaker's Apocalypse▶
Hell's Angels Forever
The Hellstrom Chronicle▶
Here's Looking at You, Warner Bros.▶
Hide and Seek
Hollywood Clowns
Hollywood Home Movies
Hollywood Scandals and Tragedies
Hollywood Uncensored
Hoop Dreams▶
The Horror of It All
Hugh Hefner: Once Upon a Time
Incident at Oglala: The Leonard Peltier Story▶
Indomitable Teddy Roosevelt
Irving Berlin's America
It Happened in the Park
It's All True
James Dean
James Dean Story
James Stewart: A Wonderful Life
The JFK Conspiracy
JFK Remembered
The Kennedys Don't Cry
Kidco
Kino Pravda/Enthusiasm
The Lash of the Penitents
The Last Waltz
LBJ: A Biography
Le Joli Mai
The Legend of Valentino
Let It Be
Let's Get Lost
Lightning Over Water
Long Shadows
Louisiana Story▶
The Love Goddesses
Love Meetings
Love Without Fear
Malcolm X: Make It Plain
Man in the Silk Hat▶
Man of Aran▶
The Man Who Skied Down Everest
The Man with a Movie Camera▶
Many Faces of Sherlock Holmes
Marjoe
Marlon Brando
Mein Kampf: Hitler's Rise and Fall
Memphis Belle: A Story of a Flying Fortress
MGM: When the Lion Roars
Moana, a Romance of the Golden Age▶
Mondo Cane
Mondo Cane 2
Mondo Magic
Night of the Living Dead, 25th Anniversary Documentary
Oscar's Greatest Moments: 1971-1991
Paris is Burning▶
Prelude to War
Pumping Iron
Pumping Iron 2: The Women
Punk Rock Movie
Rascal Dazzle
Rate It X
The Real Buddy Holly Story
Revolution
Roger & Me▶
Sasquatch
Sex and Buttered Popcorn
Shocking Asia
The Show
Signals Through the Flames▶
Slave Trade in the World Today
Soft and Hard
The Sorrow and the Pity▶
Streetwise▶
Stripper
Superstar: The Life and Times of Andy Warhol▶
Swimming to Cambodia▶
Taxi zum Klo▶
Thank You & Good Night
Theremin: An Electronic Odyssey▶
The Thin Blue Line▶
Tokyo-Ga▶
Tokyo Olympiad
Triumph of the Will
Truth or Dare
Unzipped▶
Vanishing Prairie▶
Vanishing Wilderness
Vietnam: Chronicle of a War
Visions of Light: The Art of Cinematography▶
War in the Sky▶
The War Room▶
Wigstock: The Movie
Wild, Wild World of Jayne Mansfield
Wisecracks▶
The Wonderful, Horrible Life of Leni Riefenstahl

Dogs

see King of Beasts (Dogs)

Dolls That Kill

see Killer Toys

Down Under

The Adventures of Priscilla, Queen of the Desert▶
Alvin Purple
Anzacs: The War Down Under▶
Around the World in 80 Ways
Between Wars
The Blue Lightning
Born to Run
Botany Bay
Boulevard of Broken Dreams
Brides of Christ
Burke & Wills
Caddie
The Cars That Ate Paris▶
Cass
Cool Change
Country Life
Crocodile Dundee 2
A Cry in the Dark▶
The Custodian
Dark Age
Dead Easy
Death of a Soldier
The Desert Rats▶
Down Under
The Dunera Boys▶
Dusty
Eureka Stockade
Fair Game
Fast Talking
Forty Thousand Horsemen
Freedom
The Fringe Dwellers
Gallagher's Travels
Gallipoli▶
The Getting of Wisdom
The Good Wife

Great Gold Swindle
Ground Zero▶
Heavenly Creatures▶
Hurricane Smith
The Irishman
Kitty and the Bagman
The Lighthorsemen▶
Little Boy Lost
The Long Weekend
Mad Dog Morgan
The Man from Snowy River
Miracle Down Under
Money Movers
Monkey Grip▶
Moving Out
Muriel's Wedding▶
My Brilliant Career▶
The Naked Country
Ned Kelly
Nevil Shute's The Far Country
On the Beach▶
One Crazy Night
Only the Brave
Over the Hill
Overlanders▶
Palm Beach
Phar Lap
Prince and the Great Race
Prisoners of the Sun▶
The Quest
Quigley Down Under
Race the Sun
Rebel
Reckless Kelly
The Rescuers Down Under
Return to Snowy River▶
Ride a Wild Pony▶
The Right Hand Man
Robbery Under Arms
Run, Rebecca, Run
Sara Dane
Savage Attraction
The Shrimp on the Barbie
Silver City
The Silver Stallion: King of the Wild Brumbies
Sirens
Sister Kenny▶
Snowy River, the MacGregor Saga: The Race
Sorrento Beach
Squizzy Taylor
Stones of Death
Strictly Ballroom▶
The Sum of Us▶
Summer City
The Sundowners▶
Sweet Talker
Talk
The Thorn Birds▶
Under Capricorn
The Wacky World of Wills & Burke
A Waltz Through the Hills
Waterfront
We of the Never Never▶
Where the Green Ants Dream
The Winds of Jarrah
The Winter of Our Dreams

Dragons

see also Medieval Romps

Captain Sinbad
Dragonheart
Dragonslayer▶
Dragonworld
Erik the Viking
Ghidrah the Three Headed Monster
Goliath and the Dragon
Jabberwocky
Jack the Giant Killer▶
Jason and the Argonauts▶
The Magic Sword
The NeverEnding Story▶
Pete's Dragon
The Reluctant Dragon
The Seventh Voyage of Sinbad▶
Sleeping Beauty▶
Sword & the Dragon
The Wonderful World of the Brothers Grimm

Drama

see also Adventure Drama; Comedy Drama; Historical Drama; Musical Drama; Romantic Drama; Tearjerkers; Tragedy

A Nos Amours▶
ABC Stage 67: Truman Capote's A Christmas Memory
Abducted
The Abduction of Allison Tate
The Abduction of Kari Swenson
The Abe Lincoln of Ninth Avenue
Above the Rim
Above Us the Waves▶
Abraham
Abraham Lincoln
Absence of Malice
Accatone!▶
Acceptable Risks
Accident
The Accused
The Accused▶
Acla's Descent into Floristella
Across 110th Street
Across the Tracks
Act of Aggression
Act of Passion: The Lost Honor of Kathryn Beck
Act of Vengeance
Action for Slander
Actors and Sin
An Actor's Revenge
Adam▶
Adam at 6 a.m.
Adam Had Four Sons
The Adjuster
Adomas Nori Buti Zmogumi
Adoption▶
The Adultress
Adventure Island
The Adventures of Mark Twain▶
The Adventures of Nellie Bly
The Adventures of Rusty
The Adventures of the Flying Cadets
The Adventurous Knights
The Adversary
Affair in Trinidad
Africa Texas Style
An African Dream
African Journey
After the Rehearsal▶
Afterburn▶
Against the Wall▶
Against the Wind
Age Old Friends▶
The Agency
Agent on Ice
Agnes of God
Aguirre, the Wrath of God▶
Airborne
Akira Kurosawa's Dreams
Alamo Bay
Alan & Naomi
Albino
Alex
Alexander: The Other Side of Dawn
Alfred Hitchcock's Aventure Malgache
Alfred Hitchcock's Bon Voyage
Alias, La Gringa
Alice in the Cities▶
All About Eve▶
All Creatures Great and Small▶
All God's Children
All I Desire
All My Sons▶
All Quiet on the Western Front▶
All Quiet on the Western Front
All the King's Men▶
All the President's Men▶
All the Right Moves
All the Young Men▶
All Things Fair
Allonsanfan▶
Almost Human
Almost Royal Family
Alone in the Neon Jungle
Alpha Beta
Alphabet City
Alpine Fire
Alsino and the Condor▶
Alternative
Amazing Grace & Chuck
The Amazing Howard Hughes
Amber Waves
Amelia Earhart: The Final Flight
America First
America/The Fall of Babylon▶
The American Angels: Baptism of Blood
American Anthem
American Blue Note
An American Christmas Carol
American Dream▶
American Flyers
American Heart▶
American Me▶
American Nightmare
The American Soldier
An American Story
An American Summer
Americana
The Americano/Variety
America's Dream▶
Amin: The Rise and Fall
Among the Cinders
Amongst Friends
Amor Bandido
Amore▶
Amos
Amy
Anatomy of a Murder▶
Anatomy of Terror
And God Created Woman
And Hope to Die
And Justice for All
And Nothing But the Truth
And Now Miguel
And the Band Played On▶
And the Ship Sails On▶
Andersonville▶
The Andersonville Trial▶
Andre
Andy Warhol's Bad▶
Angel
An Angel at My Table▶
Angel Baby
Angel City
Angel with the Trumpet
Angela
Angele▶
Angelo My Love▶
Angels with Dirty Faces▶
AngKor: Cambodia Express
Angry Harvest▶
Angry Joe Bass
The Ann Jillian Story
Anna▶
Anna and the King of Siam▶
Anne of Green Gables▶
Annie O
Another Country
Another Woman▶
Antonia and Jane▶
Antonio Das Mortes
Any Number Can Play
Anything for a Thrill
Anzio
Aparajito▶
Applause▶
Aria
Arizona
Armored Car Robbery
Armored Command
The Arrangement
Arrowsmith
Art for Teachers of Children
Arthur's Hallowed Ground
Artist's Studio Secrets
As You Desire Me▶
Ash Wednesday
Ashes and Diamonds▶
Ashes and Embers
Ashik Kerib▶
The Asphalt Jungle▶
Assassin of Youth
The Assault▶
Assault at West Point: The Court-Martial of Johnson Whittaker
Assault of the Rebel Girls
The Assignment
The Assisi Underground
At Gunpoint
At Play in the Fields of the Lord▶
Atlantic City▶
Atomic Attack
Attack Squadron
Attica▶
Au Revoir Les Enfants▶
August
Augustine of Hippo▶
Autobiography of a Princess
An Autumn Afternoon▶
Autumn Born
Autumn Leaves
Autumn Sonata▶
Avenging Angel
Away All Boats
An Awfully Big Adventure
Baba▶
Babe!▶
The Babe
Babe Ruth Story
Baby Doll▶
Baby Girl Scott
The Baby Maker
Baby, the Rain Must Fall
Babyfever
The Babylon Story from "Intolerance"▶
The Bacchantes
The Bachelor▶
Back Door to Heaven▶
Back Home
Backbeat▶
Backstairs
The Bad and the Beautiful▶
Bad Blood
Bad Boy
Bad Boys▶
Bad Bunch
Bad Georgia Road
Bad Girls Do Cry
Bad Girls Go to Hell
Bad Girls in the Movies
Bad Lieutenant▶
The Bad Sleep Well▶
Badge of the Assassin
Badlands▶
Bail Out at 43,000
Baker's Hawk
The Balcony▶
Ballad of a Soldier▶
Ballet Shoes
Baltic Deputy▶
Bandit Queen
Bandits
Bandits of Orgosolo
Barbarians at the Gate▶
Bare Knees
The Barefoot Contessa▶
Barfly▶
Baritone
Barnum
The Baron and the Kid
Barry Lyndon▶
Basileus Quartet▶
The Basketball Diaries
Battle Circus
Battle Cry▶
Battle Hymn
The Battle of Austerlitz
The Battle of Blood Island
Battleground▶
Battling Bunyon
Battling Orioles
The Bay Boy
The Bear▶
The Bears & I
The Beat
Beat Girl
The Beatniks
Beatrice▶
Beau Brummel
Beau Brummel▶
Beautiful Dreamers
Beauty for the Asking
Becky Sharp
Becoming Colette
Bed and Sofa▶
Beethoven
Beethoven Lives Upstairs
Before and After
Before the Revolution
Beggars in Ermine
The Beguiled▶
Behind Enemy Lines
Behind Office Doors
Behind the Rising Sun
Behold a Pale Horse
Belfast Assassin
Belizaire the Cajun
Bell Diamond
The Bell Jar
Bell Ringer of Antigua
Belle de Jour▶
Bellissima▶
Bellman and True
The Belly of an Architect▶
Below the Belt
Below the Deadline
The Beniker Gang
The Benny Goodman Story
Bergonzi Hand
Berlin Alexanderplatz▶
Bernadette
The Best Christmas Pageant Ever
Best Enemies
Best Kept Secrets
The Best Little Girl in the World▶
The Best Man▶
The Best Years of Our Lives▶
Bethune
Betrayal
Betrayal from the East
Betrayed▶
Betrayed
The Betsy
Better Off Dead
Betty
Between Friends
Between Heaven and Earth
Between Two Women
Between Wars
Beulah Land
Beverly Hills Madam
Beverly Hills 90210
Beverly Hills 90210: The Graduation
Beware of a Holy Whore
Beyond Fear
Beyond Innocence
Beyond Obsession
Beyond Reason
Beyond Reasonable Doubt
Beyond the Forest
Beyond the Limit
Beyond the Next Mountain
Beyond the Time Barrier
Beyond the Walls
The Bible...In the Beginning▶
The Bicycle Thief▶
Big Bad Mama 2
The Big Bird Cage
The Big Blue
Big Boss
Big Combo▶
The Big Hangover
The Big Knife▶
The Big Lift
The Big Man: Crossing the Line▶
Big Mo
Big Red
Big Score
Big Town
Big Trees▶
Bilitis
Bill▶
A Bill of Divorcement
Bill: On His Own▶
Billionaire Boys Club
Billy Bathgate
Billy Galvin

Conspirator
Contempt▶
Control
Conversation Piece▶
Convicted
Convicted: A Mother's Story
Convoy
Cool Hand Luke▶
The Cool Surface
Cooley High▶
Cop
Copkillers
Copycat
Cordelia
The Corn is Green▶
Cornbread, Earl & Me
Cornered▶
The Corridor: Death
Corrupt▶
Corruption
Cosh Boy
Cottage to Let
Cotton Candy
The Count of the Old Town
Countdown
Counterblast
The Counterfeit Traitor▶
Country▶
The Country Diary of an Edwardian Lady
Country Girl▶
Country Girl
Country Lovers, City Lovers
Countryman
County Fair
Courage▶
Courage of Lassie
Courage Under Fire▶
Courageous Dr. Christian
The Courier
Courier of Death
The Court Martial of Jackie Robinson▶
The Courtesans of Bombay▶
Courtship▶
Covergirl
Coward of the County
Cowboys Don't Cry
The Cracker Factory
Crash
Crashout
Cria▶
Cricket on the Hearth
Cries and Whispers▶
Crime and Punishment▶
Crime and Punishment
Crime of Honor
The Crime of Monsieur Lange▶
Crime of Passion
Crimes of Passion▶
Criminal Act
Criminal Code
Crisscross
Crooked Hearts
The Cross & the Switchblade
Cross Creek
Cross Examination
Cross My Heart
Crossbar
Crossfire▶
The Crossing Guard▶
Crossover
Crossroads
The Crowd▶
Crows and Sparrows▶
The Crucible▶
The Crucified Lovers▶
Cruel Sea▶
The Cruel Story of Youth▶
Cruisin' High
Crush
A Cry for Love
Cry Freedom
A Cry from the Mountain
A Cry from the Streets
A Cry in the Dark▶
Cry of a Prostitute: Love Kills
Cry of the Penguins
Cry, the Beloved Country▶
Cry Vengeance
The Crying Game▶
Cup Final

The Cure
The Curfew Breakers
The Curse of King Tut's Tomb
Curse of the Starving Class
The Custodian
Cut and Run
Cyrano de Bergerac
Cyrano de Bergerac▶
D-Day, the Sixth of June▶
Da
Dad
Daddy Nostalgia▶
Daddy-O
Daens
Daisy Miller
Dakota
Damien: The Leper Priest
The Damned
The Dance Goes On
Dance Me Outside
Dance or Die
Dance with a Stranger▶
Dancing in the Dark
Dancing Man
Dancing Mothers
Dandelions
Danger in the Skies
Danger Lights
Danger UXB
Dangerous
A Dangerous Age
Dangerous Game
Dangerous Holiday
Dangerous Hours
Dangerous Liaisons
Dangerous Life
Dangerous Moves▶
Dangerous Passion
Dangerous Relations
A Dangerous Woman
Dangerous Youth
Dangerously Close
Daniel
Daniel and the Towers
Danny
Danny Boy▶
Dante's Inferno▶
Dante's Inferno: Life of Dante Gabriel Rossetti
Danzon▶
Dark Horse
The Dark Hour
Dark Obsession
Dark River: A Father's Revenge
The Dark Side of Love
Dark Victory▶
Darling▶
Das Boot▶
Das Testament des Dr. Mabuse▶
Date Bait
Daughter of Death
Daughter of the Dragon
Daughter of the Tong
Daughters of the Dust▶
David▶
David and Lisa▶
Dawn!
Dawn Express
Dawn Patrol▶
The Day After▶
The Day and the Hour
Day for Night▶
A Day for Thanks on Walton's Mountain
A Day in the Country▶
The Day of the Locust▶
Day of Triumph
Day One▶
Day with Conrad Green
Days of Glory
Days of Heaven▶
Days of Wine and Roses
Days of Wine and Roses▶
The Dead▶
Dead Boyz Can't Fly
Dead End▶
Dead End Street
Dead Man Out▶
Dead Man Walking▶
Dead Poets Society▶
Dead Presidents

Dead Right
Dead Silence
Dead Wrong: The John Evans Story
Deadline
Deadly Business▶
Deadly Darling
Deadly Encounter
Deadly Game
Deadly Twins
Dealers
Dear Boys
Dear Murderer
Death and the Maiden▶
Death Be Not Proud▶
Death Blow
Death Driver
Death Drug
Death Force
Death in Deep Water
Death in Venice▶
Death is Called Engelchen▶
Death of a Centerfold
Death of a Salesman▶
Death of a Soldier
The Death of Adolf Hitler
Death of an Angel
The Death of Richie
Death Scream
Death Wish Club
December
December Bride
Decoration Day▶
Deep End▶
Deep in the Heart
Deep Six
The Deer Hunter▶
The Defender
The Defense Never Rests
Defiance
The Defiant Ones▶
The Defilers
The Deliberate Stranger▶
Delinquent Daughters
Delta of Venus
Demented
Demons in the Garden▶
Demonstrator
Dempsey
Denial: The Dark Side of Passion
Department Store
Desert Bloom▶
The Desert Fox▶
The Desert Rats▶
The Deserters
Desire Under the Elms
Despair▶
Desperate Characters▶
Desperate Lives
Detective Story▶
Detour▶
Deutschland im Jahre Null▶
Devi▶
The Devil at 4 O'Clock
The Devil in Silk
The Devil on Wheels
The Devil's Harvest
The Devil's Playground▶
The Devil's Sleep
Devil's Son-in-Law
D.I.
Diamond Head
Diamonds of the Night▶
Diana: Her True Story
Diane
Diary of a Country Priest▶
Diary of a Lost Girl▶
Diary of a Mad Old Man
Diary of a Teenage Hitchhiker
Diary of a Young Comic
The Diary of Anne Frank▶
Dick Barton, Special Agent
Dick Barton Strikes Back
Didn't You Hear?
Dillinger
Dillinger and Capone
Dingaka
Dino
Dirt Gang
Dirty Dancing▶
Dirty Gertie from Harlem U.S.A.

The Disappearance of Aimee▶
Disclosure
Discontent
Dishonored
Disraeli▶
Distant Thunder▶
Distant Thunder
Distant Voices, Still Lives▶
Diving In
Divorce His, Divorce Hers
D.O.A.
Docks of New York▶
The Doctor
Dr. Bethune▶
Doctor Faustus
Dr. Kildare's Strange Case
Dr. Petiot
Dr. Strange
Doctors' Wives
Dodes 'ka-den▶
Dodsworth▶
A Dog of Flanders
The Dog Soldier
The Dog Who Stopped the War
The Doll
The Dollmaker
A Doll's House
A Doll's House▶
Dominick & Eugene▶
The Domino Principle
Don Segundo Sombra
Don't Cry, It's Only Thunder
Don't Look Back: The Story of Leroy "Satchel" Paige
Don't Mess with My Sister!
Doomed Love
Doomsday Gun
The Doors
Double-Crossed
Double Deal
Double Edge
Double Exposure: The Story of Margaret Bourke-White
A Double Life▶
The Double Life of Veronique
Double Standard
Double Suicide▶
Down Came a Blackbird
Downhill Racer
D.P.
Drachenfutter▶
Dragnet
Dragon Seed
Dragon: The Bruce Lee Story▶
Dragstrip Girl
The Drake Case
A Dream for Christmas▶
A Dream of Passion
Dream Street
Dream to Believe
Dreamchild▶
Dreamer
Dreaming Lips
Dreams
The Dresser▶
Drifting
Drifting Souls
Drifting Weeds▶
Driving Miss Daisy▶
Drowning by Numbers▶
Drug Wars 2: The Cocaine Cartel
Drum
Drums O'Voodoo
Drunken Angel▶
A Dry White Season▶
Drying Up the Streets
Dual Alibi
Dubeat-E-O
The Duellists▶
Duet for One
Duke of the Derby
The Dunera Boys▶
Dupont Lajoie
Dusty
Dutchman▶
D.W. Griffith Triple Feature
The Dwelling Place
The Dybbuk▶
Dynamite Dan
An Early Frost▶
Early Summer▶

The Earrings of Madame De...▶
Earth Entranced
Earthling
East End Hustle
East of Eden▶
East of Eden
East of Elephant Rock
The Easy Life▶
Easy Living
Easy Rider▶
Ebony Tower
Echoes in the Darkness
Echoes of Paradise
The Eclipse▶
Eddie and the Cruisers
Eddie and the Cruisers 2: Eddie Lives!
Eddie Macon's Run
Eden
Eden 2
Eden 3
Eden 4
Edge of Darkness▶
Edge of the World▶
Edie in Ciao! Manhattan
The Education of Sonny Carson
Edvard Munch
The Effect of Gamma Rays on Man-in-the-Moon Marigolds▶
The Egyptian
8 1/2▶
Eight Men Out▶
8 Million Ways to Die
1860
The Eighth Day
Eijanaika▶
El Bruto
El Muerto
El Norte▶
El Super▶
Ele, My Friend
The Elegant Criminal
Eleni
The Elephant Man▶
Elisa, Vida Mia
Elizabeth, the Queen
Elke
Elmer
Elmer Gantry▶
The Elusive Corporal▶
Elvis: The Movie
Emergency▶
The Emigrants▶
Emily
Eminent Domain
Emmanuelle
Emmanuelle 5
Emmanuelle 6
Emmanuelle & Joanna
Emmanuelle in Bangkok
Emmanuelle in Soho
Emmanuelle in the Country
Emmanuelle on Taboo Island
Emmanuelle, the Joys of a Woman
Emmanuelle, the Queen
Emmanuelle's Daughter
Emma's Shadow▶
Emperor Jones
Emperor Jones/Paul Robeson: Tribute to an Artist
The Empire of Passion▶
Empire of the Sun▶
Employees' Entrance▶
An Empty Bed▶
Encore▶
End of Desire
The End of Innocence
The End of St. Petersburg▶
End of the Road
The Endless Game
Enemy of Women
Enemy Territory
The Enemy Within
An Englishman Abroad▶
Enigma Secret
Enjo
Enola Gay: The Men, the Mission, the Atomic Bomb
The Entertainer▶
Entre-Nous▶
Equinox

Journey
The Journey of August King
Journey of Hope▶
Journey to Spirit Island
Journeys from Berlin/1971
The Joy Luck Club▶
Joyful Laughter
Joyride
Ju Dou▶
Juarez
Jud
Jud Suess▶
The Judas Project: The Ultimate Encounter
Judex
The Judge
The Judge and the Assassin▶
Judgment▶
Judgment at Nuremberg▶
Judgment in Berlin
The Juggler of Notre Dame
Juice
Julia▶
July Group
Jumpin' at the Boneyard
June Night
The Jungle Trap
The Juniper Tree
Juno and the Paycock
Just a Gigolo
Just Another Girl on the I.R.T.
Just for the Hell of It
Just Like Weather▶
Justice
Justine
Kalifornia
Kameradschaft▶
Kamikaze Hearts
Kandyland
Kangaroo▶
Kansas
Kansas City Confidential▶
Kansas City Massacre
Kaos▶
Kapo▶
Katherine
Keeper of the Flame
Keeping On
Keetje Tippel
Kennedy
Kent State
The Key Man
The Keys of the Kingdom▶
A Kid for Two Farthings
Kid from Not-So-Big
The Kid Who Loved Christmas
Kidnapping of Baby John Doe
Kids
Kill Castro
Kill Me Again
The Kill Reflex
Killer
Killer on Board
Killer's Kiss
The Killing▶
The Killing Beach
Killing 'em Softly
The Killing Fields▶
Killing Floor
The Killing of a Chinese Bookie
Killing of Angel Street
Killing of Randy Webster
Killing Zoe
A Kind of Loving▶
Kindergarten▶
King▶
King of America
King of Kings
The King of Kings▶
The King of Marvin Gardens
King of the Gypsies
King of the Hill▶
The King of the Roaring '20s: The Story of Arnold Rothstein
King of the Wind
King Rat▶
Kingfish: A Story of Huey P. Long
Kings and Desperate Men
Kings of the Road—In the Course of Time▶
Kings Row▶

Kipps▶
Kismet▶
The Kiss▶
Kiss of Death▶
Kiss of Death
Kiss of the Spider Woman▶
Kiss the Night
Kiss Tomorrow Goodbye
The Kissing Place
Kissinger and Nixon
The Kitchen Toto▶
The Klansman
Knife in the Head
Knock on Any Door
Knute Rockne: All American▶
Kojak: The Belarus File
Korczak▶
Kramer vs. Kramer▶
The Krays▶
Kung Fu
Kurt Vonnegut's Monkey House
L.627▶
L.A. Bad
La Balance▶
La Belle Noiseuse▶
La Boca del Lobo
La Cicada
L.A. Crackdown
L.A. Crackdown 2
La Femme Nikita▶
L.A. Law▶
La Merveilleuse Visite
La Puritaine
La Salamandre
La Scorta▶
La Signora di Tutti▶
La Symphonie Pastorale▶
La Terra Trema▶
La Truite▶
La Vie Continue
The Lacemaker▶
L'Addition
The Ladies Club
Ladies of the Lotus
Ladies on the Rocks
Ladies They Talk About
Lady Chatterley's Lover
Lady for a Night
Lady from Nowhere
Lady from Yesterday
Lady Grey
Lady Ice
Lady in Distress
Lady in Red
Lady in the Lake
Lady Mobster
Lady of the House
Lady on the Bus
Lady Windermere's Fan
Ladybird, Ladybird▶
Lai Shi: China's Last Eunuch
Lake Consequence
Lakota Woman: Siege at Wounded Knee
Lamb
Lamerica▶
Lamp at Midnight
Lancelot of the Lake
Land and Freedom▶
Land of Fury
Land of Promise
Landscape in the Mist▶
Lantern Hill
Lap Dancing
L'Appat
L'Argent
Larry
Las Vegas Lady
The Las Vegas Story
Lassie
Lassie's Great Adventure
The Last Angry Man▶
The Last Bastion
The Last Best Year
The Last Butterfly
Last Call
The Last Chance▶
Last Command▶
Last Cry for Help
Last Dance
Last Day of the War
The Last Days of Dolwyn

The Last Days of Patton
Last Exit to Brooklyn▶
The Last Fight
The Last Five Days
Last Flight Out: A True Story
Last Game
The Last Good Time
Last Hurrah
The Last Innocent Man
The Last Laugh▶
Last Light
The Last Metro▶
The Last Mile
The Last Movie
The Last of England▶
The Last of His Tribe
The Last of Mrs. Lincoln
The Last Picture Show▶
The Last Safari
Last Summer
The Last Supper▶
Last Tango in Paris▶
The Last Temptation of Christ▶
Last Time Out
The Last Tycoon▶
The Last Wave▶
The Last Winter
The Last Word
Last Year at Marienbad▶
L'Atalante▶
Late Chrysanthemums
Late Extra
The Late Shift
Late Spring▶
Late Summer Blues
Latino
Laughing at Life
Laughing Sinners
Laurel Avenue
L'Avventura▶
Law of the Underworld
Lawrence of Arabia▶
The Lawrenceville Stories
Laws of Gravity▶
Lazarillo
The Lazarus Syndrome
LBJ: The Early Years▶
Le Bal▶
Le Cas du Dr. Laurent▶
Le Chat▶
Le Crabe Tambour▶
Le Dernier Combat▶
Le Doulos▶
Le Grand Chemin▶
Le Plaisir
Le Sexe des Etoiles
Lean on Me▶
The Learning Tree
Leather Boys
Leather Jackets
Leaves from Satan's Book
Leaving Las Vegas▶
Leaving Normal
L'Ecole Buisoniere
Legal Tender
The Legend of Sleepy Hollow
Legend of Valentino
Legend of Walks Far Woman
Legs
L'Enfant d'Eau
Lenny▶
Leonor
The Leopard Woman
Lepke
Les Assassins de L'Ordre
Les Biches▶
Les Bons Debarras
Les Carabiniers▶
Les Enfants Terrible▶
Les Miserables▶
Les Miserables
Les Miserables▶
Les Mistons▶
Les Nuits Fauves▶
Les Rendez-vous D'Anna
Les Violons du Bal
Less Than Zero
Let 'er Go Gallegher
Let Him Have It▶
Let It Rock
L'Etat Sauvage▶
Lethal Charm

Lethal Obsession
Let's Get Married
The Letter▶
Letter of Introduction
A Letter to Three Wives▶
Letters to an Unknown Lover
Letting the Birds Go Free
L'Homme Blesse▶
Liar's Moon
The Liberation of L.B. Jones
Liberators
License to Kill
L'Idiot
Lies My Father Told Me▶
The Life and Assassination of the Kingfish
The Life and Death of Colonel Blimp▶
A Life in the Theater
Life Is Beautiful
The Life of Emile Zola▶
Life of Oharu▶
A Life of Sin
Life on a String
Lifeboat▶
Lifeguard
The Light Ahead
The Light in the Jungle
The Light of Faith
Light Sleeper
Lightning: The White Stallion
The Lightship
Lilies of the Field▶
Liliom▶
Lillie▶
Lily in Winter
Limelight▶
The Line
A Lion Is in the Streets▶
Lipstick
Lisztomania
Little Ballerina
Little Boy Lost
Little Buddha
Little Church Around the Corner
Little Dorrit, Film 1: Nobody's Fault▶
The Little Foxes▶
Little Girl ... Big Tease
Little Gloria...Happy at Last
Little Heroes
Little House on the Prairie▶
The Little Kidnappers
Little Ladies of the Night
Little Lord Fauntleroy▶
Little Lord Fauntleroy
Little Man Tate▶
Little Men
Little Miss Innocence
Little Odessa
Little Orphan Annie
The Little Princess
Little Sweetheart
Little Tough Guys
The Little Valentino
Little Vera▶
Little Women▶
Little Women
Little Women▶
The Littlest Outlaw
Live! From Death Row
The Living End
Living Proof: The Hank Williams Jr. Story
Loaded
Loan Shark
Lock Up
L'Odeur des Fauves
Lois Gibbs and the Love Canal
Lola Montes▶
Lolita▶
London Kills Me
Lone Star Kid
The Loneliest Runner
The Loneliness of the Long Distance Runner▶
The Lonely Lady
The Lonely Passion of Judith Hearne▶
Lonelyhearts
Loners
The Long Dark Hall

The Long Day Closes▶
Long Day's Journey into Night▶
Long Day's Journey into Night
The Long Days of Summer
Long Gone
The Long Good Friday▶
The Long Gray Line▶
The Long Haul
The Long Island Four
Long Journey Back
Long Road Home
The Long Voyage Home▶
The Long Walk Home▶
A Long Way Home
The Long Weekend
The Longest Day▶
Longtime Companion▶
Look Back in Anger▶
Look Back in Anger
Look Back in Anger▶
The Lookalike
Looking for Miracles
Looking for Mr. Goodbar
The Looking Glass War
Lord Jim▶
Lord of the Flies▶
Lord of the Flies
The Lords of Discipline
The Lords of Flatbush
Lorenzo's Oil▶
Lorna Doone
Los Olvidados▶
The Losers
Losing Isaiah▶
Lost Angels
Lost Boundaries
The Lost Honor of Katharina Blum▶
Lost Horizon▶
Lost in the Barrens
The Lost Language of Cranes▶
Lost Legacy: A Girl Called Hatter Fox
Lost Moment
The Lost One
The Lost Weekend▶
The Lost World
Lotna
The Lotus Eaters
Love▶
Love and a .45
Love Child
Love Field
Love Film
Love for Lydia▶
Love Leads the Way
The Love Machine
Love Matters
Love on the Dole▶
Love Strange Love
Love Under Pressure
Love Your Mama
Loveless
Lovely ... But Deadly
The Loves of Edgar Allen Poe
Lovey: A Circle of Children 2
The Lower Depths▶
Loyalties
Loyola, the Soldier Saint
Lucky Luciano
Lucy and Desi: Before the Laughter
Lumiere
Luna Park
Lush Life▶
Lust for Freedom
Lust for Life▶
Luzia
M. Butterfly
Ma Barker's Killer Brood
Mac▶
MacArthur
MacArthur's Children▶
Machine Gun Kelly
Machine to Kill Bad People
Mack
Macon County Line
Macumba Love
Mad About Music▶
Mad Death
Mad Dog Morgan
The Mad Whirl

The Raven
The Razor's Edge▶
The Razor's Edge
Reach for the Sky
A Real American Hero
A Reason to Believe
Rebel
Rebel Rousers
The Rebel Set
Rebel Vixens
Rebel Without a Cause▶
Reborn
Reckless Disregard
The Reckless Way
The Rector's Wife
The Red and the White▶
The Red Badge of Courage▶
Red Beard▶
The Red Desert▶
The Red Half-Breed
Red Hot
Red Line 7000
The Red Menace
Red Nightmare
Red Nights
The Red Pony▶
Red Shoe Diaries
Red Shoe Diaries 2: Double Dare
Red Shoe Diaries 3: Another Woman's Lipstick
Red Shoe Diaries 4: Auto Erotica
Red Shoe Diaries 5: Weekend Pass
Red Shoe Diaries 6: How I Met My Husband
The Red Stallion
Red Surf
Red, White & Busted
Reds▶
Redwood Curtain
Reefer Madness
The Reflecting Skin
Reflections in a Golden Eye
Reflections in the Dark
Reform School Girl
Reform School Girls
Regarding Henry▶
The Reincarnation of Golden Lotus▶
The Remains of the Day▶
Rembrandt▶
Rembrandt—1669
Rendez-vous▶
Requiem for Dominic▶
Reservoir Dogs▶
The Respectful Prostitute
Resurrection▶
Return to Earth
Return to Peyton Place
Reunion▶
Revenge of a Kabuki Actor
Reversal of Fortune▶
The Revolt of Job▶
Rhapsody in August
Rhodes
Rhythm Thief
Rich Kids
Rich Man, Poor Man▶
Richard III▶
Richard Petty Story
Richard's Things
Riddance▶
Ride a Wild Pony▶
Ride in a Pink Car
Riel
Riff Raff
The Right Hand Man
Right of Way
The Right to Remain Silent
The Ring
Ring of Bright Water▶
Ringside
Riot
Riot Squad
Riptide▶
Rising Son▶
Risky Business
Rita Hayworth: The Love Goddess
The Rite
Rivals
The River▶
The River
River Beat
The River Niger
River of Unrest
The River Rat
A River Runs Through It▶
Riverbend
River's Edge▶
The Road Home
Road House
Road Racers
The Road to Galveston▶
The Road to Life
Roadhouse Girl
Roadhouse 66
Roadside Prophets
Roaring Roads
Roaring Speedboats
Robert Kennedy and His Times
Robot Pilot
Rocco and His Brothers▶
Rock All Night
Rock, Pretty Baby
Rocket to the Moon
The Rocking Horse Winner
Rocky▶
Rocky 2
Rocky 3
Rocky 4
Rocky 5
Rodrigo D.: No Future
Roe vs. Wade▶
RoGoPaG
Roll of Thunder, Hear My Cry
Rolling Home
Rolling Thunder
Rollover
Rome '78
Romero
The Roof
The Room
Rooster: Spurs of Death!
Roosters
Rosa Luxemburg
The Rose and the Jackal
The Rose Garden
Roseanne: An Unauthorized Biography
Roseland▶
Rosie: The Rosemary Clooney Story
Roswell: The U.F.O. Cover-Up
Round Midnight▶
The Round Up
R.P.M.* (*Revolutions Per Minute)
Ruby
Ruby Gentry
Ruby in Paradise▶
Ruby's Dream
Rudy
Rumble Fish▶
The Rumor Mill
A Rumor of War▶
Rumpole of the Bailey: Rumpole's Return▶
Run for the Roses
Run Silent, Run Deep▶
Runaway
Runaway Father
The Runaways
The Runner Stumbles
Running Brave
Running Free
Running Mates▶
Running on Empty▶
Rush▶
The Russia House
Rusty's Birthday
The Rutherford County Line
Sabre Jet
The Sacrifice▶
Sacrilege
Sadat
Safe▶
Safe Passage
Saigon: Year of the Cat
St. Elmo's Fire
St. Ives
Saint Jack▶
The Saint of Fort Washington
Sakharov▶
Salaam Bombay!▶
Salammbo
Salmonberries
Salo, or the 120 Days of Sodom
Salome
Salome/Queen Elizabeth
Salome, Where She Danced
Salt of the Earth▶
Salute John Citizen▶
Samaritan: The Mitch Snyder Story▶
Sam's Son
Samson and Delilah▶
Samson and Delilah
Sandakan No. 8▶
Sandra of a Thousand Delights
Sanshiro Sugata▶
Sansho the Bailiff▶
Santa Sangre▶
Sara Dane
Satan Met a Lady
Satan's Brew
Satan's Harvest
Savage Attraction
Savage Is Loose
Savage Run▶
The Savage Seven
The Savage Woman
Savages from Hell
Savannah Smiles
Save the Lady
Save the Tiger▶
Sawdust & Tinsel▶
Say Goodbye, Maggie Cole
Scandal
Scandal▶
Scandal in a Small Town
The Scar
Scarecrow
Scarface Mob
The Scarlet Letter
The Scarlet Letter▶
The Scarlet Pimpernel▶
Scarred
Scenes from a Marriage▶
Scent of a Woman▶
The Scent of Green Papaya▶
Schindler's List▶
School Ties▶
The Scorpion Woman
Scott Turow's The Burden of Proof
Scout's Honor
Scrooge▶
Scrubbers
Scruples
Scum▶
Sea Lion
Sea Racketeers
The Seagull▶
The Search▶
The Search for Bridey Murphy
Searching for Bobby Fischer▶
Season for Assassins
Season of Change
Sebastian
Second Best▶
Second Chance
Second Coming of Suzanne
Second Victory
The Secret
Secret File of Hollywood
The Secret Four
The Secret Garden▶
The Secret Garden
The Secret Garden▶
The Secret Garden
Secret Honor▶
The Secret of Roan Inish▶
The Secret of the Loch
Secret Places
The Secret Rapture
A Secret Space
Secret Weapons
Secrets
Secrets and Lies
Secrets of a Soul
Seduce Me: Pamela Principle 2
The Seducers
The Seduction of Joe Tynan
Seduction: The Cruel Woman
See How She Runs▶
Seize the Day▶
A Sense of Freedom▶
Sensual Partners
Sensuous Summer
The Sensuous Teenager
A Separate Peace
Separate Tables▶
Separate Tables
Separate Ways
September
September 30, 1955
Sergeant Matlovich vs. the U.S. Air Force
Sergeant Ryker
The Serpent's Egg
Serpico▶
The Servant▶
Sessions
The Set-Up▶
Seven Days in May▶
Seven Deadly Sins▶
Seven Miles from Alcatraz/Flight from Glory
The Seventeenth Bride
The 7th Commandment
The Seventh Cross▶
The Seventh Seal▶
The Seventh Veil▶
Severance
Sex and the College Girl
Sex, Drugs, and Rock-n-Roll
sex, lies and videotape▶
Sex Through a Window
S.F.W.
Shack Out on 101▶
The Shadow Box▶
Shadow Dancing▶
Shadow of Angels
Shadow on the Sun
Shadowlands▶
Shadows
Shadows▶
Shadows of the Orient
Shadows Over Shanghai
Shake Hands with the Devil▶
Shakespeare Wallah▶
Shaking the Tree
Shame▶
The Shame▶
The Shaming
Shanghai Express▶
The Shanghai Gesture
Shanghai Triad▶
Shanty Tramp
Sharma & Beyond
Shattered▶
Shattered
Shattered Dreams
Shattered Spirits
Shattered Vows
The Shawshank Redemption▶
She and He
She-Devils on Wheels
Sheer Madness▶
She'll Be Wearing Pink Pajamas
The Shell Seekers
The Sheltering Sky▶
Shifting Sands
Shiokari Pass
Ship of Fools▶
Shock Corridor▶
The Shoes of the Fisherman
Shoeshine▶
Shogun▶
Shoot It Black, Shoot It Blue
Shoot the Moon
Shoot to Kill
Shooting
The Shooting Party
The Shooting Party▶
The Shop on Main Street▶
Short Eyes▶
Short Fuse
Showgirls
The Shrieking
Shy People▶
Siberiade▶
Sicilian Connection
The Sicilian Connection
Sid & Nancy▶
Sidewalks of London▶
Signal 7
Signs of Life
Silas Marner▶
The Silence▶
Silence
Silence Like Glass
Silence of the Heart▶
Silence of the North
The Silent One
Silent Rebellion
The Silent Touch
Silent Victim
Silent Victory: The Kitty O'Neil Story▶
Silent Witness
Silkwood▶
The Silver Chalice
Silver Dream Racer
The Silver Streak
Simba▶
Simon Bolivar
Simple Justice
A Simple Story▶
Sin of Adam & Eve
Sin You Sinners
Sinatra
Sinbad
Sing Sing Nights
The Singing Blacksmith
The Singing Nun
Singing the Blues in Red▶
Single Room Furnished
The Single Standard
Sinners in Paradise
Sins
Sins of Jezebel
Sirocco
Sister Kenny▶
Sister My Sister
The Sisters▶
Sisters of Gion▶
Six Degrees of Separation
Sixteen
'68
Sizzle
Skag▶
Skateboard
Skeezer
Skier's Dream
Skin
Skin Art
Skin Game
Skinheads: The Second Coming of Hate
Skullduggery
The Sky Pilot
Skylark
Skyscraper Souls▶
Slacker▶
Slash
Slashed Dreams
Slaughterday
Slavers
Sleeping Dogs
The Sleeping Tiger
The Slender Thread▶
The Small Back Room▶
A Small Circle of Friends
Small Sacrifices
Small Time
Small Town Boy
A Small Town in Texas
Smash Palace
Smash-Up: The Story of a Woman▶
Smith!
Smithereens
Smoke
Smoking/No Smoking
A Smoky Mountain Christmas
Smooth Talk▶
Smouldering Fires
The Snake Pit▶
Sniper▶
Snow Treasure
The Snows of Kilimanjaro▶
So Dear to My Heart▶
So Ends Our Night▶
So Proudly We Hail▶
Sofie
Soldier's Revenge

Drama

Tornado
Torpedo Alley
Torpedo Attack
Torpedo Run
Torrents of Spring
Tortilla Flat▶
Torture Ship
Total Eclipse
Totally F***ed Up
Touch and Go
Touched
Touched by Love
Tough Enough
Tough Kid
Tough to Handle
Toughlove
Touki Bouki
Tournament
Tous les Matins du Monde▶
A Town Like Alice
Toys in the Attic
Tracks
Traenen in Florenz
Traffik▶
Trahir▶
The Train▶
Train of Events
Train Station Pickups
Trained to Kill, U.S.A.
Tramp at the Door
Transport from Paradise
Trapped
Trapped in Silence
Traps
Traveling Man
Travelling North
Treasure of Arne
Treasure of the Lost Desert
A Tree Grows in Brooklyn▶
The Tree of Wooden Clogs▶
Trespasser
The Trial▶
The Trial
The Trial of Billy Jack
The Trial of Lee Harvey Oswald
Trial of the Catonsville Nine
The Trials of Oscar Wilde▶
Tribes
Tribute
Tricheurs
The Trigger Effect
Trilby▶
Trio▶
The Trip
The Trip to Bountiful▶
Triple Echo
Triumph of the Spirit▶
Trois Couleurs: Bleu▶
Trois Couleurs: Rouge▶
Tromba, the Tiger Man
Tropic of Cancer▶
Trucker's Woman
True Colors
True Confessions▶
True West▶
Truman
Trumps
Tucker: The Man and His Dream▶
Tuff Turf
Tunes of Glory▶
Turf Boy
The Turning Point
Turtle Diary▶
The Tuskegee Airmen▶
Tuxedo Warrior
Twelve Angry Men▶
Twelve O'Clock High▶
21 Hours at Munich▶
Twenty-Four Eyes▶
25 Fireman's Street▶
Twice a Woman
Twice in a Lifetime▶
Twin Peaks
Twin Peaks: Fire Walk with Me
Twirl
Two Bits
Two Kinds of Love
Two Men & a Wardrobe
Two of a Kind
The Two of Us▶
The Two Sisters
Two Small Bodies
Two Weeks in Another Town
Two Women▶
Tycoon
Tyson
The Ugly American
Ulysses
Ulysses' Gaze
Umberto D▶
Un Singe en Hiver
The Unapproachable
Uncaged
Uncertain Glory
The Unchastened Woman
Uncle Moses
Uncle Tom's Cabin
Uncommon Valor
Under Fire▶
Under Milk Wood
Under Satan's Sun▶
Under the Earth▶
Under the Volcano▶
Undercover Cop
Underground U.S.A.
Une Jeunesse▶
Unfinished Business
An Unforgettable Summer
Unicorn
The Unknown▶
Unknown Powers
An Unmarried Woman▶
Unnatural Causes▶
Unsettled Land
The Unstoppable Man
Unstrung Heroes
The Untamable
Until They Sail
Up Against the Wall
Up to a Certain Point
Upper Crust
The Uprising▶
Uptown Angel
Urban Cowboy
Users
Utamaro and His Five Women
Vagabond▶
Valentino
Valentino Returns
The Valley Obscured by the Clouds
Valley of the Dolls
Valmont▶
Van Gogh▶
Vanishing Point
Vanya on 42nd Street▶
Variety
Variety Lights▶
The Vegas Strip Wars
Velvet Smooth
Vendetta
Vendetta for the Saint
Vengeance
Verdi
Verne Miller
Veronico Cruz
Veronika Voss▶
A Very Natural Thing
A Very Old Man with Enormous Wings
Via Appia
Vice Squad
Victim▶
Victimless Crimes
Victory
Video Wars
Vietnam War Story 1
Vietnam War Story 2
Vietnam War Story 3
Vigil▶
Vigilante
Vincent & Theo▶
Vincent, Francois, Paul and the Others▶
Vincent: The Life and Death of Vincent van Gogh▶
Violated
Violence at Noon▶
Violent Ones
Violent Women
The Violent Years
The V.I.P.'s▶
The Virginia Hill Story
Viridiana▶
Virtue's Revolt
Vision Quest
Vital Signs
Vortex
Voyage en Douce
Voyage of Terror: The Achille Lauro Affair
Voyage of the Damned▶
A Voyage' Round My Father▶
Voyage to Italy
The Voyeur
Wager of Love
Wages of Fear▶
Wagner: The Complete Epic
Wagner: The Movie
Waiting for the Moon
Waiting to Exhale▶
The Walking Dead
Walking on Air
Walking Tall
Walking Tall: Part 2
Walking Tall: The Final Chapter
Walking the Edge
Walking Through the Fire
The Wall▶
Wall Street▶
The Waltons: The Christmas Carol
Wanda, The Sadistic Hypnotist
Wanderers▶
Wandering Jew
Wanted: The Perfect Guy
The War
War & Remembrance, Part 1
War & Remembrance, Part 2
War & Remembrance: The Final Chapter, Part 8
War & Remembrance: The Final Chapter, Part 9
War Between the Tates
War Brides
War of the Buttons
War Victims
Ward Six
WarGames
The Warning
Warning Shadows▶
The Wash▶
Washington Affair
Watch on the Rhine▶
The Water Engine
The Waterdance▶
Waterfront
Waterland
Way Back Home
The Wayward Wife
We are the Children
We of the Never Never▶
We Will Not Enter the Forest▶
The Wedding Gift▶
A Wedding in Galilee▶
Wedding in White
Wee Willie Winkie▶
Weeds▶
Weekend▶
Weekend of Shadows▶
Welcome to L.A.▶
The Well▶
Well-Digger's Daughter▶
Wend Kuuni
Westfront 1918▶
Wetherby▶
Whale for the Killing
Whale Music
Whale of a Tale
The Whales of August▶
The Wharf Rat
What Comes Around
What Happened Was...
What Price Glory?▶
What Price Hollywood?▶
What the Moon Saw
What's Eating Gilbert Grape▶
When a Man Loves a Woman
When a Woman Ascends the Stairs
When Every Day was the Fourth of July
When Father was Away on Business▶
When Gangland Strikes
When Hell Was in Session▶
When He's Not a Stranger▶
When the Greeks
When the Line Goes Through
When the Party's Over
When the Whales Came
When Wolves Cry
Where
Where Angels Fear to Tread▶
Where Have All the People Gone?
Where Is My Child?
Where Love Has Gone
Where the Day Takes You
Where the Eagle Flies
Where the Green Ants Dream
Where the Hot Wind Blows
Where the Lilies Bloom▶
Where the Red Fern Grows: Part 2
Where the Rivers Flow North
While the City Sleeps▶
Whistle Down the Wind▶
The White Balloon▶
White Heat▶
White Hunter, Black Heart▶
The White Legion
White Lie
White Mama▶
White Mane▶
White Man's Burden
White Mile
White Nights
White Shadows in the South Seas
The White Sin
White Tiger
Who Shot Pat?
Who'll Save Our Children?▶
Who'll Stop the Rain?▶
Whore
Whore 2
Who's Afraid of Virginia Woolf?▶
Who's That Knocking at My Door?▶
Whose Child Am I?
Why Has Bodhi-Darma Left for the East
Why Shoot the Teacher▶
The Wicked Lady
The Widow
Wifemistress
The Wilby Conspiracy▶
The Wild Child▶
The Wild Duck
Wild Engine/Mistaken Orders
Wild Guitar
Wild Horse Hank
Wild in the Country
The Wild One▶
Wild Ones on Wheels
Wild Orchid
Wild Orchid 2: Two Shades of Blue
Wild Orchids
Wild Party
Wild Pony
Wild Reeds▶
The Wild Ride
Wild Strawberries▶
Wild Style
Wild Wheels
Wildcat
Wildflower▶
Wildrose▶
Will: G. Gordon Liddy
Willa
Wilma
Wilson▶
Windom's Way▶
Windows
Windrunner
The Winds of War
Windwalker▶
Windy City
A Winner Never Quits
Winner Takes All
The Winning Team
The Winslow Boy▶
The Winter Light▶
The Winter of Our Dreams
Winterset
Without Anesthesia
Without Love
Without Warning: The James Brady Story▶
Witness▶
Witness to the Execution
Wittgenstein
Wives Under Suspicion
The Wizard of Loneliness
Wolf Lake
The Wolves▶
A Woman and a Woman
A Woman, Her Men and Her Futon
Woman in Brown
A Woman in Flames▶
Woman in the Dunes▶
Woman in the Shadows
The Woman Inside
A Woman Named Jackie
A Woman Obsessed
A Woman of Rome
A Woman Rebels
A Woman Under the Influence▶
The Woman Who Willed a Miracle
Woman With a Past
A Woman's Secret
A Woman's Tale▶
A Woman's World▶
Women & Men: In Love There Are No Rules
Women & Men: Stories of Seduction
Women From the Lake of Scented Souls
Women in Cell Block 7
Women in Love▶
The Women of Brewster Place▶
Women of Valor
Women Unchained
Wonsan Operation
The Wooden Gun
The Wooden Man's Bride
Words by Heart
Workin' for Peanuts
Working Girls
A World Apart▶
The World Gone Mad
The World of Apu▶
A World of Strangers▶
World War II: When Lions Roared
The Worldly Madonna
Woyzeck▶
The Wrestler
Wrestling Ernest Hemingway
Wrestling Racket Girls
The Wrong Move
The Wrong Road
X Marks the Spot
Xica▶
Yanco
A Yank in the R.A.F.
Year of the Dragon
Year of the Gun
The Yearling
Yellow Cargo
Yellow Earth
Yol▶
You Must Remember This
You Only Live Once
The Young Americans
Young Aphrodites
Young Charlie Chaplin
The Young Graduates
The Young in Heart▶
The Young Lions▶
Young Love, First Love
The Young Nurses
The Young One
The Young Philadelphians▶
The Young Teacher
Young Tom Edison
Young Winston▶
Youngblood
Your Ticket Is No Longer Valid
Youth Aflame
You've Ruined Me, Eddie
Yuri Nosenko, KGB
Zabriskie Point▶

Dream Girls

Drugs

Earthquakes

Eating

Eco-Vengeance!

Edibles

Elevators

Emerging Viruses

The Empire State Building

Erotic Thrillers

Ethics & Morals

see also Big Ideas

All the King's Men▶
And Justice for All
Any Man's Death
The Assault▶
Barbarians at the Gate▶
The Best Man▶
Blame It on Rio
Blue Chips
The Border▶
The Boy with the Green Hair▶
The Bridge on the River Kwai▶
Casualties of War▶
Chinese Roulette
Chloe in the Afternoon▶
Circle of Power
The Citadel▶
City Hall▶
The Conversation▶
Crimes & Misdemeanors▶
Cutter's Way
A Dangerous Woman
Deep Six
The Defiant Ones▶
The Doctor
The Dog Soldier
Double Identity
El: This Strange Passion▶
The Elephant Man▶
Elmer Gantry▶
Fifth Day of Peace
The Fifth Seal
Force of Evil▶
Fortunes of War
The Funeral▶
Fury▶
Getting Away With Murder
The Image
It Could Happen to You
Jezebel▶
The Judge and the Assassin▶
Judgment at Nuremberg▶
The Juggler of Notre Dame
Kings Row▶
La Ronde▶
La Truite▶
The Last of England▶
L'Avventura▶
The Lazarus Syndrome
License to Kill
Love with the Proper Stranger▶
Malicious
The Man Inside
The Man Who Shot Liberty Valance▶
Manhattan Melodrama▶
Marihuana
A Matter of Dignity
Midnight
The Millionairess
Mindwalk: A Film for Passionate Thinkers▶
Mr. Smith Goes to Washington▶
Mom & Dad
Muriel▶
Network▶
News at Eleven
The Next Voice You Hear
Nixon▶
No Man's Land
Oedipus Rex▶
One Flew Over the Cuckoo's Nest▶
Other People's Money
Overture to Glory
The Ox-Bow Incident▶
Paris Trout
Penalty Phase
A Place in the Sun▶
Platoon▶
The Ploughman's Lunch▶
Prime Suspect
Private Hell 36
Question 7
Quiz Show▶
Ran▶
Reckless Disregard
Riel
The Sacrifice▶
Scandal Man
The Scarlet Letter
The Scarlet Letter▶
Shampoo
The Shootist▶
Silent Witness
Soul Man
S*P*Y*S
SS Girls
The Star Chamber
The Story of Women▶
Strangers When We Meet
Survival of Spaceship Earth
Sweet Smell of Success▶
Test Tube Babies
The Things of Life▶
To Live & Die in L.A.
A Touch of Class▶
The Toy
Tulsa▶
Twelve Angry Men▶
Twenty-One
Tycoon
Under Fire▶
Viridiana▶
Wall Street▶
The Wheeler Dealers▶
With Honors
Zabriskie Point▶

Etiquette

Born Yesterday▶
Educating Rita▶
My Fair Lady▶
Papa's Delicate Condition▶
Phantom of Liberty▶
Pleasure
Pygmalion▶
The Ruling Class▶
True Love▶

Evil Doctors

see also Doctors & Nurses; Mad Scientists

The Abominable Dr. Phibes▶
The Awful Dr. Orlof
Body Melt
The Curious Dr. Humpp
Dead Ringers▶
Death and the Maiden▶
Dr. Alien
The Doctor and the Devils
Dr. Black, Mr. Hyde
Doctor Blood's Coffin
Doctor Butcher M.D.
Dr. Caligari
Dr. Cyclops
Dr. Death, Seeker of Souls
Dr. Frankenstein's Castle of Freaks
Dr. Giggles
Dr. Goldfoot and the Bikini Machine
Dr. Hackenstein
Dr. Jekyll and Mr. Hyde▶
Dr. Jekyll and Mr. Hyde
Dr. Jekyll and Sister Hyde
Dr. Jekyll and the Wolfman
Dr. Jekyll's Dungeon of Death
Dr. Mabuse, Parts 1 & 2▶
Dr. Mabuse vs. Scotland Yard
Dr. No▶
Dr. Otto & the Riddle of the Gloom Beam
Doctor Phibes Rises Again
Doctor Satan's Robot
Dr. Tarr's Torture Dungeon
Dr. Terror's House of Horrors
Doctor X
Jekyll and Hyde
Mad Doctor of Blood Island
Malice
Night of the Bloody Apes
Night of the Bloody Transplant
Slaughter Hotel
Strange World of Coffin Joe
The Two Faces of Dr. Jekyll

Existentialism

see The Meaning of Life

Experimental

see Avant-Garde

Exploitation

see also Sexploitation

Abduction
Agony of Love
American Nightmare
Angel of H.E.A.T.
Angels of the City
Armed Response
Artist's Studio Secrets
Assassin of Youth
Bachelor Party
Bad Girls from Mars
Barn of the Naked Dead
Basic Training
Beatrice▶
Betrayal
Beyond the Valley of the Dolls
The Black Maid
Black Shampoo
Blackenstein
Blood Games
The Bloody Brood
Blue Movies
Blue Ribbon Babes
Boss
The Cage
Caged Terror
Certain Sacrifice
Chained for Life
Come Back, Africa▶
Common Law Wife
Confessions of a Vice Baron
Cover Girl Models
The Curfew Breakers
The Cut Throats
Cycle Psycho
Cycle Vixens
Dance Hall Racket
Dangerous Obsession
The Dark Side of Love
Deadly Sanctuary
Death of a Centerfold
Devil's Wedding Night
Escape from Safehaven
Exterminator 2
Eyes of a Stranger
Film House Fever
Five Minutes to Love
The Flaming Teen-Age
For Ladies Only
Fox and His Friends▶
Foxy Brown
Ghoulies 3: Ghoulies Go to College
Girl on a Chain Gang
Gun Girls
Harlow
Heat of the Flame
High School Caesar
Hitler's Children▶
Hollywood After Dark
Hollywood Confidential
Hollywood Dreams
The Hollywood Strangler Meets the Skid Row Slasher
Honky Tonk Girl
House of Whipcord
I Accuse My Parents
In Trouble
Island of Lost Girls
Jock Petersen
Kidnapped
Kinjite: Forbidden Subjects
L.A. Heat
L.A. Vice
The Lash of the Penitents
Last Call
Little Girl ... Big Tease
Little Miss Innocence
The Lonely Sex
Love Camp
Mack
Malibu Express
Mandinga
M'Lady's Court
My Wonderful Life
The Naked Flame
Naked in the Night
Naked Vengeance
The Narcotics Story
Night Friend
Night of Evil
Nightmare in Red China
Nomugi Pass
One Down, Two to Go!
One Night Only
One Plus One
One Too Many
Overexposed
Paradise Motel
Party Incorporated
Pin Down Girls
Policewoman Centerfold
Poor Pretty Eddie
Protect Your Daughters
Rate It X
Reefer Madness
Revenge of the Zombies
The Road to Ruin
Samurai
Satan's Cheerleaders
Saturday Night Sleazies, Vol. 1
Savages from Hell
Secrets of Sweet Sixteen
Sensual Partners
Sex Adventures of the Three Musketeers
Sin You Sinners
Single Room Furnished
Slaughter
Slaughter's Big Ripoff
Slaves in Bondage
Sleazemania
Sleazemania III: The Good, the Bad & the Sleazy
S.O.B.
Something Weird
SS Girls
Star 80
Street of Forgotten Women
Student Confidential
Suite 16
Summer School Teachers
Sunset Strip
Swamp Women
Sweet Spirits
Taxi Dancers
The Teacher
Test Tube Babies
Therese & Isabelle
They're Playing with Fire
Three in the Attic
Thunder & Mud
Tomorrow's Children
Unmarried Mothers
Violated
Warrior Queen
Weekend with the Babysitter
Weird World of LSD
Wild Rapture
Wild Weed
Wild, Wild World of Jayne Mansfield
Woman Hunt
Women's Club
The Worst of Faces of Death
Wrestling Racket Girls
Yesterday's Hero
Young Lady Chatterly 2
Youth Aflame

Explorers

The Adventures of Marco Polo
Apollo 13▶
Cabeza de Vaca▶
Call Me Bwana
Christopher Columbus
Christopher Columbus: The Discovery
Congo
Conqueror & the Empress
1492: Conquest of Paradise
How Tasty Was My Little Frenchman
King Solomon's Mines▶
King Solomon's Mines
The Last Place on Earth
The Live Wire
The Lost World
The Magic Voyage
Mountains of the Moon▶
She
The Sky Above, the Mud Below
The Valley Obscured by the Clouds
The Wacky World of Wills & Burke
Wagon Wheels
Wake of the Red Witch

Extraordinary Pairings

Abbott and Costello Meet Frankenstein▶
Bela Lugosi Meets a Brooklyn Gorilla
Billy the Kid Versus Dracula
Dracula vs. Frankenstein
Frankenstein Meets the Space Monster
Frankenstein Meets the Wolfman▶
The Hollywood Strangler Meets the Skid Row Slasher
Jesse James Meets Frankenstein's Daughter
King Kong vs. Godzilla
Santa Claus Conquers the Martians
Wrestling Women vs. the Aztec Ape
Wrestling Women vs. the Aztec Mummy

Eyeballs!

see also Hearts!

Anguish
The Birds▶
A Clockwork Orange▶
The Crawling Eye
Damien: Omen 2
Demolition Man
Die Hard 2: Die Harder▶
Evil Dead 2: Dead by Dawn
The Eye Creatures
Eyeball
Eyes of Laura Mars
Friday the 13th, Part 3
The Fury
The Godfather▶
Headless Eyes
Peeping Tom▶
The Phantom
Rocky▶
Scanners
Strange Behavior
True Lies
Un Chien Andalou▶
X: The Man with X-Ray Eyes▶
Zombie

Fairs & Expositions

see also Amusement Parks; Carnivals & Circuses

Howling 6: The Freaks
Ma and Pa Kettle at the Fair
My Girl
Shag: The Movie▶
State Fair▶
Swap Meet

Family Ties

see also Dads; Moms; Parenthood

ABC Stage 67: Truman Capote's A Christmas Memory
Above Suspicion
Above the Rim
Abraham
The Accidental Tourist▶
Adam Had Four Sons
The Addams Family
Addams Family Values
The Adventures of Rusty

Roommates
Roosters
Roses Bloom Twice
The Royal Bed
Rulers of the City
Rumble Fish▶
The Run of the Country▶
Runaway Father
Running Mates▶
Running on Empty▶
Running Wild
Sabrina
The Sacketts
Sacred Ground
Safe Passage
Sallah▶
Samantha
Sandra of a Thousand Delights
The Santa Clause
Santa Sangre▶
The Saphead
Sardinia Kidnapped
Satan in High Heels
Savage Is Loose
Scandal in a Small Town
Scarlett
Scent of a Woman▶
Scott Turow's The Burden of Proof
Scream for Help
Sea Devils
The Search▶
Searching for Bobby Fischer▶
Season of Change
Season of Fear
Second Best▶
The Secret
Secret Ceremony
The Secret Garden▶
The Secret of Roan Inish▶
The Secret Passion of Robert Clayton
The Secret Rapture
Secrets and Lies
Secrets of Women▶
Seduced and Abandoned▶
The Seducers
See How She Runs▶
See You in the Morning
The Seekers
Sense & Sensibility
Sense and Sensibility▶
Sensuous Summer
Separate Vacations
Separate Ways
Seven Alone
Seven Beauties▶
7 Faces of Dr. Lao▶
Severance
Sex and the Single Parent
Shadow of a Doubt▶
The Shadow Riders
Shadows▶
The Shanghai Gesture
Shark River
Shattered▶
The Sheep Has Five Legs
The Shell Seekers
Shenandoah▶
Sherman's March: An Improbable Search for Love
The Shining Hour
Shoot the Moon
Shy People▶
Siberiade▶
The Sibling
Sibling Rivalry
The Sicilian Connection
Sidewalks of New York
The Silence▶
Silence
Silent Rebellion
Silent Tongue
Silent Witness
The Silver Stallion: King of the Wild Brumbies
Simple Justice
Simple Men▶
The Sin of Madelon Claudet▶
Since You Went Away▶
A Sinful Life
Sinners
Sioux City
The Sister-in-Law
Sister My Sister
The Sisters▶
Sisters▶
Six in Paris
Sixteen Candles▶
'68
Skag▶
Skin Game
Skylark
Slaughter of the Innocents
The Sleazy Uncle
Slightly Scarlet
The Slingshot▶
Small Sacrifices
Smilin' Through▶
Smoke
The Snapper▶
Snowy River, the MacGregor Saga: The Race
Sofie
The Solitary Man
Solo
Something to Talk About
Sometimes a Great Notion▶
Son-in-Law
Son of Flubber
Son of Frankenstein▶
Son of Fury▶
The Son of the Shark
Song of the Exile
Song of the Islands
Sons
Sons of Katie Elder▶
Sons of Steel
Sorceress
Sorrento Beach
Sorrows of Gin
The Sound of Music▶
South Central
South of Hell Mountain
The Southerner▶
Souvenir
The Spanish Gardener▶
Spanking the Monkey▶
Special Olympics
Spencer's Mountain
Spider Baby
Spirit Rider▶
Spitfire
Split Decisions
Split Image▶
Splitting Heirs
Spraggue
Star Spangled Rhythm▶
State Fair▶
State Fair
State of Grace▶
Steal Big, Steal Little
Stealing Beauty
Stella
Stella Dallas▶
The Stepfather▶
Stepfather 2: Make Room for Daddy
Stepfather 3: Father's Day
Stepmonster
Stepsisters
Still Not Quite Human
The Stolen Children▶
The Stone Boy▶
Stop! or My Mom Will Shoot
The Storm Within▶
The Story of Boys & Girls▶
The Story of Jacob & Joseph▶
Storyville
Strange Interlude▶
Strange Interlude
Strange Shadows in an Empty Room
Strangers in the City
Strangers: The Story of a Mother and Daughter▶
Strapless
Street Girls
Street Hero
Street Hitz
Street Justice
A Streetcar Named Desire▶
Striking Distance
Stuck on You
The Stupids
The Substitute Wife
Suddenly, Last Summer▶
Suffering Bastards
Sugar Cane Alley▶
Sugar Hill
The Sum of Us▶
Summer Holiday
Summer Magic
Summer of Fear
Summer Snow
Summer Wishes, Winter Dreams
A Sunday in the Country▶
Sunday's Children▶
The Sundowners▶
Sure Fire
Susan and God▶
Susana▶
Suture
Suzanne
Swedenhielms
The Sweeper
Sweet Smell of Success▶
Sweetie▶
The Swiss Family Robinson▶
Switched at Birth
Sylvester
Table Settings
The Tale of Ruby Rose▶
A Tale of Winter
Tales from Avonlea, Vol. 1: The Journey Begins
Tank
Tatie Danielle▶
Tears in the Rain
Teenage Exorcist
The Tempest▶
Teorema
Termini Station
Terms of Endearment▶
Testament▶
Tevye
Tex
Texas Jack
Texas Lightning
Thank You & Good Night
That Eye, The Sky
That Man Is Pregnant
That Was Then...This Is Now
There's No Business Like Show Business▶
They Watch
Things in Their Season
The Third Sex
Third Walker▶
This Boy's Life▶
This Happy Breed▶
This Is My Life
This Property is Condemned
A Thousand Clowns▶
Threads▶
Three Brothers▶
Three Daring Daughters
The Three Lives of Thomasina▶
Three Men and a Cradle▶
3 Ninjas
3 Ninjas Kick Back
Three Smart Girls▶
Three Violent People
The Three Weird Sisters
Three Wishes
Three's Trouble
Thrillkill
Through a Glass Darkly▶
Thursday's Child
Ticket to Heaven▶
The Tie That Binds
Tiger Warsaw
Till Marriage Do Us Part
Till There was You
Time Flies When You're Alive
Time Indefinite
A Time of Destiny
Time Stands Still▶
A Time to Live
A Time to Live and a Time to Die
Time Without Pity
Timemaster
'Tis a Pity She's a Whore
Titanic▶
Tito and Me▶
To All My Friends on Shore▶
To Dance with the White Dog▶
To Die for 2: Son of Darkness
To Grandmother's House We Go
To Live▶
To Paris with Love
To Sleep with Anger▶
Toby McTeague
Tokyo Story▶
Toll of the Desert
Tollbooth
Tommy Boy
Toughlove
Toys
Toys in the Attic
Track 29
Trade Secrets
Trading Mom
Traenen in Florenz
Traffic Jam
Trained to Kill
Tramp at the Door
Trapped In Paradise
Traps
Travels with My Aunt
Treacherous Crossing
Treasure of the Sierra Madre▶
The Tree of Wooden Clogs▶
The Trip to Bountiful▶
Trois Couleurs: Blanc▶
Trois Couleurs: Bleu▶
Troublemakers
True Blood
True Confessions▶
True Love▶
True West▶
Trusting Beatrice
The Tuttles of Tahiti▶
29th Street
Twice in a Lifetime▶
Twister
Two Bits
Two Kinds of Love
The Two Sisters
Two Small Bodies
The Ugly Dachshund
Uncle Buck▶
Uncle Moses
Uncommon Valor
Under the Boardwalk
Under the Hula Moon
Under the Volcano▶
Undergrads▶
Uneasy Terms
The Unforgiven▶
An Unremarkable Life
Unstrung Heroes
Until They Sail
Up the Sandbox
The Uprising▶
Used People
Vengeance
Vengeance Valley
A Very Brady Christmas
A Very Brady Sequel
Vigil▶
Vincent & Theo▶
Violette▶
Viridiana▶
Voyage en Balloon
A Voyage' Round My Father▶
Voyage to Italy
Voyager▶
Vultures
Wagon Tracks
Wait Till Your Mother Gets Home
A Walk in the Clouds
Walk in the Spring Rain
The Waltons: A Thanksgiving Story
The Waltons: The Christmas Carol
The War
War & Remembrance, Part 1
War & Remembrance, Part 2
War & Remembrance: The Final Chapter, Part 8
War & Remembrance: The Final Chapter, Part 9
Waterfront
The Wedding Banquet▶
Wedding in White
Weep No More My Lady
Welcome Home
Welcome to the Dollhouse
Whale Music
The Whales of August▶
What About Bob?▶
What Ever Happened To...
What Ever Happened to Baby Jane?▶
What the Peeper Saw
What's Eating Gilbert Grape▶
When a Man Loves a Woman
When Nature Calls
When Wolves Cry
Where East Is East
Where Have All the People Gone?
Where Love Has Gone
Where the Heart Is
Where the Lilies Bloom▶
Where's Poppa?▶
While You Were Sleeping▶
The White Balloon▶
The White Cliffs of Dover▶
White Mane▶
Why Does Herr R. Run Amok?
Wicked Stepmother
Widow's Kiss
Wild at Heart▶
The Wild Country
The Wild Duck
Wild Pony
Wild West
Wild Zone
Wilder Napalm
Wildflower▶
The Winds of War
Winter Kills▶
Winter People
Winterset
The Wistful Widow of Wagon Gap
With Six You Get Eggroll
The Wizard
The Wizard of Loneliness
A Woman Under the Influence▶
Women on the Verge of a Nervous Breakdown▶
Woodchipper Massacre
The World Accuses
A World Apart▶
The World of Apu▶
The Worldly Madonna
Wyatt Earp
The Yearling
Yellow Earth
You Can't Take It with You▶
The Young Detectives on Wheels
Younger & Younger
Your Ticket Is No Longer Valid
Yours, Mine & Ours
Zertigo Diamond Caper
Zooman▶

Fantasy

see also ***Animation & Cartoons; Musical Fantasy***

A Nous la Liberte▶
The Acid Eaters
Adventures in Dinosaur City
The Adventures of a Gnome Named Gnorm
The Adventures of Baron Munchausen▶
The Adventures of Mark Twain▶
The Adventures of Pinocchio
Afrita Hanen▶
Aladdin
Aladdin and His Wonderful Lamp
Alice▶
Alice Through the Looking Glass
Alice's Adventures in Wonderland
Alien from L.A.
...Almost
Alone Against Rome

Sherlock Holmes in Washington
Shredder Orpheus
Siegfried▶
Sinbad and the Eye of the Tiger
Sinbad of the Seven Seas
Slave Girls from Beyond Infinity
Sleepwalk
Solarbabies
Some Call It Loving
Something Wicked This Way Comes
Son of Kong
Son of Samson
Son of Sinbad
Song Spinner
Sons of Hercules in the Land of Darkness
Sorceress
Space Raiders
Space Soldiers Conquer the Universe
Splash
The Spring
Stalker▶
Stand Up and Cheer
The Steagle
Steel Dawn
Story of a Cowboy Angel
Storybook
Strange Tales
Strange Tales/Ray Bradbury Theatre
Striptease
Student of Prague▶
Super Mario Bros.
Supergirl
Superman: The Movie▶
Superman 2▶
Superman 3
Superman 4: The Quest for Peace
Superman & the Mole Men
Superman: The Serial, Vol. 1
Survival of a Dragon
Sword & the Dragon
Sword & the Sorcerer
The Sword in the Stone▶
Sword of the Valiant
Sylvia and the Phantom▶
Tales of Beatrix Potter▶
Tall Tale: The Unbelievable Adventures of Pecos Bill
Tammy and the T-Rex
Tank Girl
Tanya's Island
Teenage Mutant Ninja Turtles: The Movie
The Tempest
Terror of Rome Against the Son of Hercules
Terror of the Steppes
Test Tube Teens from the Year 2000
The Testament of Dr. Cordelier▶
The Testament of Orpheus▶
The Thief of Bagdad▶
The Thief of Baghdad▶
Thief of Baghdad
The Thief of Baghdad
Thor and the Amazon Women
A Thousand and One Nights
Three Wishes
The Three Worlds of Gulliver
Throne of Fire
Thumbelina
Time Bandits
Time Burst: The Final Alliance
Time Fighters
The Time of Their Lives
Timestalkers
Tobor the Great
Tom Thumb▶
Toy Story▶
Trading Mom
Train to Hollywood▶
Transformers: The Movie
The Trip
Triumph of the Son of Hercules
A Troll in Central Park
Trouble in Mind▶
The Tune
20,000 Leagues Under the Sea▶
The Twilight Zone
The Two Worlds of Jenny Logan
Tyrant of Lydia Against the Son of Hercules
Ultra Flash
Undersea Kingdom
Unidentified Flying Oddball
Ursus in the Valley of the Lions
The Valley of Gwangi▶
Venus Against the Son of Hercules
A Very Old Man with Enormous Wings
Vibes
Vice Versa▶
Vulcan God of Fire
Walking on Air
The Warrior & the Sorceress
Warrior Queen
Watership Down
Wax, or the Discovery of Television Among the Bees
Waxworks▶
Welcome to Blood City
The White Sheik▶
Wild Women of Wongo
Wildest Dreams
Willow
Window to Paris
Wings of Desire▶
Wings of Fame
Witch Hunt
A Witch Without a Broom
The Witching of Ben Wagner
The Wizard of Oz
The Wizard of Speed and Time
Wizards
Wizards of the Lost Kingdom
Wizards of the Lost Kingdom 2
Wombling Free
The Wonderful World of the Brothers Grimm
Woof!
The Worst Witch
Yor, the Hunter from the Future
Zapped!
Zardoz
Zero for Conduct▶
Zone Troopers

Farming

see Crop Dusters

Fast Cars

see also Motor Vehicle Dept.

American Graffiti▶
Baffled
Banzai Runner
The Big Wheel
Bobby Deerfield
Born to Race
Born to Run
Brewster McCloud▶
Bullitt▶
Burn 'Em Up Barnes
Cannonball
Cannonball Run
Cannonball Run 2
Car Crash
Catch Me...If You Can
The Checkered Flag
Daddy-O
Days of Thunder
Death Driver
Death Race 2000
Death Sport
Desert Steel
The Devil on Wheels
Diamonds Are Forever▶
Dirty Mary Crazy Larry▶
Dragstrip Girl
Eat My Dust
The Fast and the Furious
Fast Company
Fast Lane Fever
Faster Pussycat! Kill! Kill!
Fury on Wheels
Genevieve▶
Goldfinger▶
Grand Prix
Grandview U.S.A.
Greased Lightning
Great Race
Gumball Rally
Hard Drivin'
Heart Like a Wheel
The Heavenly Kid
Hell on Wheels
Herbie Goes Bananas
Herbie Goes to Monte Carlo
High Gear
Hot Rod
Hot Rod Girl
King of the Mountain
The Last American Hero▶
Last Chase
Le Mans▶
A Man and a Woman: 20 Years Later
The Pinchcliffe Grand Prix
Private Road: No Trespassing
Race for Life
Race the Sun
The Racers
Rebel Without a Cause▶
Red Line 7000
Return to Macon County
Richard Petty Story
Road Racers
Roaring Roads
Safari 3000
Sahara
Shaker Run
Six Pack
Smash Palace
Smokey and the Bandit
Speed Zone
Speedway
Spinout
Stroker Ace
Those Daring Young Men in Their Jaunty Jalopies
To Please a Lady
Van Nuys Blvd.
Vanishing Point
Viva Las Vegas
Winning▶
The Wraith

Feds

see also Detectives; Spies & Espionage

American Yakuza
Assassin
Betrayed
Black Widow▶
Bloodfist 5: Human Target
Boiling Point
Broken Trust
Burning Vengeance
Capone
Captain Nuke and the Bomber Boys
Children of Fury
Chu Chu & the Philly Flash
C.I.A.: Code Name Alexa
C.I.A. 2: Target Alexa
Class of 1999 2: The Substitute
Clear and Present Danger
The Client
Code Name Alpha
Crime Killer
Daughter of the Tong
Deadly Spygames
Dillinger and Capone
The Eiger Sanction
Eraser
Exterminator
Fast Getaway 2
FBI Girl
The FBI Murders▶
The FBI Story▶
Federal Agents vs. Underworld, Inc.
Feds
Femme Fontaine: Killer Babe for the C.I.A.
Fifty/Fifty
The Fix
Flashback▶
Flight to Nowhere
Follow That Car
"G" Men▶
G-Men Never Forget
The Glass Jungle
Golden Gate
Government Agents vs. Phantom Legion
Guarding Tess
Gun Grit
Hit Woman: The Double Edge
Honor and Glory
House on 92nd Street▶
I Was a Zombie for the FBI
I'll Get You
In the Line of Fire▶
J. Edgar Hoover
Johnnie Gibson F.B.I.
Kelly of the Secret Service
Kill Castro
Killer Likes Candy
Let 'Em Have It
Live Wire
Live Wire: Human Timebomb
Manhunter▶
Mankillers
Married to the Mob▶
Me and the Mob
Melvin Purvis: G-Man
Memoirs of an Invisible Man
Midnight Murders
Mission: Impossible▶
Mississippi Burning▶
Nixon▶
No Safe Haven
The Outfit
The P.A.C.K.
Panther
Patriot Games▶
Plughead Rewired: Circuitry Man 2
Point Break
President's Target
The Private Files of J. Edgar Hoover
Raiders of Ghost City
Raw Deal
The Reluctant Agent
The Return of Eliot Ness
Revolver
Robin of Locksley
The Rock▶
Rosebud
Royce
S.A.S. San Salvador
Scam
Shattered Image
Silence of the Hams
The Silence of the Lambs▶
The Silencers
Silk Degrees
Sky High
Slaughter of the Innocents
Special Investigator
The Spook Who Sat By the Door
Street Hawk
Street Justice
Sugartime
Target
That Darn Cat
357 Magnum
Thunderheart▶
To Live & Die in L.A.
To the Limit
Triplecross
The Untouchables▶
Violent Breed
White Ghost
White Sands
The X-Files: Pilot Episode/Deep Throat
Zero Tolerance

Female Bonding

see also Women; Wonder Women

Across the Moon
Antonia's Line
Beaches▶
Boys on the Side
The Buccaneers▶
Camilla
The Cemetery Club
The Craft
Desert Hearts▶
Fried Green Tomatoes▶
Girls Town
The Heidi Chronicles
How to Make an American Quilt
The Joy Luck Club▶
Live Nude Girls
Moonlight and Valentino
9 to 5
Now and Then
Passion Fish▶
Steel Magnolias▶
Talk
Thelma & Louise▶
Waiting to Exhale▶
A Woman's Guide to Adultery

Feminism

see Women; Wonder Women

Femme Fatale

see also Wonder Women

The Accused
Addams Family Values
Algiers▶
All About Eve▶
The Amy Fisher Story
Armored Command
Auntie Lee's Meat Pies
Backstab
Basic Instinct
Beverly Hills Vamp
Bitter Harvest
Black Magic Woman
Black Widow▶
Blood of Dracula
The Blood Spattered Bride
Blown Away
The Blue Angel▶
Body Heat▶
Body of Evidence
Body Trouble
Bulletproof Heart▶
The Cabin in the Cotton
Caesar and Cleopatra
Carried Away
Casino▶
Casque d'Or▶
Casualties of Love: The "Long Island Lolita" Story
Cat on a Hot Tin Roof
Champagne for Caesar▶
Clash by Night▶
Clean Slate
Cleopatra
Crime of Passion
Crush
The Crush
The Dallas Connection
Dance Hall
Dangerous Liaisons▶
Daughter of the Tong
Dead Reckoning▶
Deadly Past
Death in Deep Water
Deceptions
Detour▶
The Devil's Daughter
Disclosure
Dishonored Lady
Dr. Caligari
Dr. Jekyll and Sister Hyde
Double Indemnity▶
Double Jeopardy
Dream Lover
Drowning by Numbers▶
Emmanuelle, the Queen
Eve of Destruction
Fangs of the Living Dead
Far from the Madding Crowd▶
Faster Pussycat! Kill! Kill!
Federal Agents vs. Underworld, Inc.
Final Analysis
First Name: Carmen▶
Flame of the Islands

The Flesh and the Devil▶
A Fool There Was
Frankenhooker
The Girl from Tobacco Row
Girl Hunters
Girl in His Pocket
A Girl to Kill For
Girlfriend from Hell
Great Flamarion
Grievous Bodily Harm
Hedda
Hellgate
Human Desire
I Spit on Your Corpse
Illusions
Impact▶
Impulse
Inner Sanctum
Intersection
Into the Fire
Invasion of the Bee Girls▶
The Jayne Mansfield Story
Jezebel▶
Kill Cruise
L'Addition
Lady and the Tramp▶
Lady for a Night
Lady Frankenstein
The Lady from Shanghai▶
The Lair of the White Worm▶
The Last Seduction▶
Leave Her to Heaven▶
The Legend of the Wolf Woman
Lemora, Lady Dracula
The Leopard Woman
Lethal Lolita—Amy Fisher: My Story
The Lifetaker
Linda
Love Is a Gun
Mado▶
The Malibu Beach Vampires
Malice
Malicious
The Maltese Falcon▶
Mantis in Lace
Married to the Mob▶
Mata Hari▶
Mata Hari
Medusa Against the Son of Hercules
Mesa of Lost Women
Mirage
Ms. 45▶
Mountaintop Motel Massacre
Nana▶
Nana
The Natural▶
Night Angel
The Night Evelyn Came Out of the Grave
Night of the Cobra Woman
Night Tide
No Way Out▶
Of Human Bondage▶
Of Human Bondage
On Her Majesty's Secret Service▶
Out Cold
Out of the Past▶
The Pamela Principle
Party Girls
Pepe Le Moko▶
Perfect Alibi
Planet of Blood
Play Murder for Me
Point of No Return
Poison Ivy
Poison Ivy 2: Lily
Possession: Until Death Do You Part
The Postman Always Rings Twice▶
Praying Mantis
Prey of the Chameleon
The Quick and the Dead
A Rage in Harlem▶
Ran▶
Range Renegades
Reckless
Ring of Steel
Roadhouse Girl
Salome
Samson and Delilah▶
Samson and Delilah
Satanik
Scandal▶
Scarlet Street▶
Scorned
Sea of Love▶
Secret Weapons
The Secretary
Seven Sinners▶
Sexpot
Shadows in the Storm
Sins of Jezebel
Sleep of Death
Snow White and the Seven Dwarfs▶
Some Came Running▶
Something Wild
The Specialist
The Strange Woman
Sunrise▶
Sunset Boulevard▶
The Temp
The Temptress
A Thin Line Between Love and Hate
Third Degree Burn
Tomb
Too Late for Tears▶
Truth or Dare
Under Suspicion
The Untamable
Valmont▶
Vanity Fair
The Velvet Vampire
Venus Against the Son of Hercules
Venus in Furs
Victim of Desire
The Wasp Woman
White Cargo
Who Framed Roger Rabbit▶
Witchcraft 3: The Kiss of Death
Woman of Desire

Fencing

see also Swashbucklers

By the Sword
Ring of Steel
Rob Roy▶

Fifties

see Nifty '50s

Film History

America at the Movies
American Cinema
Assunta Spina
The Bad and the Beautiful▶
Battle of Elderbush Gulch
The Battleship Potemkin▶
Bellissimo: Images of the Italian Cinema
The Big Picture
Bombshell▶
Burden of Dreams
The Busby Berkeley Disc
Buster Keaton Rides Again/The Railrodder
Camp Classics #1
The Celluloid Closet▶
Chaplin: A Character Is Born
Cinema Paradiso▶
Cinema Shrapnel
The Comic▶
Crimes & Misdemeanors▶
Custer's Last Fight
Doctor X
Early Cinema Vol. 1
Early Sound Films
Ed Wood▶
Ed Wood: Look Back in Angora
8 1/2▶
Fangoria's Weekend of Horrors
Flying Saucers Over Hollywood: The Plan 9 Companion
Forever James Dean
Frank and Ollie▶
From "Star Wars" to "Jedi": The Making of a Saga
Golden Age of Hollywood
Great Chase
Great Movie Stunts & the Making of Raiders of the Lost Ark
The Great Train Robbery: Cinema Begins
Griffith Biograph Program
Guilty by Suspicion
Happy Anniversary 007: 25 Years of James Bond
Heavy Petting
Hepburn & Tracy
Here's Looking at You, Warner Bros.▶
History of the World: Part 1
Hollywood Boulevard
Hollywood Come Home
Hollywood Crime Wave
Hollywood Home Movies
Hollywood in Trouble
Hollywood Outtakes & Rare Footage
Hollywood Scandals and Tragedies
Hollywood Uncensored
Hollywood without Makeup
Intervista▶
James Dean: The First American Teenager
A Kiss for Mary Pickford
Kisses
The Lady Without Camelias
Last Command▶
The Last Tycoon▶
Lies
Lightning Over Water
The Little Theatre of Jean Renoir▶
Lobster Man from Mars
Lost Squadron
The Love Goddesses
Many Faces of Sherlock Holmes
Marlon Brando
MGM: When the Lion Roars
Modern Romance▶
Movie Maker
The Oscar
Oscar's Greatest Moments: 1971-1991
Paris When It Sizzles
The Perils of Pauline
Prurient Interest
Rented Lips
Scenario du Film Passion▶
Scherzo
Sex and Buttered Popcorn
Signals Through the Flames▶
S.O.B.
A Star is Born▶
Stardust Memories
State of Things▶
Story of William S. Hart/Sad Clowns
Strangers Kiss
The Stunt Man▶
That's Adequate
Visions of Light: The Art of Cinematography▶
Way Down East▶
When Comedy was King
The Wonderful, Horrible Life of Leni Riefenstahl
You Must Remember This

Film Noir

see also Contemporary Noir

The Accused
Al Capone▶
Amateur▶
The Asphalt Jungle▶
Beware, My Lovely
Beyond a Reasonable Doubt
Big Combo▶
The Big Heat▶
The Big Sleep▶
Black Lizard
The Blue Dahlia▶
Bob le Flambeur▶
Body Heat▶
Boomerang▶
Born to Kill▶
Bulletproof Heart▶
Cornered▶
Crack-Up
Criss Cross▶
Crossfire▶
Dark Corner▶
Dark Mirror▶
Dark Passage
Dead Again▶
Dead Silence
Deadline at Dawn
Delusion
Desperate
Detour▶
The Devil Thumbs a Ride▶
The Devil Thumbs a Ride/Having Wonderful Crime
D.O.A.▶
Don't Bother to Knock
Double Indemnity▶
The Element of Crime
The Enforcer
Fallen Angels 1▶
Fallen Angels 2▶
Farewell, My Lovely▶
Force of Evil▶
Frantic▶
Gilda▶
The Glass Key▶
Gotham▶
Gun Crazy▶
High & Low▶
High Sierra▶
The Hitch-Hiker▶
Human Desire
In a Lonely Place▶
Jigsaw▶
Johnny Angel▶
Key Largo▶
Killer's Kiss
The Killing▶
King Creole
Kiss Me Deadly▶
Kiss of Death▶
The Lady from Shanghai▶
Lady in the Death House
Lady in the Lake
The Las Vegas Story
Laura▶
Le Doulos▶
Leave Her to Heaven▶
Macao▶
The Maltese Falcon▶
Mikey & Nicky
Mildred Pierce▶
Murder, My Sweet▶
The Naked City▶
Naked Kiss
The Narrow Margin▶
Niagara
Night and the City▶
Nightfall▶
Nocturne
On Dangerous Ground▶
Out of the Past▶
Panic in the Streets▶
Pickup on South Street▶
Pitfall▶
Plunder Road
The Postman Always Rings Twice▶
The Postman Always Rings Twice
Postmark for Danger/Quicksand
Prowler
The Red House▶
Rendez-vous▶
Rope▶
The Scar
Scarlet Street▶
The Set-Up▶
Shoot to Kill
Signal 7
Slow Moves
Sorry, Wrong Number▶
Station
Strange Illusion
The Strange Love of Martha Ivers▶
Sudden Fear▶
Sunset Boulevard▶
Sweet Smell of Success▶
Tchao Pantin▶
They Live by Night▶
The Third Man▶
This Gun for Hire▶
Too Late for Tears▶
Touch of Evil▶
The Underneath▶
Vortex
While the City Sleeps▶
White Heat▶
The Window▶
A Woman's Secret
The Wrong Man▶

Film Stars

see also Price of Fame

Acting on Impulse
Actor: The Paul Muni Story
Bela Lugosi Scrapbook
The Best of Bogart▶
Blonde Cobra/The Doctor's Dream
Bogie: The Last Hero
Bombshell▶
The Bretts▶
Bruce Lee: Curse of the Dragon▶
Bud and Lou
Calendar Girl
Chaplin▶
Count/Adventurer
Cult People
Dear Brigitte
Death at Love House
Deep in My Heart
Duke: The Films of John Wayne
Ed Wood▶
Emperor Jones/Paul Robeson: Tribute to an Artist
Frances▶
Go West, Young Man
Grosse Fatigue▶
Hedda Hopper's Hollywood
Hepburn & Tracy
Hollywood Clowns
Hollywood Goes to War
Hollywood Home Movies
The Horror of It All
Hurricane Express
In Person
James Dean
James Stewart: A Wonderful Life
The Jayne Mansfield Story
The Josephine Baker Story▶
The King of Kings▶
Kisses
L.A. Goddess
Legend of Valentino
The Legend of Valentino
The Love Goddesses
Man of a Thousand Faces▶
Marilyn & Bobby: Her Final Affair
Marlon Brando
The Meateater
Merton of the Movies
My Favorite Year▶
My Wicked, Wicked Ways
The Oscar
Oscar's Greatest Moments: 1971-1991
Overexposed
Perfect Furlough
The Perils of Pauline
Play It Again, Sam▶
The Player▶
Power, Passion & Murder
The Purple Rose of Cairo▶
Queenie
Rainbow
Rascal Dazzle
Rita Hayworth: The Love Goddess
Rock Hudson's Home Movies
Sinatra
Sophia Loren: Her Own Story
Superstar: The Life and Times of Andy Warhol▶
Targets▶
That's Entertainment
That's Entertainment, Part 2

That's Entertainment, Part 3
Thursday's Child
Users
Valentino
Veronika Voss▶
W.C. Fields: Flask of Fields
What Ever Happened to Baby Jane?▶
White Hot: The Mysterious Murder of Thelma Todd
Wild, Wild World of Jayne Mansfield
Work/Police▶

Filmmaking

see also At the Movies; Behind the Scenes

Abbott and Costello Meet the Keystone Kops
The Adjuster
An Almost Perfect Affair
...And God Spoke
Barton Fink▶
Big Show
Black Cat
Bloodbath in Psycho Town
Body Chemistry 3: Point of Seduction
Bombay Talkie
Cass
Children Shouldn't Play with Dead Things
Chuck Amuck: The Movie
Ciao Federico! Fellini Directs Satyricon
Comment Ca Va?
Contempt▶
The Cool Surface
Dangerous Game
David Holzman's Diary▶
Day for Night▶
Dead Silence
Dracula: A Cinematic Scrapbook
Drifting
Dubeat-E-O
Ed Wood▶
Ed Wood: Look Back in Angora
The Ed Wood Story: The Plan 9 Companion
84 Charlie Mopic▶
Elsa, Elsa
Elvis in Hollywood▶
F/X 2: The Deadly Art of Illusion
Final Cut
Finnegan's Wake
Frankenstein: A Cinematic Scrapbook
Get Shorty▶
Good Morning, Babylon▶
Hearts of Darkness: A Filmmaker's Apocalypse▶
Hi, Mom!▶
Hollywood Chaos
Hollywood Mystery
The Horror of It All
The House of Seven Corpses
How to Make a Monster
I'll Do Anything
In a Moment of Passion
Intervista▶
Invasion Force
Iron Cowboy
Island of Blood
It's All True
Jacquot
Kamikaze Hearts
The King of the Kickboxers
The Last Porno Flick
Les Violons du Bal
Living in Oblivion▶
Loaded
A Man, a Woman and a Killer
A Man Like Eva▶
The Mirror Crack'd
Mistress
Mute Witness
My Dream Is Yours
My Life's In Turnaround
Nightmare in Blood
Nightmare in Wax
Notes for an African Orestes
Nudity Required
On an Island with You
Once in Paris...
The Pickle
Pictures
The Player▶
The Red Raven Kiss-Off
Secret File of Hollywood
She Must Be Seeing Things
Silent Motive
A Slave of Love▶
Special Effects
Stand-In
The Stunt Man▶
Sullivan's Travels▶
The Swap
Sweet Liberty
Swimming with Sharks▶
Two Weeks in Another Town
Ulysses' Gaze
Understudy: The Graveyard Shift 2
Visions of Light: The Art of Cinematography▶
Wes Craven's New Nightmare▶
White Hunter, Black Heart▶
The Wizard of Speed and Time
The Wonderful, Horrible Life of Leni Riefenstahl
You Must Remember This

Firemen

see also Fires

Always
Backdraft
Backfire!
Club Paradise
Fahrenheit 451▶
Fire Alarm
Fireballs
Firehouse
The Fireman
The Firemen's Ball▶
Hellfighters
Inferno in Paradise
Roxanne▶
Trespass
Turk 182!

Fires

see also Boom!; Disaster Flicks; Firemen

Always
Backdraft
Burning Rage
City on Fire
The Cremators
Dinosaurus!
Don't Go in the House
Endless Love
Erendira
Fire
Fire Alarm
Firehead
The Fireman
Firestarter
Firestorm: 72 Hours in Oakland
The Flaming Urge
Flashfire
Frankenstein▶
In Old Chicago▶
Island of the Burning Doomed
The Michigan Kid
Mighty Joe Young
Nice Girls Don't Explode
Oil
Pretty Poison▶
Pyrates
A Pyromaniac's Love Story
Quest for Fire▶
Save the Tiger▶
Sounds of Silence
Speeding Up Time
Spontaneous Combustion
Terror on the 40th Floor
Ticks
The Towering Inferno
The Triangle Factory Fire Scandal
Wilder Napalm

Flashback

Antonia's Line
Being at Home with Claude
Betrayal
Boys
Broken Harvest
Carried Away
Casablanca▶
Citizen Kane▶
The Confessional
Courage Under Fire▶
Dogfight▶
Dolores Claiborne▶
Edward Scissorhands▶
Exotica▶
A Family Thing▶
Frankie Starlight
Helas Pour Moi
Hellraiser 4: Bloodline
Jacob's Ladder
Johnny Dangerously
Kicking and Screaming▶
Leave Her to Heaven▶
Liebestraum
The Neon Bible
Nina Takes a Lover
The Ninth Configuration▶
Now and Then
Passage to Marseilles▶
The Razor's Edge▶
The Razor's Edge
Reservoir Dogs▶
Sergeant Rutledge▶
Shattered
Stealing Home
301, 302
Total Eclipse
The Underneath▶
The Usual Suspects▶
Valentino
Wild Bill
The Wild Bunch▶

Flatulence

Blazing Saddles▶
Dumb & Dumber
Ed
Grumpier Old Men
National Lampoon's Senior Trip
The Road to Wellville

Flight

see Airborne

Flower Children

see also Boomer Reunions

Adam at 6 a.m.
Alice's Restaurant
American Blue Note
Angels Hard as They Come
Awakenings of the Beast
Best Enemies
Best Revenge
The Big Chill▶
The Big Fix▶
Blast-Off Girls
Bob & Carol & Ted & Alice
Born on the Fourth of July▶
Children Shouldn't Play with Dead Things
The Compleat Beatles▶
Conspiracy: The Trial of the Chicago Eight▶
The Crimson Cult
Dogfight▶
The Doors
Dreamwood▶
Dynamite Chicken
Easy Rider▶
Even Cowgirls Get the Blues
Flashback▶
Four Friends▶
Free Grass
Fritz the Cat▶
Gimme Shelter
The Glory Stompers
Greetings▶
Hair▶
Head▶
Help Wanted Female
High Hopes▶
I Drink Your Blood
I Love You, Alice B. Toklas!
Mantis in Lace
Married to It
The Mod Squad
More
More American Graffiti
Off Limits
Out
Petit Con
Property
Psych-Out
Psychedelic Fever
Rainbow Bridge
The Rebel Set
Revolution
R.P.M.* (*Revolutions Per Minute)
Rude Awakening
The Sandpiper
Satan's Sadists
Sea Devils
Second Thoughts
Slashed Dreams
A Small Circle of Friends
The Snake People
The Speed Lovers
The Stoned Age
The Strawberry Statement
There Goes My Baby
There's a Girl in My Soup
Thumb Tripping
The Trip
Where Angels Go, Trouble Follows
Where the Eagle Flies
Who'll Stop the Rain?▶
Wild in the Streets
Woodstock▶
Yellow Submarine▶

Flying Saucers

see Alien Beings—Benign; Alien Beings—Vicious; Space Operas

Folklore & Mythology

see also Storytelling

Antonio Das Mortes
Atlantis, the Lost Continent
Atlas in the Land of the Cyclops
The Ballad of Paul Bunyan
Beauty and the Devil
Black Orpheus▶
Candyman
Candyman 2: Farewell to the Flesh
Clash of the Titans
Colossus and the Amazon Queen
Crossroads
Darby O'Gill & the Little People▶
Disney's Storybook Classics
Donkey Skin▶
Down to Earth
Dreamwood▶
Early Russian Cinema, Vol. 2: Folklore & Legend
Erik the Viking
Faust▶
The Fool Killer
Force on Thunder Mountain
The Fury of Hercules
The Giant of Marathon
The Giant of Metropolis
The Giants of Thessaly
Golden Voyage of Sinbad
Goliath Against the Giants
Goliath and the Barbarians
Goliath and the Dragon
Goliath and the Sins of Babylon
The Gorgon
Grendel, Grendel, Grendel
Helen of Troy
Hercules
Hercules 2
Hercules Against the Moon Men
Hercules and the Captive Women
Hercules in the Haunted World
Hercules Unchained
Into the West▶
Invincible Gladiators
Invitation to the Dance
Iphigenia▶
Jason and the Argonauts▶
Johnny Appleseed
Kismet▶
Kriemhilde's Revenge▶
Leapin' Leprechauns
The Legend of Sleepy Hollow
The Legend of Suram Fortress
Leprechaun 2
Life on a String
The Loves of Hercules
Magic in the Water
Medea
Merlin and the Sword
Messalina vs. the Son of Hercules
A Midsummer Night's Dream
Monty Python and the Holy Grail▶
My Darlin' Clementine
Pancho Villa Returns
Pandora and the Flying Dutchman
Pathfinder▶
Pecos Bill
Phedre
Phoenix
The Phoenix and the Magic Carpet
Rudyard Kipling's Classic Stories
The Secret of Navajo Cave
The Secret of Roan Inish▶
The Secret of the Loch
Siegfried▶
Son of Samson
Sons of Hercules in the Land of Darkness
Tall Tale: The Unbelievable Adventures of Pecos Bill
Terror of Rome Against the Son of Hercules
Thor and the Amazon Women
Ulysses
Ursus in the Valley of the Lions
Vulcan God of Fire
Wend Kuuni
The Wonderful World of the Brothers Grimm
Young Aphrodites
Zvenigora▶

Food

see Edibles

Football

Ace Ventura: Pet Detective
All the Right Moves
Backfield in Motion
The Best of Times
Black Sunday
Brian's Song▶
Cheering Section
Cheerleaders' Wild Weekend
Diner▶
The Dropkick▶
Easy Living
Everybody's All American
Father Was a Fullback
First & Ten
First & Ten: The Team Scores Again
The Fortune Cookie▶
The Freshman▶
The Galloping Ghost
Good News
Grambling's White Tiger
Gus
The Halfback of Notre Dame
Harmon of Michigan
Heaven Can Wait▶
Hold 'Em Jail
Horse Feathers▶
Jim Thorpe: All American

Johnny Be Good
Knute Rockne: All American▶
The Last Boy Scout
Last Game
Last Time Out
Little Giants
The Longest Yard
Midnight Heat
Navy Blue and Gold
Necessary Roughness
North Dallas Forty▶
The O.J. Simpson Story
One Night Only
Paper Lion
The Program
Quarterback Princess
Roberta▶
Rudy
School Ties▶
Semi-Tough
The Spirit of West Point
Trouble Along the Way
Two Minute Warning
Wildcats
Windrunner

Foreign Intrigue

***see also** Spies & Espionage*

Above Suspicion▶
Ambassador Bill
American Roulette
Battle Beneath the Earth
Bulldog Drummond at Bay
Call Him Mr. Shatter
Catch Me a Spy
Chinese Boxes
Chinese Web
Cover-Up
Crimson Tide▶
The Day of the Jackal▶
Deadly Alliance
Defense Play
The Destructors
Devil Wears White
Diamonds Are Forever▶
Diplomatic Courier▶
Dr. No▶
The Dogs of War
Don't Drink the Water
The Eiger Sanction
An Englishman Abroad▶
Enigma
The Equalizer: Memories of Manon
Erik
Escapade in Florence
Escape from the KGB
Escape to Love
Escape to the Sun
The Executioner
The Experts
Exposed
Exposure
Eye of the Needle
Federal Agent
Foreign Correspondent▶
The Fourth Protocol▶
A Global Affair
Gunpowder
Half Moon Street
The Human Factor
The Hunt for Red October▶
Jaguar Lives
Jumpin' Jack Flash
The Key to Rebecca
La Passante▶
Lady L
License to Kill▶
The Little Drummer Girl▶
Man from Headquarters
The Man Who Knew Too Much▶
The Man Who Knew Too Much
Marathon Man▶
Natural Causes
The Odessa File
Overthrow
Panama Hattie
Postmark for Danger
Puzzle
Reilly: Ace of Spies▶
Return of the Man from U.N.C.L.E.
Return of the Tall Blond Man With One Black Shoe
Rollover
The Russia House
Saigon: Year of the Cat
Sebastian
The Spy Who Came in from the Cold▶
Strangers
Sweet Country
They Met in Bombay
The Third Man▶
Tokyo Joe
Topaz▶
Torn Curtain
Undeclared War
Windmills of the Gods

Frame-Ups

Abbott and Costello Meet the Invisible Man▶
Another Pair of Aces: Three of a Kind▶
Backfire
Bedroom Eyes
Below the Deadline
Best Revenge
Big Score
The Big Sweat
The Big Switch
Bitter Vengeance
Blind Man's Bluff
The Blum Affair
Breakdown
Buried Alive
Caged Fear
Caught in the Act
Chain Reaction
City Hall▶
Class of Fear
Consenting Adults
Cop-Out
Covered Wagon Days
Cry of the Black Wolves
Cry Vengeance
Dancing Man
Deadline at Dawn
Death Sentence
The Disappearance of Christina
Escape from DS-3
F/X▶
Fast Getaway 2
The Fighting Rookie
Fingerprints Don't Lie
Fleshtone
Frame by Frame
Framed
Free to Love
The Fugitive▶
Get Rita
The Ghost Camera
The Gilded Cage
Girls in Prison
Hi-Jacked
The Inner Circle
An Innocent Man
Judicial Consent
Kentucky Blue Streak
Killing 'em Softly
The Lady Confesses
Lady in the Death House
Left for Dead
Les Miserables
The Life & Times of the Chocolate Killer
The Life of Emile Zola▶
Linda
Louisiana Purchase
Macon County Line
Man Outside
The Manhunt
The Mighty Quinn
Mr. Wise Guy
Murder▶
Murphy's Law
My Cousin Vinny▶
Nasty Hero
Nightmare in Badham County
No Escape, No Return
North by Northwest▶
Now and Forever
The Obsessed
Off the Wall
Presumed Innocent▶
Prime Suspect
Prison Break
Rubdown
Shakes the Clown
The Sphinx
Stir Crazy
Sunset Heat
Suspended Alibi
Tank
TekWar
Today I Hang
Voulez-Vous Danser Avec Moi?
White Fire
The Wrong Man
The Wrong Woman

France

***see also** Paris*

A la Mode
The Accompanist
The Advocate▶
The Ambassador's Daughter
An American in Paris▶
And Soon the Darkness
Arch of Triumph▶
Arch of Triumph
Bedtime Story
Bluebeard's Eighth Wife
Borsalino▶
Breathless▶
Buffet Froid▶
Can-Can
Captain Scarlett
Carnival in Flanders▶
Carve Her Name with Pride
Catherine & Co.
Cesar▶
Charade▶
Chasing Butterflies
Cloud Waltzing
Danton▶
Desiree
Diane
Dirty Rotten Scoundrels▶
Dr. Petiot
Dubarry
The Duellists▶
Dupont Lajoie
The Elusive Corporal▶
The Fatal Image
The Foreman Went to France
Forget Paris
Frantic▶
French Connection 2▶
French Intrigue
French Kiss
The French Lesson
French Postcards
The French Woman
Gentlemen Prefer Blondes▶
Gigi▶
Harvest▶
Hate▶
Heart of a Nation▶
Hellraiser 4: Bloodline
The Horseman on the Roof
How to Steal a Million▶
Is Paris Burning?▶
Jefferson in Paris
Joan of Paris▶
Killer Tomatoes Eat France
Killing Zoe
Kings Go Forth
La Collectionneuse
La Marseillaise▶
La Passante▶
La Vie de Boheme▶
The Lacemaker▶
Ladies Man
Lafayette Escadrille
The Last Metro▶
Last Tango in Paris▶
The Last Time I Saw Paris
The Last Train
Le Bal▶
Le Complot▶
Le Corbeau▶
Le Gendarme de Saint-Tropez
Le Joli Mai
Le Million▶
Les Grandes Manoeuvres▶
Les Miserables▶
The Life of Emile Zola▶
The Longest Day▶
Lovely to Look At▶
Loves & Times of Scaramouche
Ma and Pa Kettle on Vacation
Madame Bovary▶
Mademoiselle Fifi
The Man in the Iron Mask▶
Man on the Eiffel Tower▶
Maniac
Manon
Marie Antoinette
Marius▶
May Fools▶
Me and the Colonel
Mr. Klein▶
The Moderns▶
Monkeys, Go Home!
Monsieur Beaucaire
Monsieur Verdoux▶
The Moonraker
Moulin Rouge▶
The Mountain
My Father's Glory▶
Napoleon▶
Napoleon
A New Kind of Love
The Old Lady Who Walked in the Sea
Paths of Glory▶
Piaf
Prisoner of Honor▶
The Private Affairs of Bel Ami▶
Quality Street
Quatorze Juliet
Queen Margot▶
Ready to Wear
The Red Inn
Reign of Terror
Reunion in France
Round Midnight▶
The Rules of the Game▶
Saint Joan
The Scarlet Pimpernel▶
Silk Stockings▶
Sister My Sister
Spy of Napoleon
Suite 16
A Tale of Two Cities▶
A Tale of Two Cities
A Tale of Winter
Theatre of Death
This Land is Mine▶
Those Magnificent Men in Their Flying Machines▶
To Catch a Thief▶
Total Eclipse
Tropic of Cancer▶
True Colors
Uncertain Glory
Until September
Uranus▶
Valmont▶
Waterloo
What Price Glory?▶
Window to Paris
A Year in Provence▶

Friendship

***see** Buddies*

Front Page

***see also** Mass Media; Shutterbugs*

Absence of Malice
Act of Passion: The Lost Honor of Kathryn Beck
Action in Arabia
The Adventures of Nellie Bly
Alice in the Cities▶
All Over Town
All the President's Men▶
Ambition
American Autobahn
And Nothing But the Truth
AngKor: Cambodia Express
Another Time, Another Place
Anzio
The Average Woman
The Barcelona Kill
Barton Fink▶
The Beniker Gang
Between the Lines▶
The Big Hurt
Big News
The Big Slice
Big Town
Big Town After Dark
Blankman
Blessed Event▶
Boca
Boeing Boeing
Brenda Starr
Broadcast News▶
Broadway Melody of 1936▶
Bulldog Edition
A Bunny's Tale
Call Northside 777▶
Caroline at Midnight
Chill Factor
The China Syndrome▶
Circumstantial Evidence
Citizen Kane▶
City in Fear▶
Cobb▶
Concrete Beat
Continental Divide
Cover Story
Criminal Act
Cry Freedom
Cut and Run
Dark Side of Genius
Dead Air
Dead Connection
Deadline
Deadly Exposure
Defense of the Realm▶
Delirious
Demonstone
The Devil's Commandment
Diamond Trail
Double Cross
Double Edge
Double Exposure
Double Exposure: The Story of Margaret Bourke-White
Down Came a Blackbird
Eternity
Everything Happens at Night▶
Eyes Behind the Stars
Eyes of a Stranger
A Face in the Fog
Far East
Father Hood
Fatherland
Fever Pitch
Final Extra
Finnegan Begin Again
Fit for a King
A Flash of Green
Fletch
Fletch Lives
Foreign Correspondent▶
Francis Covers the Big Town
Freeze Frame
The Front Page▶
The Front Page
Gentleman's Agreement▶
The Ghost and Mr. Chicken
The Great Muppet Caper▶
Grown Ups
Headline Woman
Heads
Heat Wave▶
Her Life as a Man
Hero▶
His Girl Friday▶
Hit the Ice
Hour of Decision
The Hudsucker Proxy▶
Hue and Cry▶
Hustling▶
I Cover the Waterfront
I Love Trouble
The Image
An Inconvenient Woman
The Infiltrator
Invasion of Privacy
Istanbul

Johnny Come Lately
Journey for Margaret▶
Just One of the Guys
Keeper of the City
Keeper of the Flame
Kid from Not-So-Big
Kill Slade
The Killing Beach
The Killing Device
The Killing Fields▶
Killing Stone
La Dolce Vita▶
Lana in Love
The Last Word
Late Extra
Let 'er Go Gallegher
Lethal Charm
Libeled Lady▶
Lip Service▶
L'Odeur des Fauves
Lonelyhearts
Love Is a Many-Splendored Thing
The Love Machine
Malarek
The Man Inside
Man of Iron▶
Mean Season
Meet John Doe▶
Midnight Edition
Midnight Warrior
Mrs. Parker and the Vicious Circle
Murder on the Campus
Murrow
Mystic Circle Murder
Natas...The Reflection
News at Eleven
Newsfront▶
Newsies
Night Hunter
The Nightmare Years
Nina Takes a Lover
No Time to Die
Not for Publication
Nothing Sacred▶
Novel Desires
The Odessa File
One Man Out
The Outlaws is Coming!
The Paper▶
Paper Lion
Paralyzed
The Payoff
The Pelican Brief
Perfect
The Philadelphia Story▶
Platinum Blonde▶
The Ploughman's Lunch▶
Primary Motive
Private Investigations
Profile
Qui Etes Vous, Mr. Sorge?
Reckless Disregard
Resurrection of Zachary Wheeler
Revenge of the Radioactive Reporter
Riding on Air
Roman Holiday▶
Roxie Hart
The Rumor Mill
Safari 3000
Salome, Where She Danced
Salvador▶
Savage Capitalism
Scandal
The Secrets of Wu Sin
Sex and the Single Girl
Sex Through a Window
Shock Corridor▶
Short Fuse
Shriek in the Night
Shy People▶
Somewhere I'll Find You▶
Soul Patrol
Special Bulletin▶
Speed Reporter
Star Reporter
Stavisky▶
Stay Tuned for Murder
Straight Talk
The Strange Love of Molly Louvain
Stranger on the Third Floor▶
Street Smart
Sucker Money
Sweet Rosie O'Grady
Sweet Smell of Success▶
Switching Channels
Tainted Blood
Tarnished Angels▶
Teacher's Pet▶
That Lucky Touch
They Got Me Covered
The Thirteenth Man
Thirteenth Reunion
Those Glory, Glory Days
Three O'Clock High
Tomorrow at Seven
Too Hot to Handle▶
Tough Assignment
Trahir▶
Transylvania 6-5000
Traps
Under Fire▶
The Underworld Story
Unexplained Laughter
Up to a Certain Point
Up Your Alley
The Wharf Rat
Where the Buffalo Roam
While the City Sleeps▶
Whispering City▶
Without Love
Woman Condemned
Woman of the Year▶
A World Apart▶
The World Gone Mad
The Year of Living Dangerously▶

Fugitives

***see also* Lovers on the Lam**

Agent on Ice
Bad Girls
Bail Jumper
Ball of Fire▶
Ballad of Gregorio Cortez▶
Bandits of Orgosolo
Bed & Breakfast
The Big Fix▶
Bobbie Jo and the Outlaw
The Boldest Job in the West
A Boy Called Hate
Boys on the Side
Brannigan
Breathless
Bushwhacked
Butch and Sundance: The Early Days
Butch Cassidy and the Sundance Kid▶
Captured in Chinatown
Chain Reaction
The Chase
Cyber-Tracker 2
Danger: Diabolik
Dead Easy
The Deserters
Desperate
The Desperate Trail
Eddie Macon's Run
Escape 2000
Father Hood
Fled
Frank and Jesse
Free Grass
The Fugitive▶
Fugitive Among Us
The Fugitive: Premiere Episode
The Fugitive: The Final Episode
Good Girls Don't
The Great Texas Dynamite Chase
Hard Knocks
Hiding Out
Hold Me, Thrill Me, Kiss Me
I Died a Thousand Times
I Met a Murderer
The Jesus Trip
Jungle Inferno
Keeping Track
Kiss of Death▶
Klondike Annie
Le Doulos▶
Leather Jackets
Liberators
Loners
The Love Flower
The Man Upstairs
Manhunt
Miami Cops
Miles from Home
Moving Target
Moving Violation
North by Northwest▶
Northwest Trail
Nowhere to Hide
On the Run
One Away
The Outlaw and His Wife
Outlaw Riders
Paris Express
A Perfect World
Posse▶
The Pursuit of D.B. Cooper
The Red Half-Breed
Rider on the Rain▶
Rough Cut
The Savage Woman
Sea Devils
Shallow Grave
Shoot to Kill▶
Simple Men▶
Slate, Wyn & Me
Sonny and Jed
The Spy Within
Stray Dog▶
Strike Back
Suspect Device
Teenage Bonnie & Klepto Clyde
Three Days of the Condor▶
Three Fugitives
Thunder County
Time is Running Out
The Walls of Malapaga
The Way Out
Woman With a Past
The Wrong Man

Funerals

***see also* Death & the Afterlife**

The Addams Family
The Big Chill▶
City Hall▶
First Knight
Four Weddings and a Funeral▶
The Funeral▶
Funeral Home
Gardens of Stone
Harold and Maude▶
Heathers▶
Mr. Saturday Night
My Girl
My Girl 2
Only the Lonely
The Pallbearer
Roommates
Sleepless in Seattle▶
Terms of Endearment▶
Tom and Huck▶
What's Eating Gilbert Grape▶

Future Cop

***see also* Cops**

Apprentice to Murder
The Believers
The Dying Truth
The First Power
God Told Me To
Maniac Cop
Maniac Cop 2
Maniac Cop 3: Badge of Silence
Split Second
Wolfen▶

Gambling

***see also* Viva Las Vegas!**

Aces and Eights
Action for Slander
Any Number Can Play
Atlantic City▶
Back to the Future, Part 2
A Big Hand for the Little Lady
Big Town
A Billion for Boris
Birds & the Bees
Bitter Sweet
Bob le Flambeur▶
Bugsy▶
Casino
Casino▶
Catch Me...If You Can
The Cheaters
The Cincinnati Kid
Cockfighter▶
The Color of Money▶
The Dark Dealer
Dead Lucky
Deadly Impact
Diamonds Are Forever▶
Diggstown
Dona Flor and Her Two Husbands▶
Double Dynamite
Draw!
The Duchess and the Dirtwater Fox
Duke of the Derby
Easy Money
Eight Men Out▶
Eyes of an Angel
Family Prayers
Fever Pitch
A Fine Mess
Firepower
Five Card Stud
Flame of the Barbary Coast
Flame of the Islands
The Flamingo Kid▶
Force of Evil▶
Four Rooms
Frankie and Johnny
The Gamble
Gamble on Love
The Gambler▶
The Gambler & the Lady
The Gambler Returns: The Luck of the Draw
Get Shorty▶
Gilda▶
Glory Years
Golden Rendezvous
The Great Mike
Gun Crazy
Guys and Dolls▶
Half a Lifetime
The Harder They Fall▶
Havana
Heat▶
Hell's Angels '69
Here Come the Marines
Honeymoon in Vegas
The Honeymoon Machine
House of Games▶
Household Saints▶
Huck and the King of Hearts
The Hustler▶
In Like Flint
Indecent Proposal
Inn of Temptation
Inside Out
Jinxed
Kenny Rogers as the Gambler
Kenny Rogers as the Gambler, Part 2: The Adventure Continues
Kenny Rogers as the Gambler, Part 3: The Legend Continues
Lady for a Night
Lady from Louisiana
Las Vegas Hillbillys
Las Vegas Lady
The Las Vegas Story
Las Vegas Weekend
Le Million▶
The Lemon Drop Kid
Let It Ride
Let's Do It Again
Let's Make It Legal
Little Miss Marker▶
Little Miss Marker
Little Vegas
Living to Die
Lookin' to Get Out
Lost in America▶
Manhattan Melodrama▶
The Marrying Man
Maverick
McCabe & Mrs. Miller▶
Meet Me in Las Vegas
Melodie en Sous-Sol
Mickey One
Mr. Lucky▶
Money Train
Mother and Son
Murderers' Row
The Music of Chance
My Darling Clementine▶
My Little Chickadee▶
Ninja, the Violent Sorcerer
No Man of Her Own
Oklahoma Kid▶
Order to Kill
Our Man Flint
Paradise Island
Pink Cadillac
Pleasure Palace
Poker Alice
The Queen of Spades▶
Quintet
Rain Man▶
Riders of the Range
Rimfire
The Roaring Twenties▶
Robbery
The Rocking Horse Winner
Ruggles of Red Gap▶
Say Yes!
Sgt. Bilko
The Shadow Man
The Shanghai Gesture
Shoot
Showgirls
Silver Queen
Sno-Line
Song of the Thin Man
Sorrowful Jones
The Squeeze
Stacy's Knights
The Sting▶
Strike It Rich
Support Your Local Sheriff▶
Swing Time▶
Tall Story
Talons of the Eagle
Tax Season
Taxi Dancers
Tennessee's Partner
Thief
Things Change▶
This Is a Hijack
Thoroughbreds Don't Cry
Three Men on a Horse▶
Trading Places
29th Street
The Underneath▶
Uphill All the Way
Uptown Saturday Night
The Vegas Strip Wars
Walking Tall
Wanda Nevada
Welcome to 18
The Westerner▶
Wheel of Fortune
Who's Got the Action?
Wise Guys

Game Shows

Champagne for Caesar▶
Deathrow Gameshow
For Love or Money
Mallrats
Prize of Peril
Queen for a Day
Quiz Show▶
Reckless
The Running Man
Shock Treatment

Gangs

see also Crime & Criminals; Organized Crime

Abduction of St. Anne
Al Capone▶
Alien Private Eye
All Dogs Go to Heaven
Alley Cat
Alvin Rides Again
American Me▶
Angel Town
Angels Die Hard
Apache Woman
Assassin
Assault on Precinct 13▶
Baby Face Morgan
Bad Bunch
Bad Guys
Ballbuster
Behave Yourself!
Bells of Death
A Better Tomorrow
A Better Tomorrow, Part 2
Beyond the Law
Big Bad Mama
Big Bad Mama 2
The Big Brawl
Black Bikers from Hell
Black Caesar
The Black Cobra
Black Gestapo
Blood In...Blood Out: Bound by Honor
The Bloody Brood
Bloody Mama
Blue
Blues Busters
Bonnie & Clyde▶
Borderline
Borsalino▶
Boss of Big Town
Boulevard Nights
Bowery Blitzkrieg
Boyz N the Hood▶
Breaking Loose
Bring Me the Head of Alfredo Garcia
Broadway Danny Rose▶
The Bronx War
Brother Orchid▶
Buckeye and Blue
Buddy Buddy
Bulldog Drummond's Bride
Bulldog Edition
Bulldog Jack▶
Bullets or Ballots▶
Cartouche▶
Chains
Chains of Gold
The Chase
China Girl
China O'Brien
Chrome and Hot Leather
Chrome Hearts
City Heat
Class of 1984
Class of 1999
Class of 1999 2: The Substitute
Clipped Wings
Code of Silence
Colors▶
Commando Squad
The Concentratin' Kid
Confidential
Contraband
Cookie
Cop in Blue Jeans
Corruption
Corsair
Cosh Boy
The Cross & the Switchblade
Cruisin' High
Cry of a Prostitute: Love Kills
Cry Terror
Danger Zone
Danger Zone 2
Dangerous Mission
Dark Rider
Darktown Strutters
The Day It Came to Earth
Dead End City
Deadly Encounter▶
Deadly Revenge
Defenders of the Law
Defiance
Defiant
Delta Fox
Designing Woman▶
Devil's Angels
Diamonds on Wheels
Dick Tracy vs. Cueball
Dillinger▶
Dillinger
Dirt Gang
Dirty Laundry
Disorganized Crime
Diva▶
The Divine Enforcer
Dixie Jamboree
The Doberman Gang
The Dog Who Stopped the War
The Don is Dead
Each Dawn I Die
East L.A. Warriors
East Side Kids
The Education of Sonny Carson
Emil and the Detectives
Enemy Territory
The Enforcer
Escape from L.A.
Escape from the Bronx
Every Which Way But Loose
Exterminator
Eye of the Tiger
Fear in the City
The Final Alliance
Forced Vengeance
Forever, Lulu
Four Deuces
Four Jacks and a Jill
Foxy Brown
Full Eclipse
"G" Men▶
The Gambler & the Lady
Gambler's Choice
Game of Death
Gang Bullets
Gang Justice
Gang Wars
Gangbusters
The Gangster
Gangster Wars
Gangway
The George McKenna Story
Ghetto Blaster
The Ghost and the Guest
Ghost Chasers
Gimme Shelter
Girls of the White Orchid
The Glory Stompers
Golden Lady
The Golden Triangle
Gone are the Days
Goodfellas▶
The Great Mike
The Great Skycopter Rescue
The Grissom Gang▶
The Gumshoe Kid
Gun Girls
The Gunrunner
Guns Don't Argue
Hard-Boiled Mahoney
Harley
Heartbreaker
Heat Street
Hell on Frisco Bay
Hellcats
High Ballin'
High Sierra▶
Hit Men
Hitz
Homeboy
Homeboys
Hoodlum Empire
I Died a Thousand Times
I, Mobster
I'd Give My Life
Impulse
Inside the Law
Jinxed
Johnny Apollo
Johnny Dangerously
Jungleground
Just William's Luck
Kansas City Massacre
Key Largo▶
Killer Dill
King Boxer
The King of the Roaring '20s: The Story of Arnold Rothstein
Knights of the City
L.A. Bad
La Balance▶
L.A. Gangs Rising
Lady from Nowhere
Lady in a Cage▶
Lady in Red
Lady Killer▶
Last Flight to Hell
The Last Ride of the Dalton Gang
The Last Riders
Law of the Underworld
Leather Jackets
Lepke
Lethal Games
Lethal Obsession
Little Dragons
Little Laura & Big John
The Longshot
The Lost Capone▶
Love Me or Leave Me▶
Lucky Luciano
Ma Barker's Killer Brood
Machine Gun Kelly
Manhattan Merry-Go-Round
Marked Woman▶
Marshal Law
The Masters of Menace
Master's Revenge
The Maverick Queen
Meet the Mob
Melvin Purvis: G-Man
Men of Respect
Menace II Society▶
The Meteor Man
Mi Vida Loca
Midnight
Miller's Crossing▶
Million Dollar Kid
Miracle in Harlem
Mr. Majestyk
Mob Boss
Mob Story
Mob War
Mobsters
The Monster and the Stripper
Motorcycle Squad
My Samurai
Mystery Date
The Naked Angels
Nashville Beat
'Neath Brooklyn Bridge
The Neon Empire
Never a Dull Moment
Never Let Go
Never Love a Stranger
The New Kids
99 & 44/100 Dead
Ninja Brothers of Blood
Nitti: The Enforcer
No Trace
The Noose Hangs High▶
One Man's Justice
Original Gangstas
The Outsiders
Paco
Paradise in Harlem
Parole, Inc.
Party Girl▶
The Payoff
Peacekillers
Performance▶
Petrified Forest▶
Pickup on South Street▶
Pierrot le Fou▶
Play Murder for Me
Postmark for Danger/Quicksand
The Power of the Ninjitsu
Prime Cut
The Prime Time
Prize Fighter
Public Enemy▶
Pulp
Punk Vacation
Quatorze Juliet
The Racket▶
The Racketeer
Rapid Fire
Renegades
Return of the Dragon
Return of the Rebels
Return of the Tiger
Revenge
Revenge of the Ninja
Revolt of the Dragon
Ricco
Riot Squad
The Rise and Fall of Legs Diamond
The Ritz▶
The Roaring Twenties▶
Robin and the 7 Hoods
Rooftops
Rumble Fish▶
Rumble in the Bronx
The St. Valentine's Day Massacre
Satan's Sadists
The Savage Seven
Scared Stiff▶
Scarface▶
The Sea Serpent
Second Chance
The Set-Up▶
Sexton Blake and the Hooded Terror
Shaft▶
Shark Hunter
She's Back
Shining Star
Shoot the Piano Player▶
Showdown
Showdown in Little Tokyo
Sidewalks of New York
Smart Alecks
SnakeEater 3: His Law
Sno-Line
Some Like It Hot▶
South Central
Speedy▶
Spike of Bensonhurst
Spook Busters
Star Reporter
Stavisky▶
Sticky Fingers
Stingray
Stone Cold
Straight Line
Street Crimes
Street Hitz
Street Knight
Street Soldiers
Street Warriors
Street Warriors, Part 2
The Street with No Name▶
The Streets of L.A.
The Substitute
Sunnyside
The Sun's Burial▶
T-Bird Gang
Tattoo Connection
Tattooed Hit Man
Teenage Gang Debs
Teenage Wolfpack
This Time I'll Make You Rich
Timber Queen
The Tin Soldier
The Tip-Off
Tongs: An American Nightmare
Too Late for Tears▶
Topaze▶
Tough Assignment
Tough Kid
Tough to Handle
Tropical Snow
Trouble in Store
Truck Stop Women
True Believer
True Blood
Tuff Turf
Two to Tango
Underground Terror
The Underworld Story
Urban Crossfire
Variety
Vengeance
Verne Miller
Vietnam, Texas
Violent Professionals
The Violent Years
The Virginia Hill Story
Wanderers▶
The Warriors
West Side Story▶
When Gangland Strikes
The Wild One▶
Wilding
The Wolves▶
Wonder Man
Wonderland▶
The Wrong Arm of the Law▶
The Yakuza
Year of the Dragon
Young Warriors
Zooman▶

Gays

see also AIDS; Bisexuality; Gender Bending; Lesbians

American Fabulous
And the Band Played On▶
Another Country
Apart from Hugh
Arabian Nights▶
Armistead Maupin's Tales of the City
As Is
The Best Way
The Birdcage▶
Blue
The Boys in the Band
Boys Life
Carrington
The Celluloid Closet▶
City in Panic
Colonel Redl▶
The Conformist▶
Consenting Adult
Creation of Adam
Cruising
The Crying Game▶
Curse of the Queerwolf
Dear Boys
Death in Venice▶
The Detective▶
Different Story
Drifting
An Early Frost▶
Edward II
El Diputado▶
An Empty Bed▶
Entertaining Mr. Sloane
Ernesto
The Everlasting Secret Family
Flirt
For a Lost Soldier
Forbidden Passion: The Oscar Wilde Movie
Fortune and Men's Eyes
Four Weddings and a Funeral▶
Fox and His Friends▶
Fun Down There
The Garden
Go Fish▶
Grief
Hearing Voices
Heaven's a Drag
The Hours and Times▶
I Can't Sleep
It's My Party
Jeffrey
Joey Breaker▶
Kiss of the Spider Woman▶
La Cage aux Folles▶
La Cage aux Folles 2
La Cage aux Folles 3: The Wedding
Les Nuits Fauves▶
L'Homme Blesse▶
Lie Down with Dogs
The Living End
Longtime Companion▶
The Lost Language of Cranes▶
Love and Human Remains▶
Making Love
A Man of No Importance▶

Maurice▶
Maybe...Maybe Not
Men in Love
Menage▶
Midnight Cowboy▶
Midnight Dancers
Mouth to Mouth
The Music Lovers
My Beautiful Laundrette▶
My Father Is Coming
My Own Private Idaho▶
The Naked Civil Servant▶
Naked Lunch▶
Nijinsky
Norman, Is That You?
Okoge
Our Sons
Paris is Burning▶
Parting Glances▶
Partners
Philadelphia▶
Prick Up Your Ears▶
Priest
Querelle
Ready to Wear
Reflections in a Golden Eye
The Ritz▶
Rock Hudson's Home Movies
The Rocky Horror Picture Show▶
Rope▶
Sand and Blood
Satan's Brew
Sergeant Matlovich vs. the U.S. Air Force
Smoke
The Sprinter
Straight for the Heart
Strawberry and Chocolate▶
The Sum of Us▶
Sunday, Bloody Sunday▶
Swoon▶
Taxi zum Klo▶
The Third Sex
This Special Friendship
Threesome
Tidy Endings
Times of Harvey Milk
To Forget Venice
To Play or To Die
Too Much Sun
Torch Song Trilogy
Total Eclipse
Totally F***ed Up
A Very Natural Thing
Via Appia
Victim▶
Victor/Victoria▶
We Think the World of You▶
The Wedding Banquet▶
Wild Reeds▶
Withnail and I▶
Wittgenstein
Wonderland▶
Zero Patience

Gender Bending

***see also** Gays; Lesbians; Role Reversal*

Abroad with Two Yanks
The Adventures of Priscilla, Queen of the Desert▶
Anything for Love
At War with the Army
Auntie
Blue Murder at St. Trinian's▶
Boy! What a Girl
The Crying Game▶
The Damned
Desperate Living
Dr. Jekyll and Ms. Hyde
Dressed to Kill
Ed Wood▶
Forever Mary▶
Glen or Glenda: Confessions of Ed Wood
Hairspray▶
Happily Ever After
Her Life as a Man
He's My Girl
I Like It Like That▶
I Wanna Be a Beauty Queen
I Want What I Want
I Was a Male War Bride▶
In a Year of 13 Moons
It's Pat: The Movie
Just Like a Woman
Just One of the Girls
La Cage aux Folles▶
La Cage aux Folles 2
La Cage aux Folles 3: The Wedding
Law of Desire▶
Le Sexe des Etoiles
Lust in the Dust▶
M. Butterfly
Mascara
Mrs. Doubtfire
Mixed Nuts
Mutant on the Bounty
My Son, the Vampire
Myra Breckinridge
The Mystery of Alexina
The Newlydeads
Nobody's Perfect
Nuns on the Run
Old Mother Riley's Ghosts
Outrageous!▶
Paris is Burning▶
Pink Flamingos
Polyester
Prime Suspect 3▶
Psycho▶
The Rocky Horror Picture Show▶
Shadey
The Silence of the Lambs▶
Some Like It Hot▶
Sonny Boy
Switch▶
To Wong Foo, Thanks for Everything, Julie Newmar
Tootsie▶
Torch Song Trilogy
Trash
Vegas in Space
Victor/Victoria▶
Wigstock: The Movie
Wild Party
Wild, Wild World of Jayne Mansfield
The Woman Inside
The World According to Garp▶
The Year of Living Dangerously▶
Yentl
Zazie dans le Metro▶

Generation X

Before Sunrise
Bio-Dome
Bodies, Rest & Motion
Bottle Rocket
Clerks▶
Don't Do It
Floundering
Kicking and Screaming▶
A Little Stiff
Live Bait
Loaded
Mad Love
Mallrats
The Pallbearer
Party Girl
Reality Bites
S.F.W.
Singles▶
Slacker▶
Sleep with Me
When the Party's Over

Genetics

***see also** Mad Scientists; Metamorphosis*

Biohazard: The Alien Force
The Boys from Brazil
The Fly▶
The Fly▶
The Fly 2
Forbidden World
Metamorphosis: The Alien Factor
Rats
Tomcat: Dangerous Desires
Wes Craven Presents Mind Ripper

Genies

***see also** Magic Carpet Rides*

Aladdin▶
Aladdin and His Wonderful Lamp
Aladdin and the King of Thieves
Bernard and the Genie
Kazaam
Miracle Beach
The Outing
Priceless Beauty
The Return of Jafar
The Thief of Bagdad▶
The Thief of Baghdad▶
The Thief of Baghdad
A Thousand and One Nights
Three Wishes
Wildest Dreams
Wish Me Luck
Wishman
The Wonders of Aladdin

Genre Spoofs

***see also** Credits Chaos!; Satire & Parody*

The Adventures of Hairbreadth Harry
Airplane!▶
Airplane 2: The Sequel
All Through the Night▶
All You Need Is Cash▶
April Fool's Day
Based on an Untrue Story
The Big Bus
The Big Crimewave
Blazing Saddles▶
Blondes Have More Guns
Bloodbath at the House of Death
Bordello
Bugsy Malone
Casino Royale
Closet Cases of the Nerd Kind
Code Name: Chaos
Creature from the Haunted Sea
Dead Men Don't Wear Plaid
Dragnet
Drive-In
Fatal Instinct
Fear of a Black Hat
Ferocious Female Freedom Fighters
Flesh Gordon
Frankenstein General Hospital
Frankenstein's Great Aunt Tillie
Galactic Gigolo
Galaxina
Ganjasaurus Rex
Get Crazy
Ghoul School
Grunt! The Wrestling Movie
Hell Comes to Frogtown
High Anxiety
The Hollywood Detective
Hollywood Harry
Hot Shots!▶
Hot Shots! Part Deux
The Hound of the Baskervilles
Hysterical
I'm Gonna Git You Sucka▶
J-Men Forever!▶
Jake Speed
Jet Benny Show
Kentucky Fried Movie▶
Last Action Hero
Lust in the Dust▶
The Man with Two Brains▶
Mob Boss
Monster in the Closet
Monty Python and the Holy Grail▶
Murder by Death
Mutant on the Bounty
The Naked Gun: From the Files of Police Squad▶
Naked Gun 33 1/3: The Final Insult
Naked Gun 2 1/2: The Smell of Fear
National Lampoon's Loaded Weapon 1
99 & 44/100 Dead
Once Bitten
Pandemonium
A Perfect Little Murder
Phantom of the Paradise
The Pink Chiquitas
Plan 10 from Outer Space
Repossessed
Return of Captain Invincible
The Return of Spinal Tap
Ricky 1
Robin Hood: Men in Tights
Robin of Locksley
Rustler's Rhapsody
Saturday the 14th
Saturday the 14th Strikes Back
Soapdish▶
Spaceballs
Spaceship
Spy Hard
Strange Invaders▶
The Stuff
Supersonic Man
Support Your Local Gunfighter▶
Support Your Local Sheriff▶
Surf Ninjas
Teenage Exorcist
Terror Eyes
That Man from Rio
They Call Me Bruce?
They Call Me Trinity
They Live
They Still Call Me Bruce
This Is Spinal Tap▶
Three Amigos
Too Many Crooks
Top Secret!▶
Transylvania 6-5000
Trinity is Still My Name
2069: A Sex Odyssey
UHF
Union City
Unmasked Part 25
Vegas in Space
The Video Dead
Video Violence
Video Violence Part 2...The Exploitation!
The Villain
Voyage of the Rock Aliens
Wacko
Werewolf of Washington
Who Framed Roger Rabbit▶
Young Frankenstein▶
The Zany Adventures of Robin Hood

Germany

***see also** Berlin*

Ali: Fear Eats the Soul▶
Alice in the Cities▶
Backbeat▶
The Battle of Russia
Berlin Alexanderplatz▶
The Blue Angel▶
The Bridge
Carnival Story
The Damned
The Desert Fox▶
Die Grosse Freiheit Nr. 7
Dr. Mabuse, Parts 1 & 2▶
Faraway, So Close!
Flirt
Geheimakte WB1
G.I. Blues
Hitler: The Last Ten Days
The Infiltrator
Isn't Life Wonderful▶
Jud Suess▶
Kapo▶
Knife in the Head
Marianne and Juliane▶
The Marriage of Maria Braun▶
Mein Kampf: Hitler's Rise and Fall
Mephisto▶
The Merchant of Four Seasons▶
Mr. Emmanuel
The Odessa File
Once Upon a Honeymoon
Periphery
Porcile
Prelude to War
Prince Brat and the Whipping Boy▶
The Promise
The Sound of Music▶
SS Girls
The Stationmaster's Wife
Strikeback
Swing Kids
They Were So Young
Three Comrades▶
Tiefland
Triumph of the Will
Wings of Desire▶
Woyzeck▶

Ghosts, Ghouls, & Goblins

***see also** Death & the Afterlife; Demons & Wizards; Occult*

Amazing Mr. Blunden
Beetlejuice▶
Beyond Tomorrow
Blondie Has Trouble
The Canterville Ghost
Casper▶
The Changeling
Charlie's Ghost: The Secret of Coronado
Children Shouldn't Play with Dead Things
A Christmas Carol▶
The Club
Cold Sweat
Curse of the Blue Lights
Deadly Advice
Death Dreams
Death Magic
Dona Flor and Her Two Husbands▶
The Empire of Passion▶
Encounter with the Unknown
Fatally Yours
Feet Foremost
The Fog
Forever: A Ghost of a Love Story
The Forgotten One
The Frighteners
The Gate
Genghis Cohn
Ghost▶
The Ghost and Mr. Chicken
The Ghost Breakers▶
The Ghost Brigade
Ghost Dad
The Ghost Goes West▶
Ghost of Hanley House
The Ghost of Rashmon Hall
Ghost on the Loose
Ghost Rider
Ghost Ship
Ghost Story
Ghostbusters▶
Ghostbusters 2
Ghosts of Berkeley Square
The Ghoul
The Green Man▶
Haunted
Haunted Honeymoon
The Haunting of Barney Palmer
Heart and Souls
Heart Condition
Heaven's a Drag
High Spirits
Hollywood's New Blood
The House of Dies Drear
House Where Evil Dwells
In the Realm of Passion
The Innocents▶
The Kingdom
Kiss Me Goodbye
Kwaidan▶

Last Reunion
Little Orphan Annie
Lurking Fear
The Midnight Phantom
The Mummy's Ghost
My Friend Walter
Mystic Circle Murder
Night of the Scarecrow
No End
O'Hara's Wife
Phantasm III: Lord of the Dead
The Phantom
Poltergeist▶
Poltergeist 2: The Other Side
Poltergeist 3
The Princess and the Goblin
Revenge of the Red Baron
Seven Keys to Baldplate
Shadow Dancing▶
Silent Tongue
Somewhere Tomorrow
Soultaker
The Speed Spook
Stormswept
The Supernaturals
Sylvia and the Phantom▶
Things
13 Ghosts
The Time of Their Lives
Topper▶
Topper Returns▶
Topper Takes a Trip▶
Twice Dead
Ugetsu▶
The Uninvited▶
Visitor from the Grave
The Visitors
The Watcher in the Woods
Whale Music
Windrunner
Woman in Black
Younger & Younger
Zero Patience

Giants

see also Monsters, General

The Amazing Colossal Man
Attack of the 50 Foot Woman
Attack of the 50 Ft. Woman
Beanstalk
Boggy Creek II
Bride of the Monster
Cyclops
Digby, the Biggest Dog in the World
Dr. Cyclops
Giant from the Unknown
Godzilla vs. Megalon
Honey, I Blew Up the Kid
Humongous
Josh Kirby...Time Warrior: Chapter 2, The Human Pets
Kronos
Mothra▶
The Mysterians
The Phantom Planet
The Princess Bride▶
The Spy Who Loved Me
Teenage Mutant Ninja Turtles: The Movie
Them!▶
Tremors
Tremors 2: Aftershocks
Village of the Giants
The War of the Colossal Beast

Gifted Children

see also Childhood Visions

And You Thought Your Parents Were Weird!
Dangerous Holiday
Dear Brigitte
Escape to Witch Mountain▶
Little Man Tate▶
Matilda
On the Right Track
Powder
Real Genius▶
Rookie of the Year
Searching for Bobby Fischer▶

Gigolos

see also Happy Hookers; Oldest Profession

American Gigolo
Midnight Cowboy▶
Roman Spring of Mrs. Stone▶

Go Fish

see also Deep Blue; Sea Critter Attack

Alamo Bay
Around the World Under the Sea
Black Water
Captains Courageous▶
The Day of the Dolphin
Detour to Danger
Doomwatch
A Fish Called Wanda▶
Flipper▶
Forrest Gump▶
Free Willy
Grumpier Old Men
Grumpy Old Men▶
The Islander
It Came from Beneath the Sea▶
Jaws▶
Jaws 2
Jaws 3
Jaws: The Revenge
Killer Fish
La Terra Trema▶
Man of Aran▶
Man's Favorite Sport?
Mr. Peabody & the Mermaid
Moby Dick▶
My Summer Story
92 in the Shade▶
Northern Extremes
The Old Man and the Sea
On Golden Pond▶
Orca
Riff Raff
A River Runs Through It▶
Scorpion with Two Tails
Shark Hunter
Sixteen Fathoms Deep
Tabu: A Story of the South Seas▶
Thunder Bay▶
The Treasure of Jamaica Reef
Up from the Depths
Wallaby Jim of the Islands
Whale for the Killing
Where the Hot Wind Blows

Going Native

Apocalypse Now▶
The Blue Lagoon
The Bounty▶
Congo
Dances with Wolves▶
The Emerald Forest▶
Farewell to the King
Grizzly Adams: The Legend Continues
Jeremiah Johnson▶
Little Indian, Big City
Lord of the Flies▶
Lord of the Flies
A Man Called Horse▶
The Mosquito Coast
Pagan Island
Paradise
The Return of a Man Called Horse
Robinson Crusoe
A Stranger Among Us
The Swiss Family Robinson▶

Golf

Babe!▶
Blades
The Caddy
Caddyshack▶
Caddyshack 2
Dead Solid Perfect
Goof Balls
Happy Gilmore
The Man with the Perfect Swing
Prehysteria 3
Tin Cup▶
W.C. Fields: Flask of Fields

Good Earth

see also Trees & Forests; Wilderness

Baraka▶
Bio-Dome
A Cry in the Wild▶
Dead Man
Deadly Harvest
Doctor Dolittle
Don't Change My World
A Flash of Green
Fly with the Hawk
Free Willy 2: The Adventure Home
Godzilla vs. the Smog Monster
The Great Adventure▶
Green Horizon
Impulse
Jonathan Livingston Seagull
Lassie: Adventures of Neeka
The Legend of Black Thunder Mountain
The Long Weekend
Man of Aran▶
Nothing Personal
The Overlanders
Pocahontas▶
Silent Running▶
Slipstream
Spirit of the Eagle
Vanishing Prairie▶
Vanishing Wilderness
Whale for the Killing
When the North Wind Blows

Grand Hotel

see also No-Exit Motel

Ants
The Avenging Hand
Billy Madison
Blame It on the Bellboy
Blondie Takes a Vacation
Bloody Wednesday
Bugsy▶
Come September
Crawlspace
Dirty Dancing▶
Dunston Checks In
Eden
Eden 2
Eden 3
Eden 4
Fawlty Towers
For Love or Money
40 Pounds of Trouble
Four Rooms
French Kiss
Girl in Black Stockings
The Girl with the Hungry Eyes
Grand Hotel▶
The Green Man▶
Holiday Hotel
Holiday Inn▶
Hook, Line and Sinker
Hotel
Hotel du Lac
Hotel Imperial
Hotel Room
It Happened at Nightmare Inn
Mistaken Identity
Mystery Train▶
Nick of Time
A Night in Casablanca▶
The Night Porter
Nightmare on the 13th Floor
One Crazy Night
Plaza Suite▶
Psycho▶
Psycho 2
Psycho 3
The Queen of Mean
The Red Inn
Roadside Prophets
Room Service
Rosebud Beach Hotel
Secret of the Black Trunk
Separate Tables▶
Separate Tables
The Shining
Sleeping with Strangers
Snowball Express
Somewhere in Time
Spare Parts
Suite 16
Sweet Lorraine▶
The Terror
Terror at Red Wolf Inn
This Property is Condemned
Weekend at the Waldorf▶
Witchery

Great Britain

see also Ireland; London; Scotland

The Affair
Alien Prey
Amazing Mr. Blunden
American Friends
And a Nightingale Sang
Angels and Insects▶
Angels One Five
Anne of the Thousand Days▶
August
An Awfully Big Adventure
Back Home
Barry Lyndon▶
Beau Brummel▶
Bhaji on the Beach
The Big Scam
Black Panther
The Black Velvet Gown
The Black Windmill
Blue Jeans
Bonnie Prince Charlie
Brighton Rock▶
Brother Cadfael
The Browning Version
The Buccaneers▶
Bullshot
Camelot
The Canterville Ghost
Carrington
The Charge of the Light Brigade
Charles & Diana: A Palace Divided
Chicago Joe & the Showgirl
A Chump at Oxford
The Cinder Path
Cold Comfort Farm▶
Cold Light of Day
The Corn is Green▶
The Courtney Affair
Cromwell
A Cry from the Streets
Danger UXB
Devices and Desires▶
Devotion
Diamonds on Wheels
Diana: Her True Story
Dick Turpin
Disraeli▶
Distant Voices, Still Lives▶
The Dwelling Place
The Eagle Has Landed▶
Edge of the World▶
Edward and Mrs. Simpson
Elizabeth of Ladymead▶
Elizabeth R▶
Elizabeth, the Queen
Emma▶
Emmanuelle in Soho
The Englishman Who Went Up a Hill But Came Down a Mountain▶
Everybody Wins
Excalibur▶
Fame Is the Spur
Feast of July
Fergie & Andrew: Behind Palace Doors
The Fifteen Streets
The Final Cut▶
Flambards
Foreign Affairs▶
Forever and a Day▶
Four Weddings and a Funeral▶
Funny Bones▶
Gallowglass▶
Goodbye, Mr. Chips
Great Expectations: The Untold Story
The Great Muppet Caper▶
The Green Man▶
Gulliver's Travels
Haunted
The Hellfire Club
High Hopes▶
House of Cards▶
The House of Eliott
The House of Secrets
How Green Was My Valley▶
The Innocents▶
Invincible Mr. Disraeli
The Iron Duke
Jamaica Inn
King Ralph
The King's Thief
The Krays▶
Lady Jane▶
The Lady's Not for Burning
The Last of England▶
Lillie▶
The Lion in Winter▶
Lipstick On Your Collar
Lloyds of London▶
The Long Day Closes▶
The Long Good Friday▶
Lorna Doone
Love for Lydia▶
Made in Heaven
The Madness of King George▶
A Man for All Seasons▶
The Man from the Pru
The Man in Grey▶
Mary of Scotland▶
A Midwinter's Tale
The Mill on the Floss
Mrs. Miniver▶
The Moonraker
Murder Elite
Naked▶
The Naked Civil Servant▶
Nine Days a Queen▶
No Surrender▶
None But the Lonely Heart▶
Passport to Pimlico
Persuasion▶
Pictures
Pink Strings and Sealing Wax
Plenty
Poldark▶
Pride and Prejudice▶
Princess Caraboo
A Question of Attribution
The Return of the Native
Richard III▶
The Riddle of the Sands
Riff Raff▶
Robbery
Room to Let
Royal Wedding▶
The Ruling Class▶
The Saint in London
Say Hello to Yesterday
Scandal▶
The Secret Garden▶
Secret of the Black Trunk
Sense and Sensibility▶
The Servant▶
Shadowlands▶
Silver Dream Racer
Six Wives of Henry VIII▶
Soldier in Love
Split Second
The Stick-Up
That Sinking Feeling▶
This England
Those Magnificent Men in Their Flying Machines▶
To Play the King▶
A Touch of Class▶
Tunes of Glory▶
A Very British Coup▶
Victoria Regina
The Virgin Queen▶
We Think the World of You▶
Whiskey Galore▶
The Whistle Blower▶
The White Cliffs of Dover▶

White Mischief▶
The Woman He Loved
Woman in Black
Wuthering Heights▶
Yanks
Year of the Comet
The Young Americans
Young Bess▶
Young Winston▶

Great Death Scenes

***see also** Death & the Afterlife; Funerals*

Bonnie & Clyde▶
Breaker Morant▶
Bring Me the Head of Alfredo Garcia
Buffy the Vampire Slayer▶
Butch Cassidy and the Sundance Kid▶
Camille▶
The Champ
Coquette
Dangerous Liaisons▶
Dark Victory▶
Die Hard: With a Vengeance
From Dusk Till Dawn
Gallipoli▶
Gettysburg▶
Glory▶
Highlander▶
Highlander: The Gathering
Johnny Mnemonic
Julius Caesar▶
Jurassic Park▶
Mimi
Monty Python and the Holy Grail▶
Pat Garrett & Billy the Kid▶
Psycho▶
Public Enemy▶
Shadowlands▶
A Song to Remember▶
Strangers on a Train▶
Things to Do In Denver When You're Dead▶
Valmont▶
The Wizard of Oz▶

Great Depression

***see also** Hard Knock Life; Homeless*

After the Promise
All the King's Men▶
The Ballad of the Sad Cafe
Big Bad Mama
Big Bad Mama 2
Billy Bathgate
Bloody Mama
Bonnie & Clyde▶
Bound for Glory▶
Broadway Melody of 1938
Charley and the Angel
A Christmas to Remember
Dance Fools Dance▶
Dream Chasers
Eleanor & Franklin▶
Fatty Finn
Four Deuces
Fresh Horses
The Grapes of Wrath▶
The Group
Hallelujah, I'm a Bum
Hard Times▶
Hard Traveling
Homecoming: A Christmas Story
Honkytonk Man
Ironweed▶
It Happened One Night▶
The Journey of Natty Gann▶
Just Around the Corner
Kansas City Massacre
King of the Hill▶
Kingfish: A Story of Huey P. Long
Laurel & Hardy: Below Zero
Long Road Home
Love on the Dole▶
Melvin Purvis: G-Man
Modern Times▶
Morning Glory
Of Mice and Men▶
Our Daily Bread▶
Paper Moon▶
Pennies From Heaven▶
Places in the Heart▶
Possessed
The Postman Always Rings Twice▶
The Postman Always Rings Twice
Rambling Rose▶
Reaching for the Moon
The Road Home
Sounder▶
The Stars Fell on Henrietta
Street Scene▶
Sullivan's Travels▶
The Tale of Ruby Rose▶
They Shoot Horses, Don't They?▶
Thieves Like Us▶
Two Bits
Victor/Victoria▶
The Water Engine
Who Has Seen the Wind?
Why Shoot the Teacher▶
Wild Hearts Can't Be Broken▶
Wildflower▶
Winter People
You Only Live Once

Great Escapes

***see also** Men in Prison; POW/MIA; War, General; Women in Prison*

Alias, La Gringa
The Ascent
Assassination
Berlin Tunnel 21
The Big Doll House
Blood on the Mountain
Born to Be Wild
Brady's Escape
Breakout
Butch Cassidy and the Sundance Kid▶
Caged Fear
The Chase
Chasers
The Colditz Story
Crashout
A Day in October
Deadlock 2
Deadly Mission
Deadly Target
The Deer Hunter▶
Desperate
Diamonds of the Night▶
Die Hard▶
Die Hard: With a Vengeance
Dirty Heroes
Down by Law▶
Era Notte a Roma▶
Escape
The Escape Artist▶
Escape from Alcatraz▶
Escape from Cell Block 3
Escape from Death Row
Escape from El Diablo
Escape from Fort Bravo
Escape from Galaxy Three
Escape from Hell
Escape from L.A.
Escape from New York
Escape from Safehaven
Escape from Sobibor▶
Escape from the KGB
Escape to Love
Escape to Witch Mountain▶
Escapist
Fantastic Voyage▶
Fast Walking
Flame Over India▶
Fled
Follow the River
Fortress
Gang Busters
Girls in Prison
The Great Escape▶
The Great Escape 2: The Untold Story
The Great Train Robbery▶
Hangfire
The Horseman on the Roof
Hostile Intentions
Houdini
The Ice Runner
In Hot Pursuit
Inside Out
Iron Eagle
Jailbreakin'
La Nuit de Varennes▶
Ladyhawke
The Last Samurai
Leaving Normal
Les Miserables▶
Les Violons du Bal
Lonely Are the Brave▶
The Long Riders▶
Macho Callahan
A Man Escaped▶
The Man Who Broke 1,000 Chains
The Manhunt
McKenzie Break▶
McVicar
Midnight Edition
Midnight Express▶
Missing in Action
Mrs. Soffel
The Mole People
Murder In the First
Murder One
The Muthers
Mysterious Island▶
Naked Youth
Night Crossing
No Escape
North by Northwest▶
Not Without My Daughter
On Wings of Eagles
One That Got Away▶
Operation Thunderbolt
Pacific Inferno
Papillon▶
Passage to Marseilles▶
A Perfect World
Prison Break
The Prize▶
The Promise
Raiders of the Lost Ark▶
Raising Arizona▶
Rob Roy▶
The Rock▶
Romancing the Stone▶
Run
Runaway Train▶
Samar
The Secret War of Harry Frigg
The Seventh Cross▶
The Seventh Floor
The Shining
Skin Game▶
The Sound of Music▶
The Spy Who Came in from the Cold▶
Stalag 17▶
Stalag Luft
Strange Cargo
Strike Back
The Sugarland Express▶
Sweet Poison
Tequila Sunrise
Teresa's Tattoo
Texas Payback
Three Days of the Condor▶
Thunder County
To Catch a Thief▶
Torn Curtain
Toy Story▶
Venus Rising
Victory
Violent Women
Von Ryan's Express▶
Warbus
We're No Angels
White Nights
Women Unchained
Wooden Horse▶
Zebra in the Kitchen

Growing Older

***see also** Death & the Afterlife; Late Bloomin' Love*

After the Rehearsal▶
Age Isn't Everything
Age Old Friends▶
Amos
Anna▶
Around the World in 80 Ways
As Young As You Feel▶
Atlantic City▶
Autumn Leaves
The Ballad of Narayama▶
*batteries not included
The Best of Times
Better Late Than Never
Breathing Lessons▶
Camilla
Captain Kronos: Vampire Hunter▶
The Cemetery Club
Chasing Butterflies
The Cheyenne Social Club
Children of Nature
Chimes at Midnight▶
Choices
Citizen Kane▶
City Slickers▶
Cocoon▶
Cocoon: The Return
The Color of Evening
Come Along with Me
The Conductor
Cooperstown
Dad
Daddy Nostalgia▶
Death of a Salesman▶
Dorian Gray
Draw!
Dream a Little Dream
Dream Chasers
Dreaming of Rita
Driving Miss Daisy▶
Early Days
Easy Living
Eating
Ebony Tower
An Empty Bed▶
The Enchanted Forest
Family Upside Down▶
Fantasy Man
Father of the Bride Part II
The Field▶
The Firemen's Ball▶
Folks!
A Foreign Field
Forever Young
Forty Carats
Foxfire▶
Getting Up and Going Home
Gin Game▶
Ginger & Fred▶
The Godfather, Part 3▶
Going in Style▶
The Good Guys and the Bad Guys
The Good Old Boys
The Goodbye People
Grace Quigley
Great Smokey Roadblock
Greedy
Grumpier Old Men
Grumpy Old Men▶
Hard Labour
Hardbodies
Harry and Tonto▶
Home Free All
Home Is Where the Hart Is
Home to Stay
Homebodies
The Hunger
Hurry Up or I'll Be Thirty
Hush, Hush, Sweet Charlotte▶
I Can't Sleep
I, Claudius, Vol. 7: Old King Log
In Custody
Iron Horsemen
Kotch▶
Lamerica▶
Larry McMurtry's Streets of Laredo▶
The Last Good Time
The Last Laugh▶
Late Chrysanthemums
The Leech Woman
Lifeguard
Light Sleeper
Lightning Jack
Lip Service▶
The Magic Bubble
Mama Turns a Hundred▶
The Man Upstairs
Marathon
Middle Age Crazy
Miss Firecracker▶
Mister Halpren & Mister Johnson
Mr. Saturday Night
Money to Burn
Monte Walsh▶
My Heroes Have Always Been Cowboys
Next of Kin
Nobody's Fool▶
Off Your Rocker
Old Explorers
The Old Lady Who Walked in the Sea
The Old Man and the Sea
Oldest Living Graduate▶
On Golden Pond▶
Over the Hill
Pals
Pastime▶
Pelle the Conqueror▶
A Piano for Mrs. Cimino▶
The Pickle
Picture of Dorian Gray▶
The Portrait▶
The Private Life of Henry VIII▶
Pushing Hands
Queens Logic
Rabid Grannies
Ran▶
The Rejuvenator
Return of the Rebels
Rhapsody in August
Rocket Gibraltar▶
Roommates
Rooster Cogburn
Roses Bloom Twice
The Rounders
Satanik
The Set-Up▶
Seven Thieves▶
The Shell Seekers
Shirley Valentine▶
A Shock to the System▶
The Shootist▶
Side By Side
The Silent Touch
Stephen King's Golden Years
Strangers in Good Company▶
Street Music
Summer Snow
Summer Solstice
Summer Wishes, Winter Dreams
The Sunshine Boys▶
Taking My Turn
Tatie Danielle▶
Tell Me a Riddle
Texas Guns
That's Life!
Things Change▶
30 Is a Dangerous Age, Cynthia
Three Strange Loves▶
To Dance with the White Dog▶
To Forget Venice
Tokyo Story▶
Toto le Heros▶
Tough Guys
Two for the Road▶
Two of a Kind
Two Weeks in Another Town
Umberto D▶
Unforgiven▶
Voyage of the Heart
The Wasp Woman
The Whales of August▶

When a Woman Ascends the Stairs
The Wild Bunch▶
Wild Strawberries▶
A Woman's Tale▶
Wrestling Ernest Hemingway

Guys in Kilts

***see also** Scotland*

Bonnie Prince Charlie
Braveheart▶
The Master of Ballantrae
Rob Roy▶
Rob Roy—The Highland Rogue
Tunes of Glory▶

Gymnastics

American Anthem
Breaking Free
Dream to Believe
I Was a Teenage Werewolf
Nadia

Happy Hookers

***see also** Gigolos; Oldest Profession*

Arthur▶
Bank Robber
Dixie: Changing Habits▶
Doctor Detroit
The Duchess and the Dirtwater Fox
For Pete's Sake
The Happy Hooker
The Happy Hooker Goes Hollywood
The Happy Hooker Goes to Washington
Irma La Douce
The Last Prostitute
McCabe & Mrs. Miller▶
Mighty Aphrodite
Milk Money
Night Shift
The Owl and the Pussycat▶
Pretty Woman▶
Risky Business▶
Sweet Charity▶
Working Girls

Hard Knock Life

***see also** Great Depression; Homeless*

Beggars in Ermine
Black Tower
Blessing
A Brivele der Mamen▶
Cafe Express
Captain Scarlett
Carrie▶
City of Joy
Clockers▶
Crisscross
Crows and Sparrows▶
Dolores Claiborne▶
Elena and Her Men▶
Forbidden Choices
The Good Earth▶
The Grim Reaper▶
A Home of Our Own
Italian
Jude the Obscure
Juno and the Paycock
Lamerica▶
Laughing Sinners
Les Miserables▶
Lies My Father Told Me▶
Little Heroes
Little Women▶
The Match Factory Girl▶
Moll Flanders▶
None But the Lonely Heart▶
The Old Curiosity Shop
One Third of a Nation
Pocketful of Miracles▶
The Pope of Greenwich Village
Restoration▶
Salaam Bombay!▶
The Stars Fell on Henrietta
The Story of Fausta
Street Scene▶
The Super
White Man's Burden
Yellow Earth

Hard Knuckle Sandwich

***see** Boxing*

Hawaii

***see also** Island Fare*

Hawaii▶
Hercules
Magnum P.I.: Don't Eat the Snow in Hawaii
Picture Bride
Race the Sun
A Very Brady Sequel
Waikiki Wedding▶

Hearts!

***see also** Eyeballs!*

Angel Heart
Brainstorm
Dumb & Dumber
Indiana Jones and the Temple of Doom▶
The Last of the Mohicans▶
Legends of the Fall
Mary Shelley's Frankenstein
Pulp Fiction▶

Heaven Sent

***see also** Angels*

All Dogs Go to Heaven
All Dogs Go to Heaven 2
All of Me
Almost an Angel
Always
Angel on My Shoulder▶
Angel on My Shoulder
The Bishop's Wife▶
Brewster McCloud▶
Brother John▶
Carousel▶
Chances Are▶
Charley and the Angel
Clarence
Date with an Angel
Defending Your Life▶
Field of Dreams▶
Forever Darling
Ghost▶
Ghost Dad
A Guy Named Joe
Heading for Heaven
Heart Condition
Heaven
Heaven Can Wait▶
The Heavenly Kid
Hello Again
Here Comes Mr. Jordan▶
The Horn Blows at Midnight▶
I Married an Angel
It Came Upon a Midnight Clear
It's a Wonderful Life▶
Kiss Me Goodbye
Liliom▶
The Littlest Angel
Made in Heaven
Miracle in Milan▶
Mr. Destiny
The Next Voice You Hear
Oh, God!
Oh, God! Book 2
Oh, God! You Devil
One Magic Christmas
The Return of Peter Grimm
Static
The Three Lives of Thomasina▶
Truly, Madly, Deeply▶
Two of a Kind
White Light
Xanadu

Heists

***see also** Scams, Stings & Cons*

Alberto Express
Almost Partners
The Amazing Transparent Man
The Anderson Tapes▶
The Apple Dumpling Gang
Armored Car Robbery
The Armour of God
Army of One
The Asphalt Jungle▶
Assault of the Rebel Girls
At Gunpoint
Back in the USSR
Bad Boys
B.A.D. Cats
The Badlanders▶
Bandits
The Bank Dick▶
Bank Robber
Bank Shot▶
Bellman and True
Bells of Coronado
Beyond Fear
The Bicycle Thief▶
Big Chase
Big Deal on Madonna Street▶
The Big Scam
Bitter Vengeance
The Black Lash
Black Moon Rising
Blind Justice
The Boatniks
Bob le Flambeur▶
Bonnie & Clyde▶
Bottle Rocket
Bound
The Brain
Breathing Fire
Butch and Sundance: The Early Days
Canvas: The Fine Art of Crime
Captain Blackjack
Casino▶
The Catamount Killing
C.I.A. 2: Target Alexa
The Cobra Strikes
Crackerjack
Crime Broker
Crooks & Coronets
Daring Dobermans
Dead Presidents
Deadly Diamonds
Death Tide
The Deputy Drummer
Desperate Cargo
The Desperate Trail
Destiny Turns on the Radio
Diamond Fleece
Diamond Trail
The Diamond Trap
Die Hard: With a Vengeance
Dillinger and Capone
Dog Eat Dog
Dollars▶
Double Deal
Double Trouble
Dunston Checks In
11 Harrowhouse▶
Five Golden Dragons
The Florida Connection
Four Ways Out
Free Ride
French Kiss
Gambit
The Getaway
Getting Even with Dad
Going in Style▶
Grand Larceny
Great Bank Hoax
Great Gold Swindle
The Great St. Louis Bank Robbery
The Great Train Robbery▶
The Green Glove
Grisbi
Gun Crazy▶
Gun Girls
Guns Don't Argue
Gypsy
Hand Gun
Happy New Year
Hard Hunted
The Hard Truth
Harley Davidson and the Marlboro Man
Heat▶
The Heist
High Risk
Holy Matrimony
The Hoodlum
The Horse Without a Head
Hot Money
Hot Target
Hot Touch
How to Steal a Million▶
I Died a Thousand Times
Ice
The Immortals
Incident at Deception Ridge
Inside Information
Interceptor
The Italian Job
Joy Ride to Nowhere
Kansas City Confidential▶
Killer
Killer Force
The Killing▶
Killing in the Sun
Killing Zoe
King's Ransom
Lassiter
The Last of Mrs. Cheyney▶
Late Extra
The League of Gentlemen▶
Letting the Birds Go Free
Lightning Jack
The Lion's Share
Loophole
Mad Mission 3
A Man, a Woman, and a Bank
Man Trouble
Marbella
Marked Money
Master Touch
Melodie en Sous-Sol
Midnight Limited
Million Dollar Haul
Mission Batangas
Money Movers
Money to Burn
Money Train
Motor Patrol
Motorama
Murph the Surf
My Dog, the Thief
No Man's Land
Normal Life
Ocean's 11
The Old Lady Who Walked in the Sea
Operation Amsterdam
Pardon My Sarong
Passionate Thief
The Pink Panther▶
Point Break
Professionals
Queen of Diamonds
The Real McCoy
The Rebel Set
Reservoir Dogs▶
The Return of Boston Blackie
Rififi▶
The Rip Off
Robbery
Rough Cut
Scarlet Street▶
Seven Thieves▶
Shadow Man
Slaughterday
Sneakers
The Squeaker
The Squeeze
Super Soul Brother
They Met in Bombay
Thief▶
The Thief Who Came to Dinner
To Catch a Thief▶
Too Many Crooks
Topkapi▶
Tough Guys
Trapped In Paradise
Two If by Sea
Two-Way Stretch
The Underneath▶
The Usual Suspects▶
White Fire
White Tiger
Who'll Stop the Rain?▶
The Wrong Arm of the Law▶
The Wrong Road
X Marks the Spot

Hell High School

***see also** Campus Capers; School Daze; Teen Angst*

Angus
Anything for Love
The Beat
Beverly Hills 90210
Big Bully
Bill & Ted's Excellent Adventure
Billy Madison
Blackboard Jungle▶
Blood of Dracula
Bloodmoon
Born Innocent
Boy's Reformatory
The Brady Bunch Movie▶
Brutal Fury
Buffy the Vampire Slayer▶
Carrie▶
Cemetery High
Cheering Section
Cherry Hill High
The Chicken Chronicles
Class Act
Class of Fear
The Class of Miss MacMichael
Class of 1984
Class of 1999
Class of 1999 2: The Substitute
Class of Nuke 'Em High
Class of Nuke 'Em High 2: Subhumanoid Meltdown
Class of Nuke 'Em High 3: The Good, the Bad and the Subhumanoid
Class Reunion Massacre
The Club
Clueless▶
Coach
Coneheads
Cooley High▶
The Craft
Creepers
Crisis at Central High▶
Cry-Baby▶
Cutting Class
Dangerously Close
Dazed and Confused▶
Deadly Fieldtrip
Death Goes to School
Echoes in the Darkness
Ernest Goes to School
The Ernest Green Story
Fast Times at Ridgemont High▶
Ferris Bueller's Day Off▶
Finishing School
The George McKenna Story
The Girl, the Body and the Pill
Girls in Chains
Girls Town
Grad Night
Graduation Day
Grease 2
Great Love Experiment
The Great St. Trinian's Train Robbery
Hadley's Rebellion
Hard Knox
Heathers▶
Hell High
Hide and Go Shriek
Hiding Out
High School Caesar
High School Confidential
High School High
High School USA
Hollywood High
Homework
Hoosiers▶
I Was a Teenage Werewolf
I Was a Teenage Zombie
If...▶
The Imposter
The Invisible Kid
The Invisible Maniac

Joy of Sex
Just One of the Girls
The Lawrenceville Stories
Lone Wolf
Loose Screws
Lust for a Vampire
Major Payne
The Majorettes
Massacre at Central High
Maya
Mirror, Mirror
Monster High
My Bodyguard▶
National Lampoon's Senior Trip
Night Visitor
Nowhere to Run
On the Edge: The Survival of Dana
One Night Only
Only the Strong
Pandemonium
Peggy Sue Got Married
Platinum High School
Porky's
Porky's 2: The Next Day
The Positively True Adventures of the Alleged Texas Cheerleader-Murdering Mom▶
Princess Academy
Prison for Children
Prom Night
Prom Night 3: The Last Kiss
Prom Night 4: Deliver Us From Evil
Pump Up the Volume
Rebel High
Return to Horror High
Rock 'n' Roll High School▶
Rock 'n' Roll High School Forever
Rock, Pretty Baby
Satan's Cheerleaders
School Ties▶
Screwballs
Senior Trip
Showdown
Sidekicks
Sister Act 2: Back in the Habit
Sixteen Candles▶
Slaughter High
Some Kind of Wonderful
Stay Awake
Student Affairs
Student Bodies
The Substitute
Summer School
Teenage Strangler
Terror Squad
3:15—The Moment of Truth
Three O'Clock High
Tom Brown's School Days▶
Trick or Treat
Twisted Brain
Undercover
Urusei Yatsura Movie 2: Beautiful Dreamer
Wanderers▶
Werewolf in a Girl's Dormitory
White Squall
Zombie High

Hispanic America

Hitz
I Like It Like That▶
Lone Star▶
Maricela
Mi Vida Loca
Miami Rhapsody
My Family▶
The Ring
Roosters
Salsa
Steal Big, Steal Little
Sweet 15
Zoot Suit▶

Historical Drama

see also Medieval Romps; Period Piece

Abe Lincoln in Illinois▶
Across the Wide Missouri
The Adventures of Tom Sawyer
The Agony and the Ecstasy
The Alamo▶
The Alamo: Thirteen Days to Glory
Alexander the Great
Alone Against Rome
Amadeus▶
Anastasia▶
Anastasia: The Mystery of Anna
Andrei Rublev▶
Anne of the Thousand Days▶
Antony and Cleopatra
Assassination of Trotsky
Assunta Spina
The Attic: The Hiding of Anne Frank
Augustine of Hippo▶
The Autobiography of Miss Jane Pittman▶
The Ballad of Narayama▶
Barabbas
Barefoot in Athens
The Bastard
The Battle of Algiers▶
Battle of Britain
Battle of the Bulge
Battle of Valiant
The Battleship Potemkin▶
Beau Brummel▶
Becket▶
Beethoven's Nephew
Ben-Hur▶
Bhowani Junction
The Big Red One▶
The Birth of a Nation▶
Black Robe▶
Blaise Pascal▶
The Blue Yonder
Bonnie Prince Charlie
Braveheart▶
A Bridge Too Far
Brigham Young: Frontiersman
Brother Sun, Sister Moon
The Bushido Blade
Cabeza de Vaca▶
Cabiria
Caesar and Cleopatra
Captain Caution
Carthage in Flames
Catherine the Great
The Charge of the Light Brigade▶
The Charge of the Light Brigade
Children of Paradise▶
Christopher Columbus
Christopher Columbus: The Discovery
Cleopatra
Condemned to Live
A Connecticut Yankee▶
Conquest▶
The Court Martial of Billy Mitchell▶
Crisis at Central High▶
Cromwell
The Crusades
Dances with Wolves▶
A Dangerous Man: Lawrence after Arabia▶
Danton▶
David and Bathsheba▶
David Copperfield▶
David Copperfield
The Day That Shook the World
Demetrius and the Gladiators
Desiree
The Devils▶
The Devil's Disciple▶
Diane
Doctor Zhivago▶
Drums in the Deep South
Dynasty
Edward II
El Cid▶
Eleanor & Franklin▶
Eleanor: First Lady of the World
Elizabeth R▶
Elizabeth, the Queen
Erik, the Viking
The Eternal Waltz
Eureka Stockade
Extramuros
Fabiola▶
The Fall of the Roman Empire▶
Fellini Satyricon▶
Fire Over England▶
The First Olympics: Athens 1896
Forever and a Day▶
Forty Days of Musa Dagh
47 Ronin, Part 1▶
47 Ronin, Part 2▶
1492: Conquest of Paradise
Freedom Road
Gallipoli▶
Gate of Hell▶
The Gathering Storm
Geheimakte WB1
Geronimo: An American Legend
Gettysburg▶
Giants of Rome
Gladiator of Rome
Glory▶
Gonza the Spearman
The Great Commandment
The Greatest Story Ever Told
Guilty by Suspicion
Hawaii▶
The Hellfire Club
Henry V▶
Hill Number One
Hiroshima▶
Hitler
The Horseman on the Roof
The Howards of Virginia
The Hunchback of Notre Dame▶
Hunter in the Dark
I Beheld His Glory
Imperial Venus
In Old Chicago▶
Independence
The Invaders
The Iron Crown
The Iron Duke
Ironclads
Ivan the Terrible, Part 1▶
Ivan the Terrible, Part 2▶
Ivanhoe▶
Ivanhoe
Jefferson in Paris
Jesus of Nazareth▶
The Jewel in the Crown
JFK▶
Joan of Arc
Johnny Tremain & the Sons of Liberty
Judith of Bethulia▶
Julius Caesar▶
Justin Morgan Had a Horse
Khartoum
King David
King Richard and the Crusaders
Kolberg
La Marseillaise▶
La Nuit de Varennes▶
Lady Jane▶
Last Days of Pompeii
The Last Emperor▶
Last Four Days
The Last of the Mohicans
The Last Valley
Lawrence of Arabia▶
Le Complot▶
Les Miserables
The Lighthorsemen▶
The Lindbergh Kidnapping Case▶
The Lion in Winter▶
The Lion of Thebes▶
Lionheart
Little House on the Prairie▶
Lloyds of London▶
Long Shadows
Luther
The Magician of Lublin
The Mahabharata
Mahler▶
A Man for All Seasons▶
Mandela▶
Marie Antoinette
Martin Luther
Mary of Scotland▶
Masada▶
Mata Hari
Mayerling
Missiles of October▶
The Mission▶
Mockery
Moll Flanders▶
The Moonraker
Mountain Man
Mutiny on the Bounty▶
Napoleon▶
Nefertiti, Queen of the Nile
Nicholas and Alexandra
Nine Days a Queen▶
Nixon▶
Norseman
Omar Khayyam
Once Upon a Time...When We Were Colored▶
The Ordeal of Dr. Mudd▶
Orphan Train▶
Orphans of the Storm▶
Overlanders▶
The Passion of Joan of Arc▶
The Passover Plot
Peter the First: Part 1
Peter the First: Part 2
Peter the Great▶
Pharoah's Army
Portrait of a Rebel: Margaret Sanger
The Power of One
Pride and Prejudice▶
The Private Life of Henry VIII▶
The Private Lives of Elizabeth & Essex▶
Queen Christina▶
Queen Margot▶
Quo Vadis
Quo Vadis▶
Quo Vadis
Ragtime▶
Raintree County
Rasputin▶
Rasputin and the Empress▶
The Rebels
The Red and the Black▶
Reign of Terror
Restoration▶
Revolt of the Barbarians
Revolution
Richard III▶
The Right Stuff▶
Rikyu▶
The Rise of Louis XIV▶
Road to Yesterday/The Yankee Clipper
Roanoak
Rob Roy—The Highland Rogue
The Robe
Robin and Marian
Roots▶
Roots: The Gift
Roots: The Next Generation▶
Saint Joan
Salome
Samurai Reincarnation
Scarlet Empress▶
The Scarlet Letter
The Scarlet Pimpernel▶
Sebastiane▶
The Seekers
Senso▶
Separate But Equal▶
Shaka Zulu▶
Shenandoah▶
Shin Heike Monogatari▶
The Sicilian
The Sign of the Cross
The Silk Road
Sins of Rome
Six Wives of Henry VIII▶
Soldier in Love
Soldier of Orange▶
Spartacus▶
Spy of Napoleon
Sunrise at Campobello▶
The Sword of El Cid
Tai-Pan
A Tale of Two Cities▶
Tale of Two Cities/In the Switch Tower
Tamango
The Ten Commandments
The Ten Commandments▶
Ten Days That Shook the World▶
Ten Who Dared
Tharus Son of Attila
That Hamilton Woman▶
Therese▶
They Died with Their Boots On▶
'38: Vienna Before the Fall
This England
The Thorn Birds▶
Three Sovereigns for Sarah
The Tower of London
Tower of London
Tower of Screaming Virgins
The Triangle Factory Fire Scandal
Uncle Tom's Cabin
Uranus▶
Vanina Vanini▶
Victoria Regina
The Virgin Queen▶
Viva Zapata!▶
The Wannsee Conference▶
The War Lord▶
The Warriors
Waterloo
Where the Sky Begins
White Mischief▶
The White Rose▶
Who Has Seen the Wind?
The Winds of Kitty Hawk
The Wolf at the Door
A Woman Called Golda▶
A Woman Called Moses
Young Bess▶
Young Catherine▶
Young Mr. Lincoln▶

Hit Men

see also Assassinations

African Rage
Amateur▶
Assassins
Baja
Body Count
Breakaway
Bulletproof Heart▶
Cold Sweat
Confessions of a Hit Man
DaVinci's War
Deja Vu
Desperado▶
Diary of a Hitman
Direct Hit
Dumb & Dumber
El Mariachi▶
Faithful
The Family
Fatal Chase
Fatal Justice
Fight to the Death
Final Mission
Firepower
The Hit List
Hit Woman: The Double Edge
Honor and Glory
The Killer▶
La Femme Nikita▶
The Last Hit
Little Odessa
Man with a Gun
The Mechanic
Mr. Nice Guy
The Naked City▶
Night of the Running Man
The Outside Man
Over the Wire
Paid to Kill
Perfect Killer
Point of No Return
Portrait of a Hitman
The Positively True Adventures of the Alleged Texas Cheerleader-Murdering Mom▶
Prizzi's Honor▶
The Professional

The Professional: Golgo 13
Project: Kill!
Pulp Fiction▶
Quick
Red King, White Knight
Red Rock West▶
Savage Hearts
Season for Assassins
The Specialist
Stiletto
Strangers on a Train▶
Suddenly▶
Things to Do In Denver When You're Dead▶

Hockey

***see also* Skating**

Accident
The Cutting Edge
D2: The Mighty Ducks
Dutch Girls
Happy Gilmore
Hockey Night
The Mighty Ducks
Miracle on Ice
Mystery of the Million Dollar Hockey Puck
Paperback Hero
Slap Shot▶
Sudden Death
Touch and Go
Youngblood

Holidays

***see also* Christmas; Horrible Holidays**

Bloody New Year
Carry On Behind
A Charlie Brown Thanksgiving
Clown Murders
A Day for Thanks on Walton's Mountain
Double Double Toil and Trouble
Easter Parade▶
Fourth Wise Man
Frankenstein Sings...The Movie
Groundhog Day▶
A Happy New Year!
Happy New Year, Charlie Brown
The Hoboken Chicken Emergency
Hocus Pocus
Home for the Holidays
It's the Great Pumpkin, Charlie Brown
Jack-O
The Legend of Sleepy Hollow
Mrs. Wiggs of the Cabbage Patch
New Year's Evil
Night of the Demons 2
Planes, Trains & Automobiles
Spaced Invaders
Squanto: A Warrior's Tale▶
Strange Days▶
Turumba▶
Two Weeks with Love
The Waltons: A Thanksgiving Story
The White Balloon▶

The Holocaust

***see also* Germany; Judaism; Nazis & Other Paramilitary Slugs; World War II**

Alan & Naomi
The Assault▶
The Assisi Underground
The Attic: The Hiding of Anne Frank
Au Revoir Les Enfants▶
Border Street
The Boxer and Death▶
Charlie Grant's War
Christabel
Cold Days
David▶
A Day in October
Diamonds of the Night▶
The Diary of Anne Frank▶
Enemies, a Love Story▶
Era Notte a Roma▶
Europa, Europa▶
The Execution
Forced March
The Garden of the Finzi-Continis▶
Genghis Cohn
Getting Away With Murder
Good Evening, Mr. Wallenberg
Hanna's War
The Hiding Place
Hitler
The Holcroft Covenant
Holocaust▶
Holocaust Survivors...Remembrance of Love
Hunted!
In a Glass Cage
Kanal▶
Kapo▶
Korczak▶
The Last Butterfly
The Last Metro▶
Les Miserables
Les Violons du Bal
Max and Helen
Murderers among Us: The Simon Wiesenthal Story▶
Never Forget
The Pawnbroker▶
Playing for Time▶
Reunion▶
The Revolt of Job▶
The Rose Garden
Schindler's List▶
The Shop on Main Street▶
Sophie's Choice▶
Transport from Paradise
Triumph of the Spirit▶
The Wannsee Conference▶
War & Love
The White Rose▶

Home Alone

***see also* Childhood Visions**

Adventures in Babysitting
And You Thought Your Parents Were Weird!
Anything for a Thrill
The Apple Dumpling Gang
Baby's Day Out
Blank Check
Bless the Beasts and Children
The Blue Lagoon
Camp Nowhere
Children's Island
Cloak & Dagger
Cohen and Tate
Courage Mountain
Cross My Heart
Dirkham Detective Agency
Dirt Bike Kid
Don't Tell Mom the Babysitter's Dead
Explorers
Famous Five Get into Trouble
A Far Off Place
Fatal Skies
Four Rooms
Gleaming the Cube
The Goonies
He is My Brother
Home Alone▶
Home Alone 2: Lost in New York
Honey, I Shrunk the Kids
Hook
The Horse Without a Head
Invaders from Mars
Island Trader
Just William's Luck
Legend of Billie Jean
The Littlest Horse Thieves
Lord of the Flies▶
Lord of the Flies
Mr. Wise Guy
Monkey Trouble
The Monster Squad
Paradise
The Rescue
Return to the Blue Lagoon
Shipwrecked
Snow Treasure
3 Ninjas
3 Ninjas Kick Back
A Waltz Through the Hills
The Window▶
Young Sherlock Holmes

Homeless

***see also* Great Depression; Hard Knock Life; Yuppie Nightmares**

Accatone!▶
All Mine to Give
The Billion Dollar Hobo
Billy: Portrait of a Street Kid
Bums
Children of Sanchez
City Lights▶
Curly Sue
Distant Thunder▶
Dodes 'ka-den▶
Down, Out and Dangerous
Emanon
The Fisher King▶
God Bless the Child▶
The Grapes of Wrath▶
Home for Christmas
Home of Angels
Homecoming
Into the West▶
Kanal▶
The Kid▶
The Kid/Idle Class▶
Life Stinks
Los Olvidados▶
The Lower Depths▶
The Man from Left Field
Midnight Cowboy▶
None But the Lonely Heart▶
Oliver!▶
Oliver Twist▶
Oliver Twist
Oliver Twist▶
Oliver Twist
Original Intent
An Orphan Boy of Vienna
Pardon My Trunk
The Prince of Central Park▶
The Saint of Fort Washington
Salaam Bombay!▶
Samaritan: The Mitch Snyder Story▶
Scarecrow
Silas Marner▶
Sounder▶
Streetwise▶
Sullivan's Travels▶
Summer Magic
They Shall Have Music
Times Square
Up Your Alley
The Vagrant
Where the Day Takes You
With Honors

Homosexuality

***see* Bisexuality; Gays; Lesbians**

Horrible Holidays

***see also* Christmas; Holidays**

April Fool's Day
Black Christmas
Bloodbeat
Bloody New Year
Don't Open Till Christmas
Dorm That Dripped Blood
Frankenstein Sings...The Movie
Halloween▶
Halloween 2: The Nightmare Isn't Over!
Halloween 3: Season of the Witch
Halloween 4: The Return of Michael Myers
Halloween 5: The Revenge of Michael Myers
Halloween 6: The Curse of Michael Myers
Halloween Night
Happy Birthday to Me
Home for the Holidays
Home Sweet Home
Jack-O
Mixed Nuts
Mother's Day
My Bloody Valentine
New Year's Evil
The Night After Halloween
Night of the Demons
Reckless
The Ref▶
Silent Night, Bloody Night
Silent Night, Deadly Night
Silent Night, Deadly Night 2
Silent Night, Deadly Night 3: Better Watch Out!
Silent Night, Deadly Night 4: Initiation
Silent Night, Deadly Night 5: The Toymaker
Teen Alien
Trick or Treats
Wacko

Horror

***see also* Bloody Mayhem; Cannibalism; Classic Horror; Horror Comedy; Killer Appliances; Killer Beasts; Killer Bugs; Killer Plants; Killer Toys; Mad Scientists; Monsters, General; Occult; Phone Terror; Renegade Body Parts; Satanism; Supernatural Horror; Vampire Spoof; Vampires; Werewolves; Zombies**

Abducted 2: The Reunion
The Abomination
The Addiction
After Midnight
Afterward
Alice Sweet Alice
Alien Dead
Alien Prey
Alien Seed
Alligator▶
Alligator 2: The Mutation
Alone in the Dark
The Amazing Transplant
The Ambulance
American Gothic
An American Werewolf in London▶
An Angel for Satan
Anguish
Ants
A*P*E*
At Midnight, I'll Take Your Soul
Autopsy
The Avenger
Awakenings of the Beast
The Awful Dr. Orlof
The Baby
Backwoods
Bad Girls Dormitory
The Bad Seed
Barracuda
Basket Case▶
Basket Case 2
Basket Case 3: The Progeny
The Beach Girls and the Monster
Beaks: The Movie
Beast in the Cellar
Beast of Morocco
Beast of the Yellow Night
The Beast that Killed Women
The Beast with Five Fingers
The Beast Within
The Beautiful, the Bloody and the Bare
Because of the Cats
The Being
Ben
Berserker
Beware! Children at Play
Beyond Darkness
Beyond Dream's Door
Beyond the Door
Beyond the Door 2
Beyond the Door 3
Big Foot
Bio Hazard
The Birds 2: Land's End
The Black Castle
Black Cat
Black Christmas
Black Devil Doll from Hell
Black Friday
Black Magic Terror
Black Pit of Dr. M
The Black Room
Black Roses
Black Vampire
Blackenstein
Blackout
Blacula
A Blade in the Dark
Blade of the Ripper
Blades
Blind Faith
Blood and Black Lace
Blood Bride
Blood Cult
Blood Diner
Blood Feast
Blood Freak
Blood Games
Blood Lake
Blood Legacy
Blood Lust
Blood Mania
Blood of Ghastly Horror
The Blood on Satan's Claw▶
Blood Rage
Blood Salvage
Blood Screams
Blood Sisters
Blood Song
The Blood Spattered Bride
Blood Thirst
Blood Tide
Blood Tracks
Blood Voyage
Bloodbath in Psycho Town
Bloodlink
Bloodlust: Subspecies 3
Bloodmoon
Bloodshed
Bloodspell
Bloodstalkers
Bloodstone: Subspecies 2
Bloodsuckers from Outer Space
Bloodsucking Freaks
Bloodsucking Pharoahs of Pittsburgh
Bloody Birthday
Bloody Moon
Bloody New Year
The Bloody Pit of Horror
The Bloody Vampire
Bloody Wednesday
Blue Blood
Blue Sunshine
Boarding House
The Body Beneath
Body Count
Body Melt
Body Parts
The Body Shop
Body Snatcher from Hell
Boggy Creek II
The Boogey Man
Boogey Man 2
The Borrower
Bowery at Midnight
The Brain
Brain Dead▶
Brain of Blood
The Brain That Wouldn't Die
Brainscan
Bram Stoker's Dracula
Bride of Killer Nerd
The Brides of Dracula
Brides of the Beast

Lunatic
Lurking Fear
Luther the Geek
Macabre
The Mad Butcher
Mad Doctor of Blood Island
The Mad Ghoul
Mad Love▶
Madhouse
Madhouse Mansion
Madman
The Majorettes
Man Beast
Man Made Monster
The Man Who Lived Again
Man with Two Heads
The Man with Two Lives
The Mangler
Mania
Maniac
Maniac Cop
Maniac Cop 2
Maniac Cop 3: Badge of Silence
Man's Best Friend
Mantis in Lace
Mary Reilly
The Mask
The Mask of Fu Manchu
Mausoleum
Maximum Overdrive
Maximum Thrust
The Meateater
Memorial Valley Massacre
Metamorphosis: The Alien Factor
Midnight
Midnight 2: Sex, Death, and Videotape
The Midnight Hour
Midnight Kiss
The Midnight Phantom
Mikey
Mill of the Stone Women
The Milpitas Monster
Mirror, Mirror 2: Raven Dance
Mr. Stitch
Mommy
Mongrel
Monkey Shines
The Monster▶
Monster
The Monster and the Girl
The Monster and the Stripper
The Monster Club
Monster Dog
Monster High
The Monster of London City
The Monster Squad
Monsters Crash the Pajama Party
Moon of the Wolf
Mortuary
Mother's Day
Mountaintop Motel Massacre
The Movie House Massacre
Multiple Maniacs
Murder-in-Law
Murder Mansion
Murder Motel
Murder on Line One
Murderer's Keep
Murders in the Zoo
Mutant
My Bloody Valentine
My Daughter's Keeper
Nail Gun Massacre
The Naked Witch
The Nanny
Needful Things
The New Kids
The Newlydeads
Next of Kin
The Night After Halloween
Night Breed
The Night Brings Charlie
Night Creature
The Night God Screamed
Night Hunter
Night Monster
Night of Bloody Horror
Night of Terror
Night of the Bloody Apes
Night of the Bloody Transplant
Night of the Cobra Woman
Night of the Demon
Night of the Howling Beast
Night of the Living Dead▶
Night of the Living Dead
Night of the Scarecrow
Night of the Strangler
Night of the Zombies
Night Ripper
Night Screams
Night Slasher
Night Terror
Night Train to Terror
Night Warning
Nightmare
Nightmare in Wax
A Nightmare on Elm Street
A Nightmare on Elm Street 2: Freddy's Revenge
A Nightmare on Elm Street 3: Dream Warriors
A Nightmare on Elm Street 4: Dream Master
A Nightmare on Elm Street 5: Dream Child
Nightmare on the 13th Floor
Nightmares
Nightscare
976-EVIL
976-EVIL 2: The Astral Factor
Oasis of the Zombies
Offerings
One Dark Night
One Deadly Owner
125 Rooms of Comfort
One Minute Before Death
The Orphan
The Outcast
The Pack
Pagan Island
Pale Blood
Panic
Paralyzed
Paranoiac
The Passing
Patrick
Pay Off
The Penalty
The People Under the Stairs
The Perverse Countess
Phantasm III: Lord of the Dead
The Phantom
Phantom of Death
Phantom of the Mall: Eric's Revenge
The Phantom of the Opera
Pieces
Pigs
Pin
The Pit
Play Dead
Playroom
Pledge Night
Plutonium Baby
Point of Terror
Popcorn
Possession
Possession: Until Death Do You Part
The Power
Premature Burial
The Prey
Primal Rage
Prime Evil
Prince of Darkness
Prison
Project: Nightmare
Project Vampire
Prom Night
Prom Night 3: The Last Kiss
Prom Night 4: Deliver Us From Evil
Prophecy
The Prowler
The Psychic
Psychic Killer
Psycho Cop
Psycho Cop 2
Psycho from Texas
Psychopath
Pumpkinhead 2: Blood Wings
Puppet Master
Puppet Master 2
Puppet Master 3: Toulon's Revenge
Puppet Master 4
Puppet Master 5: The Final Chapter
The Pyx▶
Rabid
Race with the Devil
Raging Angels
Rana: The Legend of Shadow Lake
Rape
The Rats are Coming! The Werewolves are Here!
Rattled
Rattlers
The Raven▶
Razorback
Red Blooded American Girl
The Redeemer
The Reincarnate
The Rejuvenator
Relative Fear
Rest In Pieces
The Resurrected
Retribution
The Return of Count Yorga
Return of Dracula
Return of the Ape Man
Return of the Evil Dead
Return of the Family Man
Return to Boggy Creek
Return to Horror High
Return to Salem's Lot
Revenge
Revenge in the House of Usher
Revenge of Doctor X
The Revenge of Frankenstein
Revenge of the Dead
Revenge of the Living Zombies
Revenge of the Radioactive Reporter
Revenge of the Zombies
Ring of Terror
The Ripper
The Robot vs. the Aztec Mummy
Rock 'n' Roll Nightmare
Rocktober Blood
Rodan
Rogue
Rosemary's Baby▶
Ruby
The Rue Morgue Massacres
Run, Stranger, Run
The Runestone
Rush Week
Sabaka
The Sadist
The Saga of the Draculas
Salem's Lot
Samson in the Wax Museum
Samson vs. the Vampire Women
Satan in High Heels
The Satanic Rites of Dracula
Satanik
Satan's Black Wedding
Satan's Blade
Satan's Cheerleaders
Satan's Princess
Satan's School for Girls
Satan's Touch
Satanwar
Saturday Night Shockers
Saturday Night Shockers, Vol. 2
Saturday Night Shockers, Vol. 3
Saturday Night Shockers, Vol. 4
The Savage Bees
Savage Intruder
Savage Weekend
Savages
Sawbones
Scalpel
Scanners
Scanners 2: The New Order
Scanners 3: The Takeover
Scanners: The Showdown
Scared Stiff
Scared to Death
The Scars of Dracula
Schizo
Schizoid
Science Crazed
Scorpion with Two Tails
The Scorpion's Tail
Scream, Baby, Scream
Scream Blacula Scream
Scream Dream
Scream of Fear▶
Scream of the Demon Lover
Screamers
The Screaming Dead
The Screaming Skull
Screams of a Winter Night
Screamtime
Season of the Witch
The Secret Cinema
Seducers
See No Evil▶
Seedpeople
Seeds of Evil
Seizure
The Sender
The Sentinel
The Serpent and the Rainbow
The Serpent of Death
Servants of Twilight
Seven Deaths in the Cat's Eye
Seven Doors of Death
The Seventh Victim▶
The Severed Arm
Severed Ties
Sex Is Crazy
Shadow of Chinatown
Shadows Run Black
Shakma
The Shaman
Shark's Paradise
The She-Beast
She Came on the Bus
She Demons
She-Freak
Shock 'Em Dead
Shock! Shock! Shock!
Shock Waves
Shocker
Shriek of the Mutilated
The Sibling
Silent Madness
Silent Night, Bloody Night
Silent Night, Deadly Night
Silent Night, Deadly Night 2
Silent Night, Deadly Night 3: Better Watch Out!
Silent Night, Deadly Night 4: Initiation
Silent Night, Deadly Night 5: The Toymaker
Silent Scream
Silver Bullet
The Sinister Invasion
Sinner's Blood
The Sins of Dorian Gray
Sinthia: The Devil's Doll
Sisters▶
Sisters of Satan
Skinned Alive
Skinner
The Skull
Skullduggery
Slashdance
Slaughter High
Slaughter Hotel
The Slaughter of the Vampires
Slaughterhouse
Slaughterhouse Rock
The Slayer
The Slayer/The Scalps
Sleazemania III: The Good, the Bad & the Sleazy
Sledgehammer
Sleep of Death
Sleepaway Camp
Sleepaway Camp 2: Unhappy Campers
Sleepaway Camp 3: Teenage Wasteland
Sleepwalkers
Slime City
The Slime People
Slithis
Slugs
The Slumber Party Massacre
Slumber Party Massacre 2
Slumber Party Massacre 3
The Snake Hunter Strangler
The Snake People
The Snake Woman
Snowbeast
Society
Sole Survivor
Something Weird
Sometimes Aunt Martha Does Dreadful Things
Sometimes They Come Back
Son of Blob
Sorority House Massacre
Sorority House Massacre 2: Nighty Nightmare
Sound of Horror
Sounds of Silence
Spasms
The Spawning
The Spectre of Edgar Allen Poe
The Speed Lovers
The Spell
The Spellbinder
Spellcaster
Spiritism
Spirits
Spirits of the Dead▶
Splatter University
Spontaneous Combustion
Spookies
Squirm
Stage Fright
Stagefright
Stanley
Stay Awake
Stephen King's Golden Years
Stephen King's It
Stephen King's The Stand
Stephen King's The Tommyknockers
Steps from Hell
Stepsisters
Stones of Death
Strait-Jacket
Strange Behavior
Strange Case of Dr. Jekyll & Mr. Hyde
Strange World of Coffin Joe
The Strangeness
Strangers
Strays
Stuff Stephanie in the Incinerator
Subspecies
Sugar Cookies
Suicide Cult
Summer of Fear
Summer of Secrets
Sundown
Superstition
The Surgeon
Survivor
Suspiria▶
Swamp of the Lost Monster
The Swarm
Sweet 16
Tainted Image
Tales from the Crypt▶
Tales from the Crypt
Tales from the Gimli Hospital
Tales of Terror
Tales That Witness Madness
Tarantulas: The Deadly Cargo
Taste the Blood of Dracula
Teenage Gang Debs
Teenage Strangler
Teenage Zombies
The Tell-Tale Heart
The Tempter
Tentacles
The Terror
Terror at Red Wolf Inn
Terror at Tenkiller
Terror at the Opera
Terror Beach
Terror Eyes
Terror in the Haunted House
Terror in the Swamp
Terror in the Wax Museum
Terror in Toyland

Horror Anthologies

see also Horror

Horror Comedy

see also Horror

Horse Racing

see Gambling; Horses

Horses

Devil on Horseback
The Devil's Cargo
Duke of the Derby
Eagle's Wing
The Electric Horseman
Equus
Ex-Mrs. Bradford▶
Far North
The Fighting Stallion▶
A Fine Mess
The Flying Deuces▶
Forbidden Trails
Francis Goes to the Races
A Girl in Every Port
Glory
The Golden Stallion
Great Dan Patch
The Great Mike
Gypsy Colt
Heart of the Rockies
Hell's Hinges
Hit the Saddle
A Horse for Danny
The Horse in the Gray Flannel Suit
Horsemasters
The Horsemen
Hot to Trot!
In Pursuit of Honor
Indian Paint
International Velvet
Into the West▶
Italian Straw Hat▶
It's a Great Life
Justin Morgan Had a Horse
Kentucky Blue Streak
King of the Sierras
King of the Stallions
King of the Wild Horses▶
King of the Wind
Law of the Wild
Le Gentleman D'Epsom
The Lemon Drop Kid
The Lighthorsemen▶
Lightning: The White Stallion
The Littlest Horse Thieves
The Littlest Outlaw
The Longshot
Lotna
Lucky Luke
Ma and Pa Kettle at the Fair
The Man from Snowy River
Marshal of Cedar Rock
The Miracle of the White Stallions
The Misfits▶
Misty
My Friend Flicka▶
My Old Man
My Pal Trigger
National Lampoon's Animal House▶
National Velvet▶
On the Right Track
Phar Lap
Primo Baby
Prince and the Great Race
The Quiet Man▶
Racing Luck
A Rare Breed
The Red Fury
The Red Pony▶
The Red Stallion
Return of Wildfire
Return to Snowy River▶
Ride a Wild Pony▶
Ride Him, Cowboy▶
Riding High
Rolling Home
The Rounders
Run for the Roses
Running Wild
Saddle Buster
Saratoga
Silver Stallion
The Silver Stallion: King of the Wild Brumbies
Something to Talk About
Speedy▶
The Story of Seabiscuit
Sundown Saunders
Sylvester
Tennessee Stallion
Texas to Bataan
Thoroughbreds Don't Cry
Three Men on a Horse▶
Turf Boy
Two Bits & Pepper
The Undefeated
Western Double Feature 16
When the West Was Young
White Mane▶
Wild Hearts Can't Be Broken▶
Wild Horse Hank
Wild Horses
Wild Pony
Win, Place, or Steal
Winds of the Wasteland

Hospitals & Medicine

***see also** Disease of the Week; Doctors & Nurses; Emerging Viruses; Sanity Check; Shrinks*

Article 99
B.O.R.N.
Britannia Hospital
Carry On Nurse
A Child is Waiting▶
China Beach▶
City of Joy
The Clonus Horror
Coma▶
Come to the Stable▶
Critical Condition
Dead Ringers▶
Disorderlies
Disorderly Orderly
Doctor at Large
Dr. Kildare's Strange Case
Doctors' Wives
East of Kilimanjaro
The Egyptian
ER
Frankenstein General Hospital
Green for Danger
Gross Anatomy
Hard-Boiled
The Hasty Heart
Horror Hospital
The Hospital▶
Hospital Massacre
Hospital of Terror
In for Treatment▶
The Interns
Invasion
Junior
The Kingdom
Lifespan
Naked Is Better
Nine Months
Nurse
One Flew Over the Cuckoo's Nest▶
State of Emergency
A Stolen Face
The Surgeon
Tales from the Gimli Hospital
Tender Loving Care
Threshold
12 Monkeys▶
Vital Signs
Welcome Stranger
While You Were Sleeping▶
Whose Life Is It Anyway?▶
Young Doctors in Love

Hostage!

***see also** Kidnapped!; Missing Persons*

Against the Wall▶
Airheads
Amos and Andrew
Autumn Born
Black Cobra 2
Blackout
Blood of the Hunter
Cadillac Man
Codename: Vengeance
Cold Sweat
Cul de Sac▶
Days of Hell
Death and the Maiden▶
Death Stalk
Die Hard▶
Die Hard 2: Die Harder▶
Distortions
Dog Day Afternoon▶
Door to Door Maniac
Escape from New York
Fall Time
Fatal Mission
Field of Fire
48 Hours to Live
Headless Body in Topless Bar
Hostages▶
Housewife
Iron Eagle
The Jesus Trip
King of Comedy▶
The Last Samurai
The Legend of Wolf Mountain
Live! From Death Row
Midnight Fear
Nick of Time
No Contest
Open Fire
Operation Thunderbolt
A Perfect World
Provoked
Quake
The Ref▶
Rock All Night
The Seventh Floor
S.F.W.
Skyscraper
Snatched
Spaghetti House
Split Second
A Stranger is Watching
Stranglehold
Stripteaser
Sudden Death
Suddenly▶
Sweet Hostage
The Taking of Pelham One Two Three▶
Terror Stalks the Class Reunion
The Trap
12 Monkeys▶
Vengeance

Houston

Apollo 13▶
The Bad News Bears in Breaking Training
Brewster McCloud▶
Full Fathom Five
Jason's Lyric
Last Night at the Alamo▶
Night Game
Reality Bites
The Swarm
Tin Cup▶
Urban Cowboy
Vietnam, Texas

Hunted!

***see also** Survival*

Arctic Blue
Beyond Fear
Beyond Rangoon
Bigfoot: The Unforgettable Encounter
Bounty Hunter 2002
The Cursed Mountain Mystery
Cyborg 2
Damned River
Deadly Game
Death Hunt
Decoy
Deliverance▶
Desperate Prey
Diary of a Hitman
Dominion
Ex-Cop
Eyes of the Beholder
Fair Game
Final Round
Fortress
Freejack
The Ghost of Fletcher Ridge
Goetz von Berlichingen
The Good Guys and the Bad Guys
Hard Target
The Hunted
Hunter's Blood
Illegal Entry: Formula for Fear
Incident at Deception Ridge
Jungleground
Killing at Hell's Gate
Ladykillers
The Last of the Dogmen
Last Witness
Midnight Murders
The Most Dangerous Game▶
The Naked Prey▶
Nightmare at Bittercreek
Prey for the Hunter
Project Shadowchaser 3000
Shadowhunter
Shoot to Kill▶
Southern Comfort▶
Survival Quest
Surviving the Game
Trial and Error
Uncivilized
Warriors

Hunting

***see also** Go Fish*

The Amazing Panda Adventure
The Bear▶
The Belstone Fox
The Bridge to Nowhere
Caddyshack▶
Dan Candy's Law
Deadly Prey
First Blood
Forest of Little Bear
Frostbiter: Wrath of the Wendigo
Gaiety
Git!
Harry Black and the Tiger
The Hunt▶
The Last Hunt
The Last Safari
Mogambo▶
Night of the Grizzly
Shoot
Shooting
Those Calloways
White Hunter, Black Heart▶

Hurling

Blood Simple▶
Car Wash
The Crying Game▶
The Cutting Edge
Dogfight▶
Eating Raoul▶
The Exorcist▶
52 Pick-Up
Jaws▶
Monty Python's The Meaning of Life▶
National Lampoon's Animal House▶
Parenthood▶
The Sandlot▶
Sirens
Stand By Me▶
This Is Spinal Tap▶
The Verdict▶

I Love Detroit

***see also** Fast Cars; Motor Vehicle Dept.*

Aspen Extreme
Beverly Hills Cop
Beverly Hills Cop 2
Beverly Hills Cop 3
Bird on a Wire
Chameleon Street▶
Collision Course
Coupe de Ville
Crimewave
Crossing the Bridge
Detroit 9000
The Dollmaker
Hoffa▶
Indian Summer
The Last Word
Let's Kill All the Lawyers
Mirrors
Mr. Mom▶
One in a Million: The Ron LeFlore Story
Paper Lion
Presumed Innocent▶
Renaissance Man
RoboCop▶
RoboCop 2
RoboCop 3
RoboCop the Series: The Future of Law Enforcement
Roger & Me▶
The Rosary Murders
Scarecrow
Tiger Town
True Romance
Tucker: The Man and His Dream▶
Zebrahead▶

Identity

***see also** Amnesia; Role Reversal*

Babyfever
Boys
Brainwaves
The Broken Chain
Changes
The Crimes of Stephen Hawke
The Dark Half
Dark Passage
Diabolically Yours
Dr. Heckyl and Mr. Hype
Don Juan DeMarco
Dumbo▶
The Effect of Gamma Rays on Man-in-the-Moon Marigolds▶
Far Out Man
The Great Gabbo
High Country
Higher Learning
Joe Versus the Volcano
Leon the Pig Farmer
Marnie▶
Middle Age Crazy
Midnight▶
Mrs. Winterbourne
Montenegro▶
Moving Out
My Brilliant Career▶
My Dinner with Andre▶
Nevil Shute's The Far Country
Next Year If All Goes Well
The Nutty Professor▶
Old Boyfriends
Olivier, Olivier▶
Orlando▶
Partner▶
Pocketful of Miracles▶
Point of No Return
The Promise
Rebel Without a Cause▶
Return of the Secaucus 7▶
Ruby in Paradise▶
Secrets and Lies
Sorrows of Gin
Timothy and the Angel
Torment
Touki Bouki
Vincent, Francois, Paul and the Others▶
Woof!
The Wrong Move
Zelig▶

Immigration

An American Tail
Arizona
Avalon▶
Blood Red
Borderline
Bread and Chocolate▶
Buck Privates Come Home▶
Combination Platter
Coming to America▶
The Cowboy Way
Does This Mean We're Married?
Drachenfutter▶

Driving Me Crazy
El Super▶
The Emigrants▶
Enemies, a Love Story▶
Far and Away
Green Card
Hester Street▶
I Can't Sleep
I Cover the Waterfront
The Immigrant▶
Italian
Journey of Hope▶
A King in New York
Living on Tokyo Time
The Manions of America
Maricela
Miami Rhapsody
Midnight Auto Supply
Monkey Business▶
Moscow on the Hudson▶
My Girl Tisa
My Sweet Victim
The New Land▶
O Quatrilho
Pelle the Conqueror▶
Sky High
Skyline▶
Wait Until Spring, Bandini
Where Is My Child?

Incest

see also Family Ties

Against the Wind
Angels and Insects▶
The Grifters▶
Innocent Lies
My Sister, My Love
Spanking the Monkey▶
'Tis a Pity She's a Whore
Waterland

India

see also Calcutta

The Adversary
Aparajito▶
Autobiography of a Princess
Bandit Queen
Bhowani Junction
The Black Devils of Kali
Black Narcissus▶
City of Joy
Company Limited
Conduct Unbecoming
The Courtesans of Bombay▶
The Deceivers
Distant Thunder▶
Drums
Ele, My Friend
The Far Pavilions
Flame Over India▶
Gandhi▶
Gunga Din▶
Heat and Dust▶
The Home and the World▶
Hullabaloo Over Georgie & Bonnie's Pictures
In Custody
The Jewel in the Crown
Journey to the Lost City
Jungle Hell
Kim▶
Kim
The Lives of a Bengal Lancer▶
The Mahabharata
The Man Who Would Be King▶
Masala
Maya
Octopussy
A Passage to India▶
Pather Panchali▶
The Rains Came
The Razor's Edge▶
The River▶
Rudyard Kipling's The Jungle Book
Sabaka
Shakespeare Wallah▶
Spices▶
Staying On
Two Daughters▶
Wee Willie Winkie▶

The World of Apu▶

Interracial Affairs

Cafe au Lait▶
Come See the Paradise▶
Corrina, Corrina
Guess Who's Coming to Dinner▶
Jungle Fever▶
Love Field
Machine Gun Blues
Miami Rhapsody
Mississippi Masala▶
Mr. & Mrs. Loving▶
Norman, Is That You?
A Patch of Blue
Pocahontas▶
The Story of a Three Day Pass
Taxi Blues▶
The Wedding Banquet▶

Interviews

see also This is Your Life

Bugs Bunny Superstar
Chuck Berry: Hail! Hail! Rock 'n' Roll▶
The Compleat Beatles▶
Cult People
Hearts of Darkness: A Filmmaker's Apocalypse▶
Hedda Hopper's Hollywood
Hollywood Ghost Stories
James Dean
The JFK Conspiracy
La Salamandre
Roger & Me▶
Sometimes It Works, Sometimes It Doesn't
Stripper
Wisecracks▶
The Wonderful, Horrible Life of Leni Riefenstahl

Inventors & Inventions

see also Mad Scientists; Science & Scientists

Chitty Chitty Bang Bang
C.H.O.M.P.S.
The Demi-Paradise▶
Edison the Man
The Great Moment
Hidden Enemy
Homer Comes Home
Homewrecker
Honey, I Blew Up the Kid
Honey, I Shrunk the Kids
The Man in the White Suit▶
The Man Who Fell to Earth▶
The Mosquito Coast
Mystery Plane
Not Quite Human
Not Quite Human 2
The Nut
The Pinchcliffe Grand Prix
Roaring Speedboats
Rogue's Gallery
So This is Washington
The Sound and the Silence
Spitfire▶
Still Not Quite Human
The Story of Alexander Graham Bell▶
Theremin: An Electronic Odyssey▶
Time Chasers
Under the Hula Moon
The Water Engine
Where's Willie?
The Whole Shootin' Match▶
The Yellow Cab Man
Young Tom Edison

Ireland

see also Great Britain

Belfast Assassin
Beloved Enemy▶
Blown Away
Broken Harvest
Cal▶
Children in the Crossfire
Circle of Deceit
Circle of Friends
The Commitments▶
The Crying Game▶
Danny Boy▶
Darby O'Gill & the Little People▶
The Dawning
The Dead▶
December Bride
Far and Away
The Field▶
The Fighting Prince of Donegal
Fools of Fortune
Four Days in July
Frankie Starlight
Hear My Song▶
Hennessy
I See a Dark Stranger▶
In the Name of the Father▶
The Informer
The Informer▶
Into the West▶
Irish Cinderella
James Joyce: A Portrait of the Artist as a Young Man
Johnny Nobody
Lamb
Leprechaun
The Lonely Passion of Judith Hearne▶
Man of Aran▶
A Man of No Importance▶
The Manions of America
Men of Ireland
My Left Foot▶
Odd Man Out▶
Oh, Mr. Porter
The Playboys▶
Prayer for the Dying
The Purple Taxi
Quiet Day In Belfast▶
The Quiet Man▶
Rawhead Rex
River of Unrest
The Run of the Country▶
Ryan's Daughter
Scarlett
The Secret of Roan Inish▶
Shake Hands with the Devil▶
The Snapper▶
Song O' My Heart▶
Taffin
Ulysses
The Van▶
War of the Buttons
Widow's Peak

Islam

see also Middle East

Hamsin▶
Malcolm X: Make It Plain
Mohammed: Messenger of God
The Suitors

Island Fare

see also Pacific Islands; Sex on the Beach

The Adventures of Sadie
All the Brothers Were Valiant
Atlantis, the Lost Continent
Bare Essentials
Baywatch the Movie: Forbidden Paradise
Bikini Island
Bird of Paradise
Blacksnake!
The Blue Lagoon
Body Trouble
Cabin Boy
Captain Ron
The Castaway Cowboy
Chandu on the Magic Island
Club Paradise
Conqueror & the Empress
The Cover Girl Murders
Crusoe
Cutthroat Island
Cyber Bandits
Deadly Currents
Dinosaur Island
Dungeon of Harrow
Echoes of Paradise
Emmanuelle on Taboo Island
Exit to Eden
Father Goose
Flipper▶
F.P. 1
Gilligan's Island: Meet the Crew
Hawk of the Wilderness
Horrors of Spider Island
Hurricane
The Idol Dancer
The Island
Island in the Sun
Island of Adventure
The Island of Dr. Moreau
Island of Lost Souls▶
Island of the Blue Dolphins
Island of the Lost
Joe Versus the Volcano
Jurassic Park▶
Kilma, Queen of the Amazons
King of the Damned
L'Enfant d'Eau
The Lunatic
Ma and Pa Kettle at Waikiki
Magic on Love Island
A Man of Passion
Mediterraneo▶
Melody in Love
Men of War
My Father the Hero
Mysterious Island of Beautiful Women
National Lampoon's Last Resort
No Escape
Northern Extremes
On an Island with You
One Night in the Tropics
Pagan Island
Paradise
Passion in Paradise
The Passion of Anna▶
Pearl of the South Pacific
Pippi in the South Seas
The Postman▶
PT 109
The Quest
Rapa Nui
Return to Paradise
Return to the Blue Lagoon
Savage Is Loose
The Seducers
Signs of Life
The Snake People
Somewhere in Time
Son of Fury▶
The Story of Dr. Wassell
Summer Affair
Swept Away...▶
A Swingin' Summer
Terror in Paradise
Trouble in Paradise
The Tuttles of Tahiti▶
Utopia
Waikiki Wedding▶
Week-End In Havana
We're Not Dressing▶
When Time Ran Out
Wide Sargasso Sea
Wings Over the Pacific
Xtro 3: Watch the Skies

Israel

see also The Holocaust; Judaism

Cast a Giant Shadow
Children of Rage
Cup Final
Diamonds
Double Edge
Eagles Attack at Dawn
Echoes of Conflict
Exodus▶
Hide and Seek
Hill 24 Doesn't Answer▶
Intimate Story
Late Summer Blues
The Little Drummer Girl▶
Operation Thunderbolt
The Seventh Coin
Sinai Commandos
Soldier of the Night

Italy

see also Venice

Accatone!▶
Acla's Descent into Floristella
Acqua e Sapone
All Screwed Up▶
Amarcord▶
The Assisi Underground
Assunta Spina
Avanti!
The Bicycle Thief▶
A Blade in the Dark
Blame It on the Bellboy
Blood Feud
Cemetery Man
The Children
Christ Stopped at Eboli▶
Ciao, Professore!
Cinema Paradiso▶
Cobra
Come September
The Conformist▶
Cry of a Prostitute: Love Kills
Divorce—Italian Style▶
1860
Enchanted April
Escapade in Florence
Europa '51
Executioner of Venice
Fellini's Roma
Fiances
Final Justice
Francesco
Gallowglass▶
The Garden of the Finzi-Continis▶
The Godfather, Part 3▶
Hornet's Nest
It Started in Naples▶
Kaos▶
La Chartreuse de Parme
La Dolce Vita▶
La Scorta▶
La Terra Trema▶
The Lion of Venice
Lost Moment
Love and Anarchy▶
Love in the City▶
Macaroni
Mamma Roma▶
A Man About the House
Massacre in Rome
A Month by the Lake
Mussolini & I
1900▶
Obsession
Only You
Open City▶
Ossessione▶
Paisan▶
Passion of Love▶
The Postman▶
A Rare Breed
Roman Spring of Mrs. Stone▶
Rome Adventure
The Scent of a Woman
Season for Assassins
The Seven Hills of Rome
Shoeshine▶
The Sicilian
A Special Day▶
Stealing Beauty
Three Coins in the Fountain
The Tree of Wooden Clogs▶
Von Ryan's Express▶
The Walls of Malapaga
What Did You Do in the War, Daddy?
Where Angels Fear to Tread▶
Women in Prison
Year of the Gun

Jail

see Great Escapes; Men in Prison; Women in Prison

Japan

see also Asia; Tokyo

Akira
The Ballad of Narayama▶
Barbarian and the Geisha
Battle of China
The Battle of the Japan Sea
Behind the Rising Sun
Black Rain▶
Black Rain
Blood on the Sun
Captive Hearts
The Cruel Story of Youth▶
Destination Tokyo
Dodes 'ka-den▶
Eijanaika▶
Enjo
Escapade in Japan
Flirt
47 Ronin, Part 1▶
47 Ronin, Part 2▶
Geisha Girl
Girls of the White Orchid
Heaven & Earth▶
Hiroshima▶
Hiroshima Maiden
Hiroshima, Mon Amour▶
The Hunted
The Idiot▶
The Imperial Japanese Empire
Imperial Navy
Journey of Honor
King's Ransom
Life of Oharu▶
Love and Faith▶
MacArthur's Children▶
A Majority of One
The Makioka Sisters▶
The Men Who Tread on the Tiger's Tail
Midway
Minbo—Or the Gentle Art of Japanese Extortion
Mishima: A Life in Four Chapters▶
Mr. Baseball
Mother▶
Ninja Wars
No Regrets for Our Youth▶
Nomugi Pass
Objective, Burma!▶
Okoge
Osaka Elegy
Prisoners of the Sun▶
Professional Killers 1
Ran▶
Rashomon▶
Red Beard▶
Revenge of a Kabuki Actor
Rikyu▶
Rising Sun▶
Saga of the Vagabond
Samurai Cowboy
Samurai Reincarnation
Sansho the Bailiff▶
Sayonara▶
Seven Samurai▶
She and He
Shin Heike Monogatari▶
Shogun▶
Shogun's Ninja
Showdown in Little Tokyo
Snow Country
The Sun's Burial▶
Sword of Fury II
Thirty Seconds Over Tokyo▶
3 Ninjas Kick Back
Tokyo Decadence
Tokyo-Ga▶
Tokyo Pop
Tora! Tora! Tora!
Traffic Jam
Twenty-Four Eyes▶
Ugetsu▶
Utamaro and His Five Women
Walk, Don't Run
What's Up, Tiger Lily?▶
The Wolves▶
The Yakuza
You Only Live Twice
Zatoichi vs. Yojimbo▶

Japanimation

see also Animation & Cartoons

Akira
Alakazam the Great!
Arcadia of My Youth
The Dagger of Kamui
Demon City Shinjuku
GUY: Awakening of the Devil
Lensman
My Neighbor Totoro
Otaku no Video
Planet Busters
The Professional: Golgo 13
Project A-ko
Starvengers
Toward the Terra
Urotsukidoj 1: Legend of the Overfiend
Urotsukidoj 2: Legend of the Demon Womb
Urusei Yatsura Movie 1: Only You
Urusei Yatsura Movie 2: Beautiful Dreamer
Urusei Yatsura Movie 3: Remember My Love
Urusei Yatsura Movie 4: Lum the Forever
Urusei Yatsura Movie 5: The Final Chapter
Urusei Yatsura Movie 6: Always My Darling
A Wind Named Amnesia

Journalism

see Front Page

Judaism

see also The Holocaust; Israel

American Matchmaker
Angry Harvest▶
The Apprenticeship of Duddy Kravitz▶
The Assisi Underground
Atalia
The Attic: The Hiding of Anne Frank
Au Revoir Les Enfants▶
The Blum Affair
Border Street
A Brivele der Mamen▶
Brussels Transit▶
The Cantor's Son
Charlie Grant's War
The Chosen▶
Commissar▶
Conspiracy of Hearts▶
The Corridor: Death
Crossfire▶
Crossing Delancey▶
David▶
A Day in October
The Diary of Anne Frank▶
Drifting
The Dunera Boys▶
The Dybbuk▶
East and West▶
Eli Eli
Enemies, a Love Story▶
Every Time We Say Goodbye
Exodus▶
Fiddler on the Roof▶
The Fixer▶
A Friendship in Vienna
The Frisco Kid
Funny Girl▶
The Garden of the Finzi-Continis▶
Gentleman's Agreement▶
God, Man and Devil
The Golem▶
Good Evening, Mr. Wallenberg
Goodbye, New York
Green Fields
Hamsin▶
Hanna's War
Hester Street▶
Hill 24 Doesn't Answer▶
Holocaust▶
Homicide▶
The House on Chelouche Street
Hunted!
I Love You, Alice B. Toklas!
I Love You Rosa
The Infiltrator
The Jazz Singer
Jud Suess▶
King David
Kuni Lemel in Tel Aviv
The Last Metro▶
The Last Winter
Leon the Pig Farmer
Les Violons du Bal
Lies My Father Told Me▶
The Light Ahead
Madman
Martha and I▶
Masada▶
Me and the Colonel
Miracle at Moreaux
Miss Rose White▶
Mr. Emmanuel
My Michael▶
No Way to Treat a Lady▶
Noa at Seventeen▶
The Only Way
Outside Chance of Maximillian Glick
Over the Brooklyn Bridge
The Pawnbroker▶
Power
The Quarrel
Radio Days▶
The Revolt of Job▶
Sallah▶
Schindler's List▶
School Ties▶
A Secret Space
The Serpent's Egg
The Shop on Main Street▶
Sofie
The Sorrow and the Pity▶
A Stranger Among Us
The Summer of My German Soldier▶
Table Settings
Tevye
They Were Ten
'38: Vienna Before the Fall
Transport from Paradise
The Two of Us▶
Uncle Moses
Under the Earth▶
Unsettled Land
Unstrung Heroes
Used People
Voyage of the Damned▶
Wandering Jew
War & Love
Where Is My Child?
Where's Poppa?▶
The Wooden Gun
Yentl
Zalmen or the Madness of God

Jungle Stories

see also Monkeyshines; Treasure Hunt

Ace Ventura: When Nature Calls
Africa Screams
Aguirre, the Wrath of God▶
All the Way, Boys
Amazon
Amazon Jail
At Play in the Fields of the Lord▶
Baby ... Secret of the Lost Legend
Back from Eternity
Bat 21
Bela Lugosi Meets a Brooklyn Gorilla
Beyond Rangoon
Beyond the Carribean
Black Cobra 3: The Manila Connection
The Black Devils of Kali
Blonde Savage
Brenda Starr
Bride of the Gorilla
Cannibal Women in the Avocado Jungle of Death
Cobra Woman
Codename: Terminate
The Colombian Connection
Commando Invasion
Congo
Death in the Garden
Delta Force Commando
Diplomatic Immunity
Dr. Cyclops
East of Borneo
Elephant Boy▶
Elephant Walk
The Emerald Forest▶
Emerald Jungle
Emmanuelle 6
Enemy Unseen
Escape from Hell
Escape to Burma
Escape 2000
Farewell to the King
Fatal Mission
Field of Fire
Field of Honor
Final Mission
Firehawk
Firewalker
Fitzcarraldo▶
Five Came Back
Flight from Singapore
Found Alive
The Further Adventures of Tennessee Buck
Fury
Gold of the Amazon Women
Gold Raiders
Goliathon
Gorillas in the Mist▶
Green Fire
Green Inferno
Green Mansions
Greystoke: The Legend of Tarzan, Lord of the Apes
Harry Black and the Tiger
Heart of Darkness
Hell's Headquarters
How Tasty Was My Little Frenchman
Indio
Indio 2: The Revolt
Invincible Barbarian
Jacare
Jane & the Lost City
Jumanji
Jungle
The Jungle Book
The Jungle Book▶
Jungle Bride
Jungle Drums of Africa
Jungle Goddess
Jungle Heat
Jungle Hell
Jungle Inferno
Jungle Master
Jungle Patrol
Jungle Raiders
Jungle Siren
The Jungle Trap
Jungle Warriors
Killers
Killing Heat
King of the Kongo
King Solomon's Treasure
The Land Unknown
Law of the Jungle
Liana, Jungle Goddess
The Lion King▶
The Lion Man
Lion Man
The Lost City
Lost City of the Jungle
The Lost Continent
The Lost Jungle
The Lost Tribe
Lure of the Islands
Medicine Man
Merrill's Marauders
Mighty Jungle
Miracles
Missing in Action
The Mission▶
Mistress of the Apes
Mogambo▶
The Mosquito Coast
The Muthers
Mysterious Island of Beautiful Women
Nabonga
Naked Jungle▶
The Naked Prey▶
The New Adventures of Tarzan
Night Creature
Nightforce
Objective, Burma!▶
Omoo Omoo, the Shark God
Operation Dumbo Drop
Options
Perils of the Darkest Jungle
The Phantom
Predator
Queen of the Amazons
Queen of the Jungle
Red Dust▶
Revenge of Doctor X
River of Death
River of Evil
The Road to Zanzibar▶
Robbers of the Sacred Mountain
Romancing the Stone▶
Rudyard Kipling's The Jungle Book
Samar
The Savage Girl
Shame of the Jungle
Sheena
Sniper
Son of Kong
Stormquest
Sweet Revenge
Tarzan and His Mate▶
Tarzan and the Green Goddess
Tarzan and the Trappers
Tarzan Escapes▶
Tarzan Finds a Son▶
Tarzan of the Apes
Tarzan, the Ape Man▶
Tarzan, the Ape Man
Tarzan the Fearless
Tarzan the Tiger
Tarzana, the Wild Girl
Tarzan's Revenge
Tarzan's Secret Treasure
Terror in the Jungle
Terror of the Bloodhunters
The Thirsty Dead
Tiger Fangs
Trader Horn
Trap Them & Kill Them
The Treasure of the Amazon
Troma's War
Tropical Heat
Typhoon Treasure
Virgin Sacrifice
Volunteers
Voodoo Woman
The Voyage of Tanai
Wages of Fear▶
Warkill
Warriors of the Apocalypse
Watchers 3
West of Zanzibar
Where the River Runs Black
White Cannibal Queen
White Cargo
White Ghost
White Gorilla
White Huntress
The White Legion
The White Orchid
White Pongo
Wild Women
Woman Hunt
The World's Greatest Athlete
Zombie Island Massacre

Justice Prevails...?

see also Order in the Court

Above Suspicion
Absence of Malice
The Accused▶
The Advocate▶
All-American Murder
And Justice for All
Assault at West Point: The Court-Martial of Johnson Whittaker
The Avenging Angel
Beau Geste▶
Better Off Dead
Beyond Reasonable Doubt
The Burning Season▶
A Case for Murder
Circumstantial Evidence
Creature with the Blue Hand
Cross Examination
A Cry in the Dark▶
Cyber-Tracker
Dark Justice
The Day the Sun Turned Cold▶
Dead Right
Dingaka
A Dry White Season▶
Eddie Macon's Run
The Execution of Private Slovik▶
An Eye for an Eye
False Arrest
Forgotten Prisoners
The Good Fight
Guilty as Charged
Guilty as Sin
A Gun in the House
The Hanging Tree▶
Honor Thy Father and Mother: The True Story of the Menendez Brothers
In Self Defense
In the Name of the Father▶
Indictment: The McMartin Trial▶
The Jagged Edge
JFK▶
Judge Dredd
Judicial Consent
Jury Duty
Just Cause
Last Dance
Lawman▶
Let Him Have It▶
Life & Times of Judge Roy Bean
Losing Isaiah▶
The Magnificent Yankee▶
Mr. & Mrs. Loving▶
Murder In the First
Music Box
Nuts▶
The Paper▶
Presumed Innocent▶
Prime Suspect: The Scent of Darkness▶
Prisoners of the Sun▶
Reversal of Fortune▶
Roe vs. Wade▶
Separate But Equal▶
Shoot to Kill
The Shooting Party
Showdown
Skin
The Story of Qui Ju▶
A Time to Kill▶
Trial and Error
The Trials of Oscar Wilde▶
An Unforgettable Summer
The Verdict▶
Weekend of Shadows▶
White Lie
Woman Undone
The Wrong Man▶
The Young Land
The Young One

Kidnapped!

see also Hostage!; Missing Persons

Abducted
Abducted 2: The Reunion
Abduction
The Abduction of Allison Tate
The Abduction of Kari Swenson
Ace Ventura: Pet Detective
Act of Piracy
Adam▶
African Rage
Against A Crooked Sky
American Kickboxer 2: To the Death
And Hope to Die
The Armour of God
Ashanti, Land of No Mercy
The Atomic City
Autumn Born
Baby's Day Out
Beach Blanket Bingo▶
Beethoven's 2nd
Benji▶
Best Revenge
Beverly Hills Brats
Beyond Fear
Beyond Justice
Black Samurai
Blood at Sundown
Blown Away
Bound and Gagged: A Love Story
Celtic Pride
The Chase
The City of Lost Children
Cohen and Tate
Cold Blood
Commando▶
The Concentratin' Kid
Crimebusters
The Crying Game▶
Dead Air
Distant Justice
Door to Door Maniac
Dumb & Dumber
Fargo▶
Fire in the Sky
Fireback
Follow the River
Gallowglass▶
The Grissom Gang▶
Guarding Tess
Gun Fury
Hangfire
Harem
Hearts & Armour
Hollywood Cop
Hostage for a Day
In a Stranger's Hand
Incident at Deception Ridge
Island Monster
Jack and His Friends
Jailbait
Kickboxer 3: The Art of War
Kid Colter
Kidnapped
Lake Consequence
The Light in the Forest
The Lightning Incident
The Lindbergh Kidnapping Case▶
Lorna Doone
Ma and Pa Kettle at Waikiki
Manipulator
Martin's Day
Memphis
Mr. Nanny
The Money
Moran of the Lady Letty
Never Say Die
Nick of Time
The Night of the Following Day
The Nightmare Before Christmas▶
Nightstick
No Deposit, No Return
The Only Way Home
Orphans▶
Outlaw Force
Parker
A Perfect World
Prime Suspect: The Lost Child▶
Prince of Pennsylvania
Private Obsession
The Quest
Rage of Wind
Raising Arizona▶
Ransom Money
The Real McCoy
Remote Control
Rescue Me
The Revenger
Riders of the Purple Sage
Ring of Fire 2: Blood and Steel
Ring of the Musketeers
Rio Diablo
The Road Killers
Rosebud
Runaway Nightmare
Ruthless People▶
Sahara
Savage Abduction
Second Sight
Seven Hours to Judgment
Sharpe's Enemy
Shattered Image
Singapore
Slate, Wyn & Me
Sloane
SnakeEater
Soldier Boyz
Son of the Pink Panther
The Squeeze
Still Not Quite Human
Street Fighter
Sunstroke
Sweet Poison
Tarzan's New York Adventure
Teresa's Tattoo
Terror Stalks the Class Reunion
That Man from Rio
Thou Shalt Not Kill...Except
Three Days to a Kill
3 Ninjas
3 Ninjas Knuckle Up
Tie Me Up! Tie Me Down!
Till the End of the Night
To Grandmother's House We Go
The Trap
Trapped Alive
Try and Get Me
Twinsitters
Two Bits & Pepper
Under the Hula Moon
Unlawful Passage
The Vanishing
A Vow to Kill
Waikiki Wedding▶
When the Greeks
Whistling in the Dark▶

Killer Apes

see also Monkeyshines

The Ape
A*P*E*
The Ape Man
Battle for the Planet of the Apes
Beneath the Planet of the Apes
Congo
Conquest of the Planet of the Apes
In the Shadow of Kilimanjaro
King Kong▶
King Kong
King Kong Lives
King Kong vs. Godzilla
King of Kong Island
Link
Mighty Joe Young
Monkey Shines
Planet of the Apes▶
Primal Rage
Return of the Ape Man
Son of Ingagi
Son of Kong

Killer Appliances

see also Technology-Rampant

Attack of the Killer Refrigerator
Ghost in the Machine
The Mangler
Microwave Massacre
The Refrigerator

Killer Beasts

see also Killer Apes; Killer Dogs; Killer Kats; Killer Pigs; Killer Rodents

The Abomination
Alligator▶
Alligator 2: The Mutation
The Angry Red Planet
The Ape
A*P*E*
The Ape Man
Attack of the Beast Creatures
Attack of the Giant Leeches
Beaks: The Movie
Ben
Berserker
Big Foot
Bog
The Brain Eaters
The Bride & the Beast
Claws
Copperhead
Creepshow
Crocodile
Dark Age
Day of the Animals
The Devil Bat
The Devil Bat's Daughter
Devil Dog: The Hound of Hell
Devil Monster
Dinosaurus!
Dragonslayer▶
Fangs
Fer-De-Lance
Food of the Gods
Frogs
Gamera, the Invincible
Gamera vs. Barugon
Gamera vs. Gaos
The Giant Gila Monster
Godzilla on Monster Island
Godzilla Raids Again
Godzilla vs. Biollante
Godzilla vs. Megalon
Godzilla vs. the Cosmic Monster
Godzilla vs. the Sea Monster
Gorilla
Grizzly
In the Shadow of Kilimanjaro
Island of Terror▶
It Came from Beneath the Sea▶
It Conquered the World
Jabberwocky
Jaws of Satan
Jurassic Park▶
The Killer Shrews
King Kong▶
King Kong
King Kong Lives
Legend of Big Foot
The Leopard Man
Link
Mad Death
Mighty Joe Young
The Mole People
The Monster Walks
Monty Python and the Holy Grail▶
Mutator
Mysterious Island▶
Night Creature
Night of the Grizzly
Night of the Howling Beast
Nightwing
Pigs
Q (The Winged Serpent)▶
Rana: The Legend of Shadow Lake
The Rats are Coming! The Werewolves are Here!
Rattlers
Razorback
Return to Boggy Creek
Rodan
Shakma
Shriek of the Mutilated
Sleepwalkers
The Slime People
Slithis
Snowbeast
Son of Kong
Spasms
Stanley
Subspecies
Swamp of the Lost Monster
Tremors
Tremors 2: Aftershocks
Tromba, the Tiger Man
Venom
Vulture
The Wild Beasts
Winterbeast
Wrestling Women vs. the Aztec Ape
X from Outer Space
Yongkari Monster of the Deep

Killer Brains

see also Renegade Body Parts

Black Friday
Blood of Ghastly Horror
The Brain
Brain Damage
The Brain from Planet Arous
Brain of Blood
The Brain That Wouldn't Die
Donovan's Brain▶
Fiend Without a Face
Mindkiller

Killer Bugs

Ants
The Applegates
Arachnophobia
The Bees
Beginning of the End
The Black Scorpion
Blood Beast Terror
Blue Monkey
Bug
The Cosmic Monsters
Creepers
Creepshow
Curse of the Black Widow
The Deadly Mantis
Earth vs. the Spider
Empire of the Ants
Evil Spawn
Food of the Gods
The Giant Spider Invasion
Horrors of Spider Island
Kingdom of the Spiders
Kiss of the Tarantula
The Lair of the White Worm▶
Last Days of Planet Earth
Man of the House
Monster from Green Hell
The Monster That Challenged the World
Mosquito
Mothra▶
Naked Jungle▶
The Nest
Parasite
Phase 4
Return of the Fly
The Savage Bees
The Scorpion's Tail
Skeeter
Slugs
Son of Godzilla
Spider Woman▶
Squirm
The Swarm
Tarantula▶
Tarantulas: The Deadly Cargo
Terror Out of the Sky
Them!▶
They Came from Within
Ticks
The Wasp Woman
The Worm Eaters

Killer Cars

see also Motor Vehicle Dept.

The Cars That Ate Paris▶
Christine
Dark of the Night
Death Race 2000
Death Sport

Duel▶
The Hearse
Mad Max▶
Mad Max: Beyond Thunderdome
Maximum Overdrive
One Deadly Owner
The Road Warrior▶
Wheels of Terror

Killer Dogs

see also King of Beasts (Dogs)

Cujo
Devil Dog: The Hound of Hell
Dogs of Hell
The Hound of the Baskervilles▶
The Hound of the Baskervilles
Mongrel
Monster Dog
The Omen
The Pack
Pet Sematary 2
Play Dead
Revenge
Zoltan...Hound of Dracula

Killer Dreams

Alias John Preston
Bad Dreams
Blood Rage
Dario Argento's Trauma
Dead of Night▶
Deadly Dreams
Dream No Evil
Freddy's Dead: The Final Nightmare
Mirrors
A Nightmare on Elm Street
A Nightmare on Elm Street 2: Freddy's Revenge
A Nightmare on Elm Street 3: Dream Warriors
A Nightmare on Elm Street 4: Dream Master
A Nightmare on Elm Street 5: Dream Child
Paperhouse▶
Phantasm
Twisted Nightmare
Wes Craven's New Nightmare▶

Killer Kats

see also Cats

Batman Returns
The Black Cat
Cat People▶
Cat People
Cat Women of the Moon
Claws
The Corpse Grinders
The Creeper
Curse of the Cat People▶
The Leopard Man
Mutator
Night of a Thousand Cats
Pet Sematary
Seven Deaths in the Cat's Eye
Strays
The Uncanny
The Uninvited

Killer Pigs

see also Pigs

The Amityville Horror
Evilspeak
Pigs
Razorback

Killer Plants

Attack of the Killer Tomatoes
Attack of the Mushroom People
Body Snatchers
Day of the Triffids▶
Dr. Terror's House of Horrors
The Freakmaker
Invasion of the Body Snatchers▶
Killer Tomatoes Eat France
Killer Tomatoes Strike Back
Little Shop of Horrors▶
Navy vs. the Night Monsters
Please Don't Eat My Mother
Return of the Killer Tomatoes!
Seedpeople
Seeds of Evil

Killer Rodents

The Bat
The Bat People
Ben
Burial of the Rats
Deadly Eyes
Food of the Gods
Food of the Gods: Part 2
The Killer Shrews
Of Unknown Origin
Rats
The Rats are Coming! The Werewolves are Here!
Willard

Killer Toys

Black Devil Doll from Hell
Child's Play
Child's Play 2
Child's Play 3
Dance of Death
Demonic Toys
Devil Doll▶
Devil Doll
Devil's Gift
Dollman vs Demonic Toys
Dolls
Dolly Dearest
Halloween 3: Season of the Witch
Magic
Poltergeist▶
Puppet Master
Puppet Master 2
Puppet Master 3: Toulon's Revenge
Puppet Master 4
Puppet Master 5: The Final Chapter
Silent Night, Deadly Night 5: The Toymaker
Trilogy of Terror
Wired to Kill

Kindness of Strangers

Angels Over Broadway▶
The Big Push
Forrest Gump▶
Good Sam
Lilies of the Field▶
Major Barbara▶
Mr. Deeds Goes to Town▶
Mr. Lucky▶
Mr. North
Powder
She Couldn't Say No
Sincerely Yours
Toll Gate
Touch & Go
The Vals

King of Beasts (Dogs)

see also Killer Dogs

The Accidental Tourist▶
Across the Bridge
The Adventures of Milo & Otis▶
The Adventures of Rex & Rinty
The Adventures of Rin Tin Tin
The Adventures of Rusty
After the Thin Man▶
All Dogs Go to Heaven
All Dogs Go to Heaven 2
The Amazing Dobermans
Antarctica
The Awful Truth▶
Balto
Baxter
Beethoven
Beethoven's 2nd
Behave Yourself!
Benji▶
Benji the Hunted
Benji's Very Own Christmas Story
Big Red
Bingo
Blondie in Society
A Boy and His Dog
A Boy Named Charlie Brown▶
Call of the Wild
Captured in Chinatown
Challenge To Be Free
Challenge to Lassie
Challenge to White Fang
A Charlie Brown Celebration
Children of the Wild
Chips, the War Dog
C.H.O.M.P.S.
Clean Slate
Come Back Little Reba
Complex
Cool Hand Luke▶
Courage of Lassie
Courage of Rin Tin Tin
Courage of the North
A Cry in the Dark▶
Cujo
Danny Boy
Daring Dobermans
The Dawson Patrol
Devil Dog: The Hound of Hell
Digby, the Biggest Dog in the World
Dirkham Detective Agency
The Doberman Gang
A Dog of Flanders
Dog Pound Shuffle▶
The Dog Who Stopped the War
Dogs of Hell
Down and Out in Beverly Hills
Dumb & Dumber
Dusty
Elmer
Eyes of an Angel
Eyes of Texas
Fabulous Joe
Family Dog: Complete Series
Famous Five Get into Trouble
Fangs of the Wild
Far from Home: The Adventures of Yellow Dog
Flaming Signal
Fluke
For the Love of Benji
The Fox and the Hound▶
Frankenweenie
George!
Git!
God's Country
The Good, the Bad, and Huckleberry Hound
Goodbye, My Lady
A Goofy Movie
Great Adventure
Greyfriars Bobby
Hambone & Hillie
Heart of the Rockies
Heck's Way Home
He's Your Dog, Charlie Brown!
Hollow Gate
Homeward Bound 2: Lost in San Francisco
Homeward Bound: The Incredible Journey▶
The Hound of the Baskervilles
The Incredible Journey
Inside Information
Iron Will
It's a Dog's Life
It's a Mystery, Charlie Brown
K-9
K-9000
Kavik the Wolf Dog
Lady and the Tramp▶
Lassie
Lassie: Adventures of Neeka
Lassie, Come Home
Lassie: The Miracle
Lassie: Well of Love
Lassie's Great Adventure
Laurel & Hardy: Laughing Gravy
Legend of the Northwest
Life is a Circus, Charlie Brown/ You're the Greatest, Charlie Brown
Lightning Warrior
Little Heroes
The Lone Defender
Look Who's Talking Now
Love Leads the Way
Magic of Lassie
Man Trouble
The Man Who Wagged His Tail
Man's Best Friend
The Meeting: Eddie Finds a Home
Million Dollar Haul
Milo & Otis
Mrs. Brown, You've Got a Lovely Daughter
Mr. Superinvisible
Mom, the Wolfman and Me
Mongrel
Monster Dog
My Dog Shep
My Dog, the Thief
The Night Cry
Nikki, the Wild Dog of the North
Oh, Heavenly Dog!
Old Yeller▶
Oliver & Company
101 Dalmatians▶
The Pack
The Painted Hills
The Plague Dogs
Play Dead
Poco
Pound Puppies and the Legend of Big Paw
The Return of Grey Wolf
The Return of Our Gang
Reuben, Reuben▶
Rin Tin Tin, Hero of the West
Rover Dangerfield
Rusty's Birthday
The Sandlot▶
Savage Sam
Scruffy
Shadow of the Thin Man▶
The Shaggy D.A.
The Shaggy Dog
Shep Comes Home
Sherlock Hound: Tales of Mystery
Sherlock: Undercover Dog
Silver Stallion
Skeezer
Skull & Crown
Smoke
Son of Lassie
Son of Rusty
Song of the Thin Man
Sputnik
Spy with a Cold Nose
Storm in a Teacup
Summerdog
Teddy at the Throttle
The Tender Years
They Only Kill Their Masters
The Thin Man▶
The Thin Man Goes Home
Three Wishes
To Dance with the White Dog▶
Toby McTeague
Tom and Jerry: The Movie
Top Dog
The Truth About Cats and Dogs▶
Turner and Hooch
The Ugly Dachshund
Umberto D▶
The Underdog
Watchers
Watchers 2
We Think the World of You▶
When Lightning Strikes
Where the Red Fern Grows
Where the Red Fern Grows: Part 2
White Fang 2: The Myth of the White Wolf
White Fang and the Hunter
Whitewater Sam
The Wizard of Oz▶
Wolf Dog
Wolfheart's Revenge
Woof!
Zoltan...Hound of Dracula

Kings

see Royalty

Korean War

All the Young Men▶
Battle Circus
Battle Hymn
The Bridges at Toko-Ri▶
The Canon Operation
Dragonfly Squadron
Field of Honor
For the Boys
The Hunters
Iron Angel
Jet Attack/Paratroop Command
The Last Picture Show▶
MacArthur
The Manchurian Candidate▶
M*A*S*H▶
M*A*S*H: Goodbye, Farewell & Amen▶
M*A*S*H: The Collector's Edition
Men in War
Men of the Fighting Lady▶
Mission Inferno
Mr. Walkie Talkie
One Minute to Zero
Operation Dames
Operation Inchon
Pork Chop Hill▶
Pueblo Affair▶
Retreat, Hell!
Sabre Jet
Sayonara▶
Sergeant Ryker
The Steel Helmet▶
Torpedo Alley
Wonsan Operation

Kung Fu

see Martial Arts

L.A.

see also Earthquakes

Abbott and Costello in Hollywood
Assault on Precinct 13▶
The Beverly Hillbillies
Beverly Hills Bodysnatchers
Beverly Hills Brats
Beverly Hills Cop
Beverly Hills Cop 2
Beverly Hills Cop 3
Beverly Hills Knockouts
Beverly Hills Madam
Beverly Hills 90210
A Boy Called Hate
Color of a Brisk and Leaping Day
Come See the Paradise▶
Cool Blue
Cover Me
The Craft
The Crow 2: City of Angels▶
Dead Again▶
Delta Heat
Devil In a Blue Dress▶
The Doom Generation▶
Down and Out in Beverly Hills
Dunston Checks In
Escape from L.A.
Four Rooms
Freeway
Get Shorty▶
Heat▶
It's My Party
Jimmy Hollywood
L.A. Bad
L.A. Bounty
L.A. Crackdown
L.A. Crackdown 2
L.A. Goddess
L.A. Law▶
L.A. Story▶

L.A. Vice
Lawnmower Man 2: Beyond Cyberspace
Marshal Law
Nick of Time
Night Hunter
Night on Earth▶
Raging Angels
Rave Review
Skyscraper
Speed▶
Stand and Deliver▶
Strange Days▶
The Streets of L.A.
Talking About Sex
To Live & Die in L.A.
Totally F***ed Up
The Trigger Effect

Labor & Unions

see also Miners & Mining

Act of Vengeance
Black Fury▶
Blue Collar▶
Boxcar Bertha
Brother John▶
The Burning Season▶
Canada's Sweetheart: The Saga of Hal C. Banks
Daens
Deadly Stranger
The Devil & Miss Jones▶
The End of St. Petersburg▶
End of the Line
Fame Is the Spur
F.I.S.T.
The $5.20 an Hour Dream
Gung Ho
Hoffa▶
I'm All Right Jack▶
Joyride
Keeping On
Killing Floor
Land of Promise
Last Exit to Brooklyn▶
Long Road Home
Mac▶
Man of Iron▶
Man of Marble▶
Matewan▶
Molly Maguires
Moonlighting▶
Never Steal Anything Small
Newsies
Norma Rae▶
North Dallas Forty▶
On the Waterfront▶
The Pajama Game▶
Riff Raff▶
Salt of the Earth▶
Silkwood▶
Singleton's Pluck▶
Sons of Steel
Strike▶
Take This Job & Shove It
Teamster Boss: The Jackie Presser Story▶
The Triangle Factory Fire Scandal
Waterfront

Late Bloomin' Love

see also Growing Older

Adorable Julia
The African Queen▶
Ali: Fear Eats the Soul▶
Atlantic City▶
Bed & Breakfast
Breakfast in Paris
The Bridges of Madison County▶
Brief Encounter▶
Camilla
Cass Timberlane
Charly▶
Children of Nature
The Christmas Wife
Circle of Two
Cold Sassy Tree▶
Crazy from the Heart▶
Devil in the Flesh▶
Devil in the Flesh
Digger
Doctor in Distress
End of August
A Fine Romance
Finnegan Begin Again
Forbidden Love
Foreign Affairs▶
Forty Carats
Gal Young 'Un▶
Gin Game▶
Grumpy Old Men▶
Harold and Maude▶
If Ever I See You Again
La Symphonie Pastorale▶
The Last Winters
Lonely Hearts▶
The Lonely Passion of Judith Hearne▶
Love Among the Ruins▶
Macaroni
A Majority of One
A Man and a Woman▶
Mrs. 'Arris Goes to Paris
A Month by the Lake
The Night of the Iguana▶
Other People's Money
The Pamela Principle
Players
Queen of the Stardust Ballroom▶
The Rainmaker▶
Roman Spring of Mrs. Stone▶
San Antonio
Shadowlands▶
Shirley Valentine▶
The Shock
The Shop Around the Corner▶
Shore Leave▶
A Small Killing
Something in Common
Stay As You Are
Stormy Waters
Stroszek▶
Summertime▶
To Love Again
Travelling North
24 Hours in a Woman's Life
Twice in a Lifetime▶
Used People
With Six You Get Eggroll

Law & Lawyers

see also Order in the Court

Adam's Rib▶
The Advocate▶
Afterburn▶
Anatomy of a Murder▶
And Justice for All
Angel on My Shoulder
Assault at West Point: The Court-Martial of Johnson Whittaker
Before and After
Better Off Dead
Beyond a Reasonable Doubt
Beyond the Silhouette
Bleak House
Blood Brothers
Body Chemistry 4: Full Exposure
Body Language
Boomerang▶
Brain Donors
Brothers in Law
Brother's Keeper▶
The Candidate▶
Cape Fear▶
Carlito's Way▶
A Case for Murder
A Case of Libel
Chase
Circonstances Attenuantes
Citizen Cohn
Class Action▶
The Client
Compulsion▶
The Conqueror Worm▶
Criminal Law
Dark Justice
Death and the Maiden▶
Death of a Soldier
Defenders of the Law
Dirty Mary Crazy Larry▶
Disorganized Crime
The Divorce of Lady X
Down the Drain
Ebbtide
The Enforcer
Evelyn Prentice
Eye Witness
Fair Game
False Witness
A Few Good Men▶
Final Appeal
Final Verdict
The Firm▶
First Monday in October
The Franchise Affair
A Free Soul
From the Hip
Georgia
Getting Gotti
Gideon's Trumpet
The Glass Shield
The Good Fight
The Great American Sex Scandal
Guilty as Sin
Honor Thy Father and Mother: The True Story of the Menendez Brothers
I Am the Law▶
Illegal
I'm No Angel▶
In the Name of the Father▶
The Incident▶
The Island of Dr. Moreau
JAG
The Jagged Edge
The Judge
Judge Dredd
Judge Priest▶
Judicial Consent
The Juror
Jury Duty
Just Cause
Justice
L.A. Law▶
Last Dance
The Last Innocent Man
Legal Eagles
Legend of Billie Jean
Let Freedom Ring
Let's Kill All the Lawyers
Life & Times of Judge Roy Bean
Losing Isaiah▶
Love Crimes
Madame X
The Magnificent Yankee▶
Man from Colorado
Man of the House
Manhattan Melodrama▶
Marked Woman▶
Minbo—Or the Gentle Art of Japanese Extortion
Misbehaving Husbands
Mr. & Mrs. Loving▶
Murder In the First
My Cousin Vinny▶
The Narrow Margin▶
Night and the City▶
Nixon▶
North
Ordeal by Innocence
Original Intent
The Paper Chase▶
The Pelican Brief
Penthouse▶
Perfect Witness
Perry Mason Returns▶
Philadelphia▶
Physical Evidence
Portraits of a Killer
Power of Attorney
Presumed Innocent▶
Primal Fear
Promised a Miracle
Reet, Petite and Gone▶
Regarding Henry▶
Road Agent
Roxie Hart
Rumpole of the Bailey
Rumpole of the Bailey: Rumpole's Return▶
Runaway Father
Rustler's Valley
Scandal
Scott Turow's The Burden of Proof
Sharon's Secret
Shoot to Kill
A Simple Twist of Fate
Slightly Honorable
The Star Chamber
State's Attorney
The Sun Shines Bright
Swoon▶
A Time to Kill▶
To Kill a Mockingbird▶
Too Young to Die
The Trial
Trial and Error
Trial by Jury
Trois Couleurs: Rouge▶
True Believer
True Colors
Truth or Die
Twelve Angry Men▶
The Verdict▶
Victim▶
Web of Deceit
The Winslow Boy▶
The Wistful Widow of Wagon Gap
Woman of Desire
The World's Oldest Living Bridesmaid
The Young Philadelphians▶

Lesbians

see also Bisexuality; Gays; Gender Bending

Alien Prey
Another Way▶
Bar Girls
The Berlin Affair
The Bitter Tears of Petra von Kant
Black Cobra
The Blood Spattered Bride
Bound
Boys on the Side
Butterfly Kiss
Carmilla
The Celluloid Closet▶
The Children's Hour
Claire of the Moon
Daughters of Darkness▶
Desert Hearts▶
Desperate Remedies
Different Story
Double Face
Entre-Nous▶
Even Cowgirls Get the Blues
Extramuros
French Twist
Higher Learning
The Hunger
The Incredibly True Adventure of Two Girls in Love
I've Heard the Mermaids Singing▶
Kamikaze Hearts
The Killing of Sister George
Law of Desire▶
Lianna▶
Maedchen in Uniform▶
My Father Is Coming
My Sister, My Love
Nadja▶
Only the Brave
Personal Best▶
A Question of Love▶
The Rainbow▶
The Scorpion Woman
Seducers
She Must Be Seeing Things
The Silence▶
Sugar Cookies
Therese & Isabelle
These Three▶
Three of Hearts
Totally F***ed Up
The Vampire Lovers
Vampyres
Walk on the Wild Side
When Night is Falling▶
Wild Side
Windows
X, Y & Zee

Libraries and Librarians

Desk Set▶
Foul Play▶
Ghostbusters▶
Goodbye Columbus▶
The Gun in Betty Lou's Handbag
Kicking and Screaming▶
The Music Man▶
The Name of the Rose
No Man of Her Own
Off Beat
The Pagemaster
Party Girl
The Shawshank Redemption▶
With Honors

Life Imitates Art

The Deer Hunter▶
Menace II Society▶
Money Train
The Program
Taxi Driver▶

Lifeguards

see also Beach Blanket Bingo; Swimming

Baywatch the Movie: Forbidden Paradise
Caddyshack▶
Fun in Acapulco
Lifeguard
That Summer of White Roses
Wet and Wild Summer

London

see also Great Britain; Royalty

Abbott and Costello Meet Dr. Jekyll and Mr. Hyde
Alfie▶
American Roulette
Annie: A Royal Adventure
The Assassination Bureau▶
Autobiography of a Princess
Bad Behavior
Bedlam▶
Broken Blossoms▶
Carpet of Horror
Century
Chicago Joe & the Showgirl
Claudia
Curse of the Yellow Snake
Danger UXB
Dick Barton, Special Agent
Double Vision
Dracula's Daughter▶
Dream Street
The Elephant Man▶
11 Harrowhouse▶
Emmanuelle in Soho
Fanny Hill: Memoirs of a Woman of Pleasure
Foreign Affairs▶
Foreign Correspondent▶
Forever and a Day▶
Frenzy▶
Full Moon in Paris
The Gambler & the Lady
Gaslight▶
The Gay Lady
Great Expectations
The Great Muppet Caper▶
Hands of a Murderer
Heaven's a Drag
Hope and Glory▶
The Horse's Mouth▶
The House of Eliott
In the Name of the Father▶
Journey for Margaret▶
Just Like a Woman

Loneliness

see Only the Lonely

Loner Cops

see also Cops

Lost Worlds

see also Parallel Universes

Lovable Loonies

see also Shrinks

Lovers on the Lam

see also Fugitives

Macho Men

see also Action Adventure

Too Late the Hero▶
Tor
Total Recall▶
Tough Guy
Triumph of the Son of Hercules
Two Mules for Sister Sara▶
Tyrant of Lydia Against the Son of Hercules
Under Siege
Under Siege 2: Dark Territory
Venus Against the Son of Hercules
Viva Villa!▶
Vulcan God of Fire
Warlords 3000
Where Eagles Dare▶
White Lightning
Wild Bill
The Wild Bunch▶
Windjammer

Mad Scientists

see also Inventors & Inventions; Science & Scientists

Alien Terminator
The Ape Man
Atom Age Vampire
Attack of the 60-Foot Centerfold
Attack of the Swamp Creature
Before I Hang▶
Bela Lugosi Meets a Brooklyn Gorilla
Beverly Hills Bodysnatchers
Bloodbath at the House of Death
Bloodlust
The Body Shop
Bowery Boys Meet the Monsters
The Brain That Wouldn't Die
Brenda Starr
Bride of Re-Animator
Bride of the Monster
Captain America
Captive Wild Woman
The Cars That Ate Paris▶
Castle of Evil
Castle of the Creeping Flesh
The City of Lost Children
The Cobweb
The Corpse Vanishes
Creator
Creature of the Walking Dead
The Creeper
The Creeping Flesh
The Crime of Dr. Crespi
Crimes of Dr. Mabuse▶
The Curse of the Aztec Mummy
Cyborg Cop
Darkman 2: The Return of Durant
Darkman 3: Die Darkman Die
The Dead Next Door
Dead Pit
Dead Sleep
Death Warmed Up
Deep Red
Devil Doll▶
Dr. Black, Mr. Hyde
Doctor Blood's Coffin
Doctor Butcher M.D.
Dr. Caligari
Dr. Cyclops
Dr. Death, Seeker of Souls
Dr. Frankenstein's Castle of Freaks
Dr. Goldfoot and the Bikini Machine
Dr. Jekyll and Mr. Hyde▶
Dr. Jekyll and Mr. Hyde
Dr. Jekyll and Sister Hyde
Dr. Jekyll and the Wolfman
Dr. Jekyll's Dungeon of Death
Dr. No▶
Dr. Orloff's Monster
Doctor X
Donovan's Brain▶
The Double O Kid
Embryo
Evil Town
The Flesh Eaters
Frankenhooker
Frankenstein▶
Frankenstein
Frankenstein and the Monster from Hell
Frankenstein '80
Frankenstein General Hospital
Frankenstein Unbound▶
Frankenstein's Daughter
Freaked
The Freakmaker
Geisha Girl
The Giant Spider Invasion
Girl in His Pocket
The Head
Hellmaster
Hideous Sun Demon
House of Frankenstein
Hyena of London
The Immortalizer
The Incredible Two-Headed Transplant
The Indestructible Man
Invasion of the Zombies
The Invisible Dr. Mabuse▶
The Invisible Man▶
The Invisible Ray
The Invisible Terror
Island of Dr. Moreau
The Island of Dr. Moreau
Island of Lost Souls▶
Jekyll and Hyde
Jurassic Park▶
Kids In the Hall Brain Candy
The Killing Device
King of Kong Island
King of the Zombies
Lady Frankenstein
The Lawnmower Man
Lawnmower Man 2: Beyond Cyberspace
Lightblast
The Living Dead
The Lost City
The Mad Ghoul
Man Made Monster
The Man They Could Not Hang
The Man Who Lived Again
The Man with Two Lives
Mandroid
Maniac
The Manster
Mary Shelley's Frankenstein
Master Minds
Metamorphosis
Miami Horror
Mr. Stitch
The Monster▶
The Monster Maker
Monsters Crash the Pajama Party
The Mosaic Project
The Munsters' Revenge
Murders in the Rue Morgue
Mystery Science Theater 3000: The Movie
Naked Souls
Nightmare Castle
Nightmare Weekend
The Outer Limits: Sandkings▶
Philadelphia Experiment 2
The Pink Panther Strikes Again▶
Re-Animator▶
Red Blooded American Girl
Return of the Killer Tomatoes!
Revenge of the Zombies
Revolt of the Zombies
Samson in the Wax Museum
Scanner Cop
Science Crazed
Screamers
Severed Ties
Shadow of Chinatown
She Demons
Shock Waves
Silent Killers
Star Trek Generations▶
Strange Behavior
Strange Case of Dr. Jekyll & Mr. Hyde
Superargo
Supersonic Man
Tammy and the T-Rex
Teenage Zombies
Terror Is a Man
Testament of Dr. Mabuse
Torture Ship
Transmutations
The Unearthly
The Vampire Bat
Vulture
Werewolf of London
Wes Craven Presents Mind Ripper
The Worst of Hollywood: Vol. 1

Made for Television

see TV Movies; TV Pilot Movies; TV Series

Mafia

see Organized Crime

Magic

see also Genies; Magic Carpet Rides; Occult

Alabama's Ghost
The Alchemist
Bedknobs and Broomsticks
Black Magic Terror
The Butcher's Wife
Chandu on the Magic Island
Chandu the Magician
The Craft
Cthulhu Mansion
The Day the Earth Froze
Death Magic
Deathstalker 3
The Devil Thumbs a Ride/ Having Wonderful Crime
Doctor Mordrid: Master of the Unknown
Dream a Little Dream 2
Escape to Witch Mountain▶
Eternally Yours
Gryphon
Houdini
Lady in Distress
The Linguini Incident
Lord of Illusions
Magic Moments
Magic Serpent▶
The Magician▶
The Magician of Lublin
The Man in the Santa Claus Suit
Merlin
Merlin of the Crystal Cave
Mondo Magic
My Chauffeur
The Mysterious Stranger
Penn and Teller Get Killed
Prospero's Books▶
Quicker Than the Eye
Stunt Rock
Sword & the Sorcerer
Teen Witch
Turnaround
Tut & Tuttle
Wedding Band
The Wizard of Gore
Zotz!

Magic Carpet Rides

see also Genies

Aladdin▶
Golden Voyage of Sinbad
1001 Arabian Nights
The Seventh Voyage of Sinbad▶
Sinbad and the Eye of the Tiger
Sinbad of the Seven Seas
Sinbad, the Sailor▶
The Thief of Bagdad▶
The Thief of Baghdad▶
Thief of Baghdad
The Thief of Baghdad

Marriage

see also Divorce; Otherwise Engaged; War Between the Sexes; Wedding Bells; Wedding Hell

Absent Without Leave
Accused
Across the Wide Missouri
The Adjuster
The Adultress
The Adventures of Mark Twain▶
An Affair in Mind
The Age of Innocence▶
Alfredo, Alfredo
All Things Fair
All This and Heaven Too▶
Almost You
Always▶
American Matchmaker
Angel
Any Wednesday
Arnold
Arrivederci, Baby!
As You Desire Me▶
Ash Wednesday
Ask Any Girl
Assault and Matrimony
Attack of the 50 Ft. Woman
Autumn Leaves
Autumn Marathon
Baby Doll▶
The Baby Maker
Bachelor in Paradise
Bachelor Party
Back to the Wall
Backstreet Dreams
Bad Behavior
Barefoot in the Park▶
Barjo
The Barkleys of Broadway▶
The Bat People
Battle Shock
Bedroom Eyes 2
Best Enemies
Best Friends
The Best Intentions▶
Betrayal
Betsy's Wedding
Big Business Girl
A Black Veil for Lisa
Blindfold: Acts of Obsession
The Bliss of Mrs. Blossom▶
Blonde Venus▶
Blondie
Blondie Hits the Jackpot
Blondie in Society
Blondie Knows Best
Blood of Jesus
Blood Wedding▶
Blue Heaven
Blue In the Face
Blue Sky▶
Bluebeard's Eighth Wife
Blume in Love▶
Body Chemistry
Brand New Life
Breaking the Waves▶
Breathing Lessons▶
The Bride & the Beast
The Bride Walks Out
The Brides Wore Blood
The Browning Version
The Buccaneers▶
Bulldog Drummond's Bride
Bullwhip
Burn Witch, Burn!▶
The Burning Bed▶
A Business Affair
By Love Possessed
By the Light of the Silvery Moon
Calendar▶
Captain's Paradise▶
Car Trouble
Casanova Brown
Cast a Dark Shadow▶
Cause for Alarm
Chained
A Change of Seasons
Charles & Diana: A Palace Divided
Cheaters
Cheatin' Hearts
Child Bride of Short Creek
China Moon
Chinese Roulette
Chloe in the Afternoon▶
The Chocolate Soldier
Choices
Christina
Circumstances Unknown
Claire's Knee▶
Clash by Night▶
Coast to Coast
Cold Heaven
Come Back, Little Sheba▶
Coming to America▶
Common Law Wife
Conflict▶
Consenting Adults
Consolation Marriage
Conspiracy of Terror
Cosmic Slop
Country Girl▶
The Cowboy and the Lady
Crash
Crazy in Love
Crime & Passion
A Cry in the Night
Cul de Sac▶
Dancing in the Dark
Dangerous Game
Dangerous Liaisons
Danielle Steel's Changes
The Dead▶
Dead in the Water
Dead Mate
Dead On
Death Kiss
Deception
Designing Woman▶
Desire and Hell at Sunset Motel
Desire Under the Elms
Desperate Characters▶
Desperate Hours
Desperate Remedies
The Devil in Silk
Diabolically Yours
Dial "M" for Murder▶
Diary of a Mad Housewife▶
Diary of the Dead
Dirty Hands
The Disappearance of Christina
Divorce American Style
Divorce—Italian Style▶
The Divorce of Lady X
Doctors' Wives
Dodsworth▶
Dollar
A Doll's House
A Doll's House▶
Dominique is Dead
Don Juan DeMarco
Dona Flor and Her Two Husbands▶
Donkey Skin▶
Don't Raise the Bridge, Lower the River
Don't Talk to Strangers
Doomsday
Double Deal
Double Exposure
Double Indemnity▶
Double Standard
Doubting Thomas
Dream Lover
Dressmaker
Drifting Souls
Drowning by Numbers▶
Drums Along the Mohawk▶
East Side, West Side
Easy Living
Eat a Bowl of Tea▶
Eating Raoul▶
Ecstasy
Edward and Mrs. Simpson
Effi Briest▶
Egg and I▶
El: This Strange Passion▶
Elizabeth of Ladymead▶
Ellie
Elvis and Me
Emmanuelle

Tell Me That You Love Me
Tender Is the Night
The Tender Trap
Test Pilot▶
That Certain Thing
That Uncertain Feeling
Thicker Than Water
Third Walker▶
30 Is a Dangerous Age, Cynthia
Three Broadway Girls▶
Three Daring Daughters
Three Husbands
Three Smart Girls▶
Thursday's Game▶
Till Death Do Us Part
Till Marriage Do Us Part
Till Murder Do Us Part
Till the End of the Night
Tin Men
To Joy▶
Tom & Viv▶
Too Beautiful for You
Too Far to Go▶
Torchlight
The Torture of Silence
A Touch of Class▶
Trade Off
Traps
Tricks of the Trade
True Lies
True Love▶
The Tunnel
The Tunnel of Love
Twice a Woman
Two for the Road▶
The Two Mrs. Carrolls
Ulysses
The Unchastened Woman
Under Capricorn
Under the Volcano▶
Undercover Blues
Une Jeunesse▶
Unfaithfully Yours▶
Unfaithfully Yours
Unholy Wife
The Unkissed Bride
Until September
Uptown New York
The Van▶
Vanishing Act
Vasectomy: A Delicate Matter
Violets Are Blue
The Virgin of Nuremberg
Vivacious Lady▶
Voulez-Vous Danser Avec Moi?
A Vow to Kill
Voyage to Italy
W
A Walk in the Clouds
Walk in the Spring Rain
Waltz of the Toreadors▶
War Brides
The Wash▶
Waterland
Way Down East▶
The Wayward Wife
A Wedding
The Wedding Gift▶
Wedding in Blood▶
A Wedding in Galilee▶
We're Not Married▶
What's Good for the Goose
When a Man Loves a Woman
Where Angels Fear to Tread▶
Where Were You When the Lights Went Out?
White Gold▶
Who's Afraid of Virginia Woolf?▶
Who's Got the Action?
Widow's Kiss
Wife Versus Secretary▶
Wifemistress
Without Anesthesia
A Woman Named Jackie
The Woman Next Door▶
Woman of the Year▶
A Woman Under the Influence▶
Woman Undone
Woman With a Past
A Woman's Guide to Adultery
A Woman's World▶
The Women▶
Women From the Lake of Scented Souls
The Wooden Man's Bride
The World is Full of Married Men
World's Greatest Lover
Worth Winning
X, Y & Zee
A Year in Provence▶
You Can't Fool Your Wife
Younger & Younger
Yours, Mine & Ours
You've Got to Have Heart
Zandy's Bride

Martial Arts

Above the Law
Against the Drunken Cat Paws
Alley Cat
Aloha Summer
American Kickboxer 1
American Kickboxer 2: To the Death
American Ninja
American Ninja 2: The Confrontation
American Ninja 3: Blood Hunt
American Ninja 4: The Annihilation
American Samurai
American Shaolin: King of the Kickboxers 2
The Amsterdam Connection
Angel of Fury
Angel Town
Assassin
Baby Cart 1: Lend a Child...Lend an Arm
Baby Cart at the River Styx
Baby Cart to Hades
Back in Action
Bells of Death
Best of the Best
Best of the Best 2
Best of the Best 3: No Turning Back
The Big Brawl
Big Trouble in Little China
Black Belt
Black Belt Jones
Black Dragon
Black Dragon's Revenge
Black Eagle
Black Samurai
Blackbelt 2: Fatal Force
Blind Fists of Bruce
Blind Fury
Blind Rage
Blood for Blood
Blood Ring
Blood Warriors
Bloodfight
Bloodfist
Bloodfist 2
Bloodfist 3: Forced to Fight
Bloodfist 4: Die Trying
Bloodfist 5: Human Target
Bloodfist 6: Ground Zero
Bloodmatch
Bloodsport
Bloodsport 2: The Next Kumite
The Bloody Fight
The Bodyguard
Born Invincible
Born Losers
Bounty Tracker
Braddock: Missing in Action 3
Brain Smasher...A Love Story
Breaker! Breaker!
Breathing Fire
Bronson Lee, Champion
The Bronx Executioner
Bruce Lee: Curse of the Dragon▶
Bruce Lee Fights Back From the Grave
Bruce Lee's Ways of Kung Fu
Bruce Le's Greatest Revenge
Bruce Li in New Guinea
Bruce Li the Invincible
Bruce the Superhero
Bruce's Deadly Fingers
Bruce's Fists of Vengeance
Buddha Assassinator
The Bushido Blade
Cage 2: The Arena of Death
Cantonen Iron Kung Fu
Catch the Heat
The Cavalier
Challenge of the Masters
Challenge the Ninja
Champion Operation
China O'Brien
China O'Brien 2
China White
The Chinatown Kid
Chinese Connection
Chinese Connection 2
Circle of Iron
Clash of the Ninja
Cleopatra Jones
Cleopatra Jones & the Casino of Gold
Clones of Bruce Lee
The Cobra
Cobra Against Ninja
Counter Attack
Crack Shadow Boxers
Cyber Ninja
Dance of Death
A Dangerous Place
Day of the Panther
The Deadliest Art: The Best of the Martial Arts Films
Deadly Bet
Deadly Target
Death Challenge
Death Machines
Death Mask of the Ninja
Death Match
Death Ring
Death Warrant
Deathfight
Desert Kickboxer
Diamond Ninja Force
The Divine Enforcer
Dolemite
Double Dragon
Double Impact
Dragon Force
Dragon Fury
Dragon Princess
Dragon: The Bruce Lee Story▶
Dragon the Odds
Dragon vs. Needles of Death
Dragon's Claw
The Dragon's Showdown
Dreadnaught Rivals
Dual Flying Kicks
Duel of Fists
Duel of the Iron Fist
Duel of the Seven Tigers
The Dynamite Brothers
Dynamo
Dynasty
Eagle Claws Champion
Eagle's Shadow
Eighteen Jade Arhats
The Eliminators
Empire of the Dragon
Enter the Dragon▶
Enter the Ninja
Enter the Panther
Enter Three Dragons
Exit the Dragon, Enter the Tiger
An Eye for an Eye
Fearless Tiger
Ferocious Female Freedom Fighters
Fight for Survival
Fight to the Death
The Fighter
Fighting Black Kings
Fighting Life
Final Impact
Firecracker
Fist of Fear, Touch of Death
Fist of Glory
Fist of Steel
The Fist, the Kicks, and the Evils
Fists of Blood
Fists of Dragons
Fists of Fury▶
Fists of Fury 2
Fists of Iron
Five Fighters from Shaolin
Force of One
Forced Vengeance
Forgotten Warrior
Four Robbers
Full Contact
Full Metal Ninja
Furious
The Furious Avenger
Futurekick
The Gambling Samurai
Game of Death
Gang Justice
Gang Wars
Ghostwarrior
Gladiator Cop: The Swordsman 2
Golden Exterminators
Golden Ninja Warrior
Golden Sun
Goldfinger▶
Good Guys Wear Black
The Great Hunter
Green Dragon Inn
Guardian Angel
Gymkata
Half a Loaf of Kung Fu
Hands of Death
Hard to Kill
Heatseeker
Hell's Wind Staff
Hero and the Terror
The Heroic Trio
Hot Potato
The Hot, the Cool, and the Vicious
Hurricane Sword
Image of Bruce Lee
Immortal Combat
In Your Face
Incredible Master Beggars
Instant Kung-Fu Man
The Instructor
Invasion U.S.A.
Invincible
Iron Dragon Strikes Back
Iron Thunder
Ironheart
Jackie Chan's Police Force
Jaguar Lives
Japanese Connection
Karate Cop
The Karate Kid▶
The Karate Kid: Part 2
The Karate Kid: Part 3
Karate Warrior
Karate Warriors
The Kick Fighter
Kick of Death: The Prodigal Boxer
Kickboxer
Kickboxer 2: The Road Back
Kickboxer 3: The Art of War
Kickboxer 4: The Aggressor
Kickboxer the Champion
Kill and Kill Again
Kill Line
Kill or Be Killed
Kill Squad
Kill the Golden Goose
Killer Elephants
King Boxer
King Boxers
The King of the Kickboxers
Kingfisher the Killer
Knights
Kung Fu
Kung Fu Avengers
Kung Fu Commandos
Kung Fu Massacre
Kung Fu Rebels
Kung Fu: The Movie
Lady Dragon
Lady Dragon 2
The Last Dragon
Leopard Fist Ninja
Lethal Ninja
Lionheart
Little Dragons
Little Heroes of Shaolin Temple
Little Ninjas
Low Blow
Machoman
Mafia vs. Ninja
Magic Kid
Magic Kid 2
Magnum Killers
Manchurian Avenger
Marked for Death
Martial Law
Martial Law 2: Undercover
Martial Outlaw
Marvelous Stunts of Kung Fu
Master Killer
Master Ninja
Master of Kung Fu
Master's Revenge
Mission of Justice
Mortal Kombat: The Movie
The Mosaic Project
My Name Called Bruce
My Samurai
Naked Killer
New Fist of Fury
New York Cop
The Next Karate Kid
Night Hunter
Night Master
Night of the Kickfighters
Night of the Warrior
9 1/2 Ninjas
Nine Deaths of the Ninja
Ninja 3: The Domination
Ninja Academy
Ninja: American Warrior
Ninja Brothers of Blood
Ninja Champion
Ninja Checkmate
Ninja Commandments
Ninja Condors
Ninja Connection
Ninja Death Squad
Ninja Demon's Massacre
Ninja Destroyer
Ninja Dragon
Ninja Exterminators
Ninja Fantasy
Ninja Hunt
Ninja Massacre
Ninja Masters of Death
Ninja Mission
Ninja Nightmare
Ninja of the Magnificence
Ninja Operation: Licensed to Terminate
Ninja Phantom Heroes
The Ninja Pirates
Ninja Powerforce
Ninja Showdown
Ninja Squad
Ninja Strike Force
Ninja Supremo
Ninja Swords of Death
Ninja Terminator
Ninja the Battalion
Ninja the Protector
Ninja, the Violent Sorcerer
Ninja Turf
Ninja Vengeance
Ninja vs. Ninja
Ninja vs. the Shaolin
Ninja Wars
Ninja's Extreme Weapons
No Retreat, No Surrender
No Retreat, No Surrender 2
No Retreat, No Surrender 3: Blood Brothers
The Noble Ninja
Octagon
Of Cooks and Kung-Fu
Omega Cop
The One Arm Swordsmen
One Down, Two to Go!
One-Eyed Swordsman
One Man Army
Only the Strong
Open Fire
Operation Golden Phoenix
Operation Orient
Out for Blood
Out for Justice
Overkill
The Perfect Weapon

Phoenix the Ninja
The Power of the Ninjitsu
The Power Within
Pray for Death
Prodigal Boxer: The Kick of Death
Professional Killers 1
Protector
Pursuit
Pushed to the Limit
Queen Boxer
The Quest
Rage and Honor
Rage and Honor 2: Hostile Takeover
Rage of Honor
Rage of Wind
Ragin' Cajun
Rapid Fire
Raw Force
Real Bruce Lee
Red Sun Rising
Remo Williams: The Adventure Begins
Renegade Monk
Renegade Ninja
Retrievers
Return of the Chinese Boxer
Return of the Dragon
Return of the Scorpion
Return of the Street Fighter
Return of the Tiger
Revenge of the Ninja
Revolt of the Dragon
Ring of Fire
Ring of Fire 2: Blood and Steel
Ring of Fire 3: Lion Strike
Ring of Steel
Rivals of the Silver Fox
Roller Blade
Rumble in the Bronx
Sakura Killers
Sanshiro Sugata▶
Scorpion
Seven Blows of the Dragon
The 7 Brothers Meet Dracula
Shadow Killers
Shao Lin Popeye
Shaolin Ex-Monk
Shaolin Executioner
Shaolin Kids
Shaolin Kung Fu Mystagogue
Shaolin Temple Strikes Back
Shaolin Traitor
Shaolin Vengence
Shinobi Ninja
Shogun's Ninja
Shootfighter: Fight to the Death
Showdown
Showdown at the Equator
Showdown in Little Tokyo
Sidekicks
Silent Assassins
Silent Rage
Sister Street Fighter
Slaughter in San Francisco
Sloane
Snake in the Eagle's Shadow 2
Snuff-Bottle Connection
Space Ninja: Sword of the Space Ark
Steel Fisted Dragon
Stickfighter
Sting of the Dragon Masters
Story of the Dragon
The Stranger and the Gunfighter
Stranglehold
The Street Fighter
The Street Fighter's Last Revenge
Street Hunter
Street Soldiers
Super Ninjas
Surf Ninjas
Survival Game
Survival of a Dragon
Sword of Doom▶
Sword of Fury II
Sword of Honor
Swords of Death
Talons of the Eagle
Tattoo Connection
Ten Brothers of Shao-lin
They Call Me Bruce?
They Still Call Me Bruce
The Three Avengers
3 Ninjas
3 Ninjas Kick Back
3 Ninjas Knuckle Up
Thundering Ninja
Tiger Claws
Tiger Heart
Tigershark
Timecop
TNT Jackson
To Be the Best
To the Death
Tongs: An American Nightmare
Top Dog
Tough Guy
Trancers 3: Deth Lives
Triple Impact
The True Game of Death
24 Hours to Midnight
Twister Kicker
Two Assassins in the Dark
Two Graves to Kung-Fu
The Two Great Cavaliers
Two Wondrous Tigers
The Unbeaten 28
Undefeatable
Unmasking the Idol
Vampire Raiders—Ninja Queen
Vengeance of the Snowmaid
Venus the Ninja
Warrior Within
Way of the Black Dragon
Weapons of Death
When Taekwondo Strikes
White Phantom: Enemy of Darkness
White Tiger
Wing Chun
Without Mercy
Wolfen Ninja
The Young Bruce Lee
Young Dragon
Young Tiger
Zatoichi: Master Ichi and a Chest of Gold
Zatoichi: The Blind Swordsman and the Chess Expert
Zatoichi: The Blind Swordsman's Vengeance
Zatoichi vs. Yojimbo▶

Martyred Pop Icons

see also Rock Stars on Film

Beatlemania! The Movie
Blue Hawaii
Bob Dylan: Don't Look Back▶
The Buddy Holly Story▶
Bus Stop▶
Clambake
The Doors
The Doors: Soft Parade, a Retrospective
Elvis and Me
Elvis Stories
Elvis: The Movie
Forever James Dean
Fun in Acapulco
James Dean Story
John & Yoko: A Love Story
King Creole
Kissin' Cousins
La Bamba▶
Lenny▶
Live a Little, Love a Little
Love Me Tender
Marilyn: The Untold Story▶
Paradise, Hawaiian Style
The Real Buddy Holly Story
Rebel Without a Cause▶
The Rose▶
Roustabout
Sgt. Pepper's Lonely Hearts Club Band
The Seven Year Itch▶
Speedway
Spinout
Stardust Memories
Stay Away, Joe
This Is Elvis
Train to Hollywood▶
The Trouble with Girls (and How To Get Into It)▶

Mass Media

see also Front Page; Radio

America
At Home with the Webbers
Behind the Rising Sun
Bigfoot: The Unforgettable Encounter
Broadcast News▶
A Case of Libel
Chill Factor
The China Syndrome▶
A Cry in the Dark▶
Dead Men Don't Die
Death Watch▶
E. Nick: A Legend in His Own Mind
Eternity
Exiled to Shanghai
Eyewitness
A Face in the Crowd▶
France/Tour/Detour/Deux/Enfants▶
The Gladiators
The Groove Tube
Groundhog Day▶
Hero▶
Hollywood Scandals and Tragedies
I Was a Teenage TV Terrorist
The Image
Indictment: The McMartin Trial▶
International House
Lipstick Camera
Live! From Death Row
Livin' Large
The Lost Honor of Katharina Blum▶
Love and a .45
Loving You
Max Headroom, the Original Story
Medium Cool▶
My Favorite Year▶
National Lampoon's Attack of the 5 Ft. 2 Women
Natural Born Killers
Network▶
News at Eleven
Nothing Sacred▶
The Passenger▶
Pray TV
Prime Suspect
Prime Time Murder
Quiz Show▶
Ratings Game
Ready to Wear
Riders of the Storm
Scrooged
The Seduction
Sex Through a Window
S.F.W.
Six Fois Deux/Sur et Sous la Communication▶
Soft and Hard
The Stuff
Superstar: The Life and Times of Andy Warhol▶
Switching Channels
Tabloid!
The Thrill of It All!
Tunnelvision
UHF
Up Close and Personal▶
Videodrome
Witness to the Execution
Zelig▶

May-December Romance

see also Coming of Age; Growing Older; Romantic Adventures; Romantic Comedy; Romantic Drama

Atlantic City▶
Cass Timberlane
The Color of Evening
Goodbye Again
The Graduate▶
Harold and Maude▶
Live Bait
Love in the Afternoon
Nelly et Monsieur Arnaud▶
The Pallbearer
Roman Spring of Mrs. Stone▶
Sabrina▶
That Obscure Object of Desire▶
Tim

The Meaning of Life

At Home with the Webbers
Badlands▶
Being Human
The Blood of Others
Breathing Lessons▶
The Castle▶
The Collector▶
End of the Road
Field of Dreams▶
The French Lieutenant's Woman▶
Full Body Massage
Funny Face▶
Galaxies are Colliding
Gospa
Heaven Can Wait▶
Here Comes Mr. Jordan▶
Joey Breaker▶
Land and Freedom▶
Love and Death▶
Monty Python's The Meaning of Life▶
My Life
My Own Private Idaho▶
The Razor's Edge▶
The Razor's Edge
The Remains of the Day▶
Shadowlands▶
The Sheltering Sky▶
The Trial
Why Has Bodhi-Darma Left for the East
Wings of Desire▶
Zabriskie Point▶

Medieval Romps

see also Camelot (Old); Historical Drama; Period Piece; Swashbucklers

The Adventures of Robin Hood▶
Beatrice▶
Becket▶
Being Human
The Beloved Rogue▶
Braveheart▶
Brother Cadfael
Camelot
Choice of Weapons
The Company of Wolves▶
Conquest of the Normans
Deathstalker
Deathstalker 2: Duel of the Titans
The Decameron▶
Decameron Nights
Diane
Donkey Skin▶
Dragonslayer▶
El Cid▶
Excalibur▶
The Fighting Prince of Donegal
Fire and Sword
First Knight
The Flame & the Arrow▶
Flesh and Blood
Goetz von Berlichingen
Hawk and Castile
Hawk the Slayer
Inquisition
Ivanhoe▶
Ivanhoe
Jabberwocky
Jack the Giant Killer▶
The Juniper Tree
King Arthur, the Young Warlord
Knights of the Round Table
Kojiro▶
Ladyhawke
The Lady's Not for Burning
Lancelot of the Lake
Legend
Leonor
The Lion in Winter▶
Lionheart
Magdalene
Magic Serpent▶
The Magic Sword
Mark of the Devil
Mark of the Devil 2
The Mongols
Monty Python and the Holy Grail▶
The Name of the Rose
Naughty Knights
The Navigator▶
Onibaba▶
Pippin▶
The Prince of Thieves
Ran▶
Rashomon▶
The Return of Martin Guerre▶
Rikyu▶
Robin and Marian
Robin Hood▶
Robin Hood: Men in Tights
Robin Hood: Prince of Thieves
Robin Hood...The Legend: Herne's Son
Robin Hood...The Legend: Robin Hood and the Sorcerer
Robin Hood...The Legend: The Swords of Wayland
Robin Hood...The Legend: The Time of the Wolf
The Scalawag Bunch
The Secret of El Zorro
Seven Samurai▶
The Seventh Seal▶
Skullduggery
Stealing Heaven
Sword & the Dragon
Sword & the Sorcerer
The Sword in the Stone▶
Sword of Lancelot
Sword of Sherwood Forest
Sword of the Valiant
Tales of Robin Hood
Tharus Son of Attila
Time Bandits
Time Trackers
Tor
The Undead▶
Unidentified Flying Oddball
The Vikings
The Warrior & the Sorceress
When Knights were Bold
Wholly Moses!
Wizards of the Lost Kingdom
Young Warlord
The Zany Adventures of Robin Hood

Meltdown

see also Disaster Flicks

Above and Beyond▶
Access Code
Amazing Grace & Chuck
Atomic Attack
The Atomic Cafe▶
The Atomic Kid
Black Rain▶
Bloodfist 6: Ground Zero
Bombs Away!
Broken Arrow
Chain Reaction
The China Syndrome▶
Cloak and Dagger
Control
Crimson Tide▶
Cyclotrode "X"
The Day After▶
The Day the Earth Caught Fire▶
The Death Merchant
Desert Bloom▶
Dick Barton Strikes Back
Disaster at Silo 7

Dr. Strangelove, or: How I Learned to Stop Worrying and Love the Bomb▶
Enola Gay: The Men, the Mission, the Atomic Bomb
Fail-Safe▶
Fat Man and Little Boy
Final Sanction
First Spaceship on Venus▶
First Strike
First Yank into Tokyo
Flight of Black Angel
The Fourth Protocol▶
Full Fathom Five
Future Kill
Geisha Girl
Glen and Randa
Ground Zero▶
H-Man
Hiroshima▶
Hiroshima Maiden
Hiroshima: Out of the Ashes▶
I Live in Fear▶
In the King of Prussia
Incident at Map-Grid 36-80
Invasion U.S.A.
A Man Called Rage
The Manhattan Project
Massive Retaliation
Miracle Mile▶
Modern Problems
Night Siege Project: Shadowchaser 2
Nuclear Conspiracy
Omega Man
On the Beach▶
One Night Stand▶
Panic in the Year Zero!
The Patriot
Plutonium Incident
Prisoner in the Middle
Radioactive Dreams
Rats
Reactor
The Reflecting Skin
Refuge of Fear
Rhapsody in August
Rocket Attack U.S.A.
The Sacrifice▶
Seven Days in May▶
The Shoes of the Fisherman
Silkwood▶
Slugs
Special Bulletin▶
Split Second
The Spy Who Loved Me
State of Things▶
Superman 4: The Quest for Peace
TC 2000
Testament▶
This Is Not a Test
Threads▶
True Lies
The 27 Day
Unknown World
Utopia
Voyage to the Bottom of the Sea▶
WarGames
When the Wind Blows▶
Young Lady Chatterly 2

Men

***see also** Dads; Macho Men; Repressed Men; War Between the Sexes*

Bachelor Apartment
Carnal Knowledge▶
City Hall▶
City Slickers▶
The Incredible Shrinking Man▶
La Grande Bouffe▶
The Men's Club
Mr. Mom▶
90 Days▶
Patti Rocks▶
Planet of the Apes▶
Raging Bull▶
Rate It X
The Saint of Fort Washington
Three Men and a Baby▶
Three Men and a Cradle▶
Thursday's Game▶
Truth or Die
Up to a Certain Point
Watch It▶
The Young Poisoner's Handbook▶

Men in Prison

***see also** Fugitives; Great Escapes; POW/MIA; Women in Prison*

Against the Wall▶
Alias, La Gringa
American Me▶
Andersonville▶
Angels with Dirty Faces▶
Appointment with Crime
Attica▶
Baba▶
Bad Boys▶
Band of the Hand
Behind Prison Walls
Beyond the Walls
Birdman of Alcatraz▶
Black Lemons
Blind Faith
Bloodsport 2: The Next Kumite
Botany Bay
Boy's Reformatory
Breaker Morant▶
Breakout
The Brig▶
Broken Melody
Brubaker▶
Buried Alive
Buy & Cell
The Cable Guy
Caged Heat 2: Stripped of Freedom
Caged in Paradiso
Call Northside 777▶
Captives
Chain Gang Killings
The Chair
City Without Men
Club Fed
Colonel Chabert
Coming Out of the Ice▶
Convict Cowboy
Cool Hand Luke▶
The Count of Monte Cristo
The Count of Monte Cristo▶
The Count of Monte Cristo
Crashout
Criminal Code
Cry Danger▶
Das Testament des Dr. Mabuse▶
Dead Man Out▶
Dead Right
Deadlock
Deadlock 2
Death House
Death Warrant
Deathrow Gameshow
The Defiant Ones▶
Devil's Canyon
The Devil's Cargo
The Dirty Dozen▶
The Dirty Dozen: The Deadly Mission
The Dirty Dozen: The Fatal Mission
The Dirty Dozen: The Next Mission
Doin' Time
The Domino Principle
Down by Law▶
Each Dawn I Die
Eagles Attack at Dawn
Embassy
Empire of the Sun▶
Ernest Goes to Jail
Escape from Alcatraz▶
Escape from Death Row
Escape from DS-3
Escape from El Diablo
Escape from New York
Execution of Raymond Graham
The Executioner's Song
Fast Walking
The Fence
Fled
Fortress
Framed
Gang Busters
Gideon's Trumpet
The Glass House▶
Gulag
Hangfire
Hard Frame
Hard Justice
Hold 'Em Jail
House Across the Bay
I Am a Fugitive from a Chain Gang▶
In Hot Pursuit
In the Name of the Father▶
An Innocent Man
Invasion
The Invisible Strangler
Jailbreakin'
Jailhouse Rock▶
The Jericho Mile
Johnny Handsome▶
Kansas City Confidential▶
King of the Damned
Kiss of the Spider Woman▶
L'Addition
The Last Detail▶
The Last Mile
Les Miserables
The Life of Emile Zola▶
The Line
Little Red Schoolhouse
Live! From Death Row
Lock Up
The Longest Yard
A Man Escaped▶
Man of La Mancha
The Man Who Broke 1,000 Chains
Maximum Security
McKenzie Break▶
McVicar
Mean Frank and Crazy Tony
Midnight Express▶
Mrs. Soffel
Mr. Frost
Moon 44
Murder In the First
Mutiny in the Big House
My Boys Are Good Boys
New Crime City: Los Angeles 2020
New Eden
The Night Visitor
984: Prisoner of the Future
No Escape
Off the Wall
On the Yard
Papillon▶
Pardon Us
Payback
Penitentiary
Penitentiary 2
Penitentiary 3
Phantom Empire
Pressure Point▶
Prison
Prison Break
Prison Planet
Prison Train
The Pursuit of Happiness
Real Bullets
Riot
Riot in Cell Block 11▶
The Rock▶
Runaway Train▶
Samar
Scum▶
A Sense of Freedom▶
The Shawshank Redemption▶
Shoeshine▶
Short Eyes▶
Slaughterhouse Rock
Soul Vengeance
Space Rage
Stir Crazy
Tank
Terminal Island
Terror of the Bloodhunters
Terror on Alcatraz
There was a Crooked Man▶
They Never Come Back
They Went That-a-Way & That-a-Way
Tomb of the Undead
Torture Ship
Triumph of the Spirit▶
Truth or Die
Two-Way Stretch
Weeds▶
Women's Prison Massacre
Yol▶

Mental Retardation

***see also** Physical Problems; Savants*

Bill▶
Bill: On His Own▶
Charly▶
A Child is Waiting▶
A Dangerous Woman
Dark Night of the Scarecrow
A Day in the Death of Joe Egg▶
Dominick & Eugene▶
The Eighth Day
Family Pictures▶
Homer and Eddie
Larry
L'Enfant d'Eau
Lovey: A Circle of Children 2
Malcolm
Of Mice and Men▶
Rain Man▶
The Rain People▶
Slipping into Darkness
Square Dance
Sweetie▶
Tim
Two of a Kind
What's Eating Gilbert Grape▶
The Wizard
The Woman Who Willed a Miracle

Metamorphosis

***see also** Genetics; Werewolves*

An American Werewolf in London▶
Cat People▶
Cat People
The Company of Wolves▶
The Curse of the Werewolf
The Fly▶
The Fly▶
The Fly 2
The Howling▶
I Was a Teenage Werewolf
The Lair of the White Worm▶
Naked Lunch▶
Silver Bullet
Species
Vampire in Brooklyn
Wolfen▶
The Wolfman
Woof!

Mexico

***see also** Central America*

Across the Bridge
Against All Odds
The Black Scorpion
The Border▶
Borderline
Breakout
A Bullet for the General
Bullfighter & the Lady
Bullfighters
The Cisco Kid
Commando Squad
Crazy from the Heart▶
Danzon▶
Desperado▶
Django
Escape from Cell Block 3
The Falcon in Mexico
Five Giants from Texas
Found Alive
From Dusk Till Dawn
Fun in Acapulco
His Kind of Woman▶
Holiday in Mexico
A Home of Our Own
In 'n Out
Interval
Juarez
Los Olvidados▶
Love Has Many Faces
The Magnificent Seven▶
The Masked Rider
Mexican Hayride
The Night of the Iguana▶
Octaman
Old Gringo
On the Line
The Pearl▶
The Professionals▶
The Proud Ones
Pure Luck
Que Viva Mexico▶
The Scout
Shoot the Living, Pray for the Dead
Sonny and Jed
South of Santa Fe
Survival Run
The Torch
Touch of Evil▶
Treasure of the Sierra Madre▶
Two Mules for Sister Sara▶
Valdez is Coming
Vera Cruz
Villa Rides
Viva Villa!▶
Viva Zapata!▶
Warlords from Hell
The White Orchid
Wild Rovers

Miami

***see also** American South*

Ace Ventura: Pet Detective
Band of the Hand
The Birdcage▶
Fair Game
Fires Within
Get Shorty▶
Miami Beach Cops
Miami Blues
Miami Cops
Miami Horror
Miami Rhapsody
Miami Supercops
Miami Vendetta
Miami Vice
Miami Vice 2: The Prodigal Son
The Perez Family
Scarface▶
Two Much

Middle East

***see also** Desert War/Foreign Legion; Deserts; Genies; Islam; Israel; Persian Gulf War; Terrorism*

Abbott and Costello Meet the Mummy
Ali Baba and the Forty Thieves
Ali Baba and the 40 Thieves▶
The Ambassador
The Arab Conspiracy
Arabian Nights
Bloodstone
A Casualty of War
Cleopatra
Counterforce
The Crusades
Cup Final
Eagles Attack at Dawn
The Egyptian
Fictitious Marriage
The Flight of the Phoenix▶
The Glory Boys
The Great Armored Car Swindle
The Guns and the Fury
Hamsin▶
Hanna K.
Harum Scarum
Held Hostage
Honeybaby
Hostages▶

Ilsa, Harem Keeper of the Oil Sheiks
The Invincible Six
Iran: Days of Crisis
Iron Eagle
Iron Eagle 2
Ishtar
The Jewel of the Nile
Joseph
Khartoum
Killing Streets
King Richard and the Crusaders
Lawrence of Arabia▶
The Lighthorsemen▶
The Lone Runner
A Matter of WHO
Not Without My Daughter
On Wings of Eagles
Paradise
Raiders of the Lost Ark▶
Rescue Force
The Road to Morocco▶
The Robe
Rosebud
Sadat
The Sheik▶
Sirocco
Son of Ali Baba
The Spy Who Loved Me
Three Days in Beirut
Through the Olive Trees▶
Torn Apart
Trident Force
Unveiled
Warbirds
A Wedding in Galilee▶
The White Balloon▶

Military Comedy

see also Comedy; War, General

Abbott and Costello in the Foreign Legion
Abroad with Two Yanks
Article 99
As You Were
At War with the Army
The Baby and the Battleship
Basic Training
Best Defense
Best Foot Forward
Biloxi Blues
Black and White in Color▶
The Captain from Koepenick
Caught in the Draft▶
Chesty Anderson USN
Clipped Wings
Combat Academy
Don't Go Near the Water
Down Periscope
Ensign Pulver
The Flying Deuces▶
Follow That Camel
Follow the Leader
Francis Goes to West Point
Francis in the Navy
Francis Joins the WACs
Getting Wasted
G.I. Blues
G.I. Jane
Going Under
Here Come the Marines
Hillbilly Blitzkrieg
Hot Shots!▶
Hot Shots! Part Deux
In the Army Now
Jumping Jacks
Le Gendarme de Saint-Tropez
Leave It to the Marines
Major Payne
A Man Called Sarge
M*A*S*H▶
M*A*S*H: Goodbye, Farewell & Amen▶
Miracle of Morgan's Creek▶
Mr. Walkie Talkie
The Mouse That Roared▶
Never Wave at a WAC
No Time for Sergeants▶
The Odd Squad
Off Limits
Operation Dames
Perfect Furlough
Private Benjamin
Private Manoeuvres
Privates on Parade
Renaissance Man
The Sad Sack
Sgt. Bilko
She's in the Army Now
Snuffy Smith, Yard Bird
Soldier in the Rain
Stripes
Suppose They Gave a War and Nobody Came?
Tanks a Million
Three Legionnaires
23 1/2 Hours Leave
The Virgin Soldiers
Viva Max
Weekend Pass
Weekend Warriors
We're in the Legion Now
We're in the Navy Now
The West Point Story

Miners & Mining

Act of Vengeance
The Adventures of Bullwhip Griffin
Angels Die Hard
Backlash: Oblivion 2
Ballad of Cable Hogue▶
The Big Man: Crossing the Line▶
Black Fury▶
Burning Rage
Challenge to White Fang
The Christmas Coal Mine Miracle
Eureka Stockade
Fighting Cowboy
Fighting Valley
Flaming Frontiers
Gangster's Den
Gangsters of the Frontier
Germinal▶
Ghost Town Renegades
Girl Rush
Grand Canyon Trail
Green Fire
The Hallelujah Trail
Haunted Gold
Hills of Utah
How Green Was My Valley▶
Human Hearts
Kameradschaft▶
King Solomon's Mines
Little Church Around the Corner
The Man from Music Mountain
Margaret's Museum
Matewan▶
McCabe & Mrs. Miller▶
Molly Maguires
My Darlin' Clementine
'Neath Canadian Skies
No Man's Law
North to Alaska▶
Paint Your Wagon
Pale Rider▶
Phantom Gold
Poldark▶
Poldark 2▶
The Rainbow Gang
Red Earth
Rider from Tucson
The Ruthless Four
Salt of the Earth▶
Sands of Sacrifice
Silver Bandit
The Spoilers▶
Springhill
The Stars Look Down▶
The Strangeness
The War Wagon▶
Way Out West▶
Where the Green Ants Dream
Where Trails End
Wildrose▶
Xica▶

Minnesota

see also America's Heartland

Beautiful Girls
D2: The Mighty Ducks
The Emigrants▶
Far North
Fargo▶
The Good Son
The Great Northfield Minnesota Raid
Grumpier Old Men
Grumpy Old Men▶
The Heartbreak Kid▶
Ice Castles
Iron Will
Little Big League
The Long Riders▶
The Mighty Ducks
The New Land▶
Patti Rocks▶
The Personals
Purple Rain
Slaughterhouse Five
That Was Then...This Is Now
Untamed Heart
Wildrose▶

Missing Persons

see also Hostage!; Kidnapped!

Adam▶
Agatha
Almost Human
American Nightmare
Anastasia▶
Anastasia: The Mystery of Anna
AngKor: Cambodia Express
Big Jake
Bureau of Missing Persons
Cavalcade of the West
Christina
Coming Out Alive
Curse of the Pink Panther
Disappearance
Dying Room Only
The Emerald Forest▶
Empire State
The Empty Beach
Equinox▶
Escapade in Japan
Experiment in Terror▶
Eye Witness
Final Cut
Foxtrap
Frantic▶
From Hollywood to Deadwood
Girl Hunters
Grayeagle
Green Eyes▶
Grievous Bodily Harm
Harem
Harper▶
Heading for Heaven
Hell Squad
Hide in Plain Sight▶
High Road to China
The Hit List
Hollywood Chaos
Home Is Where the Hart Is
Hurricane Smith
In the Mouth of Madness
Into Thin Air▶
The Island at the Top of the World
Jungle Goddess
Kentucky Jubilee
Kidnap Syndicate
The Lady Vanishes▶
The Lady Vanishes
The Last Winter
Little Miss Millions
A Low Down Dirty Shame
Midnight Warning
Misery▶
Missing▶
The Missing Corpse
Murder, My Sweet▶
Nickel & Dime
Night of the Cyclone
Norseman
Old Gringo
Picnic at Hanging Rock▶
The Port of Missing Girls
Prisoner of Zenda▶
The Professionals▶
Psych-Out
Psycho from Texas
Pure Luck
Raising Arizona▶
Romancing the Stone▶
Scandalous
Seance on a Wet Afternoon▶
The Searchers▶
Skull: A Night of Terror
Stark
Street Girls
Street Justice
Surfacing
Tarzan the Fearless
Terminal Force
Tokyo Joe
Tony Rome
The Vanishing▶
Wanted: Babysitter
Where Are the Children?
Where's Piccone▶
White Fire
The Wicker Man▶
Without a Trace

Missionaries

see also Nuns & Priests; Religion; Religious Epics

At Play in the Fields of the Lord▶
Beyond the Next Mountain
Black Robe▶
Ethan
Hawaii▶
The Inn of the Sixth Happiness▶
The Keys of the Kingdom▶
The Mission▶
Mission to Glory
The Missionary

Misspelled Titles

The 'Burbs
Charly▶
Cheech and Chong: Still Smokin'
C.H.O.M.P.S.
Class of Nuke 'Em High
Class of Nuke 'Em High 2: Subhumanoid Meltdown
The Concentratin' Kid
Doin' Time
Doin' Time on Planet Earth
Feelin' Up
Fightin' Ranch
Fyre
Git Along Little Dogies
Hittin' the Trail
I Dood It
I Live with Me Dad
I Wanna Be a Beauty Queen
Lightnin' Carson Rides Again
Li'l Abner
Livin' Large
Lock 'n' Load
The Mirror Crack'd
Mo' Better Blues
Mo' Money
'Neath Canadian Skies
Nobody's Perfekt
Old Swimmin' Hole
Packin' It In
Peddlin' in Society
Pete 'n' Tillie
Pudd'nhead Wilson
Puss 'n Boots
Rappin'
Rat Pfink a Boo-Boo
Reg'lar Fellers
Ride 'Em Cowgirl
Ridin' on a Rainbow
Ridin' the California Trail
Ridin' the Trail
Roamin' Wild
Roarin' Lead
Rockin' Road Trip
Rootin' Tootin' Rhythm
Singin' in the Rain▶
Six Shootin' Sheriff
Smilin' Through
Snowballin'
Spittin' Image
Straight Shootin'
Streetwalkin'
Sweet Sweetback's Baadasssss Song▶
Thrashin'
Tol'able David
We're Talkin' Serious Money
Workin' for Peanuts

Mistaken Identity

see also Amnesia; Gender Bending; Role Reversal

Across the Bridge
The Adventurer
The Adventures of Bullwhip Griffin
Along Came Jones▶
Alvin Rides Again
American Cop
Amore!
Amos and Andrew
Another You
As Good as Dead
As You Desire Me▶
As You Like It
As Young As You Feel▶
Bachelor Mother▶
The Ballad of Little Jo
The Beautiful Blonde from Bashful Bend
Being There▶
Betrayed▶
Billy the Kid Returns
Bittersweet Love
Black Glove
Blackjack
Blame It on the Bellboy
Blind Justice
Blondie Knows Best
Body Snatchers
Borderline
Boy's Reformatory
Brighton Strangler
Broadway Limited
Broken Melody
Bullets or Ballots▶
Bullseye!
Bundle of Joy
Buona Sera, Mrs. Campbell
Bushwhacked
Butler's Dilemma
Camp Cucamonga: How I Spent My Summer Vacation
The Capture▶
Caroline?▶
Carry On Admiral
A Case of Deadly Force▶
CB4: The Movie
Center of the Web
The Challengers
Chameleon Street▶
Charade▶
Charley's Aunt
The Chase
Colonel Chabert
Convicted
Convicts at Large
Cornbread, Earl & Me
The Couch Trip
Counterblast
Court Jester▶
Dave▶
Deadwood
Deconstructing Sarah
The Desert Song
Don Juan DeMarco
Don't Tell Her It's Me
Double Vision
El Mariachi▶
Ernest Goes to Jail
Erotic Touch of Hot Skin
Evergreen
Every Man's Law
Execution of Raymond Graham
F/X 2: The Deadly Art of Illusion
Family Reunion
Fargo Express

Modern Cowboys

***see also** Western Comedy; Westerns*

Moms

***see also** Bad Dads; Dads; Monster Moms; Parenthood*

Monkeyshines

***see also** Jungle Stories; Wild Kingdom*

Monster Moms

***see also** Bad Dads; Dads; Moms; Parenthood*

Monsters, General

***see also** Ghosts, Ghouls, & Goblins; Giants; Killer Beasts; Killer Bugs; Killer Plants; Killer Toys; Mad Scientists; Robots & Androids; Sea Critter Attack; Vampires; Werewolves; Zombies*

Montreal

see also Canada

Moscow

see also Russia/USSR

Motor Vehicle Dept.

see also Bikers; Fast Cars; Killer Cars

Mountaineering

Movie & TV Trailers

Mummies

see also Horror; Zombies

Murderous Children

see also Childhood Visions

Music

see also Martyred Pop Icons; Musician Biopics; Nashville Narratives; Rock Stars on Film; Roll Over Beethoven; Struggling Musicians

Music

Musical Comedy

You'll Never Get Rich▶
Ziegfeld Follies
Zis Boom Bah

Musical Drama

see also Musicals

Actor: The Paul Muni Story
The Band Wagon▶
The Barkleys of Broadway▶
Beatlemania! The Movie
The Belle of New York
Bells are Ringing▶
Beware
Blonde Venus▶
Blue Hawaii
Body Moves
Body Rock
Broadway Serenade
The Buddy Holly Story▶
Cabaret▶
Camelot
Can-Can
The Cantor's Son
Carmen Jones▶
Carnival Rock
The Cat and the Fiddle▶
The Chocolate Soldier
A Christmas Carol
Clambake
Club Havana
Coal Miner's Daughter▶
Concrete Angels
Congress Dances
Cool Mikado
The Cotton Club▶
Crossover Dreams
Curly Top
Daddy Long Legs▶
A Damsel in Distress▶
Dance Hall
Dance of Life
Dancing Lady
Dancing Pirate
A Date with Judy
Deadman's Curve
The Deputy Drummer
Dimples
Dogs in Space
Don Quixote▶
Double Trouble
Down Argentine Way▶
The Duke is Tops
The Farmer Takes a Wife
Fast Forward
Fiddler on the Roof▶
The Firefly
Fisherman's Wharf
The Five Pennies
Flashdance
Follow the Boys▶
Footloose
The Forbidden Dance
42nd Street▶
Frankie and Johnny
Funny Girl▶
Funny Lady
Gangway
George Balanchine's The Nutcracker
The Glenn Miller Story▶
Go, Johnny Go!
Goodbye, Mr. Chips
Graffiti Bridge
Great Balls of Fire
The Great Caruso
The Great Waltz▶
The Great Ziegfeld▶
Greek Street
Hard to Hold
The Harder They Come
Harmony Lane
Harum Scarum
Heart's Desire
Hello, Frisco, Hello
Honeysuckle Rose
Honkytonk Nights
I Could Go on Singing
Idolmaker
If You Knew Susie
I'll Cry Tomorrow▶
I'll See You in My Dreams
The In Crowd
It Happened at the World's Fair
It's Always Fair Weather
Jailbird Rock
Jailhouse Rock▶
The Jazz Singer
Jesus Christ, Superstar▶
Jolson Sings Again
The Jolson Story▶
The Josephine Baker Story▶
Jungle Patrol
Just Around the Corner
The King and I▶
King Creole
Knights of the City
La Bamba▶
Ladies of the Chorus
Lady Sings the Blues
Lambada
Life of Verdi
Light of Day
The Little Colonel▶
Little Miss Broadway
The Littlest Angel
The Littlest Rebel
Lottery Bride
Love Me or Leave Me▶
Love Me Tender
Mack the Knife
The Mambo Kings▶
The Man I Love▶
Man of La Mancha
Marco
A Matter of Time
Meet Danny Wilson
Melody Master
Miss Sadie Thompson▶
Murder at the Vanities
Murder with Music
The Music Lovers
The Music Man▶
Musica Proibita
My Fair Lady▶
Never Steal Anything Small
New Moon
New York, New York▶
Night and Day
No, No Nanette
Northwest Outpost
The Old Curiosity Shop
Oliver!▶
The One and Only, Genuine, Original Family Band▶
One Night of Love▶
One Trick Pony
Opera do Malandro
Orchestra Wives▶
An Orphan Boy of Vienna
Paradise, Hawaiian Style
Paradise in Harlem
Paradise Island
Paris Blues
Pennies From Heaven▶
Pete Kelly's Blues
Pete Townshend: White City
Piaf
The Poor Little Rich Girl
Princess Tam Tam▶
Purple Rain
Quadrophenia▶
Rainbow
Rappin'
Reckless
The Red Shoes▶
Rhapsody in Blue▶
Rock, Baby, Rock It
Rock, Rock, Rock
Rooftops
The Rose▶
Rose Marie▶
Rose of Washington Square
Roustabout
Sailing Along
Salsa
Sarafina!▶
Satisfaction
Scrooge
Senora Tentacion
Shining Star
Shout
Show Boat▶
Show Boat
Sincerely Yours
Sing
Smilin' Through
Something to Sing About
Song O' My Heart▶
Song of Freedom
Song of Norway
Song Without End
Songwriter
The Sound of Music▶
Sparkle
Star!
Stars and Stripes Forever▶
Stay Away, Joe
Stepping Out▶
Stowaway▶
Sunday in the Park with George▶
Sweet Charity▶
Sweet Dreams
Sweetheart of the Navy
Tap
They Shall Have Music
This Is the Army
The Three Penny Opera▶
Thunder Alley
Till the Clouds Roll By/A Star Is Born▶
Tommy
Transatlantic Merry-Go-Round
Umbrellas of Cherbourg▶
Waltz King
Way Down South
West Side Story▶
What's Love Got to Do with It?
Yankee Doodle Dandy▶
Yentl
Young at Heart
Young Caruso
Young Man with a Horn▶
Ziegfeld Girl▶
Zoot Suit▶
Zou Zou

Musical Fantasy

see also Musicals

Alice
Alice in Wonderland
Babes in Toyland
Bedknobs and Broomsticks
Brigadoon▶
Butterfly Ball
Cabin in the Sky▶
Carousel▶
Chitty Chitty Bang Bang
Cinderella
Cinderella 2000
Comic Book Kids
A Connecticut Yankee in King Arthur's Court
Damn Yankees▶
Doctor Dolittle
Down to Earth
Fairy Tales
The 5000 Fingers of Dr. T▶
Kismet
Labyrinth▶
The Little Match Girl
The Little Prince
Magical Mystery Tour
March of the Wooden Soldiers▶
Mary Poppins▶
The New Adventures of Pippi Longstocking
Once Upon a Brothers Grimm
Peter Pan▶
Rumpelstiltskin
Sleeping Beauty
Willy Wonka & the Chocolate Factory▶
The Wizard of Oz▶
Wonderwall: The Movie
Zero Patience

Musicals

see also Animated Musicals; Contemporary Musicals; Disco Musicals; Musical Comedy; Musical Drama; Musical Fantasy

Alexander's Ragtime Band▶
An American in Paris▶
Anchors Aweigh▶
Annie
Babes in Toyland
Balalaika
Beat Street
Bitter Sweet
Black Tights
Blue Skies▶
Born to Dance
Breaking the Ice
Broadway Melody
Broadway Melody of 1938
Broadway Melody of 1940
Bugsy Malone
By the Light of the Silvery Moon
Calamity Jane▶
Charm of La Boheme
Deep in My Heart
The Desert Song
Dogs in Space
The Dolly Sisters
Easter Parade▶
Easy to Love
Emperor Waltz
Flying Down to Rio
Follies Girl
Follies in Concert
Follow the Fleet▶
Footlight Parade▶
Footlight Serenade
For Me and My Gal
For the First Time
Frankenstein Sings...The Movie
Gaiety
Hair▶
Half a Sixpence
Hands Across the Border
Hans Brinker
Hans Christian Andersen
Happy Landing
Harlem on the Prairie
Harvest Melody
Hats Off
Hawaii Calls
Hi-De-Ho
Higher and Higher
Hillbillies in a Haunted House
Iceland
Incident at Channel Q
Invitation to the Dance
Junction 88
Killer Diller
Krush Groove
The Last Radio Station
Let Freedom Ring
Let's Sing Again
Little Johnny Jones
A Little Night Music
London Melody
Look for the Silver Lining
Madam Satan
Manhattan Merry-Go-Round
Maytime▶
Meet Me in St. Louis▶
Meet the Navy
Mrs. Brown, You've Got a Lovely Daughter
Moon over Harlem
Moon over Miami▶
Music in My Heart
Music Shoppe
My Lucky Star
Oh! Calcutta!
Oklahoma!▶
On Moonlight Bay
On the Town
100 Men and a Girl▶
Pagan Love Song
Pinocchio
Pippin▶
Private Buckaroo
Rainbow Over Broadway
Red Garters
Reet, Petite and Gone▶
Rhapsody
Rhythm Parade
Rich, Young and Pretty
Rosalie
Second Chorus
Sepia Cinderella
The Seven Hills of Rome
The Seven Little Foys▶
She Shall Have Music
South Pacific▶
Stage Door Canteen
Stormy Weather
The Story of Vernon and Irene Castle▶
The Student Prince
Sweeney Todd: The Demon Barber of Fleet Street
Sweet Adeline
Swing
Swing Parade of 1946
Take It Big
Taking My Turn
Terror of Tiny Town
Thank Your Lucky Stars▶
That Midnight Kiss
That's Dancing!
That's Entertainment
That's Entertainment, Part 2
That's Entertainment, Part 3
That's Singing: The Best of Broadway
Thousands Cheer
Three Little Words
The Threepenny Opera
Thrill of a Romance
Till the Clouds Roll By
Tin Pan Alley
The Toast of New Orleans
Tonight and Every Night
The Trouble with Girls (and How To Get Into It)▶
Under the Cherry Moon
Vagabond Lover
The Vampyr
Velnio Nuotaka
Viva Las Vegas
Week-End In Havana
Welcome Stranger
Wigstock: The Movie
Window Shopping
Wintertime
Words and Music
Yes, Sir, Mr. Bones
Young People

Musician Biopics

see also Nashville Narratives; Roll Over Beethoven

Amadeus▶
Bird▶
The Buddy Holly Story▶
Coal Miner's Daughter▶
The Doors
Elvis: The Movie
The Gene Krupa Story
The Glenn Miller Story▶
Great Balls of Fire
Immortal Beloved
John & Yoko: A Love Story
La Bamba▶
Lady Sings the Blues
Living Proof: The Hank Williams Jr. Story
Sweet Dreams
Whale Music
What's Love Got to Do with It?

Mutiny

see also Deep Blue; Sail Away; Sea Disasters; Shipwrecked

The Bounty▶
Crimson Tide▶
The Legend of the Sea Wolf
Mutiny
The Mutiny of the Elsinore
Mutiny on the Bounty▶
Mutiny on the Bounty
Pirate Ship
The Sea Wolf▶
The Sea Wolf

Mystery & Suspense

see also Psycho-Thriller

Abduction of St. Anne
Above Suspicion▶
Above Suspicion

Absolution
Accidental Meeting
Accidents
Accomplice
Accused
Ace Crawford, Private Eye
Ace Drummond
Ace of Hearts
Across the Bridge
Across the Pacific▶
Acting on Impulse
Adrift
Adventures of a Private Eye
The Adventures of Sherlock Holmes
The Adventures of Sherlock Holmes: Hound of the Baskervilles
An Affair in Mind
The Affair of the Pink Pearl
African Rage
After Dark, My Sweet▶
After Pilkington
After the Thin Man▶
Agatha
Agatha Christie's Miss Marple
Alias John Preston
All-American Murder
All the Kind Strangers
Alligator Eyes
Almost Partners
The Alphabet Murders
Alphaville▶
The Amateur
Amazing Mr. Blunden
The Amazing Mr. X
The Ambassador
The American Friend▶
American Gigolo
Amsterdamned
And Soon the Darkness
And Then There Were None▶
The Anderson Tapes▶
Android
The Andromeda Strain
Angel Heart
Animal Instincts
Animal Instincts 2
Another Thin Man
Any Man's Death
Apology
Appointment with Death
Appointment with Fear
Apprentice to Murder
Arabesque
Are You in the House Alone?
Arizona Stagecoach
The Arsenal Stadium Mystery
The Art of Crime
As Good as Dead
Assassin
The Assassination Run
Assault
At Close Range▶
The Atomic City
Autopsy
The Avenging Hand
The Baby Doll Murders
The Babysitter
Back from Eternity
Back to Hannibal: The Return of Tom Sawyer and Huckleberry Finn
Back to the Wall
Backfire
Backstab
Backstreet Justice
Backtrack▶
B.A.D. Cats
Bad Company
Bad Influence
Bad Ronald▶
The Banker
The Barcelona Kill
Basic Instinct
The Bat Whispers
Battle Shock
Bedford Incident
Bedroom Eyes
Bedroom Eyes 2
The Bedroom Window
Before Morning
Behind Locked Doors
Bell from Hell
Bellamy
Benefit of the Doubt
Berlin Express▶
Berserk!
The Best of Cracker Mysteries▶
The Best of Lovejoy Mysteries
Best Seller▶
Betrayal of the Dove
Betrayed
Beyond a Reasonable Doubt
Beyond the Bermuda Triangle
Beyond the Silhouette
Big Deadly Game
The Big Easy▶
The Big Fix▶
The Big Heat▶
The Big Hurt
Big News
The Big Sleep▶
The Big Sleep
The Big Switch
Big Town After Dark
Bikini Island
The Bird with the Crystal Plumage
Birgitt Haas Must Be Killed
Bits and Pieces
Bitter Harvest
Bitter Vengeance
The Black Abbot
Black Bird
Black Box Affair
The Black Cat
Black Cobra
Black Glove
Black Gold
The Black Hand▶
Black Hand
Black Ice
Black Limelight
Black Magic Woman
Black Panther
Black Rainbow▶
The Black Raven
Black Sunday
Black Tide
Black Tower
A Black Veil for Lisa
Black Water
Black Widow▶
The Black Windmill
Blackmail▶
Blackout
Blind Date
Blind Fear
Blind Justice
Blind Man's Bluff
Blind Side
Blind Vision
Blind Witness
Blindfold: Acts of Obsession
Blindside
Blindsided
Blink
Blonde Blackmailer
Blood Frenzy
Blood on the Sun
Blood Relations
Blood Relatives
Blood Simple▶
Bloody Avenger
Blow Out▶
Blown Away
Blue City
The Blue Dahlia▶
Blue Desert▶
Blue Ice
Blue Steel
Blue Tornado
Blue Velvet▶
Bodily Harm
Body Chemistry
Body Chemistry 3: Point of Seduction
Body Double▶
Body Heat▶
The Body in the Library
Body Language
Body of Influence
Body Parts
Body Shot
The Body Vanished
Boomerang▶
Borderline
B.O.R.N.
Born to Kill▶
The Boston Strangler
Bounty Hunters
The Bourne Identity▶
Bowery at Midnight/Dick Tracy vs. Cueball
The Boys from Brazil
Brass Target
Breakheart Pass
Breaking All the Rules
The Bride Wore Black▶
Bright Smiler
Brighton Strangler
The Brighton Strangler/Before Dawn
Broken Trust
Broken Vows
Brother Cadfael
Brotherly Love
Bulldog Drummond
Bulldog Drummond at Bay
Bulldog Drummond Comes Back
Bulldog Drummond in Africa/ Arrest Bulldog Drummond
Bulldog Drummond's Bride
Bulldog Drummond's Peril
Bulldog Drummond's Revenge
Bulldog Drummond's Revenge/ Bulldog Drummond's Peril
Bulldog Drummond's Secret Police
Bums
Burndown
Buying Time
By Dawn's Early Light
By the Blood of Others▶
Calendar Girl Murders
The Caller
Calling Paul Temple
Candles at Nine
Caper of the Golden Bulls
Cardiac Arrest
Caribe
Carnival Lady
Caroline at Midnight
A Case for Murder
Case of the Baby Sitter
The Case of the Lucky Legs
The Case of the Missing Lady
Cast a Dark Shadow▶
Cast a Deadly Spell▶
Castle in the Desert
Cat and Mouse▶
The Cat and the Canary▶
The Cat and the Canary
Cat Chaser
The Cat o' Nine Tails
Catacombs
The Catamount Killing
Catch Me a Spy
Caught in the Act
Cause for Alarm
Center of the Web
The Centerfold Girls
Chain of Desire
Challenge of McKenna
Charlie Chan and the Curse of the Dragon Queen
Charlie Chan at the Opera▶
Charlie Chan at the Wax Museum
The Charlie Chan Collection
Charlie Chan in Paris
Charlie Chan in Rio
Charlie Chan in the Secret Service
Charlie Chan's Secret
Child in the Night
Child of Glass
Chill Factor
The China Lake Murders
China Moon
Chinatown▶
The Chinese Cat
Choice of Arms
Christina
City in Panic
City Killer
City of Blood
City of Shadows
City on Fire
The Clay Pigeon
The Clergyman's Daughter
A Climate for Killing
Cloak and Dagger
The Clouded Yellow▶
Clouds Over Europe▶
Clown Murders
The Clutching Hand
The Cobra Strikes
The Cobweb
Code Name Alpha
Code Name: Diamond Head
Codename: Foxfire
Codename: Icarus
Cohen and Tate
Cold Comfort
Cold Eyes of Fear
Cold Sweat
The Colony
Color Me Dead
Color of Night
Columbo: Murder By the Book
Columbo: Prescription Murder
Coma▶
Coming Out Alive
Compromising Positions
Concealed Weapon
Concrete Beat
The Confession
Confessions of a Hit Man
Confidentially Yours▶
Consenting Adults
The Conversation▶
Convicted
The Corpse Vanishes
Cosmo Jones, Crime Smasher
Counter Punch
The Cover Girl Murders
Cover Me
Cover Story
Crack-Up
The Crackler
The Cradle Will Fall
Crime Broker
Criminal Court
Criminal Law
Criminals Within
Criss Cross▶
Cross Country
Crow Hollow
The Crucifer of Blood
The Crude Oasis
Cruise into Terror
Cruise Missile
Cruising
Cry Danger▶
A Cry in the Night
The Cry of the Owl
Cry Panic
Cry Terror
Cry Wolf
Curiosity Kills
Curse of the Yellow Snake
Cutter's Way
Cycle Psycho
Dagger Eyes
The Dain Curse
Damned River
Dance Macabre
Dance with Death
Dancing with Danger
Danger Man
Danger of Love
Danger on the Air
Danger Zone
The Dangerous
Dangerous Appointment
Dangerous Game
Dangerous Heart
Dangerous Love
Dangerous Mission
Dangerous Obsession
Dangerous Summer
Danielle Steel's Kaleidoscope
The Dark Angel▶
Dark Corner▶
Dark Forces
Dark Night of the Scarecrow
Dark of the Night
Dark Passage
Dark Side of Genius
Dark Side of Midnight
The Dark Wind
Darker than Amber
The Darkside
Daughter of Horror
The Day of the Jackal▶
Day of the Maniac
Dead Again▶
Dead Air
Dead Certain
Dead Connection
Dead Eyes of London
Dead Funny
Dead Heat on a Merry-Go-Round▶
Dead in the Water
Dead Lucky
Dead of Winter▶
Dead On
Dead on Sight
Dead on the Money
Dead Pigeon on Beethoven Street
Dead Reckoning▶
Dead Reckoning
Dead Women in Lingerie
Dead Zone▶
Deadfall
Deadline
Deadline Assault
Deadline at Dawn
Deadly Business
Deadly Currents
Deadly Dancer
Deadly Embrace
Deadly Exposure
Deadly Fieldtrip
Deadly Force
The Deadly Game
Deadly Games
Deadly Illusion
Deadly Impact
Deadly Innocence
Deadly Intent
Deadly Passion
Deadly Possession
Deadly Rivals
The Deadly Secret
Deadly Sins
Deadly Spygames
Deadly Sting
Deadly Strangers
Deadly Surveillance
Dear Dead Delilah
Dear Detective
Death at Love House
Death by Prescription
Death Cruise
Death Dreams
Death from a Distance
Death Games
Death Goes to School
The Death Kiss
Death Kiss
Death Magic
Death of a Scoundrel
Death on the Nile
Death Rage
Death Ray 2000
Death Sentence
Death Train
Death Valley
Death Warrant
Death Weekend
Deathmask
Deceived
December Flower
Deception
Deceptions
The Deep
Deep Cover
Defense of the Realm▶
Defenseless
Deja Vu
Delusion
Deranged
Descending Angel▶
Desire and Hell at Sunset Motel

Jigsaw Murders
Johnny Angel▶
Johnny Nobody
Journey into Fear▶
Journey into Fear
Joy House
Judicial Consent
Juggernaut▶
Julia and Julia
Jungle Bride
The Junkman
Just Another Pretty Face
Just Cause
Kafka
Kelly's Heroes
Kemek
The Kennel Murder Case
Kentucky Jubilee
The KGB: The Secret War
Kid
Kidnapped
The Kidnapping of the President
Kill Cruise
Killer Fish
Killer Image
A Killer in Every Corner
Killer Likes Candy
Killer Looks
Killer with Two Faces
The Killers
A Killing Affair
Killing Cars
The Killing Game
Killing Hour
The Killing Kind
The Killing Mind
Killing Obsession
Killing Stone
The Killing Time
Killjoy
Killpoint
The King Murder
A Kiss Before Dying
Kiss Daddy Goodnight
Kiss Me a Killer
Kiss Me, Kill Me
Klute▶
La Ceremonie▶
L.A. Goddess
La Passante▶
Lady Beware
The Lady Confesses
The Lady from Shanghai▶
Lady in a Cage▶
Lady in Cement
Lady in the Death House
The Lady in White▶
Lady of Burlesque
Lady Scarface
The Lady Vanishes▶
The Lady Vanishes
Ladykiller
Ladykillers
The Lady's Maid's Bell
Laguna Heat
Last Dance
Last Embrace▶
The Last of Philip Banter
The Last of Sheila
Last Reunion
Last Rites
Last Song
The Late Show▶
The Laughing Policeman
Laura▶
Le Corbeau▶
Le Magnifique
Le Secret▶
Left for Dead
Legacy of Lies
Letter to My Killer
The Liars
Liar's Edge
Lie Down with Lions
Liebestraum
Lies
Lies Before Kisses
Lifespan
The Lift
The Lightning Incident
Lights! Camera! Murder!
Lily Was Here

The Limping Man
Linda
Lipstick Camera
Lisa
Lisbon
The List of Adrian Messenger▶
The Little Drummer Girl▶
The Little Girl Who Lives Down the Lane
Little Nikita
Living to Die
The Lodger▶
Lonely Hearts
The Long Goodbye▶
Long Time Gone
Loose Cannons
The Lost Jungle
The Lost Tribe
Love and Hate: A Marriage Made in Hell
Love & Murder
Love at Large▶
Love Camp
Love from a Stranger
Love Kills
Love on the Run
Lower Level
Lure of the Islands
Lying Lips
Mackintosh Man
The Mad Executioners
Madame Sin
Madeleine
Madigan▶
Magic Moments
Malibu Express
Malice
Malicious
The Maltese Falcon▶
A Man About the House
Man Bait
Man from Headquarters
The Man from the Pru
The Man in the Mist
The Man Inside
Man on Fire
Man on the Eiffel Tower▶
Man on the Run
Man Outside
The Man Who Haunted Himself
The Man Who Knew Too Much▶
The Man Who Knew Too Much
The Man Who Would Not Die
Man with a Gun
The Manchurian Candidate▶
The Mandarin Mystery
Manfish
The Manhattan Project
Manhunter▶
Mania
Maniac
Marathon Man▶
Margin for Murder
Marie Galante▶
Mark of Cain
Mark of the Beast
Marked for Murder
Marlowe
Marnie▶
Maroc 7
Mascara
Mask of the Dragon
Masks of Death
Masquerade▶
Master Touch
A Matter of WHO
Maya
The Maze▶
Mazes and Monsters
The McGuffin
Medusa
Meeting at Midnight
Melodie en Sous-Sol
Memories of Murder
Men at Work
Messenger of Death
Miami Blues
Midnight
Midnight at the Wax Museum
Midnight Faces
Midnight Girl

Midnight Heat
Midnight Limited
Midnight Warning
Midnight Witness
Mike's Murder
Million Dollar Haul
Million Dollar Mystery
Mind, Body & Soul
A Mind to Kill
Mind Twister
Mindfield
Mirage▶
Mirage
The Mirror Crack'd
Mirror Images
Mirror Images 2
Missing Pieces
Mission: Monte Carlo
Mistaken Identity
Mr. Frost
Mr. Moto's Last Warning▶
Mr. Moto's Last Warning/ Meeting at Midnight
Mr. Reeder in Room 13
Mr. Scarface
Mr. Wong, Detective
Mr. Wong in Chinatown
Money Madness
Monique
Monsieur Hire▶
The Monster Walks
Moon in Scorpio
Moonlighting
The Morning After
Mortal Passions
The Most Dangerous Game▶
Mother's Boys
Motor Patrol
Motorcycle Squad
Mulholland Falls
Murder▶
Murder Ahoy
Murder at 45 R.P.M.
Murder at Midnight
Murder at the Baskervilles
Murder at the Gallop▶
Murder by Decree▶
Murder by Natural Causes▶
Murder by Night
Murder by Numbers
Murder by Phone
Murder by Television
Murder by the Book
Murder in Space
Murder in the Doll House
Murder in the Footlights
A Murder Is Announced
Murder Most Foul▶
Murder, My Sweet▶
Murder of a Moderate Man
Murder on Approval
Murder on the Campus
Murder on the High Seas
Murder on the Midnight Express
Murder on the Orient Express▶
Murder Once Removed
Murder 101
Murder over New York
Murder Rap
Murder She Said
Murder So Sweet
Murder Story
Murder: Ultimate Grounds for Divorce
Murdered Innocence
Murderers' Row
Murderlust
Murderous Vision
Murders at Lynch Cross
Murders in the Rue Morgue
The Murders in the Rue Morgue▶
Mute Witness
My Man Adam
My Sister, My Love
My Sweet Victim
Mysterious Doctor Satan
The Mysterious Magician
Mysterious Mr. Wong
Mystery at Castle House
Mystery at Fire Island
Mystery in Swing

Mystery Liner
The Mystery Man
Mystery Mansion
The Mystery of Edwin Drood
Mystery of Mr. Wong
The Mystery of Rampo▶
The Mystery of the Mary Celeste
Mystery of the Riverboat
Mystery Plane
Mystic Circle Murder
The Naked Edge
The Naked Face
Naked Obsession
The Name of the Rose
Nancy Drew, Reporter
The Narrow Margin▶
Narrow Margin
Natural Causes
Nature's Playmates
The Neighbor
Neutron vs. the Maniac
Never Say Die
New Year's Evil
New York Ripper
Newman's Law
The Next Victim
Next Victim
Niagara
Night and the City▶
Night Angel
Night Birds
Night Cries
Night Eyes
Night Eyes 2
Night Eyes 3
Night Fire
A Night for Crime
The Night Has Eyes
Night Moves▶
Night of Terror
Night of the Assassin
Night of the Cyclone
The Night of the Hunter▶
Night of the Juggler
Night Rhythms
Night School
Night Shadow
Night Stalker
Night Terror
A Night to Remember▶
Night Train to Munich▶
The Night Visitor
Night Watch
The Nightcomers
Nighthawks
Nightkill
The Nightman
Nightmare in Badham County
Nightwing
No Comebacks
No Mercy
No Place to Hide
No Problem
No Secrets
No Way Out▶
No Way to Treat a Lady▶
Nocturne
Non-Stop New York
Norman Conquest
North by Northwest▶
Nothing Underneath
Notorious▶
Nowhere to Hide
Nuclear Conspiracy
No. 17▶
The Oblong Box
The Obsessed
Obsession
Obsession: A Taste for Fear
Obsessive Love
The Occult Experience
Octagon
The October Man▶
The Odessa File
On Dangerous Ground▶
On the Edge
One Frightened Night
One Night Stand
One of My Wives Is Missing
One Shoe Makes It Murder
Open House
Open Secret

Operation Amsterdam
Ordeal by Innocence
Orion's Belt
The Osterman Weekend
Out of Annie's Past
Out of Bounds
Out of Order
Out of Sight, Out of Her Mind
Out of the Darkness▶
Out of the Past▶
Out on Bail
The Outside Man
Outside the Law
The Oval Portrait
Over Indulgence
Overexposed
Paid to Kill
Paint It Black
Painted Hero
The Pamela Principle
Panic in the Streets▶
Panic on the 5:22
Panique▶
The Panther's Claw
Paperhouse▶
The Parallax View▶
Paranoia
Paris Belongs to Us
Paris Express
Parker
Party Girls for Sale
Party Line
Passion Flower
Passion in Paradise
Past Midnight
Past Tense
Payback
The Payoff
The Pearl of Death
The Pelican Brief
Pendulum
Penthouse▶
The Perfect Bride
Perfect Crime
Perfect Family
A Perfect Spy
Perfect Strangers
Perfect Victims
Peril
Perry Mason Returns▶
Perry Mason: The Case of the Lost Love
Personals
Peter Gunn
The Phantom Broadcast
The Phantom Creeps
Phantom Express
Phantom Fiend
Phantom Killer
The Phantom Light
Phantom of Chinatown
The Phantom of 42nd Street
The Phantom of Soho
Phobia
Phoenix Team
The Phone Call
Photographer
Physical Evidence
Picnic at Hanging Rock▶
Picture Mommy Dead
Pier 23
Plain Clothes
Play Misty for Me▶
Play Nice
Plumber
A Pocketful of Rye
Point Blank
Poor Girl, A Ghost Story
Portraits of a Killer
Posed For Murder
Positive I.D.
Postmark for Danger/Quicksand
Power of Attorney
Power Play
The Practice of Love
Praying Mantis
President's Mistress
The President's Mystery
The Presidio
Presumed Innocent▶
Prey of the Chameleon
Primal Secrets

Union Station
Unsane
Unsuitable Job for a Woman
Unveiled
Up in the Air
Urge to Kill
The Usual Suspects▶
Utz
The Vagrant
Vamping
The Vanishing▶
The Vanishing
Vanishing Act
Vatican Conspiracy
Vegas
Velvet Touch▶
Vertigo▶
The Very Edge
Vicious
The Vicious Circle
Victim of Beauty
Victim of Desire
Victim of Love
Video Murders
Violette▶
The Vision
Visions
Visiting Hours
Voulez-Vous Danser Avec Moi?
A Vow to Kill
Vultures
W
Waikiki
Wanted: Babysitter
Warm Nights on a Slow-Moving Train
Warning Sign
Watched
The Way Out
Wayne Murder Case▶
Weep No More My Lady
Whatever Happened to Aunt Alice?▶
When a Stranger Calls
When a Stranger Calls Back
When Angels Fly
When the Bough Breaks
Where Are the Children?
Where Sleeping Dogs Lie
A Whisper to a Scream
Whispering City▶
Whispering Shadow
Whispers in the Dark
The Whistle Blower▶
White Fire
White Hot: The Mysterious Murder of Thelma Todd
White Mischief▶
White of the Eye▶
White Sands
Who Is the Black Dahlia?▶
Who Killed Baby Azaria?
Who Killed Mary What's 'Er Name?
Whodunit
Widow Couderc▶
Widow's Kiss
Widow's Nest
Wild Cactus
Wild West
Wildcard
The Wind
The Window▶
Witch Hunt
Witchfire
Without Warning
Witness for the Prosecution▶
Woman Condemned
Woman Hunt
The Woman Hunter
Woman in Black
The Woman in Green
Woman of Desire
Woman Undone
The Woman Who Came Back
A Woman's Face▶
Wonderland▶
The Word
Writer's Block
The Wrong Man▶
The Wrong Man
The Wrong Woman
Yellowstone
Young and Innocent▶
The Young Detectives on Wheels
Young Sherlock Holmes
Z▶
Zentropa
Zero Boys
Zertigo Diamond Caper
The Zodiac Killer

Nashville

see also American South; Nashville Narratives

The Concrete Cowboys
Honkytonk Man
Nashville▶
Nashville Beat
Nashville Girl
The Night the Lights Went Out in Georgia
Sweet Country Road
The Thing Called Love

Nashville Narratives

see also American South; Musician Biopics; Southern Belles

Baja Oklahoma
Cassie
The City
Coal Miner's Daughter▶
Falling from Grace
Hard Part Begins
Honeysuckle Rose
Honkytonk Man
Honkytonk Nights
Lady Grey
Living Proof: The Hank Williams Jr. Story
Nashville▶
Nashville Girl
The Night the Lights Went Out in Georgia
Paradise Park
Payday
Pure Country
Rhinestone
Rikky and Pete
Road to Nashville
Saturday Night Special
A Smoky Mountain Christmas
Songwriter
Sweet Dreams
Tender Mercies▶
The Thing Called Love
Wild West

Native America

The Abduction of Allison Tate
Across the Wide Missouri
Angry Joe Bass
Apache Blood
Apache Chief
Apache Woman
Bad Lands
The Bears & I
Billy Jack
Black Fox: The Price of Peace
Black Robe▶
Blood Horse
Born Losers
Braveheart
Broken Arrow
The Broken Chain
Buffalo Bill Rides Again
Bugles in the Afternoon
Captain Apache
The Captive: The Longest Drive 2
Cavalier of the West
Cavalry Charge
Chato's Land
Cheyenne Autumn
Cheyenne Warrior
Chuka
Circle of Death
Clearcut
The Comancheros▶
Conquest of Cochise
Cotter
Crazy Horse and Custer: "The Untold Story"
Crypt of Dark Secrets
Custer's Last Fight
Dakota Incident
Dalva
Dan Candy's Law
Dance Me Outside
Dances with Wolves▶
The Dark Wind
Dead Man
Diplomaniacs
Escape from Fort Bravo
Eyes of Fire
Fish Hawk
Flaming Star▶
Fleshburn
Follow the River
The Gatling Gun
Geronimo
Geronimo▶
Geronimo: An American Legend
Ghost Dance
The Glory Trail
A Good Day to Die
Hawkeye: Premiere Episode
Hondo▶
I Heard the Owl Call My Name
I Will Fight No More Forever▶
Incident at Oglala: The Leonard Peltier Story▶
The Indian Fighter▶
The Indian in the Cupboard
Island of the Blue Dolphins
Jim Thorpe: All American
Joe Panther▶
Johnny Firecloud
Johnny Tiger
Journey Through Rosebud
Journey to Spirit Island
Lakota Woman: Siege at Wounded Knee
The Last of His Tribe
The Last of the Dogmen
The Last of the Mohicans▶
The Last of the Mohicans
The Last of the Mohicans▶
The Last of the Redmen
Legend of Walks Far Woman
The Legend of Wolf Mountain
The Light in the Forest
Little Big Man▶
Lost Legacy: A Girl Called Hatter Fox
A Man Called Horse▶
Man of the House
The Manitou
Map of the Human Heart
Mission to Glory
A Mormon Maid
Naked in the Sun
Natas...The Reflection
Northern Passage
On Top of the Whale
Pocahontas▶
Pocahontas: The Legend
Poltergeist 2: The Other Side
Powwow Highway▶
The Prophecy
The Red Fury
The Red Half-Breed
Renegades
Requiem for a Heavyweight▶
Roanoak
Running Brave
Savage Sam
The Savage Seven
Savage Wilderness
The Secret of Navajo Cave
Shadow of the Wolf
Shadowhunter
Silent Tongue
Sioux City
The Slayer/The Scalps
Smith!
Spirit Rider▶
Squanto: A Warrior's Tale▶
Tecumseh: The Last Warrior
Tell Them Willie Boy Is Here▶
Terror in the Jungle
Texas John Slaughter: Geronimo's Revenge
3 Ninjas Knuckle Up
Three Warriors
Thunder Warrior
Thunder Warrior 2
Thunderheart▶
Tonka
Track of the Moonbeast
Unconquered
Uninvited
The Villain
Wagon Wheels
War Party
Where the Spirit Lives
White Fang 2: The Myth of the White Wolf
Windrunner
Windwalker▶

Nazis & Other Paramilitary Slugs

see also Germany; The Holocaust; Judaism; World War II

All Through the Night▶
Angel of Death
Angel with the Trumpet
Angry Harvest▶
Any Man's Death
Ark of the Sun God
The Assisi Underground
Background to Danger▶
Bedknobs and Broomsticks
The Berlin Affair
Berlin Express▶
Betrayed▶
The Black Klansman
The Boxer and Death▶
The Boys from Brazil
Brady's Escape
Cabaret▶
Cabo Blanco
Casablanca▶
Casablanca Express
Charlie Grant's War
Clipped Wings
Closet Land
Cold Days
Commandos Strike at Dawn
The Conformist▶
Cottage to Let
Counterblast
The Counterfeit Traitor▶
The Cut Throats
Dam Busters▶
Dawn Express
A Day in October
Dead Bang
Death is Called Engelchen▶
The Death of Adolf Hitler
Descending Angel▶
Desert Commandos
The Desert Fox▶
Despair▶
The Devil's Brigade
The Diary of Anne Frank▶
The Dirty Dozen▶
The Dirty Dozen: The Deadly Mission
The Dirty Dozen: The Fatal Mission
The Dirty Dozen: The Next Mission
Dirty Heroes
Edge of Darkness▶
Elves
Enemy of Women
Enigma Secret
Equalizer 2000
Escape from Sobibor▶
Europa, Europa▶
The Execution
Eye of the Needle
The Fallen Sparrow▶
Father
Fatherland
Firewalker
Five Fingers▶
Flesh Feast
Forbidden
Force 10 from Navarone
Foreign Correspondent▶
The Forty-Ninth Parallel▶
Four Bags Full
The Four Horsemen of the Apocalypse
A Friendship in Vienna
Genghis Cohn
Getting Away With Murder
Ghost on the Loose
Goldengirl
Good Evening, Mr. Wallenberg
The Great Dictator▶
The Great Escape▶
Hanna's War
Hanussen▶
He Lives: The Search for the Evil One
Hell Commandos
Hell Hunters
Hell River
Hell Squad
Heroes in Hell
The Hiding Place
Higher Learning
Hitler
Hitler: Dead or Alive
Hitler's Children▶
Hitler's Daughter
Holocaust▶
Hornet's Nest
Hotel Reserve▶
The House on Carroll Street
The House on Garibaldi Street
House on 92nd Street▶
Ilsa, Harem Keeper of the Oil Sheiks
Ilsa, She-Wolf of the SS
In a Glass Cage
The Incredible Mr. Limpet
Indiana Jones and the Last Crusade▶
Indiana Jones and the Temple of Doom▶
The Infiltrator
Inside Out
Inside the Third Reich
Into the Homeland
Invisible Agent
Jenny's War
Judgment at Nuremberg▶
Julia▶
Jungle Siren
Kanal▶
Kapo▶
The Keep
The Key to Rebecca
The Klansman
Kojak: The Belarus File
Korczak▶
La Passante▶
Lassiter
The Last Butterfly
The Last Five Days
The Last Metro▶
The Last Train
Law of the Jungle
Les Miserables
Les Violons du Bal
Lifeboat▶
The Long Island Four
The Longest Day▶
The Lucifer Complex
Madame Rosa▶
A Man Escaped▶
The Man in the Glass Booth▶
Marathon Man▶
Martha and I▶
Massacre in Rome
Master Key
Master Race
Me and the Colonel
The Mediterranean in Flames
Mein Kampf: Hitler's Rise and Fall
Mephisto▶
Miracle at Moreaux
Mission Corbari
Mr. Klein▶
The Mortal Storm▶
Music Box
The Nasty Girl▶
Night Ambush
A Night in Casablanca▶

Night of the Fox
Night of the Generals▶
The Night Porter
Night Train to Munich▶
Night Train to Venice
No Dead Heroes
The North Star▶
Northern Pursuit
Notorious▶
Oasis of the Zombies
The Odessa File
Old Gun▶
Once Upon a Honeymoon
One of Our Aircraft Is Missing▶
The Only Way
Open City▶
Operation Amsterdam
Operation Crossbow▶
Passage to Marseilles▶
The Pedestrian▶
Pimpernel Smith
A Prayer for Katarina Horovitzova▶
Prayer of the Rollerboys
Pressure Point▶
Puppet Master 3: Toulon's Revenge
The Quiller Memorandum▶
Raid on Rommel
Raiders of the Lost Ark▶
Reunion in France
The Revolt of Job▶
Richard III▶
Rio Rita
River of Death
River of Diamonds
The Rocketeer▶
The Rose Garden
The Salzburg Connection
Savage Attraction
The Scarlet & the Black
Schindler's List▶
Scream and Scream Again
Sea of Sand
The Secret Code
Secret Mission
The Secret War of Harry Frigg
Seven Miles from Alcatraz/Flight from Glory
The Seventh Cross▶
Severed Ties
She Demons
Shining Through
Shock Waves
Silent Scream
633 Squadron
Skinheads: The Second Coming of Hate
Snow Treasure
So Ends Our Night▶
Soldier of Orange▶
A Soldier's Tale
Son of Lassie
The Sorrow and the Pity▶
The Sound of Music▶
S.S. Experiment Camp 2
S.S. Love Camp No. 27
Stalag 17▶
Stalag Luft
The Stranger▶
Strangers in Paradise
Sundown
Surf Nazis Must Die
Sweet Light in a Dark Room▶
Swing Kids
A Taxing Woman's Return▶
That Summer of White Roses
They Saved Hitler's Brain
13 Rue Madeleine▶
'38: Vienna Before the Fall
This Land is Mine▶
Tiger Fangs
Tigershark
To Be or Not to Be▶
To Be or Not to Be
To Catch a King
Top Dog
Top Secret!▶
The Tormentors
Transport from Paradise
Triumph of the Spirit▶
Triumph of the Will
True Colors
U-Boat Prisoner
Uranus▶
War & Love
War & Remembrance, Part 1
War & Remembrance, Part 2
War & Remembrance: The Final Chapter, Part 8
War & Remembrance: The Final Chapter, Part 9
Watch on the Rhine▶
Waterfront
Where Eagles Dare▶
Where Trails End
Wild Geese 2
The Winds of War
Wings Over the Pacific
Wizards
A Woman at War
Wooden Horse▶
Yank in Libya
The Yesterday Machine
Zentropa
Zombie Lake
Zone Troopers

Negative Utopia

***see also** Post Apocalypse; Technology-Rampant*

Alphaville▶
Animal Farm▶
Brazil▶
El Norte▶
Futureworld
Metropolis▶
Moonraker
The Mosquito Coast
984: Prisoner of the Future
1984▶
The Prisoner: Arrival
Rollerball
Soylent Green
10th Victim▶
THX 1138▶
Whodunit
Zardoz

New Black Cinema

***see also** African America; Blaxploitation*

Boyz N the Hood▶
Clockers▶
Crooklyn▶
Do the Right Thing▶
The Five Heartbeats▶
Girl 6
Hangin' with the Homeboys▶
Hollywood Shuffle
I'm Gonna Git You Sucka▶
Joe's Bed-Stuy Barbershop: We Cut Heads
Jungle Fever▶
Just Another Girl on the I.R.T.
Livin' Large
Menace II Society▶
The Meteor Man
Mo' Better Blues
Poetic Justice
Posse▶
A Rage in Harlem▶
School Daze▶
She's Gotta Have It▶
Straight Out of Brooklyn
Sweet Sweetback's Baadasssss Song▶
To Sleep with Anger▶

New Orleans

***see also** American South*

Angel Heart
Band of Angels
The Big Easy▶
Birth of the Blues
Boxcar Blues
Candyman 2: Farewell to the Flesh
Child of Glass
Cry of the Werewolf
The Cure
The Dangerous
The Dark Side of Love
Dead Man Walking▶
Dixie: Changing Habits▶
Easy Rider▶
End of August
False Witness
The Family
French Quarter
French Quarter Undercover
French Silk
Heaven's Prisoners
Hotel
Interview with the Vampire
The Invisible Avenger
It Happened in New Orleans
J.D.'s Revenge
King Creole
Mardi Gras for the Devil
Mardi Gras Massacre
Mirrors
My Forbidden Past
New Orleans After Dark
Night of the Strangler
Panic in the Streets▶
Pretty Baby▶
Saratoga Trunk
The Savage Bees
Storyville
A Streetcar Named Desire▶
Suddenly, Last Summer▶
Thunderground
Tightrope▶
Toys in the Attic
Tune in Tomorrow
Undercover Blues
The Unholy
Walk on the Wild Side

New Year's Eve

***see also** Christmas; Holidays; Horrible Holidays*

About Last Night...▶
Bloody New Year
Doctor Who
The Enforcer
Happy New Year▶
A Happy New Year!
Happy New Year
The Hudsucker Proxy▶
The January Man
New Year's Day▶
New Year's Evil
The Poseidon Adventure
Strange Days▶
Waiting to Exhale▶
When Harry Met Sally...▶

New York, New York

***see also** The Empire State Building*

Across 110th Street
The Addiction
An Affair to Remember
After Hours▶
Alice▶
All About Eve▶
All That Jazz▶
All the Vermeers in New York▶
Alphabet City
Angelo My Love▶
Angels with Dirty Faces▶
Annie
Annie Hall▶
Another Woman▶
The Apartment▶
Arthur▶
Arthur 2: On the Rocks
Awakenings▶
Bad Lieutenant▶
Barefoot in the Park▶
The Basketball Diaries
Bed of Roses
Big▶
The Big Bus
Big Business
Big Night
Big Street
Blackboard Jungle▶
Blade
Blink
Blue In the Face
Blue Skies▶
The Bonfire of the Vanities
Born to Win
The Bostonians
Breakfast at Tiffany's▶
Bright Lights, Big City
Brighton Beach Memoirs
Broadway Bound
Broadway Danny Rose▶
The Broadway Drifter
Broadway Limited
Broadway Melody
Broadway Melody of 1936▶
Broadway Melody of 1938
Broadway Melody of 1940
Broadway Rhythm
Broadway Serenade
The Bronx Executioner
A Bronx Tale▶
The Bronx War
The Brother from Another Planet▶
Bullets Over Broadway▶
Carlito's Way▶
Carnal Knowledge▶
Cat People
A Chorus Line
City Hall▶
City Slickers▶
Clockers▶
Cocktail
The Cocoanuts
Coming to America▶
Compromising Positions
Coogan's Bluff▶
The Cotton Club▶
The Cowboy Way
Crimes & Misdemeanors▶
Crocodile Dundee▶
Crocodile Dundee 2
Crooklyn▶
Crossing Delancey▶
The Crowd▶
Cruising
Dead Funny
Dead Presidents
Desperate Characters▶
Desperately Seeking Susan
Detective Story▶
Die Hard: With a Vengeance
Do the Right Thing▶
Dog Day Afternoon▶
The Dream Team
Dressed to Kill
Escape from New York
Eyes of Laura Mars
Eyewitness
F/X▶
Falling in Love
Fame▶
Fatal Attraction▶
Fear, Anxiety and Depression
Fingers▶
First Love
The Fisher King▶
Fleshpot on 42nd Street
Flirt
For Love or Money
The Foreigner
Fort Apache, the Bronx▶
42nd Street▶
Frankie and Johnny▶
The French Connection▶
The Freshman
Funny Girl▶
Ghost▶
Ghostbusters▶
Ghostbusters 2
The Godfather▶
The Godfather, Part 2▶
The Godfather, Part 3▶
The Goodbye Girl▶
Goodbye, New York
Goodfellas▶
The Great Gatsby
Green Card
Greetings▶
The Guardian
Guys and Dolls▶
Hair▶
Hangin' with the Homeboys▶
Hannah and Her Sisters▶
Harlem Nights
Harry and Tonto▶
Headless Body in Topless Bar
Heartburn▶
Heartstrings
Heaven Help Us
Hello Again
Hester Street▶
Hi, Mom!▶
Highlander▶
His Butler's Sister
His Girl Friday▶
Home Alone 2: Lost in New York
The Hunger
Husbands and Wives▶
It Could Happen to You
It Happened in Brooklyn
It Should Happen to You▶
It's My Turn
The January Man
Jeffrey
Joe
Joe's Apartment
Joe's Bed-Stuy Barbershop: We Cut Heads
Johnny Suede
Juice
Jungle Fever▶
Key Exchange
Kids
King Kong▶
King of Comedy▶
King of New York▶
King of the Gypsies
Kramer vs. Kramer▶
Lady On a Train▶
Last Exit to Brooklyn▶
The Last Seduction▶
Laws of Gravity▶
Legal Eagles
A Life of Her Own
Light Sleeper
Liquid Sky▶
Little Miss Marker▶
Living in Oblivion▶
Lonely in America
The Long Island Four
Look Who's Talking, Too
The Lords of Flatbush
Lost in Yonkers
Love Affair
Love at First Bite
Love Is Better Than Ever
Love Story▶
Lullaby of Broadway
Ma and Pa Kettle Go to Town
Mad Dog and Glory▶
Malcolm X▶
The Manchurian Candidate▶
Manhattan▶
Manhattan Melodrama▶
Manhattan Merry-Go-Round
Manhattan Murder Mystery▶
Marathon Man▶
Marty▶
Mean Streets▶
Metropolitan▶
Midnight Cowboy▶
Mighty Aphrodite
Miracle on 34th Street▶
Miracle on 34th Street
Mirrors
Misery▶
Mr. Blandings Builds His Dream House▶
Mo' Better Blues
Money Train
Morning Glory
Mortal Thoughts
Moscow on the Hudson▶
The Muppets Take Manhattan▶
My Favorite Year▶
My Man Godfrey▶
My Sister Eileen▶
Nadja▶
The Naked City▶
Naked in New York
The Natural▶
Network▶
New Jack City
New York Cop

New York, New York▶
New York Nights
New York Ripper
New York Stories▶
New York's Finest
News from Home
Next Stop, Greenwich Village▶
Night and the City▶
Night on Earth▶
The Night They Raided Minsky's▶
The Night We Never Met
9 1/2 Weeks
1931: Once Upon a Time in New York
The Odd Couple▶
Off Beat
Oliver & Company
On the Town▶
On the Waterfront▶
Once Upon a Time in America▶
Only When I Laugh▶
The Out-of-Towners▶
Outrageous!▶
Panic in Needle Park▶
The Paper▶
Paradise Alley
Paradise in Harlem
Paris is Burning▶
The Park is Mine
Party Girl
Permanent Vacation
The Phantom
The Pick-Up Artist
Pillow Talk▶
Plaza Suite▶
Portrait of Jennie▶
Postcards from America
The Prince of Central Park▶
Prince of the City▶
The Prince of Tides▶
Prisoner of Second Avenue
The Public Eye▶
The Quest
Quick Change
Radio Days▶
A Rage in Harlem▶
Raging Bull▶
Ragtime▶
A Raisin in the Sun▶
The Rat Race▶
Ready to Wear
Rear Window▶
Risk▶
The Roaring Twenties▶
Rosemary's Baby▶
Rumble in the Bronx
Saturday Night Fever
Scent of a Woman▶
Searching for Bobby Fischer▶
Serpico▶
Seven▶
The Seven-Ups
The Seven Year Itch▶
Shadows and Fog
She-Devil
She's Gotta Have It▶
Shining Star
Single White Female
Six Degrees of Separation
Slaves of New York
Sliver
Smithereens
Something Short of Paradise
Something Wild
Sophie's Choice▶
Speedy▶
Splash
Stage Door▶
State of Grace▶
Staying Alive
Stepping Out▶
Still of the Night
Straight Out of Brooklyn
Stranger than Paradise▶
Street Scene▶
Street Smart
Street Trash
Sugar Hill
The Super
Superfly
Sweet Charity▶
Sweet Smell of Success▶
The Taking of Pelham One Two Three▶
Talk to Me
Tarzan's New York Adventure
Taxi Driver▶
They Call It Sin
Three Days of the Condor▶
Three Men and a Baby▶
Through the Eyes of a Killer
Times Square
Tootsie▶
Torch Song Trilogy
Trash
A Tree Grows in Brooklyn▶
A Troll in Central Park
29th Street
Underground U.S.A.
An Unmarried Woman▶
Untamed Heart
Unzipped▶
Uptown New York
Vampire in Brooklyn
A Very Natural Thing
Wall Street▶
Walls of Glass
The Way We Were▶
The Wedding Party
We're Back! A Dinosaur's Story
West Side Story▶
When Harry Met Sally...▶
Where Were You When the Lights Went Out?
Who's That Knocking at My Door?▶
Wild Style
Wise Guys
Wolf
Wolfen▶
Working Girl▶
Year of the Dragon

New Zealand

see Down Under

Newspapers

see Front Page

Nifty '50s

Absolute Beginners
The Affairs of Dobie Gillis
Alex
As Summers Die
Back to the Future▶
Back to the Future, Part 2
Badlands▶
Big Night
Book of Love
Born Reckless
The Buddy Holly Story▶
Bye, Bye, Birdie▶
Celia: Child Of Terror
Child Bride of Short Creek
Circle of Friends
Corrina, Corrina
Crazy Mama
Cry-Baby▶
Dance with a Stranger▶
Dead Poets Society▶
Desire and Hell at Sunset Motel
Dirty Dancing▶
Elvis: The Movie
Father of the Bride▶
Fellow Traveler▶
For the Boys
The Front▶
Girls' Town
Grease▶
Grease 2
Ground Zero▶
Guilty by Suspicion
The Heart of Dixie
Hometown U.S.A.
Housekeeping▶
The Hudsucker Proxy▶
I.Q.
A King in New York
The Kitchen Toto▶
La Bamba▶
Last Exit to Brooklyn▶
The Last Picture Show▶
The Long Day Closes▶
Long Gone
The Long Walk Home▶
The Lords of Flatbush
Lost, Lonely, and Vicious
Loveless
Mac▶
The Man in the Moon▶
Matinee
Mischief
Mrs. 'Arris Goes to Paris
Moscow Does Not Believe in Tears▶
Mulholland Falls
My Favorite Year▶
My Michael▶
Newsfront▶
Nightbreaker▶
Oh, What a Night
One Plus One
Ordeal by Innocence
Our Time
Parents▶
Peggy Sue Got Married
Perfect Harmony
Pillow Talk▶
The Playboys▶
Porky's
Quiz Show▶
A Rage in Harlem▶
A Raisin in the Sun▶
Red Hot
The Reflecting Skin
Rock All Night
Rock, Baby, Rock It
Round Midnight▶
School Ties▶
Shag: The Movie▶
Shake, Rattle and Rock
Shout
Sparkle
Stacking
Strange Invaders▶
The Summer House
Superdad
Suzanne
That'll Be the Day
This Boy's Life▶
Three Wishes
Trading Hearts
Visitants
The War of the Worlds▶
The Way We Were▶
When Father was Away on Business▶
Who Shot Pat?
The Wild One▶
The Wooden Gun
You've Ruined Me, Eddie

Nightclubs

Amateur Night
Animal Instincts
Backbeat▶
Bar Girls
Before Sunrise
Berlin Blues
Birth of the Blues
Black Glove
The Blue Angel▶
The Bride Wore Red
Bucktown
A Bunny's Tale
Bus Stop▶
Cabaret▶
Can-Can
Carnival Rock
Casablanca▶
CB4: The Movie
Club Havana
Cocktail
Copacabana
The Cotton Club▶
Dance, Girl, Dance
Dance Hall Racket
Dark Secrets
Deadly Revenge
Death in Brunswick
Desperate Cargo
Dick Tracy▶
Dracula Blows His Cool
The Fabulous Baker Boys▶
Fake Out
Femmes de Paris
Flaming Lead
Foxstyle
Framed
French Can-Can▶
The French Way
Fun in Acapulco
G.I. Blues
Girls! Girls! Girls!
Harlem Nights
It Started in Naples▶
Jive Junction
The Killing of a Chinese Bookie
King Creole
La Cage aux Folles▶
La Cage aux Folles 2
La Cage aux Folles 3: The Wedding
Lady On a Train▶
Lambada
Last Night at the Alamo▶
Lenny▶
Lenny Bruce Performance Film
Liquid Dreams
Lullaby of Broadway
Mad Dog and Glory▶
The Mambo Kings▶
Marked Woman▶
Martial Law 2: Undercover
Mickey One
Midnight Warrior
Mighty Joe Young
Morocco▶
Night After Night
A Night in Heaven
The Night They Raided Minsky's▶
No Surrender▶
Not Quite Love
The Nutty Professor▶
Pandora and the Flying Dutchman
Party Girl
Pete Kelly's Blues
Play Murder for Me
The Public Eye▶
Rebel
Ruby
Ruby's Dream
Sea Racketeers
Sex, Drugs, and Rock-n-Roll
Shanghai Triad▶
The Shining Hour
Showgirls
Smash-Up: The Story of a Woman▶
Suffering Bastards
That Naughty Girl
30 Is a Dangerous Age, Cynthia
To Catch a King
Treasure of the Moon Goddess
Underground U.S.A.
Uptown Saturday Night
Whistle Stop
A Woman is a Woman▶
Wonderland▶
Xanadu
The Zoo Gang

Ninjitsu

see Martial Arts

No-Exit Motel

see also Grand Hotel

Cheap Shots
Eaten Alive
Motel Hell
Mountaintop Motel Massacre
The Newlydeads
Pink Motel
Poor Pretty Eddie
Psycho▶
Psycho 2
Psycho 3
Psycho 4: The Beginning
Slaughter Hotel

Not-So-True Identity

Black Like Me
The Cotton Club▶
Europa, Europa▶
Gentleman's Agreement▶
Imitation of Life▶
Lost Boundaries
Mrs. Winterbourne
Pinky▶
Shadows▶
Soul Man
True Identity

Nuclear Disaster

see Disaster Flicks; Meltdown

Nuns & Priests

see also Missionaries; Religion; Religious Epics

Absolution
Agnes of God
The Agony and the Ecstasy
Amateur▶
Angels with Dirty Faces▶
Anna
The Assisi Underground
The Atonement of Gosta Berling▶
Becket▶
The Bells of St. Mary's▶
Black Narcissus▶
Black Robe▶
The Boys of St. Vincent▶
Brides of Christ
The Bridge of San Luis Rey▶
Camila▶
The Cardinal
Catholic Hour
Change of Habit
Child of Darkness, Child of Light
Cold Justice
Come to the Stable▶
The Confession
The Confessional
Conspiracy of Hearts▶
The Cross & the Switchblade
Cry, the Beloved Country▶
Curse 4: The Ultimate Sacrifice
Daens
Damien: The Leper Priest
Dead Man Walking▶
Death of an Angel
The Detective▶
The Devils▶
The Devil's Playground▶
Diary of a Country Priest▶
The Divine Enforcer
Dixie: Changing Habits▶
Elmer Gantry▶
End of the World
The Exorcist▶
The Exorcist 2: The Heretic
Extramuros
The Father Clements Story
Fighting Father Dunne
First Legion
For Better and For Worse
Forever Young
The Fugitive▶
Gentleman Bandit
Going My Way▶
Goodnight God Bless
Gospa
A Home of Our Own
Hot Under the Collar
I Confess
I Heard the Owl Call My Name
I, the Worst of All
In the Region of Ice▶
In This House of Brede▶
Jesus of Montreal▶
Judgment▶
Last Rites
The Left Hand of God▶
Leon Morin, Priest
Lilies of the Field▶
Loyola, the Soldier Saint
Mass Appeal
Massacre in Rome
Mission to Glory
Monsignor
Mortal Sins
Most Wanted

Mother Joan of the Angels▶
The Name of the Rose
Nasty Habits
Nazarin▶
Night of the Assassin
Night of the Demons 2
The Nun
Nuns on the Run
The Nun's Story▶
Pier 23
Pope John Paul II
The Pope Must Diet
The Possessed
Prayer for the Dying
Priest
The Prisoner▶
The Red Inn
The Rosary Murders
The Runner Stumbles
Saving Grace
The Scarlet & the Black
Second Sight
Secret Ingredient
September Gun
Shattered Vows
The Shoes of the Fisherman
The Singing Nun
Sister Act
Sister Act 2: Back in the Habit
Sisters of Satan
Sorceress▶
The Sound of Music▶
Spirits
Therese▶
To Kill a Priest
Trouble Along the Way
The Trouble with Angels
True Confessions▶
Under Satan's Sun▶
Under the Red Robe
The Unholy
Vatican Conspiracy
We're No Angels
Where Angels Go, Trouble Follows
The White Sister▶

Nuns With Guns

Girlfriend from Hell
Ms. 45▶
Nuns on the Run
Two Mules for Sister Sara▶
We're No Angels

Nursploitation!

see also Doctors & Nurses; Sexploitation

Candy Stripe Nurses
Emmanuelle in the Country
Hospital of Terror
Inner Sanctum
Naked Massacre
Night Call Nurses
Nurse on Call
Private Duty Nurses
The Sensuous Nurse
The Student Nurses
Tender Loving Care
The Young Nurses
Young Nurses in Love

Obsessive Love

Aaron Loves Angela
Against All Odds
Anna Karenina▶
Anna Karenina
Betty Blue▶
Brief Encounter▶
Can't Buy Me Love
Chungking Express▶
Crazy Moon
The Crush
Cyrano de Bergerac▶
Cyrano de Bergerac
Cyrano de Bergerac▶
Endless Love
Fatal Attraction▶
Fear
Ghost▶
The Heartbreak Kid▶
Mad Love
Mr. Wrong
The Phantom of the Opera▶
The Phantom of the Opera
A Place in the Sun▶
Romeo and Juliet▶
Romeo and Juliet
Romeo and Juliet▶
Roxanne▶
Sabrina▶
Sabrina
Show Boat▶
Show Boat
Some Kind of Wonderful
10
A Thin Line Between Love and Hate
Truly, Madly, Deeply▶
West Side Story▶
Wuthering Heights▶
Wuthering Heights

Occult

see also Demons & Wizards; Satanism; Witchcraft

Afterward
Alabama's Ghost
The Amazing Mr. X
The American Scream
Apprentice to Murder
Army of Darkness▶
Bad Dreams
Barbarian Queen
Because of the Cats
The Believers
Beyond Dream's Door
Beyond Evil
Beyond the Door 3
The Black Cat
Black Magic Terror
Black Magic Woman
Blackbeard's Ghost
Blood Diner
The Blood on Satan's Claw▶
Blood Orgy of the She-Devils
Bloodspell
Born of Fire
The Brainiac
Brimstone & Treacle▶
The Brotherhood of Satan
The Burning Court
Cabin in the Sky▶
Cat Girl
Cat in the Cage
The Cellar
Chandu on the Magic Island
Child of Glass
Children Shouldn't Play with Dead Things
Come Along with Me
The Craft
Craze
The Curse of the Crying Woman
Curse of the Demon▶
Curse of the Devil
Damien: Omen 2
Damn Yankees▶
The Dark Secret of Harvest Home
Dead Men Don't Die
Deathstalker 4: Match of Titans
Deep Red: Hatchet Murders
Demon Possessed
Demon Rage
Demon Wind
Demonoid, Messenger of Death
Demons 2
Demons of Ludlow
The Devil
The Devil & Daniel Webster▶
Devil Dog: The Hound of Hell
Devil Doll▶
Devil Doll
Devil Kiss
The Devils▶
The Devil's Daughter
The Devil's Eye
Devil's Gift
The Devil's Hand
The Devil's Mistress
The Devil's Nightmare
Devil's Rain
Devil's Son-in-Law
Diary of a Madman
Dick Tracy, Detective
Doctor Faustus
Dr. Strange
Dominique is Dead
Dona Flor and Her Two Husbands▶
Donovan's Brain▶
Don't Be Afraid of the Dark
Dream Man
The Dreaming
Dreamscape
The Dunwich Horror
The Dybbuk▶
The Dying Truth
Encounter with the Unknown
The Entity
Equinox▶
Erotic Dreams
Eternal Evil
The Evictors
The Evil
Evil Altar
Evil Dead
Evil Dead 2: Dead by Dawn
The Evil Mind
Evilspeak
Excalibur▶
Exorcism
The Exorcist▶
The Exorcist 2: The Heretic
Eye of the Demon
Eyes of Fire
Feast for the Devil
The Final Conflict
The First Power
The Fish that Saved Pittsburgh
Four Rooms
Fright House
Full Circle
Genie of Darkness
Ghosts That Still Walk
The Girl in a Swing
God Told Me To
Grave Secrets
The Guardian
Half of Heaven▶
Hanussen▶
Haunted Symphony
The Hearse
Horror Hotel
House of the Yellow Carpet
The House on Skull Mountain
The House that Bled to Death
I Don't Want to Be Born
I'm Dangerous Tonight
Inferno
Inner Sanctum
Into the Badlands
The Invasion of Carol Enders
Invasion of the Blood Farmers
Journey into the Beyond
Kill, Baby, Kill▶
Killing Hour
The Kingdom
The Kiss
KISS Meets the Phantom of the Park
Lady Terminator
The Lady's Maid's Bell
Land of the Minotaur
The Legacy
The Legend of Hell House▶
Leonor
The Living Head
Low Blow
The Magician▶
Making Contact
The Mangler
Manos, the Hands of Fate
Mardi Gras for the Devil
Mardi Gras Massacre
Maxim Xul
Medea
Men of Two Worlds
Midnight
Midnight Cabaret
Mirror, Mirror
Mirror, Mirror 2: Raven Dance
Mirror of Death
Mirrors
The Monster Demolisher
Mystic Circle Murder
Natas...The Reflection
Necromancer: Satan's Servant
Necropolis
The Night Stalker: Two Tales of Terror
Ninja, the Violent Sorcerer
The Occult Experience
The Occultist
Omoo Omoo, the Shark God
One Step Beyond
Only You
The Oracle
Orgy of the Dead
Out on a Limb
Phantasm
Phantasm II
Phantasm III: Lord of the Dead
Poltergeist▶
Poltergeist 2: The Other Side
Poltergeist 3
Possession: Until Death Do You Part
The Power
The Psychic
Psychic
Psychic Killer
Psychomania
Puppet Master
Quest of the Delta Knights
Race with the Devil
The Raven▶
A Reflection of Fear
The Reincarnate
Rendez-Moi Ma Peau
Repossessed
Rest In Pieces
Retribution
Return
Return from Witch Mountain
Return of Chandu
Rosemary's Baby▶
Ruby
Run If You Can
The Runestone
Sabaka
Satan's Princess
Satan's Touch
Scared Stiff
Season of the Witch
Second Sight
Seduced by Evil
Seizure
Sensation
The Sentinel
The Seventh Sign
The Seventh Victim▶
The Shaman
Shock 'Em Dead
Silent Night, Deadly Night 3: Better Watch Out!
Sorceress
The Spaniard's Curse
Speak of the Devil
The Spellbinder
Spellbound
Spiritism
Student of Prague▶
Summer of Fear
Supergirl
Teen Witch
The Tempter
Temptress
Terror Beach
Terror Creatures from the Grave
That Darn Sorceress
Three Sovereigns for Sarah
To the Devil, A Daughter
The Torture Chamber of Dr. Sadism
The Touch of Satan
Treasure of the Four Crowns
The Undead▶
Unknown Powers
Venus in Furs
Vibes
The Visitor
Warlock Moon
White Gorilla
Who Killed Doc Robbin?
The Wicker Man▶
Wild Man
Witch Hunt
Witch Who Came from the Sea
Witchboard
Witchboard 2: The Devil's Doorway
Witchboard 3: The Possession
Witchcraft 2: The Temptress
Witchcraft 4: Virgin Heart
Witchcraft 5: Dance with the Devil
Witchcraft Through the Ages▶
The Witches of Eastwick
The Witching
Witching Time
The Witchmaker
The Witch's Mirror
The Wizard of Oz▶
Wizards
The Woman Who Came Back
Zapped Again
The Zodiac Killer

Oceans

see Deep Blue; Go Fish; Mutiny; Scuba; Sea Critter Attack; Shipwrecked; Submarines

Oedipal Allegories

see also Family Ties; Incest

Angela
The Brothers Karamazov▶
Die! Die! My Darling!
Hamlet▶
Hamlet
Hamlet▶
I Dismember Mama
The Manchurian Candidate▶
Matters of the Heart
Murmur of the Heart▶
New York Stories▶
Oedipus Rex▶
Paddy
Phedre
Psycho▶
Rivals
Savage Is Loose
The Secret Diary of Sigmund Freud
Stay As You Are
The Strangler
Trespasser
Walk in the Spring Rain
Waltz of the Toreadors▶
White Heat▶
Wild Bill
Wild Pony
A Woman Obsessed

Oil

see Black Gold

Oldest Profession

see also Gigolos; Happy Hookers; Women in Prison

Accatone!▶
Alexander: The Other Side of Dawn
Alien Warrior
The Allnighter
American Justice
American Nightmare
Amor Bandido
The Amsterdam Connection
Angel
Angel 3: The Final Chapter
Anna Christie▶
Anna Christie
Aroused
Auntie
Avenging Angel
Back Roads
Bad Girls
The Balcony▶
Being at Home with Claude
Belle de Jour▶

The Best Little Whorehouse in Texas
Beverly Hills Madam
Beverly Hills Vamp
Beyond Desire
Blood Money: The Story of Clinton and Nadine
Blow Out▶
The Blue Hour
Boiling Point
Bordello
Boulevard
Broken Mirrors
Butterfield 8▶
Candy Tangerine Man
Caravaggio▶
Casino▶
Catherine & Co.
Chained Heat 2
The Cheyenne Social Club
Christiane F.▶
Cinderella Liberty▶
Class of 1984
Club Life
Coffy
Confessions of a Vice Baron
The Courtesans of Bombay▶
Crimes of Passion▶
Cross Country
Cry of a Prostitute: Love Kills
Cry, the Beloved Country▶
Dead End Street
Deadly Sanctuary
Death Shot
Death Target
Dedee d'Anvers
Desperate Crimes
The Desperate Trail
Diary of a Lost Girl▶
Diva▶
Dixie: Changing Habits▶
Doctor Detroit
Dr. Jekyll and Sister Hyde
Double Cross
Dressed to Kill
Drying Up the Streets
East End Hustle
8 Million Ways to Die
Elmer Gantry▶
Emily
Emmanuelle & Joanna
Erendira
Everybody Wins
Fall from Innocence
Firepower
Flesh▶
Fleshpot on 42nd Street
Forbidden Fruit▶
Forever Amber
Foxy Brown
Frankenhooker
Frankie and Johnny
French Quarter
Full Exposure: The Sex Tape Scandals
Fyre
Get Rita
The Gift
Gigi▶
Girls of the White Orchid
Half Moon Street
The Happy Hooker
The Happy Hooker Goes Hollywood
The Happy Hooker Goes to Washington
Hard Bounty
Hard Vice
Help Wanted Female
High Stakes
Hollywood Chainsaw Hookers
Hollywood Vice Sqaud
Honky Tonk Girl
Hotel Room
The Hustle
Hustler Squad
Hustling▶
I Want to Live!▶
Impulse
Irma La Douce
Jack's Back▶
Jade
Jamon, Jamon
Just a Gigolo
Justine
Keetje Tippel
Killing Zoe
Kinjite: Forbidden Subjects
Kiss the Night
Kitty and the Bagman
Klute▶
La Chienne▶
L.A. Crackdown
L.A. Crackdown 2
Ladies of the Lotus
Lady in Waiting
Lady of the Evening
Lady of the House
The Last Prostitute
The Last Temptation of Christ▶
Leaving Las Vegas▶
Life of Oharu▶
A Life of Sin
Little Ladies of the Night
Lola Montes▶
Love by Appointment
Love Strange Love
Mack
Madame Rosa▶
Magdalene
Malibu High
Mamma Roma▶
Man of Flowers
Manon
Marriage Italian Style▶
Mayflower Madam
McCabe & Mrs. Miller▶
Miami Blues
Mid Knight Rider
Midnight Auto Supply
Midnight Cop
Midnight Cowboy▶
Midnight Dancers
Miss Sadie Thompson▶
The Missionary
Moll Flanders▶
Mona Lisa▶
Murderlust
Murphy's Law
My Life to Live▶
My Mother's Secret Life
My Own Private Idaho▶
My Pleasure Is My Business
Naked Kiss
Nana▶
Nana
Never on Sunday▶
New York's Finest
Night Friend
Night of the Generals▶
Night Shift
Night Slasher
The Night They Robbed Big Bertha's
Nightmare in Badham County
Nights of Cabiria▶
No One Cries Forever
No Prince for My Cinderella
The Nun
Nuts▶
Off Limits
Oldest Profession
Olivia
One Night Only
Out of the Dark
Padre Nuestro
Pandora's Box▶
Panic in Needle Park▶
Party Girls
The Passing of Evil
Pennies From Heaven▶
Personal Services
Poker Alice
Postcards from America
Pretty Baby▶
Pretty Woman▶
Prettykill
Prime Cut
Prime Suspect 3▶
The Pyx▶
Queen Kelly▶
Quick, Let's Get Married
Rain
Raw Justice
Reason to Die
Red Kimono
Risky Business▶
Room 43
Roots of Evil
Saint Jack▶
Sandakan No. 8▶
Sansho the Bailiff▶
Scarred
Schnelles Geld
Scorchers
Secret Games
Secrets of a Married Man
Sessions
Sex, Love and Cold Hard Cash
Shadow of Angels
Sharky's Machine
The Silencer
Single Room Furnished
Sisters of Gion▶
Sketches of a Strangler
Skin Art
Spenser: Ceremony
SS Girls
S.S. Love Camp No. 27
Stone Cold Dead
Storyville
Street Girls
Street of Forgotten Women
Street of Shame▶
Street Smart
Streetwalkin'
The Substitute Wife
The Sun's Burial▶
Sweet Charity▶
Sweet Revenge
Sweet Sweetback's Baadasssss Song▶
Sweet Trash
The Sword and the Cross
Talons of the Eagle
Taxi Driver▶
They Were So Young
Things
Things to Do In Denver When You're Dead▶
Thousand Pieces of Gold▶
Tightrope▶
Tokyo Decadence
Trading Places
Traffic in Souls▶
Train Station Pickups
Tricks of the Trade
Truck Stop Women
Twenty Dollar Star
Twin Peaks: Fire Walk with Me
Ultimate Desires
Uncaged
Utamaro and His Five Women
The Vampire Hookers
Via Appia
Vice Squad
Walk on the Wild Side
Warm Nights on a Slow-Moving Train
Warrior Queen
Waterloo Bridge▶
Whore
Whore 2
Wild Bill
Wild Orchid 2: Two Shades of Blue
Wild Side
The Winter of Our Dreams
A Woman in Flames▶
A Woman of Rome
Working Girls
Working Girls▶
The World of Suzie Wong
Wrestling Racket Girls

The Olympics

see also Sports Dramas

Alex
American Anthem
Best of the Best
Blades of Courage
Chariots of Fire▶
Cool Runnings
Crossbar
The Cutting Edge
The First Olympics: Athens 1896
Going for the Gold: The Bill Johnson Story
International Velvet
The Jesse Owens Story
Life is a Circus, Charlie Brown/ You're the Greatest, Charlie Brown
A Million to One
Miracle on Ice
Pentathlon
Personal Best▶
Running Brave
Special Olympics
Sword of Gideon
Tokyo Olympiad
21 Hours at Munich▶
Walk, Don't Run
Wilma

On the Rocks

see also Pill Poppin'

Arthur 2: On the Rocks
Barfly▶
Betty
The Big Hangover
Blue Heaven
Break of Hearts
Casino▶
Clean and Sober▶
Cocktail
Come Back, Little Sheba▶
Country Girl▶
Country Girl
Country Life
The Crossing Guard▶
A Cry for Love
Dance of Life
Danger in the Skies
Dangerous
Days of Wine and Roses
Days of Wine and Roses▶
Desert Bloom▶
The Devil at 4 O'Clock
The Devil Thumbs a Ride▶
The Devil Thumbs a Ride/ Having Wonderful Crime
Dona Flor and Her Two Husbands▶
Drunken Angel▶
Educating Rita▶
El Dorado▶
The Electric Horseman
The Entertainer▶
Fat City▶
The Fire Within▶
Fish Hawk
The Flaming Teen-Age
Flesh and Bone▶
Frances▶
A Free Soul
Georgia▶
Gervaise▶
The Great Man Votes▶
The Green Man▶
Heaven's Prisoners
Honkytonk Man
Hot Summer in Barefoot County
I Live with Me Dad
I'll Cry Tomorrow▶
The Informer▶
Ironweed▶
Izzy & Moe
Jack and Sarah
Jack the Bear
Kill Cruise
The Last American Hero▶
Last Time Out
Le Beau Serge▶
Leaving Las Vegas▶
License to Kill
Living Proof: The Hank Williams Jr. Story
Long Day's Journey into Night▶
Long Day's Journey into Night
The Lost Weekend▶
M.A.D.D.: Mothers Against Drunk Driving
Marvin & Tige
Mean Dog Blues
Mrs. Parker and the Vicious Circle
The Morning After
My Favorite Year▶
Once Were Warriors▶
One Too Many
Only When I Laugh▶
Papa's Delicate Condition▶
Police Court
Reuben, Reuben▶
The Robe
Scent of a Woman▶
The Secret Rapture
Shakes the Clown
The Sin of Harold Diddlebock
The Singing Blacksmith
Skin Deep
Smash-Up: The Story of a Woman▶
A Star is Born▶
A Star is Born
Straight Up
Stranded
Strange Brew
Stuart Saves His Family
Tales of Ordinary Madness
Ten Nights in a Bar Room
Ten Nights in a Bar-Room
Termini Station
Under Capricorn
Under the Volcano▶
Unnatural Pursuits
The Verdict▶
Wagons East
What Price Hollywood?▶
When a Man Loves a Woman
Whiskey Galore▶
White Lightning
Willa
The Winning Team

Only the Lonely

Abducted
The Abduction of Kari Swenson
An Autumn Afternoon▶
The Ballad of Little Jo
Bed of Roses
Betrayal
Birdman of Alcatraz▶
The Body Shop
Breakfast in Paris
The Browning Version▶
The Cemetery Club
Choose Me▶
A Chorus of Disapproval
A Christmas Without Snow
Citizen Kane▶
Cotter
Cowboys Don't Cry
Cyrano de Bergerac▶
Cyrano de Bergerac
Cyrano de Bergerac▶
A Day in the Country▶
Desperately Seeking Susan
Didn't You Hear?
Dirty Dishes▶
Distant Thunder
Docks of New York▶
Doin' Time on Planet Earth
The Doll
A Doll's House
A Doll's House▶
Eat Drink Man Woman▶
The Eclipse▶
El Super▶
An Empty Bed▶
The Enchanted Cottage
Escapade in Japan
E.T.: The Extra-Terrestrial▶
Every Man for Himself & God Against All▶
Eye of the Needle
Fiances
The Final Alliance
Full Moon in Blue Water
Full Moon in Paris
The Game of Love
The Gun in Betty Lou's Handbag
Harold and Maude▶
The Heart is a Lonely Hunter▶
Heavy

Opera

see also Musicals

Order in the Court

see also Justice Prevails...?; Law & Lawyers

Organized Crime

see also Crime & Criminals; Disorganized Crime; Gangs

The Godfather, Part 3▶
Goldeneye▶
Goodfellas▶
Gunblast
Hard-Boiled
The Harder They Fall▶
Harlem Nights
Heat
Hell on Frisco Bay
Hell Up in Harlem
Heroes in Blue
Hiding Out
High Stakes
Hired to Kill
Hit Lady
The Hit List
Hit the Dutchman
Hollywood Cop
Hollywood Crime Wave
Hollywood Man
Hong Kong Nights
Honor Thy Father
Hooch
The Hunted Lady
Hurricane Smith
I Died a Thousand Times
I, Mobster
Ice
In the Kingdom of the Blind the Man with One Eye is King
Innocent Blood
Internes Can't Take Money
Johnny Mnemonic
Johnny Stecchino▶
Jornada de Muerte
The Juror
Kansas City Massacre
Keaton's Cop
Keeper of the City
The Key Man
Kill Me Again
The Kill Reflex
The Killer▶
Killer Bait
Killer Instinct
Killing in the Sun
The Killing Man
The Killing of a Chinese Bookie
The King of the Roaring '20s: The Story of Arnold Rothstein
Kiss of Death
Kiss Tomorrow Goodbye
The Krays▶
La Scorta▶
L.A. Wars
Ladies of the Lotus
Lady Mobster
Lady of the Evening
Lady Scarface
The Last Contract
Last Exit to Brooklyn▶
Last Rites
The Last Word
Legacy of Lies
Lepke
Lethal Games
Little Caesar▶
Little Odessa
Little Vegas
Loan Shark
The Long Good Friday▶
Lucky Luciano
Ma and Pa Kettle Go to Town
Machine Gun Blues
Mad Dog and Glory▶
Madigan's Millions
Mafia Princess
Mafia vs. Ninja
Magic Kid
Making the Grade
The Man I Love▶
Man on a String
Man with a Gun
The Manhandlers
Manhunt
Manhunter
Married to the Mob▶
Me and the Mob
Mean Machine
Mean Streets▶
Meet Danny Wilson
Men of Respect
The Messenger
Mickey One
Mikey & Nicky
Minbo—Or the Gentle Art of Japanese Extortion
Mr. Majestyk
Mister Mean
Mob Boss
Mobsters
The Monster and the Girl
Moon over Harlem
Movie ... In Your Face
Moving Target
Mulholland Falls
My Blue Heaven
The Narrow Margin▶
Never Steal Anything Small
New Mafia Boss
1931: Once Upon a Time in New York
Nitti: The Enforcer
Odd Jobs
Once Upon a Time in America▶
Organized Crime & Triad Bureau
Our Family Business
Out for Justice
The Outfit
The Outside Man
Overkill
Palais Royale
The Palermo Connection
Panic Button
Passion for Power
Payoff
Penthouse▶
Perfect Killer
Perfect Witness
The Plot Against Harry▶
Point Blank
Police Academy: Mission to Moscow
The Pope Must Diet
Port of New York
Power of Attorney
Pray for Death
Prime Target
Prizzi's Honor▶
The Public Eye▶
Pulp Fiction▶
Quick
Rapid Fire
Raw Deal
Red Heat
The Red Light Sting
Remote Control
The Revenger
Ricco
Ring of Fire 3: Lion Strike
Ring of the Musketeers
The Rise and Fall of Legs Diamond
The Roaring Twenties▶
Rock, Baby, Rock It
Romeo Is Bleeding
Ruby
Rulers of the City
Run
Savage Hearts
Scarface▶
Scarface Mob
Sex, Love and Cold Hard Cash
Shaft's Big Score
Shoot to Kill
Sicilian Connection
The Sicilian Connection
Sitting Ducks▶
Sizzle
Slaughter
Slaughter's Big Ripoff
Sloane
Slow Burn
Smokescreen
Sno-Line
Special Investigator
Squizzy Taylor
Stand-In
Stark
State of Grace▶
Stiletto
The Stone Killer
Street Hero
Street People
Street War
Sugartime
The Takeover
Taking the Heat
Target for Killing
Terminal Force
They Call Me Bruce?
They Paid with Bullets: Chicago 1929
Thief▶
Things Change▶
This Could Be the Night
The Three Penny Opera▶
The Threepenny Opera
Ticket of Leave Man
To Die For▶
To the Limit
Tony Rome
The Trap
Trial by Jury
TripleCross
True Identity
True Romance
Ulterior Motives
Underworld▶
Underworld, U.S.A.▶
The Untouchables▶
Velvet Smooth
Vendetta for the Saint
Verne Miller
We're Talkin' Serious Money
What! No Beer?
White Heat▶
White Hot: The Mysterious Murder of Thelma Todd
White Sands
Who's Got the Action?
Wise Guys
The Wrestler
Zatoichi: The Life and Opinion of Masseur Ichi
Zatoichi: Zatoichi's Flashing Sword
Zebra Force

Otherwise Engaged

***see also** Romantic Triangles; Wedding Bells; Wedding Hell*

An Affair to Remember
The Age of Innocence▶
Aladdin▶
The Birdcage▶
Blind Date
Come September
Coming to America▶
Fandango
Fiances
Four Weddings and a Funeral▶
French Kiss
Gone with the Wind▶
The Graduate▶
High Society▶
His Girl Friday▶
I.Q.
It Takes Two
Love Affair▶
Love Affair
Miami Rhapsody
Moonstruck▶
Only You
The Philadelphia Story▶
Pride and Prejudice▶
The Princess Bride▶
Robin Hood: Prince of Thieves
Running Wild
Sabrina
Shag: The Movie▶
Sleepless in Seattle▶
Son-in-Law
Speechless
Vermont Is for Lovers

Outtakes & Bloopers

Bela Lugosi Scrapbook
Cinema Shrapnel
Hollywood Bloopers
Hollywood Outtakes & Rare Footage
Hollywood Uncensored
Salute to the "King of the Cowboys," Roy Rogers
Star Trek Bloopers
Voice of Hollywood
What Do You Say to a Naked Lady?
Zombiethon

Overlooked Gems

Cross Creek
Crossing Delancey▶
Dazed and Confused▶
Diner▶
Dogfight▶
Gallipoli▶
Housekeeping▶
Joey Breaker▶
Johnny Nobody
The Joy Luck Club▶
The Lighthorsemen▶
Local Hero▶
Matewan▶
Metropolitan▶
Miss Firecracker▶
Raising Arizona▶
Road House
Searching for Bobby Fischer▶
Shag: The Movie▶
The Silent Partner▶
Stay Hungry▶
Stealing Home
Strictly Ballroom▶
The Tall Guy▶

Pacific Islands

***see also** Island Fare*

Aloha Summer
Balboa
Blue Hawaii
Carlton Browne of the F.O.
Castaway
Cry of Battle
Dangerous Life
Don't Go Near the Water
Enchanted Island
Ethan
Eye of the Octopus
Fighting Marines
Flaming Signal
Fog Island
Food of the Gods
From Hell to Borneo
From Here to Eternity▶
Hell in the Pacific▶
Hell Raiders
His Majesty O'Keefe
Hula
The Island▶
Island of Dr. Moreau
The Last Flight of Noah's Ark
The Last Warrior
Lt. Robin Crusoe, U.S.N.
Mad Doctor of Blood Island
The Mermaids of Tiburon
Miss Sadie Thompson▶
Mission Manila
Mr. Robinson Crusoe
Moana, a Romance of the Golden Age▶
Mysterious Island▶
Noon Sunday
Paradise, Hawaiian Style
Pardon My Sarong
Rain
South Pacific▶
Tabu: A Story of the South Seas▶
Till There was You
Tora! Tora! Tora!
Wackiest Ship in the Army
White Shadows in the South Seas
Windom's Way▶
The Year of Living Dangerously▶

Painting

***see** Art & Artists*

Paperboys

Better Off Dead
Newsies
While You Were Sleeping▶

Parades & Festivals

***see also** Carnivals & Circuses*

Easter Parade▶
Ferris Bueller's Day Off▶
Miracle on 34th Street▶
Miracle on 34th Street
National Lampoon's Animal House▶
Sweet Beat

Parallel Universes

***see also** Lost Worlds*

Alice in Wonderland
Alice in Wonderland▶
Alice in Wonderland
Blue Flame
Cool World
Journey to the Center of the Earth▶
Journey to the Center of the Earth
Jumanji
Last Action Hero
The Little Mermaid▶
Logan's Run
The Purple Rose of Cairo▶
Splash
Super Mario Bros.
Who Framed Roger Rabbit▶

Parenthood

***see also** Bad Dads; Bringing Up Baby; Dads; Moms; Monster Moms; Stepparents*

Adam▶
Addams Family Values
Alice in the Cities▶
Aliens▶
All the Kind Strangers
Amazing Grace
American Heart▶
An Autumn Afternoon▶
Baby Boom
Baby Girl Scott
Bachelor Mother▶
Backfield in Motion
The Ballad of Narayama▶
Battling for Baby
Being Two Isn't Easy
Between Two Women
Big Girls Don't Cry...They Get Even
The Big Wheel
Blind Fools
Blondie's Blessed Event
Blue City
Boys Town▶
Bush Mama
Bye Bye, Love
Cahill: United States Marshal
Careful, He Might Hear You▶
Casanova Brown
Chapter in Her Life
Cheaper by the Dozen▶
The Children of Times Square
Cody
Cold River
Commissar▶
Cowboys Don't Cry
Crisscross
Crooklyn▶
A Cry in the Dark▶
Da
Daddy Nostalgia▶
Danielle Steel's "Daddy"
The Day My Parents Ran Away
Distant Voices, Still Lives▶
Dona Herlinda & Her Son
Drop-Out Mother
Dutch
East of Eden▶
East of Eden
Eat Drink Man Woman▶
The Emerald Forest▶
Endless Love

Paris

see also France

Party Hell

see also Horror

Patriotism & Paranoia

see also Propaganda

Peace

Peculiar Partners

see also Buddies; Buddy Cops; Cops

Period Piece

see also Historical Drama; Medieval Romps; Royalty

Monsieur Beaucaire▶
Monsieur Vincent▶
Morning Glory
Mother Joan of the Angels▶
Much Ado about Nothing▶
The Music Man▶
Mutiny on the Bounty
My Antonia
My Apprenticeship▶
My Childhood▶
My Fair Lady▶
My Summer Story
My Twentieth Century▶
My Universities▶
The Mystery of Edwin Drood
The Mystery of Rampo▶
The Neon Bible
The New Land▶
New Moon
Newsies
Nicholas and Alexandra
Nicholas Nickleby▶
No Drums, No Bugles
No Time for Romance
Northanger Abbey
O Pioneers!
O Quatrilho
Odd Birds
Of Human Hearts
Of Love and Shadows
Old Gringo
Oliver!▶
Oliver Twist▶
Oliver Twist
Oliver Twist▶
Oliver Twist
Omar Khayyam
On a Clear Day You Can See Forever
On Moonlight Bay
On Valentine's Day
Once Upon a Time in America▶
Once Upon a Time...When We Were Colored▶
One Crazy Night
Orlando▶
Oscar
Othello
Our Time
Our Town▶
The Outfit
The Ox
Palais Royale
Pancho Barnes
Pandora and the Flying Dutchman
Pantaloons
Party Girl▶
A Passage to India▶
Passion
Passion in Paradise
Passion of Love▶
Peg O' My Heart
Pelle the Conqueror▶
Peppermint Soda▶
The Perez Family
A Perfect World
Persuasion▶
The Phantom of the Opera
The Piano▶
The Piano Lesson▶
Picture Bride
Pictures
Pink Strings and Sealing Wax
The Playboys▶
Poldark▶
Poldark 2▶
Pollyanna▶
Portrait of a Lady
Portrait of Jennie▶
Power
The Power of One
Pride and Prejudice▶
Pride and Prejudice
Pride and Prejudice▶
Prince Brat and the Whipping Boy▶
Prince Valiant
Princess Caraboo
Princess Yang Kwei Fei▶
The Private Affairs of Bel Ami▶
The Private Life of Henry VIII▶

The Private Lives of Elizabeth & Essex▶
The Public Eye▶
The Quarrel
Queen Christina▶
The Quest
Race to Freedom: The Story of the Underground Railroad
Racing with the Moon▶
Radioland Murders
Rambling Rose▶
Ran▶
Rapa Nui
Rasputin and the Empress▶
Rebel Love
Red Firecracker, Green Firecracker
Red Sorghum▶
The Remains of the Day▶
Rembrandt—1669
Restoration▶
The Return of Eliot Ness
The Return of Martin Guerre▶
The Return of the Musketeers
The Return of the Native
Return to Paradise
Rich Man, Poor Man▶
Richard III▶
The Right Hand Man
Rikyu▶
A River Runs Through It▶
The Road to Wellville
The Road to Yesterday
Rob Roy▶
The Robe
Robin Hood▶
Robin Hood: Prince of Thieves
The Rocketeer▶
Romance
Rome '78
A Room with a View▶
Rosa Luxemburg
The Rose and the Jackal
Roxie Hart
Ruyblas
Saga of the Vagabond
The St. Valentine's Day Massacre
Salome
Samurai Reincarnation
San Francisco▶
The Sandlot▶
Sansho the Bailiff▶
The Saragossa Manuscript
Sarah, Plain and Tall▶
Saratoga Trunk
Savage Messiah▶
Scarlett
The Scent of Green Papaya▶
School for Scandal
School Ties▶
Sea Devils
The Sea Hawk▶
Season of Change
The Secret Garden▶
The Secret Garden
The Seekers
Sense & Sensibility
Sense and Sensibility▶
Senso▶
Sergeant Rutledge▶
Shadow on the Sun
Shadowlands▶
Shag: The Movie▶
Shake Hands with the Devil▶
Shanghai Triad▶
Sharpe's Battle
Sharpe's Company
Sharpe's Eagle
Sharpe's Enemy
Sharpe's Gold
Sharpe's Honour
Sharpe's Rifles
Sharpe's Sword
Sherlock Holmes: The Master Blackmailer
Shogun▶
The Shooting Party▶
Shopworn Angel▶
Show Boat
The Sign of Four
Silas Marner▶

Sirens
Sister Dora
Sister My Sister
Skin Game▶
Skylark
The Slingshot▶
Smart-Aleck Kill
Snowy River, the MacGregor Saga: The Race
Sofie
Something for Everyone
Sommersby
Son of Fury▶
Song Without End
Sorceress▶
The Sound and the Silence
Splendor in the Grass▶
Spring Symphony
Squanto: A Warrior's Tale▶
Star!
The Star Maker
Stars and Stripes Forever▶
The Stars Fell on Henrietta
The Stationmaster's Wife
The Stick-Up
The Story of Alexander Graham Bell▶
The Strange Woman
Strawberry and Chocolate▶
The Substitute Wife
Sudie & Simpson▶
Sugartime
A Summer Story▶
Sunday's Children▶
Swing Kids
Swing Shift
Swoon▶
Swords of Death
Tai-Pan
A Tale of Two Cities▶
A Tale of Two Cities
A Tale of Two Cities▶
Tales from Avonlea, Vol. 1: The Journey Begins
Tales from the Gimli Hospital
Tamango
Taras Bulba
Tchaikovsky
Temptation of a Monk
Tess▶
The Texans
That Forsyte Woman
That Night
That'll Be the Day
They Came to Cordura
They Shoot Horses, Don't They?▶
Thieves Like Us▶
Three Comrades▶
The Three Musketeers
Throne of Blood▶
The Tigress
A Time to Live and a Time to Die
Tito and Me▶
Tom and Huck▶
Tom & Viv▶
Tom Sawyer
Torrents of Spring
Total Eclipse
Tous les Matins du Monde▶
Trading Hearts
Trahir▶
Traps
Tune in Tomorrow
20,000 Leagues Under the Sea▶
Twenty-Four Eyes▶
Two Bits
The Two Jakes
Two Nights with Cleopatra
Under Capricorn
Under the Biltmore Clock
Under the Volcano▶
An Unfinished Piece for a Player Piano▶
An Unforgettable Summer
Used People
Utamaro and His Five Women
Valentino
Valentino Returns
The Valley of Decision▶

Valmont▶
Van Gogh▶
Victoria Regina
The Vikings
The Virgin Queen▶
Viva Villa!▶
The War
War and Peace
The Warriors
The Water Engine
We of the Never Never▶
Wend Kuuni
What's the Matter with Helen?
When the Greeks
Where Angels Fear to Tread▶
Where the Rivers Flow North
White Hot: The Mysterious Murder of Thelma Todd
The Wicked Lady
Wide Sargasso Sea
Wild Bill
Wild Hearts Can't Be Broken▶
Wild Party
Wild Reeds▶
A Winner Never Quits
Witch Hunt
The Wolves▶
A Woman at Her Window
Woman in Black
A Woman Rebels
Women in Love▶
The Wooden Man's Bride
Wrangler
Xica▶
The Yearling
Yellow Earth
Yentl
Young Bess▶
Young Sherlock Holmes

Persian Gulf War

see also Desert War/ Foreign Legion

Courage Under Fire▶
The Heroes of Desert Storm
The Human Shield

Philanthropy

see Kindness of Strangers

Phobias!

Arachnophobia
Body Double▶
Copycat
High Anxiety
Home Remedy
Inside Out
Pontiac Moon
Vertigo▶

Phone Sex

see also Sex & Sexuality; Sexploitation

Girl 6
Mouth to Mouth
Short Cuts▶
The Truth About Cats and Dogs▶

Phone Terror

Are You Lonesome Tonight
Black Sabbath▶
Call Me
Dead Connection
Don't Answer the Phone
The Jerky Boys
Lady Beware
Lisa
Midnight Lace
976-EVIL
976-EVIL 2: The Astral Factor
Party Line
Smooth Talker
Sorry, Wrong Number▶
Sorry, Wrong Number
Telefon
When a Stranger Calls
When a Stranger Calls Back

Photography

see Shutterbugs

Physical Problems

see also Blindness; Deafness; Mental Retardation; Savants

Acorn People
The Affair▶
An Affair to Remember
Amy
Autumn Sonata▶
Big Street
Born on the Fourth of July▶
Breaking the Waves▶
A Brief History of Time▶
Broken Strings
The Brute Man
Chained for Life
Chinese Roulette
Choices
Coming Home▶
Crossbar
A Day in the Death of Joe Egg▶
El Cochecito▶
The Elephant Man▶
Endgame
Even Cowgirls Get the Blues
Fighting Life
Frankie Starlight
The Glass Menagerie▶
Hearing Voices
The Hunchback of Notre Dame▶
I Don't Want to Talk About It
Inside Moves
It's Good to Be Alive
Joni
Knife in the Head
Lightning Jack
Long Journey Back
Love Affair▶
Love Affair
Mac and Me
The Man with the Golden Arm▶
The Man Without a Face
Mask▶
The Men▶
The Miracle Worker▶
Mrs. Munck
Monkey Shines
Mute Witness
My Left Foot▶
Next Victim
Night Monster
Of Human Bondage▶
Off the Mark
One-Eyed Swordsman
The Other Side of the Mountain
The Other Side of the Mountain, Part 2
Passion Fish▶
The Penalty
The Phantom of the Opera▶
The Pit
Powder
Ratboy
Reach for the Sky
Rear Window▶
Revolver
Richard III▶
Ride a Wild Pony▶
The River▶
Rumble in the Bronx
Scent of a Woman▶
The Secret
Seizure: The Story of Kathy Morris
The Seventh Veil▶
Silence
Silence Like Glass
Skag▶
The Sky Pilot
The Small Back Room▶
Sound of Love
Special Olympics
The Spiral Staircase▶
Spiral Staircase
The Steel Claw
Stella Maris▶
The Stratton Story▶

Suite 16
Talk to Me
The Terry Fox Story▶
A Test of Love
Things to Do In Denver When You're Dead▶
To All My Friends on Shore▶
Untamed Heart
Vibrations
Walking on Air
The Waterdance▶
What Ever Happened to Baby Jane?▶
What's Eating Gilbert Grape▶
Whose Life Is It Anyway?▶
A Winner Never Quits
A Woman's Face▶

Pigs

see also Killer Pigs

The Advocate▶
Babe▶
Charlotte's Web
Gordy
Leon the Pig Farmer
A Private Function
Waikiki Wedding▶

Pill Poppin'

see also On the Rocks

Above the Law
Aces: Iron Eagle 3
The Acid Eaters
Across the Tracks
Adventures in Spying
Air America
All That Jazz▶
Alphabet City
Altered States▶
American Fabulous
Amongst Friends
The Amsterdam Connection
The Amsterdam Kill
And Then You Die▶
Angel's Brigade
Armistead Maupin's Tales of the City
Assassin of Youth
Avenging Disco Godfather
Awakenings of the Beast
Back in Action
Bad Boys
Bad Lieutenant▶
Bad Medicine
Baja
The Basketball Diaries
The Beatniks
Beretta's Island
Best Revenge
Bird▶
Black Snow
Black Starlet
Blast-Off Girls
Blind Spot
Blindside
Blood & Concrete: A Love Story
Blood Freak
Blood In...Blood Out: Bound by Honor
Bloodbath
The Bloody Brood
Blue Sunshine
The Boost
Borderline
Born to Win
Bright Lights, Big City
Brotherhood of Justice
Burning Vengeance
Busting
Camp Double Feature
Captain Blackjack
Captive Rage
Carlito's Way▶
Caroline at Midnight
Cartel
Casino▶
Catch the Heat
Cause of Death
Chained Heat 2
Chains of Gold
Chameleon
Cheech and Chong: Still Smokin'
Cheech and Chong: Things Are Tough All Over
Cheech and Chong's Next Movie
Cheech and Chong's Nice Dreams
Cheech and Chong's Up in Smoke
The Children of Times Square
China White
Chinatown Connection
Christiane F.▶
Chrome Soldiers
Chungking Express▶
Class of 1984
Clean and Sober▶
Clockers▶
Club Life
Cocaine Cowboys
Cocaine Fiends
Cocaine: One Man's Seduction
Cocaine Wars
Codename: Wildgeese
Coffy
Coldfire
The Colombian Connection
Commando Squad
Comrades in Arms
Confessions of a Vice Baron
The Connection▶
Contra Company
Contraband
A Cop for the Killing
Corridors of Blood
Countryman
Courage▶
Covert Action
Crack House
Crossing the Bridge
A Cry for Love
The Curfew Breakers
Cut and Run
Dance or Die
Dangerous Game
Dangerous Heart
Darkman 3: Die Darkman Die
Day of Atonement
Day of the Cobra
Day of the Maniac
Dazed and Confused▶
Dead Aim
Dead Presidents
Dead Ringers▶
Deadly Surveillance
Death Drug
The Death of Richie
Death Shot
Death Wish 4: The Crackdown
Deep Cover
Delta Heat
Desert Snow
Desperado▶
Desperate Lives
The Destructors
The Devil's Harvest
The Devil's Sleep
Dirty Laundry
Distant Justice
Dr. Jekyll and Mr. Hyde▶
Dr. Jekyll and Mr. Hyde
Dogs in Space
The Doom Generation▶
Dope Mania
Double-Crossed
Down & Dirty▶
Drug Wars 2: The Cocaine Cartel
Drugstore Cowboy▶
Drying Up the Streets
Easy Kill
Easy Rider▶
Ed Wood▶
Edge of Sanity
Edie in Ciao! Manhattan
8 Million Ways to Die
The End of Innocence
Enter the Dragon▶
Exposure
Extreme Prejudice
Fall from Innocence
Fast Money
Fatal Beauty
Fatal Fix
Federal Hill
Feelin' Screwy
Fever
The Fifth Floor
Fire Birds
First Born
The Five Heartbeats▶
The Fix
The Flaming Teen-Age
Flashback▶
Flatfoot
Flesh▶
Fletch
Four Friends▶
Frances▶
The French Connection▶
French Connection 2▶
French Intrigue
Fresh
Fresh Kill
Friday
The Fury of the Wolfman
Ganjasaurus Rex
The Gene Krupa Story
Georgia▶
The Gift
The Golden Triangle
Goodfellas▶
Gordon's War
Gothic▶
Gunmen
H
Hallucination
Hard Evidence
Haunted Summer
Heat▶
Heaven's Prisoners
Help Wanted Female
A Hero Ain't Nothin' But a Sandwich
Heroes for Sale▶
High Crime
High Risk
High School Confidential
Hit!
The Hooked Generation
How Come Nobody's On Our Side?
Hussy
I Come in Peace
I Drink Your Blood
I Love You, Alice B. Toklas!
I'm Dancing as Fast as I Can
The Imposter
In Hot Pursuit
Inside Edge
Iron Horsemen
Island Monster
Jaguar Lives
Jekyll and Hyde
Jekyll & Hyde...Together Again
Jo Jo Dancer, Your Life is Calling
Jumpin' at the Boneyard
Kamikaze Hearts
Kandyland
Kemek
Kickboxer the Champion
Kids
Kids In the Hall Brain Candy
Kill or Be Killed
Killing Zoe
The Killing Zone
Kowloon Assignment
L.627▶
La Bamba▶
L.A. Wars
Lady Sings the Blues
Last Flight to Hell
The Last of the Finest
Lenny▶
Less Than Zero
Lethal Obsession
Lethal Weapon▶
Let's Get Harry
Let's Get Lost
License to Kill▶
Light Sleeper
Live and Let Die
Loaded
Loaded Guns
London Kills Me
Long Day's Journey into Night▶
Long Day's Journey into Night
Lost Angels
Lovely ... But Deadly
The Man Inside
The Man with the Golden Arm▶
Marihuana
Marked for Death
Martial Outlaw
Maybe I'll Be Home in the Spring
McBain▶
McQ
The Messenger
Miami Vendetta
Midnight Cop
Midnight Express▶
Mike's Murder
Mindfield
Mission Manila
Mrs. Parker and the Vicious Circle
Mixed Blood
Mob War
The Moneytree
Monkey Grip▶
More
My Life and Times with Antonin Artaud▶
Naked Lunch▶
The Narcotics Story
National Lampoon's Senior Trip
New Jack City
Newman's Law
Night Friend
The Night of the Iguana▶
Night Zoo
Ninja Turf
Ninja vs. Ninja
No Escape, No Return
Not My Kid
On the Edge
On the Edge: The Survival of Dana
One False Move▶
One Man's Justice
The Organization▶
Out of Sync
Out of the Rain
Over the Edge▶
Pace That Kills
The Palermo Connection
Panic in Needle Park▶
Passion for Power
The People Next Door
Performance▶
Pharmacist
Platoon the Warriors
Playing with Fire
Point of No Return
Police
The Poppy Is Also a Flower
Postcards from the Edge▶
Pot, Parents, and Police
Premonition
Pretty Smart
Prime Cut
Private Investigations
Professionals
Protector
Psych-Out
Pulp Fiction▶
Puppet on a Chain
Question of Honor
Quiet Cool
Rage and Honor
Rapid Fire
Reckless Disregard
Red Blooded American Girl
Red Heat
Red Surf
Reefer Madness
Return of the Tiger
Revenge of the Ninja
Revenge of the Stepford Wives
Rip-Off
River's Edge▶
Rock House
Rodrigo D.: No Future
The Rose▶
Running Scared
Rush▶
Saigon Commandos
Saints and Sinners
Satan's Harvest
Savage Instinct
Scarface▶
Schnelles Geld
Scorchy
Secret Agent Super Dragon
The Seducers
The Seven-Per-Cent Solution▶
Severance
The Show
Showdown in Little Tokyo
Sicilian Connection
Sid & Nancy▶
Silk
The Slender Thread▶
The Snake People
SnakeEater 2: The Drug Buster
Sno-Line
Sorry, Wrong Number
Spenser: Pale Kings & Princes
Stand Alone
The Stoned Age
Straight Up
Strange Days▶
Street Girls
Street Hawk
Street Wars
Streetwalkin'
Strike Force
The Substitute
Sugar Hill
Sunset Heat
Sunset Strip
Super Bitch
Superfly
The Take
Talons of the Eagle
Target Eagle
Tchao Pantin▶
Teenage Devil Dolls
TekWar
Tequila Sunrise
The Third Man▶
This Time I'll Make You Rich
Thunder Alley
Timothy and the Angel
To Die Standing
Tombstone▶
The Tong Man
Tongs: An American Nightmare
Torchlight
Tough and Deadly
Toughlove
Toxic Zombies
Traffik▶
Trainspotting▶
Transmutations
Trash
Trespass
The Trip
Tropical Snow
Trouble in Paradise
True Romance
Twenty-One
Twin Peaks: Fire Walk with Me
Undercover
The Usual Suspects▶
Valley of the Dolls
Vanishing Point
Wait Until Dark▶
Wanda, The Sadistic Hypnotist
Warlords from Hell
Warlords 3000
Watched
Weekend with the Babysitter
Weird World of LSD
What Have I Done to Deserve This?▶
Whispers of White
Who'll Stop the Rain?▶
Wild Bill
Wild in the Streets
The Wild Pair
Wild Weed
The Winter of Our Dreams
Wired
Withnail and I▶

Women on the Verge of a Nervous Breakdown▶
Woodstock▶
The Young Americans
Zero Tolerance

Pirates

see also Island Fare; Sail Away; Swashbucklers

Abbott and Costello Meet Captain Kidd
Against All Flags▶
The Black Pirate▶
The Black Swan▶
Blackbeard the Pirate
Blackbeard's Ghost
The Buccaneer
Captain Blood▶
Captain Kidd
Captain Ron
Crimson Pirate▶
Cutthroat Island
Dancing Pirate
His Majesty O'Keefe
Hook
Ice Pirates
Long John Silver
The Master of Ballantrae
Morgan the Pirate
Muppet Treasure Island
Old Ironsides▶
Peter Pan▶
The Phantom
The Pirate▶
Pirate Movie
The Pirates of Penzance
The Princess and the Pirate▶
The Princess Bride▶
The Sea Hawk▶
Shipwrecked
Son of Captain Blood
The Spanish Main
Swashbuckler
The Swiss Family Robinson▶
Tiger of the Seven Seas
Treasure Island▶
Treasure Island
Yellowbeard

Pittsburgh

Alone in the Neon Jungle
Angels in the Outfield▶
Angels in the Outfield
Backstreet Justice
Bloodsucking Pharoahs of Pittsburgh
Bob Roberts▶
The Cemetery Club
Diabolique
Dominick & Eugene▶
The Fish that Saved Pittsburgh
Flashdance
Houseguest
Innocent Blood
Lady Beware
Mrs. Soffel
The Piano Lesson▶
Roommates
Silent Witness
Striking Distance
Sudden Death
The Valley of Decision▶

Poetry

The Barretts of Wimpole Street▶
The Color of Pomegranates▶
Hedd Wyn
I, the Worst of All
In Custody
Lady Caroline Lamb
My Life and Times with Antonin Artaud▶
Poetic Justice
The Postman▶
Satan's Brew
Tales of Ordinary Madness
Tom & Viv▶
Total Eclipse

Poisons

Arsenic and Old Lace▶
Barracuda
Color Me Dead
The Crazies
D.O.A.▶
D.O.A.
Doomwatch
The Invisible Killer
Juggernaut
Kiss and Kill
Safe▶
Surf 2
The Young Poisoner's Handbook▶

Political Conspiracy

see also Capitol Capers; Mystery & Suspense

All the President's Men▶
Chain Reaction
City Hall▶
Company Business
Eraser
The Fourth Protocol▶
JFK▶
Mulholland Falls
Nixon▶
No Way Out▶
The Package
The Parallax View▶
Seven Days in May▶
The Star Chamber
Winter Kills▶

Politics

see also Presidency

The Act
The American President▶
An American Story
The Americano
Americathon
And the Band Played On▶
Animal Instincts
Antonio Das Mortes
Article 99
Beggars in Ermine
Being There▶
Beyond Obsession
Beyond Rangoon
The Big Hurt
The Birdcage▶
Black Ice
Black Sheep
Blaze
Blood Money: The Story of Clinton and Nadine
The Blue Kite▶
Bob Roberts▶
Bophal▶
Buried Alive
The Burning Season▶
Burnt by the Sun▶
Call Him Mr. Shatter
Canadian Bacon
The Candidate▶
Carry On Emmanuelle
Casino▶
China Gate▶
Citizen Cohn
City Hall▶
Clear and Present Danger
Code Name: Chaos
The Colombian Connection
The Comedians
Complex World
Confessing to Laura
Conspiracy
Conspiracy: The Trial of the Chicago Eight▶
Corporate Affairs
Country▶
Country Life
A Dangerous Man: Lawrence after Arabia▶
Dave▶
Dead Center
Deadly Exposure
Death and the Maiden▶
Death of a Bureaucrat▶
Defense of the Realm▶
Demonstone
Devil In a Blue Dress▶
The Devils▶
Devlin
Disraeli▶
The Distinguished Gentleman
Don's Party▶
Double Cross
Double Edge
Down Came a Blackbird
Earth Entranced
Echoes of Conflict
Eijanaika▶
Elizabeth R▶
Eminent Domain
The Enemy Within
Eye of the Stranger
Eyes of a Witness
Fame Is the Spur
The Farmer's Daughter▶
Fever Mounts at El Pao
The Final Cut▶
The Final Days
Fires Within
First Family
First Monday in October
A Flash of Green
Foreplay
The French Detective▶
The French Woman
Friday Foster
Friends
Gabriel Over the White House▶
Germany in Autumn
A Girl on Her Own
A Good Man in Africa
The Gorgeous Hussy
The Great Man's Lady
The Great McGinty▶
Guilty by Suspicion
Hangar 18
The Home and the World▶
Hoodlum Empire
Hostages▶
Hour of the Assassin
House of Cards▶
The House of the Spirits
I Am Cuba
In the Line of Duty: Ambush in Waco
In the Line of Fire▶
In the Name of the Father▶
Indochine▶
Jefferson in Paris
JFK▶
JFK: Reckless Youth
John and the Missus
A Joke of Destiny, Lying in Wait Around the Corner Like a Bandit
Just Like Weather▶
Killer Image
The Killing Beach
The Killing Device
Kingfish: A Story of Huey P. Long
Kissinger and Nixon
Knife in the Head
Kurt Vonnegut's Harrison Bergeron
Lamerica▶
Land and Freedom▶
Larks on a String▶
The Last Supper
Laurel & Hardy: Chickens Come Home
Le Complot▶
The Life and Assassination of the Kingfish
A Lion Is in the Streets▶
The Little Drummer Girl▶
Lone Star Kid
Louisiana Purchase
M. Butterfly
Mandela▶
Marianne and Juliane▶
Marilyn & Bobby: Her Final Affair
The Mating Game▶
Mayerling
Medium Cool▶
Meeting Venus
Mission of Justice
Mr. Smith Goes to Washington▶
My Universities▶
Naked Obsession
National Lampoon's Senior Trip
Nick of Time
Nightbreaker▶
Nixon▶
Northern Extremes
Of Love and Shadows
Open Doors▶
Palombella Rossa
The Pelican Brief
The Perez Family
Pizza Man
A Place in the World▶
Presumed Innocent▶
Primary Motive
The Promise
Quiet Fire
Rage of Angels: The Story Continues
Rain Without Thunder
Red Hot
Red Kiss▶
Report to the Commissioner▶
Richard III▶
Robert Kennedy and His Times
Rosa Luxemburg
Running Mates▶
Salt of the Earth▶
Samaritan: The Mitch Snyder Story▶
The Secret
Seduced
The Seduction of Joe Tynan
Special Police
Speechless
Stalin
State of the Union▶
Storyville
Strawberry and Chocolate▶
Superfly T.N.T.
Tanner '88
Taxi Blues▶
Temptation of a Monk
Three Cases of Murder▶
Timecop
Tito and Me▶
To Live▶
To Play the King▶
Truman
Under Western Stars
An Unforgettable Summer
Unnatural Causes▶
Upper Crust
A Very British Coup▶
Viva Villa!▶
Viva Zapata!▶
The War Room▶
Washington Mistress
Werewolf of Washington
Whoops Apocalypse
Wild in the Streets
Wild Reeds▶
A Woman Named Jackie
World War II: When Lions Roared
Zero Population Growth

Pool

see also Gambling

The Baltimore Bullet
The Baron and the Kid
The Color of Money▶
The Hustler▶
Kiss Shot
Pool Hustlers

Pornography

see also Sex & Sexuality; Sexploitation

Amateur▶
Body Double▶
Defenseless
Fallen Angel
The Glitter Dome
Hardcore
Heavy Traffic▶
Hi, Mom!▶
Hollywood Vice Sqaud
Inserts
It's Called Murder, Baby
Kamikaze Hearts
Kidnapped
The Last Porno Flick
The Love God?
M'Lady's Court
The Pornographers▶
Rented Lips
The Sinister Urge
South Bronx Heroes
Variety

Post Apocalypse

see also Negative Utopia; Technology-Rampant

After the Fall of New York
Aftermath
Armageddon: The Final Challenge
Battle for the Planet of the Apes
Beneath the Planet of the Apes
The Blood of Heroes
A Boy and His Dog
Circuitry Man
City Limits
Class of 1999
Crash and Burn
The Creation of the Humanoids
Crime Zone
Cyborg
Damnation Alley
Day of the Dead
Day the World Ended
Daybreak
Dead Man Walking
Deadly Reactor
Def-Con 4
Double Dragon
Dragon Fury
Driving Force
Dune Warriors
The Element of Crime
Endgame
Equalizer 2000
Escape from Safehaven
Exterminators of the Year 3000
The Final Executioner
Final Sanction
Firefight
First Spaceship on Venus▶
Fortress of Amerikka
Future Hunters
Future Kill
Glen and Randa
The Handmaid's Tale
Hardware
Hell Comes to Frogtown
In the Aftermath: Angels Never Sleep
Interzone
Judge Dredd
Karate Cop
The Killing Edge
Knights
Land of Doom
The Last Man on Earth
The Lawless Land
Le Dernier Combat▶
Lord of the Flies▶
Mad Max▶
Mad Max: Beyond Thunderdome
A Man Called Rage
Maniac Warriors
Nemesis
Neon City
Night of the Comet
984: Prisoner of the Future
1990: The Bronx Warriors
Omega Cop
Omega Man
On the Beach▶
Osa
Panic in the Year Zero!
People Who Own the Dark
Phoenix the Warrior
Planet Earth
Planet of the Apes▶
Plughead Rewired: Circuitry Man 2
Prayer of the Rollerboys

Prison Planet
The Quiet Earth▶
Quintet
Radioactive Dreams
Raiders of the Sun
Rats
Rebel Storm
Refuge of Fear
The Road Warrior▶
RoboCop▶
Robot Holocaust
RoGoPaG
Roller Blade
Rush
Screamers
The Seventh Sign
She
Silent Running▶
The Sisterhood
The Slime People
Star Quest
Steel Dawn
Steel Frontier
Stephen King's The Stand
Strange New World
Survival Earth
Survival Zone
Survivor
Tank Girl
Teenage Caveman
Terminator 2: Judgment Day▶
The Terror Within 2
Testament▶
Things to Come▶
The Time Travelers
Time Troopers
12 Monkeys▶
2020 Texas Gladiators
Ultra Warrior
Urban Warriors
Virus
WarCat
Warlords
Warlords of the 21st Century
Warlords 3000
Warriors of the Apocalypse
Warriors of the Wasteland
Waterworld
Wheels of Fire
Where Have All the People Gone?
World Gone Wild

Postwar

see also Veterans

An American Story
Americana
An Awfully Big Adventure
Back Home
Baltic Deputy▶
Behold a Pale Horse
Berlin Express▶
The Best Years of Our Lives▶
Bitter Rice▶
Black Rain▶
Bloody Trail
The Blum Affair
Born on the Fourth of July▶
Brussels Transit▶
The Burmese Harp▶
The Bushwackers
Cabo Blanco
Chattahoochee
Cinema Paradiso▶
The Cruel Story of Youth▶
Demons in the Garden▶
Deutschland im Jahre Null▶
Distant Thunder
Distant Voices, Still Lives▶
Dixie Lanes
D.P.
Early Summer▶
Eat a Bowl of Tea▶
Ebony Dreams
Europa '51
Exodus▶
Father▶
The Fighting Kentuckian
First Blood
Foolish Wives▶
Four in a Jeep
Frieda
Grave of the Fireflies▶
Green Eyes▶
Gun Fury
Heroes
Hiroshima, Mon Amour▶
Hiroshima: Out of the Ashes▶
Horizons West
House▶
I Am a Fugitive from a Chain Gang▶
I Don't Give a Damn
In a Glass Cage
The Indian Runner
The Innocent
Inside Out
Isn't Life Wonderful▶
It Happened in New Orleans
Jacob's Ladder
Judgment at Nuremberg▶
The Last Reunion
The Last Time I Saw Paris
Le Dernier Combat▶
The Left Hand of God▶
Les Rendez-vous D'Anna
Lilies of the Field▶
The Limping Man
Love Is a Many-Splendored Thing
Love Nest
MacArthur's Children▶
The Man in the Glass Booth▶
Man of Marble▶
The Man Who Broke 1,000 Chains
Manon
Maria's Day▶
Maria's Lovers
The Marriage of Maria Braun▶
Master Race
Mine Own Executioner▶
The Miniver Story
Miss Rose White▶
A Month in the Country▶
Mother▶
My Life and Times with Antonin Artaud▶
My Old Man's Place
Nevil Shute's The Far Country
Night Stage to Galveston
Night Wars
1900▶
Notorious▶
The Odessa File
Panique▶
Plenty
A Private Function
QB VII▶
Quality Street
Rambo: First Blood, Part 2
Random Harvest▶
The Razor's Edge▶
Reunion▶
Rich Man, Poor Man▶
Rio Conchos▶
Robin Hood of the Pecos
The Rose Garden
Savage Dawn
The Search▶
Sergeant Ryker
Shoeshine▶
Sommersby
Sophie's Choice▶
Souvenir
Strategic Air Command
The Teahouse of the August Moon
The Texans
The Third Man▶
Three Comrades▶
Till the End of Time
Time of Indifference
Torpedo Alley
Trained to Kill, U.S.A.
Uranus▶
Verboten!
Vietnam, Texas
A Walk in the Clouds
We All Loved Each Other So Much▶
Who'll Stop the Rain?▶
Wish You Were Here▶
Wolf Lake
Women in Prison
The Yakuza
Year of the Quiet Sun▶
Zentropa

POW/MIA

see also Vietnam War; War, General; World War II

Against the Wind
All My Sons▶
American Commandos
Andersonville▶
The Andersonville Trial▶
Another Time, Another Place▶
The Ascent
Au Revoir Les Enfants▶
Ay, Carmela!▶
Bat 21
The Beast
Blockhouse
Bomb at 10:10
The Boxer and Death▶
Brady's Escape
The Bridge on the River Kwai▶
Bridge to Hell
Bye Bye Blues
Captive Heart▶
Captive Hearts
Charlie Bravo
Codename: Terminate
The Colditz Story
Come See the Paradise▶
Cornered▶
Crossfire
Dirty Heroes
The Dunera Boys▶
The Elusive Corporal▶
Empire of the Sun▶
Era Notte a Roma▶
Escape
Escape from Sobibor▶
Escape to Athena
Fighting Mad
The Forgotten
Generale Della Rovere▶
Grand Illusion▶
The Great Escape▶
The Great Escape 2: The Untold Story
The Hand
Hanoi Hilton
Hell to Eternity
Heroes in Hell
Homecoming▶
The Human Condition: A Soldier's Prayer▶
Hunted
In Gold We Trust
In Love and War
The Incident▶
The Iron Triangle
Jenny's War
King Rat▶
A Love in Germany
McKenzie Break▶
Merry Christmas, Mr. Lawrence▶
Mine Own Executioner▶
Missing in Action
Nam Angels
Night Wars
Objective, Burma!▶
On Wings of Eagles
One That Got Away▶
Operation 'Nam
Operation War Zone
Pacific Inferno
Porridge
P.O.W. Deathcamp
The P.O.W. Escape
Prisoners of the Sun▶
The Purple Heart
Rolling Thunder
The Seventh Cross▶
Stalag 17▶
Stalag Luft
The Summer of My German Soldier▶
Three Came Home▶
Three Wishes
Victory
Von Ryan's Express▶
War Victims
When Hell Was in Session▶
Women of Valor
Wooden Horse▶

Pregnant Men

Enemy Mine
Junior
Rabbit Test
That Man Is Pregnant

Pregnant Pauses

see also Bringing Up Baby

Angel Baby▶
Angie
Baby of the Bride
Babyfever
Between Heaven and Earth
Butterfly Wings
Cafe au Lait▶
Cast the First Stone
Choices
Danielle Steel's Heartbeat
Down, Out and Dangerous
The Dwelling Place
Fargo▶
Father of the Bride Part II
Father's Little Dividend▶
Friends
Just Another Girl on the I.R.T.
Lily Was Here
Maybe...Maybe Not
Micki & Maude
My Life
Nine Months
Our Time
Outrageous!▶
Parenthood▶
She's Having a Baby
Twogether
The Unearthing
A Walk in the Clouds
You've Ruined Me, Eddie
Zero Population Growth

Presidency

see also Camelot (New); Politics

Abe Lincoln in Illinois▶
Advise and Consent▶
All the President's Men▶
The American President▶
Assassination
The Best Man▶
Black Sunday
Dave▶
Dirty Tricks
Eleanor & Franklin▶
Eleanor: First Lady of the World
The Enemy Within
Escape from New York
Executive Action
The Final Days
First Family
Foreplay
Forrest Gump▶
Gabriel Over the White House▶
Gore Vidal's Lincoln
Guarding Tess
Hail
Imagemaker
In the Line of Fire▶
Independence Day▶
Indomitable Teddy Roosevelt
Jefferson in Paris
JFK▶
The JFK Conspiracy
JFK: Reckless Youth
JFK Remembered
Kennedy
The Kidnapping of the President
Kisses for My President
Kissinger and Nixon
The Last Bastion
LBJ: A Biography
LBJ: The Early Years▶
Meteor
Missiles of October▶
Nixon▶
The President's Analyst▶
President's Mistress
The President's Plane is Missing
Prince Jack
Ruby
Sadat
Secret Honor▶
Suddenly▶
Sunrise at Campobello▶
Truman
The War Room▶
Wild in the Streets
Wilson▶
Winter Kills▶
Young Mr. Lincoln▶

Price of Fame

see also Rags to Riches

Abraham Lincoln
All About Eve▶
All That Jazz▶
American Blue Note
The Bad and the Beautiful▶
Bank Robber
Bert Rigby, You're a Fool
Beyond the Valley of the Dolls
The Big Knife▶
Black Starlet
The Bodyguard
The Buddy Holly Story▶
By the Sword
The Cantor's Son
Cassie
Champion▶
A Chorus Line
Citizen Kane▶
Coal Miner's Daughter▶
Comeback
The Comic▶
The Commitments▶
The Cotton Club▶
Country Girl
Covergirl
Crossover Dreams
Darling▶
Dead Ringers▶
Echo Park
Eddie and the Cruisers
Eddie and the Cruisers 2: Eddie Lives!
Edie in Ciao! Manhattan
Elmer Gantry▶
Elvis and Me
Elvis: The Movie
Eureka!
Extra Girl
Fame▶
The Fan
Fellow Traveler▶
The Five Heartbeats▶
Flashdance
Frances▶
Gemini Affair
The Gene Krupa Story
The Goddess▶
Goodbye, Norma Jean
Goodnight, Sweet Marilyn
Gore Vidal's Lincoln
Grosse Fatigue▶
The Gunfighter▶
Hail Caesar
A Hard Day's Night▶
Hard Part Begins
Harvest Melody
Hero at Large
Hollywood Heartbreak
I, Claudius, Vol. 3: Poison is Queen/Some Justice
I, Claudius, Vol. 4: Queen of Heaven/Reign of Terror
I Ought to Be in Pictures
Idolmaker
I'll Cry Tomorrow▶
Imitation of Life▶
Inside Daisy Clover
Irreconcilable Differences
It Could Happen to You
It Should Happen to You▶
The Jacksons: An American Dream
Jacqueline Bouvier Kennedy
James Dean

The Jayne Mansfield Story
The Jazz Singer
Jimmy Hollywood
Jo Jo Dancer, Your Life is Calling
John & Yoko: A Love Story
Keep Punching
King of Comedy▶
La Bamba▶
La Dolce Vita▶
Lady Grey
Lady Jane▶
Lady Sings the Blues
The Lady Without Camelias
Lenny▶
Let It Rock
Little Caesar▶
The Lonely Lady
Love Me or Leave Me▶
Lucy and Desi: Before the Laughter
The Magnificent Ambersons▶
Mahogany
The Main Event
The Man Who Would Be King▶
Marilyn: The Untold Story▶
Mephisto▶
Miss All-American Beauty
Mistress
Mommie Dearest
My Fair Lady▶
My Favorite Year▶
Naked in New York
Oh, God! You Devil
The One and Only
One Trick Pony
The Oscar
Payday
Police Court
Postcards from the Edge▶
Prisoner of Rio
Provincial Actors
Pure Country
Purple Rain
The Queen of Mean
Raging Bull▶
Rocky▶
Rocky 2
Rocky 3
Rocky 4
Rocky 5
The Rose▶
The Seduction
Shadow of China▶
Shakes the Clown
Shop Angel
Show People▶
Sins
Small Town Boy
Smash-Up: The Story of a Woman▶
Smithereens
S.O.B.
Soldier in Love
Star 80
A Star is Born▶
Stardust Memories
Sunset Boulevard▶
Svengali
Sweet Dreams
Sweet Love, Bitter
Sweet Perfection
Sweethearts▶
The Thing Called Love
True Colors
Tucker: The Man and His Dream▶
Twenty Dollar Star
Two Weeks in Another Town
Valley of the Dolls
A Very Private Affair
What Ever Happened to Baby Jane?▶
What Price Hollywood?▶
What's Love Got to Do with It?
While the City Sleeps▶
Winning▶
Wired
A Woman Named Jackie
You Light Up My Life
Ziegfeld Girl▶

Princes/Princesses

see Royalty

Prison

see Great Escapes; Men in Prison; POW/MIA; Women in Prison

Production Problems

Blown Away
Brainstorm
Cannonball Run
The Crow
Cutthroat Island
Eraser
The Island of Dr. Moreau
Seven▶
Twilight Zone: The Movie
Under Siege 2: Dark Territory
Vampire in Brooklyn
Waterworld
Wicked Stepmother

Propaganda

see also Patriotism & Paranoia; Politics

Air Force▶
Alfred Hitchcock's Aventure Malgache
Alfred Hitchcock's Bon Voyage
Arsenal▶
The Atomic Cafe▶
Baltic Deputy▶
Behind the Rising Sun
The Black King
Blood on the Sun
Born American
Breaking with Old Ideas
Chapayev▶
The Commies are Coming, the Commies are Coming
Corregidor
Dangerous Hours
Desperate Journey
The Devil's Harvest
Dope Mania
The End of St. Petersburg▶
Fighting Seabees
The General Line▶
The Green Berets
Guadalcanal Diary
Invasion U.S.A.
Jud Suess▶
Mrs. Miniver▶
A Mormon Maid
No Greater Love
Passage to Marseilles▶
Que Viva Mexico▶
The Red Menace
Red Nightmare
Reefer Madness
Reunion in France
Rocket Attack U.S.A.
Shack Out on 101▶
Stamp Day for Superman
Strike▶
Teenage Devil Dolls
Ten Days That Shook the World▶
Ten Nights in a Bar-Room
The Thief
Threads▶
To the Shores of Tripoli
Tomorrow's Children
Trapped by the Mormons
Zvenigora▶

Prostitutes

see Gigolos; Happy Hookers; Oldest Profession

Protests

see also Rebel With a Cause

Born on the Fourth of July▶
Forrest Gump▶
Hairspray▶
In the Name of the Father▶
The Long Walk Home▶
Malcolm X▶
Matewan▶
Norma Rae▶
Panther
Silkwood▶

Psychiatry

see Shrinks

Psycho-Thriller

see also Mystery & Suspense

Afraid of the Dark
After Darkness
After Midnight
Alligator Eyes
Almanac of Fall
Almost Dead
Ambition
Anatomy of a Psycho
Apartment Zero▶
Apology
Are You Lonesome Tonight
The Arousers
The Art of Dying▶
The Attic
Awakening of Candra
The Babysitter
Bad Influence
The Bad Seed
Baffled
The Barretts of Wimpole Street▶
Being at Home with Claude
The Berlin Affair
Betrayal
Beware, My Lovely
Beyond Erotica
Bitter Moon
Bizarre
Black and White as Day and Night
Bloodknot
Blow-Up▶
Body Chemistry 2: Voice of a Stranger
Bound
Breach of Conduct
Breaking Point
Brighton Strangler
A Brilliant Disguise
Brimstone & Treacle▶
By the Blood of Others▶
Call Me
Cape Fear▶
The Case of the Frightened Lady
Cat's Play
Cause for Alarm
Circumstances Unknown
Cold Heaven
Cold Light of Day
Cold Room
The Collector▶
The Comfort of Strangers▶
Conflict▶
The Courtyard
The Crew
The Crush
Cul de Sac▶
Curse of the Stone Hand
Daddy's Gone A-Hunting▶
Dangerous Pursuit
Dangerous Touch
A Dark Adapted Eye▶
Dark Mirror▶
The Dark Past▶
The Dark Ride
Dark Waters
Darkroom
Day of Wrath▶
The Day the Sun Turned Cold▶
Dead as a Doorman
Dead Calm▶
Deadbolt
Deadly Daphne's Revenge
Deadly Game
Deadly Hero▶
Deadly Lessons
Deadly Sunday
Deconstructing Sarah
Deep Down
Deranged
Desperate Prey
Diabolique▶
Diabolique
Disturbance
Disturbed
Dolores Claiborne▶
The Donor
Don't Answer the Phone
Don't Talk to Strangers
Doppelganger: The Evil Within
Down, Out and Dangerous
Dream Lover
The Dreaming
Dressed for Death
The Drifter
Dynasty of Fear
El: This Strange Passion▶
Entangled
Every Breath
Evil Judgement
Eye of the Storm
Eyes of the Beholder
Fair Game
Falling Down
The Fan
Fatal Attraction▶
Fatally Yours
Fear
The Fear Inside
Final Approach
Fingers▶
The Flaming Urge
Flinch
Force of Evil
Freeway
Frenchman's Farm
Fright
Gallowglass▶
Gaslight▶
Girl in Black Stockings
Girly
Gross Misconduct
Hallucination
The Hand
The Hand that Rocks the Cradle
Haunted
Hellbent
The Hitch-Hiker▶
Honeymoon
House of Games▶
The House on Todville Road
Hush, Hush, Sweet Charlotte▶
I Never Promised You a Rose Garden▶
In a Glass Cage
In the Heat of Passion
In the Heat of Passion 2: Unfaithful
In the Realm of Passion
The Incident
Innocent Prey
Intimate Stranger
Investigation
The Invisible Ghost
Jack Be Nimble
Jacob's Ladder
Jade
Juggernaut
Julia and Julia
The Juror
Killer Inside Me
The Killing Mind
A Kiss Goodnight
Kiss of a Killer
Knife in the Water▶
Knight Moves
La Rupture
La Vengeance d'une Femme
Lady in Waiting
Laser Moon
The Last of Sheila
The Last Seduction▶
Le Boucher▶
Leave Her to Heaven▶
Les Bonnes Femmes▶
Love, Cheat & Steal
Love Crimes
Love Is a Gun
Love, Lies and Murder
M▶
The Maddening
Magic
Make Haste to Live
Man on the Eiffel Tower▶
The Man Who Haunted Himself
The Mark▶
Marnie▶
Mayalunta
The Meal
Mean Season
Memories of Murder
Midnight Edition
Midnight Fear
Midnight Lace
Midnight Tease
Mind Games
Misery▶
Mrs. Munck
Mortal Sins
The Most Dangerous Game▶
Mother
Moving Targets
Murphy's Law
My Brother Has Bad Dreams
My Neighborhood
Naked Massacre
A Name for Evil
Nature of the Beast
The Net
Never Talk to Strangers
The Night of the Following Day
Night Train to Venice
The Night Walker
Nightmare at Bittercreek
Number One Fan
The Offence▶
One Night Stand
Opposing Force
Outrage
Pacific Heights▶
The Paint Job
Panic Station
The Paperboy
The Passion of Anna▶
A Passion to Kill
Peephole
Peeping Tom▶
The Penthouse
Perfect Alibi
Performance▶
Play Misty for Me▶
Playgirl Killer
Playmaker
Poison Ivy
Portrait in Terror
Posed For Murder
Praying Mantis
Pretty Poison▶
Prey of the Chameleon
Psycho 3
Psychomania
A Pure Formality
Rage
Raising Cain
Reason to Die
A Reflection of Fear
Relentless
Repulsion▶
Ricochet▶
Rituals
Room to Let
Rorret▶
Sapphire▶
Sarah's Child
Savage Abduction
Secret Beyond the Door
Secret Ceremony
Secret Games
Secret Games 2: The Escort
Secret Games 3
The Secretary
Secrets of Three Hungry Wives
Seduced
Seduced by Evil
The Seduction
Sensation
Separate Lives
Serial Killer
Seven▶
The Seventh Floor
Shadows in the Storm

Shallow Grave
Sharon's Secret
The Shining
Siesta
The Silence of the Lambs▶
Single White Female
The Sister-in-Law
Sleeping with the Enemy
A Small Killing
Snapdragon
The Soft Kill
Someone to Die For
Sorry, Wrong Number▶
Sorry, Wrong Number
The Spiral Staircase▶
Spiral Staircase
Stalked
Stalking Laura
Stardust Memories
The Stepfather▶
Stepfather 2: Make Room for Daddy
Stepfather 3: Father's Day
Storm
Strange Illusion
The Stranger▶
Stranger by Night
Striking Distance
Stripteaser
Suture
Svengali▶
Svengali
Sweet Killing
Tails You Live, Heads You're Dead
Tall, Dark and Deadly
A Taste for Killing
Tattoo
The Temp
The Tenant▶
Terrified
Thicker Than Water
Through a Glass Darkly▶
Through the Eyes of a Killer
The Tie That Binds
Till the End of the Night
Timebomb
To Play or To Die
Tower of Terror
Trapped
Trauma
Tryst
Tunnel Vision
Twisted Love
The Two Mrs. Carrolls
Undertow
Unforgettable
Unlawful Entry
The Vanishing▶
Vengeance Is Mine▶
Victim of Love
Violated
Voyage
Wait Until Dark▶
Web of Deceit
What Ever Happened To...
When Hell Was in Session▶
When the Bough Breaks
When the Dark Man Calls
Where Are the Children?
While I Live
Wild Side
The Wind
Woman In the Window▶
The Young Poisoner's Handbook▶

Psychotics/ Sociopaths

see also Roommates from Hell

Accidental Meeting
The Avenger
Bad Ronald▶
The Bad Seed
Badlands▶
Bellamy
Berserk!
Black Eliminator
Black Panther
Black Pit of Dr. M
Blind Side
Blind Vision
Blue Steel
Body Bags
The Boston Strangler
Boxing Helena
The Boys Next Door
Broken Arrow
The Cable Guy
Cape Fear▶
Carrie▶
The Centerfold Girls
City Killer
Cold Eyes of Fear
Cold Steel
Consenting Adults
Crimes of Dr. Mabuse▶
The Crush
Damned River
Dario Argento's Trauma
The Dark Past▶
The Dark Ride
Das Testament des Dr. Mabuse▶
Dead as a Doorman
Dead Boyz Can't Fly
Deadbolt
Deadly Daphne's Revenge
Deadly Game
Death of a Soldier
Death Sentence
Demolition Man
Demon Hunter
Deranged▶
Deranged
Desperate Motives
Diary of a Teenage Hitchhiker
Dr. Giggles
Don't Answer the Phone
Don't Talk to Strangers
Doppelganger: The Evil Within
Down, Out and Dangerous
The Drifter
Ex-Cop
Eyes of the Beholder
Fade to Black
Fair Game
Falling Down
The Fan
Fast Gun
Fatal Attraction▶
Fear
Fear City
The Fear Inside
The Fool Killer
Force of Evil
From Dusk Till Dawn
Gallowglass▶
Girl in Black Stockings
Guardian Angel
Guilty as Sin
Headless Body in Topless Bar
Heat▶
Helter Skelter
Homer and Eddie
Honeymoon
The Hostage
Hot Potato
Hot Touch
House of Terror
The Housekeeper
Hush Little Baby, Don't You Cry
In the Line of Fire▶
In the Mouth of Madness
The Invisible Terror
Kalifornia
Killer Inside Me
Killing Obsession
Killing Zoe
Killzone
Lightning Bolt
The Lightship
The Little Girl Who Lives Down the Lane
Live Wire
Lunatic
The Mad Bomber
The Mad Executioners
Mademoiselle
A Man in Uniform
Maniac Warriors
Midnight 2: Sex, Death, and Videotape
Midnight Edition
Midnight Fear
Midnight Ride
Mommie Dearest
Mondo Balardo
Most Wanted
Mother's Boys
Moving Targets
Murder Elite
Murderlust
The Naked Flame
Naked Massacre
The Neighbor
Pacific Heights▶
The Paperboy
Past Midnight
Perfect Family
Perfect Victims
Play Nice
Playgirl Killer
Poison Ivy
Pretty Poison▶
Prime Time Murder
Psycho▶
Psycho 2
Psycho 3
Psycho 4: The Beginning
Psycho Girls
Psychos in Love
Quake
Rampage
Relentless
Repulsion▶
Reservoir Dogs▶
Ricochet▶
The River Wild
The Road Killers
Roadkill
The Sadist
Savage Abduction
The Sea Wolf▶
The Secretary
The Seduction
Seven Hours to Judgment
The Seventh Floor
The Shining
The Silencer
Single White Female
The Sister-in-Law
Skinner
Small Kill
Speed▶
Stalked
The Stepfather▶
Stepfather 2: Make Room for Daddy
Stepfather 3: Father's Day
Still Life
Stripped to Kill
Stripteaser
Sweet Hostage
Tainted Blood
The Taking of Beverly Hills
Tall, Dark and Deadly
Ted & Venus
The Temp
The Tenant▶
Tetsuo: The Iron Man
A Thin Line Between Love and Hate
Thirteenth Day of Christmas
Three the Hard Way
Through the Eyes of a Killer
To Die For▶
Twin Peaks: Fire Walk with Me
The Two Mrs. Carrolls
Unlawful Entry
The Vanishing
Vice Squad
Violence at Noon▶
Voyage
What Ever Happened to Baby Jane?▶
When a Stranger Calls Back
Whispers
White Heat▶
Writer's Block
The Young Poisoner's Handbook▶
The Zombie Army

Puppets

see also Killer Toys; Toys

The Adventures of Pinocchio
Alice in Wonderland
The Dark Crystal▶
Devil Doll
Early Russian Cinema, Vol. 3: Starewicz's Fantasies
Faust
The Great Gabbo
The Great Rupert▶
Lili▶
Magic
Meet the Feebles
Pinocchio▶
Puppet Master
Puppet Master 2
Puppet Master 4
Puppet Master 5: The Final Chapter

Pure Ego Vehicles

see also Big Budget Stinkers; Macho Men; Rock Stars on Film

The Adventures of Ford Fairlane
Air America
Assault of the Rebel Girls
Charade
Conan the Destroyer
The Dead Pool
Harlem Nights
Hello, Dolly!
Hudson Hawk
The Jazz Singer
Last Action Hero
Le Repos du Guerrier
Marie Antoinette
Modern Love
On Deadly Ground
Purple Rain
Rambo 3
Richard Petty Story
Running Out of Luck
The Scarlet Letter
Sidekicks
SnakeEater
Sophia Loren: Her Own Story
Staying Alive
Sweet Country Road
Tarzan, the Ape Man
Thank Your Lucky Stars▶
A Thin Line Between Love and Hate
To Hell and Back
Torch Song
200 Motels
Under the Cherry Moon
Vampire in Brooklyn
Waterworld
What Comes Around
Wildcats
The Wizard of Speed and Time
Yes, Giorgio

Queens

see Royalty

Race Against Time

Acceptable Risks
Alien Space Avenger
The Andromeda Strain
Apollo 13▶
Balto
Bitter Harvest▶
Blown Away
Broken Arrow
Chain Reaction
The China Syndrome▶
Coma▶
D.O.A.▶
D.O.A.
Escape from L.A.
Fail-Safe▶
Free Willy 2: The Adventure Home
Germicide
Grand Tour: Disaster in Time
Hell Commandos
In Pursuit of Honor
Jet Over the Atlantic
Killer on Board
Last Flight Out: A True Story
Lorenzo's Oil▶
Nick of Time
Octopussy
Once Upon a Forest
Outbreak▶
Panic in Echo Park
Panic in the Streets▶
Prisoner in the Middle
Pursuit▶
Robot in the Family
The Silver Streak
Somebody Has to Shoot the Picture▶
Sudden Death
The Taking of Beverly Hills
Things to Do In Denver When You're Dead▶
Time is Running Out
Time Lock
Time Without Pity
WarGames

Radio

see also Mass Media

Airheads
Bad Channels
Breakfast in Hollywood
Carefree▶
Choose Me▶
Citizens Band▶
City in Panic
Comfort and Joy▶
The Couch Trip
Danger on the Air
Dead Air
Dirty Mind of Young Sally
The Fisher King▶
FM
Freeway
Girls Night Out
Good Morning, Vietnam▶
The Great American Broadcast▶
The Hucksters▶
The Jackpot
The Key Man
Laser Moon
The Last Radio Station
Look Who's Laughing
The Man Who Came to Dinner▶
Midnight Confessions
My Dream Is Yours
The Next Voice You Hear
Night Rhythms
No Trace
Old Barn Dance
On the Air Live with Captain Midnight
Once Upon a Honeymoon
Open House
People Are Funny
People's Choice
The Phantom Broadcast
Play Misty for Me▶
Pot O' Gold
Psycho 4: The Beginning
Pump Up the Volume
Rachel River
Radio Days▶
Radioland Murders
Rebecca of Sunnybrook Farm
Sexual Response
Sleepless in Seattle▶
Straight Talk
Strike Up the Band
Talk Radio▶
There Goes Kelly
The Truth About Cats and Dogs▶
Tune in Tomorrow
Up in the Air
Whistling in Brooklyn
Who Done It?
WKRP in Cincinnati, Vol. 1
Zoo Radio

Rags to Riches

***see also** Price of Fame; Wrong Side of the Tracks*

The Abe Lincoln of Ninth Avenue
Aladdin▶
All the King's Men▶
The Amorous Adventures of Moll Flanders
Annie
Better Late Than Never
The Beverly Hillbillies
Blank Check
Body Slam
Breaking Glass
Brewster's Millions
The Buddy Holly Story▶
Callie and Son
Can You Hear the Laughter? The Story of Freddie Prinze
Christmas in July▶
Citizen Kane▶
Coal Miner's Daughter▶
Covergirl
Craig's Wife▶
Daddy Long Legs▶
Dangerous When Wet
Darling▶
Dodsworth▶
Dreamer
Drifting Souls
Emperor Jones
Fifth Avenue Girl
Footlight Parade▶
For Richer, For Poorer
Forever Amber
Give a Girl a Break
The Great Rupert▶
Hero▶
Honeyboy
The Hudsucker Proxy▶
I Love Melvin
It Could Happen to You
Jailhouse Rock▶
The Jerk
Jimmy Hollywood
Joseph Andrews
Kept Husbands
A Kid for Two Farthings
Kipps▶
La Vie est Belle
Lady for a Day▶
Lady Grey
The Last American Hero▶
The Last Laugh▶
Laurel & Hardy: Below Zero
Lenny▶
Lili▶
Little Lord Fauntleroy▶
Little Lord Fauntleroy
Livin' Large
Lots of Luck
Love Nest
Lucky Partners
The Mambo Kings▶
The Manions of America
Mannequin
Meet John Doe▶
A Million to Juan
Miss Melody Jones
Mrs. Parkington
Mrs. Winterbourne
Mr. Billion
Money for Nothing
My Fair Lady▶
New York's Finest
The Object of Beauty▶
One in a Million: The Ron LeFlore Story
Only One Night
The Patsy
The Pearl▶
Peddlin' in Society
Possessed
Power
Pride of the Clan
The Prince and the Pauper▶
The Prince and the Pauper
The Prince and the Showgirl
Princess Tam Tam▶
Pygmalion▶
Rebecca of Sunnybrook Farm
Rocky▶
Scarlet Dawn
Scruples
The Secret of My Success
Sepia Cinderella
The Sin of Harold Diddlebock
The Sin of Madelon Claudet▶
Sing Your Worries Away
Speak Easily
The Stars Fell on Henrietta
The Stork Club
Straight Talk
Striker's Mountain
Sweet Adeline
Sweet Hearts Dance
The Tall Guy▶
Tennessee Stallion
Three Coins in the Fountain
The Toast of New Orleans
Toast of New York▶
Trading Places
Trois Couleurs: Blanc▶
The Unsinkable Molly Brown▶
What Price Hollywood?▶
Working Girl▶
Ziegfeld Girl▶

Rape

***see also** Sexual Abuse*

The Accused▶
Act of Vengeance
The Adventurers
American Commandos
And Justice for All
Awakening of Candra
Backlash
Bad Lieutenant▶
Bandit Queen
The Beast Within
Blind Justice
Blue Desert▶
Born Innocent
Broken Badge▶
Bullies
Caged Heat 2: Stripped of Freedom
Caged Terror
Cast the First Stone
Casualties of War▶
Certain Sacrifice
Chain Gang Women
Class of 1984
Code of Honor
Convicted
Coward of the County
Dead Man Walking▶
Deadline Assault
Deadly Daphne's Revenge
Deadly Darling
Deadly Twins
Death and the Maiden▶
Death Blow
Death Wish
Deep in the Heart
Demented
The Desperados
Diary of a Lost Girl▶
Diary of a Teenage Hitchhiker
Emmanuelle's Daughter
The Entity
Extremities
An Eye for an Eye
Flesh and Blood
Forbidden Sun
Forced Entry
Free, White, and 21
From the Life of the Marionettes▶
Fugitive Among Us
The Furious Avenger
Gentle Savage
Girls Town
Guncrazy
Hands of a Stranger
Hannie Caulder
Heat of the Flame
His Name was King
Home Before Midnight
The Hooked Generation
The Hotel New Hampshire
I Spit on Your Grave
I'm the One You're Looking For
In Trouble
It's Alive▶
Jackson County Jail
Jailbait: Betrayed By Innocence
Judge Horton and the Scottsboro Boys
Kika
Kiss of a Killer
The Ladies Club
Landscape in the Mist▶
Lethal Woman
Lipstick
Liquid Sky▶
Ms. 45▶
Mrs. R's Daughter
Most Wanted
Motor Psycho
Multiple Maniacs
Naked Vengeance
Necromancer: Satan's Servant
Night of the Demon
Northville Cemetery Massacre
Olivier, Olivier▶
Open Doors▶
Outrage
A Passage to India▶
The Phantom of Soho
Positive I.D.
Postcards from America
Purgatory
Rage▶
The Ramrodder
Rape and Marriage: The Rideout Case
Rape of Love
Rashomon▶
A Reason to Believe
Rider on the Rain▶
Rob Roy▶
Screamer
Sex Crimes
Shame
The Shaming
She Came on the Bus
Short Fuse
Showgirls
Silent Witness
Sketch Artist 2: Hands That See
Slashed Dreams
A Stranger is Watching
Straw Dogs▶
Streets
Sudden Death
Sudden Impact
Tainted
Time to Kill
A Time to Kill▶
To Kill a Mockingbird▶
To Kill a Stranger
The Tormentors
Trespasses
Vengeance of the Snowmaid
Violated
Violent Ones
The Violent Years
When He's Not a Stranger▶
Wild Riders
The Wind▶
The Young One

Rebel With a Cause

***see also** Rebel Without a Cause; The Resistance*

Acceptable Risks
The Accused▶
Ace High
The Adventures of Robin Hood▶
Afterburn▶
Alice's Restaurant
American Tiger
Ann Vickers
The Applegates
Armageddon: The Final Challenge
As Young As You Feel▶
The Attic: The Hiding of Anne Frank
Billy Jack
The Blob
Blue Collar▶
Born Losers
Boyz N the Hood▶
Braveheart▶
Brubaker▶
Burglar▶
The Burmese Harp▶
The China Syndrome▶
Courage▶
Courageous Dr. Christian
Crime of Honor
Dark Rider
Daybreak
Dead Poets Society▶
Deadly Business▶
Deadly Stranger
Die Hard▶
Die Hard 2: Die Harder▶
Dragon Fury
A Dream for Christmas▶
Dust▶
East of Eden▶
East of Eden
Easy Wheels
Exiled in America
The Fighter▶
The Fighter
The Final Alliance
The Firing Line
The $5.20 an Hour Dream
Flesh and the Spur
Flight of the Intruder
The Fugitive▶
The Gambling Samurai
Game of Survival
Gandhi▶
Gorillas in the Mist▶
Guess Who's Coming to Dinner▶
Hair▶
Hardcore
Hidden City
In the Name of the Father▶
Iron Horsemen
Iron Thunder
James Dean Story
Jesse
Joe Kidd
Johnny Firecloud
Katherine
Killing of Randy Webster
Knights of the City
Kung Fu
La Marseillaise▶
The Last American Hero▶
Lawrence of Arabia▶
Legend of Billie Jean
Legend of Earl Durand
Legend of the Lone Ranger
Little Tough Guys
Lois Gibbs and the Love Canal
The Loneliness of the Long Distance Runner▶
Lust for Life▶
Luther
Man of Marble▶
The Manhattan Project
Marie▶
Memories of Underdevelopment
Mr. Smith Goes to Washington▶
Mountain Man
Network▶
Night of Evil
Norma Rae▶
Northern Lights▶
Odd Man Out▶
One-Eyed Jacks▶
One Man Jury
One Man's War
Original Intent
Outbreak▶
Overdrawn at the Memory Bank
Paths of Glory▶
Patty Hearst
Plutonium Baby
The Principal
Project X
Punk Rock Movie
Quarantine
A Raisin in the Sun▶
Rob Roy▶
Robin Hood: Prince of Thieves
The Rock▶
Roe vs. Wade▶
Rooster: Spurs of Death!
Sakharov▶
Samaritan: The Mitch Snyder Story▶
The Sand Pebbles▶
Sansho the Bailiff▶
Save the Lady
The Scarlet Pimpernel▶
Serpico▶
The Shock
Silkwood▶
Sins of Rome
Somebody Has to Shoot the Picture▶
Stay Away, Joe
Steel Frontier
The Stranger
The Stranger Wore a Gun
Sympathy for the Devil
Taffin
Tank Girl
This Land is Mine▶
The Tin Star▶
To Kill a Priest
Trial of the Catonsville Nine
True Believer
Under Western Stars
V: The Final Battle
Vengeance
WarGames
The Westerner▶
When a Man Rides Alone
Wisdom

Rebel Without a Cause

***see also** Rebel With a Cause*

Across the Tracks
All Night Long▶
Badlands▶
A Boy and His Dog
The Boys Next Door
Breathless▶
Breathless
Cheech and Chong's Up in Smoke
A Clockwork Orange▶
Cool As Ice
The Cruel Story of Youth▶
Dino
Easy Rider▶
The Electric Horseman
The Fence
Ferris Bueller's Day Off▶
Five Easy Pieces▶
The Fugitive Kind
Fury to Freedom: The Life Story of Raul Ries
Girls' Town
Going Places▶
Gore Vidal's Billy the Kid
Great Missouri Raid
Guncrazy
Heart Beat
Hud▶
I Was a Teenage Werewolf
If...▶
James Dean
Just for the Hell of It
Leather Jackets
The Little Valentino
Lost Angels
On the Edge: The Survival of Dana
Over the Edge▶
Petit Con
Presumed Guilty
Pump Up the Volume
Rambo: First Blood, Part 2
Rambo 3
Rebel High
Rebel Rousers
Rebel Without a Cause▶
Reckless
Road House
Rocky 4
September 30, 1955
sex, lies and videotape▶
Snow Kill

Suburbia
Summer Camp Nightmare
That Was Then...This Is Now
3:15—The Moment of Truth
Thunder Road▶
Top Gun
The Violent Years
West Side Story▶
The Wild Angels
The Wild One▶
The Wild Ride

Red Scare

see also Russia/USSR

Arsenal▶
Baltic Deputy▶
The Bamboo Saucer
Battle Beneath the Earth
Chapayev▶
China Cry
China, My Sorrow
Coming Out of the Ice▶
Comment Ca Va?
The Commies are Coming, the Commies are Coming
Commissar▶
Comrade X
Conspirator
Death of a Bureaucrat▶
Earth▶
Eminent Domain
Fellow Traveler▶
Golden Gate
The Great Armored Car Swindle
Guilty by Suspicion
Guilty of Treason
Hands Up▶
Hawthorne of the USA
Indochine▶
The Inner Circle▶
The Interrogation▶
Invasion U.S.A.
Jet Pilot
Little World of Don Camillo▶
Man of Iron▶
Man of Marble▶
Mandela▶
Mother Kusters Goes to Heaven▶
Mother of Kings
Never Let Me Go
Nicholas and Alexandra
Night Crossing
Night Flight from Moscow
The Oak
Oh, Bloody Life!
Open Doors▶
The Red Menace
Red Nightmare
Reds▶
Requiem for Dominic▶
Revolution! A Red Comedy▶
The She-Beast
Sideburns
Strike▶
The Theme▶
Thoughts are Free▶
Tito and Me▶
Tobor the Great
Trahir▶
The Ugly American
Uranus▶
When Father was Away on Business▶

Religion

see also Buddhism; Islam; Judaism; Missionaries; Nuns & Priests; Religious Epics; Saints

Abduction of St. Anne
Absolution
The Addiction
Androcles and the Lion
Angel Baby
Angela
Anna
Augustine of Hippo▶
The Avenging Angel
Before the Rain▶
Bernadette
The Birch Interval
The Blasphemer
Blood of Jesus
Body and Soul
Breaking the Waves▶
Brides of Christ
Brigham Young: Frontiersman
Broken Vows
Brother Cadfael
Brother Sun, Sister Moon
Brothers in Arms
Caligari's Cure▶
Camila▶
Catholics▶
Chariots of Fire▶
Children of Fury
The Church▶
Come to the Stable▶
The Confessional
Conquest of Space
Cosmic Slop
The Courageous Mr. Penn
Crimes of Passion▶
The Crucible▶
A Cry from the Mountain
Day of Judgment
Day of Triumph
Dead Man Walking▶
Def by Temptation
Devi▶
The Devil at 4 O'Clock
The Disappearance of Aimee▶
Dr. Syn
Dr. Syn, Alias the Scarecrow
A Dream for Christmas▶
El Cid▶
El: This Strange Passion▶
Emanon
Enjo
Extramuros
The Favor, the Watch, & the Very Big Fish
The Fiend
Final Judgement
The Flowers of St. Francis▶
A Fool and His Money
Francesco
Friendly Persuasion▶
The Garden
The Ghoul
Glory! Glory!▶
Go Down Death
The Godfather, Part 3▶
God's Gun
Gospa
Greaser's Palace
The Greatest Story Ever Told
Green Pastures▶
The Guyana Tragedy: The Story of Jim Jones
Hail Mary
Hallelujah!▶
Hazel's People
Heavens Above▶
Helas Pour Moi
Hellfire
Holy Matrimony
The Hoodlum Priest▶
Household Saints▶
I, the Worst of All
I'd Climb the Highest Mountain▶
In the Line of Duty: Ambush in Waco
Inherit the Wind▶
The Inquiry
Invasion of the Space Preachers
Iron Horsemen
Jesus
Jesus Christ, Superstar▶
Jesus of Nazareth
Jesus of Nazareth▶
The Jesus Trip
Joan of Arc
Joni
The Judas Project: The Ultimate Encounter
Klondike Annie
La Chartreuse de Parme
Lamb
The Last Temptation of Christ▶
Laughing Sinners
Leap of Faith
Leaves from Satan's Book
The Light of Faith
Little Buddha
Little Church Around the Corner
The Littlest Angel
Love and Faith▶
Luther
Major Barbara▶
A Man Called Peter▶
Marjoe
Martin Luther
The Meeting: Eddie Finds a Home
The Messenger of the Blessed Virgin
The Milky Way▶
The Miracle▶
Miracle in Rome
Miracle of Our Lady of Fatima
Mohammed: Messenger of God
Monsieur Vincent▶
Monsignor Quixote
Monty Python's Life of Brian▶
A Mormon Maid
Mother Joan of the Angels▶
The Neon Bible
The Next Voice You Hear
The Night of the Iguana▶
One Man's Way
Ordet▶
Padre Nuestro
Pass the Ammo
The Passion of Joan of Arc▶
The Passover Plot
The Penitent
Pray TV
Preacherman
Priest
Prisoner of Rio
The Private Secretary
The Prodigal Planet
Promised a Miracle
Queen Margot▶
Quo Vadis▶
Quo Vadis
Rain
The Rapture
The Rector's Wife
Red Planet Mars
Resurrection▶
Return to Paradise
The Robe
RoGoPaG
Romero
Sacrilege
St. Benny the Dip
Saint Joan
Salome
Salvation!
Sanctuary of Fear
Sebastiane▶
Shadowlands▶
Shiokari Pass
The Sky Pilot
The Song of Bernadette▶
Susan and God▶
Tales from the Crypt Presents Bordello of Blood
That Eye, The Sky
This Stuff'll Kill Ya!
Through a Glass Darkly▶
Tournament
Trapped by the Mormons
The Vision
When Night is Falling▶
Where Angels Go, Trouble Follows
Whistle Down the Wind▶
Whistling in the Dark▶
Whitcomb's War
The White Rose▶
Wholly Moses!
Why Has Bodhi-Darma Left for the East
The Winter Light▶
Wise Blood▶
Witness▶
The Word
The Worldly Madonna

Religious Epics

see also Religion

Abraham
The Agony and the Ecstasy
...And God Spoke
Barabbas
Ben-Hur▶
The Bible...In the Beginning▶
Cleopatra
David and Bathsheba▶
Demetrius and the Gladiators
The Egyptian
El Cid▶
From the Manger to the Cross
The Gospel According to St. Matthew▶
In the Name of the Pope-King▶
Jacob
Jesus of Nazareth
Joseph
Judith of Bethulia▶
A Man for All Seasons▶
Moses
The Prodigal
The Robe
The Sign of the Cross
Sodom and Gomorrah
The Song of Bernadette▶
The Story of David▶
The Story of Jacob & Joseph▶
The Story of Ruth
The Sword and the Cross
The Ten Commandments
The Ten Commandments▶

Renegade Body Parts

see also Horror; Killer Brains

The Addams Family
Addams Family Values
The Beast with Five Fingers
Blood of Ghastly Horror
Body Parts
The Brain That Wouldn't Die
The Crawling Eye
The Crawling Hand
Demonoid, Messenger of Death
Doctor Butcher M.D.
The Hand▶
Hands of a Stranger
The Hands of Orlac
How to Get Ahead in Advertising▶
The Kingdom
The Man with Two Brains▶
Mindkiller
Severed Ties
Waxwork 2: Lost in Time

Repressed Men

see also Men

The Age of Innocence▶
Bitter Moon
The Eighth Day
Falling Down
Maurice▶
The Remains of the Day▶
Shadowlands▶
Sirens

Rescue Missions

see also Rescue Missions Involving Time Travel

The Amazing Panda Adventure
Apollo 13▶
Balto
Berlin Tunnel 21
Boomerang
Born to Be Wild
Breakout
Caged Fear
The Children
The City of Lost Children
Commando▶
Crossfire
Daredevils of the Red Circle
Dark Mountain
Desperate Women
Die Hard▶
Die Hard 2: Die Harder▶
Die Hard: With a Vengeance
The Dirty Dozen: The Deadly Mission
Dragonworld
Ernest Scared Stupid
Escape from L.A.
The Ewok Adventure
Executioner of Venice
Executive Decision
Expect No Mercy
Far from Home: The Adventures of Yellow Dog
Force: Five
Free Willy
Free Willy 2: The Adventure Home
Hard Ticket to Hawaii
High Velocity
Hired to Kill
Honeybaby
The Inn of the Sixth Happiness▶
Jenny's War
Killing Streets
The Lone Runner
The Losers
Losing Isaiah▶
The Magnificent Seven▶
Mercy Mission
Missing in Action
Missing in Action 2: The Beginning
Naked Souls
Navy SEALS
Oliver & Company
Operation Dumbo Drop
Outbreak▶
Pray for Death
Raid on Entebbe▶
Rambo: First Blood, Part 2
The Rescue
Rescue Me
Return of Chandu
Revenge of the Barbarians
The Rock▶
The Sea Shall Not Have Them
The Searchers▶
Seven Samurai▶
The Slender Thread▶
Soldier Boyz
The Story of Dr. Wassell
Stranglehold
Street Fighter
Sudden Death
The Taking of Flight 847: The Uli Derickson Story▶
A Thousand Heroes
Three Days to a Kill
Thunder in Paradise
Thunder in Paradise 2
Toy Story▶
Two Bits & Pepper
Uncommon Valor
Waikiki Wedding▶
The Yakuza

Rescue Missions Involving Time Travel

see also Rescue Missions

Back to the Future▶
Back to the Future, Part 2
Back to the Future, Part 3▶
Bill & Ted's Excellent Adventure
Jumanji
Maximum Breakout
Millenium
The Navigator▶
Star Trek 4: The Voyage Home▶
Superman: The Movie▶
The Terminator▶
Terminator 2: Judgment Day▶
Time After Time▶
Timemaster
Trancers 2: The Return of Jack Deth

The Resistance

see also World War II

Action in the North Atlantic

Alfred Hitchcock's Bon Voyage
Casablanca▶
A Day in October
Holocaust▶
The Last Metro▶
Les Miserables
Manon
One Against the Wind▶
Passage to Marseilles▶
Soldier of Orange▶
That Summer of White Roses
The Train▶
The White Rose▶

Revealing Swimwear

The American Angels: Baptism of Blood
Beach Babes from Beyond Infinity
Beach Girls
Best Buns on the Beach
The Bikini Car Wash Company
The Bikini Car Wash Company 2
Bikini Island
Bikini Summer
Bikini Summer 2
Blood of Dracula's Castle
Blue Ribbon Babes
Body Waves
Buford's Beach Bunnies
California Girls
The Cover Girl Murders
Dark Tide
The Dolls
Fit to Kill
Frankenstein Island
Fun in Acapulco
Girls Next Door
Great Bikini Off-Road Adventure
Hardbodies
Hollywood High, Part 2
Hollywood Hot Tubs
Hollywood Hot Tubs 2: Educating Crystal
Horrors of Spider Island
Hot Resort
The House that Vanished
Island of Lost Girls
L'Annee des Meduses
Malibu Beach
The Malibu Beach Vampires
Malibu Bikini Shop
Malibu Express
Mugsy's Girls
Ocean Drive Weekend
Our Man Flint
Pauline at the Beach▶
Pin-Up Girl
Playgirl Killer
Private Lessons, Another Story
Slumber Party Massacre 2
Sorority House Party
Starhops
Summer City
Summer Fantasy
Summer's Games
Swimsuit: The Movie
Tarzan, the Ape Man
They Were So Young
Tintorera...Tiger Shark
Vice Academy 3
Welcome to Spring Break
When Dinosaurs Ruled the Earth

Revenge

see also Vigilantes

Act of Aggression
Act of Passion: The Lost Honor of Kathryn Beck
Act of Vengeance
An Actor's Revenge
Adios, Hombre
The Adventurers
Against the Drunken Cat Paws
The Alchemist
Alien Seed
All Dogs Go to Heaven
American Commandos
American Eagle
American Samurai
Anatomy of a Psycho
Angel and the Badman▶
Angel of Destruction
Angel Square
Angels from Hell
Appointment with Crime
Archer: The Fugitive from the Empire
Arizona Terror
Asylum
Attack of the 50 Ft. Woman
Avenging Angel
Avenging Force
Back in Action
Back to Back
Bad Blood
Ballad of Cable Hogue▶
The Ballad of the Sad Cafe
Bandits
Banzai Runner
The Baron
Basket Case▶
The Beast with Five Fingers
The Beguiled▶
Bell from Hell
Benefit of the Doubt
Best of the Best 2
Beyond Forgiveness
Big Bully
Big Jake
Bitter Vengeance
Black Arrow▶
The Black Arrow
Black Cobra
Black Dragon's Revenge
The Black Hand▶
The Black Klansman
The Black Pirate▶
The Black Raven
Black Scorpion
The Black Six
Black Sunday▶
A Black Veil for Lisa
Blackbelt 2: Fatal Force
Blind Vengeance
Blood and Guns
Blood for a Silver Dollar
Blood on the Mountain
Blood Red
Blood Ring
Bloodfist
Bloodknot
Bloodmatch
Bloody Birthday
The Bloody Fight
The Blue Knight
The Blue Lamp▶
Blue Tiger
Body Count
Boiling Point
Border Rangers
Born Invincible
Bounty Hunters
Bounty Tracker
Branded a Coward
Bride of Killer Nerd
Broken Harvest
Bronze Buckaroo
Brotherhood of Justice
Bruce Li the Invincible
The Brute Man
Bulldance
Bulldog Courage
Bullet for Sandoval
Bullies
The Burning
Bury Me an Angel
Cadillac Man
Caged Heat 2: Stripped of Freedom
Caged Terror
Cape Fear▶
The Caravan Trail
Carolina Skeletons
Carson City Kid
Cartouche▶
Certain Sacrifice
Chain Gang Women
The Chair
Challenge
Chameleon
Chan is Missing▶
The Chase
Chisum
Chrome and Hot Leather
Circumstances Unknown
Class of 1984
Clayton County Line
Cobra
Cobra Against Ninja
Code Name: Zebra
Code of Honor
Coffy
Cold Eyes of Fear
Cold Justice
Cold Steel
Cold Sweat
Cole Justice
Commando Invasion
Conflict of Interest
Conqueror & the Empress
A Cop for the Killing
Cornered▶
The Count of Monte Cristo
The Count of Monte Cristo▶
The Count of Monte Cristo
The Count of the Old Town
The Courier
Covert Assassin
The Cowboys▶
Crack House
The Craft
Crazed Cop
Creepers
Crimebusters
The Crossing Guard▶
The Crow
The Crow 2: City of Angels▶
Cry Danger▶
Cry of the Innocent▶
The Cry of the Owl
Cry Vengeance
Curse of the Devil
Daddy-O
Daddy's Gone A-Hunting▶
Danger Zone 2
Dangerous Obsession
Dangerous Orphans
Dark August
Dark River: A Father's Revenge
Darkman▶
Daughter of the Dragon
DaVinci's War
Dawn Rider
The Day the Women Got Even
Dead Boyz Can't Fly
Dead Man's Revenge
Dead on the Money
Deadly Daphne's Revenge
Deadly Darling
Deadly Game
Deadly Lessons
Deadly Reactor
The Deadly Secret
Deadly Sting
The Deadly Trackers
Deadly Twins
Deadly Vengeance
Deadly Weapon
Death and the Maiden▶
Death Blow
Death Magic
Death Row Diner
Death Wish
Death Wish 2
Death Wish 3
Deep in the Heart
Demented
Demon Witch Child
The Demons
Demonwarp
Desperado▶
The Desperados
Desperate Crimes
Devastator
Devil Times Five
Devil Woman
Devil's Canyon
The Devil's Mistress
The Devil's Possessed
Devonsville Terror
The Diabolical Dr. Z
Diamond Ninja Force
Die! Die! My Darling!
Die Hard: With a Vengeance
Dingaka
Dinner at the Ritz
Diplomatic Immunity
Dirty Harry▶
Disclosure
The Divine Enforcer
Dixie Dynamite
Do or Die
Dr. Syn, Alias the Scarecrow
Dr. Terror's House of Horrors
Dolemite
Double Exposure
The Double Negative
Double Revenge
Driven to Kill
Drop Zone
Drums of Jeopardy
Dudes
Dynasty
Eagles Attack at Dawn
Easy Kill
Edge of Darkness
The Eiger Sanction
El Barbaro
The Eliminators
Emmanuelle, the Queen
The Empire of Passion▶
The Equalizer: Memories of Manon
Escape
The Evil That Men Do
Evilspeak
Ex-Cop
The Execution
The Executioner, Part 2: Frozen Scream
The Expert
Exterminator
Exterminator 2
Extreme Vengeance
Extremities
An Eye for an Eye
Eye of the Eagle 2
Eye of the Tiger
Fair Game
Faithful
The Fall of the House of Usher
The Fall of the House of Usher▶
The Fall of the House of Usher
Falling Down
Far Country▶
Fight for Us
Fight for Your Life
The Fighter▶
Fighting Back
The Fighting Legion
Fighting Mad
Final Impact
Final Mission
Fine Gold
Fiorile▶
Firecracker
Fist Fighter
Fist of Honor
Fists of Blood
Fists of Iron
Flesh and Blood
Flesh and the Spur
Flesh Feast
Fleshburn
Fog Island
For Your Eyes Only▶
Forbidden Sun
Force of Evil
Forced Vengeance
Forgotten Warrior
The Four Musketeers▶
Frame Up
Framed
Freaks▶
Freeway
Frightmare
Frogs
The Fugitive: The Final Episode
Full Contact
Full Metal Ninja
Funland
The Furious Avenger
Future Kill
"G" Men▶
Galloping Dynamite
The Gambling Samurai
Gangs, Inc.
Garringo
Gator Bait 2: Cajun Justice
Genghis Cohn
Gentleman from Dixie
Getting Even
The Ghost
Ghost Dance
The Ghost of Yatsuya
Ghostriders
The Girl with the Hungry Eyes
The Godfather▶
The Godfather 1902-1959: The Complete Epic▶
The Godfather, Part 2▶
God's Gun
Gone with the West
Good Men and Bad
Grave of the Vampire
The Graveyard
The Great Hunter
Green Mansions
Gunplay
Gunsmoke: Return to Dodge
Halloween▶
Halloween 6: The Curse of Michael Myers
Hamlet▶
Hang 'Em High
Hannie Caulder
Hard Bounty
Hard to Kill
Hardcase and Fist
The Haunted Palace
HauntedWeen
Hawkeye
He Who Gets Slapped▶
Headless Eyes
Heat Street
The Heist
Hell Hunters
Hell on Frisco Bay
Hellbent
Hello Mary Lou: Prom Night 2
Hell's Angels '69
Hell's Belles
Hennessy
Hi-Riders
The Hidden Room▶
High Command
High Noon▶
Hired Hand
Hit!
Hit & Run
Hog Wild
Homeboy
Hornet's Nest
Horror Rises from the Tomb
The Horror Show
Hot Lead
Hour of the Gun
House Across the Bay
A House In The Hills
House of Horrors
House of Strangers▶
How to Make a Monster
Human Beasts
The Human Factor
Hunter
I Drink Your Blood
I Married a Witch▶
I Met a Murderer
I Spit on Your Grave
Igor & the Lunatics
Illicit Behavior
I'm the One You're Looking For
In a Glass Cage
In Deadly Heat
In the Realm of Passion
In Your Face
The Indestructible Man
Inn of the Damned
An Innocent Man
Innocent Victim
Inquisition
Instant Justice
The Invisible Man's Revenge
Iron Dragon Strikes Back
Ironheart
Jailbird's Vacation

Revolutionary War

Rio

Road Trip

see also Bikers; Chases; Fast Cars; Motor Vehicle Dept.

Roaring '20s

Robots & Androids

see also Technology-Rampant

Rock Stars on Film

see also Concert Films; Martyred Pop Icons; Pure Ego Vehicles

Kissin' Cousins
La Bamba▶
The Last Temptation of Christ▶
The Legacy
Let It Be
Lisztomania
Live a Little, Love a Little
Love Me Tender
Loving You
The Magic Christian▶
Magical Mystery Tour
The Man Who Fell to Earth▶
McVicar
Merry Christmas, Mr. Lawrence▶
Mrs. Brown, You've Got a Lovely Daughter
Monster Dog
Nomads
One Trick Pony
Paradise, Hawaiian Style
Pat Garrett & Billy the Kid▶
Performance▶
Pink Floyd: The Wall
Poetic Justice
Quadrophenia▶
Rock 'n' Roll High School▶
Roustabout
Speedway
Spinout
Stay Away, Joe
That'll Be the Day
This Is Elvis
Tickle Me
Tommy
The Trouble with Girls (and How To Get Into It)▶
Viva Las Vegas
Wild in the Country
Woodstock▶
Yellow Submarine▶

Rodeos

see also Westerns

The Adventures of Gallant Bess
Arizona Cowboy
Born Reckless
Convict Cowboy
The Cowboy Way
Desert Trail
8 Seconds
Feud of the West
Girl from Calgary
Goldenrod
Junior Bonner▶
Kid from Gower Gulch
Lady Takes a Chance▶
The Last Ride
Lights of Old Santa Fe
The Lusty Men▶
Luzia
Man from Utah
The Misfits▶
My Heroes Have Always Been Cowboys
Never a Dull Moment
Oklahoma Cyclone
Painted Hero
Rhythm on the Range
Rider from Tucson
Rodeo Girl
Rolling Home
Saddle Buster
Trouble in Texas
Western Double Feature 5
Wild Horse
Wild Horse Rodeo

Role Reversal

see also Gender Bending; Identity

Age Isn't Everything
All of Me
Anastasia▶
Anastasia: The Mystery of Anna
Angel
Angel on My Shoulder▶
Angel on My Shoulder
Babe▶
Bad Manners
The Bank Dick▶
Before Morning
Belfast Assassin
Big▶
Biggles
Billy Madison
Blood of Dracula
Bloodlink
The Captain from Koepenick
Captive Heart▶
Cheech and Chong's The Corsican Brothers
Christmas in Connecticut▶
Cinderfella
Clambake
Class Act
Cleo/Leo
Coming to America▶
Condorman
The Couch Trip
Courage▶
Dave▶
The Deputy Drummer
Desperately Seeking Susan
Devil's Canyon
Dr. Black, Mr. Hyde
Doctor Detroit
Doctor Dolittle
Dr. Heckyl and Mr. Hype
Dr. Jekyll and Mr. Hyde▶
Dr. Jekyll and Mr. Hyde
Doctors and Nurses
Down and Out in Beverly Hills
Dream a Little Dream
A Dream of Passion
18 Again!
Extremities
The $5.20 an Hour Dream
For Ladies Only
48 Hrs.▶
Freaky Friday
The Gladiator▶
The Grand Duchess and the Waiter▶
The Great Gabbo
Greystoke: The Legend of Tarzan, Lord of the Apes
Guest Wife
Gunfire
Heart Like a Wheel
Her Life as a Man
Hero▶
Hiding Out
Identity Crisis
The Incredible Mr. Limpet
Iron Maze
Jekyll and Hyde
Johnny Guitar▶
Junior
Just One of the Guys
Kagemusha▶
Kim▶
Kings and Desperate Men
La Femme Nikita▶
La Ronde▶
The Lady Vanishes▶
The Lady Vanishes
Ladybugs
Law and Order
Liana, Jungle Goddess
Like Father, Like Son
Liquid Sky▶
Lonely Wives
Maid to Order
Male and Female▶
The Man Who Haunted Himself
The Man Who Wagged His Tail
Man with Two Heads
Mrs. Winterbourne
Monkey Business▶
Moon over Parador
My Blue Heaven
My Fair Lady▶
My Neighborhood
Now, Voyager▶
Opportunity Knocks
Overboard
Panamint's Bad Man
Paris When It Sizzles
People's Choice
Performance▶
Persona▶
Pocketful of Miracles▶
Point of No Return
Posse▶
The Prince and the Pauper▶
The Prince and the Pauper
Prisoner of Zenda▶
Prisoner of Zenda
Psycho▶
Quicksilver
Rabbit Test
The Raggedy Rawney
Raid on Rommel
Red Lion
Red Rock Outlaw
Rendez-Moi Ma Peau
Rider of the Law
The Road to Yesterday
Roman Holiday▶
Satanik
Savages
Scalpel
The Scarlet Pimpernel▶
September Affair
The Shaggy D.A.
The Shaggy Dog
The Shakiest Gun in the West
Showdown in Little Tokyo
Silent Night, Deadly Night
Slapstick of Another Kind
A Slightly Pregnant Man
Small Town Boy
Something Special
Sometimes Aunt Martha Does Dreadful Things
Sommersby
Song of Texas
A Stolen Face
Stoogemania
Straight Talk
Summer Night with Greek Profile, Almond Eyes & Scent of Basil
Super Soul Brother
Sweet Revenge
Switch▶
Sylvia Scarlett
Taking Care of Business
A Tale of Two Cities▶
That Man Is Pregnant
That's My Baby!
Tomboy
Tootsie▶
Trading Places
Triple Echo
The Two Faces of Dr. Jekyll
Ultimate Desires
Vice Versa▶
Victor/Victoria▶
Wait Till Your Mother Gets Home
Watermelon Man
White Man's Burden
White Sands
Wonder Man
Yankee Zulu
Yentl
Yidl Mitn Fidl

Roll Over Beethoven

see also Musician Biopics

Beethoven Lives Upstairs
Beethoven's Nephew
Bill & Ted's Excellent Adventure
Immortal Beloved

Romance

see Late Bloomin' Love; Lovers on the Lam; Romantic Adventures; Romantic Comedy; Romantic Drama; Romantic Triangles

Romantic Adventures

The African Queen▶
Arabian Nights
Baby ... Secret of the Lost Legend
Destiny Turns on the Radio
Gun Crazy▶
Guncrazy
Gypsy Angels
The Jewel of the Nile
Joe Versus the Volcano
Lie Down with Lions
Mogambo▶
Pocahontas▶
Red Dust▶
Romancing the Stone▶
Son of Ali Baba
A Thousand and One Nights

Romantic Comedy

Abdulla the Great
About Last Night...▶
Acqua e Sapone
Adam's Rib▶
The Admiral Was a Lady
Adorable Julia
The Adventures of Sadie
Aggie Appleby, Maker of Men
Alfredo, Alfredo
All Night Long▶
All Tied Up
The Allnighter
All's Fair
...Almost
Almost an Angel
Almost Pregnant
Almost You
The Ambassador's Daughter
American Dreamer
American Friends
American Matchmaker
The American President▶
Amore!
The Amorous Adventures of Moll Flanders
And You Thought Your Parents Were Weird!
Animal Behavior
Anna Christie
Anna Karenina▶
Annabel Takes a Tour/Maid's Night Out
Annie Hall▶
Another Chance
Another Thin Man
The Apartment▶
April Fools
Are Parents People?
Arthur▶
Arthur 2: On the Rocks
Ask Any Girl
Avanti!
Baby Boom
Babycakes
Bachelor Apartment
Bachelor Bait
Bachelor in Paradise
Bachelor Party
Back to the Beach
Bahama Passage
Baja Oklahoma
Ball of Fire▶
The Balloonatic/One Week
Bar Girls
Bare Essentials
Barefoot in the Park▶
Barnaby and Me
The Bashful Bachelor
Battling Butler
Beachcomber▶
Bed & Breakfast
Belle Epoque▶
Bells are Ringing▶
Benny & Joon
Best Legs in the 8th Grade
Betsy's Wedding
Beyond Tomorrow
Birds & the Bees
Blame It on Rio
Blind Date
Blonde Crazy
Blue Country
Bluebeard's Eighth Wife
Bobo
Bombshell▶
Boom Town
Boomerang
Born Yesterday▶
Born Yesterday
Boyfriends & Girlfriends
Breakfast at Tiffany's▶
Breath of Scandal
The Bride Came C.O.D.
Bull Durham▶
But Not for Me
The Butcher's Wife
Butterflies
Bye Bye Baby
Cactus Flower
Cafe au Lait▶
Cafe Romeo
California Casanova
California Suite▶
Came a Hot Friday
The Cameraman▶
Can She Bake a Cherry Pie?
Can't Buy Me Love
Captain's Paradise▶
Car Trouble
Career Opportunities
Cartier Affair
Casanova
Casanova Brown
Casanova '70
The Cemetery Club
Chances Are▶
A Change of Seasons
Charley's Aunt
The Cheerful Fraud
Chilly Scenes of Winter
Christmas in Connecticut▶
Christmas in Connecticut
Class of '44
The Clock▶
Closely Watched Trains▶
Clueless▶
Cold Feet
Come Blow Your Horn▶
Come September
Comeback Kid
Coming to America▶
Continental Divide
Cool Blue
A Countess from Hong Kong
Couples and Robbers
The Cowboy and the Lady
Crazy in Love
Crazy Moon
Creator
Crocodile Dundee▶
Cross My Heart
Crossing Delancey▶
Curly Sue
Date with an Angel
Dear Brigitte
Dear Detective
Decameron Nights
Defending Your Life▶
The Demi-Paradise▶
Designing Woman▶
Desk Set▶
Desperate Moves
Desperately Seeking Susan
The Devil & Miss Jones▶
Different Story
Dirty Rotten Scoundrels▶
The Divorce of Lady X
Doc Hollywood
Doctor in Distress
Dr. Jack/For Heaven's Sake
Does This Mean We're Married?
Dollar
Dona Flor and Her Two Husbands▶
Dona Herlinda & Her Son
Don't Do It
Don't Hang Up
Don't Tell Her It's Me
Dream Date
Dream Trap
Dreaming of Rita
Dreams Come True
East and West▶
Electric Dreams
Elsa, Elsa
The Englishman Who Went Up a Hill But Came Down a Mountain▶
Eversmile New Jersey
Every Girl Should Be Married
Every Which Way But Loose

Face the Music
The Farmer's Daughter▶
The Farmer's Other Daughter
Fate
Father Goose
The Favor
Feelin' Screwy
Feet First
Fifth Avenue Girl
A Fine Romance
First Time
Flirt
Foolin' Around
For Better or Worse
For Heaven's Sake▶
For Love of Ivy
For Love or Money
Forget Paris
A Forgotten Tune for the Flute▶
Forty Carats
Four Weddings and a Funeral▶
Framed
Frankie and Johnny▶
French Kiss
The French Lesson
French Twist
Fridays of Eternity
Friends, Lovers & Lunatics
Full of Life
Funny About Love
Gabriela
The Gay Lady
Get Out Your Handkerchiefs▶
Getting It Right
The Ghost and the Guest
Gidget
Gidget Goes Hawaiian
Gidget Goes to Rome
Ginger in the Morning
A Girl, a Guy and a Gob
The Girl from Missouri▶
The Girl from Petrovka
The Girl in the Picture
Girl Shy▶
Girl Under the Sheet
The Glass Bottom Boat
Go Fish▶
The Gold of Naples▶
The Goodbye Girl▶
Goodbye, New York
The Grand Duchess and the Waiter▶
The Grass is Greener
The Great Gildersleeve
Green Card
Groundhog Day▶
The Halfback of Notre Dame
Hammersmith is Out
Hanky Panky
Happy New Year▶
Happy Together
Hardhat & Legs
Having It All
Having Wonderful Crime
Having Wonderful Time
He Said, She Said
Hear My Song▶
Heartaches▶
Heartbeat
Heartstrings
Heaven's a Drag
Her Alibi
Her First Romance
Herbie Goes to Monte Carlo
Hi Diddle Diddle
High Spirits
Higher Education
His First Flame▶
His Wife's Lover▶
Hobson's Choice▶
Hobson's Choice
Honeymoon Academy
Honeymoon in Vegas
Hook, Line and Sinker
The Horizontal Lieutenant
Hot Chocolate
House Calls▶
Houseboat
Housesitter
How to Marry a Millionaire
How to Steal a Million▶
How U Like Me Now?▶

Hurry, Charlie, Hurry
Hurry Up or I'll Be Thirty
I Don't Buy Kisses Anymore
I Know Where I'm Going▶
I Love Trouble
I Married a Centerfold
I Married a Witch▶
I Married a Woman
I Will, I Will for Now
Idiot's Delight▶
If Lucy Fell
Il Bell'Antonio
I'll Take Sweden
Imposters
Impromptu▶
In Love with an Older Woman
In Person
The Incredible Mr. Limpet
The Incredibly True Adventure of Two Girls in Love
Indiscreet
Indiscreet▶
Indiscreet
Innerspace
Instant Karma
Invitation to the Wedding
I.Q.
Irma La Douce
It
It Could Happen to You
It Happened One Night▶
It Should Happen to You▶
It Started with a Kiss
It Started with Eve▶
It Takes Two
It's My Turn
I've Heard the Mermaids Singing▶
Jeffrey
Jersey Girl
Jit
Jock Petersen
Joe Versus the Volcano
Joey Breaker▶
The Judge Steps Out
Julia Has Two Lovers
June Bride▶
Jupiter's Thigh
Just Like a Woman
Just Me & You
Just One of the Girls
Just Tell Me What You Want
Just the Way You Are
Key Exchange
Key to the City
The King on Main Street
King Ralph
A Kiss for Mary Pickford
Kiss Me Goodbye
Kiss Shot
Kuni Lemel in Tel Aviv
La Collectionneuse
La Lectrice
L.A. Story▶
La Vie de Boheme▶
The Lady Eve▶
The Lady is Willing
Lady L
Lady On a Train▶
Lady Takes a Chance▶
The Lady's Not for Burning
L'Annee des Meduses
Lassie from Lancashire
The Last Fling
The Last Married Couple in America
Late for Dinner
Le Beau Mariage▶
Le Magnifique
Legal Eagles
Lena's Holiday
Les Grandes Manoeuvres▶
Let's Make It Legal
Let's Make Love
Lt. Robin Crusoe, U.S.N.
The Linguini Incident
Listen to Your Heart
Little Noises
A Little Romance▶
Little Sister
A Little Stiff
Little White Lies

Live Bait
The Lonely Guy
Lonely Hearts▶
Lonely in America
Look Who's Talking▶
Look Who's Talking, Too
Loose in New York
Lost and Found
Lost in Yonkers
The Love Affair, or The Case of the Missing Switchboard Operator▶
Love Among the Ruins▶
Love at First Sight
Love by Appointment
Love Hurts
Love in the Afternoon
Love Is Better Than Ever
Love Laughs at Andy Hardy
Love on the Run
Love or Money?
Love Potion #9
Lovelines
Lover Come Back
Loverboy
Lovers and Liars
Lovers Like Us
Lovers' Lovers
Loves & Times of Scaramouche
Loving Couples
The Lunatic
Lunatics: A Love Story▶
Made in America
Made in Heaven
Magic on Love Island
The Magnificent Dope
The Maid
Maid's Night Out
The Main Event
Main Street to Broadway
A Majority of One
Making Mr. Right
Male and Female▶
Mama, There's a Man in Your Bed▶
A Man, a Woman, and a Bank
Man Trouble
The Man Who Loved Women▶
The Man Who Loved Women
Manhattan▶
Mannequin
Marriage Italian Style▶
Married?
Married to the Mob▶
The Marrying Man
The Matchmaker▶
Matrimaniac
May Wine
Me, Myself & I
Meeting Venus
Miami Rhapsody
Micki & Maude
A Midsummer Night's Dream▶
A Midsummer Night's Dream
Milk Money
The Millionairess
Miracle Beach
The Misadventures of Merlin Jones
Miss Right
Mrs. Winterbourne
Mr. Boggs Steps Out
Mr. Love
Mr. Lucky▶
Mr. Peabody & the Mermaid
Mr. Wonderful
Mr. Write
Modern Love
Modern Romance▶
Monaco Forever
A Month by the Lake
The Moon Is Blue
Moon Pilot
Moonstruck▶
Morgan!
Mouth to Mouth
Much Ado about Nothing▶
Murphy's Romance▶
My Best Friend's Girl
My Brother's Wife
My Dear Secretary
My Girl 2

My Love For Yours
My Man Godfrey
My Night at Maud's▶
My Stepmother Is an Alien
My Tutor
Mystery Date
The Mystery Man
Naked in New York
Never on Sunday▶
A New Kind of Love
A New Leaf
Next Time I Marry
Next Year If All Goes Well
Nice Girl Like Me
Nice Girls Don't Explode
Night and Day▶
The Night Club
The Night We Never Met
Nina Takes a Lover
Ninotchka▶
Nobody's Fool
The Norman Conquests, Part 1: Table Manners▶
The Norman Conquests, Part 2: Living Together▶
The Norman Conquests, Part 3: Round and Round the Garden▶
North to Alaska▶
Nothing Personal
The Nutty Professor▶
Off Beat
Okoge
On Approval▶
Once Around
One Rainy Afternoon
One, Two, Three▶
One Wild Moment
Only the Lonely
Only with Married Men
Only You
The Opposite Sex and How to Live With Them
Our Miss Brooks
Outrageous Fortune
Overboard
The Owl and the Pussycat▶
The Pallbearer
Panama Lady
Pantaloons
Paper Marriage
Pardon Mon Affaire▶
Paris Holiday
Pat and Mike▶
Peggy Sue Got Married
The Perfect Gift
Perfect Match
Perfectly Normal
Personal Property
The Personals
Phffft!
The Pick-Up Artist
Pillow Talk▶
Play It Again, Sam▶
Playmates
Pool Hustlers
Pool Sharks
Pop Always Pays
Prelude to a Kiss
Pretty Woman▶
Priceless Beauty
The Prince and the Showgirl
The Princess and the Pirate▶
Prisoner of Zenda
Private Lives▶
Probation
Promise Her Anything
Promises! Promises!
Protocol
The Purple Rose of Cairo▶
A Pyromaniac's Love Story
Quackser Fortune Has a Cousin in the Bronx▶
Queens Logic
Quick Change
The Quiet Man▶
The Raffle
The Rage of Paris▶
The Ranch
The Rat Race▶
Rattle of a Simple Man
Reaching for the Moon

Reality Bites
The Reluctant Debutante▶
Remember the Night▶
Rich in Love
The Ritz▶
Road to Ruin
Roads to the South
The Roaring Road
Roman Holiday▶
Romantic Comedy
Roses Bloom Twice
Round Numbers
Roxanne▶
Roxie Hart
Running Mates▶
Sabrina▶
Sabrina
Sacred Mountain/White Flame▶
Saratoga
Scorchers
Seaside Swingers
Secret Admirer
Secret Ingredient
Secret Life of an American Wife
The Secret of My Success
See You in the Morning
Seems Like Old Times
Send Me No Flowers▶
The Sensual Man
The Sensuous Nurse
Separate Vacations
Seven Days Ashore/Hurry, Charlie, Hurry
Seven Minutes in Heaven
The Seven Year Itch▶
Sex and the Single Girl
Sex and the Single Parent
Shadow of the Thin Man▶
Shanghai Surprise
She Done Him Wrong▶
She's Gotta Have It▶
She's Having a Baby
The Shop Around the Corner▶
Shore Leave▶
Short Circuit
The Shrimp on the Barbie
Sibling Rivalry
Singles▶
Sixteen Candles▶
Skin Deep
Sleepless in Seattle▶
Smiles of a Summer Night▶
Smokescreen
Snow: The Movie
Snowballin'
So This is Paris▶
Soapdish▶
The Social Secretary
Soldat Duroc...Ca Va Etre Ta Fete!
Something Short of Paradise
Soup for One
Speechless
Spite Marriage▶
Stand-In▶
State of the Union▶
The Station
The Sterile Cuckoo▶
Stolen Kisses▶
The Story of Boys & Girls▶
Straight Talk
Strange Bedfellows
Strictly Ballroom▶
Strictly Business
Stroke of Midnight
Summer School
Sunset Limousine
Surf Party
Surrender
Surviving Desire▶
Suzy
The Swan
The Swan▶
Sweet Lies
Sweet Talker
The Tall Guy▶
The Taming of the Shrew
The Taming of the Shrew▶
The Taming of the Shrew
Tammy and the Bachelor
Tammy and the Doctor

The Teahouse of the August Moon
Ted & Venus
The Tender Trap
That Certain Thing
That Lucky Touch
That Touch of Mink
That Uncertain Feeling
Theodora Goes Wild▶
There's a Girl in My Soup
They All Laughed
They Got Me Covered
The Thing Called Love
The Things of Life▶
30 Is a Dangerous Age, Cynthia
This Could Be the Night
This Happy Feeling
Thomas Graal's Best Film▶
Thomas Graal's First Child▶
Those Endearing Young Charms
Three Broadway Girls▶
Three Coins in the Fountain
Three for Bedroom C
Three Guys Named Mike
Three Husbands
Three of Hearts
Three Smart Girls Grow Up▶
Three Way Weekend
Threesome
Tiger and the Pussycat
Till Marriage Do Us Part
Tillie's Punctured Romance
Time of the Gypsies▶
Tin Cup▶
To Cross the Rubicon
To Paris with Love
Togetherness
Tom, Dick, and Harry
Tom Jones▶
Tomboy
Too Beautiful for You
Topsy Turvy
A Touch of Class▶
The Truth About Cats and Dogs▶
Tulips
Tune in Tomorrow
Two-Faced Woman▶
Two If by Sea
Two Nights with Cleopatra
Two of a Kind
Underground Aces
The Unkissed Bride
Up Your Alley
Utilities
Valley Girl
Victor/Victoria▶
Vivacious Lady▶
Waiting for the Light
Walk, Don't Run
Warm Summer Rain
Watch It▶
Wavelength
We All Loved Each Other So Much▶
The Wedding Banquet▶
The Wedding Party
We're Not Married▶
What Happened to Rosa?▶
What's Good for the Goose
What's New Pussycat?▶
When Harry Met Sally...▶
When Ladies Meet
Where the Boys Are
While You Were Sleeping▶
Who Am I This Time?▶
The Whoopee Boys
Why Change Your Wife?
Wildest Dreams
Wimps
Wishful Thinking
With Six You Get Eggroll
Without Love
Without Reservations
The Woman in Red
Woman of the Year▶
Working Girl▶
The World's Oldest Living Bridesmaid
Worth Winning
You Can't Fool Your Wife
Younger & Younger
Your Place or Mine
You've Got to Have Heart

Romantic Drama

Aaron Loves Angela
Absent Without Leave
The Accidental Tourist▶
The Accompanist
The Adorable Cheat
The Affair▶
The Affair
An Affair to Remember
The African Queen▶
After Julius
After Midnight
Against All Odds
Against the Wind
The Age of Innocence▶
Algiers▶
Ali: Fear Eats the Soul▶
Alice▶
Alice Adams
All the Vermeers in New York▶
All This and Heaven Too▶
Almost Blue
Always
Anatomy of a Seduction
And a Nightingale Sang
And Now My Love
Angel
Angel Baby▶
Angel Square
Angels and Insects▶
The Animal Kingdom▶
Ann Vickers
Anna
Anna Christie▶
Anna Karenina
Annapolis
The Annapolis Story
Anne of Avonlea▶
Another Time, Another Place▶
Another Way▶
Anthony Adverse
Apart from Hugh
Arch of Triumph▶
Arch of Triumph
As Is
Aspen Extreme
Atalia
The Atonement of Gosta Berling▶
Autumn Moon
The Average Woman
Back Street
Backstreet Dreams
Bad Love
The Ballad of the Sad Cafe
Band of Angels
Barbarian and the Geisha
The Barretts of Wimpole Street▶
Bayou Romance
Beau Revel▶
Beauty and the Beast▶
Bed of Roses
Before Sunrise
Before the Rain▶
Beloved Enemy▶
Beloved Infidel
Berlin Blues
The Best Intentions▶
The Best of Everything▶
Betty Blue▶
Beware of Pity
The Big Parade▶
Big Street
The Bigamist
Bird of Paradise
Birds of Paradise
Bitter Sweet
The Bitter Tea of General Yen▶
The Bitter Tears of Petra von Kant
The Black Marble▶
Black Orchid
Blind Husbands▶
Blood and Sand
Blood and Sand/Son of the Sheik
Blood Feud
The Blood of Others
The Blue Hour
The Blue Light▶
The Bodyguard
Bolero
Bombay Talkie
Born to Be Bad
The Boss Is Served
Boy Takes Girl
Boys
Breakfast in Paris
Breathless▶
The Bride Wore Red
The Bridges of Madison County▶
Brief Encounter▶
Buffalo Jump▶
Bullfighter & the Lady
Burning Secret
Buster and Billie
By Love Possessed
Bye Bye Blues
Cabiria
Cabo Blanco
Cactus
Cactus in the Snow
Caddie
Calendar▶
Camila▶
Camille▶
Camille Claudel▶
Captive Hearts
Captives
Carmen▶
Carnival Story
The Carpetbaggers
Carrington
Casablanca▶
Cash McCall
Casino
Cass Timberlane
Castaway
The Castaway Cowboy
Caught▶
Chain Lightning
Chained
Chanel Solitaire
Chapter Two
Charles & Diana: A Palace Divided
The Children
Children of a Lesser God▶
Christopher Strong
Cinderella Liberty▶
Circle of Friends
Circle of Love
Circle of Two
Circus World
City for Conquest▶
City Girl
Claire of the Moon
Clash by Night▶
Close My Eyes
Cobra
Cocktail
A Coeur Joie
Cold Sassy Tree▶
Collector's Item▶
The Color of Evening
Come See the Paradise▶
The Coming of Amos▶
Coming Through
The Competition▶
Conquest▶
Consolation Marriage
Cool Change
Corregidor
Corrina, Corrina
The Cousins▶
The Cowboy & the Ballerina
The Cranes are Flying▶
Creation of Adam
The Crossing
Crystal Heart
The Cutting Edge
Cyrano de Bergerac▶
Dalva
Damage▶
Dance
Dancers
Dangerous Liaisons▶
Danielle Steel's Changes
Danielle Steel's "Daddy"
Danielle Steel's Heartbeat
Danielle Steel's Palomino
Danielle Steel's Star
Dark Eyes▶
Dark Journey▶
The Dawning
A Day in October
Daybreak
Days and Nights in the Forest
Dead Beat
Deadly Desire
Deception▶
A Dedicated Man
Deja Vu
Desert Hearts▶
Desire▶
Desire
Desperate Remedies
Devil in the Flesh▶
Devil in the Flesh
Devil's Wanton
Devotion
Die Grosse Freiheit Nr. 7
A Different Kind of Love
The Divorcee
Doctor Zhivago▶
Dogfight▶
The Dolls
The Dolphin
Don Juan DeMarco
Doomsday
A Dream of Kings▶
Dreams Lost, Dreams Found
The Dressmaker
Dubarry
Duel of Hearts
Dying Young
Dynasty
The Eagle Has Two Heads▶
East Side, West Side
Ecstasy
Edward and Mrs. Simpson
Effi Briest▶
8 Seconds
84 Charing Cross Road▶
El Diputado▶
Elena and Her Men▶
Elephant Walk
Eliza's Horoscope
Emma▶
Empty Canvas
Enchanted April
End of August
Endless Love
Escape to Love
Ethan
Ethan Frome
Evangeline
Every Time We Say Goodbye
Everybody's All American
Everything Happens at Night▶
Ex-Lady
The Eyes, the Mouth
Falling in Love
The Family Man
Fanny▶
Far and Away
Far from the Madding Crowd▶
The Far Pavilions
A Farewell to Arms▶
The Farmer Takes a Wife
Fatal Attraction
Feast of July
Fergie & Andrew: Behind Palace Doors
Fiances
The Fifteen Streets
Fire and Ice
Fire and Sword
Fire with Fire
Fires Within
First Affair
First Knight
First Love
Five Days One Summer
The Flame Is Love
Flor Silvestre
The Flying Fool
Fool for Love
Fools
For Love Alone
For Love or Money
For the Love of Angela
For the Moment
Forbidden
Forbidden Fruit▶
Foreign Affairs▶
Foreign Student
Forever
Forever: A Ghost of a Love Story
Forever Emmanuelle
Foxfire Light
Franz
The French Lieutenant's Woman▶
French Postcards
Fresh Horses
The Fugitive Kind
Fulfillment
Full Moon in Paris
Gal Young 'Un▶
Gamble on Love
The Game of Love
A Gentle Woman
Georgia, Georgia
Ghost▶
The Gift of Love
Girl in Black
The Girl in Blue
The Go-Between▶
Golden Demon
Golden Gate
Gone with the Wind▶
Goodbye Again
The Gorgeous Hussy
Grand Isle
The Great Lie▶
Green Dolphin Street
Green Fields
Green Fire
Green Mansions
Griffin and Phoenix: A Love Story
The Hairdresser's Husband
Hanover Street
Harem
Havana
Head Over Heels▶
Hearing Voices
The Hearst and Davies Affair
Heart of Humanity
Heartbreakers▶
Heat and Dust▶
The Heiress▶
Heroes
Hide-Out
His Private Secretary
History is Made at Night▶
Hold the Dream
Holiday Affair
Holocaust Survivors...Remembrance of Love
The Home and the World▶
Home Before Midnight
Home Sweet Home
Homecoming
Honky
Hotel Room
Humoresque▶
Husbands and Wives▶
I Can't Escape
I Conquer the Sea
I Live in Grosvenor Square
I Love All of You
I Love N.Y.
I Love You
I Never Sang For My Father▶
Ice Castles
Iguana
Image of Passion
In a Shallow Grave
In Dangerous Company
In Search of Anna
In Too Deep
An Indecent Obsession
Indecent Proposal
Independence Day
Indiscretion of an American Wife
Indochine▶
Interval
Iron Cowboy
Island of Desire

Yesterday's Hero
You Light Up My Life
The Young and the Guilty
Young Lady Chatterly 2
Youth on Parole

Romantic Triangles

see also Otherwise Engaged

The Age of Innocence▶
Aladdin▶
All Things Fair
Amateur▶
Angie
Anna
Baja
Bitter Moon
Blue Skies▶
Body Heat▶
Broadcast News▶
Bull Durham▶
A Business Affair
Cafe au Lait▶
Calendar▶
Carnal Knowledge▶
Carried Away
Carrington
Casablanca▶
Casino▶
The Color of Evening
The Cook, the Thief, His Wife & Her Lover▶
Country Life
Dalva
Damage▶
The Dangerous
Dangerous Indiscretion
Dangerous Passion
Dead Beat
Dead Ringers▶
Death in Brunswick
December Bride
Diabolique
The Doom Generation▶
Elephant Walk
Ethan Frome
The Favor
Feast of July
First Knight
Flirt
French Kiss
French Twist
The Getaway
Hard Evidence
The Hard Truth
Henry & June▶
High Society▶
Indecent Proposal
Intersection
It Could Happen to You
Jason's Lyric
Jules and Jim▶
Killer Looks
The Ladies of the Bois de Bologne
The Last Days of Chez Nous
The Last of the Mohicans▶
Legends of the Fall
Lloyds of London▶
The Lovers▶
Making Love
The Man in the Attic
Man in the Saddle
Maybe...Maybe Not
Mildred Pierce▶
Mo' Better Blues
Money Train
Moonshine Highway
Mouth to Mouth
My Favorite Wife▶
Only You
Out of Africa▶
The Pallbearer
The Perfect Gift
The Philadelphia Story▶
Possessed by the Night
Radio Inside
Reality Bites
Restoration▶
Revenge
A Room with a View▶
Sabrina▶
Sabrina
Sand and Blood
Saturday Night Special
Savage Capitalism
The Separation
She's Gotta Have It▶
Sleep with Me
Sleepless in Seattle▶
Sommersby
Summer Lovers
A Tale of Winter
Tequila Sunrise
A Thin Line Between Love and Hate
Three of Hearts
Threesome
Tilai
Tin Cup▶
Tollbooth
The Truth About Cats and Dogs▶
Two Much
The Unbearable Lightness of Being▶
The Underneath▶
Waiting to Exhale▶
Wavelength
The Wedding Banquet▶
While You Were Sleeping▶
Willie & Phil
X, Y & Zee

Roommates from Hell

see also Psychotics/ Sociopaths

Deadbolt
The Fear Inside
Malice
The Night We Never Met
Pacific Heights▶
Shallow Grave
Single White Female
Sweet Murder

Royalty

see also Historical Drama; Medieval Romps; Period Piece

Abdulla the Great
The Adventures of Marco Polo
Aladdin▶
Alexander Nevsky▶
Ali Baba and the Forty Thieves
Ali Baba and the 40 Thieves▶
Anna and the King of Siam▶
Annie: A Royal Adventure
Arabian Nights
Autobiography of a Princess
Balalaika
Barbarian Queen 2: The Empress Strikes Back
Bonnie Prince Charlie
Boots & Saddles
Caligula
Carlton Browne of the F.O.
Carry On Henry VIII
Case of the Baby Sitter
Charlemagne
Charles & Diana: A Palace Divided
Chimes at Midnight▶
Cleopatra
Cobra Woman
The Coming of Amos▶
Coming to America▶
A Connecticut Yankee in King Arthur's Court
Conquest of the Normans
Court Jester▶
The Crusades
Death Mask of the Ninja
Desiree
Diana: Her True Story
Dr. Syn, Alias the Scarecrow
Donkey Skin▶
Dragonheart
DuBarry Was a Lady
The Eagle Has Two Heads▶
East of Borneo
The Egyptian
Elena and Her Men▶
Emperor Jones
Emperor Jones/Paul Robeson: Tribute to an Artist
Emperor Waltz
The Emperor's New Clothes
Excalibur▶
Fairy Tales
Farinelli
Fergie & Andrew: Behind Palace Doors
The Fifth Musketeer
The Fighting Prince of Donegal
First Knight
Fit for a King
Forever Amber
Goetz von Berlichingen
The Grace Kelly Story
The Grand Duchess and the Waiter▶
Hennessy
His Majesty, the American
The Iron Mask
Joseph
Julius Caesar▶
Julius Caesar
Just Suppose
A Kid in King Arthur's Court
Kind Hearts and Coronets▶
The King and I▶
A King in New York
King Lear▶
The King on Main Street
King Ralph
The King's Rhapsody
The King's Thief
The King's Whore
La Nuit de Varennes▶
Lancelot of the Lake
The Last Emperor▶
Lillie▶
Lion Man
Lorna Doone
Lost in a Harem
Macbeth▶
Macbeth
The Magic Fountain
The Man in the Iron Mask▶
The Man Who Would Be King▶
Mannequin 2: On the Move
Marbella
Marie Antoinette
The Master of Ballantrae
Mayerling▶
Mayerling
A Midsummer Night's Dream▶
Mom and Dad Save the World
Monsieur Beaucaire
My Pal, The King
A Night of Love
Nostradamus
Once Upon a Time
Options
Phedre
Phoenix
The Polar Bear King
Power
The Prince and the Pauper▶
The Prince and the Pauper
The Prince and the Showgirl
Prince Brat and the Whipping Boy▶
The Princess and the Pea
Princess Caraboo
The Princess Comes Across▶
Princess Tam Tam▶
Princess Yang Kwei Fei▶
Prisoner of Zenda▶
Prisoner of Zenda
Queen Christina▶
Queen Kelly▶
Queen Margot▶
The Rape of the Sabines
Rasputin and the Empress▶
The Return of the Musketeers
Return to Oz
The Rise of Louis XIV▶
Roman Holiday▶
The Royal Bed
Ruyblas
Salome/Queen Elizabeth
The Saragossa Manuscript
Shin Heike Monogatari▶
The Sign of the Cross
Snow White and the Seven Dwarfs▶
Snow White and the Seven Dwarfs
Soldier in Love
Solomon and Sheba
Son of Ali Baba
Song Spinner
Splitting Heirs
Spy of Napoleon
Storm Over Asia▶
The Story of David▶
Storybook
Surf Ninjas
The Swan
The Swan▶
The Sword & the Rose
Sword & the Sorcerer
The Sword of El Cid
A Thousand and One Nights
The Three Musketeers▶
Throne of Blood▶
To Play the King▶
The Tower of London
Tower of London
Tower of Screaming Virgins
The Virgin Queen▶
The War Lord▶
The Warriors
The Wedding March▶
Where There's Life
Willow

Royalty, British

see also Great Britain; Royalty

Anne of the Thousand Days▶
Becket▶
Braveheart▶
Edward and Mrs. Simpson
Edward II
Elizabeth R▶
Elizabeth, the Queen
Henry IV
Henry V▶
King Richard and the Crusaders
Lady Jane▶
The Lion in Winter▶
The Madness of King George▶
A Man for All Seasons▶
Mary of Scotland▶
Nine Days a Queen▶
Orlando▶
The Private Life of Henry VIII▶
The Private Lives of Elizabeth & Essex▶
Restoration▶
Richard III▶
Six Wives of Henry VIII▶
Victoria Regina
The Woman He Loved
Young Bess▶

Royalty, Russian

see also Royalty; Russia/USSR

Anastasia▶
Anastasia: The Mystery of Anna
Catherine the Great
I Killed Rasputin
Ivan the Terrible, Part 1▶
Ivan the Terrible, Part 2▶
Nicholas and Alexandra
Peter the Great▶
Rasputin▶
Scarlet Empress▶
Young Catherine▶

Running

Across the Tracks
Billie
Chariots of Fire▶
College▶
Finish Line
Forrest Gump▶
Go for the Gold
The Gold & Glory
Goldengirl
The Jericho Mile
The Jesse Owens Story
Jim Thorpe: All American
The Loneliest Runner
The Loneliness of the Long Distance Runner▶
Marathon
Marathon Man▶
Off the Mark
On the Edge
Raw Courage
Running Brave
Sam's Son
See How She Runs▶
A Shining Season▶
The Sprinter
The Terry Fox Story▶

Russia/USSR

see also Moscow; Red Scare

American Cop
Anastasia▶
Anastasia: The Mystery of Anna
Anna Karenina▶
Anna Karenina
Assassination of Trotsky
Back in the USSR
Balalaika
Baltic Deputy▶
The Battle of Russia
The Battleship Potemkin▶
The Brothers Karamazov▶
Burglar▶
Burnt by the Sun▶
Citizen X▶
Come and See▶
Coming Out of the Ice▶
The Commies are Coming, the Commies are Coming
Commissar▶
Comrade X
Creation of Adam
Crimson Tide▶
Days of Glory
Dersu Uzala▶
Doctor Zhivago▶
Don't Drink the Water
Drums of Jeopardy
The Eagle▶
The End of St. Petersburg▶
The Extraordinary Adventures of Mr. West in the Land of the Bolsheviks
Final Assignment
Final Warning
First Strike
The Fixer▶
For Those About to Rock: Monsters in Moscow
Freeze-Die-Come to Life▶
The Girl from Petrovka
Goldeneye▶
Gorky Park▶
Gulag
The Hunt for Red October▶
I Killed Rasputin
The Ice Runner
The Inner Circle▶
Ivan the Terrible, Part 1▶
Ivan the Terrible, Part 2▶
Kindergarten▶
Laser Mission
Last Command▶
The Light Ahead
Little Vera▶
Love and Death▶
The Man with a Movie Camera▶
The Mirror▶
Moscow Does Not Believe in Tears▶
Mother▶
The Music Lovers
Mute Witness
My Family Treasure
My Name is Ivan▶
Never Let Me Go
Nicholas and Alexandra
One Day in the Life of Ivan Denisovich▶
One Russian Summer
Peter the Great▶
Rasputin▶

Rasputin and the Empress▶
The Red and the White▶
Red Heat
Red Hot
Reds▶
The Road to Life
The Russia House
Russian Roulette
Sakharov▶
Scarlet Dawn
Scarlet Empress▶
The Seagull▶
Siberiade▶
Sideburns
A Slave of Love▶
Solo Voyage: The Revenge
Stalin
Taxi Blues▶
Terminal Velocity
Theremin: An Electronic Odyssey▶
The Ultimate Imposter
War and Peace
War and Peace▶
We the Living
White Nights
Window to Paris
World War III
Young Catherine▶

Sail Away

see also Deep Blue; Go Fish; Mutiny; Scuba; Sea Critter Attack; Shipwrecked; Submarines

Adrift
Adventure Island
The Adventures of Huckleberry Finn▶
An Affair to Remember
The African Queen▶
All the Brothers Were Valiant
And the Ship Sails On▶
Anna Christie
Annapolis
Assault on a Queen
Away All Boats
The Baby and the Battleship
The Battleship Potemkin▶
Beat the Devil▶
Beyond the Poseidon Adventure
The Big Braodcast of 1938
Billy Budd▶
Birds of Paradise
Bitter Moon
Blood Voyage
The Boatniks
Botany Bay
The Bounty▶
Boy in Blue
Cabin Boy
The Caine Mutiny▶
The Caine Mutiny Court Martial▶
Captain Caution
Captain Horatio Hornblower▶
Captain Ron
Captains Courageous▶
Captain's Paradise▶
The Captain's Table
Carry On Admiral
Carry On Cruising
China Seas▶
Christopher Columbus
The Coast Patrol
Convoy
A Countess from Hong Kong
The Crew
Crimson Tide▶
Cruise into Terror
Damn the Defiant▶
Dangerous Charter
Dangerous Passage
Dark Tide
Das Boot▶
Day of the Assassin
The Day Will Dawn▶
Dead Ahead: The Exxon Valdez Disaster▶
Dead Calm▶
Dead Reckoning
Death Cruise
Death Ship
Death Tide
The Deep
Destroyer▶
Die Hard: With a Vengeance
Disney's Storybook Classics
Dixie Jamboree
Doctor at Sea
Don Winslow of the Coast Guard
The Dove
Down Periscope
Down to the Sea in Ships
Ensign Pulver
Erik, the Viking
The Evil Below
Far from Home: The Adventures of Yellow Dog
Feet First
Ferry to Hong Kong
The Fighting Sullivans▶
The Final Countdown▶
Flat Top
Flight of the Intruder
Flipper▶
Francis in the Navy
Friday the 13th, Part 8: Jason Takes Manhattan
Gangway
Geheimakte WB1
Ghost Ship
The Gift Horse
A Girl in Every Port
Give Me a Sailor
Going Overboard
Going Under
Golden Rendezvous
Goliath Awaits
Gray Lady Down
The Great Lover
Gun Cargo
The Hairy Ape
Haunted Harbor
Hawaii Calls
He is My Brother
Hell-Ship Morgan
History is Made at Night▶
Horror of the Zombies
The Hunt for Red October▶
I Conquer the Sea
In Which We Serve▶
The Incredible Mr. Limpet
The Incredible Petrified World
Ironclads
Isle of Forgotten Sins
JAG
Jaws▶
Jaws 2
The Jewel of the Nile
John Paul Jones
Juggernaut▶
Kill Cruise
Killer on Board
King Kelly of the U.S.A.
Knife in the Water▶
The Last of Sheila
The Last Voyage
Law of the Sea
Le Crabe Tambour▶
The Legend of Sea Wolf
The Legend of the Sea Wolf
Lifeboat▶
Light at the Edge of the World
The Lightship
Live and Let Die
Long John Silver
The Long Voyage Home▶
Lord Jim▶
Love Affair▶
A Majority of One
Manfish
The Mermaids of Tiburon
Mister Roberts▶
Monkey Business▶
Moon in Scorpio
Moran of the Lady Letty
Muppet Treasure Island
Murder on the High Seas
Mutiny
The Mutiny of the Elsinore
Mutiny on the Bounty▶
Mutiny on the Bounty
Mystery Liner
The Mystery of the Mary Celeste
The Navigator▶
The Navy Comes Through
New Moon
A Night to Remember▶
Old Ironsides▶
Operation Petticoat▶
Oxford Blues
Pirate Ship
The Port of Missing Girls
The Poseidon Adventure
The Princess Comes Across▶
PT 109
Pueblo Affair▶
Pursuit of the Graf Spee
Rainbow Warrior
Reaching for the Moon
Reap the Wild Wind
Rich and Strange
Roaring Speedboats
Romancing the Stone▶
Run Silent, Run Deep▶
The Sand Pebbles▶
Save the Lady
Sea Chase
Sea Devils
Sea Racketeers
The Sea Wolf▶
The Sea Wolf
Sharks' Treasure
She Shall Have Music
Ship Ahoy
Ship of Fools▶
Ships in the Night
Shout at the Devil
Sinbad, the Sailor▶
Sink the Bismarck▶
South Seas Massacre
Steamboat Bill, Jr.▶
Submarine Seahawk
Swashbuckler
Tamango
Task Force
Temptation
Tentacles of the North
They Were Expendable▶
Three Daring Daughters
Thunder in Paradise
Till There was You
Titanic▶
To Have & Have Not▶
Today We Live
Torpedo Run
Transatlantic Merry-Go-Round
Treacherous Crossing
The Treasure of Jamaica Reef
U-Boat Prisoner
Under Siege
The Unsinkable Molly Brown▶
Up the Creek
Voyage
Voyage of Terror: The Achille Lauro Affair
Voyage of the Damned▶
Wake of the Red Witch
Waterworld
We're Not Dressing▶
White Squall
Wild Orchids
Wind
Windjammer
Windrider
Witch Who Came from the Sea
Woman of Desire
Wonderland Cove
The Wreck of the Mary Deare
Yankee Clipper

Saints

see also Religion

Augustine of Hippo▶
Bernadette
Brother Sun, Sister Moon
The Flowers of St. Francis▶
Francesco
Joan of Arc
The Messenger of the Blessed Virgin
Miracle in Rome
Miracle of Our Lady of Fatima
The Passion of Joan of Arc▶
Saint Joan
Sebastiane▶
The Song of Bernadette▶
Therese▶
A Time for Miracles

Salespeople

see also Corporate Shenanigans

Adventures in Babysitting
Cadillac Man
Death of a Salesman▶
Glengarry Glen Ross▶
Miss Rose White▶
The Music Man▶
Pennies From Heaven▶
The Rainmaker▶
Tin Men

San Francisco

see also Earthquakes

After the Shock
All Dogs Go to Heaven 2
Armistead Maupin's Tales of the City
Barbary Coast▶
The Barbary Coast
Beyond the Door
Big Trouble in Little China
Cardiac Arrest
Chan is Missing▶
The Chinatown Kid
Clowning Around 2
Copycat
The Dead Pool
Desperate Moves
Dim Sum: A Little Bit of Heart▶
Dirty Harry▶
Dr. Jekyll's Dungeon of Death
Doctor Who
Dogfight▶
Dying to Remember
The Enforcer
An Eye for an Eye
The Fan
Final Analysis
Fisherman's Wharf
Flame of the Barbary Coast
Flower Drum Song
Fools
48 Hrs.▶
Foul Play▶
Freebie & the Bean
The Frisco Kid
Golden Gate
Ground Zero
Hello, Frisco, Hello
Homeward Bound 2: Lost in San Francisco
I Remember Mama▶
Invasion of the Body Snatchers▶
It Came from Beneath the Sea▶
Key to the City
Kicks
Kuffs
Lady from Louisiana
Lady of the House
The Laughing Policeman
Lightblast
Magnum Force
Monster in the Closet
Mysterious Mr. Wong
Nightmare in Blood
Nina Takes a Lover
Nine Months
Pacific Heights▶
The Presidio
Revolution
The Rock▶
The Saint Strikes Back
Salome, Where She Danced
San Francisco▶
Serial▶
The Shock
The Single Standard
The Sisters▶
Stealing Heaven
Sudden Impact
Time After Time▶
Times of Harvey Milk
Weapons of Death
Whatever Happened to Susan Jane?
What's Up, Doc?▶
Wild West
The Zodiac Killer

Sanity Check

see also Doctors & Nurses; Hospitals & Medicine; Shrinks

Aguirre, the Wrath of God▶
Alone in the Dark
American Eagle
Amos
An Angel at My Table▶
Anguish
Another Time, Another Place
Appointment with Fear
Arsenic and Old Lace▶
Asylum
Asylum of Satan
Bad Dreams
Beauty on the Beach
Bedlam▶
Behind Locked Doors
The Bell Jar
Beyond Therapy
A Blade in the Dark
Blood Frenzy
Blood Salvage
Blood Song
Bloody Wednesday
Body Chemistry
Boxing Helena
Buried Alive
Camille Claudel▶
Captain Newman, M.D.
The Carpenter
Cat in the Cage
Cause for Alarm
Chattahoochee
Clockwise
Coast to Coast
The Cobweb
The Collector▶
Committed
The Couch Trip
The Cracker Factory
Crazed
Crazy Fat Ethel II
Crazy People
Crime and Punishment▶
The Crime of Dr. Crespi
Criminally Insane
Crow Hollow
Cry Wolf
Cutting Class
Dark Obsession
Dark Places
Dark Sanity
Dark Waters
Darkroom
A Day at the Races▶
Dead Man Out▶
Dead of Night▶
Dead Pit
Deadly Innocence
Deadly Intruder
Deadly Strangers
The Deadly Trap
Death Kiss
Death Nurse
Dementia 13
A Demon in My View
Demons of the Mind
Deranged
Despair▶
Desperate Living
Deutschland im Jahre Null▶
Devi▶
The Devil Bat
The Devil Bat's Daughter
Devil Doll▶
The Devil in Silk
Devil in the Flesh
Devil Times Five
Devil Wears White
Diary of a Mad Housewife▶
Diary of a Madman

Diary of a Young Comic
Diary of Forbidden Dreams▶
Dick Barton, Special Agent
Die! Die! My Darling!
Die Screaming, Marianne
Disturbance
Disturbed
The Doctor and the Devils
Doctor Blood's Coffin
Doctor Butcher M.D.
Dr. Caligari
Dr. Frankenstein's Castle of Freaks
Dr. Hackenstein
Dr. Jekyll and Mr. Hyde▶
Dr. Jekyll and Mr. Hyde
Dr. Jekyll and the Wolfman
Dr. Mabuse, Parts 1 & 2▶
Dr. Mabuse vs. Scotland Yard
Dr. Strangelove, or: How I Learned to Stop Worrying and Love the Bomb▶
Dr. Tarr's Torture Dungeon
Doctor X
Dog Day Afternoon▶
The Doll
Dominique is Dead
Don't Go in the Woods
Don't Look in the Basement
Don't Look Now▶
Don't Mess with My Sister!
Don't Open Till Christmas
Doom Asylum
A Double Life▶
Dream Lover
Dream No Evil
The Dream Team
Easy Rider▶
Eaten Alive
Echoes
Edge of Sanity
El: This Strange Passion▶
The End of Innocence
End of the Road
Endless Love
Endless Night
Entr'acte
Equus
Escape from Safehaven
Estate of Insanity
Europa '51
Exorcism's Daughter
Eyeball
The Eyes of the Amaryllis
The Fall of the House of Usher
The Fall of the House of Usher▶
The Fall of the House of Usher
False Identity
The Fan
Fat Guy Goes Nutzoid
Fear Strikes Out▶
The Fifth Floor
The Fisher King▶
The Five of Me
Follow Me Quietly▶
Forced March
The 4th Man▶
Frances▶
Fright
From the Life of the Marionettes▶
Frozen Terror
The Girl in Room 2A
The Goalie's Anxiety at the Penalty Kick▶
Gulliver's Travels
The Hairdresser's Husband
Hamlet▶
Hammersmith is Out
Harvey▶
The Haunting▶
Haunting of Sarah Hardy
Haunts
Heart of Midnight
Heat and Sunlight
Heavenly Creatures▶
Henry IV
Heroes
Hider in the House
The Horrible Dr. Hichcock
The Horror Chamber of Dr. Faustus▶
Horror Hospital
Horror House on Highway 5
The Hospital▶
Hotline
The Housekeeper
How to Get Ahead in Advertising▶
How to Make a Monster
Hush, Hush, Sweet Charlotte▶
Hysteria
I Am the Cheese
I Dismember Mama
I Never Promised You a Rose Garden▶
Icy Breasts▶
If Things Were Different
Illusions
Impulse
In the Mouth of Madness
The Incredible Two-Headed Transplant
Innocent Victim
Insanity
Interiors▶
The Invisible Ghost
It Happened at Nightmare Inn
It's Alive!
Jekyll and Hyde
Juggernaut
Keeper
Killer's Moon
The King of Hearts▶
Lassie from Lancashire
The Last of Philip Banter
The Last Ride
The Last Seduction▶
Leave Her to Heaven▶
Lethal Weapon▶
Lethal Weapon 2▶
Let's Scare Jessica to Death
Lilith▶
The Lonely Sex
Lost Angels
Lower Level
Lunatics: A Love Story▶
Luther the Geek
Mad Love▶
Mad Love
Man Facing Southeast▶
Manhunter▶
Marat/Sade▶
Midnight Warning
Mind Games
Mine Own Executioner▶
Mr. Jones
Mixed Nuts
Morgan!
Mother Kusters Goes to Heaven▶
Murder In the First
My First Wife
Network▶
Night of Bloody Horror
Night of Terror
The Night Visitor
Night Wars
Night Watch
The Ninth Configuration▶
Nobody's Perfekt
Nuts▶
The October Man▶
Offerings
One Flew Over the Cuckoo's Nest▶
125 Rooms of Comfort
One Summer Love
The Onion Field▶
Out of Sight, Out of Her Mind
Overexposed
Pale Blood
Paperback Hero
Pay Off
Peeping Tom▶
Performance▶
A Piano for Mrs. Cimino▶
Picture Mommy Dead
Pigs
The Pink Panther Strikes Again▶
The Pit and the Pendulum▶
The Pit & the Pendulum
Play Misty for Me▶
Poison▶
The Possessed▶
The President's Analyst▶
Prettykill
Prime Suspect
Private Parts
Psychic Killer
Psycho▶
Psycho 2
Psycho Cop
Psycho Cop 2
Psychos in Love
Question of Silence▶
Raising Cain
Rasputin▶
The Rejuvenator
Remember Me
Return of the Ape Man
Revolt of the Zombies
Richard III▶
Room to Let
The Ruling Class▶
Scarlet Empress▶
Scissors
The Scout
Scream Bloody Murder
Scream for Help
Screamer
Seance on a Wet Afternoon▶
Secret Beyond the Door
The Sender
Sessions
Seven Days in May▶
Shadow Play
Shattered
Shattered Silence
Shattered Spirits
The Shining
Shock Corridor▶
The Silence of the Lambs▶
Silent Night, Bloody Night
Sisters▶
Sketches of a Strangler
Slaughter Hotel
Sledgehammer
Sniper▶
Solaris
Sophie's Choice▶
South of Reno
Spectre of the Rose
Spellbound▶
Story of Adele H.▶
Strait-Jacket
Strange Illusion
Strangers on a Train▶
Street Asylum
A Streetcar Named Desire▶
Strong Medicine
Stuart Saves His Family
Summer of Secrets
The Survivalist
Svengali
Sybil▶
Tainted Image
Teenage Frankenstein
The Tenant▶
The Testament of Dr. Cordelier▶
They Might Be Giants▶
The Three Faces of Eve▶
Three Nuts in Search of a Bolt
Torture Train
Touched
Tracks
Trapped in Silence
12 Monkeys▶
Twin Peaks: Fire Walk with Me
Twinsanity
Twister
The Two Faces of Dr. Jekyll
Urge to Kill
Vampire's Kiss▶
Vengeance Is Mine▶
Violated
Ward Six
Watched
What About Bob?▶
What Ever Happened to Baby Jane?▶
Whatever Happened to Susan Jane?
What's the Matter with Helen?
While I Live
White Heat▶
The Wind
Witchfire
Woman in Black
A Woman Under the Influence▶
You Are Not I
The Young Ones

Satanism

***see also** Demons & Wizards; Devils; Occult*

Alison's Birthday
Amazon Jail
Angel on My Shoulder
Asylum of Satan
Bad Dreams
Beast of the Yellow Night
Beyond the Door 3
The Black Cat▶
Black Roses
Black Sunday▶
The Blood on Satan's Claw▶
Blood Orgy of the She-Devils
The Bloodsuckers
The Brotherhood of Satan
Child of Darkness, Child of Light
The Chosen
The Crimson Cult
Damien: Omen 2
The Demon Lover
Demonoid, Messenger of Death
The Devil & Daniel Webster▶
Devil Rider
The Devils▶
The Devil's Daughter
The Devil's Eye
The Devil's Mistress
The Devil's Nightmare
The Devil's Partner
The Devil's Possessed
Devil's Rain
Devil's Son-in-Law
The Devil's Web
Disciple of Death
Doctor Faustus
Equinox▶
Erotic Dreams
Eternal Evil
Evil Altar
Evilspeak
Exorcism
The Exorcist▶
The Exorcist 2: The Heretic
Eye of the Demon
Fear No Evil
The Final Conflict
Ghoulies 4
Guardian of the Abyss
Hack O'Lantern
Halloween Night
Highway to Hell
House of the Black Death
I Don't Want to Be Born
I Drink Your Blood
Inferno
Invitation to Hell
Jaws of Satan
Land of the Minotaur
Leaves from Satan's Book
The Legend of Hillbilly John
Leonor
The Man and the Monster
The Mangler
Masque of the Red Death/ Premature Burial
Maxim Xul
The Mephisto Waltz▶
Midnight
Midnight Cabaret
Midnight's Child
Mind, Body & Soul
Mysterious Doctor Satan
Necromancer: Satan's Servant
Night Visitor
976-EVIL
976-EVIL 2: The Astral Factor
The Occultist
Oh, God! You Devil
The Omen
Other Hell
Prime Evil
Prince of Darkness
The Pyx▶
Race with the Devil
Raging Angels
Rest In Pieces
Revenge
Rosemary's Baby▶
The Satanic Rites of Dracula
Satan's Black Wedding
Satan's Blade
Satan's Cheerleaders
Satan's Princess
Satan's School for Girls
Satan's Touch
Satanwar
The Sentinel
Servants of Twilight
The Seventh Victim▶
Shock 'Em Dead
Sisters of Satan
Speak of the Devil
Specters
The Spellbinder
Sugar Cookies
Suicide Cult
The Tempter
Terror Beach
To the Devil, A Daughter
Tombs of the Blind Dead
The Visitor
Warlock
Warlock: The Armageddon
Witchcraft
Witchcraft 3: The Kiss of Death
Witchcraft 5: Dance with the Devil
Witchcraft 6: The Devil's Mistress
WitchTrap

Satire & Parody

***see also** Black Comedy; Comedy; Genre Spoofs*

Abbott and Costello Go to Mars
ABC's of Love & Sex, Australia Style
Abduction
The Act
The Adventures of Hairbreadth Harry
The Adventures of Picasso
The Adventures of Sherlock Holmes' Smarter Brother▶
The Affairs of Annabel
Aftershock
Airplane!▶
Airplane 2: The Sequel
Alex in Wonderland
Alien Women
All Through the Night▶
All You Need Is Cash▶
The Alphabet Murders
Amazon Women on the Moon
America 3000
American Tickler
America's Deadliest Home Video
Americathon
...And God Spoke
Andy Warhol's Dracula▶
Angel City
Animal Farm▶
Any Wednesday
The Apartment▶
As Young As You Feel▶
Attack of the Robots
Auntie Mame▶
Backfire!
Bad Manners
Bad Medicine
Bananas▶
Bank Robber
Barjo
Barry McKenzie Holds His Own
Based on an Untrue Story
Basic Training
The Bawdy Adventures of Tom Jones
Beau Pere▶
Being There▶
The Best Man▶
Beyond the Valley of the Dolls

Beyond Therapy
The Big Bus
Big Deal on Madonna Street▶
The Big Picture
Big Trouble in Little China
Bill & Ted's Bogus Journey
Bill & Ted's Excellent Adventure
Bingo Inferno
Black and White in Color▶
Black Bird
Bob & Carol & Ted & Alice
Bob Roberts▶
The Bonfire of the Vanities
Born in East L.A.
Boss
Boy Meets Girl▶
The Brady Bunch Movie▶
Bread and Chocolate▶
Britannia Hospital
Bullshot
The 'Burbs
Camera Buff
Canadian Bacon
The Candidate▶
Carry On Cleo
Carry On Dick
Casino Royale
Caveman
CB4: The Movie
Champagne for Caesar▶
The Cheap Detective▶
Clockwise
A Clockwork Orange▶
Closet Cases of the Nerd Kind
The Coca-Cola Kid▶
Code Name: Chaos
Cold Turkey▶
The Committee
Coup de Grace
Crainquebille▶
Creature from the Haunted Sea
Crimewave
Curtain Up
Dark Habits
Dark Star▶
Darktown Strutters
Darling Lili
Dead Men Don't Die
Dead Men Don't Wear Plaid
Deal of the Century
Death of a Bureaucrat▶
Deathrow Gameshow
Diary of a Chambermaid▶
Dirty Dishes▶
The Discreet Charm of the Bourgeoisie▶
Dr. Heckyl and Mr. Hype
Doctors and Nurses
Dope Mania
The Dove▶
Down & Dirty▶
Down and Out in Beverly Hills
Down to Earth
Down Under
Dracula: Dead and Loving It
Dracula Sucks
Dragnet
E. Nick: A Legend in His Own Mind
Easy Wheels
11 Harrowhouse▶
Ella Cinders▶
Erik the Viking
The Extraordinary Adventures of Mr. West in the Land of the Bolsheviks
The Family Game▶
Fat and the Lean▶
Fatal Instinct
Fear of a Black Hat
Ferocious Female Freedom Fighters
First Family
The Flaming Teen-Age
Flesh Gordon
Flicks
Floundering
Footlight Frenzy
The Fortune Cookie▶
Frankenstein General Hospital
Frankenstein Sings...The Movie
Frankenweenie
The French Touch
The Freshman
From Here to Maternity
The Front▶
Funny Money
Gabriel Over the White House▶
Galactic Gigolo
Galaxina
Ganjasaurus Rex
Gas
Geek Maggot Bingo
Genevieve▶
Gentlemen Prefer Blondes▶
Glory! Glory!▶
Going Berserk
Going Places▶
Greaser's Palace
Great American Traffic Jam
The Great Dictator▶
The Great Madcap
Great McGonagall
The Great White Hype
The Groove Tube
Grunt! The Wrestling Movie
Gulliver's Travels
Gumshoe
Gypsy
Hail
Hail the Conquering Hero▶
Hairspray▶
Half a Sixpence
Happiness
Hardware Wars & Other Film Farces
Heaven Can Wait▶
Heavens Above▶
Hell Comes to Frogtown
Hexed
High Anxiety
High Hopes▶
High School High
High Season
History of the World: Part 1
The History of White People in America
The History of White People in America: Vol. 2
Hollywood Harry
Home Movies
The Horror of Frankenstein
The Hospital▶
Hot Shots!▶
Hot Shots! Part Deux
The Hound of the Baskervilles
How I Got into College
I Love You, Alice B. Toklas!
I Married a Vampire
I Was a Zombie for the FBI
The Icicle Thief▶
I'll Do Anything
I'm All Right Jack▶
I'm Gonna Git You Sucka▶
The Incredible Shrinking Woman
Incredibly Strange Creatures Who Stopped Living and Became Mixed-Up Zombies
The Inspector General
Invasion Earth: The Aliens Are Here!
Is There Sex After Death?▶
It Couldn't Happen Here
It's a Bundyful Life
J-Men Forever!▶
Jabberwocky
Jack and His Friends
Jamon, Jamon
Jekyll & Hyde...Together Again
Jet Benny Show
Johnny Dangerously
A Joke of Destiny, Lying in Wait Around the Corner Like a Bandit
Kentucky Fried Movie▶
Kids In the Hall Brain Candy
The King of Hearts▶
Kurt Vonnegut's Harrison Bergeron
The Ladies' Man
L'Age D'Or▶
The Last Polka▶
Le Schpountz
Leon the Pig Farmer
Let's Kill All the Lawyers
Lincoln County Incident
Lip Service▶
Look Out Sister▶
Loose Shoes
Love and a .45
Love and Death▶
Love at Stake
Mad Mission 3
Mad Monster Party
Man Bites Dog
The Man in the White Suit▶
The Man Who Came to Dinner▶
Man Who Had Power Over Women
The Man with Bogart's Face
The Man with Two Brains▶
Marihuana
Me and the Colonel
Men...▶
The Meteor Man
Mickey
The Milky Way▶
Minbo—Or the Gentle Art of Japanese Extortion
The Missionary
Mr. Write
Mob Boss
Modern Times▶
Monster in a Box▶
Monty Python and the Holy Grail▶
Monty Python's Flying Circus
Monty Python's Life of Brian▶
Monty Python's Parrot Sketch Not Included
Monty Python's The Meaning of Life▶
More! Police Squad
The Mouse That Roared▶
Movers and Shakers
Movie, Movie
Murder by Death
Mutant on the Bounty
My Best Friend Is a Vampire
My Best Girl
Myra Breckinridge
Mystery Science Theater 3000: The Movie
The Naked Gun: From the Files of Police Squad▶
Naked Gun 33 1/3: The Final Insult
Naked Gun 2 1/2: The Smell of Fear
Naked in New York
Nasty Habits
National Lampoon Goes to the Movies
National Lampoon's Animal House▶
National Lampoon's Attack of the 5 Ft. 2 Women
National Lampoon's Loaded Weapon 1
Natural Born Killers
Night Patrol
99 & 44/100 Dead
Nocturna
Northanger Abbey
The Nutty Professor▶
On the Avenue▶
Oscar
Overdrawn at the Memory Bank
Padre Nuestro
Pajama Tops
Pandemonium
Paramedics
Pardners
Partners
Pass the Ammo
P.C.U.
Personal Services
Phantom of Liberty▶
Pictures
The Pink Chiquitas
Plan 10 from Outer Space
The Player▶
Police Squad! Help Wanted!
The Positively True Adventures of the Alleged Texas Cheerleader-Murdering Mom▶
Pray TV
The President's Analyst▶
Prime Time
The Princess Bride▶
Prisoner of Rio
A Private Function
Prize of Peril
The Producers▶
A Propos de Nice▶
Putney Swope▶
The Ramrodder
Rat Pfink a Boo-Boo
Ready to Wear
Real Men
Really Weird Tales
Red Desert Penitentiary
Red Earth
Red Garters
Rentadick
Repentance▶
The Report on the Party and the Guests▶
Repossessed
Return of Captain Invincible
The Return of Spinal Tap
Revolution! A Red Comedy▶
Ricky 1
Ring of the Musketeers
The Road to Lebanon
Robin Hood: Men in Tights
The Rocky Horror Picture Show▶
Romeo Is Bleeding
Rosalie Goes Shopping▶
The Royal Bed
Rude Awakening
The Ruling Class▶
Running Mates▶
Sallah▶
Salvation!
Sammy & Rosie Get Laid▶
Saturday Night Live
Scenes from the Class Struggle in Beverly Hills
School for Scandal
Scrambled Feet
Scrooged
Search and Destroy
Second Time Lucky
Secret Agent 00-Soul
The Secret Diary of Sigmund Freud
Seduction of Mimi▶
The Senator was Indiscreet▶
Serial▶
Serial Mom▶
Sex Adventures of the Three Musketeers
Sex with a Smile
Shame of the Jungle
Shampoo
A Shock to the System▶
Sideburns
Silence of the Hams
Silent Movie
Simon of the Desert▶
Slammer Girls
Sleeper▶
Smile▶
S.O.B.
Spaced Out
Spaceship
Spirit of '76
Spy Hard
State of Things▶
Stay Tuned
Straight to Hell
Strange Invaders▶
Streetfight
Sullivan's Travels▶
Sunset
Suppose They Gave a War and Nobody Came?
Surf Nazis Must Die
Swimming with Sharks▶
Sympathy for the Devil
Tanner '88
Tapeheads
Tartuffe
A Taste for Flesh and Blood
That's Adequate
They Call Me Bruce?
They Live
They Still Call Me Bruce
This Is Spinal Tap▶
The Thorn
Three Ages▶
The Thrill of It All!
To Be or Not to Be
Too Many Crooks
Top Secret!▶
Transylvania 6-5000
Trash
Traxx
True Stories▶
Trust Me
Tunnelvision
Turumba▶
Uforia
UHF
Unmasking the Idol
Up from the Depths
Up the Academy
A Very Brady Sequel
A Very Curious Girl
The Villain Still Pursued Her
Virgin High
Voyage of the Rock Aliens
Walker
Watermelon Man
Way He Was
What's Up, Tiger Lily?▶
The Wheeler Dealers▶
When Nature Calls
Where the Buffalo Roam
Where the Bullets Fly
White Mischief▶
The White Sheik▶
Whoops Apocalypse
Who's Who
Wild, Wild West Revisited
Will Success Spoil Rock Hunter?
Window to Paris
Without a Clue
World Gone Wild
The Worm Eaters
The Worst of Hollywood: Vol. 1
The Worst of Hollywood: Vol. 2
The Worst of Hollywood: Vol. 3
The Would-Be Gentleman
Yin & Yang of Mr. Go
You'll Find Out
Young Doctors in Love
Young Frankenstein▶
Young Nurses in Love
Zachariah
The Zany Adventures of Robin Hood
Zelig▶
Zoo Radio
Zorro, the Gay Blade

Savants

see also Mental Retardation

Being There▶
Champagne for Caesar▶
Charly▶
Doctor Dolittle
Forrest Gump▶
King Lear▶
Malcolm
Rain Man▶
Tony Draws a Horse

Scams, Stings & Cons

see also Heists

Abbott and Costello Meet the Keystone Kops
Adios Amigo
After the Fox
The Amazing Mr. X
Another You
Assault on a Queen
Barnaby and Me
Bedtime Story
Bergonzi Hand
Best of the Badmen

Beyond a Reasonable Doubt
The Big Grab
Big Trouble
Billionaire Boys Club
Birds & the Bees
Black Oak Conspiracy
Blackmail▶
Blackout
Blonde Crazy
Blood on the Moon
Blue Murder at St. Trinian's▶
Border Phantom
Border Saddlemates
Bottle Rocket
Buffalo Stampede
Buona Sera, Mrs. Campbell
Butterfly Affair
Came a Hot Friday
Candleshoe
Caper of the Golden Bulls
Capricorn One▶
The Captain from Koepenick
Cartier Affair
Casino▶
Catch Me a Spy
Cause for Alarm
Chameleon Street▶
The Charmer
Cheap Shots
Cheech and Chong: Things Are Tough All Over
Chinatown▶
Club Fed
Cold Justice
The Color of Money▶
The Con Artists
Con Man
Consenting Adults
The Conversation▶
Convicts at Large
Cops and Robbers
Cotton Comes to Harlem▶
Country Gentlemen
Couples and Robbers
Crack-Up
Curly Sue
Dangerous Summer
Dead Heat on a Merry-Go-Round▶
The Dead Pool
Deadfall
Deception
The Desperate Trail
Destiny Turns on the Radio
Diggstown
Dirty Rotten Scoundrels▶
The Distinguished Gentleman
Dr. Christian Meets the Women
Dollar
Elmer Gantry▶
Every Day's a Holiday
F/X▶
F/X 2: The Deadly Art of Illusion
The Falcon Takes Over/Strange Bargain
Fargo▶
Federal Agents vs. Underworld, Inc.
A Fish Called Wanda▶
Flim-Flam Man
For Better or Worse
Forger of London
Formula for a Murder
The Fortune Cookie▶
The Fourth Protocol▶
Framed
Frauds
The Frighteners
The Gang's All Here
Get Shorty▶
A Girl in Every Port
Girl Under the Sheet
Glengarry Glen Ross▶
Glory! Glory!▶
Going to Town
Good Neighbor Sam▶
Great Bank Hoax
The Great Impostor
The Great White Hype
Green Card
The Grifters▶
Harlem Rides the Range
Harry & Walter Go to New York
The Heat's On
Hi Diddle Diddle
Hold Your Man▶
The Honeymoon Machine
Hopscotch▶
The Hot Rock▶
House of Errors
House of Games▶
Housesitter
I Love Melvin
I Love You Again▶
If I Were Rich
In the Soup
Infernal Trio
Invasion of the Space Preachers
Kid from Not-So-Big
Killer
The Killing▶
Kind Hearts and Coronets▶
The King and Four Queens
The King of Marvin Gardens
The Lady Eve▶
Lamerica▶
The Last of Mrs. Cheyney▶
Law and Order
Le Gentleman D'Epsom
Leap of Faith
The Lemon Drop Kid
Les Aventuriers
Let's Do It Again
The Liars
Lies
Life Stinks
Lonely Hearts
Lovers: A True Story▶
The Madwoman of Chaillot
The Magician of Lublin
Malone
Manhattan Melodrama▶
Marshal of Cedar Rock
The Mask of Dijon
Maverick
Me and the Kid
Medicine Man
Mexican Hayride
Mexican Spitfire at Sea
Millions
Mistaken Identity
Mr. Boggs Steps Out
Mr. Lucky▶
Mo' Money
Murder for Sale
Murder on Approval
Murder on the Yukon
Never Give a Sucker an Even Break▶
Never Say Never Again
Nickel & Dime
Night and the City▶
No Way Out▶
None But the Lonely Heart▶
Nothing Sacred▶
The Old Lady Who Walked in the Sea
Old Spanish Custom
One of My Wives Is Missing
Opportunity Knocks
Ossessione▶
Panic Button
Paper Man
Paper Moon▶
The Parallax View▶
Parole, Inc.
Pass the Ammo
Phantom Gold
Piece of the Action
The Pope Must Diet
Popi▶
The President's Plane is Missing
Prisoner of Rio
The Producers▶
The Promoter▶
The Quest
Quiz Show▶
Reborn
The Red Light Sting
Remedy for Riches
Risky Business▶
The Road to Zanzibar▶
Roaring Speedboats
Rule #3
Ruthless People▶
Sands of Sacrifice
Save the Tiger▶
Scam
Scandalous
Sgt. Bilko
Sexual Intent
Shattered Image
Silk n' Sabotage
Silver Bears
Six Degrees of Separation
Skin Game▶
Sky Hei$t
Slither▶
Small Hotel
Something for Everyone
The Squeeze
Stacy's Knights
Stagecoach to Denver
The Star Maker
Stavisky▶
The Sting▶
The Sting 2
The Story of a Cheat▶
Sucker Money
Sunburn
Support Your Local Gunfighter▶
Sweet Talker
The Swindle
Swindle
The Switch
Tall in the Saddle
A Taste for Killing
Tax Season
The Ten Million Dollar Getaway
Tequila Sunrise
Things Change▶
Things to Do In Denver When You're Dead▶
The Third Key
This Is a Hijack
Thrilled to Death
The Tigress
Title Shot
Too Pretty to Be Honest
Tootsie▶
Train Robbers
Tricheurs
Trust Me
Underworld Scandal
The Unholy Three▶
Walpurgis Night▶
The Warrior & the Sorceress
Watch the Birdie
We're Talkin' Serious Money
The Wharf Rat
White Men Can't Jump
Why Me?
Write to Kill

School Daze

see also Campus Capers; Hell High School

Absolution
Accident
All God's Children
All Things Fair
American Friends
Amy
Anna and the King of Siam▶
Au Revoir Les Enfants▶
Back to School
Backfield in Motion
The Beguiled▶
The Belles of St. Trinian's▶
The Bells of St. Mary's▶
Beverly Hills 90210: The Graduation
Billy Madison
Black Narcissus▶
Blue Jeans
Bluffing It
Boarding School
Boys
The Broadway Drifter
The Browning Version▶
The Browning Version
Brutal Fury
Buried Alive
Cheers for Miss Bishop
Children of a Lesser God▶
The Children's Hour
The Chocolate War▶
Christy
Ciao, Professore!
The Corn is Green▶
The Craft
Crazy for Love
Crazy from the Heart▶
Dangerous Minds
Dead Poets Society▶
Deadly Sins
The Devil's Playground▶
Diabolique
Doctor Dolittle
Dream to Believe
Educating Rita▶
Encino Man
The Ernest Green Story
Europa, Europa▶
Eyes Right!
Fame▶
Flirting▶
Forever Mary▶
The French Lesson
French Postcards
Games Girls Play
The George McKenna Story
Getting It On
The Getting of Wisdom
Getting Straight
Getting Wasted
The Girl, the Body and the Pill
The Girl Who Spelled Freedom▶
The Girls of Huntington House
The Goodbye Bird
Goodbye, Mr. Chips▶
Goodbye, Mr. Chips
Goodnight God Bless
The Gospel According to Vic
Grease▶
Grown Ups
Guess What We Learned in School Today?
The Guinea Pig
The Halfback of Notre Dame
The Happiest Days of Your Life▶
Hard Knox
Heavenly Creatures▶
Here Come the Co-Eds
High School High
High School USA
Homework
Horsemasters
How I Got into College
Impure Thoughts
Iron & Silk
Is There Life Out There?
Jack
Johnny Tiger
The Kid with the 200 I.Q.
Kindergarten Cop
Kurt Vonnegut's Harrison Bergeron
Lambada
Last Time Out
Leader of the Band
Lean on Me▶
L'Ecole Buisoniere
The Little Princess▶
A Little Princess▶
Little Red Schoolhouse
The Long Gray Line▶
The Lords of Discipline
Maedchen in Uniform▶
Major Payne
Married to It
Matilda
A Minor Miracle
Murder in New Hampshire: The Pamela Smart Story
Murder 101
National Lampoon's Class Reunion
National Lampoon's Senior Trip
The NeverEnding Story▶
Not Quite Human 2
Oleanna
Oxford Blues
Passion for Life
The People
Perfect Harmony
Platinum High School
Porky's
The Possessed
Powder
Prep School
Pride of Jesse Hallum
The Prime of Miss Jean Brodie▶
The Principal
The Pure Hell of St. Trinian's
Rachel, Rachel▶
The Rascals
Real Genius▶
Rebel
Renaissance Man
Robin of Locksley
Sabrina the Teenage Witch
The St. Tammany Miracle
The Sandpiper
Satan's School for Girls
Secret Places
A Separate Peace
September Gun
Shao Lin Popeye
Shout
Sing
Stand and Deliver▶
Stanley and Iris
Student Confidential
The Student Teachers
The Substitute
Summer School
Summer School Teachers
Tea and Sympathy▶
Teachers
There Goes My Baby
To Sir, with Love
Tom Brown's School Days
Tom Brown's School Days▶
Tommy Boy
Topaze▶
Toy Soldiers
The Trouble with Angels
Twenty-Four Eyes▶
The Underachievers
Undergrads▶
Up the Academy
Up the Down Staircase▶
Virgin Queen of St. Francis High
Vital Signs
Waterland
Why Shoot the Teacher▶
Wild Reeds▶
The Winslow Boy▶
With Honors
The Worst Witch
Yentl
The Young Teacher
Zebrahead▶

Sci Fi

see also Fantasy

Abbott and Costello Go to Mars
Abraxas: Guardian of the Universe
The Abyss▶
Access Code
Aelita: Queen of Mars
After the Fall of New York
Aftermath
Aftershock
Akira
Alien▶
Alien 3
Alien Contamination
The Alien Factor
Alien from L.A.
Alien Intruder
Alien Nation
Alien Nation: Dark Horizon
Alien Predators
Alien Private Eye
Alien Space Avenger
Alien Terminator
Alien Warrior
Alien Women
Alienator
Aliens▶
Aliens Are Coming
Aliens from Spaceship Earth
The Alpha Incident
Alphaville▶
Altered States▶
The Amazing Colossal Man

Science & Scientists

see also Genetics; Inventors & Inventions; Mad Scientists

Altered States▶
Android
The Andromeda Strain
Around the World Under the Sea
Arrowsmith
Assassin
The Atomic City
The Atomic Man
Attack of the Robots
Beach Party
A Brief History of Time▶
Caravan to Vaccares
Chain Reaction
Children of the Damned
The Dallas Connection
Dam Busters▶
Dark Star▶
Darkman▶
The Day of the Dolphin
Day One▶
Dead Men Don't Wear Plaid
The Dead Next Door
Deadly Friend
Demon Seed▶
Dick Barton, Special Agent
Dick Tracy, Detective/The Corpse Vanishes
Die Laughing
Die, Monster, Die!
Dirty Games
Dr. Alien
Doctor Dolittle
Dr. Jekyll and Ms. Hyde
The Eliminators
Fantastic Voyage▶
Fat Man and Little Boy
Feast for the Devil
The Fly▶
The Fly▶
The Fly 2
Forbidden World
Forever Darling
Four Sided Triangle
The 4D Man
From the Earth to the Moon
Geheimakte WB1
Glory Enough for All: The Discovery of Insulin
The Henderson Monster
How to Make a Doll
Human Gorilla
Humanoid Defender
Illegal Entry: Formula for Fear
Illumination
The Incredible Hulk Returns
International House
The Invisible Man Returns▶
I.Q.
Junior
Jurassic Park▶
Last Day of the War
Laughing at Danger
Link
The Lost World
Love Potion #9
The Man with Two Brains▶
Mary Reilly
Max Fleischer's Documentary Features
Medicine Man
Miracle Mile▶
Mr. Superinvisible
Monkey Boy
Monkey Business▶
Monkey's Uncle
My Science Project
My Stepmother Is an Alien
Neptune Factor
Outbreak▶
Phantom Empire
Project X
Prototype X29A
The Quiet Earth▶
Real Genius▶
Return of Captain Invincible
Return of the Ape Man
Return of the Fly
The Rocky Horror Picture Show▶
The Secret of the Telegian
The Sex Machine
Shaker Run
Shakma
Simon
Son of Flubber
Spaceways
Species
Stephen King's Golden Years
The Story of Louis Pasteur▶
The Structure of Crystals
Surf 2
Swamp Thing
The Thing
Things to Come▶
This Island Earth
Threshold
Tidal Wave
Time Trackers
The Time Travelers
Tomcat: Dangerous Desires
12:01
Unforgettable
Unknown Island
Unknown World
Where Time Began
The Wild and the Free
Woman in the Dunes▶
The Yesterday Machine

Scotland

see also Great Britain; Guys in Kilts

Another Time, Another Place▶
The Big Man: Crossing the Line▶
Blood Clan
Bonnie Prince Charlie
Bonnie Scotland
Braveheart▶
Breaking the Waves▶
Brigadoon▶
Challenge to Lassie
Comfort and Joy▶
Devil Girl from Mars
The Devil's Undead
Dragonworld
Dreams Lost, Dreams Found
Escape
The Gospel According to Vic
Gregory's Girl▶
Greystoke: The Legend of Tarzan, Lord of the Apes
I Know Where I'm Going▶
Lady of the Lake
Little Minister▶
Local Hero▶
Madeleine
Mary of Scotland▶
The Master of Ballantrae
The Pointsman
Pride of the Clan
The Prime of Miss Jean Brodie▶
Ring of Bright Water▶
Rob Roy▶
Rob Roy—The Highland Rogue
The Secret of the Loch
The Three Lives of Thomasina▶
Tragedy of Flight 103: The Inside Story▶
Trainspotting▶
Trouble in the Glen
Whiskey Galore▶
Year of the Comet

Screwball Comedy

see also Comedy; Romantic Comedy; Slapstick Comedy

All in a Night's Work
Amazing Adventure
Ambassador Bill
America
And Baby Makes Six
Angel on My Shoulder▶
Angel on My Shoulder
Antonio
As You Like It
As You Were
Assault of the Party Nerds
The Associate
Auntie
The Awful Truth▶
The Baby and the Battleship
The Bachelor and the Bobby-Soxer▶
Bachelor Mother▶
Bachelor of Hearts
Back to School
Bank Shot▶
Bedazzled▶
Bedtime Story
Beer
Best of W.C. Fields
Big Business
Blame It on the Bellboy
The Bliss of Mrs. Blossom▶
Blue Murder at St. Trinian's▶
Boeing Boeing
Boss Foreman
Bringing Up Baby▶
Bullseye!
Buona Sera, Mrs. Campbell
Camp Cucamonga: How I Spent My Summer Vacation
Carry On Admiral
Chaplin: A Character Is Born
Chaplin Essanay Book 1
The Chaplin Revue
Charlie Chaplin: Night at the Show▶
Charlie Chaplin...Our Hero!
Charlie Chaplin's Keystone Comedies #1
Charlie Chaplin's Keystone Comedies #2
Charlie Chaplin's Keystone Comedies #3
Charlie Chaplin's Keystone Comedies #4
Charlie Chaplin's Keystone Comedies #5
The Circus▶
Combat Academy
The Couch Trip
The Count
Crackers
Days of Thrills and Laughter▶
Doctor in the House▶
Dr. Otto & the Riddle of the Gloom Beam
Doctor Takes a Wife▶
Don Juan, My Love▶
Double Wedding▶
Doubting Thomas
Down Among the Z Men
Down the Drain
Easy Money
Easy Street▶
Egg and I▶
Everything You Always Wanted to Know about Sex (But Were Afraid to Ask)▶
The Favor, the Watch, & the Very Big Fish
Fireballs
The Fireman
Fit for a King
The Floorwalker▶
The Floorwalker/By the Sea▶
Forever Darling
Forsaking All Others
The Geisha Boy
Get Crazy
Gold Rush/Payday
Hands Across the Table▶
A Hard Day's Night▶
Harvey▶
Her Husband's Affairs
He's My Girl
Holiday▶
Hot to Trot!
How I Learned to Love Women
How Sweet It Is!
I Love My...Wife
I Love You Again▶
I Wanna Be a Beauty Queen
Inspector Hornleigh
Italian Straw Hat▶
It's the Old Army Game
Joy of Living▶
La Chevre▶
Labyrinth of Passion
The Lady Eve▶
Libeled Lady▶
Life Stinks
Little Rascals Christmas Special
Lobster Man from Mars
The Long, Long Trailer
Lots of Luck
The Love Bug
Love Crazy▶
Lucky Partners
Lunatics & Lovers
Madhouse
Make Mine Mink▶
Malibu Beach
Malibu Bikini Shop
The Marriage Circle▶
The Marx Brothers in a Nutshell▶
The Mating Game▶
Me and Him
Meatballs
Meatballs 2
A Midsummer Night's Sex Comedy▶
Minsky's Follies
Miracle of Morgan's Creek▶
Mr. & Mrs. Smith▶
Modern Girls
The Money Pit
Monkey Business▶
Monkeys, Go Home!
The Moon's Our Home
The More the Merrier▶
Morons from Outer Space
Mugsy's Girls
The Munsters' Revenge
My American Cousin▶
My Chauffeur
My Favorite Brunette
My Favorite Wife▶
My Man Godfrey▶
Naked Is Better
National Lampoon's Christmas Vacation
National Lampoon's European Vacation
National Lampoon's Vacation▶
Nervous Ticks
Noises Off
Not for Publication
Nothing Sacred▶
The Nude Bomb
Ollie Hopnoodle's Haven of Bliss
One Woman or Two
The Palm Beach Story▶
Pink Flamingos
Platinum Blonde▶
Police Academy
Police Academy 2: Their First Assignment
Police Academy 3: Back in Training
Police Academy 4: Citizens on Patrol
Police Academy 5: Assignment Miami Beach
Polyester
Reaching for the Moon
Recruits
The Rink▶
Romance with a Double Bass▶
Running Wild
See No Evil, Hear No Evil
Simon
The Smallest Show on Earth▶
Some Like It Hot▶
A Southern Yankee
Spaced Invaders
Spring Break
Stan Without Ollie, Vol. 1
Stan Without Ollie, Vol. 2
Stan Without Ollie, Vol. 3
Stan Without Ollie, Vol. 4
Starhops
Starring Bugs Bunny!
Start the Revolution Without Me▶
The Statue
Stewardess School
Still Not Quite Human
Stir Crazy
Stitches
Stocks and Blondes
The Stoogephile Trivia Movie
Strange Brew
Stripes
Stroker Ace
Stuckey's Last Stand
Student Affairs
The Student Teachers
Summer School Teachers
Sundance
Superdad
Supergrass
Swap Meet
Sweet Revenge
Sweet Young Thing
Swing It, Sailor!
The Swinging Cheerleaders
Swinging Wives
Switching Channels
Takin' It All Off
Talk of the Town▶
Teen Vamp
Teen Witch
Tell It to the Judge
That Naughty Girl
They Went That-a-Way & That-a-Way
Three in the Cellar
Thunder & Mud
Tigers in Lipstick
Tramp & a Woman
Tricks of the Trade
Triple Trouble/Easy Street
Truck Stop
Twist
Two Weeks to Live
The Underachievers
The Vagabond
Vibes
Vice Versa▶
Waitress
Waltz of the Toreadors▶
Watch the Birdie
W.C. Fields Comedy Bag
What's Up, Doc?▶
When Women Had Tails
When Women Lost Their Tails
Where Were You When the Lights Went Out?
Which Way Is Up?
Whoops Apocalypse
Who's That Girl?
Wild Women of Wongo
Witches' Brew
Woman of Paris/Sunnyside▶
Work/Police▶
World's Greatest Lover
You Can't Cheat an Honest Man▶
You Can't Take It with You▶
Zotz!

Scuba

see also Deep Blue

The Abyss▶
Beneath the 12-Mile Reef
The Big Blue
Daring Game
The Deep
Easy Come, Easy Go
The Evil Below
ffolkes
Flipper▶
Flipper's New Adventure▶
Full Fathom Five
Isle of Forgotten Sins
Leviathan
The Man from Atlantis
Navy SEALS
Neptune Factor
Never Say Never Again
Night of the Sharks
Oceans of Fire
The Sea Serpent
Thunderball
The Treasure Seekers
Underwater!

Sea Critter Attack

see also Deep Blue; Go Fish; Killer Beasts

Alligator▶
Around the World Under the Sea
Attack of the Giant Leeches
Attack of the Swamp Creature
Barracuda
The Beach Girls and the Monster
The Beast from 20,000 Fathoms
Beyond Atlantis
Blood Beach
Bloodstalkers
Creature from Black Lake
Creature from the Black Lagoon▶
Creature from the Haunted Sea
Creature of Destruction
The Creature Walks Among Us
Curse of the Swamp Creature
Deepstar Six
Demon of Paradise
Devil Monster
Devilfish
The Flesh Eaters
Godzilla vs. the Sea Monster
Gorgo
The Great Alligator
Horror of Party Beach
Island Claw
Jason and the Argonauts▶
Jaws▶
Jaws 2
Jaws 3
Jaws of Death
Jaws: The Revenge
Killer Fish
The Loch Ness Horror
The Man from Atlantis
The McConnell Story
Mean Streets▶
Memphis Belle▶
Monster from the Ocean Floor
The Monster of Piedras Blancas
The Monster That Challenged the World
New York, New York▶
None But the Brave
Obsession
Octaman
Orca
The Phantom from 10,000 Leagues
Piranha
Piranha 2: The Spawning
Reap the Wild Wind
Revenge of the Creature
Scorpion with Two Tails
Screams of a Winter Night
The Sea Serpent
Serpent Island
Shark!
Shark's Paradise
The Spawning
Swamp Thing
Tentacles
Terror in the Swamp
They Bite
Tintorera...Tiger Shark
20,000 Leagues Under the Sea▶
Up from the Depths
What Waits Below

Sea Disasters

see also Air Disasters; Deep Blue; Disaster Flicks; Shipwrecked

The Abyss▶
Airport '77
Beyond the Poseidon Adventure
Das Boot▶
Deepstar Six
Far from Home: The Adventures of Yellow Dog
Goliath Awaits
Juggernaut▶
The Last Voyage
Leviathan
A Night to Remember▶
The Poseidon Adventure
Raise the Titanic
The Seducers
S.O.S. Titanic
Titanic▶
The Unsinkable Molly Brown▶
Waterworld

Seattle

Bombs Away!
Breaking Point
Dream Man
Georgia▶
The Hitman
It Happened at the World's Fair
Little Buddha
My Own Private Idaho▶
Singles▶
Sleepless in Seattle▶
The Slender Thread▶
Stakeout
Streetwise▶

Serial Killers

see also Crime & Criminals; Crime Sprees

Addams Family Values
Ambition
Amsterdamned
Aroused
The Awful Dr. Orlof
The Baby Doll Murders
The Banker
Blondes Have More Guns
Bluebeard▶
Body Parts
The Boston Strangler
Breaking Point
Broken Mirrors
Bums
Butterfly Kiss
The China Lake Murders
Citizen X▶
Cold Front
Cold Light of Day
Confessions of a Serial Killer
Cop
Copycat
Cosh Boy
Dancing with Danger
Dangerous Love
The Dark Ride
Dead Certain
Dead Girls
Dead on Sight
Dead to Rights
Deadly Force
Deadly Games
Deadly Neighbor
The Deliberate Stranger▶
A Demon in My View
Desire
Destroyer
The Element of Crime
Evil Laugh
Eyes of a Stranger
Eyes of Laura Mars
Eyes of the Beholder
Fatal Charm
Fathers and Sons
Fear
Final Notice
The First Power
The Freeway Maniac
The Frighteners
Ghost in the Machine
The Hawk
Henry: Portrait of a Serial Killer▶
Hidden Obsession
Hideaway
The Hillside Strangler
Honeymoon Killers▶
The Horror Show
The Hunt for the Night Stalker
I Can't Sleep
Impulse
In the Deep Woods
Inn on the River
The Invisible Strangler
Jack the Ripper
Jack the Ripper▶
The January Man
Jennifer 8
Kalifornia
L.A. Crackdown 2
Lady in Waiting
Laser Moon
The Laughing Policeman
Love and Human Remains▶
M▶
The Mad Executioners
Man Bites Dog
Maniac Cop
A Mind to Kill
Mr. Frost
Mixed Nuts
Mortal Sins
Natural Born Killers
Nature of the Beast
Never Talk to Strangers
Night Shadow
Night Stalker
Nightscare
No Way to Treat a Lady▶
The Paint Job
Pale Blood
Portraits of a Killer
Prey of the Chameleon
Prime Suspect▶
Prime Suspect: The Scent of Darkness▶
Probable Cause
Psychic
The Rain Killer
Relentless 3
Relentless 4
The Rosary Murders
The Satan Killer
Serial Killer
Serial Mom▶
Seven▶
The Silence of the Lambs▶
Slaughter of the Innocents
Sleepstalker: The Sandman's Last Rites
Snapdragon
So I Married an Axe Murderer
Split Second
Stagefright
Stamp of a Killer
Star Time
Still Life
Stranger by Night
Strangler of Blackmoor Castle
Striking Distance
Tails You Live, Heads You're Dead
10 Rillington Place▶
Ten to Midnight
Terror at London Bridge
To Catch a Killer▶
The Todd Killings
True Crime
Tunnel Vision
Undefeatable
When the Bough Breaks
While the City Sleeps▶
Without Warning
Writer's Block
Zipperface

Serials

Ace Drummond
The Adventures of Captain Marvel
The Adventures of Frank and Jesse James
Adventures of Red Ryder
The Adventures of Rex & Rinty
Adventures of Smilin' Jack
The Adventures of Tarzan
The Adventures of the Flying Cadets
The Adventures of the Masked Phantom
Amazing Stories
Battling with Buffalo Bill
The Black Coin
The Black Widow
Blake of Scotland Yard
Bugs Bunny Superstar
Burn 'Em Up Barnes
Canadian Mounties vs. Atomic Invaders
Captain America
Casey Jones and Fury (Brave Stallion)
Cheyenne Rides Again
The Clutching Hand
Custer's Last Stand
Cyclotrode "X"
D-Day on Mars
Daredevils of the Red Circle
Darkest Africa
Daughter of Don Q
Destination Saturn
Devil Horse
Dick Tracy
Dick Tracy Returns
Dick Tracy: The Original Serial, Vol. 1▶
Dick Tracy: The Original Serial, Vol. 2▶
Dick Tracy vs. Crime Inc.
Doctor Satan's Robot
Don Daredevil Rides Again
Don Winslow of the Coast Guard
Don Winslow of the Navy
Drums of Fu Manchu▶
East Side Kids/The Lost City
Federal Agents vs. Underworld, Inc.
Federal Operator 99
Fighting Devil Dogs
Fighting Marines
Fighting with Kit Carson
Flaming Frontiers
Flash Gordon Conquers the Universe
Flash Gordon: Mars Attacks the World
Flash Gordon: Vol. 1
Flash Gordon: Vol. 2
Flash Gordon: Vol. 3
Flying Discman from Mars
G-Men Never Forget
G-Men vs. the Black Dragon
The Galloping Ghost
Genie of Darkness
Government Agents vs. Phantom Legion
Green Archer
The Green Hornet
Haunted Harbor
Hawk of the Wilderness
Heroes of the West
Holt of the Secret Service
Hurricane Express
In Old New Mexico
The Invisible Monster
Jesse James Rides Again
Jungle Drums of Africa
Junior G-Men
Junior G-Men of the Air
King of the Congo
King of the Forest Rangers
King of the Kongo
King of the Rocketmen
King of the Texas Rangers
Last Frontier
The Last of the Mohicans
Law of the Wild
A Lawman Is Born▶
Lightning Warrior
The Lone Defender
The Lone Ranger
Lone Ranger
The Lost City
Lost City of the Jungle
The Lost Jungle
Lost Planet Airmen
Manhunt in the African Jungle
Manhunt of Mystery Island
Mansfield Park
The Masked Marvel
Master Key
Masters of Venus
The Miracle Rider
Mission: Monte Carlo
The Monster Demolisher
Mysterious Doctor Satan
Mystery Mountain
Mystery of the Riverboat
Mystery Squadron
Mystery Trooper
The New Adventures of Tarzan
Nyoka and the Tigermen
Oregon Trail
The Original Flash Gordon Collection
Overland Mail
The Painted Stallion
The Perils of Pauline
Perils of the Darkest Jungle
The Phantom Creeps
The Phantom Empire
Phantom of the Air
Phantom of the West
The Phantom Rider
Pirates of the High Seas
The Purple Monster Strikes
Queen of the Jungle
Radar Men from the Moon
Radio Patrol
Raiders of Ghost City
Red Barry
Return of Chandu
Riders of Death Valley
Robinson Crusoe of Clipper Island
Robinson Crusoe of Mystery Island
Rustlers of Red Dog
Saturday Night Serials
Savage Fury
Sea Hound
The Secret Code
Shadow of Chinatown
Shadow of the Eagle
Son of Zorro
S.O.S. Coast Guard
Space Soldiers Conquer the Universe
Spy Smasher
Spy Smasher Returns
Stone Cold Dead
Sunset on the Desert
Superman: The Serial, Vol. 1
Tailspin Tommy
Tarzan the Tiger
Texas to Bataan
The Three Musketeers
Tim Tyler's Luck
Tom Mix Compilation 1
Tom Mix Compilation 2
Trader Tom of the China Seas
Trail of the Silver Spurs
Trail Riders
Tumbledown Ranch in Arizona
Undersea Kingdom
Vanishing Legion
The Vigilantes are Coming
Whispering Shadow
Winners of the West
Wolf Dog
Woman in Grey
Young Eagles
Zombies of the Stratosphere
Zorro Rides Again
Zorro's Black Whip
Zorro's Fighting Legion

Sex & Sexuality

see also Crimes of Passion; Erotic Thrillers; Pornography; Sex on the Beach; Sexploitation

ABC's of Love & Sex, Australia Style
Accident
Acting on Impulse
The Adjuster
The Adultress
Adventures of a Private Eye
Adventures of a Taxi Driver
The Adventures of Sadie
The Advocate▶
Alfie▶
All Things Fair
The Allnighter
Almost Pregnant
Alpine Fire
Alvin Purple

Alvin Rides Again
The Amazing Transplant
American Gigolo
The Amorous Adventures of Moll Flanders
The Amy Fisher Story
And God Created Woman
Andy Warhol's Dracula▶
Andy Warhol's Frankenstein
Angel Heart
Angel of H.E.A.T.
Angels and Insects▶
Animal Instincts
Animal Instincts 2
Animal Instincts 3: The Seductress
Any Wednesday
The Apartment▶
Armistead Maupin's Tales of the City
The Arousers
Arrivederci, Baby!
Art for Teachers of Children
Assault
Baby Doll▶
The Baby Doll Murders
Baby Face
Baby Love
The Baby Maker
The Bachelor▶
Bachelor in Paradise
Bachelor Party
Bad Company
Bad Girls from Mars
Bad Lieutenant▶
Bank Robber
Barbarella
Basic Training
The Bawdy Adventures of Tom Jones
Beach Girls
Becoming Colette
Bedroom Eyes
Bedroom Eyes 2
Before Sunrise
Being at Home with Claude
Belle de Jour▶
Belle Epoque▶
Belle of the Nineties
Beneath the Valley of the Ultra-Vixens
The Best Little Whorehouse in Texas
Betrayal
Betty Blue▶
Beverly Hills Madam
Beyond Erotica
Beyond the Silhouette
The Big Bet
The Big Dis
Bilitis
The Bitch
Bitter Harvest
Bitter Moon
Bitter Rice▶
The Black Room
Black Starlet
Blind Vision
Blindfold: Acts of Obsession
Blood and Sand▶
Bloodbath
Blown Away
The Blue Angel▶
Blue Jeans
The Blue Lagoon
Blue Movies
Blue Velvet▶
Boarding School
Bob & Carol & Ted & Alice
Boccaccio '70
Bodily Harm
Body Chemistry
Body Chemistry 2: Voice of a Stranger
Body Chemistry 3: Point of Seduction
Body Double▶
Body Language
Body Waves
Boeing Boeing
Bonjour Tristesse▶
The Boss' Wife
Boxing Helena
A Boy and His Dog
Boys' Night Out▶
Bram Stoker's Dracula
Breaking the Waves▶
Breathless
The Bride Is Much Too Beautiful
Brides of the Beast
Broken Trust
Buford's Beach Bunnies
Business as Usual
Butterfield 8▶
Butterfly
Bye Bye Baby
Cactus in the Snow
Caligula
Can I Do It...Till I Need Glasses?
The Canterbury Tales
Captives
Carnal Crimes
Carnal Knowledge▶
Carnival in Flanders▶
Carried Away
Carry On Camping
Carry On Emmanuelle
Carry On Henry VIII
Casanova
Casanova '70
Casual Sex?
Cat on a Hot Tin Roof▶
Cat People
Cave Girl
Cesar & Rosalie▶
Chain of Desire
Champagne for Breakfast
Chatterbox
Cheaters
Cheech and Chong's Up in Smoke
Cherry 2000
The Chicken Chronicles
Chinese Roulette
Choose Me▶
Cinderella 2000
Claire's Knee▶
Class
Class of '63
Class Reunion
Cleo/Leo
Close My Eyes
Closely Watched Trains▶
Cold Sweat
Collector's Item▶
Color of Night
The Comfort of Strangers▶
Compromising Positions
Conspiracy
Contagion
The Cook, the Thief, His Wife & Her Lover▶
The Cool Surface
Cool World
Corruption
The Courtesans of Bombay▶
Crash
Crimes of Passion▶
The Cruel Story of Youth▶
Crush
Cry Uncle
Damage▶
Dangerous Game
Dangerous Indiscretion
Dangerous Liaisons▶
Dangerous Touch
The Dark Side of Love
Dark Tide
Daughters of Satan
Dead On
Dead Weekend
Dear Boys
Death of a Centerfold
The Decameron▶
Decameron Nights
Deceit
Deceptions
The Decline of the American Empire▶
Deep Down
Delta of Venus
Denial: The Dark Side of Passion
Desire
Desire and Hell at Sunset Motel
Desk Set▶
Devil in the Flesh▶
Devil in the Flesh
The Devils▶
The Devil's Eye
The Devil's Nightmare
The Devil's Playground▶
Devil's Wedding Night
Diary of a Chambermaid▶
Diary of a Mad Housewife▶
Diary of a Mad Old Man
Die Watching
Diner▶
Discretion Assured
Divine Nymph
Divorce—Italian Style▶
Dr. Alien
Dr. Caligari
Dog Day Afternoon▶
Doll Face
Dollar
Domino
Dona Herlinda & Her Son
Don's Party▶
Double Cross
Double Suicide▶
Dracula Sucks
Dreams
Dreams Come True
Dreams of Desire
Driver's Seat
Drum
East End Hustle
Eating Raoul▶
Ebbtide
Ebony Tower
Echoes of Paradise
The Eclipse▶
Ecstasy
Eddie Murphy: Raw
Eden
Eden 2
Eden 3
Eden 4
El: This Strange Passion▶
Elke
Elmer Gantry▶
Elvira, Mistress of the Dark
Embrace of the Vampire
Emily
Emmanuelle
Emmanuelle 4
Emmanuelle & Joanna
Emmanuelle in Bangkok
Emmanuelle in Soho
Emmanuelle in the Country
Emmanuelle, the Joys of a Woman
Emmanuelle, the Queen
Emmanuelle's Daughter
End of August
Endless Love
Enemies, a Love Story▶
Enormous Changes▶
Enrapture
Ernesto
Erotic Escape
Erotic Images
Erotic Touch of Hot Skin
Et La Tenoresse?...Bordel!
Every Breath
Everything You Always Wanted to Know about Sex (But Were Afraid to Ask)▶
Evils of the Night
Exit to Eden
Exotica▶
Fairy Tales
Fanny Hill
Fanny Hill: Memoirs of a Woman of Pleasure
The Fantasist
Fast Food
Fast Times at Ridgemont High▶
Fatal Attraction
Fatal Attraction▶
Fatal Bond
Fatal Charm
Fatal Instinct
Fatal Past
The Favor
Feelin' Screwy
Fellini Satyricon▶
Female Trouble
Final Judgement
The Finishing Touch
First Affair
The First Time
First Time
First Turn On
Flesh▶
Flesh Gordon
A Flight of Rainbirds
Flirt
Forbidden Zone: Alien Abduction
Foreign Body
Foreplay
Forever Emmanuelle
The 4th Man▶
Foxes
Frankenstein Unbound▶
Frasier the Sensuous Lion
Fraternity Vacation
French Fried Vacation
The French Woman
Frenzy▶
Fritz the Cat▶
The Fugitive Kind
Full Exposure: The Sex Tape Scandals
Gabriela
Galactic Gigolo
The Game is Over
Games Girls Play
The Garden
Gas Pump Girls
Gentlemen Prefer Blondes▶
Genuine Risk
Georgy Girl▶
Get Out Your Handkerchiefs▶
Ghosts Can Do It
The Gift
Gilda▶
Ginger Ale Afternoon
The Girl
Girl 6
The Girl on a Motorcycle
Glen or Glenda: Confessions of Ed Wood
Go West, Young Man
The Goddess▶
The Good Mother
Goodbye Emmanuelle
Gorp
Gothic▶
The Graduate▶
The Great American Sex Scandal
Gross Misconduct
The Handmaid's Tale
Happily Ever After
Hard Drive
Hardbodies 2
Harrad Experiment
Harrad Summer
Heart of the Stag
Heaven Can Wait▶
Heavy Petting
Hell Comes to Frogtown
Henry & June▶
Higher Education
The Hit List
Hold Me, Thrill Me, Kiss Me
Hollywood Confidential
Homework
Honey
The Horseplayer
Hot Child in the City
The Hot Spot
Hot Target
Hot Under the Collar
The Hotel New Hampshire
Hotel Paradiso
Hotel Room
Hourglass
How Funny Can Sex Be?
How to Pick Up Girls
How to Seduce a Woman
Hugh Hefner: Once Upon a Time
Husbands and Lovers
I Am Curious (Yellow)
I Like to Play Games
I Posed for Playboy
I Will, I Will for Now
Illegal in Blue
Illicit Dreams
Ilsa, Harem Keeper of the Oil Sheiks
I'm No Angel▶
Impure Thoughts
In Praise of Older Women
In the Heat of Passion
In the Heat of Passion 2: Unfaithful
In the Realm of the Senses▶
An Inconvenient Woman
Indecency
Indecent Behavior
Indecent Behavior 2
Indecent Behavior 3
Indecent Proposal
Inner Sanctum 2
Inside Out
Invasion of Privacy
Invasion of the Bee Girls▶
Irezumi▶
Is There Sex After Death?▶
Isadora▶
It
The Italian Stallion
It's Not the Size That Counts
Jade
Jailbait
Jamon, Jamon
Jeffrey
Justine
Kandyland
Kids
Kika
Killer Looks
Killer Workout
The Killing Game
A Kiss Goodnight
Kiss Me, Stupid!
Kiss of a Killer
The Knack▶
La Cicada
La Collectionneuse
L.A. Goddess
La Ronde▶
Labyrinth of Passion
Lady Caroline Lamb
Lady Chatterley's Lover
Lady Frankenstein
Lady on the Bus
Ladykiller
Ladykillers
Lake Consequence
L'Annee des Meduses
Lap Dancing
The Laserman
Last Call
Last of the Red Hot Lovers
Last Resort
Last Summer
Last Tango in Paris▶
Le Boucher▶
Le Cavaleur
Le Sex Shop▶
Les Nuits Fauves▶
Lethal Lolita—Amy Fisher: My Story
Liebestraum
Lies Before Kisses
A Life of Sin
Lifeforce
The Lifetaker
Like Water for Chocolate▶
Lipstick Camera
Liquid Sky▶
Little Darlings
A Little Sex
Live Nude Girls
Lolita▶
Looking for Mr. Goodbar
Loulou▶
The Love Affair, or The Case of the Missing Switchboard Operator▶
Love After Love
Love and Human Remains▶
The Love Boat
Love Crimes

Sex on the Beach

see also Island Fare

Sexploitation

see also Erotic Thrillers; Exploitation

Sexual Abuse

Sexual Harrassment

Ships

Shipwrecked

Showbiz Comedies

Showbiz Dramas

Showbiz Musicals

Showbiz Thrillers

Shrinks

Shutterbugs

see also Front Page

Silent Films

see also Silent Horror/Fantasy Classics

Kriemhilde's Revenge▶
La Chute de la Maison Usher▶
Lady of the Lake
Lady Windermere's Fan
The Lamb
Last Command▶
The Last Laugh▶
The Last of the Mohicans▶
The Last Outlaw
Laugh with Linder!
Laughfest
Laughing at Danger
Leap Year
The Leatherneck
Leaves from Satan's Book
The Leopard Woman
Let 'er Go Gallegher
Let's Go!
The Light of Faith
Linda
The Little American
Little Annie Rooney
Little Church Around the Corner
The Lizzies of Mack Sennett
The Lodger▶
The Lost World
Love 'Em and Leave 'Em▶
The Love Flower
Lucky Devil
Mabel & Fatty
Mack & Carole
Mack Sennett Comedies: Vol. 1
Mack Sennett Comedies: Vol. 2
The Mad Whirl
Male and Female▶
The Man from Beyond
The Man from Painted Post
Man in the Silk Hat
Man in the Silk Hat▶
The Man on the Box
The Man Who Laughs▶
The Man with a Movie Camera▶
Manhandled
Mantrap
The Manxman
Mark of Zorro▶
Marked Money
The Marriage Circle▶
Married?
Master of the House▶
Matrimaniac
Max
Merry-Go-Round▶
The Messenger of the Blessed Virgin
Metropolis▶
The Michigan Kid
Mickey
Mid-Channel
Midnight Faces
Moana, a Romance of the Golden Age▶
Modern Times▶
Monsieur Beaucaire
Moran of the Lady Letty
A Mormon Maid
Mother▶
My Best Girl
My Boy
My Lady of Whims
The Mysterious Lady
Mystery of the Leaping Fish/ Chess Fever
Napoleon▶
Narrow Trail▶
The Navigator▶
The Nervous Wreck▶
Nevada
Never Weaken/Why Worry?▶
The Night Club
The Night Cry
The Night Patrol
No Man's Law
Nomads of the North
Nosferatu▶
The Notorious Lady
The Nut
Old Ironsides▶
Oliver Twist▶
On the Night Stage
One A.M.
One Arabian Night▶
One-Punch O'Day
Orphans of the Storm▶
Othello
Our Dancing Daughters
Our Gang
Our Gang Comedy Festival
Our Gang Comedy Festival 2
Our Hospitality▶
The Outlaw and His Wife
Outside the Law
Pace That Kills
Pandora's Box▶
Passion
The Passion of Joan of Arc▶
Patchwork Girl of Oz
Paths to Paradise▶
Pawnshop
The Peacock Fan
Peck's Bad Boy
Peg O' My Heart
The Phantom Chariot
The Phantom Flyer
The Phantom of the Opera▶
Playing Dead
Pollyanna
The Pony Express
Pool Sharks
A Poor Little Rich Girl▶
Pop Goes the Cork
Power
The Prairie King
The Prairie Pirate
Pride of the Clan
The Primitive Lover
A Propos de Nice▶
Q Ships
Queen Kelly▶
Quo Vadis
Ranson's Folly
The Raven
Reaching for the Moon
Rebecca of Sunnybrook Farm
Red Kimono
Red Signals
Regeneration
Reggie Mixes In▶
Renoir Shorts▶
The Return of Boston Blackie
Return of Draw Egan
The Return of Grey Wolf
Riders of the Purple Sage
Riders of the Range
The Ring
The Rink▶
Rink/Immigrant
Risky Business
The Road to Ruin
The Road to Yesterday
Road to Yesterday/The Yankee Clipper
The Roaring Road
Robin Hood▶
Robinson Crusoe
Romola
Rounding Up the Law
Running Wild
Sacred Mountain/White Flame▶
Sadie Thompson▶
Sailor-Made Man/Grandma's Boy▶
Salammbo
Sally of the Sawdust
Salome
Salome/Queen Elizabeth
Sands of Sacrifice
The Saphead
Sawmill/The Dome Doctor
Scar of Shame
The Scarlet Car
Sea Lion
Secrets of a Soul
Seven Chances▶
Seven Years Bad Luck▶
Sex
Shadows
Shattered▶
She
The Sheik▶
Shifting Sands
Ships in the Night
The Shock
Show People▶
Siegfried▶
Silent Laugh Makers, No. 1▶
Silent Laugh Makers, No. 2▶
Silent Laugh Makers, No. 3
The Silent Mr. Sherlock Holmes
Silent Movie
Silent Movies...Just For the Fun of It!
The Single Standard
Skinner's Dress Suit
Sky High
Smiling Madame Beudet/The Seashell and the Clergyman▶
So This is Paris▶
The Social Secretary
Son of a Gun
Son of the Sheik▶
The Sorrows of Satan▶
Soul-Fire
Soul of the Beast
Spangles
Sparrows▶
The Speed Spook
Spiders▶
Spies▶
Spite Marriage▶
The Spoilers
Square Shoulders
Stan Without Ollie, Vol. 1
Stand and Deliver
Steamboat Bill, Jr.▶
Stella Maris▶
Storm Over Asia▶
Straight Shootin'
The Street
Street of Forgotten Women
Strike▶
Student of Prague▶
The Student Prince in Old Heidelberg
Suds
Sunny Side Up
Sunrise▶
The Swan
Sweet Adeline
Tabu: A Story of the South Seas▶
Tale of Two Cities/In the Switch Tower
Tarzan of the Apes
Tarzan the Tiger
The Taxi Mystery
Teddy at the Throttle
Teddy at the Throttle/Speeding Along
The Tempest▶
The Tempest/The Eagle▶
The Ten Commandments
Ten Days That Shook the World▶
Ten Nights in a Bar Room
Tentacles of the North
Test of Donald Norton
That Certain Thing
These Girls Won't Talk
The Thief
The Thief of Baghdad▶
Thomas Graal's Best Film▶
Thomas Graal's First Child▶
Three Ages▶
Three Charlies and One Phoney!
The Three Musketeers
The Three Musketeers▶
Three Word Brand
Through the Breakers
Tillie Wakes Up
Tillie's Punctured Romance
Tol'able David
Toll Gate
Tom Mix Compilation 1
Tom Mix Compilation 2
The Tomboy
The Tong Man
Too Wise Wives
The Torture of Silence
Tournament
Traffic in Souls▶
Trailin'
Tramp & a Woman
Trapped by the Mormons
Treasure of Arne
Triple Trouble/Easy Street
True Heart Susie
20,000 Leagues Under the Sea▶
Two Men & a Wardrobe
Un Chien Andalou▶
The Unchastened Woman
Uncle Tom's Cabin
Underworld▶
The Unholy Three▶
The Unknown▶
The Untamable
Until They Get Me
The Vagabond
Vanishing American
Variety▶
The Virginian
Virtue's Revolt
Wagon Tracks
Walking Back
The Walloping Kid
Warning Shadows▶
Waxworks▶
Way Down East▶
The Wedding March▶
We're in the Navy Now
West-Bound Limited
West of Zanzibar
What Happened to Rosa?▶
When the Clouds Roll By▶
Where East Is East
White Gold▶
The White Rose▶
The White Sin
The White Sister▶
White Tiger
Why Change Your Wife?
Wild Horse Canyon
Wild Orchids
The Wind▶
Wings
The Wishing Ring▶
Witchcraft Through the Ages▶
With Kit Carson Over the Great Divide
The Wizard of Oz
Wolf Blood
Wolfheart's Revenge
Woman in Grey
Woman in the Moon
A Woman of Affairs
Woman of Paris/Sunnyside▶
Work/Police▶
Working Winnie/Oh So Simple
The Worldly Madonna
Yankee Clipper
Yankee Doodle in Berlin
Zvenigora▶

Silent Horror/ Fantasy Classics

see also Silent Films

Aelita: Queen of Mars
The Cabinet of Dr. Caligari▶
Dante's Inferno▶
Dr. Jekyll and Mr. Hyde▶
The Golem▶
The Hunchback of Notre Dame▶
La Chute de la Maison Usher▶
Metropolis▶
Million Dollar Mystery
The Monster▶
Nosferatu▶
The Penalty
The Phantom of the Opera▶
The Thief of Baghdad▶
20,000 Leagues Under the Sea▶
Vampyr▶
The Wizard of Oz

Singles

see also Dates From Hell

About Last Night...▶
Before Sunrise
Boys' Night Out▶
Breakfast at Tiffany's▶
Bye Bye, Love
Crossing Delancey▶
Forget Paris
He Said, She Said
Kicking and Screaming▶
Metropolitan▶
Mr. Wonderful
Mr. Wrong
Mystic Pizza▶
The Opposite Sex and How to Live With Them
Pillow Talk▶
Reality Bites
St. Elmo's Fire
Singles▶
Sleepless in Seattle▶
That Touch of Mink
The Thing Called Love
When Harry Met Sally...▶
The Wild Life

Sixties

see Flower Children

Skateboarding

Gleaming the Cube
Skateboard

Skating

see also Hockey

Airborne
Blades of Courage
Breaking the Ice
The Cutting Edge
Derby▶
Everything Happens at Night▶
Frolics on Ice
Hans Brinker
Happy Landing
Ice Castles
Ice Pawn
Iceland
My Lucky Star
Nutcracker, A Fantasy on Ice
One in a Million▶
Roller Boogie
Schizo
Sun Valley Serenade
Unholy Rollers
Wintertime
Xanadu

Skiing

Aspen Extreme
Avalanche
Better Off Dead
Club Med
Downhill Racer
Dumb & Dumber
Fire and Ice
Fire, Ice and Dynamite
For Your Eyes Only▶
Going for the Gold: The Bill Johnson Story
Hot Dog...The Movie!
Iced
Lost and Found
The Man Who Skied Down Everest
On Her Majesty's Secret Service▶
One Last Run
The Other Side of the Mountain
The Other Side of the Mountain, Part 2
Red Snow
Reno and the Doc
Ski Bum
Ski Patrol
Ski School
Ski School 2
Ski Troop Attack
Skier's Dream
Snow: The Movie
Snowball Express
Snowballin'
Snowballing
Snowblind
Striker's Mountain
Tales from the Snow Zone

Skinheads

see also Nazis & Other Paramilitary Slugs

The Infiltrator
Luna Park
Red Scorpion 2
Romper Stomper
Skin
Surf Nazis Must Die

Skydiving

Drop Zone
Fandango
Honeymoon in Vegas
Point Break
Terminal Velocity

Slapstick Comedy

see also Comedy; Screwball Comedy

Abbott and Costello Go to Mars
Abbott and Costello in Hollywood
Abbott and Costello in the Foreign Legion
Abbott and Costello Meet Captain Kidd
Abbott and Costello Meet Dr. Jekyll and Mr. Hyde
Abbott and Costello Meet Frankenstein▶
Abbott and Costello Meet the Invisible Man▶
Abbott and Costello Meet the Keystone Kops
Abbott and Costello Meet the Killer, Boris Karloff
Abbott and Costello Meet the Mummy
Abroad with Two Yanks
Ace Crawford, Private Eye
Ace Ventura: Pet Detective
Ace Ventura: When Nature Calls
The Adventurer
The Adventures of Buckaroo Banzai Across the Eighth Dimension▶
Africa Screams
After the Fox
Air Raid Wardens
All Night Long/Smile Please
All of Me
Alvin Purple
Alvin Rides Again
American Aristocracy
American Pluck
Amos and Andrew
Animal Crackers▶
Any Which Way You Can
Armed and Dangerous
Around the World in 80 Ways
Around the World in a Daze
Assault and Matrimony
At the Circus
At War with the Army
Baby's Day Out
The Bad News Bears▶
The Bad News Bears Go to Japan
The Bad News Bears in Breaking Training
Bakery/Grocery Clerk
The Bank Dick▶
The Barber Shop▶
The Barefoot Executive
The Battle of the Sexes▶
Bedtime for Bonzo
Beethoven
Beethoven's 2nd
The Bellboy
Bellhop/The Noon Whistle
Big Mouth
Big Store
Block-heads▶
Bohemian Girl▶
Bonnie Scotland
Bowery Boys Meet the Monsters
Boy, Did I Get a Wrong Number!
Brain Donors
Buck Privates
Buck Privates Come Home▶
Bullfighters
Buster Keaton Rides Again/The Railrodder
The Caddy
Caddyshack▶
Caddyshack 2
Candleshoe
Cannonball/Dizzy Heights and Daring Hearts
Carry On at Your Convenience
Carry On Behind
Carry On Camping
Carry On Cruising
Carry On Doctor▶
Carry On Emmanuelle
Carry On England
Carry On Henry VIII
Carry On Nurse
Carry On 'Round the Bend
Casanova's Big Night
The Case of the Mukkinese Battle Horn
The Champion/His New Job▶
Charlie Chaplin: The Early Years, Vol. 1
Charlie Chaplin: The Early Years, Vol. 2
Charlie Chaplin: The Early Years, Vol. 3
Charlie Chaplin: The Early Years, Vol. 4
Cheech and Chong: Still Smokin'
Cheech and Chong: Things Are Tough All Over
Cheech and Chong's Next Movie
Cheech and Chong's The Corsican Brothers
Cheech and Chong's Up in Smoke
Christmas in July▶
A Chump at Oxford
Cinderfella
Cockeyed Cavaliers
College▶
Comin' Round the Mountain
Cord & Dischords/Naughty Nurse
Count/Adventurer
Cracking Up
The Cure
Dance with Me, Henry
A Day at the Races▶
The Delicate Delinquent
The Dentist▶
Detective School Dropouts
Disorderly Orderly
Don't Raise the Bridge, Lower the River
Don't Shove/Two Gun Gussie
Doughboys
Duck Soup▶
Dumb & Dumber
Ernest Goes to Camp
Ernest Goes to Jail
Ernest Goes to School
Ernest Rides Again
Ernest Scared Stupid
The Errand Boy
Family Jewels
The Fatal Glass of Beer
The Feud
Finders Keepers
A Fine Mess
Flim-Flam Man
The Flying Deuces▶
Folks!
Follow That Camel
For Auld Lang Syne: The Marx Brothers
Francis Covers the Big Town
Francis Goes to the Races
Francis Goes to West Point
Francis in the Haunted House
Francis in the Navy
Francis Joins the WACs
Francis the Talking Mule▶
Free and Easy
The Fuller Brush Girl
The Fuller Brush Man
Funny Farm
George Washington Slept Here▶
Get Smart, Again!
The Ghost and Mr. Chicken
Ghost in the Noonday Sun
Ghost on the Loose
Gilligan's Island: Meet the Crew
A Girl in Every Port
The Gods Must Be Crazy▶
The Gods Must Be Crazy 2
Going Bananas
The Gorilla
Great Guns
The Great Lover
Great Race
A Guide for the Married Man▶
Gus
Half-Shot at Sunrise
Hands Up
Hardly Working
A Hash House Fraud/The Sultan's Wife
Have Rocket Will Travel
Here Come the Co-Eds
Hold That Ghost▶
Hollywood or Bust
Home Alone▶
Home Alone 2: Lost in New York
The Horn Blows at Midnight▶
Horse Feathers▶
Hot Lead & Cold Feet
I Hate Blondes
In Society
Ishtar
It's a Mad, Mad, Mad, Mad World
Jack & the Beanstalk
The Jerk
Jour de Fete▶
Julia Misbehaves▶
Jumping Jacks
Kentucky Kernels
The Kettles in the Ozarks
The Kettles on Old MacDonald's Farm
The Klutz
The Last Remake of Beau Geste
Laughfest
Laurel & Hardy and the Family
Laurel & Hardy: Another Fine Mess
Laurel & Hardy: At Work
Laurel & Hardy: Be Big
Laurel & Hardy: Below Zero
Laurel & Hardy: Berth Marks
Laurel & Hardy: Blotto
Laurel & Hardy: Brats
Laurel & Hardy: Chickens Come Home
Laurel & Hardy Comedy Classics, Vol. 7
Laurel & Hardy: Hog Wild
Laurel & Hardy: Laughing Gravy
Laurel & Hardy: Men O'War
Laurel & Hardy: Night Owls
Laurel & Hardy On the Lam
Laurel & Hardy: Perfect Day
Laurel & Hardy Spooktacular
Laurel & Hardy: Stan "Helps" Ollie
Laurel & Hardy: The Hoose-Gow
Let's Go!
Little Giant
Lost in a Harem
Lost in Alaska
The Lost Stooges
Love Happy
Ma and Pa Kettle
Ma and Pa Kettle at the Fair
Ma and Pa Kettle at Waikiki
Ma and Pa Kettle Back On the Farm
Ma and Pa Kettle Go to Town
Man of the House
Man's Favorite Sport?
Matilda
Meatballs 3
Meatballs 4
Menage▶
Mexican Hayride
Milky Way
Mr. Bill's Real Life Adventures
Mr. Hulot's Holiday▶
Monkey Business▶
Monkey Trouble
Music Box/Helpmates
My Friend Irma
The Naughty Nineties
The Navigator▶
Never Give a Sucker an Even Break▶
A Night at the Opera▶
A Night in Casablanca▶
The Noose Hangs High▶
The North Avenue Irregulars
Not Quite Human
Not Quite Human 2
Nothing But Trouble
Nuns on the Run
Odd Jobs
Off Limits
Off the Wall
One A.M.
Our Relations▶
Out of the Blue
The Outlaws is Coming!
Pack Up Your Troubles
Pardon My Sarong
Pardon My Trunk
Pardon Us
The Party▶
The Patsy
Pawnshop
Pharmacist
Playtime▶
Police Academy 6: City Under Siege
Problem Child 2
Quick, Let's Get Married
Railrodder▶
Reckless Kelly
Rio Rita
The Road to Hong Kong
Robin Hood: Men in Tights
Rockin' Road Trip
Room Service
Saps at Sea
Seven Years Bad Luck▶
Show People▶
Sidewalks of New York
Silent Laugh Makers, No. 1▶
Silent Laugh Makers, No. 2▶
Silent Laugh Makers, No. 3
Slapstick
Slapstick of Another Kind
Snow White and the Three Stooges
Son of the Pink Panther
Sons of the Desert▶
The Speed Spook
Spies Like Us
Stooges Shorts Festival
The Stooges Story▶
The Stupids
Swiss Miss
Take the Money and Run▶
Tanks a Million
The 30-Foot Bride of Candy Rock
Three Charlies and One Phoney!
Three Stooges Comedy Capers: Vol. 1
Three Stooges Comedy Classics
Three Stooges: Cookoo Cavaliers and Other Nyuks
Three Stooges Festival
Three Stooges: From Nurse to Worse and Other Nyuks
The Three Stooges: Half-Wit's Holiday and Other Nyuks
The Three Stooges: Idiots Deluxe and Other Nyuks
Three Stooges in Orbit
The Three Stooges Meet Hercules
The Three Stooges: Nutty but Nice and Other Nyuks
The Three Stooges: They Stooge to Conga and Other Nyuks
Tillie Wakes Up
Too Shy to Try
A Tribute to the Boys
Two Much
Two-Way Stretch
Up the Creek
Utopia
Voyage-Suprise▶
Walk Like a Man
W.C. Fields: Flask of Fields
Weekend at Bernie's
Weekend at Bernie's 2
What! No Beer?
Who Done It?
Who Killed Doc Robbin?
Why Me?
Wide Open Faces
A Woman of Distinction▶
The Wonders of Aladdin
Yankee Doodle in Berlin
The Yellow Cab Man
Yellowbeard

Slavery

see also Civil Rights

The Abductors
Acla's Descent into Floristella
The Adventures of Huckleberry Finn
Angel City
The Association
Band of Angels
The Big Bust Out
Black Fox: The Price of Peace
Blacksnake!
Brother Future
Buck and the Preacher
Burn!▶
Candyman 2: Farewell to the Flesh
The Civil War, Episode 1: The Cause—1861▶
The Civil War, Episode 2: A Very Bloody Affair—1862▶
The Civil War, Episode 3: Forever Free—1862▶
The Civil War, Episode 4: Simply Murder—1863▶
The Civil War, Episode 5: The Universe of Battle—1863▶
The Civil War, Episode 6: Valley of the Shadow of Death—1864▶
The Civil War, Episode 7: Most Hallowed Ground—1864▶
The Civil War, Episode 8: War is All Hell—1865▶
The Civil War, Episode 9: The Better Angels of Our Nature—1865▶
The Colombian Connection
Dragonard
Gone are the Days
Half Slave, Half Free
Hell's Wind Staff
The House of Dies Drear
The House of 1000 Dolls
Intimate Power
Island of Lost Girls
Jefferson in Paris
Joseph
The Journey of August King
The Last Supper▶
Lust for Freedom
Man Friday
Man from Deep River
Mandinga
Mandingo
Naked in the Sun
Naked Warriors
Pudd'nhead Wilson
Quilombo
Race to Freedom: The Story of the Underground Railroad
The Road to Morocco▶
The Robe
Roots▶
Roots: The Gift
Sansho the Bailiff▶

Shaft in Africa
The Silencer
Skin Game▶
Slave Trade in the World Today
Slavers
Spartacus▶
Sunshine Run
Tamango
Traffic in Souls▶
Uncle Tom's Cabin
Wanda, The Sadistic Hypnotist
White Slave
A Woman Called Moses
Xica▶

Slice of Life

see also America's Heartland; True Stories

The Adventures of Huck Finn▶
The Adventures of Huckleberry Finn▶
Ah, Wilderness!▶
Alice Doesn't Live Here Anymore
All Creatures Great and Small▶
All I Desire
Amarcord▶
American Graffiti▶
Andy Hardy Gets Spring Fever
Andy Hardy's Double Life
Andy Hardy's Private Secretary
Angie
Arizona Dream
Autumn Moon
Avalon▶
Babycakes
Bad Behavior
The Basketball Diaries
Before Sunrise
The Bicycle Thief▶
Billy Galvin
Black God & White Devil
Bloodbrothers
The Blot
Blueberry Hill
Bodies, Rest & Motion
Breaking In▶
Breathing Lessons▶
Bright Angel
The Brothers McMullen▶
Bus Stop▶
Camilla
Captains Courageous▶
Car Wash
Cesar▶
Christy
Circle of Friends
Citizens Band▶
Coming Up Roses
Cotter
Courtship▶
Crisscross
Crooklyn▶
Cross Creek
Crossing Delancey▶
The Crowd▶
Crows and Sparrows▶
Dance Me Outside
Dance of Life
A Dangerous Woman
Days of Heaven▶
Delicatessen▶
Desperate Characters▶
Dim Sum: A Little Bit of Heart▶
Diner▶
The Dining Room
Dinner at Eight
Dodes 'ka-den▶
Double Happiness▶
Early Summer▶
Earthworm Tractors
Eat a Bowl of Tea▶
Eat Drink Man Woman▶
Eating
Echo Park
Edge of the World▶
Egg
El Super▶
An Empty Bed▶
End of the Line
The Englishman Who Went Up a Hill But Came Down a Mountain▶
The Errors of Youth
Every Man for Himself & God Against All▶
Everybody's All American
The Family Game▶
Family Secrets
Fanny and Alexander▶
Federal Hill
Five Corners▶
Fleshpot on 42nd Street
The Flintstones
Fried Green Tomatoes▶
The Funeral▶
Girlfriends▶
Go Fish▶
God's Little Acre▶
The Graduate▶
Grand Canyon▶
Gregory's Girl▶
The Group
Hannah and Her Sisters▶
Heavy Traffic▶
Here Comes Kelly
Hester Street▶
High Hopes▶
Honor Thy Father
The Horse of Pride
How U Like Me Now?▶
I Don't Buy Kisses Anymore
I Like It Like That▶
I Remember Mama▶
I Wanna Hold Your Hand
I'd Climb the Highest Mountain▶
The Inheritors
Innocent Sorcerers
Ironweed▶
Jacknife▶
Joyless Street▶
Judge Priest▶
Key Exchange
Kings Row▶
La Terra Trema▶
Ladybird, Ladybird▶
The Last American Hero▶
The Last Days of Dolwyn
The Last Picture Show▶
Late Spring▶
Laws of Gravity▶
Le Grand Chemin▶
Leather Boys
Life Begins for Andy Hardy▶
Life with Father▶
The Little Thief▶
Little Women▶
Little Women
Living on Tokyo Time
Local Hero▶
London Kills Me
Look Back in Anger▶
The Lords of Flatbush
Love on the Run▶
Lumiere
Mac▶
MacArthur's Children▶
Madame Sousatzka▶
Mamma Roma▶
The Mango Tree
Marius▶
Mean Streets▶
Meet Me in St. Louis▶
Memories of a Marriage▶
Metropolitan▶
Middlemarch▶
Mississippi Masala▶
A Mongolian Tale
Moonrise
Moonstruck▶
More American Graffiti
The Music Man▶
My Family▶
My Sister Eileen▶
My Summer Story
My Sweet Little Village
Mystic Pizza▶
Naked▶
Nashville▶
The New Age
1918
90 Days▶
No Fear, No Die
Nobody's Fool
Nobody's Fool▶
Now and Then
Offnight
Oklahoma!▶
Old Swimmin' Hole
Once Were Warriors▶
One More Saturday Night
One Third of a Nation
Our Town▶
Our Town
Our Vines Have Tender Grapes▶
The Out-of-Towners▶
Over the Brooklyn Bridge
Papa's Delicate Condition▶
The Paper Chase▶
The Patriots▶
Pete 'n' Tillie
Pharmacist
Phenomenon
The Playboys▶
The Pope of Greenwich Village
Priest
Prisoner of Second Avenue
Queens Logic
Rachel River
Raggedy Man▶
Raging Bull▶
Rainy Day
Rambling Rose▶
Real Life▶
Return of the Secaucus 7▶
Return to Mayberry
Reuben, Reuben▶
Rhythm Thief
Riff Raff▶
A River Runs Through It▶
The Road to Life
Room at the Top▶
Roommates
Rosalie Goes Shopping▶
The Rules of the Game▶
Same Time, Next Year▶
Short Cuts▶
Sinners
Sinners in Paradise
The Smallest Show on Earth▶
Smithereens
Smoke
Some Came Running▶
The Southerner▶
The Star Maker
State Fair▶
State Fair
Steamboat Bill, Jr.▶
Steel Magnolias▶
Stranger than Paradise▶
Strong Medicine
Stroszek▶
Sugarbaby▶
The Sun Shines Bright
Tex
That Sinking Feeling▶
The Time of Your Life▶
Tin Men
To Kill a Mockingbird▶
Toni▶
Tonio Kroger
A Touch of Class▶
The Tree of Wooden Clogs▶
Trouble in the Glen
True Love▶
Twenty Bucks▶
29th Street
Twice in a Lifetime▶
Twist & Shout▶
The Two Sisters
Urban Cowboy
Used People
Walls of Glass
Wanderers▶
Watch It▶
A Wedding
When the Party's Over
The White Balloon▶
The Whole Shootin' Match▶
Who's That Knocking at My Door?▶
Why Shoot the Teacher▶
Wild Style
Wish You Were Here▶
Women From the Lake of Scented Souls

Snakes

see also Wild Kingdom

Black Cobra
Copperhead
Curse 2: The Bite
Fer-De-Lance
Indiana Jones and the Last Crusade▶
Indiana Jones and the Temple of Doom▶
Jennifer
Journey to the Lost City
Raiders of the Lost Ark▶
Rattled
Rattlers
The Road Warrior▶
Silver Stallion
The Snake People
Stanley
Women's Prison Escape

Soccer

The Big Green
The Club▶
Cup Final
The Goalie's Anxiety at the Penalty Kick▶
Gregory's Girl▶
The Hero
Hot Shot
Hothead
Ladybugs
Long Shot
Those Glory, Glory Days
Victory
Yesterday's Hero

South America

see also Central America

Aguirre, the Wrath of God▶
Amazon
The Americano
Americano
At Play in the Fields of the Lord▶
Bananas▶
Black Orpheus▶
Boca
Burden of Dreams
The Burning Season▶
Bye Bye Brazil
Catch the Heat
Clear and Present Danger
The Colombian Connection
Death and the Maiden▶
Death in the Garden
Diplomatic Immunity
800 Leagues Down the Amazon
El Muerto
The Emerald Forest▶
Fitzcarraldo▶
Five Came Back
The Fugitive▶
Fury
Green Fire
Green Mansions
The Hour of the Star▶
The House of the Spirits
I Don't Want to Talk About It
It's All True
Last Flight to Hell
The Last Movie
Latin Lovers
Let's Get Harry
Max is Missing
Mighty Jungle
Miracles
Miss Mary
Missing▶
The Mission▶
Monster
Moon over Parador
The Muthers
Naked Jungle▶
Nancy Goes to Rio
Night Gallery▶
O Quatrilho
Of Love and Shadows
One Man Out
Only Angels Have Wings▶
A Place in the World▶
The Plague
Quilombo
Rodrigo D.: No Future
Romancing the Stone▶
Shoot to Kill
Simon Bolivar
The Story of Fausta
Sweet Country
Terror in the Jungle
The Three Caballeros
To Kill a Stranger
Wild Orchid
Xica▶
You Were Never Lovelier▶

Southern Belles

see also American South; Nashville Narratives

Blaze
Cat on a Hot Tin Roof▶
Cat on a Hot Tin Roof
Crimes of the Heart
Dear Dead Delilah
Driving Miss Daisy▶
The Glass Menagerie▶
Gone with the Wind▶
Hush, Hush, Sweet Charlotte▶
Jezebel▶
Miss Firecracker▶
Nashville▶
North and South Book 1▶
North and South Book 2▶
Queen Bee
Rich in Love
Scarlett
Scorchers
Steel Magnolias▶
A Streetcar Named Desire▶
The Trip to Bountiful▶

Space Operas

see also Alien Beings—Benign; Alien Beings—Vicious

Alien▶
Apollo 13▶
Assignment Outer Space
Battle Beyond the Stars
Battle Beyond the Sun
Battlestar Galactica
The Black Hole
Buck Rogers Conquers the Universe
Capricorn One▶
Cat Women of the Moon
Conquest of Space
Countdown
Creature
Dark Side of the Moon
Dark Star▶
The Day the Sky Exploded
Destination Moon
Destination Moonbase Alpha
Destination Saturn
Doctor Who and the Daleks
Escape from Planet Earth
Explorers
Fire Maidens from Outer Space
First Men in the Moon
First Spaceship on Venus▶
Flight to Mars
Forbidden Planet▶
From the Earth to the Moon
Galaxy of Terror
The Green Slime
Hangar 18
Have Rocket Will Travel
Heavens Above▶
Hellraiser 4: Bloodline
Horror Planet
Horrors of the Red Planet
Journey to the Far Side of the Sun▶
Killings at Outpost Zeta
Laser Mission
The Last Starfighter
Lifepod

Marooned
Megaforce
Mission Galactica: The Cylon Attack
Mission Mars
Mom and Dad Save the World
Moon 44
Moonraker
Moontrap
Murder in Space
Mutant on the Bounty
Mystery Science Theater 3000: The Movie
Nude on the Moon
Outland
Planet Burg
Planet of Dinosaurs
Planet of the Apes▶
Planet of the Vampires
Project Moon Base
PSI Factor
The Reluctant Astronaut
Return of the Jedi▶
Return to Earth
The Right Stuff▶
Robinson Crusoe on Mars
Rocketship X-M
Silent Running▶
Solar Crisis
Solaris
Space Mutiny
Space Rage
Space Raiders
Spaceballs
Star Crash
Star Slammer
Star Trek: The Motion Picture
Star Trek 2: The Wrath of Khan▶
Star Trek 3: The Search for Spock
Star Trek 4: The Voyage Home▶
Star Trek 5: The Final Frontier
Star Trek 6: The Undiscovered Country
Star Trek Generations▶
Star Trek the Next Generation: Encounter at Farpoint
Star Wars▶
Starship
The Terronauts
Three Stooges in Orbit
Transformations
Trapped in Space
2001: A Space Odyssey▶
2010: The Year We Make Contact▶
Vegas in Space
Voyage to the Planet of Prehistoric Women
Voyage to the Prehistoric Planet
Walking on Air
Warlords of the 21st Century
Woman in the Moon
Women of the Prehistoric Planet

Spaghetti Western

see also Western Comedy; Westerns

Ace High
Beyond the Law
Boot Hill
Bullet for Sandoval
Chino
A Fistful of Dollars▶
A Fistful of Dynamite▶
Five Giants from Texas
For a Few Dollars More
The Good, the Bad and the Ugly▶
The Grand Duel
Gun Fight at Red Sands
Hang 'Em High
Hellbenders
A Minute to Pray, A Second to Die
My Name is Nobody
Once Upon a Time in the West▶
Rough Justice
The Ruthless Four
Spaghetti Western
Straight to Hell
The Stranger and the Gunfighter
Stranger in Paso Bravo
Take a Hard Ride
Tramplers
Trinity is Still My Name
You're Jinxed, Friend, You've Met Sacramento

Spain

Against the Wind
Ay, Carmela!▶
Barcelona▶
The Barcelona Kill
Behold a Pale Horse
Belle Epoque▶
Blood and Sand▶
Caper of the Golden Bulls
The Castilian
Desire▶
Extramuros
For Whom the Bell Tolls▶
I'm the One You're Looking For
Land and Freedom▶
Lazarillo
Marbella
The Naked Maja
Pandora and the Flying Dutchman
The Pride and the Passion
Sand and Blood
Siesta
The Spanish Gardener▶
Surprise Attack
The Sword of El Cid
A Touch of Class▶

Speculation

Sasquatch

Spies & Espionage

see also Feds; Foreign Intrigue; Terrorism

Above Suspicion▶
Access Code
Across the Pacific▶
Action in Arabia
Adventures in Spying
The Adventures of Tartu
Against the Wind
Agent on Ice
Air Raid Wardens
Alamut Ambush
Alfred Hitchcock's Aventure Malgache
Alfred Hitchcock's Bon Voyage
Alien Women
All Through the Night▶
The Amateur
Arabesque
Armored Command
Artists and Models
As If It Were Raining
Assassin
The Assassination Run
The Atomic Kid
Attack of the Robots
Avalanche Express
Background to Danger▶
Bad Company
Bear Island
Behind Enemy Lines
The Berlin Conspiracy
Berlin Express▶
Betrayed▶
Big Deadly Game
Big Jim McLain
The Big Lift
Black Box Affair
Black Brigade
The Black Dragons
Black Eagle
The Black Windmill
Blue Ice
Boris and Natasha: The Movie
The Bourne Identity▶
British Intelligence
Bulldog Drummond at Bay
Bulldog Drummond Escapes
Bulletproof
Cairo
Call Me Bwana
Canadian Mounties vs. Atomic Invaders
The Canon Operation
Caravan to Vaccares
Carve Her Name with Pride
Casablanca▶
Casino Royale
A Casualty of War
Charge of the Model T's
Chu Chu & the Philly Flash
Clear and Present Danger
Clipped Wings
Cloak and Dagger
Cloak & Dagger
Code Name Alpha
Code Name: Chaos
Code Name: Dancer
Code Name: Diamond Head
Code Name: Emerald
Codename: Foxfire
Codename: Icarus
Codename Kyril
Codename: Wildgeese
Cold War Killers
Company Business
Comrades in Arms
Condorman
Conspirator
Counterblast
The Counterfeit Traitor▶
Cowboy Commandos
Criminals Within
Dandy in Aspic
Danger Man
Daniel
Dark Journey▶
Darling Lili
Dawn Express
The Day and the Hour
The Day of the Dolphin
The Day of the Jackal▶
The Day Will Dawn▶
Dead Aim
Deadly Currents
The Deadly Game
Deadly Recruits
Deadly Rivals
Deadly Spygames
The Deadly Trap
Death Ray 2000
Death Rides the Range
Deathcheaters
Defense Play
Delta Force Commando 2
Desperate Cargo
Diamonds Are Forever▶
Diplomatic Courier▶
Dishonored
Dr. No▶
The Doll Squad
Don't Drink the Water
Don't Raise the Bridge, Lower the River
Doomsday Gun
Double Agents
Double Deal
The Double O Kid
Down Among the Z Men
Duck Soup▶
The Dunera Boys▶
Edge of Darkness▶
Edge of Darkness
The Eiger Sanction
Embassy
Emissary
The Endless Game
Enforcer from Death Row
An Englishman Abroad▶
Enigma
Erik
Escape from Fort Bravo
Escape from the KGB
The Executioner
The Experts
Eye of the Needle
Eyewitness
The Falcon and the Snowman▶
The Falcon's Brother
Fall from Grace
The Fallen Sparrow▶
False Faces
The Fantastic World of D.C. Collins
Federal Agent
Final Assignment
The Final Option
Fire Over England▶
Firefall
Firefox
Firehead
First Yank into Tokyo
Five Fingers▶
Five for Hell
Flight from Vienna
Flight to Nowhere
Flying Blind
For Your Eyes Only▶
Foreign Correspondent▶
The Foreigner
The Formula
The Fourth Protocol▶
Francis Gary Powers: The True Story of the U-2 Spy
French Intrigue
From Russia with Love▶
Funeral in Berlin▶
The General Died at Dawn▶
A Generation▶
Get Smart, Again!
Girl Hunters
Girls Are for Loving
The Glass Bottom Boat
Golden Earrings
Goldeneye▶
Goldfinger▶
Gotcha!
The Great Armored Car Swindle
Green Inferno
The Groundstar Conspiracy▶
Gunpowder
Hanky Panky
Happy Anniversary 007: 25 Years of James Bond
Hard Ticket to Hawaii
Harriet the Spy
The Heat of the Day
Heroes in Hell
Heroes Stand Alone
Hidden Enemy
Hillbillies in a Haunted House
The Holcroft Covenant
Holt of the Secret Service
Honeybaby
Honeymoon Academy
Hopscotch▶
Hostage
The Hot Line
Hotel Reserve▶
Hour of the Assassin
The House on Carroll Street
The House on Garibaldi Street
House on 92nd Street▶
The Human Factor
The Hunt for Red October▶
Hunter
I Dood It
I See a Dark Stranger▶
I Stand Condemned
The Ice Runner
Ice Station Zebra
If Looks Could Kill
The Impossible Spy▶
The In-Laws▶
In the Secret State
Incident at Map-Grid 36-80
The Innocent
The Inside Man
Inside the Lines
Internecine Project
Intrigue
Invisible Agent
The Ipcress File▶
Ishtar
It Means That to Me
J-Men Forever!▶
Jakarta
Jet Pilot
The Jigsaw Man
Joan of Paris▶
Journey into Fear▶
Journey into Fear
Jumpin' Jack Flash
Jungle Drums of Africa
Keep Talking Baby
The KGB: The Secret War
Kill Castro
Kill Factor
Kim▶
Kim
Koroshi
La Cage aux Folles 2
Ladies Man
Laser Mission
Last Embrace▶
Le Magnifique
License to Kill
License to Kill▶
Lie Down with Lions
Lightning Bolt
Lipstick Camera
Lisbon
The Little Drummer Girl▶
Live and Let Die
The Living Daylights▶
Loaded Guns
The Looking Glass War
Lost Diamond
The Lost One
Love on the Run
M. Butterfly
Ma and Pa Kettle on Vacation
Mackintosh Man
Madame Sin
Malone
Man from Headquarters
The Man from U.N.C.L.E.
The Man on the Box
The Man Outside
The Man Who Never Was▶
The Man Who Wasn't There
The Man with One Red Shoe
The Man with the Golden Gun
Marie Galante▶
Maroc 7
Mata Hari▶
Mata Hari
The Mediterranean in Flames
The Mercenaries
Mind Trap
Mindfield
Mission: Impossible▶
Mission Phantom
Mission to Venice
Mr. Superinvisible
The Monocle
Monte Carlo
Moonraker
Morituri▶
Murder for Sale
Murder on the Midnight Express
Murderers' Row
My Favorite Blonde▶
My Favorite Brunette
My Name is Ivan▶
The Mysterious Lady
Mystery Plane
Nasty Rabbit
Never Say Never Again
Never Too Young to Die
Night Flight from Moscow
A Night in Casablanca▶
Night Train to Munich▶
Ninja Champion
No Dead Heroes
No Way Out▶
North by Northwest▶
Notorious▶
The Nude Bomb
Number 1 of the Secret Service
Octopussy
The Odessa File
Old Mother Riley's Ghosts
On Her Majesty's Secret Service▶
On the Edge
Once Upon a Honeymoon
One Armed Executioner
One of Our Dinosaurs Is Missing
Operation C.I.A.
Operation Crossbow▶
The Osterman Weekend
Overture
The Package
Panama Hattie

Panama Menace
Panama Patrol
Paper Tiger
Paradisio
Pascali's Island▶
Patriot Games▶
The Peking Blond
A Perfect Spy
Permission To Kill
The Persuaders
Philby, Burgess and MacLean: Spy Scandal of the Century
Phoenix Team
Picasso Trigger
Pickup on South Street▶
President's Mistress
Prime Risk
The Prize▶
Protocol
Pueblo Affair▶
A Question of Attribution
Qui Etes Vous, Mr. Sorge?
The Quiller Memorandum▶
Ravishing Idiot
Rebel Love
Reilly: Ace of Spies▶
Retrievers
Return of the Man from U.N.C.L.E.
Rio Rita
Robinson Crusoe of Mystery Island
Roboman
Robot Pilot
Running Blind
Running Delilah
Running Scared
The Russia House
Russian Roulette
The Rutanga Tapes
Sabotage▶
Saboteur▶
The Saint's Vacation/The Narrow Margin
Samurai
S.A.S. San Salvador
Scorpio
Sea Devils
Sebastian
Second Best Secret Agent in the Whole Wide World
The Secret Agent▶
Secret Agent
Secret Agent 00
Secret Agent 00-Soul
Secret Agent Super Dragon
Secret Mission
Secret Weapon
Secret Weapons
Sell Out
Shack Out on 101▶
Shadows Over Shanghai
S*H*E
Shining Through
Ship Ahoy
A Show of Force
Sky High
Sky Liner
Sneakers
Snuff-Bottle Connection
The Soldier
A Southern Yankee
Soviet Spy
Spies▶
Spies, Lies and Naked Thighs
Spitfire
Spy
Spy Hard
Spy in Black▶
Spy of Napoleon
Spy Smasher
Spy Smasher Returns
Spy Story
Spy Trap
The Spy Who Came in from the Cold▶
The Spy Who Loved Me
Spy with a Cold Nose
The Spy Within
Spymaker: The Secret Life of Ian Fleming
S*P*Y*S
Stalag 17▶
State Department File 649
Steal the Sky
Stopover Tokyo
The Stranger▶
Strike Commando
Subterfuge
The Tall Blond Man with One Black Shoe▶
The Tamarind Seed
Tangiers
Target for Killing
Telefon
Terminal Entry
Terminal Velocity
Texas to Bataan
There Goes Barder
They Got Me Covered
The Thief
The Third Man▶
13 Rue Madeleine▶
The Thirty-Nine Steps
The 39 Steps▶
Three Days in Beirut
Three Days of the Condor▶
Three Kinds of Heat
Thunderball
Tiffany Jones
To Live and Die in Hong Kong
Tokyo Joe
Top Secret!▶
Topaz▶
Torn Curtain
Trader Tom of the China Seas
Trenchcoat
Trident Force
Triple Cross▶
Tripwire
The Trouble with Spies
The Ultimate Imposter
Undeclared War
Under the Rainbow
Undercover Blues
Up Periscope
The Uranium Conspiracy
A View to a Kill
Viper
Wanted Dead or Alive
Watch on the Rhine▶
Waterfront
What's Up, Tiger Lily?▶
Where Eagles Dare▶
Where the Bullets Fly
The Whistle Blower▶
White Ghost
White Nights
WhiteForce
Wonsan Operation
Yin & Yang of Mr. Go
You Only Live Twice
Young Nurses in Love
Your Turn Darling
Yuri Nosenko, KGB
Zeppelin
Zotz!

Sports

***see** Baseball; Basketball; Bicycling; Boxing; Football; Golf; Hockey; The Olympics; Running; Scuba; Skating; Skiing; Skydiving; Soccer; Sports Comedies; Sports Dramas; Surfing; Swimming; Tennis; Volleyball*

Sports Comedies

The Air Up There
Angels in the Outfield
The Bad News Bears▶
The Bad News Bears Go to Japan
The Bad News Bears in Breaking Training
The Best of Times
The Big Green
Billie
Bingo Long Traveling All-Stars & Motor Kings▶
Blue Skies Again
Body Slam
Bowery Blitzkrieg
Bull Durham▶
Celtic Pride
Comeback Kid
The Comrades of Summer
Cool Runnings
Day the Bookies Wept
Diggstown
D2: The Mighty Ducks
Ed
Eddie
Fast Break
First & Ten
First & Ten: The Team Scores Again
The Fish that Saved Pittsburgh
For Heaven's Sake
The Freshman▶
Goof Balls
The Great White Hype
Happy Gilmore
Hold 'Em Jail
Hot Dog...The Movie!
Hothead
It Happens Every Spring▶
Jocks
Johnny Be Good
Kingpin
Ladybugs
A League of Their Own▶
Little Big League
Little Giants
The Longest Yard
The Longshot
Major League
Major League 2
The Man with the Perfect Swing
The Mighty Ducks
Mr. Baseball
Monty Python's The Meaning of Life▶
Necessary Roughness
North Dallas Forty▶
Off the Mark
The One and Only
One-Punch O'Day
Paper Lion
Pat and Mike▶
Prehysteria 3
Prize Fighter
Rookie of the Year
The St. Tammany Miracle
The Sandlot▶
The Scout
Semi-Tough
Ski School
Slam Dunk Ernest
Slap Shot▶
Splitz
Spring Fever
Squeeze Play
Sunset Park
Swim Team
Tin Cup▶
Trading Hearts
White Men Can't Jump
Wildcats
The World's Greatest Athlete

Sports Dramas

Above the Rim
Airborne
Alex
All the Right Moves
American Anthem
American Flyers
American Kickboxer 1
Babe!▶
The Babe
Babe Ruth Story
Bang the Drum Slowly
Bang the Drum Slowly▶
The Big Blue
Big Mo
Billyboy
Blades of Courage
Blue Chips
Body and Soul▶
Body & Soul
Boy in Blue
The Break
Breaking Away▶
Breaking Free
Brian's Song▶
Brutal Glory
Challenge of a Lifetime
Champion▶
Champions
Chariots of Fire▶
Chasing Dreams
The Club▶
Coach
Cobb▶
The Color of Money▶
Crossbar
The Cutting Edge
Dawn!
Days of Thunder
Dempsey
Diving In
Don't Look Back: The Story of Leroy "Satchel" Paige
Downhill Racer
Dream to Believe
Dreamer
Dynamite Dan
Eight Men Out▶
8 Seconds
The Fan
Fat City▶
Field of Dreams▶
Fight for the Title
Final Shot: The Hank Gathers Story
Finish Line
The First Olympics: Athens 1896
Gentleman Jim▶
Gladiator
Go for the Gold
Going for the Gold: The Bill Johnson Story
The Gold & Glory
Goldengirl
Grambling's White Tiger
Heart Like a Wheel
Heaven is a Playground
The Hero
Hockey Night
Honeyboy
Hoosiers▶
Hot Shot
The Hustler▶
Ice Castles
Ice Pawn
International Velvet
The Jericho Mile
The Jesse Owens Story
Jim Thorpe: All American
The Joe Louis Story
Kid Galahad▶
Knute Rockne: All American▶
The Last American Hero▶
The Last Fight
Last Time Out
The Loneliest Runner
Long Gone
Marciano
A Matter of Honor
Miracle on Ice
My Champion
Nadia
The Natural▶
On the Edge
One in a Million: The Ron LeFlore Story
One Last Run
One on One
Over the Top
Paperback Hero
Pastime▶
Personal Best▶
Pistol: The Birth of a Legend
Players
Pride of St. Louis
The Pride of the Yankees▶
The Program
Pulsebeat
Raging Bull▶
Red Line 7000
Red Surf
Requiem for a Heavyweight▶
Rocky▶
Rocky 2
Rocky 3
Rocky 4
Rocky 5
Rudy
Running Brave
Side Out
Skier's Dream
The Spirit of West Point
The Stratton Story▶
Talent for the Game
That Championship Season
This Sporting Life▶
Tiger Town
Touch and Go
21 Hours at Munich▶
Victory
Vision Quest
Wilma
Wind
A Winner Never Quits
The Winning Team
Youngblood

Spousal Abuse

***see also** Sexual Abuse*

The Burning Bed▶
Dangerous Game
Falling Down
Far Cry from Home
Independence Day
Intimate Strangers
Mesmerized
Mortal Thoughts
Olivia
Remember Me
Shattered Dreams
Sleeping with the Enemy
This Boy's Life▶
What's Love Got to Do with It?
Woman Undone
Woman With a Past

Stagestruck

***see also** Showbiz Comedies; Showbiz Dramas; Showbiz Thrillers*

All About Eve▶
Broadway Danny Rose▶
Broadway Limited
Broadway Melody
Broadway Rhythm
Bullets Over Broadway▶
The Dolly Sisters
Fame▶
Gypsy▶
Gypsy
Let's Make Love
A Midwinter's Tale
Morning Glory
Stage Door▶
Stage Struck
Stagefright
Tea for Two▶

Stalked!

***see also** Horror*

Breach of Conduct
Dying Game
The Fan
A Kiss Goodnight
Mr. Wrong
The Seduction
Stalking Laura

Star Gazing

The Arrival
Eliza's Horoscope
The Fish that Saved Pittsburgh
How Come Nobody's On Our Side?
Lamp at Midnight
Local Hero▶

Stepparents

***see also** Family Ties; Parenthood*

The Adventures of Rusty
Big Girls Don't Cry...They Get Even

Cinderella▶
Cinderella
Ellie
Fear
Hard Frame
Lassie
Lost
Night of the Twisters
The Orphan
Out on a Limb
Private Passions
Rivals
The Stepfather▶
Stepfather 2: Make Room for Daddy
Stepfather 3: Father's Day
The Stepmother
A Summer to Remember▶
This Boy's Life▶

Stewardesses

see also Airborne

Blazing Stewardesses
Stewardess School
Three Guys Named Mike

Stolen from Asia

A Fistful of Dollars▶
The Magnificent Seven▶
Reservoir Dogs▶
Star Wars▶

Stolen from Europe

Kiss Me Goodbye
Last House on the Left
Scent of a Woman▶
The Vanishing
A Walk in the Clouds

Stolen from France

The Birdcage▶
Blame It on Rio
Breathless
Buddy Buddy
Cousins▶
Diabolique
Down and Out in Beverly Hills
Happy New Year
The Man Who Loved Women
The Man with One Red Shoe
Men Don't Leave
Mixed Nuts
My Father the Hero
Nine Months
Paradise▶
Point of No Return
Pure Luck
Quick Change
Scenes from the Class Struggle in Beverly Hills
Sommersby
Sorcerer
Three Fugitives
Three Men and a Baby▶
The Toy
12 Monkeys▶
The Woman in Red

Storytelling

Babyfever
The Company of Wolves▶
Grim Prairie Tales
Monster in a Box▶
My Dinner with Andre▶
The Neverending Story 3
Paper Tiger
The Princess Bride▶
The Story Lady
The Willies
Windwalker▶

Strained Suburbia

see also Yuppie Nightmares

Adventures in Spying
The Amityville Horror
Amongst Friends
Amos and Andrew
Blue Velvet▶
The Brady Bunch Movie▶
The 'Burbs
Clown House
Coneheads
Consenting Adults
The Crude Oasis
Deadly Neighbor
Dennis the Menace
Desperate Hours▶
Desperate Hours
Don't Talk to Strangers
Don't Tell Mom the Babysitter's Dead
Edward Scissorhands▶
Faithful
The Graduate▶
Grand Canyon▶
The Grass is Always Greener Over the Septic Tank
Hocus Pocus
House▶
How to Beat the High Cost of Living
Hush Little Baby, Don't You Cry
I Love My...Wife
Jaws▶
Jaws 2
Madhouse
Marked for Death
The Meal
Mr. Blandings Builds His Dream House▶
The Money Pit
My Blue Heaven
My New Gun
Neighbors
Opportunity Knocks
The Osterman Weekend
Over the Edge▶
Parents▶
The People Next Door
Please Don't Eat the Daisies
The Positively True Adventures of the Alleged Texas Cheerleader-Murdering Mom▶
Return of the Living Dead 2
Revenge of the Stepford Wives
Serial Mom▶
Shattered Spirits
Short Cuts▶
The Stranger▶
The Swimmer▶
Terrorvision
Three Wishes
The Trigger Effect
Twice in a Lifetime▶
The Underworld Story
A Very Brady Sequel
The War of the Roses▶
When Every Day was the Fourth of July

Strippers

Blaze
Body Language
The Dark Dancer
Exit
Exotica▶
For Ladies Only
From Dusk Till Dawn
Gypsy▶
Gypsy
Headless Body in Topless Bar
Kiss of Death
Lady of Burlesque
Lap Dancing
The Last Word
Lenny▶
Midnight Tease
Midnight Tease 2
A Night in Heaven
Showgirls
The Stripper
Stripper
Stripshow
Striptease
Stripteaser
True Lies
Working Girls

Struggling Musicians

see also Music

American Blue Note
Backbeat▶
Beyond the Valley of the Dolls
Bikini Summer
Blast-Off Girls
The Brady Bunch Movie▶
Breaking Glass
Bye Bye Blues
The Competition▶
Cotton Candy
Crossover Dreams
Crossroads
Dangerous Holiday
Dangerous Moonlight▶
Desperate Teenage Lovedolls
Dogs in Space
Eddie and the Cruisers
Eddie and the Cruisers 2: Eddie Lives!
The Eternal Waltz
The Fabulous Dorseys
Falling from Grace
Fear of a Black Hat
The Five Heartbeats▶
Heaven Tonight
Killing 'em Softly
Knights of the City
Light of Day
A Man Called Adam
Mo' Better Blues
Murder Rap
Oh, God! You Devil
One Trick Pony
Purple Rain
The Return of Spinal Tap
Rhinestone
Rock & Rule
The Rose▶
Satisfaction
Sparkle
A Star is Born
Streets of Fire
Tender Mercies▶
This Is Spinal Tap▶
Vibrations
You Light Up My Life

Stupid Is...

Being There▶
Big Top Pee Wee
Bill & Ted's Bogus Journey
Bill & Ted's Excellent Adventure
Billy Madison
Bio-Dome
Black Sheep
Caddyshack▶
Dumb & Dumber
Fast Times at Ridgemont High▶
Forrest Gump▶
Happy Gilmore
The Jerk
The Jerky Boys
National Lampoon's Animal House▶
The Nutty Professor▶
Pee Wee's Big Adventure▶
Son-in-Law
The Stupids
Tommy Boy
Wayne's World▶
White Mile

Submarines

see also Deep Blue

Above Us the Waves▶
The Abyss▶
Action in the North Atlantic
Assault on a Queen
Atomic Submarine
Crash Dive
Crimson Tide▶
Das Boot▶
The Day Will Dawn▶
Destination Tokyo
Down Periscope
Enemy Below▶
Fer-De-Lance
First Strike
For Your Eyes Only▶
Full Fathom Five
Going Under
The Hunt for Red October▶
Ice Station Zebra
The Inside Man
Leviathan
Mysterious Island▶
Operation Petticoat▶
Q Ships
Raise the Titanic
Run Silent, Run Deep▶
The Spy Who Loved Me
Submarine Seahawk
Torpedo Alley
Torpedo Attack
Torpedo Run
20,000 Leagues Under the Sea▶
Up Periscope
Voyage to the Bottom of the Sea▶
We Dive at Dawn▶
Yellow Submarine▶
You Only Live Twice

Subways

see also Trains

Adventures in Babysitting
Carlito's Way▶
Dutchman▶
Eve of Destruction
The French Connection▶
The Fugitive▶
Highlander 2: The Quickening
The Incident
Lethal Weapon 3
Money Train
Predator 2
Quatermass and the Pit
Risky Business▶
Speed▶
Subway
The Taking of Pelham One Two Three▶
The Warriors
Zazie dans le Metro▶

Suicide

see also Death & the Afterlife

Absence of Malice
Angels Over Broadway▶
The Arrangement
Attack Squadron
Autopsy
Bad Girls Dormitory
Bedazzled▶
The Bell Jar
Better Off Dead
The Big Chill▶
Buddy Buddy
Can You Hear the Laughter? The Story of Freddie Prinze
Club Extinction
Crimes of the Heart
The Crude Oasis
Crumb▶
Dead Poets Society▶
Death Wish Club
Delinquent Daughters
Demon Witch Child
Deutschland im Jahre Null▶
The Devil in Silk
Docks of New York▶
Dominique is Dead
Double Suicide▶
The End▶
Europa '51
The Eyes, the Mouth
Faithful
The Fire Within▶
Fuzz
A Gentle Woman
Golden Gate
Goodbye Cruel World
Harold and Maude▶
Heading for Heaven
Heat▶
Heathers▶
The Hudsucker Proxy▶
The Hustle
It's a Wonderful Life▶
Kamikaze
Last Cry for Help
Last Tango in Paris▶
Le Corbeau▶
Leaving Las Vegas▶
Maedchen in Uniform▶
Memorial Day
Mixed Nuts
Mortal Danger
Mother Kusters Goes to Heaven▶
Mouchette▶
Nais▶
Natural Enemies
'night, Mother
The Odd Job
Ode to Billy Joe
One Flew Over the Cuckoo's Nest▶
Ordinary People▶
Pain in the A—▶
The Pallbearer
Peeping Tom▶
Permanent Record
Retribution
Return of Frank Cannon
Reuben, Reuben▶
Right of Way
Romeo and Juliet▶
Romeo and Juliet
Romeo and Juliet▶
Scent of a Woman▶
Silence of the Heart▶
The Slender Thread▶
Stealing Home
Stella Maris▶
The Tenant▶
Warm Summer Rain
Wetherby▶
Whose Life Is It Anyway?▶

Summer Camp

Addams Family Values
Backwoods
Berserker
The Best Way
The Burning
Bushwhacked
Camp Cucamonga: How I Spent My Summer Vacation
Camp Nowhere
Cannibal Campout
A Cry from the Mountain
Deliverance▶
Don't Go in the Woods
Ernest Goes to Camp
Evil Dead
Evils of the Night
Father and Scout
The Final Terror
The Forest
Forever Evil
Friday the 13th
Friday the 13th, Part 2
Friday the 13th, Part 3
Friday the 13th, Part 4: The Final Chapter
The Ghost of Fletcher Ridge
Gimme an F
Gorp
The Great Outdoors
Grim Prairie Tales
Grizzly
Heavyweights
The Hills Have Eyes
Hot Resort
Indian Summer
Little Darlings
Man of the House
Meatballs
Meatballs 2
Meatballs 3
Meatballs 4
Memorial Valley Massacre
Mother's Day
Nuts in May
Oddballs
Party Camp
A Pig's Tale
Poison Ivy

The Prey
Princes in Exile
Race for Your Life, Charlie Brown
Race with the Devil
Redwood Forest Trail
Rituals
The River Wild
Sleepaway Camp
Sleepaway Camp 2: Unhappy Campers
Sleepaway Camp 3: Teenage Wasteland
Storm
Stuckey's Last Stand
Summer Camp Nightmare
There's Nothing Out There
Three Way Weekend
Ticks
Troop Beverly Hills
The Willies

Super Heroes

The Amazing Spider-Man
Batman
Batman▶
Batman Forever▶
Batman: Mask of the Phantasm
Batman Returns
Black Scorpion
Blankman
Captain America
Captain America 2: Death Too Soon
Chinese Web
Cloak & Dagger
Death of the Incredible Hulk
Dr. Strange
The Flash
The Flash 2: Revenge of the Trickster
Flash Gordon
Freddie the Frog
The Incredible Hulk
The Incredible Hulk Returns
Infra-Man
The Mask▶
The Meteor Man
Mighty Morphin Power Rangers: The Movie
The Original Flash Gordon Collection
The Phantom
Phantom 2040 Movie: The Ghost Who Walks
Phenomenal and the Treasure of Tutankamen
The Puma Man
The Punisher
Return of Captain Invincible
The Shadow
Spiderman: The Deadly Dust
Super Fuzz
Supergirl
Superman: The Movie▶
Superman 2▶
Superman 3
Superman 4: The Quest for Peace
Superman & the Mole Men
Supersonic Man
The Trial of the Incredible Hulk
TV's Best Adventures of Superman
VIP, My Brother Superman
The Wild World of Batwoman

Supernatural Comedies

see also Comedy

Angels in the Outfield
Beetlejuice▶
Bell, Book and Candle
Bernard and the Genie
Blackbeard's Ghost
The Craft
Dead Heat
The Devil & Max Devlin
Fridays of Eternity
The Frighteners
Ghost Chasers
Ghost Dad
Ghost Fever
The Ghost Goes West▶
The Ghost Train
Ghost Writer
Ghostbusters▶
Ghostbusters 2
Ghosts Can Do It
Ghosts of Berkeley Square
Haunted Honeymoon
Heart and Souls
High Spirits
Hillbillies in a Haunted House
Hocus Pocus
Limit Up
Love at Stake
The Man in the Santa Claus Suit
Matilda
My Best Friend Is a Vampire
Oh, God!
Oh, God! Book 2
Oh, God! You Devil
Rockula
Saturday the 14th
Saturday the 14th Strikes Back
She-Devil
Spook Busters
Spooks Run Wild
Teen Wolf
Teen Wolf Too
Topper▶
Topper Returns▶
Topper Takes a Trip▶
Who Killed Doc Robbin?
Wicked Stepmother
Wishful Thinking
A Witch Without a Broom

Supernatural Horror

see also Classic Horror; Horror

Afterward
Alabama's Ghost
Alison's Birthday
The Amityville Horror
Amityville 2: The Possession
Amityville 3: The Demon
Amityville 4
Amityville: A New Generation
Amityville 1992: It's About Time
The Appointment
Audrey Rose
Bad Dreams
The Believers
Beyond Evil
The Black Cat
Blood Orgy of the She-Devils
Bloodbeat
Bloodlust
Born of Fire
The Brainiac
Candyman
Cassandra
Charlie Boy
Children of the Night
Christine
Crimes of Dr. Mabuse▶
Crypt of Dark Secrets
Curse of the Aztec Mummy/ Robot vs. the Aztec Mummy
Curse of the Black Widow
Curse of the Blue Lights
The Curse of the Crying Woman
Curse of the Demon▶
Curse of the Headless Horseman
Curse of the Living Corpse
Curse of the Stone Hand
The Curse of the Werewolf
The Cursed Mountain Mystery
Damien: Omen 2
Dance of Death
The Dark
Dark Places
The Dark Secret of Harvest Home
Dark Shadows: Episode 1
Dark Tower
The Daughter of Dr. Jekyll
Daughters of Satan
Dawn of the Mummy
Dead and Buried
The Dead Don't Die
The Death Curse of Tartu
Death Ship
Deathdream
Deathhead Virgin
Deathmoon
Deep Red: Hatchet Murders
Def by Temptation
The Demon Lover
Demon of Paradise
Demon Rage
Demon Wind
Demon Witch Child
Demonoid, Messenger of Death
The Demons
Demons
Demons 2
Demons of Ludlow
Demonstone
Demonwarp
Destroyer
The Devil
Devil Dog: The Hound of Hell
Devil Doll
Devil Woman
The Devil's Daughter
Devil's Gift
The Devil's Hand
The Devil's Nightmare
The Devil's Partner
The Devil's Possessed
Devil's Rain
The Devil's Web
Devil's Wedding Night
Devonsville Terror
The Diabolical Dr. Z
Diary of a Madman
Diary of the Dead
Die, Monster, Die!
Disciple of Death
The Doctor and the Devils
Doctor Butcher M.D.
Dr. Frankenstein's Castle of Freaks
Doctor Phibes Rises Again
Dr. Tarr's Torture Dungeon
Dr. Terror's House of Horrors
Don't Be Afraid of the Dark
Don't Go to Sleep
The Dunwich Horror
Dust Devil
Edge of Sanity
Embrace of the Vampire
Equinox▶
The Evil
Evil Altar
Evil Town
Evilspeak
Exorcism
The Exorcist▶
The Exorcist 2: The Heretic
Feast for the Devil
Feet Foremost
The Final Conflict
Firestarter
The First Power
Fright House
From Beyond the Grave
From Dusk Till Dawn
The Gate
Gate 2
The Ghastly Ones
The Ghost
The Ghost Brigade
Ghost Dance
Ghost Keeper
The Ghost of Rashmon Hall
The Ghost of Yatsuya
Ghost Stories: Graveyard Thriller
Ghost Story
Ghosthouse
Ghostriders
The Ghosts of Hanley House
Ghosts That Still Walk
Giant from the Unknown
God Told Me To
Grave Secrets: The Legacy of Hilltop Drive
The Haunted Palace
The Hearse
Hellbound: Hellraiser 2
Hellraiser
Hellraiser 3: Hell on Earth
Hellraiser 4: Bloodline
The Horrible Dr. Hichcock
Horror Express
Horror Hotel
Horror of the Blood Monsters
Horror Rises from the Tomb
The House by the Cemetery
The House in Marsh Road
The House of Seven Corpses
House of the Yellow Carpet
The House on Skull Mountain
The House that Bled to Death
House Where Evil Dwells
The Howling▶
Howling 2: Your Sister is a Werewolf
Howling 3: The Marsupials
Howling 4: The Original Nightmare
Howling 5: The Rebirth
Howling 6: The Freaks
Immortal Sins
The Indestructible Man
Inferno
Initiation of Sarah
Inquisition
Invasion of the Blood Farmers
Invasion of the Zombies
Invitation to Hell
It's Alive!
Jaws of Satan
J.D.'s Revenge
Jennifer
Judgment Day
Kill and Go Hide
Kill, Baby, Kill▶
The Kiss
Kiss Daddy Goodbye
Kwaidan▶
Land of the Minotaur
The Last Man on Earth
The Legacy
The Legend of Hell House▶
Let's Scare Jessica to Death
Lisa and the Devil
The Living Head
Lord of Illusions
The Loves of Irina
Lurkers
Lust for a Vampire
The Man and the Monster
Manhattan Baby
Maniac
The Manitou
Manos, the Hands of Fate
Mardi Gras for the Devil
Mardi Gras Massacre
Mark of the Devil
Mark of the Devil 2
Mary, Mary, Bloody Mary
Maxim Xul
The Medusa Touch
The Mephisto Waltz▶
Meridian: Kiss of the Beast
Messiah of Evil
Midnight
Midnight Cabaret
Midnight's Child
Mirror, Mirror
Mirror of Death
The Monster Demolisher
The Mummy's Revenge
Near Dark▶
Necromancer: Satan's Servant
Necropolis
Neon Maniacs
The Nesting
Netherworld
The Night Evelyn Came Out of the Grave
Night Life
Night Nurse
Night of Horror
Night of the Death Cult
Night of the Demons
Night of the Demons 2
Night of the Ghouls
Night of the Sorcerers
The Night Stalker: Two Tales of Terror
Night Vision
Night Visitor
Nightmare Castle
Nightmare in Blood
Nightmare Sisters
Nightmare Weekend
Nightstalker
Nightwish
Nomads
Nothing But the Night
The Occultist
Of Unknown Origin
The Offspring
The Omen
Omen 4: The Awakening
The Oracle
Orgy of the Dead
Orgy of the Vampires
The Other▶
Other Hell
Out of the Body
The Outing
Patrick
Pet Sematary
Pet Sematary 2
Phantasm
Phantasm II
Phantom of the Ritz
Poltergeist▶
Poltergeist 2: The Other Side
Poltergeist 3
The Possessed
The Possession of Joel Delaney
The Premonition
The Prophecy
The Psychic
Psychomania
Pumpkinhead
Rawhead Rex
Revolt of the Zombies
Sarah's Child
The Sleeping Car
Sleepstalker: The Sandman's Last Rites
Sorceress
Specters
Supernatural
The Supernaturals
Terror Creatures from the Grave
They Watch
13 Ghosts
The Turn of the Screw
The Visitors
Witchcraft 4: Virgin Heart
The Wraith

Supernatural Martial Arts

Baby Cart at the River Styx
Baby Cart to Hades
The Crow
Hellbound
The Heroic Trio
Ninja, the Violent Sorcerer
Remo Williams: The Adventure Begins
The 7 Brothers Meet Dracula
Vampire Raiders—Ninja Queen

Supernatural Westerns

Back to the Future, Part 3▶
Billy the Kid Versus Dracula
The Devil's Mistress
Ghostriders
Grim Prairie Tales
Into the Badlands
Jesse James Meets Frankenstein's Daughter
Mad at the Moon
Sundown
Timerider

Surfing

see also Beach Blanket Bingo

Aloha Summer
Beach Blanket Bingo▶
Beach Party
Big Wednesday
Bikini Beach

California Dreaming
Computer Beach Party
The Endless Summer▶
The Endless Summer 2▶
Follow Me
Gidget
How to Stuff a Wild Bikini
Lauderdale
Mad Wax: The Surf Movie
Muscle Beach Party
North Shore
Point Break
Puberty Blues
Red Surf
Ride the Wild Surf
Summer City
Sundance
Surf Nazis Must Die
Surf Party
Surf 2

Survival

***see also** Hunted!; Negative Utopia; Post Apocalypse*

Adrift
Adventure Island
Adventures of Eliza Fraser
The Alaska Wilderness Adventure
Alive
Alive: 20 Years Later
Alpine Fire
And I Alone Survived
Antarctica
Arctic Blue
Attack of the Beast Creatures
The Aviator
Back from Eternity
Bat 21
Black Rain▶
Born Killer
Born Wild
The Bridge on the River Kwai▶
Buffalo Rider
A Bullet Is Waiting
Cage 2: The Arena of Death
Caged in Paradiso
Captain January
A Captive in the Land
Challenge To Be Free
Cheyenne Warrior
Clearcut
Cliffhanger▶
Clown
Cold River
Cool Hand Luke▶
Damned River
Das Boot▶
The Dawson Patrol
The Day After▶
Dead Calm▶
Deadly Harvest
Deadly Prey
Death Hunt
Def-Con 4
Deliverance▶
Delos Adventure
Delusion
Desperate Target
The Devil
The Devil at 4 O'Clock
Diamonds of the Night▶
The Dive
Dust Devil
Earthling
Edge of Honor
Empire of the Sun▶
Endangered
Endgame
Enemy Mine
Enemy Territory
Erendira
Eric▶
Escape from Hell
Escapist
Far from Home: The Adventures of Yellow Dog
Fearless▶
Fight for Your Life
Firehawk
Five Came Back
Flight from Glory
Flight from Singapore
Flight of the Eagle
The Flight of the Phoenix▶
Fortress
Found Alive
Gas-s-s-s!
The Ghost of Fletcher Ridge
Grave of the Fireflies▶
He is My Brother
Heaven and Earth
Heck's Way Home
Heroes for Sale▶
High Ice
High Noon▶
Hunter's Blood
The Incredible Journey
The Interrogation▶
The Island▶
The Island at the Top of the World
Island of the Blue Dolphins
Island of the Lost
Jeremiah Johnson▶
Jungle Inferno
Just Before Dawn
Kameradschaft▶
Killing at Hell's Gate
The Killing Fields▶
King Rat▶
The Land That Time Forgot
The Last Chance▶
Last Exit to Brooklyn▶
The Last Flight of Noah's Ark
Le Dernier Combat▶
Legend of Alfred Packer
The Legend of Wolf Mountain
L'Enfant d'Eau
The Life and Death of Colonel Blimp▶
Lifeboat▶
Lily Was Here
Little Dorrit, Film 1: Nobody's Fault▶
Little Dorrit, Film 2: Little Dorrit's Story▶
Lord of the Flies▶
Lord of the Flies
Lost
Love on the Dole▶
Male and Female▶
Man in the Wilderness
Manon
Melody
Merry Christmas, Mr. Lawrence▶
Mr. Robinson Crusoe
The Mosquito Coast
The Most Dangerous Game▶
My Side of the Mountain
Mysterious Island▶
The Naked Prey▶
Nightmare at Bittercreek
Nightmare at Noon
Objective, Burma!▶
On the Beach▶
Once Before I Die
Osa
Out of Control
The Overlanders
Packin' It In
Pagan Island
Panic in the Year Zero!
Paradise
Perfect Witness
Phone Call from a Stranger
Pioneer Woman
The Poseidon Adventure
Quest for Fire▶
The Return of Grey Wolf
Return of the Jedi▶
The Revolt of Job▶
Robby
Robinson Crusoe
Sahara▶
Savage Hunger
Savage Is Loose
Sea Gypsies
The Sea Shall Not Have Them
Seven Days in May▶
Shadow of the Wolf
She'll Be Wearing Pink Pajamas
Shipwreck Island
Silence
Silence of the North
Skyline▶
Sniper
S.O.S. Pacific
Sourdough
Springhill
Stagecoach▶
Starbird and Sweet William
Storm and Sorrow
Survival of Spaceship Earth
Survival Quest
Survival Run
The Survivalist
Sweet Sweetback's Baadasssss Song▶
The Swiss Family Robinson▶
The Terror
Testament▶
Thief▶
Three Came Home▶
Trouble in Paradise
Tundra
Unsettled Land
Voyage
The Voyage of the Yes
Wagon Master▶
Warriors of the Apocalypse
Waterworld
The White Dawn
White Fang and the Hunter
White Water Summer

Suspended Animation

Buck Rogers in the 25th Century
Chances Are▶
Coma▶
Encino Man
Forever Young

Swashbucklers

***see also** Action Adventure; Fencing; Medieval Romps*

Abbott and Costello Meet Captain Kidd
Adventures of Captain Fabian
Adventures of Don Juan▶
The Adventures of Robin Hood▶
Against All Flags▶
Ali Baba and the Forty Thieves
Ali Baba and the 40 Thieves▶
Anthony Adverse
Arabian Nights
At Sword's Point
The Black Pirate▶
The Black Swan▶
Blackbeard the Pirate
Blackbeard's Ghost
Bluebeard
The Bold Caballero
The Buccaneer
Captain Blood▶
Captain Horatio Hornblower▶
Captain Kidd
Captain Kronos: Vampire Hunter▶
Captain Ron
Cartouche▶
The Challenge
Cheech and Chong's The Corsican Brothers
China Seas▶
Conqueror & the Empress
Corsair
The Corsican Brothers
The Count of Monte Cristo
The Count of Monte Cristo▶
The Count of Monte Cristo
Court Jester▶
Crimson Pirate▶
Cutthroat Island
Dancing Pirate
Dr. Syn
Dr. Syn, Alias the Scarecrow
Don Juan DeMarco
Don Q., Son of Zorro
The Elusive Pimpernel
Executioner of Venice
Fearless Tiger
The Fifth Musketeer
Fighting Marines
The Fighting Prince of Donegal
First Knight
The Flame & the Arrow▶
The Four Musketeers▶
Ghost in the Noonday Sun
Gun Cargo
Gypsy
Hawk of the Wilderness
Hell Ship Mutiny
Highlander: The Gathering
His Majesty O'Keefe
Hook
The Iron Mask
The Island
Island Trader
Ivanhoe
The King's Thief
Kojiro▶
The Lamb
The Lives of a Bengal Lancer▶
Long John Silver
Magic Island
The Man in the Iron Mask▶
Marauder
Mark of Zorro▶
The Mark of Zorro▶
The Master of Ballantrae
Master of Dragonard Hill
Monty Python's The Meaning of Life▶
Mooncussers
Moonfleet
Moran of the Lady Letty
Morgan the Pirate
Muppet Treasure Island
My Favorite Year▶
My Wicked, Wicked Ways
The Naked Sword of Zorro
Nate and Hayes
Naughty Marietta
New Moon
The Ninja Pirates
Old Ironsides▶
The Phantom
The Pirate▶
Pirate Movie
Pirate Warrior
Pirates
The Pirates of Penzance
Pirates of the Coast
Pirates of the Seven Seas
The Princess and the Pirate▶
The Princess Bride▶
Prisoner of Zenda▶
Prisoner of Zenda
Quest of the Delta Knights
The Return of the Musketeers
Ring of the Musketeers
Robin Hood▶
Romola
Royal Flash▶
Scaramouche▶
The Scarlet Pimpernel▶
The Sea Hawk▶
Sea Hound
The Secret of El Zorro
Shipwrecked
The Sign of Zorro
Sinbad and the Eye of the Tiger
Sinbad, the Sailor▶
Smuggler's Cove
Son of Ali Baba
Son of Captain Blood
Son of Fury▶
The Son of Monte Cristo
Son of Zorro
South of Pago Pago
South Seas Massacre
The Spanish Main
The Story of Robin Hood & His Merrie Men▶
Swashbuckler
The Swiss Family Robinson▶
Sword & the Sorcerer
Sword of Sherwood Forest
The Swordsman
Tharus Son of Attila
Three Amigos
The Three Musketeers
The Three Musketeers▶
The Three Musketeers
The Three Musketeers▶
The Three Musketeers
Tiger of the Seven Seas
Treasure Island▶
Treasure Island
Treasure of the Golden Condor
Treasure of the Moon Goddess
Two Lost Worlds
Under the Red Robe
Wallaby Jim of the Islands
The Warriors
The Wicked Lady
Yellowbeard
Zorro, the Gay Blade

Swimming

***see also** Deep Blue; Go Fish; Island Fare; Lifeguards; Pacific Islands; Sea Critter Attack*

Alex
Barracuda
Bathing Beauty
The Bridges at Toko-Ri▶
Cocoon▶
Dangerous When Wet
Dawn!
Easy to Love
Gremlins▶
Jaws▶
The Man from Atlantis
Million Dollar Mermaid
Neptune's Daughter
Off the Mark
Splash
Swim Team
The Swimmer▶
Thrill of a Romance

Swingers

Barfly▶
Bob & Carol & Ted & Alice
A Change of Seasons
Group Marriage
Invasion of the Bee Girls▶
Looking for Mr. Goodbar
9 1/2 Weeks
The Party▶
The Swap
The Swinging Cheerleaders
Swinging Wives

Sword & Sandal

Ali Baba and the Forty Thieves
Ali Baba and the 40 Thieves▶
Alone Against Rome
Arabian Nights
The Avenger
Colossus and the Amazon Queen
Colossus of the Arena
Coriolanus, Man without a Country
Fabiola▶
Fire Monsters Against the Son of Hercules
Giants of Rome
Gladiator of Rome
Gladiators 7
Goliath Against the Giants
Goliath and the Barbarians
Goliath and the Dragon
Goliath and the Sins of Babylon
Gor
Hercules
Hercules Against the Moon Men
Hercules and the Captive Women
Hercules and the Princess of Troy
Hercules in the Haunted World
Hercules, Prisoner of Evil
Hercules Unchained
Hero of Rome
The Invincible Gladiator
The Last Days of Pompeii
Revenge of the Barbarians
Revolt of the Barbarians

Roland the Mighty
Samson
Samson Against the Sheik
Samson and His Mighty Challenge
Samson and the 7 Miracles of the World
Sins of Rome
Son of Ali Baba
Sons of Hercules in the Land of Darkness
Sword of Venus
Terror of the Steppes
Thor and the Amazon Women

Tattoos

Blue Tiger
Cape Fear▶
Cyber Bandits
Down Periscope
The Illustrated Man▶
Lust in the Dust▶
The Night of the Hunter▶
Tattoo
Teresa's Tattoo
Waterworld
The Yakuza

Team Efforts

The Alamo▶
The Bad News Bears Go to Japan
The Bad News Bears in Breaking Training
Breaking Away▶
The Club▶
Coach
Codename: Foxfire
Codename: Wildgeese
Crossfire
The Cutting Edge
The Dirty Dozen▶
The Dirty Dozen: The Deadly Mission
The Dirty Dozen: The Fatal Mission
The Dirty Dozen: The Next Mission
Dirty Hands
The Doll Squad
D2: The Mighty Ducks
Finger on the Trigger
Force Five
Force 10 from Navarone
The Guns of Navarone▶
Hoosiers▶
Kill and Kill Again
Ladybugs
Let's Get Harry
The Losers
The Magnificent Seven▶
Memphis Belle▶
The Mighty Ducks
Miracle on Ice
Race the Sun
Renaissance Man
Seven Magnificent Gladiators
Seven Samurai▶
Silverado▶
Soldier Boyz
Three the Hard Way
Uncommon Valor
The Untouchables▶
Victory
Wild Geese
Wild Geese 2
Wind

Tearjerkers

Acorn People
An Affair to Remember
After the Promise
All Dogs Go to Heaven
All Fall Down
All Mine to Give
Another Time, Another Place
Baby Face
Back Street
Balboa
Ballad in Blue
Bang the Drum Slowly
Bang the Drum Slowly▶
Beaches▶
Big Bluff
Bittersweet Love
Black Eyes
Blind Spot
Blood of Jesus
Blossoms in the Dust
Bonjour Tristesse▶
Bouquet of Barbed Wire
Breaking the Rules
Brian's Song▶
The Cabin in the Cotton
Camille
Carrie▶
Carry On Cruising
Cast the First Stone
The Champ▶
The Champ
Chantilly Lace
The Cheat▶
Chinatown After Dark
Choices
Christmas Comes to Willow Creek
City That Never Sleeps
City Without Men
Claudia
Coquette
The Country Kid▶
The Courtney Affair
Craig's Wife▶
Crawlspace
Curly Sue
Dance Fools Dance▶
Dead Wrong
Death Be Not Proud▶
Dedee d'Anvers
Delinquent Parents
A Different Kind of Love
A Dog of Flanders
Dog Pound Shuffle▶
An Early Frost▶
Easy Virtue
The Eddy Duchin Story
Eric▶
Escape Me Never
Fine Things
Fire Down Below
Flamingo Road▶
The Forbidden City
Fortune's Fool
Found Alive
Fourth Wish
Free Willy
Fulfillment
Gangs, Inc.
The Garden of Allah▶
The Gathering
The Gathering: Part 2
Ghost▶
Girl from Chicago
The Girl Who Had Everything
Goodbye, Mr. Chips▶
Goodbye, My Lady
Great Day
The Greatest Question
Griffin and Phoenix: A Love Story
Harlow
Hearts of Humanity
Heaven and Earth
Heaven's a Drag
Hell-Ship Morgan
Her Silent Sacrifice
High Gear
A Home of Our Own
Honky Tonk▶
Hot Spell
Human Desire
Human Hearts
I Conquer the Sea
I Sent a Letter to My Love▶
Ice Castles
If Ever I See You Again
In This Our Life
Inside Daisy Clover
Intermezzo▶
Jack the Bear
Johnny Belinda▶
Johnny Belinda
Johnny Eager▶
Journey for Margaret▶
Keep Punching
The Kid with the Broken Halo
La Bete Humaine▶
La Chienne▶
Lady Caroline Lamb
The Lady Without Camelias
The Last Best Year
Le Jour Se Leve▶
Legends of the Fall
Leopard in the Snow
Leper
Letter from an Unknown Woman▶
The Little Match Girl
The Little Princess▶
A Little Princess▶
Look Who's Talking Now
Love Affair▶
Love Affair
Love Affair: The Eleanor & Lou Gehrig Story▶
Love Butcher
The Love Flower
Love Has Many Faces
Love in the Present Tense
Love Songs
Love Story▶
Lovers of Their Time
Loving
Lure of the Sila
Madame X
Magnificent Obsession
Man of Evil
The Manxman
Matters of the Heart
Mayerling
Mildred Pierce▶
Miles to Go
Millie
Mimi
The Miniver Story
Miss Julie
Mrs. Silly
Mr. Holland's Opus▶
Mr. Skeffington▶
Mistress
Moment in Time
Moon over Harlem
A Mormon Maid
Mother and Son
Murder on Lenox Avenue
The Nest
The Night Cry
Night Life in Reno
Nomads of the North
Now, Voyager▶
Old Yeller▶
Only Angels Have Wings▶
An Orphan Boy of Vienna
The Other Side of the Mountain
The Other Side of the Mountain, Part 2
Our Sons
Our Time
The Passing of the Third Floor Back
Pattes Blanches
Peg O' My Heart
Penny Serenade▶
A Place in the Sun▶
The Pride of the Yankees▶
The Promise
Question of Faith
A Question of Guilt
Quicksand
The Racket▶
Rage of Angels
The Rains Came
Random Harvest▶
Rebecca of Sunnybrook Farm
Red Kimono
Remolina de Pasiones
Rikisha-Man▶
The Road to Ruin
Romola
Scar of Shame
Secrets of a Married Man
Seizure: The Story of Kathy Morris
Sex
Shadowlands▶
She Goes to War
A Shining Season▶
The Shock
Shopworn Angel▶
Silent Night, Lonely Night
The Sin of Madelon Claudet▶
Since You Went Away▶
Six Weeks
Smilin' Through▶
Sommersby
Sooner or Later
Sparrows▶
Steel Magnolias▶
Stella
Stella Dallas▶
Stella Maris▶
Stolen Hours
Strangers: The Story of a Mother and Daughter▶
Stromboli
Suds
Summer and Smoke
A Summer Place
Sunny
Sunny Skies
Susan Lenox: Her Fall and Rise
Tango
Tell Me That You Love Me
Tender Comrade
Terms of Endearment▶
Test Tube Babies
That Certain Woman
They Drive by Night▶
Things in Their Season
This Boy's Life▶
Three Secrets
Thursday's Child
Tiefland
A Time to Live
Tomorrow's Children
The Tong Man
Torch Song
Toute Une Nuit▶
Traffic in Souls▶
Trapped by the Mormons
Under the Roofs of Paris▶
The Underdog
The Unholy Three▶
Untamed Heart
Uptown New York
Walk on the Wild Side
Walpurgis Night▶
Waterfront
Waterloo Bridge▶
Way Down East▶
The Weaker Sex
Welcome Home
West-Bound Limited
West of Zanzibar
When Wolves Cry
Where East Is East
Where the Red Fern Grows
The White Cliffs of Dover▶
The White Rose▶
Wide Sargasso Sea
Winter Meeting
Without a Trace
A Woman of Affairs
The World Accuses
The World is Full of Married Men
The World Owes Me a Living
Written on the Wind▶
X, Y & Zee
The Yearling▶

Technology-Rampant

see also Computers; Killer Appliances; Robots & Androids

A Nous la Liberte▶
The Android Affair
Armageddon: The Final Challenge
Assassin
Attack of the Killer Refrigerator
Attack of the Robots
Baby Girl Scott
Back to the Future▶
Best Defense
The Bionic Woman
Black Cobra 3: The Manila Connection
The Black Hole
Blade Runner▶
Blades
Bloodlust
Brainscan
Chandu the Magician
Charly▶
Chopping Mall
Circuitry Man
Colossus: The Forbin Project▶
The Companion
Computer Beach Party
Computer Wizard
Crash and Burn
The Creation of the Humanoids
Cyber Bandits
Cyber-Tracker 2
Death of the Rat
Death Ray 2000
Defense Play
Demon Seed▶
Denise Calls Up
Detonator 2: Night Watch
Diamonds Are Forever▶
Digital Man
Dr. Goldfoot and the Bikini Machine
Dungeonmaster
Duplicates
Electric Dreams
The Eliminators
Eve of Destruction
Evolver
Fail-Safe▶
Fair Game
Family Viewing▶
Final Mission
The Final Programme
The Fly▶
The Fly▶
The Fly 2
Future Cop
Futureworld
Geheimakte WB1
Ghost in the Machine
Goldeneye▶
Hackers
Hide and Seek
Hologram Man
Improper Channels
Interface
Johnny Mnemonic
A Joke of Destiny, Lying in Wait Around the Corner Like a Bandit
Judge Dredd
A King in New York
Lawnmower Man 2: Beyond Cyberspace
The Lift
Live Wire: Human Timebomb
Lost Legacy: A Girl Called Hatter Fox
Maximum Overdrive
Metropolis▶
Microwave Massacre
Modern Times▶
Mon Oncle▶
Moonraker
The Mosaic Project
The Munsters' Revenge
Murder by Phone
Murder by Television
Mutant Hunt
Mutant Species
The Net
New Crime City: Los Angeles 2020
Night of the Kickfighters
Nightflyers
One Deadly Owner
Out of Order
Panique▶
The Philadelphia Experiment
Plughead Rewired: Circuitry Man 2
The Power Within
Project: Eliminator
Project: Shadowchaser
The Quiet Earth▶

Rage
Remote
Replikator: Cloned to Kill
RoboCop▶
RoboCop 2
RoboCop 3
RoboCop the Series: The Future of Law Enforcement
Robot Holocaust
Robot Jox
Rock & Roll Cowboys
R.O.T.O.R.
Runaway
Screamers
Search and Destroy
The Seventh Floor
Shadowzone
Shaker Run
Shocker
Short Circuit
Short Circuit 2
Sneakers
Space: 1999
Speaking Parts▶
The Spy Who Loved Me
Stay Tuned
Steel and Lace
Strange New World
Terminal Choice
Terminal Entry
Terminal Impact
The Terminal Man
The Terminator▶
Terrorvision
Things to Come▶
Thrillkill
Touki Bouki
Tron
12:01
Twisted
2001: A Space Odyssey▶
The Ultimate Imposter
The Unborn
Under Siege 2: Dark Territory
The Vindicator
Virtuosity
WarGames
Warning Sign
Weird Science
Westworld▶
Wild Palms
Wired to Kill
Wrestling Women vs. the Aztec Ape
Zardoz

Teen Angst

see also Coming of Age; Hell High School

Above the Rim
Across the Tracks
Adventures in Dinosaur City
Age Isn't Everything
Ah, Wilderness!▶
Airborne
Alex
All Things Fair
American Graffiti▶
An American Summer
Amor Bandido
Andy Hardy Gets Spring Fever
Andy Hardy Meets Debutante
Andy Hardy's Double Life
Andy Hardy's Private Secretary
Angel
Angels with Dirty Faces▶
Angus
Annie O
Anything for Love
Art for Teachers of Children
Autumn Moon
Baby It's You▶
The Baby-Sitters Club
The Bachelor and the Bobby-Soxer▶
Backstreet Dreams
Bad Boys▶
Bad Ronald▶
The Basketball Diaries
Battle of the Bullies
The Bay Boy
Beach Blanket Bingo▶
Beach House
Beach Party
The Beat
Before and After
The Beniker Gang
Berserker
The Best Little Girl in the World▶
Better Off Dead
Beverly Hills 90210
Beverly Hills 90210: The Graduation
Beyond Innocence
The Big Bet
Big Bully
Big Girls Don't Cry...They Get Even
Big Town
Bikini Beach
Bill & Ted's Excellent Adventure
Blackboard Jungle▶
BMX Bandits
Body Snatchers
Book of Love
Born Innocent
Born to Be Wild
A Boy Called Hate
Boys
Boys Life
Boy's Reformatory
Boyz N the Hood▶
The Brady Bunch Movie▶
Brainscan
The Break
The Breakfast Club▶
Breaking All the Rules
Breaking Away▶
Breaking Free
The Bridge
Brotherhood of Justice
Buffy the Vampire Slayer▶
Burglar▶
Buster and Billie
Buying Time
Bye, Bye, Birdie▶
Cadillac Girls
Can You Feel Me Dancing?
Can't Buy Me Love
The Canterville Ghost
Captain Nuke and the Bomber Boys
Career Opportunities
Carrie▶
Carried Away
Cave Girl
The Chalk Garden▶
The Chicken Chronicles
Children of the Corn 2: The Final Sacrifice
China, My Sorrow
Choices
The Choppers
The Chosen▶
Christine
Class
The Class of Miss MacMichael
Clayton County Line
The Club
Clueless▶
Condemned to Hell
Coneheads
Corvette Summer
Cotton Candy
The Craft
The Cruel Story of Youth▶
The Crush
Cry-Baby▶
A Cry in the Wild▶
The Cure
The Curfew Breakers
Dance Me Outside
A Dangerous Age
Dangerous Curves
Dangerous Minds
A Dangerous Place
Dangerous Youth
Dangerously Close
Dario Argento's Trauma
Dark Horse
Date Bait
A Date with Judy
Daughter of Death
The Day My Parents Ran Away
Dazed and Confused▶
Dead Beat
Dead End▶
Dead Poets Society▶
Deadly Weapon
Death Wish Club
Defense Play
The Defilers
Delinquent Daughters
Delivery Boys
Desert Bloom▶
Desperate Lives
The Devil on Wheels
The Devil's Sleep
The Diary of Anne Frank▶
Diner▶
Dino
Diving In
Dogs in Space
Doin' Time on Planet Earth
Don't Tell Mom the Babysitter's Dead
The Doom Generation▶
Dream Date
Dream Machine
Dream to Believe
Drive-In
Dudes
Dutch
Dutch Girls
East of Eden▶
East of Eden
East Side Kids
The Effect of Gamma Rays on Man-in-the-Moon Marigolds▶
Emma▶
Empire Records
Encino Man
Endless Love
The Ernest Green Story
The Escape Artist▶
Escape from El Diablo
E.T.: The Extra-Terrestrial▶
Evils of the Night
Eyes of the Panther
Eyes Right!
Fall Time
Fame▶
Fast Talking
Fast Times at Ridgemont High▶
Fear
Fear No Evil
Fellini's Roma
Ferris Bueller's Day Off▶
Fire with Fire
The First Time
First Turn On
The Flamingo Kid▶
Flipper▶
Flirting▶
The Fly 2
Fly with the Hawk
Footloose
For Keeps
Force of Impulse
Forever
Foxes
The Franchise Affair
Freeze Frame
Friends
Friends Forever▶
A Friendship in Vienna
Gas Food Lodging▶
Gate 2
Girl from Hunan▶
A Girl of the Limberlost
The Girl, the Body and the Pill
Girlfriend from Hell
Girls Just Want to Have Fun
Girls Town
Gleaming the Cube
The Goodbye Bird
Goodbye, Miss 4th of July
A Goofy Movie
Grease▶
Grease 2
Gregory's Girl▶
The Guinea Pig
Hackers
Hadley's Rebellion
Hairspray▶
Halloween▶
Halloween 6: The Curse of Michael Myers
Hard Knocks
Hardcore
Harley
Heathers▶
Heavenly Creatures▶
The Heavenly Kid
Heavyweights
Hide and Go Shriek
High School Caesar
High School Confidential
High School USA
Hollywood High
Hollywood High, Part 2
A Home of Our Own
Hometown U.S.A.
Homework
Hoop Dreams▶
Hoosiers▶
Hornet's Nest
Hot Bubblegum
Hot Times
How I Got into College
How to Stuff a Wild Bikini
I Accuse My Parents
I Am the Cheese
I Never Promised You a Rose Garden▶
I Wanna Hold Your Hand
I Was a Teenage Werewolf
If....▶
If Looks Could Kill
Imaginary Crimes▶
The Impossible Years
The In Crowd
In the Land of the Owl Turds
The Incredibly True Adventure of Two Girls in Love
Inga
The Inkwell
The Invisible Kid
Iron Eagle 4
Jennifer
Junior High School
Just Another Girl on the I.R.T.
Just for the Hell of It
Just One of the Girls
Kansas
Kid Dynamite
A Kid in King Arthur's Court
Kids
Kim
King Creole
Knights & Emeralds
La Bamba▶
La Petite Sirene
L'Amour en Herbe
Lantern Hill
Last Cry for Help
Last Summer
Lauderdale
The Lawrenceville Stories
Les Enfants Terrible▶
Les Mistons▶
Liar's Edge
License to Drive
Life Begins for Andy Hardy▶
Lisa
Little Darlings
The Little Mermaid▶
A Little Romance▶
Little Sweetheart
The Little Thief▶
The Little Valentino
The Loneliest Runner
The Loneliness of the Long Distance Runner▶
Loners
Looking for Miracles
Loose Screws
Losin' It
Lost Angels
The Lost Boys
Love Laughs at Andy Hardy
Love Under Pressure
Lovelines
Lucas▶
Mad About You
Mad Love
Mad Youth
Made in USA
Magic Kid 2
Major Payne
Making the Grade
Malibu Beach
Man from Texas
The Man in the Attic
The Man in the Moon▶
The Manhattan Project
Married Too Young
Meatballs
Meatballs 2
Meatballs 3
Meatballs 4
The Member of the Wedding▶
The Member of the Wedding
Mermaids▶
Metropolitan▶
Min & Bill
The Miracle
Mirror, Mirror
Mischief
Misfits of Science
Miss A & Miss M
Miss Annie Rooney
Mon Oncle Antoine▶
Monika
Monkey Business▶
Morgan Stewart's Coming Home
Mortal Danger
Motorcycle Gang
Mouchette▶
Murder in New Hampshire: The Pamela Smart Story
Muscle Beach Party
My American Cousin▶
My Antonia
My Best Friend Is a Vampire
My Boyfriend's Back
My Boys Are Good Boys
My Father, My Rival
My Father the Hero
My Girl 2
My Own Private Idaho▶
My Science Project
Mystery Date
Mystic Pizza▶
Naked Youth
National Lampoon's Senior Trip
The Neon Bible
New Jersey Drive
The Next Karate Kid
Nice Girls Don't Explode
Nickel Mountain
The Night Before
Night Breed
Night Friend
A Night in the Life of Jimmy Reardon
Night Life
Night of Evil
Night of the Twisters
A Nightmare on Elm Street 2: Freddy's Revenge
A Nightmare on Elm Street 3: Dream Warriors
A Nightmare on Elm Street 4: Dream Master
A Nightmare on Elm Street 5: Dream Child
1969▶
Ninja Supremo
No Big Deal
Nobody's Perfect
Not My Kid
Now and Then
Nowhere to Run
O.C. and Stiggs
Odd Birds
On the Edge: The Survival of Dana
One Crazy Night
One Crazy Summer
One Dark Night
Only the Brave
Only the Strong
Ordinary Magic
Our Time
Outside Chance of Maximillian Glick
The Outsiders

Over the Edge▶
Over the Summer
Pajama Party
Palm Springs Weekend
Paradise Motel
Parenthood▶
Party! Party!
Pathfinder▶
Peggy Sue Got Married
The People Next Door
Peppermint Soda▶
Phantom 2040 Movie: The Ghost Who Walks
A Pig's Tale
Pin
Pippin▶
Platypus Cove
Playing for Keeps
Playing with Fire
Poison Ivy
Pom Pom Girls
Porky's
Porky's 2: The Next Day
The Positively True Adventures of the Alleged Texas Cheerleader-Murdering Mom▶
Pot, Parents, and Police
Powder
The Power Within
Prayer of the Rollerboys
Pretty in Pink
Pretty Smart
The Prime of Miss Jean Brodie▶
The Prime Time
Primo Baby
Princes in Exile
Prison for Children
Puberty Blues
Pump Up the Volume
Quadrophenia▶
Quarterback Princess
Race the Sun
Racing with the Moon▶
Rad
Rambling Rose▶
Rebel Without a Cause▶
Reckless
Red Kiss▶
Return to Horror High
Return to the Blue Lagoon
Revenge of the Living Zombies
River's Edge▶
Roadhouse 66
Robin of Locksley
Rock 'n' Roll High School Forever
Rock, Rock, Rock
Rockula
Rodrigo D.: No Future
Romeo and Juliet
Romeo and Juliet▶
Rooftops
Roustabout
The Run of the Country▶
Running Mates▶
Sabrina the Teenage Witch
Say Anything▶
Scarred
Scream for Help
Screen Test
Screwballs
Season of Change
Secret Admirer
Secrets of Sweet Sixteen
Seizure: The Story of Kathy Morris
Senior Trip
Seven Minutes in Heaven
The Seventh Coin
S.F.W.
Shag: The Movie▶
Shake, Rattle and Rock
Shao Lin Popeye
Sharma & Beyond
Sharon's Secret
She's Out of Control
Shooting
Shout
Silence of the Heart▶
The Silent One
Sing
Sixteen Candles▶
Skateboard
Smokey Bites the Dust
Smugglers' Cove▶
Snowballing
Solarbabies
Some Kind of Wonderful
Something Special
Sooner or Later
The Spell
Spetters
Spirit Rider▶
Splendor in the Grass▶
Spring Fever
Stand and Deliver▶
Starchaser: The Legend of Orin
Stealing Beauty
Sticky Fingers
Still Not Quite Human
Stones of Death
Straight Out of Brooklyn
Straight Up
Strange Illusion
Streets
The Stripper
Student Bodies
Suburbia
Summer Camp Nightmare
Summer Holiday
Summer of '42▶
The Summer of My German Soldier▶
Summer School
Sunnyside
Swap Meet
Sweet 16
Swim Team
Swing Kids
A Swingin' Summer
Tainted Blood
Tammy and the T-Rex
Tearaway
Teen Mothers
Teen Wolf
Teenage
Teenage Bad Girl
Teenage Bonnie & Klepto Clyde
Teenage Caveman
Teenage Crime Wave
Teenage Mother
Teenage Mutant Ninja Turtles 2: The Secret of the Ooze
Teenage Strangler
Teenage Wolfpack
Teenager
Teenagers from Outer Space
The Tender Age
Terminal Bliss
Tex
That Night
That Was Then...This Is Now
There Goes My Baby
They Made Me a Criminal
36 Fillete▶
This Boy's Life▶
This Special Friendship
Thrashin'
3:15—The Moment of Truth
Three O'Clock High
Time Stands Still▶
Times Square
To Die For▶
To Play or To Die
Tom Brown's School Days▶
Too Young to Die
Totally F***ed Up
Toughlove
Toy Soldiers
Treasure Island
Troop Beverly Hills
The Trouble with Angels
True Crime
Trust
Twirl
Twist & Shout▶
Twisted
Twisted Love
Uncle Buck▶
Under the Boardwalk
Unfinished Business
Unstrung Heroes
Up Against the Wall
Uptown Angel
Urusei Yatsura Movie 1: Only You
Urusei Yatsura Movie 2: Beautiful Dreamer
Urusei Yatsura Movie 3: Remember My Love
Valley Girl
The Vals
The Van
A Very Brady Sequel
Village of the Giants
Virgin High
Vision Quest
The Voyage of the Yes
Walking Back
Wanderers▶
Weird Science
Welcome Home, Roxy Carmichael
Welcome to 18
Where Angels Go, Trouble Follows
Where the Boys Are '84
Where the Day Takes You
White Squall
White Wolves 2: Legend of the Wild
The Wild Life
Wild Ones on Wheels
Wild Pony
Windrunner
Wish You Were Here▶
The Wooden Gun
The Wraith
The Year My Voice Broke▶
The Young Graduates
Young Guns
Young Love, First Love
The Young Poisoner's Handbook▶
Youngblood
Youth Aflame
Youth on Parole
You've Ruined Me, Eddie
Zebrahead▶
Zero Boys
Zombie Nightmare
The Zoo Gang

Television

see Mass Media; TV Movies; TV Pilot Movies; TV Series

Tennis

The Break
Jocks
Nobody's Perfect
Players
Racquet
Spring Fever

Terror in Tall Buildings

see also Elevators; Mystery & Suspense

Blackout
Die Hard▶
Hard to Die
Project: Shadowchaser
Speed▶
Terror on the 40th Floor
Tower of Terror
The Towering Inferno

Terrorism

see also Crime & Criminals; Foreign Intrigue; Spies & Espionage

Act of Passion: The Lost Honor of Kathryn Beck
Act of Piracy
Airheads
The Amateur
Angel of Fury
The Applegates
The Assassination Run
Assignment Skybolt
Barcelona▶
Belfast Assassin
Black Cobra 2
Black Cobra 3: The Manila Connection
Black Sunday
Black Terrorist
Blink of an Eye
Blood on the Badge
Bloodfist 6: Ground Zero
Blown Away
Captain America 2: Death Too Soon
Captive
Captive Rage
The Cassandra Crossing
Children of Rage
C.I.A. 2: Target Alexa
Circle of Deceit
Codename: Vengeance
Commando▶
Contra Company
Could It Happen Here?
Cover-Up
Covert Assassin
Crash and Burn
Cry of the Innocent▶
The Crying Game▶
Dark Rider
Deadline
Death Before Dishonor
The Death Merchant
Death of the Incredible Hulk
Death Ray
Delta Force
Delta Force 3: The Killing Game
Delta Force Commando
Delta Force Commando 2
Dick Barton, Special Agent
Die Hard▶
Die Hard 2: Die Harder▶
Die Hard: With a Vengeance
Dirty Games
Dr. Otto & the Riddle of the Gloom Beam
Dog Day Afternoon▶
The Dogfighters
The Enforcer
Eraser
The Evil That Men Do
Executive Decision
Exposed
Fast Kill
A Father's Revenge
ffolkes
The Final Option
Flashpoint Africa
Fortress of Amerikka
48 Hours to Live
French Quarter Undercover
Full Fathom Five
Galyon
Germicide
The Glass Jungle
The Glory Boys
Held Hostage
Hell Squad
Hidden Agenda
Hologram Man
Hostage
In the Name of the Father▶
Invasion Force
Invasion U.S.A.
Iran: Days of Crisis
Jericho Fever
Journeys from Berlin/1971
Judgment in Berlin
Juggernaut▶
July Group
Jungle Assault
Kamikaze '89▶
Katherine
The Kidnapping of the President
Kings and Desperate Men
L'Anne Sainte
The Little Drummer Girl▶
Live Wire
The Lost Command
The Mad Bomber
Marianne and Juliane▶
Merchants of War
Molly Maguires
Murder on Flight 502
Naked Gun 33 1/3: The Final Insult
Navy SEALS
Night of the Assassin
Nightstick
Ninja Connection
Ninja the Battalion
No Contest
No Dead Heroes
Odd Man Out▶
Omega Syndrome
Open Fire
Operation Thunderbolt
Panic in the Streets▶
Panic on the 5:22
The Passenger▶
Passenger 57
The Patriot
Patriot Games▶
Patty Hearst
Programmed to Kill
Project: Alien
Pursuit▶
Python Wolf
Raid on Entebbe▶
The Railway Station Man▶
Rebel
Rescue Force
The Rock▶
Rollercoaster
Rosebud
Running Delilah
The Rutanga Tapes
Secret Agent 00
Secret Agent Super Dragon
Silk Degrees
Skeleton Coast
Skull: A Night of Terror
Special Bulletin▶
Stalking Danger
Sudden Death
Summer Night
The Taking of Flight 847: The Uli Derickson Story▶
The Taking of Pelham One Two Three▶
Terminal Entry
Terror in Beverly Hills
Terror in Paradise
Terror Squad
The Terrorists
Terrorists
Thunder Run
Thunderball
A Town Called Hell
Toy Soldiers
The Tragedy of a Ridiculous Man
Tragedy of Flight 103: The Inside Story▶
Trained to Kill, U.S.A.
Treasure of the Lost Desert
Trident Force
Troma's War
True Lies
Turk 182!
21 Hours at Munich▶
Undeclared War
The Vernonia Incident
Viper
Voyage of Terror: The Achille Lauro Affair
Wanted Dead or Alive
Women on the Verge of a Nervous Breakdown▶
Wrong is Right
Year of the Gun
You Only Live Twice

This is Your Life

see also Camelot (New); Musician Biopics; Nashville Narratives; Roll Over Beethoven

Abe Lincoln in Illinois▶
Above and Beyond▶
Abraham Lincoln
Actor: The Paul Muni Story
The Adventures of Mark Twain▶

Agatha
Al Capone▶
Alex in Wonderland
Alexander the Great
All That Jazz▶
Amadeus▶
Amarcord▶
The Amazing Howard Hughes
American Graffiti▶
Amin: The Rise and Fall
An Angel at My Table▶
Anita, Dances of Vice
The Ann Jillian Story
Annie Oakley▶
Annie Oakley
Antony and Cleopatra
Au Revoir Les Enfants▶
The Autobiography of Miss Jane Pittman▶
Babe!▶
The Babe
Babe Ruth Story
Backbeat▶
Bandit Queen
Barefoot in Athens
Barnum
The Barretts of Wimpole Street▶
Battle Hymn
Becoming Colette
Beethoven
Beethoven Lives Upstairs
The Benny Goodman Story
The Best Intentions▶
Bethune
Big Mo
The Big Red One▶
Bird▶
Bix
Blades of Courage
Blaze
Blind Ambition
Blossoms in the Dust
Bluebeard▶
Bogie: The Last Hero
Bonnie & Clyde▶
Bonnie Prince Charlie
Born Again
Born on the Fourth of July▶
Bound for Glory▶
Boy in Blue
Bruce Lee: Curse of the Dragon▶
The Buccaneer
Bud and Lou
The Buddy Holly Story▶
Bugsy▶
The Burning Season▶
Buster Keaton Rides Again/The Railrodder
Cabeza de Vaca▶
Caddie
Calamity Jane
Camille Claudel▶
Can You Hear the Laughter? The Story of Freddie Prinze
Canada's Sweetheart: The Saga of Hal C. Banks
Caravaggio▶
Caro Diario▶
Carrington
Casanova
Cast a Giant Shadow
Catherine the Great
Catholic Hour
Celeste▶
Cesare Borgia
Chain Lightning
Champions
Chanel Solitaire
Chapayev▶
Chaplin▶
Chariots of Fire▶
Charlemagne
Christopher Columbus
Christopher Columbus: The Discovery
Churchill and the Generals
Citizen Cohn
Coal Miner's Daughter▶
Cobb▶
The Color of Pomegranates▶
Coming Through
Conrack▶
The Country Diary of an Edwardian Lady
The Courageous Mr. Penn
The Court Martial of Jackie Robinson▶
Cowboy▶
Crime Lords
Cromwell
Cross Creek
Crumb▶
Damien: The Leper Priest
Dance with a Stranger▶
A Dangerous Man: Lawrence after Arabia▶
Daniel Boone
Dante's Inferno: Life of Dante Gabriel Rossetti
Dawn!
The Death of Adolf Hitler
Deep in My Heart
Dempsey
The Desert Fox▶
Diana: Her True Story
The Diary of Anne Frank▶
Dick Turpin
Dillinger▶
Dillinger
The Disappearance of Aimee▶
Disraeli▶
The Doctor
Dr. Bethune▶
The Dolly Sisters
Don't Look Back: The Story of Leroy "Satchel" Paige
The Doors
Double Exposure: The Story of Margaret Bourke-White
Dragon: The Bruce Lee Story▶
Dreamchild▶
Ed Wood▶
Ed Wood: Look Back in Angora
The Ed Wood Story: The Plan 9 Companion
The Eddy Duchin Story
Edie in Ciao! Manhattan
Edison the Man
Edith & Marcel
The Education of Sonny Carson
Edvard Munch
Edward and Mrs. Simpson
8 Seconds
Eleanor & Franklin▶
Eleanor: First Lady of the World
The Elegant Criminal
Eleni
The Elephant Man▶
Elizabeth R▶
Elizabeth, the Queen
Elvis and Me
Elvis Stories
Elvis: The Movie
Enemy of Women
Enter Laughing
Ernie Kovacs: Between the Laughter
The Eternal Waltz
Eubie!
Europa, Europa▶
Evel Knievel
Exit the Dragon, Enter the Tiger
F. Scott Fitzgerald in Hollywood
The Fabulous Dorseys
Fallen Champ: The Untold Story of Mike Tyson▶
Fanny and Alexander▶
Farinelli
Fast Company
Final Shot: The Hank Gathers Story
The Five of Me
The Five Pennies
For Us, the Living▶
Forbidden Passion: The Oscar Wilde Movie
Ford: The Man & the Machine
Forever James Dean
The Fountainhead▶
1492: Conquest of Paradise
Francesco
Frank and Ollie▶
Frida
Funny Girl▶
Funny Lady
The Gallant Hours▶
Gandhi▶
The Gathering Storm
The Gene Krupa Story
Gentleman Jim▶
George Washington
George Washington: The Forging of a Nation
Geronimo▶
Give 'Em Hell, Harry!
The Glenn Miller Story▶
The Goddess▶
Going for the Gold: The Bill Johnson Story
Goodbye, Norma Jean
Goodnight, Sweet Marilyn
Gore Vidal's Lincoln
The Gorgeous Hussy
Gorillas in the Mist▶
Gothic▶
The Grace Kelly Story
Grambling's White Tiger
Greased Lightning
Great Balls of Fire
The Great Caruso
The Great Impostor
Great Missouri Raid
The Great Moment
The Great Wallendas
The Great Waltz▶
The Great White Hope
The Great Ziegfeld▶
The Greatest
The Greatest Story Ever Told
The Greek Tycoon
Gypsy▶
Gypsy
Hammett
Hank Aaron: Chasing the Dream▶
Hans Christian Andersen
The Happy Hooker Goes Hollywood
Harlow
Harmon of Michigan
Harmony Lane
Haunted Summer
Heading Home
Heart Beat
Heart Like a Wheel
Heart of a Champion: The Ray Mancini Story
Heaven and Earth
Hedda Hopper's Hollywood
Henry & June▶
Hitler
Hitler: The Last Ten Days
Hoffa▶
Holy Terror
Home Sweet Home
The Hoodlum Priest▶
Hoodoo Ann
Houdini
The Hours and Times▶
Hugh Hefner: Once Upon a Time
Hughes & Harlow: Angels in Hell
The Hunter
I'Am a Fugitive from a Chain Gang▶
I Dream of Jeannie
I Shot Billy the Kid
I, the Worst of All
Ike
I'll Cry Tomorrow▶
I'll See You in My Dreams
Immortal Beloved
Imperial Venus
In Love and War
The Incredible Sarah
The Inn of the Sixth Happiness▶
Inside the Third Reich
Interrupted Melody▶
Invincible Mr. Disraeli
Iris
The Iron Duke
Isadora▶
It's Good to Be Alive
J. Edgar Hoover
Jack Frost
Jack London
The Jackie Robinson Story▶
The Jacksons: An American Dream
Jacqueline Bouvier Kennedy
James Dean
James Dean Story
James Dean: The First American Teenager
James Joyce: A Portrait of the Artist as a Young Man
James Joyce's Women▶
Janis: A Film
The Jayne Mansfield Story
Jefferson in Paris
Jesse James Under the Black Flag
The Jesse Owens Story
Jesus
Jesus Christ, Superstar▶
JFK: Reckless Youth
Jim Thorpe: All American
Joan of Arc
The Joe Louis Story
John & Yoko: A Love Story
John Paul Jones
Johnny We Hardly Knew Ye
Jolson Sings Again
The Jolson Story▶
Joni
The Josephine Baker Story▶
Juarez
Judith of Bethulia▶
Kennedy
King▶
The King of Kings▶
The King of the Roaring '20s: The Story of Arnold Rothstein
Kingfish: A Story of Huey P. Long
Kissinger and Nixon
Knute Rockne: All American▶
Korczak▶
La Bamba▶
La Signora di Tutti▶
Lady Jane▶
Lady Sings the Blues
Lakota Woman: Siege at Wounded Knee
Lamp at Midnight
Last Days of Frank & Jesse James
The Last Days of Patton
The Last Emperor▶
Last Four Days
The Last of Mrs. Lincoln
Lawrence of Arabia▶
LBJ: The Early Years▶
The Learning Tree
The Left-Handed Gun▶
Legend of Valentino
The Legend of Valentino
Lenny▶
Lepke
Let's Get Lost
The Life and Assassination of the Kingfish
The Life and Loves of Mozart
The Life of Emile Zola▶
Life of Verdi
The Light in the Jungle
Lightning Over Water
Lillie▶
Lisztomania
Living Proof: The Hank Williams Jr. Story
The Loneliest Runner
The Long Gray Line▶
Long Journey Back
Look for the Silver Lining
Love Affair: The Eleanor & Lou Gehrig Story▶
Love Me or Leave Me▶
The Loves of Edgar Allen Poe
Loyola, the Soldier Saint
Lucky Luciano
Lucy and Desi: Before the Laughter
Lust for Life▶
MacArthur
Madame Curie▶
Madman
Madonna: Innocence Lost
Mae West
Mafia Princess
Magnificent Adventurer
The Magnificent Yankee▶
Mahler▶
Malcolm X▶
Malcolm X: Make It Plain
A Man Called Peter▶
Man of a Thousand Faces▶
Mandela▶
Marciano
Marco
Marie▶
Marie Antoinette
Marilyn: The Untold Story▶
Marjoe
Marlon Brando
Martin Luther
Mary of Scotland▶
Mary White
A Matter of Life and Death
McVicar
Melody Master
The Miracle Worker▶
Mishima: A Life in Four Chapters▶
Mrs. Parker and the Vicious Circle
Mo' Better Blues
Modigliani
Mommie Dearest
Monsieur Vincent▶
Moulin Rouge▶
Mozart: A Childhood Chronicle▶
The Mozart Story
Murderers among Us: The Simon Wiesenthal Story▶
Murrow
The Music Lovers
Mussolini & I
My Apprenticeship▶
My Childhood▶
My Father's Glory▶
My Left Foot▶
My Universities▶
My Wicked, Wicked Ways
Nadia
The Naked Civil Servant▶
The Naked Maja
Nancy Astor
Napoleon▶
Napoleon
Ned Kelly
Nicholas and Alexandra
Night and Day
Nijinsky
Nixon▶
Nostradamus
Nurse Edith Cavell▶
Onassis
One in a Million: The Ron LeFlore Story
One Man's Way
The Outlaw
Padre Padrone▶
Pancho Barnes
Pancho Villa
Papa's Delicate Condition▶
Patton▶
Patty Hearst
Paul Robeson
Perfumed Nightmare▶
The Perils of Pauline
Personal Services
Peter the Great▶
Piaf
Pistol: The Birth of a Legend
Poor Little Rich Girl: The Barbara Hutton Story
Pope John Paul II
Portrait of a Rebel: Margaret Sanger
Postcards from America
Prick Up Your Ears▶
Pride of St. Louis
The Pride of the Yankees▶
Priest of Love
Prince Jack
PT 109
The Queen of Mean
Queenie

Raging Bull▶
Rainbow
Rasputin▶
The Raven
A Real American Hero
The Real Buddy Holly Story
Reilly: Ace of Spies▶
Rembrandt▶
Rembrandt—1669
Return to Earth
Rhapsody in Blue▶
Rhodes
Richard Petty Story
Riel
Ring of Bright Water▶
The Rise and Fall of Legs Diamond
The Rise of Louis XIV▶
Rita Hayworth: The Love Goddess
Robert Kennedy and His Times
Rodeo Girl
Romero
Rosa Luxemburg
Roseanne: An Unauthorized Biography
Rosie: The Rosemary Clooney Story
Ruby
Rush▶
Sadat
Sakharov▶
Samaritan: The Mitch Snyder Story▶
Savage Messiah▶
Schindler's List▶
Sebastiane▶
The Secret Diary of Sigmund Freud
Secret Honor▶
A Sense of Freedom▶
The Seven Little Foys▶
Shadow on the Sun
Shadowlands▶
The Sicilian
Sid & Nancy▶
Silent Victory: The Kitty O'Neil Story▶
Simon Bolivar
Sinatra
Sister Kenny▶
Six Wives of Henry VIII▶
Soldier in Love
Somebody Up There Likes Me▶
Song of Norway
A Song to Remember▶
Song Without End
Sophia Loren: Her Own Story
The Sound and the Silence
The Spectre of Edgar Allen Poe
Spirit of St. Louis▶
Spitfire▶
Spring Symphony
Spymaker: The Secret Life of Ian Fleming
Squizzy Taylor
Stalin
Star!
Stars and Stripes Forever▶
Stevie
Story of Adele H.▶
The Story of Alexander Graham Bell▶
The Story of Dr. Wassell
The Story of Louis Pasteur▶
The Story of Vernon and Irene Castle▶
The Stratton Story▶
Striker's Mountain
Sugartime
Sunday's Children▶
Sunrise at Campobello▶
Sweet Dreams
Sweet Love, Bitter
Sylvia
Taxi zum Klo▶
Tchaikovsky
Teamster Boss: The Jackie Presser Story▶
The Ten Commandments▶
The Testament of Orpheus▶
That Hamilton Woman▶
Theremin: An Electronic Odyssey▶
Therese▶
32 Short Films about Glenn Gould▶
This Boy's Life▶
This Is Elvis
Three Came Home▶
Three Little Words
Till the Clouds Roll By
Till the Clouds Roll By/A Star Is Born▶
A Time for Miracles
To Hell and Back
To Kill a Priest
To Race the Wind
Tom & Viv▶
Tom Horn
Total Eclipse
The Trials of Oscar Wilde▶
Truman
Tyson
Valentino
Van Gogh▶
Veronika Voss▶
Victoria Regina
Vincent & Theo▶
Vincent: The Life and Death of Vincent van Gogh▶
The Virgin Queen▶
The Virginia Hill Story
Viva Villa!▶
Viva Zapata!▶
A Voyage' Round My Father▶
Wagner: The Complete Epic
Wagner: The Movie
Wait Until Spring, Bandini
Waiting for the Moon
Waltz King
Weeds▶
What's Love Got to Do with It?
White Hunter, Black Heart▶
Who's That Knocking at My Door?▶
Wild Bill
Wild Hearts Can't Be Broken▶
Wild, Wild World of Jayne Mansfield
Will: G. Gordon Liddy
Wilma
Wilson▶
The Winds of Kitty Hawk
Wings of Eagles
A Winner Never Quits
The Winning Team
Wired
Without Warning: The James Brady Story▶
Wittgenstein
The Wolf at the Door
A Woman Called Golda▶
A Woman Called Moses
The Woman He Loved
A Woman Named Jackie
The Wonderful, Horrible Life of Leni Riefenstahl
The Wonderful World of the Brothers Grimm
Words and Music
Wyatt Earp
Yankee Doodle Dandy▶
Young Bill Hickok
Young Buffalo Bill
Young Caruso
Young Charlie Chaplin
Young Einstein
Young Mr. Lincoln▶
Young Tom Edison
Young Winston▶
Zora Is My Name!

3-D Flicks

Amityville 3: The Demon
Andy Warhol's Frankenstein
Cat Women of the Moon
Creature from the Black Lagoon▶
The Creature Walks Among Us
Devil's Canyon
Dogs of Hell
Dynasty
Flesh and Blood Show
The French Line
Friday the 13th, Part 3
Gun Fury
House of Wax▶
It Came From Outer Space▶
Jaws 3
Kiss Me Kate▶
The Man Who Wasn't There
The Mask
Miss Sadie Thompson▶
Paradisio
Parasite
Revenge of the Creature
Robot Monster
Spacehunter: Adventures in the Forbidden Zone
Starchaser: The Legend of Orin
The Stranger Wore a Gun

Thumbs Up

Alligator Eyes
Blood Simple▶
Diary of a Teenage Hitchhiker
Even Cowgirls Get the Blues
The Hitcher
The Hitchhiker
Hitchhiker 2
Hitchhiker 3
Hitchhiker 4
Hitchhikers
The Hitchhiker's Guide to the Galaxy
Josh and S.A.M.
Kalifornia
Melvin and Howard▶
My Own Private Idaho▶
The Sure Thing▶
Thelma & Louise▶

Time Travel

see also Rescue Missions Involving Time Travel

Adventures in Dinosaur City
Amazing Mr. Blunden
A.P.E.X.
Army of Darkness▶
The Arrival
Back to the Future▶
Back to the Future, Part 2
Back to the Future, Part 3▶
Battle for the Planet of the Apes
Beastmaster 2: Through the Portal of Time
Being Human
Beneath the Planet of the Apes
Beyond the Time Barrier
Biggles
Bill & Ted's Bogus Journey
Bill & Ted's Excellent Adventure
Blue Flame
The Blue Yonder
Brother Future
Buck Rogers in the 25th Century
A Connecticut Yankee▶
A Connecticut Yankee in King Arthur's Court
Conquest of the Planet of the Apes
Day Time Ended
Doctor Mordrid: Master of the Unknown
Doctor Who
Doctor Who: An Unearthly Child
Doctor Who and the Daleks
Doctor Who: Cybermen—The Early Years
The Eliminators
Escape from the Planet of the Apes▶
Escapes
The Final Countdown▶
Frankenstein Unbound▶
Freejack
Future Zone
Galaxis
Grand Tour: Disaster in Time
Groundhog Day▶
Hercules in New York
Highlander 2: The Quickening
Highlander: The Final Dimension
Hocus Pocus
Idaho Transfer
The Indian in the Cupboard
The Jetsons Meet the Flintstones
Josh Kirby...Time Warrior: Chapter 1, Planet of the Dino-Knights
Josh Kirby...Time Warrior: Chapter 2, The Human Pets
Josh Kirby...Time Warrior: Chapter 3, Trapped on Toyworld
Josh Kirby...Time Warrior: Chapter 4, Eggs from 70 Million B.C.
Josh Kirby...Time Warrior: Chapter 5, Journey to the Magic Cavern
Josh Kirby...Time Warrior: Chapter 6, Last Battle for the Universe
Journey to the Center of Time
Lords of Magick
Mannequin 2: On the Move
Millenium
The Navigator▶
Next One
Night of Dark Shadows
Peggy Sue Got Married
The Philadelphia Experiment
Philadelphia Experiment 2
Planet of the Apes▶
Roman Scandals
Running Against Time
Somewhere in Time
Spirit of '76
Star Trek 4: The Voyage Home▶
Star Trek the Next Generation, the Final Episode: All Good Things...
Stargate
The Swordsman
Teenage Mutant Ninja Turtles 3
The Terminator▶
Terminator 2: Judgment Day▶
Test Tube Teens from the Year 2000
The Three Stooges Meet Hercules
Time After Time▶
Time Bandits
Time Chasers
Time Fighters
The Time Guardian
The Time Machine▶
Time Machine
Time Runner
Time Trackers
The Time Travelers
Timecop
Timemaster
Timerider
Timestalkers
Trancers
Trancers 2: The Return of Jack Deth
Trancers 3: Deth Lives
Trancers 4: Jack of Swords
Trancers 5: Sudden Deth
12 Monkeys▶
12:01
Unidentified Flying Oddball
Warlock
Waxwork 2: Lost in Time
A Witch Without a Broom
Yor, the Hunter from the Future

Toilets

see Bathroom Scenes

Tokyo

see also Japan

Akira
An Autumn Afternoon▶
The Bad News Bears Go to Japan
Black Lizard
Black Rain
Demon City Shinjuku
Dodes 'ka-den▶
Escapade in Japan
Gamera vs. Barugon
Gappa the Trifibian Monster
Ghidrah the Three Headed Monster
Godzilla, King of the Monsters
Godzilla vs. Megalon
H-Man
Hiroshima, Mon Amour▶
The Human Vapor
Mothra▶
Okoge
Proof of the Man
Running Brave
Sisters of Gion▶
Street of Shame▶
A Taxing Woman's Return▶
Thirty Seconds Over Tokyo▶
Tokyo Decadence
Tokyo-Ga▶
Tokyo Joe
Tokyo Pop
Tokyo Story▶
War of the Gargantuas

Torn in Two (or More)

Abbott and Costello Meet Dr. Jekyll and Mr. Hyde
Dr. Heckyl and Mr. Hype
Dr. Jekyll and Ms. Hyde
Dr. Jekyll and Mr. Hyde▶
Dr. Jekyll and Mr. Hyde
Dr. Jekyll and Sister Hyde
Edge of Sanity
Jekyll and Hyde
Mary Reilly
Mirage
Multiplicity
Primal Fear
Raising Cain
Separate Lives
Sybil▶
The Three Faces of Eve▶

Torrid Love Scenes

see also Sex & Sexuality; Sex on the Beach; Sexploitation

The Adventurers
Against All Odds
Alien Prey
Angel Heart
Atlantic City▶
Basic Instinct
The Berlin Affair
Betty Blue▶
The Big Easy▶
Bitter Moon
Black Ice
Blue Velvet▶
Body Double▶
Body Heat▶
Body of Evidence
Bram Stoker's Dracula
Breathless
Bull Durham▶
Cat Chaser
Cat on a Hot Tin Roof▶
Close My Eyes
The Cook, the Thief, His Wife & Her Lover▶
Crimes of Passion▶
Dark Obsession
Deadly Desire
The Dolphin
Dona Flor and Her Two Husbands▶
Don't Look Now▶
The Executioner's Song
Exit to Eden
The Fabulous Baker Boys▶
Fatal Attraction▶
Five Easy Pieces▶
From Here to Eternity▶
Green Fire
The Harvest
Heat of Desire
Henry & June▶
The Hunting

In the Realm of the Senses▶
Kiss Me a Killer
Lady Godiva Rides
Last Tango in Paris▶
Law of Desire▶
The Lawnmower Man
The Lover
The Lovers▶
Mad Dog and Glory▶
The Mambo Kings▶
Men in Love
Moon in the Gutter
Moonstruck▶
Night Eyes 2
Night Eyes 3
9 1/2 Weeks
1900▶
An Officer and a Gentleman▶
The Pamela Principle
The Postman Always Rings Twice
Prizzi's Honor▶
Pyrates
Rage of Angels
Revenge
Risky Business▶
Sea of Love▶
Secrets
Sexual Response
Siesta
Sliver
Something Wild
The Story of O
Swept Away...▶
Tattoo
Tequila Sunrise
Threesome
The Unbearable Lightness of Being▶
White Palace
Wild at Heart▶
Wild Orchid
Wild Orchid 2: Two Shades of Blue
The Woman Next Door▶
Women & Men: In Love There Are No Rules
Women in Love▶
Year of the Gun
Zandalee

Toys

see also Killer Toys

Babes in Toyland
Child's Play 2
Dance of Death
Demonic Toys
Devil Doll▶
Dolls
Dolly Dearest
Josh Kirby...Time Warrior: Chapter 3, Trapped on Toyworld
Not Quite Human
Silent Night, Deadly Night 5: The Toymaker
The Toy
Toy Story▶
Toys
Wired to Kill

Tragedy

see also Drama; Tearjerkers

Against the Wind
Angel with the Trumpet
Anna Karenina▶
Baba▶
Bitter Sweet
Camille
Camille▶
Celebrity
Charly▶
The Crucified Lovers▶
Damage▶
Danielle Steel's Palomino
Deadman's Curve
Deep End▶
A Different Kind of Love
The Discovery Program
Dying Young
East of Eden▶
East of Eden
Effi Briest▶
El Amor Brujo▶
El Bruto
End of the Road
Enemies, a Love Story▶
Ernie Kovacs: Between the Laughter
Ethan Frome
Evangeline
Everybody's All American
The Fifteen Streets
The Fighting Sullivans▶
First Knight
Flowers of Reverie
Forbidden Choices
Franz
The French Lieutenant's Woman▶
Gandhi▶
Gate of Hell▶
Girl in Black
Golden Boy▶
A Good Day to Die
Hamlet▶
Hamlet
Harmony Lane
Henry IV
House of Cards
Howard's End▶
I, Claudius, Vol. 6: Fool's Luck/A God in Colchester
Il Grido
In Memoriam
Jude the Obscure
Jules and Jim▶
Julius Caesar▶
Julius Caesar
King Lear▶
King Lear
Law of Desire▶
Love Is a Many-Splendored Thing
Love Story▶
Lovespell
Lush Life▶
Macbeth▶
Macbeth
Madame Bovary▶
Margaret's Museum
Maria Candelaria
Marilyn & Bobby: Her Final Affair
Martha and I▶
Mary of Scotland▶
Medea
The Merchant of Venice▶
The Mummy▶
The Nest
The Notorious Lady
Oedipus Rex▶
Othello
Othello▶
Othello
Our Time
Pennies From Heaven▶
Phaedra
Piece of Cake
A Place in the Sun▶
Princess Yang Kwei Fei▶
Queen Bee
Ran▶
The Return of the Native
Romeo and Juliet▶
Romeo and Juliet
Romeo and Juliet▶
Shadowlands▶
Shadows of Forgotten Ancestors▶
Shattered▶
The Shooting Party
Silent Tongue
Stella
Sure Fire
Tess▶
Three Comrades▶
Throne of Blood▶
Tilai
Titanic▶
Tragedy of Flight 103: The Inside Story▶
Trois Couleurs: Bleu▶
Trojan Women
Turkish Delights
Variety▶
A Very Private Affair
The Virgin Spring▶
Voyager▶
The Walls of Malapaga
The Wedding Gift▶
Where Angels Fear to Tread▶
The White Cliffs of Dover▶
White Mile
The White Sister▶
A Woman at Her Window
The Woman Next Door▶
The Wooden Man's Bride
The World According to Garp▶

Trains

see also Subways

Across the Bridge
Alberto Express
Avalanche Express
Before Sunrise
Berlin Express▶
Blood and Steel
Boxcar Bertha
The Brain
Breakheart Pass
Broken Arrow
Cafe Express
Cajon Pass
The Cassandra Crossing
Chattanooga Choo Choo
Closely Watched Trains▶
Color of a Brisk and Leaping Day
Dakota
Danger Lights
Death Train
The Denver & Rio Grande
Detonator
The Dirty Dozen: The Fatal Mission
End of the Line
Express to Terror
Finders Keepers
Flame Over India▶
The Flying Scotsman
From Russia with Love▶
The Fugitive▶
The General▶
The Ghost Train
The Glory Trail
Go Kill and Come Back
Great K & A Train Robbery
The Great Locomotive Chase
The Great Train Robbery▶
The Grey Fox▶
Grit of the Girl Telegrapher/In the Switch Tower
The Harvey Girls▶
Horror Express
Hot Lead & Cold Feet
The Illusion Travels by Streetcar▶
Indiscretion of an American Wife
Inner Sanctum
Interrupted Journey
Jesse James at Bay
The Journey of Natty Gann▶
La Bete Humaine▶
The Lady Eve▶
Lady On a Train▶
The Lady Vanishes▶
The Lady Vanishes
Malcolm
Man Who Loved Cat Dancing
Man Without a Star▶
Midnight Limited
Murder on the Midnight Express
Murder on the Orient Express▶
My Twentieth Century▶
Mystery Mountain
Narrow Margin
Night Train to Munich▶
Night Train to Terror
Night Train to Venice
No. 17▶
The Odyssey of the Pacific
Oh, Mr. Porter
Once Upon a Time in the West▶
Panic on the 5:22
Paris Express
Phantom Express
Plunder Road
Prison Train
Railroaded
Railrodder▶
Red Signals
The Return of Casey Jones
Rhythm on the Range
The Road Home
The Road to Yesterday
Robbery
Romance on the Orient Express
Runaway Train▶
Running Scared
The Saint's Vacation/The Narrow Margin
Saratoga Trunk
Shanghai Express▶
The Silver Streak
Silver Streak▶
The Sleeping Car
Sleeping Car to Trieste
Some Like It Hot▶
Strangers on a Train▶
Subway
A Tale of Winter
Terror Train
Three for Bedroom C
3:10 to Yuma▶
Throw Momma from the Train▶
Thunder Over Texas
Torture Train
Tough Guys
Tracks
The Train▶
The Train Killer
Train Robbers
Train to Tombstone
Two Weeks to Live
Under Siege 2: Dark Territory
Union Pacific▶
Von Ryan's Express▶
Warm Nights on a Slow-Moving Train
Wild Engine/Mistaken Orders
Without Reservations
Zentropa

Transvestites & Transsexuals

see Gender Bending

Trapped with a Killer!

see also Psychotics/ Sociopaths

Adrift
Alien Terminator
Blind Witness
Blink
Blood at Sundown
Blood Bride
Copycat
Dead Calm▶
Deadbolt
Extremities
Eye of the Needle
Eyes of the Beholder
Fatal Attraction▶
Headless Body in Topless Bar
Hider in the House
Kalifornia
Lifepod
The Maddening
Manhunter▶
Misery▶
Mute Witness
Narrow Margin
Pacific Heights▶
The Penthouse
The Shining
The Silence of the Lambs▶
Slaughter of the Innocents
The Terror
Through the Eyes of a Killer
The Tie That Binds
Tracks of a Killer
Undertow
Unveiled
Voyage
Wait Until Dark▶
What's the Matter with Helen?
When a Stranger Calls
When a Stranger Calls Back

Treasure Hunt

Abbott and Costello Meet the Mummy
Adventure of the Action Hunters
The Adventurers
All the Brothers Were Valiant
Blue Jeans and Dynamite
Cabo Blanco
Call of the Wild
City Slickers 2: The Legend of Curly's Gold
Comin' Round the Mountain
Curse of the Crystal Eye
Cutthroat Island
Enemy Gold
Ernest Rides Again
Finger on the Trigger
Girls in Prison
Gold Diggers: The Secret of Bear Mountain
The Goonies
Greedy
Green Fire
Hear No Evil
Hunters of the Golden Cobra
Inside Out
The Jewel of the Nile
Kelly's Heroes
Klondike Fever
Legends of the North
Les Aventuriers
Lust in the Dust▶
Max is Missing
The Mermaids of Tiburon
Muppet Treasure Island
My Family Treasure
One-Eyed Soldiers
Operation Golden Phoenix
Pattern for Plunder
The Phantom of the Range
Romancing the Stone▶
Rudyard Kipling's The Jungle Book
The Secret of the Golden Eagle
Secret of the Ice Cave
Shadow of Chikara
Tarzan's Secret Treasure
Terror on Alcatraz
That Man from Rio
There Goes the Neighborhood
Thieves of Fortune
Tom and Huck▶
Treasure Island▶
Treasure Island
The Treasure of Jamaica Reef
The Treasure of Matecumbe
The Treasure of the Amazon
Treasure of the Four Crowns
Treasure of the Golden Condor
Treasure of the Sierra Madre▶
Treasure of the Yankee Zephyr
The Treasure Seekers
Trespass
Uninvited
Warrior Spirit
Whistling in Dixie
The Wrong Road

Trees & Forests

see also Good Earth; Wilderness

Big Trees▶
The Burning Season▶
Dr. Tarr's Torture Dungeon
Equinox▶
Evil Dead
Fatal Passion
Himatsuri▶
Hole in the Sky
The Ice Flood
King of the Forest Rangers
Lassie: Adventures of Neeka
Les Grandes Gueules
Lunatic

Mr. Sycamore
The Night Brings Charlie
Redwood Curtain
Redwood Forest Trail
Surfacing
Where the Rivers Flow North
The Wizard of Oz▶

True Crime

see also Crime & Criminals; This is Your Life; True Stories

At Close Range▶
Ballad of Gregorio Cortez▶
Beyond Reasonable Doubt
Billionaire Boys Club
Black Oak Conspiracy
Black Panther
Bluebeard▶
Boomerang▶
The Boston Strangler
Chicago Joe & the Showgirl
Citizen X▶
Compulsion▶
Cordelia
Danger of Love
Dead Wrong: The John Evans Story
Death Scream
The Deliberate Stranger▶
Dick Turpin
Dillinger
Dr. Petiot
Double-Crossed
Echoes in the Darkness
The Elegant Criminal
The Executioner's Song
The Falcon and the Snowman▶
Final Appeal
Getting Gotti
Great Gold Swindle
The Great St. Louis Bank Robbery
Headless Body in Topless Bar
Helter Skelter
The Hillside Strangler
Honor Thy Father and Mother: The True Story of the Menendez Brothers
I Can't Sleep
L'Appat
Mad Dog Morgan
The Man from the Pru
The Man in the Attic
McVicar
Mrs. Soffel
Money Movers
Murder in Coweta County
Murder in New Hampshire: The Pamela Smart Story
Murder in Texas▶
Murder So Sweet
Murph the Surf
Normal Life
Nowhere to Run
The O.J. Simpson Story
The Onion Field▶
The People vs. Jean Harris▶
The Preppie Murder
Prince of the City▶
The Pursuit of D.B. Cooper
Rainbow Warrior
Rampage
Rule #3
Sister My Sister
Squizzy Taylor
Stalking Laura
Swoon▶
Till Murder Do Us Part
Too Young to Die
Triple Cross▶
Undercover Cop
The Untouchables▶
Verne Miller
The Zodiac Killer

True Stories

see also This is Your Life; True Crime

The Abduction of Kari Swenson
Above and Beyond▶
The Accused▶
Act of Vengeance
Adam▶
The Adventures of Nellie Bly
After the Promise
After the Shock
Afterburn▶
Against the Wall▶
Al Capone▶
The Alamo▶
Alamo Bay
Alive
All Mine to Give
All the President's Men▶
Alvarez Kelly
The Ambush Murders
Amelia Earhart: The Final Flight
An American Story
The Amityville Horror
Amor Bandido
The Amy Fisher Story
And I Alone Survived
And the Band Played On▶
Andersonville▶
Andre
The Ann Jillian Story
Anna and the King of Siam▶
Apollo 13▶
Apprentice to Murder
Archer's Adventure
Art for Teachers of Children
The Ascent
Assault at West Point: The Court-Martial of Johnson Whittaker
The Assisi Underground
At Close Range▶
The Attic: The Hiding of Anne Frank
Attica▶
Au Revoir Les Enfants▶
Awakening of Candra
Awakenings▶
Away All Boats
Backbeat▶
Bad Blood
Badge of the Assassin
Badlands▶
Ballad in Blue
Ballad of Gregorio Cortez▶
The Ballad of Little Jo
Balto
The Basketball Diaries
Bataan
Battle Hell
Battle Hymn
Battle of the Eagles
Beautiful Dreamers
Beloved Infidel
Beyond Reasonable Doubt
Beyond the Next Mountain
Big Mo
The Big Red One▶
Bill▶
Bill: On His Own▶
Bitter Harvest▶
Black Oak Conspiracy
Black Panther
Blind Ambition
Blood Clan
Bonnie & Clyde▶
The Boston Strangler
The Boys of St. Vincent▶
The Bridge
The Bridge at Remagen
Brink's Job▶
Brutal Glory
Burke & Wills
The Burning Bed▶
The Burning Season▶
Cabeza de Vaca▶
Call Northside 777▶
Camel Boy
Camila▶
Can You Hear the Laughter? The Story of Freddie Prinze
Canada's Sweetheart: The Saga of Hal C. Banks
The Canon Operation
The Cantor's Son
The Captain from Koepenick
Carve Her Name with Pride
A Case of Deadly Force▶
Cast the First Stone
Castaway
Casualties of Love: The "Long Island Lolita" Story
Casualties of War▶
Chameleon Street▶
Champions
Chariots of Fire▶
Charlie Grant's War
Charlotte Forten's Mission: Experiment in Freedom▶
The Chase
Chattahoochee
Cheaper by the Dozen▶
Cheyenne Autumn
The Children of An Lac
Children of Fury
China Cry
Christabel
Christian the Lion
Christiane F.▶
Churchill and the Generals
Circle of Power
Citizen X▶
The Climb
Coming Out of the Ice▶
Coming Through
Communion
Confessions of a Serial Killer
Confessions of Tom Harris
Conrack▶
Convicted
Cool Runnings
Cordelia
The Counterfeit Traitor▶
Courage▶
The Court Martial of Billy Mitchell▶
The Court Martial of Jackie Robinson▶
Cowboy▶
The Crash of Flight 401
Crime of Honor
Cry Freedom
A Cry in the Dark▶
Dance with a Stranger▶
Dangerous Life
Dangerous Minds
David and Lisa▶
Dawn!
Day One▶
Dead Ahead: The Exxon Valdez Disaster▶
Dead Ringers▶
Dead Wrong: The John Evans Story
Deadly Business▶
Death of a Centerfold
Death of a Soldier
The Death of Adolf Hitler
The Death of Richie
Death Scream
The Deliberate Stranger▶
Delta Force
Deranged▶
The Diary of Anne Frank▶
Dillinger▶
Dillinger
The Doctor
Dr. Bethune▶
Dog Day Afternoon▶
Donner Pass: The Road to Survival
Don't Cry, It's Only Thunder
Doomsday Gun
Double-Crossed
Double Exposure: The Story of Margaret Bourke-White
The Dove
Drugstore Cowboy▶
Drum Beat
Echoes in the Darkness
Eddie Macon's Run
Edie in Ciao! Manhattan
Edison the Man
The Education of Sonny Carson
Edward and Mrs. Simpson
Egg and I▶
Eight Men Out▶
8 Seconds
84 Charing Cross Road▶
Eleni
The Elephant Man▶
Elvira Madigan▶
Elvis and Me
Elvis: The Movie
The Emerald Forest▶
Eminent Domain
Empire of the Sun▶
Encounter with the Unknown
Endangered Species
Enemy of Women
The Enforcer
An Englishman Abroad▶
Enigma Secret
Enjo
Enola Gay: The Men, the Mission, the Atomic Bomb
Enter Laughing
The Entity
Eric▶
The Ernest Green Story
Escape from Sobibor▶
Europa, Europa▶
Evel Knievel
Every Man for Himself & God Against All▶
The Execution of Private Slovik▶
Execution of Raymond Graham
The Executioner's Song
Exodus▶
Extreme Justice
Eye of the Octopus
Eye on the Sparrow
The Falcon and the Snowman▶
False Arrest
Farinelli
Fast Company
Fat Man and Little Boy
Fatal Vision
The Father Clements Story
The FBI Murders▶
The FBI Story▶
Fear Strikes Out▶
Fifth Day of Peace
Fighting Father Dunne
Fighting Seabees
The Fighting Sullivans▶
The Final Days
Final Warning
Fire and Rain
Fire in the Sky
Fitzcarraldo▶
The Fixer▶
Flight of the Eagle
Forty Days of Musa Dagh
Foul Play
Frances▶
Francis Gary Powers: The True Story of the U-2 Spy
Gaby: A True Story▶
Gentleman Bandit
The George McKenna Story
Geronimo▶
Gideon's Trumpet
The Girl Who Spelled Freedom▶
Girls of the White Orchid
Glory Enough for All: The Discovery of Insulin
Going for the Gold: The Bill Johnson Story
Going Home
Good Evening, Mr. Wallenberg
Goodbye, Miss 4th of July
Goodfellas▶
Gospa
Grain of Sand▶
Grambling's White Tiger
Grave Secrets: The Legacy of Hilltop Drive
The Great Escape▶
Great Gold Swindle
The Great Impostor
The Great Locomotive Chase
The Great Riviera Bank Robbery
The Great Train Robbery▶
The Great Wallendas
The Greek Tycoon
The Grey Fox▶
Gross Misconduct
Guilty of Innocence
Guns of War
The Guyana Tragedy: The Story of Jim Jones
Hanna's War
Hard Choices▶
The Hatfields & the McCoys
He Walked by Night▶
He Who Walks Alone
Heart Like a Wheel
Heartland▶
Heavenly Creatures▶
Heaven's Heroes
Hedd Wyn
Held Hostage
Hell to Eternity
Hellcats of the Navy
Helter Skelter
Henry & June▶
Henry: Portrait of a Serial Killer▶
Hide in Plain Sight▶
The Hiding Place
The Highest Honor
The Hindenburg
Holy Terror
A Home of Our Own
Honeymoon Killers▶
Honor Thy Father
Honor Thy Father and Mother: The True Story of the Menendez Brothers
Hoodlum Empire
The Hoodlum Priest▶
The Horse Soldiers
Hostages▶
The House on Garibaldi Street
The House on Todville Road
The Hunt for the Night Stalker
The Hunter
I Am a Fugitive from a Chain Gang▶
I Love You to Death
I, the Worst of All
I Will Fight No More Forever▶
If You Could See What I Hear
I'm Dancing as Fast as I Can
The Impossible Spy▶
In Cold Blood▶
In Pursuit of Honor
In the Line of Duty: Ambush in Waco
In the Mood
In the Name of the Father▶
In Which We Serve▶
Indictment: The McMartin Trial▶
Infernal Trio
The Infiltrator
Inherit the Wind▶
The Inn of the Sixth Happiness▶
The Inner Circle▶
Inside the Third Reich
Interrupted Melody▶
Iron Will
Ironclads
Island of the Blue Dolphins
It's Good to Be Alive
It's My Party
Izzy & Moe
The Jayne Mansfield Story
Jenny's War
The Jesse Owens Story
Jesus Christ, Superstar▶
JFK▶
Jo Jo Dancer, Your Life is Calling
Joni
Journey of Hope▶
Journeys from Berlin/1971
Judge Horton and the Scottsboro Boys
Judgment in Berlin
Julia▶
Justin Morgan Had a Horse
Kidco
The Killing Fields▶
A Killing in a Small Town▶
King of the Wind
Knute Rockne: All American▶
Korczak▶
The Krays▶
Ladies They Talk About
Lady Jane▶
Lady of the House
Ladybird, Ladybird▶

Larry
The Last American Hero▶
The Last Days of Dolwyn
The Last Five Days
Last Flight Out: A True Story
The Last Place on Earth
The Last Supper▶
The Late Shift
Lean on Me▶
The Legend of Blood Castle
Legend of Boggy Creek
Let Him Have It▶
Lethal Lolita—Amy Fisher: My Story
Life & Times of Grizzly Adams
Little Boy Lost
Little Gloria...Happy at Last
Little Heroes
Little Laura & Big John
A Little Stiff
Lone Star Kid
The Long Island Four
Lorenzo's Oil▶
Lost
Lost Boundaries
The Lost One
Love Leads the Way
Love, Lies and Murder
Lovey: A Circle of Children 2
M. Butterfly
Ma Barker's Killer Brood
Machine Gun Kelly
Mad Dog Morgan
M.A.D.D.: Mothers Against Drunk Driving
Madeleine
Madman
Malaya
A Man Escaped▶
The Man Who Never Was▶
Manhunt for Claude Dallas
Marciano
Marianne and Juliane▶
Marie▶
Mark Twain and Me
Marked Woman▶
Mary White
Mask▶
Massacre in Rome
Mata Hari▶
Matewan▶
A Matter of Life and Death
Mayerling▶
Mayerling
The McConnell Story
Melvin and Howard▶
Memphis Belle▶
Midnight Express▶
Miracle of Our Lady of Fatima
The Miracle Worker▶
Missing▶
Mission of the Shark▶
Mrs. R's Daughter
Mrs. Soffel
Mr. & Mrs. Loving▶
Mr. Horn
Molly Maguires
Money for Nothing
Money Movers
Mother Joan of the Angels▶
A Mother's Prayer
Mountain Man
The Mozart Story
Murder in Coweta County
Murder In the First
Murder in the Old Red Barn
The Murder of Mary Phagan▶
Murder One
Murder Ordained
Murph the Surf
Mutiny on the Bounty▶
My Darling Clementine▶
My Left Foot▶
My Pleasure Is My Business
The Mystery of Alexina
The Mystery of the Mary Celeste
Naked in the Sun
Nancy Astor
The Nasty Girl▶
The Neon Empire
Night Ambush
Night Crossing
A Night to Remember▶
Nightmare at 43 Hillcrest
Nitti: The Enforcer
Norma Rae▶
Normal Life
Not Without My Daughter
Nowhere to Run
Nurse Edith Cavell▶
Old Gringo
Olivier, Olivier▶
On Wings of Eagles
One Against the Wind▶
One in a Million: The Ron LeFlore Story
One That Got Away▶
The Onion Field▶
Operation Amsterdam
Operation Haylift
Operation Thunderbolt
Opposing Force
The Ordeal of Dr. Mudd▶
The Other Side of the Mountain
The Ox
Pancho Barnes
Passion in Paradise
The Passion of Joan of Arc▶
Pat Garrett & Billy the Kid▶
Paths of Glory▶
Patton▶
Patty Hearst
Pete Townshend: White City
Phar Lap
Philby, Burgess and MacLean: Spy Scandal of the Century
A Place for Annie
Playing for Time▶
Portrait of a Rebel: Margaret Sanger
The Positively True Adventures of the Alleged Texas Cheerleader-Murdering Mom▶
The Preppie Murder
Pressure Point▶
Prick Up Your Ears▶
Prince of the City▶
Princess Caraboo
A Private Matter▶
The Prize Pulitzer
Promised a Miracle
PT 109
Quarterback Princess
A Question of Attribution
Question of Faith
Question of Honor
Qui Etes Vous, Mr. Sorge?
Quilombo
Raid on Entebbe▶
Rainbow Drive
Rape and Marriage: The Rideout Case
Reach for the Sky
A Real American Hero
Reckless Disregard
Reds▶
Reilly: Ace of Spies▶
The Return of Martin Guerre▶
Reversal of Fortune▶
Ring of Bright Water▶
Ring of Terror
Riot in Cell Block 11▶
River's Edge▶
The Road to Galveston▶
Rodeo Girl
Roe vs. Wade▶
Roswell: The U.F.O. Cover-Up
Ruby
Rudy
The Rumor Mill
A Rumor of War▶
Runaway Father
The Runner Stumbles
Running Brave
Sacco & Vanzetti
Sadat
St. Helen's, Killer Volcano
The St. Valentine's Day Massacre
Sakharov▶
Samaritan: The Mitch Snyder Story▶
Samurai 1: Musashi Miyamoto▶
Samurai 2: Duel at Ichijoji Temple▶
Samurai 3: Duel at Ganryu Island▶
Savage Attraction
Scandal▶
The Scarlet & the Black
Schindler's List▶
Sea Gypsies
Sea Wolves
The Search for Bridey Murphy
Searching for Bobby Fischer▶
Secret Weapon
Seizure: The Story of Kathy Morris
Separate But Equal▶
Sergeant Matlovich vs. the U.S. Air Force
Sergeant York▶
Sexual Intent
Shadow on the Sun
Shadowlands▶
Shattered Dreams
Shattered Vows
A Shining Season▶
Shout at the Devil
The Sicilian
Sid & Nancy▶
Silence of the North
Silent Victim
Silent Victory: The Kitty O'Neil Story▶
Silkwood▶
The Singing Nun
Six Degrees of Separation
633 Squadron
Skeezer
Skin
The Slender Thread▶
Small Sacrifices
Sniper▶
So Proudly We Hail▶
Soldier Blue
Solo
The Son of the Shark
The Sound of Music▶
Spartacus▶
Spirit of St. Louis▶
The Spirit of West Point
Springfield Rifle
Springhill
Squizzy Taylor
Stand and Deliver▶
Star 80
Stealing Heaven
Stevie
Storm and Sorrow
The Story of Dr. Wassell
The Stratton Story▶
Street Smart
The Sugarland Express▶
Sugartime
Switched at Birth
The Taking of Flight 847: The Uli Derickson Story▶
Teamster Boss: The Jackie Presser Story▶
The Ten Million Dollar Getaway
10 Rillington Place▶
Ten Who Dared
The Terry Fox Story▶
The Thin Blue Line▶
Thirty Seconds Over Tokyo▶
A Thousand Heroes
Thousand Pieces of Gold▶
Three Came Home▶
The Three Faces of Eve▶
Till Death Do Us Part
Till the Clouds Roll By
Time Flies When You're Alive
Titanic▶
To Catch a Killer▶
To Heal a Nation
To Kill a Priest
Toast of New York▶
Touched by Love
Town that Dreaded Sundown
Tragedy of Flight 103: The Inside Story▶
The Triangle Factory Fire Scandal
Triple Cross▶
Triumph of the Spirit▶
True Confessions▶
The Tuskegee Airmen▶
29th Street
Tyson
Vengeance Is Mine▶
Violette▶
Voyage of Terror: The Achille Lauro Affair
Voyage of the Damned▶
Walking Tall
Walking Tall: Part 2
Walking Tall: The Final Chapter
Walking Through the Fire
The Wall▶
The Wannsee Conference▶
The Wedding Gift▶
Wedding in Blood▶
Weeds▶
What's Love Got to Do with It?
When Hell Was in Session▶
White Mile
White Mischief▶
The White Rose▶
The Wild Child▶
Wild Hearts Can't Be Broken▶
Will: G. Gordon Liddy
A Winner Never Quits
Without a Trace
A Woman at War
A Woman Called Golda▶
The Woman He Loved
Woman With a Past
Wooden Horse▶
A World Apart▶
The Wrong Man▶
The Young Poisoner's Handbook▶
Yours, Mine & Ours
Yuri Nosenko, KGB
The Zodiac Killer
Zoot Suit▶
Zulu

TV Movies

ABC Stage 67: Truman Capote's A Christmas Memory
The Abduction of Kari Swenson
Abduction of St. Anne
Abigail's Party
Above Suspicion
Abraham
Acceptable Risks
Acorn People
Act of Passion: The Lost Honor of Kathryn Beck
Act of Vengeance
Acting on Impulse
Adam▶
Adrift
The Adultress
The Adventures of Huckleberry Finn
The Adventures of Nellie Bly
The Adventures of Tom Sawyer
The Affair▶
The Affair
An Affair in Mind
The Affair of the Pink Pearl
African Journey
After Pilkington
After the Promise
After the Rehearsal▶
After the Shock
Afterburn▶
Afterward
Against the Wall▶
Air Hawk
The Alamo: Thirteen Days to Glory
Alexander: The Other Side of Dawn
Alice to Nowhere
Alien Nation: Dark Horizon
Aliens Are Coming
All God's Children
All My Sons▶
All Quiet on the Western Front
All the Kind Strangers
All the Rivers Run
All You Need Is Cash▶
Almost Partners
Alone in the Neon Jungle
Amanda and the Alien
The Amazing Howard Hughes
The Amazing Spider-Man
Amazing Stories
The Amazons
Amber Waves
The Ambush Murders
Amelia Earhart: The Final Flight
An American Christmas Carol
America's Dream▶
Amityville 4
Amos
The Amy Fisher Story
Anastasia: The Mystery of Anna
Anatomy of a Seduction
Anatomy of Terror
And a Nightingale Sang
And Baby Makes Six
And I Alone Survived
And the Band Played On▶
And the Children Shall Lead
Andersonville▶
The Andersonville Trial▶
An Angel at My Table▶
Angel City
Angel on My Shoulder
The Ann Jillian Story
Anna Karenina
Anne of Avonlea▶
Anne of Green Gables▶
Annie: A Royal Adventure
Annie O
Annie Oakley
Another Pair of Aces: Three of a Kind▶
Antonia and Jane▶
Ants
Anzacs: The War Down Under▶
Apology
Arch of Triumph
Archer: The Fugitive from the Empire
Are You in the House Alone?
Are You Lonesome Tonight
Around the World in 80 Days
As Is
As Summers Die
Assassin
The Assassination Run
Assault and Matrimony
Assault at West Point: The Court-Martial of Johnson Whittaker
Attack of the 50 Ft. Woman
The Attic: The Hiding of Anne Frank
Attica▶
The Autobiography of Miss Jane Pittman▶
The Avenging Angel
Awakening of Candra
Babel▶
Babes in Toyland
Baby Girl Scott
Baby of the Bride
Babycakes
The Babysitter
Back Home
Back to Hannibal: The Return of Tom Sawyer and Huckleberry Finn
Backfield in Motion
Backtrack▶
Bad Ronald▶
The Bad Seed
Badge of the Assassin
Baffled
Baja Oklahoma
Bang the Drum Slowly
Barbarians at the Gate▶
The Barbary Coast
Bare Essentials
Barefoot in Athens
The Baron and the Kid
Based on an Untrue Story
The Bastard
Battle of the Bullies
Battling for Baby
Baywatch the Movie: Forbidden Paradise

Fer-De-Lance
Fergie & Andrew: Behind Palace Doors
Fever
A Few Moments with Buster Keaton and Laurel and Hardy▶
The Fifteen Streets
The Fig Tree
A Fight for Jenny
Final Appeal
The Final Cut▶
The Final Days
Final Shot: The Hank Gathers Story
Final Verdict
Final Warning
Fine Things
Finessing the King
Finish Line
Finnegan Begin Again
Fire
Fire and Rain
The Fire Next Time
Fireball Forward
Firehouse
Firesign Theatre Presents Nick Danger in the Case of the Missing Yolks
First Affair
First & Ten
First & Ten: The Team Scores Again
First Degree
The First Olympics: Athens 1896
Five Miles to Midnight
The Five of Me
The $5.20 an Hour Dream
The Flame Is Love
The Flame Trees of Thika▶
A Flash of Green
Flatbed Annie and Sweetiepie: Lady Truckers
Flight of Black Angel
Flood!
Florida Straits
Follow the River
For Better or Worse
For Heaven's Sake
For Ladies Only
For Love or Money
For Richer, For Poorer
For the Love of It
For Us, the Living▶
For Your Love Only
Forbidden
Forbidden Love
Force Five
Force of Evil
Foreign Affairs▶
Forever
Forever Young
The Forgotten
Forgotten Prisoners
Fortress
Fortunes of War▶
Four Days in July
Four Eyes and Six Guns
The Four Feathers
Foxfire▶
Frame by Frame
France/Tour/Detour/Deux/Enfants▶
The Franchise Affair
Francis Gary Powers: The True Story of the U-2 Spy
Frankenstein
Freedom Road
French Silk
Friendly Fire▶
A Friendship in Vienna
Frog
Frogs!
From Here to Eternity
From Here to Maternity
From the Dead of Night▶
From the Mixed-Up Files of Mrs. Basil E. Frankweiler
Fugitive Among Us
Fulfillment
Full Body Massage
Full Exposure: The Sex Tape Scandals
Future Cop
Gallowglass▶
The Gambler Returns: The Luck of the Draw
Gangster Wars
The Gathering
The Gathering: Part 2
Genghis Cohn
Gentleman Bandit
The George McKenna Story
George Washington
George Washington: The Forging of a Nation
Geronimo▶
Get Christie Love!
Get Smart, Again!
Getting Gotti
Getting Out
Getting Physical
Ghostwriter
Gideon's Trumpet
The Gift of Love
A Girl of the Limberlost
The Girl Who Spelled Freedom▶
The Girls of Huntington House
Girls of the White Orchid
The Gladiator
The Glass House▶
The Glitter Dome
Glitz
Glory Enough for All: The Discovery of Insulin
God Bless the Child▶
Gold of the Amazon Women
Goldenrod
Goliath Awaits
Gone are the Days
A Good Day to Die
The Good Father▶
The Good Fight
The Good Old Boys
Goodbye, Miss 4th of July
Gore Vidal's Billy the Kid
Gore Vidal's Lincoln
Gotham▶
The Grace Kelly Story
Grambling's White Tiger
Grand Isle
Grand Tour: Disaster in Time
The Grass is Always Greener Over the Septic Tank
The Great American Sex Scandal
Great American Traffic Jam
The Great Elephant Escape
The Great Escape 2: The Untold Story
Great Expectations
Great Expectations▶
The Great Los Angeles Earthquake
Great Movie Stunts & the Making of Raiders of the Lost Ark
The Great Wallendas
Green Eyes▶
Griffin and Phoenix: A Love Story
Grown Ups
Gryphon
The Guardian
A Guide for the Married Woman
Guilty of Innocence
Gulag
Gulliver's Travels
A Gun in the House
Gunsmoke: Return to Dodge
The Guyana Tragedy: The Story of Jim Jones
Gypsy
The Gypsy Warriors
The Habitation of Dragons
Half Slave, Half Free
The Halfback of Notre Dame
Halloween with the Addams Family
Hands of a Murderer
Hands of a Stranger
The Hanged Man
Happily Ever After
Happy Since I Met You▶
Hard Frame
Hard Knox
Hard Labour
Hard Rain-The Tet 1968
Hardhat & Legs
Harem
The Hatfields & the McCoys
The Haunting of Barney Palmer
Haunting of Harrington House
Haunting of Sarah Hardy
The Haunting Passion
Haunts of the Very Rich
Having It All
He Who Walks Alone
Heads
The Hearst and Davies Affair
Heart of a Champion: The Ray Mancini Story
Heart of Darkness
Heartbreak House
Heat Wave▶
Heck's Way Home
Hector's Bunyip
Heidi
Heidi▶
The Heidi Chronicles
The Heist
Held Hostage
Help Wanted: Male
Helter Skelter
The Henderson Monster
Her Life as a Man
Hercules, Prisoner of Evil
Hi-Di-Hi
High Desert Kill
High Noon: Part 2
High School USA
Hill Number One
The Hillside Strangler
Hired Hand
Hiroshima▶
Hiroshima Maiden
The History of White People in America
The History of White People in America: Vol. 2
Hit Lady
Hit Woman: The Double Edge
Hitchhiker 2
Hitchhiker 3
Hitchhiker 4
Hitler's Daughter
The Hobbit▶
The Hoboken Chicken Emergency
Hobo's Christmas
Hobson's Choice
Hold the Dream
Hole in the Sky
The Hollywood Detective
Holocaust▶
Holocaust Survivors...Remembrance of Love
Home at Last
Home for Christmas
Home for the Holidays
Home Sweet Home
Home to Stay
Homecoming
Homecoming: A Christmas Story
Homeward Bound
Honeyboy
Honor Thy Father
Honor Thy Father and Mother: The True Story of the Menendez Brothers
A Horse for Danny
The Horse Without a Head
Horsemasters
Hostage for a Day
The Hostage Tower
Hostages▶
Hotel du Lac
Hotel Room
Hotline
The Hound of London
House of Cards▶
The House of Dies Drear
The House of Eliott
The House of Lurking Death
The House on Garibaldi Street
A House Without a Christmas Tree
How Many Miles to Babylon?
How the West was Fun
How to Be a Perfect Person in Just Three Days
How to Break Up a Happy Divorce
How to Pick Up Girls
Huckleberry Finn
Hullabaloo Over Georgie & Bonnie's Pictures
Humanoid Defender
The Hunchback of Notre Dame▶
The Hunt for the Night Stalker
Hunter
Hurricane
Hush Little Baby, Don't You Cry
Hustling▶
I, Claudius, Vol. 1: A Touch of Murder/Family Affairs
I, Claudius, Vol. 2: Waiting in the Wings/What Shall We Do With Claudius?
I, Claudius, Vol. 3: Poison is Queen/Some Justice
I, Claudius, Vol. 4: Queen of Heaven/Reign of Terror
I, Claudius, Vol. 5: Zeus, By Jove!/Hail Who?
I, Claudius, Vol. 6: Fool's Luck/A God in Colchester
I, Claudius, Vol. 7: Old King Log
I Heard the Owl Call My Name
I Know Why the Caged Bird Sings▶
I Married a Centerfold
I Posed for Playboy
I Will Fight No More Forever▶
Ike
The Image
The Impossible Spy▶
The Imposter
In a Stranger's Hand
In Love with an Older Woman
In the Custody of Strangers▶
In the Line of Duty: Ambush in Waco
In This House of Brede▶
The Incident▶
Incident at Deception Ridge
An Inconvenient Woman
The Incredible Hulk Returns
The Incredible Journey of Dr. Meg Laurel▶
The Incredible Rocky Mountain Race
Indictment: The McMartin Trial▶
Indiscreet
The Infiltrator
Initiation of Sarah
Inside the Third Reich
Intimate Contact▶
Intimate Power
Intimate Stranger
Intimate Strangers
Into the Badlands
Into the Homeland
Into Thin Air▶
Intrigue
Intruder Within
The Invaders
Invasion of Privacy
Invincible Mr. Disraeli
Invitation to Hell
Iran: Days of Crisis
Ironclads
Is There Life Out There?
Islands
It Came Upon a Midnight Clear
It's a Bundyful Life
It's Good to Be Alive
Ivanhoe
Ivory Hunters
Izzy & Moe
J. Edgar Hoover
Jack the Ripper▶
Jackson County Jail
The Jacksons: An American Dream
Jacob
Jacob Have I Loved
Jacqueline Bouvier Kennedy
Jailbait: Betrayed By Innocence
Jamaica Inn
James Dean
Jane Doe
Jane Eyre▶
The Jayne Mansfield Story
Jealousy
Jekyll and Hyde
Jenny's War
The Jericho Mile
Jesse
The Jesse Owens Story
Jesus of Nazareth▶
The Jewel in the Crown
The JFK Conspiracy
JFK: Reckless Youth
John & Yoko: A Love Story
Johnny Appleseed
Johnny Belinda
Johnny Shiloh
Johnny We Hardly Knew Ye
Johnny's Girl
Joseph
Journey
Judge Horton and the Scottsboro Boys
Judgment▶
Just Me & You
Justice
K-9000
Kansas City Massacre
Katherine
Kavik the Wolf Dog
Keep the Change
Keeping On
Kennedy
Kenny Rogers as the Gambler
Kenny Rogers as the Gambler, Part 2: The Adventure Continues
Kenny Rogers as the Gambler, Part 3: The Legend Continues
Kent State
The Key to Rebecca
Kicks
The Kid from Left Field
The Kid Who Loved Christmas
The Kid with the 200 I.Q.
Killer on Board
Killer with Two Faces
Killing at Hell's Gate
Killing Floor
A Killing in a Small Town▶
The Killing Mind
Killing Stone
Killjoy
Kim
King▶
Kingfish: A Story of Huey P. Long
Kiss of a Killer
Kiss of Death
Kissinger and Nixon
Kojak: The Belarus File
Konrad
Kung Fu: The Movie
Kurt Vonnegut's Harrison Bergeron
Kurt Vonnegut's Monkey House
Lady from Yesterday
Lady Mobster
The Lady's Not for Burning
Laguna Heat
Lakota Woman: Siege at Wounded Knee
Lantern Hill
Larry
Larry McMurtry's Streets of Laredo▶
Lassie: The Miracle
Lassie's Great Adventure
The Last Best Year
Last Chase
Last Cry for Help
Last Days of Frank & Jesse James

Queen of the Stardust Ballroom▶
Queenie
A Question of Attribution
A Question of Guilt
Question of Honor
A Question of Love▶
The Quick and the Dead
Quo Vadis
Race to Freedom: The Story of the Underground Railroad
Radio Inside
Rage▶
Rage of Angels
Rage of Angels: The Story Continues
Raid on Entebbe▶
The Railway Station Man▶
Rainbow
Rainbow Drive
A Raisin in the Sun▶
Rape and Marriage: The Rideout Case
Ratings Game
Rattlers
A Real American Hero
The Rebels
Reckless Disregard
Red Alert
Red Flag: The Ultimate Game
Red King, White Knight
The Red Pony▶
Red Shoe Diaries
Red Shoe Diaries 3: Another Woman's Lipstick
Red Shoe Diaries 4: Auto Erotica
Redwood Curtain
Reflections of Murder
Rehearsal for Murder
Reilly: Ace of Spies▶
The Return of Eliot Ness
Return of Frank Cannon
The Return of the King
Return of the Man from U.N.C.L.E.
The Return of the Native
Return of the Rebels
Return to Earth
Return to Fantasy Island
Return to Lonesome Dove
Return to Mayberry
Revenge of the Nerds 4: Nerds in Love
Revenge of the Stepford Wives
Rich Man, Poor Man▶
Ride the Wind
Riders of the Purple Sage
Riding High
Right of Way
Rio Diablo
The Rise & Rise of Daniel Rocket
The Rise of Louis XIV▶
Rising Son▶
Rita Hayworth: The Love Goddess
The Rite
Riverbend
The Road to Galveston▶
Robbers of the Sacred Mountain
Robin Hood▶
Robin Hood...The Legend: Herne's Son
Robin Hood...The Legend: Robin Hood and the Sorcerer
Robin Hood...The Legend: The Swords of Wayland
Robin Hood...The Legend: The Time of the Wolf
Rocket to the Moon
Rodeo Girl
Roe vs. Wade▶
Rogue Male
Roll of Thunder, Hear My Cry
Romance on the Orient Express
The Room
Roommate
Roots▶
Roots: The Gift
Roots: The Next Generation▶
The Rose and the Jackal
Roseanne: An Unauthorized Biography
Rosie: The Rosemary Clooney Story
Roswell: The U.F.O. Cover-Up
Roughnecks
The Rousters
Rubberface
Rudolph the Red-Nosed Reindeer
The Rumor Mill
A Rumor of War▶
Runaway
The Runaway Barge
Runaway Father
Running Against Time
Running Blind
Running Mates▶
The Sacketts
Sadat
Saigon: Year of the Cat
Sakharov▶
Samaritan: The Mitch Snyder Story▶
Samson and Delilah
Sarah, Plain and Tall▶
Satan's School for Girls
The Savage Bees
Savage Run▶
Savages
Say Goodbye, Maggie Cole
Scandal in a Small Town
The Scarlet & the Black
The Scarlet Pimpernel▶
Scarlett
Scene of the Crime
Scott Turow's The Burden of Proof
Scout's Honor
Scruples
The Sea Wolf
Second Chance
The Secret Garden
The Secret Garden▶
Secret Passions
Secret Weapon
Secret Weapons
Secrets
Secrets of a Married Man
Secrets of Three Hungry Wives
Seduced
See How She Runs▶
The Seekers
Senior Trip
Sense & Sensibility
Separate But Equal▶
Separate Tables
September Gun
Sergeant Matlovich vs. the U.S. Air Force
Servants of Twilight
Sessions
Sex and the Single Parent
The Shadow Box▶
The Shadow Riders
Shame
Sharon's Secret
Sharpe's Battle
Sharpe's Company
Sharpe's Eagle
Sharpe's Enemy
Sharpe's Gold
Sharpe's Honour
Sharpe's Rifles
Sharpe's Sword
Shattered Dreams
Shattered Image
Shattered Silence
Shattered Vows
S*H*E
She Waits
The Shell Seekers
Sherlock Holmes: The Master Blackmailer
She's Dressed to Kill
A Shining Season▶
Shogun▶
Shooting Stars
Side Show
Silas Marner▶
Silent Night, Lonely Night
Silent Victory: The Kitty O'Neil Story▶
Silent Witness
Silhouette
Sinatra
Single Bars, Single Women
The Sins of Dorian Gray
The Sister-in-Law
Six Fois Deux/Sur et Sous la Communication▶
Six Wives of Henry VIII▶
Sizzle
Skeezer
Sketch Artist
Sketch Artist 2: Hands That See
Sketches of a Strangler
Skin
Sky Hei$t
Slow Burn
A Small Killing
Small Sacrifices
Smoke
A Smoky Mountain Christmas
Smooth Talk▶
Snatched
Sniper▶
The Snow Queen
Snow White and the Seven Dwarfs
Snowbeast
Snowblind
Sodbusters
Soft and Hard
Soldier in Love
The Solitary Man
Someone I Touched
Something in Common
Sometimes They Come Back
Son of the Morning Star▶
Sooner or Later
Sophia Loren: Her Own Story
Sophisticated Gents▶
Sorry, Wrong Number
S.O.S. Titanic
The Sound and the Silence
Special Bulletin▶
Special Olympics
The Spell
Spenser: Ceremony
Spenser: Pale Kings & Princes
The Spider and the Fly
Spiderman: The Deadly Dust
Spiral Staircase
Spy
Spymaker: The Secret Life of Ian Fleming
Stagecoach
Stalag Luft
Stalin
Stalking Laura
Stamp of a Killer
Standing Tall
Star Trek Bloopers
Starflight One
State of Emergency
Steal the Sky
Steel Cowboy
Stephen King's Golden Years
Stephen King's It
Stephen King's The Langoliers
Stephen King's The Stand
Stephen King's The Tommyknockers
Stigma
Still Not Quite Human
Stone Fox
The Story of David▶
The Story of Jacob & Joseph▶
A Strange and Deadly Occurence
Strange Case of Dr. Jekyll & Mr. Hyde
Strange Interlude
The Stranger
A Stranger is Watching
The Stranger Who Looks Like Me
The Stranger Within
Strangers: The Story of a Mother and Daughter▶
Strapped
A Streetcar Named Desire▶
The Streets of L.A.
Strike Force
The Substitute Wife
Sudie & Simpson▶
Summer Fantasy
Summer of Fear
The Summer of My German Soldier▶
Summer Solstice
A Summer to Remember
Sunburn
Suspect Device
Svengali
Sweet Bird of Youth
Sweet 15
Sweet Hostage
Swimsuit: The Movie
Switched at Birth
Sword of Gideon
Sybil▶
T Bone N Weasel
Tagget
Tails You Live, Heads You're Dead
Tailspin: Behind the Korean Airline Tragedy
Take Your Best Shot
Taken Away
The Taking of Flight 847: The Uli Derickson Story▶
Taking the Heat
A Tale of Two Cities
A Tale of Two Cities▶
Tales from the Crypt
Tales from the Crypt, Vol. 3
Tall, Dark and Deadly
Tarantulas: The Deadly Cargo
Target: Favorite Son
The Tattered Web
Teamster Boss: The Jackie Presser Story▶
Tears in the Rain
Tecumseh: The Last Warrior
Tell Me Where It Hurts
The Ten Million Dollar Getaway
Tender Is the Night
The Tenth Man
Tenth Month
Terror at London Bridge
Terror on the 40th Floor
Terror Out of the Sky
The Terry Fox Story▶
The Testament of Dr. Cordelier▶
Texas
Texas Guns
Texas John Slaughter: Geronimo's Revenge
Texas John Slaughter: Stampede at Bitter Creek
They Watch
Thicker Than Water
Thief
The Thief of Baghdad
Third Degree Burn
Thirteenth Day of Christmas
This Lightning Always Strikes Twice
Thompson's Last Run
The Thorn Birds▶
Threads▶
The Three Little Pigs
Through Naked Eyes
Through the Eyes of a Killer
Thumbelina
Thursday's Game▶
Tidy Endings
Tiger Town
Till Death Do Us Part
Till Murder Do Us Part
Time Flies When You're Alive
A Time for Miracles
Time for Murder
A Time to Live
Timestalkers
The Tin Soldier
To All My Friends on Shore▶
To Catch a Killer▶
To Catch a King
To Dance with the White Dog▶
To Grandmother's House We Go
To Heal a Nation
To Play the King▶
To Race the Wind
Tomorrow's Child
Too Far to Go▶
Too Young to Die
Torn Between Two Lovers
Tornado!
Toughlove
A Town Like Alice
The Tracker
The Trackers
Traffik▶
Trapped
Trapped in Silence
Traveling Man
Treasure Island
The Trial of Lee Harvey Oswald
The Trial of the Incredible Hulk
The Triangle Factory Fire Scandal
Tribes
Tricks of the Trade
Trilogy of Terror
Triplecross
Trouble in Paradise
True West▶
Truman
Truth or Die
The Tuskegee Airmen▶
12:01
21 Hours at Munich▶
24 Hours in a Woman's Life
Twin Peaks
Twirl
Two Fathers' Justice
Two Kinds of Love
Two of a Kind
The Two Worlds of Jenny Logan
Tyson
The Ultimate Imposter
The Unbreakable Alibi
Uncle Tom's Cabin
Under the Biltmore Clock
Undergrads▶
Undertow
Unexplained Laughter
Unnatural Causes▶
Unnatural Pursuits
Uphill All the Way
Urge to Kill
Users
V: The Final Battle
Vanishing Act
The Vegas Strip Wars
Vendetta for the Saint
Vengeance
A Very Brady Christmas
A Very British Coup▶
Victim of Beauty
Victim of Love
Victoria Regina
Vietnam War Story 1
Vietnam War Story 2
Vietnam War Story 3
The Virginia Hill Story
A Vow to Kill
Voyage
Voyage of Terror: The Achille Lauro Affair
The Voyage of the Yes
A Voyage' Round My Father▶
Wagner: The Complete Epic
Wagner: The Movie
Wait Till Your Mother Gets Home
Waiting for the Moon
Walking on Air
Walking Through the Fire
The Waltons: The Christmas Carol
A Waltz Through the Hills
War & Remembrance, Part 1
War & Remembrance, Part 2
War & Remembrance: The Final Chapter, Part 8
War & Remembrance: The Final Chapter, Part 9
War Between the Tates
Washington Mistress
The Water Engine

We are the Children
Web of Deceit
The Wedding Gift▶
Weekend War
Welcome Home
Wet Gold
Whale for the Killing
The Wharf Rat
When a Stranger Calls Back
When Every Day was the Fourth of July
When Hell Was in Session▶
When He's Not a Stranger▶
When the Bough Breaks
When the Dark Man Calls
When the Time Comes
When Your Lover Leaves
Where the Spirit Lives
Which Way Home
White Hot: The Mysterious Murder of Thelma Todd
White Mama▶
White Mile
Who Am I This Time?▶
Who Is the Black Dahlia?▶
Who Killed Baby Azaria?
Who'll Save Our Children?▶
Whoops Apocalypse
Who's Who
The Widow
The Wild and the Free
Wild & Wooly
Wild Horses
Wild Palms
Wild Times
Wild, Wild West Revisited
Wild Women
Wildflower▶
Will: G. Gordon Liddy
Willa
Wilma
Windmills of the Gods
The Winds of Kitty Hawk
The Winds of War
A Winner Never Quits
Witch Hunt
Without Warning: The James Brady Story▶
Witness to the Execution
A Woman Called Golda▶
A Woman Called Moses
The Woman He Loved
The Woman Hunter
Woman in Black
A Woman Named Jackie
A Woman of Substance, Episode 1: Nest of Vipers
A Woman of Substance, Episode 2: The Secret is Revealed
A Woman of Substance, Episode 3: Fighting for the Dream
Woman Undone
The Woman Who Willed a Miracle
Woman With a Past
A Woman's Guide to Adultery
Women & Men: Stories of Seduction
Women of Valor
Words by Heart
World War II: When Lions Roared
World War III
The World's Oldest Living Bridesmaid
The Wrestler
Writer's Block
The Wrong Man
Wyatt Earp: Return to Tombstone
A Year in Provence▶
The Yearling
You Must Remember This
Young Catherine▶
Young Charlie Chaplin
Young Love, First Love
The Young Ones
Your Place or Mine
Yuri Nosenko, KGB
The Zany Adventures of Robin Hood
Zooman▶

TV Pilot Movies

Africa Texas Style
American Dream▶
The Art of Crime
Balboa
Battlestar Galactica
Beverly Hills 90210
The Bionic Woman
Blade in Hong Kong
Blue De Ville
Brass
Buck Rogers in the 25th Century
Call to Glory
China Beach▶
Christy
Columbo: Prescription Murder
The Concrete Cowboys
Conspiracy of Terror
Daring Game
Death Ray 2000
Destination Moonbase Alpha
Doctor Quinn, Medicine Woman
Dr. Strange
ER
Express to Terror
The Flash
Force Five
The Gunfighters
Hawkeye: Premiere Episode
Hercules and the Princess of Troy
Highlander: The Gathering
The Hunted Lady
Hunter
The Incredible Hulk
JAG
Jigsaw
The Kid with the Broken Halo
Kung Fu
L.A. Law▶
Little House on the Prairie▶
Loving
Magnum P.I.: Don't Eat the Snow in Hawaii
Miami Vice
Misfits of Science
Moonlighting
Nick Knight
Night Gallery▶
Our Family Business
Probe
Rags to Riches
Remington Steele, Vol. 1: License to Steele
Riding with Death
RoboCop the Series: The Future of Law Enforcement
Sabrina the Teenage Witch
Sanctuary of Fear
Scarface Mob
Search for the Gods
The Secret Adversary
She's in the Army Now
Skag▶
Smile, Jenny, You're Dead
Space: 1999—Alien Attack▶
Spraggue
Stalk the Wild Child
Star Trek Deep Space Nine: Emissary
Star Trek Voyager: Caretaker
Stark
Strange New World
The Streets of San Francisco▶
Strike Force
Superman & the Mole Men
TekWar
Terraces
Thunder in Paradise
Tour of Duty
V▶
Vegas
Waikiki
Walker: Texas Ranger: One Riot, One Ranger
White Dwarf
The Women of Brewster Place▶

TV Series

The Addams Family
Adventures of Kit Carson
The Adventures of Ozzie & Harriet
The Adventures of Robin Hood
The Adventures of Sherlock Holmes: Hound of the Baskervilles
The Affair of the Pink Pearl
And Now for Something Completely Different▶
Andy Griffith Show
Beauty and the Beast, Episode 1: Once Upon a Time in New York
Best of Eddie Murphy
Best of Ernie Kovacs
The Best of Soap: Jessica's Wonderful Life
The Best of Soap: Who Killed Peter?
The Best of the Kids in the Hall
The Best of the Two Ronnies
The Beverly Hillbillies
Beverly Hills 90210
Beverly Hills 90210: The Graduation
Blake's Seven
Bonanza
Bosom Buddies
The Brady Bunch
The Burns and Allen Show
Car 54, Where Are You?
The Cisco Kid
Combat!
Crime Story: The Complete Saga
Danger Man
Dark Justice
Dark Shadows
Dark Shadows: Episode 1
Davy Crockett and the River Pirates
Davy Crockett, King of the Wild Frontier▶
Death Valley Days: No Gun Behind His Badge
The Defender
The Devlin Connection
Doctor Who: An Unearthly Child
Doctor Who: Cybermen—The Early Years
Dragnet
The Equalizer: Memories of Manon
Family Dog: Complete Series
Fawlty Towers
The Flash 2: Revenge of the Trickster
Flipper
Fu Manchu
The Fugitive: Premiere Episode
The Fugitive: The Final Episode
Gilligan's Island: Meet the Crew
Gunfight at Sandoval
Hill Street Blues, Vol. 1: Hill Street Station
The Hitchhiker
The Honeymooners "Classic 39": TV or Not TV/ Honeymooners Highlights
Honeymooners Hidden Episodes, Vol. 1
I Love Lucy
The Invaders
Jeeves & Wooster: Jeeves' Arrival
Judge Roy Bean
Little Rascals, Book 1
Lone Ranger and the Lost City of Gold
The Loretta Young Show
Lucy and Desi: A Home Movie
The Man from U.N.C.L.E.
M*A*S*H: The Collector's Edition
Maverick: The Collector's Edition
The Mod Squad
Monty Python's Flying Circus
Mork & Mindy
One Step Beyond
Our Gang Comedies
The Outer Limits: Galaxy Being
The Prisoner: Arrival
Prisoner Cell Block H
Professionals
Queen for a Day
Requiem for a Heavyweight▶
Ripping Yarns
Robin Hood: The Movie
The Rockford Files: Backlash of the Hunter
Rocky Jones, Space Ranger
Rocky Jones, Space Ranger: Renegade Satellite
Rumpole of the Bailey
Saturday Night Live
Secret Agent
Smart-Aleck Kill
Snowy River, the MacGregor Saga: The Race
Space: 1999
Space Patrol
Star Trek: The Cage
Star Trek the Next Generation: Encounter at Farpoint
Star Trek 25th Anniversary Special
Tales from Avonlea, Vol. 1: The Journey Begins
Tales from the Darkside
The Trouble with Father
TV's Best Adventures of Superman
The Twilight Zone
Twin Peaks
The Waltons: A Thanksgiving Story
Wanted: Dead or Alive
The White Shadow, Vol. 1
Wild, Wild West Revisited
WKRP in Cincinnati, Vol. 1
Your Show of Shows

Twins

see also Family Ties

After Darkness
Basket Case▶
Basket Case 2
Basket Case 3: The Progeny
Big Business
Bloodlink
Brotherly Love
Chained for Life
City of Shadows
Class of Nuke 'Em High 3: The Good, the Bad and the Subhumanoid
Cobra Woman
The Corsican Brothers
The Crazysitter
Dead Ringers▶
Deadly Twins
Devil's Wedding Night
Double Double Toil and Trouble
The Double Life of Veronique
Double Trouble
Double Vision
Dual Alibi
Equinox
The Eyes, the Mouth
Here Come the Waves▶
How the West was Fun
Instant Kung-Fu Man
Invitation au Voyage
It Takes Two
The Krays▶
Lies of the Twins
Lost Honeymoon
The Man in the Iron Mask▶
Man with a Gun
Mirror Images
Mirror Images 2
Mother Lode
Mountain Fury
Nukie
The Nutt House
The Other▶
Out on a Limb
The Parent Trap
Raising Cain
The Reluctant Agent
Sisters▶
The Sphinx
Start the Revolution Without Me▶
Steal Big, Steal Little
A Stolen Life
Thicker Than Water
To Grandmother's House We Go
Twins
Twins of Evil
Twinsanity
Twinsitters
Wagon's Westward
The Worldly Madonna

Twister!

see also Disaster Flicks

Night of the Twisters
Places in the Heart▶
Tornado!
Twister
The Wizard of Oz
The Wizard of Oz▶

UFOs

see Alien Beings—Benign; Alien Beings—Vicious; Space Operas

Underground

see Avant-Garde

Unexplained Phenomena

The Adventures of Sherlock Holmes: Hound of the Baskervilles
The Amityville Curse
Angel Baby
Beyond the Bermuda Triangle
Black Rainbow▶
Blue Tornado
The Carpathian Eagle
The Carpenter
Carrie▶
Catacombs
Daffy Duck's Quackbusters
Dead Again▶
Dead Zone▶
Delusion
Destiny Turns on the Radio
Die, Monster, Die!
Dream a Little Dream 2
Dying to Remember
Encounter with the Unknown
Endgame
The Entity
Escapes
E.S.P.
Eternal Evil
The Evil Mind
Eyes of Laura Mars
Fire in the Sky
Firestarter
The 4D Man
The Fury
Ghost Chasers
Ghost Town
The Ghosts of Hanley House
Grandma's House
Hangar 18
The Haunting Passion
The House of Seven Corpses
Lisa and the Devil
Lurkers
Maximum Overdrive
Miracle in Rome
Miracle of Our Lady of Fatima
Mondo Balardo
Murphy's Fault
A Name for Evil
The Night Stalker: Two Tales of Terror
Nomads
Out There
Phenomenon
Psychic
The Psychotronic Man

Retribution
Return from Witch Mountain
Roswell: The U.F.O. Cover-Up
Salem's Lot
Scared Stiff▶
Shattered Silence
The Sleeping Car
Spook Busters
The Stranger
Things Happen at Night
The Three Lives of Thomasina▶
The Tin Drum▶
Truly, Madly, Deeply▶
Twin Peaks
The Undead▶
Visions
Visions of Evil
Waiting for the Light
Web of the Spider
The X-Files: Pilot Episode/Deep Throat
X: The Man with X-Ray Eyes▶

Up All Night

see also Vampire Babes; Vampires

After Hours▶
American Graffiti▶
Batman▶
Before Sunrise
Blade Runner▶
Dazed and Confused▶
Escape from New York
From Dusk Till Dawn
Hocus Pocus
Into the Night
Judgment Night
Little Nemo: Adventures in Slumberland
Mannequin

Urban Drama

Above the Rim
American Heart▶
American Me▶
The Asphalt Jungle▶
Bad Attitude
Bad Lieutenant▶
Boyz N the Hood▶
The Bronx War
Carlito's Way▶
City Hall▶
Crossing the Bridge
Cry, the Beloved Country▶
Dangerous Minds
Dead Boyz Can't Fly
Do the Right Thing▶
The Fence
Fly by Night
Fresh
The George McKenna Story
Grand Canyon▶
Heaven is a Playground
Jason's Lyric
Juice
Jungleground
Just Another Girl on the I.R.T.
Love Your Mama
Menace II Society▶
Mi Vida Loca
Money for Nothing
Naked▶
New Jack City
New Jersey Drive
Once Were Warriors▶
Original Gangstas
Out of Sync
Poetic Justice
South Central
Straight Out of Brooklyn
Strange Days▶
Strapped
Street Wars
Sugar Hill
Urban Crossfire
White Man's Burden
Zebrahead▶
Zooman▶

Vacations

American Gothic
The American Scream
An American Werewolf in London▶
Backwoods
Beyond the Door 3
Blame It on Rio
Blondie Takes a Vacation
Body Trouble
Cabin Boy
California Suite▶
Camilla
Cancel My Reservation
Captain Ron
Casual Sex?
City Slickers▶
Claire's Knee▶
Come September
Crackerjack
Dangerous Prey
Dead Cold
Deadly Intruder
Death Stalk
Death Weekend
Deliverance▶
Demon Lust
Devil Wears White
Dirty Dancing▶
Don't Drink the Water
Enchanted April
Far from Home
A Far Off Place
The Fatal Image
Frantic▶
Fraternity Vacation
Gidget Goes Hawaiian
Gidget Goes to Rome
Grotesque
Harry and the Hendersons
The Hills Have Eyes
Home Alone▶
Home Alone 2: Lost in New York
Hot Pursuit
The Inkwell
Judgment Day
Killing at Hell's Gate
La Collectionneuse
Lena's Holiday
Lie Down with Dogs
The Long, Long Trailer
The Lunatic
Magic in the Water
Magic Kid
The Man Who Knew Too Much▶
The Man Who Knew Too Much
Mr. Hobbs Takes a Vacation▶
Mr. Hulot's Holiday▶
A Month by the Lake
My Father the Hero
My Grandpa is a Vampire
National Lampoon's Christmas Vacation
National Lampoon's European Vacation
National Lampoon's Vacation▶
Nightmare at Bittercreek
Ollie Hopnoodle's Haven of Bliss
The Out-of-Towners▶
Pauline at the Beach▶
Poor White Trash 2
Ring of Fire 3: Lion Strike
The River Wild
Russian Roulette
The Slayer/The Scalps
Spring Break
Stealing Beauty
The Sucker
Summer Rental
A Tale of Winter
Target
Terror at Red Wolf Inn
Terror at Tenkiller
Tracks of a Killer
Twitch of the Death Nerve
The Two Faces of Evil
Two If by Sea
Uncivilized
Unlawful Passage
Week-End In Havana
Weekend at Bernie's
Welcome to Spring Break
Where the Boys Are '84
The Wild Life
Witchery

Vampire Babes

see also Up All Night; Vampires

The Addiction
The Brides of Dracula
Buffy the Vampire Slayer▶
Captain Kronos: Vampire Hunter▶
The Craving
Crypt of the Living Dead
Daughters of Darkness▶
Demon Queen
Dracula's Daughter▶
Fangs of the Living Dead
The Fearless Vampire Killers▶
Fright Night
From Dusk Till Dawn
The Girl with the Hungry Eyes
Interview with the Vampire
The Kiss
Lemora, Lady Dracula
Lust for a Vampire
Mary, Mary, Bloody Mary
Nadja▶
Night of the Sorcerers
Nightlife
Once Bitten
Tales from the Crypt Presents Bordello of Blood
Twins of Evil
Vamp
The Vampire Lovers
Vampyres
The Velvet Vampire

Vampire Spoof

see also Horror Comedy; Vampires

Andy Warhol's Dracula▶
Beverly Hills Vamp
Buffy the Vampire Slayer▶
Dracula & Son
Dracula Blows His Cool
Dracula: Dead and Loving It
Dracula Sucks
Dracula: Up in Harlem
Dracula vs. Frankenstein
The Fearless Vampire Killers▶
Gore-Met Zombie Chef From Hell
I Married a Vampire
Love at First Bite
The Malibu Beach Vampires
My Best Friend Is a Vampire
My Grandpa is a Vampire
Near Dark▶
Once Bitten
A Polish Vampire in Burbank
Rockula
Teen Vamp
Vamp
The Vampire Happening

Vampires

see also Up All Night; Vampire Babes; Vampire Spoof

The Addiction
Alien Massacre
The Bat People
Beast of Morocco
Bela Lugosi Scrapbook
Billy the Kid Versus Dracula
Black Sabbath▶
Black Vampire
Blacula
Blood and Roses
Blood Freak
Blood of Dracula's Castle
Blood of the Vampire
The Blood Spattered Bride
Blood Thirst
Blood Ties
Bloodlust: Subspecies 3
Bloodstone: Subspecies 2
The Bloodsuckers
Bloodsuckers from Outer Space
The Bloody Vampire
Body Snatcher from Hell
Bram Stoker's Dracula
The Brides of Dracula
The Brides Wore Blood
Bring Me the Vampire
Buffy the Vampire Slayer▶
Captain Kronos: Vampire Hunter▶
Carmilla
Cave of the Living Dead
Children of the Night
Condemned to Live
Count Dracula
Count Yorga, Vampire
The Craving
Cronos
Crypt of the Living Dead
Dance of the Damned
Dark Shadows
Dark Shadows: Episode 1
Daughter of Darkness
Daughters of Darkness▶
Dead Men Walk
Demon Queen
The Devil Bat
The Devil Bat's Daughter
Devil's Wedding Night
Dr. Terror's House of Horrors
Dracula▶
Dracula
Dracula: A Cinematic Scrapbook
Dracula: Dead and Loving It
Dracula/Garden of Eden
Dracula Has Risen from the Grave
Dracula Rising
Dracula (Spanish Version)
Dracula vs. Frankenstein
Dracula's Daughter▶
Dracula's Great Love
Dracula's Last Rites
Dracula's Widow
Elvira, Mistress of the Dark
Embrace of the Vampire
Evil's Commandment
Evils of the Night
Fangs of the Living Dead
Fright Night
Fright Night 2
From Dusk Till Dawn
Genie of Darkness
Ghost Stories: Graveyard Thriller
Grave of the Vampire
Graveyard Shift
Heartstopper
The Horror of Dracula▶
Horror of the Blood Monsters
House of Dark Shadows
House of Frankenstein
The House that Dripped Blood
Howling 6: The Freaks
The Hunger
I Like Bats
Innocent Blood
Interview with the Vampire
Invasion of the Vampires
Isle of the Dead
Kiss of the Vampire
The Last Man on Earth
Lemora, Lady Dracula
Let's Scare Jessica to Death
Lifeforce
The Lost Boys
The Lost Platoon
The Loves of Irina
Lust for a Vampire
Mark of the Vampire▶
Martin▶
Mary, Mary, Bloody Mary
Midnight Kiss
The Monster Club
The Monster Demolisher
The Monster Squad
My Grandpa is a Vampire
My Son, the Vampire
Nadja▶
Near Dark▶
Nick Knight
Night Hunter
Night of Dark Shadows
Night of the Sorcerers
The Night Stalker: Two Tales of Terror
Nightlife
Nightmare in Blood
Ninja, the Violent Sorcerer
Nocturna
Not of This Earth
Once Bitten
Orgy of the Vampires
Pale Blood
Planet of Blood
Planet of the Vampires
Project Vampire
Rabid
Red Blooded American Girl
The Reflecting Skin
The Return of Count Yorga
Return of the Vampire
Return to Salem's Lot
The Saga of the Draculas
Salem's Lot
Samson vs. the Vampire Women
The Satanic Rites of Dracula
The Scars of Dracula
Scream Blacula Scream
The 7 Brothers Meet Dracula
The Slaughter of the Vampires
Sleepwalkers
Son of Dracula▶
Subspecies
Sundown
Tale of a Vampire
Tales from the Crypt Presents Bordello of Blood
Taste the Blood of Dracula
Theatre of Death
Thirst
The Thirsty Dead
To Die for
To Die for 2: Son of Darkness
To Sleep with a Vampire
Track of the Vampire
Transylvania Twist
Twins of Evil
Uncle Was a Vampire
Understudy: The Graveyard Shift 2
The Unearthing
Vamp
The Vampire
Vampire at Midnight
The Vampire Bat
Vampire Circus
Vampire Cop
The Vampire Happening
The Vampire Hookers
Vampire in Brooklyn
The Vampire Lovers
The Vampire People
The Vampire's Coffin
The Vampire's Ghost
Vampire's Kiss▶
Vampyr▶
The Vampyr
Vampyres
The Velvet Vampire
The Werewolf vs. the Vampire Woman
The Wicked
Witchcraft 7: Judgement Hour
Zoltan...Hound of Dracula

Variety

Doctor Duck's Super Secret All-Purpose Sauce
Flying Karamazov Brothers Comedy Hour
Follow the Boys▶
Give a Girl a Break
Heller in Pink Tights
Hollywood Goes to War
Hollywood Varieties
If You Don't Stop It...You'll Go Blind
In the Money
International House
Minsky's Follies
Mr. Mike's Mondo Video

Parade▶
The Pee Wee Herman Show
Pee Wee's Playhouse Festival of Fun
Sleazemania
Strictly G.I.
That's Dancing!
That's Singing: The Best of Broadway
Varieties on Parade
Your Show of Shows
Ziegfeld Follies

Venice

see also Italy

Blame It on the Bellboy
The Children
Death in Venice▶
Don't Look Now▶
Indiana Jones and the Last Crusade▶
A Little Romance▶
Night Train to Venice
Only You
Othello
Panic Button
Summertime▶
Walk, Don't Run

Veterans

see also Postwar

Alamo Bay
American Eagle
Americana
Anatomy of Terror
Angels from Hell
The Annihilators
Article 99
Ashes and Embers
Backfire
Bad Company▶
Bell Diamond
The Best Years of Our Lives▶
Billy Jack
Birds of Prey
Birdy▶
The Black Six
Braddock: Missing in Action 3
The Bushwackers
The Cage
Cease Fire
Chattahoochee
Child Bride of Short Creek
Chrome Soldiers
Combat Shock
Cry of the Innocent▶
Dark Before Dawn
Distant Thunder
The Enchanted Cottage
Fear
Fireback
First Blood
Fleshburn
Forced Vengeance
The Forgotten
Ghetto Revenge
G.I. Executioner
The Great American Broadcast▶
Heated Vengeance
Heroes
Heroes for Sale▶
House▶
Identity Unknown
In a Shallow Grave
In Country
Jud
Jungle Assault
Kill Alex Kill
Killcrazy
The Killer's Edge
Killzone
Last Mercenary
Lethal Weapon▶
Liberty & Bash
The Line
Memorial Day
Mr. Majestyk
Moon in Scorpio
The Park is Mine
Rambo 3
Red, White & Busted
Redwood Curtain
Ride in a Pink Car
Riders of the Storm
Robbery
Rolling Thunder
Savage Dawn
Scent of a Woman▶
Shark River
Skin Art
Soldier's Revenge
Stand Alone
Stanley
Steele Justice
Tagget
To Heal a Nation
To Kill a Clown
Tracks
The War
Who'll Stop the Rain?▶
The Woman Inside

Vietnam War

see also Postwar; POW/MIA

After the Fall of Saigon
Air America
American Commandos
Americana
The Annihilators
Apocalypse Now▶
Ashes and Embers
Autopsy
Bat 21
Bell Diamond
Beyond the Call of Duty
Birdy▶
The Black Six
Born on the Fourth of July▶
The Boys in Company C
Braddock: Missing in Action 3
Cactus in the Snow
Casualties of War▶
Cease Fire
Charlie Bravo
The Children of An Lac
China Beach▶
China Gate▶
Combat Shock
Coming Home▶
Commando Invasion
Conspiracy: The Trial of the Chicago Eight▶
Crossfire
Dead Presidents
Dear America: Letters Home from Vietnam▶
Deathdream
The Deer Hunter▶
The Deserters
Dogfight▶
Don't Cry, It's Only Thunder
84 Charlie Mopic▶
Explosion
Eye of the Eagle
Eye of the Eagle 2
Eye of the Eagle 3
Fatal Mission
Fear
Fighting Mad
Firehawk
First Blood
Fist of Glory
Flight of the Intruder
For the Boys
The Forgotten
Forgotten Warrior
Forrest Gump▶
Four Friends▶
Friendly Fire▶
Full Metal Jacket▶
Gardens of Stone
Ghetto Revenge
Go Tell the Spartans▶
Good Morning, Vietnam▶
The Green Berets
Green Eyes▶
Hail, Hero!
Hair▶
Hamburger Hill
Hanoi Hilton
Hard Rain-The Tet 1968
The Hard Ride
Heated Vengeance
Heaven and Earth
In Country
In Gold We Trust
In Love and War
Invasion of the Flesh Hunters
The Iron Triangle
Jacknife▶
Jacob's Ladder
Jenny
Jud
Jungle Assault
Kent State
The Killing Fields▶
Kissinger and Nixon
Lady from Yesterday
Last Flight Out: A True Story
The Last Hunter
Memorial Day
Missing in Action
Missing in Action 2: The Beginning
More American Graffiti
Nam Angels
Night Wars
1969▶
No Dead Heroes
The Odd Angry Shot
Off Limits
Once Upon a Time in Vietnam
Operation C.I.A.
Operation Dumbo Drop
Operation 'Nam
Operation War Zone
Ordinary Heroes
Platoon▶
Platoon Leader
P.O.W. Deathcamp
The P.O.W. Escape
Primary Target
Private War
Purple Hearts
Rambo: First Blood, Part 2
Rambo 3
Red, White & Busted
Return of the Secaucus 7▶
Ride in a Pink Car
Rolling Thunder
A Rumor of War▶
Running on Empty▶
Saigon Commandos
Saigon: Year of the Cat
Search and Destroy
The Siege of Firebase Gloria
Skin Art
Soldier's Revenge
Some Kind of Hero
Streamers
Strike Commando
Summertree
Thou Shalt Not Kill...Except
To Heal a Nation
To the Shores of Hell
Tornado
Tour of Duty
Trial of the Catonsville Nine
Twilight's Last Gleaming
Uncommon Valor
Unnatural Causes▶
Vietnam: Chronicle of a War
Vietnam War Story 1
Vietnam War Story 2
Vietnam War Story 3
The Walking Dead
The War
Warbus
Wardogs
Welcome Home
When Hell Was in Session▶
Which Way Home
The Wild Aces
Winner Takes All
Woodstock▶

Vigilantes

see also Revenge

American Commandos
The Avenging Angel
Best of the Best 3: No Turning Back
Blood Horse
Brutal Fury
Combat Shock
Dark Angel: The Ascent
The Death Squad
Death Wish
Death Wish 2
Death Wish 3
Death Wish 5: The Face of Death
Defiance
Dirty Harry▶
DROP Squad
An Eye for an Eye
Falling Down
Force Five
Jimmy Hollywood
Keeper of the City
One Man Jury
Original Gangstas
Out for Blood
The Outlaw Josey Wales▶
Quiet Cool
Raw Deal
Self-Defense
Shadows and Fog
SnakeEater
SnakeEater 2: The Drug Buster
The Sniper
Soldier of the Night
Steele Justice
The Stranger Wore a Gun
Street Hunter
Target Eagle
To Protect and Serve
Zebra Force

Viva Las Vegas!

see also Gambling

Beyond Desire
Bodily Harm
Casino▶
Destiny Turns on the Radio
Gamble on Love
Get Shorty▶
The Great White Hype
Happily Ever After
Hard Vice
Hell Squad
Honeymoon in Vegas
Indecent Proposal
Jinxed
Jocks
Kingpin
Kiss Me, Stupid!
Lady Cocoa
Las Vegas Hillbillys
Las Vegas Lady
Las Vegas Serial Killer
The Las Vegas Story
Las Vegas Weekend
Leaving Las Vegas▶
Leprechaun 3
The Marrying Man
Meet Me in Las Vegas
Nature of the Beast
Rock-a-Doodle
Showgirls
Sister Act
Stripshow
Sugartime
Sword of Honor
Texas Payback
The Vegas Strip Wars
Viva Las Vegas

Volcanos

see also Disaster Flicks

The Devil at 4 O'Clock
Joe Versus the Volcano
Last Days of Pompeii
The Last Days of Pompeii
Nutcase
St. Helen's, Killer Volcano
Waikiki Wedding▶
When Time Ran Out

Volleyball

Side Out
Top Gun

Voodoo

see also Occult

Angel Heart
Asylum
Beyond the Carribean
Black Devil Doll from Hell
Black Magic Woman
Caribe
Curse 3: Blood Sacrifice
Curse of the Living Dead
The Devil's Daughter
Dr. Terror's House of Horrors
Headhunter
The House on Skull Mountain
Household Saints▶
How to Stuff a Wild Bikini
I Walked with a Zombie▶
Jungle Drums of Africa
Live and Let Die
Macumba Love
The Offspring
The Possession of Joel Delaney
Scared Stiff
Scream Blacula Scream
The Serpent and the Rainbow
Shrunken Heads
The Snake People
Theatre of Death
Voodoo
Voodoo Black Exorcist
Voodoo Dawn
Weekend at Bernie's 2

Waitresses

Alice Doesn't Live Here Anymore
Atlantic City▶
Bikini Bistro
Come Back to the Five & Dime Jimmy Dean, Jimmy Dean▶
Five Easy Pieces▶
Frankie and Johnny▶
Heavy
It Could Happen to You
Joey Breaker▶
Mystic Pizza▶
The Postman Always Rings Twice▶
The Postman Always Rings Twice
The Spitfire Grill
Thelma & Louise▶
Untamed Heart
Waitress
White Palace
Willa

War Between the Sexes

see also Divorce; Marriage; Singles

About Last Night...▶
Adam's Rib▶
The Adventures of Robin Hood▶
The African Queen▶
All of Me
All Tied Up
All's Fair
Alternative
Always▶
America 3000
Annie Hall▶
Around the World Under the Sea
Autumn Marathon
The Awful Truth▶
The Ballad of the Sad Cafe
Bare Essentials
Basic Training
Behind Office Doors
The Best Intentions▶
Beware of Pity
The Bigamist
Blood and Sand▶
Blue Paradise
The Bodyguard
Boomerang
The Bride Walks Out
Bringing Up Baby▶

Buffalo Jump▶
Bull Durham▶
Cannibal Women in the Avocado Jungle of Death
Carmen▶
Carmen Jones▶
Carrington, V.C.▶
Carry On Nurse
Casablanca▶
Casanova's Big Night
Castaway
Casual Sex?
Chained
Cold Heat
Concrete Beat
The Cry of the Owl
The Cutting Edge
Dangerous Liaisons
Dear Murderer
Dear Wife
Designing Woman▶
Disclosure
Divorce His, Divorce Hers
Divorce—Italian Style▶
Dogfight▶
Don Juan, My Love▶
Easy Wheels
El: This Strange Passion▶
Far and Away
The Favor
The Female Bunch
Fever
The Fighting Sheriff
First Monday in October
Forever Darling
Forget Paris
Frankie and Johnny▶
Fury is a Woman▶
A Girl in a Million
Gone with the Wind▶
The Good Father▶
Goodbye Love
Guarding Tess
The Happy Ending
Hardhat & Legs
Having It All
He Said, She Said
Hearing Voices
Heartburn▶
His Girl Friday▶
Hotel Room
Housesitter
I, Claudius, Vol. 1: A Touch of Murder/Family Affairs
I Live My Life
I Love All of You
I Love My...Wife
I Love Trouble
I Love You
In the Good Old Summertime▶
In the Line of Fire▶
Intimate Story
Irreconcilable Differences
It Happened One Night▶
The Jewel of the Nile
Juliet of the Spirits▶
June Bride▶
Just Tell Me What You Want
Key Exchange
Kill My Wife...Please!
The King and I▶
Kiss Me Kate▶
Kramer vs. Kramer▶
La Discrete▶
L.A. Story▶
The Lady Says No
The Last Woman on Earth
Le Chat▶
Legion of Iron
Letters to an Unknown Lover
Lily in Love
The Lion in Winter▶
Love Crazy▶
Love in the Afternoon
Love Nest
Lover Come Back
Loyalties
Lucky Partners
Man of Destiny
The Man Who Guards the Greenhouse
Manhattan▶
Maria's Lovers
The Marriage of Maria Braun▶
The Marrying Man
A Matter of Love
Maverick
McLintock!▶
Men...▶
Menschenfrauen
A Midsummer Night's Dream▶
Moonlighting
Moonstruck▶
Mortal Thoughts
Much Ado about Nothing▶
Murphy's Law
My Brilliant Career▶
Near Misses
A New Leaf
9 to 5
Nothing in Common
One Woman or Two
The Opposite Sex and How to Live With Them
Pajama Tops
Pat and Mike▶
Patti Rocks▶
Pauline at the Beach▶
A Piece of Pleasure▶
Pillow Talk▶
Places in the Heart▶
Portrait of Teresa▶
The Practice of Love
Private Lives▶
Prizzi's Honor▶
Public Enemy▶
Queen of Outer Space
Question of Silence▶
The Quiet Man▶
Ramrod
The Ref▶
Romancing the Stone▶
Rooster Cogburn
Running Mates▶
Sabrina▶
Sabrina
Scenes from a Mall
Seance on a Wet Afternoon▶
The Sensual Man
Sex and the College Girl
She-Devil
Shore Leave▶
The Single Standard
The Social Secretary
Sotto, Sotto
Speechless
Speedtrap
Spies, Lies and Naked Thighs
Star 80
The Story of Fausta
Summer Night with Greek Profile, Almond Eyes & Scent of Basil
Switch▶
Switching Channels
The Taming of the Shrew
The Taming of the Shrew▶
The Taming of the Shrew
A Taxing Woman▶
Teacher's Pet▶
Ted & Venus
That's My Baby!
Thelma & Louise▶
The Thing▶
Thor and the Amazon Women
Three of Hearts
Thunder in the Pines
Tiger and the Pussycat
To Have & Have Not▶
To Wong Foo, Thanks for Everything, Julie Newmar
Tony Draws a Horse
True Love▶
Two-Faced Woman▶
Vasectomy: A Delicate Matter
War Between the Tates
The War of the Roses▶
When Harry Met Sally...▶
When Ladies Meet
When Women Lost Their Tails
Who's Afraid of Virginia Woolf?▶
Wife Versus Secretary▶
The Witches of Eastwick
Without Love
A Woman of Distinction▶
Woman of the Year▶
Women & Men: In Love There Are No Rules
Women & Men: Stories of Seduction
Women on the Verge of a Nervous Breakdown▶
The World According to Garp▶
Year of the Comet
Yesterday, Today and Tomorrow▶
You're a Big Boy Now▶

War, General

***see also* Anti-War War Movies; Big Battles; Civil War; Korean War; Persian Gulf War; Postwar; POW/MIA; Revolutionary War; Terrorism; Veterans; Vietnam War; World War I; World War II**

The Adventures of the Flying Cadets
The Alamo▶
The Alamo: Thirteen Days to Glory
Alexander Nevsky▶
Alexander the Great
Alone Against Rome
Alsino and the Condor▶
Anna Karenina
Atlas
The Avenger
Ay, Carmela!▶
Ballad of a Soldier▶
Battle Hell
The Battle of Algiers▶
The Battle of Austerlitz
The Beast
Beau Geste▶
Before the Rain▶
Behind the Front
Behold a Pale Horse
The Bitter Tea of General Yen▶
Braveheart▶
The Buccaneer
Bugles in the Afternoon
A Bullet for the General
By Dawn's Early Light
Captain Caution
Captain Horatio Hornblower▶
Carthage in Flames
Cast a Giant Shadow
Cavalry Command
Chapayev▶
The Charge of the Light Brigade▶
The Charge of the Light Brigade
Civilization▶
Codename: Terminate
Colonel Chabert
Colonel Wolodyjowski
The Conqueror
Conquest of the Normans
Coup de Grace
The Court Martial of Billy Mitchell▶
Cromwell
Cup Final
Danton▶
Days of Hell
Deadline
The Desert of the Tartars
Devil Wears White
Distant Drums
Doctor Zhivago▶
Dragon Seed
Eagles Attack at Dawn
1860
El Cid▶
El Paso Stampede
Elizabeth of Ladymead▶
Emissary
The Enchanted Cottage
The End of St. Petersburg▶
The Expendables
The Fall of the Roman Empire▶
Field of Honor
The Fighter▶
Fighting Marines
Fighting Pilot
The Fighting Prince of Donegal
The Finest Hour
Fire Over England▶
The Firing Line
Flor Silvestre
Flowers of Reverie
For Whom the Bell Tolls▶
Forever and a Day▶
Fort Apache▶
Forty Days of Musa Dagh
The Four Feathers▶
The Four Feathers
F.P. 1
Funny, Dirty Little War
Guerilla Brigade
Gunga Din▶
Guns at Batasi
Hail the Conquering Hero▶
Harry's War
Hawkeye: Premiere Episode
Heart of a Nation▶
Heartbreak Ridge▶
Hearts & Armour
Heaven & Earth▶
Hell in the Pacific▶
Hell on the Battleground
Hell Raiders
Henry V▶
Hero Bunker
The Hidden Fortress▶
Hill 24 Doesn't Answer▶
Holy Terror
Homecoming▶
How I Won the War
In the Name of the Pope-King▶
The Informer▶
The Invincible Gladiator
Johnny Got His Gun
Judith of Bethulia▶
Khartoum
Killers
Kolberg
La Marseillaise▶
La Nuit de Varennes▶
Land and Freedom▶
The Last Command
The Last of the Mohicans
The Last of the Mohicans▶
The Last Valley
Late Summer Blues
Latino
Laughing at Life
Legion of Missing Men
The Life and Death of Colonel Blimp▶
Lion of the Desert▶
Lipstick On Your Collar
The Longest Day▶
The Lost Command
The Lost Idol/Shock Troop
Mademoiselle Fifi
Man from the Alamo▶
Man with a Cross
Massive Retaliation
Megaforce
Mercenary Fighters
Mission to Glory
Mission to Kill
The Mongols
The Moonraker
Mother▶
Mountain Fury
The Mouse That Roared▶
Napoleon▶
An Occurrence at Owl Creek Bridge/Coup de Grace
Old Gringo
One Night Stand▶
Orphans of the Storm▶
The Phantom Planet
Port Arthur
Prehistoric Bimbos in Armageddon City
The Pride and the Passion
Project: Alien
Rage to Kill
The Rape of the Sabines
The Real Glory▶
A Reason to Live, A Reason to Die
The Red and the Black▶
The Red and the White▶
Red Dawn
Reds▶
Reign of Terror
Revenge of the Barbarians
Rhodes
Richard III▶
Ride to Glory
River of Unrest
Ryan's Daughter
Saga of the Vagabond
Salome, Where She Danced
Sanders of the River▶
Scarlet Dawn
Senso▶
The Seventeenth Bride
Shake Hands with the Devil▶
The Shame▶
Sharpe's Battle
Sharpe's Company
Sharpe's Eagle
Sharpe's Enemy
Sharpe's Gold
Sharpe's Honour
Sharpe's Rifles
Sharpe's Sword
She Wore a Yellow Ribbon▶
Simon Bolivar
Sinai Commandos
Smugglers
Something of Value▶
Storm Over Asia▶
Striker
Surprise Attack
The Tempest/The Eagle▶
This England
This Island Earth
The 317th Platoon▶
Tiger Joe
Time to Kill
The Torch
Torn Allegiance
Treasure of the Lost Desert
The Ugly American
Ulysses' Gaze
Under Fire▶
The Uprising▶
Vera Cruz
Villa Rides
Walker
War and Peace
War and Peace▶
War Bus Commando
Warbirds
Waterloo
Weekend War
White Dwarf
Wild Geese 2
The World Owes Me a Living
World War III
Yank in Libya
Young Winston▶
Zulu Dawn▶

Wedding Bells

***see also* Marriage; Otherwise Engaged; Wedding Hell**

Betsy's Wedding
Blind Date
The Bride Came C.O.D.
The Bride Walks Out
Date Bait
Easy Money
8 Seconds
Father of the Bride▶
Father of the Bride
Foolin' Around
For Better and For Worse
Forget Paris
Four Weddings and a Funeral▶
Full of Life
Give Me a Sailor
Hard Promises
Holy Matrimony
Honeymoon in Vegas
House Party 3
Housesitter
It Started with Eve▶

Jack and Sarah
The Jewel of the Nile
Lovers and Other Strangers▶
The Marrying Man
Miami Rhapsody
Moonstruck▶
Murders in the Rue Morgue
Muriel's Wedding▶
My Favorite Wife▶
Nine Months
Only You
The Philadelphia Story▶
Prelude to a Kiss
Revenge of the Nerds 4: Nerds in Love
Rhythm on the Range
Roommates
Royal Wedding▶
She's Having a Baby
Sixteen Candles▶
The Summer House
The 30-Foot Bride of Candy Rock
Three Smart Girls Grow Up▶
Waikiki Wedding▶
A Wedding
Wedding Band
The Wedding March▶
The Wedding Party
Wedding Rehearsal
When Harry Met Sally...▶
Where There's Life
The World's Oldest Living Bridesmaid

Wedding Hell

see also Marriage; Otherwise Engaged; Wedding Bells

Black Vampire
Blood Bride
The Blood Spattered Bride
The Bride
The Bride & the Beast
The Bride of Frankenstein▶
Bride of Killer Nerd
Bride of Re-Animator
Bride of the Gorilla
Bride of the Monster
The Bride Wore Black▶
Brides of the Beast
The Brides Wore Blood
The Catered Affair▶
Cheatin' Hearts
The Graduate▶
He Knows You're Alone
Highway to Hell
Honeymoon
Honeymoon Horror
Honeymoon Killers▶
I Married a Monster from Outer Space
My New Gun
The Newlydeads
Niagara
The Perfect Bride
True Love▶
The Wedding Banquet▶
Wedding in Blood▶
Wedding in White

Werewolves

see also Metamorphosis

An American Werewolf in London▶
Black Werewolf
Blood of Dracula's Castle
Bride of the Gorilla
Children of the Full Moon
The Company of Wolves▶
The Craving
Cry of the Werewolf
Curse of the Devil
Curse of the Queerwolf
The Curse of the Werewolf
Deathmoon
Dr. Jekyll and the Wolfman
Dr. Jekyll vs. the Werewolf
Dr. Terror's House of Horrors
Dracula vs. Frankenstein
Face of the Screaming Werewolf
Frankenstein Meets the Wolfman▶
Full Eclipse
The Fury of the Wolfman
Hercules, Prisoner of Evil
House of Frankenstein
The Howling▶
Howling 2: Your Sister is a Werewolf
Howling 3: The Marsupials
Howling 4: The Original Nightmare
Howling 6: The Freaks
The Howling: New Moon Rising
I Was a Teenage Werewolf
Legend of the Werewolf
The Legend of the Wolf Woman
Lone Wolf
The Mad Monster
Meridian: Kiss of the Beast
Monster Dog
The Monster Squad
Moon of the Wolf
My Mom's a Werewolf
Night of the Howling Beast
Orgy of the Dead
Project Metalbeast: DNA Overload
The Rats are Coming! The Werewolves are Here!
Return of the Vampire
Silver Bullet
Teen Wolf
Teen Wolf Too
The Undying Monster
Werewolf in a Girl's Dormitory
Werewolf of London
Werewolf of Washington
The Werewolf vs. the Vampire Woman
Werewolves on Wheels
Wolf
Wolf Blood
The Wolf Man▶
Wolfen▶
The Wolfman

Western Comedy

see also Comedy; Westerns

Adios Amigo
Along Came Jones▶
The Apple Dumpling Gang
The Apple Dumpling Gang Rides Again
Bad Man's River
Ballad of Cable Hogue▶
Bang Bang Kid
The Beautiful Blonde from Bashful Bend
Beyond the Trail
Blazing Saddles▶
Bordello
Border Phantom
Boss
Bowery Buckaroos
Branded Men
Bronco Billy
Bus Stop▶
Carry On Cowboy
Cat Ballou▶
Catlow
Check & Double Check
The Cheyenne Social Club
The Cisco Kid
City Slickers▶
City Slickers 2: The Legend of Curly's Gold
Cold Feet
The Cowboy Way
Desperate Women
Destry Rides Again▶
The Duchess and the Dirtwater Fox
El Diablo Rides
Four Eyes and Six Guns
Four for Texas
The Frisco Kid
From Noon Till Three
Go West
Goin' South▶
Gold Raiders
The Good Guys and the Bad Guys
Greaser's Palace
Great Scout & Cathouse Thursday
Gun Crazy
The Hallelujah Trail
Hangman's Knot
Hearts of the West▶
How the West was Fun
I'm from Arkansas
The Incredible Rocky Mountain Race
The Kid Brother▶
Life & Times of Judge Roy Bean
Lightning Jack
Lincoln County Incident
Local Badman
Lucky Luke
Maverick
McLintock!▶
More Wild, Wild West
The Nervous Wreck▶
Oklahoma Kid▶
The Outlaws is Coming!
The Paleface▶
Pardners
Pocket Money
Rancho Deluxe▶
Rhythm on the Range
Ride 'Em Cowboy
The Rounders
Rustler's Rhapsody
Samurai Cowboy
The Scalphunters
Scandalous John
September Gun
The Shakiest Gun in the West
Shame, Shame on the Bixby Boys
Sodbusters
Son of Paleface▶
Sting of the West
Support Your Local Gunfighter▶
Support Your Local Sheriff▶
Take Me Back to Oklahoma
Texas▶
Texas Across the River
Texas Layover
There was a Crooked Man▶
They Call Me Trinity
Three Godfathers▶
Ticket to Tomahawk
Trinity is Still My Name
Troublemakers
Under Montana Skies
The Villain
Wackiest Wagon Train in the West
Wagons East
Waterhole #3
Way Out West▶
Wild & Wooly
Wild Horse Phantom
Wild Rovers
The Wistful Widow of Wagon Gap
Yellow Hair & the Fortress of Gold

Westerns

see also Spaghetti Western; Western Comedy; Westrogens

Abilene Town▶
Aces and Eights
Aces Wild
Across the Plains
Adios Gringo
Adios, Hombre
The Adventures of Gallant Bess
Adventures of Kit Carson
Adventures of Red Ryder
Against A Crooked Sky
The Alamo▶
Alias Billy the Kid
Alias John Law
Allegheny Uprising
Along the Great Divide
Along the Sundown Trail
Alvarez Kelly
Ambush at Tomahawk Gap
Ambush Trail
American Empire
Americano
And God Said to Cain
Angel and the Badman▶
Animal Called Man
Annie Oakley▶
Another Man, Another Chance
Another Pair of Aces: Three of a Kind▶
Any Gun Can Play
Apache
Apache Blood
Apache Chief
Apache Kid's Escape
Apache Rose
Apache Uprising
Apache Woman
Apaches Last Battle
The Appaloosa
Arizona
Arizona Badman
Arizona Bound
Arizona Bushwackers
Arizona Cowboy
Arizona Days
Arizona Gangbusters
Arizona Gunfighter
Arizona Kid
Arizona Mahoney
Arizona Raiders
Arizona Roundup
Arizona Stagecoach
Arizona Terror
Arizona Whirlwind
Arrowhead
At Gunpoint
The Avenging Angel
Backfire
Backlash: Oblivion 2
Bad Company▶
Bad Day at Black Rock▶
Bad Girls
Bad Guys
Bad Jim
Bad Lands
Bad Man of Deadwood
Bad Men of the Border
The Badlanders▶
Badman's Territory▶
Badmen of Nevada
Ballad of a Gunfighter
Ballad of Gregorio Cortez▶
The Ballad of Little Jo
Bandit King of Texas
Bandit Queen
Bandits
Bandolero!
Bar-20
Barbarosa▶
The Bargain
Baron of Arizona▶
Battle of Elderbush Gulch
Battling Marshal
Battling Outlaws
Battling with Buffalo Bill
Belle Starr
Bells of Coronado
Bells of Rosarita
Bells of San Angelo
Bells of San Fernando
Below the Border
Bend of the River▶
Beneath Arizona Skies/Paradise Canyon
Best of the Badmen
Between Fighting Men
Between God, the Devil & a Winchester
Between Men
Beyond the Law
Beyond the Rockies
Beyond the Trail
Big Calibre
The Big Cat
The Big Country
A Big Hand for the Little Lady
Big Jake
Big Show
The Big Sky▶
The Big Sombrero
Big Stakes
The Big Stampede
Big Trail▶
Big Valley
Billy the Kid
Billy the Kid in Texas
Billy the Kid Returns
Billy the Kid Trapped
Bite the Bullet▶
Black Fox: The Price of Peace
Black Hills
The Black Lash
Black Market Rustlers
Blazing Guns
Blind Justice
Blood at Sundown
Blood for a Silver Dollar
Blood Horse
Blood on the Moon
Bloody Trail
Blue
Blue Canadian Rockies
Blue Steel
Boiling Point
The Boldest Job in the West
Bonanza
Bonanza: The Return
Boot Hill Bandits
Boothill Brigade
Boots & Saddles
Boots of Destiny
Border Badmen
Border Bandits
Border Caballero
Border Devils
Border Feud
Border Law
The Border Legion
Border Patrol
Border Rangers
Border Romance
Border Roundup
Border Saddlemates
Border Shootout
Border Vengeance
Border Vigilantes
Bordertown Gunfighters
Born in America
Boss Cowboy
Boss of Bullion City
Boss of Rawhide
The Bounty Man
Brand of Fear
Brand of Hate
Brand of the Outlaws
Branded
Branded a Bandit
Branded a Coward
The Bravados▶
Breakheart Pass
Breed of the Border
Broadway to Cheyenne
Broken Arrow
Broken Lance▶
Bronson's Revenge
Bronze Buckaroo
Brothers of the West
Brothers O'Toole
Buck and the Preacher
Buckeye and Blue
Buckskin
Buckskin Frontier
Buffalo Bill
Buffalo Bill & the Indians▶
Buffalo Bill Rides Again
Buffalo Girls
Buffalo Rider
Buffalo Stampede
Bugles in the Afternoon
Bull of the West
Bulldog Courage
Bullet Code
Bullet for Sandoval
A Bullet for the General
Bullwhip
The Burning Hills
Bury Me Not On the Lone Prairie
The Bushwackers
Butch and Sundance: The Early Days

Butch Cassidy and the Sundance Kid▶
Buzzy Rides the Range
Cahill: United States Marshal
Cain's Cutthroats
Calamity Jane
California Joe
Call of the Canyon
Call of the Forest
Call of the Rockies
Calling Wild Bill Elliott
Captain Apache
The Captive: The Longest Drive 2
The Capture▶
The Caravan Trail
The Cariboo Trail
Carson City Kid
Cattle Queen of Montana
Cavalcade of the West
Cavalier of the West
Cavalry
Cavalry Charge
Cavalry Command
Challenge of McKenna
Charro!
Chato's Land
Check Your Guns
Cheyenne Autumn
Cheyenne Kid
Cheyenne Rides Again
Cheyenne Takes Over
Cheyenne Warrior
Child of the Prairie
Chino
The Chisholms
Chisum
The Christmas Kid
Chuka
Cimarron
Circle Canyon
Circle of Death
The Cisco Kid
Clearing the Range
Code of the Fearless
Colorado
Colorado Serenade
Colorado Sundown
Colt Comrades
Comanche Territory
The Comancheros▶
Come On, Cowboys
Come On Danger!
Come On Rangers
Come On Tarzan
Comes a Horseman
Conagher
The Concentratin' Kid
Conquest of Cochise
Convict Cowboy
Copper Canyon
Cornered
Coroner Creek
Cotter
Courage of the North
Courageous Avenger
Courtin' Wildcats
The Covered Wagon
Covered Wagon Days
Covered Wagon Trails
Cow Town
Cowboy
Cowboy▶
Cowboy & the Bandit
Cowboy & the Senorita
Cowboy Commandos
Cowboy Counselor
Cowboy Millionaire
The Cowboys▶
Cowboys from Texas
Cowboys of the Saturday Matinee
Coyote Trails
Crazy Horse and Custer: "The Untold Story"
The Crimson Trail
Crooked Trail
Crossfire
Culpepper Cattle Co.
Custer's Last Fight
Custer's Last Stand
Cyclone of the Saddle

Dakota
Dakota Incident
Dan Candy's Law
Danger Ahead
Danger Trails
Daniel Boone
Daniel Boone: Trail Blazer
Daring Danger
Dark Command▶
Dawn on the Great Divide
Dawn Rider
Dawn Rider/Frontier Horizon
Dead for a Dollar
Dead Man
Dead Man's Revenge
Dead or Alive
Deadly Companions
The Deadly Trackers
Deadwood
Deadwood Pass
Death of a Gunfighter
Death Rides the Plains
Death Rides the Range
Death Valley
Death Valley Manhunt
Death Valley Rangers
The Deerslayer
Demon for Trouble
The Denver & Rio Grande
Deputy Marshall
Desert Gold
Desert Guns/Six-Shootin' Sheriff
Desert Phantom
Desert Snow
Desert Trail
Desperados
The Desperados
The Desperate Trail
Devil & Leroy Basset
Devil Horse
Devil Riders
Devil's Canyon
The Devil's Mistress
Diamond Trail
The Disciple
Distant Drums
Django
Django Shoots First
Doctor Quinn, Medicine Woman
Dodge City▶
Don Amigo/Stage to Chino
Don Daredevil Rides Again
Donner Pass: The Road to Survival
The Doolins of Oklahoma
Doomed at Sundown
Doomed Caravan▶
Down Dakota Way
Down Mexico Way
Down Texas Way
Down the Wyoming Trail
Draw!
Drift Fence
The Drifter
The Driftin' Kid
Driftin' River
Drum Beat
Drum Taps
Drums Along the Mohawk▶
Dude Bandit
Dude Ranger
Duel at Diablo▶
Duel in the Sun▶
Duke: The Films of John Wayne
Durango Valley Raiders
Dynamite and Gold
Dynamite Canyon
Dynamite Pass
Dynamite Ranch
Eagle's Wing
El Condor
El Diablo
El Dorado▶
El Paso Stampede
The Electric Horseman
Enemy of the Law
Escape from Fort Bravo
Every Man's Law
Extreme Prejudice
Eyes of Texas
False Colors
Fangs of Fate

Far Country▶
Far Frontier
Fargo Express
Fast Bullets
Fastest Guitar Alive
Fastest Gun Alive▶
Feud Maker
Feud of the Trail
Feud of the West
The Fiddlin' Buckaroo
$50,000 Reward
Fight for Gold
The Fighter
Fightin' Ranch
Fighting Caballero
Fighting Caravans
Fighting Champ
Fighting Cowboy
Fighting Fists of Shanghai Joe
Fighting Fool
Fighting Jack
The Fighting Kentuckian
The Fighting Legion
Fighting Mad
The Fighting Marshal
Fighting Parson
The Fighting Redhead
Fighting Renegade
Fighting Shadows
The Fighting Sheriff
The Fighting Stallion▶
Fighting Texans
Fighting Thru
The Fighting Trooper
Fighting Valley
Fighting Vigilantes
Fighting with Kit Carson
Finger on the Trigger
Firecreek
The First Movie Cowboy
Fistful of Death
Five Card Stud
Flame of the Barbary Coast
Flaming Bullets
Flaming Frontiers
Flaming Lead
Flaming Star▶
Flesh and the Spur
Forbidden Trails
Forlorn River
Fort Apache▶
The Forty-Niners
Four Faces West
Four Rode Out
Frank and Jesse
Frontier Days
Frontier Fugitives
Frontier Horizon
Frontier Justice
Frontier Law
Frontier Outlaws
Frontier Pony Express
Frontier Scout
Frontier Uprising
Frontier Vengeance
The Frontiersmen
The Fugitive: Taking of Luke McVane
Fugitive Valley
The Gallant Fool
Galloping Dynamite
Galloping Romeo
The Gambler Returns: The Luck of the Draw
The Gambling Terror
Gangster's Den
Gangsters of the Frontier
Garringo
The Gatling Gun
The Gay Ranchero
Gene Autry Matinee Double Feature #1
Gene Autry Matinee Double Feature #2
Gene Autry Matinee Double Feature #3
Gentle Savage
The Gentleman from California
Gentleman from Dixie
Gentleman from Texas
The Gentleman Killer
Geronimo

Geronimo: An American Legend
Geronimo's Revenge
Get That Girl
Ghost City
Ghost Patrol
Ghost Rider
Ghost Town
Ghost Town Gold
Ghost Town Law
Ghost Town Renegades
Ghost Town Riders
Ghost Valley
Ghostriders
Girl from Calgary
Girl of the Golden West
Git Along Little Dogies
The Glory Trail
God's Country and the Man
God's Gun
The Golden Stallion
Gone with the West
A Good Day to Die
Good Men and Bad
The Good Old Boys
The Good, the Bad and the Ugly▶
Gore Vidal's Billy the Kid
Grand Canyon Trail
The Grand Duel
Grayeagle
The Great American Western Collection: Roy Rogers
Great Day in the Morning
The Great Gundown
Great Jesse James Raid
Great Missouri Raid
The Great Northfield Minnesota Raid
Great Treasure Hunt
Gun Code
Gun Fight at Red Sands
Gun Fury
Gun Glory
Gun Grit
Gun Law
Gun Lords of Stirrup Basin
Gun Packer
Gun Play
The Gun Ranger
Gun Riders
Gun Smugglers/Hot Lead
A Gunfight
Gunfight at Sandoval
Gunfight at the O.K. Corral▶
The Gunfighter▶
The Gunfighters
Gunfire
Gunman from Bodie
Gunners & Guns
Gunplay
Guns for Dollars
Guns in the Dark
Guns of Diablo
Guns of Fury
Guns of Justice
Guns of the Law
Guns of the Magnificent Seven
The Gunslinger
Gunslinger
Gunsmoke: Return to Dodge
Gunsmoke Trail
The Half-Breed
Hands Across the Border
The Hanged Man
The Hanging Tree▶
Hannie Caulder
Hard Bounty
Hard Hombre
Harlem on the Prairie
Harlem Rides the Range
Harmony Trail
Harry Tracy
The Harvey Girls▶
Haunted Gold
Haunted Ranch
Hawaiian Buckaroo
The Hawk of Powder River
Hawken's Breed
Headin' for the Rio Grande
Heart of Texas Ryan
Heart of the Golden West
Heart of the Rio Grande

Heart of the Rockies
Heaven's Gate
Hell Fire Austin
Helldorado
Heller in Pink Tights
Hellfire
Hello Trouble
Hell's Hinges
Helltown
Heritage of the Desert
Heroes of the Alamo
Heroes of the Hills
Heroes of the West
Hidden Gold
Hidden Guns▶
Hidden Valley
High Lonesome
High Noon▶
High Noon: Part 2
High Plains Drifter
Hills of Oklahoma
Hills of Utah
Hired Hand
His Brother's Ghost
His Fighting Blood
His Name was King
Hit the Saddle
Hittin' the Trail
Hole in the Sky
Hombre▶
Home in Oklahoma
Homesteaders of Paradise Valley
Hondo▶
Honor of the Range
Hopalong Cassidy▶
Hopalong Cassidy: Borrowed Trouble
Hopalong Cassidy: Dangerous Venture
Hopalong Cassidy: False Paradise
Hopalong Cassidy: Hoppy's Holiday
Hopalong Cassidy: Renegade Trail
Hopalong Cassidy: Riders of the Deadline
Hopalong Cassidy: Silent Conflict
Hopalong Cassidy: Sinister Journey
Hopalong Cassidy: The Dead Don't Dream
Hopalong Cassidy: The Devil's Playground
Hopalong Cassidy: The Marauders
Hopalong Cassidy: Unexpected Guest
Hoppy Serves a Writ
Horizons West
Hostile Guns
Hot Lead
Hour of the Gun
How the West Was Won▶
Hurricane Express
I Shot Billy the Kid
I Shot Jesse James▶
I Will Fight No More Forever▶
Idaho
In Old Caliente
In Old California
In Old Cheyenne
In Old Colorado
In Old Montana
In Old New Mexico
In Old Santa Fe
In the Days of the Thundering Herd & the Law & the Outlaw
The Indian Fighter▶
Indian Paint
Indian Uprising
Into the Badlands
Invitation to a Gunfighter
The Jayhawkers
Jeremiah Johnson▶
Jesse James▶
Jesse James at Bay
Jesse James Meets Frankenstein's Daughter
Jesse James Rides Again

Rio Grande▶
Rio Grande Raiders
Rio Lobo
Rio Rattler
River of No Return
Road Agent
The Roamin' Cowboy
Roamin' Wild
Roarin' Lead
Roaring Guns
Roaring Ranch
Roaring Six Guns
Robbery Under Arms
Robin Hood of Texas
Robin Hood of the Pecos
Rock River Renegades
Rockwell: A Legend of the Wild West
Rocky Mountain Rangers
Rodeo Girl
Rogue of the Range
Rogue of the Rio Grande
Roll Along Cowboy
Roll on Texas Moon
Roll, Wagons, Roll
Rollin' Plains
Romance on the Range
Rooster Cogburn
Rootin' Tootin' Rhythm
Rose of Rio Grande
Rough Night in Jericho
Rough Riders of Cheyenne
Rough Riders' Roundup
Rough Ridin' Rhythm
Rough Riding Rangers
Round-Up Time in Texas
Rounding Up the Law
Run of the Arrow
Running Wild
Rustler's Hideout
Rustlers of Red Dog
Rustler's Paradise
Rustler's Roundup
Rustler's Valley
The Sacketts
Sacred Ground
Saddle Buster
Saddle Mountain Round-Up
Saga of Death Valley
Sagebrush Law
Sagebrush Trail▶
Salute to the "King of the Cowboys," Roy Rogers
San Antonio
San Fernando Valley
Sandflow
Santa Fe
Santa Fe Bound
Santa Fe Marshal
Santa Fe Stampede
Santa Fe Trail
Santa Fe Uprising
Santee
Sartana's Here...Trade Your Pistol for a Coffin
Savage Guns
Savage Journey
Savage Land
Savage Wilderness
Scalps
The Searchers▶
Sergeant Rutledge▶
Seven Cities of Gold
Seven Sixgunners
Seventh Cavalry
The Shadow Riders
Shadows of Death
Shalako
Shane▶
She Wore a Yellow Ribbon▶
Sheriff of Tombstone
Shine on, Harvest Moon
Shoot the Living, Pray for the Dead
Shoot the Sun Down
The Shooting▶
The Shootist▶
Shotgun
The Showdown
Showdown
Showdown at Boot Hill
Showdown at Williams Creek
Silent Code
Silent Tongue
Silent Valley
Silver Bandit
The Silver Bullet
Silver City Bonanza
Silver City Kid
Silver Lode
Silver Queen
Silver River
Silver Spurs
Silver Stallion
Silver Star
Silverado▶
Sing, Cowboy, Sing
Singing Buckaroo
Singing Cowboys, Vol. 2
The Singing Cowgirl
Siringo
Six Gun Gospel
Six Gun Rhythm
Six Shootin' Sheriff
Sky Bandits
Sky High
Slaughter Trail
Smoke in the Wind
Smokey Smith
Sodbusters
Soldier Blue
The Sombrero Kid
Somewhere in Sonora
Son of a Gun
Son of God's Country
Son of the Morning Star▶
Song of Arizona
Song of Nevada
Song of Old Wyoming
Song of Texas
Song of the Gringo
Song of the Trail
Songs and Bullets
Sonora Stagecoach
Sons of Katie Elder▶
Sons of the Pioneers
South of Monterey
South of St. Louis
South of Santa Fe
South of the Border
South of the Rio Grande
Southward Ho!
Spirit of the West
Springfield Rifle
Springtime in the Rockies
Springtime in the Sierras
Spurs
Square Dance Jubilee
Stage to Mesa City
Stagecoach▶
Stagecoach
Stagecoach to Denver
The Stalking Moon
Standing Tall
The Star Packer
Station West▶
Storm Over Wyoming
Storm Rider
Stormy Trails
Straight Shooter
Straight Shootin'
The Stranger from Pecos
The Stranger Wore a Gun
Stranger's Gold
Strawberry Roan
Sudden Death
Sundance and the Kid
Sundown Fury
Sundown Kid
Sundown Riders
Sundown Saunders
Sunrise Trail
Sunset
Sunset in El Dorado
Sunset on the Desert
Sunset Range
Sunset Serenade
Sunset Trail
Susanna Pass
Sweet Georgia
Swifty
Talion
Tall in the Saddle
The Tall Men
The Tall T
Tall Tale: The Unbelievable Adventures of Pecos Bill
Taste of Death
Telegraph Trail
Tell Them Willie Boy Is Here▶
Ten Wanted Men
Tennessee's Partner
Tension at Table Rock
Terror of Tiny Town
Terror Trail
Test of Donald Norton
Tex Rides with the Boy Scouts
The Texans
Texas
Texas Bad Man
Texas Buddies
Texas Cyclone
Texas Gunfighter
Texas Guns
Texas Jack
Texas John Slaughter: Geronimo's Revenge
Texas John Slaughter: Stampede at Bitter Creek
Texas Justice
Texas Kid
Texas Lady
Texas Legionnaires
Texas Masquerade
Texas Pioneers
The Texas Rangers
The Texas Rangers Ride Again
Texas Terror
Texas to Bataan
Texas Trouble
Texas Wildcats
They Died with Their Boots On▶
Thousand Pieces of Gold▶
Three Bullets for a Long Gun
Three Desperate Men
Three Faces West
Three in the Saddle
3:10 to Yuma▶
Three Texas Steers
Three Violent People
Three Word Brand
The Throwback
Thunder in God's Country
Thunder in the Desert
Thunder Mountain
Thunder Over Texas
Thunder Pass
Thunder River Feud
Thunder Trail
Thundering Gunslingers
Thundering Trail
Timber Terrors
The Tin Star▶
The Tioga Kid
To the Last Man
Today We Kill, Tomorrow We Die
Toll Gate
Toll of the Desert
Tom Horn
Tom Mix Compilation 1
Tom Mix Compilation 2
Tombstone▶
Tombstone Canyon
Tombstone Terror
Tonto Basin Outlaws
The Tonto Kid
The Topeka Terror
The Tracker
The Trackers
Trail Beyond
Trail Drive
Trail of Robin Hood
Trail of Terror
Trail of the Hawk
Trail of the Mounties
Trail of the Silver Spurs
Trail Riders
Trail Street
Trailin'
Trailing Double Trouble
Trailing Trouble
Trails West
Train Robbers
Train to Tombstone
The Traitor
Tramplers
Treasure of Pancho Villa
Tribute to a Bad Man▶
Trigger, Jr.
Trigger Men
Trigger Pals
Trigger Tricks
The Trigger Trio
Triumphs of a Man Called Horse
Trouble Busters
Trouble in Texas
True Grit▶
Tulsa▶
Tumbledown Ranch in Arizona
Tumbleweed Trail
Tumbleweeds▶
Twice a Judas
Twilight in the Sierras
Twilight on the Rio Grande
Twilight on the Trail
Two Fisted Justice
Two-Fisted Justice
Two-Fisted Law
Two Gun Man
Two-Gun Man from Harlem
Two-Gun Troubador
Two Mules for Sister Sara▶
Two Rode Together
Ulzana's Raid▶
The Undefeated
Under California Stars
Under Nevada Skies
Under Western Stars
Undercover Man
Underground Rustlers
The Unforgiven▶
Unforgiven▶
Uninvited
Union Pacific▶
The Unknown Ranger
Up River
Utah
Utah Trail
Valdez is Coming
Valley of Fire
Valley of Terror
Valley of the Lawless
Valley of the Sun▶
Vanishing American
Vanishing Legion
The Vanishing Westerner
Vengeance Valley
Vigilantes of Boom Town
Villa Rides
The Violent Men
Virginia City▶
The Virginian
The Virginian▶
The Virginian
Wagon Master▶
Wagon Tracks
Wagon Trail
Wagon Wheels
Wagon's Westward
Wall Street Cowboy
The Walloping Kid
Wanda Nevada
Wanted: Dead or Alive
War Arrow
War of the Wildcats
The War Wagon▶
Warlock▶
Water Rustlers
Way of the West
The Way West
Welcome to Blood City
West of Nevada
West of Pinto Basin
West of the Divide
West of the Law
West of the Pecos
West to Glory
Western Double Feature 1
Western Double Feature 1: Wild Bill & Sunset Carson
Western Double Feature 2
Western Double Feature 2: Wayne & Hale
Western Double Feature 3
Western Double Feature 3: Rogers & Allen
Western Double Feature 4
Western Double Feature 4: Rogers & Evans
Western Double Feature 5
Western Double Feature 5: Rogers & Autry
Western Double Feature 6: Rogers & Trigger
Western Double Feature 7: Wild Bill & Crabbe
Western Double Feature 8: Hale & Carradine
Western Double Feature 9: LaRue & Beery
Western Double Feature 10: Roy, Dale, & Trigger
Western Double Feature 11
Western Double Feature 12
Western Double Feature 13
Western Double Feature 14
Western Double Feature 15
Western Double Feature 16
Western Double Feature 17
Western Double Feature 18
Western Double Feature 19
Western Double Feature 21
Western Double Feature 22
Western Double Feature 24
Western Frontier
Western Gold
Western Justice
Western Mail
Western Pacific Agent
Western Trails
Western Union▶
The Westerner▶
Westward Ho
Westward Ho, the Wagons!
Westward the Women▶
When a Man Rides Alone
When a Man Sees Red
When the Legends Die▶
When the West Was Young
Where the North Begins
Where Trails Divide
Where Trails End
Whirlwind Horseman
Whistlin' Dan
Whistling Bullets
White Apache
The White Buffalo
White Comanche
White Eagle
White Gold▶
Wild Bill
The Wild Bunch▶
Wild Country
The Wild Country
Wild Frontier
Wild Horse
Wild Horse Canyon
Wild Horse Rodeo
Wild Mustang
Wild Times
Wild West
Wild, Wild West Revisited
Wild Women
Wildfire
Will Penny▶
Winchester '73▶
The Wind▶
Winds of the Wasteland
Winners of the West
Winning of the West
With Kit Carson Over the Great Divide
Without Honors
Wolf Call
Wolfheart's Revenge
The Woman of the Town
Wrangler
Wyatt Earp
Wyatt Earp: Return to Tombstone
Wyoming Outlaw
Yellow Dust
The Yellow Rose of Texas
Yodelin' Kid From Pine Ridge
Young Bill Hickok
Young Blood
Young Buffalo Bill
Young Guns
Young Guns 2

The Young Land
Yukon Flight
Yuma
Zachariah
Zandy's Bride
Zorro Rides Again
Zorro's Black Whip
Zorro's Fighting Legion

Westrogens

***see also* Westerns; Wonder Women**

Angel and the Badman▶
Annie Oakley▶
Annie Oakley
Bad Girls
The Beautiful Blonde from Bashful Bend
Belle Starr
A Big Hand for the Little Lady
Calamity Jane▶
Calamity Jane
Cat Ballou▶
Even Cowgirls Get the Blues
The Gunslinger
Hannie Caulder
Heartland▶
Johnny Guitar▶
The Maverick Queen
McCabe & Mrs. Miller▶
Poker Alice
The Quick and the Dead
Ramrod
Riders of the Purple Sage
Texas Lady
Two Mules for Sister Sara▶

Whitewater Rafting

A Cry from the Mountain
Deliverance▶
Race for Your Life, Charlie Brown
The River Wild
Scream
White Water Summer

Wild Kingdom

***see also* Birds; Cats; Dinosaurs; Killer Beasts; Killer Bugs; King of Beasts (Dogs); Monkeyshines; Sea Critter Attack; Wilderness**

Ace Ventura: When Nature Calls
The Adventures of Tarzan
Africa Texas Style
Alaska
All Creatures Great and Small▶
All Dogs Go to Heaven 2
The Amazing Panda Adventure
Andre
Animal Farm▶
Ava's Magical Adventure
Babe▶
Bambi▶
The Barefoot Executive
The Bear▶
The Bears & I
The Beast that Killed Women
Beastmaster
Beastmaster 2: Through the Portal of Time
Beasts
Bedtime for Bonzo
The Belstone Fox
Black Cobra
Bless the Beasts and Children
Born Free▶
Born to Be Wild
Born Wild
The Brave One▶
A Breed Apart
Bringing Up Baby▶
Buffalo Rider
Bugs Bunny Superstar
Call of the Wild
Captive Wild Woman
The Carnivores
Catch as Catch Can
Charlie, the Lonesome Cougar
Cheetah
Christian the Lion
The Chronicles of Narnia
Clarence, the Cross-eyed Lion▶
Courage of the North
A Cry in the Dark▶
A Cry in the Wild▶
Dark Age
Darkest Africa
Day of the Animals
The Day of the Dolphin
Doctor Dolittle
Dumbo▶
Dunston Checks In
Eaten Alive
Ed
Ele, My Friend
The Electric Horseman
Elephant Boy▶
Every Which Way But Loose
Eye of the Wolf
Eyes of the Panther
Far from Home: The Adventures of Yellow Dog
The Fifth Monkey
Flight of the Grey Wolf
Flipper▶
Flipper
Flipper▶
The Fox and the Hound▶
Francis Covers the Big Town
Francis Goes to the Races
Francis Goes to West Point
Francis in the Haunted House
Francis in the Navy
Francis Joins the WACs
Francis the Talking Mule▶
Frasier the Sensuous Lion
Free Willy
Futz
Gaiety
Gentle Giant
Going Ape!
Going Bananas
The Golden Seal
Goldy: The Last of the Golden Bears
Goldy 2: The Saga of the Golden Bear
Goliathon
Gordy
Gorilla
Gorillas in the Mist▶
The Great Adventure▶
The Great Elephant Escape
The Great Rupert▶
Grizzly Adams: The Legend Continues
Gus
Harry and the Hendersons
Hatari!▶
Hawmps!
High Country Calling
Homeward Bound 2: Lost in San Francisco
In the Shadow of Kilimanjaro
The Island of Dr. Moreau
Island of Lost Souls▶
Island of the Blue Dolphins
Jumanji
Jungle
The Jungle Book▶
Jungle Drums of Africa
King Kung Fu
King of the Grizzlies
Lassie, Come Home
Lassie: The Miracle
The Last Safari
Legend of Lobo
Leonard Part 6
The Lion King▶
Living Free
The Magic of the Golden Bear: Goldy 3
Matilda
Max, Mon Amour
The Misadventures of Merlin Jones
Mr. Kingstreet's War
Monkey Trouble
Monkeys, Go Home!
Monkey's Uncle
The Monster and the Girl
Mountain Family Robinson
Mountain Man
Mouse and His Child
Murders in the Rue Morgue
My Sister, My Love
Napoleon and Samantha▶
Never Cry Wolf▶
Night of the Grizzly
Nikki, the Wild Dog of the North
Once Upon a Forest
Operation Dumbo Drop
Operation Haylift
Pardon My Trunk
Pet Sematary 2
Pippi Longstocking
Planet of the Apes▶
The Polar Bear King
Project X
Razorback
Red Earth
The Rescuers▶
The Rescuers Down Under
Ring of Bright Water▶
Rock-a-Doodle
Rogue Lion
Rudyard Kipling's The Jungle Book
The Runaways
Running Free
Sammy, the Way-Out Seal
The Secret of NIMH▶
Shakma
Shaolin Traitor
Silver Streak▶
Soul of the Beast
Stalk the Wild Child
Starring Bugs Bunny!
A Summer to Remember
Super Seal
Survival of Spaceship Earth
Tarka the Otter
The Tender Warrior
Those Calloways
Thumbelina
A Tiger Walks
Time of the Apes
Tomboy & the Champ
Trap on Cougar Mountain
Vampire Circus
Vanishing Wilderness
Walk Like a Man
Watership Down
Whale of a Tale
When the North Wind Blows
When the Whales Came
The White Buffalo
White Gorilla
White Pongo
White Wolves 2: Legend of the Wild
Wild Horses
Wolfen Ninja
The Yearling▶
The Yearling
Zebra in the Kitchen

Wilderness

***see also* Good Earth; Trees & Forests**

Abducted
Across the Great Divide
The Adventures of Frontier Fremont
The Adventures of the Wilderness Family
Alaska
The Alaska Wilderness Adventure
All Mine to Give
Arctic Blue
Backwoods
The Bear▶
Beyond Fear
Black Robe▶
Blood Brothers
Blood of the Hunter
The Bridge to Nowhere
Bullies
Cajon Pass
The Capture of Grizzly Adams
Claws
Clearcut
Cold River
Continental Divide
Cross Creek
Davy Crockett and the River Pirates
Davy Crockett, King of the Wild Frontier▶
Death Hunt
Decoy
Dominion
Earthling
Edge of Honor
Endangered
Eyes of Fire
Far from Home: The Adventures of Yellow Dog
The Fatal Glass of Beer
Father and Scout
Ferngully: The Last Rain Forest
Flight from Glory
Further Adventures of the Wilderness Family, Part 2
God's Country
Goldy 2: The Saga of the Golden Bear
Great Adventure
The Great Outdoors
Grizzly
Grizzly Adams: The Legend Continues
Heaven on Earth
Hunter's Blood
Ice Palace
Jeremiah Johnson▶
Just Before Dawn
Kid Colter
The Legend of Wolf Mountain
Life & Times of Grizzly Adams
Lost
Lost in the Barrens
Man in the Wilderness
Man of the House
Mountain Charlie
Mountain Family Robinson
Mountain Man
Napoleon and Samantha▶
Never Cry Wolf▶
Northwest Passage▶
Northwest Trail
Orion's Belt
Orphans of the North
Quest for Fire▶
Shoot to Kill▶
Silence
Silence of the North
Slashed Dreams
Sourdough
Spirit of the Eagle
Starbird and Sweet William
The Tale of Ruby Rose▶
Tales of the Klondike: In a Far Country
Tales of the Klondike: Race for Number One
Tales of the Klondike: The Scorn of Women
Tales of the Klondike: The Unexpected
Timber Queen
Tundra
Vanishing Prairie▶
Vanishing Wilderness
Violent Zone
The Voyage of Tanai
Warrior Spirit
White Fang▶
White Fang and the Hunter
The White Tower▶
White Water Summer
White Wolves 2: Legend of the Wild
Whitewater Sam
Young & Free

Witchcraft

***see also* Demons & Wizards; Occult**

Bell, Book and Candle
Bewitched
Beyond Darkness
Black Magic
Black Sunday▶
Burn Witch, Burn!▶
Cast a Deadly Spell▶
The Conqueror Worm▶
The Craft
The Crucible▶
Cry of the Banshee
The Curse of the Crying Woman
Curse of the Devil
Dark Shadows: Episode 1
Daughters of Satan
Day of Wrath▶
The Day the Earth Froze
Demon Witch Child
The Demons
The Devils▶
Devonsville Terror
Dr. Strange
Double Double Toil and Trouble
Eye of the Demon
Eyes of Fire
Four Rooms
The Haunted Palace
The Haunting of Morella
Hercules, Prisoner of Evil
Hocus Pocus
Horror Hotel
Horror Rises from the Tomb
The Hospital▶
House of the Black Death
I Married a Witch▶
Inquisition
The Juniper Tree
Kill, Baby, Kill▶
The Lady's Not for Burning
Lisa and the Devil
Lost Legacy: A Girl Called Hatter Fox
Love at Stake
Maciste in Hell
Mark of the Devil
Mark of the Devil 2
My Little Pony: The Movie
The Naked Witch
Netherworld
Night of the Scarecrow
The Polar Bear King
Quartier Mozart
The Resurrected
Return to Oz
Sabrina the Teenage Witch
Season of the Witch
The She-Beast
The Shrieking
Something Weird
Sorceress▶
Sorceress
The Terror
Terror Beach
That Darn Sorceress
Three Sovereigns for Sarah
The Touch of Satan
Troll 2
The Undead▶
The Virgin Witch
Warlock
Warlock Moon
Warlock: The Armageddon
The Werewolf vs. the Vampire Woman
Wicked Stepmother
The Witch
Witch Who Came from the Sea
A Witch Without a Broom
Witchcraft
Witchcraft 3: The Kiss of Death
Witchcraft 4: Virgin Heart
Witchcraft 7: Judgement Hour
Witchery
The Witches▶
Witches' Brew
Witches' Mountain
The Witches of Eastwick
The Witching of Ben Wagner
The Witchmaker
The Witch's Mirror
WitchTrap
The Wizard of Oz▶
The Woman Who Came Back
The Worst Witch

Women

see also Dream Girls; Femme Fatale; Moms; Westrogens; Women in Prison; Wonder Women

Accidental Meeting
Alice Doesn't Live Here Anymore
Amelia Earhart: The Final Flight
Anna▶
Another Way▶
Another Woman▶
Antonia and Jane▶
Antonia's Line
Arizona
The Astounding She-Monster
Babyfever
Bachelor Mother▶
Backstreet Justice
The Ballad of Little Jo
Bandit Queen
Bar Girls
Beaches▶
Betty
Bhaji on the Beach
Black Scorpion
Blood and Sand▶
Blood Games
Blue De Ville
Born in Flames
The Bostonians
Boulevard
Boys on the Side
The Buccaneers▶
Buffalo Girls
A Bunny's Tale
Business as Usual
Camilla
A Century of Women
Certain Fury
Challenge of a Lifetime
Chantilly Lace
The Children's Hour
China Beach▶
City Without Men
Claire of the Moon
The Color Purple▶
Come Back to the Five & Dime Jimmy Dean, Jimmy Dean▶
Commissar▶
Courage Under Fire▶
Crazy Mama
Crimes of the Heart
Cry of the Werewolf
Daisy Miller
The Dallas Connection
Dames Ahoy
Dangerous Prey
A Dangerous Woman
Darktown Strutters
Daughters of the Dust▶
The Day the Women Got Even
Defenseless
The Desperate Trail
Dirty Dishes▶
Doctor Quinn, Medicine Woman
A Doll's House
A Doll's House▶
Dolores Claiborne▶
Double Obsession
Dreams
Early Summer▶
Easy Virtue
Eating
Ebony Dreams
Eddie
Eleanor: First Lady of the World
Elizabeth R▶
Enchanted April
Enid Is Sleeping
Enormous Changes▶
Even Cowgirls Get the Blues
The Execution
An Eye for an Eye
Faces of Women
Family Secrets
Feast of July
Feds
Fire in the Night
Flatbed Annie and Sweetiepie: Lady Truckers
The Flower of My Secret▶
Follow the River
Fran
Fried Green Tomatoes▶
Friends
Gangs, Inc.
Gas Food Lodging▶
A Geisha▶
Gentlemen Prefer Blondes▶
Girl 6
Girlfriends▶
Good Girls Don't
The Great Man's Lady
The Group
Guardian Angel
The Happy Ending
Hard Country
Head of the Family
Heat and Dust▶
Heaven and Earth
The Heidi Chronicles
Hellcats
The Heroic Trio
Horror of the Zombies
House of Whipcord
Household Saints▶
How to Make an American Quilt
How to Marry a Millionaire
I Like It Like That▶
In This House of Brede▶
The Insect Woman▶
Is There Life Out There?
Island of Lost Girls
Jamon, Jamon
Je Tu Il Elle
The Joy Luck Club▶
Joy Ride to Nowhere
Judicial Consent
Juliet of the Spirits▶
Just Another Girl on the I.R.T.
Kamikaze Hearts
Keetje Tippel
The Ladies Club
Ladies on the Rocks
Ladybird, Ladybird▶
The Last Best Year
Late Chrysanthemums
A League of Their Own▶
Leaving Normal
The Legend of Blood Castle
Les Bonnes Femmes▶
Little Women▶
Little Women
Little Women▶
Live Nude Girls
Lola Montes▶
Losing Isaiah▶
Love After Love
The Love Goddesses
Lumiere
Madame Bovary▶
Mademoiselle Striptease
Madonna: Innocence Lost
Maedchen in Uniform▶
The Magic Bubble
Malou
Marianne and Juliane▶
Marilyn: The Untold Story▶
Mars Needs Women
Memories of Murder
Messidor
Mi Vida Loca
Miles to Go
Mina Tannenbaum
Miss Firecracker▶
Moll Flanders▶
Monkey Grip▶
Moonlight and Valentino
Mortal Thoughts
Moscow Does Not Believe in Tears▶
Mother & Daughter: A Loving War
My Brilliant Career▶
My Twentieth Century▶
9 to 5
Nomugi Pass
Now and Then
The Nun
One Sings, the Other Doesn't
The Opposite Sex
Oriane
Osaka Elegy
Overseas: Three Women with Man Trouble▶
Pancho Barnes
Passion Fish▶
Patti Rocks▶
Perfume
Poetic Justice
Poor Little Rich Girl: The Barbara Hutton Story
Portrait of a Showgirl
Portrait of Teresa▶
Prime Suspect▶
Prime Suspect 2▶
Prime Suspect 3▶
Prime Suspect: Inner Circles
Prime Suspect: The Lost Child▶
Prime Suspect: The Scent of Darkness▶
Pumping Iron 2: The Women
Quartier Mozart
Queen of Diamonds
Question of Silence▶
The Rector's Wife
Revenge of the Teenage Vixens from Outer Space
Rich and Famous
The Road to Galveston▶
Rosa Luxemburg
Roseanne: An Unauthorized Biography
Ruby in Paradise▶
Salmonberries
Samson vs. the Vampire Women
Sandra of a Thousand Delights
The Scent of Green Papaya▶
Sexual Intent
She-Devil
The Shooter
Sifted Evidence
Sister Street Fighter
The Sisterhood
Snapdragon
Sorceress▶
Spices▶
The Spitfire Grill
Stage Door▶
Star!
Steaming
Steel and Lace
Steel Magnolias▶
The Story of Qui Ju▶
The Story of Women▶
The Stranger
Strangers in Good Company▶
Strangers: The Story of a Mother and Daughter▶
Street of Shame▶
Stripper
Sudden Death
Sunset Strip
Talk
Talking About Sex
The Taxi Mystery
Tell Me Where It Hurts
Tender Comrade
301, 302
Three Secrets
Tomorrow's Children
Trojan Women
Trumps
Twenty-One
An Unmarried Woman▶
Unnatural
Utamaro and His Five Women
Visiting Hours
Viva Maria!
Voyage en Douce
Waiting to Exhale▶
Walpurgis Night▶
Westward the Women▶
What's Love Got to Do with It?
When a Woman Ascends the Stairs
Whose Child Am I?
Widow's Peak
Wildrose▶
Wing Chun
Witchfire
A Woman and a Woman
A Woman Named Jackie
A Woman Rebels
The Women▶
Women From the Lake of Scented Souls
Women in Prison
The Women of Brewster Place▶
Women on the Verge of a Nervous Breakdown▶
The Wonderful, Horrible Life of Leni Riefenstahl
Working Girl▶
Working Girls▶
The Wrong Woman

Women Cops

see also Cops

Arizona Heat
Black Widow▶
Blue Steel
China O'Brien
Copycat
Dear Detective
Do or Die
The Enforcer
Fargo▶
Fatal Beauty
Get Christie Love!
L.A. Crackdown
L.A. Crackdown 2
Policewoman Centerfold
Policewomen
Prey of the Chameleon
Scorchy
The Silence of the Lambs▶
Silk 2
A Stranger Among Us
Tereza▶
V.I. Warshawski

Women in Prison

see also Exploitation; Men in Prison; Sexploitation

Alien 3
Amazon Jail
Bad Girls Dormitory
Bad Girls in the Movies
Better Off Dead
The Big Bird Cage
The Big Bust Out
The Big Doll House
Born Innocent
Caged Fear
Caged Fury
Caged Hearts
Caged Heat
Caged Heat 2: Stripped of Freedom
Caged in Paradiso
Caged Women
Chained Heat
Chained Heat 2
Chasers
The Concrete Jungle
Condemned to Hell
Condition Red
Convicted: A Mother's Story
Deadlock
Deadlock 2
Desperate Women
Escape from Cell Block 3
Escape from Hell
False Arrest
Getting Out
Girl on a Chain Gang
Girls in Chains
Girls in Prison
Girls Riot
Hot Box
Human Experiments
I Want to Live!▶
Ilsa, the Wicked Warden
Jailbird Rock
Ladies They Talk About
Lady in the Death House
Last Dance
Love Child
Lust for Freedom
Me & Veronica
Midnight
The Muthers
Naked Cage
Nightmare in Badham County
99 Women
Off the Wall
Outside Chance
Playing for Time▶
Prison Stories: Women on the Inside▶
Prisoner Cell Block H
Purgatory
Red Heat
Reflections in the Dark
Reform School Girl
Reform School Girls
Savage Island
Scrubbers
Slammer Girls
Star Slammer
Sweet Sugar
10 Violent Women
Terminal Island
Vendetta
Violent Women
Women in Cell Block 7
Women in Fury
Women Unchained
Women's Prison Escape
Women's Prison Massacre

Wonder Women

see also Dream Girls

The Abductors
Act of Vengeance
Alien▶
Alien 3
Aliens▶
Alley Cat
The Amazons
Amazons
The American Angels: Baptism of Blood
Angel's Brigade
Annie Oakley
Attack of the 50 Foot Woman
Attack of the 50 Ft. Woman
Attack of the 60-Foot Centerfold
Backfire!
Bad Georgia Road
Bad Girls
Barbarian Queen
Barbarian Queen 2: The Empress Strikes Back
Basic Training
Batman Returns
Beauty for the Asking
Belle Starr
Big Bad Mama 2
The Big Bust Out
Billie
Bimini Code
The Bionic Woman
Blonde in Black Leather
Blonde Savage
Blue Tiger
Born in Flames
Buffy the Vampire Slayer▶
Bury Me an Angel
Business as Usual
China O'Brien 2
Chopper Chicks in Zombietown
The Clan of the Cave Bear
Cleopatra
Cleopatra Jones
Colossus and the Amazon Queen
Comes a Horseman
Cutthroat Island
Dance of Death
Danger Zone
The Deadly and the Beautiful
Deadly Weapons
The Demolitionist
Do or Die
The $5.20 an Hour Dream
Galaxis
Get Christie Love!
Girl from Calgary
Golden Lady
Golden Ninja Warrior
Grand Larceny
The Great Texas Dynamite Chase

World War I

World War II

see also The Holocaust; Postwar; POW/MIA; The Resistance

Hell is for Heroes▶
Hell River
Hell Squad
Hell to Eternity
Hellcats of the Navy
Hell's Brigade: The Final Assault
Heroes Die Young
Heroes in Hell
The Hiding Place
The Highest Honor
Hillbilly Blitzkrieg
Hiroshima▶
Hiroshima Maiden
Hiroshima: Out of the Ashes▶
Hitler
Hitler: The Last Ten Days
Hitler's Children▶
Hollywood Canteen▶
Holocaust▶
Homecoming
Hope and Glory▶
The Horizontal Lieutenant
Hornet's Nest
Hotel Reserve▶
The Human Comedy▶
The Human Condition: A Soldier's Prayer▶
The Human Condition: No Greater Love▶
The Human Condition: Road to Eternity▶
Hunted!
Hunted
Hunters of the Golden Cobra
Hustler Squad
I See a Dark Stranger▶
I Was a Male War Bride▶
Identity Unknown
Ike
Immortal Battalion▶
Immortal Sergeant
The Imperial Japanese Empire
Imperial Navy
In a Shallow Grave
In Harm's Way
In Which We Serve▶
The Incident▶
The Incredible Mr. Limpet
The Inheritors
Inside the Third Reich
Is Paris Burning?▶
Jenny's War
Jet Attack/Paratroop Command
Jive Junction
Joan of Paris▶
Journey for Margaret▶
Journey into Fear▶
Judgment at Nuremberg▶
Julia▶
Jungle Patrol
Kamikaze
Kanal▶
Kapo▶
Kelly's Heroes
The Key
The Key to Rebecca
Kindergarten▶
King Rat▶
Kings Go Forth
La Grande Vadrouille▶
Lassiter
The Last Bastion
The Last Butterfly
The Last Chance▶
Last Day of the War
The Last Days of Patton
The Last Five Days
The Last Metro▶
The Last Train
The Last Warrior
Law of the Jungle
A League of Their Own▶
Leon Morin, Priest
Les Miserables
Les Violons du Bal
Letters to an Unknown Lover
The Life and Death of Colonel Blimp▶
Lifeboat▶
The Lion Has Wings
The Little Thief▶
The Long Island Four
The Longest Day▶
The Lost One
Lotna
A Love in Germany
MacArthur
MacArthur's Children▶
Malaya
Malta Story
A Man Called Sarge
A Man Escaped▶
The Man Who Never Was▶
Manhunt in the African Jungle
Manon
Map of the Human Heart
Maria's Lovers
Marine Raiders
Massacre in Rome
Max and Helen
The McConnell Story
McKenzie Break▶
Me and the Colonel
The Mediterranean in Flames
Mediterraneo▶
Meet Sexton Blake
Mein Kampf: Hitler's Rise and Fall
Memories of Hell
Memphis Belle▶
Memphis Belle: A Story of a Flying Fortress
The Men▶
Mephisto▶
Merrill's Marauders
Merry Christmas, Mr. Lawrence▶
A Midnight Clear▶
Midway
Miracle at Moreaux
The Miracle of the White Stallions
The Mirror▶
The Misfit Brigade
Mission Batangas
Mission Corbari
Mission of the Shark▶
Mrs. Miniver▶
Mr. Kingstreet's War
Mr. Klein▶
Mister Roberts▶
Mr. Skeffington▶
Mr. Winkle Goes to War
Monte Carlo
The More the Merrier▶
Morituri▶
The Mortal Storm▶
Mother of Kings
The Mountain Road
Murderers among Us: The Simon Wiesenthal Story▶
Murphy's War
Music Box
Mussolini & I
My Name is Ivan▶
The Naked and the Dead
The Nasty Girl▶
The Navy Comes Through
Navy Way
The Neon Bible
Never So Few
Never Wave at a WAC
Night Ambush
Night of the Fox
The Night of the Shooting Stars▶
The Nightmare Years
No Greater Love
No Regrets for Our Youth▶
None But the Brave
The North Star▶
Nous N'Irons Plus au Bois
The Nun's Story▶
Objective, Burma!▶
The Odd Squad
Once Before I Die
Once Upon a Honeymoon
One Against the Wind▶
One of Our Aircraft Is Missing▶
One That Got Away▶
The Only Way
Open City▶
Operation Amsterdam
Operation Cross Eagles
Operation Crossbow▶
The Oppermann Family
Overlanders▶
Pacific Inferno
Paisan▶
Panama Hattie
Passage to Marseilles▶
Patton▶
The Pawnbroker▶
The Philadelphia Experiment
Piece of Cake
Pimpernel Smith
Pin-Up Girl
Place in Hell
Playing for Time▶
Prelude to War
Prisoners of the Sun▶
Private Buckaroo
Private Contentment
PT 109
The Purple Heart
Pursuit of the Graf Spee
Qui Etes Vous, Mr. Sorge?
Racing with the Moon▶
Rage of Wind
Raggedy Man▶
Raid on Rommel
Raiders in Action
Raiders of Sunset Pass
Reach for the Sky
Rebel
Red Ball Express
The Reflecting Skin
Reunion▶
Reunion in France
The Revolt of Job▶
Robot Pilot
Run Silent, Run Deep▶
Running Away
Saboteur▶
Sahara▶
Salo, or the 120 Days of Sodom
Salute John Citizen▶
San Demetrio, London
Sands of Iwo Jima▶
The Scarlet & the Black
Schindler's List▶
Sea Chase
Sea of Sand
The Sea Shall Not Have Them
Sea Wolves
The Search▶
Second Victory
The Secret Code
Secret Mission
The Secret War of Harry Frigg
Seven Beauties▶
Seven Days' Leave
The Seventh Cross▶
Shadows Over Shanghai
Shell Shock
Sherlock Holmes and the Secret Weapon▶
Sherlock Holmes: The Voice of Terror
Shining Through
Ship of Fools▶
The Shop on Main Street▶
Signs of Life
The Silent Enemy
Silent Raiders
Since You Went Away▶
Sink the Bismarck▶
633 Squadron
Ski Troop Attack
The Small Back Room▶
Snow Treasure
So Proudly We Hail▶
So This is Washington
Soldat Duroc...Ca Va Etre Ta Fete!
Soldier of Orange▶
A Soldier's Story▶
A Soldier's Tale
Somewhere I'll Find You▶
Son of Lassie
The Sorrow and the Pity▶
The Sound of Music▶
South Pacific▶
Special Forces
Spitfire▶
Spy Smasher Returns
S.S. Experiment Camp 2
SS Girls
Stage Door Canteen
Stalag 17▶
Stalag Luft
Star Spangled Rhythm▶
The Steel Claw
The Story of Dr. Wassell
Strictly G.I.
Submarine Seahawk
Suicide Battalion/Hell Squad
Suicide Patrol
The Summer of My German Soldier▶
Sundown
Sweet Light in a Dark Room▶
Swing Shift
Tank Commando
Task Force
A Taste of Hell
The Teahouse of the August Moon
Tender Comrade
The Tenth Man
Thank Your Lucky Stars▶
That Long Night in '43
That Summer of White Roses
They Were Expendable▶
13 Rue Madeleine▶
Thirty Seconds Over Tokyo▶
Thirty-Six Hours of Hell
This Is the Army
This Land is Mine▶
Thousands Cheer
Three Came Home▶
Tides of War
Tiger Fangs
A Time of Destiny
A Time to Love & a Time to Die
The Tin Drum▶
To Be or Not to Be▶
To Be or Not to Be
To Have & Have Not▶
To Hell and Back
To the Shores of Tripoli
Tobruk
Tomorrow Is Forever
Tonight and Every Night
Too Late the Hero▶
Tora! Tora! Tora!
Torpedo Attack
Torpedo Run
Tower of Terror
The Train▶
Transport from Paradise
Triple Cross▶
Triple Echo
Triumph of the Spirit▶
Triumph of the Will
True Colors
The Tuskegee Airmen▶
Twelve O'Clock High▶
25 Fireman's Street▶
Two Girls and a Sailor▶
The Two of Us▶
Two Women▶
U-Boat Prisoner
Uncertain Glory
Under the Earth▶
The Underdog
Underground▶
Until They Sail
Up in Arms
Up Periscope
Victory
Von Ryan's Express▶
Voyage of the Damned▶
Wackiest Ship in the Army
Wake Island▶
A Walk in the Sun▶
The Wannsee Conference▶
War & Love
War & Remembrance, Part 1
War & Remembrance, Part 2
War & Remembrance, Part 3
War & Remembrance, Part 4
War & Remembrance, Part 5
War & Remembrance, Part 6
War & Remembrance, Part 7
War & Remembrance: The Final Chapter, Part 8
War & Remembrance: The Final Chapter, Part 9
War & Remembrance: The Final Chapter, Part 10
War & Remembrance: The Final Chapter, Part 11
War & Remembrance: The Final Chapter, Part 12
The War Boy
War in the Sky▶
War Lover
War Victims
Warkill
Watch on the Rhine▶
Waterfront
We Dive at Dawn▶
We Will Not Enter the Forest▶
The Weaker Sex
Wedding in White
Well-Digger's Daughter▶
What Did You Do in the War, Daddy?
When Hell Broke Loose
When Taekwondo Strikes
Where Eagles Dare▶
The White Cliffs of Dover▶
The White Rose▶
The Winds of War
A Wing and a Prayer▶
Wings Over the Pacific
The Wizard of Loneliness
A Woman at War
Women of Valor
Wooden Horse▶
World War II: When Lions Roared
A Yank in Australia
A Yank in the R.A.F.
Yanks
You'll Never Get Rich▶
The Young Lions▶
Zero
Zero Pilot
Zone Troopers

Wrestling

...All the Marbles
The American Angels: Baptism of Blood
Bad Guys
Below the Belt
Body Slam
Grunt! The Wrestling Movie
Hadley's Rebellion
Invasion of the Zombies
Mad Bull
Mugsy's Girls
My Breakfast with Blassie
No Holds Barred
The One and Only
Paradise Alley
Park Avenue Logger
Pin Down Girls
Samson in the Wax Museum
Summer's Games
Superargo
Take Down
Think Big
Thunder & Mud
Vision Quest
Women in Love▶
The World According to Garp▶
The Wrestler
Wrestling Racket Girls
Wrestling Women vs. the Aztec Ape
Wrestling Women vs. the Aztec Mummy

Writers

see also This is Your Life

The Adventures of Mark Twain▶
Agatha
American Dreamer
Author! Author!
Barton Fink▶
The Basketball Diaries
Beloved Infidel
Best Seller▶
Breakfast at Tiffany's▶
A Business Affair

Chapter Two
Cross Creek
Dante's Inferno: Life of Dante Gabriel Rossetti
The Dark Half
Deathtrap
Delirious
F. Scott Fitzgerald in Hollywood
The Flower of My Secret▶
Forbidden Passion: The Oscar Wilde Movie
Ghostwriter
Gothic▶
Haunted Summer
Heart Beat
Heartburn▶
Henry & June▶
Her Alibi
In the Deep Woods
In the Mouth of Madness
James Joyce: A Portrait of the Artist as a Young Man
James Joyce's Women▶
Joshua Then and Now▶
Kafka
Lady On a Train▶
The Life of Emile Zola▶
The Lonely Lady
The Loves of Edgar Allen Poe
Misery▶
Mrs. Parker and the Vicious Circle
My Apprenticeship▶
My Brilliant Career▶
My Universities▶
Naked Lunch▶
Out of Africa▶
The Prize▶
Reds▶
Romancing the Stone▶
Shadowlands▶
The Snows of Kilimanjaro▶
Spymaker: The Secret Life of Ian Fleming
Street Smart
Theodora Goes Wild▶
The Third Man▶
301, 302
Tom & Viv▶
The Trials of Oscar Wilde▶
Unsane
The Wonderful World of the Brothers Grimm
The World According to Garp▶
Zora Is My Name!

Wrong Side of the Tracks

see also Rags to Riches

Aaron Loves Angela
Algiers▶
Alice Adams
Angel and the Badman▶
Angels with Dirty Faces▶
Anna Christie
Bachelor Party
Back Door to Heaven▶
Breaking Away▶
The Bride Wore Red
Camille▶
Cannery Row
Captains Courageous▶
Captives
Carbon Copy
Careful, He Might Hear You▶
Carrie▶
Cat Ballou▶
Chains
China Girl
Claudia
Cool As Ice
The Courtney Affair
Courtship▶
The Crucified Lovers▶
Cry-Baby▶
The Dark Side of Love
Diary of a Chambermaid▶
Dirty Dancing▶
Dr. Jack/For Heaven's Sake
Eegah!
Far and Away
Federal Hill
The Fence
Fire with Fire
The Flamingo Kid▶
Foxfire Light
Fresh Horses
Future Kill
Grease▶
The Great Gatsby
The Hairy Ape
Hearts of Humanity
Iron Maze
It
It Could Happen to You
It Happened One Night▶
Jersey Girl
Jungle Fever▶
King Ralph
The Lacemaker▶
Last Exit to Brooklyn▶
Liar's Moon
Little Minister▶
The Loves of Carmen
Luzia
The Man from Snowy River
Manhattan Melodrama▶
Masquerade▶
A Million to One
Min & Bill
My Forbidden Past
My Man Godfrey▶
Naked Youth
Night Beat
Off Beat
Outpost in Morocco
Over the Brooklyn Bridge
The Phantom in the House
The Phantom of the Opera▶
Picnic on the Grass
A Place in the Sun▶
The Pope of Greenwich Village
Port of New York
Pretty in Pink
Primrose Path
Princess Tam Tam▶
Probation
Pygmalion▶
Reckless
Reform School Girl
Return to Snowy River▶
Rich Girl
Riff Raff▶
Rocky▶
Room at the Top▶
Ruby Gentry
Rumble Fish▶
San Francisco▶
The Servant▶
sex, lies and videotape▶
Show People▶
Snow Country
Some Kind of Wonderful
Somebody Up There Likes Me▶
Stay Hungry▶
The Story of the Late Chrysanthemum▶
Suburbia
The Swan
The Swan▶
Sweet Light in a Dark Room▶
The Tamarind Seed
Tango
That Night
This Sporting Life▶
Tortilla Flat▶
A Tree Grows in Brooklyn▶
Under the Boardwalk
Uptown Angel
Valley Girl
The Valley of Decision▶
Virtue's Revolt
Vivacious Lady▶
Waterloo Bridge▶
White Palace
The White Sin
The World of Suzie Wong
The Young Philadelphians▶

You Lose, You Die

see also Post Apocalypse

Arcade
Arena
Death Race 2000
Deathrow Gameshow
Dominion
Mad Max: Beyond Thunderdome
Naked Warriors
Prayer of the Rollerboys
Robot Jox
Roller Blade
Roller Blade Warriors: Taken By Force
Rollerball
The Running Man
Solarbabies
Tron

Yuppie Nightmares

see also Strained Suburbia

Addams Family Values
Alice▶
Almost You
Amos and Andrew
Baby Boom
Bad Influence
Barbarians at the Gate▶
Bare Essentials
Bedroom Eyes
Beetlejuice▶
The Big Chill▶
Blind Date
Blind Side
The Bonfire of the Vanities
The Boost
Bright Lights, Big City
Cape Fear▶
City of Hope▶
Clara's Heart
Clean and Sober▶
Coma▶
Consenting Adults
Curly Sue
Dead Calm▶
Denise Calls Up
Desperately Seeking Susan
Diary of a Mad Housewife▶
Down and Out in Beverly Hills
Drop Dead Fred
Edge of Honor
The End of Innocence
Eye of the Demon
Fatal Attraction▶
The Fisher King▶
Folks!
Fun with Dick and Jane
The Further Adventures of Tennessee Buck
Goodbye, New York
The Guardian
The Hand that Rocks the Cradle
The Hard Way▶
He Said, She Said
Heartburn▶
Hiding Out
In the Spirit
Indian Summer
Jungle Fever▶
Key Exchange
Kicks
L.A. Story▶
Let's Kill All the Lawyers
Limit Up
Looking for Mr. Goodbar
Lost in America▶
Love or Money?
Madhouse
Maid to Order
The Malibu Beach Vampires
Maniac
Micki & Maude
The Mighty Ducks
The Money Pit
Mother's Boys
Moving
My Daughter's Keeper
My New Gun
Neighbors
New Year's Day▶
Next Door
Night of the Living Babes
Nothing But Trouble
Nothing in Common
Oasis of the Zombies
The Object of Beauty▶
Pacific Heights▶
Perfect Family
Permanent Vacation
Preppies
Private Benjamin
Quicksilver
Reversal of Fortune▶
Roadhouse 66
Rude Awakening
Ruthless People▶
St. Elmo's Fire
The Secret of My Success
The Secretary
September
sex, lies and videotape▶
Shattered
A Shock to the System▶
Six Degrees of Separation
Something Wild
Stay Tuned
Straw Dogs▶
Summer Rental
Taking Care of Business
Taking the Heat
The Temp
Three Men and a Little Lady
Through the Eyes of a Killer
The Tie That Binds
The Toxic Avenger, Part 3: The Last Temptation of Toxie
Trading Places
Trapped
The Trigger Effect
Unlawful Entry
The Vagrant
Video Americana
Voodoo Dawn
Wall Street▶
The War of the Roses▶
Westworld▶
What About Bob?▶
When a Man Loves a Woman
Windy City
Wolf

Zombie Soldiers

see also Zombies

Akira Kurosawa's Dreams
The Dark Power
Deathdream
Hard Rock Zombies
Oasis of the Zombies
Revenge of the Zombies
Revolt of the Zombies
Scream and Scream Again
She Demons
Shock Waves
The Supernaturals
They Saved Hitler's Brain
The Zombie Army
Zombie Lake

Zombies

see also Death & the Afterlife; Ghosts, Ghouls, & Goblins; Zombie Soldiers

The Alchemist
Alien Massacre
Almost Dead
The Astro-Zombies
Bowery at Midnight
Bride of Re-Animator
Carnival of Souls▶
Cast a Deadly Spell▶
Cemetery Man
Children Shouldn't Play with Dead Things
The Chilling
Chopper Chicks in Zombietown
C.H.U.D. 2: Bud the Chud
City of the Walking Dead
Creature of the Walking Dead
The Curse of the Aztec Mummy
Curse of the Screaming Dead
Dawn of the Dead▶
Dawn of the Mummy
Day of the Dead
Dead Alive
The Dead Don't Die
Dead Heat
Dead Men Don't Die
The Dead Next Door
Dead Pit
Death Becomes Her▶
The Death Curse of Tartu
Deathdream
Demon Wind
Destroyer
Devil Kiss
Ed and His Dead Mother
Evil Town
The Ghost Brigade
The Ghoul
The Granny
The Hanging Woman
Haunting Fear
Hellgate
The Hereafter
Horror of the Zombies
Horror Rises from the Tomb
The House of Seven Corpses
House of the Dead
I Eat Your Skin
I Walked with a Zombie▶
Invisible Invaders
Isle of the Dead
The Jitters
King of the Zombies
Kiss Daddy Goodbye
The Mad Ghoul
Messiah of Evil
The Mummy▶
Mummy & Curse of the Jackal
The Mummy's Revenge
My Boyfriend's Back
Neon Maniacs
Night Life
Night of Horror
Night of the Comet
Night of the Creeps
Night of the Death Cult
Night of the Ghouls
Night of the Living Babes
Night of the Living Dead▶
Night of the Living Dead
Night of the Living Dead, 25th Anniversary Documentary
Nightmare Weekend
Oasis of the Zombies
Orgy of the Dead
The Outing
Pet Sematary 2
Phantasm III: Lord of the Dead
Plan 9 from Outer Space
Prison
Quatermass 2▶
Re-Animator▶
Redneck Zombies
Return of the Evil Dead
Return of the Living Dead
Return of the Living Dead 2
Return of the Living Dead 3
Revenge of the Dead
Revenge of the Living Zombies
Revenge of the Zombies
Revolt of the Zombies
The Robot vs. the Aztec Mummy
Seedpeople
Seven Doors of Death
Shock Waves
Sole Survivor
Steps from Hell
The Stuff
Svengali▶
Teenage Zombies
Tomb of the Undead
Tombs of the Blind Dead
Torture Chamber of Baron Blood
The Vampire's Ghost
Vengeance of the Zombies
Virgin Among the Living Dead
Voodoo Dawn
Voodoo Woman
The White Zombie▶
Winterbeast
Zombie
The Zombie Army
Zombie High

Zombies

Zombie Island Massacre
Zombie Lake
Zombie Nightmare
Zombies of Moratau
Zombies of the Stratosphere
Zombies on Broadway
Zombiethon

Kibbles and Series Index

The **Kibbles** and **Series** indexes have been combined into one index in this edition. This is where you'll find info on where your favorite movies came from—literary, theatrical, cartoon, and television adaptations to name a few, as well as the behind the scenes talents that make movies possible, such as producers and special effects wizards. Another important feature of this index is the quality check it provides with categories like **Woofs!**, **4 Bones**, and **Top Grossing Films** by year. This index also provides information on recurring characters like James Bond or Mike Hammer, as well as notable screen partnerships. Some examples include Abbott & Costello, Hope & Crosby, and De Niro & Scorsese. **A tipped triangle denotes a three-bone or higher rating** The categories are as follows, with an asterisk (*) denoting a new category:

Kibbles and Series Index

Abbott & Costello

Adapted from a Book

Adapted

Land of Promise
The Land That Time Forgot
Lantern Hill
L'Appat
Larry McMurtry's Streets of Laredo▶
The Last Butterfly
Last Days of Pompeii
The Last Detail▶
Last Exit to Brooklyn▶
The Last Hit
The Last Hunt
Last Hurrah
The Last of the Mohicans▶
The Last of the Mohicans
The Last of the Mohicans▶
The Last of the Redmen
The Last Safari
Last Summer
The Last Temptation of Christ▶
The Last Tycoon▶
The Late Shift
Lathe of Heaven
The Laughing Policeman
Laura▶
A Lawless Street
Le Sexe des Etoiles
The Learning Tree
Leave Her to Heaven▶
A Legacy for Leonette
The Legend of Hell House▶
The Legend of Sea Wolf
The Legend of Sleepy Hollow
The Legend of the Sea Wolf
Legend of Walks Far Woman
Legends of the Fall
Lensman
Leon Morin, Priest
The Leopard Man
Les Miserables▶
Les Miserables
Les Miserables▶
Les Miserables
Less Than Zero
L'Etat Sauvage▶
The Letter▶
A Letter to Three Wives▶
License to Kill▶
L'Idiot
Lie Down with Lions
A Life of Her Own
Life of Oharu▶
Life with Father▶
Lifeboat▶
The Light in the Forest
Light Years
Like Water for Chocolate▶
Linda
Little Big Man▶
The Little Colonel▶
The Little Drummer Girl▶
Little Gloria...Happy at Last
Little House on the Prairie▶
The Little Match Girl
Little Men
The Little Mermaid
The Little Mermaid▶
Little Minister▶
The Little Princess
A Little Princess▶
A Little Romance▶
Little Women▶
Little Women
Little Women▶
Living Free
Living Proof: The Hank Williams Jr. Story
Logan's Run
Lola Montes▶
Lolita▶
Lonely Are the Brave▶
The Lonely Guy
The Lonely Lady
The Lonely Passion of Judith Hearne▶
Lonelyhearts
The Long, Hot Summer▶
The Longest Day▶
The Lookalike
Looking for Miracles
Looking for Mr. Goodbar
Lord Jim▶
Lord of the Flies▶
Lord of the Flies
The Lord of the Rings
The Lords of Discipline
Lorna Doone
Losing Isaiah▶
The Lost Command
The Lost Honor of Katharina Blum▶
Lost Horizon▶
Lost in the Barrens
The Lost Language of Cranes▶
The Lost Patrol▶
Love for Lydia▶
Love in the Present Tense
The Lover
The Loves of Carmen
Lucky Jim
Lust for Life▶
The Mad Executioners
Madame Bovary▶
Madigan▶
Mafia Princess
Magic
The Magnificent Ambersons▶
Magnificent Obsession
Make Me an Offer
Malarek
Malcolm X▶
The Maltese Falcon▶
The Mambo Kings▶
Man Friday
Man from Nowhere
The Man I Love▶
The Man in the Gray Flannel Suit
The Man in the Iron Mask▶
The Man in the Mist
Man in the Saddle
Man of Destiny
Man of Evil
Man of the Forest
Man on the Eiffel Tower▶
The Man Outside
The Man Who Cried
The Man Who Fell to Earth▶
The Man Who Never Was▶
The Man Who Would Be King▶
The Man Who Would Not Die
Man with a Gun
The Man with the Golden Arm▶
The Man Without a Face
The Manchurian Candidate▶
Mandingo
Manhunt for Claude Dallas
Manhunter▶
Manon
Manon of the Spring▶
Mansfield Park
The Many Adventures of Winnie the Pooh
Marathon Man▶
Margin for Murder
Marie▶
Marie Antoinette
Marilyn: The Untold Story▶
The Mark of Zorro▶
The Martian Chronicles: Part 1
The Martian Chronicles: Part 3
Mary Poppins▶
Mary Reilly
Mary Shelley's Frankenstein
Masada▶
M*A*S*H▶
The Mask of Fu Manchu
The Master of Ballantrae
Master of the World
Matewan▶
Matilda
Matters of the Heart
Mazes and Monsters
McCabe & Mrs. Miller▶
McKenzie Break▶
McVicar
Memphis
The Men's Club
Mephisto▶
The Mephisto Waltz▶
Merry Christmas, Mr. Lawrence▶
Middlemarch▶
Midnight
A Midnight Clear▶
Midnight Cowboy▶
Midnight Edition
Mildred Pierce▶
Mimi
Mindwalk: A Film for Passionate Thinkers▶
Miracle at Moreaux
Miracle in the Wilderness
The Miracle of the Bells
The Mirror Crack'd
Misery▶
Miss Sadie Thompson▶
Missing Pieces
Mission Stardust
Mississippi Mermaid▶
Missouri Traveler▶
Mrs. 'Arris Goes to Paris
Mrs. Doubtfire
Mrs. Miniver▶
Mrs. Munck
Mrs. Parkington
Mrs. Winterbourne
Mr. & Mrs. Bridge▶
Mr. Horn
Mister Johnson▶
Mr. North
Mr. Peabody & the Mermaid
Mr. Skeffington▶
Mr. Winkle Goes to War
Mistral's Daughter
Mistress Pamela
Misty
Moby Dick▶
Moll Flanders▶
Monkey Boy
Monkey Grip▶
Monkey Shines
Monsieur Beaucaire▶
Monsignor
Monsignor Quixote
Monte Walsh▶
A Month in the Country▶
The Moon and Sixpence▶
Moon in the Gutter
Moonfleet
Morning Glory
Morocco▶
The Mortal Storm▶
The Mosquito Coast
Mother▶
Mother's Boys
The Mountain
Mountain Fury
Mountains of the Moon▶
The Mouse That Roared▶
The Muppet Christmas Carol
Muppet Treasure Island
Murder by the Book
Murder in Coweta County
Murder in Texas▶
A Murder Is Announced
Murder, My Sweet▶
Murder of a Moderate Man
Murder on the Bayou▶
The Music of Chance
The Mutiny of the Elsinore
Mutiny on the Bounty▶
Mutiny on the Bounty
My African Adventure
My Antonia
My Brilliant Career▶
My Father's Glory▶
My Friend Walter
My Girl Tisa
My Left Foot▶
My Man Godfrey▶
My Man Godfrey
My Michael▶
My Old Man
My Summer Story
Myra Breckinridge
Mysteries
Mysterious Island▶
The Mysterious Stranger
The Mystery of Edwin Drood
The Naked and the Dead
The Naked Edge
The Naked Face
Naked Lunch▶
The Name of the Rose
Nana▶
Nana
The Nanny
Nasty Habits
National Velvet▶
Native Son
The Natural▶
Necessary Parties
Needful Things
Neighbors
The Neon Empire
Never Cry Wolf▶
Never Let Me Go
Never Love a Stranger
Never Say Never Again
Never So Few
The NeverEnding Story▶
Nevil Shute's The Far Country
The New Adventures of Pippi Longstocking
The New Invisible Man
The New Land▶
Nice Girl Like Me
Nicholas and Alexandra
Nicholas Nickleby▶
Nickel Mountain
Night After Night
Night Ambush
Night and the City▶
Night Breed
A Night in the Life of Jimmy Reardon
'night, Mother
The Night of the Following Day
Night of the Generals▶
The Night of the Hunter▶
Night of the Twisters
A Night to Remember▶
Night Train to Munich▶
Nightfall▶
Nightscare
Nikki, the Wild Dog of the North
1984▶
92 in the Shade▶
No Escape
No Highway in the Sky▶
No Love for Johnnie▶
Nobody's Fool▶
North
North and South Book 1▶
North and South Book 2▶
North Dallas Forty▶
North to Alaska▶
Northanger Abbey
Northern Pursuit
Northwest Passage▶
Nosferatu▶
Not as a Stranger
Not Quite Human
Now and Forever
Now, Voyager▶
The Nun's Story▶
O Pioneers!
O Quatrilho
The Oak
Oblomov▶
Octopussy
The Odessa File
Of Human Bondage▶
Of Human Bondage
Of Love and Shadows
Of Mice and Men▶
The Old Curiosity Shop
The Old Dark House▶
Old Gringo
The Old Lady Who Walked in the Sea
The Old Maid▶
The Old Man and the Sea
Oldest Confederate Widow Tells All▶
Oliver!▶
Oliver & Company
Oliver Twist▶
Oliver Twist
Oliver Twist▶
Oliver Twist
Omega Man
The Omen
On the Beach▶
On the Comet▶
On Wings of Eagles
Onassis
Once Upon a Time...When We Were Colored▶
Once Were Warriors▶
One Day in the Life of Ivan Denisovich▶
One Deadly Summer▶
One Flew Over the Cuckoo's Nest▶
One in a Million: The Ron LeFlore Story
One Man's Way
One Night in the Tropics
One Russian Summer
One Shoe Makes It Murder
Ordeal by Innocence
Ordinary Magic
Orlando▶
Orphan Train▶
The Osterman Weekend
The Other▶
The Other Side of Midnight
Our Vines Have Tender Grapes▶
Out
Out of Africa▶
Out of the Past▶
Out on a Limb
Outbreak▶
The Outlaw Josey Wales▶
Outlaw of Gor
Outrage!
The Outsiders
The Overcoat▶
Overnight Sensation
The Painted Veil
Pal Joey▶
Panique▶
Papa's Delicate Condition▶
The Paper Chase▶
Paper Moon▶
Paperhouse▶
The Paradine Case
Paris Express
Paris, France
Paris Trout
Parrish
A Passage to India▶
Past the Bleachers
Paths of Glory▶
Patriot Games▶
Patty Hearst
The Pawnbroker▶
The Pearl▶
The Pelican Brief
Pelle the Conqueror▶
The Penthouse
The People
The Perez Family
A Perfect Spy
Peril
Persuasion▶
Pet Sematary
Pete 'n' Tillie
Peter Pan▶
Petulia▶
Phantom Fiend
The Phantom of the Opera▶
The Phantom of the Opera
Phantom Tollbooth▶
The Phoenix and the Magic Carpet
The Pickwick Papers
Picnic at Hanging Rock▶
Picture of Dorian Gray▶
Piece of Cake
Pinky▶
Pippi Goes on Board
Pippi Longstocking
Pippi on the Run
A Place in the Sun▶
The Plague
The Plague Dogs
Planet of the Apes▶
The Player▶
A Pocketful of Rye
Poldark▶
Poldark 2▶
Police
Pollyanna▶
Poor Little Rich Girl: The Barbara Hutton Story
The Poppy Is Also a Flower
Portnoy's Complaint
Portrait of a Lady
Postcards from America

Postcards from the Edge▶
The Postman▶
The Postman Always Rings Twice▶
The Postman Always Rings Twice
Power
The Power of One
A Prayer for Katarina Horovitzova▶
Presenting Lily Mars
The President's Mystery
Pride and Prejudice▶
Pride and Prejudice
Pride and Prejudice▶
Primal Fear
Primal Secrets
Prime Suspect▶
The Prince and the Pauper▶
The Prince and the Pauper
Prince Brat and the Whipping Boy▶
The Prince of Central Park▶
The Prince of Thieves
The Prince of Tides▶
The Princess and the Goblin
The Princess Bride▶
The Princess Comes Across▶
Princess Daisy
Prisoner of Zenda▶
Prisoner of Zenda
The Private Affairs of Bel Ami▶
The Private History of a Campaign That Failed
Private War
The Prize▶
The Prize Pulitzer
Prizzi's Honor▶
Promised a Miracle
The Proud Ones
Prudential Family Playhouse
Psycho▶
The Pumpkin Eater▶
The Puppet Masters
Puppet on a Chain
The Purple Taxi
Pursuit▶
Quartet▶
Queen Bee
Queen Margot▶
Queenie
Querelle
Question of Honor
The Quick and the Dead
Quick Change
The Quiller Memorandum▶
Quo Vadis▶
Quo Vadis
Rachel, Rachel▶
A Rage in Harlem▶
Rage of Angels
Rage of Angels: The Story Continues
Ragtime▶
The Railway Children▶
The Railway Station Man▶
Rain
Rainbow
The Rainbow▶
Rainbow Drive
The Rains Came
Raintree County
Raise the Titanic
Rampage
Random Harvest▶
Rattled
The Razor's Edge▶
The Razor's Edge
Rebecca▶
Rebecca of Sunnybrook Farm
The Rebels
The Rector's Wife
The Red and the Black▶
The Red Badge of Courage▶
The Red House▶
The Red Pony▶
The Red Raven Kiss-Off
Reflections in a Golden Eye
The Reincarnation of Peter Proud
The Reivers▶
The Remains of the Day▶

Remo Williams: The Adventure Begins
The Resurrected
The Return of the King
The Return of the Musketeers
The Return of the Native
Return of the Soldier▶
Return to Earth
Return to Oz
Reuben, Reuben▶
Reunion▶
Revenge
Reversal of Fortune▶
Rhapsody
Rhapsody in August
Rich in Love
Rich Man, Poor Man▶
The Riddle of the Sands
Ride a Wild Pony▶
Riders of the Purple Sage
The Right Stuff▶
Ring of Bright Water▶
Rip van Winkle
Rising Sun▶
The River Pirates
A River Runs Through It▶
The Robe
Robert Kennedy and His Times
Robin Hood▶
Robinson Crusoe
Rogue Male
Roll Along Cowboy
Roll of Thunder, Hear My Cry
Room Service
A Room with a View▶
Roommates
Roots▶
Roots: The Gift
Roots: The Next Generation▶
The Rosary Murders
Rosebud
Rosemary's Baby▶
Roswell: The U.F.O. Cover-Up
Roxanne▶
Royal Flash▶
Rudyard Kipling's The Jungle Book
Rumble Fish▶
The Rumor Mill
A Rumor of War▶
Rumpole of the Bailey
Runaway
Running Against Time
The Running Man
Rush▶
The Russia House
The Russians are Coming, the Russians are Coming▶
Ruyblas
The Sacketts
Sadie Thompson▶
Safe Passage
The Sailor Who Fell from Grace with the Sea
The Saint
Saint Jack▶
Salo, or the 120 Days of Sodom
Salome
The Salzburg Connection
Sanctuary of Fear
Santa Fe
The Saragossa Manuscript
Sarah, Plain and Tall▶
Saratoga Trunk
Satan Met a Lady
Savage Wilderness
Sayonara▶
The Scar
The Scarlet & the Black
Scarlet Dawn
The Scarlet Letter
The Scarlet Letter▶
The Scarlet Letter
The Scarlet Pimpernel▶
Scarlett
Schindler's List▶
Scott Turow's The Burden of Proof
Scrooge▶
Scrooge
Scruples
The Sea Wolf▶

The Sea Wolf
The Search for Bridey Murphy
Searching for Bobby Fischer▶
Second Best▶
Second Victory
The Secret Adversary
The Secret Four
The Secret Garden▶
The Secret Garden
The Secret Garden▶
The Secret Garden
The Secret of NIMH▶
The Secret of Roan Inish▶
Seduced by Evil
Seduction: The Cruel Woman
The Seekers
Seize the Day▶
Sense & Sensibility
Sense and Sensibility▶
A Sense of Freedom▶
A Separate Peace
The Separation
Sergeant Rutledge▶
The Serpent and the Rainbow
Serpico▶
The Servant▶
Servants of Twilight
The Set Up
Seven Blows of the Dragon
7 Faces of Dr. Lao▶
The Seven-Per-Cent Solution▶
Seven Sixgunners
Seven Thieves▶
The Seventh Cross▶
S.F.W.
Shadow of China▶
Shadow of the Thin Man▶
Shadow of the Wolf
The Shadow Riders
Shaft▶
Shalako
Shane▶
Sharky's Machine
Sharpe's Battle
Sharpe's Company
Sharpe's Eagle
Sharpe's Enemy
Sharpe's Gold
Sharpe's Honour
Sharpe's Rifles
Sharpe's Sword
Shattered Vows
She
She Came to the Valley
She-Devil
The Shell Seekers
The Sheltering Sky▶
Sherlock Holmes: The Silver Blaze
Sherlock Holmes: The Voice of Terror
Sherlock Hound: Tales of Mystery
The Shining
Shining Through
Ship of Fools▶
Shipwrecked
A Shock to the System▶
The Shoes of the Fisherman
Shogun▶
Shoot the Piano Player▶
The Shooting Party▶
The Shootist▶
The Shout▶
Shout at the Devil
Sidney Sheldon's Bloodline
Silas Marner▶
The Silence of the Lambs▶
The Silk Road
Silver Bears
Silver Bullet
The Silver Chalice
The Silver Horde
Silver River
The Silver Stallion: King of the Wild Brumbies
A Simple Twist of Fate
Single White Female
The Sins of Dorian Gray
The Sisters▶
Ski Bum
Skyscraper Souls▶

Slapstick of Another Kind
Slaughterhouse Five
Slaves of New York
Slightly Honorable
Slightly Scarlet
The Slingshot▶
Sliver
Slow Burn
A Small Killing
Smart-Aleck Kill
Smith!
The Snake Pit▶
SnakeEater 3: His Law
The Snapper▶
Snow Country
Snow Treasure
Sofie
Solaris
Soldier Blue
Soldier in the Rain
Solomon and Sheba
Something of Value▶
Something Wicked This Way Comes
Sometimes a Great Notion▶
Somewhere in Sonora
Son of Fury▶
Son of the Morning Star▶
Sophie's Choice▶
Sounder▶
South Central
South Pacific▶
The Spanish Gardener▶
Special Investigator
Spencer's Mountain
Spenser: Ceremony
Spenser: Pale Kings & Princes
Spirit Rider▶
Spirits of the Dead▶
The Spoilers▶
The Spook Who Sat By the Door
Spy in Black▶
Spy of Napoleon
Spy Story
The Spy Who Came in from the Cold▶
The Squeaker
Stars and Bars
Stars in My Crown▶
The Stars Look Down▶
State Fair▶
State Fair
Staying On
Steaming
Stella
Stella Dallas▶
Stephen King's The Langoliers
Stephen King's The Stand
Stephen King's The Tommyknockers
Steppenwolf
Stick
Stiletto
Stopover Tokyo
Storm and Sorrow
The Story of Dr. Wassell
The Story of O
The Story of Qui Ju▶
Straight Time▶
Strange Case of Dr. Jekyll & Mr. Hyde
Strange Fruit
Strange Tales/Ray Bradbury Theatre
The Stranger Wore a Gun
Strangers on a Train▶
Strangers When We Meet
The Streets of San Francisco▶
Striptease
Stuart Saves His Family
Studs Lonigan
The Stunt Man▶
The Stupids
Sudden Fear▶
Sudie & Simpson▶
Sugartime
Summer Heat
The Summer House
The Summer of My German Soldier▶
A Summer Place
The Sundowners▶

Suzy
Svengali▶
Svengali
Swann in Love
Sweet Hostage
Sweet Killing
Sweet Love, Bitter
The Swiss Family Robinson▶
Sword of Gideon
Tai-Pan
A Tale of Two Cities▶
A Tale of Two Cities
A Tale of Two Cities▶
Tall Story
Taras Bulba
Tarnished Angels▶
Tarzan, the Ape Man▶
Tarzan, the Ape Man
Tecumseh: The Last Warrior
TekWar
Temptation of a Monk
Ten Days That Shook the World▶
Ten Days Wonder
Ten Little Indians
Ten North Frederick
The Tenant▶
Tender Is the Night
The Tenth Man
10th Victim▶
The Terminal Man
Terror Is a Man
Terror Stalks the Class Reunion
Tess▶
Tex
Texas
The Texas Rangers
That Darn Cat
That Eye, The Sky
That Forsyte Woman
That Night
That Obscure Object of Desire▶
That Uncertain Feeling
That Was Then...This Is Now
They Call It Sin
They Came to Cordura
They Live by Night▶
They Won't Forget▶
Thicker Than Water
The Thief Who Came to Dinner
Thieves Like Us▶
The Thing▶
Things to Come▶
The Third Man▶
Third Man on the Mountain
This Gun for Hire
This Sweet Sickness
The Thorn Birds▶
Those Calloways
Three Came Home▶
Three Comrades▶
Three Days of the Condor▶
The Three Musketeers
The Three Musketeers▶
The Three Musketeers
The Three Musketeers▶
3:10 to Yuma▶
The Three Worlds of Gulliver
Thumbelina
Thunder Mountain
Thunder Pass
Till Death Do Us Part
Till the End of Time
Tim
Time for Murder
The Time Machine▶
Time Machine
Time of Indifference
A Time to Kill▶
A Time to Love & a Time to Die
The Tin Drum▶
To Catch a Thief▶
To Dance with the White Dog▶
To Die For▶
To Have & Have Not▶
To Hell and Back
To Kill a Mockingbird▶
To Play the King▶
To Sir, with Love
To the Devil, A Daughter
To the Last Man
To the Lighthouse
Tokyo Decadence

Tom and Huck▶
Tom Brown's School Days
Tom Brown's School Days▶
Tom Jones▶
Tom Sawyer
Tomb
Topaz▶
Topkapi▶
Torn Apart
Tortilla Flat▶
Total Recall▶
Tough Guys Don't Dance
A Town Like Alice
Toy Soldiers
Trader Horn
Trading Mom
Trainspotting▶
Transport from Paradise
Traps
Treasure Island▶
Treasure Island
Treasure of the Sierra Madre▶
A Tree Grows in Brooklyn▶
Trespasser
The Trial▶
The Trial
Trial by Jury
The Trials of Oscar Wilde▶
Triple Cross▶
Tristana▶
The Triumph of Sherlock Holmes
Trojan Women
Tropic of Cancer▶
True Confessions▶
True Grit▶
Truman
Tune in Tomorrow
Tunes of Glory▶
20,000 Leagues Under the Sea▶
29th Street
The 27 Day
Twice-Told Tales▶
Twilight's Last Gleaming
Two English Girls▶
Two Kinds of Love
2001: A Space Odyssey▶
2010: The Year We Make Contact▶
Two to Tango
The Two Worlds of Jenny Logan
Tyson
Ugetsu▶
The Ugly American
Ulysses
The Unbearable Lightness of Being▶
The Unbreakable Alibi
Uncle Moses
Uncle Tom's Cabin
Unconquered
Under Capricorn
Under Satan's Sun▶
Under the Volcano▶
Uneasy Terms
Union Pacific▶
The Unnamable
The Unsinkable Molly Brown▶
Unstrung Heroes
Unsuitable Job for a Woman
Until They Sail
Up the Down Staircase▶
Users
Utz
The Valley of Decision▶
Valley of the Dolls
Valmont▶
The Vampire Lovers
Vampyr▶
The Vanishing
Vanity Fair
A Very Old Man with Enormous Wings
V.I. Warshawski
Village of the Damned▶
Village of the Damned
Village of the Giants
The Violent Men
The Virgin and the Gypsy
The Virgin Soldiers
The Virginian
The Virginian▶
The Virginian
Vision Quest
Viva Zapata!▶
Voyage of the Damned▶
Voyager▶
The Voyeur
Wages of Fear▶
Wagon Wheels
Walk on the Wild Side
Walking on Air
Wanderers▶
War & Love
War and Peace
War and Peace▶
War & Remembrance, Part 1
War & Remembrance, Part 2
War & Remembrance, Part 3
War & Remembrance, Part 4
War & Remembrance, Part 5
War & Remembrance, Part 6
War & Remembrance, Part 7
War & Remembrance: The Final Chapter, Part 8
War & Remembrance: The Final Chapter, Part 9
War & Remembrance: The Final Chapter, Part 10
War & Remembrance: The Final Chapter, Part 11
War & Remembrance: The Final Chapter, Part 12
War Between the Tates
War Lover
War of the Buttons
The War of the Roses▶
The War of the Worlds▶
The War Wagon▶
Warlock▶
Watchers
Waterland
Watership Down
The Way We Were▶
The Way West
The Wayward Wife
We the Living
We Think the World of You▶
The Wedding Gift▶
Weep No More My Lady
We're Back! A Dinosaur's Story
West of the Pecos
Whale for the Killing
Whale Music
What Price Hollywood?▶
What's Eating Gilbert Grape▶
What's Love Got to Do with It?
When the Bough Breaks
When the Dark Man Calls
When the West Was Young
When the Whales Came
When the Wind Blows▶
Where Angels Fear to Tread▶
Where Are the Children?
Where the Buffalo Roam
Where the Lilies Bloom▶
Where the Red Fern Grows
Where the Red Fern Grows: Part 2
Where the Rivers Flow North
Where Time Began
Where's Poppa?▶
Whispers
Whistle Down the Wind▶
White Cargo
White Fang▶
White Fang and the Hunter
White Hot: The Mysterious Murder of Thelma Todd
White Lie
White Nights▶
Who Am I This Time?▶
Who Framed Roger Rabbit▶
Who Is Killing the Great Chefs of Europe?▶
Who'll Stop the Rain?▶
Why Shoot the Teacher▶
The Wicked Lady
Wide Sargasso Sea
The Widow
Wild Bill
The Wild Country
Wild Times
Wildflower▶
Will: G. Gordon Liddy
Willy Wonka & the Chocolate Factory▶
The Wind▶
Windom's Way▶
The Winds of Jarrah
Winter People
Wise Blood▶
The Witches of Eastwick
Without Reservations
Without Warning: The James Brady Story▶
Witness for the Prosecution▶
The Wizard of Loneliness
The Wizard of Oz▶
Wolf Call
Wolfen▶
A Woman at Her Window
A Woman Called Moses
Woman in Black
Woman in the Shadows
Woman In the Window▶
A Woman Named Jackie
A Woman of Substance, Episode 1: Nest of Vipers
A Woman of Substance, Episode 2: The Secret is Revealed
A Woman of Substance, Episode 3: Fighting for the Dream
A Woman Rebels
A Woman's Guide to Adultery
Women in Love▶
Wooden Horse▶
Words by Heart
The World According to Garp▶
The World is Full of Married Men
The World of Apu▶
The World of Henry Orient▶
A World of Strangers▶
The World Owes Me a Living
The Worst Witch
The Wreck of the Mary Deare
The Wrong Box▶
The Wrong Move
Wuthering Heights▶
Wuthering Heights
A Year in Provence▶
Year of the Dragon
The Yearling▶
The Yearling
Yentl
Yesterday's Hero
You Only Live Twice
Young at Heart
Young Bess▶
The Young in Heart▶
Young Lady Chatterly 2
Young Man with a Horn▶
Young Winston▶
Your Ticket Is No Longer Valid
Zandy's Bride
Zatoichi: Master Ichi and a Chest of Gold
Zotz!

Adapted from a Cartoon

The Addams Family
Addams Family Values
The Adventures of Captain Marvel
Adventures of Red Ryder
Adventures of Smilin' Jack
The Amazing Spider-Man
Arcadia of My Youth
Barbarella
The Belles of St. Trinian's▶
Big Zapper
Blondie
Blondie Has Trouble
Blondie Hits the Jackpot
Blondie in Society
Blondie Knows Best
Blondie Takes a Vacation
Blondie's Blessed Event
Casper▶
Cool World
Crimewave
Dennis the Menace
Dennis the Menace: Dinosaur Hunter
Dick Tracy
Dick Tracy vs. Cueball
Dick Tracy's Dilemma
Dr. Strange
Edward Scissorhands▶
Elvira, Mistress of the Dark
Fatty Finn
The Fighting Redhead
The Flash
The Flash 2: Revenge of the Trickster
Flash Gordon
Flesh Gordon 2: Flesh Gordon Meets the Cosmic Cheerleaders
The Flintstones
Friday Foster
Frostbiter: Wrath of the Wendigo
The Great St. Trinian's Train Robbery
The Guyver
Guyver 2: Dark Hero
Heavy Metal▶
Hillbilly Blitzkrieg
Home Alone▶
Howard the Duck
It's a Great Life
Jane & the Lost City
Kowloon Assignment
Li'l Abner
Little Nemo: Adventures in Slumberland
Little Orphan Annie
The Mask▶
Maybe...Maybe Not
Mighty Morphin Power Rangers: The Movie
Pee Wee's Big Adventure▶
The Perils of Gwendoline
Petit Con
Phantom 2040 Movie: The Ghost Who Walks
The Pink Panther▶
The Pink Panther Strikes Again▶
Prince Valiant
The Pure Hell of St. Trinian's
Reg'lar Fellers
The Return of Swamp Thing
Richie Rich
Sabrina the Teenage Witch
The Sad Sack
Supergirl
Superman 2▶
Tank Girl
Teenage Mutant Ninja Turtles: The Movie
Teenage Mutant Ninja Turtles 2: The Secret of the Ooze
Teenage Mutant Ninja Turtles 3
Timecop
Tom and Jerry: The Movie
Vault of Horror
The Villain
Wicked City
Wild Palms
The Wild World of Batwoman

Adapted from a Fairy Tale

The Adventures of Pinocchio
Aladdin
Aladdin▶
Aladdin and His Wonderful Lamp
Alice in Wonderland
Alice's Adventures in Wonderland
Beanstalk
Beauty and the Beast▶
Beauty and the Beast
Beauty and the Beast▶
The Blue Light▶
The Boy Who Left Home to Find Out About the Shivers
Butterfly Ball
Cannon Movie Tales: Red Riding Hood
Cannon Movie Tales: Sleeping Beauty
Cannon Movie Tales: The Emperor's New Clothes
Casey at the Bat
Cinderella▶
Cinderella
Cinderella 2000
Cinderfella
The Company of Wolves▶
The Dancing Princesses
Deadtime Stories
Donkey Skin▶
Dos Cruces en Danger Pass▶
The Emperor's New Clothes
Fairy Tales
Frog
George Balanchine's The Nutcracker
The Glass Slipper
Goldilocks & the Three Bears
Hans Christian Andersen
Hansel and Gretel
Happily Ever After
A Hungarian Fairy Tale▶
Irish Cinderella
Jack & the Beanstalk
La Petite Sirene
Les Visiteurs du Soir▶
The Little Match Girl
The Little Mermaid
The Little Mermaid▶
Little Red Riding Hood
The Magic Fountain
The Magic Legend of the Golden Goose
The Magic Sword
Magical Wonderland
March of the Wooden Soldiers▶
Mother Goose Rock 'n' Rhyme
The NeverEnding Story▶
The Neverending Story 3
The Nightingale
Nutcracker, A Fantasy on Ice
The Nutcracker Prince
Nutcracker: The Motion Picture
Once Upon a Brothers Grimm
Peter Pan▶
The Pied Piper of Hamelin
Pinocchio▶
Pinocchio
Pinocchio's Storybook Adventures
The Princess and the Pea
The Princess and the Swineherd
The Princess Bride▶
Princess Cinderella
The Princess Who Never Laughed
Puss 'n Boots
Rapunzel
Red Riding Hood
The Red Shoes
Rip van Winkle
Rudyard Kipling's Classic Stories
Rumpelstiltskin
The Scalawag Bunch
Sleeping Beauty▶
Sleeping Beauty
The Snow Queen
Snow White
Snow White and the Seven Dwarfs
Snow White and the Three Stooges
Storytime Classics
The Swan▶
The Swan Princess
The Tale of the Frog Prince▶
The Three Little Pigs
Thumbelina
The Tin Soldier
Tom Thumb▶
Who Slew Auntie Roo?
The Wishmaker
The Witches▶
The Wonderful World of the Brothers Grimm
The Wonders of Aladdin

Adapted from a Game

Clue
Double Dragon

Mortal Kombat: The Movie
Street Fighter
Super Mario Bros.
Tag: The Assassination Game

Adapted from a Play or Musical

Abe Lincoln in Illinois▶
The Adventures of Robin Hood▶
Age Old Friends▶
Agnes of God
Ah, Wilderness!▶
Alfie▶
Alice
All My Sons▶
Amadeus▶
Anastasia▶
Animal Crackers▶
The Animal Kingdom▶
Anna Christie▶
Anna Christie
Annie
The Anniversary
Another Country
Any Wednesday
Arsenic and Old Lace▶
As Is
As You Desire Me▶
August
The Avenger
The Awful Truth▶
Babes in Arms
Babes in Toyland
Baby Doll▶
Baby, the Rain Must Fall
The Bacchantes
The Bad Seed
The Balcony▶
The Ballad of the Sad Cafe
Bar Girls
Barefoot in the Park▶
Beatlemania! The Movie
Beau Brummel
Beau Brummel▶
Becket▶
Becky Sharp
Being at Home with Claude
Bells are Ringing▶
Best Foot Forward
The Best Little Whorehouse in Texas
The Best Man▶
Betrayal
Beyond Therapy
The Big Knife▶
Big News
Billie
Biloxi Blues
The Birth of a Nation▶
Bitter Sweet
Black Limelight
Black Lizard
Black Orpheus▶
Blessed Event▶
Blithe Spirit▶
Blood Wedding▶
Bluebeard's Eighth Wife
Bodies, Rest & Motion
Bophal!▶
Born Yesterday▶
Born Yesterday
Boy Meets Girl▶
The Boys in the Band
The Boys Next Door
Breath of Scandal
The Brig▶
Brigadoon▶
Brighton Beach Memoirs
Broadway Bound
A Bronx Tale▶
The Browning Version▶
The Browning Version
Bus Stop▶
Butterflies Are Free▶
Bye, Bye, Birdie▶
Cabaret▶
Cactus Flower
Caesar and Cleopatra
California Suite▶
Can-Can
Casablanca▶
Casanova Brown
Cast a Dark Shadow▶
Casual Sex?
Cat on a Hot Tin Roof▶
Cat on a Hot Tin Roof
Cavalcade▶
Cease Fire
Ceiling Zero▶
The Chalk Garden▶
Chapter Two
Charm of La Boheme
The Chase
The Cheap Detective▶
Children of a Lesser God▶
The Children's Hour
Chimes at Midnight▶
The Chocolate Soldier
A Chorus Line
A Chorus of Disapproval
Circle of Love
Clarence Darrow▶
Clarence, the Cross-eyed Lion▶
Clash by Night▶
Columbo: Prescription Murder
Come Back, Little Sheba▶
Come Back to the Five & Dime Jimmy Dean, Jimmy Dean▶
Come Blow Your Horn▶
Command Decision
Conduct Unbecoming
The Connection▶
Cool Mikado
Coquette
The Corn is Green▶
The Count of the Old Town
Country Girl▶
County Fair
Craig's Wife▶
Crimes of the Heart
The Crucible▶
Curse of the Starving Class
Cyrano de Bergerac
Cyrano de Bergerac▶
Da
Daddy's Dyin'...Who's Got the Will?
Damn Yankees▶
A Day in the Death of Joe Egg▶
Day of Wrath▶
Daybreak
Dead End▶
Death and the Maiden▶
Death of a Salesman▶
Deathtrap
The Desert Song
Desire Under the Elms
Desk Set▶
Desperate Hours▶
Detective Story▶
Devil Girl from Mars
The Devil's Brother
The Devil's Disciple▶
Dial "M" for Murder▶
Diary of a Hitman
The Dining Room
Dinner at Eight▶
Disraeli▶
The Divorce of Lady X
The Doctor and the Devils
Doll Face
A Doll's House
A Doll's House▶
Don't Drink the Water
Double Wedding▶
The Dresser▶
Driving Miss Daisy▶
DuBarry Was a Lady
Duet for One
Dumb Waiter
Dutchman▶
The Eagle Has Two Heads▶
Easy Virtue
Educating Rita▶
Edward II
The Effect of Gamma Rays on Man-in-the-Moon Marigolds▶
Emperor Jones
Emperor Jones/Paul Robeson: Tribute to an Artist
Employees' Entrance▶
The Enchanted Cottage
Ensign Pulver
The Entertainer▶
Entertaining Mr. Sloane
Equus
Escapade▶
Escape Me Never
Everybody Wins
Faithful
The Farmer Takes a Wife
The Farmer's Wife
A Few Good Men▶
Fiddler on the Roof▶
The Field▶
A Fine Romance
Finian's Rainbow▶
Flower Drum Song
Follies in Concert
Fool for Love
Footlight Serenade
Footsteps in the Dark
Forbidden Planet▶
Forever Female▶
Fortune and Men's Eyes
Forty Carats
Foxfire▶
Frankenstein Sings...The Movie
Frankie and Johnny▶
The Front Page▶
The Fugitive Kind
A Funny Thing Happened on the Way to the Forum▶
Fury is a Woman▶
Futz
Gaslight▶
The Gay Divorcee▶
The Gazebo▶
Generation
Gentlemen Prefer Blondes▶
George Washington Slept Here▶
George White's Scandals
Getting Out
The Ghost Breakers▶
Give Me a Sailor
The Glass Menagerie▶
Glengarry Glen Ross▶
Golden Boy▶
The Golden Coach▶
Gone are the Days
The Goodbye Girl▶
The Gorilla
Grease▶
Grease 2
The Great White Hope
Green Pastures▶
Grown Ups
The Guardsman▶
Gypsy▶
Gypsy
Hair▶
The Hairy Ape
Hamlet▶
Hamlet
Hamlet▶
The Happiest Days of Your Life▶
Happy Birthday, Gemini
Harriet Craig▶
He Who Gets Slapped▶
Heartbreak House
Heaven Can Wait▶
Hedda
The Heidi Chronicles
Hello, Dolly!
Henry IV
Henry V▶
His Double Life
His Girl Friday▶
Hit the Deck
Holiday▶
The Honey Pot
Hotel Paradiso
The Hound of London
I Confess
I Do! I Do!
I Married an Angel
I Never Sang For My Father▶
I Ought to Be in Pictures
I Remember Mama▶
Idiot's Delight▶
Illicit
Illusions
The Impossible Years
In Celebration▶
In Search of the Castaways▶
In the Good Old Summertime▶
Indiscreet
Inherit the Wind▶
Iphigenia▶
Irma La Douce
Italian Straw Hat▶
Jacknife▶
Jeffrey
Jesus Christ, Superstar▶
Joan of Arc
Johnny Belinda
Jubal
Julius Caesar▶
Julius Caesar
Key Exchange
Key Largo▶
The Killing of Sister George
The King and I▶
King Lear▶
King Lear
Kiss Me Kate▶
Kiss Me, Stupid!
The Knack▶
K2: The Ultimate High
La Cage aux Folles▶
La Cage aux Folles 2
La Cage aux Folles 3: The Wedding
La Ronde▶
Ladies They Talk About
Lady Be Good
The Lady's Not for Burning
The Last of Mrs. Cheyney▶
Last of the Red Hot Lovers
Laughing Sinners
Lenny▶
Les Enfants Terrible▶
A Life in the Theater
Li'l Abner
The Lion in Winter▶
The Little Foxes▶
Little Johnny Jones
Little Murders▶
A Little Night Music
Little Shop of Horrors▶
Long Day's Journey into Night▶
Long Day's Journey into Night
The Long Voyage Home▶
Look Back in Anger▶
Look Back in Anger
Look Back in Anger▶
Loot...Give Me Money, Honey!
Lost in Yonkers
Louisiana Purchase
The Lovable Cheat
Love and Human Remains▶
The Lower Depths▶
M. Butterfly
Macbeth▶
Macbeth
Madame X
The Madwoman of Chaillot
The Magnificent Yankee▶
The Mahabharata
Major Barbara▶
A Majority of One
Male and Female▶
Mame
A Man for All Seasons▶
The Man in the Glass Booth▶
Man of La Mancha
The Man Who Came to Dinner▶
Marat/Sade▶
Marius▶
Marriage Italian Style▶
Mary of Scotland▶
Mass Appeal
Master Harold and the Boys▶
The Matchmaker▶
Maytime▶
Me and the Colonel
Medea
The Merry Widow▶
The Merry Widow
Merton of the Movies
Mexican Hayride
Midnight Lace
A Midsummer Night's Dream▶
A Midsummer Night's Dream
The Migrants▶
The Millionairess
The Miracle Worker▶
Miss Firecracker▶
Miss Julie
Miss Rose White▶
Mr. Music
Mister Roberts▶
Mr. Write
Monster in a Box▶
Morning Glory
Much Ado about Nothing▶
Murder▶
Murder at the Vanities
Murder by Death
The Music Man▶
My Brother's Wife
My Fair Lady▶
My Sister Eileen▶
Nell
Never Steal Anything Small
Never Too Late to Mend
New Faces of 1952
New Moon
The Night of the Iguana▶
No, No Nanette
No Time for Sergeants▶
Noises Off
The Norman Conquests, Part 1: Table Manners▶
The Norman Conquests, Part 2: Living Together▶
The Norman Conquests, Part 3: Round and Round the Garden▶
Norman, Is That You?
No. 17▶
The Odd Couple▶
Oedipus Rex▶
Oh! Calcutta!
Oh Dad, Poor Dad (Momma's Hung You in the Closet & I'm Feeling So Sad)
Oklahoma!▶
Oleanna
On a Clear Day You Can See Forever
On Approval▶
On Borrowed Time▶
On Golden Pond▶
On the Town▶
One of My Wives Is Missing
One Touch of Venus
One Trick Pony
Only When I Laugh▶
Opera do Malandro
Ordet▶
Orphans▶
Orphans of the Storm▶
Orpheus Descending
Oscar
Othello
Othello▶
Othello
Other People's Money
Our Town▶
Our Town
Out of Season
The Owl and the Pussycat▶
Paint Your Wagon
The Pajama Game▶
Panama Hattie
The Passing of the Third Floor Back
Patterns▶
Peephole
People Will Talk▶
The Perfect Marriage
Period of Adjustment▶
Personal Property
Petrified Forest▶
Phaedra
The Phantom of the Opera
Phantom of the Paradise
The Philadelphia Story▶
The Piano Lesson▶
Pippin▶
The Pirates of Penzance
Play It Again, Sam▶
Playboy of the Western World
Plaza Suite▶
Plenty
The Portrait▶
Prelude to a Kiss

The Prime of Miss Jean Brodie▶
Princess Tam Tam▶
Prisoner of Second Avenue
Private Lives▶
The Private Secretary
Privates on Parade
Purlie Victorious
Pygmalion▶
Quality Street
A Question of Attribution
Quiet Day In Belfast▶
A Quiet Duel
The Rainmaker▶
A Raisin in the Sun▶
Ran▶
Reckless
Red Planet Mars
Redwood Curtain
The Return of Peter Grimm
Richard III▶
Riders to the Sea
The Right to Remain Silent
The Ritz▶
Roman Spring of Mrs. Stone▶
Romance
Romantic Comedy
Romeo and Juliet▶
Romeo and Juliet
Romeo and Juliet▶
The Room
Roosters
Rope▶
Rosencrantz & Guildenstern Are Dead▶
Roxie Hart
Ruby
The Runner Stumbles
Sabrina▶
Sabrina
Saint Joan
Same Time, Next Year▶
The Saphead
Sarafina!▶
School for Scandal
Scorchers
Scum▶
The Seagull▶
Search and Destroy
Secret Honor▶
The Secret Rapture
Separate Tables▶
Separate Tables
1776▶
Sextette
The Shadow Box▶
Shadowlands▶
The Shanghai Gesture
Shirley Valentine▶
The Shop Around the Corner▶
Short Eyes▶
Show Boat▶
Show Boat
The Show-Off
The Sicilian
The Sign of the Cross
Silent Night, Lonely Night
Silk Stockings▶
A Sinful Life
The Singing Blacksmith
Six Degrees of Separation
Skin Game
Sleuth▶
Small Hotel
Smoking/No Smoking
So Ends Our Night▶
A Soldier's Story▶
Solid Gold Cadillac▶
Sorrento Beach
South Pacific▶
Stage Door▶
Star Spangled Girl
State of the Union▶
Stevie
Stolen Hours
The Storm Within▶
Strange Interlude▶
Strange Interlude
The Strange Love of Molly Louvain
Streamers
Street Scene▶
A Streetcar Named Desire▶
A Streetcar Named Desire
The Stripper
Suddenly, Last Summer▶
The Sum of Us▶
Summer and Smoke
Summertime▶
Summertree
Sunday in the Park with George▶
Sunrise at Campobello▶
The Sunshine Boys▶
Susan Slept Here
Sweeney Todd: The Demon Barber of Fleet Street
Sweet Bird of Youth▶
Sweet Bird of Youth
Sweet Charity▶
Sylvia and the Phantom▶
Talk Radio▶
Tall Story
The Taming of the Shrew
The Taming of the Shrew▶
The Taming of the Shrew
Tartuffe
A Taste of Honey▶
Tea and Sympathy▶
Tea for Two▶
The Teahouse of the August Moon
The Tempest
The Tempest▶
The Terror
That Championship Season
That's Singing: The Best of Broadway
There's a Girl in My Soup
These Three▶
They Knew What They Wanted▶
Thin Ice▶
This Happy Breed▶
This Is the Army
This Property is Condemned
Thoroughly Modern Millie
Those Endearing Young Charms
A Thousand Clowns▶
Three Daring Daughters
Three Men on a Horse▶
The Three Penny Opera▶
The Threepenny Opera
Throne of Blood▶
Tidy Endings
Time Lock
The Time of Your Life▶
Time Without Pity
Tom & Viv▶
Too Many Girls
Topaze▶
Torch Song Trilogy
Tough Guy
Toys in the Attic
The Trials of Oscar Wilde▶
The Trip to Bountiful▶
True West▶
The Tunnel of Love
Twelve Angry Men▶
21 Days
Two for the Seesaw▶
Two Small Bodies
The Unapproachable
Under Milk Wood
Under the Biltmore Clock
An Unfinished Piece for a Player Piano▶
Vanya on 42nd Street▶
Velnio Nuotaka
Volpone▶
A Voyage' Round My Father▶
Wait Until Dark▶
The War Lord▶
Watch on the Rhine▶
The Water Engine
Waterfront
Weekend at the Waldorf▶
We're No Angels
We're Not Dressing▶
West Side Story▶
The Whales of August▶
Where Were You When the Lights Went Out?
Whoopee!
Who's Afraid of Virginia Woolf?▶
Whose Life Is It Anyway?▶
Wild Bill
The Wild Duck
Will Success Spoil Rock Hunter?
Window Shopping
The Winslow Boy▶
Winterset
Without Love
The Wiz
The Women▶
Woyzeck▶
Yellow Dust
You Can't Take It with You▶
Young & Willing
You're a Good Man, Charlie Brown
Zooman▶
Zoot Suit▶

Adapted from a Poem

Braveheart▶
Casey at the Bat
The Castilian
Evangeline
Gunga Din▶
The Man from Snowy River
Old Ironsides▶
The Set-Up▶
Ulysses
The White Cliffs of Dover▶
Wild Party

Adapted from a Song

Alice's Restaurant
The Baron and the Kid
Born in East L.A.
Convoy
Coward of the County
Frankie and Johnny
The Gambler Returns: The Luck of the Draw
Girls Just Want to Have Fun
The Indian Runner
Is There Life Out There?
Kenny Rogers as the Gambler
Kenny Rogers as the Gambler, Part 2: The Adventure Continues
Kenny Rogers as the Gambler, Part 3: The Legend Continues
Legend of Tom Dooley
Love Potion #9
My Darlin' Clementine
The Night the Lights Went Out in Georgia
Ode to Billy Joe
Purple People Eater
Single Bars, Single Women
Take This Job & Shove It
Yellow Submarine▶
You Light Up My Life

Adapted from a Story

ABC Stage 67: Truman Capote's A Christmas Memory
The Adventures of Ichabod and Mr. Toad▶
The Affair of the Pink Pearl
Alice in Wonderland▶
Alice in Wonderland
Amanda and the Alien
Ambassador Bill
America's Dream▶
Androcles and the Lion
The Android Affair
Angels in the Outfield▶
Angels with Dirty Faces▶
Appointment with Crime
Arizona Bushwackers
As Young As You Feel▶
Ashik Kerib▶
The Assassination Bureau▶
Ava's Magical Adventure
Babette's Feast▶
The Babysitter
The Ballad of the Sad Cafe
Bartleby
The Beast from 20,000 Fathoms
Benefit of the Doubt
Big Business Girl
The Big Stampede
Billy the Kid
The Birds▶
The Black Abbot
Blackmail▶
Boots of Destiny
Border Caballero
Boss of Bullion City
A Boy and His Dog
Boys
Boys' Night Out▶
Breakfast at Tiffany's▶
Brief Encounter▶
Brigham Young: Frontiersman
Bright Angel
Burial of the Rats
Bury Me Not On the Lone Prairie
By the Light of the Silvery Moon
Call of the Wild
Candyman
Candyman 2: Farewell to the Flesh
The Canterville Ghost
Carmilla
Casanova's Big Night
Cat's Eye
Caught in the Draft▶
Charade▶
Cinderella
Cinderella 2000
The Cisco Kid
College Swing
Comanche Territory
Come to the Stable▶
Comrade X
Cosmic Slop
Country Lovers, City Lovers
Crash Dive
Creature from the Black Lagoon▶
Creature with the Blue Hand
Cricket on the Hearth
Cult of the Cobra
Dark Eyes▶
Daughter of the Dragon
David and Bathsheba▶
A Day in the Country▶
The Day the Earth Stood Still▶
The Dead▶
The Decameron▶
Decameron Nights
Department Store
Detonator 2: Night Watch
The Devil & Daniel Webster▶
Diary of a Madman
Die, Monster, Die!
Dive Bomber▶
Doomed at Sundown
Door with the Seven Locks
Double Trouble
Double Vision
D.P.
Drift Fence
DROP Squad
The Dropkick▶
Eat a Bowl of Tea▶
The Eyes of the Amaryllis
Eyes of the Panther
A Face in the Crowd▶
Face to Face
Fallen Angels 1▶
Fallen Angels 2▶
Feud Maker
The Fig Tree
The Fighter▶
Fighting Caravans
First Love
Five Days One Summer
The 5000 Fingers of Dr. T▶
Flirtation Walk
Forger of London
Frontier Uprising
Galloping Romeo
Gangway
A Gentle Woman
The Ghost of Frankenstein
Ghost Valley
The Gift of Love
The Girl with the Hungry Eyes
The Glass House▶
The Go-Between▶
Great Adventure
The Great Man's Lady
Gunfight at the O.K. Corral▶
Guys and Dolls▶
Hands Across the Table▶
The Hard Way▶
Haunting Fear
The Haunting of Morella
Highlander▶
Hills of Oklahoma
Hole in the Sky
Home for the Holidays
Homecoming
Hondo▶
Hostile Guns
The House of Usher
How the Grinch Stole Christmas▶
How to Steal a Million▶
I Don't Want to Talk About It
I'm the One You're Looking For
Importance of Being Earnest▶
In Memoriam
In Old Chicago▶
The Incredible Sarah
The Indian Scarf
Internes Can't Take Money
Invasion U.S.A.
The Invisible Boy
The Invisible Woman▶
Isle of Forgotten Sins
It Started with Eve▶
It's a Date
It's a Dog's Life
Jigsaw▶
Johnny Eager▶
Johnny Mnemonic
Johnny Reno
Jonathan Livingston Seagull
Judgment Night
The Jungle Book
The Juniper Tree
Kaos▶
Key to the City
Kim▶
Kurt Vonnegut's Harrison Bergeron
Kurt Vonnegut's Monkey House
La Chute de la Maison Usher▶
La Merveilleuse Visite
The Ladies of the Bois de Bologne
The Lady Eve▶
Lady Killer▶
Lady On a Train▶
The Lady with the Dog▶
The Lady's Maid's Bell
The Land Unknown
Late Chrysanthemums
The Lawnmower Man
The Lawrenceville Stories
Le Plaisir
The Leech Woman
Legends of the North
Life on a String
Little Miss Marker
The Little Prince
Lone Star
Lord of Illusions
The Lost World
Love on the Run
Loyalties
Lurking Fear
The Magic Fountain
The Magic Legend of the Golden Goose
The Magnificent Dope
Main Street to Broadway
Manfish
The Mangler
Margaret's Museum
The Masked Rider
Masque of the Red Death▶
Masque of the Red Death
Maximum Overdrive
Menace II Society▶
Midnight▶
A Million to Juan
Miracle in Rome
Mr. Reeder in Room 13
A Month by the Lake
The Most Dangerous Game▶

The Mummy's Curse
The Mummy's Tomb
Murders in the Rue Morgue
The Murders in the Rue Morgue▶
My Apprenticeship▶
My Childhood▶
My Favorite Blonde▶
My Lucky Star
My Mother's Castle▶
My Sister Eileen▶
My Universities▶
The Mysterious Magician
Mystic Circle Murder
Naked Jungle▶
The Naked Maja
Nevada
Never Say Goodbye
Nightfall
Nightflyers
No Comebacks
Noir et Blanc
Noon Wine▶
Objective, Burma!▶
The Oblong Box
O.C. and Stiggs
An Occurrence at Owl Creek Bridge/Coup de Grace
Of Human Hearts
On Moonlight Bay
100 Men and a Girl▶
Our Modern Maidens
Our Relations▶
The Outlaw Deputy
The Oval Portrait
Peck's Bad Boy
The Pied Piper of Hamelin
The Pit and the Pendulum▶
The Pit & the Pendulum
Pittsburgh
Play Misty for Me▶
Pocketful of Miracles▶
The Possessed▶
Premature Burial
The Prince and the Pauper
The Princess and the Swineherd
Pudd'nhead Wilson
The Purchase Price
The Quarrel
The Queen of Spades▶
Quest for Love
Rawhead Rex
Re-Animator▶
Rear Window▶
Red Balloon/Occurrence at Owl Creek Bridge▶
The Red Shoes▶
The Red Shoes
The Redhead from Wyoming
The Reluctant Dragon
The Report on the Party and the Guests▶
Return to Paradise
Return to the Lost World
Revenge of the Creature
Ride Him, Cowboy▶
Ridin' Down the Canyon
Ridin' the Lone Trail
Robbers of the Sacred Mountain
Rocket to the Moon
The Rocking Horse Winner
Roman Holiday▶
Roommate
Rough Ridin' Rhythm
Ruggles of Red Gap▶
Rumpelstiltskin
Sabotage▶
Salome
Santa Fe
Saturday Night Fever
Screamers
Secret of the Black Trunk
Seven Brides for Seven Brothers▶
The Seven Hills of Rome
Shadow of a Doubt▶
Shanghai Express▶
The Shawshank Redemption▶
Sherlock Holmes: The Master Blackmailer
Shinbone Alley
The Shooting Party
Shopworn Angel▶
Short Cuts▶
The Skull
Sleep of Death
Sleeping Car to Trieste
Smooth Talk▶
The Snow Queen
Snow White and the Seven Dwarfs▶
The Snows of Kilimanjaro▶
Somewhere I'll Find You▶
Song of the Thin Man
Sorrows of Gin
Sorry, Wrong Number
The Southerner▶
The Spectre of Edgar Allen Poe
Stagecoach▶
Station West▶
The Strange Countess
Strawberry and Chocolate▶
A Summer Story▶
A Summer to Remember
Sunset Boulevard▶
The Swimmer▶
Tails You Live, Heads You're Dead
Tales from Avonlea, Vol. 1: The Journey Begins
Tales from the Darkside: The Movie
Tales of Terror
Tales of the Klondike: In a Far Country
Tales of the Klondike: Race for Number One
Tales of the Klondike: The Scorn of Women
Tales of the Klondike: The Unexpected
The Tell-Tale Heart
Tennessee's Partner
They Met in Bombay
They Watch
The Thin Man▶
The Thin Man Goes Home
The Thing
Three Brothers▶
Three Cases of Murder▶
The Three Little Pigs
Three Smart Girls▶
Through the Eyes of a Killer
Thunder Pass
The Tin Soldier
Today We Live
Tomb of Ligeia▶
Tomorrow▶
Tonto Basin Outlaws
Too Far to Go▶
The Topeka Terror
Torture Garden
Torture Ship
Trailin'
Transmutations
Trapped in Space
Tribute to a Bad Man▶
Trio▶
Tropical Heat
Trumps
Twelve Chairs▶
12:01
Two by Forsyth
Two Evil Eyes
Uncertain Glory
An Unforgettable Summer
Vanina Vanini▶
Ward Six
Wee Willie Winkie▶
Who Slew Auntie Roo?
Who's the Man?
The Window▶
Wintertime
A Woman Without Love▶
A Woman's World▶
Women & Men: In Love There Are No Rules
Women & Men: Stories of Seduction
Young at Heart
The Young Land
The Young One
Youth Aflame

Adapted from an Article

All Mine to Give
Christiane F.▶
The Last American Hero▶
Olivier, Olivier▶
Streetwise▶

Adapted from an Opera

Aria
Balalaika
Baritone
Broken Melody
Burlesque of Carmen
Carmen▶
Carmen Jones▶
The Chocolate Soldier
Farewell My Concubine
Faust
Fitzcarraldo▶
For the First Time
The Great Caruso
The Great Waltz▶
Gypsy Blood
I Dream Too Much
Jesus Christ, Superstar▶
La Grande Vadrouille▶
Life of Verdi
The Magic Flute▶
The Medium
Meeting Venus
Midnight Girl
The Mozart Brothers▶
Otello▶
The Panther's Claw
The Phantom of the Opera▶
Rose Marie▶
The Tales of Hoffmann
Terror at the Opera
The Toast of New Orleans
The Tsar's Bride▶
The Vampyr
Verdi
Wagner: The Complete Epic
Wagner: The Movie

Adapted from Comics

Annie
Barb Wire
Batman
Batman▶
Batman Forever▶
Batman Returns
Brenda Starr
Captain America
Captain America 2: Death Too Soon
Casper▶
Creepshow
Creepshow 2
The Crow
The Crow 2: City of Angels▶
Dennis the Menace
Dick Tracy▶
The Incredible Hulk
The Incredible Hulk Returns
Judge Dredd
The Phantom
Richie Rich
Superman: The Movie▶
Superman 2▶
Superman 3
Superman 4: The Quest for Peace
Superman & the Mole Men
Tales from the Crypt▶
Tales from the Crypt
Tales from the Crypt Presents Bordello of Blood

Adapted from Memoirs or Diaries

Bandit Queen
The Basketball Diaries
A Business Affair
Caro Diario▶
Celeste▶
Churchill and the Generals
Cowboy▶
Danger UXB
The Diary of Anne Frank▶
Edvard Munch
The Elegant Criminal
The Flame Trees of Thika▶
A Free Soul
The Gathering Storm
Goodbye, Miss 4th of July
Gypsy▶
The Happy Hooker
The Happy Hooker Goes Hollywood
The Happy Hooker Goes to Washington
Heart Beat
Heartland▶
Henry & June▶
I Remember Mama▶
I'll Cry Tomorrow▶
I'm Dancing as Fast as I Can
In the Name of the Father▶
Inside the Third Reich
Jacquot
Julia▶
Just Like a Woman
Maids of Wilko
Meetings with Remarkable Men
Mommie Dearest
My Life and Times with Antonin Artaud▶
Sister Kenny▶
Stars and Stripes Forever▶
This Boy's Life▶
What's Love Got to Do with It?
Wish You Were Here▶

Adapted from Television

The Addams Family
Addams Family Values
Alien Nation: Dark Horizon
Batman
Batman: Mask of the Phantasm
Baywatch the Movie: Forbidden Paradise
The Beverly Hillbillies
The Blues Brothers
Bonanza: The Return
Boris and Natasha: The Movie
The Brady Bunch Movie▶
Car 54, Where Are You?
Coneheads
Cooley High▶
The Crawling Eye
Days of Wine and Roses▶
Dennis the Menace
Doctor Who
Dragnet
The Flintstones
Flipper▶
The Fugitive▶
Gargoyles, The Movie: The Heroes Awaken
Get Smart, Again!
Gunfight at Sandoval
Here Come the Littles: The Movie
The Invaders
It's Pat: The Movie
Jetsons: The Movie
Joe's Apartment
The Key to Rebecca
Kids In the Hall Brain Candy
Lassie
The Left-Handed Gun▶
Maverick
Mission: Impossible▶
Mystery Science Theater 3000: The Movie
The Naked Gun: From the Files of Police Squad▶
Naked Gun 33 1/3: The Final Insult
Naked Gun 2 1/2: The Smell of Fear
The Nude Bomb
One Night Stand
Our Miss Brooks
Pennies From Heaven▶
The People Next Door
Phantom 2040 Movie: The Ghost Who Walks
Queen for a Day
The Saint
Sgt. Bilko
Sergeant Ryker
Star Trek: The Motion Picture
Star Trek 2: The Wrath of Khan▶
Star Trek 3: The Search for Spock
Star Trek 4: The Voyage Home▶
Star Trek 5: The Final Frontier
Star Trek 6: The Undiscovered Country
Star Trek Generations▶
Stuart Saves His Family
Tales from the Crypt Presents Demon Knight
Thunder in Paradise 2
Thunder in Paradise 3
Twin Peaks: Fire Walk with Me
The Untouchables▶
Wackiest Wagon Train in the West
Walker: Texas Ranger: Deadly Reunion
Wayne's World▶
Wayne's World 2

Adapted from the Radio

Behind the Mask
Big Town
Check & Double Check
Cosmo Jones, Crime Smasher
The Devil's Eye
Dreaming Out Loud
Gang Busters
Gangbusters
Going to Town
Goon Movie
The Great Gildersleeve
Here We Go Again!
Inner Sanctum
International Crime
The Invisible Avenger
Mr. Arkadin▶
My Friend Irma
Queen for a Day
Renfrew of the Royal Mounted
The Shadow
The Shadow Strikes
Sorry, Wrong Number▶
Treacherous Crossing
The War of the Worlds▶

"Alien" & Rip-Offs

Alien▶
Alien 3
Alien Prey
Alien Seed
Alien Space Avenger
Aliens▶
Blue Monkey
Creature
Deep Space
Deepstar Six
Forbidden World
Galaxy of Terror
Horror Planet
Leviathan
Nightflyers
Predator
Star Crystal
Xtro 2: The Second Encounter

Allen & Farrow

Alice▶
Another Woman▶
Broadway Danny Rose▶
Crimes & Misdemeanors▶
Hannah and Her Sisters▶
Husbands and Wives▶

A Midsummer Night's Sex Comedy▶
New York Stories▶
The Purple Rose of Cairo▶
Radio Days▶
September
Shadows and Fog
Zelig▶

Allen & Keaton

Annie Hall▶
Interiors▶
Love and Death▶
Manhattan▶
Manhattan Murder Mystery▶
Play It Again, Sam▶
Sleeper▶

Amy Fisher

The Amy Fisher Story
Casualties of Love: The "Long Island Lolita" Story
Lethal Lolita—Amy Fisher: My Story

Andy Hardy

Andy Hardy Gets Spring Fever
Andy Hardy Meets Debutante
Andy Hardy's Double Life
Andy Hardy's Private Secretary
Life Begins for Andy Hardy▶
Love Finds Andy Hardy▶
Love Laughs at Andy Hardy

Astaire & Rogers

The Barkleys of Broadway▶
Carefree▶
Flying Down to Rio
Follow the Fleet▶
The Gay Divorcee▶
Roberta▶
Shall We Dance▶
The Story of Vernon and Irene Castle▶
Swing Time▶
Top Hat▶

B/W & Color Combos

And Now My Love
The Blue Bird▶
Dead Again▶
Dixiana
D.O.A.
If...▶
Kafka
Kiss of the Spider Woman▶
Made in Heaven
A Man and a Woman▶
Martin▶
Mishima: A Life in Four Chapters▶
The Moon and Sixpence▶
Movie, Movie
Natural Born Killers
Portrait of Jennie▶
Rumble Fish▶
Schindler's List▶
She's Gotta Have It▶
Stalker▶
Transylvania Twist
Truth or Dare
Unzipped▶
Wings of Desire▶
The Wizard of Oz▶
Zelig▶

"Basic Instinct" & Rip-Offs

Basic Instinct
Fatal Instinct
Jade
Showgirls
Sliver

BBC TV Productions

The Affair
An Affair in Mind
After Pilkington
Agatha Christie's Miss Marple
And a Nightingale Sang
And Now for Something Completely Different▶
The Assassination Run
The Best of Lovejoy Mysteries
The Borrowers▶
The Buccaneers▶
Christabel
The Chronicles of Narnia
Cold Comfort Farm▶
Danger Man
A Dark Adapted Eye▶
The Dark Angel▶
Doctor Who
Doctor Who: Cybermen—The Early Years
Edge of Darkness
Elizabeth R▶
An Englishman Abroad▶
The Final Cut▶
The Flame Trees of Thika▶
Fortunes of War▶
The Franchise Affair
Gallowglass▶
Genghis Cohn
The Hitchhiker's Guide to the Galaxy
House of Cards▶
The House of Eliott
How Many Miles to Babylon?
Jude the Obscure
The Lost Language of Cranes▶
Mad Death
The Man from the Pru
Mansfield Park
Maria's Child
Merlin of the Crystal Cave
Middlemarch▶
Murder of a Moderate Man
Northanger Abbey
A Perfect Spy
Persuasion▶
Poldark▶
Poldark 2▶
Portrait of a Lady
Pride and Prejudice▶
Priest
A Question of Attribution
Robin Hood...The Legend: Herne's Son
Robin Hood...The Legend: Robin Hood and the Sorcerer
Robin Hood...The Legend: The Swords of Wayland
Robin Hood...The Legend: The Time of the Wolf
Rogue Male
Running Blind
School for Scandal
The Secret Garden
Sense & Sensibility
Shadowlands▶
Six Wives of Henry VIII▶
A Tale of Two Cities▶
Thicker Than Water
To Play the King▶
Unexplained Laughter
Unnatural Pursuits
The Vampyr
The Wedding Gift▶
A Year in Provence▶

Beach Party

Back to the Beach
Beach Blanket Bingo▶
Beach Party
Bikini Beach
How to Stuff a Wild Bikini
Muscle Beach Party
Pajama Party

Billy the Kid

Billy the Kid
Billy the Kid in Texas
Billy the Kid Returns
Billy the Kid Trapped
Billy the Kid Versus Dracula
Border Badmen
Deadwood
Devil Riders
Frontier Outlaws
Gangster's Den
Gore Vidal's Billy the Kid
I Shot Billy the Kid
Law and Order
The Left-Handed Gun▶
The Mysterious Rider
Oath of Vengeance
Outlaw of the Plains
Pat Garrett & Billy the Kid▶
Prairie Badmen
Rustler's Hideout
Shadows of Death
Thundering Gunslingers
Trigger Men
Wild Horse Phantom
Young Guns
Young Guns 2

Blondie

Blondie
Blondie Has Trouble
Blondie Hits the Jackpot
Blondie in Society
Blondie Knows Best
Blondie Takes a Vacation
Blondie's Blessed Event
It's a Great Life

Bogart & Bacall

The Big Sleep▶
Dark Passage
To Have & Have Not▶

Books to Film: Louisa May Alcott

Little Men
Little Women▶
Little Women
Little Women▶

Books to Film: Eric Ambler

Background to Danger▶
Hotel Reserve▶
Journey into Fear▶

Books to Film: Kingsley Amis

Lucky Jim
That Uncertain Feeling

Books to Film: Hans Christian Andersen

The Red Shoes▶
The Red Shoes

Books to Film: Maya Angelou

Georgia, Georgia
I Know Why the Caged Bird Sings▶

Books to Film: Isaac Asimov

Nightfall

Books to Film: Jane Austen

Emma▶
Mansfield Park
Northanger Abbey
Persuasion▶
Pride and Prejudice▶
Pride and Prejudice
Pride and Prejudice▶
Sense & Sensibility
Sense and Sensibility▶

Books to Film: Clive Barker

Candyman
Candyman 2: Farewell to the Flesh
Hellbound: Hellraiser 2
Hellraiser
Hellraiser 3: Hell on Earth
Night Breed
Rawhead Rex
Transmutations

Books to Film: J.M. Barrie

Hook
Peter Pan▶

Books to Film: Ambrose Bierce

Eyes of the Panther
An Occurrence at Owl Creek Bridge/Coup de Grace
Red Balloon/Occurrence at Owl Creek Bridge▶

Books to Film: Maeve Binchy

Circle of Friends

Books to Film: Robert Bloch

The Skull
Torture Garden

Books to Film: Judy Blume

Forever

Books to Film: Ray Bradbury

The Beast from 20,000 Fathoms
Fahrenheit 451▶
The Illustrated Man▶
It Came From Outer Space▶
The Martian Chronicles: Part 1
The Martian Chronicles: Part 2
The Martian Chronicles: Part 3
Something Wicked This Way Comes
Strange Tales/Ray Bradbury Theatre
Walking on Air

Books to Film: Barbara Taylor Bradford

Hold the Dream
A Woman of Substance, Episode 1: Nest of Vipers
A Woman of Substance, Episode 2: The Secret is Revealed
A Woman of Substance, Episode 3: Fighting for the Dream

Books to Film: Pearl S. Buck

China Sky
Dragon Seed
The Good Earth▶

Books to Film: Frances Hodgson Burnett

Little Lord Fauntleroy▶
Little Lord Fauntleroy
The Little Princess▶
The Little Princess
A Little Princess▶
The Secret Garden▶
The Secret Garden
The Secret Garden▶
The Secret Garden

Books to Film: Edgar Rice Burroughs

At the Earth's Core
Greystoke: The Legend of Tarzan, Lord of the Apes
The Land That Time Forgot
The People That Time Forgot
Tarzan and His Mate▶
Tarzan and the Green Goddess
Tarzan and the Trappers
Tarzan Escapes▶
Tarzan Finds a Son▶
Tarzan, the Ape Man▶
Tarzan, the Ape Man
Tarzan the Fearless
Tarzan's New York Adventure
Tarzan's Revenge
Tarzan's Secret Treasure

Books to Film: William Burroughs

Naked Lunch▶

Books to Film: James M. Cain

Butterfly
Double Indemnity▶
Girl in the Cadillac
Mildred Pierce▶
The Postman Always Rings Twice▶
The Postman Always Rings Twice
Slightly Scarlet

Books to Film: Truman Capote

ABC Stage 67: Truman Capote's A Christmas Memory
Breakfast at Tiffany's▶
The Glass House▶
In Cold Blood▶

Books to Film: Barbara Cartland

Duel of Hearts
The Flame Is Love

Books to Film: Willa Cather

My Antonia
O Pioneers!

Books to Film: Raymond Chandler

The Big Sleep▶
The Big Sleep

Farewell, My Lovely▶
The Finger Man
Lady in the Lake
The Long Goodbye▶
Marlowe
Murder, My Sweet▶
Smart-Aleck Kill
Strangers on a Train▶

Books to Film: Paddy Chayefsky

Altered States▶
As Young As You Feel▶
The Catered Affair▶

Books to Film: John Cheever

Sorrows of Gin
The Swimmer▶

Books to Film: Anton Chekhov

August
Country Life
The Lady with the Dog▶
The Seagull▶
The Shooting Party
Vanya on 42nd Street▶
Ward Six

Books to Film: Agatha Christie

The Affair of the Pink Pearl
Agatha Christie's Miss Marple
The Alphabet Murders
And Then There Were None▶
Appointment with Death
The Body in the Library
The Case of the Missing Lady
The Clergyman's Daughter
The Crackler
Death on the Nile
Endless Night
Evil under the Sun
Finessing the King
The House of Lurking Death
Love from a Stranger
The Man in the Mist
The Mirror Crack'd
Murder Ahoy
Murder at the Gallop▶
A Murder Is Announced
Murder Most Foul▶
Murder on the Orient Express▶
Murder She Said
Ordeal by Innocence
A Pocketful of Rye
The Secret Adversary
Ten Little Indians
The Unbreakable Alibi
Witness for the Prosecution▶

Books to Film: Tom Clancy

Clear and Present Danger
The Hunt for Red October▶
Patriot Games▶

Books to Film: Mary Higgins Clark

The Cradle Will Fall
A Cry in the Night
Double Vision
Terror Stalks the Class Reunion

Books to Film: Arthur C. Clarke

Trapped in Space
2001: A Space Odyssey▶
2010: The Year We Make Contact▶

Books to Film: James Clavell

King Rat▶
Noble House
Shogun▶
Tai-Pan

Books to Film: Jackie Collins

The Bitch
The World is Full of Married Men
Yesterday's Hero

Books to Film: Richard Condon

Gun Crazy
The Manchurian Candidate▶
Prizzi's Honor▶
Winter Kills▶

Books to Film: Joseph Conrad

Apocalypse Now▶
The Duellists▶
Face to Face
Heart of Darkness
Lord Jim▶

Books to Film: Pat Conroy

Conrack▶
The Great Santini▶
The Lords of Discipline
The Prince of Tides▶

Books to Film: Robin Cook

Coma▶
Sphinx

Books to Film: Catherine Cookson

The Black Velvet Gown
The Cinder Path
The Dwelling Place
The Fifteen Streets
The Man Who Cried

Books to Film: James Fenimore Cooper

The Deerslayer
The Last of the Mohicans▶
The Last of the Mohicans
The Last of the Mohicans▶
The Last of the Redmen

Books to Film: Stephen Crane

Face to Face
The Red Badge of Courage▶

Books to Film: Michael Crichton

The Andromeda Strain
Congo
The Great Train Robbery▶
Jurassic Park▶
Rising Sun▶
The Terminal Man
Westworld▶

Books to Film: Clive Cussler

Raise the Titanic

Books to Film: Roald Dahl

James and the Giant Peach▶
Matilda
Willy Wonka & the Chocolate Factory▶
The Witches▶

Books to Film: Miguel de Cervantes

Don Quixote▶
Man of La Mancha

Books to Film: Guy de Maupassant

A Day in the Country▶
Diary of a Madman
Le Plaisir
The Private Affairs of Bel Ami▶
A Woman Without Love▶

Books to Film: Daniel Defoe

The Amorous Adventures of Moll Flanders
Crusoe
Man Friday
Moll Flanders▶
Robinson Crusoe
Robinson Crusoe on Mars

Books to Film: Phillip K. Dick

Barjo
Blade Runner▶
Screamers
Total Recall▶

Books to Film: Charles Dickens

An American Christmas Carol
Bleak House
A Christmas Carol▶
A Christmas Carol
A Christmas Carol▶
Cricket on the Hearth
David Copperfield▶
David Copperfield
Great Expectations▶
Great Expectations
Great Expectations▶
Great Expectations: The Untold Story
The Life and Adventures of Nicholas Nickleby▶
Little Dorrit, Film 1: Nobody's Fault▶
Little Dorrit, Film 2: Little Dorrit's Story▶
The Muppet Christmas Carol
The Mystery of Edwin Drood
Nicholas Nickleby▶
The Old Curiosity Shop
Oliver!▶
Oliver & Company
Oliver Twist▶
Oliver Twist
Oliver Twist▶
Oliver Twist
The Pickwick Papers
Scrooge▶
Scrooge
A Tale of Two Cities▶
A Tale of Two Cities
A Tale of Two Cities▶
Tale of Two Cities/In the Switch Tower

Books to Film: E.L. Doctorow

Billy Bathgate
Daniel
Ragtime▶

Books to Film: Fyodor Dostoyevski

The Brothers Karamazov▶
Crime and Punishment▶
Crime and Punishment
A Gentle Woman
La Vengeance d'une Femme
L'Idiot
White Nights▶

Books to Film: Sir Arthur Conan Doyle

The Adventures of Sherlock Holmes
The Adventures of Sherlock Holmes: Hound of the Baskervilles
The Crucifer of Blood
Dressed to Kill
The Hound of the Baskervilles▶
The Hound of the Baskervilles
House of Fear
The Lost World
Masks of Death
Murder at the Baskervilles
The Pearl of Death
Return to the Lost World
Robbers of the Sacred Mountain
Scarlet Claw▶
Sherlock Holmes and the Deadly Necklace
Sherlock Holmes and the Secret Weapon▶
Sherlock Holmes: The Master Blackmailer
Sherlock Hound: Tales of Mystery
The Sign of Four
The Silent Mr. Sherlock Holmes
Tales from the Darkside: The Movie
The Triumph of Sherlock Holmes
The Woman in Green

Books to Film: Daphne Du Maurier

The Birds▶
Don't Look Now▶
Jamaica Inn
Rebecca▶

Books to Film: Alexandre Dumas

At Sword's Point
Black Magic
Camille
Camille▶
The Corsican Brothers
The Count of Monte Cristo
The Count of Monte Cristo▶
The Count of Monte Cristo
The Four Musketeers▶
The Iron Mask
The Man in the Iron Mask▶
Mountain Fury
The Prince of Thieves
Queen Margot▶
The Return of the Musketeers
Robin Hood▶
Sword of Monte Cristo
The Three Musketeers
The Three Musketeers▶
The Three Musketeers
The Three Musketeers▶

Books to Film: Dominick Dunne

An Inconvenient Woman

Books to Film: George Eliot

Middlemarch▶
The Mill on the Floss
Silas Marner▶
A Simple Twist of Fate

Books to Film: Bret Easton Ellis

Less Than Zero

Books to Film: Howard Fast

Freedom Road

Books to Film: William Faulkner

Intruder in the Dust▶
The Long, Hot Summer▶
The Reivers▶
Tarnished Angels▶
Today We Live
Tomorrow▶

Books to Film: Edna Ferber

Cimarron
Dinner at Eight▶
Dinner at Eight
Giant▶
Saratoga Trunk
Show Boat▶
Show Boat
Stage Door▶

Books to Film: Henry Fielding

Joseph Andrews
Tom Jones▶

Books to Film: F. Scott Fitzgerald

The Great Gatsby
The Last Time I Saw Paris
The Last Tycoon▶
Tender Is the Night

Books to Film: Gustov Flaubert

Madame Bovary▶
Salammbo

Books to Film: Ian Fleming

Casino Royale
Chitty Chitty Bang Bang
Diamonds Are Forever▶
Dr. No▶
For Your Eyes Only▶
From Russia with Love▶
Goldfinger▶
License to Kill▶
Live and Let Die
The Living Daylights▶
The Man with the Golden Gun
Moonraker
Never Say Never Again
Octopussy
On Her Majesty's Secret Service▶
The Poppy Is Also a Flower

The Spy Who Loved Me
Thunderball
A View to a Kill
You Only Live Twice

Books to Film: Ken Follett

Capricorn One▶
Eye of the Needle
The Key to Rebecca
Lie Down with Lions

Books to Film: E.M. Forster

Howard's End▶
Maurice▶
A Passage to India▶
A Room with a View▶
Where Angels Fear to Tread▶

Books to Film: Frederick Forsyth

The Day of the Jackal▶
The Dogs of War
The Fourth Protocol▶
No Comebacks
The Odessa File
Two by Forsyth

Books to Film: Rumer Godden

Black Narcissus▶
In This House of Brede▶
The River▶

Books to Film: Nikolai Gogol

The Overcoat▶
Taras Bulba

Books to Film: William Goldman

Heat
Magic
Marathon Man▶
Mr. Horn
The Princess Bride▶

Books to Film: David Goodis

Dark Passage
Moon in the Gutter
Nightfall▶
Shoot the Piano Player▶

Books to Film: Elizabeth Goudge

Green Dolphin Street

Books to Film: Kenneth Grahame

The Adventures of Ichabod and Mr. Toad▶
The Reluctant Dragon

Books to Film: Graham Greene

Across the Bridge
Beyond the Limit
Brighton Rock▶
The Fallen Idol▶
The Fugitive▶
The Human Factor
Monsignor Quixote
Strike It Rich
The Tenth Man
The Third Man▶
This Gun for Hire▶
This Gun for Hire
Travels with My Aunt

Books to Film: Zane Grey

Arizona Mahoney
The Border Legion
Desert Gold
Drift Fence
Dude Ranger
Fighting Caravans
Forlorn River
The Great American Western Collection: Roy Rogers
Helltown
The Light of Western Stars
Man of the Forest
Nevada
Riders of the Purple Sage
Roll Along Cowboy
Thunder Mountain
Thunder Pass
To the Last Man
Wagon Wheels
West of the Pecos
When the West Was Young

Books to Film: John Grisham

The Client
The Firm▶
The Pelican Brief
A Time to Kill▶

Books to Film: H. Rider Haggard

Allan Quatermain and the Lost City of Gold
King Solomon's Mines▶
King Solomon's Mines
She

Books to Film: Arthur Hailey

Airport▶
Hotel
Time Lock

Books to Film: Alex Haley

Malcolm X▶
Roots▶
Roots: The Gift
Roots: The Next Generation▶

Books to Film: Dashiell Hammett

After the Thin Man▶
Another Thin Man
The Dain Curse
Hammett
The Maltese Falcon▶
Satan Met a Lady
Shadow of the Thin Man▶
Song of the Thin Man
The Thin Man▶
The Thin Man Goes Home
Woman in the Shadows

Books to Film: Thomas Hardy

Far from the Madding Crowd▶
Jude the Obscure
The Return of the Native
Tess▶

Books to Film: Harlequin Romances

Dreams Lost, Dreams Found
Love with a Perfect Stranger
The Winds of Jarrah

Books to Film: Jim Harrison

Carried Away
Dalva
Legends of the Fall
Revenge
Wolf

Books to Film: Nathaniel Hawthorne

The Scarlet Letter▶
The Scarlet Letter
Twice-Told Tales▶

Books to Film: Ernest Hemingway

A Farewell to Arms▶
For Whom the Bell Tolls▶
Islands in the Stream
The Killers
My Old Man
The Old Man and the Sea
The Snows of Kilimanjaro▶
To Have & Have Not▶
Women & Men: Stories of Seduction

Books to Film: O. Henry

The Cisco Kid
The Gift of Love
Ruthless People▶

Books to Film: James Hilton

Lost Horizon▶
Random Harvest▶
The Story of Dr. Wassell

Books to Film: S.E. Hinton

The Outsiders
Rumble Fish▶
Tex
That Was Then...This Is Now

Books to Film: Victor Hugo

Delusions of Grandeur
The Halfback of Notre Dame
The Hunchback of Notre Dame▶
Les Miserables▶
Les Miserables
Les Miserables▶
Les Miserables
Ruyblas

Books to Film: Fanny Hurst

Back Street
The Castle▶
Imitation of Life▶
Young at Heart

Books to Film: John Irving

The Hotel New Hampshire
The World According to Garp▶

Books to Film: Washington Irving

The Adventures of Ichabod and Mr. Toad▶
The Legend of Sleepy Hollow
Rip van Winkle

Books to Film: Susan Isaacs

Compromising Positions
Shining Through

Books to Film: Rona Jaffe

Mazes and Monsters

Books to Film: John Jakes

The Bastard
North and South Book 1▶
North and South Book 2▶
The Rebels
The Seekers

Books to Film: Henry James

The Bostonians
Daisy Miller
The Europeans▶
The Green Room
The Heiress▶
The Innocents▶
Lost Moment
The Nightcomers
Portrait of a Lady
Some Came Running▶
The Turn of the Screw

Books to Film: James Jones

From Here to Eternity▶
From Here to Eternity

Books to Film: James Joyce

The Dead▶
James Joyce: A Portrait of the Artist as a Young Man
Ulysses

Books to Film: Franz Kafka

The Trial▶
The Trial

Books to Film: Stephen King

Carrie▶
Cat's Eye
Children of the Corn
Christine
Creepshow
Creepshow 2
Cujo
The Dark Half
Dead Zone▶
Dolores Claiborne▶
Firestarter
Graveyard Shift
The Lawnmower Man
The Mangler
Maximum Overdrive
Misery▶
Needful Things
Pet Sematary
Return to Salem's Lot
The Running Man
Salem's Lot
The Shawshank Redemption▶
The Shining
Silver Bullet
Sleepwalkers
Sometimes They Come Back
Stand By Me▶
Stephen King's Golden Years
Stephen King's It
Stephen King's The Langoliers
Stephen King's The Stand
Stephen King's The Tommyknockers
Tales from the Darkside: The Movie

Books to Film: Rudyard Kipling

Captains Courageous▶
A Fool There Was
Gunga Din▶
The Jungle Book
Kim▶
Kim
The Man Who Would Be King▶
Rudyard Kipling's The Jungle Book
They Watch
Wee Willie Winkie▶

Books to Film: Dean R. Koontz

Hideaway
Servants of Twilight
Watchers
Whispers

Books to Film: Judith Krantz

Mistral's Daughter
Princess Daisy
Scruples

Books to Film: Louis L'Amour

The Burning Hills
Cancel My Reservation
Conagher
Heller in Pink Tights
Hondo▶
The Quick and the Dead
The Sacketts
The Shadow Riders
Shalako

Books to Film: D.H. Lawrence

Kangaroo▶
Lady Chatterley's Lover
The Rainbow▶
The Rocking Horse Winner
Trespasser
The Virgin and the Gypsy
Women in Love▶
Young Lady Chatterly 2

Books to Film: John Le Carre

The Little Drummer Girl▶
The Looking Glass War
A Perfect Spy
The Russia House
The Spy Who Came in from the Cold▶

Books to Film: Harper Lee

To Kill a Mockingbird▶

Books to Film: Elmore Leonard

The Ambassador
Cat Chaser
52 Pick-Up
Get Shorty▶
Glitz
Hombre▶
Stick
3:10 to Yuma▶
Valdez is Coming

Books to Film: Sinclair Lewis

Ann Vickers
Arrowsmith
Dodsworth▶
Elmer Gantry▶

Books to Film: Astrid Lindgren

The Land of Faraway
The New Adventures of Pippi Longstocking
Pippi Goes on Board
Pippi in the South Seas
Pippi Longstocking
Pippi on the Run

Books to Film: Jack London

The Assassination Bureau▶
Call of the Wild
The Fighter▶
Great Adventure
The Legend of Sea Wolf
The Legend of the Sea Wolf
Legends of the North
The Mutiny of the Elsinore
The Sea Wolf▶
The Sea Wolf
Tales of the Klondike: In a Far Country
Tales of the Klondike: Race for Number One
Tales of the Klondike: The Scorn of Women
Tales of the Klondike: The Unexpected
Torture Ship
White Fang▶
White Fang and the Hunter
Wolf Call

Books to Film: H.P. Lovecraft

Blood Island
Bride of Re-Animator
Cthulhu Mansion
The Curse
Die, Monster, Die!
The Dunwich Horror
From Beyond▶
The Haunted Palace
Lurking Fear
Re-Animator▶
The Resurrected
The Sinister Invasion
The Unnamable
The Unnamable 2: The Statement of Randolph Carter

Books to Film: Robert Ludlum

The Bourne Identity▶
The Holcroft Covenant
The Osterman Weekend

Books to Film: Peter Maas

King of the Gypsies
Marie▶
Serpico▶

Books to Film: Alistair MacLean

Bear Island
Breakheart Pass
Caravan to Vaccares
Detonator
Detonator 2: Night Watch
Force 10 from Navarone
Golden Rendezvous
The Guns of Navarone▶
Ice Station Zebra
Puppet on a Chain
River of Death
Where Eagles Dare▶

Books to Film: Norman Mailer

The Executioner's Song
Marilyn: The Untold Story▶
The Naked and the Dead
Pursuit▶
Tough Guys Don't Dance

Books to Film: W. Somerset Maugham

Adorable Julia
Beachcomber▶
Dirty Gertie from Harlem U.S.A.
Encore▶
The Letter▶
Miss Sadie Thompson▶
The Moon and Sixpence▶
Of Human Bondage▶
Of Human Bondage
Overnight Sensation
The Painted Veil
Rain
The Razor's Edge▶
The Razor's Edge
Sadie Thompson▶
Trio▶

Books to Film: Colleen McCullough

An Indecent Obsession
The Thorn Birds▶
Tim

Books to Film: Larry McMurtry

The Best Little Whorehouse in Texas
The Last Picture Show▶
Lonesome Dove▶
Terms of Endearment▶
Texasville

Books to Film: Herman Melville

Bartleby
Enchanted Island
Moby Dick▶

Books to Film: James Michener

The Bridges at Toko-Ri▶
Dynasty
Hawaii▶
Return to Paradise
Sayonara▶
Texas
Until They Sail

Books to Film: L.M. Montgomery

Anne of Avonlea▶
Anne of Green Gables▶
Lantern Hill
Tales from Avonlea, Vol. 1: The Journey Begins

Books to Film: Vladimir Nabokov

Despair▶
Lolita▶

Books to Film: Joyce Carol Oates

Smooth Talk▶

Books to Film: Marcel Pagnol

The Baker's Wife▶
Fanny▶
Jean de Florette▶
Manon of the Spring▶
Marius▶
My Father's Glory▶
My Mother's Castle▶
Topaze▶

Books to Film: Nicholas Pileggi

Casino▶
Goodfellas▶

Books to Film: Edgar Allan Poe

The Black Cat▶
The Black Cat
Dr. Tarr's Torture Dungeon
The Fall of the House of Usher
The Fall of the House of Usher▶
The Fall of the House of Usher
The Haunted Palace
Haunting Fear
The Haunting of Morella
The House of Usher
Jaws of Justice
La Chute de la Maison Usher▶
The Living Coffin
Manfish
Masque of the Red Death▶
Masque of the Red Death
Murders in the Rue Morgue
The Murders in the Rue Morgue▶
The Oblong Box
The Oval Portrait
The Pit and the Pendulum▶
The Pit & the Pendulum
Premature Burial
The Raven
The Raven▶
The Spectre of Edgar Allen Poe
Spirits of the Dead▶
Tales of Terror
The Tell-Tale Heart
Tomb of Ligeia▶
The Torture Chamber of Dr. Sadism
Two Evil Eyes
Web of the Spider

Books to Film: Katherine Anne Porter

Noon Wine▶
Ship of Fools▶

Books to Film: Mario Puzo

The Godfather▶
The Godfather, Part 2▶
The Godfather, Part 3▶
The Sicilian

Books to Film: Anne Rice

Exit to Eden
Interview with the Vampire

Books to Film: Harold Robbins

The Adventurers
The Betsy
The Carpetbaggers
King Creole
The Lonely Lady
Nevada Smith
Never Love a Stranger
Stiletto
Where Love Has Gone

Books to Film: Sir Walter Scott

Ivanhoe▶
Ivanhoe
King Richard and the Crusaders

Books to Film: Sidney Sheldon

The Naked Face
The Other Side of Midnight
Rage of Angels
Rage of Angels: The Story Continues
Sidney Sheldon's Bloodline
Windmills of the Gods

Books to Film: Mary Shelley

The Bride of Frankenstein▶
Frankenstein▶
Frankenstein
Frankenstein Unbound▶
Mary Shelley's Frankenstein

Books to Film: Danielle Steel

Danielle Steel's Changes
Danielle Steel's "Daddy"
Danielle Steel's Heartbeat
Danielle Steel's Kaleidoscope
Danielle Steel's Palomino
Danielle Steel's Star
Fine Things
Now and Forever
The Promise

Books to Film: John Steinbeck

Cannery Row
East of Eden▶
East of Eden
The Grapes of Wrath▶
Lifeboat▶
Of Mice and Men▶
The Pearl▶
The Red Pony▶
Tortilla Flat▶

Books to Film: Stendhal

La Chartreuse de Parme
The Red and the Black▶
Vanina Vanini▶

Books to Film: Robert Louis Stevenson

Abbott and Costello Meet Dr. Jekyll and Mr. Hyde
Adventure Island
Black Arrow▶
The Body Snatcher▶
Dr. Jekyll and Mr. Hyde▶
Dr. Jekyll and Mr. Hyde
Dr. Jekyll and Sister Hyde
Jekyll and Hyde
Jekyll & Hyde...Together Again
Kidnapped
Man with Two Heads
The Master of Ballantrae
Muppet Treasure Island
Strange Case of Dr. Jekyll & Mr. Hyde
Treasure Island▶
Treasure Island
The Wrong Box▶

Books to Film: Bram Stoker

Bram Stoker's Dracula
Burial of the Rats
Count Dracula
Dracula▶
Dracula
Dracula (Spanish Version)
The Horror of Dracula▶
The Lair of the White Worm▶
Nosferatu▶
Tomb

Books to Film: Harriet Beecher Stowe

Uncle Tom's Cabin

Books to Film: Jacqueline Susann

The Love Machine
Once is Not Enough

Books to Film: Jonathan Swift

Gulliver's Travels
The Three Worlds of Gulliver

Books to Film: Paul Theroux

Half Moon Street
The Mosquito Coast
Saint Jack▶

Books to Film: Jim Thompson

After Dark, My Sweet▶
Coup de Torchon▶
The Getaway
The Grifters▶

Books to Film: James Thurber

The Battle of the Sexes▶
Billy Liar▶
The Secret Life of Walter Mitty▶

Books to Film: J.R.R. Tolkien

The Hobbit▶
The Lord of the Rings
The Return of the King

Books to Film: Leo Tolstoy

War and Peace▶

Books to Film: Scott Turow

Presumed Innocent▶

Books to Film: Mark Twain

The Adventures of Huck Finn▶
The Adventures of Huckleberry Finn▶
The Adventures of Huckleberry Finn
The Adventures of Tom Sawyer▶
The Adventures of Tom Sawyer
Ava's Magical Adventure
A Connecticut Yankee▶
A Connecticut Yankee in King Arthur's Court
Huck and the King of Hearts
Huckleberry Finn
The Innocents Abroad
A Kid in King Arthur's Court
A Million to Juan
The Mysterious Stranger
The Prince and the Pauper▶
The Prince and the Pauper
The Private History of a Campaign That Failed
Pudd'nhead Wilson
Tom and Huck▶
Tom Sawyer▶
Tom Sawyer
Unidentified Flying Oddball

Books to Film: John Updike

Roommate
Too Far to Go▶
The Witches of Eastwick

Books to Film: Leon Uris

Battle Cry▶
Exodus▶
QB VII▶
Topaz▶

Books to Film: Jules Verne

Around the World in 80 Days▶
Around the World in 80 Days
Around the World in a Daze
800 Leagues Down the Amazon
Five Weeks in a Balloon
From the Earth to the Moon
In Search of the Castaways▶
Journey to the Center of the Earth▶
Journey to the Center of the Earth
Light at the Edge of the World
Master of the World
Mysterious Island▶
On the Comet▶
Those Fantastic Flying Fools
20,000 Leagues Under the Sea▶
Where Time Began

Books to Film: Kurt Vonnegut

D.P.
Kurt Vonnegut's Harrison Bergeron
Slapstick of Another Kind
Slaughterhouse Five
Who Am I This Time?▶

Books to Film: Alice Walker

The Color Purple▶

Books to Film: Edgar Wallace

The Black Abbot
Chamber of Horrors
Creature with the Blue Hand
Curse of the Yellow Snake
Dead Eyes of London
Door with the Seven Locks
Forger of London
The Human Monster
The Indian Scarf
Mr. Reeder in Room 13
The Mysterious Magician
The Secret Four
Secret of the Black Trunk
The Squeaker
The Strange Countess
The Terror

Books to Film: Joseph Wambaugh

The Black Marble▶
The Choirboys
Echoes in the Darkness
The Glitter Dome
The New Centurions
The Onion Field▶

Books to Film: Evelyn Waugh

Brideshead Revisited▶
A Handful of Dust▶
The Loved One▶

Books to Film: H.G. Wells

Empire of the Ants
First Men in the Moon
Food of the Gods
Food of the Gods: Part 2
Half a Sixpence
The Invisible Man▶
The Invisible Man's Revenge
Island of Dr. Moreau
The Island of Dr. Moreau
Kipps▶
La Merveilleuse Visite
The Man Who Could Work Miracles▶
The New Invisible Man
Terror Is a Man
Things to Come▶
The Time Machine▶
Time Machine
Village of the Giants
The War of the Worlds▶

Books to Film: Edith Wharton

The Age of Innocence▶
The Buccaneers▶
The Children
Ethan Frome
The Lady's Maid's Bell
The Old Maid▶

Books to Film: William Wharton

Birdy▶
Dad
A Midnight Clear▶

Books to Film: Oscar Wilde

The Canterville Ghost
Dorian Gray
Importance of Being Earnest▶
Lady Windermere's Fan
Picture of Dorian Gray▶
Salome
The Sins of Dorian Gray

Books to Film: Thornton Wilder

The Bridge of San Luis Rey▶
Hello, Dolly!
The Matchmaker▶
Mr. North
Our Town▶
Our Town

Books to Film: Virginia Woolf

To the Lighthouse

Books to Film: Cornell Woolrich

The Bride Wore Black▶
Mississippi Mermaid▶
Mrs. Winterbourne
Rear Window▶
The Window▶

Books to Film: Herman Wouk

The Caine Mutiny▶
The Caine Mutiny Court Martial▶
Marjorie Morningstar
War & Remembrance, Part 1
War & Remembrance, Part 2
War & Remembrance, Part 3
War & Remembrance, Part 4
War & Remembrance, Part 5
War & Remembrance, Part 6
War & Remembrance, Part 7
War & Remembrance: The Final Chapter, Part 8
War & Remembrance: The Final Chapter, Part 9
War & Remembrance: The Final Chapter, Part 10
War & Remembrance: The Final Chapter, Part 11
War & Remembrance: The Final Chapter, Part 12
The Winds of War

The Bowery Boys

Angels with Dirty Faces▶
Blues Busters
Bowery Blitzkrieg
Bowery Boys Meet the Monsters
Bowery Buckaroos
Boys of the City
Clipped Wings
Dead End▶
East Side Kids
East Side Kids/The Lost City
Flying Wild
Follow the Leader
Ghost Chasers
Ghost on the Loose
Hard-Boiled Mahoney
Here Come the Marines
Kid Dynamite
Let's Get Tough
Little Tough Guys
Master Minds
Million Dollar Kid
Mr. Wise Guy
'Neath Brooklyn Bridge
Pride of the Bowery
Smart Alecks
Smugglers' Cove▶
Spook Busters
Spooks Run Wild
That Gang of Mine
They Made Me a Criminal

Bulldog Drummond

Arrest Bulldog Drummond
Bulldog Drummond
Bulldog Drummond at Bay
Bulldog Drummond Comes Back
Bulldog Drummond Escapes
Bulldog Drummond in Africa/Arrest Bulldog Drummond
Bulldog Drummond's Bride
Bulldog Drummond's Peril
Bulldog Drummond's Revenge
Bulldog Drummond's Revenge/Bulldog Drummond's Peril
Bulldog Drummond's Secret Police
Bulldog Jack▶

Burton & Taylor

Cleopatra
The Comedians
Divorce His, Divorce Hers
Doctor Faustus
Hammersmith is Out
The Sandpiper
The Taming of the Shrew▶
Under Milk Wood
The V.I.P.'s▶
Who's Afraid of Virginia Woolf?▶

Carry On

Carry On at Your Convenience
Carry On Behind
Carry On Camping
Carry On Cleo
Carry On Cowboy
Carry On Cruising
Carry On Dick
Carry On Doctor▶
Carry On Emmanuelle
Carry On England
Carry On Henry VIII
Carry On Nurse
Carry On 'Round the Bend
Carry On Screaming
Follow That Camel

Charlie Brown and the Peanuts Gang

Be My Valentine, Charlie Brown
Bon Voyage, Charlie Brown▶
A Boy Named Charlie Brown▶
A Charlie Brown Celebration
A Charlie Brown Christmas
A Charlie Brown Thanksgiving
Charlie Brown's All-Stars
He's Your Dog, Charlie Brown!
It Was a Short Summer, Charlie Brown
It's a Mystery, Charlie Brown
It's Arbor Day, Charlie Brown
It's Magic, Charlie Brown/Charlie Brown's All Star
It's the Great Pumpkin, Charlie Brown
Play It Again, Charlie Brown
Race for Your Life, Charlie Brown
Snoopy, Come Home▶
Snoopy's Getting Married, Charlie Brown
Someday You'll Find Her, Charlie Brown
There's No Time for Love, Charlie Brown
You're a Good Man, Charlie Brown
You're in Love, Charlie Brown

Charlie Chan

Castle in the Desert
Charlie Chan and the Curse of the Dragon Queen
Charlie Chan at the Opera▶
Charlie Chan at the Wax Museum
The Charlie Chan Collection
Charlie Chan in Paris
Charlie Chan in Rio
Charlie Chan in the Secret Service
Charlie Chan's Secret
The Chinese Cat
The Jade Mask
Meeting at Midnight
Murder over New York
The Scarlet Clue
The Shanghai Cobra
Terror by Night/Meeting at Midnight

Cheech & Chong

After Hours▶
Cheech and Chong: Still Smokin'
Cheech and Chong: Things Are Tough All Over
Cheech and Chong's Next Movie
Cheech and Chong's Nice Dreams
Cheech and Chong's The Corsican Brothers
Cheech and Chong's Up in Smoke

Classics

A Nous la Liberte▶
Abe Lincoln in Illinois▶
Across the Pacific▶
Adam's Rib▶
The Adventures of Robin Hood▶
The Adventures of Tarzan
The Adventures of Tom Sawyer▶
The African Queen▶
Aguirre, the Wrath of God▶
Airplane!▶
Alexander Nevsky▶
Alice in Wonderland▶
All About Eve▶
All Quiet on the Western Front▶
All the King's Men▶
All This and Heaven Too▶
Amarcord▶
American Graffiti▶
An American in Paris▶
Anastasia▶
Anatomy of a Murder▶
Anchors Aweigh▶
Angels with Dirty Faces▶
Animal Crackers▶
Anna Christie
Anna Karenina▶
Annie Hall▶
The Apartment▶
Apocalypse Now▶
Applause▶
Arsenal▶
Arsenic and Old Lace▶
The Asphalt Jungle▶
At the Circus
Avenging Conscience
The Awful Truth▶
Baby Face
The Bad and the Beautiful▶
Badlands▶
Bahama Passage
Bambi▶
The Bank Dick▶
Bathing Beauty
The Battleship Potemkin▶
Beau Geste▶
Beauty and the Beast▶
Ben-Hur▶
The Best Years of Our Lives▶
Beyond the Forest
Beyond the Trail
The Bicycle Thief▶
The Big Parade▶
The Big Sleep▶
Big Trail▶
The Birth of a Nation▶
Black Beauty▶
The Black Cat▶
The Black Pirate▶
Blade Runner▶
Blind Husbands▶
Block-heads▶
Blood and Sand
The Blood of a Poet
Blow-Up▶

Classics

The Thirteenth Man
Thirty Seconds Over Tokyo▶
Three Charlies and One Phoney!
The Three Musketeers
Three on a Match▶
Throne of Blood▶
Thunder Trail
The Tin Star▶
The Tip-Off
To Have & Have Not▶
To Kill a Mockingbird▶
Tom Sawyer▶
Topper▶
Touch of Evil▶
Tramp & a Woman
Treasure of the Sierra Madre▶
True Heart Susie
Tumbleweeds▶
Twentieth Century▶
Ugetsu▶
Un Chien Andalou▶
Under the Roofs of Paris▶
The Vagabond
Vampyr▶
Variety▶
Vertigo▶
The Virginian▶
Wages of Fear▶
The War of the Worlds▶
Warning Shadows▶
Waxworks▶
Way Down East▶
The Wedding March▶
West Side Story▶
Western Gold
Westfront 1918▶
When Ladies Meet
White Christmas▶
The White Zombie▶
The Wild Bunch▶
The Wild One▶
Wild Strawberries▶
The Wind▶
Wings
The Wizard of Oz▶
A Woman of Affairs
Woman of the Year▶
The World of Apu▶
Wuthering Heights▶
Yankee Doodle Dandy▶
The Yearling▶
Yojimbo▶
You Can't Cheat an Honest Man▶
Young Mr. Lincoln▶
Zero for Conduct▶
Zvenigora▶

Corman's Mama

Big Bad Mama
Big Bad Mama 2
Bloody Mama
Crazy Mama

Dirty Harry

The Dead Pool
Dirty Harry▶
The Enforcer
Magnum Force
Sudden Impact

Disney Animated Movies

Aladdin▶
Alice in Wonderland▶
The Aristocats▶
Bambi▶
Beauty and the Beast▶
Cinderella▶
DuckTales the Movie: Treasure of the Lost Lamp
Dumbo▶
Fantasia▶
The Fox and the Hound▶
A Goofy Movie
The Great Mouse Detective▶
The Hunchback of Notre Dame▶
The Jungle Book▶
Lady and the Tramp▶
The Lion King▶
The Little Mermaid▶
The Many Adventures of Winnie the Pooh
The Nightmare Before Christmas▶
101 Dalmatians▶
Peter Pan▶
Pinocchio▶
Pocahontas▶
The Rescuers▶
The Rescuers Down Under
The Return of Jafar
Robin Hood▶
Sleeping Beauty▶
Snow White and the Seven Dwarfs▶
The Sword in the Stone▶
The Three Caballeros
Toy Story▶

Disney Family Movies

The Absent-Minded Professor▶
The Adventures of Bullwhip Griffin
The Adventures of Huck Finn▶
The Adventures of Ichabod and Mr. Toad▶
The Air Up There
Almost Angels
Amy
Angels in the Outfield
The Apple Dumpling Gang
The Apple Dumpling Gang Rides Again
Babes in Toyland
The Barefoot Executive
The Bears & I
Bedknobs and Broomsticks
Benji the Hunted
Big Red
Black Arrow▶
The Black Arrow
The Black Hole
Blackbeard's Ghost
Blank Check
The Blue Yonder
Bon Voyage!
Born to Run
Breakin' Through
Candleshoe
The Castaway Cowboy
The Cat from Outer Space
Charley and the Angel
Charlie, the Lonesome Cougar
Cheetah
Child of Glass
The Computer Wore Tennis Shoes
Condorman
Darby O'Gill & the Little People▶
Davy Crockett and the River Pirates
Davy Crockett, King of the Wild Frontier▶
The Devil & Max Devlin
Diamonds on Wheels
Dr. Syn, Alias the Scarecrow
Emil and the Detectives
Escapade in Florence
Escape to Witch Mountain▶
A Far Off Place
The Fighting Prince of Donegal
Flight of the Grey Wolf
Flight of the Navigator
Freaky Friday
The Girl Who Spelled Freedom▶
The Gnome-Mobile
Gone are the Days
A Goofy Movie
The Great Locomotive Chase
Greyfriars Bobby
Gus
Heavyweights
Herbie Goes Bananas
Herbie Goes to Monte Carlo
Herbie Rides Again
Homeward Bound: The Incredible Journey▶
Honey, I Blew Up the Kid
Honey, I Shrunk the Kids
The Horse in the Gray Flannel Suit
The Horse Without a Head
Horsemasters
Hot Lead & Cold Feet
The Hunchback of Notre Dame▶
In Search of the Castaways▶
The Incredible Journey
Iron Will
The Island at the Top of the World
Johnny Shiloh
Johnny Tremain & the Sons of Liberty
The Journey of Natty Gann▶
Justin Morgan Had a Horse
King of the Grizzlies
The Last Flight of Noah's Ark
Lt. Robin Crusoe, U.S.N.
The Light in the Forest
The Littlest Horse Thieves
The Littlest Outlaw
Lots of Luck
The Love Bug
Love Leads the Way
Mary Poppins▶
Menace on the Mountain
Mickey's Christmas Carol▶
Million Dollar Duck
Miracle Down Under
The Miracle of the White Stallions
The Misadventures of Merlin Jones
Monkeys, Go Home!
Monkey's Uncle
Moon Pilot
The Moon-Spinners
Mooncussers
Mosby's Marauders
My Dog, the Thief
Napoleon and Samantha▶
Never a Dull Moment
Newsies
Night Crossing
Nikki, the Wild Dog of the North
The Nine Lives of Elfego Baca
No Deposit, No Return
The North Avenue Irregulars
Now You See Him, Now You Don't
Old Yeller▶
The One and Only, Genuine, Original Family Band▶
One Little Indian
One Magic Christmas
One of Our Dinosaurs Is Missing
The Parent Trap
Pete's Dragon
Pocahontas▶
Pollyanna▶
Return from Witch Mountain
Return to Oz
Ride a Wild Pony▶
Rob Roy—The Highland Rogue
The Rocketeer▶
Sammy, the Way-Out Seal
Savage Sam
Scandalous John
The Secret of El Zorro
The Shaggy D.A.
The Shaggy Dog
The Sign of Zorro
Smith!
Smoke
Snowball Express
So Dear to My Heart▶
Son of Flubber
The Story of Robin Hood & His Merrie Men▶
Summer Magic
Superdad
The Swiss Family Robinson▶
The Sword & the Rose
Tall Tale: The Unbelievable Adventures of Pecos Bill
Ten Who Dared
That Darn Cat
Third Man on the Mountain
Those Calloways
The Three Lives of Thomasina▶
3 Ninjas
3 Ninjas Kick Back
A Tiger Walks
Toby Tyler▶
Tom and Huck▶
Tonka
Toy Story▶
Treasure Island▶
The Treasure of Matecumbe
20,000 Leagues Under the Sea▶
The Ugly Dachshund
Undergrads▶
Unidentified Flying Oddball
Waltz King
The Watcher in the Woods
Westward Ho, the Wagons!
White Fang▶
White Fang 2: The Myth of the White Wolf
The Wild Country
Wild Hearts Can't Be Broken▶
The World's Greatest Athlete

Dr. Christian

Courageous Dr. Christian
Dr. Christian Meets the Women
Meet Dr. Christian
Melody for Three
Remedy for Riches
They Meet Again

Dr. Mabuse

Das Testament des Dr. Mabuse▶
Dr. Mabuse, Parts 1 & 2▶
Dr. Mabuse vs. Scotland Yard
The Invisible Dr. Mabuse▶
The Return of Dr. Mabuse
The Thousand Eyes of Dr. Mabuse

Dr. Seuss

The 5000 Fingers of Dr. T▶
How the Grinch Stole Christmas▶

Dracula

Abbott and Costello Meet Frankenstein▶
Bela Lugosi Scrapbook
The Best of the Two Ronnies
Blood of Dracula
Blood of Dracula's Castle
Bram Stoker's Dracula
The Brides of Dracula
Count Dracula
Count Dracula's Great Love
Dracula▶
Dracula
Dracula: A Cinematic Scrapbook
Dracula & Son
Dracula: Dead and Loving It
Dracula/Garden of Eden
Dracula Has Risen from the Grave
Dracula Rising
Dracula (Spanish Version)
Dracula Sucks
Dracula: Up in Harlem
Dracula vs. Frankenstein
Dracula's Daughter▶
Dracula's Great Love
Dracula's Last Rites
Dracula's Widow
The Horror of Dracula▶
House of Dracula
House of Frankenstein
Hysterical
Love at First Bite
The Monster Squad
Nocturna
Return of Dracula
Return of the Vampire
The Satanic Rites of Dracula
The Scars of Dracula
The Screaming Dead
Son of Dracula▶
Taste the Blood of Dracula
To Die for
Transylvania 6-5000
Vampire Circus
Waxwork
Zoltan...Hound of Dracula

Eddy & McDonald

Bitter Sweet
Girl of the Golden West
I Married an Angel
Maytime▶
Naughty Marietta
New Moon
Rose Marie▶
Sweethearts▶

Elvisfilm

Blue Hawaii
Change of Habit
Charro!
Clambake
Double Trouble
Easy Come, Easy Go
Elvis and Me
Elvis in Hollywood▶
Elvis Stories
Elvis: The Movie
Flaming Star▶
Follow That Dream
Frankie and Johnny
Fun in Acapulco
G.I. Blues
Girl Happy
Girls! Girls! Girls!
Harum Scarum
Heartbreak Hotel
Honeymoon in Vegas
It Happened at the World's Fair
Jailhouse Rock▶
Kid Galahad
King Creole
Kissin' Cousins
Live a Little, Love a Little
Love Me Tender
Loving You
Paradise, Hawaiian Style
Rock-a-Doodle
Roustabout
Speedway
Spinout
Stay Away, Joe
This Is Elvis
Tickle Me
Top Secret!▶
The Trouble with Girls (and How To Get Into It)▶
True Romance
Viva Las Vegas
Wild in the Country

"E.T." & Rip-Offs

E.T.: The Extra-Terrestrial▶
Mac and Me
Magic in the Water

Faerie Tale Theatre

Aladdin and His Wonderful Lamp
Beauty and the Beast
The Boy Who Left Home to Find Out About the Shivers
Cinderella
The Dancing Princesses
The Emperor's New Clothes
Goldilocks & the Three Bears
Hansel and Gretel
Jack & the Beanstalk
The Little Mermaid
Little Red Riding Hood
The Nightingale
The Pied Piper of Hamelin
Pinocchio
The Princess and the Pea
The Princess Who Never Laughed
Puss 'n Boots

Rapunzel
Rip van Winkle
Rumpelstiltskin
Sleeping Beauty
The Snow Queen
Snow White and the Seven Dwarfs
The Tale of the Frog Prince▶
The Three Little Pigs
Thumbelina

The Falcon

The Amityville Curse
The Devil's Cargo
The Falcon in Hollywood
The Falcon in Mexico
The Falcon Takes Over/Strange Bargain
The Falcon's Adventure/Armored Car Robbery
The Falcon's Brother

Family Viewing

The Absent-Minded Professor▶
Adventures in Dinosaur City
Adventures in Spying
The Adventures of Bullwhip Griffin
The Adventures of Huckleberry Finn
The Adventures of Mark Twain▶
The Adventures of Pinocchio
African Journey
Aladdin▶
Aladdin and His Wonderful Lamp
Alaska
All Dogs Go to Heaven 2
Almost Partners
The Amazing Dobermans
The Amazing Panda Adventure
An American Tail
An American Tail: Fievel Goes West
Amy
And the Children Shall Lead
And You Thought Your Parents Were Weird!
Andre
Angels in the Outfield
Anne of Avonlea▶
Anne of Green Gables▶
Annie Oakley
The Apple Dumpling Gang
The Apple Dumpling Gang Rides Again
The Aristocats▶
Ava's Magical Adventure
Babar: The Movie
Babe▶
Babes in Toyland
Baby's Day Out
Back to Hannibal: The Return of Tom Sawyer and Huckleberry Finn
The Ballad of Paul Bunyan
Bambi▶
The Barefoot Executive
Batman▶
Batman Forever▶
Be My Valentine, Charlie Brown
Beauty and the Beast▶
Beethoven
Beethoven's 2nd
Behave Yourself!
Bell, Book and Candle
Benji▶
Benji the Hunted
Benji's Very Own Christmas Story
Bernard and the Genie
The Best Christmas Pageant Ever
The Big Green
Big Red
Bigfoot: The Unforgettable Encounter
The Billion Dollar Hobo
Bingo
The Black Arrow
Black Beauty
Black Beauty▶
Black Beauty/Courage of Black Beauty
The Black Hole
Blackbeard's Ghost
The Blue Yonder
Bon Voyage!
Born Free▶
Born to Be Wild
Born to Run
The Borrowers▶
A Boy Named Charlie Brown▶
The Boy Who Loved Trolls
The Brain
The Brave Little Frog
Breakin' Through
Brewster's Millions
Bridge to Terabithia
Brother Future
The Bulldozer Brigade
Candleshoe
The Canterville Ghost
The Capture of Grizzly Adams
The Care Bears Movie
The Care Bears Movie 2: A New Generation
Casey at the Bat
The Castaway Cowboy
The Cat from Outer Space
Challenge to Lassie
The Challengers
Charley and the Angel
A Charlie Brown Christmas
Charlie Brown's All-Stars
Charlie, the Lonesome Cougar
Cheetah
Child of Glass
Chips, the War Dog
The Chronicles of Narnia
Cinderella▶
Clarence
Clarence, the Cross-eyed Lion▶
Clowning Around
The Computer Wore Tennis Shoes
Condorman
Courage Mountain
Courage of Lassie
Cross Creek
A Cry from the Mountain
Daniel and the Towers
Darby O'Gill & the Little People▶
The Dark Crystal▶
Davy Crockett and the River Pirates
Davy Crockett, King of the Wild Frontier▶
A Day for Thanks on Walton's Mountain
The Devil & Max Devlin
Diamond's Edge
Diamonds on Wheels
Disney's Storybook Classics
Dr. Syn, Alias the Scarecrow
A Dog of Flanders
The Dog Who Stopped the War
Donner Pass: The Road to Survival
D2: The Mighty Ducks
DuckTales the Movie: Treasure of the Lost Lamp
Dumbo▶
Dusty
Ele, My Friend
Emil and the Detectives
The Enchanted Forest
Escapade in Florence
Escape to Witch Mountain▶
Eyes of an Angel
Father of the Bride
Felix the Cat: The Movie
Ferngully: The Last Rain Forest
The Fig Tree
The Fighting Prince of Donegal
Flight of the Grey Wolf
Flight of the Navigator
Flipper▶
Flipper's New Adventure▶
Flipper's Odyssey
Follow Me, Boys!▶
For the Love of Benji
The Fox and the Hound▶
Freaky Friday
Free Willy
Freeze Frame
Frog
Frogs!
Gay Purr-ee
George's Island▶
The Gift of Love
A Girl of the Limberlost
The Girl Who Spelled Freedom▶
The Gnome-Mobile
Goin' Coconuts
Gone are the Days
The Good, the Bad, and Huckleberry Hound
The Great Land of Small
The Great Locomotive Chase
Greyfriars Bobby
Gryphon
Gus
Happily Ever After
Harriet the Spy
The Haunting of Barney Palmer
Heavyweights
Hector's Bunyip
Heidi
Heidi▶
Herbie Goes Bananas
Herbie Goes to Monte Carlo
Herbie Rides Again
Here Comes Santa Claus
He's Your Dog, Charlie Brown!
The Hideaways
The Hills of Home▶
Hiroshima Maiden
The Hoboken Chicken Emergency
Hockey Night
Home Alone▶
Home at Last
Home for Christmas
Home of Angels
Honey, I Blew Up the Kid
Honey, I Shrunk the Kids
The Horse in the Gray Flannel Suit
The Horse Without a Head
Horsemasters
Hot Lead & Cold Feet
The House of Dies Drear
How to Be a Perfect Person in Just Three Days
Huck and the King of Hearts
Huckleberry Finn
Hugo the Hippo
I Love Lucy
The Incredible Journey
Into the West▶
The Invisible Boy
Is This Goodbye, Charlie Brown?
The Island at the Top of the World
It Was a Short Summer, Charlie Brown
It's an Adventure, Charlie Brown!
It's the Great Pumpkin, Charlie Brown
Jack & the Beanstalk
Jacob Have I Loved
The Jetsons Meet the Flintstones
Joe Panther▶
Johnny Appleseed
Johnny Shiloh
Johnny Tremain & the Sons of Liberty
Journey Back to Oz
The Journey of Natty Gann▶
Journey to Spirit Island
The Jungle Book
The Jungle Book▶
Justin Morgan Had a Horse
Kazaam
Kid Colter
A Kid for Two Farthings
The Kid Who Loved Christmas
King of the Grizzlies
King of the Wind
Konrad
The Land Before Time 2: The Great Valley Adventure
The Land of Faraway
Lantern Hill
Lassie: Adventures of Neeka
Lassie: Well of Love
The Last Flight of Noah's Ark
The Last Winter
The Lawrenceville Stories
Legend of Lobo
The Legend of Sleepy Hollow
Lt. Robin Crusoe, U.S.N.
The Light in the Forest
The Lion King▶
Little Big League
Little Giants
Little Heroes
Little Indian, Big City
Little Miss Marker▶
Little Nemo: Adventures in Slumberland
The Little Princess▶
The Little Princess
A Little Princess▶
The Little Rascals
Little Rascals, Vol. 1
Little Rascals, Vol. 2
The Littlest Horse Thieves
The Littlest Outlaw
Lone Star Kid
Look Who's Talking Now
Looking for Miracles
Lots of Luck
The Love Bug
Love Leads the Way
Magic of Lassie
The Magic of the Golden Bear: Goldy 3
The Magic Sword
Magical Wonderland
Man of the House
Maricela
Mark Twain and Me
Mary Poppins▶
Matilda
Men of Boys Town
Menace on the Mountain
Mickey's Christmas Carol▶
The Mighty Ducks
The Mighty Pawns
Million Dollar Duck
Miracle at Moreaux
Miracle Down Under
The Miracle of the White Stallions
The Misadventures of Merlin Jones
Mr. Superinvisible
Misty
Monkey Trouble
Monkeys, Go Home!
Monkey's Uncle
Moon Pilot
The Moon-Spinners
Mooncussers
Mosby's Marauders
Mother Goose Rock 'n' Rhyme
Munchie
The Muppet Movie▶
Muppet Treasure Island
The Muppets Take Manhattan▶
My Darlin' Clementine
My Dog, the Thief
My Family Treasure
My Friend Flicka▶
My Neighbor Totoro
The Mysterious Stranger
Napoleon and Samantha▶
Necessary Parties
Never a Dull Moment
The NeverEnding Story▶
NeverEnding Story 2: The Next Chapter
Newsies
Night Crossing
The Nightingale
Nikki, the Wild Dog of the North
The Nine Lives of Elfego Baca
No Deposit, No Return
No Grumps Allowed!
The North Avenue Irregulars
Not Quite Human
Not Quite Human 2
Now You See Him, Now You Don't
Nukie
The Nutcracker Prince
Old Yeller▶
Ollie Hopnoodle's Haven of Bliss
Once Upon a Forest
The One and Only, Genuine, Original Family Band▶
101 Dalmatians▶
One Little Indian
One Magic Christmas
One of Our Dinosaurs Is Missing
The Out-of-Towners▶
The Pebble and the Penguin
Pecos Bill
Pete's Dragon
Pinocchio▶
Pippi Goes on Board
Pippi in the South Seas
Pippi Longstocking
Pippi on the Run
Pistol: The Birth of a Legend
Poco
Pollyanna▶
Prancer
Prehysteria 2
Primo Baby
Prince and the Great Race
Prince Brat and the Whipping Boy▶
The Princess and the Goblin
A Rare Breed
The Red Fury
The Red Pony▶
The Reluctant Dragon
The Rescuers▶
The Rescuers Down Under
Return from Witch Mountain
The Return of the King
Return to Oz
Ride a Wild Pony▶
Ring of Bright Water▶
The River Pirates
Rob Roy—The Highland Rogue
Rock-a-Doodle
The Rocketeer▶
Rover Dangerfield
Rudolph the Red-Nosed Reindeer
Rumpelstiltskin
Run for the Roses
Runaway
The Runaways
The St. Tammany Miracle
Sammy, the Way-Out Seal
Santa Claus
Santa Claus Is Coming to Town
Santa Claus: The Movie
Sarah, Plain and Tall▶
Savage Sam
Savannah Smiles
Save the Lady
Scandalous John
The Secret Garden▶
The Secret Garden
The Secret of El Zorro
The Secret of Navajo Cave
The Secret of the Golden Eagle
Seven Alone
The Shaggy D.A.
The Shaggy Dog
She's a Good Skate, Charlie Brown
The Sign of Zorro
The Silver Stallion: King of the Wild Brumbies
Skeezer
Sleeping Beauty▶
Sleeping Beauty
Smith!
Smoke
A Smoky Mountain Christmas
Snoopy, Come Home▶
Snow White and the Seven Dwarfs▶
Snowball Express
Solo
Son of Flubber
Spirit of the Eagle
Spy Trap
Squanto: A Warrior's Tale▶
Starbird and Sweet William
Starring Bugs Bunny!
Still Not Quite Human
Stone Fox

The Story Lady
The Story of Robin Hood & His Merrie Men▶
Summer Magic
A Summer to Remember
The Sun Comes Up
Superdad
Sweet 15
The Swiss Family Robinson▶
The Sword & the Rose
The Sword in the Stone▶
Tales from Avonlea, Vol. 1: The Journey Begins
Tall Tale: The Unbelievable Adventures of Pecos Bill
Ten Who Dared
That Darn Cat
The Thief of Bagdad▶
Third Man on the Mountain
Those Calloways
The Three Little Pigs
The Three Lives of Thomasina▶
Thumbelina
Tiger Town
A Tiger Walks
Toby Tyler▶
Tom and Jerry: The Movie
Tom Sawyer▶
Tom Sawyer
Tonka
Trading Mom
Treasure Island▶
The Treasure of Matecumbe
The Ugly Dachshund
Unidentified Flying Oddball
Up Against the Wall
A Very Brady Christmas
Walking on Air
The Waltons: A Thanksgiving Story
Waltz King
A Waltz Through the Hills
The Watcher in the Woods
Westward Ho, the Wagons!
What the Moon Saw
Where the Lilies Bloom▶
Where the Red Fern Grows
Where the Red Fern Grows: Part 2
White Fang▶
White Fang 2: The Myth of the White Wolf
Whitewater Sam
Who Has Seen the Wind?
The Wild Country
Wild Hearts Can't Be Broken▶
Wild Horse Hank
The Witches▶
Woof!
Words by Heart
The World's Greatest Athlete
The Yearling▶
The Yearling
You Must Remember This
The Young Detectives on Wheels

Flynn & de Havilland

The Adventures of Robin Hood▶
Captain Blood▶
The Charge of the Light Brigade▶
Dodge City▶
The Private Lives of Elizabeth & Essex▶
Santa Fe Trail
They Died with Their Boots On▶

Ford & Wayne

Donovan's Reef▶
Fort Apache▶
The Horse Soldiers
How the West Was Won▶
The Long Voyage Home▶
The Man Who Shot Liberty Valance▶
The Quiet Man▶
Rio Grande▶
The Searchers▶
She Wore a Yellow Ribbon▶
Stagecoach▶
They Were Expendable▶
Three Godfathers▶
Wings of Eagles

4 Bones

A Nous la Liberte▶
Abe Lincoln in Illinois▶
Adam's Rib▶
The Adventures of Robin Hood▶
The African Queen▶
All About Eve▶
All Quiet on the Western Front▶
All the King's Men▶
An American in Paris▶
Anatomy of a Murder▶
Andrei Rublev▶
An Angel at My Table▶
Angels with Dirty Faces▶
Annie Hall▶
Apocalypse Now▶
The Asphalt Jungle▶
Au Revoir Les Enfants▶
The Awful Truth▶
The Ballad of Narayama▶
Bambi▶
The Bank Dick▶
The Battleship Potemkin▶
Beauty and the Beast▶
Ben-Hur▶
The Best Years of Our Lives▶
The Bicycle Thief▶
The Big Parade▶
The Big Sleep▶
The Birth of a Nation▶
The Blue Angel▶
The Boys of St. Vincent▶
Breathless▶
Brian's Song▶
The Bride of Frankenstein▶
The Bridge on the River Kwai▶
Brief Encounter▶
Bringing Up Baby▶
The Burmese Harp▶
Butch Cassidy and the Sundance Kid▶
The Cabinet of Dr. Caligari▶
The Caine Mutiny▶
The Cameraman▶
Casablanca▶
Cesar▶
Children of Paradise▶
Chimes at Midnight▶
Chinatown▶
Christ Stopped at Eboli▶
A Christmas Carol▶
Citizen Kane▶
City Lights▶
The Civil War, Episode 1: The Cause—1861▶
The Civil War, Episode 2: A Very Bloody Affair—1862▶
The Civil War, Episode 3: Forever Free—1862▶
The Civil War, Episode 4: Simply Murder—1863▶
The Civil War, Episode 5: The Universe of Battle—1863▶
The Civil War, Episode 6: Valley of the Shadow of Death—1864▶
The Civil War, Episode 7: Most Hallowed Ground—1864▶
The Civil War, Episode 8: War is All Hell—1865▶
The Civil War, Episode 9: The Better Angels of Our Nature—1865▶
A Clockwork Orange▶
Close Encounters of the Third Kind▶
Colonel Redl▶
Come and See▶
Commissar▶
The Conformist▶
Crime and Punishment▶
The Crowd▶
Cyrano de Bergerac▶
Danton▶
Das Boot▶
David Copperfield▶
Day for Night▶
Day of Wrath▶
Dead of Night▶
The Deer Hunter▶
Deliverance▶
Destry Rides Again▶
Diamonds of the Night▶
Dinner at Eight▶
The Discreet Charm of the Bourgeoisie▶
Dr. Strangelove, or: How I Learned to Stop Worrying and Love the Bomb▶
Don Quixote▶
Double Indemnity▶
Duck Soup▶
Dumbo▶
The Earrings of Madame De...▶
Earth▶
East of Eden▶
8 1/2▶
El Norte▶
The Elephant Man▶
The Empire Strikes Back▶
E.T.: The Extra-Terrestrial▶
Every Man for Himself & God Against All▶
Fanny▶
Fanny and Alexander▶
Fantasia▶
Fitzcarraldo▶
Five Easy Pieces▶
Forbidden Games▶
Foreign Correspondent▶
Forever and a Day▶
Forrest Gump▶
42nd Street▶
The Four Feathers▶
The 400 Blows▶
Frankenstein▶
The Freshman▶
From Here to Eternity▶
The Fugitive▶
Gallipoli▶
The Garden of the Finzi-Continis▶
The General▶
The General Line▶
Gigi▶
The Godfather▶
The Godfather 1902-1959: The Complete Epic▶
The Godfather, Part 2▶
The Gold Rush▶
Gone with the Wind▶
Goodfellas▶
The Gospel According to St. Matthew▶
The Graduate▶
Grand Illusion▶
The Great Dictator▶
Great Expectations▶
Greed▶
Gunga Din▶
Hamlet▶
Harold and Maude▶
Harvest▶
Hearts of Darkness: A Filmmaker's Apocalypse▶
Henry V▶
Henry: Portrait of a Serial Killer▶
Here Comes Mr. Jordan▶
High Noon▶
Hiroshima, Mon Amour▶
His Girl Friday▶
Hollywood Canteen▶
Hoop Dreams▶
How Green Was My Valley▶
Howard's End▶
Hud▶
The Hunchback of Notre Dame▶
The Hustler▶
I Am a Fugitive from a Chain Gang▶
The Idiot▶
If...▶
Ikiru▶
The Informer▶
Intolerance▶
The Invisible Man▶
Isn't Life Wonderful▶
It Happened One Night▶
It's a Wonderful Life▶
Ivan the Terrible, Part 1▶
Ju Dou▶
Judgment at Nuremberg▶
Jules and Jim▶
The King and I▶
King Kong▶
Knife in the Water▶
Koyaanisqatsi▶
Kriemhilde's Revenge▶
Kwaidan▶
La Chienne▶
La Dolce Vita▶
La Strada▶
Lady and the Tramp▶
The Lady Eve▶
The Lady Vanishes▶
L'Age D'Or▶
Last Command▶
The Last Detail▶
The Last Emperor▶
The Last Picture Show▶
The Last Seduction▶
Late Spring▶
Laura▶
Lawrence of Arabia▶
Les Miserables▶
The Letter▶
A Letter to Three Wives▶
The Life and Death of Colonel Blimp▶
The Lion in Winter▶
The Lion King▶
Little Women▶
The Lives of a Bengal Lancer▶
Local Hero▶
Lola Montes▶
Long Day's Journey into Night▶
Lost Horizon▶
The Lost Weekend▶
M▶
The Magnificent Ambersons▶
The Magnificent Seven▶
Male and Female▶
The Maltese Falcon▶
A Man for All Seasons▶
The Man Who Would Be King▶
The Manchurian Candidate▶
Manhattan▶
Marius▶
The Marriage of Maria Braun▶
M*A*S*H▶
McCabe & Mrs. Miller▶
Mean Streets▶
Metropolis▶
Miracle of Morgan's Creek▶
Miracle on 34th Street▶
Mrs. Miniver▶
Mr. & Mrs. Bridge▶
Mister Roberts▶
Mr. Smith Goes to Washington▶
Modern Times▶
Mon Oncle▶
The Music Man▶
Mutiny on the Bounty▶
My Left Foot▶
My Life as a Dog▶
My Life to Live▶
My Man Godfrey▶
Napoleon▶
Nashville▶
National Velvet▶
A Night at the Opera▶
The Night of the Hunter▶
The Night of the Shooting Stars▶
North by Northwest▶
Nosferatu▶
Notorious▶
O Lucky Man!▶
Objective, Burma!▶
Of Mice and Men▶
Oliver Twist▶
On the Waterfront▶
One Flew Over the Cuckoo's Nest▶
Only Angels Have Wings▶
Open City▶
Our Hospitality▶
The Ox-Bow Incident▶
Pandora's Box▶
The Passion of Joan of Arc▶
Pather Panchali▶
Paths of Glory▶
Pelle the Conqueror▶
Persona▶
Petulia▶
The Philadelphia Story▶
Pinocchio▶
Pixote▶
Poltergeist▶
The Private Life of Henry VIII▶
Psycho▶
Pulp Fiction▶
The Quiet Man▶
Quiz Show▶
Raging Bull▶
Raiders of the Lost Ark▶
A Raisin in the Sun▶
Ran▶
Rashomon▶
Rear Window▶
Rebecca▶
Rebel Without a Cause▶
Red River▶
The Red Shoes▶
The Reincarnation of Golden Lotus▶
The Report on the Party and the Guests▶
Ride the High Country▶
The River▶
A Room with a View▶
Roots▶
Rosemary's Baby▶
Ruggles of Red Gap▶
The Rules of the Game▶
Sansho the Bailiff▶
Scenes from a Marriage▶
Schindler's List▶
The Searchers▶
Sergeant York▶
Seven Beauties▶
Seven Samurai▶
The Seventh Seal▶
Shane▶
Shin Heike Monogatari▶
Shoeshine▶
Shoot the Piano Player▶
The Shop on Main Street▶
Show Boat▶
Siegfried▶
Singin' in the Rain▶
Small Change▶
Snow White and the Seven Dwarfs▶
Some Like It Hot▶
The Sound of Music▶
Sounder▶
The Southerner▶
Spartacus▶
Stagecoach▶
Stalag 17▶
Star Wars▶
Storm Over Asia▶
Strangers on a Train▶
A Streetcar Named Desire▶
The Stunt Man▶
Sullivan's Travels▶
Sunrise▶
A Tale of Two Cities▶
The Third Man▶
The 39 Steps▶
Throne of Blood▶
The Tin Drum▶
To Kill a Mockingbird▶
To Live▶
Tokyo Story▶
Tom Jones▶
Tootsie▶
Top Hat▶
Touch of Evil▶
The Train▶
Treasure of the Sierra Madre▶
Tristana▶
Twelve Angry Men▶
Twentieth Century▶
2001: A Space Odyssey▶
Two Women▶
Umberto D▶
Un Chien Andalou▶
Vampyr▶
Variety▶
Vertigo▶
Viridiana▶
Viva Zapata!▶

Wages of Fear▶
The Wedding March▶
Who's Afraid of Virginia Woolf?▶
The Wild Bunch▶
Wild Strawberries▶
The Wind▶
The Wizard of Oz▶
Woman in the Dunes▶
Woman of the Year▶
Woodstock▶
The World of Apu▶
Wuthering Heights▶
Yankee Doodle Dandy▶
Yojimbo▶
Young Frankenstein▶
Z▶
Zero for Conduct▶
Zvenigora▶

Francis the Talking Mule

Francis Covers the Big Town
Francis Goes to the Races
Francis Goes to West Point
Francis in the Haunted House
Francis in the Navy
Francis Joins the WACs
Francis the Talking Mule▶

Frankenstein

Abbott and Costello Meet Frankenstein▶
Andy Warhol's Frankenstein
Blackenstein
The Bride
The Bride of Frankenstein▶
The Curse of Frankenstein
Dr. Frankenstein's Castle of Freaks
Dracula vs. Frankenstein
The Evil of Frankenstein
Frankenstein▶
Frankenstein
Frankenstein: A Cinematic Scrapbook
Frankenstein and the Monster from Hell
Frankenstein '80
Frankenstein General Hospital
Frankenstein Island
Frankenstein Meets the Space Monster
Frankenstein Meets the Wolfman▶
Frankenstein Sings...The Movie
Frankenstein Unbound▶
Frankenstein's Daughter
Frankenstein's Great Aunt Tillie
Frankenweenie
The Ghost of Frankenstein
Gothic▶
The Horror of Frankenstein
House of Frankenstein
Jesse James Meets Frankenstein's Daughter
Lady Frankenstein
Mary Shelley's Frankenstein
Mr. Stitch
The Munsters' Revenge
Nosferatu▶
Prototype▶
The Revenge of Frankenstein
The Screaming Dead
Son of Frankenstein▶
Teenage Frankenstein
The Vindicator
Young Frankenstein▶

Gable & Crawford

Chained
Dance Fools Dance▶
Dancing Lady
Forsaking All Others
Laughing Sinners
Love on the Run
Possessed
Strange Cargo

Garland & Rooney

Andy Hardy Meets Debutante
Babes in Arms
Babes on Broadway
Girl Crazy▶
Life Begins for Andy Hardy▶
Love Finds Andy Hardy▶
Strike Up the Band
Thoroughbreds Don't Cry
Thousands Cheer
Words and Music

Garson & Pidgeon

Blossoms in the Dust
Julia Misbehaves▶
Madame Curie▶
The Miniver Story
Mrs. Miniver▶
Mrs. Parkington
That Forsyte Woman

Gibson & Glover

Lethal Weapon▶
Lethal Weapon 2▶
Lethal Weapon 3
Maverick

Godzilla and Friends

Dagora, the Space Monster
Destroy All Monsters
Destroy All Planets
Gamera, the Invincible
Gamera vs. Barugon
Gamera vs. Gaos
Gamera vs. Guiron
Gamera vs. Zigra
Gappa the Trifibian Monster
Ghidrah the Three Headed Monster
Godzilla, King of the Monsters
Godzilla 1985
Godzilla on Monster Island
Godzilla Raids Again
Godzilla vs. Biollante
Godzilla vs. Megalon
Godzilla vs. Monster Zero
Godzilla vs. Mothra
Godzilla vs. the Cosmic Monster
Godzilla vs. the Sea Monster
Godzilla vs. the Smog Monster
Godzilla's Revenge
King Kong vs. Godzilla
Mothra▶
Rodan
Son of Godzilla
Terror of Mechagodzilla
Varan the Unbelievable
War of the Gargantuas
X from Outer Space
Yog, Monster from Space

"Gremlins" & Rip-Offs

Critters
Critters 2: The Main Course
Critters 3
Critters 4
Ghoulies
Ghoulies 2
Ghoulies 3: Ghoulies Go to College
Ghoulies 4
Gremlins▶
Gremlins 2: The New Batch▶
Munchie
Munchies
Spookies

Hallmark Hall of Fame

An American Story
Blind Spot
The Boys Next Door
Breathing Lessons▶
Caroline?▶
Decoration Day▶
Foxfire▶
Journey
Miss Rose White▶
O Pioneers!
One Against the Wind▶
The Piano Lesson▶
A Place for Annie
Redwood Curtain
The Return of the Native
Sarah, Plain and Tall▶
The Secret Garden▶
The Shell Seekers
Skylark
To Dance with the White Dog▶

Hammer Films: Horror

Asylum
Blood of the Vampire
The Blood on Satan's Claw▶
The Brides of Dracula
Captain Kronos: Vampire Hunter▶
Count Dracula's Great Love
The Creeping Flesh
The Curse of Frankenstein
The Curse of the Werewolf
Die Screaming, Marianne
Dr. Jekyll and Sister Hyde
Dracula Has Risen from the Grave
The Evil of Frankenstein
Frankenstein and the Monster from Hell
The Ghoul
The Gorgon
Hands of the Ripper
The Horror of Dracula▶
The Horror of Frankenstein
The Hound of the Baskervilles
Hysteria
Kiss of the Vampire
Lust for a Vampire
Maniac
The Mummy▶
The Nanny
Nightmare
Paranoiac
The Phantom of the Opera
The Revenge of Frankenstein
The Satanic Rites of Dracula
The Scars of Dracula
The 7 Brothers Meet Dracula
Tales from the Crypt▶
Tales That Witness Madness
Taste the Blood of Dracula
Theatre of Blood▶
To the Devil, A Daughter
Twins of Evil
The Two Faces of Dr. Jekyll
Vampire Circus
The Vampire Lovers
Vault of Horror

Hammer Films: Sci Fi & Fantasy

Creatures the World Forgot
Four Sided Triangle
Men of Sherwood Forest
One Million Years B.C.
Quatermass 2▶
Quatermass and the Pit
The Quatermass Experiment▶
Spaceways
Sword of Sherwood Forest
When Dinosaurs Ruled the Earth

Hawks & Wayne

El Dorado▶
Hatari!▶
Red River▶
Rio Bravo▶
Rio Lobo

Hepburn & Grant

Bringing Up Baby▶
Holiday▶
The Philadelphia Story▶
Sylvia Scarlett

Hepburn & Tracy

Adam's Rib▶
Desk Set▶
Guess Who's Coming to Dinner▶
Hepburn & Tracy
Pat and Mike▶
State of the Union▶
Without Love
Woman of the Year▶

Hercules

Conquest of Mycene
The Fury of Hercules
Hercules
Hercules 2
Hercules Against the Moon Men
Hercules and the Captive Women
Hercules in New York
Hercules in the Haunted World
Hercules, Prisoner of Evil
Hercules Unchained
Jason and the Argonauts▶
The Loves of Hercules
Samson and His Mighty Challenge
The Three Stooges Meet Hercules

Hopalong Cassidy

Bar-20
Border Patrol
Border Vigilantes
Colt Comrades
Doomed Caravan▶
False Colors
The Frontiersmen
Hopalong Cassidy▶
Hopalong Cassidy: Borrowed Trouble
Hopalong Cassidy: Dangerous Venture
Hopalong Cassidy: False Paradise
Hopalong Cassidy: Hoppy's Holiday
Hopalong Cassidy: Renegade Trail
Hopalong Cassidy: Riders of the Deadline
Hopalong Cassidy: Silent Conflict
Hopalong Cassidy: Sinister Journey
Hopalong Cassidy: The Dead Don't Dream
Hopalong Cassidy: The Devil's Playground
Hopalong Cassidy: The Marauders
Hopalong Cassidy: Unexpected Guest
Hoppy Serves a Writ
In Old Colorado
Law of the Pampas
Leather Burners
Lost Canyon
Mystery Man
Outlaws of the Desert
Renegade Trail
Riders of the Timberline
Rustler's Valley
Santa Fe Marshal
The Showdown
Texas Masquerade
Twilight on the Trail
Undercover Man

Hope & Crosby

Cancel My Reservation
My Favorite Blonde▶
My Favorite Brunette
The Princess and the Pirate▶
The Road to Bali▶
The Road to Hong Kong
The Road to Morocco▶
The Road to Rio▶
The Road to Singapore
The Road to Utopia▶
The Road to Zanzibar▶
Scared Stiff▶
Star Spangled Rhythm▶

Jack the Ripper

Blade of the Ripper
Cosh Boy
Deadly Advice
Hands of the Ripper
He Kills Night After Night After Night
Jack the Ripper
Jack the Ripper▶
Jack's Back▶
The Monster of London City
Murder by Decree▶
Night Ripper
Phantom Fiend
The Ripper
Room to Let
A Study in Terror▶
Terror at London Bridge
Terror in the Wax Museum
Time After Time▶

James Bond

Diamonds Are Forever▶
Dr. No▶
For Your Eyes Only▶
From Russia with Love▶
Goldeneye▶
Goldfinger▶
License to Kill▶
Live and Let Die
The Living Daylights▶
The Man with the Golden Gun
Moonraker
Never Say Never Again
Octopussy
On Her Majesty's Secret Service▶
The Spy Who Loved Me
Thunderball
A View to a Kill
You Only Live Twice

James Bond Spoofs

The Ambushers
Casino Royale
If Looks Could Kill
In Like Flint
Murderers' Row
Number 1 of the Secret Service
Our Man Flint
Second Best Secret Agent in the Whole Wide World
Where the Bullets Fly

Jesse James

Frank and Jesse
I Shot Jesse James▶
Jesse James▶
Jesse James at Bay
Jesse James Meets Frankenstein's Daughter
Jesse James Rides Again
Last Days of Frank & Jesse James
The Long Riders▶
Return of Jesse James

Lassie

Challenge to Lassie
Courage of Lassie
The Hills of Home▶
Lassie: Adventures of Neeka
Lassie, Come Home
Lassie: The Miracle

Lassie: Well of Love
Lassie's Great Adventure
Magic of Lassie
The Painted Hills
Son of Lassie
The Sun Comes Up

Laurel & Hardy

Air Raid Wardens
Bellhop/The Noon Whistle
Block-heads▶
Bohemian Girl▶
Bonnie Scotland
Bullfighters
A Chump at Oxford
The Devil's Brother
A Few Moments with Buster Keaton and Laurel and Hardy▶
The Flying Deuces▶
Golden Age of Comedy
Great Guns
Hollywood Party
Laurel & Hardy and the Family
Laurel & Hardy: Another Fine Mess
Laurel & Hardy: At Work
Laurel & Hardy: Be Big
Laurel & Hardy: Below Zero
Laurel & Hardy: Berth Marks
Laurel & Hardy: Blotto
Laurel & Hardy: Brats
Laurel & Hardy: Chickens Come Home
Laurel & Hardy Comedy Classics, Vol. 1
Laurel & Hardy Comedy Classics, Vol. 2
Laurel & Hardy Comedy Classics, Vol. 3
Laurel & Hardy Comedy Classics, Vol. 4
Laurel & Hardy Comedy Classics, Vol. 5
Laurel & Hardy Comedy Classics, Vol. 6
Laurel & Hardy Comedy Classics, Vol. 7
Laurel & Hardy Comedy Classics, Vol. 8
Laurel & Hardy Comedy Classics, Vol. 9
Laurel & Hardy: Hog Wild
Laurel & Hardy: Laughing Gravy
Laurel & Hardy: Men O'War
Laurel & Hardy: Night Owls
Laurel & Hardy On the Lam
Laurel & Hardy: Perfect Day
Laurel & Hardy Special
Laurel & Hardy Spooktacular
Laurel & Hardy: Stan "Helps" Ollie
Laurel & Hardy: The Hoose-Gow
Nothing But Trouble
Our Relations▶
Pack Up Your Troubles
Pardon Us
Pick a Star
Saps at Sea
Silent Laugh Makers, No. 1▶
Sons of the Desert▶
Swiss Miss
A Tribute to the Boys
Utopia
Way Out West▶

Lemmon & Matthau

Buddy Buddy
The Fortune Cookie▶
The Front Page
Grumpier Old Men
Grumpy Old Men▶
JFK▶
The Odd Couple▶

Live Action/ Animation Combos

Alice▶
Alice in Wonderland
Anchors Aweigh▶
Bedknobs and Broomsticks
Butterfly Ball
Cool World
Dangerous When Wet
Fabulous Adventures of Baron Munchausen
Hollywood Party
The Incredible Mr. Limpet
James and the Giant Peach▶
Mary Poppins▶
The Pagemaster
Pete's Dragon
So Dear to My Heart▶
Tank Girl
The Three Caballeros
Tron
Volere Volare
Who Framed Roger Rabbit▶
Xanadu

The Lone Rider

Border Roundup
Death Rides the Plains
Law of the Saddle
The Lone Rider in Cheyenne
The Lone Rider in Ghost Town
Raiders of Red Gap
Rangeland Racket

Loy & Powell

After the Thin Man▶
Another Thin Man
Double Wedding▶
Evelyn Prentice
The Great Ziegfeld▶
I Love You Again▶
Libeled Lady▶
Love Crazy▶
Manhattan Melodrama▶
Shadow of the Thin Man▶
Song of the Thin Man
The Thin Man▶
The Thin Man Goes Home

Ma and Pa Kettle

Egg and I▶
The Kettles in the Ozarks
The Kettles on Old MacDonald's Farm
Ma and Pa Kettle
Ma and Pa Kettle at Home
Ma and Pa Kettle at the Fair
Ma and Pa Kettle at Waikiki
Ma and Pa Kettle Back On the Farm
Ma and Pa Kettle Go to Town
Ma and Pa Kettle on Vacation

Martin & Lewis

Artists and Models
At War with the Army
The Caddy
Hollywood or Bust
Jumping Jacks
My Friend Irma
Pardners
The Road to Bali▶
Scared Stiff▶
The Stooge

The Marx Brothers

Animal Crackers▶
At the Circus
Big Store
The Cocoanuts
A Day at the Races▶
Duck Soup▶
Go West
Horse Feathers▶
Love Happy
The Marx Brothers in a Nutshell▶
Monkey Business▶
A Night at the Opera▶
A Night in Casablanca▶
Room Service

MGM Musicals

An American in Paris▶
Anchors Aweigh▶
Athena
The Band Wagon▶
The Barkleys of Broadway▶
Because You're Mine
Bells are Ringing▶
Big Store
Born to Dance
Broadway Melody
Broadway Melody of 1936▶
Broadway Melody of 1938
Broadway Melody of 1940
Broadway Rhythm
Broadway Serenade
The Chocolate Soldier
Dancing Lady
Deep in My Heart
Double Trouble
The Duchess of Idaho
Easter Parade▶
Easy to Love
Everybody Sing
The Firefly
For Me and My Gal
Gigi▶
Girl of the Golden West
Give a Girl a Break
Going Hollywood▶
Good News
Goodbye, Mr. Chips
The Great Ziegfeld▶
Harum Scarum
Holiday in Mexico
Honolulu
I Love Melvin
I Married an Angel
In the Good Old Summertime▶
It Happened at the World's Fair
It Happened in Brooklyn
Lady Be Good
Les Girls
Little Nellie Kelly
Live a Little, Love a Little
Love Me or Leave Me▶
Lovely to Look At▶
Madam Satan
Maytime▶
Meet Me in Las Vegas
Meet Me in St. Louis▶
The Merry Widow▶
The Merry Widow
Million Dollar Mermaid
Mrs. Brown, You've Got a Lovely Daughter
On an Island with You
On the Town▶
Pagan Love Song
Rich, Young and Pretty
Rosalie
Rose Marie▶
Royal Wedding▶
Seven Brides for Seven Brothers▶
Ship Ahoy
Show Boat
Singin' in the Rain▶
Skirts Ahoy!
Small Town Girl
Spinout
Stay Away, Joe
Strike Up the Band
The Student Prince
Summer Stock▶
Sweethearts▶
Take Me Out to the Ball Game
Texas Carnival
That Midnight Kiss
That's Dancing!
That's Entertainment
That's Entertainment, Part 2
That's Entertainment, Part 3
Three Little Words
Thrill of a Romance
Till the Clouds Roll By
Till the Clouds Roll By/A Star Is Born▶
The Toast of New Orleans
The Trouble with Girls (and How To Get Into It)▶
The Unsinkable Molly Brown▶
Viva Las Vegas
The Wizard of Oz▶
Words and Music
Yankee Doodle Dandy▶
Yolanda and the Thief
Ziegfeld Follies
Ziegfeld Girl▶

Mike Hammer

Girl Hunters
I, the Jury
Kiss Me Deadly▶
Margin for Murder

Mr. Wong

Doomed to Die
The Fatal Hour
Mr. Wong, Detective
Mr. Wong in Chinatown
Mysterious Mr. Wong
Mystery of Mr. Wong
Phantom of Chinatown

Modern Shakespeare

Chimes at Midnight▶
A Double Life▶
Forbidden Planet▶
Fury is a Woman▶
The Godfather▶
The Godfather, Part 2▶
The Godfather, Part 3▶
Jubal
King Lear
Kiss Me Kate▶
Men Are Not Gods
Men of Respect
A Midsummer Night's Sex Comedy▶
My Own Private Idaho▶
Otello▶
Prospero's Books▶
Ran▶
Richard III▶
Ring of Fire
Rosencrantz & Guildenstern Are Dead▶
Shakespeare Wallah▶
Throne of Blood▶
West Side Story▶

Monty Python

The Adventures of Baron Munchausen▶
All You Need Is Cash▶
And Now for Something Completely Different▶
Brazil▶
Clockwise
Consuming Passions
Down Among the Z Men
Erik the Viking
A Fish Called Wanda▶
The Fisher King▶
Jabberwocky
The Missionary
Monty Python and the Holy Grail▶
Monty Python Live at the Hollywood Bowl▶
Monty Python's Life of Brian▶
Monty Python's Parrot Sketch Not Included
Monty Python's The Meaning of Life▶
Nuns on the Run
The Odd Job
Personal Services
A Private Function
Privates on Parade
Rentadick
Ripping Yarns
Romance with a Double Bass▶
The Secret Policeman's Other Ball▶
Secret Policeman's Private Parts
Time Bandits
Whoops Apocalypse
Yellowbeard

The Muppets

The Adventures of a Gnome Named Gnorm
The Great Muppet Caper▶
Labyrinth▶
The Muppet Christmas Carol
The Muppet Movie▶
Muppet Treasure Island
The Muppets Take Manhattan▶
Sesame Street Presents: Follow That Bird

National Lampoon

National Lampoon's Animal House▶
National Lampoon's Attack of the 5 Ft. 2 Women
National Lampoon's Christmas Vacation
National Lampoon's Class of '86
National Lampoon's Class Reunion
National Lampoon's European Vacation
National Lampoon's Last Resort
National Lampoon's Loaded Weapon 1
National Lampoon's Senior Trip
National Lampoon's Vacation▶

A Night at the Movies

Auntie Mame▶
Battle Cry▶
Days of Wine and Roses▶
Dial "M" for Murder▶
Fanny▶
Ocean's 11
The Prince and the Showgirl
PT 109
The Wrong Man▶
The Young Philadelphians▶

Our Gang

General Spanky
The Little Rascals
Little Rascals, Book 1
Little Rascals Christmas Special
Little Rascals, Vol. 1
Little Rascals, Vol. 2
Our Gang
Our Gang Comedies
Our Gang Comedy Festival
Our Gang Comedy Festival 2
Rascal Dazzle
The Return of Our Gang

The Pink Panther

Curse of the Pink Panther
The Pink Panther▶
The Pink Panther Strikes Again▶
Return of the Pink Panther
Revenge of the Pink Panther
A Shot in the Dark▶
Son of the Pink Panther
Trail of the Pink Panther

The Planet of the Apes

Battle for the Planet of the Apes
Beneath the Planet of the Apes
Conquest of the Planet of the Apes
Escape from the Planet of the Apes▶
Planet of the Apes▶

Plays to Film: Horton Foote
Baby, the Rain Must Fall
The Chase
Courtship▶
1918
The Trip to Bountiful▶

Plays to Film: Beth Henley
Crimes of the Heart
Miss Firecracker▶
Nobody's Fool
True Stories▶

Plays to Film: Eugene O'Neill
Ah, Wilderness!▶
Anna Christie▶
Anna Christie
Desire Under the Elms
Emperor Jones
Emperor Jones/Paul Robeson: Tribute to an Artist
The Hairy Ape
Long Day's Journey into Night▶
Long Day's Journey into Night
The Long Voyage Home▶
On Borrowed Time▶
Strange Interlude▶
Strange Interlude
Summer Holiday

Plays to Film: Rodgers & Hammerstein
Carousel▶
Flower Drum Song
The King and I▶
Oklahoma!▶
The Sound of Music▶
South Pacific▶

Plays to Film: William Shakespeare
Antony and Cleopatra
As You Like It
Carry On Cleo
Hamlet▶
Hamlet
Hamlet▶
Henry V▶
Julius Caesar▶
Julius Caesar
King Lear▶
King Lear
Macbeth▶
Macbeth
The Merchant of Venice▶
A Midsummer Night's Dream▶
A Midsummer Night's Dream
Much Ado about Nothing▶
Othello
Othello▶
Othello
Prospero's Books▶
Ran▶
Richard III▶
Romeo and Juliet▶
Romeo and Juliet
Romeo and Juliet▶
The Taming of the Shrew
The Taming of the Shrew▶
The Taming of the Shrew
The Tempest
The Tempest▶
West Side Story▶

Plays to Film: George Bernard Shaw
Androcles and the Lion
Caesar and Cleopatra
The Devil's Disciple▶
Heartbreak House
Major Barbara▶
The Millionairess
Pygmalion▶
Saint Joan

Plays to Film: Sam Shepard
Curse of the Starving Class
Fool for Love
True West▶

Plays to Film: Neil Simon
Barefoot in the Park▶
Biloxi Blues
Brighton Beach Memoirs
Broadway Bound
California Suite▶
Chapter Two
The Cheap Detective▶
Come Blow Your Horn▶
The Goodbye Girl▶
The Heartbreak Kid▶
I Ought to Be in Pictures
Last of the Red Hot Lovers
Lost in Yonkers
The Marrying Man
Max Dugan Returns
Murder by Death
The Odd Couple▶
One Trick Pony
Only When I Laugh▶
The Out-of-Towners▶
Plaza Suite▶
Prisoner of Second Avenue
Seems Like Old Times
The Slugger's Wife
Star Spangled Girl
The Sunshine Boys▶
Sweet Charity▶

Plays to Film: Tom Stoppard
Rosencrantz & Guildenstern Are Dead▶

Plays to Film: Tennessee Williams
Baby Doll▶
Cat on a Hot Tin Roof▶
Cat on a Hot Tin Roof
The Fugitive Kind
The Glass Menagerie▶
The Migrants▶
The Night of the Iguana▶
Orpheus Descending
Period of Adjustment▶
Roman Spring of Mrs. Stone▶
The Rose Tattoo▶
A Streetcar Named Desire▶
A Streetcar Named Desire
Suddenly, Last Summer▶
Summer and Smoke
Sweet Bird of Youth▶
Sweet Bird of Youth
This Property is Condemned

Producers: Robert Altman
Buffalo Bill & the Indians▶
James Dean Story
The Late Show▶
Nashville▶
Quintet
Rich Kids
A Wedding
Welcome to L.A.▶

Producers: William Castle
Bug
House on Haunted Hill
Macabre
Riot
Rosemary's Baby▶
Strait-Jacket
13 Ghosts
Zotz!

Producers: Coppola/American Zoetrope
American Graffiti▶
The Black Stallion▶
The Conversation▶
The Escape Artist▶
The Godfather, Part 2▶
Hammett

Producers: Roger Corman/New World
Atlas
Attack of the Giant Leeches
Avalanche
Battle Beyond the Stars
Battle Beyond the Sun
Beyond the Call of Duty
Big Bad Mama
Big Bad Mama 2
The Big Bird Cage
The Big Doll House
Bloodfist
Bloodfist 2
Bloody Mama
Body Waves
Boxcar Bertha
A Bucket of Blood▶
Caged Heat
Candy Stripe Nurses
Carnival Rock
Cocaine Wars
Cockfighter▶
Crazy Mama
Daddy's Boys
Day the World Ended
Death Race 2000
Death Sport
Dementia 13
Dinosaur Island
The Dunwich Horror
Eat My Dust
Eye of the Eagle 3
The Fall of the House of Usher▶
Field of Fire
Fighting Mad
Firehawk
Forbidden World
Futurekick
Galaxy of Terror
Gas-s-s-s!
Grand Theft Auto
The Gunslinger
The Haunted Palace
Humanoids from the Deep
I, Mobster
I Never Promised You a Rose Garden▶
In the Heat of Passion
It Conquered the World
Jackson County Jail
Lady in Red
The Last Woman on Earth
Little Shop of Horrors▶
Lords of the Deep
Lumiere
Machine Gun Kelly
Masque of the Red Death▶
Masque of the Red Death
Monster from the Ocean Floor
Munchies
Nam Angels
Night of the Blood Beast
Piranha
The Pit and the Pendulum▶
Premature Burial
Primary Target
Private Duty Nurses
Raiders of the Sun
The Raven▶
Rock 'n' Roll High School Forever
The St. Valentine's Day Massacre
Ski Troop Attack
Small Change▶
Smokey Bites the Dust
Stripped to Kill
The Student Nurses
T-Bird Gang
Tales of Terror
Targets▶
Teenage Caveman
The Terror
Thunder and Lightning
Time Trackers
Tomb of Ligeia▶
Too Hot to Handle
The Trip
The Undead▶
Unholy Rollers
Voyage to the Planet of Prehistoric Women
The Wasp Woman
The Wild Angels
The Wild Ride
X: The Man with X-Ray Eyes▶
The Young Nurses

Producers: Val Lewton
Bedlam▶
Cat People▶
Isle of the Dead

Producers: George Lucas
The Empire Strikes Back▶
The Ewok Adventure
More American Graffiti
Raiders of the Lost Ark▶
Return of the Jedi▶

Producers: Merchant Ivory
Autobiography of a Princess
The Ballad of the Sad Cafe
Bombay Talkie
The Courtesans of Bombay▶
The Europeans▶
Fast Talking
Feast of July
Howard's End▶
Hullabaloo Over Georgie & Bonnie's Pictures
Jane Austen in Manhattan
Jefferson in Paris
Maurice▶
Mr. & Mrs. Bridge▶
The Remains of the Day▶
A Room with a View▶
Roseland▶
Shakespeare Wallah▶

Producers: George Pal
Atlantis, the Lost Continent
Conquest of Space
Destination Moon
Doc Savage
The Great Rupert▶
Naked Jungle▶
7 Faces of Dr. Lao▶
Time Machine
The War of the Worlds▶
When Worlds Collide

Producers: Steven Spielberg
Amazing Stories
An American Tail
An American Tail: Fievel Goes West
Back to the Future▶
The Color Purple▶
Empire of the Sun▶
The Goonies
Gremlins▶
Honey, I Shrunk the Kids
Innerspace
Jurassic Park▶
Poltergeist▶
Twilight Zone: The Movie
Who Framed Roger Rabbit▶
Young Sherlock Holmes

Producers: Andy Warhol
Andy Warhol's Bad▶
Cocaine Cowboys
Flesh▶
Heat▶
Trash

Raiders of the Lost Ark
Indiana Jones and the Last Crusade▶
Indiana Jones and the Temple of Doom▶
Raiders of the Lost Ark▶

Rambo
First Blood
Rambo: First Blood, Part 2
Rambo 3

The Rangebusters
Arizona Stagecoach
Black Market Rustlers
Boot Hill Bandits
Cowboy Commandos
Fugitive Valley
Haunted Ranch
Kid's Last Ride
Land of Hunted Men
Range Busters
Rock River Renegades
Saddle Mountain Round-Up
Texas to Bataan
Thunder River Feud
Tonto Basin Outlaws
Trail of the Silver Spurs
Trail Riders
Trailing Double Trouble
Tumbledown Ranch in Arizona
Two-Fisted Justice
Underground Rustlers
West of Pinto Basin

Redford & Newman
Butch Cassidy and the Sundance Kid▶
The Sting▶

Renfrew of the Mounties
Danger Ahead
Fighting Mad
Murder on the Yukon
Renfrew of the Royal Mounted
Renfrew on the Great White Trail
Sky Bandits
Yukon Flight

Restored Footage
Beau Revel▶
Crimes of Passion▶
Dr. Jekyll and Mr. Hyde▶
Foolish Wives▶
Frankenstein▶
Isadora▶
Lawrence of Arabia▶

Lost Horizon▶
The Lost World
New York, New York▶
Othello▶
Que Viva Mexico▶
Red River▶
The Rules of the Game▶
Sadie Thompson▶
Spartacus▶
Spiders▶
A Star is Born▶
Star Trek: The Motion Picture
Star Trek: The Cage
Sunny Side Up
Tarzan and His Mate▶
Twelve O'Clock High▶
Two English Girls▶
Wages of Fear▶
When Time Ran Out

The Ritz Brothers

Blazing Stewardesses
The Goldwyn Follies
The Gorilla

"Road Warrior" & Rip-Offs

City Limits
Dead Man Walking
Driving Force
Dune Warriors
Endgame
Escape from Safehaven
Exterminators of the Year 3000
Firefight
Future Hunters
Future Kill
The Killing Edge
Never Too Young to Die
Phoenix the Warrior
Prison Planet
Radioactive Dreams
The Road Warrior▶
Solarbabies
Steel Dawn
Survival Zone
2020 Texas Gladiators
Ultra Warrior
Warlords 3000
Warriors of the Apocalypse
Warriors of the Wasteland
Wheels of Fire
World Gone Wild

Robin Hood

The Adventures of Robin Hood▶
The Adventures of Robin Hood
Men of Sherwood Forest
The Prince of Thieves
Robin and Marian
Robin Hood▶
Robin Hood: Men in Tights
Robin Hood: Prince of Thieves
Robin Hood: The Movie
Robin Hood...The Legend: Herne's Son
Robin Hood...The Legend: Robin Hood and the Sorcerer
Robin Hood...The Legend: The Swords of Wayland
Robin Hood...The Legend: The Time of the Wolf
Robin of Locksley
The Story of Robin Hood & His Merrie Men▶
Sword of Sherwood Forest
Tales of Robin Hood
Time Bandits
The Zany Adventures of Robin Hood

The Rough Riders

Arizona Bound
Below the Border
Dead Man
Down Texas Way
Forbidden Trails
Ghost Town Law
Gunman from Bodie
Riders of the West

Rusty the Dog

The Adventures of Rusty
Rusty's Birthday
Son of Rusty

The Saint

The Saint
The Saint in London
The Saint in New York
The Saint Strikes Back
The Saint Takes Over
The Saint's Double Trouble
The Saint's Vacation/The Narrow Margin
Vendetta for the Saint

Scorsese & De Niro

Cape Fear▶
Casino▶
Goodfellas▶
King of Comedy▶
Mean Streets▶
New York, New York▶
Raging Bull▶
Taxi Driver▶

Sexton Blake

Echo Murders
Meet Sexton Blake
Sexton Blake and the Hooded Terror
Stage Struck

Shelly Duvall's Tall Tales & Legends

Annie Oakley
Casey at the Bat
Johnny Appleseed
The Legend of Sleepy Hollow
My Darlin' Clementine
Pecos Bill

Sherlock Holmes

The Adventures of Sherlock Holmes
The Adventures of Sherlock Holmes: Hound of the Baskervilles
The Adventures of Sherlock Holmes' Smarter Brother▶
The Crucifer of Blood
Dressed to Kill
Hands of a Murderer
The Hound of London
The Hound of the Baskervilles▶
The Hound of the Baskervilles
House of Fear
Masks of Death
Murder at the Baskervilles
Murder by Decree▶
The Pearl of Death
The Private Life of Sherlock Holmes▶
Pursuit to Algiers
Scarlet Claw▶
The Seven-Per-Cent Solution▶
Sherlock Holmes and the Deadly Necklace
Sherlock Holmes and the Incident at Victoria Falls
Sherlock Holmes and the Secret Weapon▶
Sherlock Holmes Faces Death▶
Sherlock Holmes in Washington
Sherlock Holmes: The Master Blackmailer
Sherlock Holmes: The Sign of Four
Sherlock Holmes: The Silver Blaze
Sherlock Holmes: The Voice of Terror
The Sign of Four
The Silent Mr. Sherlock Holmes
The Speckled Band▶
Spider Woman▶
The Strange Case of the End of Civilization as We Know It
A Study in Scarlet
A Study in Terror▶
Terror by Night
Terror by Night/Meeting at Midnight
They Might Be Giants▶
The Triumph of Sherlock Holmes
Without a Clue
The Woman in Green
Young Sherlock Holmes

Snipes & Harrelson

Money Train
White Men Can't Jump
Wildcats

Special FX Extravaganzas

The Abyss▶
Aliens▶
The Arrival
Batman▶
Batman Forever▶
Beetlejuice▶
Big Trouble in Little China
The Black Hole
Blithe Spirit▶
Captain Sinbad
Crash Dive
Dragonheart
The Ewok Adventure
The Exorcist▶
The Exorcist 2: The Heretic
Fantastic Voyage▶
Forbidden Planet▶
Hideaway
Highlander: The Final Dimension
Innerspace
Judge Dredd
Jurassic Park▶
Lifeforce
Mary Shelley's Frankenstein
The Mask▶
Poltergeist▶
The Rains Came
Return of the Jedi▶
The Shadow
Solar Crisis
Species
Star Trek 2: The Wrath of Khan▶
Star Trek 4: The Voyage Home▶
Star Trek Generations▶
Star Wars▶
Superman 2▶
The Terminator▶
Terminator 2: Judgment Day▶
The Thing
Total Recall▶
Twister
2001: A Space Odyssey▶
2010: The Year We Make Contact▶
Virtuosity
Who Framed Roger Rabbit▶
Wolfen▶

Special FX Extravaganzas: Make-Up

An American Werewolf in London▶
Battle for the Planet of the Apes
Beetlejuice▶
Beneath the Planet of the Apes
Body Melt
Conquest of the Planet of the Apes
Darkman 2: The Return of Durant
Darkman 3: Die Darkman Die
Dawn of the Dead▶
Day of the Dead
Escape from the Planet of the Apes▶
The Exorcist▶
The Fly▶
The Fly 2
Freaked
Hocus Pocus
The Howling▶
The Island of Dr. Moreau
The Man Without a Face
Mary Shelley's Frankenstein
The Nutty Professor▶
Planet of the Apes▶
Scanner Cop
Scanners
The Thing
Vampire in Brooklyn
Wolf

Special FX Wizards: Rick Baker

An American Werewolf in London▶
Food of the Gods
The Funhouse
The Fury
Greystoke: The Legend of Tarzan, Lord of the Apes
Incredible Melting Man
The Incredible Shrinking Woman
It's Alive▶
King Kong
The Nutty Professor▶
Octaman
Schlock
Squirm
Star Wars▶
Tanya's Island
Track of the Moonbeast
Videodrome
Wolf

Special FX Wizards: Rob Bottin

Bugsy▶
Explorers
The Fog
The Howling▶
Humanoids from the Deep
Innerspace
Legend
Mission: Impossible▶
RoboCop▶
Tanya's Island
The Thing
Total Recall▶
Twilight Zone: The Movie
The Witches of Eastwick

Special FX Wizards: Anton Furst

Alien▶
Batman▶
The Company of Wolves▶
Full Metal Jacket▶
Moonraker
Star Wars▶

Special FX Wizards: Ray Harryhausen

The Beast from 20,000 Fathoms
Clash of the Titans
Earth vs. the Flying Saucers
First Men in the Moon
Golden Voyage of Sinbad
It Came from Beneath the Sea▶
Jason and the Argonauts▶
Mighty Joe Young
Mysterious Island▶
One Million Years B.C.
The Seventh Voyage of Sinbad▶
Sinbad and the Eye of the Tiger
The Three Worlds of Gulliver
20 Million Miles to Earth
The Valley of Gwangi▶

Special FX Wizards: Herschell Gordon Lewis

Blood Feast
Color Me Blood Red
Gruesome Twosome
Just for the Hell of It
Moonshine Mountain
The Psychic
She-Devils on Wheels
Suburban Roulette
This Stuff'll Kill Ya!
2000 Maniacs
The Wizard of Gore

Special FX Wizards: Tom Savini

Creepshow
Dawn of the Dead▶
Day of the Dead
Deathdream
Deranged▶
Friday the 13th
Friday the 13th, Part 4: The Final Chapter
Knightriders
Maniac
Martin▶
Midnight
Monkey Shines
The Prowler
The Ripper
Texas Chainsaw Massacre, Part 2

Special FX Wizards: Dick Smith

Altered States▶
Amadeus▶
The Exorcist▶
Ghost Story
The Godfather▶
House of Dark Shadows
Little Big Man▶
Marathon Man▶
Midnight Cowboy▶
Scanners
The Sentinel
Spasms
The Sunshine Boys▶
Taxi Driver▶
The World of Henry Orient▶

Special FX Wizards: Douglas Trumball

The Andromeda Strain
Blade Runner▶
Brainstorm
Close Encounters of the Third Kind▶
Silent Running▶
Star Trek: The Motion Picture
2001: A Space Odyssey▶

Star Wars

The Empire Strikes Back▶
The Ewok Adventure
The Ewoks: Battle for Endor
Return of the Jedi▶
Star Wars▶

Tarzan

Greystoke: The Legend of Tarzan, Lord of the Apes
The New Adventures of Tarzan
Tarzan and His Mate▶
Tarzan and the Green Goddess

Tarzan and the Trappers
Tarzan Escapes▶
Tarzan Finds a Son!▶
Tarzan of the Apes
Tarzan, the Ape Man▶
Tarzan, the Ape Man
Tarzan the Fearless
Tarzan the Tiger
Tarzan's New York Adventure
Tarzan's Revenge
Tarzan's Secret Treasure
Walk Like a Man

The Texas Rangers

Boss of Rawhide
Dead or Alive
Enemy of the Law
Fighting Valley
Flaming Bullets
Frontier Fugitives
Gangsters of the Frontier
Guns of the Law
Marked for Murder
Outlaw Roundup
Ranger's Roundup
Rangers Take Over
Three in the Saddle
Wild West

The Thin Man

After the Thin Man▶
Another Thin Man
Shadow of the Thin Man▶
Song of the Thin Man
The Thin Man▶
The Thin Man Goes Home

The Three Mequiteers

Come On, Cowboys
Covered Wagon Days
Cowboys from Texas
Frontier Horizon
Ghost Town Gold
Heart of the Rockies
Heroes of the Hills
Hit the Saddle
The Kansas Terrors
Lonely Trail/Three Texas Steers
Outlaws of Sonora
Overland Stage Raiders▶
Pals of the Saddle
Powdersmoke Range
Purple Vigilantes
Riders of the Whistling Skull
Roarin' Lead
Rocky Mountain Rangers
Santa Fe Stampede
Three Texas Steers
The Trigger Trio
Wild Horse Rodeo
Wyoming Outlaw

The Three Musketeers

The Four Musketeers▶
Ring of the Musketeers
The Three Musketeers
The Three Musketeers▶
The Three Musketeers
The Three Musketeers▶
The Three Musketeers

3 Stooges

Around the World in a Daze
Dancing Lady
Gold Raiders
Have Rocket Will Travel
Hollywood Party
It's a Mad, Mad, Mad, Mad World
The Lost Stooges
The Outlaws is Coming!
Snow White and the Three Stooges
Stoogemania
The Stoogephile Trivia Movie
Stooges Shorts Festival
The Stooges Story▶
Stop! Look! and Laugh!
Three Stooges Comedy Capers: Vol. 1
Three Stooges Comedy Classics
Three Stooges: Cookoo Cavaliers and Other Nyuks
Three Stooges Festival
Three Stooges: From Nurse to Worse and Other Nyuks
The Three Stooges: Half-Wit's Holiday and Other Nyuks
The Three Stooges: Idiots Deluxe and Other Nyuks
Three Stooges in Orbit
The Three Stooges Meet Hercules
The Three Stooges: Nutty but Nice and Other Nyuks
The Three Stooges: They Stooge to Conga and Other Nyuks

Top Grossing Films of 1939

Gone with the Wind▶
The Hunchback of Notre Dame▶
Jesse James▶
Mr. Smith Goes to Washington▶
The Wizard of Oz▶

Top Grossing Films of 1940

Boom Town
Fantasia▶
Pinocchio▶
Rebecca▶
Santa Fe Trail

Top Grossing Films of 1941

Honky Tonk▶
The Philadelphia Story▶
Sergeant York▶
A Yank in the R.A.F.

Top Grossing Films of 1942

Bambi▶
Casablanca▶
Mrs. Miniver▶
Random Harvest▶
Yankee Doodle Dandy▶

Top Grossing Films of 1943

The Outlaw
The Song of Bernadette▶
Stage Door Canteen
This Is the Army

Top Grossing Films of 1944

Going My Way▶
Meet Me in St. Louis▶
Since You Went Away▶
Thirty Seconds Over Tokyo▶

Top Grossing Films of 1945

Anchors Aweigh▶
The Bells of St. Mary's▶
Spellbound▶
Weekend at the Waldorf▶

Top Grossing Films of 1946

The Best Years of Our Lives▶
Duel in the Sun▶
The Jolson Story▶

Top Grossing Films of 1947

Egg and I▶
Life with Father▶

Top Grossing Films of 1948

Johnny Belinda▶
On an Island with You
The Paleface▶
Red River▶
The Red Shoes▶
The Three Musketeers

Top Grossing Films of 1949

Battleground▶
Jolson Sings Again
Samson and Delilah▶
Sands of Iwo Jima▶

Top Grossing Films of 1950

Cinderella▶
Father of the Bride▶
King Solomon's Mines▶

Top Grossing Films of 1951

Alice in Wonderland▶
David and Bathsheba▶
The Great Caruso
Quo Vadis▶
Show Boat

Top Grossing Films of 1952

The Greatest Show on Earth▶
Hans Christian Andersen
Ivanhoe▶
The Snows of Kilimanjaro▶

Top Grossing Films of 1953

From Here to Eternity▶
How to Marry a Millionaire
Peter Pan▶
The Robe
Shane▶

Top Grossing Films of 1954

The Caine Mutiny▶
The Glenn Miller Story▶
Rear Window▶
20,000 Leagues Under the Sea▶
White Christmas▶

Top Grossing Films of 1955

Battle Cry▶
Lady and the Tramp▶
Mister Roberts▶
Oklahoma!▶

Top Grossing Films of 1956

Around the World in 80 Days▶
Giant▶
The King and I▶
The Ten Commandments▶

Top Grossing Films of 1957

The Bridge on the River Kwai▶
Old Yeller▶
Peyton Place▶
Raintree County
Sayonara▶

Top Grossing Films of 1958

Auntie Mame▶
Cat on a Hot Tin Roof▶
Gigi▶
No Time for Sergeants▶
South Pacific▶

Top Grossing Films of 1959

Ben-Hur▶
Darby O'Gill & the Little People▶
Operation Petticoat▶
The Shaggy Dog
Sleeping Beauty▶

Top Grossing Films of 1960

The Alamo▶
Exodus▶
Psycho▶
Spartacus▶
The Swiss Family Robinson▶

Top Grossing Films of 1961

The Absent-Minded Professor▶
El Cid▶
The Guns of Navarone▶
West Side Story▶

Top Grossing Films of 1962

How the West Was Won▶
In Search of the Castaways▶
Lawrence of Arabia▶
The Longest Day▶
The Music Man▶

Top Grossing Films of 1963

Cleopatra
Irma La Douce
It's a Mad, Mad, Mad, Mad World
The Sword in the Stone▶
Tom Jones▶

Top Grossing Films of 1964

The Carpetbaggers
From Russia with Love▶
Goldfinger▶
Mary Poppins▶
My Fair Lady▶

Top Grossing Films of 1965

Doctor Zhivago▶
The Sound of Music▶
That Darn Cat
Those Magnificent Men in Their Flying Machines▶
Thunderball

Top Grossing Films of 1966

The Bible...In the Beginning▶
Hawaii▶
Lt. Robin Crusoe, U.S.N.
A Man for All Seasons▶
Who's Afraid of Virginia Woolf?▶

Top Grossing Films of 1967

Bonnie & Clyde▶
The Dirty Dozen▶
The Graduate▶
Guess Who's Coming to Dinner▶
The Jungle Book▶

Top Grossing Films of 1968

Bullitt▶
Funny Girl▶
The Odd Couple▶
Romeo and Juliet▶
2001: A Space Odyssey▶

Top Grossing Films of 1969

Butch Cassidy and the Sundance Kid▶
Easy Rider▶
Hello, Dolly!
The Love Bug
Midnight Cowboy▶

Top Grossing Films of 1970

Airport▶
Love Story▶
M*A*S*H▶
Patton▶

Top Grossing Films of 1971

Billy Jack
Diamonds Are Forever▶
Fiddler on the Roof▶
The French Connection▶
Summer of '42▶

Top Grossing Films of 1972

Deliverance▶
The Godfather▶
Jeremiah Johnson▶
The Poseidon Adventure
What's Up, Doc?▶

Top Grossing Films of 1973

American Graffiti▶
The Exorcist▶
Papillon▶
The Sting▶
The Way We Were▶

Top Grossing Films of 1974

Blazing Saddles▶
Earthquake
The Towering Inferno
The Trial of Billy Jack
Young Frankenstein▶

Top Grossing Films of 1975

Dog Day Afternoon▶

Jaws▶
One Flew Over the Cuckoo's Nest▶

Top Grossing Films of 1976

All the President's Men▶
King Kong
Rocky▶
Silver Streak▶
A Star is Born

Top Grossing Films of 1977

Close Encounters of the Third Kind▶
The Goodbye Girl▶
Saturday Night Fever
Smokey and the Bandit
Star Wars▶

Top Grossing Films of 1978

Every Which Way But Loose
Grease▶
Jaws 2
National Lampoon's Animal House▶
Superman: The Movie▶

Top Grossing Films of 1979

Alien▶
The Jerk
Kramer vs. Kramer▶
Rocky 2
Star Trek: The Motion Picture

Top Grossing Films of 1980

Airplane!▶
Any Which Way You Can
The Empire Strikes Back▶
9 to 5
Stir Crazy

Top Grossing Films of 1981

Arthur▶
Cannonball Run
On Golden Pond▶
Raiders of the Lost Ark▶
Stripes
Superman 2▶

Top Grossing Films of 1982

E.T.: The Extra-Terrestrial▶
An Officer and a Gentleman▶
Porky's
Rocky 3

Top Grossing Films of 1983

Return of the Jedi▶
Superman 3
Terms of Endearment▶
Trading Places
WarGames

Top Grossing Films of 1984

Beverly Hills Cop
Ghostbusters▶
Gremlins▶
Indiana Jones and the Temple of Doom▶
The Karate Kid▶

Top Grossing Films of 1985

Back to the Future▶
The Color Purple▶
Out of Africa▶
Rambo: First Blood, Part 2
Rocky 4

Top Grossing Films of 1986

Crocodile Dundee▶
The Karate Kid: Part 2
Platoon▶
Star Trek 4: The Voyage Home▶
Top Gun

Top Grossing Films of 1987

Beverly Hills Cop 2
Fatal Attraction▶
Good Morning, Vietnam▶
Lethal Weapon▶
Three Men and a Baby▶
The Untouchables▶

Top Grossing Films of 1988

Coming to America▶
Crocodile Dundee 2
Die Hard▶
Rain Man▶
Twins
Who Framed Roger Rabbit▶

Top Grossing Films of 1989

Batman▶
Driving Miss Daisy▶
Ghostbusters 2
Honey, I Shrunk the Kids
Indiana Jones and the Last Crusade▶
Lethal Weapon 2▶

Top Grossing Films of 1990

Dances with Wolves▶
Dick Tracy▶
Die Hard 2: Die Harder▶
Ghost▶
Home Alone▶
The Hunt for Red October▶
Pretty Woman▶
Teenage Mutant Ninja Turtles: The Movie
Total Recall▶

Top Grossing Films of 1991

The Addams Family
Backdraft
Boyz N the Hood▶
City Slickers▶
Doc Hollywood
Dying Young
Hot Shots!▶
Naked Gun 2 1/2: The Smell of Fear
New Jack City
101 Dalmatians▶
Robin Hood: Prince of Thieves
The Rocketeer▶
The Silence of the Lambs▶
Sleeping with the Enemy
Teenage Mutant Ninja Turtles 2: The Secret of the Ooze
Terminator 2: Judgment Day▶
What About Bob?▶

Top Grossing Films of 1992

Aladdin▶
Alien 3
Basic Instinct
Batman Returns
The Bodyguard
Boomerang
Bram Stoker's Dracula
Fried Green Tomatoes▶
The Hand that Rocks the Cradle
Home Alone 2: Lost in New York
The Last of the Mohicans▶
A League of Their Own▶
Lethal Weapon 3
Patriot Games▶
Sister Act
Under Siege
Unforgiven▶
Wayne's World▶
White Men Can't Jump

Top Grossing Films of 1993

Aladdin▶
Cliffhanger▶
A Few Good Men▶
The Firm▶
Free Willy
The Fugitive▶
In the Line of Fire▶
Indecent Proposal
Jurassic Park▶
Sleepless in Seattle▶

Top Grossing Films of 1994

Ace Ventura: Pet Detective
Clear and Present Danger
The Client
The Flintstones
Forrest Gump▶
The Lion King▶
The Mask▶
Maverick
Speed▶
True Lies

Top Grossing Films of 1995

Ace Ventura: When Nature Calls
Apollo 13▶
Batman Forever▶
Casper▶
Die Hard: With a Vengeance
Goldeneye▶
Jumanji
Pocahontas▶
Seven▶
Toy Story▶

The Trail Blazers

Arizona Whirlwind
Death Valley Rangers
The Law Rides Again
Outlaw Trail

Trash

The Adventurers
The Alien Factor
Alien Massacre
Alien Prey
All the Lovin' Kinfolk
The Allnighter
Alone in the T-Shirt Zone
Amazon Women on the Moon
America
American Tickler
Andy Warhol's Bad▶
Andy Warhol's Dracula▶
Andy Warhol's Frankenstein
Angel of H.E.A.T.
Assassin of Youth
Assault of the Killer Bimbos
The Astounding She-Monster
The Astro-Zombies
Attack of the Beast Creatures
Attack of the Giant Leeches
Attack of the Killer Tomatoes
Bad Girls Go to Hell
Barn of the Naked Dead
The Beast of Yucca Flats
The Beast that Killed Women
The Beautiful, the Bloody and the Bare
Bela Lugosi Meets a Brooklyn Gorilla
The Bellboy and the Playgirls
Best Buns on the Beach
Beverly Hills Bodysnatchers
Beverly Hills Knockouts
The Big Gag
Bikini Drive-In
The Bitch
Black Venus
Blazing Stewardesses
Blood Freak
Blood of Ghastly Horror
Bloodlust
Bloodsucking Freaks
Body of Evidence
Bottoms Up
Brain of Blood
Camp Double Feature
Candy Tangerine Man
The Carpetbaggers
Casting Call
The Castle of Fu Manchu
Cheerleader Camp
Cocaine Fiends
The Commies are Coming, the Commies are Coming
The Conqueror
The Corpse Grinders
Corruption
The Crater Lake Monster
Creature of Destruction
Creeping Terror
Crypt of the Living Dead
Curse of the Blue Lights
Curse of the Living Dead
Cyborg
Cycle Vixens
Dead Aim
The Dead Next Door
Delinquent School Girls
Demons
Desperate Living
Desperate Teenage Lovedolls
Detour to Danger
Dolemite
Dolemite 2: Human Tornado
Dracula vs. Frankenstein
Drop Dead Fred
Drum
Drums O'Voodoo
Dungeon of Harrow
Eegah!
Escape from Planet Earth
Fat Guy Goes Nutzoid
Female Trouble
The Fifth Floor
Film House Fever
Five Minutes to Love
Flesh and Blood Show
Frankenstein '80
Frankenstein Meets the Space Monster
Frostbiter: Wrath of the Wendigo
Fun Down There
Galactic Gigolo
Ghoul School
Glen or Glenda: Confessions of Ed Wood
Gore-Met Zombie Chef From Hell
Gun Cargo
Heartstopper
Hitchhikers
Hold Me, Thrill Me, Kiss Me
Hollywood After Dark
Hollywood Chainsaw Hookers
The Hollywood Strangler Meets the Skid Row Slasher
Honkytonk Nights
Horror of Party Beach
The House of Usher
I Spit on Your Grave
I Was a Zombie for the FBI
Ilsa, Harem Keeper of the Oil Sheiks
Ilsa, She-Wolf of the SS
Ilsa, the Tigress of Siberia
Impulse
In the Cold of the Night
Incredibly Strange Creatures Who Stopped Living and Became Mixed-Up Zombies
Infra-Man
Invasion of the Bee Girls▶
Island of Lost Girls
It's Not the Size That Counts
Jail Bait
Jungle Master
Killer Tomatoes Eat France
Killer Tomatoes Strike Back
Lady Godiva Rides
The Last Season
The Lonely Lady
Lost, Lonely, and Vicious
A Man Called Rage
Man with Two Heads
Manos, the Hands of Fate
Master Blaster
Microwave Massacre
Midnight 2: Sex, Death, and Videotape
Mind Trap
Mondo Balardo
Mondo Trasho
Motel Hell
Multiple Maniacs
The Naked Flame
A Night in Heaven
Night of the Cobra Woman
Night of the Demon
Night of the Ghouls
Nightmare
Oasis of the Zombies
On the Edge: The Survival of Dana
Once is Not Enough
One Down, Two to Go!
One More Saturday Night
Orgy of the Dead
Out of the Body
The Outcast
Pagan Island
The Perverse Countess
Phantasm
Pink Flamingos
Plan 9 from Outer Space
Please Don't Eat My Mother
Pot, Parents, and Police
The Power
The Psychic
Queen of Outer Space
Rabid Grannies
Rat Pfink a Boo-Boo
The Rats are Coming! The Werewolves are Here!
Reform School Girl
Return of the Family Man
Return of the Killer Tomatoes!
Return to the Blue Lagoon
Revenge of the Virgins
Robot Monster
Rush
Satan in High Heels
Satan's Cheerleaders
Saturday the 14th Strikes Back
Savage Intruder
Screen Test
She Demons
She-Devils on Wheels
The Sinister Invasion
The Sinister Urge
Slaves in Bondage
Sleazemania III: The Good, the Bad & the Sleazy
Some Call It Loving
Sorority Girl
Space Monster
The Speed Lovers

Streetfight
Sweet Georgia
Sweet Trash
Tarzan, the Ape Man
Teenage Gang Debs
Teenage Mother
Teenage Strangler
Teenagers from Outer Space
Terror in the Jungle
Texas Layover
They Saved Hitler's Brain
Tomboy
Torture Dungeon
Train Station Pickups
The Trial of Billy Jack
Troma's War
Unholy Rollers
Valley of the Dolls
Vampire Vixens from Venus
Vegas in Space
Violated
The Violent Years
White Pongo
Wild Ones on Wheels
Wild Women of Wongo
Winterbeast
World of the Depraved
The Worst of Faces of Death
Youth Aflame
You've Ruined Me, Eddie
The Zombie Army

Troma Films

Beware! Children at Play
Blades
Blondes Have More Guns
Bloodsucking Freaks
Chopper Chicks in Zombietown
Class of Nuke 'Em High
Class of Nuke 'Em High 2: Subhumanoid Meltdown
Class of Nuke 'Em High 3: The Good, the Bad and the Subhumanoid
Combat Shock
Cry Uncle
Deadly Daphne's Revenge
Evil Clutch
Ferocious Female Freedom Fighters
Frostbiter: Wrath of the Wendigo
I Married a Vampire
I Was a Teenage TV Terrorist
Malibu Hot Summer
Monster in the Closet
Preacherman
Rabid Grannies
Redneck Zombies
Splatter University
Squeeze Play
Stuck on You
Student Confidential
Surf Nazis Must Die
The Toxic Avenger
The Toxic Avenger, Part 2
The Toxic Avenger, Part 3: The Last Temptation of Toxie
Troma's War
Vegas in Space

Turner & Douglas

The Jewel of the Nile
Romancing the Stone▶
The War of the Roses▶

20 Highest Grossing Films of All Time

Aladdin▶
Back to the Future▶
Batman▶
Beverly Hills Cop
The Empire Strikes Back▶
E.T.: The Extra-Terrestrial▶
Forrest Gump▶
Ghost▶
Ghostbusters▶
Gone with the Wind▶
Home Alone▶
Indiana Jones and the Last Crusade▶
Jaws▶
Jurassic Park▶
The Lion King▶
Mrs. Doubtfire
Raiders of the Lost Ark▶
Return of the Jedi▶
Star Wars▶
Terminator 2: Judgment Day▶

Universal Studios' Classic Horror

Abbott and Costello Meet Dr. Jekyll and Mr. Hyde
Abbott and Costello Meet Frankenstein▶
Abbott and Costello Meet the Killer, Boris Karloff
The Black Cat▶
The Bride of Frankenstein▶
Creature from the Black Lagoon▶
The Creature Walks Among Us
Dracula▶
Dracula (Spanish Version)
Dracula's Daughter▶
Frankenstein▶
Frankenstein Meets the Wolfman▶
The Ghost of Frankenstein
House of Dracula
House of Frankenstein
The Hunchback of Notre Dame▶
Invisible Agent
The Invisible Man▶
The Invisible Man Returns▶
The Invisible Woman▶
Island of Lost Souls▶
The Mummy▶
The Mummy's Curse
The Mummy's Ghost
The Mummy's Hand
The Mummy's Tomb
Murders in the Rue Morgue
The Phantom of the Opera▶
The Raven▶
Revenge of the Creature
Son of Dracula▶
Son of Frankenstein▶
Werewolf of London
The Wolf Man▶

Wilder & Pryor

Another You
See No Evil, Hear No Evil
Silver Streak▶
Stir Crazy

Wonderworks Family Movies

African Journey
Almost Partners
And the Children Shall Lead
Anne of Avonlea▶
Anne of Green Gables▶
The Boy Who Loved Trolls
Bridge to Terabithia
Brother Future
The Canterville Ghost
The Chronicles of Narnia
City Boy▶
Clowning Around
Clowning Around 2
Daniel and the Towers
The Fig Tree
Frog
Frogs!
A Girl of the Limberlost
Gryphon
The Haunting of Barney Palmer
Hector's Bunyip
Hiroshima Maiden
The Hoboken Chicken Emergency
Home at Last
The House of Dies Drear
How to Be a Perfect Person in Just Three Days
Jacob Have I Loved
Konrad
Lantern Hill
The Little Princess
Lone Star Kid
Looking for Miracles
Maricela
The Mighty Pawns
Miracle at Moreaux
My Friend Walter
Necessary Parties
Runaway
Spirit Rider▶
Sweet 15
Walking on Air
A Waltz Through the Hills
Words by Heart
You Must Remember This

Woofs!

The Adventurers
Adventures of a Taxi Driver
The Adventures of Ford Fairlane
The Adventurous Knights
After the Fall of New York
Albino
The Alchemist
Alien Contamination
Alien from L.A.
Alien Massacre
Alien Predators
Alien Warrior
Almost Human
The Amazing Transparent Man
The Amazing Transplant
The Ambushers
American Gothic
American Ninja 3: Blood Hunt
American Ninja 4: The Annihilation
Americathon
Amin: The Rise and Fall
Amityville 2: The Possession
The Amityville Curse
Angel 3: The Final Chapter
Angel of Death
Angel of H.E.A.T.
Angels' Wild Women
The Annihilators
A*P*E*
The Appointment
The Astounding She-Monster
The Astro-Zombies
Atlas in the Land of the Cyclops
Atom Age Vampire
The Atomic Brain
Ator the Fighting Eagle
Attack of the Beast Creatures
Attack of the Killer Refrigerator
Attack of the Killer Tomatoes
Attack of the Mayan Mummy
Attack of the Swamp Creature
Auntie
Avenging Angel
Awakening of Candra
Baby Love
Bad Charleston Charlie
Bad Girls Do Cry
Bad Girls from Mars
Bad Girls Go to Hell
Bad Medicine
Balboa
Bananas Boat
Barn of the Naked Dead
Barracuda
Basic Training
Battle of the Bullies
Beaks: The Movie
Beast of the Yellow Night
The Beast of Yucca Flats
The Bees
Bela Lugosi Meets a Brooklyn Gorilla
The Bellboy and the Playgirls
Best Buns on the Beach
Beyond Atlantis
Beyond Evil
Beyond the Door
Beyond the Door 3
The Big Bust Out
Big Foot
The Bikini Car Wash Company
The Birds 2: Land's End
Birds of Paradise
The Bitch
The Black Cat
Black Cobra
The Black Cobra
Black Gestapo
Black Magic Woman
The Black Maid
Black Shampoo
Black Venus
Blackenstein
Blade of the Ripper
Blastfighter
Blazing Stewardesses
Blockhouse
Blood Beach
Blood Diner
Blood Freak
Blood Games
Blood Lake
Blood of Ghastly Horror
Blood Orgy of the She-Devils
Blood Rage
Blood Screams
Blood Sisters
Blood Voyage
Bloodmoon
Bloodstalkers
Bloodsuckers from Outer Space
Bloodsucking Freaks
Bloodsucking Pharoahs of Pittsburgh
The Bloody Brood
Bloody Moon
The Blue Lagoon
Blue Movies
Blue Paradise
Blue Ribbon Babes
The Body Beneath
Body of Evidence
Body Rock
The Body Shop
Bolero
Boogey Man 2
Boom in the Moon
Border Radio
Boss Foreman
Bottoms Up
Brain of Blood
The Bride & the Beast
Bride of the Monster
Brides of the Beast
The Brides Wore Blood
Bug
Bullies
Bummer
Cabin Boy
Caged Terror
California Casanova
Caligula
Can I Do It...Till I Need Glasses?
Can't Stop the Music
Cartel
Castle of Evil
Castle of the Creeping Flesh
Cave Girl
Cave of the Living Dead
Cellar Dweller
The Centerfold Girls
Chain Gang Women
Chained for Life
Challenge
Cheaper to Keep Her
Cheech and Chong's The Corsican Brothers
Cheering Section
Cheerleader Camp
The Cheerleaders
Cheerleaders' Wild Weekend
Cherry Hill High
The Children
Child's Play 2
The Chilling
The Chosen
Chu Chu & the Philly Flash
C.H.U.D.
C.H.U.D 2: Bud the Chud
City on Fire
Clash of the Titans
Class of 1984
Class of Nuke 'Em High 3: The Good, the Bad and the Subhumanoid
Class Reunion
Class Reunion Massacre
Claws
Clifford
Color Me Blood Red
Comic Cabby
Condemned to Hell
Confidential
The Conqueror
Conqueror & the Empress
Conqueror of the World
Copkillers
The Corpse Grinders
Corruption
Cosh Boy
Cosmos: War of the Planets
The Cradle Will Fall
The Crater Lake Monster
The Crawling Hand
Crazed
Crazy Fat Ethel II
The Creation of the Humanoids
Creatures the World Forgot
Creeping Terror
The Cremators
Crocodile
Crucible of Terror
Cruise into Terror
Crypt of the Living Dead
Cthulhu Mansion
Curse of the Alpha Stone
The Curse of the Aztec Mummy
Curse of the Aztec Mummy/Robot vs. the Aztec Mummy
Curse of the Blue Lights
Curse of the Screaming Dead
Curse of the Stone Hand
Curtains
Cycle Psycho
Cycle Vixens
Dagora, the Space Monster
Dance of Death
Danger Zone
Dangerous Love
Dark Sanity
Dawn of the Mummy
The Day It Came to Earth
Dead Aim
Dead Pit
Dead Women in Lingerie
Deadly Darling
Deadly Embrace
Deadly Encounter
Deadly Prey
Deadly Sanctuary
Deadly Twins
The Death Curse of Tartu
Death Ray
Death Spa
Death Wish 2
Death Wish 5: The Face of Death
Deathstalker
Delinquent School Girls
Delirium
The Demon Lover
Demon of Paradise
Demon Witch Child
Demonwarp
Detour to Danger
Devil Woman
Devil's Gift
The Devil's Harvest
Devil's Son-in-Law
Devil's Wedding Night
Diamond Ninja Force
Die Laughing
Digging Up Business
Dirty Laundry
Dirty Mind of Young Sally
Doctor Butcher M.D.
Dr. Orloff's Monster
Dr. Tarr's Torture Dungeon
The Dolls
Don't Go in the Woods
Don't Look in the Attic
Don't Open the Door!
Don't Open Till Christmas

Doom Asylum
Dorm That Dripped Blood
Dracula: Up in Harlem
Dracula vs. Frankenstein
Dracula's Great Love
Dracula's Last Rites
Driller Killer
Drive-In
Drive-In Massacre
Driver's Seat
Drop Dead Fred
Drum
Drums O'Voodoo
Dutch Girls
Ecstasy
Eegah!
Emily
End of the World
Endless Descent
Erotic Dreams
Erotic Images
Escape from Hell
Escape from Safehaven
Escape from the KGB
Escape 2000
Escapist
Eve of Destruction
The Evictors
Evil Laugh
The Evil Within
Evilspeak
Exterminators of the Year 3000
Eyeball
Eyes of a Stranger
Fade to Black
Fair Game
Fanny Hill: Memoirs of a Woman of Pleasure
Fantasies
Far Out Man
Fat Guy Goes Nutzoid
Fatal Pulse
The Fear Chamber
Feelin' Up
The Female Bunch
Fever Pitch
Fiend
The Fiendish Plot of Dr. Fu Manchu
The Fifth Floor
Final Exam
Flesh Feast
Flight to Nowhere
Food of the Gods
Food of the Gods: Part 2
The Forbidden Dance
Forbidden World
Foreplay
Fowl Play
Frankenstein '80
Frankenstein General Hospital
Frankenstein Island
Frankenstein Meets the Space Monster
Frankenstein's Great Aunt Tillie
Friday the 13th, Part 2
Friday the 13th, Part 3
Friday the 13th, Part 4: The Final Chapter
Friday the 13th, Part 5: A New Beginning
Friday the 13th, Part 6: Jason Lives
Friday the 13th, Part 7: The New Blood
Frostbiter: Wrath of the Wendigo
Fugitive Alien
Fun Down There
Galactic Gigolo
The Gamma People
Gangster's Law
The Garbage Pail Kids Movie
Gas
Gates of Hell
The Ghastly Ones
Ghost Fever
Ghost in the Noonday Sun
Ghoulies 3: Ghoulies Go to College
Giant from the Unknown
Giants of Rome
Gimme an F
The Girl in Room 2A
Girl on a Chain Gang
Glen or Glenda: Confessions of Ed Wood
The Glory Stompers
Goblin
God's Bloody Acre
Godzilla vs. the Sea Monster
Goliath and the Dragon
Goliathon
Goof Balls
Gore-Met Zombie Chef From Hell
Gorp
The Green Berets
The Green Slime
Grotesque
Grunt! The Wrestling Movie
Guess What We Learned in School Today?
H-Bomb
H-Man
Halloween with the Addams Family
Hallucination
Hands of Steel
Hangmen
Hardbodies 2
Hawmps!
The Hearse
Heavenly Bodies
Hell Night
Hell Up in Harlem
Hellcats
Hellgate
Hellriders
Hell's Brigade: The Final Assault
Hillbillies in a Haunted House
The Hills Have Eyes
His Name was King
Hitchhikers
The Hollywood Strangler Meets the Skid Row Slasher
Hollywood Zap
Hometown U.S.A.
Horror House on Highway 5
Horror of Party Beach
Horror of the Blood Monsters
Horror Planet
Hospital Massacre
Hot Box
Hot T-Shirts
Hot Touch
The Hound of the Baskervilles
House of Psychotic Women
House of Whipcord
House on the Edge of the Park
How to Seduce a Woman
Humanoids from the Deep
Humongous
Hurricane
I Dismember Mama
I Eat Your Skin
I Spit on Your Corpse
I Spit on Your Grave
I Was a Teenage TV Terrorist
Icebox Murders
Idaho Transfer
Ilsa, Harem Keeper of the Oil Sheiks
Ilsa, She-Wolf of the SS
Ilsa, the Tigress of Siberia
Ilsa, the Wicked Warden
Impulse
In Search of Anna
In the Shadow of Kilimanjaro
In Trouble
Incredible Melting Man
The Incredible Petrified World
The Incredible Two-Headed Transplant
Incredibly Strange Creatures Who Stopped Living and Became Mixed-Up Zombies
Incubus
Infra-Man
Inner Sanctum
Invasion of the Animal People
Invasion of the Blood Farmers
Invasion of the Body Stealers
Invasion of the Flesh Hunters
Invasion of the Girl Snatchers
Invincible Barbarian
Invincible Gladiators
The Invisible Maniac
Invitation to Hell
The Island
Island Claw
Island of Lost Girls
It's Alive 2: It Lives Again
It's Not the Size That Counts
It's Pat: The Movie
Jason Goes to Hell: The Final Friday
Jaws of Satan
The Jazz Singer
The Jerky Boys
Joy Sticks
Junior
Just for the Hell of It
Kidnapped
Kill Alex Kill
Kill Factor
Killer Party
Killers from Space
Kilma, Queen of the Amazons
King of Kong Island
The King of the Kickboxers
King of the Zombies
King's Ransom
Las Vegas Serial Killer
The Las Vegas Story
Laserblast
Last Days of Planet Earth
The Last Horror Film
Last House on Dead End Street
Last Mercenary
The Last Season
The Last Slumber Party
The Last Woman on Earth
Lauderdale
A Legacy for Leonette
Legacy of Horror
Legend of the Dinosaurs
Leprechaun
The Lifetaker
Link
Lipstick
Lisa and the Devil
Lisztomania
Little Darlings
Loaded Guns
The Loch Ness Horror
The Lone Runner
The Lonely Lady
The Longshot
Lords of the Deep
Love Thrill Murders
The Loves of Hercules
Love's Savage Fury
Lurkers
Luther the Geek
Mack the Knife
Mad About You
The Mad Bomber
Mad Doctor of Blood Island
Mad Dog
Mad Youth
Madigan's Millions
Mama Dracula
A Man Called Rage
Man from Deep River
Maniac
Mannequin 2: On the Move
Manos, the Hands of Fate
Mardi Gras Massacre
A Matter of Time
Maxim Xul
Maximum Thrust
Maya
Meatballs 3
The Meateater
Megaforce
Mesa of Lost Women
Meteor
Meteor Monster
Midnight Cabaret
Mistress of the Apes
Mob War
Mom
Mondo Trasho
Mongrel
Monsignor
Monster a Go-Go!
Monster Dog
The Monster of Piedras Blancas
Moonshine Mountain
Moses
Motor Psycho
Mountaintop Motel Massacre
Mummy & Curse of the Jackal
Murderer's Keep
Murderlust
Mutant Hunt
Mutants In Paradise
The Mutilator
My African Adventure
My Therapist
Myra Breckinridge
Nail Gun Massacre
Naked Cage
The Naked Flame
Naked Vengeance
Naked Youth
The Narcotics Story
National Lampoon's Class Reunion
Navy vs. the Night Monsters
Neon Maniacs
The New Gladiators
New Year's Evil
New York Ripper
The Night God Screamed
A Night in Heaven
Night of Dark Shadows
Night of the Bloody Apes
Night of the Bloody Transplant
Night of the Demon
Night of the Ghouls
Night of the Living Babes
Night of the Sharks
Night of the Sorcerers
Night of the Zombies
Night Patrol
Night Train to Terror
Nightmare
Nightmare in Red China
Nightmare Sisters
Nightstalker
Nine Deaths of the Ninja
1990: The Bronx Warriors
Ninja Champion
Ninja Exterminators
Ninja Fantasy
Ninja Hunt
Ninja Terminator
Ninja Wars
No One Cries Forever
Nobody's Perfekt
Nocturna
Norman's Awesome Experience
Nude on the Moon
The Occultist
Ocean Drive Weekend
Oddballs
On Deadly Ground
One Brief Summer
One Down, Two to Go!
One Russian Summer
Orca
Orgy of the Dead
The Other Side of Midnight
Parasite
Party Favors
People Who Own the Dark
Perfect Timing
Phobia
Pieces
Pink Motel
Plan 9 from Outer Space
Please Don't Eat My Mother
Police Academy 5: Assignment Miami Beach
Prehistoric Bimbos in Armageddon City
Prehistoric Women
Pretty Smart
Prettykill
The Prime Time
Private Manoeuvres
The Psychic
Psychos in Love
Pulsebeat
The Puma Man
Queen of Outer Space
Quick, Let's Get Married
Rabid Grannies
Raise the Titanic
The Rape of the Sabines
Rat Pfink a Boo-Boo
The Rats are Coming! The Werewolves are Here!
Rebel Vixens
The Red Menace
The Return
Revenge
Revenge of Doctor X
Ridin' the Lone Trail
The Ripper
The Robot vs. the Aztec Mummy
Rocket Attack U.S.A.
Roller Boogie
Rooster: Spurs of Death!
Sahara
Santa Claus
Sasquatch
Satan's Blade
Satan's Cheerleaders
Satan's Touch
Satanwar
Savage!
Savage Is Loose
Savage Weekend
Scarlet Spear
Scream Bloody Murder
Scream of the Demon Lover
Screen Test
Secrets of Sweet Sixteen
Senior Week
Sensual Partners
The Sensuous Teenager
The Serpent and the Rainbow
The Severed Arm
Sex Adventures of the Three Musketeers
Sex, Drugs, and Rock-n-Roll
The Sex Machine
Sex on the Run
Sextette
She Came on the Bus
She Demons
She-Devils on Wheels
Sheena
Shriek of the Mutilated
Sidney Sheldon's Bloodline
The Simple Truth
Sincerely Yours
The Sinister Urge
Sinner's Blood
Skinned Alive
Skullduggery
Sky Pirates
Slashdance
The Slasher
The Slaughter of the Vampires
Slaughterhouse
Slaughterhouse Rock
Slave of the Cannibal God
The Slayer
Sledgehammer
Sleepaway Camp 3: Teenage Wasteland
The Slime People
Slithis
Sloane
Slugs
Slumber Party Massacre 2
Slumber Party Massacre 3
Smooth Talker
The Snow Creature
Something Weird
Sonny Boy
Sorceress
Sorority House Massacre
Sorority House Massacre 2: Nighty Nightmare
Soul Hustler
South Seas Massacre
Space Monster
Space Riders
Spaced Out
Spare Parts
Spasms
Sphinx
Splatter University
Splitz
Spookies
The Sporting Club
The Squeeze

Squeeze Play
SS Girls
Stepsisters
Stewardess School
Stocks and Blondes
Stone Cold
Stormquest
The Strangeness
The Stranger from Venus
Street Hero
Street Hunter
Street People
Street Trash
Street Warriors
Street Warriors, Part 2
Strike Commando
Stroker Ace
Stryker
The Stud
Student Affairs
Student Bodies
Sugar Cookies
Suicide Cult
Summer School Teachers
Sunnyside
Sunset Strip
Superchick
Superfly T.N.T.
Supersonic Man
Surf 2
Surfacing
Survival Zone
Sweater Girls
Sweet Murder
Sweet Spirits
Sweet Trash
Switchblade Sisters
Tarzan, the Ape Man
Teenage Mother
Teenage Strangler
Teenage Zombies
Teenagers from Outer Space
The Telephone
The Temp
10 Violent Women
Tentacles
The Terror
Terror in Beverly Hills
Terror in the Wax Museum
Terror on Tour
The Terrornauts
Terrorvision
Test Tube Babies
Texas Chainsaw Massacre, Part 2
Texas Layover
They Saved Hitler's Brain
They Went That-a-Way & That-a-Way
They're Playing with Fire
Thieves of Fortune
The Thirsty Dead
This Stuff'll Kill Ya!
Three on a Meathook
Threesome
The Thrill Killers
Throne of Fire
Tintorera...Tiger Shark
TNT Jackson
To All a Goodnight
Tomb of Torture
Tomboy
The Tormentors
Torso
Tower of Evil
Treasure of the Moon Goddess
The Trial of Billy Jack
Trick or Treats
Troma's War
Twice Dead
Twilight People
Two Lost Worlds
2020 Texas Gladiators
The Uncanny
Under the Rainbow
Underground Aces
The Uninvited
Unknown Powers
Vampire Raiders—Ninja Queen
Vasectomy: A Delicate Matter
Vegas in Space
Vengeance Is Mine
Venom
Vice Academy 3
Vice Squad
The Video Dead
Video Wars
Vigilante
Violated
Violent Ones
The Violent Years
Viva Knievel
Voyage to the Planet of Prehistoric Women
Vulcan God of Fire
Wacko
Waitress
Wanted: Babysitter
Warlords from Hell
Warrior of the Lost World
Warriors of the Apocalypse
Warriors of the Wasteland
Weekend with the Babysitter
Werewolves on Wheels
Wet and Wild Summer
When Lightning Strikes
When Nature Calls
Where the Boys Are '84
White Cannibal Queen
White Gorilla
White Pongo
Wholly Moses!
The Wild Beasts
Wild Guitar
Wild Ones on Wheels
Wild Orchid 2: Two Shades of Blue
Wild Riders
Wild Wheels
The Wildest Office Party
Wired to Kill
Witchcraft
The Witching
Woman Hunt
Women in Cell Block 7
Women in Fury
Women of the Prehistoric Planet
Women Unchained
Women's Prison Massacre
Woodchipper Massacre
The World is Full of Married Men
The Worm Eaters
The Worst of Faces of Death
Wrestling Racket Girls
Wrestling Women vs. the Aztec Ape
Wrestling Women vs. the Aztec Mummy
Xanadu
Xtro
The Yesterday Machine
You Light Up My Life
Youth Aflame
Zandalee
Zero Boys
Zero Pilot
Zombie Nightmare
Zombies of Moratau

Wyatt Earp

Cheyenne Autumn
Four Eyes and Six Guns
Gunfight at the O.K. Corral▶
Hour of the Gun
My Darling Clementine▶
Sunset
Tombstone▶
Wyatt Earp
Wyatt Earp: Return to Tombstone

Zucker/Abrahams/Zucker

Airplane!▶
Kentucky Fried Movie▶
More! Police Squad
The Naked Gun: From the Files of Police Squad▶
Naked Gun 33 1/3: The Final Insult
Naked Gun 2 1/2: The Smell of Fear
Police Squad! Help Wanted!
Top Secret!▶

Awards Index

The **Awards Index** lists films honored by over 20 national and international award bodies, representing over 100 categories of recognition. This information can also be found in the reviews, following the credits. **Only features available on video and reviewed in the main section are listed in this index; movies not yet released on video are not covered here.** As award-winning films find their way to video, they will be added to the review section and covered in this index. The awards covered include:

Academy Awards
Australia Film Institute
Blockbuster Entertainment Awards
British Academy of Film and Television Arts
Cannes Film Festival
Cesar Awards (French)
Directors Guild of America
Edgar Allan Poe Awards
Genie Awards (Canadian)
Golden Globe
Golden Raspberries
Independent Spirit Awards
Los Angeles Film Critics Association Awards
Montreal Film Festival
MTV Movie Awards
National Board of Review Awards
National Society of Film Critics Awards
New York Film Critics Awards
Sundance Film Festival
Toronto-City Awards
Writers Guild of America

ACADEMY AWARDS

ACTOR

1928 ● Emil Jannings
Last Command

1930 ● George Arliss
Disraeli

1931 ● Lionel Barrymore
A Free Soul

1932 ● Wallace Beery
The Champ
Fredric March
Dr. Jekyll and Mr. Hyde

1933 ● Charles Laughton
The Private Life of Henry VIII

1934 ● Clark Gable
It Happened One Night

1935 ● Victor McLaglen
The Informer

1936 ● Paul Muni
The Story of Louis Pasteur

1937 ● Spencer Tracy
Captains Courageous

1938 ● Spencer Tracy
Boys Town

1939 ● Robert Donat
Goodbye, Mr. Chips

1940 ● James Stewart
The Philadelphia Story

1941 ● Gary Cooper
Sergeant York

1942 ● James Cagney
Yankee Doodle Dandy

1943 ● Paul Lukas
Watch on the Rhine

1944 ● Bing Crosby
Going My Way

1945 ● Ray Milland
The Lost Weekend

1946 ● Fredric March
The Best Years of Our Lives

1947 ● Ronald Colman
A Double Life

1948 ● Laurence Olivier
Hamlet

1949 ● Broderick Crawford
All the King's Men

1950 ● Jose Ferrer
Cyrano de Bergerac

1951 ● Humphrey Bogart
The African Queen

1952 ● Gary Cooper
High Noon

1953 ● William Holden
Stalag 17

1954 ● Marlon Brando
On the Waterfront

1955 ● Ernest Borgnine
Marty

1956 ● Yul Brynner
The King and I

1957 ● Alec Guinness
The Bridge on the River Kwai

1958 ● David Niven
Separate Tables

1959 ● Charlton Heston
Ben-Hur

1960 ● Burt Lancaster
Elmer Gantry

1961 ● Maximilian Schell
Judgment at Nuremberg

1962 ● Gregory Peck
To Kill a Mockingbird

1963 ● Sidney Poitier
Lilies of the Field

1964 ● Rex Harrison
My Fair Lady

1965 ● Lee Marvin
Cat Ballou

1966 ● Paul Scofield
A Man for All Seasons

1967 ● Rod Steiger
In the Heat of the Night

1968 ● Cliff Robertson
Charly

1969 ● John Wayne
True Grit

1970 ● George C. Scott
Patton

1971 ● Gene Hackman
The French Connection

1972 ● Marlon Brando
The Godfather

1973 ● Jack Lemmon
Save the Tiger

1974 ● Art Carney
Harry and Tonto

1975 ● Jack Nicholson
One Flew Over the Cuckoo's Nest

1976 ● Peter Finch
Network

1977 ● Richard Dreyfuss
The Goodbye Girl

1978 ● Jon Voight
Coming Home

1979 ● Dustin Hoffman
Kramer vs. Kramer

1980 ● Robert De Niro
Raging Bull

1981 ● Henry Fonda
On Golden Pond

1982 ● Ben Kingsley
Gandhi

1983 ● Robert Duvall
Tender Mercies

1984 ● F. Murray Abraham
Amadeus

1985 ● William Hurt
Kiss of the Spider Woman

1986 ● Paul Newman
The Color of Money

1987 ● Michael Douglas
Wall Street

1988 ● Dustin Hoffman
Rain Man

1989 ● Daniel Day-Lewis
My Left Foot

1990 ● Jeremy Irons
Reversal of Fortune

1991 ● Anthony Hopkins
The Silence of the Lambs

1992 ● Al Pacino
Scent of a Woman

1993 ● Tom Hanks
Philadelphia

1994 ● Tom Hanks
Forrest Gump

1995 ● Nicolas Cage
Leaving Las Vegas

ACTOR—SUPPORTING

1936 ● Walter Brennan
Come and Get It

1937 ● Joseph Schildkraut
The Life of Emile Zola

1939 ● Thomas Mitchell
Stagecoach

1940 ● Walter Brennan
The Westerner

1941 ● Donald Crisp
How Green Was My Valley

1942 ● Van Heflin
Johnny Eager

1943 ● Charles Coburn
The More the Merrier

1944 ● Barry Fitzgerald
Going My Way

1945 ● James Dunn
A Tree Grows in Brooklyn

1946 ● Harold Russell
The Best Years of Our Lives

1947 ● Edmund Gwenn
Miracle on 34th Street

1948 ● Walter Huston
Treasure of the Sierra Madre

1949 ● Dean Jagger
Twelve O'Clock High

1950 ● George Sanders
All About Eve

ACTOR—SUPPORTING ▶cont.

1951 ● Karl Malden
A Streetcar Named Desire

1952 ● Anthony Quinn
Viva Zapata!

1953 ● Frank Sinatra
From Here to Eternity

1954 ● Edmond O'Brien
The Barefoot Contessa

1955 ● Jack Lemmon
Mister Roberts

1956 ● Anthony Quinn
Lust for Life

1957 ● Red Buttons
Sayonara

1958 ● Burl Ives
The Big Country

1959 ● Hugh Griffith
Ben-Hur

1960 ● Peter Ustinov
Spartacus

1961 ● George Chakiris
West Side Story

1962 ● Ed Begley, Sr.
Sweet Bird of Youth

1963 ● Melvyn Douglas
Hud

1964 ● Peter Ustinov
Topkapi

1965 ● Martin Balsam
A Thousand Clowns

1966 ● Walter Matthau
The Fortune Cookie

1967 ● George Kennedy
Cool Hand Luke

1969 ● Gig Young
They Shoot Horses, Don't They?

1970 ● John Mills
Ryan's Daughter

1971 ● Ben Johnson
The Last Picture Show

1972 ● Joel Grey
Cabaret

1973 ● John Houseman
The Paper Chase

1974 ● Robert De Niro
The Godfather, Part 2

1975 ● George Burns
The Sunshine Boys

1976 ● Jason Robards, Jr.
All the President's Men

1977 ● Jason Robards, Jr.
Julia

1978 ● Christopher Walken
The Deer Hunter

1979 ● Melvyn Douglas
Being There

1980 ● Timothy Hutton
Ordinary People

1981 ● John Gielgud
Arthur

1982 ● Louis Gossett, Jr.
An Officer and a Gentleman

1983 ● Jack Nicholson
Terms of Endearment

1984 ● Haing S. Ngor
The Killing Fields

1985 ● Don Ameche
Cocoon

1986 ● Michael Caine
Hannah and Her Sisters

1987 ● Sean Connery
The Untouchables

1988 ● Kevin Kline
A Fish Called Wanda

1989 ● Denzel Washington
Glory

1990 ● Joe Pesci
Goodfellas

1991 ● Jack Palance
City Slickers

1992 ● Gene Hackman
Unforgiven

1993 ● Tommy Lee Jones
The Fugitive

1994 ● Martin Landau
Ed Wood

1995 ● Kevin Spacey
The Usual Suspects

ACTRESS

1928 ● Janet Gaynor
Sunrise

1929 ● Mary Pickford
Coquette

1930 ● Norma Shearer
The Divorcee

1931 ● Marie Dressler
Min & Bill

1932 ● Helen Hayes
The Sin of Madelon Claudet

1933 ● Katharine Hepburn
Morning Glory

1934 ● Claudette Colbert
It Happened One Night

1935 ● Bette Davis
Dangerous

1936 ● Luise Rainer
The Great Ziegfeld

1937 ● Luise Rainer
The Good Earth

1938 ● Bette Davis
Jezebel

1939 ● Vivien Leigh
Gone with the Wind

1940 ● Ginger Rogers
Kitty Foyle

1941 ● Joan Fontaine
Suspicion

1942 ● Greer Garson
Mrs. Miniver

1943 ● Jennifer Jones
The Song of Bernadette

1944 ● Ingrid Bergman
Gaslight

1945 ● Joan Crawford
Mildred Pierce

1947 ● Loretta Young
The Farmer's Daughter

1948 ● Jane Wyman
Johnny Belinda

1949 ● Olivia de Havilland
The Heiress

1950 ● Judy Holliday
Born Yesterday

1951 ● Vivien Leigh
A Streetcar Named Desire

1952 ● Shirley Booth
Come Back, Little Sheba

1953 ● Audrey Hepburn
Roman Holiday

1954 ● Grace Kelly
Country Girl

1955 ● Anna Magnani
The Rose Tattoo

1956 ● Ingrid Bergman
Anastasia

1957 ● Joanne Woodward
The Three Faces of Eve

1958 ● Susan Hayward
I Want to Live!

1959 ● Simone Signoret
Room at the Top

1960 ● Elizabeth Taylor
Butterfield 8

1961 ● Sophia Loren
Two Women

1962 ● Anne Bancroft
The Miracle Worker

1963 ● Patricia Neal
Hud

1964 ● Julie Andrews
Mary Poppins

1965 ● Julie Christie
Darling

1966 ● Elizabeth Taylor
Who's Afraid of Virginia Woolf?

1967 ● Katharine Hepburn
Guess Who's Coming to Dinner

1968 ● Barbra Streisand
Funny Girl
Katharine Hepburn
The Lion in Winter

1969 ● Maggie Smith
The Prime of Miss Jean Brodie

1970 ● Glenda Jackson
Women in Love

1971 ● Jane Fonda
Klute

1972 ● Liza Minnelli
Cabaret

1973 ● Glenda Jackson
A Touch of Class

1974 ● Ellen Burstyn
Alice Doesn't Live Here Anymore

1975 ● Louise Fletcher
One Flew Over the Cuckoo's Nest

1976 ● Faye Dunaway
Network

1977 ● Diane Keaton
Annie Hall

1978 ● Jane Fonda
Coming Home

1979 ● Sally Field
Norma Rae

1980 ● Sissy Spacek
Coal Miner's Daughter

1981 ● Katharine Hepburn
On Golden Pond

1982 ● Meryl Streep
Sophie's Choice

1983 ● Shirley MacLaine
Terms of Endearment

1984 ● Sally Field
Places in the Heart

1985 ● Geraldine Page
The Trip to Bountiful

1986 ● Marlee Matlin
Children of a Lesser God

1987 ● Cher
Moonstruck

1988 ● Jodie Foster
The Accused

1989 ● Jessica Tandy
Driving Miss Daisy

1990 ● Kathy Bates
Misery

1991 ● Jodie Foster
The Silence of the Lambs

1992 ● Emma Thompson
Howard's End

1993 ● Holly Hunter
The Piano

1994 ● Jessica Lange
Blue Sky

1995 ● Susan Sarandon
Dead Man Walking

ACTRESS—SUPPORTING

1936 ● Gale Sondergaard
Anthony Adverse

1938 ● Fay Bainter
Jezebel

1939 ● Hattie McDaniel
Gone with the Wind

1940 ● Jane Darwell
The Grapes of Wrath

1941 ● Mary Astor
The Great Lie

1942 ● Teresa Wright
Mrs. Miniver

1943 ● Katina Paxinou
For Whom the Bell Tolls

1944 ● Ethel Barrymore
None But the Lonely Heart

1945 ● Anne Revere
National Velvet

1946 ● Anne Baxter
The Razor's Edge

1947 ● Celeste Holm
Gentleman's Agreement

1948 ● Claire Trevor
Key Largo

1949 ● Mercedes McCambridge
All the King's Men

1950 ● Josephine Hull
Harvey

1951 ● Kim Hunter
A Streetcar Named Desire

1952 ● Gloria Grahame
The Bad and the Beautiful

1953 ● Donna Reed
From Here to Eternity

1954 ● Eva Marie Saint
On the Waterfront

1955 ● Jo Van Fleet
East of Eden

1956 ● Dorothy Malone
Written on the Wind

1957 ● Miyoshi Umeki
Sayonara

1958 ● Wendy Hiller
Separate Tables

1959 ● Shelley Winters
The Diary of Anne Frank

1960 ● Shirley Jones
Elmer Gantry

1961 ● Rita Moreno
West Side Story

1962 ● Patty Duke
The Miracle Worker

1963 ● Margaret Rutherford
The V.I.P.'s

1964 ● Lila Kedrova
Zorba the Greek

1965 ● Shelley Winters
A Patch of Blue

1966 ● Sandy Dennis
Who's Afraid of Virginia Woolf?

1967 ● Estelle Parsons
Bonnie & Clyde

1968 ● Ruth Gordon
Rosemary's Baby

1969 ● Goldie Hawn
Cactus Flower

1970 ● Helen Hayes
Airport

1971 ● Cloris Leachman
The Last Picture Show

1972 ● Eileen Heckart
Butterflies Are Free

1973 ● Tatum O'Neal
Paper Moon

1974 ● Ingrid Bergman
Murder on the Orient Express

1975 ● Lee Grant
Shampoo

1976 ● Beatrice Straight
Network

1977 ● Vanessa Redgrave
Julia

1978 ● Maggie Smith
California Suite

1979 ● Meryl Streep
Kramer vs. Kramer

1980 ● Mary Steenburgen
Melvin and Howard

1981 ● Maureen Stapleton
Reds

1982 ● Jessica Lange
Tootsie

1983 ● Linda Hunt
The Year of Living Dangerously

1984 ● Peggy Ashcroft
A Passage to India

1985 ● Anjelica Huston
Prizzi's Honor

1986 ● Dianne Wiest
Hannah and Her Sisters
1987 ● Olympia Dukakis
Moonstruck
1988 ● Geena Davis
The Accidental Tourist
1989 ● Brenda Fricker
My Left Foot
1990 ● Whoopi Goldberg
Ghost
1991 ● Mercedes Ruehl
The Fisher King
1992 ● Marisa Tomei
My Cousin Vinny
1993 ● Anna Paquin
The Piano
1994 ● Dianne Wiest
Bullets Over Broadway
1995 ● Mira Sorvino
Mighty Aphrodite

ART DIRECTION

1946
Anna and the King of Siam
1957
Sayonara
1958
Gigi
1967
Camelot
1968
Oliver!
1969
Hello, Dolly!
1970
Patton
1971
Nicholas and Alexandra
1972
Cabaret
1973
The Sting
1974
The Godfather, Part 2
1975
Barry Lyndon
1976
All the President's Men
1977
Star Wars
1978
Heaven Can Wait
1979
All That Jazz
1980
Tess
1981
Raiders of the Lost Ark
1982
Gandhi
1983
Fanny and Alexander
1984
Amadeus
1985
Out of Africa
1986
A Room with a View
1987
The Last Emperor
1988
Dangerous Liaisons
1989
Batman
1990
Dick Tracy
1991
Bugsy
1992
Howard's End
1993
Schindler's List
1994
The Madness of King George
1995
Restoration

ART DIRECTION (B & W)

1947
Great Expectations
1948
Hamlet
1949
The Heiress
1950
Sunset Boulevard
1951
A Streetcar Named Desire
1952
The Bad and the Beautiful
1953
Julius Caesar
1954
On the Waterfront
1955
The Rose Tattoo
1956
Somebody Up There Likes Me
1959
The Diary of Anne Frank
1960
The Apartment
1961
The Hustler
1962
To Kill a Mockingbird
1964
Zorba the Greek
1965
Ship of Fools
1966
Who's Afraid of Virginia Woolf?

ART DIRECTION (COLOR)

1947
Black Narcissus
1948
The Red Shoes
1949
Little Women
1950
Samson and Delilah
1951
An American in Paris
1952
Moulin Rouge
1953
The Robe
1954
20,000 Leagues Under the Sea
1955
Picnic
1956
The King and I
1959
Ben-Hur
1960
Spartacus
1961
West Side Story
1962
Lawrence of Arabia
1963
Cleopatra
1964
My Fair Lady
1965
Doctor Zhivago
1966
Fantastic Voyage

CINEMATOGRAPHY

1928
Sunrise
1931
Tabu: A Story of the South Seas
1932 ● Lee Garmes
Shanghai Express
1933
A Farewell to Arms
1934
Cleopatra
1935
A Midsummer Night's Dream
1936
Anthony Adverse
1937
The Good Earth
1945
Leave Her to Heaven
1967
Bonnie & Clyde
1968
Romeo and Juliet
1969
Butch Cassidy and the Sundance Kid
1970
Ryan's Daughter
1971
Fiddler on the Roof
1972
Cabaret
1973
Cries and Whispers
1974
The Towering Inferno
1975
Barry Lyndon
1976
Bound for Glory
1977
Close Encounters of the Third Kind
1978
Days of Heaven
1979
Apocalypse Now
1980
Tess
1981
Reds
1982
Gandhi
1983
Fanny and Alexander
1984
The Killing Fields
1985
Out of Africa
1986
The Mission
1987
The Last Emperor
1988
Mississippi Burning
1989
Glory
1990
Dances with Wolves
1991
JFK
1992
A River Runs Through It
1993
Schindler's List
1994
Legends of the Fall
1995
Braveheart

CINEMATOGRAPHY (B & W)

1939
Wuthering Heights
1940
Rebecca
1941
How Green Was My Valley
1942
Mrs. Miniver
1943
The Song of Bernadette
1944
Laura
1945
Picture of Dorian Gray
1946
Anna and the King of Siam
1947
Great Expectations
1948
The Naked City
1949
Battleground
1950
The Third Man
1951
A Place in the Sun
1952
The Bad and the Beautiful
1953
From Here to Eternity
1954
On the Waterfront
1955
The Rose Tattoo
1956
Somebody Up There Likes Me
1958
The Defiant Ones
1959
The Diary of Anne Frank
1961
The Hustler
1962
The Longest Day
1963
Hud
1964
Zorba the Greek
1965
Ship of Fools
1966
Who's Afraid of Virginia Woolf?

CINEMATOGRAPHY (COLOR)

1939
Gone with the Wind
1941
Blood and Sand
1942
The Black Swan
1943
The Phantom of the Opera
1944
Wilson
1946
The Yearling
1947
Black Narcissus
1948
Joan of Arc
1949
She Wore a Yellow Ribbon
1950
King Solomon's Mines
1951
An American in Paris
1952
The Quiet Man
1953
Shane
1954
Three Coins in the Fountain
1955
To Catch a Thief

CINEMATOGRAPHY (COLOR) ▶cont.

1956
Around the World in 80 Days

1957
The Bridge on the River Kwai

1958
Gigi

1959
Ben-Hur

1960
Spartacus

1961
West Side Story

1962
Lawrence of Arabia

1963
Cleopatra

1964
My Fair Lady

1965
Doctor Zhivago

1966
A Man for All Seasons

COSTUME DESIGN

1948
Joan of Arc

1957
Les Girls

1958
Gigi

1967
Camelot

1968
Romeo and Juliet

1969
Anne of the Thousand Days

1970
Cromwell

1971
Nicholas and Alexandra

1972
Travels with My Aunt

1973
The Sting

1974
The Great Gatsby

1975
Barry Lyndon

1977
Star Wars

1978
Death on the Nile

1979
All That Jazz

1980
Tess

1981
Chariots of Fire

1982
Gandhi

1983
Fanny and Alexander

1984
Amadeus

1985
Ran

1986
A Room with a View

1987
The Last Emperor

1988
Dangerous Liaisons

1989
Henry V

1990
Cyrano de Bergerac

1991
Bugsy

1992
Bram Stoker's Dracula

1993
The Age of Innocence

1994
The Adventures of Priscilla, Queen of the Desert

1995
Restoration

COSTUME DESIGN (B & W)

1948
Hamlet

1949
The Heiress

1951
A Place in the Sun

1952
The Bad and the Beautiful

1953
Roman Holiday

1954
Sabrina

1955
I'll Cry Tomorrow

1956
Solid Gold Cadillac

1959
Some Like It Hot

1961
La Dolce Vita

1963
8 1/2

1964
The Night of the Iguana

1965
Darling

1966
Who's Afraid of Virginia Woolf?

COSTUME DESIGN (COLOR)

1949
Adventures of Don Juan

1950
Samson and Delilah

1951
An American in Paris

1952
Moulin Rouge

1953
The Robe

1954
Gate of Hell

1955
Love Is a Many-Splendored Thing

1956
The King and I

1959
Ben-Hur

1960
Spartacus

1961
West Side Story

1962
The Wonderful World of the Brothers Grimm

1963
Cleopatra

1964
My Fair Lady

1965
Doctor Zhivago

1966
A Man for All Seasons

DIRECTOR

1930 ● Lewis Milestone
All Quiet on the Western Front

1933 ● Frank Lloyd
Cavalcade

1934 ● Frank Capra
It Happened One Night

1935 ● John Ford
The Informer

1936 ● Frank Capra
Mr. Deeds Goes to Town

1937 ● Leo McCarey
The Awful Truth

1938 ● Frank Capra
You Can't Take It with You

1939 ● Victor Fleming
Gone with the Wind

1940 ● John Ford
The Grapes of Wrath

1941 ● John Ford
How Green Was My Valley

1942 ● William Wyler
Mrs. Miniver

1943 ● Michael Curtiz
Casablanca

1944 ● Leo McCarey
Going My Way

1945 ● Billy Wilder
The Lost Weekend

1946 ● William Wyler
The Best Years of Our Lives

1947 ● Elia Kazan
Gentleman's Agreement

1948 ● John Huston
Treasure of the Sierra Madre

1949 ● Joseph L. Mankiewicz
A Letter to Three Wives

1950 ● Joseph L. Mankiewicz
All About Eve

1951 ● George Stevens
A Place in the Sun

1952 ● John Ford
The Quiet Man

1953 ● Fred Zinnemann
From Here to Eternity

1954 ● Elia Kazan
On the Waterfront

1955 ● Delbert Mann
Marty

1956 ● George Stevens
Giant

1957 ● David Lean
The Bridge on the River Kwai

1958 ● Vincente Minnelli
Gigi

1959 ● William Wyler
Ben-Hur

1960 ● Billy Wilder
The Apartment

1961 ● Robert Wise
West Side Story

1962 ● David Lean
Lawrence of Arabia

1963 ● Tony Richardson
Tom Jones

1964 ● George Cukor
My Fair Lady

1965 ● Robert Wise
The Sound of Music

1966 ● Fred Zinnemann
A Man for All Seasons

1967 ● Mike Nichols
The Graduate

1968 ● Carol Reed
Oliver!

1969 ● John Schlesinger
Midnight Cowboy

1970 ● Franklin J. Schaffner
Patton

1971 ● William Friedkin
The French Connection

1972 ● Bob Fosse
Cabaret

1973 ● George Roy Hill
The Sting

1974 ● Francis Ford Coppola
The Godfather, Part 2

1975 ● Milos Forman
One Flew Over the Cuckoo's Nest

1976 ● John G. Avildsen
Rocky

1977 ● Woody Allen
Annie Hall

1978 ● Michael Cimino
The Deer Hunter

1979 ● Robert Benton
Kramer vs. Kramer

1980 ● Robert Redford
Ordinary People

1981 ● Warren Beatty
Reds

1982 ● Richard Attenborough
Gandhi

1983 ● James L. Brooks
Terms of Endearment

1984 ● Milos Forman
Amadeus

1985 ● Sydney Pollack
Out of Africa

1986 ● Oliver Stone
Platoon

1987 ● Bernardo Bertolucci
The Last Emperor

1988 ● Barry Levinson
Rain Man

1989 ● Oliver Stone
Born on the Fourth of July

1990 ● Kevin Costner
Dances with Wolves

1991 ● Jonathan Demme
The Silence of the Lambs

1992 ● Clint Eastwood
Unforgiven

1993 ● Steven Spielberg
Schindler's List

1994 ● Robert Zemeckis
Forrest Gump

1995 ● Mel Gibson
Braveheart

FILM

1927
Wings

1929
Broadway Melody

1930
All Quiet on the Western Front

1931
Cimarron

1932
Grand Hotel

1933
Cavalcade

1934
It Happened One Night

1935
Mutiny on the Bounty

1936
The Great Ziegfeld

1937
The Life of Emile Zola

1938
You Can't Take It with You

1939
Gone with the Wind

1940
Rebecca

1941
How Green Was My Valley

1942
Mrs. Miniver

1943
Casablanca

1944
Going My Way

1945
The Lost Weekend

1946
The Best Years of Our Lives

1947
Gentleman's Agreement

1948
Hamlet

1949
All the King's Men

1950
All About Eve

1951
An American in Paris

1952
The Greatest Show on Earth

1953
From Here to Eternity

1954
On the Waterfront

1955
Marty

1956
Around the World in 80 Days

1957
The Bridge on the River Kwai

1958
Gigi

1959
Ben-Hur

1960
The Apartment

1961
West Side Story

1962
Lawrence of Arabia

1963
Tom Jones

1964
My Fair Lady

1965
The Sound of Music

1966
A Man for All Seasons

1967
In the Heat of the Night

1968
Oliver!

1969
Midnight Cowboy

1970
Patton

1971
The French Connection

1972
The Godfather

1973
The Sting

1974
The Godfather, Part 2

1975
One Flew Over the Cuckoo's Nest

1976
Rocky

1977
Annie Hall

1978
The Deer Hunter

1979
Kramer vs. Kramer

1980
Ordinary People

1981
Chariots of Fire

1982
Gandhi

1983
Terms of Endearment

1984
Amadeus

1985
Out of Africa

1986
Platoon

1987
The Last Emperor

1988
Rain Man

1989
Driving Miss Daisy

1990
Dances with Wolves

1991
The Silence of the Lambs

1992
Unforgiven

1993
Schindler's List

1994
Forrest Gump

1995
Braveheart

FEATURE DOCUMENTARY

1942
Prelude to War

1954
Vanishing Prairie

1961
The Sky Above, the Mud Below

1970
Woodstock

1971
The Hellstrom Chronicle

1972
Marjoe

1975
The Man Who Skied Down Everest

1976
Harlan County, U.S.A.

1983
Times of Harvey Milk

1989
Common Threads: Stories from the Quilt

FILM EDITING

1935
A Midsummer Night's Dream

1936
Anthony Adverse

1937
Lost Horizon

1938
The Adventures of Robin Hood

1939
Gone with the Wind

1941
Sergeant York

1942
The Pride of the Yankees

1943
Air Force

1944
Wilson

1945
National Velvet

1946
The Best Years of Our Lives

1947
Body and Soul

1948
The Naked City

1949
Champion

1950
King Solomon's Mines

1951
A Place in the Sun

1952
High Noon

1953
From Here to Eternity

1954
On the Waterfront

1955
Picnic

1956
Around the World in 80 Days

1957
The Bridge on the River Kwai

1958
Gigi

1959
Ben-Hur

1960
The Apartment

1961
West Side Story

1962
Lawrence of Arabia

1963
How the West Was Won

1964
Mary Poppins

1965
The Sound of Music

1966
Grand Prix

1967
In the Heat of the Night

1968
Bullitt

1969
Z

1970
Patton

1971
The French Connection

1972
Cabaret

1973
The Sting

1974
The Towering Inferno

1975
Jaws

1976
Rocky

1977
Star Wars

1978
The Deer Hunter

1979
All That Jazz

1980
Raging Bull

1981
Raiders of the Lost Ark

1982
Gandhi

1983
The Right Stuff

1984
The Killing Fields

1985
Witness

1986
Platoon

1987
The Last Emperor

1988
Who Framed Roger Rabbit

1989
Born on the Fourth of July

1990
Dances with Wolves

1991
JFK

1992
Unforgiven

1993
Schindler's List

1994
Forrest Gump

1995
Apollo 13

FILM—FOREIGN LANGUAGE

1949
The Bicycle Thief

1951
Rashomon

1952
Forbidden Games

1954
Gate of Hell

1955
Samurai 1: Musashi Miyamoto

1956
La Strada

1957
Nights of Cabiria

1958
Mon Oncle

1959
Black Orpheus

1960
The Virgin Spring

1961
Through a Glass Darkly

1962
Sundays & Cybele

1963
8 1/2

1964
Yesterday, Today and Tomorrow

1965
The Shop on Main Street

1966
A Man and a Woman

1967
Closely Watched Trains

1968
War and Peace

1969
Z

1971
The Garden of the Finzi-Continis

1972
The Discreet Charm of the Bourgeoisie

1973
Day for Night

1974
Amarcord

1975
Dersu Uzala

1976
Black and White in Color

1977
Madame Rosa

1978
Get Out Your Handkerchiefs

1979
The Tin Drum

1980
Moscow Does Not Believe in Tears

1981
Mephisto

1983
Fanny and Alexander

1984
Dangerous Moves

1985
The Official Story

1986
The Assault

FILM—FOREIGN LANGUAGE ▶cont.

1987
Babette's Feast

1988
Pelle the Conqueror

1989
Cinema Paradiso

1990
Journey of Hope

1991
Mediterraneo

1992
Indochine

1993
Belle Epoque

1994
Burnt by the Sun

1995
Antonia's Line

MAKEUP

1981
An American Werewolf in London

1982
Quest for Fire

1984
Amadeus

1985
Mask

1986
The Fly

1987
Harry and the Hendersons

1988
Beetlejuice

1989
Driving Miss Daisy

1990
Dick Tracy

1991
Terminator 2: Judgment Day

1992
Bram Stoker's Dracula

1993
Mrs. Doubtfire

1994
Ed Wood

1995
Braveheart

MUSIC

1934
One Night of Love

1935
The Informer

1936
Anthony Adverse

1937
100 Men and a Girl

1938
The Adventures of Robin Hood
Alexander's Ragtime Band

1939
Stagecoach
The Wizard of Oz

1940
Pinocchio
Tin Pan Alley

1941
Dumbo

1942
Now, Voyager
Yankee Doodle Dandy

1943
The Song of Bernadette
This Is the Army

1944
Cover Girl
Since You Went Away

1945
Anchors Aweigh
Spellbound

1946
The Best Years of Our Lives
The Jolson Story

1947
A Double Life

1948
Easter Parade
The Red Shoes

1949
The Heiress
On the Town

1950
Sunset Boulevard

1951
An American in Paris
A Place in the Sun

1952
High Noon

1953
Lili

1954
Seven Brides for Seven Brothers

1955
Love Is a Many-Splendored Thing
Oklahoma!

1956
Around the World in 80 Days
The King and I

1957
The Bridge on the River Kwai

1958
Gigi

1959
Ben-Hur

1960
Exodus
Song Without End

1961
Breakfast at Tiffany's
West Side Story

1962
Lawrence of Arabia
The Music Man

1963
Irma La Douce
Tom Jones

1964
Mary Poppins
My Fair Lady

1965
Doctor Zhivago
The Sound of Music

1966
Born Free
A Funny Thing Happened on the Way to the Forum

1967
Camelot
Thoroughly Modern Millie

1968
The Lion in Winter
Oliver!

1969
Butch Cassidy and the Sundance Kid
Hello, Dolly!

1970
Let It Be
Love Story

1971
Fiddler on the Roof
Summer of '42

1972
Cabaret

1973
The Sting
The Way We Were

1974
The Godfather, Part 2
The Great Gatsby

1975
Barry Lyndon
Jaws

1976
Bound for Glory
The Omen

1977
A Little Night Music
Star Wars

1978
The Buddy Holly Story
Midnight Express

1979
All That Jazz
A Little Romance

1980
Fame

1981
Chariots of Fire

1982
E.T.: The Extra-Terrestrial
Victor/Victoria

1983
The Right Stuff
Yentl

1984
A Passage to India
Purple Rain

1985
Out of Africa

1986
Round Midnight

1987
The Last Emperor

1988
The Milagro Beanfield War

1989
The Little Mermaid

1990
Dances with Wolves

1991
Beauty and the Beast

1992
Aladdin

1993
Schindler's List

1994
The Lion King

1995
Pocahontas

ORIGINAL DRAMATIC SCORE

1995
The Postman

SONG

1934 ● "The Continental"
The Gay Divorcee

1936 ● "The Way You Look Tonight"
Swing Time

1937 ● "Sweet Leilani"
Waikiki Wedding

1938 ● "Thanks for the Memories"
The Big Braodcast of 1938

1939 ● "Over the Rainbow"
The Wizard of Oz

1940 ● "When You Wish Upon a Star"
Pinocchio

1941 ● "The Last Time I Saw Paris"
Lady Be Good

1942 ● "White Christmas"
Holiday Inn

1943 ● "You'll Never Know"
Hello, Frisco, Hello

1944 ● "Swinging on a Star"
Going My Way

1945 ● "It Might as Well Be Spring"
State Fair

1946 ● "On the Atchison, Topeka and Santa Fe"
The Harvey Girls

1948 ● "Buttons and Bows"
The Paleface

1949 ● "Baby It's Cold Outside"
Neptune's Daughter

1951 ● "In the Cool, Cool, Cool of the Evening"
Here Comes the Groom

1952 ● "High Noon (Do Not Forsake Me, Oh My Darlin')"
High Noon

1953 ● "Secret Love"
Calamity Jane

1954 ● "Three Coins in the Fountain"
Three Coins in the Fountain

1955 ● "Love Is a Many-Splendored Thing"
Love Is a Many-Splendored Thing

1956 ● "Que Sera, Sera"
The Man Who Knew Too Much

1958 ● "Gigi"
Gigi

1959 ● "High Hopes"
A Hole in the Head

1960 ● "Never on Sunday"
Never on Sunday

1961 ● "Moon River"
Breakfast at Tiffany's

1962 ● "Days of Wine and Roses"
Days of Wine and Roses

1963 ● "Call Me Irresponsible"
Papa's Delicate Condition

1964 ● "Chim Chim Cher-ee"
Mary Poppins

1965 ● "The Shadow of Your Smile"
The Sandpiper

1966 ● "Born Free"
Born Free

1967 ● "Talk to the Animals"
Doctor Dolittle

1968 ● "The Windmills of Your Mind"
The Thomas Crown Affair

1969 ● "Raindrops Keep Fallin' on My Head"
Butch Cassidy and the Sundance Kid

1970 ● "For All We Know"
Lovers and Other Strangers

1971 ● "Theme from Shaft"
Shaft

1972 ● "The Morning After"
The Poseidon Adventure

1973 ● "The Way We Were"
The Way We Were

1974 ● "We May Never Love Like This Again"
The Towering Inferno

1975 ● "I'm Easy"
Nashville

1976 ● "Evergreen"
A Star is Born

1977 ● "You Light Up My Life"
You Light Up My Life

1978 ● "Last Dance"
Thank God It's Friday

1979 ● "It Goes Like It Goes"
Norma Rae

1980 ● "Fame"
Fame

1981 ● "Arthur's Theme"
Arthur

1982 ● "Up Where We Belong"
An Officer and a Gentleman

1983 ● "Flashdance...What a Feeling"
Flashdance

1984 ● "I Just Called to Say I Love You"
The Woman in Red

1985 ● "Say You, Say Me"
White Nights

1986 ● "Take My Breath Away"
Top Gun

1987 ● "(I've Had) the Time of My Life"
Dirty Dancing

1988 ● "Let the River Run"
Working Girl

1989 ● "Under the Sea"
The Little Mermaid

1990 ● "Sooner or Later"
Dick Tracy

1991 ● "Beauty and the Beast"
Beauty and the Beast

1992 ● "A Whole New World"
Aladdin

1993 ● "Streets of Philadelphia"
Philadelphia

1994 ● "Can You Feel the Love Tonight"
The Lion King

1995 ● "Colors of the Wind"
Pocahontas

SOUND

1933
A Farewell to Arms

1934
One Night of Love

1935
Naughty Marietta

1936
San Francisco

1937
The Hurricane

1938
The Cowboy and the Lady

1940
Strike Up the Band

1941
That Hamilton Woman

1942
Yankee Doodle Dandy

1943
This Land is Mine

1944
Wilson

1945
The Bells of St. Mary's

1946
The Jolson Story

1947
The Bishop's Wife

1948
The Snake Pit

1949
Twelve O'Clock High

1950
All About Eve

1951
The Great Caruso

1953
From Here to Eternity

1954
The Glenn Miller Story

1955
Oklahoma!

1956
The King and I

1957
Sayonara

1958
South Pacific

1959
Ben-Hur

1960
The Alamo

1961
West Side Story

1962
Lawrence of Arabia

1963
How the West Was Won

1964
My Fair Lady

1965
The Sound of Music

1966
Grand Prix

1967
In the Heat of the Night

1968
Oliver!

1969
Hello, Dolly!

1970
Patton

1971
Fiddler on the Roof

1972
Cabaret

1973
The Exorcist

1974
Earthquake

1975
Jaws

1976
All the President's Men

1977
Star Wars

1978
The Deer Hunter

1979
Apocalypse Now

1980
The Empire Strikes Back

1981
Raiders of the Lost Ark

1982
E.T.: The Extra-Terrestrial

1983
The Right Stuff

1984
Amadeus

1985
Out of Africa

1986
Platoon

1987
The Last Emperor

1988
Bird

1989
Glory

1990
Dances with Wolves

1991
Terminator 2: Judgment Day

1992
The Last of the Mohicans

1993
Jurassic Park

1994
Speed

1995
Apollo 13

WRITING

1931
Cimarron

1932
The Champ

1933
Little Women

1934
It Happened One Night

1935
The Informer

1936
The Story of Louis Pasteur

1937
The Life of Emile Zola
A Star is Born

1938
Boys Town
Pygmalion

1939
Gone with the Wind
Mr. Smith Goes to Washington

1940
The Great McGinty
The Philadelphia Story

1941
Citizen Kane
Here Comes Mr. Jordan

1942
Mrs. Miniver
Woman of the Year

1943
Casablanca
The Human Comedy

1944
Going My Way
Wilson

1945
House on 92nd Street
The Lost Weekend

1946
The Best Years of Our Lives
The Seventh Veil

1947
The Bachelor and the Bobby-Soxer
Miracle on 34th Street

1948
The Search
Treasure of the Sierra Madre

1949
Battleground
Joseph L. Mankiewicz
A Letter to Three Wives
The Stratton Story

1950
All About Eve
Panic in the Streets
Sunset Boulevard

1951
An American in Paris
A Place in the Sun

1952
The Bad and the Beautiful
The Greatest Show on Earth
The Lavender Hill Mob

1953
From Here to Eternity
Roman Holiday
Titanic
Titanic

1954
Broken Lance
Country Girl
On the Waterfront

1955
Love Me or Leave Me
Marty

1956
Around the World in 80 Days
The Brave One
The Red Balloon

1957
The Bridge on the River Kwai
Designing Woman

1958
The Defiant Ones
Gigi

1959
Pillow Talk
Room at the Top

1960
The Apartment
Elmer Gantry

1961
Judgment at Nuremberg
Splendor in the Grass

1962
Divorce—Italian Style
To Kill a Mockingbird

1963
How the West Was Won
Tom Jones

1964
Becket
Father Goose

1965
Darling
Doctor Zhivago

1966
A Man and a Woman
A Man for All Seasons

1967
Guess Who's Coming to Dinner

1968
The Lion in Winter
The Producers

1969
Butch Cassidy and the Sundance Kid
Midnight Cowboy

1970
*M*A*S*H*
Patton

1971
The French Connection
The Hospital

1972
The Candidate
The Godfather

1973
The Exorcist
The Sting

1974
Chinatown
The Godfather, Part 2

1975
Dog Day Afternoon
One Flew Over the Cuckoo's Nest

1976
All the President's Men
Network

1977
Annie Hall
Julia

1978
Coming Home
Midnight Express

1979
Breaking Away
Kramer vs. Kramer

1980
Melvin and Howard
Ordinary People

1981
Chariots of Fire
On Golden Pond

1982
Gandhi
Missing

1983
Tender Mercies
Terms of Endearment

1984
Amadeus
Places in the Heart

1985
Out of Africa
Witness

1986
Hannah and Her Sisters
A Room with a View

WRITING ▸cont.

1987
The Last Emperor
Moonstruck

1988
Dangerous Liaisons
Rain Man

1989
Dead Poets Society
Driving Miss Daisy

1990
Dances with Wolves
Ghost

1991
The Silence of the Lambs
Thelma & Louise

1992
The Crying Game
Howard's End

1993
The Piano
Schindler's List

1994
Forrest Gump
Pulp Fiction

1995
Sense and Sensibility
The Usual Suspects

AUSTRALIAN FILM INSTITUTE

ACTOR

1974 • Jack Thompson
Sunday Too Far Away

1975 • John Meillon
Fourth Wish

1976 • Nick Tate
The Devil's Playground
Simon Burke
The Devil's Playground

1978 • Bill Hunter
Newsfront

1979 • Mel Gibson
Tim

1980 • Jack Thompson
Breaker Morant

1981 • Mel Gibson
Gallipoli

1983 • Norman Kaye
Man of Flowers

1984 • John Hargreaves
My First Wife

1986 • Colin Friels
Malcolm

1987 • Leo McKern
Travelling North

1989 • Sam Neill
A Cry in the Dark

1990 • Max von Sydow
Father

1991 • Hugo Weaving
Proof

1992 • Russell Crowe
Romper Stomper

1993 • Harvey Keitel
The Piano

1994 • Nicholas Hope
Bad Boy Bubby

1995 • John Lynch
Angel Baby

ACTOR—SUPPORTING

1991 • Russell Crowe
Proof

1992 • Barry Otto
Strictly Ballroom

1995 • Ray Barrett
Sorrento Beach

ACTRESS

1977 • Pat Bishop
Don's Party

1980 • Tracey Mann
Hard Knocks

1981 • Judy Davis
The Winter of Our Dreams

1982 • Noni Hazlehurst
Monkey Grip

1983 • Wendy Hughes
Careful, He Might Hear You

1985 • Noni Hazlehurst
Fran

1986 • Judy Davis
Kangaroo

1987 • Judy Davis
High Tide

1989 • Meryl Streep
A Cry in the Dark

1990 • Julia Blake
Father

1991 • Sheila Florence
A Woman's Tale

1992 • Lisa Harrow
The Last Days of Chez Nous

1993 • Holly Hunter
The Piano

1994 • Toni Collette
Muriel's Wedding

1995 • Jacqueline McKenzie
Angel Baby

ACTRESS—SUPPORTING

1992 • Pat Thomsen
Strictly Ballroom

1994 • Rachel Griffiths
Muriel's Wedding

1995 • Amanda Douge
That Eye, The Sky

CINEMATOGRAPHY

1988
The Navigator

1992
Black Robe

1993
The Piano

1995
Angel Baby

COSTUME DESIGN

1992
Strictly Ballroom

1993
The Piano

1994
The Adventures of Priscilla, Queen of the Desert

DIRECTOR

1988 • Vincent Ward
The Navigator

1991 • Jocelyn Moorhouse
Proof

1992 • Baz Luhrmann
Strictly Ballroom

1993 • Jane Campion
The Piano

1994 • Rolf de Heer
Bad Boy Bubby

1995 • Michael Rymer
Angel Baby

FILM

1974
Sunday Too Far Away

1976
The Devil's Playground

1978
Newsfront

1979
My Brilliant Career

1980
Breaker Morant

1981
Gallipoli

1982
Lonely Hearts

1983
Careful, He Might Hear You

1984
A Test of Love

1985
Bliss

1986
Malcolm

1987
The Year My Voice Broke

1988
The Navigator

1989
A Cry in the Dark

1990
Flirting

1991
Proof

1992
Strictly Ballroom

1993
The Piano

1994
Muriel's Wedding

1995
Angel Baby

FILM EDITING

1991
Proof

1992
Strictly Ballroom

1993
The Piano

1994
Bad Boy Bubby

1995
Angel Baby

MUSIC

1992
Romper Stomper

1993
The Piano

SOUND

1992
Romper Stomper

1993
The Piano

1994
Muriel's Wedding

WRITING

1991
Proof

1992
Strictly Ballroom

1993
The Piano

1994
Bad Boy Bubby
The Sum of Us

1995
Angel Baby
Sorrento Beach

FILM—FOREIGN LANGUAGE

1992
Truly, Madly, Deeply

1993
The Crying Game

1994
Four Weddings and a Funeral

1995
Once Were Warriors

BLOCKBUSTER ENTERTAINMENT AWARDS

MOVIE, THEATRICAL

1995
Forrest Gump

MOVIE, VIDEO

1995
Speed

FAMILY MOVIE, THEATRICAL

1995
The Lion King

FAMILY MOVIE, VIDEO

1995
Rookie of the Year

ACTION ACTOR, THEATRICAL

1995 • Harrison Ford
Clear and Present Danger

1996 • Pierce Brosnan
Goldeneye

ACTION ACTOR, VIDEO

1995 • Harrison Ford
The Fugitive

1996 • Harrison Ford
Clear and Present Danger

ACTION ACTRESS, THEATRICAL

1995 • Sandra Bullock
Speed

1996 • Nicole Kidman
Batman Forever

ACTION ACTRESS, VIDEO

1995 • Sandra Bullock
Speed

1996 • Jamie Lee Curtis
True Lies

COMEDY ACTOR, THEATRICAL

1995 • Jim Carrey
The Mask

1996 • Jim Carrey
Ace Ventura: When Nature Calls

COMEDY ACTOR, VIDEO

1995 • Jim Carrey
Ace Ventura: Pet Detective

1996 • Jim Carrey
Dumb & Dumber
Jim Carrey
The Mask

COMEDY ACTRESS, THEATRICAL

1995 • Jodie Foster
Maverick

1996 • Sandra Bullock
While You Were Sleeping

COMEDY ACTRESS, VIDEO

1995 • Whoopi Goldberg
Sister Act 2: Back in the Habit

1996 • Sandra Bullock
While You Were Sleeping

DRAMA ACTOR, THEATRICAL

1995 • Tom Hanks
Forrest Gump

1996 • Tom Hanks
Apollo 13

DRAMA ACTOR, VIDEO

1995 • Tom Hanks
Philadelphia

1996 • Tom Hanks
Forrest Gump

DRAMA ACTRESS, THEATRICAL

1995 • Demi Moore
Disclosure

1996 • Michelle Pfeiffer
Dangerous Minds

DRAMA ACTRESS, VIDEO

1995 • Meg Ryan
When a Man Loves a Woman

1996 • Demi Moore
Disclosure

FEMALE NEWCOMER, THEATRICAL

1995 • Cameron Diaz
The Mask

1996 • Alicia Silverstone
Clueless

FEMALE NEWCOMER, VIDEO

1995 • Angela Bassett
What's Love Got to Do with It?

MALE NEWCOMER, THEATRICAL

1995 • Tim Allen
The Santa Clause

1996 • Will Smith
Bad Boys

MALE NEWCOMER, VIDEO

1995 • Jim Carrey
Ace Ventura: Pet Detective

BEST SOUNDTRACK

1995
The Lion King

BRITISH ACADEMY OF FILM AND TELEVISION ARTS

ACTOR

1952 • Marlon Brando
Viva Zapata!

1953 • Marlon Brando
Julius Caesar
John Gielgud
Julius Caesar

1954 • Kenneth More
Doctor in the House
Marlon Brando
On the Waterfront

1955 • Ernest Borgnine
Marty
Laurence Olivier
Richard III

1956 • Francois Perier
Gervaise

1957 • Alec Guinness
The Bridge on the River Kwai
Henry Fonda
Twelve Angry Men

1958 • Sidney Poitier
The Defiant Ones
Trevor Howard
The Key

1959 • Peter Sellers
I'm All Right Jack
Jack Lemmon
Some Like It Hot

1960 • Jack Lemmon
The Apartment

1961 • Paul Newman
The Hustler
Peter Finch
No Love for Johnnie

1962 • Burt Lancaster
Birdman of Alcatraz
Peter O'Toole
Lawrence of Arabia

1963 • Marcello Mastroianni
Divorce—Italian Style
Dirk Bogarde
The Servant

1964 • Richard Attenborough
Seance on a Wet Afternoon
Marcello Mastroianni
Yesterday, Today and Tomorrow

1965 • Lee Marvin
Cat Ballou
Dirk Bogarde
Darling

1966 • Rod Steiger
The Pawnbroker
Richard Burton
Who's Afraid of Virginia Woolf?

1967 • Rod Steiger
In the Heat of the Night
Paul Scofield
A Man for All Seasons

1968 • Spencer Tracy
Guess Who's Coming to Dinner

1969 • Dustin Hoffman
Midnight Cowboy

1970 • Robert Redford
Butch Cassidy and the Sundance Kid

1971 • Peter Finch
Sunday, Bloody Sunday

1972 • Gene Hackman
The French Connection

1973 • Walter Matthau
Pete 'n' Tillie

1974 • Jack Nicholson
Chinatown
Jack Nicholson
The Last Detail

1975 • Al Pacino
Dog Day Afternoon

1976 • Jack Nicholson
One Flew Over the Cuckoo's Nest

1977 • Peter Finch
Network

1978 • Richard Dreyfuss
The Goodbye Girl

1979 • Jack Lemmon
The China Syndrome

1980 • John Hurt
The Elephant Man

1981 • Burt Lancaster
Atlantic City

1982 • Ben Kingsley
Gandhi

1983 • Michael Caine
Educating Rita
Dustin Hoffman
Tootsie

1984 • Haing S. Ngor
The Killing Fields

1985 • William Hurt
Kiss of the Spider Woman

1986 • Bob Hoskins
Mona Lisa

1987 • Sean Connery
The Name of the Rose

1988 • John Cleese
A Fish Called Wanda

1989 • Daniel Day-Lewis
My Left Foot

1990 • Philippe Noiret
Cinema Paradiso

1991 • Anthony Hopkins
The Silence of the Lambs

1992 • Robert Downey, Jr.
Chaplin

1993 • Anthony Hopkins
The Remains of the Day

1994 • Hugh Grant
Four Weddings and a Funeral

1995 • Nigel Hawthorne
The Madness of King George

ACTOR—SUPPORTING

1971 • Edward Fox
The Go-Between

1972 • Ben Johnson
The Last Picture Show

1973 • Arthur Lowe
O Lucky Man!

1974 • John Gielgud
Murder on the Orient Express

1975 • Fred Astaire
The Towering Inferno

1976 • Brad Dourif
One Flew Over the Cuckoo's Nest

1977 • Edward Fox
A Bridge Too Far

1978 • John Hurt
Midnight Express

1979 • Robert Duvall
Apocalypse Now

1981 • Ian Holm
Chariots of Fire

1982 • Jack Nicholson
Reds

1983 • Denholm Elliott
Trading Places

1984 • Denholm Elliott
A Private Function

1985 • Denholm Elliott
Defense of the Realm

1986 • Ray McAnally
The Mission

1987 • Daniel Auteuil
Jean de Florette

1988 • Michael Palin
A Fish Called Wanda

1989 • Ray McAnally
My Left Foot

1990 • Salvatore Cascio
Cinema Paradiso

1991 • Alan Rickman
Robin Hood: Prince of Thieves

1992 • Gene Hackman
Unforgiven

1993 • Ralph Fiennes
Schindler's List

1994 • Samuel L. Jackson
Pulp Fiction

1995 • Tim Roth
Rob Roy

ACTRESS

1952 • Vivien Leigh
A Streetcar Named Desire

1953 • Leslie Caron
Lili
Audrey Hepburn
Roman Holiday

1955 • Katie Johnson
The Ladykillers
Betsy Blair
Marty

1956 • Anna Magnani
The Rose Tattoo

1958 • Simone Signoret
Room at the Top

1959 • Shirley MacLaine
Ask Any Girl
Audrey Hepburn
The Nun's Story

1960 • Shirley MacLaine
The Apartment

1961 • Sophia Loren
Two Women

1962 • Anne Bancroft
The Miracle Worker

1963 • Patricia Neal
Hud
Rachel Roberts
This Sporting Life

1964 • Audrey Hepburn
Charade

1965 • Julie Christie
Darling
Patricia Neal
In Harm's Way

1966 • Elizabeth Taylor
Who's Afraid of Virginia Woolf?

1967 • Anouk Aimee
A Man and a Woman

1968 • Katharine Hepburn
Guess Who's Coming to Dinner

1969 • Maggie Smith
The Prime of Miss Jean Brodie

ACTRESS ▶*cont.*

1970 ● Katharine Ross
Butch Cassidy and the Sundance Kid

1971 ● Glenda Jackson
Sunday, Bloody Sunday

1972 ● Liza Minnelli
Cabaret

1973 ● Delphine Seyrig
The Discreet Charm of the Bourgeoisie

1974 ● Joanne Woodward
Summer Wishes, Winter Dreams

1975 ● Ellen Burstyn
Alice Doesn't Live Here Anymore

1976 ● Louise Fletcher
One Flew Over the Cuckoo's Nest

1977 ● Diane Keaton
Annie Hall

1978 ● Jane Fonda
Julia

1979 ● Jane Fonda
The China Syndrome

1980 ● Judy Davis
My Brilliant Career

1981 ● Meryl Streep
The French Lieutenant's Woman

1982 ● Katharine Hepburn
On Golden Pond

1983 ● Julie Walters
Educating Rita

1984 ● Maggie Smith
A Private Function

1985 ● Peggy Ashcroft
A Passage to India

1986 ● Maggie Smith
A Room with a View

1987 ● Anne Bancroft
84 Charing Cross Road

1988 ● Maggie Smith
The Lonely Passion of Judith Hearne

1989 ● Pauline Collins
Shirley Valentine

1990 ● Jessica Tandy
Driving Miss Daisy

1991 ● Jodie Foster
The Silence of the Lambs

1992 ● Emma Thompson
Howard's End

1993 ● Holly Hunter
The Piano

1994 ● Susan Sarandon
The Client

1995 ● Emma Thompson
Sense and Sensibility

ACTRESS—SUPPORTING

1961 ● Dora Bryan
A Taste of Honey

1969 ● Celia Johnson
The Prime of Miss Jean Brodie

1970 ● Susannah York
They Shoot Horses, Don't They?

1971 ● Margaret Leighton
The Go-Between

1972 ● Cloris Leachman
The Last Picture Show

1973 ● Valentina Cortese
Day for Night

1974 ● Ingrid Bergman
Murder on the Orient Express

1975 ● Diane Ladd
Alice Doesn't Live Here Anymore

1976 ● Jodie Foster
Taxi Driver

1977 ● Jenny Agutter
Equus

1978 ● Geraldine Page
Interiors
Vanessa Redgrave
Julia

1979 ● Rachel Roberts
Yanks

1982 ● Rohini Hattangady
Gandhi
Maureen Stapleton
Reds

1983 ● Jamie Lee Curtis
Trading Places

1984 ● Liz Smith
A Private Function

1985 ● Rosanna Arquette
Desperately Seeking Susan

1986 ● Judi Dench
A Room with a View

1987 ● Susan Wooldridge
Hope and Glory

1988 ● Judi Dench
A Handful of Dust

1989 ● Michelle Pfeiffer
Dangerous Liaisons

1990 ● Whoopi Goldberg
Ghost

1991 ● Kate Nelligan
Frankie and Johnny

1992 ● Miranda Richardson
Damage

1993 ● Miriam Margolyes
The Age of Innocence

1994 ● Kristin Scott Thomas
Four Weddings and a Funeral

1995 ● Kate Winslet
Sense and Sensibility

CINEMATOGRAPHY

1995
Braveheart

DIRECTOR

1955 ● Laurence Olivier
Richard III

1968 ● Mike Nichols
The Graduate

1969 ● John Schlesinger
Midnight Cowboy

1970 ● George Roy Hill
Butch Cassidy and the Sundance Kid

1971 ● John Schlesinger
Sunday, Bloody Sunday

1972 ● Bob Fosse
Cabaret

1973 ● Francois Truffaut
Day for Night

1974 ● Roman Polanski
Chinatown

1975 ● Stanley Kubrick
Barry Lyndon

1976 ● Milos Forman
One Flew Over the Cuckoo's Nest

1977 ● Woody Allen
Annie Hall

1978 ● Alan Parker
Midnight Express

1979 ● Francis Ford Coppola
Apocalypse Now

1980 ● Akira Kurosawa
Kagemusha

1981 ● Louis Malle
Atlantic City

1982 ● Richard Attenborough
Gandhi

1983 ● Bill Forsyth
Local Hero

1984 ● Wim Wenders
Paris, Texas

1986 ● Woody Allen
Hannah and Her Sisters

1987 ● Oliver Stone
Platoon

1988 ● Louis Malle
Au Revoir Les Enfants

1989 ● Kenneth Branagh
Henry V

1990 ● Martin Scorsese
Goodfellas

1991 ● Alan Parker
The Commitments

1992 ● Clint Eastwood
Unforgiven

1993 ● Steven Spielberg
Schindler's List

1994 ● Mike Newell
Four Weddings and a Funeral

1995 ● Michael Radford
The Postman

FILM

1947
The Best Years of Our Lives
Odd Man Out

1948
The Fallen Idol
Hamlet

1949
The Bicycle Thief
The Third Man

1950
All About Eve
The Blue Lamp

1951
La Ronde
The Lavender Hill Mob

1953
Forbidden Games
Genevieve

1954
Hobson's Choice
Wages of Fear

1955
Richard III

1956
Gervaise
Reach for the Sky

1957
The Bridge on the River Kwai

1958
Room at the Top

1959
Ben-Hur
Sapphire

1960
The Apartment

1961
Ballad of a Soldier
The Hustler
A Taste of Honey

1962
Lawrence of Arabia

1963
Tom Jones

1964
Dr. Strangelove, or: How I Learned to Stop Worrying and Love the Bomb

1965
The Ipcress File
My Fair Lady

1966
The Spy Who Came in from the Cold
Who's Afraid of Virginia Woolf?

1967
A Man for All Seasons

1968
The Graduate

1969
Midnight Cowboy

1970
Butch Cassidy and the Sundance Kid

1971
Sunday, Bloody Sunday

1972
Cabaret

1973
Day for Night

1975
Alice Doesn't Live Here Anymore

1976
One Flew Over the Cuckoo's Nest

1977
Annie Hall

1978
Julia

1979
Manhattan

1980
The Elephant Man

1981
Chariots of Fire

1982
Gandhi

1983
Educating Rita

1984
The Killing Fields

1985
The Purple Rose of Cairo

1986
A Room with a View

1987
Hope and Glory
Jean de Florette

1988
The Last Emperor

1989
Dead Poets Society

1990
Goodfellas

1991
The Commitments

1992
Unforgiven

1993
Schindler's List
Shadowlands

1994
Four Weddings and a Funeral

1995
Sense and Sensibility

MUSIC

1995
The Postman

WRITING

1955
The Ladykillers

1956
The Man Who Never Was

1957
The Bridge on the River Kwai

1959
I'm All Right Jack

1961
The Day the Earth Caught Fire

1962
Lawrence of Arabia
A Taste of Honey

1963
Tom Jones

1964
The Pumpkin Eater

1965
Darling
1966
Morgan!
1967
A Man for All Seasons
1968
The Graduate
1969
Midnight Cowboy
1970
Butch Cassidy and the Sundance Kid
1971
The Go-Between
1972
The Hospital
The Last Picture Show
1973
The Discreet Charm of the Bourgeoisie
1974
Chinatown
The Last Detail
1975
Alice Doesn't Live Here Anymore
1976
Bugsy Malone
1977
Annie Hall
1978
Julia
1979
Manhattan
1981
Gregory's Girl
1982
Missing
1983
Heat and Dust
King of Comedy
1984
Broadway Danny Rose
The Killing Fields
1985
Prizzi's Honor
The Purple Rose of Cairo
1986
Hannah and Her Sisters
Out of Africa
1987
Jean de Florette
Wish You Were Here
1988
The Unbearable Lightness of Being
A World Apart
1989
Dangerous Liaisons
When Harry Met Sally...
1990
Being There
Cinema Paradiso
Goodfellas
1991
The Commitments
Truly, Madly, Deeply
1992
Husbands and Wives
The Player
1993
Groundhog Day
Schindler's List
1994
Pulp Fiction
Quiz Show
1995
Trainspotting
The Usual Suspects

FILM—FOREIGN LANGUAGE

1982
Christ Stopped at Eboli
1983
Danton
1984
Carmen
1985
Colonel Redl
1986
Ran
1987
The Sacrifice
1988
Babette's Feast
1989
Life and Nothing But
1990
Cinema Paradiso
1991
The Nasty Girl
1992
Raise the Red Lantern
1993
Farewell My Concubine
1994
To Live
1995
The Postman

CANADIAN GENIE

ACTOR

1980 ● Christopher Plummer
Murder by Decree
1982 ● Nick Mancuso
Ticket to Heaven
1983 ● Donald Sutherland
Threshold
1984 ● Eric Fryer
The Terry Fox Story
1986 ● John Wildman
My American Cousin
1987 ● Gordon Pinsent
John and the Missus
1988 ● Roger Le Bel
Night Zoo
1989 ● Jeremy Irons
Dead Ringers
1990 ● Remy Girard
Jesus of Montreal
1993 ● Tom McCamus
A Man in Uniform
1994 ● Maury Chaykin
Whale Music
1995 ● David La Haye
L'Enfant d'Eau

ACTOR—SUPPORTING

1981 ● German Houde
Les Bons Debarras
1982 ● Saul Rubinek
Ticket to Heaven
1983 ● R.H. Thomson
If You Could See What I Hear
1984 ● Michael Zelniker
The Terry Fox Story
1985 ● Alan Scarfe
The Bay Boy
1986 ● Alan Arkin
Joshua Then and Now
1987 ● Gabriel Arcand
The Decline of the American Empire
1988 ● German Houde
Night Zoo
1990 ● Remy Girard
Jesus of Montreal
1993 ● Kevin Tighe
A Man in Uniform
1994 ● Don McKellar
Exotica
1995 ● Kenneth Welsh
Margaret's Museum

ACTRESS

1980 ● Kate Lynch
Meatballs
1981 ● Marie Tifo
Les Bons Debarras
1982 ● Margot Kidder
Heartaches
1983 ● Rae Dawn Chong
Quest for Fire
1986 ● Margaret Langrick
My American Cousin
1987 ● Martha Henry
Dancing in the Dark
1988 ● Sheila McCarthy
I've Heard the Mermaids Singing
1990 ● Rebecca Jenkins
Bye Bye Blues
1993 ● Sheila McCarthy
The Lotus Eaters
1994 ● Sandra Oh
Double Happiness
1995 ● Helena Bonham Carter
Margaret's Museum

ACTRESS—SUPPORTING

1980 ● Genevieve Bujold
Murder by Decree
1981 ● Kate Reid
Atlantic City
1983 ● Jackie Burroughs
The Grey Fox
1986 ● Linda Sorensen
Joshua Then and Now
1987 ● Louise Portal
The Decline of the American Empire
1988 ● Paule Baillargeon
I've Heard the Mermaids Singing
1989 ● Colleen Dewhurst
Obsessed
1990 ● Robyn Stevan
Bye Bye Blues
1992 ● Monique Mercure
Naked Lunch
1995 ● Kate Nelligan
Margaret's Museum

ART DIRECTION

1992
Naked Lunch
1993
Shadow of the Wolf
1994
Exotica
1995
The Confessional

CINEMATOGRAPHY

1992
Naked Lunch
1993
32 Short Films about Glenn Gould
1994
Exotica
1995
Magic in the Water

COSTUME DESIGN

1992
Leolo
1993
Shadow of the Wolf
1994
Exotica
1995
Margaret's Museum

DIRECTOR

1980 ● Bob (Benjamin) Clark
Murder by Decree
1981 ● Francis Mankiewicz
Les Bons Debarras
1983 ● Phillip Borsos
The Grey Fox
1984 ● Bob (Benjamin) Clark
A Christmas Story
David Cronenberg
Videodrome
1986 ● Sandy Wilson
My American Cousin
1987 ● Denys Arcand
The Decline of the American Empire
1988 ● Jean-Claude Lauzon
Night Zoo
1989 ● David Cronenberg
Dead Ringers
1990 ● Denys Arcand
Jesus of Montreal
1992 ● David Cronenberg
Naked Lunch
1993 ● Francois Girard
32 Short Films about Glenn Gould
1994 ● Atom Egoyan
Exotica
1995 ● Robert Lepage
The Confessional

FILM

1980
The Changeling
1981
Les Bons Debarras
1982
Ticket to Heaven
1983
The Grey Fox
1984
The Terry Fox Story
1985
The Bay Boy
1986
My American Cousin
1987
The Decline of the American Empire
1988
Night Zoo
1989
Dead Ringers
1990
Jesus of Montreal
1992
Naked Lunch
1993
32 Short Films about Glenn Gould
1994
Exotica
1995
The Confessional

FILM EDITING

1992
Leolo
1993
32 Short Films about Glenn Gould
1994
Double Happiness
1995
Dance Me Outside

MUSIC

1994
Exotica

1995
Margaret's Museum

SONG

1994 ● "Claire"
Whale Music

SOUND

1992
Naked Lunch

1993
Le Sexe des Etoiles
The Lotus Eaters

1994
Whale Music

1995
Magic in the Water

WRITING

1992
Leolo
Naked Lunch

1993
The Lotus Eaters

1994
Exotica
Love and Human Remains

1995
Margaret's Museum

CANNES

ACTOR

1946 ● Ray Milland
The Lost Weekend

1949 ● Edward G. Robinson
House of Strangers

1951 ● Michael Redgrave
The Browning Version

1952 ● Marlon Brando
Viva Zapata!

1953 ● Charles Vanel
Wages of Fear

1955 ● Spencer Tracy
Bad Day at Black Rock

1958 ● Paul Newman
The Long, Hot Summer

1961 ● Anthony Perkins
Goodbye Again

1962 ● Murray Melvin
A Taste of Honey

1963 ● Richard Harris
This Sporting Life

1964 ● Saro Urzi
Seduced and Abandoned

1965 ● Terence Stamp
The Collector

1966 ● Per Oscarsson
Hunger

1969 ● Jean-Louis Trintignant
Z

1971 ● Riccardo Cucciolla
Sacco & Vanzetti

1973 ● Giancarlo Giannini
Love and Anarchy

1974 ● Jack Nicholson
The Last Detail

1977 ● Fernando Rey
Elisa, Vida Mia

1978 ● Jon Voight
Coming Home

1979 ● Jack Lemmon
The China Syndrome

1981 ● Ugo Tognazzi
The Tragedy of a Ridiculous Man

1982 ● Jack Lemmon
Missing

1984 ● Alfredo Landa
The Holy Innocents
Francesco Rabal
The Holy Innocents

1985 ● William Hurt
Kiss of the Spider Woman

1986 ● Michel Blanc
Menage
Bob Hoskins
Mona Lisa

1987 ● Marcello Mastroianni
Dark Eyes

1988 ● Forest Whitaker
Bird

1989 ● James Spader
sex, lies and videotape

1990 ● Gerard Depardieu
Cyrano de Bergerac

1991 ● John Turturro
Barton Fink

1992 ● Tim Robbins
The Player

1993 ● David Thewlis
Naked

1994 ● Ge You
To Live

1995 ● Jonathan Pryce
Carrington

1996 ● Daniel Auteuil
The Eighth Day
Pascal Duquenne
The Eighth Day

ACTRESS

1946 ● Michele Morgan
La Symphonie Pastorale

1951 ● Bette Davis
All About Eve

1952 ● Lee Grant
Detective Story

1953 ● Shirley Booth
Come Back, Little Sheba

1956 ● Susan Hayward
I'll Cry Tomorrow

1957 ● Giulietta Masina
Nights of Cabiria

1958 ● Eva Dahlbeck
Brink of Life
Bibi Andersson
Brink of Life
Ingrid Thulin
Brink of Life

1959 ● Simone Signoret
Room at the Top

1960 ● Melina Mercouri
Never on Sunday

1961 ● Sophia Loren
Two Women

1962 ● Katharine Hepburn
Long Day's Journey into Night
Rita Tushingham
A Taste of Honey

1965 ● Samantha Eggar
The Collector

1966 ● Vanessa Redgrave
Morgan!

1967 ● Pia Degermark
Elvira Madigan

1969 ● Vanessa Redgrave
Isadora

1971 ● Kitty Winn
Panic in Needle Park

1973 ● Joanne Woodward
The Effect of Gamma Rays on Man-in-the-Moon Marigolds

1974 ● Marie-Jose Nat
Les Violons du Bal

1975 ● Valerie Perrine
Lenny

1976 ● Dominique Sanda
The Inheritance

1978 ● Jill Clayburgh
An Unmarried Woman
Isabelle Huppert
Violette

1979 ● Sally Field
Norma Rae

1981 ● Isabelle Adjani
Quartet

1982 ● Jadwiga Jankowska Cieslak
Another Way

1984 ● Helen Mirren
Cal

1985 ● Cher
Mask
Norma Aleandro
The Official Story

1986 ● Barbara Sukowa
Rosa Luxemburg

1987 ● Barbara Hershey
Shy People

1988 ● Barbara Hershey
A World Apart
Jodhi May
A World Apart
Linda Mvusi
A World Apart

1989 ● Meryl Streep
A Cry in the Dark

1991 ● Irene Jacob
The Double Life of Veronique

1992 ● Pernilla August
The Best Intentions

1993 ● Holly Hunter
The Piano

1994 ● Virna Lisi
Queen Margot

1995 ● Helen Mirren
The Madness of King George

1996 ● Brenda Blethyn
Secrets and Lies

DIRECTOR

1951 ● Luis Bunuel
Los Olvidados

1955 ● Jules Dassin
Rififi

1957 ● Robert Bresson
A Man Escaped

1958 ● Ingmar Bergman
Brink of Life

1959 ● Francois Truffaut
The 400 Blows

1969 ● Vojtech Jasny
All My Good Countrymen

1976 ● Ettore Scola
Down & Dirty

1978 ● Nagisa Oshima
The Empire of Passion

1979 ● Terence Malick
Days of Heaven

1982 ● Werner Herzog
Fitzcarraldo

1983 ● Robert Bresson
L'Argent

1984 ● Bertrand Tavernier
A Sunday in the Country

1985 ● Andre Techine
Rendez-vous

1986 ● Martin Scorsese
After Hours

1989 ● Emir Kusturica
Time of the Gypsies

1990 ● Pavel Lounguine
Taxi Blues

1991 ● Joel Coen
Barton Fink

1992 ● Robert Altman
The Player

1993 ● Mike Leigh
Naked

1994 ● Nanni Moretti
Caro Diario

1995 ● Mathieu Kassovitz
Hate

1996 ● Joel Coen
Fargo

FILM

1946
The Lost Weekend

1949
The Third Man

1951
Los Olvidados
Miracle in Milan
Miss Julie

1952
Othello
White Mane

1953
Wages of Fear

1954
Gate of Hell

1957
Friendly Persuasion

1958
The Cranes are Flying

1959
Black Orpheus

1960
La Dolce Vita

1961
Viridiana

1964
Umbrellas of Cherbourg

1966
A Man and a Woman

1967
Blow-Up
Dutchman

1969
If...

1970
*M*A*S*H*

1971
The Go-Between

1973
Scarecrow

1974
The Conversation

1976
Taxi Driver

1977
Padre Padrone

1978
The Tree of Wooden Clogs

1979
Apocalypse Now
The Tin Drum

1980
All That Jazz
Kagemusha

1981
Man of Iron

1982
Missing
Yol

1983
The Ballad of Narayama

1984
Paris, Texas

1985
Dance with a Stranger
When Father was Away on Business

1986
The Mission

1987
Under Satan's Sun

1988
Pelle the Conqueror

1989
sex, lies and videotape

1990
Overseas: Three Women with Man Trouble
Wild at Heart

1991
Barton Fink

1992
The Best Intentions
My New Gun

1993
Farewell My Concubine
The Piano

1994
Pulp Fiction

1995
Underground

1996
Secrets and Lies

GRAND JURY PRIZE

1951
All About Eve

1957
Kanal
The Seventh Seal

1958
Mon Oncle

1961
Mother Joan of the Angels

1964
Woman in the Dunes

1965
Kwaidan

1967
Accident
Alfie

1971
Johnny Got His Gun

1972
Solaris

1976
Cria

1978
The Shout

1979
Siberiade

1980
Mon Oncle D'Amerique

1982
The Night of the Shooting Stars

1983
Monty Python's The Meaning of Life

1985
Birdy

1987
Repentance

1988
A World Apart

1989
Cinema Paradiso
Too Beautiful for You

1990
Tilai

1991
La Belle Noiseuse

1992
The Stolen Children

1993
Faraway, So Close!

1994
Burnt by the Sun
To Live

1995
Ulysses' Gaze

1996
Breaking the Waves

SPECIAL JURY PRIZE

1960
L'Avventura

1969
Z

1970
The Strawberry Statement

1972
Slaughterhouse Five

1985
Colonel Redl

1986
Therese

1989
Jesus of Montreal

1990
Hidden Agenda

1993
Raining Stones

1994
Queen Margot

1995
Carrington

1996
Crash

CESAR

ACTOR

1978 • Jean Rochefort
Le Crabe Tambour

1979 • Michel Serrault
La Cage aux Folles

1981 • Gerard Depardieu
The Last Metro

1983 • Philippe Leotard
La Balance

1984 • Coluche
Tchao Pantin

1986 • Christopher Lambert
Subway

1987 • Daniel Auteuil
Jean de Florette

1988 • Richard Bohringer
Le Grand Chemin

1990 • Philippe Noiret
Life and Nothing But

1991 • Gerard Depardieu
Cyrano de Bergerac

1992 • Jacques Dutronc
Van Gogh

1994 • Pierre Arditti
Smoking/No Smoking

1995 • Gerard Lanvin
The Favorite Son

1996 • Michel Serrault
Nelly et Monsieur Arnaud

ACTOR—SUPPORTING

1977 • Claude Brasseur
Pardon Mon Affaire

1978 • Jacques Dufilho
Le Crabe Tambour

1979 • Jacques Villeret
Robert et Robert

1980 • Jean Bouise
Hothead

1984 • Richard Anconina
Tchao Pantin

1986 • Michel Boujenah
Three Men and a Cradle

1989 • Patrick Chesnais
La Lectrice

1991 • Jacques Weber
Cyrano de Bergerac

1993 • Andre Dussollier
Un Coeur en Hiver

1995 • Jean-Hugues Anglade
Queen Margot

ACTRESS

1978 • Simone Signoret
Madame Rosa

1981 • Catherine Deneuve
The Last Metro

1982 • Isabelle Adjani
Possession

1983 • Nathalie Baye
La Balance

1984 • Isabelle Adjani
One Deadly Summer

1985 • Sabine Azema
A Sunday in the Country

1986 • Sandrine Bonnaire
Vagabond

1988 • Anemone
Le Grand Chemin

1989 • Isabelle Adjani
Camille Claudel

1990 • Carole Bouquet
Too Beautiful for You

1991 • Anne Parillaud
La Femme Nikita

1993 • Catherine Deneuve
Indochine

1994 • Juliette Binoche
Trois Couleurs: Bleu

1995 • Isabelle Adjani
Queen Margot

1996 • Isabelle Huppert
La Ceremonie

ACTRESS—SUPPORTING

1976 • Marie-France Pisier
Cousin, Cousine

1979 • Stephane Audran
Violette

1984 • Suzanne Flon
One Deadly Summer

1987 • Emmanuelle Beart
Jean de Florette

1989 • Helene Vincent
Life Is a Long Quiet River

1991 • Dominique Blanc
May Fools

1992 • Anne Brochet
Tous les Matins du Monde

1993 • Dominique Blanc
Indochine

1995 • Virna Lisi
Queen Margot

ART DIRECTION

1978
Providence

1981
The Last Metro

1984
Moon in the Gutter

1985
Swann in Love

1986
Subway

1987
Pirates

1988
Au Revoir Les Enfants

1989
Camille Claudel

1990
Valmont

1991
Cyrano de Bergerac

1992
Delicatessen

1993
Indochine

1994
Smoking/No Smoking

1995
Farinelli

CINEMATOGRAPHY

1978
Le Crabe Tambour

1980
Tess

1981
The Last Metro

1982
Diva

1983
La Truite

1984
Tchao Pantin

1985
A Sunday in the Country

1987
Therese

1988
Au Revoir Les Enfants

1989
Camille Claudel

1991
Cyrano de Bergerac

1992
Tous les Matins du Monde

1993
Indochine

1994
Germinal

1995
Queen Margot

COSTUME DESIGN

1985
Swann in Love

1987
Pirates

1988
Beatrice

1989
Camille Claudel

1990
Valmont

1991
Cyrano de Bergerac

1994
Germinal

1995
Queen Margot

DIRECTOR

1978 • Alain Resnais
Providence

1980 • Roman Polanski
Tess

1981 • Francois Truffaut
The Last Metro

1983 • Andrzej Wajda
Danton

1984 • Ettore Scola
Le Bal

1986 • Michel DeVille
Peril

1987 • Alain Cavalier
Therese

1988 • Louis Malle
Au Revoir Les Enfants

1990 • Bertrand Blier
Too Beautiful for You

1991 • Jean-Paul Rappeneau
Cyrano de Bergerac

1992 • Alain Corneau
Tous les Matins du Monde

1993 • Claude Sautet
Un Coeur en Hiver

1994 • Alain Resnais
Smoking/No Smoking

1995 • Andre Techine
Wild Reeds

DIRECTOR ▶cont.

1996 • Claude Sautet
Nelly et Monsieur Arnaud

FILM

1978
Providence

1980
Tess

1981
The Last Metro

1983
La Balance

1984
Le Bal

1986
Three Men and a Cradle

1987
Therese

1988
Au Revoir Les Enfants

1989
Camille Claudel

1990
Too Beautiful for You

1991
Cyrano de Bergerac

1992
Tous les Matins du Monde

1993
Les Nuits Fauves

1994
Smoking/No Smoking

1995
Wild Reeds

1996
Hate

FILM EDITING

1994
Trois Couleurs: Bleu

1996
Hate

MUSIC

1977
The Judge and the Assassin

1978
Providence

1979
Get Out Your Handkerchiefs

1980
Love on the Run

1981
The Last Metro

1982
Diva

1983
The Return of Martin Guerre

1984
Le Bal

1988
Field of Honor

1989
The Big Blue

1990
Life and Nothing But

1991
Cyrano de Bergerac

1992
Tous les Matins du Monde

1993
The Lover

1994
Trois Couleurs: Rouge

SOUND

1977
Mado

1978
Providence

1979
L'Etat Sauvage

1981
The Last Metro

1982
Diva

1983
La Passante

1984
Tchao Pantin

1986
Subway

1988
Au Revoir Les Enfants

1989
The Big Blue

1990
Monsieur Hire

1991
Cyrano de Bergerac

1993
Indochine

1994
Trois Couleurs: Bleu

1995
Farinelli

WRITING

1977
The Judge and the Assassin

1978
Providence

1980
Buffet Froid

1981
The Last Metro

1983
The Return of Martin Guerre

1984
L'Homme Blesse
One Deadly Summer

1985
A Sunday in the Country

1986
Three Men and a Cradle

1987
Therese

1988
Au Revoir Les Enfants

1989
Life Is a Long Quiet River

1990
Too Beautiful for You

1991
La Discrete

1992
Delicatessen

1994
Smoking/No Smoking

1995
Wild Reeds

FILM—FOREIGN LANGUAGE

1980
Manhattan

1981
Kagemusha

1982
The Elephant Man

1983
Victor/Victoria

1984
Fanny and Alexander

1985
Amadeus

1986
The Purple Rose of Cairo

1987
The Name of the Rose

1988
The Last Emperor

1989
Bagdad Cafe

1990
Dangerous Liaisons

1991
Dead Poets Society
Toto le Heros

1993
High Heels

1996
Land and Freedom

DIRECTORS GUILD OF AMERICA

DIRECTOR

1948 • Joseph L. Mankiewicz
A Letter to Three Wives

1949 • Carol Reed
The Third Man

1950 • Joseph L. Mankiewicz
All About Eve

1951 • George Stevens
A Place in the Sun

1952 • John Ford
The Quiet Man

1953 • Fred Zinnemann
From Here to Eternity

1954 • Elia Kazan
On the Waterfront
Billy Wilder
Sabrina

1955 • Delbert Mann
Marty

1956 • George Stevens
Giant

1957 • David Lean
The Bridge on the River Kwai

1958 • Vincente Minnelli
Gigi

1959 • William Wyler
Ben-Hur

1960 • Billy Wilder
The Apartment

1961 • Robert Wise
West Side Story
Jerome Robbins
West Side Story

1962 • David Lean
Lawrence of Arabia

1963 • Tony Richardson
Tom Jones

1964 • George Cukor
My Fair Lady

1965 • Robert Wise
The Sound of Music

1966 • Fred Zinnemann
A Man for All Seasons

1967 • Mike Nichols
The Graduate

1968 • Anthony Harvey
The Lion in Winter

1969 • John Schlesinger
Midnight Cowboy

1970 • Charles Jarrott
Anne of the Thousand Days
Franklin J. Schaffner
Patton

1971 • William Friedkin
The French Connection

1972 • Francis Ford Coppola
The Godfather

1973 • George Roy Hill
The Sting

1974 • Francis Ford Coppola
The Godfather, Part 2

1975 • Milos Forman
One Flew Over the Cuckoo's Nest

1976 • John G. Avildsen
Rocky

1977 • Woody Allen
Annie Hall

1978 • Michael Cimino
The Deer Hunter

1979 • Robert Benton
Kramer vs. Kramer

1980 • Robert Redford
Ordinary People

1981 • Warren Beatty
Reds

1982 • Richard Attenborough
Gandhi

1983 • James L. Brooks
Terms of Endearment

1984 • Milos Forman
Amadeus

1985 • Steven Spielberg
The Color Purple

1986 • Oliver Stone
Platoon

1987 • Bernardo Bertolucci
The Last Emperor

1988 • Barry Levinson
Rain Man

1989 • Oliver Stone
Born on the Fourth of July

1990 • Kevin Costner
Dances with Wolves

1991 • Jonathan Demme
The Silence of the Lambs

1992 • Clint Eastwood
Unforgiven

1993 • Steven Spielberg
Schindler's List

1994 • Robert Zemeckis
Forrest Gump

1995 • Ron Howard
Apollo 13

GOLDEN GLOBE AWARDS

ACTOR—DRAMA

1944 • Paul Lukas
Watch on the Rhine

1945 • Alexander Knox
Wilson

1946 • Ray Milland
The Lost Weekend

1947 • Gregory Peck
The Yearling

1948 • Ronald Colman
A Double Life

1949 • Laurence Olivier
Hamlet

1950 • Broderick Crawford
All the King's Men

1951 • Jose Ferrer
Cyrano de Bergerac

1953 • Gary Cooper
High Noon

1955 • Marlon Brando
On the Waterfront

1956 • Ernest Borgnine
Marty

1957 • Kirk Douglas
Lust for Life

1958 • Alec Guinness
The Bridge on the River Kwai

1959 • David Niven
Separate Tables

1960 • Anthony (Tony) Franciosa
Career

1961 ● Burt Lancaster
Elmer Gantry

1962 ● Maximilian Schell
Judgment at Nuremberg

1963 ● Gregory Peck
To Kill a Mockingbird

1964 ● Sidney Poitier
Lilies of the Field

1965 ● Peter O'Toole
Becket

1966 ● Omar Sharif
Doctor Zhivago

1967 ● Paul Scofield
A Man for All Seasons

1968 ● Rod Steiger
In the Heat of the Night

1969 ● Peter O'Toole
The Lion in Winter

1970 ● John Wayne
True Grit

1971 ● George C. Scott
Patton

1972 ● Gene Hackman
The French Connection

1973 ● Marlon Brando
The Godfather

1974 ● Al Pacino
Serpico

1975 ● Jack Nicholson
Chinatown

1976 ● Jack Nicholson
One Flew Over the Cuckoo's Nest

1977 ● Peter Finch
Network

1978 ● Richard Burton
Equus

1979 ● Jon Voight
Coming Home

1980 ● Dustin Hoffman
Kramer vs. Kramer

1981 ● Robert De Niro
Raging Bull

1982 ● Henry Fonda
On Golden Pond

1983 ● Ben Kingsley
Gandhi
Robert Duvall
Tender Mercies

1984 ● Tom Courtenay
The Dresser

1985 ● F. Murray Abraham
Amadeus

1986 ● Jon Voight
Runaway Train

1987 ● Bob Hoskins
Mona Lisa

1988 ● Michael Douglas
Wall Street

1989 ● Dustin Hoffman
Rain Man

1990 ● Tom Cruise
Born on the Fourth of July

1991 ● Jeremy Irons
Reversal of Fortune

1992 ● Nick Nolte
The Prince of Tides

1993 ● Al Pacino
Scent of a Woman

1994 ● Tom Hanks
Philadelphia

1995 ● Tom Hanks
Forrest Gump

1996 ● Nicolas Cage
Leaving Las Vegas

ACTOR—MUSICAL/COMEDY

1951 ● Fred Astaire
Three Little Words

1953 ● Donald O'Connor
Singin' in the Rain

1954 ● David Niven
The Moon Is Blue

1955 ● James Mason
A Star is Born

1956 ● Tom Ewell
The Seven Year Itch

1957 ● Cantinflas
Around the World in 80 Days

1958 ● Frank Sinatra
Pal Joey

1960 ● Jack Lemmon
Some Like It Hot

1961 ● Jack Lemmon
The Apartment

1962 ● Glenn Ford
Pocketful of Miracles

1963 ● Marcello Mastroianni
Divorce—Italian Style

1965 ● Rex Harrison
My Fair Lady

1966 ● Lee Marvin
Cat Ballou

1967 ● Alan Arkin
The Russians are Coming, the Russians are Coming

1968 ● Richard Harris
Camelot

1969 ● Ron Moody
Oliver!

1970 ● Peter O'Toole
Goodbye, Mr. Chips

1971 ● Albert Finney
Scrooge

1972 ● Chaim Topol
Fiddler on the Roof

1974 ● George Segal
A Touch of Class

1975 ● Art Carney
Harry and Tonto

1976 ● Walter Matthau
The Sunshine Boys

1977 ● Kris Kristofferson
A Star is Born

1978 ● Richard Dreyfuss
The Goodbye Girl

1979 ● Warren Beatty
Heaven Can Wait

1980 ● Peter Sellers
Being There

1981 ● Ray Sharkey
Idolmaker

1982 ● Dudley Moore
Arthur

1983 ● Dustin Hoffman
Tootsie

1984 ● Michael Caine
Educating Rita

1985 ● Dudley Moore
Micki & Maude

1986 ● Jack Nicholson
Prizzi's Honor

1987 ● Paul Hogan
Crocodile Dundee

1988 ● Robin Williams
Good Morning, Vietnam

1989 ● Tom Hanks
Big

1990 ● Morgan Freeman
Driving Miss Daisy

1991 ● Gerard Depardieu
Green Card

1992 ● Robin Williams
The Fisher King

1993 ● Tim Robbins
The Player

1994 ● Robin Williams
Mrs. Doubtfire

1995 ● Hugh Grant
Four Weddings and a Funeral

1996 ● John Travolta
Get Shorty

ACTOR—SUPPORTING

1945 ● Barry Fitzgerald
Going My Way

1947 ● Clifton Webb
The Razor's Edge

1948 ● Edmund Gwenn
Miracle on 34th Street

1949 ● Walter Huston
Treasure of the Sierra Madre

1950 ● James Whitmore
Battleground

1952 ● Peter Ustinov
Quo Vadis

1954 ● Frank Sinatra
From Here to Eternity

1955 ● Edmond O'Brien
The Barefoot Contessa

1957 ● Earl Holliman
The Rainmaker

1958 ● Red Buttons
Sayonara

1959 ● Burl Ives
The Big Country

1960 ● Stephen Boyd
Ben-Hur

1961 ● Sal Mineo
Exodus

1962 ● George Chakiris
West Side Story

1963 ● Omar Sharif
Lawrence of Arabia

1964 ● John Huston
The Cardinal

1965 ● Edmond O'Brien
Seven Days in May

1966 ● Oskar Werner
The Spy Who Came in from the Cold

1967 ● Richard Attenborough
The Sand Pebbles

1968 ● David Attenborough
Doctor Dolittle

1970 ● Gig Young
They Shoot Horses, Don't They?

1971 ● John Mills
Ryan's Daughter

1972 ● Ben Johnson
The Last Picture Show

1973 ● Joel Grey
Cabaret

1974 ● John Houseman
The Paper Chase

1975 ● Fred Astaire
The Towering Inferno

1976 ● Richard Benjamin
The Sunshine Boys

1977 ● Laurence Olivier
Marathon Man

1978 ● Peter Firth
Equus

1979 ● John Hurt
Midnight Express

1980 ● Robert Duvall
Apocalypse Now
Melvyn Douglas
Being There

1981 ● Timothy Hutton
Ordinary People

1982 ● John Gielgud
Arthur

1983 ● Louis Gossett, Jr.
An Officer and a Gentleman

1984 ● Jack Nicholson
Terms of Endearment

1985 ● Haing S. Ngor
The Killing Fields

1986 ● Klaus Maria Brandauer
Out of Africa

1987 ● Tom Berenger
Platoon

1988 ● Sean Connery
The Untouchables

1989 ● Martin Landau
Tucker: The Man and His Dream

1990 ● Denzel Washington
Glory

1991 ● Bruce Davison
Longtime Companion

1992 ● Jack Palance
City Slickers

1993 ● Gene Hackman
Unforgiven

1994 ● Tommy Lee Jones
The Fugitive

1995 ● Martin Landau
Ed Wood

1996 ● Brad Pitt
12 Monkeys

ACTRESS—DRAMA

1944 ● Jennifer Jones
The Song of Bernadette

1945 ● Ingrid Bergman
Gaslight

1946 ● Ingrid Bergman
The Bells of St. Mary's

1947 ● Rosalind Russell
Sister Kenny

1949 ● Jane Wyman
Johnny Belinda

1950 ● Olivia de Havilland
The Heiress

1951 ● Gloria Swanson
Sunset Boulevard

1953 ● Shirley Booth
Come Back, Little Sheba

1954 ● Audrey Hepburn
Roman Holiday

1955 ● Grace Kelly
Country Girl

1956 ● Anna Magnani
The Rose Tattoo

1957 ● Ingrid Bergman
Anastasia

1958 ● Joanne Woodward
The Three Faces of Eve

1959 ● Susan Hayward
I Want to Live!

1960 ● Elizabeth Taylor
Suddenly, Last Summer

1961 ● Greer Garson
Sunrise at Campobello

1962 ● Geraldine Page
Summer and Smoke

1963 ● Geraldine Page
Sweet Bird of Youth

1966 ● Samantha Eggar
The Collector

1967 ● Anouk Aimee
A Man and a Woman

1969 ● Joanne Woodward
Rachel, Rachel

1970 ● Genevieve Bujold
Anne of the Thousand Days

1971 ● Ali MacGraw
Love Story

1972 ● Jane Fonda
Klute

1974 ● Marsha Mason
Cinderella Liberty

1975 ● Gena Rowlands
A Woman Under the Influence

1976 ● Louise Fletcher
One Flew Over the Cuckoo's Nest

1977 ● Faye Dunaway
Network

1978 ● Jane Fonda
Julia

1979 ● Jane Fonda
Coming Home

1980 ● Sally Field
Norma Rae

1981 ● Mary Tyler Moore
Ordinary People

ACTRESS—DRAMA ▶cont.

1982 • Meryl Streep
The French Lieutenant's Woman

1983 • Meryl Streep
Sophie's Choice

1984 • Shirley MacLaine
Terms of Endearment

1985 • Sally Field
Places in the Heart

1986 • Whoopi Goldberg
The Color Purple

1987 • Marlee Matlin
Children of a Lesser God

1988 • Sally Kirkland
Anna
Sigourney Weaver
Gorillas in the Mist

1989 • Jodie Foster
The Accused
Shirley MacLaine
Madame Sousatzka

1990 • Michelle Pfeiffer
The Fabulous Baker Boys

1991 • Kathy Bates
Misery

1992 • Jodie Foster
The Silence of the Lambs

1993 • Emma Thompson
Howard's End

1994 • Debra Winger
A Dangerous Woman
Holly Hunter
The Piano

1995 • Jessica Lange
Blue Sky

1996 • Sharon Stone
Casino

ACTRESS—MUSICAL/COMEDY

1951 • Judy Holliday
Born Yesterday

1955 • Judy Garland
A Star is Born

1956 • Jean Simmons
Guys and Dolls

1957 • Deborah Kerr
The King and I

1958 • Kay Kendall
Les Girls

1959 • Rosalind Russell
Auntie Mame

1960 • Marilyn Monroe
Some Like It Hot

1961 • Shirley MacLaine
The Apartment

1963 • Rosalind Russell
Gypsy

1964 • Shirley MacLaine
Irma La Douce

1965 • Julie Andrews
Mary Poppins

1966 • Julie Andrews
The Sound of Music

1967 • Lynn Redgrave
Georgy Girl

1968 • Anne Bancroft
The Graduate

1969 • Barbra Streisand
Funny Girl

1971 • Carrie Snodgress
Diary of a Mad Housewife

1972 • Twiggy
The Boy Friend

1973 • Liza Minnelli
Cabaret

1974 • Glenda Jackson
A Touch of Class

1975 • Raquel Welch
The Three Musketeers

1976 • Ann-Margret
Tommy

1977 • Barbra Streisand
A Star is Born

1978 • Diane Keaton
Annie Hall
Marsha Mason
The Goodbye Girl

1979 • Maggie Smith
California Suite
Ellen Burstyn
Same Time, Next Year

1980 • Bette Midler
The Rose

1981 • Sissy Spacek
Coal Miner's Daughter

1982 • Bernadette Peters
Pennies From Heaven

1983 • Julie Andrews
Victor/Victoria

1984 • Julie Walters
Educating Rita

1985 • Kathleen Turner
Romancing the Stone

1986 • Kathleen Turner
Prizzi's Honor

1987 • Sissy Spacek
Crimes of the Heart

1988 • Cher
Moonstruck

1989 • Melanie Griffith
Working Girl

1990 • Jessica Tandy
Driving Miss Daisy

1991 • Julia Roberts
Pretty Woman

1992 • Bette Midler
For the Boys

1993 • Miranda Richardson
Enchanted April

1994 • Angela Bassett
What's Love Got to Do with It?

1995 • Jamie Lee Curtis
True Lies

1996 • Nicole Kidman
To Die For

ACTRESS—SUPPORTING

1945 • Agnes Moorehead
Mrs. Parkington

1946 • Angela Lansbury
Picture of Dorian Gray

1947 • Anne Baxter
The Razor's Edge

1948 • Celeste Holm
Gentleman's Agreement

1949 • Ellen Corby
I Remember Mama

1950 • Mercedes McCambridge
All the King's Men

1951 • Josephine Hull
Harvey

1952 • Kim Hunter
A Streetcar Named Desire

1953 • Katy Jurado
High Noon

1954 • Grace Kelly
Mogambo

1956 • Marisa Pavan
The Rose Tattoo

1957 • Eileen Heckart
The Bad Seed

1958 • Elsa Lanchester
Witness for the Prosecution

1959 • Hermione Gingold
Gigi

1960 • Susan Kohner
Imitation of Life

1961 • Janet Leigh
Psycho

1962 • Rita Moreno
West Side Story

1963 • Angela Lansbury
The Manchurian Candidate

1964 • Margaret Rutherford
The V.I.P.'s

1965 • Agnes Moorehead
Hush, Hush, Sweet Charlotte

1966 • Ruth Gordon
Inside Daisy Clover

1967 • Jocelyn Lagarde
Hawaii

1968 • Carol Channing
Thoroughly Modern Millie

1969 • Ruth Gordon
Rosemary's Baby

1970 • Goldie Hawn
Cactus Flower

1971 • Maureen Stapleton
Airport
Karen Black
Five Easy Pieces

1972 • Ann-Margret
Carnal Knowledge

1973 • Shelley Winters
The Poseidon Adventure

1974 • Linda Blair
The Exorcist

1975 • Karen Black
The Great Gatsby

1976 • Brenda Vaccaro
Once is Not Enough

1977 • Katharine Ross
Voyage of the Damned

1978 • Vanessa Redgrave
Julia

1979 • Dyan Cannon
Heaven Can Wait

1980 • Meryl Streep
Kramer vs. Kramer

1981 • Mary Steenburgen
Melvin and Howard

1982 • Joan Hackett
Only When I Laugh

1983 • Jessica Lange
Tootsie

1984 • Cher
Silkwood

1985 • Peggy Ashcroft
A Passage to India

1986 • Meg Tilly
Agnes of God

1987 • Maggie Smith
A Room with a View

1988 • Olympia Dukakis
Moonstruck

1989 • Sigourney Weaver
Working Girl

1990 • Julia Roberts
Steel Magnolias

1991 • Whoopi Goldberg
Ghost

1992 • Mercedes Ruehl
The Fisher King

1993 • Joan Plowright
Enchanted April

1994 • Winona Ryder
The Age of Innocence

1995 • Dianne Wiest
Bullets Over Broadway

1996 • Mira Sorvino
Mighty Aphrodite

BEST FILM—DRAMA

1944
The Song of Bernadette

1945
Going My Way

1946
The Lost Weekend

1947
The Best Years of Our Lives

1948
Gentleman's Agreement

1949
Johnny Belinda
Treasure of the Sierra Madre

1950
All the King's Men

1951
Sunset Boulevard

1952
A Place in the Sun

1953
The Greatest Show on Earth

1954
The Robe

1955
On the Waterfront

1956
East of Eden

1957
Around the World in 80 Days

1958
The Bridge on the River Kwai

1959
The Defiant Ones

1960
Ben-Hur

1961
Spartacus

1962
The Guns of Navarone

1963
Lawrence of Arabia

1964
The Cardinal

1965
Becket

1966
Doctor Zhivago

1967
A Man for All Seasons

1968
In the Heat of the Night

1969
The Lion in Winter

1970
Anne of the Thousand Days

1971
Love Story

1972
The French Connection

1973
The Godfather

1974
The Exorcist

1975
Chinatown

1976
One Flew Over the Cuckoo's Nest

1977
Rocky

1978
The Turning Point

1979
Midnight Express

1980
Kramer vs. Kramer

1981
Ordinary People

1982
On Golden Pond

1983
E.T.: The Extra-Terrestrial

1984
Terms of Endearment

1985
Amadeus

1986
Out of Africa

1987
Platoon

1988
The Last Emperor

1989
Rain Man

1990
Born on the Fourth of July
1991
Dances with Wolves
1992
Bugsy
1993
Scent of a Woman
1994
Schindler's List
1995
Forrest Gump
1996
Sense and Sensibility

BEST FILM—MUSICAL/COMEDY

1952
An American in Paris
1955
Carmen Jones
1956
Guys and Dolls
1957
The King and I
1958
Les Girls
1959
Gigi
1960
Some Like It Hot
1961
The Apartment
Song Without End
1962
West Side Story
1963
The Music Man
That Touch of Mink
1964
Tom Jones
1965
My Fair Lady
1966
The Sound of Music
1967
The Russians are Coming, the Russians are Coming
1968
The Graduate
1969
Oliver!
1971
*M*A*S*H*
1972
Fiddler on the Roof
1973
Cabaret
1974
American Graffiti
1975
The Longest Yard
1976
The Sunshine Boys
1977
A Star is Born
1978
The Goodbye Girl
1979
Heaven Can Wait
1980
Breaking Away
1981
Coal Miner's Daughter
1982
Arthur
1983
Tootsie
1984
Yentl
1985
Romancing the Stone
1986
Prizzi's Honor
1987
Hannah and Her Sisters
1988
Hope and Glory
1989
Working Girl
1990
Driving Miss Daisy
1991
Green Card
1992
Beauty and the Beast
1993
The Player
1994
Mrs. Doubtfire
1995
The Lion King
1996
Babe

DIRECTOR

1944 ● Henry King
The Song of Bernadette
1945 ● Leo McCarey
Going My Way
1946 ● Billy Wilder
The Lost Weekend
1947 ● Frank Capra
It's a Wonderful Life
1948 ● Elia Kazan
Gentleman's Agreement
1949 ● John Huston
Treasure of the Sierra Madre
1950 ● Robert Rossen
All the King's Men
1951 ● Billy Wilder
Sunset Boulevard
1953 ● Cecil B. DeMille
The Greatest Show on Earth
1955 ● Elia Kazan
On the Waterfront
1956 ● Joshua Logan
Picnic
1957 ● Elia Kazan
Baby Doll
1958 ● David Lean
The Bridge on the River Kwai
1959 ● Vincente Minnelli
Gigi
1960 ● William Wyler
Ben-Hur
1962 ● Stanley Kramer
Judgment at Nuremberg
1963 ● David Lean
Lawrence of Arabia
1965 ● George Cukor
My Fair Lady
1966 ● David Lean
Doctor Zhivago
1967 ● Fred Zinnemann
A Man for All Seasons
1968 ● Mike Nichols
The Graduate
1969 ● Paul Newman
Rachel, Rachel
1970 ● Charles Jarrott
Anne of the Thousand Days
1971 ● Arthur Hiller
Love Story
1972 ● William Friedkin
The French Connection
1973 ● Francis Ford Coppola
The Godfather
1974 ● William Friedkin
The Exorcist
1975 ● Roman Polanski
Chinatown
1976 ● Milos Forman
One Flew Over the Cuckoo's Nest
1977 ● Sidney Lumet
Network
1978 ● Herbert Ross
The Turning Point
1979 ● Michael Cimino
The Deer Hunter
1980 ● Francis Ford Coppola
Apocalypse Now
1981 ● Robert Redford
Ordinary People
1982 ● Warren Beatty
Reds
1983 ● Richard Attenborough
Gandhi
1984 ● Barbra Streisand
Yentl
1985 ● Milos Forman
Amadeus
1986 ● John Huston
Prizzi's Honor
1987 ● Oliver Stone
Platoon
1988 ● Bernardo Bertolucci
The Last Emperor
1989 ● Clint Eastwood
Bird
1990 ● Oliver Stone
Born on the Fourth of July
1991 ● Kevin Costner
Dances with Wolves
1992 ● Oliver Stone
JFK
1993 ● Clint Eastwood
Unforgiven
1994 ● Steven Spielberg
Schindler's List
1995 ● Robert Zemeckis
Forrest Gump
1996 ● Mel Gibson
Braveheart

MUSIC

1948
Life with Father
1949
The Red Shoes
1950
The Inspector General
1951
Sunset Boulevard
1952
September Affair
1953
High Noon
1960
On the Beach
1961
The Alamo
1962
The Guns of Navarone
1963
To Kill a Mockingbird
1965
The Fall of the Roman Empire
1966
Doctor Zhivago
1967
Hawaii
1968
Camelot
1969
The Shoes of the Fisherman
1970
Butch Cassidy and the Sundance Kid
1971
Love Story
1972
Shaft
1973
The Godfather
1974
Jonathan Livingston Seagull
1975
The Little Prince
1976
Jaws
1977
A Star is Born
1978
Star Wars
1979
Midnight Express
1980
Apocalypse Now
1981
The Stunt Man
1983
E.T.: The Extra-Terrestrial
1984
Flashdance
1985
A Passage to India
1986
Out of Africa
1987
The Mission
1988
The Last Emperor
1989
Gorillas in the Mist
1990
The Little Mermaid
1991
The Sheltering Sky
1993
Aladdin
1994
Heaven and Earth
1995
The Lion King
1996
A Walk in the Clouds

SONG

1965 ● "Circus World"
Circus World
1968 ● "If Ever I Should Leave You"
Camelot
1969 ● "The Windmills of Your Mind"
The Thomas Crown Affair
1970 ● "Jean"
The Prime of Miss Jean Brodie
1971 ● "Whistling Away the Dark"
Darling Lili
1972 ● "Life Is What You Make It"
Kotch
1973 ● "Ben"
Ben
1974 ● "The Way We Were"
The Way We Were
1975 ● "I Feel Love"
Benji
1976 ● "I'm Easy"
Nashville
1977 ● "Evergreen"
A Star is Born
1978 ● "You Light Up My Life"
You Light Up My Life
1980 ● "The Rose"
The Rose
1981 ● "Fame"
Fame
1982 ● "Arthur's Theme"
Arthur
1983 ● "Up Where We Belong"
An Officer and a Gentleman

SONG ▶*cont.*

1984 ● "Flashdance...What a Feeling"
Flashdance

1985 ● "I Just Called to Say I Love You"
The Woman in Red

1986 ● "Say You, Say Me"
White Nights

1987 ● "Take My Breath Away"
Top Gun

1988 ● "(I've Had) the Time of My Life"
Dirty Dancing

1989 ● "Let the River Run"
Working Girl

1990 ● "Under the Sea"
The Little Mermaid

1991 ● "Blaze of Glory"
Young Guns 2

1993 ● "A Whole New World"
Aladdin

1994 ● "Streets of Philadelphia"
Philadelphia

1995 ● "Can You Feel the Love Tonight?"
The Lion King

1996 ● "Colors of the Wind"
Pocahontas

WRITING

1948
Miracle on 34th Street

1949
The Search

1950
Battleground

1951
All About Eve

1953
Five Fingers

1954
Lili

1955
Sabrina

1966
Doctor Zhivago

1967
A Man for All Seasons

1968
In the Heat of the Night

1969
Charly

1970
Anne of the Thousand Days

1971
Love Story

1972
The Hospital

1973
The Godfather

1974
The Exorcist

1975
Chinatown

1976
One Flew Over the Cuckoo's Nest

1977
Network

1978
The Goodbye Girl

1979
Midnight Express

1980
Kramer vs. Kramer

1981
The Ninth Configuration

1982
On Golden Pond

1983
Gandhi

1984
Terms of Endearment

1985
Amadeus

1986
The Purple Rose of Cairo

1987
The Mission

1988
The Last Emperor

1989
Running on Empty

1990
Born on the Fourth of July

1991
Dances with Wolves

1993
Scent of a Woman

1994
Schindler's List

1995
Pulp Fiction

1996
Sense and Sensibility

FILM—FOREIGN LANGUAGE

1950
The Bicycle Thief

1955
Genevieve

1956
Ordet

1957
Richard III
War and Peace

1959
A Night to Remember

1960
Black Orpheus
Odd Obsession
Wild Strawberries

1961
The Virgin Spring

1962
Two Women

1963
Divorce—Italian Style

1964
Tom Jones

1965
Marriage Italian Style
Sallah

1966
Darling

1967
Alfie
A Man and a Woman

1969
Romeo and Juliet
War and Peace

1970
Z

1971
Rider on the Rain
Women in Love

1972
Sunday, Bloody Sunday

1973
Young Winston

1974
The Pedestrian

1975
Scenes from a Marriage

1976
Lies My Father Told Me

1977
Face to Face

1978
A Special Day

1979
Autumn Sonata

1980
La Cage aux Folles

1981
Tess

1982
Chariots of Fire

1983
Gandhi

1984
Fanny and Alexander

1985
A Passage to India

1986
The Official Story

1987
The Assault

1988
My Life as a Dog

1989
Pelle the Conqueror

1990
Cinema Paradiso

1991
Cyrano de Bergerac

1992
Europa, Europa

1993
Indochine

1994
Farewell My Concubine

1995
Farinelli

1996
Les Miserables

INDEPENDENT SPIRIT AWARDS

ACTOR

1986 ● M. Emmet Walsh
Blood Simple

1987 ● James Woods
Salvador

1988 ● Dennis Quaid
The Big Easy

1989 ● Edward James Olmos
Stand and Deliver

1990 ● Matt Dillon
Drugstore Cowboy

1991 ● Danny Glover
To Sleep with Anger

1992 ● River Phoenix
My Own Private Idaho

1993 ● Harvey Keitel
Bad Lieutenant

1994 ● Jeff Bridges
American Heart

1995 ● Samuel L. Jackson
Pulp Fiction

1996 ● Sean Penn
Dead Man Walking

ACTOR—SUPPORTING

1988 ● Morgan Freeman
Street Smart

1989 ● Lou Diamond Phillips
Stand and Deliver

1990 ● Max Perlich
Drugstore Cowboy

1991 ● Bruce Davison
Longtime Companion

1992 ● David Strathairn
City of Hope

1993 ● Steve Buscemi
Reservoir Dogs

1994 ● Christopher Lloyd
Twenty Bucks

1995 ● Chazz Palminteri
Bullets Over Broadway

1996 ● Benicio Del Toro
The Usual Suspects

ACTRESS

1986 ● Geraldine Page
The Trip to Bountiful

1987 ● Isabella Rossellini
Blue Velvet

1988 ● Sally Kirkland
Anna

1989 ● Jodie Foster
Five Corners

1990 ● Andie MacDowell
sex, lies and videotape

1991 ● Anjelica Huston
The Grifters

1992 ● Judy Davis
Impromptu

1993 ● Fairuza Balk
Gas Food Lodging

1994 ● Ashley Judd
Ruby in Paradise

1995 ● Linda Fiorentino
The Last Seduction

1996 ● Elisabeth Shue
Leaving Las Vegas

ACTRESS—SUPPORTING

1988 ● Anjelica Huston
The Dead

1989 ● Rosana De Soto
Stand and Deliver

1990 ● Laura San Giacomo
sex, lies and videotape

1991 ● Sheryl Lee Ralph
To Sleep with Anger

1992 ● Diane Ladd
Rambling Rose

1993 ● Alfre Woodard
Passion Fish

1994 ● Lili Taylor
Household Saints

1995 ● Dianne Wiest
Bullets Over Broadway

1996 ● Mare Winningham
Georgia

CINEMATOGRAPHY

1986
Trouble in Mind

1987
Platoon

1988
Matewan

1989
The Unbearable Lightness of Being

1990
Drugstore Cowboy

1991
Wild at Heart

1992
Kafka

1993
Night on Earth

1994
Menace II Society

1995
Barcelona

1996
Leaving Las Vegas

DIRECTOR

1986 ● Martin Scorsese
After Hours
Joel Coen
Blood Simple

1987 ● Oliver Stone
Platoon

1988 ● John Huston
The Dead

1989 ● Ramon Menendez
Stand and Deliver

1990 ● Steven Soderbergh
sex, lies and videotape

1991 ● Charles Burnett
To Sleep with Anger

1992 ● Martha Coolidge
Rambling Rose

1993 ● Carl Franklin
One False Move

1994 ● Robert Altman
Short Cuts

1995 ● Quentin Tarantino
Pulp Fiction

1996 ● Mike Figgis
Leaving Las Vegas

FILM

1986
After Hours

1987
Platoon

1988
River's Edge

1989
Stand and Deliver

1990
sex, lies and videotape

1991
The Grifters

1992
Rambling Rose

1993
The Player

1994
Short Cuts

1995
Pulp Fiction

1996
Leaving Las Vegas

FIRST FEATURE

1988
Dirty Dancing

1989
Mystic Pizza

1990
Heathers

1991
Metropolitan

1992
Straight Out of Brooklyn

1993
The Waterdance

1994
El Mariachi

1995
Spanking the Monkey

1996
The Brothers McMullen

WRITING

1986
The Trip to Bountiful

1987
Platoon

1988
River's Edge

1989
Stand and Deliver

1990
Drugstore Cowboy

1991
To Sleep with Anger

1992
My Own Private Idaho

1993
The Waterdance

1994
Short Cuts

1995
Pulp Fiction

1996
The Usual Suspects

DEBUT PERFORMANCE

1995 ● Sean Nelson
Fresh

1996 ● Justin Pierce
Kids

FILM—FOREIGN LANGUAGE

1986
Kiss of the Spider Woman

1987
A Room with a View

1988
My Life as a Dog

1989
Wings of Desire

1990
My Left Foot

1992
An Angel at My Table

1993
The Crying Game

1994
The Piano

1995
Trois Couleurs: Rouge

1996
Before the Rain

LOS ANGELES FILM CRITICS ASSOCIATION AWARDS

ACTOR

1976 ● Robert De Niro
Taxi Driver

1977 ● Richard Dreyfuss
The Goodbye Girl

1978 ● Jon Voight
Coming Home

1979 ● Dustin Hoffman
Kramer vs. Kramer

1980 ● Robert De Niro
Raging Bull

1981 ● Burt Lancaster
Atlantic City

1982 ● Ben Kingsley
Gandhi

1983 ● Robert Duvall
Tender Mercies

1984 ● Albert Finney
Under the Volcano

1985 ● William Hurt
Kiss of the Spider Woman

1986 ● Bob Hoskins
Mona Lisa

1987 ● Jack Nicholson
Ironweed
Steve Martin
Roxanne
Jack Nicholson
The Witches of Eastwick

1988 ● Tom Hanks
Big
Tom Hanks
Punchline

1989 ● Daniel Day-Lewis
My Left Foot

1990 ● Jeremy Irons
Reversal of Fortune

1991 ● Nick Nolte
The Prince of Tides

1992 ● Clint Eastwood
Unforgiven

1993 ● Anthony Hopkins
The Remains of the Day
Anthony Hopkins
Shadowlands

1994 ● John Travolta
Pulp Fiction

1995 ● Nicolas Cage
Leaving Las Vegas

ACTOR—SUPPORTING

1977 ● Jason Robards, Jr.
Julia

1978 ● Robert Morley
Who Is Killing the Great Chefs of Europe?

1979 ● Melvyn Douglas
Being There
Melvyn Douglas
The Seduction of Joe Tynan

1980 ● Timothy Hutton
Ordinary People

1981 ● John Gielgud
Arthur

1982 ● John Lithgow
The World According to Garp

1983 ● Jack Nicholson
Terms of Endearment

1984 ● Adolph Caesar
A Soldier's Story

1985 ● John Gielgud
Plenty
John Gielgud
The Shooting Party

1986 ● Dennis Hopper
Blue Velvet
Dennis Hopper
Hoosiers

1987 ● Morgan Freeman
Street Smart

1988 ● Alec Guinness
Little Dorrit, Film 1: Nobody's Fault
Alec Guinness
Little Dorrit, Film 2: Little Dorrit's Story

1989 ● Danny Aiello
Do the Right Thing

1990 ● Joe Pesci
Goodfellas

1991 ● Michael Lerner
Barton Fink

1992 ● Gene Hackman
Unforgiven

1993 ● Tommy Lee Jones
The Fugitive

1994 ● Martin Landau
Ed Wood

1995 ● Don Cheadle
Devil In a Blue Dress

ACTRESS

1976 ● Liv Ullmann
Face to Face

1978 ● Jane Fonda
Coming Home

1979 ● Sally Field
Norma Rae

1980 ● Sissy Spacek
Coal Miner's Daughter

1981 ● Meryl Streep
The French Lieutenant's Woman

1982 ● Meryl Streep
Sophie's Choice

1983 ● Shirley MacLaine
Terms of Endearment

1984 ● Kathleen Turner
Crimes of Passion
Kathleen Turner
Romancing the Stone

1985 ● Meryl Streep
Out of Africa

1986 ● Sandrine Bonnaire
Vagabond

1987 ● Sally Kirkland
Anna
Holly Hunter
Broadcast News

1988 ● Christine Lahti
Running on Empty

1989 ● Michelle Pfeiffer
The Fabulous Baker Boys
Andie MacDowell
sex, lies and videotape

1990 ● Anjelica Huston
The Grifters
Anjelica Huston
The Witches

1991 ● Mercedes Ruehl
The Fisher King

1992 ● Emma Thompson
Howard's End

1993 ● Holly Hunter
The Piano

1994 ● Jessica Lange
Blue Sky

1995 ● Elisabeth Shue
Leaving Las Vegas

ACTRESS—SUPPORTING

1977 ● Vanessa Redgrave
Julia

1978 ● Maureen Stapleton
Interiors
Mona Washbourne
Stevie

1979 ● Meryl Streep
Kramer vs. Kramer
Meryl Streep
Manhattan
Meryl Streep
The Seduction of Joe Tynan

1980 ● Mary Steenburgen
Melvin and Howard

1981 ● Maureen Stapleton
Reds

1982 ● Glenn Close
The World According to Garp

1983 ● Linda Hunt
The Year of Living Dangerously

1984 ● Peggy Ashcroft
A Passage to India

1985 ● Anjelica Huston
Prizzi's Honor

1986 ● Dianne Wiest
Hannah and Her Sisters
Cathy Tyson
Mona Lisa

1987 ● Olympia Dukakis
Moonstruck

1988 ● Genevieve Bujold
Dead Ringers
Genevieve Bujold
The Moderns

1989 ● Brenda Fricker
My Left Foot

1990 ● Lorraine Bracco
Goodfellas

1991 ● Jane Horrocks
Life Is Sweet

1992 ● Judy Davis
Husbands and Wives

1993 ● Rosie Perez
Fearless
Anna Paquin
The Piano

1994 ● Dianne Wiest
Bullets Over Broadway

1995 ● Joan Allen
Nixon

CINEMATOGRAPHY

1975
Barry Lyndon

1976
Bound for Glory

CINEMATOGRAPHY ▶cont.

1977
Julia

1978
Days of Heaven

1979
The Black Stallion

1980
Tess

1981
Reds

1982
Blade Runner

1983
Fanny and Alexander

1984
The Killing Fields

1985
Out of Africa

1986
The Mission

1987
The Last Emperor

1988
Wings of Desire

1989
The Fabulous Baker Boys

1990
Goodfellas

1991
Barton Fink

1992
Raise the Red Lantern

1993
The Piano
Schindler's List

1994
Ed Wood

DIRECTOR

1976 ● Sidney Lumet
Network

1977 ● Herbert Ross
The Turning Point

1978 ● Michael Cimino
The Deer Hunter

1979 ● Robert Benton
Kramer vs. Kramer

1980 ● Roman Polanski
Tess

1981 ● Warren Beatty
Reds

1982 ● Steven Spielberg
E.T.: The Extra-Terrestrial

1983 ● James L. Brooks
Terms of Endearment

1984 ● Milos Forman
Amadeus

1985 ● Terry Gilliam
Brazil

1986 ● David Lynch
Blue Velvet

1987 ● John Boorman
Hope and Glory

1988 ● David Cronenberg
Dead Ringers

1989 ● Spike Lee
Do the Right Thing

1990 ● Martin Scorsese
Goodfellas

1991 ● Barry Levinson
Bugsy

1992 ● Clint Eastwood
Unforgiven

1993 ● Jane Campion
The Piano

1994 ● Quentin Tarantino
Pulp Fiction

1995 ● Mike Figgis
Leaving Las Vegas

FILM

1976
Network
Rocky

1977
Star Wars

1978
Coming Home

1979
Kramer vs. Kramer

1980
Raging Bull

1981
Atlantic City

1982
E.T.: The Extra-Terrestrial

1983
Terms of Endearment

1984
Amadeus

1985
Brazil

1986
Hannah and Her Sisters

1987
Hope and Glory

1988
Little Dorrit, Film 1: Nobody's Fault
Little Dorrit, Film 2: Little Dorrit's Story

1989
Do the Right Thing

1990
Goodfellas

1991
Bugsy

1992
Unforgiven

1993
Schindler's List

1994
Pulp Fiction

1995
Leaving Las Vegas

FEATURE DOCUMENTARY

1994
Hoop Dreams

MUSIC

1983
Koyaanisqatsi

1992
Damage

1993
Olivier, Olivier
The Secret Garden
Trois Couleurs: Bleu

1994
Ed Wood

WRITING

1977
Annie Hall

1978
An Unmarried Woman

1979
Kramer vs. Kramer

1980
Return of the Secaucus 7

1981
Atlantic City

1982
Tootsie

1983
Terms of Endearment

1984
Amadeus

1985
Brazil

1986
Hannah and Her Sisters

1987
Hope and Glory

1988
Bull Durham

1989
Drugstore Cowboy

1990
Reversal of Fortune

1991
Bugsy

1992
Unforgiven

1993
The Piano

1994
Pulp Fiction

1995
Sense and Sensibility

FILM—FOREIGN LANGUAGE

1975
And Now My Love

1976
Face to Face

1977
That Obscure Object of Desire

1978
Madame Rosa

1979
Soldier of Orange

1980
The Tin Drum

1981
Pixote

1982
The Road Warrior

1983
Fanny and Alexander

1984
The 4th Man

1985
The Official Story
Ran

1986
Vagabond

1987
Au Revoir Les Enfants

1988
Wings of Desire

1989
Distant Voices, Still Lives
The Story of Women

1990
Life and Nothing But

1991
La Belle Noiseuse

1992
The Crying Game

1993
Farewell My Concubine

1994
Trois Couleurs: Rouge

1995
Wild Reeds

MONTREAL WORLD FILM FESTIVAL

ACTOR

1979 ● Giuliano Gemma
Corleone

1980 ● Robert Duvall
The Great Santini

1983 ● Gerard Depardieu
Danton

1985 ● Armin Mueller-Stahl
Angry Harvest

1987 ● Leo McKern
Travelling North

1989 ● Daniel Day-Lewis
My Left Foot

1993 ● Johan Leysen
Trahir

ACTOR—SUPPORTING

1986 ● Dennis Hopper
Blue Velvet

ACTRESS

1978 ● Glenda Jackson
Stevie

1988 ● Udvaros Dorottya
Oh, Bloody Life!

1994 ● Rena Owen
Once Were Warriors

1995 ● Jennifer Jason Leigh
Georgia

DIRECTOR

1992 ● Maurizio Nichetti
Volere Volare

1995 ● Xie Fei
A Mongolian Tale

FILM

1980
The Stunt Man

1982
Brimstone & Treacle
Time for Revenge

1983
The Go-Masters

1988
La Lectrice

1989
Freedom Is Paradise

1993
Trahir

1994
Once Were Warriors

1995
Georgia

WRITING

1994
The Sum of Us

MTV MOVIE AWARDS

ACTION SEQUENCE

1992
Terminator 2: Judgment Day

1993
Lethal Weapon 3

1994
The Fugitive

1995
Speed

1996
Braveheart

BREAKTHROUGH PERFORMANCE

1992 ● Edward Furlong
Terminator 2: Judgment Day

1993 ● Marisa Tomei
My Cousin Vinny

1994 ● Alicia Silverstone
The Crush

1995 ● Kirsten Dunst
Interview with the Vampire

1996 • George Clooney
From Dusk Till Dawn

COMEDIC PERFORMANCE

1992 • Billy Crystal
City Slickers

1993 • Robin Williams
Aladdin

1994 • Robin Williams
Mrs. Doubtfire

1995 • Jim Carrey
Dumb & Dumber

1996 • Jim Carrey
Ace Ventura: When Nature Calls

FILM

1992
Terminator 2: Judgment Day

1993
A Few Good Men

1994
Menace II Society

1995
Pulp Fiction

1996
Seven

KISS

1992 • Macaulay Culkin/ Anna Chlumsky
My Girl

1993 • Christian Slater/ Marisa Tomei
Untamed Heart

1994 • Demi Moore/Woody Harrelson
Indecent Proposal

1995 • Jim Carrey/Lauren Holly
Dumb & Dumber

1996 • Natasha Henstridge/Anthony Guidera
Species

MOST DESIRABLE FEMALE

1992 • Linda Hamilton
Terminator 2: Judgment Day

1993 • Sharon Stone
Basic Instinct

1994 • Janet Jackson
Poetic Justice

1995 • Sandra Bullock
Speed

1996 • Alicia Silverstone
Clueless

MOST DESIRABLE MALE

1992 • Keanu Reeves
Point Break

1993 • Christian Slater
Untamed Heart

1994 • William Baldwin
Sliver

1995 • Brad Pitt
Interview with the Vampire

1996 • Brad Pitt
Seven

NEW FILMMAKER

1992 • John Singleton
Boyz N the Hood

1993 • Carl Franklin
One False Move

1994 • Steven Zaillian
Searching for Bobby Fischer

1995 • Steve James
Hoop Dreams

1996 • Wes Anderson
Bottle Rocket

ON-SCREEN DUO

1992 • Mike Myers/Dana Carvey
Wayne's World

1993 • Mel Gibson/Danny Glover
Lethal Weapon 3

1994 • Harrison Ford/ Tommy Lee Jones
The Fugitive

1995 • Keanu Reeves/ Sandra Bullock
Speed

1996 • Chris Farley/David Spade
Tommy Boy

SONG

1992 • "(Everything I Do) I Do for You"
Robin Hood: Prince of Thieves

1993 • "I Will Always Love You"
The Bodyguard

1994 • "Will You Be There"
Free Willy

1995 • "Big Empty"
The Crow

1996 • "Sittin' Up in My Room"
Waiting to Exhale

VILLAIN

1992 • Rebecca DeMornay
The Hand that Rocks the Cradle

1993 • Jennifer Jason Leigh
Single White Female

1994 • Alicia Silverstone
The Crush

1995 • Dennis Hopper
Speed

1996 • Kevin Spacey
Seven

BEST DANCE SEQUENCE

1995 • John Travolta/Uma Thurman
Pulp Fiction

BEST MALE PERFORMANCE

1992 • Arnold Schwarzenegger
Terminator 2: Judgment Day

1993 • Denzel Washington
Malcolm X

1994 • Tom Hanks
Philadelphia

1995 • Brad Pitt
Interview with the Vampire

1996 • Jim Carrey
Ace Ventura: When Nature Calls

BEST FEMALE PERFORMANCE

1992 • Linda Hamilton
Terminator 2: Judgment Day

1993 • Sharon Stone
Basic Instinct

1994 • Janet Jackson
Poetic Justice

1995 • Sandra Bullock
Speed

1996 • Alicia Silverstone
Clueless

FIGHT

1996 • Adam Sandler/Bob Barker
Happy Gilmore

NATIONAL BOARD OF REVIEW AWARDS

ACTOR

1945 • Ray Milland
The Lost Weekend

1946 • Laurence Olivier
Henry V

1948 • Walter Huston
Treasure of the Sierra Madre

1949 • Ralph Richardson
The Fallen Idol
Ralph Richardson
The Heiress

1953 • James Mason
Julius Caesar

1955 • Ernest Borgnine
Marty

1957 • Alec Guinness
The Bridge on the River Kwai

1958 • Spencer Tracy
Last Hurrah

1960 • Robert Mitchum
Home from the Hill
Robert Mitchum
The Sundowners

1963 • Rex Harrison
Cleopatra

1964 • Anthony Quinn
Zorba the Greek

1965 • Lee Marvin
Cat Ballou
Lee Marvin
Ship of Fools

1966 • Paul Scofield
A Man for All Seasons

1967 • Peter Finch
Far from the Madding Crowd

1968 • Cliff Robertson
Charly

1969 • Peter O'Toole
Goodbye, Mr. Chips

1970 • George C. Scott
Patton

1971 • Gene Hackman
The French Connection

1972 • Peter O'Toole
Man of La Mancha
Peter O'Toole
The Ruling Class

1973 • Al Pacino
Serpico

1974 • Gene Hackman
The Conversation

1975 • Jack Nicholson
One Flew Over the Cuckoo's Nest

1976 • David Carradine
Bound for Glory

1977 • John Travolta
Saturday Night Fever

1978 • Laurence Olivier
The Boys from Brazil

1979 • Peter Sellers
Being There

1980 • Robert De Niro
Raging Bull

1981 • Henry Fonda
On Golden Pond

1982 • Ben Kingsley
Gandhi

1983 • Tom Conti
Merry Christmas, Mr. Lawrence
Tom Conti
Reuben, Reuben

1984 • Victor Banerjee
A Passage to India

1985 • William Hurt
Kiss of the Spider Woman
Raul Julia
Kiss of the Spider Woman

1986 • Paul Newman
The Color of Money

1987 • Michael Douglas
Wall Street

1988 • Gene Hackman
Mississippi Burning

1989 • Morgan Freeman
Driving Miss Daisy

1990 • Robert De Niro
Awakenings
Robin Williams
Awakenings

1991 • Warren Beatty
Bugsy

1992 • Jack Lemmon
Glengarry Glen Ross

1993 • Anthony Hopkins
The Remains of the Day
Anthony Hopkins
Shadowlands

1994 • Tom Hanks
Forrest Gump

1995 • Nicolas Cage
Leaving Las Vegas

ACTOR—SUPPORTING

1954 • John Williams
Sabrina

1957 • Sessue Hayakawa
The Bridge on the River Kwai

1958 • Albert Salmi
The Bravados

1961 • Jackie Gleason
The Hustler

1962 • Burgess Meredith
Advise and Consent
Jason Robards, Jr.
Long Day's Journey into Night

1963 • Melvyn Douglas
Hud

1964 • Martin Balsam
The Carpetbaggers

1965 • Harry Andrews
The Agony and the Ecstasy

1966 • Robert Shaw
A Man for All Seasons

1967 • Paul Ford
The Comedians

1968 • Leo McKern
The Shoes of the Fisherman

1969 • Philippe Noiret
Topaz

1970 • Frank Langella
Diary of a Mad Housewife

1971 • Ben Johnson
The Last Picture Show

1972 • Joel Grey
Cabaret
Al Pacino
The Godfather

ACTOR—SUPPORTING ▶cont.

1973 ● John Houseman
The Paper Chase

1975 ● Charles Durning
Dog Day Afternoon

1976 ● Jason Robards, Jr.
All the President's Men

1977 ● Tom Skerritt
The Turning Point

1978 ● Richard Farnsworth
Comes a Horseman

1979 ● Paul Dooley
Breaking Away

1980 ● Joe Pesci
Raging Bull

1981 ● Jack Nicholson
Reds

1982 ● Robert Preston
Victor/Victoria

1983 ● Jack Nicholson
Terms of Endearment

1984 ● John Malkovich
Places in the Heart

1985 ● Klaus Maria Brandauer
Out of Africa

1986 ● Daniel Day-Lewis
My Beautiful Laundrette
Daniel Day-Lewis
A Room with a View

1987 ● Sean Connery
The Untouchables

1988 ● River Phoenix
Running on Empty

1989 ● Alan Alda
Crimes & Misdemeanors

1990 ● Joe Pesci
Goodfellas

1991 ● Anthony Hopkins
The Silence of the Lambs

1992 ● Jack Nicholson
A Few Good Men

1993 ● Leonardo DiCaprio
What's Eating Gilbert Grape

1994 ● Gary Sinise
Forrest Gump

1995 ● Kevin Spacey
Seven
Kevin Spacey
The Usual Suspects

ACTRESS

1953 ● Jean Simmons
The Robe

1954 ● Grace Kelly
Country Girl

1958 ● Ingrid Bergman
The Inn of the Sixth Happiness

1960 ● Greer Garson
Sunrise at Campobello

1961 ● Geraldine Page
Summer and Smoke

1962 ● Anne Bancroft
The Miracle Worker

1963 ● Patricia Neal
Hud

1964 ● Kim Stanley
Seance on a Wet Afternoon

1965 ● Julie Christie
Darling
Julie Christie
Doctor Zhivago

1966 ● Elizabeth Taylor
Who's Afraid of Virginia Woolf?

1968 ● Liv Ullmann
Hour of the Wolf

1970 ● Glenda Jackson
Women in Love

1971 ● Irene Papas
Trojan Women

1972 ● Cicely Tyson
Sounder

1973 ● Liv Ullmann
The New Land

1974 ● Gena Rowlands
A Woman Under the Influence

1975 ● Isabelle Adjani
Story of Adele H.

1976 ● Liv Ullmann
Face to Face

1977 ● Anne Bancroft
The Turning Point

1978 ● Ingrid Bergman
Autumn Sonata

1979 ● Sally Field
Norma Rae

1980 ● Sissy Spacek
Coal Miner's Daughter

1982 ● Meryl Streep
Sophie's Choice

1983 ● Shirley MacLaine
Terms of Endearment

1984 ● Peggy Ashcroft
A Passage to India

1985 ● Whoopi Goldberg
The Color Purple

1986 ● Kathleen Turner
Peggy Sue Got Married

1987 ● Holly Hunter
Broadcast News
Lillian Gish
The Whales of August

1988 ● Jodie Foster
The Accused

1989 ● Michelle Pfeiffer
The Fabulous Baker Boys

1990 ● Mia Farrow
Alice

1991 ● Susan Sarandon
Thelma & Louise
Geena Davis
Thelma & Louise

1992 ● Emma Thompson
Howard's End

1993 ● Holly Hunter
The Piano

1994 ● Miranda Richardson
Tom & Viv

1995 ● Emma Thompson
Carrington
Emma Thompson
Sense and Sensibility

ACTRESS—SUPPORTING

1958 ● Kay Walsh
The Horse's Mouth

1959 ● Edith Evans
The Nun's Story

1960 ● Shirley Jones
Elmer Gantry

1961 ● Ruby Dee
A Raisin in the Sun

1962 ● Angela Lansbury
The Manchurian Candidate

1963 ● Margaret Rutherford
The V.I.P.'s

1964 ● Edith Evans
The Chalk Garden

1965 ● Joan Blondell
The Cincinnati Kid

1966 ● Vivien Merchant
Alfie

1969 ● Pamela Franklin
The Prime of Miss Jean Brodie

1970 ● Karen Black
Five Easy Pieces

1971 ● Cloris Leachman
The Last Picture Show

1972 ● Marisa Berenson
Cabaret

1973 ● Sylvia Sidney
Summer Wishes, Winter Dreams

1974 ● Valerie Perrine
Lenny

1975 ● Ronee Blakley
Nashville

1976 ● Talia Shire
Rocky

1977 ● Diane Keaton
Annie Hall

1978 ● Angela Lansbury
Death on the Nile

1979 ● Meryl Streep
Kramer vs. Kramer
Meryl Streep
The Seduction of Joe Tynan

1980 ● Eva LeGallienne
Resurrection

1982 ● Glenn Close
The World According to Garp

1983 ● Linda Hunt
The Year of Living Dangerously

1984 ● Sabine Azema
A Sunday in the Country

1985 ● Rosanna Arquette
Desperately Seeking Susan

1986 ● Dianne Wiest
Hannah and Her Sisters

1987 ● Olympia Dukakis
Moonstruck

1988 ● Frances McDormand
Mississippi Burning

1989 ● Mary Stuart Masterson
Immediate Family

1990 ● Winona Ryder
Mermaids

1991 ● Kate Nelligan
Frankie and Johnny

1992 ● Judy Davis
Husbands and Wives

1993 ● Winona Ryder
The Age of Innocence

1994 ● Rosemary Harris
Tom & Viv

1995 ● Mira Sorvino
Mighty Aphrodite

DIRECTOR

1943 ● William A. Wellman
The Ox-Bow Incident

1945 ● Jean Renoir
The Southerner

1946 ● William Wyler
The Best Years of Our Lives

1948 ● Federico Fellini
Paisan

1949 ● Vittorio De Sica
The Bicycle Thief

1950 ● John Huston
The Asphalt Jungle

1951 ● Akira Kurosawa
Rashomon

1953 ● George Stevens
Shane

1954 ● Renato Castellani
Romeo and Juliet

1955 ● William Wyler
Desperate Hours

1956 ● John Huston
Moby Dick

1957 ● David Lean
The Bridge on the River Kwai

1958 ● John Ford
Last Hurrah

1959 ● Fred Zinnemann
The Nun's Story

1962 ● David Lean
Lawrence of Arabia

1963 ● Tony Richardson
Tom Jones

1965 ● John Schlesinger
Darling

1966 ● Fred Zinnemann
A Man for All Seasons

1967 ● Richard Brooks
In Cold Blood

1968 ● Franco Zeffirelli
Romeo and Juliet

1969 ● Alfred Hitchcock
Topaz

1970 ● Francois Truffaut
The Wild Child

1971 ● Ken Russell
The Devils

1972 ● Bob Fosse
Cabaret

1973 ● Ingmar Bergman
Cries and Whispers

1974 ● Francis Ford Coppola
The Conversation

1975 ● Stanley Kubrick
Barry Lyndon
Robert Altman
Nashville

1976 ● Alan J. Pakula
All the President's Men

1977 ● Luis Bunuel
That Obscure Object of Desire

1978 ● Ingmar Bergman
Autumn Sonata

1979 ● John Schlesinger
Yanks

1980 ● Robert Redford
Ordinary People

1981 ● Warren Beatty
Reds

1982 ● Sidney Lumet
The Verdict

1983 ● James L. Brooks
Terms of Endearment

1984 ● David Lean
A Passage to India

1985 ● Akira Kurosawa
Ran

1986 ● Woody Allen
Hannah and Her Sisters

1987 ● Steven Spielberg
Empire of the Sun

1988 ● Alan Parker
Mississippi Burning

1989 ● Kenneth Branagh
Henry V

1990 ● Kevin Costner
Dances with Wolves

1991 ● Jonathan Demme
The Silence of the Lambs

1992 ● James Ivory
Howard's End

1993 ● Martin Scorsese
The Age of Innocence

1994 ● Quentin Tarantino
Pulp Fiction

1995 ● Ang Lee
Sense and Sensibility

FILM

1991
The Silence of the Lambs

1992
Howard's End

1993
Schindler's List

1994
Forrest Gump
Pulp Fiction

1995
Sense and Sensibility

FEATURE DOCUMENTARY

1991
Hearts of Darkness: A Filmmaker's Apocalypse

1992
Brother's Keeper

1993
The War Room

1994
Hoop Dreams

FILM—FOREIGN LANGUAGE

1991
Europa, Europa

1992
Indochine

1993
Farewell My Concubine

1994
Eat Drink Man Woman

NATIONAL SOCIETY OF FILM CRITICS AWARDS

ACTOR

1966 ● Michael Caine
Alfie

1967 ● Rod Steiger
In the Heat of the Night

1968 ● Per Oscarsson
Hunger

1969 ● Jon Voight
Midnight Cowboy

1970 ● George C. Scott
Patton

1971 ● Peter Finch
Sunday, Bloody Sunday

1972 ● Al Pacino
The Godfather

1973 ● Marlon Brando
Last Tango in Paris

1974 ● Jack Nicholson
Chinatown
Jack Nicholson
The Last Detail

1975 ● Jack Nicholson
One Flew Over the Cuckoo's Nest

1976 ● Robert De Niro
Taxi Driver

1977 ● Art Carney
The Late Show

1978 ● Gary Busey
The Buddy Holly Story

1979 ● Dustin Hoffman
Kramer vs. Kramer

1980 ● Peter O'Toole
The Stunt Man

1981 ● Burt Lancaster
Atlantic City

1982 ● Dustin Hoffman
Tootsie

1983 ● Gerard Depardieu
The Return of Martin Guerre

1984 ● Steve Martin
All of Me

1985 ● Jack Nicholson
Prizzi's Honor

1986 ● Bob Hoskins
Mona Lisa

1987 ● Steve Martin
Roxanne

1988 ● Michael Keaton
Beetlejuice
Michael Keaton
Clean and Sober

1989 ● Daniel Day-Lewis
My Left Foot

1990 ● Robert De Niro
Awakenings
Jeremy Irons
Reversal of Fortune

1991 ● River Phoenix
My Own Private Idaho

1992 ● Stephen Rea
The Crying Game

1993 ● David Thewlis
Naked

1994 ● Paul Newman
Nobody's Fool

1995 ● Nicolas Cage
Leaving Las Vegas

ACTOR—SUPPORTING

1967 ● Gene Hackman
Bonnie & Clyde

1968 ● Seymour Cassel
Faces

1969 ● Jack Nicholson
Easy Rider

1970 ● Chief Dan George
Little Big Man

1972 ● Joel Grey
Cabaret
Eddie Albert
The Heartbreak Kid

1973 ● Robert De Niro
Mean Streets

1975 ● Henry Gibson
Nashville

1976 ● Jason Robards, Jr.
All the President's Men

1977 ● Edward Fox
A Bridge Too Far

1978 ● Richard Farnsworth
Comes a Horseman

1979 ● Frederic Forrest
Apocalypse Now
Frederic Forrest
The Rose

1980 ● Joe Pesci
Raging Bull

1981 ● Robert Preston
S.O.B.

1982 ● Mickey Rourke
Diner

1983 ● Jack Nicholson
Terms of Endearment

1984 ● John Malkovich
Places in the Heart

1985 ● John Gielgud
Plenty
John Gielgud
The Shooting Party

1986 ● Dennis Hopper
Blue Velvet

1987 ● Morgan Freeman
Street Smart

1988 ● Dean Stockwell
Married to the Mob

1989 ● Beau Bridges
The Fabulous Baker Boys

1990 ● Bruce Davison
Longtime Companion

1991 ● Harvey Keitel
Mortal Thoughts
Harvey Keitel
Thelma & Louise

1992 ● Gene Hackman
Unforgiven

1993 ● Ralph Fiennes
Schindler's List

1994 ● Martin Landau
Ed Wood

1995 ● Don Cheadle
Devil In a Blue Dress

ACTRESS

1967 ● Bibi Andersson
Persona

1968 ● Liv Ullmann
The Shame

1969 ● Vanessa Redgrave
Isadora

1970 ● Glenda Jackson
Women in Love

1971 ● Jane Fonda
Klute

1972 ● Cicely Tyson
Sounder

1973 ● Liv Ullmann
The New Land

1974 ● Liv Ullmann
Scenes from a Marriage

1975 ● Isabelle Adjani
Story of Adele H.

1976 ● Sissy Spacek
Carrie

1977 ● Diane Keaton
Annie Hall

1978 ● Ingrid Bergman
Autumn Sonata

1979 ● Sally Field
Norma Rae

1980 ● Sissy Spacek
Coal Miner's Daughter

1981 ● Marilia Pera
Pixote

1982 ● Meryl Streep
Sophie's Choice

1983 ● Debra Winger
Terms of Endearment

1984 ● Vanessa Redgrave
The Bostonians

1985 ● Vanessa Redgrave
Wetherby

1986 ● Chloe Webb
Sid & Nancy

1987 ● Emily Lloyd
Wish You Were Here

1988 ● Judy Davis
High Tide

1989 ● Michelle Pfeiffer
The Fabulous Baker Boys

1990 ● Anjelica Huston
The Grifters
Anjelica Huston
The Witches

1991 ● Alison Steadman
Life Is Sweet

1992 ● Emma Thompson
Howard's End

1993 ● Holly Hunter
The Piano

1994 ● Jennifer Jason Leigh
Mrs. Parker and the Vicious Circle

1995 ● Elisabeth Shue
Leaving Las Vegas

ACTRESS—SUPPORTING

1969 ● Sian Phillips
Goodbye, Mr. Chips

1970 ● Lois Smith
Five Easy Pieces

1971 ● Ellen Burstyn
The Last Picture Show

1972 ● Jeannie Berlin
The Heartbreak Kid

1973 ● Valentina Cortese
Day for Night

1974 ● Bibi Andersson
Scenes from a Marriage

1975 ● Lily Tomlin
Nashville

1976 ● Jodie Foster
Taxi Driver

1977 ● Ann Wedgeworth
Citizens Band

1978 ● Meryl Streep
The Deer Hunter

1979 ● Meryl Streep
Kramer vs. Kramer
Meryl Streep
Manhattan
Meryl Streep
The Seduction of Joe Tynan

1980 ● Mary Steenburgen
Melvin and Howard

1981 ● Maureen Stapleton
Reds

1982 ● Jessica Lange
Tootsie

1983 ● Sandra Bernhard
King of Comedy

1984 ● Melanie Griffith
Body Double

1985 ● Anjelica Huston
Prizzi's Honor

1986 ● Dianne Wiest
Hannah and Her Sisters

1987 ● Kathy Baker
Street Smart

1988 ● Mercedes Ruehl
Married to the Mob

1989 ● Anjelica Huston
Enemies, a Love Story

1990 ● Annette Bening
The Grifters

1991 ● Jane Horrocks
Life Is Sweet

1992 ● Judy Davis
Husbands and Wives

1993 ● Madeleine Stowe
Short Cuts

1994 ● Dianne Wiest
Bullets Over Broadway

1995 ● Joan Allen
Nixon

CINEMATOGRAPHY

1967
In the Heat of the Night

1968
Bullitt

1969
The Wild Bunch

1970
My Night at Maud's
The Wild Child

1971
The Conformist

1972
Cries and Whispers

1973
The Long Goodbye

1974
The Parallax View

1975
Barry Lyndon

1976
Bound for Glory

1977
Aguirre, the Wrath of God

1978
Days of Heaven

1979
Being There
The Black Stallion

1980
Raging Bull

1981
Pennies From Heaven

1982
Diva

1983
Never Cry Wolf

1984
Comfort and Joy
The Killing Fields

1985
Ran

1986
Blue Velvet

1987
Hope and Glory

1988
Wings of Desire

CINEMATOGRAPHY ▶cont.

1989
The Fabulous Baker Boys

1990
Where the Heart Is

1991
Barton Fink

1992
Raise the Red Lantern

1993
Schindler's List

1994
Ed Wood

1995
Devil In a Blue Dress

DIRECTOR

1966 • Michelangelo Antonioni
Blow-Up

1967 • Ingmar Bergman
Persona

1968 • Ingmar Bergman
Hour of the Wolf
Ingmar Bergman
The Shame

1969 • Francois Truffaut
Stolen Kisses

1970 • Ingmar Bergman
The Passion of Anna

1971 • Bernardo Bertolucci
The Conformist

1972 • Luis Bunuel
The Discreet Charm of the Bourgeoisie

1973 • Francois Truffaut
Day for Night

1974 • Francis Ford Coppola
The Conversation
Francis Ford Coppola
The Godfather, Part 2

1975 • Robert Altman
Nashville

1976 • Martin Scorsese
Taxi Driver

1977 • Luis Bunuel
That Obscure Object of Desire

1978 • Terence Malick
Days of Heaven

1979 • Robert Benton
Kramer vs. Kramer
Woody Allen
Manhattan

1980 • Martin Scorsese
Raging Bull

1981 • Louis Malle
Atlantic City

1982 • Steven Spielberg
E.T.: The Extra-Terrestrial

1983 • Paolo Taviani
The Night of the Shooting Stars
Vittorio Taviani
The Night of the Shooting Stars

1984 • Robert Bresson
L'Argent

1985 • John Huston
Prizzi's Honor

1986 • David Lynch
Blue Velvet

1987 • John Boorman
Hope and Glory

1988 • Philip Kaufman
The Unbearable Lightness of Being

1989 • Gus Van Sant
Drugstore Cowboy

1990 • Martin Scorsese
Goodfellas

1991 • David Cronenberg
Naked Lunch

1992 • Clint Eastwood
Unforgiven

1993 • Steven Spielberg
Schindler's List

1994 • Quentin Tarantino
Pulp Fiction

1995 • Mike Figgis
Leaving Las Vegas

FILM

1966
Blow-Up

1967
Persona

1968
The Shame

1969
Z

1970
*M*A*S*H*

1971
Claire's Knee

1972
The Discreet Charm of the Bourgeoisie

1973
Day for Night

1974
Scenes from a Marriage

1975
Nashville

1976
All the President's Men

1977
Annie Hall

1978
Days of Heaven
Get Out Your Handkerchiefs

1979
Breaking Away

1980
Melvin and Howard

1981
Atlantic City

1982
Tootsie

1983
The Night of the Shooting Stars

1984
Stranger than Paradise

1985
Ran

1986
Blue Velvet

1987
The Dead
Hope and Glory

1988
The Unbearable Lightness of Being

1989
Drugstore Cowboy

1990
Goodfellas

1991
Life Is Sweet

1992
Unforgiven

1993
Schindler's List

1994
Pulp Fiction

1995
Babe

FEATURE DOCUMENTARY

1991
Paris is Burning

1993
Visions of Light: The Art of Cinematography

1994
Hoop Dreams

1995
Crumb

WRITING

1967
Bonnie & Clyde

1968
Faces

1969
Bob & Carol & Ted & Alice

1970
My Night at Maud's

1971
Sunday, Bloody Sunday

1972
Cries and Whispers

1973
American Graffiti

1974
Scenes from a Marriage

1975
Shampoo

1976
Jonah Who Will Be 25 in the Year 2000

1977
Annie Hall

1978
An Unmarried Woman

1979
Breaking Away

1980
Melvin and Howard

1981
Atlantic City

1982
Tootsie

1983
Local Hero

1984
Splash

1985
Lost in America

1986
My Beautiful Laundrette

1987
Hope and Glory

1988
Bull Durham

1989
Drugstore Cowboy

1990
To Sleep with Anger

1991
Naked Lunch

1992
Unforgiven

1993
The Piano

1994
Pulp Fiction

1995
Clueless

FILM—FOREIGN LANGUAGE

1990
Ariel

1991
The Double Life of Veronique

1992
Raise the Red Lantern

1993
The Story of Qui Ju

1994
Trois Couleurs: Rouge

1995
Wild Reeds

NEW YORK FILM CRITICS AWARDS

ACTOR

1935 • Charles Laughton
Mutiny on the Bounty
Charles Laughton
Ruggles of Red Gap

1936 • Walter Huston
Dodsworth

1937 • Paul Muni
The Life of Emile Zola

1938 • James Cagney
Angels with Dirty Faces

1939 • James Stewart
Mr. Smith Goes to Washington

1940 • Charlie Chaplin
The Great Dictator

1941 • Gary Cooper
Sergeant York

1942 • James Cagney
Yankee Doodle Dandy

1943 • Paul Lukas
Watch on the Rhine

1944 • Barry Fitzgerald
Going My Way

1945 • Ray Milland
The Lost Weekend

1946 • Laurence Olivier
Henry V

1947 • William Powell
Life with Father
William Powell
The Senator was Indiscreet

1948 • Laurence Olivier
Hamlet

1949 • Broderick Crawford
All the King's Men

1953 • Burt Lancaster
From Here to Eternity

1954 • Marlon Brando
On the Waterfront

1955 • Ernest Borgnine
Marty

1956 • Kirk Douglas
Lust for Life

1957 • Alec Guinness
The Bridge on the River Kwai

1958 • David Niven
Separate Tables

1959 • James Stewart
Anatomy of a Murder

1960 • Burt Lancaster
Elmer Gantry

1961 • Maximilian Schell
Judgment at Nuremberg

1963 • Albert Finney
Tom Jones

1964 • Rex Harrison
My Fair Lady

1965 • Oskar Werner
Ship of Fools

1966 • Paul Scofield
A Man for All Seasons

1967 • Rod Steiger
In the Heat of the Night

1968 • Alan Arkin
The Heart is a Lonely Hunter

1969 • Jon Voight
Midnight Cowboy

1970 • George C. Scott
Patton

1971 • Gene Hackman
The French Connection

1972 • Laurence Olivier
Sleuth

1973 • Marlon Brando
Last Tango in Paris

1974 ● Jack Nicholson
Chinatown
Jack Nicholson
The Last Detail

1975 ● Jack Nicholson
One Flew Over the Cuckoo's Nest

1976 ● Robert De Niro
Taxi Driver

1977 ● John Gielgud
Providence

1978 ● Jon Voight
Coming Home

1979 ● Dustin Hoffman
Kramer vs. Kramer

1980 ● Robert De Niro
Raging Bull
Robert De Niro
Raging Bull

1981 ● Burt Lancaster
Atlantic City

1982 ● Ben Kingsley
Gandhi

1983 ● Robert Duvall
Tender Mercies

1984 ● Steve Martin
All of Me

1985 ● Jack Nicholson
Prizzi's Honor

1986 ● Bob Hoskins
Mona Lisa

1987 ● Jack Nicholson
Ironweed
Jack Nicholson
The Witches of Eastwick

1988 ● Jeremy Irons
Dead Ringers

1989 ● Daniel Day-Lewis
My Left Foot

1990 ● Robert De Niro
Goodfellas

1991 ● Anthony Hopkins
The Silence of the Lambs

1992 ● Denzel Washington
Malcolm X

1993 ● David Thewlis
Naked

1994 ● Paul Newman
Nobody's Fool

1995 ● Nicolas Cage
Leaving Las Vegas

ACTOR—SUPPORTING

1969 ● Jack Nicholson
Easy Rider

1970 ● Chief Dan George
Little Big Man

1971 ● Ben Johnson
The Last Picture Show

1972 ● Robert Duvall
The Godfather

1973 ● Robert De Niro
Bang the Drum Slowly

1974 ● Charles Boyer
Stavisky

1975 ● Alan Arkin
Hearts of the West

1976 ● Jason Robards, Jr.
All the President's Men

1977 ● Maximilian Schell
Julia

1978 ● Christopher Walken
The Deer Hunter

1979 ● Melvyn Douglas
Being There

1980 ● Joe Pesci
Raging Bull
Joe Pesci
Raging Bull

1981 ● John Gielgud
Arthur

1982 ● John Lithgow
The World According to Garp

1983 ● Jack Nicholson
Terms of Endearment

1984 ● Ralph Richardson
Greystoke: The Legend of Tarzan, Lord of the Apes

1985 ● Klaus Maria Brandauer
Out of Africa

1986 ● Daniel Day-Lewis
My Beautiful Laundrette
Daniel Day-Lewis
A Room with a View

1987 ● Morgan Freeman
Street Smart

1988 ● Dean Stockwell
Married to the Mob
Dean Stockwell
Tucker: The Man and His Dream

1989 ● Alan Alda
Crimes & Misdemeanors

1990 ● Bruce Davison
Longtime Companion

1991 ● Samuel L. Jackson
Jungle Fever

1992 ● Gene Hackman
Unforgiven

1993 ● Ralph Fiennes
Schindler's List

1994 ● Martin Landau
Ed Wood

1995 ● Kevin Spacey
Outbreak
Kevin Spacey
Seven
Kevin Spacey
Swimming with Sharks
Kevin Spacey
The Usual Suspects

ACTRESS

1935 ● Greta Garbo
Anna Karenina

1936 ● Luise Rainer
The Great Ziegfeld
Luise Rainer
The Great Ziegfeld

1937 ● Greta Garbo
Camille

1938 ● Margaret Sullavan
Three Comrades

1939 ● Vivien Leigh
Gone with the Wind

1940 ● Katharine Hepburn
The Philadelphia Story

1941 ● Joan Fontaine
Suspicion

1942 ● Agnes Moorehead
The Magnificent Ambersons

1944 ● Tallulah Bankhead
Lifeboat

1945 ● Ingrid Bergman
The Bells of St. Mary's
Ingrid Bergman
Spellbound

1946 ● Celia Johnson
Brief Encounter

1947 ● Deborah Kerr
Black Narcissus

1948 ● Olivia de Havilland
The Snake Pit

1949 ● Olivia de Havilland
The Heiress

1950 ● Bette Davis
All About Eve

1951 ● Vivien Leigh
A Streetcar Named Desire

1952 ● Shirley Booth
Come Back, Little Sheba

1953 ● Audrey Hepburn
Roman Holiday

1954 ● Grace Kelly
Country Girl

1955 ● Anna Magnani
The Rose Tattoo

1956 ● Ingrid Bergman
Anastasia

1958 ● Susan Hayward
I Want to Live!

1959 ● Audrey Hepburn
The Nun's Story

1960 ● Deborah Kerr
The Sundowners

1961 ● Sophia Loren
Two Women

1963 ● Patricia Neal
Hud

1964 ● Kim Stanley
Seance on a Wet Afternoon

1965 ● Julie Christie
Darling

1966 ● Lynn Redgrave
Georgy Girl
Elizabeth Taylor
Who's Afraid of Virginia Woolf?

1968 ● Joanne Woodward
Rachel, Rachel

1969 ● Jane Fonda
They Shoot Horses, Don't They?

1970 ● Glenda Jackson
Women in Love

1971 ● Jane Fonda
Klute

1972 ● Liv Ullmann
Cries and Whispers
Liv Ullmann
The Emigrants

1973 ● Joanne Woodward
Summer Wishes, Winter Dreams

1974 ● Liv Ullmann
Scenes from a Marriage

1975 ● Isabelle Adjani
Story of Adele H.

1976 ● Liv Ullmann
Face to Face

1977 ● Diane Keaton
Annie Hall

1978 ● Ingrid Bergman
Autumn Sonata

1979 ● Sally Field
Norma Rae

1980 ● Sissy Spacek
Coal Miner's Daughter

1982 ● Meryl Streep
Sophie's Choice

1983 ● Shirley MacLaine
Terms of Endearment

1984 ● Peggy Ashcroft
A Passage to India

1985 ● Norma Aleandro
The Official Story

1986 ● Sissy Spacek
Crimes of the Heart

1987 ● Holly Hunter
Broadcast News

1988 ● Meryl Streep
A Cry in the Dark

1989 ● Michelle Pfeiffer
The Fabulous Baker Boys

1990 ● Joanne Woodward
Mr. & Mrs. Bridge

1991 ● Jodie Foster
The Silence of the Lambs

1992 ● Emma Thompson
Howard's End

1993 ● Holly Hunter
The Piano

1994 ● Linda Fiorentino
The Last Seduction

1995 ● Jennifer Jason Leigh
Georgia

ACTRESS—SUPPORTING

1969 ● Dyan Cannon
Bob & Carol & Ted & Alice

1970 ● Karen Black
Five Easy Pieces

1971 ● Ellen Burstyn
The Last Picture Show

1972 ● Jeannie Berlin
The Heartbreak Kid

1973 ● Valentina Cortese
Day for Night

1974 ● Valerie Perrine
Lenny

1975 ● Lily Tomlin
Nashville

1976 ● Talia Shire
Rocky

1978 ● Mona Washbourne
Stevie

1979 ● Meryl Streep
Kramer vs. Kramer
Meryl Streep
Manhattan
Meryl Streep
The Seduction of Joe Tynan

1980 ● Mary Steenburgen
Melvin and Howard

1982 ● Jessica Lange
Tootsie

1983 ● Linda Hunt
The Year of Living Dangerously

1984 ● Christine Lahti
Swing Shift

1985 ● Anjelica Huston
Prizzi's Honor

1986 ● Dianne Wiest
Hannah and Her Sisters

1987 ● Vanessa Redgrave
Prick Up Your Ears

1988 ● Diane Venora
Bird

1989 ● Lena Olin
Enemies, a Love Story
Jennifer Jason Leigh
Last Exit to Brooklyn

1990 ● Jennifer Jason Leigh
Miami Blues

1991 ● Judy Davis
Barton Fink
Judy Davis
Naked Lunch

1992 ● Miranda Richardson
The Crying Game

1993 ● Gong Li
Farewell My Concubine

1994 ● Dianne Wiest
Bullets Over Broadway

1995 ● Mira Sorvino
Mighty Aphrodite

CINEMATOGRAPHY

1980
Tess

1981
Chariots of Fire

1982
Sophie's Choice

1983
Zelig

1984
The Killing Fields

1985
Out of Africa

1986
A Room with a View

1987
The Last Emperor

1988
Wings of Desire

1989
Do the Right Thing

1990
The Sheltering Sky

1991
Barton Fink

1992
The Player

1993
Schindler's List

CINEMATOGRAPHY ▶cont.

1994
Ed Wood

DIRECTOR

1935 ● John Ford
The Informer

1937 ● Gregory La Cava
Stage Door

1938 ● Alfred Hitchcock
The Lady Vanishes

1939 ● John Ford
Stagecoach

1940 ● John Ford
The Grapes of Wrath
John Ford
The Long Voyage Home

1941 ● John Ford
How Green Was My Valley

1942 ● John Farrow
Wake Island

1943 ● George Stevens
The More the Merrier

1944 ● Leo McCarey
Going My Way

1945 ● Billy Wilder
The Lost Weekend

1946 ● William Wyler
The Best Years of Our Lives

1947 ● Elia Kazan
Gentleman's Agreement

1948 ● John Huston
Treasure of the Sierra Madre

1949 ● Carol Reed
The Fallen Idol

1950 ● Joseph L. Mankiewicz
All About Eve

1951 ● Elia Kazan
A Streetcar Named Desire

1952 ● Fred Zinnemann
High Noon

1953 ● Fred Zinnemann
From Here to Eternity

1954 ● Elia Kazan
On the Waterfront

1955 ● David Lean
Summertime

1956 ● John Huston
Moby Dick

1957 ● David Lean
The Bridge on the River Kwai

1958 ● Stanley Kramer
The Defiant Ones

1959 ● Fred Zinnemann
The Nun's Story

1960 ● Billy Wilder
The Apartment

1961 ● Robert Rossen
The Hustler

1963 ● Tony Richardson
Tom Jones

1964 ● Stanley Kubrick
Dr. Strangelove, or: How I Learned to Stop Worrying and Love the Bomb

1965 ● John Schlesinger
Darling

1966 ● Fred Zinnemann
A Man for All Seasons

1967 ● Mike Nichols
The Graduate
Mike Nichols
In the Heat of the Night

1968 ● Paul Newman
Rachel, Rachel

1969 ● Constantin Costa-Gavras
Z

1970 ● Bob Rafelson
Five Easy Pieces

1971 ● Stanley Kubrick
A Clockwork Orange

1972 ● Ingmar Bergman
Cries and Whispers

1973 ● Francois Truffaut
Day for Night

1974 ● Federico Fellini
Amarcord

1975 ● Robert Altman
Nashville

1976 ● Alan J. Pakula
All the President's Men

1977 ● Woody Allen
Annie Hall

1978 ● Terence Malick
Days of Heaven

1979 ● Woody Allen
Manhattan

1980 ● Jonathan Demme
Melvin and Howard

1981 ● Sidney Lumet
Prince of the City

1982 ● Sydney Pollack
Tootsie

1983 ● Ingmar Bergman
Fanny and Alexander

1984 ● David Lean
A Passage to India

1985 ● John Huston
Prizzi's Honor

1986 ● Woody Allen
Hannah and Her Sisters

1987 ● James L. Brooks
Broadcast News

1988 ● Chris Menges
A World Apart

1989 ● Paul Mazursky
Enemies, a Love Story

1990 ● Martin Scorsese
Goodfellas
Whit Stillman
Metropolitan

1991 ● Jonathan Demme
The Silence of the Lambs

1992 ● Robert Altman
The Player

1993 ● Jane Campion
The Piano

1994 ● Quentin Tarantino
Pulp Fiction

1995 ● Ang Lee
Sense and Sensibility

FILM

1935
The Informer

1936
Mr. Deeds Goes to Town

1937
The Life of Emile Zola

1938
The Citadel

1939
Wuthering Heights

1940
The Grapes of Wrath

1941
Citizen Kane

1942
In Which We Serve

1943
Watch on the Rhine

1944
Going My Way

1945
The Lost Weekend

1946
The Best Years of Our Lives

1947
Gentleman's Agreement

1948
Treasure of the Sierra Madre

1949
All the King's Men

1950
All About Eve

1951
A Streetcar Named Desire

1952
High Noon

1953
From Here to Eternity

1954
On the Waterfront

1955
Marty

1956
Around the World in 80 Days

1957
The Bridge on the River Kwai

1958
The Defiant Ones

1959
Ben-Hur

1960
The Apartment

1961
West Side Story

1963
Tom Jones

1964
My Fair Lady

1965
Darling

1966
A Man for All Seasons

1967
In the Heat of the Night

1968
The Lion in Winter

1969
Z

1970
Five Easy Pieces

1971
A Clockwork Orange

1972
Cries and Whispers

1973
Day for Night

1974
Amarcord

1975
Nashville

1976
All the President's Men

1977
Annie Hall

1978
The Deer Hunter

1979
Kramer vs. Kramer

1980
Ordinary People

1981
Reds

1982
Gandhi

1983
Terms of Endearment

1984
A Passage to India

1985
Prizzi's Honor

1986
Hannah and Her Sisters

1987
Broadcast News

1988
The Accidental Tourist

1989
My Left Foot

1990
Goodfellas

1991
The Silence of the Lambs

1992
The Player

1993
Schindler's List

1994
Quiz Show

1995
Leaving Las Vegas

FEATURE DOCUMENTARY

1992
Brother's Keeper

1993
Visions of Light: The Art of Cinematography

1994
Hoop Dreams

WRITING

1956
Around the World in 80 Days

1958
The Defiant Ones

1959
Anatomy of a Murder

1960
The Apartment

1961
Judgment at Nuremberg

1963
Hud

1964
The Servant

1966
A Man for All Seasons

1967
Bonnie & Clyde

1968
Pretty Poison

1969
Bob & Carol & Ted & Alice

1970
My Night at Maud's

1971
The Last Picture Show
Sunday, Bloody Sunday

1972
Cries and Whispers

1973
American Graffiti

1974
Scenes from a Marriage

1975
Story of Adele H.

1976
Network

1977
Annie Hall

1978
An Unmarried Woman

1979
Breaking Away

1980
Melvin and Howard

1981
Atlantic City

1982
Tootsie

1983
Local Hero

1984
Places in the Heart

1985
The Purple Rose of Cairo

1986
My Beautiful Laundrette

1987
Broadcast News

1988
Bull Durham

1989
Drugstore Cowboy

1990
Mr. & Mrs. Bridge

1991
Naked Lunch

1992
The Crying Game

1993
The Piano

1994
Pulp Fiction

FILM—FOREIGN LANGUAGE

1936
Carnival in Flanders

1937
Mayerling

1938
Grand Illusion

1939
Harvest

1940
The Baker's Wife

1946
Open City

1948
Paisan

1949
The Bicycle Thief

1951
Miracle in Milan

1952
Forbidden Games

1955
Diabolique
Umberto D

1956
La Strada

1957
Gervaise

1958
Mon Oncle

1959
The 400 Blows

1960
Hiroshima, Mon Amour

1961
La Dolce Vita

1963
8 1/2

1964
That Man from Rio

1965
Juliet of the Spirits

1966
The Shop on Main Street

1968
War and Peace

1978
Bread and Chocolate

1979
The Tree of Wooden Clogs

1980
Mon Oncle D'Amerique

1981
Pixote

1982
Time Stands Still

1983
Fanny and Alexander

1984
A Sunday in the Country

1985
Ran

1986
The Decline of the American Empire

1987
My Life as a Dog

1988
Women on the Verge of a Nervous Breakdown

1989
The Story of Women

1990
The Nasty Girl

1991
Europa, Europa

1992
Raise the Red Lantern

1993
Farewell My Concubine

1994
Trois Couleurs: Rouge

SCREEN ACTORS GUILD AWARDS

ACTOR

1994 ● Tom Hanks
Forrest Gump

1995 ● Nicolas Cage
Leaving Las Vegas

ACTOR—SUPPORTING

1994 ● Martin Landau
Ed Wood

1995 ● Ed Harris
Apollo 13

ACTRESS

1994 ● Jodie Foster
Nell

1995 ● Susan Sarandon
Dead Man Walking

ACTRESS—SUPPORTING

1994 ● Dianne Wiest
Bullets Over Broadway

1995 ● Kate Winslet
Sense and Sensibility

CAST

1995
Apollo 13

SUNDANCE FILM FESTIVAL

CINEMATOGRAPHY

1990
House Party

1991
Daughters of the Dust

1992
Swoon

1994
Suture

1995
Angela
Crumb

1996
Color of a Brisk and Leaping Day

WRITING

1991
Hangin' with the Homeboys
Trust

1992
The Waterdance

1993
Combination Platter

1994
What Happened Was...

1995
Living in Oblivion

1996
Big Night

AUDIENCE AWARD

1989
sex, lies and videotape

1990
Longtime Companion

1991
Pastime

1992
Brother's Keeper
The Waterdance

1993
El Mariachi

1994
Hoop Dreams
Spanking the Monkey

1995
Picture Bride
Unzipped

1996
The Spitfire Grill

FILMMAKERS TROPHY

1989
Powwow Highway

1992
A Brief History of Time
Zebrahead

1993
Fly by Night

1994
Clerks
Fresh

1995
Angela

1996
Girls Town

GRAND JURY PRIZE

1978
Girlfriends

1981
Gal Young 'Un
Heartland

1982
Street Music

1984
Old Enough

1985
Blood Simple

1986
Smooth Talk

1987
The Trouble with Dick
Waiting for the Moon

1988
Heat and Sunlight

1989
True Love

1990
Chameleon Street

1991
Paris is Burning
Poison

1992
In the Soup

1993
Public Access
Ruby in Paradise

1994
What Happened Was...

1995
The Brothers McMullen
Crumb

1996
Welcome to the Dollhouse

SPECIAL JURY PRIZE

1987
River's Edge

1990
To Sleep with Anger

1991
Straight Out of Brooklyn

1992
The Hours and Times

1993
Just Another Girl on the I.R.T.

1994
Fresh

1995
Heavy
Rhythm Thief

TORONTO-CITY AWARD

CANADIAN FEATURE FILM

1985
Canada's Sweetheart: The Saga of Hal C. Banks

1986
The Decline of the American Empire

1987
Family Viewing

1988
Outside Chance of Maximillian Glick

1989
Roadkill

1990
H

1991
The Adjuster

1994
Exotica

1995
Live Bait

WRITERS GUILD OF AMERICA

WRITING

1967
Bonnie & Clyde

1968
Goodbye Columbus
The Producers

1969
Bob & Carol & Ted & Alice
Butch Cassidy and the Sundance Kid
Midnight Cowboy

1970
I Never Sang For My Father
*M*A*S*H*
The Out-of-Towners
Patton

1971
The French Connection
The Hospital
Kotch
Sunday, Bloody Sunday

1972
Cabaret
The Candidate
The Godfather
What's Up, Doc?

1973
Paper Moon
Save the Tiger
Serpico
A Touch of Class

WRITING ▶*cont.*

1974
The Apprenticeship of Duddy Kravitz
Blazing Saddles
Chinatown
The Godfather, Part 2

1975
Dog Day Afternoon
One Flew Over the Cuckoo's Nest
Shampoo
The Sunshine Boys

1976
All the President's Men
The Bad News Bears
Network
The Pink Panther Strikes Again

1977
Annie Hall
Julia
Oh, God!
The Turning Point

1978
Coming Home
Heaven Can Wait
Midnight Express
Movie, Movie

1979
Being There
Breaking Away
The China Syndrome
Kramer vs. Kramer

1980
Airplane!
Melvin and Howard
Ordinary People
Private Benjamin

1981
Arthur
On Golden Pond
Reds
Rich and Famous

1982
E.T.: The Extra-Terrestrial
Missing
Tootsie
Victor/Victoria

1983
The Big Chill
Reuben, Reuben
Tender Mercies
Terms of Endearment

1984
Broadway Danny Rose
The Killing Fields

1985
Prizzi's Honor
Witness

1986
Hannah and Her Sisters
A Room with a View

1987
Moonstruck
Roxanne

1988
Bull Durham
Dangerous Liaisons

1989
Crimes & Misdemeanors
Driving Miss Daisy

1990
Avalon
Dances with Wolves

1991
The Silence of the Lambs
Thelma & Louise

1992
The Crying Game
The Player

1993
The Piano
Schindler's List

1994
Forrest Gump
Four Weddings and a Funeral

1995
Braveheart
Sense and Sensibility

GOLDEN RASPBERRY AWARDS

WORST PICTURE

1980
Can't Stop the Music

1981
Mommie Dearest

1983
The Lonely Lady

1984
Bolero

1985
Rambo: First Blood, Part 2

1986
Howard the Duck
Under the Cherry Moon

1987
Leonard Part 6

1988
Cocktail

1989
Star Trek 5: The Final Frontier

1990
The Adventures of Ford Fairlane
Ghosts Can't Do It

1991
Hudson Hawk

1992
Shining Through

1993
Indecent Proposal

1994
Color of Night

1995
Showgirls

WORST REMAKE/ SEQUEL

1994
Wyatt Earp

1995
The Scarlet Letter

WORST ACTOR

1980 • Neil Diamond
The Jazz Singer

1981 • Klinton Spilsbury
Legend of the Lone Ranger

1983 • Christopher Atkins
A Night in Heaven

1984 • Sylvester Stallone
Rhinestone

1985 • Sylvester Stallone
Rambo: First Blood, Part 2
Sylvester Stallone
Rocky 4

1986 • Prince
Under the Cherry Moon

1987 • Bill Cosby
Leonard Part 6

1988 • Sylvester Stallone
Rambo 3

1989 • William Shatner
Star Trek 5: The Final Frontier

1990 • Andrew Dice Clay
The Adventures of Ford Fairlane

1991 • Kevin Costner
Robin Hood: Prince of Thieves

1992 • Sylvester Stallone
Stop! or My Mom Will Shoot

1993 • Burt Reynolds
Cop and a Half

1994 • Kevin Costner
Wyatt Earp

1995 • Pauly Shore
Jury Duty

WORST ACTRESS

1980 • Brooke Shields
The Blue Lagoon

1981 • Faye Dunaway
Mommie Dearest
Bo Derek
Tarzan, the Ape Man

1982 • Pia Zadora
Butterfly

1983 • Pia Zadora
The Lonely Lady

1984 • Bo Derek
Bolero

1985 • Linda Blair
Night Patrol
Linda Blair
Savage Island
Linda Blair
Savage Streets

1986 • Madonna
Shanghai Surprise

1987 • Liza Minnelli
Arthur 2: On the Rocks
Madonna
Who's That Girl?

1988 • Liza Minnelli
Rent-A-Cop

1990 • Bo Derek
Ghosts Can't Do It

1991 • Sean Young
A Kiss Before Dying

1992 • Melanie Griffith
Shining Through
Melanie Griffith
A Stranger Among Us

1993 • Madonna
Body of Evidence

1994 • Sharon Stone
Intersection
Sharon Stone
The Specialist

1995 • Elizabeth Berkley
Showgirls

WORST SUPPORTING ACTOR

1980 • John Adams
Gloria
Laurence Olivier
The Jazz Singer

1981 • Steve Forrest
Mommie Dearest

1982 • Ed McMahon
Butterfly

1983 • Jim Nabors
Stroker Ace

1985 • Rob Lowe
St. Elmo's Fire

1986 • Jerome Benton
Under the Cherry Moon

1987 • David Mendenhall
Over the Top

1988 • Dan Aykroyd
Caddyshack 2

1989 • Christopher Atkins
Listen to Me

1991 • Dan Aykroyd
Nothing But Trouble

1992 • Tom Selleck
Christopher Columbus: The Discovery

1993 • Woody Harrelson
Indecent Proposal

1994 • O.J. Simpson
Naked Gun 33 1/3: The Final Insult

1995 • Dennis Hopper
Waterworld

WORST SUPPORTING ACTRESS

1980 • Amy Irving
Honeysuckle Rose

1981 • Diana Scarwid
Mommie Dearest

1982 • Aileen Quinn
Annie

1983 • Sybil Danning
Chained Heat
Sybil Danning
Hercules

1984 • Lynn-Holly Johnson
Where the Boys Are '84

1985 • Brigitte Nielsen
Rocky 4

1987 • Daryl Hannah
Wall Street

1988 • Kristy McNichol
Two Moon Junction

1989 • Brooke Shields
Speed Zone

1990 • Sofia Coppola
The Godfather, Part 3

1991 • Sean Young
A Kiss Before Dying

1992 • Estelle Getty
Stop! or My Mom Will Shoot

1993 • Faye Dunaway
The Temp

1994 • Rosie O'Donnell
Car 54, Where Are You?
Rosie O'Donnell
Exit to Eden
Rosie O'Donnell
The Flintstones

1995 • Madonna
Four Rooms

WORST DIRECTOR

1980 • Robert Greenwald
Xanadu

1981 • Michael Cimino
Heaven's Gate

1982 • Ken Annakin
Pirate Movie

1983 • Peter Sasdy
The Lonely Lady

1984 • John Derek
Bolero

1985 • Sylvester Stallone
Rocky 4

1986 • Prince
Under the Cherry Moon

1987 • Elaine May
Ishtar
Norman Mailer
Tough Guys Don't Dance

1988 • Stewart Raffill
Mac and Me
Blake Edwards
Sunset

1989 • William Shatner
Star Trek 5: The Final Frontier

1990 • John Derek
Ghosts Can't Do It

1991 • Michael Lehmann
Hudson Hawk

1992 • David Seltzer
Shining Through

1993 • Jennifer Lynch
Boxing Helena

1994 • Steven Seagal
On Deadly Ground

1995 • Paul Verhoeven
Showgirls

WORST SCREENPLAY

1980
Can't Stop the Music

1981
Mommie Dearest

1983
The Lonely Lady

1984
Bolero

1985
Rambo: First Blood, Part 2
Rocky 4

1986
Howard the Duck

1987
Leonard Part 6

1988
Cocktail

1989
Harlem Nights

1990
The Adventures of Ford Fairlane

1991
Hudson Hawk

1992
Stop! or My Mom Will Shoot

1993
Indecent Proposal

1994
The Flintstones

1995
Showgirls

WORST SONG

1980 ● "The Man with Bogart's Face"
The Man with Bogart's Face

1981 ● "Baby Talk"
Paternity

1982 ● "Pumpin' and Blowin'"
Pirate Movie

1983 ● "The Way You Do It"
The Lonely Lady

1984 ● "Drinkenstein"
Rhinestone

1985 ● "Peace In Our Life"
Rambo: First Blood, Part 2

1986 ● "Love or Money"
Under the Cherry Moon

1987 ● "I Want Your Sex"
Beverly Hills Cop 2

1988 ● "Jack Fresh"
Caddyshack 2

1989 ● "Bring Your Daughter to the Slaughter"
A Nightmare on Elm Street 5: Dream Child

1990 ● "He's Comin' Back (The Devil!)"
Repossessed

1991 ● "Addams Groove"
The Addams Family

1992 ● "High Times, Hard Times"
Newsies

1993 ● "WHOOMP! There It Is"
Addams Family Values

1994 ● "Marry the Mole"
Thumbelina

1995 ● "Walk into the Wind"
Showgirls

WORST NEW STAR

1981 ● Klinton Spilsbury
Legend of the Lone Ranger

1982 ● Pia Zadora
Butterfly

1983 ● Lou Ferrigno
Hercules

1984 ● Olivia D'Abo
Bolero
Olivia D'Abo
Conan the Destroyer

1985 ● Brigitte Nielsen
Red Sonja
Brigitte Nielsen
Rocky 4

1987 ● David Mendenhall
Over the Top

1990 ● Sofia Coppola
The Godfather, Part 3

1991 ● Vanilla Ice
Cool As Ice

1992 ● Pauly Shore
Encino Man

1993 ● Janet Jackson
Poetic Justice

1994 ● Anna Nicole Smith
Naked Gun 33 1/3: The Final Insult

1995 ● Elizabeth Berkley
Showgirls

Foreign Film Index

The **Foreign Film Index** classifies movies by the country of record in which they were produced. Since a film may be financed or produced in more than one country, some videos will appear with more than one country of origin. The codes appear in the review, immediately following the color/black and white designation before the credits. In this index, movies are listed alphabetically by country.

Key to Country Origination Tags

AL Algerian
AR Argentinian
AT Austrian
AU Australian
BE Belgian
BR Brazilian
GB British
CA Canadian
CH Chinese
CL Colombian
CU Cuban
CZ Czech
DK Danish
NL Dutch
PH Filipino
FI Finnish
FR French
GE German
GR Greek
HK Hong Kong
HU Hungarian
IC Icelandic
IN Indian
IA Iranian
IR Irish
IS Israeli
IT Italian
JP Japanese
KO Korean
LI Lithuanian
MA Macedonian
MX Mexican
NZ New Zealand
NI Nicaraguan
NO Norwegian
PL Polish
PT Portuguese
RU Russian
SA South African
SP Spanish
SW Swedish
SI Swiss
TU Turkish
TW Taiwanese
VT Vietnamese
VZ Venezuelan
YU Yugoslavian

Algerian

Argentinean

Australian

Squizzy Taylor
Starstruck
Strangers
Stranglehold
Strictly Ballroom▶
The Sum of Us▶
Summer City
Summer of Secrets
Sunday Too Far Away▶
Survivor
Sweet Talker
Sweetie▶
The Tale of Ruby Rose▶
Talk
Tearaway
A Test of Love
That Eye, The Sky
Three's Trouble
Thundering Forest
Tim
Torn Allegiance
Touch & Go
A Town Like Alice
Traps
Travelling North
Treasure of the Yankee Zephyr
Tunnel Vision
Typhoon Treasure
Under Capricorn
Vincent: The Life and Death of Vincent van Gogh▶
The Wacky World of Wills & Burke
Walk into Hell
Warm Nights on a Slow-Moving Train
Waterfront
We of the Never Never▶
Who Killed Baby Azaria?
Wide Sargasso Sea
The Wild Duck
Windrider
The Winds of Jarrah
The Winter of Our Dreams
A Woman's Tale▶
A Yank in Australia
The Year My Voice Broke▶
The Year of Living Dangerously▶
Young Einstein

Austrian

The Hands of Orlac
Heidi▶
Time Troopers
Wandering Jew

Belgian

Between Heaven and Earth
Daens
Daughters of Darkness▶
The Devil's Nightmare
Dust▶
The Eighth Day
Farinelli
Les Rendez-vous D'Anna
Man Bites Dog
Mascara
The Music Teacher
Night and Day▶
One Sings, the Other Doesn't
Rabid Grannies
Suite 16
Toute Une Nuit▶
A Wedding in Galilee▶

Brazilian

Amor Bandido
Antonio Das Mortes
At Midnight, I'll Take Your Soul
Awakenings of the Beast
Black God & White Devil
Black Orpheus▶
Bye Bye Brazil
The Dolphin
Dona Flor and Her Two Husbands▶
Earth Entranced
Gabriela
Hallucinations of a Deranged Mind
Happily Ever After
The Hour of the Star▶
How Tasty Was My Little Frenchman
I Love You
Killer Fish
Kiss of the Spider Woman▶
Lady on the Bus
Luzia
O Quatrilho
Opera do Malandro
Pixote▶
Quilombo
Savage Capitalism
The Story of Fausta
Strange World of Coffin Joe
Subway to the Stars
Via Appia
Women in Fury
Xica▶

British

Abdulla the Great
Abigail's Party
The Abominable Dr. Phibes▶
Above Us the Waves▶
Absolute Beginners
Absolution
Accident
Accused
Across the Bridge
Action for Slander
The Adventurers
Adventures of a Private Eye
Adventures of a Taxi Driver
The Adventures of Sadie
The Adventures of Sherlock Holmes: Hound of the Baskervilles
The Adventures of Tartu
The Advocate▶
The Affair
An Affair in Mind
The Affair of the Pink Pearl
After Darkness
After Julius
After Pilkington
After the Fox
Afterward
Agatha Christie's Miss Marple
Alamut Ambush
Alfie▶
Alias John Preston
Alice▶
Alice's Adventures in Wonderland
Alien Women
All Creatures Great and Small▶
American Friends
American Roulette
And Nothing But the Truth
And Now for Something Completely Different▶
And Now the Screaming Starts
And Soon the Darkness
Angel with the Trumpet
Angels and Insects▶
Anna Karenina
The Anniversary
Another Country
Another Time, Another Place
Another Time, Another Place▶
Antonia and Jane▶
Apartment Zero▶
Appointment with Crime
Aria
Armistead Maupin's Tales of the City
The Arsenal Stadium Mystery
As You Like It
The Asphyx▶
The Assassination Bureau▶
Assassination of Trotsky
The Assassination Run
Assault
Assault on Agathon
Asylum
At the Earth's Core
The Atomic Man
August
An Awfully Big Adventure
The Baby and the Battleship
Baby Love
Bachelor of Hearts
Backbeat▶
Bad Behavior
Ballad in Blue
The Ballad of the Sad Cafe
Ballet Shoes
Bananas Boat
Bandit Queen
Battle Beneath the Earth
Battle Hell
The Battle of the Sexes▶
The Bawdy Adventures of Tom Jones
Beachcomber▶
Beast in the Cellar
Beast of Morocco
Beat Girl
Bedazzled▶
Before the Rain▶
The Belles of St. Trinian's▶
Bellman and True
The Belly of an Architect▶
Benny Hill's Crazy World
Bernard and the Genie
Best Enemies
The Best of Cracker Mysteries▶
The Best of Lovejoy Mysteries
The Best of the Two Ronnies
Betrayal
Bewitched
Bhaji on the Beach
The Big Man: Crossing the Line▶
Big Zapper
Biggles
Billy Budd▶
Billy Liar▶
The Bitch
Bitter Sweet
Black Beauty
The Black Cat
Black Eyes
Black Limelight
Black Narcissus▶
The Black Velvet Gown
Black Werewolf
Blackmail▶
Blackout
Blake's Seven
Bleak House
The Bliss of Mrs. Blossom▶
Blithe Spirit▶
Blockhouse
Blonde Blackmailer
Blood Beast Terror
Blood Island
Blood of the Vampire
The Blood on Satan's Claw▶
Bloodbath at the House of Death
The Bloodsuckers
Blow-Up▶
Blue
Blue Blood
The Blue Lamp▶
Blue Money
Blue Murder at St. Trinian's▶
Bobo
The Body in the Library
The Body Vanished
Bonnie Prince Charlie
The Borrowers▶
The Boy Friend▶
The Brain
Brazil▶
Breaking Glass
The Bretts▶
The Brides of Dracula
Brideshead Revisited▶
The Bridge on the River Kwai▶
A Bridge Too Far
Brief Encounter▶
Bright Smiler
Brighton Rock▶
Brimstone & Treacle▶
Britannia Hospital
Broken Melody
Brother Cadfael
Brothers in Law
The Browning Version▶
The Buccaneers▶
Buddy's Song
Bugsy Malone
Bulldog Drummond at Bay
Bulldog Jack▶
Bullshot
Burn Witch, Burn!▶
Burning Secret
Buster
Butler's Dilemma
Butterflies
Butterfly Ball
Butterfly Kiss
Caesar and Cleopatra
Call Him Mr. Shatter
Calling Paul Temple
Candles at Nine
A Canterbury Tale▶
Captain Horatio Hornblower▶
Captain Kronos: Vampire Hunter▶
Captain's Paradise▶
The Captain's Table
Captive Heart▶
Captives
Car Trouble
Caravaggio▶
Carlton Browne of the F.O.
Carrington
Carrington, V.C.▶
Carry On Admiral
Carry On at Your Convenience
Carry On Behind
Carry On Camping
Carry On Cleo
Carry On Cowboy
Carry On Dick
Carry On Doctor▶
Carry On Emmanuelle
Carry On England
Carry On Henry VIII
Carry On Nurse
Carry On 'Round the Bend
Carry On Screaming
The Case of the Frightened Lady
The Case of the Missing Lady
The Case of the Mukkinese Battle Horn
The Cassandra Crossing
Cast a Dark Shadow▶
The Castle of Fu Manchu
The Cat and the Canary
Catch Me a Spy
Catherine the Great
Century
The Chalk Garden▶
Chamber of Horrors
Champagne
Champions
The Charge of the Light Brigade
Chariots of Fire▶
Charlemagne
Charlie Grant's War
The Charmer
Chicago Joe & the Showgirl
The Children
Children of Rage
Children of the Damned
Children of the Full Moon
Chinese Boxes
Chitty Chitty Bang Bang
Choice of Weapons
A Chorus of Disapproval
Christabel
Christian the Lion
A Christmas Carol▶
Christopher Columbus
The Chronicles of Narnia
The Cinder Path
Circle of Deceit
Circle of Iron
Circle of Power
Circus of Fear
Circus of Horrors
The Citadel▶
City Boy▶
City of Joy
Clash of the Titans
The Class of Miss MacMichael
The Clergyman's Daughter
Clockwise
A Clockwork Orange▶
The Clouded Yellow▶
Codename: Icarus
Cold Comfort Farm▶
Cold Light of Day
Cold War Killers
The Collector▶
The Comeback
Comfort and Joy▶
Coming Through
Coming Up Roses
Conduct Unbecoming
The Confessional
The Conqueror Worm▶
Conspiracy of Hearts▶
Conspirator
Consuming Passions
The Cook, the Thief, His Wife & Her Lover▶
Cool Mikado
Corridors of Blood
Cottage to Let
The Count of Monte Cristo
Counterblast
The Country Diary of an Edwardian Lady
The Courageous Mr. Penn
The Courtesans of Bombay▶
The Courtney Affair
The Crackler
The Crawling Eye
The Creeping Flesh
Crimes at the Dark House▶
The Crimes of Stephen Hawke
The Crimson Cult
Crimson Pirate▶
Cromwell
Crooks & Coronets
Crow Hollow
Crucible of Horror
Cruel Sea▶
A Cry from the Streets
Cry of the Banshee
Cry of the Penguins
Cry Terror
Cry, the Beloved Country▶
Cul de Sac▶
The Curse of Frankenstein
Curse of the Demon▶
The Curse of the Werewolf
Curtain Up
Cyrano de Bergerac
Daleks—Invasion Earth 2150 A.D.
Dam Busters▶
Damage▶
Damn the Defiant▶
Dance with a Stranger▶

Dandy in Aspic
Danger Man
Danger UXB
A Dangerous Man: Lawrence after Arabia▶
Dangerous Moonlight▶
Dangerous Youth
Dante's Inferno: Life of Dante Gabriel Rossetti
A Dark Adapted Eye▶
The Dark Angel▶
Dark Journey▶
Dark of the Sun
Dark Places
Darling▶
The Dawning
A Day in the Death of Joe Egg▶
The Day Will Dawn▶
The Dead▶
Dead Lucky
Dead of Night▶
The Deadly Game
Deadly Recruits
Deadly Strangers
Dealers
Dear Murderer
Death Goes to School
The Death of Adolf Hitler
Death on the Nile
Death Ship
Decameron Nights
The Deceivers
A Dedicated Man
Deep End▶
Deep in the Heart
Defense of the Realm▶
Deja Vu
The Demi-Paradise▶
Demon Barber of Fleet Street
Demons of the Mind
Department Store
The Deputy Drummer
The Destructors
The Detective▶
Devices and Desires▶
Devil Doll
Devil Girl from Mars
Devil on Horseback
The Devils▶
The Devil's Disciple▶
The Devil's Undead
Diamonds Are Forever▶
Dick Barton, Special Agent
Dick Barton Strikes Back
Die! Die! My Darling!
Die, Monster, Die!
Die Screaming, Marianne
Digby, the Biggest Dog in the World
Dinner at the Ritz
Disciple of Death
Distant Voices, Still Lives▶
The Divorce of Lady X
The Doctor and the Devils
Doctor at Large
Doctor at Sea
Doctor Blood's Coffin
Doctor in Distress
Doctor in the House▶
Dr. Jekyll and Sister Hyde
Dr. No▶
Doctor Phibes Rises Again
Dr. Strangelove, or: How I Learned to Stop Worrying and Love the Bomb▶
Dr. Syn
Dr. Terror's House of Horrors
Doctor Who
Doctor Who: An Unearthly Child
Doctor Who and the Daleks
Doctor Who: Cybermen—The Early Years
The Dogs of War
Don't Hang Up
Don't Open Till Christmas
Doomwatch
Down Among the Z Men
Dracula Has Risen from the Grave
The Draughtsman's Contract▶
Dream Demon
Dreamchild▶
Dreaming Lips
Dressed for Death
The Dressmaker
Drowning by Numbers▶
Drums
Dual Alibi
Duel of Hearts
The Duellists▶
The Dummy Talks
Dust to Dust
Dutch Girls
Dutchman▶
The Dwelling Place
Dynasty of Fear
Eagle's Wing
East of Elephant Rock
Easy Virtue
Eat the Rich
Ebony Tower
Edge of Darkness
Edge of Sanity
Edge of the World▶
Educating Rita▶
Edward II
The Electronic Monster
Elephant Boy▶
11 Harrowhouse▶
Elizabeth R▶
The Elusive Pimpernel
Embassy
Empire State
Enchanted April
Encore▶
The Endless Game
Endless Night
An Englishman Abroad▶
The Englishman Who Went Up a Hill But Came Down a Mountain▶
Enigma
The Entertainer▶
Erik the Viking
Escapade▶
Escape from El Diablo
Escape to Athena
Eureka!
Evergreen
The Evil Mind
The Evil of Frankenstein
Evil under the Sun
The Executioner
Experience Preferred... But Not Essential
Eye Witness
Fall and Rise of Reginald Perrin 1▶
Fall and Rise of Reginald Perrin 2▶
Fall from Grace
The Fall of the House of Usher
The Fallen Idol▶
Fame Is the Spur
Family Life
Fanny Hill
Far from the Madding Crowd▶
Farewell, My Lovely▶
The Farmer's Wife
Fatal Confinement
The Favor, the Watch, & the Very Big Fish
Fawlty Towers
The Fearless Vampire Killers▶
Feet Foremost
The Field▶
The Fiend
The Fiendish Plot of Dr. Fu Manchu
The Fifteen Streets
The Fifth Musketeer
The Final Cut▶
The Final Option
The Final Programme
Finessing the King
Fire and Sword
Fire Down Below
Fire Maidens from Outer Space
Fire Over England▶
First Men in the Moon
Five Golden Dragons
Five Miles to Midnight
Flambards
Flame Over India▶
Flame to the Phoenix
The Flame Trees of Thika▶
Flesh and Blood Show
Flight from Singapore
Follow That Camel
Fools of Fortune
Footlight Frenzy
For Your Eyes Only▶
Forbidden Passion: The Oscar Wilde Movie
Foreign Body
A Foreign Field
The Foreman Went to France
Forever Young
Fortunes of War▶
The Forty-Ninth Parallel▶
Four Days in July
The Four Feathers▶
Four Sided Triangle
Four Weddings and a Funeral▶
The Fourth Protocol▶
The Franchise Affair
The Freakmaker
Freddie the Frog
The French Lesson
Frenzy
Frenzy▶
Frieda
Friends
Fright
Frightmare
From Beyond the Grave
From Russia with Love▶
Frozen Alive
Full Circle
Funny Money
Gallowglass▶
The Gambler & the Lady
Game for Vultures
The Gamma People
Gandhi▶
Gangway
The Garden
Gaslight▶
The Gay Lady
Genevieve▶
Genghis Cohn
Georgy Girl▶
Getting It Right
The Ghost Camera
The Ghost Goes West▶
Ghost in the Noonday Sun
Ghost Ship
The Ghost Train
The Ghoul
The Gift Horse
The Gilded Cage
A Girl in a Million
The Girl in the Picture
The Girl on a Motorcycle
Girly
Give My Regards to Broad Street
The Go-Between▶
The Golden Salamander
Goldfinger▶
The Good Father▶
Gorgo
The Gorgon
The Gospel According to Vic
Great Expectations▶
Great Expectations
Great Expectations▶
Great McGonagall
The Great St. Trinian's Train Robbery
The Great Train Robbery▶
The Greed of William Hart
Greek Street
Green for Danger
Green Grow the Rushes
Green Ice
The Green Man▶
Gregory's Girl▶
Grown Ups
The Guinea Pig
Gulag
Gulliver's Travels
Gumshoe
Guns at Batasi
Hail Mary
Hamlet▶
Hamlet
The Hand
The Hand▶
A Handful of Dust▶
The Hands of Orlac
Hands of the Ripper
The Happiest Days of Your Life▶
Happy Since I Met You▶
A Hard Day's Night▶
Hard Labour
Harry Black and the Tiger
Haunted
The Haunted Strangler
Haunted: The Ferryman
The Hawk
Hawks
Hear My Song▶
Heart's Desire
Heat and Dust▶
Heat Wave
Heaven's a Drag
Heavens Above▶
Hedd Wyn
Hedda
Hellbound: Hellraiser 2
The Hellfire Club
Hellraiser
Hennessy
Henry V▶
Hi-Di-Hi
The Hidden Room▶
High Command
High Hopes▶
High Season
The Hit
The Hitchhiker's Guide to the Galaxy
Hobson's Choice▶
The Holcroft Covenant
Home Sweet Home
Hope and Glory▶
Horror Hospital
Horror Hotel
The Horror of Dracula▶
The Horror of Frankenstein
Horror Planet
The Horse's Mouth▶
Hot Millions▶
Hotel du Lac
Hotel Paradiso
Hotel Reserve▶
The Hound of the Baskervilles▶
The Hound of the Baskervilles
Hour of Decision
The House in Marsh Road
House of Cards▶
The House of Eliott
The House of Lurking Death
House of Mystery
The House of 1000 Dolls
The House of the Arrow▶
House of Whipcord
The House that Dripped Blood
The House that Vanished
How I Learned to Love Women
How I Won the War
How Many Miles to Babylon?
How to Get Ahead in Advertising▶
Howard's End▶
Hue and Cry▶
Hullabaloo Over Georgie & Bonnie's Pictures
The Human Factor
The Human Monster
Hussy
Hysteria
I Am a Camera▶
I, Claudius, Vol. 1: A Touch of Murder/Family Affairs
I Don't Want to Be Born
I Know Where I'm Going▶
I Live in Grosvenor Square
I See a Dark Stranger▶
I Stand Condemned
I Want What I Want
If...▶
If I Were Rich
The Impossible Spy▶
Impulse
In Celebration▶
In Search of the Castaways▶
In the Name of the Father▶
In the Shadow of Kilimanjaro
In Which We Serve▶
The Informer
Inheritance▶
The Innocent
Innocent Lies
The Innocents▶
Innocents in Paris
Inserts
Inside Out
Insignificance▶
Inspector Hornleigh
Instant Justice
International Velvet
Internecine Project
Interrupted Journey
Intimate Contact▶
Invasion
Invasion of the Body Stealers
The Ipcress File▶
The Iron Duke
Island of Desire
Island of Terror▶
Island of the Burning Doomed
It Couldn't Happen Here
It Takes a Thief
The Italian Job
It's Love Again
Jabberwocky
Jack and Sarah
Jack the Ripper
Jamaica Inn
Jane & the Lost City
Jane Eyre▶
Jason and the Argonauts▶
Java Head▶
Jeeves & Wooster: Jeeves' Arrival
Jericho
The Jewel in the Crown
The Jigsaw Man
Johnny Frenchman
Johnny Nobody
Joseph Andrews
Journey to the Far Side of the Sun▶
Jude the Obscure
Juggernaut▶
Julius Caesar
Just Like a Woman
Just William's Luck
The Key
The Key Man
Killer Fish
The Killing Fields▶
Killing Heat
Kind Hearts and Coronets▶
A Kind of Loving▶
A King in New York
King Lear▶

The King of Hearts▶
King of the Damned
King Solomon's Treasure
Kings and Desperate Men
The King's Rhapsody
Kipperbang
Kipps▶
Kiss of Death
Kiss of the Vampire
The Kitchen Toto▶
The Knack▶
Knight Without Armour▶
Knights & Emeralds
The Krays▶
Krull
Ladies Who Do
Lady Caroline Lamb
Lady Chatterley's Lover
Lady in Distress
Lady Jane▶
Lady of the Lake
The Lady Vanishes▶
The Lady Vanishes
Ladybird, Ladybird▶
The Ladykillers▶
The Lair of the White Worm▶
Land and Freedom▶
Land of Fury
Land of the Minotaur
The Land That Time Forgot
The Last Days of Dolwyn
Last Holiday▶
The Last of England▶
Last Reunion
Late Extra
The Lavender Hill Mob▶
Lawrence of Arabia▶
The League of Gentlemen▶
Leather Boys
The Legacy
Legend
Legend of the Werewolf
Leon the Pig Farmer
Les Carabiniers▶
Let Him Have It▶
Let's Make Up
Letter to Brezhnev▶
Letters to an Unknown Lover
License to Kill▶
Lies
The Life and Adventures of Nicholas Nickleby▶
The Life and Death of Colonel Blimp▶
Life Is Sweet▶
Lillie▶
Lily of Killarney
The Limping Man
Link
Lion of the Desert▶
Lipstick On Your Collar
Lisztomania
Little Dorrit, Film 1: Nobody's Fault▶
Little Dorrit, Film 2: Little Dorrit's Story▶
The Little Match Girl
The Little Prince
The Little Princess
Live and Let Die
The Living Dead
Loaded
Local Hero▶
The Lodger▶
Lola
Lolita▶
London Kills Me
London Melody
The Loneliness of the Long Distance Runner▶
The Lonely Passion of Judith Hearne▶
Long Ago Tomorrow
The Long Dark Hall
The Long Day Closes▶
The Long Good Friday▶
Look Back in Anger▶
The Looking Glass War
Loophole
Loose Connections
Loot...Give Me Money, Honey!
Lord of the Flies▶
Lorna Doone
The Lost Language of Cranes▶
Love and Bullets
The Love Factor
Love for Lydia▶
Love from a Stranger
Love on the Dole▶
Lucky Jim
The Lunatic
Lust for a Vampire
Mad Death
Made in Heaven
Mademoiselle
Madhouse
Madhouse Mansion
The Madness of King George▶
The Magic Christian▶
Magic Moments
Magical Mystery Tour
The Mahabharata
Major Barbara▶
Make Me an Offer
Make Mine Mink▶
A Man About the House
Man Bait
A Man for All Seasons▶
Man Friday
The Man from the Pru
The Man in Grey▶
The Man in the Mist
The Man in the White Suit▶
Man of Evil
A Man of No Importance▶
Man on the Run
The Man Outside
The Man Who Cried
The Man Who Fell to Earth▶
Man Who Had Power Over Women
The Man Who Haunted Himself
The Man Who Knew Too Much▶
The Man Who Lived Again
The Man Who Never Was▶
The Man with the Golden Gun
Mandy▶
Mania
Maniac
Mansfield Park
The Manxman
Marat/Sade▶
March or Die
Margaret's Museum
Maria's Child
The Mark▶
Mark of the Devil
Mark of the Devil 2
The Mark of the Hawk▶
A Married Man
Masque of the Red Death▶
A Matter of WHO
Maurice▶
Max and Helen
Max Headroom, the Original Story
Mayerling
The Maze▶
The McGuffin
McVicar
The Medusa Touch
Meet Sexton Blake
Melody
Men Are Not Gods
Men of Sherwood Forest
Men of Two Worlds
The Merchant of Venice▶
Merlin of the Crystal Cave
Merry Christmas, Mr. Lawrence▶
Mesmerized
Middlemarch▶
A Midsummer Night's Dream
A Midwinter's Tale
The Mill on the Floss
The Millionairess
Mimi
A Mind to Kill
Mine Own Executioner▶
The Miniver Story
The Miracle
The Mirror Crack'd
The Misadventures of Mr. Wilt
The Missionary
Mr. Arkadin▶
Mr. Love
Mohammed: Messenger of God
Mona Lisa▶
The Monster Club
A Month in the Country▶
Monty Python and the Holy Grail▶
Monty Python Live at the Hollywood Bowl▶
Monty Python's Flying Circus
Monty Python's Life of Brian▶
Monty Python's The Meaning of Life▶
The Moon Stallion
Moonlight Sonata
Moonlighting▶
The Moonraker
Moonraker
Morgan!
Morons from Outer Space
The Mouse That Roared▶
Much Ado about Nothing▶
The Mummy▶
The Muppet Movie▶
Murder▶
Murder at the Baskervilles
Murder by Moonlight
Murder in the Footlights
Murder in the Old Red Barn
A Murder Is Announced
Murder of a Moderate Man
Murder on the Campus
Murder on the Orient Express▶
Murders at Lynch Cross
Murphy's War
The Music Lovers
Mute Witness
My Friend Walter
My Son, the Vampire
Mysterious Island▶
The Mystery of Edwin Drood
Naked▶
The Naked Edge
The Naked Truth
Nancy Astor
The Nanny
Nasty Habits
Ned Kelly
Negatives
Never Let Go
Never Too Late to Mend
Next Victim
Nice Girl Like Me
Nicholas Nickleby▶
Night Ambush
Night and the City▶
Night Beat
Night Birds
Night Caller from Outer Space
The Night Has Eyes
Night of the Laughing Dead
Night Train to Munich▶
The Night Visitor
Night Watch
The Nightcomers
Nightmare
Nightscare
Nine Days a Queen▶
1984▶
99 Women
No Comebacks
No Highway in the Sky▶
No Love for Johnnie▶
No Surrender▶
No Trace
Norman Conquest
The Norman Conquests, Part 1: Table Manners▶
The Norman Conquests, Part 2: Living Together▶
The Norman Conquests, Part 3: Round and Round the Garden▶
Northanger Abbey
Nothing But the Night
Number 1 of the Secret Service
No. 17▶
Nuts in May
O Lucky Man!▶
The Oblong Box
The Obsessed
The October Man▶
Octopussy
The Odd Job
Odd Man Out▶
The Odessa File
Of Human Bondage
The Offence▶
Office Romances
Oh, Alfie
Oh, Mr. Porter
O.H.M.S.
The Old Curiosity Shop
Old Mother Riley's Ghosts
Old Spanish Custom
Oliver!▶
Oliver Twist▶
Oliver Twist
On Approval▶
On Her Majesty's Secret Service▶
One Day in the Life of Ivan Denisovich▶
One-Eyed Soldiers
One Million Years B.C.
One of Our Aircraft Is Missing▶
One Wish Too Many
Only Two Can Play▶
Open All Hours
Order of the Black Eagle
Orlando▶
Out of Season
Overture
Paid to Kill
Paper Marriage
Paper Mask
Paper Tiger
Paperhouse▶
Paranoiac
Party! Party!
Pascali's Island▶
A Passage to India▶
The Passing of the Third Floor Back
Passport to Pimlico
Pattern for Plunder
Paul and Michelle
The People That Time Forgot
A Perfect Spy
Performance▶
Permission To Kill
Personal Services
The Persuaders
Persuasion▶
Peter's Friends
Phantom Fiend
The Phantom Light
The Phantom of the Opera
Philby, Burgess and MacLean: Spy Scandal of the Century
The Pickwick Papers
Pictures
Piece of Cake
Pimpernel Smith
Pink Floyd: The Wall
The Pink Panther▶
The Pink Panther Strikes Again▶
Pink Strings and Sealing Wax
Playing Away
A Pocketful of Rye
Poldark▶
Poldark 2▶
The Pope Must Diet
Porridge
Portrait of a Lady
Postmark for Danger
Postmark for Danger/Quicksand
Power
Power Play
Prick Up Your Ears▶
Pride and Prejudice
Pride and Prejudice▶
Priest
Priest of Love
The Prime of Miss Jean Brodie▶
Prime Suspect▶
Prime Suspect 2▶
Prime Suspect 3▶
Prime Suspect: Inner Circles
Prime Suspect: The Lost Child▶
Prime Suspect: The Scent of Darkness▶
The Prince and the Pauper
The Princess and the Goblin
The Prisoner▶
The Prisoner: Arrival
A Private Function
Private Life of Don Juan
The Private Life of Henry VIII▶
The Private Life of Sherlock Holmes▶
The Private Secretary
Privates on Parade
Promise Her Anything
The Promoter▶
Providence▶
Psychomania
Psychopath
Pulp
The Pumpkin Eater▶
Puppet on a Chain
The Pure Hell of St. Trinian's
Pursuit of the Graf Spee
Pygmalion▶
Quadrophenia▶
Quartet▶
Quatermass 2▶
Quatermass and the Pit
Quatermass Conclusion
The Quatermass Experiment▶
Queen of Hearts▶
The Queen of Spades▶
Quest for Love
A Question of Attribution
Race for Life
The Railway Children▶
The Rainbow▶
Raining Stones
Rattle of a Simple Man
Reach for the Sky
The Rector's Wife
The Red Shoes▶
Redneck
Reilly: Ace of Spies▶
The Remains of the Day▶
Rembrandt▶
Rentadick
Repulsion▶
The Return of the Musketeers
Return of the Soldier▶
Reunion▶
Revenge
The Revenge of Frankenstein
Revolution
Rhodes
Rich and Strange
Richard III▶
Richard's Things
The Riddle of the Sands
Riff Raff▶
The Ring
Ring of Bright Water▶
Ripping Yarns

Rita, Sue & Bob Too▶
Roadhouse Girl
Robbery
Robbery Under Arms
Robin and Marian
Robin Hood: The Movie
Robin Hood...The Legend: Herne's Son
Robin Hood...The Legend: Robin Hood and the Sorcerer
Robin Hood...The Legend: The Swords of Wayland
Robin Hood...The Legend: The Time of the Wolf
Roboman
The Rocking Horse Winner
Rogue Male
Rogue's Yarn
Romance with a Double Bass▶
Romantic Englishwoman▶
Romeo and Juliet▶
Room at the Top▶
Room to Let
A Room with a View▶
Royal Flash▶
The Ruling Class▶
Rumpole of the Bailey
Rumpole of the Bailey: Rumpole's Return▶
The Runaway Bus
Running Blind
Ryan's Daughter
Saigon: Year of the Cat
Sailing Along
The Sailor Who Fell from Grace with the Sea
The Saint
Salaam Bombay!▶
The Salamander
Sammy & Rosie Get Laid▶
Sanders of the River▶
Sapphire▶
The Satanic Rites of Dracula
Saturn 3
Savage Messiah▶
Say Hello to Yesterday
Scandal▶
The Scarlet Pimpernel▶
The Scars of Dracula
School for Scandal
Scotland Yard Inspector
Scott of the Antarctic
Scream and Scream Again
Scream of Fear▶
Scrooge▶
Scrooge
Scrubbers
Scum▶
Sea Devils
Sea of Sand
Sea Wolves
Seance on a Wet Afternoon▶
Seaside Swingers
Sebastian
Second Best▶
Second Best Secret Agent in the Whole Wide World
Second Chance
The Secret Adversary
The Secret Agent▶
The Secret Four
The Secret Garden
Secret Mission
The Secret of the Loch
Secret Places
The Secret Policeman's Other Ball▶
Secret Policeman's Private Parts
The Secret Rapture
Secrets
Secrets and Lies
The Sender
Sense & Sensibility
Sense and Sensibility▶
A Sense of Freedom▶
The Servant▶
The 7 Brothers Meet Dracula
The Seventh Veil▶
Sexton Blake and the Hooded Terror
Shadey
The Shadow
The Shadow Man
Shadowlands▶
Shaka Zulu▶
Shallow Grave
Sharpe's Battle
Sharpe's Company
Sharpe's Eagle
Sharpe's Enemy
Sharpe's Gold
Sharpe's Honour
Sharpe's Rifles
Sharpe's Sword
Shattered
She Shall Have Music
The Shell Seekers
Sherlock Holmes and the Incident at Victoria Falls
Sherlock Holmes: The Master Blackmailer
Shirley Valentine▶
The Shooting Party▶
A Shot in the Dark
The Shout▶
Shout at the Devil
Sidewalks of London▶
The Sign of Four
Silas Marner▶
The Silent Enemy
The Silent Mr. Sherlock Holmes
The Silent Passenger
Silent Scream
The Silent Touch
Simba▶
Sinbad and the Eye of the Tiger
Singleton's Pluck▶
Sirens
Sister Dora
Sister My Sister
Six Wives of Henry VIII▶
Skin Game
Slayground
Slipstream
The Smallest Show on Earth▶
The Snake Woman
Someone at the Door
Song of Freedom
S.O.S. Pacific
Space: 1999
Space: 1999—Alien Attack▶
The Spaniard's Curse
Spellbound
Spiral Staircase
Spitfire▶
Split Second
Spy in Black▶
Spy of Napoleon
The Spy Who Loved Me
Spy with a Cold Nose
Spymaker: The Secret Life of Ian Fleming
Stage Fright▶
Stalag Luft
The Stars Look Down▶
Starship
The Statue
Staying On
Stealing Beauty
Stealing Heaven
Steaming
Stevie
A Stolen Face
Storm in a Teacup
Stormy Monday
Strange Awakening
The Strange Case of the End of Civilization as We Know It
Stranger in Town
Straw Dogs▶
The Stud
A Study in Terror▶
Subterfuge
Success is the Best Revenge
Sudden Terror
Suite 16
The Summer House
A Summer Story▶
Sunday, Bloody Sunday▶
Supergirl
Supergrass
Suspended Alibi
Svengali
Sweeney Todd: The Demon Barber of Fleet Street
Sweet William▶
Sword of Lancelot
Sword of Sherwood Forest
Sword of the Valiant
Taffin
Tale of a Vampire
A Tale of Two Cities▶
Tales from the Crypt▶
Tales of Beatrix Potter▶
Tales That Witness Madness
A Taste of Honey▶
Taste the Blood of Dracula
Tears in the Rain
The Tell-Tale Heart
The Temptress
Ten Little Indians
10 Rillington Place▶
The Terror
Terror Ship
The Terrornauts
Tess▶
That Sinking Feeling▶
Theatre of Blood▶
There's a Girl in My Soup
They Came from Beyond Space
Thicker Than Water
Things Happen at Night
Things to Come▶
Think Dirty
Thirteenth Day of Christmas
30 Is a Dangerous Age, Cynthia
The Thirty-Nine Steps
The 39 Steps▶
This England
This Happy Breed▶
This Lightning Always Strikes Twice
This Sporting Life▶
Those Daring Young Men in Their Jaunty Jalopies
Those Fantastic Flying Fools
Those Glory, Glory Days
Those Magnificent Men in Their Flying Machines▶
Threads▶
Three Cases of Murder▶
Three Stops to Murder
The Three Weird Sisters
Thunder in the City▶
Thunderball
Thursday's Child
Ticket of Leave Man
Tiger Bay▶
Time Bandits
Time for Murder
Time Lock
Time Without Pity
Tintorera...Tiger Shark
To Play the King▶
To See Such Fun
To Sir, with Love
Tom & Viv▶
Tom Brown's School Days
Tom Brown's School Days▶
Tom Jones▶
Tom Thumb▶
Tomb of Ligeia▶
Tomb of the Undead
Too Many Crooks
Torture Garden
Touch Me Not
Tough Guy
Tower of Evil
Tower of Terror
A Town Called Hell
Traffik▶
Trainspotting▶
Transatlantic Tunnel
Transmutations
Trap
Treasure Island
Treasure of Monte Cristo
The Trials of Oscar Wilde▶
Triple Cross▶
Triple Echo
The Triumph of Sherlock Holmes
Trouble in Store
Trouble in the Glen
Truth About Women
Tunes of Glory▶
Turtle Diary▶
21 Days
Twins of Evil
Twinsanity
The Two Faces of Dr. Jekyll
2001: A Space Odyssey▶
Two-Way Stretch
The Unbreakable Alibi
The Uncanny
Under Capricorn
Under Milk Wood
Under Suspicion
Under the Red Robe
The Unearthly Stranger
Uneasy Terms
Unexplained Laughter
Unholy Four
Unicorn
Unmasked Part 25
Unmasking the Idol
Unnatural Pursuits
The Unstoppable Man
Unsuitable Job for a Woman
Up the Creek
Utz
Valentino
Valley of the Eagles
Vampire Circus
The Vampire Lovers
The Vampyr
Vampyres
The Van▶
Vault of Horror
Vendetta for the Saint
Venom
Venus in Furs
Veronico Cruz
A Very British Coup▶
The Very Edge
The Vicious Circle
Victim▶
A View to a Kill
Village of the Damned▶
The V.I.P.'s▶
The Virgin and the Gypsy
The Virgin Soldiers
The Virgin Witch
The Vision
A Voyage' Round My Father▶
Wagner: The Complete Epic
Wagner: The Movie
Waltz of the Toreadors▶
War Lover
The Warriors
Water
Water Babies
Watership Down
The Way Out
We Dive at Dawn▶
We Think the World of You▶
The Weaker Sex
The Wedding Gift▶
Wetherby▶
What a Carve-Up!
What's Good for the Goose
When Dinosaurs Ruled the Earth
When the Whales Came
When the Wind Blows▶
When Thief Meets Thief
Where Angels Fear to Tread▶
Where the Bullets Fly
While I Live
Whiskey Galore▶
The Whistle Blower▶
Whistle Down the Wind▶
White Fire
White Huntress
Whoops Apocalypse
Who's Who
The Wicked Lady
Wild Geese
Wild Geese 2
Wild West
Windom's Way▶
Wings of Danger
Winner Takes All
The Winslow Boy▶
Winter Flight
Wish You Were Here▶
Withnail and I▶
Without a Clue
Wittgenstein
Woman in Black
A Woman's Guide to Adultery
Wombling Free
Women in Love▶
Wonderland▶
Wonderwall: The Movie
A World Apart▶
The World is Full of Married Men
The World of Suzie Wong
The World Owes Me a Living
The Wreck of the Mary Deare
The Wrong Arm of the Law▶
The Wrong Box▶
Wuthering Heights
Xtro
A Year in Prôvence▶
Yellow Submarine▶
Yesterday's Hero
You Only Live Twice
The Young Americans
Young and Innocent▶
The Young Ones
The Young Poisoner's Handbook▶
Young Winston▶
Yuri Nosenko, KGB
A Zed & Two Noughts▶
Zeppelin

Canadian

Abducted
The Adjuster
The Agency
American Boyfriends
The Amityville Curse
And Then You Die▶
Angel Square
Angela
Anne of Avonlea▶
Anne of Green Gables▶
The Apprenticeship of Duddy Kravitz▶
Atlantic City▶
Babar: The Movie
The Bay Boy
Beautiful Dreamers
Being at Home with Claude
The Best of the Kids in the Hall
Beyond the Silhouette
The Big Crimewave
Big Meat Eater
Black Christmas
Black Robe▶
Blades of Courage
Blood Relations
Blood Relatives
The Bloody Brood
Boy in Blue
The Boys of St. Vincent▶

Canadian

Breaking All the Rules
The Brood
Buffalo Jump▶
Bullies
Busted Up
By Design
Bye Bye Blues
Cafe Romeo
Calendar▶
Canada's Sweetheart: The Saga of Hal C. Banks
Candy Mountain
Cathy's Curse
The Changeling
Christina
Circle of Two
City Boy▶
City on Fire
Class of 1984
Clearcut
Close to Home
Cold Comfort
Cold Front
Concrete Angels
The Confessional
Confidential
Cordelia
Covergirl
Crash
Cross Country
Curtains
Dan Candy's Law
Dance Me Outside
Dancing in the Dark
Daughter of Death
Dead Ringers▶
Death Ship
Death Weekend
Deathdream
The Decline of the American Empire▶
Deranged▶
Dirty Tricks
Disappearance
Distant Thunder
Dr. Bethune▶
Doctor Who
Dog Pound Shuffle▶
The Dog Who Stopped the War
A Doll's House▶
Double Happiness▶
Double Identity
The Double Negative
Drying Up the Streets
Eddie and the Cruisers 2: Eddie Lives!
Eliza's Horoscope
Exotica▶
Family Viewing▶
Fatal Attraction
Fight for Your Life
Final Assignment
Find the Lady
Fish Hawk
Flesh Gordon 2: Flesh Gordon Meets the Cosmic Cheerleaders
For the Moment
Friends, Lovers & Lunatics
Full Circle
Funeral Home
The Funny Farm
Gas
The Girl in Blue
Girls on the Road
Glory Enough for All: The Discovery of Insulin
The Godsend
Going Berserk
Goldenrod
The Great American Sex Scandal
The Grey Fox▶
The Groundstar Conspiracy▶
The Gunfighters
The Gunrunner
H
Happy Birthday to Me
Harry Tracy
Heads
Heartaches▶
Heaven on Earth
Heavenly Bodies
Heavy Metal▶
High Ballin'
High Country
Highpoint
Hiroshima▶
Hockey Night
Hog Wild
The Hound of London
The Housekeeper
Humongous
Iceman▶
If You Could See What I Hear
In Celebration▶
In Praise of Older Women
In Trouble
Incubus
Into the Fire
Iron Eagle 2
Iron Eagle 4
I've Heard the Mermaids Singing▶
Jesus of Montreal▶
John and the Missus
Joshua Then and Now▶
Journey
Journey into Fear
Keeper
The Kidnapping of the President
Killing 'em Softly
King Solomon's Treasure
Ladies of the Lotus
Lantern Hill
Last Chase
The Last Place on Earth
The Last Winter
Le Sexe des Etoiles
L'Enfant d'Eau
Leolo
Les Bons Debarras
Lies My Father Told Me▶
The Little Girl Who Lives Down the Lane
The Little Kidnappers
Live Bait
Loose Screws
Lost
Lost in the Barrens
The Lotus Eaters
Love and Human Remains▶
Love Songs
Loyalties
A Man, a Woman, and a Bank
A Man in Uniform
The Man Inside
Margaret's Museum
Maria Chapdelaine
Martin's Day
Masala
The Mask
Mazes and Monsters
Meatballs
Melanie
Middle Age Crazy
Mindfield
Mon Oncle Antoine▶
Murder by Decree▶
Murder by Phone
My American Cousin▶
My Bloody Valentine
My Pleasure Is My Business
My Side of the Mountain
My Twentieth Century▶
'Neath Canadian Skies
Next of Kin
Night Breed
Night Zoo
Nikki, the Wild Dog of the North
90 Days▶
North of the Border
Northern Extremes
The Nutcracker Prince
The Odyssey of the Pacific
Of Unknown Origin
Oh, What a Night
One Night Stand
One Plus One
Outrageous!▶
Outside Chance of Maximillian Glick
Palais Royale
Pandemonium
A Paper Wedding▶
Paperback Hero
Paris, France
Phobia
Pick-Up Summer
Playgirl Killer
Porky's
Porky's 2: The Next Day
Porky's Revenge
Power Play
Princes in Exile
Prom Night
Psycho Girls
The Pyx▶
The Quarrel
Quiet Day In Belfast▶
Rabid
Red Blooded American Girl
The Reincarnate
Reno and the Doc
Rituals
Roadkill
Rock 'n' Roll Nightmare
Rubberface
Salmonberries
The Savage Woman
Scanners
Scanners 2: The New Order
Science Crazed
Seizure
Shadow of the Wolf
Shoot
Showdown at Williams Creek
Silence of the North
The Silent Partner▶
Slipstream
Spacehunter: Adventures in the Forbidden Zone
Spasms
Speaking Parts▶
Spirit Rider▶
Spring Fever
Starship Invasions
Storm
Straight for the Heart
Strangers in Good Company▶
Surrogate
Tales from Avonlea, Vol. 1: The Journey Begins
Termini Station
They Came from Within
32 Short Films about Glenn Gould▶
Threshold
Trap
Tribute
Tulips
Unfinished Business
Utilities
Videodrome
The Vindicator
Virgin Queen of St. Francis High
Virtual Assassin
Visiting Hours
The War Boy
Wedding in White
Whale Music
When Night is Falling▶
Where the Spirit Lives
A Whisper to a Scream
Whispering City▶
Why Shoot the Teacher▶
Wild Horse Hank
The Woman Inside
Xtro 2: The Second Encounter
Your Ticket Is No Longer Valid
Zero Patience

Cantonese

Naked Killer

Chinese

The Armour of God
A Better Tomorrow
A Better Tomorrow, Part 2
The Blue Kite▶
Breaking with Old Ideas
China, My Sorrow
Chinese Connection
Crows and Sparrows▶
The Go-Masters▶
The Horse Thief▶
Jackie Chan's Police Force
Ju Dou▶
Lai Shi: China's Last Eunuch
Life on a String
A Mongolian Tale
Paper Marriage
Raise the Red Lantern▶
Red Firecracker, Green Firecracker
Red Sorghum▶
Return of the Dragon
Shanghai Triad▶
Shao Lin Popeye
The Silk Road
Slaughter in San Francisco
Song of the Exile
The Story of Qui Ju▶
Temptation of a Monk
A Time to Live and a Time to Die
To Live▶
Women From the Lake of Scented Souls
The Wooden Man's Bride
Yellow Earth

Columbian

Confessing to Laura

Cuban

Death of a Bureaucrat▶
I Am Cuba
The Last Supper▶
Letters from the Park▶
Memories of Underdevelopment
Strawberry and Chocolate▶
Up to a Certain Point

Czech

All My Good Countrymen
Closely Watched Trains▶
Death is Called Engelchen▶
Diamonds of the Night▶
Ecstasy
The Firemen's Ball▶
Larks on a String▶
The Last Butterfly
Loves of a Blonde▶
My Sweet Little Village
New Pastures
On the Comet▶
The Original Fabulous Adventures of Baron Munchausen
A Prayer for Katarina Horovitzova▶
The Report on the Party and the Guests▶
The Shop on Main Street▶
Sweet Light in a Dark Room▶
Tereza▶
Transport from Paradise

Danish

All Things Fair
Babette's Feast▶
Breaking the Waves▶
Day of Wrath▶
The Element of Crime
Emma's Shadow▶
Friends Forever▶
Gertrud▶
Hunger
The Kingdom
Kiss Daddy Goodnight
Ladies on the Rocks
Leaves from Satan's Book
Memories of a Marriage▶
The Night Visitor
Ordet▶
Pelle the Conqueror▶
The Silent Touch
Twist & Shout▶
The Wolf at the Door
A World of Strangers▶
You Are Not Alone

Dutch

Amsterdamned
Antonia's Line
Army Brats
The Assault▶
Broken Mirrors
Cold Blood
Daens
Dear Boys
Egg
Fatal Error
A Flight of Rainbirds
For a Lost Soldier
The 4th Man▶
In for Treatment▶
Keetje Tippel
The Lift
The Man Inside
On Top of the Whale
The Pointsman
Question of Silence▶
Rembrandt—1669
Soldier of Orange▶
Spetters
To Play or To Die
Turkish Delights
The Vanishing▶

Filipino

Beast of the Yellow Night
Beyond Atlantis
Blind Rage
Brides of the Beast
Caged Fury
Circle of Fear
The Deadly and the Beautiful
Devil Woman
Horror of the Blood Monsters
Midnight Dancers
Night of the Cobra Woman
Once Before I Die
Perfumed Nightmare▶
Raw Force
Stickfighter
Stryker
Terror Is a Man
The Thirsty Dead
Turumba▶
Twilight People
The Vampire Hookers
The Vampire People

Finnish

Ariel▶
The Day the Earth Froze
Leningrad Cowboys Go America

The Match Factory Girl▶

French

A la Mode
A Nos Amours▶
A Nous la Liberte▶
The Accompanist
Act of Aggression
Adorable Julia
After the Fall of New York
Akermania, Vol. 1▶
Alberto Express
Ali Baba and the 40 Thieves▶
Alice in Wonderland
Alphaville▶
The American Friend▶
And God Created Woman
And Hope to Die
And Now My Love
Andy Warhol's Dracula▶
Andy Warhol's Frankenstein
Angele▶
Another Man, Another Chance
As If It Were Raining
Assassination of Trotsky
The Associate
Atlantic City▶
Attack of the Robots
Au Revoir Les Enfants▶
Augustin
The Avenger
Babar: The Movie
Babette's Feast▶
Back to the Wall
The Baker's Wife▶
Band of Outsiders
Bandits
Barbarella
Barjo
Basileus Quartet▶
The Battle of Austerlitz
The Battle of El Alamein
Baxter
The Bear▶
Beatrice▶
Beau Pere▶
Beauties of the Night
Beauty and the Beast▶
Beauty and the Devil
Beethoven
Beethoven's Nephew
Before the Rain▶
Belle Americaine
Belle de Jour▶
Bernadette
The Best Way
Betty
Betty Blue▶
Between Heaven and Earth
The Big Grab
Bilitis
Bim/Dream of the Wild Horses
Bizarre Bizarre▶
Black and White in Color▶
Black Orpheus▶
Black Tights
Blood and Black Lace
The Blood of Others
Blue Country
Blue Jeans
Bluebeard▶
Bob le Flambeur▶
Bonjour Tristesse▶
Borsalino▶
Boudu Saved from Drowning▶
Boy Meets Girl▶
Boyfriends & Girlfriends
The Brain
Breaking the Waves▶
Breathless▶
The Bride Is Much Too Beautiful
The Bride Wore Black▶
Buffet Froid▶
Burnt by the Sun▶
By the Blood of Others▶
Cafe au Lait▶
Caged Women
Camille Claudel▶
Candy Mountain
Captain Blackjack
Carnival in Flanders▶
Carrington
Cartouche▶
Casque d'Or▶
Castle of Blood
Castle of the Living Dead
Cat and Mouse▶
The Cat o' Nine Tails
Catch Me a Spy
Catherine & Co.
Cathy's Curse
Cesar▶
Cesar & Rosalie▶
Charles et Lucie▶
Charlie Bravo
Chasing Butterflies
Children of Paradise▶
Chloe in the Afternoon▶
Choice of Arms
Christ Stopped at Eboli▶
Circle of Love
Circonstances Attenuantes
Circus Angel▶
City of Joy
The City of Lost Children
Claire's Knee▶
Cleo from 5 to 7▶
The Clockmaker▶
Cobra
A Coeur Joie
Cold Sweat
Colonel Chabert
Comment Ca Va?
The Confessional
Confidentially Yours▶
The Conformist▶
Conquest of Mycene
Contempt▶
Conversation Piece▶
Coup de Grace
Coup de Torchon▶
Cousin, Cousine▶
The Cousins▶
Crainquebille▶
Crazy for Love
The Crazy Ray▶
The Crime of Monsieur Lange▶
Cross My Heart
The Crucible▶
The Cry of the Owl
Cyrano de Bergerac▶
Daddy Nostalgia▶
Daens
Damage▶
Dangerous Liaisons
Danton▶
Daughters of Darkness▶
The Day and the Hour
Day for Night▶
A Day in the Country▶
The Day the Sky Exploded
The Daydreamer
Deadly Sting
The Deadly Trap
Dear Detective
Death in the Garden
Death Watch▶
The Decameron▶
Delicatessen▶
Delusions of Grandeur
Devil in the Flesh▶
The Devil's Commandment
The Diabolical Dr. Z
Diabolically Yours
Diabolique▶
Diary of a Chambermaid▶
Diary of a Country Priest▶
Dirty Dishes▶
Dirty Hands
The Discreet Charm of the Bourgeoisie▶
Diva▶
Dr. Bethune▶
Dr. Petiot
Dog Day
Donkey Skin▶
Dos Cruces en Danger Pass▶
Double Agents
Double Identity
The Double Life of Veronique
Dracula & Son
Dressmaker
Duke of the Derby
Dupont Lajoie
Dust▶
The Eagle Has Two Heads▶
The Earrings of Madame De...▶
Edith & Marcel
The Eighth Day
The Eighties
The Elegant Criminal
Elena and Her Men▶
Elsa, Elsa
Emmanuelle
Emmanuelle 4
Emmanuelle 5
Emmanuelle & Joanna
Emmanuelle in Bangkok
Emmanuelle in Soho
Emmanuelle in the Country
Emmanuelle on Taboo Island
Emmanuelle, the Joys of a Woman
Empty Canvas
End of Desire
Enigma
Entr'acte
Entre-Nous▶
Erendira
Erotic Escape
Et La Tenoresse?...Bordel!
Eternal Return
The Eyes, the Mouth
Fahrenheit 451▶
Fanny▶
Fantastic Planet▶
Farinelli
Fatal Fix
The Favor, the Watch, & the Very Big Fish
The Favorite Son▶
Fellini's Roma
Femmes de Paris
Fernandel the Dressmaker
Field of Honor
The Fire Within▶
First Name: Carmen▶
The Flower of My Secret▶
Forbidden Fruit▶
Forbidden Games▶
Fort Saganne
Four Adventures of Reinette and Mirabelle▶
Four Bags Full
The 400 Blows▶
France/Tour/Detour/Deux/ Enfants▶
Frantic▶
Franz
French Can-Can▶
The French Detective▶
The French Touch
French Twist
The French Way
From Hell to Victory
Full Moon in Paris
The Game is Over
A Gentle Woman
Germinal▶
Gervaise▶
Get Out Your Handkerchiefs▶
The Gift
Girl in His Pocket
A Girl on Her Own
Godard/Truffaut Shorts
Godson▶
Going Places▶
The Golden Coach▶
Goliath and the Dragon
Grain of Sand▶
Grand Illusion▶
The Great War
The Green Room
Grisbi
Grosse Fatigue▶
Hail Mary
The Hairdresser's Husband
The Hands of Orlac
Hanna K.
Happy New Year▶
Harem
Harvest▶
Hate▶
Head of the Family
Head Over Heels▶
Heart of a Nation▶
Heat of Desire
Helas Pour Moi
Hercules Against the Moon Men
Here and Elsewhere
High Heels
Hiroshima, Mon Amour▶
The Holes
Holiday Hotel
Honor Among Thieves
The Horror Chamber of Dr. Faustus▶
The Horse of Pride
The Horseman on the Roof
Hothead
Howling 2: Your Sister is a Werewolf
I Can't Sleep
I Killed Rasputin
I Love All of You
I Sent a Letter to My Love▶
Icy Breasts▶
In the Realm of the Senses▶
Indochine▶
Infernal Trio
Innocent Lies
The Invaders
Investigation
Invitation au Voyage
Is Paris Burning?▶
Istanbul
It Happened in the Park
It Means That to Me
Italian Straw Hat▶
J'Accuse▶
Jacko & Lise
Jacquot
Jailbird's Vacation
Je Tu Il Elle
Jean de Florette▶
Jenny Lamour
Jesus of Montreal▶
Josepha▶
Jour de Fete▶
Journey Beneath the Desert
Journey to the Lost City
The Joy of Knowledge
Judex
The Judge and the Assassin▶
Jules and Jim▶
Jupiter's Thigh
Just Another Pretty Face
Kapo▶
The Killing Game
The King of Hearts▶
The Klutz
L.627▶
La Balance▶
La Belle Noiseuse▶
La Bete Humaine▶
La Boum
La Cage aux Folles▶
La Cage aux Folles 2
La Cage aux Folles 3: The Wedding
La Ceremonie▶
La Chartreuse de Parme
La Chevre▶
La Chienne▶
La Chute de la Maison Usher▶
La Collectionneuse
La Discrete▶
La Femme Nikita▶
La Grande Bouffe▶
La Grande Vadrouille▶
La Lectrice
La Marseillaise▶
La Merveilleuse Visite
La Nuit de Varennes▶
La Passante▶
La Petite Sirene
La Ronde▶
La Rupture
La Symphonie Pastorale▶
La Truite▶
La Vengeance d'une Femme
The Lacemaker▶
The Ladies of the Bois de Bologne
Lady Chatterley's Lover
Lady L
L'Age D'Or▶
L'Amour en Herbe
Lancelot of the Lake
Landscape in the Mist▶
L'Anne Sainte
L'Annee des Meduses
L'Appat
L'Argent
The Last Metro▶
Last Tango in Paris▶
The Last Winters
Last Year at Marienbad▶
L'Atalante▶
Le Bal▶
Le Beau Mariage▶
Le Beau Serge▶
Le Bonheur
Le Boucher▶
Le Bourgeois Gentilhomme
Le Cas du Dr. Laurent▶
Le Cavaleur
Le Chat▶
Le Complot▶
Le Corbeau▶
Le Crabe Tambour▶
Le Dernier Combat▶
Le Doulos▶
Le Gendarme de Saint-Tropez
Le Gentleman D'Epsom
Le Grand Chemin▶
Le Joli Mai
Le Jour Se Leve▶
Le Magnifique
Le Million▶
Le Petit Amour▶
Le Plaisir
Le Repos du Guerrier
Le Schpountz
Le Secret▶
Le Sex Shop▶
L'Ecole Buisoniere
L'Enfer▶
Leon Morin, Priest
Leonor
Les Assassins de L'Ordre
Les Aventuriers
Les Biches▶
Les Bonnes Femmes▶
Les Carabiniers▶
Les Comperes▶
Les Enfants Terrible▶
Les Grandes Gueules
Les Grandes Manoeuvres▶
Les Miserables▶
Les Mistons▶
Les Nuits Fauves▶
Les Rendez-vous D'Anna
Les Violons du Bal
Les Visiteurs du Soir▶
L'Etat Sauvage▶
Letters from My Windmill▶

Letters to an Unknown Lover
L'Homme Blesse▶
License to Kill
L'Idiot
Life and Nothing But▶
Life Is a Long Quiet River▶
Liliom▶
Little Indian, Big City
The Little Thief▶
Little World of Don Camillo▶
L'Odeur des Fauves
Lola▶
Lola Montes▶
Loulou▶
Love After Love
Love and the Frenchwoman▶
A Love in Germany
Love on the Run▶
Love Songs
Love Without Pity
The Lover
The Lovers▶
Lovers Like Us
The Loves of Hercules
The Lower Depths▶
Lucky Luciano
Lumiere
Madame Bovary▶
Madame Rosa▶
Mademoiselle
The Mahabharata
Maids of Wilko
Make Room for Tomorrow
Mama Dracula
Mama, There's a Man in Your Bed▶
A Man and a Woman▶
A Man and a Woman: 20 Years Later
Man from Nowhere
A Man in Love▶
The Man in the Raincoat
Man in the Silk Hat
Man on Fire
The Man Who Loved Women▶
Manon of the Spring▶
Maria Chapdelaine▶
Maria Chapdelaine
Marius▶
A Married Woman▶
Marry Me, Marry Me▶
Martin Luther
Masculine Feminine▶
Max, Mon Amour
May Fools▶
Mayerling
Melodie en Sous-Sol
Menage▶
The Milky Way▶
Mill of the Stone Women
Mina Tannenbaum
Minnesota Clay
Mississippi Mermaid▶
Mr. Hulot's Holiday▶
Mr. Peek-A-Boo
Modigliani
Mon Oncle▶
Mon Oncle D'Amerique▶
The Mongols
The Monocle
Monsieur Hire▶
Monsieur Vincent▶
Moon in the Gutter
Morgan the Pirate
Mouchette▶
Murder at 45 R.P.M.
Muriel▶
Murmur of the Heart▶
My Best Friend's Girl
My Father's Glory▶
My Life and Times with Antonin Artaud▶
My Life to Live▶
My Mother's Castle▶
My New Partner
My Night at Maud's▶

My Other Husband
The Mystery of Alexina
Nais▶
The Name of the Rose
Nana▶
Napoleon▶
Napoleon
Nelly et Monsieur Arnaud▶
Next Summer▶
Next Year If All Goes Well
Night and Day▶
Night Flight from Moscow
1900▶
No Fear, No Die
No Problem
Noir et Blanc
Nostradamus
Nous N'Irons Plus au Bois
Nouvelle Vague
Numero Deux
The Nun
Oasis of the Zombies
The Old Lady Who Walked in the Sea
Oldest Profession
Olivier, Olivier▶
One Deadly Summer▶
One Sings, the Other Doesn't
One Wild Moment
One Woman or Two
The Outside Man
Overseas: Three Women with Man Trouble▶
Pain in the A—▶
Panique▶
Pantaloons
Parade▶
Pardon Mon Affaire▶
Pardon Mon Affaire, Too!
Paris Belongs to Us
Paris, Texas▶
The Passion of Joan of Arc▶
Passion of Love▶
Pattes Blanches
Paul and Michelle
Pauline at the Beach▶
The Peking Blond
Pepe Le Moko▶
Peppermint Soda▶
Peril
The Perils of Gwendoline
The Perverse Countess
Petit Con
Phaedra
Phantom of Liberty▶
Pickpocket▶
Picnic on the Grass
Pierrot le Fou▶
The Plague
Planets Against Us
Playtime▶
Poil de Carotte
Police
Possession
Pouvoir Intime
Princess Academy
Princess Tam Tam▶
Prix de Beaute
Prize of Peril
The Professional
A Propos de Nice▶
The Proud Ones
A Pure Formality
The Purple Taxi
Quartet▶
Quatorze Juliet
Queen Margot▶
Quest for Fire▶
Qui Etes Vous, Mr. Sorge?
Ramparts of Clay▶
Ran▶
Rape of Love
The Rape of the Sabines
The Rascals
Ravishing Idiot
The Red and the Black▶

The Red Balloon▶
Red Balloon/Occurrence at Owl Creek Bridge▶
The Red Inn
Red Kiss▶
Red Sun
Rendez-Moi Ma Peau
Rendez-vous▶
The Respectful Prostitute
The Return of Dr. Mabuse
The Return of Martin Guerre▶
The Return of the Musketeers
Return of the Tall Blond Man With One Black Shoe
Reunion▶
Ricco
Rider on the Rain▶
Rififi▶
The Rise of Louis XIV▶
The River▶
Road to Salina▶
Roads to the South
Robert et Robert▶
Round Midnight▶
Ruyblas
The Sacrifice▶
Salut l'Artiste▶
Samson and the 7 Miracles of the World
Sand and Blood
Sans Soleil▶
Scene of the Crime▶
Scoumoune
Secret Agent Super Dragon
The Separation
Seven Deadly Sins▶
Shanghai Triad▶
The Sheep Has Five Legs
Sheer Madness▶
Shoot the Piano Player▶
A Simple Story▶
Sincerely Charlotte▶
Six Fois Deux/Sur et Sous la Communication▶
Six in Paris
The Slap
Small Change▶
Smiling Madame Beudet/The Seashell and the Clergyman▶
Smoking/No Smoking
Soft and Hard
The Soft Skin▶
Sois Belle et Tais-Toi
Soldat Duroc...Ca Va Etre Ta Fete!
Son of Samson
The Son of the Shark
The Sorrow and the Pity▶
Soviet Spy
Special Police
Spirits of the Dead▶
Spoiled Children
Sputnik
State of Siege▶
Stay As You Are
Stealing Beauty
Stolen Kisses▶
The Storm Within▶
Stormy Waters
The Story of a Cheat▶
The Story of a Love Story
Story of Adele H.▶
The Story of Women▶
Subway
The Sucker
Sugar Cane Alley▶
Summer▶
A Sunday in the Country▶
Sundays & Cybele▶
Swann in Love
Swashbuckler
Sweet Ecstasy
Swimming Pool
Sylvia and the Phantom▶
Sympathy for the Devil

A Tale of Springtime
A Tale of Winter
The Tall Blond Man with One Black Shoe▶
Tamango
Tartuffe
Tatie Danielle▶
Tchao Pantin▶
Ten Days Wonder
The Tenant▶
Terror of Rome Against the Son of Hercules
Tess▶
The Testament of Dr. Cordelier▶
The Testament of Orpheus▶
That Man from Rio
That Naughty Girl
There Goes Barder
Therese▶
The Things of Life▶
36 Fillete▶
This Man Must Die▶
This Special Friendship
This Sweet Sickness
The 317th Platoon▶
Three Men and a Cradle▶
Tiger of the Seven Seas
Time Out for Love
Toni▶
Too Beautiful for You
Too Pretty to Be Honest
Too Shy to Try
Topaze▶
Toto le Heros▶
Tournament
Tous les Matins du Monde▶
Toute Une Nuit▶
Traffic
Trahir▶
The Trial▶
Tricheurs
Triple Cross▶
Tristana▶
Trois Couleurs: Blanc▶
Trois Couleurs: Bleu▶
Trois Couleurs: Rouge▶
12 Plus 1▶
Twist
Two English Girls▶
The Two of Us▶
Ulysses' Gaze
Umbrellas of Cherbourg▶
Un Chien Andalou▶
Un Coeur en Hiver
Uncle Tom's Cabin
Under Satan's Sun▶
Under the Roofs of Paris▶
Underground▶
Une Jeunesse▶
Uranus▶
Utopia
Vagabond▶
The Valley Obscured by the Clouds
Van Gogh▶
The Vanishing▶
A Very Curious Girl
A Very Private Affair
Vincent, Francois, Paul and the Others▶
Violette▶
Viva Maria!
Volpone▶
Voulez-Vous Danser Avec Moi?
Voyage en Balloon
Voyage en Douce
Voyage-Suprise▶
Voyager▶
Wages of Fear▶
The Walls of Malapaga
The Wanderer
We Will Not Enter the Forest▶
Web of the Spider
Wedding in Blood▶
A Wedding in Galilee▶

Weekend▶
Well-Digger's Daughter▶
Where the Hot Wind Blows
Where the Sky Begins
Widow Couderc▶
The Wild Child▶
Wild Reeds▶
Window Shopping
Window to Paris
Without Warning
The Wolf at the Door
A Woman at Her Window
A Woman is a Woman▶
The Woman Next Door▶
Woman Times Seven
The Wonders of Aladdin
The Would-Be Gentleman
Yesterday, Today and Tomorrow▶
Your Turn Darling
Z▶
Zazie dans le Metro▶
Zero for Conduct▶
Zero for Conduct/Taris/A Propos de Nice
Zombie Lake
Zou Zou

German

Aguirre, the Wrath of God▶
Ali: Fear Eats the Soul▶
The American Friend▶
The American Soldier
Among the Cinders
Andy Warhol's Frankenstein
Angry Harvest▶
Anita, Dances of Vice
The Avenger
Backstairs
Bagdad Cafe▶
Baron Munchausen▶
Battleforce
The Berlin Affair
Berlin Alexanderplatz▶
Beware of a Holy Whore
The Bitter Tears of Petra von Kant
The Black Abbot
Black Beauty
A Black Veil for Lisa
Blood and Black Lace
The Blue Angel▶
The Blue Hour
The Blue Light▶
The Blum Affair
Boarding School
The Brain
The Bridge
The Cabinet of Dr. Caligari▶
The Captain from Koepenick
The Castle▶
The Castle of Fu Manchu
The Cat o' Nine Tails
The Catamount Killing
Cave of the Living Dead
Celeste▶
Cesare Borgia
Charm of La Boheme
The Children
Chinese Boxes
Chinese Roulette
Christiane F.▶
Circus of Fear
Club Extinction
Code Name Alpha
Codename: Wildgeese
Colonel Redl▶
Commandos
The Conformist▶
Congress Dances
The Cop & the Girl
Count Dracula
Coup de Grace
Creature with the Blue Hand

Greek

Hong Kong

Hungarian

Icelandic

Indian

Iranian

Irish

Israeli

Noa at Seventeen▶
Sallah▶
They Were Ten
Unsettled Land
The Wooden Gun

Italian

Accatone!▶
Ace High
Acla's Descent into Floristella
Acqua e Sapone
Adios, Hombre
After the Fall of New York
After the Fox
Aladdin
Alfredo, Alfredo
Alien Contamination
All Screwed Up▶
All the Way, Boys
Allegro Non Troppo▶
Allonsanfan▶
Almost Human
Alone Against Rome
Amarcord▶
Amore▶
And the Ship Sails On▶
Andy Warhol's Dracula▶
Andy Warhol's Frankenstein
An Angel for Satan
Angel in a Taxi
Anna
Any Gun Can Play
Arabian Nights▶
Arena
Assassination of Trotsky
Assault on Agathon
Assignment Outer Space
Assunta Spina
Atlas in the Land of the Cyclops
Atom Age Vampire
Ator the Fighting Eagle
Augustine of Hippo▶
Autopsy
The Avenger
Ay, Carmela!▶
The Bacchantes
Bad Boy Bubby
Bad Man's River
Bandits of Orgosolo
Barbarella
Barbarian Queen
Barbarian Queen 2: The Empress Strikes Back
The Barbarians
Basileus Quartet▶
The Battle of Algiers▶
The Battle of Austerlitz
The Battle of El Alamein
Battle of the Commandos
Battle of the Worlds
Beauty on the Beach
Before the Revolution
Belle Starr
Bellissima▶
Bellissimo: Images of the Italian Cinema
The Belly of an Architect▶
The Berlin Affair
Beyond Obsession
Beyond the Door
Beyond the Door 2
Beyond the Law
The Bible...In the Beginning▶
The Bicycle Thief▶
Big Boss
Big Deal on Madonna Street▶
The Bird with the Crystal Plumage
Bitter Rice▶
Bix
Bizarre
The Black Cat
Black Cat
The Black Cobra
Black Lemons
The Black Maid
The Black Pirate▶
Black Sabbath▶
Black Sunday▶
A Black Veil for Lisa
Blaise Pascal▶
Blastfighter
Blood and Black Lace
Blood Brothers
Blood Feud
Blood Ties
The Bloody Pit of Horror
Blow-Up▶
Boccaccio '70
Body Moves
The Boldest Job in the West
Boomerang
Boot Hill
The Boss Is Served
Bread and Chocolate▶
Bullet for Sandoval
A Bullet for the General
Buried Alive
Burn!▶
Bye Bye Baby
Cabiria
Cafe Express
Caged Women
Caligula
Camorra: The Naples Connection
The Canterbury Tales
Caro Diario▶
Carthage in Flames
Cartouche▶
Casanova '70
Castle of Blood
The Castle of Fu Manchu
Castle of the Living Dead
The Cat o' Nine Tails
Catch as Catch Can
Catherine & Co.
Cemetery Man
The Cheaters
The Children Are Watching Us▶
Chino
Christ Stopped at Eboli▶
The Christmas That Almost Wasn't
The Church▶
Ciao, Professore!
Cinema Paradiso▶
City of the Walking Dead
City of Women
The Clowns▶
Cobra
Code Name Alpha
Codename: Wildgeese
Cold Steel for Tortuga
Cold Sweat
Collector's Item▶
Colossus and the Amazon Queen
Commandos
The Con Artists
Condemned to Hell
Confessions of a Police Captain
The Conformist▶
Conquest
Conquest of Mycene
Contempt▶
Contraband
Control
Conversation Piece▶
Coriolanus, Man without a Country
Corleone
Corrupt▶
Cosmos: War of the Planets
Could It Happen Here?
Count Dracula
Counter Punch
Creepers
Crime Busters
The Cry of the Owl
Cyrano de Bergerac▶
The Damned
Danger: Diabolik
Dangerous Liaisons
Dangerous Obsession
Dark Eyes▶
Daughters of Darkness▶
Day of the Cobra
The Day the Sky Exploded
Deadly Impact
Deadly Revenge
The Deadly Trap
Death in Venice▶
Death Rage
The Decameron▶
Delta Force Commando 2
Demons
Demons 2
Devil in the Flesh
Devil of the Desert Against the Son of Hercules
Devilfish
Devil's Crude
The Devil's Daughter
The Devil's Nightmare
Dial Help
Diary of Forbidden Dreams▶
Divine Nymph
Divorce—Italian Style▶
Doctor Butcher M.D.
Dr. Frankenstein's Castle of Freaks
Domino
Dorian Gray
Down & Dirty▶
Dracula vs. Frankenstein
Driver's Seat
Duel of Champions
The Easy Life▶
The Eclipse▶
8 1/2▶
1860
Emerald Jungle
Empty Canvas
Era Notte a Roma▶
Ernesto
Esther and the King
Everybody's Fine
Evil Clutch
Evil's Commandment
Exterminators of the Year 3000
Eyeball
Eyes Behind the Stars
The Eyes, the Mouth
Fabiola▶
The Family
The Family▶
Fangs of the Living Dead
Farinelli
Fear in the City
Fellini Satyricon▶
Fellini's Roma
Fiances
Fifth Day of Peace
Fiorile▶
A Fistful of Dollars▶
A Fistful of Dynamite▶
Five for Hell
Flatfoot
Flight of the Innocent
The Flowers of St. Francis▶
For a Few Dollars More
Forever Mary▶
Four Ways Out
Foxtrap
Frankenstein '80
Full Hearts & Empty Pockets
The Fury of Hercules
Gangsters
The Garden of the Finzi-Continis▶
Garringo
Generale Della Rovere▶
The Ghost
The Giant of Marathon
The Giant of Metropolis
Giants of Rome
The Giants of Thessaly
Ginger & Fred▶
Gladiator of Rome
Gladiators 7
Go for It
The Gold of Naples▶
Goliath Against the Giants
Goliath and the Barbarians
Goliath and the Dragon
Goliath and the Sins of Babylon
The Good, the Bad and the Ugly▶
Goodnight, Michelangelo
The Gospel According to St. Matthew▶
The Grand Duel
Graveyard Shift
Great Adventure
The Great War
The Grim Reaper▶
Grim Reaper
Gun Fight at Red Sands
Gunfire
The Hanging Woman
Happy New Year▶
Hatchet for the Honeymoon
The Hawks & the Sparrows
Head of the Family
Hearts & Armour
Hell Commandos
Hellbenders
Henry IV
Hercules
Hercules 2
Hercules Against the Moon Men
Hercules and the Captive Women
Hercules and the Princess of Troy
Hercules in the Haunted World
Hercules, Prisoner of Evil
Hercules Unchained
Hero of Rome
Herod the Great
High Frequency
His Name was King
Homo Eroticus/Man of the Year
Honey
Honor Among Thieves
The Horrible Dr. Hichcock
Hotel Colonial
The House by the Cemetery
House on the Edge of the Park
How Funny Can Sex Be?
Howling 2: Your Sister is a Werewolf
The Human Factor
Hundra
Husband Hunting
I Hate Blondes
I Killed Rasputin
I Vitelloni▶
The Icicle Thief▶
Il Bell'Antonio
Il Grido
Il Sorpasso
Immortal Bachelor
Indiscretion of an American Wife
Infernal Trio
Inferno
The Inheritance
The Innocent▶
The Inquiry
Intermezzo▶
Intervista▶
The Invaders
Invasion of the Flesh Hunters
The Invincible Gladiator
The Invisible Dead
Island Monster
Johnny Stecchino▶
A Joke of Destiny, Lying in Wait Around the Corner Like a Bandit
Journey Beneath the Desert
Journey to the Lost City
Joyful Laughter
Judex
Juliet of the Spirits▶
Kaos▶
Kapo▶
Kidnap Syndicate
Kill, Baby, Kill▶
La Cicada
La Dolce Vita▶
La Grande Bourgeoise
La Nuit de Varennes▶
La Signora di Tutti▶
La Strada▶
La Terra Trema▶
La Vie Continue
Lady Caroline Lamb
Lady Frankenstein
Lady L
Lady of the Evening
The Lady Without Camelias
Lamerica▶
Landscape in the Mist▶
The Last Days of Pompeii
The Last Emperor▶
The Last Hunter
The Last Man on Earth
Last Tango in Paris▶
The Last Tomahawk
Last Year at Marienbad▶
L'Avventura▶
Le Bal▶
The Legend of Blood Castle
The Legend of the Wolf Woman
Leon Morin, Priest
Leonor
Les Carabiniers▶
Les Miserables
Life of Verdi
Lightning Bolt
The Lion of Thebes▶
Lisa and the Devil
Little World of Don Camillo▶
Lobster for Breakfast
Lola
Love and Anarchy▶
Love in the City▶
Love Meetings
Lovers and Liars
Loves & Times of Scaramouche
The Loves of Hercules
Lucky Luciano
L'Udienza
Lunatics & Lovers
Lure of the Sila
Macaroni
Machine to Kill Bad People
Maciste in Hell
The Mad Butcher
Malicious
Mamma Roma▶
A Man Called Rage
Man from Cairo
Man from Deep River
Man of Legend
The Man Who Wagged His Tail
Man with a Cross
Manhattan Baby
Manhunt
Marauder
Marriage Italian Style▶
Master Touch
Mean Frank and Crazy Tony
Medea
Mediterraneo▶
Medusa Against the Son of Hercules
Messalina vs. the Son of Hercules
The Messiah▶
Miami Cops
Miami Horror
Mill of the Stone Women
Millions
Minnesota Clay

Japanese

Japanese

Korean

Lithuanian

Macedonian

Mexican

New Zealand

Nicaraguan

Norwegian

Peruvian

Polish

Portuguese

Romanian

Russian

The Lady with the Dog▶
The Legend of Suram Fortress
Little Vera▶
Luna Park
The Magic Voyage of Sinbad
The Man with a Movie Camera▶
The Mirror▶
Moscow Does Not Believe in Tears▶
Mother▶
My Apprenticeship▶
My Childhood▶
My Name is Ivan▶
My Universities▶
No Greater Love
Oblomov▶
The Overcoat▶
The Patriots▶
Peter the First: Part 1
Peter the First: Part 2
Planet Burg
Private Life
Que Viva Mexico▶
Rasputin▶
Repentance▶
The Road to Life
Shadows of Forgotten Ancestors▶
The Shooting Party
Siberiade▶
Sideburns
A Slave of Love▶
Solaris
Solo Voyage: The Revenge
Stalker▶
Storm Over Asia▶
Strike▶
A Summer to Remember▶
Sword & the Dragon
Taxi Blues▶
Tchaikovsky
Ten Days That Shook the World▶
The Theme▶
The Tsar's Bride▶
An Unfinished Piece for a Player Piano▶
War and Peace▶
Waterloo
Window to Paris
Zvenigora▶

South African

African Rage
City of Blood
Cry, the Beloved Country▶
Deadly Passion
Emissary
The Evil Below
House of the Living Dead
Kill Slade
Place of Weeping
Stay Awake
Yankee Zulu

Spanish

Against the Wind
Anguish
Any Gun Can Play
Attack of the Robots
Autopsy of a Ghost
Ay, Carmela!▶
Bad Man's River
Belle Epoque▶
Between Heaven and Earth
Black Beauty
The Blood Spattered Bride
Blood Wedding▶
Bullet for Sandoval
Butterfly Wings
Cabeza de Vaca▶
Camila▶
Carmen▶
The Castle of Fu Manchu
Cauldron of Blood
Chimes at Midnight▶
The Christmas Kid
The City and the Dogs▶
City of the Walking Dead
Conquest
Count Dracula
Cria▶
The Criminal Life of Archibaldo de la Cruz▶
Curse of the Devil
Danzon▶
Dark Habits
Demons in the Garden▶
Desperados
Details of a Duel: A Question of Honor
The Devil's Possessed
The Diabolical Dr. Z
Dr. Jekyll and the Wolfman
Dr. Orloff's Monster
Don Juan, My Love▶
Don Quixote▶
Don Segundo Sombra
Dracula vs. Frankenstein
Dracula's Great Love
Duel of Champions
El Barbaro
El Cochecito▶
El Condor
El Diputado▶
El Muerto
El Norte▶
El Super▶
El: This Strange Passion▶
Elisa, Vida Mia
Endless Descent
Escape from El Diablo
Exorcism's Daughter
The Exterminating Angel▶
Exterminators of the Year 3000
Extramuros
The Fable of the Beautiful Pigeon Fancier
Fangs of the Living Dead
The Flower of My Secret▶
Frida
From Hell to Victory
The Fury of the Wolfman
The Garden of Delights▶
Garringo
Gladiators 7
Goliath Against the Giants
Grandes Amigos
Graveyard of Horror
Great Adventure
The Green Wall▶
Half of Heaven▶
The Hanging Woman
Hatchet for the Honeymoon
Hellbenders
High Heels▶
The Holy Innocents▶
Honey
Horror Express
Horror of the Zombies
Horror Rises from the Tomb
The House of 1000 Dolls
House of Psychotic Women
Human Beasts
The Hunt▶
I, the Worst of All
I'm the One You're Looking For
In a Glass Cage
In Memoriam
Inquisition
The Invincible Gladiator
It Happened at Nightmare Inn
Jamon, Jamon
Jornada de Muerte
Kashmiri Run
Kika
King of Kong Island
Labyrinth of Passion
Land and Freedom▶
Last Day of the War
Law of Desire▶
Lazarillo
The Legend of Blood Castle
Leonor
Lightning Bolt
The Lion's Share
Lovers: A True Story▶
Mama Turns a Hundred▶
Man of Legend
The Man Who Wagged His Tail
Matador
Mayalunta
Miracle in Rome
Mission Stardust
Mr. Superinvisible
Mouth to Mouth
The Mummy's Revenge
Murder Mansion
Navajo Joe
The Nest
Night of the Death Cult
Night of the Howling Beast
Night of the Zombies
99 Women
Oasis of the Zombies
On the Line
Orgy of the Vampires
Outrage
Padre Nuestro
Pancho Villa
Passion for Power
Pepi, Luci, Bom and Other Girls on the Heap
Pieces
Pistoleros Asesinos
The Plague
Princess Cinderella
Pulsebeat
Red Sun
Remolina de Pasiones
Return of the Evil Dead
The Return of the Musketeers
Ricco
The Rue Morgue Massacres
The Saga of the Draculas
Satanik
Savage Island
The Scarlet Letter▶
The Scorpion's Tail
The Screaming Dead
The Sea Serpent
Sex Is Crazy
Skyline▶
Son of Captain Blood
Sound of Horror
Spirit of the Beehive▶
The Stilts▶
Stormquest
The Summer of Miss Forbes
Superargo
Supersonic Man
The Sword of El Cid
Target Eagle
That Obscure Object of Desire▶
Tie Me Up! Tie Me Down!
Tombs of the Blind Dead
A Town Called Hell
Trahir▶
Treasure of the Four Crowns
Tristana▶
Under the Earth▶
The Uprising▶
Ursus in the Valley of the Lions
Vengeance of the Zombies
A Very Old Man with Enormous Wings
Virgin Among the Living Dead
Viridiana▶
Web of Deception
The Werewolf vs. the Vampire Woman
When the Screaming Stops
A Witch Without a Broom
Women on the Verge of a Nervous Breakdown▶
Yellow Hair & the Fortress of Gold
Zombie Lake

Swedish

The Adventures of Picasso
After the Rehearsal▶
All Things Fair
The Assignment
The Atonement of Gosta Berling▶
Autumn Sonata▶
The Best Intentions▶
Brink of Life
The Count of the Old Town
Cries and Whispers▶
The Devil's Eye
Devil's Wanton
The Doll
Dollar
Dreaming of Rita
Dreams
Elvira Madigan▶
The Emigrants▶
Face to Face▶
Fanny and Alexander▶
Flight of the Eagle
From the Life of the Marionettes▶
Good Evening, Mr. Wallenberg
Gorilla
The Great Adventure▶
Hour of the Wolf▶
House of Angels
I Am Curious (Yellow)
Inga
The Inside Man
Intermezzo▶
Invasion of the Animal People
Istanbul
June Night
Killing Heat
Lesson in Love
The Magic Flute▶
The Magician▶
The Match Factory Girl▶
Miss Julie
Monika
Montenegro▶
The Mozart Brothers▶
My Life as a Dog▶
The New Land▶
Night Is My Future
Ninja Mission
Only One Night
The Outlaw and His Wife
The Ox
The Passion of Anna▶
Pelle the Conqueror▶
Persona▶
The Phantom Chariot
Pippi Goes on Board
Pippi in the South Seas
Pippi Longstocking
Pippi on the Run
Port of Call▶
The Rite
The Sacrifice▶
Sawdust & Tinsel▶
Scenes from a Marriage▶
Secrets of Women▶
The Seventh Seal▶
The Shame▶
The Silence▶
The Slingshot▶
Smiles of a Summer Night▶
Sofie
Summer Interlude▶
Sunday's Children▶
Swedenhielms
Thomas Graal's Best Film▶
Three Strange Loves▶
Through a Glass Darkly▶
To Joy▶
Torment▶
The Touch
Treasure of Arne
Unmarried Mothers
The Virgin Spring▶
The Visitors
Walpurgis Night▶
Wardogs
Wild Strawberries▶
The Winter Light▶
Witchcraft Through the Ages▶
A Woman's Face▶

Swiss

After Darkness
Alpine Fire
Big Bluff
The Boat is Full▶
Candy Mountain
The Castle▶
Chimes at Midnight▶
Dangerous Moves▶
Drachenfutter▶
A Dream of Passion
First Love
Foxtrot
Hail Mary
Heidi
Helas Pour Moi
In the White City▶
Jonah Who Will Be 25 in the Year 2000▶
Journey of Hope▶
King Lear
La Salamandre
The Lacemaker▶
Messidor
Night and Day▶
Nouvelle Vague
The Pedestrian▶
Trahir▶
Trois Couleurs: Blanc▶
Trois Couleurs: Rouge▶

Taiwanese

The Association
Eat Drink Man Woman▶
The Outcasts▶
The Wedding Banquet▶

Turkish

Baba▶
The Horse▶
Istanbul
The Wall▶
Yol▶

Venezuelan

Shoot to Kill

Vietnamese

The Scent of Green Papaya▶

Yugoslavian

The Battle of Austerlitz
Battle of Neretva
Battleforce
Cave of the Living Dead
Guns of War
Hey, Babu Riba
Innocence Unprotected
Kapo▶
The Love Affair, or The Case of the Missing Switchboard Operator▶
Man Is Not a Bird
One-Eyed Soldiers
Operation Cross Eagles
Romance of a Horsethief

Cast Index

The Cast Index provides a complete videography for cast members with more than one appearance on video. The listings for the actor names follow an alphabetical sort by last name (although the names appear in a first name last name format). The videographies are listed chronologically, from oldest film to the most recent, making it easier to trace the development of your favorite actor's career. When a cast member appears in more than one film in the same year, these movies are listed alphabetically within the year.

Ackland ▶cont.

A Zed & Two Noughts *'88*
Lethal Weapon 2 *'89*
To Kill a Priest *'89*
The Hunt for Red October *'90*
Jekyll and Hyde *'90*
Spymaker: The Secret Life of Ian Fleming *'90*
Bill & Ted's Bogus Journey *'91*
Codename Kyril *'91*
The Object of Beauty *'91*
The Palermo Connection *'91*
A Woman Named Jackie *'91*
The Mighty Ducks *'92*
Once Upon a Crime *'92*
Project: Shadowchaser *'92*
Nowhere to Run *'93*
Jacob *'94*
Miracle on 34th Street *'94*
Mother's Boys *'94*
Citizen X *'95*
A Kid in King Arthur's Court *'95*

David Ackroyd
And I Alone Survived *'78*
The Dark Secret of Harvest Home *'78*
A Gun in the House *'81*
Cocaine: One Man's Seduction *'83*
When Your Lover Leaves *'83*
The Children of Times Square *'86*
A Smoky Mountain Christmas *'86*
Poor Little Rich Girl: The Barbara Hutton Story *'87*
Memories of Me *'88*
Windmills of the Gods *'88*
The Fear Inside *'92*
Dead On *'93*
Love, Cheat & Steal *'93*
Against the Wall *'94*

Rodolfo Acosta
Pancho Villa Returns *'50*
Hondo *'53*
Drum Beat *'54*
Savage Run *'70*

Jay Acovone
Doctor Mordrid: Master of the Unknown *'90*
Quicksand: No Escape *'91*
Born to Run *'93*

Acquanetta
Captive Wild Woman *'43*
The Lost Continent *'51*
Grizzly Adams: The Legend Continues *'90*

Eddie Acuff
Law of the Underworld *'38*
G-Men Never Forget *'48*

Deborah Adair
Gore Vidal's Lincoln *'88*
Endless Descent *'90*

Dick Adair
Blind Rage *'78*
Pay or Die *'83*

Robert Adair
The Face at the Window *'39*
Norman Conquest *'53*

Beverly Adams
Roustabout *'64*
How to Stuff a Wild Bikini *'65*
Murderers' Row *'66*
Devil's Angels *'67*
Torture Garden *'67*

Brandon Adams
The People Under the Stairs *'91*
Ghost in the Machine *'93*
The Sandlot *'93*

Brooke Adams
James Dean *'76*
Shock Waves *'77*
Days of Heaven *'78*
Invasion of the Body Snatchers *'78*
Cuba *'79*
A Man, a Woman, and a Bank *'79*
Tell Me a Riddle *'80*
Dead Zone *'83*
Utilities *'83*
The Innocents Abroad *'84*
Almost You *'85*
Key Exchange *'85*
The Stuff *'85*
The Lion of Africa *'87*
Man on Fire *'87*
Sometimes They Come Back *'91*
The Unborn *'91*
Gas Food Lodging *'92*
The Last Hit *'93*
The Baby-Sitters Club *'95*

Catlin Adams
Panic in Echo Park *'77*
The Jerk *'79*
The Jazz Singer *'80*

Claire Adams
The Penalty *'20*
Heart's Haven *'22*
The Big Parade *'25*

Don Adams
The Nude Bomb *'80*
Jimmy the Kid *'82*
Back to the Beach *'87*
Get Smart, Again! *'89*

Dorothy Adams
Laura *'44*
Streets of Sin *'49*
The Prodigal *'55*

Edie Adams
Best of Ernie Kovacs *'56*
The Apartment *'60*
Lover Come Back *'61*
Call Me Bwana *'63*
It's a Mad, Mad, Mad, Mad World *'63*
Love with the Proper Stranger *'63*
The Best Man *'64*
The Oscar *'66*
The Honey Pot *'67*
Cheech and Chong's Up in Smoke *'79*
Racquet *'79*
The Seekers *'79*
Haunting of Harrington House *'82*
Shooting Stars *'85*
Adventures Beyond Belief *'87*

Ernie Adams
Nevada *'27*
The Fighting Legion *'30*
The Tip-Off *'31*
Beyond the Rockies *'32*
Breed of the Border *'33*
Galloping Romeo *'33*
The Gun Ranger *'34*
Gun Lords of Stirrup Basin *'37*
Lightning Bill Crandall *'37*
Ridin' the Lone Trail *'37*
Sagebrush Law *'43*
Wings Over the Pacific *'43*

Jane Adams
House of Dracula *'45*
Lost City of the Jungle *'45*
The Brute Man *'46*

Jane Adams
Rising Son *'90*
Vital Signs *'90*
Father of the Bride Part II *'95*

Joey Adams
S.F.W. *'94*
Mallrats *'95*
Bio-Dome *'96*

Julie Adams
Blazing Guns *'50*
Sudden Death *'50*
Horizons West *'52*
Man from the Alamo *'53*
Creature from the Black Lagoon *'54*
Francis Joins the WACs *'54*
Away All Boats *'56*
Tickle Me *'65*
The Last Movie *'71*
The Trackers *'71*
McQ *'74*
Psychic Killer *'75*
Black Roses *'88*
Backtrack *'89*

Lynne Adams
Blood Relations *'87*
Night Zoo *'87*
The Carpenter *'89*
Silent Hunter *'94*

Mason Adams
A Shining Season *'79*
Revenge of the Stepford Wives *'80*
The Kid with the Broken Halo *'82*
Adam *'83*
Half Slave, Half Free *'85*
F/X *'86*
Rage of Angels: The Story Continues *'86*
Son-in-Law *'93*
Houseguest *'94*

Maud Adams
The Girl in Blue *'74*
The Man with the Golden Gun *'74*
Killer Force *'75*
Rollerball *'75*
The Hostage Tower *'80*
Playing for Time *'80*
Tattoo *'81*
Octopussy *'83*
Target Eagle *'84*
Hell Hunters *'87*
Jane & the Lost City *'87*
Women's Club *'87*
Angel 3: The Final Chapter *'88*
Deadly Intent *'88*
Nairobi Affair *'88*
Intimate Power *'89*
The Kill Reflex *'89*
A Man of Passion *'90s*
Silent Night, Deadly Night 4: Initiation *'90*

Nick Adams
Mister Roberts *'55*
Picnic *'55*
Rebel Without a Cause *'55*
Our Miss Brooks *'56*
No Time for Sergeants *'58*
Teacher's Pet *'58*
The FBI Story *'59*
Pillow Talk *'59*
Hell is for Heroes *'62*
The Interns *'62*
Die, Monster, Die! *'65*
Mosby's Marauders *'66*
Mission Mars *'67*
Godzilla vs. Monster Zero *'68*

Peter Adams
Bullwhip *'58*
Alternative *'76*

Stanley Adams
Hell Ship Mutiny *'57*
Lilies of the Field *'63*
The Passing of Evil *'70*

Ted Adams
Ghost Valley *'32*
The Savage Girl *'32*
Toll of the Desert *'35*
Border Caballero *'36*
Desert Phantom *'36*
The Lion Man *'36*
Undercover Man *'36*
Arizona Gunfighter *'37*
Lightnin' Carson Rides Again *'38*
Pals of the Saddle *'38*
Outlaw's Paradise *'39*
Pinto Canyon *'40*
Billy the Kid *'41*
Outlaw Country *'49*

Tom Adams
Second Best Secret Agent in the Whole Wide World *'65*
The Fighting Prince of Donegal *'66*
Where the Bullets Fly *'66*
The House that Dripped Blood *'71*
Fast Kill *'73*

Tony Addabbo
The Gunfighters *'87*
Red Shoe Diaries 5: Weekend Pass *'95*

Dawn Addams
The Robe *'53*
A King in New York *'57*
The Silent Enemy *'58*
The Thousand Eyes of Dr. Mabuse *'60*
The Two Faces of Dr. Jekyll *'60*
The Liars *'64*
Secret Agent *'64*
Ballad in Blue *'66*
Where the Bullets Fly *'66*
Alien Women *'69*
The Vampire Lovers *'70*
Vault of Horror *'73*

Nancy Addison
The Dain Curse *'78*
Somewhere Tomorrow *'85*

Wesley Addy
The Big Knife *'55*
Kiss Me Deadly *'55*
Tora! Tora! Tora! *'70*
The Grissom Gang *'71*
Network *'76*
The Europeans *'79*
The Bostonians *'84*
Hiroshima *'95*

Isabelle Adjani
Story of Adele H. *'75*
The Slap *'76*
The Tenant *'76*
The Driver *'78*
Possession *'81*
Quartet *'81*
Next Year If All Goes Well *'83*
One Deadly Summer *'83*
Subway *'85*
Ishtar *'87*
Camille Claudel *'89*
Queen Margot *'94*
Diabolique *'96*

Bill Adler
Pom Pom Girls *'76*
Van Nuys Blvd. *'79*

Jay Adler
Crime of Passion *'57*
Grave of the Vampire *'72*

Jerry Adler
The Public Eye *'92*
Manhattan Murder Mystery *'93*

Luther Adler
Cornered *'45*
The Loves of Carmen *'48*
D.O.A. *'49*
House of Strangers *'49*
Wake of the Red Witch *'49*
Kiss Tomorrow Goodbye *'50*
The Desert Fox *'51*
Hoodlum Empire *'52*
Crashout *'55*
The Last Angry Man *'59*
The Brotherhood *'68*
The Man in the Glass Booth *'75*
Mean Johnny Barrows *'75*
Murph the Surf *'75*
Voyage of the Damned *'76*
Absence of Malice *'81*

Matt Adler
Flight of the Navigator *'86*
North Shore *'87*
White Water Summer *'87*
Doin' Time on Planet Earth *'88*
Diving In *'90*

Edvin Adolphson
The Count of the Old Town *'34*
Dollar *'38*
Only One Night *'42*
Boy of Two Worlds *'70*

Renee Adoree
The Big Parade *'25*
The Michigan Kid *'28*

Mario Adorf
Paralyzed *'70s*
Hired to Kill *'73*
Hit Men *'73*
Manhunt *'73*
The Lost Honor of Katharina Blum *'75*
The Tin Drum *'79*
Invitation au Voyage *'82*
The Holcroft Covenant *'85*

Iris Adrian
The Road to Zanzibar *'41*
I Killed That Man *'42*
I'm from Arkansas *'44*
Million Dollar Kid *'44*
Shake Hands with Murder *'44*
The Stork Club *'45*
Infamous Crimes *'47*
The Paleface *'48*
The Lovable Cheat *'49*
G.I. Jane *'51*
Stop That Cab *'51*
Varieties on Parade *'52*
The Fast and the Furious *'54*
Blue Hawaii *'62*

Max Adrian
The Boy Friend *'71*
The Devils *'71*
The Music Lovers *'71*

Patricia Adriani
The Nest *'80*
I'm the One You're Looking For *'88*

Ben Affleck
School Ties *'92*
Mallrats *'95*

Casey Affleck
To Die For *'95*
Race the Sun *'96*

John Agar
Fort Apache *'48*
Sands of Iwo Jima *'49*
She Wore a Yellow Ribbon *'49*
Along the Great Divide *'51*
Revenge of the Creature *'55*
Tarantula *'55*
The Mole People *'56*
The Brain from Planet Arous *'57*
The Daughter of Dr. Jekyll *'57*
Flesh and the Spur *'57*
Jet Attack/Paratroop Command *'58*
Invisible Invaders *'59*
Cavalry Command *'63*
Curse of the Swamp Creature *'66*
Johnny Reno *'66*
Zontar, the Thing from Venus *'66*
Hell Raiders *'68*
Miracle Mile *'89*
Fear *'90*
Body Bags *'93*

Tetchie Agbayani
The Dolls *'83*
Gymkata *'85*
Rikky and Pete *'88*
Deathfight *'93*

Carlos Agosti
Invasion of the Vampires *'61*
The Bloody Vampire *'62*

Pierre Agostino
The Hollywood Strangler Meets the Skid Row Slasher *'79*
Las Vegas Serial Killer *'86*

Janet Agren
Perfect Crime *'78*
The Uranium Conspiracy *'78*
Emerald Jungle *'80*
Gates of Hell *'83*
Panic *'83*
Aladdin *'86*
Hands of Steel *'86*
Magdalene *'88*
Night of the Sharks *'89*

Kris Aguilar
Bloodfist *'89*
Fist of Steel *'93*

Jenny Agutter
Star! *'68*
The Railway Children *'70*
Logan's Run *'76*
The Eagle Has Landed *'77*
Equus *'77*
The Man in the Iron Mask *'77*
Gunfire *'78*
Dominique is Dead *'79*
The Riddle of the Sands *'79*
Sweet William *'79*
Survivor *'80*
An American Werewolf in London *'81*
Amy *'81*
Secret Places *'85*
Silas Marner *'85*
Dark Tower *'87*
Child's Play 2 *'90*
Darkman *'90*
The Buccaneers *'95*

Brian Aherne
I Live My Life *'35*
Sylvia Scarlett *'35*
Beloved Enemy *'36*
The Lady in Question *'40*
Smilin' Through *'41*
A Night to Remember *'42*
Forever and a Day *'43*
I Confess *'53*
Titanic *'53*
A Bullet Is Waiting *'54*
Prince Valiant *'54*
The Swan *'56*
The Best of Everything *'59*
Sword of Lancelot *'63*
Waltz King *'63*

Bjorje Ahistedt
Emma's Shadow *'88*
Sunday's Children *'94*

Philip Ahn
The General Died at Dawn '36
Hawaii Calls '38
Betrayal from the East '44
China Sky '44
The Story of Dr. Wassell '44
Back to Bataan '45
His Majesty O'Keefe '53
Battle Hymn '57
Shock Corridor '63
Paradise, Hawaiian Style '66

Charles Aidman
Hour of the Gun '67
Countdown '68
Adam at 6 a.m. '70
Menace on the Mountain '70
The Barbary Coast '74
The Invasion of Carol Enders '74
Picture of Dorian Gray '74
Zone of the Dead '78
House of the Dead '80
Zoot Suit '81
Prime Suspect '82

Danny Aiello
Deathmask '69
Bang the Drum Slowly '73
The Godfather, Part 2 '74
The Front '76
Hooch '76
Bloodbrothers '78
Fingers '78
Defiance '79
The Lost Idol/Shock Troop '80s
Hide in Plain Sight '80
Question of Honor '80
Chu Chu & the Philly Flash '81
Fort Apache, the Bronx '81
Old Enough '84
Once Upon a Time in America '84
Key Exchange '85
Protector '85
The Purple Rose of Cairo '85
The Stuff '85
Alone in the Neon Jungle '87
Man on Fire '87
Moonstruck '87
The Pick-Up Artist '87
Radio Days '87
White Hot '88
Do the Right Thing '89
Harlem Nights '89
The January Man '89
The Preppie Murder '89
Third Solution '89
Jacob's Ladder '90
The Closer '91
Hudson Hawk '91
Mistress '91
Once Around '91
29th Street '91
Ruby '92
The Cemetery Club '93
Me and the Kid '93
The Pickle '93
Power of Attorney '94
The Professional '94
Ready to Wear '94
City Hall '95
The Road Home '95
Two Much '96

Rick Aiello
The Closer '91
29th Street '91
Endangered '94
Uncivilized '94

Anouk Aimee
The Golden Salamander '51
Paris Express '53
Modigliani '58
La Dolce Vita '60
Lola '61
Sodom and Gomorrah '62
8 1/2 '63
A Man and a Woman '66
Justine '69
The Tragedy of a Ridiculous Man '81
Success is the Best Revenge '84
A Man and a Woman: 20 Years Later '86
Dr. Bethune '90
Ready to Wear '94

Richard Ainley
White Cargo '42
I Dood It '43

Holly Aird
The Flame Trees of Thika '81
Over Indulgence '87

Michael Aitkens
The Highest Honor '84
Moving Targets '87

Franklin Ajaye
Car Wash '76
Convoy '78
The Jazz Singer '80
Fraternity Vacation '85
The Wrong Guys '88

Chantal Akerman
Je Tu Il Elle '74
Akermania, Vol. 1 '92

Andra Akers
E. Nick: A Legend in His Own Mind '84
Desert Hearts '86

Karen Akers
The Purple Rose of Cairo '85
Heartburn '86

Claude Akins
From Here to Eternity '53
The Caine Mutiny '54
Sea Chase '55
The Kettles on Old MacDonald's Farm '57
Rio Bravo '59
Merrill's Marauders '62
The Killers '64
Return of the Seven '66
Waterhole #3 '67
The Devil's Brigade '68
A Man Called Sledge '71
Battle for the Planet of the Apes '73
The Death Squad '73
The Big Push '75
Eric '75
Killer on Board '77
Tarantulas: The Deadly Cargo '77
The Concrete Cowboys '79
Manhunt for Claude Dallas '86
Monster in the Closet '86
Pecos Bill '86
The Curse '87
Falling from Grace '92
The Gambler Returns: The Luck of the Draw '93

Marc Alaimo
Archer: The Fugitive from the Empire '81
Arena '89
Tango and Cash '89
Quicksand: No Escape '91
The Fence '94

Steve Alaimo
The Hooked Generation '69
Wild Rebels '71
Alligator Alley '72

Craig Alan
Sex Crimes '92
Endangered '94

Joe Alaskey
Lucky Stiff '88
Bank Robber '93

Maria Alba
Mr. Robinson Crusoe '32
Chandu on the Magic Island '34
Return of Chandu '34

Captain Lou Albano
Wise Guys '86
Body Slam '87

Josh Albee
The Adventures of Tom Sawyer '73
The Runaways '75

Kevin Alber
Alien Terminator '95
Burial of the Rats '95

Anna Maria Alberghetti
Here Comes the Groom '51
The Medium '51
The Last Command '55
Cinderfella '60

Luis Alberni
The Big Stampede '32
Man from Monterey '33
The Sphinx '33
Goodbye Love '34
One Night of Love '34
Dancing Pirate '36
Hats Off '37
The Great Man Votes '38
Harvest Melody '43

Hans Albers
The Blue Angel '30
F.P. 1 Doesn't Answer '33
Baron Munchausen '43
Die Grosse Freiheit Nr. 7 '45

Eddie Albert
Bombardier '43
The Perfect Marriage '46
Smash-Up: The Story of a Woman '47
The Fuller Brush Girl '50
Actors and Sin '52
Carrie '52
Roman Holiday '53
I'll Cry Tomorrow '55
Oklahoma! '55
The Teahouse of the August Moon '56
Beloved Infidel '59
The Longest Day '62
Captain Newman, M.D. '63
The Miracle of the White Stallions '63
Who's Got the Action? '63
Fireball Forward '72
The Heartbreak Kid '72
The Longest Yard '74
McQ '74
Devil's Rain '75
Escape to Witch Mountain '75
Whiffs '75
Moving Violation '76
The Birch Interval '78
The Crash of Flight 401 '78
The Word '78
The Concorde: Airport '79 '79
Beulah Land '80
Foolin' Around '80
How to Beat the High Cost of Living '80
Goliath Awaits '81
Take This Job & Shove It '81
The Act '82
Yes, Giorgio '82
Burning Rage '84
Dreamscape '84
Stitches '85
Brenda Starr '86
Dress Gray '86
Head Office '86
Turnaround '87
The Victory '88
The Big Picture '89
Out of Sight, Out of Her Mind '89

Edward Albert
The Fool Killer '65
Butterflies Are Free '72
Forty Carats '73
Death Cruise '74
The Domino Principle '77
The Purple Taxi '77
The Greek Tycoon '78
The Rip Off '78
Silent Victory: The Kitty O'Neil Story '79
The Squeeze '80
When Time Ran Out '80
Galaxy of Terror '81
Night School '81
Butterfly '82
House Where Evil Dwells '82
Time to Die '83
Ellie '84
Getting Even '86
Distortions '87
Terminal Entry '87
Fist Fighter '88
The Heist '88
The Rescue '88
The Underachievers '88
Accidents '89
Mind Games '89
Wild Zone '89
Exiled in America '90
Body Language '92
Broken Trust '93
The Ice Runner '93
Sexual Malice '93
Shootfighter: Fight to the Death '93
Guarding Tess '94
Hard Drive '94
Sorceress '94

Laura Albert
Death by Dialogue '88
Dr. Caligari '89
Blood Games '90

Guido Alberti
Casanova '70 '65
Ten Days Wonder '72

Frank Albertson
Big Business Girl '31
Way Back Home '32
Rainbow Over Broadway '33
Hollywood Mystery '34
Ah, Wilderness! '35
Fury '36
Navy Blue and Gold '37
Room Service '38
Louisiana Purchase '41
Man Made Monster '41
It's a Wonderful Life '46
Killer Dill '47
Nightfall '56
Psycho '60

Jack Albertson
Miracle on 34th Street '47
Lover Come Back '61
Days of Wine and Roses '62
Period of Adjustment '62
Who's Got the Action? '63
How to Murder Your Wife '64
Kissin' Cousins '64
The Patsy '64
Roustabout '64
Flim-Flam Man '67
Changes '69
Justine '69
Willy Wonka & the Chocolate Factory '71
The Poseidon Adventure '72
Where the Eagle Flies '72
Marriage Is Alive and Well '80
Dead and Buried '81
Charlie and the Great Balloon Chase '82

Hardie Albright
The Purchase Price '32
The Scarlet Letter '34
Champagne for Breakfast '35
Sing Sing Nights '35
The Jade Mask '45
Sunset in El Dorado '45
Mom & Dad '47

Lola Albright
Champion '49
The Tender Trap '55
The Monolith Monsters '57
Kid Galahad '62
Joy House '64
The Way West '67
The Impossible Years '68
Where Were You When the Lights Went Out? '68

Victor Alcocer
It Happened at Nightmare Inn '70
Pistoleros Asesinos '87

Alan Alda
Gone are the Days '63
Purlie Victorious '63
Paper Lion '68
Jenny '70
The Mephisto Waltz '71
The Glass House '72
M*A*S*H: The Collector's Edition '72
Playmates '72
To Kill a Clown '72
California Suite '78
Same Time, Next Year '78
The Seduction of Joe Tynan '79
The Four Seasons '81
M*A*S*H: Goodbye, Farewell & Amen '83
Sweet Liberty '86
A New Life '88
Crimes & Misdemeanors '89
Betsy's Wedding '90
Whispers in the Dark '92
And the Band Played On '93
Manhattan Murder Mystery '93
Canadian Bacon '94
White Mile '94
Flirting with Disaster '95

Antony Alda
Movie Maker '86
Homeboy '88
The Killing Device '92

Robert Alda
Rhapsody in Blue '45
The Beast with Five Fingers '46
Cloak and Dagger '46
The Man I Love '46
Hollywood Varieties '50
Force of Impulse '60
The Devil's Hand '61
Revenge of the Barbarians '64
Night Flight from Moscow '73
Lisa and the Devil '75
Bittersweet Love '76
I Will, I Will for Now '76
Love by Appointment '76
Every Girl Should Have One '78
The Rip Off '78
Express to Terror '79
The Squeeze '80
The Heist '88

Rutanya Alda
The Deer Hunter '78
Mommie Dearest '81
Amityville 2: The Possession '82
Girls Night Out '83
Vigilante '83
Racing with the Moon '84
Black Widow '87
Prancer '89
The Dark Half '91
Article 99 '92
Leaving Normal '92

Mary Alden
April Fool '26
Strange Interlude '32

Priscilla Alden
Criminally Insane '75
Crazy Fat Ethel II '85
Death Nurse '87

John Alderman
Little Miss Innocence '73
The Alpha Incident '76

Mari Aldon
Distant Drums '51
Race for Life '55

Tom Aldredge
Gentleman Bandit '81
O Pioneers! '91
Other People's Money '91
What About Bob? '91
The Adventures of Huck Finn '93
Andersonville '95

Kay Aldridge
Nyoka and the Tigermen '42
Haunted Harbor '44
The Phantom of 42nd Street '45

Kitty Aldridge
American Roulette '88
Slipstream '89
An African Dream '90
To Play the King '93

Michael Aldridge
Love for Lydia '79
Bullshot '83
Footlight Frenzy '84

Norma Aleandro
The Official Story '85
Gaby: A True Story '87
Cousins '89
One Man's War '90
Vital Signs '90

Julio Aleman
Neutron and the Black Mask '61
Neutron vs. the Amazing Dr. Caronte '61
Neutron vs. the Death Robots '62
The Green Wall '70

Aki Aleong
Hanoi Hilton '87
Braddock: Missing in Action 3 '88
Farewell to the King '89
The Quest '96

Barbara Lee Alexander
Hired to Kill '91
Illegal Entry: Formula for Fear '93
Psycho Cop 2 '94

Ben Alexander
The Little American '17
Hearts of the World '18
Little Orphan Annie '18
All Quiet on the Western Front '30
Red Lights Ahead '36

Alexander ▶cont.

Legion of Missing Men '37
Western Gold '37
Criminals Within '41
Dragnet '50s
Dragnet '54

Jace Alexander
Eight Men Out '88
City of Hope '91
Mistress '91
Love and a .45 '94

Jane Alexander
The Great White Hope '70
A Gunfight '71
The New Centurions '72
Death Be Not Proud '75
All the President's Men '76
Eleanor & Franklin '76
The Betsy '78
A Question of Love '78
Kramer vs. Kramer '79
Brubaker '80
Playing for Time '80
Night Crossing '81
Calamity Jane '82
In the Custody of Strangers '82
Lovey: A Circle of Children 2 '82
Testament '83
City Heat '84
The Rumor Mill '86
Square Dance '87
Sweet Country '87
A Friendship in Vienna '88
Glory '89
In Love and War '91

Jason Alexander
The Burning '82
Brighton Beach Memoirs '86
The Mosquito Coast '86
Jacob's Ladder '90
Pretty Woman '90
White Palace '90
I Don't Buy Kisses Anymore '92
Coneheads '93
Blankman '94
North '94
The Paper '94
Dunston Checks In '95
For Better or Worse '95

Jeff Alexander
Curse of the Swamp Creature '66
Twisted Brain '74

John Alexander
Arsenic and Old Lace '44
Mr. Skeffington '44
The Horn Blows at Midnight '45
A Tree Grows in Brooklyn '45
The Jolson Story '46
Where There's Life '47
Fancy Pants '50

Katherine Alexander
The Barretts of Wimpole Street '34
That Certain Woman '37
The Great Man Votes '38
Dance, Girl, Dance '40

Khandi Alexander
CB4: The Movie '93
What's Love Got to Do with It? '93
Greedy '94
Sugar Hill '94

Richard Alexander
The Mysterious Lady '28
Daring Danger '32
Scarlet Dawn '32
Texas Bad Man '32
Renfrew on the Great White Trail '38
The Kansas Terrors '39

Lidia Alfonsi
Black Sabbath '64
Open Doors '89

Kristian Alfonso
Army of One '94
Blindfold: Acts of Obsession '94

Chuck Alford
Commando Squad '76
The Hollywood Strangler Meets the Skid Row Slasher '79

Hans Alfredson
The Shame '68
The New Land '73
The Adventures of Picasso '80

Muhammad Ali
The Greatest '77
Freedom Road '79
Body & Soul '81
Doin' Time '85

Mary Alice
Sparkle '76
He Who Walks Alone '78
Charlotte Forten's Mission: Experiment in Freedom '85
The Women of Brewster Place '89
To Sleep with Anger '90
Laurel Avenue '93

Ana Alicia
Coward of the County '81
Romero '89

Lisa Aliff
Trained to Kill '88
Damned River '89
Playroom '90

Jeff Alin
American Tickler '76
A Matter of Love '78

Elizabeth Allan
Ace of Aces '33
Java Head '35
Mark of the Vampire '35
Phantom Fiend '35
A Tale of Two Cities '35
Camille '36
The Shadow '36
A Woman Rebels '36
No Highway in the Sky '51
The Haunted Strangler '58

Jed Allan
Lassie: Adventures of Neeka '68
Suspect Device '95

Louise Allbritton
Pittsburgh '42
Who Done It? '42
Son of Dracula '43
Egg and I '47
The Doolins of Oklahoma '49

Michael Alldredge
About Last Night... '86
Robot Jox '90

Bambi Allen
Satan's Sadists '69
Outlaw Riders '72

Bill Allen
Rad '86
Sioux City '94

Chad Allen
Camp Cucamonga: How I Spent My Summer Vacation '90
Straight Up '90
Murder in New Hampshire: The Pamela Smart Story '91
Praying Mantis '93

Corey Allen
Rebel Without a Cause '55
Darby's Rangers '58
Party Girl '58

Debbie Allen
The Fish that Saved Pittsburgh '79
Roots: The Next Generation '79
Ragtime '81
Jo Jo Dancer, Your Life is Calling '86

Elizabeth Allen
Donovan's Reef '63
Star Spangled Girl '71

Fred Allen
It's in the Bag '45
We're Not Married '52

Ginger Lynn Allen
Vice Academy '88
Buried Alive '89
Cleo/Leo '89
Hollywood Boulevard 2 '89
Wild Man '89
Leather Jackets '90
Vice Academy 2 '90
Young Guns 2 '90
Vice Academy 3 '91
Mind, Body & Soul '92
Bound and Gagged: A Love Story '93

Gracie Allen
International House '33
We're Not Dressing '34
A Damsel in Distress '37
College Swing '38
Honolulu '39
Two Girls and a Sailor '44
The Burns and Allen Show '50

India Allen
Wild Cactus '92
Seduce Me: Pamela Principle 2 '94

Jeffrey Allen
Moonshine Mountain '64
2000 Maniacs '64
This Stuff'll Kill Ya! '71

Joan Allen
All My Sons '86
Fat Guy Goes Nutzoid '86
Manhunter '86
Peggy Sue Got Married '86
Tucker: The Man and His Dream '88
In Country '89
Without Warning: The James Brady Story '91
Ethan Frome '92
Josh and S.A.M. '93
Searching for Bobby Fischer '93
Mad Love '95
Nixon '95

Jonelle Allen
The River Niger '76
The Midnight Hour '86
Penalty Phase '86
Grave Secrets: The Legacy of Hilltop Drive '92

Judith Allen
Dancing Man '33
Bright Eyes '34
Healer '36
Boots & Saddles '37
Git Along Little Dogies '37
The Port of Missing Girls '38
Tough Kid '39
Train to Tombstone '50

Karen Allen
National Lampoon's Animal House '78
Manhattan '79
Wanderers '79
Cruising '80
East of Eden '80
A Small Circle of Friends '80
Raiders of the Lost Ark '81
Shoot the Moon '82
Split Image '82
Starman '84
Until September '84
The Glass Menagerie '87
Backfire '88
Scrooged '88
Animal Behavior '89
Secret Weapon '90
Sweet Talker '91
Ghost in the Machine '93
King of the Hill '93
The Sandlot '93
Voyage '93

Keith Allen
Chicago Joe & the Showgirl '90
Small Time '91
Nightscare '93
The Young Americans '93
Captives '94
Second Best '94
Shallow Grave '94

Marty Allen
Harrad Summer '74
Whale of a Tale '76

Mike Allen
Hooch '76
Death Driver '78

Nancy Allen
The Last Detail '73
Forced Entry '75
Carrie '76
I Wanna Hold Your Hand '78
Home Movies '79
1941 '79
Dressed to Kill '80
Blow Out '81
The Buddy System '83
Strange Invaders '83
Not for Publication '84
The Philadelphia Experiment '84
The Gladiator '86
RoboCop '87
Sweet Revenge '87
Poltergeist 3 '88
Limit Up '89
Memories of Murder '90
RoboCop 2 '90
RoboCop 3 '91
Acting on Impulse '93

Patrick Allen
The Long Haul '57
Flight from Singapore '62
Island of the Burning Doomed '67
Invasion of the Body Stealers '69
When Dinosaurs Ruled the Earth '70
Puppet on a Chain '72
Thirteenth Day of Christmas '85
Full Metal Ninja '89

Rex Allen
Arizona Cowboy '49
Hills of Oklahoma '50
Redwood Forest Trail '50
Trail of Robin Hood '50
Western Double Feature 3: Rogers & Allen '50
Silver City Bonanza '51
Thunder in God's Country '51
Border Saddlemates '52
Colorado Sundown '52
I Dream of Jeannie '52

Robert Allen
The Perils of Pauline '34
The Black Room '35
Crime and Punishment '35
Fighting Shadows '35
The Revenge Rider '35
The Unknown Ranger '36
The Awful Truth '37
The Rangers Step In '37

Ronald Allen
Eat the Rich '87
Supergrass '87

Rosalind Allen
To Die for 2: Son of Darkness '91
Children of the Corn 2: The Final Sacrifice '92
Ticks '93

Sheila Allen
Children of the Damned '63
The Alphabet Murders '65
Bouquet of Barbed Wire '76
Pascali's Island '88

Steve Allen
The Benny Goodman Story '55
Where Were You When the Lights Went Out? '68
Heart Beat '80
Ratings Game '84
Amazon Women on the Moon '87
Great Balls of Fire '89

Todd Allen
Witchboard '87
Brothers in Arms '88
Storm and Sorrow '90
Wyatt Earp '94
Tall, Dark and Deadly '95

Tom Allen
Shadows '60
Clash of the Ninja '86

Woody Allen
What's New Pussycat? '65
What's Up, Tiger Lily? '66
Casino Royale '67
Take the Money and Run '69
Bananas '71
Everything You Always Wanted to Know about Sex (But Were Afraid to Ask) '72
Play It Again, Sam '72
Sleeper '73
Love and Death '75
The Front '76
Annie Hall '77
Manhattan '79
Stardust Memories '80
A Midsummer Night's Sex Comedy '82
Zelig '83
Broadway Danny Rose '84
Hannah and Her Sisters '86
King Lear '87
Crimes & Misdemeanors '89
New York Stories '89
Scenes from a Mall '91
Husbands and Wives '92
Shadows and Fog '92
Manhattan Murder Mystery '93
Mighty Aphrodite '95

Kirstie Alley
Star Trek 2: The Wrath of Khan '82
Blind Date '84
Champions '84
Runaway '84
A Bunny's Tale '85
North and South Book 1 '85
North and South Book 2 '86
Prince of Bel Air '87
Summer School '87
Shoot to Kill '88
Look Who's Talking '89
Loverboy '89
Look Who's Talking, Too '90
Madhouse '90
One More Chance '90
Sibling Rivalry '90
Look Who's Talking Now '93
It Takes Two '95
Village of the Damned '95

Sara Allgood
Blackmail '29
Juno and the Paycock '30
Storm in a Teacup '37
How Green Was My Valley '41
That Hamilton Woman '41
Roxie Hart '42
City Without Men '43
Jane Eyre '44
The Keys of the Kingdom '44
The Strange Affair of Uncle Harry '45
The Spiral Staircase '46
The Fabulous Dorseys '47
The Accused '48
Challenge to Lassie '49
Cheaper by the Dozen '50

Dorothy Allison
The Third Key '57
See No Evil '71
Rikky and Pete '88

Gregg Allman
Rush Week '88
Rush '91

Christopher Allport
Savage Weekend '80
Circle of Power '83
Special Bulletin '83
News at Eleven '86

Corbin Allred
Quest of the Delta Knights '93
Josh Kirby...Time Warrior: Chapter 1, Planet of the Dino-Knights '95
Josh Kirby...Time Warrior: Chapter 2, The Human Pets '95
Josh Kirby...Time Warrior: Chapter 3, Trapped on Toyworld '95
Josh Kirby...Time Warrior: Chapter 4, Eggs from 70 Million B.C. '95
Josh Kirby...Time Warrior: Chapter 5, Journey to the Magic Cavern '96
Josh Kirby...Time Warrior: Chapter 6, Last Battle for the Universe '96

Astrid Allwyn
Beggars in Ermine '34
Monte Carlo Nights '34
Mystery Liner '34
Charlie Chan's Secret '35
Hands Across the Table '35
Stowaway '36
International Crime '37
It Could Happen to You '37
Love Affair '39

June Allyson
Best Foot Forward '43
Girl Crazy '43
Thousands Cheer '43
Two Girls and a Sailor '44
Till the Clouds Roll By '46
Good News '47
The Three Musketeers '48
Words and Music '48
Little Women '49
The Stratton Story '49
Battle Circus '53
Executive Suite '54

The Glenn Miller Story '54
A Woman's World '54
The McConnell Story '55
Strategic Air Command '55
The Opposite Sex '56
My Man Godfrey '57
They Only Kill Their Masters '72
Curse of the Black Widow '77
Blackout '78
Vegas '78
The Kid with the Broken Halo '82

Gila Almagor
Sallah '63
The House on Chelouche Street '73
Hide and Seek '80
Every Time We Say Goodbye '86

Chelo Alonso
Girl Under the Sheet '60s
Atlas in the Land of the Cyclops '61
Son of Samson '62
The Good, the Bad and the Ugly '67

Ernesto Alonso
Wuthering Heights '53
The Criminal Life of Archibaldo de la Cruz '55

Maria Conchita Alonso
Moscow on the Hudson '84
Fear City '85
A Fine Mess '86
Touch and Go '86
Blood Ties '87
Extreme Prejudice '87
The Running Man '87
Colors '88
Vampire's Kiss '88
Predator 2 '90
McBain '91
Teamster Boss: The Jackie Presser Story '92
The House of the Spirits '93
Texas '94
Roosters '95

Corinne Alphen
Hot T-Shirts '79
C.O.D. '83
Spring Break '83
New York Nights '84

Catherine Alric
Dear Detective '77
The Associate '82

Carol Alt
Bye Bye Baby '88
Portfolio '88
Millions '90
My Wonderful Life '90
A Family Matter '91
Beyond Justice '92
Thunder in Paradise '93
Ring of Steel '94
Thunder in Paradise 2 '94
Deadly Past '95

John Altamura
New York's Finest '87
The Toxic Avenger, Part 2 '89
The Toxic Avenger, Part 3: The Last Temptation of Toxie '89
Bikini Bistro '94

Hector Alterio
The Nest '80
Fridays of Eternity '81
Basileus Quartet '82
Camila '84
The Official Story '85
I, the Worst of All '90

Bruce Altman
The Favor, the Watch, & the Very Big Fish '92
Glengarry Glen Ross '92
My New Gun '92
Mr. Jones '93
Vibrations '94
White Mile '94

Jeff Altman
In Love with an Older Woman '82
Doin' Time '85
Russian Roulette '93

Walter George Alton
The Puma Man '80
Heavenly Bodies '84

Crox Alvarado
The Curse of the Aztec Mummy '59
Curse of the Aztec Mummy/Robot vs. the Aztec Mummy '59
The Robot vs. the Aztec Mummy '59

Magali Alvarado
Salsa '88
Mi Vida Loca '94

Trini Alvarado
A Movie Star's Daughter '79
Rich Kids '79
Times Square '80
Private Contentment '83
Mrs. Soffel '84
The Chair '87
Sweet Lorraine '87
Nitti: The Enforcer '88
Satisfaction '88
American Blue Note '89
Stella '89
American Friends '91
The Babe '92
Little Women '94
The Perez Family '94
The Frighteners '96

Anicee Alvina
Friends '71
Paul and Michelle '74

Kirk Alyn
Daughter of Don Q '46
Superman: The Serial, Vol. 1 '48
Federal Agents vs. Underworld, Inc. '49

Lyle Alzado
The Lost Idol/Shock Troop '80s
Oceans of Fire '86
Tough Guys '86
Ernest Goes to Camp '87
Destroyer '88
Tapeheads '89
Who's Harry Crumb? '89
Zapped Again '89
Club Fed '90
Comrades in Arms '91
Neon City '91

Shigeru Amachi
The Ghost of Yatsuya '58
Zatoichi: The Life and Opinion of Masseur Ichi '62
Zatoichi: The Blind Swordsman's Vengeance '66

Betty Amann
Rich and Strange '32
Nancy Drew, Reporter '39

Andriana Ambesi
Secret Agent Super Dragon '66
Fangs of the Living Dead '68
Stranger in Paso Bravo '73

Don Ameche
One in a Million '36
Alexander's Ragtime Band '38
Happy Landing '38
In Old Chicago '38
Midnight '39
The Story of Alexander Graham Bell '39
The Three Musketeers '39
Down Argentine Way '40
Moon over Miami '41
The Magnificent Dope '42
Heaven Can Wait '43
A Wing and a Prayer '44
Guest Wife '45
It's in the Bag '45
Picture Mommy Dead '66
The Boatniks '70
Suppose They Gave a War and Nobody Came? '70
Trading Places '83
Cocoon '85
Harry and the Hendersons '87
Pals '87
Cocoon: The Return '88
Coming to America '88
Things Change '88
Oddball Hall '91
Oscar '91
Folks! '92
Sunstroke '92
Corrina, Corrina '94

Claudio Amendola
La Scorta '94

Queen Margot '94
The Horseman on the Roof '95

George American Horse
Kenny Rogers as the Gambler, Part 3: The Legend Continues '87
Son of the Morning Star '91

Adrienne Ames
The Death Kiss '33
Harmony Lane '35
Panama Patrol '39

Heather Ames
Blood of Dracula '57
How to Make a Monster '58

Leon Ames
Murders in the Rue Morgue '32
Uptown New York '32
Get That Man '35
Panama Patrol '39
East Side Kids '40
The Iron Major '43
Thirty Seconds Over Tokyo '44
Son of Lassie '45
They Were Expendable '45
Weekend at the Waldorf '45
Yolanda and the Thief '45
Lady in the Lake '46
The Postman Always Rings Twice '46
The Show-Off '46
Merton of the Movies '47
Song of the Thin Man '47
A Date with Judy '48
On an Island with You '48
Velvet Touch '48
Battleground '49
The Big Hangover '50
Watch the Birdie '50
On Moonlight Bay '51
By the Light of the Silvery Moon '53
Peyton Place '57
From the Terrace '60
The Absent-Minded Professor '61
The Misadventures of Merlin Jones '63
Son of Flubber '63
Monkey's Uncle '65
Tora! Tora! Tora! '70
The Big Push '75
The Meal '75
Claws '77
Deadly Encounter '78
Peggy Sue Got Married '86

Ramsay Ames
The Mummy's Ghost '44
G-Men Never Forget '48

Robert Ames
Behind Office Doors '31
Millie '31

Madchen Amick
Don't Tell Her It's Me '90
I'm Dangerous Tonight '90
Twin Peaks '90
Twin Peaks '90
Sleepwalkers '92
Dream Lover '93
Love, Cheat & Steal '93
The Great American Sex Scandal '94
Trapped In Paradise '94
The Courtyard '95

Soudad Amidou
Sorcerer '77
Petit Con '84

Suzy Amis
Fandango '85
Big Town '87
Plain Clothes '88
Rocket Gibraltar '88
Twister '89
Where the Heart Is '90
The Ballad of Little Jo '93
Rich in Love '93
Two Small Bodies '93
Watch It '93
Blown Away '94
Nadja '95
The Usual Suspects '95

Renee Ammann
Death Match '94
Number One Fan '94

Christine Amor
Now and Forever '82

Bloodmoon '90

John Amos
Sweet Sweetback's Baadasssss Song '71
The World's Greatest Athlete '73
Let's Do It Again '75
Future Cop '76
Willa '79
Touched by Love '80
Beastmaster '82
American Flyers '85
Coming to America '88
Lock Up '89
Die Hard 2: Die Harder '90
Ricochet '91
Mac '93
Mardi Gras for the Devil '93
For Better or Worse '95
Hologram Man '95

John Amplas
Martin '77
Midnight '81

Morey Amsterdam
Machine Gun Kelly '58
Beach Party '63
Muscle Beach Party '64
Sooner or Later '78

Richard Anconina
Tchao Pantin '84
Police '85

Avalon Anders
Bikini Summer 2 '92
Sorority House Party '92
Great Bikini Off-Road Adventure '94
Wish Me Luck '95

Glenn Anders
The Lady from Shanghai '48
Nancy Goes to Rio '50

Luana Anders
The Pit and the Pendulum '61
Dementia 13 '63
Night Tide '63
Sex and the College Girl '64
Manipulator '71
The Killing Kind '73
Goin' South '78
Irreconcilable Differences '84
Movers and Shakers '85
Border Radio '88
Limit Up '89

Merry Anders
Phffft! '54
The Time Travelers '64
Women of the Prehistoric Planet '66
Blood Legacy '73

Rudolph Anders
Under Nevada Skies '46
Phantom from Space '53

Elga Andersen
Your Turn Darling '63
Le Mans '71
Night Flight from Moscow '73

Bridgette Anderson
Hansel and Gretel '82
Savannah Smiles '82
A Summer to Remember '84
Fever Pitch '85
Between Two Women '86

"Broncho" Billy Anderson
The Great Train Robbery: Cinema Begins '03
The First Movie Cowboy '13
The Champion/His New Job '15
Son of a Gun '19

Cheryl Anderson
Acorn People '82
Rosie: The Rosemary Clooney Story '82
Writer's Block '91

Donna Anderson
On the Beach '59
Werewolves on Wheels '71

Eddie Anderson
False Faces '32
Green Pastures '36
Jezebel '38
You Can't Take It with You '38
Gone with the Wind '39
Honolulu '39

You Can't Cheat an Honest Man '39
Birth of the Blues '41
Topper Returns '41
Star Spangled Rhythm '42
Tales of Manhattan '42
Cabin in the Sky '43
Broadway Rhythm '44
Brewster's Millions '45
The Show-Off '46
It's a Mad, Mad, Mad, Mad World '63

Erich Anderson
Friday the 13th, Part 4: The Final Chapter '84
Bat 21 '88
Love Kills '91

Erika Anderson
Zandalee '91
Quake '92
Object of Obsession '95

Harry Anderson
Rich Hall's Vanishing America '86
Mother Goose Rock 'n' Rhyme '90
Stephen King's It '90
Spies, Lies and Naked Thighs '91

Jean Anderson
Screamtime '83
Back Home '90
Prince Brat and the Whipping Boy '95

Jo Anderson
Decoration Day '90
Season of Change '94

John Anderson
Psycho '60
Geronimo '62
Ride the High Country '62
Namu, the Killer Whale '66
Five Card Stud '68
Cotton Comes to Harlem '70
The Stepmother '71
Executive Action '73
Smile, Jenny, You're Dead '74
The Specialist '75
The Deerslayer '78
The Desperados '80s
Zoot Suit '81
Ashes and Embers '82
Donner Pass: The Road to Survival '84
Firehouse '87
Eight Men Out '88

Judith Anderson
Rebecca '40
Kings Row '41
Lady Scarface '41
All Through the Night '42
Edge of Darkness '43
Stage Door Canteen '43
Laura '44
And Then There Were None '45
Diary of a Chambermaid '46
Spectre of the Rose '46
The Strange Love of Martha Ivers '46
Pursued '47
The Red House '47
Tycoon '47
Lady Scarface/The Threat '49
Salome '53
The Ten Commandments '56
Cat on a Hot Tin Roof '58
Medea '59
Cinderfella '60
Elizabeth, the Queen '68
A Man Called Horse '70
Inn of the Damned '74
Star Trek 3: The Search for Spock '84

Kevin Anderson
Risky Business '83
Orphans '87
Pink Nights '87
Miles from Home '88
In Country '89
Liebestraum '91
Orpheus Descending '91
Sleeping with the Enemy '91
Hoffa '92
The Night We Never Met '93
Rising Sun '93
The Wrong Man '93

Lindsay Anderson
Look Back in Anger '80

Anderson ▶cont.

Chariots of Fire '81
Prisoner of Honor '91
Blame It on the Bellboy '92

Loni Anderson
WKRP in Cincinnati, Vol. 1 '78
The Jayne Mansfield Story '80
Sizzle '81
Stroker Ace '83
My Mother's Secret Life '84
Sorry, Wrong Number '89
Blown Away '90
White Hot: The Mysterious Murder of Thelma Todd '91
Munchie '92

Louie Anderson
Quicksilver '86
Coming to America '88
The Wrong Guys '88

Mary Anderson
False Faces '18
Lifeboat '44
Wilson '44
Whispering City '47
The Underworld Story '50

Melissa Sue Anderson
Little House on the Prairie '74
The Loneliest Runner '76
On the Edge: The Survival of Dana '79
Happy Birthday to Me '81
First Affair '83
Chattanooga Choo Choo '84
The Equalizer: Memories of Manon '88

Melody Anderson
Flash Gordon '80
Dead and Buried '81
Policewoman Centerfold '83
Ernie Kovacs: Between the Laughter '84
Beverly Hills Madam '86
Firewalker '86
Speed Zone '88
Final Notice '89
Hitler's Daughter '90
Landslide '92
Marilyn & Bobby: Her Final Affair '94

Michael Anderson, Jr.
The Sundowners '60
In Search of the Castaways '62
Sons of Katie Elder '65
A Legacy for Leonette '85
The Great Land of Small '86
Sunset Grill '92

Miles Anderson
A Far Off Place '93
The Rector's Wife '94

Mitchell Anderson
Deadly Dreams '88
Goodbye, Miss 4th of July '88
Back to Hannibal: The Return of Tom Sawyer and Huckleberry Finn '90
Is There Life Out There? '94

Pat Anderson
Cover Girl Models '75
Summer School Teachers '75

Richard Anderson
The Magnificent Yankee '50
The Vanishing Westerner '50
Rich, Young and Pretty '51
Scaramouche '52
Escape from Fort Bravo '53
Give a Girl a Break '53
I Love Melvin '53
Hit the Deck '55
Forbidden Planet '56
The Search for Bridey Murphy '56
Paths of Glory '57
The Long, Hot Summer '58
Compulsion '59
The Bionic Woman '75
Murder by Natural Causes '79
Perry Mason Returns '85
The Glass Shield '95

Richard Dean Anderson
Ordinary Heroes '85
Through the Eyes of a Killer '92
Past the Bleachers '95

Robert Anderson
White Shadows in the South Seas '28
The Tall T '57

Stanley Anderson
He Said, She Said '91
Son of the Morning Star '91
Primal Fear '96

Susy Anderson
Thor and the Amazon Women '60
Black Sabbath '64
Gangster's Law '86

Warner Anderson
Destination Tokyo '43
Abbott and Costello in Hollywood '45
Objective, Burma! '45
Weekend at the Waldorf '45
Song of the Thin Man '47
Destination Moon '50
Detective Story '51
Go for Broke! '51
Santa Fe '51
A Lion Is in the Streets '53
Drum Beat '54
Blackboard Jungle '55
A Lawless Street '55
Armored Command '61

Pamela Anderson Lee
Raw Justice '93
Snapdragon '93
Baywatch the Movie: Forbidden Paradise '95
Naked Souls '95
Barb Wire '96

Bibi Andersson
The Seventh Seal '56
Brink of Life '57
Wild Strawberries '57
The Magician '58
The Devil's Eye '60
Duel at Diablo '66
Persona '66
The Passion of Anna '70
The Touch '71
Scenes from a Marriage '73
Germicide '74
I Never Promised You a Rose Garden '77
The Concorde: Airport '79 '79
Quintet '79
Twice a Woman '79
Exposed '83
Law of Desire '86
Babette's Feast '87

Harriet Andersson
Monika '52
Sawdust & Tinsel '53
Lesson in Love '54
Dreams '55
Smiles of a Summer Night '55
Through a Glass Darkly '61
Cries and Whispers '72
Fanny and Alexander '83

Keith Andes
Blackbeard the Pirate '52
Away All Boats '56
Back from Eternity '56
The Ultimate Imposter '79

Eiko Ando
Barbarian and the Geisha '58
Paper Tiger '74

Peter Andorai
Mephisto '81
My Twentieth Century '90

Annette Andre
A Funny Thing Happened on the Way to the Forum '66
Mission: Monte Carlo '75

Gaby Andre
The Green Glove '52
East of Kilimanjaro '57
The Cosmic Monsters '58
Goliath and the Dragon '61

Lona Andre
The Mysterious Rider '33
Custer's Last Stand '36
Slaves in Bondage '37

Marcel Andre
Maniac '34
Beauty and the Beast '46
The Storm Within '48

Andre the Giant
Micki & Maude '84
The Princess Bride '87

Starr Andreeff
Dance of the Damned '88
Out of the Dark '88
The Terror Within '88
Syngenor '90

Ursula Andress
Dr. No '62
Four for Texas '63
Fun in Acapulco '63
Once Before I Die '65
10th Victim '65
What's New Pussycat? '65
The Blue Max '66
Casino Royale '67
Red Sun '71
Loaded Guns '75
Stateline Motel '75
Loves & Times of Scaramouche '76
The Sensuous Nurse '76
The Fifth Musketeer '79
Slave of the Cannibal God '79
Tigers in Lipstick '80
Clash of the Titans '81
Peter the Great '86
The Chinatown Murders: Man Against the Mob '92

Simon Andreu
Sharpe's Rifles '93
The Shooter '94

Simon Andrew
Surprise Attack '70s
Night of the Sorcerers '70
The Blood Spattered Bride '72
The Barcelona Kill '77
Blue Jeans and Dynamite '80s
Fist Fighter '88
Blood and Sand '89

Anthony Andrews
Brideshead Revisited '81
Danger UXB '81
Ivanhoe '82
The Scarlet Pimpernel '82
Under the Volcano '84
The Holcroft Covenant '85
The Lighthorsemen '87
Second Victory '87
Suspicion '87
Hanna's War '88
The Woman He Loved '88
Strange Case of Dr. Jekyll & Mr. Hyde '89
Hands of a Murderer '90
Haunted '95

Barry Andrews
Dracula Has Risen from the Grave '68
The Blood on Satan's Claw '71

Dana Andrews
Kit Carson '40
Lucky Cisco Kid '40
The Westerner '40
Ball of Fire '41
Crash Dive '43
The North Star '43
The Ox-Bow Incident '43
Laura '44
The Purple Heart '44
Up in Arms '44
A Wing and a Prayer '44
State Fair '45
The Best Years of Our Lives '46
A Walk in the Sun '46
Boomerang '47
Elephant Walk '54
Beyond a Reasonable Doubt '56
While the City Sleeps '56
Curse of the Demon '57
Enchanted Island '58
Battle of the Bulge '65
In Harm's Way '65
The Loved One '65
Johnny Reno '66
The Cobra '68
The Devil's Brigade '68
Airport '75 '75
The Last Tycoon '76
Born Again '78
Danger in the Skies '79
Ike '79
Prince Jack '83

David Andrews
Wild Horses '84
Cherry 2000 '88
Graveyard Shift '90
Deconstructing Sarah '94
Wyatt Earp '94
Apollo 13 '95

Edward Andrews
Tea and Sympathy '56
Elmer Gantry '60
Advise and Consent '62
40 Pounds of Trouble '62
The Thrill of It All! '63
Kisses for My President '64
A Tiger Walks '64
The Glass Bottom Boat '66
The Trouble with Girls (and How To Get Into It) '69
Avanti! '72
Sixteen Candles '84

Harry Andrews
Alexander the Great '55
Helen of Troy '56
Moby Dick '56
Saint Joan '57
The Devil's Disciple '59
633 Squadron '64
The Agony and the Ecstasy '65
The Charge of the Light Brigade '68
Dandy in Aspic '68
Nice Girl Like Me '69
Entertaining Mr. Sloane '70
Too Late the Hero '70
Wuthering Heights '70
Horrors of Burke & Hare '71
Nicholas and Alexandra '71
I Want What I Want '72
Man of La Mancha '72
The Ruling Class '72
The Final Programme '73
Internecine Project '73
Mackintosh Man '73
The Story of Jacob & Joseph '74
The Passover Plot '75
Sky Riders '76
Equus '77
The Big Sleep '78
Death on the Nile '78
The Four Feathers '78
The Medusa Touch '78
S.O.S. Titanic '79
The Curse of King Tut's Tomb '80
Hawk the Slayer '81
Mesmerized '84

Jason Andrews
Federal Hill '94
Rhythm Thief '94

Julie Andrews
The Americanization of Emily '64
Mary Poppins '64
The Sound of Music '65
Hawaii '66
Torn Curtain '66
Thoroughly Modern Millie '67
Star! '68
Darling Lili '70
The Tamarind Seed '74
10 '79
Little Miss Marker '80
S.O.B. '81
Victor/Victoria '82
The Man Who Loved Women '83
Duet for One '86
That's Life! '86
Our Sons '91
A Fine Romance '92

Slim Andrews
The Driftin' Kid '41
Riding the Sunset Trail '41

Stanley Andrews
Blondie '38
Shine on, Harvest Moon '38
In Old Colorado '41
Crash Dive '43
The Adventures of Frank and Jesse James '48

The Andrews Sisters
Buck Privates '41
Hold That Ghost '41
In the Navy '41
Private Buckaroo '42
The Road to Rio '47
Disney's Storybook Classics '82

Anemone
Le Grand Chemin '87
Twisted Obsession '90

Julie Ange
Girl on a Chain Gang '65
Teenage Mother '67

Heather Angel
Daniel Boone '34
Headline Woman '35
The Informer '35
The Three Musketeers '35
The Bold Caballero '36
The Last of the Mohicans '36
Bulldog Drummond Escapes '37
Western Gold '37
Arrest Bulldog Drummond '38
Bulldog Drummond's Bride '39
Bulldog Drummond's Secret Police '39
Half a Soldier '40
Shadows on the Stairs '41
Suspicion '41
The Undying Monster '42
Premature Burial '62

Vanessa Angel
Homicidal Impulse '92
The Cover Girl Murders '93
Kingpin '96

Pier Angeli
The Silver Chalice '54
Somebody Up There Likes Me '56
S.O.S. Pacific '60
Sodom and Gomorrah '62
Battle of the Bulge '65
One Step to Hell '68
Octaman '71

Muriel Angelus
Night Birds '31
The Great McGinty '40

Angelyne
Earth Girls Are Easy '89
The Malibu Beach Vampires '91

Jean-Hugues Anglade
L'Homme Blesse '83
Subway '85
Betty Blue '86
La Femme Nikita '91
Killing Zoe '94
Queen Margot '94
Nelly et Monsieur Arnaud '95

Philip Anglim
Haunted Summer '88
Deadly Currents '93

Sally Anglim
Thundering Trail '51
Yes, Sir, Mr. Bones '51

Ira Angustain
The White Shadow, Vol. 1 '78
Can You Hear the Laughter? The Story of Freddie Prinze '79

Christien Anholt
Reunion '88
One Against the Wind '91
Class of '61 '92

Paul Anka
Girls' Town '59
The Longest Day '62

Evelyn Ankers
The Wolf Man '41
The Ghost of Frankenstein '42
Sherlock Holmes: The Voice of Terror '42
Captive Wild Woman '43
His Butler's Sister '43
The Mad Ghoul '43
Son of Dracula '43
The Invisible Man's Revenge '44
The Pearl of Death '44
Black Beauty '46
Flight to Nowhere '46
The Last of the Redmen '47
Parole, Inc. '49

Morris Ankrum
The Light of Western Stars '40
The Showdown '40
Border Vigilantes '41
Doomed Caravan '41
In Old Colorado '41
Borderline '50
Earth vs. the Flying Saucers '56

Beginning of the End '57
The Giant Claw '57
Half Human '58
How to Make a Monster '58

Ann-Margret
Pocketful of Miracles '61
State Fair '62
Bye, Bye, Birdie '63
Viva Las Vegas '63
The Cincinnati Kid '65
Murderers' Row '66
Tiger and the Pussycat '67
Chrome Hearts '70
R.P.M.* (*Revolutions Per Minute) '70
Carnal Knowledge '71
The Outside Man '73
Train Robbers '73
Tommy '75
Twist '76
Joseph Andrews '77
The Last Remake of Beau Geste '77
The Cheap Detective '78
Magic '78
The Villain '79
Middle Age Crazy '80
I Ought to Be in Pictures '82
Lookin' to Get Out '82
Return of the Soldier '82
A Streetcar Named Desire '84
Twice in a Lifetime '85
52 Pick-Up '86
Hollywood Home Movies '87
A Tiger's Tale '87
A New Life '88
Our Sons '91
Newsies '92
Grumpy Old Men '93
Scarlett '94
Grumpier Old Men '95

Annabella
Le Million '31
Under the Red Robe '36
Dinner at the Ritz '37
13 Rue Madeleine '46

Amina Annabi
The Sheltering Sky '90
The Advocate '93

Frank Annese
House of the Rising Sun '87
Another Chance '88

Francesca Annis
Flipper's New Adventure '64
Macbeth '71
Lillie '79
Coming Out of the Ice '82
The Case of the Missing Lady '83
Krull '83
The Man in the Mist '83
The Secret Adversary '83
The Unbreakable Alibi '83
The Affair of the Pink Pearl '84
The Clergyman's Daughter '84
The Crackler '84
Dune '84
Finessing the King '84
The House of Lurking Death '84
The Maze '85
Under the Cherry Moon '86
Onassis '88
Doomsday Gun '94

Michael Ansara
Action in Arabia '44
Hill Number One '51
Abbott and Costello Meet the Mummy '55
Diane '55
Jupiter's Darling '55
Voyage to the Bottom of the Sea '61
Harum Scarum '65
And Now Miguel '66
Texas Across the River '66
Daring Game '68
Guns of the Magnificent Seven '69
Powder Keg '70
Quick, Let's Get Married '71
Dear Dead Delilah '72
The Doll Squad '73
The Barbary Coast '74
The Bears & I '74
It's Alive '74
Day of the Animals '77
Mohammed: Messenger of God '77
The Manitou '78
Mission to Glory '80
The Guns and the Fury '83
Access Code '84
The Fantastic World of D.C. Collins '84
Knights of the City '85
Bayou Romance '86
The KGB: The Secret War '86
Assassination '87
Border Shootout '90

Zachary Ansley
Christmas Comes to Willow Creek '87
Princes in Exile '90
This Boy's Life '93
The X-Files: Pilot Episode/Deep Throat '93

Susan Anspach
Five Easy Pieces '70
Deadly Encounter '72
Play It Again, Sam '72
Blume in Love '73
Mad Bull '77
The Big Fix '78
The Devil & Max Devlin '81
Gas '81
Montenegro '81
Gone are the Days '84
Misunderstood '84
Hitchhiker 2 '85
Blue Monkey '87
Blood Red '88
Into the Fire '88
Back to Back '90
The Rutanga Tapes '90

Adam Ant
Nomads '86
Cold Steel '87
Slamdance '87
World Gone Wild '88
Trust Me '89
Spellcaster '91
Sunset Heat '92
Acting on Impulse '93
Cyber Bandits '94

Gerald Anthony
Secret of the Ice Cave '89
To Die Standing '91

Lysette Anthony
Ivanhoe '82
Oliver Twist '82
Krull '83
The Bretts '88
Without a Clue '88
Dark Shadows: Episode 1 '91
Face the Music '92
Husbands and Wives '92
The Advocate '93
A Brilliant Disguise '93
Look Who's Talking Now '93
Save Me '93
The Hard Truth '94
Dr. Jekyll and Ms. Hyde '95
Dracula: Dead and Loving It '95
Dead Cold '96

Mark Anthony
Big Night '95
The Substitute '96

Ray Anthony
The Girl Can't Help It '56
High School Confidential '58
Girls' Town '59

Tony Anthony
Force of Impulse '60
Treasure of the Four Crowns '82

Steve Antin
Last American Virgin '82
Penitentiary 3 '87
The Accused '88
Survival Quest '89
Inside Monkey Zetterland '93

Susan Anton
Goldengirl '79
Spring Fever '81
The Boy Who Loved Trolls '84
Cannonball Run 2 '84
Making Mr. Right '86
Lena's Holiday '90

Laura Antonelli
Divine Nymph '71
A Man Called Sledge '71
High Heels '72
Malicious '74
Till Marriage Do Us Part '74
How Funny Can Sex Be? '76
The Innocent '76
Wifemistress '79
Tigers in Lipstick '80
Passion of Love '82
Swashbuckler '84
Collector's Item '89

Omero Antonutti
Padre Padrone '77
Basileus Quartet '82
The Night of the Shooting Stars '82
Kaos '85
Good Morning, Babylon '87
Farinelli '94

Gabrielle Anwar
A Night of Love '87
If Looks Could Kill '91
Wild Hearts Can't Be Broken '91
Scent of a Woman '92
Body Snatchers '93
Fallen Angels 2 '93
For Love or Money '93
The Three Musketeers '93
In Pursuit of Honor '95
Innocent Lies '95
Things to Do In Denver When You're Dead '95

Rocky Aoki
For Us, the Living '88
That's Adequate '90

Oscar Apfel
Rainbow's End '35
Bulldog Edition '36

Apollonia
Heartbreaker '83
Purple Rain '84
Tricks of the Trade '88
Ministry of Vengeance '89
Back to Back '90
Black Magic Woman '91

Noel Appleby
The Navigator '88
My Grandpa is a Vampire '92

Christina Applegate
Jaws of Satan '81
Streets '90
Don't Tell Mom the Babysitter's Dead '91
It's a Bundyful Life '92
Across the Moon '94
Vibrations '94
Wild Bill '95

Royce D. Applegate
Outside Chance '78
Gettysburg '93

John Aprea
The Arousers '70
The Godfather, Part 2 '74
Idolmaker '80
Picasso Trigger '89
Savage Beach '89
Cyber-Tracker '93
Direct Hit '93
To the Limit '95

Amy Aquino
Descending Angel '90
Alan & Naomi '92

Tomas Arana
Domino '88
The Last Temptation of Christ '88
The Church '90
The Devil's Daughter '91
The Bodyguard '92

Julie Araskog
In a Moment of Passion '93
Seven '95

Michiyo Aratama
The Human Condition: No Greater Love '58
The Human Condition: Road to Eternity '59
Saga of the Vagabond '59
The Gambling Samurai '60
The Human Condition: A Soldier's Prayer '61
Kwaidan '64

Alfonso Arau
Scandalous John '71
Posse '75
Romancing the Stone '84
Three Amigos '86
Dynamite and Gold '88

Fatty Arbuckle
Charlie Chaplin's Keystone Comedies #4 '14
The Knockout/Dough and Dynamite '14
The Lizzies of Mack Sennett '15
Fatty and Mabel Adrift/Mabel, Fatty and the Law '16
Mabel & Fatty '16
Mack Sennett Comedies: Vol. 2 '16
Leap Year '21

Allan Arbus
Greaser's Palace '72
Coffy '73
The Young Nurses '73
M*A*S*H: Goodbye, Farewell & Amen '83
Daniel and the Towers '90s

Anne Archer
Cancel My Reservation '72
Lifeguard '75
Good Guys Wear Black '78
Paradise Alley '78
Hero at Large '80
Raise the Titanic '80
Green Ice '81
Waltz Across Texas '83
The Naked Face '84
Check Is in the Mail '85
Too Scared to Scream '85
Fatal Attraction '87
Love at Large '89
Narrow Margin '90
Eminent Domain '91
Family Prayers '91
Body of Evidence '92
The Last of His Tribe '92
Nails '92
Patriot Games '92
Question of Faith '93
Short Cuts '93
Clear and Present Danger '94
The Man in the Attic '94

John Archer
Overland Stage Raiders '38
Gangs, Inc. '41
King of the Zombies '41
Crash Dive '43
Hello, Frisco, Hello '43
Sherlock Holmes in Washington '43
Best of the Badmen '50
High Lonesome '50
Santa Fe '51
Blue Hawaii '62

Fanny Ardant
The Woman Next Door '81
Confidentially Yours '83
Next Summer '84
Swann in Love '84
The Family '87
Afraid of the Dark '92
Colonel Chabert '94
Sabrina '95

Eve Arden
Stage Door '37
Having Wonderful Time '38
Letter of Introduction '38
At the Circus '39
Eternally Yours '39
Comrade X '40
No, No Nanette '40
Slightly Honorable '40
That Uncertain Feeling '41
Whistling in the Dark '41
Ziegfeld Girl '41
Cover Girl '44
Mildred Pierce '45
Kid from Brooklyn '46
Night and Day '46
One Touch of Venus '48
My Dream Is Yours '49
Tea for Two '50
Three Husbands '50
Phone Call from a Stranger '52
We're Not Married '52
Our Miss Brooks '56
Anatomy of a Murder '59
Grease '78
A Guide for the Married Woman '78
Under the Rainbow '81
Grease 2 '82
Pandemonium '82
Cinderella '84

George Ardisson
The Invaders '63
Hercules in the Haunted World '64

Pierre Arditti
Smoking/No Smoking '94
The Horseman on the Roof '95

Rosita Arenas
El Bruto '52
The Curse of the Aztec Mummy '59
Curse of the Aztec Mummy/Robot vs. the Aztec Mummy '59
The Robot vs. the Aztec Mummy '59
The Witch's Mirror '60
The Curse of the Crying Woman '61
Neutron and the Black Mask '61
Neutron vs. the Amazing Dr. Caronte '61
Neutron vs. the Death Robots '62

Eddi Arent
Dead Eyes of London '61
Forger of London '61
Door with the Seven Locks '62
The Mysterious Magician '65
The Squeaker '65
Circus of Fear '67

Joey Aresco
Circle of Fear '89
Primary Target '89

Niels Arestrup
Je Tu Il Elle '74
Sincerely Charlotte '86
Meeting Venus '91

Asia Argento
Demons 2 '87
Dario Argento's Trauma '93
Queen Margot '94

Fiore Argento
Creepers '85
Demons '86

Carmen Argenziano
Death Force '78
The Accused '88
Red Scorpion '89
Unlawful Entry '92
The Burning Season '94
Andersonville '95

Allison Argo
Return of Frank Cannon '80
A Cry from the Mountain '85

Victor Argo
King of New York '90
Quick Change '90
Bad Lieutenant '92
Household Saints '93
Blue In the Face '95
Smoke '95

David Argue
Gallipoli '81
BMX Bandits '83
Snow: The Movie '83
Backlash '86

Imanol Arias
Demons in the Garden '82
Labyrinth of Passion '82
Camila '84
The Flower of My Secret '95

Ineko Arima
Equinox Flower '58
The Human Condition: No Greater Love '58

Yareli Arizmendi
Like Water for Chocolate '93
The Big Green '95

Adam Arkin
Fourth Wise Man '85
Necessary Parties '88
Heat Wave '90
The Doctor '91

Alan Arkin
The Russians are Coming, the Russians are Coming '66
Wait Until Dark '67
Woman Times Seven '67
The Heart is a Lonely Hunter '68
Popi '69
Catch-22 '70
Little Murders '71
Last of the Red Hot Lovers '72

Arkin ▶cont.

Freebie & the Bean '74
Hearts of the West '75
Rafferty & the Gold Dust Twins '75
The Seven-Per-Cent Solution '76
The In-Laws '79
The Magician of Lublin '79
Simon '80
Chu Chu & the Philly Flash '81
Improper Channels '82
A Matter of Principle '83
Return of Captain Invincible '83
The Emperor's New Clothes '84
Bad Medicine '85
Fourth Wise Man '85
Joshua Then and Now '85
Big Trouble '86
Deadly Business '86
Escape from Sobibor '87
Necessary Parties '88
Coupe de Ville '90
Edward Scissorhands '90
Havana '90
The Rocketeer '91
Glengarry Glen Ross '92
Cooperstown '93
Indian Summer '93
Taking the Heat '93
Doomsday Gun '94
North '94
Heck's Way Home '95
The Jerky Boys '95
Steal Big, Steal Little '95

David Arkin
The Long Goodbye '73
Nashville '75

Alan Arkus
Brutal Fury '92
A Matter of Honor '95

Elizabeth Arlen
Lucky Stiff '88
The First Power '89
Separate Lives '94

Richard Arlen
Behind the Front '26
Wings '27
Feel My Pulse '28
The Virginian '29
The Light of Western Stars '30
Island of Lost Souls '32
Let 'Em Have It '35
Flying Blind '41
Wildcat '42
Timber Queen '44
Identity Unknown '45
Accomplice '46
Buffalo Bill Rides Again '47
Return of Wildfire '48
Hidden Guns '56
The Mountain '56
Blonde Blackmailer '58
Warlock '59
Cavalry Command '63
The Crawling Hand '63
The Human Duplicators '64
Sex and the College Girl '64
Apache Uprising '66
Johnny Reno '66
Road to Nashville '67

Arletty
Circonstances Attenuantes '36
Le Jour Se Leve '39
Les Visiteurs du Soir '42
Children of Paradise '44
The Longest Day '62

Dimitra Arliss
Ski Bum '75
Eleni '85

George Arliss
Disraeli '29
The Iron Duke '34
Transatlantic Tunnel '35
Dr. Syn '37

Pedro Armendariz, Sr.
Maria Candelaria '46
Fort Apache '48
The Fugitive '48
The Pearl '48
Three Godfathers '48
Tulsa '49
The Torch '50
El Bruto '52
The Littlest Outlaw '54
Diane '55
The Conqueror '56
Flor Silvestre '58
Captain Sinbad '63
From Russia with Love '63

Pedro Armendariz, Jr.
The Deadly Trackers '73
Don't Be Afraid of the Dark '73
La Chevre '81
Old Gringo '89
Tombstone '93

Henry Armetta
Speak Easily '32
What! No Beer? '33
The Black Cat '34
The Merry Widow '34
Let's Sing Again '36
Boss Foreman '39
Fisherman's Wharf '39

Armida
Border Romance '30
Gaiety '43
Bad Men of the Border '45
Fiesta '47
Jungle Goddess '49

Russell Arms
Captains of the Clouds '42
Fighting Vigilantes '47
Stage to Mesa City '48
By the Light of the Silvery Moon '53

Alun Armstrong
White Hunter, Black Heart '90
Split Second '92
An Awfully Big Adventure '94
Black Beauty '94

Bess Armstrong
How to Pick Up Girls '78
Walking Through the Fire '80
The Four Seasons '81
Jekyll & Hyde...Together Again '82
High Road to China '83
Jaws 3 '83
Nothing in Common '86
Second Sight '89
Dream Lover '93
The Skateboard Kid '93

Curtis Armstrong
Risky Business '83
Revenge of the Nerds '84
Bad Medicine '85
Better Off Dead '85
One Crazy Summer '86
Revenge of the Nerds 2: Nerds in Paradise '87
Revenge of the Nerds 3: The Next Generation '92
The Adventures of Huck Finn '93
Revenge of the Nerds 4: Nerds in Love '94
Big Bully '95

Jack Armstrong
Eden '92
Eden 2 '93
Eden 3 '93
Eden 4 '93

Katherine Armstrong
Ambition '91
Street Soldiers '91

Kerry Armstrong
Prisoner Cell Block H '80
The Hunting '92

Louis Armstrong
Cabin in the Sky '43
The Glenn Miller Story '54
High Society '56
The Five Pennies '59
Paris Blues '61
A Man Called Adam '66
Hello, Dolly! '69

Melinda Armstrong
Bikini Summer '91
Bikini Summer 2 '92

R.G. Armstrong
The Fugitive Kind '60
The Twilight Zone '61
Ride the High Country '62
El Dorado '67
The Great White Hope '70
Final Comedown '72
The Great Northfield Minnesota Raid '72
Boss '74
My Name is Nobody '74
Reflections of Murder '74
Dixie Dynamite '76
The Pack '77
Texas Detour '77
Dear Detective '78
Steel '80
Evilspeak '82
The Shadow Riders '82
Angels Die Hard '84
Children of the Corn '84
Predator '87
Bulletproof '88
Ghetto Blaster '89
Dick Tracy '90
Warlock: The Armageddon '93
Payback '94

R.L. Armstrong
The Hard Ride '71
Slumber Party '57 '76

Robert Armstrong
Big News '29
The Racketeer '29
Danger Lights '30
The Tip-Off '31
The Most Dangerous Game '32
King Kong '33
Son of Kong '33
Palooka '34
"G" Men '35
The Mystery Man '35
Ex-Mrs. Bradford '36
The Girl Said No '37
Three Legionnaires '37
Gangbusters '38
Dive Bomber '41
Baby Face Morgan '42
The Mad Ghoul '43
Wings Over the Pacific '43
Action in Arabia '44
Mr. Winkle Goes to War '44
Blood on the Sun '45
Criminal Court '46
The Fugitive '48
The Paleface '48
Mighty Joe Young '49

Todd Armstrong
Jason and the Argonauts '63
Dead Heat on a Merry-Go-Round '66

Desi Arnaz, Sr.
Too Many Girls '40
Four Jacks and a Jill '41
The Navy Comes Through '42
Bataan '43
Holiday in Havana '49
I Love Lucy '52
The Long, Long Trailer '54
Forever Darling '56
The Escape Artist '82

Desi Arnaz, Jr.
The Voyage of the Yes '72
Marco '73
Joyride '77
How to Pick Up Girls '78
A Wedding '78
Great American Traffic Jam '80
Fake Out '82
House of the Long Shadows '82
The Mambo Kings '92

Lucie Arnaz
Death Scream '75
Who Is the Black Dahlia? '75
The Jazz Singer '80
Mating Season '81
Washington Mistress '81
Second Thoughts '83

Adelheid Arndt
Chinese Boxes '84
Rosa Luxemburg '86

Denis Arndt
Basic Instinct '92
Amelia Earhart: The Final Flight '94

Peter Arne
The Atomic Man '56
The Moonraker '58
The Hellfire Club '61
Battle Beneath the Earth '68
The Oblong Box '69

James Arness
The Farmer's Daughter '47
Stars in My Crown '50
Two Lost Worlds '50
Wagon Master '50
The Thing '51
Big Jim McLain '52
Horizons West '52
Hondo '53
Them! '54
Flame of the Islands '55
Sea Chase '55
The Alamo: Thirteen Days to Glory '87
Gunsmoke: Return to Dodge '87

Jeanetta Arnetta
The Redeemer '76
The Shadow Riders '82
Ladybugs '92

Stefan Arngrim
Fear No Evil '80
Class of 1984 '82

Alice Arno
The Perverse Countess '73
The Loves of Irina '80s

Edward Arnold
Rasputin and the Empress '32
I'm No Angel '33
Roman Scandals '33
Hide-Out '34
Sadie McKee '34
Crime and Punishment '35
Come and Get It '36
Toast of New York '37
You Can't Take It with You '38
Idiot's Delight '39
Let Freedom Ring '39
Mr. Smith Goes to Washington '39
Johnny Apollo '40
Slightly Honorable '40
The Devil & Daniel Webster '41
Meet John Doe '41
Johnny Eager '42
Mrs. Parkington '44
Weekend at the Waldorf '45
Ziegfeld Follies '46
The Hucksters '47
Three Daring Daughters '48
Dear Wife '49
Take Me Out to the Ball Game '49
The Yellow Cab Man '50
City That Never Sleeps '53
The Ambassador's Daughter '56

Mark Arnold
Trancers 4: Jack of Swords '93
Threesome '94
Trancers 5: Sudden Deth '94

Seth Arnold
Lost Boundaries '49
The Blue Knight '75

Tom Arnold
Backfield in Motion '91
Hero '92
Undercover Blues '93
True Lies '94
Big Bully '95
Nine Months '95
The Stupids '95

Mark Arnott
Return of the Secaucus 7 '80
Not Quite Human 2 '89

Francoise Arnoul
Forbidden Fruit '52
French Can-Can '55
The Little Theatre of Jean Renoir '71

Charles Arnt
The Great Gildersleeve '43
Gambler's Choice '44
Strange Illusion '45
That Brennan Girl '46
Big Town '47

Michael J. Aronin
The Lone Runner '88
Miami Cops '89
Getting Even '92

Judie Aronson
Friday the 13th, Part 4: The Final Chapter '84
American Ninja '85
The Sleeping Car '90
Desert Kickboxer '92

Alexis Arquette
Down and Out in Beverly Hills '86
Jumpin' at the Boneyard '92
Miracle Beach '92
Don't Do It '94
Frank and Jesse '94
Grief '94
Jack Be Nimble '94
Threesome '94

David Arquette
Buffy the Vampire Slayer '92
Where the Day Takes You '92
At Home with the Webbers '94
Fall Time '94
Wild Bill '95
Beautiful Girls '96

Lewis Arquette
Syngenor '90
Book of Love '91
The Linguini Incident '92
Attack of the 50 Ft. Woman '93
Sleep with Me '94

Patricia Arquette
A Nightmare on Elm Street 3: Dream Warriors '87
Pretty Smart '87
Far North '88
Dillinger '91
The Indian Runner '91
Prayer of the Rollerboys '91
Wildflower '91
Ethan Frome '92
Trouble Bound '92
Inside Monkey Zetterland '93
True Romance '93
Ed Wood '94
Holy Matrimony '94
Beyond Rangoon '95
Flirting with Disaster '95

Rosanna Arquette
The Dark Secret of Harvest Home '78
Gorp '80
A Long Way Home '81
S.O.B. '81
Baby It's You '82
The Executioner's Song '82
Johnny Belinda '82
Off the Wall '82
One Cooks, the Other Doesn't '83
After Hours '85
The Aviator '85
Desperately Seeking Susan '85
8 Million Ways to Die '85
Silverado '85
Nobody's Fool '86
Amazon Women on the Moon '87
The Big Blue '88
Promised a Miracle '88
New York Stories '89
...Almost '90
Don't Hang Up '90
Flight of the Intruder '90
Sweet Revenge '90
Black Rainbow '91
In the Deep Woods '91
Son of the Morning Star '91
Fathers and Sons '92
The Linguini Incident '92
Nowhere to Run '93
The Wrong Man '93
Pulp Fiction '94
Search and Destroy '94
Crash '95

Rod Arrants
A*P*E* '76
Vamping '84

Jeri Arrendondo
Spirit of the Eagle '90
Silent Tongue '92
Color of a Brisk and Leaping Day '95
Tecumseh: The Last Warrior '95

Carlos Arruza
Torero '56
The Alamo '60

Antonin Artaud
Napoleon '27
The Passion of Joan of Arc '28

Beatrice Arthur
How to Commit Marriage '69
The Best of Soap: Jessica's Wonderful Life '70s
Lovers and Other Strangers '70
Mame '74
History of the World: Part 1 '81
For Better or Worse '95

Jean Arthur
Danger Lights '30
The Silver Horde '30
Ex-Mrs. Bradford '36
Mr. Deeds Goes to Town '36
History is Made at Night '37
The Plainsman '37
You Can't Take It with You '38
Mr. Smith Goes to Washington '39
Only Angels Have Wings '39
Arizona '40
The Devil & Miss Jones '41
Talk of the Town '42
Lady Takes a Chance '43
The More the Merrier '43
Shane '53

Johnny Arthur
The Monster '25
The Ghost Walks '34
Danger on the Air '38
The Road to Singapore '40
The Masked Marvel '43

Maureen Arthur
How to Succeed in Business without Really Trying '67
The Love God? '70
The Love Machine '71

Robert Arthur
September Affair '50
Just for You '52
The Ring '52
Hellcats of the Navy '57
Naked Youth '59

Michael Artura
Amongst Friends '93
Killer Looks '94

Oscar Asche
Don Quixote '35
The Private Secretary '35
Scrooge '35

Leslie Ash
Quadrophenia '79
Curse of the Pink Panther '83
Murder: Ultimate Grounds for Divorce '85
Shadey '87

Dana Ashbrook
Return of the Living Dead 2 '88
Waxwork '88
Girlfriend from Hell '89
Ghost Dad '90
Twin Peaks '90
Twin Peaks: Fire Walk with Me '92

Daphne Ashbrook
Quiet Cool '86
Intruders '92
Sunset Heat '92
Murder So Sweet '93
Automatic '94
Doctor Who '96

Linden Ashby
The Perfect Bride '91
Wyatt Earp '94

Peggy Ashcroft
The 39 Steps '35
Rhodes '36
The Nun's Story '59
Secret Ceremony '69
The Pedestrian '73
Hullabaloo Over Georgie & Bonnie's Pictures '78
The Jewel in the Crown '84
A Passage to India '84
Madame Sousatzka '88
The Heat of the Day '91

Jane Asher
The Prince and the Pauper '62
Masque of the Red Death '65
Masque of the Red Death/ Premature Burial '65
Deep End '70
Success is the Best Revenge '84
Dreamchild '85
A Voyage' Round My Father '89

Ron Asheton
Frostbiter: Wrath of the Wendigo '94
Mosquito '95

Edward Ashley
Bitter Sweet '40
The Black Swan '42
Nocturne '46
Beyond the Next Mountain '87

Elizabeth Ashley
The Carpetbaggers '64
Ship of Fools '65
Shattered Silence '71
Paperback Hero '73
Rancho Deluxe '75
Great Scout & Cathouse Thursday '76
One of My Wives Is Missing '76
War Between the Tates '76
Coma '78
Windows '80
Paternity '81
Svengali '83
Stagecoach '86
Dragnet '87
Dangerous Curves '88
Vampire's Kiss '88
A Man of Passion '90s
The Buccaneers '95

Jennifer Ashley
Hell on Wheels '67
Barn of the Naked Dead '73
Pom Pom Girls '76
Tintorera...Tiger Shark '78
Horror Planet '80

John Ashley
High School Caesar '56
Dragstrip Girl '57
Motorcycle Gang '57
Frankenstein's Daughter '58
How to Make a Monster '58
Suicide Battalion/Hell Squad '58
Beach Party '63
Hud '63
Bikini Beach '64
Muscle Beach Party '64
Beach Blanket Bingo '65
The Eye Creatures '65
How to Stuff a Wild Bikini '65
Hell on Wheels '67
Brides of the Beast '68
Mad Doctor of Blood Island '69
Beast of the Yellow Night '70
Twilight People '72
Woman Hunt '72
Beyond Atlantis '73
Smoke in the Wind '75
Revenge of Doctor X '80s

John Ashton
Beverly Hills Cop '84
The Deliberate Stranger '86
King Kong Lives '86
Beverly Hills Cop 2 '87
Some Kind of Wonderful '87
Midnight Run '88
She's Having a Baby '88
L.A. Gangs Rising '89
Love, Lies and Murder '91
Dirty Work '92
Stephen King's The Tommyknockers '93
Little Big League '94
The Shooter '94
Trapped In Paradise '94

Luke Askew
The Devil's Brigade '68
Angel Unchained '70
The Great Northfield Minnesota Raid '72
Posse '75
The Longest Drive '76
Wanda Nevada '79
The Warrior & the Sorceress '84
Kung Fu: The Movie '86
Back to Back '90
Dune Warriors '91

Leon Askin
Sherlock Holmes and the Deadly Necklace '62
Dr. Death, Seeker of Souls '73
Savage Island '85

Robin Askwith
Hans Brinker '69
Flesh and Blood Show '73
Horror Hospital '73

Gregoire Aslan
The Red Inn '51
Paris When It Sizzles '64
Golden Voyage of Sinbad '73

Ed Asner
Kid Galahad '62
The Doomsday Flight '66
El Dorado '67
Change of Habit '69
They Call Me Mr. Tibbs! '70
Skin Game '71
The Todd Killings '71
Haunts of the Very Rich '72
The Wrestler '73
Death Scream '75
Gus '76
The Life and Assassination of the Kingfish '76
Rich Man, Poor Man '76
The Gathering '77
Roots '77
The Family Man '79
Fort Apache, the Bronx '81
A Small Killing '81
O'Hara's Wife '82
A Case of Libel '83
Daniel '83
My Darlin' Clementine '86
A Friendship in Vienna '88
Moon over Parador '88
JFK '91
Silent Motive '91
Switched at Birth '91
Gypsy '93
Heads '93

Armand Assante
The Lords of Flatbush '74
Lady of the House '78
Paradise Alley '78
Prophecy '79
Little Darlings '80
Private Benjamin '80
Sophia Loren: Her Own Story '80
I, the Jury '82
Rage of Angels '83
Unfaithfully Yours '84
Belizaire the Cajun '86
Deadly Business '86
Hands of a Stranger '87
Jack the Ripper '88
The Penitent '88
Animal Behavior '89
Passion in Paradise '89
Eternity '90
Q & A '90
Fever '91
The Marrying Man '91
1492: Conquest of Paradise '92
Hoffa '92
The Mambo Kings '92
Fatal Instinct '93
Blind Justice '94
Trial by Jury '94
Judge Dredd '95
Striptease '96

Pat Ast
Heat '72
Reform School Girls '86

Fred Astaire
Dancing Lady '33
Flying Down to Rio '33
The Gay Divorcee '34
Roberta '35
Top Hat '35
Follow the Fleet '36
Swing Time '36
A Damsel in Distress '37
Shall We Dance '37
Carefree '38
The Story of Vernon and Irene Castle '39
Broadway Melody of 1940 '40
Second Chorus '40
You'll Never Get Rich '41
Holiday Inn '42
You Were Never Lovelier '42
The Sky's the Limit '43
Yolanda and the Thief '45
Blue Skies '46
Ziegfeld Follies '46
Easter Parade '48
The Barkleys of Broadway '49
Let's Dance '50
Three Little Words '50
Royal Wedding '51
The Belle of New York '52
The Band Wagon '53
Daddy Long Legs '55
Funny Face '57
Silk Stockings '57
On the Beach '59
Paris When It Sizzles '64
Finian's Rainbow '68
That's Entertainment '74
The Towering Inferno '74
The Amazing Dobermans '76
That's Entertainment, Part 2 '76
The Purple Taxi '77
Family Upside Down '78
The Man in the Santa Claus Suit '79
Ghost Story '81
Gotta Dance, Gotta Sing '84
That's Dancing! '85
Irving Berlin's America '86

Nils Asther
Our Dancing Daughters '28
Wild Orchids '28
The Single Standard '29
The Bitter Tea of General Yen '33
Make-Up '37
Night Monster '42
Bluebeard '44
Son of Lassie '45

Adrianna Asti
Before the Revolution '65
Phantom of Liberty '68

John Astin
That Touch of Mink '62
The Wheeler Dealers '63
The Addams Family '64
Viva Max '69
Pepper and His Wacky Taxi '72
Brothers O'Toole '73
Only with Married Men '74
The Barcelona Kill '77
Halloween with the Addams Family '79
National Lampoon's European Vacation '85
Adventures Beyond Belief '87
Body Slam '87
Teen Wolf Too '87
Return of the Killer Tomatoes! '88
Killer Tomatoes Strike Back '90
Night Life '90
Killer Tomatoes Eat France '91
Stepmonster '92
Huck and the King of Hearts '93
The Frighteners '96

MacKenzie Astin
The Garbage Pail Kids Movie '87
Iron Will '93
Widow's Kiss '96

Sean Astin
The Goonies '85
Like Father, Like Son '87
White Water Summer '87
Staying Together '89
The War of the Roses '89
Memphis Belle '90
The Willies '90
Toy Soldiers '91
Encino Man '92
Where the Day Takes You '92
Rudy '93
Safe Passage '94
Kurt Vonnegut's Harrison Bergeron '95
Courage Under Fire '96

Gertrude Astor
Strong Man '26
The Cat and the Canary '27
The Cheerful Fraud '27
Dames Ahoy '30
After Midnight '33

Mary Astor
Beau Brummel '24
The Fighting American '24
Don Q., Son of Zorro '25
Don Juan '26
Behind Office Doors '31
The Royal Bed '31
Red Dust '32
The Kennel Murder Case '33
Dodsworth '36
Lady from Nowhere '36
The Hurricane '37
Prisoner of Zenda '37
Listen, Darling '38
Midnight '39
Brigham Young: Frontiersman '40
The Great Lie '41
The Maltese Falcon '41
Across the Pacific '42
The Palm Beach Story '42
The Best of Bogart '43
Thousands Cheer '43
Meet Me in St. Louis '44
Cass Timberlane '47
Any Number Can Play '49
Little Women '49
This Happy Feeling '58
Return to Peyton Place '61
Hush, Hush, Sweet Charlotte '65

Patti Astor
The Foreigner '78
Underground U.S.A. '84
Assault of the Killer Bimbos '88

Nancy Moore Atchison
Midnight Edition '93
The Yearling '94

Hooper Atchley
Clearing the Range '31
Midnight Warning '32
Spirit of the West '32
I Can't Escape '34
Prescott Kid '36

Roscoe Ates
Cimarron '30
The Champ '31
Come On Danger! '32
Freaks '32
Cheyenne Kid '33
What! No Beer? '33
Woman in the Shadows '34
Three Texas Steers '39
Reg'lar Fellers '41
Robin Hood of the Pecos '41
Colorado Serenade '46
Driftin' River '46
Wild West '46
West to Glory '47
Wild Country '47
Black Hills '48
Check Your Guns '48
The Hawk of Powder River '48
The Tioga Kid '48
Thunder in the Pines '49
Hills of Oklahoma '50

William Atherton
Class of '44 '73
The Sugarland Express '74
The Day of the Locust '75
The Hindenburg '75
Looking for Mr. Goodbar '77
Tomorrow's Child '82
Ghostbusters '84
Real Genius '85
No Mercy '86
Die Hard '88
Grim Prairie Tales '89
Buried Alive '90
Die Hard 2: Die Harder '90
A Fight for Jenny '90
Intrigue '90
Chrome Soldiers '92
The Pelican Brief '93
Frank and Jesse '94
Broken Trust '95
Saints and Sinners '95
Bio-Dome '96

Harvey Atkin
Meatballs '79
SnakeEater 2: The Drug Buster '89

Christopher Atkins
The Blue Lagoon '80
Child Bride of Short Creek '81
Pirate Movie '82
A Night in Heaven '83
Secret Weapons '85
Beaks: The Movie '87
Listen to Me '89
Shakma '89
King's Ransom '91
Mortuary Academy '91
Fatal Charm '92
Shoot '92
Wet and Wild Summer '92
Die Watching '93
Dracula Rising '93
It's My Party '95
Project Shadowchaser 3000 '95

David Atkins
Squizzy Taylor '84
Personal Services '87
Prick Up Your Ears '87

Eileen Atkins
I Don't Want to Be Born '75
Oliver Twist '82
The Dresser '83
Bewitched '85
The Vision '87
Let Him Have It '91
The Lost Language of Cranes '92
Cold Comfort Farm '94
Wolf '94
Jack and Sarah '96

Tom Atkins
Special Delivery '76
Tarantulas: The Deadly Cargo '77
Desperate Lives '82
Halloween 3: Season of the Witch '82
Skeezer '82
Blind Justice '86
Night of the Creeps '86
Lethal Weapon '87
Maniac Cop '88
Dead Man Out '89

Jayne Atkinson
Free Willy '93
Free Willy 2: The Adventure Home '95

Rowan Atkinson
Never Say Never Again '83
The Tall Guy '89
Bernard and the Genie '90s
The Witches '90
Hot Shots! Part Deux '93
Four Weddings and a Funeral '94

Richard Attenborough
In Which We Serve '43
Brighton Rock '47
The Guinea Pig '48
The Gift Horse '52
The Baby and the Battleship '56
Brothers in Law '57
Sea of Sand '58
The League of Gentlemen '60
S.O.S. Pacific '60
Only Two Can Play '62
The Great Escape '63
Guns at Batasi '64
Seance on a Wet Afternoon '64
The Flight of the Phoenix '65
The Sand Pebbles '66
Doctor Dolittle '67
The Bliss of Mrs. Blossom '68
The Magic Christian '69
David Copperfield '70
Loot...Give Me Money, Honey! '70
10 Rillington Place '71
Brannigan '75
Conduct Unbecoming '75
Rosebud '75
Ten Little Indians '75
The Human Factor '79
Jurassic Park '93
Miracle on 34th Street '94
Wavelength '96

Malcolm Atterbury
Blood of Dracula '57
Crime of Passion '57
I Was a Teenage Werewolf '57
How to Make a Monster '58

Edith Atwater
The Body Snatcher '45
It Happened at the World's Fair '63
The Love Machine '71
Die Sister, Die! '74
Our Time '74

Lionel Atwill
Doctor X '32
The Vampire Bat '32
Murders in the Zoo '33
Mystery of the Wax Museum '33
The Sphinx '33
The Sphinx '33
Beggars in Ermine '34
Captain Blood '35
High Command '37
The Wrong Road '37
The Great Waltz '38
Three Comrades '38
Balalaika '39
The Gorilla '39
The Hound of the Baskervilles '39
Son of Frankenstein '39
The Three Musketeers '39
Boom Town '40
Johnny Apollo '40
Man Made Monster '41
Cairo '42
Frankenstein Meets the Wolfman '42
The Ghost of Frankenstein '42
Night Monster '42
Pardon My Sarong '42
Sherlock Holmes and the Secret Weapon '42
To Be or Not to Be '42
Captain America '44
House of Frankenstein '44
Lady in the Death House '44
Raiders of Ghost City '44
Fog Island '45
House of Dracula '45
Lost City of the Jungle '45
The Horror of It All '91

Anat Atzman
Dead End Street '83
Every Time We Say Goodbye '86
Double Edge '92

Rene Auberjonois
Petulia '68
Brewster McCloud '70
M*A*S*H '70
McCabe & Mrs. Miller '71
Pete 'n' Tillie '72
King Kong '76
The Dark Secret of Harvest Home '78
Eyes of Laura Mars '78
Wild, Wild West Revisited '79
A Smoky Mountain Christmas '86
3:15—The Moment of Truth '86
Walker '87
My Best Friend Is a Vampire '88
Police Academy 5: Assignment Miami Beach '88
A Connecticut Yankee in King Arthur's Court '89
Gore Vidal's Billy the Kid '89
The Feud '90
Once Upon a Midnight Scary '90
Wildcard '92
The Ballad of Little Jo '93
Lone Justice '93
Star Trek Deep Space Nine: Emissary '93

Lenore Aubert
Action in Arabia '44
Having Wonderful Crime '45
Abbott and Costello Meet Frankenstein '48
Abbott and Costello Meet the Killer, Boris Karloff '49

James Aubrey
Lord of the Flies '63
Bouquet of Barbed Wire '76
The Terror '79
Home Before Midnight '84
Forever Young '85
Riders of the Storm '88

Jimmy Aubrey
Courage of the North '35
Go-Get-'Em-Haines '35
Aces and Eights '36
Legion of Missing Men '37

Juliet Aubrey
Middlemarch '93
Jacob '94

Danielle Aubry
Bikini Beach '64
Operation C.I.A. '65

Jacques Aubuchon
Gun Glory '57
Thunder Road '58

Michel Auclair
Beauty and the Beast '46
Manon '50
Murder at 45 R.P.M. '65
The Story of a Love Story '73
Swashbuckler '84

Maxine Audley
A King in New York '57
The Trials of Oscar Wilde '60
Peeping Tom '63

Stephane Audran
Les Bonnes Femmes '60
Les Biches '68
Six in Paris '68
Le Boucher '69
La Rupture '70
The Discreet Charm of the Bourgeoisie '72
Wedding in Blood '74
Black Bird '75
Ten Little Indians '75
Twist '76
Vincent, Francois, Paul and the Others '76
Blood Relatives '77
Silver Bears '78
Violette '78
Eagle's Wing '79
The Big Red One '80
Brideshead Revisited '81
Coup de Torchon '81
The Blood of Others '84
La Cage aux Folles 3: The Wedding '86
Babette's Feast '87
Poor Little Rich Girl: The Barbara Hutton Story '87
Betty '92
The Turn of the Screw '92

Mischa Auer
Inside the Lines '30
Drums of Jeopardy '31
The Monster Walks '32
Flaming Signal '33
Woman Condemned '33
Sucker Money '34
Condemned to Live '35
The Crusades '35
I Dream Too Much '35
My Man Godfrey '36
The Princess Comes Across '36
That Girl from Paris '36
Three Smart Girls '36
100 Men and a Girl '37
Pick a Star '37
Vogues of 1938 '37
The Rage of Paris '38
Sweethearts '38
You Can't Take It with You '38
Destry Rides Again '39
Seven Sinners '40
Hold That Ghost '41
Around the World '43
And Then There Were None '45
Brewster's Millions '45
Mr. Arkadin '55
Sputnik '61
Arrivederci, Baby! '66
The Christmas That Almost Wasn't '66

Claudine Auger
The Road to Lebanon '60
Thunderball '65
The Killing Game '67
Triple Cross '67
Head of the Family '71
Twitch of the Death Nerve '71
Ricco '74
The Associate '82
Lobster for Breakfast '82
Secret Places '85

Lance August
Terror Eyes '87
Stripteaser '95

Robert August
The Endless Summer '66
The Endless Summer 2 '94

Ewa Aulin
Start the Revolution Without Me '70
The Legend of Blood Castle '72

Jean-Pierre Aumont
Maria Chapdelaine '34
Heartbeat '46
Lili '53
Napoleon '55
John Paul Jones '59
The Devil at 4 O'Clock '61
The Horse Without a Head '63
Cauldron of Blood '67
Day for Night '73
The Happy Hooker '75
Mahogany '75
Catherine & Co. '76
Blackout '78
Cat and Mouse '78
Something Short of Paradise '79
A Time for Miracles '80
Don't Look in the Attic '81
Nana '82
The Blood of Others '84
Sweet Country '87
Windmills of the Gods '88
A Tale of Two Cities '91
Becoming Colette '92
Jefferson in Paris '94

Michel Aumont
Spoiled Children '77
Hothead '78
La Vie Continue '82
Les Comperes '83
Grain of Sand '84
A Sunday in the Country '84
One Woman or Two '85
Alberto Express '92

Tina Aumont
Texas Across the River '66
Partner '68
Man of Legend '71
Torso '73
La Grande Bourgeoise '74
Malicious '74
Lifespan '75
A Matter of Time '76

Marcus Aurelius
A.P.E.X. '94
Suspect Device '95

Albert Austin
Charlie Chaplin: The Early Years, Vol. 3 '16
Charlie Chaplin: The Early Years, Vol. 4 '16
The Vagabond '16
Charlie Chaplin: The Early Years, Vol. 2 '17
The Cure '17
Three Charlies and One Phoney! '18

Charlotte Austin
Daddy Long Legs '55
The Bride & the Beast '58

Julie Austin
Elves '89
Fatal Exposure '90

Karen Austin
The Jagged Edge '85
Summer Rental '85
Assassin '86
The Ladies Club '86
Far from Home '89
A Girl to Kill For '90
When the Time Comes '91
When a Stranger Calls Back '93

Terri Austin
The Vindicator '85
False Witness '89

Daniel Auteuil
Le Sex Shop '73
Jean de Florette '87
Manon of the Spring '87
Mama, There's a Man in Your Bed '89
The Elegant Criminal '92
Un Coeur en Hiver '93
Queen Margot '94
The Separation '94
The Eighth Day '95

Alan Autry
At Close Range '86
Blue De Ville '86
Proud Men '87

Gene Autry
Singing Cowboys, Vol. 2 '30s
In Old Santa Fe '34
Mystery Mountain '34
Melody Trail '35
The Phantom Empire '35
Old Corral '36
Red River Valley '36
Ride, Ranger, Ride '36
Big Show '37
Boots & Saddles '37
Git Along Little Dogies '37
Manhattan Merry-Go-Round '37
Public Cowboy No. 1 '37
Round-Up Time in Texas '37
Springtime in the Rockies '37
Western Double Feature 4 '37
Western Double Feature 5: Rogers & Autry '37
Yodelin' Kid From Pine Ridge '37
The Man from Music Mountain '38
Oh Susannah '38
Old Barn Dance '38
Prairie Moon '38
Rootin' Tootin' Rhythm '38
Western Double Feature 1 '38
South of the Border '39
Melody Ranch '40
Saturday Night Serials '40
Down Mexico Way '41
Ridin' on a Rainbow '41
Twilight on the Rio Grande '41
Call of the Canyon '42
Heart of the Rio Grande '42
Sioux City Sue '46
Western Double Feature 16 '46
Robin Hood of Texas '47
Loaded Pistols '48
The Big Sombrero '49
Riders of the Whistling Pines '49
Rim of the Canyon '49
Cow Town '50
Hills of Utah '51
Valley of Fire '51
Blue Canadian Rockies '52
Night Stage to Galveston '52
Gene Autry Matinee Double Feature #1 '53
Gene Autry Matinee Double Feature #2 '53
Gene Autry Matinee Double Feature #3 '53
Last of the Pony Riders '53
On Top of Old Smoky '53
Winning of the West '53
Cowboys of the Saturday Matinee '84
Bad Girls in the Movies '86

Frankie Avalon
The Alamo '60
Voyage to the Bottom of the Sea '61
Panic in the Year Zero! '62
Beach Party '63
The Castilian '63
Bikini Beach '64
Muscle Beach Party '64
Beach Blanket Bingo '65
How to Stuff a Wild Bikini '65
I'll Take Sweden '65
Dr. Goldfoot and the Bikini Machine '66
Grease '78
Blood Song '82
Back to the Beach '87

Phillip Avalon
Summer City '77
The Cursed Mountain Mystery '93

Luis Avalos
Ghost Fever '87
Lone Justice '93
Lone Justice 2 '93

Erik Avari
The Beast '88
Stargate '94

Loren Avedon
No Retreat, No Surrender 2 '89
The King of the Kickboxers '91
No Retreat, No Surrender 3: Blood Brothers '91
Operation Golden Phoenix '94
Virtual Combat '95

Brian Avery
The Graduate '67
Forced to Kill '93

James Avery
Kicks '85
Beastmaster 2: Through the Portal of Time '91

Linda Avery
Noon Sunday '71
Hitchhikers '72

Margaret Avery
Terror at Red Wolf Inn '72
Hell Up in Harlem '73
Which Way Is Up? '77
The Fish that Saved Pittsburgh '79
Lathe of Heaven '80
The Color Purple '85
Blueberry Hill '88
For Us, the Living '88
Riverbend '89
Heat Wave '90
Return of Superfly '90
The Jacksons: An American Dream '92
Mardi Gras for the Devil '93
White Man's Burden '95

Val Avery
Faces '68
A Dream of Kings '69
Firehouse '72
Black Caesar '73
Choices '81
The Chosen '81
Continental Divide '81
Courage '86

Angel Aviles
Chain of Desire '93
Mi Vida Loca '94

Rick Aviles
Spike of Bensonhurst '88

Mystery Train '89
Ghost '90
The Saint of Fort Washington '93
Stephen King's The Stand '94

Mili Avital
Stargate '94
Dead Man '95

Chikage Awashima
Early Summer '51
The Human Condition: No Greater Love '58

Eddie Axberg
The Emigrants '72
The New Land '73

Nina Axelrod
Motel Hell '80
Cross Country '83

Hanne Axman
The Red Menace '49
Five Fingers '52

Hoyt Axton
Endangered Species '82
The Junkman '82
Deadline Auto Theft '83
Goldilocks & the Three Bears '83
Heart Like a Wheel '83
Gremlins '84
Act of Vengeance '86
Christmas Comes to Willow Creek '87
Guilty of Innocence '87
Dixie Lanes '88
Retribution '88
Disorganized Crime '89
We're No Angels '89
Buried Alive '90
The Rousters '90
Number One Fan '94
Season of Change '94
Kingfish: A Story of Huey P. Long '95

Ann Ayars
Reunion in France '42
Gaiety '43
Fiesta '47

Dan Aykroyd
Saturday Night Live '70s
Love at First Sight '76
All You Need Is Cash '78
Mr. Mike's Mondo Video '79
1941 '79
The Blues Brothers '80
Neighbors '81
Doctor Detroit '83
Trading Places '83
Twilight Zone: The Movie '83
Ghostbusters '84
Into the Night '85
Spies Like Us '85
The Couch Trip '87
Dragnet '87
Caddyshack 2 '88
The Great Outdoors '88
My Stepmother Is an Alien '88
Driving Miss Daisy '89
Ghostbusters 2 '89
Loose Cannons '90
The Masters of Menace '90
My Girl '91
Nothing But Trouble '91
Chaplin '92
Sneakers '92
This Is My Life '92
Coneheads '93
Exit to Eden '94
My Girl 2 '94
North '94
Sgt. Bilko '95
Tommy Boy '95
Celtic Pride '96
Getting Away With Murder '96

Peter Aykroyd
Gas '81
The Funny Farm '82

Felix Aylmer
The Evil Mind '34
The Iron Duke '34
Nine Days a Queen '34
As You Like It '36
The Shadow '36
Dreaming Lips '37
Action for Slander '38
The Case of the Frightened Lady '39
Spellbound '41
Henry V '44
Mr. Emmanuel '44
The Wicked Lady '45
Ghosts of Berkeley Square '47
A Man About the House '47
Hamlet '48
The October Man '48
Eye Witness '49
Alice in Wonderland '50
Trio '50
Quo Vadis '51
Ivanhoe '52
Knights of the Round Table '53
The Master of Ballantrae '53
Paris Express '53
Saint Joan '57
Separate Tables '58
The Mummy '59
Exodus '60
From the Terrace '60
The Hands of Orlac '60
Victoria Regina '61
The Chalk Garden '64
School for Scandal '65

Agnes Ayres
The Sheik '21
Son of the Sheik '26

Leah Ayres
The Burning '82
Eddie Macon's Run '83
Bloodsport '88

Lew Ayres
Big News '29
The Kiss '29
All Quiet on the Western Front '30
Holiday '38
Broadway Serenade '39
Dr. Kildare's Strange Case '40
Dark Mirror '46
Johnny Belinda '48
The Capture '50
Donovan's Brain '53
Advise and Consent '62
The Carpetbaggers '64
Battle for the Planet of the Apes '73
The Stranger '73
End of the World '76
Francis Gary Powers: The True Story of the U-2 Spy '76
Damien: Omen 2 '78
Salem's Lot '79
Of Mice and Men '81
Cast the First Stone '89

Robert Ayres
River Beat '54
Cat Girl '57
Battle Beneath the Earth '68

Hank Azaria
Cool Blue '88
Quiz Show '94
The Birdcage '95
Heat '95

Sabine Azema
A Sunday in the Country '84
Life and Nothing But '89
Smoking/No Smoking '94

Ayu Azhari
Diamond Run '90
Without Mercy '95

Tony Azito
Chattanooga Choo Choo '84
Private Resort '84
Bloodhounds of Broadway '89

Shabana Azmi
Madame Sousatzka '88
City of Joy '92
Son of the Pink Panther '93
In Custody '94

Charles Aznavour
The Testament of Orpheus '59
Shoot the Piano Player '62
The Adventurers '70
Blockhouse '73
Ten Little Indians '75
Sky Riders '76
Twist '76
The Tin Drum '79
Edith & Marcel '83

Candice Azzara
House Calls '78
Fatso '80
Easy Money '83
Doin' Time on Planet Earth '88

Karin Baal
Teenage Wolfpack '57
Dead Eyes of London '61
Berlin Alexanderplatz '80

Obba Babatunde
God Bless the Child '88
Miami Blues '90
Philadelphia '93
Undercover Blues '93
A Reason to Believe '95

Barbara Babcock
The Christmas Coal Mine Miracle '77
The Black Marble '79
On the Edge: The Survival of Dana '79
Hill Street Blues, Vol. 1: Hill Street Station '81
The Lords of Discipline '83
That Was Then...This Is Now '85
News at Eleven '86
Happy Together '89
The Heart of Dixie '89
Far and Away '92

Lauren Bacall
To Have & Have Not '44
The Big Sleep '46
Dark Passage '47
Key Largo '48
Hollywood Bloopers '50s
Young Man with a Horn '50
How to Marry a Millionaire '53
A Woman's World '54
Blood Alley '55
The Cobweb '55
Written on the Wind '56
Designing Woman '57
Flame Over India '60
Sex and the Single Girl '64
Harper '66
Murder on the Orient Express '74
The Shootist '76
The Fan '81
Appointment with Death '88
Mr. North '88
Dinner at Eight '89
Innocent Victim '90
Misery '90
All I Want for Christmas '91
A Foreign Field '93
The Portrait '93
Ready to Wear '94
From the Mixed-Up Files of Mrs. Basil E. Frankweiler '95

Barbara Bach
The Legend of Sea Wolf '75
Stateline Motel '75
The Spy Who Loved Me '77
Force 10 from Navarone '78
Jaguar Lives '79
Street Law '79
Screamers '80
The Unseen '80
Up the Academy '80
Caveman '81
The Great Alligator '81
Princess Daisy '83
Give My Regards to Broad Street '84

Catherine Bach
Nicole '72
Strange New World '75
Cannonball Run 2 '84
Criminal Act '88
Driving Force '88
Street Justice '89
The Masters of Menace '90
Rage and Honor '92

John Bach
Wild Horses '82
Georgia '87
The Lost Tribe '89
The Sound and the Silence '93

Hans Bachman
Star Quest '89
Invader '91

Brian Backer
Fast Times at Ridgemont High '82
Talk to Me '82
Moving Violations '85

Jim Backus
Father Was a Fullback '49
The Great Lover '49
His Kind of Woman '51
I'll See You in My Dreams '51
Don't Bother to Knock '52
Pat and Mike '52
Above and Beyond '53
I Love Melvin '53
Francis in the Navy '55
Rebel Without a Cause '55
Meet Me in Las Vegas '56
Naked Hills '56
Man of a Thousand Faces '57
The Pied Piper of Hamelin '57
Ask Any Girl '59
Ice Palace '60
The Horizontal Lieutenant '62
The Wonderful World of the Brothers Grimm '62
Zotz! '62
It's a Mad, Mad, Mad, Mad World '63
The Wheeler Dealers '63
Gilligan's Island: Meet the Crew '64
Billie '65
Where Were You When the Lights Went Out? '68
Myra Breckinridge '70
Now You See Him, Now You Don't '72
Crazy Mama '75
Pete's Dragon '77
Angel's Brigade '79
C.H.O.M.P.S. '79
The Rebels '79
Slapstick of Another Kind '84

Olga Baclanova
The Man Who Laughs '27
Docks of New York '28
Freaks '32

Irving Bacon
Branded Men '31
Internes Can't Take Money '37
Blondie Takes a Vacation '39
Blondie Has Trouble '40
Dreaming Out Loud '40
The Howards of Virginia '40
Caught in the Draft '41
Western Union '41
The Bashful Bachelor '42
Blondie's Blessed Event '42
It's a Great Life '43
Monsieur Verdoux '47
Dynamite '49
Cause for Alarm '51
Ma and Pa Kettle at Home '54

Kevin Bacon
National Lampoon's Animal House '78
Starting Over '79
Friday the 13th '80
Hero at Large '80
Only When I Laugh '81
Diner '82
Enormous Changes '83
Trumps '83
Footloose '84
Quicksilver '86
Planes, Trains & Automobiles '87
White Water Summer '87
End of the Line '88
She's Having a Baby '88
The Big Picture '89
Criminal Law '89
Tremors '89
Flatliners '90
He Said, She Said '91
JFK '91
Pyrates '91
Queens Logic '91
A Few Good Men '92
The Air Up There '94
The River Wild '94
Apollo 13 '95
Murder In the First '95

Lloyd Bacon
Charlie Chaplin...Our Hero! '15
Charlie Chaplin: The Early Years, Vol. 4 '16
Wagon Tracks '19

Michael Badalucco
Mac '93
The Professional '94
Two If by Sea '95

Hermione Baddeley
Brighton Rock '47
Passport to Pimlico '49
A Christmas Carol '51
The Belles of St. Trinian's '53
The Pickwick Papers '54
Room at the Top '59
Mary Poppins '64
The Unsinkable Molly Brown '64

Alan Badel
Three Cases of Murder '55
Children of the Damned '63
This Sporting Life '63
The Adventurers '70
The Day of the Jackal '73
Luther '74
The Medusa Touch '78
The Riddle of the Sands '79
Nijinsky '80

Rupert Baderman
1984 '84
Shadowlands '85

Mary Badham
To Kill a Mockingbird '62
This Property is Condemned '66

Annette Badland
Pictures '80s
Captives '94
Angels and Insects '95

Jane Badler
V '83
Fine Gold '88
Easy Kill '89
Black Snow '93

Buddy Baer
Quo Vadis '51
The Big Sky '52
Jack & the Beanstalk '52
Giant from the Unknown '58

Harry Baer
Rulers of the City '71
Fox and His Friends '75
Big Boss '77
Mr. Scarface '77

John Baer
Indian Uprising '51
Night of the Blood Beast '58
Wanted: Dead or Alive '59

Max Baer, Sr.
The Prizefighter and the Lady '33
The Navy Comes Through '42
Buckskin Frontier '43
Riding High '50
The Harder They Fall '56

Max Baer, Jr.
The Beverly Hillbillies '62
Macon County Line '74

Meredith Baer
The Sister-in-Law '74
The Chicken Chronicles '77

Parley Baer
The Adventures of Huckleberry Finn '60
Cash McCall '60
Gypsy '62
The Ugly Dachshund '65
Sixteen '72
Rodeo Girl '80
Dave '93

Joan Baez
Dynamite Chicken '70
Bob Dylan: Don't Look Back '91

Carol Bagdasarian
Charge of the Model T's '76
The Aurora Encounter '85

Vernel Bagneris
Pennies From Heaven '81
Down by Law '86

Blake Bahner
Sensations '87
Thrilled to Death '88
Deadly Breed '89
Fatal Exposure '90
Blackbelt 2: Fatal Force '93

Chuck Bail
The Stunt Man '80
L.A. Bad '85

Bill Bailey
On the Edge '86
Heat and Sunlight '87

Bunty Bailey
Dolls '87
Spellcaster '91

G.W. Bailey
Rustler's Rhapsody '85
A Winner Never Quits '86
Burglar '87
Mannequin '87

Bailey ▶cont.

Police Academy 6: City Under Siege '89
Double-Crossed '91
Held Hostage '91
Write to Kill '91
An American Story '92
Police Academy: Mission to Moscow '94

Jim Bailey
Vultures '84
Penitentiary 3 '87

Mark Bailey
The Unbelievable Truth '90
Simple Men '92

Pearl Bailey
Carmen Jones '54
Norman, Is That You? '76
The Member of the Wedding '83
Peter Gunn '89

Raymond Bailey
Picnic '55
The Incredible Shrinking Man '57
Vertigo '58
The Gallant Hours '60
The Beverly Hillbillies '62

Richard Bailey
Manhunt of Mystery Island '45
Forever Amber '47

Robin Bailey
See No Evil '71
Screamtime '83

Barbara Bain
Murder Once Removed '71
Destination Moonbase Alpha '75
Space: 1999 '75
Space: 1999—Alien Attack '79
Skinheads: The Second Coming of Hate '88
Trust Me '89
Spirit of '76 '91

Conrad Bain
Bananas '71
Who Killed Mary What's 'Er Name? '71
C.H.O.M.P.S. '79
A Pleasure Doing Business '79
Child Bride of Short Creek '81
Postcards from the Edge '90

Cynthia Bain
Pumpkinhead '88
Vietnam War Story 2 '88
Spontaneous Combustion '89
Danielle Steel's Changes '91
Hometown Boy Makes Good '93

Sherry Bain
The Hard Ride '71
Wild Riders '71
Pipe Dreams '76
Wild & Wooly '78

Fay Bainter
Quality Street '37
Jezebel '38
The Shining Hour '38
Our Town '40
Young Tom Edison '40
Babes on Broadway '41
Journey for Margaret '42
Woman of the Year '42
The Human Comedy '43
Presenting Lily Mars '43
Dark Waters '44
State Fair '45
Kid from Brooklyn '46
The Virginian '46
The Secret Life of Walter Mitty '47
June Bride '48
The Children's Hour '61

Jimmy Baio
The Bad News Bears in Breaking Training '77
Playing for Keeps '86
Kiss and Be Killed '91

Scott Baio
Bugsy Malone '76
Foxes '80
Senior Trip '81
Zapped! '82
I Love N.Y. '87

Harry Baird
Tor '64
The Story of a Three Day Pass '68
The Oblong Box '69

Jimmie Baird
Return of Dracula '58
Black Orchid '59
Brass '85

Richard Bakalayan
Jet Attack/Paratroop Command '58
Up Periscope '59
The St. Valentine's Day Massacre '67
The Computer Wore Tennis Shoes '69

Art Baker
Homecoming '48
A Southern Yankee '48
Task Force '49
The Underworld Story '50

Blanche Baker
French Postcards '79
Mary and Joseph: A Story of Faith '79
Awakening of Candra '81
Cold Feet '84
Sixteen Candles '84
Embassy '85
Shakedown '88
The Handmaid's Tale '90
Livin' Large '91
Dead Funny '94

Bob Baker
Ghost Town Riders '38
Outlaw Express '38
Western Trails '38
Riders of Pasco Basin '40

Carroll Baker
Easy to Love '53
Baby Doll '56
Giant '56
The Big Country '58
But Not for Me '59
How the West Was Won '63
The Carpetbaggers '64
Cheyenne Autumn '64
The Greatest Story Ever Told '65
Harlow '65
Kiss Me, Kill Me '69
Paranoia '69
Captain Apache '71
Next Victim '74
Andy Warhol's Bad '77
You've Got to Have Heart '77
The World is Full of Married Men '80
The Watcher in the Woods '81
Star 80 '83
The Secret Diary of Sigmund Freud '84
Native Son '86
Ironweed '87
Kindergarten Cop '90
Dalva '95
Bloodbath
Private Lessons

Diane Baker
The Best of Everything '59
The Diary of Anne Frank '59
Journey to the Center of the Earth '59
The Prize '63
Stolen Hours '63
Marnie '64
Strait-Jacket '64
Mirage '66
The Fugitive: The Final Episode '67
The Invaders '67
The Horse in the Gray Flannel Suit '68
Baker's Hawk '76
Danger in the Skies '79
The Closer '91
The Silence of the Lambs '91
The Joy Luck Club '93
Twenty Bucks '93
Imaginary Crimes '94
The Net '95
The Cable Guy '96

Dylan Baker
Planes, Trains & Automobiles '87
The Wizard of Loneliness '88
The Long Walk Home '89
Delirious '91
Love Potion #9 '92
Disclosure '94

Frank Baker
The New Adventures of Tarzan '35
Tarzan and the Green Goddess '38

George Baker
Dangerous Youth '58
The Moonraker '58
Sword of Lancelot '63
The Prisoner: Arrival '68
Goodbye, Mr. Chips '69
Robin Hood...The Legend: Herne's Son '85
The Charmer '89

Jay Baker
April Fool's Day '86
Storm and Sorrow '90

Jill Baker
Hope and Glory '87
Prime Suspect: Inner Circles '95

Joe Don Baker
Cool Hand Luke '67
Guns of the Magnificent Seven '69
Adam at 6 a.m. '70
Wild Rovers '71
Junior Bonner '72
Charley Varrick '73
Walking Tall '73
Framed '75
Mitchell '75
The Pack '77
Shadow of Chikara '77
Speedtrap '78
Joy Sticks '83
Wacko '83
Final Justice '84
The Natural '84
Fletch '85
Edge of Darkness '86
Getting Even '86
The Abduction of Kari Swenson '87
The Killing Time '87
Leonard Part 6 '87
The Living Daylights '87
Criminal Law '89
The Children '90
Cape Fear '91
Citizen Cohn '92
The Distinguished Gentleman '92
Reality Bites '94
Ring of Steel '94
Congo '95
Felony '95
Goldeneye '95
Panther '95

Jolyon Baker
Duel of Hearts '92
Final Analysis '92

Josephine Baker
Zou Zou '34
Princess Tam Tam '35
The French Way '40

Kai Baker
Stormquest '87
American Eagle '90

Kathy Baker
The Right Stuff '83
A Killing Affair '85
Street Smart '87
Clean and Sober '88
Permanent Record '88
Dad '89
The Image '89
Jacknife '89
Mr. Frost '89
Edward Scissorhands '90
Article 99 '92
Jennifer 8 '92
Mad Dog and Glory '93
Lush Life '94

Kenny Baker
Star Wars '77
The Elephant Man '80
The Empire Strikes Back '80
Time Bandits '81
Return of the Jedi '83
Amadeus '84
Cannon Movie Tales: Sleeping Beauty '89
Sleeping Beauty '89

Kenny L. Baker
At the Circus '39
The Harvey Girls '46

Kirsten Baker
Gas Pump Girls '79
Girls Next Door '79

Ray Baker
Everybody's All American '88
Heart Condition '90
Camp Nowhere '94
The Hard Truth '94
Speechless '94

Scott Thompson Baker
New York's Finest '87
Rest In Pieces '87
Cleo/Leo '89

Sharon Baker
Captive Planet '78
Metallica '85

Stanley Baker
Cruel Sea '53
Knights of the Round Table '53
Richard III '55
Helen of Troy '56
The Guns of Navarone '61
Sodom and Gomorrah '62
Zulu '64
Dingaka '65
Accident '67
Robbery '67
Butterfly Affair '71
Queen of Diamonds '80s

Timothy Baker
Bloodfist 2 '90
Out for Blood '93

Tom Baker
Nicholas and Alexandra '71
The Freakmaker '73
Golden Voyage of Sinbad '73
Vault of Horror '73
Candy Stripe Nurses '74
Fyre '78
Angels Die Hard '84
The Zany Adventures of Robin Hood '84
The Chronicles of Narnia '89

William "Billy" Bakewell
Annapolis '28
Dance Fools Dance '31
Sons of Steel '35
Exiled to Shanghai '37
Roaring Speedboats '37
Gone with the Wind '39
Dawn Express '42
Romance on the High Seas '48
The Capture '50
Radar Men from the Moon '52
Lucky Me '54
Davy Crockett, King of the Wild Frontier '55

Brenda Bakke
Hardbodies 2 '86
Dangerous Love '87
Death Spa '87
Scavengers '87
Fist Fighter '88
Fast Gun '93
Hot Shots! Part Deux '93
Lone Justice 2 '93
Star Quest '94
Tales from the Crypt Presents Demon Knight '94
Twogether '94
Under Siege 2: Dark Territory '95

Brigitte Bako
Red Shoe Diaries '92
Dark Tide '93
A Man in Uniform '93
Replikator: Cloned to Kill '94
Strange Days '95

Muhamad Bakri
Hanna K. '83
Beyond the Walls '84
Double Edge '92

Scott Bakula
The Last Fling '86
Sibling Rivalry '90
Necessary Roughness '91
Mercy Mission '93
Color of Night '94
My Family '94
A Passion to Kill '94
The Invaders '95
Lord of Illusions '95

Bob Balaban
Midnight Cowboy '69
The Strawberry Statement '70
Bank Shot '74
Close Encounters of the Third Kind '77
Girlfriends '78
Altered States '80
Absence of Malice '81
Whose Life Is It Anyway? '81
2010: The Year We Make Contact '84
End of the Line '88
Dead Bang '89
Alice '90
Unnatural Pursuits '91
Amos and Andrew '93
For Love or Money '93
Greedy '94
The Late Shift '96

Belinda Balaski
The Howling '81
Proud Men '87

Josiane Balasko
French Fried Vacation '79
Too Beautiful for You '88
Grosse Fatigue '94
French Twist '95

Nick Baldasare
Beyond Dream's Door '88
They Bite '95

Renalto Baldini
The Wayward Wife '52
Four Ways Out '57

Adam Baldwin
My Bodyguard '80
Ordinary People '80
D.C. Cab '84
Hadley's Rebellion '84
Reckless '84
Bad Guys '86
3:15—The Moment of Truth '86
Full Metal Jacket '87
The Chocolate War '88
Cohen and Tate '88
Next of Kin '89
Predator 2 '90
Guilty by Suspicion '91
Deadbolt '92
Radio Flyer '92
Where the Day Takes You '92
Bitter Harvest '93
Cold Sweat '93
800 Leagues Down the Amazon '93
Digital Man '94
Wyatt Earp '94
Sawbones '95
Trade Off '95

Alec Baldwin
Code of Honor '84
Love on the Run '85
Dress Gray '86
The Alamo: Thirteen Days to Glory '87
Forever, Lulu '87
Beetlejuice '88
Married to the Mob '88
She's Having a Baby '88
Talk Radio '88
Working Girl '88
Great Balls of Fire '89
Alice '90
The Hunt for Red October '90
Miami Blues '90
The Marrying Man '91
Glengarry Glen Ross '92
Prelude to a Kiss '92
The Getaway '93
Malice '93
The Shadow '94
Heaven's Prisoners '95
A Streetcar Named Desire '95
The Juror '96

Daniel Baldwin
Harley Davidson and the Marlboro Man '91
The Heroes of Desert Storm '91
Attack of the 50 Ft. Woman '93
Knight Moves '93
Lone Justice '93
Car 54, Where Are You? '94
Dead on Sight '94
Bodily Harm '95
Mulholland Falls '95

Janet Baldwin
Gator Bait '73
Ruby '77
Humongous '82

Robert Baldwin
Meet Dr. Christian '39
Courageous Dr. Christian '40

Stephen Baldwin
The Lawrenceville Stories '80s
The Beast '88
Born on the Fourth of July '89
Last Exit to Brooklyn '90
Crossing the Bridge '92
Bitter Harvest '93
Posse '93
8 Seconds '94
Fall Time '94
The Great American Sex Scandal '94
New Eden '94
A Simple Twist of Fate '94
Threesome '94
Dead Weekend '95
Under the Hula Moon '95
The Usual Suspects '95
Bio-Dome '96
Fled '96

Walter Baldwin
Winter Meeting '48
Interrupted Melody '55

William Baldwin
The Preppie Murder '89
Flatliners '90
Internal Affairs '90
Backdraft '91
Sliver '93
Three of Hearts '93
Fair Game '95
A Pyromaniac's Love Story '95

Christian Bale
Empire of the Sun '87
The Land of Faraway '87
Henry V '89
Treasure Island '89
Newsies '92
Swing Kids '93
Little Women '94

Betty Balfour
Champagne '28
Evergreen '34

Michael Balfour
Moulin Rouge '52
Murder on Approval '56
Quatermass 2 '57
Fiend Without a Face '58
Mania '60
The Canterbury Tales '71

Jennifer Balgobin
Repo Man '83
City Limits '85
Dr. Caligari '89
Roadside Prophets '92

Ina Balin
Black Orchid '59
From the Terrace '60
The Comancheros '61
The Patsy '64
Charro! '69
The Projectionist '71
The Don is Dead '73
Panic on the 5:22 '74
Galyon '77
The Children of An Lac '80
Vasectomy: A Delicate Matter '86

Andras Balint
Father '67
Love Film '70
A Happy New Year! '79
Colonel Redl '84
Stalin '92

Eszter Balint
Stranger than Paradise '84
Bail Jumper '89
The Linguini Incident '92

Fairuza Balk
Return to Oz '85
The Worst Witch '86
Outside Chance of Maximillian Glick '88
Valmont '89
Gas Food Lodging '92
Shame '92
Imaginary Crimes '94
Tollbooth '94
Things to Do In Denver When You're Dead '95
The Craft '96
The Island of Dr. Moreau '96

Frank Ball
The Forty-Niners '32
Galloping Romeo '33
When a Man Rides Alone '33
Boothill Brigade '37
Gun Lords of Stirrup Basin '37
Feud Maker '38

Lucille Ball
Roman Scandals '33
I Dream Too Much '35
Roberta '35
Top Hat '35
Follow the Fleet '36
That Girl from Paris '36
Stage Door '37
The Affairs of Annabel '38
Annabel Takes a Tour/Maid's Night Out '38
Having Wonderful Time '38
Having Wonderful Time/Carnival Boat '38
Joy of Living '38
Next Time I Marry '38
Room Service '38
Beauty for the Asking '39
Five Came Back '39
Panama Lady '39
Dance, Girl, Dance '40
Too Many Girls '40
You Can't Fool Your Wife '40
A Girl, a Guy and a Gob '41
Look Who's Laughing '41
Big Street '42
Hedda Hopper's Hollywood '42
Seven Days' Leave '42
Valley of the Sun '42
Best Foot Forward '43
DuBarry Was a Lady '43
Thousands Cheer '43
Abbott and Costello in Hollywood '45
Without Love '45
Dark Corner '46
Ziegfeld Follies '46
Her Husband's Affairs '47
Easy Living '49
Miss Grant Takes Richmond '49
Sorrowful Jones '49
Fancy Pants '50
The Fuller Brush Girl '50
I Love Lucy '52
The Long, Long Trailer '54
Forever Darling '56
Yours, Mine & Ours '68
Mame '74

Nicholas Ball
The House that Bled to Death '81
Claudia '85
Lifeforce '85

Vincent Ball
Terror Ship '54
Blonde Blackmailer '58
Blood of the Vampire '58
Sea of Sand '58
Dead Lucky '60
A Matter of WHO '62
Not Tonight Darling '72
Demolition '77
Sirens '94

Carl Ballantine
Speedway '68
Revenge of the Cheerleaders '76
World's Greatest Lover '77
Hollywood Chaos '89
Mr. Saturday Night '92

Kaye Ballard
The Girl Most Likely '57
The Ritz '76
Tiger Warsaw '87
Eternity '90
Fate '90
Modern Love '90
Ava's Magical Adventure '94

Smith Ballew
Roll Along Cowboy '37
Western Gold '37
Hawaiian Buckaroo '38
Panamint's Bad Man '38
Rawhide '38
Gun Cargo '49

Jean-Francois Balmer
Window Shopping '86
Madame Bovary '91

Martin Balsam
The Defender '57
Twelve Angry Men '57
Marjorie Morningstar '58
Al Capone '59
Psycho '60
Breakfast at Tiffany's '61
Cape Fear '61
The Carpetbaggers '64
Bedford Incident '65
Harlow '65
A Thousand Clowns '65
After the Fox '66
Hombre '67
The Good Guys and the Bad Guys '69
Spaghetti Western '69
Catch-22 '70
Hard Frame '70
Little Big Man '70
Tora! Tora! Tora! '70
The Anderson Tapes '71
Season for Assassins '71
Brand New Life '72
Confessions of a Police Captain '72
Eyes Behind the Stars '72
The Stone Killer '73
Summer Wishes, Winter Dreams '73
Miles to Go before I Sleep '74
Murder on the Orient Express '74
The Taking of Pelham One Two Three '74
Mitchell '75
All the President's Men '76
The Lindbergh Kidnapping Case '76
Two Minute Warning '76
Death Rage '77
Raid on Entebbe '77
Silver Bears '78
The House on Garibaldi Street '79
The Warning '80
The People vs. Jean Harris '81
The Salamander '82
The Goodbye People '83
Little Gloria...Happy at Last '84
Death Wish 3 '85
Murder in Space '85
St. Elmo's Fire '85
Delta Force '86
Grown Ups '86
P.I. Private Investigations '87
Queenie '87
Innocent Prey '88
Silence of the Hams '93

Talia Balsam
On the Edge: The Survival of Dana '79
Sunnyside '79
Kent State '81
Calamity Jane '82
Mass Appeal '84
Nadia '84
Consenting Adult '85
Crawlspace '86
In the Mood '87
The Kindred '87
Private Investigations '87
Trust Me '89
The Companion '94

Kirk Baltz
Reservoir Dogs '92
Skin Art '93
Kingfish: A Story of Huey P. Long '95
Probable Cause '95

David Bamber
High Hopes '88
Pride and Prejudice '95

Gerry Bamman
Lightning Over Water '80
The Chase '91
The Ten Million Dollar Getaway '91
Home Alone 2: Lost in New York '92
Lorenzo's Oil '92

Anne Bancroft
Don't Bother to Knock '52
Treasure of the Golden Condor '53
Demetrius and the Gladiators '54
Savage Wilderness '55
Nightfall '56
Girl in Black Stockings '57
The Restless Breed '58
The Miracle Worker '62
The Pumpkin Eater '64
The Slender Thread '65
The Graduate '67
Young Winston '72
Prisoner of Second Avenue '74
The Hindenburg '75
Lipstick '76
Silent Movie '76
Jesus of Nazareth '77
The Turning Point '77
The Bell Jar '79
The Elephant Man '80
Fatso '80
To Be or Not to Be '83
Garbo Talks '84
Agnes of God '85
84 Charing Cross Road '86
'night, Mother '86
Torch Song Trilogy '88
Bert Rigby, You're a Fool '89
Broadway Bound '92
Honeymoon in Vegas '92
Malice '93
Mr. Jones '93
Point of No Return '93
Dracula: Dead and Loving It '95
Home for the Holidays '95
How to Make an American Quilt '95
Oldest Confederate Widow Tells All '95
Homecoming '96

Bradford Bancroft
Damned River '89
A Time to Die '91

Cameron Bancroft
Just One of the Girls '93
Love and Human Remains '93

George Bancroft
The Pony Express '25
Old Ironsides '26
Underworld '27
Docks of New York '28
White Gold '28
Hell-Ship Morgan '36
Mr. Deeds Goes to Town '36
Angels with Dirty Faces '38
Each Dawn I Die '39
Stagecoach '39
Little Men '40
Young Tom Edison '40
Texas '41
Whistling in Dixie '42

Antonio Banderas
Labyrinth of Passion '82
Law of Desire '86
Matador '86
Women on the Verge of a Nervous Breakdown '88
Against the Wind '90
Tie Me Up! Tie Me Down! '90
The Mambo Kings '92
The House of the Spirits '93
Outrage '93
Philadelphia '93
Interview with the Vampire '94
Of Love and Shadows '94
Assassins '95
Desperado '95
Four Rooms '95
Miami Rhapsody '95
Never Talk to Strangers '95
Two Much '96

Kanu Banerjee
Pather Panchali '54
Aparajito '58

Karuna Banerjee
Pather Panchali '54
Aparajito '58

Victor Banerjee
Hullabaloo Over Georgie & Bonnie's Pictures '78
The Home and the World '84
A Passage to India '84
Foreign Body '86
Bitter Moon '92

Lisa Banes
Look Back in Anger '80
The Hotel New Hampshire '84
Marie '85
Cocktail '88

Joy Bang
Night of the Cobra Woman '72
Play It Again, Sam '72
Messiah of Evil '74

Tallulah Bankhead
Stage Door Canteen '43
Lifeboat '44
Die! Die! My Darling! '65

Aaron Banks
The Bodyguard '76
Fist of Fear, Touch of Death '77

Jonathan Banks
Beverly Hills Cop '84
Nadia '84
Armed and Dangerous '86
Assassin '86
Cold Steel '87
Freejack '92
There Goes the Neighborhood '92
Boiling Point '93
Marilyn & Bobby: Her Final Affair '94
Walker: Texas Ranger: Deadly Reunion '94
Last Man Standing '95
Flipper '96

Leslie Banks
The Most Dangerous Game '32
The Man Who Knew Too Much '34
Sanders of the River '35
Transatlantic Tunnel '35
Fire Over England '37
21 Days '37
The Arsenal Stadium Mystery '39
Jamaica Inn '39
Chamber of Horrors '40
Cottage to Let '41
Henry V '44
Eye Witness '49
Madeleine '50

Vilma Banky
The Eagle '25
Blood and Sand/Son of the Sheik '26
Son of the Sheik '26

Ian Bannen
The Third Key '57
A Tale of Two Cities '58
Carlton Browne of the F.O. '59
The Flight of the Phoenix '65
Too Late the Hero '70
Fright '71
Ride to Glory '71
Doomwatch '72
Driver's Seat '73
From Beyond the Grave '73
Mackintosh Man '73
The Offence '73
The Gathering Storm '74
Bite the Bullet '75
Eye of the Needle '81
The Watcher in the Woods '81
The Prodigal '83
Defense of the Realm '85
Lamb '85
Hope and Glory '87
The Courier '88
The Fifteen Streets '90
Ghost Dad '90
The Big Man: Crossing the Line '91
George's Island '91
Blue Ice '92
Damage '92
The Sound and the Silence '93

John Banner
The Fallen Sparrow '43
Guilty of Treason '50
Togetherness '70

Reggie Bannister
Phantasm '79
Phantasm II '88
Survival Quest '89
Silent Night, Deadly Night 4: Initiation '90
Phantasm III: Lord of the Dead '94

Jack Bannon
Take Your Best Shot '82
Miracle of the Heart: A Boys Town Story '86
DaVinci's War '92

Jim Bannon
Man from Colorado '49
The Fighting Redhead '50
Unknown World '51

Ildiko Bansagi
Mephisto '81
Meeting Venus '91

Li Bao-Tian
Ju Dou '90
Shanghai Triad '95

Nina Bara
Black Hills '48
Missile to the Moon '59

Theda Bara
A Fool There Was '14
The Unchastened Woman '25
The Love Goddesses '65

John Baragrey
Pardners '56
Gamera, the Invincible '66

Christine Baranski
Crackers '84
9 1/2 Weeks '86
Reversal of Fortune '90
Addams Family Values '93
The Night We Never Met '93
The Ref '93
To Dance with the White Dog '93
The War '94
The Birdcage '95

Olivia Barash
Child of Glass '78
Repo Man '83
Tuff Turf '85
Dr. Alien '88
Grave Secrets '89

Richie Barathy
Caged Fury '90
Body Trouble '92

Luca Barbareschi
Bye Bye Baby '88
Private Affairs '89

Adrienne Barbeau
Red Alert '77
Return to Fantasy Island '77
The Crash of Flight 401 '78
The Fog '78
Magic on Love Island '80
Cannonball Run '81
Escape from New York '81
Charlie and the Great Balloon Chase '82
Creepshow '82
Swamp Thing '82
Next One '84
Seduced '85
Terror at London Bridge '85
Back to School '86
Open House '86
Cannibal Women in the Avocado Jungle of Death '89
Two Evil Eyes '90
Double-Crossed '91
Scott Turow's The Burden of Proof '92
Silk Degrees '94
Burial of the Rats '95

Ellen Barber
The Premonition '75
Born Beautiful '82
Blood Bride

Frances Barber
Home Sweet Home '82
Pete Townshend: White City '85
Castaway '87
Prick Up Your Ears '87
Sammy & Rosie Get Laid '87
We Think the World of You '88
A Zed & Two Noughts '88

Glynis Barber
Yesterday's Hero '79
The Wicked Lady '83
Edge of Sanity '89

Katie Barberi
The Garbage Pail Kids Movie '87
Not Quite Human 2 '89

Urbano Barberini
Demons '86
Outlaw of Gor '87
Gor '88
Terror at the Opera '88
Torrents of Spring '90

George Barbier
The Merry Widow '34
The Crusades '35
The Princess Comes Across '36
Wife Versus Secretary '36
On the Avenue '37
Waikiki Wedding '37
The Adventures of Marco Polo '38
Little Miss Broadway '38
My Lucky Star '38
The Man Who Came to Dinner '41
Week-End In Havana '41

Paula Barbieri
The Dangerous '95
Night Eyes 4: Fatal Passion '95
Red Shoe Diaries 5: Weekend Pass '95

Don Barclay
Border Phantom '37
Sweetheart of the Navy '37
Outlaw Express '38
Thunder in the Desert '38

Joan Barclay
Finishing School '33
Feud of the West '35
Blake of Scotland Yard '36
The Glory Trail '36
Phantom Patrol '36
Prison Shadows '36
Shadow of Chinatown '36
West of Nevada '36
Lightnin' Carson Rides Again '38
Whirlwind Horseman '38
Outlaw's Paradise '39
Flying Wild '41
The Black Dragons '42
The Corpse Vanishes '42
Sagebrush Law '43
The Shanghai Cobra '45

Roy Barcroft
The Frontiersmen '38
Hopalong Cassidy: Renegade Trail '39
Renegade Trail '39
Don Amigo/Stage to Chino '40s
The Showdown '40
Below the Border '42
Dawn on the Great Divide '42
Sunset on the Desert '42
Calling Wild Bill Elliott '43
Hoppy Serves a Writ '43
Raiders of Sunset Pass '43
Sagebrush Law '43
Six Gun Gospel '43
Haunted Harbor '44
Bells of Rosarita '45
D-Day on Mars '45
Manhunt of Mystery Island '45
The Purple Monster Strikes '45
Sunset in El Dorado '45
The Topeka Terror '45
Stagecoach to Denver '46
Vigilantes of Boom Town '46
Jesse James Rides Again '47
Son of Zorro '47
Eyes of Texas '48
G-Men Never Forget '48
Arizona Cowboy '49
Down Dakota Way '49
Federal Agents vs. Underworld, Inc. '49
North of the Great Divide '50
The Vanishing Westerner '50
Don Daredevil Rides Again '51
Hoodlum Empire '52
Radar Men from the Moon '52
Marshal of Cedar Rock '53
The Last Hunt '56
The Kettles on Old MacDonald's Farm '57
Billy the Kid Versus Dracula '66

Javier Bardem
Jamon, Jamon '93
Mouth to Mouth '95

Trevor Bardette
Doomed Caravan '41
The Secret Code '42
Gun Crazy '49
Omoo Omoo, the Shark God '49
Hills of Oklahoma '50
The Monolith Monsters '57
Thunder Road '58

Aleksander Bardini
No End '84
The Double Life of Veronique '91

The Silent Touch '94

Brigitte Bardot
Crazy for Love '52
Les Grandes Manoeuvres '55
Doctor at Sea '56
Helen of Troy '56
And God Created Woman '57
Mademoiselle Striptease '57
The Bride Is Much Too Beautiful '58
That Naughty Girl '58
Voulez-Vous Danser Avec Moi? '59
Le Repos du Guerrier '62
A Very Private Affair '62
Contempt '64
Ravishing Idiot '64
Dear Brigitte '65
Viva Maria! '65
A Coeur Joie '67
Head Over Heels '67
Shalako '68
Spirits of the Dead '68
Legend of Frenchie King '71

Edda Barends
Question of Silence '83
Broken Mirrors '85

Lynn Bari
Kit Carson '40
Sun Valley Serenade '41
The Magnificent Dope '42
Orchestra Wives '42
Hello, Frisco, Hello '43
The Bridge of San Luis Rey '44
Nocturne '46
Shock! '46
The Amazing Mr. X '48
I'd Climb the Highest Mountain '51
I Dream of Jeannie '52
Abbott and Costello Meet the Keystone Kops '54
Francis Joins the WACs '54
Trauma '62

Sophie Barjae
Holiday Hotel '77
Alice '86

Jess Barker
Dragonfly Squadron '54
Kentucky Rifle '55

Lex Barker
The Farmer's Daughter '47
Mr. Blandings Builds His Dream House '48
Velvet Touch '48
The Black Devils of Kali '55
Away All Boats '56
Girl in Black Stockings '57
Strange Awakening '58
Mission in Morocco '59
La Dolce Vita '60
Pirates of the Coast '61
The Return of Dr. Mabuse '61
The Invisible Dr. Mabuse '62
Executioner of Venice '63
Apaches Last Battle '64
A Place Called Glory '66
Woman Times Seven '67
The Torture Chamber of Dr. Sadism '69

Ronnie Barker
The Man Outside '68
The Best of the Two Ronnies '70s
Robin and Marian '76
Open All Hours '83
Porridge '91

Steve Barkett
Aftermath '85
Dark Universe '93
Dinosaur Island '93
Bikini Drive-In '94

Ellen Barkin
Kent State '81
Diner '82
Daniel '83
Eddie and the Cruisers '83
Enormous Changes '83
Tender Mercies '83
Trumps '83
The Adventures of Buckaroo Banzai Across the Eighth Dimension '84
Harry & Son '84
The Princess Who Never Laughed '84

Terminal Choice '85
Act of Vengeance '86
Desert Bloom '86
Down by Law '86
The Big Easy '87
Siesta '87
Blood Money: The Story of Clinton and Nadine '88
Johnny Handsome '89
Sea of Love '89
Switch '91
Into the West '92
Man Trouble '92
Mac '93
This Boy's Life '93
Bad Company '94
Wild Bill '95
The Fan '96

Peter Barkworth
The Littlest Horse Thieves '76
Champions '84

Binnie Barnes
The Private Life of Henry VIII '33
Private Life of Don Juan '34
The Last of the Mohicans '36
Three Smart Girls '36
Broadway Melody of 1938 '37
The Adventures of Marco Polo '38
The Divorce of Lady X '38
Holiday '38
The Three Musketeers '39
Melody Master '41
Call Out the Marines '42
I Married an Angel '42
In Old California '42
It's in the Bag '45
The Spanish Main '45
The Time of Their Lives '46
Decameron Nights '53
The Trouble with Angels '66
Where Angels Go, Trouble Follows '68
Forty Carats '73

Christopher Barnes
Tut & Tuttle '82
Battle of the Bullies '85
Angel of Fury '93

Christopher Daniel Barnes
Murder without Motive '92
The Brady Bunch Movie '95
A Very Brady Sequel '96

Joanna Barnes
Spartacus '60
The War Wagon '67
I Wonder Who's Killing Her Now? '76
Kill My Wife...Please!

Priscilla Barnes
Beyond Reason '77
Delta Fox '77
Texas Detour '77
The Seniors '78
Time Machine '78
The Last Married Couple in America '80
Traxx '87
License to Kill '89
Lords of the Deep '89
Body Trouble '92
Stepfather 3: Father's Day '92
Talons of the Eagle '92
Ava's Magical Adventure '94
The Crossing Guard '94
National Lampoon's Attack of the 5 Ft. 2 Women '94
Mallrats '95

Charlie Barnett
D.C. Cab '84
My Man Adam '86
They Bite '95

Chester Barnett
The Wishing Ring '14
Trilby '17

Vince Barnett
The Death Kiss '33
The Prizefighter and the Lady '33
Crimson Romance '34
East Side Kids/The Lost City '35
I Live My Life '35
Yellow Cargo '36
Boots of Destiny '37
We're in the Legion Now '37
The Singing Cowgirl '39
Gangs, Inc. '41

Ride 'Em Cowgirl '41
Baby Face Morgan '42
The Corpse Vanishes '42
I Killed That Man '42
X Marks the Spot '42
Captive Wild Woman '43
Shoot to Kill '47
Thunder in the Pines '49
Red Planet Mars '52
Charade '53

Jean Marie Barnwell
Blue River '95
Born to Be Wild '95
From the Mixed-Up Files of Mrs. Basil E. Frankweiler '95

Bruce Baron
Ninja Destroyer '70s
Fireback '78
Challenge the Ninja '80s
Ninja Champion '80s
Ninja Hunt '80s

Joannne Baron
Crazy in Love '92
Pet Shop '94

Sandy Baron
If It's Tuesday, This Must Be Belgium '69
The Out-of-Towners '70
Birdy '84
Broadway Danny Rose '84
Motorama '91
Leprechaun 2 '94

Elizabeth Barondes
Full Body Massage '95
Night of the Scarecrow '95

Byron Barr
Double Indemnity '44
Big Town '47
Pitfall '48
Down Dakota Way '49

Jean-Marc Barr
Hope and Glory '87
The Big Blue '88
The Plague '92
Zentropa '92
The Favorite Son '94
Breaking the Waves '95

Patrick Barr
Sailing Along '38
The Case of the Frightened Lady '39
Flesh and Blood Show '73
The Satanic Rites of Dracula '73
House of Whipcord '75
The Godsend '79

Sharon Barr
Archer: The Fugitive from the Empire '81
Spittin' Image '83
The Reluctant Agent '95

Maria Barranco
Women on the Verge of a Nervous Breakdown '88
Don Juan, My Love '90
Tie Me Up! Tie Me Down! '90
Mouth to Mouth '95

Robert Barrat
Heroes for Sale '33
Devil Dogs of the Air '35
Mary of Scotland '36
Shadows Over Shanghai '38
The Texans '38
Bad Lands '39
Union Pacific '39
Captain Caution '40
Northwest Passage '40
The Adventures of Mark Twain '44
Strangler of the Swamp '46
Distant Drums '51

Jean-Louis Barrault
Beethoven '36
Children of Paradise '44
La Ronde '51
The Testament of Dr. Cordelier '59
The Longest Day '62
La Nuit de Varennes '82

Marie-Christine Barrault
My Night at Maud's '69
Chloe in the Afternoon '72
The Daydreamer '75
Cousin, Cousine '76

L'Etat Sauvage '78
The Medusa Touch '78
Stardust Memories '80
Table for Five '83
Swann in Love '84
Jesus of Montreal '89

Edith Barrett
Lady for a Night '42
I Walked with a Zombie '43
Jane Eyre '44

Jane Barrett
Eureka Stockade '49
The Sword & the Rose '53

John Barrett
Lights! Camera! Murder! '89
American Kickboxer 1 '91
To the Death '93

Judith Barrett
Yellowstone '36
The Road to Singapore '40

Majel Barrett
Star Trek: The Cage '65
Westworld '73
Mommy '95

Nancy Barrett
House of Dark Shadows '70
Night of Dark Shadows '71
Belizaire the Cajun '86

Nitchie Barrett
Preppies '82
A Time to Die '91

Ray Barrett
Revenge '71
Waterfront '83
Where the Green Ants Dream '84
Rebel '85
Sorrento Beach '95

Barbara Barrie
Child of Glass '78
The Bell Jar '79
Breaking Away '79
Private Benjamin '80
To Race the Wind '80
Two of a Kind '82
The Execution '85
Real Men '87
End of the Line '88
Scarlett '94

Judith Barrie
Party Girls '29
Hidden Gold '33

Mona Barrie
One Night of Love '34
Dawn on the Great Divide '42
Today I Hang '42
Cass Timberlane '47

Wendy Barrie
Wedding Rehearsal '32
If I Were Rich '33
The Private Life of Henry VIII '33
Dead End '37
Vengeance '37
I Am the Law '38
Five Came Back '39
The Hound of the Baskervilles '39
The Saint Strikes Back '39
The Saint Takes Over '40
Follies Girl '43
The Saint Strikes Back: Criminal Court '46

Edgar Barrier
Arabian Nights '42
The Phantom of the Opera '43
Cobra Woman '44
The Giant Claw '57

Pat Barringer
Orgy of the Dead '65
The Acid Eaters '67

Phyliss Barrington
The Drifter '32
Sucker Money '34

Bob Barron
Guns of the Law '44
Song of Old Wyoming '45
The Caravan Trail '46
Sea Hound '47
Tank Commando '59
Ballad of a Gunfighter '64

Keith Barron
Baby Love '69
Nothing But the Night '72
At the Earth's Core '76
Con Man '92

Bruce Barry
Plunge Into Darkness '77
The Good Wife '86

Donald (Don "Red") Barry
Sinners in Paradise '38
Panama Patrol '39
Saga of Death Valley '39
Wyoming Outlaw '39
Western Double Feature 9: LaRue & Beery '40s
Adventures of Red Ryder '40
Frontier Vengeance '40
The Sombrero Kid '42
Sundown Fury '42
California Joe '43
Sundown Kid '43
The Purple Heart '44
Trail of the Mounties '47
Outlaw Gang '49
Ringside '49
Tough Assignment '49
Border Rangers '50
Gunfire '50
I Shot Billy the Kid '50
Red Desert '50
Train to Tombstone '50
Western Double Feature 15 '50
Square Dance Jubilee '51
Born Reckless '59
Iron Angel '64
The Shakiest Gun in the West '68
Hard Frame '70
Blazing Stewardesses '75
Texas Layover '75

Gene Barry
The Atomic City '52
The War of the Worlds '53
Red Garters '54
Soldier of Fortune '55
Back from Eternity '56
China Gate '57
The 27 Day '57
Thunder Road '58
Columbo: Prescription Murder '67
Maroc 7 '67
Subterfuge '68
A Cry for Love '80
Second Coming of Suzanne '80
Suzanne '80
The Adventures of Nellie Bly '81
Perry Mason: The Case of the Lost Love '87
The Gambler Returns: The Luck of the Draw '93

Leon Barry
The Three Musketeers '21
King of the Wild Horses '24

Neill Barry
Old Enough '84
Joey '85
O.C. and Stiggs '87

Patricia Barry
Sammy, the Way-Out Seal '62
Bogie: The Last Hero '80
Twilight Zone: The Movie '83

Phyllis Barry
What! No Beer? '33
Goodbye Love '34

Raymond J. Barry
Year of the Dragon '85
Daddy's Boys '87
Cop '88
Born on the Fourth of July '89
K2: The Ultimate High '92
Rapid Fire '92
Cool Runnings '93
Falling Down '93
Dead Man Walking '95
Sudden Death '95
Headless Body in Topless Bar '96

Tony Barry
Little Boy Lost '78
Hard Knocks '80
Goodbye Pork Pie '81
We of the Never Never '82
The Quest '86
Shame '87

Wesley Barry
The Country Kid '23
Battling Bunyon '24
Sunny Skies '30

Deborah Barrymore
Lionheart '87

Bullseye! '90

Drew Barrymore
Altered States '80
E.T.: The Extra-Terrestrial '82
Firestarter '84
Irreconcilable Differences '84
Cat's Eye '85
Babes in Toyland '86
Strange Tales/Ray Bradbury Theatre '86
A Conspiracy of Love '87
Far from Home '89
See You in the Morning '89
Doppelganger: The Evil Within '90
Motorama '91
Guncrazy '92
Poison Ivy '92
Sketch Artist '92
The Amy Fisher Story '93
No Place to Hide '93
Wayne's World 2 '93
Bad Girls '94
Boys on the Side '94
Batman Forever '95
Mad Love '95

Ethel Barrymore
Rasputin and the Empress '32
None But the Lonely Heart '44
The Spiral Staircase '46
The Farmer's Daughter '47
The Paradine Case '47
Moonrise '48
Portrait of Jennie '48
Pinky '49
That Midnight Kiss '49
Just for You '52
Young at Heart '54

John Barrymore
Dr. Jekyll and Mr. Hyde '20
Beau Brummel '24
Don Juan '26
The Beloved Rogue '27
The Tempest/The Eagle '27
The Tempest '28
State's Attorney '31
Svengali '31
A Bill of Divorcement '32
Grand Hotel '32
Rasputin and the Empress '32
Dinner at Eight '33
Topaze '33
Twentieth Century '34
Romeo and Juliet '36
Bulldog Drummond Comes Back '37
Bulldog Drummond's Revenge '37
Maytime '37
Bulldog Drummond's Peril '38
Bulldog Drummond's Revenge/ Bulldog Drummond's Peril '38
The Great Man Votes '38
Marie Antoinette '38
Midnight '39
The Invisible Woman '40
Playmates '41
The Horror of It All '91

John Blythe Barrymore, Jr.
High Lonesome '50
High School Confidential '58
Never Love a Stranger '58
A Game of Crime '60
Americana '81
Smokey Bites the Dust '81

Lionel Barrymore
America/The Fall of Babylon '24
Sadie Thompson '28
West of Zanzibar '28
A Free Soul '31
Grand Hotel '32
Mata Hari '32
Rasputin and the Empress '32
Dinner at Eight '33
The Girl from Missouri '34
Treasure Island '34
Ah, Wilderness! '35
David Copperfield '35
The Little Colonel '35
Mark of the Vampire '35
The Return of Peter Grimm '35
Camille '36
Devil Doll '36
The Gorgeous Hussy '36
Captains Courageous '37
Navy Blue and Gold '37

Saratoga '37
Test Pilot '38
You Can't Take It with You '38
Let Freedom Ring '39
On Borrowed Time '39
Dr. Kildare's Strange Case '40
Lady Be Good '41
Thousands Cheer '43
A Guy Named Joe '44
Since You Went Away '44
The Valley of Decision '45
Duel in the Sun '46
It's a Wonderful Life '46
Key Largo '48
Malaya '49
Lone Star '52

Paul Bartel
Hollywood Boulevard '76
Piranha '78
Rock 'n' Roll High School '79
Eating Raoul '82
Frankenweenie '84
Chopping Mall '86
Killer Party '86
Amazon Women on the Moon '87
Out of the Dark '88
Far Out Man '89
Pucker Up and Bark Like a Dog '89
Scenes from the Class Struggle in Beverly Hills '89
Mortuary Academy '91
The Pope Must Diet '91
Desire and Hell at Sunset Motel '92
Liquid Dreams '92
Number One Fan '94
The Jerky Boys '95
The Usual Suspects '95

Eddie Barth
Thunder and Lightning '77
Twenty Dollar Star '91
Mr. Write '92

Richard Barthelmess
Broken Blossoms '19
The Idol Dancer '20
The Love Flower '20
Way Down East '20
Tol'able David '21
Shore Leave '25
Soul-Fire '25
Just Suppose '26
Ranson's Folly '26
The Dropkick '27
The Cabin in the Cotton '32
Heroes for Sale '33
Spy of Napoleon '36
Only Angels Have Wings '39
The Spoilers '42

Freddie Bartholomew
Anna Karenina '35
David Copperfield '35
Little Lord Fauntleroy '36
Lloyds of London '36
Captains Courageous '37
Listen, Darling '38
Tom Brown's School Days '40
Sepia Cinderella '47
St. Benny the Dip '51

Bennie Bartlett
Master Minds '49
Clipped Wings '53
Bowery Boys Meet the Monsters '54

Bonnie Bartlett
Rape and Marriage: The Rideout Case '80
A Long Way Home '81
Dempsey '83
Love Letters '83
The Deliberate Stranger '86
Twins '88
Dave '93
Dead to Rights '93

Robin Bartlett
Baby Boom '87
Lean on Me '89
Alice '90
Deceived '91
If Looks Could Kill '91
Regarding Henry '91
Fallen Angels 1 '93
Dangerous Minds '95

Eva Bartok
Crimson Pirate '52

Norman Conquest '53
Spaceways '53
The Gamma People '56
Naked in the Night '58
Operation Amsterdam '60
S.O.S. Pacific '60
Blood and Black Lace '64

Luciano Bartoli
Henry IV '85
Bizarre '87

Buzz Barton
Apache Kid's Escape '30
The Lone Defender '32
Mystery Trooper '32
Feud of the West '35
Powdersmoke Range '35
The Tonto Kid '35
The Riding Avenger '36

Diana Barton
Body of Influence '93
Sexual Malice '93

Gregg Barton
West to Glory '47
Silver City Bonanza '51

James Barton
The Time of Your Life '48
Here Comes the Groom '51
Naked Hills '56
The Misfits '61

Peter Barton
Hell Night '81
Friday the 13th, Part 4: The Final Chapter '84

Billy Barty
A Midsummer Night's Dream '35
Mickey the Great '39
Roustabout '64
Harum Scarum '65
The Day of the Locust '75
The Amazing Dobermans '76
Foul Play '78
Under the Rainbow '81
Night Patrol '85
Legend '86
Rumpelstiltskin '86
Tough Guys '86
Body Slam '87
Masters of the Universe '87
Willow '88
Lobster Man from Mars '89
Snow White '89
Digging Up Business '91
Life Stinks '91
Wishful Thinking '92
Ace Crawford, Private Eye

Mikhail Baryshnikov
The Turning Point '77
That's Dancing! '85
White Nights '85
Dancers '87
Company Business '91

Gary Basaraba
One Magic Christmas '85
Fried Green Tomatoes '91
Midnight Murders '91
The War '94
A Horse for Danny '95

Richard Basehart
Cry Wolf '47
He Walked by Night '48
Reign of Terror '49
Titanic '53
La Strada '54
The Swindle '55
Moby Dick '56
The Brothers Karamazov '58
Hitler '62
Hans Brinker '69
The Andersonville Trial '70
Chato's Land '71
The Bounty Man '72
Rage '72
Flood! '76
Island of Dr. Moreau '77
Great Bank Hoax '78
Being There '79
The Rebels '79
Marilyn: The Untold Story '80

Count Basie
Cinderfella '60
Sex and the Single Girl '64

Toni Basil
Pajama Party '64
Easy Rider '69
Mother, Jugs and Speed '76

Waiting to Exhale '95
A Family Thing '96

Stephanie Beacham
The Nightcomers '72
And Now the Screaming Starts '73
The Confessional '75
Horror Planet '80
Super Bitch '89
Troop Beverly Hills '89
The Dying Truth '91
Foreign Affairs '93

John Beal
Little Minister '34
Break of Hearts '35
Les Miserables '35
Double Wedding '37
Madame X '37
I Am the Law '38
The Great Commandment '41
Edge of Darkness '43
Ten Who Dared '60
Amityville 3: The Demon '83
The Kid Who Loved Christmas '90
The Firm '93

Jennifer Beals
Flashdance '83
Cinderella '84
The Bride '85
That's Dancing! '85
The Gamble '88
Split Decisions '88
Vampire's Kiss '88
Club Extinction '89
Blood & Concrete: A Love Story '90
In the Soup '92
Indecency '92
Day of Atonement '93
Terror Stalks the Class Reunion '93
Dead on Sight '94
Mrs. Parker and the Vicious Circle '94
Devil In a Blue Dress '95
Four Rooms '95

Lee Ann Beaman
Tropical Heat '93
Improper Conduct '94

Orson Bean
Anatomy of a Murder '59
Lola '69
Movie Maker '86
Innerspace '87
Instant Karma '90
Final Judgement '92

Robert Bean
Creature from the Haunted Sea '60
The Wild Ride '60

Sean Bean
Caravaggio '86
Stormy Monday '88
The Field '90
The Fifteen Streets '90
Lorna Doone '90
Patriot Games '92
Sharpe's Eagle '93
Sharpe's Rifles '93
A Woman's Guide to Adultery '93
Black Beauty '94
Jacob '94
Scarlett '94
Sharpe's Battle '94
Sharpe's Company '94
Sharpe's Enemy '94
Sharpe's Gold '94
Sharpe's Honour '94
Sharpe's Sword '94
Goldeneye '95

Matthew "Stymie" Beard
Little Rascals, Vol. 1 '29
Little Rascals, Book 1 '30s
Two-Gun Man from Harlem '38
Broken Strings '40
Little Rascals Christmas Special '79
East of Eden '80

Amanda Bearse
Protocol '84
Fraternity Vacation '85
Fright Night '85
It's a Bundyful Life '92

Emmanuelle Beart
Date with an Angel '87
Manon of the Spring '87
La Belle Noiseuse '90
L'Enfer '93
Un Coeur en Hiver '93
Nelly et Monsieur Arnaud '95
Mission: Impossible '96

Allyce Beasley
Moonlighting '85
Silent Night, Deadly Night 4: Initiation '90
Motorama '91
Stephen King's The Tommyknockers '93

Norman Beaton
Growing Pains '82
Playing Away '87
The Mighty Quinn '89

Clyde Beatty
The Lost Jungle '34
Darkest Africa '36
Africa Screams '49

Ned Beatty
Deliverance '72
Dying Room Only '73
The Last American Hero '73
The Thief Who Came to Dinner '73
White Lightning '73
The Execution of Private Slovik '74
Nashville '75
Sniper '75
The Big Bus '76
Mikey & Nicky '76
Network '76
Silver Streak '76
The Exorcist 2: The Heretic '77
Gray Lady Down '77
Our Town '77
Great Bank Hoax '78
A Question of Love '78
Superman: The Movie '78
Friendly Fire '79
1941 '79
Promises in the Dark '79
Wise Blood '79
All God's Children '80
The Guyana Tragedy: The Story of Jim Jones '80
Hopscotch '80
Superman 2 '80
The Incredible Shrinking Woman '81
Pray TV '82
Rumpelstiltskin '82
Touched '82
The Toy '82
A Woman Called Golda '82
Stroker Ace '83
Charlotte Forten's Mission: Experiment in Freedom '85
Back to School '86
The Big Easy '87
The Fourth Protocol '87
Midnight Crossing '87
Rolling Vengeance '87
The Trouble with Spies '87
Purple People Eater '88
Shadows in the Storm '88
Switching Channels '88
Time Trackers '88
The Unholy '88
Captain America '89
Chattahoochee '89
Ministry of Vengeance '89
Physical Evidence '89
Spy '89
The Haunting of Barney Palmer '90s
Konrad '90s
Back to Hannibal: The Return of Tom Sawyer and Huckleberry Finn '90
Big Bad John '90
A Cry in the Wild '90
Repossessed '90
Robert Kennedy and His Times '90
Blind Vision '91
Going Under '91
Hear My Song '91
Illusions '91
Tragedy of Flight 103: The Inside Story '91
Angel Square '92
Prelude to a Kiss '92
Ed and His Dead Mother '93
Rudy '93
Black Water '94
Just Cause '94
Radioland Murders '94
Replikator: Cloned to Kill '94
The Affair '95
Gulliver's Travels '95
Larry McMurtry's Streets of Laredo '95

Robert Beatty
Appointment with Crime '45
San Demetrio, London '47
Against the Wind '48
Counterblast '48
Captain Horatio Hornblower '51
Wings of Danger '52
The Love of Three Queens '54
Postmark for Danger '56
Postmark for Danger/Quicksand '56
Time Lock '57
Where Eagles Dare '68

Warren Beatty
Roman Spring of Mrs. Stone '61
Splendor in the Grass '61
All Fall Down '62
Lilith '64
Mickey One '65
Promise Her Anything '66
Bonnie & Clyde '67
Dollars '71
McCabe & Mrs. Miller '71
The Parallax View '74
Shampoo '75
Heaven Can Wait '78
Reds '81
Ishtar '87
Dick Tracy '90
Bugsy '91
Love Affair '94

Michelle Beaudoin
Live Bait '95
Sabrina the Teenage Witch '96

Hugh Beaumont
Panama Menace '41
To the Shores of Tripoli '42
The Fallen Sparrow '43
The Seventh Victim '43
The Lady Confesses '45
Objective, Burma! '45
The Blue Dahlia '46
Money Madness '47
Railroaded '47
Cavalry Charge '51
Danger Zone '51
The Lost Continent '51
Pier 23 '51
Roaring City '51
Phone Call from a Stranger '52
The Mole People '56
The Human Duplicators '64

Lucy Beaumont
The Crowd '28
A Free Soul '31
Condemned to Live '35

Nicholas Beauvy
Rage '72
The Toolbox Murders '78

Jim Beaver
In Country '89
Twogether '94

Terry Beaver
Impure Thoughts '86
To Dance with the White Dog '93

Louise Beavers
Coquette '29
She Done Him Wrong '33
In the Money '34
General Spanky '36
Bullets or Ballots '38
Big Street '42
Reap the Wild Wind '42
DuBarry Was a Lady '43
Dixie Jamboree '44
Delightfully Dangerous '45
Mr. Blandings Builds His Dream House '48
Tell It to the Judge '49
The Jackie Robinson Story '50
Goodbye, My Lady '56
Tammy and the Bachelor '57

Jennifer Beck
Tightrope '84
Gypsy '93

John Beck
Three in the Attic '68
Lawman '71
Paperback Hero '73
Sleeper '73
Rollerball '75
The Big Bus '76
Sky Riders '76
Audrey Rose '77
The Other Side of Midnight '77
Time Machine '78
Great American Traffic Jam '80
Deadly Illusion '87
Fire and Rain '89
In the Cold of the Night '89
A Climate for Killing '91
Honor Thy Father and Mother: The True Story of the Menendez Brothers '94
Last Time Out '94
Suspect Device '95

Julian Beck
Oedipus Rex '67
Emergency '68
Signals Through the Flames '83
Poltergeist 2: The Other Side '86

Kimberly Beck
Massacre at Central High '76
Roller Boogie '79
Friday the 13th, Part 4: The Final Chapter '84
Nightmare at Noon '87
Private War '90
In the Deep Woods '91

Michael Beck
Holocaust '78
Madman '79
The Warriors '79
Xanadu '80
Megaforce '82
Warlords of the 21st Century '82
The Golden Seal '83
Blackout '85
Celebrity '85
Deadly Game '91
Fade to Black '93

Thomas Beck
Charlie Chan in Paris '35
Charlie Chan at the Opera '36

Graham Beckel
The Paper Chase '73
Hazel's People '75
The Money '75
Lost Angels '89
Rising Son '90
O Pioneers! '91
Separate But Equal '91
Jennifer 8 '92

Gerry Becker
Legacy of Lies '92
The Public Eye '92
Eraser '96

Gretchen Becker
Firehead '90
Huck and the King of Hearts '93
Maniac Cop 3: Badge of Silence '93

Hartmut Becker
Jenny's War '85
Escape from Sobibor '87

Scotty Beckett
Stand Up and Cheer '34
I Dream Too Much '35
Anthony Adverse '36
The Charge of the Light Brigade '36
Conquest '37
Devil's Party '38
Listen, Darling '38
Marie Antoinette '38
Love Affair '39
My Favorite Wife '40
Kings Row '41
Ali Baba and the Forty Thieves '43
Heaven Can Wait '43
The Jolson Story '46
Battleground '49
Nancy Goes to Rio '50
Rocky Jones, Space Ranger '54
The Oklahoman '56

Kate Beckinsale
One Against the Wind '91
Much Ado about Nothing '93
Cold Comfort Farm '94

Haunted '95

Tony Beckley
The Italian Job '69
Assault '70
The Fiend '71

Henry Beckman
Family Reunion '88
The Man Upstairs '93

Reginald Beckwith
Men of Sherwood Forest '57
Burn Witch, Burn! '62

William Beckwith
Escape from Safehaven '88
Prime Evil '88

Irene Bedard
Lakota Woman: Siege at Wounded Knee '94
Squanto: A Warrior's Tale '94

Don Beddoe
Golden Boy '39
Buck Privates Come Home '47
Welcome Stranger '47
The Enforcer '51
The Narrow Margin '52
The Night of the Hunter '55
Jack the Giant Killer '62
Nickel Mountain '85

Bonnie Bedelia
They Shoot Horses, Don't They? '69
Lovers and Other Strangers '70
The Big Fix '78
A Question of Love '78
Salem's Lot '79
Walking Through the Fire '80
Heart Like a Wheel '83
Memorial Day '83
Lady from Yesterday '85
The Boy Who Could Fly '86
Death of an Angel '86
Violets Are Blue '86
The Stranger '87
Die Hard '88
Prince of Pennsylvania '88
Fat Man and Little Boy '89
Die Hard 2: Die Harder '90
Presumed Innocent '90
Somebody Has to Shoot the Picture '90
Switched at Birth '91
When the Time Comes '91
Fallen Angels 2 '93
The Fire Next Time '93
Needful Things '93
Judicial Consent '94
Speechless '94
Homecoming '96

Barbara Bedford
The Last of the Mohicans '20
The Mad Whirl '25
Tumbleweeds '25
Mockery '27
The Notorious Lady '27
The Broken Mask '28
Found Alive '34

Brian Bedford
Grand Prix '66
The Last Best Year '90
Scarlett '94
Nixon '95

Kabir Bedi
Archer: The Fugitive from the Empire '81
Demon Rage '82
Octopussy '83
Terminal Entry '87
The Beast '88
Lie Down with Lions '94

Guy Bedos
Pardon Mon Affaire '76
Pardon Mon Affaire, Too! '77

Alfonso Bedoya
Treasure of the Sierra Madre '48
The Stranger Wore a Gun '53

Janet Beecher
I'd Give My Life '36
The Mark of Zorro '40

David Beecroft
Shadowzone '89
The Rain Killer '90

Daniel Beer
Creepshow 2 '87
Point Break '91
Talking About Sex '94

Noah Beery, Sr.
A Mormon Maid '17
Mark of Zorro '20
Soul of the Beast '23
The Coming of Amos '25
Vanishing American '26
Linda '29
The Big Stampede '32
Cornered '32
Devil Horse '32
The Drifter '32
Buffalo Stampede '33
Fighting with Kit Carson '33
Flaming Signal '33
Man of the Forest '33
She Done Him Wrong '33
To the Last Man '33
Kentucky Kernels '34
Mystery Liner '34
Trail Beyond '34
King of the Damned '36
Zorro Rides Again '37
Panamint's Bad Man '38
Western Double Feature 9: LaRue & Beery '40s
Adventures of Red Ryder '40

Noah Beery, Jr.
Heroes of the West '32
Fighting with Kit Carson '33
Rustler's Roundup '33
Savage Fury '33
Tailspin Tommy '34
Ace Drummond '36
Bad Lands '39
Of Mice and Men '39
Only Angels Have Wings '39
Sergeant York '41
Tanks a Million '41
'Neath Brooklyn Bridge '42
The Avenging Hand '43
Gung Ho! '43
Million Dollar Kid '44
Red River '48
The Doolins of Oklahoma '49
Rocketship X-M '50
Cavalry Charge '51
The Texas Rangers '51
War Arrow '53
Fastest Gun Alive '56
Jubal '56
Great Chase '63
7 Faces of Dr. Lao '63
Richard Petty Story '72
Walking Tall '73
Savages '75
Walking Tall: Part 2 '75
Francis Gary Powers: The True Story of the U-2 Spy '76
The Bastard '78
Great American Traffic Jam '80
The Capture of Grizzly Adams '82
Mysterious Two '82

Wallace Beery
Teddy at the Throttle '16
Teddy at the Throttle/Speeding Along '17
The Last of the Mohicans '20
Charlie Chase and Ben Turpin '21
The Four Horsemen of the Apocalypse '21
Robin Hood '22
Three Ages '23
White Tiger '23
The Lost World '25
The Night Club '25
The Pony Express '25
Behind the Front '26
Old Ironsides '26
We're in the Navy Now '27
The Big House '30
Min & Bill '30
The Champ '31
Grand Hotel '32
Dinner at Eight '33
Treasure Island '34
Viva Villa! '34
Ah, Wilderness! '35
China Seas '35
A Date with Judy '48

Ed Begley, Sr.
Boomerang '47
Sorry, Wrong Number '48
The Street with No Name '48
It Happens Every Spring '49
Tulsa '49
Stars in My Crown '50
On Dangerous Ground '51
Boots Malone '52
Lone Star '52
Patterns '56
Twelve Angry Men '57
Sweet Bird of Youth '62
The Unsinkable Molly Brown '64
The Oscar '66
Hang 'Em High '67
Firecreek '68
Road to Salina '68
Wild in the Streets '68
The Dunwich Horror '70

Ed Begley, Jr.
Showdown '73
Citizens Band '77
Dead of Night '77
Blue Collar '78
Goin' South '78
Elvis: The Movie '79
The In-Laws '79
A Shining Season '79
Cat People '82
Eating Raoul '82
Get Crazy '83
Protocol '84
Streets of Fire '84
This Is Spinal Tap '84
Transylvania 6-5000 '85
The Legend of Sleepy Hollow '86
The Accidental Tourist '88
The Applegates '89
Scenes from the Class Struggle in Beverly Hills '89
She-Devil '89
The Great Los Angeles Earthquake '91
Spies, Lies and Naked Thighs '91
Dark Horse '92
Running Mates '92
Cooperstown '93
The Story Lady '93
Children of Fury '94
The Crazysitter '94
Greedy '94
Incident at Deception Ridge '94
The Pagemaster '94
Renaissance Man '94
Sensation '94
World War II: When Lions Roared '94
Hourglass '95
Rave Review '95
The Late Shift '96

Brionny Behets
Alvin Rides Again '74
Cassandra '87

Sam Behrens
American Blue Note '89
Murder by Numbers '89
And You Thought Your Parents Were Weird! '91
Alive '93

Richard Bekins
Model Behavior '82
George Washington: The Forging of a Nation '86

Barbara Bel Geddes
Blood on the Moon '48
I Remember Mama '48
Caught '49
Panic in the Streets '50
Vertigo '58
The Five Pennies '59
Summertree '71
The Todd Killings '71

Doris Belack
Opportunity Knocks '90
What About Bob? '91

Harry Belafonte
Carmen Jones '54
Island in the Sun '57
Buck and the Preacher '72
Uptown Saturday Night '74
Grambling's White Tiger '81
White Man's Burden '95

Shari Belafonte
If You Could See What I Hear '82
Overnight Sensation '83
The Midnight Hour '86
Speed Zone '88
Murder by Numbers '89
Fire, Ice and Dynamite '91
French Silk '94
The Heidi Chronicles '95

Leon Belasco
Fisherman's Wharf '39
It's a Date '40
Infamous Crimes '47
Abbott and Costello in the Foreign Legion '50
Can-Can '60

Christine Belford
The Groundstar Conspiracy '72
Pocket Money '72
Kenny Rogers as the Gambler '80

Ann Bell
The Statue '71
Champions '84

Christopher Bell
Sarah, Plain and Tall '91
Without Warning: The James Brady Story '91
Skylark '93

Darryl M. Bell
School Daze '88
Mr. Write '92

Edward Bell
The Premonition '75
Image of Passion '86

Hank Bell
Beyond the Rockies '32
The Big Stampede '32
South of Santa Fe '32
Whistlin' Dan '32
The Fiddlin' Buckaroo '33
Border Vengeance '35
Valley of the Sun '42

James Bell
The Leopard Man '43
My Friend Flicka '43
A Lawless Street '55
Teenage Crime Wave '55
Tribute to a Bad Man '56

Jeanne Bell
Policewomen '73
TNT Jackson '75
The Muthers '76
Fass Black '77

Marie Bell
Sandra of a Thousand Delights '65
Hotel Paradiso '66
Phedre '68

Marshall Bell
No Way Out '87
Johnny Be Good '88
Tucker: The Man and His Dream '88
Twins '88
Wildfire '88
Air America '90
Leather Jackets '90
Total Recall '90
The Heroes of Desert Storm '91
The Vagrant '92
Payback '94

Rex Bell
Battling with Buffalo Bill '31
Broadway to Cheyenne '32
Diamond Trail '33
Fighting Texans '33
Rainbow Ranch '33
The Tonto Kid '35
Stormy Trails '36
West of Nevada '36
Law of the Sea '38

Tobin Bell
False Identity '90
Ruby '92
The Firm '93
New Eden '94
Serial Killer '95

Tom Bell
Ballad in Blue '66
Quest for Love '71
Dressed for Death '74
Royal Flash '75
Wish You Were Here '87
Let Him Have It '91
Prospero's Books '91
Prime Suspect '92
Prime Suspect 3 '93
The Cinder Path '94
Feast of July '95

Vanessa Bell
Coming to America '88
Memphis '91

Diana Bellamy
The Nest '88
Amelia Earhart: The Final Flight '94

Madge Bellamy
Lorna Doone '22
Soul of the Beast '23
The White Sin '24
The White Zombie '32
Northwest Trail '46

Ned Bellamy
Writer's Block '91
Carnosaur '93

Ralph Bellamy
Ace of Aces '33
Spitfire '34
Woman in the Shadows '34
Hands Across the Table '35
Healer '36
The Awful Truth '37
Boy Meets Girl '38
Carefree '38
Brother Orchid '40
Dance, Girl, Dance '40
His Girl Friday '40
Dive Bomber '41
Footsteps in the Dark '41
The Wolf Man '41
The Ghost of Frankenstein '42
Delightfully Dangerous '45
Guest in the House '45
Lady On a Train '45
The Court Martial of Billy Mitchell '55
The Defender '57
Sunrise at Campobello '60
The Professionals '66
Rosemary's Baby '68
Doctors' Wives '70
Cancel My Reservation '72
Missiles of October '74
Murder on Flight 502 '75
Search for the Gods '75
The Boy in the Plastic Bubble '76
Nightmare in Badham County '76
Return to Earth '76
Oh, God! '77
Trading Places '83
The Winds of War '83
Love Leads the Way '84
Fourth Wise Man '85
Disorderlies '87
The Good Mother '88
War & Remembrance, Part 1 '88
War & Remembrance, Part 2 '89
War & Remembrance: The Final Chapter, Part 8 '89
Pretty Woman '90

Harry Bellaver
House on 92nd Street '45
The Lemon Drop Kid '51

Annie Belle
Naked Paradise '78
Forever Emmanuelle '82
House on the Edge of the Park '84

Kathleen Beller
The Godfather, Part 2 '74
Mary White '77
Are You in the House Alone? '78
The Betsy '78
Promises in the Dark '79
Mother & Daughter: A Loving War '80
Fort Apache, the Bronx '81
The Manions of America '81
No Place to Hide '81
Sword & the Sorcerer '82
Touched '82
Surfacing '84
Cloud Waltzing '87
Time Trackers '88

Agostina Belli
The Sex Machine '76
The Chosen '77

Cynthia Belliveau
A New Life '88
The Dream Team '89
The Dark '94
The Spider and the Fly '94

Sara Bellomo
Beach Babes from Beyond Infinity '93
Bikini Drive-In '94

Gil Bellows
Love and a .45 '94
The Shawshank Redemption '94
Miami Rhapsody '95
Silver Strand '95

Pamela Bellwood
Deadman's Curve '78
Hangar 18 '80
Cocaine: One Man's Seduction '83
Cellar Dweller '87
Double Standard '88

Jean-Paul Belmondo
Sois Belle et Tais-Toi '58
Breathless '59
Love and the Frenchwoman '60
A Woman is a Woman '60
Le Doulos '61
Leon Morin, Priest '61
Two Women '61
Cartouche '62
Un Singe en Hiver '62
That Man from Rio '64
Pierrot le Fou '65
Casino Royale '67
Is Paris Burning? '68
The Brain '69
Mississippi Mermaid '69
Borsalino '70
High Heels '72
Scoumoune '74
Stavisky '74
Le Magnifique '76
Stuntwoman '81
Swashbuckler '84
Les Miserables '95

Robert Beltran
Eating Raoul '82
Night of the Comet '84
Latino '85
Gaby: A True Story '87
Scenes from the Class Struggle in Beverly Hills '89
El Diablo '90
Bugsy '91
The Chase '91
Kiss Me a Killer '91
To Die Standing '91
Star Trek Voyager: Caretaker '95

Mark Beltzman
Mo' Money '92
Billy Madison '94

James Belushi
Mutant Video '76
Thief '81
Trading Places '83
Best Legs in the 8th Grade '84
Birthday Boy '85
The Man with One Red Shoe '85
About Last Night... '86
Jumpin' Jack Flash '86
Little Shop of Horrors '86
Salvador '86
The Principal '87
Real Men '87
Red Heat '88
Homer and Eddie '89
K-9 '89
Wedding Band '89
Who's Harry Crumb? '89
The Masters of Menace '90
Mr. Destiny '90
Taking Care of Business '90
Curly Sue '91
Diary of a Hitman '91
Only the Lonely '91
The Palermo Connection '91
Once Upon a Crime '92
Traces of Red '92
Royce '93
Wild Palms '93
Parallel Lives '94
Separate Lives '94
Destiny Turns on the Radio '95
Race the Sun '96

John Belushi
Saturday Night Live '70s
All You Need Is Cash '78
Goin' South '78
National Lampoon's Animal House '78
1941 '79
Old Boyfriends '79
The Blues Brothers '80
Continental Divide '81
Neighbors '81

Richard Belzer
The Groove Tube '72
Fame '80
Night Shift '82
Flicks '85
America '86
Freeway '88
The Wrong Guys '88
The Big Picture '89
The Flash 2: Revenge of the Trickster '91
Mad Dog and Glory '93
The Puppet Masters '94
The Invaders '95
Girl 6 '96

Brian Benben
Gangster Wars '81
Clean and Sober '88
I Come in Peace '90
Mortal Sins '90
Radioland Murders '94

Robert Benchley
China Seas '35
Foreign Correspondent '40
You'll Never Get Rich '41
Young & Willing '42
The Sky's the Limit '43
It's in the Bag '45
The Stork Club '45
Weekend at the Waldorf '45
The Road to Utopia '46

Russ Bender
It Conquered the World '56
The Amazing Colossal Man '57
Suicide Battalion/Hell Squad '58
The War of the Colossal Beast '58
Anatomy of a Psycho '61
Navy vs. the Night Monsters '66

Michael C. Bendetti
Netherworld '90
Amanda and the Alien '95

William Bendix
The Glass Key '42
Star Spangled Rhythm '42
Wake Island '42
Who Done It? '42
Woman of the Year '42
Guadalcanal Diary '43
Abroad with Two Yanks '44
The Hairy Ape '44
Lifeboat '44
It's in the Bag '45
The Blue Dahlia '46
Dark Corner '46
Where There's Life '47
Babe Ruth Story '48
The Time of Your Life '48
Big Steal '49
A Connecticut Yankee in King Arthur's Court '49
Detective Story '51
Blackbeard the Pirate '52
A Girl in Every Port '52
Macao '52
Dangerous Mission '54
Crashout '55
Deep Six '58
Johnny Nobody '61
For Love or Money '63

Leonor Benedetto
Condemned to Hell '80s
A Place in the World '95

Billy Benedict
Wildcat '42
Follow the Leader '44
Bowery Buckaroos '47
Hard-Boiled Mahoney '47
Spook Busters '48
Master Minds '49
Ghost Chasers '51

Brooks Benedict
The Freshman '25
Ranson's Folly '26
The Dropkick '27

Dirk Benedict
Georgia, Georgia '72
W '74
Battlestar Galactica '78
Cruise into Terror '78
Mission Galactica: The Cylon Attack '79
Scavenger Hunt '79
Follow That Car '80
Underground Aces '80
Ruckus '81
Body Slam '87
Blue Tornado '90
Shadow Force '92
Official Denial '93
Alaska '96

Paul Benedict
Mandingo '75
Desperate Moves '86
The Chair '87
Cocktail '88
Babycakes '89
The Freshman '90
The Addams Family '91
Attack of the 50 Ft. Woman '93

Richard Benedict
Omoo Omoo, the Shark God '49
Breakdown '53
Beginning of the End '57

Yves Beneyton
Weekend '67
The Lacemaker '77
Letters to an Unknown Lover '84

John Benfield
Hidden Agenda '90
In the Name of the Father '93
Prime Suspect: The Lost Child '94
Prime Suspect: Inner Circles '95
Prime Suspect: The Scent of Darkness '95

Wilson Benge
Robin Hood '22
The Bat Whispers '30

Norman Bengell
Planet of the Vampires '65
Hellbenders '67

Jean Benguigui
Buffet Froid '79
Control '87

Roberto Benigni
Down by Law '86
Night on Earth '91
Johnny Stecchino '92
Son of the Pink Panther '93

Annette Bening
The Great Outdoors '88
Valmont '89
The Grifters '90
Postcards from the Edge '90
Bugsy '91
Guilty by Suspicion '91
Regarding Henry '91
Love Affair '94
The American President '95
Richard III '95

Paul Benjamin
Across 110th Street '72
The Deadly Trackers '73
The Education of Sonny Carson '74
I Know Why the Caged Bird Sings '79
The Five Heartbeats '91
The Fence '94

Richard Benjamin
Goodbye Columbus '69
Catch-22 '70
Diary of a Mad Housewife '70
The Steagle '71
Portnoy's Complaint '72
The Last of Sheila '73
Westworld '73
The Sunshine Boys '75
House Calls '78
No Room to Run '78
Love at First Bite '79
Scavenger Hunt '79
Witches' Brew '79
First Family '80
How to Beat the High Cost of Living '80
The Last Married Couple in America '80
Saturday the 14th '81
Packin' It In '83

Benji
Benji '74
For the Love of Benji '77
Benji the Hunted '87

David Bennent
The Tin Drum '79
Legend '86

Heinz Bennent
Nea '78
The Tin Drum '79
From the Life of the Marionettes '80
The Last Metro '80
Possession '81

Bruce (Herman Brix) Bennett
The New Adventures of Tarzan '35
Shadow of Chinatown '36
A Million to One '37
Daredevils of the Red Circle '38
Fighting Devil Dogs '38
Hawk of the Wilderness '38
Tarzan and the Green Goddess '38
Before I Hang '40
The More the Merrier '43
Sahara '43
I'm from Arkansas '44
U-Boat Prisoner '44
Mildred Pierce '45
The Man I Love '46
A Stolen Life '46
Dark Passage '47
Silver River '48
Treasure of the Sierra Madre '48
Task Force '49
Angels in the Outfield '51
Cavalry Charge '51
Sudden Fear '52
Dragonfly Squadron '54
Daniel Boone: Trail Blazer '56
Hidden Guns '56
Three Violent People '57
The Cosmic Man '59

Constance Bennett
Married? '26
Sin Takes a Holiday '30
What Price Hollywood? '32
Topper '37
Topper Takes a Trip '39
Two-Faced Woman '41
As Young As You Feel '51
Madame X '66

Hywel Bennett
The Virgin Soldiers '69
Loot...Give Me Money, Honey! '70
Endless Night '71
Murder Elite '86
Deadline '87
A Mind to Kill '95

Jill Bennett
Lust for Life '56
The Nanny '65
The Skull '65
The Charge of the Light Brigade '68
I Want What I Want '72
The Old Curiosity Shop '75
Full Circle '77
For Your Eyes Only '81
Murders at Lynch Cross '85
Hawks '89
The Sheltering Sky '90

Joan Bennett
Power '28
Bulldog Drummond '29
Disraeli '29
Little Women '33
Vogues of 1938 '37
The Texans '38
The Man in the Iron Mask '39
House Across the Bay '40
The Son of Monte Cristo '41
Woman In the Window '44
Colonel Effingham's Raid '45
Scarlet Street '45
The Scar '48
Secret Beyond the Door '48
Reckless Moment '49
Father of the Bride '50
Father's Little Dividend '51
We're No Angels '55
Dark Shadows '67
House of Dark Shadows '70
Suspiria '77

John Bennett
It Takes a Thief '59
The House that Dripped Blood '71
Antonia and Jane '91
Priest '94

Marjorie Bennett
Kiss Me Deadly '55
The Love God? '70
Stacey '73

Nigel Bennett
Back in Action '94
Soft Deceit '94
Darkman 3: Die Darkman Die '95
Kurt Vonnegut's Harrison Bergeron '95
Madonna: Innocence Lost '95

Ray Bennett
Death Rides the Plains '44
Border Badmen '45
Thundering Trail '51
Lovers' Lovers '94

Tony Bennett
The Oscar '66
The Scout '94

Jack Benny
Medicine Man '30
Transatlantic Merry-Go-Round '34
Broadway Melody of 1936 '35
George Washington Slept Here '42
To Be or Not to Be '42
Hollywood Canteen '44
The Horn Blows at Midnight '45
It's in the Bag '45
It's a Mad, Mad, Mad, Mad World '63

Abraham Benrubi
The Program '93
Magic Island '95
Twister '96

Amber Benson
The Crush '93
King of the Hill '93

Deborah Benson
September 30, 1955 '77
Just Before Dawn '80
Mutant on the Bounty '89

George Benson
Convoy '40
The Creeping Flesh '72

Lucille Benson
Duel '71
Cactus in the Snow '72
Private Parts '72
Huckleberry Finn '74
Reflections of Murder '74

Martin Benson
The King and I '56
Istanbul '57
The Cosmic Monsters '58
Exodus '60
A Matter of WHO '62
Tiffany Jones '75

Robby Benson
Jory '72
All the Kind Strangers '74
Death Be Not Proud '75
The Death of Richie '76
The Last of Mrs. Lincoln '76
Ode to Billy Joe '76
The Virginia Hill Story '76
One on One '77
Our Town '77
The End '78
Ice Castles '79
Die Laughing '80
Tribute '80
The Chosen '81
National Lampoon Goes to the Movies '81
Two of a Kind '82
Running Brave '83
Harry & Son '84
City Limits '85
Rent-A-Cop '88
White Hot '88
Modern Love '90
Homewrecker '92
Invasion of Privacy '92
Deadly Exposure '93
At Home with the Webbers '94

Timothy Bentinck
Year of the Comet '92
Sharpe's Rifles '93

Michael Bentine
Down Among the Z Men '52
Rentadick '72

Dana Bentley
Sorority House Massacre 2: Nighty Nightmare '92
Karate Cop '93

John Bentley
Calling Paul Temple '48
The Happiest Days of Your Life '50
Profile '54
River Beat '54
Scarlet Spear '54
The Way Out '56
Istanbul '57
White Huntress '57
Flight from Vienna '58
Submarine Seahawk '59
The Chair '87

Barbi Benton
For the Love of It '80
Hospital Massacre '81
Deathstalker '83

Jerome Benton
Under the Cherry Moon '86
Graffiti Bridge '90

Suzanne Benton
That Cold Day in the Park '69
A Boy and His Dog '75

Daniel Benzali
Messenger of Death '88
A Day in October '92
The Last of His Tribe '92

John Beradino
Moon of the Wolf '72
Don't Look Back: The Story of Leroy "Satchel" Paige '81

Ady Berber
Dead Eyes of London '61
Door with the Seven Locks '62

Luca Bercovici
Frightmare '81
Parasite '82
American Flyers '85
Clean and Sober '88
Mortal Passions '90
Pacific Heights '90
K2: The Ultimate High '92
Mission of Justice '92
Mirror Images 2 '93
Drop Zone '94
Scanner Cop '94

Tom Berenger
The Sentinel '76
Johnny We Hardly Knew Ye '77
Looking for Mr. Goodbar '77
Rush It '77
In Praise of Older Women '78
Butch and Sundance: The Early Days '79
The Dogs of War '81
Beyond Obsession '82
The Big Chill '83
Eddie and the Cruisers '83
Fear City '85
Rustler's Rhapsody '85
Platoon '86
Someone to Watch Over Me '87
Betrayed '88
Last Rites '88
Shoot to Kill '88
Born on the Fourth of July '89
Love at Large '89
Major League '89
The Field '90
At Play in the Fields of the Lord '91
Shattered '91
Sniper '92
Gettysburg '93
Sliver '93
Chasers '94
Major League 2 '94
The Avenging Angel '95
Body Language '95
The Last of the Dogmen '95
The Substitute '96

Marisa Berenson
Death in Venice '71
Cabaret '72
Barry Lyndon '75
Sex on the Run '78
Killer Fish '79
S.O.B. '81
The Secret Diary of Sigmund Freud '84
Trade Secrets '90s
Night of the Cyclone '90
White Hunter, Black Heart '90

Harry Beresford
The Sign of the Cross '32
Murders in the Zoo '33
Klondike Annie '36

Peter Berg
Never on Tuesday '88
Genuine Risk '89
Going Overboard '89
Race for Glory '89
Shocker '89
Crooked Hearts '91
Late for Dinner '91
A Midnight Clear '92
Aspen Extreme '93
A Case for Murder '93
Fire in the Sky '93
Across the Moon '94
The Last Ride '94
The Last Seduction '94
Girl 6 '96
The Great White Hype '96

Judith-Marie Bergan
Abduction '75
Never Pick Up a Stranger '79

Francine Berge
Circle of Love '64
Judex '64
The Nun '66

Candice Bergen
The Group '66
The Sand Pebbles '66
The Adventurers '70
Getting Straight '70
Soldier Blue '70
Carnal Knowledge '71
11 Harrowhouse '74
Bite the Bullet '75
The Wind and the Lion '75
The Domino Principle '77
A Night Full of Rain '78
Oliver's Story '78
Starting Over '79
Rich and Famous '81
Gandhi '82
Merlin and the Sword '85
My Sweet Victim '85
Stick '85
Mayflower Madam '87

Edgar Bergen
The Goldwyn Follies '38
Letter of Introduction '38
You Can't Cheat an Honest Man '39
Look Who's Laughing '41
Here We Go Again! '42
I Remember Mama '48
Homecoming: A Christmas Story '71

Frances Bergen
The Morning After '86
Eating '90

Polly Bergen
At War with the Army '50
The Stooge '51
Escape from Fort Bravo '53
Cape Fear '61
Kisses for My President '64
Anatomy of Terror '74
Death Cruise '74
Murder on Flight 502 '75
How to Pick Up Girls '78
Born Beautiful '82
The Winds of War '83
Making Mr. Right '86
War & Remembrance, Part 1 '88
War & Remembrance, Part 3 '88
War & Remembrance, Part 4 '88
War & Remembrance, Part 5 '88
War & Remembrance, Part 6 '88
War & Remembrance, Part 7 '88
Haunting of Sarah Hardy '89
My Brother's Wife '89
War & Remembrance, Part 2 '89
War & Remembrance: The Final Chapter, Part 8 '89
War & Remembrance: The Final Chapter, Part 9 '89
War & Remembrance: The Final Chapter, Part 10 '89
War & Remembrance: The Final Chapter, Part 11 '89
War & Remembrance: The Final Chapter, Part 12 '89
Cry-Baby '90
The Lightning Incident '91
Dr. Jekyll and Ms. Hyde '95
Once Upon a Time...When We Were Colored '95

Tushka Bergen
Wrangler '88
Swing Kids '93
Barcelona '94

Deborah Berger
La Merveilleuse Visite '74
Rosebud '75

Helmut Berger
The Damned '69
Dorian Gray '70
The Garden of the Finzi-Continis '71
Ash Wednesday '73
Order to Kill '73
Conversation Piece '75
Romantic Englishwoman '75
Battleforce '78
Fatal Fix '80s
Deadly Game '83
Mad Dog '84
Code Name: Emerald '85
The Godfather, Part 3 '90

Joachim Berger
Curse of the Yellow Snake '63
Carpet of Horror '64

Katya Berger
Nana '82
Tales of Ordinary Madness '83

Nicole Berger
Shoot the Piano Player '62
The Story of a Three Day Pass '68

Senta Berger
The Boss Is Served '60s
Mother Doesn't Always Know Best '60s
Secret of the Black Trunk '62
Sherlock Holmes and the Deadly Necklace '62
Testament of Dr. Mabuse '62
Full Hearts & Empty Pockets '63
Waltz King '63
Cast a Giant Shadow '66
The Quiller Memorandum '66
The Ambushers '67
Diabolically Yours '67
When Women Had Tails '70
Cobra '71
The Scarlet Letter '73
Smugglers '75
When Women Lost Their Tails '75
Cross of Iron '76
Swiss Conspiracy '77
Killing Cars '85

William Berger
What a Way to Die '70
Today We Kill, Tomorrow We Die '71
Superfly T.N.T. '73
Slaughterday '77
Oil '78
Hercules '83
Day of the Cobra '84
Hercules 2 '85
Hell Hunters '87

Thommy Berggren
Elvira Madigan '67
The Adventurers '70
Sunday's Children '94

Herbert Berghof
Five Fingers '52
Red Planet Mars '52
Master Mind '73

Patrick Bergin
The Courier '88
Taffin '88
Mountains of the Moon '90
Robin Hood '91
Sleeping with the Enemy '91
Highway to Hell '92
Love Crimes '92
Patriot Games '92
Frankenstein '93
Map of the Human Heart '93
They Watch '93
Double Cross '94
Soft Deceit '94
Lawnmower Man 2: Beyond Cyberspace '95
Triplecross '95

Erik Berglund
Walpurgis Night '41
Only One Night '42

Henry Bergman
Charlie Chaplin: The Early Years, Vol. 2 '17
City Lights '31
Modern Times '36

Ingrid Bergman
The Count of the Old Town '34
Swedenhielms '35
Intermezzo '36
Dollar '38
A Woman's Face '38
Intermezzo '39
June Night '40
Adam Had Four Sons '41
Dr. Jekyll and Mr. Hyde '41
Walpurgis Night '41
Casablanca '42
Only One Night '42
The Best of Bogart '43
For Whom the Bell Tolls '43
Gaslight '44
The Bells of St. Mary's '45
Saratoga Trunk '45
Spellbound '45
Notorious '46
Arch of Triumph '48
Joan of Arc '48
Under Capricorn '49
Stromboli '50
Europa '51 '52
Voyage to Italy '53
Anastasia '56
Elena and Her Men '56
Indiscreet '58
The Inn of the Sixth Happiness '58
Goodbye Again '61
24 Hours in a Woman's Life '61
Cactus Flower '69
Walk in the Spring Rain '70
The Hideaways '73
Murder on the Orient Express '74
A Matter of Time '76
Autumn Sonata '78
A Woman Called Golda '82
The Cary Grant Collection '90

Peter Bergman
J-Men Forever! '79
Firesign Theatre Presents Nick Danger in the Case of the Missing Yolks '83
Phantom of the Ritz '88

Sandahl Bergman
All That Jazz '79
Xanadu '80
Airplane 2: The Sequel '82
Conan the Barbarian '82
She '83
Getting Physical '84
Red Sonja '85
Programmed to Kill '86
Stewardess School '86
Kandyland '87
Hell Comes to Frogtown '88
Raw Nerve '91
Body of Influence '93
Lipstick Camera '93
Possessed by the Night '93
Inner Sanctum 2 '94
Ice Cream Man '95
The P.A.C.K. '96

Elisabeth Bergner
Catherine the Great '34
As You Like It '36
Dreaming Lips '37
Cry of the Banshee '70
The Pedestrian '73

Luis Beristain
El: This Strange Passion '52
The Exterminating Angel '62

Busby Berkeley
42nd Street '33
Roman Scandals '33
Dames '34
Fashions of 1934 '34
Babes on Broadway '41
Million Dollar Mermaid '52

Xander Berkeley
Deadly Dreams '88
The Lawless Land '88
Assassin '89
Short Time '90
Candyman '92
A Few Good Men '92
The Gun in Betty Lou's Handbag '92
Attack of the 50 Ft. Woman '93
Dead to Rights '93
Roswell: The U.F.O. Cover-Up '94
Poison Ivy 2: Lily '95
Safe '95
Barb Wire '96

Elizabeth Berkley
White Wolves 2: Legend of the Wild '94
Showgirls '95

Steven Berkoff
A Clockwork Orange '71
The Passenger '75
Beverly Hills Cop '84
Rambo: First Blood, Part 2 '85
Revolution '85
Transmutations '85
War & Remembrance, Part 1 '88
Prisoner of Rio '89
War & Remembrance: The Final Chapter, Part 8 '89
The Krays '90
Intruders '92

Terri Berland
Pink Motel '82
The Strangeness '85

Milton Berle
Sun Valley Serenade '41
Let's Make Love '60
It's a Mad, Mad, Mad, Mad World '63
The Loved One '65
The Oscar '66
Who's Minding the Mint? '67
Legend of Valentino '75
Lepke '75
Off Your Rocker '80
Cracking Up '83
Broadway Danny Rose '84
Side By Side '88
Driving Me Crazy '91
Storybook '95

Francois Berleand
Au Revoir Les Enfants '87
May Fools '90

Jeannie Berlin
The Baby Maker '70
Getting Straight '70
The Strawberry Statement '70
The Heartbreak Kid '72
Housewife '72
Portnoy's Complaint '72
In the Spirit '90

Peter Berling
Aguirre, the Wrath of God '72
Francesco '93

Warren Berlinger
Platinum High School '60
Billie '65
Spinout '66
The Long Goodbye '73
Four Deuces '75
Sex and the Single Parent '82
The World According to Garp '82
Take Two '87
Hero '92

Shelley Berman
The Wheeler Dealers '63
The Best Man '64
Divorce American Style '67
Think Dirty '70
Son of Blob '72
Rented Lips '88
Motorama '91

Crystal Bernard
Slumber Party Massacre 2 '87
Siringo '94
As Good as Dead '95

Ed Bernard
Across 110th Street '72
Reflections of Murder '74
The White Shadow, Vol. 1 '78

Jason Bernard
No Way Out '87
Cosmic Slop '94
While You Were Sleeping '95

Paul Bernard
The Ladies of the Bois de Bologne '44
Pattes Blanches '49

Susan Bernard
Faster Pussycat! Kill! Kill! '66
Teenager '74

Herschel Bernardi
Green Fields '37
Irma La Douce '63
Love with the Proper Stranger '63
No Place to Run '72
The Story of Jacob & Joseph '74
The Front '76
Actor: The Paul Muni Story '78

Sandra Bernhard
King of Comedy '82
Sesame Street Presents: Follow That Bird '85
Track 29 '88
Heavy Petting '89
Hudson Hawk '91
Inside Monkey Zetterland '93
The Late Shift '96

Kevin Bernhardt
Counterforce '87
Midnight Warrior '89
Hellraiser 3: Hell on Earth '92
Beauty School '93
The Immortals '95

Mara Berni
The Fury of Hercules '61
Samson '61

Corbin Bernsen
Eat My Dust '76
L.A. Law '86
Dead Aim '87
Hello Again '87
Bert Rigby, You're a Fool '89
Disorganized Crime '89
Major League '89
Dead on the Money '91
Shattered '91
Frozen Assets '92
A Brilliant Disguise '93
Final Mission '93
The Ghost Brigade '93
Ring of the Musketeers '93
Major League 2 '94
The New Age '94
Radioland Murders '94
Savage Land '94
The Soft Kill '94
Baja '95
Cover Me '95
Operation Intercept '95
Someone to Die For '95
Tails You Live, Heads You're Dead '95
Tales from the Hood '95
Temptress '95
The Great White Hype '96

Claude Berri
Marry Me, Marry Me '69
Le Sex Shop '73

Elizabeth Berridge
The Funhouse '81
Amadeus '84
Five Corners '88
Montana '90
When the Party's Over '91

Rev. Daniel Berrigan
In the King of Prussia '83
The Mission '86

Chuck Berry
Rock, Rock, Rock '56
Go, Johnny Go! '59
Chuck Berry: Hail! Hail! Rock 'n' Roll '87

Halle Berry
Jungle Fever '91
The Last Boy Scout '91
Strictly Business '91
Boomerang '92
Father Hood '93
The Program '93
The Flintstones '94
Losing Isaiah '94
Executive Decision '96
Girl 6 '96
Race the Sun '96

Jules Berry
The Crime of Monsieur Lange '36
Le Jour Se Leve '39
Les Visiteurs du Soir '42

Ken Berry
Herbie Rides Again '74
Mountain Man '77
The Cat from Outer Space '78

Richard Berry
L'Addition '85
Special Police '85
A Man and a Woman: 20 Years Later '86
Honeymoon '87
Day of Atonement '93
L'Appat '94

Dorothee Berryman
The Decline of the American Empire '86
A Paper Wedding '89
Scanners 2: The New Order '91

Michael Berryman
One Flew Over the Cuckoo's Nest '75
The Hills Have Eyes '77
The Hills Have Eyes, Part 2 '84
Cut and Run '85
The Barbarians '87
Voyage of the Rock Aliens '87
Aftershock '88
Beastmaster 2: Through the Portal of Time '91
Evil Spirits '91
The Guyver '91
Haunting Fear '91
The Secret of the Golden Eagle '91
Auntie Lee's Meat Pies '92
Teenage Exorcist '93

Dehl Berti
Sweet Hostage '75
Bullies '86

Roland Bertin
Diva '82
L'Homme Blesse '83
Cyrano de Bergerac '90
The Hairdresser's Husband '92

Valerie Bertinelli
C.H.O.M.P.S. '79
Young Love, First Love '79
Aladdin and His Wonderful Lamp '84
Shattered Vows '84
Ordinary Heroes '85
Silent Witness '85
Number One with a Bullet '87
Pancho Barnes '88
Taken Away '89

Juliet Berto
The Joy of Knowledge '65
Le Sex Shop '73

Bibi Besch
Peter Lundy and the Medicine Hat Stallion '77
Death of a Centerfold '81
The Beast Within '82
The Lonely Lady '83
Date with an Angel '87
Kill Me Again '89
Tremors '89
Betsy's Wedding '90
Crazy from the Heart '91
Rattled '96

Ted Bessell
Billie '65
Don't Drink the Water '69
Breaking Up Is Hard to Do '79
Acorn People '82

Joe Besser
Africa Screams '49
Savage Intruder '68

Eugenie Besserer
Little Orphan Annie '18
The Greatest Question '19
What Happened to Rosa? '21
Anna Christie '23
The Flesh and the Devil '27
The Jazz Singer '27

Edna Best
The Man Who Knew Too Much '34
Intermezzo '39
The Ghost and Mrs. Muir '47

James Best
Ma and Pa Kettle at the Fair '52
The Naked and the Dead '58
The Killer Shrews '59
Ride Lonesome '59
Verboten! '59
Shock Corridor '63
Savage Run '70
Mind Warp '72
Sounder '72
The Runaway Barge '75
Ode to Billy Joe '76

Willie Best
The Monster Walks '32
Kentucky Kernels '34
The Littlest Rebel '35
The Bride Walks Out '36
The Ghost Breakers '40
The Trouble with Father '50

Martine Beswick
From Russia with Love '63
Thunderball '65
One Million Years B.C. '66
A Bullet for the General '68
Dr. Jekyll and Sister Hyde '71
Strange New World '75
The Happy Hooker Goes Hollywood '80
Balboa '82
Cyclone '87
The Offspring '87
Miami Blues '90
Trancers 2: The Return of Jack Deth '90
Evil Spirits '91
Wide Sargasso Sea '92

Sabine Bethmann
Journey to the Lost City '58
Dr. Mabuse vs. Scotland Yard '64

Lyle Bettger
Union Station '50
All I Desire '53
Carnival Story '54
Sea Chase '55
Lone Ranger '56
Johnny Reno '66

Laura Betti
Teorema '68
Hatchet for the Honeymoon '70
The Canterbury Tales '71
Allonsanfan '73
Sonny and Jed '73
1900 '76
Lovers and Liars '81

Robert Bettles
Fourth Wish '75
Ride a Wild Pony '75

Franca Bettoya
The Last Man on Earth '64
Marauder '65

Jack Betts
The Bloody Brood '59
Dead Men Don't Die '91

Carl Betz
Spinout '66
The Meal '75
Deadly Encounter '78

Matthew Betz
The Unholy Three '25
The Wedding March '28
Broadway to Cheyenne '32
The Fighting Marshal '32
Tarzan the Fearless '33
The Black Coin '36

Jack Beutel
The Outlaw '43
Judge Roy Bean '55

Billy Bevan
The Lizzies of Mack Sennett '15
Silent Laugh Makers, No. 2 '17
The White Sin '24
High Voltage '29
Vanity Fair '32
Cavalcade '33
The Wrong Road '37
Girl of the Golden West '38
The Woman in Green '45

Clem Bevans
Abe Lincoln in Illinois '40
Highway 13 '48
Rim of the Canyon '49
Gold Raiders '51
Silver City Bonanza '51

Helen Beverly
Green Fields '37
The Light Ahead '39
Overture to Glory '40
Meeting at Midnight '44

Turhan Bey
Footsteps in the Dark '41
Shadows on the Stairs '41
Arabian Nights '42
The Mummy's Tomb '42
Ali Baba and the Forty Thieves '43
Background to Danger '43
The Mad Ghoul '43
Dragon Seed '44
Out of the Blue '47
The Amazing Mr. X '48
The Falcon Takes Over/Strange Bargain '49
Parole, Inc. '49
Virtual Combat '95

Troy Beyer
Rooftops '89
Weekend at Bernie's 2 '93

Richard Beymer
Indiscretion of an American Wife '54
Johnny Tremain & the Sons of Liberty '58
The Diary of Anne Frank '59
West Side Story '61
The Longest Day '62
The Stripper '63
Free Grass '69
Cross Country '83
Silent Night, Deadly Night 3: Better Watch Out! '89
Twin Peaks '90
Twin Peaks '90
Black Belt '92
Under Investigation '93

Didier Bezace
The Little Thief '89
L.627 '92
Between Heaven and Earth '93

Bhasker
I Drink Your Blood '71
Drachenfutter '87

Daniela Bianchi
The Sword of El Cid '62
From Russia with Love '63
Secret Agent 00 '67
Dirty Heroes '71

Charles K. Bibby
Unmasking the Idol '86
Order of the Black Eagle '87

Abner Biberman
Gunga Din '39
Panama Patrol '39
The Rains Came '39
His Girl Friday '40
Betrayal from the East '44
The Keys of the Kingdom '44
Elephant Walk '54

Robert Bice
Bandit King of Texas '49
Invasion U.S.A. '52

Charles Bickford
Anna Christie '30
East of Borneo '31
Little Miss Marker '34
The Farmer Takes a Wife '35
The Plainsman '37
Thunder Pass '37
Thunder Trail '37
Mutiny in the Big House '39
Of Mice and Men '39
Reap the Wild Wind '42
Tarzan's New York Adventure '42
Mr. Lucky '43
The Song of Bernadette '43
A Wing and a Prayer '44
Duel in the Sun '46
The Farmer's Daughter '47
Babe Ruth Story '48
Command Decision '48
Four Faces West '48
Johnny Belinda '48
Branded '50
Guilty of Treason '50
Riding High '50
Jim Thorpe: All American '51
A Star is Born '54
The Court Martial of Billy Mitchell '55
Not as a Stranger '55
The Unforgiven '60
Days of Wine and Roses '62
Fatal Confinement '64
A Big Hand for the Little Lady '66

Andrew Bicknell
Heidi '93
Buffalo Girls '95
Prince Brat and the Whipping Boy '95

Jean-Luc Bideau
La Salamandre '71
Jonah Who Will Be 25 in the Year 2000 '76

Michael Biehn
Coach '78
Hog Wild '80
The Fan '81
The Lords of Discipline '83
The Terminator '84
Aliens '86
Rampage '87
In a Shallow Grave '88
The Seventh Sign '88
The Abyss '89
Navy SEALS '90
Timebomb '91
K2: The Ultimate High '92
A Taste for Killing '92
Deadfall '93
Strapped '93
Tombstone '93
Blood of the Hunter '94
Deep Red '94
In the Kingdom of the Blind the Man with One Eye is King '94
Breach of Trust '95
Frame by Frame '95
Jade '95
The Rock '96

Dick Biel
Splatter University '84
Slime City '89

Josef Bierbichler
Heart of Glass '74
Woyzeck '78

Ramon Bieri
The Passing of Evil '70
Nicole '72
Love Affair: The Eleanor & Lou Gehrig Story '77
Panic in Echo Park '77
Sorcerer '77
The Frisco Kid '79
A Christmas Without Snow '80
A Matter of Life and Death '81
Grandview U.S.A. '84
Love, Lies and Murder '91

Craig Bierko
Victimless Crimes '90
Danielle Steel's Star '93

Adam Biesk
The Applegates '89
Leprechaun 2 '94

Claudio Bigagli
The Night of the Shooting Stars '82
Kaos '85
Mediterraneo '91
Fiorile '93

Scott "Bam Bam" Bigelow
SnakeEater 3: His Law '92
Major Payne '95

Roxann Biggs
Broken Angel '88
Darkman 3: Die Darkman Die '95
Dirty Work '92
Guilty by Suspicion '91
Midnight's Child '93
Star Trek Voyager: Caretaker '95

Theodore Bikel
The African Queen '51
Never Let Me Go '53
Above Us the Waves '56
Enemy Below '57
The Defiant Ones '58
Flight from Vienna '58
I Bury the Living '58
I Want to Live! '58
A Dog of Flanders '59
My Fair Lady '64
The Russians are Coming, the Russians are Coming '66
My Side of the Mountain '69
Darker than Amber '70
Murder on Flight 502 '75
Very Close Quarters '84
Dark Tower '87
The Final Days '89
See You in the Morning '89
Shattered '91
Benefit of the Doubt '93
My Family Treasure '93

Fernando Bilbao
Fangs of the Living Dead '68
The Screaming Dead '72

Tony Bill
Come Blow Your Horn '63
Soldier in the Rain '63
None But the Brave '65
You're a Big Boy Now '66
Ice Station Zebra '68
Never a Dull Moment '68
Haunts of the Very Rich '72
Shampoo '75
Are You in the House Alone? '78
Initiation of Sarah '78
Heart Beat '80
Little Dragons '80
Washington Mistress '81
Pee Wee's Big Adventure '85
The Killing Mind '90
Barb Wire '96

Raoul Billerey
Le Grand Chemin '87
The Little Thief '89

Dawn Ann Billings
Trancers 3: Deth Lives '92
Warlock: The Armageddon '93

Earl Billings
Stakeout '87
One False Move '91

Barbara Billingsley
Back to the Beach '87
Eye of the Demon '87

Jennifer Billingsley
Lady in a Cage '64
Chrome Hearts '70
White Lightning '73
The Thirsty Dead '74
Hollywood Man '76

Peter Billingsley
Death Valley '81
A Christmas Story '83
The Hoboken Chicken Emergency '84
Dirt Bike Kid '86
Russkies '87
Beverly Hills Brats '89
Arcade '93

Sybilla Binder
Counterblast '48
The Golden Salamander '51

Herman Bing
The Guardsman '31
Crimson Romance '34
The Merry Widow '34
Tango '36
That Girl from Paris '36
Maytime '37
Bluebeard's Eighth Wife '38
Every Day's a Holiday '38
The Great Waltz '38
Bitter Sweet '40

Barbara Bingham
Friday the 13th, Part 8: Jason Takes Manhattan '89
Soldier's Fortune '91
Beyond Darkness '92

Geoffrey Binney
Hot Potato '76
Raw Force '81

Edward Binns
Without Warning '52
Beyond a Reasonable Doubt '56
Twelve Angry Men '57
Compulsion '59
A Public Affair '62
The Americanization of Emily '64
Hunter '73
Night Moves '75
Oliver's Story '78
Danger in the Skies '79
Return to Eden '89

Juliette Binoche
Hail Mary '85
Rendez-vous '85
The Unbearable Lightness of Being '88
Women & Men: In Love There Are No Rules '91
Damage '92
Trois Couleurs: Bleu '93
The Horseman on the Roof '95

Thelma Biral
El Muerto '75
Fridays of Eternity '81

Paul Birch
Apache Woman '55
Day the World Ended '55
Queen of Outer Space '58

Thora Birch
All I Want for Christmas '91
Paradise '91
Patriot Games '92

Birch ►cont.

Hocus Pocus '93
Clear and Present Danger '94
Monkey Trouble '94
Now and Then '95
Alaska '96

Billie Bird
Ernest Saves Christmas '88
The End of Innocence '90
Home Alone '90
Dennis the Menace '93

Jesse Birdsall
Wish You Were Here '87
Getting It Right '89
Nightscare '93

Tala Birell
Crime and Punishment '35
The White Legion '36
The Purple Heart '44

Jane Birkin
Blow-Up '66
Wonderwall: The Movie '69
Swimming Pool '70
Romance of a Horsethief '71
Seven Deaths in the Cat's Eye '72
Too Pretty to Be Honest '72
Catherine & Co. '76
Death on the Nile '78
Make Room for Tomorrow '81
Evil under the Sun '82
Dust '85
Le Petit Amour '87
Beethoven's Nephew '88
Daddy Nostalgia '90
La Belle Noiseuse '90
French Intrigue

Len Birman
Lies My Father Told Me '75
Captain America '79
Captain America 2: Death Too Soon '79
Undergrads '85
Web of Deceit '90

Serafina Birman
The Girl with the Hat Box '27
Ivan the Terrible, Part 1 '44
Ivan the Terrible, Part 2 '46

David Birney
Caravan to Vaccares '74
Murder or Mercy '74
Only with Married Men '74
Choice of Weapons '76
Mom, the Wolfman and Me '80
Oh, God! Book 2 '80
The Five of Me '81
Prettykill '87
Nightfall '88

Reed Birney
Four Friends '81
Crimewave '85

Debbie Bishop
Scrubbers '82
Sid & Nancy '86

Ed Bishop
Journey to the Far Side of the Sun '69
The Devil's Web '74
Brass Target '78
Saturn 3 '80

Jennifer Bishop
The Female Bunch '69
Horror of the Blood Monsters '70
Impulse '74
Jessie's Girls '75
Jaws of Death '76
House of Terror '87

Joey Bishop
Deep Six '58
The Naked and the Dead '58
Texas Across the River '66
Valley of the Dolls '67
Who's Minding the Mint? '67
Delta Force '86
Betsy's Wedding '90

Julie Bishop
Action in the North Atlantic '43
Northern Pursuit '43
Rhapsody in Blue '45
The Last of the Redmen '47
Westward the Women '51

Kelly Bishop
Dirty Dancing '87
Queens Logic '91
Miami Rhapsody '95

Larry Bishop
The Savage Seven '68
Angel Unchained '70
How Come Nobody's On Our Side? '73
Soul Hustler '76

Pat Bishop
Don's Party '76
Women of Valor '86

Wes Bishop
Chrome and Hot Leather '71
Dixie Dynamite '76

William Bishop
Harriet Craig '50
Breakdown '53
The Redhead from Wyoming '53

Steve Bisley
Chain Reaction '80
Mad Max '80
The Highest Honor '84
Fast Talking '86

Whit Bissell
He Walked by Night '48
The Lost Continent '51
Boots Malone '52
Devil's Canyon '53
Creature from the Black Lagoon '54
Shack Out on 101 '55
I Was a Teenage Werewolf '57
Teenage Frankenstein '58
The Time Machine '60
Spencer's Mountain '63

Jacqueline Bisset
Cul de Sac '66
Casino Royale '67
Two for the Road '67
Bullitt '68
The Detective '68
The First Time '69
Airport '70
The Passing of Evil '70
The Mephisto Waltz '71
Secrets '71
Life & Times of Judge Roy Bean '72
Day for Night '73
The Thief Who Came to Dinner '73
Murder on the Orient Express '74
Spiral Staircase '75
Le Magnifique '76
St. Ives '76
The Deep '77
The Greek Tycoon '78
Who Is Killing the Great Chefs of Europe? '78
Together? '79
When Time Ran Out '80
Rich and Famous '81
Class '83
Under the Volcano '84
Anna Karenina '85
Forbidden '85
Choices '86
High Season '88
Scenes from the Class Struggle in Beverly Hills '89
The Maid '90
Wild Orchid '90
Crime Broker '94
La Ceremonie '95

Josie Bissett
All-American Murder '91
Book of Love '91
Mikey '92

Bill Bixby
Clambake '67
Speedway '68
The Barbary Coast '74
The Apple Dumpling Gang '75
Fantasy Island '76
Rich Man, Poor Man '76
The Incredible Hulk '77
Kentucky Fried Movie '77
The Incredible Hulk Returns '88
The Trial of the Incredible Hulk '89
Death of the Incredible Hulk '90

Anita Bjork
Miss Julie '50
Secrets of Women '52

Halvar Bjork
The New Land '73
Autumn Sonata '78

Anna Bjorn
More American Graffiti '79
Sword & the Sorcerer '82

Gunnar Bjornstrand
Lesson in Love '54
Dreams '55
Smiles of a Summer Night '55
The Seventh Seal '56
Wild Strawberries '57
The Magician '58
Through a Glass Darkly '61
The Winter Light '62
Persona '66
The Shame '68
The Rite '69
Face to Face '76
Autumn Sonata '78

Jack Black
The Neverending Story 3 '94
The Cable Guy '96

Karen Black
The Prime Time '60
You're a Big Boy Now '66
Easy Rider '69
Five Easy Pieces '70
Born to Win '71
A Gunfight '71
Portnoy's Complaint '72
Little Laura & Big John '73
The Pyx '73
The Great Gatsby '74
Law and Disorder '74
Airport '75 '75
Crime & Passion '75
The Day of the Locust '75
Nashville '75
Trilogy of Terror '75
Burnt Offerings '76
Family Plot '76
Capricorn One '78
In Praise of Older Women '78
The Rip Off '78
Killer Fish '79
Mr. Horn '79
Love Under Pressure '80s
The Last Word '80
The Squeeze '80
Chanel Solitaire '81
Miss Right '81
Come Back to the Five & Dime Jimmy Dean, Jimmy Dean '82
Separate Ways '82
Can She Bake a Cherry Pie? '83
Bad Manners '84
Killing Heat '84
The Little Mermaid '84
Savage Dawn '84
Cut and Run '85
The Hitchhiker '85
Martin's Day '85
Invaders from Mars '86
Eternal Evil '87
Hostage '87
It's Alive 3: Island of the Alive '87
Dixie Lanes '88
The Heist '88
The Invisible Kid '88
Out of the Dark '88
Homer and Eddie '89
Twisted Justice '89
Zapped Again '89
The Children '90
Club Fed '90
The Killer's Edge '90
Mirror, Mirror '90
Night Angel '90
Overexposed '90
Evil Spirits '91
Haunting Fear '91
Quiet Fire '91
Auntie Lee's Meat Pies '92
Caged Fear '92
Children of the Night '92
The Double O Kid '92
Final Judgement '92
Hitz '92
Rubin & Ed '92
Bound and Gagged: A Love Story '93
Plan 10 from Outer Space '95

Maurice Black
Marked Money '28
Sixteen Fathoms Deep '34

Ryan Black
Geronimo '93
Dance Me Outside '95

Richard Blackburn
Lemora, Lady Dracula '73
Sugartime '95

Honor Blackman
Conspirator '49
Green Grow the Rushes '51
Glass Tomb '55
Suspended Alibi '56
A Night to Remember '58
A Matter of WHO '62
Jason and the Argonauts '63
Goldfinger '64
Shalako '68
Lola '69
The Virgin and the Gypsy '70
Fright '71
To the Devil, A Daughter '76
The Cat and the Canary '79
The First Olympics: Athens 1896 '84

Joan Blackman
Career '59
Blue Hawaii '62
Kid Galahad '62
Daring Game '68
Macon County Line '74

Sidney Blackmer
Little Caesar '30
Deluge '33
The Count of Monte Cristo '34
Goodbye Love '34
Transatlantic Merry-Go-Round '34
The Little Colonel '35
The President's Mystery '36
The House of Secrets '37
In Old Chicago '38
Law of the Pampas '39
Love Crazy '41
The Panther's Claw '42
War of the Wildcats '43
Buffalo Bill '44
Wilson '44
People Will Talk '51
Beyond a Reasonable Doubt '56
High Society '56
Tammy and the Bachelor '57
How to Murder Your Wife '64
Rosemary's Baby '68

Taurean Blacque
The $5.20 an Hour Dream '80
Hill Street Blues, Vol. 1: Hill Street Station '81
Deepstar Six '89

Ruben Blades
The Last Fight '82
Crossover Dreams '85
Critical Condition '86
Fatal Beauty '87
Homeboy '88
The Milagro Beanfield War '88
Dead Man Out '89
Disorganized Crime '89
The Josephine Baker Story '90
The Lemon Sisters '90
Mo' Better Blues '90
One Man's War '90
Predator 2 '90
The Two Jakes '90
Crazy from the Heart '91
The Super '91
Color of Night '94

Estella Blain
Pirates of the Coast '61
The Diabolical Dr. Z '65

Gerard Blain
Le Beau Serge '58
The Cousins '59
Hatari! '62
The American Friend '77

Vivian Blaine
State Fair '45
Doll Face '46
Skirts Ahoy! '52
Guys and Dolls '55
The Cracker Factory '79
The Dark '79
Parasite '82

Betsy Blair
Marty '55
Il Grido '57
Scarlett '94

Isla Blair
Taste the Blood of Dracula '70
The Final Cut '95

Janet Blair
Tonight and Every Night '45
The Fabulous Dorseys '47
Black Arrow '48
The Fuller Brush Man '48
Boys' Night Out '62
Burn Witch, Burn! '62
The One and Only, Genuine, Original Family Band '68

Kevin Blair
The Hills Have Eyes, Part 2 '84
Friday the 13th, Part 7: The New Blood '88
Bloodstone: Subspecies 2 '92
Bloodlust: Subspecies 3 '93

Linda Blair
The Sporting Club '72
The Exorcist '73
Born Innocent '74
Airport '75 '75
Sweet Hostage '75
The Exorcist 2: The Heretic '77
Summer of Fear '78
Roller Boogie '79
Wild Horse Hank '79
Hell Night '81
Ruckus '81
Chained Heat '83
Savage Streets '83
Night Patrol '85
Red Heat '85
Savage Island '85
Nightforce '86
Grotesque '87
Silent Assassins '88
Witchery '88
A Woman Obsessed '88
Bedroom Eyes 2 '89
The Chilling '89
Moving Target '89
Up Your Alley '89
Zapped Again '89
Bail Out '90
Repossessed '90
Dead Sleep '91
Fatal Bond '91
Sorceress '94

Tom Blair
The Game '89
Sure Fire '90

Deborah Blaisdell
Wimps '87
Student Affairs '88
Wildest Dreams '90

Amanda Blake
The Duchess of Idaho '50
Stars in My Crown '50
Sabre Jet '53
The Glass Slipper '55
Betrayal '74
Gunsmoke: Return to Dodge '87
The Boost '88
B.O.R.N. '88

Andre B. Blake
Philadelphia '93
Who's the Man? '93

Geoffrey Blake
The Abduction of Kari Swenson '87
Fatal Exposure '91
Philadelphia Experiment 2 '93
Dominion '94
Marilyn & Bobby: Her Final Affair '94

Jon Blake
Freedom '81
Early Frost '84
Anzacs: The War Down Under '85
The Lighthorsemen '87

Julia Blake
Lonely Hearts '82
Under Capricorn '82
Man of Flowers '84
Georgia '87
Travelling North '87
Father '90

Marie Blake
Love Finds Andy Hardy '38
Sensations of 1945 '44

Pamela Blake
Kid Dynamite '43
Case of the Baby Sitter '47
Hat Box Mystery '47
Sea Hound '47
Highway 13 '48
Rolling Home '48
Son of God's Country '48
Sky Liner '49
Border Rangers '50
Gunfire '50

Robert (Bobby) Blake
Our Gang Comedies '40s
Western Double Feature 13 '40s
Western Double Feature 21 '40s
Andy Hardy's Double Life '42
Western Double Feature 12 '44
Woman In the Window '44
Humoresque '46
Santa Fe Uprising '46
Stagecoach to Denver '46
Vigilantes of Boom Town '46
The Adventures of Rin Tin Tin '47
Homesteaders of Paradise Valley '47
Treasure of the Sierra Madre '48
Treasure of the Golden Condor '53
Pork Chop Hill '59
PT 109 '63
This Property is Condemned '66
In Cold Blood '67
Tell Them Willie Boy Is Here '69
Counter Punch '71
Electra Glide in Blue '73
Busting '74
Coast to Coast '80
Of Mice and Men '81
Heart of a Champion: The Ray Mancini Story '85
Money Train '95

Colin Blakely
This Sporting Life '63
The Private Life of Sherlock Holmes '70
Shattered '72
Murder on the Orient Express '74
Love Among the Ruins '75
The Pink Panther Strikes Again '76
Equus '77
The Big Sleep '78
Little Lord Fauntleroy '80
Nijinsky '80
The Dogs of War '81
Evil under the Sun '82
Loophole '83
Operation Julie '85

Donald Blakely
Strike Force '75
Short Eyes '79
In the Shadow of Kilimanjaro '86

Susan Blakely
Savages '72
The Lords of Flatbush '74
Report to the Commissioner '74
The Towering Inferno '74
Rich Man, Poor Man '76
Secrets '77
The Concorde: Airport '79 '79
Dreamer '79
A Cry for Love '80
Make Me an Offer '80
Over the Top '86
The Survivalist '87
Broken Angel '88
Hiroshima Maiden '88
Ladykillers '88
Dead Reckoning '89
The Incident '89
My Mom's a Werewolf '89
Out of Sight, Out of Her Mind '89
Blackmail '91
Wildflower '91
Intruders '92
Russian Roulette '93
Honor Thy Father and Mother: The True Story of the Menendez Brothers '94

Olive Blakeney
Gangway '37
Billy the Kid '41

Ronee Blakley
Nashville '75
The Private Files of J. Edgar Hoover '77
She Came to the Valley '77
Desperate Women '78
The Driver '78
The Baltimore Bullet '80
Lightning Over Water '80
A Nightmare on Elm Street '84
Return to Salem's Lot '87
Someone to Love '87
Student Confidential '87
Murder by Numbers '89

Dominique Blanc
May Fools '90
Indochine '92
Queen Margot '94
Total Eclipse '95

Erika Blanc
Kill, Baby, Kill '66
Special Forces '68
Sartana's Here...Trade Your Pistol for a Coffin '70
The Devil's Nightmare '71
The Night Evelyn Came Out of the Grave '71
Mark of the Devil 2 '72
Sweet Spirits '80s

Mel Blanc
Neptune's Daughter '49
Kiss Me, Stupid! '64

Michel Blanc
French Fried Vacation '79
Menage '86
Monsieur Hire '89
Prospero's Books '91
Uranus '91
The Favor, the Watch, & the Very Big Fish '92
Grosse Fatigue '94
Ready to Wear '94

Jewel Blanch
Baffled '72
Against A Crooked Sky '75

Pierre Blanchar
Crime and Punishment '35
Man from Nowhere '37
La Symphonie Pastorale '46

Mari Blanchard
Abbott and Costello Go to Mars '53
Son of Sinbad '55

Susan Blanchard
President's Mistress '78
She's in the Army Now '81

Dorothee Blanck
Cleo from 5 to 7 '61
Umbrellas of Cherbourg '64

Sandrine Blancke
Toto le Heros '91
The Son of the Shark '93

Peter Bland
Came a Hot Friday '85
Dangerous Orphans '86
Tearaway '87

Clara Blandick
Romance '30
Murder at Midnight '31
The Bitter Tea of General Yen '33
The Girl from Missouri '34
Small Town Boy '37
The Adventures of Tom Sawyer '38
The Wizard of Oz '39
Dreaming Out Loud '40
It Started with Eve '41
Infamous Crimes '47

Sally Blane
Vagabond Lover '29
Cross Examination '32
Phantom Express '32
Probation '32
When the West Was Young '32
Heritage of the Desert '33
Night of Terror '33
The Silver Streak '34
Law of the Sea '38
Fighting Mad '39
The Story of Alexander Graham Bell '39
Way Down South '39

Mark Blankfield
Jekyll & Hyde...Together Again '82
Jack & the Beanstalk '83
The Midnight Hour '86
Angel 3: The Final Chapter '88
Frankenstein General Hospital '88
Robin Hood: Men in Tights '93
The Great American Sex Scandal '94

Billy Blanks
Bloodfist '89
The King of the Kickboxers '91
Timebomb '91
Talons of the Eagle '92
Showdown '93
TC 2000 '93
Back in Action '94
Tough and Deadly '94
Expect No Mercy '95

Arell Blanton
Wild Riders '71
House of Terror '87
Assault of the Killer Bimbos '88

Hans-Christian Blech
The Blum Affair '48
The Scarlet Letter '73
Dirty Hands '76
The Wrong Move '78
Colonel Redl '84

Jonah Blechman
This Boy's Life '93
Fall Time '94

Debra Blee
Beach Girls '82
Savage Streets '83
Sloane '84
Malibu Bikini Shop '86

Brian Blessed
Trojan Women '71
Man of La Mancha '72
King Arthur, the Young Warlord '75
Young Warlord '75
Flash Gordon '80
I, Claudius, Vol. 2: Waiting in the Wings/What Shall We Do With Claudius? '80
I, Claudius, Vol. 3: Poison is Queen/Some Justice '80
High Road to China '83
The Hound of the Baskervilles '83
Henry V '89
I, Claudius, Vol. 1: A Touch of Murder/Family Affairs '91
Prisoner of Honor '91
Robin Hood: Prince of Thieves '91
Back in the USSR '92
Much Ado about Nothing '93

Billy Bletcher
Branded Men '31
God's Country and the Man '37

Brenda Blethyn
Grown Ups '80
The Witches '90
A River Runs Through It '92
Secrets and Lies '95

Jason Blicker
African Journey '89
American Boyfriends '89

Bernard Blier
Jenny Lamour '47
Passion for Life '48
Dedee d'Anvers '49
Les Miserables '57
The Man in the Raincoat '57
Casanova '70 '65
Catch Me a Spy '71
The Tall Blond Man with One Black Shoe '72
The Daydreamer '75
Buffet Froid '79

Hunt Block
Secret Weapons '85
The Dirty Dozen: The Fatal Mission '88

Dan Blocker
The Errand Boy '61
Bonanza '64
Ride the Wind '66
Lady in Cement '68

Dirk Blocker
Bonanza: The Return '93
Night of the Scarecrow '95

Michael Blodgett
The Velvet Vampire '71
The Ultimate Thrill '74

Joan Blondell
Big Business Girl '31
Blonde Crazy '31
Illicit '31
Millie '31
Night Nurse '31
Public Enemy '31
Three Broadway Girls '32
Three on a Match '32
Footlight Parade '33
Gold Diggers of 1933 '33
Dames '34
Three Men on a Horse '36
Stand-In '37
Bullets or Ballots '38
Topper Returns '41
Lady for a Night '42
Adventure '45
A Tree Grows in Brooklyn '45
Hollywood Bloopers '50s
The Opposite Sex '56
Desk Set '57
This Could Be the Night '57
Will Success Spoil Rock Hunter? '57
Angel Baby '61
The Cincinnati Kid '65
Waterhole #3 '67
Stay Away, Joe '68
Support Your Local Gunfighter '71
The Dead Don't Die '75
Death at Love House '75
Opening Night '77
The Glove '78
The Champ '79
The Rebels '79
The Woman Inside '83
The Baron '88

Anne Bloom
Dirt Bike Kid '86
That's Adequate '90

Brian Bloom
Walls of Glass '85
Voyage of Terror: The Achille Lauro Affair '90
At Home with the Webbers '94

Claire Bloom
Limelight '52
Innocents in Paris '53
Alexander the Great '55
Richard III '55
The Brothers Karamazov '58
The Buccaneer '58
Look Back in Anger '58
The Wonderful World of the Brothers Grimm '62
The Haunting '63
The Spy Who Came in from the Cold '65
Soldier in Love '67
Charly '68
The Illustrated Man '69
Islands in the Stream '77
Brideshead Revisited '81
Clash of the Titans '81
Separate Tables '83
Deja Vu '84
Ghostwriter '84
Shadowlands '85
This Lightning Always Strikes Twice '85
Anastasia: The Mystery of Anna '86
Intimate Contact '87
Queenie '87
Sammy & Rosie Get Laid '87
Shadow on the Sun '88
Crimes & Misdemeanors '89
A Doll's House '89
Mighty Aphrodite '95

John Bloom
Brain of Blood '71
Dracula vs. Frankenstein '71
The Incredible Two-Headed Transplant '71
Bachelor Party '84
The Hills Have Eyes, Part 2 '84
Casino '95

Lindsay Bloom
Cover Girl Models '75
Hughes & Harlow: Angels in Hell '77
Texas Detour '77
French Quarter '78

Verna Bloom
Medium Cool '69
Hired Hand '71
Badge 373 '73
High Plains Drifter '73
Where Have All the People Gone? '74
The Blue Knight '75
National Lampoon's Animal House '78
Playing for Time '80
Honkytonk Man '82
After Hours '85
The Journey of Natty Gann '85
The Last Temptation of Christ '88

Eric Blore
Flying Down to Rio '33
The Gay Divorcee '34
I Dream Too Much '35
I Live My Life '35
Top Hat '35
Ex-Mrs. Bradford '36
Swing Time '36
Quality Street '37
Shall We Dance '37
Joy of Living '38
Swiss Miss '38
Music in My Heart '40
The Lady Eve '41
Lady Scarface '41
The Road to Zanzibar '41
Sullivan's Travels '41
The Shanghai Gesture '42
The Moon and Sixpence '43
Romance on the High Seas '48
Lady Scarface/The Threat '49
Fancy Pants '50

Roberts Blossom
Deranged '74
Citizens Band '77
Escape from Alcatraz '79
Resurrection '80
Johnny Belinda '82
Reuben, Reuben '83
Flashpoint '84
Vision Quest '85
Candy Mountain '87
The Last Temptation of Christ '88
Always '89
Home Alone '90
Doc Hollywood '91
The Quick and the Dead '94

Lisa Blount
September 30, 1955 '77
Dead and Buried '81
An Officer and a Gentleman '82
What Waits Below '83
Cease Fire '85
Cut and Run '85
Radioactive Dreams '86
Nightflyers '87
Prince of Darkness '87
South of Reno '87
Great Balls of Fire '89
Blind Fury '90
Femme Fatale '90
An American Story '92
Judicial Consent '94
Stalked '94

Kurtis Blow
Krush Groove '85
The Show '95

Ben Blue
The Big Braodcast of 1938 '38
College Swing '38
For Me and My Gal '42
Panama Hattie '42
Broadway Rhythm '44
Two Girls and a Sailor '44
The Russians are Coming, the Russians are Coming '66
Where Were You When the Lights Went Out? '68

Monte Blue
The Man from Painted Post '17
Orphans of the Storm '21
The Marriage Circle '24
So This is Paris '26
White Shadows in the South Seas '28
Wagon Wheels '34
The Lives of a Bengal Lancer '35
Desert Gold '36
Prison Shadows '36
Ride, Ranger, Ride '36
Song of the Gringo '36
A Million to One '37
Thunder Pass '37
Thunder Trail '37

Blue ▶cont.

Rootin' Tootin' Rhythm *'38*
Silver River *'48*

Jack Blum
Happy Birthday to Me *'81*
SnakeEater 2: The Drug Buster *'89*

Mark Blum
Desperately Seeking Susan *'85*
Crocodile Dundee *'86*
Blind Date *'87*
The Presidio *'88*
Worth Winning *'89*
Indictment: The McMartin Trial *'95*

Alan Blumenfeld
Worth Winning *'89*
Dark Side of the Moon *'90*
Instant Karma *'90*
Night Life *'90*
Problem Child 2 *'91*
Black Belt *'92*

Graeme Blundell
Alvin Purple *'73*
Alvin Rides Again *'74*
Weekend of Shadows *'77*
Doctors and Nurses *'82*
The Year My Voice Broke *'87*

Lothaire Bluteau
Jesus of Montreal *'89*
Black Robe *'91*
Mrs. 'Arris Goes to Paris *'92*
Orlando *'92*
The Silent Touch *'94*
The Confessional *'95*

Margaret Blye
Waterhole #3 *'67*
The Italian Job *'69*
The Sporting Club *'72*
Ash Wednesday *'73*
Melvin Purvis: G-Man *'74*
Little Darlings *'80*
Mischief *'85*
Silhouette *'91*

Stanley Blystone
The Fighting Legion *'30*
Man of Action *'33*
Fighting Parson *'35*

Ann Blyth
Mildred Pierce *'45*
Mr. Peabody & the Mermaid *'48*
The Great Caruso *'51*
One Minute to Zero *'52*
All the Brothers Were Valiant *'53*
Rose Marie *'54*
The Student Prince *'54*
The King's Thief *'55*
Kismet *'55*

Betty Blythe
Nomads of the North *'20*
She *'21*
The Scarlet Letter *'34*
Honky Tonk *'41*
Misbehaving Husbands *'41*
Dawn on the Great Divide *'42*
House of Errors *'42*
Miracle Kid *'42*

Janus Blythe
The Hills Have Eyes, Part 2 *'84*
Soldier's Fortune *'91*

Bruce Boa
Murder Story *'89*
White Light *'90*
The Neighbor *'93*

Eleanor Boardman
The Crowd *'28*
She Goes to War *'29*

Virginia True Boardman
Test of Donald Norton *'26*
Brand of the Outlaws *'36*

Michael Boatman
Hamburger Hill *'87*
China Beach *'88*
Urban Crossfire *'94*
The Glass Shield *'95*

Anne Bobby
Night Breed *'90*
Baby of the Bride *'91*
Scott Turow's The Burden of Proof *'92*
Beautiful Girls *'96*

Hart Bochner
East of Eden *'80*
Terror Train *'80*
Rich and Famous *'81*
Having It All *'82*
Supergirl *'84*
The Wild Life *'84*
Making Mr. Right *'86*
Apartment Zero *'88*
Die Hard *'88*
War & Remembrance, Part 1 *'88*
War & Remembrance, Part 3 *'88*
War & Remembrance, Part 4 *'88*
War & Remembrance, Part 5 *'88*
War & Remembrance, Part 6 *'88*
War & Remembrance, Part 7 *'88*
Fellow Traveler *'89*
War & Remembrance, Part 2 *'89*
War & Remembrance: The Final Chapter, Part 8 *'89*
War & Remembrance: The Final Chapter, Part 9 *'89*
War & Remembrance: The Final Chapter, Part 10 *'89*
War & Remembrance: The Final Chapter, Part 11 *'89*
War & Remembrance: The Final Chapter, Part 12 *'89*
Mr. Destiny *'90*
Mad at the Moon *'92*
The Innocent *'93*
A Good Day to Die *'95*

Lloyd Bochner
The Night Walker *'64*
Point Blank *'67*
Tony Rome *'67*
The Horse in the Gray Flannel Suit *'68*
The Dunwich Horror *'70*
Ulzana's Raid *'72*
Satan's School for Girls *'73*
Terraces *'77*
Mary and Joseph: A Story of Faith *'79*
Mazes and Monsters *'82*
The Lonely Lady *'83*
Crystal Heart *'87*
Louisiana *'87*
Fine Gold *'88*
Millenium *'89*
Naked Gun 2 1/2: The Smell of Fear *'91*
Landslide *'92*
Morning Glory *'93*

Wolfgang Bodison
A Few Good Men *'92*
Little Big League *'94*
The Expert *'95*

Erika Bodnar
A Happy New Year! *'79*
Almanac of Fall

Karl-Heinz Boehm
Unnatural *'52*
The Wonderful World of the Brothers Grimm *'62*
Peeping Tom *'63*
Fox and His Friends *'75*

Dirk Bogarde
The Blue Lamp *'49*
Doctor in the House *'53*
The Sleeping Tiger *'54*
Cast a Dark Shadow *'55*
The Sea Shall Not Have Them *'55*
Simba *'55*
Doctor at Sea *'56*
Doctor at Large *'57*
Night Ambush *'57*
The Spanish Gardener *'57*
A Tale of Two Cities *'58*
Song Without End *'60*
Damn the Defiant *'62*
Victim *'62*
Doctor in Distress *'63*
I Could Go on Singing *'63*
The Servant *'63*
Darling *'65*
Accident *'67*
The Fixer *'68*
Sebastian *'68*
The Damned *'69*
Justine *'69*
Death in Venice *'71*
Night Flight from Moscow *'73*
The Night Porter *'74*
Permission To Kill *'75*
A Bridge Too Far *'77*
Providence *'77*
Despair *'78*
To See Such Fun *'81*
The Vision *'87*
Daddy Nostalgia *'90*

Humphrey Bogart
Three on a Match *'32*
Midnight *'34*
Petrified Forest *'36*
Dead End *'37*
Kid Galahad *'37*
Marked Woman *'37*
Stand-In *'37*
Angels with Dirty Faces *'38*
Bullets or Ballots *'38*
Dark Victory *'39*
Oklahoma Kid *'39*
The Roaring Twenties *'39*
Brother Orchid *'40*
They Drive by Night *'40*
Virginia City *'40*
High Sierra *'41*
The Maltese Falcon *'41*
Across the Pacific *'42*
All Through the Night *'42*
Casablanca *'42*
Action in the North Atlantic *'43*
The Best of Bogart *'43*
Sahara *'43*
Thank Your Lucky Stars *'43*
Passage to Marseilles *'44*
To Have & Have Not *'44*
Conflict *'45*
The Big Sleep *'46*
Dark Passage *'47*
Dead Reckoning *'47*
The Two Mrs. Carrolls *'47*
Key Largo *'48*
Treasure of the Sierra Madre *'48*
Knock on Any Door *'49*
Tokyo Joe *'49*
Chain Lightning *'50*
In a Lonely Place *'50*
The African Queen *'51*
The Enforcer *'51*
Sirocco *'51*
Battle Circus *'53*
Beat the Devil *'53*
The Barefoot Contessa *'54*
The Caine Mutiny *'54*
Sabrina *'54*
Desperate Hours *'55*
The Left Hand of God *'55*
We're No Angels *'55*
The Harder They Fall *'56*
Hollywood Outtakes & Rare Footage *'83*

Eric Bogosian
Special Effects *'85*
The Caine Mutiny Court Martial *'88*
Talk Radio *'88*
Last Flight Out: A True Story *'90*
Suffering Bastards *'90*
Sex, Drugs, Rock & Roll: Eric Bogosian *'91*
Witch Hunt *'94*
Under Siege 2: Dark Territory *'95*

Roman Bohnen
The Hairy Ape *'44*
The Best Years of Our Lives *'46*
Open Secret *'48*

Corinne Bohrer
Stewardess School *'86*
Dead Solid Perfect *'88*
Vice Versa *'88*
Revenge of the Nerds 4: Nerds in Love *'94*

Richard Bohringer
Diva *'82*
L'Addition *'85*
Peril *'85*
Le Grand Chemin *'87*
The Cook, the Thief, His Wife & Her Lover *'90*
The Accompanist *'93*
Barjo *'93*

Romane Bohringer
Les Nuits Fauves *'92*
The Accompanist *'93*
Mina Tannenbaum *'94*
Total Eclipse *'95*

Curt Bois
The Great Waltz *'38*
The Hunchback of Notre Dame *'39*
Bitter Sweet *'40*
Boom Town *'40*
The Lady in Question *'40*
The Tuttles of Tahiti *'42*
Caught *'49*
The Boat is Full *'81*
Wings of Desire *'88*

Christine Boisson
Sorceress *'88*
Unsettled Land *'88*

James Bolam
The Loneliness of the Long Distance Runner *'62*
Crucible of Terror *'72*
Dressed for Death *'74*
In Celebration *'75*
The Maze *'85*

Mary Boland
Ruggles of Red Gap *'35*
The Women *'39*
New Moon *'40*
One Night in the Tropics *'40*
Pride and Prejudice *'40*
Nothing But Trouble *'44*
Julia Misbehaves *'48*

John Boles
King of Jazz *'30*
Frankenstein *'31*
Stand Up and Cheer *'34*
Curly Top *'35*
The Littlest Rebel *'35*
Craig's Wife *'36*
Stella Dallas *'37*
Sinners in Paradise *'38*
Thousands Cheer *'43*

Ray Bolger
The Great Ziegfeld *'36*
Rosalie *'38*
Sweethearts *'38*
The Wizard of Oz *'39*
Four Jacks and a Jill *'41*
Sunny *'41*
Stage Door Canteen *'43*
The Harvey Girls *'46*
Look for the Silver Lining *'49*
April In Paris *'52*
Babes in Toyland *'61*
For Heaven's Sake *'79*
The Runner Stumbles *'79*
That's Dancing! *'85*

Florinda Bolkan
The Last Valley *'71*
Ring of Death *'72*
Master Touch *'74*
Royal Flash *'75*
The Day That Shook the World *'78*
The Word *'78*
Black Lemons *'80s*
Acqua e Sapone *'83*
Some Girls *'88*
Collector's Item *'89*

Tiffany Bolling
Bonnie's Kids *'73*
The Centerfold Girls *'74*
Wild Party *'74*
Kingdom of the Spiders *'77*
Ecstasy *'84*

Ryan Bollman
Children of the Corn 2: The Final Sacrifice *'92*
The Neverending Story 3 *'94*

Joseph Bologna
Cops and Robbers *'73*
Honor Thy Father *'73*
The Big Bus *'76*
Chapter Two *'79*
Torn Between Two Lovers *'79*
My Favorite Year *'82*
One Cooks, the Other Doesn't *'83*
Blame It on Rio *'84*
The Woman in Red *'84*
Transylvania 6-5000 *'85*
Not Quite Human *'87*
Rags to Riches *'87*
Alligator 2: The Mutation *'90*
Coupe de Ville *'90*
Citizen Cohn *'92*
Deadly Rivals *'92*
Jersey Girl *'92*
Revenge of the Nerds 4: Nerds in Love *'94*
Danger of Love *'95*

Jon Bon Jovi
Young Guns 2 *'90*
Moonlight and Valentino *'95*

Paolo Bonacelli
Salo, or the 120 Days of Sodom *'75*
Christ Stopped at Eboli *'79*
Henry IV *'85*
Night on Earth *'91*
Johnny Stecchino *'92*
Francesco *'93*

Danny Bonaduce
H.O.T.S. *'79*
America's Deadliest Home Video *'91*

Louie Bonanno
Night of the Living Babes *'87*
Wimps *'87*
Student Affairs *'88*

Fortunio Bonanova
The Black Swan *'42*
Ali Baba and the Forty Thieves *'43*
For Whom the Bell Tolls *'43*
Double Indemnity *'44*
An Affair to Remember *'57*

Ivan Bonar
MacArthur *'77*
The Haunting Passion *'83*

Derek Bond
Nicholas Nickleby *'46*
Inheritance *'47*
Scott of the Antarctic *'48*
The Weaker Sex *'49*
Tony Draws a Horse *'51*
The Stranger from Venus *'54*
Svengali *'55*
Rogue's Yarn *'56*
Black Tide *'58*
The Hand *'60*

James Bond, III
The Fish that Saved Pittsburgh *'79*
Go Tell It On the Mountain *'84*
Def by Temptation *'90*

Renee Bond
Please Don't Eat My Mother *'72*
Class Reunion *'87*

Steve Bond
Massacre at Central High *'76*
Gas Pump Girls *'79*
H.O.T.S. *'79*
The Prey *'80*
Magdalene *'88*
L.A. Gangs Rising *'89*
Picasso Trigger *'89*
To Die for *'89*
To Die for 2: Son of Darkness *'91*
Tryst *'94*

Sudie Bond
Tomorrow *'72*
Where the Lilies Bloom *'74*
Come Back to the Five & Dime Jimmy Dean, Jimmy Dean *'82*
I Am the Cheese *'83*
Trumps *'83*

Tommy "Butch" Bond
Our Gang Comedies *'40s*
Superman: The Serial, Vol. 1 *'48*

Ward Bond
Big Trail *'30*
Hello Trouble *'32*
White Eagle *'32*
Heroes for Sale *'33*
It Happened One Night *'34*
The Crimson Trail *'35*
Devil Dogs of the Air *'35*
Fighting Shadows *'35*
Park Avenue Logger *'37*
You Only Live Once *'37*
Born to Be Wild *'38*
Bringing Up Baby *'38*
Hawaii Calls *'38*
Prison Break *'38*
Drums Along the Mohawk *'39*
Gone with the Wind *'39*
Oklahoma Kid *'39*
Waterfront *'39*
Young Mr. Lincoln *'39*
Kit Carson *'40*
The Maltese Falcon *'41*
Sergeant York *'41*
Wheel of Fortune *'41*

The Fighting Sullivans '42
Gentleman Jim '42
Hello, Frisco, Hello '43
Hitler: Dead or Alive '43
A Guy Named Joe '44
Tall in the Saddle '44
Dakota '45
They Were Expendable '45
It's a Wonderful Life '46
My Darling Clementine '46
Unconquered '47
Fort Apache '48
The Fugitive '48
Three Godfathers '48
The Time of Your Life '48
The Falcon Takes Over/Strange Bargain '49
Kiss Tomorrow Goodbye '50
Only the Valiant '50
Riding High '50
Wagon Master '50
Great Missouri Raid '51
On Dangerous Ground '51
The Quiet Man '52
Hondo '53
Johnny Guitar '53
Blowing Wild '54
Gypsy Colt '54
The Long Gray Line '55
A Man Alone '55
Mister Roberts '55
Dakota Incident '56
The Searchers '56
Wings of Eagles '57
Rio Bravo '59

Sergei Bondarchuk
A Summer to Remember '61
War and Peace '68
Battle of Neretva '69

Beulah Bondi
Street Scene '31
Rain '32
Finishing School '33
The Invisible Ray '36
The Moon's Our Home '36
Of Human Hearts '38
The Sisters '38
Vivacious Lady '38
Mr. Smith Goes to Washington '39
On Borrowed Time '39
Our Town '40
Remember the Night '40
Penny Serenade '41
Watch on the Rhine '43
Back to Bataan '45
The Southerner '45
Breakfast in Hollywood '46
It's a Wonderful Life '46
Sister Kenny '46
The Snake Pit '48
So Dear to My Heart '49
Baron of Arizona '51
Lone Star '52
Latin Lovers '53
Unholy Wife '57
A Summer Place '59
The Wonderful World of the Brothers Grimm '62

Peter Bonerz
The Committee '68
Medium Cool '69
A Session with the Committee '69
How to Break Up a Happy Divorce '76
Serial '80
Your Place or Mine '83

Ken Bones
Bellman and True '88
Jack the Ripper '88

Charles Bonet
Black Dragon's Revenge '75
Death Promise '78
Way of the Black Dragon '81

Lisa Bonet
Angel Heart '87
Bank Robber '93
Dead Connection '94
New Eden '94

Nai Bonet
Devil's Angels '67
Fairy Tales '76
Soul Hustler '76
Gangsters '79
Nocturna '79

Massimo Bonetti
The Night of the Shooting Stars '82
Kaos '85
The Story of Boys & Girls '91

Helena Bonham Carter
Lady Jane '85
A Room with a View '86
Maurice '87
The Vision '87
Getting It Right '89
Hamlet '90
Where Angels Fear to Tread '91
Howard's End '92
A Dark Adapted Eye '93
Francesco '93
Mary Shelley's Frankenstein '94
Margaret's Museum '95
Mighty Aphrodite '95

Sandrine Bonnaire
A Nos Amours '84
Police '85
Vagabond '85
La Puritaine '86
Under Satan's Sun '87
Monsieur Hire '89
The Plague '92
La Ceremonie '95

Lee Bonnell
Look Who's Laughing '41
The Navy Comes Through '42

Vivian Bonnell
The Josephine Baker Story '90
Christmas in Connecticut '92

Bill Bonner
Satan's Sadists '69
Outlaw Riders '72

Frank Bonner
Equinox '71
WKRP in Cincinnati, Vol. 1 '78
You Can't Hurry Love '88
The Colony '95

Tony Bonner
Creatures the World Forgot '70
Sudden Terror '70
Inn of the Damned '74
Alternative '76
Money Movers '78
The Lighthorsemen '87
Quigley Down Under '90
Dead Sleep '91
Hurricane Smith '92

Sonny Bono
Murder on Flight 502 '75
Escape to Athena '79
Airplane 2: The Sequel '82
Balboa '82
The Vals '85
Troll '86
Dirty Laundry '87
Hairspray '88
Under the Boardwalk '89

Brian Bonsall
Desperate Motives '92
Mikey '92
Blank Check '93
Father Hood '93
Lily in Winter '94
Father and Scout '95

Sorrell Booke
Gone are the Days '63
Up the Down Staircase '67
Bank Shot '74
Devil Times Five '74
Special Delivery '76
The Other Side of Midnight '77

Pat Boone
Journey to the Center of the Earth '59
State Fair '62
The Cross & the Switchblade '72
Roger & Me '89

Richard Boone
The Halls of Montezuma '50
Beneath the 12-Mile Reef '53
The Robe '53
Dragnet '54
Ten Wanted Men '54
Away All Boats '56
The Tall T '57
I Bury the Living '58
The Alamo '60
Rio Conchos '64
The War Lord '65
Hombre '67
The Arrangement '69
The Night of the Following Day '69
Madron '70
Big Jake '71
Against A Crooked Sky '75
God's Gun '75
The Shootist '76
The Big Sleep '78
Winter Kills '79
The Bushido Blade '80

Charley Boorman
Deliverance '72
Excalibur '81
The Emerald Forest '85
Hope and Glory '87
Picture Windows '95

Katrine Boorman
Hope and Glory '87
Camille Claudel '89

Elayne Boosler
Meatballs 2 '84
Mother Goose Rock 'n' Rhyme '90

Adrian Booth
The Man They Could Not Hang '39
Ridin' Down the Canyon '42
Captain America '44
Daughter of Don Q '46
Son of God's Country '48

Connie Booth
John Cleese on How to Irritate People '68
Monty Python's Flying Circus '71
Romance with a Double Bass '74
Monty Python and the Holy Grail '75
Fawlty Towers '77
Little Lord Fauntleroy '80
Nairobi Affair '88
Hawks '89
American Friends '91
Leon the Pig Farmer '93
The Strange Case of the End of Civilization as We Know It '93
The Buccaneers '95

Edwina Booth
Trader Horn '31
The Last of the Mohicans '32

James Booth
The Trials of Oscar Wilde '60
Robbery '67
The Bliss of Mrs. Blossom '68
Darker than Amber '70
Man Who Had Power Over Women '70
Revenge '71
Rentadick '72
Brannigan '75
Hotline '82
Pray for Death '85
Bad Guys '86
Programmed to Kill '86
American Ninja 4: The Annihilation '91

Karin Booth
Tobor the Great '54
Beloved Infidel '59

Shirley Booth
Come Back, Little Sheba '52
Hot Spell '58
The Matchmaker '58

Powers Boothe
Skag '79
Cruising '80
A Cry for Love '80
The Guyana Tragedy: The Story of Jim Jones '80
Southern Comfort '81
Plutonium Incident '82
A Breed Apart '84
Red Dawn '84
The Emerald Forest '85
Smart-Aleck Kill '85
Extreme Prejudice '87
Into the Homeland '87
By Dawn's Early Light '89
Blue Sky '91
Rapid Fire '92
Wildcard '92
Tombstone '93
Dalva '95
Mutant Species '95
Nixon '95
Sudden Death '95

Cornell Borchers
The Big Lift '50
Istanbul '57

Lynn Borden
Frogs '72
This Is a Hijack '75

Carla Borelli
Asylum of Satan '72
Charlotte Forten's Mission: Experiment in Freedom '85

Veda Ann Borg
False Faces '32
Kid Galahad '37
Dr. Christian Meets the Women '40
I Take This Oath '40
Melody Ranch '40
Honky Tonk '41
The Corsican Brothers '42
I Married an Angel '42
Isle of Forgotten Sins '43
Revenge of the Zombies '43
The Falcon in Hollywood '44
Marked Trails '44
Fog Island '45
Treasure of Fear '45
Accomplice '46
The Bachelor and the Bobby-Soxer '47
Big Town '47
Blonde Savage '47
Julia Misbehaves '48
Rider from Tucson '50
Big Jim McLain '52
Guys and Dolls '55
I'll Cry Tomorrow '55
Love Me or Leave Me '55
Wings of Eagles '57
The Alamo '60

Nelly Borgeaud
Mississippi Mermaid '69
The Accompanist '93

Sal Borgese
Thundersquad '85
Flight of the Innocent '93

Ernest Borgnine
From Here to Eternity '53
Johnny Guitar '53
The Stranger Wore a Gun '53
Vera Cruz '53
Bad Day at Black Rock '54
Demetrius and the Gladiators '54
The Last Command '55
Marty '55
The Catered Affair '56
Jubal '56
The Badlanders '58
Torpedo Run '58
The Vikings '58
Barabbas '62
The Flight of the Phoenix '65
The Oscar '66
Chuka '67
The Dirty Dozen '67
Ice Station Zebra '68
The Wild Bunch '69
The Adventurers '70
Bullet for Sandoval '70
Suppose They Gave a War and Nobody Came? '70
Counter Punch '71
The Trackers '71
Willard '71
Hannie Caulder '72
The Poseidon Adventure '72
Neptune Factor '73
Law and Disorder '74
Devil's Rain '75
Future Cop '76
High Risk '76
Love by Appointment '76
Fire '77
The Greatest '77
Jesus of Nazareth '77
Convoy '78
The Prince and the Pauper '78
All Quiet on the Western Front '79
The Black Hole '79
The Double McGuffin '79
When Time Ran Out '80
Deadly Blessing '81
Escape from New York '81
Super Fuzz '81
Young Warriors '83
Codename: Wildgeese '84
Love Leads the Way '84
Vengeance Is Mine '84
The Dirty Dozen: The Next Mission '85
Shoot '85
The Manhunt '86
The Dirty Dozen: The Deadly Mission '87
The Dirty Dozen: The Fatal Mission '88
Spike of Bensonhurst '88
Moving Target '89
The Opponent '89
Skeleton Coast '89
Any Man's Death '90
Laser Mission '90

Roscoe Born
Lady Mobster '88
Haunting of Sarah Hardy '89

Katherine Borowitz
Fellow Traveler '89
Men of Respect '91
Mac '93

Jesse Borrego
Blood In...Blood Out: Bound by Honor '93
I Like It Like That '94
Mi Vida Loca '94
Tecumseh: The Last Warrior '95

Dieter Borsche
Ali Baba and the 40 Thieves '54
Dead Eyes of London '61
The Black Abbot '63
The Phantom of Soho '64
The Mad Executioners '65

Jean-Mark Bory
The Lovers '59
Le Repos du Guerrier '62
RoGoPaG '62

Frank Borzage
Grit of the Girl Telegrapher/In the Switch Tower '15
Tale of Two Cities/In the Switch Tower '15
A Mormon Maid '17

Philip Bosco
Heaven Help Us '85
Walls of Glass '85
Children of a Lesser God '86
The Mission '86
The Money Pit '86
Suspect '87
Three Men and a Baby '87
Another Woman '88
Working Girl '88
The Dream Team '89
Blue Steel '90
Quick Change '90
F/X 2: The Deadly Art of Illusion '91
The Return of Eliot Ness '91
Shadows and Fog '92
Straight Talk '92
Against the Wall '94
Angie '94
Milk Money '94
Nobody's Fool '94
Safe Passage '94
It Takes Two '95

Lucia Bose
The Legend of Blood Castle '72
Lumiere '76

Miguel Bose
High Heels '91
Queen Margot '94

Andrea Bosic
Maciste in Hell '60
Pirates of the Seven Seas '62
Hornet's Nest '70

Tom Bosley
Love with the Proper Stranger '63
The World of Henry Orient '64
Bang Bang Kid '67
Divorce American Style '67
The Secret War of Harry Frigg '68
Yours, Mine & Ours '68
Night Gallery '69
The Streets of San Francisco '72
Death Cruise '74
Gus '76
The Bastard '78
The Rebels '79

Bosley ▶cont.

The Triangle Factory Fire Scandal '79
For the Love of It '80
O'Hara's Wife '82
The Jesse Owens Story '84
Million Dollar Mystery '87
Fire and Rain '89
Wicked Stepmother '89

Barbara Bosson
The Committee '68
A Session with the Committee '69
The Last Starfighter '84
Little Sweetheart '90
The Great American Sex Scandal '94

Barry Bostwick
The Rocky Horror Picture Show '75
Movie, Movie '78
Murder by Natural Causes '79
Scruples '80
Red Flag: The Ultimate Game '81
Megaforce '82
George Washington '84
A Woman of Substance, Episode 1: Nest of Vipers '84
A Woman of Substance, Episode 2: The Secret is Revealed '84
A Woman of Substance, Episode 3: Fighting for the Dream '84
George Washington: The Forging of a Nation '86
Jailbait: Betrayed By Innocence '86
Hitchhiker 3 '87
War & Remembrance, Part 1 '88
War & Remembrance, Part 2 '89
800 Leagues Down the Amazon '93
Praying Mantis '93
Russian Roulette '93
Weekend at Bernie's 2 '93
In the Heat of Passion 2: Unfaithful '94
Project Metalbeast: DNA Overload '94
The Secretary '94
Spy Hard '96

Jackson Bostwick
Escape from DS-3 '80s
A Matter of Honor '95

Brian Bosworth
Stone Cold '91
One Man's Justice '95

Hobart Bosworth
The Little American '17
A Mormon Maid '17
Sea Lion '21
Little Church Around the Corner '23
The Big Parade '25
The Nervous Wreck '26
Spangles '26
Annapolis '28
A Woman of Affairs '28
Abraham Lincoln '30
Dubarry '30
The Last of the Mohicans '32
Phantom Express '32
The Crusades '35
The Dark Hour '36
King of the Sierras '38

Wade Boteler
Let 'er Go Gallegher '28
Big News '29
Come On Danger! '32
The Mandarin Mystery '37
The Green Hornet '39

Sara Botsford
By Design '82
Deadly Eyes '82
Murder by Phone '82
Still of the Night '82
The Gunrunner '84

Benjamin Bottoms
Stalk the Wild Child '76
A Shining Season '79

Joseph Bottoms
The Dove '74
Crime & Passion '75
Stalk the Wild Child '76
High Rolling in a Hot Corvette '77
Holocaust '78
Return Engagement '78
The Black Hole '79
Cloud Dancer '80
Intruder Within '81
King of the Mountain '81
The Sins of Dorian Gray '82
Blind Date '84
Surfacing '84
Celebrity '85
Open House '86
Born to Race '88
Inner Sanctum '91
Liar's Edge '92
Treacherous Crossing '92

Sam Bottoms
The Last Picture Show '71
Class of '44 '73
Zandy's Bride '74
Savages '75
The Outlaw Josey Wales '76
Apocalypse Now '79
Up from the Depths '79
Bronco Billy '80
East of Eden '80
Desperate Lives '82
Prime Risk '84
In 'n Out '86
Gardens of Stone '87
Hunter's Blood '87
Return to Eden '89
Ragin' Cajun '90
Hearts of Darkness: A Filmmaker's Apocalypse '91
Dolly Dearest '92
Project Shadowchaser 3000 '95
The Witching of Ben Wagner '95

Timothy Bottoms
Johnny Got His Gun '71
The Last Picture Show '71
The Paper Chase '73
The White Dawn '75
A Small Town in Texas '76
The Story of David '76
Rollercoaster '77
The Other Side of the Mountain, Part 2 '78
Hurricane '79
A Shining Season '79
East of Eden '80
High Country '81
Tin Man '83
What Waits Below '83
Hambone & Hillie '84
Love Leads the Way '84
The Sea Serpent '85
Husbands, Wives, Money, and Murder '86
In the Shadow of Kilimanjaro '86
Invaders from Mars '86
The Land of Faraway '87
The Drifter '88
The Fantasist '89
The Gift of Love '90
Istanbul '90
Texasville '90
Ava's Magical Adventure '94
Digger '94
Hourglass '95
Top Dog '95

Savannah Smith Boucher
The Applegates '89
Last Summer In the Hamptons '96

Barbara Bouchet
In Harm's Way '65
Cry of a Prostitute: Love Kills '72
Mean Machine '73
Surabaya Conspiracy '75
Rogue '76

Patrick Bouchitey
The Best Way '82
Life Is a Long Quiet River '88

Jean Bouise
I Am Cuba '64
Old Gun '76
Hothead '78
Le Dernier Combat '84
La Femme Nikita '91

Michel Boujenah
Three Men and a Cradle '85
Les Miserables '95

Ingrid Boulting
The Last Tycoon '76
Deadly Passion '85

Carole Bouquet
That Obscure Object of Desire '77
Buffet Froid '79
Dagger Eyes '80s
For Your Eyes Only '81
Special Police '85
Too Beautiful for You '88
New York Stories '89
A Business Affair '93
Grosse Fatigue '94

Michel Bouquet
Pattes Blanches '49
This Special Friendship '67
The Bride Wore Black '68
Mississippi Mermaid '69
Borsalino '70
La Rupture '70
Le Complot '73
Toto le Heros '91
Tous les Matins du Monde '92

Bourvil
Mr. Peek-A-Boo '50
Crazy for Love '52
Four Bags Full '56
Les Miserables '57
Jailbird's Vacation '65
Les Grandes Gueules '65
The Sucker '65
La Grande Vadrouille '66
The Brain '69

Dennis Boutsikaris
*batteries not included '87
The Dream Team '89

Brunella Bova
Miracle in Milan '51
The White Sheik '52

Julie Bovasso
Willie & Phil '80
Gentleman Bandit '81
Wise Guys '86
Moonstruck '87
Betsy's Wedding '90
Article 99 '92

Clara Bow
Down to the Sea in Ships '22
Free to Love '25
My Lady of Whims '25
Dancing Mothers '26
Mantrap '26
It '27
Wings '27
Hula '28

Dorris Bowdon
Drums Along the Mohawk '39
The Grapes of Wrath '40

Christopher Bowen
The Shell Seekers '89
Cold Comfort Farm '94

Dennis Bowen
Gas Pump Girls '79
Van Nuys Blvd. '79

Michael Bowen
Night of the Comet '84
Echo Park '86
Iron Eagle '86
The Abduction of Kari Swenson '87
Season of Fear '89
Mortal Passions '90
The Taking of Beverly Hills '91
Casualties of Love: The "Long Island Lolita" Story '93
New Eden '94

Roger Bowen
M*A*S*H '70
Zapped! '82
What About Bob? '91

Malick Bowens
Out of Africa '85
The Believers '87
Bopha! '93

Antoinette Bower
Die Sister, Die! '74
Blood Song '82
The Evil That Men Do '84

Tom Bower
Ballad of Gregorio Cortez '83
Massive Retaliation '85
Wildrose '85
The Lightship '86
Family Sins '87
River's Edge '87
Promised a Miracle '88
True Believer '89
Love, Lies and Murder '91
Raising Cain '92
Relentless 3 '93
Against the Wall '94
Far from Home: The Adventures of Yellow Dog '94
The Avenging Angel '95
White Man's Burden '95

John Bowers
The Sky Pilot '21
Lorna Doone '22
The White Sin '24

David Bowie
The Man Who Fell to Earth '76
Just a Gigolo '79
Christiane F. '82
The Hunger '83
Merry Christmas, Mr. Lawrence '83
Yellowbeard '83
Into the Night '85
Absolute Beginners '86
Labyrinth '86
The Last Temptation of Christ '88
UHF '89
The Linguini Incident '92

Judi Bowker
Brother Sun, Sister Moon '73
East of Elephant Rock '76
Clash of the Titans '81
Anna Karenina '85
The Shooting Party '85

Peter Bowles
The Charge of the Light Brigade '68
A Day in the Death of Joe Egg '71
Endless Night '71
The Offence '73

Laura Bowman
Drums O'Voodoo '34
Son of Ingagi '40

Lee Bowman
Internes Can't Take Money '37
Next Time I Marry '38
Love Affair '39
Buck Privates '41
Bataan '43
Cover Girl '44
Tonight and Every Night '45
Smash-Up: The Story of a Woman '47
My Dream Is Yours '49

Bruce Boxleitner
The Baltimore Bullet '80
East of Eden '80
Kenny Rogers as the Gambler '80
Tron '82
Kenny Rogers as the Gambler, Part 2: The Adventure Continues '83
Passion Flower '86
Kenny Rogers as the Gambler, Part 3: The Legend Continues '87
From the Dead of Night '89
Diplomatic Immunity '91
Murderous Vision '91
The Babe '92
Double Jeopardy '92
Kuffs '92
Perfect Family '92
The Secret '93
Wyatt Earp: Return to Tombstone '94

Alan Boyce
Permanent Record '88
Totally F***ed Up '94

Todd Boyce
Great Expectations: The Untold Story '87
Jefferson in Paris '94

Beverly Boyd
Ghost Rider '43
Jive Junction '43

Blake Boyd
Dune Warriors '91
Raiders of the Sun '92

Guy Boyd
Keeping On '81
The Eyes of the Amaryllis '82
Body Double '84
Eyes of Fire '84
The Jagged Edge '85
Murder Ordained '87
The Last of the Finest '90
Kiss Me a Killer '91
Past Midnight '92

Stephen Boyd
The Man Who Never Was '55
The Bravados '58
Ben-Hur '59
The Best of Everything '59
Billy Rose's Jumbo '62
The Fall of the Roman Empire '64
The Bible...In the Beginning '66
Fantastic Voyage '66
The Oscar '66
Caper of the Golden Bulls '67
Shalako '68
Black Brigade '69
Imperial Venus '71
Hannie Caulder '72
The Treasure of Jamaica Reef '74
The Squeeze '77

William Boyd
The Road to Yesterday '25
King of Kings '27
Road to Yesterday/The Yankee Clipper '27
Yankee Clipper '27
The Leatherneck '28
Power '28
The Flying Fool '29
High Voltage '29
His First Command '29
Painted Desert '31
Midnight Warning '32
Go-Get-'Em-Haines '35
Hopalong Cassidy '35
Racing Luck '35
Federal Agent '36
Rustler's Valley '37
The Frontiersmen '38
Having Wonderful Time/Carnival Boat '38
Hopalong Cassidy: Renegade Trail '39
Law of the Pampas '39
Renegade Trail '39
Santa Fe Marshal '40
The Showdown '40
Border Vigilantes '41
Doomed Caravan '41
In Old Colorado '41
Outlaws of the Desert '41
Riders of the Timberline '41
Twilight on the Trail '41
Along the Sundown Trail '42
Prairie Pals '42
Tumbleweed Trail '42
Bar-20 '43
Border Patrol '43
Colt Comrades '43
False Colors '43
Hopalong Cassidy: Riders of the Deadline '43
Hoppy Serves a Writ '43
Leather Burners '43
Lost Canyon '43
Mystery Man '44
Texas Masquerade '44
Hopalong Cassidy: The Devil's Playground '46
Hopalong Cassidy: Hoppy's Holiday '47
Hopalong Cassidy: The Marauders '47
Hopalong Cassidy: Unexpected Guest '47
Hopalong Cassidy: Borrowed Trouble '48
Hopalong Cassidy: Dangerous Venture '48
Hopalong Cassidy: False Paradise '48
Hopalong Cassidy: Silent Conflict '48
Hopalong Cassidy: Sinister Journey '48
Hopalong Cassidy: The Dead Don't Dream '48

William "Stage" Boyd
State's Attorney '31
Laughing at Life '33
Oliver Twist '33
The Lost City '34
East Side Kids/The Lost City '35

Sally Boyden
Barnaby and Me '77
Little Dragons '80

Charles Boyer
Red Headed Woman '32
Break of Hearts '35
Liliom '35
The Garden of Allah '36
Mayerling '36
Conquest '37
History is Made at Night '37
Algiers '38
Love Affair '39
All This and Heaven Too '40
Tales of Manhattan '42
Gaslight '44
Arch of Triumph '48
First Legion '51
The Earrings of Madame De... '54
The Cobweb '55
Nana '55
Around the World in 80 Days '56
The Buccaneer '58
Fanny '61
Adorable Julia '62
The Four Horsemen of the Apocalypse '62
How to Steal a Million '66
Barefoot in the Park '67
Casino Royale '67
Is Paris Burning? '68
April Fools '69
The Hot Line '69
The Madwoman of Chaillot '69
Stavisky '74
A Matter of Time '76

Katy Boyer
Long Gone '87
Tapeheads '89
Trapped '89
White Dwarf '95

Miriam Boyer
Jonah Who Will Be 25 in the Year 2000 '76
Window Shopping '86
Tous les Matins du Monde '92
Un Coeur en Hiver '93

Sully Boyer
Car Wash '76
The Manhattan Project '86

Lara Flynn Boyle
Poltergeist 3 '88
Dead Poets Society '89
How I Got into College '89
The Preppie Murder '89
May Wine '90
The Rookie '90
Twin Peaks '90
Twin Peaks '90
The Dark Backward '91
Eye of the Storm '91
Mobsters '91
Wayne's World '92
Where the Day Takes You '92
Equinox '93
Red Rock West '93
The Temp '93
Baby's Day Out '94
Jacob '94
Past Tense '94
The Road to Wellville '94
Threesome '94

Lisa Boyle
Elke '95
I Like to Play Games '95

Peter Boyle
Medium Cool '69
Joe '70
The Candidate '72
Slither '73
Steelyard Blues '73
Ghost in the Noonday Sun '74
Young Frankenstein '74
Swashbuckler '76
Taxi Driver '76
Brink's Job '78
F.I.S.T. '78
Beyond the Poseidon Adventure '79
From Here to Eternity '79
Hardcore '79
Where the Buffalo Roam '80
Outland '81
Hammett '82
Yellowbeard '83
Johnny Dangerously '84
Turk 182! '85
Conspiracy: The Trial of the Chicago Eight '87
Echoes in the Darkness '87
Surrender '87
Walker '87
Disaster at Silo 7 '88
Red Heat '88
Speed Zone '88
The Dream Team '89
Kickboxer 2: The Road Back '90
Men of Respect '91
Tragedy of Flight 103: The Inside Story '91
Honeymoon in Vegas '92
Solar Crisis '92
Nervous Ticks '93
Royce '93
Taking the Heat '93
The Shadow '94
The Surgeon '94
Urban Crossfire '94
Born to Be Wild '95
Bulletproof Heart '95
While You Were Sleeping '95

Max Bozyk
Yidl Mitn Fidl '36
The Jolly Paupers '38
Mamele '38

Marcel Bozzuffi
Z '69
The French Connection '71
La Cage aux Folles 2 '81

Teda Bracci
Chrome Hearts '70
The Big Bird Cage '72

Elizabeth Bracco
Mystery Train '89
In the Soup '92
Money for Nothing '93

Lorraine Bracco
Camorra: The Naples Connection '85
The Pick-Up Artist '87
Someone to Watch Over Me '87
The Dream Team '89
Sing '89
Goodfellas '90
Switch '91
Talent for the Game '91
Medicine Man '92
Radio Flyer '92
Traces of Red '92
Scam '93
The Basketball Diaries '94
Being Human '94
Even Cowgirls Get the Blues '94
Getting Gotti '94
Hackers '95

Eddie Bracken
Too Many Girls '40
Caught in the Draft '41
Star Spangled Rhythm '42
Young & Willing '42
Hail the Conquering Hero '44
Miracle of Morgan's Creek '44
Summer Stock '50
We're Not Married '52
National Lampoon's Vacation '83
Home Alone 2: Lost in New York '92

Sidney Bracy
The Cameraman '28
Tangled Destinies '32

Lane Bradbury
Maybe I'll Be Home in the Spring '70
The Ultimate Warrior '75

Kim Braden
Billyboy '79
Bloodsuckers from Outer Space '83

Greg Bradford
Zapped! '82
Lovelines '84

Jesse Bradford
King of the Hill '93
Far from Home: The Adventures of Yellow Dog '94
Hackers '95

Lane Bradford
The Hawk of Powder River '48
Bandit King of Texas '49
The Fighting Redhead '50
The Invisible Monster '50
Gun Glory '57

Richard Bradford
Goin' South '78
More American Graffiti '79
A Rumor of War '80
Running Hot '83
Badge of the Assassin '85
Legend of Billie Jean '85
Mean Season '85
The Trip to Bountiful '85
The Untouchables '87
Little Nikita '88
The Milagro Beanfield War '88
Permanent Record '88
Sunset '88
The Heart of Dixie '89
Internal Affairs '90
Ambition '91
Servants of Twilight '91
The Chinatown Murders: Man Against the Mob '92
Cold Heaven '92
Arctic Blue '93
The Crossing Guard '94
Indictment: The McMartin Trial '95

David Bradley
American Ninja 3: Blood Hunt '89
American Ninja 4: The Annihilation '91
Lower Level '91
American Samurai '92
Blood Warriors '93
Cyborg Cop '93
Cyborg Soldier '94
Exit '95
Hard Justice '95
Outside the Law '95

Doug Bradley
Hellbound: Hellraiser 2 '88
Hellraiser 3: Hell on Earth '92
Hellraiser 4: Bloodline '95

Carl Bradshaw
The Harder They Come '72
The Lunatic '92

Alice Brady
Her Silent Sacrifice '18
The Gay Divorcee '34
Gold Diggers of 1935 '35
Go West, Young Man '36
My Man Godfrey '36
Three Smart Girls '36
100 Men and a Girl '37
In Old Chicago '38
Joy of Living '38
Young Mr. Lincoln '39

Pat Brady
Call of the Canyon '42
Sunset on the Desert '42
Song of Texas '43
Texas Legionnaires '43
Western Double Feature 19 '45
Down Dakota Way '49
The Golden Stallion '49
Bells of Coronado '50
Trigger, Jr. '50
Twilight in the Sierras '50

Scott Brady
He Walked by Night '48
Port of New York '49
Montana Belle '52
Johnny Guitar '53
White Fire '53
Party Girls for Sale '54
The Maverick Queen '55
They Were So Young '55
Mohawk '56
Storm Rider '57
The Restless Breed '58
Castle of Evil '66
Arizona Bushwackers '67
Journey to the Center of Time '67
Gun Riders '69
Satan's Sadists '69
Cain's Cutthroats '71
Dollars '71
Loners '72
Bonnie's Kids '73
Kansas City Massacre '75
When Every Day was the Fourth of July '78
The China Syndrome '79
Strange Behavior '81

Eric (Hans Gudegast) Braeden
Dayton's Devils '68
Colossus: The Forbin Project '70
Escape from the Planet of the Apes '71
Lady Ice '73
The Ultimate Thrill '74
Death Scream '75
The Adultress '77
The Power Within '79
Aliens Are Coming '80
Happily Ever After '82
The Ambulance '90

Sonia Braga
Dona Flor and Her Two Husbands '78
Lady on the Bus '78
I Love You '81
Gabriela '84
Kiss of the Spider Woman '85
The Man Who Broke 1,000 Chains '87
The Milagro Beanfield War '88
Moon over Parador '88
The Rookie '90
The Last Prostitute '91
The Burning Season '94
Larry McMurtry's Streets of Laredo '95
Roosters '95

Wilfrid Brambell
The Conqueror Worm '68
The Adventures of Picasso '80
Sword of the Valiant '83

Francisco (Frank) Brana
Graveyard of Horror '71
Crypt of the Living Dead '73
Street Warriors '87
Cthulhu Mansion '91

Kenneth Branagh
Fortunes of War '87
A Month in the Country '87
High Season '88
Henry V '89
Look Back in Anger '89
Coming Through '90
Dead Again '91
Peter's Friends '92
Much Ado about Nothing '93
Swing Kids '93
Mary Shelley's Frankenstein '94
The Lady's Not for Burning '95
Othello '95

Lillo Brancato
A Bronx Tale '93
Renaissance Man '94
Crimson Tide '95

Neville Brand
D.O.A. '49
The Halls of Montezuma '50
Only the Valiant '50
Kansas City Confidential '52
Stalag 17 '53
Riot in Cell Block 11 '54
The Prodigal '55
Love Me Tender '56
Mohawk '56
Lonely Man '57
The Tin Star '57
The Adventures of Huckleberry Finn '60
Birdman of Alcatraz '62
Scarface Mob '62
That Darn Cat '65
Desperados '69
The Mad Bomber '72
No Place to Run '72
Cahill: United States Marshal '73
The Deadly Trackers '73
The Barbary Coast '74
Death Stalk '74
Psychic Killer '75
This Is a Hijack '75
Eaten Alive '76
The Longest Drive '76
Hi-Riders '77
The Ninth Configuration '79
The Seekers '79
The Return '80
Evils of the Night '85

Klaus Maria Brandauer
The Salzburg Connection '72
Mephisto '81
Never Say Never Again '83
Colonel Redl '84
Kindergarten '84
Out of Africa '85
Quo Vadis '85
The Lightship '86
Streets of Gold '86
Hanussen '88
Burning Secret '89
The Russia House '90
White Fang '91
Becoming Colette '92

Larry Brandenburg
Victimless Crimes '90
Mo' Money '92

Walter Brandi
The Slaughter of the Vampires '62
The Bloody Pit of Horror '65
Terror Creatures from the Grave '66

Jonathan Brandis
Stepfather 2: Make Room for Daddy '89
Stephen King's It '90
NeverEnding Story 2: The Next Chapter '91
Ladybugs '92
Sidekicks '93

Jocelyn Brando
The Big Heat '53
Ten Wanted Men '54
Nightfall '56
A Question of Love '78

Luisina Brando
The Lion's Share '79
Miss Mary '86
I Don't Want to Talk About It '94

Marlon Brando
The Men '50
A Streetcar Named Desire '51
Viva Zapata! '52
Julius Caesar '53
Desiree '54
On the Waterfront '54
The Wild One '54
Guys and Dolls '55
The Teahouse of the August Moon '56
Sayonara '57
The Young Lions '58
The Fugitive Kind '60
One-Eyed Jacks '61
Mutiny on the Bounty '62
Bedtime Story '63
The Ugly American '63
Morituri '65
The Appaloosa '66
The Chase '66
A Countess from Hong Kong '67
Reflections in a Golden Eye '67
The Night of the Following Day '69
Burn! '70
The Godfather '72
The Nightcomers '72
Last Tango in Paris '73
Missouri Breaks '76
Superman: The Movie '78
Apocalypse Now '79
The Formula '80
The Godfather 1902-1959: The Complete Epic '81
Marlon Brando '85
A Dry White Season '89
The Freshman '90
Christopher Columbus: The Discovery '92
Don Juan DeMarco '94
The Island of Dr. Moreau '96

Rikki Brando
The Bikini Car Wash Company 2 '92
Buford's Beach Bunnies '92

Clark Brandon
My Tutor '82
Fast Food '89

David Brandon
Good Morning, Babylon '87
Stagefright '87
Beyond Darkness '92

Henry Brandon
Drums of Fu Manchu '40
War Arrow '53
The Searchers '56
The Land Unknown '57
When the North Wind Blows '74
Assault on Precinct 13 '76

Michael Brandon
Lovers and Other Strangers '70
James Dean '76
Red Alert '77
Promises in the Dark '79
A Change of Seasons '80
Rich and Famous '81

Carolyn Brandt
Incredibly Strange Creatures Who Stopped Living and Became Mixed-Up Zombies '63
The Thrill Killers '65
Rat Pfink a Boo-Boo '66
The Hollywood Strangler Meets the Skid Row Slasher '79

Betsy Brantley
Five Days One Summer '82
Another Country '84
Dreams Lost, Dreams Found '87
The Fourth Protocol '87
Havana '90
I Come in Peace '90
Final Appeal '93

Nicoletta Braschi
Down by Law '86
Mystery Train '89
Johnny Stecchino '92

Keefe Brasselle
Streets of Sin '49
Skirts Ahoy! '52

Claude Brasseur
The Elusive Corporal '62
Band of Outsiders '64
Act of Aggression '73
Pardon Mon Affaire '76
Pardon Mon Affaire, Too! '77
L'Etat Sauvage '78
A Simple Story '79
La Boum '81
Josepha '82
Lobster for Breakfast '82

Pierre Brasseur
Children of Paradise '44
The Horror Chamber of Dr. Faustus '59
Carthage in Flames '60
Il Bell'Antonio '60

Benjamin Bratt
Bright Angel '91
One Good Cop '91
Blood In...Blood Out: Bound by Honor '93
Demolition Man '93
The River Wild '94
Texas '94
Woman Undone '95

Andre Braugher
Glory '89
The Court Martial of Jackie Robinson '90
Somebody Has to Shoot the Picture '90
Class of '61 '92
Striking Distance '93
The Tuskegee Airmen '95
Primal Fear '96

Pinkas Braun
The Man Outside '68
Mission Stardust '68
Praying Mantis '83

Asher Brauner
Boss' Son '79
B.A.D. Cats '80
Treasure of the Moon Goddess '88
American Eagle '90
Merchants of War '90
Living to Die '91

Bart Braverman
The Great Texas Dynamite Chase '76
Hollywood Hot Tubs 2: Educating Crystal '89

Rossano Brazzi
We the Living '42
The Barefoot Contessa '54
Three Coins in the Fountain '54
Summertime '55
Legend of the Lost '57
South Pacific '58
Rome Adventure '62
The Christmas That Almost Wasn't '66
Bobo '67
Woman Times Seven '67
One Step to Hell '68
The Italian Job '69
The Adventurers '70
Mr. Kingstreet's War '71
Dr. Frankenstein's Castle of Freaks '74
A Time for Miracles '80
The Final Conflict '81
The Far Pavilions '84
Final Justice '84
Fear City '85
Formula for a Murder '85
Third Solution '89

Peter Breck
The Beatniks '60
The Crawling Hand '63
Shock Corridor '63
Benji '74
Highway 61 '91
Decoy '95

Larry Breeding
A Matter of Life and Death '81
Street Music '81

Bobby Breen
It Happened in New Orleans '36
Let's Sing Again '36
Make a Wish '37
Breaking the Ice '38
Hawaii Calls '38
Escape to Paradise '39
Fisherman's Wharf '39
Way Down South '39

Patrick Breen
Nobody's Perfect '90
Passed Away '92
Fallen Angels 2 '93
For Love or Money '93

Paulette Breen
The Clonus Horror '79
The Wizard of Speed and Time '88

Tracy Bregman
Happy Birthday to Me '81
The Concrete Jungle '82

Jana Brejchova
Fabulous Adventures of Baron Munchausen '61
The Original Fabulous Adventures of Baron Munchausen '61
Loves of a Blonde '65

Jacques Brel
Les Assassins de L'Ordre '71
Franz '72
Pain in the A— '77

Lucille Bremer
Meet Me in St. Louis '44
Yolanda and the Thief '45
Till the Clouds Roll By '46
Till the Clouds Roll By/A Star Is Born '46
Ziegfeld Follies '46
Behind Locked Doors '48
Human Gorilla '48

Ewen Bremmer
Naked '93
Trainspotting '95

El Brendel
Big Trail '30
Happy Landing '38
I'm from Arkansas '44
The Beautiful Blonde from Bashful Bend '49

Eileen Brennan
Divorce American Style '67
The Last Picture Show '71
Playmates '72
Scarecrow '73
The Sting '73
Daisy Miller '74
My Father's House '75
The Death of Richie '76
Great Smokey Roadblock '76
Murder by Death '76
The Cheap Detective '78
FM '78
My Old Man '79
Private Benjamin '80
The Funny Farm '82
Pandemonium '82
Clue '85
Fourth Wise Man '85
Babes in Toyland '86
Blood Vows: The Story of a Mafia Wife '87
The New Adventures of Pippi Longstocking '88
Rented Lips '88
Sticky Fingers '88
Stella '89
Texasville '90
White Palace '90
I Don't Buy Kisses Anymore '92
Murder So Sweet '93
Reckless '95

Walter Brennan
The Range Feud/Two Fisted Law '31
Texas Cyclone '32
Two-Fisted Law '32
Man of Action '33
Phantom of the Air '33
Barbary Coast '35
Come and Get It '36
Fury '36
The Moon's Our Home '36
Prescott Kid '36
These Three '36
The Adventures of Tom Sawyer '38
The Cowboy and the Lady '38
The Texans '38
Stanley and Livingstone '39
The Story of Vernon and Irene Castle '39
They Shall Have Music '39
Northwest Passage '40
The Westerner '40
Meet John Doe '41
Sergeant York '41
The Pride of the Yankees '42
The North Star '43
The Princess and the Pirate '44
To Have & Have Not '44
Dakota '45
My Darling Clementine '46
A Stolen Life '46
Blood on the Moon '48
Red River '48
The Green Promise '49
Task Force '49
Best of the Badmen '50
The Showdown '50
Ticket to Tomahawk '50
Along the Great Divide '51
Bad Day at Black Rock '54
At Gunpoint '55
Far Country '55
Glory '56
Goodbye, My Lady '56
Tammy and the Bachelor '57
Rio Bravo '59
How the West Was Won '63
Those Calloways '65
The Oscar '66
The Gnome-Mobile '67
Who's Minding the Mint? '67
The One and Only, Genuine, Original Family Band '68
Support Your Local Sheriff '69
Home for the Holidays '72
Smoke in the Wind '75

Amy Brenneman
Casper '95
Heat '95
Fear '96

Dori Brenner
Summer Wishes, Winter Dreams '73
Altered States '80
Sex and the Single Parent '82
Baby Boom '87
For the Boys '91
Silent Victim '92

Evelyn Brent
Trapped by the Mormons '22
Love 'Em and Leave 'Em '26
Underworld '27
Last Command '28
The Silver Horde '30
The President's Mystery '36
Song of the Trail '36
Law West of Tombstone '38
Daughter of the Tong '39
Panama Lady '39
Robot Pilot '41
Holt of the Secret Service '42
The Payoff '43
The Seventh Victim '43

George Brent
Lightning Warrior '31
The Purchase Price '32
They Call It Sin '32
Baby Face '33
Female '33
42nd Street '33
The Painted Veil '34
In Person '35
Jezebel '38
Dark Victory '39
The Old Maid '39
The Rains Came '39
The Fighting 69th '40
The Great Lie '41
In This Our Life '42
Silver Queen '42
Experiment Perilous '45
The Spiral Staircase '46
Tomorrow Is Forever '46
Out of the Blue '47
FBI Girl '52
Man Bait '52
Montana Belle '52
Born Again '78

Linda Brent
Below the Border '42
Death Valley Rangers '44

Romney Brent
Under the Red Robe '36
Dreaming Lips '37
Adventures of Don Juan '49
The Virgin Queen '55
The Sign of Zorro '60

Timothy Brent
Sting of the West '76
Tornado '83
Warriors of the Wasteland '83
Escape from the Bronx '85

Edmund Breon
Casanova Brown '44
Gaslight '44
Woman In the Window '44
Dressed to Kill '46
Forever Amber '47

Bobbie Bresee
Mausoleum '83
Ghoulies '84
Evil Spawn '87
Surf Nazis Must Die '87
Pre-Madonnas: Rebels Without a Clue '95

Felix Bressart
Ninotchka '39
Bitter Sweet '40
Comrade X '40
Edison the Man '40
The Shop Around the Corner '40
Blossoms in the Dust '41
Ziegfeld Girl '41
Iceland '42
To Be or Not to Be '42
The Seventh Cross '44
Without Love '45
Portrait of Jennie '48
A Song is Born '48

Jean Bretonniere
The Green Glove '52
That Naughty Girl '58

Jeremy Brett
The Very Edge '63
My Fair Lady '64
The Merchant of Venice '73
Haunted: The Ferryman '74
One Deadly Owner '74
The Medusa Touch '78
The Adventures of Sherlock Holmes: Hound of the Baskervilles '89
Sherlock Holmes: The Master Blackmailer '92
Moll Flanders '96

Diane Brewster
Courage of Black Beauty '57
The Invisible Boy '57
Torpedo Run '58

Maia Brewton
Back to the Future '85
Adventures in Babysitting '87

Tom Breznahan
The Brain '88
Twice Dead '88
Ski School '91

Jean-Claude Brialy
Le Beau Serge '58
The Cousins '59
The 400 Blows '59
Paris Belongs to Us '60
A Woman is a Woman '60
Cleo from 5 to 7 '61
The Burning Court '62
Circle of Love '64
Tonio Kroger '65
The Bride Wore Black '68
Phantom of Liberty '68
Claire's Knee '71
The Judge and the Assassin '75
Catherine & Co. '76
L'Anne Sainte '78
Robert et Robert '79
La Nuit de Varennes '82
No Fear, No Die '90
Queen Margot '94

David Brian
Beyond the Forest '49
Flamingo Road '49
Intruder in the Dust '49
Million Dollar Mermaid '52
Springfield Rifle '52
Ambush at Tomahawk Gap '53
Pocketful of Miracles '61
Castle of Evil '66
Confessions of Tom Harris '72

Mary Brian
Behind the Front '26
Running Wild '27
The Light of Western Stars '30
Blessed Event '32
Monte Carlo Nights '34
Charlie Chan in Paris '35
Amazing Adventure '37

Shane Briant
Demons of the Mind '72
Captain Kronos: Vampire Hunter '74
Dressed for Death '74
Frankenstein and the Monster from Hell '74
Picture of Dorian Gray '74
The Flame Is Love '79
Lady Chatterley's Lover '81
Cassandra '87
Moving Targets '87
True Colors '87
Wrangler '88
Till There was You '91

Fanny Brice
Everybody Sing '38
Ziegfeld Follies '46

Pierre Brice
Mill of the Stone Women '60
Sweet Ecstasy '62
The Bacchantes '63
Apaches Last Battle '64
A Place Called Glory '66

Ron Brice
Fly by Night '93
A Horse for Danny '95

Beth Brickell
The Only Way Home '72
Seducers '77

Alan Bridge
Broadway to Cheyenne '32
The Forty-Niners '32
Man's Land '32
When a Man Rides Alone '33
Outlaw Rule '36
Sullivan's Travels '41
Miracle of Morgan's Creek '44
Gene Autry Matinee Double Feature #2 '53

Beau Bridges
The Red Pony '49
Village of the Giants '65
The Incident '67
For Love of Ivy '68
Hammersmith is Out '72
The Stranger Who Looks Like Me '74
The Other Side of the Mountain '75
One Summer Love '76
Swashbuckler '76
Two Minute Warning '76
Greased Lightning '77
Mutual Respect '77
The Four Feathers '78
President's Mistress '78
The Fifth Musketeer '79
Norma Rae '79
The Runner Stumbles '79
Honky Tonk Freeway '81
Night Crossing '81

Love Child '82
Heart Like a Wheel '83
Silver Dream Racer '83
The Hotel New Hampshire '84
The Red Light Sting '84
Outrage! '86
The Killing Time '87
The Wild Pair '87
Seven Hours to Judgment '88
The Fabulous Baker Boys '89
The Iron Triangle '89
Signs of Life '89
The Wizard '89
Daddy's Dyin'...Who's Got the Will? '90
Women & Men: Stories of Seduction '90
Wildflower '91
Without Warning: The James Brady Story '91
Married to It '93
The Positively True Adventures of the Alleged Texas Cheerleader-Murdering Mom '93
Sidekicks '93
The Outer Limits: Sandkings '95
Kissinger and Nixon '96

Jeff Bridges
Silent Night, Lonely Night '69
The Last Picture Show '71
Yin & Yang of Mr. Go '71
Bad Company '72
Fat City '72
The Last American Hero '73
Thunderbolt & Lightfoot '74
Hearts of the West '75
Rancho Deluxe '75
King Kong '76
Stay Hungry '76
Winter Kills '79
Cutter's Way '81
Heaven's Gate '81
Kiss Me Goodbye '82
Rapunzel '82
Tron '82
Against All Odds '84
Starman '84
8 Million Ways to Die '85
The Jagged Edge '85
The Morning After '86
Nadine '87
Tucker: The Man and His Dream '88
The Fabulous Baker Boys '89
See You in the Morning '89
Texasville '90
The Fisher King '91
American Heart '92
Fearless '93
The Vanishing '93
Blown Away '94
Wild Bill '95
White Squall '96

Lloyd Bridges
Harmon of Michigan '41
The Heat's On '43
Sahara '43
Master Race '44
Strange Confession '45
Abilene Town '46
A Walk in the Sun '46
Ramrod '47
Moonrise '48
Home of the Brave '49
Trapped '49
Rocketship X-M '50
Try and Get Me '50
The White Tower '50
Little Big Horn '51
High Noon '52
Last of the Comanches '52
The Limping Man '53
Tall Texan '53
Big Deadly Game '54
Apache Woman '55
The Rainmaker '56
The Goddess '58
Around the World Under the Sea '65
Daring Game '68
The Happy Ending '69
Silent Night, Lonely Night '69
The Tattered Web '71
Haunts of the Very Rich '72
Running Wild '73
Force of Evil '77
Mutual Respect '77
Roots '77
The Great Wallendas '78
Mission Galactica: The Cylon Attack '79
Airplane! '80
Bear Island '80
East of Eden '80
Airplane 2: The Sequel '82
The Grace Kelly Story '83
George Washington '84
Loving '84
The Blue and the Gray '85
Dress Gray '86
North and South Book 2 '86
Weekend Warriors '86
The Wild Pair '87
Tucker: The Man and His Dream '88
Cousins '89
Winter People '89
Joe Versus the Volcano '90
The Queen of Mean '90
Hot Shots! '91
Devlin '92
Honey, I Blew Up the Kid '92
Hot Shots! Part Deux '93
Blown Away '94
The Outer Limits: Sandkings '95

Todd Bridges
Twice Dead '88
Homeboys '92

Richard Briers
A Matter of WHO '62
Rentadick '72
The Norman Conquests, Part 1: Table Manners '80
The Norman Conquests, Part 2: Living Together '80
The Norman Conquests, Part 3: Round and Round the Garden '80
A Chorus of Disapproval '89
Henry V '89
Peter's Friends '92
Mary Shelley's Frankenstein '94
A Midwinter's Tale '95

Richard Bright
Panic in Needle Park '75
Rancho Deluxe '75
Idolmaker '80
Red Heat '88
The Ambulance '90
The Godfather, Part 3 '90
Who's the Man? '93
Beautiful Girls '96

Charlie Brill
Bloodstone '88
Bail Out '90

Fran Brill
Look Back in Anger '80
Old Enough '84
What About Bob? '91

Patti Brill
Girl Rush '44
Hard-Boiled Mahoney '47

Steven Brill
sex, lies and videotape '89
The Mighty Ducks '92

Nick Brimble
Frankenstein Unbound '90
Robin Hood: Prince of Thieves '91
The Final Cut '95

Cynthia Brimhall
Hard Ticket to Hawaii '87
Hard Hunted '92
Fit to Kill '93

Wilford Brimley
The China Syndrome '79
The Electric Horseman '79
Borderline '80
Rodeo Girl '80
Roughnecks '80
Absence of Malice '81
Death Valley '81
The Thing '82
High Road to China '83
Ten to Midnight '83
Tender Mercies '83
Tough Enough '83
Country '84
Harry & Son '84
The Hotel New Hampshire '84
The Natural '84
The Stone Boy '84
Cocoon '85
The Ewoks: Battle for Endor '85
Murder in Space '85
Remo Williams: The Adventure Begins '85
Act of Vengeance '86
American Justice '86
Cocoon: The Return '88
End of the Line '88
Gore Vidal's Billy the Kid '89
Eternity '90
Thompson's Last Run '90
Where the Red Fern Grows: Part 2 '92
The Firm '93
Hard Target '93
The Good Old Boys '95
Mutant Species '95

Michele Brin
Secret Games '92
Sexual Intent '94

Paul Brinegar
How to Make a Monster '58
Charro! '69
Wyatt Earp: Return to Tombstone '94

Mark Bringleson
The Lawnmower Man '92
Dead Man '95

Ritch Brinkley
Silhouette '91
Cabin Boy '94

Charles Brinley
Moran of the Lady Letty '22
The Crimson Trail '35

David Brisbin
Kiss Daddy Goodnight '87
Leaving Las Vegas '95

Danielle Brisebois
The Premonition '75
Mom, the Wolfman and Me '80
Big Bad Mama 2 '87
Killcrazy '89

Carl Brisson
The Ring '27
The Manxman '29
Murder at the Vanities '34

May Britt
The Hunters '58
There Goes Barder '64
Haunts '77

Morgan Brittany
Initiation of Sarah '78
The Prodigal '83
LBJ: The Early Years '88
Sundown '91

Barbara Britton
Louisiana Purchase '41
Mrs. Wiggs of the Cabbage Patch '42
Reap the Wild Wind '42
Wake Island '42
Young & Willing '42
So Proudly We Hail '43
The Story of Dr. Wassell '44
Captain Kidd '45
The Virginian '46
Loaded Pistols '48
I Shot Jesse James '49
Champagne for Caesar '50
Bandit Queen '51
Ride the Man Down '53
Dragonfly Squadron '54

Pamela Britton
Anchors Aweigh '45
D.O.A. '49
If It's Tuesday, This Must Be Belgium '69

Tony Britton
Operation Amsterdam '60
Horsemasters '61
Dr. Syn, Alias the Scarecrow '64
Cry of the Penguins '71
The Day of the Jackal '73
Agatha '79

Jim Broadbent
The Good Father '87
Life Is Sweet '90
The Crying Game '92
Enchanted April '92
The Wedding Gift '93
Bullets Over Broadway '94
Princess Caraboo '94
Widow's Peak '94
Richard III '95

Peter Brocco
Ma and Pa Kettle on Vacation '53
The Balcony '63
Homebodies '74
One Flew Over the Cuckoo's Nest '75

Anne Brochet
Cyrano de Bergerac '90
Tous les Matins du Monde '92
Barjo '93

Phil Brock
A Climate for Killing '91
Dollman vs Demonic Toys '93

Stan Brock
Galyon '77
Tin Men '87
Return to Africa '89

Roy Brocksmith
King of the Gypsies '78
Killer Fish '79
Tales of Ordinary Madness '83
Big Business '88
Arachnophobia '90
Total Recall '90
Bill & Ted's Bogus Journey '91
Nickel & Dime '92
The Road to Wellville '94

Gladys Brockwell
Oliver Twist '22
Spangles '26
The Drake Case '29

Beth Broderick
Thousand Pieces of Gold '91
Are You Lonesome Tonight '92

Helen Broderick
Top Hat '35
The Bride Walks Out '36
Swing Time '36
The Rage of Paris '38

James Broderick
The Group '66
Alice's Restaurant '69
The Taking of Pelham One Two Three '74
Dog Day Afternoon '75
The Shadow Box '80
Keeping On '81

Matthew Broderick
Max Dugan Returns '83
WarGames '83
Cinderella '84
Master Harold and the Boys '84
Ladyhawke '85
1918 '85
Ferris Bueller's Day Off '86
On Valentine's Day '86
Project X '87
Biloxi Blues '88
Torch Song Trilogy '88
Family Business '89
Glory '89
The Freshman '90
Out on a Limb '92
A Life in the Theater '93
The Night We Never Met '93
Mrs. Parker and the Vicious Circle '94
The Road to Wellville '94
The Cable Guy '96

Steve Brodie
Badman's Territory '46
Criminal Court '46
The Saint Strikes Back: Criminal Court '46
Desperate '47
Out of the Past '47
Tough Assignment '49
The Admiral Was a Lady '50
Armored Car Robbery '50
Kiss Tomorrow Goodbye '50
Treasure of Monte Cristo '50
The Steel Helmet '51
Three for Bedroom C '52
The Beast from 20,000 Fathoms '53
Donovan's Brain '53
Blue Hawaii '62
Roustabout '64
The Wild World of Batwoman '66
The Giant Spider Invasion '75
The Wizard of Speed and Time '88

Adrien Brody
Home at Last '88
King of the Hill '93

Harry Brogan
Broth of a Boy '59
Shake Hands with the Devil '59

James Brolin
Von Ryan's Express '65
Fantastic Voyage '66
Our Man Flint '66
The Boston Strangler '68
Class of '63 '73
Westworld '73
High Risk '76
Capricorn One '78
Steel Cowboy '78
The Amityville Horror '79
Night of the Juggler '80
The Ambush Murders '82
Mae West '84
Hold the Dream '85
Pee Wee's Big Adventure '85
Bad Jim '89
Finish Line '89
Backstab '90
Nightmare on the 13th Floor '90
Gas Food Lodging '92
Cheatin' Hearts '93
City Boy '93
Ted & Venus '93
Indecent Behavior 2 '94
Parallel Lives '94
The Expert '95
The Fighter '95
Relative Fear '95
Tracks of a Killer '95

Josh Brolin
The Goonies '85
Thrashin' '86
Finish Line '89
Prison for Children '93
Bed of Roses '95
Flirting with Disaster '95

J. Edward Bromberg
The Mark of Zorro '40
Return of Frank James '40
Strange Cargo '40
Invisible Agent '42
Reunion in France '42
The Phantom of the Opera '43
Son of Dracula '43
The Missing Corpse '45
Cloak and Dagger '46
Queen of the Amazons '47
A Song is Born '48

John Bromfield
Flat Top '52
Easy to Love '53
Big Bluff '55
Revenge of the Creature '55
Manfish '56

Valri Bromfield
Mr. Mom '83
Home Is Where the Hart Is '88
Who's Harry Crumb? '89
Nothing But Trouble '91

Sheila Bromley
Nancy Drew, Reporter '39
Torture Ship '39
Waterfront '39

Sydney Bromley
The NeverEnding Story '84
Crystalstone '88

Eleanor Bron
Help! '65
Two for the Road '67
Bedazzled '68
Women in Love '70
Turtle Diary '86
The Attic: The Hiding of Anne Frank '88
Little Dorrit, Film 1: Nobody's Fault '88
Little Dorrit, Film 2: Little Dorrit's Story '88
Intrigue '90
Black Beauty '94
A Little Princess '95

Brick Bronsky
Class of Nuke 'Em High 2: Subhumanoid Meltdown '91
Class of Nuke 'Em High 3: The Good, the Bad and the Subhumanoid '94

Betty Bronson
Are Parents People? '25
Ben-Hur '26
Medicine Man '30

Bronson ▶cont.

Yodelin' Kid From Pine Ridge '37
Naked Kiss '64

Charles Bronson
Pat and Mike '52
House of Wax '53
Miss Sadie Thompson '53
Vera Cruz '53
Drum Beat '54
Jubal '56
Run of the Arrow '56
Machine Gun Kelly '58
Showdown at Boot Hill '58
When Hell Broke Loose '58
Never So Few '59
The Magnificent Seven '60
Master of the World '61
Kid Galahad '62
Four for Texas '63
The Great Escape '63
Guns of Diablo '64
Battle of the Bulge '65
The Sandpiper '65
This Property is Condemned '66
The Dirty Dozen '67
Honor Among Thieves '68
Once Upon a Time in the West '68
Villa Rides '68
Lola '69
Rider on the Rain '70
Chato's Land '71
Red Sun '71
Someone Behind the Door '71
The Mechanic '72
The Family '73
The Stone Killer '73
Cold Sweat '74
Death Wish '74
Mr. Majestyk '74
Breakout '75
Chino '75
Hard Times '75
Breakheart Pass '76
From Noon Till Three '76
The Meanest Men in the West '76
St. Ives '76
Raid on Entebbe '77
Telefon '77
The White Buffalo '77
Love and Bullets '79
Borderline '80
Cabo Blanco '81
Death Hunt '81
Death Wish 2 '82
Ten to Midnight '83
The Evil That Men Do '84
Death Wish 3 '85
Act of Vengeance '86
Murphy's Law '86
Assassination '87
Death Wish 4: The Crackdown '87
Wild West '87
Messenger of Death '88
Bull of the West '89
Kinjite: Forbidden Subjects '89
The Indian Runner '91
Dead to Rights '93
The Sea Wolf '93
Death Wish 5: The Face of Death '94

Lillian Bronson
The Next Voice You Hear '50
Spencer's Mountain '63

Claudio Brook
Daniel Boone: Trail Blazer '56
Neutron and the Black Mask '61
The Young One '61
Samson in the Wax Museum '63
Viva Maria! '65
Simon of the Desert '66
The Peking Blond '68
Dr. Tarr's Torture Dungeon '75
Sisters of Satan '75
The Bees '78
Cronos '94

Clive Brook
Underworld '27
Hula '28
Shanghai Express '32
Cavalcade '33
Action for Slander '38
Convoy '40
On Approval '44

Faith Brook
Uneasy Terms '48
To Sir, with Love '67
After Julius '78
Bloodbath

Irina Brook
Transmutations '85
The Girl in the Picture '86
Captive '87

Jayne Brook
Kindergarten Cop '90
Clean Slate '94
Ed '96
Last Dance '96

Lyndon Brook
Above Us the Waves '56
The Spanish Gardener '57
Invasion '65

Elwyn Brook-Jones
Bonnie Prince Charlie '48
The Gilded Cage '54
Rogue's Yarn '56

Hillary Brooke
The Philadelphia Story '40
Rangeland Racket '41
Sherlock Holmes: The Voice of Terror '42
To the Shores of Tripoli '42
Sherlock Holmes Faces Death '43
Jane Eyre '44
The Enchanted Cottage '45
The Woman in Green '45
The Road to Utopia '46
The Strange Woman '46
Big Town '47
Big Town After Dark '47
Underworld Scandal '47
Africa Screams '49
The Lost Continent '51
Abbott and Costello Meet Captain Kidd '52
Never Wave at a WAC '52
Heat Wave '54
The Man Who Knew Too Much '56

Sandy Brooke
Terror on Alcatraz '86
Miami Vendetta '87
Star Slammer '87
Crazed Cop '88

Walter Brooke
Conquest of Space '55
The Return of Count Yorga '71

Richard Brooker
Friday the 13th, Part 3 '82
Deathstalker '83

Jacqueline Brookes
Hardhat & Legs '80
Rodeo Girl '80
Silent Witness '85
Naked Gun 2 1/2: The Smell of Fear '91

Aimee Brooks
Say Anything '89
Critters 3 '91

Albert Brooks
Taxi Driver '76
Real Life '79
Private Benjamin '80
Modern Romance '81
Twilight Zone: The Movie '83
Unfaithfully Yours '84
Lost in America '85
Broadcast News '87
Defending Your Life '91
I'll Do Anything '93
The Scout '94

Avery Brooks
Half Slave, Half Free '85
Uncle Tom's Cabin '87
Roots: The Gift '88
The Ernest Green Story '93
Spenser: Ceremony '93
Star Trek Deep Space Nine: Emissary '93
Spenser: Pale Kings & Princes '94

Clarence Brooks
Bronze Buckaroo '39
Harlem Rides the Range '39

Elisabeth Brooks
The Howling '81
The Forgotten One '89

Foster Brooks
Super Seal '77
The Villain '79
Cracking Up '83
Oddballs '84

Geraldine Brooks
Cry Wolf '47
The Possessed '47
Challenge to Lassie '49
Reckless Moment '49
The Green Glove '52
Johnny Tiger '66

Hildy Brooks
The Chosen '81
Forbidden Love '82

Jean Brooks
Boot Hill Bandits '42
Boss of Big Town '43
The Leopard Man '43
The Seventh Victim '43

Joel Brooks
Are You Lonesome Tonight '92
Indecent Proposal '93

Leslie Brooks
You Were Never Lovelier '42
City Without Men '43
Tonight and Every Night '45
The Cobra Strikes '48
Romance on the High Seas '48
The Scar '48

Louise Brooks
It's the Old Army Game '26
Love 'Em and Leave 'Em '26
Pandora's Box '28
Diary of a Lost Girl '29
Prix de Beaute '30
Overland Stage Raiders '38

Mel Brooks
Putney Swope '69
Twelve Chairs '70
Blazing Saddles '74
Silent Movie '76
High Anxiety '77
History of the World: Part 1 '81
To Be or Not to Be '83
Spaceballs '87
Life Stinks '91
Robin Hood: Men in Tights '93
Dracula: Dead and Loving It '95

Phyllis Brooks
In Old Chicago '38
Little Miss Broadway '38
Rebecca of Sunnybrook Farm '38
Slightly Honorable '40
The Shanghai Gesture '42
Silver Spurs '43
Dangerous Passage '44

Rand Brooks
Gone with the Wind '39
The Sombrero Kid '42
Hopalong Cassidy: The Devil's Playground '46
Hopalong Cassidy: Hoppy's Holiday '47
Hopalong Cassidy: The Marauders '47
Hopalong Cassidy: Unexpected Guest '47
Hopalong Cassidy: Borrowed Trouble '48
Hopalong Cassidy: Dangerous Venture '48
Hopalong Cassidy: False Paradise '48
Hopalong Cassidy: Silent Conflict '48
Hopalong Cassidy: Sinister Journey '48
Hopalong Cassidy: The Dead Don't Dream '48
Ladies of the Chorus '49
The Vanishing Westerner '50

Randi Brooks
Forbidden Love '82
Tightrope '84
Hamburger...The Motion Picture '86
Colors '88
Cop '88

Ray Brooks
The Knack '65
Daleks—Invasion Earth 2150 A.D. '66
Flesh and Blood Show '73
House of Whipcord '75
Tiffany Jones '75
Office Romances '86

Richard Brooks
The Crow 2: City of Angels '96
The Substitute '96

Richard Brooks
The Hidden '87
Shakedown '88
Short Fuse '88
84 Charlie Mopic '89
Shocker '89
To Sleep with Anger '90
Memphis '91

Edward Brophy
The Cameraman '28
Doughboys '30
The Champ '31
Speak Easily '32
What! No Beer? '33
Evelyn Prentice '34
Hide-Out '34
Mad Love '35
Show Them No Mercy '35
Great Guy '36
Kelly the Second '36
Dance, Girl, Dance '40
The Invisible Woman '40
Destroyer '43
Cover Girl '44
The Thin Man Goes Home '44
Renegade Girl '46
Swing Parade of 1946 '46
Roaring City '51
Last Hurrah '58

Kevin Brophy
Hell Night '81
The Seduction '82
Delos Adventure '86

Pierce Brosnan
The Long Good Friday '79
The Mirror Crack'd '80
The Carpathian Eagle '81
The Manions of America '81
Remington Steele, Vol. 1: License to Steele '82
Nomads '86
The Fourth Protocol '87
The Deceivers '88
Noble House '88
Taffin '88
Around the World in 80 Days '89
The Heist '89
Mister Johnson '91
Murder 101 '91
Victim of Love '91
The Lawnmower Man '92
Live Wire '92
The Broken Chain '93
Detonator '93
Entangled '93
Mrs. Doubtfire '93
Don't Talk to Strangers '94
Love Affair '94
Detonator 2: Night Watch '95
Goldeneye '95

Collette Brosset
Femmes de Paris '53
Belle Americaine '61

Dr. Joyce Brothers
Embryo '76
Desperate Lives '82
The Lonely Guy '84

Liliane Brousse
Paranoiac '62
Maniac '63

Amelda Brown
Little Dorrit, Film 1: Nobody's Fault '88
Little Dorrit, Film 2: Little Dorrit's Story '88

Barbara Brown
The Fighting Sullivans '42
Hollywood Canteen '44
Ma and Pa Kettle Go to Town '50
Home Town Story '51
Ma and Pa Kettle Back On the Farm '51
Ma and Pa Kettle on Vacation '53
My Sister Eileen '55

Barry Brown
Bad Company '72
The Ultimate Thrill '74
The Disappearance of Aimee '76
He Who Walks Alone '78

Blair Brown
The Choirboys '77
And I Alone Survived '78
Altered States '80
One Trick Pony '80
Continental Divide '81
Kennedy '83
The Bad Seed '85
A Flash of Green '85
Hands of a Stranger '87
Stealing Home '88
Strapless '90
Passed Away '92
The Day My Parents Ran Away '93

Bobby Brown
Mother Goose Rock 'n' Rhyme '90
A Thin Line Between Love and Hate '96

Bryan Brown
The Irishman '78
Money Movers '78
Newsfront '78
Palm Beach '79
Blood Money '80
Breaker Morant '80
The Winter of Our Dreams '82
The Thorn Birds '83
Give My Regards to Broad Street '84
Kim '84
Parker '84
The Empty Beach '85
Far East '85
Rebel '85
A Town Like Alice '85
F/X '86
The Good Wife '86
Tai-Pan '86
Cocktail '88
Gorillas in the Mist '88
Dead in the Water '91
F/X 2: The Deadly Art of Illusion '91
Prisoners of the Sun '91
Sweet Talker '91
Blame It on the Bellboy '92
Devlin '92
The Last Hit '93
Full Body Massage '95

Charles D. Brown
Dance of Life '29
Shopworn Angel '38
Brother Orchid '40
Old Swimmin' Hole '40
Merton of the Movies '47
Follow Me Quietly '49

Clancy Brown
Bad Boys '83
The Bride '85
Highlander '86
Shoot to Kill '88
Season of Fear '89
Blue Steel '90
Ambition '91
Cast a Deadly Spell '91
Love, Lies and Murder '91
Past Midnight '92
Pet Sematary 2 '92
Last Light '93
The Shawshank Redemption '94
Donor Unknown '95

David G. Brown
Deadly Harvest '72
Chasing Dreams '81

D.W. Brown
Weekend Pass '84
Mischief '85

Dwier Brown
The Guardian '90
The Cutting Edge '92
Galaxies are Colliding '92
Mom and Dad Save the World '92
Deconstructing Sarah '94
Lily in Winter '94

Eric Brown
Private Lessons '81
They're Playing with Fire '84
Video Murders '87

Gary Brown
The Glory Boys '84
Invasion of the Space Preachers '90

Georg Stanford Brown
Dayton's Devils *'68*
Colossus: The Forbin Project *'70*
Roots: The Next Generation *'79*
The Night the City Screamed *'80*
The Kid with the Broken Halo *'82*
The Jesse Owens Story *'84*
North and South Book 1 *'85*
Alone in the Neon Jungle *'87*
House Party 2: The Pajama Jam *'91*
Murder without Motive *'92*
Ava's Magical Adventure *'94*
Tyson *'95*

Georgia Brown
The Fixer *'68*
Long Ago Tomorrow *'71*
Nothing But the Night *'72*
Tales That Witness Madness *'73*
Actor: The Paul Muni Story *'78*
Love at Stake *'87*
Victim of Love *'91*

Henry Brown
The Man in the Glass Booth *'75*
Uncaged *'91*

James Brown
Objective, Burma! *'45*
Rin Tin Tin, Hero of the West *'55*
Targets *'68*
Adios Amigo *'75*
The Blues Brothers *'80*
Courage of Rin Tin Tin *'83*
Doctor Detroit *'83*

Jim Brown
Rio Conchos *'64*
The Dirty Dozen *'67*
Dark of the Sun *'68*
Ice Station Zebra *'68*
100 Rifles *'69*
Riot *'69*
El Condor *'70*
The Passing of Evil *'70*
Slaughter *'72*
Slaughter's Big Ripoff *'73*
Three the Hard Way *'74*
Kid Vengeance *'75*
Take a Hard Ride *'75*
Fingers *'78*
One Down, Two to Go! *'82*
Pacific Inferno *'85*
I'm Gonna Git You Sucka *'88*
L.A. Heat *'88*
Crack House *'89*
L.A. Vice *'89*
Twisted Justice *'89*
The Divine Enforcer *'91*
Original Gangstas *'96*

Joe E. Brown
Lottery Bride *'30*
A Midsummer Night's Dream *'35*
Earthworm Tractors *'36*
Fit for a King *'37*
Riding on Air *'37*
When's Your Birthday? *'37*
The Gladiator *'38*
Wide Open Faces *'38*
Pin-Up Girl *'44*
The Tender Years *'47*
Show Boat *'51*
Around the World in 80 Days *'56*
Some Like It Hot *'59*
It's a Mad, Mad, Mad, Mad World *'63*
The Comedy of Terrors *'64*

Johnny Mack Brown
Annapolis *'28*
Our Dancing Daughters *'28*
A Woman of Affairs *'28*
Coquette *'29*
The Single Standard *'29*
Voice of Hollywood *'29*
Female *'33*
Fighting with Kit Carson *'33*
Belle of the Nineties *'34*
Between Men *'35*
Branded a Coward *'35*
Courageous Avenger *'35*
Every Man's Law *'35*
Rustlers of Red Dog *'35*
Crooked Trail *'36*
Desert Phantom *'36*
Rogue of the Range *'36*
Undercover Man *'36*
Valley of the Lawless *'36*
Western Double Feature 3 *'36*
Boothill Brigade *'37*
The Gambling Terror *'37*
Guns in the Dark *'37*
A Lawman Is Born *'37*
Fire Alarm *'38*
Flaming Frontiers *'38*
Oregon Trail *'39*
Pony Post *'40*
Riders of Pasco Basin *'40*
Boss of Bullion City *'41*
Bury Me Not On the Lone Prairie *'41*
Man from Montana *'41*
The Masked Rider *'41*
Ride 'Em Cowboy *'42*
Ghost Rider *'43*
Six Gun Gospel *'43*
Texas Kid *'43*
Lawmen *'44*
Partners of the Trail *'44*
Raiders of the Border *'44*
Range Law *'44*
The Stranger from Pecos *'45*
Border Bandits *'46*
Gentleman from Texas *'46*
Apache Uprising *'66*

Juanita Brown
Black Starlet *'74*
Caged Heat *'74*

Judy Brown
The Big Doll House *'71*
The Manhandlers *'73*

Julie Brown
Bloody Birthday *'80*
Earth Girls Are Easy *'89*
Spirit of '76 *'91*
Shakes the Clown *'92*
Nervous Ticks *'93*
The Opposite Sex and How to Live With Them *'93*
Raining Stones *'93*
National Lampoon's Attack of the 5 Ft. 2 Women *'94*
Clueless *'95*
Out There *'95*

Lou Brown
The Irishman *'78*
Alison's Birthday *'79*
Death Games *'82*

Pamela Brown
One of Our Aircraft Is Missing *'41*
I Know Where I'm Going *'45*
Alice in Wonderland *'50*
Lust for Life *'56*
Victoria Regina *'61*
Cleopatra *'63*
Secret Ceremony *'69*
Wuthering Heights *'70*

Paul Brown
Morons from Outer Space *'85*
Transmutations *'85*
Butterfly Kiss *'94*

Peter Brown
The Commies are Coming, the Commies are Coming *'57*
Darby's Rangers *'58*
Merrill's Marauders *'62*
Red Nightmare *'62*
Ride the Wild Surf *'64*
A Tiger Walks *'64*
Hard Frame *'70*
Chrome and Hot Leather *'71*
Act of Vengeance *'74*
Eagles Attack at Dawn *'74*
Memory of Us *'74*
Slashed Dreams *'74*
The Concrete Jungle *'82*
The Aurora Encounter *'85*

Phil Brown
Without Reservations *'46*
The Hidden Room *'49*
Operation Cross Eagles *'69*
Tropic of Cancer *'70*

Philip Brown
Special Olympics *'78*
Eye of the Needle *'81*
Wild Zone *'89*

Ralph Brown
Buster *'88*
Impromptu *'90*
Alien 3 *'92*
The Crying Game *'92*
Wayne's World 2 *'93*

Reb Brown
Captain America *'79*
Captain America 2: Death Too Soon *'79*
Uncommon Valor *'83*
Yor, the Hunter from the Future *'83*
Death of a Soldier *'85*
Howling 2: Your Sister is a Werewolf *'85*
Strike Commando *'87*
Mercenary Fighters *'88*
Space Mutiny *'88*
White Ghost *'88*
The Cage *'89*
Street Hunter *'90*
The Firing Line *'91*
Cage 2: The Arena of Death *'94*
Last Flight to Hell

Ritza Brown
Ator the Fighting Eagle *'83*
The McGuffin *'85*

Robert Brown
Shake Hands with the Devil *'59*
Tower of London *'62*
One Million Years B.C. *'66*
Pilgrim, Farewell *'82*
The Living Daylights *'87*

Roger Brown
Venus Against the Son of Hercules *'62*
Paper Lion *'68*
Don't Cry, It's Only Thunder *'82*
Tall Tale: The Unbelievable Adventures of Pecos Bill *'95*

Ron Brown
Charlie, the Lonesome Cougar *'67*
The Legend of Black Thunder Mountain *'79*

Sara Suzanne Brown
Secret Games 2: The Escort *'93*
Test Tube Teens from the Year 2000 *'93*
Killer Looks *'94*

Stephen Brown
Metamorphosis *'90*
Beyond Darkness *'92*

Thomas Wilson Brown
Honey, I Shrunk the Kids *'89*
Welcome Home *'89*
Diggstown *'92*

Tim Brown
A Place Called Today *'72*
Code Name: Zebra *'84*
Pacific Inferno *'85*

Timothy Brown
Sweet Sugar *'72*
Girls Are for Loving *'73*
The Dynamite Brothers *'74*

Tom Brown
Anne of Green Gables *'34*
I'd Give My Life *'36*
Maytime *'37*
Navy Blue and Gold *'37*
In Old Chicago *'38*
Adventures of Smilin' Jack *'43*
The Payoff *'43*
Buck Privates Come Home *'47*
Ringside *'49*
Operation Haylift *'50*
The Choppers *'61*

Vanessa Brown
The Ghost and Mrs. Muir *'47*
Three Husbands *'50*
The Fighter *'52*
Witch Who Came from the Sea *'76*

W. Earl Brown
Excessive Force *'93*
Dead Air *'94*

Wally Brown
Girl Rush *'44*
Zombies on Broadway *'44*

Woody Brown
The Accused *'88*
Alligator 2: The Mutation *'90*
The Rain Killer *'90*
Animal Instincts 2 *'94*
Dominion *'94*
Secret Games 3 *'94*

Charles A. Browne
Tailspin Tommy *'34*
Federal Agent *'36*

Coral Browne
The Courtney Affair *'47*
Auntie Mame *'58*
The Killing of Sister George *'69*
The Ruling Class *'72*
Eleanor: First Lady of the World *'82*
An Englishman Abroad *'83*
American Dreamer *'84*
Dreamchild *'85*

Leslie Browne
The Turning Point *'77*
Nijinsky *'80*
Dancers *'87*

Lucille Browne
The Devil's Brother *'33*
Mystery Squadron *'33*
Brand of Hate *'34*
Law of the Wild *'34*
Texas Terror *'35*
Western Frontier *'35*
Cheyenne Rides Again *'38*

Roscoe Lee Browne
The Connection *'61*
Black Like Me *'64*
The Liberation of L.B. Jones *'70*
The Cowboys *'72*
Superfly T.N.T. *'73*
The World's Greatest Athlete *'73*
Logan's Run *'76*
Twilight's Last Gleaming *'77*
King *'78*
Nothing Personal *'80*
Unknown Powers *'80*
Haunting of Harrington House *'82*
Legal Eagles *'86*
For Us, the Living *'88*
Moon 44 *'90*
The Mambo Kings *'92*
Naked in New York *'93*
Last Summer In the Hamptons *'96*

Suzanne Browne
The Bikini Car Wash Company *'90*
The Bikini Car Wash Company 2 *'92*

Ricou Browning
Creature from the Black Lagoon *'54*
Flipper's New Adventure *'64*

Brenda Bruce
Nightmare *'63*
Peeping Tom *'63*
The Tenth Man *'88*
Back Home *'90*
Antonia and Jane *'91*
December Bride *'91*
Splitting Heirs *'93*

Cheryl Lynn Bruce
Music Box *'89*
Victimless Crimes *'90*
Daughters of the Dust *'91*

Colin Bruce
Gotham *'88*
Crusoe *'89*
Chicago Joe & the Showgirl *'90*

David Bruce
The Sea Wolf *'41*
The Mad Ghoul *'43*
Lady On a Train *'45*
Salome, Where She Danced *'45*
Pier 23 *'51*
Jungle Hell *'55*

Kate Bruce
Judith of Bethulia *'14*
The Idol Dancer *'20*

Lenny Bruce
Dance Hall Racket *'58*
Lenny Bruce Performance Film *'68*
Dynamite Chicken *'70*

Nigel Bruce
The Scarlet Pimpernel *'34*
Stand Up and Cheer *'34*
Treasure Island *'34*
Becky Sharp *'35*
She *'35*
The Charge of the Light Brigade *'36*
The Last of Mrs. Cheyney *'37*
Thunder in the City *'37*
The Adventures of Sherlock Holmes *'39*
The Hound of the Baskervilles *'39*
The Rains Came *'39*
The Blue Bird *'40*
Rebecca *'40*
Susan and God *'40*
The Chocolate Soldier *'41*
Suspicion *'41*
Journey for Margaret *'42*
Roxie Hart *'42*
Sherlock Holmes and the Secret Weapon *'42*
Sherlock Holmes: The Voice of Terror *'42*
Lassie, Come Home *'43*
Sherlock Holmes Faces Death *'43*
Sherlock Holmes in Washington *'43*
The Pearl of Death *'44*
Scarlet Claw *'44*
Spider Woman *'44*
The Corn is Green *'45*
House of Fear *'45*
Pursuit to Algiers *'45*
Son of Lassie *'45*
The Woman in Green *'45*
Dressed to Kill *'46*
Terror by Night *'46*
Terror by Night/Meeting at Midnight *'46*
The Two Mrs. Carrolls *'47*
Julia Misbehaves *'48*
Limelight *'52*

Virginia Bruce
Jane Eyre *'34*
Let 'Em Have It *'35*
Born to Dance *'36*
The Great Ziegfeld *'36*
Let Freedom Ring *'39*
The Invisible Woman *'40*
Pardon My Sarong *'42*
Action in Arabia *'44*
State Department File 649 *'49*
Strangers When We Meet *'60*

Patrick Bruel
Bandits *'86*
Secret Obsession *'88*
Sabrina *'95*

Eddie Brugman
Keetje Tippel *'75*
Broken Mirrors *'85*

Beau Brummel
Village of the Giants *'65*
Three Bullets for a Long Gun *'73*

Bo Brundin
Russian Roulette *'75*
Shoot the Sun Down *'81*
Headless Eyes *'83*

Fernando Bruno
Two Nights with Cleopatra *'54*
Time Out for Love *'61*

Philip Bruns
The Stunt Man *'80*
Return of the Living Dead 2 *'88*
Dead Men Don't Die *'91*
The Opposite Sex and How to Live With Them *'93*

Dora Bryan
No Trace *'50*
My Son, the Vampire *'52*
Small Hotel *'57*
A Taste of Honey *'61*
The Great St. Trinian's Train Robbery *'66*
Screamtime *'83*

Jane Bryan
Kid Galahad *'37*
Marked Woman *'37*
The Sisters *'38*
Each Dawn I Die *'39*
The Old Maid *'39*

Zachery Ty Bryan
Bigfoot: The Unforgettable Encounter *'94*
Magic Island *'95*

Joyce Bryant
Across the Plains *'39*
East Side Kids *'40*

Lee Bryant
Half Slave, Half Free *'85*
Alien Nation: Dark Horizon *'94*

Michael Bryant
Goodbye, Mr. Chips *'69*
Girly *'70*

Bryant ▶cont.

Sakharov '84

Nana Bryant
Give Me a Sailor '38
Sinners in Paradise '38
Big Town '47
The Possessed '47
Eyes of Texas '48
Inner Sanctum '48
Ladies of the Chorus '49
Harvey '50

Pamela Bryant
Lunch Wagon '81
Tigershark '87

Virginia Bryant
The Barbarians '87
Demons 2 '87

William Bryant
Corvette Summer '78
Mountain Family Robinson '79

Scott Bryce
Stalking Laura '93
Up Close and Personal '96

Andrew Bryniarski
Batman Returns '92
The Program '93
Cyborg 3: The Recycler '95

Yul Brynner
Port of New York '49
Anastasia '56
The King and I '56
The Ten Commandments '56
The Brothers Karamazov '58
The Buccaneer '58
Solomon and Sheba '59
The Testament of Orpheus '59
The Magnificent Seven '60
Taras Bulba '62
Invitation to a Gunfighter '64
Morituri '65
Cast a Giant Shadow '66
The Poppy Is Also a Flower '66
Return of the Seven '66
Triple Cross '67
Villa Rides '68
Battle of Neretva '69
The Madwoman of Chaillot '69
The Magic Christian '69
Catlow '71
Light at the Edge of the World '71
Romance of a Horsethief '71
Fuzz '72
Night Flight from Moscow '73
Westworld '73
The Ultimate Warrior '75
Futureworld '76
Death Rage '77

Edgar Buchanan
Arizona '40
Penny Serenade '41
Texas '41
Talk of the Town '42
City Without Men '43
Destroyer '43
Buffalo Bill '44
Abilene Town '46
Black Arrow '48
Coroner Creek '48
Lust for Gold '49
Man from Colorado '49
The Big Hangover '50
Cheaper by the Dozen '50
Rawhide '50
Big Trees '52
She Couldn't Say No '52
Shane '53
Human Desire '54
Make Haste to Live '54
Judge Roy Bean '55
Rage at Dawn '55
Silver Star '55
The Devil's Partner '58
It Started with a Kiss '59
Ride the High Country '62
McLintock! '63
The Rounders '65
Yuma '70

Ian Buchanan
The Cool Surface '92
Blue Flame '93
Double Exposure '93
Marilyn & Bobby: Her Final Affair '94

Jack Buchanan
When Knights were Bold '36
The Band Wagon '53

Sherry Buchanan
Eyes Behind the Stars '72
Emmanuelle & Joanna '86

Simone Buchanan
Run, Rebecca, Run '81
Shame '87

Christopher Buchholz
No Fear, No Die '90
Covert Assassin '94

Horst Buchholz
Teenage Wolfpack '57
Tiger Bay '59
The Magnificent Seven '60
Fanny '61
One, Two, Three '61
Empty Canvas '64
The Catamount Killing '74
The Savage Bees '76
Raid on Entebbe '77
Return to Fantasy Island '77
Avalanche Express '79
From Hell to Victory '79
Berlin Tunnel 21 '81
Sahara '83
Code Name: Emerald '85
Aces: Iron Eagle 3 '92
Faraway, So Close! '93

Buck
Robinson Crusoe of Clipper Island '36
Robinson Crusoe of Mystery Island '36

Frank Buck
Jacare '42
Tiger Fangs '43

John Buckler
The Black Room '35
Tarzan Escapes '36

Betty Buckley
Carrie '76
Tender Mercies '83
Wild Thing '87
Another Woman '88
Frantic '88
Babycakes '89
Rain Without Thunder '93
Last Time Out '94
Wyatt Earp '94

Keith Buckley
The Virgin Witch '70
Half Moon Street '86

Helen Buday
Mad Max: Beyond Thunderdome '85
For Love Alone '86

Jack Buetel
Best of the Badmen '50
The Half-Breed '51

Marilyn Buferd
Machine to Kill Bad People '48
Queen of Outer Space '58

Buffalo Bill, Jr.
Deadwood Pass '33
Fighting Cowboy '33
Terror Trail '33
Rawhide Romance '34
Lightning Bill '35
Powdersmoke Range '35
Riding Speed '35

Jimmy Buffett
Rancho Deluxe '75
FM '78
Doctor Duck's Super Secret All-Purpose Sauce '85

Joe Bugner
Fatal Bond '91
The Cursed Mountain Mystery '93

Valerie Buhagiar
Roadkill '89
Highway 61 '91

Genevieve Bujold
The King of Hearts '66
Anne of the Thousand Days '69
Trojan Women '71
Earthquake '74
Obsession '76
Swashbuckler '76
Another Man, Another Chance '77
Journey '77
Coma '78
Murder by Decree '79
Final Assignment '80
The Last Flight of Noah's Ark '80
Monsignor '82
Choose Me '84
Tightrope '84
Trouble in Mind '86
Dead Ringers '88
The Moderns '88
A Paper Wedding '89
False Identity '90
The Dance Goes On '92
Oh, What a Night '92

Donald Buka
The Street with No Name '48
Stolen Identity '53

Raymond Buktenica
The Jayne Mansfield Story '80
The Adventures of Nellie Bly '81
Wait Till Your Mother Gets Home '83
My Girl '91

Peter Bull
Marie Antoinette '38
The African Queen '51
A Christmas Carol '51
Tom Jones '63
Dr. Strangelove, or: How I Learned to Stop Worrying and Love the Bomb '64
Second Best Secret Agent in the Whole Wide World '65
Doctor Dolittle '67

Richard Bull
Lawman '71
Different Story '78

Sandra Bullock
A Fool and His Money '88
When the Party's Over '91
Love Potion #9 '92
Who Shot Pat? '92
Demolition Man '93
The Thing Called Love '93
The Vanishing '93
Wrestling Ernest Hemingway '93
Me and the Mob '94
Speed '94
The Net '95
Two If by Sea '95
While You Were Sleeping '95
A Time to Kill '96

William Bumiller
Death Spa '87
The Heroes of Desert Storm '91

Brooke Bundy
Francis Gary Powers: The True Story of the U-2 Spy '76
The Crash of Flight 401 '78
Explorers '85
Two Fathers' Justice '85
A Nightmare on Elm Street 4: Dream Master '88
Twice Dead '88
Beverly Hills Bodysnatchers '89

Avis Bunnage
The Loneliness of the Long Distance Runner '62
Forbidden '85
No Surrender '86

Cara Buono
Gladiator '92
Waterland '92
The Cowboy Way '94
Kicking and Screaming '95

Victor Buono
What Ever Happened to Baby Jane? '62
Four for Texas '63
The Strangler '64
Boot Hill '69
Beneath the Planet of the Apes '70
The Mad Butcher '72
Northeast of Seoul '72
Arnold '73
The Man from Atlantis '77
The Evil '78
Better Late Than Never '79
The Man with Bogart's Face '80
More Wild, Wild West '80

Sonny Bupp
Hopalong Cassidy: Renegade Trail '39
Renegade Trail '39
Three Faces West '40
Citizen Kane '41

Hugh Burden
Fame Is the Spur '47
Ghost Ship '53

Suzanne Burden
Sharma & Beyond '84
Office Romances '86
Strapless '90

Kim Burfield
The Hero '71
Treasure Island '72

Christopher Burgard
Twice Dead '88
84 Charlie Mopic '89
Full Body Massage '95

Gregg Burge
A Chorus Line '85
School Daze '88

Dorothy Burgess
Hold Your Man '33
Ladies They Talk About '33
Girls in Chains '43

Gary Burghoff
M*A*S*H '70
M*A*S*H: The Collector's Edition '72
The Man in the Santa Claus Suit '79
Casino '80
Small Kill '93

Alfred Burke
Dead Lucky '60
Children of the Damned '63
The Nanny '65
Night Caller from Outer Space '66
One Day in the Life of Ivan Denisovich '71
The House on Garibaldi Street '79

Billie Burke
A Bill of Divorcement '32
Christopher Strong '33
Dinner at Eight '33
Finishing School '33
Becky Sharp '35
Doubting Thomas '35
Forsaking All Others '35
Craig's Wife '36
The Bride Wore Red '37
Navy Blue and Gold '37
Topper '37
Everybody Sing '38
The Young in Heart '38
Eternally Yours '39
Topper Takes a Trip '39
The Wizard of Oz '39
The Man Who Came to Dinner '41
Topper Returns '41
In This Our Life '42
Breakfast in Hollywood '46
The Barkleys of Broadway '49
Father of the Bride '50
Father's Little Dividend '51
Small Town Girl '53
The Young Philadelphians '59
Sergeant Rutledge '60

Delta Burke
The Seekers '79
A Bunny's Tale '85
First & Ten '85
First & Ten: The Team Scores Again '85
Dynamite and Gold '88

J. Frank Burke
Italian '15
Angels with Dirty Faces '38

James Burke
Lady by Choice '34
The Mystery Man '35
Ruggles of Red Gap '35
Down to Earth '47
Cavalry Charge '51
Lucky Me '54

Kathleen Burke
Island of Lost Souls '32
Murders in the Zoo '33
The Lives of a Bengal Lancer '35

Michelle Burke
Coneheads '93
Dazed and Confused '93
Major League 2 '94
The Last Word '95

Paul Burke
Francis Goes to West Point '52
Francis in the Navy '55
Fatal Confinement '64
Valley of the Dolls '67
Daddy's Gone A-Hunting '69
Anatomy of Terror '74
Psychic Killer '75
Wild & Wooly '78
The Red Light Sting '84

Robert Burke
The Unbelievable Truth '90
Rambling Rose '91
RoboCop 3 '91
Simple Men '92
Dust Devil '93
A Far Off Place '93
Tombstone '93

Simon Burke
The Devil's Playground '76
The Irishman '78
Slate, Wyn & Me '87

Laura Burkett
Overkill '86
Daddy's Boys '87

Scott Burkholder
House 4: Home Deadly Home '91
Class of '61 '92
Sketch Artist 2: Hands That See '94

Dennis Burkley
Bummer '73
Murphy's Romance '85
Pass the Ammo '88
Lambada '89
The Doors '91
Stop! or My Mom Will Shoot '92
Son-in-Law '93

Tom Burlinson
The Man from Snowy River '82
Phar Lap '84
Flesh and Blood '85
Windrider '86
The Time Guardian '87
Return to Snowy River '88
Piece of Cake '90
Showdown at Williams Creek '91
Landslide '92

Leo Burmester
The Abyss '89
Passion Fish '92
A Perfect World '93
The Great Elephant Escape '95
The Neon Bible '95
Truman '95

Caesar Burner
Tombs of the Blind Dead '72
Green Inferno '80s

Carol Burnett
Pete 'n' Tillie '72
The Front Page '74
The Grass is Always Greener Over the Septic Tank '78
A Wedding '78
Friendly Fire '79
Tenth Month '79
Chu Chu & the Philly Flash '81
The Four Seasons '81
Annie '82
Between Friends '83
Follies in Concert '85
Noises Off '92

Smiley Burnette
Dude Ranger '34
In Old Santa Fe '34
Mystery Mountain '34
The Adventures of Rex & Rinty '35
Harmony Lane '35
Melody Trail '35
The Phantom Empire '35
Old Corral '36
Red River Valley '36
Ride, Ranger, Ride '36
Big Show '37
Boots & Saddles '37
Dick Tracy '37
Dick Tracy: The Original Serial, Vol. 1 '37

Dick Tracy: The Original Serial, Vol. 2 *'37*
Git Along Little Dogies *'37*
Round-Up Time in Texas *'37*
Springtime in the Rockies *'37*
Western Double Feature 4 *'37*
Western Double Feature 5: Rogers & Autry *'37*
Yodelin' Kid From Pine Ridge *'37*
Billy the Kid Returns *'38*
Hollywood Stadium Mystery *'38*
The Man from Music Mountain *'38*
Oh Susannah *'38*
Old Barn Dance *'38*
Prairie Moon *'38*
Rootin' Tootin' Rhythm *'38*
Western Double Feature 1 *'38*
South of the Border *'39*
Down Mexico Way *'41*
Ridin' on a Rainbow *'41*
Call of the Canyon *'42*
Heart of the Golden West *'42*
Heart of the Rio Grande *'42*
Idaho *'43*
King of the Cowboys *'43*
Raiders of Sunset Pass *'43*
Silver Spurs *'43*
Call of the Rockies *'44*
Under Western Stars *'45*
Western Double Feature 16 *'46*
Gene Autry Matinee Double Feature #2 *'53*
Gene Autry Matinee Double Feature #3 *'53*
Last of the Pony Riders *'53*
On Top of Old Smoky *'53*
Winning of the West *'53*

Bob Burns
Rhythm on the Range *'36*
Waikiki Wedding *'37*

Carol Burns
Prisoner Cell Block H *'80*
Dusty *'85*
Bad Blood *'87*

Edmund Burns
Made for Love *'26*
Sunny Side Up *'28*
Sea Devils *'31*

George Burns
International House *'33*
We're Not Dressing *'34*
A Damsel in Distress *'37*
College Swing *'38*
Honolulu *'39*
The Burns and Allen Show *'50*
The Sunshine Boys *'75*
Oh, God! *'77*
Sgt. Pepper's Lonely Hearts Club Band *'78*
Going in Style *'79*
Oh, God! Book 2 *'80*
Two of a Kind *'82*
Oh, God! You Devil *'84*
18 Again! *'88*
Radioland Murders *'94*

Jennifer Burns
The Liar's Club *'93*
Haunted Symphony *'94*
Josh Kirby...Time Warrior: Chapter 1, Planet of the Dino-Knights *'95*
Josh Kirby...Time Warrior: Chapter 2, The Human Pets *'95*
Josh Kirby...Time Warrior: Chapter 3, Trapped on Toyworld *'95*
Josh Kirby...Time Warrior: Chapter 4, Eggs from 70 Million B.C. *'95*
Josh Kirby...Time Warrior: Chapter 5, Journey to the Magic Cavern *'96*
Josh Kirby...Time Warrior: Chapter 6, Last Battle for the Universe *'96*

Jere Burns
Wired *'89*
The Gambler Returns: The Luck of the Draw *'93*
Greedy *'94*

Marilyn Burns
The Texas Chainsaw Massacre *'74*
Eaten Alive *'76*
Helter Skelter *'76*
Kiss Daddy Goodbye *'81*
Future Kill *'85*

Marion Burns
Dawn Rider *'35*
Paradise Canyon *'35*
Dawn Rider/Frontier Horizon *'39*

Mark Burns
The Charge of the Light Brigade *'68*
The Virgin and the Gypsy *'70*
Death in Venice *'71*
House of the Living Dead *'73*
Bullseye! *'90*

Michael Burns
That Cold Day in the Park *'69*
Thumb Tripping *'72*

Robert Burns
South of Santa Fe *'32*
Gun Law *'33*
When a Man Rides Alone *'33*
Western Trails *'38*

Robert Burns
Terror in the Jungle *'68*
Confessions of a Serial Killer *'87*

Raymond Burr
Desperate *'47*
Pitfall *'48*
Station West *'48*
Adventures of Don Juan *'49*
Black Magic *'49*
Borderline *'50*
Key to the City *'50*
Love Happy *'50*
Bride of the Gorilla *'51*
His Kind of Woman *'51*
A Place in the Sun *'51*
FBI Girl *'52*
Horizons West *'52*
Meet Danny Wilson *'52*
Casanova's Big Night *'54*
Party Girls for Sale *'54*
Passion *'54*
Rear Window *'54*
Thunder Pass *'54*
A Man Alone *'55*
They Were So Young *'55*
Godzilla, King of the Monsters *'56*
Great Day in the Morning *'56*
Crime of Passion *'57*
Tomorrow Never Comes *'77*
Love's Savage Fury *'79*
The Curse of King Tut's Tomb *'80*
The Night the City Screamed *'80*
Out of the Blue *'80*
The Return *'80*
Airplane 2: The Sequel *'82*
Godzilla 1985 *'85*
Perry Mason Returns *'85*
Perry Mason: The Case of the Lost Love *'87*
The Defense Never Rests *'90*
Delirious *'91*
Showdown at Williams Creek *'91*

Robert Burr
The Possession of Joel Delaney *'72*
Netherworld *'90*

Jackie Burroughs
The Grey Fox *'83*
125 Rooms of Comfort *'83*
Anne of Green Gables *'85*
Undergrads *'85*
The Housekeeper *'86*
John and the Missus *'87*
Final Notice *'89*
Tales from Avonlea, Vol. 1: The Journey Begins *'90*
Careful *'94*

William S. Burroughs
Bloodhounds of Broadway *'89*
Drugstore Cowboy *'89*
Wax, or the Discovery of Television Among the Bees *'93*

Darren E. Burrows
Class of 1999 *'90*
Cry-Baby *'90*

Ellen Burstyn
Alex in Wonderland *'70*
Tropic of Cancer *'70*
The Last Picture Show *'71*
The King of Marvin Gardens *'72*
The Exorcist *'73*
Alice Doesn't Live Here Anymore *'74*
Harry and Tonto *'74*
Thursday's Game *'74*
Providence *'77*
A Dream of Passion *'78*
Same Time, Next Year *'78*
Resurrection *'80*
The People vs. Jean Harris *'81*
Silence of the North *'81*
The Ambassador *'84*
Into Thin Air *'85*
Twice in a Lifetime *'85*
Act of Vengeance *'86*
Something in Common *'86*
Hanna's War *'88*
Dying Young *'91*
Grand Isle *'92*
The Cemetery Club *'93*
Getting Gotti *'94*
Getting Out *'94*
Primal Secrets *'94*
When a Man Loves a Woman *'94*
The Baby-Sitters Club *'95*
The Color of Evening *'95*
Follow the River *'95*
How to Make an American Quilt *'95*
Roommates *'95*
The Spitfire Grill *'95*

Benny Burt
Sea Racketeers *'37*
Hawaiian Buckaroo *'38*

Kate Burton
Big Trouble in Little China *'86*
Uncle Tom's Cabin *'87*
Love Matters *'93*
August *'95*

LeVar Burton
Billy: Portrait of a Street Kid *'77*
Roots *'77*
One in a Million: The Ron LeFlore Story *'78*
The Guyana Tragedy: The Story of Jim Jones *'80*
The Hunter *'80*
Grambling's White Tiger *'81*
Acorn People *'82*
The Jesse Owens Story *'84*
And the Children Shall Lead *'85*
The Midnight Hour *'86*
The Supernaturals *'86*
Star Trek the Next Generation: Encounter at Farpoint *'87*
Roots: The Gift *'88*
Firestorm: 72 Hours in Oakland *'93*
Parallel Lives *'94*
Star Trek Generations *'94*
Star Trek the Next Generation, the Final Episode: All Good Things... *'94*

Norman Burton
Fright *'56*
Attack of the Mayan Mummy *'63*
Diamonds Are Forever *'71*
Jud *'71*
Simon, King of the Witches *'71*
Save the Tiger *'73*
The Terminal Man *'74*
Mausoleum *'83*
Crimes of Passion *'84*
Bad Guys *'86*
Bloodsport *'88*

Richard Burton
The Last Days of Dolwyn *'49*
Green Grow the Rushes *'51*
The Desert Rats *'53*
The Robe *'53*
Alexander the Great *'55*
Look Back in Anger *'58*
The Bramble Bush *'60*
Ice Palace *'60*
The Longest Day *'62*
Cleopatra *'63*
The Tempest *'63*
The V.I.P.'s *'63*
Becket *'64*
The Night of the Iguana *'64*
The Sandpiper *'65*
The Spy Who Came in from the Cold *'65*
Who's Afraid of Virginia Woolf? *'66*
The Comedians *'67*
The Taming of the Shrew *'67*
Doctor Faustus *'68*
Where Eagles Dare *'68*
Anne of the Thousand Days *'69*
Raid on Rommel *'71*
Assassination of Trotsky *'72*
Bluebeard *'72*
Divorce His, Divorce Hers *'72*
Hammersmith is Out *'72*
Massacre in Rome *'73*
Under Milk Wood *'73*
The Gathering Storm *'74*
The Klansman *'74*
Equus *'77*
The Exorcist 2: The Heretic *'77*
Breakthrough *'78*
The Medusa Touch *'78*
Wild Geese *'78*
Lovespell *'79*
Circle of Two *'80*
Absolution *'81*
1984 *'84*
Wagner: The Complete Epic *'85*
Wagner: The Movie *'85*

Robert Burton
Above and Beyond *'53*
All the Brothers Were Valiant *'53*
The Girl Who Had Everything *'53*
A Man Called Peter *'55*
The Tall T *'57*
Teenage Frankenstein *'58*
Compulsion *'59*
The Gallant Hours *'60*
Invasion of the Animal People *'62*
The Slime People *'63*
A Reason to Live, A Reason to Die *'73*
Trilogy of Terror *'75*

Tony Burton
Assault on Precinct 13 *'76*
Blackjack *'78*
Armed and Dangerous *'86*
Oceans of Fire *'86*
House Party 2: The Pajama Jam *'91*
Mission of Justice *'92*

Wendell Burton
The Sterile Cuckoo *'69*
Fortune and Men's Eyes *'71*
East of Eden *'80*

Sean Bury
Friends *'71*
Paul and Michelle *'74*

Steve Buscemi
Parting Glances *'86*
Heart *'87*
Mystery Train *'89*
New York Stories *'89*
King of New York *'90*
Barton Fink *'91*
Billy Bathgate *'91*
Crisscross *'92*
In the Soup *'92*
Reservoir Dogs *'92*
Trusting Beatrice *'92*
Ed and His Dead Mother *'93*
The Last Outlaw *'93*
Twenty Bucks *'93*
Airheads *'94*
Floundering *'94*
Living in Oblivion *'94*
Pulp Fiction *'94*
Desperado *'95*
Things to Do In Denver When You're Dead *'95*
Escape from L.A. *'96*
Fargo *'96*

Mae Busch
Foolish Wives *'22*
The Unholy Three *'25*
Laurel & Hardy Comedy Classics, Vol. 7 *'30s*
Defenders of the Law *'31*
Without Honors *'32*
Laurel & Hardy Comedy Classics, Vol. 1 *'33*
Sons of the Desert *'33*
Laurel & Hardy Comedy Classics, Vol. 3 *'34*
Sucker Money *'34*
Laurel & Hardy Comedy Classics, Vol. 6 *'35*
Bohemian Girl *'36*
Marie Antoinette *'38*
Ziegfeld Girl *'41*
The Mad Monster *'42*

Gary Busey
Angels Hard as They Come *'71*
The Last American Hero *'73*
The Shrieking *'73*
The Execution of Private Slovik *'74*
Thunderbolt & Lightfoot *'74*
Gumball Rally *'76*
A Star is Born *'76*
Big Wednesday *'78*
The Buddy Holly Story *'78*
Straight Time *'78*
Carny *'80*
Foolin' Around *'80*
Barbarosa *'82*
Didn't You Hear? *'83*
D.C. Cab *'84*
The Hitchhiker *'85*
Insignificance *'85*
Silver Bullet *'85*
Eye of the Tiger *'86*
Half a Lifetime *'86*
Lethal Weapon *'87*
Let's Get Harry *'87*
Bulletproof *'88*
Act of Piracy *'89*
Dangerous Life *'89*
The Neon Empire *'89*
Hider in the House *'90*
Predator 2 *'90*
My Heroes Have Always Been Cowboys *'91*
Point Break *'91*
Canvas: The Fine Art of Crime *'92*
Chrome Soldiers *'92*
South Beach *'92*
Under Siege *'92*
Fallen Angels 1 *'93*
The Firm *'93*
Rookie of the Year *'93*
Breaking Point *'94*
Drop Zone *'94*
Surviving the Game *'94*
Warriors *'94*
Carried Away *'95*
Man with a Gun *'95*
Black Sheep *'96*

Jake Busey
P.C.U. *'94*
S.F.W. *'94*
Windrunner *'94*
The Frighteners *'96*
Twister *'96*

Timothy Busfield
Revenge of the Nerds *'84*
Revenge of the Nerds 2: Nerds in Paradise *'87*
Field of Dreams *'89*
Strays *'91*
Sneakers *'92*
Fade to Black *'93*
The Skateboard Kid *'93*
Striking Distance *'93*
Little Big League *'94*

Billy Green Bush
Five Easy Pieces *'70*
Culpepper Cattle Co. *'72*
Electra Glide in Blue *'73*
Alice Doesn't Live Here Anymore *'74*
Tom Horn *'80*
The River *'84*
Critters *'86*
The Deliberate Stranger *'86*
Elvis and Me *'88*
Conagher *'91*
Jason Goes to Hell: The Final Friday *'93*

Grand Bush
Streets of Fire *'84*
Colors *'88*
Blind Vengeance *'90*
Freejack *'92*

James Bush
Beggars in Ermine *'34*
Crimson Romance *'34*
The Return of Peter Grimm *'35*
A Shot in the Dark *'35*
The Glory Trail *'36*
King of the Cowboys *'43*

Jovita Bush
The Cheerleaders *'72*
Foxstyle *'73*

Anthony Bushell
Disraeli *'29*
The Royal Bed *'31*
Vanity Fair *'32*
The Ghoul *'34*
The Scarlet Pimpernel *'34*

Bushell ▶cont.

Dark Journey '37
The Arsenal Stadium Mystery '39
The Small Back Room '49
Angel with the Trumpet '50
The Miniver Story '50
A Night to Remember '58

Francis X. Bushman
Ben-Hur '26
Eyes Right! '26
Midnight Faces '26
Last Frontier '32
When Lightning Strikes '34
Dick Tracy: The Original Serial, Vol. 1 '37
Dick Tracy: The Original Serial, Vol. 2 '37
Dick Tracy: The Spider Strikes '37
Honky Tonk '41
David and Bathsheba '51
Sabrina '54
The Phantom Planet '61

Akosua Busia
The Final Terror '83
The Color Purple '85
The George McKenna Story '86
Native Son '86
The Seventh Sign '88

Marion Busia
Gone in 60 Seconds '74
Deadline Auto Theft '83

Raymond Bussieres
Beauties of the Night '52
Casque d'Or '52
Paris When It Sizzles '64
Jonah Who Will Be 25 in the Year 2000 '76

Budd Buster
The Gun Ranger '34
Texas Jack '35
Gun Grit '36
Feud Maker '38
Songs and Bullets '38
Thunder in the Desert '38
Covered Wagon Trails '40
Pinto Canyon '40
The Lone Rider in Ghost Town '41
Trigger Men '41
Cowboy Commandos '43
Raiders of Sunset Pass '43
Frontier Outlaws '44
Border Badmen '45
Outlaw of the Plains '46

Dick Butkus
Mother, Jugs and Speed '76
The Legend of Sleepy Hollow '79
Deadly Games '80
Cracking Up '83
Johnny Dangerously '84
Hamburger...The Motion Picture '86

Calvin Butler
July Group '70s
Drying Up the Streets '76

Cindy Butler
Grayeagle '77
Boggy Creek II '83

David Butler
County Fair '20
The Sky Pilot '21
The Man on the Box '25

Dean Butler
Forever '78
The Kid with the 200 I.Q. '83
Desert Hearts '86

Frank Butler
King of the Wild Horses '24
Made for Love '26

Lois Butler
Mickey '48
High Lonesome '50

Paul Butler
Crime Story: The Complete Saga '86
To Sleep with Anger '90
Zebrahead '92
Romeo Is Bleeding '93

Tom Butler
Confidential '86
Tales of the Klondike: The Scorn of Women '87
Scanners 2: The New Order '91
Ernest Rides Again '93

William Butler
Leatherface: The Texas Chainsaw Massacre 3 '89
Inner Sanctum '91

Yancy Butler
Hard Target '93
The Hit List '93
Drop Zone '94

Merritt Butrick
Star Trek 2: The Wrath of Khan '82
Zapped! '82
Code of Honor '84
Star Trek 3: The Search for Spock '84
When the Bough Breaks '86
Wired to Kill '86
Death Spa '87
Shy People '87
From the Dead of Night '89

Lawson Butt
Dante's Inferno '24
Lady of the Lake '28

Charles Butterworth
Illicit '31
Penthouse '33
The Cat and the Fiddle '34
Hollywood Party '34
Forsaking All Others '35
The Moon's Our Home '36
Swing High, Swing Low '37
Every Day's a Holiday '38
Let Freedom Ring '39
Second Chorus '40
Road Show '41
Dixie Jamboree '44
Follow the Boys '44

Donna Butterworth
Family Jewels '65
Paradise, Hawaiian Style '66

Red Buttons
13 Rue Madeleine '46
Sayonara '57
Five Weeks in a Balloon '62
Hatari! '62
The Longest Day '62
Harlow '65
They Shoot Horses, Don't They? '69
Who Killed Mary What's 'Er Name? '71
The Poseidon Adventure '72
Pete's Dragon '77
Viva Knievel '77
Movie, Movie '78
Users '78
C.H.O.M.P.S. '79
Off Your Rocker '80
When Time Ran Out '80
Leave 'Em Laughing '81
Side Show '84
18 Again! '88
The Ambulance '90
It Could Happen to You '94

Pat Buttram
Hills of Utah '51
Valley of Fire '51
Blue Canadian Rockies '52
Night Stage to Galveston '52
Roustabout '64
The Gatling Gun '72
Back to the Future, Part 3 '90

Sarah Buxton
Primal Rage '90
Rock 'n' Roll High School Forever '91
Fast Getaway 2 '94

Margherita Buy
The Station '92
The Favorite Son '94

Ruth Buzzi
Freaky Friday '76
Once Upon a Brothers Grimm '77
The North Avenue Irregulars '79
Scavenger Hunt '79
The Villain '79
Chu Chu & the Philly Flash '81
The Being '83
Surf 2 '84
Bad Guys '86
Dixie Lanes '88
My Mom's a Werewolf '89
Up Your Alley '89
Digging Up Business '91
Wishful Thinking '92

Bobbie Byers
Savages from Hell '68
Wild Rebels '71

Spring Byington
Little Women '33
Ah, Wilderness! '35
Mutiny on the Bounty '35
Werewolf of London '35
Theodora Goes Wild '36
Jezebel '38
You Can't Take It with You '38
The Story of Alexander Graham Bell '39
The Blue Bird '40
Lucky Partners '40
The Devil & Miss Jones '41
Meet John Doe '41
When Ladies Meet '41
Roxie Hart '42
Heaven Can Wait '43
The Enchanted Cottage '45
Thrill of a Romance '45
Singapore '47
The Big Wheel '49
In the Good Old Summertime '49
Walk Softly, Stranger '50
Angels in the Outfield '51
Because You're Mine '52
Please Don't Eat the Daisies '60

Rolan Bykov
The Overcoat '59
Commissar '68

John Byner
Great Smokey Roadblock '76
The Man in the Santa Claus Suit '79
A Pleasure Doing Business '79
Transylvania 6-5000 '85

Ralph Byrd
Blake of Scotland Yard '36
Border Caballero '36
Hell-Ship Morgan '36
Dick Tracy '37
Dick Tracy: The Original Serial, Vol. 1 '37
Dick Tracy: The Original Serial, Vol. 2 '37
Dick Tracy: The Spider Strikes '37
S.O.S. Coast Guard '37
The Trigger Trio '37
Born to Be Wild '38
Dick Tracy Returns '38
The Howards of Virginia '40
Desperate Cargo '41
Dick Tracy vs. Crime Inc. '41
Life Begins for Andy Hardy '41
Misbehaving Husbands '41
The Son of Monte Cristo '41
The Jungle Book '42
Guadalcanal Diary '43
Dick Tracy Double Feature #1 '45
Dick Tracy Double Feature #2 '47
Dick Tracy Meets Gruesome '47
Dick Tracy's Dilemma '47
Scared to Death/Dick Tracy's Dilemma '47
Jungle Goddess '49
Thunder in the Pines '49
Radar Secret Service '50

Bill Byrge
Ernest Goes to Jail '90
Ernest Goes to School '94

Anne Byrne
A Night Full of Rain '78
Manhattan '79

Barbara Byrne
Mystery at Fire Island '81
Svengali '83
Sunday in the Park with George '86

David Byrne
True Stories '86
Heavy Petting '89

Gabriel Byrne
Excalibur '81
Hanna K. '83
The Keep '83
Christopher Columbus '85
Defense of the Realm '85
Gothic '87
Hello Again '87
Julia and Julia '87
Lionheart '87
Siesta '87
The Courier '88
Dark Obsession '90
Miller's Crossing '90
Shipwrecked '90
A Soldier's Tale '91
Cool World '92
Into the West '92
A Dangerous Woman '93
Point of No Return '93
Little Women '94
A Simple Twist of Fate '94
Trial by Jury '94
Buffalo Girls '95
Dead Man '95
Frankie Starlight '95
The Usual Suspects '95

Martha Byrne
The Eyes of the Amaryllis '82
Anna to the Infinite Power '84

Michael Byrne
The Good Father '87
Over Indulgence '87
Indiana Jones and the Last Crusade '89
Sharpe's Enemy '94
Sharpe's Honour '94
The Infiltrator '95

Edd Byrnes
Darby's Rangers '58
Any Gun Can Play '67
Go Kill and Come Back '68
Twirl '81
Erotic Images '85
Back to the Beach '87
Mankillers '87
Troop Beverly Hills '89

Jim Byrnes
Dirty Work '92
Suspicious Agenda '94

Josephine Byrnes
Brides of Christ '91
Frauds '93

David Byron
My Brother's Wife '89
Fade to Black '93

Jeffrey Byron
The Seniors '78
Dungeonmaster '83
Metalstorm: The Destruction of Jared Syn '83

Kathleen Byron
Black Narcissus '47
The Small Back Room '49
The Gambler & the Lady '52
Young Bess '53
Profile '54
Burn Witch, Burn! '62
Twins of Evil '71

Marion Byron
Steamboat Bill, Jr. '28
Breed of the Border '33

Walter Byron
Queen Kelly '29
The Savage Girl '32
Vanity Fair '32
Mr. Boggs Steps Out '38

Susan Byun
Crime Lords '91
Deadly Target '94

James Caan
Lady in a Cage '64
Red Line 7000 '65
El Dorado '67
Countdown '68
The Rain People '69
Brian's Song '71
The Godfather '72
Gone with the West '72
Cinderella Liberty '73
Slither '73
Freebie & the Bean '74
The Gambler '74
The Godfather, Part 2 '74
Funny Lady '75
The Killer Elite '75
Rollerball '75
Harry & Walter Go to New York '76
Silent Movie '76
Another Man, Another Chance '77
A Bridge Too Far '77
Comes a Horseman '78
Little Moon & Jud McGraw '78
Chapter Two '79
Hide in Plain Sight '80
The Godfather 1902-1959: The Complete Epic '81
Thief '81
Bolero '82
Kiss Me Goodbye '82
Gardens of Stone '87
Alien Nation '88
Dick Tracy '90
Misery '90
The Dark Backward '91
For the Boys '91
Honeymoon in Vegas '92
Flesh and Bone '93
The Program '93
Bottle Rocket '95
Eraser '96

Katia Caballero
Beyond Innocence '87
Sharpe's Eagle '93

Bruce Cabot
Ann Vickers '33
Finishing School '33
King Kong '33
Let 'Em Have It '35
Show Them No Mercy '35
Fury '36
The Last of the Mohicans '36
Renegade Ranger/Scarlet River '38
Sinners in Paradise '38
Dodge City '39
Captain Caution '40
Susan and God '40
Sundown '41
Silver Queen '42
Angel and the Badman '47
Sorrowful Jones '49
Best of the Badmen '50
Fancy Pants '50
Lost in Alaska '52
John Paul Jones '59
Goliath and the Barbarians '60
The Comancheros '61
Goliath and the Dragon '61
Hatari! '62
McLintock! '63
In Harm's Way '65
The War Wagon '67
Hellfighters '68
The Undefeated '69
Chisum '70
Diamonds Are Forever '71

Sebastian Cabot
Dual Alibi '47
Dick Barton Strikes Back '48
Captain's Paradise '53
Romeo and Juliet '54
Westward Ho, the Wagons! '56
Omar Khayyam '57
Johnny Tremain & the Sons of Liberty '58
The Time Machine '60
Twice-Told Tales '63
Family Jewels '65

Susan Cabot
Son of Ali Baba '52
Carnival Rock '57
Sorority Girl '57
Machine Gun Kelly '58
The Wasp Woman '59

Jean Cadell
Love from a Stranger '37
The Obsessed '51

Adolph Caesar
Fist of Fear, Touch of Death '77
The Hitter '79
A Soldier's Story '84
The Color Purple '85
Club Paradise '86
Fortune Dane '86

Harry Caesar
The Offspring '87
Ghetto Blaster '89

Sid Caesar
It's a Mad, Mad, Mad, Mad World '63
Airport '75 '75
Silent Movie '76
Barnaby and Me '77
Curse of the Black Widow '77

The Cheap Detective '78
Grease '78
The Fiendish Plot of Dr. Fu Manchu '80
History of the World: Part 1 '81
The Munsters' Revenge '81
Grease 2 '82
Over the Brooklyn Bridge '83
Cannonball Run 2 '84
Stoogemania '85
Side By Side '88
Cannon Movie Tales: The Emperor's New Clothes '89

Cheri Caffaro
The Abductors '72
Ginger '72
A Place Called Today '72
Girls Are for Loving '73
Too Hot to Handle '76

Stephen Caffrey
Tour of Duty '87
Hard Rain-The Tet 1968 '89
Longtime Companion '90
The Babe '92

Andrea Cagan
Hot Box '72
Teenager '74

Nicolas Cage
Rumble Fish '83
Valley Girl '83
Birdy '84
The Cotton Club '84
Racing with the Moon '84
Boy in Blue '86
Peggy Sue Got Married '86
Moonstruck '87
Raising Arizona '87
Vampire's Kiss '88
Time to Kill '89
Fire Birds '90
Wild at Heart '90
Zandalee '91
Honeymoon in Vegas '92
Amos and Andrew '93
Deadfall '93
Red Rock West '93
Guarding Tess '94
It Could Happen to You '94
Kiss of Death '94
Trapped In Paradise '94
Leaving Las Vegas '95
The Rock '96

James Cagney
Blonde Crazy '31
Public Enemy '31
Footlight Parade '33
Lady Killer '33
Ceiling Zero '35
Devil Dogs of the Air '35
"G" Men '35
A Midsummer Night's Dream '35
Great Guy '36
Something to Sing About '36
Angels with Dirty Faces '38
Boy Meets Girl '38
Each Dawn I Die '39
Oklahoma Kid '39
The Roaring Twenties '39
City for Conquest '40
The Fighting 69th '40
The Bride Came C.O.D. '41
Strawberry Blonde '41
Captains of the Clouds '42
Yankee Doodle Dandy '42
Johnny Come Lately '43
Blood on the Sun '45
13 Rue Madeleine '46
The Time of Your Life '48
White Heat '49
Kiss Tomorrow Goodbye '50
The West Point Story '50
What Price Glory? '52
A Lion Is in the Streets '53
Love Me or Leave Me '55
Mister Roberts '55
The Seven Little Foys '55
Tribute to a Bad Man '56
Man of a Thousand Faces '57
Never Steal Anything Small '59
Shake Hands with the Devil '59
The Gallant Hours '60
One, Two, Three '61
Ragtime '81

Jeanne Cagney
Yankee Doodle Dandy '42
The Time of Your Life '48
Quicksand '50
Don't Bother to Knock '52
A Lion Is in the Streets '53
Kentucky Rifle '55
Postmark for Danger/Quicksand '56

William Cagney
Ace of Aces '33
Palooka '34

Howard Caine
Pressure Point '62
Watermelon Man '70

Michael Caine
Room 43 '58
Zulu '64
The Ipcress File '65
Alfie '66
Funeral in Berlin '66
Gambit '66
The Wrong Box '66
Woman Times Seven '67
Battle of Britain '69
The Italian Job '69
Too Late the Hero '70
The Last Valley '71
Pulp '72
Sleuth '72
X, Y & Zee '72
The Black Windmill '74
The Destructors '74
The Man Who Would Be King '75
Romantic Englishwoman '75
The Wilby Conspiracy '75
Harry & Walter Go to New York '76
A Bridge Too Far '77
The Eagle Has Landed '77
California Suite '78
Silver Bears '78
The Swarm '78
Ashanti, Land of No Mercy '79
Beyond the Poseidon Adventure '79
Dressed to Kill '80
The Island '80
The Hand '81
Victory '81
Deathtrap '82
Beyond the Limit '83
Educating Rita '83
Blame It on Rio '84
The Jigsaw Man '84
The Holcroft Covenant '85
Water '85
Half Moon Street '86
Hannah and Her Sisters '86
Mona Lisa '86
Sweet Liberty '86
The Fourth Protocol '87
Jaws: The Revenge '87
Surrender '87
The Whistle Blower '87
Dirty Rotten Scoundrels '88
Jack the Ripper '88
Without a Clue '88
Bullseye! '90
Jekyll and Hyde '90
Mr. Destiny '90
A Shock to the System '90
Blue Ice '92
Death Becomes Her '92
The Muppet Christmas Carol '92
Noises Off '92
On Deadly Ground '94
World War II: When Lions Roared '94

Anna Calder-Marshall
Wuthering Heights '70
The Two Faces of Evil '82

Sergio Calderon
Old Gringo '89
Border Shootout '90

Paul Calderone
Q & A '90
Bad Lieutenant '92
Crisscross '92
The Addiction '95
Four Rooms '95

L. Scott Caldwell
God Bless the Child '88
Down Came a Blackbird '94

Zoe Caldwell
Medea '59
The Purple Rose of Cairo '85
Lantern Hill '90

Don Calfa
The Rainbow Gang '73
E. Nick: A Legend in His Own Mind '84
Return of the Living Dead '85
Treasure of the Moon Goddess '88
Weekend at Bernie's '89
Chopper Chicks in Zombietown '91
Me, Myself & I '92

Louis Calhern
The Blot '21
Too Wise Wives '21
Blonde Crazy '31
Night After Night '32
They Call It Sin '32
Duck Soup '33
The World Gone Mad '33
The Count of Monte Cristo '34
Last Days of Pompeii '35
Sweet Adeline '35
The Gorgeous Hussy '36
Heaven Can Wait '43
The Bridge of San Luis Rey '44
Up in Arms '44
Notorious '46
Arch of Triumph '48
The Red Pony '49
The Asphalt Jungle '50
A Life of Her Own '50
The Magnificent Yankee '50
Nancy Goes to Rio '50
Two Weeks with Love '50
Prisoner of Zenda '52
We're Not Married '52
Julius Caesar '53
Latin Lovers '53
Athena '54
Betrayed '54
Executive Suite '54
Men of the Fighting Lady '54
Rhapsody '54
The Student Prince '54
Blackboard Jungle '55
The Prodigal '55
Forever Darling '56
High Society '56

Alice Calhoun
The Man on the Box '25
Tentacles of the North '26

Rory Calhoun
Adventure Island '47
The Red House '47
Ticket to Tomahawk '50
I'd Climb the Highest Mountain '51
A Bullet Is Waiting '54
River of No Return '54
Treasure of Pancho Villa '55
Hard Drivin' '60
Finger on the Trigger '65
Apache Uprising '66
Emerald of Artama '67
Dayton's Devils '68
Operation Cross Eagles '69
Midnight Auto Supply '78
Flatbed Annie and Sweetiepie: Lady Truckers '79
The Rebels '79
Mission to Glory '80
Motel Hell '80
Angel '84
Avenging Angel '85
Hell Comes to Frogtown '88
Bad Jim '89
Roller Blade Warriors: Taken By Force '90
Pure Country '92

Joseph Cali
The Competition '80
The Lonely Lady '83

Brandon Call
The Adventures of Ford Fairlane '90
Blind Fury '90
For the Boys '91

R.D. Call
Young Guns 2 '90
Other People's Money '91
Stephen King's Golden Years '91
Waterworld '95

James Callahan
Tropic of Cancer '70
Lady Sings the Blues '72
Outlaw Blues '77
Prison for Children '93
Blood for Blood '95

K. Callan
A Touch of Class '73
Frankie and Johnny '91
The Unborn '91

Michael Callan
Gidget Goes Hawaiian '61
Mysterious Island '61
Bon Voyage! '62
The Interns '62
Cat Ballou '65
Frasier the Sensuous Lion '73
Lepke '75
Photographer '75
The Cat and the Canary '79
Double Exposure '82
Donner Pass: The Road to Survival '84
Freeway '88
Leprechaun 3 '95

Charlie Callas
Big Mouth '67
Vampire Vixens from Venus '94

Joseph Calleia
Riff Raff '35
After the Thin Man '36
Algiers '38
Marie Antoinette '38
Five Came Back '39
Golden Boy '39
My Little Chickadee '40
The Monster and the Girl '41
Sundown '41
The Glass Key '42
The Jungle Book '42
Deadline at Dawn '46
Gilda '46
The Noose Hangs High '48
Branded '50
The Caddy '53
The Littlest Outlaw '54
The Light in the Forest '58
Touch of Evil '58

Simon Callow
Amadeus '84
A Room with a View '86
The Good Father '87
Maurice '87
Mr. & Mrs. Bridge '90
The Crucifer of Blood '91
Four Weddings and a Funeral '94
Street Fighter '94
Ace Ventura: When Nature Calls '95

Cab Calloway
International House '33
Hi-De-Ho '35
Manhattan Merry-Go-Round '37
Stormy Weather '43
Sensations of 1945 '44
The Cincinnati Kid '65
The Littlest Angel '69
The Blues Brothers '80

Kirk Calloway
Summertree '71
Cinderella Liberty '73

Vanessa Bell Calloway
What's Love Got to Do with It? '93
America's Dream '95
Crimson Tide '95

Donald Calthrop
No. 17 '32
The Phantom Light '35
Scrooge '35

Bill Calvert
Terror Squad '87
C.H.U.D. 2: Bud the Chud '89
Body Waves '92

Phyllis Calvert
Kipps '41
The Man in Grey '45
Men of Two Worlds '46
Man of Evil '48
Mandy '53
Indiscreet '58
The Young and the Guilty '58
The Woman He Loved '88

Corinne Calvet
What Price Glory? '52
Far Country '55
Apache Uprising '66
Too Hot to Handle '76
Dr. Heckyl and Mr. Hype '80

Henry Calvin
Toby Tyler '59
The Sign of Zorro '60

John Calvin
California Dreaming '79
Ghostwarrior '86
Primary Target '89
The Magic Bubble '93
Dragonworld '94

Armando Calvo
The Witch's Mirror '60
Satanik '69

Godfrey Cambridge
Gone are the Days '63
Purlie Victorious '63
The President's Analyst '67
Cotton Comes to Harlem '70
Watermelon Man '70
Son of Blob '72
Friday Foster '75
Whiffs '75

Juan Jose Camero
Far Away and Long Ago '74
El Muerto '75
Veronico Cruz '87

Candace Cameron
Frankenstein Sings...The Movie '95
Sharon's Secret '95

Dean Cameron
Summer School '87
Bad Dreams '88
Rockula '90
Ski School '91
Miracle Beach '92
Ski School 2 '94
Sleep with Me '94

Jane Cameron
Pair of Aces '90
The Unborn '91

Kirk Cameron
The Best of Times '86
Like Father, Like Son '87
Listen to Me '89

Rod Cameron
The Monster and the Girl '41
Wake Island '42
G-Men vs. the Black Dragon '43
Salome, Where She Danced '45
Jungle '52
Ride the Man Down '53
Manhunt in the African Jungle '54
The Electronic Monster '57
The Last Movie '71
Evel Knievel '72
Psychic Killer '75
Midnight Auto Supply '78

Jesse Cameron-Glickenhaus
Slaughter of the Innocents '93
Timemaster '95

Terry Camillieri
The Cars That Ate Paris '74
Bill & Ted's Excellent Adventure '89

Colleen Camp
Cat in the Cage '68
The Last Porno Flick '74
The Swinging Cheerleaders '74
Smile '75
Seducers '77
Lady of the House '78
Midnight Auto Supply '78
Apocalypse Now '79
Game of Death '79
Cloud Dancer '80
Deadly Games '80
They All Laughed '81
The Seduction '82
Smokey and the Bandit, Part 3 '83
Valley Girl '83
Joy of Sex '84
Clue '85
D.A.R.Y.L. '85
Doin' Time '85
Police Academy 2: Their First Assignment '85
Rosebud Beach Hotel '85
Screwball Academy '86
Illegally Yours '87
Police Academy 4: Citizens on Patrol '87

Camp ▶cont.

Walk Like a Man '87
Track 29 '88
Wicked Stepmother '89
Backfield in Motion '91
Wayne's World '92
The Magic Bubble '93
Sliver '93
Greedy '94
Die Hard: With a Vengeance '95
She Devils in Chains

Hamilton Camp
Under Fire '83
Meatballs 2 '84
Casey at the Bat '85
Lots of Luck '85
Rosebud Beach Hotel '85
Arena '89
Attack of the 50 Ft. Woman '93

Frank Campanella
Chesty Anderson USN '76
Blood Red '88

Joseph Campanella
The Fugitive: The Final Episode '67
The St. Valentine's Day Massacre '67
Murder Once Removed '71
The President's Plane is Missing '71
Ben '72
Terror on the 40th Floor '74
Sky Hei$t '75
Return to Fantasy Island '77
Meteor '79
Hangar 18 '80
Comic Book Kids '82
Plutonium Incident '82
Steele Justice '87
Down the Drain '89
Body Chemistry '90
Club Fed '90
Last Call '90
No Retreat, No Surrender 3: Blood Brothers '91
Original Intent '91
Magic Kid '92

Beatrice Campbell
Last Holiday '50
The Master of Ballantrae '53

Bill Campbell
Crime Story: The Complete Saga '86
The Rocketeer '91
Bram Stoker's Dracula '92
Armistead Maupin's Tales of the City '93
The Night We Never Met '93
Out There '95
Under the Hula Moon '95

Bruce Campbell
Evil Dead '83
Going Back '83
Crimewave '85
Evil Dead 2: Dead by Dawn '87
Maniac Cop '88
Moontrap '89
Maniac Cop 2 '90
Mindwarp '91
Sundown '91
Waxwork 2: Lost in Time '91
Army of Darkness '92
Lunatics: A Love Story '92
The Hudsucker Proxy '93
Tornado! '96

Cheryl Campbell
Lillie '79
McVicar '80
Chariots of Fire '81
Greystoke: The Legend of Tarzan, Lord of the Apes '84
The Shooting Party '85

Christian Campbell
Born to Run '93
City Boy '93

David James Campbell
Killzone '85
Killer Workout '86

Eric Campbell
The Floorwalker/By the Sea '15
Charlie Chaplin: The Early Years, Vol. 3 '16
Charlie Chaplin: The Early Years, Vol. 4 '16
The Fireman '16
The Vagabond '16
Charlie Chaplin: The Early Years, Vol. 1 '17
Charlie Chaplin: The Early Years, Vol. 2 '17
Count/Adventurer '17
The Cure '17
Triple Trouble/Easy Street '18

Glen Campbell
True Grit '69
Uphill All the Way '85

Judy Campbell
Convoy '40
The World Owes Me a Living '47
Bonnie Prince Charlie '48
Cry of the Penguins '71
Dust to Dust '85

Julia Campbell
Opportunity Knocks '90
Livin' Large '91
Lone Justice '93

Kate Campbell
Ghost Valley '32
Monte Carlo Nights '34

Ken Campbell
Joshua Then and Now '85
Letter to Brezhnev '86
Smart Money '88
Down Periscope '96

Louise Campbell
Bulldog Drummond Comes Back '37
Bulldog Drummond's Revenge '37
Bulldog Drummond's Peril '38
Bulldog Drummond's Revenge/ Bulldog Drummond's Peril '38

Naomi Campbell
Cool As Ice '91
Miami Rhapsody '95
Girl 6 '96

Neve Campbell
Northern Passage '95
The Canterville Ghost '96
The Craft '96

Nicholas Campbell
July Group '70s
Fast Company '78
Certain Fury '85
Knights of the City '85
Going Home '86
Rampage '87
The Victory '88
The Big Slice '90
Naked Lunch '91
No Contest '94
Guitarman '95

Peggy Campbell
When a Man Sees Red '34
Big Calibre '35

Rob Campbell
Unforgiven '92
Lone Justice 2 '93

Tisha Campbell
Rags to Riches '87
School Daze '88
Rooftops '89
House Party '90
House Party 2: The Pajama Jam '91
Boomerang '92
House Party 3 '94

Torquil Campbell
The Golden Seal '83
Heaven on Earth '89

William Campbell
Battle Circus '53
Escape from Fort Bravo '53
Man Without a Star '55
Night of Evil '62
Dementia 13 '63
Portrait in Terror '66
Track of the Vampire '66

Frank Campeau
The Man from Painted Post '17
His Majesty, the American '19
When the Clouds Roll By '19

Cris Campion
Pirates '86
Field of Honor '87

Wally Campo
Hell Squad '58
Machine Gun Kelly '58
Suicide Battalion/Hell Squad '58
Tank Commando '59
The Beast from Haunted Cave '60

Rafael Campos
This Could Be the Night '57
Lady in a Cage '64
The Astro-Zombies '67
The Hanged Man '74
Slumber Party '57 '76
V '83
A Streetcar Named Desire '84
The Return of Josey Wales '86

Ron Canada
Lone Star '95
Man of the House '95

Gianna Maria Canale
Go for Broke! '51
Man from Cairo '54
Sins of Rome '54
The Devil's Commandment '56
Evil's Commandment '56
Hercules '58
Tiger of the Seven Seas '62
Marauder '65

Lee Canalito
Paradise Alley '78
The Glass Jungle '88

David Canary
Melvin Purvis: G-Man '74
Johnny Firecloud '75
Posse '75
Sharks' Treasure '75

John Candy
Class of '44 '73
Find the Lady '75
Tunnelvision '76
The Silent Partner '78
Lost and Found '79
1941 '79
The Best of John Candy on SCTV '80s
The Blues Brothers '80
The Double Negative '80
Stripes '81
Clown Murders '83
Going Berserk '83
National Lampoon's Vacation '83
The Last Polka '84
Splash '84
Brewster's Millions '85
Sesame Street Presents: Follow That Bird '85
Summer Rental '85
Volunteers '85
Armed and Dangerous '86
Little Shop of Horrors '86
Really Weird Tales '86
Planes, Trains & Automobiles '87
Spaceballs '87
Tales of the Klondike: The Unexpected '87
The Great Outdoors '88
Speed Zone '88
Uncle Buck '89
Who's Harry Crumb? '89
Home Alone '90
The Masters of Menace '90
Delirious '91
JFK '91
Nothing But Trouble '91
Only the Lonely '91
Once Upon a Crime '92
Cool Runnings '93
Canadian Bacon '94
Wagons East '94

Charles Cane
Dead Reckoning '47
Native Son '51
Lucky Me '54

Dyan Cannon
Bob & Carol & Ted & Alice '69
Doctors' Wives '70
The Anderson Tapes '71
The Love Machine '71
The Last of Sheila '73
Shamus '73
The Virginia Hill Story '76
Heaven Can Wait '78
Lady of the House '78
Revenge of the Pink Panther '78
Coast to Coast '80
Honeysuckle Rose '80
Author! Author! '82
Deathtrap '82
Having It All '82
Jenny's War '85
Merlin and the Sword '85
Caddyshack 2 '88
The End of Innocence '90
Christmas in Connecticut '92
Based on an Untrue Story '93
The Pickle '93

J.D. Cannon
Cool Hand Luke '67
The Invaders '67
Cotton Comes to Harlem '70
Lawman '71
Scorpio '73
Killing Stone '78
Pleasure Palace '80
Raise the Titanic '80
Walking Through the Fire '80
The Adventures of Nellie Bly '81
Death Wish 2 '82
Street Justice '89

Kathy Cannon
The Red Fury '70s
Private Duty Nurses '71
High Noon: Part 2 '80
Will: G. Gordon Liddy '82
Matters of the Heart '90

Wanda Cannon
The Last Winter '89
For the Moment '94

Diana Canova
The First Nudie Musical '75
The Best of Soap: Who Killed Peter? '77
Night Partners '83

Judy Canova
Oklahoma Annie '51
The Adventures of Huckleberry Finn '60

Anne Canovos
High Frequency '88
Ready to Wear '94

Antonio Cantafora
Gabriela '84
Intervista '87

Luis Aceves Cantaneda
Curse of the Aztec Mummy/ Robot vs. the Aztec Mummy '59
The Robot vs. the Aztec Mummy '59

Eddie Cantor
Glorifying the American Girl '30
Whoopee! '30
Roman Scandals '33
Kid Millions '34
Thank Your Lucky Stars '43
Hollywood Canteen '44
Show Business '44
If You Knew Susie '48
Hollywood Goes to War '54

Yakima Canutt
Branded a Bandit '24
Wild Horse Canyon '25
The Fighting Stallion '26
Last Frontier '32
Sagebrush Trail '33
Telegraph Trail '33
Lucky Texan '34
The Man from Hell '34
Man from Utah '34
The Star Packer '34
West of the Divide '34
Branded a Coward '35
Cyclone of the Saddle '35
Dawn Rider '35
Paradise Canyon '35
Circle of Death '36
King of the Pecos '36
Outlaw Rule '36
Winds of the Wasteland '36
Heart of the Rockies '37
Hit the Saddle '37
The Painted Stallion '37
Riders of the Rockies '37
Riders of the Whistling Skull '37
Trouble in Texas '37
Overland Stage Raiders '38
Santa Fe Stampede '38
Gone with the Wind '39
The Kansas Terrors '39
Wyoming Outlaw '39
Calling Wild Bill Elliott '43
The Showdown '50

Peter Capaldi
Local Hero '83
John & Yoko: A Love Story '85
Dangerous Liaisons '88
The Lair of the White Worm '88
Prime Suspect 3 '93
Captives '94

Jad Capelja
Freedom '81
Puberty Blues '81

Virginia Capers
The North Avenue Irregulars '79
White Mama '80
Ferris Bueller's Day Off '86
Jo Jo Dancer, Your Life is Calling '86

Carmine Capobianco
Galactic Gigolo '87
Psychos in Love '87

John Capodice
The Hard Way '91
Honeymoon in Vegas '92

Lino Capolicchio
The Garden of the Finzi-Continis '71
Fiorile '93

Nadia Capone
Skull: A Night of Terror '88
A Whisper to a Scream '88

Carl Capotorto
American Blue Note '89
Mac '93

Jordanna Capra
Hired to Kill '91
Watch It '93

Tony Caprari
River of Diamonds '90
Armageddon: The Final Challenge '94

Ahna Capri
Darker than Amber '70
The Brotherhood of Satan '71
Payday '72
The Specialist '75

Kate Capshaw
A Little Sex '82
Best Defense '84
Dreamscape '84
Indiana Jones and the Temple of Doom '84
Windy City '84
Power '86
Code Name: Dancer '87
The Quick and the Dead '87
Black Rain '89
Love at Large '89
Private Affairs '89
My Heroes Have Always Been Cowboys '91
Just Cause '94
Love Affair '94
Next Door '94
How to Make an American Quilt '95

Capucine
North to Alaska '60
Song Without End '60
Walk on the Wild Side '62
The Pink Panther '64
What's New Pussycat? '65
The Honey Pot '67
Fellini Satyricon '69
From Hell to Victory '79
Jaguar Lives '79
The Con Artists '80
Trail of the Pink Panther '82
Curse of the Pink Panther '83
Scandalous '88
The Switch '89

Irene Cara
Aaron Loves Angela '75
Sparkle '76
Roots: The Next Generation '79
Fame '80
City Heat '84
D.C. Cab '84
Certain Fury '85
Killing 'em Softly '85
Busted Up '86

Carney ▶cont.

Miracle of the Heart: A Boys Town Story '86
Night Friend '87
The Night They Saved Christmas '87
Last Action Hero '93

George Carney
Love on the Dole '41
Brighton Rock '47

Morris Carnovsky
Our Vines Have Tender Grapes '45
Rhapsody in Blue '45
Dead Reckoning '47
Gun Crazy '49
Cyrano de Bergerac '50
Joe's Bed-Stuy Barbershop: We Cut Heads '83

Cindy Carol
Gidget Goes to Rome '63
Dear Brigitte '65

Linda Carol
Reform School Girls '86
Future Hunters '88
Carnal Crimes '91

Martine Carol
Voyage-Suprise '46
Beauties of the Night '52
Lola Montes '55
Nana '55
Around the World in 80 Days '56
The Battle of Austerlitz '60

Sheila Carol
The Beast from Haunted Cave '60
Ski Troop Attack '60

Sue Carol
Captain Swagger '25
Walking Back '26
The Lone Star Ranger '30

Leslie Caron
An American in Paris '51
Lili '53
Daddy Long Legs '55
The Glass Slipper '55
Gigi '58
The Battle of Austerlitz '60
Fanny '61
Father Goose '64
Promise Her Anything '66
Is Paris Burning? '68
Madron '70
Head of the Family '71
Nicole '72
QB VII '74
The Man Who Loved Women '77
Valentino '77
Goldengirl '79
The Unapproachable '82
Dangerous Moves '84
Courage Mountain '89
The Cary Grant Collection '90
Damage '92
Funny Bones '94

Carleton Carpenter
Lost Boundaries '49
Summer Stock '50
Two Weeks with Love '50
Up Periscope '59

David Carpenter
Warlock '91
Amelia Earhart: The Final Flight '94

Fred Carpenter
Small Kill '93
Murdered Innocence '94

Horace Carpenter
Maniac '34
The Worst of Hollywood: Vol. 1 '90

John Carpenter
Song of Old Wyoming '45
Night of the Ghouls '59

Paul Carpenter
Heat Wave '54
Paid to Kill '54
Unholy Four '54
Fire Maidens from Outer Space '56
Call Me Bwana '63

Peter Carpenter
Blood Mania '70
Point of Terror '71

Camilla Carr
Don't Look in the Basement '73
Poor White Trash 2 '75
Logan's Run '76
Keep My Grave Open '80
Making Love '82

Carole Carr
Down Among the Z Men '52
Scream Dream '89

Mary Carr
Red Kimono '25
The Night Patrol '26
Kept Husbands '31
The Fighting Marshal '32
Gun Law '33
The World Accuses '35

Paul Carr
Dirt Gang '71
The Severed Arm '73
The Bat People '74
Truck Stop Women '74
Sniper '75
Sisters of Death '76

Thomas Carr
The Idol Dancer '20
Superman: The Serial, Vol. 1 '48

David Carradine
Violent Ones '68
The Good Guys and the Bad Guys '69
Macho Callahan '70
Maybe I'll Be Home in the Spring '70
The McMasters '70
Boxcar Bertha '72
Kung Fu '72
Mean Streets '73
Death Race 2000 '75
Bound for Glory '76
Cannonball '76
Gray Lady Down '77
Thunder and Lightning '77
Circle of Iron '78
Death Sport '78
The Serpent's Egg '78
Mr. Horn '79
Cloud Dancer '80
High Noon: Part 2 '80
The Long Riders '80
Americana '81
Q (The Winged Serpent) '82
Safari 3000 '82
Trick or Treats '82
Lone Wolf McQuade '83
On the Line '83
Jealousy '84
The Warrior & the Sorceress '84
The Bad Seed '85
North and South Book 1 '85
Armed Response '86
Bad Girls in the Movies '86
Kung Fu: The Movie '86
Oceans of Fire '86
The P.O.W. Escape '86
The Misfit Brigade '87
Sonny Boy '87
Crime Zone '88
Nowhere to Run '88
Tropical Snow '88
Warlords '88
Future Force '89
Night Children '89
Wizards of the Lost Kingdom 2 '89
Bird on a Wire '90
Evil Toons '90
Future Zone '90
Martial Law '90
Midnight Fear '90
Think Big '90
Deadly Surveillance '91
Double Trouble '91
Dune Warriors '91
The Dying Truth '91
Project: Eliminator '91
Sundown '91
Animal Instincts '92
Distant Justice '92
Field of Fire '92
Night Rhythms '92
Roadside Prophets '92
The Gambler Returns: The Luck of the Draw '93
Karate Cop '93

John Carradine
To the Last Man '33
Daniel Boone '34
The Bride of Frankenstein '35
Les Miserables '35
Dimples '36
The Garden of Allah '36
Mary of Scotland '36
Winterset '36
Captains Courageous '37
The Hurricane '37
Alexander's Ragtime Band '38
Of Human Hearts '38
Drums Along the Mohawk '39
Five Came Back '39
The Hound of the Baskervilles '39
Mr. Moto's Last Warning '39
Stagecoach '39
The Three Musketeers '39
Western Double Feature 8: Hale & Carradine '40s
Brigham Young: Frontiersman '40
The Grapes of Wrath '40
Return of Frank James '40
Blood and Sand '41
Western Union '41
Reunion in France '42
Son of Fury '42
Captive Wild Woman '43
Isle of Forgotten Sins '43
Revenge of the Zombies '43
Silver Spurs '43
The Adventures of Mark Twain '44
Bluebeard '44
House of Frankenstein '44
The Invisible Man's Revenge '44
The Mummy's Ghost '44
Return of the Ape Man '44
Waterfront '44
Captain Kidd '45
House of Dracula '45
The Private Affairs of Bel Ami '47
The C-Man '49
Johnny Guitar '53
Casanova's Big Night '54
The Egyptian '54
Thunder Pass '54
The Kentuckian '55
Around the World in 80 Days '56
Court Jester '56
The Female Jungle '56
Hidden Guns '56
The Ten Commandments '56
Hell Ship Mutiny '57
The Unearthly '57
Half Human '58
The Incredible Petrified World '58
Last Hurrah '58
Showdown at Boot Hill '58
The Cosmic Man '59
Invisible Invaders '59
The Adventures of Huckleberry Finn '60
Invasion of the Animal People '62
The Man Who Shot Liberty Valance '62
Cheyenne Autumn '64
Curse of the Stone Hand '64
Horrors of the Red Planet '64
The Patsy '64
House of the Black Death '65
Billy the Kid Versus Dracula '66
Alien Massacre '67
The Astro-Zombies '67
Autopsy of a Ghost '67
Hillbillies in a Haunted House '67
The Hostage '67
Mummy & Curse of the Jackal '67
Blood of Dracula's Castle '69
The Good Guys and the Bad Guys '69
Gun Riders '69
The Trouble with Girls (and How To Get Into It) '69
Horror of the Blood Monsters '70
The McMasters '70
Myra Breckinridge '70
Cain's Cutthroats '71
Big Foot '72
Blood of Ghastly Horror '72
Boxcar Bertha '72
Everything You Always Wanted to Know about Sex (But Were Afraid to Ask) '72
The Gatling Gun '72
Bad Charleston Charlie '73
Blood Legacy '73
The House of Seven Corpses '73
The Shrieking '73
Silent Night, Bloody Night '73
Terror in the Wax Museum '73
Death at Love House '75
Killer Inside Me '76
The Last Tycoon '76
Mary, Mary, Bloody Mary '76
The Sentinel '76
The Shootist '76
The Christmas Coal Mine Miracle '77
Golden Rendezvous '77
Satan's Cheerleaders '77
Shock Waves '77
The White Buffalo '77
The Bees '78
Monster '78
The Vampire Hookers '78
Nocturna '79
The Seekers '79
The Boogey Man '80
The Nesting '80
Frankenstein Island '81
Goliath Awaits '81
The Howling '81
Demon Rage '82
House of the Long Shadows '82
Boogey Man 2 '83
Ice Pirates '84
Evils of the Night '85
The Monster Club '85
The Vals '85
Monster in the Closet '86
Peggy Sue Got Married '86
Revenge '86
Tomb '86
Evil Spawn '87
Star Slammer '87
Buried Alive '89
The Horror of It All '91
Jack-O '95

Keith Carradine
A Gunfight '71
Man on a String '71
McCabe & Mrs. Miller '71
Kung Fu '72
Idaho Transfer '73
The Shrieking '73
Thieves Like Us '74
Nashville '75
Lumiere '76
The Duellists '77
Welcome to L.A. '77
Pretty Baby '78
An Almost Perfect Affair '79
Old Boyfriends '79
The Long Riders '80
A Rumor of War '80
Southern Comfort '81
Chiefs '83
Choose Me '84
Maria's Lovers '84
Blackout '85
Half a Lifetime '86
Trouble in Mind '86
A Winner Never Quits '86
The Inquiry '87
Murder Ordained '87
Backfire '88
The Moderns '88
Capone '89
Cold Feet '89
The Forgotten '89
Daddy's Dyin'...Who's Got the Will? '90
Judgment '90
The Ballad of the Sad Cafe '91
Eye on the Sparrow '91
Payoff '91
Crisscross '92
The Bachelor '93
Andre '94
Is There Life Out There? '94
The Tie That Binds '95
Wild Bill '95

Robert Carradine
The Cowboys '72
Mean Streets '73
Aloha, Bobby and Rose '74
Cannonball '76
Jackson County Jail '76
Massacre at Central High '76
Pom Pom Girls '76
Joyride '77
Blackout '78
Coming Home '78
On the Edge: The Survival of Dana '79
The Big Red One '80
The Long Riders '80
Heartaches '82
Tag: The Assassination Game '82
Wavelength '83
Aladdin and His Wonderful Lamp '84
Just the Way You Are '84
Revenge of the Nerds '84
As Is '85
Monte Carlo '86
Conspiracy: The Trial of the Chicago Eight '87
Number One with a Bullet '87
Revenge of the Nerds 2: Nerds in Paradise '87
Tales of the Klondike: In a Far Country '87
All's Fair '89
Buy & Cell '89
The Incident '89
Rude Awakening '89
Somebody Has to Shoot the Picture '90
Clarence '91
Double-Crossed '91
Illusions '91
Revenge of the Nerds 3: The Next Generation '92
Body Bags '93
The Disappearance of Christina '93
Stephen King's The Tommyknockers '93
Revenge of the Nerds 4: Nerds in Love '94

Barbara Carrera
Embryo '76
Island of Dr. Moreau '77
When Time Ran Out '80
Condorman '81
Masada '81
I, the Jury '82
Lone Wolf McQuade '83
Never Say Never Again '83
Wild Geese 2 '85
Love at Stake '87
The Underachievers '88
Loverboy '89
Wicked Stepmother '89
Point of Impact '93
Tryst '94
Sawbones '95

Tia Carrere
Zombie Nightmare '86
Aloha Summer '88
Noble House '88
Fatal Mission '89
Showdown in Little Tokyo '91
Wayne's World '92
Quick '93
Rising Sun '93
Wayne's World 2 '93
True Lies '94
Hostile Intentions '95
The Immortals '95
Jury Duty '95
High School High '96

Jim Carrey
Rubberface '81
Club Med '83
Finders Keepers '84
Once Bitten '85
Peggy Sue Got Married '86
Earth Girls Are Easy '89
Pink Cadillac '89
High Strung '91
Ace Ventura: Pet Detective '93
Dumb & Dumber '94
The Mask '94
Ace Ventura: When Nature Calls '95
Batman Forever '95
The Cable Guy '96

Corey Carrier
Men Don't Leave '89
After Dark, My Sweet '90
Savage Land '94

Matthieu Carriere
An Occurrence at Owl Creek Bridge/Coup de Grace '62
Coup de Grace '78
Naked Massacre '80s
La Passante '83
A Woman in Flames '84
The Bay Boy '85

Christopher Columbus: The Discovery '92

Elpidia Carrillo
The Border '82
Beyond the Limit '83
Salvador '86
Let's Get Harry '87
Predator '87
Assassin '89
The Lightning Incident '91
My Family '94

Leo Carrillo
Before Morning '33
Manhattan Melodrama '34
Viva Villa! '34
Fit for a King '37
History is Made at Night '37
Girl of the Golden West '38
Too Hot to Handle '38
Fisherman's Wharf '39
Don Amigo/Stage to Chino '40s
One Night in the Tropics '40
Riders of Death Valley '41
American Empire '42
The Phantom of the Opera '43
The Fugitive '48
The Cisco Kid '50
Pancho Villa Returns '50

Debbie Lee Carrington
Club Fed '90
Spaced Invaders '90

Regina Carrol
The Female Bunch '69
Satan's Sadists '69
Brain of Blood '71
Dracula vs. Frankenstein '71
Angels' Wild Women '72
Blood of Ghastly Horror '72
Blazing Stewardesses '75
Jessie's Girls '75
Texas Layover '75

Barbara Carroll
The Last Days of Pompeii '60
Goliath Against the Giants '63

Brandon Carroll
Hell Squad '58
Suicide Battalion/Hell Squad '58

Diahann Carroll
Carmen Jones '54
Goodbye Again '61
Paris Blues '61
Death Scream '75
I Know Why the Caged Bird Sings '79
From the Dead of Night '89
The Five Heartbeats '91

Helen Carroll
The Dead '87
The Man Upstairs '93

Janet Carroll
Risky Business '83
Bluffing It '87
Memories of Me '88
Family Business '89

John Carroll
Zorro Rides Again '37
Rose of Rio Grande '38
Only Angels Have Wings '39
Wolf Call '39
Go West '40
Susan and God '40
Lady Be Good '41
Sunny '41
Flying Tigers '42
Rio Rita '42
The Farmer Takes a Wife '53
Rock, Baby, Rock It '57

Leo G. Carroll
A Christmas Carol '38
Bulldog Drummond's Secret Police '39
The Private Lives of Elizabeth & Essex '39
The Tower of London '39
Wuthering Heights '39
Rebecca '40
Suspicion '41
Bahama Passage '42
House on 92nd Street '45
Spellbound '45
Forever Amber '47
The Paradine Case '47
Father of the Bride '50
First Legion '51
Strangers on a Train '51
The Snows of Kilimanjaro '52
Treasure of the Golden Condor '53
Tarantula '55
We're No Angels '55
North by Northwest '59
One Plus One '61
The Parent Trap '61
The Prize '63
The Man from U.N.C.L.E. '64

Madeleine Carroll
The 39 Steps '35
The General Died at Dawn '36
Lloyds of London '36
The Secret Agent '36
On the Avenue '37
Prisoner of Zenda '37
My Love For Yours '39
Bahama Passage '42
My Favorite Blonde '42
Hitchcock Collection '87

Nancy Carroll
Dance of Life '29
Scarlet Dawn '32
Transatlantic Merry-Go-Round '34

Pat Carroll
With Six You Get Eggroll '68
Brothers O'Toole '73

Peter Carroll
Cass '78
Who Killed Baby Azaria? '83

Rocky Carroll
Crimson Tide '95
The Great White Hype '96

Ben Carruthers
Shadows '60
Riot '69

Charles Carson
Broken Melody '34
Dreaming Lips '37
The Courageous Mr. Penn '41
Cry, the Beloved Country '51
Beau Brummel '54

Crystal Carson
Killer Tomatoes Strike Back '90
Kiss and Be Killed '91

Glen Carson
Ninja Death Squad '87
Ninja Phantom Heroes '87

Hunter Carson
Paris, Texas '83
Invaders from Mars '86
Mr. North '88

Jack Carson
Stage Door '37
Stand-In '37
Carefree '38
The Saint in New York '38
Vivacious Lady '38
Destry Rides Again '39
Mr. Smith Goes to Washington '39
Lucky Partners '40
The Bride Came C.O.D. '41
Love Crazy '41
Mr. & Mrs. Smith '41
Strawberry Blonde '41
Gentleman Jim '42
Thank Your Lucky Stars '43
Arsenic and Old Lace '44
Hollywood Canteen '44
Mildred Pierce '45
Romance on the High Seas '48
It's a Great Feeling '49
My Dream Is Yours '49
Dangerous When Wet '53
Phffft! '54
Red Garters '54
A Star is Born '54
Tarnished Angels '57
Cat on a Hot Tin Roof '58
The Bramble Bush '60
The King of the Roaring '20s: The Story of Arnold Rothstein '61

John Carson
Taste the Blood of Dracula '70
Captain Kronos: Vampire Hunter '74
After Julius '78
An African Dream '90

John David Carson
Savage Is Loose '74
Charge of the Model T's '76
Creature from Black Lake '76
Empire of the Ants '77

L.M. Kit Carson
David Holzman's Diary '67
Running on Empty '88

Sunset Carson
Western Double Feature 1: Wild Bill & Sunset Carson '40s
Western Double Feature 17 '40s
Stage Door Canteen '43
Call of the Rockies '44
Bells of Rosarita '45
Rough Riders of Cheyenne '45
Alias Billy the Kid '46
Rio Grande Raiders '46
Battling Marshal '48

Peter Carsten
Secret of the Black Trunk '62
Dark of the Sun '68
Web of the Spider '70
Zeppelin '71
Black Lemons '80s

Margit Carstensen
The Bitter Tears of Petra von Kant '72
Mother Kusters Goes to Heaven '76
Satan's Brew '76
Possession '81
Angry Harvest '85
Chinese Roulette '86

Alice Carter
Gross Anatomy '89
Dangerous Heart '93

Ann Carter
Curse of the Cat People '44
The Two Mrs. Carrolls '47

Ben Carter
Kentucky Blue Streak '35
Crash Dive '43

Bill Carter
Battle of the Worlds '61
Flatbed Annie and Sweetiepie: Lady Truckers '79

Finn Carter
How I Got into College '89
Tremors '89
Sweet Justice '92

Gary Carter
Cobra Against Ninja '87
Ninja Strike Force '88

Helena Carter
Kiss Tomorrow Goodbye '50
Bugles in the Afternoon '52
Invaders from Mars '53

Jack Carter
The Horizontal Lieutenant '62
Viva Las Vegas '63
Resurrection of Zachary Wheeler '71
The Amazing Dobermans '76
The Happy Hooker Goes to Washington '77
The Glove '78
Rainbow '78
Alligator '80
Octagon '80
Heartbeeps '81
History of the World: Part 1 '81
Ecstasy '84
Hambone & Hillie '84
Death Blow '87
Red Nights '87
Deadly Embrace '88
Sexpot '88
Arena '89
Robo-Chic '89
In the Heat of Passion '91

Janis Carter
I Married an Angel '42
Lady of Burlesque '43
Miss Grant Takes Richmond '49
Flying Leathernecks '51
The Half-Breed '51
Santa Fe '51

Jim Carter
Haunted Honeymoon '86
A Month in the Country '87
Stalin '92
The Advocate '93
Black Beauty '94

Karen Carter
The Big Bust Out '73
The Legend of the Wolf Woman '77

Lynda Carter
Bobbie Jo and the Outlaw '76
Last Song '80
Hotline '82
Rita Hayworth: The Love Goddess '83
I Posed for Playboy '91
Danielle Steel's "Daddy" '92
Hawkeye: Premiere Episode '95

Nell Carter
Modern Problems '81
Final Shot: The Hank Gathers Story '92

Terry Carter
Foxy Brown '74
Man on the Run '74
Battlestar Galactica '78
Black Force 2 '78

Thomas Carter
Monkey Hustle '77
The White Shadow, Vol. 1 '78
Whose Life Is It Anyway? '81

T.K. Carter
Seems Like Old Times '80
Southern Comfort '81
The Thing '82
Doctor Detroit '83
Runaway Train '85
He's My Girl '87
Ski Patrol '89
A Rage in Harlem '91

Anna Carteret
The Shell Seekers '89
The Heat of the Day '91

Gabrielle Carteris
Beverly Hills 90210 '90
Raising Cain '92
Beverly Hills 90210: The Graduation '93

Katrin Cartlidge
Naked '93
Before the Rain '94
Breaking the Waves '95

Angela Cartwright
The Sound of Music '65
Scout's Honor '80
High School USA '84

Veronica Cartwright
The Children's Hour '61
The Birds '63
One Man's Way '63
Spencer's Mountain '63
Inserts '76
Goin' South '78
Invasion of the Body Snatchers '78
Kid from Not-So-Big '78
Alien '79
Prime Suspect '82
Nightmares '83
The Right Stuff '83
Flight of the Navigator '86
My Man Adam '86
Wisdom '87
The Witches of Eastwick '87
Valentino Returns '88
False Identity '90
Hitler's Daughter '90
Robert Kennedy and His Times '90
Dead in the Water '91
Man Trouble '92
Candyman 2: Farewell to the Flesh '94
Dead Air '94
Mirror, Mirror 2: Raven Dance '94

Anthony Caruso
Objective, Burma! '45
The Asphalt Jungle '50
Cattle Queen of Montana '54
Drum Beat '54
When Gangland Strikes '56
Legend of Earl Durand '74
Zebra Force '76
Claws '77

David Caruso
First Blood '82
An Officer and a Gentleman '82
Blue City '86
China Girl '87
King of New York '90
Rainbow Drive '90
Mad Dog and Glory '93
Kiss of Death '94
Jade '95

Betty Carvalho
Halloween 5: The Revenge of Michael Myers '89
Best of the Best 2 '93

Brent Carver
One Night Stand '77
Crossbar '79
Millenium '89

Lynne Carver
The Bride Wore Red '37
Madame X '37
Maytime '37
A Christmas Carol '38
Everybody Sing '38
The Adventures of Huckleberry Finn '39
Sunset on the Desert '42

Dana Carvey
Racing with the Moon '84
This Is Spinal Tap '84
Tough Guys '86
Moving '88
Opportunity Knocks '90
Wayne's World '92
Wayne's World 2 '93
Clean Slate '94
The Road to Wellville '94
Trapped In Paradise '94

Maria Casares
Children of Paradise '44
The Ladies of the Bois de Bologne '44
La Chartreuse de Parme '48
Orpheus '49
The Testament of Orpheus '59
Sand and Blood '87
La Lectrice '88

Antonio Casas
Tristana '70
Blood at Sundown '88

Salvatore Cascio
Cinema Paradiso '88
Everybody's Fine '90
The Pope Must Diet '91

Nicholas Cascone
Vietnam War Story 1 '88
84 Charlie Mopic '89

Kathleen Case
Last of the Pony Riders '53
Human Desire '54

Max Casella
Newsies '92
Windrunner '94
Sgt. Bilko '95

Chiara Caselli
My Own Private Idaho '91
Fiorile '93

Bernie Casey
Guns of the Magnificent Seven '69
Big Mo '73
Cleopatra Jones '73
Panic on the 5:22 '74
Cornbread, Earl & Me '75
Dr. Black, Mr. Hyde '76
The Man Who Fell to Earth '76
Ants '77
The Martian Chronicles: Part 1 '79
The Martian Chronicles: Part 2 '79
The Martian Chronicles: Part 3 '79
Sharky's Machine '81
Sophisticated Gents '81
Never Say Never Again '83
The Fantastic World of D.C. Collins '84
Revenge of the Nerds '84
Spies Like Us '85
Steele Justice '87
Backfire '88
I'm Gonna Git You Sucka '88
Rent-A-Cop '88
Bill & Ted's Excellent Adventure '89
Another 48 Hrs. '90
Chains of Gold '92
The Cemetery Club '93
Street Knight '93
In the Mouth of Madness '95

Lawrence Casey
The Student Nurses '70
The Hunted Lady '77

Johnny Cash
Door to Door Maniac '61
Road to Nashville '67
A Gunfight '71
Pride of Jesse Hallum '81
Murder in Coweta County '83
The Baron and the Kid '84
North and South Book 1 '85
Last Days of Frank & Jesse James '86
Stagecoach '86

June Carter Cash
Murder in Coweta County '83
The Baron and the Kid '84
Last Days of Frank & Jesse James '86

Rosalind Cash
Omega Man '71
Amazing Grace '74
Cornbread, Earl & Me '75
Dr. Black, Mr. Hyde '76
Monkey Hustle '77
The Class of Miss MacMichael '78
Keeping On '81
Sophisticated Gents '81
Wrong is Right '82
Death Drug '83
The Adventures of Buckaroo Banzai Across the Eighth Dimension '84
Go Tell It On the Mountain '84
The Mighty Pawns '87
The Offspring '87
Tales from the Hood '95

Isadore Cashier
His Wife's Lover '31
The Cantor's Son '37
The Light Ahead '39

Philip Casnoff
Gorp '80
North and South Book 2 '86
Hands of a Stranger '87
Ironclads '90
Red Wind '91
Sinatra '92
Temptation '94

John Cason
Outlaw of the Plains '46
Last Bullet '50
Rangeland Empire '50
Jungle Drums of Africa '53

Katrina Caspary
Mac and Me '88
My Mom's a Werewolf '89

Maurice Cass
Thin Ice '37
Spook Busters '48
Rocky Jones, Space Ranger: Renegade Satellite '54

Peggy Cass
Auntie Mame '58
Gidget Goes Hawaiian '61
If It's Tuesday, This Must Be Belgium '69
Paddy '70
Cheaters '84

John Cassavetes
The Killers '64
Devil's Angels '67
The Dirty Dozen '67
Rosemary's Baby '68
Mikey & Nicky '76
Two Minute Warning '76
Opening Night '77
Brass Target '78
The Fury '78
Whose Life Is It Anyway? '81
Incubus '82
The Tempest '82
Love Streams '84
Marvin & Tige '84

Nick Cassavetes
The Wraith '87
Assault of the Killer Bimbos '88
Backstreet Dreams '90
Blind Fury '90
Delta Force 3: The Killing Game '91
Sins of Desire '92
Body of Influence '93
Broken Trust '93
Class of 1999 2: The Substitute '93
Sins of the Night '93
Mrs. Parker and the Vicious Circle '94
Twogether '94
Machine Gun Blues '95

Jean-Pierre Cassel
The Elusive Corporal '62
Those Magnificent Men in Their Flying Machines '65
The Killing Game '67
Is Paris Burning? '68
La Rupture '70
The Discreet Charm of the Bourgeoisie '72
Murder on the Orient Express '74
The Three Musketeers '74
The Four Musketeers '75
That Lucky Touch '75
The Killing of a Chinese Bookie '76
Twist '76
Les Rendez-vous D'Anna '78
Who Is Killing the Great Chefs of Europe? '78
From Hell to Victory '79
La Vie Continue '82
La Truite '83
Nudo di Donna '83
Alice '86
Mr. Frost '89
The Return of the Musketeers '89
The Fatal Image '90
The Maid '90
The Phantom of the Opera '90
The Favor, the Watch, & the Very Big Fish '92
Between Heaven and Earth '93
Ready to Wear '94
La Ceremonie '95

Seymour Cassel
Faces '68
Black Oak Conspiracy '77
Seducers '77
Valentino '77
California Dreaming '79
The Mountain Men '80
Double Exposure '82
Love Streams '84
Eye of the Tiger '86
Best Seller '87
Survival Game '87
Tin Men '87
Johnny Be Good '88
Plain Clothes '88
Track 29 '88
Sweet Bird of Youth '89
Wicked Stepmother '89
Dick Tracy '90
Diary of a Hitman '91
White Fang '91
Adventures in Spying '92
Honeymoon in Vegas '92
In the Soup '92
There Goes My Baby '92
Trouble Bound '92
Boiling Point '93
Chain of Desire '93
Hand Gun '93
Indecent Proposal '93
Dark Side of Genius '94
Imaginary Crimes '94
It Could Happen to You '94
Tollbooth '94
Bad Love '95

Vincent Cassel
Cafe au Lait '94
Hate '95

Alan Cassell
Money Movers '78
The Club '81
Squizzy Taylor '84

Wally Cassell
Breakdown '53
Until They Sail '57

Andrew Cassese
Revenge of the Nerds '84
Revenge of the Nerds 2: Nerds in Paradise '87

David Cassidy
The Night the City Screamed '80
Instant Karma '90
Spirit of '76 '91

Edward Cassidy
Feud of the West '35
Toll of the Desert '35
A Face in the Fog '36
Aces Wild '37
Boothill Brigade '37
Boots of Destiny '37
Roaring Six Guns '37
Santa Fe Bound '37
Sagebrush Law '43
Devil Riders '44
Frontier Outlaws '44
Rustler's Hideout '44
Wild Horse Phantom '44
Buffalo Bill Rides Again '47
Son of Zorro '47

Jack Cassidy
The Andersonville Trial '70
Columbo: Murder By the Book '71
The Eiger Sanction '75

Joanna Cassidy
Bank Shot '74
The Late Show '77
Stunts '77
The Glove '78
Night Games '80
Blade Runner '82
Under Fire '83
Invitation to Hell '84
Codename: Foxfire '85
The Children of Times Square '86
Club Paradise '86
The Fourth Protocol '87
A Father's Revenge '88
Who Framed Roger Rabbit '88
1969 '89
The Package '89
A Girl of the Limberlost '90
May Wine '90
Wheels of Terror '90
Where the Heart Is '90
All-American Murder '91
Don't Tell Mom the Babysitter's Dead '91
Lonely Hearts '91
Nightmare at Bittercreek '91
Landslide '92
Live! From Death Row '92
Perfect Family '92
Barbarians at the Gate '93
Stephen King's The Tommyknockers '93

Patrick Cassidy
Off the Wall '82
Just the Way You Are '84
Fever Pitch '85
Nickel Mountain '85
Dress Gray '86
Something in Common '86
Love at Stake '87
Hitler's Daughter '90
Longtime Companion '90
How the West was Fun '95

Shaun Cassidy
Roots: The Gift '88
Texas Guns '90

Ted Cassidy
The Addams Family '64
Butch Cassidy and the Sundance Kid '69
MacKenna's Gold '69
Poor Pretty Eddie '73
Planet Earth '74
Thunder County '74
Goin' Coconuts '78
Halloween with the Addams Family '79
Sunshine Run '79
Women's Prison Escape

Claudio Cassinelli
Allonsanfan '73
Slave of the Cannibal God '79
Hercules 2 '85
Hands of Steel '86
The New Gladiators '87

Nadia Cassini
Pulp '72
Star Crash '78

John Cassisi
Bugsy Malone '76
Man's Best Friend '93

Jean-Pierre Castaldi
La Merveilleuse Visite '74
A Fine Romance '92

Lou Castel
A Bullet for the General '68
Paranoia '69
Beware of a Holy Whore '70
The Scarlet Letter '73
The Eyes, the Mouth '83
Rorret '87

Dan Castellaneta
Nothing in Common '86
The War of the Roses '89

Richard Castellano
Lovers and Other Strangers '70
The Godfather '72
Honor Thy Father '73
Night of the Juggler '80
The Godfather 1902-1959: The Complete Epic '81

Sergio Castellitto
The Big Blue '88
Alberto Express '92
The Star Maker '95

Willy Castello
Mad Youth '40
Confessions of a Vice Baron '42

Christopher Castile
Beethoven '92
Beethoven's 2nd '93

Gloria Castillo
Invasion of the Saucer Men '57
Meteor Monster '57
Reform School Girl '57

Don Castle
Who Killed Doc Robbin? '48
Motor Patrol '50

John Castle
The Lion in Winter '68
Man of La Mancha '72
Lillie '79
The Bretts '88
The Crucifer of Blood '91
RoboCop 3 '91

Peggy Castle
Invasion U.S.A. '52
The White Orchid '54
The Finger Man '55
Beginning of the End '57
The Seven Hills of Rome '58

Roy Castle
Doctor Who and the Daleks '65
Alice Through the Looking Glass '66

William Castle
Rosemary's Baby '68
Bug '75
Shampoo '75

Georgina Cates
An Awfully Big Adventure '94
Frankie Starlight '95

Phoebe Cates
Fast Times at Ridgemont High '82
Paradise '82
Private School '83
Gremlins '84
Date with an Angel '87
Bright Lights, Big City '88
The Heart of Dixie '89
Shag: The Movie '89
Gremlins 2: The New Batch '90
Drop Dead Fred '91
Bodies, Rest & Motion '93
Princess Caraboo '94

Reg E. Cathey
Tank Girl '94
Seven '95

Brigitte Catillon
La Lectrice '88
Un Coeur en Hiver '93

Walter Catlett
The Front Page '31
Rain '32
A Tale of Two Cities '35
Mr. Deeds Goes to Town '36
On the Avenue '37
Bringing Up Baby '38
Every Day's a Holiday '38
Pop Always Pays '40
Remedy for Riches '40
It Started with Eve '41
Yankee Doodle Dandy '42
His Butler's Sister '43
They Got Me Covered '43
The Inspector General '49

Victoria Catlin
Howling 5: The Rebirth '89
Mutant on the Bounty '89

Juliette Caton
The Last Temptation of Christ '88
Courage Mountain '89

Christine Cattall
Bedroom Eyes '86
Screwball Academy '86

Kim Cattrall
Deadly Harvest '72
Rosebud '75
The Bastard '78
The Rebels '79
Scruples '80
Tribute '80
Ticket to Heaven '81
Porky's '82
Police Academy '84
City Limits '85
Turk 182! '85
Big Trouble in Little China '86
Mannequin '87
Midnight Crossing '87
Masquerade '88
Palais Royale '88
Goodnight, Michelangelo '89
The Return of the Musketeers '89
The Bonfire of the Vanities '90
Honeymoon Academy '90
Smokescreen '90
Miracle in the Wilderness '91
Star Trek 6: The Undiscovered Country '91
Double Vision '92
Split Second '92
Running Delilah '93
Wild Palms '93
Breaking Point '94
Above Suspicion '95
The Heidi Chronicles '95
Live Nude Girls '95
Unforgettable '96

Philippe Caubere
My Father's Glory '91
My Mother's Castle '91

Daniel Cauchy
Grisbi '53
Bob le Flambeur '55

Lane Caudell
Hanging on a Star '78
Archer: The Fugitive from the Empire '81

Joan Caulfield
Blue Skies '46
Monsieur Beaucaire '46
Welcome Stranger '47
Dear Wife '49
The Lady Says No '51
Buckskin '68
Daring Dobermans '73
Pony Express Rider '76

Maxwell Caulfield
Grease 2 '82
Electric Dreams '84
The Boys Next Door '85
The Supernaturals '86
Mind Games '89
Project: Alien '89
Exiled in America '90
Dance with Death '91
Sundown '91
Animal Instincts '92
Alien Intruder '93
Gettysburg '93
In a Moment of Passion '93
Midnight Witness '93
No Escape, No Return '93
Backlash: Oblivion 2 '95
Empire Records '95

Valeria Cavalli
Everybody's Fine '90
Joseph '95

Victor Cavallo
The Tragedy of a Ridiculous Man '81
Dial Help '88

Megan Cavanagh
A League of Their Own '92
Robin Hood: Men in Tights '93

Paul Cavanagh
A Bill of Divorcement '32
Tarzan and His Mate '34
Goin' to Town '35
Shadows on the Stairs '41
Captains of the Clouds '42
House of Fear '45
The Woman in Green '45

Humoresque '46
Black Arrow '48
Hi-Jacked '50
Bride of the Gorilla '51
Charade '53
House of Wax '53
The Prodigal '55
Francis in the Haunted House '56

Hobart Cavanaugh
I Cover the Waterfront '33
Wife Versus Secretary '36
Rose of Washington Square '39
The Magnificent Dope '42

Elise Cavanna
W.C. Fields: Flask of Fields '30
The Dentist '32
Pharmacist '32
The Barber Shop '33
Best of W.C. Fields '33

Lumi Cavazos
Like Water for Chocolate '93
Bottle Rocket '95

Ingrid Caven
Beware of a Holy Whore '70
Mother Kusters Goes to Heaven '76
Satan's Brew '76
In a Year of 13 Moons '78
Malou '83

Dick Cavett
A Nightmare on Elm Street 3: Dream Warriors '87
Beetlejuice '88
Moon over Parador '88
The Marx Brothers in a Nutshell '90

James Caviezel
Wyatt Earp '94
Ed '96

Joseph Cawthorn
The Taming of the Shrew '29
They Call It Sin '32
Harmony Lane '35
Sweet Adeline '35

Elizabeth Cayton
Silent Night, Deadly Night 2 '87
Slave Girls from Beyond Infinity '87
Necromancer: Satan's Servant '88

John Cazale
The Godfather '72
The Conversation '74
The Godfather, Part 2 '74
Dog Day Afternoon '75
The Deer Hunter '78
The Godfather 1902-1959: The Complete Epic '81

Christopher Cazenove
Royal Flash '75
East of Elephant Rock '76
Eye of the Needle '81
Heat and Dust '82
Children of the Full Moon '84
Until September '84
Jenny's War '85
Mata Hari '85
The Man Who Guards the Greenhouse '88
Souvenir '88
Tears in the Rain '88
Windmills of the Gods '88
The Fantasist '89
Three Men and a Little Lady '90
Aces: Iron Eagle 3 '92

Daniel Ceccaldi
Chloe in the Afternoon '72
Holiday Hotel '77
Charles et Lucie '79
Twisted Obsession '90

Carlo Cecchi
La Scorta '94
Stealing Beauty '96

Edward Cecil
Wild Horse Canyon '25
Desert of the Lost '27

Jon Cedar
Day of the Animals '77
Kiss Daddy Goodbye '81

Larry Cedar
Feds '88
C.H.U.D. 2: Bud the Chud '89

Boris and Natasha: The Movie '92

Violeta Cela
Conquest '83
El Barbaro '84

Clementine Celarie
Betty Blue '86
Sand and Blood '87
Les Miserables '95

Henry Cele
Shaka Zulu '83
Rage to Kill '88
Curse 3: Blood Sacrifice '90
The Last Samurai '90
The Rutanga Tapes '90

Adriano Celentano
The Con Artists '80
The Switch '89

Adolfo Celi
The Agony and the Ecstasy '65
Thunderball '65
Von Ryan's Express '65
The King of Hearts '66
Target for Killing '66
Bobo '67
The Honey Pot '67
Secret Agent 00 '67
Phantom of Liberty '68
Dirty Heroes '71
Murders in the Rue Morgue '71
1931: Once Upon a Time in New York '72
Ring of Death '72
Hired to Kill '73
Hit Men '73
Hitler: The Last Ten Days '73
Ten Little Indians '75
The Arab Conspiracy '76
Intruder '77
Cafe Express '83

Teresa Celli
The Asphalt Jungle '50
The Black Hand '50

Antoinette Cellier
Late Extra '35
River of Unrest '37

Caroline Cellier
This Man Must Die '70
Pain in the A— '77
Petit Con '84
Farinelli '94

Frank Cellier
The Man Who Lived Again '36
The Passing of the Third Floor Back '36
Rhodes '36
Non-Stop New York '37
O.H.M.S. '37
Cottage to Let '41

Peter Cellier
Man Friday '75
Sister Dora '77
And the Ship Sails On '83
Fergie & Andrew: Behind Palace Doors '93

Nicholas Celozzi
Slaughterhouse Rock '88
Hidden Obsession '92

Daniel Cerney
Demonic Toys '90
Children of the Corn 3: Urban Harvest '95

Gino Cervi
Fabiola '48
Little World of Don Camillo '51
Les Miserables '52
Mistress of the World '59
The Naked Maja '59
Full Hearts & Empty Pockets '63

Renzo Cesana
Stromboli '50
For the First Time '59
The Naked Maja '59

Michael Ceveris
Rock 'n' Roll High School Forever '91
A Woman, Her Men and Her Futon '92

June Chadwick
Golden Lady '79
Forbidden World '82
This Is Spinal Tap '84
The Evil Below '87
Quiet Thunder '87

Headhunter '89
Rebel Storm '90

Sarah Chadwick
Gross Misconduct '93
The Adventures of Priscilla, Queen of the Desert '94

Suzy Chaffee
Snowblind '78
Fire and Ice '87

George Chakiris
West Side Story '61
Diamond Head '62
633 Squadron '64
Is Paris Burning? '68
The Hot Line '69
Return to Fantasy Island '77
Pale Blood '91

Feodor Chaliapin, Jr
The Name of the Rose '86
Moonstruck '87
The Church '90
The King's Whore '90
Stanley and Iris '90
The Inner Circle '91

Sarah Chalke
City Boy '93
Robin of Locksley '95

Georges Chamarat
The French Touch '54
Fernandel the Dressmaker '57

Richard Chamberlain
Portrait of a Lady '67
Petulia '68
The Madwoman of Chaillot '69
Julius Caesar '70
The Music Lovers '71
Lady Caroline Lamb '73
The Count of Monte Cristo '74
The Three Musketeers '74
The Towering Inferno '74
The Four Musketeers '75
The Last Wave '77
The Man in the Iron Mask '77
The Swarm '78
Shogun '80
Murder by Phone '82
The Thorn Birds '83
King Solomon's Mines '85
Allan Quatermain and the Lost City of Gold '86
Casanova '87
The Bourne Identity '88
The Return of the Musketeers '89

Wilt Chamberlain
Conan the Destroyer '84
Rich Hall's Vanishing America '86

Carrie Chambers
The Divine Enforcer '91
Karate Cop '93

Marilyn Chambers
Rabid '77
Angel of H.E.A.T. '82
My Therapist '84
Cassie '87
Party Incorporated '89
Bikini Bistro '94

Michael "Boogaloo Shrimp" Chambers
Breakin' '84
Breakin' 2: Electric Boogaloo '84

Gower Champion
Mr. Music '50
Show Boat '51
Lovely to Look At '52
Give a Girl a Break '53
Jupiter's Darling '55

Marge Champion
Mr. Music '50
Lovely to Look At '52
Give a Girl a Break '53
Jupiter's Darling '55
The Party '68
The Swimmer '68

Michael Champion
One Man Out '89
The Heroes of Desert Storm '91
The Swordsman '92
Private Wars '93
Dead Cold '96

Irene Champlin
Flash Gordon: Vol. 1 '53
Flash Gordon: Vol. 2 '53

Dennis Chan
Kickboxer '89
Kickboxer 3: The Art of War '92

Jackie Chan
The Big Brawl '80
Young Tiger '80
Eagle's Shadow '84
Half a Loaf of Kung Fu '85
Jackie Chan's Police Force '85
New Fist of Fury '85
Protector '85
The Armour of God '86
The Deadliest Art: The Best of the Martial Arts Films '90
Rumble in the Bronx '96

Kim Chan
American Shaolin: King of the Kickboxers 2 '92
Who's the Man? '93

Michael Paul Chan
Thousand Pieces of Gold '91
Rapid Fire '92
Falling Down '93
The Joy Luck Club '93

Naomi Chance
The Gambler & the Lady '52
Wings of Danger '52
Three Stops to Murder '53
Terror Ship '54

Chick Chandler
Melody Cruise '32
Circumstantial Evidence '35
Mistaken Identity '36
Tango '36
Blondie in Society '41
Baby Face Morgan '42
Rhythm Parade '43
Seven Doors to Death '44
The Lost Continent '51

George Chandler
The Light of Western Stars '30
The Fatal Glass of Beer '33
Lady Killer '33
W.C. Fields Comedy Bag '33
Arizona '40
Roxie Hart '42
Behind the Mask '46
The Next Voice You Hear '50
Westward the Women '51

Helen Chandler
Dracula '31
Christopher Strong '33
Mr. Boggs Steps Out '38

Janet Chandler
Million Dollar Haul '35
Rough Riding Rangers '35

Jeff Chandler
Broken Arrow '50
Red Ball Express '52
War Arrow '53
Away All Boats '56
The Jayhawkers '59
Return to Peyton Place '61
Merrill's Marauders '62

John Davis Chandler
Alligator Alley '72
The Ultimate Thrill '74

Karen Mayo Chandler
Death Feud '89
Stripped to Kill II: Live Girls '89

Kyle Chandler
Pure Country '92
Convict Cowboy '95

Lane Chandler
The Single Standard '29
Deluge '33
Lone Bandit '33
The Outlaw Tamer '33
Trouble Busters '33
The Lawless Nineties '36
Winds of the Wasteland '36
Heroes of the Alamo '37
Sea Racketeers '37
Pony Post '40
Laura '44
Rustler's Hideout '44
Wild Horse Phantom '44

Simon Chandler
Who's Who '78
Middlemarch '93

Helene Chanel
Maciste in Hell '60

Samson and the 7 Miracles of the World '62
Place in Hell '65

Lon Chaney, Sr.
Oubliette '14
The Scarlet Car '17
False Faces '18
Nomads of the North '20
The Penalty '20
Outside the Law '21
Flesh and Blood '22
The Light of Faith '22
Oliver Twist '22
Shadows '22
The Trap '22
The Hunchback of Notre Dame '23
The Shock '23
He Who Gets Slapped '24
The Monster '25
The Phantom of the Opera '25
The Unholy Three '25
Mockery '27
The Unknown '27
West of Zanzibar '28
Where East Is East '29
The Unholy Three '30
The Bushwackers '52
The Horror of It All '91

Lon Chaney, Jr.
Bird of Paradise '32
Last Frontier '32
The Three Musketeers '33
Sixteen Fathoms Deep '34
Undersea Kingdom '36
Cheyenne Rides Again '38
Renegade Ranger/Scarlet River '38
Of Mice and Men '39
One Million B.C. '40
Saturday Night Serials '40
Billy the Kid '41
Man Made Monster '41
Overland Mail '41
Riders of Death Valley '41
The Wolf Man '41
Frankenstein Meets the Wolfman '42
The Ghost of Frankenstein '42
The Mummy's Tomb '42
Son of Dracula '43
Cobra Woman '44
House of Frankenstein '44
The Mummy's Curse '44
The Mummy's Ghost '44
Here Come the Co-Eds '45
House of Dracula '45
Strange Confession '45
My Favorite Brunette '47
Abbott and Costello Meet Frankenstein '48
Only the Valiant '50
Bride of the Gorilla '51
Behave Yourself! '52
The Black Castle '52
High Noon '52
Springfield Rifle '52
A Lion Is in the Streets '53
Big Chase '54
Passion '54
I Died a Thousand Times '55
The Indian Fighter '55
Not as a Stranger '55
Cyclops '56
Daniel Boone: Trail Blazer '56
The Indestructible Man '56
Manfish '56
Pardners '56
The Defiant Ones '58
Face of the Screaming Werewolf '59
The Haunted Palace '63
Spider Baby '64
House of the Black Death '65
Apache Uprising '66
Johnny Reno '66
Alien Massacre '67
Hillbillies in a Haunted House '67
Buckskin '68
The Female Bunch '69
Dracula vs. Frankenstein '71
Film House Fever '86

Sylvia Chang
Mad Mission 3 '84
Eat Drink Man Woman '94

Stockard Channing
The Hospital '71
The Big Bus '76

Channing ▶cont.

The Cheap Detective '78
Grease '78
The Fish that Saved Pittsburgh '79
Silent Victory: The Kitty O'Neil Story '79
Safari 3000 '82
Without a Trace '83
Table Settings '84
Not My Kid '85
Heartburn '86
The Men's Club '86
Echoes in the Darkness '87
Tidy Endings '88
A Time of Destiny '88
The Applegates '89
Perfect Witness '89
Staying Together '89
Married to It '93
Six Degrees of Separation '93
Smoke '95
To Wong Foo, Thanks for Everything, Julie Newmar '95
Moll Flanders '96
Up Close and Personal '96

Rosalind Chao
Chinese Web '78
The Big Brawl '80
Twirl '81
The Terry Fox Story '83
White Ghost '88
Thousand Pieces of Gold '91
Memoirs of an Invisible Man '92
The Joy Luck Club '93

Winston Chao
The Wedding Banquet '93
Eat Drink Man Woman '94

Damian Chapa
Blood In...Blood Out: Bound by Honor '93
Street Fighter '94
Saints and Sinners '95

Billy Chapin
Tobor the Great '54
The Night of the Hunter '55

Jonathan Chapin
Twice Dead '88
Prison for Children '93

Miles Chapin
Bless the Beasts and Children '71
French Postcards '79
The Funny Farm '82
Pandemonium '82

Robert Chapin
Ring of Steel '94
Dragon Fury '95

Ben Chaplin
Feast of July '95
The Truth About Cats and Dogs '96

Charles Chaplin, Jr.
Fangs of the Wild '54
High School Confidential '58
Girls' Town '59

Charlie Chaplin
Laughfest '10s
Rink/Immigrant '10s
Charlie Chaplin's Keystone Comedies #1 '14
Charlie Chaplin's Keystone Comedies #2 '14
Charlie Chaplin's Keystone Comedies #3 '14
Charlie Chaplin's Keystone Comedies #4 '14
Charlie Chaplin's Keystone Comedies #5 '14
The Knockout/Dough and Dynamite '14
Tillie's Punctured Romance '14
The Champion/His New Job '15
Chaplin Essanay Book 1 '15
Charlie Chaplin: Night at the Show '15
Charlie Chaplin...Our Hero! '15
The Floorwalker/By the Sea '15
His Prehistoric Past/The Bank '15
Kid's Auto Race/Mabel's Married Life '15
Silent Laugh Makers, No. 1 '15
Tramp & a Woman '15
Burlesque of Carmen '16
Charlie Chaplin: The Early Years, Vol. 3 '16
Charlie Chaplin: The Early Years, Vol. 4 '16
The Count '16
Easy Street '16
The Fireman '16
One A.M. '16
Pawnshop '16
The Rink '16
The Vagabond '16
Work/Police '16
The Adventurer '17
Charlie Chaplin: The Early Years, Vol. 1 '17
Charlie Chaplin: The Early Years, Vol. 2 '17
Count/Adventurer '17
The Cure '17
The Floorwalker '17
The Immigrant '17
The Best of Chaplin '18
Three Charlies and One Phoney! '18
Triple Trouble/Easy Street '18
The Circus '19
The Kid '21
The Kid/Idle Class '21
The Gold Rush '25
Gold Rush/Payday '25
Slapstick '30s
City Lights '31
Modern Times '36
The Great Dictator '40
Monsieur Verdoux '47
Limelight '52
A King in New York '57
The Chaplin Revue '58
When Comedy was King '59
Days of Thrills and Laughter '61
Chaplin: A Character Is Born '79
Man in the Silk Hat '83
Hollywood Clowns '85

Geraldine Chaplin
Doctor Zhivago '65
I Killed Rasputin '67
Zero Population Growth '72
The Three Musketeers '74
The Four Musketeers '75
Nashville '75
Buffalo Bill & the Indians '76
Cria '76
In Memoriam '76
Elisa, Vida Mia '77
Roseland '77
Welcome to L.A. '77
A Wedding '78
The Word '78
Mama Turns a Hundred '79
The Mirror Crack'd '80
Voyage en Douce '81
Bolero '82
The Moderns '88
White Mischief '88
The Return of the Musketeers '89
The Children '90
Chaplin '92
Duel of Hearts '92
The Age of Innocence '93
A Foreign Field '93
Gulliver's Travels '95
Home for the Holidays '95
Jane Eyre '96

Josephine Chaplin
L'Odeur des Fauves '66
The Canterbury Tales '71
Escape to the Sun '72
Shadow Man '75
Jack the Ripper '80

Lita Grey Chaplin
The Kid/Idle Class '21
The Devil's Sleep '51

Sydney Chaplin
Three Charlies and One Phoney! '18
Charley's Aunt '25
The Man on the Box '25
Land of the Pharaohs '55
Abdulla the Great '56
The Chaplin Revue '58
A Countess from Hong Kong '67
The Sibling '72
The Woman Hunter '72
Satan's Cheerleaders '77

Daniel Chapman
Exquisite Corpses '88
Death Collector '89
Philadelphia '93

Edward Chapman
Juno and the Paycock '30
Convoy '40
The October Man '48
Man on the Run '49
Bhowani Junction '56
The Young and the Guilty '58

Graham Chapman
John Cleese on How to Irritate People '68
The Magic Christian '69
Monty Python's Flying Circus '71
And Now for Something Completely Different '72
Monty Python and the Holy Grail '75
The Odd Job '78
Monty Python's Life of Brian '79
Monty Python Live at the Hollywood Bowl '82
The Secret Policeman's Other Ball '82
Monty Python's The Meaning of Life '83
Yellowbeard '83
Monty Python's Parrot Sketch Not Included '90

Helen Chapman
Outlaw Roundup '44
Hopalong Cassidy: Borrowed Trouble '48

Judith Chapman
Scalpel '76
And God Created Woman '88
Dead Space '90

Lonny Chapman
Where the Red Fern Grows '74
Moving Violation '76
Witch Who Came from the Sea '76
Alexander: The Other Side of Dawn '77
He Who Walks Alone '78
52 Pick-Up '86
The China Lake Murders '90

Marguerite Chapman
Charlie Chan at the Wax Museum '40
Spy Smasher '42
Spy Smasher Returns '42
Destroyer '43
Coroner Creek '48
The Green Promise '49
Flight to Mars '52
Man Bait '52
The Amazing Transparent Man '60

Mark Lindsay Chapman
Separate Lives '94
Stephen King's The Langoliers '95

Sean Chapman
Hellraiser '87
Hellbound: Hellraiser 2 '88

Dave Chappelle
Robin Hood: Men in Tights '93
Getting In '94
The Nutty Professor '96

Patricia Charbonneau
Desert Hearts '86
Stalking Danger '86
Call Me '88
Disaster at Silo 7 '88
Shakedown '88
Brain Dead '89
RoboCop 2 '90
K2: The Ultimate High '92
Portraits of a Killer '95

Cyd Charisse
The Harvey Girls '46
Till the Clouds Roll By/A Star Is Born '46
On an Island with You '48
Words and Music '48
Singin' in the Rain '52
The Band Wagon '53
Brigadoon '54
Deep in My Heart '54
It's Always Fair Weather '55
Meet Me in Las Vegas '56
Silk Stockings '57
Party Girl '58
Black Tights '60
Two Weeks in Another Town '62
Maroc 7 '67
That's Dancing! '85
Swimsuit: The Movie '89

Josh Charles
Dead Poets Society '89
Don't Tell Mom the Babysitter's Dead '91
Crossing the Bridge '92
Cooperstown '93
Coldblooded '94
Threesome '94

Ray Charles
Ballad in Blue '66
The Blues Brothers '80
Limit Up '89

Ian Charleson
Chariots of Fire '81
Gandhi '82
Greystoke: The Legend of Tarzan, Lord of the Apes '84
Car Trouble '86
Louisiana '87
Terror at the Opera '88
Codename Kyril '91

Charo
The Concorde: Airport '79 '79
Moon over Parador '88

Charpin
Marius '31
Fanny '32
The Baker's Wife '33
Cesar '36
Le Schpountz '38
Well-Digger's Daughter '46

Henri Charriere
Butterfly Affair '71
Queen of Diamonds '80s

Spencer Charters
The Bat Whispers '30
The Ghost Walks '34
Lady from Nowhere '36
Mr. Boggs Steps Out '38
Three Comrades '38

Melanie Chartoff
Having It All '82
Doin' Time '85
Stoogemania '85
Kenny Rogers as the Gambler, Part 3: The Legend Continues '87

Alden Chase
Cowboy Millionaire '35
Prescott Kid '36
Buried Alive '39

Annazette Chase
Truck Turner '74
Fist '79

Charley Chase
Silent Laugh Makers, No. 1 '15
Silent Laugh Makers, No. 2 '17
Three Charlies and One Phoney! '18
Charlie Chase and Ben Turpin '21
Charley Chase Festival, Vol. 1 '23
King of the Wild Horses '24
Slapstick '30s
Sons of the Desert '33
Kelly the Second '36
Block-heads '38

Chevy Chase
Saturday Night Live '70s
The Groove Tube '72
Tunnelvision '76
Foul Play '78
Caddyshack '80
Oh, Heavenly Dog! '80
Seems Like Old Times '80
Modern Problems '81
Under the Rainbow '81
Deal of the Century '83
National Lampoon's Vacation '83
Fletch '85
National Lampoon's European Vacation '85
Sesame Street Presents: Follow That Bird '85
Spies Like Us '85
Three Amigos '86
Caddyshack 2 '88
Funny Farm '88
Fletch Lives '89
National Lampoon's Christmas Vacation '89
Nothing But Trouble '91
Hero '92
Memoirs of an Invisible Man '92
Cops and Robbersons '94
Man of the House '95

Ilka Chase
The Animal Kingdom '32
The Big Knife '55

Jennifer Chase
Balboa '82
House of Death '82
Death Screams '83

Stephan Chase
The Black Arrow '84
The Dying Truth '91

Steve Chase
Eden '92
Eden 2 '93
Eden 3 '93
Eden 4 '93

Soumitra Chatterjee
The World of Apu '59
Devi '60
Distant Thunder '73
The Home and the World '84

Ruth Chatterton
Female '33
Dodsworth '36
Prudential Family Playhouse '50

Daniel Chatto
Little Dorrit, Film 1: Nobody's Fault '88
Little Dorrit, Film 2: Little Dorrit's Story '88

Francois Chau
Vietnam War Story 3 '89
Teenage Mutant Ninja Turtles 2: The Secret of the Ooze '91

Emmanuelle Chaulet
Boyfriends & Girlfriends '88
All the Vermeers in New York '91

Lilyan Chauvin
Bloodlust '59
Lost, Lonely, and Vicious '59
Silent Night, Deadly Night '84
Tyson '95

Richard Chaves
Predator '87
Night Eyes 2 '91

Maury Chaykin
July Group '70s
Mrs. Soffel '84
Canada's Sweetheart: The Saga of Hal C. Banks '85
Def-Con 4 '85
Wild Thing '87
Higher Education '88
Iron Eagle 2 '88
Stars and Bars '88
Breaking In '89
Millenium '89
Cold Comfort '90
Dances with Wolves '90
Mr. Destiny '90
The Adjuster '91
George's Island '91
Hero '92
Leaving Normal '92
Money for Nothing '93
Northern Extremes '93
Sommersby '93
Camilla '94
Whale Music '94
Cutthroat Island '95
Devil In a Blue Dress '95
Sugartime '95
Unstrung Heroes '95

Mariann Chazel
French Fried Vacation '79
Next Year If All Goes Well '83

Don Cheadle
Hamburger Hill '87
Colors '88
Lush Life '94
Devil In a Blue Dress '95

Andrea Checchi
The Walls of Malapaga '49
Black Sunday '60
The Invaders '63

Micheline Cheirel
Carnival in Flanders '35

Cornered '45

Michael Chekhov
Spellbound '45
Spectre of the Rose '46
Rhapsody '54

Tsilla Chelton
Peppermint Soda '77
Tatie Danielle '91

Joan Chen
Dim Sum: A Little Bit of Heart '85
Tai-Pan '86
The Last Emperor '87
Night Stalker '87
The Blood of Heroes '89
Twin Peaks '90
Twin Peaks '90
Deadlock '91
Strangers '91
The Killing Beach '92
Golden Gate '93
Heaven and Earth '93
The Hunted '94
On Deadly Ground '94
Temptation of a Monk '94
Judge Dredd '95
Wild Side '95

Tina Chen
Paper Man '71
Lady from Yesterday '85

Jacky Cheng
Of Cooks and Kung-Fu '80s
Ninja Exterminators '81

Cher
Come Back to the Five & Dime Jimmy Dean, Jimmy Dean '82
Silkwood '83
Mask '85
Moonstruck '87
Suspect '87
The Witches of Eastwick '87
Mermaids '90
Faithful '95

Patrice Chereau
Danton '82
The Last of the Mohicans '92

Nikolai Cherkassov
Baltic Deputy '37
Alexander Nevsky '38
Ivan the Terrible, Part 1 '44
Ivan the Terrible, Part 2 '46
Don Quixote '57

Virginia Cherrill
City Lights '31
Late Extra '35

George Chesebro
Wolf Blood '25
Fighting Champ '33
In Old Santa Fe '34
The Silver Bullet '34
Laramie Kid '35
The Miracle Rider '35
Red River Valley '36
Roamin' Wild '36
Trigger Men '41
Holt of the Secret Service '42
Devil Riders '44
Cheyenne Takes Over '47
Fighting Vigilantes '47
Return of the Lash '47
Check Your Guns '48
Stage to Mesa City '48

Craig Chester
Swoon '91
Grief '94

Vanessa Lee Chester
A Little Princess '95
Harriet the Spy '96

Morris Chestnut
Boyz N the Hood '91
The Ernest Green Story '93
Under Siege 2: Dark Territory '95

Jacky Cheung
A Bullet in the Head '90
Wicked City '92

Leslie Cheung
A Better Tomorrow '86
A Better Tomorrow, Part 2 '88
Farewell My Concubine '93

Maggie Cheung
Jackie Chan's Police Force '85
Paper Marriage '88
Song of the Exile '90
The Heroic Trio '93

Kevin Timothy Chevalia
Folks! '92
Homeward Bound: The Incredible Journey '93
Homeward Bound 2: Lost in San Francisco '96

Maurice Chevalier
The Merry Widow '34
Love in the Afternoon '57
Gigi '58
Breath of Scandal '60
Can-Can '60
Fanny '61
In Search of the Castaways '62
Panic Button '62
A New Kind of Love '63
Monkeys, Go Home! '66

Laureen Chew
Chan is Missing '82
Dim Sum: A Little Bit of Heart '85

Yuen Man Chi
Young Dragon '77
Bruce's Deadly Fingers '80

Sun Chia-Lin
The Hot, the Cool, and the Vicious '80s
Eighteen Jade Arhats '84

Liu Chia-Yung
Two Graves to Kung-Fu '82
Challenge of the Masters '89

Minoru Chiaki
Seven Samurai '54
Throne of Blood '57
The Hidden Fortress '58
Godzilla Raids Again '59
The Human Condition: Road to Eternity '59

Dominic Chianese
The Public Eye '92
The Night We Never Met '93

David Chiang
Duel of the Iron Fist '72
Seven Blows of the Dragon '73
Duel of Fists '89

Roy Chiao
Bloodsport '88
Summer Snow '94

Walter Chiari
Bonjour Tristesse '57
Girl Under the Sheet '60s
Husband Hunting '60s

Sofiko Chiaureli
The Color of Pomegranates '69
Ashik Kerib '88

Sonny Chiba
Terror Beneath the Sea '66
Dragon Princess '70s
Karate Warriors '70s
Return of the Street Fighter '70s
The Street Fighter '75
The Bodyguard '76
Kowloon Assignment '77
Assassin '79
The Street Fighter's Last Revenge '79
Hunter in the Dark '80
Virus '82
Shogun's Ninja '83
Aces: Iron Eagle 3 '92
Immortal Combat '94
Body Count '95

Etienne Chicot
Osa '85
36 Fillete '88

Linden Chiles
Texas Across the River '66
Death Be Not Proud '75
Who Is the Black Dahlia? '75
Red Flag: The Ultimate Game '81
Forbidden World '82
To Heal a Nation '88
Deadline Assault '90

Lois Chiles
Coma '78
Death on the Nile '78
Moonraker '79
Raw Courage '84
Broadcast News '87
Creepshow 2 '87
Twister '89
Diary of a Hitman '91
Lush Life '94

The Babysitter '95

Simon Chilvers
The Dunera Boys '85
Windrider '86
The Big Hurt '87
Ground Zero '88

Joey Chin
China Girl '87
King of New York '90

Tsai Chin
Invasion '65
You Only Live Twice '67
The Castle of Fu Manchu '68
Kiss and Kill '68
The Virgin Soldiers '69
Enter the Panther '79
The Joy Luck Club '93

William Ching
The Wistful Widow of Wagon Gap '47
Never Wave at a WAC '52
Pat and Mike '52
Give a Girl a Break '53
Terror in the Haunted House '58

Kieu Chinh
Operation C.I.A. '65
The Children of An Lac '80
The Girl Who Spelled Freedom '86
The Joy Luck Club '93

Nicholas Chinlund
The Ambulance '90
Red Shoe Diaries 4: Auto Erotica '93
Unveiled '94
Letter to My Killer '95
Eraser '96

Anna Chlumsky
My Girl '91
My Girl 2 '94
Trading Mom '94
Gold Diggers: The Secret of Bear Mountain '95

Tim Choate
First Time '82
Def-Con 4 '85
Blind Witness '89
Spy '89
Live Nude Girls '95

Jun Chong
Ninja Turf '86
Silent Assassins '88
Street Soldiers '91

Rae Dawn Chong
Quest for Fire '82
Beat Street '84
Cheech and Chong's The Corsican Brothers '84
Choose Me '84
American Flyers '85
Badge of the Assassin '85
City Limits '85
The Color Purple '85
Commando '85
Fear City '85
Running Out of Luck '86
Soul Man '86
The Principal '87
The Squeeze '87
The Borrower '89
Far Out Man '89
Amazon '90
Curiosity Kills '90
Tales from the Darkside: The Movie '90
Common Bonds '91
Denial: The Dark Side of Passion '91
Prison Stories: Women on the Inside '91
When the Party's Over '91
Time Runner '92
Dangerous Relations '93
Boca '94
Boulevard '94
Hideaway '94
Power of Attorney '94
The Break '95

Thomas Chong
Cheech and Chong's Up in Smoke '79
Cheech and Chong's Next Movie '80
Cheech and Chong's Nice Dreams '81

Cheech and Chong: Things Are Tough All Over '82
Cheech and Chong: Still Smokin' '83
Yellowbeard '83
Cheech and Chong's The Corsican Brothers '84
Far Out Man '89
Tripwire '89
Spirit of '76 '91
National Lampoon's Senior Trip '95

Sarita Choudhury
Mississippi Masala '92
The House of the Spirits '93
Wild West '93
Down Came a Blackbird '94

Etchika Choureau
Darby's Rangers '58
Lafayette Escadrille '58

Navin Chowdhry
Madame Sousatzka '88
The Seventh Coin '92

Ranjit Chowdhry
Lonely in America '90
Mississippi Masala '92
The Night We Never Met '93

Claudia Christian
The Hidden '87
Clean and Sober '88
Never on Tuesday '88
Arena '89
Mom '89
Tale of Two Sisters '89
Mad About You '90
Maniac Cop 2 '90
The Dark Backward '91
Strays '91
The Adventures of a Gnome Named Gnorm '93
Hexed '93

John Christian
Covert Action '88
Mob War '88
Comrades in Arms '91
The Outfit '93

Linda Christian
Athena '54
The Devil's Hand '61
Full Hearts & Empty Pockets '63
The V.I.P.'s '63

Michael Christian
Poor Pretty Eddie '73
The Legend of Frank Woods '77
Mid Knight Rider '84
Private Obsession '94
Hard Knocks

Paul Christian
The Beast from 20,000 Fathoms '53
Journey to the Lost City '58

Mady Christians
Tender Comrade '43
Letter from an Unknown Woman '48

Audrey Christie
Keeper of the Flame '42
Splendor in the Grass '61
Frankie and Johnny '65
Harper Valley P.T.A. '78

Julie Christie
Billy Liar '63
Darling '65
Doctor Zhivago '65
Fahrenheit 451 '66
Far from the Madding Crowd '67
Petulia '68
The Go-Between '71
McCabe & Mrs. Miller '71
Don't Look Now '73
Shampoo '75
Demon Seed '77
Heaven Can Wait '78
Heat and Dust '82
Return of the Soldier '82
Separate Tables '83
Miss Mary '86
Power '86
Secret Obsession '88
Fools of Fortune '90
The Railway Station Man '92
Dragonheart '96

Katia Christine
Spirits of the Dead '68

Cosmos: War of the Planets '80

Virginia Christine
The Mummy's Curse '44
The Inner Circle '46
The Cobweb '55
One Man's Way '63
Billy the Kid Versus Dracula '66

Eric Christmas
Attack of the Killer Tomatoes '77
Middle Age Crazy '80
The Philadelphia Experiment '84
Home Is Where the Hart Is '88
Child of Darkness, Child of Light '91
The Challengers '93

Francoise Christophe
Walk into Hell '57
The Invaders '63
The King of Hearts '66
Borsalino '70

Bojesse Christopher
Point Break '91
Meatballs 4 '92

Dennis Christopher
The Young Graduates '71
September 30, 1955 '77
A Wedding '78
Breaking Away '79
California Dreaming '79
Elvis: The Movie '79
Alien Predators '80
Fade to Black '80
The Last Word '80
Chariots of Fire '81
Don't Cry, It's Only Thunder '82
Didn't You Hear? '83
Jack & the Beanstalk '83
Jake Speed '86
A Sinful Life '89
Circuitry Man '90
Doppelganger: The Evil Within '90
Stephen King's It '90
False Arrest '92
Boys Life '94
Plughead Rewired: Circuitry Man 2 '94
It's My Party '95
Operation Intercept '95
The Silencers '95

Kay Christopher
Dick Tracy's Dilemma '47
Scared to Death/Dick Tracy's Dilemma '47

Thom Christopher
Wizards of the Lost Kingdom '85
Deathstalker 3 '89

William Christopher
With Six You Get Eggroll '68
M*A*S*H: The Collector's Edition '72
For the Love of It '80
M*A*S*H: Goodbye, Farewell & Amen '83

Dorothy Christy
Big Business Girl '31
Night Life in Reno '31
Convicted '32
Sons of the Desert '33

Lung Chun-Eng
Two Assassins in the Dark '80s
Shaolin Traitor '82

David Chung
The Ballad of Little Jo '93
Combination Platter '93
Color of a Brisk and Leaping Day '95

Thomas Haden Church
Tombstone '93
Tales from the Crypt Presents Demon Knight '94

Berton Churchill
The Big Stampede '32
False Faces '32
The Mysterious Rider '33
Sing Sing Nights '35
The Dark Hour '36
Dimples '36
Mistaken Identity '36
Danger on the Air '38
In Old Chicago '38
Wide Open Faces '38
Stagecoach '39

Marguerite Churchill
Big Trail '30
Ambassador Bill '31
Dracula's Daughter '36

Julien Ciamaca
My Father's Glory '91
My Mother's Castle '91

Jo Ciampa
Salome '85
The Family '87

Eduardo Ciannelli
Marked Woman '37
Law of the Underworld '38
Bulldog Drummond's Bride '39
Gunga Din '39
Doctor Satan's Robot '40
Foreign Correspondent '40
Kitty Foyle '40
The Mummy's Hand '40
Mysterious Doctor Satan '40
Strange Cargo '40
They Met in Bombay '41
Cairo '42
They Got Me Covered '43
Passage to Marseilles '44
Heartbeat '46
The Creeper '48
Mambo '55
Houseboat '58
Monster from Green Hell '58
MacKenna's Gold '69

Jude Ciccolella
Shakedown '88
Glengarry Glen Ross '92
Mad Love '95

Phyllis Cicero
Steele's Law '91
America's Dream '95

Jennifer Ciesar
Inner Sanctum 2 '94
Lovers' Lovers '94

Diane Cilento
The Naked Edge '61
Tom Jones '63
Rattle of a Simple Man '64
The Agony and the Ecstasy '65
Hombre '67
Negatives '68
Zero Population Growth '72
The Wicker Man '75
Winner Takes All '86

Leonardo Cimino
Penn and Teller Get Killed '90
Trusting Beatrice '92

Kelly Cinnante
True Love '89
Christmas in Connecticut '92

Charles Cioffi
Klute '71
Shaft '71
The Don is Dead '73
The Thief Who Came to Dinner '73
The Arab Conspiracy '76
Return to Earth '76
Time After Time '79
Missing '82
Peter Gunn '89
Newsies '92
Used People '92
The X-Files: Pilot Episode/Deep Throat '93

Franco Citti
Accatone! '61
Mamma Roma '62
Oedipus Rex '67
Porcile '69
The Decameron '70

Jany Clair
Planets Against Us '61
Conquest of Mycene '63
Hercules Against the Moon Men '64

Cyrielle Claire
Sword of the Valiant '83
Code Name: Emerald '85
Control '87

Ina Claire
Three Broadway Girls '32
Ninotchka '39

Rony Clanton
The Education of Sonny Carson '74
Def by Temptation '90

Gordon Clapp
Return of the Secaucus 7 '80
Eight Men Out '88
Small Sacrifices '89
Termini Station '89

Eric Clapton
Tommy '75
Chuck Berry: Hail! Hail! Rock 'n' Roll '87

Diane Clare
Murder on the Campus '52
The Reluctant Debutante '58
Vulture '67

Mary Clare
Lorna Doone '34
Power '34
The Mill on the Floss '37
The Night Has Eyes '42
The Three Weird Sisters '48
Mambo '55

O.B. Clarence
A Shot in the Dark '33
The Courageous Mr. Penn '41

Aime Clarimond
La Marseillaise '37
Monsieur Vincent '48

Angela Clark
Miracle of Our Lady of Fatima '52
Houdini '53
The Seven Little Foys '55

Anthony Clark
Dogfight '91
The Thing Called Love '93
Hourglass '95

Blake Clark
Johnny Handsome '89
Grave Secrets: The Legacy of Hilltop Drive '92
Ladybugs '92
Shakes the Clown '92

Bobby Clark
Clark & McCullough '33
The Goldwyn Follies '38

Brett Clark
Alien Warrior '85
Eye of the Eagle '87
Inner Sanctum '91

Brian Patrick Clark
Sleepaway Camp 2: Unhappy Campers '88
Private Wars '93

Candy Clark
Fat City '72
American Graffiti '73
James Dean '76
The Man Who Fell to Earth '76
Citizens Band '77
The Big Sleep '78
More American Graffiti '79
Rodeo Girl '80
National Lampoon Goes to the Movies '81
Johnny Belinda '82
Q (The Winged Serpent) '82
Amityville 3: The Demon '83
Blue Thunder '83
Hambone & Hillie '84
Cat's Eye '85
At Close Range '86
The Blob '88
Cool As Ice '91
Original Intent '91
Buffy the Vampire Slayer '92

Dane Clark
The Glass Key '42
Action in the North Atlantic '43
Destination Tokyo '43
Hollywood Canteen '44
A Stolen Life '46
Moonrise '48
The Gambler & the Lady '52
Blackout '54
Paid to Kill '54
Thunder Pass '54
The McMasters '70
Say Goodbye, Maggie Cole '72
Murder on Flight 502 '75
James Dean '76
Blood Song '82
Last Rites '88

Dave Clark
Time is Running Out '52
The Woman Inside '83

Davison Clark
Dishonored '31
Rogue's Gallery '44

Eugene C. Clark
Trial and Error '92
TekWar '94

Frank Clark
The Spoilers '14
Roaring Ranch '30

Fred Clark
Flamingo Road '49
The Jackpot '50
Sunset Boulevard '50
The Lemon Drop Kid '51
Three for Bedroom C '52
The Caddy '53
Here Come the Girls '53
Abbott and Costello Meet the Keystone Kops '54
The Court Martial of Billy Mitchell '55
Daddy Long Legs '55
Solid Gold Cadillac '56
Don't Go Near the Water '57
It Started with a Kiss '59
The Mating Game '59
Bells are Ringing '60
Passionate Thief '60
Zotz! '62
Dr. Goldfoot and the Bikini Machine '66
The Horse in the Gray Flannel Suit '68

Greydon Clark
Satan's Sadists '69
Bad Bunch '76

Harvey Clark
Red Headed Woman '32
Shriek in the Night '33
Peck's Bad Boy '34

Judy Clark
South of Santa Fe '42
Kid Sister '45

Kenneth Clark
Between Heaven and Hell '56
Desert Commandos '60s
Tarzana, the Wild Girl '72

Liddy Clark
Kitty and the Bagman '82
Deadly Possession '88

Marlene Clark
Night of the Cobra Woman '72
Slaughter '72
Black Vampire '73
The Baron '88

Matt Clark
The Great Northfield Minnesota Raid '72
The Execution of Private Slovik '74
Melvin Purvis: G-Man '74
Kansas City Massacre '75
The Outlaw Josey Wales '76
The Driver '78
Brubaker '80
Chasing Dreams '81
An Eye for an Eye '81
Legend of the Lone Ranger '81
Ruckus '81
In the Custody of Strangers '82
Love Letters '83
Country '84
Out of the Darkness '85
Return to Oz '85
Tuff Turf '85
Kenny Rogers as the Gambler, Part 3: The Legend Continues '87
Let's Get Harry '87
The Quick and the Dead '87
Blind Witness '89
The Horror Show '89
Back to the Future, Part 3 '90
Class Action '91
Frozen Assets '92
The Harvest '92
Barbarians at the Gate '93

Oliver Clark
Mikey & Nicky '76
A Star is Born '76
One Cooks, the Other Doesn't '83
Ernest Saves Christmas '88
Nightlife '90

Petula Clark
Made in Heaven '52
The Promoter '52
The Runaway Bus '54
Finian's Rainbow '68
Goodbye, Mr. Chips '69

Roger Clark
The Lady is Willing '42
Girls in Chains '43

Steve Clark
West of Nevada '36
Boothill Brigade '37
Gun Lords of Stirrup Basin '37
Pinto Canyon '40
Range Law '44
The Stranger from Pecos '45
Border Bandits '46
Fighting Vigilantes '47
Range Renegades '48

Susan Clark
Coogan's Bluff '68
Madigan '68
Tell Them Willie Boy Is Here '69
Colossus: The Forbin Project '70
Skullduggery '70
Skin Game '71
Valdez is Coming '71
Showdown '73
Airport '75 '75
The Apple Dumpling Gang '75
Babe! '75
Night Moves '75
City on Fire '78
Murder by Decree '79
Nobody's Perfekt '79
The North Avenue Irregulars '79
Promises in the Dark '79
The Double Negative '80
The Choice '81

Wallis Clark
Postal Inspector '36
Star Reporter '39

Andrew Clarke
Anzacs: The War Down Under '85
Les Patterson Saves the World '90
Snowy River, the MacGregor Saga: The Race '93

Caitlin Clarke
Dragonslayer '81
Penn and Teller Get Killed '90

Gary Clarke
How to Make a Monster '58
Missile to the Moon '59
Date Bait '60
Confessions of Tom Harris '72

Graham Clarke
Laser Mission '90
Armageddon: The Final Challenge '94

Mae Clarke
Frankenstein '31
The Front Page '31
Public Enemy '31
Lady Killer '33
Penthouse '33
Great Guy '36
Hats Off '37
Flying Tigers '42
Here Come the Waves '44
King of the Rocketmen '49
Lost Planet Airmen '49
Pat and Mike '52

Mindy Clarke
Hot Under the Collar '91
Return of the Living Dead 3 '93
Return to Two Moon Junction '93

Robert Clarke
The Enchanted Cottage '45
Tales of Robin Hood '52
Sword of Venus '53
The Astounding She-Monster '58
Hideous Sun Demon '59
Beyond the Time Barrier '60
Secret File of Hollywood '62
Terror of the Bloodhunters '62
Midnight Movie Massacre '88
Alienator '89

Warren Clarke
A Clockwork Orange '71
O Lucky Man! '73
The Great Riviera Bank Robbery '79
Enigma '82
Firefox '82
Cold Room '84
Lassiter '84
Gulag '85
Mandela '87
Hands of a Murderer '90
Joseph '95

Lana Clarkson
Deathstalker '83
Blind Date '84
Barbarian Queen '85
Barbarian Queen 2: The Empress Strikes Back '89
Wizards of the Lost Kingdom 2 '89
The Haunting of Morella '91

Patricia Clarkson
The Dead Pool '88
Rocket Gibraltar '88
The Old Man and the Sea '90
Tune in Tomorrow '90
Blind Man's Bluff '91
An American Story '92
Legacy of Lies '92
Caught in the Act '93
Four Eyes and Six Guns '93
Pharoah's Army '95

Robert Clary
New Faces of 1952 '54
Holocaust Survivors...Remembrance of Love '83

Andrew Dice Clay
Wacko '83
Making the Grade '84
Private Resort '84
Night Patrol '85
Pretty in Pink '86
Amazon Women on the Moon '87
Casual Sex? '88
The Adventures of Ford Fairlane '90
Brain Smasher...A Love Story '93
No Contest '94
National Lampoon's Favorite Deadly Sins '95

Nicholas Clay
Lovespell '79
Excalibur '81
Lady Chatterley's Lover '81
Evil under the Sun '82
The Hound of the Baskervilles '83
Lionheart '87
Cannon Movie Tales: Sleeping Beauty '89
Sleeping Beauty '89

Jill Clayburgh
The Wedding Party '69
Portnoy's Complaint '72
The Thief Who Came to Dinner '73
The Terminal Man '74
The Art of Crime '75
Hustling '75
Griffin and Phoenix: A Love Story '76
Silver Streak '76
Semi-Tough '77
An Unmarried Woman '78
Starting Over '79
It's My Turn '80
First Monday in October '81
I'm Dancing as Fast as I Can '82
Hanna K. '83
Where Are the Children? '85
Miles to Go '86
Shy People '87
Whispers in the Dark '92
Day of Atonement '93
Firestorm: 72 Hours in Oakland '93
Naked in New York '93
Rich in Love '93
Honor Thy Father and Mother: The True Story of the Menendez Brothers '94

John Clayton
Freedom '81
High Tide '87
Warm Nights on a Slow-Moving Train '87

John Cleese
The Bliss of Mrs. Blossom '68
John Cleese on How to Irritate People '68
The Magic Christian '69

Monty Python's Flying Circus '71
The Statue '71
And Now for Something Completely Different '72
Romance with a Double Bass '74
Monty Python and the Holy Grail '75
Fawlty Towers '77
Monty Python's Life of Brian '79
Secret Policeman's Private Parts '81
Time Bandits '81
Monty Python Live at the Hollywood Bowl '82
The Secret Policeman's Other Ball '82
Monty Python's The Meaning of Life '83
Whoops Apocalypse '83
Yellowbeard '83
Privates on Parade '84
Silverado '85
Clockwise '86
A Fish Called Wanda '88
The Big Picture '89
Erik the Viking '89
Bullseye! '90
Monty Python's Parrot Sketch Not Included '90
Splitting Heirs '93
The Strange Case of the End of Civilization as We Know It '93
Mary Shelley's Frankenstein '94
Rudyard Kipling's The Jungle Book '94

Paul Clemens
The Family Man '79
Promises in the Dark '79
The Beast Within '82
They're Playing with Fire '84

Christian Clemenson
Bad Influence '90
Hero '92
And the Band Played On '93

Aurore Clement
Le Crabe Tambour '77
Les Rendez-vous D'Anna '78
Invitation au Voyage '82
Toute Une Nuit '82
The Eighties '83
Paris, Texas '83

Pierre Clementi
Belle de Jour '67
Partner '68
Porcile '69
The Conformist '71
Sweet Movie '75

Hal Clements
Grit of the Girl Telegrapher/In the Switch Tower '15
Let's Go! '23

John Clements
The Four Feathers '39
Convoy '40
This England '42
Train of Events '49
The Silent Enemy '58

David Clennon
Go Tell the Spartans '78
Missing '82
The Thing '82
Hanna K. '83
The Right Stuff '83
Star 80 '83
Falling in Love '84
Sweet Dreams '85
Legal Eagles '86
Conspiracy: The Trial of the Chicago Eight '87
The Couch Trip '87
Light Sleeper '92
Man Trouble '92
Matinee '92
Tecumseh: The Last Warrior '95

Corinne Clery
The Story of O '75
Love by Appointment '76
Moonraker '79
Fatal Fix '80s
The Con Artists '80
Insanity '82
Yor, the Hunter from the Future '83
Dangerous Obsession '88
The Switch '89

Carol Cleveland
Monty Python's Flying Circus '71
Monty Python and the Holy Grail '75
Monty Python's The Meaning of Life '83

George Cleveland
Monte Carlo Nights '34
I Conquer the Sea '36
Revolt of the Zombies '36
Ghost Town Riders '38
The Abe Lincoln of Ninth Avenue '39
Mutiny in the Big House '39
Drums of Fu Manchu '40
Hidden Enemy '40
Midnight Limited '40
Playmates '41
Two-Faced Woman '41
Valley of the Sun '42
Texas Legionnaires '43
Abroad with Two Yanks '44
Little Giant '46
The Show-Off '46
The Wistful Widow of Wagon Gap '47
Miss Grant Takes Richmond '49
Trigger, Jr. '50

Jimmy Cliff
The Harder They Come '72
Club Paradise '86

Jack Clifford
Sweet Adeline '26
Sunrise Trail '31
South of Santa Fe '32
The Revenge Rider '35
King of the Pecos '36
The Man from Gun Town '36

Richard Clifford
Much Ado about Nothing '93
Carrington '95

Faith Clift
Cataclysm '81
Savage Journey '83

Montgomery Clift
Red River '48
The Search '48
The Heiress '49
The Big Lift '50
A Place in the Sun '51
From Here to Eternity '53
I Confess '53
Indiscretion of an American Wife '54
Raintree County '57
Lonelyhearts '58
The Young Lions '58
Suddenly, Last Summer '59
Judgment at Nuremberg '61
The Misfits '61

Elmer Clifton
Intolerance '16
America/The Fall of Babylon '24

Renee Cline
Fatal Exposure '90
Invasion Force '90

Colin Clive
Frankenstein '31
Christopher Strong '33
Jane Eyre '34
The Bride of Frankenstein '35
Mad Love '35
History is Made at Night '37

E.E. Clive
The Invisible Man '33
The Bride of Frankenstein '35
The Charge of the Light Brigade '36
The Dark Hour '36
Libeled Lady '36
Bulldog Drummond Escapes '37
Personal Property '37
Arrest Bulldog Drummond '38
Bulldog Drummond's Peril '38
Bulldog Drummond's Revenge/ Bulldog Drummond's Peril '38
The Adventures of Sherlock Holmes '39
Bulldog Drummond's Bride '39
Bulldog Drummond's Secret Police '39
The Hound of the Baskervilles '39
The Little Princess '39

Teagan Clive
Alienator '89

Sinbad of the Seven Seas '89
Vice Academy 2 '90

Al Cliver
Rulers of the City '71
Big Boss '77
Mr. Scarface '77
Zombie '80
The Black Cat '81
Forever Emmanuelle '82
2020 Texas Gladiators '85

George Clooney
Return of the Killer Tomatoes! '88
Red Surf '90
ER '94
From Dusk Till Dawn '95

Rosemary Clooney
Here Come the Girls '53
Deep in My Heart '54
Red Garters '54
White Christmas '54

Del Close
Ferris Bueller's Day Off '86
Opportunity Knocks '90

Glenn Close
Orphan Train '79
Too Far to Go '79
The World According to Garp '82
The Big Chill '83
The Natural '84
The Stone Boy '84
The Jagged Edge '85
Maxie '85
Fatal Attraction '87
Dangerous Liaisons '88
Immediate Family '89
Hamlet '90
Reversal of Fortune '90
Meeting Venus '91
Sarah, Plain and Tall '91
The House of the Spirits '93
Skylark '93
The Paper '94
Mary Reilly '95

John Scott Clough
Fast Forward '84
Gross Anatomy '89
What Ever Happened To... '93

Vera Clouzot
Diabolique '55
Wages of Fear '55

David Clover
Ten Speed '76
Zipperface '92

Francois Cluzet
The Horse of Pride '80
Round Midnight '86
Chocolat '88
The Story of Women '88
Olivier, Olivier '92
L'Enfer '93
Ready to Wear '94
French Kiss '95
The Horseman on the Roof '95

Andy Clyde
Ships in the Night '28
Shirley Temple Festival '33
Annie Oakley '35
Red Lights Ahead '36
Yellow Dust '36
Bad Lands '39
Border Vigilantes '41
Doomed Caravan '41
In Old Colorado '41
Outlaws of the Desert '41
Riders of the Timberline '41
Twilight on the Trail '41
Bar-20 '43
Border Patrol '43
Colt Comrades '43
False Colors '43
Hopalong Cassidy: Riders of the Deadline '43
Hoppy Serves a Writ '43
Leather Burners '43
Lost Canyon '43
Mystery Man '44
Texas Masquerade '44
Hopalong Cassidy: The Devil's Playground '46
Hopalong Cassidy: Hoppy's Holiday '47
Hopalong Cassidy: The Marauders '47
Hopalong Cassidy: Unexpected Guest '47

Hopalong Cassidy: Borrowed Trouble '48
Hopalong Cassidy: Dangerous Venture '48
Hopalong Cassidy: False Paradise '48
Hopalong Cassidy: Silent Conflict '48
Hopalong Cassidy: Sinister Journey '48
Hopalong Cassidy: The Dead Don't Dream '48
Sundown Riders '48

June Clyde
Branded Men '31
Morals for Women '31
A Study in Scarlet '33
Hollywood Mystery '34
She Shall Have Music '36
Make-Up '37
Wayne Murder Case '38
Seven Doors to Death '44
Behind the Mask '46

Kim Coates
Blind Fear '89
Cold Front '89
The Amityville Curse '90
Red Blooded American Girl '90
Smokescreen '90
Innocent Blood '92
The Club '94
Good Men and Bad '94
The Spider and the Fly '94
Breach of Trust '95
The Outer Limits: Sandkings '95
Unforgettable '96

Phyllis Coates
Blues Busters '50
Superman & the Mole Men '51
TV's Best Adventures of Superman '51
Invasion U.S.A. '52
El Paso Stampede '53
Jungle Drums of Africa '53
Marshal of Cedar Rock '53
The Incredible Petrified World '58
Teenage Frankenstein '58

Edmund Cobb
Riders of the Range '24
Wild Horse '31
Gun Law '33
Gunners & Guns '34
Danger Trails '35
Rustler's Paradise '35
Tonto Basin Outlaws '41
Texas Kid '43
Sunset in El Dorado '45
Buffalo Bill Rides Again '47

Joe Cobb
The Return of Our Gang '25
Our Gang '26
Little Rascals, Book 1 '30s
Our Gang Comedy Festival '88
Our Gang Comedy Festival 2 '89

Lee J. Cobb
Rustler's Valley '37
Danger on the Air '38
Golden Boy '39
Men of Boys Town '41
Buckskin Frontier '43
The Song of Bernadette '43
Anna and the King of Siam '46
Boomerang '47
Call Northside 777 '48
The Miracle of the Bells '48
The Dark Past '49
Sirocco '51
The Fighter '52
Tall Texan '53
Day of Triumph '54
On the Waterfront '54
The Left Hand of God '55
The Racers '55
The Man in the Gray Flannel Suit '56
The Three Faces of Eve '57
Twelve Angry Men '57
The Brothers Karamazov '58
Man of the West '58
Party Girl '58
But Not for Me '59
Green Mansions '59
The Trap '59
Exodus '60
The Four Horsemen of the Apocalypse '62
Come Blow Your Horn '63

How the West Was Won '63
Our Man Flint '66
In Like Flint '67
Coogan's Bluff '68
MacKenna's Gold '69
The Liberation of L.B. Jones '70
Macho Callahan '70
Lawman '71
The Exorcist '73
Man Who Loved Cat Dancing '73
That Lucky Touch '75
The Meanest Men in the West '76
Bull of the West '89

Randall "Tex" Cobb
Uncommon Valor '83
The Golden Child '86
Raising Arizona '87
Buy & Cell '89
Blind Fury '90
Ernest Goes to Jail '90
Raw Nerve '91
Diggstown '92

Bill Cobbs
Dominick & Eugene '88
Decoration Day '90
The Bodyguard '92
Carolina Skeletons '92
The Hudsucker Proxy '93
Fluke '95
Kingfish: A Story of Huey P. Long '95
Man with a Gun '95
Out There '95
Ed '96

Roberto Cobo
Los Olvidados '50
Cabeza de Vaca '90

Charles Coburn
Of Human Hearts '38
Vivacious Lady '38
Bachelor Mother '39
Idiot's Delight '39
Made for Each Other '39
Stanley and Livingstone '39
The Story of Alexander Graham Bell '39
Edison the Man '40
The Road to Singapore '40
Three Faces West '40
The Devil & Miss Jones '41
Kings Row '41
The Lady Eve '41
George Washington Slept Here '42
In This Our Life '42
Heaven Can Wait '43
The More the Merrier '43
Wilson '44
Colonel Effingham's Raid '45
Rhapsody in Blue '45
The Paradine Case '47
Mr. Music '50
Monkey Business '52
Gentlemen Prefer Blondes '53
Trouble Along the Way '53
Around the World in 80 Days '56
John Paul Jones '59

James Coburn
Ride Lonesome '59
Wanted: Dead or Alive '59
The Magnificent Seven '60
Hell is for Heroes '62
Charade '63
The Great Escape '63
The Americanization of Emily '64
The Loved One '65
Major Dundee '65
Dead Heat on a Merry-Go-Round '66
Our Man Flint '66
What Did You Do in the War, Daddy? '66
In Like Flint '67
The President's Analyst '67
Waterhole #3 '67
A Fistful of Dynamite '72
Internecine Project '73
The Last of Sheila '73
Pat Garrett & Billy the Kid '73
A Reason to Live, A Reason to Die '73
Bite the Bullet '75
Hard Times '75
Cross of Iron '76
High Risk '76
Midway '76
Sky Riders '76
The Dain Curse '78

Coburn ▶cont.

Firepower '79
Goldengirl '79
The Baltimore Bullet '80
Loving Couples '80
Draw! '81
Looker '81
Crossover '82
Pinocchio '83
Death of a Soldier '85
Martin's Day '85
Young Guns 2 '90
Hudson Hawk '91
Deadfall '93
The Hit List '93
Sister Act 2: Back in the Habit '93
Maverick '94
A Thousand Heroes '94
The Avenging Angel '95
The Set Up '95
Eraser '96
The Nutty Professor '96

Michael Coby
The Bitch '78
Supersonic Man '78

Imogene Coca
Rabbit Test '78
National Lampoon's Vacation '83

Richard Coca
Street Knight '93
The Truth About Cats and Dogs '96

Robert Cochran
Sanders of the River '35
Scrooge '35
I Stand Condemned '36

Steve Cochran
Wonder Man '45
The Best Years of Our Lives '46
The Chase '46
Copacabana '47
A Song is Born '48
White Heat '49
Jim Thorpe: All American '51
The Desert Song '53
Shark River '53
Carnival Story '54
Private Hell 36 '54
Il Grido '57
I, Mobster '58
Deadly Companions '61

Rory Cochrane
Fathers and Sons '92
Dazed and Confused '93
Love and a .45 '94
Empire Records '95

James Coco
Ensign Pulver '64
Generation '69
End of the Road '70
The Strawberry Statement '70
A New Leaf '71
Man of La Mancha '72
Wild Party '74
Murder by Death '76
The Cheap Detective '78
Scavenger Hunt '79
Wholly Moses! '80
Only When I Laugh '81
You Can't Take It with You '84
The Chair '87
Hunk '87
That's Adequate '90

Jean Cocteau
The Blood of a Poet '30
The Testament of Orpheus '59

Camille Coduri
Hawks '89
Nuns on the Run '90
Strapless '90
King Ralph '91

Bill Cody
Ghost City '32
Mason of the Mounted '32
Texas Pioneers '32
Frontier Days '34
Outlaws of the Range '36

Iron Eyes Cody
The Road to Yesterday '25
Whistlin' Dan '32
King of the Stallions '42
Under Nevada Skies '46
Bowery Buckaroos '47
Son of Paleface '52
El Condor '70
The Longest Drive '76
Grayeagle '77
Ernest Goes to Camp '87
Spirit of '76 '91

Kathleen Cody
Charley and the Angel '73
Girls on the Road '73
Superdad '73

Lew Cody
Mickey '17
Dishonored '31

Barry Coe
Love Me Tender '56
Peyton Place '57
The Bravados '58
But Not for Me '59
The Cat '66
Dr. Death, Seeker of Souls '73
The Oval Portrait '88

George Coe
Bustin' Loose '81
Red Flag: The Ultimate Game '81
Rage of Angels '83
Sessions '83
A Flash of Green '85
Best Seller '87
Blind Date '87
Uncle Tom's Cabin '87
The Hollywood Detective '89
The End of Innocence '90

Peter Coe
House of Frankenstein '44
The Mummy's Curse '44

Paul Coeur
Cool Runnings '93
White Fang 2: The Myth of the White Wolf '94

Colleen Coffey
Relentless 4 '94
Indecent Behavior 3 '95

Scott Coffey
Zombie High '87
Satisfaction '88
Shag: The Movie '89
Montana '90
Shout '91
Dream Lover '93
The Temp '93
Tank Girl '94

Frederick Coffin
One Summer Love '76
Manhunt for Claude Dallas '86
The Bedroom Window '87
Shoot to Kill '88
Hard to Kill '89
There Goes My Baby '92
Andersonville '95
A Streetcar Named Desire '95

Tristram Coffin
Up in the Air '40
Tonto Basin Outlaws '41
The Corpse Vanishes '42
Dick Tracy, Detective/The Corpse Vanishes '42
Holt of the Secret Service '42
Meet the Mob '42
Spy Smasher '42
Spy Smasher Returns '42
Under Nevada Skies '46
Jesse James Rides Again '47
Land of the Lawless '47
King of the Rocketmen '49
Lost Planet Airmen '49
Pirates of the High Seas '50
Queen for a Day '51
Ma Barker's Killer Brood '60

Nikki Coghill
The Time Guardian '87
Dark Age '88

Frank "Junior" Coghlan
Yankee Clipper '27
Let 'er Go Gallegher '28
Marked Money '28
Square Shoulders '29
Hell's House '32
The Last of the Mohicans '32
Drum Taps '33
In the Money '34
Kentucky Blue Streak '35
Little Red Schoolhouse '36
Red Lights Ahead '36
The Adventures of Captain Marvel '41

Emma Cohen
Horror Rises from the Tomb '72
Bronson's Revenge '79

J.J. Cohen
Back to the Future '85
The Principal '87
Back to the Future, Part 2 '89
Back to the Future, Part 3 '90

Lynn Cohen
Manhattan Murder Mystery '93
Vanya on 42nd Street '94

Scott Cohen
Vibrations '94
The Wharf Rat '95

Nicholas Colasanto
Fat City '72
Mad Bull '77
Raging Bull '80

Catero Colbert
Sweet Perfection '90
Up Against the Wall '91

Claudette Colbert
The Sign of the Cross '32
I Cover the Waterfront '33
Cleopatra '34
It Happened One Night '34
Bluebeard's Eighth Wife '38
Drums Along the Mohawk '39
Midnight '39
Boom Town '40
The Palm Beach Story '42
So Proudly We Hail '43
Since You Went Away '44
Guest Wife '45
Tomorrow Is Forever '46
Without Reservations '46
Egg and I '47
Three Came Home '50
Let's Make It Legal '51
Texas Lady '56
Parrish '61
The Love Goddesses '65

Dennis Cole
Powder Keg '70
The Connection '73
The Barbary Coast '74
Amateur Night '85
Pretty Smart '87
Dead End City '88
Death House '88

Gary Cole
Fatal Vision '84
Echoes in the Darkness '87
The Old Man and the Sea '90
Son of the Morning Star '91
In the Line of Fire '93
Fall from Grace '94
The Brady Bunch Movie '95
A Very Brady Sequel '96

George Cole
Cottage to Let '41
A Christmas Carol '51
The Belles of St. Trinian's '53
The Adventures of Sadie '55
Blue Murder at St. Trinian's '56
Too Many Crooks '59
The Pure Hell of St. Trinian's '61
Dr. Syn, Alias the Scarecrow '64
The Vampire Lovers '70
Fright '71
Gone in 60 Seconds '74
Deadline Auto Theft '83
Mary Reilly '95

Jacqulin Cole
Bad Bunch '76
Satan's Cheerleaders '77

Michael Cole
Chuka '67
The Mod Squad '68
Nickel Mountain '85

Nat King Cole
Killer Diller '48
Small Town Girl '53
China Gate '57
Istanbul '57
Cat Ballou '65

Olivia Cole
Some Kind of Hero '82
Go Tell It On the Mountain '84
North and South Book 1 '85
The Fig Tree '87
The Women of Brewster Place '89

Robert Coleby
Plumber '79
Now and Forever '82
The Blue Lightning '86
Hector's Bunyip '86
Great Expectations: The Untold Story '87
In Pursuit of Honor '95
The Phantom '96

Charles Coleman
Bachelor Apartment '31
First Love '39
It Started with Eve '41
Grand Canyon Trail '48

Charlotte Coleman
Four Weddings and a Funeral '94
The Young Poisoner's Handbook '94

Dabney Coleman
The Scalphunters '68
Downhill Racer '69
The Trouble with Girls (and How To Get Into It) '69
The President's Plane is Missing '71
Cinderella Liberty '73
Dying Room Only '73
Bad Ronald '74
The Dove '74
Bite the Bullet '75
The Other Side of the Mountain '75
Viva Knievel '77
Fist '79
North Dallas Forty '79
Homeboy '80s
How to Beat the High Cost of Living '80
Melvin and Howard '80
9 to 5 '80
Nothing Personal '80
Pray TV '80
Callie and Son '81
Modern Problems '81
On Golden Pond '81
Tootsie '82
Young Doctors in Love '82
WarGames '83
Cloak & Dagger '84
The Man with One Red Shoe '85
Murrow '86
Dragnet '87
Guilty of Innocence '87
Hot to Trot! '88
The Applegates '89
Short Time '90
Where the Heart Is '90
Never Forget '91
Clifford '92
There Goes the Neighborhood '92
Amos and Andrew '93
The Beverly Hillbillies '93
Judicial Consent '94

Gary Coleman
The Kid from Left Field '79
Scout's Honor '80
On the Right Track '81
Jimmy the Kid '82
The Kid with the Broken Halo '82
The Kid with the 200 I.Q. '83
The Fantastic World of D.C. Collins '84

Jack Coleman
Daughter of Darkness '89
The Return of Eliot Ness '91
Rubdown '93
Foreign Student '94
Trapped in Space '94

Jimmy Coleman
Riff Raff '92
Priest '94

Nancy Coleman
Kings Row '41
Desperate Journey '42
Edge of Darkness '43

Renee Coleman
Return to Eden '89
Who's Harry Crumb? '89
A League of Their Own '92
Pentathlon '94

Mildred Coles
Lady Scarface '41
Seven Days Ashore/Hurry, Charlie, Hurry '44
Oklahoma Badlands '48

John Colicos
Murder on Approval '56
Anne of the Thousand Days '69
Doctors' Wives '70
Raid on Rommel '71
Scorpio '73
Battlestar Galactica '78
The Postman Always Rings Twice '81
Shadow Dancing '88
Love and Hate: A Marriage Made in Hell '90

David Colin, Jr.
Beyond the Door '75
Beyond the Door 2 '79

Gregoire Colin
Olivier, Olivier '92
Before the Rain '94

Ian Colin
Late Extra '35
Never Too Late to Mend '37

Margaret Colin
Pretty in Pink '86
Something Wild '86
Like Father, Like Son '87
Three Men and a Baby '87
Traveling Man '89
True Believer '89
Martians Go Home! '90
The Butcher's Wife '91
Amos and Andrew '93

Christopher Collet
Sleepaway Camp '83
First Born '84
The Manhattan Project '86
Prayer of the Rollerboys '91
Stephen King's The Langoliers '95

Toni Collette
The Efficiency Expert '92
Muriel's Wedding '94
The Pallbearer '95
Emma '96

Kenneth Colley
The Music Lovers '71
And Nothing But the Truth '82
Firefox '82
Casanova '87
A Summer Story '88
The Rainbow '89
Prisoner of Honor '91

Constance Collier
Thunder in the City '37
Wee Willie Winkie '37
Dark Corner '46
Monsieur Beaucaire '46
The Perils of Pauline '47
Rope '48

Lois Collier
Cobra Woman '44
The Naughty Nineties '45

William Collier, Jr.
Cimarron '30
Street Scene '31
Phantom Express '32

John Collin
Star! '68
Tess '80

Patricia Collinge
Tender Comrade '43
Casanova Brown '44

Anne Collings
The Mask '61
Return to Africa '89

Alan Collins
The Last Hunter '80
Ark of the Sun God '82
Hunters of the Golden Cobra '82
Exterminators of the Year 3000 '83
Tornado '83
Tiger Joe '85

Cora Sue Collins
Evelyn Prentice '34
The Scarlet Letter '34
The World Accuses '35

Eddie Collins
Drums Along the Mohawk '39
Young Mr. Lincoln '39
The Blue Bird '40

Joan Collins
Decameron Nights '53
Tough Guy '53
The Adventures of Sadie '55
Land of the Pharaohs '55
The Virgin Queen '55
The Opposite Sex '56
Stopover Tokyo '57
The Bravados '58
Esther and the King '60
Seven Thieves '60
Cosh Boy '61
The Road to Hong Kong '62
Subterfuge '68
The Executioner '70
Three in the Cellar '70
The Persuaders '71
Quest for Love '71
Revenge '71
Dynasty of Fear '72
Tales from the Crypt '72
Dark Places '73
Tales That Witness Madness '73
Great Adventure '75
I Don't Want to Be Born '75
Oh, Alfie '75
The Bawdy Adventures of Tom Jones '76
Empire of the Ants '77
The Big Sleep '78
The Bitch '78
Fearless '78
The Stud '78
Zero to Sixty '78
Sunburn '79
Five Miles to Midnight '80
Hansel and Gretel '82
Homework '82
Her Life as a Man '83
Cartier Affair '84
Nutcracker Sweet '84
Sins '85
Game for Vultures '86
Monte Carlo '86
Annie: A Royal Adventure '95
A Midwinter's Tale '95

Kevin Collins
The Garden '90
Edward II '92

Lewis Collins
Professionals '76
The Final Option '82
Codename: Wildgeese '84
Jack the Ripper '88

Patrick Collins
The Juggler of Notre Dame '84
Dirt Bike Kid '86

Pauline Collins
Shirley Valentine '89
City of Joy '92

Phil Collins
Buster '88
Hook '91
Frauds '93

Ray Collins
Citizen Kane '41
The Magnificent Ambersons '42
The Navy Comes Through '42
Commandos Strike at Dawn '43
The Human Comedy '43
Whistling in Brooklyn '43
The Seventh Cross '44
Leave Her to Heaven '45
Crack-Up '46
The Bachelor and the Bobby-Soxer '47
A Double Life '47
Good Sam '48
Homecoming '48
The Fountainhead '49
Francis the Talking Mule '49
It Happens Every Spring '49
Man from Colorado '49
Ma and Pa Kettle Go to Town '50
Summer Stock '50
Ma and Pa Kettle Back On the Farm '51
The Racket '51
The Desert Song '53
Ma and Pa Kettle on Vacation '53
Solid Gold Cadillac '56

Rick Collins
The Toxic Avenger, Part 2 '89
The Toxic Avenger, Part 3: The Last Temptation of Toxie '89

Roberta Collins
The Arousers '70
The Big Doll House '71
Unholy Rollers '72
The Deadly and the Beautiful '73
Caged Heat '74
Whiskey Mountain '77
Hardbodies '84

Russell Collins
Savage Wilderness '55
Soldier of Fortune '55
Enemy Below '57
The Matchmaker '58

Ruth Collins
Galactic Gigolo '87
New York's Finest '87
Doom Asylum '88
Exquisite Corpses '88
Sexpot '88
Cemetery High '89
Death Collector '89
Wildest Dreams '90
Dead Boyz Can't Fly '93

Stephen Collins
All the President's Men '76
Between the Lines '77
The Promise '78
The Henderson Monster '80
Loving Couples '80
Star Trek: The Motion Picture '80
Summer Solstice '81
Inside the Third Reich '82
Chiefs '83
Brewster's Millions '85
Hold the Dream '85
Choke Canyon '86
Jumpin' Jack Flash '86
Hitchhiker 3 '87
Weekend War '88
The Big Picture '89
Stella '89
A Woman Named Jackie '91
My New Gun '92
Till Murder Do Us Part '92
Scarlett '94

Madeleine Collinson
The Love Machine '71
Twins of Evil '71

Mary Collinson
The Love Machine '71
Twins of Evil '71

Frank Collison
Wired to Kill '86
Dollman '90

Mark Collver
Bix '90
There's Nothing Out There '90

June Collyer
Drums of Jeopardy '31
The Ghost Walks '34
A Face in the Fog '36

Pamela Collyer
Evil Judgement '85
The Kiss '88

Ronald Colman
The White Sister '23
Romola '25
Lady Windermere's Fan '26
Bulldog Drummond '29
Arrowsmith '31
A Tale of Two Cities '35
Lost Horizon '37
Prisoner of Zenda '37
Lucky Partners '40
Random Harvest '42
Talk of the Town '42
A Double Life '47
Champagne for Caesar '50
Around the World in 80 Days '56

Scott Colomby
Are You in the House Alone? '78
Porky's '82
Porky's 2: The Next Day '83
Porky's Revenge '85

Alex Colon
Invasion U.S.A. '85
Death of an Angel '86

Miriam Colon
A Life of Sin '92
Lone Star '95
Sabrina '95

Jerry Colonna
Rosalie '38
The Road to Singapore '40
Strictly G.I. '44
Kentucky Jubilee '51
Meet Me in Las Vegas '56

Vince Colosimo
Moving Out '83
Street Hero '84

Louisa Colpeyn
Band of Outsiders '64
Marry Me, Marry Me '69

Marshall Colt
The Jagged Edge '85
Beverly Hills Madam '86
Guilty of Innocence '87
To Heal a Nation '88

Robbie Coltrane
Chinese Boxes '84
Defense of the Realm '85
Mona Lisa '86
Loose Connections '87
Wonderland '88
Bert Rigby, You're a Fool '89
Henry V '89
Let It Ride '89
Slipstream '89
Nuns on the Run '90
Perfectly Normal '91
The Pope Must Diet '91
Oh, What a Night '92
The Adventures of Huck Finn '93
The Best of Cracker Mysteries '93
Goldeneye '95

Coluche
My Best Friend's Girl '84
Tchao Pantin '84

Franco Columbo
Pumping Iron '76
Last Man Standing '87

Franco Columbu
Beretta's Island '92
Desperate Crimes '93

Jack Colvin
The Incredible Hulk '77
Child's Play '88
The Incredible Hulk Returns '88

Michael Colyar
Hot Shots! Part Deux '93
House Party 3 '94

Holly Marie Combs
Sweet Hearts Dance '88
Dr. Giggles '92
Chain of Desire '93

Jeffrey Combs
Re-Animator '84
From Beyond '86
Cellar Dweller '87
Cyclone '87
Phantom Empire '87
Dead Man Walking '88
Bride of Re-Animator '89
Doctor Mordrid: Master of the Unknown '90
Trancers 2: The Return of Jack Deth '90
The Guyver '91
The Pit & the Pendulum '91
Love and a .45 '94
Lurking Fear '94
Castle Freak '95
The Frighteners '96

Anjanette Comer
The Loved One '65
The Appaloosa '66
The Baby '72
Night of a Thousand Cats '72
Death Stalk '74
Terror on the 40th Floor '74
Dead of Night '77
Netherworld '90
Larry McMurtry's Streets of Laredo '95

Dorothy Comingore
Citizen Kane '41
The Hairy Ape '44

Perry Como
Doll Face '46
Words and Music '48

Betty Compson
These Girls Won't Talk '20s
Hot Foot/A Happy Married Couple '20
Paths to Paradise '25
The Pony Express '25
Docks of New York '28
The Great Gabbo '29
Inside the Lines '30
The Lady Refuses '31
Bulldog Edition '36
God's Country and the Man '37
The Port of Missing Girls '38
Mystic Circle Murder '39
Mad Youth '40
Hard-Boiled Mahoney '47

Fay Compton
The Mill on the Floss '37
Othello '52

Joyce Compton
False Faces '32
King Kelly of the U.S.A. '34
Let 'Em Have It '35
Rustlers of Red Dog '35
Country Gentlemen '36
The Awful Truth '37
Sea Racketeers '37
Small Town Boy '37
Balalaika '39
Escape to Paradise '39
Rose of Washington Square '39
I Take This Oath '40
Silver Spurs '43
Christmas in Connecticut '45
Scared to Death '47
A Southern Yankee '48

Oliver Conant
Summer of '42 '71
Class of '44 '73

Cristi Conaway
Batman Returns '92
Attack of the 50 Ft. Woman '93
Nina Takes a Lover '94

Jeff Conaway
Pete's Dragon '77
Grease '78
Breaking Up Is Hard to Do '79
For the Love of It '80
Covergirl '83
The Patriot '86
The Dirty Dozen: The Fatal Mission '88
Elvira, Mistress of the Dark '88
The Banker '89
Ghost Writer '89
Tale of Two Sisters '89
The Sleeping Car '90
Almost Pregnant '91
Mirror Images '91
Sunset Strip '91
A Time to Die '91
Total Exposure '91
Bikini Summer 2 '92
L.A. Goddess '92
Bounty Hunter 2002 '94

James Congdon
The 4D Man '59
Summerdog '78

Chester Conklin
Charlie Chaplin's Keystone Comedies #3 '14
Charlie Chaplin's Keystone Comedies #4 '14
Tillie's Punctured Romance '14
Cannon Ball/Eyes Have It '15
Charlie Chaplin...Our Hero! '15
A Hash House Fraud/The Sultan's Wife '15
The Lizzies of Mack Sennett '15
Cannonball/Dizzy Heights and Daring Hearts '16
Mack Sennett Comedies: Vol. 1 '21
Anna Christie '23
Battling Bunyon '24
Greed '24
Behind the Front '26
The Nervous Wreck '26
The Virginian '29
Hallelujah, I'm a Bum '33
Modern Times '36
Forlorn River '37
Harmon of Michigan '41
Sullivan's Travels '41
Miracle of Morgan's Creek '44

Joe Conley
The Waltons: The Christmas Carol '80
A Day for Thanks on Walton's Mountain '82

Brigid Conley Walsh
The Day My Parents Ran Away '93
Quest of the Delta Knights '93

Jimmy Conlin
Sullivan's Travels '41
Miracle of Morgan's Creek '44
Dick Tracy's Dilemma '47

Didi Conn
You Light Up My Life '77
Grease 2 '82

Christopher Connelly
The Other '72
They Only Kill Their Masters '72
Benji '74
The Invasion of Carol Enders '74
Hawmps! '76
The Incredible Rocky Mountain Race '77
The Crash of Flight 401 '78
Norseman '78
The Martian Chronicles: Part 3 '79
Return of the Rebels '81
Fantastic Seven '82
Liar's Moon '82
Manhattan Baby '82
1990: The Bronx Warriors '83
Raiders of Atlantis '83
Foxtrap '85
Jungle Raiders '85
Operation 'Nam '85
The Messenger '87
Mines of Kilimanjaro '87
Strike Commando '87
Night of the Sharks '89

Edward Connelly
The Saphead '21
The Mysterious Lady '28

Jennifer Connelly
Once Upon a Time in America '84
Creepers '85
Labyrinth '86
Seven Minutes in Heaven '86
Some Girls '88
The Hot Spot '90
Career Opportunities '91
The Rocketeer '91
Higher Learning '94
Of Love and Shadows '94
Mulholland Falls '95

Marc Connelly
Spirit of St. Louis '57
Tall Story '60

Jason Connery
The First Olympics: Athens 1896 '84
Robin Hood...The Legend: Herne's Son '85
Robin Hood...The Legend: The Time of the Wolf '85
Winner Takes All '86
Bye Bye Baby '88
Casablanca Express '89
Spymaker: The Secret Life of Ian Fleming '90
Double Cross '92

Sean Connery
Time Lock '57
Another Time, Another Place '58
Darby O'Gill & the Little People '59
Dr. No '62
The Longest Day '62
From Russia with Love '63
Goldfinger '64
Marnie '64
Thunderball '65
A Fine Madness '66
You Only Live Twice '67
Shalako '68
Red Tent '69
Molly Maguires '70
The Anderson Tapes '71
Diamonds Are Forever '71
The Offence '73
Zardoz '73
Murder on the Orient Express '74
The Terrorists '74
The Man Who Would Be King '75
The Wind and the Lion '75
The Arab Conspiracy '76
Robin and Marian '76
A Bridge Too Far '77
Cuba '79
The Great Train Robbery '79
Meteor '79
Outland '81
Time Bandits '81

Dr. Heckyl and Mr. Hype '80
The Prey '80
The Escape Artist '82

Keith Coogan
Adventures in Babysitting '87
Hiding Out '87
Cheetah '89
Cousins '89
Under the Boardwalk '89
Book of Love '91
Don't Tell Mom the Babysitter's Dead '91
Toy Soldiers '91
Forever: A Ghost of a Love Story '92
Life 101 '95
The Power Within '95

Carole Cook
The Incredible Mr. Limpet '64
Sixteen Candles '84

Clyde Cook
Through the Breakers '28
White Gold '28
White Cargo '42

Dale "Apollo" Cook
Triple Impact '92
American Kickboxer 2: To the Death '93
Blood Ring '93
Fist of Steel '93
Fist of Glory '95

Donald Cook
Baby Face '33
Viva Villa! '34
Confidential '35
Show Boat '36
Here Come the Co-Eds '45

Elisha Cook, Jr.
They Won't Forget '37
Stranger on the Third Floor '40
Tin Pan Alley '40
The Maltese Falcon '41
Wildcat '42
Dark Mountain '44
Dark Waters '44
Dillinger '45
The Big Sleep '46
Born to Kill '47
Behave Yourself! '52
Don't Bother to Knock '52
Shane '53
Drum Beat '54
The Indian Fighter '55
The Killing '56
Plunder Road '57
Platinum High School '60
One-Eyed Jacks '61
The Haunted Palace '63
Papa's Delicate Condition '63
Rosemary's Baby '68
El Condor '70
The Great Northfield Minnesota Raid '72
Electra Glide in Blue '73
Messiah of Evil '74
Black Bird '75
St. Ives '76
The Champ '79
1941 '79
Salem's Lot '79
Carny '80
Leave 'Em Laughing '81
Hammett '82

Peter Cook
The Wrong Box '66
Bedazzled '68
Dandy in Aspic '68
Those Daring Young Men in Their Jaunty Jalopies '69
Find the Lady '75
The Hound of the Baskervilles '77
Yellowbeard '83
The Princess Bride '87
Whoops Apocalypse '88
Without a Clue '88
Getting It Right '89
Great Balls of Fire '89
Black Beauty '94

Rachel Leigh Cook
The Baby-Sitters Club '95
Tom and Huck '95

Roderick Cook
Our Time '74
9 1/2 Weeks '86

Ron Cook
Sharpe's Honour '94
Secrets and Lies '95

Tommy Cook
Teenage Crime Wave '55
Missile to the Moon '59

Jennifer Cooke
Gimme an F '85
Friday the 13th, Part 6: Jason Lives '86

Keith Cooke
China O'Brien '88
China O'Brien 2 '89
The King of the Kickboxers '91
Heatseeker '95

Peter Cookson
Fear '46
Black Tower '50

Spade Cooley
Kid from Gower Gulch '47
Silver Bandit '47
Everybody's Dancin' '50

Alice Cooper
Sextette '78
Roadie '80
Monster Dog '82
Decline of Western Civilization 2: The Metal Years '88
Freddy's Dead: The Final Nightmare '91

Cami Cooper
The Applegates '89
Shocker '89

Chris Cooper
Matewan '87
City of Hope '91
Guilty by Suspicion '91
Thousand Pieces of Gold '91
Lone Justice '93
Return to Lonesome Dove '93
This Boy's Life '93
Lone Star '95
Money Train '95
Pharoah's Army '95

Clancy Cooper
The Secret Code '42
Girls in Chains '43
Naked Youth '59

Gary Cooper
Dark Before Dawn '89
Naked Gun 33 1/3: The Final Insult '94

Gary Cooper
It '27
The Last Outlaw '27
Nevada '27
Wings '27
Doomsday '28
The Virginian '29
Kings, Queens, Jokers '30s
Morocco '30
Fighting Caravans '31
A Farewell to Arms '32
Today We Live '33
The Lives of a Bengal Lancer '35
Desire '36
The General Died at Dawn '36
Mr. Deeds Goes to Town '36
The Plainsman '37
The Adventures of Marco Polo '38
Bluebeard's Eighth Wife '38
The Cowboy and the Lady '38
Beau Geste '39
The Real Glory '39
The Westerner '40
Ball of Fire '41
Meet John Doe '41
Sergeant York '41
Hedda Hopper's Hollywood '42
The Pride of the Yankees '42
For Whom the Bell Tolls '43
Casanova Brown '44
The Story of Dr. Wassell '44
Along Came Jones '45
Saratoga Trunk '45
Cloak and Dagger '46
Unconquered '47
Good Sam '48
The Fountainhead '49
It's a Great Feeling '49
Task Force '49
Distant Drums '51
High Noon '52
Springfield Rifle '52
Return to Paradise '53
Vera Cruz '53
Blowing Wild '54
The Court Martial of Billy Mitchell '55
Friendly Persuasion '56
Love in the Afternoon '57
Man of the West '58
Ten North Frederick '58
The Hanging Tree '59
They Came to Cordura '59
The Wreck of the Mary Deare '59
The Naked Edge '61

George Cooper
Little Church Around the Corner '23
Smouldering Fires '25
Uptown New York '32
Federal Agent '36

Gladys Cooper
The Iron Duke '34
Kitty Foyle '40
Rebecca '40
That Hamilton Woman '41
Now, Voyager '42
Mr. Lucky '43
The Song of Bernadette '43
Mrs. Parkington '44
The White Cliffs of Dover '44
The Valley of Decision '45
Beware of Pity '46
The Bishop's Wife '47
Homecoming '48
The Pirate '48
Madame Bovary '49
The Secret Garden '49
Separate Tables '58
The Twilight Zone '61
My Fair Lady '64
Nice Girl Like Me '69

Inez Cooper
I Married an Angel '42
Wings Over the Pacific '43
'Neath Canadian Skies '46
North of the Border '46

Jack Cooper
All Night Long/Smile Please '24
Cord & Dischords/Naughty Nurse '28

Jackie Cooper
The Champ '31
Peck's Bad Boy '34
Treasure Island '34
The Abe Lincoln of Ninth Avenue '39
Return of Frank James '40
Ziegfeld Girl '41
The Navy Comes Through '42
Maybe I'll Be Home in the Spring '70
The Love Machine '71
Superman: The Movie '78
Superman 2 '80
Superman 3 '83
Surrender '87

Jeanne Cooper
The Redhead from Wyoming '53
Plunder Road '57
Shame '61
Red Nightmare '62
Sweet Hostage '75

Jeff Cooper
The Impossible Years '68
Circle of Iron '78
Fantastic Balloon Voyage '80s

Maggie Cooper
And Baby Makes Six '79
Death Ray 2000 '81
An Eye for an Eye '81

Melville Cooper
Private Life of Don Juan '34
Thin Ice '37
The Adventures of Robin Hood '38
Dawn Patrol '38
Murder over New York '40
Rebecca '40
The Lady Eve '41
Immortal Sergeant '43
Heartbeat '46
13 Rue Madeleine '46
Let's Dance '50
The Underworld Story '50
The King's Thief '55

Ralph Cooper
The Duke is Tops '38
Gang War '40

Stan Cooper
Hell Commandos '69
Great Treasure Hunt '70s
The Hanging Woman '72

Robert Coote
Bad Lands '39
Gunga Din '39
Mr. Moto's Last Warning '39
Nurse Edith Cavell '39
You Can't Fool Your Wife '40
Commandos Strike at Dawn '43
Forever Amber '47
The Ghost and Mrs. Muir '47
Macbeth '48
The Three Musketeers '48
The Elusive Pimpernel '50
The Merry Widow '52
Othello '52
Scaramouche '52
The Horse's Mouth '58
Tunes of Glory/Horse's Mouth '60
My Fair Lady '64
Alice Through the Looking Glass '66

Joan Copeland
Roseland '77
Happy New Year '87
Her Alibi '88
The Laserman '90

Teri Copley
I Married a Centerfold '84
The FBI Murders '88
Down the Drain '89
Transylvania Twist '89
Brain Donors '92
Frozen Assets '92

Sofia Coppola
The Godfather '72
Peggy Sue Got Married '86
The Godfather, Part 3 '90
Inside Monkey Zetterland '93

Glenn Corbett
The Violent Years '56
All the Young Men '60
The Mountain Road '60
Shenandoah '65
Chisum '70
Dead Pigeon on Beethoven Street '72
The Stranger '73
Ride in a Pink Car '74
Shadow Force '92

Gretchen Corbett
Let's Scare Jessica to Death '71
The Savage Bees '76
Secrets of Three Hungry Wives '78
PSI Factor '80
Jaws of Satan '81

Harry H. Corbett
The Unstoppable Man '59
Ladies Who Do '63
Rattle of a Simple Man '64
Carry On Screaming '66
Silver Dream Racer '83

Barry Corbin
Urban Cowboy '80
Bitter Harvest '81
Prime Suspect '82
Six Pack '82
Ballad of Gregorio Cortez '83
Hard Traveling '85
My Science Project '85
What Comes Around '85
Nothing in Common '86
Undercover '87
Critters 2: The Main Course '88
It Takes Two '88
LBJ: The Early Years '88
Permanent Record '88
Who's Harry Crumb? '89
The Hot Spot '90
Short Time '90
Career Opportunities '91
The Chase '91
Conagher '91

Ellen Corby
It's a Wonderful Life '46
Forever Amber '47
I Remember Mama '48
Harriet Craig '50
Ma and Pa Kettle Go to Town '50
Angels in the Outfield '51
On Moonlight Bay '51
Illegal '55
All Mine to Give '56
Vertigo '58
The Strangler '64
The Glass Bottom Boat '66
The Invaders '67
Homecoming: A Christmas Story '71
Support Your Local Gunfighter '71
The Waltons: A Thanksgiving Story '73
A Day for Thanks on Walton's Mountain '82

Donna Corcoran
Angels in the Outfield '51
Don't Bother to Knock '52
Gypsy Colt '54

Kevin Corcoran
Old Yeller '57
The Shaggy Dog '59
Toby Tyler '59
Pollyanna '60
Mooncussers '62
Johnny Shiloh '63
Savage Sam '63
A Tiger Walks '64

Alex Cord
A Minute to Pray, A Second to Die '67
The Brotherhood '68
Stiletto '69
Inn of the Damned '74
Fire '77
Grayeagle '77
Sidewinder One '77
Goliath Awaits '81
Jungle Warriors '84
The Dirty Dozen: The Fatal Mission '88
The Uninvited '88
A Girl to Kill For '90
Street Asylum '90
Roots of Evil '91
C.I.A.: Code Name Alexa '92
To Be the Best '93

Mara Corday
Francis Joins the WACs '54
Tarantula '55
The Black Scorpion '57
The Giant Claw '57

Rita (Paula) Corday
The Leopard Man '43
The Falcon in Hollywood '44
The Body Snatcher '45
West of the Pecos '45
Sword of Monte Cristo '51
Because You're Mine '52
The Black Castle '52

Allan Corduner
Yentl '83
Mandela '87
Heart of Darkness '93

Annie Cordy
La Rupture '70
Le Chat '75

Raymond Cordy
A Nous la Liberte '31
Beauty and the Devil '50
Beauties of the Night '52

Brigitte Corey
The Fury of Hercules '61
Samson '61

Prof. Irwin Corey
How to Commit Marriage '69
Fairy Tales '76
Stuck on You '84
Jack '96

Isabel Corey
Bob le Flambeur '55
The Invincible Gladiator '63

Jeff Corey
My Friend Flicka '43
Hopalong Cassidy: Hoppy's Holiday '47
A Southern Yankee '48
Follow Me Quietly '49
Home of the Brave '49
The Nevadan '50
The Next Voice You Hear '50
Rawhide '50
Superman & the Mole Men '51
The Balcony '63
Lady in a Cage '64
Mickey One '65
The Boston Strangler '68

Corey ▶cont.

Butch Cassidy and the Sundance Kid '69
Beneath the Planet of the Apes '70
Getting Straight '70
Little Big Man '70
They Call Me Mr. Tibbs! '70
Catlow '71
The Premonition '75
Curse of the Black Widow '77
Moonshine County Express '77
Oh, God! '77
Wild Geese '78
Butch and Sundance: The Early Days '79
Up River '79
Sword & the Sorcerer '82
Conan the Destroyer '84
Creator '85
Messenger of Death '88
Payoff '91
Deception '92
Secret Ingredient '92
Sinatra '92
Color of Night '94
Surviving the Game '94

Wendell Corey
The Accused '48
The Search '48
Sorry, Wrong Number '48
Any Number Can Play '49
Holiday Affair '49
Harriet Craig '50
Great Missouri Raid '51
Rich, Young and Pretty '51
Rear Window '54
The Big Knife '55
The Rainmaker '56
Loving You '57
The Light in the Forest '58
Women of the Prehistoric Planet '66
The Astro-Zombies '67
Buckskin '68

Danny Corkill
Mrs. Soffel '84
D.A.R.Y.L. '85
Between Two Women '86

Anthony Corlan
Something for Everyone '70
Vampire Circus '71

Al Corley
Squeeze Play '79
Torchlight '85
Incident at Channel Q '86
A Kiss Goodnight '94

Pat Corley
The Two Worlds of Jenny Logan '79
Of Mice and Men '81
Night Shift '82
Silent Witness '85
Poker Alice '87
Mr. Destiny '90

Sharron Corley
New Jersey Drive '95
The Substitute '96

Maddie Corman
Seven Minutes in Heaven '86
The Adventures of Ford Fairlane '90
My New Gun '92

Roger Corman
The Godfather, Part 2 '74
The Godfather 1902-1959: The Complete Epic '81
State of Things '82
Swing Shift '84
The Silence of the Lambs '91
Philadelphia '93

Don Cornelius
No Way Back '74
Tapeheads '89

Ellie Cornell
Halloween 4: The Return of Michael Myers '88
Halloween 5: The Revenge of Michael Myers '89
Chips, the War Dog '90

Charlotte Cornwell
The Krays '90
White Hunter, Black Heart '90

Judy Cornwell
Think Dirty '70
Wuthering Heights '70
Santa Claus: The Movie '85
Persuasion '95

Georges Corraface
Impromptu '90
Not Without My Daughter '90
Christopher Columbus: The Discovery '92
Escape from L.A. '96

Mady Correll
Texas Masquerade '44
Monsieur Verdoux '47

Adrienne Corri
The River '51
Devil Girl from Mars '54
Make Me an Offer '55
Corridors of Blood '58
The Hellfire Club '61
The Tell-Tale Heart '62
A Clockwork Orange '71
Vampire Circus '71
Madhouse '74
Rosebud '75

Nick Corri
A Nightmare on Elm Street '84
Gotcha! '85
The Lawless Land '88
Tropical Snow '88
Slaves of New York '89
In the Heat of Passion '91

Sergio Corrieri
I Am Cuba '64
Memories of Underdevelopment '68

Lloyd Corrigan
The Lady in Question '40
Young Tom Edison '40
A Girl, a Guy and a Gob '41
Captive Wild Woman '43
Hitler's Children '43
Gambler's Choice '44
Since You Went Away '44
The Thin Man Goes Home '44
The Chase '46
Blondie Hits the Jackpot '49
Cavalry Charge '51
Ghost Chasers '51
Bowery Boys Meet the Monsters '54

Ray Corrigan
Country Gentlemen '36
Ghost Town Gold '36
Undersea Kingdom '36
Come On, Cowboys '37
Heart of the Rockies '37
Hit the Saddle '37
The Painted Stallion '37
Riders of the Whistling Skull '37
Roarin' Lead '37
The Trigger Trio '37
Wild Horse Rodeo '37
Heroes of the Hills '38
Outlaws of Sonora '38
Overland Stage Raiders '38
Pals of the Saddle '38
Purple Vigilantes '38
Santa Fe Stampede '38
Frontier Horizon '39
Lonely Trail/Three Texas Steers '39
Three Texas Steers '39
Wyoming Outlaw '39
Range Busters '40
Saturday Night Serials '40
Trailing Double Trouble '40
West of Pinto Basin '40
Fugitive Valley '41
Kid's Last Ride '41
Saddle Mountain Round-Up '41
Tonto Basin Outlaws '41
Trail of the Silver Spurs '41
Tumbledown Ranch in Arizona '41
Underground Rustlers '41
Arizona Stagecoach '42
Boot Hill Bandits '42
Rock River Renegades '42
Thunder River Feud '42
Black Market Rustlers '43
Cowboy Commandos '43
Land of Hunted Men '43
Renegade Girl '46
White Gorilla '47
Trail of Robin Hood '50
It! The Terror from Beyond Space '58

Shirley Corrigan
The Devil's Nightmare '71
Dr. Jekyll and the Wolfman '71

Aneta Corsaut
The Blob '58
The Toolbox Murders '78
Return to Mayberry '85

Silvana Corsini
Accatone! '61
Mamma Roma '62

Bud Cort
Sweet Charity '69
Brewster McCloud '70
Gas-s-s-s! '70
M*A*S*H '70
The Strawberry Statement '70
Harold and Maude '71
Why Shoot the Teacher '79
Die Laughing '80
Rumpelstiltskin '82
Hysterical '83
Love Letters '83
The Nightingale '83
Electric Dreams '84
Maria's Lovers '84
The Secret Diary of Sigmund Freud '84
Invaders from Mars '86
Love at Stake '87
The Chocolate War '88
Out of the Dark '88
Brain Dead '89
Going Under '91
Ted & Venus '93
Girl in the Cadillac '94

Rowena Cortes
Heroes Three '84
To Live and Die in Hong Kong '89

Joe Cortese
Family Enforcer '76
Windows '80
Evilspeak '82
Letting Go '85
Stalking Danger '86
Assault and Matrimony '87
Deadly Illusion '87
Python Wolf '88
The Closer '91
Ruby '92
To Protect and Serve '92
Born to Run '93

Valentina Cortese
Malaya '49
Les Miserables '52
The Barefoot Contessa '54
Juliet of the Spirits '65
First Love '70
Assassination of Trotsky '72
Brother Sun, Sister Moon '73
Day for Night '73
Kidnap Syndicate '76
Widow's Nest '77
When Time Ran Out '80
The Adventures of Baron Munchausen '89

Bella Cortez
The Giant of Metropolis '61
Vulcan God of Fire '62
Tor '64

Ricardo Cortez
The Pony Express '25
The Swan '25
The Sorrows of Satan '26
Mockery '27
Lost Zeppelin '29
The Phantom in the House '29
Behind Office Doors '31
Big Business Girl '31
Illicit '31
The Maltese Falcon '31
The Gentleman from California '37
Mr. Moto's Last Warning '39
Murder over New York '40
I Killed That Man '42
The Inner Circle '46
Last Hurrah '58

Bill Cosby
Man & Boy '71
To All My Friends on Shore '71
Uptown Saturday Night '74
Let's Do It Again '75
Mother, Jugs and Speed '76
Piece of the Action '77
California Suite '78
The Devil & Max Devlin '81
Leonard Part 6 '87
Ghost Dad '90
Jack '96

Howard Cosell
Bananas '71
Sleeper '73
Broadway Danny Rose '84
Casey at the Bat '85

James Cosmo
Stormy Monday '88
Braveheart '95
Emma '96

Ernest Cossart
Desire '36
The Great Ziegfeld '36
Three Smart Girls Grow Up '39
Kitty Foyle '40
Kings Row '41
Love from a Stranger '47

James Cossins
The Anniversary '68
Wuthering Heights '70
Dynasty of Fear '72

Marina Costa
The Final Executioner '83
Jungle Raiders '85

Robert Costanzo
Honeyboy '82
The Vegas Strip Wars '84
Die Hard 2: Die Harder '90
Delusion '91
Honeymoon in Vegas '92
The Cemetery Club '93
Man's Best Friend '93
Relentless 3 '93
Lady in Waiting '94
Ring of Fire 3: Lion Strike '94
For Better or Worse '95
Storybook '95

Dolores Costello
Little Lord Fauntleroy '36
Breaking the Ice '38
The Magnificent Ambersons '42

Don Costello
Whistling in the Dark '41
Mystery Man '44
Texas Masquerade '44
The Blue Dahlia '46

Elvis Costello
Americathon '79
No Surrender '86
Straight to Hell '87

Helene Costello
The Man on the Box '25
Don Juan '26

Lou Costello
One Night in the Tropics '40
Buck Privates '41
Hold That Ghost '41
In the Navy '41
Keep 'Em Flying '41
Pardon My Sarong '42
Ride 'Em Cowboy '42
Rio Rita '42
Who Done It? '42
Hit the Ice '43
In Society '44
Lost in a Harem '44
Abbott and Costello in Hollywood '45
Here Come the Co-Eds '45
The Naughty Nineties '45
Little Giant '46
The Time of Their Lives '46
Buck Privates Come Home '47
The Wistful Widow of Wagon Gap '47
Abbott and Costello Meet Frankenstein '48
Mexican Hayride '48
The Noose Hangs High '48
Abbott and Costello Meet the Killer, Boris Karloff '49
Africa Screams '49
Abbott and Costello in the Foreign Legion '50
Abbott and Costello Meet the Invisible Man '51
Comin' Round the Mountain '51
Abbott and Costello Meet Captain Kidd '52
Abbott and Costello Meet Dr. Jekyll and Mr. Hyde '52
Jack & the Beanstalk '52
Lost in Alaska '52
Abbott and Costello Go to Mars '53
Abbott and Costello Meet the Keystone Kops '54
The Best of Abbott & Costello Live '54
Hollywood Goes to War '54
Abbott and Costello Meet the Mummy '55
Dance with Me, Henry '56
The 30-Foot Bride of Candy Rock '59
The World of Abbott & Costello '64
Hollywood Clowns '85

Mariclare Costello
The Execution of Private Slovik '74
Conspiracy of Terror '75
All God's Children '80
Coward of the County '81
Skeezer '82
Heart of a Champion: The Ray Mancini Story '85

Ward Costello
The Gallant Hours '60
The City '76
MacArthur '77

John Costelloe
Billy Bathgate '91
Me and the Mob '94
Kazaam '96

Nicolas Coster
The Sporting Club '72
MacArthur '77
The Electric Horseman '79
Stir Crazy '80
The Solitary Man '82
Betsy's Wedding '90

George Costigan
Rita, Sue & Bob Too '87
The Hawk '93

Kevin Costner
Malibu Hot Summer '74
Chasing Dreams '81
Night Shift '82
Stacy's Knights '83
Table for Five '83
Testament '83
The Gunrunner '84
Shadows Run Black '84
Amazing Stories '85
American Flyers '85
Fandango '85
Silverado '85
No Way Out '87
The Untouchables '87
Bull Durham '88
Field of Dreams '89
Dances with Wolves '90
Revenge '90
JFK '91
Robin Hood: Prince of Thieves '91
The Bodyguard '92
A Perfect World '93
The War '94
Wyatt Earp '94
Waterworld '95
Tin Cup '96

Kami Cotler
The Waltons: A Thanksgiving Story '73
The Waltons: The Christmas Carol '80
A Day for Thanks on Walton's Mountain '82

Joseph Cotten
Citizen Kane '41
Lydia '41
Journey into Fear '42
The Magnificent Ambersons '42
Shadow of a Doubt '43
Gaslight '44
Since You Went Away '44
Duel in the Sun '46
The Farmer's Daughter '47
Portrait of Jennie '48
Beyond the Forest '49
The Third Man '49
Under Capricorn '49
September Affair '50
Walk Softly, Stranger '50
Niagara '52
Othello '52

From the Earth to the Moon '58
Hush, Hush, Sweet Charlotte '65
The Oscar '66
Tramplers '66
Brighty of the Grand Canyon '67
Hellbenders '67
White Comanche '67
Petulia '68
The Passing of Evil '70
Tora! Tora! Tora! '70
The Abominable Dr. Phibes '71
Lady Frankenstein '72
Torture Chamber of Baron Blood '72
Soylent Green '73
The Big Push '75
The Lindbergh Kidnapping Case '76
Airport '77 '77
Return to Fantasy Island '77
Twilight's Last Gleaming '77
Perfect Crime '78
Casino '80
The Hearse '80
Screamers '80
Survivor '80
Churchill and the Generals '81
Heaven's Gate '81
Delusion '84

Fanny Cottencon
Special Police '85
Window Shopping '86

Catherine Cotter
Outlaws of the Range '36
Pinto Rustlers '36

Ralph Cotterill
Burke & Wills '85
Howling 3: The Marsupials '87
Starship '87
Bad Boy Bubby '93

Oliver Cotton
Eleni '85
Robin Hood...The Legend: Herne's Son '85
Christopher Columbus: The Discovery '92

Paul Coufos
The Lost Empire '83
Busted Up '86
City of Shadows '86
Food of the Gods: Part 2 '88
Thunderground '89
Boxcar Blues '90
Dragonfight '92
Mortal Danger '94

George Coulouris
The Lady in Question '40
Citizen Kane '41
This Land is Mine '43
Watch on the Rhine '43
Master Race '44
Mr. Skeffington '44
None But the Lonely Heart '44
Lady On a Train '45
A Song to Remember '45
Where There's Life '47
A Southern Yankee '48
Doctor in the House '53
The Runaway Bus '54
Race for Life '55
The Skull '65
Arabesque '66
Tower of Evil '72
Papillon '73
The Stranger '73
Murder on the Orient Express '74
The Tempter '74
The Long Good Friday '79

Keith Coulouris
Dead Man's Revenge '93
Beastmaster 3: The Eye of Braxus '95

Bernie Coulson
The Accused '88
Eddie and the Cruisers 2: Eddie Lives! '89
Adventures in Spying '92

Catherine Coulson
Twin Peaks '90
Twin Peaks '90

Nicole Courcel
Le Cas du Dr. Laurent '57
Sundays & Cybele '62

Hazel Court
Dear Murderer '47
Ghost Ship '53
Devil Girl from Mars '54
The Curse of Frankenstein '57
Hour of Decision '57
Doctor Blood's Coffin '62
Premature Burial '62
The Raven '63
Masque of the Red Death '65
Masque of the Red Death/ Premature Burial '65

Jason Court
Grandview U.S.A. '84
A Night in the Life of Jimmy Reardon '88

Tom Courtenay
The Loneliness of the Long Distance Runner '62
Billy Liar '63
Doctor Zhivago '65
King Rat '65
Operation Crossbow '65
Night of the Generals '67
Dandy in Aspic '68
Catch Me a Spy '71
One Day in the Life of Ivan Denisovich '71
I Heard the Owl Call My Name '73
The Dresser '83
Happy New Year '87
Leonard Part 6 '87
Let Him Have It '91
The Last Butterfly '92
The Old Curiosity Shop '94

Jerome Courtland
Battleground '49
Man from Colorado '49
Tokyo Joe '49
Santa Fe '51
The Texas Rangers '51
Tonka '58
Tharus Son of Attila '87

Alex Courtney
Enter the Ninja '81
Fatal Pulse '88

Chuck Courtney
Meteor Monster '57
Billy the Kid Versus Dracula '66

Inez Courtney
Let's Sing Again '36
The Reckless Way '36
Suzy '36
The Thirteenth Man '37

Brian Cousins
Longtime Companion '90
Invisible: The Chronicles of Benjamin Knight '93
Mandroid '93

Christian Cousins
Danielle Steel's Heartbeat '93
Twinsitters '95

Jerome Cowan
The Saint Strikes Back '39
The Great Lie '41
The Maltese Falcon '41
Who Done It? '42
Silver Spurs '43
Fog Island '45
Blondie Knows Best '46
The Perfect Marriage '46
Cry Wolf '47
Riff-Raff '47
June Bride '48
Blondie Hits the Jackpot '49
The West Point Story '50
Have Rocket Will Travel '59

Noel Coward
Hearts of the World '18
In Which We Serve '43
Paris When It Sizzles '64
The Italian Job '69

Bruce Cowling
Battleground '49
The Stratton Story '49
Cause for Alarm '51
The Painted Hills '51

Nicola Cowper
Winter Flight '84
Dreamchild '85
Transmutations '85
Lionheart '87
Journey to the Center of the Earth '88

Alan Cox
Young Sherlock Holmes '85
An Awfully Big Adventure '94

Brian Cox
In Celebration '75
Pope John Paul II '84
Silent Scream '84
Manhunter '86
Hidden Agenda '90
Secret Weapon '90
Murder by Moonlight '91
The Lost Language of Cranes '92
Sharpe's Eagle '93
Sharpe's Rifles '93
Rob Roy '95
Chain Reaction '96

Courteney Cox
Misfits of Science '85
Masters of the Universe '87
Cocoon: The Return '88
Down Twisted '89
The Prize Pulitzer '89
Curiosity Kills '90
Mr. Destiny '90
Blue Desert '91
Battling for Baby '92
Shaking the Tree '92
Ace Ventura: Pet Detective '93
The Opposite Sex and How to Live With Them '93
Sketch Artist 2: Hands That See '94

Jennifer Elise Cox
The Brady Bunch Movie '95
A Very Brady Sequel '96

Mitchell Cox
Red Snow '91
Rule #3 '93
A.P.E.X. '94

Richard Cox
King of the Mountain '81
The Vindicator '85
Zombie High '87
Street Justice '89

Ronny Cox
Deliverance '72
Mind Snatchers '72
The Connection '73
Who Is the Black Dahlia? '75
Bound for Glory '76
Gray Lady Down '77
Lost Legacy: A Girl Called Hatter Fox '77
Our Town '77
Harper Valley P.T.A. '78
The Onion Field '79
Last Song '80
Fallen Angel '81
Taps '81
The Beast Within '82
Some Kind of Hero '82
Two of a Kind '82
When Hell Was in Session '82
Tangiers '83
Beverly Hills Cop '84
Kavik the Wolf Dog '84
Raw Courage '84
Reckless Disregard '84
Vision Quest '85
Hollywood Vice Sqaud '86
The Abduction of Kari Swenson '87
Beverly Hills Cop 2 '87
RoboCop '87
Steele Justice '87
Target: Favorite Son '87
The FBI Murders '88
Scandal in a Small Town '88
Captain America '89
One Man Force '89
Loose Cannons '90
Martians Go Home! '90
Total Recall '90
Scissors '91

Ruth Cox
Swap Meet '79
The Attic '80

Wally Cox
State Fair '62
Spencer's Mountain '63
Bedford Incident '65
Morituri '65
The One and Only, Genuine, Original Family Band '68
The Boatniks '70
The Barefoot Executive '71

Peter Coyote
Die Laughing '80
Tell Me a Riddle '80
The People vs. Jean Harris '81
Southern Comfort '81
Endangered Species '82
E.T.: The Extra-Terrestrial '82
Cross Creek '83
Strangers Kiss '83
Timerider '83
Heartbreakers '84
Slayground '84
Hitchhiker 2 '85
The Jagged Edge '85
Legend of Billie Jean '85
The Blue Yonder '86
Baja Oklahoma '87
Echoes in the Darkness '87
A Man in Love '87
Outrageous Fortune '87
Stacking '87
Best Kept Secrets '88
Out '88
Heart of Midnight '89
The Man Inside '90
Crooked Hearts '91
Exposure '91
Bitter Moon '92
Keeper of the City '92
Breach of Conduct '94
Kika '94
That Eye, The Sky '94
Buffalo Girls '95
Dalva '95
Moonlight and Valentino '95
Unforgettable '96

Buster Crabbe
Buffalo Stampede '33
Tarzan the Fearless '33
To the Last Man '33
Desert Gold '36
Drift Fence '36
Flash Gordon: Rocketship '36
Rocketship '36
Forlorn River '37
Flash Gordon: Mars Attacks the World '38
Red Barry '38
Buck Rogers Conquers the Universe '39
Destination Saturn '39
Flash Gordon Conquers the Universe '40
Space Soldiers Conquer the Universe '40
Thundering Gunslingers '40
Billy the Kid Trapped '42
Jungle Siren '42
Law and Order '42
The Mysterious Rider '42
Wildcat '42
Devil Riders '44
Frontier Outlaws '44
Nabonga '44
Oath of Vengeance '44
Rustler's Hideout '44
Wild Horse Phantom '44
Border Badmen '45
Gangster's Den '45
His Brother's Ghost '45
Lightning Raiders '45
Shadows of Death '45
Western Double Feature 7: Wild Bill & Crabbe '45
Outlaw of the Plains '46
Prairie Badmen '46
Swamp Fire '46
The Last of the Redmen '47
Sea Hound '47
Pirates of the High Seas '50
King of the Congo '52
Arizona Raiders '65
Swim Team '79
Alien Dead '85
The Original Flash Gordon Collection '91

Ruth Cracknell
Island Trader '71
Alice to Nowhere '86

Daniel Craig
The Power of One '92
A Kid in King Arthur's Court '95

Diane Craig
Ned Kelly '70
The Mango Tree '77
Roses Bloom Twice '77
All the Rivers Run '84

Helen Craig
The Snake Pit '48
They Live by Night '49

James Craig
Thunder Trail '37
Kitty Foyle '40
Winners of the West '40
The Devil & Daniel Webster '41
Valley of the Sun '42
The Human Comedy '43
Seven Miles from Alcatraz/Flight from Glory '43
Our Vines Have Tender Grapes '45
Drums in the Deep South '51
Cyclops '56
Naked in the Sun '57
Man or Gun '58
The Devil's Brigade '68
The Tormentors '80s

Michael Craig
Sea of Sand '58
The Silent Enemy '58
Sapphire '59
Mysterious Island '61
Stolen Hours '63
Sandra of a Thousand Delights '65
Star! '68
Lola '69
Vault of Horror '73
Inn of the Damned '74
Ride a Wild Pony '75
Night of the Assassin '77
Roses Bloom Twice '77
The Irishman '78
Escape 2000 '81
Robin Hood...The Legend: Herne's Son '85

Wendy Craig
The Servant '63
The Nanny '65

Yvonne Craig
The Young Land '59
It Happened at the World's Fair '63
Kissin' Cousins '64
Mars Needs Women '66
Digging Up Business '91

Jeanne Crain
Leave Her to Heaven '45
State Fair '45
A Letter to Three Wives '49
Pinky '49
Cheaper by the Dozen '50
People Will Talk '51
Man Without a Star '55
Fastest Gun Alive '56
Nefertiti, Queen of the Nile '64
The Night God Screamed '80s

Grant Cramer
Hardbodies '84
Killer Klowns from Outer Space '88
Leapin' Leprechauns '95

Joey Cramer
Flight of the Navigator '86
Stone Fox '87

Marc Cramer
First Yank into Tokyo '45
Isle of the Dead '45

Richard Cramer
The Fatal Glass of Beer '33
Frontier Justice '35
Speed Reporter '36
Santa Fe Bound '37
Saps at Sea '40

Barbara Crampton
Body Double '84
Re-Animator '84
Fraternity Vacation '85
From Beyond '86
Kidnapped '87
Puppet Master '89
Trancers 2: The Return of Jack Deth '90
Robot Wars '93
Castle Freak '95

Bob Crane
Return to Peyton Place '61
Superdad '73
Gus '76

Norma Crane
Tea and Sympathy '56

Crane ▶cont.

They Call Me Mr. Tibbs! '70
Fiddler on the Roof '71

Richard Crane
Dynamite '49
Cavalry Charge '51
Winning of the West '53
Rocky Jones, Space Ranger '54
Rocky Jones, Space Ranger: Renegade Satellite '54
Guns Don't Argue '57
The Devil's Partner '58

Kenneth Cranham
Brother Sun, Sister Moon '73
Danger UXB '81
Chocolat '88
Hellbound: Hellraiser 2 '88
Stealing Heaven '88
Monkey Boy '90
Prospero's Books '91
Tale of a Vampire '92
Under Suspicion '92

Bryan Cranston
Dead Space '90
The Companion '94

Nick Cravat
The Flame & the Arrow '50
Crimson Pirate '52
The Scalphunters '68

Noel Cravat
G-Men vs. the Black Dragon '43
Pirate Ship '49

Frank Craven
City for Conquest '40
Dreaming Out Loud '40
Our Town '40
In This Our Life '42
Keeper of the Flame '42
Pittsburgh '42
Son of Dracula '43
Jack London '44

James Craven
Green Archer '40
Sherlock Holmes and the Secret Weapon '42
Today I Hang '42
D-Day on Mars '45

Matt Craven
Till Death Do Us Part '72
Happy Birthday to Me '81
Agent on Ice '86
Palais Royale '88
Chattahoochee '89
Jacob's Ladder '90
Smokescreen '90
A Few Good Men '92
K2: The Ultimate High '92
Indian Summer '93
Double Cross '94
Breach of Trust '95
Bulletproof Heart '95
Crimson Tide '95
Kingfish: A Story of Huey P. Long '95
White Tiger '95
The Juror '96

Mimi Craven
Open Fire '94
Midnight Heat '95

Wes Craven
Fangoria's Weekend of Horrors '86
Wes Craven's New Nightmare '94

Andrew Crawford
Dear Murderer '47
The Gay Lady '49

Anne Crawford
Night Beat '48
Tony Draws a Horse '51
Knights of the Round Table '53

Broderick Crawford
Eternally Yours '39
The Real Glory '39
Seven Sinners '40
Slightly Honorable '40
The Texas Rangers Ride Again '40
I Married a Witch '42
The Time of Your Life '48
All the King's Men '49
Born Yesterday '50
Last of the Comanches '52
Lone Star '52
Human Desire '54
Not as a Stranger '55
The Swindle '55
Between Heaven and Hell '56
Fastest Gun Alive '56
Goliath and the Dragon '61
The Castilian '63
The Oscar '66
Vulture '67
The Tattered Web '71
Yin & Yang of Mr. Go '71
Embassy '72
Terror in the Wax Museum '73
Hunter '77
The Private Files of J. Edgar Hoover '77
Express to Terror '79
A Little Romance '79
Dark Forces '83
Proof of the Man '84
Ransom Money '88
Upper Crust '88

H. Marion Crawford
Man on the Run '49
The Castle of Fu Manchu '68
Kiss and Kill '68

Joan Crawford
The Unknown '27
Our Dancing Daughters '28
Our Modern Maidens '29
Kings, Queens, Jokers '30s
Dance Fools Dance '31
Laughing Sinners '31
Possessed '31
Grand Hotel '32
Rain '32
Dancing Lady '33
The Lost Stooges '33
Today We Live '33
Chained '34
Sadie McKee '34
Forsaking All Others '35
I Live My Life '35
The Gorgeous Hussy '36
Love on the Run '36
The Bride Wore Red '37
The Last of Mrs. Cheyney '37
Mannequin '37
The Shining Hour '38
The Women '39
Strange Cargo '40
Susan and God '40
When Ladies Meet '41
A Woman's Face '41
Reunion in France '42
Above Suspicion '43
Hollywood Canteen '44
Mildred Pierce '45
Humoresque '46
The Possessed '47
Flamingo Road '49
It's a Great Feeling '49
Harriet Craig '50
Sudden Fear '52
Johnny Guitar '53
Torch Song '53
Queen Bee '55
Autumn Leaves '56
The Best of Everything '59
What Ever Happened to Baby Jane? '62
Fatal Confinement '64
Strait-Jacket '64
Berserk! '67
Night Gallery '69
Hollywood Outtakes & Rare Footage '83

John Crawford
The Invisible Monster '50
Zombies of the Stratosphere '52
John Paul Jones '59
Red Line 7000 '65
The Severed Arm '73
Hard Knocks

Johnny Crawford
Black Beauty/Courage of Black Beauty '57
Courage of Black Beauty '57
Indian Paint '64
Village of the Giants '65
El Dorado '67
The Great Texas Dynamite Chase '76
Outlaw Blues '77
Kenny Rogers as the Gambler, Part 2: The Adventure Continues '83
The Gambler Returns: The Luck of the Draw '93

Katherine Crawford
The Doomsday Flight '66
Walk in the Spring Rain '70
Riding with Death '76

Kathryn Crawford
King of the Rodeo '28
The Concentratin' Kid '30
Mountain Justice '30

Michael Crawford
The Knack '65
A Funny Thing Happened on the Way to the Forum '66
How I Won the War '67
Hello, Dolly! '69
Alice's Adventures in Wonderland '72
Condorman '81

Wayne Crawford
Barracuda '78
Jake Speed '86
The Evil Below '87
Quiet Thunder '87
White Ghost '88
Headhunter '89
Rebel Storm '90
Crime Lords '91
American Cop '94

Laird Cregar
I Wake Up Screaming '41
The Black Swan '42
Joan of Paris '42
This Gun for Hire '42
Heaven Can Wait '43
Hello, Frisco, Hello '43

Joseph Crehan
Stanley and Livingstone '39
Star Reporter '39
Music in My Heart '40
Hands Across the Border '43
Meeting at Midnight '44
Night Time in Nevada '48
Red Desert '50

Francis Creighton
The Malibu Beach Vampires '91
Barcelona '94

Bruno Cremer
The 317th Platoon '65
Is Paris Burning? '68
Sorcerer '77
A Simple Story '79
Josepha '82
Menage '86

Richard Crenna
Pride of St. Louis '52
Our Miss Brooks '56
The Sand Pebbles '66
Wait Until Dark '67
Star! '68
Marooned '69
Doctors' Wives '70
Catlow '71
Ride to Glory '71
Thief '71
Breakheart Pass '76
War Between the Tates '76
Devil Dog: The Hound of Hell '78
The Evil '78
Wild Horse Hank '79
Death Ship '80
Stone Cold Dead '80
Body Heat '81
First Blood '82
Table for Five '83
The Flamingo Kid '84
Broken Badge '85
Rambo: First Blood, Part 2 '85
Summer Rental '85
A Case of Deadly Force '86
On Wings of Eagles '86
Rambo 3 '88
The Hillside Strangler '89
Leviathan '89
Last Flight Out: A True Story '90
Montana '90
Intruders '92
Hot Shots! Part Deux '93
Jade '95
A Pyromaniac's Love Story '95
Sabrina '95

Laura Hope Crews
Camille '36
Angel '37
Gone with the Wind '39
The Rains Came '39

Wendy Crewson
Skullduggery '79
Mazes and Monsters '82
Mark of Cain '84
Hobo's Christmas '87
Buffalo Jump '90
The Doctor '91
Spies, Lies and Naked Thighs '91
Folks! '92
The Good Son '93
Corrina, Corrina '94
The Santa Clause '94

Bernard Cribbins
The Wrong Arm of the Law '63
The Railway Children '70
The Adventures of Picasso '80

Ed Crick
Eye of the Eagle '87
Future Hunters '88

Missy Crider
A Boy Called Hate '95
Powder '95

Lawrence Criner
Gang War '40
Miracle in Harlem '48

Donald Crisp
Home Sweet Home '14
The Birth of a Nation '15
Broken Blossoms '19
The Black Pirate '26
Stand and Deliver '28
Svengali '31
Red Dust '32
Little Minister '34
Mutiny on the Bounty '35
Beloved Enemy '36
The Charge of the Light Brigade '36
A Woman Rebels '36
That Certain Woman '37
Dawn Patrol '38
Jezebel '38
The Sisters '38
Oklahoma Kid '39
The Old Maid '39
The Private Lives of Elizabeth & Essex '39
Wuthering Heights '39
Brother Orchid '40
City for Conquest '40
Knute Rockne: All American '40
The Sea Hawk '40
Dr. Jekyll and Mr. Hyde '41
How Green Was My Valley '41
Lassie, Come Home '43
The Adventures of Mark Twain '44
National Velvet '44
The Uninvited '44
Son of Lassie '45
The Valley of Decision '45
Ramrod '47
The Hills of Home '48
Challenge to Lassie '49
Home Town Story '51
Prince Valiant '54
The Long Gray Line '55
The Man from Laramie '55
Last Hurrah '58
A Dog of Flanders '59
Pollyanna '60
Greyfriars Bobby '61
Spencer's Mountain '63

Linda Cristal
Perfect Furlough '59
Two Rode Together '61
Mr. Majestyk '74
The Dead Don't Die '75
Hughes & Harlow: Angels in Hell '77
Midnight Auto Supply '78

Perla Cristal
White Comanche '67
The Christmas Kid '68
A Witch Without a Broom '68
The Fury of the Wolfman '70

Anthony Crivello
The Lost Capone '90
Frankenstein Sings...The Movie '95

Karlene Crockett
Eyes of Fire '84
Massive Retaliation '85
Return '88

Peter Croft
King of the Damned '36
O.H.M.S. '37

Jonathan Crombie
Anne of Green Gables '85
Bullies '86
The Housekeeper '86
Anne of Avonlea '87
Cafe Romeo '91
The Good Fight '92

Peter Crombie
Smooth Talker '90
Seven '95

James Cromwell
A Christmas Without Snow '80
Spraggue '84
The Babe '92
Romeo Is Bleeding '93
Babe '95
Eraser '96

Richard Cromwell
The Strange Love of Molly Louvain '32
The Lives of a Bengal Lancer '35
The Wrong Road '37
Young Mr. Lincoln '39
Riot Squad '41
Baby Face Morgan '42

Claudia Cron
Hit & Run '82
Running Brave '83

Laurel Cronin
Beethoven '92
Housesitter '92

Hume Cronyn
The Phantom of the Opera '43
Shadow of a Doubt '43
Lifeboat '44
The Seventh Cross '44
The Postman Always Rings Twice '46
Ziegfeld Follies '46
People Will Talk '51
A Doll's House '59
Sunrise at Campobello '60
Cleopatra '63
The Arrangement '69
There was a Crooked Man '70
Conrack '74
The Parallax View '74
Honky Tonk Freeway '81
Rollover '81
The World According to Garp '82
Gin Game '84
Impulse '84
Brewster's Millions '85
Cocoon '85
*batteries not included '87
Foxfire '87
Cocoon: The Return '88
Age Old Friends '89
Day One '89
Broadway Bound '92
To Dance with the White Dog '93
Camilla '94

Tandy Cronyn
Twisted '86
Age Old Friends '89
Getting Out '94

Leland Crooke
Dead Man Walking '88
Scorchers '92

Annette Crosbie
Six Wives of Henry VIII '70s
Ordeal by Innocence '84

Bing Crosby
King of Jazz '30
Reaching for the Moon '31
Going Hollywood '33
We're Not Dressing '34
Rhythm on the Range '36
Waikiki Wedding '37
Rhythm on the River '40
The Road to Singapore '40
Birth of the Blues '41
The Road to Zanzibar '41
Holiday Inn '42
The Road to Morocco '42
Star Spangled Rhythm '42
Going My Way '44
Here Come the Waves '44
Strictly G.I. '44
The Bells of St. Mary's '45
Blue Skies '46

The Road to Utopia *'46*
My Favorite Brunette *'47*
The Road to Rio *'47*
Welcome Stranger *'47*
Emperor Waltz *'48*
A Connecticut Yankee in King Arthur's Court *'49*
Mr. Music *'50*
Riding High *'50*
Here Comes the Groom *'51*
Just for You *'52*
The Road to Bali *'53*
Country Girl *'54*
Hollywood Goes to War *'54*
White Christmas *'54*
High Society *'56*
Let's Make Love *'60*
The Road to Lebanon *'60*
The Road to Hong Kong *'62*
Robin and the 7 Hoods *'64*
That's Entertainment *'74*

Cathy Lee Crosby
Coach *'78*
The Dark *'79*
Roughnecks *'80*
World War III *'86*

David Crosby
Backdraft *'91*
Thunderheart *'92*

Denise Crosby
48 Hrs. *'82*
Curse of the Pink Panther *'83*
Desert Hearts *'86*
The Eliminators *'86*
Arizona Heat *'87*
Star Trek the Next Generation: Encounter at Farpoint *'87*
Miracle Mile *'89*
Pet Sematary *'89*
Skin Deep *'89*
Dolly Dearest *'92*
Red Shoe Diaries 2: Double Dare *'92*
Desperate Crimes *'93*
Black Water *'94*
Star Trek the Next Generation, the Final Episode: All Good Things... *'94*
Mutant Species *'95*
Relative Fear *'95*

Gary Crosby
Girl Happy *'65*
Justin Morgan Had a Horse *'81*
Music Shoppe *'82*
Night Stalker *'87*
Chill Factor *'90*

Lucinda Crosby
Naked Cage *'86*
Blue Movies *'88*

Mary Crosby
Last Plane Out *'83*
Ice Pirates *'84*
Stagecoach *'86*
Deadly Innocence *'88*
Quicker Than the Eye *'88*
Tapeheads *'89*
Body Chemistry *'90*
Corporate Affairs *'90*
Eating *'90*
The Berlin Conspiracy *'91*
Desperate Motives *'92*

Henrietta Crosman
Charlie Chan's Secret *'35*
Personal Property *'37*

Ben Cross
Chariots of Fire *'81*
The Flame Trees of Thika *'81*
Coming Out of the Ice *'82*
The Assisi Underground *'84*
The Far Pavilions *'84*
Steal the Sky *'88*
The Unholy *'88*
Paperhouse *'89*
The Jeweller's Shop *'90*
Nightlife *'90*
Dark Shadows: Episode 1 *'91*
Diamond Fleece *'92*
Live Wire *'92*
Cold Sweat *'93*
The Criminal Mind *'93*
The Ascent *'94*
Haunted Symphony *'94*
First Knight *'95*
Temptress *'95*

Dennis Cross
Crime of Passion *'57*
How to Make a Monster *'58*

Harley Cross
Where Are the Children? *'85*
The Believers *'87*
Cohen and Tate *'88*
The Fly 2 *'89*
Stanley and Iris *'90*
To Dance with the White Dog *'93*

Rupert Crosse
Shadows *'60*
The Reivers *'69*

Syd Crossley
That Certain Thing *'28*
The Deputy Drummer *'35*

Scatman Crothers
Yes, Sir, Mr. Bones *'51*
Between Heaven and Hell *'56*
Lady in a Cage *'64*
The Patsy *'64*
Bloody Mama *'70*
The Great White Hope *'70*
The King of Marvin Gardens *'72*
Detroit 9000 *'73*
Black Belt Jones *'74*
Truck Turner *'74*
One Flew Over the Cuckoo's Nest *'75*
Streetfight *'75*
Chesty Anderson USN *'76*
The Shootist *'76*
Silver Streak *'76*
Stay Hungry *'76*
Mean Dog Blues *'78*
Scavenger Hunt *'79*
Bronco Billy *'80*
The Shining *'80*
Deadly Eyes *'82*
Zapped! *'82*
Twilight Zone: The Movie *'83*
Two of a Kind *'83*
The Journey of Natty Gann *'85*

Lindsay Crouse
All the President's Men *'76*
Eleanor & Franklin *'76*
Between the Lines *'77*
Slap Shot *'77*
Prince of the City *'81*
Summer Solstice *'81*
The Verdict *'82*
Daniel *'83*
Iceman *'84*
Places in the Heart *'84*
House of Games *'87*
Communion *'89*
Desperate Hours *'90*
Chantilly Lace *'93*
Final Appeal *'93*
Being Human *'94*
Bye Bye, Love *'94*
Parallel Lives *'94*
The Indian in the Cupboard *'95*
The Arrival *'96*
The Juror *'96*

Ashley Crow
Final Appeal *'93*
Little Big League *'94*

Emilia Crow
Grand Tour: Disaster in Time *'92*
Hitz *'92*

Graham Crowden
If... *'69*
Naughty Knights *'71*
Romance with a Double Bass *'74*
Britannia Hospital *'82*
Code Name: Emerald *'85*
The Company of Wolves *'85*
Out of Africa *'85*
Monsignor Quixote *'91*

Russell Crowe
Proof *'91*
The Crossing *'92*
The Efficiency Expert *'92*
Romper Stomper *'92*
The Silver Stallion: King of the Wild Brumbies *'93*
For the Moment *'94*
The Quick and the Dead *'94*
The Sum of Us *'94*
Virtuosity *'95*

Josephine Crowell
Hearts of the World *'18*
The Greatest Question *'19*
The Man Who Laughs *'27*

Kathleen Crowley
The Female Jungle *'56*
Westward Ho, the Wagons! *'56*
The Rebel Set *'59*

Pat Crowley
Forever Female *'53*
Red Garters *'54*
Hollywood or Bust *'56*
Wild Women of Wongo *'59*
Force of Evil *'77*
Return to Fantasy Island *'77*

Tom Cruise
Endless Love *'81*
Taps *'81*
Losin' It *'82*
All the Right Moves *'83*
The Outsiders *'83*
Risky Business *'83*
The Color of Money *'86*
Legend *'86*
Top Gun *'86*
Cocktail *'88*
Rain Man *'88*
Born on the Fourth of July *'89*
Days of Thunder *'90*
Far and Away *'92*
A Few Good Men *'92*
The Firm *'93*
Interview with the Vampire *'94*
Mission: Impossible *'96*

Rosalie Crutchley
Make Me an Offer *'55*
Six Wives of Henry VIII *'70s*
Creatures the World Forgot *'70*
Wuthering Heights *'70*
Elizabeth R *'72*
Night of the Laughing Dead *'75*
The Hunchback of Notre Dame *'82*
Eleni *'85*
Monsignor Quixote *'91*
The Franchise Affair

Abigail Cruttenden
Kipperbang *'82*
Intimate Contact *'87*

Alexis Cruz
Gryphon *'88*
The Old Man and the Sea *'90*
Stargate *'94*
Larry McMurtry's Streets of Laredo *'95*

Celia Cruz
The Mambo Kings *'92*
The Perez Family *'94*

Penelope Cruz
Belle Epoque *'92*
Jamon, Jamon *'93*

Raymond Cruz
Vietnam War Story 3 *'89*
Clear and Present Danger *'94*
The Substitute *'96*
Up Close and Personal *'96*

Jon Cryer
No Small Affair *'84*
Noon Wine *'84*
Pretty in Pink *'86*
Dudes *'87*
Hiding Out *'87*
Morgan Stewart's Coming Home *'87*
O.C. and Stiggs *'87*
Superman 4: The Quest for Peace *'87*
Hot Shots! *'91*
Heads *'93*

Billy Crystal
The Best of Soap: Jessica's Wonderful Life *'70s*
The Best of Soap: Who Killed Peter? *'77*
Rabbit Test *'78*
Breaking Up Is Hard to Do *'79*
Enola Gay: The Men, the Mission, the Atomic Bomb *'80*
The Three Little Pigs *'84*
Running Scared *'86*
The Princess Bride *'87*
Throw Momma from the Train *'87*
Memories of Me *'88*
When Harry Met Sally... *'89*
City Slickers *'91*
Mr. Saturday Night *'92*
City Slickers 2: The Legend of Curly's Gold *'94*
Forget Paris *'95*

Gyorgy Cserhalmi
Hungarian Rhapsody *'78*
Mephisto *'81*

Xavier Cugat
You Were Never Lovelier *'42*
Two Girls and a Sailor *'44*
Holiday in Mexico *'46*
A Date with Judy *'48*
Neptune's Daughter *'49*

Kieran Culkin
Home Alone *'90*
Father of the Bride *'91*
Home Alone 2: Lost in New York *'92*
Nowhere to Run *'93*
My Summer Story *'94*
Father of the Bride Part II *'95*

Macaulay Culkin
Rocket Gibraltar *'88*
See You in the Morning *'89*
Uncle Buck *'89*
Home Alone *'90*
Jacob's Ladder *'90*
My Girl *'91*
Only the Lonely *'91*
Home Alone 2: Lost in New York *'92*
George Balanchine's The Nutcracker *'93*
The Good Son *'93*
Getting Even with Dad *'94*
The Pagemaster *'94*
Richie Rich *'94*

Brett Cullen
Dead Solid Perfect *'88*
In a Stranger's Hand *'92*
Leaving Normal *'92*
Prehysteria *'93*
A Kiss Goodnight *'94*
Apollo 13 *'95*
Something to Talk About *'95*

Max Cullen
Hard Knocks *'80*
Lightning Jack *'94*

John Cullum
The Day After *'83*
The Prodigal *'83*
Marie *'85*
Morgan Stewart's Coming Home *'87*
Sweet Country *'87*
Glory *'89*
Ambition *'91*

Joseph Culp
Dream Lover *'85*
The Arrival *'90*

Robert Culp
Sammy, the Way-Out Seal *'62*
PT 109 *'63*
Demon with a Glass Hand *'64*
Bob & Carol & Ted & Alice *'69*
A Name for Evil *'70*
Hannie Caulder *'72*
The Castaway Cowboy *'74*
Inside Out *'75*
Flood! *'76*
Great Scout & Cathouse Thursday *'76*
Sky Riders *'76*
Goldengirl *'79*
Hot Rod *'79*
The Night the City Screamed *'80*
Killjoy *'81*
Her Life as a Man *'83*
Calendar Girl Murders *'84*
The Key to Rebecca *'85*
Turk 182! *'85*
The Blue Lightning *'86*
The Gladiator *'86*
Big Bad Mama 2 *'87*
Pucker Up and Bark Like a Dog *'89*
Silent Night, Deadly Night 3: Better Watch Out! *'89*
Voyage of Terror: The Achille Lauro Affair *'90*
Murderous Vision *'91*
Timebomb *'91*
The Pelican Brief *'93*
Xtro 3: Watch the Skies *'95*

Michael Culver
Fast Kill *'73*
The Devil's Web *'74*
Conduct Unbecoming *'75*
Philby, Burgess and MacLean: Spy Scandal of the Century *'84*
Alamut Ambush *'86*
Deadly Recruits *'86*
The Green Man *'91*

Roland Culver
The Day Will Dawn *'42*
Secret Mission *'42*
Spitfire *'42*
On Approval *'44*
Dead of Night *'45*
Down to Earth *'47*
Singapore *'47*
Emperor Waltz *'48*
The Great Lover *'49*
The Obsessed *'51*
Encore *'52*
Betrayed *'54*

Ji Tu Cumbuka
Mandingo *'75*
Glitch! *'88*
Midnight Edition *'93*

Alan Cumming
Bernard and the Genie *'90s*
Second Best *'94*
Circle of Friends *'94*
Goldeneye *'95*
Emma *'96*

Dorothy Cumming
King of Kings *'27*
The Wind *'28*
Applause *'29*

Constance Cummings
Criminal Code *'31*
Night After Night *'32*
The Foreman Went to France *'42*
This England *'42*
Blithe Spirit *'45*
The Battle of the Sexes *'60*

Irving Cummings
Uncle Tom's Cabin *'14*
Sex *'20*
The Saphead *'21*

Quinn Cummings
Night Terror *'76*
The Goodbye Girl *'77*
Intimate Strangers *'77*
The Babysitter *'80*

Robert Cummings
Arizona Mahoney *'36*
Desert Gold *'36*
The Texans *'38*
Everything Happens at Night *'39*
Three Smart Girls Grow Up *'39*
One Night in the Tropics *'40*
The Devil & Miss Jones *'41*
It Started with Eve *'41*
Kings Row *'41*
Moon over Miami *'41*
Saboteur *'42*
Forever and a Day *'43*
The Chase *'46*
Lost Moment *'47*
The Accused *'48*
Reign of Terror *'49*
Tell It to the Judge *'49*
Dial "M" for Murder *'54*
Lucky Me *'54*
My Geisha *'62*
Beach Party *'63*
The Carpetbaggers *'64*
Promise Her Anything *'66*
Five Golden Dragons *'67*

Susan Cummings
Swamp Women *'55*
Verboten! *'59*

Eli Cummins
Dakota *'88*
Harley *'90*

Greg Cummins
Dead End City *'88*
Action U.S.A. *'89*
Caged Fury *'90*

Gregory Scott Cummins
Lone Justice 2 *'93*
Watchers 3 *'94*
The Last of the Dogmen *'95*

Juliette Cummins
Running Hot *'83*
Friday the 13th, Part 5: A New Beginning *'85*
Slumber Party Massacre 2 *'87*
Deadly Dreams *'88*

Peggy Cummins
Salute John Citizen *'42*
Gun Crazy *'49*

Cummins ▶cont.

Carry On Admiral '57
Curse of the Demon '57
The Captain's Table '60

Peter Cummins
Blue Fire Lady '78
Ground Zero '88

Rusty Cundieff
Fear of a Black Hat '94
Tales from the Hood '95

Liam Cundill
Return of the Family Man '89
Reason to Die '90

John Cunningham
Lost and Found '79
Twisted '86

Liam Cunningham
First Knight '95
A Little Princess '95
War of the Buttons '95

Peter "Sugarfoot" Cunningham
Bloodmatch '91
Bloodfist 3: Forced to Fight '92

Alain Cuny
Les Visiteurs du Soir '42
The Lovers '59
La Dolce Vita '60
The Milky Way '68
Emmanuelle '74
Christ Stopped at Eboli '79
Basileus Quartet '82
Camille Claudel '89

Barbara Cupisti
Stagefright '87
Terror at the Opera '88

Lynette Curran
Bliss '85
The Year My Voice Broke '87

Cherie Currie
Foxes '80
Parasite '82
Twilight Zone: The Movie '83
Wavelength '83
Rosebud Beach Hotel '85

Finlay Currie
Edge of the World '37
The Forty-Ninth Parallel '41
The Day Will Dawn '42
I Know Where I'm Going '45
Sleeping Car to Trieste '45
Great Expectations '46
Bonnie Prince Charlie '48
Treasure Island '50
Trio '50
People Will Talk '51
Quo Vadis '51
Ivanhoe '52
Stars and Stripes Forever '52
Big Deadly Game '54
The King's Rhapsody '55
Make Me an Offer '55
Corridors of Blood '58
Ben-Hur '59
The Adventures of Huckleberry Finn '60
Billy Liar '63

Gordon Currie
Puppet Master 4 '93
Puppet Master 5: The Final Chapter '94

Louise Currie
The Adventures of Captain Marvel '41
The Bashful Bachelor '42
The Masked Marvel '43
Million Dollar Kid '44
Wild West '46

Michael Currie
Pray TV '82
The Dead Pool '88

Sondra Currie
Policewomen '73
Mama's Dirty Girls '74
Jessie's Girls '75
The Concrete Jungle '82
Runaways '84

Tim Curry
The Rocky Horror Picture Show '75
The Shout '78
Times Square '80
Annie '82
Oliver Twist '82
The Ploughman's Lunch '83
Blue Money '84
Clue '85
Legend '86
The Worst Witch '86
Pass the Ammo '88
The Hunt for Red October '90
Stephen King's It '90
Oscar '91
Home Alone 2: Lost in New York '92
Passed Away '92
National Lampoon's Loaded Weapon 1 '93
The Three Musketeers '93
The Shadow '94
Congo '95
Muppet Treasure Island '96

Jane Curtin
Saturday Night Live '70s
Mr. Mike's Mondo Video '79
How to Beat the High Cost of Living '80
O.C. and Stiggs '87
Suspicion '87
Coneheads '93

Valerie Curtin
Different Story '78
A Christmas Without Snow '80
Maxie '85
Big Trouble '86
Down and Out in Beverly Hills '86

Alan Curtis
Last Outlaw '36
Mannequin '37
Shopworn Angel '38
Buck Privates '41
Melody Master '41
Gung Ho! '43
The Invisible Man's Revenge '44
The Naughty Nineties '45
Flight to Nowhere '46
Renegade Girl '46
Apache Chief '50

Dick Curtis
Racing Luck '35
Boothill Brigade '37
A Lawman Is Born '37
Valley of Terror '38
Billy the Kid '41
Government Agents vs. Phantom Legion '51

Donald Curtis
Criminals Within '41
Son of Lassie '45
The Amazing Mr. X '48
It Came from Beneath the Sea '55
Earth vs. the Flying Saucers '56
Seventh Cavalry '56

Jamie Lee Curtis
The Fog '78
Halloween '78
Prom Night '80
Terror Train '80
Death of a Centerfold '81
Halloween 2: The Nightmare Isn't Over! '81
Road Games '81
She's in the Army Now '81
Love Letters '83
Trading Places '83
The Adventures of Buckaroo Banzai Across the Eighth Dimension '84
Grandview U.S.A. '84
Annie Oakley '85
Perfect '85
As Summers Die '86
Film House Fever '86
Amazing Grace & Chuck '87
A Man in Love '87
Dominick & Eugene '88
A Fish Called Wanda '88
Blue Steel '90
My Girl '91
Queens Logic '91
Forever Young '92
Mother's Boys '94
My Girl 2 '94
True Lies '94
The Heidi Chronicles '95
House Arrest '96

Keene Curtis
Strange New World '75
The Buddy System '83
Sliver '93

Ken Curtis
Call of the Forest '49
Don Daredevil Rides Again '51
The Quiet Man '52
Mister Roberts '55
Wings of Eagles '57
The Killer Shrews '59
The Young Land '59
Pony Express Rider '76
California Gold Rush '81
Lost '83
Texas Guns '90
Conagher '91

Liane Curtis
Hard Choices '84
Sixteen Candles '84
Critters 2: The Main Course '88
Girlfriend from Hell '89
Wild Orchid 2: Two Shades of Blue '92

Robin Curtis
Star Trek 3: The Search for Spock '84
The Unborn 2 '94

Tony Curtis
Criss Cross '48
Francis the Talking Mule '49
Winchester '73 '50
Son of Ali Baba '52
Houdini '53
Trapeze '56
Sweet Smell of Success '57
The Defiant Ones '58
Kings Go Forth '58
The Vikings '58
Operation Petticoat '59
Perfect Furlough '59
Some Like It Hot '59
The Rat Race '60
Spartacus '60
The Great Impostor '61
40 Pounds of Trouble '62
Taras Bulba '62
Captain Newman, M.D. '63
Paris When It Sizzles '64
Sex and the Single Girl '64
Boeing Boeing '65
The Great Race '65
Arrivederci, Baby! '66
The Boston Strangler '68
Those Daring Young Men in Their Jaunty Jalopies '69
Suppose They Gave a War and Nobody Came? '70
The Persuaders '71
The Count of Monte Cristo '74
Lepke '75
Mission: Monte Carlo '75
Overture '75
The Last Tycoon '76
The Bad News Bears Go to Japan '78
It Rained All Night the Day I Left '78
The Manitou '78
Sex on the Run '78
Sextette '78
Users '78
Vegas '78
Five Miles to Midnight '80
Little Miss Marker '80
The Mirror Crack'd '80
Title Shot '81
Balboa '82
Brainwaves '82
Portrait of a Showgirl '82
Insignificance '85
Club Life '86
Mafia Princess '86
The Last of Philip Banter '87
Lobster Man from Mars '89
Midnight '89
The Cary Grant Collection '90
Prime Target '91
Center of the Web '92
Christmas in Connecticut '92
Naked in New York '93
The Immortals '95

Vondie Curtis-Hall
Coming to America '88
In a Stranger's Hand '92
The Mambo Kings '92
Passion Fish '92
Fallen Angels 2 '93
Falling Down '93
Crooklyn '94
DROP Squad '94
Sugar Hill '94
Heaven's Prisoners '95
Zooman '95

George Curzan
Java Head '35
The Living Dead '36

Pierre Curzi
Maria Chapdelaine '84
Pouvoir Intime '87

Ann Cusack
A League of Their Own '92
Tank Girl '94

Cyril Cusack
Late Extra '35
Odd Man Out '47
The Small Back Room '49
The Elusive Pimpernel '50
Night Ambush '57
The Spanish Gardener '57
Johnny Nobody '61
Waltz of the Toreadors '62
The Spy Who Came in from the Cold '65
Fahrenheit 451 '66
The Taming of the Shrew '67
Street War '70s
David Copperfield '70
Harold and Maude '71
King Lear '71
Sacco & Vanzetti '71
All the Way, Boys '73
The Day of the Jackal '73
Children of Rage '75
Les Miserables '78
Lovespell '79
Cry of the Innocent '80
True Confessions '81
1984 '84
No Comebacks '85
Two by Forsyth '86
Little Dorrit, Film 1: Nobody's Fault '88
Little Dorrit, Film 2: Little Dorrit's Story '88
The Tenth Man '88
My Left Foot '89
Far and Away '92

Joan Cusack
My Bodyguard '80
Grandview U.S.A. '84
Sixteen Candles '84
The Allnighter '87
Broadcast News '87
Married to the Mob '88
Stars and Bars '88
Working Girl '88
Men Don't Leave '89
Say Anything '89
My Blue Heaven '90
Hero '92
Toys '92
Addams Family Values '93
Mr. Wrong '95
Nine Months '95
Two Much '96

John Cusack
Class '83
Grandview U.S.A. '84
Sixteen Candles '84
Better Off Dead '85
The Journey of Natty Gann '85
The Sure Thing '85
One Crazy Summer '86
Stand By Me '86
Hot Pursuit '87
Eight Men Out '88
Stars and Bars '88
Elvis Stories '89
Fat Man and Little Boy '89
Say Anything '89
Tapeheads '89
The Grifters '90
True Colors '91
Shadows and Fog '92
Map of the Human Heart '93
Money for Nothing '93
Bullets Over Broadway '94
Floundering '94
The Road to Wellville '94
City Hall '95

Sinead Cusack
Revenge '71
Cyrano de Bergerac '85
Rocket Gibraltar '88
Bad Behavior '92
Waterland '92
Stealing Beauty '96

Peter Cushing
A Chump at Oxford '40
Hamlet '48
Moulin Rouge '52
Alexander the Great '55
The Curse of Frankenstein '57
Time Without Pity '57
The Horror of Dracula '58
The Revenge of Frankenstein '58
The Hound of the Baskervilles '59
John Paul Jones '59
The Mummy '59
The Brides of Dracula '60
Mania '60
Sword of Sherwood Forest '60
The Hellfire Club '61
The Naked Edge '61
The Evil of Frankenstein '64
The Gorgon '64
Dr. Terror's House of Horrors '65
Doctor Who and the Daleks '65
The Skull '65
Daleks—Invasion Earth 2150 A.D. '66
Island of Terror '66
Blood Beast Terror '67
Island of the Burning Doomed '67
Torture Garden '67
The Bloodsuckers '70
Scream and Scream Again '70
The Vampire Lovers '70
The House that Dripped Blood '71
Twins of Evil '71
Asylum '72
The Creeping Flesh '72
Doctor Phibes Rises Again '72
Dynasty of Fear '72
Horror Express '72
Nothing But the Night '72
Tales from the Crypt '72
And Now the Screaming Starts '73
From Beyond the Grave '73
The Satanic Rites of Dracula '73
The 7 Brothers Meet Dracula '73
Call Him Mr. Shatter '74
Frankenstein and the Monster from Hell '74
Madhouse '74
Black Werewolf '75
The Devil's Undead '75
The Ghoul '75
Legend of the Werewolf '75
At the Earth's Core '76
Choice of Weapons '76
Land of the Minotaur '77
Shock Waves '77
Star Wars '77
The Uncanny '78
A Tale of Two Cities '80
House of the Long Shadows '82
Sword of the Valiant '83
Silent Scream '84
Top Secret! '84
Biggles '85
Masks of Death '86

Bob Custer
Mark of the Spur '32
Law of the Wild '34

Jon Cuthbert
Deadlock 2 '94
Virtual Assassin '95

Iain Cuthbertson
The Railway Children '70
Danger UXB '81
Gorillas in the Mist '88

Lise Cutter
Buy & Cell '89
Havana '90
Nickel & Dime '92
Shadow Force '92
Fleshtone '94

Zbigniew Cybulski
A Generation '54
Ashes and Diamonds '58
Innocent Sorcerers '60
The Saragossa Manuscript '65

Jon Cypher
Valdez is Coming '71
Memory of Us '74
Food of the Gods '76
Kid and the Killers '80s

Off the Mark '87
Elvis and Me '88
Accidents '89
Spontaneous Combustion '89
The Invaders '95

Charles Cyphers
Halloween 2: The Nightmare Isn't Over! '81
Major League '89

Miriam Cyr
Gothic '87
Savage Hearts '95

Henry Czerny
The Boys of St. Vincent '93
Northern Extremes '93
Clear and Present Danger '94
When Night is Falling '95
Mission: Impossible '96

Chris D
No Way Out '87
Border Radio '88

Eric Da Re
Silent Night, Deadly Night 3: Better Watch Out! '89
Twin Peaks '90
Twin Peaks '90
Number One Fan '94
The Takeover '94

Erick Da Silva
The Son of the Shark '93
Delta of Venus '95

Howard da Silva
Abe Lincoln in Illinois '40
The Sea Wolf '41
Keeper of the Flame '42
Reunion in France '42
The Lost Weekend '45
The Blue Dahlia '46
Unconquered '47
They Live by Night '49
Three Husbands '50
The Underworld Story '50
David and Lisa '62
1776 '72
The Great Gatsby '74
Missiles of October '74
Smile, Jenny, You're Dead '74
Mommie Dearest '81
Garbo Talks '84

Augusta Dabney
Violets Are Blue '86
Running on Empty '88
The Portrait '93

Maryam D'Abo
Xtro '83
The Living Daylights '87
Nightlife '90
Immortal Sins '91
Double Obsession '93
Leon the Pig Farmer '93
Red Shoe Diaries 3: Another Woman's Lipstick '93
Shootfighter: Fight to the Death '93
Tomcat: Dangerous Desires '93
Tropical Heat '93
The Browning Version '94
Stalked '94
Savage Hearts '95

Olivia D'Abo
Bolero '84
Conan the Destroyer '84
Dream to Believe '85
Mission to Kill '85
Bullies '86
Into the Fire '88
Beyond the Stars '89
Spirit of '76 '91
Bank Robber '93
Midnight's Child '93
Point of No Return '93
Wayne's World 2 '93
Clean Slate '94
Greedy '94
The Last Good Time '94
The Big Green '95
Kicking and Screaming '95
Live Nude Girls '95

Mark Dacascos
American Samurai '92
Only the Strong '93
Double Dragon '94
Deadly Past '95

Andrew Daddo
A Kink in the Picasso '90
Body Melt '93

Willem Dafoe
The Hunger '83
Loveless '83
New York Nights '84
Roadhouse 66 '84
Streets of Fire '84
To Live & Die in L.A. '85
Platoon '86
Hitchhiker 3 '87
Off Limits '87
The Last Temptation of Christ '88
Mississippi Burning '88
Born on the Fourth of July '89
Triumph of the Spirit '89
Cry-Baby '90
Flight of the Intruder '90
Wild at Heart '90
Body of Evidence '92
Light Sleeper '92
White Sands '92
Faraway, So Close! '93
Clear and Present Danger '94
Tom & Viv '94

Jean-Michel Dagory
Clowning Around '92
Clowning Around 2 '93

Lil Dagover
Spiders '18
The Cabinet of Dr. Caligari '19
Dr. Mabuse, Parts 1 & 2 '22
The Strange Countess '61
The Pedestrian '73

Arlene Dahl
A Southern Yankee '48
Reign of Terror '49
Three Little Words '50
Watch the Birdie '50
Here Come the Girls '53
A Woman's World '54
Slightly Scarlet '56
Journey to the Center of the Earth '59
Kisses for My President '64
Land Raiders '69
Night of the Warrior '91

Eva Dahlbeck
Secrets of Women '52
Lesson in Love '54
Dreams '55
Smiles of a Summer Night '55
Brink of Life '57
The Counterfeit Traitor '62

Paul Dahlke
The Head '59
The Third Sex '59

Dan Dailey
Lady Be Good '41
Ziegfeld Girl '41
Panama Hattie '42
Pride of St. Louis '52
What Price Glory? '52
There's No Business Like Show Business '54
It's Always Fair Weather '55
Meet Me in Las Vegas '56
Wings of Eagles '57
The Private Files of J. Edgar Hoover '77

Bill Daily
Magic on Love Island '80
Alligator 2: The Mutation '90

Elizabeth Daily
Street Music '81
Funny Money '82
No Small Affair '84
Streets of Fire '84
Fandango '85
Pee Wee's Big Adventure '85
Bad Dreams '88

Esther Dale
Curly Top '35
The Awful Truth '37
Blondie Has Trouble '40
A Stolen Life '46
Holiday Affair '49
Ma and Pa Kettle '49
Ma and Pa Kettle Go to Town '50
On Moonlight Bay '51
Ma and Pa Kettle at the Fair '52

Jennifer Dale
When Angels Fly '82
Of Unknown Origin '83
Separate Vacations '86
The Adjuster '91
Cadillac Girls '93
Whale Music '94

Jim Dale
Carry On Cleo '65
Carry On Cowboy '66
Carry On Screaming '66
Follow That Camel '67
Carry On Doctor '68
Digby, the Biggest Dog in the World '73
Joseph Andrews '77
Pete's Dragon '77
Hot Lead & Cold Feet '78
Unidentified Flying Oddball '79
Scandalous '84
The Adventures of Huckleberry Finn '85

Virginia Dale
Holiday Inn '42
Danger Zone '51

Fabienne Dali
Erotic Touch of Hot Skin '65
Kill, Baby, Kill '66
Mayerling '68

David Dalie
Virgin Sacrifice '59
Mighty Jungle '64

Marcel Dalio
Beethoven '36
Grand Illusion '37
The Rules of the Game '39
Casablanca '42
To Have & Have Not '44
Dedee d'Anvers '49
Captain Blackjack '51
Rich, Young and Pretty '51
Lovely to Look At '52
The Merry Widow '52
The Snows of Kilimanjaro '52
Lucky Me '54
Sabrina '54
China Gate '57
Lafayette Escadrille '58
Can-Can '60
The Monocle '64
Lady L '65
How to Steal a Million '66
How Sweet It Is! '68

Ewa Dalkowska
Without Anesthesia '78
Provincial Actors '79
Korczak '90

John Dall
The Corn is Green '45
Rope '48
Gun Crazy '49
Atlantis, the Lost Continent '61

Charlene Dallas
Rancho Deluxe '75
Criminal Act '88

Beatrice Dalle
Betty Blue '86
La Vengeance d'une Femme '89
Night on Earth '91
I Can't Sleep '93

Joe Dallesandro
Flesh '68
Trash '70
Season for Assassins '71
Heat '72
Andy Warhol's Dracula '74
Andy Warhol's Frankenstein '74
Seeds of Evil '76
The Cotton Club '84
Sunset '88
Double Revenge '89
The Hollywood Detective '89
Cry-Baby '90
Private War '90
Guncrazy '92
Wild Orchid 2: Two Shades of Blue '92
Sugar Hill '94

Abby Dalton
Rock All Night '57
Whale of a Tale '76
Roller Blade Warriors: Taken By Force '90
Cyber-Tracker '93

Audrey Dalton
Titanic '53
Casanova's Big Night '54
The Prodigal '55
The Monster That Challenged the World '57

Darren Dalton
Brotherhood of Justice '86
Montana '90

Dorothy Dalton
The Disciple '15
The Three Musketeers '16
Moran of the Lady Letty '22

Timothy Dalton
The Lion in Winter '68
Cromwell '70
Wuthering Heights '70
Permission To Kill '75
Sextette '78
Agatha '79
The Flame Is Love '79
Flash Gordon '80
Chanel Solitaire '81
Jane Eyre '83
Mistral's Daughter '84
The Doctor and the Devils '85
Sins '85
Brenda Starr '86
Happy Anniversary 007: 25 Years of James Bond '87
The Living Daylights '87
Hawks '89
License to Kill '89
The King's Whore '90
The Rocketeer '91
Naked in New York '93
Lie Down with Lions '94
Scarlett '94

Roger Daltrey
Lisztomania '75
Tommy '75
The Legacy '79
McVicar '80
Murder: Ultimate Grounds for Divorce '85
The Little Match Girl '87
Cold Justice '89
Mack the Knife '89
Forgotten Prisoners '90
Buddy's Song '91
If Looks Could Kill '91
Lightning Jack '94

Candice Daly
Hell Hunters '87
Liquid Dreams '92

James Daly
The Court Martial of Billy Mitchell '55
Tender Is the Night '55
The Invaders '67
Planet of the Apes '68
Resurrection of Zachary Wheeler '71

Timothy Daly
Diner '82
I Married a Centerfold '84
Just the Way You Are '84
Mirrors '85
The Rise & Rise of Daniel Rocket '86
Made in Heaven '87
For Love or Money '88
Love or Money? '88
The Spellbinder '88
Year of the Comet '92
Caroline at Midnight '93
Dangerous Heart '93
In the Line of Duty: Ambush in Waco '93
Witness to the Execution '94
Denise Calls Up '95
Dr. Jekyll and Ms. Hyde '95

Tyne Daly
Angel Unchained '70
Larry '74
The Enforcer '76
The Adultress '77
Intimate Strangers '77
Telefon '77
Speedtrap '78
Better Late Than Never '79
A Matter of Life and Death '81
Zoot Suit '81
Your Place or Mine '83
The Aviator '85
Movers and Shakers '85
On the Town '91
Christy '94

Jacqueline Dalya
Behind Prison Walls '43
Miss Melody Jones '73

William Dame
In Deadly Heat '87
Stuff Stephanie in the Incinerator '89

Leo Damian
Ghosts Can't Do It '90
Hard Drive '94

Cathryn Damon
The Best of Soap: Jessica's Wonderful Life '70s
How to Beat the High Cost of Living '80
First Time '82
She's Having a Baby '88

Gabriel Damon
Call to Glory '84
RoboCop 2 '90
Iron Maze '91
Journey to Spirit Island '92

Mark Damon
Between Heaven and Hell '56
The Fall of the House of Usher '60
Black Sabbath '64
Anzio '68
Great Treasure Hunt '70s
Crypt of the Living Dead '73
Devil's Wedding Night '73
The Scalawag Bunch '75

Matt Damon
Rising Son '90
School Ties '92
Geronimo: An American Legend '93
The Good Old Boys '95
Courage Under Fire '96

Vic Damone
Rich, Young and Pretty '51
Athena '54
Hit the Deck '55
Kismet '55
Hell to Eternity '60

Barbara Dana
A Matter of Principle '83
Necessary Parties '88

Bill Dana
Harrad Summer '74
I Wonder Who's Killing Her Now? '76
Lena's Holiday '90
Kill My Wife...Please!

Leora Dana
Kings Go Forth '58
Baby It's You '82
Amityville 3: The Demon '83

Viola Dana
The Ice Flood '26
That Certain Thing '28

Malcolm Danare
Heaven Help Us '85
The Curse '87
Popcorn '89

Charles Dance
For Your Eyes Only '81
The Jewel in the Crown '84
The McGuffin '85
Plenty '85
This Lightning Always Strikes Twice '85
The Golden Child '86
Good Morning, Babylon '87
Hidden City '87
Out on a Limb '87
Pascali's Island '88
White Mischief '88
The Phantom of the Opera '90
China Moon '91
Tales of the Unexpected '91
Alien 3 '92
Last Action Hero '93
Century '94
The Surgeon '94
Undertow '95

Tom D'Andrea
Humoresque '46
Never Say Goodbye '46
Dark Passage '47
Silver River '48
The Next Voice You Hear '50

Dorothy Dandridge
Sun Valley Serenade '41
Sundown '41
Lady from Louisiana '42
Since You Went Away '44

Dandridge ▶cont.

Carmen Jones '54
Island in the Sun '57
Tamango '59

Karl Dane
The Big Parade '25
The Big House '30

Lawrence Dane
Find the Lady '75
Rituals '79
Fatal Attraction '80
Scanners '81
Clown Murders '83
Of Unknown Origin '83
Rolling Vengeance '87
The Good Fight '92
Lethal Lolita—Amy Fisher: My Story '92
It Takes Two '95
National Lampoon's Senior Trip '95

Patricia Dane
Johnny Eager '42
Rio Rita '42
Somewhere I'll Find You '42
I Dood It '43

Paul Daneman
Time Without Pity '57
Tears in the Rain '88

Claire Danes
Little Women '94
Home for the Holidays '95
How to Make an American Quilt '95

Beverly D'Angelo
The Sentinel '76
Annie Hall '77
First Love '77
Every Which Way But Loose '78
Hair '79
Coal Miner's Daughter '80
Highpoint '80
Honky Tonk Freeway '81
Paternity '81
National Lampoon's Vacation '83
Sleeping Beauty '83
Finders Keepers '84
A Streetcar Named Desire '84
National Lampoon's European Vacation '85
Big Trouble '86
The Legend of Sleepy Hollow '86
Slow Burn '86
Hands of a Stranger '87
In the Mood '87
Maid to Order '87
Trading Hearts '87
Aria '88
High Spirits '88
Cold Front '89
National Lampoon's Christmas Vacation '89
Daddy's Dyin'...Who's Got the Will? '90
Pacific Heights '90
Lonely Hearts '91
The Miracle '91
The Pope Must Diet '91
Man Trouble '92
The Crazysitter '94
Lightning Jack '94
An Eye for an Eye '95
Widow's Kiss '96

Carlo D'Angelo
The Devil's Commandment '56
Secret Agent Super Dragon '66

Rodney Dangerfield
The Projectionist '71
Caddyshack '80
Easy Money '83
Back to School '86
Moving '88
Ladybugs '92
Natural Born Killers '94

Isa Danieli
Macaroni '85
Ciao, Professore! '94

Henry Daniell
Camille '36
The Firefly '37
Madame X '37
All This and Heaven Too '40
The Great Dictator '40
The Philadelphia Story '40
The Sea Hawk '40
A Woman's Face '41
Castle in the Desert '42
Reunion in France '42
Sherlock Holmes in Washington '43
Watch on the Rhine '43
Jane Eyre '44
The Body Snatcher '45
The Woman in Green '45
Wake of the Red Witch '49
The Egyptian '54
Diane '55
The Prodigal '55
Lust for Life '56
The Man in the Gray Flannel Suit '56
Les Girls '57
Witness for the Prosecution '57

Suzanne Danielle
Carry On Emmanuelle '78
Golden Lady '79
The Carpathian Eagle '81

Anthony Daniels
Star Wars '77
The Empire Strikes Back '80
Return of the Jedi '83

Bebe Daniels
I'm on My Way/The Non-Stop Kid '18
Don't Shove/Two Gun Gussie '19
Male and Female '19
Silent Laugh Makers, No. 3 '19
Why Change Your Wife? '20
Monsieur Beaucaire '24
Feel My Pulse '28
Dixiana '30
The Maltese Falcon '31
Reaching for the Moon '31
42nd Street '33

Gary Daniels
Firepower '93
Knights '93
Deadly Target '94
Heatseeker '95
Rage '95
White Tiger '95

J.D. Daniels
Man's Best Friend '93
Beanstalk '94
Roswell: The U.F.O. Cover-Up '94

Jeff Daniels
A Rumor of War '80
Ragtime '81
Terms of Endearment '83
Marie '85
The Purple Rose of Cairo '85
Heartburn '86
Something Wild '86
Radio Days '87
The Caine Mutiny Court Martial '88
The House on Carroll Street '88
Love Notes '88
Sweet Hearts Dance '88
Checking Out '89
Arachnophobia '90
Welcome Home, Roxy Carmichael '90
The Butcher's Wife '91
Love Hurts '91
Grand Tour: Disaster in Time '92
Teamster Boss: The Jackie Presser Story '92
There Goes the Neighborhood '92
Gettysburg '93
Rain Without Thunder '93
Dumb & Dumber '94
Speed '94
Redwood Curtain '95

John Daniels
Candy Tangerine Man '75
Black Shampoo '76
Bare Knuckles '77
Getting Over '81

Mickey Daniels
The Return of Our Gang '25
Our Gang '26
The Adventurous Knights '35
The Great Ziegfeld '36
Our Gang Comedy Festival '88
Our Gang Comedy Festival 2 '89

Phil Daniels
Quadrophenia '79
Scum '79
Breaking Glass '80
The Bride '85
Bad Behavior '92

William Daniels
A Thousand Clowns '65
The Graduate '67
The President's Analyst '67
Two for the Road '67
Marlowe '69
1776 '72
The Parallax View '74
Black Sunday '77
Killer on Board '77
Oh, God! '77
The Bastard '78
The One and Only '78
Sergeant Matlovich vs. the U.S. Air Force '78
The Rebels '79
Sunburn '79
The Blue Lagoon '80
City in Fear '80
Damien: The Leper Priest '80
All Night Long '81
Reds '81
Rehearsal for Murder '82
Blind Date '87
Her Alibi '88
Skin '89

Lynn Danielson
Out of the Dark '88
Mortuary Academy '91
Nickel & Dime '92

Eli Danker
The Taking of Flight 847: The Uli Derickson Story '88
The Flight '89
Impulse '90

Blythe Danner
1776 '72
To Kill a Clown '72
Hearts of the West '75
Futureworld '76
Love Affair: The Eleanor & Lou Gehrig Story '77
Are You in the House Alone? '78
Too Far to Go '79
The Great Santini '80
Inside the Third Reich '82
Man, Woman & Child '83
Brighton Beach Memoirs '86
Another Woman '88
Alice '90
Judgment '90
Mr. & Mrs. Bridge '90
Never Forget '91
The Prince of Tides '91
Getting Up and Going Home '92
Husbands and Wives '92
Oldest Confederate Widow Tells All '95
To Wong Foo, Thanks for Everything, Julie Newmar '95

Sybil Danning
Cat in the Cage '68
Bluebeard '72
God's Gun '75
Albino '76
The Prince and the Pauper '78
The Concorde: Airport '79 '79
Battle Beyond the Stars '80
Kill Castro '80
The Man with Bogart's Face '80
The Mercenaries '80
Nightkill '80
Daughter of Death '82
The Salamander '82
Separate Ways '82
Chained Heat '83
Hercules '83
Day of the Cobra '84
Jungle Warriors '84
Panther Squad '84
Seven Magnificent Gladiators '84
They're Playing with Fire '84
Howling 2: Your Sister is a Werewolf '85
Malibu Express '85
Private Passions '85
Young Lady Chatterly 2 '85
Reform School Girls '86
Tomb '86
Amazon Women on the Moon '87
Hitchhiker 4 '87
Phantom Empire '87
Warrior Queen '87
L.A. Bounty '89

Royal Dano
The Red Badge of Courage '51
Bend of the River '52
Johnny Guitar '53
The Trouble with Harry '55
All Mine to Give '56
Tribute to a Bad Man '56
Crime of Passion '57
Man of the West '58
The Adventures of Huckleberry Finn '60
Electra Glide in Blue '73
Big Bad Mama '74
Messiah of Evil '74
Wild Party '74
Huckleberry Finn '75
Bad Georgia Road '77
Hughes & Harlow: Angels in Hell '77
The Right Stuff '83
Teachers '84
Cocaine Wars '86
Ghoulies 2 '87
House 2: The Second Story '87
Killer Klowns from Outer Space '88
Spaced Invaders '90
Texas Guns '90
The Dark Half '91

Leslie Danon
Hail Caesar '94
The Whispering '94

Cesare Danova
Gidget Goes to Rome '63
Viva Las Vegas '63
Boy, Did I Get a Wrong Number! '66
Mean Streets '73
Scorchy '76
Tentacles '77
St. Helen's, Killer Volcano '82

Ted Danson
Chinese Web '78
The Onion Field '79
Body Heat '81
Our Family Business '81
Creepshow '82
Little Treasure '85
A Fine Mess '86
Just Between Friends '86
When the Bough Breaks '86
Three Men and a Baby '87
We are the Children '87
Cousins '89
Dad '89
Three Men and a Little Lady '90
Made in America '93
Getting Even with Dad '94
Pontiac Moon '94
Gulliver's Travels '95

Michael Dante
Naked Kiss '64
Cruise Missile '78
Beyond Evil '80
Big Score '83
The Cage '89
Crazy Horse and Custer: "The Untold Story" '90

Helmut Dantine
Casablanca '42
Desperate Journey '42
Mrs. Miniver '42
The Navy Comes Through '42
To Be or Not to Be '42
Edge of Darkness '43
Northern Pursuit '43
Watch on the Rhine '43
Hollywood Canteen '44
Passage to Marseilles '44
Whispering City '47
The Stranger from Venus '54
Alexander the Great '55
War and Peace '56
Operation Crossbow '65
Bring Me the Head of Alfredo Garcia '74
The Killer Elite '75
The Wilby Conspiracy '75
The Fifth Musketeer '79

Ray Danton
I'll Cry Tomorrow '55
A Majority of One '56
The Rise and Fall of Legs Diamond '60
The Longest Day '62
Conqueror & the Empress '64
Secret Agent Super Dragon '66
The Centerfold Girls '74
Apache Blood '75

Tony Danza
Going Ape! '81
Single Bars, Single Women '84
Truth or Die '86
She's Out of Control '89
Angels in the Outfield '94

Maia Danzinger
Dr. Heckyl and Mr. Hype '80
Last Exit to Brooklyn '90

Ho Chung Dao
Bruce Li in New Guinea '80
Bruce Li the Invincible '80
Invincible '80

Sun Dao-Lin
Crows and Sparrows '49
The Go-Masters '82

Patti D'Arbanville
Flesh '68
Bilitis '77
Big Wednesday '78
Time After Time '79
The Fifth Floor '80
Hog Wild '80
Modern Problems '81
The Boys Next Door '85
Real Genius '85
Call Me '88
Fresh Horses '88
Wired '89
Snow Kill '90
Deadly Conspiracy '91
Blind Spot '93
The Fan '96

Patrika Darbo
Daddy's Dyin'...Who's Got the Will? '90
Leaving Normal '92

Kim Darby
Generation '69
True Grit '69
The Strawberry Statement '70
The Grissom Gang '71
The People '71
The Streets of San Francisco '72
Don't Be Afraid of the Dark '73
Rich Man, Poor Man '76
The One and Only '78
Flatbed Annie and Sweetiepie: Lady Truckers '79
Enola Gay: The Men, the Mission, the Atomic Bomb '80
The Capture of Grizzly Adams '82
Better Off Dead '85
Embassy '85
Teen Wolf Too '87

Mireille Darc
Weekend '67
The Peking Blond '68
The Tall Blond Man with One Black Shoe '72
Return of the Tall Blond Man With One Black Shoe '74
Icy Breasts '75
Intruder '77

Denise Darcel
Thunder in the Pines '49
Westward the Women '51
Vera Cruz '53

Alexander D'Arcy
The Awful Truth '37
Prisoner of Zenda '37
Soldier of Fortune '55
Horrors of Spider Island '59
Fanny Hill: Memoirs of a Woman of Pleasure '64
Blood of Dracula's Castle '69
Dead Pigeon on Beethoven Street '72

Jake D'Arcy
A Sense of Freedom '78
Gregory's Girl '80

Roy D'Arcy
Revolt of the Zombies '36
Legion of Missing Men '37

Sheila Darcy
Irish Luck '39
Zorro's Fighting Legion '39
Tumbledown Ranch in Arizona '41

Severn Darden
Dead Heat on a Merry-Go-Round '66
The President's Analyst '67
Hired Hand '71
Vanishing Point '71
Werewolves on Wheels '71
Conquest of the Planet of the Apes '72
Playmates '72
Battle for the Planet of the Apes '73
The Day of the Dolphin '73
The Legend of Hillbilly John '73
The Disappearance of Aimee '76
Jackson County Jail '76
Wanda Nevada '79
Saturday the 14th '81
Real Genius '85
Back to School '86
Once Upon a Midnight Scary '90

Florence Darel
The Stolen Children '92
A Tale of Springtime '92
A la Mode '94

Bobby Darin
Come September '61
Hell is for Heroes '62
Pressure Point '62
State Fair '62
Captain Newman, M.D. '63
The Happy Ending '69
Run, Stranger, Run '73

Johnny Dark
Rip-Off '77
Up Your Alley '89
Wishful Thinking '92

Joan Darling
Sunnyside '79
The Two Worlds of Jenny Logan '79

Linda Darlow
Immediate Family '89
The Amy Fisher Story '93

Gerard Darmon
Diva '82
Betty Blue '86
Obsession: A Taste for Fear '89

Linda Darnell
Brigham Young: Frontiersman '40
The Mark of Zorro '40
Blood and Sand '41
The Loves of Edgar Allen Poe '42
City Without Men '43
Buffalo Bill '44
Anna and the King of Siam '46
My Darling Clementine '46
Forever Amber '47
Unfaithfully Yours '48
A Letter to Three Wives '49
Blackbeard the Pirate '52
Island of Desire '52
Second Chance '53
Dakota Incident '56

Steve Darrell
Lightning Raiders '45
The Adventures of Frank and Jesse James '48

James Darren
The Gene Krupa Story '59
Gidget '59
All the Young Men '60
Gidget Goes Hawaiian '61
The Guns of Navarone '61
Diamond Head '62
Gidget Goes to Rome '63
Venus in Furs '70
Boss' Son '79

Danielle Darrieux
Mayerling '36
The Rage of Paris '38
Ruyblas '48
La Ronde '51
Rich, Young and Pretty '51
Five Fingers '52
Le Plaisir '52
The Earrings of Madame De... '54
Alexander the Great '55
Lady Chatterley's Lover '55
The Red and the Black '57
Bluebeard '63
Murder at 45 R.P.M. '65
L'Anne Sainte '78
Le Cavaleur '78
Scene of the Crime '87

Frankie Darro
Lightning Warrior '31
Vanishing Legion '31
Devil Horse '32
Wolf Dog '33
Broadway Bill '34
Burn 'Em Up Barnes '34
The Phantom Empire '35
Valley of Wanted Men '35
Black Gold '36
Anything for a Thrill '37
Devil Diamond '37
Tough to Handle '37
Boy's Reformatory '39
Irish Luck '39
Tough Kid '39
The Gang's All Here '40
Up in the Air '40
Let's Go Collegiate '41
Riding High '50
Westward the Women '51

Henry Darrow
Computer Wizard '77
Where's Willie? '77
Death Blow '87
In Dangerous Company '88
L.A. Bounty '89
The Last of the Finest '90

John Darrow
Hell's Angels '30
The Lady Refuses '31
Ten Nights in a Bar-Room '31
Monte Carlo Nights '34

Oliver Darrow
The Channeler '89
Bad Girls from Mars '90
Spirits '90

Paul Darrow
Blake's Seven '78
Guardian of the Abyss '82

Tony Darrow
Goodfellas '90
Me and the Mob '94

Lili Darvas
Meet Me in Las Vegas '56
24 Hours in a Woman's Life '61
Love '71

Bella Darvi
The Egyptian '54
The Racers '55

Jane Darwell
Finishing School '33
One Night of Love '34
Curly Top '35
Captain January '36
Craig's Wife '36
The Poor Little Rich Girl '36
Little Miss Broadway '38
Gone with the Wind '39
Jesse James '39
The Rains Came '39
Brigham Young: Frontiersman '40
The Grapes of Wrath '40
The Devil & Daniel Webster '41
All Through the Night '42
The Loves of Edgar Allen Poe '42
The Great Gildersleeve '43
The Ox-Bow Incident '43
Tender Comrade '43
I Live in Grosvenor Square '46
The Red Stallion '47
Three Godfathers '48
Redwood Forest Trail '50
Three Husbands '50
Wagon Master '50
The Lemon Drop Kid '51
We're Not Married '52
The Bigamist '53
Girls in Prison '56
Last Hurrah '58

Stacey Dash
Moving '88
Mo' Money '92
Black Water '94
Renaissance Man '94
Clueless '95
Illegal in Blue '95

Jules Dassin
Rififi '54
Never on Sunday '60

Jean Daste
Boudu Saved from Drowning '32
Zero for Conduct '33
L'Atalante '34
The Crime of Monsieur Lange '36
Grand Illusion '37
The Green Room '78

Alex Datcher
Passenger 57 '92
Rage and Honor '92
Body Bags '93
The Expert '95

Kristin Datillo
Mirror, Mirror '90
Child of Darkness, Child of Light '91
Pyrates '91

James Daughton
Malibu Beach '78
Swim Team '79
Blind Date '84
Girlfriend from Hell '89

Claude Dauphin
April In Paris '52
Casque d'Or '52
Le Plaisir '52
Tiara Tahiti '62
Lady L '65
Two for the Road '67
Is Paris Burning? '68
The Madwoman of Chaillot '69
Rosebud '75
Madame Rosa '77
Les Miserables '78

Elyssa Davalos
Wild & Wooly '78
Jericho Fever '93

Richard Davalos
East of Eden '54
Sea Chase '55
Cool Hand Luke '67
Something Wicked This Way Comes '83

Harry Davenport
Fit for a King '37
The Cowboy and the Lady '38
Marie Antoinette '38
You Can't Take It with You '38
Gone with the Wind '39
The Hunchback of Notre Dame '39
The Story of Alexander Graham Bell '39
All This and Heaven Too '40
Foreign Correspondent '40
Lucky Partners '40
Kings Row '41
That Uncertain Feeling '41
Son of Fury '42
The Ox-Bow Incident '43
Jack London '44
Meet Me in St. Louis '44
The Thin Man Goes Home '44
The Enchanted Forest '45
Courage of Lassie '46
The Bachelor and the Bobby-Soxer '47
The Farmer's Daughter '47
Three Daring Daughters '48
Tell It to the Judge '49
Riding High '50
That Forsyte Woman '50
December 7th: The Movie '91

Nigel Davenport
Ladies Who Do '63
Peeping Tom '63
A Man for All Seasons '66
Sebastian '68
The Virgin Soldiers '69
The Last Valley '71
Living Free '72
Dracula '73
Phase 4 '74
Picture of Dorian Gray '74
Island of Dr. Moreau '77
Zulu Dawn '79
Death by Prescription '80s
Cry of the Innocent '80
The Ordeal of Dr. Mudd '80
Soul Patrol '80
Chariots of Fire '81
Nighthawks '81
Greystoke: The Legend of Tarzan, Lord of the Apes '84
Upper Crust '88
Without a Clue '88

Robert Davi
The $5.20 an Hour Dream '80
Gangster Wars '81
The Goonies '85
Traxx '87
Wild Thing '87
Die Hard '88
License to Kill '89
Amazon '90
Legal Tender '90
Maniac Cop 2 '90
Peacemaker '90
Predator 2 '90
Illicit Behavior '91
The Taking of Beverly Hills '91
White Hot: The Mysterious Murder of Thelma Todd '91
Center of the Web '92
Christopher Columbus: The Discovery '92
Wild Orchid 2: Two Shades of Blue '92
Maniac Cop 3: Badge of Silence '93
Mardi Gras for the Devil '93
Quick '93
Son of the Pink Panther '93
Blind Justice '94
Cops and Robbersons '94
No Contest '94
Body Count '95
The Dangerous '95
The Dogfighters '95
Showgirls '95

Angel David
Mixed Blood '84
The Crow '93

Clifford David
Resurrection '80
Agent on Ice '86
Matters of the Heart '90

Eleanor David
The Scarlet Pimpernel '82
Comfort and Joy '84
84 Charing Cross Road '86
Sylvia '86
Slipstream '89

Keith David
The Thing '82
Platoon '86
Off Limits '87
Bird '88
They Live '88
Always '89
Marked for Death '90
Men at Work '90
Article 99 '92
Final Analysis '92
The Last Outlaw '93
The Puppet Masters '94
The Quick and the Dead '94
Blue In the Face '95
Clockers '95
Dead Presidents '95
An Eye for an Eye '95

Thayer David
The Legend of the Sea Wolf '58
Journey to the Center of the Earth '59
The Story of Ruth '60
House of Dark Shadows '70
Savages '72
Save the Tiger '73
The Eiger Sanction '75
The Duchess and the Dirtwater Fox '76

Lolita Davidovich
Recruits '86
Adventures in Babysitting '87
Blindside '88
Blaze '89
The Inner Circle '91
The Object of Beauty '91
Prison Stories: Women on the Inside '91
Keep the Change '92
Leap of Faith '92
Raising Cain '92
Boiling Point '93
Intersection '93
Cobb '94
Younger & Younger '94
For Better or Worse '95
Indictment: The McMartin Trial '95
Now and Then '95

Ben Davidson
The Black Six '74
Conan the Barbarian '82

Davey Davidson
No Drums, No Bugles '71
When the Line Goes Through '71

Diana Davidson
Scared to Death '80
Around the World in 80 Ways '86

Eileen Davidson
The House on Sorority Row '83
Easy Wheels '89
Eternity '90

Jaye Davidson
The Crying Game '92
Stargate '94

John Davidson
Monsieur Beaucaire '24
Tailspin Tommy '34

John Davidson
The Happiest Millionaire '67
The Concorde: Airport '79 '79
The Squeeze '87
Edward Scissorhands '90

Max Davidson
Hotel Imperial '27
Daring Danger '32
Roamin' Wild '36

Tommy Davidson
Strictly Business '91
Ace Ventura: When Nature Calls '95

William B. Davidson
Vice Squad '31
Held for Murder '32
I'm No Angel '33

Embeth Davidtz
Army of Darkness '92
Schindler's List '93
Sweet Murder '93
Feast of July '95
Murder In the First '95
Matilda '96

Betty Ann Davies
The Blue Lamp '49
Blackout '54
Alias John Preston '56

Jackson Davies
Dead Wrong '83
Jane Doe '83
Dead Ahead: The Exxon Valdez Disaster '92

James Davies
Young Nurses in Love '89
Wildest Dreams '90

John Davies
Interface '84
Positive I.D. '87

John Howard Davies
Oliver Twist '48
The Rocking Horse Winner '49
Tom Brown's School Days '51

Marion Davies
Show People '28
Going Hollywood '33

Rudi Davies
The Lonely Passion of Judith Hearne '87
The Object of Beauty '91
Maria's Child '93
Frankie Starlight '95

Rupert Davies
The Spy Who Came in from the Cold '65
Target for Killing '66
The Conqueror Worm '68
The Crimson Cult '68
Dracula Has Risen from the Grave '68
Waterloo '71
Zeppelin '71
Frightmare '74

Stephen Davies
Hanoi Hilton '87
The Nest '88
The Berlin Conspiracy '91
Dillinger and Capone '95

Luis Davila
Pancho Villa '72
The Scalawag Bunch '75

Alex Davion
Paranoiac '62
Valley of the Dolls '67

Ann B. Davis
Lover Come Back '61
The Brady Bunch '69
A Very Brady Christmas '88

Art Davis
Phantom Gold '38
Along the Sundown Trail '42
Prairie Pals '42
Tumbleweed Trail '42

Bette Davis
The Cabin in the Cotton '32
Hell's House '32
Three on a Match '32
Way Back Home '32
Bureau of Missing Persons '33
Ex-Lady '33
Fashions of 1934 '34
Of Human Bondage '34
Dangerous '35
Petrified Forest '36
Satan Met a Lady '36
Kid Galahad '37
Marked Woman '37
That Certain Woman '37
Jezebel '38
The Sisters '38
Dark Victory '39
Juarez '39
The Old Maid '39
The Private Lives of Elizabeth & Essex '39
All This and Heaven Too '40
The Letter '40
The Bride Came C.O.D. '41
The Great Lie '41
The Little Foxes '41
The Man Who Came to Dinner '41
In This Our Life '42
Now, Voyager '42
Thank Your Lucky Stars '43
Watch on the Rhine '43
Hollywood Canteen '44
Mr. Skeffington '44
The Corn is Green '45
Deception '46
A Stolen Life '46
June Bride '48
Winter Meeting '48
Beyond the Forest '49
All About Eve '50
Phone Call from a Stranger '52
The Virgin Queen '55
The Catered Affair '56
Pocketful of Miracles '61
What Ever Happened to Baby Jane? '62
Empty Canvas '64
Where Love Has Gone '64
Hush, Hush, Sweet Charlotte '65
The Nanny '65
The Anniversary '68
Madame Sin '71
Burnt Offerings '76
The Disappearance of Aimee '76
The Dark Secret of Harvest Home '78
Death on the Nile '78
Return from Witch Mountain '78
Strangers: The Story of a Mother and Daughter '79
White Mama '80
The Watcher in the Woods '81
A Piano for Mrs. Cimino '82
Hollywood Outtakes & Rare Footage '83
Little Gloria...Happy at Last '84
Right of Way '84
As Summers Die '86
The Whales of August '87
Wicked Stepmother '89

Brad Davis
Sybil '76
The Campus Corpse '77
Midnight Express '78
A Rumor of War '80
A Small Circle of Friends '80
Chariots of Fire '81
Chiefs '83
Querelle '83
Blood Ties '87
Cold Steel '87
Heart '87
The Caine Mutiny Court Martial '88
Rosalie Goes Shopping '89
Vengeance '89
Robert Kennedy and His Times '90
Child of Darkness, Child of Light '91
The Habitation of Dragons '91
Hangfire '91
When the Time Comes '91

Bud Davis
House of the Rising Sun '87
Andersonville '95

Carole Davis
C.O.D. '83
The Flamingo Kid '84
Mannequin '87
Princess Academy '87
The Shrimp on the Barbie '90
If Looks Could Kill '91

Chet Davis
Yes, Sir, Mr. Bones '51
The Eye Creatures '65

Clifton Davis
Little Ladies of the Night '77
The Night the City Screamed '80
Don't Look Back: The Story of Leroy "Satchel" Paige '81
Dream Date '93

Duane Davis
Diggstown '92
Final Shot: The Hank Gathers Story '92
The Program '93

Eddie Davis
Gunners & Guns '34
Fighting Pilot '35

Gail Davis
Brand of Fear '49
Cow Town '50
Valley of Fire '51
Blue Canadian Rockies '52
On Top of Old Smoky '53
Winning of the West '53

Geena Davis
Tootsie '82
Fletch '85
Secret Weapons '85
Transylvania 6-5000 '85
The Fly '86
The Accidental Tourist '88
Beetlejuice '88
Earth Girls Are Easy '89
Quick Change '90
Thelma & Louise '91
Hero '92
A League of Their Own '92
Angie '94
Speechless '94
Cutthroat Island '95

Gene Davis
Night Games '80
Messenger of Death '88

Jim Davis
Hellfire '48
Hi-Jacked '50
The Showdown '50
Three Desperate Men '50
Little Big Horn '51
The Big Sky '52
Big Chase '54
The Outcast '54
The Maverick Queen '55
Guns Don't Argue '57
Monster from Green Hell '58
The Restless Breed '58
Frontier Uprising '61
Iron Angel '64
Jesse James Meets Frankenstein's Daughter '65
Zebra in the Kitchen '65
El Dorado '67
Gun Riders '69
Monte Walsh '70
Dracula vs. Frankenstein '71
The Trackers '71
Bad Company '72
The Runaway Barge '75
Law of the Land '76
The Choirboys '77
Comes a Horseman '78
Killing Stone '78
Day Time Ended '80
Don't Look Back: The Story of Leroy "Satchel" Paige '81
Inferno in Paradise '88

Joan Davis
On the Avenue '37
Thin Ice '37
Just Around the Corner '38
My Lucky Star '38
Hold That Ghost '41
Sun Valley Serenade '41
Around the World '43
Show Business '44
George White's Scandals '45
If You Knew Susie '48
The Outcast '54

Judy Davis
High Rolling in a Hot Corvette '77
My Brilliant Career '79
The Final Option '82
The Winter of Our Dreams '82
A Woman Called Golda '82
Heatwave '83
A Passage to India '84
Kangaroo '86
Rocket to the Moon '86
Georgia '87
High Tide '87
Alice '90
Impromptu '90
Barton Fink '91
Naked Lunch '91
One Against the Wind '91
Where Angels Fear to Tread '91
Husbands and Wives '92
The Ref '93
The New Age '94

Mac Davis
North Dallas Forty '79
Cheaper to Keep Her '80
The Sting 2 '83
Blackmail '91

Nancy Davis
East Side, West Side '49
The Next Voice You Hear '50
Donovan's Brain '53
Hellcats of the Navy '57

Nathan Davis
Code of Silence '85
Shaking the Tree '92
Dunston Checks In '95

Ossie Davis
Gone are the Days '63
Purlie Victorious '63
A Man Called Adam '66
The Scalphunters '68
Night Gallery '69
Let's Do It Again '75
Billy: Portrait of a Street Kid '77
King '78
All God's Children '80
Hot Stuff '80
Don't Look Back: The Story of Leroy "Satchel" Paige '81
Harry & Son '84
Avenging Angel '85
School Daze '88
Do the Right Thing '89
Joe Versus the Volcano '90
Jungle Fever '91
Gladiator '92
The Ernest Green Story '93
Grumpy Old Men '93
The Client '94
Stephen King's The Stand '94
The Android Affair '95

Owen Davis, Jr.
Special Investigator '36
It Could Happen to You '37

Patricia Davis
For Ladies Only '81
Night Partners '83

Philip Davis
Who's Who '78
Quadrophenia '79
Grown Ups '80
The Bounty '84
High Hopes '88
Howling 5: The Rebirth '89

Phyllis E. Davis
Sweet Sugar '72
Terminal Island '73

Roger Davis
House of Dark Shadows '70
Flash & Firecat '75
Ruby '77

Sammi Davis
Mona Lisa '86
Hope and Glory '87
Prayer for the Dying '87
Consuming Passions '88
The Lair of the White Worm '88
The Rainbow '89
Final Warning '90
The Horseplayer '91
The Perfect Bride '91
Shadow of China '91
Indecency '92
Four Rooms '95

Sammy Davis, Jr.
Ocean's 11 '60
The Three Penny Opera '62
Robin and the 7 Hoods '64
A Man Called Adam '66
Sweet Charity '69
The Trackers '71
Gone with the West '72
James Dean: The First American Teenager '76
Little Moon & Jud McGraw '78
Cannonball Run '81
Cracking Up '83
Cannonball Run 2 '84
That's Dancing! '85
Moon over Parador '88
Tap '89
The Kid Who Loved Christmas '90

Scott Davis
The Abomination '88
Tabloid! '88

Sonny Carl Davis
The Whole Shootin' Match '79
Fast Money '83
Last Night at the Alamo '83
Verne Miller '88
Pair of Aces '90
Seedpeople '92

Tom Davis
Tunnelvision '76
One More Saturday Night '86

Viveka Davis
Shoot the Moon '82
Not My Kid '85
Morgan Stewart's Coming Home '87
The End of Innocence '90
Man Trouble '92
A Dangerous Woman '93
Stalking Laura '93

Warwick Davis
The Ewok Adventure '84
The Ewoks: Battle for Endor '85
Willow '88
Leprechaun '93
Leprechaun 2 '94
Gulliver's Travels '95
Leprechaun 3 '95

Bruce Davison
Last Summer '69
The Strawberry Statement '70
Willard '71
Ulzana's Raid '72
The Affair '73
Mame '74
High Risk '76
Mother, Jugs and Speed '76
The Gathering '77
Portrait of Grandpa Doc '77
Brass Target '78
Deadman's Curve '78
French Quarter '78
The Summer of My German Soldier '78
The Gathering: Part 2 '79
Short Eyes '79
Lathe of Heaven '80
Kiss My Grits '82
Tomorrow's Child '82
Lies '83
Crimes of Passion '84
Spies Like Us '85
The Ladies Club '86
The Misfit Brigade '87
Poor Little Rich Girl: The Barbara Hutton Story '87
Longtime Companion '90
Steel and Lace '90
Live! From Death Row '92
Short Cuts '93
Six Degrees of Separation '93
Far from Home: The Adventures of Yellow Dog '94
The Baby-Sitters Club '95
The Cure '95
Down, Out and Dangerous '95
It's My Party '95
Widow's Kiss '96

Peter Davison
Love for Lydia '79
Black Beauty '94

Ninetto Davoli
The Hawks & the Sparrows '67
The Decameron '70
The Canterbury Tales '71
Arabian Nights '74

Evelyn Daw
Something to Sing About '36
Panamint's Bad Man '38

Marjorie Daw
Rebecca of Sunnybrook Farm '17
His Majesty, the American '19

Pam Dawber
Mork & Mindy '78
Holocaust Survivors...Remembrance of Love '83
The Little Mermaid '84
Wild Horses '84
Through Naked Eyes '87
Stay Tuned '92

Sugar Dawn
Dynamite Canyon '41
Riding the Sunset Trail '41
Arizona Roundup '42
Lone Star Law Men '42

Anthony Dawson
The Queen of Spades '49
The Long Dark Hall '51
Dial "M" for Murder '54
Hour of Decision '57
The Haunted Strangler '58
The Curse of the Werewolf '61
Dr. No '62

Kamala Dawson
The Burning Season '94
Lightning Jack '94

Kim Dawson
The Voyeur '94
The Perfect Gift '95

Richard Dawson
The Devil's Brigade '68
How to Pick Up Girls '78
The Running Man '87

Vicky Dawson
Carbon Copy '81
The Prowler '81

Doris Day
Saga of Death Valley '39
Lady Be Good '41
Turf Boy '42

Doris Day
Romance on the High Seas '48
It's a Great Feeling '49
My Dream Is Yours '49
Tea for Two '50
The West Point Story '50
Young Man with a Horn '50
I'll See You in My Dreams '51
Lullaby of Broadway '51
On Moonlight Bay '51
April In Paris '52
The Winning Team '52
By the Light of the Silvery Moon '53
Calamity Jane '53
Lucky Me '54
Young at Heart '54
Love Me or Leave Me '55
The Man Who Knew Too Much '56
The Pajama Game '57
Teacher's Pet '58
The Tunnel of Love '58
Pillow Talk '59
Midnight Lace '60
Please Don't Eat the Daisies '60
Lover Come Back '61
Billy Rose's Jumbo '62
That Touch of Mink '62
The Thrill of It All! '63
Send Me No Flowers '64
The Glass Bottom Boat '66
Where Were You When the Lights Went Out? '68
With Six You Get Eggroll '68

Gary Day
Night Nurse '77
Crime Broker '94

Josette Day
Beauty and the Beast '46
Well-Digger's Daughter '46
The Storm Within '48

Laraine Day
Doomed at Sundown '37
Dr. Kildare's Strange Case '40
Foreign Correspondent '40

Journey for Margaret '42
Mr. Lucky '43
The Story of Dr. Wassell '44
Those Endearing Young Charms '45
Tycoon '47
My Dear Secretary '49
Murder on Flight 502 '75
Return to Fantasy Island '77

Marceline Day
The Beloved Rogue '27
The Cameraman '28
Paradise Island '30
Sunny Skies '30
The Pocatello Kid '31
Broadway to Cheyenne '32
Fighting Fool '32
The King Murder '32
Flaming Signal '33
Telegraph Trail '33
Fighting Parson '35

Morris Day
Purple Rain '84
The Adventures of Ford Fairlane '90
Graffiti Bridge '90

Patrick Day
The Adventures of Huckleberry Finn '85
Hollywood Hot Tubs 2: Educating Crystal '89

Stuart Garrison Day
Covert Action '88
Search and Destroy '88

Vera Day
Quatermass 2 '57
Up the Creek '58

Daniel Day-Lewis
Sunday, Bloody Sunday '71
Gandhi '82
How Many Miles to Babylon? '82
The Bounty '84
My Beautiful Laundrette '85
A Room with a View '86
Stars and Bars '88
The Unbearable Lightness of Being '88
Eversmile New Jersey '89
My Left Foot '89
The Last of the Mohicans '92
The Age of Innocence '93
In the Name of the Father '93

Assaf Dayan
Operation Thunderbolt '77
The Uranium Conspiracy '78

Margit Dayka
Cat's Play '74
Nice Neighbor '79

Joaquim de Almeida
Good Morning, Babylon '87
Clear and Present Danger '94
Only You '94
Desperado '95

Maria de Aragon
Blood Mania '70
The Cremators '72
The Deadly and the Beautiful '73

Jean De Baer
84 Charing Cross Road '86
Broken Vows '87

Isaach de Bankole
Chocolat '88
No Fear, No Die '90
Heart of Darkness '93

Brenda de Banzie
Hobson's Choice '53
The Man Who Knew Too Much '56
Too Many Crooks '59
The Entertainer '60
Come September '61
The Mark '61
The Pink Panther '64

Burr de Benning
Iron Horsemen '71
Incredible Melting Man '77

Andre de Beranger
The Bat '26
So This is Paris '26

Nigel de Brulier
The Four Horsemen of the Apocalypse '21
The Three Musketeers '21
Salome/Queen Elizabeth '23
Ben-Hur '26
The Iron Mask '29

Celia de Burgh
Sound of Love '77
Phar Lap '84

Yvonne De Carlo
The Road to Morocco '42
Rhythm Parade '43
Salome, Where She Danced '45
Criss Cross '48
Captain's Paradise '53
Sea Devils '53
Passion '54
Flame of the Islands '55
Shotgun '55
Death of a Scoundrel '56
The Ten Commandments '56
Band of Angels '57
The Sword and the Cross '58
A Global Affair '63
McLintock! '63
Arizona Bushwackers '67
Hostile Guns '67
Blazing Stewardesses '75
Texas Layover '75
Satan's Cheerleaders '77
Nocturna '79
Silent Scream '80
The Munsters' Revenge '81
Play Dead '81
House of Shadows '83
Vultures '84
Bad Girls in the Movies '86
Cellar Dweller '87
American Gothic '88
Mirror, Mirror '90

Pedro de Cordoba
Condemned to Live '35
The Crusades '35
Law of the Pampas '39
The Ghost Breakers '40
Son of Fury '42
In Old New Mexico '45
Swamp Fire '46
Mexican Hayride '48
Omoo Omoo, the Shark God '49

Arturo de Cordova
For Whom the Bell Tolls '43
El: This Strange Passion '52
The New Invisible Man '58

Ted de Corsia
The Lady from Shanghai '48
The Naked City '48
It Happens Every Spring '49
Neptune's Daughter '49
The Enforcer '51
Dance with Me, Henry '56
The Kettles in the Ozarks '56
The Killing '56
Slightly Scarlet '56
The Outside Man '73

Eduardo de Filippo
Seven Deadly Sins '53
The Gold of Naples '54

Louis de Funes
Femmes de Paris '53
Seven Deadly Sins '53
The Sheep Has Five Legs '54
Four Bags Full '56
Belle Americaine '61
The Sucker '65
La Grande Vadrouille '66
Le Gendarme de Saint-Tropez '67
Delusions of Grandeur '76

Julio de Grazia
The Lion's Share '79
Time for Revenge '82
Deadly Revenge '83
Funny, Dirty Little War '83
The Stranger '87

Gloria De Haven
Modern Times '36
Susan and God '40
Best Foot Forward '43
Broadway Rhythm '44
Step Lively '44
The Thin Man Goes Home '44
Two Girls and a Sailor '44
Summer Holiday '48
Summer Stock '50
Three Little Words '50
The Yellow Cab Man '50
Two Tickets to Broadway '51
Bog '84

Consuelo de Haviland
Betty Blue '86
Barjo '93

Olivia de Havilland
Captain Blood '35
A Midsummer Night's Dream '35
Anthony Adverse '36
The Charge of the Light Brigade '36
The Adventures of Robin Hood '38
Dodge City '39
Gone with the Wind '39
The Private Lives of Elizabeth & Essex '39
Santa Fe Trail '40
Strawberry Blonde '41
They Died with Their Boots On '41
In This Our Life '42
Thank Your Lucky Stars '43
Dark Mirror '46
The Snake Pit '48
The Heiress '49
Not as a Stranger '55
The Ambassador's Daughter '56
Proud Rebel '58
Lady in a Cage '64
Hush, Hush, Sweet Charlotte '65
The Adventurers '70
Airport '77 '77
The Swarm '78
The Fifth Musketeer '79
Roots: The Next Generation '79
Anastasia: The Mystery of Anna '86
The Woman He Loved '88

Frank De Kova
Machine Gun Kelly '58
Teenage Caveman '58
The Jayhawkers '59
Atlantis, the Lost Continent '61
Cat in the Cage '68
Frasier the Sensuous Lion '73
Johnny Firecloud '75
Jive Turkey '76

Simon de la Brosse
The Little Thief '89
Strike It Rich '90

Marguerite de la Motte
Mark of Zorro '20
The Nut '21
Final Extra '27
The Iron Mask '29

Danny De La Paz
Boulevard Nights '79
3:15—The Moment of Truth '86
Miracle Mile '89
American Me '92

George de la Pena
Nijinsky '80
The Cowboy & the Ballerina '84
Brain Donors '92
Kuffs '92

John de Lancie
The Fisher King '91
The Hand that Rocks the Cradle '92
Arcade '93
Fearless '93
Deep Red '94
Evolver '94
Star Trek the Next Generation, the Final Episode: All Good Things... '94

Derek De Lint
The Assault '86
Mascara '87
Three Men and a Baby '87
Diary of a Mad Old Man '88
Stealing Heaven '88
The Unbearable Lightness of Being '88
The Endless Game '89

Terence de Marney
Dual Alibi '47
Die, Monster, Die! '65
Beast of Morocco '66

Maria De Medeiros
Henry & June '90
Meeting Venus '91
Akermania, Vol. 1 '92
Pulp Fiction '94

Carlo De Meyo
The Outside Man '73
Other Hell '85

Robert De Niro
Greetings '68
The Wedding Party '69
Bloody Mama '70
Hi, Mom! '70
Born to Win '71
The Swap '71
Bang the Drum Slowly '73
Mean Streets '73
The Godfather, Part 2 '74
America at the Movies '76
The Last Tycoon '76
1900 '76
Taxi Driver '76
New York, New York '77
The Deer Hunter '78
Raging Bull '80
The Godfather 1902-1959: The Complete Epic '81
True Confessions '81
King of Comedy '82
Falling in Love '84
Once Upon a Time in America '84
Brazil '85
The Mission '86
Angel Heart '87
The Untouchables '87
Midnight Run '88
Jacknife '89
We're No Angels '89
Awakenings '90
Goodfellas '90
Stanley and Iris '90
Backdraft '91
Cape Fear '91
Guilty by Suspicion '91
Mistress '91
Night and the City '92
A Bronx Tale '93
Mad Dog and Glory '93
This Boy's Life '93
Mary Shelley's Frankenstein '94
Casino '95
Heat '95
The Fan '96

Rossy de Palma
Women on the Verge of a Nervous Breakdown '88
Don Juan, My Love '90
Tie Me Up! Tie Me Down! '90
Kika '94
Ready to Wear '94
The Flower of My Secret '95

Lya de Putti
Othello '22
Variety '25
The Sorrows of Satan '26
The Informer '29

Chris De Rose
Aftershock '88
Breakaway '95

Anthony De Sando
The Return of Eliot Ness '91
Grand Isle '92
Federal Hill '94
Party Girl '94

Joe De Santis
Marty '55
Al Capone '59
And Now Miguel '66
Blue '68

Lorraine De Selle
Caged Women '84
House on the Edge of the Park '84
The Wild Beasts '85
Women's Prison Massacre '85

Christian de Sica
An Almost Perfect Affair '79
Detective School Dropouts '85

Vittorio De Sica
Peddlin' in Society '47
Pardon My Trunk '52
The Earrings of Madame De... '54
The Gold of Naples '54
Angel in a Taxi '59
The Battle of Austerlitz '60
Generale Della Rovere '60
It Started in Naples '60
The Millionairess '60
The Wonders of Aladdin '61
The Amorous Adventures of Moll Flanders '65
L'Odeur des Fauves '66
The Shoes of the Fisherman '68
Andy Warhol's Dracula '74
Bellissimo: Images of the Italian Cinema '87

Guiliana de Sio
Pool Hustlers '83
Private Affairs '89

Rosana De Soto
The In-Laws '79
Ballad of Gregorio Cortez '83
La Bamba '87
Stand and Deliver '88
Family Business '89
Star Trek 6: The Undiscovered Country '91

Edward De Souza
Kiss of the Vampire '62
The Phantom of the Opera '62
A Question of Attribution '91

Jose-Luis De Villalonga
The Lovers '59
Blood and Sand '89

Brandon de Wilde
The Member of the Wedding '52
Shane '53
Goodbye, My Lady '56
Missouri Traveler '58
All Fall Down '62
Hud '63
In Harm's Way '65
Those Calloways '65

Brian Deacon
Vampyres '74
Triple Echo '77
Jesus '79
A Zed & Two Noughts '88

Richard Deacon
Abbott and Costello Meet the Mummy '55
Carousel '56
Francis in the Haunted House '56
The Kettles in the Ozarks '56
The Patsy '64
Billie '65
Blackbeard's Ghost '67
The Gnome-Mobile '67
The One and Only, Genuine, Original Family Band '68
Bad Manners '84

Lucy Deakins
The Boy Who Could Fly '86
The Great Outdoors '88
Little Nikita '88
Cheetah '89
There Goes My Baby '92

Allison Dean
Coming to America '88
Ruby in Paradise '93

Eddie Dean
Law of the Pampas '39
Renegade Trail '39
Western Double Feature 24 '40s
Knights of the Range '40
Santa Fe Marshal '40
Song of Old Wyoming '45
Wildfire '45
The Caravan Trail '46
Colorado Serenade '46
Driftin' River '46
Wild West '46
West to Glory '47
Wild Country '47
Black Hills '48
Check Your Guns '48
The Hawk of Powder River '48
The Tioga Kid '48

Felicity Dean
The Whistle Blower '87
Persuasion '95

James Dean
Hill Number One '51
East of Eden '54
Rebel Without a Cause '55
Giant '56
James Dean Story '57
America at the Movies '76
James Dean: The First American Teenager '76
Hollywood Outtakes & Rare Footage '83

Dean ▶cont.

James Dean '85
Forever James Dean '88

Jimmy Dean
Diamonds Are Forever '71
The City '76
Big Bad John '90

Loren Dean
Say Anything '89
Billy Bathgate '91
1492: Conquest of Paradise '92
JFK: Reckless Youth '93
How to Make an American Quilt '95
Mrs. Winterbourne '96

Margia Dean
Rimfire '49
Fangs of the Wild '54
The Quatermass Experiment '56

Priscilla Dean
Outside the Law '21
White Tiger '23
Law of the Sea '38

Rick Dean
Heroes Stand Alone '89
Naked Obsession '91
Bloodfist 3: Forced to Fight '92
Raiders of the Sun '92
Saturday Night Special '92
Peephole '93
Cheyenne Warrior '94
Max is Missing '95
Stripteaser '95

Ron Dean
Big Score '83
Above the Law '88
Cocktail '88
Cold Justice '89
Legacy of Lies '92
Rudy '93

Leslie Deane
976-EVIL '88
Girlfriend from Hell '89
Freddy's Dead: The Final Nightmare '91
To Protect and Serve '92

Justin Deas
Dream Lover '85
Montana '90

Kristine DeBell
Lifepod '80
Willie & Phil '80
Tag: The Assassination Game '82
Rooster: Spurs of Death! '83
Cheerleaders' Wild Weekend '85

Lee DeBroux
Sweet Hostage '75
Hangfire '91
Open Fire '94

Jean Debucourt
La Chute de la Maison Usher '28
Seven Deadly Sins '53
The Earrings of Madame De... '54
The Crucible '57

Rosemary DeCamp
Cheers for Miss Bishop '41
The Jungle Book '42
Yankee Doodle Dandy '42
Commandos Strike at Dawn '43
Rhapsody in Blue '45
Look for the Silver Lining '49
The Story of Seabiscuit '49
On Moonlight Bay '51
By the Light of the Silvery Moon '53
Main Street to Broadway '53
13 Ghosts '60

Eugene Deckers
The Golden Salamander '51
Flame Over India '60
Lady L '65

Jan Decleir
Daens '92
Antonia's Line '95

Guy Decomble
Jour de Fete '48
The 400 Blows '59

Catherine Dee
In Deadly Heat '87
Stuff Stephanie in the Incinerator '89

Frances Dee
Finishing School '33
Little Women '33
Of Human Bondage '34
Becky Sharp '35
So Ends Our Night '41
Wheel of Fortune '41
I Walked with a Zombie '43
The Private Affairs of Bel Ami '47
Four Faces West '48
Gypsy Colt '54

Ruby Dee
The Jackie Robinson Story '50
A Raisin in the Sun '61
The Balcony '63
Gone are the Days '63
Purlie Victorious '63
The Incident '67
Buck and the Preacher '72
It's Good to Be Alive '74
I Know Why the Caged Bird Sings '79
Roots: The Next Generation '79
All God's Children '80
Cat People '82
Go Tell It On the Mountain '84
Gore Vidal's Lincoln '88
Windmills of the Gods '88
Do the Right Thing '89
Love at Large '89
The Court Martial of Jackie Robinson '90
Decoration Day '90
Zora Is My Name! '90
Jungle Fever '91
Cop and a Half '93
The Ernest Green Story '93
Just Cause '94
Stephen King's The Stand '94
Mr. & Mrs. Loving '96

Sandra Dee
Until They Sail '57
The Reluctant Debutante '58
Gidget '59
Imitation of Life '59
A Summer Place '59
Come September '61
Tammy and the Doctor '63
The Dunwich Horror '70
Fantasy Island '76
Lost '83

Eddie Deezen
I Wanna Hold Your Hand '78
Midnight Madness '80
A Polish Vampire in Burbank '80
Surf 2 '84
Mugsy's Girls '85
Rosebud Beach Hotel '85
Desperate Moves '86
Million Dollar Mystery '87
Assault of the Killer Bimbos '88
Beverly Hills Vamp '88
Hollywood Boulevard 2 '89
Teenage Exorcist '93

Don DeFore
The Stork Club '45
Without Reservations '46
Ramrod '47
Romance on the High Seas '48
Killer Bait '49
My Friend Irma '49
Too Late for Tears '49
A Girl in Every Port '52
Jumping Jacks '52
Battle Hymn '57
A Rare Breed '81

Calvert Deforest
Heaven Help Us '85
Leader of the Band '87
Mr. Write '92

Pia Degermark
Elvira Madigan '67
The Looking Glass War '69

Sam DeGrasse
The Scarlet Car '17
Robin Hood '22

John Dehner
Vigilantes of Boom Town '46
Hot Lead '51
The King's Thief '55
The Prodigal '55
Fastest Gun Alive '56
Girl in Black Stockings '57
The Left-Handed Gun '58
Man of the West '58
Support Your Local Gunfighter '71
The Day of the Dolphin '73
Killer Inside Me '76
Mountain Man '77
Nothing Personal '80
California Gold Rush '81
Creator '85
The Jagged Edge '85

David DeKeyser
Valentino '77
Yentl '83
Leon the Pig Farmer '93

Albert Dekker
Marie Antoinette '38
Dr. Cyclops '40
Seven Sinners '40
Strange Cargo '40
The Great Commandment '41
Honky Tonk '41
In Old California '42
Once Upon a Honeymoon '42
Wake Island '42
Buckskin Frontier '43
The Kansan '43
War of the Wildcats '43
The Woman of the Town '44
Experiment Perilous '45
Cass Timberlane '47
Gentleman's Agreement '47
As Young As You Feel '51
East of Eden '54
Illegal '55
Kiss Me Deadly '55
Suddenly, Last Summer '59
Gamera, the Invincible '66
The Wild Bunch '69

Louis Del Grande
Of Unknown Origin '83
Northern Extremes '93
Sugartime '95

Dulio Del Prete
Alfredo, Alfredo '72
Redneck '73
How Funny Can Sex Be? '76
The Sensuous Nurse '76

Dolores Del Rio
Evangeline '29
Bird of Paradise '32
Flying Down to Rio '33
Accused '36
Journey into Fear '42
Maria Candelaria '46
The Fugitive '48
Torero '56
Flor Silvestre '58
Flaming Star '60
Cheyenne Autumn '64
Children of Sanchez '79

Laura Del Sol
Carmen '83
The Stilts '84
The Hit '85
El Amor Brujo '86
The Crew '95

Benicio Del Toro
License to Kill '89
China Moon '91
Christopher Columbus: The Discovery '92
Fearless '93
Money for Nothing '93
Swimming with Sharks '94
The Usual Suspects '95
The Fan '96

Suzy Delair
Jenny Lamour '47
Pattes Blanches '49
Utopia '51
Gervaise '56
Fernandel the Dressmaker '57
Is Paris Burning? '68

Lisa Delamare
La Marseillaise '37
Monsieur Vincent '48
Baxter '89

Cassandra Delaney
One Night Stand '84
Fair Game '85
Hurricane Smith '92

Charles Delaney
Hearts of Humanity '32
Captured in Chinatown '35

Joan Delaney
The President's Analyst '67
Don't Drink the Water '69

Kim Delaney
That Was Then...This Is Now '85
Delta Force '86
Campus Man '87
Christmas Comes to Willow Creek '87
Hunter's Blood '87
The Drifter '88
Body Parts '91
Hangfire '91
The Disappearance of Christina '93
Darkman 2: The Return of Durant '94
The Force '94
Project Metalbeast: DNA Overload '94
Serial Killer '95
Tall, Dark and Deadly '95
Temptress '95

Pat Delaney
Zontar, the Thing from Venus '66
Creature of Destruction '67

Michael Delano
Catlow '71
Ring of Fire '91
Ring of Fire 2: Blood and Steel '92
Out for Blood '93
Private Wars '93

Dana Delany
Almost You '85
A Winner Never Quits '86
China Beach '88
Masquerade '88
Moon over Parador '88
Patty Hearst '88
Housesitter '92
Light Sleeper '92
Dead to Rights '93
Tombstone '93
Wild Palms '93
The Enemy Within '94
Exit to Eden '94
Live Nude Girls '95

Debra Deliso
The Slumber Party Massacre '82
Iced '88

Claudia Dell
Bachelor Apartment '31
Hearts of Humanity '32
Midnight Warning '32
Woman Condemned '33
The Lost City '34
Yellow Cargo '36
Boots of Destiny '37

Gabriel Dell
Angels with Dirty Faces '38
Little Tough Guys '38
Pride of the Bowery '41
Let's Get Tough '42
'Neath Brooklyn Bridge '42
Smart Alecks '42
Kid Dynamite '43
Follow the Leader '44
Million Dollar Kid '44
Bowery Buckaroos '47
Hard-Boiled Mahoney '47
Smugglers' Cove '48
Spook Busters '48
Master Minds '49
Blues Busters '50
Framed '75
The Escape Artist '82

Myrna Dell
Nocturne '46
Fighting Father Dunne '48
The Judge Steps Out '49
The Bushwackers '52
Naked Hills '56
Ma Barker's Killer Brood '60

Michael DellaFemina
Bloodlust: Subspecies 3 '93
Invisible: The Chronicles of Benjamin Knight '93
Mandroid '93

Edouard Delmont
Angele '34
Toni '34
Harvest '37
Passion for Life '48
The Sheep Has Five Legs '54

Genevieve Deloir
The Red Half-Breed '70
The Screaming Dead '72

Alain Delon
Sois Belle et Tais-Toi '58
Rocco and His Brothers '60
The Big Grab '63
Melodie en Sous-Sol '63
Joy House '64
The Eclipse '66
The Lost Command '66
Texas Across the River '66
Diabolically Yours '67
The Girl on a Motorcycle '68
Honor Among Thieves '68
Is Paris Burning? '68
Spirits of the Dead '68
Borsalino '70
Swimming Pool '70
Red Sun '71
Assassination of Trotsky '72
Godson '72
Scorpio '73
Widow Couderc '74
Gypsy '75
Icy Breasts '75
Mr. Klein '75
Boomerang '76
Les Aventuriers '77
The Concorde: Airport '79 '79
Swann in Love '84
Nouvelle Vague '90

Nathalie Delon
Bluebeard '72
Eyes Behind the Stars '72
Godson '72
Le Sex Shop '73
Game of Seduction '86

Jennifer Delora
Deranged '87
New York's Finest '87
Robot Holocaust '87
Sensations '87
Bedroom Eyes 2 '89

Daniele Delorme
Les Miserables '57
Pardon Mon Affaire '76

Julie Delpy
Beatrice '88
Europa, Europa '91
Voyager '91
The Three Musketeers '93
Before Sunrise '94
Killing Zoe '94
Trois Couleurs: Blanc '94
Younger & Younger '94

Rene Deltgen
The Mozart Story '48
Tromba, the Tiger Man '52
Journey to the Lost City '58

Rudy DeLuca
The Return of Count Yorga '71
Life Stinks '91

Dom DeLuise
Fail-Safe '64
The Glass Bottom Boat '66
Twelve Chairs '70
Blazing Saddles '74
Silent Movie '76
World's Greatest Lover '77
The Adventures of Sherlock Holmes' Smarter Brother '78
The Cheap Detective '78
The End '78
Sextette '78
Diary of a Young Comic '79
Fatso '80
Hot Stuff '80
The Last Married Couple in America '80
Smokey and the Bandit, Part 2 '80
Wholly Moses! '80
Cannonball Run '81
History of the World: Part 1 '81
The Best Little Whorehouse in Texas '82
Cannonball Run 2 '84
Johnny Dangerously '84
Haunted Honeymoon '86
My African Adventure '87
Spaceballs '87
Going Bananas '88
Loose Cannons '90
Almost Pregnant '91
Driving Me Crazy '91

Silence of the Hams '93
The Tin Soldier '95

Michael DeLuise
Encino Man '92
Midnight Edition '93

Peter DeLuise
Free Ride '86
The Midnight Hour '86
Children of the Night '92
Rescue Me '93
National Lampoon's Attack of the 5 Ft. 2 Women '94

Gordon DeMain
Fighting Texans '33
High Gear '33
Rainbow Ranch '33
The Mad Monster '42

William Demarest
The Jazz Singer '27
Hands Across the Table '35
Charlie Chan at the Opera '36
The Great Ziegfeld '36
Love on the Run '36
The Great Man Votes '38
Rebecca of Sunnybrook Farm '38
Christmas in July '40
The Great McGinty '40
The Devil & Miss Jones '41
The Lady Eve '41
Sullivan's Travels '41
All Through the Night '42
The Palm Beach Story '42
Pardon My Sarong '42
The Great Moment '44
Hail the Conquering Hero '44
Miracle of Morgan's Creek '44
Along Came Jones '45
The Jolson Story '46
The Perils of Pauline '47
Jolson Sings Again '49
Sorrowful Jones '49
Never a Dull Moment '50
Riding High '50
First Legion '51
Behave Yourself! '52
What Price Glory? '52
Dangerous When Wet '53
Escape from Fort Bravo '53
Here Come the Girls '53
Hell on Frisco Bay '55
Jupiter's Darling '55
The Mountain '56
Sincerely Yours '56
It's a Mad, Mad, Mad, Mad World '63
Viva Las Vegas '63
Don't Be Afraid of the Dark '73

Derrick DeMarney
Things to Come '36
Young and Innocent '37
Dangerous Moonlight '41
Frenzy '46
Inheritance '47

Orane Demazis
Marius '31
Fanny '32
Angele '34
Cesar '36
Harvest '37
Le Schpountz '38

Alla Demidova
The Seagull '71
Tchaikovsky '71

Cecil B. DeMille
Star Spangled Rhythm '42
Sunset Boulevard '50

Katherine DeMille
Belle of the Nineties '34
Viva Villa! '34
The Black Room '35
The Crusades '35
Drift Fence '36
The Gentleman from California '37
Unconquered '47
The Judge '49

Mylene Demongeot
Bonjour Tristesse '57
The Crucible '57
Just Another Pretty Face '58
Sois Belle et Tais-Toi '58
The Giant of Marathon '60
The Rape of the Sabines '61
Uncle Tom's Cabin '69
12 Plus 1 '70

Rebecca DeMornay
One from the Heart '82
Risky Business '83
Testament '83
Runaway Train '85
The Slugger's Wife '85
The Trip to Bountiful '85
The Murders in the Rue Morgue '86
Pecos Bill '86
And God Created Woman '88
Feds '88
By Dawn's Early Light '89
Dealers '89
Backdraft '91
An Inconvenient Woman '91
The Hand that Rocks the Cradle '92
Blind Side '93
Guilty as Sin '93
The Three Musketeers '93
Getting Out '94
Never Talk to Strangers '95

Darcy Demoss
Living to Die '91
Pale Blood '91
Eden '92
Eden 2 '93
Eden 3 '93
Eden 4 '93
Forbidden Zone: Alien Abduction '96

Patrick Dempsey
Heaven Help Us '85
Can't Buy Me Love '87
In the Mood '87
Meatballs 3 '87
In a Shallow Grave '88
Some Girls '88
Happy Together '89
Loverboy '89
Coupe de Ville '90
Mobsters '91
Run '91
Face the Music '92
For Better and For Worse '92
Bank Robber '93
JFK: Reckless Youth '93
Ava's Magical Adventure '94
With Honors '94
Bloodknot '95
The Right to Remain Silent '95

Carol Dempster
The Love Flower '20
Dream Street '21
The White Rose '23
Isn't Life Wonderful '24
Sally of the Sawdust '25
The Sorrows of Satan '26

Jeffrey DeMunn
Sessions '83
Trumps '83
Windy City '84
Terror in Toyland '85
A Time to Live '85
The Hitcher '86
Betrayed '88
The Blob '88
Gore Vidal's Lincoln '88
Windmills of the Gods '88
Blaze '89
Eyes of an Angel '91
Treacherous Crossing '92
Barbarians at the Gate '93
Down Came a Blackbird '94
Citizen X '95
Hiroshima '95

Judi Dench
A Study in Terror '66
A Midsummer Night's Dream '68
Wetherby '85
84 Charing Cross Road '86
A Room with a View '86
Saigon: Year of the Cat '87
A Handful of Dust '88
Henry V '89
Goldeneye '95
Jack and Sarah '96

Catherine Deneuve
Umbrellas of Cherbourg '64
Repulsion '65
Belle de Jour '67
Mayerling '68
April Fools '69
Mississippi Mermaid '69
Donkey Skin '70
Tristana '70
Dos Cruces en Danger Pass '71
Act of Aggression '73
La Grande Bourgeoise '74
The Hustle '75
Lovers Like Us '75
March or Die '77
A Slightly Pregnant Man '79
The Last Metro '80
Choice of Arms '83
The Hunger '83
I Love All of You '83
Fort Saganne '84
Love Songs '85
Scene of the Crime '87
Indochine '92

Jake Dengel
Ironweed '87
Bloodsucking Pharoahs of Pittsburgh '90
Prayer of the Rollerboys '91

Maurice Denham
Curse of the Demon '57
Sink the Bismarck '60
The Mark '61
Damn the Defiant '62
Paranoiac '62
Hysteria '64
The Alphabet Murders '65
The Nanny '65
Night Caller from Outer Space '66
Negatives '68
84 Charing Cross Road '86
Mr. Love '86
Monsignor Quixote '91

Marianne Denicourt
La Belle Noiseuse '90
Doomsday Gun '94

Lydie Denier
Blood Relations '87
Midnight Cabaret '90
Satan's Princess '90
Invasion of Privacy '92
Mardi Gras for the Devil '93
Red Shoe Diaries 3: Another Woman's Lipstick '93
Under Investigation '93
Guardian Angel '94

Jacques Denis
La Salamandre '71
The Clockmaker '76
Jonah Who Will Be 25 in the Year 2000 '76

Anthony John Denison
Crime Story: The Complete Saga '86
The Great Escape 2: The Untold Story '88
Full Exposure: The Sex Tape Scandals '89
Little Vegas '90
Child of Darkness, Child of Light '91
City of Hope '91
The Harvest '92
The Amy Fisher Story '93
A Brilliant Disguise '93
Full Eclipse '93
Sex, Love and Cold Hard Cash '93
Getting Gotti '94
Men of War '94

Leslie Denison
Sherlock Holmes and the Secret Weapon '42
The Snow Creature '54

Michael Denison
The Franchise Affair '52
Importance of Being Earnest '52
Angels One Five '54
Shadowlands '93

Brian Dennehy
Ants '77
Johnny We Hardly Knew Ye '77
Semi-Tough '77
F.I.S.T. '78
Foul Play '78
A Real American Hero '78
Butch and Sundance: The Early Days '79
The Jericho Mile '79
North Dallas Forty '79
Silent Victory: The Kitty O'Neil Story '79
10 '79
Little Miss Marker '80
A Rumor of War '80
To Love Again '80
First Blood '82
Split Image '82
Gorky Park '83
Never Cry Wolf '83
Finders Keepers '84
The Little Mermaid '84
The River Rat '84
Annie Oakley '85
Check Is in the Mail '85
Cocoon '85
Silverado '85
Twice in a Lifetime '85
Acceptable Risks '86
F/X '86
Legal Eagles '86
Best Seller '87
The Lion of Africa '87
Cocoon: The Return '88
A Father's Revenge '88
Miles from Home '88
Return to Snowy River '88
Day One '89
Perfect Witness '89
Indio '90
A Killing in a Small Town '90
The Last of the Finest '90
Presumed Innocent '90
Rising Son '90
The Belly of an Architect '91
F/X 2: The Deadly Art of Illusion '91
Diamond Fleece '92
Gladiator '92
Scott Turow's The Burden of Proof '92
Teamster Boss: The Jackie Presser Story '92
To Catch a Killer '92
Final Appeal '93
Foreign Affairs '93
The Stars Fell on Henrietta '94
Tommy Boy '95

Charles Denner
Bluebeard '63
The Two of Us '68
Z '69
Les Assassins de L'Ordre '71
The Holes '72
Mado '76
The Man Who Loved Women '77
Robert et Robert '79
Window Shopping '86

Richard Denning
Adam Had Four Sons '41
The Glass Key '42
Black Beauty '46
Unknown Island '48
Double Deal '50
Hangman's Knot '52
Creature from the Black Lagoon '54
Day the World Ended '55
Girls in Prison '56
An Affair to Remember '57
The Black Scorpion '57
Alice Through the Looking Glass '66

Sandy Dennis
Splendor in the Grass '61
Who's Afraid of Virginia Woolf? '66
Up the Down Staircase '67
That Cold Day in the Park '69
The Out-of-Towners '70
Mr. Sycamore '74
God Told Me To '76
Nasty Habits '77
The Four Seasons '81
Come Back to the Five & Dime Jimmy Dean, Jimmy Dean '82
The Execution '85
Another Woman '88
976-EVIL '88
Parents '89
The Indian Runner '91

Reginald Denny
California Straight Ahead '25
Skinner's Dress Suit '26
The Cheerful Fraud '27
Madam Satan '30
Parlor, Bedroom and Bath '31
Private Lives '31
Dancing Man '33
The Lost Patrol '34
Of Human Bondage '34
Anna Karenina '35
The Midnight Phantom '35
Bulldog Drummond Comes Back '37
Bulldog Drummond Escapes '37
Bulldog Drummond's Revenge '37
We're in the Legion Now '37
Arrest Bulldog Drummond '38
Bulldog Drummond's Peril '38
Bulldog Drummond's Revenge/ Bulldog Drummond's Peril '38
Bulldog Drummond's Bride '39
Bulldog Drummond's Secret Police '39
Rebecca '40
Captains of the Clouds '42
Sherlock Holmes: The Voice of Terror '42
Escape Me Never '47
My Favorite Brunette '47
Mr. Blandings Builds His Dream House '48
Abbott and Costello Meet Dr. Jekyll and Mr. Hyde '52
Escape to Burma '55
Sabaka '55
Cat Ballou '65
Assault on a Queen '66

Vernon Dent
Extra Girl '23
Baby Face Harry Langdon '26
His First Flame '26
The Cameraman '28
Texas Cyclone '32

Christa Denton
Convicted: A Mother's Story '87
The Gate '87
Scandal in a Small Town '88

Donna Denton
Death Blow '87
Glory Years '87
Outlaw of Gor '87
Slaughterhouse Rock '88

Graham Denton
The Great St. Louis Bank Robbery '59
The Young One '61

Bob Denver
Gilligan's Island: Meet the Crew '64
Who's Minding the Mint? '67
Wackiest Wagon Train in the West '77
High School USA '84
Back to the Beach '87

John Denver
Oh, God! '77
Foxfire '87

Elisabeth Depardieu
Tartuffe '84
Jean de Florette '87

Gerard Depardieu
The Holes '72
Going Places '74
Stavisky '74
Maitresse '76
1900 '76
Vincent, Francois, Paul and the Others '76
This Sweet Sickness '77
Get Out Your Handkerchiefs '78
Buffet Froid '79
The Last Metro '80
Loulou '80
Mon Oncle D'Amerique '80
La Chevre '81
The Woman Next Door '81
Danton '82
Choice of Arms '83
I Love All of You '83
Les Comperes '83
Moon in the Gutter '83
The Return of Martin Guerre '83
Fort Saganne '84
Tartuffe '84
One Woman or Two '85
Police '85
Menage '86
Jean de Florette '87
Under Satan's Sun '87
Too Beautiful for You '88
Camille Claudel '89
Cyrano de Bergerac '90
Green Card '90
Uranus '91
1492: Conquest of Paradise '92

Depardieu ▶cont.

Tous les Matins du Monde *'92*
Germinal *'93*
My Father the Hero *'93*
Colonel Chabert *'94*
Helas Pour Moi *'94*
A Pure Formality *'94*

Johnny Depp
A Nightmare on Elm Street *'84*
Private Resort *'84*
Platoon *'86*
Cry-Baby *'90*
Edward Scissorhands *'90*
Freddy's Dead: The Final Nightmare *'91*
Benny & Joon *'93*
What's Eating Gilbert Grape *'93*
Arizona Dream *'94*
Don Juan DeMarco *'94*
Ed Wood *'94*
Dead Man *'95*
Nick of Time *'95*

Bo Derek
Fantasies *'73*
Orca *'77*
10 *'79*
A Change of Seasons *'80*
Tarzan, the Ape Man *'81*
Bolero *'84*
Ghosts Can't Do It *'90*
Hot Chocolate *'92*
Shattered Image *'93*
Woman of Desire *'93*
Tommy Boy *'95*

John Derek
All the King's Men *'49*
Knock on Any Door *'49*
Ambush at Tomahawk Gap *'53*
The Outcast *'54*
The Annapolis Story *'55*
The Ten Commandments *'56*
Omar Khayyam *'57*
Exodus *'60*
Once Before I Die *'65*

Joe DeRita
Have Rocket Will Travel *'59*
The Three Stooges Meet Hercules *'61*
Three Stooges in Orbit *'62*
Around the World in a Daze *'63*
It's a Mad, Mad, Mad, Mad World *'63*
The Outlaws is Coming! *'65*

Edouard Dermithe
Les Enfants Terrible *'50*
The Testament of Orpheus *'59*

Bruce Dern
Marnie *'64*
Hush, Hush, Sweet Charlotte *'65*
The Wild Angels *'66*
The St. Valentine's Day Massacre *'67*
The Trip *'67*
The War Wagon *'67*
Waterhole #3 *'67*
Will Penny *'67*
Psych-Out *'68*
Rebel Rousers *'69*
Support Your Local Sheriff *'69*
They Shoot Horses, Don't They? *'69*
Bloody Mama *'70*
The Incredible Two-Headed Transplant *'71*
Silent Running *'71*
The Cowboys *'72*
The King of Marvin Gardens *'72*
Thumb Tripping *'72*
The Great Gatsby *'74*
The Laughing Policeman *'74*
Posse *'75*
Smile *'75*
Family Plot *'76*
Twist *'76*
Black Sunday *'77*
Coming Home *'78*
The Driver *'78*
Middle Age Crazy *'80*
Tattoo *'81*
That Championship Season *'82*
Harry Tracy *'83*
Toughlove *'85*
On the Edge *'86*
Big Town *'87*
Uncle Tom's Cabin *'87*
World Gone Wild *'88*
The 'Burbs *'89*
1969 *'89*
After Dark, My Sweet *'90*
The Court Martial of Jackie Robinson *'90*
Carolina Skeletons *'92*
Diggstown *'92*
Into the Badlands *'92*
Dead Man's Revenge *'93*
Amelia Earhart: The Final Flight *'94*
Mrs. Munck *'95*
A Mother's Prayer *'95*
Mulholland Falls *'95*
Wild Bill *'95*
Down Periscope *'96*

Laura Dern
Foxes *'80*
Teachers *'84*
Mask *'85*
Smooth Talk *'85*
Blue Velvet *'86*
Haunted Summer *'88*
Fat Man and Little Boy *'89*
Strange Case of Dr. Jekyll & Mr. Hyde *'89*
Wild at Heart *'90*
Rambling Rose *'91*
Afterburn *'92*
Fallen Angels 1 *'93*
Jurassic Park *'93*
A Perfect World *'93*
Down Came a Blackbird *'94*

Barbara DeRossi
Mussolini & I *'85*
Quo Vadis *'85*
Blood Ties *'87*

Richard Derr
Castle in the Desert *'42*
Guilty of Treason *'50*
When Worlds Collide *'51*
The Invisible Avenger *'58*
Terror Is a Man *'59*
Adam at 6 a.m. *'70*

Cleavant Derricks
Moscow on the Hudson *'84*
The Slugger's Wife *'85*
Off Beat *'86*
Bluffing It *'87*

Michael Des Barres
Nightflyers *'87*
Pink Cadillac *'89*
Midnight Cabaret *'90*
Waxwork 2: Lost in Time *'91*
Silk Degrees *'94*
A Simple Twist of Fate *'94*

Jean Desailly
La Symphonie Pastorale *'46*
Les Grandes Manoeuvres *'55*
The Soft Skin *'64*
Assassination of Trotsky *'72*

Anne DeSalvo
My Favorite Year *'82*
Bad Manners *'84*
D.C. Cab *'84*
Compromising Positions *'85*
Perfect *'85*
Burglar *'87*
Spike of Bensonhurst *'88*
Taking Care of Business *'90*
Dead in the Water *'91*
Casualties of Love: The "Long Island Lolita" Story *'93*
National Lampoon's Attack of the 5 Ft. 2 Women *'94*

Stanley DeSantis
Candyman *'92*
Armistead Maupin's Tales of the City *'93*
National Lampoon's Attack of the 5 Ft. 2 Women *'94*
Broken Trust *'95*
The Truth About Cats and Dogs *'96*

Gerard Desarthe
Uranus *'91*
Daens *'92*

Alex Descas
No Fear, No Die *'90*
I Can't Sleep *'93*

Mary Jo Deschanel
The Right Stuff *'83*
2010: The Year We Make Contact *'84*

Sandy Descher
The Cobweb *'55*
The Prodigal *'55*

Robert Desiderio
Oh, God! You Devil *'84*
Maximum Security *'87*
Gross Anatomy *'89*

William Desmond
Blood and Steel *'25*
Phantom of the West *'31*
Phantom of the Air *'33*
Rustler's Roundup *'33*
Tailspin Tommy *'34*
Courage of the North *'35*
Cowboy & the Bandit *'35*
Cyclone of the Saddle *'35*
Powdersmoke Range *'35*
Rustlers of Red Dog *'35*
Way of the West *'35*

Ivan Desny
Madeleine *'50*
The Respectful Prostitute *'52*
Lola Montes *'55*
Song Without End *'60*
End of Desire *'62*
Escapade in Florence *'62*
Sherlock Holmes and the Deadly Necklace *'62*
The Snake Hunter Strangler *'66*
Mayerling *'68*
Touch Me Not *'74*
The Marriage of Maria Braun *'79*
Berlin Alexanderplatz *'80*
Escape from the KGB *'87*
Quicker Than the Eye *'88*

Nada Despotovich
Babycakes *'89*
Taken Away *'89*

Maruschka Detmers
First Name: Carmen *'83*
Devil in the Flesh *'87*
Hanna's War *'88*
The Mambo Kings *'92*
The Shooter *'94*

Geoffrey Deuel
Chisum *'70*
Amateur Night *'85*

William Devane
McCabe & Mrs. Miller *'71*
My Old Man's Place *'71*
Missiles of October *'74*
Family Plot *'76*
Marathon Man *'76*
The Bad News Bears in Breaking Training *'77*
Red Alert *'77*
Rolling Thunder *'77*
The Dark *'79*
From Here to Eternity *'79*
Yanks *'79*
Honky Tonk Freeway *'81*
Red Flag: The Ultimate Game *'81*
Jane Doe *'83*
Testament *'83*
Hadley's Rebellion *'84*
Urge to Kill *'84*
Timestalkers *'87*
The Preppie Murder *'89*
Chips, the War Dog *'90*
Vital Signs *'90*
A Woman Named Jackie *'91*
Rubdown *'93*
Lady in Waiting *'94*
Detonator 2: Night Watch *'95*

Alan Deveau
Loose Screws *'85*
Recruits *'86*

Renee Devillers
J'Accuse *'37*
Heart of a Nation *'43*
The French Touch *'54*

Andy Devine
Yellowstone *'36*
A Star is Born *'37*
In Old Chicago *'38*
Stagecoach *'39*
Western Double Feature 18 *'40s*
The Gay Ranchero *'42*
Ali Baba and the Forty Thieves *'43*
Till the Clouds Roll By/A Star Is Born *'46*
On the Old Spanish Trail *'47*
Springtime in the Sierras *'47*
Eyes of Texas *'48*
Far Frontier *'48*
Grand Canyon Trail *'48*
Night Time in Nevada *'48*
Under California Stars *'48*
Never a Dull Moment *'50*
The Red Badge of Courage *'51*
Slaughter Trail *'51*
Montana Belle *'52*
Thunder Pass *'54*
The Adventures of Huckleberry Finn *'60*
Two Rode Together *'61*
The Man Who Shot Liberty Valance *'62*
How the West Was Won *'63*
Zebra in the Kitchen *'65*
Myra Breckinridge *'70*
Smoke *'70*
Whale of a Tale *'76*

George Devine
Time Without Pity *'57*
Tom Jones *'63*

Loretta Devine
Stanley and Iris *'90*
Caged Fear *'92*
Waiting to Exhale *'95*

Danny DeVito
Hurry Up or I'll Be Thirty *'73*
The Money *'75*
One Flew Over the Cuckoo's Nest *'75*
The Van *'77*
Goin' South *'78*
Going Ape! *'81*
Terms of Endearment *'83*
Johnny Dangerously *'84*
Ratings Game *'84*
Romancing the Stone *'84*
Amazing Stories *'85*
The Jewel of the Nile *'85*
Head Office *'86*
Ruthless People *'86*
Wise Guys *'86*
Throw Momma from the Train *'87*
Tin Men *'87*
Twins *'88*
The War of the Roses *'89*
Other People's Money *'91*
Batman Returns *'92*
Hoffa *'92*
Jack the Bear *'93*
Junior *'94*
Renaissance Man *'94*
Get Shorty *'95*
Matilda *'96*

Alan Devlin
The Lonely Passion of Judith Hearne *'87*
The Playboys *'92*

J.G. Devlin
The Raggedy Rawney *'90*
The Miracle *'91*

Richard Devon
The Prodigal *'55*
The Battle of Blood Island *'60*

Dorothy Devore
The Tomboy *'24*
Silent Movies...Just For the Fun of It! *'26*

Jon DeVries
The 4th Man *'79*
Act of Passion: The Lost Honor of Kathryn Beck *'83*
Lianna *'83*
Truth or Die *'86*
Rachel River *'87*
Sarah, Plain and Tall *'91*
Grand Isle *'92*
Skylark *'93*

Elaine Devry
A Guide for the Married Man *'67*
The Cheyenne Social Club *'70*

Eddie Dew
Raiders of Sunset Pass *'43*
Six Gun Gospel *'43*
Pagan Island *'60*

Patrick Dewaere
Going Places *'74*
The French Detective *'75*
Catherine & Co. *'76*
Get Out Your Handkerchiefs *'78*
Hothead *'78*
Beau Pere *'81*
The Best Way *'82*
Heat of Desire *'84*

Colleen Dewhurst
Medea *'59*
The Nun's Story *'59*
A Fine Madness *'66*
The Cowboys *'72*
McQ *'74*
The Story of Jacob & Joseph *'74*
Annie Hall *'77*
And Baby Makes Six *'79*
Ice Castles *'79*
Mary and Joseph: A Story of Faith *'79*
Silent Victory: The Kitty O'Neil Story *'79*
Third Walker *'79*
When a Stranger Calls *'79*
Final Assignment *'80*
The Guyana Tragedy: The Story of Jim Jones *'80*
Dead Zone *'83*
The Glitter Dome *'84*
You Can't Take It with You *'84*
Anne of Green Gables *'85*
The Blue and the Gray *'85*
Between Two Women *'86*
The Boy Who Could Fly *'86*
Sword of Gideon *'86*
Anne of Avonlea *'87*
Obsessed *'88*
Termini Station *'89*
Lantern Hill *'90*
Dying Young *'91*
Bed & Breakfast *'92*
Danielle Steel's Kaleidoscope *'92*

Billy DeWolfe
Blue Skies *'46*
The Perils of Pauline *'47*
Dear Wife *'49*
Tea for Two *'50*
Lullaby of Broadway *'51*
Billie *'65*

Anthony Dexter
Fire Maidens from Outer Space *'56*
Married Too Young *'62*

Brad Dexter
The Las Vegas Story *'52*
Between Heaven and Hell *'56*
The Oklahoman *'56*
Run Silent, Run Deep *'58*
Last Train from Gun Hill *'59*
The Magnificent Seven *'60*
None But the Brave *'65*
Von Ryan's Express *'65*
Winter Kills *'79*
Secret Ingredient *'92*

Susan Dey
First Love *'77*
Little Women *'78*
Comeback Kid *'80*
Looker *'81*
Sunset Limousine *'83*
Love Leads the Way *'84*
Echo Park *'86*
L.A. Law *'86*
The Trouble with Dick *'88*
That's Adequate *'90*
Blue River *'95*

Cliff DeYoung
The Lindbergh Kidnapping Case *'76*
King *'78*
Awakening of Candra *'81*
Shock Treatment *'81*
The Hunger *'83*
Independence Day *'83*
Protocol *'84*
Reckless *'84*
Annie Oakley *'85*
Secret Admirer *'85*
F/X *'86*
Flight of the Navigator *'86*
Code Name: Dancer *'87*
The Survivalist *'87*
Bulldance *'88*
Fear *'88*
In Dangerous Company *'88*
Pulse *'88*
Flashback *'89*
Forbidden Sun *'89*
Glory *'89*
Rude Awakening *'89*
Fourth Story *'90*
Robert Kennedy and His Times *'90*

Immortal Sins '91
To Die Standing '91
Dr. Giggles '92
Nails '92
Revenge of the Red Baron '93
Stephen King's The Tommyknockers '93
The X-Files: Pilot Episode/Deep Throat '93
Carnosaur 2 '94
RoboCop the Series: The Future of Law Enforcement '94
Star Quest '94
Andersonville '95
The Craft '96
The Substitute '96

Robert Dhery
Femmes de Paris '53
Belle Americaine '61

Dalia di Lazzaro
Andy Warhol's Frankenstein '74
Creepers '85

Don Diamond
Borderline '50
Adventures of Kit Carson '51

Reed Edward Diamond
Ironclads '90
Memphis Belle '90
O Pioneers! '91
Blind Spot '93

Selma Diamond
Bang the Drum Slowly '73
Twilight Zone: The Movie '83
All of Me '84

John DiAquino
Pumpkinhead '88
Slipping into Darkness '88

Cameron Diaz
The Mask '94
The Last Supper '96

Vic Diaz
Flight to Fury '66
Beast of the Yellow Night '70
Night of the Cobra Woman '72
The Deadly and the Beautiful '73
Savage! '73
Deathhead Virgin '74
Too Hot to Handle '76
The Children of An Lac '80
Caged Heat 2: Stripped of Freedom '94

Leonardo DiCaprio
Critters 3 '91
This Boy's Life '93
What's Eating Gilbert Grape '93
The Basketball Diaries '94
The Quick and the Dead '94
Total Eclipse '95

George DiCenzo
Helter Skelter '76
The Frisco Kid '79
The Ninth Configuration '79
The Night the City Screamed '80
Back to the Future '85
About Last Night... '86
Omega Syndrome '87
Walk Like a Man '87
18 Again! '88
The Equalizer: Memories of Manon '88
The New Adventures of Pippi Longstocking '88
Sing '89
Exorcist 3: Legion '90

Bobby DiCicco
I Wanna Hold Your Hand '78
Night Shift '82
The Philadelphia Experiment '84
Splash '84
Tiger Warsaw '87
Frame Up '91
The Last Hour '91

Andy Dick
...And God Spoke '94
In the Army Now '94
The Cable Guy '96

Douglas Dick
The Accused '48
The Red Badge of Courage '51
The Oklahoman '56

Beach Dickerson
T-Bird Gang '59
Creature from the Haunted Sea '60

George Dickerson
Cutter's Way '81
Blue Velvet '86
After Dark, My Sweet '90
Death Warrant '90

Lucinda Dickey
Breakin' '84
Breakin' 2: Electric Boogaloo '84
Ninja 3: The Domination '84
Cheerleader Camp '88

Angie Dickinson
Lucky Me '54
Hidden Guns '56
China Gate '57
Rio Bravo '59
The Bramble Bush '60
Ocean's 11 '60
Rome Adventure '62
Captain Newman, M.D. '63
The Killers '64
Cast a Giant Shadow '66
The Chase '66
The Poppy Is Also a Flower '66
Point Blank '67
Resurrection of Zachary Wheeler '71
Thief '71
The Outside Man '73
Big Bad Mama '74
Pray for the Wildcats '74
Klondike Fever '79
Dressed to Kill '80
Charlie Chan and the Curse of the Dragon Queen '81
Death Hunt '81
One Shoe Makes It Murder '82
Jealousy '84
Big Bad Mama 2 '87
Fire and Rain '89
Texas Guns '90
Treacherous Crossing '92
Wild Palms '93
Even Cowgirls Get the Blues '94
The Maddening '95
Sabrina '95

Neil Dickson
Biggles '85
The Murders in the Rue Morgue '86
It Couldn't Happen Here '88

Bo Diddley
Hell's Angels Forever '83
Chuck Berry: Hail! Hail! Rock 'n' Roll '87
Rockula '90

Gabino Diego
Ay, Carmela! '90
Belle Epoque '92

Juan Diego
Cabeza de Vaca '90
Jamon, Jamon '93

John Diehl
Angel '84
Miami Vice '84
Cool Blue '88
Glitz '88
Dark Side of the Moon '90
Kickboxer 2: The Road Back '90
Madhouse '90
A Climate for Killing '91
Motorama '91
Mikey '92
Mo' Money '92
Falling Down '93
Remote '93
Almost Dead '94
Stargate '94
Buffalo Girls '95
Color of a Brisk and Leaping Day '95
Three Wishes '95
Wes Craven Presents Mind Ripper '95

John Dierkes
The Daughter of Dr. Jekyll '57
The Haunted Palace '63

Charles Dierkop
The Fix '84
Banzai Runner '86
Roots of Evil '91

Gustav Diesl
Westfront 1918 '30
Crimes of Dr. Mabuse '32
Das Testament des Dr. Mabuse '33

William Dieterle
Backstairs '21
Waxworks '24

Marlene Dietrich
The Blue Angel '30
Morocco '30
Dishonored '31
Blonde Venus '32
Shanghai Express '32
Scarlet Empress '34
Desire '36
The Garden of Allah '36
Angel '37
Knight Without Armour '37
Destry Rides Again '39
Seven Sinners '40
The Lady is Willing '42
Pittsburgh '42
The Spoilers '42
Golden Earrings '47
Stage Fright '50
No Highway in the Sky '51
Rancho Notorious '52
Witness for the Prosecution '57
Touch of Evil '58
Judgment at Nuremberg '61
Paris When It Sizzles '64
The Love Goddesses '65
Just a Gigolo '79

Frank Dietz
Zombie Nightmare '86
The Jitters '88

Anton Diffring
The Colditz Story '55
Circus of Horrors '60
Fahrenheit 451 '66
Where Eagles Dare '68
Zeppelin '71
Dead Pigeon on Beethoven Street '72
Mark of the Devil 2 '72
Seven Deaths in the Cat's Eye '72
Call Him Mr. Shatter '74
Black Werewolf '75
Valentino '77
The Winds of War '83

Dudley Digges
Devotion '31
The Maltese Falcon '31
Emperor Jones '33
Emperor Jones/Paul Robeson: Tribute to an Artist '33
The Invisible Man '33
China Seas '35
Mutiny on the Bounty '35
The General Died at Dawn '36
Son of Fury '42

Arthur Dignam
Between Wars '74
The Devil's Playground '76
Strange Behavior '81
We of the Never Never '82
The Wild Duck '84
The Right Hand Man '87
The Everlasting Secret Family '88
The Nostradamus Kid '92

Stephen Dillane
The Rector's Wife '94
Two If by Sea '95

Victoria Dillard
Ricochet '91
Deep Cover '92
Out of Sync '95

Phyllis Diller
Splendor in the Grass '61
Boy, Did I Get a Wrong Number! '66
A Pleasure Doing Business '79
Pink Motel '82
Minsky's Follies '83
The Bone Yard '90
The Worst of Hollywood: Vol. 1 '90
Heartstrings '95

Bradford Dillman
Compulsion '59
Sergeant Ryker '68
Black Water Gold '69
The Bridge at Remagen '69
Brother John '70
Suppose They Gave a War and Nobody Came? '70
Escape from the Planet of the Apes '71
The Mephisto Waltz '71
Resurrection of Zachary Wheeler '71
Moon of the Wolf '72
Master Mind '73
The Way We Were '73
Death in Deep Water '74
Murder or Mercy '74
99 & 44/100 Dead '74
Bug '75
Force Five '75
The Enforcer '76
The Widow '76
The Amsterdam Kill '78
Piranha '78
The Swarm '78
Love and Bullets '79
Running Scared '79
One Away '80
Legend of Walks Far Woman '82
Sudden Impact '83
The Treasure of the Amazon '84
Man Outside '88
Heroes Stand Alone '89
Lords of the Deep '89

Kevin Dillon
No Big Deal '83
Heaven Help Us '85
Platoon '86
The Blob '88
Remote Control '88
The Rescue '88
Immediate Family '89
War Party '89
When He's Not a Stranger '89
The Doors '91
A Midnight Clear '92
No Escape '94
Criminal Hearts '95
True Crime '95

Matt Dillon
Over the Edge '79
Little Darlings '80
My Bodyguard '80
Liar's Moon '82
Tex '82
The Outsiders '83
Rumble Fish '83
The Flamingo Kid '84
Rebel '85
Target '85
Native Son '86
Big Town '87
Kansas '88
Bloodhounds of Broadway '89
Drugstore Cowboy '89
A Kiss Before Dying '91
Women & Men: In Love There Are No Rules '91
Singles '92
Golden Gate '93
Mr. Wonderful '93
The Saint of Fort Washington '93
Frankie Starlight '95
To Die For '95
Beautiful Girls '96

Melinda Dillon
Bound for Glory '76
Close Encounters of the Third Kind '77
Slap Shot '77
F.I.S.T. '78
Marriage Is Alive and Well '80
The Shadow Box '80
Absence of Malice '81
Fallen Angel '81
A Christmas Story '83
The Juggler of Notre Dame '84
Right of Way '84
Songwriter '84
Harry and the Hendersons '87
Captain America '89
Nightbreaker '89
Spontaneous Combustion '89
Staying Together '89
The Prince of Tides '91
Shattered Spirits '91
Sioux City '94
How to Make an American Quilt '95
To Wong Foo, Thanks for Everything, Julie Newmar '95

Paul Dillon
Kiss Daddy Goodnight '87
The Beat '88
Blink '93

Stephen Dillon
An Affair in Mind '89
Christabel '89

Tom Dillon
Dressed to Kill '46
Night Tide '63

Victor Dimattia
Danielle Steel's Heartbeat '93
Dennis the Menace: Dinosaur Hunter '93

Alan Dinehart
After Midnight '33
A Study in Scarlet '33
Supernatural '33
Baby, Take a Bow '34
Everything Happens at Night '39
Second Fiddle '39
The Heat's On '43
It's a Great Life '43
Sweet Rosie O'Grady '43

Charles Dingle
The Little Foxes '41
Johnny Eager '42
Somewhere I'll Find You '42
Guest Wife '45
Here Come the Co-Eds '45
The Beast with Five Fingers '46
If You Knew Susie '48
A Southern Yankee '48
The Court Martial of Billy Mitchell '55

Ernie Dingo
The Fringe Dwellers '86
Crocodile Dundee 2 '88
A Waltz Through the Hills '88
Until The End of The World '91
Clowning Around '92
Clowning Around 2 '93

Kelly Dingwall
Around the World in 80 Ways '86
The Custodian '94

Reece Dinsdale
Winter Flight '84
Threads '85
Young Catherine '91

Rose Dione
Suds '20
Salome '22

Stefano Dionisi
Farinelli '94
Joseph '95

John Disanti
Eyes of a Stranger '81
Man of the House '95

Bob Dishy
Lovers and Other Strangers '70
I Wonder Who's Killing Her Now? '76
Brighton Beach Memoirs '86
Used People '92
My Boyfriend's Back '93
Don Juan DeMarco '94
Kill My Wife...Please!

Divine
Mondo Trasho '69
Multiple Maniacs '70
Pink Flamingos '72
Female Trouble '74
Polyester '81
I Wanna Be a Beauty Queen '85
Lust in the Dust '85
Trouble in Mind '86
Hairspray '88
Out of the Dark '88
Divine '90

Andrew Divoff
Toy Soldiers '91
Back in the USSR '92
Interceptor '92
Running Cool '93
A Low Down Dirty Shame '94
Oblivion '94
Backlash: Oblivion 2 '95
Magic Island '95
The Stranger '95
Xtro 3: Watch the Skies '95

Richard Dix
The Ten Commandments '23
Lucky Devil '25
Vanishing American '26
Seven Keys to Baldplate '29
Cimarron '30
Lost Squadron '32
Ace of Aces '33

Dix ▶cont.

Transatlantic Tunnel '35
Special Investigator '36
Yellow Dust '36
American Empire '42
Buckskin Frontier '43
The Kansan '43

Robert Dix
Deadwood '65
Blood of Dracula's Castle '69
Satan's Sadists '69
Horror of the Blood Monsters '70
Cain's Cutthroats '71
Wild Wheels '75
Killers '88

Donna Dixon
Bosom Buddies '80
Margin for Murder '81
Doctor Detroit '83
Spies Like Us '85
Beverly Hills Madam '86
The Couch Trip '87
Lucky Stiff '88
Speed Zone '88
Wayne's World '92

Ivan Dixon
A Raisin in the Sun '61
Nothing But a Man '64
A Patch of Blue '65
Suppose They Gave a War and Nobody Came? '70
Fer-De-Lance '74
Car Wash '76

James Dixon
It's Alive '74
It's Alive 3: Island of the Alive '87
Return to Salem's Lot '87

Joan Dixon
Gunplay '51
Hot Lead '51

MacIntyre Dixon
Ghostwriter '84
Funny Farm '88

Pamela Dixon
Hollywood in Trouble '87
L.A. Crackdown '87
Mayhem '87
L.A. Crackdown 2 '88
Chance '89
C.I.A.: Code Name Alexa '92
Magic Kid '92
C.I.A. 2: Target Alexa '94

Steve Dixon
The Carrier '87
Mosquito '95

Badja Djola
The Serpent and the Rainbow '87
Mississippi Burning '88
An Innocent Man '89
A Rage in Harlem '91
Who's the Man? '93
Heaven's Prisoners '95

Mauricio Do Valle
Antonio Das Mortes '68
Amazon Jail '85

Heidi Dobbs
Death Journey '76
Jornada de Muerte '80s

Valeria D'Obici
Passion of Love '82
Escape from the Bronx '85

Alan Dobie
The Charge of the Light Brigade '68
White Mischief '88

Lawrence Dobkin
Geronimo '62
Patton '70

Gosia Dobrowolska
Silver City '84
Around the World in 80 Ways '86
A Woman's Tale '92
Careful '94
The Custodian '94

Kevin Dobson
Midway '76
Orphan Train '79
Hardhat & Legs '80
All Night Long '81
Margin for Murder '81
Code of Honor '84
Dirty Work '92

Peter Dobson
Sing '89
The Marrying Man '91
Where the Day Takes You '92
Dead Cold '96
The Frighteners '96

Tamara Dobson
Cleopatra Jones '73
Cleopatra Jones & the Casino of Gold '75
Norman, Is That You? '76
Chained Heat '83
The Amazons '84

Vernon Dobtcheff
The Assassination Bureau '69
Darling Lili '70
Nijinsky '80
Pascali's Island '88
M. Butterfly '93

Jack Dodson
The Getaway '72
Return to Mayberry '85
A Climate for Killing '91

John Doe
Slamdance '87
Great Balls of Fire '89
A Matter of Degrees '90
Pure Country '92
Roadside Prophets '92
Georgia '95

Matt Doherty
The Mighty Ducks '92
So I Married an Axe Murderer '93

Shannen Doherty
Night Shift '82
Girls Just Want to Have Fun '85
Heathers '89
Beverly Hills 90210 '90
Freeze Frame '92
Beverly Hills 90210: The Graduation '93
Almost Dead '94
Blindfold: Acts of Obsession '94
Mallrats '95

Michael Dolan
Hamburger Hill '87
Light of Day '87
Biloxi Blues '88

Guy Doleman
The Ipcress File '65
Thunderball '65
The Prisoner: Arrival '68

Ami Dolenz
Children of the Night '92
Faith '92
Miracle Beach '92
Stepmonster '92
Rescue Me '93
Ticks '93
Witchboard 2: The Devil's Doorway '93
Mortal Danger '94
Pumpkinhead 2: Blood Wings '94
Life 101 '95

Mickey Dolenz
Head '68
Night of the Strangler '73

Dora Doll
Black and White in Color '76
Boomerang '76

Patrick Dollaghan
Murphy's Fault '88
Circle of Fear '89
Kill Slade '89

Larry Domasin
Fun in Acapulco '63
Island of the Blue Dolphins '64

Arielle Dombasle
Le Beau Mariage '82
Pauline at the Beach '83
The Boss' Wife '86
Around the World in 80 Days '89
Trade Secrets '90s
Twisted Obsession '90
Little Indian, Big City '95
Raging Angels '95

Faith Domergue
Cult of the Cobra '55
It Came from Beneath the Sea '55
This Island Earth '55
The Atomic Man '56
Voyage to the Prehistoric Planet '65
The Sibling '72
Blood Legacy '73
The House of Seven Corpses '73

Arturo Dominici
Hercules '58
Black Sunday '60

Solveig Dommartin
Wings of Desire '88
No Fear, No Die '90
Until The End of The World '91
Faraway, So Close! '93

Angelica Domrose
Girls Riot '88
The Scorpion Woman '89

Linda Dona
Delta Heat '92
Final Embrace '92

Elinor Donahue
Three Daring Daughters '48
Love Is Better Than Ever '52
Girls' Town '59
High School USA '84
Pretty Woman '90
Freddy's Dead: The Final Nightmare '91
The Invaders '95

Troy Donahue
Tarnished Angels '57
Imitation of Life '59
Monster on the Campus '59
A Summer Place '59
Parrish '61
Rome Adventure '62
Palm Springs Weekend '63
Those Fantastic Flying Fools '67
Love Thrill Murders '71
Cockfighter '74
The Godfather, Part 2 '74
The Legend of Frank Woods '77
The Godfather 1902-1959: The Complete Epic '81
Tin Man '83
Grandview U.S.A. '84
Cyclone '87
Deadly Prey '87
Hollywood Cop '87
Dr. Alien '88
Hawkeye '88
Sexpot '88
Terminal Force '88
A Woman Obsessed '88
Assault of the Party Nerds '89
The Chilling '89
Deadly Spygames '89
Cry-Baby '90
Nudity Required '90
Omega Cop '90
Shock 'Em Dead '90
Deadly Diamonds '91
The Pamela Principle '91
Sounds of Silence '91
Showdown '93
South Seas Massacre

James Donald
In Which We Serve '43
Immortal Battalion '44
The Gay Lady '49
Beau Brummel '54
The Pickwick Papers '54
Lust for Life '56
The Bridge on the River Kwai '57
The Vikings '58
Third Man on the Mountain '59
Victoria Regina '61
The Great Escape '63
King Rat '65
Cast a Giant Shadow '66
The Big Sleep '78

Norma Donaldson
9 to 5 '80
Staying Alive '83
The Five Heartbeats '91
Poetic Justice '93

Ted Donaldson
The Adventures of Rusty '45
A Tree Grows in Brooklyn '45
The Red Stallion '47
Son of Rusty '47
Rusty's Birthday '49

Peter Donat
Different Story '78
F.I.S.T. '78
Mirrors '78
Return Engagement '78
The China Syndrome '79
Mazes and Monsters '82
The Bay Boy '85
Massive Retaliation '85
Honeymoon '87
Tucker: The Man and His Dream '88
The War of the Roses '89
The Babe '92
School Ties '92

Robert Donat
If I Were Rich '33
The Private Life of Henry VIII '33
The Count of Monte Cristo '34
The 39 Steps '35
The Ghost Goes West '36
Knight Without Armour '37
The Citadel '38
Goodbye, Mr. Chips '39
The Adventures of Tartu '43
The Winslow Boy '48
The Inn of the Sixth Happiness '58
Hitchcock Collection '87

Ludwig Donath
The Secret Code '42
The Jolson Story '46
The Lovable Cheat '49

Manuel Donde
Savage Wilderness '55
Swamp of the Lost Monster '65

Yolande Donlan
The Devil Bat '41
The Adventurers '70

Brian Donlevy
Barbary Coast '35
In Old Chicago '38
Allegheny Uprising '39
Beau Geste '39
Destry Rides Again '39
Jesse James '39
Union Pacific '39
Brigham Young: Frontiersman '40
The Great McGinty '40
Billy the Kid '41
Birth of the Blues '41
The Glass Key '42
The Great Man's Lady '42
Wake Island '42
Miracle of Morgan's Creek '44
The Virginian '46
Kiss of Death '47
Command Decision '48
A Southern Yankee '48
Impact '49
Slaughter Trail '51
Hoodlum Empire '52
Ride the Man Down '53
Big Combo '55
The Quatermass Experiment '56
Quatermass 2 '57
Cowboy '58
The Errand Boy '61
How to Stuff a Wild Bikini '65
Gamera, the Invincible '66
Arizona Bushwackers '67
Five Golden Dragons '67

Steve Donmyer
Glitch! '88
Terminal Exposure '89

Barnard Pierre Donnadieu
The Return of Martin Guerre '83
Beatrice '88
The Vanishing '88

Jeff Donnell
The Fuller Brush Girl '50
In a Lonely Place '50
Redwood Forest Trail '50
Walk Softly, Stranger '50
Three Guys Named Mike '51
Because You're Mine '52
My Man Godfrey '57
Gidget Goes to Rome '63

Donal Donnelly
The Knack '65
Waterloo '71
The Dead '87
The Godfather, Part 3 '90
Squanto: A Warrior's Tale '94

Ruth Donnelly
Blessed Event '32
Bureau of Missing Persons '33
Female '33
Footlight Parade '33
Ladies They Talk About '33
Hands Across the Table '35
Mr. Deeds Goes to Town '36
The Affairs of Annabel '38
Annabel Takes a Tour/Maid's Night Out '38
Holiday '38
I'd Climb the Highest Mountain '51
A Lawless Street '55

Tim Donnelly
The Toolbox Murders '78
The Clonus Horror '79

Robert Donner
Vanishing Point '71
Man Who Loved Cat Dancing '73
Under the Rainbow '81
Lassie: Well of Love '90

Vincent D'Onofrio
First Turn On '83
Adventures in Babysitting '87
Full Metal Jacket '87
Mystic Pizza '88
The Blood of Heroes '89
Signs of Life '89
Crooked Hearts '91
Dying Young '91
Fires Within '91
JFK '91
The Player '92
Desire '93
Household Saints '93
Mr. Wonderful '93
Being Human '94
Ed Wood '94
Imaginary Crimes '94
Stuart Saves His Family '94
Strange Days '95

Amanda Donohoe
Foreign Body '86
Castaway '87
The Lair of the White Worm '88
An Affair in Mind '89
The Rainbow '89
Dark Obsession '90
Paper Mask '91
Double Cross '92
Shame '92
The Substitute '93
A Woman's Guide to Adultery '93
The Madness of King George '94

Donovan
Aliens from Spaceship Earth '77
Bob Dylan: Don't Look Back '91

King Donovan
The Enforcer '51
The Merry Widow '52
Singin' in the Rain '52
Easy to Love '53
Forever Female '53
Invasion of the Body Snatchers '56
Cowboy '58
The Hanging Tree '59

Martin Donovan
Surviving Desire '91
Trust '91
Simple Men '92
Quick '93
Amateur '94
Nadja '95
Flirt '95

Tate Donovan
Into Thin Air '85
Not My Kid '85
Clean and Sober '88
Dangerous Curves '88
Vietnam War Story 2 '88
Dead Bang '89
Memphis Belle '90
Little Noises '91
Ethan Frome '92
Love Potion #9 '92
Equinox '93
Inside Monkey Zetterland '93
Holy Matrimony '94
America's Dream '95

Terence Donovan
Money Movers '78
The Man from Snowy River '82
The Winds of Jarrah '83

Alison Doody
Prayer for the Dying '87
Taffin '88

Indiana Jones and the Last Crusade '89
Duel of Hearts '92
Ring of the Musketeers '93
Major League 2 '94
Temptation '94

James Doohan
Star Trek Bloopers '69
Man in the Wilderness '71
Star Trek: The Motion Picture '80
Star Trek 2: The Wrath of Khan '82
Star Trek 3: The Search for Spock '84
Star Trek 4: The Voyage Home '86
Star Trek 5: The Final Frontier '89
Double Trouble '91
Star Trek 6: The Undiscovered Country '91
Amore! '93
Star Trek Generations '94
Storybook '95

Paul Dooley
A Wedding '78
Breaking Away '79
Rich Kids '79
Popeye '80
Paternity '81
Endangered Species '82
Hansel and Gretel '82
Kiss Me Goodbye '82
Rumpelstiltskin '82
Going Berserk '83
Strange Brew '83
Sixteen Candles '84
Big Trouble '86
The Murder of Mary Phagan '87
O.C. and Stiggs '87
Last Rites '88
Lip Service '88
Flashback '89
When He's Not a Stranger '89
The Court Martial of Jackie Robinson '90
White Hot: The Mysterious Murder of Thelma Todd '91
Shakes the Clown '92
Armistead Maupin's Tales of the City '93
Cooperstown '93
A Dangerous Woman '93
My Boyfriend's Back '93
Evolver '94
State of Emergency '94
Out There '95
The Underneath '95

Lucinda Dooling
The Alchemist '81
Miracle on Ice '81
Lovely ... But Deadly '82

Patric Doonan
The Blue Lamp '49
Train of Events '49
Blackout '50

Robert DoQui
Coffy '73
A Dream for Christmas '73
Nashville '75
RoboCop '87
Short Fuse '88
Miracle Mile '89
Original Intent '91

Karin Dor
Forger of London '61
The Invisible Dr. Mabuse '62
Strangler of Blackmoor Castle '63
Carpet of Horror '64
The Last Tomahawk '65
You Only Live Twice '67
Dracula vs. Frankenstein '69
Topaz '69
The Torture Chamber of Dr. Sadism '69
Die Screaming, Marianne '73
Prisoner in the Middle '74

Ann Doran
Little Red Schoolhouse '36
Blondie '38
Criminals Within '41
Meet John Doe '41
Mr. Wise Guy '42
The More the Merrier '43
Here Come the Waves '44
Fear in the Night '47
The Accused '48
Pitfall '48
Holiday in Havana '49
Rusty's Birthday '49
Never a Dull Moment '50
The Painted Hills '51
Love Is Better Than Ever '52
Rebel Without a Cause '55
It! The Terror from Beyond Space '58

Jesse Doran
Heart '87
Street Asylum '90

Mary Doran
Broadway Melody '29
The Divorcee '30
Criminal Code '31
The Strange Love of Molly Louvain '32
Sing Sing Nights '35

Johnny Dorelli
How to Kill 400 Duponts '65
Bread and Chocolate '74
The Odd Squad '86

Stephen Dorff
The Gate '87
The Power of One '92
Judgment Night '93
Rescue Me '93
Backbeat '94
S.F.W. '94
Innocent Lies '95
Reckless '95

Pierre Doris
The Story of a Three Day Pass '68
Overseas: Three Women with Man Trouble '90

Francoise Dorleac
The Soft Skin '64
That Man from Rio '64
Cul de Sac '66

Dolores Dorn
Lucky Me '54
Underworld, U.S.A. '60
Truck Stop Women '74

Michael Dorn
The Jagged Edge '85
Star Trek the Next Generation: Encounter at Farpoint '87
Star Trek 6: The Undiscovered Country '91
Star Trek Generations '94
Star Trek the Next Generation, the Final Episode: All Good Things... '94
Amanda and the Alien '95
Timemaster '95

Philip Dorn
Tarzan's Secret Treasure '41
Ziegfeld Girl '41
Random Harvest '42
Reunion in France '42
I've Always Loved You '46
The Fighting Kentuckian '49

Robert Dornan
The Starfighters '63
Hell on Wheels '67

Sandra Dorne
Roadhouse Girl '53
Alias John Preston '56
The House in Marsh Road '60
Eat the Rich '87

Lester Dorr
Panama Menace '41
Meet the Mob '42

Diana Dors
Oliver Twist '48
Man Bait '52
I Married a Woman '56
The Long Haul '57
Unholy Wife '57
Room 43 '58
The King of the Roaring '20s: The Story of Arnold Rothstein '61
Berserk! '67
Baby Love '69
Deep End '70
There's a Girl in My Soup '70
Amazing Mr. Blunden '72
Hannie Caulder '72
Nothing But the Night '72
From Beyond the Grave '73
A Man with a Maid '73
Theatre of Blood '73
Craze '74
The Devil's Web '74
Adventures of a Taxi Driver '76
Unicorn '83
Children of the Full Moon '84
Steaming '86

Fifi d'Orsay
Girl from Calgary '32
Going Hollywood '33
Three Legionnaires '37
Delinquent Daughters '44
Nabonga '44
The Gangster '47

Jimmy Dorsey
Hollywood Canteen '44
The Fabulous Dorseys '47

Tommy Dorsey
Presenting Lily Mars '43
The Fabulous Dorseys '47

Susana Dosamantes
Target Eagle '84
Counterforce '87
Remolina de Pasiones '87

John Dossett
Longtime Companion '90
That Night '93

Karen Dotrice
The Three Lives of Thomasina '63
The Gnome-Mobile '67
The Thirty-Nine Steps '79

Michele Dotrice
And Soon the Darkness '70
The Blood on Satan's Claw '71

Roy Dotrice
Space: 1999—Alien Attack '79
Amadeus '84
Cheech and Chong's The Corsican Brothers '84
The Dancing Princesses '84
The Eliminators '86
Beauty and the Beast, Episode 1: Once Upon a Time in New York '87
Carmilla '89
Suburban Commando '91
The Cutting Edge '92
The Scarlet Letter '95

John Doucette
Seven Cities of Gold '55
Paradise, Hawaiian Style '66
Fighting Mad '76

Doug E. Doug
Class Act '91
Hangin' with the Homeboys '91
Cool Runnings '93
Operation Dumbo Drop '95

Angela Douglas
Carry On Screaming '66
Digby, the Biggest Dog in the World '73

Brandon Douglas
The Children of Times Square '86
Chips, the War Dog '90
Journey to Spirit Island '92

Burt Douglas
High School Confidential '58
The Law and Jake Wade '58
Hush Little Baby, Don't You Cry '86

Don Douglas
The Great Gabbo '29
Tomorrow's Children '34
Law of the Texan '38
Whistling in the Dark '41
Behind the Rising Sun '43
Club Havana '46

Donna Douglas
Career '59
The Beverly Hillbillies '62
Frankie and Johnny '65

Eric Douglas
Tomboy '85
Student Confidential '87
Delta Force 3: The Killing Game '91

Illeana Douglas
Cape Fear '91
Alive '93
Household Saints '93
Grief '94
Search and Destroy '94
To Die For '95

John Douglas
Hell's Brigade: The Final Assault '80
Violent Zone '89

Kirk Douglas
The Strange Love of Martha Ivers '46
Out of the Past '47
Champion '49
A Letter to Three Wives '49
My Dear Secretary '49
Hollywood Bloopers '50s
Young Man with a Horn '50
Along the Great Divide '51
Detective Story '51
The Bad and the Beautiful '52
The Big Sky '52
Big Trees '52
20,000 Leagues Under the Sea '54
The Indian Fighter '55
Man Without a Star '55
The Racers '55
Ulysses '55
Lust for Life '56
Gunfight at the O.K. Corral '57
Paths of Glory '57
The Vikings '58
The Devil's Disciple '59
Last Train from Gun Hill '59
Spartacus '60
Strangers When We Meet '60
Lonely Are the Brave '62
Two Weeks in Another Town '62
For Love or Money '63
The List of Adrian Messenger '63
Seven Days in May '64
In Harm's Way '65
Cast a Giant Shadow '66
The War Wagon '67
The Way West '67
The Brotherhood '68
Is Paris Burning? '68
The Arrangement '69
There was a Crooked Man '70
Catch Me a Spy '71
A Gunfight '71
Light at the Edge of the World '71
Dr. Jekyll and Mr. Hyde '73
Master Touch '74
Once is Not Enough '75
Posse '75
The Chosen '77
The Fury '78
Home Movies '79
The Villain '79
The Final Countdown '80
Saturn 3 '80
Draw! '81
The Man from Snowy River '82
Eddie Macon's Run '83
Holocaust Survivors...Remembrance of Love '83
Amos '85
Tough Guys '86
Queenie '87
Oscar '91
The Secret '93
Greedy '94

Mark Douglas
Moonshine Mountain '64
2000 Maniacs '64

Melvyn Douglas
As You Desire Me '32
The Old Dark House '32
The Vampire Bat '32
Woman in the Shadows '34
Annie Oakley '35
The Gorgeous Hussy '36
Theodora Goes Wild '36
Angel '37
Captains Courageous '37
The Shining Hour '38
Ninotchka '39
That Uncertain Feeling '41
Two-Faced Woman '41
A Woman's Face '41
Mr. Blandings Builds His Dream House '48
A Woman's Secret '49
My Forbidden Past '51
Billy Budd '62
Hud '63
The Americanization of Emily '64
Lamp at Midnight '66
Hotel '67
Hard Frame '70
I Never Sang For My Father '70
The Candidate '72
The Death Squad '73
Murder or Mercy '74
The Tenant '76
Portrait of Grandpa Doc '77
Twilight's Last Gleaming '77
Being There '79
The Seduction of Joe Tynan '79
Hot Touch '80s
The Changeling '80
Tell Me a Riddle '80
Ghost Story '81

Michael Douglas
Hail, Hero! '69
Adam at 6 a.m. '70
Shattered Silence '71
Summertree '71
Napoleon and Samantha '72
The Streets of San Francisco '72
Coma '78
The China Syndrome '79
It's My Turn '80
The Star Chamber '83
Romancing the Stone '84
A Chorus Line '85
The Jewel of the Nile '85
Fatal Attraction '87
Wall Street '87
Black Rain '89
The War of the Roses '89
Basic Instinct '92
Shining Through '92
Falling Down '93
Disclosure '94
The American President '95

Paul Douglas
It Happens Every Spring '49
A Letter to Three Wives '49
The Big Lift '50
Panic in the Streets '50
Angels in the Outfield '51
Clash by Night '52
Never Wave at a WAC '52
We're Not Married '52
Forever Female '53
Executive Suite '54
Green Fire '55
The Gamma People '56
Solid Gold Cadillac '56
This Could Be the Night '57
The Mating Game '59

Robert Douglas
London Melody '37
The Challenge '38
Adventures of Don Juan '49
The Flame & the Arrow '50
At Sword's Point '51
The Desert Rats '53
King Richard and the Crusaders '54
Helen of Troy '56

Sarah Douglas
The Final Programme '73
The People That Time Forgot '77
Superman: The Movie '78
Superman 2 '80
Conan the Destroyer '84
Solarbabies '86
Steele Justice '87
Nightfall '88
The Return of Swamp Thing '89
The Art of Dying '90
Puppet Master 3: Toulon's Revenge '90
Tagget '90
Beastmaster 2: Through the Portal of Time '91
Meatballs 4 '92
Spitfire '94
Voodoo '95

Shirley Douglas
Dead Ringers '88
Shadow Dancing '88
Johnny's Girl '95

Susan Douglas
The Private Affairs of Bel Ami '47
Lost Boundaries '49

Suzanne Douglas
Tap '89
Jason's Lyric '94

Warren Douglas
The Inner Circle '46
The Man I Love '46

Robyn Douglass
Partners '82
Her Life as a Man '83
The Lonely Guy '84
Freeze Frame '92

Brad Dourif
One Flew Over the Cuckoo's Nest '75
Eyes of Laura Mars '78
Sergeant Matlovich vs. the U.S. Air Force '78
Wise Blood '79
The Guyana Tragedy: The Story of Jim Jones '80
Heaven's Gate '81
Ragtime '81
Dune '84
Istanbul '85
Blue Velvet '86
Impure Thoughts '86
Rage of Angels: The Story Continues '86
Fatal Beauty '87
Sonny Boy '87
Child's Play '88
Mississippi Burning '88
Grim Prairie Tales '89
Spontaneous Combustion '89
Vengeance '89
Exorcist 3: Legion '90
Graveyard Shift '90
Hidden Agenda '90
Body Parts '91
Common Bonds '91
Critters 4 '91
The Horseplayer '91
Jungle Fever '91
London Kills Me '91
Dead Certain '92
Final Judgement '92
Amos and Andrew '93
Dario Argento's Trauma '93
Wild Palms '93
Color of Night '94
Death Machine '95
Murder In the First '95
Phoenix '95

Billie Dove
The Black Pirate '26
All the Brothers Were Valiant '53

Tony Dow
Death Scream '75
High School USA '84
Back to the Beach '87

Ann Dowd
Philadelphia '93
It Could Happen to You '94
Bushwhacked '95
Kingfish: A Story of Huey P. Long '95

Don Dowe
Evil Toons '90
Test Tube Teens from the Year 2000 '93

Raye Dowell
She's Gotta Have It '86
Landlord Blues '87

Garrick Dowhen
Land of Doom '84
Appointment with Fear '85

Doris Dowling
The Lost Weekend '45
The Blue Dahlia '46
Othello '52

Joan Dowling
Hue and Cry '47
Train of Events '49

Lesley-Anne Down
Assault '70
From Beyond the Grave '73
Brannigan '75
The Pink Panther Strikes Again '76
A Little Night Music '77
The Betsy '78
The Great Train Robbery '79
Hanover Street '79
Rough Cut '80
Sphinx '81
The Hunchback of Notre Dame '82
Arch of Triumph '85
North and South Book 1 '85
Nomads '86
North and South Book 2 '86
Scenes from the Goldmine '87
Indiscreet '88
Ladykillers '88
Mardi Gras for the Devil '93
Death Wish 5: The Face of Death '94
In the Heat of Passion 2: Unfaithful '94
Beastmaster 3: The Eye of Braxus '95

Morton Downey, Jr.
Legal Tender '90
Predator 2 '90
Body Chemistry 2: Voice of a Stranger '91
Driving Me Crazy '91
Revenge of the Nerds 3: The Next Generation '92
The Silencer '92

Robert Downey
To Live & Die in L.A. '85
That's Adequate '90

Robert Downey, Jr.
Baby It's You '82
First Born '84
Tuff Turf '85
Weird Science '85
America '86
Back to School '86
Less Than Zero '87
The Pick-Up Artist '87
Johnny Be Good '88
Rented Lips '88
Chances Are '89
1969 '89
True Believer '89
Air America '90
Too Much Sun '90
Soapdish '91
Chaplin '92
Heart and Souls '93
Short Cuts '93
Hail Caesar '94
Natural Born Killers '94
Only You '94
Restoration '94
Home for the Holidays '95
Richard III '95

Roma Downey
A Woman Named Jackie '91
Devlin '92
Getting Up and Going Home '92

J. Downing
Ghoulies 2 '87
Robot Wars '93

Cathy Downs
Dark Corner '46
The Noose Hangs High '48
The Flaming Urge '53
Kentucky Rifle '55
The Phantom from 10,000 Leagues '56
The Amazing Colossal Man '57
The Curfew Breakers '57
Missile to the Moon '59

Johnny Downs
March of the Wooden Soldiers '34
Bad Boy '39
The Mad Monster '42
Harvest Melody '43
The Adventures of the Flying Cadets '44
Rhapsody in Blue '45

David Doyle
Paper Lion '68
Who Killed Mary What's 'Er Name? '71
The Comeback '77
My Boys Are Good Boys '78
Wild & Wooly '78
The Line '80
Wait Till Your Mother Gets Home '83
Love or Money? '88
Ghost Writer '89

John Doyle
Contagion '87
The Wicked '89
Rock & Roll Cowboys '92

Maxine Doyle
Condemned to Live '35
The Mystery Man '35
S.O.S. Coast Guard '37

Tony Doyle
The Final Option '82
Eat the Peach '86
Adventures in Dinosaur City '92

Brian Doyle-Murray
Caddyshack '80
Modern Problems '81
National Lampoon's Vacation '83
The Razor's Edge '84
Sixteen Candles '84
Club Paradise '86
Scrooged '88
The Experts '89
How I Got into College '89
National Lampoon's Christmas Vacation '89
JFK '91
Bob Roberts '92
Wayne's World '92
Groundhog Day '93
Cabin Boy '94
Jury Duty '95

Heinz Drache
The Avenger '60
Door with the Seven Locks '62
The Indian Scarf '63
The Mysterious Magician '65
The Squeaker '65
Circus of Fear '67

Billy Drago
Invasion U.S.A. '85
The Untouchables '87
Freeway '88
Hero and the Terror '88
Prime Suspect '88
Dark Before Dawn '89
Delta Force 2: Operation Stranglehold '90
China White '91
Diplomatic Immunity '91
Martial Law 2: Undercover '91
Guncrazy '92
Secret Games '92
Cyborg 2 '93
Death Ring '93
In Self Defense '93
Lady Dragon 2 '93
The Outfit '93
Never Say Die '94
Solar Force '94
The Takeover '94
Phoenix '95

Betsy Drake
Every Girl Should Be Married '48
Second Woman '51
Will Success Spoil Rock Hunter? '57
Clarence, the Cross-eyed Lion '65

Charles Drake
Air Force '43
Conflict '45
A Night in Casablanca '46
The Tender Years '47
Comanche Territory '50
Harvey '50
Winchester '73 '50
Red Ball Express '52
It Came From Outer Space '53
Tobor the Great '54
Until They Sail '57
Valley of the Dolls '67
Hail, Hero! '69

Claudia Drake
Border Patrol '43
Enemy of Women '44
The Lady Confesses '45
Detour '46
Gentleman from Texas '46

Dona Drake
Louisiana Purchase '41
The Road to Morocco '42

Frances Drake
Forsaking All Others '35
Les Miserables '35
Mad Love '35
I'd Give My Life '36
The Invisible Ray '36

Larry Drake
Dark Night of the Scarecrow '81
Tales from the Crypt '89
Darkman '90
Murder in New Hampshire: The Pamela Smart Story '91
Dr. Giggles '92
Darkman 2: The Return of Durant '94
The Journey of August King '95

Tom Drake
The Howards of Virginia '40
Meet Me in St. Louis '44
Two Girls and a Sailor '44
The White Cliffs of Dover '44
Courage of Lassie '46
Cass Timberlane '47
The Hills of Home '48
Words and Music '48
The Great Rupert '50
FBI Girl '52
Cyclops '56
The Bramble Bush '60
House of the Black Death '65
Warkill '65
Johnny Reno '66
The Singing Nun '66
Cycle Psycho '72
Savage Abduction '73
The Spectre of Edgar Allen Poe '73

Polly Draper
Making Mr. Right '86
The Pick-Up Artist '87
Danielle Steel's Heartbeat '93
A Million to Juan '94
Gold Diggers: The Secret of Bear Mountain '95

Milena Dravic
Man Is Not a Bird '65
WR: Mysteries of the Organism '71

Alfred Drayton
Nicholas Nickleby '46
Things Happen at Night '48

Alex Dreier
Loners '72
Lady Cocoa '75

Fran Drescher
Doctor Detroit '83
This Is Spinal Tap '84
Rosebud Beach Hotel '85
Wedding Band '89
Cadillac Man '90
We're Talkin' Serious Money '92
Car 54, Where Are You? '94
Jack '96

Sonia Dresdel
While I Live '47
The Fallen Idol '49
The Clouded Yellow '51

Curly Dresden
Rough Ridin' Rhythm '37
Pals of the Saddle '38
Santa Fe Stampede '38
Wyoming Outlaw '39
Arizona Gangbusters '40
Trigger Men '41
Fighting Valley '43

John Dresden
Raw Force '81
Final Mission '84
No Dead Heroes '87

Louise Dresser
The Eagle '25
The Tempest/The Eagle '27
Dracula/Garden of Eden '28
The Garden of Eden '28
Scarlet Empress '34

Lieux Dressler
Grave of the Vampire '72
Truck Stop Women '74

Marie Dressler
Tillie's Punctured Romance '14
Tillie Wakes Up '17
Vagabond Lover '29
Kings, Queens, Jokers '30s
Anna Christie '30
Min & Bill '30
Dinner at Eight '33

Ellen Drew
Christmas in July '40
The Texas Rangers Ride Again '40
The Monster and the Girl '41
China Sky '44
Dark Mountain '44
Isle of the Dead '45
Man from Colorado '49
Stars in My Crown '50
Baron of Arizona '51
Great Missouri Raid '51
Man in the Saddle '51

Gene Drew
Steel Arena '72
Truck Stop Women '74

Griffin Drew
Dinosaur Island '93
Elke '95
Masseuse '95
Over the Wire '95

Roland Drew
Evangeline '29
The Invisible Killer '40

Sidney Drew
Playing Dead '15
Early Cinema Vol. 1 '19

Nancy Drexel
Man from Hell's Edges '32
Mason of the Mounted '32
Texas Buddies '32

Jean Claude Dreyfus
Delicatessen '92
The City of Lost Children '95

Lorin Dreyfuss
Detective School Dropouts '85
Dutch Treat '86

Richard Dreyfuss
The Graduate '67
The Mod Squad '68
American Graffiti '73
Dillinger '73
The Apprenticeship of Duddy Kravitz '74
Jaws '75
Inserts '76
Close Encounters of the Third Kind '77
The Goodbye Girl '77
The Big Fix '78
The Competition '80
Second Coming of Suzanne '80
Suzanne '80
Whose Life Is It Anyway? '81
The Buddy System '83
Down and Out in Beverly Hills '86
Stand By Me '86
Nuts '87
Stakeout '87
Tin Men '87
Moon over Parador '88
Always '89
Let It Ride '89
Postcards from the Edge '90
Rosencrantz & Guildenstern Are Dead '90
Once Around '91
Prisoner of Honor '91
What About Bob? '91
Another Stakeout '93
Lost in Yonkers '93
Silent Fall '94
The American President '95
Mr. Holland's Opus '95

Moosie Drier
Ants '77
Homeward Bound '80
Charlie and the Great Balloon Chase '82

Deborah Driggs
Total Exposure '91
Night Rhythms '92

Carol Drinkwater
Father '90
An Awfully Big Adventure '94

Bobby Driscoll
The Fighting Sullivans '42
Identity Unknown '45
So Dear to My Heart '49
The Window '49
Treasure Island '50

Minnie Driver
Circle of Friends '94
Big Night '95

Jean-Claude Drouot
Le Bonheur '65
La Rupture '70

Joanne Dru
Red River '48
All the King's Men '49
She Wore a Yellow Ribbon '49
Wagon Master '50
Vengeance Valley '51
Pride of St. Louis '52
Thunder Bay '53

Hell on Frisco Bay '55
The Warriors '55
Sincerely Yours '56
The Light in the Forest '58
Super Fuzz '81

James Drury
The Tender Trap '55
Love Me Tender '56
Ten Who Dared '60
Ride the High Country '62
The Meanest Men in the West '76
The Gambler Returns: The Luck of the Draw '93
Walker: Texas Ranger: One Riot, One Ranger '93

Fred Dryer
The Fantastic World of D.C. Collins '84
Death Before Dishonor '87

Robert Dryer
Heartbreaker '83
Savage Streets '83
Fast Gun '93

Jeanie Drynan
Fantasy Man '84
Muriel's Wedding '94

Gerald du Maurier
Power '34
The Living Dead '36

Carmen Du Sautoy
Praying Mantis '83
Deadly Recruits '86
It Couldn't Happen Here '88

Michael Duane
City Without Men '43
The Prince of Thieves '48

Frances Dubay
The Body Vanished '39
Wild Women '53

Don Dubbins
Tribute to a Bad Man '56
D.I. '57
From the Earth to the Moon '58
The Illustrated Man '69
Savage Run '70

Jessica Dublin
The Rejuvenator '88
The Toxic Avenger, Part 3: The Last Temptation of Toxie '89

Ja'net DuBois
Piece of the Action '77
I'm Gonna Git You Sucka '88
Heart Condition '90
Magic Island '95

Marie DuBois
A Woman is a Woman '60
Jules and Jim '62
Shoot the Piano Player '62
Circle of Love '64
Jailbird's Vacation '65
Les Grandes Gueules '65
Night Flight from Moscow '73
La Petite Sirene '80
Mon Oncle D'Amerique '80

Marta DuBois
Boulevard Nights '79
The Grace Kelly Story '83
The Trial of the Incredible Hulk '89
Fear '90
Dead Badge '94

Paulette Dubost
The Rules of the Game '39
The Sheep Has Five Legs '54
Viva Maria! '65
The Last Metro '80
May Fools '90

Paul Dubov
Apache Woman '55
Day the World Ended '55
China Gate '57
Atomic Submarine '59
Verboten! '59
Ma Barker's Killer Brood '60
Underworld, U.S.A. '60

Kristie Ducati
The Bikini Car Wash Company '90
The Bikini Car Wash Company 2 '92

Michael Duchaussoy
The Killing Game '67
This Man Must Die '70

Return of the Tall Blond Man With One Black Shoe '74
Fort Saganne '84
May Fools '90
Road to Ruin '91

David Duchovny
New Year's Day '89
Julia Has Two Lovers '91
The Rapture '91
Beethoven '92
Chaplin '92
Red Shoe Diaries '92
Red Shoe Diaries 2: Double Dare '92
Ruby '92
Kalifornia '93
Red Shoe Diaries 3: Another Woman's Lipstick '93
Red Shoe Diaries 4: Auto Erotica '93
The X-Files: Pilot Episode/Deep Throat '93
Red Shoe Diaries 6: How I Met My Husband '95

Rick Ducommun
No Small Affair '84
Die Hard '88
The 'Burbs '89
Little Monsters '89
Class Act '91
Encino Man '92
Blank Check '93
Ghost in the Machine '93

Louis Ducreux
A Sunday in the Country '84
The Story of Women '88
The Double Life of Veronique '91

Michael Dudikoff
The Black Marble '79
Bloody Birthday '80
I Ought to Be in Pictures '82
Making Love '82
Bachelor Party '84
American Ninja '85
Avenging Force '86
Radioactive Dreams '86
American Ninja 2: The Confrontation '87
Platoon Leader '87
River of Death '90
American Ninja 4: The Annihilation '91
The Human Shield '92
Midnight Ride '92
Rescue Me '93
Soldier Boyz '95
Virtual Assassin '95

William Duell
Police Squad! Help Wanted! '82
Grace Quigley '84

Denice Duff
Bloodstone: Subspecies 2 '92
Bloodfist 5: Human Target '93
Bloodlust: Subspecies 3 '93

Howard Duff
The Naked City '48
Spaceways '53
Private Hell 36 '54
Flame of the Islands '55
While the City Sleeps '56
Boys' Night Out '62
Snatched '72
Snowblind '78
A Wedding '78
Kramer vs. Kramer '79
The Double Negative '80
East of Eden '80
Magic on Love Island '80
Oh, God! Book 2 '80
Love on the Run '85
Monster in the Closet '86
No Way Out '87

Kevin Duffis
Nam Angels '88
The Expendables '89

Julia Duffy
Night Warning '82
Children in the Crossfire '84

Karen Duffy
Blank Check '93
Dumb & Dumber '94
Synapse '95

Patrick Duffy
The Last of Mrs. Lincoln '76
The Man from Atlantis '77

Enola Gay: The Men, the Mission, the Atomic Bomb '80
Vamping '84
Danielle Steel's "Daddy" '92
Texas '94

Thomas F. Duffy
Eye of the Stranger '93
Wagons East '94

Jacques Dufilho
Black and White in Color '76
Le Crabe Tambour '77
The Horse of Pride '80

Dennis Dugan
Night Call Nurses '72
Night Moves '75
Norman, Is That You? '76
Unidentified Flying Oddball '79
The Howling '81
Can't Buy Me Love '87
The New Adventures of Pippi Longstocking '88
She's Having a Baby '88
Parenthood '89
Happy Gilmore '96

Tom Dugan
Medicine Man '30
The Galloping Ghost '31
Blessed Event '32
Pick a Star '37
To Be or Not to Be '42
Gambler's Choice '44
Accomplice '46
Take Me Out to the Ball Game '49

Andrew Duggan
The Commies are Coming, the Commies are Coming '57
Merrill's Marauders '62
Palm Springs Weekend '63
The Incredible Mr. Limpet '64
In Like Flint '67
The Secret War of Harry Frigg '68
Jigsaw '71
Skin Game '71
Firehouse '72
Housewife '72
The Streets of San Francisco '72
Pueblo Affair '73
The Bears & I '74
It's Alive '74
The Hunted Lady '77
It's Alive 2: It Lives Again '78
Time Machine '78
The Long Days of Summer '80
Frankenstein Island '81
Doctor Detroit '83
The Winds of War '83
J. Edgar Hoover '87
Return to Salem's Lot '87

Olympia Dukakis
Death Wish '74
Rich Kids '79
Idolmaker '80
Walls of Glass '85
Moonstruck '87
Working Girl '88
Dad '89
Look Who's Talking '89
Steel Magnolias '89
In the Spirit '90
Look Who's Talking, Too '90
Sinatra '92
Armistead Maupin's Tales of the City '93
The Cemetery Club '93
Look Who's Talking Now '93
Over the Hill '93
A Century of Women '94
Dead Badge '94
Digger '94
Mother '94
Jeffrey '95
Mighty Aphrodite '95
Mr. Holland's Opus '95

Bill Duke
Commando '85
Killing Floor '85
Predator '87
Bird on a Wire '90
Menace II Society '93

Patty Duke
The Goddess '58
The 4D Man '59
The Miracle Worker '62
Billie '65
Valley of the Dolls '67
My Sweet Charlie '70

She Waits '71
Curse of the Black Widow '77
Fire '77
Killer on Board '77
Family Upside Down '78
The Swarm '78
The Miracle Worker '79
The Babysitter '80
Mom, the Wolfman and Me '80
By Design '82
September Gun '83
George Washington '84
George Washington: The Forging of a Nation '86
Something Special '86
Best Kept Secrets '88
Amityville 4 '89
Grave Secrets: The Legacy of Hilltop Drive '92
Prelude to a Kiss '92

Robin Duke
The Last Polka '84
Club Paradise '86
Best of Eddie Murphy '89
Motorama '91
Hostage for a Day '94

David Dukes
The Strawberry Statement '70
Wild Party '74
The Triangle Factory Fire Scandal '79
The First Deadly Sin '80
Only When I Laugh '81
Miss All-American Beauty '82
Portrait of a Rebel: Margaret Sanger '82
The Winds of War '83
Without a Trace '83
Cat on a Hot Tin Roof '84
George Washington '84
The Men's Club '86
My Darlin' Clementine '86
Catch the Heat '87
Date with an Angel '87
Rawhead Rex '87
War & Remembrance, Part 1 '88
War & Remembrance, Part 3 '88
War & Remembrance, Part 4 '88
War & Remembrance, Part 5 '88
War & Remembrance, Part 6 '88
War & Remembrance, Part 7 '88
See You in the Morning '89
War & Remembrance, Part 2 '89
War & Remembrance: The Final Chapter, Part 8 '89
War & Remembrance: The Final Chapter, Part 9 '89
War & Remembrance: The Final Chapter, Part 10 '89
War & Remembrance: The Final Chapter, Part 11 '89
War & Remembrance: The Final Chapter, Part 12 '89
The Josephine Baker Story '90
The Rutanga Tapes '90
Snow Kill '90
Strange Interlude '90
Held Hostage '91
Me and the Kid '93

Caitlin Dulany
Class of 1999 2: The Substitute '93
Maniac Cop 3: Badge of Silence '93

Keir Dullea
The Hoodlum Priest '61
David and Lisa '62
Madame X '66
2001: A Space Odyssey '68
Black Water Gold '69
Paperback Hero '73
Paul and Michelle '74
Black Christmas '75
Full Circle '77
Welcome to Blood City '77
Leopard in the Snow '78
Love Under Pressure '80s
The Hostage Tower '80
No Place to Hide '81
Brainwaves '82
Blind Date '84
Next One '84
2010: The Year We Make Contact '84
Oh, What a Night '92

Douglass Dumbrille
Baby Face '33
Heroes for Sale '33

Rustler's Roundup '33
Treasure Island '34
Crime and Punishment '35
The Lives of a Bengal Lancer '35
Naughty Marietta '35
Mr. Deeds Goes to Town '36
The Princess Comes Across '36
A Day at the Races '37
The Firefly '37
The Mysterious Rider '38
The Three Musketeers '39
Virginia City '40
Castle in the Desert '42
I Married an Angel '42
Ride 'Em Cowboy '42
Lost in a Harem '44
Uncertain Glory '44
The Road to Utopia '46
Under Nevada Skies '46
Blonde Savage '47
Spook Busters '48
Abbott and Costello in the Foreign Legion '50
Riding High '50
Son of Paleface '52
Jupiter's Darling '55
The Ten Commandments '56
Shake, Rattle and Rock '57

Denise Dumont
Kiss of the Spider Woman '85
Heart of Midnight '89

Margaret Dumont
The Cocoanuts '29
Animal Crackers '30
Duck Soup '33
A Night at the Opera '35
A Day at the Races '37
At the Circus '39
The Women '39
Big Store '41
Never Give a Sucker an Even Break '41
Sing Your Worries Away '42
Tales of Manhattan '42
Rhythm Parade '43
Seven Days Ashore/Hurry, Charlie, Hurry '44
Up in Arms '44
The Horn Blows at Midnight '45
Three for Bedroom C '52
Shake, Rattle and Rock '57

Ulises Dumont
The Lion's Share '79
Time for Revenge '82

Dennis Dun
Big Trouble in Little China '86
The Last Emperor '87
Prince of Darkness '87
Thousand Pieces of Gold '91

Steffi Duna
Dancing Pirate '36
I Conquer the Sea '36
Law of the Pampas '39
Way Down South '39

Faye Dunaway
Bonnie & Clyde '67
The Thomas Crown Affair '68
The Arrangement '69
Little Big Man '70
The Deadly Trap '71
Oklahoma Crude '73
Chinatown '74
The Three Musketeers '74
The Towering Inferno '74
The Four Musketeers '75
Three Days of the Condor '75
The Disappearance of Aimee '76
Network '76
Voyage of the Damned '76
Eyes of Laura Mars '78
The Champ '79
The First Deadly Sin '80
Mommie Dearest '81
Country Girl '82
The Wicked Lady '83
Ordeal by Innocence '84
Supergirl '84
Christopher Columbus '85
Beverly Hills Madam '86
Barfly '87
Casanova '87
Midnight Crossing '87
The Gamble '88
Burning Secret '89
Cold Sassy Tree '89
The Handmaid's Tale '90
Wait Until Spring, Bandini '90

Dunaway ▶cont.

Silhouette '91
Double Edge '92
Scorchers '92
The Temp '93
Arizona Dream '94
Don Juan DeMarco '94
Dunston Checks In '95

Adrian Dunbar
My Left Foot '89
Hear My Song '91
The Crying Game '92
The Playboys '92
The Best of Cracker Mysteries '93
A Woman's Guide to Adultery '93
Widow's Peak '94
Innocent Lies '95

Andrew Duncan
The Gig '85
Morgan Stewart's Coming Home '87

Angus Duncan
Hard Frame '70
How to Seduce a Woman '74

Arletta Duncan
Fighting Champ '33
The Gallant Fool '33
Roaring Speedboats '37

Bob Duncan
Colorado Serenade '46
Border Feud '47

Bud Duncan
Hillbilly Blitzkrieg '42
Snuffy Smith, Yard Bird '42

Carmen Duncan
Now and Forever '82
Dark Forces '83
Moving Targets '87

Julie Duncan
Fugitive Valley '41
Along the Sundown Trail '42
Haunted Ranch '43

Kenne Duncan
Make-Up '37
Pinto Canyon '40
Dynamite Canyon '41
Riding the Sunset Trail '41
Raiders of Sunset Pass '43
Manhunt of Mystery Island '45
Cyclotrode "X" '46
Flesh and the Spur '57
The Astounding She-Monster '58
Night of the Ghouls '59
The Sinister Urge '60

Lindsay Duncan
Grown Ups '80
Loose Connections '87
Prick Up Your Ears '87
A Year in Provence '89
Traffik '90
Body Parts '91
The Reflecting Skin '91
The Rector's Wife '94
City Hall '95

Mary Duncan
City Girl '30
Morning Glory '33

Neil Duncan
Murder on Line One '90
Split Second '92
Sleeping with Strangers '94

Peter Duncan
The Old Curiosity Shop '75
The Lifetaker '89

Sandy Duncan
Million Dollar Duck '71
Star Spangled Girl '71
Pinocchio '76
Roots '77
The Cat from Outer Space '78

Jennie Dundas
The Beniker Gang '83
Mrs. Soffel '84
Heaven Help Us '85
Legal Eagles '86

Robert Dunham
The Green Slime '68
Godzilla vs. Megalon '76

Dawn Dunlap
Forbidden World '82
Heartbreaker '83
Barbarian Queen '85

Lesley Dunlop
Haunted: The Ferryman '74
The Dying Truth '91

Vic Dunlop
Jud '71
Martians Go Home! '90
Wishful Thinking '92

Carolyn Dunn
Breaking All the Rules '85
Hitler's Daughter '90

Eddie Dunn
Sunrise Trail '31
South of Santa Fe '32
Billy the Kid '41
Mexican Spitfire at Sea '42
Call Northside 777 '48

Emma Dunn
Morals for Women '31
Blessed Event '32
Hell's House '32
Madame X '37
Son of Frankenstein '39
You Can't Fool Your Wife '40
Talk of the Town '42

James Dunn
Baby, Take a Bow '34
Bright Eyes '34
Stand Up and Cheer '34
Shadows Over Shanghai '38
The Ghost and the Guest '43
A Tree Grows in Brooklyn '45
That Brennan Girl '46
The Bramble Bush '60
The Oscar '66

Josephine Dunn
Our Modern Maidens '29
Between Fighting Men '32

Kevin Dunn
Mississippi Burning '88
Taken Away '89
Hot Shots! '91
Only the Lonely '91
Chaplin '92
Dave '93
Little Big League '94
Mad Love '95
Nixon '95

Michael Dunn
Ship of Fools '65
You're a Big Boy Now '66
Madigan '68
House of the Damned '71
Murders in the Rue Morgue '71
The Freakmaker '73
Dr. Frankenstein's Castle of Freaks '74

Nora Dunn
Working Girl '88
How I Got into College '89
Miami Blues '90
Stepping Out '91
Passion Fish '92
Born Yesterday '93

Dominique Dunne
Magic on Love Island '80
Haunting of Harrington House '82
Poltergeist '82
The Shadow Riders '82

Griffin Dunne
The Other Side of the Mountain '75
Chilly Scenes of Winter '79
An American Werewolf in London '81
The Fan '81
Cold Feet '84
Johnny Dangerously '84
After Hours '85
Almost You '85
From Here to Maternity '85
Amazon Women on the Moon '87
Who's That Girl? '87
The Big Blue '88
Lip Service '88
Me and Him '89
Secret Weapon '90
White Palace '90
My Girl '91
Once Around '91

Big Girls Don't Cry...They Get Even '92
Straight Talk '92
Hotel Room '93
Love Matters '93
I Like It Like That '94
Quiz Show '94
Search and Destroy '94
The Android Affair '95

Irene Dunne
Cimarron '30
Bachelor Apartment '31
Consolation Marriage '31
Ann Vickers '33
Roberta '35
Sweet Adeline '35
Show Boat '36
Theodora Goes Wild '36
The Awful Truth '37
Joy of Living '38
Love Affair '39
My Favorite Wife '40
Penny Serenade '41
A Guy Named Joe '44
The White Cliffs of Dover '44
Anna and the King of Siam '46
Life with Father '47
I Remember Mama '48
Never a Dull Moment '50

Steve Dunne
The Big Sombrero '49
The Underworld Story '50

Mildred Dunnock
The Corn is Green '45
Viva Zapata! '52
The Trouble with Harry '55
Baby Doll '56
Love Me Tender '56
Peyton Place '57
The Nun's Story '59
Butterfield 8 '60
Sweet Bird of Youth '62
Behold a Pale Horse '64
Whatever Happened to Aunt Alice? '69
Brand New Life '72
Murder or Mercy '74
Spiral Staircase '75
One Summer Love '76
And Baby Makes Six '79
The Pick-Up Artist '87

Rosemary Dunsmore
Dancing in the Dark '86
After the Promise '87
Anne of Avonlea '87
Blades of Courage '88
Personals '90

Kirsten Dunst
Interview with the Vampire '94
Little Women '94
Jumanji '95

Wilson Dunster
Swift Justice '88
The Rutanga Tapes '90
Yankee Zulu '95

Anny Duperey
Stavisky '74
Pardon Mon Affaire '76
Bobby Deerfield '77
From Hell to Victory '79
Les Comperes '83
Germinal '93

Starletta DuPois
Hollywood Shuffle '87
A Raisin in the Sun '89
The Road to Galveston '96

June Duprez
The Four Feathers '39
Spy in Black '39
The Lion Has Wings '40
The Thief of Bagdad '40
Tiger Fangs '43
None But the Lonely Heart '44
And Then There Were None '45
Brighton Strangler '45
The Brighton Strangler/Before Dawn '45
That Brennan Girl '46

Roy Dupuis
Being at Home with Claude '92
Entangled '93

David Durand
Viva Villa! '34
Boy's Reformatory '39

Christopher Durang
Heaven Help Us '85
Mr. North '88
In the Spirit '90
The Butcher's Wife '91
Housesitter '92

Jimmy Durante
Speak Easily '32
The Lost Stooges '33
What! No Beer? '33
Hollywood Party '34
Palooka '34
Little Miss Broadway '38
Melody Ranch '40
The Man Who Came to Dinner '41
Two Girls and a Sailor '44
Ziegfeld Follies '46
It Happened in Brooklyn '47
On an Island with You '48
The Great Rupert '50
Hollywood Goes to War '54
Billy Rose's Jumbo '62
It's a Mad, Mad, Mad, Mad World '63
Alice Through the Looking Glass '66

Deanna Durbin
Three Smart Girls '36
100 Men and a Girl '37
Mad About Music '38
First Love '39
Three Smart Girls Grow Up '39
It's a Date '40
It Started with Eve '41
His Butler's Sister '43
Lady On a Train '45
Summer Stock '50

John Durbin
Dr. Caligari '89
King of the Hill '93

Minta Durfee
Fatty and Mabel Adrift/Mabel, Fatty and the Law '16
Mickey '17
Mack Sennett Comedies: Vol. 1 '21
Miracle Kid '42
Savage Intruder '68

Anna Marie Duringer
The Lacemaker '77
Veronika Voss '82

Charles Durning
The Connection '73
Sisters '73
The Sting '73
The Front Page '74
Dog Day Afternoon '75
The Hindenburg '75
Queen of the Stardust Ballroom '75
Breakheart Pass '76
Harry & Walter Go to New York '76
The Choirboys '77
Twilight's Last Gleaming '77
The Fury '78
Special Olympics '78
Tilt '78
North Dallas Forty '79
When a Stranger Calls '79
Attica '80
Crisis at Central High '80
Die Laughing '80
The Final Countdown '80
The Best Little Girl in the World '81
Dark Night of the Scarecrow '81
Sharky's Machine '81
True Confessions '81
The Best Little Whorehouse in Texas '82
Tootsie '82
To Be or Not to Be '83
Two of a Kind '83
Hadley's Rebellion '84
Mass Appeal '84
The Man with One Red Shoe '85
Stand Alone '85
Stick '85
Big Trouble '86
Brenda Starr '86
Death of a Salesman '86
The Legend of Sleepy Hollow '86
Solarbabies '86
Tough Guys '86
Where the River Runs Black '86

Happy New Year '87
Kenny Rogers as the Gambler, Part 3: The Legend Continues '87
The Man Who Broke 1,000 Chains '87
The Rosary Murders '87
A Tiger's Tale '87
Cop '88
Far North '88
Dinner at Eight '89
Project: Alien '89
Cat Chaser '90
Dick Tracy '90
The Return of Eliot Ness '91
V.I. Warshawski '91
The Water Engine '92
The Hudsucker Proxy '93
The Music of Chance '93
The Story Lady '93
When a Stranger Calls Back '93
Home for the Holidays '95
Spy Hard '96

Dick Durock
Swamp Thing '82
The Return of Swamp Thing '89

Jason Durr
A Dark Adapted Eye '93
Sharpe's Battle '94

Michael Durrell
V '83
Family Sins '87
Illegal in Blue '95

Ian Dury
The Raggedy Rawney '90
Split Second '92
The Crow 2: City of Angels '96

Dan Duryea
Ball of Fire '41
The Little Foxes '41
The Pride of the Yankees '42
Sahara '43
None But the Lonely Heart '44
Woman In the Window '44
Along Came Jones '45
Great Flamarion '45
Lady On a Train '45
Scarlet Street '45
The Valley of Decision '45
Criss Cross '48
Killer Bait '49
Too Late for Tears '49
The Underworld Story '50
Winchester '73 '50
Thunder Bay '53
Silver Lode '54
Terror Street '54
Battle Hymn '57
Gunfight at Sandoval '59
Platinum High School '60
The Flight of the Phoenix '65
Five Golden Dragons '67
The Bamboo Saucer '68

George Duryea
Marked Money '28
Pardon My Gun '30

Marj Dusay
Pendulum '69
Made in Heaven '87

Ann Dusenberry
The Possessed '77
Desperate Women '78
Little Women '78
Heart Beat '80
Cutter's Way '81
Killjoy '81
Lies '83
Basic Training '86
Long Time Gone '86
The Men's Club '86

Eliza Dushku
That Night '93
This Boy's Life '93
True Lies '94
Journey '95
Race the Sun '96

Andre Dussollier
And Now My Love '74
Le Beau Mariage '82
Three Men and a Cradle '85
Sand and Blood '87
Un Coeur en Hiver '93
Colonel Chabert '94

Jacques Dutronc
L'Etat Sauvage '78

Tricheurs '84
Van Gogh '92

Charles S. Dutton
Cat's Eye '85
The Murder of Mary Phagan '87
Crocodile Dundee 2 '88
Jacknife '89
Runaway '89
An Unremarkable Life '89
Q & A '90
Alien 3 '92
The Distinguished Gentleman '92
Mississippi Masala '92
Menace II Society '93
Rudy '93
Foreign Student '94
A Low Down Dirty Shame '94
The Piano Lesson '94
Surviving the Game '94
Cry, the Beloved Country '95
Nick of Time '95
Zooman '95
A Time to Kill '96

James Duval
Totally F***ed Up '94
The Doom Generation '95

Josey Duval
Sex, Drugs, and Rock-n-Roll '84
New York's Finest '87

Maria Duval
The Living Coffin '58
Samson vs. the Vampire Women '61

Robert Duvall
To Kill a Mockingbird '62
Captain Newman, M.D. '63
The Chase '66
Bullitt '68
Countdown '68
The Detective '68
The Rain People '69
True Grit '69
M*A*S*H '70
Lawman '71
THX 1138 '71
The Godfather '72
The Great Northfield Minnesota Raid '72
Joe Kidd '72
Tomorrow '72
Badge 373 '73
Lady Ice '73
The Conversation '74
The Godfather, Part 2 '74
Breakout '75
The Killer Elite '75
Network '76
The Seven-Per-Cent Solution '76
The Eagle Has Landed '77
The Greatest '77
The Betsy '78
Apocalypse Now '79
Ike '79
The Great Santini '80
The Godfather 1902-1959: The Complete Epic '81
The Pursuit of D.B. Cooper '81
True Confessions '81
Tender Mercies '83
The Terry Fox Story '83
The Natural '84
The Stone Boy '84
Belizaire the Cajun '86
The Lightship '86
Let's Get Harry '87
Colors '88
Hotel Colonial '88
Lonesome Dove '89
Days of Thunder '90
The Handmaid's Tale '90
A Show of Force '90
Hearts of Darkness: A Filmmaker's Apocalypse '91
Rambling Rose '91
Newsies '92
The Plague '92
Stalin '92
Falling Down '93
Geronimo: An American Legend '93
Wrestling Ernest Hemingway '93
The Paper '94
The Stars Fell on Henrietta '94
The Scarlet Letter '95
Something to Talk About '95
A Family Thing '96
Phenomenon '96

Shelley Duvall
Brewster McCloud '70
McCabe & Mrs. Miller '71
Thieves Like Us '74
Nashville '75
Annie Hall '77
Popeye '80
The Shining '80
Time Bandits '81
Rapunzel '82
Rumpelstiltskin '82
Frankenweenie '84
My Darlin' Clementine '86
Roxanne '87
Frog '89
Frogs! '90s
Mother Goose Rock 'n' Rhyme '90
Suburban Commando '91

Wayne Duvall
Final Approach '91
Warlords 3000 '93

Pierre Dux
Les Grandes Manoeuvres '55
The Day and the Hour '63
La Vie Continue '82
La Lectrice '88

Ann Dvorak
The Guardsman '31
Scarface '31
The Strange Love of Molly Louvain '32
Three on a Match '32
"G" Men '35
Manhattan Merry-Go-Round '37
Flame of the Barbary Coast '45
Abilene Town '46
Out of the Blue '47
The Private Affairs of Bel Ami '47
A Life of Her Own '50
Return of Jesse James '50

Peter Dvorsky
Videodrome '83
The Kiss '88

Dorothy Dwan
Sawmill/The Dome Doctor '22
The Wizard of Oz '25
Great K & A Train Robbery '26
The Fighting Legion '30

Earl Dwire
The Star Packer '34
Between Men '35
Big Calibre '35
Lawless Frontier '35
Lawless Range '35
Toll of the Desert '35
Cavalcade of the West '36
Lightning Bill Crandall '37
Riding On '37
Trouble in Texas '37

Hilary Dwyer
The Conqueror Worm '68
The Oblong Box '69
Cry of the Banshee '70
Wuthering Heights '70

Leslie Dwyer
Roadhouse Girl '53
Hi-Di-Hi '88

Valentine Dyall
Hotel Reserve '44
Frenzy '46
The Ghost of Rashmon Hall '47
Room to Let '49
The Golden Salamander '51
Suspended Alibi '56
Horror Hotel '60

Cameron Dye
Body Rock '84
Joy of Sex '84
The Last Starfighter '84
Fraternity Vacation '85
Heated Vengeance '87
Scenes from the Goldmine '87
Stranded '87
Out of the Dark '88

Dale Dye
Fire Birds '90
Blue Sky '91
Heaven and Earth '93
Endangered '94

John Dye
Campus Man '87
Best of the Best '89

Bob Dylan
Pat Garrett & Billy the Kid '73
Hearts of Fire '87
Backtrack '89
Bob Dylan: Don't Look Back '91

Peter Dyneley
Beau Brummel '54
Strange Awakening '58
The Manster '59
Soul Patrol '80

Richard Dysart
Petulia '68
The Hospital '71
The Autobiography of Miss Jane Pittman '74
The Terminal Man '74
The Day of the Locust '75
The Hindenburg '75
Riding with Death '76
Being There '79
Meteor '79
Prophecy '79
Bogie: The Last Hero '80
The Ordeal of Dr. Mudd '80
Bitter Harvest '81
Churchill and the Generals '81
The People vs. Jean Harris '81
The Thing '82
The Falcon and the Snowman '85
Mask '85
Pale Rider '85
Warning Sign '85
L.A. Law '86
The Last Days of Patton '86
The Rumor Mill '86
Wall Street '87
Day One '89
Back to the Future, Part 3 '90
Marilyn & Bobby: Her Final Affair '94
Panther '95
Truman '95

Dick Dyszel
The Alien Factor '78
Night Beast '83

George Dzundza
The Deer Hunter '78
A Long Way Home '81
Act of Passion: The Lost Honor of Kathryn Beck '83
Streamers '83
Best Defense '84
Broken Badge '85
Brotherly Love '85
No Mercy '86
Glory Years '87
No Way Out '87
The Beast '88
Impulse '90
White Hunter, Black Heart '90
The Butcher's Wife '91
Basic Instinct '92
The Enemy Within '94
Crimson Tide '95
Dangerous Minds '95

Nicholas Eadie
Return to Snowy River '88
Celia: Child Of Terror '89

Edward Earle
The Wind '28
Spite Marriage '29
The Revenge Rider '35

Harry Earles
The Unholy Three '25
The Unholy Three '30
Freaks '32

Bo Eason
Miami Rhapsody '95
Tornado! '96

Carlos East
The Fear Chamber '68
The Snake People '68
Fearmaker '89

Jeff East
Tom Sawyer '73
Huckleberry Finn '74
Flight of the Grey Wolf '76
The Campus Corpse '77
Mary and Joseph: A Story of Faith '79
Deadly Blessing '81
Another Chance '88
Pumpkinhead '88

Leslie Easterbrook
Police Academy '84
Private Resort '84
Police Academy 3: Back in Training '86
Police Academy 5: Assignment Miami Beach '88
The Taking of Flight 847: The Uli Derickson Story '88
Police Academy 6: City Under Siege '89
Police Academy: Mission to Moscow '94

George Eastman
Kiss Me, Kill Me '69
Call of the Wild '72
Belle Starr '79
Bloody Avenger '80s
Grim Reaper '81
Ironmaster '83
After the Fall of New York '85
Blastfighter '85
Detective School Dropouts '85
Hands of Steel '86

Rodney Eastman
Deadly Weapon '88
A Nightmare on Elm Street 4: Dream Master '88

Robert Easton
When Hell Broke Loose '58
The Giant Spider Invasion '75
Working Girl '88

Clint Eastwood
Francis in the Navy '55
Revenge of the Creature '55
Tarantula '55
Escapade in Japan '57
Lafayette Escadrille '58
A Fistful of Dollars '64
For a Few Dollars More '65
The Good, the Bad and the Ugly '67
Hang 'Em High '67
Coogan's Bluff '68
Where Eagles Dare '68
Paint Your Wagon '69
The Beguiled '70
Kelly's Heroes '70
Two Mules for Sister Sara '70
Dirty Harry '71
Play Misty for Me '71
Joe Kidd '72
High Plains Drifter '73
Magnum Force '73
Thunderbolt & Lightfoot '74
The Eiger Sanction '75
The Enforcer '76
The Outlaw Josey Wales '76
The Gauntlet '77
Every Which Way But Loose '78
Escape from Alcatraz '79
Any Which Way You Can '80
Bronco Billy '80
Firefox '82
Honkytonk Man '82
Sudden Impact '83
City Heat '84
Tightrope '84
Pale Rider '85
Heartbreak Ridge '86
Wild West '87
The Dead Pool '88
Pink Cadillac '89
The Rookie '90
White Hunter, Black Heart '90
Unforgiven '92
In the Line of Fire '93
A Perfect World '93
The Bridges of Madison County '95

Jayne Eastwood
My Pleasure Is My Business '74
Night Friend '87
Hostile Takeover '88
Kidnapping of Baby John Doe '88

Marjorie Eaton
Night Tide '63
The Atomic Brain '64
The Attic '80

Mary Eaton
The Cocoanuts '29
Glorifying the American Girl '30

Roberta Eaton
Split Second '92
The Crude Oasis '95

Shirley Eaton
Doctor in the House '53
Doctor at Large '57
The Naked Truth '58
Carry On Nurse '59
What a Carve-Up! '62
Girl Hunters '63
Goldfinger '64
Around the World Under the Sea '65
Kiss and Kill '68

John Eaves
Fire and Ice '87
Skier's Dream '88

Christine Ebersole
Tootsie '82
Amadeus '84
Thief of Hearts '84
Acceptable Risks '86
Mac and Me '88
Ghost Dad '90
Dead Again '91
Folks! '92
Gypsy '93
My Girl 2 '94
Richie Rich '94
Black Sheep '96

Buddy Ebsen
Broadway Melody of 1936 '35
Born to Dance '36
Captain January '36
Broadway Melody of 1938 '37
Girl of the Golden West '38
My Lucky Star '38
Sing Your Worries Away '42
Silver City Bonanza '51
Red Garters '54
Davy Crockett, King of the Wild Frontier '55
Between Heaven and Hell '56
Davy Crockett and the River Pirates '56
Breakfast at Tiffany's '61
The Beverly Hillbillies '62
The Interns '62
The One and Only, Genuine, Original Family Band '68
The Andersonville Trial '70
The President's Plane is Missing '71
The Adventures of Tom Sawyer '73
The Bastard '78
Stone Fox '87

Maude Eburne
The Guardsman '31
The Vampire Bat '32
Ladies They Talk About '33
Ruggles of Red Gap '35
Doughnuts & Society '36
The Border Legion '40
Courageous Dr. Christian '40

Aimee Eccles
Little Big Man '70
Group Marriage '72
The Concrete Jungle '82
Lovelines '84
Humanoid Defender '85

Christopher Eccleston
Let Him Have It '91
The Best of Cracker Mysteries '93
Shallow Grave '94

Guy Ecker
Devil Wears White '86
Night Terror '89

James Eckhouse
Blue Heaven '84
The Christmas Wife '88
Leaving Normal '92
Junior '94

Billy Eckstine
Skirts Ahoy! '52
Jo Jo Dancer, Your Life is Calling '86

Helen Jerome Eddy
Rebecca of Sunnybrook Farm '17
The Tong Man '19
County Fair '20
The Country Kid '23
A Shot in the Dark '35
Klondike Annie '36

Nelson Eddy
Dancing Lady '33
Naughty Marietta '35
Rose Marie '36
Maytime '37

Eddy ▶cont.

Girl of the Golden West '38
Rosalie '38
Sweethearts '38
Balalaika '39
Let Freedom Ring '39
Bitter Sweet '40
New Moon '40
The Chocolate Soldier '41
I Married an Angel '42
The Phantom of the Opera '43
Northwest Outpost '47

Herb Edelman
The Odd Couple '68
The Way We Were '73
A Strange and Deadly Occurence '74
The Yakuza '75
Charge of the Model T's '76
Goin' Coconuts '78
Special Olympics '78
A Cry for Love '80
Marathon '80
On the Right Track '81
Strike Force '81
Cracking Up '83

Barbara Eden
Flaming Star '60
From the Terrace '60
Voyage to the Bottom of the Sea '61
Five Weeks in a Balloon '62
The Wonderful World of the Brothers Grimm '62
7 Faces of Dr. Lao '63
Ride the Wild Surf '64
Quick, Let's Get Married '71
The Woman Hunter '72
The Stranger Within '74
The Amazing Dobermans '76
How to Break Up a Happy Divorce '76
Harper Valley P.T.A. '78
Return of the Rebels '81
Chattanooga Choo Choo '84
Lethal Charm '90

Jerome Eden
2000 Maniacs '64
The Defilers '65

Mark Eden
Seance on a Wet Afternoon '64
The Crimson Cult '68

Richard Eden
Liberty & Bash '90
RoboCop the Series: The Future of Law Enforcement '94

Robert Edeson
On the Night Stage '15
Walking Back '26

George Edgely
Free, White, and 21 '62
Common Law Wife '63

Elizabeth Edmonds
Scrubbers '82
Experience Preferred... But Not Essential '83

Beatie Edney
Highlander '86
Diary of a Mad Old Man '88
The Dark Angel '91
Mister Johnson '91
In the Name of the Father '93
Prime Suspect: The Lost Child '94
The Affair '95

Richard Edson
Stranger than Paradise '84
Platoon '86
Good Morning, Vietnam '87
Eight Men Out '88
Tougher than Leather '88
Do the Right Thing '89
Let It Ride '89
Attack of the 50 Ft. Woman '93
Joey Breaker '93
Love, Cheat & Steal '93
Posse '93
Super Mario Bros. '93
Bad Love '95
Strange Days '95

Allan Edwall
The Emigrants '72
The New Land '73
Fanny and Alexander '83
Brothers Lionheart '85
The Sacrifice '86

Anthony Edwards
Fast Times at Ridgemont High '82
Heart Like a Wheel '83
Revenge of the Nerds '84
Going for the Gold: The Bill Johnson Story '85
Gotcha! '85
The Sure Thing '85
Top Gun '86
Revenge of the Nerds 2: Nerds in Paradise '87
Summer Heat '87
Mr. North '88
Downtown '89
Hawks '89
How I Got into College '89
Miracle Mile '89
El Diablo '90
Delta Heat '92
Landslide '92
Pet Sematary 2 '92
Hometown Boy Makes Good '93
Charlie's Ghost: The Secret of Coronado '94
The Client '94
ER '94

Barbara Edwards
Malibu Express '85
Another Chance '88
House Party 3 '94

Bill Edwards
Ladies of the Chorus '49
First Man into Space '59
War Lover '62

Bruce Edwards
The Fallen Sparrow '43
Hitler: Dead or Alive '43
The Iron Major '43
The Black Widow '47
Federal Agents vs. Underworld, Inc. '49

Cliff Edwards
Doughboys '30
Dance Fools Dance '31
Laughing Sinners '31
Parlor, Bedroom and Bath '31
Sidewalks of New York '31
The Sin of Madelon Claudet '31
Saratoga '37
Girl of the Golden West '38
Gone with the Wind '39
His Girl Friday '40
Sagebrush Law '43

Gail Edwards
Get Crazy '83
A Perfect Little Murder '90

James Edwards
Home of the Brave '49
The Set-Up '49
The Steel Helmet '51
Pork Chop Hill '59
Patton '70

Jennifer Edwards
Heidi '67
S.O.B. '81
The Man Who Loved Women '83
That's Life! '86
Perfect Match '88
Sunset '88
All's Fair '89
Peter Gunn '89
Overexposed '90

Lance Edwards
Peacemaker '90
A Woman, Her Men and Her Futon '92

Luke Edwards
The Wizard '89
Guilty by Suspicion '91
Newsies '92
Little Big League '94
Mother's Boys '94

Mark Edwards
The Boldest Job in the West '71
Tower of Evil '72

Penny Edwards
North of the Great Divide '50
Trail of Robin Hood '50
Western Double Feature 11 '50
Western Double Feature 15 '50
Heart of the Rockies '51

Ronnie Clair Edwards
Future Cop '76
A Day for Thanks on Walton's Mountain '82
8 Seconds '94

Snitz Edwards
The Thief of Baghdad '24
Seven Chances '25
April Fool '26
Battling Butler '26

Vince Edwards
The Killing '56
The Three Faces of Eve '57
The Devil's Brigade '68
Desperados '69
Firehouse '72
The Mad Bomber '72
Death Stalk '74
The Seduction '82
Space Raiders '83
The Fix '84
Sno-Line '85
Cellar Dweller '87
The Dirty Dozen: The Deadly Mission '87
Return to Horror High '87
Andy and the Airwave Rangers '89
The Gumshoe Kid '89
Dillinger '91
Motorama '91
Original Intent '91
The Fear '94

Walter Edwards
Grit of the Girl Telegrapher/In the Switch Tower '15
Tale of Two Cities/In the Switch Tower '15

Marshall Efron
Is There Sex After Death? '71
First Time '82

Aeryk Egan
Book of Love '91
Keeper of the City '92
Shrunken Heads '94

Eddie Egan
The French Connection '71
Badge 373 '73
Out of the Darkness '85

Peter Egan
One Brief Summer '70
Hennessy '75
Lillie '79
A Perfect Spy '88

Richard Egan
Blackbeard the Pirate '52
One Minute to Zero '52
Split Second '53
Demetrius and the Gladiators '54
Seven Cities of Gold '55
Underwater! '55
Love Me Tender '56
Tension at Table Rock '56
The Hunters '58
A Summer Place '59
Esther and the King '60
Pollyanna '60
The Amsterdam Kill '78
Mission to Glory '80
Sweet Creek County War '82

Will Egan
Glitch! '88
Ninja Academy '90

Julie Ege
On Her Majesty's Secret Service '69
Creatures the World Forgot '70
Rentadick '72
The Freakmaker '73
The 7 Brothers Meet Dracula '73
Craze '74

Samantha Eggar
Doctor in Distress '63
The Collector '65
Walk, Don't Run '66
Doctor Dolittle '67
Molly Maguires '70
A Name for Evil '70
Light at the Edge of the World '71
Man of Destiny '73
All the Kind Strangers '74
The Seven-Per-Cent Solution '76
Welcome to Blood City '77
Battleforce '78
The Uncanny '78
The Brood '79
Why Shoot the Teacher '79
Hot Touch '80s
Exterminator '80
Unknown Powers '80
Demonoid, Messenger of Death '81
Curtains '83
Ragin' Cajun '90
Round Numbers '91
Tales of the Unexpected '91
Dark Horse '92
The Phantom '96

Nicole Eggert
The Haunting of Morella '91
The Double O Kid '92
Blown Away '93
Just One of the Girls '93
Amanda and the Alien '95
The Demolitionist '95

Martha Eggerth
Charm of La Boheme '36
For Me and My Gal '42

Stan Egi
Come See the Paradise '90
Hiroshima: Out of the Ashes '90
Golden Gate '93
Rising Sun '93

Jennifer Ehle
Backbeat '94
Pride and Prejudice '95

Lisa Eichhorn
The Europeans '79
Yanks '79
Cutter's Way '81
Weather in the Streets '84
Wildrose '85
Blind Justice '86
Opposing Force '87
Moon 44 '90
King of the Hill '93
The Vanishing '93

Christopher Eigeman
Metropolitan '90
Barcelona '94
Kicking and Screaming '95

Jill Eikenberry
Between the Lines '77
Rush It '77
Butch and Sundance: The Early Days '79
Orphan Train '79
Rich Kids '79
Hide in Plain Sight '80
Arthur '81
Sessions '83
Grace Quigley '84
L.A. Law '86
The Manhattan Project '86
Assault and Matrimony '87
Family Sins '87
Cast the First Stone '89
An Inconvenient Woman '91
Chantilly Lace '93
Parallel Lives '94

Lisa Eilbacher
The Amazing Spider-Man '77
Run for the Roses '78
To Race the Wind '80
On the Right Track '81
An Officer and a Gentleman '82
Ten to Midnight '83
Beverly Hills Cop '84
Monte Carlo '86
Deadly Intent '88
Leviathan '89
The Last Samurai '90
Never Say Die '90
Blind Man's Bluff '91
The Hunt for the Night Stalker '91
Live Wire '92

Sally Eilers
Doughboys '30
Roaring Ranch '30
Trigger Tricks '30
Clearing the Range '31
Strange Illusion '45
Coroner Creek '48

Aron Eisenberg
The Horror Show '89
Playroom '90

Ike Eisenmann
Escape to Witch Mountain '75
Return from Witch Mountain '78

Debra Eisenstadt
Oleanna '94
The Heidi Chronicles '95

Anthony Eisley
The Wasp Woman '59
Naked Kiss '64
Frankie and Johnny '65
Navy vs. the Night Monsters '66
Journey to the Center of Time '67
Lightning Bolt '67
Mummy & Curse of the Jackal '67
Star! '68
The Witchmaker '69
Dracula vs. Frankenstein '71
The Doll Squad '73
Secrets '77
Monster '78
The Tormentors '80s
Killer Commandos

Anita Ekberg
Abbott and Costello Go to Mars '53
Artists and Models '55
Blood Alley '55
Back from Eternity '56
Hollywood or Bust '56
War and Peace '56
Paris Holiday '57
How I Learned to Love Women '60s
La Dolce Vita '60
The Mongols '60
Boccaccio '70 '62
Call Me Bwana '63
Four for Texas '63
The Alphabet Murders '65
Woman Times Seven '67
The Cobra '68
Fangs of the Living Dead '68
Northeast of Seoul '72
Gold of the Amazon Women '79
S*H*E '79
Intervista '87

Britt Ekland
After the Fox '66
Bobo '67
The Night They Raided Minsky's '69
Stiletto '69
Endless Night '71
Asylum '72
What the Peeper Saw '72
The Man with the Golden Gun '74
The Ultimate Thrill '74
Royal Flash '75
The Wicker Man '75
High Velocity '76
King Solomon's Treasure '76
Slavers '77
The Great Wallendas '78
Sex on the Run '78
The Hostage Tower '80
Demon Rage '82
Dead Wrong '83
Ecstasy '84
Erotic Images '85
Fraternity Vacation '85
Marbella '85
The Monster Club '85
Moon in Scorpio '86
Beverly Hills Vamp '88
Scandal '89
The Children '90
Cold Heat '90

Gosta Ekman
Faust '26
Swedenhielms '35
Intermezzo '36

Gosta Ekman
The Adventures of Picasso '80
The Inside Man '84

Jack Elam
Wild Weed '49
High Lonesome '50
Rawhide '50
The Bushwackers '52
Kansas City Confidential '52
Rancho Notorious '52
The Ring '52
Vera Cruz '53
Cattle Queen of Montana '54
Artists and Models '55

Kiss Me Deadly '55
The Man from Laramie '55
Pardners '56
The Girl in Lover's Lane '60
Pocketful of Miracles '61
Four for Texas '63
The Rare Breed '66
The Way West '67
Firecreek '68
Never a Dull Moment '68
Once Upon a Time in the West '68
Support Your Local Sheriff '69
Rio Lobo '70
Support Your Local Gunfighter '71
Hannie Caulder '72
Huckleberry Finn '75
Creature from Black Lake '76
Pony Express Rider '76
The Red Pony '76
Grayeagle '77
Norseman '78
The Apple Dumpling Gang Rides Again '79
The Sacketts '79
The Villain '79
Cannonball Run '81
Lost '83
Sacred Ground '83
Cannonball Run 2 '84
The Aurora Encounter '85
Hawken's Breed '87
Dynamite and Gold '88
Big Bad John '90
Suburban Commando '91
Shadow Force '92
Bonanza: The Return '93
Uninvited '93

Dana Elcar
The Fool Killer '65
The Learning Tree '69
Adam at 6 a.m. '70
Soldier Blue '70
A Gunfight '71
Fireball Forward '72
Dying Room Only '73
The Nude Bomb '80
Condorman '81
Forbidden Love '82
Help Wanted: Male '82
Blue Skies Again '83
All of Me '84
Code of Honor '84
Toughlove '85
Inside Out '91

Ron Eldard
True Love '89
Drop Dead Fred '91
The Last Supper '96

Florence Eldridge
Les Miserables '35
Mary of Scotland '36
Christopher Columbus '49
Inherit the Wind '60

George Eldridge
Take Me Back to Oklahoma '40
Sherlock Holmes and the Secret Weapon '42
Sonora Stagecoach '44
Mom & Dad '47

John Eldridge
Dangerous '35
Bad Men of the Border '45
Square Dance Jubilee '51
I Married a Monster from Outer Space '58

Erika Eleniak
Broken Angel '88
Under Siege '92
The Beverly Hillbillies '93
Chasers '94
Girl in the Cadillac '94
A Pyromaniac's Love Story '95
Tales from the Crypt Presents Bordello of Blood '96

Sandor Eles
The Evil of Frankenstein '64
And Soon the Darkness '70

Taina Elg
Diane '55
The Prodigal '55
Les Girls '57
The Bacchantes '63

Alix Elias
Citizens Band '77
Rock 'n' Roll High School '79

Christine Elise
Child's Play 2 '90
Boiling Point '93

Hector Elizondo
Born to Win '71
Valdez is Coming '71
Pocket Money '72
Report to the Commissioner '74
The Taking of Pelham One Two Three '74
The Dain Curse '78
American Gigolo '79
Cuba '79
Diary of the Dead '80s
The Fan '81
Young Doctors in Love '82
The Flamingo Kid '84
Private Resort '84
Out of the Darkness '85
Courage '86
Nothing in Common '86
Leviathan '89
Forgotten Prisoners '90
Pretty Woman '90
Taking Care of Business '90
Final Approach '91
Frankie and Johnny '91
Necessary Roughness '91
Chains of Gold '92
Samantha '92
Scott Turow's The Burden of Proof '92
There Goes the Neighborhood '92
Backstreet Justice '93
Being Human '94
Beverly Hills Cop 3 '94
Exit to Eden '94
Getting Even with Dad '94
Perfect Alibi '94

Duke Ellington
Check & Double Check '30
Murder at the Vanities '34
Cabin in the Sky '43

Ramblin' Jack Elliot
Honkytonk Nights '70s
Roadie '80

Alison Elliott
Home Before Midnight '84
The Buccaneers '95
Indictment: The McMartin Trial '95
The Spitfire Grill '95
The Underneath '95

Bob Elliott
Vengeance '80
Quick Change '90
Cabin Boy '94

Chris Elliott
The Abyss '89
New York Stories '89
CB4: The Movie '93
Groundhog Day '93
Cabin Boy '94

Denholm Elliott
Cruel Sea '53
Holy Terror '65
King Rat '65
Strange Case of Dr. Jekyll & Mr. Hyde '68
The Night They Raided Minsky's '69
Too Late the Hero '70
The House that Dripped Blood '71
Quest for Love '71
Vault of Horror '73
The Apprenticeship of Duddy Kravitz '74
It's Not the Size That Counts '74
Russian Roulette '75
Robin and Marian '76
To the Devil, A Daughter '76
Voyage of the Damned '76
The Hound of the Baskervilles '77
The Boys from Brazil '78
Cuba '79
Saint Jack '79
Zulu Dawn '79
Raiders of the Lost Ark '81
Rude Awakening '81
Brimstone & Treacle '82
The Missionary '82
The Two Faces of Evil '82
The Hound of the Baskervilles '83
Trading Places '83
The Wicked Lady '83
A Private Function '84
The Razor's Edge '84
Bleak House '85
Defense of the Realm '85
Transmutations '85
Hotel du Lac '86
A Room with a View '86
Maurice '87
Over Indulgence '87
The Bourne Identity '88
Deep Cover '88
Hanna's War '88
September '88
Stealing Heaven '88
A Doll's House '89
Indiana Jones and the Last Crusade '89
Codename Kyril '91
One Against the Wind '91
Toy Soldiers '91
Noises Off '92
Scorchers '92

John Elliott
Mother and Son '31
The Gallant Fool '33
Big Calibre '35
Bulldog Courage '35
Danger Trails '35
Toll of the Desert '35
A Face in the Fog '36
Rogue's Tavern '36
Riding On '37
The Phantom of the Range '38
Death Rides the Range '40

Robert Elliott
The Maltese Falcon '31
Murder at Midnight '31
White Eagle '32
The Return of Casey Jones '34

Ross Elliott
Hot Lead '51
Ma and Pa Kettle at Home '54
Tarantula '55
Paper Man '71

Sam Elliott
Butch Cassidy and the Sundance Kid '69
Frogs '72
Molly & Lawless John '72
I Will Fight No More Forever '75
Lifeguard '75
The Legacy '79
The Sacketts '79
Wild Times '79
Murder in Texas '81
The Shadow Riders '82
Mask '85
The Blue Lightning '86
Fatal Beauty '87
The Quick and the Dead '87
Shakedown '88
Prancer '89
Road House '89
Sibling Rivalry '90
Conagher '91
Rush '91
Gettysburg '93
Tombstone '93
The Desperate Trail '94
Blue River '95
Buffalo Girls '95
Hole in the Sky '95
Woman Undone '95

Shawn Elliott
Short Eyes '79
Crossover Dreams '85
Bloodsucking Pharoahs of Pittsburgh '90
Impulse '90

Stephen Elliott
Report to the Commissioner '74
Betrayal '78
Sergeant Matlovich vs. the U.S. Air Force '78
Can You Hear the Laughter? The Story of Freddie Prinze '79
Mrs. R's Daughter '79
Arthur '81
Cutter's Way '81
Jacqueline Bouvier Kennedy '81
Beauty and the Beast '83
Beverly Hills Cop '84
Days of Hell '84
Roadhouse 66 '84
Assassination '87
Perry Mason: The Case of the Lost Love '87
Arthur 2: On the Rocks '88
Taking Care of Business '90

Wild Bill Elliott
Western Double Feature 1: Wild Bill & Sunset Carson '40s
Bordertown Gunfighters '43
Calling Wild Bill Elliott '43
Death Valley Manhunt '43
Man from Thunder River '43
Western Double Feature 12 '44
Western Double Feature 7: Wild Bill & Crabbe '45
The Showdown '50

Desmond Walter Ellis
The Hellfire Club '61
The Great St. Trinian's Train Robbery '66

Edward Ellis
I Am a Fugitive from a Chain Gang '32
The Thin Man '34
The Return of Peter Grimm '35
Fury '36
The Texas Rangers '36
Wheel of Fortune '41

Frank Ellis
The Big Stampede '32
Whistlin' Dan '32
Wildfire '45

Jack Ellis
Prime Suspect 2 '93
Prime Suspect: The Lost Child '94

James Ellis
No Surrender '86
Priest '94
Leapin' Leprechauns '95

Patricia Ellis
Three on a Match '32
The Case of the Lucky Legs '35
Postal Inspector '36
Block-heads '38
Back Door to Heaven '39

Robert Ellis
The Fighting Sheriff '31
Broadway to Cheyenne '32
Come On Danger! '32
Daring Danger '32
Fighting Fool '32
White Eagle '32
Captured in Chinatown '35

Robin Ellis
Elizabeth R '72
Poldark '75
Poldark 2 '75
The Europeans '79
The Curse of King Tut's Tomb '80
A Dark Adapted Eye '93

Tracey Ellis
This Boy's Life '93
The Neverending Story 3 '94

James Ellison
Hopalong Cassidy '35
23 1/2 Hours Leave '37
Next Time I Marry '38
Vivacious Lady '38
Fifth Avenue Girl '39
You Can't Fool Your Wife '40
The Undying Monster '42
I Walked with a Zombie '43
Last of the Wild Horses '49
Guns of Justice '50
Last Bullet '50
Marshal of Heldorado '50
Outlaw Fury '50
Rangeland Empire '50
Sudden Death '50
Kentucky Jubilee '51

Rebekah Elmaloglou
In Too Deep '90
The Sum of Us '94

Michael Elphick
Arthur's Hallowed Ground '84
The Element of Crime '84
Ordeal by Innocence '84
Little Dorrit, Film 1: Nobody's Fault '88
Little Dorrit, Film 2: Little Dorrit's Story '88
Let Him Have It '91

Isobel Elsom
Casanova Brown '44
Escape Me Never '47
The Ghost and Mrs. Muir '47
Love from a Stranger '47
Monsieur Verdoux '47
Love Is a Many-Splendored Thing '55

Cary Elwes
Another Country '84
Oxford Blues '84
Lady Jane '85
The Princess Bride '87
Glory '89
Days of Thunder '90
Leather Jackets '90
Hot Shots! '91
Bram Stoker's Dracula '92
The Crush '93
Robin Hood: Men in Tights '93
Rudyard Kipling's The Jungle Book '94
Twister '96

Ron Ely
Once Before I Die '65
Cry of the Black Wolves '70s
Doc Savage '75
Slavers '77

Sallee Elyse
Demented '80
Home Sweet Home '80

Faye Emerson
Destination Tokyo '43
Uncertain Glory '44

Hope Emerson
Adam's Rib '50
Westward the Women '51
All Mine to Give '56

Karrie Emerson
Evils of the Night '85
Chopping Mall '86

Gilbert Emery
The Lady Refuses '31
The Royal Bed '31
Goin' to Town '35
Wife Versus Secretary '36

John Emery
Here Comes Mr. Jordan '41
Ship Ahoy '42
Mademoiselle Fifi '44
The Spanish Main '45
Rocketship X-M '50
A Lawless Street '55
Forever Darling '56
Kronos '57

David Emge
Dawn of the Dead '78
Hellmaster '92

Robert Emhardt
Underworld, U.S.A. '60
Shame '61
Die Sister, Die! '74

Michael Emil
Sitting Ducks '80
Can She Bake a Cherry Pie? '83
Always '85
Insignificance '85
Someone to Love '87
New Year's Day '89
In the Spirit '90
Adventures in Spying '92

Daniel Emilfork
Lady L '65
The Devil's Nightmare '71
The City of Lost Children '95

Alphonsia Emmanuel
Peter's Friends '92
Under Suspicion '92

Michael Emmet
Night of the Blood Beast '58
Attack of the Giant Leeches '59

Lena Endre
The Visitors '89
The Best Intentions '92
Sunday's Children '94

Georgia Engel
The Outside Man '73
The Day the Women Got Even '80
Signs of Life '89

Tina Engel
The Boat is Full '81

Engel ▶*cont.*

The Promise '95

Wera Engels
Fugitive Road '34
Hong Kong Nights '35

Audie England
Delta of Venus '95
Venus Rising '95

Marla English
Flesh and the Spur '57
Voodoo Woman '57

Robert Englund
Buster and Billie '74
Slashed Dreams '74
Eaten Alive '76
A Star is Born '76
Stay Hungry '76
Mysterious Two '82
V '83
A Nightmare on Elm Street '84
V: The Final Battle '84
A Nightmare on Elm Street 2: Freddy's Revenge '85
Fangoria's Weekend of Horrors '86
A Nightmare on Elm Street 3: Dream Warriors '87
A Nightmare on Elm Street 4: Dream Master '88
A Nightmare on Elm Street 5: Dream Child '89
The Phantom of the Opera '89
The Adventures of Ford Fairlane '90
Dance Macabre '91
Freddy's Dead: The Final Nightmare '91
The Mangler '94
Wes Craven's New Nightmare '94

John Enos
Till the End of the Night '94
Red Shoe Diaries 6: How I Met My Husband '95

Rene Enriquez
Ants '77
Hill Street Blues, Vol. 1: Hill Street Station '81
The Evil That Men Do '84
Bulletproof '88

Michael Ensign
House '86
Life Stinks '91
Born Yesterday '93

Brenda Epperson
Amore! '93
Storybook '95

Dieter Eppler
The Slaughter of the Vampires '62
The Torture Chamber of Dr. Sadism '69

Omar Epps
Juice '92
Daybreak '93
The Program '93
Higher Learning '94
Major League 2 '94

Kathryn Erbe
What About Bob? '91
Rich in Love '93
Breathing Lessons '94
D2: The Mighty Ducks '94
The Addiction '95

Richard Erdman
Objective, Burma! '45
Cry Danger '51
The Stooge '51
Stalag 17 '53
Namu, the Killer Whale '66
Tomboy '85

Leif Erickson
Desert Gold '36
Conquest '37
Waikiki Wedding '37
The Big Broadcast of 1938 '38
One Third of a Nation '39
Arabian Nights '42
Night Monster '42
Pardon My Sarong '42
Blonde Savage '47
Joan of Arc '48
The Snake Pit '48
The Showdown '50
Three Secrets '50
Hill Number One '51
Abbott and Costello Meet Captain Kidd '52
Never Wave at a WAC '52
Invaders from Mars '53
Trouble Along the Way '53
On the Waterfront '54
Fastest Gun Alive '56
Tea and Sympathy '56
Istanbul '57
A Gathering of Eagles '63
Roustabout '64
Strait-Jacket '64
Abduction '75
Force Five '75
Twilight's Last Gleaming '77
Penitentiary 2 '82
Rocky 3 '82
D.C. Cab '84

Devon Ericson
The Runaway Barge '75
Can You Hear the Laughter? The Story of Freddie Prinze '79

John Ericson
Bad Day at Black Rock '54
Rhapsody '54
The Student Prince '54
Green Fire '55
7 Faces of Dr. Lao '63
The Bamboo Saucer '68
The Bounty Man '72
Hustler Squad '76
Zone of the Dead '78
House of the Dead '80
Primary Target '89

R. Lee Ermey
The Boys in Company C '77
Full Metal Jacket '87
Mississippi Burning '88
Demonstone '89
Fletch Lives '89
The Siege of Firebase Gloria '89
Endless Descent '90
I'm Dangerous Tonight '90
Kid '90
The Take '90
The Terror Within 2 '91
Body Snatchers '93
Hexed '93
Sommersby '93
French Silk '94
Love Is a Gun '94
Dead Man Walking '95
The Fighter '95
Murder In the First '95
Seven '95
The Frighteners '96

Krista Errickson
First Time '82
Jekyll & Hyde...Together Again '82
Mortal Passions '90
Killer Image '92
Martial Outlaw '93

Leon Errol
We're Not Dressing '34
The Great Ziegfeld '36
Make a Wish '37
The Flustered Comedy of Leon Errol '39
Mexican Spitfire/Smartest Girl in Town '40
Pop Always Pays '40
Hurry, Charlie, Hurry '41
Never Give a Sucker an Even Break '41
Mexican Spitfire at Sea '42
Higher and Higher '44
The Invisible Man's Revenge '44
Seven Days Ashore/Hurry, Charlie, Hurry '44
The Noose Hangs High '48
Joe's Bed-Stuy Barbershop: We Cut Heads '83

Patrick Ersgard
The Visitors '89
Mandroid '93
Dreaming of Rita '94

Victor Ertmanis
Brainscan '94
Paris, France '94

Bill Erwin
Huckleberry Finn '75
Hard Knox '83
Fallen Angels 1 '93

Stuart Erwin
Going Hollywood '33
Hold Your Man '33
Bachelor Bait '34
Chained '34
Palooka '34
Viva Villa! '34
Ceiling Zero '35
Small Town Boy '37
Mr. Boggs Steps Out '38
Back Door to Heaven '39
It Could Happen to You '39
The Bride Came C.O.D. '41
The Great Mike '44
Heading for Heaven '47
Killer Dill '47
The Trouble with Father '50
The Misadventures of Merlin Jones '63

Norman Eshley
The Confessional '75
Brother Cadfael '94

Carl Esmond
The Navy Comes Through '42
Panama Hattie '42
The Story of Dr. Wassell '44
Without Love '45

Jill Esmond
Skin Game '31
State's Attorney '31
F.P. 1 '33
Journey for Margaret '42
Casanova Brown '44
The White Cliffs of Dover '44
A Man Called Peter '55

Bella Esperance
Lady Dragon '92
Lady Dragon 2 '93

Giancarlo Esposito
Sweet Lorraine '87
School Daze '88
Do the Right Thing '89
King of New York '90
Mo' Better Blues '90
Night on Earth '91
Bob Roberts '92
Malcolm X '92
Amos and Andrew '93
Fresh '94
Blue In the Face '95
Reckless '95
Smoke '95
The Usual Suspects '95

Gianni Esposito
Les Miserables '57
Paris Belongs to Us '60

David Essex
Octaman '71
That'll Be the Day '73
Silver Dream Racer '83
Journey of Honor '91

Christine Estabrook
Almost You '85
Second Sight '89
Presumed Innocent '90

Robert Estes
Trapper County War '89
Aces: Iron Eagle 3 '92

Emilio Estevez
In the Custody of Strangers '82
Tex '82
Nightmares '83
The Outsiders '83
Repo Man '83
The Breakfast Club '85
St. Elmo's Fire '85
That Was Then...This Is Now '85
Maximum Overdrive '86
Stakeout '87
Wisdom '87
Young Guns '88
Nightbreaker '89
Men at Work '90
Young Guns 2 '90
Freejack '92
The Mighty Ducks '92
Another Stakeout '93
Judgment Night '93
National Lampoon's Loaded Weapon 1 '93
D2: The Mighty Ducks '94
Mission: Impossible '96

Joe Estevez
Fatal Justice '90s
Lockdown '90
Soultaker '90
Dark Rider '91
Armed for Action '92
L.A. Goddess '92
Murder-in-Law '92
Beach Babes from Beyond Infinity '93
Dark Universe '93
Eye of the Stranger '93
In a Moment of Passion '93
The Deadly Secret '94
Money to Burn '94
Breakaway '95
The Mosaic Project '95

Ramon Estevez
Cadence '89
Blood on the Badge '92

Renee Estevez
Bulldance '88
Intruder '88
Sleepaway Camp 2: Unhappy Campers '88
Forbidden Sun '89
Marked for Murder '89
Single White Female '92
Endangered '94
Good Girls Don't '95

Erik Estrada
The Cross & the Switchblade '72
Jailbreakin' '72
The New Centurions '72
The Lost Idol/Shock Troop '80s
The Line '80
Honeyboy '82
Lightblast '85
Hour of the Assassin '86
The Dirty Dozen: The Fatal Mission '88
Alien Seed '89
Andy and the Airwave Rangers '89
Twisted Justice '89
Caged Fury '90
Guns '90
The Last Riders '90
Night of the Wilding '90
A Show of Force '90
Spirits '90
The Divine Enforcer '91
Do or Die '91
Gang Justice '94

Pat Estrin
America First '70
Act of Vengeance '74
Dennis the Menace: Dinosaur Hunter '93

Ruth Etting
Roman Scandals '33
Hips, Hips, Hooray '34

Shari Eubank
Supervixens '75
Chesty Anderson USN '76

Bob Eubanks
Johnny Dangerously '84
The History of White People in America '85
Roger & Me '89

Corey Michael Eubanks
Payback '90
Forced to Kill '93

Wesley Eure
Jennifer '78
The Toolbox Murders '78
C.H.O.M.P.S. '79

Art Evans
King '78
The In-Laws '79
A Soldier's Story '84
Jo Jo Dancer, Your Life is Calling '86
Native Son '86
School Daze '88
White of the Eye '88
The Mighty Quinn '89
Mom '89
Die Hard 2: Die Harder '90
The Finishing Touch '92
Trespass '92
CB4: The Movie '93

Clifford Evans
The Mutiny of the Elsinore '39
The Courageous Mr. Penn '41
Love on the Dole '41
The Foreman Went to France '42
While I Live '47
I'll Get You '53
The Gilded Cage '54
The Curse of the Werewolf '61
Kiss of the Vampire '62
One Brief Summer '70

Dale Evans
Western Double Feature 1 '38
The Great American Western Collection: Roy Rogers '40s
Western Double Feature 4: Rogers & Evans '40s
Western Double Feature 18 '40s
Western Double Feature 21 '40s
Western Double Feature 24 '40s
Cowboy & the Senorita '44
San Fernando Valley '44
Song of Nevada '44
The Yellow Rose of Texas '44
Bells of Rosarita '45
Sunset in El Dorado '45
Utah '45
Western Double Feature 19 '45
Helldorado '46
My Pal Trigger '46
Roll on Texas Moon '46
Song of Arizona '46
Under Nevada Skies '46
Apache Rose '47
Bells of San Angelo '47
Home in Oklahoma '47
Lights of Old Santa Fe '47
Down Dakota Way '49
The Golden Stallion '49
Susanna Pass '49
Bells of Coronado '50
Trigger, Jr. '50
Twilight in the Sierras '50
Western Double Feature 3: Rogers & Allen '50
Western Double Feature 6: Rogers & Trigger '50
Western Double Feature 10: Roy, Dale, & Trigger '80s

Douglas Evans
The Green Hornet '39
The Golden Stallion '49
North of the Great Divide '50
Sky High '51

Edith Evans
The Last Days of Dolwyn '49
The Queen of Spades '49
Importance of Being Earnest '52
Look Back in Anger '58
The Nun's Story '59
Tom Jones '63
The Chalk Garden '64
Crooks & Coronets '69
The Madwoman of Chaillot '69
David Copperfield '70
Scrooge '70
Craze '74
Nasty Habits '77
A Doll's House '89

Evans Evans
The Story of a Love Story '73
Dead Bang '89

Gene Evans
It Happens Every Spring '49
The Steel Helmet '51
Mutiny '52
Donovan's Brain '53
Cattle Queen of Montana '54
Crashout '55
The Sad Sack '57
Operation Petticoat '59
Shock Corridor '63
Apache Uprising '66
The Bounty Man '72
Gentle Savage '73
Walking Tall '73
Devil Times Five '74
The Concrete Cowboys '79
The Shadow Riders '82

John Evans
I've Heard the Mermaids Singing '87
Long Road Home '91

Josh Evans
Born on the Fourth of July '89
The Doors '91
Ricochet '91

Linda Evans
Beach Blanket Bingo '65
Those Calloways '65
Big Valley '68

Confessions of Tom Harris '72
The Klansman '74
Mitchell '75
Hunter '77
Standing Tall '78
Avalanche Express '79
Tom Horn '80
Kenny Rogers as the Gambler, Part 2: The Adventure Continues '83
The Gambler Returns: The Luck of the Draw '93

Madge Evans
Three Broadway Girls '32
Dinner at Eight '33
Hallelujah, I'm a Bum '33
Stand Up and Cheer '34
David Copperfield '35
Transatlantic Tunnel '35
Sinners in Paradise '38

Maurice Evans
Wedding Rehearsal '32
Scrooge '35
Androcles and the Lion '52
The Tempest '63
The War Lord '65
Planet of the Apes '68
Rosemary's Baby '68
Invasion of the Body Stealers '69
Beneath the Planet of the Apes '70
Terror in the Wax Museum '73

Mike Evans
The Voyage of the Yes '72
The House on Skull Mountain '74

Muriel Evans
The Prizefighter and the Lady '33
Manhattan Melodrama '34
The New Frontier '35
The Throwback '35
King of the Pecos '36
The House of Secrets '37

Rex Evans
The Wrong Road '37
The Matchmaker '58

Robert Evans
Man of a Thousand Faces '57
The Best of Everything '59

Robin Evans
One Dark Night '82
Rage of Honor '87

Terry Evans
Cody '67
Mongrel '83

Troy Evans
Article 99 '92
Kuffs '92
My Summer Story '94
Bodily Harm '95
Father and Scout '95
The Frighteners '96

Edith Evanson
The Jade Mask '45
Forever Amber '47
The Magnificent Yankee '50

Judith Evelyn
The Egyptian '54
Rear Window '54

Kimberly Evenson
The Big Bet '85
Porky's Revenge '85
Kandyland '87

Barbara Everest
Phantom Fiend '35
Gaslight '44
Jane Eyre '44
The Valley of Decision '45
Tony Draws a Horse '51

Chad Everett
Rome Adventure '62
Johnny Tiger '66
The Singing Nun '66
The Impossible Years '68
Intruder Within '81
Airplane 2: The Sequel '82
Fever Pitch '85
Heroes Stand Alone '89
Jigsaw Murders '89
The Rousters '90
Official Denial '93

Francine Everett
Dirty Gertie from Harlem U.S.A. '46
Tall, Tan and Terrific '46

Kenny Everett
The Best of the Kenny Everett Video Show '81
Bloodbath at the House of Death '85

Rupert Everett
Another Country '84
Dance with a Stranger '85
Hearts of Fire '87
The Right Hand Man '87
The Comfort of Strangers '91
Inside Monkey Zetterland '93
The Madness of King George '94
Ready to Wear '94
Cemetery Man '95
Dunston Checks In '95

Tom Everett
Friday the 13th, Part 4: The Final Chapter '84
Prison '88
Best of the Best '89

Nancy Everhard
Deepstar Six '89
Demonstone '89
Double Revenge '89
The Trial of the Incredible Hulk '89
The China Lake Murders '90
This Gun for Hire '90

Jason Evers
Fer-De-Lance '74
Claws '77
Barracuda '78
Basket Case 2 '90

Cory Everson
Double Impact '91
Felony '95

Greg Evigan
Private Road: No Trespassing '87
Stripped to Kill '87
Deepstar Six '89
Lies Before Kisses '92
TekWar '94

Pat Evison
Tim '79
Starstruck '82
What the Moon Saw '90

John Ewart
Island Trader '71
Newsfront '78
Prince and the Great Race '83
The Quest '86
Which Way Home '90

Tom Ewell
Adam's Rib '50
A Life of Her Own '50
Mr. Music '50
Lost in Alaska '52
The Seven Year Itch '55
The Girl Can't Help It '56
State Fair '62
They Only Kill Their Masters '72
Easy Money '83

Barbara Ewing
Dracula Has Risen from the Grave '68
Guardian of the Abyss '82

Richard Eyer
Desperate Hours '55
The Kettles in the Ozarks '56
The Invisible Boy '57
The Seventh Voyage of Sinbad '58

Peter Eyre
Hedda '75
Diamond's Edge '88
Princess Caraboo '94
Scarlett '94
Sharpe's Gold '94
Joseph '95

William Eythe
The Ox-Bow Incident '43
Wilson '44
A Wing and a Prayer '44
Colonel Effingham's Raid '45
House on 92nd Street '45

Maynard Eziashi
Mister Johnson '91
Twenty-One '91
Bopha! '93
Ace Ventura: When Nature Calls '95

Shelley Fabares
Ride the Wild Surf '64
Girl Happy '65
Spinout '66
Clambake '67
Brian's Song '71
Sky Hei$t '75
Great American Traffic Jam '80
Memorial Day '83
Love or Money? '88

Fabian
North to Alaska '60
Five Weeks in a Balloon '62
The Longest Day '62
Mr. Hobbs Takes a Vacation '62
Ride the Wild Surf '64
Dear Brigitte '65
Little Laura & Big John '73
Soul Hustler '76
Kiss Daddy Goodbye '81

Ava Fabian
To Die for '89
Welcome Home, Roxy Carmichael '90
Ski School '91
Last Man Standing '95

Francoise Fabian
Dressmaker '56
Fernandel the Dressmaker '57
That Naughty Girl '58
Belle de Jour '67
My Night at Maud's '69
Happy New Year '74
Salut l'Artiste '74
Love by Appointment '76
The French Woman '79
Reunion '88

Joel Fabiani
President's Mistress '78
Reuben, Reuben '83

Nanette Fabray
The Private Lives of Elizabeth & Essex '39
The Band Wagon '53
Alice Through the Looking Glass '66
The Happy Ending '69
Harper Valley P.T.A. '78
The Man in the Santa Claus Suit '79
Amy '81
Personal Exemptions '88

Franco Fabrizi
I Vitelloni '53
The Swindle '55
A Woman of Rome '56
Ginger & Fred '86

Valeria Fabrizi
Beauty on the Beach '60s
Women in Cell Block 7 '77

Robert Factor
Fear '88
Ninja Academy '90

Bill Fagerbakke
Stephen King's The Stand '94
The Reluctant Agent '95

Jeff Fahey
Execution of Raymond Graham '85
Silverado '85
Psycho 3 '86
Backfire '88
Split Decisions '88
Wrangler '88
True Blood '89
Curiosity Kills '90
Impulse '90
The Last of the Finest '90
White Hunter, Black Heart '90
Body Parts '91
Iran: Days of Crisis '91
Iron Maze '91
The Lawnmower Man '92
Sketch Artist '92
Blindsided '93
The Hit List '93
Quick '93
Woman of Desire '93
Firefall '94
Sketch Artist 2: Hands That See '94
Temptation '94
Wyatt Earp '94
Darkman 3: Die Darkman Die '95
Eye of the Wolf '95

Northern Passage '95
The Sweeper '95

Mary-Anne Fahey
The Dunera Boys '85
Mutant Hunt '87
Celia: Child Of Terror '89

Elinor Fair
Kismet '20
Big Stakes '22
Road to Yesterday/The Yankee Clipper '27
Yankee Clipper '27
Let 'er Go Gallegher '28

Jody Fair
The Brain Eaters '58
High School Confidential '58

Bruce Fairbairn
The Vampire Hookers '78
Cyclone '87
Nightstick '87

Douglas Fairbanks, Sr.
The Lamb '15
Flirting with Fate '16
His Picture in the Papers '16
Matrimaniac '16
Reggie Mixes In '16
American Aristocracy '17
The Americano '17
Down to Earth '17
The Man from Painted Post '17
Reaching for the Moon '17
His Majesty, the American '19
When the Clouds Roll By '19
Mark of Zorro '20
The Nut '21
The Three Musketeers '21
Robin Hood '22
The Thief of Baghdad '24
The Americano/Variety '25
Don Q., Son of Zorro '25
Mystery of the Leaping Fish/Chess Fever '25
The Black Pirate '26
A Kiss for Mary Pickford '27
The Iron Mask '29
The Taming of the Shrew '29
Reaching for the Moon '31
Mr. Robinson Crusoe '32
Private Life of Don Juan '34
Camp Classics #1 '50s
Days of Thrills and Laughter '61

Douglas Fairbanks, Jr.
A Woman of Affairs '28
Our Modern Maidens '29
Party Girls '29
Little Caesar '30
Scarlet Dawn '32
Morning Glory '33
Catherine the Great '34
Mimi '35
Accused '36
Prisoner of Zenda '37
When Thief Meets Thief '37
Having Wonderful Time '38
Having Wonderful Time/Carnival Boat '38
Joy of Living '38
The Rage of Paris '38
The Young in Heart '38
Gunga Din '39
Angels Over Broadway '40
The Corsican Brothers '42
Sinbad, the Sailor '47
The Hostage Tower '80
Ghost Story '81

Craig Fairbrass
Cliffhanger '93
Nightscare '93
Prime Suspect 2 '93
Galaxis '95

Morgan Fairchild
Initiation of Sarah '78
The Concrete Cowboys '79
Honeyboy '82
The Seduction '82
The Zany Adventures of Robin Hood '84
Pee Wee's Big Adventure '85
North and South Book 2 '86
Campus Man '87
Deadly Illusion '87
Red Headed Stranger '87
Midnight Cop '88

Cannon Movie Tales: Sleeping Beauty '89
Haunting of Sarah Hardy '89
Phantom of the Mall: Eric's Revenge '89
Sleeping Beauty '89
Even Angels Fall '90
Mob Boss '90
Writer's Block '91
Based on an Untrue Story '93
Body Chemistry 3: Point of Seduction '93
Freaked '93
Test Tube Teens from the Year 2000 '93
Gospa '94
Criminal Hearts '95
Venus Rising '95

Heather Fairfield
The War of the Roses '89
A Girl of the Limberlost '90
No Secrets '91

Donald A. Faison
Clueless '95
New Jersey Drive '95
Waiting to Exhale '95

Frankie Faison
Exterminator 2 '84
Coming to America '88
Mississippi Burning '88
Do the Right Thing '89
City of Hope '91
Freejack '92
Sommersby '93
The Spider and the Fly '94
Stephen King's The Langoliers '95

Matthew Faison
Taken Away '89
Lily in Winter '94

Adam Faith
Yesterday's Hero '79
McVicar '80

Dolores Faith
The Phantom Planet '61
The Human Duplicators '64

Marianne Faithfull
The Girl on a Motorcycle '68
Hamlet '69
Madhouse Mansion '74
Assault on Agathon '75
The Turn of the Screw '92

Lola Falana
A Man Called Adam '66
The Liberation of L.B. Jones '70
The Klansman '74
Lady Cocoa '75

Edie Falco
Sweet Lorraine '87
Trust '91
Laws of Gravity '92
The Addiction '95

Peter Falk
The Bloody Brood '59
Pocketful of Miracles '61
Pressure Point '62
The Balcony '63
It's a Mad, Mad, Mad, Mad World '63
Robin and the 7 Hoods '64
The Great Race '65
Columbo: Prescription Murder '67
Luv '67
Anzio '68
Columbo: Murder By the Book '71
A Woman Under the Influence '74
Griffin and Phoenix: A Love Story '76
Mikey & Nicky '76
Murder by Death '76
Brink's Job '78
The Cheap Detective '78
The In-Laws '79
...All the Marbles '81
Big Trouble '86
Happy New Year '87
The Princess Bride '87
Vibes '88
Wings of Desire '88
Cookie '89
In the Spirit '90
Tune in Tomorrow '90
Faraway, So Close! '93
Roommates '95

Mary Fanaro
Demon Queen '80s
Truth or Dare? '86

Al Fann
Parasite '82
Frankie and Johnny '91

Ennio Fantastichini
Open Doors '89
The Station '92

Sergio Fantoni
Esther and the King '60
The Giant of Marathon '60
Atom Age Vampire '61
The Prize '63
Von Ryan's Express '65
What Did You Do in the War, Daddy? '66
Hornet's Nest '70

Stephanie Faracy
Blind Date '87
The Great Outdoors '88
Hocus Pocus '93

Daniel Faraldo
Above the Law '88
Full Fathom Five '90

Debrah Farentino
Capone '89
Mortal Sins '90
Bugsy '91
Son of the Pink Panther '93
Dead Air '94

James Farentino
Psychomania '63
Ensign Pulver '64
The War Lord '65
The Possessed '77
Silent Victory: The Kitty O'Neil Story '79
The Final Countdown '80
Dead and Buried '81
The Cradle Will Fall '83
License to Kill '84
A Summer to Remember '84
Sins '85
Family Sins '87
Her Alibi '88
Naked Lie '89
A Cop for the Killing '94
Honor Thy Father and Mother: The True Story of the Menendez Brothers '94

Antonio Fargas
Milo Milo '60s
Across 110th Street '72
Busting '74
Foxy Brown '74
Cornbread, Earl & Me '75
Huckleberry Finn '75
Car Wash '76
Pretty Baby '78
Nurse '80
The Ambush Murders '82
Firestarter '84
Streetwalkin' '85
Florida Straits '87
I'm Gonna Git You Sucka '88
Shakedown '88
The Borrower '89
Night of the Sharks '89
Howling 6: The Freaks '90

Betty Faria
Bye Bye Brazil '79
The Story of Fausta '88

Dennis Farina
Code of Silence '85
Crime Story: The Complete Saga '86
Jo Jo Dancer, Your Life is Calling '86
Manhunter '86
Midnight Run '88
The Hillside Strangler '89
Men of Respect '91
Drug Wars 2: The Cocaine Cartel '92
Street Crimes '92
We're Talkin' Serious Money '92
Another Stakeout '93
Mac '93
Striking Distance '93
Little Big League '94
Out of Annie's Past '94
Get Shorty '95
Eddie '96

Chris Farley
Coneheads '93
Wayne's World 2 '93
Airheads '94
Tommy Boy '95
Black Sheep '96

Frances Farmer
Come and Get It '36
Rhythm on the Range '36
Toast of New York '37
South of Pago Pago '40
Son of Fury '42

Gary Farmer
Powwow Highway '89
Sioux City '94
Tales from the Crypt Presents Demon Knight '94
Dead Man '95
Moonshine Highway '96

Mimsy Farmer
Spencer's Mountain '63
Devil's Angels '67
Road to Salina '68
More '69
Allonsanfan '73
Autopsy '78
The Black Cat '81
Codename: Wildgeese '84

Suzan Farmer
Die, Monster, Die! '65
Death in Deep Water '74
The Graveyard '74

Alberto Farnese
The Giants of Thessaly '60
Gladiator of Rome '63
Conqueror & the Empress '64

Richard Farnsworth
Texas Across the River '66
Strange New World '75
Comes a Horseman '78
Resurrection '80
Tom Horn '80
Legend of the Lone Ranger '81
Ruckus '81
The Grey Fox '83
Independence Day '83
Waltz Across Texas '83
The Natural '84
Rhinestone '84
Anne of Green Gables '85
Chase '85
Into the Night '85
Sylvester '85
Space Rage '86
Witchery '88
Havana '90
Misery '90
The Two Jakes '90
Highway to Hell '92
The Fire Next Time '93
Lassie '94
The River Pirates '94

Franklyn Farnum
The Scarlet Car '17
Battling with Buffalo Bill '31
Mark of the Spur '32
The Silver Bullet '34
Ghost Rider '35
Hopalong Cassidy '35
Powdersmoke Range '35
Prison Train '38

William Farnum
The Spoilers '14
Dubarry '30
A Connecticut Yankee '31
Painted Desert '31
Ten Nights in a Bar-Room '31
The Drifter '32
Mr. Robinson Crusoe '32
Supernatural '33
The Silver Streak '34
Between Men '35
The Crusades '35
Million Dollar Haul '35
Powdersmoke Range '35
Custer's Last Stand '36
Kid Ranger '36
The Vigilantes are Coming '36
Git Along Little Dogies '37
Public Cowboy No. 1 '37
Law of the Sea '38
Santa Fe Stampede '38
Today I Hang '42
Wildfire '45
God's Country '46
My Dog Shep '46
Gun Cargo '49
Trail of Robin Hood '50
Lone Star '52

Derek Farr
Spellbound '41
Man on the Run '49
Truth About Women '58

Felicia Farr
Jubal '56
3:10 to Yuma '57
Kiss Me, Stupid! '64
Kotch '71
Charley Varrick '73

Jamie Farr
No Time for Sergeants '58
Who's Minding the Mint? '67
With Six You Get Eggroll '68
M*A*S*H: The Collector's Edition '72
Cannonball Run '81
Return of the Rebels '81
M*A*S*H: Goodbye, Farewell & Amen '83
Cannonball Run 2 '84
For Love or Money '84
Combat Academy '86
Happy Hour '87
Curse 2: The Bite '88
Scrooged '88
Speed Zone '88
Fearless Tiger '94

Patricia Farr
Tailspin Tommy '34
Mistaken Identity '36

David Farrar
Meet Sexton Blake '44
Echo Murders '45
Black Narcissus '47
Frieda '47
The World Owes Me a Living '47
The Small Back Room '49
The Obsessed '51
Let's Make Up '55
Pearl of the South Pacific '55
Sea Chase '55
John Paul Jones '59
Beat Girl '60

Charles Farrell
Old Ironsides '26
City Girl '30
Aggie Appleby, Maker of Men '33
Just Around the Corner '38
Moonlight Sonata '38

Glenda Farrell
Little Caesar '30
I Am a Fugitive from a Chain Gang '32
Bureau of Missing Persons '33
Lady for a Day '33
Mystery of the Wax Museum '33
Gold Diggers of 1935 '35
Prison Break '38
Johnny Eager '42
A Night for Crime '42
Talk of the Town '42
City Without Men '43
Heading for Heaven '47
Bonanza '64
Disorderly Orderly '64
Kissin' Cousins '64

Mike Farrell
Escape from Planet Earth '67
The Graduate '67
Damien: The Leper Priest '80
Prime Suspect '82
Sex and the Single Parent '82
M*A*S*H: Goodbye, Farewell & Amen '83
Memorial Day '83
Vanishing Act '88
Dark River: A Father's Revenge '90
Lockdown '90
Silent Motive '91

Nicholas Farrell
To Play the King '93
A Midwinter's Tale '95
Othello '95

Sharon Farrell
40 Pounds of Trouble '62
Marlowe '69
The Reivers '69
The Love Machine '71
It's Alive '74
The Premonition '75
Rage '80
The Stunt Man '80
Night of the Comet '84
One Man Force '89
Arcade '93
Beyond Desire '94

Terry Farrell
Back to School '86
Beverly Hills Madam '86
Off the Mark '87
Hellraiser 3: Hell on Earth '92
Danielle Steel's Star '93
Star Trek Deep Space Nine: Emissary '93
Red Sun Rising '94

Timothy Farrell
Test Tube Babies '48
The Devil's Sleep '51
Jail Bait '54
Gun Girls '56

Tommy Farrell
Pirates of the High Seas '50
Meet Danny Wilson '52
Kissin' Cousins '64

Mia Farrow
Guns at Batasi '64
Dandy in Aspic '68
Rosemary's Baby '68
Secret Ceremony '69
See No Evil '71
High Heels '72
The Great Gatsby '74
Full Circle '77
Avalanche '78
Death on the Nile '78
A Wedding '78
Hurricane '79
A Midsummer Night's Sex Comedy '82
Zelig '83
Broadway Danny Rose '84
Supergirl '84
The Purple Rose of Cairo '85
Hannah and Her Sisters '86
Radio Days '87
Another Woman '88
September '88
Crimes & Misdemeanors '89
New York Stories '89
Alice '90
Husbands and Wives '92
Shadows and Fog '92
Widow's Peak '94
Miami Rhapsody '95
Reckless '95

Tisa Farrow
And Hope to Die '72
Some Call It Loving '73
Strange Shadows in an Empty Room '76
Fingers '78
Initiation of Sarah '78
Manhattan '79
Winter Kills '79
The Last Hunter '80
Zombie '80
Grim Reaper '81
Search and Destroy '81

Rainer Werner Fassbinder
Beware of a Holy Whore '70
Fox and His Friends '75
Kamikaze '89 '83

Chow Yung Fat
A Better Tomorrow '86
A Better Tomorrow, Part 2 '88

James Faulkner
Conduct Unbecoming '75
Albino '76
Flashpoint Africa '84
The Maid '90
Wavelength '96

Sally Faulkner
Vampyres '74
Alien Prey '83

Stephanie Faulkner
The Bus Is Coming '72
Death Journey '76
Virus '82

David Faustino
Perfect Harmony '91
It's a Bundyful Life '92

Jon Favreau
Rudy '93
P.C.U. '94

Alan Fawcett
A Conspiracy of Love '87
Blindside '88

Farrah Fawcett
Myra Breckinridge '70
Murder on Flight 502 '75
Logan's Run '76
Sunburn '79
Saturn 3 '80
Cannonball Run '81
Murder in Texas '81
The Red Light Sting '84
The Burning Bed '85
Between Two Women '86
Extremities '86
Poor Little Rich Girl: The Barbara Hutton Story '87
Double Exposure: The Story of Margaret Bourke-White '89
See You in the Morning '89
Small Sacrifices '89
The Substitute Wife '94
Dalva '95
A Good Day to Die '95
Man of the House '95

George Fawcett
The Greatest Question '19
The Mad Whirl '25
The Flesh and the Devil '27
The Wedding March '28
Drums of Jeopardy '31

William "Bill" Fawcett
Driftin' River '46
Wild Country '47
Black Hills '48
Check Your Guns '48
The Tioga Kid '48
Gun Glory '57
Storm Rider '57
Jesse James Meets Frankenstein's Daughter '65

Dorothy Fay
Law of the Texan '38
Trigger Pals '39

Frank Fay
Spotlight Scandals '43
Love Nest '51

Alice Faye
The Range Feud/Two Fisted Law '31
The Poor Little Rich Girl '36
Stowaway '36
On the Avenue '37
Alexander's Ragtime Band '38
In Old Chicago '38
Rose of Washington Square '39
Tin Pan Alley '40
The Great American Broadcast '41
Week-End In Havana '41
Hello, Frisco, Hello '43
State Fair '62
Every Girl Should Have One '78
Magic of Lassie '78

Frank Faylen
The Flustered Comedy of Leon Errol '39
Waterfront '39
Tanks a Million '41
The Lost Weekend '45
Blue Skies '46
It's a Wonderful Life '46
The Road to Rio '47
Welcome Stranger '47
Francis the Talking Mule '49
Copper Canyon '50
The Nevadan '50
Detective Story '51
Hangman's Knot '52
Red Garters '54
Riot in Cell Block 11 '54
The McConnell Story '55
Seventh Cavalry '56
Gunfight at the O.K. Corral '57

Louise Fazenda
A Hash House Fraud/The Sultan's Wife '15
The Night Club '25
The Bat '26
Doughnuts & Society '36
The Old Maid '39

Ron Fazio
The Toxic Avenger, Part 2 '89

The Toxic Avenger, Part 3: The Last Temptation of Toxie '89

Melinda Fee
Aliens Are Coming '80
Fade to Black '80
Doin' Time '85

Bekim Fehmiu
The Adventurers '70
Ride to Glory '71
Battle of the Eagles '81

Lung Fei
Shaolin Temple Strikes Back '72
Return of the Chinese Boxer '74
The Cavalier '80s
Buddha Assassinator '82
Shaolin Traitor '82
Marvelous Stunts of Kung Fu '83
Snake in the Eagle's Shadow 2 '83

Meng Fei
Prodigal Boxer: The Kick of Death '73
The Unbeaten 28 '80s
Venus the Ninja '80s

Alan Feinstein
Joe Panther '76
The Hunted Lady '77
The Two Worlds of Jenny Logan '79
Bunco '83
The Hunt for the Night Stalker '91

Fritz Feld
Last Command '28
The Affairs of Annabel '38
Bringing Up Baby '38
At the Circus '39
Everything Happens at Night '39
Four Jacks and a Jill '41
Iceland '42
Mexican Hayride '48
The Noose Hangs High '48
The Lovable Cheat '49
Kentucky Jubilee '51
The Errand Boy '61
Promises! Promises! '63
World's Greatest Lover '77
Herbie Goes Bananas '80
History of the World: Part 1 '81
Get Smart, Again! '89

Clarence Felder
Killing Floor '85
The Hidden '87

Corey Feldman
Friday the 13th, Part 4: The Final Chapter '84
Gremlins '84
Friday the 13th, Part 5: A New Beginning '85
The Goonies '85
Stand By Me '86
The Lost Boys '87
License to Drive '88
The 'Burbs '89
Dream a Little Dream '89
Edge of Honor '91
Rock 'n' Roll High School Forever '91
Meatballs 4 '92
Round Trip to Heaven '92
Stepmonster '92
Blown Away '93
Lipstick Camera '93
A Dangerous Place '94
Dream a Little Dream 2 '94
National Lampoon's Last Resort '94
Voodoo '95
Tales from the Crypt Presents Bordello of Blood '96

Marty Feldman
Think Dirty '70
Young Frankenstein '74
Sex with a Smile '76
Silent Movie '76
The Last Remake of Beau Geste '77
The Adventures of Sherlock Holmes' Smarter Brother '78
To See Such Fun '81
Yellowbeard '83
Slapstick of Another Kind '84

Barbara Feldon
The Man from U.N.C.L.E. '64
Playmates '72
Smile '75
No Deposit, No Return '76
A Guide for the Married Woman '78
Children of Divorce '80
Get Smart, Again! '89

Tovah Feldshuh
The Amazing Howard Hughes '77
Holocaust '78
The Triangle Factory Fire Scandal '79
Cheaper to Keep Her '80
Idolmaker '80
Brewster's Millions '85
Blue Iguana '88
A Day in October '92

Norman Fell
Pork Chop Hill '59
The Killers '64
The Graduate '67
Bullitt '68
If It's Tuesday, This Must Be Belgium '69
The Boatniks '70
Charley Varrick '73
The Stone Killer '73
Death Stalk '74
Cleopatra Jones & the Casino of Gold '75
The End '78
For the Love of It '80
On the Right Track '81
Paternity '81
Transylvania 6-5000 '85
Stripped to Kill '87
The Bone Yard '90
For the Boys '91
Hexed '93

Federico Fellini
The Miracle '48
The Flowers of St. Francis '50
Ciao Federico! Fellini Directs Satyricon '69
We All Loved Each Other So Much '77
Bellissimo: Images of the Italian Cinema '87
Intervista '87

Julian Fellowes
Baby ... Secret of the Lost Legend '85
Damage '92
Sharpe's Rifles '93
The Final Cut '95

Edith Fellows
Her First Romance '40
Music in My Heart '40
Heart of the Rio Grande '42
The Grace Kelly Story '83
In the Mood '87

Hansjorg Felmy
The Monster of London City '64
The Mad Executioners '65

Verna Felton
Picnic '55
The Oklahoman '56

Freddy Fender
She Came to the Valley '77
The Milagro Beanfield War '88

Edwige Fenech
The Seducers '70
Sex with a Smile '76
Blade of the Ripper '84
Phantom of Death '87

Ku Feng
Crack Shadow Boxers '70s
Incredible Master Beggars '82
Kung Fu Avengers '85

Zhang Fengyi
Farewell My Concubine '93
Temptation of a Monk '94

Tanya Fenmore
My Stepmother Is an Alien '88
Lisa '90

Sherilyn Fenn
The Wild Life '84
Just One of the Guys '85
The Wraith '87
Zombie High '87
Crime Zone '88
Two Moon Junction '88
True Blood '89
Backstreet Dreams '90
Meridian: Kiss of the Beast '90
Twin Peaks '90
Wild at Heart '90
Diary of a Hitman '91
Dillinger '91
Desire and Hell at Sunset Motel '92
Of Mice and Men '92
Ruby '92
Boxing Helena '93
Fatal Instinct '93
Three of Hearts '93

George Fenneman
How to Succeed in Business without Really Trying '67
The Marx Brothers in a Nutshell '90

Frank Fenton
Isle of Forgotten Sins '43
Mexican Hayride '48
The Golden Stallion '49
Naked Hills '56

Lance Fenton
Night of the Demons '88
Heathers '89

Leslie Fenton
Murder at Midnight '31
Public Enemy '31
The Strange Love of Molly Louvain '32
F.P. 1 '33
Lady Killer '33
Fugitive Road '34
Marie Galante '34
The House of Secrets '37

Simon Fenton
Matinee '92
The Rector's Wife '94

Colm Feore
Blades of Courage '88
Dr. Bethune '90
Personals '90
Beautiful Dreamers '92
32 Short Films about Glenn Gould '93
The Spider and the Fly '94
Truman '95

Tawny Fere
Angel 3: The Final Chapter '88
Night Children '89
Rockula '90

Al Ferguson
Tentacles of the North '26
Tarzan the Tiger '29
Near the Rainbow's End '30
Laramie Kid '35
Roamin' Wild '36
Lightning Raiders '45
Rose Marie '54

J. Don Ferguson
Loveless '83
Running Mates '86

Matthew Ferguson
Love and Human Remains '93
The Club '94

Tom Ferguson
Dark Universe '93
Biohazard: The Alien Force '95

Fernandel
Angele '34
Harvest '37
Le Schpountz '38
Nais '45
Well-Digger's Daughter '46
Little World of Don Camillo '51
The Red Inn '51
Topaze '51
Forbidden Fruit '52
The French Touch '54
The Sheep Has Five Legs '54
Dressmaker '56
Fernandel the Dressmaker '57
The Man in the Raincoat '57
Pantaloons '57
Paris Holiday '57

Emilio Fernandez
The Wild Bunch '69
Bring Me the Head of Alfredo Garcia '74

Jesus Fernandez
Nazarin '58
Tristana '70

Juan Fernandez
The Amazing Transplant '70
Crocodile Dundee 2 '88
Kinjite: Forbidden Subjects '89
Cat Chaser '90
Liquid Dreams '92

Miguel Fernandez
The Kidnapping of the President '80
Sorry, Wrong Number '89
True Believer '89

Ashley Ferrare
Revenge of the Ninja '83
Cyclone '87

Christina Ferrare
The Impossible Years '68
Mary, Mary, Bloody Mary '76

Rebecca Ferratti
Outlaw of Gor '87
Cheerleader Camp '88
Gor '88
Small Kill '93
Hard Vice '94
To the Limit '95

Conchata Ferrell
Deadly Hero '75
Lost Legacy: A Girl Called Hatter Fox '77
Rape and Marriage: The Rideout Case '80
To Love Again '80
Heartland '81
Who'll Save Our Children? '82
Where the River Runs Black '86
Goodbye, Miss 4th of July '88
Mystic Pizza '88
Portrait of a White Marriage '88
Edward Scissorhands '90
Backfield in Motion '91
Eye on the Sparrow '91
Family Prayers '91
Heaven and Earth '93
Samurai Cowboy '93
True Romance '93
The Buccaneers '95

Tyra Ferrell
Lady Beware '87
School Daze '88
Boyz N the Hood '91
Jungle Fever '91
Ulterior Motives '92
White Men Can't Jump '92
Equinox '93
Poetic Justice '93
Better Off Dead '94

Andrea Ferreol
La Grande Bouffe '73
Despair '78
The Tin Drum '79
The Last Metro '80
Three Brothers '80
Control '87
A Zed & Two Noughts '88
The Sleazy Uncle '89
The Phantom of the Opera '90
Stroke of Midnight '90
Francesco '93
Sweet Killing '93

Jose Ferrer
Joan of Arc '48
Cyrano de Bergerac '50
Moulin Rouge '52
Miss Sadie Thompson '53
The Caine Mutiny '54
Deep in My Heart '54
Lawrence of Arabia '62
The Greatest Story Ever Told '65
Ship of Fools '65
Enter Laughing '67
Order to Kill '73
The Art of Crime '75
Paco '75
The Big Bus '76
The Sentinel '76
Voyage of the Damned '76
The Private Files of J. Edgar Hoover '77
Who Has Seen the Wind? '77
The Swarm '78
Zoltan...Hound of Dracula '78
The Fifth Musketeer '79
Natural Enemies '79
The Big Brawl '80
Bloody Birthday '80
Gideon's Trumpet '80
Pleasure Palace '80
Berlin Tunnel 21 '81
Blood Tide '82
A Midsummer Night's Sex Comedy '82
The Being '83
To Be or Not to Be '83
Dune '84
The Evil That Men Do '84
George Washington '84
Samson and Delilah '84
Christopher Columbus '85
Seduced '85
Old Explorers '90
Strange Interlude '90
Hired to Kill '91
A Life of Sin '92

Leilani Sarelle Ferrer
Neon Maniacs '86
Shag: The Movie '89
Basic Instinct '92
The Harvest '92
Barbarians at the Gate '93
Sketch Artist 2: Hands That See '94
Breach of Trust '95

Lupita Ferrer
Children of Sanchez '79
Balboa '82

Mel Ferrer
Lost Boundaries '49
Born to Be Bad '50
Rancho Notorious '52
Scaramouche '52
Knights of the Round Table '53
Lili '53
Elena and Her Men '56
War and Peace '56
The Hands of Orlac '60
Blood and Roses '61
The Longest Day '62
The Fall of the Roman Empire '64
Paris When It Sizzles '64
Sex and the Single Girl '64
The Tempter '74
Brannigan '75
Eaten Alive '76
Hi-Riders '77
Norseman '78
Emerald Jungle '80
The Fifth Floor '80
The Visitor '80
The Great Alligator '81
One Shoe Makes It Murder '82
City of the Walking Dead '83
Deadly Game '83
Outrage! '86

Miguel Ferrer
Flashpoint '84
Lovelines '84
Star Trek 3: The Search for Spock '84
RoboCop '87
Python Wolf '88
Deepstar Six '89
Revenge '90
The Harvest '92
Another Stakeout '93
Blank Check '93
Hot Shots! Part Deux '93
Point of No Return '93
Royce '93
Scam '93
Incident at Deception Ridge '94
Stephen King's The Stand '94

Martin Ferrero
Planes, Trains & Automobiles '87
High Spirits '88
Stop! or My Mom Will Shoot '92
Jurassic Park '93

Noel Ferrier
Adventures of Eliza Fraser '76
Return of Captain Invincible '83
Great Expectations: The Untold Story '87

Carla Ferrigno
Seven Magnificent Gladiators '84
Black Roses '88

Lou Ferrigno
Pumping Iron '76
The Incredible Hulk '77
Hercules '83
Seven Magnificent Gladiators '84
Hercules 2 '85
Desert Warrior '88
The Incredible Hulk Returns '88
All's Fair '89
The Cage '89
Sinbad of the Seven Seas '89

Ferrigno ▶cont.

The Trial of the Incredible Hulk '89
Death of the Incredible Hulk '90
Liberty & Bash '90
...And God Spoke '94
Cage 2: The Arena of Death '94

Barbara Ferris
Children of the Damned '63
Nice Girl Like Me '69
A Chorus of Disapproval '89

John Ferris
Torpedo Attack '72
Monique '83

David Ferry
Tales of the Klondike: Race for Number One '87
Men of Steel '88
The Last Winter '89
Project: Genesis '93

Gabriele Ferzetti
The Wayward Wife '52
Angel in a Taxi '59
L'Avventura '60
On Her Majesty's Secret Service '69
Counter Punch '71
The Night Porter '74
The Psychic '78
Basileus Quartet '82
Quo Vadis '85
Julia and Julia '87
Voyage of Terror: The Achille Lauro Affair '90
Othello '95

Stepin Fetchit
Wild Horse '31
Judge Priest '34
Stand Up and Cheer '34
On the Avenue '37
Miracle in Harlem '48
The Sun Shines Bright '53
Amazing Grace '74

Debra Feuer
Red Flag: The Ultimate Game '81
To Live & Die in L.A. '85
Homeboy '88
Night Angel '90

Edwige Feuillere
Topaze '33
L'Idiot '46
The Eagle Has Two Heads '48

Peggy Feury
Witch Who Came from the Sea '76
The Orphan '79

Norman Feusier
Diamond Trail '33
Border Vengeance '35

William Fichtner
Heat '95
Strange Days '95
The Underneath '95
Virtuosity '95

Shelby Fiddis
Cheech and Chong: Things Are Tough All Over '82
Cheech and Chong's The Corsican Brothers '84

John Fiedler
Twelve Angry Men '57
A Raisin in the Sun '61
Kiss Me, Stupid! '64
A Fine Madness '66
The Odd Couple '68
Bad Ronald '74
Harper Valley P.T.A. '78
Sharky's Machine '81

Betty Field
Of Mice and Men '39
Kings Row '41
The Great Moment '44
The Southerner '45
Picnic '55
Bus Stop '56
Peyton Place '57
Butterfield 8 '60
Birdman of Alcatraz '62
Coogan's Bluff '68

Chelsea Field
Prison '88
Skin Deep '89
The Dark Half '91
Harley Davidson and the Marlboro Man '91
The Last Boy Scout '91
Dust Devil '93
Extreme Justice '93
Hotel Room '93
Royce '93
Snapdragon '93
Andre '94
The Birds 2: Land's End '94
A Passion to Kill '94
Texas '94
Indictment: The McMartin Trial '95
The Wrong Woman '95
Flipper '96

Karin Field
Cave of the Living Dead '65
Web of the Spider '70
The Mad Butcher '72

Sally Field
The Way West '67
Maybe I'll Be Home in the Spring '70
Home for the Holidays '72
Stay Hungry '76
Sybil '76
Heroes '77
Smokey and the Bandit '77
The End '78
Hooper '78
Beyond the Poseidon Adventure '79
Norma Rae '79
Smokey and the Bandit, Part 2 '80
Absence of Malice '81
Back Roads '81
Kiss Me Goodbye '82
Places in the Heart '84
Murphy's Romance '85
Surrender '87
Punchline '88
Steel Magnolias '89
Not Without My Daughter '90
Soapdish '91
Mrs. Doubtfire '93
Forrest Gump '94
An Eye for an Eye '95

Shirley Anne Field
Beat Girl '60
The Entertainer '60
War Lover '62
Peeping Tom '63
House of the Living Dead '73
My Beautiful Laundrette '85
Two by Forsyth '86
Getting It Right '89
Shag: The Movie '89
Hear My Song '91

Todd Field
Eye of the Eagle 2 '89
Gross Anatomy '89
Back to Back '90
Full Fathom Five '90
Ruby in Paradise '93
Sleep with Me '94

Virginia Field
Lloyds of London '36
Mr. Moto's Last Warning '39
Dance, Girl, Dance '40
Waterloo Bridge '40
A Connecticut Yankee in King Arthur's Court '49

Dorothy Fielding
Fright Night '85
The Abduction of Kari Swenson '87
The Preppie Murder '89

Fenella Fielding
Arrivederci, Baby! '66
Carry On Screaming '66

Marjorie Fielding
Conspirator '49
The Lavender Hill Mob '51
The Franchise Affair '52

Charlie Fields
Fish Hawk '79
The Beniker Gang '83

Christopher John Fields
Alien 3 '92
The Gun in Betty Lou's Handbag '92
Indecency '92

Robert Fields
The Sporting Club '72
Anna '87

Stanley Fields
Cimarron '30
Island of Lost Souls '32
Wide Open Faces '38

Tony Fields
Trick or Treat '86
Body Beat '88
Backstreet Dreams '90
Across the Moon '94

W.C. Fields
Pool Sharks '15
Sally of the Sawdust '25
It's the Old Army Game '26
Running Wild '27
W.C. Fields: Flask of Fields '30
The Dentist '32
Pharmacist '32
The Barber Shop '33
Best of W.C. Fields '33
The Fatal Glass of Beer '33
International House '33
W.C. Fields Comedy Bag '33
It's A Gift '34
David Copperfield '35
The Big Braodcast of 1938 '38
You Can't Cheat an Honest Man '39
The Bank Dick '40
My Little Chickadee '40
Never Give a Sucker an Even Break '41
Mrs. Wiggs of the Cabbage Patch '42
Tales of Manhattan '42
Hollywood Clowns '85

Ralph Fiennes
A Dangerous Man: Lawrence after Arabia '91
Prime Suspect '92
Schindler's List '93
Quiz Show '94
Strange Days '95

Harvey Fierstein
Garbo Talks '84
Apology '86
Tidy Endings '88
Torch Song Trilogy '88
The Harvest '92
Mrs. Doubtfire '93
Bullets Over Broadway '94
Dr. Jekyll and Ms. Hyde '95
Independence Day '96

Kaisa Figura
Fatal Past '94
Ready to Wear '94

Dennis Fimple
Truck Stop Women '74
Creature from Black Lake '76
The Evictors '79
The $5.20 an Hour Dream '80
Of Mice and Men '81
My Heroes Have Always Been Cowboys '91

Jon Finch
Macbeth '71
Frenzy '72
The Final Programme '73
Lady Caroline Lamb '73
Death on the Nile '78
Breaking Glass '80
And Nothing But the Truth '82
Witching Time '84
Game of Seduction '86
Unexplained Laughter '89
Lurking Fear '94

Peter Finch
Eureka Stockade '49
Train of Events '49
Wooden Horse '50
The Story of Robin Hood & His Merrie Men '52
The Detective '54
Elephant Walk '54
Make Me an Offer '55
The Warriors '55
Pursuit of the Graf Spee '57
Robbery Under Arms '57
Windom's Way '57
The Nun's Story '59
Kidnapped '60
No Love for Johnnie '60
Operation Amsterdam '60
The Trials of Oscar Wilde '60
First Men in the Moon '64
The Pumpkin Eater '64
The Flight of the Phoenix '65
Far from the Madding Crowd '67
Red Tent '69
Sunday, Bloody Sunday '71
Shattered '72
Network '76
Raid on Entebbe '77

Larry Fine
Dancing Lady '33
The Lost Stooges '33
Hollywood Party '34
The Three Stooges: Half-Wit's Holiday and Other Nyuks '35
The Three Stooges: Nutty but Nice and Other Nyuks '36
Three Stooges Comedy Capers: Vol. 1 '40s
Three Stooges: Cookoo Cavaliers and Other Nyuks '40
The Three Stooges: Idiots Deluxe and Other Nyuks '40
The Three Stooges: They Stooge to Conga and Other Nyuks '40
Three Stooges: From Nurse to Worse and Other Nyuks '45
Three Stooges Comedy Classics '49
Three Stooges Festival '49
Gold Raiders '51
Have Rocket Will Travel '59
Stop! Look! and Laugh! '60
Snow White and the Three Stooges '61
The Three Stooges Meet Hercules '61
Three Stooges in Orbit '62
Around the World in a Daze '63
It's a Mad, Mad, Mad, Mad World '63
The Outlaws is Coming! '65
The Stooges Story '90

Travis Fine
Child's Play 3 '91
My Antonia '94

Anthony Finetti
The Expendables '89
Prime Time Murder '92

Frank Finlay
The Loneliness of the Long Distance Runner '62
A Study in Terror '66
Robbery '67
Assault '70
Cromwell '70
Molly Maguires '70
Gumshoe '72
Shaft in Africa '73
The Three Musketeers '74
The Four Musketeers '75
Bouquet of Barbed Wire '76
The Thief of Baghdad '78
Wild Geese '78
Murder by Decree '79
Enigma '82
Return of the Soldier '82
The Ploughman's Lunch '83
The Death of Adolf Hitler '84
Arch of Triumph '85
Lifeforce '85
Casanova '87
The Return of the Musketeers '89
Cthulhu Mansion '91
Stalin '92
Gospa '94
In the Secret State

James Finlayson
Eyes of Turpin Are Upon You! '21
Stan Without Ollie, Vol. 3 '23
Stan Without Ollie, Vol. 4 '25
No Man's Law '27
Laurel & Hardy Comedy Classics, Vol. 7 '30s
Laurel & Hardy: Chickens Come Home '31
Laurel & Hardy Comedy Classics, Vol. 5 '31
Pardon Us '31
Laurel & Hardy Comedy Classics, Vol. 4 '32
Pack Up Your Troubles '32
Clark & McCullough '33
The Devil's Brother '33
Bonnie Scotland '35
Laurel & Hardy Comedy Classics, Vol. 6 '35
Bohemian Girl '36
Our Relations '36
All Over Town '37
Pick a Star '37
Way Out West '37
Block-heads '38
The Flying Deuces '39
A Chump at Oxford '40
Saps at Sea '40

Jon Finlayson
Lonely Hearts '82
A Kink in the Picasso '90

Evelyn Finley
Dynamite Canyon '41
Trail Riders '42

William Finley
The Wedding Party '69
Phantom of the Paradise '74

John Finn
Glory '89
Cover-Up '91
Quicksand: No Escape '91

Warren Finnerty
The Connection '61
The Brig '64
Free Grass '69
Panic in Needle Park '75

Albert Finney
The Entertainer '60
Tom Jones '63
Two for the Road '67
Scrooge '70
Gumshoe '72
Alpha Beta '73
Murder on the Orient Express '74
The Duellists '77
Looker '81
Wolfen '81
Annie '82
Shoot the Moon '82
The Dresser '83
Loophole '83
Pope John Paul II '84
Under the Volcano '84
Orphans '87
The Endless Game '89
The Image '89
Miller's Crossing '90
The Green Man '91
The Playboys '92
Rich in Love '93
The Browning Version '94
A Man of No Importance '94
The Run of the Country '95

Shirley Jo Finney
Wilma '77
Echo Park '86

Linda Fiorentino
After Hours '85
Gotcha! '85
Vision Quest '85
The Moderns '88
Wildfire '88
The Neon Empire '89
Queens Logic '91
Shout '91
Strangers '91
Beyond the Law '92
Acting on Impulse '93
Chain of Desire '93
Charlie's Ghost: The Secret of Coronado '94
The Desperate Trail '94
The Last Seduction '94
Bodily Harm '95
Jade '95
Unforgettable '96

Ann Firbank
Lillie '79
Flame to the Phoenix '85

Eddie Firestone
The Law and Jake Wade '58
Two for the Seesaw '62
Duel '71

Colin Firth
Another Country '84
Dutch Girls '87
A Month in the Country '87
The Secret Garden '87
Apartment Zero '88
Valmont '89
Femme Fatale '90
The Advocate '93

Hostages '93
Wings of Fame '93
Circle of Friends '94
Playmaker '94
Pride and Prejudice '95

Jonathan Firth
Middlemarch '93
Brother Cadfael '94

Peter Firth
King Arthur, the Young Warlord '75
Equus '77
Joseph Andrews '77
Tess '80
Fire and Sword '82
Lifeforce '85
Letter to Brezhnev '86
Born of Fire '87
Northanger Abbey '87
Burndown '89
The Incident '89
The Hunt for Red October '90
Innocent Victim '90
Prisoner of Honor '91
Shadowlands '93
An Awfully Big Adventure '94

Kai Fischer
The Hellfire Club '61
The Goalie's Anxiety at the Penalty Kick '71

Vera Fischer
I Love You '81
Love Strange Love '82
Quilombo '84

Nancy Fish
Exorcist 3: Legion '90
Death Becomes Her '92
Ghost in the Machine '93
Reflections in the Dark '94

Laurence "Larry" Fishburne
Apocalypse Now '79
Willie & Phil '80
Quicksilver '86
Gardens of Stone '87
A Nightmare on Elm Street 3: Dream Warriors '87
For Us, the Living '88
Red Heat '88
School Daze '88
Cadence '89
Decoration Day '90
King of New York '90
Boyz N the Hood '91
Class Action '91
Hearts of Darkness: A Filmmaker's Apocalypse '91
Deep Cover '92
Searching for Bobby Fischer '93
What's Love Got to Do with It? '93
Bad Company '94
Higher Learning '94
Just Cause '94
Othello '95
The Tuskegee Airmen '95
Fled '96

Carrie Fisher
Shampoo '75
Star Wars '77
Mr. Mike's Mondo Video '79
The Blues Brothers '80
The Empire Strikes Back '80
Under the Rainbow '81
Frankenstein '82
Thumbelina '82
From "Star Wars" to "Jedi": The Making of a Saga '83
Return of the Jedi '83
Garbo Talks '84
From Here to Maternity '85
The Man with One Red Shoe '85
Hannah and Her Sisters '86
Hollywood Vice Sqaud '86
Amazon Women on the Moon '87
The Time Guardian '87
Appointment with Death '88
She's Back '88
The 'Burbs '89
Loverboy '89
When Harry Met Sally... '89
Sibling Rivalry '90
Sweet Revenge '90
Drop Dead Fred '91
Soapdish '91
This Is My Life '92

Cindy Fisher
Hometown U.S.A. '79
Liar's Moon '82

Eddie Fisher
All About Eve '50
Bundle of Joy '56
Butterfield 8 '60

Frances Fisher
Can She Bake a Cherry Pie? '83
Heart '87
Tough Guys Don't Dance '87
Patty Hearst '88
Cold Sassy Tree '89
Sudie & Simpson '90
Deadly Conspiracy '91
Frame Up '91
Lucy and Desi: Before the Laughter '91
Unforgiven '92
Attack of the 50 Ft. Woman '93
Praying Mantis '93
Babyfever '94
Molly and Gina '94
The Stars Fell on Henrietta '94

Gregory Fisher
1984 '84
The Girl in the Picture '86

Shug Fisher
The Giant Gila Monster '59
Huckleberry Finn '75

Tricia Leigh Fisher
Pretty Smart '87
C.H.U.D. 2: Bud the Chud '89
Hollywood Chaos '89
Book of Love '91
Arizona Dream '94
Hostile Intentions '95

Robert Fiske
Mystic Circle Murder '39
Green Archer '40

Alan Fisler
If Looks Could Kill '86
New York's Finest '87
Student Affairs '88

Rick Fitts
Hanoi Hilton '87
Platoon Leader '87

Peter Fitz
Au Revoir Les Enfants '87
Club Extinction '89

Lewis Fitz-gerald
A Cry in the Dark '88
Rikky and Pete '88

Barry Fitzgerald
Bringing Up Baby '38
Dawn Patrol '38
Marie Antoinette '38
The Saint Strikes Back '39
The Long Voyage Home '40
How Green Was My Valley '41
The Sea Wolf '41
Tarzan's Secret Treasure '41
Going My Way '44
None But the Lonely Heart '44
And Then There Were None '45
The Stork Club '45
The Saint Strikes Back: Criminal Court '46
Welcome Stranger '47
The Naked City '48
The Story of Seabiscuit '49
Union Station '50
The Quiet Man '52
The Catered Affair '56
Broth of a Boy '59

Ciaran Fitzgerald
Into the West '92
The Canterville Ghost '96

Ella Fitzgerald
Ride 'Em Cowboy '42
Pete Kelly's Blues '55

Geraldine Fitzgerald
Department Store '35
The Mill on the Floss '37
Dark Victory '39
Wuthering Heights '39
Watch on the Rhine '43
Wilson '44
The Strange Affair of Uncle Harry '45
The Obsessed '51
Ten North Frederick '58
The Pawnbroker '65
Rachel, Rachel '68
The Last American Hero '73
Harry and Tonto '74
The Mango Tree '77
Lovespell '79
Diary of the Dead '80s
Arthur '81
Easy Money '83
Kennedy '83
Dixie: Changing Habits '85
Bloodlink '86
Poltergeist 2: The Other Side '86
Arthur 2: On the Rocks '88

Sean Fitzgerald
The Power Within '95
Storybook '95

Tara Fitzgerald
Hear My Song '91
Brother Cadfael '94
A Man of No Importance '94
Sirens '94
The Englishman Who Went Up a Hill But Came Down a Mountain '95

Walter Fitzgerald
Great Day '46
San Demetrio, London '47
Treasure Island '50
The Adventures of Sadie '55

Ian Fitzgibbon
A Fine Romance '92
Prime Suspect 2 '93

Kate Fitzpatrick
Night Nurse '77
Return of Captain Invincible '83
Fantasy Man '84

Michael Fitzpatrick
Blood Tracks '86
Pay Off '89

Neil Fitzpatrick
A Cry in the Dark '88
Ground Zero '88

Emily Fitzroy
The Bat '26
The Cheerful Fraud '27
Mockery '27
Don Quixote '35
The Frontiersmen '38

Paul Fix
The Fighting Sheriff '31
Fargo Express '32
Gun Law '33
Somewhere in Sonora '33
Desert Trail '35
The Throwback '35
Phantom Patrol '36
Mannequin '37
Star Reporter '39
Black Friday '40
Sherlock Holmes and the Secret Weapon '42
South of Santa Fe '42
Captive Wild Woman '43
Hitler: Dead or Alive '43
Red River '48
Hondo '53
Blood Alley '55
The Bad Seed '56
Jet Pilot '57
Lafayette Escadrille '58
To Kill a Mockingbird '62
Sons of Katie Elder '65
El Dorado '67
Zabriskie Point '70
Grayeagle '77
Wanda Nevada '79

Cash Flagg
Incredibly Strange Creatures Who Stopped Living and Became Mixed-Up Zombies '63
The Thrill Killers '65

Fannie Flagg
Five Easy Pieces '70
My Best Friend Is a Vampire '88

Joe Flaherty
Tunnelvision '76
Used Cars '80
Stripes '81
Going Berserk '83
Sesame Street Presents: Follow That Bird '85
One Crazy Summer '86
Really Weird Tales '86
Blue Monkey '87
Speed Zone '88
Back to the Future, Part 2 '89
Wedding Band '89
Who's Harry Crumb? '89
Looking for Miracles '90
A Pig's Tale '94
Happy Gilmore '96

Lanny Flaherty
The Ballad of the Sad Cafe '91
Sommersby '93
Tom and Huck '95

Georges Flament
La Chienne '31
The 400 Blows '59

Fionnula Flanagan
Picture of Dorian Gray '74
In the Region of Ice '76
Mary White '77
Young Love, First Love '79
The Ewok Adventure '84
James Joyce's Women '85
A Winner Never Quits '86
Youngblood '86
Death Dreams '92
Mad at the Moon '92
Money for Nothing '93
White Mile '94

Ed Flanders
The Passing of Evil '70
Trial of the Catonsville Nine '72
Things in Their Season '74
Eleanor & Franklin '76
The Amazing Howard Hughes '77
Mary White '77
The Ninth Configuration '79
Salem's Lot '79
Sophia Loren: Her Own Story '80
The Pursuit of D.B. Cooper '81
True Confessions '81
Tomorrow's Child '82
Special Bulletin '83
The Final Days '89
Exorcist 3: Legion '90
Citizen Cohn '92
Bye Bye, Love '94

Sean Patrick Flanery
Powder '95
Raging Angels '95

Susan Flannery
Gumball Rally '76
Anatomy of a Seduction '79

John Flaus
Blood Money '80
In Too Deep '90

James Flavin
King Kong '33
Brand of Hate '34
Abroad with Two Yanks '44
Hollywood Canteen '44
Uncertain Glory '44
The Shanghai Cobra '45
Cloak and Dagger '46
Abbott and Costello Meet the Killer, Boris Karloff '49
Blondie Hits the Jackpot '49
Francis in the Haunted House '56

Flea
Dudes '87
Back to the Future, Part 2 '89
Motorama '91
My Own Private Idaho '91
The Chase '93

John Fleck
Mutant on the Bounty '89
The Comrades of Summer '92

James Fleet
Four Weddings and a Funeral '94
Sense and Sensibility '95

Mick Fleetwood
The Running Man '87
Zero Tolerance '93

Susan Fleetwood
Murder of a Moderate Man '70s
The Sacrifice '86
White Mischief '88
The Krays '90
Persuasion '95

Charles Fleischer
A Nightmare on Elm Street '84
Bad Dreams '88
Back to the Future, Part 2 '89
Straight Talk '92
Tales from the Crypt Presents Demon Knight '94

Noah Fleiss
Josh and S.A.M. '93
A Mother's Prayer '95

Eric Fleming
Conquest of Space '55
Fright '56
Queen of Outer Space '58
The Glass Bottom Boat '66

Ian Fleming
The Triumph of Sherlock Holmes '35
Murder at the Baskervilles '37
When Thief Meets Thief '37
Sherlock Holmes: The Silver Blaze '41
Butler's Dilemma '43
Norman Conquest '53
Land of Fury '55
The Trials of Oscar Wilde '60

Lone Fleming
It Happened at Nightmare Inn '70
Tombs of the Blind Dead '72

Rhonda Fleming
Since You Went Away '44
Spellbound '45
Abilene Town '46
The Spiral Staircase '46
Adventure Island '47
Out of the Past '47
A Connecticut Yankee in King Arthur's Court '49
The Great Lover '49
Cavalry Charge '51
Cry Danger '51
Pony Express '53
Tennessee's Partner '55
Slightly Scarlet '56
While the City Sleeps '56
Gun Glory '57
Gunfight at the O.K. Corral '57
Bullwhip '58
The Nude Bomb '80

Susan Fleming
Range Feud '31
The Range Feud/Two Fisted Law '31

Jason Flemyng
A Question of Attribution '91
Stealing Beauty '96

Robert Flemyng
The Guinea Pig '48
The Blue Lamp '49
Conspirator '49
Cast a Dark Shadow '55
The Man Who Never Was '55
The Horrible Dr. Hichcock '62
Blood Beast Terror '67
Kafka '91

Alan Fletcher
Fran '85
Gross Misconduct '93

Bramwell Fletcher
Daughter of the Dragon '31
Random Harvest '42
The Undying Monster '42
White Cargo '42

Dexter Fletcher
Lionheart '87
The Rachel Papers '89
The Raggedy Rawney '90
Twisted Obsession '90

Diane Fletcher
To Play the King '93
The Final Cut '95

Dusty Fletcher
Boardinghouse Blues '48
Killer Diller '48

Louise Fletcher
Thieves Like Us '74
One Flew Over the Cuckoo's Nest '75
Russian Roulette '75
The Exorcist 2: The Heretic '77
The Cheap Detective '78
Lady in Red '79
The Magician of Lublin '79
Natural Enemies '79
Mama Dracula '80
Strange Behavior '81
Talk to Me '82
Brainstorm '83
Overnight Sensation '83
Strange Invaders '83
Firestarter '84

Fletcher ▶cont.

A Summer to Remember '84
The Boy Who Could Fly '86
Invaders from Mars '86
Nobody's Fool '86
Flowers in the Attic '87
Islands '87
J. Edgar Hoover '87
Two Moon Junction '88
Best of the Best '89
Final Notice '89
Shadowzone '89
Blue Steel '90
Nightmare on the 13th Floor '90
Blind Vision '91
Return to Two Moon Junction '93
The Haunting of Seacliff Inn '94
Tollbooth '94
Tryst '94
Virtuosity '95
High School High '96

Suzanne Fletcher
Sleepwalk '88
Bloodsucking Pharoahs of Pittsburgh '90

Sam Flint
Evelyn Prentice '34
A Face in the Fog '36
The Lawless Nineties '36
Red Lights Ahead '36
Red River Valley '36
Spy Smasher '42
Spy Smasher Returns '42
The Chinese Cat '44

Jay C. Flippen
Marie Galante '34
They Live by Night '49
A Woman's Secret '49
Winchester '73 '50
The Yellow Cab Man '50
The Lemon Drop Kid '51
Devil's Canyon '53
The Wild One '54
Far Country '55
Oklahoma! '55
The Killing '56
The King and Four Queens '56
Seventh Cavalry '56
Jet Pilot '57
The Restless Breed '58
Firecreek '68
Hellfighters '68

Suzanne Flon
Un Singe en Hiver '62
The Train '65
One Deadly Summer '83

Michael Flood
Criminally Insane '75
Crazy Fat Ethel II '85
Death Nurse '87

Florelle
Liliom '35
The Crime of Monsieur Lange '36

Sheila Florence
Cactus '86
A Woman's Tale '92

Holly Floria
Netherworld '90
Bikini Island '91
Presumed Guilty '91
Private Wars '93

George Flower
Devil & Leroy Basset '73
Candy Tangerine Man '75
Across the Great Divide '76
Further Adventures of the Wilderness Family, Part 2 '77
The Capture of Bigfoot '79
Mountain Family Robinson '79
In Search of a Golden Sky '84
Cheerleader Camp '88
They Live '88
Relentless '89

Darlanne Fluegel
Eyes of Laura Mars '78
Battle Beyond the Stars '80
The Last Fight '82
Concrete Beat '84
Once Upon a Time in America '84
To Live & Die in L.A. '85
Crime Story: The Complete Saga '86
Running Scared '86
Tough Guys '86
Bulletproof '88
Deadly Stranger '88
Freeway '88
Lock Up '89
Project: Alien '89
Pet Sematary 2 '92
Slaughter of the Innocents '93
Breaking Point '94
Scanner Cop '94
Darkman 3: Die Darkman Die '95
Relative Fear '95

Joel Fluellen
The Jackie Robinson Story '50
The Great White Hope '70
A Dream for Christmas '73
Man Friday '75

The Flying Karamazov Brothers
Flying Karamazov Brothers Comedy Hour '83
The Jewel of the Nile '85

Colleen Flynn
The Temp '93
Incident at Deception Ridge '94

Errol Flynn
Captain Blood '35
The Charge of the Light Brigade '36
The Prince and the Pauper '37
The Adventures of Robin Hood '38
Dawn Patrol '38
The Sisters '38
Dodge City '39
The Private Lives of Elizabeth & Essex '39
Santa Fe Trail '40
The Sea Hawk '40
Virginia City '40
Dive Bomber '41
Footsteps in the Dark '41
They Died with Their Boots On '41
Desperate Journey '42
Gentleman Jim '42
Edge of Darkness '43
Northern Pursuit '43
Thank Your Lucky Stars '43
Uncertain Glory '44
Objective, Burma! '45
San Antonio '45
Never Say Goodbye '46
Cry Wolf '47
Escape Me Never '47
Silver River '48
Adventures of Don Juan '49
It's a Great Feeling '49
Hollywood Bloopers '50s
Kim '50
That Forsyte Woman '50
Adventures of Captain Fabian '51
Against All Flags '52
The Master of Ballantrae '53
The King's Rhapsody '55
Let's Make Up '55
The Warriors '55
Istanbul '57
Assault of the Rebel Girls '59

Jerome Flynn
A Summer Story '88
Edward II '92

Joe Flynn
Lover Come Back '61
Divorce American Style '67
The Computer Wore Tennis Shoes '69
My Dog, the Thief '69
The Barefoot Executive '71
Million Dollar Duck '71
Now You See Him, Now You Don't '72
Gentle Savage '73
Superdad '73

Kimberly Flynn
Revolution! A Red Comedy '91
Boys Life '94
Rhythm Thief '94

Miriam Flynn
18 Again! '88
National Lampoon's Christmas Vacation '89

Sean Flynn
Son of Captain Blood '62
Mission to Venice '63

Spiros Focas
The Jewel of the Nile '85
Rambo 3 '88
White Palace '90

Nina Foch
Return of the Vampire '43
Cry of the Werewolf '44
A Song to Remember '45
The Dark Past '49
An American in Paris '51
St. Benny the Dip '51
Scaramouche '52
Executive Suite '54
Illegal '55
The Ten Commandments '56
Cash McCall '60
Spartacus '60
Columbo: Prescription Murder '67
Salty '73
Mahogany '75
Child of Glass '78
Jennifer '78
Dixie Lanes '88
Skin Deep '89
Armistead Maupin's Tales of the City '93
Morning Glory '93
Sliver '93

Brenda Fogarty
Deadly Fieldtrip '74
Fairy Tales '76

Vladimar Fogel
Bed and Sofa '27
The Girl with the Hat Box '27

Dave Foley
The Best of the Kids in the Hall '93
It's Pat: The Movie '94
Kids In the Hall Brain Candy '96

Ellen Foley
Fatal Attraction '87
Married to the Mob '88

Macka Foley
Las Vegas Weekend '85
WarCat '88

Michael Foley
The Divine Enforcer '91
Prison Planet '92
Karate Cop '93

Alison Folland
Before and After '95
To Die For '95

Megan Follows
Hockey Night '84
Anne of Green Gables '85
Silver Bullet '85
Anne of Avonlea '87
Stacking '87
A Time of Destiny '88
Termini Station '89
Back to Hannibal: The Return of Tom Sawyer and Huckleberry Finn '90
The Chase '91

Bridget Fonda
Aria '88
Jacob Have I Loved '88
You Can't Hurry Love '88
Scandal '89
Shag: The Movie '89
Frankenstein Unbound '90
The Godfather, Part 3 '90
Leather Jackets '90
Out of the Rain '90
Strapless '90
Doc Hollywood '91
Iron Maze '91
Single White Female '92
Singles '92
Bodies, Rest & Motion '93
Little Buddha '93
Point of No Return '93
Camilla '94
It Could Happen to You '94
The Road to Wellville '94
City Hall '95

Henry Fonda
The Farmer Takes a Wife '35
I Dream Too Much '35
The Moon's Our Home '36
That Certain Woman '37
You Only Live Once '37
Jezebel '38
Mad Miss Manton '38
Drums Along the Mohawk '39
Jesse James '39
The Story of Alexander Graham Bell '39
Young Mr. Lincoln '39
The Grapes of Wrath '40
Return of Frank James '40
The Lady Eve '41
Big Street '42
The Magnificent Dope '42
Tales of Manhattan '42
Immortal Sergeant '43
The Ox-Bow Incident '43
My Darling Clementine '46
Fort Apache '48
The Fugitive '48
Mister Roberts '55
War and Peace '56
The Wrong Man '56
Stage Struck '57
The Tin Star '57
Twelve Angry Men '57
Warlock '59
Advise and Consent '62
The Longest Day '62
How the West Was Won '63
Spencer's Mountain '63
The Best Man '64
Fail-Safe '64
Sex and the Single Girl '64
Battle of the Bulge '65
In Harm's Way '65
The Rounders '65
A Big Hand for the Little Lady '66
The Boston Strangler '68
Firecreek '68
Madigan '68
Once Upon a Time in the West '68
Yours, Mine & Ours '68
The Cheyenne Social Club '70
There was a Crooked Man '70
Too Late the Hero '70
Sometimes a Great Notion '71
Ash Wednesday '73
Night Flight from Moscow '73
My Name is Nobody '74
Great Smokey Roadblock '76
Midway '76
The Red Pony '76
Golden Age of Hollywood '77
Last Four Days '77
Rollercoaster '77
Tentacles '77
Battleforce '78
City on Fire '78
Clarence Darrow '78
The Swarm '78
Home to Stay '79
Meteor '79
Roots: The Next Generation '79
Wanda Nevada '79
Gideon's Trumpet '80
On Golden Pond '81
Summer Solstice '81
Oldest Living Graduate '82

Jane Fonda
Tall Story '60
Period of Adjustment '62
Walk on the Wild Side '62
Circle of Love '64
Joy House '64
Cat Ballou '65
Any Wednesday '66
The Chase '66
The Game is Over '66
Barefoot in the Park '67
Barbarella '68
Spirits of the Dead '68
They Shoot Horses, Don't They? '69
Klute '71
A Doll's House '73
Steelyard Blues '73
Fun with Dick and Jane '77
Julia '77
California Suite '78
Comes a Horseman '78
Coming Home '78
The China Syndrome '79
The Electric Horseman '79
9 to 5 '80
On Golden Pond '81
Rollover '81
The Dollmaker '84
Agnes of God '85
The Morning After '86
Old Gringo '89
Stanley and Iris '90

Peter Fonda
Tammy and the Doctor '63
Lilith '64
The Wild Angels '66
The Trip '67
Spirits of the Dead '68
Easy Rider '69
Hired Hand '71
The Last Movie '71
Dirty Mary Crazy Larry '74
Killer Force '75
Race with the Devil '75
Fighting Mad '76
Futureworld '76
92 in the Shade '76
Outlaw Blues '77
High Ballin' '78
Wanda Nevada '79
The Hostage Tower '80
Cannonball Run '81
Spasms '82
Split Image '82
Jungle Heat '84
Certain Fury '85
Hawken's Breed '87
Mercenary Fighters '88
Fatal Mission '89
The Rose Garden '89
South Beach '92
Deadfall '93
Love and a .45 '94
Molly and Gina '94
Nadja '95
Escape from L.A. '96

Phil Fondacaro
Ghoulies 2 '87
Meridian: Kiss of the Beast '90
Dollman vs Demonic Toys '93

Benson Fong
Charlie Chan in the Secret Service '44
The Chinese Cat '44
The Purple Heart '44
The Scarlet Clue '45
The Shanghai Cobra '45
Deception '46
His Majesty O'Keefe '53
Conquest of Space '55
Girls! Girls! Girls! '62
Our Man Flint '66
Kung Fu: The Movie '86

Leo Fong
Blind Rage '78
Enforcer from Death Row '78
The Last Reunion '80
Killpoint '84
Low Blow '85
Ninja Nightmare '88
Showdown '93

Joan Fontaine
A Damsel in Distress '37
A Million to One '37
Annabel Takes a Tour/Maid's Night Out '38
Maid's Night Out '38
Gunga Din '39
The Women '39
Rebecca '40
Suspicion '41
Jane Eyre '44
Emperor Waltz '48
Letter from an Unknown Woman '48
Born to Be Bad '50
September Affair '50
Ivanhoe '52
Othello '52
The Bigamist '53
Decameron Nights '53
Casanova's Big Night '54
Beyond a Reasonable Doubt '56
Island in the Sun '57
Until They Sail '57
Voyage to the Bottom of the Sea '61

Hallie Foote
1918 '85
On Valentine's Day '86
Courtship '87
The Habitation of Dragons '91

Horton Foote, Jr.
1918 '85
On Valentine's Day '86
Blood Red '88

Dick Foran
Dangerous '35
Earthworm Tractors '36

Petrified Forest '36
Boy Meets Girl '38
Four Daughters '38
The Sisters '38
The Fighting 69th '40
The Mummy's Hand '40
My Little Chickadee '40
Winners of the West '40
Riders of Death Valley '41
The Mummy's Tomb '42
Private Buckaroo '42
Ride 'Em Cowboy '42
Guest Wife '45
Deputy Marshall '50
Atomic Submarine '59
Brighty of the Grand Canyon '67

Bryan Forbes
Wooden Horse '50
The Colditz Story '55
The Baby and the Battleship '56
Quatermass 2 '57
The League of Gentlemen '60
A Shot in the Dark '64
December Flower

Mary Forbes
Vanity Fair '32
The Awful Truth '37
You Can't Take It with You '38
You Can't Cheat an Honest Man '39
Tender Comrade '43

Michele Forbes
Kalifornia '93
Swimming with Sharks '94

Ralph Forbes
Inside the Lines '30
Smilin' Through '32
The Phantom Broadcast '33
Riptide '34
Twentieth Century '34
I'll Name the Murderer '36
Legion of Missing Men '37
Make a Wish '37
Convicts at Large '38

Anitra Ford
The Big Bird Cage '72
Invasion of the Bee Girls '73
Stacey '73

Ann Ford
The Love Machine '71
Logan's Run '76

Constance Ford
The Last Hunt '56
A Summer Place '59
Home from the Hill '60
All Fall Down '62
Rome Adventure '62

Faith Ford
You Talkin' to Me? '87
Murder So Sweet '93
North '94

Francis Ford
Man from Monterey '33
The Texans '38
Stagecoach '39
Lucky Cisco Kid '40
Accomplice '46
The Quiet Man '52

Glenn Ford
The Lady in Question '40
So Ends Our Night '41
Texas '41
Destroyer '43
Gilda '46
A Stolen Life '46
The Loves of Carmen '48
Lust for Gold '49
Man from Colorado '49
The White Tower '50
Affair in Trinidad '52
The Green Glove '52
Appointment in Honduras '53
The Big Heat '53
Man from the Alamo '53
Human Desire '54
Americano '55
Blackboard Jungle '55
Interrupted Melody '55
The Violent Men '55
Fastest Gun Alive '56
Jubal '56
The Teahouse of the August Moon '56
Don't Go Near the Water '57
3:10 to Yuma '57
Cowboy '58
Torpedo Run '58
The Gazebo '59
It Started with a Kiss '59
Cimarron '60
Pocketful of Miracles '61
The Courtship of Eddie's Father '62
Experiment in Terror '62
The Four Horsemen of the Apocalypse '62
The Rounders '65
Is Paris Burning? '68
Smith! '69
Santee '73
Midway '76
Superman: The Movie '78
The Sacketts '79
The Visitor '80
Day of the Assassin '81
Happy Birthday to Me '81
Virus '82
Casablanca Express '89
Border Shootout '90
Final Verdict '91
Raw Nerve '91

Harrison Ford
The Primitive Lover '16
Hawthorne of the USA '19
Foolish Wives '22
Shadows '22
The Average Woman '24
The Nervous Wreck '26

Harrison Ford
Dead Heat on a Merry-Go-Round '66
Getting Straight '70
Zabriskie Point '70
American Graffiti '73
The Conversation '74
Heroes '77
Star Wars '77
Force 10 from Navarone '78
Apocalypse Now '79
The Frisco Kid '79
Hanover Street '79
The Empire Strikes Back '80
Great Movie Stunts & the Making of Raiders of the Lost Ark '81
Raiders of the Lost Ark '81
Blade Runner '82
From "Star Wars" to "Jedi": The Making of a Saga '83
Return of the Jedi '83
Indiana Jones and the Temple of Doom '84
Witness '85
The Mosquito Coast '86
Frantic '88
Working Girl '88
Indiana Jones and the Last Crusade '89
Presumed Innocent '90
Regarding Henry '91
Patriot Games '92
The Fugitive '93
Clear and Present Danger '94
Sabrina '95

Maria Ford
Masque of the Red Death '89
Stripped to Kill II: Live Girls '89
The Rain Killer '90
Slumber Party Massacre 3 '90
The Haunting of Morella '91
Naked Obsession '91
Ring of Fire '91
Deathstalker 4: Match of Titans '92
Final Judgement '92
Ring of Fire 2: Blood and Steel '92
Saturday Night Special '92
The Unnamable 2: The Statement of Randolph Carter '92
Angel of Destruction '94
Alien Terminator '95
Machine Gun Blues '95
Night Hunter '95
Stripteaser '95

Mick Ford
Scum '79
How to Get Ahead in Advertising '89

Paul Ford
Lust for Gold '49
The Teahouse of the August Moon '56
The Matchmaker '58
Missouri Traveler '58
Advise and Consent '62
The Music Man '62
Who's Got the Action? '63
The Russians are Coming, the Russians are Coming '66
The Comedians '67
Lola '69

Ross Ford
Jungle Patrol '48
Blue Canadian Rockies '52
Reform School Girl '57

Ruth Ford
The Lady is Willing '42
The Woman Who Came Back '45
The Eyes of the Amaryllis '82

Steven Ford
Body Count '87
When Harry Met Sally... '89

Wallace Ford
Mad About Money '30
Possessed '31
Freaks '32
Skyscraper Souls '32
Employees' Entrance '33
Night of Terror '33
The Lost Patrol '34
Get That Man '35
The Informer '35
Mysterious Mr. Wong '35
One Frightened Night '35
Rogue's Tavern '36
Exiled to Shanghai '37
O.H.M.S. '37
Swing It, Sailor! '37
Jericho '38
Back Door to Heaven '39
The Mummy's Hand '40
Wheel of Fortune '41
Inside the Law '42
The Mummy's Tomb '42
Seven Days' Leave '42
The Ape Man '43
Shadow of a Doubt '43
Blood on the Sun '45
Spellbound '45
Crack-Up '46
Dead Reckoning '47
T-Men '47
Coroner Creek '48
Great Jesse James Raid '49
The Set-Up '49
Harvey '50
She Couldn't Say No '52
A Lawless Street '55
The Man from Laramie '55
The Maverick Queen '55
The Rainmaker '56
Last Hurrah '58
The Matchmaker '58
Warlock '59
A Patch of Blue '65

Ken Foree
Dawn of the Dead '78
From Beyond '86
Glitz '88
Leatherface: The Texas Chainsaw Massacre 3 '89

Deborah Foreman
Valley Girl '83
April Fool's Day '86
My Chauffeur '86
3:15—The Moment of Truth '86
Destroyer '88
Waxwork '88
The Experts '89
Friends, Lovers & Lunatics '89
Lobster Man from Mars '89
Sundown '91
Lunatics: A Love Story '92

Mark Forest
Colossus of the Arena '60
Goliath and the Dragon '61
Mole Men against the Son of Hercules '61
Son of Samson '62
Goliath and the Sins of Babylon '64
The Lion of Thebes '64
Terror of Rome Against the Son of Hercules '64

Michael Forest
Atlas '60
The Beast from Haunted Cave '60
Ski Troop Attack '60
Dirt Gang '71
Mohammed: Messenger of God '77
Body of Evidence '92

Claire Forlani
Mallrats '95
The Rock '96

Carol Forman
The Black Widow '47
Federal Agents vs. Underworld, Inc. '49

Milos Forman
Heartburn '86
New Year's Day '89

Richard Foronjy
Prince of the City '81
The Morning After '86
Midnight Run '88
DaVinci's War '92
The Public Eye '92
Man of the House '95

Frederic Forrest
When the Legends Die '72
The Don is Dead '73
The Conversation '74
Larry '74
Permission To Kill '75
Missouri Breaks '76
It's Alive 2: It Lives Again '78
Apocalypse Now '79
The Rose '79
Calamity Jane '82
Hammett '82
One from the Heart '82
Valley Girl '83
The Stone Boy '84
The Adventures of Huckleberry Finn '85
Quo Vadis '85
Where Are the Children? '85
The Deliberate Stranger '86
Saigon: Year of the Cat '87
Stacking '87
Best Kept Secrets '88
Gotham '88
Return '88
Shadow on the Sun '88
Tucker: The Man and His Dream '88
Valentino Returns '88
Double Exposure: The Story of Margaret Bourke-White '89
Lonesome Dove '89
Music Box '89
Cat Chaser '90
The Two Jakes '90
The Habitation of Dragons '91
Hearts of Darkness: A Filmmaker's Apocalypse '91
Citizen Cohn '92
Dario Argento's Trauma '93
Double Obsession '93
Falling Down '93
Hidden Fears '93
Rain Without Thunder '93
Against the Wall '94
Lassie '94
Andersonville '95
One Night Stand '95

Sally Forrest
Streets of Sin '49
Vengeance Valley '51
Son of Sinbad '55

Steve Forrest
Clown '53
Flaming Star '60
Heller in Pink Tights '60
The Wild Country '71
The Hanged Man '74
The Hatfields & the McCoys '75
The Deerslayer '78
Captain America '79
North Dallas Forty '79
Roughnecks '80
A Rumor of War '80
Mommie Dearest '81
Hotline '82
Sahara '83
The Last of the Mohicans '85
Spies Like Us '85
Gunsmoke: Return to Dodge '87

William Forrest
The Masked Marvel '43
I'll See You in My Dreams '51
Jailhouse Rock '57

Constance Forslund
Dear Detective '78
A Shining Season '79
River's Edge '87
Village of the Damned '95

Robert Forster
Medium Cool '69
The Stalking Moon '69
Journey Through Rosebud '72
The Death Squad '73
The Don is Dead '73
The City '76
Stunts '77
Avalanche '78
Standing Tall '78
The Black Hole '79
Alligator '80
Goliath Awaits '81
Vigilante '83
Walking the Edge '83
Delta Force '86
Hollywood Harry '86
Once a Hero '88
The Banker '89
Peacemaker '90
Satan's Princess '90
Committed '91
Diplomatic Immunity '91
29th Street '91
In Between '92
Cover Story '93
Scanners: The Showdown '94

Rudolph Forster
The Threepenny Opera '31
The Return of Dr. Mabuse '61
The Mad Executioners '65

Bruce Forsyth
Star! '68
Bedknobs and Broomsticks '71

Rosemary Forsyth
Shenandoah '65
The War Lord '65
Texas Across the River '66
Whatever Happened to Aunt Alice? '69
Columbo: Murder By the Book '71
My Father's House '75
Gray Lady Down '77
The Gladiator '86
A Friendship in Vienna '88
Disclosure '94

Drew Forsythe
Doctors and Nurses '82
A Test of Love '84
Burke & Wills '85
Wrangler '88

Henderson Forsythe
Crisis at Central High '80
Sessions '83
Midnight Murders '91
Carolina Skeletons '92
Teamster Boss: The Jackie Presser Story '92

John Forsythe
Destination Tokyo '43
Escape from Fort Bravo '53
The Trouble with Harry '55
The Ambassador's Daughter '56
Madame X '66
In Cold Blood '67
The Happy Ending '69
Topaz '69
Murder Once Removed '71
Cry Panic '74
Terror on the 40th Floor '74
Sniper '75
Cruise into Terror '78
Users '78
And Justice for All '79
A Time for Miracles '80
Sizzle '81
Mysterious Two '82
Scrooged '88

William Forsythe
Savage Dawn '84
The Lightship '86
The Long, Hot Summer '86
Raising Arizona '87
Weeds '87
Patty Hearst '88
Dead Bang '89
Dick Tracy '90
Torrents of Spring '90
Career Opportunities '91
Out for Justice '91
Stone Cold '91
The Waterdance '91
American Me '92

Forsythe ▶cont.

The Gun in Betty Lou's Handbag *'92*
Direct Hit *'93*
Relentless 3 *'93*
Beyond Desire *'94*
The Immortals *'95*
Things to Do In Denver When You're Dead *'95*
Virtuosity *'95*
The Rock *'96*
The Substitute *'96*

Albert Fortell
Nuclear Conspiracy *'85*
Scandalous *'88*
Time Troopers *'89*

Bob Fosse
The Affairs of Dobie Gillis *'53*
Give a Girl a Break *'53*
Kiss Me Kate *'53*
My Sister Eileen *'55*
The Little Prince *'74*

Nicole Fosse
All That Jazz *'79*
A Chorus Line *'85*

Brigitte Fossey
Forbidden Games *'52*
The Wanderer *'67*
Honor Among Thieves *'68*
Going Places *'74*
Blue Country *'77*
The Man Who Loved Women *'77*
Quintet *'79*
Chanel Solitaire *'81*
La Boum *'81*
Enigma *'82*
The Last Butterfly *'92*

Barry Foster
Robbery *'67*
Frenzy *'72*
Quiet Day In Belfast *'74*
Beyond the Next Mountain *'87*
Maurice *'87*
The Whistle Blower *'87*
After Pilkington *'88*

Dianne Foster
The Kentuckian *'55*
The Violent Men *'55*
Last Hurrah *'58*
The King of the Roaring '20s: The Story of Arnold Rothstein *'61*

Frances Foster
Enemy Territory *'87*
Crooklyn *'94*

Gloria Foster
Nothing But a Man *'64*
Man & Boy *'71*
To All My Friends on Shore *'71*
Leonard Part 6 *'87*
The House of Dies Drear *'88*
City of Hope *'91*
Percy & Thunder *'93*

Helen Foster
The Road to Ruin *'28*
Linda *'29*
Ghost City *'32*
Saddle Buster *'32*
Young Blood *'33*

Jodie Foster
Napoleon and Samantha *'72*
One Little Indian *'73*
Tom Sawyer *'73*
Alice Doesn't Live Here Anymore *'74*
Smile, Jenny, You're Dead *'74*
Bugsy Malone *'76*
Freaky Friday *'76*
The Little Girl Who Lives Down the Lane *'76*
Taxi Driver *'76*
Candleshoe *'78*
Carny *'80*
Foxes *'80*
O'Hara's Wife *'82*
Svengali *'83*
The Blood of Others *'84*
The Hotel New Hampshire *'84*
Mesmerized *'84*
Siesta *'87*
The Accused *'88*
Five Corners *'88*
Stealing Home *'88*
Backtrack *'89*
Little Man Tate *'91*
The Silence of the Lambs *'91*
Shadows and Fog *'92*
Sommersby *'93*
Maverick *'94*
Nell *'94*

Julia Foster
The Loneliness of the Long Distance Runner *'62*
Half a Sixpence *'67*
Great McGonagall *'75*
F. Scott Fitzgerald in Hollywood *'76*
Thirteenth Reunion *'81*

Kimberly Foster
It Takes Two *'88*
Broken Trust *'93*

Meg Foster
Adam at 6 a.m. *'70*
Thumb Tripping *'72*
Things in Their Season *'74*
James Dean *'76*
Different Story *'78*
The Legend of Sleepy Hollow *'79*
Carny *'80*
Ticket to Heaven *'81*
The Osterman Weekend *'83*
The Emerald Forest *'85*
Masters of the Universe *'87*
The Wind *'87*
They Live *'88*
Leviathan *'89*
Relentless *'89*
Stepfather 2: Make Room for Daddy *'89*
Tripwire *'89*
Backstab *'90*
Blind Fury *'90*
Jezebel's Kiss *'90*
Diplomatic Immunity *'91*
Futurekick *'91*
Relentless 2: Dead On *'91*
Project: Shadowchaser *'92*
To Catch a Killer *'92*
Best of the Best 2 *'93*
Hidden Fears *'93*
Immortal Combat *'94*
Lady in Waiting *'94*
Oblivion *'94*
Shrunken Heads *'94*
Undercover *'94*
Backlash: Oblivion 2 *'95*

Norman Foster
Skyscraper Souls *'32*
Journey into Fear *'42*

Phil Foster
Conquest of Space *'55*
Bang the Drum Slowly *'73*
Hail *'73*

Preston Foster
Doctor X *'32*
I Am a Fugitive from a Chain Gang *'32*
The Last Mile *'32*
Ladies They Talk About *'33*
Annie Oakley *'35*
The Informer *'35*
Last Days of Pompeii *'35*
Sea Devils *'37*
American Empire *'42*
Guadalcanal Diary *'43*
My Friend Flicka *'43*
The Valley of Decision *'45*
The Harvey Girls *'46*
Ramrod *'47*
The Big Cat *'49*
I Shot Jesse James *'49*
Three Desperate Men *'50*
Kansas City Confidential *'52*
The Marshal's Daughter *'53*
The Time Travelers *'64*

Stacie Foster
Steel Frontier *'94*
Cyber-Tracker 2 *'95*

Byron Foulger
Prisoner of Zenda *'37*
Sullivan's Travels *'41*
The Panther's Claw *'42*
Hoppy Serves a Writ *'43*
Bells of San Fernando *'47*
The Devil's Partner *'58*

Derek Fowlds
Hotel Paradiso *'66*
Over the Hill *'93*

Harry Fowler
Fire Maidens from Outer Space *'56*
Flight from Singapore *'62*

Douglas Fowley
On the Avenue *'37*
It Could Happen to You *'39*
Wagon's Westward *'40*
Tanks a Million *'41*
Meet the Mob *'42*
Mr. Wise Guy *'42*
Sunset on the Desert *'42*
Bar-20 *'43*
Colt Comrades *'43*
Lost Canyon *'43*
Shake Hands with Murder *'44*
North of the Border *'46*
Desperate *'47*
Scared to Death *'47*
Wild Country *'47*
Behind Locked Doors *'48*
Battleground *'49*
Susanna Pass *'49*
Rider from Tucson *'50*
Singin' in the Rain *'52*
Cat Women of the Moon *'53*
Poor White Trash *'57*
The Good Guys and the Bad Guys *'69*
From Noon Till Three *'76*
The White Buffalo *'77*

Bernard Fox
Strange Bedfellows *'65*
Arnold *'73*
Zone of the Dead *'78*
House of the Dead *'80*
The Private Eyes *'80*

Colin Fox
My Pleasure Is My Business *'74*
Beautiful Dreamers *'92*

David Fox
Ordinary Magic *'93*
When Night is Falling *'95*

Edward Fox
Portrait of a Lady *'67*
Battle of Britain *'69*
Skullduggery *'70*
The Go-Between *'71*
The Day of the Jackal *'73*
A Doll's House *'73*
A Bridge Too Far *'77*
The Duellists *'77*
The Squeeze *'77*
The Big Sleep *'78*
Force 10 from Navarone *'78*
Soldier of Orange *'78*
The Cat and the Canary *'79*
Edward and Mrs. Simpson *'80*
The Mirror Crack'd *'80*
Gandhi *'82*
The Dresser *'83*
Never Say Never Again *'83*
Shaka Zulu *'83*
The Bounty *'84*
The Shooting Party *'85*
Wild Geese 2 *'85*
Anastasia: The Mystery of Anna *'86*
The Crucifer of Blood *'91*
Robin Hood *'91*
Gulliver's Travels *'95*
A Month by the Lake *'95*

Huckleberry Fox
Misunderstood *'84*
The Blue Yonder *'86*
A Winner Never Quits *'86*
Konrad *'90s*
Pharoah's Army *'95*

James Fox
The Servant *'63*
King Rat *'65*
Those Magnificent Men in Their Flying Machines *'65*
The Chase *'66*
Thoroughly Modern Millie *'67*
Isadora *'68*
Performance *'70*
Nancy Astor *'82*
Greystoke: The Legend of Tarzan, Lord of the Apes *'84*
A Passage to India *'84*
Absolute Beginners *'86*
The Whistle Blower *'87*
High Season *'88*
Shadow on the Sun *'88*
Farewell to the King *'89*
The Mighty Quinn *'89*
The Dwelling Place *'90s*
The Russia House *'90*
A Question of Attribution *'91*
Afraid of the Dark *'92*
Hostage *'92*
Patriot Games *'92*
Heart of Darkness *'93*
The Remains of the Day *'93*
Doomsday Gun *'94*
Fall from Grace *'94*
The Old Curiosity Shop *'94*

Kerry Fox
An Angel at My Table *'89*
The Last Days of Chez Nous *'92*
Rainbow Warrior *'94*
Shallow Grave *'94*
The Affair *'95*
Country Life *'95*
Friends *'95*

Michael J. Fox
Midnight Madness *'80*
Class of 1984 *'82*
High School USA *'84*
Back to the Future *'85*
Poison Ivy *'85*
Teen Wolf *'85*
Light of Day *'87*
The Secret of My Success *'87*
Bright Lights, Big City *'88*
Back to the Future, Part 2 *'89*
Casualties of War *'89*
Back to the Future, Part 3 *'90*
Doc Hollywood *'91*
The Hard Way *'91*
For Love or Money *'93*
Life with Mikey *'93*
Greedy *'94*
The American President *'95*
Blue In the Face *'95*
The Frighteners *'96*

Peter Fox
A Minor Miracle *'83*
Diamond Run *'90*

Samantha Fox
Delivery Boys *'84*
Violated *'84*
Warrior Queen *'87*

Sidney Fox
Murders in the Rue Morgue *'32*
Midnight *'34*
Don Quixote *'35*

Virginia Fox
The Blacksmith/The Cops *'22*
The Blacksmith/The Balloonatic *'23*

Robert Foxworth
Frankenstein *'73*
The Invisible Strangler *'76*
The Treasure of Matecumbe *'76*
Ants *'77*
Damien: Omen 2 *'78*
Deathmoon *'78*
The Black Marble *'79*
Prophecy *'79*
Double Standard *'88*
Beyond the Stars *'89*

Jamie Foxx
The Great White Hype *'96*
The Truth About Cats and Dogs *'96*

Redd Foxx
Cotton Comes to Harlem *'70*
Norman, Is That You? *'76*
Harlem Nights *'89*

Eddie Foy, Jr.
Four Jacks and a Jill *'41*
Yankee Doodle Dandy *'42*
Wilson *'44*
The Farmer Takes a Wife *'53*
Lucky Me *'54*
The Pajama Game *'57*
Bells are Ringing *'60*
Gidget Goes Hawaiian *'61*
30 Is a Dangerous Age, Cynthia *'68*

Carla Fracci
Nijinsky *'80*
Life of Verdi *'84*

Tracy Fraim
Dream Machine *'91*
Fear *'96*

Jonathon Frakes
North and South Book 1 *'85*
Star Trek the Next Generation: Encounter at Farpoint *'87*
Star Trek Generations *'94*
Star Trek the Next Generation, the Final Episode: All Good Things... *'94*

Victor Francen
J'Accuse *'37*
The Tuttles of Tahiti *'42*
Madame Curie *'43*
San Antonio *'45*
The Beast with Five Fingers *'46*

Anthony (Tony) Franciosa
A Face in the Crowd *'57*
This Could Be the Night *'57*
The Long, Hot Summer *'58*
Career *'59*
The Naked Maja *'59*
Period of Adjustment *'62*
Rio Conchos *'64*
Assault on a Queen *'66*
Web of the Spider *'70*
Across 110th Street *'72*
Ghost in the Noonday Sun *'74*
The Drowning Pool *'75*
Curse of the Black Widow *'77*
The World is Full of Married Men *'80*
Daughter of Death *'82*
Death Wish 2 *'82*
Kiss My Grits *'82*
Unsane *'82*
La Cicada *'83*
Side Show *'84*
Stagecoach *'86*
Blood Vows: The Story of a Mafia Wife *'87*
Death House *'88*
Ghost Writer *'89*
Backstreet Dreams *'90*
Double Threat *'92*
City Hall *'95*

Alec B. Francis
The Wishing Ring *'14*
Little Church Around the Corner *'23*
Beau Brummel *'24*
Charley's Aunt *'25*
The Mad Whirl *'25*
Evangeline *'29*
Mata Hari *'32*
His Private Secretary *'33*

Anne Francis
Portrait of Jennie *'48*
Summer Holiday *'48*
A Lion Is in the Streets *'53*
Bad Day at Black Rock *'54*
Susan Slept Here *'54*
Battle Cry *'55*
Blackboard Jungle *'55*
Forbidden Planet *'56*
Don't Go Near the Water *'57*
Funny Girl *'68*
The Love God? *'70*
Wild Women *'70*
Fireball Forward *'72*
Haunts of the Very Rich *'72*
Pancho Villa *'72*
Cry Panic *'74*
Born Again *'78*
The Rebels *'79*
Mazes and Monsters *'82*
Laguna Heat *'87*
Poor Little Rich Girl: The Barbara Hutton Story *'87*
Return *'88*
Little Vegas *'90*

Arlene Francis
Murders in the Rue Morgue *'32*
One, Two, Three *'61*
The Thrill of It All! *'63*

Clive Francis
Man Who Had Power Over Women *'70*
Poldark *'75*
The Bretts *'88*
Sharpe's Company *'94*

Genie Francis
North and South Book 1 *'85*
North and South Book 2 *'86*

Ivor Francis
Hard Frame *'70*
Zone of the Dead *'78*
House of the Dead *'80*

Kay Francis
The Cocoanuts '29
Vice Squad '31
In Name Only '39
It's a Date '40
Little Men '40

Noel Francis
Bachelor Apartment '31
My Pal, The King '32
Fire Alarm '38

Robert Francis
The Caine Mutiny '54
The Long Gray Line '55

James Franciscus
Snow Treasure '67
Marooned '69
The Valley of Gwangi '69
Beneath the Planet of the Apes '70
The Cat o' Nine Tails '71
Jonathan Livingston Seagull '73
The Amazing Dobermans '76
The Man Inside '76
One of My Wives Is Missing '76
Hunter '77
Good Guys Wear Black '78
The Greek Tycoon '78
Puzzle '78
Secrets of Three Hungry Wives '78
Killer Fish '79
Nightkill '80
Jacqueline Bouvier Kennedy '81
Butterfly '82
Secret Weapons '85

Don Francks
Finian's Rainbow '68
Drying Up the Streets '76
Fast Company '78
Phoenix Team '80
984: Prisoner of the Future '84
The Christmas Wife '88
Madonna: Innocence Lost '95

Ramon Franco
Tour of Duty '87
Kiss Me a Killer '91
Shattered Image '93

Jacques Francois
The Barkleys of Broadway '49
The Gift '82

Billy Franey
Ghost Valley '32
Somewhere in Sonora '33

Ben Frank
Don't Answer the Phone '80
Hollywood Vice Sqaud '86
Hollywood Zap '86

Charles Frank
Tarantulas: The Deadly Cargo '77
A Guide for the Married Woman '78
Snowblind '78
The Chisholms '79
The Right Stuff '83
LBJ: The Early Years '88
Lucky Stiff '88
Danielle Steel's Changes '91

Diana Frank
The Glass Jungle '88
Monster High '89
Pale Blood '91

Gary Frank
Enola Gay: The Men, the Mission, the Atomic Bomb '80
The Night the City Screamed '80
Enemy Territory '87
Deadly Weapon '88
Getting Up and Going Home '92

Horst Frank
The Head '59
Desert Commandos '60s
Code Name Alpha '67
The Grand Duel '73
Albino '76

Joanna Frank
The Savage Seven '68
Always '85
Say Anything '89

Tony Frank
Riverbend '89
Rush '91

Mark Frankel
Young Catherine '91
Leon the Pig Farmer '93

Al Franken
Tunnelvision '76
One More Saturday Night '86
Stuart Saves His Family '94

Steve Franken
Which Way to the Front? '70
Ants '77
Freeway '88

Paul Frankeur
Le Gentleman D'Epsom '62
Un Singe en Hiver '62
License to Kill '64
The Milky Way '68

William Frankfather
Defense Play '88
Born Yesterday '93

Bonnie Franklin
Breaking Up Is Hard to Do '79
Portrait of a Rebel: Margaret Sanger '82
Your Place or Mine '83

David Franklin
Early Frost '84
Rock & Roll Cowboys '92

Diane Franklin
Last American Virgin '82
Second Time Lucky '84
Better Off Dead '85
Terrorvision '86

Gloria Franklin
Drums of Fu Manchu '40
Without Warning '52

Joe Franklin
Ghoul School '90
29th Street '91

John Franklin
Children of the Corn '84
The Addams Family '91
Tammy and the T-Rex '94

Pamela Franklin
The Innocents '61
The Horse Without a Head '63
Flipper's New Adventure '64
A Tiger Walks '64
The Nanny '65
The Night of the Following Day '69
The Prime of Miss Jean Brodie '69
And Soon the Darkness '70
David Copperfield '70
The Witching '72
The Legend of Hell House '73
Satan's School for Girls '73
Screamer '74
Eleanor & Franklin '76
Food of the Gods '76

William Franklyn
Quatermass 2 '57
The Satanic Rites of Dracula '73
Splitting Heirs '93

Chloe Franks
The House that Dripped Blood '71
Ivanhoe '82

Mary Frann
I'm Dangerous Tonight '90
Fatal Charm '92

Arthur Franz
Jungle Patrol '48
Abbott and Costello Meet the Invisible Man '51
Flight to Mars '52
The Member of the Wedding '52
Invaders from Mars '53
Beyond a Reasonable Doubt '56
Hellcats of the Navy '57
Atomic Submarine '59
Monster on the Campus '59
Dream No Evil '75
The Human Factor '75
Sisters of Death '76
Bogie: The Last Hero '80

Dennis Franz
Dressed to Kill '80
Blow Out '81
Psycho 2 '83
Body Double '84
Kiss Shot '89
The Package '89
Die Hard 2: Die Harder '90
Children of Fury '94

Eduard Franz
The Scar '48
Francis the Talking Mule '49
Outpost in Morocco '49
The Magnificent Yankee '50
One Minute to Zero '52
Latin Lovers '53
Sins of Jezebel '54
The Indian Fighter '55
The Burning Hills '56
The Story of Ruth '60

Bill Fraser
Alias John Preston '56
Naughty Knights '71
Ripping Yarns '75
Pirates '86
Little Dorrit, Film 1: Nobody's Fault '88
Little Dorrit, Film 2: Little Dorrit's Story '88

Brendan Fraser
Dogfight '91
Encino Man '92
School Ties '92
Twenty Bucks '93
Airheads '94
Dark Side of Genius '94
The Scout '94
With Honors '94
Younger & Younger '94
Now and Then '95
Mrs. Winterbourne '96

Duncan Fraser
Call of the Wild '93
Timecop '94
Unforgettable '96

Elisabeth Fraser
The Man Who Came to Dinner '41
Hills of Oklahoma '50
Young at Heart '54
The Tunnel of Love '58
Ask Any Girl '59
Two for the Seesaw '62
A Patch of Blue '65

Hugh Fraser
The Draughtsman's Contract '82
The Bretts '88
Sharpe's Battle '94
Sharpe's Company '94
Sharpe's Enemy '94
Sharpe's Gold '94
Sharpe's Honour '94

John Fraser
The Trials of Oscar Wilde '60
Horsemasters '61
Repulsion '65
Isadora '68

Liz Fraser
Two-Way Stretch '60
Carry On Cruising '62
The Americanization of Emily '64
Adventures of a Taxi Driver '76
Chicago Joe & the Showgirl '90

Phyllis Fraser
Western Double Feature 3 '36
Winds of the Wasteland '36
Tough to Handle '37

Richard Fraser
Bedlam '45
White Pongo '45
The Private Affairs of Bel Ami '47
The Cobra Strikes '48

Ronald Fraser
The Killing of Sister George '69
Rentadick '72
The Mystery of Edwin Drood '93

Sally Fraser
It Conquered the World '56
Giant from the Unknown '58
The War of the Colossal Beast '58
Dangerous Charter '62

Stuart Fratkin
Dr. Alien '88
Ski School '91
Prehysteria '93
Remote '93

William Frawley
Harmony Lane '35
Desire '36
The General Died at Dawn '36
The Princess Comes Across '36
Something to Sing About '36
Mad About Music '38
The Adventures of Huckleberry Finn '39
Rose of Washington Square '39
One Night in the Tropics '40
Rhythm on the River '40
Blondie in Society '41
The Bride Came C.O.D. '41
Footsteps in the Dark '41
Gentleman Jim '42
Roxie Hart '42
Wildcat '42
Whistling in Brooklyn '43
Fighting Seabees '44
Flame of the Barbary Coast '45
Lady On a Train '45
The Inner Circle '46
The Virginian '46
Down to Earth '47
Miracle on 34th Street '47
Monsieur Verdoux '47
Babe Ruth Story '48
East Side, West Side '49
Abbott and Costello Meet the Invisible Man '51
The Lemon Drop Kid '51
I Love Lucy '52
Rancho Notorious '52

Jane Frazee
The Gay Ranchero '42
On the Old Spanish Trail '47
Springtime in the Sierras '47
Grand Canyon Trail '48
Under California Stars '48
Last of the Wild Horses '49

Robert Frazer
The Drake Case '29
Ten Nights in a Bar-Room '31
Mystery Trooper '32
Saddle Buster '32
Found Alive '34
Monte Carlo Nights '34
Fighting Parson '35
Fighting Pilot '35
The Miracle Rider '35
Death from a Distance '36
Renfrew on the Great White Trail '38
Dawn Express '42
Partners of the Trail '44

Rupert Frazer
Empire of the Sun '87
The Girl in a Swing '89
Back Home '90

Sheila Frazier
Firehouse '72
Superfly '72
Superfly T.N.T. '73
Three the Hard Way '74
The Hitter '79

Peter Frechette
No Small Affair '84
The Kindred '87
Paint It Black '89

Blanche Frederici
Sadie Thompson '28
Night Nurse '31
A Farewell to Arms '32

Lynne Frederick
Vampire Circus '71
Amazing Mr. Blunden '72
Phase 4 '74
Voyage of the Damned '76
Schizo '77
Prisoner of Zenda '79

Vicki Frederick
...All the Marbles '81
Body Rock '84
A Chorus Line '85
Chopper Chicks in Zombietown '91

Alan Freed
Rock, Rock, Rock '56
Go, Johnny Go! '59

Bert Freed
The Halls of Montezuma '50
Detective Story '51
Men of the Fighting Lady '54
The Cobweb '55
Paths of Glory '57
The Gazebo '59
Evel Knievel '72

Al Freeman, Jr.
Ensign Pulver '64
Dutchman '67
The Detective '68
Finian's Rainbow '68
My Sweet Charlie '70
Perry Mason Returns '85
Seven Hours to Judgment '88
The Defense Never Rests '90
Malcolm X '92
Assault at West Point: The Court-Martial of Johnson Whittaker '94
Once Upon a Time...When We Were Colored '95

Howard Freeman
Air Raid Wardens '43
The Blue Dahlia '46
House of Horrors '46
Double Dynamite '51
Million Dollar Mermaid '52
Scaramouche '52

J.E. Freeman
Hard Traveling '85
Miller's Crossing '90
Wild at Heart '90
Memphis '91
Aces: Iron Eagle 3 '92
There Goes My Baby '92
Casualties of Love: The "Long Island Lolita" Story '93
Fallen Angels 2 '93
It Could Happen to You '94
Mother's Boys '94

Joan Freeman
Panic in the Year Zero! '62
Tower of London '62
Roustabout '64
The Rounders '65
The Reluctant Astronaut '67
Fastest Guitar Alive '68

Kathleen Freeman
Love Is Better Than Ever '52
The Errand Boy '61
The Nutty Professor '63
Disorderly Orderly '64
The Rounders '65
Malibu Bikini Shop '86
In the Mood '87
Innerspace '87
Hollywood Chaos '89
The Willies '90
Reckless Kelly '93
Naked Gun 33 1/3: The Final Insult '94
At First Sight '95

Mona Freeman
Black Beauty '46
That Brennan Girl '46
Dear Wife '49
Branded '50
Copper Canyon '50
Jumping Jacks '52
Battle Cry '55
The Way Out '56
Black Beauty/Courage of Black Beauty '57

Morgan Freeman
Roll of Thunder, Hear My Cry '78
Brubaker '80
Eyewitness '81
Harry & Son '84
Teachers '84
Execution of Raymond Graham '85
Marie '85
That Was Then...This Is Now '85
Street Smart '87
Blood Money: The Story of Clinton and Nadine '88
Clean and Sober '88
Driving Miss Daisy '89
Glory '89
Johnny Handsome '89
Lean on Me '89
The Bonfire of the Vanities '90
Robin Hood: Prince of Thieves '91
The Power of One '92
Unforgiven '92
Outbreak '94
The Shawshank Redemption '94
Seven '95
Chain Reaction '96
Moll Flanders '96

Paul Freeman
Whose Child Am I? '75
The Dogs of War '81
Raiders of the Lost Ark '81
The Sender '82

Freeman ▶cont.

Unsuitable Job for a Woman '82
Shanghai Surprise '86
Without a Clue '88
A World Apart '88
Murderers among Us: The Simon Wiesenthal Story '89
Prisoner of Rio '89
A Dangerous Man: Lawrence after Arabia '91
Eminent Domain '91
Aces: Iron Eagle 3 '92
The Final Cut '95
Just Like a Woman '95
Mighty Morphin Power Rangers: The Movie '95

Tony Freeman
Invincible Gladiators '64
Ocean Drive Weekend '85

Paul Frees
Hunt the Man Down/Smashing the Rackets '50
Suddenly '54

Alice Freindlikh
Stalker '79
Rasputin '85

Stephane Freiss
Vagabond '85
Does This Mean We're Married? '90

Bruce French
Pipe Dreams '76
Ants '77

Charles French
King of the Rodeo '28
Man of Action '33
The Live Wire '34
The Man from Hell '34
When a Man Sees Red '34
The Crimson Trail '35
Trail of Terror '35
Gun Play '36
Where Trails Divide '37

Edwige French
The Next Victim '71
You've Got to Have Heart '77

Valerie French
Jubal '56
The 27 Day '57

Victor French
Spencer's Mountain '63
Charro! '69
Chato's Land '71
The Other '72
The House on Skull Mountain '74
Little House on the Prairie '74
Choices '81

Pierre Fresnay
Marius '31
Fanny '32
The Man Who Knew Too Much '34
Cesar '36
Grand Illusion '37
Le Corbeau '43
Monsieur Vincent '48

Bernard Fresson
Hiroshima, Mon Amour '59
Honor Among Thieves '68
French Connection 2 '75
The Tenant '76
Germinal '93

Matt Frewer
Supergirl '84
Max Headroom, the Original Story '86
The Fourth Protocol '87
Speed Zone '88
Far from Home '89
Honey, I Shrunk the Kids '89
Short Time '90
The Taking of Beverly Hills '91
The Day My Parents Ran Away '93
The Positively True Adventures of the Alleged Texas Cheerleader-Murdering Mom '93
Twenty Bucks '93
Stephen King's The Stand '94
Lawnmower Man 2: Beyond Cyberspace '95
National Lampoon's Senior Trip '95
Kissinger and Nixon '96

Leonard Frey
The Magic Christian '69
The Boys in the Band '70
Fiddler on the Roof '71
Tattoo '81

Sami Frey
Cleo from 5 to 7 '61
Band of Outsiders '64
Cesar & Rosalie '72
Sweet Movie '75
Nea '78
The Little Drummer Girl '84
Black Widow '87
Sand and Blood '87
War & Remembrance, Part 1 '88
War & Remembrance: The Final Chapter, Part 8 '89
My Life and Times with Antonin Artaud '93

Brenda Fricker
My Left Foot '89
The Field '90
Brides of Christ '91
Home Alone 2: Lost in New York '92
Deadly Advice '93
So I Married an Axe Murderer '93
The Sound and the Silence '93
Utz '93
Angels in the Outfield '94
A Man of No Importance '94
Journey '95
Moll Flanders '96
A Time to Kill '96

Jonathan Frid
Dark Shadows '67
House of Dark Shadows '70
Seizure '74

Tom Fridley
Summer Camp Nightmare '86
Vietnam War Story 1 '88

Peter Friedman
The Seventh Sign '88
Single White Female '92
Blink '93
The Heidi Chronicles '95
Safe '95

John Friedrich
Forever '78
Wanderers '79
A Rumor of War '80
The Final Terror '83

Colin Friels
Monkey Grip '82
Kangaroo '86
Malcolm '86
High Tide '87
Warm Nights on a Slow-Moving Train '87
The Gold & Glory '88
Ground Zero '88
Grievous Bodily Harm '89
Darkman '90
Class Action '91
A Good Man in Africa '94
Angel Baby '95

Philip Friend
Great Day '46
Vulture '67

Willy Fritsch
Spies '28
Woman in the Moon '29
Congress Dances '31

Gert Frobe
The Eternal Waltz '54
The Thousand Eyes of Dr. Mabuse '60
The Return of Dr. Mabuse '61
The Longest Day '62
Testament of Dr. Mabuse '62
The Three Penny Opera '62
Goldfinger '64
Those Magnificent Men in Their Flying Machines '65
Tonio Kroger '65
I Killed Rasputin '67
Those Fantastic Flying Fools '67
Triple Cross '67
Chitty Chitty Bang Bang '68
Is Paris Burning? '68
Those Daring Young Men in Their Jaunty Jalopies '69
Dollars '71
Shadow Man '75
Ten Little Indians '75
The Serpent's Egg '78
Sidney Sheldon's Bloodline '79

Gustav Froehlich
Metropolis '26
Homecoming '28

Ewa Froling
Fanny and Alexander '83
The Ox '91

Milton Frome
Ride 'Em Cowgirl '41
Pardners '56

Lindsay Frost
Dead Heat '88
Danielle Steel's Palomino '91
Monolith '93

Sadie Frost
Dark Obsession '90
Bram Stoker's Dracula '92
Paper Marriage '93
Splitting Heirs '93
The Cisco Kid '94
A Pyromaniac's Love Story '95

Terry Frost
The Monster Maker '44
Waterfront '44
Black Hills '48
The Hawk of Powder River '48

Warren Frost
Psycho 4: The Beginning '90
Twin Peaks '90
Twin Peaks '90

Stephen Fry
Jeeves & Wooster: Jeeves' Arrival '91
Peter's Friends '92
Cold Comfort Farm '94
I.Q. '94
Stalag Luft

Taylor Fry
Necessary Parties '88
Lone Justice '93
A Little Princess '95

Brittain Frye
Hide and Go Shriek '87
Slumber Party Massacre 3 '90

Dwight Frye
Dracula '31
Frankenstein '31
The Maltese Falcon '31
The Vampire Bat '32
The Invisible Man '33
The Bride of Frankenstein '35
The Crime of Dr. Crespi '35
Sinners in Paradise '38
Drums of Fu Manchu '40
The Ghost of Frankenstein '42
Dead Men Walk '43
The Worst of Hollywood: Vol. 2 '90

Sean Frye
E.T.: The Extra-Terrestrial '82
Deadline Assault '90

Soleil Moon Frye
Invitation to Hell '84
The Liar's Club '93
The St. Tammany Miracle '94
Twisted Love '95

Virgil Frye
Up from the Depths '79
Dr. Heckyl and Mr. Hype '80
Revenge of the Ninja '83
Running Hot '83
Hot Moves '84
Secret of the Ice Cave '89
Born in America '90

Gaby Fuchs
Mark of the Devil '69
The Werewolf vs. the Vampire Woman '70

Leo Fuchs
American Matchmaker '40
Avalon '90

Joachim Fuchsberger
Dead Eyes of London '61
The Strange Countess '61
Inn on the River '62
The Black Abbot '63
The Last Tomahawk '65
The Mysterious Magician '65

Alan Fudge
Bug '75
The Children of An Lac '80
Nightmare on the 13th Floor '90
Too Young to Die '90

Miguel Angel Fuentes
The Puma Man '80
Fitzcarraldo '82

Athol Fugard
Gandhi '82
The Killing Fields '84

Tatsuya Fuji
The Empire of Passion '76
In the Realm of the Senses '76
In the Realm of Passion '80

Hiroshi Fujioka
Tidal Wave '75
Ghostwarrior '86
K2: The Ultimate High '92

John Fujioka
A Conspiracy of Love '87
The Last Samurai '90
American Samurai '92

Christopher Fulford
Prayer for the Dying '87
Immortal Beloved '94
Prime Suspect: The Scent of Darkness '95

Dale Fuller
Greed '24
The Marriage Circle '24
The Unchastened Woman '25

Jonathan Fuller
The Pit & the Pendulum '91
Arcade '93
Castle Freak '95
Last Man Standing '95
Suspect Device '95

Kurt Fuller
Miracle Mile '89
No Holds Barred '89
Bingo '91
Wayne's World '92
Calendar Girl '93
Reflections in the Dark '94

Lance Fuller
Cattle Queen of Montana '54
Apache Woman '55
Kentucky Rifle '55
Girls in Prison '56
Voodoo Woman '57
The Bride & the Beast '58

Nancy Belle Fuller
Sky Heist '75
Hard Part Begins '80s

Penny Fuller
Lois Gibbs and the Love Canal '82
A Piano for Mrs. Cimino '82
Your Place or Mine '83
License to Kill '84
As Summers Die '86
George Washington: The Forging of a Nation '86
Fire and Rain '89
Lies Before Kisses '92
Miss Rose White '92
The Beverly Hillbillies '93
Danielle Steel's Star '93

Robert Fuller
The Brain from Planet Arous '57
Return of the Seven '66
Sinai Commandos '68
Whatever Happened to Aunt Alice? '69
The Hard Ride '71
The Gatling Gun '72
Donner Pass: The Road to Survival '84

Samuel Fuller
Pierrot le Fou '65
The Young Nurses '73
The American Friend '77
State of Things '82
Slapstick of Another Kind '84
Return to Salem's Lot '87
La Vie de Boheme '93

Fiona Fullerton
Alice's Adventures in Wonderland '72
Shaka Zulu '83
The Charmer '89
Spymaker: The Secret Life of Ian Fleming '90

Brad Fulton
Journey Beneath the Desert '61
The Undertaker and His Pals '67

Christina Fulton
Red Shoe Diaries 3: Another Woman's Lipstick '93
The Girl with the Hungry Eyes '94
Hard Drive '94

Eiji Funakoshi
Fires on the Plain '59
Being Two Isn't Easy '62
Gamera, the Invincible '66
Gamera vs. Guiron '69

Annette Funicello
The Shaggy Dog '59
Babes in Toyland '61
Horsemasters '61
Beach Party '63
The Misadventures of Merlin Jones '63
Bikini Beach '64
Muscle Beach Party '64
Pajama Party '64
Beach Blanket Bingo '65
How to Stuff a Wild Bikini '65
Monkey's Uncle '65
Dr. Goldfoot and the Bikini Machine '66
Head '68
Lots of Luck '85
Back to the Beach '87

John Furey
Friday the 13th, Part 2 '81
Mutant on the Bounty '89

Edward Furlong
Terminator 2: Judgment Day '91
American Heart '92
Pet Sematary 2 '92
A Home of Our Own '93
Brainscan '94
Little Odessa '94
Before and After '95

Yvonne Furneaux
The House of the Arrow '53
The Master of Ballantrae '53
The Warriors '55
The Mummy '59*
La Dolce Vita '60
The Lion of Thebes '64
Repulsion '65
Frankenstein's Great Aunt Tillie '83

Betty Furness
Beggars in Ermine '34
The President's Mystery '36
Swing Time '36
Renegade Ranger/Scarlet River '38

Deborra-Lee Furness
Shame '87
The Last of the Finest '90
Voyager '91
Angel Baby '95

Joseph Furst
Diamonds Are Forever '71
The Dunera Boys '85

Stephen Furst
National Lampoon's Animal House '78
Swim Team '79
Getting Wasted '80
Midnight Madness '80
The Unseen '80
Up the Creek '84
The Dream Team '89
Magic Kid '92
Magic Kid 2 '94

George Furth
Butch Cassidy and the Sundance Kid '69
Norman, Is That You? '76
Doctor Detroit '83

Ed Fury
Wild Women of Wongo '59
Samson Against the Sheik '62
Ursus in the Valley of the Lions '62
Colossus and the Amazon Queen '64

Dan Futterman
Class of '61 '92
The Birdcage '95

Marianne Gaba
The Choppers '61
How to Stuff a Wild Bikini '65

Richard Gabai
Assault of the Party Nerds '89
Virgin High '90
Hot Under the Collar '91
Dinosaur Island '93
Bikini Drive-In '94
Assault of the Party Nerds 2: Heavy Petting Detective '95

Martin Gabel
The Thief '52
Divorce American Style '67
Lady in Cement '68
Smile, Jenny, You're Dead '74

Scilla Gabel
Colossus of the Arena '60
Mill of the Stone Women '60

Jean Gabin
Maria Chapdelaine '34
Zou Zou '34
The Lower Depths '36
Grand Illusion '37
Pepe Le Moko '37
La Bete Humaine '38
Le Jour Se Leve '39
Stormy Waters '41
The Walls of Malapaga '49
Le Plaisir '52
Grisbi '53
French Can-Can '55
Napoleon '55
Four Bags Full '56
Le Cas du Dr. Laurent '57
Les Miserables '57
Duke of the Derby '62
Le Gentleman D'Epsom '62
Un Singe en Hiver '62
The Big Grab '63
Melodie en Sous-Sol '63
Le Chat '75
L'Anne Sainte '78

Christopher Gable
The Boy Friend '71
The Music Lovers '71
The Lair of the White Worm '88
The Rainbow '89

Clark Gable
Dance Fools Dance '31
A Free Soul '31
Laughing Sinners '31
Night Nurse '31
Painted Desert '31
Possessed '31
Susan Lenox: Her Fall and Rise '31
No Man of Her Own '32
Red Dust '32
Strange Interlude '32
Dancing Lady '33
Hold Your Man '33
The Lost Stooges '33
Chained '34
It Happened One Night '34
Manhattan Melodrama '34
China Seas '35
Forsaking All Others '35
Mutiny on the Bounty '35
Love on the Run '36
San Francisco '36
Wife Versus Secretary '36
Saratoga '37
Test Pilot '38
Too Hot to Handle '38
Gone with the Wind '39
Idiot's Delight '39
Boom Town '40
Comrade X '40
Strange Cargo '40
Honky Tonk '41
They Met in Bombay '41
Somewhere I'll Find You '42
Adventure '45
The Hucksters '47
Command Decision '48
Homecoming '48
Any Number Can Play '49
Key to the City '50
To Please a Lady '50
Across the Wide Missouri '51
Lone Star '52
Mogambo '53
Never Let Me Go '53
Betrayed '54
Soldier of Fortune '55
The Tall Men '55
The King and Four Queens '56
Band of Angels '57
Run Silent, Run Deep '58
Teacher's Pet '58
But Not for Me '59
It Started in Naples '60
The Misfits '61

Eva Gabor
The Last Time I Saw Paris '54
Artists and Models '55
Don't Go Near the Water '57
My Man Godfrey '57
Gigi '58
Truth About Women '58
It Started with a Kiss '59
A New Kind of Love '63
Princess Academy '87
Tales of the Klondike: The Scorn of Women '87

Zsa Zsa Gabor
Lovely to Look At '52
Moulin Rouge '52
We're Not Married '52
Lili '53
Death of a Scoundrel '56
Queen of Outer Space '58
Touch of Evil '58
For the First Time '59
Boys' Night Out '62
Arrivederci, Baby! '66
Picture Mommy Dead '66
Every Girl Should Have One '78
Frankenstein's Great Aunt Tillie '83
Movie Maker '86

Monique Gabrielle
Bachelor Party '84
Hard to Hold '84
Hot Moves '84
Amazon Women on the Moon '87
Deathstalker 2: Duel of the Titans '87
Emmanuelle 5 '87
Silk 2 '89
Evil Toons '90

Gabriel Gabrio
Harvest '37
Pepe Le Moko '37

Antonio Gades
Blood Wedding '81
Carmen '83
El Amor Brujo '86

Anna Gael
Therese & Isabelle '68
Alien Women '69

Jenny Gago
Old Gringo '89
Sweet 15 '90
My Family '94

Max Gail
Cardiac Arrest '74
Night Moves '75
Aliens Are Coming '80
D.C. Cab '84
Heartbreakers '84
Where Are the Children? '85
Judgment in Berlin '88
The Game of Love '90
Street Crimes '92
Deadly Target '94
Pontiac Moon '94
Sodbusters '94

Boyd Gaines
The Sure Thing '85
Heartbreak Ridge '86
Call Me '88
Piece of Cake '90

Jim Gaines
Blood Debts '83
Commando Invasion '87
Codename: Terminate '90
Fist of Steel '93

Richard Gaines
The More the Merrier '43
The Enchanted Cottage '45
Humoresque '46

M.C. Gainey
El Diablo '90
Leap of Faith '92

Courtney Gains
Children of the Corn '84
Hardbodies '84
Back to the Future '85
Lust in the Dust '85
Can't Buy Me Love '87
The 'Burbs '89
Memphis Belle '90

Charlotte Gainsbourg
Le Petit Amour '87
The Little Thief '89
Jane Eyre '96

Serge Gainsbourg
The Fury of Hercules '61
Samson '61
Too Pretty to Be Honest '72
I Love All of You '83

Janusz Gajos
The Interrogation '82
Trois Couleurs: Blanc '94

Michel Galabru
Soldat Duroc...Ca Va Etre Ta Fete! '60s
Le Gendarme de Saint-Tropez '67
The Judge and the Assassin '75
La Cage aux Folles '78
La Cage aux Folles 2 '81
La Cage aux Folles 3: The Wedding '86
Uranus '91
Belle Epoque '92

David Gale
Re-Animator '84
The Brain '88
Bride of Re-Animator '89
Syngenor '90
The Guyver '91

Eddra Gale
8 1/2 '63
Revenge of the Cheerleaders '76

June Gale
Rainbow's End '35
It Could Happen to You '39

Johnny Galecki
National Lampoon's Christmas Vacation '89
Backfield in Motion '91

Anna Galiena
Rorret '87
The Hairdresser's Husband '92
Jamon, Jamon '93
Being Human '94

Kelly Galindo
Angels of the City '89
The Malibu Beach Vampires '91

Nacho Galindo
Borderline '50
Green Fire '55
Born Reckless '59

Frank Gallacher
Waterfront '83
Proof '91

Bronagh Gallagher
The Commitments '91
Mary Reilly '95

Megan Gallagher
The Ambulance '90
In a Stranger's Hand '92
The Birds 2: Land's End '94
Breaking Free '95
Trade Off '95
Crosscut '96

Peter Gallagher
Skag '79
Idolmaker '80
Summer Lovers '82
Private Contentment '83
Dreamchild '85
The Murder of Mary Phagan '87
My Little Girl '87
The Caine Mutiny Court Martial '88
High Spirits '88
Long Day's Journey into Night '88
sex, lies and videotape '89
Tune in Tomorrow '90
An Inconvenient Woman '91
Late for Dinner '91
The Player '92
Fallen Angels 1 '93
Fallen Angels 2 '93
Malice '93
Short Cuts '93
Watch It '93
Mother's Boys '94
White Mile '94
The Underneath '95
While You Were Sleeping '95
Last Dance '96

Richard "Skeets" Gallagher
Possessed '31
Bachelor Bait '34
Riptide '34
Hats Off '37
Danger on the Air '38

Camillo Gallardo
Singles '92
Of Love and Shadows '94

Silvania Gallardo
Out of the Dark '88
Prison Stories: Women on the Inside '91

Gina Gallego
Lust in the Dust '85
My Demon Lover '87
Personals '90

Rosina Galli
Escape to Paradise '39
Fisherman's Wharf '39

Zach Galligan
The Lawrenceville Stories '80s
Gremlins '84
Waxwork '88
Gremlins 2: The New Batch '90
Mortal Passions '90
Rebel Storm '90
Psychic '91
Waxwork 2: Lost in Time '91
Zandalee '91
All Tied Up '92
Round Trip to Heaven '92
Caroline at Midnight '93
Ice '93
Warlock: The Armageddon '93
Cyborg 3: The Recycler '95

Robert Gallo
Mayhem '87
Sinners '89

Vincent Gallo
The House of the Spirits '93
Angela '94
Arizona Dream '94

Don Galloway
Rough Night in Jericho '67
Snowblind '78
Demon Rage '82
Two Moon Junction '88

Rita Gam
The Thief '52
Mohawk '56
The King of Kings '61
Klute '71
Seeds of Evil '76
Distortions '87
Midnight '89

Michael Gambon
Turtle Diary '86
Forbidden Passion: The Oscar Wilde Movie '87
Missing Link '88
The Rachel Papers '89
The Cook, the Thief, His Wife & Her Lover '90
The Heat of the Day '91
Mobsters '91
Toys '92
The Browning Version '94
Clean Slate '94
A Man of No Importance '94
Squanto: A Warrior's Tale '94
Mary Reilly '95

Robin Gammell
Full Circle '77
Panic in Echo Park '77
Missing Pieces '83
Project X '87
Gore Vidal's Lincoln '88
Guilty by Suspicion '91
Sinatra '92

James Gammon
Deadly Encounter '72
Ballad of Gregorio Cortez '83
Hard Traveling '85
Ironweed '87
Gore Vidal's Lincoln '88
The Milagro Beanfield War '88
Major League '89
Roe vs. Wade '89
Coupe de Ville '90
I Love You to Death '90
Revenge '90
Crisscross '92
Leaving Normal '92
The Adventures of Huck Finn '93
Running Cool '93
Cabin Boy '94
Hard Vice '94
Major League 2 '94
Larry McMurtry's Streets of Laredo '95
Truman '95
Wild Bill '95

Ken Gampu
Dingaka '65
The Naked Prey '66
African Rage '78
Soul Patrol '80
Kill and Kill Again '81
Chain Gang Killings '85
Scavengers '87
American Ninja 4: The Annihilation '91
Enemy Unseen '91

James Gandolfini
Money for Nothing '93
True Romance '93
Angie '94
Terminal Velocity '94
Crimson Tide '95
Get Shorty '95
The Juror '96

Tony Ganios
Continental Divide '81
Porky's '82
Porky's 2: The Next Day '83
Porky's Revenge '85

Richard Gant
The Freshman '90
Jason Goes to Hell: The Final Friday '93

Paul Ganus
Crash and Burn '90
The Silencer '92

Bruno Ganz
Black and White as Day and Night '63
The American Friend '77
Knife in the Head '78
In the White City '83
Wings of Desire '88
Strapless '90
Children of Nature '91
The Last Days of Chez Nous '92
Faraway, So Close! '93

Yehoram Gaon
Operation Thunderbolt '77
Dead End Street '83

Kaz Garas
The Last Safari '67
Final Mission '84
Naked Vengeance '85
Fast Gun '93
Puppet Master 5: The Final Chapter '94

Matthew Garber
The Three Lives of Thomasina '63
The Gnome-Mobile '67

Terri Garber
North and South Book 1 '85
North and South Book 2 '86

Victor Garber
Life with Mikey '93
Sleepless in Seattle '93
Exotica '94

Greta Garbo
The Atonement of Gosta Berling '24
Joyless Street '25
The Flesh and the Devil '27
The Mysterious Lady '28
Wild Orchids '28
A Woman of Affairs '28
The Kiss '29
The Single Standard '29
Anna Christie '30
Romance '30
Susan Lenox: Her Fall and Rise '31
As You Desire Me '32
Grand Hotel '32
Mata Hari '32
Queen Christina '33

Garbo ▶cont.

The Painted Veil '34
Anna Karenina '35
Camille '36
Conquest '37
Ninotchka '39
Two-Faced Woman '41
The Love Goddesses '65

Mauricio Garces
The Living Head '59
The Brainiac '61

Andy Garcia
Blue Skies Again '83
A Night in Heaven '83
8 Million Ways to Die '85
Mean Season '85
The Untouchables '87
American Roulette '88
Blood Money: The Story of Clinton and Nadine '88
Stand and Deliver '88
Black Rain '89
The Godfather, Part 3 '90
Internal Affairs '90
A Show of Force '90
Dead Again '91
Hero '92
Jennifer 8 '92
When a Man Loves a Woman '94
Steal Big, Steal Little '95
Things to Do In Denver When You're Dead '95

Darnell Garcia
Blind Rage '78
Enforcer from Death Row '78

Eddie Garcia
Beast of the Yellow Night '70
Woman Hunt '72

Nicole Garcia
Le Cavaleur '78
Mon Oncle D'Amerique '80
Bolero '82
Corrupt '84
Peril '85
Overseas: Three Women with Man Trouble '90

Ginette Garcin
Cousin, Cousine '76
Charles et Lucie '79

Henri Garcin
Someone Behind the Door '71
The Eighth Day '95

Vincent Gardenia
The Hustler '61
Parrish '61
Jenny '70
Where's Poppa? '70
Cold Turkey '71
Little Murders '71
Bang the Drum Slowly '73
Death Wish '74
The Front Page '74
Lucky Luciano '74
Greased Lightning '77
Home Movies '79
Marciano '79
The Last Flight of Noah's Ark '80
Death Wish 2 '82
Kennedy '83
Brass '85
Movers and Shakers '85
Little Shop of Horrors '86
The Odd Squad '86
Moonstruck '87
Age Old Friends '89
Skin Deep '89
The Super '91
Tragedy of Flight 103: The Inside Story '91

Reginald Gardiner
Born to Dance '36
A Damsel in Distress '37
Everybody Sing '38
Marie Antoinette '38
The Flying Deuces '39
Doctor Takes a Wife '40
The Great Dictator '40
The Man Who Came to Dinner '41
Sundown '41
A Yank in the R.A.F. '41
Captains of the Clouds '42
Immortal Sergeant '43
Sweet Rosie O'Grady '43
Christmas in Connecticut '45
The Dolly Sisters '45
The Horn Blows at Midnight '45
The Halls of Montezuma '50
Birds & the Bees '56
Mr. Hobbs Takes a Vacation '62

Arthur Gardner
Assassin of Youth '35
Mystic Circle Murder '39

Ava Gardner
Reunion in France '42
Whistle Stop '46
The Hucksters '47
Singapore '47
One Touch of Venus '48
East Side, West Side '49
My Forbidden Past '51
Pandora and the Flying Dutchman '51
Show Boat '51
Lone Star '52
The Snows of Kilimanjaro '52
Knights of the Round Table '53
Mogambo '53
The Barefoot Contessa '54
Bhowani Junction '56
The Naked Maja '59
On the Beach '59
55 Days at Peking '63
The Night of the Iguana '64
Seven Days in May '64
The Bible...In the Beginning '66
Mayerling '68
Life & Times of Judge Roy Bean '72
Earthquake '74
Permission To Kill '75
The Cassandra Crossing '76
The Sentinel '76
City on Fire '78
The Kidnapping of the President '80
Regina '83
Harem '86
The Long, Hot Summer '86

Joan Gardner
Wedding Rehearsal '32
Private Life of Don Juan '34
The Scarlet Pimpernel '34
Dark Journey '37
The Man Who Could Work Miracles '37

Allen (Goorwitz) Garfield
Greetings '68
Hi, Mom! '70
The Owl and the Pussycat '70
Cry Uncle '71
The Candidate '72
Slither '73
Busting '74
The Conversation '74
Nashville '75
Paco '75
Mother, Jugs and Speed '76
The Virginia Hill Story '76
Skateboard '77
Brink's Job '78
Fyre '78
Sketches of a Strangler '78
One Trick Pony '80
The Stunt Man '80
Continental Divide '81
Leave 'Em Laughing '81
State of Things '82
Get Crazy '83
The Cotton Club '84
Irreconcilable Differences '84
Desert Bloom '86
Beverly Hills Cop 2 '87
Let It Ride '89
Night Visitor '89
Club Fed '90
Family Prayers '91
Jack and His Friends '92
Destiny Turns on the Radio '95
Diabolique '96

John Garfield
Four Daughters '38
Juarez '39
They Made Me a Criminal '39
The Sea Wolf '41
Tortilla Flat '42
Air Force '43
Destination Tokyo '43
The Fallen Sparrow '43
Thank Your Lucky Stars '43
Hollywood Canteen '44
Humoresque '46
The Postman Always Rings Twice '46
Body and Soul '47
Gentleman's Agreement '47
Force of Evil '49

John David Garfield
Savage Intruder '68
The Swimmer '68
MacKenna's Gold '69
That Cold Day in the Park '69
The Stepmother '71
Golden Voyage of Sinbad '73
The Other Side of the Mountain '75
White Line Fever '75

Art Garfunkel
Catch-22 '70
Carnal Knowledge '71
Short Fuse '88
Mother Goose Rock 'n' Rhyme '90
Boxing Helena '93

Edward Gargan
Belle of the Nineties '34
Hands Across the Table '35
The Saint Strikes Back '39

William Gargan
The Animal Kingdom '32
Rain '32
Aggie Appleby, Maker of Men '33
Milky Way '36
You Only Live Once '37
Devil's Party '38
Broadway Serenade '39
They Knew What They Wanted '40
Cheers for Miss Bishop '41
I Wake Up Screaming '41
Miss Annie Rooney '42
Who Done It? '42
The Canterville Ghost '44
Till the End of Time '46
Dynamite '49

Gianni "John" Garko
Kapo '59
The Mongols '60
The Avenger '62
Five for Hell '67
Saul and David '68
Gunslinger '70s
Stranger's Gold '71
Waterloo '71
The Psychic '78

Beverly Garland
D.O.A. '49
The Go-Getter '54
Swamp Women '55
The Gunslinger '56
It Conquered the World '56
Gunfight at Sandoval '59
Pretty Poison '68
The Voyage of the Yes '72
Where the Red Fern Grows '74
Roller Boogie '79
It's My Turn '80
Gamble on Love '86
The World's Oldest Living Bridesmaid '92
Haunted Symphony '94

Judy Garland
Broadway Melody of 1938 '37
Thoroughbreds Don't Cry '37
Everybody Sing '38
Listen, Darling '38
Love Finds Andy Hardy '38
Babes in Arms '39
The Wizard of Oz '39
Andy Hardy Meets Debutante '40
Little Nellie Kelly '40
Strike Up the Band '40
Babes on Broadway '41
Life Begins for Andy Hardy '41
Ziegfeld Girl '41
For Me and My Gal '42
Girl Crazy '43
Presenting Lily Mars '43
Thousands Cheer '43
Meet Me in St. Louis '44
Strictly G.I. '44
The Clock '45
The Harvey Girls '46
Till the Clouds Roll By '46
Till the Clouds Roll By/A Star Is Born '46
Ziegfeld Follies '46
Easter Parade '48
The Pirate '48
Words and Music '48
In the Good Old Summertime '49
Summer Stock '50
A Star is Born '54
Judgment at Nuremberg '61
A Child is Waiting '63
I Could Go on Singing '63
That's Entertainment '74
Hollywood Outtakes & Rare Footage '83

Richard Garland
The Undead '57
Panic in the Year Zero! '62

Lee Garlington
The Seventh Sign '88
Cold Sassy Tree '89
A Killing in a Small Town '90
My Life '93
Reflections in the Dark '94
The Babysitter '95

James Garner
Maverick: The Collector's Edition '50s
Sayonara '57
Darby's Rangers '58
Up Periscope '59
Cash McCall '60
The Children's Hour '61
Boys' Night Out '62
The Great Escape '63
The Thrill of It All! '63
The Wheeler Dealers '63
The Americanization of Emily '64
Duel at Diablo '66
Grand Prix '66
Hour of the Gun '67
How Sweet It Is! '68
Marlowe '69
Support Your Local Sheriff '69
A Man Called Sledge '71
Skin Game '71
Support Your Local Gunfighter '71
They Only Kill Their Masters '72
One Little Indian '73
The Castaway Cowboy '74
The Rockford Files: Backlash of the Hunter '74
The Fan '81
Victor/Victoria '82
Tank '83
The Glitter Dome '84
Murphy's Romance '85
Sunset '88
Decoration Day '90
The Distinguished Gentleman '92
Barbarians at the Gate '93
Fire in the Sky '93
Breathing Lessons '94
Maverick '94
Larry McMurtry's Streets of Laredo '95

Peggy Ann Garner
Jane Eyre '44
The Keys of the Kingdom '44
A Tree Grows in Brooklyn '45
The Big Cat '49
The Lovable Cheat '49
Eight Witnesses '54
The Cat '66
Betrayal '78
A Wedding '78

Gale Garnett
The Children '80
Mr. & Mrs. Bridge '90
32 Short Films about Glenn Gould '93

Janeane Garofalo
Bye Bye, Love '94
Coldblooded '94
Reality Bites '94
The Cable Guy '96
Kids In the Hall Brain Candy '96
The Truth About Cats and Dogs '96

Teri Garr
Pajama Party '64
Head '68
The Conversation '74
Young Frankenstein '74
Close Encounters of the Third Kind '77
Oh, God! '77
Once Upon a Brothers Grimm '77
The Black Stallion '79
Mr. Mike's Mondo Video '79
Witches' Brew '79
Honky Tonk Freeway '81
The Escape Artist '82
One from the Heart '82
Prime Suspect '82
Tootsie '82
The Black Stallion Returns '83
Mr. Mom '83
The Sting 2 '83
The Tale of the Frog Prince '83
First Born '84
To Catch a King '84
After Hours '85
The History of White People in America '85
Steve Martin Live '85
Miracles '86
Full Moon in Blue Water '88
Let It Ride '89
Out Cold '89
Mother Goose Rock 'n' Rhyme '90
A Perfect Little Murder '90
Short Time '90
Waiting for the Light '90
Mom and Dad Save the World '92
Dumb & Dumber '94
Perfect Alibi '94
Ready to Wear '94

Martin Garralaga
Boots of Destiny '37
In Old New Mexico '45
South of Monterey '47
Susanna Pass '49
The Fighter '52

Ivo Garrani
The Day the Sky Exploded '57
Black Sunday '60
The Giant of Marathon '60
Great Leaders of the Bibles '70s
Waterloo '71
Street People '76

Maurice Garrel
La Discrete '90
Un Coeur en Hiver '93

Betty Garrett
Words and Music '48
Neptune's Daughter '49
On the Town '49
Take Me Out to the Ball Game '49
My Sister Eileen '55

Eliza Garrett
Schlock '73
Terraces '77
Love Is a Gun '94

Hank Garrett
The Boys Next Door '85
Rosebud Beach Hotel '85
Blood Frenzy '87

Leif Garrett
Kid Vengeance '75
Peter Lundy and the Medicine Hat Stallion '77
Skateboard '77
Walking Tall: The Final Chapter '77
The Outsiders '83
Shaker Run '85
Thunder Alley '85
Cheerleader Camp '88
Party Line '88
The Banker '89
Spirit of '76 '91
The Whispering '94

Patsy Garrett
Benji '74
For the Love of Benji '77
Dennis the Menace: Dinosaur Hunter '93

Roger Garrett
The Passing of Evil '70
Night of the Cobra Woman '72

Barbara Garrick
Armistead Maupin's Tales of the City '93
The Firm '93
Sleepless in Seattle '93
Miami Rhapsody '95

John Garrick
Song O' My Heart '29
Lottery Bride '30
Broken Melody '34
Lily of Killarney '34

David Garrison
On the Town '91
Homeboys '92

Riccardo Garrone
Two Nights with Cleopatra '54
Terror Creatures from the Grave '66

Greer Garson
Goodbye, Mr. Chips '39
Pride and Prejudice '40
Blossoms in the Dust '41
When Ladies Meet '41
Mrs. Miniver '42
Random Harvest '42
Madame Curie '43
Mrs. Parkington '44
Adventure '45
The Valley of Decision '45
Julia Misbehaves '48
The Miniver Story '50
That Forsyte Woman '50
Julius Caesar '53
Sunrise at Campobello '60
Invincible Mr. Disraeli '63
The Singing Nun '66
The Happiest Millionaire '67
Little Women '78

Jennie Garth
Beverly Hills 90210 '90
Beverly Hills 90210: The Graduation '93
Danielle Steel's Star '93

Christopher Gartin
No Big Deal '83
Matters of the Heart '90
Danielle Steel's Changes '91
Tremors 2: Aftershocks '96

Steve Garvey
Bloodfist 6: Ground Zero '94
The Scout '94
Ice Cream Man '95

Elizabeth Garvie
Pride and Prejudice '85
Diana: Her True Story '93

John Garwood
Hell's Angels on Wheels '67
A Taste of Hell '73

Lorraine Gary
Pray for the Wildcats '74
Jaws '75
The Crash of Flight 401 '78
Jaws 2 '78
1941 '79
Jaws: The Revenge '87

Alessandro Gassman
Sacrilege '86
A Month by the Lake '95

Vittorio Gassman
Bitter Rice '49
Lure of the Sila '49
Anna '51
Rhapsody '54
Mambo '55
War and Peace '56
Big Deal on Madonna Street '58
The Great War '59
The Easy Life '63
Il Sorpasso '63
Tiger and the Pussycat '67
Woman Times Seven '67
Catch as Catch Can '68
12 Plus 1 '70
The Scent of a Woman '75
We All Loved Each Other So Much '77
A Wedding '78
Quintet '79
Immortal Bachelor '80
Sharky's Machine '81
The Tempest '82
The Family '87
The Sleazy Uncle '89
The Palermo Connection '91
Abraham '94

Lisa Gastoni
The Baby and the Battleship '56
RoGoPaG '62
The Great Armored Car Swindle '64
Messalina vs. the Son of Hercules '64
Wild, Wild Planet '65
Submission '77
Tharus Son of Attila '87

Larry Gates
Above and Beyond '53
Francis Covers the Big Town '53
Underworld, U.S.A. '60
The Hoodlum Priest '61
Toys in the Attic '63
The Sand Pebbles '66
Death of a Gunfighter '69
Funny Lady '75
The Henderson Monster '80

Nancy Gates
The Great Gildersleeve '43
Master Race '44
Nevada '44
Check Your Guns '48
The Atomic City '52
Torch Song '53
Suddenly '54
The Search for Bridey Murphy '56
Some Came Running '58

Marjorie Gateson
Goin' to Town '35
Arizona Mahoney '36

John Gatins
Witchboard 2: The Devil's Doorway '93
Leprechaun 3 '95

Jill Gatsby
Return to Salem's Lot '87
The Ambulance '90

Jennifer Gatti
Double Exposure '93
Street Knight '93

Valerie Gaunt
The Curse of Frankenstein '57
The Horror of Dracula '58

Mikkel Gaup
Pathfinder '87
Breaking the Waves '95

Dan Gauthier
Teen Witch '89
Shame '92
Son-in-Law '93
Excessive Force 2: Force on Force '95
Illegal in Blue '95

Dick Gautier
Divorce American Style '67
Marathon '80
Glitch! '88
Get Smart, Again! '89

John Gavin
A Time to Love & a Time to Die '58
Imitation of Life '59
Breath of Scandal '60
Midnight Lace '60
Psycho '60
Spartacus '60
Back Street '61
Thoroughly Modern Millie '67
The Madwoman of Chaillot '69
Murder for Sale '70
Jennifer '78
Sophia Loren: Her Own Story '80
History of the World: Part 1 '81
House of Shadows '83

Cassandra Gaviola
The Black Room '82
Conan the Barbarian '82

William Gaxton
It's the Old Army Game '26
Best Foot Forward '43
The Heat's On '43

Gregory Gay
The Secret Code '42
Seven Doors to Death '44

Ramon Gay
The Curse of the Aztec Mummy '59
Curse of the Aztec Mummy/Robot vs. the Aztec Mummy '59
The Robot vs. the Aztec Mummy '59

Howard Gaye
Flirting with Fate '16
Dante's Inferno '24

Lisa Gaye
Shake, Rattle and Rock '57
The Sign of Zorro '60
Night of Evil '62
Castle of Evil '66
The Toxic Avenger, Part 3: The Last Temptation of Toxie '89
Class of Nuke 'Em High 2: Subhumanoid Meltdown '91
Class of Nuke 'Em High 3: The Good, the Bad and the Subhumanoid '94

Jackie Gayle
Pepper and His Wacky Taxi '72
Tin Men '87
Plain Clothes '88
Bert Rigby, You're a Fool '89
Mr. Saturday Night '92

Monica Gayle
Switchblade Sisters '75
Nashville Girl '76

Mitch Gaylord
American Anthem '86
American Tiger '89
Animal Instincts '92

George Gaynes
Breaking Up Is Hard to Do '79
Dead Men Don't Wear Plaid '82
Tootsie '82
It Came Upon a Midnight Clear '84
Micki & Maude '84
Police Academy '84
Police Academy 2: Their First Assignment '85
Police Academy 3: Back in Training '86
Police Academy 4: Citizens on Patrol '87
Police Academy 5: Assignment Miami Beach '88
Police Academy 6: City Under Siege '89
Stepmonster '92
Police Academy: Mission to Moscow '94
Vanya on 42nd Street '94

Janet Gaynor
Sunrise '27
The Farmer Takes a Wife '35
A Star is Born '37
The Young in Heart '38
Till the Clouds Roll By/A Star Is Born '46

Mitzi Gaynor
We're Not Married '52
There's No Business Like Show Business '54
Birds & the Bees '56
Les Girls '57
South Pacific '58
For Love or Money '63

Eunice Gayson
Carry On Admiral '57
The Revenge of Frankenstein '58
Dr. No '62
From Russia with Love '63

Wendy Gazelle
Hot Pursuit '87
Sammy & Rosie Get Laid '87
Understudy: The Graveyard Shift 2 '88
Triumph of the Spirit '89
The Net '95

Ben Gazzara
Anatomy of a Murder '59
Passionate Thief '60
The Bridge at Remagen '69
Shattered Silence '71
Fireball Forward '72
Pursuit '72
Neptune Factor '73
QB VII '74
Sicilian Connection '74
The Death of Richie '76
High Velocity '76
The Killing of a Chinese Bookie '76
Voyage of the Damned '76
Opening Night '77
The Trial of Lee Harvey Oswald '77
Saint Jack '79
Sidney Sheldon's Bloodline '79
Question of Honor '80
They All Laughed '81
Tales of Ordinary Madness '83
An Early Frost '85
Control '87
Quicker Than the Eye '88
Secret Obsession '88
Road House '89
Lies Before Kisses '92
Blindsided '93
Parallel Lives '94
Convict Cowboy '95
The Dogfighters '95

Michael V. Gazzo
The Godfather, Part 2 '74
Black Sunday '77
Fingers '78
King of the Gypsies '78
Gangsters '79
Love and Bullets '79
Kill Castro '80
The Mercenaries '80
The Godfather 1902-1959: The Complete Epic '81
Cookie '89

Anthony Geary
The Imposter '84
Kicks '85
Dangerous Love '87
Penitentiary 3 '87
Pass the Ammo '88
You Can't Hurry Love '88
Crack House '89
UHF '89
High Desert Kill '90
Night of the Warrior '91
Scorchers '92

Bud Geary
D-Day on Mars '45
The Topeka Terror '45

Cynthia Geary
8 Seconds '94
To Grandmother's House We Go '94

Jason Gedrick
The Heavenly Kid '85
Massive Retaliation '85
The Zoo Gang '85
Iron Eagle '86
Stacking '87
Promised Land '88
Rooftops '89
Backdraft '91
Crossing the Bridge '92
Still Life '92
The Force '94

Prunella Gee
The Wilby Conspiracy '75
Never Say Never Again '83
Witching Time '84

Ellen Geer
Harold and Maude '71
Silence '73
Memory of Us '74
Babe! '75
A Shining Season '79
Bloody Birthday '80
Hard Traveling '85

Will Geer
Lust for Gold '49
Broken Arrow '50
Comanche Territory '50
To Please a Lady '50
Winchester '73 '50
Salt of the Earth '54
Black Like Me '64
The President's Analyst '67
Bandolero! '68
The Reivers '69
Brother John '70
Dear Dead Delilah '72
Jeremiah Johnson '72
Napoleon and Samantha '72
Executive Action '73
Silence '73
The Waltons: A Thanksgiving Story '73
The Hanged Man '74
Hurricane '74
Memory of Us '74
Moving Violation '76
The Billion Dollar Hobo '78
My Sister, My Love '78
A Woman Called Moses '78
Unknown Powers '80
Bunco '83

Judy Geeson
Berserk! '67
To Sir, with Love '67
The Executioner '70
It Happened at Nightmare Inn '70
Twinsanity '70
10 Rillington Place '71
Doomwatch '72
Dynasty of Fear '72
Murder on the Midnight Express '74
Poldark '75
Poldark 2 '75
Adventures of a Taxi Driver '76
Carry On England '76
Horror Planet '80
Danger UXB '81

Sally Geeson
The Oblong Box '69
What's Good for the Goose '69
Cry of the Banshee '70

Martha Gehman
The Flamingo Kid '84
F/X '86
Father of the Bride '91
A Kiss Before Dying '91
Threesome '94
Unveiled '94

Bob Geldof
Pink Floyd: The Wall '82
The Secret Policeman's Other Ball '82

Daniel Gelin
La Ronde '51
The Man Who Knew Too Much '56
A Woman of Rome '56
Mademoiselle Striptease '57
The Testament of Orpheus '59
Is Paris Burning? '68
Murmur of the Heart '71
Life Is a Long Quiet River '88
Iran: Days of Crisis '91

Larry Gelman
Chatterbox '76
Slumber Party '57 '76

Grant Gelt
Avalon '90
Mutant Species '95

Giuliano Gemma
Goliath and the Sins of Babylon '64
Erik, the Viking '72
Master Touch '74
Smugglers '75
Battleforce '78
Corleone '79
The Warning '80
Unsane '82
Blood at Sundown '88

Laura Gemser
Emmanuelle, the Queen '75
Emmanuelle on Taboo Island '76
Love Camp '76
Crime Busters '78
Emmanuelle in the Country '78
Naked Paradise '78
Emmanuelle's Daughter '79
Fury '80s
Ator the Fighting Eagle '83
Black Cobra '83
Caged Women '84
Women's Prison Massacre '85

Francois-Eric Gendron
Cloud Waltzing '87
Boyfriends & Girlfriends '88

Bryan Genesse
Loose Screws '85
California Casanova '89
Night Siege Project: Shadowchaser 2 '94
Live Wire: Human Timebomb '95
Terminal Impact '95

Leo Genn
When Thief Meets Thief '37
Henry V '44
Green for Danger '47
The Snake Pit '48
Velvet Touch '48
The Miniver Story '50
Wooden Horse '50
Lady Chatterley's Lover '55
Moby Dick '56
The Longest Day '62
Circus of Fear '67

Genn ▶cont.

Strange Case of Dr. Jekyll & Mr. Hyde '68
Mackintosh Man '73

Minnie Gentry
Georgia, Georgia '72
Def by Temptation '90

Roger Gentry
Horrors of the Red Planet '64
Alien Massacre '67

Paul Geoffrey
Excalibur '81
Flame to the Phoenix '85

Stephen Geoffreys
Fraternity Vacation '85
Fright Night '85
The Chair '87
976-EVIL '88
Moon 44 '90

Chief Dan George
Little Big Man '70
Cancel My Reservation '72
Dan Candy's Law '73
The Bears & I '74
Harry and Tonto '74
The Outlaw Josey Wales '76
Americathon '79

Christopher George
El Dorado '67
Chisum '70
Man on a String '71
Train Robbers '73
Dixie Dynamite '76
Grizzly '76
Midway '76
Day of the Animals '77
Whiskey Mountain '77
Cruise into Terror '78
Exterminator '80
AngKor: Cambodia Express '81
Enter the Ninja '81
Graduation Day '81
Mortuary '81
Gates of Hell '83
Pieces '83

Gladys George
Madame X '37
Marie Antoinette '38
The Roaring Twenties '39
House Across the Bay '40
The Maltese Falcon '41
The Best Years of Our Lives '46
Flamingo Road '49
Detective Story '51
Lullaby of Broadway '51

Heinrich George
Jud Suess '40
Kolberg '45

Lynda Day George
The Barbary Coast '74
Panic on the 5:22 '74
Aliens from Spaceship Earth '77
Ants '77
Day of the Animals '77
Roots '77
Cruise into Terror '78
Racquet '79
Beyond Evil '80
Casino '80
Mortuary '81
The Junkman '82
Pieces '83
Young Warriors '83

Maude George
Foolish Wives '22
The Wedding March '28

Rita George
Hollywood Boulevard '76
On the Run '85

Susan George
Lola '69
The Looking Glass War '69
Sudden Terror '70
Fright '71
Straw Dogs '72
Die Screaming, Marianne '73
Dr. Jekyll and Mr. Hyde '73
Sonny and Jed '73
Dirty Mary Crazy Larry '74
Mandingo '75
Mission: Monte Carlo '75
Out of Season '75
A Small Town in Texas '76
Tomorrow Never Comes '77
Tintorera...Tiger Shark '78
Enter the Ninja '81
House Where Evil Dwells '82
Kiss My Grits '82
Venom '82
Pajama Tops '83
The Jigsaw Man '84
Lightning: The White Stallion '86
Jack the Ripper '88
That Summer of White Roses '90

Olga Georges-Picot
Honor Among Thieves '68
The Man Who Haunted Himself '70
The Day of the Jackal '73
The Graveyard '74
Children of Rage '75

Tom Georgeson
No Surrender '86
A Fish Called Wanda '88

Carmelita Geraghty
My Lady of Whims '25
Rogue of the Rio Grande '30
Night Life in Reno '31
Flaming Signal '33

Marita Geraghty
Groundhog Day '93
Past Tense '94

Danny Gerard
Drop-Out Mother '88
Desperate Hours '90
Robot in the Family '94

Gil Gerard
Hooch '76
Killing Stone '78
Buck Rogers in the 25th Century '79
Help Wanted: Male '82
For Love or Money '84
Fury to Freedom: The Life Story of Raul Ries '85
Final Notice '89
Soldier's Fortune '91

Steve Geray
Inspector Hornleigh '39
The Moon and Sixpence '43
In Society '44
The Seventh Cross '44
Blondie Knows Best '46
Gilda '46
Ladies of the Chorus '49
Affair in Trinidad '52
The Big Sky '52
Tobor the Great '54
Jesse James Meets Frankenstein's Daughter '65

Richard Gere
Report to the Commissioner '74
Strike Force '75
Looking for Mr. Goodbar '77
Bloodbrothers '78
Days of Heaven '78
American Gigolo '79
Yanks '79
An Officer and a Gentleman '82
Beyond the Limit '83
Breathless '83
The Cotton Club '84
King David '85
No Mercy '86
Power '86
Miles from Home '88
Internal Affairs '90
Pretty Woman '90
Rhapsody in August '91
Final Analysis '92
Intersection '93
Mr. Jones '93
Sommersby '93
First Knight '95
Primal Fear '96

Georges Geret
Diary of a Chambermaid '64
A Very Curious Girl '69
Z '69

Gaia Germani
Your Turn Darling '63
Castle of the Living Dead '64

Greg Germann
Once Around '91
The Night We Never Met '93

Charles Gerrard
Down to Earth '17
The Nervous Wreck '26

Daniel Gerroll
84 Charing Cross Road '86
Big Business '88
Drop Dead Fred '91
A Far Off Place '93

Savina Gersak
Iron Warrior '87
Sonny Boy '87
Curse 2: The Bite '88
War Bus Commando '89
Beyond the Door 3 '91
Midnight Ride '92

Gina Gershon
Pretty in Pink '86
Cocktail '88
Red Heat '88
Voodoo Dawn '89
City of Hope '91
The Player '92
Sinatra '92
Joey Breaker '93
Love Matters '93
Flinch '94
Best of the Best 3: No Turning Back '95
Showgirls '95
Bound '96

Jeanne Gerson
She Gods of Shark Reef '56
The Touch of Satan '70

Berta Gersten
A Brivele der Mamen '38
Mirele Efros '38

Frank Gerstle
Gang Busters '55
Submarine Seahawk '59
The Wasp Woman '59
The Atomic Brain '64
Hell on Wheels '67

Valeska Gert
The Threepenny Opera '31
An Occurrence at Owl Creek Bridge/Coup de Grace '62

Jami Gertz
Endless Love '81
Alphabet City '84
Sixteen Candles '84
Mischief '85
Crossroads '86
Quicksilver '86
Solarbabies '86
Less Than Zero '87
The Lost Boys '87
Listen to Me '89
Renegades '89
Don't Tell Her It's Me '90
Sibling Rivalry '90
Silence Like Glass '90
Jersey Girl '92
Twister '96

Balthazar Getty
Lord of the Flies '90
Young Guns 2 '90
December '91
My Heroes Have Always Been Cowboys '91
The Pope Must Diet '91
Where the Day Takes You '92
Dead Beat '94
Don't Do It '94
Red Hot '95
White Squall '96

Estelle Getty
Tootsie '82
Mask '85
Mannequin '87
Stop! or My Mom Will Shoot '92

John Getz
Kent State '81
Tattoo '81
Concrete Beat '84
Thief of Hearts '84
Blood Simple '85
The Fly '86
Born on the Fourth of July '89
The Fly 2 '89
Curly Sue '91
Don't Tell Mom the Babysitter's Dead '91
A Passion to Kill '94
Playmaker '94
The Late Shift '96

Alice Ghostley
New Faces of 1952 '54
To Kill a Mockingbird '62
The Graduate '67
With Six You Get Eggroll '68
Gator '76
Blue Sunshine '78
Not for Publication '84

Louis Giambalvo
The Ambush Murders '82
The Devlin Connection '82
The Jagged Edge '85
Weekend at Bernie's '89
Dead to Rights '93
Fade to Black '93
Question of Faith '93
Illegal in Blue '95

Joseph Gian
Night Stalker '87
Blackout '88
Mad About You '90

Rick Gianasi
Mutant Hunt '87
Robot Holocaust '87
Escape from Safehaven '88
Maximum Thrust '88
The Occultist '89
Posed For Murder '89

Giancarlo Giannini
Seduction of Mimi '72
Love and Anarchy '73
La Grande Bourgeoise '74
The Sensual Man '74
Swept Away... '75
How Funny Can Sex Be? '76
The Innocent '76
Seven Beauties '76
A Night Full of Rain '78
Blood Feud '79
Life Is Beautiful '79
Immortal Bachelor '80
Lovers and Liars '81
American Dreamer '84
Where's Piccone '84
Fever Pitch '85
Saving Grace '86
Bellissimo: Images of the Italian Cinema '87
Blood Red '88
Goodnight, Michelangelo '89
New York Stories '89
The Sleazy Uncle '89
Time to Kill '89
Once Upon a Crime '92
Jacob '94
A Walk in the Clouds '95

Cynthia Gibb
Stardust Memories '80
Modern Girls '86
Salvador '86
Youngblood '86
Jack's Back '87
Malone '87
Short Circuit 2 '88
Death Warrant '90
Gypsy '93

Donald Gibb
Bloodsport '88
Magic Kid 2 '94
Revenge of the Nerds 4: Nerds in Love '94

Robyn Gibbes
Gone to Ground '76
Wild Horses '82

Marla Gibbs
Up Against the Wall '91
The Meteor Man '93
Lily in Winter '94

Timothy Gibbs
The Kindred '87
Witchboard 2: The Devil's Doorway '93

Rebecca Gibney
Among the Cinders '83
Jigsaw '90

Henry Gibson
Kiss Me, Stupid! '64
The Outlaws is Coming! '65
The Long Goodbye '73
Nashville '75
Kentucky Fried Movie '77
The Blues Brothers '80
For the Love of It '80
The Incredible Shrinking Woman '81
Tulips '81
Brenda Starr '86
Monster in the Closet '86
Innerspace '87
Long Gone '87
Switching Channels '88
Around the World in 80 Days '89
Night Visitor '89
Tune in Tomorrow '90
Color of a Brisk and Leaping Day '95
Bio-Dome '96

Hoot Gibson
Straight Shootin' '17
Wild Engine/Mistaken Orders '23
The Phantom Bullet '26
The Prairie King '27
King of the Rodeo '28
Courtin' Wildcats '29
The Concentratin' Kid '30
Roaring Ranch '30
Spurs '30
Trailing Trouble '30
Trigger Tricks '30
Clearing the Range '31
Hard Hombre '31
Wild Horse '31
Boiling Point '32
Dude Bandit '32
Local Badman '32
Man's Land '32
Spirit of the West '32
Cowboy Counselor '33
Feud of the West '35
Fighting Parson '35
Frontier Justice '35
Powdersmoke Range '35
Rainbow's End '35
Sunset Range '35
Cavalcade of the West '36
Last Outlaw '36
Lucky Terror '36
The Riding Avenger '36
Swifty '36
The Painted Stallion '37
The Law Rides Again '43
Arizona Whirlwind '44
Death Valley Rangers '44
Marked Trails '44
Outlaw Trail '44
Sonora Stagecoach '44
The Marshal's Daughter '53
The Horse Soldiers '59

Margaret Gibson
Never a Dull Moment '50
Last Days of Frank & Jesse James '86

Mel Gibson
Summer City '77
Tim '79
Mad Max '80
Gallipoli '81
The Road Warrior '82
The Year of Living Dangerously '82
Attack Force Z '84
The Bounty '84
Mrs. Soffel '84
The River '84
Mad Max: Beyond Thunderdome '85
Lethal Weapon '87
Tequila Sunrise '88
Lethal Weapon 2 '89
Air America '90
Bird on a Wire '90
Hamlet '90
Forever Young '92
Lethal Weapon 3 '92
The Man Without a Face '93
Maverick '94
Braveheart '95

Mimi Gibson
Courage of Black Beauty '57
The Monster That Challenged the World '57

Thomas Gibson
Far and Away '92
Armistead Maupin's Tales of the City '93
Love and Human Remains '93
Barcelona '94
Sleep with Me '94

Virginia Gibson
Tea for Two '50
Athena '54
Seven Brides for Seven Brothers '54

Wynne Gibson
Night After Night '32
Aggie Appleby, Maker of Men '33
Motorcycle Squad '37

Bond Gideon
Storyville '74
Gold of the Amazon Women '79
Stepsisters '85

Pamela Gidley
Thrashin' '86
Blue Iguana '88
Permanent Record '88
Disturbed '90
Liebestraum '91
Highway to Hell '92
Cheatin' Hearts '93
Firefall '94
S.F.W. '94
Bad Love '95
The Crew '95

John Gielgud
The Secret Agent '36
Julius Caesar '53
Romeo and Juliet '54
Richard III '55
Saint Joan '57
Becket '64
The Loved One '65
Chimes at Midnight '67
The Charge of the Light Brigade '68
Sebastian '68
The Shoes of the Fisherman '68
Julius Caesar '70
Probe '72
Invitation to the Wedding '73
11 Harrowhouse '74
Murder on the Orient Express '74
QB VII '74
James Joyce: A Portrait of the Artist as a Young Man '77
Providence '77
Les Miserables '78
The Human Factor '79
Murder by Decree '79
Caligula '80
The Conductor '80
The Elephant Man '80
The Formula '80
Arthur '81
Brideshead Revisited '81
Chariots of Fire '81
Lion of the Desert '81
Priest of Love '81
Sphinx '81
Frankenstein '82
Gandhi '82
The Hunchback of Notre Dame '82
Inside the Third Reich '82
The Scarlet & the Black '83
The Wicked Lady '83
Scandalous '84
Plenty '85
The Shooting Party '85
Wagner: The Complete Epic '85
Wagner: The Movie '85
The Whistle Blower '87
Appointment with Death '88
Arthur 2: On the Rocks '88
A Man for All Seasons '88
War & Remembrance, Part 1 '88
Getting It Right '89
Romance on the Orient Express '89
War & Remembrance, Part 2 '89
War & Remembrance: The Final Chapter, Part 8 '89
Strike It Rich '90
Prospero's Books '91
The Power of One '92
Shining Through '92
Scarlett '94
First Knight '95
Gulliver's Travels '95

Stefan Gierasch
Dave '93
Murder in the First '95

Frances Gifford
Border Vigilantes '41
American Empire '42
Our Vines Have Tender Grapes '45
Thrill of a Romance '45
Riding High '50

Gloria Gifford
D.C. Cab '84
Vice Versa '88

Roland Gift
Sammy & Rosie Get Laid '87
Scandal '89

Elaine Giftos
Gas-s-s-s! '70
The Student Nurses '70
The Wrestler '73
Angel '84

Sandro Giglio
The War of the Worlds '53
For the First Time '59

Vincent Gil
Solo '77
Body Melt '93

Billy Gilbert
Laurel & Hardy Comedy Classics, Vol. 2 '30
Laurel & Hardy Comedy Classics, Vol. 1 '33
Laurel & Hardy Comedy Classics, Vol. 3 '34
Laurel & Hardy Comedy Classics, Vol. 6 '35
Kelly the Second '36
The Firefly '37
100 Men and a Girl '37
Toast of New York '37
Block-heads '38
Breaking the Ice '38
Happy Landing '38
Joy of Living '38
Maid's Night Out '38
Peck's Bad Boy with the Circus '38
Destry Rides Again '39
The Great Dictator '40
His Girl Friday '40
No, No Nanette '40
Seven Sinners '40
Tin Pan Alley '40
Melody Master '41
Week-End In Havana '41
Mr. Wise Guy '42
Song of the Islands '42
Valley of the Sun '42
Spotlight Scandals '43
Cooking Up Trouble '44
Ghost Crazy '44

Eugenia Gilbert
Test of Donald Norton '26
Courtin' Wildcats '29

Helen Gilbert
Andy Hardy Gets Spring Fever '39
Death Valley '46
God's Country '46
Girls in Prison '56

John Gilbert
The Busher '19
He Who Gets Slapped '24
The Big Parade '25
The Flesh and the Devil '27
A Woman of Affairs '28
Queen Christina '33

Melissa Gilbert
Little House on the Prairie '74
The Christmas Coal Mine Miracle '77
The Miracle Worker '79
The Snow Queen '83
Family Secrets '84
Sylvester '85
Choices '86
Penalty Phase '86
Blood Vows: The Story of a Mafia Wife '87
Ice House '89
The Lookalike '90
Dying to Remember '93

Sara Gilbert
Sudie & Simpson '90
Poison Ivy '92
Dead Beat '94

Taylor Gilbert
Torment '85
Alone in the T-Shirt Zone '86

Connie Gilchrist
Tortilla Flat '42
Nothing But Trouble '44
A Letter to Three Wives '49
Stars in My Crown '50
Ticket to Tomahawk '50
The Half-Breed '51
Here Comes the Groom '51
Houdini '53
Long John Silver '53
The Misadventures of Merlin Jones '63

Richard Gilden
Lost, Lonely, and Vicious '59
The Black Klansman '66

Sandra Giles
Daddy-O '59
Lost, Lonely, and Vicious '59

Jack Gilford
A Funny Thing Happened on the Way to the Forum '66
Enter Laughing '67
The Incident '67
Catch-22 '70
They Might Be Giants '71
Save the Tiger '73
Harry & Walter Go to New York '76
Max '79
Cheaper to Keep Her '80
Wholly Moses! '80
Caveman '81
Cocoon '85
Arthur 2: On the Rocks '88
Cocoon: The Return '88

Dana Gillespie
The People That Time Forgot '77
Scrubbers '82

Anita Gillette
Ants '77
Marathon '80
Brass '85
Moonstruck '87
Bob Roberts '92
Boys on the Side '94

David Gilliam
Frogs '72
Sharks' Treasure '75
Gunpowder '84

Seth Gilliam
Assault at West Point: The Court-Martial of Johnson Whittaker '94
Jefferson in Paris '94
Courage Under Fire '96

Terry Gilliam
Monty Python's Flying Circus '71
And Now for Something Completely Different '72
Monty Python and the Holy Grail '75
Monty Python's Life of Brian '79
Monty Python Live at the Hollywood Bowl '82
Monty Python's The Meaning of Life '83
Monty Python's Parrot Sketch Not Included '90

Richard Gilliland
Bug '75
A Day for Thanks on Walton's Mountain '82
Challenge of a Lifetime '85
Embassy '85
Acceptable Risks '86
Happy Hour '87
A Killing in a Small Town '90

Linda Gillin
Terror at Red Wolf Inn '72
Windows '80

Rebecca Gilling
The Naked Country '85
The Blue Lightning '86
Heaven Tonight '93

Claude Gillingwater
My Boy '21
Illicit '31
Green Eyes '34

Ann Gillis
The Adventures of Tom Sawyer '38
Peck's Bad Boy with the Circus '38
'Neath Brooklyn Bridge '42
Texas Legionnaires '43
In Society '44
Big Town After Dark '47

James Gillis
Dracula Sucks '79
Night of the Zombies '81
Deranged '87
Alien Space Avenger '91

Margalo Gillmore
Cause for Alarm '51
A Woman's World '54

Kenneth Gilman
Bedroom Eyes '86
Nights in White Satin '87
Scavengers '87

Lowell Gilmore
Days of Glory '43
Johnny Angel '45
Picture of Dorian Gray '45
King Solomon's Mines '50
Lone Star '52
Ma and Pa Kettle at Waikiki '55

Virginia Gilmore
Western Union '41
The Loves of Edgar Allen Poe '42
Orchestra Wives '42

Jack Gilpin
Something Wild '86
Funny Farm '88
Reversal of Fortune '90
Unnatural Pursuits '91
Barcelona '94
White Mile '94

Marc Gilpin
Computer Wizard '77
Where's Willie? '77

Clarence Gilyard, Jr.
Off the Mark '87
Walker: Texas Ranger: One Riot, One Ranger '93
Walker: Texas Ranger: Deadly Reunion '94

Teresa Gimpera
Black Box Affair '66
Feast for the Devil '70s
Crypt of the Living Dead '73
Spirit of the Beehive '73
Macabre '77

Jack Ging
Mosby's Marauders '66
Play Misty for Me '71
Die Sister, Die! '74
Where the Red Fern Grows '74
Dear Detective '78

Hermione Gingold
Butler's Dilemma '43
Tough Guy '53
The Pickwick Papers '54
The Adventures of Sadie '55
Bell, Book and Candle '58
Gigi '58
The Naked Edge '61
The Music Man '62
Promise Her Anything '66
Those Fantastic Flying Fools '67
A Little Night Music '77
Garbo Talks '84
How to Be a Perfect Person in Just Three Days '84

Bob Ginnaven
Hootch Country Boys '75
The Day It Came to Earth '77

Robert Ginty
Coming Home '78
Exterminator '80
The Alchemist '81
The Act '82
White Fire '83
Exterminator 2 '84
Gold Raiders '84
Warrior of the Lost World '84
Mission to Kill '85
Programmed to Kill '86
Codename: Vengeance '87
Three Kinds of Heat '87
Bounty Hunters '89
Loverboy '89
Out on Bail '89
Madhouse '90
Vietnam, Texas '90
Harley Davidson and the Marlboro Man '91
Lady Dragon '92

Rocky Giordani
After Dark, My Sweet '90
Cop and a Half '93

Daniela Giordano
Stranger's Gold '71
The Girl in Room 2A '76
Inquisition '76

Domiziana Giordano
Nouvelle Vague '90
Interview with the Vampire '94

Florence Giorgetti
The Lacemaker '77
Monique '83

Elenora Giorgi
Inferno '78
To Forget Venice '79
Beyond Obsession '82
Nudo di Donna '83
Creepers '85

Cindy Girard
Operation Dames '59
Raising Cain '92

Joseph Girard
Laughing at Danger '24
Tentacles of the North '26
King of the Rodeo '28
Defenders of the Law '31
Hurricane Express '32
The Tonto Kid '35
Aces and Eights '36
Mystery of the Hooded Horseman '37

Michele Girardon
Death in the Garden '56
Devil of the Desert Against the Son of Hercules '62

Annie Girardot
Love and the Frenchwoman '60
Rocco and His Brothers '60
Gypsy '75
Dear Detective '77
Le Cavaleur '78
Jupiter's Thigh '81
Jacko & Lise '82
La Vie Continue '82
Mussolini & I '85
Les Miserables '95

Hippolyte Girardot
Manon of the Spring '87
Love Without Pity '91
Barjo '93
Love After Love '94

Roland Giraud
Three Men and a Cradle '85
Mr. Frost '89

Bernard Giraudeau
Bilitis '77
La Boum '81
Passion of Love '82
The Favorite Son '94

Massimo Girotti
Ossessione '42
Senso '54
Sins of Rome '54
The Giants of Thessaly '60
Teorema '68
Red Tent '69
Torture Chamber of Baron Blood '72
Quo Vadis '85

Jackie Giroux
The Cross & the Switchblade '72
Trick or Treats '82

Annabeth Gish
Desert Bloom '86
Hiding Out '87
Mystic Pizza '88
Shag: The Movie '89
When He's Not a Stranger '89
Coupe de Ville '90
Scarlett '94
Wyatt Earp '94
Nixon '95
Beautiful Girls '96
The Last Supper '96

Dorothy Gish
Griffith Biograph Program '09
Home Sweet Home '14
Judith of Bethulia '14
Hearts of the World '18
Orphans of the Storm '21
Romola '25
The Cardinal '63

Lillian Gish
Griffith Biograph Program '09
Battle of Elderbush Gulch '13
D.W. Griffith Triple Feature '13
Home Sweet Home '14
Judith of Bethulia '14
The Birth of a Nation '15
Intolerance '16
Hearts of the World '18
Broken Blossoms '19

Gish ▶cont.

The Greatest Question '19
True Heart Susie '19
Way Down East '20
Orphans of the Storm '21
The White Sister '23
Romola '25
The Wind '28
His Double Life '33
Commandos Strike at Dawn '43
Duel in the Sun '46
Portrait of Jennie '48
The Cobweb '55
The Night of the Hunter '55
The Unforgiven '60
Great Chase '63
Follow Me, Boys! '66
The Comedians '67
A Wedding '78
Hobson's Choice '83
Hambone & Hillie '84
The Adventures of Huckleberry Finn '85
Sweet Liberty '86
The Whales of August '87

Sheila Gish
A Day in the Death of Joe Egg '71
Highlander '86

Robert Gist
Jigsaw '49
One Minute to Zero '52
Jack the Giant Killer '62

Paul Giusti
Dirty Hands '76
Emmanuelle on Taboo Island '76
L'Anne Sainte '78

Robin Givens
Beverly Hills Madam '86
The Women of Brewster Place '89
A Rage in Harlem '91
Boomerang '92
The Penthouse '92
Blankman '94
Foreign Student '94

George Givot
Hollywood Party '34
Thin Ice '37
DuBarry Was a Lady '43
Leather Burners '43
April In Paris '52
China Gate '57

Paul Michael Glaser
Phobia '80
Wait Till Your Mother Gets Home '83
Jealousy '84
Single Bars, Single Women '84

Ned Glass
Fright '56
Requiem for a Heavyweight '56
The Rebel Set '59
West Side Story '61
Kid Galahad '62
Street Music '81

Ron Glass
The Crash of Flight 401 '78
Deep Space '87
Houseguest '94
It's My Party '95

Isabel Glasser
Forever Young '92
Pure Country '92
Death Ring '93
The Surgeon '94
Circumstances Unknown '95

Bob Glaudini
The Alchemist '81
Chameleon '81
Angel City '84

Louise Glaum
Return of Draw Egan '16
The Three Musketeers '16
The Leopard Woman '20
Sex '20

Eugene Glazer
Dollman '90
The Substitute '93

Jackie Gleason
All Through the Night '42
Orchestra Wives '42
Springtime in the Rockies '42
Tales of Manhattan '42
Honeymooners Hidden Episodes, Vol. 1 '53
The Hustler '61
Papa's Delicate Condition '63
Soldier in the Rain '63
Don't Drink the Water '69
How to Commit Marriage '69
Mr. Billion '77
Smokey and the Bandit '77
Smokey and the Bandit, Part 2 '80
The Toy '82
Mister Halpren & Mister Johnson '83
Smokey and the Bandit, Part 3 '83
The Sting 2 '83
Izzy & Moe '85
Nothing in Common '86

James Gleason
A Free Soul '31
The Crooked Circle '32
Ex-Mrs. Bradford '36
Here Comes Mr. Jordan '41
Meet John Doe '41
Tanks a Million '41
Footlight Serenade '42
Crash Dive '43
Arsenic and Old Lace '44
A Guy Named Joe '44
The Keys of the Kingdom '44
The Clock '45
A Tree Grows in Brooklyn '45
The Bishop's Wife '47
Down to Earth '47
Tycoon '47
The Falcon Takes Over/Strange Bargain '49
Miss Grant Takes Richmond '49
The Jackpot '50
Key to the City '50
Riding High '50
The Yellow Cab Man '50
I'll See You in My Dreams '51
We're Not Married '52
What Price Glory? '52
Forever Female '53
Movie Stuntmen '53
Suddenly '54
The Night of the Hunter '55
Loving You '57
Last Hurrah '58
Man or Gun '58

Joanna Gleason
Heartburn '86
Crimes & Misdemeanors '89
F/X 2: The Deadly Art of Illusion '91
For Richer, For Poorer '92

Pat Gleason
Swing It, Professor '37
I Killed That Man '42
Rogue's Gallery '44
Criminal Court '46

Paul Gleason
Private Duty Nurses '71
Doc Savage '75
He Knows You're Alone '80
Trading Places '83
The Breakfast Club '85
Challenge of a Lifetime '85
The Ewoks: Battle for Endor '85
Forever, Lulu '87
Morgan Stewart's Coming Home '87
Die Hard '88
Ghost Chase '88
Johnny Be Good '88
She's Having a Baby '88
Night Game '89
Fourth Story '90
Miami Blues '90
Rich Girl '91
There Goes My Baby '92
Wild Cactus '92
Boiling Point '93
Maniac Cop 3: Badge of Silence '93
Running Cool '93
Wishman '93
Digital Man '94

Russell Gleason
The Flying Fool '29
All Quiet on the Western Front '30
I Can't Escape '34
Condemned to Live '35

Iain Glen
Fools of Fortune '90
Mountains of the Moon '90
Rosencrantz & Guildenstern Are Dead '90
The Young Americans '93

Roy Glenn
Jungle Drums of Africa '53
Carmen Jones '54

Scott Glenn
The Baby Maker '70
Angels Hard as They Come '71
The Shrieking '73
Nashville '75
Fighting Mad '76
She Came to the Valley '77
Apocalypse Now '79
More American Graffiti '79
Urban Cowboy '80
The Challenge '82
Personal Best '82
The Keep '83
The Right Stuff '83
The River '84
Silverado '85
Wild Geese 2 '85
As Summers Die '86
Man on Fire '87
Off Limits '87
Verne Miller '88
Miss Firecracker '89
The Hunt for Red October '90
Intrigue '90
Backdraft '91
My Heroes Have Always Been Cowboys '91
The Silence of the Lambs '91
Women & Men: In Love There Are No Rules '91
Extreme Justice '93
Shadowhunter '93
Slaughter of the Innocents '93
Night of the Running Man '94
Past Tense '94
The Spy Within '94
Reckless '95
Tall Tale: The Unbelievable Adventures of Pecos Bill '95
Courage Under Fire '96

Sharon Gless
The Crash of Flight 401 '78
Hardhat & Legs '80
Revenge of the Stepford Wives '80
Hobson's Choice '83
The Star Chamber '83
Letting Go '85
Tales of the Unexpected '91

Stacey Glick
Brighton Beach Memoirs '86
Three O'Clock High '87

Brian Glover
An American Werewolf in London '81
The Company of Wolves '85
The McGuffin '85
Kafka '91
Alien 3 '92
Leon the Pig Farmer '93

Bruce Glover
Chrome Hearts '70
Diamonds Are Forever '71
Stunts '77
Ghost Town '88
Killcrazy '89
Hider in the House '90
Warlock: The Armageddon '93
Night of the Scarecrow '95

Crispin Glover
My Tutor '82
Friday the 13th, Part 4: The Final Chapter '84
Racing with the Moon '84
Teachers '84
Back to the Future '85
At Close Range '86
River's Edge '87
Back to the Future, Part 2 '89
Twister '89
Where the Heart Is '90
Wild at Heart '90
The Doors '91
Little Noises '91
Rubin & Ed '92
Hotel Room '93
What's Eating Gilbert Grape '93
Dead Man '95

Danny Glover
Escape from Alcatraz '79
Chu Chu & the Philly Flash '81
Keeping On '81
Memorial Day '83
Iceman '84
Places in the Heart '84
And the Children Shall Lead '85
The Color Purple '85
Silverado '85
Stand-In '85
Witness '85
Lethal Weapon '87
Mandela '87
Bat 21 '88
Out '88
Dead Man Out '89
Lethal Weapon 2 '89
Lonesome Dove '89
A Raisin in the Sun '89
Flight of the Intruder '90
Predator 2 '90
To Sleep with Anger '90
Grand Canyon '91
Pure Luck '91
A Rage in Harlem '91
Lethal Weapon 3 '92
Bopha! '93
The Saint of Fort Washington '93
Angels in the Outfield '94
America's Dream '95
Operation Dumbo Drop '95

John Glover
Annie Hall '77
Last Embrace '79
The Mountain Men '80
A Little Sex '82
Ernie Kovacs: Between the Laughter '84
The Evil That Men Do '84
An Early Frost '85
A Killing Affair '85
Apology '86
52 Pick-Up '86
Something Special '86
The Chocolate War '88
Masquerade '88
Rocket Gibraltar '88
Scrooged '88
Meet the Hollowheads '89
Traveling Man '89
El Diablo '90
Gremlins 2: The New Batch '90
Dead on the Money '91
Drug Wars 2: The Cocaine Cartel '92
Ed and His Dead Mother '93
What Ever Happened To... '93
Assault at West Point: The Court-Martial of Johnson Whittaker '94
Automatic '94
Night of the Running Man '94
In the Mouth of Madness '95

Julian Glover
Tom Jones '63
Theatre of Death '67
The Story of Jacob & Joseph '74
The Empire Strikes Back '80
For Your Eyes Only '81
Ivanhoe '82
Kim '84
The Fourth Protocol '87
Hearts of Fire '87
Mandela '87
The Secret Garden '87
Indiana Jones and the Last Crusade '89
Treasure Island '89
Tusks '89
The Infiltrator '95

Kara Glover
Caribe '87
The Beat '88

Carlin Glynn
Continental Divide '81
Sixteen Candles '84
The Trip to Bountiful '85
Blood Red '88
Night Game '89
Blessing '94

Mathias Gnaedinger
The Boat is Full '81
Journey of Hope '90

Hiromi Go
MacArthur's Children '85
Samurai Cowboy '93

Harry Goaz
Twin Peaks '90
Twin Peaks '90

George Gobel
Birds & the Bees '56
I Married a Woman '56
Rabbit Test '78
Better Late Than Never '79
Ellie '84
The Fantastic World of D.C. Collins '84

Justin Gocke
My Grandpa is a Vampire '92
The Witching of Ben Wagner '95

Jean-Luc Godard
Cleo from 5 to 7 '61
First Name: Carmen '83
King Lear '87

John Goddard
Storm Rider '57
Naked Youth '59

Mark Goddard
The Death Squad '73
Blue Sunshine '78
Roller Boogie '79
Strange Invaders '83

Paulette Goddard
Modern Times '36
The Young in Heart '38
The Women '39
The Ghost Breakers '40
The Great Dictator '40
Second Chorus '40
Pot O' Gold '41
Reap the Wild Wind '42
Star Spangled Rhythm '42
So Proudly We Hail '43
Diary of a Chambermaid '46
Unconquered '47
The Torch '50
Sins of Jezebel '54
Unholy Four '54
Time of Indifference '64

Arthur Godfrey
The Glass Bottom Boat '66
Great Bank Hoax '78
Angel's Brigade '79
Flatbed Annie and Sweetiepie: Lady Truckers '79

Jacques Godin
The Man Inside '76
The Victory '88
Double Identity '89
Being at Home with Claude '92

Alexander Godunov
Witness '85
The Money Pit '86
Die Hard '88
The Runestone '91
Waxwork 2: Lost in Time '91
North '94
The Dogfighters '95

Angela Goethals
Heartbreak Hotel '88
Home Alone '90
V.I. Warshawski '91

Michael C. Goetz
Village of the Damned '60
Deadly Encounter '72

Peter Michael Goetz
Beer '85
King Kong Lives '86
Tagget '90
Father of the Bride '91
My Girl '91
The Water Engine '92
The Buccaneers '95
Father of the Bride Part II '95

John Goff
Devil & Leroy Basset '73
The Alpha Incident '76
The Capture of Bigfoot '79
Getting Over '81
Night Stalker '87
Party Plane '90

Norris Goff
Dreaming Out Loud '40
The Bashful Bachelor '42

Joanna Going
Dark Shadows: Episode 1 '91
Wyatt Earp '94
A Good Day to Die '95

How to Make an American Quilt '95

Gila Golan
Our Man Flint '66
Catch as Catch Can '68
The Valley of Gwangi '69

Whoopi Goldberg
The Color Purple '85
Doctor Duck's Super Secret All-Purpose Sauce '85
Jumpin' Jack Flash '86
Burglar '87
Fatal Beauty '87
The Telephone '87
Clara's Heart '88
Homer and Eddie '89
Kiss Shot '89
The Long Walk Home '89
Ghost '90
Soapdish '91
The Player '92
Sarafina! '92
Sister Act '92
Made in America '93
Sister Act 2: Back in the Habit '93
Boys on the Side '94
Corrina, Corrina '94
Star Trek Generations '94
Moonlight and Valentino '95
Theodore Rex '95
Eddie '96

Jeff Goldblum
Death Wish '74
Nashville '75
The Sentinel '76
Special Delivery '76
Annie Hall '77
Between the Lines '77
Invasion of the Body Snatchers '78
Thank God It's Friday '78
The Legend of Sleepy Hollow '79
Rehearsal for Murder '82
The Big Chill '83
The Right Stuff '83
Threshold '83
The Adventures of Buckaroo Banzai Across the Eighth Dimension '84
Ernie Kovacs: Between the Laughter '84
The Three Little Pigs '84
Into the Night '85
Silverado '85
Transylvania 6-5000 '85
Beyond Therapy '86
The Fly '86
Strange Tales/Ray Bradbury Theatre '86
Vibes '88
Earth Girls Are Easy '89
Mr. Frost '89
The Tall Guy '89
Framed '90
Twisted Obsession '90
Deep Cover '92
Fathers and Sons '92
The Favor, the Watch, & the Very Big Fish '92
Shooting Elizabeth '92
Jurassic Park '93
Hideaway '94
Lush Life '94
Nine Months '95
Powder '95
The Great White Hype '96
Independence Day '96

Annie Golden
Hair '79
Desperately Seeking Susan '85
Key Exchange '85
Streetwalkin' '85
National Lampoon's Class of '86 '86
Baby Boom '87
Forever, Lulu '87
Love at Stake '87

Norman D. Golden, II
Cop and a Half '93
America's Dream '95

Devin Goldenberg
Guess What We Learned in School Today? '70
Cry Uncle '71

Ricky Paull Goldin
Hyper-Sapien: People from Another Star '86
The Blob '88
Lambada '89
Mirror, Mirror '90

Lelia Goldoni
Shadows '60
Secret Agent '64
Theatre of Death '67
The Disappearance of Aimee '76
Fatal Chase '77
The Spell '77
Bloodbrothers '78
Choices '81

Clio Goldsmith
Honey '81
The Gift '82
La Cicada '83
Heat of Desire '84

Jenette Goldstein
Aliens '86
Near Dark '87
The Presidio '88
Dead to Rights '93
Fair Game '95

Bob(cat) Goldthwait
One Crazy Summer '86
Police Academy 3: Back in Training '86
Burglar '87
Police Academy 4: Citizens on Patrol '87
Hot to Trot! '88
Scrooged '88
Little Vegas '90
Shakes the Clown '92
Destiny Turns on the Radio '95
Out There '95

Tony Goldwyn
Gaby: A True Story '87
Ghost '90
Iran: Days of Crisis '91
Kuffs '92
Traces of Red '92
Love Matters '93
The Pelican Brief '93
Taking the Heat '93
Doomsday Gun '94
The Last Word '95
Nixon '95
Pocahontas: The Legend '95
Reckless '95
Truman '95
The Boys Next Door '96

Valeria Golino
A Joke of Destiny, Lying in Wait Around the Corner Like a Bandit '84
Rain Man '88
The King's Whore '90
Torrents of Spring '90
Hot Shots! '91
The Indian Runner '91
Year of the Gun '91
Hot Shots! Part Deux '93
Clean Slate '94
Immortal Beloved '94
Four Rooms '95
Leaving Las Vegas '95
Escape from L.A. '96

Lisa Golm
The Hoodlum '51
Come Back, Little Sheba '52

Arlene Golonka
The In-Laws '79
My Tutor '82
The Hoboken Chicken Emergency '84
Foxtrap '85
Dr. Alien '88
Trained to Kill '88
The Gumshoe Kid '89

Marina Golovine
Olivier, Olivier '92
The Stolen Children '92

Minna Gombell
The Merry Widow '34
The Thin Man '34
The Great Waltz '38
Second Fiddle '39
Doomed Caravan '41
Pagan Love Song '50
I'll See You in My Dreams '51

Carlos Gomez
Silhouette '91
Bitter Vengeance '94
Desperado '95
Hostile Intentions '95

Fernando Gomez
Spirit of the Beehive '73
Mama Turns a Hundred '79
The Stilts '84
Belle Epoque '92

Panchito Gomez
Paco '75
Sweet 15 '90
Mi Vida Loca '94
Saints and Sinners '95

Thomas Gomez
Pittsburgh '42
In Society '44
Singapore '47
Force of Evil '49
Sorrowful Jones '49
The Merry Widow '52
The Magnificent Matador '55
The Conqueror '56
Trapeze '56
But Not for Me '59
Summer and Smoke '61
Stay Away, Joe '68

Milton Goncalves
Kiss of the Spider Woman '85
Subway to the Stars '87

Mascha Gonska
Infernal Trio '74
Tea For Three '84

Pedro Gonzalez-Gonzalez
The Young Land '59
Lust in the Dust '85

Caroline Goodall
The Moon Stallion '85
Hook '91
Cliffhanger '93
Schindler's List '93
The Silver Stallion: King of the Wild Brumbies '93
At Home with the Webbers '94
Disclosure '94
Sorrento Beach '95
White Squall '96

Grant Goodeve
Hot Rod '79
Last Cry for Help '79
Take Two '87

Cuba Gooding, Jr.
Coming to America '88
Boyz N the Hood '91
A Few Good Men '92
Gladiator '92
Hitz '92
Murder without Motive '92
Daybreak '93
Judgment Night '93
Lightning Jack '94
Losing Isaiah '94
Outbreak '94
The Tuskegee Airmen '95

Michael Goodliffe
The Way Out '56
A Night to Remember '58
Up the Creek '58
The Gorgon '64
To the Devil, A Daughter '76

Dody Goodman
Bedtime Story '63
Magic on Love Island '80
Private Resort '84
Splash '84
Cool As Ice '91
Frozen Assets '92

John Goodman
Eddie Macon's Run '83
Survivors '83
C.H.U.D. '84
Maria's Lovers '84
Revenge of the Nerds '84
True Stories '86
The Big Easy '87
Burglar '87
Raising Arizona '87
Everybody's All American '88
Punchline '88
The Wrong Guys '88
Always '89
Sea of Love '89
Stella '89
Arachnophobia '90
Barton Fink '91
King Ralph '91
The Babe '92
Matinee '92
Born Yesterday '93
The Flintstones '94
Kingfish: A Story of Huey P. Long '95
A Streetcar Named Desire '95

Deborah Goodrich
April Fool's Day '86
Survival Game '87
Remote Control '88

Garry Goodrow
The Connection '61
The Committee '68
A Session with the Committee '69
Steelyard Blues '73
Cardiac Arrest '74

Angela Goodwin
Autopsy '78
Julia and Julia '87

Bill Goodwin
Bathing Beauty '44
The Stork Club '45
House of Horrors '46
The Jolson Story '46
Mickey '48
It's a Great Feeling '49
Jolson Sings Again '49
Tea for Two '50
The Atomic Kid '54
Lucky Me '54

Harold Goodwin
Suds '20
College '27
The Cameraman '28
Tanks a Million '41
Abbott and Costello Meet the Keystone Kops '54

Laurel Goodwin
Girls! Girls! Girls! '62
Papa's Delicate Condition '63

Michael Goodwin
Sizzle '81
Date with an Angel '87
The Dead Pool '88
Deadline Assault '90

Bernard Gorcey
Bowery Buckaroos '47
Hard-Boiled Mahoney '47
Spook Busters '48
Blues Busters '50
Ghost Chasers '51
Clipped Wings '53
Bowery Boys Meet the Monsters '54

David Gorcey
Flying Wild '41
Pride of the Bowery '41
Mr. Wise Guy '42
Bowery Buckaroos '47
Hard-Boiled Mahoney '47
Spook Busters '48
Master Minds '49
Wild Weed '49
Blues Busters '50
Ghost Chasers '51

Elizabeth Gorcey
Kidco '83
Iced '88

Leo Gorcey
Dead End '37
Mannequin '37
Angels with Dirty Faces '38
Little Tough Guys '38
They Made Me a Criminal '39
Boys of the City '40
That Gang of Mine '40
Bowery Blitzkrieg '41
Flying Wild '41
Pride of the Bowery '41
Spooks Run Wild '41
Let's Get Tough '42
Mr. Wise Guy '42
'Neath Brooklyn Bridge '42
Smart Alecks '42
Destroyer '43
Ghost on the Loose '43
Kid Dynamite '43
Follow the Leader '44
Million Dollar Kid '44
Bowery Buckaroos '47
Hard-Boiled Mahoney '47
Smugglers' Cove '48
Spook Busters '48
Master Minds '49
Blues Busters '50
Ghost Chasers '51
Here Come the Marines '52
Clipped Wings '53
Bowery Boys Meet the Monsters '54
It's a Mad, Mad, Mad, Mad World '63

Barry Gordon
Pressure Point '62
A Thousand Clowns '65
Body Slam '87

Ben Gordon
Utilities '83
Goof Balls '87

C. Henry Gordon
The Crooked Circle '32
Mata Hari '32
Rasputin and the Empress '32
The Strange Love of Molly Louvain '32
Gabriel Over the White House '33
Penthouse '33
The Crusades '35
Charlie Chan at the Wax Museum '40

Colin Gordon
The Key Man '57
One That Got Away '57
Burn Witch, Burn! '62
The Body Beneath '70

Don Gordon
Bullitt '68
Slaughter '72
Zero Population Growth '72
Mack '73
The Education of Sonny Carson '74
The Beast Within '82
Bruce's Fists of Vengeance '84
The Borrower '89

Eve Gordon
Avalon '90
Paradise '91
Switched at Birth '91
Leaving Normal '92
The Secret Passion of Robert Clayton '92
The Heidi Chronicles '95

Gale Gordon
Here We Go Again! '42
Francis Covers the Big Town '53
Our Miss Brooks '56
The 30-Foot Bride of Candy Rock '59
Speedway '68
The 'Burbs '89

Gavin Gordon
His First Command '29
Romance '30
The Silver Horde '30
The Bitter Tea of General Yen '33
Female '33
The Bride of Frankenstein '35
I Killed That Man '42
Turf Boy '42
The Matchmaker '58
The Bat '59

Gerald Gordon
Hell Up in Harlem '73
Force Five '75
Ants '77

Glenn Gordon
The Finger Man '55
Fu Manchu '56

James Gordon
The Last of the Mohicans '20
Trailin' '21

Keith Gordon
All That Jazz '79
Home Movies '79
Dressed to Kill '80
Kent State '81
Silent Rebellion '82
Christine '84
Single Bars, Single Women '84
Legend of Billie Jean '85
Back to School '86
Combat Academy '86
Static '87

Leo Gordon
Hondo '53
Riot in Cell Block 11 '54
Ten Wanted Men '54
Soldier of Fortune '55
Seventh Cavalry '56
The Jayhawkers '59
Shame '61
The Haunted Palace '63
Devil's Angels '67
Bog '84
Alienator '89

Mary Gordon
Texas Cyclone '32
Double Wedding '37
The Adventures of Sherlock Holmes '39
Riot Squad '41
Sherlock Holmes and the Secret Weapon '42
Boss of Big Town '43
Follow the Leader '44
Million Dollar Kid '44
The Woman in Green '45
Little Giant '46

Pamela Gordon
Bloodstone: Subspecies 2 '92
Bloodlust: Subspecies 3 '93

Philip Gordon
Came a Hot Friday '85
The Bridge to Nowhere '86

Roy Gordon
The Great Man Votes '38
Attack of the 50 Foot Woman '58

Ruth Gordon
Abe Lincoln in Illinois '40
Two-Faced Woman '41
Action in the North Atlantic '43
Edge of Darkness '43
Inside Daisy Clover '65
Rosemary's Baby '68
Whatever Happened to Aunt Alice? '69
Where's Poppa? '70
Harold and Maude '71
The Big Bus '76
The Prince of Central Park '77
Every Which Way But Loose '78
Any Which Way You Can '80
My Bodyguard '80
Don't Go to Sleep '82
Jimmy the Kid '82
Maxie '85
Mugsy's Girls '85
The Trouble with Spies '87
Voyage of the Rock Aliens '87

Serena Gordon
A Tale of Two Cities '91
Goldeneye '95

Susan Gordon
Tormented '60
Picture Mommy Dead '66

Joseph Gordon-Levitt
Angels in the Outfield '94
Holy Matrimony '94
The Great Elephant Escape '95
The Juror '96

Sandy Gore
Street Hero '84
Wrangler '88
Brides of Christ '91

Galyn Gorg
Malibu Bikini Shop '86
Body Beat '88
RoboCop 2 '90

Mel Gorham
Blue In the Face '95
Smoke '95

Marius Goring
The Case of the Frightened Lady '39
Spy in Black '39
The Red Shoes '48
Paris Express '53
Night Ambush '57
The Moonraker '58
The Unstoppable Man '59
Exodus '60
Zeppelin '71
Holocaust '78
Charlie Boy '81

Cliff Gorman
The Boys in the Band '70
Class of '63 '73
Cops and Robbers '73
Rosebud '75
Strike Force '75
An Unmarried Woman '78
All That Jazz '79
Night of the Juggler '80
Angel '84
Hoffa '92
Night and the City '92
Down Came a Blackbird '94

Jonathan Gorman
Street Soldiers '91
Gang Justice '94

Robert Gorman
Leprechaun '93
Mr. Nanny '93

Karen Gorney
Saturday Night Fever '77
The Hard Way '91

Frank Gorshin
Between Heaven and Hell '56
Dragstrip Girl '57
Invasion of the Saucer Men '57
Studs Lonigan '60
The Great Impostor '61
That Darn Cat '65
Batman '66
Star Trek Bloopers '69
Sky Hei$t '75
Underground Aces '80
Hot Resort '85
Hollywood Vice Sqaud '86
Upper Crust '88
Beverly Hills Bodysnatchers '89
Midnight '89
Body Trouble '92
Sweet Justice '92
Amore! '93
The Meteor Man '93
Hail Caesar '94
12 Monkeys '95

Marjoe Gortner
Marjoe '72
Earthquake '74
Pray for the Wildcats '74
Bobbie Jo and the Outlaw '76
Food of the Gods '76
Sidewinder One '77
Viva Knievel '77
Star Crash '78
Mausoleum '83
Jungle Warriors '84
Hellhole '85
The Survivalist '87
American Ninja 3: Blood Hunt '89
Fire, Ice and Dynamite '91
Wild Bill '95

David Goss
She '83
Hollywood Cop '87

Mark Paul Gosselaar
Necessary Parties '88
The St. Tammany Miracle '94
Twisted Love '95

Louis Gossett, Jr.
A Raisin in the Sun '61
The Bushbaby '70
Skin Game '71
Travels with My Aunt '72
It's Good to Be Alive '74
The Laughing Policeman '74
The White Dawn '75
J.D.'s Revenge '76
The River Niger '76
The Choirboys '77
The Deep '77
Little Ladies of the Night '77
He Who Walks Alone '78
It Rained All Night the Day I Left '78
The Lazarus Syndrome '79
Don't Look Back: The Story of Leroy "Satchel" Paige '81
An Officer and a Gentleman '82
Jaws 3 '83
Sadat '83
Finders Keepers '84
The Guardian '84
Enemy Mine '85
Firewalker '86
Iron Eagle '86
The Father Clements Story '87
The Principal '87
Goodbye, Miss 4th of July '88
Iron Eagle 2 '88
Roots: The Gift '88
El Diablo '90
The Josephine Baker Story '90
The Punisher '90
Straight Up '90
Sudie & Simpson '90
Zora Is My Name! '90
Cover-Up '91
Murder on the Bayou '91
Toy Soldiers '91
Aces: Iron Eagle 3 '92
Carolina Skeletons '92
Diggstown '92
Keeper of the City '92
Dangerous Relations '93
Monolith '93
Return to Lonesome Dove '93
Curse of the Starving Class '94
Flashfire '94
A Good Man in Africa '94
Iron Eagle 4 '95
Zooman '95

Roland Got
Across the Pacific '42
G-Men vs. the Black Dragon '43

Walter Gotell
The African Queen '51
From Russia with Love '63
Lord Jim '65
The Spy Who Loved Me '77
Moonraker '79
For Your Eyes Only '81
Basic Training '86
The Living Daylights '87
Sleepaway Camp 2: Unhappy Campers '88
Puppet Master 3: Toulon's Revenge '90

Michael Gothard
King Arthur, the Young Warlord '75
Young Warlord '75
For Your Eyes Only '81
Lifeforce '85

Gilbert Gottfried
Bad Medicine '85
The Adventures of Ford Fairlane '90
Problem Child '90
Problem Child 2 '91
Silk Degrees '94

Carl Gottlieb
The Committee '68
A Session with the Committee '69
Jaws '75

Ferdinand Gottschalk
Ex-Lady '33
Female '33
King Kelly of the U.S.A. '34
Sing Sing Nights '35

Thomas Gottschalk
Driving Me Crazy '91
Ring of the Musketeers '93
Sister Act 2: Back in the Habit '93

Jetta Goudal
The Coming of Amos '25
The Road to Yesterday '25
Road to Yesterday/The Yankee Clipper '27
White Gold '28

Michael Gough
The Small Back Room '49
Rob Roy—The Highland Rogue '53
The Sword & the Rose '53
Last Reunion '55
Richard III '55
The Horror of Dracula '58
The Horse's Mouth '58
The Phantom of the Opera '62
What a Carve-Up! '62
The Skull '65
They Came from Beyond Space '67
The Crimson Cult '68
Crucible of Horror '69
Women in Love '70
The Go-Between '71
Savage Messiah '72
Horror Hospital '73
Venom '82
The Dresser '83
Oxford Blues '84
Top Secret! '84
Out of Africa '85
The Fourth Protocol '87
Batman '89
The Shell Seekers '89
Strapless '90
Batman Returns '92
The Advocate '93
The Age of Innocence '93
Nostradamus '93
Wittgenstein '93
Batman Forever '95

Elliott Gould
Bob & Carol & Ted & Alice '69
The Night They Raided Minsky's '69
Getting Straight '70
I Love My...Wife '70
M*A*S*H '70
Little Murders '71
Quick, Let's Get Married '71
The Touch '71
The Long Goodbye '73
Busting '74
S*P*Y*S '74
Mean Johnny Barrows '75
Roboman '75
Whiffs '75
Harry & Walter Go to New York '76
I Will, I Will for Now '76
A Bridge Too Far '77
Capricorn One '78
Matilda '78
The Silent Partner '78
Escape to Athena '79
The Lady Vanishes '79
Falling in Love Again '80
The Last Flight of Noah's Ark '80
The Devil & Max Devlin '81
Dirty Tricks '81
Jack & the Beanstalk '83
Over the Brooklyn Bridge '83
The Naked Face '84
Casey at the Bat '85
Conspiracy: The Trial of the Chicago Eight '87
Dangerous Love '87
Lethal Obsession '87
The Telephone '87
Vanishing Act '88
Frog '89
Night Visitor '89
Frogs! '90s
The Lemon Sisters '90
My Wonderful Life '90
Bugsy '91
Dead Men Don't Die '91
Inside Out '91
Beyond Justice '92
Hitz '92
Wet and Wild Summer '92
Amore! '93
A Boy Called Hate '95
Cover Me '95
The Dangerous '95
The Glass Shield '95
Kicking and Screaming '95

Harold Gould
The Sting '73
Love and Death '75
How to Break Up a Happy Divorce '76
Actor: The Paul Muni Story '78
The One and Only '78
Better Late Than Never '79
Kenny Rogers as the Gambler '80
Seems Like Old Times '80
Help Wanted: Male '82
Kenny Rogers as the Gambler, Part 2: The Adventure Continues '83
Dream Chasers '84
The Red Light Sting '84
Fourth Wise Man '85
Playing for Keeps '86
Get Smart, Again! '89
Romero '89

Jason Gould
The Big Picture '89
Say Anything '89
The Prince of Tides '91

William Gould
The Phantom '31
Phantom Thunderbolt '33
Rio Rattler '35
Man from Montana '41
Tanks a Million '41

Robert Goulet
Scrooged '88
Naked Gun 2 1/2: The Smell of Fear '91
Based on an Untrue Story '93
Mr. Wrong '95

Gibson Gowland
Greed '24
The Phantom of the Opera '25
Hell Harbor '30
Without Honors '32
The Secret of the Loch '34
Gun Cargo '49

Harry Goz
Bill '81
Mommie Dearest '81
Bill: On His Own '83
Rappin' '85

Jody Graber
The Garden '90
Edward II '92

Betty Grable
Whoopee! '30
Hold 'Em Jail '32
Probation '32
The Gay Divorcee '34
Follow the Fleet '36
College Swing '38
Give Me a Sailor '38
Day the Bookies Wept '39
Down Argentine Way '40
Tin Pan Alley '40
I Wake Up Screaming '41
Moon over Miami '41
A Yank in the R.A.F. '41
Footlight Serenade '42
Song of the Islands '42
Springtime in the Rockies '42
Sweet Rosie O'Grady '43
Pin-Up Girl '44
Strictly G.I. '44
The Dolly Sisters '45
The Beautiful Blonde from Bashful Bend '49
The Farmer Takes a Wife '53
How to Marry a Millionaire '53
Hollywood Goes to War '54
The Love Goddesses '65
Gotta Dance, Gotta Sing '84
The Worst of Hollywood: Vol. 3 '90

Sofie Graboel
The Wolf at the Door '87
The Silent Touch '94

Nickolas Grace
Heat and Dust '82
Robin Hood...The Legend: Robin Hood and the Sorcerer '83
Robin Hood...The Legend: The Swords of Wayland '83
Robin Hood...The Legend: Herne's Son '85
Robin Hood...The Legend: The Time of the Wolf '85
Max Headroom, the Original Story '86
Diamond's Edge '88
Salome's Last Dance '88
The Green Man '91
Tom & Viv '94
The Final Cut '95

Wayne Grace
Heroes Stand Alone '89
Fallen Angels 2 '93
My Summer Story '94

Elizabeth Gracen
Death of the Incredible Hulk '90
Lower Level '91
Discretion Assured '93
Final Mission '93
The Expert '95

Paulo Gracindo
Earth Entranced '66
Amor Bandido '79

Paul Graetz
Power '34
Bulldog Jack '35
Mimi '35
Heart's Desire '37

David Graf
Police Academy 2: Their First Assignment '85
Police Academy 3: Back in Training '86

Police Academy 4: Citizens on Patrol '87
Police Academy 5: Assignment Miami Beach '88
Police Academy 6: City Under Siege '89
Suture '93
Police Academy: Mission to Moscow '94
Roseanne: An Unauthorized Biography '94
The Brady Bunch Movie '95
Father and Scout '95

Ilene Graff
Ladybugs '92
The Great American Sex Scandal '94

Todd Graff
Sweet Lorraine '87
Dominick & Eugene '88
Five Corners '88
The Abyss '89
Vietnam War Story 3 '89
Framed '90
Opportunity Knocks '90
City of Hope '91

Wilton Graff
The Mozart Story '48
The West Point Story '50
Bloodlust '59
Compulsion '59

Aimee Graham
Amos and Andrew '93
Fallen Angels 1 '93

Bill Graham
Gardens of Stone '87
Bugsy '91
The Doors '91

Fred Graham
The Fuller Brush Girl '50
Heart of the Rockies '51
Escape from Fort Bravo '53
Trader Tom of the China Seas '54
The Last Hunt '56

Gary Graham
No Place to Hide '81
The Dirty Dozen: The Deadly Mission '87
The Last Warrior '89
Robot Jox '90
Alien Nation: Dark Horizon '94

Gerrit Graham
Greetings '68
Hi, Mom! '70
Son of Blob '72
Phantom of the Paradise '74
Cannonball '76
Special Delivery '76
Tunnelvision '76
Demon Seed '77
Home Movies '79
Used Cars '80
Spaceship '81
National Lampoon's Class Reunion '82
Soup for One '82
Ratings Game '84
The Annihilators '85
The Man with One Red Shoe '85
Terrorvision '86
It's Alive 3: Island of the Alive '87
C.H.U.D. 2: Bud the Chud '89
Child's Play 2 '90
Martians Go Home! '90
Night of the Cyclone '90
Frozen Assets '92
Philadelphia Experiment 2 '93
This Boy's Life '93

Heather Graham
Drugstore Cowboy '89
I Love You to Death '90
O Pioneers! '91
Shout '91
Diggstown '92
Guilty as Charged '92
The Ballad of Little Jo '93
Six Degrees of Separation '93
Terrified '94

Morland Graham
Tower of Terror '42
Bonnie Prince Charlie '48

Ronny Graham
New Faces of 1952 '54
World's Greatest Lover '77
Ratings Game '84

Gloria Grahame
It's a Wonderful Life '46
Crossfire '47
It Happened in Brooklyn '47
Merton of the Movies '47
Song of the Thin Man '47
A Woman's Secret '49
In a Lonely Place '50
The Bad and the Beautiful '52
Macao '52
Sudden Fear '52
The Big Heat '53
Human Desire '54
The Cobweb '55
The Man Who Never Was '55
Not as a Stranger '55
Oklahoma! '55
Autopsy '70s
The Todd Killings '71
Loners '72
Mama's Dirty Girls '74
The Big Scam '79
Chilly Scenes of Winter '79
The Nesting '80

Margot Grahame
Broken Melody '34
The Informer '35
The Three Musketeers '35
Fabulous Joe '47

Kelsey Grammer
Galaxies are Colliding '92
Down Periscope '96

Sam Grana
90 Days '86
The Boys of St. Vincent '93

Alexander Granach
Nosferatu '22
Dracula/Garden of Eden '28
Kameradschaft '31
Joan of Paris '42
The Seventh Cross '44

Daisy Granados
Memories of Underdevelopment '68
Portrait of Teresa '79
A Very Old Man with Enormous Wings '88

Rosario Granados
The Great Madcap '49
A Woman Without Love '51

Bjorn Granath
Pelle the Conqueror '88
The Ox '91

Dorothy Granger
Fighting Fool '32
W.C. Fields Comedy Bag '33
The Flustered Comedy of Leon Errol '39
Killer Dill '47

Farley Granger
The North Star '43
The Purple Heart '44
Rope '48
They Live by Night '49
Strangers on a Train '51
Behave Yourself! '52
Hans Christian Andersen '52
Small Town Girl '53
Senso '54
Deathmask '69
They Call Me Trinity '72
Arnold '73
Night Flight from Moscow '73
The Slasher '74
The Widow '76
Sweet Spirits '80s
The Prowler '81
Very Close Quarters '84
Imagemaker '86

Stewart Granger
Convoy '40
Secret Mission '42
Thursday's Child '43
The Man in Grey '45
Caesar and Cleopatra '46
Man of Evil '48
King Solomon's Mines '50
Prisoner of Zenda '52
Scaramouche '52
All the Brothers Were Valiant '53
Salome '53
Young Bess '53
Beau Brummel '54
Green Fire '55
Moonfleet '55
Bhowani Junction '56
The Last Hunt '56
Gun Glory '57
Harry Black and the Tiger '58
North to Alaska '60
Sodom and Gomorrah '62
Target for Killing '66
Code Name Alpha '67
The Last Safari '67
Wild Geese '78
Hell Hunters '87
Fine Gold '88

Nils T. Granlund
Rhythm Parade '43
Take It Big '44

William Grannell
The Abductors '72
Ginger '72

Beth Grant
Rain Man '88
The Dark Half '91
Love Field '91
White Sands '92
Speed '94

Cary Grant
Blonde Venus '32
I'm No Angel '33
She Done Him Wrong '33
Sylvia Scarlett '35
Suzy '36
Amazing Adventure '37
The Awful Truth '37
Toast of New York '37
Topper '37
Bringing Up Baby '38
Holiday '38
Gunga Din '39
In Name Only '39
Only Angels Have Wings '39
His Girl Friday '40
The Howards of Virginia '40
My Favorite Wife '40
The Philadelphia Story '40
Penny Serenade '41
Suspicion '41
Once Upon a Honeymoon '42
Talk of the Town '42
Destination Tokyo '43
Mr. Lucky '43
Arsenic and Old Lace '44
None But the Lonely Heart '44
Night and Day '46
Notorious '46
The Bachelor and the Bobby-Soxer '47
The Bishop's Wife '47
Every Girl Should Be Married '48
Mr. Blandings Builds His Dream House '48
I Was a Male War Bride '49
People Will Talk '51
Monkey Business '52
To Catch a Thief '55
An Affair to Remember '57
The Pride and the Passion '57
Houseboat '58
Indiscreet '58
North by Northwest '59
Operation Petticoat '59
The Grass is Greener '61
That Touch of Mink '62
Charade '63
Father Goose '64
Walk, Don't Run '66
The Cary Grant Collection '90

Charles Grant
Lady in Waiting '94
Playback '95

David Marshall Grant
Happy Birthday, Gemini '80
End of August '82
Sessions '83
American Flyers '85
Bat 21 '88
Air America '90
Forever Young '92
Through the Eyes of a Killer '92
Three Wishes '95

Faye Grant
Senior Trip '81
V '83
Omen 4: The Awakening '91
Vibrations '94

Frances Grant
Cavalry '36
Red River Valley '36
Oh Susannah '38

Hugh Grant
Maurice '87
The Dawning '88
The Lair of the White Worm '88
White Mischief '88
Impromptu '90
The Big Man: Crossing the Line '91
Our Sons '91
Bitter Moon '92
Night Train to Venice '93
The Remains of the Day '93
An Awfully Big Adventure '94
Four Weddings and a Funeral '94
Restoration '94
Sirens '94
The Englishman Who Went Up a Hill But Came Down a Mountain '95
Nine Months '95
Sense and Sensibility '95

James Grant
Prick Up Your Ears '87
The Innocent '93

Kathryn Grant
The Seventh Voyage of Sinbad '58
Anatomy of a Murder '59

Kirby Grant
In Society '44
Bad Men of the Border '45
The Stranger from Pecos '45
Comin' Round the Mountain '51

Lawrence Grant
The Grand Duchess and the Waiter '26
Doomsday '28
The Mask of Fu Manchu '32
Shanghai Express '32
Speak Easily '32
Son of Frankenstein '39

Lee Grant
Detective Story '51
The Balcony '63
Divorce American Style '67
In the Heat of the Night '67
Valley of the Dolls '67
Buona Sera, Mrs. Campbell '68
The Mod Squad '68
Marooned '69
There was a Crooked Man '70
Plaza Suite '71
Portnoy's Complaint '72
Internecine Project '73
Shampoo '75
Voyage of the Damned '76
Airport '77 '77
The Spell '77
Damien: Omen 2 '78
My Sister, My Love '78
The Swarm '78
Little Miss Marker '80
Charlie Chan and the Curse of the Dragon Queen '81
For Ladies Only '81
Visiting Hours '82
Teachers '84
Big Town '87
A Billion for Boris '90
Defending Your Life '91
Citizen Cohn '92
It's My Party '95

Leon Grant
Beat Street '84
Playing for Keeps '86

Richard E. Grant
Withnail and I '87
How to Get Ahead in Advertising '89
Henry & June '90
Mountains of the Moon '90
Codename Kyril '91
Hudson Hawk '91
L.A. Story '91
Warlock '91
Bram Stoker's Dracula '92
The Player '92
The Age of Innocence '93
Ready to Wear '94
Cold Light of Day '95
Jack and Sarah '96

Rodney Grant
Dances with Wolves '90
Son of the Morning Star '91
Geronimo: An American Legend '93

The Last Ride '94
Wagons East '94
Hawkeye: Premiere Episode '95
The Substitute '96

Schuyler Grant
Anne of Green Gables '85
Anne of Avonlea '87

Shelby Grant
Our Man Flint '66
The Witchmaker '69

Allan Granville
Black Terrorist '85
Prey for the Hunter '92

Bonita Granville
These Three '36
Quality Street '37
Nancy Drew, Reporter '39
The Mortal Storm '40
The Glass Key '42
Now, Voyager '42
Hitler's Children '43
Seven Miles from Alcatraz/Flight from Glory '43
Breakfast in Hollywood '46
Love Laughs at Andy Hardy '46
Guilty of Treason '50
Lone Ranger '56

Charley Grapewin
Hell's House '32
Heroes for Sale '33
Ah, Wilderness! '35
One Frightened Night '35
Libeled Lady '36
Petrified Forest '36
Captains Courageous '37
The Good Earth '37
Of Human Hearts '38
Shopworn Angel '38
Three Comrades '38
The Wizard of Oz '39
The Grapes of Wrath '40
Johnny Apollo '40
Rhythm on the River '40
The Texas Rangers Ride Again '40
They Died with Their Boots On '41
Follow the Boys '44

Karen Grassle
Little House on the Prairie '74
President's Mistress '78
Cocaine: One Man's Seduction '83
Harry's War '84
The Best Christmas Pageant Ever '86
Wyatt Earp '94

Ernest Graves
One Plus One '61
Hercules in New York '70

Peter Graves
Encore '52
Maytime in Mayfair '52
The Magic Christian '69
The Adventurers '70

Peter Graves
Red Planet Mars '52
Beneath the 12-Mile Reef '53
Stalag 17 '53
Killers from Space '54
The Court Martial of Billy Mitchell '55
Let's Make Up '55
The Night of the Hunter '55
It Conquered the World '56
Beginning of the End '57
Casey Jones and Fury (Brave Stallion) '57
Poor White Trash '57
The Legend of the Sea Wolf '58
Texas Across the River '66
Sergeant Ryker '68
The President's Plane is Missing '71
Where Have All the People Gone? '74
Cruise Missile '78
The Clonus Horror '79
The Rebels '79
Airplane! '80
Survival Run '80
Airplane 2: The Sequel '82
Savannah Smiles '82
The Guns and the Fury '83
The Winds of War '83
Number One with a Bullet '87

Ralph Graves
The Greatest Question '19
Dream Street '21
Extra Girl '23
That Certain Thing '28
The Black Coin '36
Three Texas Steers '39

Rupert Graves
A Room with a View '86
Fortunes of War '87
Maurice '87
A Handful of Dust '88
The Children '90
Where Angels Fear to Tread '91
Damage '92
The Madness of King George '94

Fernand Gravet
The Great Waltz '38
La Ronde '51
How to Steal a Million '66
The Madwoman of Chaillot '69

Carla Gravina
Alfredo, Alfredo '72
And Now My Love '74
Salut l'Artiste '74
The Tempter '74
Boomerang '76

Cesare Gravina
Foolish Wives '22
Merry-Go-Round '23
The Wedding March '28

Billy Gray
The Day the Earth Stood Still '51
On Moonlight Bay '51
By the Light of the Silvery Moon '53
Two for the Seesaw '62
Werewolves on Wheels '71

Charles Gray
You Only Live Twice '67
The Man Outside '68
The Executioner '70
Diamonds Are Forever '71
Murder on the Midnight Express '74
Black Werewolf '75
The Seven-Per-Cent Solution '76
Silver Bears '78
The House on Garibaldi Street '79
The Mirror Crack'd '80
Shock Treatment '81
An Englishman Abroad '83
The Jigsaw Man '84
Dreams Lost, Dreams Found '87
Mr. & Mrs. Loving '96

Coleen Gray
Kiss of Death '47
Red River '48
Riding High '50
Kansas City Confidential '52
The Killing '56
The Leech Woman '59
The Phantom Planet '61
A Cry from the Mountain '85

David Barry Gray
Cops and Robbersons '94
S.F.W. '94
Soldier Boyz '95

Dolores Gray
Kismet '55
The Opposite Sex '56
Designing Woman '57

Donald Gray
The Four Feathers '39
Island of Desire '52
Murder on the Campus '52
Flight from Vienna '58

Dorian Gray
Il Grido '57
Colossus and the Amazon Queen '64

Dulcie Gray
A Man About the House '47
Mine Own Executioner '47
The Franchise Affair '52
Angels One Five '54

Erin Gray
Buck Rogers in the 25th Century '79
The Ultimate Imposter '79
Born Beautiful '82
Six Pack '82
Breaking Home Ties '87

Jason Goes to Hell: The Final Friday '93
Official Denial '93
A Dangerous Place '94
Honor Thy Father and Mother: The True Story of the Menendez Brothers '94
T-Force '94

Eve Gray
Night Birds '31
Department Store '35

Gary Gray
Rachel and the Stranger '48
The Next Voice You Hear '50
Two Weeks with Love '50
The Painted Hills '51

Lawrence Gray
Love 'Em and Leave 'Em '26
A Face in the Fog '36

Linda Gray
The Grass is Always Greener Over the Septic Tank '78
The Two Worlds of Jenny Logan '79
The Wild and the Free '80
Kenny Rogers as the Gambler, Part 3: The Legend Continues '87
Accidental Meeting '93
Bonanza: The Return '93

Marc Gray
Flirting '89
Which Way Home '90

Nadia Gray
Valley of the Eagles '51
The Captain's Table '60
La Dolce Vita '60
Maniac '63
Two for the Road '67

Sally Gray
Lady in Distress '39
The Saint in London '39
Dangerous Moonlight '41
The Hidden Room '49
The Saint's Vacation/The Narrow Margin '52
I'll Get You '53
Keeper '84

Spalding Gray
Hard Choices '84
The Killing Fields '84
Almost You '85
True Stories '86
Swimming to Cambodia '87
Beaches '88
Clara's Heart '88
Spalding Gray: Terrors of Pleasure '88
Stars and Bars '88
Heavy Petting '89
The Image '89
Our Town '89
Monster in a Box '92
Straight Talk '92
King of the Hill '93
Twenty Bucks '93
Bad Company '94
The Paper '94
Beyond Rangoon '95
Diabolique '96

Kathryn Grayson
Andy Hardy's Private Secretary '41
Rio Rita '42
Thousands Cheer '43
Anchors Aweigh '45
Till the Clouds Roll By '46
Till the Clouds Roll By/A Star Is Born '46
It Happened in Brooklyn '47
That Midnight Kiss '49
The Toast of New Orleans '50
Show Boat '51
Lovely to Look At '52
The Desert Song '53
Kiss Me Kate '53

Jose Greco
Goliath and the Sins of Babylon '64
Ship of Fools '65

Juliette Greco
The Green Glove '52
Elena and Her Men '56
Uncle Tom's Cabin '69

Adolph Green
Simon '80
My Favorite Year '82
Follies in Concert '85
Lily in Love '85

Brian Austin Green
An American Summer '90
Beverly Hills 90210 '90
Kid '90
Beverly Hills 90210: The Graduation '93

Harry Green
The Light of Western Stars '30
A King in New York '57

Janet-Laine Green
Bullies '86
Cowboys Don't Cry '88
Kidnapping of Baby John Doe '88
When the Dark Man Calls '95

Kerri Green
The Goonies '85
Summer Rental '85
Lucas '86
Three for the Road '87
Blue Flame '93
Tainted Blood '93

Marika Green
Pickpocket '59
Emmanuelle '74

Mitzie Green
Tom Sawyer '30
Little Orphan Annie '32
Lost in Alaska '52

Nigel Green
Reach for the Sky '56
Corridors of Blood '58
Sword of Sherwood Forest '60
Mysterious Island '61
Jason and the Argonauts '63
Zulu '64
The Ipcress File '65
Masque of the Red Death/Premature Burial '65
The Skull '65
Khartoum '66
Tobruk '66
Africa Texas Style '67
The Ruling Class '72

Seth Green
The Hotel New Hampshire '84
Something Special '86
Radio Days '87
My Stepmother Is an Alien '88
Airborne '93
Arcade '93

Esther Greenberg
Sallah '63
Lupo '70

Shon Greenblatt
Freddy's Dead: The Final Nightmare '91
There Goes My Baby '92

Angela Greene
Night of the Blood Beast '58
The Cosmic Man '59

Daniel Greene
Pulsebeat '85
Hands of Steel '86
Weekend Warriors '86
Elvira, Mistress of the Dark '88
American Tiger '89
The Opponent '89
Skeleton Coast '89

Ellen Greene
Next Stop, Greenwich Village '76
Little Shop of Horrors '86
Talk Radio '88
Dinner at Eight '89
Me and Him '89
Glory! Glory! '90
Pump Up the Volume '90
Stepping Out '91
Fathers and Sons '92
Murdered Innocence '94
The Professional '94
Wagons East '94

Graham Greene
Powwow Highway '89
Dances with Wolves '90
Lost in the Barrens '91
Clearcut '92
The Last of His Tribe '92
Thunderheart '92
Benefit of the Doubt '93

The Broken Chain '93
Cooperstown '93
Huck and the King of Hearts '93
Rain Without Thunder '93
Spirit Rider '93
Camilla '94
Maverick '94
Medicine River '94
North '94
Savage Land '94
Die Hard: With a Vengeance '95

James Greene
The Moon Stallion '85
Pals '87
Philadelphia Experiment 2 '93

Joe "Mean Joe" Greene
The Black Six '74
Twisted Brain '74
Lady Cocoa '75

Jon Greene
Alley Cat '84
Swift Justice '88

Kim Morgan Greene
Scorned '93
The Soft Kill '94

Lorne Greene
The Silver Chalice '54
Autumn Leaves '56
Peyton Place '57
The Buccaneer '58
The Trap '59
The Errand Boy '61
Bonanza '64
Ride the Wind '66
Earthquake '74
Tidal Wave '75
Roots '77
The Trial of Lee Harvey Oswald '77
The Bastard '78
Battlestar Galactica '78
Klondike Fever '79
Mission Galactica: The Cylon Attack '79
A Time for Miracles '80
Vasectomy: A Delicate Matter '86
The Alamo: Thirteen Days to Glory '87

Michael Greene
The Naked Angels '69
The Clones '73
Americana '81
Lost in America '85
Johnny Be Good '88
Moon over Parador '88
The Night Before '88
White of the Eye '88
Nightmare on the 13th Floor '90
In the Heat of Passion '91
Rubin & Ed '92
Last Man Standing '95

Michelle Greene
Double Standard '88
Danielle Steel's Palomino '91
I Posed for Playboy '91
Silent Victim '92
Stranger by Night '94
The Unborn 2 '94
How the West was Fun '95

Peter Greene
Laws of Gravity '92
Clean, Shaven '93
Judgment Night '93
The Mask '94

Richard Greene
My Lucky Star '38
The Hound of the Baskervilles '39
The Little Princess '39
Stanley and Livingstone '39
Forever Amber '47
The Black Castle '52
Captain Scarlett '53
The Adventures of Robin Hood '55
Robin Hood: The Movie '55
Sword of Sherwood Forest '60
The Castle of Fu Manchu '68
Island of the Lost '68
Kiss and Kill '68
Tales from the Crypt '72
Special Effects '85

Shecky Greene
The Love Machine '71
Lovelines '84

Splash '84

Kate Greenfield
Robinson Crusoe of Clipper Island '36
Night Gallery '69

Raymond Greenleaf
Harriet Craig '50
Pier 23 '51
When Gangland Strikes '56

Brad Greenquist
The Bedroom Window '87
Mutants In Paradise '88
The Yearling '94

Sydney Greenstreet
The Maltese Falcon '41
They Died with Their Boots On '41
Across the Pacific '42
Casablanca '42
Background to Danger '43
The Best of Bogart '43
Hollywood Canteen '44
Passage to Marseilles '44
Christmas in Connecticut '45
Conflict '45
The Hucksters '47
Velvet Touch '48
Flamingo Road '49
It's a Great Feeling '49
Malaya '49

Bruce Greenwood
Malibu Bikini Shop '86
The Climb '87
Striker's Mountain '87
Another Chance '88
The FBI Murders '88
Spy '89
The Little Kidnappers '90
Wild Orchid '90
Servants of Twilight '91
Passenger 57 '92
Adrift '93
Rio Diablo '93
Bitter Vengeance '94
The Companion '94
Dream Man '94
Exotica '94

Charlotte Greenwood
Parlor, Bedroom and Bath '31
Down Argentine Way '40
Young People '40
Moon over Miami '41
Springtime in the Rockies '42
Dangerous When Wet '53
Oklahoma! '55
Glory '56

Joan Greenwood
Frenzy '46
A Girl in a Million '46
The October Man '48
Whiskey Galore '48
Kind Hearts and Coronets '49
Mr. Peek-A-Boo '50
The Man in the White Suit '51
Importance of Being Earnest '52
The Detective '54
Moonfleet '55
Stage Struck '57
Mysterious Island '61
Tom Jones '63
The Hound of the Baskervilles '77
Little Dorrit, Film 1: Nobody's Fault '88
Little Dorrit, Film 2: Little Dorrit's Story '88

Dabbs Greer
Trouble Along the Way '53
Rose Marie '54
It! The Terror from Beyond Space '58
Cash McCall '60
Roustabout '64
Rage '72
Two Moon Junction '88

Jane Greer
Dick Tracy, Detective/The Corpse Vanishes '42
Dick Tracy, Detective '45
George White's Scandals '45
Out of the Past '47
Sinbad, the Sailor '47
They Won't Believe Me '47
Station West '48
Big Steal '49
Prisoner of Zenda '52
Clown '53

Man of a Thousand Faces '57
Where Love Has Gone '64
Billie '65
Against All Odds '84
Just Between Friends '86
Immediate Family '89

Michael Greer
Fortune and Men's Eyes '71
Messiah of Evil '74

Bradley Gregg
Class of 1999 '90
Madhouse '90
Eye of the Storm '91

Clark Gregg
Lana in Love '92
Tyson '95

John Gregg
Heatwave '83
Trouble in Paradise '88
Ebbtide '94

Julie Gregg
From Hell to Borneo '64
The Seekers '79

Virginia Gregg
The Amazing Mr. X '48
Love Is a Many-Splendored Thing '55
D.I. '57
The Hanging Tree '59
Operation Petticoat '59
Spencer's Mountain '63
Columbo: Prescription Murder '67
Walk in the Spring Rain '70
No Way Back '74

Pascal Greggory
Pauline at the Beach '83
Queen Margot '94

Rose Gregorio
The Swimmer '68
Desperate Characters '71
The Last Innocent Man '87
Five Corners '88
City of Hope '91

Andre Gregory
My Dinner with Andre '81
Author! Author! '82
Protocol '84
Always '85
Follies in Concert '85
The Mosquito Coast '86
Street Smart '87
The Last Temptation of Christ '88
Some Girls '88
The Bonfire of the Vanities '90
The Linguini Incident '92
Vanya on 42nd Street '94
Last Summer In the Hamptons '96

Celia Gregory
Agatha '79
Children of the Full Moon '84

James Gregory
Nightfall '56
Gun Glory '57
Al Capone '59
The Manchurian Candidate '62
Two Weeks in Another Town '62
Captain Newman, M.D. '63
PT 109 '63
Sons of Katie Elder '65
Murderers' Row '66
The Ambushers '67
Clambake '67
Beneath the Planet of the Apes '70
The Love God? '70
Great American Traffic Jam '80
Wait Till Your Mother Gets Home '83

Mark Gregory
Escape from the Bronx '85
Thunder Warrior '85
Thunder Warrior 2 '85
Blue Paradise '86
Thunder Warrior 3 '88
War Bus Commando '89

Sebastian Gregory
Help Wanted Female '68
Sweet Trash '89

Thea Gregory
Paid to Kill '54
Profile '54

John Gregson
The Lavender Hill Mob '51
Genevieve '53
Angels One Five '54
Three Cases of Murder '55
Above Us the Waves '56
Sea of Sand '58
The Captain's Table '60
S.O.S. Pacific '60
Night of the Generals '67
Hans Brinker '69
Fright '71

Stephen Greif
The Great Riviera Bank Robbery '79
The Dying Truth '91

Robert Greig
Animal Crackers '30
The Great Ziegfeld '36
Sullivan's Travels '41

Kim Greist
C.H.U.D. '84
Brazil '85
Manhunter '86
Throw Momma from the Train '87
Punchline '88
Why Me? '90
Payoff '91
Duplicates '92
Homeward Bound: The Incredible Journey '93
Houseguest '94
Roswell: The U.F.O. Cover-Up '94
Homeward Bound 2: Lost in San Francisco '96

Joyce Grenfell
The Happiest Days of Your Life '50
The Belles of St. Trinian's '53
Blue Murder at St. Trinian's '56
The Pure Hell of St. Trinian's '61
The Americanization of Emily '64

Googy Gress
First Turn On '83
Babes in Toyland '86
Promised Land '88
Vibes '88
Bloodhounds of Broadway '89

Laurent Grevill
Camille Claudel '89
I Can't Sleep '93

Anne Grey
No. 17 '32
Kiss of Death '47

Denise Grey
Devil in the Flesh '46
Sputnik '61
La Boum '81

Jennifer Grey
The Cotton Club '84
Reckless '84
Red Dawn '84
American Flyers '85
Ferris Bueller's Day Off '86
Dirty Dancing '87
Bloodhounds of Broadway '89
Criminal Justice '90
Stroke of Midnight '90
Wind '92
A Case for Murder '93
Eyes of a Witness '94
Portraits of a Killer '95

Joel Grey
Come September '61
Man on a String '71
Cabaret '72
Buffalo Bill & the Indians '76
The Seven-Per-Cent Solution '76
Remo Williams: The Adventure Begins '85
Queenie '87
Kafka '91
The Music of Chance '93
The Dangerous '95

Nan Grey
Dracula's Daughter '36
Three Smart Girls '36
Danger on the Air '38
Three Smart Girls Grow Up '39
The Tower of London '39
The Invisible Man Returns '40

Shirley Grey
Cornered '32
Drifting Souls '32
Get That Girl '32
Hurricane Express '32
The Riding Tornado '32
Texas Cyclone '32
Uptown New York '32
Green Eyes '34
Circumstantial Evidence '35
The Mystery of the Mary Celeste '37

Virginia Grey
The Michigan Kid '28
Another Thin Man '39
Broadway Serenade '39
Big Store '41
Whistling in the Dark '41
Tarzan's New York Adventure '42
Idaho '43
Sweet Rosie O'Grady '43
House of Horrors '46
Swamp Fire '46
Unconquered '47
Mexican Hayride '48
Unknown Island '48
Who Killed Doc Robbin? '48
Lady Scarface/The Threat '49
Threat '49
Bullfighter & the Lady '50
Three Desperate Men '50
Slaughter Trail '51
The Last Command '55
The Rose Tattoo '55
Crime of Passion '57
Naked Kiss '64
Love Has Many Faces '65
Madame X '66
Bachelor in Paradise '69

Michael Greyeyes
Geronimo '93
Dance Me Outside '95

Clinton Greyn
The Love Machine '71
Raid on Rommel '71

Bill Gribble
The Wild and the Free '80
Dogs of Hell '83

Eddie Gribbon
Dames Ahoy '30
Rio Rattler '35

Harry Gribbon
Ben Turpin: An Eye for an Eye '24
The Tomboy '24
The Cameraman '28
Ride Him, Cowboy '32

Richard Grieco
If Looks Could Kill '91
Mobsters '91
Born to Run '93
Tomcat: Dangerous Desires '93
Suspicious Agenda '94
A Vow to Kill '94
The Demolitionist '95

Helmut Griem
The Damned '69
McKenzie Break '70
Children of Rage '75
Les Rendez-vous D'Anna '78
La Passante '83
Malou '83
Escape '90

David Alan Grier
A Soldier's Story '84
Beer '85
Off Limits '87
I'm Gonna Git You Sucka '88
Loose Cannons '90
Boomerang '92
Blankman '94
In the Army Now '94
Jumanji '95
Tales from the Hood '95

Pam Grier
The Big Doll House '71
The Big Bird Cage '72
Twilight People '72
Coffy '73
Naked Warriors '73
Scream Blacula Scream '73
Foxy Brown '74
Bucktown '75
Friday Foster '75
Sheba, Baby '75
Drum '76
Greased Lightning '77
Fort Apache, the Bronx '81
Something Wicked This Way Comes '83
Tough Enough '83
Badge of the Assassin '85
Stand Alone '85
The Vindicator '85
On the Edge '86
Above the Law '88
The Package '89
Class of 1999 '90
Bill & Ted's Bogus Journey '91
Serial Killer '95
Escape from L.A. '96
Original Gangstas '96

Roosevelt Grier
The Treasure of Jamaica Reef '74
The Big Push '75
The Glove '78
The Seekers '79
Sophisticated Gents '81

Jonathan Gries
Swap Meet '79
Joy Sticks '83
Real Genius '85
Kill Me Again '89
Pucker Up and Bark Like a Dog '89

Joe Grifasi
On the Yard '79
Gentleman Bandit '81
Still of the Night '82
Bad Medicine '85
F/X '86
Ironweed '87
Chances Are '89
Perfect Witness '89
The Feud '90
Presumed Innocent '90
City of Hope '91
Benny & Joon '93
Household Saints '93
Heavy '94
Money Train '95
Two Bits '96

Simone Griffeth
Sixteen '72
Death Race 2000 '75
Delusion '84
Hot Target '85
The Patriot '86

Josephine Griffin
The Man Who Never Was '55
Postmark for Danger '56
The Spanish Gardener '57

Lorie Griffin
Aloha Summer '88
Cheerleader Camp '88

Robert Griffin
Crime of Passion '57
I Was a Teenage Werewolf '57
Monster from Green Hell '58

Tony Griffin
Evil Laugh '86
Robin Hood: Men in Tights '93

Andy Griffith
A Face in the Crowd '57
No Time for Sergeants '58
Andy Griffith Show '60
Pray for the Wildcats '74
Hearts of the West '75
Savages '75
From Here to Eternity '79
Murder in Texas '81
Murder in Coweta County '83
Fatal Vision '84
Return to Mayberry '85
Rustler's Rhapsody '85
Spy Hard '96

Anthony Griffith
Panther '95
Tales from the Hood '95

Corine Griffith
Dracula/Garden of Eden '28
The Garden of Eden '28

Eva Griffith
The Turn of the Screw '74
Ride a Wild Pony '75

Gordon Griffith
Little Annie Rooney '25
Outlaws of the Range '36

Hugh Griffith
The Last Days of Dolwyn '49
The Sleeping Tiger '54
Lucky Jim '58
Ben-Hur '59
Exodus '60
The Counterfeit Traitor '62
Mutiny on the Bounty '62
Tom Jones '63
How to Steal a Million '66
Oh Dad, Poor Dad (Momma's Hung You in the Closet & I'm Feeling So Sad) '67
The Fixer '68
Oliver! '68
Cry of the Banshee '70
Start the Revolution Without Me '70
Wuthering Heights '70
The Abominable Dr. Phibes '71
The Canterbury Tales '71
Who Slew Auntie Roo? '71
Doctor Phibes Rises Again '72
Diary of Forbidden Dreams '73
The Final Programme '73
Craze '74
Luther '74
Legend of the Werewolf '75
The Passover Plot '75
The Big Scam '79

James Griffith
Tribute to a Bad Man '56
Bullwhip '58
The Amazing Transparent Man '60
The Legend of Sleepy Hollow '79

Kenneth Griffith
Circus of Horrors '60
Koroshi '67
The Assassination Bureau '69
Revenge '71
Night of the Laughing Dead '75
The Final Option '82
The Englishman Who Went Up a Hill But Came Down a Mountain '95

Melanie Griffith
Harrad Experiment '73
The Drowning Pool '75
Night Moves '75
Smile '75
Joyride '77
One on One '77
Steel Cowboy '78
Underground Aces '80
She's in the Army Now '81
Body Double '84
Fear City '85
Something Wild '86
Cherry 2000 '88
The Milagro Beanfield War '88
Stormy Monday '88
Working Girl '88
The Bonfire of the Vanities '90
In the Spirit '90
Pacific Heights '90
Women & Men: Stories of Seduction '90
Paradise '91
Shining Through '92
A Stranger Among Us '92
Born Yesterday '93
Milk Money '94
Nobody's Fool '94
Buffalo Girls '95
Mulholland Falls '95
Now and Then '95
Two Much '96

Raymond Griffith
White Tiger '23
The Night Club '25
Paths to Paradise '25
Hands Up '26
All Quiet on the Western Front '30

Thomas Ian Griffith
The Karate Kid: Part 3 '89
Ulterior Motives '92
Excessive Force '93
Beyond Forgiveness '94
Crackerjack '94

Tom Griffith
The Alien Factor '78
Night Beast '83
Hawk and Castile

Tracy Griffith
The Good Mother '88
Fast Food '89
The First Power '89
Sleepaway Camp 3: Teenage Wasteland '89
The Finest Hour '91
All Tied Up '92
Skeeter '93

Linda Griffiths
Lianna '83
Overdrawn at the Memory Bank '83
Reno and the Doc '84

Richard Griffiths
Whoops Apocalypse '83
Shanghai Surprise '86
Withnail and I '87
Naked Gun 2 1/2: The Smell of Fear '91
Blame It on the Bellboy '92
Guarding Tess '94

Jeff Griggs
Eden '92
Eden 2 '93
Eden 3 '93
Eden 4 '93
Breaking Point '94

Johanna Grika
Visitants '87
Vice Academy 3 '91

Frank Grimes
Crystalstone '88
The Dive '89

Gary Grimes
Summer of '42 '71
Culpepper Cattle Co. '72
Cahill: United States Marshal '73
Class of '44 '73

Scott Grimes
It Came Upon a Midnight Clear '84
Critters '86
Critters 2: The Main Course '88
Frog '89
Frogs! '90s
Night Life '90

Tammy Grimes
The Runner Stumbles '79
No Big Deal '83
America '86
Mr. North '88
Backstreet Justice '93

Herbert Grimwood
When the Clouds Roll By '19
Romola '25

Nikolai Grinko
Andrei Rublev '66
Stalker '79

Stephen Grives
Horror Planet '80
Flambards

George Grizzard
From the Terrace '60
Advise and Consent '62
Pueblo Affair '73
The Stranger Within '74
Comes a Horseman '78
Attica '80
Seems Like Old Times '80
Oldest Living Graduate '82
Wrong is Right '82
Bachelor Party '84
Embassy '85
The Deliberate Stranger '86
False Witness '89
Caroline? '90
Iran: Days of Crisis '91
Scarlett '94

Charles Grodin
Sex and the College Girl '64
Rosemary's Baby '68
Catch-22 '70
The Heartbreak Kid '72
11 Harrowhouse '74
King Kong '76
The Meanest Men in the West '76
The Grass is Always Greener Over the Septic Tank '78
Heaven Can Wait '78
Just Me & You '78
Real Life '79
Sunburn '79
It's My Turn '80
Seems Like Old Times '80
The Great Muppet Caper '81
The Incredible Shrinking Woman '81
The Lonely Guy '84
The Woman in Red '84
Movers and Shakers '85
Grown Ups '86
Last Resort '86
The Couch Trip '87
Ishtar '87
Midnight Run '88
You Can't Hurry Love '88
Taking Care of Business '90
Beethoven '92
Clifford '92
Beethoven's 2nd '93
Dave '93
Heart and Souls '93
So I Married an Axe Murderer '93
My Summer Story '94

Kathryn Grody
Parents '89
The Lemon Sisters '90
Quick Change '90

David Groh
A Hero Ain't Nothin' But a Sandwich '78
Zertigo Diamond Caper '82
Hot Shot '86
Broken Vows '87
Illegal in Blue '95

Ake Gronberg
Monika '52
Sawdust & Tinsel '53

Herbert Gronemeyer
Das Boot '81
Spring Symphony '86

Sam Groom
The Baby Maker '70
Betrayal '74
Beyond the Bermuda Triangle '75
Run for the Roses '78
Deadly Games '80
Deadly Eyes '82

Arye Gross
Soul Man '86
The Couch Trip '87
House 2: The Second Story '87
Tequila Sunrise '88
The Experts '89
Coupe de Ville '90
A Matter of Degrees '90
For the Boys '91
Boris and Natasha: The Movie '92
A Midnight Clear '92
Shaking the Tree '92
Hexed '93
The Opposite Sex and How to Live With Them '93

Edan Gross
And You Thought Your Parents Were Weird! '91
Best of the Best 2 '93

Mary Gross
Club Paradise '86
Baby Boom '87
The Couch Trip '87
Big Business '88
Casual Sex? '88
Feds '88
Best of Eddie Murphy '89
Troop Beverly Hills '89
There Goes the Neighborhood '92
The Santa Clause '94

Michael Gross
Summer Fantasy '84
Big Business '88
The FBI Murders '88
A Connecticut Yankee in King Arthur's Court '89
Tremors '89
Cool As Ice '91
Midnight Murders '91
Alan & Naomi '92
Firestorm: 72 Hours in Oakland '93
In the Heat of Passion 2: Unfaithful '94
Tremors 2: Aftershocks '96

Paul Gross
Buffalo Jump '90
Armistead Maupin's Tales of the City '93
Aspen Extreme '93
Northern Extremes '93
Whale Music '94

Brigitte Grothum
The Strange Countess '61
Inn on the River '62

Deborah Grover
Mania '80s
The Christmas Wife '88

Robert Grubb
Gallipoli '81
Mad Max: Beyond Thunderdome '85
Remember Me '85

Gary Grubbs
Foxfire '87
Without Warning: The James Brady Story '91
The Ernest Green Story '93

Franz Gruber
Deutschland im Jahre Null '47
Terror Beneath the Sea '66
X from Outer Space '67

Olivier Gruner
Angel Town '89
Nemesis '93
Automatic '94
The Fighter '95

Dominic Guard
The Go-Between '71
Picnic at Hanging Rock '75
Absolution '81

Kit Guard
Fighting Champ '33
El Diablo Rides '39

Pippa Guard
Unsuitable Job for a Woman '82
Scarlett '94

Harry Guardino
Houseboat '58
The Five Pennies '59
Pork Chop Hill '59
Hell is for Heroes '62
The Adventures of Bullwhip Griffin '66
Madigan '68
Lovers and Other Strangers '70
Dirty Harry '71
Octaman '71
They Only Kill Their Masters '72
Get Christie Love! '74
Whiffs '75
The Enforcer '76
St. Ives '76
Rollercoaster '77
Matilda '78
Goldengirl '79
Any Which Way You Can '80
The Neon Empire '89
Fist of Honor '92

Irina Gubanova
War and Peace '68
Private Life '82

Blanca Guerra
Santa Sangre '90
Danzon '91

Evelyn Guerrero
The Toolbox Murders '78
Cheech and Chong's Next Movie '80
Cheech and Chong's Nice Dreams '81
Cheech and Chong: Things Are Tough All Over '82

Franco Guerrero
One Armed Executioner '80
American Commandos '84
Warriors of the Apocalypse '85
The Kick Fighter '91
Deathfight '93

Monica Guerritore
Together? '79
The Endless Game '89

Fausto Guerzoni
The Bicycle Thief '48
Black Orpheus '58

Christopher Guest
Girlfriends '78
The Last Word '80
The Long Riders '80
Heartbeeps '81
A Piano for Mrs. Cimino '82
This Is Spinal Tap '84
Beyond Therapy '86
Little Shop of Horrors '86
The Princess Bride '87
Sticky Fingers '88
A Few Good Men '92
The Return of Spinal Tap '92

Lance Guest
Halloween 2: The Nightmare Isn't Over! '81
I Ought to Be in Pictures '82
Just the Way You Are '84
The Last Starfighter '84
Roommate '84
My Father, My Rival '85
Jaws: The Revenge '87
The Wizard of Loneliness '88

Nicholas Guest
The Long Riders '80
Criminal Act '88
Assassin '89
National Lampoon's Christmas Vacation '89
Strange Case of Dr. Jekyll & Mr. Hyde '89
Dollman '90
Chrome Soldiers '92
Forever: A Ghost of a Love Story '92
Grand Tour: Disaster in Time '92
My Daughter's Keeper '93
Nemesis '93
Kickboxer 4: The Aggressor '94
Puppet Master 5: The Final Chapter '94
Night Hunter '95

Carla Gugino
Murder without Motive '92
Son-in-Law '93
This Boy's Life '93
The Buccaneers '95
Miami Rhapsody '95
Red Hot '95

Wandisa Guida
The Devil's Commandment '56
Gladiator of Rome '63

Giovanni Guidelli
Where Angels Fear to Tread '91
Fiorile '93

Nancy Guild
Black Magic '49
Abbott and Costello Meet the Invisible Man '51
Francis Covers the Big Town '53

Paul Guilfoyle
The Crime of Dr. Crespi '35
Law of the Underworld '38
The Saint Takes Over '40
The Missing Corpse '45
Follow Me Quietly '49
The Judge '49

Paul Guilfoyle
Billy Galvin '86
Cadillac Man '90
Class of '61 '92
Curiosity Kills '90
Dead Ahead: The Exxon Valdez Disaster '92
Final Analysis '92
Fallen Angels 2 '93
Amelia Earhart: The Final Flight '94
Little Odessa '94
Mother's Boys '94
Celtic Pride '96

Robert Guillaume
Superfly T.N.T. '73
The Best of Soap: Who Killed Peter? '77
The Kid from Left Field '79
Seems Like Old Times '80
The Kid with the Broken Halo '82
The Kid with the 200 I.Q. '83
Prince Jack '83
North and South Book 1 '85
They Still Call Me Bruce '86
Wanted Dead or Alive '86
Fire and Rain '89
Lean on Me '89
You Must Remember This '90s
Death Warrant '90
The Penthouse '92
The Meteor Man '93
Cosmic Slop '94
A Good Day to Die '95

Fernando Guillen
Women on the Verge of a Nervous Breakdown '88
Mouth to Mouth '95

Tim Guinee
Tai-Pan '86
Vietnam War Story 2 '88
American Blue Note '89
Once Around '91
Chain of Desire '93
The Night We Never Met '93
Breathing Lessons '94
Men of War '94
Follow the River '95
How to Make an American Quilt '95

Rick Guinn
Buffalo Rider '78
Mountain Charlie '80

Alec Guinness
Great Expectations '46
Oliver Twist '48
Kind Hearts and Coronets '49
Last Holiday '50
The Lavender Hill Mob '51
The Man in the White Suit '51
The Promoter '52
Captain's Paradise '53
Malta Story '53
The Detective '54
The Ladykillers '55
The Prisoner '55
To Paris with Love '55
A Majority of One '56
The Swan '56
The Bridge on the River Kwai '57
The Horse's Mouth '58
Tunes of Glory '60
Tunes of Glory/Horse's Mouth '60
Damn the Defiant '62
Lawrence of Arabia '62
The Fall of the Roman Empire '64
Doctor Zhivago '65
Hotel Paradiso '66
The Quiller Memorandum '66
The Comedians '67
Cromwell '70
Scrooge '70
Brother Sun, Sister Moon '73
Hitler: The Last Ten Days '73
Murder by Death '76
Star Wars '77
The Empire Strikes Back '80
Little Lord Fauntleroy '80
Raise the Titanic '80
To See Such Fun '81
From "Star Wars" to "Jedi": The Making of a Saga '83
Lovesick '83
A Passage to India '84
A Handful of Dust '88
Little Dorrit, Film 1: Nobody's Fault '88
Little Dorrit, Film 2: Little Dorrit's Story '88
Kafka '91
Monsignor Quixote '91
A Foreign Field '93

Julien Guiomar
My New Partner '84
Swashbuckler '84
Leolo '92

Tom Guiry
The Sandlot '93
Lassie '94

Tito Guizar
The Gay Ranchero '42
On the Old Spanish Trail '47

Clu Gulager
The Killers '64
And Now Miguel '66
Winning '69
The Last Picture Show '71
The Glass House '72
Hit Lady '74
McQ '74
Smile, Jenny, You're Dead '74
Wonderland Cove '75
The Other Side of Midnight '77
He Who Walks Alone '78
A Question of Love '78
Snowblind '78
Force of One '79
Willa '79
Kenny Rogers as the Gambler '80
Touched by Love '80
Kenny Rogers as the Gambler, Part 2: The Adventure Continues '83
Lies '83
Living Proof: The Hank Williams Jr. Story '83
Chattanooga Choo Choo '84
The Initiation '84
Into the Night '85
A Nightmare on Elm Street 2: Freddy's Revenge '85

Return of the Living Dead '85
The Hidden '87
Hunter's Blood '87
The Offspring '87
I'm Gonna Git You Sucka '88
Teen Vamp '88
The Uninvited '88
Tapeheads '89
My Heroes Have Always Been Cowboys '91
The Killing Device '92

Dorothy Gulliver
Under Montana Skies '30
The Galloping Ghost '31
The Fighting Marshal '32
Outlaw Justice '32
Shadow of the Eagle '32
Faces '68

Leo Gullotta
Sinbad of the Seven Seas '89
La Scorta '94

David Gulpilil
Mad Dog Morgan '76
The Last Wave '77
Crocodile Dundee '86
Dark Age '88

Moses Gunn
The Great White Hope '70
The Hot Rock '70
Shaft '71
Wild Rovers '71
Haunts of the Very Rich '72
Shaft's Big Score '72
Amazing Grace '74
Aaron Loves Angela '75
Cornbread, Earl & Me '75
Rollerball '75
Ragtime '81
Amityville 2: The Possession '82
Firestarter '84
The NeverEnding Story '84
Certain Fury '85
Charlotte Forten's Mission: Experiment in Freedom '85
Killing Floor '85
Heartbreak Ridge '86
The House of Dies Drear '88
The Women of Brewster Place '89
Memphis '91
Perfect Harmony '91

Bob Gunton
Rollover '81
Lois Gibbs and the Love Canal '82
Static '87
Cookie '89
Glory '89
Judgment '90
Mission of the Shark '91
Dead Ahead: The Exxon Valdez Disaster '92
Sinatra '92
Demolition Man '93
Father Hood '93
Lone Justice '93
Wild Palms '93
Roswell: The U.F.O. Cover-Up '94
The Shawshank Redemption '94
Ace Ventura: When Nature Calls '95
Broken Arrow '95
In Pursuit of Honor '95
Kingfish: A Story of Huey P. Long '95

Alizia Gur
From Russia with Love '63
Beast of Morocco '66

Sigrid Gurie
The Adventures of Marco Polo '38
Algiers '38
Three Faces West '40
Enemy of Women '44

Eric Gurry
Mystery at Fire Island '81
Bad Boys '83
The Zoo Gang '85
Something Special '86

Louis Guss
Willie & Phil '80
Moonstruck '87
Nitti: The Enforcer '88
American Blue Note '89
The Cemetery Club '93

Arlo Guthrie
Alice's Restaurant '69
Roadside Prophets '92

Tani Phelps Guthrie
Daughters of Satan '72
The Thirsty Dead '74

Steve Guttenberg
The Chicken Chronicles '77
The Boys from Brazil '78
Can't Stop the Music '80
To Race the Wind '80
Miracle on Ice '81
Diner '82
The Day After '83
The Man Who Wasn't There '83
Police Academy '84
Bad Medicine '85
Cocoon '85
Police Academy 2: Their First Assignment '85
Pecos Bill '86
Police Academy 3: Back in Training '86
Short Circuit '86
Amazon Women on the Moon '87
The Bedroom Window '87
Police Academy 4: Citizens on Patrol '87
Surrender '87
Three Men and a Baby '87
Cocoon: The Return '88
High Spirits '88
Don't Tell Her It's Me '90
Three Men and a Little Lady '90
The Big Green '95
Home for the Holidays '95
It Takes Two '95

Lucy Gutteridge
Top Secret! '84
The Secret Garden '87
The Trouble with Spies '87
The Woman He Loved '88
Tusks '89
Grief '94

Ronald Guttman
Iran: Days of Crisis '91
Josh and S.A.M. '93

DeJuan Guy
Candyman '92
One Man's Justice '95

Jasmine Guy
School Daze '88
Harlem Nights '89
Runaway '89
A Century of Women '94
America's Dream '95

Sheila Guyse
Boy! What a Girl '45
Sepia Cinderella '47
Miracle in Harlem '48

Joe Guzaldo
Smooth Talker '90
Bingo '91

Luis Guzman
Q & A '90
The Hard Way '91
Jumpin' at the Boneyard '92
Carlito's Way '93
Guilty as Sin '93
Mr. Wonderful '93
The Burning Season '94
The Substitute '96

Teri Guzman
Women Unchained '70s
Escape from Cell Block 3 '78

Jack Gwaltney
Vital Signs '90
Risk '94

Edmund Gwenn
Skin Game '31
If I Were Rich '33
Java Head '35
Sylvia Scarlett '35
Doctor Takes a Wife '40
Foreign Correspondent '40
Pride and Prejudice '40
Cheers for Miss Bishop '41
The Devil & Miss Jones '41
Forever and a Day '43
Lassie, Come Home '43
The Keys of the Kingdom '44
Green Dolphin Street '47
Life with Father '47
Miracle on 34th Street '47
The Hills of Home '48
Challenge to Lassie '49
A Woman of Distinction '50
The Bigamist '53
The Student Prince '54
Them! '54
It's a Dog's Life '55
The Trouble with Harry '55

Jack Gwillim
Flame Over India '60
Sword of Sherwood Forest '60
The Bushbaby '70

Michael Gwynn
The Revenge of Frankenstein '58
Jason and the Argonauts '63
The Scars of Dracula '70

Anne Gwynne
Black Friday '40
Ride 'Em Cowboy '42
House of Frankenstein '44
Fear '46
Killer Dill '47
Black Tower '50
King of the Bullwhip '51
Breakdown '53
Meteor Monster '57
Adam at 6 a.m. '70

Fred Gwynne
Car 54, Where Are You? '61
The Littlest Angel '69
Sanctuary of Fear '79
Day with Conrad Green '80
Simon '80
The Munsters' Revenge '81
The Mysterious Stranger '82
The Cotton Club '84
The Boy Who Could Fly '86
Off Beat '86
Fatal Attraction '87
Ironweed '87
Murder by the Book '87
Vanishing Act '88
Disorganized Crime '89
Pet Sematary '89
My Cousin Vinny '92
Shadows and Fog '92

Michael C. Gwynne
Payday '72
Special Delivery '76
The Streets of L.A. '79
Harry Tracy '83
Seduced '85
Cherry 2000 '88
The Last of the Finest '90

Peter Gwynne
The Dove '74
Puzzle '78
Tim '79

Kim Gyngell
The Wacky World of Wills & Burke '85
Boulevard of Broken Dreams '88
Heaven Tonight '93

Greta Gynt
The Hooded Terror '38
Sexton Blake and the Hooded Terror '38
The Arsenal Stadium Mystery '39
The Human Monster '39
Mr. Emmanuel '44
Dear Murderer '47

Hugo Haas
Days of Glory '43
Holiday in Mexico '46
Merton of the Movies '47
Northwest Outpost '47
The Private Affairs of Bel Ami '47
My Girl Tisa '48
The Fighting Kentuckian '49
King Solomon's Mines '50

Lukas Haas
Witness '85
Solarbabies '86
The Lady in White '88
The Wizard of Loneliness '88
Music Box '89
See You in the Morning '89
Rambling Rose '91
Shattered Spirits '91
Alan & Naomi '92
Leap of Faith '92
Warrior Spirit '94
Boys '95

Matthias Habich
An Occurrence at Owl Creek Bridge/Coup de Grace '62
Coup de Grace '78
Straight for the Heart '88
The Savage Woman '91

Olivia Hack
The Brady Bunch Movie '95
A Very Brady Sequel '96

Shelley Hack
Annie Hall '77
If Ever I See You Again '78
King of Comedy '82
Single Bars, Single Women '84
Kicks '85
Troll '86
The Stepfather '87
Blind Fear '89
A Casualty of War '90
The Finishing Touch '92
Me, Myself & I '92

George Hackathorne
The Last of the Mohicans '20
The Worldly Madonna '22
Merry-Go-Round '23

Joseph Hacker
The Ultimate Imposter '79
Little Treasure '85

Buddy Hackett
God's Little Acre '58
The Music Man '62
The Wonderful World of the Brothers Grimm '62
It's a Mad, Mad, Mad, Mad World '63
Muscle Beach Party '64
Bud and Lou '78
Loose Shoes '80
Scrooged '88

Joan Hackett
The Group '66
Will Penny '67
Support Your Local Sheriff '69
Rivals '72
Class of '63 '73
The Last of Sheila '73
Reflections of Murder '74
The Terminal Man '74
The Treasure of Matecumbe '76
Dead of Night '77
The Possessed '77
The Long Days of Summer '80
One Trick Pony '80
Only When I Laugh '81
The Escape Artist '82
Flicks '85

Karl Hackett
Cavalry '36
Border Phantom '37
Gun Lords of Stirrup Basin '37
The Red Rope '37
Feud Maker '38
Phantom Ranger '38
Songs and Bullets '38
Take Me Back to Oklahoma '40
Sagebrush Law '43
Sonora Stagecoach '44
His Brother's Ghost '45
Lightning Raiders '45
Outlaw of the Plains '46

Sandy Hackett
Hamburger...The Motion Picture '86
Ex-Cop '93

Gene Hackman
Lilith '64
Hawaii '66
Bonnie & Clyde '67
Downhill Racer '69
Marooned '69
Riot '69
Doctors' Wives '70
I Never Sang For My Father '70
The French Connection '71
The Poseidon Adventure '72
Prime Cut '72
Scarecrow '73
The Conversation '74
Zandy's Bride '74
Bite the Bullet '75
French Connection 2 '75
Night Moves '75
America at the Movies '76
A Bridge Too Far '77
The Domino Principle '77
March or Die '77
Superman: The Movie '78
Superman 2 '80
All Night Long '81
Eureka! '81
Reds '81
Uncommon Valor '83
Under Fire '83
Misunderstood '84
Target '85
Twice in a Lifetime '85
Hoosiers '86
Power '86
No Way Out '87
Superman 4: The Quest for Peace '87
Another Woman '88
Bat 21 '88
Full Moon in Blue Water '88
Mississippi Burning '88
Split Decisions '88
The Package '89
Loose Cannons '90
Narrow Margin '90
Postcards from the Edge '90
Class Action '91
Company Business '91
Unforgiven '92
The Firm '93
Geronimo: An American Legend '93
The Quick and the Dead '94
Wyatt Earp '94
The Birdcage '95
Crimson Tide '95
Get Shorty '95

Jonathan Hadary
As Is '85
The New Age '94

Dayle Haddon
Paperback Hero '73
The World's Greatest Athlete '73
The Cheaters '76
North Dallas Forty '79
Bedroom Eyes '86
Hitchhiker 3 '87
Cyborg '89

Ron Haddrick
Great Expectations: The Untold Story '87
Quigley Down Under '90

Sara Haden
Finishing School '33
Mad Love '35
The Poor Little Rich Girl '36
Andy Hardy Gets Spring Fever '39
Andy Hardy Meets Debutante '40
The Shop Around the Corner '40
Andy Hardy's Private Secretary '41
Andy Hardy's Double Life '42
Somewhere I'll Find You '42
Our Vines Have Tender Grapes '45
Love Laughs at Andy Hardy '46
Mr. Ace '46
The Great Rupert '50
A Life of Her Own '50

Reed Hadley
Hollywood Stadium Mystery '38
Zorro's Fighting Legion '39
The Bank Dick '40
Whistling in the Dark '41
Ziegfeld Girl '41
Guadalcanal Diary '43
Dark Corner '46
Doll Face '46
A Southern Yankee '48
I Shot Jesse James '49
Rimfire '49
Return of Jesse James '50
Baron of Arizona '51
The Half-Breed '51
Little Big Horn '51
Kansas Pacific '53
Brain of Blood '71

Molly Hagan
Code of Silence '85
Some Kind of Wonderful '87

Jean Hagen
Adam's Rib '50
The Asphalt Jungle '50
A Life of Her Own '50
Singin' in the Rain '52
Latin Lovers '53
The Big Knife '55
The Shaggy Dog '59

Hagen ▶cont.

Sunrise at Campobello *'60*
Panic in the Year Zero! *'62*
Alexander: The Other Side of Dawn *'77*

Ross Hagen
Hellcats *'68*
Speedway *'68*
Angels' Wild Women *'72*
Bad Charleston Charlie *'73*
The Deadly and the Beautiful *'73*
Night Creature *'79*
Angel *'84*
Avenging Angel *'85*
Armed Response *'86*
Commando Squad *'87*
Phantom Empire *'87*
Star Slammer *'87*
B.O.R.N. *'88*
Warlords *'88*
Alienator *'89*
Marked for Murder *'89*
Blood Games *'90*
Dinosaur Island *'93*
Bikini Drive-In *'94*
Midnight Tease 2 *'95*

Uta Hagen
The Other *'72*
The Boys from Brazil *'78*
Reversal of Fortune *'90*

Julie Hagerty
Airplane! *'80*
The Day the Women Got Even *'80*
Airplane 2: The Sequel *'82*
A Midsummer Night's Sex Comedy *'82*
Bad Medicine *'85*
Goodbye, New York *'85*
Lost in America *'85*
Beyond Therapy *'86*
Necessary Parties *'88*
Bloodhounds of Broadway *'89*
Rude Awakening *'89*
Reversal of Fortune *'90*
What About Bob? *'91*
Noises Off *'92*

Dan Haggerty
Bury Me an Angel *'71*
The Tender Warrior *'71*
The Shrieking *'73*
Starbird and Sweet William *'73*
Life & Times of Grizzly Adams *'74*
When the North Wind Blows *'74*
The Adventures of Frontier Fremont *'75*
Blood Brothers *'77*
Desperate Women *'78*
Terror Out of the Sky *'78*
California Gold Rush *'81*
King of the Mountain *'81*
The Capture of Grizzly Adams *'82*
Angels Die Hard *'84*
Abducted *'86*
Night Wars *'88*
Chance *'89*
The Channeler *'89*
The Chilling *'89*
Elves *'89*
The Inheritor *'90*
Repo Jake *'90*
Spirit of the Eagle *'90*
Deadly Diamonds *'91*
Mind Trap *'91*
Soldier's Fortune *'91*
Ice Pawn *'92*
Abducted 2: The Reunion *'94*
Cheyenne Warrior *'94*

Kenichi Hagiwara
Kagemusha *'80*
Traffic Jam *'91*

Michael Hagiwara
Prehysteria 2 *'94*
Josh Kirby...Time Warrior: Chapter 5, Journey to the Magic Cavern *'96*

Marvin Hagler
Indio *'90*
Indio 2: The Revolt *'92*

Larry Hagman
Ensign Pulver *'64*
Fail-Safe *'64*
In Harm's Way *'65*
The Group *'66*
Three in the Cellar *'70*
Deadly Encounter *'72*
No Place to Run *'72*
Son of Blob *'72*
Antonio *'73*
Harry and Tonto *'74*
Hurricane *'74*
The Big Bus *'76*
Mother, Jugs and Speed *'76*
The Eagle Has Landed *'77*
Intimate Strangers *'77*
President's Mistress *'78*
S.O.B. *'81*
Nixon *'95*

Archie Hahn
Pray TV *'80*
Meatballs 2 *'84*
Protocol *'84*
Glory Years *'87*

Eric Hahn
Crossfire *'89*
Fist of Glory *'95*

Gisela Hahn
Big Boss *'77*
Mr. Scarface *'77*

Jess Hahn
Secret Agent Super Dragon *'66*
Triple Cross *'67*
The Night of the Following Day *'69*
The Grand Duel *'73*
Mean Frank and Crazy Tony *'75*
Mama Dracula *'80*

Jessica Hahn
Thunder & Mud *'89*
Bikini Summer 2 *'92*

Mang Hai
Buddha Assassinator *'82*
Hell's Wind Staff *'82*

Charles Haid
The Choirboys *'77*
Deathmoon *'78*
Oliver's Story *'78*
Who'll Stop the Rain? *'78*
Altered States *'80*
Hill Street Blues, Vol. 1: Hill Street Station *'81*
Twirl *'81*
Children in the Crossfire *'84*
Cop *'88*
The Great Escape 2: The Untold Story *'88*
The Rescue *'88*
Weekend War *'88*
Fire and Rain *'89*
Night Breed *'90*
The Chinatown Murders: Man Against the Mob *'92*
Freeze Frame *'92*
Storyville *'92*
Cooperstown *'93*
The Fire Next Time *'93*
A Cop for the Killing *'94*
Broken Trust *'95*

Ion Haiduc
Bloodstone: Subspecies 2 *'92*
Bloodlust: Subspecies 3 *'93*

Sid Haig
Spider Baby *'64*
Track of the Vampire *'66*
Chrome Hearts *'70*
The Big Doll House *'71*
The Big Bird Cage *'72*
The Deadly and the Beautiful *'73*
Busting *'74*
Commando Squad *'87*
Warlords *'88*
Wizards of the Lost Kingdom 2 *'89*
The Forbidden Dance *'90*

Kenneth Haigh
Teenage Bad Girl *'59*
Cleopatra *'63*
The Bitch *'78*

Louisa Haigh
Murderers among Us: The Simon Wiesenthal Story *'89*
Shipwrecked *'90*

Marian Hailey
Jenny *'70*
Lovers and Other Strangers *'70*

Corey Haim
First Born *'84*
Murphy's Romance *'85*
Secret Admirer *'85*
Silver Bullet *'85*
A Time to Live *'85*
Lucas *'86*
The Lost Boys *'87*
License to Drive *'88*
Watchers *'88*
Dream a Little Dream *'89*
Dream Machine *'91*
Fast Getaway *'91*
Prayer of the Rollerboys *'91*
The Double O Kid *'92*
Oh, What a Night *'92*
Anything for Love *'93*
Blown Away *'93*
Just One of the Girls *'93*
Dream a Little Dream 2 *'94*
Fast Getaway 2 *'94*
National Lampoon's Last Resort *'94*
Life 101 *'95*

Patricia Haines
Night Caller from Outer Space *'66*
The Virgin Witch *'70*

Richard Haines
Alien from L.A. *'87*
An African Dream *'90*

William Haines
Little Annie Rooney *'25*
Show People *'28*
The Girl Said No *'37*
Way Out West *'37*

Khrystyne Haje
Scanners: The Showdown *'94*
Cyborg 3: The Recycler *'95*

Haji
Motor Psycho *'65*
Faster Pussycat! Kill! Kill! *'66*

Alan Hale
The Four Horsemen of the Apocalypse *'21*
Robin Hood *'22*
The Trap *'22*
The Covered Wagon *'23*
Dick Turpin *'25*
The Leatherneck *'28*
Power *'28*
The Sin of Madelon Claudet *'31*
Susan Lenox: Her Fall and Rise *'31*
It Happened One Night *'34*
Little Minister *'34*
The Lost Patrol *'34*
Of Human Bondage *'34*
The Scarlet Letter *'34*
The Crusades *'35*
Last Days of Pompeii *'35*
Our Relations *'36*
The Prince and the Pauper *'37*
Stella Dallas *'37*
Thin Ice *'37*
When Thief Meets Thief *'37*
The Adventures of Marco Polo *'38*
The Adventures of Robin Hood *'38*
Algiers *'38*
Listen, Darling *'38*
Dodge City *'39*
The Man in the Iron Mask *'39*
The Private Lives of Elizabeth & Essex *'39*
The Fighting 69th *'40*
Santa Fe Trail *'40*
The Sea Hawk *'40*
They Drive by Night *'40*
Virginia City *'40*
Footsteps in the Dark *'41*
Strawberry Blonde *'41*
Captains of the Clouds *'42*
Desperate Journey *'42*
Gentleman Jim *'42*
Action in the North Atlantic *'43*
Destination Tokyo *'43*
Thank Your Lucky Stars *'43*
This Is the Army *'43*
The Adventures of Mark Twain *'44*
The Man I Love *'46*
Night and Day *'46*
Pursued *'47*
My Girl Tisa *'48*
South of St. Louis *'48*
Adventures of Don Juan *'49*
The Inspector General *'49*
Stars in My Crown *'50*

Alan Hale, Jr.
To the Shores of Tripoli *'42*
The Spirit of West Point *'47*
It Happens Every Spring *'49*
Rim of the Canyon *'49*
The Underworld Story *'50*
The West Point Story *'50*
At Sword's Point *'51*
Home Town Story *'51*
Big Trees *'52*
Young at Heart *'54*
The Indian Fighter *'55*
All Mine to Give *'56*
Battle Hymn *'57*
Casey Jones and Fury (Brave Stallion) *'57*
Up Periscope *'59*
Hard Drivin' *'60*
The Crawling Hand *'63*
Gilligan's Island: Meet the Crew *'64*
There was a Crooked Man *'70*
The Giant Spider Invasion *'75*
The Fifth Musketeer *'79*
The North Avenue Irregulars *'79*
Hambone & Hillie *'84*
Johnny Dangerously *'84*

Barbara Hale
The Falcon in Hollywood *'44*
Going to Town *'44*
First Yank into Tokyo *'45*
West of the Pecos *'45*
The Boy with the Green Hair *'48*
The Clay Pigeon *'49*
Jolson Sings Again *'49*
The Window *'49*
The Jackpot *'50*
Last of the Comanches *'52*
A Lion Is in the Streets *'53*
The Oklahoman *'56*
Seventh Cavalry *'56*
Buckskin *'68*
The Giant Spider Invasion *'75*
Flight of the Grey Wolf *'76*
Perry Mason Returns *'85*
Perry Mason: The Case of the Lost Love *'87*
The Defense Never Rests *'90*

Binnie Hale
The Phantom Light *'35*
Love from a Stranger *'37*

Creighton Hale
The Idol Dancer *'20*
Way Down East *'20*
Broken Hearts of Broadway *'23*
The Marriage Circle *'24*
The Cat and the Canary *'27*
Shop Angel *'32*

Georgia Hale
The Gold Rush *'25*
Gold Rush/Payday *'25*

Georgina Hale
The Boy Friend *'71*
Mahler *'74*
Castaway *'87*

Jean Hale
Psychomania *'63*
In Like Flint *'67*
The St. Valentine's Day Massacre *'67*

Jonathan Hale
Exiled to Shanghai *'37*
Saratoga *'37*
Blondie *'38*
Bringing Up Baby *'38*
The Saint Strikes Back *'39*
The Story of Alexander Graham Bell *'39*
Blondie Has Trouble *'40*
The Saint Takes Over *'40*
The Saint's Double Trouble *'40*
Blondie in Society *'41*
Blondie's Blessed Event *'42*
It's a Great Life *'43*
Hollywood Canteen *'44*
Blondie Knows Best *'46*
Call Northside 777 *'48*
Silver River *'48*
The Judge *'49*

Louise Closser Hale
Devotion *'31*
Platinum Blonde *'31*
Shanghai Express *'32*
Today We Live *'33*

Monte Hale
Western Double Feature 8: Hale & Carradine *'40s*
Son of God's Country *'48*
Pioneer Marshal *'49*
Missourians *'50*
Trail of Robin Hood *'50*
The Vanishing Westerner *'50*
Western Double Feature 2: Wayne & Hale *'80s*

Sonnie Hale
Evergreen *'34*
It's Love Again *'36*

Jack Haley
The Poor Little Rich Girl *'36*
Pick a Star *'37*
Alexander's Ragtime Band *'38*
Rebecca of Sunnybrook Farm *'38*
The Wizard of Oz *'39*
Moon over Miami *'41*
Higher and Higher *'44*
One Body Too Many *'44*
Take It Big *'44*
George White's Scandals *'45*
Treasure of Fear *'45*
People Are Funny *'46*

Jackie Earle Haley
The Bad News Bears *'76*
The Bad News Bears in Breaking Training *'77*
Damnation Alley *'77*
The Bad News Bears Go to Japan *'78*
Breaking Away *'79*
Losin' It *'82*
The Zoo Gang *'85*
Dollman *'90*

H.B. Halicki
Gone in 60 Seconds *'74*
The Junkman *'82*
Deadline Auto Theft *'83*

Albert Hall
Apocalypse Now *'79*
The Long, Hot Summer *'86*
Uncle Tom's Cabin *'87*
Betrayed *'88*
Hearts of Darkness: A Filmmaker's Apocalypse *'91*
Separate But Equal *'91*
Malcolm X *'92*
Devil In a Blue Dress *'95*
Major Payne *'95*

Anthony Michael Hall
Six Pack *'82*
National Lampoon's Vacation *'83*
Sixteen Candles *'84*
The Breakfast Club *'85*
Weird Science *'85*
Out of Bounds *'86*
Johnny Be Good *'88*
Edward Scissorhands *'90*
Into the Sun *'92*
The Adventures of a Gnome Named Gnorm *'93*
Six Degrees of Separation *'93*
Hail Caesar *'94*
Me and the Mob *'94*
Texas *'94*

Arch Hall, Jr.
The Choppers *'61*
Eegah! *'62*
Wild Guitar *'62*
The Sadist *'63*
Nasty Rabbit *'64*
Deadwood *'65*

Archie Hall
Border Badmen *'45*
His Brother's Ghost *'45*

Arsenio Hall
Amazon Women on the Moon *'87*
Coming to America *'88*
Harlem Nights *'89*

Brad Hall
Best of Eddie Murphy *'89*
Limit Up *'89*
Worth Winning *'89*

Bug Hall
The Little Rascals *'94*
The Big Green *'95*
The Stupids *'95*

Hamilton ▶cont.

If It's Tuesday, This Must Be Belgium '69
The Tattered Web '71
The Way We Were '73
The Drowning Pool '75
Jaws '75
Casey's Shadow '78
Jaws 2 '78
The Amityville Horror '79
Last Cry for Help '79
1941 '79
Brubaker '80
Mazes and Monsters '82
Too Scared to Scream '85
The Last Days of Patton '86

Neil Hamilton
The White Rose '23
America/The Fall of Babylon '24
Isn't Life Wonderful '24
Laughing Sinners '31
The Sin of Madelon Claudet '31
The Animal Kingdom '32
Tarzan, the Ape Man '32
What Price Hollywood? '32
Tarzan and His Mate '34
Hollywood Stadium Mystery '38
The Saint Strikes Back '39
King of the Texas Rangers '41
X Marks the Spot '42
The Devil's Hand '61
The Patsy '64

Patricia Hamilton
Anne of Green Gables '85
Anne of Avonlea '87
The Christmas Wife '88

Richard Hamilton
In Country '89
Sommersby '93

Suzanna Hamilton
Brimstone & Treacle '82
1984 '84
Out of Africa '85
Wetherby '85
Duel of Hearts '92
Tale of a Vampire '92

Tony Hamilton
Nocturna '79
Fatal Instinct '92

Wendy Hamilton
The Scars of Dracula '70
The Dallas Connection '94
Ski School 2 '94

Harry Hamlin
Movie, Movie '78
Clash of the Titans '81
King of the Mountain '81
Making Love '82
Blue Skies Again '83
The Hitchhiker '85
Maxie '85
L.A. Law '86
Laguna Heat '87
Target: Favorite Son '87
Dinner at Eight '89
Deceptions '90
Murder So Sweet '93
Save Me '93
Under Investigation '93
Ebbtide '94

Warren Hammack
The Eye Creatures '65
Zontar, the Thing from Venus '66

Ben Hammer
Invasion of the Bee Girls '73
The Execution of Private Slovik '74
Survival Quest '89
Crazy People '90

John Hammond
Enforcer from Death Row '78
The Prodigal '83
The Blue and the Gray '85

Kay Hammond
Abraham Lincoln '30
Blithe Spirit '45

Nicholas Hammond
The Sound of Music '65
The Amazing Spider-Man '77
Chinese Web '78
Spiderman: The Deadly Dust '78

The Martian Chronicles: Part 1 '79
The Martian Chronicles: Part 3 '79
Trouble in Paradise '88

Olivia Hamnett
The Last Wave '77
Plunge Into Darkness '77
Earthling '80
Deadly Possession '88

Walter Hampden
The Hunchback of Notre Dame '39
Reap the Wild Wind '42
The Adventures of Mark Twain '44
Five Fingers '52
Sabrina '54
The Prodigal '55

Susan Hampshire
The Three Lives of Thomasina '63
The Fighting Prince of Donegal '66
Those Daring Young Men in Their Jaunty Jalopies '69
David Copperfield '70
Baffled '72
Living Free '72
Cry Terror '74
The Story of David '76

James Hampton
Force Five '75
Hawmps! '76
The Amazing Howard Hughes '77
The China Syndrome '79
Hangar 18 '80
Condorman '81
Teen Wolf '85
World War III '86

Lionel Hampton
The Benny Goodman Story '55
Force of Impulse '60

Paul Hampton
Private Duty Nurses '71
Lady Sings the Blues '72
Hit! '73
They Came from Within '75
Deadly Exposure '93

Master Bong Soo Han
Kill the Golden Goose '79
Force: Five '81

John Hancock
The Black Marble '79
Archer: The Fugitive from the Empire '81
In the Custody of Strangers '82
Traxx '87
Why Me? '90

Sheila Hancock
The Anniversary '68
Buster '88
Hawks '89
Three Men and a Little Lady '90
A Business Affair '93
The Buccaneers '95

Irene Handl
Small Hotel '57
Morgan! '66
Wonderwall: The Movie '69
The Private Life of Sherlock Holmes '70
Riding High '78
Adventures of a Private Eye '87

James Handy
Burglar '87
Bird '88
K-9 '89
The Preppie Murder '89
Arachnophobia '90
The Rocketeer '91
False Arrest '92
The O.J. Simpson Story '94
Rave Review '95

Daryl Haney
Daddy's Boys '87
Lords of the Deep '89
Concealed Weapon '94

Helen Hanft
Stardust Memories '80
Used People '92

Roger Hanin
Rocco and His Brothers '60

My Other Husband '85
Day of Atonement '93

Larry Hankin
Armed and Dangerous '86
Black Magic Woman '91
Out on a Limb '92
Billy Madison '94
Prehysteria 2 '94

Jim Hanks
Buford's Beach Bunnies '92
Xtro 3: Watch the Skies '95

Tom Hanks
Bosom Buddies '80
He Knows You're Alone '80
Mazes and Monsters '82
Bachelor Party '84
Splash '84
The Man with One Red Shoe '85
Volunteers '85
Every Time We Say Goodbye '86
The Money Pit '86
Nothing in Common '86
Dragnet '87
Big '88
Punchline '88
The 'Burbs '89
Turner and Hooch '89
The Bonfire of the Vanities '90
Joe Versus the Volcano '90
A League of Their Own '92
Philadelphia '93
Sleepless in Seattle '93
Forrest Gump '94
Apollo 13 '95

Jenny Hanley
On Her Majesty's Secret Service '69
The Scars of Dracula '70
Flesh and Blood Show '73

Jimmy Hanley
Housemaster '38
Salute John Citizen '42
Captive Heart '47
The Blue Lamp '49
Room to Let '49

Adam Hann-Byrd
Little Man Tate '91
Digger '94
Diabolique '96

Daryl Hannah
The Fury '78
Hard Country '81
Blade Runner '82
Summer Lovers '82
The Final Terror '83
The Pope of Greenwich Village '84
Reckless '84
Splash '84
The Clan of the Cave Bear '86
Legal Eagles '86
Roxanne '87
Wall Street '87
High Spirits '88
Steel Magnolias '89
Crazy People '90
At Play in the Fields of the Lord '91
Memoirs of an Invisible Man '92
Attack of the 50 Ft. Woman '93
Grumpy Old Men '93
The Little Rascals '94
Grumpier Old Men '95
The Tie That Binds '95
Two Much '96

Page Hannah
Racing with the Moon '84
My Man Adam '86
Creepshow 2 '87
Shag: The Movie '89

Gale Hansen
The Deadly and the Beautiful '73
Dead Poets Society '89
The Finest Hour '91
Double Vision '92
Shaking the Tree '92

Gunnar Hansen
The Texas Chainsaw Massacre '74
The Demon Lover '77
Hollywood Chainsaw Hookers '88
Freakshow '95
Mosquito '95

Joachim Hansen
Secret of the Black Trunk '62

Frozen Alive '64

Patti Hansen
They All Laughed '81
Hard to Hold '84

Lars Hanson
The Atonement of Gosta Berling '24
The Flesh and the Devil '27
Homecoming '28
The Wind '28
The Informer '29
Walpurgis Night '41

Peter Hanson
Cavalry Charge '51
When Worlds Collide '51

Setsuko Hara
No Regrets for Our Youth '46
Late Spring '49
Early Summer '51
The Idiot '51
Tokyo Story '53

Meiko Harada
Nomugi Pass '79
Ran '85
Akira Kurosawa's Dreams '90

Haya Harareet
Hill 24 Doesn't Answer '55
Ben-Hur '59
Journey Beneath the Desert '61
The Interns '62

Clement Harari
Monkeys, Go Home! '66
Flight of the Eagle '82

Ernest Harden
White Mama '80
The Final Terror '83
White Men Can't Jump '92

Marcia Gay Harden
Miller's Crossing '90
Fever '91
Late for Dinner '91
Sinatra '92
Used People '92
Crush '93
Safe Passage '94
Convict Cowboy '95
The Spitfire Grill '95
Spy Hard '96

Kate Hardie
Mona Lisa '86
Conspiracy '89

Jerry Hardin
Wolf Lake '79
Wanted Dead or Alive '86
Blaze '89
The Hot Spot '90
The Firm '93
The X-Files: Pilot Episode/Deep Throat '93

Melora Hardin
The North Avenue Irregulars '79
Iron Eagle '86
Big Man on Campus '89
Dead Poets Society '89
Lambada '89
The Rocketeer '91
Reckless Kelly '93
Chameleon '95

Ty Hardin
I Married a Monster from Outer Space '58
Merrill's Marauders '62
Palm Springs Weekend '63
PT 109 '63
Battle of the Bulge '65
Berserk! '67
One Step to Hell '68
You're Jinxed, Friend, You've Met Sacramento '70
Rooster: Spurs of Death! '83
Bad Jim '89

Ann Harding
Devotion '31
The Animal Kingdom '32
Love from a Stranger '37
The Magnificent Yankee '50
Two Weeks with Love '50
The Man in the Gray Flannel Suit '56
Promise to Murder '56

John Harding
This Property is Condemned '66
The Impossible Years '68

Kay Harding
The Mummy's Curse '44
Scarlet Claw '44

Lyn Harding
The Speckled Band '31
The Man Who Lived Again '36
Old Spanish Custom '36
Murder at the Baskervilles '37
The Mutiny of the Elsinore '39
Sherlock Holmes: The Silver Blaze '41

Kadeem Hardison
Beat Street '84
I'm Gonna Git You Sucka '88
School Daze '88
Def by Temptation '90
White Men Can't Jump '92
Dream Date '93
Gunmen '93
Renaissance Man '94
Panther '95
Vampire in Brooklyn '95

Cedric Hardwicke
The Ghoul '34
Nine Days a Queen '34
Power '34
Becky Sharp '35
Les Miserables '35
Things to Come '36
King Solomon's Mines '37
The Hunchback of Notre Dame '39
On Borrowed Time '39
Stanley and Livingstone '39
The Howards of Virginia '40
The Invisible Man Returns '40
Tom Brown's School Days '40
Sundown '41
Suspicion '41
The Ghost of Frankenstein '42
Invisible Agent '42
Valley of the Sun '42
Commandos Strike at Dawn '43
The Keys of the Kingdom '44
Wilson '44
A Wing and a Prayer '44
Beware of Pity '46
Nicholas Nickleby '46
Tycoon '47
I Remember Mama '48
Rope '48
The Winslow Boy '48
A Connecticut Yankee in King Arthur's Court '49
The White Tower '50
The Desert Fox '51
The Green Glove '52
Botany Bay '53
Salome '53
Diane '55
Richard III '55
Helen of Troy '56
The Ten Commandments '56
The Magic Fountain '61
Five Weeks in a Balloon '62
The Pumpkin Eater '64

Edward Hardwicke
The Adventures of Sherlock Holmes: Hound of the Baskervilles '89
Sherlock Holmes: The Master Blackmailer '92
Shadowlands '93
The Scarlet Letter '95

Jonathon Hardy
The Devil's Playground '76
Lonely Hearts '82
The Wacky World of Wills & Burke '85

Oliver Hardy
Silent Laugh Makers, No. 1 '15
Silent Laugh Makers, No. 2 '17
Bakery/Grocery Clerk '21
Bellhop/The Noon Whistle '22
Three Ages '23
The Wizard of Oz '25
No Man's Law '27
Laurel & Hardy: Berth Marks '29
Laurel & Hardy: Men O'War '29
Laurel & Hardy: Perfect Day '29
Laurel & Hardy Comedy Classics, Vol. 7 '30s
Laurel & Hardy Comedy Classics, Vol. 8 '30s
Laurel & Hardy Comedy Classics, Vol. 9 '30s

Laurel & Hardy: Another Fine Mess '30
Laurel & Hardy: Below Zero '30
Laurel & Hardy: Blotto '30
Laurel & Hardy: Brats '30
Laurel & Hardy Comedy Classics, Vol. 2 '30
Laurel & Hardy: Hog Wild '30
Laurel & Hardy: Night Owls '30
Laurel & Hardy On the Lam '30
Laurel & Hardy: Be Big '31
Laurel & Hardy: Chickens Come Home '31
Laurel & Hardy Comedy Classics, Vol. 5 '31
Laurel & Hardy: Laughing Gravy '31
Pardon Us '31
Laurel & Hardy: At Work '32
Laurel & Hardy Comedy Classics, Vol. 4 '32
Music Box/Helpmates '32
Pack Up Your Troubles '32
The Devil's Brother '33
Laurel & Hardy and the Family '33
Laurel & Hardy Comedy Classics, Vol. 1 '33
Laurel & Hardy: Stan "Helps" Ollie '33
Sons of the Desert '33
Hollywood Party '34
Laurel & Hardy Comedy Classics, Vol. 3 '34
March of the Wooden Soldiers '34
Bonnie Scotland '35
Laurel & Hardy Comedy Classics, Vol. 6 '35
Bohemian Girl '36
Our Relations '36
Pick a Star '37
Way Out West '37
Block-heads '38
Swiss Miss '38
The Flying Deuces '39
A Chump at Oxford '40
Saps at Sea '40
Great Guns '41
Air Raid Wardens '43
Nothing But Trouble '44
Bullfighters '45
The Fighting Kentuckian '49
Riding High '50
Utopia '51
Golden Age of Comedy '58
Days of Thrills and Laughter '61
A Few Moments with Buster Keaton and Laurel and Hardy '63
Hollywood Clowns '85
Laurel & Hardy Special

Robert Hardy
Demons of the Mind '72
Elizabeth R '72
Dark Places '73
Jenny's War '85
The Shooting Party '85
Northanger Abbey '87
War & Remembrance, Part 1 '88
The Woman He Loved '88
War & Remembrance: The Final Chapter, Part 8 '89
Sherlock Holmes: The Master Blackmailer '92
Middlemarch '93
Mary Shelley's Frankenstein '94
Gulliver's Travels '95
Sense and Sensibility '95

Sam Hardy
Big News '29
King Kong '33
Break of Hearts '35
Powdersmoke Range '35

Sophie Hardy
Erotic Touch of Hot Skin '65
The Mysterious Magician '65

Lumsden Hare
The Crusades '35
The Lives of a Bengal Lancer '35
The Princess Comes Across '36
Gunga Din '39
Northwest Passage '40
Shadows on the Stairs '41
That Forsyte Woman '50
Rose Marie '54

Robertson Hare
Things Happen at Night '48
Murder on the Campus '52
The Adventures of Sadie '55

Dorian Harewood
Sparkle '76
Panic in Echo Park '77
An American Christmas Carol '79
Roots: The Next Generation '79
Beulah Land '80
Strike Force '81
The Ambush Murders '82
Tank '83
Against All Odds '84
The Jesse Owens Story '84
The Falcon and the Snowman '85
Full Metal Jacket '87
Guilty of Innocence '87
God Bless the Child '88
Kiss Shot '89
Pacific Heights '90
Getting Up and Going Home '92
Shattered Image '93
Sudden Death '95

Mariska Hargitay
Ghoulies '84
Welcome to 18 '87
Finish Line '89
Hotel Room '93

Mickey Hargitay
Will Success Spoil Rock Hunter? '57
The Loves of Hercules '60
The Bloody Pit of Horror '65
Lady Frankenstein '72

Doris Hargrave
The Whole Shootin' Match '79
Last Night at the Alamo '83

John Hargreaves
Deathcheaters '76
Don's Party '76
Little Boy Lost '78
Beyond Reasonable Doubt '80
Killing of Angel Street '81
Careful, He Might Hear You '84
Great Gold Swindle '84
My First Wife '84
Malcolm '86
Cry Freedom '87
Sky Pirates '87
Country Life '95
Sorrento Beach '95

Gordon Harker
The Ring '27
Champagne '28
The Farmer's Wife '28
The Phantom Light '35
Inspector Hornleigh '39
Things Happen at Night '48
Small Hotel '57

Susannah Harker
A Dry White Season '89
House of Cards '90
The Crucifer of Blood '91
The Lady's Not for Burning '95
Pride and Prejudice '95

John Harkins
Absence of Malice '81
Amityville 3: The Demon '83
Birdy '84
City Killer '87
Rampage '87
Slaves of New York '89
This Gun for Hire '90

Kenneth Harlan
The Primitive Lover '16
The Penalty '20
Little Church Around the Corner '23
The Virginian '23
The Ice Flood '26
Paradise Island '30
Under Montana Skies '30
A Million to One '37
Renfrew of the Royal Mounted '37
Law of the Texan '38
Santa Fe Marshal '40
Dawn Express '42
Phantom Killer '42
Death Valley Rangers '44

Otis Harlan
Dames Ahoy '30
Mountain Justice '30
Ride Him, Cowboy '32
Telegraph Trail '33
I Can't Escape '34
King Kelly of the U.S.A. '34
Western Gold '37
Mr. Boggs Steps Out '38
Outlaws of Sonora '38

Jean Harlow
Hell's Angels '30
City Lights '31
Platinum Blonde '31
Public Enemy '31
Red Dust '32
Red Headed Woman '32
Bombshell '33
Dinner at Eight '33
Hold Your Man '33
The Girl from Missouri '34
China Seas '35
Reckless '35
Riff Raff '35
Libeled Lady '36
Suzy '36
Wife Versus Secretary '36
Personal Property '37
Saratoga '37
Golden Age of Comedy '58
The Love Goddesses '65

Deborah Harmon
Used Cars '80
Bachelor Party '84
Prince of Bel Air '87

Mark Harmon
Comes a Horseman '78
Beyond the Poseidon Adventure '79
Goliath Awaits '81
The Deliberate Stranger '86
After the Promise '87
Let's Get Harry '87
Prince of Bel Air '87
Summer School '87
The Presidio '88
Stealing Home '88
Sweet Bird of Youth '89
Worth Winning '89
Fourth Story '90
Dillinger '91
Long Road Home '91
Till There was You '91
Cold Heaven '92
Wyatt Earp '94
Magic in the Water '95

Renee Harmon
The Executioner, Part 2: Frozen Scream '84
Lady Street Fighter '86
Night of Terror '87

Tom Harmon
Harmon of Michigan '41
The Spirit of West Point '47

Elisabeth Harnois
One Magic Christmas '85
Where Are the Children? '85

Christina Harnos
The Rescue '88
Denial: The Dark Side of Passion '91
ER '94
Hellraiser 4: Bloodline '95

Ralf Harolde
Hook, Line and Sinker '30
Night Nurse '31
I'm No Angel '33
The Sea Wolf '41
Baby Face Morgan '42
I Killed That Man '42
Behind Locked Doors '48

David W. Harper
The Waltons: A Thanksgiving Story '73
A Day for Thanks on Walton's Mountain '82

Jessica Harper
Phantom of the Paradise '74
Inserts '76
Suspiria '77
The Evictors '79
Stardust Memories '80
Pennies From Heaven '81
Shock Treatment '81
My Favorite Year '82
Imagemaker '86
Blue Iguana '88
Big Man on Campus '89
Eat a Bowl of Tea '89

Robert Harper
Not Quite Human '87
Held Hostage '91
Final Analysis '92
Running Mates '92
The Wrong Man '93

Tess Harper
Amityville 3: The Demon '83
Chiefs '83
Tender Mercies '83
Flashpoint '84
Reckless Disregard '84
A Summer to Remember '84
Crimes of the Heart '86
Far North '88
Her Alibi '88
Criminal Law '89
Daddy's Dyin'...Who's Got the Will? '90
Dark River: A Father's Revenge '90
The Man in the Moon '91
My Heroes Have Always Been Cowboys '91
My New Gun '92
Children of Fury '94
Christy '94
The Road to Galveston '96

Valerie Harper
Freebie & the Bean '74
Thursday's Game '74
Night Terror '76
Chapter Two '79
The Last Married Couple in America '80
The Shadow Box '80
Don't Go to Sleep '82
Blame It on Rio '84
The Execution '85
Drop-Out Mother '88

Cindy Harrel
Model Behavior '82
The Final Terror '83

Jim Harrell
Don't Open the Door! '74
A Family Thing '96

Woody Harrelson
Wildcats '86
Eye of the Demon '87
Cool Blue '88
Mother Goose Rock 'n' Rhyme '90
Doc Hollywood '91
White Men Can't Jump '92
Indecent Proposal '93
The Cowboy Way '94
Natural Born Killers '94
Money Train '95
Kingpin '96

William Harrigan
The Invisible Man '33
"G" Men '35
Exiled to Shanghai '37

Laura Harrington
Maximum Overdrive '86
Perfect Witness '89
Vietnam War Story 3 '89
Linda '93
The Secret '93
What's Eating Gilbert Grape '93
Dead Air '94

Pat Harrington
Easy Come, Easy Go '67
The President's Analyst '67
The Affair '73

Barbara Harris
A Thousand Clowns '65
Oh Dad, Poor Dad (Momma's Hung You in the Closet & I'm Feeling So Sad) '67
Plaza Suite '71
Nashville '75
Family Plot '76
Freaky Friday '76
Movie, Movie '78
The North Avenue Irregulars '79
The Seduction of Joe Tynan '79
Peggy Sue Got Married '86
Nice Girls Don't Explode '87
Dirty Rotten Scoundrels '88

Brad Harris
The Fury of Hercules '61
Samson '61
Goliath Against the Giants '63
Jungle Inferno '70s
Rattler Kid '70s
The Mad Butcher '72
The Freakmaker '73
Island of Lost Girls '73
King of Kong Island '78
Hercules '83
Seven Magnificent Gladiators '84

Cynthia Harris
Edward and Mrs. Simpson '80
Reuben, Reuben '83
Izzy & Moe '85
Three Men and a Baby '87
Pancho Barnes '88

Danielle Harris
Halloween 4: The Return of Michael Myers '88
Halloween 5: The Revenge of Michael Myers '89
Marked for Death '90
The Last Boy Scout '91
Roseanne: An Unauthorized Biography '94

David Harris
Badge of the Assassin '85
Undercover '87
Vietnam War Story 1 '88

Ed Harris
Coma '78
The Seekers '79
Borderline '80
Knightriders '81
Creepshow '82
The Right Stuff '83
Under Fire '83
Places in the Heart '84
Swing Shift '84
Alamo Bay '85
Code Name: Emerald '85
A Flash of Green '85
Sweet Dreams '85
The Last Innocent Man '87
Walker '87
The Abyss '89
Jacknife '89
To Kill a Priest '89
State of Grace '90
China Moon '91
Paris Trout '91
Glengarry Glen Ross '92
Running Mates '92
The Firm '93
Needful Things '93
Just Cause '94
Milk Money '94
Apollo 13 '95
An Eye for an Eye '95
Nixon '95
Riders of the Purple Sage '96
The Rock '96

Edna Mae Harris
Lying Lips '39
Paradise in Harlem '40

Fox Harris
Repo Man '83
Warlords '88
Alienator '89
Dr. Caligari '89

Jared Harris
The Public Eye '92
Blue In the Face '95
Dead Man '95
Nadja '95
Smoke '95
Tall Tale: The Unbelievable Adventures of Pecos Bill '95

Jo Ann Harris
The Beguiled '70
Act of Vengeance '74
Deadly Games '80

Julie Harris
The Member of the Wedding '52
East of Eden '54
I Am a Camera '55
Truth About Women '58
A Doll's House '59
Victoria Regina '61
The Haunting '63
Holy Terror '65
Harper '66
You're a Big Boy Now '66
Reflections in a Golden Eye '67
The People Next Door '70
Home for the Holidays '72
The Hiding Place '75
America at the Movies '76
James Dean: The First American Teenager '76
The Last of Mrs. Lincoln '76
Voyage of the Damned '76
The Bell Jar '79

Harris ▶cont.

The Christmas Wife '88
Forever James Dean '88
Gorillas in the Mist '88
The Woman He Loved '88
The Dark Half '91
Housesitter '92
Scarlett '94
Carried Away '95

Julius W. Harris
Nothing But a Man '64
Shaft's Big Score '72
Superfly '72
Black Caesar '73
Hell Up in Harlem '73
Live and Let Die '73
The Taking of Pelham One Two Three '74
Missing Pieces '83
Crimewave '85
Murder on the Bayou '91
Prayer of the Rollerboys '91
Shrunken Heads '94

Lara Harris
No Man's Land '87
Blood Red '88
The Fourth War '90
All Tied Up '92
The Dogfighters '95

Leigh Anne Harris
I, the Jury '82
Sorceress '82

Lynette Harris
I, the Jury '82
Sorceress '82

Mel Harris
Wanted Dead or Alive '86
Cameron's Closet '89
K-9 '89
My Brother's Wife '89
Desperate Motives '92
Raising Cain '92
Scott Turow's The Burden of Proof '92
Suture '93
The Pagemaster '94
The Secretary '94
The Spider and the Fly '94
Sharon's Secret '95

Michael Harris
Shriek of the Mutilated '74
Shattered Image '93
Suture '93
Dead Air '94
Sleepstalker: The Sandman's Last Rites '94
The Soft Kill '94
Mr. Stitch '95

M.K. Harris
Genuine Risk '89
Slumber Party Massacre 3 '90
The Horseplayer '91

Neil Patrick Harris
Clara's Heart '88
Purple People Eater '88
Cold Sassy Tree '89
The Man in the Attic '94
My Antonia '94

Phil Harris
Melody Cruise '32
Dreaming Out Loud '40
Goodbye, My Lady '56
The Wheeler Dealers '63
The Patsy '64
The Gatling Gun '72

Richard Harris
The Wreck of the Mary Deare '59
The Guns of Navarone '61
Mutiny on the Bounty '62
This Sporting Life '63
The Red Desert '64
Major Dundee '65
The Bible...In the Beginning '66
Hawaii '66
Camelot '67
Cromwell '70
A Man Called Horse '70
Molly Maguires '70
The Hero '71
Man in the Wilderness '71
The Deadly Trackers '73
Juggernaut '74
99 & 44/100 Dead '74
The Cassandra Crossing '76
The Return of a Man Called Horse '76
Robin and Marian '76
Golden Rendezvous '77
Gulliver's Travels '77
Orca '77
Wild Geese '78
Highpoint '80
The Last Word '80
Tarzan, the Ape Man '81
Triumphs of a Man Called Horse '83
Your Ticket Is No Longer Valid '84
Martin's Day '85
Game for Vultures '86
Mack the Knife '89
The Field '90
Patriot Games '92
Silent Tongue '92
Unforgiven '92
King of the Wind '93
Wrestling Ernest Hemingway '93
Abraham '94
Cry, the Beloved Country '95
Savage Hearts '95

Robert Harris
How to Make a Monster '58
Apache Uprising '66
Valley of the Dolls '67

Robin Harris
I'm Gonna Git You Sucka '88
Hard to Die '90
House Party '90
Mo' Better Blues '90
Sorority House Massacre 2: Nighty Nightmare '92

Rosemary Harris
Beau Brummel '54
The Chisholms '79
The Ploughman's Lunch '83
To the Lighthouse '83
Heartbreak House '86
Crossing Delancey '88
Tom & Viv '94

Ross Harris
Scream, Baby, Scream '69
Testament '83

Stacy Harris
The Redhead from Wyoming '53
New Orleans After Dark '58

Zelda Harris
Crooklyn '94
The Piano Lesson '94
The Baby-Sitters Club '95

Cathryn Harrison
Blue Fire Lady '78
The Dresser '83
Empire State '87
A Handful of Dust '88

George Harrison
A Hard Day's Night '64
Help! '65
Magical Mystery Tour '67
Let It Be '70
All You Need Is Cash '78
Monty Python's Life of Brian '79
The Compleat Beatles '82

Gregory Harrison
Trilogy of Terror '75
The Gathering '77
Enola Gay: The Men, the Mission, the Atomic Bomb '80
For Ladies Only '81
Razorback '84
Seduced '85
The Hasty Heart '86
Oceans of Fire '86
North Shore '87
Dangerous Pursuit '89
Bare Essentials '91
Body Chemistry 2: Voice of a Stranger '91
Duplicates '92
Cadillac Girls '93
Caught in the Act '93
Hard Evidence '94
It's My Party '95

Jenilee Harrison
Tank '83
Curse 3: Blood Sacrifice '90
Prime Target '91
Fists of Iron '94

Kathleen Harrison
The Ghost Train '41
The Winslow Boy '48
Trio '50
A Christmas Carol '51
The Pickwick Papers '54
Cast a Dark Shadow '55
Let's Make Up '55
A Cry from the Streets '57

Linda Harrison
Planet of the Apes '68
Beneath the Planet of the Apes '70
Cocoon '85

Lottie Harrison
Lost in a Harem '44
Driftin' River '46

Rex Harrison
Men Are Not Gods '37
Storm in a Teacup '37
The Citadel '38
Night Train to Munich '40
Sidewalks of London '40
Major Barbara '41
Blithe Spirit '45
Anna and the King of Siam '46
I Live in Grosvenor Square '46
The Ghost and Mrs. Muir '47
Unfaithfully Yours '48
The Long Dark Hall '51
King Richard and the Crusaders '54
The Reluctant Debutante '58
Midnight Lace '60
Cleopatra '63
My Fair Lady '64
The Agony and the Ecstasy '65
Doctor Dolittle '67
The Honey Pot '67
Deadly Thief '78
The Prince and the Pauper '78
Ashanti, Land of No Mercy '79
The Fifth Musketeer '79
Time to Die '83
Anastasia: The Mystery of Anna '86
Heartbreak House '86

Richard Harrison
Gladiators 7 '62
Medusa Against the Son of Hercules '62
Giants of Rome '63
Gun Fight at Red Sands '63
The Invincible Gladiator '63
Messalina vs. the Son of Hercules '64
Between God, the Devil & a Winchester '72
Thirty-Six Hours of Hell '77
Fireback '78
Ninja Champion '80s
Ninja Dragon '80s
Ninja Squad '80s
Ninja the Protector '80s
Blood Debts '83
His Name was King '85
Ninja Commandments '87
Ninja Operation: Licensed to Terminate '87
Hands of Death '88
Ninja Strike Force '88
Terminal Force '88
The Channeler '89
Ninja Powerforce '90
Ninja Showdown '90
Rescue Force '90

David Harrod
Armed for Action '92
Blood on the Badge '92
The House on Todville Road '95

Kathryn Harrold
Nightwing '79
Bogie: The Last Hero '80
The Hunter '80
Modern Romance '81
The Pursuit of D.B. Cooper '81
The Sender '82
Yes, Giorgio '82
Best Legs in the 8th Grade '84
Heartbreakers '84
Into the Night '85
Raw Deal '86
Someone to Love '87
Dead Solid Perfect '88
Rainbow Drive '90
Deadly Desire '91
The Companion '94

John Harron
West-Bound Limited '23
The Night Cry '26
Midnight Warning '32
The White Zombie '32

Robert "Bobbie" Harron
Home Sweet Home '14
Judith of Bethulia '14
The Birth of a Nation '15
Hoodoo Ann '16
Hearts of the World '18
The Greatest Question '19
True Heart Susie '19

Lisa Harrow
All Creatures Great and Small '74
The Final Conflict '81
Nancy Astor '82
Under Capricorn '82
Shaker Run '85
The Last Days of Chez Nous '92
That Eye, The Sky '94

Deborah Harry
The Foreigner '78
Mr. Mike's Mondo Video '79
Union City '81
Videodrome '83
Forever, Lulu '87
Hairspray '88
Satisfaction '88
New York Stories '89
Mother Goose Rock 'n' Rhyme '90
Tales from the Darkside: The Movie '90
Intimate Stranger '91
Body Bags '93
Dead Beat '94
Heavy '94

Christina Hart
Games Girls Play '75
Johnny Firecloud '75
The Runaway Barge '75

Christopher Hart
Lady Terminator '89
The Addams Family '91
Addams Family Values '93

Dianne Lee Hart
The Giant Spider Invasion '75
Pom Pom Girls '76

Dolores Hart
Loving You '57
King Creole '58
Lonelyhearts '58
Where the Boys Are '60

Ian Hart
The Hours and Times '92
Backbeat '94
The Englishman Who Went Up a Hill But Came Down a Mountain '95
Land and Freedom '95

John Hart
The Fighting Redhead '50
Blackenstein '73

Kevin Hart
Mindkiller '87
Lone Wolf '88

Linda Hart
Gypsy '93
A Perfect World '93
Tin Cup '96

Neal Hart
Sands of Sacrifice '21
Trigger Tricks '30

Roxanne Hart
Special Bulletin '83
Oh, God! You Devil '84
Old Enough '84
The Tender Age '84
Highlander '86
Samaritan: The Mitch Snyder Story '86
The Last Innocent Man '87
Pulse '88
Vengeance '89
Tagget '90
Once Around '91

Susan Hart
The Slime People '63
Pajama Party '64
Ride the Wild Surf '64
Dr. Goldfoot and the Bikini Machine '66

Teddy Hart
Ma and Pa Kettle at Waikiki '55
Mickey One '65

William S. Hart
The Bargain '15
The Disciple '15
The Fugitive: Taking of Luke McVane '15
On the Night Stage '15
Hell's Hinges '16
Return of Draw Egan '16
Narrow Trail '17
Blue Blazes Rawden '18
Wagon Tracks '19
Story of William S. Hart/Sad Clowns '20s
Toll Gate '20
Three Word Brand '21
Tumbleweeds '25
Show People '28

Douglas Hartier
Invasion Force '90
White Fury '90

Pat Hartigan
King of the Wild Horses '24
Ranson's Folly '26

Clare Hartley
Trancers 4: Jack of Swords '93
Trancers 5: Sudden Deth '94

Mariette Hartley
Ride the High Country '62
The Return of Count Yorga '71
Nightmare at 43 Hillcrest '74
Rainy Day '79
No Place to Hide '81
Improper Channels '82
O'Hara's Wife '82
M.A.D.D.: Mothers Against Drunk Driving '83
Silence of the Heart '84
1969 '89
Passion in Paradise '89
Encino Man '92

Elizabeth Hartman
A Patch of Blue '65
The Group '66
You're a Big Boy Now '66
The Fixer '68
The Beguiled '70
Walking Tall '73

Phil Hartman
Cheech and Chong's Next Movie '80
The Pee Wee Herman Show '82
Weekend Pass '84
Blind Date '87
How I Got into College '89
Quick Change '90
CB4: The Movie '93
Coneheads '93
The Crazysitter '94
Greedy '94
Houseguest '94
Sgt. Bilko '95

Lisa Hartman Black
Just Tell Me You Love Me '80
Magic on Love Island '80
Deadly Blessing '81
The Seventeenth Bride '84
Where the Boys Are '84 '84
Full Exposure: The Sex Tape Scandals '89
The Take '90
Bare Essentials '91
Red Wind '91
The Return of Eliot Ness '91

William Hartnell
Immortal Battalion '44
Appointment with Crime '45
Brighton Rock '47
The Mouse That Roared '59
Doctor Who: An Unearthly Child '63
This Sporting Life '63

Rainbow Harvest
Old Enough '84
Mirror, Mirror '90

Don Harvey
The Beast '88
Eight Men Out '88
Casualties of War '89
Mission of the Shark '91
Prey of the Chameleon '91

American Heart '92
Men of War '94
Tank Girl '94
Sawbones '95
Last Dance '96

Harry Harvey
The Reckless Way '36
King of the Sierras '38
Code of the Fearless '39
In Old Montana '39
Ridin' the Trail '40
I'm from Arkansas '44
Tea for Two '50
The Narrow Margin '52

Laurence Harvey
Man on the Run '49
Innocents in Paris '53
King Richard and the Crusaders '54
Romeo and Juliet '54
I Am a Camera '55
The Silent Enemy '58
Truth About Women '58
Room at the Top '59
The Alamo '60
Butterfield 8 '60
Summer and Smoke '61
The Manchurian Candidate '62
Walk on the Wild Side '62
The Wonderful World of the Brothers Grimm '62
Of Human Bondage '64
Darling '65
Spy with a Cold Nose '66
Dandy in Aspic '68
The Magic Christian '69
Escape to the Sun '72
Night Watch '72

Paul Harvey
23 1/2 Hours Leave '37
Meet Dr. Christian '39
Arizona '40
Blondie's Blessed Event '42
Helldorado '46
Call Northside 777 '48
A Southern Yankee '48
Riding High '50
The Yellow Cab Man '50
April In Paris '52

Rodney Harvey
Five Corners '88
Salsa '88
My Own Private Idaho '91
Guncrazy '92

Kazuo Hasegawa
The Crucified Lovers '54
Gate of Hell '54
An Actor's Revenge '63

Peter Haskell
Christina '74
Legend of Earl Durand '74
The Cracker Factory '79
Child's Play 3 '91
Robot Wars '93

O.E. Hasse
The Big Lift '50
Betrayed '54
Above Us the Waves '56
The Elusive Corporal '62
State of Siege '73

Danny Hassel
A Nightmare on Elm Street 4: Dream Master '88
A Nightmare on Elm Street 5: Dream Child '89

David Hasselhoff
Revenge of the Cheerleaders '76
Star Crash '78
Cartier Affair '84
Terror at London Bridge '85
Witchery '88
The Final Alliance '89
Fire and Rain '89
Bail Out '90
Ring of the Musketeers '93
Baywatch the Movie: Forbidden Paradise '95

Marilyn Hassett
The Other Side of the Mountain '75
Two Minute Warning '76
The Other Side of the Mountain, Part 2 '78
The Bell Jar '79
Body Count '87
Messenger of Death '88

Twenty Dollar Star '91

Signe Hasso
Journey for Margaret '42
Heaven Can Wait '43
The Seventh Cross '44
The Story of Dr. Wassell '44
House on 92nd Street '45
Johnny Angel '45
A Double Life '47
Where There's Life '47

Bob Hastings
Harper Valley P.T.A. '78
The Munsters' Revenge '81
Snowballing '85
Shadow Force '92

Richard Hatch
The Hatfields & the McCoys '75
Battlestar Galactica '78
Deadman's Curve '78
Mission Galactica: The Cylon Attack '79
Charlie Chan and the Curse of the Dragon Queen '81
Prisoners of the Lost Universe '84
Heated Vengeance '87
Party Line '88
Ghetto Blaster '89
Delta Force Commando 2 '90

Mary Hatcher
The Big Wheel '49
Holiday in Havana '49
Tales of Robin Hood '52

Teri Hatcher
The Big Picture '89
Tango and Cash '89
Dead in the Water '91
Soapdish '91
All Tied Up '92
The Cool Surface '92
Straight Talk '92
Brain Smasher...A Love Story '93
Heaven's Prisoners '95

Hurd Hatfield
Dragon Seed '44
Picture of Dorian Gray '45
Diary of a Chambermaid '46
El Cid '61
The King of Kings '61
Invincible Mr. Disraeli '63
Mickey One '65
Lamp at Midnight '66
The Boston Strangler '68
Thief '71
The Word '78
King David '85
Crimes of the Heart '86
Her Alibi '88

Noah Hathaway
The NeverEnding Story '84
Troll '86
Mortal Danger '94

Raymond Hatton
The Little American '17
Male and Female '19
Peck's Bad Boy '21
The Virginian '23
The Fighting American '24
Behind the Front '26
We're in the Navy Now '27
Rogue of the Rio Grande '30
The Silver Horde '30
Cornered '32
The Crooked Circle '32
Drifting Souls '32
Uptown New York '32
Buffalo Stampede '33
Hidden Gold '33
Lady Killer '33
Terror Trail '33
The Three Musketeers '33
Rustlers of Red Dog '35
Desert Gold '36
The Vigilantes are Coming '36
The Texans '38
Cowboys from Texas '39
Frontier Horizon '39
The Kansas Terrors '39
Lonely Trail/Three Texas Steers '39
Rough Riders' Roundup '39
Wyoming Outlaw '39
Covered Wagon Days '40
Rocky Mountain Rangers '40
Arizona Bound '41
Forbidden Trails '41
Gunman from Bodie '41

Below the Border '42
Dawn on the Great Divide '42
Down Texas Way '42
Ghost Town Law '42
Reap the Wild Wind '42
Riders of the West '42
West of the Law '42
Ghost Rider '43
Six Gun Gospel '43
Texas Kid '43
Lawmen '44
Partners of the Trail '44
Raiders of the Border '44
Range Law '44
The Stranger from Pecos '45
Border Bandits '46
Gentleman from Texas '46
Northwest Trail '46
Land of the Lawless '47
Rolling Home '48
Blazing Guns '50
Guns of Justice '50
Marshal of Heldorado '50
Sudden Death '50
Kentucky Jubilee '51
Day the World Ended '55
Girls in Prison '56
Flesh and the Spur '57
Motorcycle Gang '57
Shake, Rattle and Rock '57

Rondo Hatton
The Pearl of Death '44
The Brute Man '46
House of Horrors '46

Rutger Hauer
Cold Blood '70s
Turkish Delights '73
Dandelions '74
Keetje Tippel '75
The Wilby Conspiracy '75
Soldier of Orange '78
Spetters '80
Chanel Solitaire '81
Eureka! '81
Nighthawks '81
Blade Runner '82
Inside the Third Reich '82
Fatal Error '83
The Osterman Weekend '83
A Breed Apart '84
Mysteries '84
Flesh and Blood '85
Ladyhawke '85
The Hitcher '86
Wanted Dead or Alive '86
Escape from Sobibor '87
The Blood of Heroes '89
Bloodhounds of Broadway '89
Blind Fury '90
Deadlock '91
Beyond Justice '92
Buffy the Vampire Slayer '92
Past Midnight '92
Split Second '92
Arctic Blue '93
Blind Side '93
Nostradamus '93
Voyage '93
Amelia Earhart: The Final Flight '94
Beyond Forgiveness '94
Fatherland '94
Forbidden Choices '94
Surviving the Game '94
Mr. Stitch '95

Angelika Hauff
Tromba, the Tiger Man '52
The Life and Loves of Mozart '59

Ullrich Haupt
Captain Swagger '25
Morocco '30

Cole Hauser
School Ties '92
Higher Learning '94

Fay Hauser
Jimmy the Kid '82
Christmas Lilies of the Field '84
Marvin & Tige '84
Jo Jo Dancer, Your Life is Calling '86
Candyman 2: Farewell to the Flesh '94

Wings Hauser
Homework '82
Vice Squad '82
Deadly Force '83
Mutant '83

Code of Honor '84
A Soldier's Story '84
Jo Jo Dancer, Your Life is Calling '86
The Long, Hot Summer '86
Hostage '87
Nightmare at Noon '87
No Safe Haven '87
Tough Guys Don't Dance '87
The Wind '87
Dead Man Walking '88
Bedroom Eyes 2 '89
The Carpenter '89
L.A. Bounty '89
Marked for Murder '89
Out of Sight, Out of Her Mind '89
The Siege of Firebase Gloria '89
The Art of Dying '90
Coldfire '90
Exiled in America '90
The Killer's Edge '90
Reason to Die '90
Street Asylum '90
Wilding '90
Beastmaster 2: Through the Portal of Time '91
Deadly Conspiracy '91
Frame Up '91
Living to Die '91
Pale Blood '91
In Between '92
Mind, Body & Soul '92
Watchers 3 '94
Tales from the Hood '95

Richie Havens
Boss' Son '79
Street Hunter '90
Perfect Harmony '91

June Haver
The Dolly Sisters '45
Look for the Silver Lining '49
Love Nest '51

Phyllis Haver
The Balloonatic/One Week '23
The Blacksmith/The Balloonatic '23
The Nervous Wreck '26

Nigel Havers
Who Is Killing the Great Chefs of Europe? '78
Chariots of Fire '81
A Passage to India '84
Burke & Wills '85
Empire of the Sun '87
The Little Princess '87
The Whistle Blower '87
The Charmer '89
Farewell to the King '89
The Burning Season '94
Lie Down with Lions '94

Thom Haverstock
Skullduggery '79
Fall from Innocence '88

Allen Havey
Love or Money? '88
Checking Out '89

June Havoc
Four Jacks and a Jill '41
Sing Your Worries Away '42
Hello, Frisco, Hello '43
Timber Queen '44
Brewster's Millions '45
Gentleman's Agreement '47
Return to Salem's Lot '87

Robin Hawdon
Alien Women '69
The Love Factor '69
When Dinosaurs Ruled the Earth '70

Ethan Hawke
Explorers '85
Dad '89
Dead Poets Society '89
Mystery Date '91
White Fang '91
A Midnight Clear '92
Waterland '92
Alive '93
Rich in Love '93
Before Sunrise '94
Floundering '94
Reality Bites '94
Search and Destroy '94

John Hawkes
Murder Rap '87
Night of the Scarecrow '95

Jack Hawkins
A Shot in the Dark '33
Phantom Fiend '35
Bonnie Prince Charlie '48
The Fallen Idol '49
The Small Back Room '49
The Elusive Pimpernel '50
The Adventurers '51
No Highway in the Sky '51
Cruel Sea '53
Malta Story '53
Mandy '53
Angels One Five '54
Land of Fury '55
Land of the Pharaohs '55
The Prisoner '55
The Bridge on the River Kwai '57
The Third Key '57
Ben-Hur '59
The League of Gentlemen '60
Lawrence of Arabia '62
Guns at Batasi '64
Zulu '64
Lord Jim '65
Lola '69
Those Daring Young Men in Their Jaunty Jalopies '69
Nicholas and Alexandra '71
Waterloo '71
Escape to the Sun '72
Restless '72
Young Winston '72
Tales That Witness Madness '73

Jay Hawkins
Two Moon Junction '88
Mystery Train '89
A Rage in Harlem '91

Monte Hawley
Double Deal '39
Gang War '40
Mystery in Swing '40
Tall, Tan and Terrific '46
Look Out Sister '48
Miracle in Harlem '48

Richard Hawley
Paper Marriage '93
Captives '94
Prime Suspect: The Lost Child '94
Prime Suspect: Inner Circles '95
Prime Suspect: The Scent of Darkness '95

Wanda Hawley
American Pluck '25
Smouldering Fires '25

Goldie Hawn
The One and Only, Genuine, Original Family Band '68
Cactus Flower '69
There's a Girl in My Soup '70
Dollars '71
Butterflies Are Free '72
The Girl from Petrovka '74
The Sugarland Express '74
Shampoo '75
The Duchess and the Dirtwater Fox '76
Foul Play '78
Private Benjamin '80
Seems Like Old Times '80
Lovers and Liars '81
Best Friends '82
Protocol '84
Swing Shift '84
Wildcats '86
Overboard '87
Bird on a Wire '90
Deceived '91
Crisscross '92
Death Becomes Her '92
Housesitter '92

Jill Haworth
Exodus '60
In Harm's Way '65
Tower of Evil '72
The Freakmaker '73

Nigel Hawthorne
S*P*Y*S '74
Firefox '82
Pope John Paul II '84
Jenny's War '85
Tartuffe '90
Demolition Man '93
The Madness of King George '94
Richard III '95

Charles Hawtrey
A Canterbury Tale '44
Room to Let '49
Carry On Cleo '65
Carry On Screaming '66
The Terrornauts '67
Alien Women '69
Carry On at Your Convenience '71
Carry On Camping '71
Carry On Henry VIII '71

Alexandra Hay
The Love Machine '71
How Come Nobody's On Our Side? '73

Christian Hay
Autopsy '70s
You're Jinxed, Friend, You've Met Sacramento '70

Sessue Hayakawa
The Cheat '15
The Tong Man '19
Daughter of the Dragon '31
Tokyo Joe '49
Three Came Home '50
The Bridge on the River Kwai '57
The Geisha Boy '58
Green Mansions '59
Hell to Eternity '60
The Swiss Family Robinson '60

Marc Hayashi
Chan is Missing '82
White of the Eye '88
The Laserman '90

Harry Hayden
The Rains Came '39
Merton of the Movies '47
Double Dynamite '51

Linda Hayden
Baby Love '69
Taste the Blood of Dracula '70
The Blood on Satan's Claw '71
Madhouse '74
The House on Straw Hill '76
The Barcelona Kill '77

Russell Hayden
The Frontiersmen '38
The Mysterious Rider '38
Hopalong Cassidy: Renegade Trail '39
Law of the Pampas '39
Renegade Trail '39
Knights of the Range '40
The Light of Western Stars '40
Santa Fe Marshal '40
The Showdown '40
Border Vigilantes '41
Doomed Caravan '41
In Old Colorado '41
Frontier Law '43
Gambler's Choice '44
Lost City of the Jungle '45
'Neath Canadian Skies '46
North of the Border '46
Trail of the Mounties '47
Where the North Begins '47
Rolling Home '48
Apache Chief '50
Blazing Guns '50
Guns of Justice '50
Last Bullet '50
Marshal of Heldorado '50
Outlaw Fury '50
Rangeland Empire '50
Sudden Death '50

Sterling Hayden
Bahama Passage '42
The Asphalt Jungle '50
The Denver & Rio Grande '51
Flat Top '52
Fighter Attack '53
Johnny Guitar '53
Kansas Pacific '53
Prince Valiant '54
Suddenly '54
The Last Command '55
Shotgun '55
The Killing '56
Crime of Passion '57
Dr. Strangelove, or: How I Learned to Stop Worrying and Love the Bomb '64
Spaghetti Western '69
Cobra '71
The Godfather '72
The Final Programme '73
The Long Goodbye '73
1900 '76
King of the Gypsies '78
Winter Kills '79
9 to 5 '80
Gas '81
The Godfather 1902-1959: The Complete Epic '81
Deadly Strangers '82
Venom '82
The Blue and the Gray '85

Richard Haydn
Adventure '45
Forever Amber '47
Singapore '47
Emperor Waltz '48
The Merry Widow '52
Pride of St. Louis '52
Never Let Me Go '53
Jupiter's Darling '55
Please Don't Eat the Daisies '60
Clarence, the Cross-eyed Lion '65
The Sound of Music '65
Young Frankenstein '74

Julie Haydon
Come On Danger! '32
It's Pat: The Movie '94

Helen Haye
Skin Game '31
The Case of the Frightened Lady '39
Spy in Black '39
Man of Evil '48

Salma Hayek
Mi Vida Loca '94
Desperado '95
Fair Game '95
From Dusk Till Dawn '95
Fled '96

Jeff Hayenga
Prince of Pennsylvania '88
The Unborn '91

Allan Hayes
Sam's Son '84
Neon Maniacs '86

Allison Hayes
Francis Joins the WACs '54
The Gunslinger '56
The Undead '57
The Unearthly '57
Zombies of Moratau '57
Attack of the 50 Foot Woman '58
The Crawling Hand '63

Bernadene Hayes
Sweetheart of the Navy '37
Heroes in Blue '39
Santa Fe Marshal '40

George "Gabby" Hayes
Cavalier of the West '31
Border Devils '32
Broadway to Cheyenne '32
Man from Hell's Edges '32
Night Rider '32
Texas Buddies '32
Without Honors '32
Breed of the Border '33
Fighting Champ '33
The Gallant Fool '33
Galloping Romeo '33
The Outlaw Tamer '33
The Phantom Broadcast '33
Riders of Destiny '33
The Sphinx '33
Western Double Feature 2 '33
Beggars in Ermine '34
Blue Steel '34
Brand of Hate '34
House of Mystery '34
In Old Santa Fe '34
The Lost City '34
Lucky Texan '34
The Man from Hell '34
Man from Utah '34
Monte Carlo Nights '34
Mystery Liner '34
'Neath the Arizona Skies '34
Randy Rides Alone '34
The Return of Casey Jones '34
The Star Packer '34
West of the Divide '34
Hopalong Cassidy '35
Lawless Frontier '35
Texas Terror '35
The Throwback '35
The Lawless Nineties '36
Smokey Smith '36
Song of the Trail '36
The Texas Rangers '36
The Plainsman '37
Rustler's Valley '37
Billy the Kid Returns '38
Come On Rangers '38
The Frontiersmen '38
Western Double Feature 1 '38
Hopalong Cassidy: Renegade Trail '39
In Old Caliente '39
Lonely Trail/Three Texas Steers '39
Renegade Trail '39
Saga of Death Valley '39
Southward Ho! '39
The Great American Western Collection: Roy Rogers '40s
Western Double Feature 4: Rogers & Evans '40s
The Border Legion '40
Colorado '40
Dark Command '40
Melody Ranch '40
Ranger and the Lady '40
Wagon's Westward '40
Young Bill Hickok '40
Young Buffalo Bill '40
Bad Man of Deadwood '41
In Old Cheyenne '41
Jesse James at Bay '41
Robin Hood of the Pecos '41
Heart of the Golden West '42
Man from Cheyenne '42
Ridin' Down the Canyon '42
Romance on the Range '42
Sons of the Pioneers '42
South of Santa Fe '42
Sunset on the Desert '42
Sunset Serenade '42
Calling Wild Bill Elliott '43
Death Valley Manhunt '43
Man from Thunder River '43
War of the Wildcats '43
Tall in the Saddle '44
Bells of Rosarita '45
Sunset in El Dorado '45
Utah '45
Badman's Territory '46
Helldorado '46
My Pal Trigger '46
Roll on Texas Moon '46
Song of Arizona '46
Under Nevada Skies '46
Western Double Feature 16 '46
Home in Oklahoma '47
Lights of Old Santa Fe '47
Trail Street '47
Return of the Bad Men '48
The Cariboo Trail '50
Western Double Feature 11 '50

Gloria Hayes
Witchboard '87
Judgment Day '88

Grace Hayes
Rainbow Over Broadway '33
Zis Boom Bah '42

Helen Hayes
Arrowsmith '31
The Sin of Madelon Claudet '31
A Farewell to Arms '32
Anastasia '56
Airport '70
Herbie Rides Again '74
One of Our Dinosaurs Is Missing '75
Candleshoe '78
Family Upside Down '78

Isaac Hayes
Truck Turner '74
Escape from New York '81
Jailbait: Betrayed By Innocence '86
Counterforce '87
Dead Aim '87
Nightstick '87
I'm Gonna Git You Sucka '88
Prime Target '91
Final Judgement '92
Guilty as Charged '92
Deadly Exposure '93
Robin Hood: Men in Tights '93
It Could Happen to You '94
Oblivion '94
Backlash: Oblivion 2 '95
Flipper '96

Linda Hayes
Danger on the Air '38
Ridin' Down the Canyon '42
South of Santa Fe '42

Margaret Hayes
In Old Colorado '41
Sullivan's Travels '41
Blackboard Jungle '55
Omar Khayyam '57

Patricia Hayes
The NeverEnding Story '84
A Fish Called Wanda '88
Little Dorrit, Film 1: Nobody's Fault '88
Little Dorrit, Film 2: Little Dorrit's Story '88
Willow '88
Super Bitch '89

Peter Lind Hayes
Playmates '41
Seven Days' Leave '42
Zis Boom Bah '42
The 5000 Fingers of Dr. T '53

Tony Haygarth
A Month in the Country '87
The Infiltrator '95

Lisa Hayland
Novel Desires '92
Fatal Passion '94

Cyd Hayman
Rogue Male '76
After Julius '78
The Godsend '79

David Hayman
A Sense of Freedom '78
Sid & Nancy '86
Hope and Glory '87
Rob Roy '95

Dick Haymes
DuBarry Was a Lady '43
State Fair '45
One Touch of Venus '48
St. Benny the Dip '51
Betrayal '74

Cal Haynes
Fyre '78
Kemek '88

Linda Haynes
Rolling Thunder '77
Human Experiments '79

Roberta Haynes
The Fighter '52
Return to Paradise '53
Hell Ship Mutiny '57
The Adventurers '70

Jim Haynie
Bitter Harvest '81
Hard Traveling '85
On the Edge '86
Jack's Back '87
Out '88
From Hollywood to Deadwood '89
Men Don't Leave '89
Too Much Sun '90
Grand Tour: Disaster in Time '92
Sleepwalkers '92
Danielle Steel's Star '93
The Bridges of Madison County '95

Robert Hays
Initiation of Sarah '78
Airplane! '80
The Fall of the House of Usher '80
California Gold Rush '81
Take This Job & Shove It '81
Airplane 2: The Sequel '82
Touched '82
Trenchcoat '83
Utilities '83
Scandalous '84
Cat's Eye '85
Murder by the Book '87
Honeymoon Academy '90
Running Against Time '90
Hot Chocolate '92
Fifty/Fifty '93
Homeward Bound: The Incredible Journey '93
Cyber Bandits '94
No Dessert Dad, 'Til You Mow the Lawn '94
Homeward Bound 2: Lost in San Francisco '96

Dennis Haysbert
Major League '89
Navy SEALS '90
Love Field '91
Mr. Baseball '92
Return to Lonesome Dove '93
Suture '93
Major League 2 '94
Heat '95
Waiting to Exhale '95
Widow's Kiss '96

James Hayter
Trio '50
Tom Brown's School Days '51
Four Sided Triangle '53
Beau Brummel '54
The Pickwick Papers '54

Chad Hayward
The Killing Game '87
Violent Zone '89

David Hayward
Who'll Save Our Children? '82
Delusion '84
Thousand Pieces of Gold '91
Accidental Meeting '93

Louis Hayward
Anthony Adverse '36
The Saint in New York '38
The Man in the Iron Mask '39
Dance, Girl, Dance '40
The Son of Monte Cristo '41
And Then There Were None '45
The Strange Woman '46
Black Arrow '48
Promise to Murder '56
The Search for Bridey Murphy '56
Chuka '67
The Christmas Kid '68
Terror in the Wax Museum '73

Susan Hayward
Beau Geste '39
Adam Had Four Sons '41
I Married a Witch '42
Reap the Wild Wind '42
Star Spangled Rhythm '42
Young & Willing '42
Jack Frost '43
Fighting Seabees '44
The Hairy Ape '44
Jack London '44
Deadline at Dawn '46
Lost Moment '47
Smash-Up: The Story of a Woman '47
They Won't Believe Me '47
House of Strangers '49
Tulsa '49
Rawhide '50
David and Bathsheba '51
I'd Climb the Highest Mountain '51
The Lusty Men '52
The Snows of Kilimanjaro '52
Demetrius and the Gladiators '54
I'll Cry Tomorrow '55
Soldier of Fortune '55
The Conqueror '56
I Want to Live! '58
Back Street '61
Stolen Hours '63
Where Love Has Gone '64
The Honey Pot '67
Valley of the Dolls '67
Say Goodbye, Maggie Cole '72

Chris Haywood
Newsfront '78
Heatwave '83
Waterfront '83
Attack Force Z '84
Man of Flowers '84
Razorback '84
Burke & Wills '85
Malcolm '86
The Tale of Ruby Rose '87
The Navigator '88
Quigley Down Under '90
Sweet Talker '91
Alex '92
A Woman's Tale '92

Rita Hayworth
Hit the Saddle '37
Trouble in Texas '37
Renegade Ranger/Scarlet River '38
Only Angels Have Wings '39

Angels Over Broadway '40
The Lady in Question '40
Music in My Heart '40
Susan and God '40
Blood and Sand '41
Strawberry Blonde '41
You'll Never Get Rich '41
Tales of Manhattan '42
You Were Never Lovelier '42
Cover Girl '44
Tonight and Every Night '45
Gilda '46
Down to Earth '47
The Lady from Shanghai '48
The Loves of Carmen '48
Affair in Trinidad '52
Miss Sadie Thompson '53
Salome '53
Fire Down Below '57
Pal Joey '57
Separate Tables '58
They Came to Cordura '59
Circus World '64
The Love Goddesses '65
The Poppy Is Also a Flower '66
Road to Salina '68

Jonathan Haze
Apache Woman '55
The Gunslinger '56
It Conquered the World '56
Poor White Trash '57
Rock All Night '57
Little Shop of Horrors '60
X: The Man with X-Ray Eyes '63
Track of the Vampire '66

Noni Hazlehurst
Monkey Grip '82
Waterfront '83
Fran '85
True Colors '87

Murray Head
Sunday, Bloody Sunday '71
White Mischief '88

Lena Headey
Waterland '92
Century '94
Rudyard Kipling's The Jungle Book '94
The Summer House '94

Glenne Headly
Doctor Detroit '83
Fandango '85
The Purple Rose of Cairo '85
Making Mr. Right '86
Seize the Day '86
Nadine '87
Dirty Rotten Scoundrels '88
Stars and Bars '88
Paperhouse '89
Dick Tracy '90
Mortal Thoughts '91
Grand Isle '92
And the Band Played On '93
Hotel Room '93
Ordinary Magic '93
Getting Even with Dad '94
Mr. Holland's Opus '95
Sgt. Bilko '95

Anthony Heald
The Silence of the Lambs '91
Whispers in the Dark '92
The Ballad of Little Jo '93
The Client '94
Kiss of Death '94
Bushwhacked '95

Myron Healey
Down to Earth '47
Gang Busters '55
Guns Don't Argue '57
The Unearthly '57
Varan the Unbelievable '61
Cavalry Command '63
Smoke in the Wind '75
Claws '77
Pulse '88

David Healy
The Sign of Four '83
Supergirl '84
Unnatural Pursuits '91

Mary Healy
Second Fiddle '39
Zis Boom Bah '42
The 5000 Fingers of Dr. T '53

Ted Healy
Dancing Lady '33
Hollywood Party '34
Mad Love '35
Reckless '35
Three Stooges Comedy Classics '49

Darin Heames
The Fear '94
Night of the Demons 2 '94

John Heard
Between the Lines '77
First Love '77
Chilly Scenes of Winter '79
On the Yard '79
Heart Beat '80
Cutter's Way '81
Cat People '82
Best Revenge '83
Legs '83
C.H.U.D. '84
Violated '84
After Hours '85
Heaven Help Us '85
Too Scared to Scream '85
The Trip to Bountiful '85
Out on a Limb '87
The Telephone '87
Beaches '88
Betrayed '88
Big '88
The Milagro Beanfield War '88
The Seventh Sign '88
The Package '89
Awakenings '90
Blown Away '90
The End of Innocence '90
Home Alone '90
Deceived '91
Mindwalk: A Film for Passionate Thinkers '91
Rambling Rose '91
Dead Ahead: The Exxon Valdez Disaster '92
Gladiator '92
Home Alone 2: Lost in New York '92
Radio Flyer '92
Waterland '92
Me & Veronica '93
The Pelican Brief '93
Before and After '95

Ann Hearn
The Accused '88
Lorenzo's Oil '92

George Hearn
Sanctuary of Fear '79
A Piano for Mrs. Cimino '82
Sweeney Todd: The Demon Barber of Fleet Street '84
See You in the Morning '89
Sneakers '92
The Vanishing '93
Annie: A Royal Adventure '95

Clifford Heatherly
Champagne '28
Bitter Sweet '33
If I Were Rich '33

Joey Heatherton
Where Love Has Gone '64
Bluebeard '72
The Happy Hooker Goes to Washington '77
Cry-Baby '90

Patricia Heaton
Beethoven '92
Memoirs of an Invisible Man '92
The New Age '94

David Heavener
Outlaw Force '87
Deadly Reactor '89
Killcrazy '89
Twisted Justice '89
Ragin' Cajun '90
Prime Target '91
L.A. Goddess '92
Eye of the Stranger '93
Kill or Be Killed '93

Anne Heche
O Pioneers! '91
The Adventures of Huck Finn '93
Against the Wall '94
Milk Money '94
A Simple Twist of Fate '94
Kingfish: A Story of Huey P. Long '95
Wild Side '95
The Juror '96

Paul Hecht
The Savage Bees '76
Mary and Joseph: A Story of Faith '79

Eileen Heckart
The Bad Seed '56
Bus Stop '56
Somebody Up There Likes Me '56
Hot Spell '58
A Doll's House '59
Up the Down Staircase '67
No Way to Treat a Lady '68
Butterflies Are Free '72
Zandy's Bride '74
The Hiding Place '75
Sorrows of Gin '79
White Mama '80
Table Settings '84
Heartbreak Ridge '86
Breathing Lessons '94

Dan Hedaya
The Prince of Central Park '77
Endangered Species '82
The Hunger '83
The Adventures of Buckaroo Banzai Across the Eighth Dimension '84
Reckless '84
Tightrope '84
Blood Simple '85
Commando '85
Courage '86
Running Scared '86
Slow Burn '86
A Smoky Mountain Christmas '86
Wise Guys '86
Joe Versus the Volcano '90
Pacific Heights '90
Tune in Tomorrow '90
The Addams Family '91
Based on an Untrue Story '93
Benny & Joon '93
Boiling Point '93
Fallen Angels 2 '93
For Love or Money '93
Four Eyes and Six Guns '93
Mr. Wonderful '93
Rookie of the Year '93
Clueless '95
The Reluctant Agent '95
To Die For '95
The Usual Suspects '95

Serene Hedin
Boggy Creek II '83
Hawken's Breed '87

David Hedison
Enemy Below '57
The Fly '58
Live and Let Die '73
The Art of Crime '75
The Power Within '79
ffolkes '80
Kenny Rogers as the Gambler, Part 2: The Adventure Continues '83
The Naked Face '84
Kemek '88
License to Kill '89
Undeclared War '91

Jack Hedley
The Anniversary '68
Goodbye, Mr. Chips '69
For Your Eyes Only '81

Tippi Hedren
The Birds '63
Marnie '64
Satan's Harvest '65
A Countess from Hong Kong '67
Mr. Kingstreet's War '71
Harrad Experiment '73
Foxfire Light '84
Deadly Spygames '89
In the Cold of the Night '89
Pacific Heights '90
Through the Eyes of a Killer '92
The Birds 2: Land's End '94

Kyle T. Heffner
Flashdance '83
Mutant on the Bounty '89

Marta Heflin
A Star is Born '76
Come Back to the Five & Dime Jimmy Dean, Jimmy Dean '82

Nora Heflin
Our Time '74
Chilly Scenes of Winter '79

Van Heflin
A Woman Rebels '36
Flight from Glory '37
Back Door to Heaven '39
Santa Fe Trail '40
Johnny Eager '42
Presenting Lily Mars '43
Seven Miles from Alcatraz/Flight from Glory '43
The Strange Love of Martha Ivers '46
Till the Clouds Roll By '46
Till the Clouds Roll By/A Star Is Born '46
Green Dolphin Street '47
The Possessed '47
The Three Musketeers '48
East Side, West Side '49
Madame Bovary '49
Prowler '51
Shane '53
A Woman's World '54
Battle Cry '55
Patterns '56
3:10 to Yuma '57
They Came to Cordura '59
Cry of Battle '63
The Greatest Story Ever Told '65
The Man Outside '68
Airport '70
The Ruthless Four '70

O.P. Heggie
Devotion '31
Smilin' Through '32
Anne of Green Gables '34
The Count of Monte Cristo '34
Midnight '34
Peck's Bad Boy '34
The Bride of Frankenstein '35

Robert Hegyes
Just Tell Me You Love Me '80
Underground Aces '80

Peter Hehir
Fast Talking '86
I Live with Me Dad '86
Sweet Talker '91

Katherine Heigl
King of the Hill '93
My Father the Hero '93
Under Siege 2: Dark Territory '95

Elayne Heilveil
Birds of Prey '72
The Adventures of Nellie Bly '81

Brit Helfer
Alley Cat '84
Body Trouble '92

Marg Helgenberger
China Beach '88
After Midnight '89
Always '89
Blind Vengeance '90
Death Dreams '92
Desperate Motives '92
Through the Eyes of a Killer '92
Fallen Angels 2 '93
Stephen King's The Tommyknockers '93
The Cowboy Way '94
Lie Down with Lions '94
Bad Boys '95
Frame by Frame '95
Species '95

Erik Hell
Port of Call '48
The Rite '69
The Passion of Anna '70

Richard Hell
Smithereens '82
Geek Maggot Bingo '83
Desperately Seeking Susan '85

Randee Heller
Can You Hear the Laughter? The Story of Freddie Prinze '79
Fast Break '79
The Karate Kid '84
Danielle Steel's Changes '91

Anne Helm
Follow That Dream '61
The Unkissed Bride '66
Nightmare in Wax '69

Levon Helm
Coal Miner's Daughter '80
Best Revenge '83
The Right Stuff '83
The Dollmaker '84
Smooth Talk '85
End of the Line '88
Man Outside '88

Charlotte J. Helmkamp
Posed For Murder '89
Frankenhooker '90

Katherine Helmond
The Best of Soap: Jessica's Wonderful Life '70s
The Autobiography of Miss Jane Pittman '74
Larry '74
Family Plot '76
The Best of Soap: Who Killed Peter? '77
Scout's Honor '80
Time Bandits '81
Rosie: The Rosemary Clooney Story '82
Jack & the Beanstalk '83
Brazil '85
World War III '86
Overboard '87
Shadey '87
The Lady in White '88
Amore! '93
Inside Monkey Zetterland '93
The Spy Within '94

Tom Helmore
Trouble Along the Way '53
The Tender Trap '55
Designing Woman '57
This Could Be the Night '57
Vertigo '58
Flipper's New Adventure '64

Robert Helpmann
The Red Shoes '48
The Tales of Hoffmann '51
Alice's Adventures in Wonderland '72
The Mango Tree '77
Patrick '78
Puzzle '78

Sheila Helpmann
The Getting of Wisdom '77
Image of Death '77

David Hemblen
Family Viewing '87
The Room '87
Short Circuit 2 '88
Speaking Parts '89
The Adjuster '91
A Man in Uniform '93
Brainscan '94

Mark Hembrow
High Tide '87
Out of the Body '88
Return to Snowy River '88

Margaux Hemingway
Lipstick '76
Killer Fish '79
They Call Me Bruce? '82
Over the Brooklyn Bridge '83
Deadly Conspiracy '91
Inner Sanctum '91
Deadly Rivals '92
Double Obsession '93
Inner Sanctum 2 '94
Bad Love '95

Mariel Hemingway
Lipstick '76
Manhattan '79
Personal Best '82
Star 80 '83
Creator '85
Mean Season '85
Superman 4: The Quest for Peace '87
Steal the Sky '88
The Suicide Club '88
Sunset '88
Delirious '91
Falling from Grace '92
Into the Badlands '92

David Hemmings
Blow-Up '66
Camelot '67
Barbarella '68
The Charge of the Light Brigade '68
The Love Machine '71
Juggernaut '74

Hemmings ▶cont.

Deep Red: Hatchet Murders *'75*
The Old Curiosity Shop *'75*
Blood Relatives *'77*
Islands in the Stream *'77*
The Squeeze *'77*
Beyond Erotica *'79*
Just a Gigolo *'79*
Murder by Decree *'79*
The Deadly Game *'80s*
Beyond Reasonable Doubt *'80*
Disappearance *'81*
Power Play *'81*
Calamity Jane *'82*
Dark Forces *'83*
Man, Woman & Child *'83*
The Snow Queen *'83*
The Key to Rebecca *'85*
Thirst *'87*
The Rainbow *'89*
The Turn of the Screw *'89*

Anouska Hempel
On Her Majesty's Secret Service *'69*
The Scars of Dracula *'70*
Blacksnake! *'73*
Tiffany Jones *'75*

John Hemphill
Hostage for a Day *'94*
Sodbusters *'94*

Sherman Hemsley
Love at First Bite *'79*
Ghost Dance *'83*
Combat Academy *'86*
Ghost Fever *'87*
Camp Cucamonga: How I Spent My Summer Vacation *'90*
Club Fed *'90*
Mr. Nanny *'93*
Home of Angels *'94*

Richard Hench
Bio Hazard *'85*
Tomb *'86*
Endangered *'94*

Bill Henderson
Get Crazy *'83*
Clue *'85*
Movie Maker *'86*
Murphy's Law *'86*
City Slickers *'91*
Ace Crawford, Private Eye

Dell Henderson
The Crowd *'28*
Show People *'28*
Rainbow Over Broadway *'33*
Love Affair *'39*

Don Henderson
The Ghoul *'75*
The Island *'80*

Florence Henderson
The Brady Bunch *'69*
Song of Norway *'70*
A Very Brady Christmas *'88*
Shakes the Clown *'92*

Jo Henderson
Lianna *'83*
Rachel River *'87*

Marcia Henderson
Thunder Bay *'53*
Naked Hills *'56*

Ty Henderson
The Competition *'80*
Happy Hour *'87*

Tony Hendra
This Is Spinal Tap *'84*
Life with Mikey *'93*

Wanda Hendrix
Welcome Stranger *'47*
The Admiral Was a Lady *'50*
My Outlaw Brother *'51*

Gloria Hendry
Black Caesar *'73*
Hell Up in Harlem *'73*
Live and Let Die *'73*
Slaughter's Big Ripoff *'73*
Black Belt Jones *'74*
Bare Knuckles *'77*

Ian Hendry
Children of the Damned *'63*
Repulsion *'65*
The Saint *'68*
Journey to the Far Side of the Sun *'69*
McKenzie Break *'70*
Tales from the Crypt *'72*
Theatre of Blood *'73*
Captain Kronos: Vampire Hunter *'74*
Killer with Two Faces *'74*
The Passenger *'75*
The Bitch *'78*

Sonja Henie
One in a Million *'36*
Thin Ice *'37*
Happy Landing *'38*
My Lucky Star *'38*
Everything Happens at Night *'39*
Second Fiddle *'39*
Sun Valley Serenade *'41*
Iceland *'42*
Wintertime *'43*

Marilu Henner
Between the Lines *'77*
Bloodbrothers *'78*
Hammett *'82*
The Man Who Loved Women *'83*
Cannonball Run 2 *'84*
Johnny Dangerously *'84*
Perfect *'85*
Rustler's Rhapsody *'85*
Stark *'85*
Grown Ups *'86*
Love with a Perfect Stranger *'86*
Ladykillers *'88*
L.A. Story *'91*
Chains of Gold *'92*
Grand Larceny *'92*
Noises Off *'92*

Eva Henning
Devil's Wanton *'49*
Three Strange Loves *'49*

Sam Hennings
Seedpeople *'92*
Drop Zone *'94*
Indecent Behavior 3 *'95*

Paul Henreid
Goodbye, Mr. Chips *'39*
Night Train to Munich *'40*
Casablanca *'42*
Joan of Paris *'42*
Now, Voyager *'42*
The Spanish Main *'45*
Deception *'46*
The Scar *'48*
A Stolen Face *'52*
Tall Lie *'53*
Deep in My Heart *'54*
Battle Shock *'56*
Never So Few *'59*
The Four Horsemen of the Apocalypse *'62*
The Madwoman of Chaillot *'69*

Lance Henriksen
Dog Day Afternoon *'75*
Damien: Omen 2 *'78*
The Visitor *'80*
Prince of the City *'81*
Piranha 2: The Spawning *'82*
Nightmares *'83*
The Right Stuff *'83*
Savage Dawn *'84*
The Terminator *'84*
The Jagged Edge *'85*
Aliens *'86*
Choke Canyon *'86*
Near Dark *'87*
Deadly Intent *'88*
The Hit List *'88*
Pumpkinhead *'88*
The Horror Show *'89*
Johnny Handsome *'89*
Survival Quest *'89*
The Last Samurai *'90*
Tales from the Crypt, Vol. 3 *'90*
Comrades in Arms *'91*
The Pit & the Pendulum *'91*
Stone Cold *'91*
Alien 3 *'92*
Delta Heat *'92*
Jennifer 8 *'92*
The Criminal Mind *'93*
Excessive Force *'93*
Hard Target *'93*
Knights *'93*
Man's Best Friend *'93*
The Outfit *'93*
Super Mario Bros. *'93*
Boulevard *'94*
Color of Night *'94*
Nature of the Beast *'94*
No Escape *'94*
The Quick and the Dead *'94*
Spitfire *'94*
Baja *'95*
Dead Man *'95*
Felony *'95*
Operation Intercept *'95*
Powder *'95*
Wes Craven Presents Mind Ripper *'95*

Anders Henrikson
A Woman's Face *'38*
Miss Julie *'50*

Buck Henry
The Graduate *'67*
Catch-22 *'70*
Is There Sex After Death? *'71*
The Man Who Fell to Earth *'76*
Old Boyfriends *'79*
Gloria *'80*
Eating Raoul *'82*
Steve Martin Live *'85*
Aria *'88*
Dark Before Dawn *'89*
Rude Awakening *'89*
Tune in Tomorrow *'90*
Defending Your Life *'91*
Keep the Change *'92*
The Linguini Incident *'92*
Grumpy Old Men *'93*
Short Cuts *'93*
Kurt Vonnegut's Harrison Bergeron *'95*

Charlotte Henry
March of the Wooden Soldiers *'34*
Charlie Chan at the Opera *'36*
God's Country and the Man *'37*
The Mandarin Mystery *'37*
Bowery Blitzkrieg *'41*

Gloria Henry
Miss Grant Takes Richmond *'49*
Phantasm III: Lord of the Dead *'94*

Greg Henry
Mean Dog Blues *'78*
Hot Rod *'79*
Just Before Dawn *'80*
Funny Money *'82*
Body Double *'84*
The Patriot *'86*
Hitchhiker 4 *'87*
The Last of Philip Banter *'87*
Fair Game *'89*
Kiss of a Killer *'93*
The Positively True Adventures of the Alleged Texas Cheerleader-Murdering Mom *'93*
Bodily Harm *'95*
Sharon's Secret *'95*

Justin Henry
Kramer vs. Kramer *'79*
Tiger Town *'83*
Sixteen Candles *'84*
Martin's Day *'85*
Sweet Hearts Dance *'88*
Andersonville *'95*

Lenny Henry
The Suicide Club *'88*
Bernard and the Genie *'90s*
True Identity *'91*

Martha Henry
Dancing in the Dark *'86*
White Light *'90*
Glory Enough for All: The Discovery of Insulin *'92*

Mike Henry
Adios Amigo *'75*
Smokey and the Bandit *'77*
Smokey and the Bandit, Part 2 *'80*
Smokey and the Bandit, Part 3 *'83*

Robert "Buzzy" Henry
Western Frontier *'35*
The Unknown Ranger *'36*
Buzzy Rides the Range *'40*
Turf Boy *'42*
The Great Mike *'44*
Wild West *'46*

Tim Henry
The Dawson Patrol *'78*
125 Rooms of Comfort *'83*

William Henry
Tarzan Escapes *'36*
Madame X *'37*
Dance Hall *'41*
The Adventures of Mark Twain *'44*
Canadian Mounties vs. Atomic Invaders *'53*
Marshal of Cedar Rock *'53*
Movie Stuntmen *'53*

Lisa Hensley
The 13th Floor *'88*
Brides of Christ *'91*

Pamela Hensley
Doc Savage *'75*
Buck Rogers in the 25th Century *'79*
The Rebels *'79*
The Nude Bomb *'80*
Double Exposure *'82*

Nicky Henson
Psychomania *'73*
Number 1 of the Secret Service *'77*

Audrey Hepburn
Roman Holiday *'53*
Sabrina *'54*
War and Peace *'56*
Funny Face *'57*
Love in the Afternoon *'57*
Green Mansions *'59*
The Nun's Story *'59*
The Unforgiven *'60*
Breakfast at Tiffany's *'61*
The Children's Hour *'61*
Charade *'63*
My Fair Lady *'64*
Paris When It Sizzles *'64*
How to Steal a Million *'66*
Two for the Road *'67*
Wait Until Dark *'67*
Robin and Marian *'76*
Sidney Sheldon's Bloodline *'79*
They All Laughed *'81*
Always *'89*

Katharine Hepburn
A Bill of Divorcement *'32*
Christopher Strong *'33*
Little Women *'33*
Morning Glory *'33*
Little Minister *'34*
Spitfire *'34*
Alice Adams *'35*
Break of Hearts *'35*
Sylvia Scarlett *'35*
Mary of Scotland *'36*
A Woman Rebels *'36*
Quality Street *'37*
Stage Door *'37*
Bringing Up Baby *'38*
Holiday *'38*
The Philadelphia Story *'40*
Keeper of the Flame *'42*
Woman of the Year *'42*
Stage Door Canteen *'43*
Dragon Seed *'44*
Without Love *'45*
State of the Union *'48*
Adam's Rib *'50*
The African Queen *'51*
Pat and Mike *'52*
Summertime *'55*
The Rainmaker *'56*
Desk Set *'57*
Suddenly, Last Summer *'59*
Long Day's Journey into Night *'62*
Guess Who's Coming to Dinner *'67*
The Lion in Winter *'68*
The Madwoman of Chaillot *'69*
Trojan Women *'71*
Love Among the Ruins *'75*
Rooster Cogburn *'75*
Olly Olly Oxen Free *'78*
On Golden Pond *'81*
Grace Quigley *'84*
Hepburn & Tracy *'84*
The Man Upstairs *'93*
Love Affair *'94*

Bernard Hepton
Mansfield Park *'85*
Shadey *'87*
Stealing Heaven *'88*
The Charmer *'89*
Eminent Domain *'91*
The Lady's Not for Burning *'95*

Charles Herbert
Gun Glory *'57*
13 Ghosts *'60*

Holmes Herbert
Through the Breakers *'28*
The Kiss *'29*
Daughter of the Dragon *'31*
Dr. Jekyll and Mr. Hyde *'31*
Shop Angel *'32*
Sons of Steel *'35*
The House of Secrets *'37*
Bad Boy *'39*
Stanley and Livingstone *'39*
British Intelligence *'40*
Invisible Agent *'42*
Sherlock Holmes and the Secret Weapon *'42*

Hugh Herbert
Hook, Line and Sinker *'30*
Bureau of Missing Persons *'33*
Diplomaniacs *'33*
Fashions of 1934 *'34*
Gold Diggers of 1935 *'35*
A Midsummer Night's Dream *'35*
Sweet Adeline *'35*
One Rainy Afternoon *'36*
The Great Waltz *'38*
Eternally Yours *'39*
The Villain Still Pursued Her *'41*
Sherlock Holmes and the Secret Weapon *'42*
It's a Great Life *'43*
A Song is Born *'48*
The Beautiful Blonde from Bashful Bend *'49*

Percy Herbert
Mysterious Island *'61*
Call Me Bwana *'63*
One Million Years B.C. *'66*
The Fiend *'71*
Man in the Wilderness *'71*
Blacksnake! *'73*

Becky Herbst
Shrunken Heads *'94*
Donor Unknown *'95*

Carla Herd
Deathstalker 3 *'89*
Wild Zone *'89*

Richard Herd
Wolf Lake *'79*
Lovely ... But Deadly *'82*
V *'83*
Cosmic Slop *'94*
The Judas Project: The Ultimate Encounter *'94*

Eileen Herlie
Hamlet *'48*
Angel with the Trumpet *'50*

Roberto Herlitzka
Summer Night *'87*
Summer Night with Greek Profile, Almond Eyes & Scent of Basil *'87*
The Favorite Son *'94*

Jimmy Herman
Dances with Wolves *'90*
Geronimo *'93*
Medicine River *'94*
Warrior Spirit *'94*

Paul Herman
The Squeeze *'87*
The Last Temptation of Christ *'88*
New York Stories *'89*

Woody Herman
Wintertime *'43*
Sensations of 1945 *'44*

Irm Hermann
The Merchant of Four Seasons *'71*
The Bitter Tears of Petra von Kant *'72*
Ali: Fear Eats the Soul *'74*
Mother Kusters Goes to Heaven *'76*
The Last Five Days *'82*

Juano Hernandez
Intruder in the Dust *'49*
Stars in My Crown *'50*
The Mark of the Hawk *'57*
Something of Value *'57*
Sergeant Rutledge *'60*

They Call Me Mr. Tibbs! '70

Marcel Herrand
Les Visiteurs du Soir '42
Children of Paradise '44

Mark Herrier
Porky's '82
Porky's 2: The Next Day '83
Tank '83
Spraggue '84

Laura Herring
Silent Night, Deadly Night 3: Better Watch Out! '89
The Forbidden Dance '90

Edward Herrmann
The Day of the Dolphin '73
The Paper Chase '73
The Great Gatsby '74
The Great Waldo Pepper '75
Eleanor & Franklin '76
Love Affair: The Eleanor & Lou Gehrig Story '77
The Betsy '78
Brass Target '78
Freedom Road '79
The North Avenue Irregulars '79
Portrait of a Stripper '79
Sorrows of Gin '79
Take Down '79
The Lawrenceville Stories '80s
Death Valley '81
Reds '81
A Little Sex '82
Memorial Day '83
Harry's War '84
Mrs. Soffel '84
Compromising Positions '85
The Man with One Red Shoe '85
The Purple Rose of Cairo '85
Murrow '86
The Lost Boys '87
Overboard '87
The Private History of a Campaign That Failed '87
Big Business '88
Sweet Poison '91
Born Yesterday '93
A Foreign Field '93
My Boyfriend's Back '93
Foreign Student '94
Richie Rich '94
Nixon '95

Mark Herron
8 1/2 '63
Girl in Gold Boots '69

Gary Hershberger
Paradise Motel '84
Free Ride '86

Barbara Hershey
With Six You Get Eggroll '68
Last Summer '69
The Baby Maker '70
The Liberation of L.B. Jones '70
The Pursuit of Happiness '70
Boxcar Bertha '72
Diamonds '72
Choice of Weapons '76
Flood! '76
From Here to Eternity '79
Angel on My Shoulder '80
The Stunt Man '80
Americana '81
Take This Job & Shove It '81
The Entity '83
The Nightingale '83
The Right Stuff '83
My Wicked, Wicked Ways '84
The Natural '84
Hannah and Her Sisters '86
Hoosiers '86
Passion Flower '86
Shy People '87
Tin Men '87
Beaches '88
The Last Temptation of Christ '88
A World Apart '88
A Killing in a Small Town '90
Tune in Tomorrow '90
Defenseless '91
Paris Trout '91
The Public Eye '92
A Dangerous Woman '93
Falling Down '93
Return to Lonesome Dove '93
Splitting Heirs '93
Swing Kids '93
Abraham '94
The Last of the Dogmen '95
The Pallbearer '95

Jean Hersholt
The Disciple '15
Heart's Haven '22
Greed '24
Hell Harbor '30
Private Lives '31
The Sin of Madelon Claudet '31
Susan Lenox: Her Fall and Rise '31
Grand Hotel '32
Hearts of Humanity '32
The Mask of Fu Manchu '32
Skyscraper Souls '32
Dinner at Eight '33
The Painted Veil '34
Break of Hearts '35
One in a Million '36
Heidi '37
Alexander's Ragtime Band '38
Happy Landing '38
Meet Dr. Christian '39
Courageous Dr. Christian '40
Dr. Christian Meets the Women '40
Remedy for Riches '40
Melody for Three '41
They Meet Again '41

Gerard Herter
Any Gun Can Play '67
Last Day of the War '69
Hornet's Nest '70

Irene Hervey
The Count of Monte Cristo '34
Dude Ranger '34
The Girl Said No '37
Gangbusters '38
Destry Rides Again '39
Night Monster '42
Mickey '48
Mr. Peabody & the Mermaid '48
Play Misty for Me '71

Jason Hervey
Back to the Future '85
Back to School '86

Werner Herzog
Burden of Dreams '82
Man of Flowers '84

Grant Heslov
True Lies '94
Congo '95
Black Sheep '96

David Hess
Last House on the Left '72
Avalanche Express '79
House on the Edge of the Park '84
Let It Rock '86

Sandra Hess
Endangered '94
Beastmaster 3: The Eye of Braxus '95

Howard Hesseman
The Committee '68
Steelyard Blues '73
Shampoo '75
The Sunshine Boys '75
The Big Bus '76
Jackson County Jail '76
Tunnelvision '76
Tarantulas: The Deadly Cargo '77
WKRP in Cincinnati, Vol. 1 '78
Americathon '79
Great American Traffic Jam '80
Loose Shoes '80
Honky Tonk Freeway '81
Private Lessons '81
One Shoe Makes It Murder '82
Doctor Detroit '83
The Princess Who Never Laughed '84
Silence of the Heart '84
This Is Spinal Tap '84
Clue '85
Police Academy 2: Their First Assignment '85
Flight of the Navigator '86
My Chauffeur '86
Amazon Women on the Moon '87
Heat '87
The Diamond Trap '91
Inside Out '91
Murder in New Hampshire: The Pamela Smart Story '91
Rubin & Ed '92
Little Miss Millions '93
Out of Sync '95

Catherine Hessling
Charleston '26
Renoir Shorts '27

Charlton Heston
The Greatest Show on Earth '52
Ruby Gentry '52
Arrowhead '53
Pony Express '53
Naked Jungle '54
The Ten Commandments '56
Three Violent People '57
The Big Country '58
The Buccaneer '58
Touch of Evil '58
Ben-Hur '59
The Wreck of the Mary Deare '59
El Cid '61
Diamond Head '62
55 Days at Peking '63
The Agony and the Ecstasy '65
The Greatest Story Ever Told '65
Major Dundee '65
The War Lord '65
Khartoum '66
Will Penny '67
Elizabeth, the Queen '68
Planet of the Apes '68
Beneath the Planet of the Apes '70
Julius Caesar '70
Omega Man '71
Call of the Wild '72
Antony and Cleopatra '73
Soylent Green '73
Earthquake '74
The Three Musketeers '74
Airport '75 '75
The Four Musketeers '75
Midway '76
Two Minute Warning '76
Gray Lady Down '77
The Prince and the Pauper '78
The Awakening '80
The Mountain Men '80
Mother Lode '82
Chiefs '83
Proud Men '87
A Man for All Seasons '88
Nairobi Affair '88
Treasure Island '89
Almost an Angel '90
The Little Kidnappers '90
The Crucifer of Blood '91
Solar Crisis '92
Tombstone '93
A Thousand Heroes '94
True Lies '94
The Avenging Angel '95
In the Mouth of Madness '95
Alaska '96

Martin Hewitt
Alien Predators '80
Endless Love '81
Yellowbeard '83
Out of Control '85
Killer Party '86
White Ghost '88
Private War '90
Carnal Crimes '91
Crime Lords '91
Night Rhythms '92
Secret Games '92
Secret Games 2: The Escort '93
Night Fire '94

Sean Hewitt
Big Zapper '73
The Sender '82

David Hewlett
Pin '88
Scanners 2: The New Order '91
Desire and Hell at Sunset Motel '92
The Penthouse '92
The Boys of St. Vincent '93

Weldon Heyburn
Sea Racketeers '37
The Thirteenth Man '37
Panama Patrol '39
Criminals Within '41
The Chinese Cat '44

Louis Jean Heydt
The Great McGinty '40
Thirty Seconds Over Tokyo '44
Zombies on Broadway '44
Our Vines Have Tender Grapes '45
The Big Sleep '46

Herbert Heyes
Calling Wild Bill Elliott '43
Teenage '44
Behind Locked Doors '48
The Cobra Strikes '48

Barton Heyman
Let's Scare Jessica to Death '71
Valdez is Coming '71
He Who Walks Alone '78
Billy Galvin '86
Static '87
Raising Cain '92
Roadside Prophets '92

Anne Heywood
Doctor at Large '57
Carthage in Flames '60
The Brain '62
The Very Edge '63
The Shaming '71
I Want What I Want '72
Scenes from a Murder '72
Sadat '83

Pat Heywood
Girly '70
Rude Awakening '81
Wish You Were Here '87

Tom Hickey
Nuns on the Run '90
Unnatural Pursuits '91
Raining Stones '93

William Hickey
Invitation to a Gunfighter '64
The Boston Strangler '68
Mikey & Nicky '76
Prizzi's Honor '85
Walls of Glass '85
The Name of the Rose '86
One Crazy Summer '86
Hobo's Christmas '87
Bright Lights, Big City '88
Da '88
National Lampoon's Christmas Vacation '89
Pink Cadillac '89
Puppet Master '89
Sea of Love '89
Any Man's Death '90
Mob Boss '90
My Blue Heaven '90
Tales from the Crypt, Vol. 3 '90
Tales from the Darkside: The Movie '90
The Runestone '91
Forget Paris '95
The Jerky Boys '95
Major Payne '95

Catherine Hickland
Ghost Town '88
Witchery '88
Millions '90

Darryl Hickman
Men of Boys Town '41
Keeper of the Flame '42
Leave Her to Heaven '45
The Devil on Wheels '47
Fighting Father Dunne '48
Tea and Sympathy '56
Geronimo's Revenge '60
Texas John Slaughter: Geronimo's Revenge '60
Johnny Shiloh '63

Dwayne Hickman
The Sun Comes Up '49
Cat Ballou '65
How to Stuff a Wild Bikini '65
Dr. Goldfoot and the Bikini Machine '66
My Dog, the Thief '69
High School USA '84

Howard Hickman
Civilization '16
Hell-Ship Morgan '36
Western Gold '37
Bullet Code '40

Catherine Hicks
Marilyn: The Untold Story '80
Death Valley '81
Better Late Than Never '83
Garbo Talks '84
The Razor's Edge '84
Fever Pitch '85
Peggy Sue Got Married '86
Star Trek 4: The Voyage Home '86
Laguna Heat '87
Like Father, Like Son '87
Child's Play '88
Souvenir '88
She's Out of Control '89
Spy '89
Running Against Time '90
Secret Ingredient '92
Dillinger and Capone '95
Redwood Curtain '95

Dan Hicks
Evil Dead 2: Dead by Dawn '87
Class Action '91

Kevin Hicks
Blood Relations '87
Higher Education '88
Final Notice '89

Russell Hicks
Devil Dogs of the Air '35
Pick a Star '37
The Big Braodcast of 1938 '38
Stanley and Livingstone '39
The Bank Dick '40
Blind Fools '40
Tarzan's New York Adventure '42
Air Raid Wardens '43
Hitler: Dead or Alive '43
Seventh Cavalry '56

Seymour Hicks
The Secret of the Loch '34
Scrooge '35
Fame Is the Spur '47

William T. Hicks
Challenge '74
Day of Judgment '81
House of Death '82
Death Screams '83
Unmasking the Idol '86
Order of the Black Eagle '87

Joan Hickson
The Guinea Pig '48
Doctor in the House '53
A Day in the Death of Joe Egg '71
Agatha Christie's Miss Marple '80s
Great Expectations '81
The Body in the Library '87
A Murder Is Announced '87
A Pocketful of Rye '87
Century '94

Sachiko Hidari
The Insect Woman '63
She and He '63

Chieko Higashiyama
Early Summer '51
Tokyo Story '53

Anthony Higgins
Quartet '81
Raiders of the Lost Ark '81
The Draughtsman's Contract '82
Cold Room '84
She'll Be Wearing Pink Pajamas '84
The Bride '85
Max, Mon Amour '86
One Against the Wind '91
For Love or Money '93
Nostradamus '93
Sweet Killing '93

Clare Higgins
Hellraiser '87
Hellbound: Hellraiser 2 '88
Wonderland '88
Bad Behavior '92
Circle of Deceit '94
Fatherland '94

Joe Higgins
Milo Milo '60s
Flipper's New Adventure '64
Namu, the Killer Whale '66

John Michael Higgins
National Lampoon's Class of '86 '86
The Late Shift '96

Michael Higgins
Desperate Characters '71
The Conversation '74
Born Beautiful '82
1918 '85
On Valentine's Day '86
Angel Heart '87
Courtship '87
Crusoe '89

Higgins ▶cont.

Dead Bang '89
School Ties '92

Jane Higginson
Devil Wears White '86
Silent Night, Deadly Night 5: The Toymaker '91

Torri Higginson
Family Pictures '93
TekWar '94
Jungleground '95

Jennifer Hilary
One Brief Summer '70
Miss A & Miss M '86

Lise Hilboldt
A Married Man '84
Noon Wine '84

Arthur Hill
The Ugly American '63
Harper '66
Petulia '68
The Pursuit of Happiness '70
The Andromeda Strain '71
Death Be Not Proud '75
The Killer Elite '75
Futureworld '76
Judge Horton and the Scottsboro Boys '76
A Bridge Too Far '77
The Champ '79
Riel '79
The Ordeal of Dr. Mudd '80
Return of Frank Cannon '80
Revenge of the Stepford Wives '80
Churchill and the Generals '81
Dirty Tricks '81
The Amateur '82
Making Love '82
Tomorrow's Child '82
The Guardian '84
Love Leads the Way '84
One Magic Christmas '85
Tales of the Unexpected '91

Benny Hill
Those Magnificent Men in Their Flying Machines '65
Chitty Chitty Bang Bang '68
The Italian Job '69
Benny Hill's Crazy World '74
To See Such Fun '81

Bernard Hill
The Bounty '84
No Surrender '86
Drowning by Numbers '87
Bellman and True '88
Shirley Valentine '89
Mountains of the Moon '90

Craig Hill
Detective Story '51
What Price Glory? '52
Black Box Affair '66
Adios, Hombre '68
Animal Called Man '87

Dana Hill
The $5.20 an Hour Dream '80
The Boy Who Left Home to Find Out About the Shivers '81
Fallen Angel '81
Shoot the Moon '82
Cross Creek '83
The Member of the Wedding '83
Silence of the Heart '84
National Lampoon's European Vacation '85

Doris Hill
Tangled Destinies '32
Galloping Romeo '33

Jack Hill
The Female Jungle '56
The Brain Eaters '58
Dance of Death '68
The Sinister Invasion '68

Lauryn Hill
King of the Hill '93
Sister Act 2: Back in the Habit '93

Marianna Hill
Married Too Young '62
Roustabout '64
Red Line 7000 '65
Paradise, Hawaiian Style '66
Medium Cool '69
El Condor '70
The Baby '72
Thumb Tripping '72
High Plains Drifter '73
The Godfather, Part 2 '74
The Last Porno Flick '74
Messiah of Evil '74
The Invisible Strangler '76
Schizoid '80
Blood Beach '81

Mary Hill
Mesa of Lost Women '52
The Beast from 20,000 Fathoms '53

Nellie Hill
Mistaken Identity '41
Murder with Music '45

Richard Hill
Deathstalker '83
Devastator '85
Warrior Queen '87
Bloodfist 2 '90
Dune Warriors '91
Deathstalker 4: Match of Titans '92
Fast Gun '93

Steven Hill
A Child is Waiting '63
The Slender Thread '65
It's My Turn '80
Eyewitness '81
Rich and Famous '81
Yentl '83
Garbo Talks '84
Between Two Women '86
Heartburn '86
Legal Eagles '86
On Valentine's Day '86
Raw Deal '86
The Boost '88
Running on Empty '88
White Palace '90
Billy Bathgate '91
The Firm '93

Terence Hill
Ace High '68
Boot Hill '69
They Call Me Trinity '72
All the Way, Boys '73
My Name is Nobody '74
Trinity is Still My Name '75
March or Die '77
Mr. Billion '77
Crime Busters '78
Odds and Evens '78
Super Fuzz '81
Go for It '83
Miami Supercops '85
Lucky Luke '94
Troublemakers '94

Teresa Hill
Puppet Master 4 '93
In the Heat of Passion 2: Unfaithful '94
Puppet Master 5: The Final Chapter '94
Bio-Dome '96

Wendy Hiller
Pygmalion '38
Major Barbara '41
I Know Where I'm Going '45
Something of Value '57
Separate Tables '58
Toys in the Attic '63
A Man for All Seasons '66
David Copperfield '70
Murder on the Orient Express '74
Voyage of the Damned '76
The Cat and the Canary '79
The Curse of King Tut's Tomb '80
The Elephant Man '80
Making Love '82
Anne of Avonlea '87
The Lonely Passion of Judith Hearne '87

John Hillerman
The Last Picture Show '71
Lawman '71
The Outside Man '73
Paper Moon '73
The Thief Who Came to Dinner '73
Blazing Saddles '74
Chinatown '74
Audrey Rose '77
Betrayal '78
Magnum P.I.: Don't Eat the Snow in Hawaii '80
Marathon '80
History of the World: Part 1 '81
Little Gloria...Happy at Last '84
Up the Creek '84
Assault and Matrimony '87
Around the World in 80 Days '89
Hands of a Murderer '90

Verna Hillie
Man of the Forest '33
House of Mystery '34
Trail Beyond '34

Candace Hilligoss
Carnival of Souls '62
Curse of the Living Corpse '64

Beverly Hills
Brides of the Beast '68
Knights & Emeralds '87

Gillian Hills
Beat Girl '60
Demons of the Mind '72

Daisy Hilton
Saturday Night Shockers '50
Chained for Life '51

George Hilton
Any Gun Can Play '67
The Battle of El Alamein '68
Dead for a Dollar '70s
Bullet for Sandoval '70
The Ruthless Four '70
Sartana's Here...Trade Your Pistol for a Coffin '70
The Next Victim '71
The Scorpion's Tail '71
Guns for Dollars '73
Day of the Maniac '77
Blade of the Ripper '84

Art Hindle
Invasion of the Body Snatchers '78
The Brood '79
The Power Within '79
Octagon '80
Desperate Lives '82
The Man Who Wasn't There '83
Wild Pony '83
Raw Courage '84
Say Yes! '86
The Gunfighters '87
J. Edgar Hoover '87
Dixie Lanes '88
Into the Fire '88
Surrogate '88
The World's Oldest Living Bridesmaid '92

Earl Hindman
The Taking of Pelham One Two Three '74
Murder in Coweta County '83
The Ballad of the Sad Cafe '91

Ciaran Hinds
December Bride '91
A Dark Adapted Eye '93
Hostages '93
The Man Who Cried '93
Prime Suspect 3 '93
The Affair '95
Mary Reilly '95
Persuasion '95

Samuel S. Hinds
Deluge '33
Gabriel Over the White House '33
The Raven '35
Rhythm on the Range '36
Navy Blue and Gold '37
Devil's Party '38
Test Pilot '38
You Can't Take It with You '38
Destry Rides Again '39
It's a Date '40
Blossoms in the Dust '41
Man Made Monster '41
Pardon My Sarong '42
Ride 'Em Cowboy '42
Son of Dracula '43
Scarlet Street '45
The Strange Affair of Uncle Harry '45
Weekend at the Waldorf '45
It's a Wonderful Life '46

Gregory Hines
History of the World: Part 1 '81
Wolfen '81
Eubie! '82
Deal of the Century '83
The Cotton Club '84
Puss 'n Boots '84
White Nights '85
Running Scared '86
Off Limits '87
Tap '89
Eve of Destruction '90
A Rage in Harlem '91
White Lie '91
T Bone N Weasel '92
Dead Air '94
Renaissance Man '94
Waiting to Exhale '95

Johnny Hines
A Girl's Folly '17
Tillie Wakes Up '17
The Speed Spook '24

Pat Hingle
The Ugly American '63
Invitation to a Gunfighter '64
Hang 'Em High '67
Bloody Mama '70
Running Wild '73
Hazel's People '75
Independence '76
The Gauntlet '77
Tarantulas: The Deadly Cargo '77
Elvis: The Movie '79
Norma Rae '79
Running Scared '79
Wild Times '79
Of Mice and Men '81
The Act '82
Going Berserk '83
Running Brave '83
Sudden Impact '83
Brewster's Millions '85
Broken Badge '85
The Falcon and the Snowman '85
Lady from Yesterday '85
In 'n Out '86
Manhunt for Claude Dallas '86
Maximum Overdrive '86
Baby Boom '87
The Private History of a Campaign That Failed '87
LBJ: The Early Years '88
Batman '89
The Grifters '90
The Habitation of Dragons '91
Batman Returns '92
Citizen Cohn '92
Lightning Jack '94
The Quick and the Dead '94
Batman Forever '95
Truman '95

Darby Hinton
Firecracker '71
The Treasure of Jamaica Reef '74
Malibu Express '85

Akihiko Hirata
H-Man '59
The Secret of the Telegian '61
Godzilla vs. the Cosmic Monster '74

Thora Hird
Conspirator '49
Dangerous Youth '58
The Entertainer '60
A Kind of Loving '62
Rattle of a Simple Man '64
The Nightcomers '72
Consuming Passions '88
The Wedding Gift '93

Daniel Hirsch
Sky High '84
Zero Boys '86

Judd Hirsch
Fury on Wheels '71
Legend of Valentino '75
King of the Gypsies '78
Sooner or Later '78
Marriage Is Alive and Well '80
Ordinary People '80
The Goodbye People '83
Without a Trace '83
Teachers '84
Brotherly Love '85
The Great Escape 2: The Untold Story '88
Running on Empty '88
Independence Day '96

Alice Hirson
Miss All-American Beauty '82
Blind Date '87

Christianne Hirt
Blades of Courage '88
For the Moment '94

Patricia Hitchcock
Strangers on a Train '51
Psycho '60

Don Ho
Joe's Apartment '96

Judith Hoag
Fine Things '90
A Matter of Degrees '90
Teenage Mutant Ninja Turtles: The Movie '90
Switched at Birth '91

Doug Hobart
The Professor '58
The Death Curse of Tartu '66

Rose Hobart
Dr. Jekyll and Mr. Hyde '31
East of Borneo '31
Susan and God '40
The Mad Ghoul '43
Conflict '45
Cass Timberlane '47
The Farmer's Daughter '47

Halliwell Hobbes
Dr. Jekyll and Mr. Hyde '31
You Can't Take It with You '38
Journey for Margaret '42
Son of Fury '42
The Undying Monster '42
Sherlock Holmes Faces Death '43
Casanova Brown '44
Gaslight '44

Peter Hobbs
Next One '84
In the Mood '87

Mara Hobel
Sorrows of Gin '79
Mommie Dearest '81

Valerie Hobson
The Bride of Frankenstein '35
Werewolf of London '35
When Thief Meets Thief '37
Drums '38
Clouds Over Europe '39
Spy in Black '39
The Adventures of Tartu '43
Great Expectations '46
Interrupted Journey '49
Kind Hearts and Coronets '49
The Rocking Horse Winner '49
Train of Events '49
The Promoter '52

Kane Hodder
Jason Goes to Hell: The Final Friday '93
Pumpkinhead 2: Blood Wings '94

Douglas Hodge
Salome's Last Dance '88
Dark Obsession '90
Middlemarch '93

Kate Hodge
Leatherface: The Texas Chainsaw Massacre 3 '89
Love Kills '91
Rapid Fire '92
The Hidden 2 '94
Desire '95

Patricia Hodge
Betrayal '83
Dust to Dust '85
Diamond's Edge '88
Sunset '88
The Shell Seekers '89
Spymaker: The Secret Life of Ian Fleming '90
The Heat of the Day '91

Eddie Hodges
A Hole in the Head '59
The Adventures of Huckleberry Finn '60
Summer Magic '63
Live a Little, Love a Little '68

Tom Hodges
Vietnam War Story 3 '89
The Baby Doll Murders '92

Earle Hodgins
Aces and Eights '36
Heroes of the Alamo '37
A Lawman Is Born '37
Santa Fe Marshal '40

Boss of Bullion City '41
The Bashful Bachelor '42
Inside the Law '42
Colt Comrades '43
Hoppy Serves a Writ '43
The Topeka Terror '45

John Hodiak
Lifeboat '44
The Harvey Girls '46
Love from a Stranger '47
Command Decision '48
Homecoming '48
Battleground '49
Malaya '49
The Miniver Story '50
Across the Wide Missouri '51
Ambush at Tomahawk Gap '53
Conquest of Cochise '53
Dragonfly Squadron '54

Dennis Hoey
Power '34
Sherlock Holmes and the Secret Weapon '42
Son of Fury '42
The Pearl of Death '44
Spider Woman '44
Uncertain Glory '44
House of Fear '45
A Thousand and One Nights '45
Anna and the King of Siam '46
Roll on Texas Moon '46
Golden Earrings '47
Where There's Life '47
David and Bathsheba '51

Abbie Hoffman
Born on the Fourth of July '89
Heavy Petting '89

Basil Hoffman
Communion '89
Lambada '89
The Double O Kid '92
The Ice Runner '93

David Hoffman
A Woman's World '54
Wolf Lake '79
Children in the Crossfire '84

Dustin Hoffman
The Graduate '67
Madigan's Millions '67
Midnight Cowboy '69
Little Big Man '70
Alfredo, Alfredo '72
Straw Dogs '72
Papillon '73
Lenny '74
All the President's Men '76
Marathon Man '76
Straight Time '78
Agatha '79
Kramer vs. Kramer '79
Tootsie '82
Death of a Salesman '86
Ishtar '87
Rain Man '88
Family Business '89
Dick Tracy '90
Billy Bathgate '91
Hook '91
Hero '92
Outbreak '94

Erika Hoffman
To Play the King '93
The Final Cut '95

Gaby Hoffman
Field of Dreams '89
Uncle Buck '89
This Is My Life '92
The Man Without a Face '93
Sleepless in Seattle '93
Now and Then '95

Jane Hoffman
Up the Sandbox '72
Sybil '76
Senior Trip '81
Static '87

Philip S. Hoffman
Leap of Faith '92
Scent of a Woman '92
Joey Breaker '93
Nobody's Fool '94
When a Man Loves a Woman '94
The Yearling '94

Robert Hoffman
A Black Veil for Lisa '68
Eyes Behind the Stars '72
Joe Panther '76

Thom Hoffman
The 4th Man '79
Lily Was Here '89
Orlando '92

Marco Hofschneider
Europa, Europa '91
Foreign Student '94
Immortal Beloved '94
The Island of Dr. Moreau '96

Bosco Hogan
James Joyce: A Portrait of the Artist as a Young Man '77
In the Name of the Father '93

Hulk Hogan
No Holds Barred '89
Suburban Commando '91
Mr. Nanny '93
Thunder in Paradise '93
Thunder in Paradise 2 '94
Thunder in Paradise 3 '94

Jack Hogan
Jet Attack/Paratroop Command '58
Legend of Tom Dooley '59

Michael Hogan
The Peanut Butter Solution '85
Lost '86
Smokescreen '90
Clearcut '92

Pat Hogan
Davy Crockett, King of the Wild Frontier '55
Savage Wilderness '55
Seventh Cavalry '56
Indian Paint '64

Paul Hogan
Anzacs: The War Down Under '85
Crocodile Dundee '86
Crocodile Dundee 2 '88
Almost an Angel '90
Lightning Jack '94
Flipper '96

Robert Hogan
Memory of Us '74
Gone are the Days '84

Susan Hogan
The Brood '79
Phobia '80
Title Shot '81
White Fang '91

Arthur Hohl
The Sign of the Cross '32
Blondie Has Trouble '40
Son of Fury '42
Mystery of the Riverboat '44

David Holbrook
Creepshow 2 '87
Return to Salem's Lot '87

Hal Holbrook
The Group '66
Wild in the Streets '68
The Great White Hope '70
The People Next Door '70
They Only Kill Their Masters '72
Magnum Force '73
Pueblo Affair '73
The Girl from Petrovka '74
All the President's Men '76
Midway '76
Julia '77
Our Town '77
Capricorn One '78
The Fog '78
Murder by Natural Causes '79
Natural Enemies '79
Rituals '79
The Kidnapping of the President '80
Killing of Randy Webster '81
Creepshow '82
When Hell Was in Session '82
Girls Night Out '83
The Star Chamber '83
George Washington '84
Behind Enemy Lines '85
North and South Book 1 '85
Dress Gray '86
North and South Book 2 '86
Wall Street '87
The Unholy '88
Day One '89
Fletch Lives '89
Sorry, Wrong Number '89
A Killing in a Small Town '90
The Firm '93
Carried Away '95

Kathryn Holcomb
Our Time '74
Skag '79

Sarah Holcomb
Caddyshack '80
Happy Birthday, Gemini '80

Diane Holden
Grave of the Vampire '72
Black Starlet '74

Fay Holden
Love Finds Andy Hardy '38
Andy Hardy Gets Spring Fever '39
Andy Hardy Meets Debutante '40
Bitter Sweet '40
Andy Hardy's Private Secretary '41
Blossoms in the Dust '41
Life Begins for Andy Hardy '41
Ziegfeld Girl '41
Andy Hardy's Double Life '42
Love Laughs at Andy Hardy '46
The Big Hangover '50
Samson and Delilah '50

Frankie J. Holden
High Tide '87
Ebbtide '94

Gloria Holden
Dracula's Daughter '36
The Life of Emile Zola '37
Hawaii Calls '38
Behind the Rising Sun '43
The Adventures of Rusty '45

Jan Holden
Fire Maidens from Outer Space '56
One Brief Summer '70

Marjean Holden
Secret Agent 00-Soul '89
Stripped to Kill II: Live Girls '89
Philadelphia Experiment 2 '93
Ballistic '94

Rebecca Holden
The Sisterhood '88
Twenty Dollar Star '91

William Holden
Golden Boy '39
Arizona '40
Our Town '40
Texas '41
Young & Willing '42
Rachel and the Stranger '48
The Dark Past '49
Dear Wife '49
Man from Colorado '49
Miss Grant Takes Richmond '49
Born Yesterday '50
Sunset Boulevard '50
Union Station '50
Boots Malone '52
Escape from Fort Bravo '53
Forever Female '53
The Moon Is Blue '53
Stalag 17 '53
Country Girl '54
Executive Suite '54
Sabrina '54
The Bridges at Toko-Ri '55
Love Is a Many-Splendored Thing '55
Picnic '55
The Bridge on the River Kwai '57
The Key '58
The Horse Soldiers '59
The World of Suzie Wong '60
The Counterfeit Traitor '62
Paris When It Sizzles '64
Alvarez Kelly '66
Casino Royale '67
The Devil's Brigade '68
When Wolves Cry '69
The Wild Bunch '69
Wild Rovers '71
The Towering Inferno '74
Network '76
21 Hours at Munich '76
Damien: Omen 2 '78
Ashanti, Land of No Mercy '79
Escape to Athena '79
Earthling '80
When Time Ran Out '80
S.O.B. '81

Geoffrey Holder
Doctor Dolittle '67
Everything You Always Wanted to Know about Sex (But Were Afraid to Ask) '72
Live and Let Die '73
Swashbuckler '76
Boomerang '92

Ticky Holgado
Delicatessen '92
French Twist '95

Hope Holiday
The Apartment '60
The Rounders '65

John Holland
Hell Harbor '30
Defenders of the Law '31
Morals for Women '31
Up in the Air '40
Gentleman from Dixie '41
House of Errors '42
Girl in Black Stockings '57

Steve Holland
Flash Gordon: Vol. 1 '53
Flash Gordon: Vol. 2 '53

Judy Holliday
Adam's Rib '50
Born Yesterday '50
It Should Happen to You '54
Phffft! '54
Full of Life '56
Solid Gold Cadillac '56
Bells are Ringing '60

Polly Holliday
Gremlins '84
Lots of Luck '85
Moon over Parador '88
Konrad '90s
Mr. Wrong '95

Earl Holliman
Broken Lance '54
Big Combo '55
The Bridges at Toko-Ri '55
I Died a Thousand Times '55
Forbidden Planet '56
Giant '56
The Rainmaker '56
Don't Go Near the Water '57
Gunfight at the O.K. Corral '57
Hot Spell '58
Last Train from Gun Hill '59
The Trap '59
Armored Command '61
Summer and Smoke '61
Sons of Katie Elder '65
Anzio '68
Smoke '70
Tribes '70
I Love You ... Goodbye '73
Cry Panic '74
Alexander: The Other Side of Dawn '77
Sharky's Machine '81
The Solitary Man '82
Gunsmoke: Return to Dodge '87

Tommy Hollis
Malcolm X '92
The Piano Lesson '94

Bridget Hollman
Slumber Party '57 '76
Evils of the Night '85

Julian Holloway
Carry On Henry VIII '71
Porridge '91

Stanley Holloway
Lily of Killarney '34
Cotton Queen '37
Salute John Citizen '42
Immortal Battalion '44
Brief Encounter '46
Nicholas Nickleby '46
This Happy Breed '47
Hamlet '48
Passport to Pimlico '49
The Lavender Hill Mob '51
No Love for Johnnie '60
My Fair Lady '64
In Harm's Way '65
Mrs. Brown, You've Got a Lovely Daughter '68
The Private Life of Sherlock Holmes '70

Sterling Holloway
International House '33
The Merry Widow '34
Tomorrow's Children '34
Doubting Thomas '35
I Live My Life '35
Remember the Night '40
Cheers for Miss Bishop '41
Melody Master '41
Twilight on the Rio Grande '41
The Lady is Willing '42
Wildfire '45
Death Valley '46
Sioux City Sue '46
A Walk in the Sun '46
Robin Hood of Texas '47
The Beautiful Blonde from Bashful Bend '49
Kentucky Rifle '55
Shake, Rattle and Rock '57
The Adventures of Huckleberry Finn '60
Live a Little, Love a Little '68
Super Seal '77
Thunder and Lightning '77
Disney's Storybook Classics '82

Ellen Holly
Cops and Robbers '73
School Daze '88

Lauren Holly
Band of the Hand '86
Seven Minutes in Heaven '86
The Adventures of Ford Fairlane '90
Fugitive Among Us '92
Dangerous Heart '93
Dragon: The Bruce Lee Story '93
Dumb & Dumber '94
Sabrina '95
Beautiful Girls '96
Down Periscope '96

Celeste Holm
Gentleman's Agreement '47
Road House '48
The Snake Pit '48
Come to the Stable '49
All About Eve '50
Champagne for Caesar '50
The Tender Trap '55
High Society '56
Cinderella '64
Tom Sawyer '73
Death Cruise '74
Bittersweet Love '76
Murder by the Book '87
Three Men and a Baby '87

Ian Holm
The Fixer '68
A Midsummer Night's Dream '68
Young Winston '72
Juggernaut '74
Robin and Marian '76
Shout at the Devil '76
The Man in the Iron Mask '77
March or Die '77
Holocaust '78
The Thief of Baghdad '78
Alien '79
S.O.S. Titanic '79
Chariots of Fire '81
Time Bandits '81
Inside the Third Reich '82
Return of the Soldier '82
Greystoke: The Legend of Tarzan, Lord of the Apes '84
Singleton's Pluck '84
Brazil '85
Dance with a Stranger '85
Dreamchild '85
Wetherby '85
Another Woman '88
The Endless Game '89
Henry V '89
Hamlet '90
Kafka '91
Naked Lunch '91
The Advocate '93
The Borrowers '93
The Madness of King George '94
Mary Shelley's Frankenstein '94
Big Night '95

Clare Holman
The Fifteen Streets '90
Let Him Have It '91
Afraid of the Dark '92
Tom & Viv '94

Harry Holman
Fugitive Road '34
Inside the Law '42

Holman ▶cont.

Mexican Spitfire at Sea '42

Rex Holman
The Choppers '61
Panic in the Year Zero! '62

Helen Holmes
Wild Engine/Mistaken Orders '23
Blood and Steel '25

Luree Holmes
Pajama Party '64
How to Stuff a Wild Bikini '65

Phillips Holmes
Criminal Code '31
Dinner at Eight '33
Penthouse '33
General Spanky '36
Housemaster '38

Stuart Holmes
Beyond the Trail '26
My Pal, The King '32
People Will Talk '51

Taylor Holmes
Before Morning '33
Boomerang '47
Copper Canyon '50
Double Deal '50
Beware, My Lovely '52
Hoodlum Empire '52
Tobor the Great '54

Rosie Holotik
Don't Look in the Basement '73
Twisted Brain '74
Encounter with the Unknown '75

Charlene Holt
Man's Favorite Sport? '63
Red Line 7000 '65
El Dorado '67

Hans Holt
The Mozart Story '48
Almost Angels '62

Jack Holt
The Little American '17
The Littlest Rebel '35
San Francisco '36
Cat People '42
Holt of the Secret Service '42
They Were Expendable '45
The Chase '46
Flight to Nowhere '46
My Pal Trigger '46
Renegade Girl '46
Loaded Pistols '48
Wild Frontier '48
Task Force '49
Red Desert '50
Trail of Robin Hood '50
Across the Wide Missouri '51
King of the Bullwhip '51
Western Double Feature 14 '52

Jennifer Holt
Frontier Law '43
Raiders of Sunset Pass '43
Outlaw Trail '44
Song of Old Wyoming '45
Buffalo Bill Rides Again '47
Fighting Vigilantes '47
Ghost Town Renegades '47
Where the North Begins '47
The Hawk of Powder River '48
Range Renegades '48
Stage to Mesa City '48
The Tioga Kid '48

Patrick Holt
Unholy Four '54
Alias John Preston '56
Suspended Alibi '56
Men of Sherwood Forest '57
Flight from Singapore '62
Vulture '67
When Dinosaurs Ruled the Earth '70
Psychomania '73

Sandrine Holt
Black Robe '91
Rapa Nui '93
Pocahontas: The Legend '95

Tim Holt
Law West of Tombstone '38
Renegade Ranger/Scarlet River '38
Fifth Avenue Girl '39
Stagecoach '39
The Magnificent Ambersons '42
Hitler's Children '43
Sagebrush Law '43
My Darling Clementine '46
Treasure of the Sierra Madre '48
Mysterious Desperado '49
Mysterious Desperado/Rider From Tucson '49
Riders of the Range '49
Dynamite Pass '50
Rider from Tucson '50
Riders of the Range/Storm Over Wyoming '50
Storm Over Wyoming '50
Gun Smugglers/Hot Lead '51
Gunplay '51
His Kind of Woman '51
Hot Lead '51
Western Double Feature 14 '52
The Monster That Challenged the World '57
The Yesterday Machine '63
This Stuff'll Kill Ya! '71

Ula Holt
The New Adventures of Tarzan '35
Tarzan and the Green Goddess '38

Mark Holton
Pee Wee's Big Adventure '85
Easy Wheels '89
Leprechaun '93

Sean Holton
White Fury '90
Presumed Guilty '91

Maria Holvoe
The Last Warrior '89
Worth Winning '89

Arabella Holzbog
The Last Samurai '90
Stone Cold '91
Carnosaur 2 '94

Robert E. Homans
The Concentratin' Kid '30
Spurs '30
Trigger Tricks '30
Man from Hell's Edges '32
I Take This Oath '40
X Marks the Spot '42
Rogue's Gallery '44
The Scarlet Clue '45

David Homb
The Channeler '89
Street Soldiers '91

Skip Homeier
The Gunfighter '50
The Halls of Montezuma '50
Cry Vengeance '54
Ten Wanted Men '54
The Burning Hills '56
The Tall T '57
Johnny Shiloh '63
The Ghost and Mr. Chicken '66
The Voyage of the Yes '72
Starbird and Sweet William '73

Oscar Homolka
Rhodes '36
Sabotage '36
Comrade X '40
The Invisible Woman '40
Seven Sinners '40
Ball of Fire '41
I Remember Mama '48
The White Tower '50
The House of the Arrow '53
The Seven Year Itch '55
War and Peace '56
The Key '58
Boys' Night Out '62
Mooncussers '62
The Wonderful World of the Brothers Grimm '62
Funeral in Berlin '66
Strange Case of Dr. Jekyll & Mr. Hyde '68
The Madwoman of Chaillot '69
The Executioner '70
Song of Norway '70

James Hong
The Dynamite Brothers '74
Bethune '77
Yes, Giorgio '82
Big Trouble in Little China '86
The Golden Child '86
Black Widow '87
Revenge of the Nerds 2: Nerds in Paradise '87
The Jitters '88
The Brotherhood of the Rose '89
Shadowzone '89
Tango and Cash '89
The Vineyard '89
Caged Fury '90
Tax Season '90
Crime Lords '91
Body Trouble '92
Dragonfight '92
L.A. Goddess '92
Merlin '92
Talons of the Eagle '92
Question of Faith '93
Wayne's World 2 '93
Bad Company '94
Operation Golden Phoenix '94
Bloodsport 2: The Next Kumite '95
Femme Fontaine: Killer Babe for the C.I.A. '95

Kojiro Hongo
Gamera vs. Barugon '66
Gamera vs. Gaos '67
Destroy All Planets '68

Darla Hood
Little Rascals, Vol. 1 '29
Bohemian Girl '36
Our Gang Comedies '40s
The Bat '59
Little Rascals Christmas Special '79

Don Hood
Absence of Malice '81
Marie '85
Blind Vengeance '90

Jan Hooks
Pee Wee's Big Adventure '85
Batman Returns '92
Coneheads '93
A Dangerous Woman '93

Kevin Hooks
Sounder '72
Aaron Loves Angela '75
The White Shadow, Vol. 1 '78
Can You Hear the Laughter? The Story of Freddie Prinze '79
Innerspace '87

Robert Hooks
Sweet Love, Bitter '67
Aaron Loves Angela '75
A Woman Called Moses '78
Fast Walking '82
Words by Heart '84
The Execution '85
Heat Wave '90
Passenger 57 '92

Peter Hooten
Fantasies '73
Slashed Dreams '74
Deadly Mission '78
Dr. Strange '78
2020 Texas Gladiators '85

William Hootkins
Valentino '77
Hear My Song '91
Dust Devil '93
Death Machine '95

Phil Hoover
Policewomen '73
Black Gestapo '75

Bob Hope
The Big Braodcast of 1938 '38
College Swing '38
Give Me a Sailor '38
The Ghost Breakers '40
The Road to Singapore '40
Caught in the Draft '41
Louisiana Purchase '41
The Road to Zanzibar '41
My Favorite Blonde '42
The Road to Morocco '42
Star Spangled Rhythm '42
They Got Me Covered '43
The Princess and the Pirate '44
Strictly G.I. '44
Monsieur Beaucaire '46
The Road to Utopia '46
My Favorite Brunette '47
The Road to Rio '47
Where There's Life '47
The Paleface '48
The Great Lover '49
Sorrowful Jones '49
Fancy Pants '50
The Lemon Drop Kid '51
Son of Paleface '52
Here Come the Girls '53
Off Limits '53
The Road to Bali '53
Casanova's Big Night '54
Hollywood Goes to War '54
The Seven Little Foys '55
Paris Holiday '57
The Road to Lebanon '60
The Road to Hong Kong '62
Call Me Bwana '63
A Global Affair '63
I'll Take Sweden '65
Boy, Did I Get a Wrong Number! '66
The Oscar '66
Bachelor in Paradise '69
How to Commit Marriage '69
Cancel My Reservation '72
Hollywood Clowns '85

Leslie Hope
Prep School '81
Sword of Gideon '86
It Takes Two '88
Kansas '88
Talk Radio '88
The Big Slice '90
Doppelganger: The Evil Within '90
Men at Work '90
The Abduction of Allison Tate '92
Caught in the Act '93
Sweet Killing '93
Paris, France '94
First Degree '95

Richard Hope
Singleton's Pluck '84
Bellman and True '88
A Casualty of War '90
Piece of Cake '90
Antonia and Jane '91

Vida Hope
Roadhouse Girl '53
Angels One Five '54

Anthony Hopkins
The Lion in Winter '68
Hamlet '69
The Looking Glass War '69
Young Winston '72
All Creatures Great and Small '74
The Girl from Petrovka '74
Juggernaut '74
QB VII '74
The Lindbergh Kidnapping Case '76
Audrey Rose '77
A Bridge Too Far '77
International Velvet '78
Magic '78
A Change of Seasons '80
The Elephant Man '80
The Hunchback of Notrè Dame '82
The Bounty '84
A Married Man '84
Arch of Triumph '85
Mussolini & I '85
84 Charing Cross Road '86
The Good Father '87
The Dawning '88
The Tenth Man '88
A Chorus of Disapproval '89
A Doll's House '89
Great Expectations '89
Desperate Hours '90
One Man's War '90
The Silence of the Lambs '91
Bram Stoker's Dracula '92
Chaplin '92
The Efficiency Expert '92
Freejack '92
Howard's End '92
The Innocent '93
The Remains of the Day '93
Shadowlands '93
The Trial '93
Legends of the Fall '94
The Road to Wellville '94
August '95
Nixon '95

Bo Hopkins
The Wild Bunch '69
Culpepper Cattle Co. '72
The Getaway '72
The Only Way Home '72
American Graffiti '73
White Lightning '73
The Day of the Locust '75
Kansas City Massacre '75
The Killer Elite '75
Posse '75
The Runaway Barge '75
A Small Town in Texas '76
Tentacles '77
Midnight Express '78
More American Graffiti '79
Casino '80
The Fifth Floor '80
Rodeo Girl '80
Sweet 16 '81
Plutonium Incident '82
Mutant '83
What Comes Around '85
A Smoky Mountain Christmas '86
Nightmare at Noon '87
Bounty Hunters '89
The Final Alliance '89
Trapper County War '89
Big Bad John '90
Blood Ties '92
Center of the Web '92
The Legend of Wolf Mountain '92
The Ballad of Little Jo '93
Inside Monkey Zetterland '93
President's Target '93
Cheyenne Warrior '94
Wyatt Earp: Return to Tombstone '94
Painted Hero '95
Texas Payback '95

Harold Hopkins
Demonstrator '71
Sara Dane '81
Monkey Grip '82
Fantasy Man '84

Joan Hopkins
Man on the Run '49
The Weaker Sex '49

Katherine Hopkins
The Capture of Bigfoot '79
Legend of Big Foot '82

Miriam Hopkins
Dr. Jekyll and Mr. Hyde '31
Barbary Coast '35
Becky Sharp '35
These Three '36
Men Are Not Gods '37
The Old Maid '39
Virginia City '40
The Heiress '49
Carrie '52
The Children's Hour '61
Fanny Hill: Memoirs of a Woman of Pleasure '64
The Chase '66
Savage Intruder '68

Rhonda Leigh Hopkins
Cover Girl Models '75
Summer School Teachers '75
Tidal Wave '75

Telma Hopkins
Bosom Buddies '80
The Kid with the Broken Halo '82
Trancers '84
Vital Signs '90
Trancers 3: Deth Lives '92

Rolf Hoppe
Mephisto '81
Spring Symphony '86

Dennis Hopper
Rebel Without a Cause '55
Giant '56
The Young Land '59
Night Tide '63
Sons of Katie Elder '65
Planet of Blood '66
Cool Hand Luke '67
The Glory Stompers '67
The Trip '67
Easy Rider '69
The Last Movie '71
Mad Dog Morgan '76
Tracks '76
The American Friend '77
Reborn '78
Apocalypse Now '79
Wild Times '79
Out of the Blue '80
King of the Mountain '81
The Osterman Weekend '83
Rumble Fish '83

The Inside Man '84
My Science Project '85
Stark '85
Blue Velvet '86
Hoosiers '86
Let It Rock '86
Running Out of Luck '86
Texas Chainsaw Massacre, Part 2 '86
Black Widow '87
O.C. and Stiggs '87
The Pick-Up Artist '87
River's Edge '87
Straight to Hell '87
Blood Red '88
Riders of the Storm '88
Backtrack '89
Chattahoochee '89
Flashback '89
Superstar: The Life and Times of Andy Warhol '90
Double-Crossed '91
Eye of the Storm '91
Hearts of Darkness: A Filmmaker's Apocalypse '91
The Indian Runner '91
Paris Trout '91
Nails '92
Sunset Heat '92
Boiling Point '93
Red Rock West '93
Super Mario Bros. '93
True Romance '93
Search and Destroy '94
Speed '94
Witch Hunt '94
Carried Away '95
Waterworld '95
Bloodbath

Hedda Hopper
Don Juan '26
Skinner's Dress Suit '26
The Dropkick '27
The Racketeer '29
As You Desire Me '32
Speak Easily '32
I Live My Life '35
One Frightened Night '35
The Dark Hour '36
Doughnuts & Society '36
Dracula's Daughter '36
Dangerous Holiday '37
Vogues of 1938 '37
Annabel Takes a Tour/Maid's Night Out '38
Maid's Night Out '38
Tarzan's Revenge '38
Midnight '39
Hedda Hopper's Hollywood '42
Reap the Wild Wind '42
Breakfast in Hollywood '46

Victoria Hopper
Lorna Doone '34
The Mill on the Floss '37

William Hopper
Conquest of Space '55
Rebel Without a Cause '55
The Deadly Mantis '57
20 Million Miles to Earth '57

Russell Hopton
I'm No Angel '33
The Girl from Missouri '34
The World Accuses '35
Death from a Distance '36
Last Outlaw '36
Hopalong Cassidy: Renegade Trail '39
Renegade Trail '39
Zombies on Broadway '44
West of the Pecos '45

Barbara Horan
Bayou Romance '86
Malibu Bikini Shop '86

Gerard Horan
Look Back in Anger '89
Much Ado about Nothing '93
A Midwinter's Tale '95

James Horan
Image of Passion '86
The Haunting of Seacliff Inn '94

Roy Horan
Snuff-Bottle Connection '82
Story of the Dragon '82
Eagle's Shadow '84

Michael Hordern
Train of Events '49
A Christmas Carol '51
The Promoter '52
The Man Who Never Was '55
The Warriors '55
The Baby and the Battleship '56
The Spanish Gardener '57
The Spaniard's Curse '58
Sink the Bismarck '60
Cleopatra '63
Dr. Syn, Alias the Scarecrow '64
The Spy Who Came in from the Cold '65
A Funny Thing Happened on the Way to the Forum '66
Khartoum '66
Lamp at Midnight '66
How I Won the War '67
The Taming of the Shrew '67
Where Eagles Dare '68
Anne of the Thousand Days '69
Alice's Adventures in Wonderland '72
Demons of the Mind '72
The Possession of Joel Delaney '72
Mackintosh Man '73
The Old Curiosity Shop '75
Royal Flash '75
Joseph Andrews '77
The Medusa Touch '78
Ivanhoe '82
The Missionary '82
Oliver Twist '82
Yellowbeard '83
Lady Jane '85
Young Sherlock Holmes '85
The Secret Garden '87
The Trouble with Spies '87
Dark Obsession '90
The Green Man '91
Middlemarch '93

Camilla Horn
Faust '26
The Tempest/The Eagle '27

David Horne
Late Extra '35
Spitfire '42
Men of Two Worlds '46

Geoffrey Horne
Bonjour Tristesse '57
The Bridge on the River Kwai '57
Joseph & His Brethren '60

Lena Horne
The Duke is Tops '38
Panama Hattie '42
Cabin in the Sky '43
I Dood It '43
Stormy Weather '43
Thousands Cheer '43
Broadway Rhythm '44
Two Girls and a Sailor '44
Till the Clouds Roll By '46
Till the Clouds Roll By/A Star Is Born '46
Ziegfeld Follies '46
Words and Music '48
The Duchess of Idaho '50
Death of a Gunfighter '69
The Wiz '78

Wil Horneff
Ghost in the Machine '93
The Yearling '94
Born to Be Wild '95
Oldest Confederate Widow Tells All '95

Penelope Horner
Half a Sixpence '67
Man Who Had Power Over Women '70

David Horovitch
Piece of Cake '90
Paper Marriage '93

Adam Horovitz
Lost Angels '89
A Kiss Before Dying '91
Long Road Home '91
Roadside Prophets '92

Jane Horrocks
The Dressmaker '89
Getting It Right '89
The Fifteen Streets '90
Life Is Sweet '90
Memphis Belle '90
The Witches '90
Deadly Advice '93
Second Best '94

Michael Horse
Legend of the Lone Ranger '81
Buckeye and Blue '87
Deadly Weapon '88
Border Shootout '90
Twin Peaks '90
Twin Peaks '90
House of Cards '92
Passenger 57 '92
Lakota Woman: Siege at Wounded Knee '94
Wagons East '94

Anna Maria Horsford
Times Square '80
Charlotte Forten's Mission: Experiment in Freedom '85
St. Elmo's Fire '85
Heartburn '86
Street Smart '87
Taken Away '89
Presumed Innocent '90
Murder without Motive '92

Lee Horsley
Sword & the Sorcerer '82
Danielle Steel's Palomino '91
French Silk '94
Unlawful Passage '94
Hawkeye: Premiere Episode '95

Edward Everett Horton
The Front Page '31
Lonely Wives '31
Reaching for the Moon '31
The Gay Divorcee '34
The Merry Widow '34
The Private Secretary '35
Top Hat '35
Angel '37
Lost Horizon '37
Shall We Dance '37
Bluebeard's Eighth Wife '38
College Swing '38
Holiday '38
Here Comes Mr. Jordan '41
Sunny '41
Ziegfeld Girl '41
I Married an Angel '42
The Magnificent Dope '42
Springtime in the Rockies '42
Forever and a Day '43
Thank Your Lucky Stars '43
Arsenic and Old Lace '44
Lady On a Train '45
Down to Earth '47
Her Husband's Affairs '47
Pocketful of Miracles '61
It's a Mad, Mad, Mad, Mad World '63
Sex and the Single Girl '64
Cold Turkey '71

Peter Horton
Children of the Corn '84
Where the River Runs Black '86
Side Out '90
The Baby-Sitters Club '95

Robert Horton
Men of the Fighting Lady '54
The Green Slime '68

Bobby Hosea
French Silk '94
The O.J. Simpson Story '94

Shizuko Hoshi
Come See the Paradise '90
M. Butterfly '93

Yuriko Hoshi
Godzilla vs. Mothra '64
Ghidrah the Three Headed Monster '65
Last War '68

Bob Hoskins
Cry Terror '74
Royal Flash '75
Inserts '76
The Long Good Friday '79
Zulu Dawn '79
Pink Floyd: The Wall '82
Beyond the Limit '83
The Cotton Club '84
Lassiter '84
Brazil '85
The Dunera Boys '85
Mussolini & I '85
Mona Lisa '86
Sweet Liberty '86
The Lonely Passion of Judith Hearne '87
Prayer for the Dying '87
Who Framed Roger Rabbit '88
Heart Condition '90
Mermaids '90
The Raggedy Rawney '90
Hook '91
The Inner Circle '91
Shattered '91
Blue Ice '92
The Favor, the Watch, & the Very Big Fish '92
Passed Away '92
Super Mario Bros. '93
World War II: When Lions Roared '94
Nixon '95

Farina Hoskins
The Return of Our Gang '25
Our Gang '26
Little Rascals, Book 1 '30s
Our Gang Comedy Festival '88
Our Gang Comedy Festival 2 '89

Robert Hossein
Double Agents '59
Le Repos du Guerrier '62
The Battle of El Alamein '68
Bolero '82

German Houde
Les Bons Debarras '81
Night Zoo '87

Katharine Houghton
Guess Who's Coming to Dinner '67
Seeds of Evil '76
The Eyes of the Amaryllis '82
Mr. North '88
Billy Bathgate '91
Ethan Frome '92
The Night We Never Met '93

Ned Hourani
Triple Impact '92
Fist of Steel '93

Billy House
Bedlam '45
Egg and I '47
People Will Talk '51
Santa Fe '51
Joe's Bed-Stuy Barbershop: We Cut Heads '83

Ron House
Bullshot '83
Footlight Frenzy '84

Arthur Houseman
Manhandled '24
The Bat '26

John Houseman
Seven Days in May '64
The Paper Chase '73
Rollerball '75
Three Days of the Condor '75
St. Ives '76
Our Town '77
The Cheap Detective '78
The Fog '78
Old Boyfriends '79
The Babysitter '80
A Christmas Without Snow '80
Gideon's Trumpet '80
My Bodyguard '80
Wholly Moses! '80
Ghost Story '81
Murder by Phone '82
The Winds of War '83
Another Woman '88
Bright Lights, Big City '88
Gore Vidal's Lincoln '88
The Naked Gun: From the Files of Police Squad '88

Jerry Houser
Summer of '42 '71
Class of '44 '73
Slap Shot '77
A Very Brady Christmas '88

Donald Houston
Crow Hollow '52
Doctor in the House '53
The Mark '61
The Prince and the Pauper '62
Maniac '63
A Study in Terror '66
The Bushbaby '70
Tales That Witness Madness '73

George Houston
Let's Sing Again '36
Wallaby Jim of the Islands '37
Frontier Scout '38
The Great Waltz '38
Border Roundup '41
The Lone Rider in Ghost Town '41
Rangeland Racket '41
The Lone Rider in Cheyenne '42
Texas Justice '42

Glyn Houston
River Beat '54
Conspiracy '89

Joff Houston
Ninja Death Squad '87
Ninja: American Warrior '90

Renee Houston
The Belles of St. Trinian's '53
Time Without Pity '57
The Horse's Mouth '58
Mania '60
Tunes of Glory/Horse's Mouth '60

Whitney Houston
The Bodyguard '92
Waiting to Exhale '95

Anders Hove
Subspecies '90
Bloodstone: Subspecies 2 '92
Bloodlust: Subspecies 3 '93

Adrian Hoven
Tromba, the Tiger Man '52
Cave of the Living Dead '65
Castle of the Creeping Flesh '68
Fox and His Friends '75

Natasha Hovey
Acqua e Sapone '83
Demons '86

Adam Coleman Howard
Quiet Cool '86
Slaves of New York '89
No Secrets '91

Alan Howard
A Casualty of War '90
The Cook, the Thief, His Wife & Her Lover '90
Strapless '90
The Secret Rapture '94

Arliss Howard
The Prodigal '83
Door to Door '84
The Lightship '86
Full Metal Jacket '87
Hands of a Stranger '87
Plain Clothes '88
Tequila Sunrise '88
Men Don't Leave '89
Somebody Has to Shoot the Picture '90
Iran: Days of Crisis '91
Crisscross '92
Ruby '92
Till Death Do Us Part '92
Wilder Napalm '93
Natural Born Killers '94
The Infiltrator '95
To Wong Foo, Thanks for Everything, Julie Newmar '95

Arthur Howard
The Reckless Way '36
The Happiest Days of Your Life '50
Paradisio '61

Barbara Howard
Running Mates '86
Lucky Stiff '88

Bob Howard
Junction 88 '40
Murder with Music '45

Boothe Howard
Mystery Liner '34
Red River Valley '36
Oh Susannah '38

Brie Howard
Android '82
The Runnin' Kind '89

Clint Howard
Gentle Giant '67
The Wild Country '71
Salty '73
Huckleberry Finn '75

Howard ▶cont.

The Death of Richie '76
Eat My Dust '76
The Red Pony '76
Grand Theft Auto '77
Rock 'n' Roll High School '79
Cotton Candy '82
Evilspeak '82
Cocoon '85
Gung Ho '85
The Wraith '87
B.O.R.N. '88
End of the Line '88
Freeway '88
Disturbed '90
Silent Night, Deadly Night 4: Initiation '90
Backdraft '91
Far and Away '92
Carnosaur '93
Forced to Kill '93
Bigfoot: The Unforgettable Encounter '94
Cheyenne Warrior '94
Leprechaun 2 '94
Dillinger and Capone '95
Ice Cream Man '95
Barb Wire '96
Rattled '96

Curly Howard
The Lost Stooges '33
Hollywood Party '34
The Three Stooges: Half-Wit's Holiday and Other Nyuks '35
The Three Stooges: Nutty but Nice and Other Nyuks '36
Three Stooges Comedy Capers: Vol. 1 '40s
Three Stooges: Cookoo Cavaliers and Other Nyuks '40
The Three Stooges: Idiots Deluxe and Other Nyuks '40
The Three Stooges: They Stooge to Conga and Other Nyuks '40
Three Stooges: From Nurse to Worse and Other Nyuks '45
Three Stooges Comedy Classics '49
Three Stooges Festival '49
Stop! Look! and Laugh! '60
Snow White and the Three Stooges '61
The Stooges Story '90

Esther Howard
Vice Squad '31
Klondike Annie '36

Frank Howard
Hard Knox '83
That Was Then...This Is Now '85

John Howard
The Club '81
Prince and the Great Race '83
The Highest Honor '84
Young Einstein '89

John Howard
Bulldog Drummond Comes Back '37
Bulldog Drummond's Revenge '37
Lost Horizon '37
Arrest Bulldog Drummond '38
Bulldog Drummond in Africa/ Arrest Bulldog Drummond '38
Bulldog Drummond's Peril '38
Bulldog Drummond's Revenge/ Bulldog Drummond's Peril '38
Bulldog Drummond's Bride '39
Bulldog Drummond's Secret Police '39
The Invisible Woman '40
The Philadelphia Story '40
The Texas Rangers Ride Again '40
The Undying Monster '42
Love from a Stranger '47
The Fighting Kentuckian '49
Radar Secret Service '50
Make Haste to Live '54

Joyce Howard
The Night Has Eyes '42
Appointment with Crime '45

Kathleen Howard
It's A Gift '34
First Love '39
Young People '40
Blossoms in the Dust '41
Crash Dive '43

Ken Howard
1776 '72
Manhunter '74
The White Shadow, Vol. 1 '78
Damien: The Leper Priest '80
Country Girl '82
Rage of Angels '83
Second Thoughts '83
The Thorn Birds '83
Rage of Angels: The Story Continues '86
Pudd'nhead Wilson '87
Strange Interlude '90
Murder in New Hampshire: The Pamela Smart Story '91
Oscar '91
Ulterior Motives '92
The Net '95

Kevyn Major Howard
Full Metal Jacket '87
Alien Nation '88

Leslie Howard
Devotion '31
A Free Soul '31
The Animal Kingdom '32
Smilin' Through '32
Of Human Bondage '34
The Scarlet Pimpernel '34
Petrified Forest '36
Romeo and Juliet '36
Stand-In '37
Pygmalion '38
Gone with the Wind '39
Intermezzo '39
The Forty-Ninth Parallel '41
Pimpernel Smith '42
Spitfire '42

Lisa Howard
Sabaka '55
Rolling Vengeance '87

Mary Howard
All Over Town '37
Abe Lincoln in Illinois '40
Billy the Kid '41
The Loves of Edgar Allen Poe '42

Moe Howard
Dancing Lady '33
The Lost Stooges '33
Hollywood Party '34
The Three Stooges: Half-Wit's Holiday and Other Nyuks '35
The Three Stooges: Nutty but Nice and Other Nyuks '36
Three Stooges Comedy Capers: Vol. 1 '40s
Three Stooges: Cookoo Cavaliers and Other Nyuks '40
The Three Stooges: Idiots Deluxe and Other Nyuks '40
The Three Stooges: They Stooge to Conga and Other Nyuks '40
Three Stooges: From Nurse to Worse and Other Nyuks '45
Swing Parade of 1946 '46
Three Stooges Comedy Classics '49
Three Stooges Festival '49
Gold Raiders '51
Have Rocket Will Travel '59
Stop! Look! and Laugh! '60
Snow White and the Three Stooges '61
The Three Stooges Meet Hercules '61
Three Stooges in Orbit '62
Around the World in a Daze '63
It's a Mad, Mad, Mad, Mad World '63
The Outlaws is Coming! '65
Dr. Death, Seeker of Souls '73
The Stooges Story '90

Rance Howard
The Wild Country '71
Bloody Trail '72
Where the Lilies Bloom '74
Huckleberry Finn '75
Eat My Dust '76
B.O.R.N. '88
Dark Before Dawn '89
Far and Away '92
Forced to Kill '93
Bigfoot: The Unforgettable Encounter '94

Ron Howard
Andy Griffith Show '60
Door to Door Maniac '61
The Courtship of Eddie's Father '62
The Music Man '62
Village of the Giants '65
Smoke '70
The Wild Country '71
American Graffiti '73
Run, Stranger, Run '73
The Migrants '74
Huckleberry Finn '75
Eat My Dust '76
The Shootist '76
Grand Theft Auto '77
More American Graffiti '79
Bitter Harvest '81
Return to Mayberry '85

Ronald Howard
Night Beat '48
The Queen of Spades '49
The Naked Edge '61
Pattern for Plunder '62

Shemp Howard
Dancing Lady '33
Three Stooges Comedy Capers: Vol. 1 '40s
The Bank Dick '40
The Invisible Woman '40
Buck Privates '41
Pittsburgh '42
Private Buckaroo '42
Cooking Up Trouble '44
Ghost Crazy '44
Africa Screams '49
Three Stooges Comedy Classics '49
Three Stooges Festival '49
Gold Raiders '51
Stop! Look! and Laugh! '60
The Stooges Story '90

Susan Howard
Moonshine County Express '77
Sidewinder One '77
The Power Within '79

Terrence DaShon Howard
The Jacksons: An American Dream '92
Sunset Park '96

Trevor Howard
Brief Encounter '46
I See a Dark Stranger '46
Green for Danger '47
The Third Man '49
The Clouded Yellow '51
The Golden Salamander '51
The Gift Horse '52
The Key '58
Mutiny on the Bounty '62
Invincible Mr. Disraeli '63
Father Goose '64
Morituri '65
Operation Crossbow '65
Von Ryan's Express '65
The Poppy Is Also a Flower '66
Triple Cross '67
The Charge of the Light Brigade '68
Battle of Britain '69
Lola '69
The Night Visitor '70
Ryan's Daughter '70
Catch Me a Spy '71
Catholics '73
A Doll's House '73
The Offence '73
The Count of Monte Cristo '74
Craze '74
11 Harrowhouse '74
The Graveyard '74
Conduct Unbecoming '75
Hennessy '75
Roboman '75
Adventures of Eliza Fraser '76
Albino '76
The Bawdy Adventures of Tom Jones '76
Slavers '77
Stevie '78
Superman: The Movie '78
Hurricane '79
Meteor '79
Staying On '80
Sea Wolves '81
Windwalker '81
Deadly Game '82
Gandhi '82
Inside the Third Reich '82
The Missionary '82
Shaka Zulu '83
Sword of the Valiant '83
Flashpoint Africa '84
George Washington '84
Dust '85
This Lightning Always Strikes Twice '85
Foreign Body '86
The Dawning '88
The Unholy '88
White Mischief '88
The Cary Grant Collection '90

Vanessa Howard
Blood Beast Terror '67
Girly '70
Picture of Dorian Gray '74

Clark Howat
Fu Manchu '56
The Giant Claw '57
Billy Jack '71

C. Thomas Howell
E.T.: The Extra-Terrestrial '82
The Outsiders '83
Tank '83
Grandview U.S.A. '84
Red Dawn '84
Secret Admirer '85
The Hitcher '86
Soul Man '86
Into the Homeland '87
A Tiger's Tale '87
Far Out Man '89
The Return of the Musketeers '89
Curiosity Kills '90
Eyes of the Panther '90
Kid '90
Side Out '90
Breaking the Rules '92
Nickel & Dime '92
Tattle Tale '92
To Protect and Serve '92
Acting on Impulse '93
Gettysburg '93
Jailbait '93
That Night '93
Dangerous Indiscretion '94
Payback '94
Teresa's Tattoo '94
Hourglass '95
Suspect Device '95
The Sweeper '95

Hoke Howell
B.O.R.N. '88
Alienator '89

Ursula Howells
The Gilded Cage '54
Girly '70

Frankie Howerd
The Runaway Bus '54
Cool Mikado '63
The Great St. Trinian's Train Robbery '66
Carry On Doctor '68
Naughty Knights '71
Night of the Laughing Dead '75

Reed Howes
Cyclone Cavalier '25
Confidential '35
Feud of the West '35
Million Dollar Haul '35
Queen of the Jungle '35
Custer's Last Stand '36
A Million to One '37
Covered Wagon Days '40
Dead or Alive '41
Fugitive Valley '41

Sally Ann Howes
Thursday's Child '43
Dead of Night '45
Pink Strings and Sealing Wax '45
Nicholas Nickleby '46
Chitty Chitty Bang Bang '68
Death Ship '80

Jobyna Howland
Hook, Line and Sinker '30
Topaze '33

Olin Howlin
Earthworm Tractors '36
Satan Met a Lady '36
Girl of the Golden West '38
Nancy Drew, Reporter '39
Apache Rose '47
The Wistful Widow of Wagon Gap '47
Storm Rider '57
The Blob '58

Jack Hoxie
Backfire '22
Wild Engine/Mistaken Orders '23
Outlaw Justice '32
Gun Law '33
Law and Lawless '33
Trouble Busters '33

Christina Hoyos
Blood Wedding '81
Carmen '83
El Amor Brujo '86

Arthur Hoyt
His Private Secretary '33
In the Money '34
The Great McGinty '40

Carol Hoyt
Illegal Entry: Formula for Fear '93
Midnight Confessions '95

John Hoyt
Winter Meeting '48
Trapped '49
The Lost Continent '51
The Black Castle '52
Loan Shark '52
Julius Caesar '53
Sins of Jezebel '54
Blackboard Jungle '55
The Conqueror '56
Forever Darling '56
X: The Man with X-Ray Eyes '63
The Time Travelers '64
Star Trek: The Cage '65
Flesh Gordon '72

Rudolf Hrusinsky
Larks on a String '68
My Sweet Little Village '86

Chen Hsing
Dual Flying Kicks '82
Rage of Wind '82
Duel of Fists '89

Carter Huang
Sting of the Dragon Masters '74
The Association '80s

John Hubbard
Road Show '41
The Mummy's Tomb '42
Cowboy & the Senorita '44
Mexican Hayride '48

Cork Hubbert
Caveman '81
The Ballad of the Sad Cafe '91

Harold Huber
Ladies They Talk About '33
Kelly the Second '36
Klondike Annie '36
Charlie Chan in Rio '41

Season Hubley
Elvis: The Movie '79
Hardcore '79
Mrs. R's Daughter '79
Escape from New York '81
Vice Squad '82
The Key to Rebecca '85
Prettykill '87
Child in the Night '90
Total Exposure '91
Stepfather 3: Father's Day '92

Whip Hubley
Top Gun '86
Russkies '87
A Connecticut Yankee in King Arthur's Court '89
Desire and Hell at Sunset Motel '92
Unveiled '94
Executive Decision '96

Cooper Huckabee
Joni '79
Getting Wasted '80
The Funhouse '81
The Curse '87
Cohen and Tate '88
Night Eyes '90
Love Field '91

Walter Hudd
Rembrandt '36
Elephant Boy '37
Black Limelight '38
Housemaster '38
Cast a Dark Shadow '55

The Prince and the Pauper '62

David Huddleston

Rio Lobo '70
McQ '74
Crime Busters '78
Go for It '83
Finnegan Begin Again '84
On the Run '85
Santa Claus: The Movie '85
When the Bough Breaks '86
Frantic '88
The Tracker '88
Double Exposure: The Story of Margaret Bourke-White '89
Life with Mikey '93

Michael Huddleston

World's Greatest Lover '77
Four Friends '81
Bombs Away! '86

Ernie Hudson

The $5.20 an Hour Dream '80
Penitentiary 2 '82
Going Berserk '83
Spacehunter: Adventures in the Forbidden Zone '83
Ghostbusters '84
Joy of Sex '84
Weeds '87
The Wrong Guys '88
Ghostbusters 2 '89
Leviathan '89
Trapper County War '89
The Hand that Rocks the Cradle '92
The Crow '93
Wild Palms '93
Airheads '94
The Basketball Diaries '94
The Cowboy Way '94
In the Army Now '94
No Escape '94
Speechless '94
Sugar Hill '94
Congo '95
The Substitute '96
Tornado! '96

Gary Hudson

Wild Cactus '92
Indecent Behavior '93
Martial Outlaw '93
Mind Twister '93
The Force '94
Scanner Cop '94
Sexual Intent '94
Serial Killer '95
Texas Payback '95

John Hudson

Return to Paradise '53
When Gangland Strikes '56

Rochelle Hudson

Beyond the Rockies '32
The Savage Girl '32
Mr. Skitch '33
Bachelor Bait '34
Curly Top '35
Les Miserables '35
Show Them No Mercy '35
The Devil's Cargo '48
Rebel Without a Cause '55
The Night Walker '64
Alien Massacre '67

Rock Hudson

Winchester '73 '50
Bend of the River '52
Horizons West '52
Gun Fury '53
Sea Devils '53
Magnificent Obsession '54
Giant '56
Written on the Wind '56
Battle Hymn '57
Something of Value '57
Tarnished Angels '57
Pillow Talk '59
Come September '61
Lover Come Back '61
A Gathering of Eagles '63
Man's Favorite Sport? '63
Send Me No Flowers '64
Strange Bedfellows '65
Tobruk '66
Ice Station Zebra '68
The Undefeated '69
Darling Lili '70
Hornet's Nest '70
Showdown '73
Embryo '76
James Dean: The First American Teenager '76
Avalanche '78
The Martian Chronicles: Part 1 '79
The Martian Chronicles: Part 2 '79
The Martian Chronicles: Part 3 '79
The Mirror Crack'd '80
The Devlin Connection '82
The Ambassador '84
The Vegas Strip Wars '84
World War III '86

Toni Hudson

Prime Risk '84
Just One of the Guys '85
The Uninvited '88

William Hudson

The Amazing Colossal Man '57
Attack of the 50 Foot Woman '58
The Screaming Skull '58
Hysterical '83

Matthias Hues

Fist Fighter '88
Black Belt '92
Mission of Justice '92
Talons of the Eagle '92
Bounty Tracker '93
TC 2000 '93
Death Match '94
Digital Man '94
Fists of Iron '94
Cyberzone '95

Brent Huff

The Perils of Gwendoline '84
Deadly Passion '85
Nine Deaths of the Ninja '85
Armed Response '86
Stormquest '87
Falling from Grace '92

David Huffman

F.I.S.T. '78
The Winds of Kitty Hawk '78
Ice Castles '79
Blood Beach '81
Firefox '82
St. Helen's, Killer Volcano '82
Last Plane Out '83

Billy Hufsey

Off the Wall '82
Magic Kid '92

Daniel Hugh-Kelly

Cujo '83
Nowhere to Hide '87
The Good Son '93
Bad Company '94

Andrew Hughes

Terror Beneath the Sea '66
Destroy All Monsters '68

Barnard Hughes

Midnight Cowboy '69
Cold Turkey '71
The Hospital '71
Rage '72
Sisters '73
Oh, God! '77
Sanctuary of Fear '79
Homeward Bound '80
First Monday in October '81
Best Friends '82
Tron '82
Little Gloria...Happy at Last '84
The Adventures of Huckleberry Finn '85
Maxie '85
Under the Biltmore Clock '85
Where Are the Children? '85
Hobo's Christmas '87
The Lost Boys '87
Da '88
Day One '89
The Incident '89
Doc Hollywood '91
Sister Act 2: Back in the Habit '93
Primal Secrets '94
Past the Bleachers '95

Brendan Hughes

Return to Horror High '87
To Die for '89
Howling 6: The Freaks '90

Carol Hughes

Earthworm Tractors '36
Three Men on a Horse '36
Renfrew of the Royal Mounted '37
The Man from Music Mountain '38
Love Affair '39
The Border Legion '40
Flash Gordon Conquers the Universe '40
Space Soldiers Conquer the Universe '40
Desperate Cargo '41
Robot Pilot '41
Silver Stallion '41
Miracle Kid '42
Home in Oklahoma '47

Charles Hughes

The Frontiersmen '38
Call of the Forest '49

Finola Hughes

Staying Alive '83
Nutcracker Sweet '84
Aspen Extreme '93
Dark Side of Genius '94

Heather Hughes

Flesh Feast '69
Blood Freak '72

Helen Hughes

Off Your Rocker '80
Incubus '82
The Peanut Butter Solution '85
Kidnapping of Baby John Doe '88
The Amityville Curse '90
Night of the Twisters '95

Kay Hughes

Ride, Ranger, Ride '36
The Vigilantes are Coming '36
Dick Tracy: The Original Serial, Vol. 1 '37
Dick Tracy: The Original Serial, Vol. 2 '37
The Mandarin Mystery '37

Lloyd Hughes

Dangerous Hours '19
Beau Revel '21
The Lost World '25
Ella Cinders '26
Where East Is East '29
Drums of Jeopardy '31
Blake of Scotland Yard '36
A Face in the Fog '36
Kelly of the Secret Service '36

Mary Beth Hughes

Lucky Cisco Kid '40
Charlie Chan in Rio '41
The Great American Broadcast '41
Orchestra Wives '42
The Ox-Bow Incident '43
Take It Big '44
Timber Queen '44
Great Flamarion '45
I Accuse My Parents '45
The Lady Confesses '45
Inner Sanctum '48
Return of Wildfire '48
Last of the Wild Horses '49
Rimfire '49
Holiday Rhythm '50
Square Dance Jubilee '51

Miko Hughes

Jack the Bear '93
Cops and Robbersons '94
Wes Craven's New Nightmare '94
Apollo 13 '95

Wendy Hughes

Jock Petersen '74
Alternative '76
High Rolling in a Hot Corvette '77
Newsfront '78
Puzzle '78
Kostas '79
My Brilliant Career '79
Touch & Go '80
Dangerous Summer '82
Lonely Hearts '82
Careful, He Might Hear You '84
My First Wife '84
An Indecent Obsession '85
Remember Me '85
Echoes of Paradise '86
Happy New Year '87
Warm Nights on a Slow-Moving Train '87
The Heist '89
A Woman Named Jackie '91
Wild Orchid 2: Two Shades of Blue '92
Princess Caraboo '94

Liu Chia Hui

Master Killer '84
Challenge of the Masters '89

Claude Hulbert

Bulldog Jack '35
The Dummy Talks '43

Tom Hulce

September 30, 1955 '77
National Lampoon's Animal House '78
Those Lips, Those Eyes '80
Amadeus '84
Echo Park '86
The Rise & Rise of Daniel Rocket '86
Slamdance '87
Dominick & Eugene '88
Parenthood '89
Black Rainbow '91
The Inner Circle '91
Fearless '93
Mary Shelley's Frankenstein '94
The Heidi Chronicles '95

Dianne Hull

Girls on the Road '73
Aloha, Bobby and Rose '74
The Fifth Floor '80
The New Adventures of Pippi Longstocking '88

Henry Hull

Midnight '34
Werewolf of London '35
Boys Town '38
Three Comrades '38
Jesse James '39
Stanley and Livingstone '39
Return of Frank James '40
High Sierra '41
Lifeboat '44
The Woman of the Town '44
Objective, Burma! '45
Portrait of Jennie '48
The Fountainhead '49
Rimfire '49
Return of Jesse James '50
The Buccaneer '58
Master of the World '61
The Fool Killer '65

Josephine Hull

Arsenic and Old Lace '44
Harvey '50

Warren Hull

Hawaii Calls '38
Star Reporter '39
Hidden Enemy '40
Bowery Blitzkrieg '41

George Humbert

Hearts of Humanity '32
Music in My Heart '40

Benita Hume

Lady of the Lake '28
Power '34
Private Life of Don Juan '34
It Happened in New Orleans '36
Suzy '36
Tarzan Escapes '36

Renee Humphrey

Jailbait '93
French Kiss '95
Mallrats '95

William Humphreys

Beau Brummel '24
The Unholy Three '25

Barry Humphries

Barry McKenzie Holds His Own '74
The Getting of Wisdom '77
Les Patterson Saves the World '90
Immortal Beloved '94

Tessa Humphries

Cassandra '87
Out of the Body '88

Robert Hundar

Fighting Fists of Shanghai Joe '65
Bronson's Revenge '79

Pa Hung

Prodigal Boxer: The Kick of Death '73
Kick of Death: The Prodigal Boxer '80s

Samo Hung

Paper Marriage '88
The Deadliest Art: The Best of the Martial Arts Films '90

Arthur Hunnicutt

Wildcat '42
Abroad with Two Yanks '44
Broken Arrow '50
Stars in My Crown '50
Ticket to Tomahawk '50
Distant Drums '51
The Big Sky '52
The Lusty Men '52
She Couldn't Say No '52
Devil's Canyon '53
The French Line '54
The Kettles in the Ozarks '56
The Tall T '57
Born Reckless '59
Apache Uprising '66
El Dorado '67
The Bounty Man '72
Harry and Tonto '74

Gayle Hunnicutt

The Wild Angels '66
Marlowe '69
The Love Machine '71
The Legend of Hell House '73
Scorpio '73
Shadow Man '75
Spiral Staircase '75
Sell Out '76
Strange Shadows in an Empty Room '76
The Martian Chronicles: Part 2 '79
The Martian Chronicles: Part 3 '79
Once in Paris... '79
Return of the Man from U.N.C.L.E. '83
Flashpoint Africa '84
Dream Lover '85
No Comebacks '85
Target '85
Turnaround '87
Con Man '92

Bonnie Hunt

Rain Man '88
Beethoven '92
Beethoven's 2nd '93
Dave '93
Only You '94
Jumanji '95
Now and Then '95
Getting Away With Murder '96

David Hunt

Date with an Angel '87
The Dead Pool '88

Eleanor Hunt

Whoopee! '30
Go-Get-'Em-Haines '35
Yellow Cargo '36

Gareth Hunt

The World is Full of Married Men '80
Funny Money '82
Bloodbath at the House of Death '85
It Couldn't Happen Here '88
A Chorus of Disapproval '89

Helen Hunt

The Spell '77
Child Bride of Short Creek '81
Desperate Lives '82
Bill: On His Own '83
Code of Honor '84
Trancers '84
Girls Just Want to Have Fun '85
Quarterback Princess '85
Peggy Sue Got Married '86
Project X '87
Miles from Home '88
Stealing Home '88
Next of Kin '89
Dark River: A Father's Revenge '90
Trancers 2: The Return of Jack Deth '90
Murder in New Hampshire: The Pamela Smart Story '91
The Waterdance '91
Into the Badlands '92
Mr. Saturday Night '92
Only You '92

Hunt ▶cont.

Trancers 3: Deth Lives *'92*
Kiss of Death *'94*
Twister *'96*

Jimmy Hunt
Rusty's Birthday *'49*
The Capture *'50*
Invaders from Mars *'53*

Linda Hunt
Popeye *'80*
The Year of Living Dangerously *'82*
The Bostonians *'84*
Dune *'84*
Eleni *'85*
Silverado *'85*
The Room *'87*
Waiting for the Moon *'87*
She-Devil *'89*
Kindergarten Cop *'90*
If Looks Could Kill *'91*
Rain Without Thunder *'93*
Twenty Bucks *'93*
Ready to Wear *'94*
Younger & Younger *'94*

Marsha Hunt
Desert Gold *'36*
Western Double Feature 3 *'36*
Thunder Pass *'37*
Thunder Trail *'37*
Star Reporter *'39*
Blossoms in the Dust *'41*
The Valley of Decision *'45*
Smash-Up: The Story of a Woman *'47*
Actors and Sin *'52*
Howling 2: Your Sister is a Werewolf *'85*

Martita Hunt
When Knights were Bold *'36*
Great Expectations *'46*
Little Ballerina *'47*
The Story of Robin Hood & His Merrie Men *'52*
The King's Rhapsody *'55*
Me and the Colonel *'58*
The Brides of Dracula *'60*
Song Without End *'60*
The Wonderful World of the Brothers Grimm *'62*
The Unsinkable Molly Brown *'64*

William Dennis Hunt
Flesh Gordon 2: Flesh Gordon Meets the Cosmic Cheerleaders *'90*
Peephole *'93*

Bill Hunter
Newsfront *'78*
In Search of Anna *'79*
Hard Knocks *'80*
Heatwave *'83*
Return of Captain Invincible *'83*
The Hit *'85*
An Indecent Obsession *'85*
Rebel *'85*
Fever *'88*
Rikky and Pete *'88*
The Last Days of Chez Nous *'92*
Strictly Ballroom *'92*
The Adventures of Priscilla, Queen of the Desert *'94*
The Custodian *'94*
Muriel's Wedding *'94*
Race the Sun *'96*

Holly Hunter
The Burning *'82*
Svengali *'83*
Swing Shift *'84*
Urge to Kill *'84*
Broadcast News *'87*
Raising Arizona *'87*
End of the Line *'88*
Always *'89*
Animal Behavior *'89*
Miss Firecracker *'89*
Roe vs. Wade *'89*
Murder on the Bayou *'91*
Once Around *'91*
Crazy in Love *'92*
The Firm *'93*
The Piano *'93*
The Positively True Adventures of the Alleged Texas Cheerleader-Murdering Mom *'93*
Copycat *'95*
Crash *'95*
Home for the Holidays *'95*

Ian Hunter
Unmasking the Idol *'86*
Order of the Black Eagle *'87*

Ian Hunter
Easy Virtue *'27*
The Ring *'27*
A Midsummer Night's Dream *'35*
The Phantom Light *'35*
That Certain Woman *'37*
The Adventures of Robin Hood *'38*
The Sisters *'38*
Broadway Serenade *'39*
The Little Princess *'39*
Tarzan Finds a Son *'39*
The Tower of London *'39*
Bitter Sweet *'40*
Broadway Melody of 1940 *'40*
The Long Voyage Home *'40*
Strange Cargo *'40*
Andy Hardy's Private Secretary *'41*
Billy the Kid *'41*
Smilin' Through *'41*
Ziegfeld Girl *'41*
Pursuit of the Graf Spee *'57*
Flame Over India *'60*
Doctor Blood's Coffin *'62*

Jeffrey Hunter
Seven Cities of Gold *'55*
The Great Locomotive Chase *'56*
The Searchers *'56*
Last Hurrah *'58*
Hell to Eternity *'60*
Sergeant Rutledge *'60*
The King of Kings *'61*
The Longest Day *'62*
Star Trek: The Cage *'65*
The Christmas Kid *'68*
A Witch Without a Broom *'68*

Kaki Hunter
Roadie *'80*
Willie & Phil *'80*
Whose Life Is It Anyway? *'81*
Porky's *'82*
Just the Way You Are *'84*
Porky's Revenge *'85*

Kelly Hunter
Prime Suspect 3 *'93*
Being Human *'94*

Kim Hunter
The Seventh Victim *'43*
Tender Comrade *'43*
A Streetcar Named Desire *'51*
Requiem for a Heavyweight *'56*
Lilith *'64*
Lamp at Midnight *'66*
Planet of the Apes *'68*
The Swimmer *'68*
Beneath the Planet of the Apes *'70*
Escape from the Planet of the Apes *'71*
Bad Ronald *'74*
Born Innocent *'74*
Dark August *'76*
The Kindred *'87*
Drop-Out Mother *'88*

Ronald Hunter
Rage of Angels *'83*
Adventure of the Action Hunters *'87*
Jakarta *'88*

Stephen Hunter
Mania *'80s*
Bullies *'86*

Tab Hunter
Island of Desire *'52*
Battle Cry *'55*
Sea Chase *'55*
The Burning Hills *'56*
Damn Yankees *'58*
Lafayette Escadrille *'58*
They Came to Cordura *'59*
Ride the Wild Surf *'64*
The Loved One *'65*
Hostile Guns *'67*
One Step to Hell *'68*
The Arousers *'70*
The Big Push *'75*
The Kid from Left Field *'79*
Polyester *'81*
Grease 2 *'82*
Pandemonium *'82*
Lust in the Dust *'85*
Grotesque *'87*
Out of the Dark *'88*
Cameron's Closet *'89*

Thomas Hunter
Battle of the Commandos *'71*
Web of Deception *'71*
Escape from the KGB *'87*

Raymond Huntley
Immortal Battalion *'44*
I See a Dark Stranger *'46*
The Long Dark Hall *'51*
The Prisoner *'55*

Isabelle Huppert
Going Places *'74*
The Judge and the Assassin *'75*
Rosebud *'75*
The Lacemaker *'77*
Violette *'78*
Loulou *'80*
Coup de Torchon *'81*
Heaven's Gate *'81*
Entre-Nous *'83*
La Truite *'83*
My Best Friend's Girl *'84*
Cactus *'86*
Sincerely Charlotte *'86*
The Bedroom Window *'87*
The Story of Women *'88*
La Vengeance d'une Femme *'89*
Madame Bovary *'91*
Amateur *'94*
Love After Love *'94*
The Separation *'94*
La Ceremonie *'95*

Elizabeth Hurley
Christabel *'89*
Kill Cruise *'90*
Passenger 57 *'92*
Nightscare *'93*
Sharpe's Enemy *'94*

Brandon Hurst
Dr. Jekyll and Mr. Hyde *'20*
The Thief of Baghdad *'24*
Made for Love *'26*
The Man Who Laughs *'27*
Murder at Midnight *'31*
Murders in the Rue Morgue *'32*
House of Mystery *'34*
Stanley and Livingstone *'39*

Michael Hurst
Death Warmed Up *'85*
Desperate Remedies *'93*

Paul Hurst
Mountain Justice *'30*
Paradise Island *'30*
The Big Stampede *'32*
My Pal, The King *'32*
13th Guest *'32*
Hold Your Man *'33*
The Sphinx *'33*
The Sphinx *'33*
Legion of Missing Men *'37*
Alexander's Ragtime Band *'38*
Bad Lands *'39*
Gone with the Wind *'39*
It Could Happen to You *'39*
Caught in the Draft *'41*
Girl Rush *'44*
Pioneer Marshal *'49*
Missourians *'50*
The Vanishing Westerner *'50*

Veronica Hurst
Angels One Five *'54*
The Gilded Cage *'54*
Peeping Tom *'63*
Second Best Secret Agent in the Whole Wide World *'65*

John Hurt
A Man for All Seasons *'66*
Cry of the Penguins *'71*
10 Rillington Place *'71*
The Ghoul *'75*
The Naked Civil Servant *'75*
East of Elephant Rock *'76*
Midnight Express *'78*
The Shout *'78*
Alien *'79*
The Elephant Man *'80*
I, Claudius, Vol. 5: Zeus, By Jove!/Hail Who? *'80*
Disappearance *'81*
Heaven's Gate *'81*
History of the World: Part 1 *'81*
Night Crossing *'81*
Partners *'82*
The Osterman Weekend *'83*
Champions *'84*
1984 *'84*
Success is the Best Revenge *'84*
After Darkness *'85*
The Hit *'85*
From the Hip *'86*
Jake Speed *'86*
Spaceballs *'87*
Aria *'88*
White Mischief *'88*
Scandal *'89*
The Field *'90*
Frankenstein Unbound *'90*
Little Sweetheart *'90*
King Ralph *'91*
Monolith *'93*
Even Cowgirls Get the Blues *'94*
Second Best *'94*
Dead Man *'95*
Rob Roy *'95*
Wild Bill *'95*

Mary Beth Hurt
Interiors *'78*
Chilly Scenes of Winter *'79*
A Change of Seasons *'80*
The World According to Garp *'82*
Compromising Positions *'85*
D.A.R.Y.L. *'85*
Baby Girl Scott *'87*
Parents *'89*
Slaves of New York *'89*
Defenseless *'91*
Light Sleeper *'92*
The Age of Innocence *'93*
My Boyfriend's Back *'93*
Six Degrees of Separation *'93*

William Hurt
Altered States *'80*
Body Heat *'81*
Eyewitness *'81*
The Big Chill *'83*
Gorky Park *'83*
Kiss of the Spider Woman *'85*
Children of a Lesser God *'86*
Broadcast News *'87*
The Accidental Tourist *'88*
A Time of Destiny *'88*
Alice *'90*
I Love You to Death *'90*
The Doctor *'91*
Until The End of The World *'91*
The Plague *'92*
Mr. Wonderful *'93*
Second Best *'94*
Trial by Jury *'94*
Smoke *'95*
Jane Eyre *'96*

Ferlin Husky
Las Vegas Hillbillys *'66*
Hillbillies in a Haunted House *'67*

Olivia Hussey
Romeo and Juliet *'68*
H-Bomb *'71*
Ricco *'74*
Black Christmas *'75*
The Bastard *'78*
Death on the Nile *'78*
The Cat and the Canary *'79*
The Man with Bogart's Face *'80*
Escape 2000 *'81*
Ivanhoe *'82*
Virus *'82*
Distortions *'87*
The Jeweller's Shop *'90*
Psycho 4: The Beginning *'90*
Stephen King's It *'90*
Undeclared War *'91*
Quest of the Delta Knights *'93*
Save Me *'93*
Ice Cream Man *'95*

Ruth Hussey
Madame X *'37*
Another Thin Man *'39*
The Women *'39*
Northwest Passage *'40*
The Philadelphia Story *'40*
Susan and God *'40*
Marine Raiders *'43*
Tender Comrade *'43*
The Uninvited *'44*
Mr. Music *'50*
Hill Number One *'51*
Stars and Stripes Forever *'52*

Anjelica Huston
Hamlet *'69*
The Last Tycoon *'76*
The Postman Always Rings Twice *'81*
Beauty and the Beast *'83*
The Cowboy & the Ballerina *'84*
Ice Pirates *'84*
Prizzi's Honor *'85*
The Dead *'87*
Gardens of Stone *'87*
A Handful of Dust *'88*
Mr. North *'88*
Crimes & Misdemeanors *'89*
Enemies, a Love Story *'89*
Lonesome Dove *'89*
The Grifters *'90*
The Witches *'90*
The Addams Family *'91*
Addams Family Values *'93*
Family Pictures *'93*
Manhattan Murder Mystery *'93*
The Crossing Guard *'94*
The Perez Family *'94*
Buffalo Girls *'95*

John Huston
The Battle of San Pietro *'44*
The Cardinal *'63*
The Bible...In the Beginning *'66*
Casino Royale *'67*
Myra Breckinridge *'70*
Man in the Wilderness *'71*
Ride to Glory *'71*
Battle for the Planet of the Apes *'73*
Chinatown *'74*
Breakout *'75*
The Wind and the Lion *'75*
Angela *'77*
Tentacles *'77*
Battleforce *'78*
The Word *'78*
Jaguar Lives *'79*
Winter Kills *'79*
Wise Blood *'79*
Fatal Attraction *'80*
The Visitor *'80*
Lovesick *'83*
A Minor Miracle *'83*
Mr. Corbett's Ghost *'90*

Virginia Huston
Nocturne *'46*
The Doolins of Oklahoma *'49*
Flamingo Road *'49*
Night Stage to Galveston *'52*
Sudden Fear *'52*

Walter Huston
The Virginian *'29*
Abraham Lincoln *'30*
Criminal Code *'31*
Rain *'32*
Ann Vickers *'33*
Gabriel Over the White House *'33*
The Prizefighter and the Lady *'33*
Transatlantic Tunnel *'35*
Dodsworth *'36*
Rhodes *'36*
Of Human Hearts *'38*
The Devil & Daniel Webster *'41*
In This Our Life *'42*
The Shanghai Gesture *'42*
Yankee Doodle Dandy *'42*
Edge of Darkness *'43*
The North Star *'43*
The Outlaw *'43*
Dragon Seed *'44*
And Then There Were None *'45*
Duel in the Sun *'46*
Summer Holiday *'48*
Treasure of the Sierra Madre *'48*
December 7th: The Movie *'91*

Michael Hutchence
Dogs in Space *'87*
Frankenstein Unbound *'90*

David Hutcheson
Murder in the Footlights *'51*
No Highway in the Sky *'51*

Geoffrey Hutchings
Wish You Were Here *'87*
Heart of Darkness *'93*

Will Hutchins
Lafayette Escadrille *'58*
Merrill's Marauders *'62*
The Shooting *'66*
Spinout *'66*
Clambake *'67*

Slumber Party '57 '76

Fiona Hutchinson
American Gothic '88
Rage '95

Josephine Hutchinson
The Story of Louis Pasteur '36
Son of Frankenstein '39
Cass Timberlane '47
The Tender Years '47
Love Is Better Than Ever '52
North by Northwest '59
The Adventures of Huckleberry Finn '60

Ken Hutchison
Deadly Strangers '82
Ladyhawke '85

Betty Hutton
Star Spangled Rhythm '42
Here Come the Waves '44
Miracle of Morgan's Creek '44
The Stork Club '45
The Perils of Pauline '47
Let's Dance '50
The Greatest Show on Earth '52
Hollywood Clowns '85

Brian Hutton
Carnival Rock '57
Last Train from Gun Hill '59

Jim Hutton
A Time to Love & a Time to Die '58
Where the Boys Are '60
The Honeymoon Machine '61
The Horizontal Lieutenant '62
Period of Adjustment '62
The Hallelujah Trail '65
Major Dundee '65
Walk, Don't Run '66
Who's Minding the Mint? '67
The Green Berets '68
Hellfighters '68
Bachelor in Paradise '69
Don't Be Afraid of the Dark '73
Nightmare at 43 Hillcrest '74
Psychic Killer '75

Lauren Hutton
Paper Lion '68
The Gambler '74
Nashville '75
Gator '76
Viva Knievel '77
Welcome to L.A. '77
A Wedding '78
American Gigolo '79
Paternity '81
Zorro, the Gay Blade '81
The Cradle Will Fall '83
The Snow Queen '83
Starflight One '83
Lassiter '84
From Here to Maternity '85
Once Bitten '85
Monte Carlo '86
Malone '87
Timestalkers '87
Bulldance '88
Scandalous '88
Forbidden Sun '89
Trade Secrets '90s
Fear '90
Millions '90
Guilty as Charged '92
My Father the Hero '93

Marion Hutton
In Society '44
Love Happy '50

Robert Hutton
Destination Tokyo '43
Hollywood Canteen '44
Slaughter Trail '51
The Steel Helmet '51
Big Bluff '55
Outcasts of the City '58
Showdown at Boot Hill '58
Invisible Invaders '59
Naked Youth '59
Cinderfella '60
The Slime People '63
They Came from Beyond Space '67
Vulture '67
The Persuaders '71

Timothy Hutton
And Baby Makes Six '79
Friendly Fire '79
Young Love, First Love '79
Father Figure '80
Ordinary People '80
A Long Way Home '81
Taps '81
Oldest Living Graduate '82
Daniel '83
Iceman '84
The Falcon and the Snowman '85
Turk 182! '85
Made in Heaven '87
Everybody's All American '88
A Time of Destiny '88
Q & A '90
Torrents of Spring '90
The Dark Half '91
Strangers '91
The Temp '93
French Kiss '95
The Last Word '95
Beautiful Girls '96
Mr. & Mrs. Loving '96

Richard Huw
Getting It Right '89
The Buccaneers '95

Leila Hyams
Spite Marriage '29
The Big House '30
Freaks '32
Island of Lost Souls '32
Red Headed Woman '32
Ruggles of Red Gap '35
Yellow Dust '36

Jonathan Hyde
An Indecent Obsession '85
Fellow Traveler '89
Richie Rich '94
Jumanji '95

Alex Hyde-White
The Seekers '79
The First Olympics: Athens 1896 '84
Biggles '85
Echoes in the Darkness '87
Indiana Jones and the Last Crusade '89
The Phantom of the Opera '89
Ironclads '90
Pretty Woman '90
Silent Victim '92
Wyatt Earp: Return to Tombstone '94

Wilfrid Hyde-White
The Demi-Paradise '43
Ghosts of Berkeley Square '47
The Third Man '49
Angel with the Trumpet '50
Last Holiday '50
The Browning Version '51
The Golden Salamander '51
Betrayed '54
The Vicious Circle '57
Truth About Women '58
Up the Creek '58
Carry On Nurse '59
Teenage Bad Girl '59
Flame Over India '60
Two-Way Stretch '60
In Search of the Castaways '62
My Fair Lady '64
The Magic Christian '69
Skullduggery '70
Brand New Life '72
King Solomon's Treasure '76
The Cat and the Canary '79
The Rebels '79
Damien: The Leper Priest '80
Oh, God! Book 2 '80
Scout's Honor '80
The Toy '82
Fanny Hill '83
Heartburn '86

Martha Hyer
Gun Smugglers/Hot Lead '51
Geisha Girl '52
Abbott and Costello Go to Mars '53
Cry Vengeance '54
Lucky Me '54
Sabrina '54
Scarlet Spear '54
Francis in the Navy '55
The Delicate Delinquent '56
Battle Hymn '57
My Man Godfrey '57
Paris Holiday '57
Houseboat '58
Some Came Running '58
The Best of Everything '59
Mistress of the World '59
Ice Palace '60
Bikini Beach '64
The Carpetbaggers '64
First Men in the Moon '64
Sons of Katie Elder '65
The Chase '66
Night of the Grizzly '66
Picture Mommy Dead '66
The House of 1000 Dolls '67
Catch as Catch Can '68

Diana Hyland
One Man's Way '63
Hercules and the Princess of Troy '65
The Boy in the Plastic Bubble '76

Frances Hyland
Home to Stay '79
The Lotus Eaters '93
When the Dark Man Calls '95

Scott Hylands
Daddy's Gone A-Hunting '69
Fools '70
Earthquake '74
The Boys in Company C '77
The Winds of Kitty Hawk '78
Coming Out Alive '84
Savage Hunger '84
Tales of the Klondike: In a Far Country '87
The Halfback of Notre Dame '96

Jane Hylton
Dear Murderer '47
The Manster '59
Circus of Horrors '60

Richard Hylton
Lost Boundaries '49
The Halls of Montezuma '50

Phyllis Hyman
School Daze '88
The Kill Reflex '89

Warren Hymer
The Lone Star Ranger '30
The Mysterious Rider '33
In the Money '34
Confidential '35
Hong Kong Nights '35
Show Them No Mercy '35
Rhythm on the Range '36
Tango '36
Sea Racketeers '37
Joy of Living '38
Birth of the Blues '41
Baby Face Morgan '42
Lure of the Islands '42
Meet the Mob '42
Mr. Wise Guy '42
Phantom Killer '42
Hitler: Dead or Alive '43

Joyce Hyser
Just One of the Guys '85
Wedding Band '89

Chaing I
They Shoot Horses, Don't They? '69
Return of the Tiger '78

Mirta Ibarra
Up to a Certain Point '83
Strawberry and Chocolate '93

Ice Cube
Boyz N the Hood '91
Trespass '92
Higher Learning '94
Friday '95
The Glass Shield '95

Ice-T
New Jack City '91
Ricochet '91
Trespass '92
Who's the Man? '93
Surviving the Game '94
Tank Girl '94
Johnny Mnemonic '95

Etsuko Ichihara
Snow Country '57
Black Rain '88

Raizo Ichikawa
Shin Heike Monogatari '55
Enjo '58

Eric Idle
Monty Python's Flying Circus '71
And Now for Something Completely Different '72
Monty Python and the Holy Grail '75
Jabberwocky '77
All You Need Is Cash '78
Monty Python's Life of Brian '79
To See Such Fun '81
Monty Python Live at the Hollywood Bowl '82
Monty Python's The Meaning of Life '83
Yellowbeard '83
The Pied Piper of Hamelin '84
The Adventures of Baron Munchausen '89
Around the World in 80 Days '89
Monty Python's Parrot Sketch Not Included '90
Nuns on the Run '90
Too Much Sun '90
Mom and Dad Save the World '92
Splitting Heirs '93
Casper '95

Cinnamon Idles
Kidco '83
Sixteen Candles '84

Hisashi Igawa
Ran '85
Akira Kurosawa's Dreams '90
Rhapsody in August '91
Hiroshima '95

James Iglehart
Angels Hard as They Come '71
Savage! '73
Fighting Mad '77
Death Force '78

Steve Ihnat
Hour of the Gun '67
Countdown '68
Hunter '73

Choko Iida
Record of a Tenement Gentleman '47
Drunken Angel '48

Ryo Ikebe
Snow Country '57
War in Space '77

Peter Illing
Against the Wind '48
Eureka Stockade '49
Bhowani Junction '56
The Electronic Monster '57

Iman
The Human Factor '79
Out of Africa '85
No Way Out '87
Surrender '87
House Party 2: The Pajama Jam '91
L.A. Story '91
Lies of the Twins '91
Star Trek 6: The Undiscovered Country '91
Heart of Darkness '93
Exit to Eden '94

Roger Imhof
Riff Raff '35
Red Lights Ahead '36
Sweetheart of the Navy '37

Michael Imperioli
Household Saints '93
The Basketball Diaries '94
The Addiction '95
Postcards from America '95
Girl 6 '96

Celia Imrie
A Dark Adapted Eye '93
Mary Shelley's Frankenstein '94
The Return of the Native '94
A Midwinter's Tale '95

Ada Ince
Frontier Days '34
Rainbow's End '35

Annabella Incontrera
The Assassination Bureau '69
Double Face '70

Frieda Inescort
Beauty for the Asking '39
Tarzan Finds a Son '39
The Letter '40
Pride and Prejudice '40
Shadows on the Stairs '41
Sunny '41
Return of the Vampire '43
The Judge Steps Out '49
The Underworld Story '50

Eddie Infante
Cavalry Command '63
Warkill '65
Ethan '71

Marty Ingels
If It's Tuesday, This Must Be Belgium '69
How to Seduce a Woman '74
Instant Karma '90
Round Numbers '91

Randi Ingerman
Deadly Rivals '92
Desperate Crimes '93

Barrie Ingham
Invasion '65
Josh Kirby...Time Warrior: Chapter 3, Trapped on Toyworld '95
Josh Kirby...Time Warrior: Chapter 4, Eggs from 70 Million B.C. '95
Josh Kirby...Time Warrior: Chapter 5, Journey to the Magic Cavern '96
Josh Kirby...Time Warrior: Chapter 6, Last Battle for the Universe '96

Lloyd Ingraham
Peck's Bad Boy '34
Between Men '35
Ghost Rider '35
Go-Get-'Em-Haines '35
Sons of Steel '35
Trail of Terror '35
Red River Valley '36
Undercover Man '36
Park Avenue Logger '37
Partners of the Trail '44
Range Law '44
The Caravan Trail '46

Jack Ingram
Whistling Bullets '36
The Rangers Step In '37
The Adventures of the Masked Phantom '38
Valley of Terror '38
Wyoming Outlaw '39
Ridin' the Trail '40
Arizona Roundup '42
The Mysterious Rider '42
Frontier Law '43
Raiders of Sunset Pass '43
Devil Riders '44
Frontier Outlaws '44
Guns of the Law '44
Oath of Vengeance '44
Outlaw Roundup '44
Range Law '44
Frontier Fugitives '45
Lost in Alaska '52

Rex Ingram
Green Pastures '36
The Adventures of Huckleberry Finn '39
The Thief of Bagdad '40
Talk of the Town '42
Cabin in the Sky '43
Sahara '43
Dark Waters '44
A Thousand and One Nights '45
Moonrise '48
Elmer Gantry '60

Valeri Inkizhinov
Storm Over Asia '28
Journey to the Lost City '58
Samson and the 7 Miracles of the World '62

George Innes
Archer: The Fugitive from the Empire '81
Danger UXB '81
Ivanhoe '82

Neil Innes
Monty Python's Flying Circus '71
Monty Python and the Holy Grail '75
All You Need Is Cash '78

Harold Innocent
Robin Hood: Prince of Thieves '91

Innocent ▶cont.

Fergie & Andrew: Behind Palace Doors *'93*

Dan Inosanto
Warrior Within *'80*
Counter Attack *'84*

Tino Insana
Wedding Band *'89*
The Masters of Menace *'90*

Franco Interlenghi
Shoeshine *'47*
The Wayward Wife *'52*
I Vitelloni *'53*

Steve Inwood
Hurry Up or I'll Be Thirty *'73*
The Human Shield *'92*

Aharon Ipale
Too Hot to Handle *'76*
One Man Out *'89*
Tragedy of Flight 103: The Inside Story *'91*
Invisible: The Chronicles of Benjamin Knight *'93*

Jill Ireland
Robbery Under Arms *'57*
Villa Rides *'68*
Rider on the Rain *'70*
Someone Behind the Door *'71*
The Mechanic *'72*
The Family *'73*
Cold Sweat *'74*
Breakout *'75*
Chino *'75*
Hard Times *'75*
Breakheart Pass *'76*
From Noon Till Three *'76*
Love and Bullets *'79*
Death Wish 2 *'82*
Assassination *'87*

John Ireland
My Darling Clementine *'46*
A Walk in the Sun *'46*
The Gangster *'47*
Railroaded *'47*
Joan of Arc *'48*
Open Secret *'48*
Red River *'48*
A Southern Yankee *'48*
All the King's Men *'49*
The Doolins of Oklahoma *'49*
I Shot Jesse James *'49*
Return of Jesse James *'50*
Little Big Horn *'51*
Vengeance Valley *'51*
The Bushwackers *'52*
The Fast and the Furious *'54*
Glass Tomb *'55*
Queen Bee *'55*
The Gunslinger *'56*
Gunfight at the O.K. Corral *'57*
Black Tide *'58*
Party Girl *'58*
Spartacus *'60*
Wild in the Country *'61*
55 Days at Peking *'63*
The Fall of the Roman Empire *'64*
Arizona Bushwackers *'67*
Dead for a Dollar *'70s*
The Adventurers *'70*
Dirty Heroes *'71*
Escape to the Sun *'72*
Northeast of Seoul *'72*
The House of Seven Corpses *'73*
Farewell, My Lovely *'75*
Delta Fox *'77*
Maniac *'77*
Perfect Killer *'77*
Satan's Cheerleaders *'77*
Taste of Death *'77*
Tomorrow Never Comes *'77*
Midnight Auto Supply *'78*
Bordello *'79*
Crossbar *'79*
Marilyn: The Untold Story *'80*
Mission to Glory *'80*
Incubus *'82*
Challenge of McKenna *'83*
Diary of a Rebel *'84*
Kavik the Wolf Dog *'84*
The Treasure of the Amazon *'84*
Martin's Day *'85*
Flying from the Hawk *'86*
Thunder Run *'86*
Miami Horror *'87*
Tales of the Klondike: Race for Number One *'87*
Messenger of Death *'88*

Kathy Ireland
Alien from L.A. *'87*
Mr. Destiny *'90*
Side Out *'90*
Necessary Roughness *'91*
Mom and Dad Save the World *'92*
Amore! *'93*
National Lampoon's Loaded Weapon 1 *'93*
Backfire! *'94*

Jeremy Irons
Love for Lydia *'79*
Nijinsky *'80*
Brideshead Revisited *'81*
The French Lieutenant's Woman *'81*
Moonlighting *'82*
Betrayal *'83*
Swann in Love *'84*
The Wild Duck *'84*
The Mission *'86*
Dead Ringers *'88*
A Chorus of Disapproval *'89*
Reversal of Fortune *'90*
Kafka *'91*
Damage *'92*
Waterland *'92*
The House of the Spirits *'93*
M. Butterfly *'93*
Die Hard: With a Vengeance *'95*
Stealing Beauty *'96*

Michael Ironside
The Family Man *'79*
American Nightmare *'81*
Visiting Hours *'82*
Cross Country *'83*
Spacehunter: Adventures in the Forbidden Zone *'83*
Coming Out Alive *'84*
V: The Final Battle *'84*
The Falcon and the Snowman *'85*
Murder in Space *'85*
Top Gun *'86*
Extreme Prejudice *'87*
Ford: The Man & the Machine *'87*
Hello Mary Lou: Prom Night 2 *'87*
Nowhere to Hide *'87*
Hostile Takeover *'88*
Surrogate *'88*
Watchers *'88*
Mindfield *'89*
Murder by Night *'89*
Payback *'90*
Total Recall *'90*
Common Bonds *'91*
Deadly Surveillance *'91*
Highlander 2: The Quickening *'91*
McBain *'91*
Neon City *'91*
Black Ice *'92*
Guncrazy *'92*
Killer Image *'92*
The Vagrant *'92*
Dead Man's Revenge *'93*
Father Hood *'93*
Forced to Kill *'93*
Mardi Gras for the Devil *'93*
Point of Impact *'93*
Save Me *'93*
Sweet Killing *'93*
Fortunes of War *'94*
Red Scorpion 2 *'94*
Red Sun Rising *'94*
The Glass Shield *'95*
Portraits of a Killer *'95*
Probable Cause *'95*

Amy Irving
Carrie *'76*
James Dean *'76*
The Fury *'78*
The Competition *'80*
Honeysuckle Rose *'80*
Yentl *'83*
The Far Pavilions *'84*
Micki & Maude *'84*
Anastasia: The Mystery of Anna *'86*
Heartbreak House *'86*
Rumpelstiltskin *'86*
Crossing Delancey *'88*
The Turn of the Screw *'89*
A Show of Force *'90*
Benefit of the Doubt *'93*
Carried Away *'95*

George Irving
Coquette *'29*
The Divorcee *'30*
Captain January *'36*
The Mandarin Mystery *'37*
Maid's Night Out *'38*
The Abe Lincoln of Ninth Avenue *'39*

Penny Irving
Big Zapper *'73*
House of Whipcord *'75*

Bill Irwin
Popeye *'80*
Eight Men Out *'88*
My Blue Heaven *'90*
Hot Shots! *'91*
Scenes from a Mall *'91*
Stepping Out *'91*

Boyd Irwin
The Three Musketeers *'21*
Madam Satan *'30*

Tom Irwin
Deceived *'91*
Ladykiller *'92*
Mr. Jones *'93*

Chris Isaak
Married to the Mob *'88*
The Silence of the Lambs *'91*
Twin Peaks: Fire Walk with Me *'92*
Little Buddha *'93*

Tom Isbell
Behind Enemy Lines *'85*
A Case of Deadly Force *'86*

Juzo Itami
The Family Game *'83*
MacArthur's Children *'85*

Robert Ito
Women of the Prehistoric Planet *'66*
The Adventures of Buckaroo Banzai Across the Eighth Dimension *'84*
Pray for Death *'85*

Yunosuke Ito
Ikiru *'52*
The Burmese Harp *'56*

Jose Iturbi
Two Girls and a Sailor *'44*
Anchors Aweigh *'45*
Holiday in Mexico *'46*
Three Daring Daughters *'48*
That Midnight Kiss *'49*

Rosalind Ivan
The Corn is Green *'45*
Pursuit to Algiers *'45*

Zeljko Ivanek
The Sender *'82*
Mass Appeal *'84*
Echoes in the Darkness *'87*
Rachel River *'87*
Our Sons *'91*
School Ties *'92*
Truman *'95*
White Squall *'96*

Terri Ivens
Trancers 4: Jack of Swords *'93*
Trancers 5: Sudden Deth *'94*

Daniel Ivernel
Manon *'50*
Diary of a Chambermaid *'64*
High Heels *'72*

Robert Ivers
The Delicate Delinquent *'56*
G.I. Blues *'60*

Burl Ives
Station West *'48*
So Dear to My Heart *'49*
East of Eden *'54*
The Big Country *'58*
Cat on a Hot Tin Roof *'58*
Desire Under the Elms *'58*
Summer Magic *'63*
Ensign Pulver *'64*
Those Fantastic Flying Fools *'67*
The McMasters *'70*
Baker's Hawk *'76*
Roots *'77*
Uphill All the Way *'85*
Poor Little Rich Girl: The Barbara Hutton Story *'87*
Two Moon Junction *'88*

Dana Ivey
Explorers *'85*
Dirty Rotten Scoundrels *'88*
Postcards from the Edge *'90*
The Addams Family *'91*
Class of '61 *'92*
Home Alone 2: Lost in New York *'92*
Addams Family Values *'93*
The Adventures of Huck Finn *'93*
Guilty as Sin *'93*
Sabrina *'95*
The Scarlet Letter *'95*

Judith Ivey
Harry & Son *'84*
The Lonely Guy *'84*
The Woman in Red *'84*
Compromising Positions *'85*
Dixie: Changing Habits *'85*
Brighton Beach Memoirs *'86*
The Long, Hot Summer *'86*
Hello Again *'87*
Sister, Sister *'87*
We are the Children *'87*
Miles from Home *'88*
In Country *'89*
Frogs! *'90s*
Decoration Day *'90*
Everybody Wins *'90*
Love Hurts *'91*
There Goes the Neighborhood *'92*

Shima Iwashita
An Autumn Afternoon *'62*
Double Suicide *'69*
Red Lion *'69*
MacArthur's Children *'85*
Gonza the Spearman *'86*

Victor Izay
Premonition *'71*
The Trial of Billy Jack *'74*

Jackee
The Women of Brewster Place *'89*
Ladybugs *'92*
The Reluctant Agent *'95*

Ian Jacklin
Kickboxer 3: The Art of War *'92*
Death Match *'94*

Anne Jackson
Tall Story *'60*
Secret Life of an American Wife *'68*
Lovers and Other Strangers *'70*
Independence *'76*
Nasty Habits *'77*
The Bell Jar *'79*
The Family Man *'79*
Leave 'Em Laughing *'81*
Blinded by the Light *'82*
A Woman Called Golda *'82*
Blood Debts *'83*
Sam's Son *'84*
Out on a Limb *'87*
Funny About Love *'90*
Folks! *'92*

David Jackson
Blake's Seven *'78*
Music Shoppe *'82*
The Vernonia Incident *'89*

Eugene Jackson
The Return of Our Gang *'25*
Red River Valley *'36*

Freda Jackson
Beware of Pity *'46*
Great Expectations *'46*
Bhowani Junction *'56*
The Brides of Dracula *'60*
Die, Monster, Die! *'65*
The Valley of Gwangi *'69*

Glenda Jackson
Marat/Sade *'66*
Negatives *'68*
Women in Love *'70*
The Music Lovers *'71*
Sunday, Bloody Sunday *'71*
Elizabeth R *'72*
A Touch of Class *'73*
Hedda *'75*
Romantic Englishwoman *'75*
The Incredible Sarah *'76*
Nasty Habits *'77*
Triple Echo *'77*
The Class of Miss MacMichael *'78*
House Calls *'78*
Stevie *'78*
Lost and Found *'79*
Hopscotch *'80*
And Nothing But the Truth *'82*
Return of the Soldier *'82*
Sakharov *'84*
Beyond Therapy *'86*
Turtle Diary *'86*
Business as Usual *'88*
Salome's Last Dance *'88*
The Rainbow *'89*
Strange Interlude *'90*
King of the Wind *'93*

Gordon Jackson
Pink Strings and Sealing Wax *'45*
Against the Wind *'48*
Whiskey Galore *'48*
Death Goes to School *'53*
The Baby and the Battleship *'56*
The Great Escape *'63*
Those Magnificent Men in Their Flying Machines *'65*
The Fighting Prince of Donegal *'66*
Hamlet *'69*
The Prime of Miss Jean Brodie *'69*
Bergonzi Hand *'70*
Professionals *'76*
Gunpowder *'84*
A Town Like Alice *'85*
The Whistle Blower *'87*
Noble House *'88*

Howard Jackson
Furious *'83*
Full Contact *'93*
Out for Blood *'93*

John M. Jackson
The Hitcher *'86*
Cold Sassy Tree *'89*
Ginger Ale Afternoon *'89*
Sudie & Simpson *'90*
Career Opportunities *'91*
Love, Lies and Murder *'91*
Switched at Birth *'91*
An American Story *'92*
Roswell: The U.F.O. Cover-Up *'94*

Joshua Jackson
The Mighty Ducks *'92*
Digger *'94*
Magic in the Water *'95*
Robin of Locksley *'95*

Kate Jackson
Dark Shadows *'67*
Night of Dark Shadows *'71*
Satan's School for Girls *'73*
Death Cruise *'74*
Death at Love House *'75*
Death Scream *'75*
Thunder and Lightning *'77*
Dirty Tricks *'81*
Making Love *'82*
Listen to Your Heart *'83*
Loverboy *'89*
Adrift *'93*

Lamont Jackson
Assault with a Deadly Weapon *'82*
Class Act *'91*

Linda Jackson
Black Bikers from Hell *'70*
The Outlaw Bikers—Gang Wars *'70*

Mary Jackson
Terror at Red Wolf Inn *'72*
Skinned Alive *'89*
A Family Thing *'96*

Philip Jackson
High Hopes *'88*
Bad Behavior *'92*

Sam Jackson
Dead Man Out *'89*
Return of Superfly *'90*

Sammy Jackson
None But the Brave *'65*
Fastest Guitar Alive *'68*
Shame, Shame on the Bixby Boys *'82*

Samuel L. Jackson
Coming to America *'88*
School Daze *'88*
Def by Temptation *'90*
Goodfellas *'90*
Mo' Better Blues *'90*

Sidney James
The Lavender Hill Mob *'51*
Norman Conquest *'53*
Heat Wave *'54*
Glass Tomb *'55*
Quatermass 2 *'57*
The Silent Enemy *'58*
Carry On Cruising *'62*
What a Carve-Up! *'62*
Carry On Cleo *'65*
Carry On Cowboy *'66*
Carry On at Your Convenience *'71*
Carry On Camping *'71*
Carry On Henry VIII *'71*
Carry On 'Round the Bend *'72*
Carry On Behind *'75*
Carry On Dick *'75*

Steve James
The Brother from Another Planet *'84*
American Ninja *'85*
Avenging Force *'86*
The P.O.W. Escape *'86*
Stalking Danger *'86*
American Ninja 2: The Confrontation *'87*
Hero and the Terror *'88*
I'm Gonna Git You Sucka *'88*
Johnny Be Good *'88*
Python Wolf *'88*
American Ninja 3: Blood Hunt *'89*
Riverbend *'89*
Street Hunter *'90*
McBain *'91*
Bloodfist 5: Human Target *'93*
Weekend at Bernie's 2 *'93*

Walter James
The Idol Dancer *'20*
Little Annie Rooney *'25*
Battling Butler *'26*
The Kid Brother *'27*

Joyce Jameson
Tales of Terror *'62*
The Balcony *'63*
The Comedy of Terrors *'64*
Good Neighbor Sam *'64*
Savage Run *'70*
Pray TV *'80*
Hardbodies *'84*

Malcom Jamieson
Pictures *'80s*
Meridian: Kiss of the Beast *'90*

Bud Jamison
W.C. Fields: Flask of Fields *'30*
The Dentist *'32*

Krystyna Janda
Man of Marble *'76*
Without Anesthesia *'78*
The Conductor *'80*
Man of Iron *'81*
Mephisto *'81*
The Interrogation *'82*

Conrad Janis
The Duchess and the Dirtwater Fox *'76*
The Buddy Holly Story *'78*
Mork & Mindy *'78*
Oh, God! Book 2 *'80*
Sonny Boy *'87*
Mr. Saturday Night *'92*

Oleg Jankowskij
My Twentieth Century *'90*
Mute Witness *'95*

Leon Janney
Police Court *'37*
Charly *'68*

Emil Jannings
Passion *'19*
Fortune's Fool *'21*
Othello *'22*
The Last Laugh *'24*
Waxworks *'24*
The Americano/Variety *'25*
Variety *'25*
Faust *'26*
Last Command *'28*
The Blue Angel *'30*

Horst Janson
McKenzie Break *'70*
Captain Kronos: Vampire Hunter *'74*
To Catch a King *'84*

David Janssen
Swamp Fire *'46*
Francis Goes to West Point *'52*
Francis in the Navy *'55*
Francis in the Haunted House *'56*
Darby's Rangers *'58*
Lafayette Escadrille *'58*
Hell to Eternity *'60*
The King of the Roaring '20s: The Story of Arnold Rothstein *'61*
The Fugitive: Premiere Episode *'63*
The Fugitive: The Final Episode *'67*
The Green Berets *'68*
The Shoes of the Fisherman *'68*
Generation *'69*
Marooned *'69*
Macho Callahan *'70*
Birds of Prey *'72*
Moon of the Wolf *'72*
Pioneer Woman *'73*
Fer-De-Lance *'74*
Prisoner in the Middle *'74*
Smile, Jenny, You're Dead *'74*
Once is Not Enough *'75*
Stalk the Wild Child *'76*
Two Minute Warning *'76*
Golden Rendezvous *'77*
Swiss Conspiracy *'77*
The Word *'78*
S.O.S. Titanic *'79*
City in Fear *'80*
High Ice *'80*

Famke Janssen
Fathers and Sons *'92*
Model by Day *'94*
Relentless 4 *'94*
Goldeneye *'95*
Lord of Illusions *'95*

Lois January
Bulldog Courage *'35*
Border Caballero *'36*
Cocaine Fiends *'36*
Lightning Bill Crandall *'37*
The Red Rope *'37*
The Roamin' Cowboy *'37*

Claude Jarman, Jr.
The Yearling *'46*
Intruder in the Dust *'49*
The Sun Comes Up *'49*
Rio Grande *'50*
Hangman's Knot *'52*

Jim Jarmusch
American Autobahn *'84*
Straight to Hell *'87*
Leningrad Cowboys Go America *'89*
Blue In the Face *'95*

John Jarratt
Sound of Love *'77*
Summer City *'77*
Next of Kin *'82*
Dark Age *'88*
Talk *'94*

Catherine Jarrett
S.A.S. San Salvador *'84*
Quicker Than the Eye *'88*
A Fine Romance *'92*

Graham Jarvis
Cold Turkey *'71*
Middle Age Crazy *'80*
Draw! *'81*
Doin' Time *'85*
Mischief *'85*
Vanishing Act *'88*
Parents *'89*
Misery *'90*

Martin Jarvis
Taste the Blood of Dracula *'70*
Buster *'88*

Donna Jason
Honor and Glory *'92*
Abducted 2: The Reunion *'94*
Undefeatable *'94*

Harvey Jason
Star! *'68*
Oklahoma Crude *'73*

Peter Jason
Texas Lightning *'81*
Hyper-Sapien: People from Another Star *'86*
Alien Nation *'88*
They Live *'88*
Arachnophobia *'90*
Deconstructing Sarah *'94*
In the Mouth of Madness *'95*
Village of the Damned *'95*

Rick Jason
Combat! *'62*
Color Me Dead *'69*
Eagles Attack at Dawn *'74*
Witch Who Came from the Sea *'76*
Partners *'82*

Sybil Jason
The Little Princess *'39*
The Blue Bird *'40*

Star Jasper
True Love *'89*
Jersey Girl *'92*

Ricky Jay
House of Games *'87*
Things Change *'88*
Hole in the Sky *'95*

Michael Jayston
A Midsummer Night's Dream *'68*
Nicholas and Alexandra *'71*
Alice's Adventures in Wonderland *'72*
Craze *'74*
Dust to Dust *'85*
Macbeth *'90*

Gloria Jean
Never Give a Sucker an Even Break *'41*
Copacabana *'47*
The Ladies' Man *'61*

Zizi Jeanmarie
Hans Christian Andersen *'52*
Black Tights *'60*

Isabel Jeans
Easy Virtue *'27*
Great Day *'46*
Elizabeth of Ladymead *'48*
Gigi *'58*
Heavens Above *'63*
The Magic Christian *'69*

Ursula Jeans
Cavalcade *'33*
Dark Journey *'37*
The Life and Death of Colonel Blimp *'43*
The Weaker Sex *'49*
Dam Busters *'55*
Flame Over India *'60*

Colin Jeavons
Bartleby *'70*
To Play the King *'93*

Herbert Jefferson, Jr.
Private Duty Nurses *'71*
Detroit 9000 *'73*
World War III *'86*

Barbara Jefford
Ulysses *'67*
A Midsummer Night's Dream *'68*
Lust for a Vampire *'71*
And the Ship Sails On *'83*
Murders at Lynch Cross *'85*
Reunion *'88*
When the Whales Came *'89*
Where Angels Fear to Tread *'91*

Doug Jeffrey
Married People, Single Sex 2: For Better or Worse *'94*
Indecent Behavior 3 *'95*

Peter Jeffrey
The Fixer *'68*
Ring of Bright Water *'69*
The Horsemen *'70*
Twinsanity *'70*
Elizabeth R *'72*
The Adventures of Baron Munchausen *'89*
Hands of a Murderer *'90*
Middlemarch *'93*

Anne Jeffreys
Billy the Kid Trapped *'42*
I Married an Angel *'42*
X Marks the Spot *'42*
Bordertown Gunfighters *'43*
Calling Wild Bill Elliott *'43*
Death Valley Manhunt *'43*
Man from Thunder River *'43*
Nevada *'44*
Step Lively *'44*
Zombies on Broadway *'44*
Dick Tracy, Detective *'45*
Dick Tracy Double Feature #1 *'45*
Dillinger *'45*
Those Endearing Young Charms *'45*
Dick Tracy vs. Cueball *'46*
Dick Tracy Double Feature #2 *'47*
Riff-Raff *'47*
Trail Street *'47*
Return of the Bad Men *'48*

Chuck Jeffreys
Aftershock *'88*
Hawkeye *'88*
Honor and Glory *'92*
Deathfight *'93*

Fran Jeffries
Sex and the Single Girl *'64*
Harum Scarum *'65*

Herbert Jeffries
Harlem on the Prairie *'38*
Two-Gun Man from Harlem *'38*
Bronze Buckaroo *'39*
Harlem Rides the Range *'39*
Chrome and Hot Leather *'71*

Lang Jeffries
Alone Against Rome *'62*
Mission Stardust *'68*

Lionel Jeffries
The Colditz Story *'55*
The Baby and the Battleship *'56*
Bhowani Junction *'56*
Blue Murder at St. Trinian's *'56*
Lust for Life *'56*
Hour of Decision *'57*
The Vicious Circle *'57*
The Revenge of Frankenstein *'58*
Up the Creek *'58*
The Trials of Oscar Wilde *'60*
Fanny *'61*
Call Me Bwana *'63*
The Wrong Arm of the Law *'63*
First Men in the Moon *'64*
Murder Ahoy *'64*
Arrivederci, Baby! *'66*
Spy with a Cold Nose *'66*
Camelot *'67*
Oh Dad, Poor Dad (Momma's Hung You in the Closet & I'm Feeling So Sad) *'67*
Those Fantastic Flying Fools *'67*
Chitty Chitty Bang Bang *'68*
Lola *'69*
Sudden Terror *'70*
Who Slew Auntie Roo? *'71*
Royal Flash *'75*
Bananas Boat *'78*
Prisoner of Zenda *'79*
Letting the Birds Go Free *'86*
A Chorus of Disapproval *'89*
Jekyll and Hyde *'90*

Rudolph Jelinek
Fabulous Adventures of Baron Munchausen *'61*
The Original Fabulous Adventures of Baron Munchausen *'61*

Anna Jemison
Smash Palace *'82*
Heatwave *'83*
My First Wife *'84*

Allen Jenkins
Blessed Event *'32*
I Am a Fugitive from a Chain Gang *'32*
Bureau of Missing Persons *'33*
Employees' Entrance *'33*
Tomorrow at Seven *'33*
The Case of the Lucky Legs *'35*
Three Men on a Horse *'36*
Dead End *'37*
Marked Woman *'37*
Destry Rides Again *'39*
Brother Orchid *'40*
Tin Pan Alley *'40*
Dive Bomber *'41*
Footsteps in the Dark *'41*
Lady On a Train *'45*
Case of the Baby Sitter *'47*
Hat Box Mystery *'47*
The Big Wheel *'49*
The Falcon Takes Over/Strange Bargain *'49*
Oklahoma Annie *'51*
Robin and the 7 Hoods *'64*

Daniel H. Jenkins
Florida Straits *'87*
O.C. and Stiggs *'87*
The Caine Mutiny Court Martial *'88*

Jackie "Butch" Jenkins
The Human Comedy *'43*
National Velvet *'44*
Our Vines Have Tender Grapes *'45*
Summer Holiday *'48*

Ken Jenkins
Edge of Honor *'91*
White Mile *'94*
Hiroshima *'95*
Past the Bleachers *'95*

Megs Jenkins
Trouble in Store *'53*
The Innocents *'61*
Murder Most Foul *'65*

Rebecca Jenkins
Cowboys Don't Cry *'88*
Family Reunion *'88*
Bye Bye Blues *'89*
Bob Roberts *'92*
Clearcut *'92*
Till Death Do Us Part *'92*

Richard Jenkins
The Tender Age *'84*
On Valentine's Day *'86*
The Witches of Eastwick *'87*
Stealing Home *'88*
Blaze *'89*
Sea of Love *'89*
Descending Angel *'90*
Rising Son *'90*
Getting Out *'94*
It Could Happen to You *'94*
Trapped In Paradise *'94*
Wolf *'94*
Flirting with Disaster *'95*
The Indian in the Cupboard *'95*
The Boys Next Door *'96*
Eddie *'96*

Sam Jenkins
Twenty Bucks *'93*
Fortunes of War *'94*

Frank Jenks
That Girl from Paris *'36*
First Love *'39*
His Girl Friday *'40*
The Navy Comes Through *'42*
Corregidor *'43*
His Butler's Sister *'43*
The Falcon in Hollywood *'44*
Rogue's Gallery *'44*
Shake Hands with Murder *'44*
Zombies on Broadway *'44*
Kid Sister *'45*
The Missing Corpse *'45*
The Phantom of 42nd Street *'45*
That Brennan Girl *'46*
Blonde Savage *'47*

Si Jenks
Rawhide Romance *'34*
Fighting Shadows *'35*
The Outlaw Deputy *'35*
Captain January *'36*

Bruce Jenner
Can't Stop the Music *'80*
Grambling's White Tiger *'81*

Lucinda Jenney
Rain Man *'88*
Verne Miller *'88*
Wired *'89*
Thelma & Louise *'91*
American Heart *'92*
Matinee *'92*

Claudia Jennings
Jud *'71*
The Love Machine *'71*
The Stepmother *'71*
Group Marriage *'72*
Unholy Rollers *'72*
Gator Bait *'73*
Truck Stop Women *'74*
The Great Texas Dynamite Chase *'76*
Sisters of Death *'76*
Moonshine County Express *'77*
Death Sport *'78*
Fast Company *'78*

DeWitt Jennings
The Little American '17
The Bat Whispers '30
The Big House '30
Criminal Code '31
Kelly the Second '36

Tom Jennings
Night Master '87
Stones of Death '88

Waylon Jennings
Sesame Street Presents: Follow That Bird '85
Stagecoach '86

Rita Jenrette
Zombie Island Massacre '84
Malibu Bikini Shop '86
End of the Line '88

Salome Jens
Angel Baby '61
The Fool Killer '65
Savages '72
Diary of the Dead '80s
A Matter of Life and Death '81
Tomorrow's Child '82
The Grace Kelly Story '83

Karen Jensen
The Salzburg Connection '72
Battlestar Galactica '78
Deadly Blessing '81

Sasha Jensen
Dream Trap '90
A Girl to Kill For '90
Dazed and Confused '93

Todd Jensen
Prey for the Hunter '92
Cyborg Cop '93
Armageddon: The Final Challenge '94
Never Say Die '94

Roy Jenson
Crossfire '67
Bandits '73

Adele Jergens
A Thousand and One Nights '45
Down to Earth '47
The Fuller Brush Man '48
The Prince of Thieves '48
The Dark Past '49
Ladies of the Chorus '49
Pirate Ship '49
Armored Car Robbery '50
Blues Busters '50
The Falcon's Adventure/Armored Car Robbery '50
Radar Secret Service '50
Treasure of Monte Cristo '50
Abbott and Costello Meet the Invisible Man '51
Big Chase '54
The Cobweb '55
Day the World Ended '55
Girls in Prison '56

George Jessel
Valley of the Dolls '67
Diary of a Young Comic '79

Michael Jeter
Dead Bang '89
The Fisher King '91
Bank Robber '93
Gypsy '93
Sister Act 2: Back in the Habit '93
Drop Zone '94
Waterworld '95
The Boys Next Door '96

Joan Jett
Dubeat-E-O '84
Light of Day '87

Isabel Jewell
Blessed Event '32
Evelyn Prentice '34
Manhattan Melodrama '34
Ceiling Zero '35
A Tale of Two Cities '35
Go West, Young Man '36
Lost Horizon '37
Marked Woman '37
Swing It, Sailor! '37
Gone with the Wind '39
The Leopard Man '43
The Seventh Victim '43
The Arousers '70

Penn Jillette
Miami Vice 2: The Prodigal Son '85
Tough Guys Don't Dance '87
Penn and Teller Get Killed '90
Hackers '95

Ann Jillian
Gypsy '62
Mr. Mom '83
Mae West '84
Girls of the White Orchid '85
Convicted: A Mother's Story '87
The Ann Jillian Story '88
Little White Lies '89

Joyce Jillson
Superchick '71
Slumber Party '57 '76

Yolanda Jilot
Diving In '90
JFK: Reckless Youth '93

Jose Luis Jimenez
The Vampire '57
Spiritism '61

Ma Jingwu
Raise the Red Lantern '91
The Day the Sun Turned Cold '94

Marlene Jobert
Masculine Feminine '66
Rider on the Rain '70
Catch Me a Spy '71
Ten Days Wonder '72
Swashbuckler '84

David Johansen
Married to the Mob '88
Scrooged '88
Let It Ride '89
Tales from the Darkside: The Movie '90
Desire and Hell at Sunset Motel '92
Freejack '92
Mr. Nanny '93
Car 54, Where Are You? '94

Paul Johansson
Martial Law 2: Undercover '91
Soapdish '91
Midnight Witness '93

I.S. Johar
Flame Over India '60
Maya '66

Elton John
Born to Boogie '72
Tommy '75

Gottfried John
Mother Kusters Goes to Heaven '76
In a Year of 13 Moons '78
The Marriage of Maria Braun '79
Berlin Alexanderplatz '80
Mata Hari '85
Abraham '94
Goldeneye '95

Karl John
The Lost One '51
The Mysterious Magician '65

Rosamund John
Spitfire '42
Fame Is the Spur '47

Glynis Johns
The Forty-Ninth Parallel '41
The Adventures of Tartu '43
Frieda '47
No Highway in the Sky '51
Encore '52
The Promoter '52
Rob Roy—The Highland Rogue '53
The Sword & the Rose '53
Land of Fury '55
All Mine to Give '56
Court Jester '56
Another Time, Another Place '58
Shake Hands with the Devil '59
The Sundowners '60
Papa's Delicate Condition '63
Mary Poppins '64
Dear Brigitte '65
Under Milk Wood '73
Vault of Horror '73
Spraggue '84
Zelly & Me '88
Nukie '93
The Ref '93
While You Were Sleeping '95

Mervyn Johns
Dead of Night '45
Pink Strings and Sealing Wax '45
Captive Heart '47
San Demetrio, London '47
Counterblast '48
A Christmas Carol '51
Tony Draws a Horse '51
The Master of Ballantrae '53
Romeo and Juliet '54
No Love for Johnnie '60
Day of the Triffids '63

Stratford Johns
Great Expectations '81
The Lair of the White Worm '88
Salome's Last Dance '88
A Demon in My View '92
Splitting Heirs '93
The Strange Case of the End of Civilization as We Know It '93

Tracy C. Johns
Mo' Better Blues '90
New Jack City '91

A.J. Johnson
House Party '90
Double Trouble '91

Anne-Marie Johnson
Hollywood Shuffle '87
I'm Gonna Git You Sucka '88
Robot Jox '90
True Identity '91
Dream Date '93

Arnold Johnson
Putney Swope '69
My Demon Lover '87

Arte Johnson
Charge of the Model T's '76
Bud and Lou '78
If Things Were Different '79
Love at First Bite '79
Bunco '83
What Comes Around '85
Evil Toons '90
The Red Raven Kiss-Off '90
Tax Season '90
Evil Spirits '91
Munchie '92
Assault of the Party Nerds 2: Heavy Petting Detective '95

Ben Johnson
Three Godfathers '48
Mighty Joe Young '49
She Wore a Yellow Ribbon '49
Rio Grande '50
Wagon Master '50
Shane '53
Tomboy & the Champ '58
One-Eyed Jacks '61
Major Dundee '65
The Rare Breed '66
Will Penny '67
The Undefeated '69
The Wild Bunch '69
Chisum '70
The Last Picture Show '71
The Getaway '72
Junior Bonner '72
Dillinger '73
Train Robbers '73
The Sugarland Express '74
Bite the Bullet '75
Breakheart Pass '76
The Red Pony '76
The Savage Bees '76
Town that Dreaded Sundown '76
Grayeagle '77
The Swarm '78
The Sacketts '79
Wild Times '79
Terror Train '80
Ruckus '81
The Shadow Riders '82
Tex '82
Champions '84
Red Dawn '84
Soggy Bottom U.S.A. '84
Wild Horses '84
Trespasses '86
Let's Get Harry '87
Cherry 2000 '88
Dark Before Dawn '89
Back to Back '90
The Chase '91
My Heroes Have Always Been Cowboys '91
Radio Flyer '92
Bonanza: The Return '93

Angels in the Outfield '94

Beverly Johnson
Ashanti, Land of No Mercy '79
The Cover Girl Murders '93

Brad Johnson
The Losers '70
Nam Angels '88
Always '89
Flight of the Intruder '90
An American Story '92
Lone Justice 2 '93
Philadelphia Experiment 2 '93
The Birds 2: Land's End '94
Dominion '94
Siringo '94

Candy Johnson
Beach Party '63
Bikini Beach '64
Muscle Beach Party '64
Pajama Party '64

Celia Johnson
In Which We Serve '43
Brief Encounter '46
This Happy Breed '47
Captain's Paradise '53
The Prime of Miss Jean Brodie '69
Les Miserables '78
The Hostage Tower '80
Staying On '80
Unicorn '83

Chic Johnson
Country Gentlemen '36
All Over Town '37

Clark Johnson
Personals '90
The Finishing Touch '92
Final Round '93

Don Johnson
Zachariah '70
Harrad Experiment '73
A Boy and His Dog '75
Return to Macon County '75
The City '76
Law of the Land '76
Snowblind '78
The Rebels '79
Beulah Land '80
Revenge of the Stepford Wives '80
Melanie '82
Miami Vice '84
Soggy Bottom U.S.A. '84
Cease Fire '85
Miami Vice 2: The Prodigal Son '85
The Long, Hot Summer '86
Sweet Hearts Dance '88
Dead Bang '89
The Hot Spot '90
Harley Davidson and the Marlboro Man '91
Paradise '91
Tales of the Unexpected '91
Born Yesterday '93
Guilty as Sin '93
In Pursuit of Honor '95
Tin Cup '96

Dots Johnson
Paisan '46
Tall, Tan and Terrific '46

Helen Johnson
The Divorcee '30
Sin Takes a Holiday '30
Vice Squad '31

Jill Johnson
Party Plane '90
Wildest Dreams '90

Joey Johnson
Grad Night '81
Courier of Death '84

Kay Johnson
Madam Satan '30
Son of Fury '42

Kelly Johnson
Goodbye Pork Pie '81
Carry Me Back '82
Utu '83

Kurt Johnson
Jane Austen in Manhattan '80
Sole Survivor '84

Kyle Johnson
The Learning Tree '69
Man on the Run '74

Laura Johnson
Beyond Reason '77
Opening Night '77
Nick Knight '80s
Murderous Vision '91
Fatal Instinct '92
Red Shoe Diaries 2: Double Dare '92
Cheatin' Hearts '93
Dario Argento's Trauma '93
Deadly Exposure '93

Lynn-Holly Johnson
Ice Castles '79
Alien Predators '80
For Your Eyes Only '81
The Watcher in the Woods '81
Where the Boys Are '84 '84
The Sisterhood '88
Digging Up Business '91
The Criminal Mind '93

Mae Johnson
Keep Punching '39
The Defilers '65

Mel Johnson, Jr.
Eubie! '82
Total Recall '90

Michelle Johnson
Blame It on Rio '84
A Chorus Line '85
Gung Ho '85
Beaks: The Movie '87
Slipping into Darkness '88
Waxwork '88
Genuine Risk '89
Jigsaw Murders '89
Driving Me Crazy '91
Blood Ties '92
Death Becomes Her '92
Far and Away '92
Till Murder Do Us Part '92
Wishful Thinking '92
Body Shot '93
The Donor '94
Incident at Deception Ridge '94

Noble Johnson
The Navigator '24
King Kong '33
The Lives of a Bengal Lancer '35
The Ghost Breakers '40
North of the Great Divide '50

Penny Johnson
What's Love Got to Do with It? '93
The Road to Galveston '96

Reggie Johnson
Platoon '86
Seven Hours to Judgment '88

Richard Johnson
Never So Few '59
The Haunting '63
The Pumpkin Eater '64
Tomb of Ligeia '64
The Amorous Adventures of Moll Flanders '65
Operation Crossbow '65
Khartoum '66
The Witch '66
Fifth Day of Peace '72
Restless '72
Beyond the Door '75
Hennessy '75
The Comeback '77
The Four Feathers '78
The Big Scam '79
Screamers '80
Zombie '80
The Great Alligator '81
Lady Jane '85
Turtle Diary '86
A Man for All Seasons '88
Treasure Island '89
Diving In '90
Spymaker: The Secret Life of Ian Fleming '90
The Crucifer of Blood '91
Duel of Hearts '92

Rita Johnson
Broadway Serenade '39
Honolulu '39
Edison the Man '40
Here Comes Mr. Jordan '41
My Friend Flicka '43
The Naughty Nineties '45
The Perfect Marriage '46
They Won't Believe Me '47
All Mine to Give '56

Robin Johnson
Times Square '80
Splitz '84

Russell Johnson
It Came From Outer Space '53
Ma and Pa Kettle at Waikiki '55
This Island Earth '55
Rock All Night '57
Gilligan's Island: Meet the Crew '64
Fatal Chase '77
The Great Skycopter Rescue '82

Steve Johnson
Lemora, Lady Dracula '73
Angel of H.E.A.T. '82

Sunny Johnson
Dr. Heckyl and Mr. Hype '80
Flashdance '83
The Red Light Sting '84

Tor Johnson
Behind Locked Doors '48
Human Gorilla '48
Abbott and Costello in the Foreign Legion '50
Houdini '53
Bride of the Monster '56
Carousel '56
Plan 9 from Outer Space '56
The Unearthly '57
Night of the Ghouls '59
The Beast of Yucca Flats '61

Van Johnson
Too Many Girls '40
The Human Comedy '43
Madame Curie '43
A Guy Named Joe '44
Thirty Seconds Over Tokyo '44
Two Girls and a Sailor '44
The White Cliffs of Dover '44
Thrill of a Romance '45
Weekend at the Waldorf '45
Command Decision '48
State of the Union '48
Battleground '49
In the Good Old Summertime '49
The Big Hangover '50
The Duchess of Idaho '50
Go for Broke! '51
Three Guys Named Mike '51
Easy to Love '53
Brigadoon '54
The Caine Mutiny '54
The Last Time I Saw Paris '54
Men of the Fighting Lady '54
The Pied Piper of Hamelin '57
The Doomsday Flight '66
Divorce American Style '67
Yours, Mine & Ours '68
The Kidnapping of the President '80
Scorpion with Two Tails '82
The Purple Rose of Cairo '85
Delta Force Commando 2 '90
Three Days to a Kill '91

Victoria (Vicki) Johnson
Grizzly '76
Starship Invasions '77

Grace Johnston
God Bless the Child '88
One Good Cop '91

J.J. Johnston
Fatal Attraction '87
Things Change '88
Mad Dog and Glory '93
Stranger by Night '94

John Dennis Johnston
Dear Detective '78
KISS Meets the Phantom of the Park '78
A Breed Apart '84
Streets of Fire '84
Into Thin Air '85
Pink Cadillac '89
Miracle in the Wilderness '91
In Pursuit of Honor '95

Margaret Johnston
A Man About the House '47
Burn Witch, Burn! '62
Sebastian '68

Oliver Johnston
A King in New York '57
Tomb of Ligeia '64
A Countess from Hong Kong '67

Mirjana Jokovic
Eversmile New Jersey '89
Underground '95

Angelina Jolie
Cyborg 2 '93
Hackers '95

I. Stanford Jolley
Midnight Limited '40
Trail of the Silver Spurs '41
The Black Raven '43
Outlaw Roundup '44
Frontier Fugitives '45
Lightning Raiders '45
Ambush Trail '46
Cyclotrode "X" '46
Wild Country '47
Check Your Guns '48
King of the Rocketmen '49
The Rebel Set '59

Al Jolson
The Jazz Singer '27
Hallelujah, I'm a Bum '33
Rose of Washington Square '39
Rhapsody in Blue '45

Allan Jones
A Night at the Opera '35
Rose Marie '36
Show Boat '36
A Day at the Races '37
The Firefly '37
Everybody Sing '38
One Night in the Tropics '40
A Swingin' Summer '65

Andras Jones
Sorority Babes in the Slimeball Bowl-A-Rama '87
A Nightmare on Elm Street 4: Dream Master '88
Far from Home '89

Barry Jones
Uneasy Terms '48
The Clouded Yellow '51
Return to Paradise '53
Demetrius and the Gladiators '54
Prince Valiant '54
The Glass Slipper '55

Ben Jones
Deep in the Heart '83
Don't Change My World '83

Buck Jones
Border Law '31
The Fighting Sheriff '31
Range Feud '31
The Range Feud/Two Fisted Law '31
Hello Trouble '32
White Eagle '32
When a Man Sees Red '34
The Crimson Trail '35
The Throwback '35
The Phantom Rider '37
Sandflow '37
Law of the Texan '38
Wagon's Westward '40
Arizona Bound '41
Forbidden Trails '41
Gunman from Bodie '41
Riders of Death Valley '41
Below the Border '42
Dawn on the Great Divide '42
Down Texas Way '42
Ghost Town Law '42
Riders of the West '42
West of the Law '42

Carolyn Jones
The Big Heat '53
House of Wax '53
The Road to Bali '53
The Seven Year Itch '55
The Tender Trap '55
Invasion of the Body Snatchers '56
The Man Who Knew Too Much '56
King Creole '58
Marjorie Morningstar '58
Career '59
A Hole in the Head '59
Last Train from Gun Hill '59
Ice Palace '60
How the West Was Won '63
The Addams Family '64
Color Me Dead '69
The Shaming '71
Eaten Alive '76
Little Ladies of the Night '77
Halloween with the Addams Family '79

Catherine Zeta Jones
Christopher Columbus: The Discovery '92
Splitting Heirs '93
The Cinder Path '94
The Return of the Native '94
The Phantom '96

Christopher Jones
Three in the Attic '68
Wild in the Streets '68
The Looking Glass War '69
Ryan's Daughter '70

Chuck Jones
Innerspace '87
Chuck Amuck: The Movie '91

Claude Earl Jones
Evilspeak '82
Impulse '84
Bride of Re-Animator '89

Clyde Jones
Crack House '89
Delta Heat '92

Darby Jones
I Walked with a Zombie '43
Zombies on Broadway '44

Dean Jones
Tea and Sympathy '56
Jailhouse Rock '57
Torpedo Run '58
That Darn Cat '65
The Ugly Dachshund '65
Any Wednesday '66
Monkeys, Go Home! '66
Blackbeard's Ghost '67
The Horse in the Gray Flannel Suit '68
The Love Bug '68
Million Dollar Duck '71
Snowball Express '72
Mr. Superinvisible '73
The Shaggy D.A. '76
Herbie Goes to Monte Carlo '77
Once Upon a Brothers Grimm '77
Born Again '78
When Every Day was the Fourth of July '78
The Long Days of Summer '80
Fire and Rain '89
Other People's Money '91
Beethoven '92
Clear and Present Danger '94

Dick Jones
Trail of the Hawk '37
The Frontiersmen '38
Nancy Drew, Reporter '39

Duane Jones
Night of the Living Dead '68
Black Vampire '73
Beat Street '84
Fright House '89
To Die for '89

Eddie Jones
Apprentice to Murder '88
Sneakers '92
Final Appeal '93
Letter to My Killer '95

Freddie Jones
Accident '67
The Bliss of Mrs. Blossom '68
Assault '70
Twinsanity '70
The Satanic Rites of Dracula '73
All Creatures Great and Small '74
Juggernaut '74
Romance with a Double Bass '74
Zulu Dawn '79
The Elephant Man '80
Firefox '82
And the Ship Sails On '83
Krull '83
Dune '84
Firestarter '84
Young Sherlock Holmes '85
Consuming Passions '88
Erik the Viking '89
Wild at Heart '90
The Last Butterfly '92
Hotel Room '93
The Mystery of Edwin Drood '93
Cold Comfort Farm '94
The Neverending Story 3 '94

Gemma Jones
The Devils '71
Paperhouse '89
Feast of July '95
Sense and Sensibility '95

Gillian Jones
Echoes of Paradise '86
Shame '87

Gordon Jones
Let 'Em Have It '35
Sea Devils '37
The Green Hornet '39
I Take This Oath '40
Up in the Air '40
Flying Tigers '42
The Wistful Widow of Wagon Gap '47
Arizona Cowboy '49
North of the Great Divide '50
Trail of Robin Hood '50
Trigger, Jr. '50
Western Double Feature 11 '50
Heart of the Rockies '51
The Monster That Challenged the World '57
McLintock! '63

Grace Jones
Gordon's War '73
Deadly Vengeance '81
Conan the Destroyer '84
A View to a Kill '85
Vamp '86
Siesta '87
Straight to Hell '87
Boomerang '92
Cyber Bandits '94

Griff Rhys Jones
Morons from Outer Space '85
The Misadventures of Mr. Wilt '90

Griffith Jones
The Mill on the Floss '37
The Secret Four '40
The Day Will Dawn '42
The Wicked Lady '45

Harold W. Jones
The Crazies '73
Provoked '89

Henry Jones
The Lady Says No '51
The Bad Seed '56
Will Success Spoil Rock Hunter? '57
Vertigo '58
The Bramble Bush '60
Cash McCall '60
Angel Baby '61
Stay Away, Joe '68
Butch Cassidy and the Sundance Kid '69
Support Your Local Gunfighter '71
Napoleon and Samantha '72
Pete 'n' Tillie '72
Balboa '82
Deathtrap '82
Codename: Foxfire '85
Nowhere to Run '88
Arachnophobia '90
The Grifters '90
Breathing Lessons '94

James Earl Jones
Dr. Strangelove, or: How I Learned to Stop Worrying and Love the Bomb '64
Paul Robeson '70s
End of the Road '70
The Great White Hope '70
Deadly Hero '75
Bingo Long Traveling All-Stars & Motor Kings '76
The River Niger '76
Swashbuckler '76
The Exorcist 2: The Heretic '77
The Greatest '77
The Last Remake of Beau Geste '77
Piece of the Action '77
Star Wars '77
Roots: The Next Generation '79
The Bushido Blade '80
The Guyana Tragedy: The Story of Jim Jones '80
Blood Tide '82
Conan the Barbarian '82
Return of the Jedi '83
Aladdin and His Wonderful Lamp '84
The Vegas Strip Wars '84
City Limits '85
Allan Quatermain and the Lost City of Gold '86
Soul Man '86
Gardens of Stone '87
Matewan '87
My Little Girl '87
Coming to America '88
Lone Star Kid '88
Best of the Best '89
By Dawn's Early Light '89
Field of Dreams '89
Grim Prairie Tales '89
Three Fugitives '89
The Ambulance '90
Heat Wave '90
The Hunt for Red October '90
Ivory Hunters '90
Last Flight Out: A True Story '90
Patriot Games '92
Scorchers '92
Sneakers '92
Excessive Force '93
The Meteor Man '93
Percy & Thunder '93
The Sandlot '93
Sommersby '93
Clean Slate '94
Clear and Present Danger '94
Jefferson in Paris '94
Cry, the Beloved Country '95
A Family Thing '96

Janet Jones
The Flamingo Kid '84
A Chorus Line '85
American Anthem '86
Police Academy 5: Assignment Miami Beach '88

Jeffrey Jones
Amadeus '84
Transylvania 6-5000 '85
Ferris Bueller's Day Off '86
George Washington: The Forging of a Nation '86
Howard the Duck '86
Hanoi Hilton '87
Kenny Rogers as the Gambler, Part 3: The Legend Continues '87
Beetlejuice '88
Without a Clue '88
Valmont '89
Who's Harry Crumb? '89
The Hunt for Red October '90
Mom and Dad Save the World '92
Out on a Limb '92
Stay Tuned '92
Ed Wood '94
Houseguest '94
The Avenging Angel '95

Jennifer Jones
Dick Tracy '37
Dawn Rider/Frontier Horizon '39
Frontier Horizon '39
The Song of Bernadette '43
Since You Went Away '44
Duel in the Sun '46
Portrait of Jennie '48
Madame Bovary '49
Carrie '52
Ruby Gentry '52
Beat the Devil '53
Indiscretion of an American Wife '54
Love Is a Many-Splendored Thing '55
The Man in the Gray Flannel Suit '56
The Towering Inferno '74

Jocelyn Jones
The Great Texas Dynamite Chase '76
Tourist Trap '79

Josephine Jacqueline Jones
Black Venus '83
Warrior Queen '87

L.Q. Jones
The Annapolis Story '55
Torpedo Run '58
Flaming Star '60
Ride the High Country '62
Iron Angel '64

Stay Away, Joe '68
The Wild Bunch '69
Ballad of Cable Hogue '70
The McMasters '70
The Brotherhood of Satan '71
Fireball Forward '72
Richard Petty Story '72
Manhunter '74
A Strange and Deadly Occurence '74
White Line Fever '75
Mother, Jugs and Speed '76
Standing Tall '78
The Beast Within '82
Lone Wolf McQuade '83
Sacred Ground '83
Timerider '83
Bulletproof '88
Grizzly Adams: The Legend Continues '90
River of Death '90
Lightning Jack '94
Casino '95
Tornado! '96

Marcia Mae Jones
The Champ '31
These Three '36
The Adventures of Tom Sawyer '38
Mad About Music '38
The Little Princess '39
The Gang's All Here '40
Old Swimmin' Hole '40
Tomboy '40
Let's Go Collegiate '41
Lady in the Death House '44

Mickey Jones
Forced to Kill '93
Drop Zone '94

Morgan Jones
Apache Woman '55
The Giant Claw '57
The Bus Is Coming '72

Nicholas Jones
A Dangerous Man: Lawrence after Arabia '91
Black Beauty '94

Peter Jones
Man of Evil '48
Whoops Apocalypse '83

Richard T. Jones
Renaissance Man '94
The Trigger Effect '96

Rosie Jones
Alice to Nowhere '86
Ganjasaurus Rex '87

Sam Jones
Flash Gordon '80
My Chauffeur '86
Jane & the Lost City '87
Driving Force '88
Silent Assassins '88
Under the Gun '88
WhiteForce '88
One Man Force '89
In Gold We Trust '91
DaVinci's War '92
Fist of Honor '92
Maximum Force '92
Night Rhythms '92
Lady Dragon 2 '93
Thunder in Paradise '93
Ballistic '94
Fists of Iron '94
Hard Vice '94
Texas Payback '95

Sharon Lee Jones
Josh Kirby...Time Warrior: Chapter 3, Trapped on Toyworld '95
Leapin' Leprechauns '95

Shirley Jones
Oklahoma! '55
Carousel '56
Never Steal Anything Small '59
Elmer Gantry '60
Two Rode Together '61
The Courtship of Eddie's Father '62
The Music Man '62
Bedtime Story '63
The Happy Ending '69
Silent Night, Lonely Night '69
The Cheyenne Social Club '70
The Girls of Huntington House '73
Beyond the Poseidon Adventure '79
Last Cry for Help '79
The Children of An Lac '80
Who'll Save Our Children? '82
Tank '83
Black Devil Doll from Hell '84

Simon Jones
The Hitchhiker's Guide to the Galaxy '81
Privates on Parade '84
Club Paradise '86
Green Card '90
Miracle on 34th Street '94

Terry Jones
Monty Python's Flying Circus '71
And Now for Something Completely Different '72
Monty Python and the Holy Grail '75
Jabberwocky '77
Monty Python's Life of Brian '79
Secret Policeman's Private Parts '81
Monty Python Live at the Hollywood Bowl '82
The Secret Policeman's Other Ball '82
Monty Python's The Meaning of Life '83
Erik the Viking '89
Monty Python's Parrot Sketch Not Included '90

Tommy Lee Jones
Eliza's Horoscope '70
Love Story '70
Jackson County Jail '76
The Amazing Howard Hughes '77
Rolling Thunder '77
The Betsy '78
Eyes of Laura Mars '78
Coal Miner's Daughter '80
Back Roads '81
The Executioner's Song '82
Nate and Hayes '83
Cat on a Hot Tin Roof '84
The River Rat '84
The Park is Mine '85
Black Moon Rising '86
Yuri Nosenko, KGB '86
Big Town '87
Broken Vows '87
Gotham '88
Stormy Monday '88
Lonesome Dove '89
The Package '89
Fire Birds '90
Blue Sky '91
JFK '91
House of Cards '92
Under Siege '92
The Fugitive '93
Heaven and Earth '93
Blown Away '94
The Client '94
Cobb '94
Natural Born Killers '94
Batman Forever '95
The Good Old Boys '95

Betsy Jones-Moreland
Creature from the Haunted Sea '60
The Last Woman on Earth '61

Richard Jordahl
The Starfighters '63
To the Shores of Hell '65

Bobby Jordan
Angels with Dirty Faces '38
Boys of the City '40
That Gang of Mine '40
Young Tom Edison '40
Bowery Blitzkrieg '41
Flying Wild '41
Pride of the Bowery '41
Spooks Run Wild '41
Let's Get Tough '42
'Neath Brooklyn Bridge '42
Kid Dynamite '43
Bowery Buckaroos '47
Hard-Boiled Mahoney '47
Spook Busters '48

Dorothy Jordan
Min & Bill '30
The Cabin in the Cotton '32
The Searchers '56

James Carroll Jordan
Slashdance '89
Tales of the Unexpected '91

Jim Jordan
Look Who's Laughing '41
Here We Go Again! '42

Joanne Moore Jordan
Faces '68
I Dismember Mama '74

Leslie Jordan
Frankenstein General Hospital '88
Ski Patrol '89
Jason Goes to Hell: The Final Friday '93

Louis Jordan
Beware '46
Reet, Petite and Gone '47
Look Out Sister '48

Marian Jordan
Look Who's Laughing '41
Here We Go Again! '42

Marsha Jordan
Saturday Night Sleazies, Vol. 1 '66
Lady Godiva Rides '68
Sweet Georgia '72
Class Reunion '87

Nick Jordan
Five for Hell '67
Reactor '85

Richard Jordan
Chato's Land '71
Lawman '71
Valdez is Coming '71
Trial of the Catonsville Nine '72
Rooster Cogburn '75
The Yakuza '75
Logan's Run '76
Interiors '78
Les Miserables '78
The Big Scam '79
Old Boyfriends '79
Raise the Titanic '80
Washington Mistress '81
Dune '84
A Flash of Green '85
Mean Season '85
The Men's Club '86
Solarbabies '86
The Murder of Mary Phagan '87
The Secret of My Success '87
Romero '89
The Hunt for Red October '90
Heaven is a Playground '91
The Hunt for the Night Stalker '91
Shout '91
Timebomb '91
Primary Motive '92
Gettysburg '93

William Jordan
The Red Fury '70s
The Buddy Holly Story '78
I Wanna Hold Your Hand '78
King '78
The Doors '91

Daniel Jordano
Alphabet City '84
Playing for Keeps '86

Victor Jory
A Midsummer Night's Dream '35
Hell-Ship Morgan '36
Bulldog Drummond at Bay '37
The Adventures of Tom Sawyer '38
Dodge City '39
Each Dawn I Die '39
Gone with the Wind '39
Susannah of the Mounties '39
Green Archer '40
Knights of the Range '40
The Light of Western Stars '40
Border Vigilantes '41
Charlie Chan in Rio '41
Riders of the Timberline '41
Bar-20 '43
Buckskin Frontier '43
Colt Comrades '43
Hoppy Serves a Writ '43
The Kansan '43
Leather Burners '43
The Loves of Carmen '48
South of St. Louis '48
A Woman's Secret '49
The Capture '50
The Cariboo Trail '50
Son of Ali Baba '52
Cat Women of the Moon '53
Man from the Alamo '53
Sabaka '55
Death of a Scoundrel '56
Manfish '56
The Fugitive Kind '60
The Miracle Worker '62
Cheyenne Autumn '64
Frasier the Sensuous Lion '73
Papillon '73
Devil Dog: The Hound of Hell '78
The Mountain Men '80

Erland Josephson
Brink of Life '57
Hour of the Wolf '68
The Passion of Anna '70
Cries and Whispers '72
Scenes from a Marriage '73
Face to Face '76
To Forget Venice '79
Montenegro '81
Fanny and Alexander '83
After the Rehearsal '84
The Sacrifice '86
Saving Grace '86
Control '87
Hanussen '88
The Unbearable Lightness of Being '88
Meeting Venus '91
The Ox '91
Prospero's Books '91
Sofie '92
Good Evening, Mr. Wallenberg '93
Ulysses' Gaze '95

Larry Joshua
Svengali '83
A Midnight Clear '92
Romeo Is Bleeding '93
Sugar Hill '94

Allyn Joslyn
They Won't Forget '37
The Shining Hour '38
Only Angels Have Wings '39
I Wake Up Screaming '41
Heaven Can Wait '43
Immortal Sergeant '43
The Horn Blows at Midnight '45
If You Knew Susie '48
Moonrise '48
Harriet Craig '50
As Young As You Feel '51
I Love Melvin '53
Fastest Gun Alive '56

Jennifer Jostyn
Omega Cop '90
The Brothers McMullen '94

Louis Jourdan
The Paradine Case '47
Letter from an Unknown Woman '48
Madame Bovary '49
Decameron Nights '53
Three Coins in the Fountain '54
The Swan '56
The Bride Is Much Too Beautiful '58
Gigi '58
The Best of Everything '59
Can-Can '60
The V.I.P.'s '63
The Count of Monte Cristo '74
The Man in the Iron Mask '77
Silver Bears '78
Escape to Love '82
Swamp Thing '82
Octopussy '83
Double Deal '84
The First Olympics: Athens 1896 '84
Beverly Hills Madam '86
For the Love of Angela '86
Counterforce '87
The Return of Swamp Thing '89
Grand Larceny '92
Year of the Comet '92

Louis Jouvet
Topaze '33
Carnival in Flanders '35
The Lower Depths '36
La Marseillaise '37
Bizarre Bizarre '39
Volpone '39
Heart of a Nation '43
Jenny Lamour '47

Milla Jovovich
The Night Train to Kathmandu '88
Return to the Blue Lagoon '91
Chaplin '92
Kuffs '92

Leatrice Joy
Made for Love '26
First Love '39
Old Swimmin' Hole '40

Nicholas Joy
Gentleman's Agreement '47
Native Son '51

Robert Joy
The Lawrenceville Stories '80s
Amityville 3: The Demon '83
Desperately Seeking Susan '85
Joshua Then and Now '85
Miracle at Moreaux '86
Sword of Gideon '86
Big Shots '87
She's Back '88
The Suicide Club '88
Millenium '89
Longtime Companion '90
The Dark Half '91
Shadows and Fog '92
Waterworld '95
Harriet the Spy '96

Alice Joyce
Dancing Mothers '26
Song O' My Heart '29

Brenda Joyce
The Rains Came '39
The Enchanted Forest '45
Strange Confession '45
Little Giant '46

Elaine Joyce
Motel Hell '80
Honor Thy Father and Mother: The True Story of the Menendez Brothers '94

William Joyce
I Eat Your Skin '64
The Young Nurses '73

Yootha Joyce
Die! Die! My Darling! '65
Horrors of Burke & Hare '71

Odette Joyeux
Sylvia and the Phantom '45
La Ronde '51

Michelle Joyner
Traces of Red '92
Cliffhanger '93
Painted Hero '95

Ashley Judd
Ruby in Paradise '93
Natural Born Killers '94
Heat '95
Smoke '95
Normal Life '96
A Time to Kill '96

Carolyn Judd
Women Unchained '70s
Escape from Cell Block 3 '78

Edward Judd
The Day the Earth Caught Fire '61
Stolen Hours '63
First Men in the Moon '64
Invasion '65
Strange Bedfellows '65
Island of Terror '66
Murder Motel '74
Whose Child Am I? '75
The Kitchen Toto '87
Flambards

Naomi Judd
Living Proof: The Hank Williams Jr. Story '83
Rio Diablo '93

Robert Judd
Fight for Your Life '79
Crossroads '86

Charles Judels
Love on the Run '36
Baby Face Morgan '42

Arline Judge
Mysterious Mr. Wong '35

Judge ▶cont.

One in a Million '36
The Lady is Willing '42
Law of the Jungle '42
Wildcat '42
Girls in Chains '43
Song of Texas '43
Take It Big '44
The Crawling Hand '63

Raul Julia
The Organization '71
Death Scream '75
Panic in Needle Park '75
Gumball Rally '76
Eyes of Laura Mars '78
The Escape Artist '82
One from the Heart '82
The Tempest '82
Overdrawn at the Memory Bank '83
Strong Medicine '84
Compromising Positions '85
Kiss of the Spider Woman '85
The Morning After '86
The Alamo: Thirteen Days to Glory '87
Florida Straits '87
Trading Hearts '87
Moon over Parador '88
Onassis '88
The Penitent '88
Tango Bar '88
Tequila Sunrise '88
Mack the Knife '89
Romero '89
Frankenstein Unbound '90
Havana '90
Presumed Innocent '90
The Rookie '90
The Addams Family '91
A Life of Sin '92
The Plague '92
Addams Family Values '93
The Burning Season '94
Down Came a Blackbird '94
Street Fighter '94

Janet Julian
Smokey Bites the Dust '81
Humongous '82
Ghostwarrior '86
King of New York '90

Max Julien
Getting Straight '70
Mack '73

Julissa
Dance of Death '68
The Fear Chamber '68
The Snake People '68

Gordon Jump
WKRP in Cincinnati, Vol. 1 '78
Dirkham Detective Agency '83
Making the Grade '84
Ransom Money '88
Bitter Vengeance '94

Tito Junco
A Woman Without Love '51
Death in the Garden '56
Invasion of the Vampires '61

Calvin Jung
In the Shadow of Kilimanjaro '86
American Ninja 3: Blood Hunt '89

Katy Jurado
Bullfighter & the Lady '50
El Bruto '52
High Noon '52
Arrowhead '53
Broken Lance '54
Trapeze '56
The Badlanders '58
One-Eyed Jacks '61
Barabbas '62
Stay Away, Joe '68
Once Upon a Scoundrel '73
Pat Garrett & Billy the Kid '73
Children of Sanchez '79
Under the Volcano '84
Fearmaker '89

Peter Jurasik
Full Exposure: The Sex Tape Scandals '89
Peter Gunn '89
Problem Child '90
The Late Shift '96

Curt Jurgens
The Mozart Story '48
The Devil in Silk '56
And God Created Woman '57
Enemy Below '57
The Inn of the Sixth Happiness '58
Me and the Colonel '58
This Happy Feeling '58
Ferry to Hong Kong '59
Tamango '59
The Longest Day '62
The Three Penny Opera '62
The Miracle of the White Stallions '63
Lord Jim '65
Target for Killing '66
The Invincible Six '68
The Assassination Bureau '69
Battle of Britain '69
Battle of Neretva '69
Murder for Sale '70
Battle of the Commandos '71
Dirty Heroes '71
The Mephisto Waltz '71
Nicholas and Alexandra '71
Vault of Horror '73
Twist '76
The Spy Who Loved Me '77
Breakthrough '78
Cruise Missile '78
Goldengirl '79
Just a Gigolo '79
Sleep of Death '79
French Intrigue

Deana Jurgens
Tin Man '83
Code Name: Zebra '84

James Robertson Justice
Whiskey Galore '48
David and Bathsheba '51
The Lady Says No '51
Doctor in the House '53
Rob Roy—The Highland Rogue '53
The Sword & the Rose '53
Land of the Pharaohs '55
Above Us the Waves '56
Doctor at Sea '56
Doctor at Large '57
Le Repos du Guerrier '62
Murder She Said '62
Doctor in Distress '63
Mayerling '68
Spirits of the Dead '68
Alien Women '69
The Love Factor '69

Katherine Justice
Columbo: Prescription Murder '67
Five Card Stud '68
The Stepmother '71
Frasier the Sensuous Lion '73
Captain America 2: Death Too Soon '79

William Justine
The Bride & the Beast '58
Trauma '62

Suzanne Kaaren
Undercover Man '36
Phantom Ranger '38
The Devil Bat '41

Jane Kaczmarek
Door to Door '84
Falling in Love '84
The Heavenly Kid '85
D.O.A. '88
Vice Versa '88
All's Fair '89

Karen Kadler
It Conquered the World '56
The Beatniks '60

Piotr Kadochnikev
Ivan the Terrible, Part 1 '44
Ivan the Terrible, Part 2 '46

Diane Kagan
The Life and Assassination of the Kingfish '76
Mr. & Mrs. Bridge '90

Elaine Kagan
Babyfever '94
Sharon's Secret '95

Kyoko Kagawa
Mother '52
The Crucified Lovers '54
Sansho the Bailiff '54
The Lower Depths '57

David Kagen
Friday the 13th, Part 6: Jason Lives '86
Conspiracy: The Trial of the Chicago Eight '87
Body Chemistry '90

Steve Kahan
Lethal Weapon '87
Lethal Weapon 2 '89
Lethal Weapon 3 '92
Warlock: The Armageddon '93

Madeline Kahn
The Dove '68
What's Up, Doc? '72
The Hideaways '73
Paper Moon '73
Blazing Saddles '74
Young Frankenstein '74
High Anxiety '77
The Adventures of Sherlock Holmes' Smarter Brother '78
The Cheap Detective '78
First Family '80
Happy Birthday, Gemini '80
Simon '80
Wholly Moses! '80
History of the World: Part 1 '81
Scrambled Feet '83
Yellowbeard '83
City Heat '84
Slapstick of Another Kind '84
Clue '85
Betsy's Wedding '90
Wanted: The Perfect Guy '90
For Richer, For Poorer '92
Mixed Nuts '94
Nixon '95

Chia Kai
Empire of the Dragon '80s
Of Cooks and Kung-Fu '80s
Dance of Death '84

Khalil Kain
Juice '92
Renaissance Man '94
Zooman '95

Joel Kaiser
Home for Christmas '90
Dead Certain '92

Elizabeth Kaitan
Aftershock '88
Assault of the Killer Bimbos '88
Roller Blade Warriors: Taken By Force '90
Vice Academy 3 '91
Desperate Crimes '93

Bonita Kalem
Women Unchained '70s
Escape from Cell Block 3 '78

Toni Kalem
Silent Rage '82
Billy Galvin '86

Patricia Kalember
Jacob's Ladder '90
Big Girls Don't Cry...They Get Even '92
A Far Off Place '93

Jean-Pierre Kalfon
Weekend '67
Condorman '81
The Cry of the Owl '92

Helena Kallianiotes
Five Easy Pieces '70
Backtrack '89

Alexander Kalyagin
An Unfinished Piece for a Player Piano '77
A Slave of Love '78

Danny Kamekona
The Karate Kid: Part 2 '86
Robot Jox '90
Robot Wars '93

Stanley Kamel
Murder by Numbers '89
Honor Thy Father and Mother: The True Story of the Menendez Brothers '94

Dan Kamin
Another Pair of Aces: Three of a Kind '91
America's Dream '95

Kris Kamm
Born to Ride '91
Andersonville '95

Fritz Kampers
Westfront 1918 '30
Kameradschaft '31

Anna Kanakis
Warriors of the Wasteland '83
After the Fall of New York '85

Steve Kanaly
Balboa '82
Fleshburn '84
Headhunter '89
Double Trouble '91
Driving Me Crazy '91
Eye of the Eagle 3 '91

Sean Kanan
The Karate Kid: Part 3 '89
Rich Girl '91

Babe Kane
W.C. Fields: Flask of Fields '30
The Dentist '32
Pharmacist '32
W.C. Fields Comedy Bag '33

Carol Kane
Carnal Knowledge '71
Desperate Characters '71
Wedding in White '72
The Last Detail '73
Dog Day Afternoon '75
Hester Street '75
Harry & Walter Go to New York '76
Annie Hall '77
Valentino '77
World's Greatest Lover '77
My Sister, My Love '78
When a Stranger Calls '79
Keeping On '81
Norman Loves Rose '82
Pandemonium '82
Over the Brooklyn Bridge '83
Burning Rage '84
Racing with the Moon '84
The Secret Diary of Sigmund Freud '84
Strong Medicine '84
Casey at the Bat '85
Transylvania 6-5000 '85
Jumpin' Jack Flash '86
The Princess Bride '87
Drop-Out Mother '88
License to Drive '88
Scrooged '88
Sticky Fingers '88
Flashback '89
The Lemon Sisters '90
My Blue Heaven '90
Baby on Board '92
Addams Family Values '93
Ted & Venus '93
When a Stranger Calls Back '93
The Crazysitter '94
Big Bully '95
The Pallbearer '95
Sunset Park '96

Marjorie Kane
The Great Gabbo '29
Border Romance '30
Sunny Skies '30

Nobuo Kaneko
Ikiru '52
The Human Condition: A Soldier's Prayer '61

John Kani
Killing Heat '84
Options '88
An African Dream '90
Sarafina! '92

Alexis Kanner
Twinsanity '70
Kings and Desperate Men '83
Nightfall '88

Ivar Kants
Plumber '79
Silver City '84
The Naked Country '85
Gallagher's Travels '87

John Kapelos
The Breakfast Club '85
Nothing in Common '86
Roxanne '87
The Boost '88
All's Fair '89
Man Trouble '92
The Late Shift '96

Gabe Kaplan
Fast Break '79
Nobody's Perfekt '79
Tulips '81
The Hoboken Chicken Emergency '84

Jonathan Kaplan
Cannonball '76
Hollywood Boulevard '76

Marvin Kaplan
Adam's Rib '50
Angels in the Outfield '51
The Severed Arm '73
Fangs '75

Shashi Kapoor
The Householder '63
Shakespeare Wallah '65
Bombay Talkie '70
Heat and Dust '82
Sammy & Rosie Get Laid '87
The Deceivers '88
In Custody '94
Gulliver's Travels '95

Valerie Kaprisky
Breathless '83
L'Annee des Meduses '86
Iran: Days of Crisis '91

Mitzi Kapture
Private Road: No Trespassing '87
Angel 3: The Final Chapter '88
Liberty & Bash '90

Ron Karabatsos
Flashdance '83
Missing Pieces '83
Hollywood Heartbreak '89
Rich Girl '91
29th Street '91

Mirjana Karanovic
When Father was Away on Business '85
Underground '95

James Karen
Frankenstein Meets the Space Monster '65
Hercules in New York '70
The China Syndrome '79
Poltergeist '82
Sam's Son '84
The Jagged Edge '85
Latino '85
Return of the Living Dead '85
Hardbodies 2 '86
Billionaire Boys Club '87
Wall Street '87
Return of the Living Dead 2 '88
Cult People '89
Girlfriend from Hell '89
Vital Signs '90
The Willies '90
The Closer '91
The Unborn '91
Lies Before Kisses '92
A Kiss Goodnight '94
Up Close and Personal '96

Anna Karin
Wild Cactus '92
Body of Influence '93
The Fear '94

Rita Karin
Sophie's Choice '82
Enemies, a Love Story '89
Age Isn't Everything '91
He Said, She Said '91

Anna Karina
A Woman is a Woman '60
Cleo from 5 to 7 '61
My Life to Live '62
Les Carabiniers '63
Band of Outsiders '64
Alphaville '65
Pierrot le Fou '65
The Nun '66
The Salzburg Connection '72
Bread and Chocolate '74
Ski Bum '75
Regina '83
Chinese Roulette '86

Vassilli Karis
SS Girls '78
Animal Called Man '87

Olga Karlatos
Zombie '80

Keach ▶cont.

Brewster McCloud '70
End of the Road '70
Fat City '72
Life & Times of Judge Roy Bean '72
The New Centurions '72
Man of Destiny '73
Watched '73
All the Kind Strangers '74
Luther '74
Conduct Unbecoming '75
Killer Inside Me '76
Street People '76
Ants '77
Gray Lady Down '77
The Squeeze '77
Battleforce '78
Cheech and Chong's Up in Smoke '79
Diary of a Young Comic '79
The Ninth Configuration '79
Slave of the Cannibal God '79
The Long Riders '80
A Rumor of War '80
Cheech and Chong's Nice Dreams '81
Road Games '81
Butterfly '82
Dynasty '82
That Championship Season '82
Princess Daisy '83
Mistral's Daughter '84
The Blue and the Gray '85
The Forgotten '89
Class of 1999 '90
False Identity '90
Mission of the Shark '91
Sunset Grill '92
Body Bags '93
Raw Justice '93
Rio Diablo '93
New Crime City: Los Angeles 2020 '94
Texas '94
Amanda and the Alien '95
Escape from L.A. '96

Marie Kean
Danny Boy '84
The Dead '87
The Lonely Passion of Judith Hearne '87

Edward Keane
Heroes in Blue '39
Midnight Limited '40
Rogue's Gallery '44

Kerrie Keane
Incubus '82
Hot Pursuit '84
Kung Fu: The Movie '86
Nightstick '87
Distant Thunder '88
Obsessed '88
Malarek '89

Robert Emmett Keane
Born to Be Wild '38
Fear in the Night '47
Susanna Pass '49
Hills of Oklahoma '50

Stephen Kearney
Rikky and Pete '88
The Nutt House '95

Charles Keating
Brideshead Revisited '81
The Bodyguard '92

Fred Keating
I Live My Life '35
Prison Train '38
Tin Pan Alley '40

Larry Keating
Francis Goes to the Races '51
When Worlds Collide '51
Monkey Business '52
Above and Beyond '53
Give a Girl a Break '53
A Lion Is in the Streets '53
Gypsy Colt '54
Daddy Long Legs '55
The Incredible Mr. Limpet '64

Buster Keaton
Story of William S. Hart/Sad Clowns '20s
The Saphead '21
The Blacksmith/The Cops '22
Cops/One Week '22
The Balloonatic/One Week '23
The Blacksmith/The Balloonatic '23
Our Hospitality '23
Three Ages '23
The Navigator '24
Seven Chances '25
Battling Butler '26
College '27
The General '27
The Cameraman '28
Steamboat Bill, Jr. '28
Spite Marriage '29
Voice of Hollywood '29
Slapstick '30s
Doughboys '30
Free and Easy '30
Parlor, Bedroom and Bath '31
Sidewalks of New York '31
Speak Easily '32
What! No Beer? '33
Old Spanish Custom '36
Li'l Abner '40
New Moon '40
The Villain Still Pursued Her '41
Forever and a Day '43
Boom in the Moon '46
God's Country '46
In the Good Old Summertime '49
Sunset Boulevard '50
Limelight '52
When Comedy was King '59
The Adventures of Huckleberry Finn '60
Days of Thrills and Laughter '61
A Few Moments with Buster Keaton and Laurel and Hardy '63
Great Chase '63
It's a Mad, Mad, Mad, Mad World '63
Beach Blanket Bingo '65
Buster Keaton Rides Again/The Railrodder '65
How to Stuff a Wild Bikini '65
Railrodder '65
A Funny Thing Happened on the Way to the Forum '66
Man in the Silk Hat '83
Hollywood Clowns '85

Diane Keaton
Lovers and Other Strangers '70
The Godfather '72
Play It Again, Sam '72
Sleeper '73
The Godfather, Part 2 '74
Love and Death '75
Harry & Walter Go to New York '76
I Will, I Will for Now '76
Annie Hall '77
Looking for Mr. Goodbar '77
Interiors '78
Manhattan '79
The Godfather 1902-1959: The Complete Epic '81
Reds '81
Shoot the Moon '82
The Little Drummer Girl '84
Mrs. Soffel '84
Crimes of the Heart '86
Baby Boom '87
Radio Days '87
The Good Mother '88
The Godfather, Part 3 '90
The Lemon Sisters '90
Father of the Bride '91
Running Mates '92
Manhattan Murder Mystery '93
Amelia Earhart: The Final Flight '94
Father of the Bride Part II '95

Joe Keaton
Our Hospitality '23
The General '27

Michael Keaton
Night Shift '82
Mr. Mom '83
Johnny Dangerously '84
Gung Ho '85
Touch and Go '86
The Squeeze '87
Beetlejuice '88
Clean and Sober '88
Batman '89
The Dream Team '89
Pacific Heights '90
One Good Cop '91
Batman Returns '92
Much Ado about Nothing '93
My Life '93
The Paper '94
Speechless '94
Multiplicity '96

Ele Keats
Lipstick Camera '93
Mother '94
White Wolves 2: Legend of the Wild '94
White Dwarf '95

Steven Keats
Hester Street '75
Black Sunday '77
Mysterious Island of Beautiful Women '79
For Ladies Only '81
The Executioner's Song '82
Silent Rage '82
Badge of the Assassin '85
In Dangerous Company '88
The Spring '89
Eternity '90

Hugh Keays-Byrne
Death Train '79
Mad Max '80
Kangaroo '86

Lila Kedrova
Modigliani '58
Zorba the Greek '64
Torn Curtain '66
Escape to the Sun '72
Widow's Nest '77
Le Cavaleur '78
Tell Me a Riddle '80
Sword of the Valiant '83
Some Girls '88

James Kee
Double Standard '88
Shadow Dancing '88

Cornelius Keefe
The Adorable Cheat '28
Man from Headquarters '28
Mystery Liner '34
Hong Kong Nights '35
Death from a Distance '36
The Trigger Trio '37

Howard Keel
Pagan Love Song '50
Show Boat '51
Texas Carnival '51
Three Guys Named Mike '51
Lovely to Look At '52
Calamity Jane '53
I Love Melvin '53
Kiss Me Kate '53
Deep in My Heart '54
Rose Marie '54
Seven Brides for Seven Brothers '54
Jupiter's Darling '55
Kismet '55
Armored Command '61
Day of the Triffids '63
Arizona Bushwackers '67
The War Wagon '67
Irving Berlin's America '86

Ruby Keeler
Footlight Parade '33
42nd Street '33
Gold Diggers of 1933 '33
Dames '34
Flirtation Walk '34
That's Dancing! '85

Geoffrey Keen
The Clouded Yellow '51
Cry, the Beloved Country '51
Doctor in the House '53
Angels One Five '54
The Man Who Never Was '55
Postmark for Danger '56
The Third Key '57
Sink the Bismarck '60
A Matter of WHO '62
Dr. Syn, Alias the Scarecrow '64
Taste the Blood of Dracula '70
Sacco & Vanzetti '71
Number 1 of the Secret Service '77
The Spy Who Loved Me '77
Moonraker '79
For Your Eyes Only '81
Amin: The Rise and Fall '82
The Living Daylights '87

Tom Keene
Beyond the Rockies '32
Come On Danger! '32
Ghost Valley '32
Saddle Buster '32
Cheyenne Kid '33
Our Daily Bread '34
Hong Kong Nights '35
Desert Gold '36
Drift Fence '36
The Glory Trail '36
God's Country and the Man '37
Where Trails Divide '37
Renegade Ranger/Scarlet River '38
The Driftin' Kid '41
Dynamite Canyon '41
Riding the Sunset Trail '41
Arizona Roundup '42
Lone Star Law Men '42
Western Mail '42
Where Trails End '42
Trail of Robin Hood '50

Catherine Keener
Survival Quest '89
Johnny Suede '92
Living in Oblivion '94

Matt Keeslar
Safe Passage '94
The Run of the Country '95

Jack Kehler
Bloodstone '88
Blindsided '93
Casualties of Love: The "Long Island Lolita" Story '93
The Invaders '95

Jack Kehoe
Serpico '73
Law and Disorder '74
The Fish that Saved Pittsburgh '79
On the Nickel '80
A Winner Never Quits '86
The Untouchables '87
Young Guns 2 '90
Servants of Twilight '91
Falling Down '93

Andrew Keir
Suspended Alibi '56
Cleopatra '63
Lord Jim '65
Daleks—Invasion Earth 2150 A.D. '66
The Fighting Prince of Donegal '66
The Night Visitor '70
Zeppelin '71
The Thirty-Nine Steps '79
Absolution '81
Dragonworld '94
Rob Roy '95

Harvey Keitel
Who's That Knocking at My Door? '68
Mean Streets '73
Alice Doesn't Live Here Anymore '74
Shining Star '75
Buffalo Bill & the Indians '76
Mother, Jugs and Speed '76
Taxi Driver '76
The Virginia Hill Story '76
The Duellists '77
Welcome to L.A. '77
Blue Collar '78
Fingers '78
Eagle's Wing '79
Death Watch '80
Saturn 3 '80
The Border '82
La Nuit de Varennes '82
Exposed '83
Corrupt '84
Falling in Love '84
Camorra: The Naples Connection '85
The Men's Club '86
Off Beat '86
The Inquiry '87
The Pick-Up Artist '87
Blindside '88
The Last Temptation of Christ '88
The January Man '89
Two Evil Eyes '90
The Two Jakes '90
Bugsy '91
Mortal Thoughts '91
Thelma & Louise '91
Bad Lieutenant '92
Reservoir Dogs '92
Sister Act '92
Dangerous Game '93
The Piano '93
Point of No Return '93
Rising Sun '93
The Young Americans '93
Imaginary Crimes '94
Monkey Trouble '94
Pulp Fiction '94
Blue In the Face '95
Clockers '95
From Dusk Till Dawn '95
Smoke '95
Ulysses' Gaze '95

Brian Keith
Arrowhead '53
The Violent Men '55
Nightfall '56
Run of the Arrow '56
Dino '57
The Young Philadelphians '59
Ten Who Dared '60
Deadly Companions '61
The Parent Trap '61
Moon Pilot '62
The Fugitive: Premiere Episode '63
Johnny Shiloh '63
Savage Sam '63
A Tiger Walks '64
The Hallelujah Trail '65
Those Calloways '65
Nevada Smith '66
The Rare Breed '66
The Russians are Coming, the Russians are Coming '66
Reflections in a Golden Eye '67
With Six You Get Eggroll '68
McKenzie Break '70
Suppose They Gave a War and Nobody Came? '70
Scandalous John '71
The Wind and the Lion '75
The Yakuza '75
Joe Panther '76
The Loneliest Runner '76
The Longest Drive '76
Hooper '78
The Chisholms '79
Meteor '79
The Seekers '79
The Mountain Men '80
Charlie Chan and the Curse of the Dragon Queen '81
Sharky's Machine '81
World War III '86
The Alamo: Thirteen Days to Glory '87
Death Before Dishonor '87
Young Guns '88
Bull of the West '89
Welcome Home '89
Escape '90
The Gambler Returns: The Luck of the Draw '93
National Lampoon's Favorite Deadly Sins '95
Picture Windows '95

David Keith
The Rose '79
Brubaker '80
The Great Santini '80
Back Roads '81
Take This Job & Shove It '81
An Officer and a Gentleman '82
Independence Day '83
The Lords of Discipline '83
Firestarter '84
Gulag '85
The Curse '87
The Further Adventures of Tennessee Buck '88
Heartbreak Hotel '88
White of the Eye '88
The Two Jakes '90
Caged Fear '92
Desperate Motives '92
Liar's Edge '92
Raw Justice '93
Major League 2 '94
Temptation '94
Texas '94
Till the End of the Night '94
Born Wild '95
Deadly Sins '95

Gold Diggers: The Secret of Bear Mountain '95

Donald Keith
Free to Love '25
My Lady of Whims '25
Dancing Mothers '26
Bare Knees '28
Branded Men '31
Outlaw Justice '32

Ian Keith
Manhandled '24
The Sign of the Cross '32
Queen Christina '33
The Crusades '35
The Three Musketeers '35
Mary of Scotland '36
The White Legion '36
Corregidor '43
Man from Thunder River '43
The Payoff '43
The Chinese Cat '44
Song of Old Wyoming '45
Dick Tracy's Dilemma '47
Scared to Death/Dick Tracy's Dilemma '47
It Came from Beneath the Sea '55

Penelope Keith
Madhouse Mansion '74
The Norman Conquests, Part 1: Table Manners '80
The Norman Conquests, Part 2: Living Together '80
The Norman Conquests, Part 3: Round and Round the Garden '80

Robert Keith
Boomerang '47
Here Comes the Groom '51
Battle Circus '53
Devil's Canyon '53
Small Town Girl '53
Drum Beat '54
The Wild One '54
Young at Heart '54
Love Me or Leave Me '55
Between Heaven and Hell '56
Written on the Wind '56
Men in War '57
My Man Godfrey '57
Cimarron '60

Rosalind Keith
Theodora Goes Wild '36
Bad Boy '39

Sheila Keith
Frightmare '74
The Confessional '75
The Comeback '77
House of the Long Shadows '82

Robert Kellard
Drums of Fu Manchu '40
Gentleman from Dixie '41

Cecil Kellaway
Maid's Night Out '38
Gunga Din '39
Wuthering Heights '39
Brother Orchid '40
The Letter '40
The Mummy's Hand '40
Birth of the Blues '41
Monsieur Beaucaire '46
The Postman Always Rings Twice '46
Unconquered '47
Portrait of Jennie '48
Harvey '50
Kim '50
Francis Goes to the Races '51
The Beast from 20,000 Fathoms '53
Young Bess '53
Interrupted Melody '55
The Prodigal '55
Zotz! '62
The Cardinal '63
Spinout '66
Guess Who's Coming to Dinner '67
Getting Straight '70
Quick, Let's Get Married '71

Tina Kellegher
The Snapper '93
Scarlett '94

Hiram Keller
Ciao Federico! Fellini Directs Satyricon '69
Fellini Satyricon '69
Lifespan '75
Countryman '83

Marthe Keller
And Now My Love '74
Marathon Man '76
Black Sunday '77
Bobby Deerfield '77
The Formula '80
The Amateur '82
Red Kiss '85
Dark Eyes '87
The Nightmare Years '89
Young Catherine '91

Mary Page Keller
Scared Stiff '87
Ulterior Motives '92
The Colony '95

Barbara Kellerman
Quatermass Conclusion '79
The Chronicles of Narnia '89

Sally Kellerman
Reform School Girl '57
Hands of a Stranger '62
The Boston Strangler '68
April Fools '69
Brewster McCloud '70
M*A*S*H '70
Last of the Red Hot Lovers '72
A Reflection of Fear '72
Slither '73
Rafferty & the Gold Dust Twins '75
The Big Bus '76
Welcome to L.A. '77
It Rained All Night the Day I Left '78
Magee and the Lady '78
A Little Romance '79
Fatal Attraction '80
Foxes '80
Loving Couples '80
Serial '80
Dempsey '83
Dirkham Detective Agency '83
September Gun '83
Moving Violations '85
Secret Weapons '85
Back to School '86
The KGB: The Secret War '86
That's Life! '86
Meatballs 3 '87
Someone to Love '87
Three for the Road '87
You Can't Hurry Love '88
All's Fair '89
Secret of the Ice Cave '89
Doppelganger: The Evil Within '90
Victim of Beauty '91
Boris and Natasha: The Movie '92
Mirror, Mirror 2: Raven Dance '94
Ready to Wear '94
Younger & Younger '94

Susan Kellerman
Oh, Heavenly Dog! '80
Where the Buffalo Roam '80
Elvira, Mistress of the Dark '88

Barry Kelley
Killer Bait '49
Ma and Pa Kettle '49
Too Late for Tears '49
The Asphalt Jungle '50
Francis Goes to the Races '51
The Well '51
Carrie '52
Jack the Giant Killer '62

DeForest Kelley
Fear in the Night '47
Illegal '55
The Man in the Gray Flannel Suit '56
Gunfight at the O.K. Corral '57
The Law and Jake Wade '58
Warlock '59
Apache Uprising '66
Star Trek Bloopers '69
Star Trek: The Motion Picture '80
Star Trek 2: The Wrath of Khan '82
Star Trek 3: The Search for Spock '84
Star Trek 4: The Voyage Home '86
Bull of the West '89
Star Trek 5: The Final Frontier '89
Star Trek 6: The Undiscovered Country '91

Sheila Kelley
Breaking In '89
Mortal Passions '90
Pure Luck '91
Soapdish '91
Passion Fish '92
Singles '92
Deconstructing Sarah '94
The Secretary '94

Mike Kellin
At War with the Army '50
Lonelyhearts '58
The Mountain Road '60
The Great Impostor '61
Wackiest Ship in the Army '61
Hell is for Heroes '62
Invitation to a Gunfighter '64
The Incident '67
The Boston Strangler '68
Riot '69
Freebie & the Bean '74
The Last Porno Flick '74
Next Stop, Greenwich Village '76
On the Yard '79
Sleepaway Camp '83

John Kellogg
Hopalong Cassidy: Borrowed Trouble '48
The Enforcer '51
Violets Are Blue '86
Jacob Have I Loved '88

Brian Kelly
Flipper '64
Flipper's New Adventure '64
Around the World Under the Sea '65
Flipper's Odyssey '66

Claire Kelly
The Badlanders '58
Party Girl '58
Ask Any Girl '59
Georgy Girl '66
A Guide for the Married Man '67
And Soon the Darkness '70
Dressed for Death '74

Craig Kelly
Silence '73
Nightscare '93
The Young Americans '93

David Kelly
Into the West '92
A Man of No Importance '94
The Run of the Country '95

David Patrick Kelly
The Warriors '79
48 Hrs. '82
Dreamscape '84
The Jigsaw Man '84
Commando '85
Pirates '86
The Misfit Brigade '87
The Adventures of Ford Fairlane '90
Penn and Teller Get Killed '90
Cheap Shots '91
Malcolm X '92
The Crow '93
Crooklyn '94
Flirting with Disaster '95

Gene Kelly
For Me and My Gal '42
DuBarry Was a Lady '43
Thousands Cheer '43
Cover Girl '44
Anchors Aweigh '45
Ziegfeld Follies '46
The Pirate '48
The Three Musketeers '48
Words and Music '48
On the Town '49
Take Me Out to the Ball Game '49
The Black Hand '50
Summer Stock '50
An American in Paris '51
Singin' in the Rain '52
Brigadoon '54
Deep in My Heart '54
It's Always Fair Weather '55
Invitation to the Dance '56
Les Girls '57
Marjorie Morningstar '58
Inherit the Wind '60
Let's Make Love '60
Forty Carats '73
That's Entertainment '74
That's Entertainment, Part 2 '76
Viva Knievel '77
Xanadu '80
North and South Book 1 '85
Sins '85
That's Dancing! '85

Grace Kelly
High Noon '52
Mogambo '53
Country Girl '54
Dial "M" for Murder '54
Rear Window '54
The Bridges at Toko-Ri '55
Green Fire '55
To Catch a Thief '55
High Society '56
The Swan '56

Jack Kelly
Red Ball Express '52
The Redhead from Wyoming '53
Cult of the Cobra '55
To Hell and Back '55
Forbidden Planet '56
The Commies are Coming, the Commies are Coming '57
Red Nightmare '62
Commandos '73
The Gambler Returns: The Luck of the Draw '93

James F. Kelly
Sinatra '92
Marilyn & Bobby: Her Final Affair '94

Jean Louisa Kelly
Breathing Lessons '94
Mr. Holland's Opus '95

Jim Kelly
Black Eliminator '70s
Enter the Dragon '73
Black Belt Jones '74
Three the Hard Way '74
Take a Hard Ride '75
Hot Potato '76
Black Samurai '77
Kill Factor '78
Tattoo Connection '78
One Down, Two to Go! '82

Judy Kelly
Make-Up '37
House of Mystery '41
Dead of Night '45

Kathleen Kelly
The Deputy Drummer '35
Heart's Desire '37
The Mutiny of the Elsinore '39
The Avenging Hand '43

Kimberly Kelly
Hard Bounty '94
Midnight Tease 2 '95

Lew Kelly
Death from a Distance '36
Mistaken Identity '36
Forlorn River '37

Mike Kelly
Heroes Three '84
Sakura Killers '86
To Live and Die in Hong Kong '89

Moira Kelly
Billy Bathgate '91
Love, Lies and Murder '91
Chaplin '92
The Cutting Edge '92
Twin Peaks: Fire Walk with Me '92
Daybreak '93
Little Odessa '94
With Honors '94
The Tie That Binds '95

Nancy Kelly
Stanley and Livingstone '39
One Night in the Tropics '40
To the Shores of Tripoli '42
Betrayal from the East '44
Gambler's Choice '44
The Woman Who Came Back '45
The Bad Seed '56

Patsy Kelly
Going Hollywood '33
The Girl from Missouri '34
Kelly the Second '36
Pick a Star '37
The Cowboy and the Lady '38
Swiss Miss '38
The Gorilla '39
Broadway Limited '41
Playmates '41
Road Show '41
In Old California '42
Sing Your Worries Away '42
Please Don't Eat the Daisies '60
Naked Kiss '64
Rosemary's Baby '68
Freaky Friday '76
The North Avenue Irregulars '79

Paul Kelly
Girl from Calgary '32
Star of Midnight '35
Fit for a King '37
Navy Blue and Gold '37
Devil's Party '38
The Howards of Virginia '40
Ziegfeld Girl '41
Call Out the Marines '42
Flying Tigers '42
The Secret Code '42
Tarzan's New York Adventure '42
Texas Legionnaires '43
The Story of Dr. Wassell '44
San Antonio '45
Adventure Island '47
Crossfire '47
Fear in the Night '47
Guilty of Treason '50
The Painted Hills '51
Springfield Rifle '52
Split Second '53
Bail Out at 43,000 '57
The Curfew Breakers '57

Paula Kelly
Sweet Charity '69
The Andromeda Strain '71
Top of the Heap '72
The Spook Who Sat By the Door '73
Jo Jo Dancer, Your Life is Calling '86
Uncle Tom's Cabin '87
The Women of Brewster Place '89
Once Upon a Time...When We Were Colored '95

Rae'ven Kelly
What's Love Got to Do with It? '93
Lily in Winter '94
America's Dream '95

Roz Kelly
Curse of the Black Widow '77
New Year's Evil '78

Sheila Kelly
Some Girls '88
A Passion to Kill '94

Tommy Kelly
The Adventures of Tom Sawyer '38
Peck's Bad Boy with the Circus '38

Fred Kelsey
Paths to Paradise '25
People's Choice '46

Linda Kelsey
Picture of Dorian Gray '74
Eleanor & Franklin '76
Baby Girl Scott '87

Pert Kelton
Bachelor Bait '34
Annie Oakley '35
Kelly the Second '36
The Music Man '62
The Comic '69

Richard Kelton
Silence '73
The Ultimate Warrior '75

Edward Kemmer
Space Patrol '50
Earth vs. the Spider '58
Giant from the Unknown '58

Warren Kemmerling
Trauma '62
Hit! '73
The Execution of Private Slovik '74
Eat My Dust '76

Brandis Kemp
Goldilocks & the Three Bears '83
Surf 2 '84

Kemp ▶cont.

South of Reno '87

Elizabeth Kemp
He Knows You're Alone '80
Killing Hour '84
Eating '90

Gary Kemp
The Krays '90
The Bodyguard '92
Paper Marriage '93
Killing Zoe '94

Jeremy Kemp
Operation Crossbow '65
Darling Lili '70
The Belstone Fox '73
Blockhouse '73
Space: 1999 '75
East of Elephant Rock '76
The Seven-Per-Cent Solution '76
Prisoner of Zenda '79
The Treasure Seekers '79
Sadat '83
The Winds of War '83
Top Secret! '84
Feet Foremost '85
War & Remembrance, Part 1 '88
War & Remembrance: The Final Chapter, Part 8 '89
When the Whales Came '89
Prisoner of Honor '91
Duel of Hearts '92
Angels and Insects '95

Martin Kemp
The Krays '90
Aspen Extreme '93
Boca '94
Cyber Bandits '94
Fleshtone '94
Desire '95
Embrace of the Vampire '95

Matty Kemp
Red Lights Ahead '36
Tango '36
Law of the Texan '38

Will Kempe
Metropolitan '90
Pledge Night '90
Hit the Dutchman '92

Charles Kemper
Fighting Father Dunne '48
The Doolins of Oklahoma '49
Mr. Music '50
The Nevadan '50
Stars in My Crown '50
Ticket to Tomahawk '50
On Dangerous Ground '51

Rachel Kempson
Captive Heart '47
Georgy Girl '66
The Charge of the Light Brigade '68
The Virgin Soldiers '69
Love for Lydia '79
Little Lord Fauntleroy '80
Out of Africa '85
Stealing Heaven '88

Felicity Kendal
Shakespeare Wallah '65
Valentino '77

Cy Kendall
Bulldog Edition '36
King of the Pecos '36
The Green Hornet '39
The Saint Takes Over '40
Billy the Kid '41
Johnny Eager '42
Tarzan's New York Adventure '42
Girl Rush '44
Outlaw Trail '44

Henry Kendall
Rich and Strange '32
The Ghost Camera '33
The Shadow '36
Amazing Adventure '37

Kay Kendall
Wings of Danger '52
Doctor in the House '53
Genevieve '53
The Shadow Man '53
Abdulla the Great '56
Les Girls '57
The Reluctant Debutante '58

Suzy Kendall
Circus of Fear '67
To Sir, with Love '67
30 Is a Dangerous Age, Cynthia '68
Assault '70
The Bird with the Crystal Plumage '70
Darker than Amber '70
Tales That Witness Madness '73
Torso '73
Craze '74
Adventures of a Private Eye '87

Tony Kendall
Island of Lost Girls '73
When the Screaming Stops '73
People Who Own the Dark '75
Return of the Evil Dead '75
Oil '78

Alexa Kenin
Honkytonk Man '82
A Piano for Mrs. Cimino '82
Pretty in Pink '86

Arthur Kennedy
City for Conquest '40
High Sierra '41
They Died with Their Boots On '41
Desperate Journey '42
Air Force '43
Boomerang '47
Champion '49
Killer Bait '49
Too Late for Tears '49
The Window '49
Bend of the River '52
The Lusty Men '52
Rancho Notorious '52
Crashout '55
Desperate Hours '55
Impulse '55
The Man from Laramie '55
Peyton Place '57
Some Came Running '58
A Summer Place '59
Elmer Gantry '60
Barabbas '62
Lawrence of Arabia '62
Murder She Said '62
Cheyenne Autumn '64
Fantastic Voyage '66
Nevada Smith '66
A Minute to Pray, A Second to Die '67
Anzio '68
Shark! '68
Hail, Hero! '69
My Old Man's Place '71
The President's Plane is Missing '71
Mean Machine '73
The Tempter '74
Emmanuelle on Taboo Island '76
Signs of Life '89

Bill Kennedy
Two Lost Worlds '50
Silver City Bonanza '51

Douglas Kennedy
South of St. Louis '48
The Land Unknown '57
Lone Ranger and the Lost City of Gold '58
The Amazing Transparent Man '60

Edgar Kennedy
Laurel & Hardy: Perfect Day '29
Laurel & Hardy: Night Owls '30
Laurel & Hardy Comedy Classics, Vol. 5 '31
Hold 'Em Jail '32
Little Orphan Annie '32
Duck Soup '33
King Kelly of the U.S.A. '34
The Silver Streak '34
Twentieth Century '34
Chasing Those Depression Blues '35
Cowboy Millionaire '35
Double Wedding '37
When's Your Birthday? '37
Peck's Bad Boy with the Circus '38
Dr. Christian Meets the Women '40
Frolics on Ice '40
Remedy for Riches '40
Blondie in Society '41
Hillbilly Blitzkrieg '42
Snuffy Smith, Yard Bird '42
Air Raid Wardens '43
The Sin of Harold Diddlebock '47
Unfaithfully Yours '48
My Dream Is Yours '49

George Kennedy
Lonely Are the Brave '62
Charade '63
Island of the Blue Dolphins '64
Strait-Jacket '64
The Flight of the Phoenix '65
In Harm's Way '65
Shenandoah '65
Mirage '66
Cool Hand Luke '67
The Dirty Dozen '67
Bandolero! '68
The Boston Strangler '68
The Good Guys and the Bad Guys '69
Guns of the Magnificent Seven '69
Hot Wire '70s
Airport '70
Cahill: United States Marshal '73
Earthquake '74
Thunderbolt & Lightfoot '74
Airport '75 '75
The Blue Knight '75
The Eiger Sanction '75
The Human Factor '75
Airport '77 '77
Brass Target '78
Death on the Nile '78
Mean Dog Blues '78
The Concorde: Airport '79 '79
The Double McGuffin '79
Death Ship '80
Just Before Dawn '80
Steel '80
Archer: The Fugitive from the Empire '81
Modern Romance '81
A Rare Breed '81
Search and Destroy '81
Virus '82
Wacko '83
Bolero '84
Chattanooga Choo Choo '84
The Jesse Owens Story '84
Proof of the Man '84
Savage Dawn '84
Delta Force '86
Radioactive Dreams '86
Counterforce '87
Creepshow 2 '87
Demonwarp '87
The Gunfighters '87
Kenny Rogers as the Gambler, Part 3: The Legend Continues '87
Nightmare at Noon '87
Private Road: No Trespassing '87
Born to Race '88
The Naked Gun: From the Files of Police Squad '88
The Terror Within '88
The Uninvited '88
Brain Dead '89
Bull of the West '89
Ministry of Vengeance '89
Driving Me Crazy '91
Hangfire '91
Hired to Kill '91
Naked Gun 2 1/2: The Smell of Fear '91
Distant Justice '92
Final Shot: The Hank Gathers Story '92
Naked Gun 33 1/3: The Final Insult '94

Gerald Kennedy
The Mango Tree '77
Puzzle '78

Gerard Kennedy
Newsfront '78
Panic Station '82
Body Melt '93

Graham Kennedy
Don's Party '76
The Club '81
Return of Captain Invincible '83

Jayne Kennedy
Group Marriage '72
The Muthers '76
Fighting Mad '77
Death Force '78
Mysterious Island of Beautiful Women '79
Body & Soul '81

June Kennedy
Sorority Girl '57
Earth vs. the Spider '58
Bloodlust '59

Leon Isaac Kennedy
Fighting Mad '77
Death Force '78
Penitentiary '79
Body & Soul '81
Penitentiary 2 '82
Lone Wolf McQuade '83
Too Scared to Scream '85
Hollywood Vice Sqaud '86
Penitentiary 3 '87
Skeleton Coast '89

Merele Kennedy
Nemesis '93
Night of the Demons 2 '94

Merna Kennedy
The Circus '19
Ghost Valley '32

Mimi Kennedy
Immediate Family '89
Pump Up the Volume '90
Death Becomes Her '92

Patricia Kennedy
The Getting of Wisdom '77
Country Life '95

Sarah Kennedy
Working Girls '75
Jack Be Nimble '94

Sheila Kennedy
First Turn On '83
Ellie '84
Dead Boyz Can't Fly '93

Tom Kennedy
Mantrap '26
Marked Money '28
Big News '29
Hollywood Party '34
Day the Bookies Wept '39
The Devil's Cargo '48
Pirate Ship '49
Invasion U.S.A. '52

James Kenney
Tough Guy '53
Above Us the Waves '56

Sean Kenney
The Corpse Grinders '71
Savage Abduction '73

Patsy Kensit
The Great Gatsby '74
Monty Python and the Holy Grail '75
Silas Marner '85
Absolute Beginners '86
A Chorus of Disapproval '89
Lethal Weapon 2 '89
Blue Tornado '90
Bullseye! '90
Chicago Joe & the Showgirl '90
Does This Mean We're Married? '90
Kill Cruise '90
Timebomb '91
Twenty-One '91
Blame It on the Bellboy '92
The Turn of the Screw '92
Bitter Harvest '93
Full Eclipse '93
Dream Man '94
Fall from Grace '94
Angels and Insects '95
Tunnel Vision '95

Barbara Kent
The Dropkick '27
The Flesh and the Devil '27
No Man's Law '27
Feet First '30
Chinatown After Dark '31
Indiscreet '31
Vanity Fair '32
Oliver Twist '33

Crauford Kent
Virtue's Revolt '24
Seven Keys to Baldplate '29
Tea for Two '50

Dorothea Kent
Danger Ahead '40
Behind the Mask '46

Elizabeth Kent
Mindwarp '91
Trapped Alive '93

Jean Kent
Sleeping Car to Trieste '45
Man of Evil '48
The Gay Lady '49
The Browning Version '51
Bonjour Tristesse '57

Keneth Kent
Dangerous Moonlight '41
House of Mystery '41

Marjorie Kent
Blondie Knows Best '46
Blondie Hits the Jackpot '49

Robert Kent
Dimples '36
Gang Bullets '38
The Gladiator '38
The Phantom Creeps '39
The Phantom Rider '46

Dambisa Kente
Cry, the Beloved Country '95
Friends '95

Doris Kenyon
A Girl's Folly '17
Monsieur Beaucaire '24

Gwen Kenyon
Meet the Mob '42
Charlie Chan in the Secret Service '44
The Great Mike '44
In Old New Mexico '45

Danny Keogh
Playing with Fire '70s
Kill Slade '89

Ken Kercheval
Judge Horton and the Scottsboro Boys '76
Too Far to Go '79
Calamity Jane '82
California Casanova '89
Corporate Affairs '90
Beretta's Island '92

Joanna Kerns
Broken Badge '85
A Bunny's Tale '85
Cross My Heart '88
The Preppie Murder '89
Street Justice '89
An American Summer '90
The Great Los Angeles Earthquake '91
The Nightman '93
No Dessert Dad, 'Til You Mow the Lawn '94

Bill Kerr
Deadline '81
Gallipoli '81
Pirate Movie '82
The Coca-Cola Kid '84
Razorback '84
Vigil '84
Dusty '85
The Lighthorsemen '87
Miracle Down Under '87
Sweet Talker '91

Deborah Kerr
The Courageous Mr. Penn '41
Love on the Dole '41
Major Barbara '41
The Day Will Dawn '42
The Life and Death of Colonel Blimp '43
I See a Dark Stranger '46
Black Narcissus '47
The Hucksters '47
King Solomon's Mines '50
Quo Vadis '51
Prisoner of Zenda '52
From Here to Eternity '53
Julius Caesar '53
Young Bess '53
The King and I '56
Tea and Sympathy '56
An Affair to Remember '57
Bonjour Tristesse '57
Separate Tables '58
Beloved Infidel '59
The Sundowners '60
The Grass is Greener '61
The Innocents '61
The Naked Edge '61
The Chalk Garden '64

The Night of the Iguana '64
Casino Royale '67
The Arrangement '69
America at the Movies '76
A Woman of Substance, Episode 1: Nest of Vipers '84
A Woman of Substance, Episode 2: The Secret is Revealed '84
A Woman of Substance, Episode 3: Fighting for the Dream '84
Hold the Dream '85

E. Katherine Kerr
Reuben, Reuben '83
Children of a Lesser God '86
Power '86
Suspect '87
The Buccaneers '95

Edward Kerr
Above Suspicion '95
Magic Island '95

John Kerr
The Cobweb '55
Tea and Sympathy '56
South Pacific '58
The Pit and the Pendulum '61

Ken Kerr
Beneath the Valley of the Ultra-Vixens '79
Thundering Ninja '80s

Linda Kerridge
Fade to Black '80
Strangers Kiss '83
Mixed Blood '84
Surf 2 '84
Alien from L.A. '87
Down Twisted '89

J.M. Kerrigan
Song O' My Heart '29
The Informer '35
The Great Man Votes '38
Fastest Gun Alive '56

John Kerry
Bad Georgia Road '77
Memorial Valley Massacre '88

Norman Kerry
The Hunchback of Notre Dame '23
Merry-Go-Round '23
The Phantom of the Opera '25
The Claw '27
The Unknown '27
Bachelor Apartment '31
Tanks a Million '41

Brian Kerwin
A Real American Hero '78
Hometown U.S.A. '79
Getting Wasted '80
Miss All-American Beauty '82
Wet Gold '84
Murphy's Romance '85
Nickel Mountain '85
King Kong Lives '86
Torch Song Trilogy '88
Code Name: Chaos '90
Love Field '91
Switched at Birth '91
Hard Promises '92
Gold Diggers: The Secret of Bear Mountain '95
Getting Away With Murder '96
Jack '96

Lance Kerwin
Reflections of Murder '74
The Loneliest Runner '76
Salem's Lot '79
Children of Divorce '80
The Mysterious Stranger '82
Shooting '82
The Snow Queen '83
Side Show '84
Enemy Mine '85
Fourth Wise Man '85

Maureen Kerwin
The Destructors '74
Reunion '88

Jillian Kesner
Firecracker '71
Starhops '78
Roots of Evil '91

Quin Kessler
She '83
Wishman '93

Sara Kestelman
Zardoz '73
Lisztomania '75
Lady Jane '85

Evelyn Keyes
Gone with the Wind '39
Union Pacific '39
Before I Hang '40
The Lady in Question '40
Slightly Honorable '40
Here Comes Mr. Jordan '41
A Thousand and One Nights '45
The Jolson Story '46
Prowler '51
The Seven Year Itch '55
Return to Salem's Lot '87
Wicked Stepmother '89

Irwin Keyes
Frankenstein General Hospital '88
The Flintstones '94
Backlash: Oblivion 2 '95

Mark Keyloun
Mike's Murder '84
Gimme an F '85
Separate Vacations '86

The Keystone Cops
The Knockout/Dough and Dynamite '14
Desperate Scoundrel/The Pride of Pikeville '22
Golden Age of Comedy '58

Persis Khambatta
Conduct Unbecoming '75
The Wilby Conspiracy '75
Star Trek: The Motion Picture '80
Nighthawks '81
Megaforce '82
Warrior of the Lost World '84
First Strike '85
Deadly Intent '88
Phoenix the Warrior '88

Arsinee Khanjian
Family Viewing '87
Speaking Parts '89
The Adjuster '91
Calendar '93
Exotica '94

Leleti Khumalo
Sarafina! '92
Cry, the Beloved Country '95

Guy Kibbee
Laughing Sinners '31
Rain '32
Scarlet Dawn '32
The Strange Love of Molly Louvain '32
Footlight Parade '33
42nd Street '33
Gold Diggers of 1933 '33
Lady for a Day '33
Dames '34
Captain Blood '35
Captain January '36
Earthworm Tractors '36
Little Lord Fauntleroy '36
Three Men on a Horse '36
Joy of Living '38
Of Human Hearts '38
Three Comrades '38
Babes in Arms '39
Let Freedom Ring '39
Mr. Smith Goes to Washington '39
Our Town '40
It Started with Eve '41
Miss Annie Rooney '42
Whistling in Dixie '42
Dixie Jamboree '44
The Horn Blows at Midnight '45
Three Godfathers '48

Michael Kidd
It's Always Fair Weather '55
Smile '75

Margot Kidder
Quackser Fortune Has a Cousin in the Bronx '70
The Bounty Man '72
Sisters '73
Quiet Day In Belfast '74
Black Christmas '75
The Great Waldo Pepper '75
The Reincarnation of Peter Proud '75
92 in the Shade '76
Superman: The Movie '78
The Amityville Horror '79
Mr. Mike's Mondo Video '79
Superman 2 '80
Willie & Phil '80
Miss Right '81
Shoot the Sun Down '81
Heartaches '82
Some Kind of Hero '82
Superman 3 '83
Trenchcoat '83
The Glitter Dome '84
Hitchhiker 2 '85
Little Treasure '85
Keeping Track '86
Louisiana '87
Superman 4: The Quest for Peace '87
Vanishing Act '88
Mob Story '90
To Catch a Killer '92
Beanstalk '94
Windrunner '94
Bloodknot '95

Nicole Kidman
BMX Bandits '83
Prince and the Great Race '83
Archer's Adventure '85
Windrider '86
Night Master '87
Dead Calm '89
Flirting '89
Days of Thunder '90
Billy Bathgate '91
Far and Away '92
Malice '93
My Life '93
Batman Forever '95
To Die For '95

Richard Kiel
The Phantom Planet '61
Eegah! '62
The Human Duplicators '64
Roustabout '64
The Longest Yard '74
Flash & Firecat '75
Silver Streak '76
The Spy Who Loved Me '77
Force 10 from Navarone '78
They Went That-a-Way & That-a-Way '78
Moonraker '79
So Fine '81
War of the Wizards '81
Hysterical '83
Mad Mission 3 '84
Pale Rider '85
Think Big '90
Happy Gilmore '96

Sue Kiel
Red Heat '85
Survivor '87

Udo Kier
Mark of the Devil '69
Andy Warhol's Dracula '74
Andy Warhol's Frankenstein '74
The House on Straw Hill '76
The Stationmaster's Wife '77
Suspiria '77
Seduction: The Cruel Woman '89
My Own Private Idaho '91
Zentropa '92
For Love or Money '93
Breaking the Waves '95
Johnny Mnemonic '95
The Kingdom '95
The Adventures of Pinocchio '96
Barb Wire '96

Robbie Kiger
Table for Five '83
Children of the Corn '84
Welcome Home, Roxy Carmichael '90

Susan Kiger
H.O.T.S. '79
Seven '79
The Return '80
House of Death '82
Death Screams '83

Percy Kilbride
George Washington Slept Here '42
Keeper of the Flame '42
The Adventures of Mark Twain '44
The Woman of the Town '44
The Southerner '45
State Fair '45
Egg and I '47
Riff-Raff '47
Welcome Stranger '47
Ma and Pa Kettle '49
Ma and Pa Kettle Go to Town '50
Riding High '50
Ma and Pa Kettle Back On the Farm '51
Ma and Pa Kettle at the Fair '52
Ma and Pa Kettle on Vacation '53
Ma and Pa Kettle at Home '54
Ma and Pa Kettle at Waikiki '55

Terence Kilburn
A Christmas Carol '38
They Shall Have Music '39
National Velvet '44
Fiend Without a Face '58

Richard Kiley
Pickup on South Street '53
Blackboard Jungle '55
Pendulum '69
Jigsaw '71
Murder Once Removed '71
The Little Prince '74
Looking for Mr. Goodbar '77
Angel on My Shoulder '80
Endless Love '81
Pray TV '82
The Thorn Birds '83
George Washington '84
The Adventures of Huckleberry Finn '85
The Bad Seed '85
Chameleon Street '89
The Final Days '89
The Canterville Ghost '91
Separate But Equal '91
Phenomenon '96

Victor Kilian
Riff Raff '35
Lady from Nowhere '36
The Adventures of Tom Sawyer '38
Dr. Cyclops '40
Young Tom Edison '40
Dangerous Passage '44
Rimfire '49
One Too Many '51
Unknown World '51

Val Kilmer
Top Secret! '84
Real Genius '85
The Murders in the Rue Morgue '86
Top Gun '86
The Man Who Broke 1,000 Chains '87
Willow '88
Gore Vidal's Billy the Kid '89
Kill Me Again '89
The Doors '91
Thunderheart '92
The Real McCoy '93
Tombstone '93
True Romance '93
Batman Forever '95
Heat '95
The Island of Dr. Moreau '96

Lincoln Kilpatrick
Deadly Force '83
Prison '88
Fortress '93

Patrick Kilpatrick
Roanoak '86
The Cellar '90
Class of 1999 '90
Death Warrant '90
3 Ninjas Knuckle Up '92
Showdown '93
Open Fire '94
Scanners: The Showdown '94
Beastmaster 3: The Eye of Braxus '95

Bobby Kim
Manchurian Avenger '84
Kill Line '91

Joon Kim
Street Soldiers '91
Gang Justice '94

Charles Kimbrough
Sunday in the Park with George '86
The Good Mother '88
Switching Channels '88

Clinton Kimbrough
Bloody Mama '70
Night Call Nurses '72

Bruce Kimmel
The First Nudie Musical '75
Spaceship '81

Dana Kimmell
Sweet 16 '81
Friday the 13th, Part 3 '82

Kenneth Kimmins
Eleanor: First Lady of the World '82
My Best Friend Is a Vampire '88

Isao Kimura
Stray Dog '49
Black Lizard '68

Aron Kincaid
Creature of Destruction '67
The Proud and the Damned '72

Kevin Kindlan
The Majorettes '87
Revenge of the Living Zombies '88
Heartstopper '92

Adrienne King
Friday the 13th '80
Friday the 13th, Part 2 '81

Alan King
The Anderson Tapes '71
How to Pick Up Girls '78
Just Tell Me What You Want '80
Pleasure Palace '80
Author! Author! '82
I, the Jury '82
Cat's Eye '85
Memories of Me '88
Enemies, a Love Story '89
The Bonfire of the Vanities '90
Night and the City '92
Casino '95
The Infiltrator '95

Andrea King
The Beast with Five Fingers '46
The Man I Love '46
Mr. Peabody & the Mermaid '48
The Lemon Drop Kid '51
Red Planet Mars '52
Band of Angels '57
House of the Black Death '65
Blackenstein '73

Atlas King
Incredibly Strange Creatures Who Stopped Living and Became Mixed-Up Zombies '63
The Thrill Killers '65

Brad King
Outlaws of the Desert '41
Riders of the Timberline '41
Twilight on the Trail '41

Charles King
Broadway Melody '29
The Silver Bullet '34

Charles "Blackie" King
Oklahoma Cyclone '30
Branded Men '31
The Pocatello Kid '31
Range Law '31
Two Gun Man '31
Outlaw Justice '32
Fighting Champ '33
Young Blood '33
Fighting Parson '35
Trail of Terror '35
Desert Phantom '36
Headin' for the Rio Grande '36
Last of the Warrens '36
The Lawless Nineties '36
Lucky Terror '36
Red River Valley '36
Rip Roarin' Buckaroo '36
The Gambling Terror '37
God's Country and the Man '37
Hittin' the Trail '37
A Lawman Is Born '37
Lightning Bill Crandall '37
Mystery of the Hooded Horseman '37
The Red Rope '37
Riders of the Rockies '37
Ridin' the Lone Trail '37
Santa Fe Bound '37
Gun Packer '38
The Phantom of the Range '38
Songs and Bullets '38
Thunder in the Desert '38

King ▶cont.

Down the Wyoming Trail '39
Mesquite Buckaroo '39
Trigger Pals '39
Wild Horse Canyon '39
Death Rides the Range '40
Dead or Alive '41
Trigger Men '41
Along the Sundown Trail '42
Arizona Stagecoach '42
Below the Border '42
Prairie Pals '42
Trail Riders '42
Where Trails End '42
Texas Kid '43
Devil Riders '44
Frontier Outlaws '44
Oath of Vengeance '44
Rustler's Hideout '44
Wild Horse Phantom '44
Border Badmen '45
Gangster's Den '45
His Brother's Ghost '45
Three in the Saddle '45
Ambush Trail '46
The Caravan Trail '46
Colorado Serenade '46
Outlaw of the Plains '46

Charmion King
Who Has Seen the Wind? '77
Anne of Green Gables '85

Damu King
Black Godfather '74
Black Starlet '74
Blackjack '78

Dave King
Naughty Knights '71
The Long Good Friday '79
Revolution '85

Erik King
Casualties of War '89
Joey Breaker '93

Joe King
Shifting Sands '18
Until They Get Me '18
Woman in the Shadows '34
Alexander's Ragtime Band '38

John "Dusty" King
Ace Drummond '36
Half a Soldier '40
Midnight Limited '40
Trailing Double Trouble '40
West of Pinto Basin '40
Fugitive Valley '41
Kid's Last Ride '41
Saddle Mountain Round-Up '41
Tonto Basin Outlaws '41
Trail of the Silver Spurs '41
Tumbledown Ranch in Arizona '41
Underground Rustlers '41
Arizona Stagecoach '42
Boot Hill Bandits '42
Law of the Jungle '42
Rock River Renegades '42
Texas to Bataan '42
Thunder River Feud '42
Trail Riders '42
Haunted Ranch '43
Two-Fisted Justice '43

Kenneth King
Polyester '81
Jade '95

Leslie King
Gas Pump Girls '79
Cotton Candy '82

Mabel King
Black Vampire '73
The Wiz '78
Dead Men Don't Die '91

Meegan King
Sweater Girls '78
Money to Burn '83

Morgana King
The Godfather '72
The Godfather, Part 2 '74
A Time to Remember '90

Perry King
The Possession of Joel Delaney '72
Slaughterhouse Five '72
The Lords of Flatbush '74
Wild Party '74
Mandingo '75
Lipstick '76
Andy Warhol's Bad '77
The Choirboys '77
Different Story '78
The Cracker Factory '79
Love's Savage Fury '79
City in Fear '80
Search and Destroy '81
Class of 1984 '82
Killing Hour '84
The Hasty Heart '86
Disaster at Silo 7 '88
The Prize Pulitzer '89
Switch '91
Danielle Steel's Kaleidoscope '92
A Cry in the Night '93
Jericho Fever '93

Regina King
Poetic Justice '93
Higher Learning '94
Friday '95
A Thin Line Between Love and Hate '96

Rowena King
Wide Sargasso Sea '92
To Play the King '93

Stephen King
Creepshow '82
Creepshow 2 '87
Pet Sematary '89

Tony King
Gordon's War '73
Report to the Commissioner '74
Sparkle '76
The Last Hunter '80

Walter Woolf King
A Night at the Opera '35
Swiss Miss '38
Smart Alecks '42
Today I Hang '42
Yank in Libya '42

Wright King
Wanted: Dead or Alive '59
Dangerous Charter '62
Invasion of the Bee Girls '73

Zalman King
Some Call It Loving '73
Deadly Fieldtrip '74
Smile, Jenny, You're Dead '74
The Passover Plot '75
Ski Bum '75
Blue Sunshine '78
Galaxy of Terror '81

King John III
Black Bikers from Hell '70
The Outlaw Bikers—Gang Wars '70
Psycho from Texas '83

Walter Kingsford
The Invisible Ray '36
The Story of Louis Pasteur '36
It Could Happen to You '37
The Man in the Iron Mask '39
My Favorite Blonde '42
Velvet Touch '48

Ben Kingsley
Hard Labour '73
Gandhi '82
Betrayal '83
Harem '85
Silas Marner '85
Turtle Diary '86
Maurice '87
Pascali's Island '88
Without a Clue '88
Murderers among Us: The Simon Wiesenthal Story '89
Slipstream '89
The Children '90
The Fifth Monkey '90
Bugsy '91
Sneakers '92
Dave '93
Schindler's List '93
Searching for Bobby Fischer '93
Death and the Maiden '94
Joseph '95
Species '95

Danitza Kingsley
Amazons '86
Jack's Back '87
South of Reno '87

Susan Kingsley
The Dollmaker '84
Old Enough '84

Alex Kingston
Carrington '95
The Infiltrator '95

Natalie Kingston
All Night Long/Smile Please '24
Baby Face Harry Langdon '26
His First Flame '26
Tarzan the Tiger '29
His Private Secretary '33

Sam Kinison
Back to School '86
It's a Bundyful Life '92

Kathleen Kinmont
Hardbodies '84
Fraternity Vacation '85
Phoenix the Warrior '88
Rush Week '88
Bride of Re-Animator '89
SnakeEater 2: The Drug Buster '89
The Art of Dying '90
Roller Blade Warriors: Taken By Force '90
Final Impact '91
Night of the Warrior '91
C.I.A.: Code Name Alexa '92
Sweet Justice '92
Final Round '93
C.I.A. 2: Target Alexa '94
Stormswept '95
Texas Payback '95

Roy Kinnear
Taste the Blood of Dracula '70
Melody '71
Willy Wonka & the Chocolate Factory '71
Juggernaut '74
The Four Musketeers '75
Ripping Yarns '75
Herbie Goes to Monte Carlo '77
The Hound of the Baskervilles '77
The Adventures of Sherlock Holmes' Smarter Brother '78
Hawk the Slayer '81
The Zany Adventures of Robin Hood '84
Pirates '86
A Man for All Seasons '88
The Return of the Musketeers '89

Terry Kinney
Murder Ordained '87
Talent for the Game '91
Body Snatchers '93
The Firm '93
JFK: Reckless Youth '93
Devil In a Blue Dress '95
The Good Old Boys '95

Leonid Kinskey
Duck Soup '33
Les Miserables '35
The Great Waltz '38
Everything Happens at Night '39
Down Argentine Way '40
Broadway Limited '41
I Married an Angel '42
Lady for a Night '42
Somewhere I'll Find You '42

Klaus Kinski
A Time to Love & a Time to Die '58
And God Said to Cain '60s
Twice a Judas '60s
The Avenger '60
Dead Eyes of London '61
Door with the Seven Locks '62
Inn on the River '62
The Indian Scarf '63
Doctor Zhivago '65
Fighting Fists of Shanghai Joe '65
For a Few Dollars More '65
The Squeaker '65
Target for Killing '66
Circus of Fear '67
Fistful of Death '67
Five for Hell '67
Five Golden Dragons '67
Heroes in Hell '67
A Bullet for the General '68
Deadly Sanctuary '68
Psychopath '68
Creature with the Blue Hand '70
Double Face '70
The Ruthless Four '70
Venus in Furs '70
Web of the Spider '70
Count Dracula '71
Slaughter Hotel '71
Aguirre, the Wrath of God '72
Shoot the Living, Pray for the Dead '73
Primal Impulse '74
Lifespan '75
Liberators '77
Night of the Assassin '77
Operation Thunderbolt '77
Woyzeck '78
The French Woman '79
Jack the Ripper '80
Schizoid '80
Buddy Buddy '81
Android '82
Burden of Dreams '82
Fitzcarraldo '82
The Soldier '82
Venom '82
Beauty and the Beast '83
Codename: Wildgeese '84
The Little Drummer Girl '84
The Secret Diary of Sigmund Freud '84
Creature '85
His Name was King '85
Crawlspace '86
Gangster's Law '86
Rough Justice '87
Timestalkers '87

Nastassia Kinski
To the Devil, A Daughter '76
Stay As You Are '78
The Wrong Move '78
For Your Love Only '79
Tess '80
Cat People '82
One from the Heart '82
Boarding School '83
Exposed '83
Moon in the Gutter '83
Paris, Texas '83
The Hotel New Hampshire '84
Maria's Lovers '84
Unfaithfully Yours '84
Harem '85
Revolution '85
Spring Symphony '86
Magdalene '88
Torrents of Spring '90
Faraway, So Close! '93
Crackerjack '94
Terminal Velocity '94

Bruce Kirby
The Young Graduates '71
Cinderella Liberty '73
Fyre '78
Armed and Dangerous '86
Throw Momma from the Train '87
Getting Up and Going Home '92
Rave Review '95

Bruno Kirby
Harrad Experiment '73
The Godfather, Part 2 '74
Between the Lines '77
Borderline '80
The Godfather 1902-1959: The Complete Epic '81
Modern Romance '81
Kiss My Grits '82
Birdy '84
This Is Spinal Tap '84
Flesh and Blood '85
Good Morning, Vietnam '87
Tin Men '87
Nitti: The Enforcer '88
Bert Rigby, You're a Fool '89
We're No Angels '89
When Harry Met Sally... '89
The Freshman '90
City Slickers '91
Fallen Angels 2 '93
Golden Gate '93
The Basketball Diaries '94

Jay Kirby
Border Patrol '43
Colt Comrades '43
Hoppy Serves a Writ '43
Leather Burners '43
Lost Canyon '43
Sundown Riders '48

Michael Kirby
The Girl in Blue '74
Another Woman '88
Swoon '91
Shadows and Fog '92

Joe Kirk
Smart Alecks '42
The Naughty Nineties '45
The Noose Hangs High '48

Phyllis Kirk
A Life of Her Own '50
Two Weeks with Love '50
Three Guys Named Mike '51
House of Wax '53
River Beat '54
Back from Eternity '56
The Sad Sack '57

Tommy Kirk
Old Yeller '57
The Shaggy Dog '59
The Swiss Family Robinson '60
The Absent-Minded Professor '61
Babes in Toyland '61
Horsemasters '61
Bon Voyage! '62
Escapade in Florence '62
Moon Pilot '62
The Misadventures of Merlin Jones '63
Savage Sam '63
Son of Flubber '63
Pajama Party '64
Monkey's Uncle '65
Village of the Giants '65
Mars Needs Women '66
The Unkissed Bride '66
It's Alive! '68
Blood of Ghastly Horror '72

Donald Kirke
Country Gentlemen '36
Oh Susannah '38
A Night for Crime '42

Sally Kirkland
Blue '68
Futz '69
Cinderella Liberty '73
The Way We Were '73
The Young Nurses '73
Big Bad Mama '74
Bite the Bullet '75
Death Scream '75
Kansas City Massacre '75
Breakheart Pass '76
Pipe Dreams '76
A Star is Born '76
Hometown U.S.A. '79
Private Benjamin '80
Love Letters '83
Fatal Games '84
Talking Walls '85
Anna '87
White Hot '88
Best of the Best '89
Cold Feet '89
High Stakes '89
Paint It Black '89
Bullseye! '90
Heat Wave '90
Revenge '90
In the Heat of Passion '91
JFK '91
Double Jeopardy '92
Double Threat '92
Forever: A Ghost of a Love Story '92
Hit the Dutchman '92
Primary Motive '92
Prime Time Murder '92
Cheatin' Hearts '93
Eye of the Stranger '93
Gunmen '93

Jack Kirkwood
Fancy Pants '50
Never a Dull Moment '50

Rudiger Kirschstein
An Occurrence at Owl Creek Bridge/Coup de Grace '62
Coup de Grace '78

Mia Kirshner
Cadillac Girls '93
Love and Human Remains '93
Exotica '94
Johnny's Girl '95
Murder In the First '95
The Crow 2: City of Angels '96

Terry Kiser
Steel '80
Making Love '82
Starflight One '83

Surf 2 '84
The Offspring '87
Weekend at Bernie's '89
Mannequin 2: On the Move '91
Into the Sun '92
Weekend at Bernie's 2 '93
Pet Shop '94
Tammy and the T-Rex '94

Keiko Kishi
Snow Country '57
Qui Etes Vous, Mr. Sorge? '61
Kwaidan '64
Master Mind '73
The Makioka Sisters '83

Kyoko Kishida
The Human Condition: A Soldier's Prayer '61
Woman in the Dunes '64

Charles Kissinger
Asylum of Satan '72
Three on a Meathook '72
Sheba, Baby '75
Grizzly '76

Tawny Kitaen
Bachelor Party '84
The Perils of Gwendoline '84
Instant Justice '86
Crystal Heart '87
Glory Years '87
Happy Hour '87
Witchboard '87
White Hot '88
Playback '95

Michael Kitchen
Out of Africa '85
The Dive '89
Fools of Fortune '90
The Russia House '90
Enchanted April '92
To Play the King '93
Doomsday Gun '94
Fatherland '94
The Buccaneers '95
Goldeneye '95

Eartha Kitt
New Faces of 1952 '54
The Mark of the Hawk '57
Naughty Knights '71
The Pink Chiquitas '86
Dragonard '88
Erik the Viking '89
Master of Dragonard Hill '89
Ernest Scared Stupid '91
Boomerang '92
Harriet the Spy '96

John Kitzmiller
Jungle Master '56
Dr. No '62
Cave of the Living Dead '65
Uncle Tom's Cabin '69

Bjorn Kjellman
The Best Intentions '92
All Things Fair '95

Gerard Klein
La Passante '83
Frantic '88

Robert Klein
The Owl and the Pussycat '70
The Pursuit of Happiness '70
Rivals '72
Hooper '78
The Bell Jar '79
Nobody's Perfekt '79
Pajama Tops '83
Your Place or Mine '83
Table Settings '84
Poison Ivy '85
Dangerous Curves '88
A Secret Space '88
The Marx Brothers in a Nutshell '90
Tales from the Darkside: The Movie '90
Mixed Nuts '94

Rudolf Klein-Rogge
Dr. Mabuse, Parts 1 & 2 '22
Kriemhilde's Revenge '24
Metropolis '26
Spies '28
Crimes of Dr. Mabuse '32
Das Testament des Dr. Mabuse '33

Henry Kleinbach (Brandon)
March of the Wooden Soldiers '34
The Garden of Allah '36

Kevin Kline
Sophie's Choice '82
The Big Chill '83
The Pirates of Penzance '83
Silverado '85
Violets Are Blue '86
Cry Freedom '87
A Fish Called Wanda '88
The January Man '89
I Love You to Death '90
Grand Canyon '91
Soapdish '91
Chaplin '92
Consenting Adults '92
Dave '93
Princess Caraboo '94
French Kiss '95

Heidi Kling
The Mighty Ducks '92
Out on a Limb '92

Jack Klugman
Justice '55
Twelve Angry Men '57
Days of Wine and Roses '62
I Could Go on Singing '63
The Detective '68
Goodbye Columbus '69
One of My Wives Is Missing '76
Two Minute Warning '76
Around the World in 80 Days '89
Parallel Lives '94

Vincent Klyn
Cyborg '89
Dollman '90
Bloodmatch '91
Point Break '91
Nemesis '93

Skelton Knaggs
Bowery at Midnight/Dick Tracy vs. Cueball '42
Forever Amber '47

Evalyn Knapp
The Strange Love of Molly Louvain '32
His Private Secretary '33
In Old Santa Fe '34
The Perils of Pauline '34
Confidential '35
Bulldog Edition '36
Mistaken Identity '36
Hawaiian Buckaroo '38
Rawhide '38

Robert Knapp
Lady Scarface/The Threat '49
Mesa of Lost Women '52

David Knell
Bitter Harvest '81
Spring Break '83

Rob Knepper
That's Life! '86
Wild Thing '87
Renegades '89
Young Guns 2 '90
Gas Food Lodging '92
Where the Day Takes You '92
Getting Out '94

Christopher Knight
Studs Lonigan '60
The Brady Bunch '69
A Very Brady Christmas '88
Good Girls Don't '95

Damien Knight
The Redeemer '76
Class Reunion Massacre '77

David Knight
Across the Bridge '57
Nightmare '63
Demons 2 '87
Who Shot Pat? '92

Esmond Knight
The Arsenal Stadium Mystery '39
A Canterbury Tale '44
Henry V '44
Black Narcissus '47
Hamlet '48
The Red Shoes '48
The River '51
Sink the Bismarck '60
Peeping Tom '63

The Element of Crime '84

Fuzzy Knight
To the Last Man '33
Kelly of the Secret Service '36
Song of the Gringo '36
Song of the Trail '36
The Cowboy and the Lady '38
Oregon Trail '39
Pony Post '40
Riders of Pasco Basin '40
Boss of Bullion City '41
Bury Me Not On the Lone Prairie '41
Man from Montana '41
The Masked Rider '41
Frontier Law '43
Take It Big '44
Bad Men of the Border '45
The Adventures of Gallant Bess '48
Rimfire '49
Blazing Guns '50
Hills of Oklahoma '50
Marshal of Heldorado '50
Oklahoma Annie '51
Naked Hills '56

Gladys Knight
Pipe Dreams '76
Twenty Bucks '93

Harlan E. Knight
The Fighting Sheriff '31
Whistlin' Dan '32

Lily Knight
Static '87
An Unremarkable Life '89

Michael E. Knight
Date with an Angel '87
Hexed '93

Sandra Knight
Frankenstein's Daughter '58
Thunder Road '58
The Terror '63
Track of the Vampire '66

Shirley Knight
Ice Palace '60
Sweet Bird of Youth '62
The Group '66
Dutchman '67
Petulia '68
The Rain People '69
Secrets '71
Juggernaut '74
Return to Earth '76
21 Hours at Munich '76
Beyond the Poseidon Adventure '79
Endless Love '81
The Sender '82
Color of Night '94
Stuart Saves His Family '94
A Good Day to Die '95
Indictment: The McMartin Trial '95
Diabolique '96

Ted Knight
Psycho '60
Countdown '68
Caddyshack '80

Trenton Knight
Charlie's Ghost: The Secret of Coronado '94
The Tin Soldier '95

Tuesday Knight
A Nightmare on Elm Street 4: Dream Master '88
Cover Story '93

Wayne Knight
Dead Again '91
JFK '91
Basic Instinct '92
Fallen Angels 2 '93
Jurassic Park '93
Chameleon '95
To Die For '95

William Knight
Action U.S.A. '89
The Lost Platoon '89

Wyatt Knight
Porky's '82
Porky's 2: The Next Day '83
Porky's Revenge '85

Andrew Knott
The Secret Garden '93
Black Beauty '94

Don Knotts
No Time for Sergeants '58
Andy Griffith Show '60
The Incredible Mr. Limpet '64
The Ghost and Mr. Chicken '66
The Reluctant Astronaut '67
The Shakiest Gun in the West '68
The Love God? '70
The Apple Dumpling Gang '75
No Deposit, No Return '76
Herbie Goes to Monte Carlo '77
Hot Lead & Cold Feet '78
The Apple Dumpling Gang Rides Again '79
Prize Fighter '79
The Private Eyes '80
Return to Mayberry '85
Big Bully '95

Patric Knowles
The Charge of the Light Brigade '36
The Adventures of Robin Hood '38
The Sisters '38
Beauty for the Asking '39
Five Came Back '39
How Green Was My Valley '41
The Wolf Man '41
Frankenstein Meets the Wolfman '42
Who Done It? '42
Hit the Ice '43
Monsieur Beaucaire '46
Big Steal '49
Three Came Home '50
Mutiny '52
Band of Angels '57
Auntie Mame '58
The Devil's Brigade '68
Chisum '70

Alexander Knox
The Sea Wolf '41
Commandos Strike at Dawn '43
Wilson '44
Sister Kenny '46
The Judge Steps Out '49
Tokyo Joe '49
I'd Climb the Highest Mountain '51
Man in the Saddle '51
Europa '51 '52
The Sleeping Tiger '54
Alias John Preston '56
Reach for the Sky '56
The Vikings '58
The Wreck of the Mary Deare '59
Operation Amsterdam '60
The Longest Day '62
Khartoum '66
Accident '67
Shalako '68
Nicholas and Alexandra '71
Puppet on a Chain '72
The Chosen '77
Cry of the Innocent '80
Joshua Then and Now '85

Elyse Knox
Tanks a Million '41
The Mummy's Tomb '42
Don Winslow of the Coast Guard '43
Hit the Ice '43
Joe's Bed-Stuy Barbershop: We Cut Heads '83

Mickey Knox
Western Pacific Agent '51
Frankenstein Unbound '90

Terence Knox
Circle of Power '83
Humanoid Defender '85
Rebel Love '85
City Killer '87
Distortions '87
The Mighty Pawns '87
Murder Ordained '87
Tour of Duty '87
Hard Rain-The Tet 1968 '89
Tripwire '89
Snow Kill '90
Children of the Corn 2: The Final Sacrifice '92
Forever: A Ghost of a Love Story '92
Murder So Sweet '93
The Spy Within '94
The Invaders '95

Peggy Knudsen
The Big Sleep '46
Humoresque '46
Never Say Goodbye '46
A Stolen Life '46
Copper Canyon '50
Istanbul '57

Gustav Knuth
Tromba, the Tiger Man '52
Heidi '65

Keiju Kobayashi
Tidal Wave '75
Godzilla 1985 '85

Jeff Kober
Out of Bounds '86
Alien Nation '88
China Beach '88
Lucky Stiff '88
The First Power '89
The Baby Doll Murders '92
Keep the Change '92
Lone Justice '93
Automatic '94
Tank Girl '94
One Man's Justice '95

Marianne Koch
A Fistful of Dollars '64
Frozen Alive '64
The Monster of London City '64
A Place Called Glory '66

Walter Koenig
Star Trek Bloopers '69
Star Trek: The Motion Picture '80
Star Trek 2: The Wrath of Khan '82
Star Trek 3: The Search for Spock '84
Star Trek 4: The Voyage Home '86
Moontrap '89
Star Trek 5: The Final Frontier '89
Star Trek 6: The Undiscovered Country '91
Star Trek Generations '94

Michiyo Kogure
A Geisha '53
Shin Heike Monogatari '55
Street of Shame '56

Fred Kohler, Sr.
Anna Christie '23
Riders of the Purple Sage '25
Underworld '27
Fighting Caravans '31
Texas Bad Man '32
Deluge '33
The Fiddlin' Buckaroo '33
Honor of the Range '34
The Texas Rangers '36

Fred Kohler, Jr.
The Man from Hell '34
Pecos Kid '35
Toll of the Desert '35
Western Mail '42
Calling Wild Bill Elliott '43
Daniel Boone: Trail Blazer '56

Susan Kohner
Dino '57
The Gene Krupa Story '59
Imitation of Life '59

Hiroshi Koizumi
Attack of the Mushroom People '63
Godzilla vs. Mothra '64
Dagora, the Space Monster '65

Clarence Kolb
Give Me a Sailor '38
Honolulu '39
His Girl Friday '40
Caught in the Draft '41

Henry Kolker
Coquette '29
Rasputin and the Empress '32
Baby Face '33
The Ghost Walks '34
Charlie Chan in Paris '35
Mad Love '35
The Mystery Man '35
The Cowboy and the Lady '38
Union Pacific '39

Amos Kollek
Goodbye, New York '85
Double Edge '92
Whore 2 '94

Tetsu Komai
Hong Kong Nights '35
The Princess Comes Across '36

Hosei Komatsu
Double Suicide '69
A Taxing Woman's Return '88

Liliana Komorowska
Scanners 3: The Takeover '92
Martial Outlaw '93

Maja Komorowska
Family Life '71
Maids of Wilko '79
Year of the Quiet Sun '84

Queen Kong
Deathstalker 2: Duel of the Titans '87
Slashdance '89

Magda Konopka
Satanik '69
When Dinosaurs Ruled the Earth '70

Phyllis Konstam
Murder '30
Skin Game '31

Guich Koock
Seven '79
American Ninja '85
Square Dance '87
Picasso Trigger '89

Milos Kopecky
Fabulous Adventures of Baron Munchausen '61
The Original Fabulous Adventures of Baron Munchausen '61

Bernie Kopell
The Loved One '65
The Love Boat '70s
Combat Academy '86
Get Smart, Again! '89

Karen Kopins
Creator '85
Once Bitten '85
Jake Speed '86
Lady in Waiting '94

Arnold Korff
The Haunted Castle '21
Doughboys '30

Jon Korkes
Little Murders '71
The Day of the Dolphin '73
Jaws of Satan '81
Syngenor '90

Harvey Korman
April Fools '69
Blazing Saddles '74
Huckleberry Finn '74
High Anxiety '77
Bud and Lou '78
Americathon '79
Herbie Goes Bananas '80
History of the World: Part 1 '81
Curse of the Pink Panther '83
Gone are the Days '84
Film House Fever '86
The Longshot '86
Munchies '87
Betrayal of the Dove '92
Based on an Untrue Story '93
Dracula: Dead and Loving It '95

Mary Kornman
The Return of Our Gang '25
Our Gang '26
The Adventurous Knights '35
Desert Trail '35
Queen of the Jungle '35
Swing It, Professor '37
Our Gang Comedy Festival '88
Our Gang Comedy Festival 2 '89

Charlie Korsmo
Men Don't Leave '89
Dick Tracy '90
Heat Wave '90
The Doctor '91
Hook '91
What About Bob? '91

Robert F. (Bob) Kortman
Island of Lost Souls '32
The Lone Defender '32
The Fiddlin' Buckaroo '33
Phantom Thunderbolt '33
Rainbow Ranch '33
Terror Trail '33
When a Man Sees Red '34
The Crimson Trail '35
Feud of the West '35
Robinson Crusoe of Clipper Island '36
The Rangers Step In '37
Sandflow '37
Law of the Texan '38
Hopalong Cassidy: Renegade Trail '39
Fugitive Valley '41
Guns of the Law '44

Fritz Kortner
Backstairs '21
Warning Shadows '23
The Hands of Orlac '25
Pandora's Box '28
Woman in Brown '48

Charles Korvin
Berlin Express '48
Ship of Fools '65

Sylva Koscina
Hercules '58
Hercules Unchained '59
Juliet of the Spirits '65
Deadly Sanctuary '68
The Secret War of Harry Frigg '68
Hornet's Nest '70
The Slasher '74
Lisa and the Devil '75

Martin Kosleck
Foreign Correspondent '40
All Through the Night '42
The Mummy's Curse '44
Pursuit to Algiers '45
House of Horrors '46
The Flesh Eaters '64

Paul Koslo
Omega Man '71
Vanishing Point '71
Joe Kidd '72
Rooster Cogburn '75
Maniac '77
Roots: The Next Generation '79
The Annihilators '85
A Night in the Life of Jimmy Reardon '88
Robot Jox '90
Xtro 2: The Second Encounter '91
Chained Heat 2 '92
Project: Shadowchaser '92

David Kossoff
Svengali '55
The Mouse That Roared '59
The Two Faces of Dr. Jekyll '60
Unicorn '83

Kane Kosugi
Revenge of the Ninja '83
Pray for Death '85
Journey of Honor '91

Sho Kosugi
Shaolin Temple Strikes Back '72
Master Ninja '78
Eagle Claws Champion '80s
Kingfisher the Killer '80s
Phoenix the Ninja '80s
Enter the Ninja '81
Revenge of the Ninja '83
Ninja 3: The Domination '84
Nine Deaths of the Ninja '85
Pray for Death '85
Rage of Honor '87
Aloha Summer '88
Black Eagle '88
Blind Fury '90
The Deadliest Art: The Best of the Martial Arts Films '90
Journey of Honor '91

Elias Koteas
Some Kind of Wonderful '87
Blood Red '88
Full Moon in Blue Water '88
Tucker: The Man and His Dream '88
Friends, Lovers & Lunatics '89
Malarek '89
Almost an Angel '90
Desperate Hours '90
Look Who's Talking, Too '90
Teenage Mutant Ninja Turtles: The Movie '90
The Adjuster '91
Chain of Desire '93
Cyborg 2 '93
Teenage Mutant Ninja Turtles 3 '93
Camilla '94
Exotica '94
Power of Attorney '94
Crash '95
The Prophecy '95
Sugartime '95

Oded Kotler
My Michael '75
Hanna K. '83

Yaphet Kotto
Nothing But a Man '64
Five Card Stud '68
The Thomas Crown Affair '68
Man & Boy '71
Across 110th Street '72
Housewife '72
Live and Let Die '73
Report to the Commissioner '74
Truck Turner '74
Friday Foster '75
Sharks' Treasure '75
Drum '76
Monkey Hustle '77
Raid on Entebbe '77
Blue Collar '78
Alien '79
Brubaker '80
Rage '80
Fighting Back '82
The Star Chamber '83
Badge of the Assassin '85
The Park is Mine '85
Warning Sign '85
Eye of the Tiger '86
Harem '86
Prettykill '87
The Running Man '87
Terminal Entry '87
Midnight Run '88
A Whisper to a Scream '88
Jigsaw Murders '89
Ministry of Vengeance '89
Tripwire '89
After the Shock '90
Freddy's Dead: The Final Nightmare '91
Hangfire '91
Chrome Soldiers '92
Almost Blue '93
Extreme Justice '93
In Self Defense '93
Dead Badge '94
The Puppet Masters '94
Out of Sync '95
Two If by Sea '95

Hubert Kounde
Cafe au Lait '94
Hate '95

Nancy Kovack
Diary of a Madman '63
Jason and the Argonauts '63
Frankie and Johnny '65
The Outlaws is Coming! '65

Ernie Kovacs
Best of Ernie Kovacs '56
Bell, Book and Candle '58
North to Alaska '60
Strangers When We Meet '60

Geza Kovacs
Baby on Board '92
Return to the Lost World '93

Martin Kove
Seven '79
The Karate Kid '84
Rambo: First Blood, Part 2 '85
The Karate Kid: Part 2 '86
Steele Justice '87
The Karate Kid: Part 3 '89
White Light '90
Firehawk '92
Project: Shadowchaser '92
Future Shock '93
The Outfit '93
President's Target '93
Shootfighter: Fight to the Death '93
To Be the Best '93
Death Match '94
Endangered '94
Uncivilized '94
Wyatt Earp '94
Wyatt Earp: Return to Tombstone '94
Final Equinox '95
Without Mercy '95

Harley Jane Kozak
Parenthood '89
When Harry Met Sally... '89
Arachnophobia '90
Side Out '90
All I Want for Christmas '91
Necessary Roughness '91
The Taking of Beverly Hills '91
The Favor '92
The Amy Fisher Story '93
The Android Affair '95
Magic in the Water '95

Linda Kozlowski
Crocodile Dundee '86
Target: Favorite Son '87
Crocodile Dundee 2 '88
Pass the Ammo '88
Almost an Angel '90
Backstreet Justice '93
The Neighbor '93
Village of the Damned '95

Jeroen Krabbe
Soldier of Orange '78
The 4th Man '79
A Flight of Rainbirds '81
No Mercy '86
Turtle Diary '86
Code Name: Dancer '87
The Living Daylights '87
Crossing Delancey '88
A World Apart '88
Scandal '89
The Punisher '90
Secret Weapon '90
Kafka '91
The Prince of Tides '91
Robin Hood '91
Till There was You '91
Stalin '92
For a Lost Soldier '93
The Fugitive '93
King of the Hill '93
Farinelli '94
Immortal Beloved '94

Jane Krakowski
No Big Deal '83
Stepping Out '91

Eric Allen Kramer
Quest for the Mighty Sword '90
The Comrades of Summer '92
Robin Hood: Men in Tights '93

Jeffrey Kramer
Hollywood Boulevard '76
Halloween 2: The Nightmare Isn't Over! '81

Robert Krantz
Paradise Motel '84
Winners Take All '87

Brian Krause
December '91
Return to the Blue Lagoon '91
Sleepwalkers '92
The Liar's Club '93
Naked Souls '95

Werner Krauss
The Cabinet of Dr. Caligari '19
Shattered '21
Othello '22
Waxworks '24
Joyless Street '25
Secrets of a Soul '25
Variety '25
Jud Suess '40

Connie Kreski
The Trackers '71
Black Bird '75

Kurt Kreuger
Mademoiselle Fifi '44
Dark Corner '46
Unfaithfully Yours '48

Elisabeth Kreuzer
Alice in the Cities '74
Kings of the Road—In the Course of Time '76
The American Friend '77
Basileus Quartet '82
Birgitt Haas Must Be Killed '83
A Man Like Eva '83

David Kriegel
Alive '93
Quest of the Delta Knights '93
Speed '94

Anneline Kriel
Kill and Kill Again '81
Reason to Die '90

Alice Krige
A Tale of Two Cities '80
Chariots of Fire '81
Ghost Story '81
King David '85
Barfly '87
Haunted Summer '88
See You in the Morning '89
Code Name: Chaos '90
Max and Helen '90
Iran: Days of Crisis '91
Ladykiller '92
Sleepwalkers '92
Sharpe's Honour '94
Donor Unknown '95
Joseph '95

Sylvia Kristel
Because of the Cats '74
Emmanuelle '74
Emmanuelle, the Joys of a Woman '76
The Concorde: Airport '79 '79
The Fifth Musketeer '79
Goodbye Emmanuelle '79
The Nude Bomb '80
Tigers in Lipstick '80
Lady Chatterley's Lover '81
Private Lessons '81
Private School '83
Emmanuelle 4 '84
Mysteries '84
The Big Bet '85
Mata Hari '85
Red Heat '85
Game of Seduction '86
Casanova '87
Dracula's Widow '88
Hot Blood '89
Beauty School '93

Marta Kristen
Savage Sam '63
Beach Blanket Bingo '65
Terminal Island '73
Gemini Affair '80s

Romano Kristoff
Bruce's Fists of Vengeance '84
Warbus '85
Slash '87

Kris Kristofferson
The Last Movie '71
Blume in Love '73
Pat Garrett & Billy the Kid '73
Alice Doesn't Live Here Anymore '74
Bring Me the Head of Alfredo Garcia '74
The Sailor Who Fell from Grace with the Sea '76
A Star is Born '76
Semi-Tough '77
Convoy '78
Freedom Road '79
Heaven's Gate '81
Rollover '81
Act of Passion: The Lost Honor of Kathryn Beck '83
Flashpoint '84
Songwriter '84
Last Days of Frank & Jesse James '86
Stagecoach '86
Trouble in Mind '86
Big Top Pee Wee '88
The Tracker '88
Millenium '89
Welcome Home '89
Night of the Cyclone '90
Pair of Aces '90
Another Pair of Aces: Three of a Kind '91
Miracle in the Wilderness '91
Original Intent '91
Christmas in Connecticut '92
Cheatin' Hearts '93
Knights '93
No Place to Hide '93
Sodbusters '94
Lone Star '95
Pharoah's Army '95
The Road Home '95

Berry Kroeger
Gun Crazy '49
Guilty of Treason '50
Blood Alley '55

Yellowneck '55
The Incredible Two-Headed Transplant '71
Demon Seed '77

Gary Kroeger
Best of Eddie Murphy '89
A Man Called Sarge '90
Secret Ingredient '92

Josef Kroner
The Shop on Main Street '65
Another Way '82

Margareta Krook
Persona '66
The Adventures of Picasso '80
Pay Off '89

Alma Kruger
Craig's Wife '36
100 Men and a Girl '37
The Great Waltz '38
Forever Amber '47

Hardy Kruger
Liana, Jungle Goddess '56
One That Got Away '57
Bachelor of Hearts '58
Hatari! '62
Sundays & Cybele '62
The Flight of the Phoenix '65
Battle of Neretva '69
Red Tent '69
What the Peeper Saw '72
Paper Tiger '74
Barry Lyndon '75
A Bridge Too Far '77
Blue Fin '78
Wild Geese '78
Wrong is Right '82
The Inside Man '84

Otto Kruger
The Prizefighter and the Lady '33
Chained '34
Treasure Island '34
Dracula's Daughter '36
They Won't Forget '37
Housemaster '38
I Am the Law '38
Another Thin Man '39
Black Eyes '39
Saboteur '42
Corregidor '43
Hitler's Children '43
Cover Girl '44
Murder, My Sweet '44
The Woman Who Came Back '45
Wonder Man '45
High Noon '52
The Young Philadelphians '59
Cash McCall '60
The Wonderful World of the Brothers Grimm '62

David Krumholtz
Addams Family Values '93
Life with Mikey '93
The Santa Clause '94

Gene Krupa
Ball of Fire '41
The Glenn Miller Story '54
The Benny Goodman Story '55

Olek Krupa
Ivory Hunters '90
Mac '93

Jack Kruschen
Meet Danny Wilson '52
Abbott and Costello Go to Mars '53
Soldier of Fortune '55
Reform School Girl '57
The Angry Red Planet '59
The Apartment '60
The Last Voyage '60
Cape Fear '61
Follow That Dream '61
The Ladies' Man '61
Lover Come Back '61
McLintock! '63
Dear Brigitte '65
Freebie & the Bean '74
Mountain Man '77
Satan's Cheerleaders '77
The Devlin Connection '82
Money to Burn '83
Cheaters '84

Ou-Yang Ksiek
Against the Drunken Cat Paws '75
Eighteen Jade Arhats '84

Chen Kuan-Tai
Shaolin Executioner '80s
Challenge of the Masters '89

Alex Kubik
Carnal Crimes '91
Trapped Alive '93

Akira Kubo
Snow Country '57
Throne of Blood '57
Attack of the Mushroom People '63
Son of Godzilla '66
Destroy All Monsters '68
Yog, Monster from Space '71

Bernie Kuby
Death Journey '76
Jornada de Muerte '80s

Youki Kudoh
Mystery Train '89
Picture Bride '94

Yoshiko Kuga
The Idiot '51
Shin Heike Monogatari '55
The Cruel Story of Youth '60

Jarl Kulle
Secrets of Women '52
Smiles of a Summer Night '55
The Devil's Eye '60
Fanny and Alexander '83
Babette's Feast '87

Nancy Kulp
Forever Darling '56
The Three Faces of Eve '57
The Beverly Hillbillies '62
The Patsy '64
Strange Bedfellows '65

William J. Kulzer
Shadows Run Black '84
Lust for Freedom '87

Yasuka Kurata
King Boxers '80
Rage of Wind '82

Alwyn Kurts
Tim '79
Earthling '80
The Efficiency Expert '92

Swoosie Kurtz
Marriage Is Alive and Well '80
Walking Through the Fire '80
The World According to Garp '82
Against All Odds '84
A Time to Live '85
True Stories '86
Wildcats '86
Baja Oklahoma '87
Bright Lights, Big City '88
Dangerous Liaisons '88
Vice Versa '88
The Image '89
A Shock to the System '90
Stanley and Iris '90
The Positively True Adventures of the Alleged Texas Cheerleader-Murdering Mom '93
Reality Bites '94
Storybook '95

Katy Kurtzman
Child of Glass '78
Long Journey Back '78
When Every Day was the Fourth of July '78

Clyde Kusatsu
The Choirboys '77
Dr. Strange '78
Dream Lover '93
Made in America '93
Top Dog '95

Dylan Kussman
Dead Poets Society '89
Journey of Honor '91
Wild Hearts Can't Be Broken '91

Miyuki Kuwano
Equinox Flower '58
The Cruel Story of Youth '60

Mimi Kuzyk
Blind Justice '86
Miles to Go '86
Family Sins '87
Striker's Mountain '87
The Kiss '88
Malicious '95

Nancy Kwan
The World of Suzie Wong '60
Flower Drum Song '61
Arrivederci, Baby! '66
Lt. Robin Crusoe, U.S.N. '66
The Corrupt Ones '67
The McMasters '70
The Deadly and the Beautiful '73
Project: Kill! '77
Night Creature '79
Fowl Play '83
Walking the Edge '83
Blade in Hong Kong '85
Night Children '89
Stickfighter '89
Dragon: The Bruce Lee Story '93

Burt Kwouk
The Pink Panther Strikes Again '76
Revenge of the Pink Panther '78
Trail of the Pink Panther '82
Plenty '85
Empire of the Sun '87
Son of the Pink Panther '93

Sam Kydd
The House in Marsh Road '60
Island of Terror '66

David Kyle
Cruisin' High '75
L.A. Gangs Rising '89

Machiko Kyo
Rashomon '51
Ugetsu '53
Gate of Hell '54
Princess Yang Kwei Fei '55
Street of Shame '56
The Teahouse of the August Moon '56
Drifting Weeds '59
Odd Obsession '60
Face of Another '66

Kay Kyser
You'll Find Out '40
Playmates '41
Around the World '43
Thousands Cheer '43

Jake La Motta
The Hustler '61
Hangmen '87
Mob War '88

Alison La Placa
Fletch '85
Madhouse '90

Rosemary La Planche
The Devil Bat's Daughter '46
Strangler of the Swamp '46
Federal Agents vs. Underworld, Inc. '49

Laura La Plante
Smouldering Fires '25
Skinner's Dress Suit '26
The Cat and the Canary '27
Lonely Wives '31
Hold Your Man '33

Rod La Rocque
The Ten Commandments '23
Braveheart '25
Captain Swagger '25
The Coming of Amos '25
Show People '28
Stand and Deliver '28
Our Modern Maidens '29
International Crime '37
The Shadow Strikes '37
The Hunchback of Notre Dame '39
Beyond Tomorrow '40
Dr. Christian Meets the Women '40
Meet John Doe '41

Rita La Roy
Sin Takes a Holiday '30
The Mandarin Mystery '37

Eriq La Salle
Coming to America '88
Vietnam War Story 1 '88
Jacob's Ladder '90
Color of Night '94
DROP Squad '94
ER '94

Barbara Laage
The Respectful Prostitute '52
Therese & Isabelle '68

Patti LaBelle
A Soldier's Story '84
Unnatural Causes '86
Fire and Rain '89
Sing '89

Halina Labonarska
Provincial Actors '79
A Woman and a Woman '80

Matthew Laborteaux
A Woman Under the Influence '74
Aliens Are Coming '80
Deadly Friend '86
Shattered Spirits '91

Patrick Laborteaux
Prince of Bel Air '87
Heathers '89
3 Ninjas '92

Elina Labourdette
The Ladies of the Bois de Bologne '44
Lola '61

Catherine Lacey
The Lady Vanishes '38
Cottage to Let '41
Pink Strings and Sealing Wax '45

Margaret Lacey
Seance on a Wet Afternoon '64
Diamonds Are Forever '71

Ronald Lacey
Disciple of Death '72
Next Victim '74
Nijinsky '80
Raiders of the Lost Ark '81
Firefox '82
The Hound of the Baskervilles '83
Sahara '83
Making the Grade '84
Flesh and Blood '85
Into the Darkness '86
Jailbird Rock '88
The Lone Runner '88
Landslide '92

Stephen Lack
Fatal Attraction '80
Scanners '81
Perfect Strangers '84
Dead Ringers '88
All the Vermeers in New York '91

Frank Lackteen
The Pony Express '25
Rustler's Roundup '33
Red Barry '38
The Sea Wolf '41

Alan Ladd
Captain Caution '40
Her First Romance '40
The Howards of Virginia '40
Citizen Kane '41
Gangs, Inc. '41
They Met in Bombay '41
The Glass Key '42
Joan of Paris '42
Star Spangled Rhythm '42
This Gun for Hire '42
The Blue Dahlia '46
My Favorite Brunette '47
Branded '50
Botany Bay '53
Shane '53
Drum Beat '54
Hell on Frisco Bay '55
The McConnell Story '55
The Badlanders '58
Deep Six '58
Proud Rebel '58
All the Young Men '60
Duel of Champions '61
The Carpetbaggers '64

Cheryl Ladd
Satan's School for Girls '73
The Treasure of Jamaica Reef '74
Now and Forever '82
The Grace Kelly Story '83
Purple Hearts '84
The Hasty Heart '86
Fulfillment '89
Millenium '89
Romance on the Orient Express '89
Jekyll and Hyde '90
Lisa '90
Danielle Steel's Changes '91
Poison Ivy '92
Dancing with Danger '93

David Ladd
A Dog of Flanders '59
Misty '61
Catlow '71
The Treasure of Jamaica Reef '74

Diane Ladd
The Wild Angels '66
Rebel Rousers '69
Alice Doesn't Live Here Anymore '74
Chinatown '74
Embryo '76
Willa '79
All Night Long '81
Desperate Lives '82
The Grace Kelly Story '83
Something Wicked This Way Comes '83
I Married a Centerfold '84
Black Widow '87
Plain Clothes '88
National Lampoon's Christmas Vacation '89
Code Name: Chaos '90
The Lookalike '90
Wild at Heart '90
A Kiss Before Dying '91
Rambling Rose '91
Doctor Quinn, Medicine Woman '92
Forever: A Ghost of a Love Story '92
Carnosaur '93
The Cemetery Club '93
Father Hood '93
Hold Me, Thrill Me, Kiss Me '93
Mother '94
Mrs. Munck '95
Raging Angels '95

John Lafayette
Full Fathom Five '90
White Sands '92

Patricia Laffan
Quo Vadis '51
Devil Girl from Mars '54

Art LaFleur
Trancers '84
Zone Troopers '84
Rampage '87
Oscar '91
Forever Young '92
Live! From Death Row '92
Jack the Bear '93
The Sandlot '93
Man of the House '95

Bernadette LaFont
Le Beau Serge '58
Les Bonnes Femmes '60
A Very Curious Girl '69
Catch Me a Spy '71
Too Pretty to Be Honest '72
Violette '78
The Perils of Gwendoline '84

Marika Lagercrantz
Dreaming of Rita '94
All Things Fair '95

Caroline Lagerfelt
Iron Eagle '86
Home at Last '88

Valerie Lagrange
Morgan the Pirate '60
A Man and a Woman '66
Weekend '67

Bert Lahr
Just Around the Corner '38
The Wizard of Oz '39
Ship Ahoy '42
Sing Your Worries Away '42
Rose Marie '54
The Night They Raided Minsky's '69

Christine Lahti
And Justice for All '79
The Henderson Monster '80
Whose Life Is It Anyway? '81
The Executioner's Song '82
Single Bars, Single Women '84
Swing Shift '84
Just Between Friends '86
Housekeeping '87
Stacking '87
Running on Empty '88
Gross Anatomy '89
Miss Firecracker '89
Funny About Love '90

Lahti ▶cont.

Crazy from the Heart *'91*
The Doctor *'91*
The Fear Inside *'92*
The Good Fight *'92*
Leaving Normal *'92*
Hideaway *'94*

Jimmy Laine
Driller Killer *'74*
Ms. 45 *'81*

Alan Lake
Don't Open Till Christmas *'84*
Con Man *'92*

Alice Lake
Playing Dead *'15*
Broken Hearts of Broadway *'23*

Arthur Lake
Silent Laugh Makers, No. 1 *'15*
Skinner's Dress Suit *'26*
The Silver Streak *'34*
Exiled to Shanghai *'37*
23 1/2 Hours Leave *'37*
Blondie *'38*
Blondie Takes a Vacation *'39*
Blondie Has Trouble *'40*
Blondie in Society *'41*
Blondie's Blessed Event *'42*
It's a Great Life *'43*
Blondie Knows Best *'46*
Blondie Hits the Jackpot *'49*

Don Lake
Hostage for a Day *'94*
Sodbusters *'94*

Florence Lake
Romance *'30*
Quality Street *'37*
Next Time I Marry *'38*
Crash Dive *'43*
Going to Town *'44*
Savage Intruder *'68*

Ricki Lake
Hairspray *'88*
Working Girl *'88*
Babycakes *'89*
Cookie *'89*
Cry-Baby *'90*
Last Exit to Brooklyn *'90*
The Chase *'91*
Where the Day Takes You *'92*
Based on an Untrue Story *'93*
Inside Monkey Zetterland *'93*
Skinner *'93*
Cabin Boy *'94*
Serial Mom *'94*
Mrs. Winterbourne *'96*

Veronica Lake
Sullivan's Travels *'41*
The Glass Key *'42*
I Married a Witch *'42*
Star Spangled Rhythm *'42*
This Gun for Hire *'42*
So Proudly We Hail *'43*
The Blue Dahlia *'46*
Ramrod *'47*
Flesh Feast *'69*

Michael Lally
The Nesting *'80*
The Secret of Roan Inish *'94*

Hedy Lamarr
Ecstasy *'33*
Algiers *'38*
Boom Town *'40*
Comrade X *'40*
Ziegfeld Girl *'41*
Tortilla Flat *'42*
White Cargo *'42*
Experiment Perilous *'45*
The Strange Woman *'46*
Dishonored Lady *'47*
Copper Canyon *'50*
Samson and Delilah *'50*
The Love of Three Queens *'54*

Fernando Lamas
Rich, Young and Pretty *'51*
The Merry Widow *'52*
Dangerous When Wet *'53*
The Girl Who Had Everything *'53*
Rose Marie *'54*
Violent Ones *'68*
100 Rifles *'69*
Powder Keg *'70*
Murder on Flight 502 *'75*
The Cheap Detective *'78*

Lorenzo Lamas
Take Down *'79*
Body Rock *'84*
SnakeEater *'89*
SnakeEater 2: The Drug Buster *'89*
Final Impact *'91*
Killing Streets *'91*
Night of the Warrior *'91*
C.I.A.: Code Name Alexa *'92*
SnakeEater 3: His Law *'92*
The Swordsman *'92*
Bounty Tracker *'93*
Final Round *'93*
Bad Blood *'94*
C.I.A. 2: Target Alexa *'94*
Blood for Blood *'95*
Gladiator Cop: The Swordsman 2 *'95*

Debra Lamb
Beverly Hills Vamp *'88*
B.O.R.N. *'88*
Rock & the Money-Hungry Party Girls *'89*
Stripped to Kill II: Live Girls *'89*
The Invisible Maniac *'90*
Evil Spirits *'91*

Larry Lamb
Transmutations *'85*
Shadey *'87*
Buster *'88*

Anne Louise Lambert
The Draughtsman's Contract *'82*
Great Expectations: The Untold Story *'87*

Christopher Lambert
Greystoke: The Legend of Tarzan, Lord of the Apes *'84*
Love Songs *'85*
Subway *'85*
Highlander *'86*
The Sicilian *'87*
To Kill a Priest *'89*
Priceless Beauty *'90*
Why Me? *'90*
Highlander 2: The Quickening *'91*
Fortress *'93*
Gunmen *'93*
Highlander: The Gathering *'93*
Knight Moves *'93*
Highlander: The Final Dimension *'94*
The Hunted *'94*
Mortal Kombat: The Movie *'95*
The Road Killers *'95*

Jack Lambert
Hue and Cry *'47*
Three Cases of Murder *'55*

Jack Lambert
Dick Tracy's Dilemma *'47*
North of the Great Divide *'50*
Stars in My Crown *'50*
Montana Belle *'52*
Machine Gun Kelly *'58*

Heath Lamberts
To Kill a Clown *'72*
Ordinary Magic *'93*
Tom and Huck *'95*

Ellie Lambetti
Girl in Black *'56*
A Matter of Dignity *'57*

Karen Lamm
The Hatfields & the McCoys *'75*
Ants *'77*

Duncan Lamont
The Golden Coach *'52*
Murder at the Gallop *'63*
The Evil of Frankenstein *'64*

Marten Lamont
Son of Fury *'42*
Federal Operator 99 *'45*
Redwood Forest Trail *'50*

Molly Lamont
The Awful Truth *'37*
Somewhere I'll Find You *'42*
The Devil Bat's Daughter *'46*

Pascal Lamorisse
The Red Balloon *'56*
Voyage en Balloon *'59*
Red Balloon/Occurrence at Owl Creek Bridge *'62*

John Lamotta
Revenge of the Ninja *'83*
One More Chance *'90*
We're Talkin' Serious Money *'92*

Dorothy Lamour
Dixiana *'30*
The Hurricane *'37*
Swing High, Swing Low *'37*
The Big Broadcast of 1938 *'38*
Johnny Apollo *'40*
The Road to Singapore *'40*
Caught in the Draft *'41*
The Road to Zanzibar *'41*
The Road to Morocco *'42*
Star Spangled Rhythm *'42*
They Got Me Covered *'43*
The Road to Utopia *'46*
My Favorite Brunette *'47*
The Road to Rio *'47*
The Greatest Show on Earth *'52*
The Road to Bali *'53*
Hollywood Goes to War *'54*
The Road to Hong Kong *'62*
Donovan's Reef *'63*
Pajama Party *'64*
The Love Goddesses *'65*
Creepshow 2 *'87*

Zohra Lampert
Splendor in the Grass *'61*
Let's Scare Jessica to Death *'71*
The Connection *'73*
Opening Night *'77*
Alphabet City *'84*
Teachers *'84*
Isle of Secret Passion *'85*
Izzy & Moe *'85*
American Blue Note *'89*
Stanley and Iris *'90*
Alan & Naomi *'92*

Chus Lampreave
What Have I Done to Deserve This? *'85*
Matador *'86*
I'm the One You're Looking For *'88*
The Flower of My Secret *'95*

Gunter Lamprecht
Berlin Alexanderplatz *'80*
Red Kiss *'85*

Burt Lancaster
Criss Cross *'48*
Sorry, Wrong Number *'48*
The Flame & the Arrow *'50*
Jim Thorpe: All American *'51*
Vengeance Valley *'51*
Come Back, Little Sheba *'52*
Crimson Pirate *'52*
From Here to Eternity *'53*
His Majesty O'Keefe *'53*
Vera Cruz *'53*
Apache *'54*
The Kentuckian *'55*
The Rose Tattoo *'55*
The Rainmaker *'56*
Trapeze *'56*
Gunfight at the O.K. Corral *'57*
Sweet Smell of Success *'57*
Run Silent, Run Deep *'58*
Separate Tables *'58*
The Devil's Disciple *'59*
Elmer Gantry *'60*
The Unforgiven *'60*
Judgment at Nuremberg *'61*
Birdman of Alcatraz *'62*
A Child is Waiting *'63*
The List of Adrian Messenger *'63*
Seven Days in May *'64*
The Hallelujah Trail *'65*
The Train *'65*
The Professionals *'66*
The Scalphunters *'68*
The Swimmer *'68*
Airport *'70*
Lawman *'71*
Valdez is Coming *'71*
Ulzana's Raid *'72*
Executive Action *'73*
Scorpio *'73*
Conversation Piece *'75*
America at the Movies *'76*
Buffalo Bill & the Indians *'76*
The Cassandra Crossing *'76*
Moses *'76*
1900 *'76*
Island of Dr. Moreau *'77*
Twilight's Last Gleaming *'77*
Go Tell the Spartans *'78*
Zulu Dawn *'79*
Atlantic City *'81*
Local Hero *'83*
The Osterman Weekend *'83*
Little Treasure *'85*
Barnum *'86*
On Wings of Eagles *'86*
Tough Guys *'86*
Control *'87*
Rocket Gibraltar *'88*
Field of Dreams *'89*
The Jeweller's Shop *'90*
The Phantom of the Opera *'90*
Voyage of Terror: The Achille Lauro Affair *'90*
Separate But Equal *'91*

James Lancaster
Gettysburg *'93*
Leprechaun 2 *'94*

Stuart Lancaster
Faster Pussycat! Kill! Kill! *'66*
Mantis in Lace *'68*
Beneath the Valley of the Ultra-Vixens *'79*
Mistress of the Apes *'79*

Elsa Lanchester
The Private Life of Henry VIII *'33*
The Bride of Frankenstein *'35*
David Copperfield *'35*
Naughty Marietta *'35*
The Ghost Goes West *'36*
Rembrandt *'36*
Beachcomber *'38*
Son of Fury *'42*
Tales of Manhattan *'42*
Forever and a Day *'43*
Lassie, Come Home *'43*
The Razor's Edge *'46*
The Spiral Staircase *'46*
The Bishop's Wife *'47*
Northwest Outpost *'47*
Come to the Stable *'49*
The Inspector General *'49*
The Secret Garden *'49*
The Glass Slipper *'55*
Witness for the Prosecution *'57*
Bell, Book and Candle *'58*
Pajama Party *'64*
That Darn Cat *'65*
Blackbeard's Ghost *'67*
Easy Come, Easy Go *'67*
My Dog, the Thief *'69*
Willard *'71*
Arnold *'73*
Terror in the Wax Museum *'73*
Murder by Death *'76*
Die Laughing *'80*

Micheline Lanctot
The Apprenticeship of Duddy Kravitz *'74*
Blood Relatives *'77*

Geoffrey Land
The Female Bunch *'69*
Against A Crooked Sky *'75*
Hospital of Terror *'78*

Paul Land
Idolmaker *'80*
Spring Break *'83*

Rodolfo Landa
The Criminal Life of Archibaldo de la Cruz *'55*
Neutron vs. the Amazing Dr. Caronte *'61*

David Landau
Street Scene *'31*
False Faces *'32*
Horse Feathers *'32*
The Purchase Price *'32*
Gabriel Over the White House *'33*

Juliet Landau
Neon City *'91*
Direct Hit *'93*
Theodore Rex *'95*

Martin Landau
The Gazebo *'59*
North by Northwest *'59*
Pork Chop Hill *'59*
Cleopatra *'63*
The Hallelujah Trail *'65*
They Call Me Mr. Tibbs! *'70*
A Town Called Hell *'72*
Destination Moonbase Alpha *'75*
Space: 1999 *'75*
Strange Shadows in an Empty Room *'76*
Meteor *'79*
Space: 1999—Alien Attack *'79*
The Fall of the House of Usher *'80*
The Last Word *'80*
The Return *'80*
Alone in the Dark *'82*
The Being *'83*
Access Code *'84*
Kung Fu: The Movie *'86*
Cyclone *'87*
Death Blow *'87*
Empire State *'87*
Run If You Can *'87*
Sweet Revenge *'87*
Tucker: The Man and His Dream *'88*
By Dawn's Early Light *'89*
Crimes & Misdemeanors *'89*
The Neon Empire *'89*
Paint It Black *'89*
Firehead *'90*
Max and Helen *'90*
Real Bullets *'90*
Mistress *'91*
Legacy of Lies *'92*
Eye of the Stranger *'93*
Intersection *'93*
No Place to Hide *'93*
Sliver *'93*
12:01 *'93*
Ed Wood *'94*
City Hall *'95*
The Color of Evening *'95*
Joseph *'95*
The Adventures of Pinocchio *'96*

Dinsdale Landen
Digby, the Biggest Dog in the World *'73*
Anatomy of Terror *'74*
Morons from Outer Space *'85*

David Lander
The Tell-Tale Heart *'62*
The Man with One Red Shoe *'85*
Funland *'89*
Steel and Lace *'90*
Betrayal of the Dove *'92*
Ava's Magical Adventure *'94*

Audrey Landers
Tennessee Stallion *'78*
Underground Aces *'80*
A Chorus Line *'85*
Deadly Twins *'85*
Getting Even *'86*
California Casanova *'89*
Ghost Writer *'89*

Harry Landers
The C-Man *'49*
Phantom from Space *'53*
The Indian Fighter *'55*
The Gallant Hours *'60*

Judy Landers
Tennessee Stallion *'78*
The Yum-Yum Girls *'78*
The Black Marble *'79*
Deadly Twins *'85*
Doin' Time *'85*
Hellhole *'85*
Armed and Dangerous *'86*
Stewardess School *'86*
Dr. Alien *'88*
Ghost Writer *'89*
Club Fed *'90*
The Divine Enforcer *'91*

Steve Landesburg
Blade *'72*
Leader of the Band *'87*
Final Notice *'89*
Mission of the Shark *'91*
Sodbusters *'94*

Clayton Landey
First & Ten: The Team Scores Again *'85*
Assault of the Killer Bimbos *'88*

Janet Landgard
The Swimmer *'68*
Land Raiders *'69*

Gudrun Landgrebe
Colonel Redl *'84*
A Woman in Flames *'84*
The Berlin Affair *'85*

Karl Landgren
Urban Warriors *'75*
The Black Cobra *'87*

Sonny Landham
48 Hrs. *'82*

Lansbury ▶cont.

The Amorous Adventures of Moll Flanders '65
The Greatest Story Ever Told '65
Harlow '65
Something for Everyone '70
Bedknobs and Broomsticks '71
Death on the Nile '78
The Lady Vanishes '79
The Pirates of Penzance '83
The First Olympics: Athens 1896 '84
Little Gloria...Happy at Last '84
Sweeney Todd: The Demon Barber of Fleet Street '84
The Company of Wolves '85
Rage of Angels: The Story Continues '86
The Shell Seekers '89
Mrs. 'Arris Goes to Paris '92

David Lansbury
Gas Food Lodging '92
Parallel Lives '94
Truman '95

Joi Lansing
Easter Parade '48
Julia Misbehaves '48
Neptune's Daughter '49
Pier 23 '51
Two Tickets to Broadway '51
The Merry Widow '52
Singin' in the Rain '52
The French Line '54
Son of Sinbad '55
The Brave One '56
Touch of Evil '58
Atomic Submarine '59
A Hole in the Head '59
Hillbillies in a Haunted House '67
Big Foot '72

Robert Lansing
The 4D Man '59
Namu, the Killer Whale '66
Talion '66
The Grissom Gang '71
Bittersweet Love '76
Scalpel '76
The Widow '76
Empire of the Ants '77
S*H*E '79
Island Claw '80
The Equalizer: Memories of Manon '88
The Nest '88

Mario Lanza
That Midnight Kiss '49
The Toast of New Orleans '50
The Great Caruso '51
Because You're Mine '52
The Seven Hills of Rome '58
For the First Time '59

Anthony LaPaglia
Nitti: The Enforcer '88
Betsy's Wedding '90
Criminal Justice '90
Mortal Sins '90
He Said, She Said '91
One Good Cop '91
29th Street '91
Black Magic '92
Innocent Blood '92
Keeper of the City '92
Whispers in the Dark '92
So I Married an Axe Murderer '93
The Client '94
The Custodian '94
Mixed Nuts '94
Past Tense '94
Bulletproof Heart '95
Chameleon '95
Empire Records '95

Francine Lapensee
Hollywood's New Blood '88
Born Killer '89
Demon Wind '90
Bounty Hunter 2002 '94

Peter Lapis
Death Blow '87
Undeclared War '91

Victor Laplace
Under the Earth '86
Letters from the Park '88

Jane Lapotaire
The Asphyx '72
Eureka! '81
Piaf '81
The Dark Angel '91
Murder by Moonlight '91

Joe Lara
American Cyborg: Steel Warrior '94
Steel Frontier '94
Final Equinox '95
Hologram Man '95
Live Wire: Human Timebomb '95

John Larch
Hail, Hero! '69
Dirty Harry '71
Play Misty for Me '71
Santee '73
Bad Ronald '74
Future Cop '76

Veronica Lario
Unsane '82
Sotto, Sotto '85

Bryan Larkin
Born on the Fourth of July '89
She-Devil '89

Mary Laroche
Gidget '59
Psychomania '73

Pierre Larquey
Le Corbeau '43
Topaze '51

John Larroquette
Altered States '80
Heart Beat '80
Green Ice '81
Stripes '81
Cat People '82
Twilight Zone: The Movie '83
Choose Me '84
Meatballs 2 '84
Star Trek 3: The Search for Spock '84
Summer Rental '85
Convicted '86
Blind Date '87
Second Sight '89
Madhouse '90
Tune in Tomorrow '90
Richie Rich '94

Erik Larsen
Trap on Cougar Mountain '72
Young & Free '78

Ham Larsen
Further Adventures of the Wilderness Family, Part 2 '77
Mountain Family Robinson '79

Keith Larsen
Flat Top '52
Mission Batangas '69
Trap on Cougar Mountain '72
Whitewater Sam '78

Bobby Larson
Leather Burners '43
The Underdog '43

Darrell Larson
The Student Nurses '70
The Girls of Huntington House '73
Red, White & Busted '75
Mike's Murder '84
City Limits '85
The Last Innocent Man '87
Murder Ordained '87
Hero '92

Eric Larson
'68 '87
The Uninvited '88
Demon Wind '90

Jack Larson
TV's Best Adventures of Superman '51
Stamp Day for Superman '53
James Dean: The First American Teenager '76

Eva LaRue
The Barbarians '87
Crash and Burn '90

Frank LaRue
Sidewalks of New York '31
The Throwback '35
Red River Valley '36
Boothill Brigade '37
Gun Lords of Stirrup Basin '37
A Lawman Is Born '37
Lightning Bill Crandall '37
Overland Stage Raiders '38
Songs and Bullets '38
Mesquite Buckaroo '39
Trigger Pals '39
Riders of Pasco Basin '40
Devil Riders '44
Border Bandits '46
Range Renegades '48

Jack LaRue
A Farewell to Arms '32
The Kennel Murder Case '33
To the Last Man '33
The Fighting Rookie '34
Headline Woman '35
Dancing Pirate '36
Yellow Cargo '36
Captains Courageous '37
Dangerous Holiday '37
Footsteps in the Dark '41
Gentleman from Dixie '41
X Marks the Spot '42
The Law Rides Again '43
The Payoff '43
Dangerous Passage '44
Follow the Leader '44
The Road to Utopia '46
Ride the Man Down '53
The Young Nurses '73

Lash LaRue
Western Double Feature 9: LaRue & Beery '40s
Gangs, Inc. '41
Master Key '44
Song of Old Wyoming '45
The Caravan Trail '46
Wild West '46
Border Feud '47
Cheyenne Takes Over '47
Fighting Vigilantes '47
Ghost Town Renegades '47
Law of the Lash '47
Return of the Lash '47
Stage to Mesa City '48
Outlaw Country '49
King of the Bullwhip '51
Thundering Trail '51
The Black Lash '52
The Dark Power '85
Pair of Aces '90

Dieter Laser
The Lost Honor of Katharina Blum '75
The Man Inside '90

Kathleen Lasky
Love & Murder '91
Lethal Lolita—Amy Fisher: My Story '92
Getting Gotti '94

Dagmar Lassander
Hatchet for the Honeymoon '70
Dandelions '74
Flatfoot '78
The Black Cat '81
S.A.S. San Salvador '84

Louise Lasser
Take the Money and Run '69
Bananas '71
Everything You Always Wanted to Know about Sex (But Were Afraid to Ask) '72
Slither '73
Just Me & You '78
For Ladies Only '81
Crimewave '85
Blood Rage '87
Surrender '87
Rude Awakening '89
Sing '89
Frankenhooker '90
Modern Love '90
The Night We Never Met '93

Sydney Lassick
The Billion Dollar Hobo '78
The Unseen '80
Monaco Forever '83
Silent Madness '84
Night Patrol '85
Sonny Boy '87
Out on Bail '89
Tale of Two Sisters '89
The Art of Dying '90
Smooth Talker '90
Committed '91
Cool As Ice '91
Deep Cover '92
Shakes the Clown '92
Money to Burn '94

Lassie
Lassie from Lancashire '38
Lassie, Come Home '43
The Painted Hills '51
Lassie's Great Adventure '62
Lassie: Adventures of Neeka '68
Lassie: The Miracle '75
Magic of Lassie '78
Lassie: Well of Love '90

Lyle Latell
Dick Tracy, Detective/The Corpse Vanishes '42
Dick Tracy, Detective '45
Dick Tracy Double Feature #1 '45
Dick Tracy Meets Gruesome '47
Dick Tracy's Dilemma '47

Anne Latham
Mind Warp '72
Thieves Like Us '74

Louise Latham
Marnie '64
Adam at 6 a.m. '70
Dying Room Only '73
White Lightning '73
Lois Gibbs and the Love Canal '82
Pray TV '82
Mass Appeal '84
Toughlove '85
Crazy from the Heart '91
Love Field '91
Paradise '91

Hugh Latimer
Someone at the Door '50
Rogue's Yarn '56
The Cosmic Monsters '58

Frank Latimore
The Dolly Sisters '45
Shock! '46
13 Rue Madeleine '46
Patton '70

Ney Latorraca
The Dolphin '87
Opera do Malandro '87
The Fable of the Beautiful Pigeon Fancier '88

Matt Lattanzi
Rich and Famous '81
My Tutor '82
Roxanne '87
Catch Me...If You Can '89
Diving In '90

Chester Lauck
Dreaming Out Loud '40
The Bashful Bachelor '42

Philippe Laudenbach
Confidentially Yours '83
Four Adventures of Reinette and Mirabelle '89

Andrew Lauer
Never on Tuesday '88
Screamers '96

John Laughlin
Crimes of Passion '84
Footloose '84
The Hills Have Eyes, Part 2 '84
Space Rage '86
Midnight Crossing '87
Memphis '91
Motorama '91
Sexual Malice '93
Improper Conduct '94
Night Fire '94

Tom Laughlin
South Pacific '58
Tall Story '60
Born Losers '67
Billy Jack '71
The Trial of Billy Jack '74

Charles Laughton
Island of Lost Souls '32
The Old Dark House '32
The Sign of the Cross '32
The Private Life of Henry VIII '33
The Barretts of Wimpole Street '34
Les Miserables '35
Mutiny on the Bounty '35
Ruggles of Red Gap '35
Rembrandt '36
Beachcomber '38
The Hunchback of Notre Dame '39
Jamaica Inn '39
Sidewalks of London '40
They Knew What They Wanted '40
It Started with Eve '41
Tales of Manhattan '42
The Tuttles of Tahiti '42
Forever and a Day '43
This Land is Mine '43
The Canterville Ghost '44
Captain Kidd '45
The Paradine Case '47
Arch of Triumph '48
Man on the Eiffel Tower '48
Abbott and Costello Meet Captain Kidd '52
Hobson's Choice '53
Salome '53
Young Bess '53
The Best of Abbott & Costello Live '54
Witness for the Prosecution '57
Spartacus '60
Advise and Consent '62

S. John Launer
Crime of Passion '57
I Was a Teenage Werewolf '57

Cyndi Lauper
Vibes '88
Mother Goose Rock 'n' Rhyme '90
Life with Mikey '93

Matthew Laurance
Eddie and the Cruisers '83
Eddie and the Cruisers 2: Eddie Lives! '89

Mitchell Laurance
The Hand that Rocks the Cradle '92
The Portrait '93

Carole Laure
Sweet Movie '75
Strange Shadows in an Empty Room '76
Get Out Your Handkerchiefs '78
Victory '81
Heartbreakers '84
Maria Chapdelaine '84
Sweet Country '87
Surrogate '88

Stan Laurel
Silent Laugh Makers, No. 1 '15
Bellhop/The Noon Whistle '22
Stan Without Ollie, Vol. 1 '23
Stan Without Ollie, Vol. 2 '23
Stan Without Ollie, Vol. 3 '23
Stan Without Ollie, Vol. 4 '25
Laurel & Hardy: Berth Marks '29
Laurel & Hardy: Men O'War '29
Laurel & Hardy: Perfect Day '29
Laurel & Hardy Comedy Classics, Vol. 7 '30s
Laurel & Hardy Comedy Classics, Vol. 8 '30s
Laurel & Hardy Comedy Classics, Vol. 9 '30s
Slapstick '30s
Laurel & Hardy: Another Fine Mess '30
Laurel & Hardy: Below Zero '30
Laurel & Hardy: Blotto '30
Laurel & Hardy: Brats '30
Laurel & Hardy Comedy Classics, Vol. 2 '30
Laurel & Hardy: Hog Wild '30
Laurel & Hardy: Night Owls '30
Laurel & Hardy: On the Lam '30
Laurel & Hardy: Be Big '31
Laurel & Hardy: Chickens Come Home '31
Laurel & Hardy Comedy Classics, Vol. 5 '31
Laurel & Hardy: Laughing Gravy '31
Pardon Us '31
Laurel & Hardy: At Work '32
Laurel & Hardy Comedy Classics, Vol. 4 '32
Music Box/Helpmates '32
Pack Up Your Troubles '32
The Devil's Brother '33
Laurel & Hardy and the Family '33

Laurel & Hardy Comedy Classics, Vol. 1 '33
Laurel & Hardy: Stan "Helps" Ollie '33
Sons of the Desert '33
Hollywood Party '34
Laurel & Hardy Comedy Classics, Vol. 3 '34
March of the Wooden Soldiers '34
Bonnie Scotland '35
Laurel & Hardy Comedy Classics, Vol. 6 '35
Bohemian Girl '36
Our Relations '36
Pick a Star '37
Way Out West '37
Block-heads '38
Swiss Miss '38
The Flying Deuces '39
A Chump at Oxford '40
Saps at Sea '40
Great Guns '41
Air Raid Wardens '43
Nothing But Trouble '44
Bullfighters '45
Utopia '51
Golden Age of Comedy '58
Days of Thrills and Laughter '61
A Few Moments with Buster Keaton and Laurel and Hardy '63
Hollywood Clowns '85
Laurel & Hardy Special

Rod Lauren
The Crawling Hand '63
Once Before I Die '65

Veronica Lauren
Homeward Bound: The Incredible Journey '93
Homeward Bound 2: Lost in San Francisco '96

Ashley Laurence
Hellraiser '87
Hellbound: Hellraiser 2 '88
One Last Run '89
Hellraiser 3: Hell on Earth '92
American Cop '94
Felony '95
The Fighter '95
Outside the Law '95
Triplecross '95

Michael Laurence
A Conspiracy of Love '87
Syngenor '90

James Laurenson
Assault '70
Rude Awakening '81
Heartbreakers '84
Rainbow Drive '90
Codename Kyril '91
Prime Suspect: Inner Circles '95

Remy Laurent
La Cage aux Folles '78
The Gift '82

Dan Lauria
Stakeout '87
Skin '89
In the Line of Duty: Ambush in Waco '93

Carol Laurie
Naked Massacre '80s
Dirty Dishes '82

Hugh Laurie
Strapless '90
Jeeves & Wooster: Jeeves' Arrival '91
Peter's Friends '92
Sense and Sensibility '95

John Laurie
Juno and the Paycock '30
The 39 Steps '35
Edge of the World '37
Dangerous Moonlight '41
Mine Own Executioner '47
The World Owes Me a Living '47
Bonnie Prince Charlie '48
Hamlet '48
Man of Evil '48
No Trace '50
Trio '50
Encore '52
Devil Girl from Mars '54

Piper Laurie
Francis Goes to the Races '51
Son of Ali Baba '52
Dangerous Mission '54
Until They Sail '57
Days of Wine and Roses '58
The Hustler '61
Carrie '76
Ruby '77
Boss' Son '79
Skag '79
Tim '79
The Thorn Birds '83
Mae West '84
Return to Oz '85
Toughlove '85
Children of a Lesser God '86
Distortions '87
Tiger Warsaw '87
Appointment with Death '88
Dream a Little Dream '89
Rising Son '90
Twin Peaks '90
Twin Peaks '90
Other People's Money '91
Storyville '92
Dario Argento's Trauma '93
Rich in Love '93
Wrestling Ernest Hemingway '93
The Crossing Guard '94
The Road to Galveston '96

Ed Lauter
Rage '72
Class of '63 '73
The Longest Yard '74
The Migrants '74
Breakheart Pass '76
Family Plot '76
King Kong '76
The Chicken Chronicles '77
Magic '78
Love's Savage Fury '79
Death Hunt '81
Eureka! '81
The Amateur '82
In the Custody of Strangers '82
Big Score '83
Cujo '83
Timerider '83
Cartier Affair '84
Finders Keepers '84
Lassiter '84
Death Wish 3 '85
Girls Just Want to Have Fun '85
Nickel Mountain '85
The Last Days of Patton '86
Youngblood '86
Yuri Nosenko, KGB '86
Revenge of the Nerds 2: Nerds in Paradise '87
Goodbye, Miss 4th of July '88
The Rocketeer '91
Stephen King's Golden Years '91
School Ties '92
Extreme Justice '93
Murder So Sweet '93
True Romance '93
Under Investigation '93
Black Water '94
Digital Man '94
Girl in the Cadillac '94
Trial by Jury '94
Breach of Trust '95
Mulholland Falls '95
The Sweeper '95
Rattled '96

Harry Lauter
Bandit King of Texas '49
Trader Tom of the China Seas '54

Kathrin Lautner
The Last Riders '90
Night of the Wilding '90
Spirits '90
Final Impact '91
Two Bits & Pepper '95

Lucille LaVerne
The White Rose '23
Hearts of Humanity '32
Kentucky Kernels '34

Daliah Lavi
The Return of Dr. Mabuse '61
Two Weeks in Another Town '62
Lord Jim '65
Spy with a Cold Nose '66
Those Fantastic Flying Fools '67

Linda Lavin
The $5.20 an Hour Dream '80
A Matter of Life and Death '81
Maricela '88
See You in the Morning '89

John Phillip Law
The Russians are Coming, the Russians are Coming '66
Barbarella '68
Danger: Diabolik '68
The Last Movie '71
The Love Machine '71
Golden Voyage of Sinbad '73
Spiral Staircase '75
The Cassandra Crossing '76
African Rage '78
No Time to Die '78
Tarzan, the Ape Man '81
Overthrow '82
American Commandos '84
Attack Force Z '84
Night Train to Terror '84
L.A. Bad '85
Moon in Scorpio '86
Space Mutiny '88
Thunder Warrior 3 '88
Alienator '89
Cold Heat '90

Phyllida Law
Peter's Friends '92
Much Ado about Nothing '93
Emma '96

Peter Lawford
Mrs. Miniver '42
The Canterville Ghost '44
The White Cliffs of Dover '44
Picture of Dorian Gray '45
Son of Lassie '45
Good News '47
It Happened in Brooklyn '47
Easter Parade '48
Julia Misbehaves '48
On an Island with You '48
Little Women '49
Royal Wedding '51
It Should Happen to You '54
Never So Few '59
Exodus '60
Ocean's 11 '60
Advise and Consent '62
The Longest Day '62
Harlow '65
A Man Called Adam '66
The Oscar '66
Buona Sera, Mrs. Campbell '68
April Fools '69
Togetherness '70
They Only Kill Their Masters '72
Rosebud '75
Fantasy Island '76
Angel's Brigade '79
Mysterious Island of Beautiful Women '79
Body & Soul '81

Yvonne Lawley
Among the Cinders '83
Death in Brunswick '90

Stephanie Lawlor
Cherry Hill High '76
Hot T-Shirts '79

Barbara Lawrence
The Street with No Name '48
A Letter to Three Wives '49
Oklahoma! '55
Kronos '57

Bruno Lawrence
Smash Palace '82
Treasure of the Yankee Zephyr '83
Utu '83
Heart of the Stag '84
An Indecent Obsession '85
The Quiet Earth '85
The Bridge to Nowhere '86
Rikky and Pete '88
Grievous Bodily Harm '89
The Efficiency Expert '92
Jack Be Nimble '94
Rainbow Warrior '94

Carol Lawrence
New Faces of 1952 '54
Shattered Image '93

Cary Lawrence
Canvas: The Fine Art of Crime '92
The Dance Goes On '92

Delphi Lawrence
Three Stops to Murder '53
Murder on Approval '56
Frozen Alive '64

Gertrude Lawrence
Mimi '35
Rembrandt '36
Men Are Not Gods '37

Joey Lawrence
Wait Till Your Mother Gets Home '83
Pulse '88
Chains of Gold '92

John Lawrence
The Asphyx '72
They Live '88

Marc Lawrence
Vengeance '37
I Am the Law '38
Charlie Chan at the Wax Museum '40
The Monster and the Girl '41
'Neath Brooklyn Bridge '42
Cloak and Dagger '46
Jigsaw '49
Abbott and Costello in the Foreign Legion '50
The Asphalt Jungle '50
The Black Hand '50
Frasier the Sensuous Lion '73
Pigs '73
The Man with the Golden Gun '74
Dream No Evil '75
Goin' Coconuts '78
King of Kong Island '78
Cataclysm '81
Night Train to Terror '84
Ruby '92

Martin Lawrence
House Party '90
House Party 2: The Pajama Jam '91
Talkin' Dirty After Dark '91
Boomerang '92
You So Crazy '94
Bad Boys '95
A Thin Line Between Love and Hate '96

Michael Lawrence
Elizabeth of Ladymead '48
Othello '52

Peter Lee Lawrence
Special Forces '68
Garringo '69
They Paid with Bullets: Chicago 1929 '70s

Rosina Lawrence
Charlie Chan's Secret '35
General Spanky '36
Pick a Star '37
Way Out West '37

Scott Lawrence
God's Bloody Acre '75
Laurel Avenue '93
Timecop '94

Stephanie Lawrence
Buster '88
The Phantom of the Opera '89

Steve Lawrence
Express to Terror '79
The Lonely Guy '84

Denis Lawson
Local Hero '83
Return of the Jedi '83

Leigh Lawson
Brother Sun, Sister Moon '73
It's Not the Size That Counts '74
Madhouse Mansion '74
Love Among the Ruins '75
Tess '80
Charlie Boy '81
Fire and Sword '82
Sword of the Valiant '83
Madame Sousatzka '88
Tears in the Rain '88
O Pioneers! '91
Battling for Baby '92

Priscilla Lawson
Flash Gordon: Rocketship '36
Girl of the Golden West '38

Richard Lawson
Foxstyle '73
Scream Blacula Scream '73
Fist '79
Poltergeist '82
Streets of Fire '84
Johnnie Gibson F.B.I. '87
The Forgotten '89
The Reluctant Agent '95

Wilfred Lawson
Pygmalion '38
The Terror '38
The Night Has Eyes '42
Tower of Terror '42
Man of Evil '48
The Prisoner '55

Frank Lawton
Skin Game '31
Cavalcade '33
David Copperfield '35
Devil Doll '36
The Invisible Ray '36
The Mill on the Floss '37
The Secret Four '40
The Winslow Boy '48
A Night to Remember '58

Evelyn Laye
Theatre of Death '67
Say Hello to Yesterday '71

John Lazar
Every Girl Should Have One '78
Deathstalker 2: Duel of the Titans '87
Attack of the 60-Foot Centerfold '95
Night of the Scarecrow '95

Paul Lazar
Philadelphia '93
Trapped In Paradise '94
Buffalo Girls '95

George Lazenby
On Her Majesty's Secret Service '69
Black Eliminator '70s
Kentucky Fried Movie '77
Kill Factor '78
Saint Jack '79
Never Too Young to Die '86
Happy Anniversary 007: 25 Years of James Bond '87
Hell Hunters '87
Eyes of the Beholder '92
Fatally Yours '95
Twinsitters '95

Bruce Le
Bruce the Superhero '79
My Name Called Bruce '80s
Bruce Le's Greatest Revenge '80
Bruce's Deadly Fingers '80
Clones of Bruce Lee '80
Bruce's Fists of Vengeance '84

Gene Le Brock
Fortress of Amerikka '89
Metamorphosis '90
Beyond Darkness '92

Kelly Le Brock
The Woman in Red '84
Weird Science '85
Hard to Kill '89
Betrayal of the Dove '92
Hard Bounty '94
Tracks of a Killer '95

Michael Le Clair
Anatomy of a Seduction '79
Leave 'Em Laughing '81

John Le Mesurier
The Baby and the Battleship '56
Brothers in Law '57
Dead Lucky '60
Jack the Ripper '60
Jabberwocky '77
The Adventures of Sherlock Holmes' Smarter Brother '78
Brideshead Revisited '81
A Married Man '84

Nicholas Lea
Xtro 2: The Second Encounter '91
The Raffle '94

Ron Lea
The Phone Call '89
Clearcut '92
The Neighbor '93

Tracy Lea
Desperate Teenage Lovedolls '84
Letter to Brezhnev '86

Rosemary Leach
That'll Be the Day '73
Ghost in the Noonday Sun '74
The Seventeenth Bride '84
D.P. '85

Leach ▶cont.

A Room with a View *'86*
Turtle Diary *'86*
The Charmer *'89*
The Children *'90*
The Hawk *'93*
The Mystery of Edwin Drood *'93*
The Buccaneers *'95*

Cloris Leachman
Kiss Me Deadly *'55*
Wanted: Dead or Alive *'59*
Butch Cassidy and the Sundance Kid *'69*
Silent Night, Lonely Night *'69*
Lovers and Other Strangers *'70*
The People Next Door *'70*
The Last Picture Show *'71*
The Steagle *'71*
Brand New Life *'72*
Haunts of the Very Rich *'72*
Charley and the Angel *'73*
Dillinger *'73*
Dying Room Only *'73*
Run, Stranger, Run *'73*
Daisy Miller *'74*
Death Sentence *'74*
The Migrants *'74*
Thursday's Game *'74*
Young Frankenstein *'74*
Crazy Mama *'75*
Death Scream *'75*
Someone I Touched *'75*
High Anxiety *'77*
Long Journey Back *'78*
Mrs. R's Daughter *'79*
The North Avenue Irregulars *'79*
Scavenger Hunt *'79*
S.O.S. Titanic *'79*
Willa *'79*
Foolin' Around *'80*
Herbie Goes Bananas *'80*
History of the World: Part 1 *'81*
Acorn People *'82*
Miss All-American Beauty *'82*
Oldest Living Graduate *'82*
The Woman Who Willed a Miracle *'83*
Ernie Kovacs: Between the Laughter *'84*
Dixie: Changing Habits *'85*
Shadow Play *'86*
Walk Like a Man *'87*
The Victory *'88*
Prancer *'89*
Fine Things *'90*
Texasville *'90*
The Beverly Hillbillies *'93*
Fade to Black *'93*
Double Double Toil and Trouble *'94*
Now and Then *'95*

Michael Learned
The Waltons: A Thanksgiving Story *'73*
The Widow *'76*
A Christmas Without Snow *'80*
Nurse *'80*
All My Sons *'86*
Deadly Business *'86*
Power *'86*
Roots: The Gift *'88*
Murder in New Hampshire: The Pamela Smart Story *'91*
Dragon: The Bruce Lee Story *'93*

Denis Leary
Gunmen *'93*
Judgment Night *'93*
The Ref *'93*
Who's the Man? *'93*
Natural Born Killers *'94*
National Lampoon's Favorite Deadly Sins *'95*
The Neon Bible *'95*
Operation Dumbo Drop *'95*
Two If by Sea *'95*

Timothy Leary
Shocker *'89*
Fatal Skies *'90*
Roadside Prophets *'92*

Rex Lease
Sunny Skies *'30*
Chinatown After Dark *'31*
The Monster Walks *'32*
Inside Information *'34*
Cowboy & the Bandit *'35*
Cyclone of the Saddle *'35*
Fighting Caballero *'35*
Ghost Rider *'35*
Pals of the Range *'35*
Rough Riding Rangers *'35*
Aces and Eights *'36*
Cavalcade of the West *'36*
The Clutching Hand *'36*
Custer's Last Stand *'36*
The Man from Gun Town *'36*
Roaring Guns *'36*
Heroes of the Alamo *'37*
Riding On *'37*
Haunted Ranch *'43*
Fast Bullets *'44*
People's Choice *'46*
Gun Cargo *'49*
Lost in Alaska *'52*

Jean-Pierre Leaud
The 400 Blows *'59*
The Testament of Orpheus *'59*
The Joy of Knowledge *'65*
Pierrot le Fou *'65*
Masculine Feminine *'66*
Weekend *'67*
Stolen Kisses *'68*
Porcile *'69*
Two English Girls *'72*
Day for Night *'73*
Last Tango in Paris *'73*
Love on the Run *'78*
36 Fillete *'88*
La Vie de Boheme *'93*

Ivan Lebedeff
Walking Back *'26*
Goin' to Town *'35*
Love on the Run *'36*

Matthew LeBlanc
Red Shoe Diaries 3: Another Woman's Lipstick *'93*
Ed *'96*

Brian Leckner
Bonanza: The Return *'93*
Sgt. Bilko *'95*

Ginette LeClerc
The Baker's Wife *'33*
Man from Nowhere *'37*
Le Corbeau *'43*

Friedrich Ledebur
Moby Dick *'56*
The 27 Day *'57*

Paul Leder
Five Minutes to Love *'63*
How to Succeed with Girls *'64*

Francis Lederer
Pandora's Box *'28*
Romance in Manhattan *'34*
One Rainy Afternoon *'36*
Midnight *'39*
The Bridge of San Luis Rey *'44*
Diary of a Chambermaid *'46*
A Woman of Distinction *'50*
Stolen Identity *'53*
The Ambassador's Daughter *'56*
Lisbon *'56*
Return of Dracula *'58*
Terror Is a Man *'59*

Suzanne Lederer
Judge Horton and the Scottsboro Boys *'76*
Women of Valor *'86*

Fernand Ledoux
La Bete Humaine *'38*
Volpone *'39*
Les Visiteurs du Soir *'42*
Pattes Blanches *'49*

Anna Lee
The Man Who Lived Again *'36*
The Passing of the Third Floor Back *'36*
King Solomon's Mines *'37*
Non-Stop New York *'37*
O.H.M.S. *'37*
The Secret Four *'40*
How Green Was My Valley *'41*
Flying Tigers *'42*
Commandos Strike at Dawn *'43*
Bedlam *'45*
The Ghost and Mrs. Muir *'47*
Fort Apache *'48*
The Horse Soldiers *'59*
Jack the Giant Killer *'62*
What Ever Happened to Baby Jane? *'62*
The Sound of Music *'65*
In Like Flint *'67*
Eleanor & Franklin *'76*

Bernard Lee
Rhodes *'36*
The Terror *'38*
The Courtney Affair *'47*
Elizabeth of Ladymead *'48*
The Blue Lamp *'49*
The Fallen Idol *'49*
The Third Man *'49*
Last Holiday *'50*
The Adventurers *'51*
The Gift Horse *'52*
The Detective *'54*
Across the Bridge *'57*
The Spanish Gardener *'57*
The Brain *'62*
Dr. No *'62*
Whistle Down the Wind *'62*
From Russia with Love *'63*
Goldfinger *'64*
Thunderball *'65*
You Only Live Twice *'67*
On Her Majesty's Secret Service *'69*
Diamonds Are Forever *'71*
Long Ago Tomorrow *'71*
Live and Let Die *'73*
The Man with the Golden Gun *'74*
The Spy Who Loved Me *'77*
Moonraker *'79*

Billy Lee
Wagon Wheels *'34*
Reg'lar Fellers *'41*

Brandon Lee
Kung Fu: The Movie *'86*
Laser Mission *'90*
Showdown in Little Tokyo *'91*
Rapid Fire *'92*
The Crow *'93*

Britton Lee
The Power of the Ninjitsu *'88*
Ironheart *'92*

Bruce Lee
Marlowe *'69*
Chinese Connection *'73*
Enter the Dragon *'73*
Fists of Fury *'73*
Return of the Dragon *'73*
Game of Death *'79*
Real Bruce Lee *'79*
The Three Avengers *'80*
The Deadliest Art: The Best of the Martial Arts Films *'90*

Canada Lee
Lifeboat *'44*
Body and Soul *'47*
Lost Boundaries *'49*
Cry, the Beloved Country *'51*

Carl Lee
The Connection *'61*
Superfly *'72*
Gordon's War *'73*
Keeping On *'81*

Christopher Lee
Hamlet *'48*
Scott of the Antarctic *'48*
Captain Horatio Hornblower *'51*
Valley of the Eagles *'51*
Crimson Pirate *'52*
Moulin Rouge *'52*
Alias John Preston *'56*
The Curse of Frankenstein *'57*
Night Ambush *'57*
Corridors of Blood *'58*
The Horror of Dracula *'58*
A Tale of Two Cities *'58*
The Hound of the Baskervilles *'59*
The Mummy *'59*
Uncle Was a Vampire *'59*
Beat Girl *'60*
The Hands of Orlac *'60*
Horror Hotel *'60*
The Two Faces of Dr. Jekyll *'60*
Scream of Fear *'61*
The Longest Day *'62*
Sherlock Holmes and the Deadly Necklace *'62*
Castle of the Living Dead *'64*
The Gorgon *'64*
Hercules in the Haunted World *'64*
Dr. Terror's House of Horrors *'65*
The Skull *'65*
The Virgin of Nuremberg *'65*
Circus of Fear *'67*
Five Golden Dragons *'67*
Island of the Burning Doomed *'67*
Theatre of Death *'67*
The Castle of Fu Manchu *'68*
The Crimson Cult *'68*
Dracula Has Risen from the Grave *'68*
Kiss and Kill *'68*
The Magic Christian *'69*
The Oblong Box *'69*
The Torture Chamber of Dr. Sadism *'69*
The Private Life of Sherlock Holmes *'70*
The Scars of Dracula *'70*
Scream and Scream Again *'70*
Taste the Blood of Dracula *'70*
Count Dracula *'71*
The House that Dripped Blood *'71*
The Creeping Flesh *'72*
Hannie Caulder *'72*
Horror Express *'72*
Nothing But the Night *'72*
Dark Places *'73*
The Satanic Rites of Dracula *'73*
The Man with the Golden Gun *'74*
The Three Musketeers *'74*
The Devil's Undead *'75*
The Four Musketeers *'75*
The Wicker Man *'75*
Albino *'76*
Dracula & Son *'76*
End of the World *'76*
To the Devil, A Daughter *'76*
Airport '77 *'77*
Starship Invasions *'77*
Circle of Iron *'78*
Return from Witch Mountain *'78*
Captain America 2: Death Too Soon *'79*
Jaguar Lives *'79*
1941 *'79*
Bear Island *'80*
Serial *'80*
The Boy Who Left Home to Find Out About the Shivers *'81*
An Eye for an Eye *'81*
Goliath Awaits *'81*
House of the Long Shadows *'82*
Safari 3000 *'82*
The Salamander *'82*
Return of Captain Invincible *'83*
Shaka Zulu *'83*
The Far Pavilions *'84*
Keeper *'84*
Howling 2: Your Sister is a Werewolf *'85*
Rosebud Beach Hotel *'85*
Desperate Moves *'86*
The Girl *'86*
Many Faces of Sherlock Holmes *'86*
Jocks *'87*
The Land of Faraway *'87*
Around the World in 80 Days *'89*
Murder Story *'89*
The Return of the Musketeers *'89*
Treasure Island *'89*
Curse 3: Blood Sacrifice *'90*
Gremlins 2: The New Batch *'90*
Journey of Honor *'91*
Sherlock Holmes and the Incident at Victoria Falls *'91*
Double Vision *'92*
Detonator *'93*
Police Academy: Mission to Moscow *'94*

Conan Lee
Gymkata *'85*
The Eliminators *'86*

Danny Lee
The Killer *'90*
Organized Crime & Triad Bureau *'93*

DeWitt Lee
The Legend of Jedediah Carver *'70s*
Apache Blood *'75*

Dorothy Lee
Half-Shot at Sunrise *'30*
Hook, Line and Sinker *'30*
Cockeyed Cavaliers *'34*
Hips, Hips, Hooray *'34*

Dragon Lee
Clones of Bruce Lee *'80*
Enter Three Dragons *'81*
The Dragon's Showdown *'83*

Eric Lee
Weapons of Death *'83*
Shinobi Ninja *'84*
Ring of Fire *'91*
Out for Blood *'93*

Etta Lee
The Untamable *'23*
The Thief of Baghdad *'24*

Gypsy Rose Lee
My Lucky Star *'38*
The Stripper *'63*
The Trouble with Angels *'66*

Hwang Jang Lee
Buddha Assassinator *'82*
Hell's Wind Staff *'82*
Snuff-Bottle Connection *'82*
Story of the Dragon *'82*
Instant Kung-Fu Man *'84*

Jason Scott Lee
Back to the Future, Part 2 *'89*
The Lookalike *'90*
Dragon: The Bruce Lee Story *'93*
Map of the Human Heart *'93*
Rapa Nui *'93*
Rudyard Kipling's The Jungle Book *'94*

Jesse Lee
Matinee *'92*
The Brady Bunch Movie *'95*
From the Mixed-Up Files of Mrs. Basil E. Frankweiler *'95*
A Very Brady Sequel *'96*

Joanna Lee
The Brain Eaters *'58*
Making the Grade *'84*
Sam's Son *'84*

Joie Lee
School Daze *'88*
Bail Jumper *'89*
Mo' Better Blues *'90*
Fathers and Sons *'92*
Crooklyn *'94*

Judy Lee
Queen Boxer *'73*
The Bodyguard *'76*

Kaiulani Lee
Zelly & Me *'88*
Before and After *'95*

Karen Lee
Roadhouse 66 *'84*
Eye on the Sparrow *'91*

Lila Lee
Hawthorne of the USA *'19*
Male and Female *'19*
Blood and Sand *'22*
Midnight Girl *'25*
Blood and Sand/Son of the Sheik *'26*
The Adorable Cheat *'28*
The Unholy Three *'30*
False Faces *'32*
I Can't Escape *'34*
Stand Up and Cheer *'34*
Champagne for Breakfast *'35*
Country Gentlemen *'36*
A Nation Aflame *'37*

Margaret Lee
Casanova '70 *'65*
How to Kill 400 Duponts *'65*
Secret Agent Super Dragon *'66*
Circus of Fear *'67*
Five for Hell *'67*
Five Golden Dragons *'67*
Murder for Sale *'70*
Slaughter Hotel *'71*
Rogue *'76*

Mark Lee
Gallipoli *'81*
The Everlasting Secret Family *'88*

Mary Lee
Nancy Drew, Reporter *'39*
Ridin' on a Rainbow *'41*

Michele Lee
How to Succeed in Business without Really Trying *'67*
The Love Bug *'68*
The Comic *'69*
Bud and Lou *'78*
The Fatal Image *'90*
Broadway Bound *'92*

Pinky Lee
Chasing Those Depression Blues '35
Lady of Burlesque '43

Robbie Lee
Big Bad Mama '74
Switchblade Sisters '75

Ruta Lee
Escape from Planet Earth '67
Rooster: Spurs of Death! '83
First & Ten '85
First & Ten: The Team Scores Again '85
Sweet Bird of Youth '89
Funny Bones '94

Sheryl Lee
Twin Peaks '90
Twin Peaks '90
Wild at Heart '90
Love, Lies and Murder '91
Jersey Girl '92
Twin Peaks: Fire Walk with Me '92
Red Shoe Diaries 4: Auto Erotica '93
Backbeat '94
Don't Do It '94
Fall Time '94
Follow the River '95

Spike Lee
She's Gotta Have It '86
School Daze '88
Do the Right Thing '89
Mo' Better Blues '90
Jungle Fever '91
Malcolm X '92
Crooklyn '94
Girl 6 '96

Stephen Lee
Steel Fisted Dragon '82
Purple Hearts '84
Dolls '87
The Pit & the Pendulum '91
Prehysteria '93
Me and the Mob '94

Waise Lee
A Bullet in the Head '90
Wing Chun '94

Richard Leech
The Third Key '57
The Moonraker '58

Andrea Leeds
Come and Get It '36
Song of the Trail '36
It Could Happen to You '37
Stage Door '37
The Goldwyn Follies '38
Letter of Introduction '38
The Real Glory '39
They Shall Have Music '39

Lila Leeds
The Show-Off '46
Wild Weed '49

Phil Leeds
Haunting of Harrington House '82
Enemies, a Love Story '89
Ghost '90
Frankie and Johnny '91
He Said, She Said '91

Jane Leeves
Mr. Write '92
Miracle on 34th Street '94

Rene Lefevre
Le Million '31
The Crime of Monsieur Lange '36

Eva LeGallienne
The Devil's Disciple '59
Resurrection '80

Lance LeGault
French Quarter '78
Kenny Rogers as the Gambler '80
Kidnapped '87
Shadow Force '92

Phoebe Legere
The Toxic Avenger, Part 2 '89
The Toxic Avenger, Part 3: The Last Temptation of Toxie '89

James LeGros
Phantasm II '88
Drugstore Cowboy '89
Hollywood Heartbreak '89
Leather Jackets '90
Point Break '91
Guncrazy '92
My New Gun '92
Singles '92
Where the Day Takes You '92
Nervous Ticks '93
Bad Girls '94
Don't Do It '94
Floundering '94
Living in Oblivion '94
Destiny Turns on the Radio '95
Safe '95
Marshal Law '96

John Leguizamo
Casualties of War '89
Die Hard 2: Die Harder '90
Street Hunter '90
Hangin' with the Homeboys '91
Regarding Henry '91
Whispers in the Dark '92
Carlito's Way '93
Super Mario Bros. '93
A Pyromaniac's Love Story '95
To Wong Foo, Thanks for Everything, Julie Newmar '95
Executive Decision '96
The Fan '96

Carla Lehmann
Cottage to Let '41
Secret Mission '42
Fame Is the Spur '47

Frederic Lehne
Coward of the County '81
Billionaire Boys Club '87
Amityville 4 '89
This Gun for Hire '90
Dream Lover '93
Man's Best Friend '93

John Lehne
Roboman '75
The Disappearance of Aimee '76
Griffin and Phoenix: A Love Story '76
A Long Way Home '81

Fritz Leiber
The Story of Louis Pasteur '36
Cry of the Werewolf '44

Ron Leibman
The Hot Rock '70
Where's Poppa? '70
Slaughterhouse Five '72
The Art of Crime '75
A Question of Guilt '78
Norma Rae '79
Up the Academy '80
Zorro, the Gay Blade '81
Romantic Comedy '83
Door to Door '84
Phar Lap '84
Rhinestone '84
Seven Hours to Judgment '88

Don Leifert
The Alien Factor '78
Fiend '83
Galaxy Invader '85
Deadly Neighbor '91

Barbara Leigh
The Student Nurses '70
Junior Bonner '72
Boss '74
Smile, Jenny, You're Dead '74
Mistress of the Apes '79
Seven '79

Cassandra Leigh
Midnight Tease '94
Alien Terminator '95

Frank Leigh
American Pluck '25
Below the Deadline '29

Janet Leigh
The Hills of Home '48
Words and Music '48
Holiday Affair '49
Little Women '49
That Forsyte Woman '50
Angels in the Outfield '51
Two Tickets to Broadway '51
Scaramouche '52
Houdini '53
The Naked Spur '53
Prince Valiant '54
My Sister Eileen '55
Pete Kelly's Blues '55
Jet Pilot '57
Touch of Evil '58
The Vikings '58
Perfect Furlough '59
Psycho '60
The Manchurian Candidate '62
Bye, Bye, Birdie '63
Harper '66
The Fog '78

Jennifer Jason Leigh
Angel City '80
The Best Little Girl in the World '81
Eyes of a Stranger '81
Killing of Randy Webster '81
Fast Times at Ridgemont High '82
Wrong is Right '82
Easy Money '83
Grandview U.S.A. '84
Flesh and Blood '85
Girls of the White Orchid '85
The Hitcher '86
The Men's Club '86
Sister, Sister '87
Undercover '87
The Big Picture '89
Heart of Midnight '89
Buried Alive '90
Last Exit to Brooklyn '90
Miami Blues '90
Backdraft '91
Crooked Hearts '91
Rush '91
Single White Female '92
The Hudsucker Proxy '93
Short Cuts '93
Dolores Claiborne '94
Mrs. Parker and the Vicious Circle '94
Georgia '95

Nelson Leigh
Texas Masquerade '44
Ma Barker's Killer Brood '60

Spencer Leigh
The Last of England '87
Smart Money '88

Steven Leigh
China White '91
Deadly Bet '91
To Be the Best '93
Sword of Honor '94

Suzanna Leigh
Boeing Boeing '65
Paradise, Hawaiian Style '66
The Fiend '71
Lust for a Vampire '71

Vivien Leigh
Dark Journey '37
Fire Over England '37
Storm in a Teacup '37
21 Days '37
Gone with the Wind '39
Sidewalks of London '40
Waterloo Bridge '40
That Hamilton Woman '41
Caesar and Cleopatra '46
Anna Karenina '48
A Streetcar Named Desire '51
Roman Spring of Mrs. Stone '61
Ship of Fools '65
Hollywood Outtakes & Rare Footage '83

Barbara Leigh-Hunt
Frenzy '72
Paper Mask '91
Pride and Prejudice '95

Lillian Leighton
The Jack Knife Man '20
Peck's Bad Boy '21
Man from Monterey '33

Margaret Leighton
Bonnie Prince Charlie '48
The Winslow Boy '48
Under Capricorn '49
The Elusive Pimpernel '50
Carrington, V.C. '54
Waltz of the Toreadors '62
The Best Man '64
The Loved One '65
The Madwoman of Chaillot '69
The Go-Between '71
X, Y & Zee '72
From Beyond the Grave '73
Choice of Weapons '76

Roberta Leighton
Barracuda '78
Covergirl '83

Harald Leipnitz
River of Evil '64
Hell Hounds of Alaska '73
Fight for Gold '86

Frederick Leister
O.H.M.S. '37
Spellbound '41
Green Grow the Rushes '51

Donovan Leitch
And God Created Woman '88
The Blob '88
The In Crowd '88
Cutting Class '89
Glory '89
Dark Horse '92
Gas Food Lodging '92

Paul LeMat
Firehouse '72
American Graffiti '73
Aloha, Bobby and Rose '74
Citizens Band '77
More American Graffiti '79
Melvin and Howard '80
Death Valley '81
Jimmy the Kid '82
Strange Invaders '83
The Burning Bed '85
P.K. and the Kid '85
Long Time Gone '86
On Wings of Eagles '86
Hanoi Hilton '87
Into the Homeland '87
The Night They Saved Christmas '87
Private Investigations '87
Blind Witness '89
Easy Wheels '89
Grave Secrets '89
Puppet Master '89
Woman With a Past '92
Wishman '93
Children of Fury '94
Sensation '94

Harvey Lembeck
Stalag 17 '53
Between Heaven and Hell '56
Beach Party '63
Love with the Proper Stranger '63
Bikini Beach '64
Pajama Party '64
Beach Blanket Bingo '65
How to Stuff a Wild Bikini '65

Michael Lembeck
The Boys in Company C '77
The In-Laws '79
Gorp '80
On the Right Track '81
Conspiracy: The Trial of the Chicago Eight '87
Danielle Steel's Heartbeat '93

Chris Lemmon
The Happy Hooker Goes Hollywood '80
Just Before Dawn '80
C.O.D. '83
Swing Shift '84
That's Life! '86
Weekend Warriors '86
Going Undercover '88
Dad '89
Corporate Affairs '90
Firehead '90
Lena's Holiday '90
Thunder in Paradise '93
Thunder in Paradise 2 '94

Jack Lemmon
It Should Happen to You '54
Phffft! '54
Mister Roberts '55
My Sister Eileen '55
Fire Down Below '57
Bell, Book and Candle '58
Cowboy '58
Some Like It Hot '59
The Apartment '60
Wackiest Ship in the Army '61
Days of Wine and Roses '62
Irma La Douce '63
Good Neighbor Sam '64
How to Murder Your Wife '64
The Great Race '65
The Fortune Cookie '66
Luv '67
The Odd Couple '68
April Fools '69
The Out-of-Towners '70
Avanti! '72
Save the Tiger '73
The Front Page '74
Prisoner of Second Avenue '74
Airport '77 '77
The China Syndrome '79
Tribute '80
Buddy Buddy '81
Missing '82
Mass Appeal '84
Macaroni '85
That's Life! '86
The Murder of Mary Phagan '87
Long Day's Journey into Night '88
Dad '89
JFK '91
For Richer, For Poorer '92
Glengarry Glen Ross '92
Grumpy Old Men '93
A Life in the Theater '93
Short Cuts '93
Grumpier Old Men '95
Getting Away With Murder '96

Kasi Lemmons
School Daze '88
Vampire's Kiss '88
Candyman '92
Hard Target '93
DROP Squad '94
Fear of a Black Hat '94

Michel Lemoine
Planets Against Us '61
The Sensuous Teenager '70

Genevieve Lemon
Sweetie '89
The Piano '93

Mark Lenard
Noon Sunday '71
Star Trek 3: The Search for Spock '84
Star Trek 4: The Voyage Home '86
Star Trek 6: The Undiscovered Country '91

Harry J. Lennix
The Five Heartbeats '91
Bob Roberts '92
Mo' Money '92

Jarrett Lennon
Servants of Twilight '91
Short Cuts '93

John Lennon
A Hard Day's Night '64
Help! '65
How I Won the War '67
Magical Mystery Tour '67
The Magic Christian '69
Let It Be '70
The Compleat Beatles '82
Chuck Berry: Hail! Hail! Rock 'n' Roll '87

Annie Lennox
Revolution '85
The Room '87
Edward II '92

Jay Leno
Silver Bears '78
Americathon '79
Doctor Duck's Super Secret All-Purpose Sauce '85
Collision Course '89

Jack Lenoir
Once in Paris... '79
Breakfast in Paris '81

Lotte Lenya
The Threepenny Opera '31
Roman Spring of Mrs. Stone '61
From Russia with Love '63
Semi-Tough '77

Kay Lenz
White Line Fever '75
Great Scout & Cathouse Thursday '76
Moving Violation '76
Rich Man, Poor Man '76
Initiation of Sarah '78
Mean Dog Blues '78
Sanctuary of Fear '79
Fast Walking '82
Prisoners of the Lost Universe '84
House '86
Death Wish 4: The Crackdown '87

Lenz ▶cont.

Stripped to Kill '87
Fear '88
Headhunter '89
Murder by Night '89
Physical Evidence '89
Hitler's Daughter '90
Falling from Grace '92
Trapped in Space '94

Rick Lenz
Cactus Flower '69
Scandalous John '71
Little Dragons '80

Melissa Leo
Always '85
Silent Witness '85
Streetwalkin' '85
Deadtime Stories '86
A Time of Destiny '88
Carolina Skeletons '92
Scarlett '94
Last Summer In the Hamptons '96

Leon
The Five Heartbeats '91
Bad Attitude '93
Cliffhanger '93
Cool Runnings '93
Above the Rim '94
Once Upon a Time...When We Were Colored '95
Waiting to Exhale '95

Loles Leon
Don Juan, My Love '90
Tie Me Up! Tie Me Down! '90

Valerie Leon
Alien Women '69
The Spy Who Loved Me '77
Never Say Never Again '83

Lu Leonard
Princess Academy '87
Shadowzone '89
Circuitry Man '90
A Climate for Killing '91

Robert Sean Leonard
Bluffing It '87
My Best Friend Is a Vampire '88
Dead Poets Society '89
Mr. & Mrs. Bridge '90
The Age of Innocence '93
Married to It '93
Much Ado about Nothing '93
Swing Kids '93
Safe Passage '94
The Boys Next Door '96

Sheldon Leonard
Week-End In Havana '41
Tortilla Flat '42
City Without Men '43
Harvest Melody '43
The Falcon in Hollywood '44
Gambler's Choice '44
Timber Queen '44
To Have & Have Not '44
Uncertain Glory '44
Zombies on Broadway '44
Captain Kidd '45
It's a Wonderful Life '46
Sinbad, the Sailor '47
Open Secret '48
Force of Evil '49
Shep Comes Home '49
Abbott and Costello Meet the Invisible Man '51
Breakdown '53
Guys and Dolls '55
The Road to Lebanon '60
Brink's Job '78

Marco Leonardi
Cinema Paradiso '88
Like Water for Chocolate '93

Al Leong
Bill & Ted's Excellent Adventure '89
Hard Hunted '92

Tea Leoni
Wyatt Earp '94
Bad Boys '95
Flirting with Disaster '95

Chauncey Leopardi
Huck and the King of Hearts '93
The Sandlot '93

Houseguest '94
The Big Green '95

Philippe Leotard
Two English Girls '72
La Petite Sirene '80
La Balance '82
Les Miserables '95

Ted Leplat
The Kirlian Witness '78
Swift Justice '88
Emissary '89
American Kickboxer 1 '91

Ken Lerner
Relentless '89
Fast Getaway '91
Unlawful Entry '92
Fallen Angels 1 '93
Mother's Boys '94
Relentless 4 '94

Michael Lerner
The Candidate '72
Firehouse '72
Busting '74
Reflections of Murder '74
F. Scott Fitzgerald in Hollywood '76
Outlaw Blues '77
Coast to Coast '80
The Postman Always Rings Twice '81
National Lampoon's Class Reunion '82
Rita Hayworth: The Love Goddess '83
Strange Invaders '83
The Execution '85
Hands of a Stranger '87
Anguish '88
Eight Men Out '88
Harlem Nights '89
Any Man's Death '90
Maniac Cop 2 '90
Barton Fink '91
The Closer '91
Omen 4: The Awakening '91
The Comrades of Summer '92
Newsies '92
Amos and Andrew '93
Blank Check '93
Girl in the Cadillac '94
No Escape '94
Radioland Murders '94
The Road to Wellville '94
A Pyromaniac's Love Story '95

Maxime LeRoux
Mama, There's a Man in Your Bed '89
The Son of the Shark '93

Phillippe LeRoy
Alone Against Rome '62
Castle of the Living Dead '64
A Married Woman '65
The Night Porter '74
Quo Vadis '85

Ed LeSaint
Range Feud '31
Texas Bad Man '32

Bethel Leslie
Ironweed '87
Long Day's Journey into Night '88

Joan Leslie
Love Affair '39
High Sierra '41
Sergeant York '41
Yankee Doodle Dandy '42
The Sky's the Limit '43
Thank Your Lucky Stars '43
This Is the Army '43
Hollywood Canteen '44
Rhapsody in Blue '45
Born to Be Bad '50
Man in the Saddle '51
Jubilee Trail '54

John Leslie
Dracula Sucks '79
It's Called Murder, Baby '82

Nan Leslie
Desperate '47
The Devil Thumbs a Ride '47
The Devil Thumbs a Ride/Having Wonderful Crime '47
Rim of the Canyon '49
Western Double Feature 14 '52
The Bamboo Saucer '68

Mimi Lesseos
The American Angels: Baptism of Blood '89
Final Impact '91
Pushed to the Limit '92
Beyond Fear '93

Len Lesser
How to Stuff a Wild Bikini '65
Joy Ride to Nowhere '78
The Ghost of Fletcher Ridge '80s
Dubeat-E-O '84

Ben Lessy
The Jackie Robinson Story '50
Pajama Party '64

Bruce Lester
Boy Meets Girl '38
British Intelligence '40
The Letter '40
Shadows on the Stairs '41
Golden Earrings '47
Charade '53

Buddy Lester
The Patsy '64
Big Mouth '67
Cracking Up '83

Jeff Lester
Once a Hero '88
In the Cold of the Night '89

Mark Lester
Oliver! '68
Sudden Terror '70
Black Beauty '71
Melody '71
Who Slew Auntie Roo? '71
What the Peeper Saw '72
Redneck '73
The Prince and the Pauper '78

David Letch
Dark of the Night '85
Death Warmed Up '85

Lori Lethin
Bloody Birthday '80
The Prey '80
Brotherly Love '85
Return to Horror High '87

Al Lettieri
The Getaway '72
The Godfather '72
Pulp '72
The Deadly Trackers '73
The Don is Dead '73
McQ '74
Mr. Majestyk '74
The Godfather 1902-1959: The Complete Epic '81

Tony Leung
A Bullet in the Head '90
The Laserman '90
Hard-Boiled '92
The Lover '92
Chungking Express '95

Lynn Levand
Hellbent '90
Kill or Be Killed '93

Oscar Levant
Dance of Life '29
Rhythm on the River '40
Humoresque '46
Romance on the High Seas '48
The Barkleys of Broadway '49
An American in Paris '51
The Band Wagon '53
The Cobweb '55

Calvin Levels
A Christmas Without Snow '80
Adventures in Babysitting '87
Johnny Suede '92
Live! From Death Row '92
Point of No Return '93
Hellbound '94

Sam Levene
Three Men on a Horse '36
Mad Miss Manton '38
Shopworn Angel '38
Golden Boy '39
Shadow of the Thin Man '41
Action in the North Atlantic '43
I Dood It '43
Whistling in Brooklyn '43
The Purple Heart '44
Boomerang '47
Babe Ruth Story '48
Designing Woman '57
Sweet Smell of Success '57

A Dream of Kings '69

Rachel Levin
Gaby: A True Story '87
White Palace '90

Jean Levine
Hollywood in Trouble '87
The Newlydeads '87

Jerry Levine
Iron Eagle '86
Casual Sex? '88
Born on the Fourth of July '89

Ted Levine
Ironweed '87
Fulfillment '89
Love at Large '89
The Silence of the Lambs '91
Detonator '93
The Last Outlaw '93
Nowhere to Run '93
The Mangler '94
Georgia '95
Heat '95

Barry Levinson
History of the World: Part 1 '81
Quiz Show '94

Emile Levisetti
Bix '90
Sexual Response '92
Alien Terminator '95

Steve Levitt
Hunk '87
Blue Movies '88
The Incredible Hulk Returns '88

Eugene Levy
The Best of John Candy on SCTV '80s
Going Berserk '83
National Lampoon's Vacation '83
The Last Polka '84
Splash '84
Armed and Dangerous '86
Club Paradise '86
Speed Zone '88
Stay Tuned '92
Father of the Bride Part II '95
Kurt Vonnegut's Harrison Bergeron '95

James Lew
Ninja Turf '86
Private Wars '93
Blood for Blood '95

Jose Lewgoy
Earth Entranced '66
Fitzcarraldo '82
Kiss of the Spider Woman '85

Al Lewis
Car 54, Where Are You? '61
Way He Was '76
The Munsters' Revenge '81
Comic Cabby '87
Married to the Mob '88
Fright House '89
My Grandpa is a Vampire '92
Car 54, Where Are You? '94

Brittney Lewis
Dream Machine '91
Rubin & Ed '92

Charlotte Lewis
The Golden Child '86
Pirates '86
Dial Help '88
Tripwire '89
Bare Essentials '91
Sketch Artist '92
Storyville '92
Excessive Force '93
Men of War '94
Decoy '95
Embrace of the Vampire '95
Red Shoe Diaries 6: How I Met My Husband '95

Dawnn Lewis
I'm Gonna Git You Sucka '88
Race to Freedom: The Story of the Underground Railroad '94

Diana Lewis
Andy Hardy Meets Debutante '40
Go West '40
Somewhere I'll Find You '42
Whistling in Dixie '42

Fiona Lewis
Blue Blood '73
Dracula '73

Lisztomania '75
Drum '76
Stunts '77
Tintorera...Tiger Shark '78
Wanda Nevada '79
Strange Behavior '81
Strange Invaders '83
Innerspace '87

Forrest Lewis
Escape from Fort Bravo '53
The Monster of Piedras Blancas '57

Geoffrey Lewis
Culpepper Cattle Co. '72
Macon County Line '74
Thunderbolt & Lightfoot '74
The Great Waldo Pepper '75
Smile '75
The Wind and the Lion '75
The Return of a Man Called Horse '76
Every Which Way But Loose '78
Tilt '78
When Every Day was the Fourth of July '78
Bronco Billy '80
Heaven's Gate '81
Shoot the Sun Down '81
I, the Jury '82
Return of the Man from U.N.C.L.E. '83
September Gun '83
Night of the Comet '84
Lust in the Dust '85
Stitches '85
Maximum Security '87
Out of the Dark '88
Pancho Barnes '88
Catch Me...If You Can '89
Pink Cadillac '89
Disturbed '90
Matters of the Heart '90
Double Impact '91
The Lawnmower Man '92
The Man Without a Face '93
Only the Strong '93
Point of No Return '93
Wishman '93
Army of One '94
Maverick '94
National Lampoon's Last Resort '94
White Fang 2: The Myth of the White Wolf '94
When the Dark Man Calls '95

George Lewis
Outlaws of the Desert '41
Perils of the Darkest Jungle '44
Zorro's Black Whip '44
Federal Operator 99 '45
The Big Sombrero '49
King of the Bullwhip '51
The Sign of Zorro '60
Indian Paint '64

Gilbert Lewis
Touched '82
The Kid Who Loved Christmas '90
Candyman '92

Greg Lewis
Frankie and Johnny '91
Prehysteria 2 '94

Jenifer Lewis
What's Love Got to Do with It? '93
Corrina, Corrina '94
Deconstructing Sarah '94
Renaissance Man '94
Girl 6 '96

Jenny Lewis
A Friendship in Vienna '88
Troop Beverly Hills '89
The Wizard '89
Runaway Father '91

Jerry Lewis
My Friend Irma '49
At War with the Army '50
The Stooge '51
Jumping Jacks '52
The Caddy '53
The Road to Bali '53
Scared Stiff '53
Artists and Models '55
The Delicate Delinquent '56
Hollywood or Bust '56
Pardners '56
The Sad Sack '57

The Geisha Boy '58
The Bellboy '60
Cinderfella '60
The Errand Boy '61
The Ladies' Man '61
It's a Mad, Mad, Mad, Mad World '63
The Nutty Professor '63
Disorderly Orderly '64
The Patsy '64
Boeing Boeing '65
Family Jewels '65
Big Mouth '67
Don't Raise the Bridge, Lower the River '68
Which Way to the Front? '70
Hardly Working '81
King of Comedy '82
Cracking Up '83
Slapstick of Another Kind '84
Hollywood Clowns '85
Trading Hearts '87
Cookie '89
Arizona Dream '94
Funny Bones '94

Jerry Lee Lewis
High School Confidential '58
Chuck Berry: Hail! Hail! Rock 'n' Roll '87

Joe Lewis
Jaguar Lives '79
Force: Five '81

Joe E. Lewis
Private Buckaroo '42
Lady in Cement '68

Juliette Lewis
My Stepmother Is an Alien '88
Meet the Hollowheads '89
National Lampoon's Christmas Vacation '89
Too Young to Die '90
Cape Fear '91
Husbands and Wives '92
Kalifornia '93
Romeo Is Bleeding '93
That Night '93
What's Eating Gilbert Grape '93
The Basketball Diaries '94
Mixed Nuts '94
Natural Born Killers '94
From Dusk Till Dawn '95
Strange Days '95

Louise Lewis
Blood of Dracula '57
I Was a Teenage Werewolf '57

Mitchell Lewis
Salome '22
Salome/Queen Elizabeth '23
Linda '29
The Wizard of Oz '39
Billy the Kid '41
Cairo '42

Phill Lewis
Brother Future '91
City Slickers '91

Ralph Lewis
When the Clouds Roll By '19
Outside the Law '21
Dante's Inferno '24
Somewhere in Sonora '33
Sucker Money '34

Richard Lewis
Diary of a Young Comic '79
The Wrong Guys '88
That's Adequate '90
Once Upon a Crime '92
Robin Hood: Men in Tights '93
Wagons East '94
Danger of Love '95
Leaving Las Vegas '95

Robert Lewis
Son of Lassie '45
Monsieur Verdoux '47
Hello Again '87

Ronald Lewis
Helen of Troy '56
Robbery Under Arms '57
Bachelor of Hearts '58
Conspiracy of Hearts '60
Scream of Fear '61
Billy Budd '62
Friends '71
Paul and Michelle '74

Sheldon Lewis
With Kit Carson Over the Great Divide '25
Beyond the Trail '26
The Phantom '31
Tombstone Canyon '35

Jacob Leygraf
The Slingshot '93
Sunday's Children '94

Johan Leysen
Hail Mary '85
Egg '88
The Music Teacher '88
Daens '92
Trahir '93

John Leyton
Guns at Batasi '64
Seaside Swingers '65
Von Ryan's Express '65

Thierry Lhermitte
Next Year If All Goes Well '83
My Best Friend's Girl '84
My New Partner '84
Until September '84
Augustin '95
Little Indian, Big City '95

Bruce Li
Blind Fists of Bruce '70s
Image of Bruce Lee '70s
Return of the Tiger '78
Enter the Panther '79
Bruce Li in New Guinea '80
Bruce Li the Invincible '80
Fists of Fury 2 '80
Enter Three Dragons '81
Story of the Dragon '82
Chinese Connection 2 '84
Counter Attack '84
Iron Dragon Strikes Back '84
Kung Fu Avengers '85

Chang Li
Enter Three Dragons '81
Fight to the Death '83

Gong Li
Red Sorghum '87
Ju Dou '90
Raise the Red Lantern '91
The Story of Qui Ju '91
Farewell My Concubine '93
To Live '94
Shanghai Triad '95

Bruce Liang
The Fist, the Kicks, and the Evils '80
Showdown at the Equator '83

Ko Shou Liang
Ninja Exterminators '81
Renegade Monk '82
Shaolin Ex-Monk '82

Tan Tao Liang
Dual Flying Kicks '82
Incredible Master Beggars '82

Peter Paul Liapis
Starhops '78
Ghoulies 4 '93
Fast Getaway 2 '94

Brian Libby
Silent Rage '82
Platoon Leader '87

Liberace
Sincerely Yours '56
The Loved One '65

Anne Libert
Virgin Among the Living Dead '71
The Demons '74

Richard Libertini
The In-Laws '79
Popeye '80
Sharky's Machine '81
Soup for One '82
Deal of the Century '83
Going Berserk '83
All of Me '84
Unfaithfully Yours '84
Fletch '85
Fourth Wise Man '85
Big Trouble '86
Animal Behavior '89
Fletch Lives '89
The Bonfire of the Vanities '90
Nell '94

Jeremy Licht
The Seekers '79
Father Figure '80
Lois Gibbs and the Love Canal '82
Twilight Zone: The Movie '83
Next One '84

Mitchell Lichtenstein
Streamers '83
The Wedding Banquet '93

Gabriella Licudi
The Unearthly Stranger '64
The Last Safari '67

G. Gordon Liddy
When Nature Calls '85
Camp Cucamonga: How I Spent My Summer Vacation '90
Street Asylum '90
Super Force '90
Adventures in Spying '92

Lo Lieh
Born Invincible '76
The Stranger and the Gunfighter '76
Shaolin Executioner '80s
Bruce's Deadly Fingers '80
The Golden Triangle '80
Showdown at the Equator '83
Ninja Massacre '84
King Boxer '90
The Ninja Pirates '90
The Noble Ninja '90

Albert Lieven
The Life and Death of Colonel Blimp '43
Sleeping Car to Trieste '45
Beware of Pity '46
The Seventh Veil '46
Frieda '47

Tina Lifford
Grand Canyon '91
Paris Trout '91
The Ernest Green Story '93
America's Dream '95

Marilyn Lightstone
Lies My Father Told Me '75
Wild Pony '83
Anne of Green Gables '85
Surrogate '88
Grand Tour: Disaster in Time '92

Tom Ligon
Fury on Wheels '71
Judge Horton and the Scottsboro Boys '76

Matthew Lillard
Serial Mom '94
Hackers '95

Beatrice Lillie
On Approval '44
Thoroughly Modern Millie '67

Bridget Lin
Jackie Chan's Police Force '85
Chungking Express '95

Abbey Lincoln
Nothing But a Man '64
For Love of Ivy '68
Mo' Better Blues '90

Elmo Lincoln
Tarzan of the Apes '17
The Adventures of Tarzan '21
Wyoming Outlaw '39

Lar Park Lincoln
Princess Academy '87
Friday the 13th, Part 7: The New Blood '88

Traci Lind
A Tiger's Tale '87
Fright Night 2 '88
Survival Quest '89
Class of 1999 '90
The Handmaid's Tale '90
No Secrets '91
Voyager '91
My Boyfriend's Back '93
The Road to Wellville '94

Gunnel Lindblom
The Seventh Seal '56
The Virgin Spring '59
Hunger '66

Doris Linden
Hillbilly Blitzkrieg '42
Snuffy Smith, Yard Bird '42

Eric Linden
Ah, Wilderness! '35
Let 'Em Have It '35
Sweetheart of the Navy '37
Gone with the Wind '39
Criminals Within '41

Hal Linden
Mr. Inside, Mr. Outside '74
How to Break Up a Happy Divorce '76
Father Figure '80
Starflight One '83
I Do! I Do! '84
My Wicked, Wicked Ways '84
A New Life '88
The Colony '95

Jennie Linden
Nightmare '63
Women in Love '70
Hedda '75

Cec Linder
Quatermass and the Pit '58
Goldfinger '64
A Touch of Class '73
The Devil's Web '74
Deadly Eyes '82
Heavenly Bodies '84

Max Linder
Laugh with Linder! '13
Man in the Silk Hat '15
Early Cinema Vol. 1 '19
Seven Years Bad Luck '20
Max '22
Pop Goes the Cork '22
Man in the Silk Hat '83

Viveca Lindfors
Adventures of Don Juan '49
Four in a Jeep '51
Moonfleet '55
The Story of Ruth '60
The King of Kings '61
Cauldron of Blood '67
The Way We Were '73
Bell from Hell '74
Welcome to L.A. '77
Girlfriends '78
A Question of Guilt '78
A Wedding '78
Natural Enemies '79
Marilyn: The Untold Story '80
Mom, the Wolfman and Me '80
The Best Little Girl in the World '81
For Ladies Only '81
The Hand '81
Creepshow '82
Inside the Third Reich '82
Silent Madness '84
Secret Weapons '85
The Sure Thing '85
Lady Beware '87
Rachel River '87
The Ann Jillian Story '88
Exiled in America '90
Exorcist 3: Legion '90
Child of Darkness, Child of Light '91
Zandalee '91
The Linguini Incident '92
Backstreet Justice '93
Stargate '94
Last Summer In the Hamptons '96

Peter Lindgren
I Am Curious (Yellow) '67
The New Land '73

Audra Lindley
The Heartbreak Kid '72
Revenge of the Stepford Wives '80
Best Friends '82
Cannery Row '82
Desert Hearts '86
Stamp of a Killer '87
The Spellbinder '88
Troop Beverly Hills '89
The New Age '94
Sudden Death '95

Delroy Lindo
Mountains of the Moon '90
Bright Angel '91
Malcolm X '92
Blood In...Blood Out: Bound by Honor '93
Mr. Jones '93
Crooklyn '94
Broken Arrow '95
Clockers '95
Get Shorty '95

Olga Lindo
Things Happen at Night '48
The Hidden Room '49

Vincent Lindon
Betty Blue '86
A Man in Love '87

Margaret Lindsay
Baby Face '33
Cavalcade '33
Lady Killer '33
Dangerous '35
Devil Dogs of the Air '35
"G" Men '35
Jezebel '38
British Intelligence '40
The Spoilers '42
The Adventures of Rusty '45
Club Havana '46
Cass Timberlane '47
Please Don't Eat the Daisies '60

Robert Lindsay
Bert Rigby, You're a Fool '89
Strike It Rich '90
Genghis Cohn '93

Stuart Lindsell
Man of Evil '48
Profile '54

George Lindsey
Andy Griffith Show '60
Return to Mayberry '85

Pierre Lindstedt
The Emigrants '72
The New Land '73

Helga Line
Nightmare Castle '65
Horror Rises from the Tomb '72
The Saga of the Draculas '72
The Mummy's Revenge '73
When the Screaming Stops '73
Pulsebeat '85

Richard Lineback
Beyond the Next Mountain '87
Woman With a Past '92
Speed '94

Stephi Lineburg
Breathing Lessons '94
Richie Rich '94

Chen Pei Ling
The Furious Avenger '76
Golden Sun '80s

Chia Ling
Against the Drunken Cat Paws '75
The Great Hunter '75
Ten Brothers of Shao-lin '80s
Eighteen Jade Arhats '84
Ninja Swords of Death '90

Shangkuan Ling-Feng
Fight for Survival '77
Kung Fu Commandos '80
Green Dragon Inn '82
Shaolin Traitor '82

Wendy Lingham
Alien Women '69
Demonstrator '71

Paul Linke
Motel Hell '80
Parenthood '89
Time Flies When You're Alive '89
The Fear Inside '92

Art Linkletter
People Are Funny '46
Champagne for Caesar '50

Rex Linn
Cliffhanger '93
Drop Zone '94
Wyatt Earp '94

Mark Linn-Baker
Manhattan '79
My Favorite Year '82
Ghostwriter '84
Bare Essentials '91
Noises Off '92

Laura Linney
Class of '61 '92
Armistead Maupin's Tales of the City '93
Blind Spot '93
Dave '93
A Simple Twist of Fate '94
Congo '95

Linney ▸cont.

Primal Fear '96

Joanne Linville
Scorpio '73
Secrets '77
From the Dead of Night '89

Larry Linville
The Stepmother '71
M*A*S*H: The Collector's Edition '72
Night Partners '83
School Spirit '85
Blue Movies '88
Earth Girls Are Easy '89
Rock 'n' Roll High School Forever '91
Body Waves '92
No Dessert Dad, 'Til You Mow the Lawn '94

Lio
The Eighties '83
Window Shopping '86
Love After Love '94

Leon M. Lion
No. 17 '32
Amazing Adventure '37

Alberto Lionello
Porcile '69
Till Marriage Do Us Part '74

Therese Liotard
One Sings, the Other Doesn't '77
Cloud Waltzing '87
My Father's Glory '91
My Mother's Castle '91

Ray Liotta
The Lonely Lady '83
Something Wild '86
Dominick & Eugene '88
Field of Dreams '89
Goodfellas '90
Women & Men: In Love There Are No Rules '91
Article 99 '92
Unlawful Entry '92
Corrina, Corrina '94
No Escape '94
Operation Dumbo Drop '95
Unforgettable '96

Eugene Lipinski
Moonlighting '82
Going Home '86
Riders of the Storm '88
Perfectly Normal '91

Maureen Lipman
Educating Rita '83
The Little Princess '87

Jonathon Lippe
Green Eyes '76
Blood Voyage '77

Dennis Lipscomb
Union City '81
Eyes of Fire '84
Slow Burn '86
Guilty of Innocence '87
Sister, Sister '87
Retribution '88
Automatic '94

Jack Lipson
Cannon Ball/Eyes Have It '15
Flash Gordon: Rocketship '36

Peggy Lipton
Mosby's Marauders '66
The Mod Squad '68
Purple People Eater '88
Kinjite: Forbidden Subjects '89
Twin Peaks '90
Twin Peaks '90
Fatal Charm '92
Twin Peaks: Fire Walk with Me '92
The Spider and the Fly '94

Joe Lisi
Come See the Paradise '90
Traces of Red '92

Virna Lisi
How to Murder Your Wife '64
Casanova 70 '65
Assault on a Queen '66
When Wolves Cry '69
The Statue '71
Bluebeard '72
Night Flight from Moscow '73
Miss Right '81
La Cicada '83
Christopher Columbus '85
I Love N.Y. '87
Queen Margot '94

Leon Lissek
Blockhouse '73
Adventures of Eliza Fraser '76
Bloodmoon '90

Moira Lister
Uneasy Terms '48
The Limping Man '53
Trouble in Store '53

Tiny Lister
Prison '88
No Holds Barred '89
Secret Agent 00-Soul '89
9 1/2 Ninjas '90
Posse '93
Immortal Combat '94
Men of War '94
Friday '95
Hologram Man '95

John Litel
Nancy Drew, Reporter '39
The Fighting 69th '40
Invisible Agent '42
Boss of Big Town '43
San Antonio '45
Northwest Trail '46
Cass Timberlane '47
Pitfall '48
Outpost in Morocco '49
Rusty's Birthday '49
The Fuller Brush Girl '50
Montana Belle '52

John Lithgow
Obsession '76
The Big Fix '78
All That Jazz '79
Rich Kids '79
Mom, the Wolfman and Me '80
Blow Out '81
I'm Dancing as Fast as I Can '82
Oldest Living Graduate '82
The World According to Garp '82
The Day After '83
Goldilocks & the Three Bears '83
Terms of Endearment '83
Twilight Zone: The Movie '83
The Adventures of Buckaroo Banzai Across the Eighth Dimension '84
Footloose '84
The Glitter Dome '84
Mesmerized '84
2010: The Year We Make Contact '84
Santa Claus: The Movie '85
The Manhattan Project '86
Baby Girl Scott '87
Harry and the Hendersons '87
Distant Thunder '88
Out Cold '89
Traveling Man '89
Ivory Hunters '90
Memphis Belle '90
At Play in the Fields of the Lord '91
Ricochet '91
Raising Cain '92
Cliffhanger '93
Love, Cheat & Steal '93
The Pelican Brief '93
The Wrong Man '93
A Good Man in Africa '94
Princess Caraboo '94
Silent Fall '94
World War II: When Lions Roared '94
Redwood Curtain '95
The Tuskegee Airmen '95

Cleavon Little
Cotton Comes to Harlem '70
Homecoming: A Christmas Story '71
Vanishing Point '71
Blazing Saddles '74
High Risk '76
Greased Lightning '77
Once Upon a Brothers Grimm '77
FM '78
Scavenger Hunt '79
Don't Look Back: The Story of Leroy "Satchel" Paige '81
Double Exposure '82
Jimmy the Kid '82
The Salamander '82
E. Nick: A Legend in His Own Mind '84
Surf 2 '84
Toy Soldiers '84
The Gig '85
Once Bitten '85
Gore Vidal's Lincoln '88
Fletch Lives '89
Murder by Numbers '89
Perfect Harmony '91
Separate But Equal '91

Mark Little
Waterfront '83
The Wacky World of Wills & Burke '85

Michelle Little
Appointment with Fear '85
Radioactive Dreams '86
Bluffing It '87
My Demon Lover '87
Blood Clan '91
Apollo 13 '95
Heartstrings '95

Rich Little
Dirty Tricks '81
Happy Hour '87
The Late Shift '96

Sacheen Little Feather
Johnny Firecloud '75
Shoot the Sun Down '81

Little Nell
The Rocky Horror Picture Show '75
I Wanna Be a Beauty Queen '85

Little Richard
Down and Out in Beverly Hills '86
Purple People Eater '88
Mother Goose Rock 'n' Rhyme '90

Eddie Little Sky
Savage Run '70
Journey Through Rosebud '72

Lucien Littlefield
The Sheik '21
Charley's Aunt '25
Tumbleweeds '25
Seven Keys to Baldplate '29
Tom Sawyer '30
Strangers of the Evening '32
The Bitter Tea of General Yen '33
Rainbow Over Broadway '33
Let's Sing Again '36
Bulldog Drummond's Revenge '37
The Gladiator '38
Hollywood Stadium Mystery '38
Wide Open Faces '38
Hillbilly Blitzkrieg '42
Zorro's Black Whip '44
Susanna Pass '49

Gary Littlejohn
Angels Hard as They Come '71
Bury Me an Angel '71

Harrison Liu
Dr. Bethune '90
Black Robe '91

John Liu
Kung Fu Commandos '80
Shaolin Ex-Monk '82
Snuff-Bottle Connection '82
Instant Kung-Fu Man '84

Jason Lively
National Lampoon's European Vacation '85
Night of the Creeps '86
Ghost Chase '88
Maximum Force '92

Robin Lively
Buckeye and Blue '87
Not Quite Human '87
Not Quite Human 2 '89
Teen Witch '89
Crazy from the Heart '91

Jack Livesey
Never Too Late to Mend '37
The World Owes Me a Living '47

Roger Livesey
Lorna Doone '34
Drums '38
The Life and Death of Colonel Blimp '43
I Know Where I'm Going '45
Green Grow the Rushes '51
The Master of Ballantrae '53
The Entertainer '60
The League of Gentlemen '60
Of Human Bondage '64

Bob Livingston
The Bold Caballero '36
Ghost Town Gold '36
The Vigilantes are Coming '36
Come On, Cowboys '37
Heart of the Rockies '37
Hit the Saddle '37
Riders of the Whistling Skull '37
Roarin' Lead '37
Heroes of the Hills '38
Outlaws of Sonora '38
Purple Vigilantes '38
Cowboys from Texas '39
The Kansas Terrors '39
Western Double Feature 13 '40s
Covered Wagon Days '40
Rocky Mountain Rangers '40
Raiders of Red Gap '43
Death Rides the Plains '44
Western Double Feature 12 '44
Law of the Saddle '45
Western Double Feature 6: Rogers & Trigger '50
Blazing Stewardesses '75
Texas Layover '75

Margaret Livingston
Sunrise '27
Through the Breakers '28
Seven Keys to Baldplate '29
The Lady Refuses '31

Stanley Livingston
Private Parts '72
Smokey & the Hotwire Gang '79

Kari Lizer
Smokey Bites the Dust '81
Private School '83

L.L. Cool J.
The Hard Way '91
Toys '92
Out of Sync '95
The Right to Remain Silent '95

Desmond Llewelyn
From Russia with Love '63
Goldfinger '64
Thunderball '65
You Only Live Twice '67
On Her Majesty's Secret Service '69
Diamonds Are Forever '71
The Man with the Golden Gun '74
The Spy Who Loved Me '77
Moonraker '79
For Your Eyes Only '81
A View to a Kill '85
The Living Daylights '87
License to Kill '89
Merlin '92
Goldeneye '95

Christopher Lloyd
One Flew Over the Cuckoo's Nest '75
Three Warriors '77
Goin' South '78
The Black Marble '79
Lady in Red '79
Legend of the Lone Ranger '81
National Lampoon Goes to the Movies '81
The Postman Always Rings Twice '81
Pilgrim, Farewell '82
Mr. Mom '83
September Gun '83
To Be or Not to Be '83
The Adventures of Buckaroo Banzai Across the Eighth Dimension '84
The Cowboy & the Ballerina '84
Joy of Sex '84
Star Trek 3: The Search for Spock '84
Street Hawk '84
Back to the Future '85
Clue '85
Miracles '86
Walk Like a Man '87
Eight Men Out '88
Track 29 '88
Who Framed Roger Rabbit '88
Back to the Future, Part 2 '89
The Dream Team '89
Back to the Future, Part 3 '90
Why Me? '90
The Addams Family '91
Suburban Commando '91
Dead Ahead: The Exxon Valdez Disaster '92
T Bone N Weasel '92
Addams Family Values '93
Dennis the Menace '93
Twenty Bucks '93
Angels in the Outfield '94
Camp Nowhere '94
The Pagemaster '94
Radioland Murders '94
Rent-A-Kid '95
The Right to Remain Silent '95
Things to Do In Denver When You're Dead '95

Danny Lloyd
The Shining '80
Will: G. Gordon Liddy '82

Doris Lloyd
Disraeli '29
The Drake Case '29
A Shot in the Dark '35
Journey for Margaret '42
The Invisible Man's Revenge '44

Emily Lloyd
Wish You Were Here '87
Cookie '89
In Country '89
Chicago Joe & the Showgirl '90
A River Runs Through It '92
Scorchers '92
Under the Hula Moon '95

Emily Ann Lloyd
Annie: A Royal Adventure '95
Apollo 13 '95

Eric Lloyd
The Santa Clause '94
Dunston Checks In '95

Harold Lloyd
I'm on My Way/The Non-Stop Kid '18
Don't Shove/Two Gun Gussie '19
Early Cinema Vol. 1 '19
Silent Laugh Makers, No. 3 '19
Sailor-Made Man/Grandma's Boy '20s
His Royal Slyness/Haunted Spooks '20
Never Weaken/Why Worry? '23
Girl Shy '24
Hot Water/Safety Last '24
The Freshman '25
Dr. Jack/For Heaven's Sake '26
For Heaven's Sake '26
The Kid Brother '27
Speedy '28
Kings, Queens, Jokers '30s
Slapstick '30s
Feet First '30
Milky Way '36
The Sin of Harold Diddlebock '47
Days of Thrills and Laughter '61
Hollywood Clowns '85

Harold Lloyd, Jr.
The Flaming Urge '53
Girls' Town '59
Platinum High School '60
Married Too Young '62

Jimmy Lloyd
The Jolson Story '46
Sea Hound '47
Miss Grant Takes Richmond '49
Riders of the Whistling Pines '49
G.I. Jane '51

John Bedford Lloyd
Sweet Lorraine '87
Tough Guys Don't Dance '87
Crossing Delancey '88
The Abyss '89
Waiting for the Light '90
Philadelphia '93
Fair Game '95

Kathleen Lloyd
Missouri Breaks '76
Skateboard '77
It's Alive 2: It Lives Again '78
Take Down '79
The Jayne Mansfield Story '80
Gangster Wars '81

Jason London
December '91
The Man in the Moon '91
Blood Ties '92
Dazed and Confused '93
Fall Time '94
Safe Passage '94
To Wong Foo, Thanks for Everything, Julie Newmar '95

Jeremy London
White Wolves 2: Legend of the Wild '94
The Babysitter '95
Breaking Free '95
Mallrats '95

Julie London
Nabonga '44
The Red House '47
Task Force '49
The Girl Can't Help It '56
Man of the West '58

Lisa London
H.O.T.S. '79
Savage Beach '89

Tom London
Two Gun Man '31
Beyond the Rockies '32
Outlaw Justice '32
Courage of the North '35
The Miracle Rider '35
Rio Rattler '35
Toll of the Desert '35
Western Gold '37
Flaming Lead '39
Fugitive Valley '41
Zorro's Black Whip '44
Sunset in El Dorado '45
Brand of Fear '49
Red Desert '50
Blue Canadian Rockies '52
Tribute to a Bad Man '56

John Lone
Iceman '84
Year of the Dragon '85
Echoes of Paradise '86
The Last Emperor '87
The Moderns '88
Shadow of China '91
M. Butterfly '93
The Hunted '94
The Shadow '94

Audrey Long
Desperate '47
The Adventures of Gallant Bess '48
Indian Uprising '51

Jodi Long
Patty Hearst '88
Amos and Andrew '93

Kathy Long
Knights '93
The Stranger '95
Under the Gun '95

Lotus Long
Mr. Wong in Chinatown '39
Mystery of Mr. Wong '39
Phantom of Chinatown '40

Melissa Long
War of the Robots '78
Reactor '85

Nia Long
Boyz N the Hood '91
Made in America '93
Friday '95

Richard Long
The Stranger '46
Tomorrow Is Forever '46
Egg and I '47
Criss Cross '48
Ma and Pa Kettle '49
Ma and Pa Kettle Go to Town '50
Ma and Pa Kettle Back On the Farm '51
Cult of the Cobra '55
House on Haunted Hill '58
Big Valley '68
Death Cruise '74

Shelley Long
The Cracker Factory '79
A Small Circle of Friends '80
Caveman '81
Losin' It '82
Night Shift '82
Irreconcilable Differences '84
The Money Pit '86
Hello Again '87
Outrageous Fortune '87
Troop Beverly Hills '89
Don't Tell Her It's Me '90
Frozen Assets '92
The Brady Bunch Movie '95
A Very Brady Sequel '96

Walter Long
The Little American '17
The Sheik '21
Blood and Sand '22
Moran of the Lady Letty '22
Little Church Around the Corner '23
Soul-Fire '25
Yankee Clipper '27
Sea Devils '31
Cornered '32
The Glory Trail '36
Man's Country '38
Six Shootin' Sheriff '38
Flaming Lead '39
Silver Stallion '41

John Longden
Blackmail '29
Juno and the Paycock '30
Tower of Terror '42
Alias John Preston '56
Quatermass 2 '57

Terence Longdon
Murder on the Campus '52
Another Time, Another Place '58

Victoria Longley
Celia: Child Of Terror '89
Talk '94

Tony Longo
Bloodhounds of Broadway '89
Worth Winning '89
Suburban Commando '91
Rapid Fire '92
Prehysteria '93
Remote '93
Houseguest '94

Emily Longstreth
Private Resort '84
Wired to Kill '86
The Big Picture '89
Rising Son '90
Too Young to Die '90
Confessions of a Hit Man '94

Ray Lonnen
Guardian of the Abyss '82
Belfast Assassin '84

Michael Lonsdale
The Bride Wore Black '68
Is Paris Burning? '68
Les Assassins de L'Ordre '71
Murmur of the Heart '71
Moonraker '79
Enigma '82
Erendira '83
The Holcroft Covenant '85
The Name of the Rose '86
Souvenir '88
The Remains of the Day '93
Nelly et Monsieur Arnaud '95

Richard Loo
The Bitter Tea of General Yen '33
Mr. Wong in Chinatown '39
Across the Pacific '42
Betrayal from the East '44
China Sky '44
The Purple Heart '44
Back to Bataan '45
First Yank into Tokyo '45
The Clay Pigeon '49
Malaya '49
The Steel Helmet '51
Five Fingers '52
Love Is a Many-Splendored Thing '55
Battle Hymn '57
The Man with the Golden Gun '74

Michael Lookinland
The Brady Bunch '69
A Very Brady Christmas '88

Nancy Loomis
Assault on Precinct 13 '76
Halloween '78

Rod Loomis
Jack's Back '87
Bill & Ted's Excellent Adventure '89

Tanya Lopert
Navajo Joe '67
Tales of Ordinary Madness '83

Jennifer Lopez
My Family '94
Money Train '95

Kamala Lopez
Born in East L.A. '87
Dollman '90
Exiled in America '90
Crazy from the Heart '91

Perry Lopez
Mister Roberts '55
Taras Bulba '62
McLintock! '63
Chinatown '74

Sal Lopez
American Me '92
The Fire Next Time '93

Trini Lopez
The Poppy Is Also a Flower '66
The Dirty Dozen '67
Antonio '73

Isabel Lorca
Lightning: The White Stallion '86
She's Having a Baby '88

Theodore Lorch
The Last of the Mohicans '20
The Man on the Box '25

Jack Lord
The Court Martial of Billy Mitchell '55
God's Little Acre '58
Man of the West '58
Dr. No '62
The Doomsday Flight '66

Justine Lord
He Kills Night After Night After Night '70
Skeezer '82

Marjorie Lord
Johnny Come Lately '43
Sherlock Holmes in Washington '43
Riding High '50
Boy, Did I Get a Wrong Number! '66

Traci Lords
Not of This Earth '88
Fast Food '89
Cry-Baby '90
Shock 'Em Dead '90
Raw Nerve '91
A Time to Die '91
Laser Moon '92
Desperate Crimes '93
Ice '93
Skinner '93
Stephen King's The Tommyknockers '93
Plughead Rewired: Circuitry Man 2 '94
Serial Mom '94
As Good as Dead '95
The Nutt House '95

Tony Lorea
The Deadly and the Beautiful '73
Smokey & the Hotwire Gang '79

Donna Loren
Bikini Beach '64
Muscle Beach Party '64
Pajama Party '64

Sophia Loren
The Gold of Naples '54
Two Nights with Cleopatra '54
Legend of the Lost '57
The Pride and the Passion '57
Desire Under the Elms '58
Houseboat '58
The Key '58
Black Orchid '59
Breath of Scandal '60
Heller in Pink Tights '60
It Started in Naples '60
The Millionairess '60
El Cid '61
Two Women '61
Boccaccio '70 '62
The Fall of the Roman Empire '64
Marriage Italian Style '64
Yesterday, Today and Tomorrow '64
Lady L '65
Operation Crossbow '65
Arabesque '66
A Countess from Hong Kong '67
Man of La Mancha '72
Get Rita '75
The Cassandra Crossing '76
Angela '77
A Special Day '77
Brass Target '78
Blood Feud '79
Firepower '79
Lady of the Evening '79
Sophia Loren: Her Own Story '80
Courage '86
Bellissimo: Images of the Italian Cinema '87
Running Away '89
Ready to Wear '94
Grumpier Old Men '95

Tray Loren
Rocktober Blood '85
Gator Bait 2: Cajun Justice '88
The American Angels: Baptism of Blood '89

Livio Lorenzon
Pirates of the Coast '61
Gladiators 7 '62
The Invincible Gladiator '63

Lisa Loring
The Addams Family '64
Blood Frenzy '87

Lynn Loring
Journey to the Far Side of the Sun '69
Kansas City Massacre '75

Teala Loring
Delinquent Daughters '44
Hard-Boiled Mahoney '47

James Lorinz
Frankenhooker '90
Punch the Clock '90
Me and the Mob '94
The Jerky Boys '95

Marion Lorne
Strangers on a Train '51
The Graduate '67

George Loros
Apology '86
Shakedown '88

Peter Lorre
M '31
F.P. 1 Doesn't Answer '33
The Man Who Knew Too Much '34
Crime and Punishment '35
Mad Love '35
The Secret Agent '36
Mr. Moto's Last Warning '39
Strange Cargo '40
Stranger on the Third Floor '40
You'll Find Out '40
The Maltese Falcon '41
They Met in Bombay '41
All Through the Night '42
Casablanca '42
Invisible Agent '42
Background to Danger '43
Arsenic and Old Lace '44
Hollywood Canteen '44
Mr. Moto's Last Warning/Meeting at Midnight '44
Passage to Marseilles '44
The Beast with Five Fingers '46
The Chase '46
My Favorite Brunette '47
Quicksand '50
The Lost One '51
Beat the Devil '53
20,000 Leagues Under the Sea '54
Postmark for Danger/Quicksand '56
Promise to Murder '56
Hell Ship Mutiny '57
The Sad Sack '57
Silk Stockings '57
Voyage to the Bottom of the Sea '61
Five Weeks in a Balloon '62
Tales of Terror '62
The Raven '63
The Comedy of Terrors '64
The Patsy '64

Joan Lorring
The Corn is Green '45
The Gangster '47
Good Sam '48

Diana Lorys
The Awful Dr. Orlof '62
Lightning Bolt '67
Fangs of the Living Dead '68
House of Psychotic Women '73

Eb Lottimer
Quicker Than the Eye '88
Lords of the Deep '89
Stripped to Kill II: Live Girls '89
Streets '90
The Finest Hour '91
Futurekick '91
Beyond the Call of Duty '92
Quake '92
Dead Center '94

Alexander Lou
Mafia vs. Ninja '84
Ninja vs. the Shaolin '84
Ninja Condors '87
Ninja the Battalion '90

Louanne
The Long Days of Summer '80
Oh, God! Book 2 '80
Missing Pieces '83
A Night in the Life of Jimmy Reardon '88

Jackie Loughery
Judge Roy Bean '55
Pardners '56
D.I. '57

Lori Loughlin
Amityville 3: The Demon '83
The New Kids '85
Secret Admirer '85
Rad '86
Back to the Beach '87
The Night Before '88

Bill Louie
The Bodyguard '76
Fist of Fear, Touch of Death '77

Joe Louis
The Spirit of Youth '37
This Is the Army '43

Justin Louis
Hello Mary Lou: Prom Night 2 '87
The Big Slice '90

Willard Louis
Robin Hood '22
Beau Brummel '24
Don Juan '26

Julia Louis-Dreyfus
Best of Eddie Murphy '89
National Lampoon's Christmas Vacation '89
Jack the Bear '93
North '94

Anita Louise
Square Shoulders '29
Millie '31
Judge Priest '34
Anthony Adverse '36
The Story of Louis Pasteur '36
That Certain Woman '37
Marie Antoinette '38
The Sisters '38
The Gorilla '39
The Little Princess '39
Wagon's Westward '40
Harmon of Michigan '41
The Villain Still Pursued Her '41
Casanova Brown '44
Retreat, Hell! '52

Tina Louise
God's Little Acre '58
The Trap '59
Armored Command '61
Gilligan's Island: Meet the Crew '64
The Good Guys and the Bad Guys '69
The Happy Ending '69
How to Commit Marriage '69
Death Scream '75
Nightmare in Badham County '76
Mean Dog Blues '78
The Day the Women Got Even '80
Hellriders '84
Evils of the Night '85
O.C. and Stiggs '87
Dixie Lanes '88
Johnny Suede '92

Alan Love
That Sinking Feeling '79

The Apple '80

Bessie Love
Intolerance '16
Reggie Mixes In '16
The King on Main Street '25
The Lost World '25
Mystery of the Leaping Fish/Chess Fever '25
Soul-Fire '25
Broadway Melody '29
Morals for Women '31
Roman Spring of Mrs. Stone '61
The Poppy Is Also a Flower '66
Isadora '68
Catlow '71

Darlene Love
Lethal Weapon '87
Lethal Weapon 2 '89
Lethal Weapon 3 '92

Lucretia Love
The She-Beast '65
Phenomenal and the Treasure of Tutankamen '70s
Naked Warriors '73
Dr. Heckyl and Mr. Hype '80

Montagu Love
Don Juan '26
Hands Up '26
The Wind '28
Bulldog Drummond '29
Inside the Lines '30
The Riding Tornado '32
Vanity Fair '32
His Double Life '33
The Crusades '35
Lloyds of London '36
One in a Million '36
A Damsel in Distress '37
The Prince and the Pauper '37
Prisoner of Zenda '37
The Adventures of Robin Hood '38
Gunga Din '39
The Mark of Zorro '40
The Son of Monte Cristo '41
Lady for a Night '42
Sherlock Holmes: The Voice of Terror '42
Wings Over the Pacific '43

Mother Love
Mr. Nanny '93
The Surgeon '94
Twinsitters '95

Suzanna Love
Cocaine Cowboys '79
The Boogey Man '80
Brainwaves '82
Boogey Man 2 '83
Devonsville Terror '83
Olivia '83

Victor Love
Native Son '86
Guilty of Innocence '87
Heaven is a Playground '91
Final Shot: The Hank Gathers Story '92

Alec Lovejoy
Moon over Harlem '39
Murder on Lenox Avenue '41

Frank Lovejoy
Home of the Brave '49
In a Lonely Place '50
Three Secrets '50
Try and Get Me '50
I'll See You in My Dreams '51
Retreat, Hell! '52
The Winning Team '52
The Hitch-Hiker '53
House of Wax '53
Men of the Fighting Lady '54
Americano '55
The Finger Man '55
Shack Out on 101 '55
Strategic Air Command '55

Raymond Lovell
King of the Damned '36
Hotel Reserve '44
Appointment with Crime '45

Ray Lovelock
One Russian Summer '73
Autopsy '78
From Hell to Victory '79

Dorothy Lovett
Courageous Dr. Christian '40
Dr. Christian Meets the Women '40
Remedy for Riches '40
They Meet Again '41
Call Out the Marines '42

Lyle Lovett
The Player '92
Short Cuts '93
Ready to Wear '94

Jon Lovitz
Jumpin' Jack Flash '86
Last Resort '86
Three Amigos '86
Big '88
My Stepmother Is an Alien '88
Mr. Destiny '90
A League of Their Own '92
Mom and Dad Save the World '92
National Lampoon's Loaded Weapon 1 '93
City Slickers 2: The Legend of Curly's Gold '94
North '94
Trapped In Paradise '94
The Great White Hype '96
High School High '96

Celia Lovsky
Rhapsody '54
I, Mobster '58

Alex Lowe
Peter's Friends '92
Haunted '95

Arthur Lowe
This Sporting Life '63
If... '69
The Ruling Class '72
O Lucky Man! '73
The Bawdy Adventures of Tom Jones '76
Sweet William '79
The Strange Case of the End of Civilization as We Know It '93

Chad Lowe
Silence of the Heart '84
Apprentice to Murder '88
True Blood '89
Nobody's Perfect '90
An Inconvenient Woman '91
Highway to Hell '92
Siringo '94

Edmund Lowe
The Eyes of Youth '19
Chandu the Magician '32
Dinner at Eight '33
The Squeaker '37
Every Day's a Holiday '38
I Love You Again '40
Call Out the Marines '42
Dillinger '45
The Enchanted Forest '45
Good Sam '48
Wings of Eagles '57
Heller in Pink Tights '60

Patrick Lowe
Slumber Party Massacre 2 '87
Primal Rage '90

Rob Lowe
Class '83
The Outsiders '83
The Hotel New Hampshire '84
Oxford Blues '84
St. Elmo's Fire '85
About Last Night... '86
Youngblood '86
Illegally Yours '87
Square Dance '87
Masquerade '88
Bad Influence '90
Stroke of Midnight '90
The Dark Backward '91
The Finest Hour '91
Wayne's World '92
Frank and Jesse '94
Stephen King's The Stand '94
First Degree '95
Tommy Boy '95

Carey Lowell
Club Paradise '86
Dangerously Close '86
Down Twisted '89
License to Kill '89
Me and Him '89
The Guardian '90
Road to Ruin '91
Sleepless in Seattle '93

Curt Lowens
Werewolf in a Girl's Dormitory '61
A Midnight Clear '92
Invisible: The Chronicles of Benjamin Knight '93
Mandroid '93

Elina Lowensohn
Simple Men '92
Amateur '94
My Antonia '94
Nadja '95

Andrew Lowery
School Ties '92
JFK: Reckless Youth '93
My Boyfriend's Back '93
Color of Night '94

Robert Lowery
Drums Along the Mohawk '39
Murder over New York '40
Dawn on the Great Divide '42
Lure of the Islands '42
Revenge of the Zombies '43
Rhythm Parade '43
Dangerous Passage '44
Dark Mountain '44
The Mummy's Ghost '44
Mystery of the Riverboat '44
Navy Way '44
Death Valley '46
God's Country '46
House of Horrors '46
Big Town '47
Queen of the Amazons '47
Trail of the Mounties '47
Highway 13 '48
Call of the Forest '49
Outlaw Gang '49
Shep Comes Home '49
Border Rangers '50
Gunfire '50
I Shot Billy the Kid '50
Train to Tombstone '50
Western Pacific Agent '51
The Rise and Fall of Legs Diamond '60
Johnny Reno '66
The Undertaker and His Pals '67

William E. Lowery
The Lamb '15
Reggie Mixes In '16
The Nut '21
Robin Hood '22

Klaus Lowitsch
Despair '78
The Marriage of Maria Braun '79

Lynn Lowry
The Crazies '73
They Came from Within '75
Fighting Mad '76
Sugar Cookies '77

Scooter Lowry
Our Gang '26
Our Gang Comedy Festival '88
Our Gang Comedy Festival 2 '89

T.J. Lowther
A Perfect World '93
Mad Love '95

Myrna Loy
Don Juan '26
So This is Paris '26
The Jazz Singer '27
Rogue of the Rio Grande '30
Arrowsmith '31
A Connecticut Yankee '31
Consolation Marriage '31
The Animal Kingdom '32
The Mask of Fu Manchu '32
Vanity Fair '32
Penthouse '33
The Prizefighter and the Lady '33
Topaze '33
Broadway Bill '34
Evelyn Prentice '34
Manhattan Melodrama '34
The Thin Man '34
After the Thin Man '36
The Great Ziegfeld '36
Libeled Lady '36
Wife Versus Secretary '36
Double Wedding '37
Renegade Ranger/Scarlet River '38
Test Pilot '38
Too Hot to Handle '38
Another Thin Man '39
The Rains Came '39
I Love You Again '40
Love Crazy '41
Shadow of the Thin Man '41
The Thin Man Goes Home '44
The Best Years of Our Lives '46
The Bachelor and the Bobby-Soxer '47
Song of the Thin Man '47
Mr. Blandings Builds His Dream House '48
The Red Pony '49
Cheaper by the Dozen '50
The Ambassador's Daughter '56
Lonelyhearts '58
From the Terrace '60
Midnight Lace '60
April Fools '69
Airport '75 '75
Ants '77
The End '78
Just Tell Me What You Want '80
Summer Solstice '81

Margarita Lozano
Lazarillo '59
Viridiana '61
The Night of the Shooting Stars '82
Kaos '85
Half of Heaven '86

Arthur Lucan
Old Mother Riley's Ghosts '41
My Son, the Vampire '52

Lisa Lucas
A House Without a Christmas Tree '72
The Migrants '74
Forbidden Love '82
Hadley's Rebellion '84

Wilfrid Lucas
Dishonored '31
The Phantom '31
Roaring Speedboats '37
A Chump at Oxford '40

Susan Lucci
Secret Passions '78
Invitation to Hell '84
Anastasia: The Mystery of Anna '86
Mafia Princess '86
Lady Mobster '88
Hit Woman: The Double Edge '93
French Silk '94

Angela Luce
The Decameron '70
'Tis a Pity She's a Whore '73

Enrique Lucero
The Woman Hunter '72
Mr. Horn '79
The Evil That Men Do '84

Fabrice Luchini
Full Moon in Paris '84
La Discrete '90
Uranus '91
Colonel Chabert '94

Chip Lucio
Hospital Massacre '81
Primary Target '89

Laurence Luckinbill
The Boys in the Band '70
Death Sentence '74
Panic on the 5:22 '74
The Money '75
The Lindbergh Kidnapping Case '76
The Promise '78
Ike '79
Mating Season '81
Not for Publication '84
Cocktail '88
Messenger of Death 88
To Heal a Nation '88
Star Trek 5: The Final Frontier '89

William Lucking
Hell's Belles '69
Doc Savage '75
Coast to Coast '80
Humanoid Defender '85
Kung Fu: The Movie '86
Naked Lie '89
Duplicates '92
Rescue Me '93
The Trigger Effect '96

Jack Luden
The Last Outlaw '27
Phantom Gold '38

Charles Ludlam
Imposters '84
The Big Easy '87

Pamela Ludwig
Over the Edge '79
Death of an Angel '86
Dead Man Walking '88
Rush Week '88
Race for Glory '89
Pale Blood '91

Laurette Luez
Prehistoric Women '50
Fu Manchu '56
Ballad of a Gunfighter '64

Lorna Luft
Grease 2 '82
Where the Boys Are '84 '84

Bela Lugosi
Midnight Girl '25
Dracula '31
Chandu the Magician '32
Island of Lost Souls '32
Murders in the Rue Morgue '32
The White Zombie '32
The Death Kiss '33
International House '33
Night of Terror '33
Whispering Shadow '33
The Black Cat '34
Chandu on the Magic Island '34
Return of Chandu '34
Mark of the Vampire '35
Murder by Television '35
The Raven '35
The Invisible Ray '36
Postal Inspector '36
Shadow of Chinatown '36
The Mystery of the Mary Celeste '37
S.O.S. Coast Guard '37
The Gorilla '39
The Human Monster '39
Ninotchka '39
The Phantom Creeps '39
Son of Frankenstein '39
Black Friday '40
The Saint's Double Trouble '40
Saturday Night Serials '40
You'll Find Out '40
The Devil Bat '41
The Invisible Ghost '41
Spooks Run Wild '41
The Wolf Man '41
The Black Dragons '42
Bowery at Midnight '42
Bowery at Midnight/Dick Tracy vs. Cueball '42
The Corpse Vanishes '42
Dick Tracy, Detective/The Corpse Vanishes '42
Frankenstein Meets the Wolfman '42
The Ghost of Frankenstein '42
Night Monster '42
The Ape Man '43
Ghost on the Loose '43
Return of the Vampire '43
One Body Too Many '44
Return of the Ape Man '44
Zombies on Broadway '44
The Body Snatcher '45
Scared to Death '47
Scared to Death/Dick Tracy's Dilemma '47
Abbott and Costello Meet Frankenstein '48
Bela Lugosi Meets a Brooklyn Gorilla '52
My Son, the Vampire '52
Glen or Glenda: Confessions of Ed Wood '53
Bride of the Monster '56
Plan 9 from Outer Space '56
Bela Lugosi Scrapbook '70s
The Horror of It All '91

James Luisi
Stunts '77
One in a Million: The Ron LeFlore Story '78
The Dark Ride '84
Murphy's Law '86
Feds '88

Paul Lukas
Vice Squad '31
Little Women '33
The Three Musketeers '35
Dodsworth '36

Lukas ▶cont.

Dinner at the Ritz '37
The Lady Vanishes '38
Lady in Distress '39
The Mutiny of the Elsinore '39
The Ghost Breakers '40
Strange Cargo '40
The Monster and the Girl '41
Watch on the Rhine '43
Uncertain Glory '44
Experiment Perilous '45
Deadline at Dawn '46
Whispering City '47
Berlin Express '48
Kim '50
20,000 Leagues Under the Sea '54
55 Days at Peking '63
Fun in Acapulco '63
Lord Jim '65
Hitchcock Collection '87

Paul Lukather
Dinosaurus! '60
Hands of a Stranger '62

Benny Luke
La Cage aux Folles '78
La Cage aux Folles 2 '81
La Cage aux Folles 3: The Wedding '86

Jorge Luke
Ulzana's Raid '72
Foxtrot '76
The Evil That Men Do '84
Shark Hunter '84

Keye Luke
Charlie Chan in Paris '35
Charlie Chan at the Opera '36
The Good Earth '37
The Green Hornet '39
The Gang's All Here '40
No, No Nanette '40
Phantom of Chinatown '40
Bowery Blitzkrieg '41
Let's Go Collegiate '41
Across the Pacific '42
The Falcon's Brother '42
Battle Hell '56
Noon Sunday '71
Kung Fu '72
The Amsterdam Kill '78
Gremlins '84
Blade in Hong Kong '85
Kung Fu: The Movie '86
Dead Heat '88
The Mighty Quinn '89
Alice '90

Wolfgang Lukschy
Dead Eyes of London '61
Frozen Alive '64

Folco Lulli
Variety Lights '51
Wages of Fear '55
The Great War '59
Lightning Bolt '67

Lum & Abner
So This is Washington '43
Two Weeks to Live '43

Carl Lumbly
The Bedroom Window '87
Everybody's All American '88
Judgment in Berlin '88
Pacific Heights '90
To Sleep with Anger '90
Brother Future '91
South Central '92
Eyes of a Witness '94
America's Dream '95

Jenny Lumet
Tougher than Leather '88
Q & A '90

Sidney Lumet
One Third of a Nation '39
Running on Empty '88

Joanna Lumley
On Her Majesty's Secret Service '69
The Satanic Rites of Dracula '73
Curse of the Pink Panther '83
Weather in the Streets '84
Shirley Valentine '89
Cold Comfort Farm '94
Innocent Lies '95

James and the Giant Peach '96

Barbara Luna
Firecreek '68
The Gatling Gun '72
Gentle Savage '73
The Hanged Man '74
The Concrete Jungle '82

Art Lund
Black Caesar '73
The Last American Hero '73
Bucktown '75

Deanna Lund
Dr. Goldfoot and the Bikini Machine '66
Hardly Working '81
Elves '89
Red Wind '91

John Lund
The Perils of Pauline '47
My Friend Irma '49
The Duchess of Idaho '50
Latin Lovers '53
Dakota Incident '56
Wackiest Ship in the Army '61

Lucille Lund
The Black Cat '34
Prison Shadows '36

Christine Lunde
Dead End City '88
Masque of the Red Death '90

Dolph Lundgren
Rocky 4 '85
A View to a Kill '85
Masters of the Universe '87
Red Scorpion '89
I Come in Peace '90
The Punisher '90
Cover-Up '91
Showdown in Little Tokyo '91
Universal Soldier '92
Army of One '94
Men of War '94
Pentathlon '94
The Shooter '94
Johnny Mnemonic '95

William Lundigan
Danger on the Air '38
Wives Under Suspicion '38
Three Smart Girls Grow Up '39
The Fighting 69th '40
Andy Hardy's Double Life '42
Dishonored Lady '47
Follow Me Quietly '49
Pinky '49
State Department File 649 '49
I'd Climb the Highest Mountain '51
Love Nest '51
Terror Ship '54
The White Orchid '54

Vic Lundin
Ma Barker's Killer Brood '60
Two for the Seesaw '62
Robinson Crusoe on Mars '64

Steve Lundquist
Return of the Killer Tomatoes! '88
Killer Tomatoes Strike Back '90
Killer Tomatoes Eat France '91

Jessica Lundy
Caddyshack 2 '88
Madhouse '90
The Stupids '95

Sihung Lung
Pushing Hands '92
The Wedding Banquet '93
Eat Drink Man Woman '94

Suma Wah Lung
Prodigal Boxer: The Kick of Death '73
Kick of Death: The Prodigal Boxer '80s

Ti Lung
Duel of the Iron Fist '72
Revenge of the Zombies '81
A Better Tomorrow '86
Duel of Fists '89

Cherie Lunghi
Excalibur '81
Oliver Twist '82
Praying Mantis '83
The Sign of Four '83
Letters to an Unknown Lover '84
King David '85
Harem '86

The Mission '86
Tales of the Klondike: The Unexpected '87
To Kill a Priest '89
Intrigue '90
Mary Shelley's Frankenstein '94
The Buccaneers '95
The Lady's Not for Burning '95
The Canterville Ghost '96
Jack and Sarah '96

Alfred Lunt
Sally of the Sawdust '25
The Guardsman '31

Roldano Lupi
The Mongols '60
The Giant of Metropolis '61

Ida Lupino
The Ghost Camera '33
One Rainy Afternoon '36
Sea Devils '37
The Adventures of Sherlock Holmes '39
They Drive by Night '40
High Sierra '41
The Sea Wolf '41
Forever and a Day '43
Thank Your Lucky Stars '43
Hollywood Canteen '44
The Man I Love '46
Escape Me Never '47
Road House '48
Lust for Gold '49
On Dangerous Ground '51
Beware, My Lovely '52
The Bigamist '53
Private Hell 36 '54
The Big Knife '55
While the City Sleeps '56
Junior Bonner '72
Devil's Rain '75
Food of the Gods '76
My Boys Are Good Boys '78

Alberto Lupo
The Giant of Marathon '60
Herod the Great '60
Atom Age Vampire '61
The Bacchantes '63
Coriolanus, Man without a Country '64
The Agony and the Ecstasy '65
Django Shoots First '74

Patti LuPone
1941 '79
Fighting Back '82
Witness '85
Wise Guys '86
LBJ: The Early Years '88
Driving Miss Daisy '89
Family Prayers '91
The Water Engine '92
Song Spinner '95

Federico Luppi
Time for Revenge '82
Funny, Dirty Little War '83
Mayalunta '86
Cronos '94
A Place in the World '95

John Lupton
All the Brothers Were Valiant '53
Escape from Fort Bravo '53
Diane '55
The Rebel Set '59
Jesse James Meets Frankenstein's Daughter '65

Peter Lupus
Muscle Beach Party '64
More! Police Squad '82
Escapist '83
Pulsebeat '85
Think Big '90

Evan Lurie
Martial Law 2: Undercover '91
American Kickboxer 2: To the Death '93
T-Force '94
Hologram Man '95

John Lurie
Permanent Vacation '84
Stranger than Paradise '84
Down by Law '86
The Last Temptation of Christ '88

Jaques Lussier
Pouvoir Intime '87
Norman's Awesome Experience '88

Franc Luz
Ecstasy '84
Ghost Town '88
The Nest '88

Jimmy Lydon
Back Door to Heaven '39
Little Men '40
Tom Brown's School Days '40
Strange Illusion '45
Life with Father '47
The Magnificent Yankee '50

Reg Lye
Walk into Hell '57
Freedom '81

Dorothy Lyman
Summer Fantasy '84
Ollie Hopnoodle's Haven of Bliss '88
Camp Cucamonga: How I Spent My Summer Vacation '90
Ruby in Paradise '93

Alfred Lynch
Blockhouse '73
Bewitched '85

David Lynch
Zelly & Me '88
Twin Peaks: Fire Walk with Me '92

Helen Lynch
The Return of Grey Wolf '22
Smouldering Fires '25

John Lynch
Cal '84
Hardware '90
Monkey Boy '90
Edward II '92
The Railway Station Man '92
In the Name of the Father '93
The Secret Garden '93
Princess Caraboo '94
The Secret of Roan Inish '94
Angel Baby '95
Moll Flanders '96

Kate Lynch
Meatballs '79
Reckless Disregard '84
Summer's Children '84
Def-Con 4 '85
Lethal Lolita—Amy Fisher: My Story '92

Kelly Lynch
Osa '85
Cocktail '88
Drugstore Cowboy '89
Road House '89
Warm Summer Rain '89
Desperate Hours '90
Curly Sue '91
For Better and For Worse '92
Three of Hearts '93
Forbidden Choices '94
Imaginary Crimes '94
Heaven's Prisoners '95
Virtuosity '95
White Man's Burden '95

Ken Lynch
I Married a Monster from Outer Space '58
Jet Attack/Paratroop Command '58
Legend of Tom Dooley '59
My Pleasure Is My Business '74

Richard Lynch
Scarecrow '73
The Premonition '75
God Told Me To '76
Delta Fox '77
Death Sport '78
The Formula '80
Steel '80
Sizzle '81
Sword & the Sorcerer '82
Savage Dawn '84
Invasion U.S.A. '85
Nightforce '86
The Barbarians '87
Aftershock '88
Bad Dreams '88
The Baron '88
Little Nikita '88
High Stakes '89
One Man Force '89
The Forbidden Dance '90
Invasion Force '90
Lockdown '90

Puppet Master 3: Toulon's Revenge '90
Trancers 2: The Return of Jack Deth '90
Double Threat '92
Inside Edge '92
Maximum Force '92
Merlin '92
Showdown '93
Scanner Cop '94
Cyborg 3: The Recycler '95
Dragon Fury '95
Midnight Confessions '95

Susan Lynch
The Best of Cracker Mysteries '93
The Secret of Roan Inish '94

Paul Lynde
New Faces of 1952 '54
Bye, Bye, Birdie '63
Son of Flubber '63
Send Me No Flowers '64
Beach Blanket Bingo '65
The Glass Bottom Boat '66
How Sweet It Is! '68
Rabbit Test '78
The Villain '79

Nicholas Lyndhurst
Gulliver's Travels '95
Stalag Luft

Carol Lynley
The Light in the Forest '58
Return to Peyton Place '61
The Cardinal '63
The Stripper '63
Blood Island '68
Cotter '72
The Poseidon Adventure '72
Son of Blob '72
Death Stalk '74
Four Deuces '75
If It's a Man, Hang Up '75
Fantasy Island '76
Flood! '76
Bad Georgia Road '77
Washington Affair '77
The Cat and the Canary '79
Balboa '82
Vigilante '83
Dark Tower '87
Blackout '88
Howling 6: The Freaks '90
Spirits '90

Ann Lynn
Baby Love '69
Estate of Insanity '70

Betty Lynn
June Bride '48
Father Was a Fullback '49
Cheaper by the Dozen '50
Meet Me in Las Vegas '56
Texas John Slaughter: Geronimo's Revenge '60
Return to Mayberry '85

Cheryl Lynn
Emanon '86
Thunder Run '86
Fate '90

Diana Lynn
Miracle of Morgan's Creek '44
Every Girl Should Be Married '48
My Friend Irma '49
Bedtime for Bonzo '51
The Annapolis Story '55
The Kentuckian '55

Emmett Lynn
Frontier Outlaws '44
Song of Old Wyoming '45
The Caravan Trail '46
The Fighting Redhead '50

Fonda Lynn
Deadly Darling '85
Ninja Brothers of Blood '89

Jeffrey Lynn
Four Daughters '38
The Roaring Twenties '39
All This and Heaven Too '40
The Fighting 69th '40
A Letter to Three Wives '49
Home Town Story '51
Tony Rome '67

Mara Lynn
Prehistoric Women '50
G.I. Jane '51
Leave It to the Marines '51

Sky High '51

Peter George Lynn
Mr. Wong in Chinatown '39
Mystery Plane '39
Wolf Call '39

Rebecca Lynn
Sensations '87
Thrilled to Death '88

Ben Lyon
Hell's Angels '30
Mad About Money '30
Indiscreet '31
Night Nurse '31
The Crooked Circle '32
I Cover the Waterfront '33
Crimson Romance '34

Richard Lyon
Anna and the King of Siam '46
The Tender Years '47

Sue Lyon
Lolita '62
The Night of the Iguana '64
Flim-Flam Man '67
Tony Rome '67
Four Rode Out '69
Evel Knievel '72
End of the World '76
The Invisible Strangler '76

Bruce Lyons
Model Behavior '82
The Navigator '88

James Lyons
Poison '91
Postcards from America '95

Robert F. Lyons
Getting Straight '70
The Todd Killings '71
Black Oak Conspiracy '77
Cease Fire '85
Murphy's Law '86
Platoon Leader '87
American Eagle '90

Susan Lyons
The Winds of Jarrah '83
Ebbtide '94

Tzi Ma
Rapid Fire '92
Golden Gate '93

Byron Mabe
The Defilers '65
The Doberman Gang '72

Kate Maberly
The Secret Garden '93
Gulliver's Travels '95
Stephen King's The Langoliers '95

Moms Mabley
Boardinghouse Blues '48
Killer Diller '48
Amazing Grace '74

Bernie Mac
Above the Rim '94
House Party 3 '94
Friday '95

Anne MacAdams
Common Law Wife '63
Don't Look in the Basement '73

James MacArthur
The Light in the Forest '58
Third Man on the Mountain '59
Kidnapped '60
The Swiss Family Robinson '60
The Interns '62
Cry of Battle '63
Spencer's Mountain '63
Bedford Incident '65
Mosby's Marauders '66
Hang 'Em High '67

Marc Macaulay
Cop and a Half '93
Hidden Fears '93

Donald MacBride
The Great Man Votes '38
Room Service '38
Blondie Takes a Vacation '39
The Invisible Woman '40
Murder over New York '40
The Saint's Double Trouble '40
A Night to Remember '42
Buck Privates Come Home '47
Egg and I '47
Holiday Rhythm '50

Meet Danny Wilson '52

Ralph Macchio
Up the Academy '80
The Outsiders '83
The Karate Kid '84
Teachers '84
Crossroads '86
The Karate Kid: Part 2 '86
Distant Thunder '88
The Karate Kid: Part 3 '89
Too Much Sun '90
My Cousin Vinny '92
Naked in New York '93

Aldo Maccione
Loves & Times of Scaramouche '76
Loose in New York '80s
Too Shy to Try '82

Katherine MacColl
Seven Doors of Death '82
Gates of Hell '83
The House by the Cemetery '83

Simon MacCorkindale
Death on the Nile '78
Quatermass Conclusion '79
The Riddle of the Sands '79
Cabo Blanco '81
The Manions of America '81
Visitor from the Grave '81
Sword & the Sorcerer '82
Jaws 3 '83
Robbers of the Sacred Mountain '83
Obsessive Love '84

Edmund MacDonald
The Lady Confesses '45
Detour '46
Shoot to Kill '47

J. Farrell MacDonald
Sky High '22
Sunrise '27
Hearts of Humanity '32
Phantom Express '32
Probation '32
13th Guest '32
Romance in Manhattan '34
Riff Raff '35
Gang Bullets '38
Susannah of the Mounties '39
I Take This Oath '40
Knights of the Range '40
Riders of the Timberline '41
Phantom Killer '42
Snuffy Smith, Yard Bird '42
Texas Masquerade '44

Jeanette MacDonald
Lottery Bride '30
The Cat and the Fiddle '34
The Merry Widow '34
Naughty Marietta '35
Rose Marie '36
San Francisco '36
The Firefly '37
Maytime '37
Girl of the Golden West '38
Sweethearts '38
Broadway Serenade '39
Bitter Sweet '40
New Moon '40
Smilin' Through '41
Cairo '42
I Married an Angel '42
Three Daring Daughters '48
The Sun Comes Up '49

Jennifer MacDonald
Clean, Shaven '93
Headless Body in Topless Bar '96

Kenneth MacDonald
Border Vengeance '35
Six Gun Gospel '43
U-Boat Prisoner '44

Michael MacDonald
Mystery of the Million Dollar Hockey Puck '80s
Mr. Nice Guy '86

Wallace MacDonald
Red Signals '27
Range Feud '31
Between Fighting Men '32
Daring Danger '32
Hello Trouble '32
The Riding Tornado '32
Texas Cyclone '32

Two-Fisted Law '32

Wendy MacDonald
Blood Frenzy '87
Heat Street '87
Mayhem '87
Dark Side of the Moon '90
Broken Trust '93

Andie MacDowell
Greystoke: The Legend of Tarzan, Lord of the Apes '84
St. Elmo's Fire '85
sex, lies and videotape '89
Green Card '90
Hudson Hawk '91
The Object of Beauty '91
Women & Men: In Love There Are No Rules '91
Deception '92
Groundhog Day '93
Short Cuts '93
Bad Girls '94
Four Weddings and a Funeral '94
Unstrung Heroes '95
Multiplicity '96

Rita Macedo
The Criminal Life of Archibaldo de la Cruz '55
Nazarin '58
The Curse of the Crying Woman '61

Moyna MacGill
The Strange Affair of Uncle Harry '45
Three Daring Daughters '48

Niall MacGinnis
Edge of the World '37
The Day Will Dawn '42
No Highway in the Sky '51
Martin Luther '53
Betrayed '54
Helen of Troy '56
Lust for Life '56
Curse of the Demon '57
Sword of Sherwood Forest '60
Secret Agent '64
The War Lord '65
Island of Terror '66

Jack MacGowran
The Quiet Man '52
The Brain '62
Lord Jim '65
Cul de Sac '66
The Fearless Vampire Killers '67
Wonderwall: The Movie '69
Start the Revolution Without Me '70
King Lear '71
The Exorcist '73

Tara MacGowran
Secret Places '85
Las Vegas Serial Killer '86
The Dawning '88

Ali MacGraw
Goodbye Columbus '69
Love Story '70
The Getaway '72
Convoy '78
Players '79
Just Tell Me What You Want '80
The Winds of War '83
Murder Elite '86
Natural Causes '94

Stephen Macht
The Choirboys '77
Enola Gay: The Men, the Mission, the Atomic Bomb '80
Galaxina '80
American Dream '81
Killjoy '81
The Monster Squad '87
A Friendship in Vienna '88
Blind Witness '89
Graveyard Shift '90
Amityville 1992: It's About Time '92
Trancers 3: Deth Lives '92
Trancers 4: Jack of Swords '93
Siringo '94
Trancers 5: Sudden Deth '94

Betty Mack
The Forty-Niners '32
Fighting Texans '33
Toll of the Desert '35
Outlaw Rule '36
Rough Ridin' Rhythm '37

Helen Mack
Fargo Express '32
Melody Cruise '32
Son of Kong '33
The Return of Peter Grimm '35
She '35
Milky Way '36
Fit for a King '37
The Wrong Road '37
His Girl Friday '40

Kerry Mack
Fair Game '82
Savage Attraction '83
Fantasy Man '84

Wayne Mack
Storyville '74
Crypt of Dark Secrets '76
Mardi Gras Massacre '78

Dorothy Mackaill
Shore Leave '25
Ranson's Folly '26
Kept Husbands '31
No Man of Her Own '32
Bulldog Drummond at Bay '37

Barry Mackay
Evergreen '34
The Private Secretary '35
Gangway '37
Sailing Along '38

Fulton Mackay
Nothing But the Night '72
A Sense of Freedom '78
Local Hero '83
Defense of the Realm '85
Porridge '91

John MacKay
Fat Guy Goes Nutzoid '86
The Rejuvenator '88
Alligator Eyes '90
Trust '91
Simple Men '92

Helen MacKellar
Delinquent Parents '38
Bad Boy '39

Giselle MacKenzie
Music Shoppe '82
One Minute Before Death '88
The Oval Portrait '88

Jan MacKenzie
Gator Bait 2: Cajun Justice '88
The American Angels: Baptism of Blood '89

Patch MacKenzie
Black Eliminator '70s
Goodbye, Norma Jean '75
Graduation Day '81
Isle of Secret Passion '85
Defense Play '88

Steven Mackintosh
London Kills Me '91
The Return of the Native '94

Jim MacKrell
Just Between Friends '86
Love at the Top '86

Janet MacLachlan
Darker than Amber '70
Sounder '72
Big Mo '73
Roll of Thunder, Hear My Cry '78
She's in the Army Now '81
Murphy's Law '86
For Us, the Living '88

Kyle MacLachlan
Dune '84
Blue Velvet '86
The Hidden '87
Don't Tell Her It's Me '90
Twin Peaks '90
Twin Peaks '90
The Doors '91
Twin Peaks: Fire Walk with Me '92
Where the Day Takes You '92
Rich in Love '93
The Trial '93
Against the Wall '94
The Flintstones '94
Roswell: The U.F.O. Cover-Up '94
Showgirls '95
Moonshine Highway '96
The Trigger Effect '96

Shirley MacLaine
Artists and Models '55

The Trouble with Harry '55
Around the World in 80 Days '56
Hot Spell '58
The Matchmaker '58
Some Came Running '58
Ask Any Girl '59
Career '59
The Apartment '60
Can-Can '60
All in a Night's Work '61
The Children's Hour '61
My Geisha '62
Two for the Seesaw '62
Irma La Douce '63
Gambit '66
Woman Times Seven '67
The Bliss of Mrs. Blossom '68
Sweet Charity '69
Two Mules for Sister Sara '70
Desperate Characters '71
The Possession of Joel Delaney '72
Golden Age of Hollywood '77
The Turning Point '77
Being There '79
A Change of Seasons '80
Loving Couples '80
Terms of Endearment '83
Cannonball Run 2 '84
That's Dancing! '85
Out on a Limb '87
Madame Sousatzka '88
Steel Magnolias '89
Postcards from the Edge '90
Waiting for the Light '90
Used People '92
Wrestling Ernest Hemingway '93
Guarding Tess '94
Mrs. Winterbourne '96

Barton MacLane
Man of the Forest '33
To the Last Man '33
Black Fury '35
The Case of the Lucky Legs '35
Ceiling Zero '35
"G" Men '35
The Prince and the Pauper '37
You Only Live Once '37
Bullets or Ballots '38
Prison Break '38
Mutiny in the Big House '39
Melody Ranch '40
The Maltese Falcon '41
Western Union '41
All Through the Night '42
Big Street '42
Bombardier '43
Marine Raiders '43
Song of Texas '43
The Underdog '43
Cry of the Werewolf '44
The Mummy's Ghost '44
Nabonga '44
The Spanish Main '45
Treasure of Fear '45
Silver River '48
Treasure of the Sierra Madre '48
Unknown Island '48
Let's Dance '50
Drums in the Deep South '51
The Half-Breed '51
Bugles in the Afternoon '52
Kansas Pacific '53
Naked in the Sun '57
Three Violent People '57
The Geisha Boy '58
Arizona Bushwackers '67
Buckskin '68

Mary MacLaren
The New Frontier '35
A Lawman Is Born '37

Gavin MacLeod
Compulsion '59
The Sand Pebbles '66
The Party '68
The Love Boat '70s
Kelly's Heroes '70
Only with Married Men '74
Scruples '80
The Cary Grant Collection '90

Michael MacLiammoir
Othello '52
What's the Matter with Helen? '71

Ellie MacLure
Alvin Purple '73

MacLure ▶cont.

Heat of the Flame '82
Air Hawk '84

Aline MacMahon
Gold Diggers of 1933 '33
Heroes for Sale '33
Ah, Wilderness! '35
I Live My Life '35
Back Door to Heaven '39
The Lady is Willing '42
Dragon Seed '44
The Search '48
The Flame & the Arrow '50
The Man from Laramie '55
I Could Go on Singing '63

Fred MacMurray
Alice Adams '35
Hands Across the Table '35
The Princess Comes Across '36
The Texas Rangers '36
Swing High, Swing Low '37
My Love For Yours '39
Remember the Night '40
Dive Bomber '41
The Lady is Willing '42
Above Suspicion '43
Double Indemnity '44
Egg and I '47
Singapore '47
The Miracle of the Bells '48
Father Was a Fullback '49
Borderline '50
Never a Dull Moment '50
The Caine Mutiny '54
A Woman's World '54
At Gunpoint '55
The Shaggy Dog '59
The Apartment '60
The Absent-Minded Professor '61
Bon Voyage! '62
Son of Flubber '63
Kisses for My President '64
Follow Me, Boys! '66
The Happiest Millionaire '67
Charley and the Angel '73
Beyond the Bermuda Triangle '75
The Swarm '78

Robert MacNaughton
E.T.: The Extra-Terrestrial '82
I Am the Cheese '83

Patrick Macnee
The Elusive Pimpernel '50
A Christmas Carol '51
Les Girls '57
The Bloodsuckers '70
King Solomon's Treasure '76
Dead of Night '77
Battlestar Galactica '78
The Howling '81
Sea Wolves '81
Spaceship '81
Sweet 16 '81
Rehearsal for Murder '82
Young Doctors in Love '82
Return of the Man from U.N.C.L.E. '83
This Is Spinal Tap '84
A View to a Kill '85
Down Under '86
Shadey '87
Transformations '88
Waxwork '88
Around the World in 80 Days '89
Cult People '89
Lobster Man from Mars '89
Masque of the Red Death '89
Sorry, Wrong Number '89
Chill Factor '90
Sherlock Holmes and the Incident at Victoria Falls '91
The Gambler Returns: The Luck of the Draw '93
The Hound of London '93
Thunder in Paradise '93
Thunder in Paradise 2 '94

Peter MacNeill
A Vow to Kill '94
Crash '95

Peter MacNicol
The Boy Who Left Home to Find Out About the Shivers '81
Dragonslayer '81
Sophie's Choice '82
Heat '87
American Blue Note '89
Ghostbusters 2 '89
Hard Promises '92
Housesitter '92
Addams Family Values '93
Roswell: The U.F.O. Cover-Up '94
Dracula: Dead and Loving It '95

Elle Macpherson
Alice '90
Sirens '94
If Lucy Fell '95
Jane Eyre '96

George MacQuarrie
The Idol Dancer '20
The Love Flower '20

Gordon MacRae
Look for the Silver Lining '49
Tea for Two '50
The West Point Story '50
On Moonlight Bay '51
By the Light of the Silvery Moon '53
The Desert Song '53
Oklahoma! '55
Carousel '56
Danger in the Skies '79

Heather MacRae
Bang the Drum Slowly '73
The Connection '73
Secrets of Three Hungry Wives '78

Meredith MacRae
Bikini Beach '64
Sketches of a Strangler '78
Vultures '84
Husbands, Wives, Money, and Murder '86

Michael MacRae
Dear Detective '78
Great Ride '78
Greedy Terror '78
Isle of Secret Passion '85
Madhouse '87

George Macready
The Seventh Cross '44
Gilda '46
Down to Earth '47
Black Arrow '48
Coroner Creek '48
The Doolins of Oklahoma '49
Knock on Any Door '49
The Nevadan '50
Detective Story '51
The Green Glove '52
I Beheld His Glory '53
Julius Caesar '53
The Stranger Wore a Gun '53
Vera Cruz '53
Paths of Glory '57
Taras Bulba '62
Two Weeks in Another Town '62
The Human Duplicators '64
Where Love Has Gone '64
The Great Race '65
Tora! Tora! Tora! '70
The Return of Count Yorga '71

Bill Macy
Oh! Calcutta! '72
The Late Show '77
Diary of a Young Comic '79
The Jerk '79
Serial '80
My Favorite Year '82
Bad Medicine '85
Casey at the Bat '85
Movers and Shakers '85
Sibling Rivalry '90
The Doctor '91
Me, Myself & I '92
Murder In the First '95

William H. Macy
Homicide '91
A Private Matter '92
The Water Engine '92
Benny & Joon '93
Searching for Bobby Fischer '93
Twenty Bucks '93
Being Human '94
Dead on Sight '94
ER '94
Oleanna '94
Andersonville '95
Mr. Holland's Opus '95
Down Periscope '96
Fargo '96

Ciaran Madden
A Married Man '84
Fortunes of War '87

John Madden
P.K. and the Kid '85
Little Giants '94

Victor Maddern
Blood of the Vampire '58
I'm All Right Jack '59

Amy Madigan
The Ambush Murders '82
Love Child '82
Love Letters '83
Places in the Heart '84
Streets of Fire '84
Alamo Bay '85
Twice in a Lifetime '85
Nowhere to Hide '87
Prince of Pennsylvania '88
Field of Dreams '89
Roe vs. Wade '89
Uncle Buck '89
The Dark Half '91
Riders of the Purple Sage '96

James Madio
Hero '92
The Basketball Diaries '94

Guy Madison
Since You Went Away '44
Till the End of Time '46
Drums in the Deep South '51
Savage Wilderness '55
Bullwhip '58
Jet Over the Atlantic '59
Executioner of Venice '63
Apaches Last Battle '64
Conqueror & the Empress '64
Cold Steel for Tortuga '65
Place in Hell '65
Five Giants from Texas '66
The Snake Hunter Strangler '66
Bang Bang Kid '67
Superargo '67
Special Forces '68
Hell Commandos '69
Computer Wizard '77
Where's Willie? '77

Noel Madison
Cocaine Fiends '36
Gangway '37
The House of Secrets '37
A Nation Aflame '37
Sailing Along '38
Footsteps in the Dark '41

Rock Madison
Man Beast '55
Creature of the Walking Dead '60

Philip Madoc
Space: 1999—Alien Attack '79
A Mind to Kill '95

Madonna
Certain Sacrifice '80
Desperately Seeking Susan '85
Shanghai Surprise '86
Who's That Girl? '87
Bloodhounds of Broadway '89
Dick Tracy '90
Truth or Dare '91
Body of Evidence '92
A League of Their Own '92
Shadows and Fog '92
Dangerous Game '93
Blue In the Face '95
Four Rooms '95
Girl 6 '96

Michael Madsen
The Natural '84
Racing with the Moon '84
Shadows in the Storm '88
Kill Me Again '89
The End of Innocence '90
The Doors '91
Thelma & Louise '91
Beyond the Law '92
Fatal Instinct '92
Inside Edge '92
Reservoir Dogs '92
Straight Talk '92
Trouble Bound '92
Almost Blue '93
Free Willy '93
The Getaway '93
A House In The Hills '93
Money for Nothing '93
Dead Connection '94
Season of Change '94
Wyatt Earp '94
Free Willy 2: The Adventure Home '95
Man with a Gun '95
Mulholland Falls '95
Species '95

Virginia Madsen
Dune '84
Electric Dreams '84
Creator '85
The Hearst and Davies Affair '85
Fire with Fire '86
Modern Girls '86
Long Gone '87
Slamdance '87
Zombie High '87
Gotham '88
Hot to Trot! '88
Mr. North '88
The Heart of Dixie '89
Third Degree Burn '89
The Hot Spot '90
Ironclads '90
Highlander 2: The Quickening '91
Love Kills '91
Victim of Love '91
Becoming Colette '92
Candyman '92
Caroline at Midnight '93
Linda '93
Bitter Vengeance '94
Blue Tiger '94
The Prophecy '95

Roma Maffia
Disclosure '94
The Heidi Chronicles '95
Nick of Time '95

Macha Magal
SS Girls '78
S.S. Experiment Camp 2 '86

Patrick Magee
Dementia 13 '63
Seance on a Wet Afternoon '64
Die, Monster, Die! '65
Masque of the Red Death '65
Masque of the Red Death/ Premature Burial '65
The Skull '65
Marat/Sade '66
Portrait in Terror '66
Anzio '68
Cromwell '70
A Clockwork Orange '71
The Fiend '71
King Lear '71
Trojan Women '71
Asylum '72
Demons of the Mind '72
Young Winston '72
And Now the Screaming Starts '73
The Final Programme '73
A Killer in Every Corner '74
Luther '74
Barry Lyndon '75
Telefon '77
Sleep of Death '79
Rough Cut '80
The Black Cat '81
Chariots of Fire '81
The Monster Club '85

Brandon Maggart
Dressed to Kill '80
The World According to Garp '82
Terror in Toyland '85
Running Mates '92

Anna Magnani
Open City '45
Peddlin' in Society '47
Amore '48
The Miracle '48
Bellissima '51
The Golden Coach '52
The Rose Tattoo '55
The Fugitive Kind '60
Passionate Thief '60
Mamma Roma '62
Bellissimo: Images of the Italian Cinema '87

Ann Magnuson
The Hunger '83
Perfect Strangers '84
Desperately Seeking Susan '85
Making Mr. Right '86
A Night in the Life of Jimmy Reardon '88
Sleepwalk '88
Tequila Sunrise '88
Checking Out '89
Heavy Petting '89
Love at Large '89
Cabin Boy '94
Before and After '95

Gerard Maguire
Demonstrator '71
Prisoner Cell Block H '80

Valerie Mahaffey
Mr. Bill's Real Life Adventures '86
The Rise & Rise of Daniel Rocket '86
Women of Valor '86
They Watch '93
Witch Hunt '94
National Lampoon's Senior Trip '95

George Maharis
Exodus '60
Desperados '69
Land Raiders '69
Last Day of the War '69
Murder on Flight 502 '75
Return to Fantasy Island '77
The Crash of Flight 401 '78
Sword & the Sorcerer '82

Bill Maher
House 2: The Second Story '87
Cannibal Women in the Avocado Jungle of Death '89
Pizza Man '91

Joseph Maher
Under the Rainbow '81
The Evil That Men Do '84
Funny Farm '88
My Stepmother Is an Alien '88
Sister Act '92
I.Q. '94
Bulletproof Heart '95

Grace Mahlaba
Bopha! '93
Being Human '94

Bruce Mahler
Funland '89
Police Academy 6: City Under Siege '89

Jock Mahoney
Rim of the Canyon '49
Cow Town '50
The Nevadan '50
Range Rider '52
Battle Hymn '57
The Land Unknown '57
A Time to Love & a Time to Die '58
The Glory Stompers '67
Bad Bunch '76

John Mahoney
The Manhattan Project '86
Trapped in Silence '86
Moonstruck '87
Suspect '87
Tin Men '87
Betrayed '88
Eight Men Out '88
Frantic '88
Dinner at Eight '89
The Image '89
Say Anything '89
The Russia House '90
Barton Fink '91
Love Hurts '91
The Ten Million Dollar Getaway '91
Unnatural Pursuits '91
Article 99 '92
The Secret Passion of Robert Clayton '92
The Water Engine '92
The Hudsucker Proxy '93
In the Line of Fire '93
Striking Distance '93
Reality Bites '94
The American President '95
Primal Fear '96

Tim Maier
Raw Courage '84
Turnaround '87

Marjorie Main
Dead End '37
Stella Dallas '37
The Wrong Road '37
Little Tough Guys '38

They Shall Have Music '39
The Women '39
Dark Command '40
Susan and God '40
Honky Tonk '41
A Woman's Face '41
Heaven Can Wait '43
Johnny Come Lately '43
The Harvey Girls '46
The Show-Off '46
Egg and I '47
The Wistful Widow of Wagon Gap '47
Ma and Pa Kettle '49
Ma and Pa Kettle Go to Town '50
Summer Stock '50
Ma and Pa Kettle Back On the Farm '51
The Belle of New York '52
Ma and Pa Kettle at the Fair '52
Ma and Pa Kettle on Vacation '53
The Long, Long Trailer '54
Ma and Pa Kettle at Home '54
Rose Marie '54
Ma and Pa Kettle at Waikiki '55
Friendly Persuasion '56
The Kettles in the Ozarks '56
The Kettles on Old MacDonald's Farm '57

Valerie Mairesse
One Sings, the Other Doesn't '77
Investigation '79
The Sacrifice '86

Marne Maitland
Bhowani Junction '56
The Bushbaby '70
Fellini's Roma '72

Tina Majorino
Andre '94
Corrina, Corrina '94
When a Man Loves a Woman '94
Waterworld '95

Lee Majors
Will Penny '67
Big Valley '68
The Bionic Woman '75
Francis Gary Powers: The True Story of the U-2 Spy '76
Norseman '78
Killer Fish '79
High Noon: Part 2 '80
Steel '80
The Agency '81
Last Chase '81
Starflight One '83
The Cowboy & the Ballerina '84
A Smoky Mountain Christmas '86
Scrooged '88
Chinatown Connection '90
Keaton's Cop '90
The Cover Girl Murders '93

Chris Makepeace
My Bodyguard '80
Last Chase '81
Mazes and Monsters '82
The Mysterious Stranger '82
The Terry Fox Story '83
Savage Hunger '84
Undergrads '85
Vamp '86
Captive Hearts '87
Aloha Summer '88
Synapse '95

Wendy Makkena
Sister Act '92
Sister Act 2: Back in the Habit '93
Camp Nowhere '94

Mako
The Sand Pebbles '66
The Streets of San Francisco '72
The Island at the Top of the World '74
The Killer Elite '75
The Big Brawl '80
An Eye for an Eye '81
Under the Rainbow '81
Conan the Barbarian '82
The Nightingale '83
Conan the Destroyer '84
Armed Response '86
Kung Fu: The Movie '86
The P.O.W. Escape '86
Tucker: The Man and His Dream '88
The Wash '88
Fatal Mission '89
An Unremarkable Life '89
Hiroshima: Out of the Ashes '90
Pacific Heights '90
Taking Care of Business '90
My Samurai '92
Rising Sun '93
Sidekicks '93
A Dangerous Place '94
Highlander: The Final Dimension '94
Red Sun Rising '94
Blood for Blood '95

Mala
Robinson Crusoe of Clipper Island '36
Robinson Crusoe of Mystery Island '36
Hawk of the Wilderness '38
The Tuttles of Tahiti '42

Patrick Malahide
Comfort and Joy '84
A Month in the Country '87
December Bride '91
Middlemarch '93
A Man of No Importance '94
Cutthroat Island '95
The Franchise Affair

Christophe MaLavoy
Peril '85
Madame Bovary '91
The Cry of the Owl '92

Karl Malden
They Knew What They Wanted '40
13 Rue Madeleine '46
Boomerang '47
Kiss of Death '47
The Gunfighter '50
The Halls of Montezuma '50
A Streetcar Named Desire '51
Diplomatic Courier '52
Ruby Gentry '52
I Confess '53
On the Waterfront '54
Baby Doll '56
Fear Strikes Out '57
The Hanging Tree '59
Pollyanna '60
The Great Impostor '61
One-Eyed Jacks '61
Parrish '61
All Fall Down '62
Birdman of Alcatraz '62
Gypsy '62
How the West Was Won '63
Cheyenne Autumn '64
The Cincinnati Kid '65
The Adventures of Bullwhip Griffin '66
Murderers' Row '66
Nevada Smith '66
Hotel '67
Blue '68
Hot Millions '68
Patton '70
The Cat o' Nine Tails '71
Wild Rovers '71
The Streets of San Francisco '72
Ricco '74
Beyond the Poseidon Adventure '79
Meteor '79
Skag '79
Miracle on Ice '81
The Sting 2 '83
Fatal Vision '84
Urge to Kill '84
Billy Galvin '86
Nuts '87

Ruth Maleczech
Anna '87
In the Soup '92
The Ballad of Little Jo '93

Arthur Malet
Beastmaster 2: Through the Portal of Time '91
Hook '91
A Little Princess '95

Laurent Malet
Blood Relatives '77
Invitation au Voyage '82
Jacko & Lise '82
Querelle '83
Sword of Gideon '86

Wendie Malick
The American President '95
Madonna: Innocence Lost '95

Art Malik
The Jewel in the Crown '84
Transmutations '85
Harem '86
The Living Daylights '87
City of Joy '92
The Killing Beach '92
Year of the Comet '92
True Lies '94
A Kid in King Arthur's Court '95

Judith Malina
Emergency '68
Signals Through the Flames '83
Enemies, a Love Story '89
The Addams Family '91
Household Saints '93

Ross Malinger
Eve of Destruction '90
Late for Dinner '91
Sleepless in Seattle '93
Sudden Death '95

John Malkovich
American Dream '81
The Killing Fields '84
Places in the Heart '84
Eleni '85
Death of a Salesman '86
Making Mr. Right '86
Rocket to the Moon '86
True West '86
Empire of the Sun '87
The Glass Menagerie '87
Dangerous Liaisons '88
Miles from Home '88
The Sheltering Sky '90
The Object of Beauty '91
Queens Logic '91
Jennifer 8 '92
Of Mice and Men '92
Shadows and Fog '92
Heart of Darkness '93
In the Line of Fire '93
Mary Reilly '95
Mulholland Falls '95

Miles Malleson
Nine Days a Queen '34
Dead of Night '45
Train of Events '49
A Christmas Carol '51
The Golden Salamander '51
Captain's Paradise '53
The King's Rhapsody '55
Brothers in Law '57

Patricia "Boots" Mallory
Carnival Lady '33
Wolf Dog '33
Powdersmoke Range '35
Sing Sing Nights '35

Jan Malmsjo
Scenes from a Marriage '73
Fanny and Alexander '83

Birger Malmsten
Night Is My Future '47
Three Strange Loves '49
Summer Interlude '50
The Silence '63

Dorothy Malone
The Big Sleep '46
Night and Day '46
South of St. Louis '48
The Nevadan '50
The Bushwackers '52
Scared Stiff '53
Torpedo Alley '53
The Fast and the Furious '54
Young at Heart '54
Artists and Models '55
At Gunpoint '55
Battle Cry '55
Sincerely Yours '56
Tension at Table Rock '56
Written on the Wind '56
Man of a Thousand Faces '57
Tarnished Angels '57
Warlock '59
The Last Voyage '60
Beach Party '63
Abduction '75
The Man Who Would Not Die '75
Winter Kills '79
Day Time Ended '80
Off Your Rocker '80
Rest In Pieces '87
Basic Instinct '92

Mollie Malone
Straight Shootin' '17
Battling Bunyon '24

Patrick Malone
Grand Canyon '91
Rock 'n' Roll High School Forever '91

Michael Maloney
Sharma & Beyond '84
Henry V '89
Truly, Madly, Deeply '91
A Midwinter's Tale '95
Othello '95

Biff Manard
Zone Troopers '84
Trancers 2: The Return of Jack Deth '90

Ray "Boom Boom" Mancini
Oceans of Fire '86
The Dirty Dozen: The Fatal Mission '88
Backstreet Dreams '90
Timebomb '91
Wishful Thinking '92

Nick Mancuso
The House on Garibaldi Street '79
Nightwing '79
Death Ship '80
Ticket to Heaven '81
Legend of Walks Far Woman '82
Mother Lode '82
Blame It on the Night '84
Heartbreakers '84
Maria Chapdelaine '84
Tell Me That You Love Me '84
Embassy '85
Death of an Angel '86
Half a Lifetime '86
Double Identity '89
Lena's Holiday '90
Fatal Exposure '91
Lies Before Kisses '92
Rapid Fire '92
Wild Palms '93
Flinch '94
Suspicious Agenda '94
The Takeover '94
Under Siege 2: Dark Territory '95

Robert Mandan
The Best of Soap: Jessica's Wonderful Life '70s
The Best of Soap: Who Killed Peter? '77
Return of the Rebels '81
In Love with an Older Woman '82
Zapped! '82
Perry Mason: The Case of the Lost Love '87
National Lampoon's Last Resort '94

Howie Mandel
Gas '81
The Princess Who Never Laughed '84
A Fine Mess '86
Walk Like a Man '87
Little Monsters '89
Mother Goose Rock 'n' Rhyme '90
Kurt Vonnegut's Harrison Bergeron '95

Miles Mander
Murder '30
The Private Life of Henry VIII '33
Don Quixote '35
The Three Musketeers '35
Mad Miss Manton '38
The Little Princess '39
Stanley and Livingstone '39
The Three Musketeers '39
The Tower of London '39
Wuthering Heights '39
Primrose Path '40
Shadows on the Stairs '41
Guadalcanal Diary '43
Return of the Vampire '43
Murder, My Sweet '44
The Pearl of Death '44
Scarlet Claw '44
Brighton Strangler '45
The Brighton Strangler/Before Dawn '45

Barbara Mandrell
The Concrete Cowboys '79
Burning Rage '84

Costas Mandylor
Triumph of the Spirit '89
The Doors '91
Mobsters '91
Soapdish '91
Almost Dead '94
Fatal Past '94
Delta of Venus '95
Portraits of a Killer '95
Venus Rising '95
Virtuosity '95
Crosscut '96

Larry Manetti
Magnum P.I.: Don't Eat the Snow in Hawaii '80
The Take '90
C.I.A. 2: Target Alexa '94
Exit '95

Nino Manfredi
Head of the Family '71
Bread and Chocolate '74
Down & Dirty '76
We All Loved Each Other So Much '77
Spaghetti House '82
Cafe Express '83
Nudo di Donna '83
In the Name of the Pope-King '85
Alberto Express '92

Silvana Mangano
Bitter Rice '49
Lure of the Sila '49
Anna '51
The Gold of Naples '54
Mambo '55
Ulysses '55
The Great War '59
Barabbas '62
Oedipus Rex '67
Teorema '68
The Decameron '70
Death in Venice '71
Conversation Piece '75
Dune '84
Dark Eyes '87

Karin Mani
Alley Cat '84
Avenging Angel '85

Cindy Manion
Preppies '82
The Toxic Avenger '86

Hank Mann
Spite Marriage '29
City Lights '31

Leonard Mann
Night School '81
Corrupt '84

Terrence Mann
A Chorus Line '85
Critters '86
Critters 2: The Main Course '88
Critters 4 '91
The Ten Million Dollar Getaway '91

Tracey Mann
Hard Knocks '80
Fast Talking '86

David Manners
Dracula '31
A Bill of Divorcement '32
The Mummy '32
They Call It Sin '32
Three Broadway Girls '32
The Death Kiss '33
The Black Cat '34

Lucie Mannheim
The 39 Steps '35
High Command '37
Hotel Reserve '44

Ettore Manni
Two Nights with Cleopatra '54
Angel in a Taxi '59
The Battle of Austerlitz '60
Giants of Rome '63
Hercules and the Captive Women '63
Mademoiselle '66
Heroes in Hell '67
The Battle of El Alamein '68
Street People '76
City of Women '81

Defense Play '88
Judgment Day '88
At First Sight '95

Ted Markland
Angels from Hell '68
Wanda Nevada '79
Fatal Mission '89
Merlin '92
American Kickboxer 2: To the Death '93

Stephen Markle
984: Prisoner of the Future '84
Perfect Timing '84

Margaret Markov
Run, Angel, Run! '69
Hot Box '72
Naked Warriors '73

Olivera Markovic
Fury is a Woman '61
Tito and Me '92

Alfred Marks
Scream and Scream Again '70
Mission: Monte Carlo '75
Valentino '77
Antonia and Jane '91

Winnie Markus
The Mozart Story '48
The Devil in Silk '56

Arnold Marle
Men of Two Worlds '46
The Snake Woman '61

John Marley
Faces '68
Love Story '70
A Man Called Sledge '71
Deathdream '72
The Godfather '72
Jory '72
Framed '75
Kid Vengeance '75
The Greatest '77
Hooper '78
It's Alive 2: It Lives Again '78
The Godfather 1902-1959: The Complete Epic '81
Robbers of the Sacred Mountain '83
Threshold '83
Utilities '83
The Glitter Dome '84
On the Edge '86

Carla Marlier
Zazie dans le Metro '61
The Avenger '62
The Big Grab '63
Spirits of the Dead '68

Lucy Marlow
My Sister Eileen '55
Queen Bee '55

Hugh Marlowe
Come to the Stable '49
Twelve O'Clock High '49
All About Eve '50
Night and the City '50
Rawhide '50
The Day the Earth Stood Still '51
Bugles in the Afternoon '52
Monkey Business '52
Casanova's Big Night '54
Illegal '55
Earth vs. the Flying Saucers '56
Elmer Gantry '60
Birdman of Alcatraz '62
Castle of Evil '66

June Marlowe
Don Juan '26
The Night Cry '26
Pardon Us '31
The Lone Defender '32

Linda Marlowe
He Kills Night After Night After Night '70
Big Zapper '73
Night Slasher '84
Mr. Love '86
The Green Man '91

Florence Marly
Tokyo Joe '49
Planet of Blood '66
Dr. Death, Seeker of Souls '73

Percy Marmont
Mantrap '26
Lady of the Lake '28
Rich and Strange '32

Young and Innocent '37
Four Sided Triangle '53
Lisbon '56

Kelli Maroney
Fast Times at Ridgemont High '82
Night of the Comet '84
Slayground '84
Chopping Mall '86
Zero Boys '86
Servants of Twilight '91

Carl Marotte
Pick-Up Summer '79
Breaking All the Rules '85
Workin' for Peanuts '85

Christian Marquand
And God Created Woman '57
End of Desire '62
The Corrupt Ones '67

Maria Elena Marques
The Pearl '48
Across the Wide Missouri '51
Ambush at Tomahawk Gap '53

Ron Marquette
Public Access '93
Deadly Past '95
Red Shoe Diaries 5: Weekend Pass '95

Margaret Marquis
Brand of the Outlaws '36
Last of the Warrens '36

Eddie Marr
Hollywood Canteen '44
I Was a Teenage Werewolf '57

Moore Marriott
The Flying Scotsman '29
Oh, Mr. Porter '37

Sylvia Marriott
Crimes at the Dark House '39
Two English Girls '72

Kenneth Mars
The Producers '68
Butch Cassidy and the Sundance Kid '69
Desperate Characters '71
What's Up, Doc? '72
The Parallax View '74
Young Frankenstein '74
Night Moves '75
Goin' Coconuts '78
The Apple Dumpling Gang Rides Again '79
Protocol '84
Beer '85
Fletch '85
Misfits of Science '85
Illegally Yours '87
Radio Days '87
For Keeps '88
Rented Lips '88
Get Smart, Again! '89
Shadows and Fog '92

Maurice Marsac
Tarzan and the Trappers '58
Werewolf in a Girl's Dormitory '61
Clarence, the Cross-eyed Lion '65

Branford Marsalis
Throw Momma from the Train '87
School Daze '88

Carol Marsh
Brighton Rock '47
Alice in Wonderland '50
A Christmas Carol '51
The Horror of Dracula '58

Garry Marsh
Department Store '35
Pink Strings and Sealing Wax '45
A Girl in a Million '46
Just William's Luck '47
Someone at the Door '50

Jean Marsh
Horsemasters '61
The Unearthly Stranger '64
Frenzy '72
The Changeling '80
Goliath Awaits '81
Return to Oz '85
Willow '88
A Connecticut Yankee in King Arthur's Court '89
Fatherland '94

Joan Marsh
High Gear '33
Rainbow Over Broadway '33
Champagne for Breakfast '35
Follow the Leader '44
Manhunt in the African Jungle '54

Mae Marsh
D.W. Griffith Triple Feature '13
Home Sweet Home '14
Judith of Bethulia '14
The Birth of a Nation '15
Hoodoo Ann '16
Intolerance '16
The White Rose '23
How Green Was My Valley '41
The Fighting Sullivans '42
Three Godfathers '48
The Gunfighter '50
The Quiet Man '52
The Tall Men '55
While the City Sleeps '56
From the Terrace '60
Sergeant Rutledge '60

Marian Marsh
Svengali '31
The Black Room '35
Crime and Punishment '35
When's Your Birthday? '37
Youth on Parole '37
Gentleman from Dixie '41
House of Errors '42

Matthew Marsh
An Affair in Mind '89
In the Secret State

Michele Marsh
Deadly Alliance '78
Evil Town '87

Alan Marshal
After the Thin Man '36
Conquest '37
The Hunchback of Notre Dame '39
The Howards of Virginia '40
Lydia '41
Tom, Dick, and Harry '41
The White Cliffs of Dover '44
House on Haunted Hill '58

Brenda Marshall
The Sea Hawk '40
Footsteps in the Dark '41
Captains of the Clouds '42
Background to Danger '43

Bryan Marshall
Because of the Cats '74
The Long Good Friday '79
Return to Snowy River '88

Dodie Marshall
Spinout '66
Easy Come, Easy Go '67

E.G. Marshall
13 Rue Madeleine '46
Call Northside 777 '48
Broken Lance '54
The Caine Mutiny '54
The Silver Chalice '54
The Left Hand of God '55
The Mountain '56
Twelve Angry Men '57
The Buccaneer '58
Compulsion '59
Cash McCall '60
The Chase '66
The Poppy Is Also a Flower '66
Is Paris Burning? '68
The Bridge at Remagen '69
The Littlest Angel '69
The Pursuit of Happiness '70
Tora! Tora! Tora! '70
Pursuit '72
Abduction of St. Anne '75
Interiors '78
The Lazarus Syndrome '79
Superman 2 '80
Creepshow '82
Eleanor: First Lady of the World '82
Kennedy '83
My Chauffeur '86
Power '86
Saigon: Year of the Cat '87
National Lampoon's Christmas Vacation '89
Ironclads '90
Consenting Adults '92
Russian Roulette '93

Stephen King's The Tommyknockers '93
Nixon '95
Oldest Confederate Widow Tells All '95

Garry Marshall
Lost in America '85
Soapdish '91
A League of Their Own '92

Herbert Marshall
Murder '30
Blonde Venus '32
The Painted Veil '34
Riptide '34
A Woman Rebels '36
Angel '37
Mad About Music '38
Foreign Correspondent '40
The Letter '40
The Little Foxes '41
When Ladies Meet '41
Forever and a Day '43
The Moon and Sixpence '43
The Enchanted Cottage '45
Crack-Up '46
Duel in the Sun '46
The Razor's Edge '46
The Secret Garden '49
The Underworld Story '50
Captain Blackjack '51
The Virgin Queen '55
Stage Struck '57
The Fly '58

James Marshall
A Few Good Men '92
Gladiator '92
Twin Peaks: Fire Walk with Me '92
Don't Do It '94
Vibrations '94

Ken Marshall
Tilt '78
Krull '83
Feds '88
Double Exposure: The Story of Margaret Bourke-White '89

Marion Marshall
I Was a Male War Bride '49
The Stooge '51

Paula Marshall
Hellraiser 3: Hell on Earth '92
Warlock: The Armageddon '93
The New Age '94
A Family Thing '96

Penny Marshall
How Come Nobody's On Our Side? '73
Challenge of a Lifetime '85
Movers and Shakers '85

Peter Marshall
Return of Jesse James '50
A Guide for the Married Woman '78

Sarah Marshall
The People vs. Jean Harris '81
French Silk '94

Sean Marshall
Wonderland Cove '75
Pete's Dragon '77

Trudy Marshall
The Fighting Sullivans '42
Crash Dive '43
Married Too Young '62
Joe's Bed-Stuy Barbershop: We Cut Heads '83

Tully Marshall
Hawthorne of the USA '19
What Happened to Rosa? '21
Broken Hearts of Broadway '23
Let's Go! '23
He Who Gets Slapped '24
Smouldering Fires '25
The Cat and the Canary '27
Queen Kelly '29
Big Trail '30
Tom Sawyer '30
Fighting Caravans '31
The Cabin in the Cotton '32
Strangers of the Evening '32
Two-Fisted Law '32
Night of Terror '33
Mr. Boggs Steps Out '38
Behind Prison Walls '43

William Marshall
State Fair '45
That Brennan Girl '46

William Marshall
Demetrius and the Gladiators '54
The Boston Strangler '68
Blacula '72
Scream Blacula Scream '73
Twilight's Last Gleaming '77
The Great Skycopter Rescue '82
Vasectomy: A Delicate Matter '86

Zena Marshall
Dr. No '62
The Terrornauts '67

Christina Marsillach
Every Time We Say Goodbye '86
Terror at the Opera '88

Tony Marsina
Tornado '83
Last Mercenary '84

Lynn Marta
Joe Kidd '72
Richard Petty Story '72

Arlene Martel
Demon with a Glass Hand '64
Angels from Hell '68

June Martel
Arizona Mahoney '36
Forlorn River '37
Santa Fe Stampede '38

K.C. Martel
The Munsters' Revenge '81
E.T.: The Extra-Terrestrial '82

Chris Martell
Gruesome Twosome '67
Flesh Feast '69
Scream, Baby, Scream '69

Donna Martell
Abbott and Costello Meet the Killer, Boris Karloff '49
Give a Girl a Break '53
Project Moon Base '53
Ten Wanted Men '54

Peter Martell
Planet on the Prowl '65
Mission Phantom '79

Cynthia Martells
Blind Spot '93
Broken Trust '95
Zooman '95

Frank Marth
Fright '56
Showdown '93

Andrea Martin
Soup for One '82
Club Paradise '86
Rude Awakening '89
Worth Winning '89
Too Much Sun '90
All I Want for Christmas '91
Stepping Out '91
Boris and Natasha: The Movie '92
Gypsy '93
Guitarman '95
Kurt Vonnegut's Harrison Bergeron '95

Chris-Pin Martin
South of Santa Fe '32
The Texans '38
Stagecoach '39
Lucky Cisco Kid '40

Christopher Martin
House Party '90
Class Act '91
House Party 2: The Pajama Jam '91
House Party 3 '94

Damon Martin
Ghoulies 2 '87
Amityville 1992: It's About Time '92

Dean Martin
My Friend Irma '49
At War with the Army '50
The Stooge '51
Jumping Jacks '52
The Caddy '53
The Road to Bali '53
Scared Stiff '53
Artists and Models '55
Hollywood or Bust '56
Pardners '56

Martin ▶cont.

Some Came Running '58
The Young Lions '58
Career '59
Rio Bravo '59
Bells are Ringing '60
Ocean's 11 '60
All in a Night's Work '61
Four for Texas '63
Toys in the Attic '63
Who's Got the Action? '63
Kiss Me, Stupid! '64
Robin and the 7 Hoods '64
Sons of Katie Elder '65
Murderers' Row '66
Texas Across the River '66
The Ambushers '67
Rough Night in Jericho '67
Bandolero! '68
Five Card Stud '68
Airport '70
Showdown '73
Cannonball Run '81
Cannonball Run 2 '84
Hollywood Clowns '85
That's Dancing! '85

Dean Paul Martin
Players '79
Misfits of Science '85
Backfire '88

Dewey Martin
The Thing '51
The Big Sky '52
Men of the Fighting Lady '54
Desperate Hours '55
Land of the Pharaohs '55
Savage Sam '63
Flight to Fury '66
Seven Alone '75

Diana Martin
Hyena of London '62
Minnesota Clay '65

Dick Martin
The Glass Bottom Boat '66
Carbon Copy '81

Duane Martin
Above the Rim '94
Down Periscope '96

D'Urville Martin
Final Comedown '72
Boss '74
Sheba, Baby '75
Death Journey '76
Blind Rage '78
Big Score '83

George Martin
Psychopath '68
The Compleat Beatles '82
Falling in Love '84
Blood at Sundown '88
Crossing Delancey '88

Helen Martin
A Hero Ain't Nothin' But a Sandwich '78
Hollywood Shuffle '87
Night Angel '90
Doc Hollywood '91
House Party 2: The Pajama Jam '91

Jared Martin
The Sea Serpent '85
Quiet Cool '86
The New Gladiators '87
Karate Warrior '88
Twinsitters '95

John Martin
The Tell-Tale Heart '62
Fire in the Night '85
Black Roses '88
Dark Before Dawn '89

Kellie Martin
Troop Beverly Hills '89
Matinee '92
Christy '94

Kiel Martin
Panic in Needle Park '75
Child Bride of Short Creek '81
Hill Street Blues, Vol. 1: Hill Street Station '81
Convicted: A Mother's Story '87

Marion Martin
Sinners in Paradise '38
The Man in the Iron Mask '39
Mexican Spitfire at Sea '42
The Great Mike '44

Mary Martin
Rhythm on the River '40
Birth of the Blues '41
Star Spangled Rhythm '42
Night and Day '46
Peter Pan '60
Irving Berlin's America '86

Mel Martin
Love for Lydia '79
White Hunter, Black Heart '90

Millicent Martin
Horsemasters '61
Those Magnificent Men in Their Flying Machines '65
Alfie '66

Nan Martin
Toys in the Attic '63
For Love of Ivy '68
Goodbye Columbus '69
The Young Nurses '73
Proud Men '87
Matters of the Heart '90

Pamela Sue Martin
The Girls of Huntington House '73
Buster and Billie '74
Our Time '74
Lady in Red '79
Flicks '85
Torchlight '85
Eye of the Demon '87
A Cry in the Wild '90

Pepper Martin
Angels from Hell '68
Scream '83
Evil Altar '89

Richard Martin
Tender Comrade '43
Nevada '44
West of the Pecos '45
Mysterious Desperado '49
Mysterious Desperado/Rider From Tucson '49
Riders of the Range '49
Dynamite Pass '50
Rider from Tucson '50
Riders of the Range/Storm Over Wyoming '50
Storm Over Wyoming '50
Gun Smugglers/Hot Lead '51
Gunplay '51

Ross Martin
Conquest of Space '55
Experiment in Terror '62
Geronimo '62
Dying Room Only '73
Wild & Wooly '78
The Seekers '79
Wild, Wild West Revisited '79
More Wild, Wild West '80

Steve Martin
Sgt. Pepper's Lonely Hearts Club Band '78
The Jerk '79
Pennies From Heaven '81
Dead Men Don't Wear Plaid '82
The Man with Two Brains '83
All of Me '84
The Lonely Guy '84
Movers and Shakers '85
Steve Martin Live '85
Little Shop of Horrors '86
Three Amigos '86
Planes, Trains & Automobiles '87
Roxanne '87
Dirty Rotten Scoundrels '88
Parenthood '89
My Blue Heaven '90
Father of the Bride '91
Grand Canyon '91
L.A. Story '91
Housesitter '92
Leap of Faith '92
Mixed Nuts '94
A Simple Twist of Fate '94
Father of the Bride Part II '95
Sgt. Bilko '95

Strother Martin
Kiss Me Deadly '55
The Horse Soldiers '59
The Man Who Shot Liberty Valance '62
McLintock! '63
Invitation to a Gunfighter '64
Cool Hand Luke '67
Butch Cassidy and the Sundance Kid '69
The Wild Bunch '69
Hot Wire '70s
Ballad of Cable Hogue '70
The Brotherhood of Satan '71
Hannie Caulder '72
Pocket Money '72
Hard Times '75
Rooster Cogburn '75
Slap Shot '77
Steel Cowboy '78
Better Late Than Never '79
The Champ '79
Cheech and Chong's Up in Smoke '79
Love and Bullets '79
Nightwing '79
The Villain '79

Tony Martin
Music in My Heart '40
Big Store '41
Ziegfeld Girl '41
Till the Clouds Roll By '46
Till the Clouds Roll By/A Star Is Born '46
Two Tickets to Broadway '51
Easy to Love '53
Here Come the Girls '53
Hit the Deck '55

Vera Martin
The Noose Hangs High '48
Loyalties '86

Vince Martin
Night Master '87
Breaking Loose '90

W.T. Martin
Hardhat & Legs '80
High Stakes '89

Margo Martindale
Lorenzo's Oil '92
Nobody's Fool '94

Elsa Martinelli
The Indian Fighter '55
Blood and Roses '61
Hatari! '62
The Trial '63
The V.I.P.'s '63
10th Victim '65
Madigan's Millions '67
Maroc 7 '67
Oldest Profession '67
Woman Times Seven '67
Belle Starr '79
Once Upon a Crime '92

A. Martinez
The Cowboys '72
Once Upon a Scoundrel '73
Starbird and Sweet William '73
Joe Panther '76
Born in East L.A. '87
Powwow Highway '89
She-Devil '89
The Hunt for the Night Stalker '91
Deconstructing Sarah '94
One Night Stand '95

Al Martino
The Godfather '72
The Godfather, Part 3 '90

Orlando Martins
Men of Two Worlds '46
Simba '55
Call Me Bwana '63

Lee Marvin
Union Station '50
Hangman's Knot '52
The Big Heat '53
Gun Fury '53
The Stranger Wore a Gun '53
Bad Day at Black Rock '54
The Caine Mutiny '54
The Wild One '54
I Died a Thousand Times '55
Pete Kelly's Blues '55
Shack Out on 101 '55
Raintree County '57
Missouri Traveler '58
The Comancheros '61
Combat! '62
The Man Who Shot Liberty Valance '62
Donovan's Reef '63
The Killers '64
Cat Ballou '65
Ship of Fools '65
The Professionals '66
The Dirty Dozen '67
Point Blank '67
Sergeant Ryker '68
Hell in the Pacific '69
Paint Your Wagon '69
Monte Walsh '70
Pocket Money '72
Prime Cut '72
The Klansman '74
Great Scout & Cathouse Thursday '76
The Meanest Men in the West '76
Shout at the Devil '76
Avalanche Express '79
The Big Red One '80
Death Hunt '81
Dog Day '83
Gorky Park '83
The Dirty Dozen: The Next Mission '85
Delta Force '86

Alan Marx
For Auld Lang Syne: The Marx Brothers '32
Gore-Met Zombie Chef From Hell '87

Chico Marx
The Cocoanuts '29
Animal Crackers '30
Monkey Business '31
For Auld Lang Syne: The Marx Brothers '32
Horse Feathers '32
Duck Soup '33
A Night at the Opera '35
A Day at the Races '37
Room Service '38
At the Circus '39
Go West '40
Big Store '41
A Night in Casablanca '46
Love Happy '50
Hollywood Clowns '85
The Marx Brothers in a Nutshell '90

Groucho Marx
The Cocoanuts '29
Animal Crackers '30
Monkey Business '31
For Auld Lang Syne: The Marx Brothers '32
Horse Feathers '32
Duck Soup '33
A Night at the Opera '35
A Day at the Races '37
Room Service '38
At the Circus '39
Go West '40
Big Store '41
A Night in Casablanca '46
Copacabana '47
Love Happy '50
Double Dynamite '51
A Girl in Every Port '52
Hollywood Clowns '85
The Marx Brothers in a Nutshell '90

Harpo Marx
The Cocoanuts '29
Animal Crackers '30
Monkey Business '31
For Auld Lang Syne: The Marx Brothers '32
Horse Feathers '32
Duck Soup '33
A Night at the Opera '35
A Day at the Races '37
Room Service '38
At the Circus '39
Go West '40
Big Store '41
Strictly G.I. '44
A Night in Casablanca '46
Love Happy '50
Hollywood Goes to War '54
Hollywood Clowns '85
The Marx Brothers in a Nutshell '90

Zeppo Marx
The Cocoanuts '29
Animal Crackers '30
Monkey Business '31
Horse Feathers '32
Duck Soup '33
The Marx Brothers in a Nutshell '90

Giulietta Masina
Variety Lights '51
Europa '51 '52
The White Sheik '52
La Strada '54
The Swindle '55
Nights of Cabiria '57
Juliet of the Spirits '65
The Madwoman of Chaillot '69
Ginger & Fred '86

Ace Mask
Not of This Earth '88
Transylvania Twist '89

Virginia Maskell
Only Two Can Play '62
The Prisoner: Arrival '68

Connie Mason
Blood Feast '63
2000 Maniacs '64

Eric Mason
Black Starlet '74
Kiss of the Tarantula '75

Hilary Mason
Don't Look Now '73
Dolls '87
Meridian: Kiss of the Beast '90
Robot Jox '90

Jackie Mason
The Jerk '79
History of the World: Part 1 '81
Caddyshack 2 '88

James Mason
For Heaven's Sake '26
The Concentratin' Kid '30
Border Law '31
Hopalong Cassidy '35
Arizona Mahoney '36
The Plainsman '37

James Mason
Late Extra '35
Fire Over England '37
High Command '37
The Mill on the Floss '37
I Met a Murderer '39
The Night Has Eyes '42
Secret Mission '42
Hotel Reserve '44
The Man in Grey '45
The Wicked Lady '45
The Seventh Veil '46
Odd Man Out '47
Man of Evil '48
Caught '49
East Side, West Side '49
Madame Bovary '49
Reckless Moment '49
The Desert Fox '51
Pandora and the Flying Dutchman '51
Face to Face '52
Five Fingers '52
Prisoner of Zenda '52
Botany Bay '53
Charade '53
The Desert Rats '53
Julius Caesar '53
Prince Valiant '54
A Star is Born '54
20,000 Leagues Under the Sea '54
Forever Darling '56
Island in the Sun '57
Journey to the Center of the Earth '59
North by Northwest '59
The Trials of Oscar Wilde '60
Lolita '62
Tiara Tahiti '62
The Fall of the Roman Empire '64
The Pumpkin Eater '64
Lord Jim '65
The Blue Max '66
Georgy Girl '66
Mayerling '68
Street War '70s
Yin & Yang of Mr. Go '71
Bad Man's River '72
The Last of Sheila '73
Mackintosh Man '73
Cold Sweat '74
The Destructors '74
11 Harrowhouse '74
Autobiography of a Princess '75
Inside Out '75
Mandingo '75
Cross of Iron '76

Kidnap Syndicate '76
Voyage of the Damned '76
Jesus of Nazareth '77
The Boys from Brazil '78
Heaven Can Wait '78
Murder by Decree '79
Salem's Lot '79
Sidney Sheldon's Bloodline '79
Water Babies '79
ffolkes '80
Dangerous Summer '82
Evil under the Sun '82
Ivanhoe '82
The Verdict '82
Yellowbeard '83
The Assisi Underground '84
George Washington '84
The Shooting Party '85

Leroy Mason
Phantom of the Air '33
When a Man Sees Red '34
Go-Get-'Em-Haines '35
The Mystery Man '35
Black Gold '36
The Painted Stallion '37
Western Gold '37
Outlaw Express '38
Santa Fe Stampede '38
Wyoming Outlaw '39
Rocky Mountain Rangers '40
Silver Stallion '41
Western Mail '42
Daughter of Don Q '46
The Phantom Rider '46

Marsha Mason
Blume in Love '73
Cinderella Liberty '73
Audrey Rose '77
The Goodbye Girl '77
The Cheap Detective '78
Chapter Two '79
Promises in the Dark '79
Only When I Laugh '81
Lois Gibbs and the Love Canal '82
Max Dugan Returns '83
Heartbreak Ridge '86
Trapped in Silence '86
Dinner at Eight '89
The Image '89
Stella '89
Drop Dead Fred '91
Broken Trust '95
Nick of Time '95

Pamela Mason
Charade '53
Door to Door Maniac '61
Navy vs. the Night Monsters '66

Tom Mason
Apocalypse Now '79
Aliens Are Coming '80
Walking Through the Fire '80
Kicks '85
Mississippi Burning '88
Men Don't Leave '89
The Amy Fisher Story '93
Final Appeal '93

Lea Massari
L'Avventura '60
The Things of Life '70
Murmur of the Heart '71
Allonsanfan '73
The Story of a Love Story '73
Les Rendez-vous D'Anna '78
Christ Stopped at Eboli '79
Vengeance '86

Michael Massee
My Father Is Coming '91
The Crow '93

Osa Massen
A Woman's Face '41
Iceland '42
Background to Danger '43
Cry of the Werewolf '44
Master Race '44
Rocketship X-M '50
Outcasts of the City '58

Anna Massey
Peeping Tom '63
Frenzy '72
Vault of Horror '73
Sweet William '79
Another Country '84
The Little Drummer Girl '84
Anna Karenina '85
Mansfield Park '85
The McGuffin '85
Foreign Body '86
Hotel du Lac '86
A Doll's House '89
The Man from the Pru '89
The Tall Guy '89
Impromptu '90
Mountains of the Moon '90
A Tale of Two Cities '91
Angels and Insects '95
Haunted '95

Athena Massey
Undercover '94
Virtual Combat '95

Daniel Massey
The Entertainer '60
Star! '68
Vault of Horror '73
The Incredible Sarah '76
The Cat and the Canary '79
Victory '81
Love with a Perfect Stranger '86
Intimate Contact '87
Scandal '89
Stalin '92
In the Name of the Father '93

Edith Massey
Multiple Maniacs '70
Pink Flamingos '72
Female Trouble '74
Desperate Living '77
Polyester '81

Ilona Massey
Rosalie '38
Balalaika '39
Melody Master '41
Invisible Agent '42
Holiday in Mexico '46
Northwest Outpost '47
Love Happy '50

Raymond Massey
The Speckled Band '31
The Old Dark House '32
The Scarlet Pimpernel '34
Things to Come '36
Under the Red Robe '36
Dreaming Lips '37
Fire Over England '37
The Hurricane '37
Prisoner of Zenda '37
Black Limelight '38
Drums '38
Abe Lincoln in Illinois '40
Santa Fe Trail '40
The Forty-Ninth Parallel '41
Desperate Journey '42
Reap the Wild Wind '42
Action in the North Atlantic '43
Arsenic and Old Lace '44
Woman In the Window '44
The Possessed '47
The Fountainhead '49
Chain Lightning '50
David and Bathsheba '51
The Desert Song '53
East of Eden '54
Battle Cry '55
Omar Khayyam '57
The Naked and the Dead '58
The Great Impostor '61
How the West Was Won '63
MacKenna's Gold '69
The President's Plane is Missing '71

Paul Massie
Sapphire '59
The Two Faces of Dr. Jekyll '60

Ben Masters
Mandingo '75
All That Jazz '79
The Shadow Box '80
Celebrity '85
Dream Lover '85
Key Exchange '85
The Deliberate Stranger '86
Making Mr. Right '86
Noble House '88
Running Mates '92

Chase Masterson
In a Moment of Passion '93
Married People, Single Sex '93

Fay Masterson
The Power of One '92
The Man Without a Face '93
Cops and Robbersons '94

Mary Stuart Masterson
Heaven Help Us '85
At Close Range '86
Gardens of Stone '87
My Little Girl '87
Some Kind of Wonderful '87
Mr. North '88
Chances Are '89
Immediate Family '89
Funny About Love '90
Fried Green Tomatoes '91
Mad at the Moon '92
Benny & Joon '93
Married to It '93
Bad Girls '94
Radioland Murders '94
Bed of Roses '95
Heaven's Prisoners '95

Mary Elizabeth Mastrantonio
Scarface '83
The Color of Money '86
Slamdance '87
The Abyss '89
The January Man '89
Fools of Fortune '90
Class Action '91
Robin Hood: Prince of Thieves '91
Consenting Adults '92
White Sands '92
Three Wishes '95
Two Bits '96

Gina Mastrogiacomo
Alien Space Avenger '91
Tall, Dark and Deadly '95

Marcello Mastroianni
White Nights '57
Big Deal on Madonna Street '58
Where the Hot Wind Blows '59
Il Bell'Antonio '60
La Dolce Vita '60
Divorce—Italian Style '62
A Very Private Affair '62
8 1/2 '63
Marriage Italian Style '64
Yesterday, Today and Tomorrow '64
Casanova '70 '65
10th Victim '65
The Poppy Is Also a Flower '66
Shoot Loud, Louder, I Don't Understand! '66
Divine Nymph '71
Allonsanfan '73
Diary of Forbidden Dreams '73
La Grande Bouffe '73
Massacre in Rome '73
Salut l'Artiste '74
Get Rita '75
Lunatics & Lovers '76
A Special Day '77
We All Loved Each Other So Much '77
Stay As You Are '78
Blood Feud '79
Lady of the Evening '79
A Slightly Pregnant Man '79
Wifemistress '79
City of Women '81
Beyond Obsession '82
La Nuit de Varennes '82
Gabriela '84
Henry IV '85
Macaroni '85
Ginger & Fred '86
Bellissimo: Images of the Italian Cinema '87
Dark Eyes '87
Intervista '87
Everybody's Fine '90
A Fine Romance '92
Used People '92
I Don't Want to Talk About It '94
Ready to Wear '94

Richard Masur
Semi-Tough '77
Betrayal '78
Who'll Stop the Rain? '78
East of Eden '80
Walking Through the Fire '80
Fallen Angel '81
Heaven's Gate '81
The Thing '82
Adam '83
Nightmares '83
Risky Business '83
Timerider '83
Under Fire '83
Wild Horses '84
The Burning Bed '85
Embassy '85
Mean Season '85
My Science Project '85
The George McKenna Story '86
Heartburn '86
When the Bough Breaks '86
The Believers '87
Walker '87
Hiroshima Maiden '88
License to Drive '88
Rent-A-Cop '88
Shoot to Kill '88
Cast the First Stone '89
Far from Home '89
Flashback '89
Third Degree Burn '89
Stephen King's It '90
My Girl '91
Encino Man '92
And the Band Played On '93
The Man Without a Face '93
Six Degrees of Separation '93
My Girl 2 '94
Forget Paris '95
Hiroshima '95

Julian Mateos
Hellbenders '67
Four Rode Out '69
Kashmiri Run '69

Aubrey Mather
The Silent Passenger '35
Mrs. Miniver '42
The Undying Monster '42
Hello, Frisco, Hello '43
Jane Eyre '44
House of Fear '45
Adventures of Don Juan '49
That Forsyte Woman '50

Jerry Mathers
Men of the Fighting Lady '54
The Trouble with Harry '55
Back to the Beach '87
Down the Drain '89

Marissa Mathes
How to Succeed with Girls '64
Track of the Vampire '66

Judy Matheson
Twins of Evil '71
The House that Vanished '73

Michelle Matheson
Howling 6: The Freaks '90
Test Tube Teens from the Year 2000 '93
Threesome '94

Tim Matheson
Yours, Mine & Ours '68
How to Commit Marriage '69
Magnum Force '73
The Runaway Barge '75
The Captive: The Longest Drive 2 '76
The Longest Drive '76
Mary White '77
National Lampoon's Animal House '78
The Apple Dumpling Gang Rides Again '79
Dreamer '79
1941 '79
A Little Sex '82
Listen to Your Heart '83
To Be or Not to Be '83
Best Legs in the 8th Grade '84
Impulse '84
Up the Creek '84
Fletch '85
Blind Justice '86
Eye of the Demon '87
Speed Zone '88
Little White Lies '89
Buried Alive '90
Drop Dead Fred '91
Quicksand: No Escape '91
Sometimes They Come Back '91
Solar Crisis '92
Trial and Error '92
Fallen Angels 1 '93
Midnight Heat '95
Tails You Live, Heads You're Dead '95
Black Sheep '96
A Very Brady Sequel '96

Carole Mathews
Shark River '53
Swamp Women '55
Strange Awakening '58

George Mathews
Last of the Comanches '52
The Man with the Golden Arm '55

Kerwin Mathews
The Seventh Voyage of Sinbad '58
The Three Worlds of Gulliver '59
The Devil at 4 O'Clock '61
Jack the Giant Killer '62
Maniac '63
Waltz King '63
Battle Beneath the Earth '68
Octaman '71
Nightmare in Blood '75
Killer Likes Candy '78

Thom Mathews
Friday the 13th, Part 6: Jason Lives '86
Alien from L.A. '87
Return of the Living Dead 2 '88
Down Twisted '89
Midnight Cabaret '90
Bloodmatch '91
Heatseeker '95

Samantha Mathis
Pump Up the Volume '90
This Is My Life '92
The Music of Chance '93
Super Mario Bros. '93
The Thing Called Love '93
Little Women '94
The American President '95
Broken Arrow '95
How to Make an American Quilt '95
Jack and Sarah '96

Jacques Mathou
Betty Blue '86
The Hairdresser's Husband '92
Year of the Comet '92

Marlee Matlin
Children of a Lesser God '86
Walker '87
Bridge to Silence '89
The Linguini Incident '92
Hear No Evil '93
It's My Party '95

John Matshikiza
Dust '85
Mandela '87
Dust Devil '93
Yankee Zulu '95

Yusaku Matsuda
Murder in the Doll House '79
The Family Game '83
Black Rain '89

Eva Mattes
The Bitter Tears of Petra von Kant '72
Stroszek '77
In a Year of 13 Moons '78
Woyzeck '78
David '79
Celeste '81
A Man Like Eva '83
The Promise '95

Pam Matteson
Punchline '88
Prehysteria 3 '95

Walter Matthau
Atomic Attack '50
The Indian Fighter '55
The Kentuckian '55
A Face in the Crowd '57
King Creole '58
Strangers When We Meet '60
Lonely Are the Brave '62
Charade '63
Who's Got the Action? '63
Ensign Pulver '64
Fail-Safe '64
The Fortune Cookie '66
Mirage '66
A Guide for the Married Man '67
The Odd Couple '68
Secret Life of an American Wife '68
Cactus Flower '69
Hello, Dolly! '69
Kotch '71
A New Leaf '71

Matthau ▶cont.

Plaza Suite '71
Pete 'n' Tillie '72
Charley Varrick '73
Earthquake '74
The Front Page '74
The Laughing Policeman '74
The Taking of Pelham One Two Three '74
The Sunshine Boys '75
The Bad News Bears '76
California Suite '78
Casey's Shadow '78
House Calls '78
Hopscotch '80
Little Miss Marker '80
Buddy Buddy '81
First Monday in October '81
I Ought to Be in Pictures '82
Survivors '83
Movers and Shakers '85
Pirates '86
The Couch Trip '87
The Incident '89
JFK '91
Dennis the Menace '93
Grumpy Old Men '93
I.Q. '94
Grumpier Old Men '95

A.E. Matthews
The Iron Duke '34
Made in Heaven '52
Carry On Admiral '57

Brian Matthews
The Burning '82
Red Nights '87

Dakin Matthews
Nuts '87
My Brother's Wife '89
Naked Lie '89
Child's Play 3 '91
In a Stranger's Hand '92
Revolver '92
The Temp '93
White Mile '94

Francis Matthews
Bhowani Junction '56
Small Hotel '57
Corridors of Blood '58
The Revenge of Frankenstein '58
The Hellfire Club '61
Murder Ahoy '64
The McGuffin '85

Fritz Matthews
Deadly Prey '87
Hell on the Battleground '88
Born Killer '89

Jessie Matthews
Evergreen '34
It's Love Again '36
Gangway '37
Sailing Along '38
Forever and a Day '43
Candles at Nine '44
The Hound of the Baskervilles '77

Lester Matthews
The Raven '35
Werewolf of London '35
The Invisible Man's Revenge '44
King Richard and the Crusaders '54

Robin Mattson
Namu, the Killer Whale '66
Bonnie's Kids '73
Candy Stripe Nurses '74
Return to Macon County '75
Captain America '79
Hot Rod '79
Wolf Lake '79
Take Two '87
In Between '92

Victor Mature
Captain Caution '40
No, No Nanette '40
One Million B.C. '40
I Wake Up Screaming '41
Footlight Serenade '42
Seven Days' Leave '42
The Shanghai Gesture '42
Song of the Islands '42
My Darling Clementine '46
Kiss of Death '47
Easy Living '49
Samson and Delilah '50
Androcles and the Lion '52
The Las Vegas Story '52
Million Dollar Mermaid '52
The Robe '53
Betrayed '54
Dangerous Mission '54
Demetrius and the Gladiators '54
The Egyptian '54
Savage Wilderness '55
The Long Haul '57
After the Fox '66
Samson and Delilah '84

John Matuszak
Semi-Tough '77
North Dallas Forty '79
Caveman '81
Ice Pirates '84
The Goonies '85
My Darlin' Clementine '86
Down the Drain '89
Ghost Writer '89
One Man Force '89

Johanna Matz
Party Girls for Sale '54
They Were So Young '55
The Life and Loves of Mozart '59

Joan Maude
Power '34
The Temptress '49

Monica Maughan
Prisoner Cell Block H '80
Cactus '86
A Woman's Tale '92

Sarah Maur-Thorp
Edge of Sanity '89
Ten Little Indians '89
River of Death '90

Carmen Maura
Pepi, Luci, Bom and Other Girls on the Heap '80
Dark Habits '84
Extramuros '85
What Have I Done to Deserve This? '85
Law of Desire '86
Matador '86
Women on the Verge of a Nervous Breakdown '88
Ay, Carmela! '90
Between Heaven and Earth '93

Joshua Maurer
Tour of Duty '87
Taken Away '89

Nicole Maurey
Rogue's Yarn '56
Me and the Colonel '58
The Jayhawkers '59
Day of the Triffids '63

Claire Maurier
Back to the Wall '56
The 400 Blows '59
Sweet Ecstasy '62
La Cage aux Folles '78

Gerda Maurus
Spies '28
Woman in the Moon '29

Edwin Maxwell
The Taming of the Shrew '29
Night of Terror '33
Mystery Liner '34
Way Down South '39
Behind Prison Walls '43
Waterfront '44
Swamp Fire '46
Woman in Brown '48

Frank Maxwell
Lonelyhearts '58
Shame '61
The Haunted Palace '63

John Maxwell
Honky Tonk '41
Boss of Big Town '43
The Payoff '43
Prowler '51

Larry Maxwell
Poison '91
Public Access '93

Lois Maxwell
Time Without Pity '57
The Unstoppable Man '59
Dr. No '62
From Russia with Love '63
Goldfinger '64
Thunderball '65
You Only Live Twice '67
On Her Majesty's Secret Service '69
Diamonds Are Forever '71
Live and Let Die '73
The Man with the Golden Gun '74
The Spy Who Loved Me '77
Moonraker '79
For Your Eyes Only '81
A View to a Kill '85
Eternal Evil '87

Marilyn Maxwell
Lost in a Harem '44
The Show-Off '46
Summer Holiday '48
Champion '49
Key to the City '50
The Lemon Drop Kid '51
Off Limits '53
Arizona Bushwackers '67
Wild Women '70

Paul Maxwell
Going Home '86
Cloud Waltzing '87

Roberta Maxwell
Lois Gibbs and the Love Canal '82
Psycho 3 '86
Philadelphia '93

Deborah May
Rage of Angels '83
Johnny Be Good '88
Caged Fear '92

Donald May
Kisses for My President '64
Bogie: The Last Hero '80

Elaine May
Enter Laughing '67
Luv '67
A New Leaf '71
California Suite '78
In the Spirit '90

Jack May
He Kills Night After Night After Night '70
Night Slasher '84

Jodhi May
A World Apart '88
Max and Helen '90
Eminent Domain '91
The Last of the Mohicans '92
Sister My Sister '94

Mathilda May
Letters to an Unknown Lover '84
Lifeforce '85
Becoming Colette '92
The Cry of the Owl '92
Prince Brat and the Whipping Boy '95

Rik Mayall
Whoops Apocalypse '83
The Young Ones '88
Drop Dead Fred '91
Little Noises '91

Anthony Mayans
Sex Is Crazy '79
Heat of the Flame '82
Zombie Lake '84

Eddie Mayehoff
The Stooge '51
Artists and Models '55
How to Murder Your Wife '64

Chip Mayer
Our Family Business '81
Survivor '87

Ray Mayer
Special Investigator '36
Swing It, Sailor! '37

Peter Mayhew
The Empire Strikes Back '80
Return of the Jedi '83

John Maynard
Dark Universe '93
Biohazard: The Alien Force '95

Ken Maynard
$50,000 Reward '25
Voice of Hollywood '29
Fightin' Ranch '30
The Fighting Legion '30
Fighting Thru '30
Mountain Justice '30
Arizona Terror '31
Branded Men '31
The Pocatello Kid '31
Range Law '31
Two Gun Man '31
Between Fighting Men '32
Come On Tarzan '32
Dynamite Ranch '32
False Faces '32
Fargo Express '32
Hell Fire Austin '32
Sunset Trail '32
Texas Gunfighter '32
Whistlin' Dan '32
Drum Taps '33
The Fiddlin' Buckaroo '33
The Lone Avenger '33
Phantom Thunderbolt '33
Strawberry Roan '33
Honor of the Range '34
In Old Santa Fe '34
Mystery Mountain '34
Tombstone Canyon '35
Trail Drive '35
Western Frontier '35
Desert Guns/Six-Shootin' Sheriff '36
Boots of Destiny '37
Six Shootin' Sheriff '38
Whirlwind Horseman '38
Flaming Lead '39
Phantom Rancher '39
Death Rides the Range '40
Lightning Strikes West '40
The Law Rides Again '43
Arizona Whirlwind '44
Death Valley Rangers '44
Harmony Trail '44

Kermit Maynard
Outlaw Justice '32
Drum Taps '33
The Fighting Trooper '34
His Fighting Blood '35
Phantom Patrol '36
Song of the Trail '36
Whistling Bullets '36
Galloping Dynamite '37
Roaring Six Guns '37
Rough Ridin' Rhythm '37
Valley of Terror '38
Pony Post '40
Riders of Pasco Basin '40
The Showdown '40
Billy the Kid '41
Bury Me Not On the Lone Prairie '41
Man from Montana '41
Along the Sundown Trail '42
Arizona Stagecoach '42
The Mysterious Rider '42
Prairie Pals '42
Texas Kid '43
Devil Riders '44
Frontier Outlaws '44
Gangster's Den '45
The Stranger from Pecos '45
Ambush Trail '46
'Neath Canadian Skies '46
Trail of Robin Hood '50
The Black Lash '52

Mimi Maynard
False Identity '90
Adventures in Dinosaur City '92

Ferdinand "Ferdy" Mayne
The Temptress '49
Captain's Paradise '53
Roadhouse Girl '53
White Fire '53
Masters of Venus '59
The Fearless Vampire Killers '67
The Adventurers '70
The Vampire Lovers '70
The Vampire Happening '71
Frightmare '81
Hawk the Slayer '81
Night Train to Terror '84
The Secret Diary of Sigmund Freud '84
Howling 2: Your Sister is a Werewolf '85
A Friendship in Vienna '88
Magdalene '88
River of Diamonds '90
Benefit of the Doubt '93

Alfredo Mayo
The Hunt '67
Bell from Hell '74

Frank Mayo
Doughboys '30
Hell's Headquarters '32
Tim Tyler's Luck '37

Virginia Mayo
Jack London '44
The Princess and the Pirate '44
Seven Days Ashore/Hurry, Charlie, Hurry '44
Wonder Man '45
The Best Years of Our Lives '46
Kid from Brooklyn '46
Out of the Blue '47
The Secret Life of Walter Mitty '47
A Song is Born '48
White Heat '49
The Flame & the Arrow '50
The West Point Story '50
Along the Great Divide '51
Captain Horatio Hornblower '51
Devil's Canyon '53
King Richard and the Crusaders '54
The Silver Chalice '54
Pearl of the South Pacific '55
Great Day in the Morning '56
Jet Over the Atlantic '59
Castle of Evil '66
French Quarter '78
The Haunted '79
Evil Spirits '91
Midnight Witness '93

Gale Mayron
Heart of Midnight '89
The Feud '90
Almost Blue '93

Melanie Mayron
Car Wash '76
You Light Up My Life '77
Girlfriends '78
Playing for Time '80
The Best Little Girl in the World '81
Heartbeeps '81
Missing '82
The Boss' Wife '86
Sticky Fingers '88
Checking Out '89
My Blue Heaven '90
Wanted: The Perfect Guy '90

Bob Maza
The Fringe Dwellers '86
Ground Zero '88
Reckless Kelly '93

Debi Mazar
Little Man Tate '91
Beethoven's 2nd '93
Inside Monkey Zetterland '93
Money for Nothing '93
Witch Hunt '94
Bad Love '95
Batman Forever '95
Empire Records '95
Girl 6 '96

Mike Mazurki
Dick Tracy, Detective/The Corpse Vanishes '42
The Shanghai Gesture '42
Behind the Rising Sun '43
The Canterville Ghost '44
Murder, My Sweet '44
Dick Tracy, Detective '45
Killer Dill '47
Sinbad, the Sailor '47
Unconquered '47
The Noose Hangs High '48
Come to the Stable '49
Neptune's Daughter '49
Night and the City '50
Blood Alley '55
Hell Ship Mutiny '57
Some Like It Hot '59
The Errand Boy '61
Donovan's Reef '63
Cheyenne Autumn '64
Challenge To Be Free '76
The Incredible Rocky Mountain Race '77
The Adventures of Huckleberry Finn '78
Doin' Time '85

Paul Mazursky
Alex in Wonderland '70
A Star is Born '76
A Man, a Woman, and a Bank '79
History of the World: Part 1 '81

Into the Night '85
Punchline '88
Enemies, a Love Story '89
Scenes from the Class Struggle in Beverly Hills '89
Man Trouble '92
Love Affair '94
Miami Rhapsody '95

Joseph Mazzello
Jersey Girl '92
Radio Flyer '92
Jurassic Park '93
Shadowlands '93
The River Wild '94
The Cure '95
Three Wishes '95

Des McAleer
Four Days in July '85
Hidden Agenda '90
Butterfly Kiss '94

Ray McAnally
Sea of Sand '58
Cal '84
Danny Boy '84
The Mission '86
No Surrender '86
Empire State '87
The Fourth Protocol '87
A Perfect Spy '88
Taffin '88
My Left Foot '89
We're No Angels '89
A Very British Coup '90s

Marianne McAndrew
Hello, Dolly! '69
The Bat People '74

Alex McArthur
Urge to Kill '84
Silent Witness '85
Rampage '87
Race for Glory '89
Drug Wars 2: The Cocaine Cartel '92
Sharon's Secret '95

Hugh McArthur
Marihuana '36
Camp Double Feature '39
Panama Patrol '39

May McAvoy
Ben-Hur '26
Lady Windermere's Fan '26
The Jazz Singer '27
Gun Glory '57

Diane McBain
Parrish '61
Spinout '66
Deathhead Virgin '74
Monster '78
Donner Pass: The Road to Survival '84
Flying from the Hawk '86
Puppet Master 5: The Final Chapter '94

Daron McBee
The Killing Zone '90
T-Force '94

Chi McBride
Cosmic Slop '94
The Frighteners '96

Jon McBride
Cannibal Campout '88
Blades '89
Woodchipper Massacre '89

Michelle McBride
Masque of the Red Death '90
Subspecies '90

Ruth McCabe
My Left Foot '89
The Snapper '93

John McCafferty
Deathrow Gameshow '88
The Perfect Gift '95

Frances Lee McCain
Real Life '79
Tex '82
Two of a Kind '82
Gremlins '84
Broken Badge '85
The Lookalike '90
Question of Faith '93

William McCall
Rounding Up the Law '22
Trailing Trouble '30
Outlaws of the Range '36

Irish McCalla
She Demons '58
Hands of a Stranger '62

Holt McCallany
Creepshow 2 '87
Alien 3 '92
Tecumseh: The Last Warrior '95
Tyson '95

Lon McCallister
Stage Door Canteen '43
The Red House '47
The Big Cat '49
The Story of Seabiscuit '49

David McCallum
Robbery Under Arms '57
A Night to Remember '58
Billy Budd '62
The Great Escape '63
The Man from U.N.C.L.E. '64
Around the World Under the Sea '65
She Waits '71
King Solomon's Treasure '76
Kingfisher Caper '76
The Watcher in the Woods '81
Return of the Man from U.N.C.L.E. '83
Behind Enemy Lines '85
Terminal Choice '85
The Wind '87
The Haunting of Morella '91
Hear My Song '91
Shattered Image '93

Joanna McCallum
Tom & Viv '94
The Franchise Affair

John McCallum
Valley of the Eagles '51
Devil on Horseback '54

Macon McCalman
The Ultimate Imposter '79
Fleshburn '84
Doc Hollywood '91

Mercedes McCambridge
All the King's Men '49
Johnny Guitar '53
Tender Is the Night '55
Giant '56
Suddenly, Last Summer '59
Cimarron '60
Angel Baby '61
Deadly Sanctuary '68
99 Women '69
The President's Plane is Missing '71
Sixteen '72
The Girls of Huntington House '73
The Concorde: Airport '79 '79
The Sacketts '79
Echoes '83

Tom McCamus
Norman's Awesome Experience '88
A Man in Uniform '93

Chuck McCann
The Heart is a Lonely Hunter '68
The Projectionist '71
Foul Play '78
They Went That-a-Way & That-a-Way '78
C.H.O.M.P.S. '79
If Things Were Different '79
Rosebud Beach Hotel '85
Thrashin' '86
Cameron's Closet '89
That's Adequate '90
Storyville '92

Donal McCann
Screamer '74
Hard Way '80
Cal '84
Danny Boy '84
Out of Africa '85
The Dead '87
December Bride '91
The Miracle '91
Stealing Beauty '96

Sean McCann
Unnatural Causes '86
Mindfield '89
Run '91
Trial and Error '92
Guilty as Sin '93
The Air Up There '94
Trapped In Paradise '94
Iron Eagle 4 '95

Fred McCarren
How to Pick Up Girls '78
Marriage Is Alive and Well '80
Red Flag: The Ultimate Game '81

Andrew McCarthy
The Beniker Gang '83
Class '83
Heaven Help Us '85
St. Elmo's Fire '85
Pretty in Pink '86
Less Than Zero '87
Mannequin '87
Waiting for the Moon '87
Fresh Horses '88
Kansas '88
Club Extinction '89
Weekend at Bernie's '89
Year of the Gun '91
Only You '92
The Joy Luck Club '93
Weekend at Bernie's 2 '93
Dead Funny '94
Dream Man '94
Getting In '94
Mrs. Parker and the Vicious Circle '94
Night of the Running Man '94
The Courtyard '95
Mulholland Falls '95

Frank McCarthy
Dead Men Don't Wear Plaid '82
A Case of Deadly Force '86

Kevin McCarthy
The Annapolis Story '55
Invasion of the Body Snatchers '56
40 Pounds of Trouble '62
A Gathering of Eagles '63
The Best Man '64
A Big Hand for the Little Lady '66
Mirage '66
Hotel '67
Ace High '68
Dead Right '68
Dan Candy's Law '73
Order to Kill '73
Buffalo Bill & the Indians '76
Invasion of the Body Snatchers '78
Piranha '78
Hero at Large '80
Those Lips, Those Eyes '80
The Howling '81
My Tutor '82
Rosie: The Rosemary Clooney Story '82
Twilight Zone: The Movie '83
Invitation to Hell '84
Ratings Game '84
The Midnight Hour '86
Dark Tower '87
Hostage '87
Innerspace '87
Poor Little Rich Girl: The Barbara Hutton Story '87
For Love or Money '88
LBJ: The Early Years '88
Love or Money? '88
Fast Food '89
UHF '89
Eve of Destruction '90
The Rose and the Jackal '90
The Sleeping Car '90
Texas Guns '90
Dead on the Money '91
Final Approach '91
Ghoulies 3: Ghoulies Go to College '91
The Distinguished Gentleman '92
Duplicates '92
Just Cause '94
The Sister-in-Law '95

Lin McCarthy
Yellowneck '55
D.I. '57

Molly McCarthy
The Great St. Louis Bank Robbery '59
The Flamingo Kid '84

Nobu McCarthy
The Geisha Boy '58
The Karate Kid: Part 2 '86
The Wash '88
Pacific Heights '90

Sheila McCarthy
I've Heard the Mermaids Singing '87
Friends, Lovers & Lunatics '89
Die Hard 2: Die Harder '90
Pacific Heights '90
Bright Angel '91
George's Island '91
Paradise '91
Stepping Out '91
Beautiful Dreamers '92
Beethoven Lives Upstairs '92
A Private Matter '92
The Lotus Eaters '93

Paul McCartney
A Hard Day's Night '64
Help! '65
Magical Mystery Tour '67
Let It Be '70
The Compleat Beatles '82
Give My Regards to Broad Street '84

Patti McCarty
Fighting Valley '43
Devil Riders '44
Outlaw of the Plains '46

Rod McCary
No Drums, No Bugles '71
A Girl to Kill For '90
Rebel Storm '90
Night of the Demons 2 '94

Constance McCashin
Special Olympics '78
The Two Worlds of Jenny Logan '79
Obsessive Love '84
Love on the Run '85
Nightmare at Bittercreek '91

Charles McCaughan
Slaves of New York '89
Impulse '90

Rue McClanahan
Five Minutes to Love '63
How to Succeed with Girls '64
Hollywood After Dark '65
Sergeant Matlovich vs. the U.S. Air Force '78
After the Shock '90
Modern Love '90
Survival of Spaceship Earth '90
Baby of the Bride '91

Sean McClory
The Quiet Man '52
Charade '53
Diane '55
The King's Thief '55
Roller Boogie '79
My Chauffeur '86
Fools of Fortune '90

Leigh McCloskey
Alexander: The Other Side of Dawn '77
Inferno '78
Hearts & Armour '83
Fraternity Vacation '85
Just One of the Guys '85
Hamburger...The Motion Picture '86
Dirty Laundry '87
Cameron's Closet '89
Double Revenge '89
Accidental Meeting '93

Doug McClure
Enemy Below '57
The Unforgiven '60
Shenandoah '65
Playmates '72
Hell Hounds of Alaska '73
The Land That Time Forgot '75
At the Earth's Core '76
The People That Time Forgot '77
Bananas Boat '78
Wild & Wooly '78
The Rebels '79
Humanoids from the Deep '80
Firebird 2015 A.D. '81
House Where Evil Dwells '82
52 Pick-Up '86
Fight for Gold '86
Omega Syndrome '87
Prime Suspect '88
Bull of the West '89
Dark Before Dawn '89
Tapeheads '89
Battling for Baby '92
The Gambler Returns: The Luck of the Draw '93

Marc McClure
I Wanna Hold Your Hand '78
Superman: The Movie '78
Superman 2 '80
Strange Behavior '81
Pandemonium '82
Superman 3 '83
Supergirl '84
Back to the Future '85
Superman 4: The Quest for Peace '87
Perfect Match '88
After Midnight '89
Grim Prairie Tales '89
Back to the Future, Part 3 '90

Molly McClure
Daddy's Dyin'...Who's Got the Will? '90
Pure Country '92

Tane McClure
Hot Under the Collar '91
Caged Hearts '95
Lap Dancing '95
Midnight Tease 2 '95
Stripshow '95

Edie McClurg
Carrie '76
Cheech and Chong's Next Movie '80
Eating Raoul '82
Pandemonium '82
Mr. Mom '83
Cheech and Chong's The Corsican Brothers '84
Back to School '86
Ferris Bueller's Day Off '86
Planes, Trains & Automobiles '87
Elvira, Mistress of the Dark '88
She's Having a Baby '88
A River Runs Through It '92
Airborne '93
Under the Hula Moon '95

Warren McCollum
Reefer Madness '38
Boy's Reformatory '39
The Great Commandment '41

Heather McComb
New York Stories '89
Stay Tuned '92

Matthew McConaughey
Boys on the Side '94
Lone Star '95
A Time to Kill '96

John McConnell
Delta Heat '92
King of the Hill '93

Marilyn McCoo
The Fantastic World of D.C. Collins '84
My Mom's a Werewolf '89

Kent McCord
For Heaven's Sake '79
Nashville Beat '89
Predator 2 '90
Illicit Behavior '91
Accidental Meeting '93
Return of the Living Dead 3 '93

Catherine McCormack
Braveheart '95
Loaded '96

Patty McCormack
All Mine to Give '56
The Bad Seed '56
The Adventures of Huckleberry Finn '60
Invitation to Hell '84
Saturday the 14th Strikes Back '88
Mommy '95

Carolyn McCormick
Enemy Mine '85
Rain Without Thunder '93

Maureen McCormick
The Brady Bunch '69
Pony Express Rider '76
Moonshine County Express '77
Take Down '79
Idolmaker '80

McCormick ▶cont.

Texas Lightning '81
A Very Brady Christmas '88

Michelle McCormick
Fatal Pulse '88
Showdown '93

Myron McCormick
One Third of a Nation '39
Jigsaw '49
Not as a Stranger '55
No Time for Sergeants '58
The Hustler '61
A Public Affair '62

Pat McCormick
If You Don't Stop It...You'll Go Blind '77
Smokey and the Bandit '77
A Wedding '78
Smokey and the Bandit, Part 2 '80
Under the Rainbow '81
The Princess and the Pea '83
Smokey and the Bandit, Part 3 '83
E. Nick: A Legend in His Own Mind '84
Doin' Time '85
Bombs Away! '86
Rented Lips '88
Chinatown Connection '90

Emer McCourt
London Kills Me '91
Riff Raff '92

Malachy McCourt
Manny's Orphans '78
JFK: Reckless Youth '93

Alec McCowen
Time Without Pity '57
A Night to Remember '58
The Silent Enemy '58
Frenzy '72
Travels with My Aunt '72
Stevie '78
Hanover Street '79
Forever Young '85
A Dedicated Man '86
Cry Freedom '87
Personal Services '87
Henry V '89
The Age of Innocence '93
Maria's Child '93

Matt McCoy
Fraternity Vacation '85
Police Academy 5: Assignment Miami Beach '88
Deepstar Six '89
Police Academy 6: City Under Siege '89
The Cool Surface '92
Eyes of the Beholder '92
The Hand that Rocks the Cradle '92
Dead On '93
Samurai Cowboy '93
Bigfoot: The Unforgettable Encounter '94
Hard Bounty '94
Hard Drive '94
The Soft Kill '94
Rent-A-Kid '95
Synapse '95

Sylvester McCoy
Leapin' Leprechauns '95
Doctor Who '96

Tim McCoy
The Range Feud/Two Fisted Law '31
Cornered '32
Daring Danger '32
Fighting Fool '32
The Fighting Marshal '32
The Riding Tornado '32
Texas Cyclone '32
Two-Fisted Law '32
Man of Action '33
Bulldog Courage '35
Fighting Shadows '35
The Outlaw Deputy '35
The Revenge Rider '35
Aces and Eights '36
Border Caballero '36
Ghost Patrol '36
Lion's Den '36
The Man from Gun Town '36
Prescott Kid '36
Roaring Guns '36
The Traitor '36
Lightnin' Carson Rides Again '38
Phantom Ranger '38
Fighting Renegade '39
Outlaw's Paradise '39
Texas Wildcats '39
Arizona Gangbusters '40
Gun Code '40
Straight Shooter '40
Arizona Bound '41
Forbidden Trails '41
Gunman from Bodie '41
Below the Border '42
Dawn on the Great Divide '42
Down Texas Way '42
Ghost Town Law '42
Riders of the West '42
West of the Law '42
Run of the Arrow '56

Paul McCrane
Fame '80
Purple Hearts '84
RoboCop '87
The Portrait '93

Jody McCrea
Force of Impulse '60
Beach Party '63
Bikini Beach '64
Muscle Beach Party '64
Pajama Party '64
Beach Blanket Bingo '65
How to Stuff a Wild Bikini '65
The Glory Stompers '67

Joel McCrea
The Silver Horde '30
Kept Husbands '31
Bird of Paradise '32
The Most Dangerous Game '32
Barbary Coast '35
Our Little Girl '35
Come and Get It '36
These Three '36
Dead End '37
Internes Can't Take Money '37
They Shall Have Music '39
Union Pacific '39
Foreign Correspondent '40
Primrose Path '40
Sullivan's Travels '41
The Great Man's Lady '42
The Palm Beach Story '42
The More the Merrier '43
Buffalo Bill '44
The Great Moment '44
The Virginian '46
Ramrod '47
Four Faces West '48
South of St. Louis '48
Stars in My Crown '50
The Oklahoman '56
Lafayette Escadrille '58
Ride the High Country '62

Bruce McCulloch
The Best of the Kids in the Hall '93
Kids In the Hall Brain Candy '96

Ian McCulloch
Doctor Butcher M.D. '80
Zombie '80
Alien Contamination '81
Witching Time '84

Kyle McCulloch
Tales from the Gimli Hospital '88
Careful '94

Julie McCullough
Big Bad Mama 2 '87
Round Trip to Heaven '92
The St. Tammany Miracle '94

Philo McCullough
Tarzan the Fearless '33
Inside Information '34
Captured in Chinatown '35
Ridin' Thru '35

Natalie McCurry
Dead End Drive-In '86
Stones of Death '88
Glass '90

Bill McCutcheon
Family Business '89
Steel Magnolias '89
Mr. Destiny '90
Tune in Tomorrow '90

Hattie McDaniel
Blonde Venus '32
Alice Adams '35
Harmony Lane '35
The Little Colonel '35
The Bride Walks Out '36
Libeled Lady '36
Show Boat '36
Saratoga '37
Carefree '38
Mad Miss Manton '38
Shopworn Angel '38
Gone with the Wind '39
The Great Lie '41
They Died with Their Boots On '41
George Washington Slept Here '42
In This Our Life '42
Johnny Come Lately '43
Since You Went Away '44
Never Say Goodbye '46
Mickey '48

James McDaniel
Malcolm X '92
The Road to Galveston '96

Dylan McDermott
Hamburger Hill '87
Blue Iguana '88
The Neon Empire '89
Steel Magnolias '89
Twister '89
Hardware '90
Where Sleeping Dogs Lie '91
The Fear Inside '92
Into the Badlands '92
Jersey Girl '92
In the Line of Fire '93
The Cowboy Way '94
Miracle on 34th Street '94
Destiny Turns on the Radio '95
Home for the Holidays '95

Hugh McDermott
The Seventh Veil '46
Devil Girl from Mars '54

Ruth McDevitt
The Shakiest Gun in the West '68
Change of Habit '69
Homebodies '74

Christopher McDonald
Breakin' '84
Chattanooga Choo Choo '84
The Boys Next Door '85
Paramedics '88
Chances Are '89
Playroom '90
Fatal Exposure '91
Red Wind '91
Thelma & Louise '91
Conflict of Interest '92
Wild Orchid 2: Two Shades of Blue '92
Benefit of the Doubt '93
Bums '93
Cover Story '93
Fatal Instinct '93
Grumpy Old Men '93
Monkey Trouble '94
Quiz Show '94
Terminal Velocity '94
Best of the Best 3: No Turning Back '95
Fair Game '95
The Tuskegee Airmen '95
Celtic Pride '96
Happy Gilmore '96
Unforgettable '96

Francis McDonald
The Confession '20
Battling Butler '26
The Notorious Lady '27
Morocco '30
Hidden Valley '32
Texas Buddies '32
Terror Trail '33
The Sea Wolf '41
Mystery Man '44
Mystery of the Riverboat '44
Texas Masquerade '44
Zorro's Black Whip '44
Bad Men of the Border '45

Garry McDonald
Pirate Movie '82
The Wacky World of Wills & Burke '85
Ghosts Can Do It '90

Grace McDonald
Gung Ho! '43
Follow the Boys '44

Kenneth McDonald
Dynamite Dan '24
The Coast Patrol '25

Kevin McDonald
The Best of the Kids in the Hall '93
National Lampoon's Senior Trip '95
Kids In the Hall Brain Candy '96

Marie McDonald
Guest in the House '45
Tell It to the Judge '49
The Geisha Boy '58
Promises! Promises! '63

Mary Ann McDonald
Far Cry from Home '70s
Love at First Sight '76

Steve McDonald
Desperate Teenage Lovedolls '84
Spirit of '76 '91

Mary McDonnell
Matewan '87
Tiger Warsaw '87
Dances with Wolves '90
Grand Canyon '91
Passion Fish '92
Sneakers '92
Blue Chips '94
Woman Undone '95
Independence Day '96

Mary McDonough
The Waltons: A Thanksgiving Story '73
The Waltons: The Christmas Carol '80
A Day for Thanks on Walton's Mountain '82
Snowballing '85
Mom '89

Neal McDonough
Blue River '95
White Dwarf '95

Frances McDormand
Blood Simple '85
Raising Arizona '87
Mississippi Burning '88
Chattahoochee '89
Darkman '90
Hidden Agenda '90
The Butcher's Wife '91
Crazy in Love '92
Passed Away '92
Short Cuts '93
Beyond Rangoon '95
The Good Old Boys '95
Lone Star '95
Fargo '96
Primal Fear '96

Betty McDowall
Time Lock '57
Dead Lucky '60
Jack the Ripper '60
Ballad in Blue '66

Roddy McDowall
How Green Was My Valley '41
Son of Fury '42
Lassie, Come Home '43
My Friend Flicka '43
The Keys of the Kingdom '44
The White Cliffs of Dover '44
Holiday in Mexico '46
Macbeth '48
Everybody's Dancin' '50
Hill Number One '51
Midnight Lace '60
The Longest Day '62
Cleopatra '63
The Tempest '63
The Greatest Story Ever Told '65
Inside Daisy Clover '65
The Loved One '65
That Darn Cat '65
The Adventures of Bullwhip Griffin '66
Five Card Stud '68
Planet of the Apes '68
Night Gallery '69
Bedknobs and Broomsticks '71
Escape from the Planet of the Apes '71
Conquest of the Planet of the Apes '72
Life & Times of Judge Roy Bean '72
The Poseidon Adventure '72
Arnold '73
Battle for the Planet of the Apes '73
The Legend of Hell House '73
Dirty Mary Crazy Larry '74
Funny Lady '75
Mean Johnny Barrows '75
Embryo '76
Flood! '76
The Cat from Outer Space '78
Circle of Iron '78
Laserblast '78
Rabbit Test '78
The Thief of Baghdad '78
The Martian Chronicles: Part 2 '79
The Martian Chronicles: Part 3 '79
Scavenger Hunt '79
Charlie Chan and the Curse of the Dragon Queen '81
Class of 1984 '82
Evil under the Sun '82
Mae West '84
The Zany Adventures of Robin Hood '84
Fright Night '85
Dead of Winter '87
Overboard '87
Doin' Time on Planet Earth '88
Fright Night 2 '88
Around the World in 80 Days '89
The Big Picture '89
Carmilla '89
Cutting Class '89
Shakma '89
Deadly Game '91
Double Trouble '91
An Inconvenient Woman '91
Heads '93
Mirror, Mirror 2: Raven Dance '94
Fatally Yours '95
It's My Party '95
Last Summer In the Hamptons '96

Claire McDowell
West-Bound Limited '23
The Big Parade '25
Ben-Hur '26

Malcolm McDowell
If... '69
A Clockwork Orange '71
Long Ago Tomorrow '71
O Lucky Man! '73
Royal Flash '75
Voyage of the Damned '76
Time After Time '79
Caligula '80
Look Back in Anger '80
Britannia Hospital '82
Cat People '82
Blue Thunder '83
Cross Creek '83
Get Crazy '83
Little Red Riding Hood '83
Gulag '85
Merlin and the Sword '85
Monte Carlo '86
The Caller '87
Sunset '88
Buy & Cell '89
Class of 1999 '90
Disturbed '90
Jezebel's Kiss '90
Moon 44 '90
The Light in the Jungle '91
Bopha! '93
Chain of Desire '93
Night Train to Venice '93
Dangerous Indiscretion '94
Milk Money '94
Star Trek Generations '94
The Surgeon '94
Tank Girl '94
Cyborg 3: The Recycler '95

Nelson McDowell
The Last of the Mohicans '20
Mason of the Mounted '32
Rustler's Roundup '33
Feud of the West '35
Texas Jack '35
Desert Phantom '36

Trevyn McDowell
Middlemarch '93
Mary Shelley's Frankenstein '94

James McEachin
The Groundstar Conspiracy '72
The Dead Don't Die '75
He Who Walks Alone '78
Honeyboy '82
Double Exposure '93

Ellen McElduff
Imposters '84
Working Girls '87

Ian McElhinney
The Playboys '92
A Woman's Guide to Adultery '93

John McEnery
Bartleby '70
One Russian Summer '73
The Land That Time Forgot '75
Pope John Paul II '84
Gulag '85
Codename Kyril '91
Black Beauty '94

Peter McEnery
Victim '62
The Moon-Spinners '64
The Fighting Prince of Donegal '66
The Game is Over '66
I Killed Rasputin '67
Negatives '68
Entertaining Mr. Sloane '70
Tales That Witness Madness '73
Pictures '80s

Annie McEnroe
Running Scared '79
The Hand '81
Warlords of the 21st Century '82
Purple Hearts '84
Howling 2: Your Sister is a Werewolf '85
True Stories '86
Cop '88

Reba McEntire
Tremors '89
The Gambler Returns: The Luck of the Draw '93
The Man from Left Field '93
Is There Life Out There? '94
North '94
Buffalo Girls '95

Geraldine McEwan
Foreign Body '86
Robin Hood: Prince of Thieves '91

Gates McFadden
Star Trek the Next Generation: Encounter at Farpoint '87
Taking Care of Business '90
Star Trek Generations '94
Star Trek the Next Generation, the Final Episode: All Good Things... '94

George "Spanky" McFarland
Little Rascals, Vol. 1 '29
Little Rascals, Book 1 '30s
Little Rascals, Vol. 2 '30
Kentucky Kernels '34
General Spanky '36
Peck's Bad Boy with the Circus '38
Our Gang Comedies '40s
The Aurora Encounter '85

William F. McGaha
The Speed Lovers '68
Iron Horsemen '71

Mark McGann
John & Yoko: A Love Story '85
Let Him Have It '91

Paul McGann
Withnail and I '87
Dealers '89
The Rainbow '89
Innocent Victim '90
Paper Mask '91
Afraid of the Dark '92
Alien 3 '92
Doctor Who '96

Darren McGavin
Queen for a Day '51
The Court Martial of Billy Mitchell '55
The Man with the Golden Arm '55
The Delicate Delinquent '56
Mission Mars '67
Tribes '70
Richard Petty Story '72
Say Goodbye, Maggie Cole '72
The Night Stalker: Two Tales of Terror '74
No Deposit, No Return '76
Airport '77 '77
Zero to Sixty '78
Ike '79
The Martian Chronicles: Part 1 '79
The Martian Chronicles: Part 2 '79
The Martian Chronicles: Part 3 '79
Hangar 18 '80
Waikiki '80
Firebird 2015 A.D. '81
A Christmas Story '83
Power, Passion & Murder '83
The Baron and the Kid '84
My Wicked, Wicked Ways '84
The Natural '84
Hitchhiker 2 '85
Turk 182! '85
Raw Deal '86
Dead Heat '88
Sunset '88
Around the World in 80 Days '89
By Dawn's Early Light '89
Captain America '89
Blood & Concrete: A Love Story '90
Child in the Night '90
Perfect Harmony '91
Billy Madison '94

Patrick McGaw
Amongst Friends '93
The Basketball Diaries '94
Forbidden Choices '94
Malicious '95

Jack McGee
Crash and Burn '90
The Quest '96

Vonetta McGee
Blacula '72
The Big Bust Out '73
Shaft in Africa '73
The Eiger Sanction '75
Repo Man '83
You Must Remember This '90s
To Sleep with Anger '90
Brother Future '91

Johnny Rae McGhee
Project X '87
Love Field '91

William Bill McGhee
Don't Look in the Basement '73
1918 '85

Bruce McGill
Citizens Band '77
National Lampoon's Animal House '78
The Hand '81
Whale for the Killing '81
Ballad of Gregorio Cortez '83
Silkwood '83
Tough Enough '83
Charlotte Forten's Mission: Experiment in Freedom '85
Into the Night '85
No Mercy '86
Wildcats '86
The Last Innocent Man '87
End of the Line '88
Out Cold '89
Little Vegas '90
The Last Boy Scout '91
My Cousin Vinny '92
Timecop '94
The Good Old Boys '95
Black Sheep '96

Everett McGill
Brubaker '80
Union City '81
Quest for Fire '82
Dune '84
Silver Bullet '85
Field of Honor '86
Heartbreak Ridge '86
Iguana '89
License to Kill '89
Jezebel's Kiss '90
Twin Peaks '90
Twin Peaks '90
The People Under the Stairs '91
Under Siege 2: Dark Territory '95

Kelly McGillis
Reuben, Reuben '83
Code of Honor '84
Witness '85
Top Gun '86
Made in Heaven '87
The Accused '88
The House on Carroll Street '88
Unsettled Land '88
Winter People '89
Cat Chaser '90
The Babe '92
Grand Isle '92
North '94

John C. McGinley
Platoon '86
Wall Street '87
Talk Radio '88
Fat Man and Little Boy '89
Lost Angels '89
Prisoners of Inertia '89
Suffering Bastards '90
Highlander 2: The Quickening '91
Little Noises '91
Point Break '91
Article 99 '92
A Midnight Clear '92
Hear No Evil '93
The Last Outlaw '93
Watch It '93
Car 54, Where Are You? '94
Mother's Boys '94
On Deadly Ground '94
Surviving the Game '94
Wagons East '94
Born to Be Wild '95
Seven '95
The Rock '96

Ted McGinley
Revenge of the Nerds '84
Physical Evidence '89
Blue Tornado '90
It's a Bundyful Life '92
Revenge of the Nerds 3: The Next Generation '92
Linda '93
Covert Assassin '94
Revenge of the Nerds 4: Nerds in Love '94
Tails You Live, Heads You're Dead '95

Scott McGinnis
Joy Sticks '83
Making the Grade '84
Odd Jobs '85
You Can't Hurry Love '88

John McGiver
Love in the Afternoon '57
The Man in the Raincoat '57
The Gazebo '59
Breakfast at Tiffany's '61
The Manchurian Candidate '62
Mr. Hobbs Takes a Vacation '62
Period of Adjustment '62
A Global Affair '63
Man's Favorite Sport? '63
Who's Got the Action? '63
The Glass Bottom Boat '66
Bachelor in Paradise '69
Midnight Cowboy '69
Lawman '71
The Adventures of Tom Sawyer '73

Mike McGlone
The Brothers McMullen '94
Ed '96

Frank McGlynn
Hopalong Cassidy '35
Custer's Last Stand '36
Western Gold '37
Rogue's Gallery '44

Patrick McGoohan
I Am a Camera '55
Danger Man '61
The Three Lives of Thomasina '63
Dr. Syn, Alias the Scarecrow '64
Secret Agent '64
Koroshi '67
Ice Station Zebra '68
The Prisoner: Arrival '68
Silver Streak '76
The Man in the Iron Mask '77
Brass Target '78
Escape from Alcatraz '79
Hard Way '80
Scanners '81
Jamaica Inn '82
Kings and Desperate Men '83
Baby ... Secret of the Lost Legend '85
Three Sovereigns for Sarah '85
Braveheart '95
The Phantom '96
A Time to Kill '96

Barry McGovern
Riders to the Sea '88
Joe Versus the Volcano '90

Elizabeth McGovern
Ordinary People '80
Ragtime '81
Lovesick '83
Snow White and the Seven Dwarfs '83
Once Upon a Time in America '84
Racing with the Moon '84
Native Son '86
The Bedroom Window '87
She's Having a Baby '88
Johnny Handsome '89
The Handmaid's Tale '90
A Shock to the System '90
Tune in Tomorrow '90
Women & Men: Stories of Seduction '90
The Favor '92
King of the Hill '93
Me & Veronica '93
Broken Trust '95

J.P. McGowan
Red Signals '27
The Outlaw Tamer '33
Somewhere in Sonora '33
Heart of the Rockies '37
Hit the Saddle '37

Michael McGrady
The Babe '92
White Dwarf '95

Walter McGrail
The Lone Star Ranger '30
Night Nurse '31
Code of the Fearless '39
The Green Hornet '39

Charles McGraw
The Mad Ghoul '43
T-Men '47
Lady Scarface/The Threat '49
Threat '49
Armored Car Robbery '50
The Falcon's Adventure/Armored Car Robbery '50
Ma and Pa Kettle Go to Town '50
His Kind of Woman '51
The Narrow Margin '52
One Minute to Zero '52
The Saint's Vacation/The Narrow Margin '52
The Bridges at Toko-Ri '55
The Defiant Ones '58
Cimarron '60
Spartacus '60
The Horizontal Lieutenant '62
Pendulum '69
Tell Them Willie Boy Is Here '69
A Boy and His Dog '75
Twilight's Last Gleaming '77

Angela Punch McGregor
Newsfront '78
The Island '80
Survivor '80
We of the Never Never '82
Double Deal '84
A Test of Love '84
The Efficiency Expert '92

Ewan McGregor
Lipstick On Your Collar '94
Shallow Grave '94
Trainspotting '95
Emma '96

Kenneth John McGregor
Primal Scream '87
The Ten Million Dollar Getaway '91

Malcolm McGregor
The Untamable '23
Smouldering Fires '25
The Reckless Way '36

Biff McGuire
Justice '55
Child of Glass '78
Deadline Assault '90

Don McGuire
The Man I Love '46
The Fuller Brush Man '48
Double Dynamite '51

Dorothy McGuire
The Enchanted Cottage '45
A Tree Grows in Brooklyn '45
The Spiral Staircase '46
Till the End of Time '46
Gentleman's Agreement '47
Make Haste to Live '54
Three Coins in the Fountain '54
Friendly Persuasion '56
Old Yeller '57
A Summer Place '59
The Swiss Family Robinson '60
Summer Magic '63
The Greatest Story Ever Told '65
She Waits '71
The Runaways '75
Rich Man, Poor Man '76
Little Women '78
The Incredible Journey of Dr. Meg Laurel '79
Amos '85
Caroline? '90
The Last Best Year '90

John McGuire
Outlaw Rule '36
Stranger on the Third Floor '40

Kathryn McGuire
The Navigator '24
Midnight Faces '26
Lost Zeppelin '29

Michael McGuire
Larry '74
Report to the Commissioner '74
Home to Stay '79
Sanctuary of Fear '79
The Long Days of Summer '80
The Ordeal of Dr. Mudd '80
Blinded by the Light '82
Bird '88

Stephen McHattie
The People Next Door '70
Search for the Gods '75
James Dean '76
Moving Violation '76
Tomorrow Never Comes '77
Mary and Joseph: A Story of Faith '79
Roughnecks '80
Death Valley '81
Belizaire the Cajun '86
Caribe '87
Salvation! '87
Call Me '88
Sticky Fingers '88
Bloodhounds of Broadway '89
One Man Out '89
Erik '90
Geronimo: An American Legend '93
Beverly Hills Cop 3 '94
The Dark '94
Deadlock 2 '94
Convict Cowboy '95

Frank McHugh
Corsair '31
Millie '31
The Strange Love of Molly Louvain '32
Ex-Lady '33
Telegraph Trail '33
Tomorrow at Seven '33
Fashions of 1934 '34
Devil Dogs of the Air '35
Gold Diggers of 1935 '35
Three Men on a Horse '36
Boy Meets Girl '38
Bullets or Ballots '38
Dodge City '39
The Roaring Twenties '39
City for Conquest '40
The Fighting 69th '40
I Love You Again '40
Virginia City '40
All Through the Night '42
Marine Raiders '43
Going My Way '44
State Fair '45
Velvet Touch '48

McHugh ▶cont.

Mighty Joe Young '49
Miss Grant Takes Richmond '49
A Lion Is in the Streets '53
There's No Business Like Show Business '54
Last Hurrah '58
A Tiger Walks '64
Easy Come, Easy Go '67

David McIlwraith
Happy Birthday, Gemini '80
The Vindicator '85
Millenium '89

John McIntire
Call Northside 777 '48
Francis the Talking Mule '49
The Asphalt Jungle '50
Walk Softly, Stranger '50
Winchester '73 '50
Westward the Women '51
Horizons West '52
A Lion Is in the Streets '53
War Arrow '53
Apache '54
Far Country '55
The Kentuckian '55
The Mark of the Hawk '57
The Tin Star '57
The Light in the Forest '58
Elmer Gantry '60
Flaming Star '60
Psycho '60
Summer and Smoke '61
Two Rode Together '61
Rough Night in Jericho '67
Herbie Rides Again '74
Rooster Cogburn '75
Mrs. R's Daughter '79
American Dream '81
Honkytonk Man '82
Cloak & Dagger '84
As Summers Die '86

Tim McIntire
The Sterile Cuckoo '69
Aloha, Bobby and Rose '74
Gumball Rally '76
The Choirboys '77
Fast Walking '82
Sacred Ground '83

Burr McIntosh
The Average Woman '24
The Adorable Cheat '28
That Certain Thing '28

Christine McIntyre
Partners of the Trail '44
The Stranger from Pecos '45
Gentleman from Texas '46
Land of the Lawless '47

Marvin J. McIntyre
Fandango '85
Wilder Napalm '93
Born to Be Wild '95

John McKay
Rocket Attack U.S.A. '58
Assault of the Rebel Girls '59

Wanda McKay
Twilight on the Trail '41
Bowery at Midnight '42
Texas Justice '42
The Black Raven '43
Corregidor '43
The Monster Maker '44
Raiders of Ghost City '44
There Goes Kelly '45
Jungle Goddess '49

Michael McKean
Used Cars '80
Young Doctors in Love '82
This Is Spinal Tap '84
Clue '85
D.A.R.Y.L. '85
Light of Day '87
Planes, Trains & Automobiles '87
Portrait of a White Marriage '88
Short Circuit 2 '88
The Big Picture '89
Earth Girls Are Easy '89
Flashback '89
Daniel and the Towers '90s
Hider in the House '90
Book of Love '91
Man Trouble '92
Memoirs of an Invisible Man '92
The Return of Spinal Tap '92
Coneheads '93
Across the Moon '94
Airheads '94
Radioland Murders '94
The Brady Bunch Movie '95

Donna McKechnie
Twirl '81
Breakin' Through '84

Lafayette McKee
Little Orphan Annie '18
Inside the Law '42

Lafe McKee
Near the Rainbow's End '30
Under Montana Skies '30
The Pocatello Kid '31
Range Law '31
Two Gun Man '31
The Big Stampede '32
The Riding Tornado '32
Deadwood Pass '33
Fighting Champ '33
Jaws of Justice '33
Lightning Range '33
Man from Monterey '33
Telegraph Trail '33
Terror Trail '33
Law of the Wild '34
Man from Utah '34
Rawhide Romance '34
The Silver Bullet '34
Boss Cowboy '35
Ghost Rider '35
The Miracle Rider '35
The Revenge Rider '35
Ridin' Thru '35
Rustlers of Red Dog '35
Last of the Warrens '36
Melody of the Plains '37
Mystery of the Hooded Horseman '37
The Rangers Step In '37
Santa Fe Bound '37
Covered Wagon Trails '40
Riders of Pasco Basin '40

Lonette McKee
Detroit 9000 '73
Sparkle '76
Which Way Is Up? '77
Cuba '79
The Cotton Club '84
Brewster's Millions '85
Round Midnight '86
Gardens of Stone '87
The Women of Brewster Place '89
Jungle Fever '91
Malcolm X '92
Dangerous Passion '95

Raymond McKee
Down to the Sea in Ships '22
Free to Love '25
Campus Knights '29

Danica McKellar
Camp Cucamonga: How I Spent My Summer Vacation '90
Sidekicks '93

Don McKellar
Roadkill '89
The Adjuster '91
Highway 61 '91
Exotica '94
When Night is Falling '95

Ian McKellen
Priest of Love '81
The Scarlet Pimpernel '82
Plenty '85
Windmills of the Gods '88
Scandal '89
And the Band Played On '93
The Ballad of Little Jo '93
Six Degrees of Separation '93
Cold Comfort Farm '94
Restoration '94
The Shadow '94
Richard III '95
Jack and Sarah '96

Siobhan McKenna
The Adventurers '51
The King of Kings '61
Playboy of the Western World '62
Of Human Bondage '64
Doctor Zhivago '65

T.P. McKenna
Ulysses '67
The Charge of the Light Brigade '68
Beast in the Cellar '70
Straw Dogs '72
All Creatures Great and Small '74
Next Victim '74
James Joyce: A Portrait of the Artist as a Young Man '77
Bleak House '85
The Doctor and the Devils '85
Red Scorpion '89
Valmont '89

Virginia McKenna
Cruel Sea '53
Simba '55
The Smallest Show on Earth '57
Carve Her Name with Pride '58
The Wreck of the Mary Deare '59
Born Free '66
Ring of Bright Water '69
Waterloo '71
The Gathering Storm '74
Christian the Lion '76
The Chosen '77
Disappearance '81
The First Olympics: Athens 1896 '84
Duel of Hearts '92

Fay McKenzie
Boss Cowboy '35
Death Rides the Range '40
Down Mexico Way '41
Heart of the Rio Grande '42

Jacqueline McKenzie
Romper Stomper '92
Traps '93
Talk '94
Angel Baby '95

Julia McKenzie
Shirley Valentine '89
The Old Curiosity Shop '94

Richard McKenzie
Corvette Summer '78
In Love and War '91

Tim McKenzie
Gallipoli '81
The Lighthorsemen '87
The 13th Floor '88

Doug McKeon
Night Crossing '81
On Golden Pond '81
Desperate Lives '82
Heart of a Champion: The Ray Mancini Story '85
Mischief '85
Breaking Home Ties '87
Turnaround '87
Where the Red Fern Grows: Part 2 '92

Nancy McKeon
High School USA '84
Poison Ivy '85
The Lightning Incident '91
Where the Day Takes You '92
Teresa's Tattoo '94
The Wrong Woman '95

Philip McKeon
Return to Horror High '87
Red Surf '90

Leo McKern
Time Without Pity '57
The Mouse That Roared '59
The Day the Earth Caught Fire '61
Doctor in Distress '63
The Horse Without a Head '63
The Amorous Adventures of Moll Flanders '65
Help! '65
The Shoes of the Fisherman '68
Ryan's Daughter '70
Massacre in Rome '73
The Adventures of Sherlock Holmes' Smarter Brother '78
Candleshoe '78
The House on Garibaldi Street '79
Rumpole of the Bailey '80s
The Blue Lagoon '80
The French Lieutenant's Woman '81
Ladyhawke '85
Travelling North '87
Rumpole of the Bailey: Rumpole's Return '90
Monsignor Quixote '91
A Foreign Field '93

Robert McKim
The Disciple '15
Hell's Hinges '16
Wagon Tracks '19
Heart's Haven '22
The Bat '26

Bill McKinney
She-Freak '67
Angel Unchained '70
Deliverance '72
The Parallax View '74
Cannonball '76
The Outlaw Josey Wales '76
The Shootist '76
The Gauntlet '77
Bronco Billy '80
St. Helen's, Killer Volcano '82
Tex '82
Heart Like a Wheel '83
Against All Odds '84
The China Lake Murders '90
Lone Justice 2 '93
City Slickers 2: The Legend of Curly's Gold '94

Gregory McKinney
A Brilliant Disguise '93
Star Quest '94

Mark McKinney
The Best of the Kids in the Hall '93
Kids In the Hall Brain Candy '96

Nina Mae McKinney
Hallelujah! '29
The Devil's Daughter '39
Pinky '49

Ray McKinnon
Paris Trout '91
Indecency '92
A Perfect World '93
The Net '95

Victor McLaglen
The Unholy Three '25
Dishonored '31
Laughing at Life '33
The Lost Patrol '34
Murder at the Vanities '34
The Informer '35
Klondike Annie '36
Sea Devils '37
Wee Willie Winkie '37
Devil's Party '38
Gunga Din '39
Let Freedom Ring '39
South of Pago Pago '40
Broadway Limited '41
Call Out the Marines '42
Forever and a Day '43
The Princess and the Pirate '44
Whistle Stop '46
Fort Apache '48
She Wore a Yellow Ribbon '49
Rio Grande '50
The Quiet Man '52
Prince Valiant '54
Trouble in the Glen '54

Hollis McLaren
Outrageous! '77
Lost and Found '79
Atlantic City '81
Vengeance Is Mine '84

Ron McLarty
Enormous Changes '83
Tiger Town '83
Trumps '83
The Feud '90
Two Bits '96

Bill McLaughlin
Naked Vengeance '85
Silk '86
Comic Cabby '87

Gibb McLaughlin
Power '34
Bulldog Jack '35
The Old Curiosity Shop '35
Mr. Reeder in Room 13 '38
Inspector Hornleigh '39

David McLean
The Strangler '64
Hughes & Harlow: Angels in Hell '77
Death Sport '78

Catherine McLeod
I've Always Loved You '46
Sword of Venus '53

Kenneth McLeod
Judgment Day '88
Out for Blood '93
Showdown '93
Deadly Target '94
Guardian Angel '94
Virtual Combat '95

Allyn Ann McLerie
Calamity Jane '53
The Desert Song '53
They Shoot Horses, Don't They? '69
Death Scream '75
Someone I Touched '75
And Baby Makes Six '79
A Shining Season '79
Living Proof: The Hank Williams Jr. Story '83

John McLiam
Showdown '73
Freedom Road '79
The Five of Me '81
The Ambush Murders '82
Split Decisions '88

Rachel McLish
Pumping Iron 2: The Women '85
Aces: Iron Eagle 3 '92

Ed McMahon
The Incident '67
Slaughter's Big Ripoff '73
Fun with Dick and Jane '77
The Kid from Left Field '79
Great American Traffic Jam '80
Butterfly '82

Horace McMahon
The Wrong Road '37
Melody Ranch '40
Birth of the Blues '41
Detective Story '51
Abbott and Costello Go to Mars '53
My Sister Eileen '55
The Delicate Delinquent '56

Michael McManus
Captain America '79
Mr. Bill's Real Life Adventures '86
Funland '89
Speaking Parts '89

John McMartin
Sweet Charity '69
Private Contentment '83
Dream Lover '85
Legal Eagles '86
Murrow '86
Native Son '86
Gore Vidal's Lincoln '88
Roots: The Gift '88
Day One '89
Little Sweetheart '90
A Shock to the System '90
Separate But Equal '91

Kenneth McMillan
The Taking of Pelham One Two Three '74
Johnny We Hardly Knew Ye '77
Bloodbrothers '78
Chilly Scenes of Winter '79
Salem's Lot '79
Borderline '80
Carny '80
Hide in Plain Sight '80
Eyewitness '81
Heartbeeps '81
Ragtime '81
True Confessions '81
Whose Life Is It Anyway? '81
In the Custody of Strangers '82
Partners '82
Blue Skies Again '83
Concrete Beat '84
Dune '84
Killing Hour '84
The Pope of Greenwich Village '84
Protocol '84
Reckless '84
Cat's Eye '85
Dixie: Changing Habits '85
Runaway Train '85
Acceptable Risks '86
Armed and Dangerous '86
Malone '87
Three Fugitives '89

W.G. McMillan
The Crazies '73

The Sister-in-Law '74

Sam McMurray
L.A. Story '91
Stone Cold '91
Getting Even with Dad '94
National Lampoon's Attack of the 5 Ft. 2 Women '94

Pamela McMyler
The Stick-Up '77
The $5.20 an Hour Dream '80

Mercedes McNab
Addams Family Values '93
Savage Land '94

Barbara McNair
Dead Right '68
Change of Habit '69
Stiletto '69
They Call Me Mr. Tibbs! '70
Venus in Furs '70
The Organization '71

Kevin McNally
Poldark 2 '75
The Berlin Affair '85
Cry Freedom '87
Jekyll and Hyde '90
Abraham '94

Stephen McNally
For Me and My Gal '42
Keeper of the Flame '42
Air Raid Wardens '43
Thirty Seconds Over Tokyo '44
Criss Cross '48
Winchester '73 '50
The Black Castle '52
Diplomatic Courier '52
Devil's Canyon '53
Split Second '53
A Bullet Is Waiting '54
Make Haste to Live '54
Tribute to a Bad Man '56
Hi-Riders '77
Dear Detective '78

Billy McNamara
Dream a Little Dream '89
Black Water '94

Brian McNamara
Detective Sadie & Son '84
Short Circuit '86
Billionaire Boys Club '87
Arachnophobia '90
Mystery Date '91
When the Party's Over '91

Julianne McNamara
Saturday the 14th Strikes Back '88
Class of Fear '91

Maggie McNamara
The Moon Is Blue '53
Three Coins in the Fountain '54
The Cardinal '63

William McNamara
The Beat '88
Stealing Home '88
Terror at the Opera '88
Texasville '90
Wildflower '91
Chasers '94
Girl in the Cadillac '94
Radio Inside '94
Surviving the Game '94
Copycat '95
Storybook '95

Julia McNeal
The Unbelievable Truth '90
The Refrigerator '93

Howard McNear
Escape from Fort Bravo '53
Andy Griffith Show '60
The Errand Boy '61
Follow That Dream '61
Fun in Acapulco '63
Kiss Me, Stupid! '64

Ian McNeice
The Lonely Passion of Judith Hearne '87
Valmont '89
The Russia House '90
Year of the Comet '92
Funny Bones '94
No Escape '94
Ace Ventura: When Nature Calls '95

The Englishman Who Went Up a Hill But Came Down a Mountain '95

Claudia McNeil
A Raisin in the Sun '61
Cry Panic '74
The Migrants '74
Roll of Thunder, Hear My Cry '78

Kate McNeil
Monkey Shines '88
Sudden Death '95

Kathy McNeil
Beach House '82
The House on Sorority Row '83

Jimmy McNichol
Smokey Bites the Dust '81
Blinded by the Light '82
Night Warning '82
Escape from El Diablo '83

Kristy McNichol
The End '78
The Summer of My German Soldier '78
My Old Man '79
Little Darlings '80
The Night the Lights Went Out in Georgia '81
Only When I Laugh '81
Blinded by the Light '82
Pirate Movie '82
Just the Way You Are '84
Dream Lover '85
Women of Valor '86
Two Moon Junction '88
You Can't Hurry Love '88
The Forgotten One '89
Baby of the Bride '91

Kevin McNulty
The Neverending Story 3 '94
Timecop '94
Live Bait '95

Sandy McPeak
Ode to Billy Joe '76
Tarantulas: The Deadly Cargo '77
My Mother's Secret Life '84
The Taking of Flight 847: The Uli Derickson Story '88
The Flight '89
Eye on the Sparrow '91
Inside Out '91

Murdock McQuarrie
Daring Danger '32
Laramie Kid '35
The New Frontier '35
The Tonto Kid '35
Ghost Town Riders '38
Man from Montana '41

Butterfly McQueen
Gone with the Wind '39
I Dood It '43
Duel in the Sun '46
Killer Diller '48
Amazing Grace '74
The Adventures of Huckleberry Finn '85
The Mosquito Coast '86

Chad McQueen
Skateboard '77
The Karate Kid '84
Fever Pitch '85
Nightforce '86
Martial Law '90
Where the Red Fern Grows: Part 2 '92
Death Ring '93
Firepower '93
Possessed by the Night '93
Sexual Malice '93
Indecent Behavior 2 '94
Money to Burn '94
New York Cop '94
Number One Fan '94

Steve McQueen
Somebody Up There Likes Me '56
The Defender '57
The Blob '58
Never Love a Stranger '58
The Great St. Louis Bank Robbery '59
Never So Few '59
Wanted: Dead or Alive '59
The Magnificent Seven '60
The Honeymoon Machine '61
Hell is for Heroes '62
War Lover '62
The Great Escape '63
Love with the Proper Stranger '63
Soldier in the Rain '63
Baby, the Rain Must Fall '64
The Cincinnati Kid '65
Nevada Smith '66
The Sand Pebbles '66
Bullitt '68
The Thomas Crown Affair '68
The Reivers '69
Le Mans '71
The Getaway '72
Junior Bonner '72
Papillon '73
The Towering Inferno '74
The Hunter '80
Tom Horn '80
Wild West '87

Elizabeth McRae
The Incredible Mr. Limpet '64
The Conversation '74

Frank McRae
Cannery Row '82
*batteries not included '87
Farewell to the King '89
License to Kill '89
Lock Up '89
Sketch Artist '92
Last Action Hero '93
Lightning Jack '94

Leslie McRae
Girl in Gold Boots '69
Blood Orgy of the She-Devils '74

Gerald McRaney
Mind Warp '72
Night of Bloody Horror '76
The Haunting Passion '83
The NeverEnding Story '84
American Justice '86
City Killer '87
Hobo's Christmas '87
Dynamite and Gold '88
Blind Vengeance '90
Murder by Moonlight '91

Peter McRobbie
Johnny Suede '92
The Neon Bible '95

Ian McShane
If It's Tuesday, This Must Be Belgium '69
The Last of Sheila '73
Journey into Fear '74
The Terrorists '74
Code Name: Diamond Head '77
The Fifth Musketeer '79
The Great Riviera Bank Robbery '79
Yesterday's Hero '79
Exposed '83
The Grace Kelly Story '83
Ordeal by Innocence '84
Too Scared to Scream '85
Torchlight '85
The Murders in the Rue Morgue '86
The Great Escape 2: The Untold Story '88
War & Remembrance, Part 1 '88
Young Charlie Chaplin '88
War & Remembrance: The Final Chapter, Part 8 '89
Con Man '92
Grand Larceny '92
The Best of Lovejoy Mysteries '93

Micheal McShane
Robin Hood: Prince of Thieves '91
Richie Rich '94
Tom and Huck '95

Gerard McSorley
In the Name of the Father '93
An Awfully Big Adventure '94
Widow's Peak '94

Bud McTaggart
Billy the Kid Trapped '42
Meet the Mob '42

Janet McTeer
Hawks '89
The Black Velvet Gown '92
Carrington '95

Patrick McVey
Desperate Characters '71
Top of the Heap '72

Paul McVey
Buried Alive '39
Phantom of Chinatown '40

Daniel McVicar
Scorned '93
Guardian Angel '94

Margaret McWade
The Confession '20
Mr. Deeds Goes to Town '36
Theodora Goes Wild '36

Robert McWade
Feet First '30
Kept Husbands '31
Healer '36

Jillian McWhirter
After Midnight '89
Dune Warriors '91
Beyond the Call of Duty '92
Stranglehold '94
Last Man Standing '95
Manhunt '95
Rage '95

Caroline McWilliams
Rage '80
Shattered Vows '84
Into Thin Air '85
Mermaids '90
Switched at Birth '91

Courtland Mead
Dragonworld '94
The Little Rascals '94
Tom and Huck '95

Audrey Meadows
Honeymooners Hidden Episodes, Vol. 1 '53
That Touch of Mink '62

Jayne Meadows
Lady in the Lake '46
Song of the Thin Man '47
David and Bathsheba '51
James Dean '76
Norman, Is That You? '76
Miss All-American Beauty '82
Ratings Game '84
Murder by Numbers '89
City Slickers '91

Joyce Meadows
The Brain from Planet Arous '57
Flesh and the Spur '57
The Girl in Lover's Lane '60
Zebra in the Kitchen '65

Stephen Meadows
A Cry in the Wild '90
The End of Innocence '90
Sunstroke '92

Karen Meagher
Experience Preferred... But Not Essential '83
Threads '85

Ray Meagher
Dark Age '88
Bootleg '89

Colm Meaney
The Commitments '91
Far and Away '92
Into the West '92
The Last of the Mohicans '92
The Snapper '93
Star Trek Deep Space Nine: Emissary '93
The Road to Wellville '94
Scarlett '94
Star Trek the Next Generation, the Final Episode: All Good Things... '94
The Englishman Who Went Up a Hill But Came Down a Mountain '95
The Van '95
War of the Buttons '95

Russell Means
The Last of the Mohicans '92
Natural Born Killers '94
Wagons East '94
Windrunner '94
Buffalo Girls '95

Anne Meara
Lovers and Other Strangers '70
The Out-of-Towners '70
Nasty Habits '77
Fame '80
The Longshot '86

My Little Girl '87
Awakenings '90
That's Adequate '90
Heavyweights '94
Kiss of Death '94

Michael Mears
Sharpe's Rifles '93
The Old Curiosity Shop '94

Meat Loaf
The Rocky Horror Picture Show '75
Americathon '79
Roadie '80
Feel the Motion '86
The Squeeze '87
Motorama '91
Leap of Faith '92

Karen Medak
A Girl to Kill For '90
Galaxies are Colliding '92
Treacherous Crossing '92

Kay Medford
Butterfield 8 '60
The Rat Race '60
Funny Girl '68
Lola '69
Windows '80

Patricia Medina
Dinner at the Ritz '37
The Day Will Dawn '42
Spitfire '42
Hotel Reserve '44
The Three Musketeers '48
Francis the Talking Mule '49
Abbott and Costello in the Foreign Legion '50
The Jackpot '50
Botany Bay '53
Mr. Arkadin '55
Snow White and the Three Stooges '61
The Killing of Sister George '69
The Big Push '75

Michael Medwin
The Courtney Affair '47
The Gay Lady '49
Someone at the Door '50
Four in a Jeep '51
Above Us the Waves '56
Rattle of a Simple Man '64
A Countess from Hong Kong '67
The Jigsaw Man '84

Lew Meehan
Backfire '22
Whistlin' Dan '32
The Silver Bullet '34
Feud of the West '35
Ridin' Thru '35
Texas Jack '35
Melody of the Plains '37
Ridin' the Lone Trail '37
Feud Maker '38
Thunder in the Desert '38

Donald Meek
The Merry Widow '34
Barbary Coast '35
The Informer '35
The Return of Peter Grimm '35
One Rainy Afternoon '36
Three Legionnaires '37
Toast of New York '37
The Adventures of Tom Sawyer '38
Little Miss Broadway '38
You Can't Take It with You '38
Blondie Takes a Vacation '39
Stagecoach '39
Young Mr. Lincoln '39
My Little Chickadee '40
Return of Frank James '40
A Woman's Face '41
Keeper of the Flame '42
Mrs. Wiggs of the Cabbage Patch '42
Tortilla Flat '42
Air Raid Wardens '43
DuBarry Was a Lady '43
They Got Me Covered '43
Bathing Beauty '44
The Thin Man Goes Home '44
Two Girls and a Sailor '44
Colonel Effingham's Raid '45
State Fair '45
Fabulous Joe '47
Magic Town '47

Jeffrey Meek
Winter People *'89*
Heart Condition *'90*
Night of the Cyclone *'90*
The St. Tammany Miracle *'94*

George Meeker
Night of Terror *'33*
Murder by Television *'35*
Tango *'36*
Danger on the Air *'38*
Seven Doors to Death *'44*
People's Choice *'46*
Apache Rose *'47*
Omoo Omoo, the Shark God *'49*
The Invisible Monster *'50*
Twilight in the Sierras *'50*

Ralph Meeker
Four in a Jeep *'51*
Kiss Me Deadly *'55*
Battle Shock *'56*
Run of the Arrow *'56*
Paths of Glory *'57*
Wanted: Dead or Alive *'59*
The Dirty Dozen *'67*
Gentle Giant *'67*
The St. Valentine's Day Massacre *'67*
The Detective *'68*
The Anderson Tapes *'71*
Birds of Prey *'72*
Mind Snatchers *'72*
Cry Panic *'74*
Brannigan *'75*
The Dead Don't Die *'75*
Johnny Firecloud *'75*
The Alpha Incident *'76*
Food of the Gods *'76*
Hi-Riders *'77*
My Boys Are Good Boys *'78*
Winter Kills *'79*

Don Megowan
A Lawless Street *'55*
The Jayhawkers *'59*
The Creation of the Humanoids *'62*
The Devil's Brigade *'68*

Blanche Mehaffey
Battling Orioles *'24*
Sunrise Trail *'31*
Devil Monster *'46*

Thomas Meighan
The Forbidden City *'18*
Male and Female *'19*
Why Change Your Wife? *'20*
Peck's Bad Boy *'21*
Peck's Bad Boy *'34*

John Meillon
Billy Budd *'62*
The Cars That Ate Paris *'74*
Inn of the Damned *'74*
Fourth Wish *'75*
Ride a Wild Pony *'75*
The Dunera Boys *'85*
The Blue Lightning *'86*
Crocodile Dundee *'86*
Frenchman's Farm *'87*
Crocodile Dundee 2 *'88*

Gunter Meisner
Between Wars *'74*
In a Glass Cage *'86*
Magdalene *'88*

Karl Meixner
Crimes of Dr. Mabuse *'32*
Das Testament des Dr. Mabuse *'33*

Isabelle Mejias
Daughter of Death *'82*
The Bay Boy *'85*
Meatballs 3 *'87*
Fall from Innocence *'88*
Higher Education *'88*
Unfinished Business *'89*
Scanners 2: The New Order *'91*

Mariangela Melato
Seduction of Mimi *'72*
By the Blood of Others *'73*
Love and Anarchy *'73*
Swept Away... *'75*
To Forget Venice *'79*
So Fine *'81*
Dancers *'87*
Summer Night *'87*
Summer Night with Greek Profile, Almond Eyes & Scent of Basil *'87*

Wendel Meldrum
Beautiful Dreamers *'92*
City Boy *'93*
Sodbusters *'94*

George Melford
Call Northside 777 *'48*
A Woman's World *'54*

Jack Melford
Department Store *'35*
When Thief Meets Thief *'37*

Marisa Mell
Secret Agent Super Dragon *'66*
Danger: Diabolik *'68*
Hostages *'79*
Mad Dog *'84*

Frank Melton
Stand Up and Cheer *'34*
The Glory Trail *'36*
Tanks a Million *'41*

Sid Melton
Leave It to the Marines *'51*
The Lost Continent *'51*
Sky High *'51*
The Steel Helmet *'51*
Stop That Cab *'51*
Lady Sings the Blues *'72*
Hit! *'73*

Sam Melville
Roughnecks *'80*
Twice Dead *'88*

Murray Melvin
A Taste of Honey *'61*
The Fixer *'68*
The Devils *'71*
Madhouse Mansion *'74*
The Bawdy Adventures of Tom Jones *'76*

George Memmoli
Mean Streets *'73*
Hot Potato *'76*

Stephen Mendel
Scanners: The Showdown *'94*
Midnight Heat *'95*

Ben Mendelsohn
The Year My Voice Broke *'87*
Quigley Down Under *'90*
The Efficiency Expert *'92*
Sirens *'94*

David Mendenhall
Space Raiders *'83*
Over the Top *'86*
Witchfire *'86*
Going Bananas *'88*
Secret of the Ice Cave *'89*
Streets *'90*

Mauro Mendonca
Dona Flor and Her Two Husbands *'78*
Love Strange Love *'82*

Victor Manuel Mendoza
Susana *'51*
The Proud Ones *'53*
Cowboy *'58*

John Mengatti
Meatballs 2 *'84*
Knights of the City *'85*

Adolphe Menjou
The Sheik *'21*
Woman of Paris/Sunnyside *'23*
The Marriage Circle *'24*
Are Parents People? *'25*
The King on Main Street *'25*
The Swan *'25*
The Grand Duchess and the Waiter *'26*
The Sorrows of Satan *'26*
Morocco *'30*
The Front Page *'31*
A Farewell to Arms *'32*
Morning Glory *'33*
Little Miss Marker *'34*
Gold Diggers of 1935 *'35*
Milky Way *'36*
One in a Million *'36*
100 Men and a Girl *'37*
Stage Door *'37*
A Star is Born *'37*
The Goldwyn Follies *'38*
Letter of Introduction *'38*
Golden Boy *'39*
Road Show *'41*
Roxie Hart *'42*
You Were Never Lovelier *'42*
Hi Diddle Diddle *'43*
Sweet Rosie O'Grady *'43*
Step Lively *'44*
Heartbeat *'46*
Till the Clouds Roll By/A Star Is Born *'46*
The Hucksters *'47*
State of the Union *'48*
My Dream Is Yours *'49*
To Please a Lady *'50*
Across the Wide Missouri *'51*
The Ambassador's Daughter *'56*
Bundle of Joy *'56*
I Married a Woman *'56*
Paths of Glory *'57*
Pollyanna *'60*

Heather Menzies
The Sound of Music *'65*
Red, White & Busted *'75*
Piranha *'78*
Captain America *'79*

Doro Merande
The Man with the Golden Arm *'55*
The Seven Year Itch *'55*
The Gazebo *'59*
Kiss Me, Stupid! *'64*
The Russians are Coming, the Russians are Coming *'66*

Beryl Mercer
All Quiet on the Western Front *'30*
Smilin' Through *'32*
Cavalcade *'33*
Supernatural *'33*
Jane Eyre *'34*

Frances Mercer
Beauty for the Asking *'39*
Hunt the Man Down/Smashing the Rackets *'50*

Vivien Merchant
Alfie *'66*
Accident *'67*
Frenzy *'72*
The Offence *'73*
Under Milk Wood *'73*

Michele Mercier
Shoot the Piano Player *'62*
A Global Affair *'63*
Black Sabbath *'64*
Casanova '70 *'65*
Oldest Profession *'67*
Web of the Spider *'70*
Call of the Wild *'72*

Melina Mercouri
Stella *'55*
Where the Hot Wind Blows *'59*
Never on Sunday *'60*
Phaedra *'61*
Topkapi *'64*
Once is Not Enough *'75*
Nasty Habits *'77*
A Dream of Passion *'78*

Monique Mercure
The Odyssey of the Pacific *'82*
Tramp at the Door *'87*
Naked Lunch *'91*

Paul Mercurio
Strictly Ballroom *'92*
Exit to Eden *'94*
Joseph *'95*

Burgess Meredith
Winterset *'36*
Idiot's Delight *'39*
Of Mice and Men *'39*
Second Chorus *'40*
That Uncertain Feeling *'41*
Tom, Dick, and Harry *'41*
Diary of a Chambermaid *'46*
Mine Own Executioner *'47*
Man on the Eiffel Tower *'48*
Advise and Consent *'62*
The Cardinal *'63*
In Harm's Way *'65*
Batman *'66*
A Big Hand for the Little Lady *'66*
Madame X *'66*
Torture Garden *'67*
Stay Away, Joe *'68*
MacKenna's Gold *'69*
There was a Crooked Man *'70*
Yin & Yang of Mr. Go *'71*
Probe *'72*
Son of Blob *'72*
The Day of the Locust *'75*
The Hindenburg *'75*
Burnt Offerings *'76*
92 in the Shade *'76*
Rocky *'76*
The Sentinel *'76*
Golden Rendezvous *'77*
Johnny We Hardly Knew Ye *'77*
Foul Play *'78*
Great Bank Hoax *'78*
Magic *'78*
The Manitou *'78*
Rocky 2 *'79*
Final Assignment *'80*
When Time Ran Out *'80*
Clash of the Titans *'81*
Last Chase *'81*
True Confessions *'81*
Rocky 3 *'82*
Thumbelina *'82*
Twilight Zone: The Movie *'83*
Wet Gold *'84*
Santa Claus: The Movie *'85*
Outrage! *'86*
King Lear *'87*
Full Moon in Blue Water *'88*
Mr. Corbett's Ghost *'90*
Rocky 5 *'90*
State of Grace *'90*
Oddball Hall *'91*
Grumpy Old Men *'93*
Across the Moon *'94*
Grumpier Old Men *'95*

Don Meredith
Terror on the 40th Floor *'74*
Sky Hei$t *'75*
Express to Terror *'79*
The Night the City Screamed *'80*
Wyatt Earp: Return to Tombstone *'94*

Iris Meredith
A Lawman Is Born *'37*
Mystery of the Hooded Horseman *'37*
Green Archer *'40*

Judi Meredith
Jack the Giant Killer *'62*
Planet of Blood *'66*

Madge Meredith
Trail Street *'47*
The Falcon's Adventure/Armored Car Robbery *'50*

Luc Merenda
Le Mans *'71*
Violent Professionals *'73*
The Cheaters *'76*
Could It Happen Here? *'80s*

Jalal Merhi
Tiger Claws *'91*
Talons of the Eagle *'92*
TC 2000 *'93*
Fearless Tiger *'94*
Operation Golden Phoenix *'94*
Expect No Mercy *'95*

Macha Meril
A Married Woman *'65*
Vagabond *'85*
Chinese Roulette *'86*
Meeting Venus *'91*

Eda Reiss Merin
Don't Tell Mom the Babysitter's Dead *'91*
For Better or Worse *'95*
The Reluctant Agent *'95*

Philip Merivale
Lady for a Night *'42*
Nothing But Trouble *'44*
Sister Kenny *'46*

Lee Meriwether
The 4D Man *'59*
Batman *'66*
Namu, the Killer Whale *'66*
The Undefeated *'69*
Brothers O'Toole *'73*

Una Merkel
Abraham Lincoln *'30*
The Bat Whispers *'30*
The Maltese Falcon *'31*
Private Lives *'31*
Red Headed Woman *'32*
They Call It Sin *'32*
Bombshell *'33*
42nd Street *'33*
Evelyn Prentice *'34*
The Merry Widow *'34*
Broadway Melody of 1936 *'35*
Riff Raff *'35*
Born to Dance *'36*
Saratoga *'37*
Destry Rides Again *'39*
On Borrowed Time *'39*
The Bank Dick *'40*
The Road to Zanzibar *'41*
It's a Joke, Son! *'47*
Rich, Young and Pretty *'51*
The Merry Widow *'52*
I Love Melvin *'53*
The Kentuckian *'55*
The Kettles in the Ozarks *'56*
The Girl Most Likely *'57*
The Mating Game *'59*
The Parent Trap *'61*
Summer and Smoke *'61*
Summer Magic *'63*
A Tiger Walks *'64*
Spinout *'66*

S. Epatha Merkerson
A Place for Annie *'94*
A Mother's Prayer *'95*

Jan Merlin
Twilight People *'72*
Silk 2 *'89*

Joanna Merlin
Fame *'80*
Baby It's You *'82*
Mystic Pizza *'88*
Class Action *'91*
Two Bits *'96*

Ethel Merman
Kid Millions *'34*
We're Not Dressing *'34*
Alexander's Ragtime Band *'38*
Happy Landing *'38*
There's No Business Like Show Business *'54*
It's a Mad, Mad, Mad, Mad World *'63*

Mary Merrall
Pink Strings and Sealing Wax *'45*
Nicholas Nickleby *'46*
The Obsessed *'51*

Charlotte Merriam
One-Punch O'Day *'26*
Night Nurse *'31*

Lynn Merrick
The Sombrero Kid *'42*
California Joe *'43*
Down to Earth *'47*
Western Double Feature 15 *'50*

Dina Merrill
Desk Set *'57*
Operation Petticoat *'59*
Butterfield 8 *'60*
The Sundowners *'60*
The Courtship of Eddie's Father *'62*
I'll Take Sweden *'65*
Running Wild *'73*
The Meal *'75*
The Greatest *'77*
Deadly Encounter *'78*
A Wedding *'78*
Tenth Month *'79*
Anna to the Infinite Power *'84*
Hot Pursuit *'84*
Twisted *'86*
Caddyshack 2 *'88*
The Cary Grant Collection *'90*
Fear *'90*
The Player *'92*
Suture *'93*

Gary Merrill
Twelve O'Clock High *'49*
All About Eve *'50*
Phone Call from a Stranger *'52*
Missouri Traveler *'58*
The Great Impostor *'61*
Mysterious Island *'61*
Around the World Under the Sea *'65*
Clambake *'67*
The Incident *'67*
Pueblo Affair *'73*
Huckleberry Finn *'74*
The Seekers *'79*

Clive Merrison
An Awfully Big Adventure *'94*
Heavenly Creatures *'94*

Theresa Merritt
All That Jazz *'79*
The Serpent and the Rainbow *'87*
Voodoo Dawn *'89*

Billy Madison '94

Jane Merrow
Island of the Burning Doomed '67
The Lion in Winter '68
Hands of the Ripper '71
The Appointment '82

John Merton
The Gun Ranger '34
Aces and Eights '36
The Rangers Step In '37
Roaring Six Guns '37
Two-Gun Troubador '37
Gang Bullets '38
Phantom Ranger '38
Valley of Terror '38
Code of the Fearless '39
Hopalong Cassidy: Renegade Trail '39
In Old Montana '39
Covered Wagon Days '40
Boot Hill Bandits '42
The Mysterious Rider '42
Prairie Pals '42
Cowboy Commandos '43
Fighting Valley '43
Devil Riders '44
Rustler's Hideout '44
Wild Horse Phantom '44
Border Bandits '46

William Mervyn
Murder Ahoy '64
The Railway Children '70

John Mese
Excessive Force 2: Force on Force '95
Night of the Scarecrow '95

Gertrude Messinger
Hidden Valley '32
The Adventurous Knights '35
Fighting Pilot '35
Roaring Roads '35
Rustler's Paradise '35
Social Error '35
Aces Wild '37
Miracle Kid '42

Laurie Metcalf
Desperately Seeking Susan '85
Execution of Raymond Graham '85
Making Mr. Right '86
Miles from Home '88
Stars and Bars '88
Uncle Buck '89
Internal Affairs '90
Pacific Heights '90
JFK '91
Mistress '91
Blink '93
A Dangerous Woman '93
Leaving Las Vegas '95

Mark Metcalf
National Lampoon's Animal House '78
The Final Terror '83
One Crazy Summer '86
Mr. North '88
Dead Ahead: The Exxon Valdez Disaster '92

Earl Metcalfe
With Kit Carson Over the Great Divide '25
The Notorious Lady '27

Aaron Michael Metchik
Trading Mom '94
The Baby-Sitters Club '95

Mayo Methot
Corsair '31
Goodbye Love '34
Marked Woman '37

Art Metrano
Rocket Attack U.S.A. '58
The Heartbreak Kid '72
They Only Kill Their Masters '72
Slaughter's Big Ripoff '73
Prisoner in the Middle '74
Seven '79
How to Beat the High Cost of Living '80
Going Ape! '81
Breathless '83
Malibu Express '85
Police Academy 2: Their First Assignment '85
Police Academy 3: Back in Training '86
Beverly Hills Bodysnatchers '89

Nancy Mette
Key Exchange '85
Meet the Hollowheads '89

Jim Metzler
Squeeze Play '79
Four Friends '81
Tex '82
On Wings of Eagles '86
River's Edge '87
Hot to Trot! '88
976-EVIL '88
Murder by Night '89
Old Gringo '89
Circuitry Man '90
Delusion '91
Love Kills '91
One False Move '91
French Silk '94
Plughead Rewired: Circuitry Man 2 '94
Children of the Corn 3: Urban Harvest '95

Paul Meurisse
Diabolique '55
Picnic on the Grass '59
The Monocle '64
Gypsy '75

Jason Mewes
Clerks '94
Mallrats '95

Dina Meyer
Johnny Mnemonic '95
Dragonheart '96

Emile Meyer
Shane '53
Riot in Cell Block 11 '54

Michael Meyer
Crossfire '89
Virtual Desire '95

Torben Meyer
Thin Ice '37
Sullivan's Travels '41
The Matchmaker '58

Ari Meyers
License to Kill '84
Shakma '89
Think Big '90
Dark Horse '92

Michelle Meyrink
Joy of Sex '84
Revenge of the Nerds '84
One Magic Christmas '85
Real Genius '85
Nice Girls Don't Explode '87
Permanent Record '88

Myriam Meziere
Jonah Who Will Be 25 in the Year 2000 '76
Mouth to Mouth '95

Vittorio Mezzogiorno
Three Brothers '80
Cafe Express '83
L'Homme Blesse '83
Moon in the Gutter '83
Car Crash

Cora Miao
Dim Sum: A Little Bit of Heart '85
Eat a Bowl of Tea '89

Nora Miao
Return of the Dragon '73
Young Dragon '77
Bruce's Deadly Fingers '80
Showdown at the Equator '83

Gertrude Michael
I'm No Angel '33
Cleopatra '34
Behind Prison Walls '43
Flamingo Road '49

Ralph Michael
Dead of Night '45
Johnny Frenchman '46
San Demetrio, London '47
Murder Most Foul '65
Diary of a Mad Old Man '88

Genia Michaela
Fallen Angels 2 '93
Is There Life Out There? '94

Dario Michaelis
The Devil's Commandment '56
The Day the Sky Exploded '57

Corinne Michaels
Laboratory '80
Consenting Adult '85

Marc Michel
Lola '61
Umbrellas of Cherbourg '64

Marcella Michelangeli
Padre Padrone '77
Could It Happen Here? '80s

Keith Michell
The Hellfire Club '61
Soldier in Love '67
Ruddigore '70s
Six Wives of Henry VIII '70s
The Executioner '70
The Story of Jacob & Joseph '74
The Story of David '76
Tenth Month '79
The Deceivers '88

Anne Michelle
The Virgin Witch '70
Mistress Pamela '74
House of Whipcord '75
French Quarter '78
The Haunted '79

Janee Michelle
Scream Blacula Scream '73
The House on Skull Mountain '74

Shelley Michelle
Bikini Summer '91
Sunset Strip '91
Married People, Single Sex '93

Maria Michi
Open City '45
Paisan '46
Redneck '73

Frank Middlemass
The Island '80
Oliver Twist '85
The Bretts '88
One Against the Wind '91

Charles Middleton
The Strange Love of Molly Louvain '32
Duck Soup '33
Mystery Ranch '34
Hopalong Cassidy '35
The Miracle Rider '35
Flash Gordon: Rocketship '36
Rocketship '36
Yodelin' Kid From Pine Ridge '37
Dick Tracy Returns '38
Flash Gordon: Mars Attacks the World '38
Oklahoma Kid '39
Wyoming Outlaw '39
Flash Gordon Conquers the Universe '40
Space Soldiers Conquer the Universe '40
Western Union '41
Northwest Trail '46
Strangler of the Swamp '46
Spook Busters '48

Guy Middleton
Dangerous Moonlight '41
A Man About the House '47
The Happiest Days of Your Life '50

Noelle Middleton
Carrington, V.C. '54
The Vicious Circle '57

Ray Middleton
Lady for a Night '42
Lady from Louisiana '42
I Dream of Jeannie '52
A Christmas Carol '54
Jubilee Trail '54

Robert Middleton
Desperate Hours '55
Court Jester '56
Tarnished Angels '57
The Law and Jake Wade '58
Career '59
Harrad Experiment '73

Dale Midkiff
Streetwalkin' '85
Nightmare Weekend '86
Elvis and Me '88
Pet Sematary '89
Blackmail '91
Love Potion #9 '92

Bette Midler
Hawaii '66
The Thorn '73
The Rose '79
Divine Madness '80
Jinxed '82
Down and Out in Beverly Hills '86
Ruthless People '86
Outrageous Fortune '87
Beaches '88
Big Business '88
Stella '89
For the Boys '91
Scenes from a Mall '91
Gypsy '93
Hocus Pocus '93

Anne-Marie Mieville
Here and Elsewhere '70s
Comment Ca Va? '76

Toshiro Mifune
Drunken Angel '48
A Quiet Duel '49
Stray Dog '49
Scandal '50
The Idiot '51
Rashomon '51
Life of Oharu '52
Seven Samurai '54
I Live in Fear '55
Samurai 1: Musashi Miyamoto '55
Samurai 2: Duel at Ichijoji Temple '55
Samurai 3: Duel at Ganryu Island '56
The Lower Depths '57
Throne of Blood '57
The Hidden Fortress '58
Rikisha-Man '58
Saga of the Vagabond '59
The Bad Sleep Well '60
The Gambling Samurai '60
Yojimbo '61
High & Low '62
Sanjuro '62
Red Beard '65
Grand Prix '66
Sword of Doom '67
Hell in the Pacific '69
Red Lion '69
The Battle of the Japan Sea '70
Zatoichi vs. Yojimbo '70
Red Sun '71
Paper Tiger '74
Midway '76
Love and Faith '78
1941 '79
Winter Kills '79
Shogun '80
The Challenge '82
Proof of the Man '84
Journey of Honor '91
Shadow of the Wolf '92

Julia Migenes-Johnson
Berlin Blues '89
Mack the Knife '89

R.A. Mihailoff
Leatherface: The Texas Chainsaw Massacre 3 '89
Pumpkinhead 2: Blood Wings '94

Tatsuya Mihashi
The Burmese Harp '56
High & Low '62
None But the Brave '65
What's Up, Tiger Lily? '66
Tora! Tora! Tora! '70

Nikita Mikhalkov
An Unfinished Piece for a Player Piano '77
Siberiade '79
Close to Eden '90
Burnt by the Sun '94

Norihei Miki
Himatsuri '85
Black Rain '88

Rentaro Mikuni
The Burmese Harp '56
Kwaidan '64
Swords of Death '71
Nomugi Pass '79
The Go-Masters '82
A Taxing Woman's Return '88
Rikyu '90

Lita Milan
Naked in the Sun '57
Poor White Trash '57
I, Mobster '58
The Left-Handed Gun '58
Never Love a Stranger '58

Alyssa Milano
Old Enough '84
Commando '85
Conflict of Interest '92
Little Sister '92
Where the Day Takes You '92
Casualties of Love: The "Long Island Lolita" Story '93
Double Dragon '94
Deadly Sins '95
Embrace of the Vampire '95
Poison Ivy 2: Lily '95
Fear '96

Adolph Milar
The Michigan Kid '28
The Savage Girl '32

Bernard Miles
In Which We Serve '43
Great Expectations '46
Nicholas Nickleby '46
Fame Is the Spur '47
The Guinea Pig '48
Never Let Me Go '53
The Man Who Knew Too Much '56
The Smallest Show on Earth '57
Sapphire '59

Betty Miles
The Driftin' Kid '41
Riding the Sunset Trail '41
Lone Star Law Men '42
The Law Rides Again '43
Sonora Stagecoach '44

Joanna Miles
Born Innocent '74
Bug '75
The Ultimate Warrior '75
The Orphan '79
Sound of Murder '82
Blackout '88
The Water Engine '92
Cooperstown '93
The Avenging Angel '95

Kevin Miles
The Cars That Ate Paris '74
Endplay '75

Lillian Miles
Get That Man '35
Reefer Madness '38

Maria Miles
The Cinder Path '94
Cold Comfort Farm '94

Peter Miles
The Red Pony '49
Trigger, Jr. '50

Rosalind Miles
Shaft's Big Score '72
The Manhandlers '73
The Black Six '74

Sarah Miles
The Servant '63
Those Magnificent Men in Their Flying Machines '65
Blow-Up '66
Ryan's Daughter '70
Lady Caroline Lamb '73
Man Who Loved Cat Dancing '73
The Sailor Who Fell from Grace with the Sea '76
The Big Sleep '78
Dynasty '82
Venom '82
Ordeal by Innocence '84
Harem '86
Steaming '86
Hope and Glory '87
Queenie '87
White Mischief '88
The Silent Touch '94

Sherry Miles
The Todd Killings '71
The Velvet Vampire '71

Sylvia Miles
Parrish '61
Psychomania '63
Midnight Cowboy '69
The Last Movie '71

Alley Mills
Rape and Marriage: The Rideout Case '80
Tainted Blood '93

Brooke Mills
The Big Doll House '71
The Student Teachers '73
Dream No Evil '75

Danny Mills
Pink Flamingos '72
Female Trouble '74

Donna Mills
The Incident '67
Play Misty for Me '71
Haunts of the Very Rich '72
Killer with Two Faces '74
One Deadly Owner '74
Beyond the Bermuda Triangle '75
Murph the Surf '75
Curse of the Black Widow '77
Fire '77
The Hunted Lady '77
Waikiki '80
Bunco '83
Runaway Father '91
False Arrest '92
The World's Oldest Living Bridesmaid '92

Hayley Mills
Tiger Bay '59
Pollyanna '60
The Parent Trap '61
In Search of the Castaways '62
Whistle Down the Wind '62
Summer Magic '63
The Chalk Garden '64
The Moon-Spinners '64
That Darn Cat '65
The Trouble with Angels '66
Cry of the Penguins '71
Endless Night '71
Kingfisher Caper '76
Bananas Boat '78
The Flame Trees of Thika '81
Deadly Strangers '82
Appointment with Death '88
Back Home '90

John Mills
The Ghost Camera '33
Nine Days a Queen '34
O.H.M.S. '37
Goodbye, Mr. Chips '39
Cottage to Let '41
In Which We Serve '43
We Dive at Dawn '43
Great Expectations '46
This Happy Breed '47
The October Man '48
Scott of the Antarctic '48
Hobson's Choice '53
The Colditz Story '55
Escapade '55
Above Us the Waves '56
The Baby and the Battleship '56
War and Peace '56
The Vicious Circle '57
Tiger Bay '59
The Swiss Family Robinson '60
Tunes of Glory '60
Tunes of Glory/Horse's Mouth '60
Tiara Tahiti '62
The Chalk Garden '64
King Rat '65
Operation Crossbow '65
The Wrong Box '66
Africa Texas Style '67
Chuka '67
A Black Veil for Lisa '68
Ryan's Daughter '70
Young Winston '72
Lady Caroline Lamb '73
Oklahoma Crude '73
The Human Factor '75
Choice of Weapons '76
The Big Sleep '78
Dr. Strange '78
Quatermass Conclusion '79
The Thirty-Nine Steps '79
Zulu Dawn '79
Gandhi '82
Sahara '83
Masks of Death '86
Who's That Girl? '87
Around the World in 80 Days '89
A Tale of Two Cities '91
Frankenstein '93

Juliet Mills
The October Man '48
The Rare Breed '66
Avanti! '72
Jonathan Livingston Seagull '73
QB VII '74
Beyond the Door '75
Alexander: The Other Side of Dawn '77
Barnaby and Me '77
The Cracker Factory '79

Martin Milner
Life with Father '47
The Halls of Montezuma '50
The Trouble with Father '50
Francis in the Navy '55
Mister Roberts '55
Pete Kelly's Blues '55
Sweet Smell of Success '57
Compulsion '59
13 Ghosts '60
Zebra in the Kitchen '65
Valley of the Dolls '67
Columbo: Murder By the Book '71
Hurricane '74
Flood! '76
The Seekers '79
Nashville Beat '89

Sandra Milo
Generale Della Rovere '60
Herod the Great '60
Vanina Vanini '61
8 1/2 '63
Bang Bang Kid '67
Dead for a Dollar '70s

Yvette Mimieux
Platinum High School '60
The Time Machine '60
Where the Boys Are '60
Diamond Head '62
The Four Horsemen of the Apocalypse '62
The Wonderful World of the Brothers Grimm '62
Toys in the Attic '63
Monkeys, Go Home! '66
Caper of the Golden Bulls '67
Dark of the Sun '68
Three in the Attic '68
Neptune Factor '73
Hit Lady '74
Journey into Fear '74
Legend of Valentino '75
Jackson County Jail '76
Snowbeast '77
Devil Dog: The Hound of Hell '78
Outside Chance '78
The Black Hole '79
Forbidden Love '82
Circle of Power '83
Night Partners '83
Obsessive Love '84

Esther Minciotti
Marty '55
Full of Life '56

Sal Mineo
Rebel Without a Cause '55
Giant '56
Rock, Pretty Baby '56
Somebody Up There Likes Me '56
Dino '57
Tonka '58
The Gene Krupa Story '59
Exodus '60
The Longest Day '62
Cheyenne Autumn '64
Escape from the Planet of the Apes '71
James Dean: The First American Teenager '76

Jan Miner
Lenny '74
Willie & Phil '80
Mermaids '90

Liza Minnelli
Hedda Hopper's Hollywood '42
In the Good Old Summertime '49
The Sterile Cuckoo '69
Cabaret '72
A Matter of Time '76
Silent Movie '76
New York, New York '77
Arthur '81
King of Comedy '82
The Princess and the Pea '83
That's Dancing! '85
A Time to Live '85
Arthur 2: On the Rocks '88
Rent-A-Cop '88
Stepping Out '91
Parallel Lives '94

Kylie Minogue
Street Fighter '94
Bio-Dome '96

Bob Minos
Black Eliminator '70s
Delinquent School Girls '84

Kelly Jo Minter
Pilot '84
Miracle Mile '89
A Nightmare on Elm Street 5: Dream Child '89
Popcorn '89

Kristin Minter
Cool As Ice '91
There Goes My Baby '92
Flashfire '94

Miou-Miou
No Problem '70s
Going Places '74
Jonah Who Will Be 25 in the Year 2000 '76
This Sweet Sickness '77
Roads to the South '78
Josepha '82
Dog Day '83
Entre-Nous '83
My Other Husband '85
Menage '86
La Lectrice '88
May Fools '90
Germinal '93
The Eighth Day '95
Little Indian, Big City '95

Brigitte Mira
Ali: Fear Eats the Soul '74
Every Man for Himself & God Against All '75
Mother Kusters Goes to Heaven '76
Berlin Alexanderplatz '80
Chinese Roulette '86

Irene Miracle
Inferno '78
In the Shadow of Kilimanjaro '86
The Last of Philip Banter '87
Puppet Master '89

Evan Mirand
Brotherhood of Justice '86
My Best Friend Is a Vampire '88
Weekend War '88

Carmen Miranda
Down Argentine Way '40
Week-End In Havana '41
Springtime in the Rockies '42
Doll Face '46
Copacabana '47
A Date with Judy '48
Nancy Goes to Rio '50
Scared Stiff '53
Hollywood Goes to War '54
Gotta Dance, Gotta Sing '84

Isa Miranda
La Signora di Tutti '34
The Walls of Malapaga '49
La Ronde '51
Seven Deadly Sins '53
Just Another Pretty Face '58
Dog Eat Dog '64
Twitch of the Death Nerve '71
The Night Porter '74

Robert Miranda
Chips, the War Dog '90
Sister Act '92
Lost in Yonkers '93
What's Love Got to Do with It? '93
Desire '95

Soledad Miranda
Sound of Horror '64
Count Dracula '71

Helen Mirren
A Midsummer Night's Dream '68
Savage Messiah '72
O Lucky Man! '73
The Long Good Friday '79
S.O.S. Titanic '79
Caligula '80
The Fiendish Plot of Dr. Fu Manchu '80
Hussy '80
Excalibur '81
Priest of Love '81
Cal '84
The Little Mermaid '84
2010: The Year We Make Contact '84
White Nights '85
The Mosquito Coast '86
The Gospel According to Vic '87
Pascali's Island '88
Red King, White Knight '89
When the Whales Came '89
Coming Through '90
The Cook, the Thief, His Wife & Her Lover '90
Dr. Bethune '90
The Comfort of Strangers '91
Where Angels Fear to Tread '91
Prime Suspect '92
The Hawk '93
Prime Suspect 2 '93
Prime Suspect 3 '93
The Madness of King George '94
Prime Suspect: The Lost Child '94
Prime Suspect: Inner Circles '95
Prime Suspect: The Scent of Darkness '95

Karen Mistal
Return of the Killer Tomatoes! '88
Cannibal Women in the Avocado Jungle of Death '89

Mr. T
Penitentiary 2 '82
Rocky 3 '82
D.C. Cab '84
Straight Line '88
Freaked '93
The Magic of the Golden Bear: Goldy 3 '94

Belle Mitchell
Crazed '82
Slipping into Darkness '88

Cameron Mitchell
They Were Expendable '45
The Adventures of Gallant Bess '48
Homecoming '48
Flight to Mars '52
How to Marry a Millionaire '53
Desiree '54
Love Me or Leave Me '55
The Tall Men '55
All Mine to Give '56
Carousel '56
Tension at Table Rock '56
Escapade in Japan '57
The Unstoppable Man '59
Conquest of the Normans '62
The Invaders '63
Blood and Black Lace '64
Dog Eat Dog '64
Last Gun '64
Minnesota Clay '65
Viking Massacre '65
Autopsy of a Ghost '67
Hombre '67
Ride in the Whirlwind '67
Nightmare in Wax '69
Rebel Rousers '69
The Andersonville Trial '70
Thief '71
Buck and the Preacher '72
Slaughter '72
The Stranger '73
The Hanged Man '74
The Klansman '74
Medusa '74
Flood! '76
The Longest Drive '76
Haunts '77
Return to Fantasy Island '77
Scalp Merchant '77
Slavers '77
Texas Detour '77
Viva Knievel '77
The Bastard '78
Enforcer from Death Row '78
Supersonic Man '78
The Swarm '78
The Toolbox Murders '78
The Last Reunion '80
Silent Scream '80
Cataclysm '81
The Demon '81
Frankenstein Island '81
Kill Squad '81
Raw Force '81
Texas Lightning '81
It's Called Murder, Baby '82
My Favorite Year '82
The Guns and the Fury '83
Prince Jack '83
Go for the Gold '84
Killpoint '84
Night Train to Terror '84
Low Blow '85
Mission to Kill '85
Bloodlink '86
Nightforce '86
Tomb '86
Codename: Vengeance '87
Deadly Prey '87
Hollywood Cop '87
The Messenger '87
The Offspring '87
Code of Honor '88
Killers '88
Memorial Valley Massacre '88
Rage to Kill '88
Space Mutiny '88
Swift Justice '88
Action U.S.A. '89
Cult People '89
Easy Kill '89
Crossing the Line '90
Terror in Beverly Hills '90
Trapped Alive '93
Jack-O '95
Killer Commandos

Chuck "Porky" Mitchell
Goodbye Cruel World '82
Porky's Revenge '85
Hollywood Zap '86
Ghost Chase '88
Swift Justice '88

Daryl Mitchell
Sgt. Bilko '95
A Thin Line Between Love and Hate '96

Donna Mitchell
Psycho 4: The Beginning '90
The Portrait '93
Two Bits '96

Duke Mitchell
Bela Lugosi Meets a Brooklyn Gorilla '52
The Executioner '78

Eric Mitchell
The Foreigner '78
Rome '78 '78
Underground U.S.A. '84

Gordon Mitchell
The Giant of Metropolis '61
Vulcan God of Fire '62
Battle of Valiant '63
Fighting Fists of Shanghai Joe '65
Beyond the Law '68
Suicide Patrol '70s
Erik, the Viking '72
The Big Bust Out '73
Slaughterday '77
Frankenstein '80 '79
Rush '84
Commando Invasion '87
Mines of Kilimanjaro '87
Operation Orient

Grant Mitchell
No Man of Her Own '32
Three on a Match '32
Heroes for Sale '33
Gold Diggers of 1935 '35
In Person '35
The Grapes of Wrath '40
Footsteps in the Dark '41
The Great Lie '41
The Man Who Came to Dinner '41
Cairo '42
Laura '44
Conflict '45

Heather Mitchell
The Everlasting Secret Family '88
Proof '91

Keith Mitchell
Bergonzi Hand '70
Memorial Day '83

Laurie Mitchell
Queen of Outer Space '58
Missile to the Moon '59

Mary Mitchell
Panic in the Year Zero! '62
A Swingin' Summer '65
Toga Party '79

Millard Mitchell
A Double Life '47
Twelve O'Clock High '49
The Gunfighter '50
Winchester '73 '50
Singin' in the Rain '52
Here Come the Girls '53
The Naked Spur '53

Red Mitchell
Forever Evil '87
8 Seconds '94

Sasha Mitchell
Spike of Bensonhurst '88
Kickboxer 2: The Road Back '90
Kickboxer 3: The Art of War '92
Class of 1999 2: The Substitute '93
Kickboxer 4: The Aggressor '94

Scoey Mitchell
The Voyage of the Yes '72
Jo Jo Dancer, Your Life is Calling '86

Steve Mitchell
Submarine Seahawk '59
The Sibling '72

Thomas Mitchell
Theodora Goes Wild '36
The Hurricane '37
Lost Horizon '37
Gone with the Wind '39
The Hunchback of Notre Dame '39
Mr. Smith Goes to Washington '39
Only Angels Have Wings '39
Stagecoach '39
Angels Over Broadway '40
The Long Voyage Home '40
Our Town '40
The Black Swan '42
The Fighting Sullivans '42
Joan of Paris '42
Song of the Islands '42
Tales of Manhattan '42
Bataan '43
Immortal Sergeant '43
The Outlaw '43
Buffalo Bill '44
Dark Waters '44
The Keys of the Kingdom '44
Wilson '44
Adventure '45
Dark Mirror '46
It's a Wonderful Life '46
Silver River '48
The Big Wheel '49
High Noon '52
While the City Sleeps '56
By Love Possessed '61
Pocketful of Miracles '61

Warren Mitchell
The Crawling Eye '58
The Unearthly Stranger '64
Arrivederci, Baby! '66
The Assassination Bureau '69
Bananas Boat '78
Norman Loves Rose '82
Waterfront '83
The Dunera Boys '85
Foreign Body '86
Knights & Emeralds '87

Yvonne Mitchell
The Queen of Spades '49
Escapade '55
Sapphire '59
Tiger Bay '59
Conspiracy of Hearts '60
The Trials of Oscar Wilde '60
Johnny Nobody '61
Crucible of Horror '69
Demons of the Mind '72
The Incredible Sarah '76

Ilan Mitchell-Smith
How to Be a Perfect Person in Just Three Days '84
Weird Science '85
The Chocolate War '88
Journey to the Center of the Earth '88
Identity Crisis '90

Bentley Mitchum
Demonic Toys '90
Deadly Exposure '93
Ruby in Paradise '93

Chris Mitchum
Rio Lobo '70
Big Jake '71
H-Bomb '71
Big Foot '72
Mean Machine '73
Ricco '74
No Time to Die '78
One Man Jury '78
Stingray '78
Day Time Ended '80
Desperate Target '80
A Rumor of War '80
American Commandos '84
The Executioner, Part 2: Frozen Scream '84
My Champion '84
Angel of Death '86
Aftershock '88
Death Feud '89
Tombstone '93
Striking Point '94
Biohazard: The Alien Force '95

Jim Mitchum
Thunder Road '58
Girls' Town '59
Ride the Wild Surf '64
In Harm's Way '65
The Invincible Six '68
Maniac '77
Blackout '78
Monster '78
Code Name: Zebra '84
Hollywood Cop '87
Mercenary Fighters '88
Fatal Mission '89
Marked for Murder '89

John Mitchum
The Devil's Sleep '51
Big Foot '72
Bloody Trail '72
The Enforcer '76
Escapes '86

Robert Mitchum
Bar-20 '43
Colt Comrades '43
False Colors '43
Gung Ho! '43
Hopalong Cassidy: Riders of the Deadline '43
Hoppy Serves a Writ '43
The Human Comedy '43
Leather Burners '43
Girl Rush '44
Nevada '44
Thirty Seconds Over Tokyo '44
West of the Pecos '45
Till the End of Time '46
Crossfire '47
Out of the Past '47
Pursued '47
Blood on the Moon '48
Rachel and the Stranger '48
Big Steal '49
Holiday Affair '49
The Red Pony '49
His Kind of Woman '51
My Forbidden Past '51
The Racket '51
The Lusty Men '52
Macao '52
One Minute to Zero '52
She Couldn't Say No '52
Second Chance '53
River of No Return '54
The Night of the Hunter '55
Not as a Stranger '55
Enemy Below '57
Fire Down Below '57
The Hunters '58
Thunder Road '58
Home from the Hill '60
The Sundowners '60
Cape Fear '61
The Grass is Greener '61
The Longest Day '62
Two for the Seesaw '62
The List of Adrian Messenger '63
El Dorado '67
The Way West '67
Anzio '68
Five Card Stud '68
Villa Rides '68
The Good Guys and the Bad Guys '69
Secret Ceremony '69
Ryan's Daughter '70
Farewell, My Lovely '75
The Yakuza '75
The Last Tycoon '76
Midway '76
The Amsterdam Kill '78
The Big Sleep '78
Breakthrough '78
Matilda '78
Nightkill '80
The Agency '81
One Shoe Makes It Murder '82
That Championship Season '82
The Winds of War '83
The Ambassador '84
Maria's Lovers '84
The Hearst and Davies Affair '85
North and South Book 1 '85
Hollywood Home Movies '87
Mr. North '88
Scrooged '88
War & Remembrance, Part 1 '88
War & Remembrance, Part 3 '88
War & Remembrance, Part 4 '88
War & Remembrance, Part 5 '88
War & Remembrance, Part 6 '88
War & Remembrance, Part 7 '88
The Brotherhood of the Rose '89
War & Remembrance, Part 2 '89
War & Remembrance: The Final Chapter, Part 8 '89
War & Remembrance: The Final Chapter, Part 9 '89
War & Remembrance: The Final Chapter, Part 10 '89
War & Remembrance: The Final Chapter, Part 11 '89
War & Remembrance: The Final Chapter, Part 12 '89
Thompson's Last Run '90
Woman of Desire '93
Backfire! '94
Dead Man '95

Art Mix
Border Devils '32
Mason of the Mounted '32
Powdersmoke Range '35
Rustlers of Red Dog '35
Way of the West '35
Yodelin' Kid From Pine Ridge '37

Ruth Mix
The Tonto Kid '35
The Black Coin '36
Custer's Last Stand '36
The Riding Avenger '36

Tom Mix
In the Days of the Thundering Herd & the Law & the Outlaw '14
Heart of Texas Ryan '16
Tom Mix Compilation 1 '16
Tom Mix Compilation 2 '16
Child of the Prairie '18
Early Cinema Vol. 1 '19
Trailin' '21
Sky High '22
Dick Turpin '25
Riders of the Purple Sage '25
Great K & A Train Robbery '26
Justice Rides Again '30s
My Pal, The King '32
Texas Bad Man '32
Hidden Gold '33
Rustler's Roundup '33
Terror Trail '33
The Miracle Rider '35

Seiji Miyaguchi
Early Summer '51
Seven Samurai '54
The Human Condition: No Greater Love '58

Nobuko Miyamoto
The Funeral '84
Tampopo '86
A Taxing Woman '87
A Taxing Woman's Return '88
Minbo—Or the Gentle Art of Japanese Extortion '92

Kim Miyori
John & Yoko: A Love Story '85
When the Bough Breaks '86
The Big Picture '89
Hiroshima: Out of the Ashes '90
The Punisher '90

Eiko Miyoshi
I Live in Fear '55
Snow Country '57

Kumi Mizuno
Attack of the Mushroom People '63
War of the Gargantuas '70

Mary Ann Mobley
Girl Happy '65
Harum Scarum '65
My Dog, the Thief '69
Crazy Horse and Custer: "The Untold Story" '90

Roger Mobley
Jack the Giant Killer '62
Emil and the Detectives '64

Jayne Modean
Spring Break '83
Street Hawk '84

Matthew Modine
Baby It's You '82
Private School '83
Streamers '83
Birdy '84
The Hotel New Hampshire '84
Mrs. Soffel '84
Vision Quest '85
Full Metal Jacket '87
Orphans '87
The Gamble '88
Married to the Mob '88
Gross Anatomy '89
Memphis Belle '90
Pacific Heights '90
Wind '92
And the Band Played On '93
Equinox '93
Short Cuts '93
The Browning Version '94
Bye Bye, Love '94
Jacob '94
Cutthroat Island '95
Fluke '95

Gaston Modot
Under the Roofs of Paris '29
L'Age D'Or '30
Grand Illusion '37
The Rules of the Game '39
Beauty and the Devil '50
Casque d'Or '52

Enrica Maria Modugno
Kaos '85
The Story of Boys & Girls '91

Donald Moffat
Rachel, Rachel '68
The Great Northfield Minnesota Raid '72
Showdown '73
Mary White '77
Mrs. R's Daughter '79
Promises in the Dark '79
Strangers: The Story of a Mother and Daughter '79
Winter Kills '79
The Long Days of Summer '80
On the Nickel '80
Jacqueline Bouvier Kennedy '81
The Thing '82
The Right Stuff '83
License to Kill '84
Alamo Bay '85
The Best of Times '86
The Bourne Identity '88
Far North '88
Necessary Parties '88
The Unbearable Lightness of Being '88
Music Box '89
The Bonfire of the Vanities '90
Class Action '91
Regarding Henry '91
When the Time Comes '91
Danielle Steel's Kaleidoscope '92
Housesitter '92
Teamster Boss: The Jackie Presser Story '92
Armistead Maupin's Tales of the City '93
Love, Cheat & Steal '93
Clear and Present Danger '94
Is There Life Out There? '94
Trapped In Paradise '94

D.W. Moffett
An Early Frost '85
Black Widow '87
The Misfit Brigade '87
Fine Things '90
Lisa '90
In the Deep Woods '91
Falling Down '93
Stealing Beauty '96

Gregory Moffett
Let's Dance '50
Robot Monster '53

Michelle Moffett
Hired to Kill '91
Deathstalker 4: Match of Titans '92
Wild Cactus '92
Indecent Behavior '93

Carl Mohner
Rififi '54
It Takes a Thief '59
Sink the Bismarck '60
Cave of the Living Dead '65
Wanted: Babysitter '75
A Woman at Her Window '77

Gerald Mohr
Love Affair '39
The Monster and the Girl '41
Hunt the Man Down '50
Hunt the Man Down/Smashing the Rackets '50
Detective Story '51
Sirocco '51
Invasion U.S.A. '52
The Ring '52
Son of Ali Baba '52
Terror in the Haunted House '58
The Angry Red Planet '59

Zia Mohyeddin
Bombay Talkie '70
We are the Children '87

Richard Moir
In Search of Anna '79
Panic Station '82
Heatwave '83
An Indecent Obsession '85
Remember Me '85
Wrangler '88

Jose Mojica Marins
At Midnight, I'll Take Your Soul '63
Awakenings of the Beast '68
Strange World of Coffin Joe '68
Hallucinations of a Deranged Mind '70

Zakes Mokae
A World of Strangers '62
The Comedians '67
Cry Freedom '87
The Serpent and the Rainbow '87
Dad '89
A Dry White Season '89
Gross Anatomy '89
Body Parts '91
A Rage in Harlem '91
Dust Devil '93
Percy & Thunder '93
Vampire in Brooklyn '95

Karin Molander
Thomas Graal's Best Film '17
Thomas Graal's First Child '18

Jeff Moldovan
Master Blaster '85
Trancers 5: Sudden Deth '94

Alfred Molina
Raiders of the Lost Ark '81
Ladyhawke '85
Letter to Brezhnev '86
A Night of Love '87
Prick Up Your Ears '87
Not Without My Daughter '90
American Friends '91
Enchanted April '92
The Trial '93
Maverick '94
The Perez Family '94
White Fang 2: The Myth of the White Wolf '94
Before and After '95
Dead Man '95
Species '95

Angela Molina
That Obscure Object of Desire '77

Demons in the Garden '82
The Eyes, the Mouth '83
Camorra: The Naples Connection '85
Half of Heaven '86
1492: Conquest of Paradise '92

Charles Moll
Cataclysm '81
Night Train to Terror '84
Combat Academy '86

Georgia Moll
Thief of Baghdad '61
Contempt '64
What a Way to Die '70

Richard Moll
Hard Country '81
Sword & the Sorcerer '82
Dungeonmaster '83
Metalstorm: The Destruction of Jared Syn '83
Savage Journey '83
House '86
Survivor '87
Wicked Stepmother '89
Think Big '90
Driving Me Crazy '91
Dream Date '93
Highlander: The Gathering '93
Sidekicks '93
Beanstalk '94
The Flintstones '94
No Dessert Dad, 'Til You Mow the Lawn '94
Galaxis '95
Storybook '95

Darbnia Molloy
Paddy '70
Frankie Starlight '95

Patrick Molloy
Plutonium Baby '87
Phantom Brother '88

Dan Monahan
Porky's '82
Porky's 2: The Next Day '83
Porky's Revenge '85

Karen Moncrieff
Deathfight '93
Midnight Witness '93
Xtro 3: Watch the Skies '95

Jorge Mondragon
The New Invisible Man '58
Spiritism '61

Richard Monette
Far Cry from Home '70s
Big Zapper '73
Dancing in the Dark '86
Hello Mary Lou: Prom Night 2 '87
Higher Education '88
Murder by Night '89

Debra Monk
Bed of Roses '95
Redwood Curtain '95

Yvonne Monlaur
The Brides of Dracula '60
Circus of Horrors '60
License to Kill '64

Lawrence Monoson
Last American Virgin '82
Mask '85
Dangerous Love '87
Gaby: A True Story '87
Machine Gun Blues '95

Marilyn Monroe
Ladies of the Chorus '49
All About Eve '50
The Asphalt Jungle '50
Love Happy '50
As Young As You Feel '51
Home Town Story '51
Let's Make It Legal '51
Love Nest '51
Clash by Night '52
Don't Bother to Knock '52
Monkey Business '52
Niagara '52
We're Not Married '52
Gentlemen Prefer Blondes '53
How to Marry a Millionaire '53
River of No Return '54
There's No Business Like Show Business '54
The Seven Year Itch '55
Bus Stop '56
The Prince and the Showgirl '57
Some Like It Hot '59
Let's Make Love '60
The Misfits '61
The Love Goddesses '65
Hollywood Outtakes & Rare Footage '83
Hollywood Home Movies '87

Lee Montague
Brother Sun, Sister Moon '73
Mahler '74
Madame Sousatzka '88
Jekyll and Hyde '90

Monte Montague
King of the Rodeo '28
Courtin' Wildcats '29
Trigger Tricks '30
Radio Patrol '37

Ricardo Montalban
On an Island with You '48
Battleground '49
Neptune's Daughter '49
Two Weeks with Love '50
Across the Wide Missouri '51
Latin Lovers '53
Sayonara '57
Cheyenne Autumn '64
Pirate Warrior '64
Alice Through the Looking Glass '66
Madame X '66
The Singing Nun '66
Blue '68
Iron Cowboy '68
Black Water Gold '69
Sweet Charity '69
Escape from the Planet of the Apes '71
Ride to Glory '71
Conquest of the Planet of the Apes '72
Fireball Forward '72
Train Robbers '73
Fantasy Island '76
Joe Panther '76
Return to Fantasy Island '77
Mission to Glory '80
Star Trek 2: The Wrath of Khan '82
Cannonball Run 2 '84
The Naked Gun: From the Files of Police Squad '88

Monte Montana
Circle of Death '36
Down Dakota Way '49

Yves Montand
Napoleon '55
Wages of Fear '55
The Crucible '57
Where the Hot Wind Blows '59
Let's Make Love '60
Goodbye Again '61
My Geisha '62
Grand Prix '66
Is Paris Burning? '68
Z '69
On a Clear Day You Can See Forever '70
Cesar & Rosalie '72
State of Siege '73
Lovers Like Us '75
Delusions of Grandeur '76
Vincent, Francois, Paul and the Others '76
Roads to the South '78
Choice of Arms '83
Jean de Florette '87
Manon of the Spring '87

Lisa Montell
She Gods of Shark Reef '56
The Nine Lives of Elfego Baca '58

Rosenda Monteros
The White Orchid '54
Tiara Tahiti '62
Cauldron of Blood '67

Enrico Montesano
Lobster for Breakfast '82
Sotto, Sotto '85

Liliane Montevecchi
Meet Me in Las Vegas '56
Me and the Colonel '58

Maria Montez
Boss of Bullion City '41
Arabian Nights '42
Ali Baba and the Forty Thieves '43
Cobra Woman '44

Belinda J. Montgomery
The Todd Killings '71
The Man from Atlantis '77
Blackout '78
Stone Cold Dead '80
Silent Madness '84
Tell Me That You Love Me '84
Stone Fox '87

Douglass Montgomery
Little Women '33
Harmony Lane '35

Elizabeth Montgomery
The Court Martial of Billy Mitchell '55
Missing Pieces '83
Amos '85
Deadline Assault '90

George Montgomery
Rough Riders' Roundup '39
Young People '40
Orchestra Wives '42
Roxie Hart '42
Indian Uprising '51
Sword of Monte Cristo '51
The Texas Rangers '51
The Steel Claw '61
Samar '62
From Hell to Borneo '64
Battle of the Bulge '65
Satan's Harvest '65
Warkill '65
Bomb at 10:10 '67
Hallucination '67
Hostile Guns '67

Julia Montgomery
Girls Night Out '83
Revenge of the Nerds '84
Up the Creek '84
Stewardess School '86
The Kindred '87
South of Reno '87
Savage Justice '88
Revenge of the Nerds 3: The Next Generation '92
Black Snow '93
Revenge of the Nerds 4: Nerds in Love '94

Lee Montgomery
Ben '72
Pete 'n' Tillie '72
Savage Is Loose '74
Mutant '83
Prime Risk '84
Girls Just Want to Have Fun '85
The Midnight Hour '86
Into the Fire '88

Robert Montgomery
The Big House '30
The Divorcee '30
Free and Easy '30
Private Lives '31
The Lost Stooges '33
Hide-Out '34
Riptide '34
Forsaking All Others '35
The Last of Mrs. Cheyney '37
Here Comes Mr. Jordan '41
Mr. & Mrs. Smith '41
They Were Expendable '45
Lady in the Lake '46
June Bride '48
Eye Witness '49

Silvia Monti
The Brain '69
Sicilian Connection '74

Anna Maria Monticelli
The Empty Beach '85
Nomads '86

Luigi Montini
Satanik '69
Mediterraneo '91

Alex Montoya
West to Glory '47
Escape from Fort Bravo '53

Michael Monty
Slash '87
The 13th Mission '91

Jim Moody
Bad Boys '83
Who's the Man? '93

King Moody
Five Minutes to Love '63
Get Smart, Again! '89

Lynne Moody
Scream Blacula Scream '73
Nightmare in Badham County '76
Roots: The Next Generation '79
Some Kind of Hero '82
Wait Till Your Mother Gets Home '83
A Fight for Jenny '90
Last Light '93

Ralph Moody
The Road to Bali '53
The Last Hunt '56

Ron Moody
Murder Most Foul '65
Oliver! '68
David Copperfield '70
Twelve Chairs '70
Dog Pound Shuffle '75
Legend of the Werewolf '75
Dominique is Dead '79
Unidentified Flying Oddball '79
Wrong is Right '82
A Kid in King Arthur's Court '95

Keith Moon
That'll Be the Day '73
Tommy '75
Sextette '78

Alvy Moore
The Wild One '54
Designing Woman '57
Three Nuts in Search of a Bolt '64
The Witchmaker '69
The Brotherhood of Satan '71
A Boy and His Dog '75
The Specialist '75
Smokey & the Hotwire Gang '79
Scream '83
They're Playing with Fire '84
Intruder '88

Archie Moore
The Adventures of Huckleberry Finn '60
The Carpetbaggers '64
My Sweet Charlie '70
Breakheart Pass '76

Ben Moore
Moonshine Mountain '64
2000 Maniacs '64

Candy Moore
Tomboy & the Champ '58
Lunch Wagon '81

Christine Moore
Lurkers '88
Prime Evil '88
Thrilled to Death '88

Clayton Moore
The Son of Monte Cristo '41
The Black Dragons '42
Nyoka and the Tigermen '42
Cyclotrode "X" '46
Jesse James Rides Again '47
The Adventures of Frank and Jesse James '48
Far Frontier '48
G-Men Never Forget '48
Radar Men from the Moon '52
Jungle Drums of Africa '53
Lone Ranger '56
Lone Ranger and the Lost City of Gold '58
Justice of the West '61

Colleen Moore
Little Orphan Annie '18
The Busher '19
These Girls Won't Talk '20s
The Sky Pilot '21
Broken Hearts of Broadway '23
Ella Cinders '26
The Scarlet Letter '34

Constance Moore
Wives Under Suspicion '38
Buck Rogers Conquers the Universe '39
Destination Saturn '39
You Can't Cheat an Honest Man '39
Delightfully Dangerous '45

Deborah Maria Moore
Chaplin '92
Into the Sun '92

Demi Moore
Choices '81
Parasite '82
Blame It on Rio '84
No Small Affair '84
St. Elmo's Fire '85
About Last Night... '86
One Crazy Summer '86
Wisdom '87
The Seventh Sign '88
We're No Angels '89
Ghost '90
Tales from the Crypt, Vol. 3 '90
The Butcher's Wife '91
Mortal Thoughts '91
Nothing But Trouble '91
A Few Good Men '92
Indecent Proposal '93
Disclosure '94
Now and Then '95
The Scarlet Letter '95
The Juror '96
Striptease '96

Dennis Moore
East Side Kids/The Lost City '35
Across the Plains '39
Mutiny in the Big House '39
Wild Horse Canyon '39
East Side Kids '40
Rocky Mountain Rangers '40
Arizona Bound '41
Border Roundup '41
Spooks Run Wild '41
Texas Justice '42
Black Market Rustlers '43
Cowboy Commandos '43
Frontier Law '43
Land of Hunted Men '43
Master Key '44
The Mummy's Curse '44
Raiders of Ghost City '44
D-Day on Mars '45
The Purple Monster Strikes '45
Colorado Serenade '46
Driftin' River '46
Range Renegades '48
The Tioga Kid '48
King of the Bullwhip '51
Tribute to a Bad Man '56

Dickie Moore
Blonde Venus '32
Gabriel Over the White House '33
Oliver Twist '33
The World Accuses '35
Little Red Schoolhouse '36
The Gladiator '38
Sergeant York '41
Miss Annie Rooney '42
Heaven Can Wait '43
Jive Junction '43
Out of the Past '47

Dudley Moore
The Wrong Box '66
Bedazzled '68
30 Is a Dangerous Age, Cynthia '68
Those Daring Young Men in Their Jaunty Jalopies '69
Alice's Adventures in Wonderland '72
The Hound of the Baskervilles '77
Foul Play '78
10 '79
Wholly Moses! '80
Arthur '81
Six Weeks '82
Lovesick '83
Romantic Comedy '83
Best Defense '84
Micki & Maude '84
Unfaithfully Yours '84
Santa Claus: The Movie '85
Like Father, Like Son '87
Arthur 2: On the Rocks '88
Crazy People '90
Blame It on the Bellboy '92
Parallel Lives '94

Duke Moore
Night of the Ghouls '59
The Sinister Urge '60

Erin O'Brien Moore
Our Little Girl '35
Destination Moon '50

Frank Moore
Rabid '77
Kings and Desperate Men '83

Moore ▶cont.

Hostage for a Day '94

Gar Moore
Paisan '46
Abbott and Costello Meet the Killer, Boris Karloff '49
The Underworld Story '50

Jeanie Moore
Vampire at Midnight '88
The Final Alliance '89
Dream Trap '90

Joanna Moore
Touch of Evil '58
Monster on the Campus '59
Follow That Dream '61
Son of Flubber '63
Countdown '68
Never a Dull Moment '68
The Dunwich Horror '70
Iron Horsemen '71
Scout's Honor '80

Juanita Moore
Imitation of Life '59
The Singing Nun '66
A Dream for Christmas '73
Foxstyle '73

Julianne Moore
Tales from the Darkside: The Movie '90
Cast a Deadly Spell '91
Body of Evidence '92
The Gun in Betty Lou's Handbag '92
The Hand that Rocks the Cradle '92
Benny & Joon '93
The Fugitive '93
Short Cuts '93
Vanya on 42nd Street '94
Assassins '95
Nine Months '95
Roommates '95
Safe '95

Kieron Moore
A Man About the House '47
Mine Own Executioner '47
Anna Karenina '48
David and Bathsheba '51
The Key '58
Doctor Blood's Coffin '62
Day of the Triffids '63

Mary Tyler Moore
Thoroughly Modern Millie '67
Change of Habit '69
Ordinary People '80
Six Weeks '82
Finnegan Begin Again '84
Just Between Friends '86
Gore Vidal's Lincoln '88
The Last Best Year '90
Flirting with Disaster '95

Matt Moore
Traffic in Souls '13
20,000 Leagues Under the Sea '16
Pride of the Clan '18
White Tiger '23
The Unholy Three '25
Coquette '29
Consolation Marriage '31
Deluge '33
That Forsyte Woman '50
An Affair to Remember '57

Melissa Moore
Scream Dream '89
Hard to Die '90
The Invisible Maniac '90
The Killing Zone '90
Vampire Cop '90
Sorority House Massacre 2: Nighty Nightmare '92
Stormswept '95

Norma Moore
Fear Strikes Out '57
Poor White Trash 2 '75

Owen Moore
Married? '26
As You Desire Me '32
She Done Him Wrong '33

Pauline Moore
The Three Musketeers '39
Young Buffalo Bill '40

R.J. Moore
Hard Hunted '92
Fit to Kill '93

Roger Moore
The Last Time I Saw Paris '54
Diane '55
Interrupted Melody '55
The King's Thief '55
The Rape of the Sabines '61
Fiction Makers '67
The Saint '68
Vendetta for the Saint '68
The Man Who Haunted Himself '70
The Persuaders '71
Live and Let Die '73
The Man with the Golden Gun '74
Mission: Monte Carlo '75
Overture '75
That Lucky Touch '75
Shout at the Devil '76
Street People '76
The Spy Who Loved Me '77
Wild Geese '78
Escape to Athena '79
Moonraker '79
ffolkes '80
Five Miles to Midnight '80
Cannonball Run '81
For Your Eyes Only '81
Sea Wolves '81
Octopussy '83
The Naked Face '84
A View to a Kill '85
Happy Anniversary 007: 25 Years of James Bond '87
Bullseye! '90
Fire, Ice and Dynamite '91
Bed & Breakfast '92
The Quest '96

Rudy Ray Moore
Dolemite '75
Avenging Disco Godfather '76
Dolemite 2: Human Tornado '76
Devil's Son-in-Law '77
Monkey Hustle '77

Stephen Moore
Clockwise '86
Under Suspicion '92

Terry Moore
Gaslight '44
Since You Went Away '44
Mighty Joe Young '49
The Great Rupert '50
Come Back, Little Sheba '52
Beneath the 12-Mile Reef '53
Daddy Long Legs '55
Shack Out on 101 '55
Between Heaven and Hell '56
Postmark for Danger '56
Postmark for Danger/Quicksand '56
Peyton Place '57
Platinum High School '60
Kill Factor '78
Hellhole '85
Death Blow '87
Beverly Hills Brats '89

Tom Moore
Manhandled '24
Mystery in Swing '40

Victor Moore
Swing Time '36
Louisiana Purchase '41
Star Spangled Rhythm '42
The Heat's On '43
Ziegfeld Follies '46
We're Not Married '52
The Seven Year Itch '55

Agnes Moorehead
Citizen Kane '41
Big Street '42
Journey into Fear '42
The Magnificent Ambersons '42
Dragon Seed '44
Jane Eyre '44
Mrs. Parkington '44
The Seventh Cross '44
Since You Went Away '44
Our Vines Have Tender Grapes '45
Dark Passage '47
Lost Moment '47
Johnny Belinda '48
Station West '48
Summer Holiday '48
The Stratton Story '49
Adventures of Captain Fabian '51
Captain Blackjack '51
Show Boat '51
Main Street to Broadway '53
Magnificent Obsession '54
The Left Hand of God '55
The Conqueror '56
Meet Me in Las Vegas '56
The Opposite Sex '56
Pardners '56
Raintree County '57
The Bat '59
Pollyanna '60
The Twilight Zone '61
How the West Was Won '63
Hush, Hush, Sweet Charlotte '65
Alice Through the Looking Glass '66
The Singing Nun '66
Bachelor in Paradise '69
What's the Matter with Helen? '71
Dear Dead Delilah '72

Natalie Moorhead
Hook, Line and Sinker '30
Illicit '31
Morals for Women '31
The King Murder '32
Murder on the High Seas '32
Dancing Man '33
The Thin Man '34

Esai Morales
Bad Boys '83
Great Love Experiment '84
L.A. Bad '85
On Wings of Eagles '86
La Bamba '87
The Principal '87
Bloodhounds of Broadway '89
Freejack '92
Rapa Nui '93
The Burning Season '94
Deadlock 2 '94
Don't Do It '94
In the Army Now '94
My Family '94

Dolores Moran
To Have & Have Not '44
The Horn Blows at Midnight '45
The Man I Love '46

Erin Moran
How Sweet It Is! '68
Watermelon Man '70
Galaxy of Terror '81
Twirl '81

Frank Moran
Ships in the Night '28
Return of the Ape Man '44

Jackie Moran
The Adventures of Tom Sawyer '38
Mad About Music '38
Buck Rogers Conquers the Universe '39
The Gang's All Here '40
Old Swimmin' Hole '40
Tomboy '40
Let's Go Collegiate '41
There Goes Kelly '45

Lee Moran
The Tomboy '24
My Lady of Whims '25
Pardon My Gun '30
High Gear '33

Patrick Moran
Dark Universe '93
Biohazard: The Alien Force '95

Peggy Moran
The Mummy's Hand '40
One Night in the Tropics '40

Polly Moran
Kings, Queens, Jokers '30s
Hollywood Party '34
Adam's Rib '50

Rick Moranis
The Best of John Candy on SCTV '80s
Strange Brew '83
Ghostbusters '84
Hockey Night '84
The Last Polka '84
Streets of Fire '84
The Wild Life '84
Brewster's Millions '85
Club Paradise '86
Head Office '86
Little Shop of Horrors '86
Spaceballs '87
Ghostbusters 2 '89
Honey, I Shrunk the Kids '89
Parenthood '89
My Blue Heaven '90
Honey, I Blew Up the Kid '92
Splitting Heirs '93
The Flintstones '94
Little Giants '94
Big Bully '95

Richard Morant
Mahler '74
Poldark '75
John & Yoko: A Love Story '85

Milburn Morante
Wolf Blood '25
Sherlock's Rivals & Where's My Wife '27
Between Men '35
Ghost Rider '43

Kenneth More
Scott of the Antarctic '48
Man on the Run '49
The Clouded Yellow '51
No Highway in the Sky '51
Doctor in the House '53
Genevieve '53
Never Let Me Go '53
The Adventures of Sadie '55
Reach for the Sky '56
A Night to Remember '58
Flame Over India '60
Sink the Bismarck '60
The Longest Day '62
Dark of the Sun '68
Battle of Britain '69
Scrooge '70
Where Time Began '77
Leopard in the Snow '78
Unidentified Flying Oddball '79
A Tale of Two Cities '80

Jeanne Moreau
Grisbi '53
Back to the Wall '56
Frantic '58
The 400 Blows '59
The Lovers '59
Dangerous Liaisons '60
Jules and Jim '62
The Trial '63
Diary of a Chambermaid '64
The Train '65
Viva Maria! '65
Mademoiselle '66
Chimes at Midnight '67
Oldest Profession '67
The Bride Wore Black '68
Alex in Wonderland '70
Monte Walsh '70
The Little Theatre of Jean Renoir '71
Going Places '74
Mr. Klein '75
The Last Tycoon '76
Lumiere '76
La Truite '83
Querelle '83
Heat of Desire '84
Your Ticket Is No Longer Valid '84
La Femme Nikita '91
The Old Lady Who Walked in the Sea '91
Until The End of The World '91
Alberto Express '92
A Foreign Field '93
Map of the Human Heart '93
The Summer House '94

Marsha Moreau
Miracle at Moreaux '86
The Last Winter '89

Nathaniel Moreau
The Last Winter '89
George's Island '91

Mantan Moreland
The Spirit of Youth '37
Frontier Scout '38
Harlem on the Prairie '38
Next Time I Marry '38
Two-Gun Man from Harlem '38
The Gang's All Here '40
Up in the Air '40
King of the Zombies '41
Let's Go Collegiate '41
Footlight Serenade '42
Law of the Jungle '42
Phantom Killer '42
Cosmo Jones, Crime Smasher '43
Revenge of the Zombies '43
Charlie Chan in the Secret Service '44
The Chinese Cat '44
Meeting at Midnight '44
Mr. Moto's Last Warning/Meeting at Midnight '44
Pin-Up Girl '44
The Jade Mask '45
The Scarlet Clue '45
The Shanghai Cobra '45
Tall, Tan and Terrific '46
Juke Joint '47
Spider Baby '64
The Young Nurses '73

Andre Morell
The Clouded Yellow '51
A Stolen Face '52
The Man Who Never Was '55
The Baby and the Battleship '56
The Bridge on the River Kwai '57
Quatermass and the Pit '58
The Hound of the Baskervilles '59
Dark of the Sun '68
10 Rillington Place '71

Antonio Moreno
It '27
Rose of Rio Grande '38
Valley of the Sun '42
Gaiety '43
Creature from the Black Lagoon '54
The Searchers '56

Jose Elias Moreno
Santa Claus '59
Night of the Bloody Apes '68

Rita Moreno
Pagan Love Song '50
The Toast of New Orleans '50
The Ring '52
Singin' in the Rain '52
Seven Cities of Gold '55
The King and I '56
Summer and Smoke '61
West Side Story '61
Cry of Battle '63
Marlowe '69
The Night of the Following Day '69
Popi '69
Carnal Knowledge '71
The Ritz '76
Anatomy of a Seduction '79
Boss' Son '79
Happy Birthday, Gemini '80
The Four Seasons '81
Portrait of a Showgirl '82
Age Isn't Everything '91
I Like It Like That '94
Angus '95
The Wharf Rat '95

George Morfogen
Deadly Business '86
Yuri Nosenko, KGB '86
Twenty Bucks '93

Debbi Morgan
Monkey Hustle '77
The Jesse Owens Story '84
Guilty of Innocence '87

Dennis (Stanley Morner) Morgan
The Great Ziegfeld '36
I Conquer the Sea '36
Waterfront '39
The Fighting 69th '40
Kitty Foyle '40
Captains of the Clouds '42
In This Our Life '42
Thank Your Lucky Stars '43
Christmas in Connecticut '45
It's a Great Feeling '49
Pearl of the South Pacific '55

Frank Morgan
Manhandled '24
Hallelujah, I'm a Bum '33
The Cat and the Fiddle '34
I Live My Life '35
Naughty Marietta '35
Dancing Pirate '36
Dimples '36
The Great Ziegfeld '36

The Last of Mrs. Cheyney '37
Saratoga '37
Rosalie '38
Sweethearts '38
Balalaika '39
Broadway Serenade '39
The Wizard of Oz '39
Boom Town '40
Broadway Melody of 1940 '40
The Mortal Storm '40
The Shop Around the Corner '40
Honky Tonk '41
Tortilla Flat '42
White Cargo '42
The Human Comedy '43
Thousands Cheer '43
Casanova Brown '44
The White Cliffs of Dover '44
Courage of Lassie '46
Summer Holiday '48
The Three Musketeers '48
Any Number Can Play '49
The Stratton Story '49
Key to the City '50

Gary Morgan
The Power Within '95
Storybook '95

Harry (Henry) Morgan
Orchestra Wives '42
To the Shores of Tripoli '42
Crash Dive '43
The Ox-Bow Incident '43
A Wing and a Prayer '44
State Fair '45
The Gangster '47
Moonrise '48
The Falcon Takes Over/Strange Bargain '49
Holiday Affair '49
The Showdown '50
The Well '51
Bend of the River '52
Boots Malone '52
High Noon '52
Torch Song '53
The Glenn Miller Story '54
Far Country '55
The Teahouse of the August Moon '56
It Started with a Kiss '59
The Mountain Road '60
How the West Was Won '63
Frankie and Johnny '65
What Did You Do in the War, Daddy? '66
Flim-Flam Man '67
Support Your Local Sheriff '69
The Barefoot Executive '71
Scandalous John '71
Support Your Local Gunfighter '71
Snowball Express '72
Charley and the Angel '73
The Apple Dumpling Gang '75
The Shootist '76
The Bastard '78
The Cat from Outer Space '78
The Apple Dumpling Gang Rides Again '79
Better Late Than Never '79
Roots: The Next Generation '79
Wild, Wild West Revisited '79
Roughnecks '80
Scout's Honor '80
M*A*S*H: Goodbye, Farewell & Amen '83
Dragnet '87
The Incident '89

Helen Morgan
Applause '29
Marie Galante '34
Frankie and Johnny '36
Show Boat '36

Jaye P. Morgan
Loose Shoes '80
Night Patrol '85

Jeffrey Dean Morgan
Uncaged '91
Undercover '94

Melissa Morgan
Nasty Rabbit '64
Deadwood '65

Michele Morgan
Stormy Waters '41
Joan of Paris '42
Heart of a Nation '43
Higher and Higher '44
Passage to Marseilles '44
The Chase '46
La Symphonie Pastorale '46
The Fallen Idol '49
The Proud Ones '53
Les Grandes Manoeuvres '55
Bluebeard '63
The Lost Command '66
Cat and Mouse '78
Everybody's Fine '90

Nancy Morgan
Grand Theft Auto '77
Americathon '79
Pray TV '80
The Nest '88
Danielle Steel's Heartbeat '93
Lucky Luke '94

Ralph Morgan
Rasputin and the Empress '32
Strange Interlude '32
The Kennel Murder Case '33
Transatlantic Merry-Go-Round '34
Condemned to Live '35
General Spanky '36
Yellowstone '36
Mannequin '37
Shadows Over Shanghai '38
Way Down South '39
Dick Tracy vs. Crime Inc. '41
Night Monster '42
Enemy of Women '44
The Monster Maker '44
Song of the Thin Man '47
The Creeper '48
Heart of the Rockies '51

Richard Morgan
Innocent Prey '88
The Wicked '89

Shelley Taylor Morgan
My Tutor '82
Malibu Express '85

Stafford Morgan
The Alpha Incident '76
The Capture of Bigfoot '79
Legend of Big Foot '82

Terence Morgan
The Love of Three Queens '54
Svengali '55
The Lifetaker '89

Maia Morgenstern
The Oak '93
Trahir '93
Ulysses' Gaze '95

Masayuki Mori
The Idiot '51
Rashomon '51
Ugetsu '53
Princess Yang Kwei Fei '55
The Bad Sleep Well '60
When a Woman Ascends the Stairs '60

Toschia Mori
The Secrets of Wu Sin '32
The Bitter Tea of General Yen '33

Pat Moriarity
Mutiny in the Big House '39
Kings Row '41

Cathy Moriarty
Raging Bull '80
Neighbors '81
White of the Eye '88
Burndown '89
Kindergarten Cop '90
Soapdish '91
The Gun in Betty Lou's Handbag '92
The Mambo Kings '92
Matinee '92
Another Stakeout '93
Me and the Kid '93
Pontiac Moon '94
Casper '95
Forget Paris '95

Michael Moriarty
My Old Man's Place '71
Bang the Drum Slowly '73
The Last Detail '73
Report to the Commissioner '74
Shoot It Black, Shoot It Blue '74
Holocaust '78
Reborn '78
Who'll Stop the Rain? '78
The Winds of Kitty Hawk '78
Too Far to Go '79
Q (The Winged Serpent) '82
Sound of Murder '82
Odd Birds '85
Pale Rider '85
The Stuff '85
Bloodlink '86
Troll '86
Dark Tower '87
Hanoi Hilton '87
It's Alive 3: Island of the Alive '87
Return to Salem's Lot '87
Nitti: The Enforcer '88
Windmills of the Gods '88
Secret of the Ice Cave '89
Tailspin: Behind the Korean Airline Tragedy '89
Full Fathom Five '90
A Good Day to Die '95
Courage Under Fire '96

Tara Morice
Strictly Ballroom '92
Sorrento Beach '95

Philippe Morier-Genoud
Confidentially Yours '83
Au Revoir Les Enfants '87
Cyrano de Bergerac '90

Patricia Morison
The Fallen Sparrow '43
Without Love '45
Dressed to Kill '46
Queen of the Amazons '47
Song of the Thin Man '47
The Prince of Thieves '48
Return of Wildfire '48
Song Without End '60

Noriyuki "Pat" Morita
Thoroughly Modern Millie '67
Cancel My Reservation '72
For the Love of It '80
When Time Ran Out '80
The Karate Kid '84
Slapstick of Another Kind '84
The Vegas Strip Wars '84
Amos '85
Night Patrol '85
Babes in Toyland '86
The Karate Kid: Part 2 '86
Captive Hearts '87
Collision Course '89
The Karate Kid: Part 3 '89
Hiroshima: Out of the Ashes '90
Lena's Holiday '90
Do or Die '91
Auntie Lee's Meat Pies '92
Honeymoon in Vegas '92
Miracle Beach '92
Even Cowgirls Get the Blues '94
The Next Karate Kid '94
North '94
Bloodsport 2: The Next Kumite '95
Timemaster '95

Louisa Moritz
One Flew Over the Cuckoo's Nest '75
New Year's Evil '78
True Confessions '81
Last American Virgin '82
Chained Heat '83

Henning Moritzen
Cries and Whispers '72
Memories of a Marriage '90
Sofie '92

Karen Morley
Scarface '31
The Sin of Madelon Claudet '31
The Mask of Fu Manchu '32
Mata Hari '32
Dinner at Eight '33
Gabriel Over the White House '33
Our Daily Bread '34
The Littlest Rebel '35
Beloved Enemy '36
Healer '36

Robert Morley
Marie Antoinette '38
Major Barbara '41
The Foreman Went to France '42
I Live in Grosvenor Square '46
Ghosts of Berkeley Square '47
The Small Back Room '49
The African Queen '51
Beat the Devil '53
Curtain Up '53
Beau Brummel '54
The Battle of the Sexes '60
Joseph & His Brethren '60
Ladies Who Do '63
Murder at the Gallop '63
Of Human Bondage '64
Topkapi '64
The Alphabet Murders '65
The Loved One '65
Those Magnificent Men in Their Flying Machines '65
A Study in Terror '66
Woman Times Seven '67
Hot Millions '68
Lola '69
Cromwell '70
Song of Norway '70
Theatre of Blood '73
Who Is Killing the Great Chefs of Europe? '78
The Human Factor '79
Scavenger Hunt '79
Oh, Heavenly Dog! '80
Deadly Game '82
High Road to China '83
Loophole '83
Second Time Lucky '84
The Trouble with Spies '87
The Wind '87
Little Dorrit, Film 1: Nobody's Fault '88
Little Dorrit, Film 2: Little Dorrit's Story '88
War & Remembrance, Part 1 '88
Around the World in 80 Days '89
War & Remembrance: The Final Chapter, Part 8 '89
Istanbul '90

Alicia Moro
Exterminators of the Year 3000 '83
Hot Blood '89

Mike Moroff
Angel Town '89
The Cage '89

Priscilla Morrill
The People vs. Jean Harris '81
Right of Way '84

Anita Morris
The Hotel New Hampshire '84
Maria's Lovers '84
Absolute Beginners '86
Blue City '86
Ruthless People '86
A Smoky Mountain Christmas '86
Aria '88
18 Again! '88
Bloodhounds of Broadway '89
A Sinful Life '89
Martians Go Home! '90
Little Miss Millions '93
Me and the Kid '93
Radioland Murders '94

Aubrey Morris
Night Caller from Outer Space '66
A Clockwork Orange '71
Lifeforce '85

Barboura Morris
Machine Gun Kelly '58
A Bucket of Blood '59
The Wasp Woman '59
Atlas '60

Chester Morris
The Bat Whispers '30
The Big House '30
The Divorcee '30
Corsair '31
Red Headed Woman '32
Tomorrow at Seven '33
Frankie and Johnny '36
Flight from Glory '37
Law of the Underworld '38
Five Came Back '39
Wagon's Westward '40
Seven Miles from Alcatraz/Flight from Glory '43
Gambler's Choice '44
Hunt the Man Down/Smashing the Rackets '50
The Great White Hope '70

Colleen Morris
Crossing the Line '90
Prehysteria '93

Garrett Morris
Saturday Night Live '70s
The Anderson Tapes '71
Cooley High '75
The Stuff '85
Husbands, Wives, Money, and Murder '86
The Underachievers '88
Motorama '91
Severed Ties '92
Almost Blue '93
Black Scorpion '95

Greg Morris
The Doomsday Flight '66
Vegas '78

Haviland Morris
Sixteen Candles '84
Who's That Girl? '87
For Love or Money '88
Love or Money? '88

Howard Morris
Andy Griffith Show '60
40 Pounds of Trouble '62
The Nutty Professor '63
High Anxiety '77
History of the World: Part 1 '81
The Munsters' Revenge '81
Portrait of a Showgirl '82
Splash '84
End of the Line '88
Life Stinks '91

Jane Morris
Nothing in Common '86
Pretty Woman '90
Frankie and Johnny '91
Pet Shop '94

Judy Morris
Between Wars '74
Cass '78
In Search of Anna '79
Plumber '79
Phar Lap '84
Razorback '84
Best Enemies '86

Kirk Morris
Maciste in Hell '60
Devil of the Desert Against the Son of Hercules '62
Triumph of the Son of Hercules '63
Terror of the Steppes '64

Lana Morris
The Gay Lady '49
The Weaker Sex '49

Mary Morris
Pimpernel Smith '42
Train of Events '49

Wayne Morris
Kid Galahad '37
Task Force '49
The Bushwackers '52
Paths of Glory '57
Plunder Road '57

Kenny Morrison
The Quick and the Dead '87
NeverEnding Story 2: The Next Chapter '91

Peter Morrison
Trailing Trouble '30
Trigger Tricks '30

Sammy Morrison
Flying Wild '41
Spooks Run Wild '41
Let's Get Tough '42
'Neath Brooklyn Bridge '42
Follow the Leader '44

Shelly Morrison
Castle of Evil '66
Devil Times Five '74

Temuera Morrison
Once Were Warriors '94
Barb Wire '96
The Island of Dr. Moreau '96

Jeff Morrow
The Robe '53
This Island Earth '55
The Creature Walks Among Us '56
Pardners '56
The Giant Claw '57
Hour of Decision '57
Kronos '57
The Story of Ruth '60

Morrow ▶cont.

Octaman '71

Jo Morrow
Legend of Tom Dooley '59
The Three Worlds of Gulliver '59
13 Ghosts '60
Dr. Death, Seeker of Souls '73

Patricia Morrow
The Kettles on Old MacDonald's Farm '57
Surf Party '64

Rob Morrow
Private Resort '84
Quiz Show '94
Last Dance '96

Susan Morrow
Canadian Mounties vs. Atomic Invaders '53
Cat Women of the Moon '53

Vic Morrow
Blackboard Jungle '55
Tribute to a Bad Man '56
Men in War '57
God's Little Acre '58
King Creole '58
Cimarron '60
Combat! '62
The Glass House '72
The Adventures of Tom Sawyer '73
Death Stalk '74
Dirty Mary Crazy Larry '74
Wanted: Babysitter '75
The Bad News Bears '76
The Treasure of Matecumbe '76
Curse of the Black Widow '77
Funeral for an Assassin '77
Wild & Wooly '78
The Evictors '79
Express to Terror '79
The Seekers '79
B.A.D. Cats '80
Humanoids from the Deep '80
1990: The Bronx Warriors '83
Twilight Zone: The Movie '83

Barry Morse
No Trace '50
The Fugitive: Premiere Episode '63
The Fugitive: The Final Episode '67
Asylum '72
Destination Moonbase Alpha '75
Space: 1999 '75
Love at First Sight '76
Welcome to Blood City '77
The Martian Chronicles: Part 2 '79
The Martian Chronicles: Part 3 '79
Space: 1999—Alien Attack '79
A Tale of Two Cities '80
Power Play '81
Sadat '83
Whoops Apocalypse '83
Glory! Glory! '90

David Morse
Inside Moves '80
Prototype '83
Shattered Vows '84
The Brotherhood of the Rose '89
Desperate Hours '90
The Indian Runner '91
Dead Ahead: The Exxon Valdez Disaster '92
The Getaway '93
The Good Son '93
The Crossing Guard '94
Stephen King's The Langoliers '95
Tecumseh: The Last Warrior '95
12 Monkeys '95
The Rock '96

Helen Morse
Picnic at Hanging Rock '75
Agatha '79
Caddie '81
Far East '85
A Town Like Alice '85
Iris '89

Robert Morse
The Matchmaker '58
The Loved One '65
A Guide for the Married Man '67
How to Succeed in Business without Really Trying '67
Oh Dad, Poor Dad (Momma's Hung You in the Closet & I'm Feeling So Sad) '67
Where Were You When the Lights Went Out? '68
The Boatniks '70
Cannon Movie Tales: The Emperor's New Clothes '89
Wild Palms '93

Glen Morshower
Drive-In '76
84 Charlie Mopic '89
Dominion '94

Viggo Mortensen
Salvation! '87
Prison '88
The Indian Runner '91
The Reflecting Skin '91
Deception '92
Boiling Point '93
Carlito's Way '93
The Young Americans '93
American Yakuza '94
The Crew '95
Crimson Tide '95
The Prophecy '95

Janne Mortil
Nightmare at Bittercreek '91
Johnny's Girl '95

Clive Morton
The Moonraker '58
A Matter of WHO '62

Joe Morton
The Brother from Another Planet '84
Crossroads '86
Trouble in Mind '86
Alone in the Neon Jungle '87
The Good Mother '88
Zelly & Me '88
Skin '89
Tap '89
City of Hope '91
Terminator 2: Judgment Day '91
Forever Young '92
Legacy of Lies '92
Of Mice and Men '92
The Inkwell '94
Speed '94
The Walking Dead '94
Lone Star '95
Executive Decision '96

Gastone Moschin
The Conformist '71
Mr. Superinvisible '73
A Woman at Her Window '77
A Joke of Destiny, Lying in Wait Around the Corner Like a Bandit '84

Maurice Moscovich
Everything Happens at Night '39
Love Affair '39
The Great Dictator '40
The Great Commandment '41

David Moscow
Big '88
Newsies '92

Bill Moseley
Osa '85
Fair Game '89
Silent Night, Deadly Night 3: Better Watch Out! '89
Crash and Burn '90

David Moses
Daring Dobermans '73
Scared to Death '80

Harry Moses
The Van '77
Sweater Girls '78

Marian Moses
Dead Heat on a Merry-Go-Round '66
Buona Sera, Mrs. Campbell '68

Mark Moses
The Tracker '88
Hollywood Heartbreak '89
Dead Men Don't Die '91
A Kiss Goodnight '94

William R. Moses
Alien from L.A. '87
Mystic Pizza '88
Double Exposure '93
Almost Dead '94
The Haunting of Seacliff Inn '94

Ivan Mosjoukine
Early Russian Cinema, Vol. 5: Chardynin's Pushkin '13
Early Russian Cinema, Vol. 10: The End of an Era '17

Roger E. Mosley
Mack '73
Darktown Strutters '74
The River Niger '76
The Greatest '77
I Know Why the Caged Bird Sings '79
The Jericho Mile '79
Attica '80
Magnum P.I.: Don't Eat the Snow in Hawaii '80
Pray TV '80
Steel '80
Heart Condition '90
Unlawful Entry '92
Pentathlon '94
A Thin Line Between Love and Hate '96

Arnold Moss
The Loves of Carmen '48
Reign of Terror '49
Viva Zapata! '52
The 27 Day '57
The Fool Killer '65

Elissabeth Moss
Midnight's Child '93
Imaginary Crimes '94
Separate Lives '94

Ron Moss
Hearts & Armour '83
Hard Ticket to Hawaii '87

Stewart Moss
Dr. Death, Seeker of Souls '73
The Bat People '74

Josh Mostel
The King of Marvin Gardens '72
Jesus Christ, Superstar '73
Harry and Tonto '74
Deadly Hero '75
Sophie's Choice '82
Star 80 '83
Windy City '84
Almost You '85
Compromising Positions '85
Stoogemania '85
The Money Pit '86
Radio Days '87
Wall Street '87
Animal Behavior '89
Heavy Petting '89
City of Hope '91
City Slickers '91
Little Man Tate '91
The Chase '93
The Basketball Diaries '94
Billy Madison '94
City Slickers 2: The Legend of Curly's Gold '94

Zero Mostel
DuBarry Was a Lady '43
Panic in the Streets '50
The Enforcer '51
Sirocco '51
A Funny Thing Happened on the Way to the Forum '66
The Producers '68
The Hot Rock '70
Marco '73
Master Mind '73
Once Upon a Scoundrel '73
Journey into Fear '74
Foreplay '75
The Front '76

Zeze Motta
Xica '76
Quilombo '84

John Moulder-Brown
Deep End '70
First Love '70
Vampire Circus '71
King, Queen, Knave '72
Killing Heat '84
Rumpelstiltskin '86

Movita
Mutiny on the Bounty '35
Rose of Rio Grande '38
Wolf Call '39
Tower of Terror '42
Panic in Echo Park '77

Alan Mowbray
A Study in Scarlet '33
The Girl from Missouri '34
In Person '35
Desire '36
It Happened in New Orleans '36
Mary of Scotland '36
My Man Godfrey '36
On the Avenue '37
Stand-In '37
Vogues of 1938 '37
Topper Takes a Trip '39
Way Down South '39
Music in My Heart '40
I Wake Up Screaming '41
That Hamilton Woman '41
That Uncertain Feeling '41
The Villain Still Pursued Her '41
Panama Hattie '42
His Butler's Sister '43
So This is Washington '43
The Phantom of 42nd Street '45
Merton of the Movies '47
The Prince of Thieves '48
Abbott and Costello Meet the Killer, Boris Karloff '49
The Lovable Cheat '49
My Dear Secretary '49
Ma and Pa Kettle at Home '54
The King's Thief '55
The King and I '56
A Majority of One '56
The Man Who Knew Too Much '56

Jack Mower
Ships in the Night '28
The Fiddlin' Buckaroo '33
Mystery Squadron '33

Patrick Mower
The Bloodsuckers '70
Cry of the Banshee '70
Catch Me a Spy '71
Carry On England '76

Maureen Mueller
In a Shallow Grave '88
The New Age '94
Oldest Confederate Widow Tells All '95

Armin Mueller-Stahl
Colonel Redl '84
A Love in Germany '84
Angry Harvest '85
Forget Mozart '85
Lethal Obsession '87
Midnight Cop '88
Music Box '89
Avalon '90
Kafka '91
Night on Earth '91
The Power of One '92
The House of the Spirits '93
Utz '93
Holy Matrimony '94
The Last Good Time '94
A Pyromaniac's Love Story '95
Red Hot '95
Theodore Rex '95

Anita Mui
The Heroic Trio '93
Rumble in the Bronx '96

Esther Muir
Racing Luck '35
Misbehaving Husbands '41

Gavin Muir
Mary of Scotland '36
Sherlock Holmes Faces Death '43
House of Fear '45
Abbott and Costello Meet the Invisible Man '51
Night Tide '63

Diana Muldaur
The Other '72
McQ '74
Planet Earth '74
Beyond Reason '77
Return of Frank Cannon '80

Kate Mulgrew
The Word '78
Lovespell '79
A Time for Miracles '80
The Manions of America '81
A Stranger is Watching '82
Remo Williams: The Adventure Begins '85
Throw Momma from the Train '87
Roots: The Gift '88
Round Numbers '91
Danielle Steel's "Daddy" '92
Camp Nowhere '94
Star Trek Voyager: Caretaker '95

Jack Mulhall
Hell's Headquarters '32
Murder on the High Seas '32
Mystery Squadron '33
Burn 'Em Up Barnes '34
Skull & Crown '35
The Clutching Hand '36
Custer's Last Stand '36
A Face in the Fog '36
Kelly of the Secret Service '36
Rogue's Tavern '36
100 Men and a Girl '37
Radio Patrol '37
Tim Tyler's Luck '37
Outlaws of Sonora '38
Desperate Cargo '41
Dawn Express '42
I Killed That Man '42
Mr. Wise Guy '42
'Neath Canadian Skies '46
North of the Border '46

Edward Mulhare
Hill 24 Doesn't Answer '55
Von Ryan's Express '65
Our Man Flint '66
Megaforce '82

Chris Mulkey
Jack's Back '87
Heartbreak Hotel '88
In Dangerous Company '88
Patti Rocks '88
Tricks of the Trade '88
K-9000 '89
Roe vs. Wade '89
Rainbow Drive '90
Runaway Father '91
Write to Kill '91
Deadbolt '92
Gas Food Lodging '92
The Silencer '92
Bound and Gagged: A Love Story '93
Ghost in the Machine '93
Dead Cold '96

Martin Mull
FM '78
My Bodyguard '80
Serial '80
Take This Job & Shove It '81
Mr. Mom '83
Bad Manners '84
Clue '85
Flicks '85
The History of White People in America '85
The History of White People in America: Vol. 2 '85
Lots of Luck '85
The Boss' Wife '86
Pecos Bill '86
O.C. and Stiggs '87
Home Is Where the Hart Is '88
Portrait of a White Marriage '88
Rented Lips '88
Cutting Class '89
Far Out Man '89
Ski Patrol '89
Think Big '90
Dance with Death '91
Miracle Beach '92
Mr. Write '92
The Day My Parents Ran Away '93
How the West was Fun '95

Jack Mullaney
The Honeymoon Machine '61
Tickle Me '65
Spinout '66
George! '70

Greg Mullavey
Chrome Hearts '70
The Love Machine '71
I Dismember Mama '74
Husbands, Wives, Money, and Murder '86
Body Count '87
Not Quite Human 2 '89
Deadly Conspiracy '91

Patty Mullen
Doom Asylum '88
Frankenhooker '90

Harrison Muller
The Final Executioner '83
She '83
Violent Breed '83
2020 Texas Gladiators '85
Miami Cops '89

Paul Muller
Two Nights with Cleopatra '54
The Black Devils of Kali '55
The Devil's Commandment '56
Four Ways Out '57
Goliath and the Sins of Babylon '64
Nightmare Castle '65
Fangs of the Living Dead '68
Virgin Among the Living Dead '71
Lady Frankenstein '72
Naked Warriors '73

Richard Mulligan
The Group '66
The Best of Soap: Jessica's Wonderful Life '70s
Little Big Man '70
The Hideaways '73
Pueblo Affair '73
The Big Bus '76
The Best of Soap: Who Killed Peter? '77
Scavenger Hunt '79
S.O.B. '81
Meatballs 2 '84
Micki & Maude '84
Teachers '84
Doin' Time '85
The Heavenly Kid '85
Babes in Toyland '86
A Fine Mess '86
Poker Alice '87
Gore Vidal's Lincoln '88

Rod Mullinar
Patrick '78
Breakfast in Paris '81
Echoes of Paradise '86
Dead Calm '89

Dermot Mulroney
Sunset '88
Young Guns '88
Staying Together '89
Survival Quest '89
Longtime Companion '90
Bright Angel '91
Career Opportunities '91
Samantha '92
Silent Tongue '92
There Goes My Baby '92
Where the Day Takes You '92
Family Pictures '93
The Last Outlaw '93
Point of No Return '93
The Thing Called Love '93
Bad Girls '94
Living in Oblivion '94
Copycat '95
How to Make an American Quilt '95
The Trigger Effect '96

Kieran Mulroney
Nowhere to Run '88
Career Opportunities '91
Sensation '94
The Immortals '95
The Spitfire Grill '95

Danny Mummert
Blondie Takes a Vacation '39
Blondie Has Trouble '40
Blondie in Society '41
Blondie's Blessed Event '42
It's a Great Life '43
Blondie Knows Best '46
Blondie Hits the Jackpot '49

Billy Mumy
Sammy, the Way-Out Seal '62
Dear Brigitte '65
Bless the Beasts and Children '71
Twilight Zone: The Movie '83

Herbert Mundin
Cavalcade '33
Mutiny on the Bounty '35
The Adventures of Robin Hood '38

Ian Mune
Sleeping Dogs '82
Dangerous Orphans '86

Paul Muni
Scarface '31
I Am a Fugitive from a Chain Gang '32
Black Fury '35
The Story of Louis Pasteur '36
The Good Earth '37
The Life of Emile Zola '37
Juarez '39
Commandos Strike at Dawn '43
Stage Door Canteen '43
A Song to Remember '45
Angel on My Shoulder '46
The Last Angry Man '59

Pep Munne
Where Time Began '77
Barcelona '94

Caroline Munro
Gun Crazy '69
The Abominable Dr. Phibes '71
Golden Voyage of Sinbad '73
Captain Kronos: Vampire Hunter '74
I Don't Want to Be Born '75
At the Earth's Core '76
The Spy Who Loved Me '77
Star Crash '78
Maniac '80
The Last Horror Film '82
Don't Open Till Christmas '84
Slaughter High '86
Black Cat '90

Janet Munro
Small Hotel '57
The Crawling Eye '58
The Young and the Guilty '58
Darby O'Gill & the Little People '59
Third Man on the Mountain '59
The Swiss Family Robinson '60
The Day the Earth Caught Fire '61
Horsemasters '61

Lochlyn Munro
Trancers 5: Sudden Deth '94
Wagons East '94

Neil Munro
Confidential '86
Dancing in the Dark '86
Beethoven Lives Upstairs '92
Gate 2 '92

Jules Munshin
Easter Parade '48
Take Me Out to the Ball Game '49
That Midnight Kiss '49

Ona Munson
Gone with the Wind '39
Wagon's Westward '40
Lady from Louisiana '42
The Shanghai Gesture '42
Idaho '43
Dakota '45
The Red House '47

Jim Henson's Muppets
The Muppet Movie '79
The Great Muppet Caper '81
The Muppets Take Manhattan '84
Sesame Street Presents: Follow That Bird '85

Jean Murat
Carnival in Flanders '35
Eternal Return '43
Rich, Young and Pretty '51

Takehiro Murata
Minbo—Or the Gentle Art of Japanese Extortion '92
Okoge '93

George Murcell
Year of the Gun '91
Cutthroat Island '95

Vince Murdocco
Flesh Gordon 2: Flesh Gordon Meets the Cosmic Cheerleaders '90
Ring of Fire '91
Ring of Fire 2: Blood and Steel '92
L.A. Wars '94

George Murdock
Breaker! Breaker! '77
In Love with an Older Woman '82
Strange Case of Dr. Jekyll & Mr. Hyde '89
Grand Tour: Disaster in Time '92
Firepower '93

Christopher Murney
The Last Dragon '85
Maximum Overdrive '86
Murder by the Book '87
Barton Fink '91
The Ten Million Dollar Getaway '91

Peter Murnik
Body Parts '91
Golden Gate '93
Andersonville '95

Audie Murphy
The Red Badge of Courage '51
To Hell and Back '55
The Unforgiven '60
Arizona Raiders '65

Barri Murphy
Action U.S.A. '89
Armed for Action '92

Ben Murphy
Riding with Death '76
The Chisholms '79
Time Walker '82
The Cradle Will Fall '83
The Winds of War '83

Eddie Murphy
48 Hrs. '82
Trading Places '83
Best Defense '84
Beverly Hills Cop '84
The Golden Child '86
Beverly Hills Cop 2 '87
Eddie Murphy: Raw '87
Coming to America '88
Best of Eddie Murphy '89
Harlem Nights '89
Another 48 Hrs. '90
Boomerang '92
The Distinguished Gentleman '92
Beverly Hills Cop 3 '94
Vampire in Brooklyn '95
The Nutty Professor '96

George Murphy
Kid Millions '34
Broadway Melody of 1938 '37
Letter of Introduction '38
Little Miss Broadway '38
Broadway Melody of 1940 '40
Little Nellie Kelly '40
A Girl, a Guy and a Gob '41
Tom, Dick, and Harry '41
For Me and My Gal '42
The Navy Comes Through '42
Bataan '43
This Is the Army '43
Broadway Rhythm '44
Show Business '44
Step Lively '44
Having Wonderful Crime '45
The Devil Thumbs a Ride/Having Wonderful Crime '47
Battleground '49

Horace Murphy
Last of the Warrens '36
Undercover Man '36
Boothill Brigade '37
Border Phantom '37
Wide Open Faces '38
Down the Wyoming Trail '39

Jimmy Murphy
Jet Attack/Paratroop Command '58
Platinum High School '60

Johnny Murphy
The Commitments '91
War of the Buttons '95

Mary Murphy
Carrie '52
Houdini '53
Main Street to Broadway '53
The Wild One '54
Desperate Hours '55
A Man Alone '55
The Maverick Queen '55
The Electronic Monster '57
40 Pounds of Trouble '62

Maurice Murphy
Found Alive '34
Tailspin Tommy '34
Delinquent Parents '38
Abe Lincoln in Illinois '40

Michael Murphy
Double Trouble '67
Countdown '68
That Cold Day in the Park '69
Brewster McCloud '70
Count Yorga, Vampire '70
McCabe & Mrs. Miller '71
The Thief Who Came to Dinner '73
The Autobiography of Miss Jane Pittman '74
Phase 4 '74
Nashville '75
The Front '76
The Class of Miss MacMichael '78
Great Bank Hoax '78
An Unmarried Woman '78
Hot Money '79
Manhattan '79
Strange Behavior '81
Talk to Me '82
The Year of Living Dangerously '82
Cloak & Dagger '84
Mesmerized '84
Salvador '86
The Caine Mutiny Court Martial '88
Tanner '88 '88
Shocker '89
Tailspin: Behind the Korean Airline Tragedy '89
Batman Returns '92
Dead Ahead: The Exxon Valdez Disaster '92
Folks! '92
Clean Slate '94

M.R. Murphy
In Deadly Heat '87
Stuff Stephanie in the Incinerator '89

Rosemary Murphy
To Kill a Mockingbird '62
Any Wednesday '66
Ben '72
Walking Tall '73
Eleanor & Franklin '76
Julia '77
The Attic '80
For the Boys '91
A Woman Named Jackie '91
The Tuskegee Airmen '95

Timothy Patrick Murphy
The Seekers '79
Sam's Son '84
Doin' Time on Planet Earth '88

Barbara Murray
Tony Draws a Horse '51
Death Goes to School '53
A Cry from the Streets '57
The Bretts '88

Bill Murray
Meatballs '79
Mr. Mike's Mondo Video '79
Caddyshack '80
Loose Shoes '80
Where the Buffalo Roam '80
Stripes '81
Tootsie '82
Ghostbusters '84
The Razor's Edge '84
Little Shop of Horrors '86
Scrooged '88
Ghostbusters 2 '89
Quick Change '90
What About Bob? '91
Groundhog Day '93
Mad Dog and Glory '93
Ed Wood '94
Kingpin '96

Don Murray
Bus Stop '56
Shake Hands with the Devil '59
The Hoodlum Priest '61
Advise and Consent '62
One Man's Way '63
Baby, the Rain Must Fall '64
Sweet Love, Bitter '67
Confessions of Tom Harris '72
Conquest of the Planet of the Apes '72
Cotter '72
Deadly Hero '75
Rainbow '78
If Things Were Different '79
Endless Love '81
Justin Morgan Had a Horse '81
Return of the Rebels '81
I Am the Cheese '83
License to Kill '84
Quarterback Princess '85
Peggy Sue Got Married '86
Radioactive Dreams '86
Scorpion '86
Something in Common '86
Made in Heaven '87
Mistress '87
Ghosts Can't Do It '90
Kickboxer the Champion '91

James Murray
The Crowd '28
Baby Face '33
High Gear '33
Skull & Crown '35

Joel Murray
One Crazy Summer '86
Elvis Stories '89

Ken Murray
The Marshal's Daughter '53
The Man Who Shot Liberty Valance '62
Follow Me, Boys! '66

Stephen Murray
Alice in Wonderland '50
Four Sided Triangle '53
Elizabeth R '72

Lionel Murton
Meet the Navy '46
Carry On Admiral '57

Tony Musante
The Incident '67
The Detective '68
The Bird with the Crystal Plumage '70
The Grissom Gang '71
Fatal Chase '77
Breaking Up Is Hard to Do '79
High Ice '80
The Pope of Greenwich Village '84
Collector's Item '89

Clarence Muse
Prison Train '38
Way Down South '39
Broken Strings '40
That Gang of Mine '40
Gentleman from Dixie '41
A Dream for Christmas '73
The Black Stallion '79

Ornella Muti
Leonor '75
Life Is Beautiful '79
Summer Affair '79
Flash Gordon '80
Tales of Ordinary Madness '83
Swann in Love '84
Casanova '87
Hitchhiker 3 '87
Wait Until Spring, Bandini '90
Oscar '91
Once Upon a Crime '92

Klaus Mutter
Thundering Ninja '80s
Clash of the Ninja '86

Carmel Myers
Beau Brummel '24
Ben-Hur '26
Chinatown After Dark '31
Pleasure '31

Harry Myers
The Marriage Circle '24
City Lights '31
Convicted '32
The Savage Girl '32
Rainbow Over Broadway '33

Kim Myers
A Nightmare on Elm Street 2: Freddy's Revenge '85
White Palace '90
Hellraiser 4: Bloodline '95

Mike Myers
Wayne's World '92
So I Married an Axe Murderer '93

Shattered Vows '84
An Unremarkable Life '89
Caroline? '90
Heidi '93

Peggy Neal
Terror Beneath the Sea '66
X from Outer Space '67

Tom Neal
Andy Hardy Meets Debutante '40
Courageous Dr. Christian '40
Bowery at Midnight '42
Miracle Kid '42
Behind the Rising Sun '43
First Yank into Tokyo '45
The Brute Man '46
Club Havana '46
Detour '46
My Dog Shep '46
Case of the Baby Sitter '47
Hat Box Mystery '47
Trail of the Mounties '47
Great Jesse James Raid '49
Apache Chief '50
I Shot Billy the Kid '50
Radar Secret Service '50
Red Desert '50
Train to Tombstone '50
Danger Zone '51
Fingerprints Don't Lie '51
G.I. Jane '51
King of the Bullwhip '51
Stop That Cab '51
Varieties on Parade '52

Kevin Nealon
Roxanne '87
All I Want for Christmas '91
Happy Gilmore '96

Christopher Neame
Steel Dawn '87
Bloodstone '88
D.O.A. '88
Transformations '88
Edge of Honor '91
Suburban Commando '91
Boris and Natasha: The Movie '92
Still Not Quite Human '92
Street Knight '93
Hellbound '94
Project Shadowchaser 3000 '95

Vaclav Neckar
Closely Watched Trains '66
Larks on a String '68

Ted Neeley
Jesus Christ, Superstar '73
Shadow of Chikara '77
Hard Country '81
Of Mice and Men '81

Liam Neeson
Excalibur '81
Krull '83
The Bounty '84
Lamb '85
Duet for One '86
The Mission '86
Prayer for the Dying '87
Suspect '87
The Dead Pool '88
The Good Mother '88
High Spirits '88
Satisfaction '88
Next of Kin '89
Darkman '90
The Big Man: Crossing the Line '91
Deception '92
Ethan Frome '92
Husbands and Wives '92
Leap of Faith '92
Shining Through '92
Under Suspicion '92
Schindler's List '93
Nell '94
Before and After '95
Rob Roy '95

Hildegarde Neff
Diplomatic Courier '52
The Snows of Kilimanjaro '52
Unnatural '52
Svengali '55
The Three Penny Opera '62
Bluebeard '63

Natalia Negoda
Little Vera '88
Back in the USSR '92
The Comrades of Summer '92

Francois Negret
Au Revoir Les Enfants '87
Night and Day '91

Pola Negri
Gypsy Blood '18
Passion '19
One Arabian Night '21
Hotel Imperial '27
Hi Diddle Diddle '43
The Moon-Spinners '64

Mary Joan Negro
The Family Man '79
No Big Deal '83

Taylor Negron
Easy Money '83
Bad Medicine '85
Better Off Dead '85
Punchline '88
The Last Boy Scout '91
Nothing But Trouble '91
Mr. Stitch '95

David Neidorf
Hoosiers '86
Undercover '87

Hildegarde Neil
The Man Who Haunted Himself '70
Antony and Cleopatra '73
A Touch of Class '73

Noel Neill
Here Come the Waves '44
The Stork Club '45
The Adventures of Frank and Jesse James '48
Superman: The Serial, Vol. 1 '48
TV's Best Adventures of Superman '51

Sam Neill
My Brilliant Career '79
The Final Conflict '81
Possession '81
Enigma '82
Ivanhoe '82
Sleeping Dogs '82
Attack Force Z '84
The Blood of Others '84
Plenty '85
For Love Alone '86
The Good Wife '86
Reilly: Ace of Spies '87
A Cry in the Dark '88
Dead Calm '89
Death in Brunswick '90
The Hunt for Red October '90
Fever '91
One Against the Wind '91
Until The End of The World '91
Hostage '92
Memoirs of an Invisible Man '92
Family Pictures '93
Jurassic Park '93
The Piano '93
Question of Faith '93
Rainbow Warrior '94
Restoration '94
Rudyard Kipling's The Jungle Book '94
Sirens '94
Country Life '95
In the Mouth of Madness '95

Stacey Nelkin
The Triangle Factory Fire Scandal '79
Children of Divorce '80
Up the Academy '80
Halloween 3: Season of the Witch '82

Nathalie Nell
Rape of Love '79
Echoes '83

Kate Nelligan
The Count of Monte Cristo '74
Romantic Englishwoman '75
Bethune '77
Dracula '79
Eye of the Needle '81
Crossover '82
Without a Trace '83
Eleni '85
Control '87
Love and Hate: A Marriage Made in Hell '90
Frankie and Johnny '91
The Prince of Tides '91
Diamond Fleece '92

Shadows and Fog '92
Fatal Instinct '93
Terror Stalks the Class Reunion '93
Wolf '94
How to Make an American Quilt '95
Margaret's Museum '95
A Mother's Prayer '95
Up Close and Personal '96

Ann Nelson
Ghosts That Still Walk '77
My Girl '91

Barry Nelson
Shadow of the Thin Man '41
Johnny Eager '42
The Human Comedy '43
Airport '70
Pete 'n' Tillie '72
Island Claw '80
The Shining '80

Bob Nelson
Sorceress '82
Miracles '86
Ryder P.I. '88
Brain Donors '92

Bobby Nelson
Roaring Ranch '30
Cowboy & the Bandit '35
Cyclone of the Saddle '35
Ghost Rider '35
Way of the West '35
Boothill Brigade '37
The Red Rope '37

Craig Richard Nelson
The Paper Chase '73
The Grass is Always Greener Over the Septic Tank '78
My Bodyguard '80

Craig T. Nelson
And Justice for All '79
Private Benjamin '80
Rage '80
Stir Crazy '80
Murder in Texas '81
Poltergeist '82
All the Right Moves '83
Man, Woman & Child '83
The Osterman Weekend '83
Silkwood '83
Call to Glory '84
The Killing Fields '84
Poltergeist 2: The Other Side '86
Rachel River '87
Action Jackson '88
Red Riding Hood '88
Cannon Movie Tales: Red Riding Hood '89
Me and Him '89
Murderers among Us: The Simon Wiesenthal Story '89
Troop Beverly Hills '89
Turner and Hooch '89
The Josephine Baker Story '90
The Fire Next Time '93
Probable Cause '95

David Nelson
The Adventures of Ozzie & Harriet '50s
Peyton Place '57
High School USA '84
Cry-Baby '90

Ed Nelson
Invasion of the Saucer Men '57
The Devil's Partner '58
Night of the Blood Beast '58
A Bucket of Blood '59
T-Bird Gang '59
Soldier in the Rain '63
Shining Star '75
For the Love of Benji '77
Anatomy of a Seduction '79
Enola Gay: The Men, the Mission, the Atomic Bomb '80
Return of Frank Cannon '80
Brenda Starr '86
Deadly Weapon '88
The Bone Yard '90

Gene Nelson
Tea for Two '50
The West Point Story '50
Lullaby of Broadway '51
Oklahoma! '55
The Atomic Man '56
The Way Out '56

Harriet Hilliard Nelson
Follow the Fleet '36
Take It Big '44
The Adventures of Ozzie & Harriet '50s
The Kid with the 200 I.Q. '83

Herbert Nelson
When the North Wind Blows '74
Future Cop '76

John Allen Nelson
Hunk '87
Killer Klowns from Outer Space '88
Saigon Commandos '88
Deathstalker 3 '89

Judd Nelson
Making the Grade '84
The Breakfast Club '85
Fandango '85
St. Elmo's Fire '85
Blue City '86
From the Hip '86
Billionaire Boys Club '87
Far Out Man '89
Relentless '89
Hiroshima: Out of the Ashes '90
The Dark Backward '91
New Jack City '91
Conflict of Interest '92
Primary Motive '92
Caroline at Midnight '93
Entangled '93
Every Breath '93
Airheads '94
Blindfold: Acts of Obsession '94
Flinch '94
Hail Caesar '94
Circumstances Unknown '95

Lloyd Nelson
Man Beast '55
The Incredible Petrified World '58
Curse of the Stone Hand '64
The Wild World of Batwoman '66

Lori Nelson
Francis Goes to West Point '52
Ma and Pa Kettle at the Fair '52
Day the World Ended '55
I Died a Thousand Times '55
Ma and Pa Kettle at Waikiki '55
Revenge of the Creature '55
Hot Rod Girl '56
Mohawk '56
Pardners '56
The Pied Piper of Hamelin '57

Margaret Nelson
Picnic at Hanging Rock '75
Scalp Merchant '77

Ozzie Nelson
Big Street '42
Take It Big '44
People Are Funny '46
The Adventures of Ozzie & Harriet '50s
The Impossible Years '68

Peter Nelson
V '83
Crime Zone '88
The Expendables '89
Silk 2 '89
Eye of the Eagle 3 '91
Sounds of Silence '91

Ricky Nelson
The Adventures of Ozzie & Harriet '50s
Rio Bravo '59
Wackiest Ship in the Army '61

Ruth Nelson
Wilson '44
Humoresque '46
A Christmas Without Snow '80
The Haunting Passion '83

Tracy Nelson
Yours, Mine & Ours '68
Maria's Lovers '84
Down and Out in Beverly Hills '86
The Game of Love '90

Willie Nelson
The Electric Horseman '79
Honeysuckle Rose '80
Thief '81
Barbarosa '82
Coming Out of the Ice '82
Hell's Angels Forever '83

Songwriter '84
Amazons '86
Last Days of Frank & Jesse James '86
Stagecoach '86
Baja Oklahoma '87
Red Headed Stranger '87
Dynamite and Gold '88
Pair of Aces '90
Texas Guns '90
Another Pair of Aces: Three of a Kind '91

Corin "Corky" Nemec
Tucker: The Man and His Dream '88
Solar Crisis '92
Drop Zone '94
Stephen King's The Stand '94
White Wolves 2: Legend of the Wild '94
Operation Dumbo Drop '95

Francesca Neri
Flight of the Innocent '93
Outrage '93

Rosalba (Sara Bay) Neri
Conquest of Mycene '63
The Castle of Fu Manchu '68
The Seducers '70
Slaughter Hotel '71
Lady Frankenstein '72
Devil's Wedding Night '73
Naked Warriors '73

David Nerman
The Scorpio Factor '90
Witchboard 3: The Possession '95

Franco Nero
Wild, Wild Planet '65
The Bible...In the Beginning '66
Camelot '67
Django '68
Battle of Neretva '69
Spaghetti Western '69
Tristana '70
The Virgin and the Gypsy '70
Devil's Crude '71
Confessions of a Police Captain '72
Fifth Day of Peace '72
Ring of Death '72
High Crime '73
Redneck '73
Blood Brothers '74
Falcon '74
Legend of Valentino '75
Sardinia Kidnapped '75
21 Hours at Munich '76
Last Four Days '77
Submission '77
Force 10 from Navarone '78
Street Law '79
The Man with Bogart's Face '80
Enter the Ninja '81
The Salamander '82
Querelle '83
Day of the Cobra '84
Shark Hunter '84
Wagner: The Movie '85
Challenge to White Fang '86
The Girl '86
Sweet Country '87
Magdalene '88
Windmills of the Gods '88
Die Hard 2: Die Harder '90
Young Catherine '91

Toni Nero
Silent Night, Deadly Night '84
No Dead Heroes '87

Cathleen Nesbitt
The Passing of the Third Floor Back '36
Men of Two Worlds '46
Nicholas Nickleby '46
Man of Evil '48
Desiree '54
An Affair to Remember '57
Separate Tables '58
Promise Her Anything '66

Derren Nesbitt
Horrors of Burke & Hare '71
Funny Money '82

Michael Nesmith
Head '68

Nesmith ▶cont.

Doctor Duck's Super Secret All-Purpose Sauce '85

Lois Nettleton
Period of Adjustment '62
The Bamboo Saucer '68
The Good Guys and the Bad Guys '69
The Man in the Glass Booth '75
Deadly Blessing '81
The Best Little Whorehouse in Texas '82
Butterfly '82
Soggy Bottom U.S.A. '84
Brass '85
Manhunt for Claude Dallas '86
Mirror, Mirror 2: Raven Dance '94

Martin Neufeld
H '90
Relative Fear '95

Jenny Neumann
Mistress of the Apes '79
Swim Team '79
Hell Night '81
Stage Fright '83
Delos Adventure '86

Bebe Neuwirth
Say Anything '89
Green Card '90
Bugsy '91
Malice '93
The Paint Job '93
Wild Palms '93
Jumanji '95
The Adventures of Pinocchio '96

Aaron Neville
Zandalee '91
The Last Ride '94

John Neville
Billy Budd '62
The Unearthly Stranger '64
A Study in Terror '66
The Adventures of Baron Munchausen '89
Baby's Day Out '94
Little Women '94
The Road to Wellville '94
Song Spinner '95

Robyn Nevin
Fourth Wish '75
The Irishman '78
Careful, He Might Hear You '84
Angel Baby '95

Claudette Nevins
The Mask '61
The Possessed '77
Take Your Best Shot '82
Child of Darkness, Child of Light '91
Sleeping with the Enemy '91

Derek Newark
The Offence '73
Bellman and True '88

George Newbern
Adventures in Babysitting '87
My Little Girl '87
It Takes Two '88
Paramedics '88
Switching Channels '88
Doppelganger: The Evil Within '90
Father of the Bride '91
Witness to the Execution '94
Father of the Bride Part II '95

Anthony Newcastle
Captive Planet '78
Metallica '85

William Newell
The Mandarin Mystery '37
Doctor Satan's Robot '40
The Invisible Killer '40
Escape from Fort Bravo '53

Bob Newhart
Hell is for Heroes '62
Hot Millions '68
Catch-22 '70
On a Clear Day You Can See Forever '70
Cold Turkey '71
Thursday's Game '74
First Family '80
Little Miss Marker '80
Marathon '80

James Newill
Renfrew of the Royal Mounted '37
Renfrew on the Great White Trail '38
Fighting Mad '39
Danger Ahead '40
Murder on the Yukon '40
Sky Bandits '40
Yukon Flight '40
The Great American Broadcast '41
Fighting Valley '43
Rangers Take Over '43
Boss of Rawhide '44
Guns of the Law '44
Outlaw Roundup '44

Anthony Newlands
Circus of Fear '67
Scream and Scream Again '70

Anthony Newley
Little Ballerina '47
Oliver Twist '48
Above Us the Waves '56
Fire Down Below '57
Let's Get Married '63
Doctor Dolittle '67
The Old Curiosity Shop '75
Blade in Hong Kong '85
Outrage! '86
Stagecoach '86
The Garbage Pail Kids Movie '87
Boris and Natasha: The Movie '92

Barry Newman
Vanishing Point '71
The Salzburg Connection '72
City on Fire '78
Amy '81
Deadline '81
Having It All '82
Fatal Vision '84

Laraine Newman
Saturday Night Live '70s
Tunnelvision '76
Mr. Mike's Mondo Video '79
Wholly Moses! '80
Her Life as a Man '83
Perfect '85
Invaders from Mars '86
Problem Child 2 '91
Coneheads '93
Revenge of the Red Baron '93
Witchboard 2: The Devil's Doorway '93

Nanette Newman
The Wrong Arm of the Law '63
The Madwoman of Chaillot '69
Long Ago Tomorrow '71
The Mystery of Edwin Drood '93

Paul Newman
The Silver Chalice '54
Bang the Drum Slowly '56
Somebody Up There Likes Me '56
Until They Sail '57
Cat on a Hot Tin Roof '58
The Left-Handed Gun '58
The Long, Hot Summer '58
The Young Philadelphians '59
Exodus '60
From the Terrace '60
The Hustler '61
Paris Blues '61
Sweet Bird of Youth '62
Hud '63
A New Kind of Love '63
The Prize '63
Lady L '65
Harper '66
Torn Curtain '66
Cool Hand Luke '67
Hombre '67
The Secret War of Harry Frigg '68
Butch Cassidy and the Sundance Kid '69
Winning '69
Sometimes a Great Notion '71
Life & Times of Judge Roy Bean '72
Pocket Money '72
Mackintosh Man '73
The Sting '73
The Towering Inferno '74
The Drowning Pool '75
Buffalo Bill & the Indians '76
Silent Movie '76
Slap Shot '77
Quintet '79
When Time Ran Out '80
Absence of Malice '81
Fort Apache, the Bronx '81
The Verdict '82
Harry & Son '84
The Color of Money '86
Blaze '89
Fat Man and Little Boy '89
Mr. & Mrs. Bridge '90
The Hudsucker Proxy '93
Nobody's Fool '94

Phyllis Newman
Picnic '55
Follies in Concert '85
A Secret Space '88

Stephen D. Newman
Sophie's Choice '82
Yuri Nosenko, KGB '86

Julie Newmar
Seven Brides for Seven Brothers '54
Li'l Abner '59
For Love or Money '63
MacKenna's Gold '69
Terraces '77
Hysterical '83
Ecstasy '84
Evils of the Night '85
Streetwalkin' '85
Deep Space '87
Nudity Required '90
Oblivion '94
Backlash: Oblivion 2 '95

John Haymes Newton
Desert Kickboxer '92
Alive '93

Margit Evelyn Newton
The Last Hunter '80
Night of the Zombies '83

Robert Newton
21 Days '37
Beachcomber '38
Jamaica Inn '39
Henry V '44
Odd Man Out '47
This Happy Breed '47
Oliver Twist '48
The Hidden Room '49
Treasure Island '50
Tom Brown's School Days '51
Androcles and the Lion '52
Blackbeard the Pirate '52
The Desert Rats '53
Long John Silver '53
Around the World in 80 Days '56

Thandie Newton
Flirting '89
The Young Americans '93
Jefferson in Paris '94
The Journey of August King '95
Loaded '96

Theodore Newton
Ace of Aces '33
The Sphinx '33
The Sphinx '33

Wayne Newton
License to Kill '89
The Adventures of Ford Fairlane '90
The Dark Backward '91
Best of the Best 2 '93

Olivia Newton-John
Grease '78
Xanadu '80
Two of a Kind '83
It's My Party '95

Richard Ney
Mrs. Miniver '42
The Lovable Cheat '49
Premature Burial '62

Marina Neyelova
The Errors of Youth '78
Autumn Marathon '79

Haing S. Ngor
The Killing Fields '84
The Iron Triangle '89
Last Flight Out: A True Story '90
Vietnam, Texas '90
Ambition '91
In Love and War '91
Heaven and Earth '93
My Life '93
Fortunes of War '94

Dustin Nguyen
Rapid Fire '92
Heaven and Earth '93
No Escape, No Return '93
3 Ninjas Kick Back '94

Michelle Nicastro
Body Rock '84
Bad Guys '86
When Harry Met Sally... '89

Maurizio Nichetti
Allegro Non Troppo '76
The Icicle Thief '89
Volere Volare '92
Stephano Quantestorie '93

Angela Nicholas
Galactic Gigolo '87
Alien Space Avenger '91

Nicholas Brothers
Stormy Weather '43
The Pirate '48

Denise Nicholas
Blacula '72
Let's Do It Again '75
Piece of the Action '77
Sophisticated Gents '81
And the Children Shall Lead '85
Ghost Dad '90

Harold Nicholas
Fass Black '77
Tap '89
The Five Heartbeats '91

Paul Nicholas
Invitation to the Wedding '73
Lisztomania '75
Yesterday's Hero '79
The World is Full of Married Men '80
Nutcracker Sweet '84
Alice '86

Thomas Ian Nicholas
The Fear Inside '92
Rookie of the Year '93
A Kid in King Arthur's Court '95

Anthony Nicholls
The Franchise Affair '52
Burn Witch, Burn! '62

George Nicholls, Jr.
The Greatest Question '19
The Country Kid '23
The Eagle '25
White Gold '28
Finishing School '33

Phoebe Nicholls
Maurice '87
Deep Cover '88
Heart of Darkness '93
Gulliver's Travels '95
Persuasion '95

Barbara Nichols
Beyond a Reasonable Doubt '56
The King and Four Queens '56
Manfish '56
Sweet Smell of Success '57
Scarface Mob '62
The Human Duplicators '64

Britt Nichols
Virgin Among the Living Dead '71
The Demons '74

Conrad Nichols
Days of Hell '84
A Man Called Rage '84
Rush '84

Nichelle Nichols
Star Trek Bloopers '69
Say Goodbye, Maggie Cole '72
Truck Turner '74
Star Trek: The Motion Picture '80
Star Trek 2: The Wrath of Khan '82
Star Trek 3: The Search for Spock '84
Star Trek 4: The Voyage Home '86
The Supernaturals '86
Star Trek 5: The Final Frontier '89
Star Trek 6: The Undiscovered Country '91

Stephen Nichols
Witchboard '87
Soapdish '91
Phoenix '95

Taylor Nichols
Metropolitan '90
Barcelona '94
Headless Body in Topless Bar '96

Jack Nicholson
Little Shop of Horrors '60
Studs Lonigan '60
The Wild Ride '60
The Raven '63
The Terror '63
Ensign Pulver '64
Flight to Fury '66
The Shooting '66
Hell's Angels on Wheels '67
Ride in the Whirlwind '67
Psych-Out '68
Easy Rider '69
Rebel Rousers '69
Five Easy Pieces '70
On a Clear Day You Can See Forever '70
Carnal Knowledge '71
The King of Marvin Gardens '72
The Last Detail '73
Chinatown '74
One Flew Over the Cuckoo's Nest '75
The Passenger '75
Tommy '75
The Last Tycoon '76
Missouri Breaks '76
Goin' South '78
The Shining '80
The Postman Always Rings Twice '81
Reds '81
The Border '82
Terms of Endearment '83
Prizzi's Honor '85
Heartburn '86
Broadcast News '87
Ironweed '87
The Witches of Eastwick '87
Batman '89
The Two Jakes '90
A Few Good Men '92
Hoffa '92
Man Trouble '92
The Crossing Guard '94
Wolf '94

Nick Nicholson
Triple Impact '92
Fist of Steel '93

Denise Nickerson
Willy Wonka & the Chocolate Factory '71
Smile '75
Zero to Sixty '78

Michael A. Nickles
Hamburger Hill '87
Baja '95

Julia Nickson-Soul
Rambo: First Blood, Part 2 '85
Glitch! '88
Noble House '88
Around the World in 80 Days '89
China Cry '91
K2: The Ultimate High '92
Amityville: A New Generation '93
Sidekicks '93
Double Dragon '94
White Tiger '95

Alex Nicol
Meet Danny Wilson '52
Red Ball Express '52
The Redhead from Wyoming '53
Black Glove '54
The Gilded Cage '54
Heat Wave '54
The Man from Laramie '55
Great Day in the Morning '56
Stranger in Town '57
The Screaming Skull '58
A Matter of WHO '62
A*P*E* '76

Daria Nicolodi
Deep Red: Hatchet Murders '75
Beyond the Door 2 '79
Unsane '82
Creepers '85
Macaroni '85
Terror at the Opera '88

Michael Nicolosi
Dream a Little Dream 2 '94

Sketch Artist 2: Hands That See '94

Brigitte Nielsen
Red Sonja '85
Rocky 4 '85
Cobra '86
Beverly Hills Cop 2 '87
Bye Bye Baby '88
Domino '88
Murder by Moonlight '91
Chained Heat 2 '92
The Double O Kid '92
Mission of Justice '92
Body Count '95
Galaxis '95

Hans Nielsen
Sherlock Holmes and the Deadly Necklace '62
The Monster of London City '64

Leslie Nielsen
Forbidden Planet '56
The Opposite Sex '56
Tammy and the Bachelor '57
Harlow '65
The Reluctant Astronaut '67
Dayton's Devils '68
Four Rode Out '69
How to Commit Marriage '69
Resurrection of Zachary Wheeler '71
Snatched '72
Day of the Animals '77
Project: Kill! '77
Viva Knievel '77
The Amsterdam Kill '78
City on Fire '78
Riel '79
Airplane! '80
Prom Night '80
Spaceship '81
Creepshow '82
More! Police Squad '82
Police Squad! Help Wanted! '82
Wrong is Right '82
Foxfire Light '84
Reckless Disregard '84
Blade in Hong Kong '85
The Patriot '86
Soul Man '86
Nightstick '87
Nuts '87
Striker's Mountain '87
Dangerous Curves '88
Home Is Where the Hart Is '88
The Naked Gun: From the Files of Police Squad '88
Repossessed '90
All I Want for Christmas '91
Naked Gun 2 1/2: The Smell of Fear '91
Surf Ninjas '93
Digger '94
Naked Gun 33 1/3: The Final Insult '94
Dracula: Dead and Loving It '95
Rent-A-Kid '95
Spy Hard '96

Lisa Niemi
Steel Dawn '87
Super Force '90

Jane Nigh
Motor Patrol '50
Operation Haylift '50

Bill Nighy
The Phantom of the Opera '89
Antonia and Jane '91

Miho Nikaidoh
Tokyo Decadence '91
Flirt '95

Jan Niklas
Colonel Redl '84
To the Camp & Back '85
Anastasia: The Mystery of Anna '86
Club Extinction '89
The Rose Garden '89

Anna Q. Nilsson
Grit of the Girl Telegrapher/In the Switch Tower '15
Regeneration '15
Seven Keys to Baldplate '17
Toll Gate '20
Riders of the Timberline '41
Fighting Father Dunne '48

Inger Nilsson
Pippi Longstocking '73
Pippi in the South Seas '74
Pippi Goes on Board '75

Maj-Britt Nilsson
Summer Interlude '50
Secrets of Women '52

Rob Nilsson
Northern Lights '79
Heat and Sunlight '87

Leonard Nimoy
Zombies of the Stratosphere '52
The Brain Eaters '58
The Balcony '63
The Man from U.N.C.L.E. '64
Star Trek: The Cage '65
Star Trek Bloopers '69
Catlow '71
Baffled '72
Invasion of the Body Snatchers '78
Star Trek: The Motion Picture '80
Seizure: The Story of Kathy Morris '82
Star Trek 2: The Wrath of Khan '82
A Woman Called Golda '82
Aladdin and His Wonderful Lamp '84
Star Trek 3: The Search for Spock '84
Star Trek 4: The Voyage Home '86
Star Trek 5: The Final Frontier '89
Never Forget '91
Star Trek 6: The Undiscovered Country '91

Annabelle Ninchi
La Dolce Vita '60
Time Out for Love '61

Yvette Nipar
Run If You Can '87
Ski Patrol '89
Doctor Mordrid: Master of the Unknown '90

John Nishio
Dim Sum: A Little Bit of Heart '85
Overkill '86

Greta Nissen
Ambassador Bill '31
Melody Cruise '32

David Niven
Barbary Coast '35
Beloved Enemy '36
The Charge of the Light Brigade '36
Dodsworth '36
Rose Marie '36
Dinner at the Ritz '37
Prisoner of Zenda '37
Bluebeard's Eighth Wife '38
Dawn Patrol '38
Bachelor Mother '39
Eternally Yours '39
The Real Glory '39
Wuthering Heights '39
Spitfire '42
Immortal Battalion '44
The Perfect Marriage '46
The Bishop's Wife '47
Bonnie Prince Charlie '48
The Elusive Pimpernel '50
The Toast of New Orleans '50
Happy Go Lovely '51
The Lady Says No '51
The Moon Is Blue '53
Carrington, V.C. '54
The King's Thief '55
Around the World in 80 Days '56
Birds & the Bees '56
Bonjour Tristesse '57
My Man Godfrey '57
Separate Tables '58
Ask Any Girl '59
Please Don't Eat the Daisies '60
The Guns of Navarone '61
Bedtime Story '63
55 Days at Peking '63
The Pink Panther '64
Lady L '65
Casino Royale '67
The Impossible Years '68
The Brain '69
The Statue '71
King, Queen, Knave '72
Paper Tiger '74
Murder by Death '76
No Deposit, No Return '76
Candleshoe '78
Death on the Nile '78
The Big Scam '79
Escape to Athena '79
Rough Cut '80
Sea Wolves '81
Trail of the Pink Panther '82
Better Late Than Never '83
Curse of the Pink Panther '83

Kip Niven
Magnum Force '73
New Year's Evil '78

Allan Nixon
Prehistoric Women '50
Mesa of Lost Women '52

Cynthia Nixon
Amadeus '84
The Manhattan Project '86
Tanner '88 '88
Let It Ride '89

Marion Nixon
Hands Up '26
Spangles '26
The Reckless Way '36
Tango '36

Mojo Nixon
Elvis Stories '89
Rock 'n' Roll High School Forever '91
Super Mario Bros. '93

James Noble
Roboman '75
One Summer Love '76
Dempsey '83
The Woman Who Willed a Miracle '83
When the Bough Breaks '86
Chances Are '89

Nancy Lee Noble
The Girl, the Body and the Pill '67
Just for the Hell of It '68
She-Devils on Wheels '68

Ray Noble
A Damsel in Distress '37
Here We Go Again! '42

Trisha Noble
The Private Eyes '80
Deadline '81

Magali Noel
Elena and Her Men '56
La Dolce Vita '60
Amarcord '74
Les Rendez-vous D'Anna '78
The Eighties '83

Noelia Noel
Sputnik '61
Night of the Bloody Apes '68

Natalija Nogulich
Sister, Sister '87
Homicide '91
Hoffa '92

Philippe Noiret
Zazie dans le Metro '61
Lady L '65
Night of the Generals '67
Woman Times Seven '67
The Assassination Bureau '69
Justine '69
Topaz '69
Murphy's War '71
The Holes '72
La Grande Bouffe '73
Night Flight from Moscow '73
Le Secret '74
The Judge and the Assassin '75
The Clockmaker '76
Old Gun '76
Dear Detective '77
The Purple Taxi '77
A Woman at Her Window '77
Who Is Killing the Great Chefs of Europe? '78
Three Brothers '80
Coup de Torchon '81
Jupiter's Thigh '81
Birgitt Haas Must Be Killed '83
Fort Saganne '84
My New Partner '84
Next Summer '84
The Family '87
Cinema Paradiso '88
Life and Nothing But '89
The Return of the Musketeers '89
The Palermo Connection '91
Uranus '91
Grosse Fatigue '94
The Postman '94

Bob Nolan
Heart of the Golden West '42
Sunset on the Desert '42
Song of Arizona '46
Lights of Old Santa Fe '47

Doris Nolan
Holiday '38
Follies Girl '43

Jeanette Nolan
Macbeth '48
Hangman's Knot '52
A Lawless Street '55
Seventh Cavalry '56
Tribute to a Bad Man '56
The Man Who Shot Liberty Valance '62
The Reluctant Astronaut '67
Babe! '75
Cloak & Dagger '84
Street Justice '89

John Nolan
In the Steps of a Dead Man '74
The Terror '79

Lloyd Nolan
"G" Men '35
The Texas Rangers '36
Internes Can't Take Money '37
Every Day's a Holiday '38
House Across the Bay '40
Johnny Apollo '40
Bataan '43
Guadalcanal Diary '43
House on 92nd Street '45
A Tree Grows in Brooklyn '45
Lady in the Lake '46
The Street with No Name '48
Easy Living '49
The Sun Comes Up '49
The Lemon Drop Kid '51
The Last Hunt '56
Peyton Place '57
Girl Hunters '63
Circus World '64
Ice Station Zebra '68
Sergeant Ryker '68
Airport '70
Earthquake '74
Abduction of St. Anne '75
Galyon '77
My Boys Are Good Boys '78
Prince Jack '83
It Came Upon a Midnight Clear '84
Hannah and Her Sisters '86

Tom Nolan
School Spirit '85
Voyage of the Rock Aliens '87

Nick Nolte
Death Sentence '74
Return to Macon County '75
The Runaway Barge '75
Rich Man, Poor Man '76
The Deep '77
Who'll Stop the Rain? '78
North Dallas Forty '79
Heart Beat '80
Cannery Row '82
48 Hrs. '82
Under Fire '83
Grace Quigley '84
Teachers '84
Down and Out in Beverly Hills '86
Extreme Prejudice '87
Weeds '87
Farewell to the King '89
New York Stories '89
Three Fugitives '89
Another 48 Hrs. '90
Everybody Wins '90
Q & A '90
Cape Fear '91
The Prince of Tides '91
Lorenzo's Oil '92
I'll Do Anything '93
Blue Chips '94
I Love Trouble '94
Jefferson in Paris '94
Mulholland Falls '95

John Ford Noonan
Adventures in Babysitting '87
Flirting with Disaster '95

Tom Noonan
Wolfen '81
The Man with One Red Shoe '85
Manhunter '86
The Monster Squad '87
Mystery Train '89
RoboCop 2 '90
Last Action Hero '93
What Happened Was... '94

Tommy Noonan
Jungle Patrol '48
Adam's Rib '50
Return of Jesse James '50
Gentlemen Prefer Blondes '53
A Star is Born '54
The Ambassador's Daughter '56
The Girl Most Likely '57
Promises! Promises! '63
Three Nuts in Search of a Bolt '64

Ghita Norby
The Wolf at the Door '87
Memories of a Marriage '90
The Best Intentions '92
Sofie '92
The Kingdom '95

Christine Norden
Mine Own Executioner '47
Night Beat '48

Tommy Norden
Flipper '64
Flipper's Odyssey '66

Jeffrey Nordling
Dangerous Heart '93
Holy Matrimony '94

Susan Norman
Poison '91
Safe '95

Zack Norman
Sitting Ducks '80
Romancing the Stone '84
America '86
Cadillac Man '90
Babyfever '94

Mabel Normand
Laughfest '10s
Charlie Chaplin's Keystone Comedies #1 '14
Charlie Chaplin's Keystone Comedies #2 '14
Charlie Chaplin's Keystone Comedies #3 '14
Charlie Chaplin's Keystone Comedies #4 '14
The Knockout/Dough and Dynamite '14
Tillie's Punctured Romance '14
Charlie Chaplin...Our Hero! '15
Kid's Auto Race/Mabel's Married Life '15
Fatty and Mabel Adrift/Mabel, Fatty and the Law '16
Mabel & Fatty '16
Mack Sennett Comedies: Vol. 2 '16
Mickey '17
Early Cinema Vol. 1 '19
What Happened to Rosa? '21
Extra Girl '23

Chuck Norris
Return of the Dragon '73
The Student Teachers '73
Breaker! Breaker! '77
Good Guys Wear Black '78
Force of One '79
Game of Death '79
Octagon '80
Warrior Within '80
An Eye for an Eye '81
Slaughter in San Francisco '81
Forced Vengeance '82
Silent Rage '82
Lone Wolf McQuade '83
Missing in Action '84
Code of Silence '85
Invasion U.S.A. '85
Missing in Action 2: The Beginning '85
Delta Force '86
Firewalker '86
Braddock: Missing in Action 3 '88
Hero and the Terror '88
Delta Force 2: Operation Stranglehold '90
The Hitman '91
Sidekicks '93
Walker: Texas Ranger: One Riot, One Ranger '93
Hellbound '94

Norris ▶cont.

Walker: Texas Ranger: Deadly Reunion '94
Top Dog '95

Dean Norris
Hard to Kill '89
The Lawnmower Man '92

Edward Norris
Show Them No Mercy '35
They Won't Forget '37
The Lady in Question '40
Road Show '41
The Man with Two Lives '42
Wings Over the Pacific '43
Heartaches '47

Mike Norris
Born American '86
Survival Game '87
Delta Force 3: The Killing Game '91
Death Ring '93

Alan North
More! Police Squad '82
Police Squad! Help Wanted! '82
Billy Galvin '86
Highlander '86
Rachel River '87
Lean on Me '89
Crazy People '90
The Jerky Boys '95

Heather North
Git! '65
The Barefoot Executive '71

Jay North
Zebra in the Kitchen '65
Maya '66
The Teacher '74
Scout's Honor '80

Noelle North
Slumber Party '57 '76
Sweater Girls '78

Sheree North
The Trouble with Girls (and How To Get Into It) '69
Lawman '71
The Organization '71
Snatched '72
Charley Varrick '73
Breakout '75
Most Wanted '76
The Shootist '76
Telefon '77
Portrait of a Stripper '79
Marilyn: The Untold Story '80
Legs '83
Only Once in a Lifetime '83
Maniac Cop '88
Defenseless '91

Ted North
Charlie Chan in Rio '41
The Devil Thumbs a Ride '47

Jeremy Northam
Carrington '95
The Net '95
Emma '96

Alex Norton
A Sense of Freedom '78
Gregory's Girl '80
Comfort and Joy '84
Hidden City '87
Squanto: A Warrior's Tale '94

Barry Norton
Dishonored '31
Dracula (Spanish Version) '31
Devil Monster '46

Edgar Norton
Dr. Jekyll and Mr. Hyde '31
Son of Frankenstein '39

Jack Norton
Finishing School '33
The Bank Dick '40

Jim Norton
Hidden Agenda '90
Memoirs of an Invisible Man '92
Midnight's Child '93

Ken Norton
Mandingo '75
Drum '76
Oceans of Fire '86
Kiss and Be Killed '91

Richard Norton
Gymkata '85
Equalizer 2000 '86
China O'Brien '88
China O'Brien 2 '89
Crossfire '89
The Kick Fighter '91
Ironheart '92
Lady Dragon '92
Rage and Honor '92
Raiders of the Sun '92
Cyber-Tracker '93
Deathfight '93
Direct Hit '93
Rage and Honor 2: Hostile Takeover '93
Under the Gun '95

Terry Norton
Emissary '89
American Kickboxer 1 '91

Judy Norton-Taylor
The Waltons: A Thanksgiving Story '73
The Waltons: The Christmas Carol '80
A Day for Thanks on Walton's Mountain '82

Jack Noseworthy
Alive '93
A Place for Annie '94
S.F.W. '94
The Brady Bunch Movie '95
Barb Wire '96

Ralph Nossek
Chicago Joe & the Showgirl '90
Citizen X '95

Christopher Noth
Smithereens '82
Apology '86
Off Beat '86
Baby Boom '87
Jakarta '88

Michael Nouri
Gangster Wars '81
Flashdance '83
Spraggue '84
Between Two Women '86
Imagemaker '86
Rage of Angels: The Story Continues '86
The Hidden '87
Project: Alien '89
Thieves of Fortune '89
Little Vegas '90
Danielle Steel's Changes '91
Psychic '91
Total Exposure '91
Black Ice '92
DaVinci's War '92
No Escape, No Return '93
American Yakuza '94
Fortunes of War '94
The Hidden 2 '94
Inner Sanctum 2 '94
Lady in Waiting '94
Shattered Dreams '94
Hologram Man '95
To the Limit '95

Eva Novak
Trailin' '21
Sky High '22
Laughing at Danger '24
Red Signals '27

Jane Novak
Wagon Tracks '19
Three Word Brand '21

Kim Novak
The French Line '54
Phffft! '54
The Man with the Golden Arm '55
Picnic '55
The Eddy Duchin Story '56
Pal Joey '57
Bell, Book and Candle '58
Vertigo '58
Strangers When We Meet '60
Boys' Night Out '62
Kiss Me, Stupid! '64
Of Human Bondage '64
The Amorous Adventures of Moll Flanders '65
Tales That Witness Madness '73
The White Buffalo '77
Just a Gigolo '79
The Mirror Crack'd '80
The Children '90
Liebestraum '91

Mel Novak
Cat in the Cage '68
Lovely ... But Deadly '82

Ramon Novarro
Eyes of Turpin Are Upon You! '21
Ben-Hur '26
The Student Prince in Old Heidelberg '27
Mata Hari '32
The Cat and the Fiddle '34
Big Steal '49
Heller in Pink Tights '60

Don Novello
Tucker: The Man and His Dream '88
New York Stories '89
The Godfather, Part 3 '90
Spirit of '76 '91
One Night Stand '95

Ivor Novello
The White Rose '23
The Lodger '26
Phantom Fiend '35

Jay Novello
The Border Legion '40
Robin Hood of the Pecos '41
Miracle of Our Lady of Fatima '52
Ma and Pa Kettle on Vacation '53
The Prodigal '55
Sabaka '55
Harum Scarum '65
What Did You Do in the War, Daddy? '66

Philomena Nowlin
Miss Melody Jones '73
Ebony Dreams '80

Zachi Noy
Hot Bubblegum '81
Private Manoeuvres '83
Young Love—Lemon Popsicle 7 '87

Bruce Nozick
Hit the Dutchman '92
Killer Instinct '92

Winston Ntshona
A Dry White Season '89
Night of the Cyclone '90

Danny Nucci
The Children of Times Square '86
Book of Love '91
Crimson Tide '95
Roosters '95
Eraser '96
The Rock '96

Eddie Nugent
Night Nurse '31
Kentucky Blue Streak '35
Doughnuts & Society '36
Prison Shadows '36

Elliott Nugent
Romance '30
The Unholy Three '30

Bill Nunn
School Daze '88
Do the Right Thing '89
Def by Temptation '90
Mo' Better Blues '90
New Jack City '91
Regarding Henry '91
White Lie '91
Sister Act '92
Save Me '93
Canadian Bacon '94
Candyman 2: Farewell to the Flesh '94
The Last Seduction '94
The Affair '95
Things to Do In Denver When You're Dead '95
Mr. & Mrs. Loving '96

Teri Nunn
Thank God It's Friday '78
Follow That Car '80

Rudolf Nureyev
Valentino '77
Exposed '83

Loredana Nusciak
Gladiators 7 '62
Django '68

Mike Nussbaum
House of Games '87
Things Change '88
The Water Engine '92

Jeff Nuttal
Robin Hood '91
Captives '94

Mayf Nutter
The $5.20 an Hour Dream '80
Hunter's Blood '87

France Nuyen
South Pacific '58
Diamond Head '62
Black Water Gold '69
Code Name: Diamond Head '77
Return to Fantasy Island '77
China Cry '91
The Joy Luck Club '93
A Passion to Kill '94

N!xau
The Gods Must Be Crazy '84
The Gods Must Be Crazy 2 '89

Carrie Nye
The Group '66
Creepshow '82
Hello Again '87

Carroll Nye
Lottery Bride '30
Gone with the Wind '39

Louis Nye
The Wheeler Dealers '63
Charge of the Model T's '76
Harper Valley P.T.A. '78
O.C. and Stiggs '87

Lena Nyman
I Am Curious (Yellow) '67
Autumn Sonata '78
The Adventures of Picasso '80

Jack Oakie
Uptown New York '32
Murder at the Vanities '34
The Texas Rangers '36
That Girl from Paris '36
Toast of New York '37
The Affairs of Annabel '38
Annabel Takes a Tour/Maid's Night Out '38
The Great Dictator '40
Little Men '40
Tin Pan Alley '40
Young People '40
The Great American Broadcast '41
Iceland '42
Song of the Islands '42
Hello, Frisco, Hello '43
Wintertime '43
The Rat Race '60
Lover Come Back '61

Simon Oakland
I Want to Live! '58
Psycho '60
The Rise and Fall of Legs Diamond '60
Follow That Dream '61
West Side Story '61
The Sand Pebbles '66
Tony Rome '67
Bullitt '68
On a Clear Day You Can See Forever '70
Chato's Land '71
The Night Stalker: Two Tales of Terror '74

Wheeler Oakman
The Spoilers '14
Outside the Law '21
Peck's Bad Boy '21
The Broken Mask '28
Roaring Ranch '30
The Riding Tornado '32
Texas Cyclone '32
Two-Fisted Law '32
Man of Action '33
Frontier Days '34
In Old Santa Fe '34
The Lost Jungle '34
Aces and Eights '36
Death from a Distance '36
Ghost Patrol '36
The Man from Gun Town '36
Roaring Guns '36
Song of the Trail '36
Slaves in Bondage '37
Wolf Call '39
Meet the Mob '42
Teenage '44

Simon Oates
The Terrornauts '67
Doomwatch '72

Warren Oates
Ride the High Country '62
Return of the Seven '66
The Shooting '66
In the Heat of the Night '67
Crooks & Coronets '69
The Wild Bunch '69
There was a Crooked Man '70
Hired Hand '71
Dillinger '73
The Thief Who Came to Dinner '73
Tom Sawyer '73
Badlands '74
Bring Me the Head of Alfredo Garcia '74
Cockfighter '74
Race with the Devil '75
The White Dawn '75
Dixie Dynamite '76
Drum '76
92 in the Shade '76
Brink's Job '78
Gunfire '78
And Baby Makes Six '79
My Old Man '79
1941 '79
East of Eden '80
Prime Time '80
Stripes '81
The Border '82
Sleeping Dogs '82
Blue Thunder '83
Tough Enough '83
The Blue and the Gray '85

Philip Ober
The Magnificent Yankee '50
Never a Dull Moment '50
Come Back, Little Sheba '52
From Here to Eternity '53
Escapade in Japan '57
Beloved Infidel '59
The Mating Game '59
North by Northwest '59
The Ghost and Mr. Chicken '66

Merle Oberon
Wedding Rehearsal '32
The Private Life of Henry VIII '33
Broken Melody '34
Private Life of Don Juan '34
The Scarlet Pimpernel '34
Beloved Enemy '36
These Three '36
The Cowboy and the Lady '38
The Divorce of Lady X '38
Wuthering Heights '39
The Lion Has Wings '40
Lydia '41
That Uncertain Feeling '41
Forever and a Day '43
Stage Door Canteen '43
Dark Waters '44
A Song to Remember '45
Berlin Express '48
Deep in My Heart '54
Desiree '54
The Oscar '66
Hotel '67
Interval '73

Anna Obregon
Treasure of the Four Crowns '82
Bolero '84
Car Crash

Rodrigo Obregon
Savage Beach '89
Tides of War '90
Hard Hunted '92
Enemy Gold '93
Fit to Kill '93
L.A. Wars '94

Hugh O'Brian
Return of Jesse James '50
Rocketship X-M '50
Little Big Horn '51
Vengeance Valley '51
Red Ball Express '52
Son of Ali Baba '52
Man from the Alamo '53
Broken Lance '54
There's No Business Like Show Business '54
In Harm's Way '65
Love Has Many Faces '65
Africa Texas Style '67

Wild Women '70
Probe '72
Killer Force '75
Murder on Flight 502 '75
Fantasy Island '76
The Shootist '76
Cruise into Terror '78
The Seekers '79
Doin' Time on Planet Earth '88
Twins '88
The Gambler Returns: The Luck of the Draw '93
Wyatt Earp: Return to Tombstone '94

Austin O'Brien
Last Action Hero '93
Prehysteria '93
My Girl 2 '94
The Baby-Sitters Club '95
Lawnmower Man 2: Beyond Cyberspace '95

Clay O'Brien
The Cowboys '72
One Little Indian '73

Dave O'Brien
The Black Coin '36
Lion's Den '36
Lightning Bill Crandall '37
Law of the Texan '38
Reefer Madness '38
Camp Double Feature '39
Daughter of the Tong '39
The Singing Cowgirl '39
Water Rustlers '39
Buzzy Rides the Range '40
Danger Ahead '40
Murder on the Yukon '40
Sky Bandits '40
That Gang of Mine '40
Yukon Flight '40
Dead or Alive '41
The Devil Bat '41
Spooks Run Wild '41
Bowery at Midnight '42
King of the Stallions '42
Fighting Valley '43
Rangers Take Over '43
Boss of Rawhide '44
Gangsters of the Frontier '44
Guns of the Law '44
Enemy of the Law '45
Frontier Fugitives '45
Marked for Murder '45
The Phantom of 42nd Street '45
Three in the Saddle '45

Donald O'Brien
Doctor Butcher M.D. '80
Trap Them & Kill Them '84
Quest for the Mighty Sword '90

Edmond O'Brien
The Hunchback of Notre Dame '39
A Girl, a Guy and a Gob '41
A Double Life '47
D.O.A. '49
White Heat '49
The Admiral Was a Lady '50
The Denver & Rio Grande '51
The Bigamist '53
The Hitch-Hiker '53
Julius Caesar '53
The Barefoot Contessa '54
Pete Kelly's Blues '55
D-Day, the Sixth of June '56
The Girl Can't Help It '56
Stopover Tokyo '57
Up Periscope '59
The Last Voyage '60
The Great Impostor '61
Birdman of Alcatraz '62
The Longest Day '62
The Man Who Shot Liberty Valance '62
Moon Pilot '62
Rio Conchos '64
Seven Days in May '64
The Doomsday Flight '66
Fantastic Voyage '66
The Wild Bunch '69
The Love God? '70
Jigsaw '71
They Only Kill Their Masters '72
Lucky Luciano '74
99 & 44/100 Dead '74
Dream No Evil '75

George O'Brien
Sunrise '27
The Lone Star Ranger '30
Painted Desert '31
Daniel Boone '34
Dude Ranger '34
Mystery Ranch '34
Cowboy Millionaire '35
Thunder Mountain '35
Park Avenue Logger '37
Windjammer '37
Renegade Ranger/Scarlet River '38
Racketeers of the Range '39
Don Amigo/Stage to Chino '40s
Bullet Code '40
Legion of the Lawless '40
She Wore a Yellow Ribbon '49
Gold Raiders '51
Cheyenne Autumn '64

Joan O'Brien
Operation Petticoat '59
Samar '62
It Happened at the World's Fair '63

Margaret O'Brien
Journey for Margaret '42
Thousands Cheer '43
The Canterville Ghost '44
Jane Eyre '44
Meet Me in St. Louis '44
Our Vines Have Tender Grapes '45
Little Women '49
The Secret Garden '49
Glory '56
Heller in Pink Tights '60
Amy '81

Maria O'Brien
Promised a Miracle '88
In a Stranger's Hand '92

Niall O'Brien
Lovespell '79
Class of '61 '92
Broken Harvest '95

Pat O'Brien
Tim Tyler's Luck '37
Hawaiian Buckaroo '38
Doomed Caravan '41

Pat O'Brien
Consolation Marriage '31
The Front Page '31
Hell's House '32
Bombshell '33
Bureau of Missing Persons '33
The World Gone Mad '33
Flirtation Walk '34
Ceiling Zero '35
Devil Dogs of the Air '35
Angels with Dirty Faces '38
Boy Meets Girl '38
The Fighting 69th '40
Knute Rockne: All American '40
Slightly Honorable '40
The Navy Comes Through '42
Bombardier '43
His Butler's Sister '43
The Iron Major '43
Marine Raiders '43
Having Wonderful Crime '45
Crack-Up '46
The Devil Thumbs a Ride/Having Wonderful Crime '47
Riff-Raff '47
The Boy with the Green Hair '48
Fighting Father Dunne '48
Jubilee Trail '54
Last Hurrah '58
Some Like It Hot '59
The End '78
Scout's Honor '80
Ragtime '81

Peter O'Brien
The Grand Duel '73
A Kink in the Picasso '90
Angel of Fury '93

Richard O'Brien
The Rocky Horror Picture Show '75
Shock Treatment '81
Robin Hood...The Legend: The Time of the Wolf '85

Shauna O'Brien
Elke '95
Over the Wire '95

Tom O'Brien
The Big Easy '87
The Accused '88

Virginia O'Brien
Big Store '41
Lady Be Good '41
Panama Hattie '42
Ship Ahoy '42
DuBarry Was a Lady '43
Thousands Cheer '43
Two Girls and a Sailor '44
The Harvey Girls '46
The Show-Off '46
Till the Clouds Roll By '46
Till the Clouds Roll By/A Star Is Born '46
Merton of the Movies '47

Jeffrey Obrow
The Power '80
The Kindred '87

Pat O'Bryan
976-EVIL '88
Relentless '89
976-EVIL 2: The Astral Factor '91

Andrea Occhipinti
A Blade in the Dark '83
Conquest '83
Bolero '84
El Barbaro '84
Control '87
The Family '87
Running Away '89

Uwe Ochsenknecht
Men... '85
Fire, Ice and Dynamite '91

Arthur O'Connell
Citizen Kane '41
Blondie's Blessed Event '42
Law of the Jungle '42
Open Secret '48
Picnic '55
Bus Stop '56
The Man in the Gray Flannel Suit '56
Solid Gold Cadillac '56
Man of the West '58
Anatomy of a Murder '59
Gidget '59
Operation Petticoat '59
Cimarron '60
Follow That Dream '61
The Great Impostor '61
Misty '61
Pocketful of Miracles '61
7 Faces of Dr. Lao '63
Kissin' Cousins '64
Monkey's Uncle '65
Fantastic Voyage '66
The Reluctant Astronaut '67
There was a Crooked Man '70
The Last Valley '71
Ben '72
They Only Kill Their Masters '72
Huckleberry Finn '74
The Hiding Place '75

Deidre O'Connell
Pastime '91
Cool World '92
Falling from Grace '92
Straight Talk '92
Fearless '93

Jerry O'Connell
Stand By Me '86
Ollie Hopnoodle's Haven of Bliss '88
Calendar Girl '93
Blue River '95
Hole in the Sky '95
Joe's Apartment '96

Carroll O'Connor
Johnny Frenchman '46
Parrish '61
Lonely Are the Brave '62
Cleopatra '63
In Harm's Way '65
Hawaii '66
What Did You Do in the War, Daddy? '66
Point Blank '67
Waterhole #3 '67
The Devil's Brigade '68
For Love of Ivy '68
Death of a Gunfighter '69
Marlowe '69
Doctors' Wives '70
Kelly's Heroes '70
Law and Disorder '74
Brass '85
Convicted '86
The Father Clements Story '87

Derrick O'Connor
Hope and Glory '87
Dealers '89
Lethal Weapon 2 '89
How to Make an American Quilt '95

Donald O'Connor
Beau Geste '39
Private Buckaroo '42
Francis the Talking Mule '49
Francis Goes to the Races '51
Francis Goes to West Point '52
Singin' in the Rain '52
Francis Covers the Big Town '53
I Love Melvin '53
Francis Joins the WACs '54
There's No Business Like Show Business '54
Francis in the Navy '55
The Wonders of Aladdin '61
Ragtime '81
Pandemonium '82
A Time to Remember '90

Glynnis O'Connor
Kid Vengeance '75
Someone I Touched '75
The Boy in the Plastic Bubble '76
Ode to Billy Joe '76
Our Town '77
California Dreaming '79
The Dark Side of Love '79
Those Lips, Those Eyes '80
Night Crossing '81
Melanie '82
Johnny Dangerously '84
The Deliberate Stranger '86
A Conspiracy of Love '87
To Heal a Nation '88
Past the Bleachers '95

Kevin J. O'Connor
Let's Scare Jessica to Death '71
Bogie: The Last Hero '80
Peggy Sue Got Married '86
Candy Mountain '87
The Caine Mutiny Court Martial '88
The Moderns '88
Love at Large '89
Signs of Life '89
Steel Magnolias '89
Hero '92
Equinox '93
Canadian Bacon '94
Color of Night '94
No Escape '94
Lord of Illusions '95
Virtuosity '95

Renee O'Connor
Darkman 2: The Return of Durant '94
Follow the River '95

Tim O'Connor
Across 110th Street '72
The Groundstar Conspiracy '72
Manhunter '74
Naked Gun 2 1/2: The Smell of Fear '91

Una O'Connor
Cavalcade '33
The Invisible Man '33
The Barretts of Wimpole Street '34
Chained '34
The Bride of Frankenstein '35
David Copperfield '35
The Informer '35
Lloyds of London '36
Personal Property '37
The Adventures of Robin Hood '38
The Sea Hawk '40
Strawberry Blonde '41
This Land is Mine '43
The Canterville Ghost '44
Christmas in Connecticut '45
Hopalong Cassidy: Unexpected Guest '47
Fighting Father Dunne '48
Witness for the Prosecution '57

Hugh O'Conor
Lamb '85
Da '88
My Left Foot '89
The Young Poisoner's Handbook '94

Nell O'Day
Pony Post '40
Bury Me Not On the Lone Prairie '41
Man from Montana '41
The Masked Rider '41

Denis O'Dea
Under Capricorn '49
Treasure Island '50
Captain Horatio Hornblower '51
The Long Dark Hall '51
Esther and the King '60

Georgia O'Dell
Cannon Ball/Eyes Have It '15
Big Calibre '35

Christophe Odent
First Name: Carmen '83
Nouvelle Vague '90

Cathy O'Donnell
The Amazing Mr. X '48
They Live by Night '49
The Miniver Story '50
Detective Story '51
The Love of Three Queens '54
The Man from Laramie '55
Terror in the Haunted House '58
Ben-Hur '59

Chris O'Donnell
Men Don't Leave '89
Blue Sky '91
Fried Green Tomatoes '91
Scent of a Woman '92
School Ties '92
The Three Musketeers '93
Circle of Friends '94
Batman Forever '95
Mad Love '95

Rosie O'Donnell
A League of Their Own '92
Another Stakeout '93
Sleepless in Seattle '93
Car 54, Where Are You? '94
Exit to Eden '94
The Flintstones '94
Now and Then '95
Beautiful Girls '96
Harriet the Spy '96

"Spec" O'Donnell
The Country Kid '23
Hello Trouble '32

Michael O'Donoghue
Mr. Mike's Mondo Video '79
The Suicide Club '88

Martha O'Driscoll
Reap the Wild Wind '42
Young & Willing '42
The Fallen Sparrow '43
Follow the Boys '44
Here Come the Co-Eds '45
House of Dracula '45
Criminal Court '46

Bernadette O'Farrell
The Happiest Days of Your Life '50
Scotland Yard Inspector '52
Robin Hood: The Movie '55

Damian O'Flynn
X Marks the Spot '42
Crack-Up '46
The Devil on Wheels '47
Daniel Boone: Trail Blazer '56

Ken Ogata
Vengeance Is Mine '79
Eijanaika '81
Virus '82
The Ballad of Narayama '83
Mishima: A Life in Four Chapters '85

Mayumi Ogawa
Zatoichi: The Blind Swordsman's Vengeance '66
The Go-Masters '82

Bulle Ogier
La Salamandre '71
The Discreet Charm of the Bourgeoisie '72
Tricheurs '84
Candy Mountain '87

Ian Ogilvy
The She-Beast '65
The Conqueror Worm '68
The Invincible Six '68
Wuthering Heights '70

Ogilvy ▶cont.

And Now the Screaming Starts '73
From Beyond the Grave '73
Ripping Yarns '75
Anna Karenina '85
Death Becomes Her '92
Invasion of Privacy '92
Puppet Master 5: The Final Chapter '94

Gail O'Grady
Blackout '88
Nobody's Perfect '90
Spellcaster '91
Celtic Pride '96

Soon-Teck Oh
The Man with the Golden Gun '74
East of Eden '80
Missing in Action 2: The Beginning '85
A Home of Our Own '93

Brian O'Halloran
Clerks '94
Mallrats '95

Jack O'Halloran
Farewell, My Lovely '75
King Kong '76
Superman: The Movie '78
The Baltimore Bullet '80
Superman 2 '80
Hero and the Terror '88

Claudia Ohana
Erendira '83
Opera do Malandro '87
The Fable of the Beautiful Pigeon Fancier '88
Luzia '88
Priceless Beauty '90

George O'Hanlon, Jr.
Our Time '74
Where Have All the People Gone? '74

Catherine O'Hara
The Best of John Candy on SCTV '80s
Nothing Personal '80
The Last Polka '84
After Hours '85
Heartburn '86
Really Weird Tales '86
Beetlejuice '88
Betsy's Wedding '90
Dick Tracy '90
Home Alone '90
Little Vegas '90
Home Alone 2: Lost in New York '92
There Goes the Neighborhood '92
The Paper '94
A Simple Twist of Fate '94
Wyatt Earp '94
Tall Tale: The Unbelievable Adventures of Pecos Bill '95

David O'Hara
WarCat '88
Maria's Child '93
Braveheart '95

Jenny O'Hara
Last Song '80
Career Opportunities '91
Angie '94
A Mother's Prayer '95

Maureen O'Hara
The Hunchback of Notre Dame '39
Jamaica Inn '39
Dance, Girl, Dance '40
How Green Was My Valley '41
The Black Swan '42
To the Shores of Tripoli '42
The Fallen Sparrow '43
Immortal Sergeant '43
This Land is Mine '43
Buffalo Bill '44
The Spanish Main '45
Miracle on 34th Street '47
Sinbad, the Sailor '47
Father Was a Fullback '49
A Woman's Secret '49
Comanche Territory '50
Rio Grande '50
At Sword's Point '51
Against All Flags '52
The Quiet Man '52
The Redhead from Wyoming '53
War Arrow '53
The Long Gray Line '55
The Magnificent Matador '55
Lisbon '56
Wings of Eagles '57
Deadly Companions '61
The Parent Trap '61
Mr. Hobbs Takes a Vacation '62
McLintock! '63
Spencer's Mountain '63
The Rare Breed '66
Big Jake '71
The Red Pony '76
Only the Lonely '91

Dan O'Herlihy
Odd Man Out '47
Macbeth '48
At Sword's Point '51
Actors and Sin '52
Invasion U.S.A. '52
Sword of Venus '53
The Virgin Queen '55
The Young Land '59
The King of the Roaring '20s: The Story of Arnold Rothstein '61
Fail-Safe '64
The People '71
Waterloo '71
The Tamarind Seed '74
MacArthur '77
Death Ray 2000 '81
Halloween 3: Season of the Witch '82
Nancy Astor '82
The Last Starfighter '84
No Comebacks '85
Two by Forsyth '86
The Dead '87
RoboCop '87
A Waltz Through the Hills '88
RoboCop 2 '90
Love, Cheat & Steal '93

Gavan O'Herlihy
Space Riders '83
Willow '88
Tailspin: Behind the Korean Airline Tragedy '89
The Shooter '94

Carol Ohmart
House on Haunted Hill '58
Born Reckless '59
Naked Youth '59
One Man's Way '63
Spider Baby '64

John O'Hurley
Mirror Images '91
The Power Within '95

Eiji Okada
Mother '52
Hiroshima, Mon Amour '59
She and He '63
The Ugly American '63
Woman in the Dunes '64
X from Outer Space '67
Traffic Jam '91

Dennis O'Keefe
Cimarron '30
Libeled Lady '36
Pop Always Pays '40
You'll Find Out '40
Broadway Limited '41
Lady Scarface '41
Topper Returns '41
Hi Diddle Diddle '43
The Leopard Man '43
Abroad with Two Yanks '44
Fighting Seabees '44
Sensations of 1945 '44
The Story of Dr. Wassell '44
Brewster's Millions '45
Doll Face '46
Dishonored Lady '47
T-Men '47
Great Dan Patch '49
Lady Scarface/The Threat '49
The Naked Flame '68

Michael O'Keefe
Gray Lady Down '77
The Dark Secret of Harvest Home '78
Caddyshack '80
The Great Santini '80
A Rumor of War '80
Split Image '82
Nate and Hayes '83
Finders Keepers '84
The Slugger's Wife '85
The Whoopee Boys '86
Hitchhiker 4 '87
Ironweed '87
Disaster at Silo 7 '88
Bridge to Silence '89
Fear '90
Out of the Rain '90
Too Young to Die '90
Me & Veronica '93
Incident at Deception Ridge '94
Nina Takes a Lover '94
Three Wishes '95

Miles O'Keeffe
Tarzan, the Ape Man '81
Ator the Fighting Eagle '83
Sword of the Valiant '83
Blade Master '84
S.A.S. San Salvador '84
Campus Man '87
Iron Warrior '87
The Drifter '88
The Lone Runner '88
Waxwork '88
Cartel '90
Liberty & Bash '90
The Colombian Connection '91
King's Ransom '91
Relentless 2: Dead On '91
Shoot '92
Zero Tolerance '93
Silent Hunter '94
Pocahontas: The Legend '95

Don O'Kelly
Frontier Uprising '61
The Hostage '67

Tim O'Kelly
Targets '68
The Passing of Evil '70

Yuji Okumoto
The Karate Kid: Part 2 '86
Aloha Summer '88
True Believer '89
Bloodfist 5: Human Target '93
Nemesis '93
Robot Wars '93
Hard Justice '95

Warner Oland
The Fighting American '24
Riders of the Purple Sage '25
Don Juan '26
The Jazz Singer '27
Stand and Deliver '28
Daughter of the Dragon '31
Dishonored '31
Drums of Jeopardy '31
Shanghai Express '32
The Painted Veil '34
Charlie Chan in Paris '35
Charlie Chan's Secret '35
Werewolf of London '35
Charlie Chan at the Opera '36

Ken Olandt
April Fool's Day '86
Super Force '90
Leprechaun '93
Digital Man '94

Daniel Olbrychski
Colonel Wolodyjowski '69
The Structure of Crystals '69
Family Life '71
Land of Promise '74
Maids of Wilko '79
The Tin Drum '79
La Truite '83
Rosa Luxemburg '86
The Unbearable Lightness of Being '88

Eric Oldfield
Island Trader '71
Gone to Ground '76
Air Hawk '84
Stones of Death '88

William Oldham
Matewan '87
Thousand Pieces of Gold '91

Gary Oldman
Sid & Nancy '86
Prick Up Your Ears '87
Track 29 '88
We Think the World of You '88
Chattahoochee '89
Criminal Law '89
Rosencrantz & Guildenstern Are Dead '90
State of Grace '90
JFK '91
Bram Stoker's Dracula '92
Fallen Angels 2 '93
Romeo Is Bleeding '93
True Romance '93
Immortal Beloved '94
The Professional '94
Murder In the First '95
The Scarlet Letter '95

Gabriel Olds
Calendar Girl '93
Andersonville '95

Sven Ole-Thorsen
Abraxas: Guardian of the Universe '90
Dragon: The Bruce Lee Story '93

William O'Leary
Nice Girls Don't Explode '87
Flight of Black Angel '91
Hot Shots! '91
In the Line of Duty: Ambush in Waco '93
Candyman 2: Farewell to the Flesh '94

Ken Olin
The Game of Love '90
Queens Logic '91

Lena Olin
After the Rehearsal '84
The Unbearable Lightness of Being '88
Enemies, a Love Story '89
Havana '90
Mr. Jones '93
Romeo Is Bleeding '93

Barret Oliver
Frankenweenie '84
The NeverEnding Story '84
Cocoon '85
D.A.R.Y.L. '85
The Secret Garden '87
Cocoon: The Return '88

Charles Oliver
Midnight at the Wax Museum '36
The Avenging Hand '43

David Oliver
Postal Inspector '36
Defense Play '88

Edna May Oliver
Lucky Devil '25
Cimarron '30
Half-Shot at Sunrise '30
Hold 'Em Jail '32
Ann Vickers '33
Little Women '33
David Copperfield '35
A Tale of Two Cities '35
Romeo and Juliet '36
Little Miss Broadway '38
Rosalie '38
Drums Along the Mohawk '39
Nurse Edith Cavell '39
Second Fiddle '39
The Story of Vernon and Irene Castle '39
Pride and Prejudice '40

Gordon Oliver
Youth on Parole '37
Blondie '38
Follies Girl '43
Seven Days Ashore/Hurry, Charlie, Hurry '44
The Spiral Staircase '46

Michael Oliver
Problem Child '90
Problem Child 2 '91

Rochelle Oliver
1918 '85
On Valentine's Day '86
Courtship '87
An Unremarkable Life '89
Scent of a Woman '92

Stephen Oliver
Motor Psycho '65
Angels from Hell '68
Werewolves on Wheels '71
Cycle Psycho '72
Savage Abduction '73

Susan Oliver
The Gene Krupa Story '59
Butterfield 8 '60
Disorderly Orderly '64
Guns of Diablo '64
Star Trek: The Cage '65
Ginger in the Morning '73
Widow's Nest '77
Hardly Working '81
Tomorrow's Child '82

Robert Oliveri
Honey, I Shrunk the Kids '89
Edward Scissorhands '90
Honey, I Blew Up the Kid '92

Laurence Olivier
As You Like It '36
I Stand Condemned '36
Fire Over England '37
21 Days '37
The Divorce of Lady X '38
Clouds Over Europe '39
Wuthering Heights '39
Pride and Prejudice '40
Rebecca '40
The Forty-Ninth Parallel '41
That Hamilton Woman '41
The Demi-Paradise '43
Henry V '44
Hamlet '48
Carrie '52
Richard III '55
The Prince and the Showgirl '57
The Devil's Disciple '59
The Entertainer '60
Spartacus '60
Khartoum '66
The Shoes of the Fisherman '68
Battle of Britain '69
David Copperfield '70
Nicholas and Alexandra '71
Sleuth '72
Lady Caroline Lamb '73
The Merchant of Venice '73
Love Among the Ruins '75
Marathon Man '76
The Seven-Per-Cent Solution '76
A Bridge Too Far '77
Jesus of Nazareth '77
The Betsy '78
The Boys from Brazil '78
Dracula '79
A Little Romance '79
The Jazz Singer '80
Brideshead Revisited '81
Clash of the Titans '81
Mister Halpren & Mister Johnson '83
The Bounty '84
The Jigsaw Man '84
Wagner: The Complete Epic '85
Wagner: The Movie '85
Wild Geese 2 '85
Ebony Tower '86
Peter the Great '86
A Voyage' Round My Father '89

Paul Olivier
A Nous la Liberte '31
Le Million '31

Silvio Oliviero
Psycho Girls '86
Graveyard Shift '87
Understudy: The Graveyard Shift 2 '88
A Whisper to a Scream '88

Walter Olkewicz
Can I Do It...Till I Need Glasses? '77
The Client '94
The Good Old Boys '95

Edward James Olmos
Aloha, Bobby and Rose '74
Wolfen '81
Zoot Suit '81
Blade Runner '82
Virus '82
Ballad of Gregorio Cortez '83
Miami Vice 2: The Prodigal Son '85
Saving Grace '86
Stand and Deliver '88
Triumph of the Spirit '89
Talent for the Game '91
American Me '92
The Burning Season '94
A Million to Juan '94
Mirage '94
My Family '94

Roosters '95

Gertrude Olmsted
California Straight Ahead '25
Cobra '25
The Monster '25
Sweet Adeline '26
The Cheerful Fraud '27

Gerald S. O'Loughlin
Ensign Pulver '64
Desperate Characters '71
The Crash of Flight 401 '78
Pleasure Palace '80
A Matter of Life and Death '81
Quicksilver '86

Ashley Olsen
Double Double Toil and Trouble '94
To Grandmother's House We Go '94
How the West was Fun '95
It Takes Two '95

Larry Olsen
Curley '47
Who Killed Doc Robbin? '48

Mary-Kate Olsen
Double Double Toil and Trouble '94
To Grandmother's House We Go '94
How the West was Fun '95
It Takes Two '95

Merlin Olsen
The Undefeated '69
Mitchell '75
The Juggler of Notre Dame '84

Moroni Olsen
The Three Musketeers '35
Mary of Scotland '36
Yellow Dust '36
Allegheny Uprising '39
Rose of Washington Square '39
Susannah of the Mounties '39
The Glass Key '42
Reunion in France '42
Ali Baba and the Forty Thieves '43
Buffalo Bill '44
Notorious '46
The Possessed '47
Call Northside 777 '48
Task Force '49
Father of the Bride '50
Father's Little Dividend '51

Ole Olsen
Country Gentlemen '36
All Over Town '37

James Olson
Rachel, Rachel '68
The Andromeda Strain '71
Paper Man '71
The Groundstar Conspiracy '72
Someone I Touched '75
Strange New World '75
The Spell '77
My Sister, My Love '78
Ragtime '81
Amityville 2: The Possession '82
Commando '85
Rachel River '87

Nancy Olson
Mr. Music '50
Sunset Boulevard '50
Union Station '50
Big Jim McLain '52
Pollyanna '60
The Absent-Minded Professor '61
Son of Flubber '63
Snowball Express '72
Making Love '82

Daragh O'Malley
Sharpe's Eagle '93
Sharpe's Rifles '93
Sharpe's Battle '94
Sharpe's Company '94
Sharpe's Enemy '94
Sharpe's Gold '94
Sharpe's Honour '94
Sharpe's Sword '94

J. Pat O'Malley
Lassie, Come Home '43
Courage of Black Beauty '57
Star! '68
A Small Killing '81

Pat O'Malley
The Virginian '23
The Fighting American '24
Spangles '26
The Fighting Marshal '32
Evelyn Prentice '34
The Perils of Pauline '34
The Miracle Rider '35
Fighting Marines '36
Stunt Pilot '39

Rex O'Malley
Camille '36
Midnight '39

Kate O'Mara
The Horror of Frankenstein '70
The Vampire Lovers '70
Whose Child Am I? '75
Nativity '78

Mollie O'Mara
Girls School Screamers '86
Escape from Safehaven '88

Judd Omen
Pee Wee's Big Adventure '85
Dollman '90

Anny Ondra
Blackmail '29
The Manxman '29

Griffin O'Neal
The Escape Artist '82
Hadley's Rebellion '84
April Fool's Day '86
The Children of Times Square '86
The Wraith '87
Assault of the Killer Bimbos '88
Night Children '89
Ghoulies 3: Ghoulies Go to College '91

Patrick O'Neal
From the Terrace '60
In Harm's Way '65
King Rat '65
Alvarez Kelly '66
A Fine Madness '66
Secret Life of an American Wife '68
Where Were You When the Lights Went Out? '68
Stiletto '69
El Condor '70
Silent Night, Bloody Night '73
The Way We Were '73
Independence '76
Make Me an Offer '80
Spraggue '84
Perry Mason Returns '85
New York Stories '89
Alice '90
The Defense Never Rests '90
Q & A '90
For the Boys '91
Under Siege '92

Ron O'Neal
Superfly '72
Superfly T.N.T. '73
Freedom Road '79
The Hitter '79
Sophisticated Gents '81
St. Helen's, Killer Volcano '82
Red Dawn '84
As Summers Die '86
Hero and the Terror '88
Mercenary Fighters '88
Trained to Kill '88
Up Against the Wall '91
Original Gangstas '96

Ryan O'Neal
Love Story '70
Wild Rovers '71
What's Up, Doc? '72
Paper Moon '73
The Thief Who Came to Dinner '73
Barry Lyndon '75
A Bridge Too Far '77
The Driver '78
Oliver's Story '78
The Main Event '79
Green Ice '81
So Fine '81
Partners '82
Irreconcilable Differences '84
Fever Pitch '85
Tough Guys Don't Dance '87
Chances Are '89
Small Sacrifices '89
The Man Upstairs '93

Faithful '95

Shaquille O'Neal
Blue Chips '94
Kazaam '96

Tatum O'Neal
Paper Moon '73
The Bad News Bears '76
International Velvet '78
Circle of Two '80
Little Darlings '80
Goldilocks & the Three Bears '83
Certain Fury '85
Little Noises '91

Barbara O'Neil
I Am the Law '38
Gone with the Wind '39
The Tower of London '39
All This and Heaven Too '40
I Remember Mama '48
Secret Beyond the Door '48
Flame of the Islands '55

Nance O'Neil
Cimarron '30
The Royal Bed '31

Sally O'Neil
Battling Butler '26
Sixteen Fathoms Deep '34

Angela O'Neill
Sorority House Massacre '86
River of Diamonds '90
Enemy Unseen '91

Chris O'Neill
James Joyce's Women '85
Backbeat '94

Dick O'Neill
Gamera, the Invincible '66
Pretty Poison '68
Hail '73
The Taking of Pelham One Two Three '74
The Mosquito Coast '86
She's Out of Control '89
Dark Justice '91
My Summer Story '94

Ed O'Neill
Deliverance '72
The Day the Women Got Even '80
When Your Lover Leaves '83
Disorganized Crime '89
K-9 '89
The Adventures of Ford Fairlane '90
Sibling Rivalry '90
Dutch '91
It's a Bundyful Life '92
Wayne's World '92
Wayne's World 2 '93
Blue Chips '94
Little Giants '94

Henry O'Neill
Lady Killer '33
Black Fury '35
The Fighting 69th '40
Billy the Kid '41
Honky Tonk '41
Men of Boys Town '41
Shadow of the Thin Man '41
Johnny Eager '42
White Cargo '42
Air Raid Wardens '43
Whistling in Brooklyn '43
Nothing But Trouble '44
The Virginian '46
Holiday Affair '49

Jennifer O'Neill
Rio Lobo '70
Summer of '42 '71
Lady Ice '73
The Reincarnation of Peter Proud '75
Whiffs '75
The Innocent '76
The Psychic '78
Force of One '79
Love's Savage Fury '79
Cloud Dancer '80
Steel '80
Scanners '81
Chase '85
I Love N.Y. '87
Full Exposure: The Sex Tape Scandals '89
Personals '90
Committed '91

Invasion of Privacy '92
Perfect Family '92
The Cover Girl Murders '93
Discretion Assured '93
Bad Love '95

Maire O'Neill
Juno and the Paycock '30
Great Day '46

Michael O'Neill
Gore-Met Zombie Chef From Hell '87
The Gun in Betty Lou's Handbag '92

Remy O'Neill
Hollywood Hot Tubs 2: Educating Crystal '89
To Die for 2: Son of Darkness '91

Yoko Ono
The Magic Christian '69
Let It Be '70

Peter Onorati
Fire Birds '90
Camp Nowhere '94
Donor Unknown '95

Lupe Ontiveros
El Norte '83
My Family '94

Michael Ontkean
Peacekillers '71
Where the Eagle Flies '72
The Witching '72
Girls on the Road '73
Slap Shot '77
Willie & Phil '80
Making Love '82
The Blood of Others '84
Just the Way You Are '84
The Allnighter '87
Maid to Order '87
Clara's Heart '88
Bye Bye Blues '89
Cold Front '89
Street Justice '89
Postcards from the Edge '90
Twin Peaks '90
Twin Peaks '90
Legacy of Lies '92

David Opatoshu
The Light Ahead '39
Exodus '60
Torn Curtain '66
The Fixer '68
Romance of a Horsethief '71
Conspiracy of Terror '75
Who'll Stop the Rain? '78
Forty Days of Musa Dagh '85

Alan Oppenheimer
Star! '68
The Groundstar Conspiracy '72
The Bionic Woman '75
A Pleasure Doing Business '79
Child of Darkness, Child of Light '91
Invisible: The Chronicles of Benjamin Knight '93
Trancers 4: Jack of Swords '93
Trancers 5: Sudden Deth '94

Don Opper
Android '82
Critters '86
Critters 2: The Main Course '88
The Forgotten '89
Critters 3 '91
Critters 4 '91

Terry O'Quinn
Mahler '74
Heaven's Gate '81
Mrs. Soffel '84
Places in the Heart '84
Mischief '85
Women of Valor '86
Black Widow '87
The Stepfather '87
Pin '88
Young Guns '88
The Forgotten One '89
Roe vs. Wade '89
Stepfather 2: Make Room for Daddy '89
Blind Fury '90
Company Business '91
Prisoners of the Sun '91
The Rocketeer '91
Son of the Morning Star '91
When the Time Comes '91

The Cutting Edge '92
The Good Fight '92
My Samurai '92
Wildcard '92
Amityville: A New Generation '93
Lipstick Camera '93
Tombstone '93
Don't Talk to Strangers '94
JAG '95
Primal Fear '96

Jerry Orbach
24 Hours in a Woman's Life '61
Foreplay '75
Underground Aces '80
Prince of the City '81
Brewster's Millions '85
F/X '86
Imagemaker '86
Dirty Dancing '87
I Love N.Y. '87
Out on a Limb '87
Someone to Watch Over Me '87
California Casanova '89
Crimes & Misdemeanors '89
Dead Women in Lingerie '90
Last Exit to Brooklyn '90
Delirious '91
Delusion '91
Out for Justice '91
Broadway Bound '92
Mr. Saturday Night '92
Straight Talk '92
Universal Soldier '92
The Adventures of a Gnome Named Gnorm '93

Roy Orbison
Fastest Guitar Alive '68
Roadie '80
Chuck Berry: Hail! Hail! Rock 'n' Roll '87

Cyril O'Reilly
Porky's '82
Porky's 2: The Next Day '83
Purple Hearts '84
On Wings of Eagles '86
Dance of the Damned '88
Navy SEALS '90
The Cool Surface '92
Philadelphia Experiment 2 '93

Liana Orfei
Mill of the Stone Women '60
The Giant of Metropolis '61
Pirates of the Coast '61
The Avenger '62
Nefertiti, Queen of the Nile '64
Pirate Warrior '64
Casanova '70 '65

Julia Ormond
Traffik '90
Young Catherine '91
Stalin '92
Nostradamus '93
Captives '94
Legends of the Fall '94
First Knight '95
Sabrina '95

Ed O'Ross
Full Metal Jacket '87
The Hidden '87
Red Heat '88
Tailspin: Behind the Korean Airline Tragedy '89
Another 48 Hrs. '90
Play Nice '92
Universal Soldier '92

Heather O'Rourke
Poltergeist '82
Poltergeist 2: The Other Side '86
Poltergeist 3 '88

Marina Orsini
Battle of the Worlds '61
Eddie and the Cruisers 2: Eddie Lives! '89

Umberto Orsini
Mademoiselle '66
Cesar & Rosalie '72
The Outside Man '73
Emmanuelle, the Joys of a Woman '76
A Woman at Her Window '77

Humberto Ortiz
Dollman '90
Arcade '93

Andrew Osborn
Spaceways '53

Osborn ▶cont.

Three Stops to Murder '53

Lyn Osborn
Space Patrol '50
The Amazing Colossal Man '57
Invasion of the Saucer Men '57

Ted Osborn
Buried Alive '39
Charlie Chan at the Wax Museum '40

Bud Osborne
The Fighting Stallion '26
Mark of the Spur '32
The Riding Tornado '32
Deadwood Pass '33
Diamond Trail '33
Rustler's Roundup '33
When a Man Rides Alone '33
The Crimson Trail '35
The Outlaw Deputy '35
Ridin' Thru '35
Rustlers of Red Dog '35
Western Gold '37
Where Trails Divide '37
Across the Plains '39
Death Rides the Range '40
Dead or Alive '41
Six Gun Gospel '43
Range Law '44
Rustler's Hideout '44
Wild Horse Phantom '44
Border Badmen '45
His Brother's Ghost '45
Border Bandits '46
The Caravan Trail '46
Outlaw of the Plains '46
Wild West '46
Tribute to a Bad Man '56
Gun Glory '57

Vivienne Osborne
The Phantom Broadcast '33
Supernatural '33
Tomorrow at Seven '33
Let's Sing Again '36
Captain Caution '40
Primrose Path '40

Ozzy Osbourne
Trick or Treat '86
Decline of Western Civilization 2: The Metal Years '88
The Jerky Boys '95

Henry Oscar
Black Limelight '38
The Terror '38
The Courageous Mr. Penn '41
The Greed of William Hart '48
Postmark for Danger '56
The Spaniard's Curse '58

Per Oscarsson
The Doll '62
Hunger '66
Dandy in Aspic '68
The Night Visitor '70
Endless Night '71
The Last Valley '71
Secrets '71
Blockhouse '73
The New Land '73
Sleep of Death '79
House of Angels '92
Dreaming of Rita '94

Brian O'Shaughnessy
Mr. Kingstreet's War '71
Claws '85

Kevin O'Shea
The Purple Heart '44
A Wing and a Prayer '44

Michael O'Shea
Jack Frost '43
Lady of Burlesque '43
Jack London '44
The Last of the Redmen '47
The Big Wheel '49
Lady Scarface/The Threat '49
Parole, Inc. '49
Threat '49
The Underworld Story '50

Milo O'Shea
Ulysses '67
Barbarella '68
Romeo and Juliet '68
Loot...Give Me Money, Honey! '70
Paddy '70
Sacco & Vanzetti '71
Theatre of Blood '73
Peter Lundy and the Medicine Hat Stallion '77
Danger in the Skies '79
A Time for Miracles '80
Portrait of a Rebel: Margaret Sanger '82
The Verdict '82
No Comebacks '85
The Purple Rose of Cairo '85
Two by Forsyth '86
Broken Vows '87
Once a Hero '88
The Dream Team '89
Opportunity Knocks '90
Only the Lonely '91
The Playboys '92

K.T. Oslin
Murder So Sweet '93
The Thing Called Love '93

Cliff Osmond
Kiss Me, Stupid! '64
The Fortune Cookie '66
Sweet Sugar '72
Invasion of the Bee Girls '73
Sharks' Treasure '75
Joe Panther '76
Mountain Man '77
Hangar 18 '80
The Adventures of Nellie Bly '81
In Search of a Golden Sky '84

Marie Osmond
Goin' Coconuts '78
The Gift of Love '90

Jeffery Osterhage
The Sacketts '79
The Shadow Riders '82
Buckeye and Blue '87
South of Reno '87
Dark Before Dawn '89
Masque of the Red Death '89
Sex Crimes '92

Bibi Osterwald
Parrish '61
Bank Shot '74

William Ostrander
Mike's Murder '84
Red Heat '85

Maureen O'Sullivan
Song O' My Heart '29
A Connecticut Yankee '31
Skyscraper Souls '32
Strange Interlude '32
Tarzan, the Ape Man '32
The Barretts of Wimpole Street '34
Hide-Out '34
Tarzan and His Mate '34
The Thin Man '34
Anna Karenina '35
David Copperfield '35
Devil Doll '36
Tarzan Escapes '36
A Day at the Races '37
Tarzan Finds a Son '39
Pride and Prejudice '40
Tarzan's Secret Treasure '41
Tarzan's New York Adventure '42
All I Desire '53
The Tall T '57
Too Scared to Scream '85
Hannah and Her Sisters '86
Peggy Sue Got Married '86
Stranded '87
The Habitation of Dragons '91
The River Pirates '94

Shoji Otake
The Funeral '84
Tampopo '86

Annette O'Toole
Smile '75
One on One '77
King of the Gypsies '78
Foolin' Around '80
Cat People '82
48 Hrs. '82
Superman 3 '83
Best Legs in the 8th Grade '84
Bridge to Terabithia '85
Broken Vows '87
Cross My Heart '88
Love at Large '89
A Girl of the Limberlost '90
Stephen King's It '90
White Lie '91
Kiss of a Killer '93
Love Matters '93
Imaginary Crimes '94

Peter O'Toole
Kidnapped '60
Lawrence of Arabia '62
Becket '64
Lord Jim '65
What's New Pussycat? '65
The Bible...In the Beginning '66
How to Steal a Million '66
Casino Royale '67
Night of the Generals '67
The Lion in Winter '68
Goodbye, Mr. Chips '69
Murphy's War '71
Man of La Mancha '72
The Ruling Class '72
Under Milk Wood '73
Man Friday '75
Rosebud '75
Foxtrot '76
Rogue Male '76
Zulu Dawn '79
Caligula '80
The Stunt Man '80
Masada '81
Power Play '81
My Favorite Year '82
Svengali '83
Kim '84
Supergirl '84
Creator '85
Club Paradise '86
Strange Tales/Ray Bradbury Theatre '86
The Last Emperor '87
High Spirits '88
The Dark Angel '91
King Ralph '91
The Seventh Coin '92
Wings of Fame '93
Gulliver's Travels '95

Nobuko Otowa
The Island '61
Onibaba '64
Last War '68

Angelica Ott
Hell Hounds of Alaska '73
Fight for Gold '86

John Ottavino
Bob Roberts '92
Malcolm X '92

Barry Otto
Bliss '85
Howling 3: The Marsupials '87
Strictly Ballroom '92
The Custodian '94

Miranda Otto
The 13th Floor '88
The Last Days of Chez Nous '92
The Nostradamus Kid '92

Andre Oumansky
Burnt by the Sun '94
Othello '95

Gerard Oury
The Love of Three Queens '54
Back to the Wall '56
The Prize '63

Maria Ouspenskaya
Dodsworth '36
Conquest '37
Love Affair '39
The Rains Came '39
Beyond Tomorrow '40
Dance, Girl, Dance '40
Waterloo Bridge '40
Kings Row '41
The Wolf Man '41
Frankenstein Meets the Wolfman '42
The Shanghai Gesture '42

Peter Outerbridge
Victim of Beauty '91
Cool Runnings '93
For the Moment '94
Paris, France '94
The Android Affair '95

Park Overall
Biloxi Blues '88
Mississippi Burning '88
Tainted '88
Lost Angels '89
Kindergarten Cop '90
House of Cards '92
The Gambler Returns: The Luck of the Draw '93
Undercover Blues '93
The Vanishing '93
The Good Old Boys '95

Lynne Overman
Little Miss Marker '34
Midnight '34
Union Pacific '39
Edison the Man '40
Caught in the Draft '41
Reap the Wild Wind '42
Roxie Hart '42

Frank Overton
Desire Under the Elms '58
To Kill a Mockingbird '62

Rick Overton
Beverly Hills Cop '84
Odd Jobs '85
Million Dollar Mystery '87
Traxx '87
Earth Girls Are Easy '89
A Sinful Life '89
Blind Fury '90
National Lampoon's Attack of the 5 Ft. 2 Women '94

Bill Owen
The Gay Lady '49
The Hellfire Club '61
Georgy Girl '66
The Comeback '77
Singleton's Pluck '84

Clive Owen
Lorna Doone '90
Close My Eyes '91
Class of '61 '92
Century '94
The Return of the Native '94

Garry Owen
Hold Your Man '33
Dark Mirror '46

Michael Owen
Dick Tracy vs. Crime Inc. '41
Youth Aflame '59

Reginald Owen
Ghost City '32
Queen Christina '33
A Study in Scarlet '33
Fashions of 1934 '34
Of Human Bondage '34
Anna Karenina '35
A Tale of Two Cities '35
The Great Ziegfeld '36
Love on the Run '36
Rose Marie '36
The Bride Wore Red '37
Conquest '37
Madame X '37
Personal Property '37
A Christmas Carol '38
Everybody Sing '38
Rosalie '38
The Real Glory '39
Tarzan's Secret Treasure '41
They Met in Bombay '41
A Woman's Face '41
Cairo '42
I Married an Angel '42
Mrs. Miniver '42
Random Harvest '42
Reunion in France '42
Somewhere I'll Find You '42
White Cargo '42
Woman of the Year '42
Above Suspicion '43
Madame Curie '43
The Canterville Ghost '44
National Velvet '44
Captain Kidd '45
The Valley of Decision '45
Diary of a Chambermaid '46
Monsieur Beaucaire '46
Julia Misbehaves '48
The Pirate '48
The Three Musketeers '48
Challenge to Lassie '49
The Miniver Story '50
Red Garters '54
The Thrill of It All! '63

Seena Owen
The Lamb '15
Intolerance '16
Queen Kelly '29

Gary Owens
I'm Gonna Git You Sucka '88
Killcrazy '89
Digging Up Business '91

Patricia Owens
The Happiest Days of Your Life '50
Sayonara '57
The Fly '58
The Law and Jake Wade '58
Hell to Eternity '60

Earl Owensby
Challenge '74
Death Driver '78
The Wolfman '82
Dogs of Hell '83
Manhunter '83
The Rutherford County Line '87

Monroe Owsley
Ex-Lady '33
Goin' to Town '35

Catherine Oxenberg
The Lair of the White Worm '88
K-9000 '89
Swimsuit: The Movie '89
Overexposed '90
Sexual Response '92
Charles & Diana: A Palace Divided '93
Rubdown '93

David Oxley
Night Ambush '57
House of the Living Dead '73

Moishe Oysher
The Cantor's Son '37
The Singing Blacksmith '38

Frank Oz
The Empire Strikes Back '80
An American Werewolf in London '81
Spies Like Us '85

Eitaro Ozawa
Record of a Tenement Gentleman '47
The Human Condition: No Greater Love '58
Sandakan No. 8 '74

Sakae Ozawa
Ugetsu '53
The Crucified Lovers '54
Princess Yang Kwei Fei '55

Shoichi Ozawa
The Pornographers '66
The Ballad of Narayama '83
Black Rain '88

Madeleine Ozeray
Crime and Punishment '35
Liliom '35

Jack Paar
Easy Living '49
Walk Softly, Stranger '50
Love Nest '51

Judy Pace
Cotton Comes to Harlem '70
Three in the Cellar '70
Brian's Song '71
Frogs '72

Tom Pace
The Astro-Zombies '67
Girl in Gold Boots '69
Blood Orgy of the She-Devils '74

Frederico Pacifici
Flight of the Innocent '93
Fluke '95

Al Pacino
The Godfather '72
Scarecrow '73
Serpico '73
The Godfather, Part 2 '74
Dog Day Afternoon '75
Panic in Needle Park '75
America at the Movies '76
Bobby Deerfield '77
And Justice for All '79
Cruising '80
The Godfather 1902-1959: The Complete Epic '81
Author! Author! '82
Scarface '83
Revolution '85
Sea of Love '89
Dick Tracy '90
The Godfather, Part 3 '90
Frankie and Johnny '91
Glengarry Glen Ross '92

Scent of a Woman '92
Carlito's Way '93
City Hall '95
Heat '95
Two Bits '96

Charles Lloyd Pack
River Beat '54
Stranger in Town '57

David Packer
You Can't Hurry Love '88
The Runnin' Kind '89
Trust Me '89
Silent Motive '91

Joanna Pacula
Gorky Park '83
Not Quite Paradise '86
Death Before Dishonor '87
Escape from Sobibor '87
The Kiss '88
Options '88
Sweet Lies '88
Marked for Death '90
Husbands and Lovers '91
Black Ice '92
Eyes of the Beholder '92
Every Breath '93
Silence of the Hams '93
Tombstone '93
Under Investigation '93
Warlock: The Armageddon '93
Deep Red '94
Captain Nuke and the Bomber Boys '95
Timemaster '95

Sarah Padden
Cross Examination '32
Tomorrow's Children '34
Exiled to Shanghai '37
Three Comrades '38
In Old Colorado '41
Reg'lar Fellers '41
The Mad Monster '42
Riders of the West '42
Snuffy Smith, Yard Bird '42
Girl Rush '44
Range Law '44
Song of Old Wyoming '45
Wildfire '45
Wild West '46

Hugh Paddick
The Killing of Sister George '69
Naughty Knights '71

Robert Padilla
The Great Gundown '75
Twisted Nightmare '87

Lea Padovani
Modigliani '58
The Naked Maja '59

Anita Page
Our Dancing Daughters '28
Broadway Melody '29
Our Modern Maidens '29
Free and Easy '30
Sidewalks of New York '31
Skyscraper Souls '32
After Midnight '33
Jungle Bride '33

Bradley Page
Champagne for Breakfast '35
Mistaken Identity '36
The Affairs of Annabel '38

Dorothy Page
The Singing Cowgirl '39
Water Rustlers '39
Ride 'Em Cowgirl '41

Gale Page
Four Daughters '38
Knute Rockne: All American '40
They Drive by Night '40

Genevieve Page
Girl in His Pocket '57
Song Without End '60
El Cid '61
The Day and the Hour '63
Belle de Jour '67
Mayerling '68
Gun Crazy '69
The Private Life of Sherlock Holmes '70
Buffet Froid '79

Geraldine Page
Hondo '53
Summer and Smoke '61
Sweet Bird of Youth '62
Toys in the Attic '63
ABC Stage 67: Truman Capote's A Christmas Memory '66
Barefoot in Athens '66
You're a Big Boy Now '66
The Happiest Millionaire '67
Whatever Happened to Aunt Alice? '69
The Beguiled '70
Pete 'n' Tillie '72
The Day of the Locust '75
Hazel's People '75
Nasty Habits '77
Interiors '78
Honky Tonk Freeway '81
I'm Dancing as Fast as I Can '82
The Dollmaker '84
Harry's War '84
Loving '84
The Pope of Greenwich Village '84
The Adventures of Huckleberry Finn '85
The Bride '85
The Hitchhiker '85
The Trip to Bountiful '85
Walls of Glass '85
White Nights '85
Native Son '86
My Little Girl '87
Riders to the Sea '88

Harrison Page
Lionheart '90
Carnosaur '93

Joy Page
Conquest of Cochise '53
Fighter Attack '53

LaWanda Page
B.A.D. Cats '80
Zapped! '82
Mausoleum '83
Shakes the Clown '92

Patti Page
Elmer Gantry '60
Boys' Night Out '62

Alfred Paget
The Lamb '15
The Babylon Story from "Intolerance" '16
Intolerance '16
America/The Fall of Babylon '24

Debra Paget
House of Strangers '49
Broken Arrow '50
Stars and Stripes Forever '52
Demetrius and the Gladiators '54
Prince Valiant '54
The Last Hunt '56
Love Me Tender '56
The Ten Commandments '56
Omar Khayyam '57
From the Earth to the Moon '58
Journey to the Lost City '58
Tales of Terror '62
The Haunted Palace '63
The Mercenaries '65

Nicola Pagett
Oliver's Story '78
Privates on Parade '84
An Awfully Big Adventure '94

Marcel Pagliero
Open City '45
Dedee d'Anvers '49

Janis Paige
Hollywood Canteen '44
Romance on the High Seas '48
Winter Meeting '48
Silk Stockings '57
Please Don't Eat the Daisies '60
Bachelor in Paradise '69
Angel on My Shoulder '80
Magic on Love Island '80
Love at the Top '86
Natural Causes '94

Mabel Paige
Nocturne '46
The Scar '48

Robert Paige
The Monster and the Girl '41
Pardon My Sarong '42
Son of Dracula '43
The Red Stallion '47
The Green Promise '49
Abbott and Costello Go to Mars '53

Geraldine Pailhas
Don Juan DeMarco '94
Suite 16 '94

Didier Pain
My Father's Glory '91
My Mother's Castle '91

Heidi Paine
New York's Finest '87
Alien Seed '89
Lethal Games '90
Wildest Dreams '90

Nestor Paiva
Prison Train '38
The Falcon in Mexico '44
The Purple Heart '44
Fear '46
Shoot to Kill '47
Follow Me Quietly '49
Double Dynamite '51
Five Fingers '52
Creature from the Black Lagoon '54
Revenge of the Creature '55
Tarantula '55
The Mole People '56
The Nine Lives of Elfego Baca '58
Outcasts of the City '58
Frontier Uprising '61
Ballad of a Gunfighter '64
Jesse James Meets Frankenstein's Daughter '65

Holly Palance
The Omen '76
Tuxedo Warrior '82
The Best of Times '86
Cast the First Stone '89

Jack Palance
The Halls of Montezuma '50
Panic in the Streets '50
Sudden Fear '52
Arrowhead '53
Second Chance '53
Shane '53
The Silver Chalice '54
The Big Knife '55
I Died a Thousand Times '55
Requiem for a Heavyweight '56
Lonely Man '57
The Battle of Austerlitz '60
The Mongols '60
Barabbas '62
Contempt '64
Alice Through the Looking Glass '66
The Professionals '66
Torture Garden '67
Deadly Sanctuary '68
Dr. Jekyll and Mr. Hyde '68
Strange Case of Dr. Jekyll & Mr. Hyde '68
Desperados '69
The Horsemen '70
The McMasters '70
Monte Walsh '70
Battle of the Commandos '71
Chato's Land '71
Rulers of the City '71
Dracula '73
Oklahoma Crude '73
Craze '74
Four Deuces '75
God's Gun '75
Great Adventure '75
The Hatfields & the McCoys '75
The Sensuous Nurse '76
Sting of the West '76
Big Boss '77
Mr. Scarface '77
Portrait of a Hitman '77
Welcome to Blood City '77
Cop in Blue Jeans '78
One Man Jury '78
Angel's Brigade '79
Cocaine Cowboys '79
The Last Ride of the Dalton Gang '79
Bloody Avenger '80s
Hell's Brigade: The Final Assault '80
Unknown Powers '80
Hawk the Slayer '81
Alone in the Dark '82
Black Cobra '83
The Last Contract '86
Outlaw of Gor '87
Bagdad Cafe '88
Gor '88
Young Guns '88
Batman '89
Tango and Cash '89
City Slickers '91
Keep the Change '92
Solar Crisis '92
Cyborg 2 '93
City Slickers 2: The Legend of Curly's Gold '94
Cops and Robbersons '94
Buffalo Girls '95

Ron Palillo
Doin' Time '85
Hellgate '89
SnakeEater '89
Committed '91

Michael Palin
John Cleese on How to Irritate People '68
Monty Python's Flying Circus '71
And Now for Something Completely Different '72
Monty Python and the Holy Grail '75
Ripping Yarns '75
Jabberwocky '77
Monty Python's Life of Brian '79
Secret Policeman's Private Parts '81
Time Bandits '81
The Missionary '82
Monty Python Live at the Hollywood Bowl '82
The Secret Policeman's Other Ball '82
Monty Python's The Meaning of Life '83
A Private Function '84
Brazil '85
A Fish Called Wanda '88
Monty Python's Parrot Sketch Not Included '90
American Friends '91

Anita Pallenberg
Barbarella '68
Performance '70

Eugene Pallette
The Birth of a Nation '15
Intolerance '16
The Three Musketeers '21
Mantrap '26
The Virginian '29
Shanghai Express '32
Strangers of the Evening '32
The Kennel Murder Case '33
The Ghost Goes West '36
My Man Godfrey '36
Stowaway '36
100 Men and a Girl '37
Topper '37
The Adventures of Robin Hood '38
First Love '39
Mr. Smith Goes to Washington '39
The Mark of Zorro '40
Young Tom Edison '40
The Bride Came C.O.D. '41
The Lady Eve '41
Big Street '42
Silver Queen '42
Heaven Can Wait '43
Pin-Up Girl '44
Sensations of 1945 '44

Gabriella Pallotti
The Roof '56
Il Grido '57
The Mongols '60
Hero of Rome '63

Ulf Palme
Miss Julie '50
Dreams '55

Betsy Palmer
The Long Gray Line '55
Mister Roberts '55
Queen Bee '55
The Tin Star '57
The Last Angry Man '59
Friday the 13th '80
Friday the 13th, Part 2 '81
Still Not Quite Human '92

Geoffrey Palmer
A Fish Called Wanda '88
Christabel '89
A Question of Attribution '91
Stalag Luft

Gregg Palmer
Francis Goes to West Point '52
The Creature Walks Among Us '56
Zombies of Moratau '57
The Rebel Set '59

Lilli Palmer
The Secret Agent '36
Chamber of Horrors '40
Beware of Pity '46
Cloak and Dagger '46
Body and Soul '47
My Girl Tisa '48
The Long Dark Hall '51
The Devil in Silk '56
Modigliani '58
But Not for Me '59
Conspiracy of Hearts '60
Adorable Julia '62
The Counterfeit Traitor '62
The Miracle of the White Stallions '63
The Amorous Adventures of Moll Flanders '65
Sebastian '68
Murders in the Rue Morgue '71
What the Peeper Saw '72
The Boys from Brazil '78
The Holcroft Covenant '85

Maria Palmer
Days of Glory '43
By the Light of the Silvery Moon '53
Outcasts of the City '58

Shirley Palmer
Campus Knights '29
Somewhere in Sonora '33

Chazz Palminteri
Oscar '91
There Goes the Neighborhood '92
A Bronx Tale '93
Bullets Over Broadway '94
The Perez Family '94
Faithful '95
Jade '95
The Last Word '95
Mulholland Falls '95
The Usual Suspects '95
Diabolique '96

Carlos Palomino
Strangers Kiss '83
Nasty Hero '89
My Samurai '92
Die Watching '93
Geronimo: An American Legend '93

Gwyneth Paltrow
Hook '91
Flesh and Bone '93
Jefferson in Paris '94
Mrs. Parker and the Vicious Circle '94
Moonlight and Valentino '95
The Pallbearer '95
Seven '95
Emma '96

Luciana Paluzzi
Journey to the Lost City '58
Carlton Browne of the F.O. '59
Return to Peyton Place '61
Muscle Beach Party '64
Thunderball '65
Chuka '67
One-Eyed Soldiers '67
A Black Veil for Lisa '68
The Green Slime '68
99 Women '69
Manhunt '73
The Klansman '74
Medusa '74

Yang Pan Pan
Duel of the Seven Tigers '80
Return of the Scorpion '80

Alessandra Panaro
The Bacchantes '63
Executioner of Venice '63

Richard Panebianco
China Girl '87
Dogfight '91

Franklin Pangborn
Flying Down to Rio '33
King Kelly of the U.S.A. '34
Doughnuts & Society '36
My Man Godfrey '36

Pangborn ▶cont.

Tango '36
All Over Town '37
Dangerous Holiday '37
Hats Off '37
The Mandarin Mystery '37
A Star is Born '37
Bluebeard's Eighth Wife '38
Carefree '38
Just Around the Corner '38
Vivacious Lady '38
Fifth Avenue Girl '39
Topper Takes a Trip '39
The Bank Dick '40
Christmas in July '40
A Girl, a Guy and a Gob '41
Never Give a Sucker an Even Break '41
Sullivan's Travels '41
Call Out the Marines '42
The Palm Beach Story '42
His Butler's Sister '43
Two Weeks to Live '43
The Great Moment '44
Hail the Conquering Hero '44
Till the Clouds Roll By/A Star Is Born '46
The Sin of Harold Diddlebock '47
Romance on the High Seas '48

Stuart Pankin
Dirt Bike Kid '86
Fatal Attraction '87
Love at Stake '87
Second Sight '89
Arachnophobia '90
That's Adequate '90
Life Stinks '91
Mannequin 2: On the Move '91
Betrayal of the Dove '92
The Vagrant '92
Beanstalk '94
Squanto: A Warrior's Tale '94
Father and Scout '95

John Pankow
To Live & Die in L.A. '85
Johnny Be Good '88
Monkey Shines '88
Talk Radio '88
Mortal Thoughts '91
Year of the Gun '91
A Stranger Among Us '92

Joe Pantoliano
Idolmaker '80
Eddie and the Cruisers '83
The Final Terror '83
Risky Business '83
The Goonies '85
Mean Season '85
Running Scared '86
Empire of the Sun '87
La Bamba '87
Scenes from the Goldmine '87
The Squeeze '87
The In Crowd '88
Midnight Run '88
Downtown '89
Nightbreaker '89
Tales from the Crypt '89
El Diablo '90
The Last of the Finest '90
Short Time '90
Zandalee '91
Through the Eyes of a Killer '92
Used People '92
Calendar Girl '93
Dangerous Heart '93
The Fugitive '93
Me and the Kid '93
Three of Hearts '93
Baby's Day Out '94
Robot in the Family '94
The Spy Within '94
Bad Boys '95
The Immortals '95
The Last Word '95
Steal Big, Steal Little '95
Bound '96

Irene Papas
Tribute to a Bad Man '56
The Guns of Navarone '61
Zorba the Greek '64
The Brotherhood '68
Anne of the Thousand Days '69
A Dream of Kings '69
Z '69
Trojan Women '71
1931: Once Upon a Time in New York '72
Moses '76
Iphigenia '77
Mohammed: Messenger of God '77
Christ Stopped at Eboli '79
Sidney Sheldon's Bloodline '79
Lion of the Desert '81
Erendira '83
The Assisi Underground '84
Into the Night '85
Sweet Country '87
High Season '88
Jacob '94

Laslo Papas
Crazed '82
Bloodshed '83
Slipping into Darkness '88

Ike Pappas
Moon over Parador '88
The Package '89

Anna Paquin
The Piano '93
Jane Eyre '96

John Paragon
Eating Raoul '82
The Pee Wee Herman Show '82
Uncensored '85

Kiri Paramore
Flirting '89
The Last Days of Chez Nous '92

Michael Pare
Eddie and the Cruisers '83
The Philadelphia Experiment '84
Streets of Fire '84
Instant Justice '86
Space Rage '86
Women's Club '87
World Gone Wild '88
Eddie and the Cruisers 2: Eddie Lives! '89
Moon 44 '90
The Closer '91
Killing Streets '91
The Last Hour '91
Blink of an Eye '92
Dragonfight '92
Into the Sun '92
Sunset Heat '92
Point of Impact '93
Solar Force '94
Warriors '94
The Dangerous '95
Raging Angels '95
Triplecross '95
Village of the Damned '95

Marisa Paredes
Dark Habits '84
In a Glass Cage '86
High Heels '91
The Flower of My Secret '95

Mila Parely
The Rules of the Game '39
Beauty and the Beast '46
Three Stops to Murder '53

Monique Parent
Buford's Beach Bunnies '92
Married People, Single Sex 2: For Better or Worse '94
Play Time '94
Dark Secrets '95
Masseuse '95
Midnight Confessions '95
The Perfect Gift '95
Stripshow '95

Judy Parfitt
Hamlet '69
The Jewel in the Crown '84
Office Romances '86
Maurice '87
The Charmer '89
Getting It Right '89
Dark Obsession '90
Midnight's Child '93
Dolores Claiborne '94

Anne Parillaud
La Femme Nikita '91
Innocent Blood '92
Map of the Human Heart '93
Frankie Starlight '95

Jerry Paris
The Wild One '54
Marty '55
D-Day, the Sixth of June '56

Reg Park
Hercules and the Captive Women '63
Hercules in the Haunted World '64
Hercules, Prisoner of Evil '64

Cecil Parker
The Man Who Lived Again '36
Storm in a Teacup '37
Housemaster '38
The Lady Vanishes '38
The Stars Look Down '39
Dangerous Moonlight '41
Caesar and Cleopatra '46
Under Capricorn '49
The Weaker Sex '49
Tony Draws a Horse '51
The Detective '54
The Ladykillers '55
Court Jester '56
A Tale of Two Cities '58
The Wreck of the Mary Deare '59
The Pure Hell of St. Trinian's '61
The Brain '62
Heavens Above '63
Lady L '65
A Study in Terror '66

Cecilia Parker
Rainbow Ranch '33
Riders of Destiny '33
Honor of the Range '34
The Lost Jungle '34
Mystery Ranch '34
Ah, Wilderness! '35
Naughty Marietta '35
Tombstone Canyon '35
Roll Along Cowboy '37
Sweetheart of the Navy '37
Love Finds Andy Hardy '38
Andy Hardy Gets Spring Fever '39
Andy Hardy Meets Debutante '40
Andy Hardy's Double Life '42

Corey Parker
Biloxi Blues '88
Big Man on Campus '89
How I Got into College '89
I'm Dangerous Tonight '90
White Palace '90
Broadway Bound '92
The Lost Language of Cranes '92
A Mother's Prayer '95
Mr. & Mrs. Loving '96

Ed Parker
Ghost Rider '35
God's Country and the Man '37
The Secret Code '42

Eleanor Parker
Hollywood Canteen '44
Never Say Goodbye '46
Escape Me Never '47
It's a Great Feeling '49
Chain Lightning '50
Three Secrets '50
Detective Story '51
Scaramouche '52
Above and Beyond '53
Escape from Fort Bravo '53
Naked Jungle '54
Interrupted Melody '55
The Man with the Golden Arm '55
The King and Four Queens '56
A Hole in the Head '59
Home from the Hill '60
Return to Peyton Place '61
Panic Button '62
The Sound of Music '65
The Oscar '66
Tiger and the Pussycat '67
Hans Brinker '69
Maybe I'll Be Home in the Spring '70
Home for the Holidays '72
Fantasy Island '76
The Bastard '78
She's Dressed to Kill '79
Dead on the Money '91

Fess Parker
Them! '54
Davy Crockett, King of the Wild Frontier '55
Davy Crockett and the River Pirates '56
The Great Locomotive Chase '56
Westward Ho, the Wagons! '56
Old Yeller '57
The Light in the Forest '58
The Jayhawkers '59
Hell is for Heroes '62

Fred Parker
Cord & Dischords/Naughty Nurse '28
Roamin' Wild '36

Jameson Parker
Anatomy of a Seduction '79
The Gathering: Part 2 '79
A Small Circle of Friends '80
Callie and Son '81
American Justice '86
Prince of Darkness '87
Spy '89
Curse of the Crystal Eye '93

Jean Parker
Rasputin and the Empress '32
Gabriel Over the White House '33
Lady for a Day '33
Little Women '33
The Ghost Goes West '36
The Texas Rangers '36
The Flying Deuces '39
Beyond Tomorrow '40
Knights of the Range '40
Flying Blind '41
Bluebeard '44
Lady in the Death House '44
Navy Way '44
One Body Too Many '44
Rolling Home '48
The Gunfighter '50
A Lawless Street '55
Apache Uprising '66

Kim Parker
Fire Maidens from Outer Space '56
Fiend Without a Face '58

Lara Parker
Hi, Mom! '70
Night of Dark Shadows '71
Race with the Devil '75
The Solitary Man '82
Foxfire Light '84

Mary-Louise Parker
Signs of Life '89
Longtime Companion '90
Fried Green Tomatoes '91
Grand Canyon '91
Mr. Wonderful '93
Naked in New York '93
Boys on the Side '94
Bullets Over Broadway '94
The Client '94
A Place for Annie '94
Reckless '95
Sugartime '95

Michael Parker
Kill Line '91
My Own Private Idaho '91

Monica Parker
Improper Channels '82
Coming Out Alive '84

Nathaniel Parker
Hamlet '90
Piece of Cake '90
Wide Sargasso Sea '92
Squanto: A Warrior's Tale '94
Othello '95

Noelle Parker
Twisted '86
Ernest Saves Christmas '88
Lethal Lolita—Amy Fisher: My Story '92

Norman Parker
Killing Hour '84
Question of Faith '93

Sachi Parker
The Dancing Princesses '84
Peggy Sue Got Married '86
Riders to the Sea '88
Welcome Home, Roxy Carmichael '90

Sarah Jessica Parker
Almost Royal Family '84
First Born '84
Footloose '84
Girls Just Want to Have Fun '85
Going for the Gold: The Bill Johnson Story '85
Somewhere Tomorrow '85
Flight of the Navigator '86
L.A. Story '91
Honeymoon in Vegas '92
Hocus Pocus '93
Striking Distance '93
Ed Wood '94
If Lucy Fell '95
Miami Rhapsody '95

Sunshine Parker
Cannery Row '82
Spittin' Image '83

Suzy Parker
Funny Face '57
Ten North Frederick '58
The Best of Everything '59
The Interns '62

Willard Parker
Great Jesse James Raid '49
Hunt the Man Down/Smashing the Rackets '50
Bandit Queen '51

Gerard Parkes
The Last Winter '89
Speaking Parts '89
It Takes Two '95

Barbara Parkins
Valley of the Dolls '67
The Deadly Trap '71
The Mephisto Waltz '71
Asylum '72
Puppet on a Chain '72
Snatched '72
Christina '74
Law of the Land '76
Shout at the Devil '76
Bear Island '80
Breakfast in Paris '81
Calendar Girl Murders '84
To Catch a King '84

Bert Parks
Shining Star '75
The Freshman '90

Larry Parks
Harmon of Michigan '41
You Were Never Lovelier '42
Destroyer '43
The Jolson Story '46
Down to Earth '47
Her Husband's Affairs '47
Jolson Sings Again '49
Love Is Better Than Ever '52

Michael Parks
The Savage Bees '76
The Private Files of J. Edgar Hoover '77
Sidewinder One '77
Breakthrough '78
Midnight Auto Supply '78
Night Cries '78
The Evictors '79
ffolkes '80
Hard Country '81
Savannah Smiles '82
Chase '85
French Quarter Undercover '85
Club Life '86
The Return of Josey Wales '86
Arizona Heat '87
Stamp of a Killer '87
Welcome to Spring Break '88
Gore Vidal's Billy the Kid '89
The China Lake Murders '90
The Hitman '91
Storyville '92
Death Wish 5: The Face of Death '94
Stranger by Night '94
From Dusk Till Dawn '95

Trina Parks
Diamonds Are Forever '71
Darktown Strutters '74
The Muthers '76

Dita Parlo
Homecoming '28
L'Atalante '34
Grand Illusion '37

Emory Parnell
Casanova Brown '44
Miracle of Morgan's Creek '44
The Show-Off '46
Trail of Robin Hood '50
Ma and Pa Kettle Back On the Farm '51
Lost in Alaska '52
Ma and Pa Kettle at the Fair '52
Ma and Pa Kettle at Home '54
Pardners '56

Man of the West '58

Helen Parrish
Big Trail '30
Little Tough Guys '38
Mad About Music '38
First Love '39
Three Smart Girls Grow Up '39
You'll Find Out '40
Overland Mail '41
Sunset Serenade '42
X Marks the Spot '42

Julie Parrish
Paradise, Hawaiian Style '66
The Doberman Gang '72

Leslie Parrish
Li'l Abner '59
The Manchurian Candidate '62
For Love or Money '63
Sex and the Single Girl '64
The Giant Spider Invasion '75
The Invisible Strangler '76

Steve Parrish
Midnight '89
Scanners 3: The Takeover '92

David Parry
Dr. Caligari '89
The Lost Platoon '89
Auntie Lee's Meat Pies '92

Nastasha Parry
Crow Hollow '52
Haunted: The Ferryman '74

Tom Parsekian
Hot Resort '85
Club Life '86

Frederick Parslow
The Last Wave '77
Wrangler '88

Estelle Parsons
Bonnie & Clyde '67
Rachel, Rachel '68
Don't Drink the Water '69
I Never Sang For My Father '70
Watermelon Man '70
For Pete's Sake '74
Foreplay '75
Gentleman Bandit '81
Come Along with Me '84
Dick Tracy '90
A Private Matter '92

Karyn Parsons
Class Act '91
Gulliver's Travels '95
Major Payne '95

Nancy Parsons
Motel Hell '80
Porky's Revenge '85
Ladybugs '92
Wishman '93
Lakota Woman: Siege at Wounded Knee '94

Percy Parsons
Power '34
Rhodes '36
Dangerous Moonlight '41

Dolly Parton
9 to 5 '80
The Best Little Whorehouse in Texas '82
Rhinestone '84
A Smoky Mountain Christmas '86
Steel Magnolias '89
Straight Talk '92

Julia Parton
Vice Academy 3 '91
Good Girls Don't '95

Christine Pascal
The Clockmaker '76
Spoiled Children '77
Maids of Wilko '79
The Best Way '82
Sincerely Charlotte '86
Le Grand Chemin '87

Mary Ann Pascal
Writer's Block '91
Lethal Lolita—Amy Fisher: My Story '92

Olivia Pascal
Bloody Moon '83
C.O.D. '83

Isabelle Pasco
High Frequency '88
Prospero's Books '91

Richard Pasco
Sword of Sherwood Forest '60
The Gorgon '64

Adrian Pasdar
Streets of Gold '86
Top Gun '86
Near Dark '87
Made in USA '88
Cookie '89
Torn Apart '89
The Lost Capone '90
Vital Signs '90
Grand Isle '92
Carlito's Way '93
The Ghost Brigade '93
The Last Good Time '94
Just Like a Woman '95

Pier Paolo Pasolini
Oedipus Rex '67
The Decameron '70
The Canterbury Tales '71
Bellissimo: Images of the Italian Cinema '87

Cyndi Pass
Bikini Island '91
Deadbolt '92
Desperate Motives '92
Mission of Justice '92
The Force '94
Scanner Cop '94
Serial Killer '95

Vinny Pastore
True Love '89
The Jerky Boys '95

Robert Pastorelli
Dances with Wolves '90
Folks! '92
The Paint Job '93
Sister Act 2: Back in the Habit '93
Striking Distance '93
Eraser '96

Willie Pastrano
Wild Rebels '71
Alligator Alley '72

Michael Pataki
Dirt Gang '71
The Baby '72
Grave of the Vampire '72
The Bat People '74
The Last Porno Flick '74
The Amazing Spider-Man '77
When Every Day was the Fourth of July '78
Zoltan...Hound of Dracula '78
On the Edge: The Survival of Dana '79
The Last Word '80
Dead and Buried '81
Delinquent School Girls '84
Rocky 4 '85
American Anthem '86
Death House '88
Halloween 4: The Return of Michael Myers '88
The Underachievers '88
One More Chance '90

Wally Patch
Don Quixote '35
Inspector Hornleigh '39
Cottage to Let '41
Calling Paul Temple '48

Michael Pate
Face to Face '52
Five Fingers '52
Hondo '53
Houdini '53
Julius Caesar '53
King Richard and the Crusaders '54
A Lawless Street '55
The Oklahoman '56
Seventh Cavalry '56
Green Mansions '59
Tower of London '62
McLintock! '63
The Singing Nun '66
Return of Captain Invincible '83
Howling 3: The Marsupials '87

Bill Paterson
The Ploughman's Lunch '83
Comfort and Joy '84
The Killing Fields '84
A Private Function '84
Defense of the Realm '85
Coming Up Roses '87
Dutch Girls '87
Hidden City '87
The Adventures of Baron Munchausen '89
The Rachel Papers '89
Traffik '90
The Witches '90
The Object of Beauty '91
Truly, Madly, Deeply '91
Chaplin '92

Mandy Patinkin
The Big Fix '78
French Postcards '79
Last Embrace '79
Night of the Juggler '80
Ragtime '81
Daniel '83
Yentl '83
Follies in Concert '85
Maxie '85
Sunday in the Park with George '86
The Princess Bride '87
Alien Nation '88
The House on Carroll Street '88
Dick Tracy '90
Impromptu '90
The Doctor '91
True Colors '91
The Music of Chance '93
Squanto: A Warrior's Tale '94

Angela Paton
Groundhog Day '93
Trapped In Paradise '94

Laurie Paton
Norman's Awesome Experience '88
The Amy Fisher Story '93

Jason Patric
Toughlove '85
Solarbabies '86
The Lost Boys '87
The Beast '88
After Dark, My Sweet '90
Frankenstein Unbound '90
Denial: The Dark Side of Passion '91
Rush '91
Geronimo: An American Legend '93
The Journey of August King '95

Dennis Patrick
The Time Travelers '64
Joe '70
Dear Dead Delilah '72
Choices '81
The Air Up There '94

Dorothy Patrick
Follow Me Quietly '49
Torch Song '53
Thunder Pass '54

Gail Patrick
Badmen of Nevada '33
Murders in the Zoo '33
The Mysterious Rider '33
The Phantom Broadcast '33
To the Last Man '33
Wagon Wheels '34
My Man Godfrey '36
Stage Door '37
Mad About Music '38
Wives Under Suspicion '38
Doctor Takes a Wife '40
My Favorite Wife '40
Love Crazy '41
Brewster's Millions '45

Gregory Patrick
Sexpot '88
A Woman Obsessed '88

Lee Patrick
Law of the Underworld '38
Fisherman's Wharf '39
Footsteps in the Dark '41
The Maltese Falcon '41
In This Our Life '42
Somewhere I'll Find You '42
Gambler's Choice '44
Mrs. Parkington '44
Inner Sanctum '48
The Fuller Brush Girl '50
Vertigo '58
Pillow Talk '59
Summer and Smoke '61
7 Faces of Dr. Lao '63
Black Bird '75

Nick Patrick
Prime Suspect: Inner Circles '95
Loaded '96

Nigel Patrick
Trio '50
The Browning Version '51
Pandora and the Flying Dutchman '51
Encore '52
The Pickwick Papers '54
Raintree County '57
Sapphire '59
The League of Gentlemen '60
The Trials of Oscar Wilde '60
Johnny Nobody '61
Battle of Britain '69
The Virgin Soldiers '69
The Executioner '70
Mackintosh Man '73

Robert Patrick
Behind Enemy Lines '85
Eye of the Eagle '87
Future Hunters '88
Die Hard 2: Die Harder '90
Terminator 2: Judgment Day '91
The Cool Surface '92
Body Shot '93
Fire in the Sky '93
Zero Tolerance '93
Double Dragon '94
Hong Kong '97 '94
Decoy '95
Striptease '96

Luana Patten
So Dear to My Heart '49
Rock, Pretty Baby '56
Johnny Tremain & the Sons of Liberty '58
Follow Me, Boys! '66

Elizabeth Patterson
A Bill of Divorcement '32
No Man of Her Own '32
Hold Your Man '33
Hide-Out '34
Go West, Young Man '36
Bluebeard's Eighth Wife '38
Remember the Night '40
The Sky's the Limit '43
Follow the Boys '44
Lady On a Train '45
Welcome Stranger '47
Intruder in the Dust '49

Jay Patterson
Heaven Help Us '85
Nadine '87
Street Smart '87
D.O.A. '88
Double Exposure: The Story of Margaret Bourke-White '89
McBain '91
Nobody's Fool '94
Excessive Force 2: Force on Force '95

Lee Patterson
Above Us the Waves '56
The Key Man '57
Time Lock '57
The Spaniard's Curse '58
Jack the Ripper '60
Chato's Land '71
He Lives: The Search for the Evil One '88
Bullseye! '90

Neva Patterson
Solid Gold Cadillac '56
An Affair to Remember '57
Desk Set '57
David and Lisa '62
The Runaways '75
V '83
Women of Valor '86

Pat Patterson
Moonshine Mountain '64
Gas-s-s-s! '70
The Body Shop '72

Rocky Patterson
Nail Gun Massacre '86
Armed for Action '92
Blood on the Badge '92
The Dark Dealer '95

Sarah Patterson
The Company of Wolves '85
Snow White '89

Scott Patterson
Alien Nation: Dark Horizon '94
Little Big League '94

Shirley Patterson
Texas Kid '43
Driftin' River '46
Black Hills '48

Bill Patton
Fangs of Fate '25
Beyond the Trail '26
Rustlers of Red Dog '35

Mark Patton
Anna to the Infinite Power '84
A Nightmare on Elm Street 2: Freddy's Revenge '85

Will Patton
Variety '83
Chinese Boxes '84
Belizaire the Cajun '86
No Way Out '87
Stars and Bars '88
Wildfire '88
Signs of Life '89
Everybody Wins '90
A Shock to the System '90
Deadly Desire '91
Dillinger '91
In the Deep Woods '91
Murder on the Bayou '91
The Rapture '91
Cold Heaven '92
In the Soup '92
Midnight Edition '93
The Paint Job '93
Romeo Is Bleeding '93
The Client '94
Judicial Consent '94
Natural Causes '94
The Puppet Masters '94
Tollbooth '94
Copycat '95
The Spitfire Grill '95
Fled '96

Adrian Paul
Masque of the Red Death '89
The Cover Girl Murders '93
Highlander: The Gathering '93

Alexandra Paul
American Nightmare '81
Christine '84
Getting Physical '84
Just the Way You Are '84
American Flyers '85
8 Million Ways to Die '85
Millions '90
Prey of the Chameleon '91
In Between '92
Sunset Grill '92
Detonator '93
Cyber Bandits '94
The Paperboy '94
Baywatch the Movie: Forbidden Paradise '95
Detonator 2: Night Watch '95

David Paul
The Barbarians '87
Ghost Writer '89
Think Big '90
Double Trouble '91
Twinsitters '95

Don Michael Paul
Lovelines '84
Brotherhood of Justice '86
Alien from L.A. '87
Rolling Vengeance '87
Winners Take All '87
Aloha Summer '88
The Heart of Dixie '89
Rich Girl '91
Robot Wars '93

Peter Paul
The Barbarians '87
Ghost Writer '89
Think Big '90
Double Trouble '91
Twinsitters '95

Richard Paul
Not for Publication '84
Princess Academy '87
Pass the Ammo '88
Bloodfist 3: Forced to Fight '92
Beanstalk '94

Richard Joseph Paul
Under the Boardwalk '89
Oblivion '94

Stuart Paul
Emanon '86

Paul ▶cont.

Fate '90

Scott Paulin
The Right Stuff '83
A Soldier's Story '84
Teen Wolf '85
The Last of Philip Banter '87
To Heal a Nation '88
Tricks of the Trade '88
Weekend War '88
Captain America '89
From Hollywood to Deadwood '89
Grim Prairie Tales '89
Turner and Hooch '89
Pump Up the Volume '90
Deceit '93
Knights '93

Pat Paulsen
Where Were You When the Lights Went Out? '68
Foreplay '75
Harper Valley P.T.A. '78
Ellie '84
Night Patrol '85
They Still Call Me Bruce '86
Auntie Lee's Meat Pies '92

Rob Paulsen
Eyes of Fire '84
Perfect Match '88

Marisa Pavan
What Price Glory? '52
Drum Beat '54
Diane '55
The Rose Tattoo '55
The Man in the Gray Flannel Suit '56
John Paul Jones '59
Solomon and Sheba '59

Muriel Pavlow
Doctor in the House '53
Malta Story '53
Doctor at Large '57
Murder She Said '62

Lennox Pawle
David Copperfield '35
Sylvia Scarlett '35

Adam Pawlikowski
Ashes and Diamonds '58
Lotna '64

Katina Paxinou
For Whom the Bell Tolls '43
Inheritance '47
Rocco and His Brothers '60

Bill Paxton
Impulse '84
Streets of Fire '84
The Terminator '84
Weird Science '85
Aliens '86
Near Dark '87
Pass the Ammo '88
Brain Dead '89
Next of Kin '89
Slipstream '89
Back to Back '90
The Last of the Finest '90
Navy SEALS '90
Predator 2 '90
The Dark Backward '91
One False Move '91
Trespass '92
The Vagrant '92
Boxing Helena '93
Future Shock '93
Indian Summer '93
Monolith '93
Tombstone '93
Frank and Jesse '94
True Lies '94
Apollo 13 '95
Twister '96

Collin Wilcox Paxton
Wildflower '91
Fluke '95

Johnny Paycheck
Sweet Country Road '81
Hell's Angels Forever '83

David Paymer
No Way Out '87
Crazy People '90
City Slickers '91
Mr. Saturday Night '92
Heart and Souls '93
Searching for Bobby Fischer '93
City Slickers 2: The Legend of Curly's Gold '94
Quiz Show '94
The American President '95
City Hall '95
Get Shorty '95
Nixon '95
Unforgettable '96

Allen Payne
New Jack City '91
CB4: The Movie '93
Jason's Lyric '94
The Walking Dead '94
The Tuskegee Airmen '95
Vampire in Brooklyn '95

Bruce Payne
Wonderland '88
Passenger 57 '92
Full Eclipse '93
The Cisco Kid '94
One Man's Justice '95

Bruce Martyn Payne
Howling 6: The Freaks '90
Pyrates '91
Switch '91

John Payne
Dodsworth '36
Hats Off '37
College Swing '38
Tin Pan Alley '40
The Great American Broadcast '41
Sun Valley Serenade '41
Week-End In Havana '41
Footlight Serenade '42
Iceland '42
Springtime in the Rockies '42
To the Shores of Tripoli '42
Hello, Frisco, Hello '43
The Dolly Sisters '45
The Razor's Edge '46
Miracle on 34th Street '47
Kansas City Confidential '52
Silver Lode '54
Tennessee's Partner '55
Slightly Scarlet '56
Bail Out at 43,000 '57

Laurence Payne
Train of Events '49
The Crawling Eye '58
The Tell-Tale Heart '62
Vampire Circus '71
One Deadly Owner '74

Sally Payne
Jesse James at Bay '41
Man from Cheyenne '42
Romance on the Range '42

Amanda Pays
Cold Room '84
Oxford Blues '84
Max Headroom, the Original Story '86
The Kindred '87
Off Limits '87
Leviathan '89
The Flash '90
Dead on the Money '91
Exposure '91
The Flash 2: Revenge of the Trickster '91

Blanche Payson
Stan Without Ollie, Vol. 4 '25
Laurel & Hardy Comedy Classics, Vol. 5 '31

Barbara Payton
Great Jesse James Raid '49
Trapped '49
Kiss Tomorrow Goodbye '50
Only the Valiant '50
Bride of the Gorilla '51
Drums in the Deep South '51
Four Sided Triangle '53

Rock Peace
Attack of the Killer Tomatoes '77
Return of the Killer Tomatoes! '88

Mary Peach
No Love for Johnnie '60
A Gathering of Eagles '63
Ballad in Blue '66

E.J. Peaker
Hello, Dolly! '69
The Banker '89

Adele Pearce
Wyoming Outlaw '39
Pop Always Pays '40

Alice Pearce
The Belle of New York '52
Dear Brigitte '65
The Glass Bottom Boat '66

Craig Pearce
Vicious '88
The Seventh Floor '93

Guy Pearce
The Hunting '92
Heaven Tonight '93
The Adventures of Priscilla, Queen of the Desert '94

Jacqueline Pearce
Don't Raise the Bridge, Lower the River '68
White Mischief '88
Princess Caraboo '94

Joanne Pearce
Whoops Apocalypse '83
Morons from Outer Space '85

Mary Vivian Pearce
Mondo Trasho '69
Multiple Maniacs '70
Pink Flamingos '72
Female Trouble '74
Desperate Living '77

Patricia Pearcy
Squirm '76
Delusion '84

Richard Pearson
Thirteenth Reunion '81
Pirates '86

Virginia Pearson
The Wizard of Oz '25
The Taxi Mystery '26

Harold Peary
Look Who's Laughing '41
Here We Go Again! '42
Seven Days' Leave '42
The Great Gildersleeve '43
Clambake '67

Patsy Pease
He Knows You're Alone '80
Improper Conduct '94

Sierra Pecheur
Bronco Billy '80
Kalifornia '93

Bob Peck
Edge of Darkness '86
The Kitchen Toto '87
After Pilkington '88
Slipstream '89
The Black Velvet Gown '92
Jurassic Park '93

Cecilia Peck
Wall Street '87
My Best Friend Is a Vampire '88
Torn Apart '89
Ambition '91
Blue Flame '93
The Portrait '93

Gregory Peck
Days of Glory '43
The Keys of the Kingdom '44
Spellbound '45
The Valley of Decision '45
Duel in the Sun '46
The Yearling '46
Gentleman's Agreement '47
The Paradine Case '47
Twelve O'Clock High '49
The Gunfighter '50
Only the Valiant '50
Captain Horatio Hornblower '51
David and Bathsheba '51
The Snows of Kilimanjaro '52
Roman Holiday '53
The Man in the Gray Flannel Suit '56
Moby Dick '56
Designing Woman '57
The Big Country '58
The Bravados '58
Beloved Infidel '59
On the Beach '59
Pork Chop Hill '59
Cape Fear '61
The Guns of Navarone '61
To Kill a Mockingbird '62
Captain Newman, M.D. '63
How the West Was Won '63
Behold a Pale Horse '64
Arabesque '66
Mirage '66
MacKenna's Gold '69
Marooned '69
The Stalking Moon '69
The Omen '76
MacArthur '77
The Boys from Brazil '78
Sea Wolves '81
The Scarlet & the Black '83
The Blue and the Gray '85
Amazing Grace & Chuck '87
Hollywood Home Movies '87
Old Gringo '89
Other People's Money '91
The Portrait '93

J. Eddie Peck
Dangerously Close '86
Curse 2: The Bite '88
Lambada '89
To Grandmother's House We Go '94

Tony Peck
Brenda Starr '86
Poor Little Rich Girl: The Barbara Hutton Story '87
Hard Hunted '92
Inside Edge '92
Fit to Kill '93
The Magic Bubble '93
Die Hard: With a Vengeance '95

Sam Peckinpah
Gunfire '78
The Visitor '80

Chris Pederson
Suburbia '83
Point Break '91

Nia Peeples
Music Shoppe '82
North Shore '87
Deepstar Six '89
Swimsuit: The Movie '89
I Don't Buy Kisses Anymore '92
Return to Lonesome Dove '93
Deadlock 2 '94
Improper Conduct '94
Mr. Stitch '95

Joan Peers
Applause '29
The Tip-Off '31

Lisa Peers
Solo '77
Glass '90

Pele
Victory '81
A Minor Miracle '83
Hot Shot '86

Lisa Pelikan
Julia '77
Jennifer '78
The Best Little Girl in the World '81
Ghoulies '84
Swing Shift '84
Lionheart '90
Return to the Blue Lagoon '91
Into the Badlands '92

Valentine Pelka
Monsignor Quixote '91
First Knight '95

Raymond Pellegrin
Napoleon '55
A Woman of Rome '56
Street War '70s
Imperial Venus '71

Mark Pellegrino
Prayer of the Rollerboys '91
Midnight Witness '93

Matti Pellonpaa
Ariel '89
Leningrad Cowboys Go America '89
Night on Earth '91
La Vie de Boheme '93

Ana Luisa Peluffo
The New Invisible Man '58
The Living Head '59

Ron Pember
Bullshot '83
Footlight Frenzy '84

George Pembroke
Buried Alive '39
The Black Dragons '42
Dawn Express '42
I Killed That Man '42

Elizabeth Pena
El Super '79
Times Square '80
They All Laughed '81
Thief '81
Crossover Dreams '85
Down and Out in Beverly Hills '86
*batteries not included '87
La Bamba '87
Vibes '88
Blue Steel '90
Jacob's Ladder '90
The Waterdance '91
Fugitive Among Us '92
Across the Moon '94
Dead Funny '94
Free Willy 2: The Adventure Home '95
The Invaders '95
Lone Star '95

Julio Pena
Satanik '69
The Werewolf vs. the Vampire Woman '70

Austin Pendleton
Petulia '68
What's Up, Doc? '72
The Thief Who Came to Dinner '73
The Front Page '74
Starting Over '79
Simon '80
Talk to Me '82
Short Circuit '86
Hello Again '87
Mr. & Mrs. Bridge '90
The Ballad of the Sad Cafe '91
My Cousin Vinny '92
Four Eyes and Six Guns '93
Mr. Nanny '93
My Boyfriend's Back '93
Rain Without Thunder '93
Guarding Tess '94

Nat Pendleton
Blonde Crazy '31
Hell Fire Austin '32
Horse Feathers '32
The Sign of the Cross '32
Penthouse '33
Manhattan Melodrama '34
The Thin Man '34
Reckless '35
The Great Ziegfeld '36
Gangway '37
Shopworn Angel '38
At the Circus '39
Northwest Passage '40
Buck Privates Come Home '47
Scared to Death '47

Thaao Penghlis
Les Patterson Saves the World '90
The Lookalike '90

Susan Penhaligon
The Confessional '75
The Land That Time Forgot '75
Bouquet of Barbed Wire '76
Nasty Habits '77
Leopard in the Snow '78
Patrick '78
Soldier of Orange '78

Bruce Penhall
Picasso Trigger '89
Savage Beach '89
Do or Die '91
Hard Hunted '92
Enemy Gold '93
Fit to Kill '93

Christopher Penn
All the Right Moves '83
Rumble Fish '83
Footloose '84
The Wild Life '84
Pale Rider '85
At Close Range '86
Made in USA '88
Best of the Best '89
Leather Jackets '90
Futurekick '91
Mobsters '91
Reservoir Dogs '92

Beethoven's 2nd '93
Best of the Best 2 '93
Josh and S.A.M. '93
The Music of Chance '93
The Pickle '93
Short Cuts '93
True Romance '93
Imaginary Crimes '94
Mulholland Falls '95
To Wong Foo, Thanks for Everything, Julie Newmar '95
Under the Hula Moon '95

Leonard Penn
Girl of the Golden West '38
Streets of Sin '49

Matthew Penn
Playing for Keeps '86
Delta Force 3: The Killing Game '91

Sean Penn
Killing of Randy Webster '81
Taps '81
Fast Times at Ridgemont High '82
Bad Boys '83
Crackers '84
Racing with the Moon '84
The Falcon and the Snowman '85
At Close Range '86
Shanghai Surprise '86
Colors '88
Judgment in Berlin '88
Casualties of War '89
We're No Angels '89
State of Grace '90
Carlito's Way '93
Dead Man Walking '95

Jonathan Penner
A Fool and His Money '88
Down Periscope '96
The Last Supper '96

Alan Penney
Gone to Ground '76
Around the World in 80 Ways '86

Jack Pennick
Stagecoach '39
Lady from Louisiana '42
Mister Roberts '55

Joe Penny
Deathmoon '78
Bloody Birthday '80
Lifepod '80
Gangster Wars '81
Blood Vows: The Story of a Mafia Wife '87
Danger of Love '95

Sydney Penny
Pale Rider '85
Hyper-Sapien: People from Another Star '86
News at Eleven '86
Running Away '89
Bernadette '90
Child of Darkness, Child of Light '91

George Peppard
Bang the Drum Slowly '56
Pork Chop Hill '59
Home from the Hill '60
Breakfast at Tiffany's '61
How the West Was Won '63
The Carpetbaggers '64
Operation Crossbow '65
The Blue Max '66
Tobruk '66
Rough Night in Jericho '67
Pendulum '69
The Executioner '70
The Groundstar Conspiracy '72
Newman's Law '74
Damnation Alley '77
From Hell to Victory '79
Torn Between Two Lovers '79
Battle Beyond the Stars '80
Treasure of the Yankee Zephyr '83
Target Eagle '84
Your Ticket Is No Longer Valid '84
Night of the Fox '90
Silence Like Glass '90
The Chinatown Murders: Man Against the Mob '92
The Tigress '93

Barbara Pepper
Our Daily Bread '34
Last Outlaw '36
Rogue's Tavern '36
Hollywood Stadium Mystery '38
Wide Open Faces '38
Girls in Chains '43
Kiss Me, Stupid! '64

Marilia Pera
Pixote '81
Mixed Blood '84

Eileen Percy
Down to Earth '17
The Man from Painted Post '17
Reaching for the Moon '17
Let's Go! '23

Esme Percy
Bitter Sweet '33
Accused '36
Old Spanish Custom '36
21 Days '37

Jose Perez
Short Eyes '79
One Shoe Makes It Murder '82
Courage '86
Miami Blues '90

Rosie Perez
Do the Right Thing '89
Criminal Justice '90
Night on Earth '91
White Men Can't Jump '92
Fearless '93
Untamed Heart '93
It Could Happen to You '94

Vincent Perez
Cyrano de Bergerac '90
Indochine '92
Queen Margot '94
The Crow 2: City of Angels '96

Francois Perier
Sylvia and the Phantom '45
Orpheus '49
Gervaise '56
The Testament of Orpheus '59
Z '69
Godson '72
Stavisky '74
Tartuffe '84

Anthony Perkins
Friendly Persuasion '56
Fear Strikes Out '57
Lonely Man '57
The Tin Star '57
Desire Under the Elms '58
The Matchmaker '58
Green Mansions '59
On the Beach '59
Psycho '60
Tall Story '60
Goodbye Again '61
Phaedra '61
The Trial '63
Ravishing Idiot '64
The Fool Killer '65
Is Paris Burning? '68
Pretty Poison '68
Catch-22 '70
Someone Behind the Door '71
Life & Times of Judge Roy Bean '72
Ten Days Wonder '72
Murder on the Orient Express '74
Mahogany '75
Les Miserables '78
The Black Hole '79
Twice a Woman '79
Winter Kills '79
The Double Negative '80
ffolkes '80
The Sins of Dorian Gray '82
Psycho 2 '83
Crimes of Passion '84
The Glory Boys '84
Psycho 3 '86
Destroyer '88
Daughter of Darkness '89
Edge of Sanity '89
I'm Dangerous Tonight '90
Psycho 4: The Beginning '90
In the Deep Woods '91
A Demon in My View '92

Elizabeth Perkins
About Last Night... '86
From the Hip '86
Big '88
Sweet Hearts Dance '88
Love at Large '89
Avalon '90
Enid Is Sleeping '90
The Doctor '91
He Said, She Said '91
Indian Summer '93
The Flintstones '94
Miracle on 34th Street '94
Moonlight and Valentino '95

Millie Perkins
The Diary of Anne Frank '59
Wild in the Country '61
Ensign Pulver '64
The Shooting '66
Ride in the Whirlwind '67
Wild in the Streets '68
Cockfighter '74
Witch Who Came from the Sea '76
The Haunting Passion '83
Table for Five '83
License to Kill '84
Shattered Vows '84
At Close Range '86
Wall Street '87
Two Moon Junction '88
Pistol: The Birth of a Legend '90
Bodily Harm '95

Osgood Perkins
Love 'Em and Leave 'Em '26
Scarface '31

Max Perlich
Ferris Bueller's Day Off '86
Drugstore Cowboy '89
The Butcher's Wife '91
Rush '91
Born Yesterday '93
Cliffhanger '93
Dead Beat '94
Maverick '94
Georgia '95
Beautiful Girls '96
Homeward Bound 2: Lost in San Francisco '96

Rhea Perlman
Intimate Strangers '77
Ratings Game '84
Amazing Stories '85
Stamp of a Killer '87
Enid Is Sleeping '90
Class Act '91
There Goes the Neighborhood '92
Ted & Venus '93
Canadian Bacon '94
To Grandmother's House We Go '94
Matilda '96
Sunset Park '96

Ron Perlman
Quest for Fire '82
Ice Pirates '84
The Name of the Rose '86
Beauty and the Beast, Episode 1: Once Upon a Time in New York '87
Beauty and the Beast: Though Lovers Be Lost '89
Blind Man's Bluff '91
Sleepwalkers '92
The Adventures of Huck Finn '93
Double Exposure '93
Romeo Is Bleeding '93
When the Bough Breaks '93
Cronos '94
Police Academy: Mission to Moscow '94
Sensation '94
The City of Lost Children '95
Fluke '95
Mr. Stitch '95

Gigi Perreau
Never a Dull Moment '50
Dance with Me, Henry '56
The Man in the Gray Flannel Suit '56
Girls' Town '59
Hell on Wheels '67
Journey to the Center of Time '67

Paul Perri
Hit & Run '82
Delta Force 2: Operation Stranglehold '90
Hellraiser 4: Bloodline '95

Mireille Perrier
Boy Meets Girl '84
Chocolat '88
Love Without Pity '91
Toto le Heros '91
Trahir '93

Jack Perrin
Midnight Faces '26
Rawhide Mail '30s
Apache Kid's Escape '30
Hell Fire Austin '32
Texas Jack '35
Gun Grit '36
The Story of Vernon and Irene Castle '39
New Moon '40
West of Pinto Basin '40
The North Star '43
I Shot Billy the Kid '50
Bandit Queen '51
Ten Wanted Men '54
Them! '54
The Court Martial of Billy Mitchell '55
When Gangland Strikes '56
Sunrise at Campobello '60

Jacques Perrin
The 317th Platoon '65
Z '69
Donkey Skin '70
Dos Cruces en Danger Pass '71
State of Siege '73
Black and White in Color '76
The Desert of the Tartars '76
Le Crabe Tambour '77
Cinema Paradiso '88
Flight of the Innocent '93

Valerie Perrine
Slaughterhouse Five '72
The Last American Hero '73
Lenny '74
Mr. Billion '77
Superman: The Movie '78
The Electric Horseman '79
The Magician of Lublin '79
Can't Stop the Music '80
Superman 2 '80
The Agency '81
The Border '82
When Your Lover Leaves '83
The Three Little Pigs '84
Water '85
Maid to Order '87
Sweet Bird of Youth '89
Bright Angel '91
Boiling Point '93
Girl in the Cadillac '94
The Break '95

Leslie Perrins
Nine Days a Queen '34
The Silent Passenger '35
Man on the Run '49

Francoise Perrot
My Best Friend's Girl '84
Women's Prison Massacre '85
Life and Nothing But '89

Felton Perry
Night Call Nurses '72
Walking Tall '73
Sudden Death '77
RoboCop '87
Checking Out '89
RoboCop 2 '90
RoboCop 3 '91
Dumb & Dumber '94

Jeffery Perry
The Chronicles of Narnia '89
Playmaker '94
Kingfish: A Story of Huey P. Long '95

John Bennett Perry
A Matter of Life and Death '81
Only When I Laugh '81
The Last Fling '86

Luke Perry
Sweet Trash '89
Terminal Bliss '91
Buffy the Vampire Slayer '92
Beverly Hills 90210: The Graduation '93
8 Seconds '94
Normal Life '96

Matthew L. Perry
The Whole Shootin' Match '79
A Night in the Life of Jimmy Reardon '88

Rod Perry
Black Godfather '74
Black Gestapo '75

Roger Perry
The Cat '66
Count Yorga, Vampire '70
The Return of Count Yorga '71
Conspiracy of Terror '75
Roller Boogie '79

Maria Perschy
Man's Favorite Sport? '63
No Survivors, Please '63
633 Squadron '64
The Mad Executioners '65
The Castle of Fu Manchu '68
A Witch Without a Broom '68
Last Day of the War '69
House of Psychotic Women '73
The Rue Morgue Massacres '73
Exorcism '74
Horror of the Zombies '74
People Who Own the Dark '75

Lisa Jane Persky
The Great Santini '80
Breathless '83
The Cotton Club '84
Shattered Vows '84
The Sure Thing '85
Peggy Sue Got Married '86
The Big Easy '87
Great Balls of Fire '89
When Harry Met Sally... '89
The Last of the Finest '90
Vital Signs '90
Coneheads '93
Dead Funny '94
Pontiac Moon '94

Nehemiah Persoff
On the Waterfront '54
The Wrong Man '56
The Badlanders '58
Al Capone '59
Green Mansions '59
Some Like It Hot '59
The Comancheros '61
A Global Affair '63
The People Next Door '70
Deadly Harvest '72
The Stranger Within '74
Eric '75
Francis Gary Powers: The True Story of the U-2 Spy '76
Voyage of the Damned '76
Killing Stone '78
The Rebels '79
The Henderson Monster '80
Sadat '83
Yentl '83
The Last Temptation of Christ '88
Twins '88

Essy Persson
Mission Stardust '68
Therese & Isabelle '68
Cry of the Banshee '70

Jon Pertwee
Ladies Who Do '63
Carry On Screaming '66
The House that Dripped Blood '71

Frank Pesce
The Pamela Principle '91
29th Street '91
Trapped In Paradise '94

Joe Pesci
Family Enforcer '76
Raging Bull '80
Eureka! '81
I'm Dancing as Fast as I Can '82
Easy Money '83
Once Upon a Time in America '84
Man on Fire '87
Lethal Weapon 2 '89
Betsy's Wedding '90
Goodfellas '90
Home Alone '90
JFK '91
The Super '91
Home Alone 2: Lost in New York '92
Lethal Weapon 3 '92
My Cousin Vinny '92
The Public Eye '92
Ruby's Dream '92
Jimmy Hollywood '94
With Honors '94
Casino '95

Lisa Pescia
Body Chemistry '90

Pescia ▶cont.

Body Chemistry 2: Voice of a Stranger '91

Donna Pescow
Saturday Night Fever '77
Policewoman Centerfold '83
Glory Years '87

Bernadette Peters
The Longest Yard '74
Silent Movie '76
The Jerk '79
The Martian Chronicles: Part 2 '79
The Martian Chronicles: Part 3 '79
Heartbeeps '81
Pennies From Heaven '81
Tulips '81
Annie '82
Sleeping Beauty '83
Sunday in the Park with George '86
Pink Cadillac '89
Slaves of New York '89
Alice '90
Impromptu '90
The Last Best Year '90

Brock Peters
Carmen Jones '54
To Kill a Mockingbird '62
The Pawnbroker '65
The Incident '67
Ace High '68
Daring Game '68
The McMasters '70
Slaughter's Big Ripoff '73
Soylent Green '73
Framed '75
The Adventures of Huckleberry Finn '78
To Heal a Nation '88
Alligator 2: The Mutation '90
Star Trek 6: The Undiscovered Country '91
The Secret '93

Clarke Peters
Mona Lisa '86
A Casualty of War '90

House Peters, Sr.
Human Hearts '22
Head Winds '25

House Peters, Jr.
Outlaw Country '49
Red Planet Mars '52

Jean Peters
It Happens Every Spring '49
As Young As You Feel '51
Niagara '52
Viva Zapata! '52
Pickup on South Street '53
Apache '54
Broken Lance '54
Three Coins in the Fountain '54
A Man Called Peter '55

Luan Peters
Man of Violence '71
Twins of Evil '71
Not Tonight Darling '72
Flesh and Blood Show '73
Land of the Minotaur '77
Con Man '92

Molly Peters
Thunderball '65
Target for Killing '66

Ralph Peters
Rough Ridin' Rhythm '37
Man's Country '38
Death Rides the Range '40
Meeting at Midnight '44

Susan Peters
Andy Hardy's Double Life '42
Random Harvest '42

Werner Peters
The Counterfeit Traitor '62
Curse of the Yellow Snake '63
The Phantom of Soho '64
The Corrupt Ones '67

Chris Petersen
When Every Day was the Fourth of July '78
Little Dragons '80
Ninja Masters of Death '85
Vampire Raiders—Ninja Queen '89

Pat Petersen
Little Dragons '80
Cold River '81

William L. Petersen
To Live & Die in L.A. '85
Manhunter '86
Amazing Grace & Chuck '87
Long Gone '87
Cousins '89
Young Guns 2 '90
Hard Promises '92
Keep the Change '92
Passed Away '92
Deadly Currents '93
Return to Lonesome Dove '93
In the Kingdom of the Blind the Man with One Eye is King '94
Fear '96

Amanda Peterson
Explorers '85
Can't Buy Me Love '87
The Lawless Land '88
Listen to Me '89
I Posed for Playboy '91
Fatal Charm '92
Windrunner '94

Cassandra Peterson
Working Girls '75
Balboa '82
Pee Wee's Big Adventure '85
Uncensored '85
Echo Park '86
Elvira, Mistress of the Dark '88

Dorothy Peterson
I'm No Angel '33
Peck's Bad Boy '34
Woman In the Window '44

Stewart Peterson
Where the Red Fern Grows '74
Against A Crooked Sky '75
Seven Alone '75
Pony Express Rider '76

Edward Petherbridge
Lovers of Their Time '85
Strange Interlude '90
An Awfully Big Adventure '94
Gulliver's Travels '95

Victor Petit
Night of the Death Cult '75
Terror Beach '80s
Street Warriors '87

Gio Petre
Gorilla '56
The Doll '62

Hay Petrie
The Old Curiosity Shop '35
21 Days '37
Crimes at the Dark House '39
Spy in Black '39
Spellbound '41
A Canterbury Tale '44
Great Expectations '46

Joanna Pettet
The Group '66
Casino Royale '67
Night of the Generals '67
Robbery '67
Blue '68
Pioneer Woman '73
A Killer in Every Corner '74
The Evil '78
Cry of the Innocent '80
Return of Frank Cannon '80
Double Exposure '82
Sweet Country '87
Terror in Paradise '90

Christopher Pettiet
Fatal Exposure '91
The Goodbye Bird '93
Carried Away '95

Lori Petty
Cadillac Man '90
Point Break '91
A League of Their Own '92
Free Willy '93
In the Army Now '94
Tank Girl '94
The Glass Shield '95

Angelique Pettyjohn
Hell's Belles '69
G.I. Executioner '71
Confessions of Tom Harris '72
Revenge of Doctor X '80s
The Lost Empire '83
Repo Man '83
Bio Hazard '85
The Wizard of Speed and Time '88

Joseph Pevney
Nocturne '46
The Street with No Name '48

Penny Peyser
The Frisco Kid '79
The In-Laws '79
Messenger of Death '88
Indecent Behavior '93

Dedee Pfeiffer
Toughlove '85
The Midnight Hour '86
Brothers in Arms '88
The Horror Show '89
Red Surf '90
A Climate for Killing '91
King's Ransom '91
Shoot '92
Double Exposure '93
Falling Down '93
Running Cool '93
Deadly Past '95
Up Close and Personal '96

Michelle Pfeiffer
B.A.D. Cats '80
Falling in Love Again '80
Callie and Son '81
Charlie Chan and the Curse of the Dragon Queen '81
Grease 2 '82
The Solitary Man '82
Power, Passion & Murder '83
Scarface '83
Into the Night '85
Ladyhawke '85
Sweet Liberty '86
Amazon Women on the Moon '87
The Witches of Eastwick '87
Dangerous Liaisons '88
Married to the Mob '88
Tequila Sunrise '88
The Fabulous Baker Boys '89
The Russia House '90
Frankie and Johnny '91
Love Field '91
Batman Returns '92
The Age of Innocence '93
Wolf '94
Dangerous Minds '95
Up Close and Personal '96

JoAnn Pflug
M*A*S*H '70
Catlow '71
The Day the Women Got Even '80

Joe Phelan
Zero Boys '86
South of Reno '87
Fatal Pulse '88
Terminal Exposure '89

Shawn Phelan
Caroline? '90
Breaking the Rules '92

Peter Phelps
The Lighthorsemen '87
Breaking Loose '90
Starlight Hotel '90
Merlin '92
Rock & Roll Cowboys '92

Mekhi Phifer
Clockers '95
High School High '96

John Philbin
North Shore '87
Shy People '87
Martians Go Home! '90
Point Break '91
The Crew '95

Mary Philbin
Human Hearts '22
Merry-Go-Round '23
The Phantom of the Opera '25
The Man Who Laughs '27

James Philbrook
Sound of Horror '64
Finger on the Trigger '65
Last Day of the War '69

Robert Philip
Children Shouldn't Play with Dead Things '72
Adios Amigo '75

Gerard Philipe
Devil in the Flesh '46
L'Idiot '46
La Chartreuse de Parme '48
Beauty and the Devil '50
La Ronde '51
Beauties of the Night '52
The Proud Ones '53
Les Grandes Manoeuvres '55
The Red and the Black '57
Modigliani '58
Fever Mounts at El Pao '59
Dangerous Liaisons '60

Bobbie Philips
TC 2000 '93
Hail Caesar '94

Lee Philips
Peyton Place '57
The Hunters '58
The Outer Limits: Galaxy Being '63
Psychomania '63

Mary Philips
A Farewell to Arms '32
Leave Her to Heaven '45
Prince Valiant '54

Barney Phillips
I Was a Teenage Werewolf '57
Savage Run '70

Bobbie Phillips
Back in Action '94
Ring of Fire 3: Lion Strike '94

Chynna Phillips
Caddyshack 2 '88
Goodbye, Miss 4th of July '88
The Invisible Kid '88
The Prize Pulitzer '89
Say Anything '89

Eddie Phillips
Probation '32
The Throwback '35
Phantom Patrol '36

Ethan Phillips
Bloodhounds of Broadway '89
Lean on Me '89
Green Card '90
Star Trek Voyager: Caretaker '95

Julianne Phillips
Summer Fantasy '84
Seven Hours to Judgment '88
Sweet Lies '88
Fletch Lives '89
Skin Deep '89
Getting Up and Going Home '92
A Vow to Kill '94
Big Bully '95

Leslie Phillips
Train of Events '49
The Limping Man '53
The Smallest Show on Earth '57
Maroc 7 '67
Empire of the Sun '87
Scandal '89
Mountains of the Moon '90
August '95
The Canterville Ghost '96

Lou Diamond Phillips
Trespasses '86
La Bamba '87
Dakota '88
Stand and Deliver '88
Young Guns '88
Disorganized Crime '89
The First Power '89
Renegades '89
Harley '90
A Show of Force '90
Young Guns 2 '90
Ambition '91
The Dark Wind '91
Shadow of the Wolf '92
Extreme Justice '93
Boulevard '94
Dangerous Touch '94
Sioux City '94
Teresa's Tattoo '94
Undertow '95
The Wharf Rat '95
Courage Under Fire '96

MacKenzie Phillips
American Graffiti '73
Miles to Go before I Sleep '74
Rafferty & the Gold Dust Twins '75
Eleanor & Franklin '76
More American Graffiti '79
Love Child '82

Michelle Phillips
The Death Squad '73
Dillinger '73
Valentino '77
Sidney Sheldon's Bloodline '79
Secrets of a Married Man '84
American Anthem '86
Assault and Matrimony '87
Let It Ride '89
Scissors '91
Rubdown '93
Army of One '94

Peg Phillips
Dogfight '91
How the West was Fun '95

Samantha Phillips
Deceit '93
Sexual Malice '93
The Dallas Connection '94

Sian Phillips
Goodbye, Mr. Chips '69
Murphy's War '71
I, Claudius, Vol. 2: Waiting in the Wings/What Shall We Do With Claudius? '80
I, Claudius, Vol. 3: Poison is Queen/Some Justice '80
I, Claudius, Vol. 4: Queen of Heaven/Reign of Terror '80
Nijinsky '80
The Carpathian Eagle '81
Clash of the Titans '81
Dune '84
The Doctor and the Devils '85
The Ewoks: Battle for Endor '85
Valmont '89
I, Claudius, Vol. 1: A Touch of Murder/Family Affairs '91
The Age of Innocence '93
Heidi '93

Sydney Coale Phillips
Cause of Death '90
Maximum Breakout '91

Wendy Phillips
Death Be Not Proud '75
Midnight Run '88
Bugsy '91

Max Phipps
Nate and Hayes '83
Return of Captain Invincible '83
The Blue Lightning '86
Sky Pirates '87
Dark Age '88

Nicholas Phipps
Elizabeth of Ladymead '48
Maytime in Mayfair '52
Captain's Paradise '53

William Phipps
The Vanishing Westerner '50
Cavalry Command '63

Joaquin Rafael (Leaf) Phoenix
Russkies '87
Parenthood '89
To Die For '95

River Phoenix
Explorers '85
The Mosquito Coast '86
Stand By Me '86
Little Nikita '88
A Night in the Life of Jimmy Reardon '88
Running on Empty '88
Indiana Jones and the Last Crusade '89
I Love You to Death '90
Dogfight '91
My Own Private Idaho '91
Silent Tongue '92
Sneakers '92
The Thing Called Love '93

Maurice Pialat
A Nos Amours '84
Under Satan's Sun '87

Jean Piat
The Would-Be Gentleman '58

Tower of Screaming Virgins '68

Ben Piazza
A Dangerous Age '57
The Hanging Tree '59
The Children of An Lac '80
The Five of Me '81
Consenting Adult '85
Scene of the Crime '85
Clean and Sober '88
Guilty by Suspicion '91

Tony Pica
Yesterday, Today and Tomorrow '64
House of Psychotic Women '73

Robert Picardo
The Howling '81
Explorers '85
Back to School '86
Innerspace '87
Jack's Back '87
China Beach '88
976-EVIL '88
Frame Up '91
Motorama '91
Matinee '92
Revenge of the Nerds 4: Nerds in Love '94
Wagons East '94
White Mile '94
Star Trek Voyager: Caretaker '95

Michel Piccoli
Death in the Garden '56
Le Doulos '61
The Day and the Hour '63
Contempt '64
Diary of a Chambermaid '64
Lady L '65
The Game is Over '66
Belle de Jour '67
Danger: Diabolik '68
The Milky Way '68
Phantom of Liberty '68
Topaz '69
The Things of Life '70
The Discreet Charm of the Bourgeoisie '72
Ten Days Wonder '72
La Grande Bouffe '73
Infernal Trio '74
Wedding in Blood '74
Leonor '75
Mado '76
Vincent, Francois, Paul and the Others '76
Spoiled Children '77
L'Etat Sauvage '78
Atlantic City '81
Beyond Obsession '82
La Passante '83
Dangerous Moves '84
Prize of Peril '84
Success is the Best Revenge '84
Peril '85
La Puritaine '86
La Belle Noiseuse '90
May Fools '90
Martha and I '91

Paul Picerni
The Scalphunters '68
Fearmaker '89

Irving Pichel
Oliver Twist '33
Dracula's Daughter '36
General Spanky '36
Dick Tracy '37
Torture Ship '39

Sorrels Pickard
Running Hot '83
Hardbodies '84

James Pickens, Jr.
Lily in Winter '94
Sodbusters '94
Sharon's Secret '95

Slim Pickens
Colorado Sundown '52
One-Eyed Jacks '61
Dr. Strangelove, or: How I Learned to Stop Worrying and Love the Bomb '64
In Harm's Way '65
Major Dundee '65
Talion '66
Flim-Flam Man '67
Rough Night in Jericho '67
Never a Dull Moment '68
Ballad of Cable Hogue '70
Iron Horsemen '71
Ride to Glory '71
The Cowboys '72
The Getaway '72
Ginger in the Morning '73
Pat Garrett & Billy the Kid '73
Poor Pretty Eddie '73
Legend of Earl Durand '74
The Apple Dumpling Gang '75
Babe! '75
Rancho Deluxe '75
White Line Fever '75
Hawmps! '76
Pony Express Rider '76
Mr. Billion '77
Shadow of Chikara '77
The White Buffalo '77
The Swarm '78
Beyond the Poseidon Adventure '79
1941 '79
Honeysuckle Rose '80
Tom Horn '80
The Howling '81
Story of a Cowboy Angel '81
Charlie and the Great Balloon Chase '82
Pink Motel '82
Sweet Creek County War '82
Crazy Horse and Custer: "The Untold Story" '90

Josh Picker
Flirting '89
Alex '92

Sarah Pickering
Little Dorrit, Film 1: Nobody's Fault '88
Little Dorrit, Film 2: Little Dorrit's Story '88

Blake Pickett
HauntedWeen '91
Dark Universe '93

Cindy Pickett
Night Games '80
Margin for Murder '81
Circle of Power '83
Hysterical '83
Call to Glory '84
Ferris Bueller's Day Off '86
The Men's Club '86
Echoes in the Darkness '87
Hot to Trot! '88
Deepstar Six '89
Crooked Hearts '91
Original Intent '91
Sleepwalkers '92
Wildcard '92
The Goodbye Bird '93
Son-in-Law '93
Evolver '94
Painted Hero '95

Mary Pickford
Griffith Biograph Program '09
D.W. Griffith Triple Feature '13
The Little American '17
A Poor Little Rich Girl '17
Rebecca of Sunnybrook Farm '17
Pride of the Clan '18
Stella Maris '18
Pollyanna '20
Suds '20
Little Annie Rooney '25
Sparrows '26
A Kiss for Mary Pickford '27
My Best Girl '27
Coquette '29
The Taming of the Shrew '29

Christina Pickles
Seizure '74
Revenge of the Nerds 4: Nerds in Love '94

Vivian Pickles
Harold and Maude '71
Elizabeth R '72
Candleshoe '78

Ronald Pickup
Nijinsky '80
Ivanhoe '82
Life of Verdi '84
Eleni '85
The Mission '86
Fortunes of War '87
The Attic: The Hiding of Anne Frank '88
Dr. Bethune '90
Jekyll and Hyde '90
Journey of Honor '91
My Friend Walter '93
The Rector's Wife '94
Scarlett '94

Molly Picon
East and West '23
Yidl Mitn Fidl '36
Mamele '38
Come Blow Your Horn '63
Fiddler on the Roof '71
For Pete's Sake '74
Murder on Flight 502 '75
Cannonball Run '81

Rebecca Pidgeon
The Dawning '88
Homicide '91

Walter Pidgeon
Saratoga '37
Girl of the Golden West '38
Listen, Darling '38
Shopworn Angel '38
Too Hot to Handle '38
Dark Command '40
House Across the Bay '40
It's a Date '40
Blossoms in the Dust '41
How Green Was My Valley '41
Mrs. Miniver '42
White Cargo '42
Madame Curie '43
Mrs. Parkington '44
Weekend at the Waldorf '45
Holiday in Mexico '46
Command Decision '48
Julia Misbehaves '48
The Miniver Story '50
That Forsyte Woman '50
The Bad and the Beautiful '52
Million Dollar Mermaid '52
Deep in My Heart '54
Executive Suite '54
The Last Time I Saw Paris '54
Men of the Fighting Lady '54
Hit the Deck '55
Forbidden Planet '56
Voyage to the Bottom of the Sea '61
Advise and Consent '62
Big Red '62
Cinderella '64
Funny Girl '68
Neptune Factor '73
Murder on Flight 502 '75
The Lindbergh Kidnapping Case '76
Two Minute Warning '76
Sextette '78

Claude Pieplu
Wedding in Blood '74
This Sweet Sickness '77
The Best Way '82

Charles B. Pierce
Grayeagle '77
Boggy Creek II '83

David Hyde Pierce
The Fisher King '91
Wolf '94
Nixon '95

Jill Pierce
Darkroom '90
Cyborg Soldier '94

Stack Pierce
Night Call Nurses '72
Murphy's Fault '88
Enemy Unseen '91
A Rage in Harlem '91
24 Hours to Midnight '92

Tony Pierce
Trancers 3: Deth Lives '92
Big Bully '95

Wendell Pierce
It Could Happen to You '94
Hackers '95
Waiting to Exhale '95

Eric Pierpont
Alien Nation: Dark Horizon '94
Blood for Blood '95
The Stranger '95

Sarah Pierse
The Navigator '88
Heavenly Creatures '94

Alexandra Pigg
Letter to Brezhnev '86
Smart Money '88
Bullseye! '90
Chicago Joe & the Showgirl '90
Strapless '90

Tim Pigott-Smith
The Hunchback of Notre Dame '82
The Jewel in the Crown '84
The Remains of the Day '93

Joseph Pilato
Day of the Dead '85
Married People, Single Sex '93
Fatal Passion '94

Nova Pilbeam
The Man Who Knew Too Much '34
Nine Days a Queen '34
Young and Innocent '37
Counterblast '48

Daniel Pilon
In Trouble '67
The Red Half-Breed '70
Brannigan '75
Starship Invasions '77
Snowballin' '85
Obsessed '88

Donald Pilon
The Pyx '73
Left for Dead '78
Keeping Track '86

Silvia Pinal
Viridiana '61
The Exterminating Angel '62
Simon of the Desert '66

Bronson Pinchot
Risky Business '83
Beverly Hills Cop '84
The Flamingo Kid '84
After Hours '85
Hot Resort '85
Second Sight '89
Blame It on the Bellboy '92
True Romance '93
Beverly Hills Cop 3 '94
The Great American Sex Scandal '94
It's My Party '95
Stephen King's The Langoliers '95
Courage Under Fire '96

Larry Pine
Hullabaloo Over Georgie & Bonnie's Pictures '78
Anna '87
Plain Clothes '88
Vanya on 42nd Street '94

Phillip Pine
The Phantom from 10,000 Leagues '56
The Lost Missile '58
Pot, Parents, and Police '71
Money to Burn '83

Robert Pine
Empire of the Ants '77
Enola Gay: The Men, the Mission, the Atomic Bomb '80
Mysterious Two '82
Are You Lonesome Tonight '92

Miguel Pinero
Short Eyes '79
Alphabet City '84
Almost You '85

Wang Ping
Duel of the Iron Fist '72
King Boxer '90

Jada Pinkett
Menace II Society '93
The Inkwell '94
Jason's Lyric '94
A Low Down Dirty Shame '94
Tales from the Crypt Presents Demon Knight '94
The Nutty Professor '96

Dominique Pinon
Diva '82
Moon in the Gutter '83
Alberto Express '92
Delicatessen '92
The City of Lost Children '95

Gordon Pinsent
Colossus: The Forbin Project '70
Newman's Law '74
John and the Missus '87
Blood Clan '91
A Vow to Kill '94

Leah K. Pinsent
The Bay Boy '85
April Fool's Day '86
Brutal Glory '89
Double Identity '89
The Little Kidnappers '90

Danny Pintauro
The Beniker Gang '83
Cujo '83
The Great American Sex Scandal '94

The Pioneers
Song of Arizona '46
Lights of Old Santa Fe '47
Under California Stars '48
Everybody's Dancin' '50

Frederick Piper
Oh, Mr. Porter '37
Johnny Frenchman '46
Hue and Cry '47
San Demetrio, London '47
The Blue Lamp '49

Kelly Piper
Maniac '80
Rawhead Rex '87

Roddy Piper
Body Slam '87
Hell Comes to Frogtown '88
They Live '88
Buy & Cell '89
Back in Action '94
Immortal Combat '94
No Contest '94
Tough and Deadly '94
Jungleground '95

Joe Piscopo
Johnny Dangerously '84
Wise Guys '86
Dead Heat '88
Best of Eddie Murphy '89
Huck and the King of Hearts '93
Sidekicks '93
Captain Nuke and the Bomber Boys '95
Two Bits & Pepper '95

Marie-France Pisier
Nous N'Irons Plus au Bois '69
Cousin, Cousine '76
The Other Side of Midnight '77
Love on the Run '78
French Postcards '79
We Will Not Enter the Forest '79
Hot Touch '80s
Chanel Solitaire '81
Miss Right '81
Prize of Peril '84

Luigi Pistilli
The Good, the Bad and the Ugly '67
The Scorpion's Tail '71
Twitch of the Death Nerve '71

Kimberly Pistone
Blue De Ville '86
WhiteForce '88

Mario Pisu
Juliet of the Spirits '65
The Sensuous Nurse '76

Maria Pitillo
Spike of Bensonhurst '88
The Lost Capone '90
Cooperstown '93
Bye Bye, Love '94

Sacha Pitoeff
Last Year at Marienbad '61
Inferno '78

Anne Pitoniak
Old Enough '84
Agnes of God '85
Best Seller '87
Sister, Sister '87
The Wizard of Loneliness '88
Old Gringo '89
The Ballad of the Sad Cafe '91
House of Cards '92

Brad Pitt
Across the Tracks '89
Cutting Class '89
Too Young to Die '90
Thelma & Louise '91
Cool World '92
The Favor '92
Johnny Suede '92
A River Runs Through It '92
Kalifornia '93

Pitt ▶*cont.*

True Romance '93
Interview with the Vampire '94
Legends of the Fall '94
Seven '95
12 Monkeys '95

Charles Pitt
Monaco Forever '83
Moving Target '89

Ingrid Pitt
Sound of Horror '64
Where Eagles Dare '68
The Vampire Lovers '70
The House that Dripped Blood '71
The Wicker Man '75
The Final Option '82
Transmutations '85
Hanna's War '88

Carl Pitti
Billy the Kid '41
Tribute to a Bad Man '56
Gun Glory '57

Tom Pittman
Verboten! '59
The Zodiac Killer '71

ZaSu Pitts
Greed '24
Risky Business '28
Sunny Side Up '28
The Wedding March '28
Lottery Bride '30
Sin Takes a Holiday '30
The Guardsman '31
The Crooked Circle '32
Strangers of the Evening '32
Aggie Appleby, Maker of Men '33
Mr. Skitch '33
Dames '34
Ruggles of Red Gap '35
Way Out West '37
Eternally Yours '39
Nurse Edith Cavell '39
No, No Nanette '40
Broadway Limited '41
The Bashful Bachelor '42
Meet the Mob '42
Mexican Spitfire at Sea '42
Mrs. Wiggs of the Cabbage Patch '42
Breakfast in Hollywood '46
The Perfect Marriage '46
Life with Father '47
Francis the Talking Mule '49
The Denver & Rio Grande '51
Francis Joins the WACs '54
This Could Be the Night '57
It's a Mad, Mad, Mad, Mad World '63
The Thrill of It All! '63

Jeremy Piven
Singles '92
Judgment Night '93
12:01 '93
Car 54, Where Are You? '94
P.C.U. '94
Twogether '94
Miami Rhapsody '95
Wavelength '96

Mary Kay Place
New York, New York '77
Starting Over '79
Private Benjamin '80
Modern Problems '81
The Big Chill '83
Waltz Across Texas '83
For Love or Money '84
Explorers '85
The History of White People in America '85
Smooth Talk '85
The Girl Who Spelled Freedom '86
A New Life '88
Portrait of a White Marriage '88
Bright Angel '91
Crazy from the Heart '91
Captain Ron '92
Samantha '92

Michele Placido
Till Marriage Do Us Part '74
Ernesto '79
Three Brothers '80
The Sicilian Connection '85
Summer Night '87
Summer Night with Greek Profile, Almond Eyes & Scent of Basil '87
Big Business '88
Forever Mary '89
Private Affairs '89
Drug Wars 2: The Cocaine Cartel '92
Lamerica '95

Tony Plana
Latino '85
Born in East L.A. '87
The Hillside Strangler '89
Romero '89
Havana '90
Sweet 15 '90
Why Me? '90
JFK '91
One Good Cop '91
The Burning Season '94
Primal Fear '96

Nigel Planer
Supergrass '87
The Young Ones '88

Scott Plank
The In Crowd '88
Pastime '91
Dying to Remember '93
Red Shoe Diaries 4: Auto Erotica '93
Saints and Sinners '95
Marshal Law '96

Dana Plato
Beyond the Bermuda Triangle '75
Return to Boggy Creek '77
High School USA '84

Edward Platt
Rebel Without a Cause '55
Rock, Pretty Baby '56
Written on the Wind '56
Designing Woman '57
North by Northwest '59
The Rebel Set '59
Atlantis, the Lost Continent '61

Louise Platt
Stagecoach '39
Captain Caution '40

Marc Platt
Tonight and Every Night '45
Down to Earth '47

Oliver Platt
Working Girl '88
Flatliners '90
Beethoven '92
Diggstown '92
Benny & Joon '93
Indecent Proposal '93
The Temp '93
The Three Musketeers '93
Funny Bones '94
The Infiltrator '95
Tall Tale: The Unbelievable Adventures of Pecos Bill '95
Executive Decision '96
A Time to Kill '96

Angela Pleasence
Six Wives of Henry VIII '70s
The Godsend '79
Stealing Heaven '88
The Favor, the Watch, & the Very Big Fish '92

Donald Pleasence
The Adventures of Robin Hood '55
A Tale of Two Cities '58
Circus of Horrors '60
The Hands of Orlac '60
Mania '60
No Love for Johnnie '60
Horsemasters '61
What a Carve-Up! '62
The Great Escape '63
The Greatest Story Ever Told '65
The Hallelujah Trail '65
Cul de Sac '66
Fantastic Voyage '66
Night of the Generals '67
Will Penny '67
You Only Live Twice '67
The Madwoman of Chaillot '69
Soldier Blue '70
House of the Damned '71
The Shaming '71
THX 1138 '71
Wedding in White '72
Dr. Jekyll and Mr. Hyde '73
The Freakmaker '73
From Beyond the Grave '73
The Rainbow Gang '73
Tales That Witness Madness '73
Barry McKenzie Holds His Own '74
The Black Windmill '74
The Count of Monte Cristo '74
Journey into Fear '74
Escape to Witch Mountain '75
Hearts of the West '75
I Don't Want to Be Born '75
The Passover Plot '75
Choice of Weapons '76
The Last Tycoon '76
Blood Relatives '77
The Eagle Has Landed '77
Goldenrod '77
Land of the Minotaur '77
Oh, God! '77
Telefon '77
Tomorrow Never Comes '77
The Bastard '78
Halloween '78
Sgt. Pepper's Lonely Hearts Club Band '78
The Uncanny '78
All Quiet on the Western Front '79
Better Late Than Never '79
Dracula '79
Gold of the Amazon Women '79
Jaguar Lives '79
Night Creature '79
The Puma Man '80
Escape from New York '81
Halloween 2: The Nightmare Isn't Over! '81
Power Play '81
Alone in the Dark '82
Devonsville Terror '83
Frankenstein's Great Aunt Tillie '83
Treasure of the Yankee Zephyr '83
The Ambassador '84
The Black Arrow '84
A Breed Apart '84
To Kill a Stranger '84
The Treasure of the Amazon '84
Warrior of the Lost World '84
Arch of Triumph '85
Creepers '85
Mansfield Park '85
The Monster Club '85
Nothing Underneath '85
Operation 'Nam '85
Into the Darkness '86
Phantom of Death '87
Prince of Darkness '87
The Room '87
Specters '87
Warrior Queen '87
Deep Cover '88
The Great Escape 2: The Untold Story '88
Ground Zero '88
Halloween 4: The Return of Michael Myers '88
Hanna's War '88
The House of Usher '88
American Tiger '89
Buried Alive '89
Casablanca Express '89
Halloween 5: The Revenge of Michael Myers '89
Ten Little Indians '89
Millions '90
River of Death '90
Shadows and Fog '92
The Advocate '93
Halloween 6: The Curse of Michael Myers '95

John Pleshette
The Trial of Lee Harvey Oswald '77
The Kid with the Broken Halo '82
Burning Rage '84
Lies of the Twins '91
Eye of the Stranger '93

Suzanne Pleshette
The Geisha Boy '58
40 Pounds of Trouble '62
Rome Adventure '62
The Birds '63
The Ugly Dachshund '65
The Adventures of Bullwhip Griffin '66
Nevada Smith '66
Blackbeard's Ghost '67
If It's Tuesday, This Must Be Belgium '69
Hard Frame '70
Suppose They Gave a War and Nobody Came? '70
Support Your Local Gunfighter '71
Legend of Valentino '75
The Shaggy D.A. '76
If Things Were Different '79
Hot Stuff '80
Oh, God! Book 2 '80
Help Wanted: Male '82
One Cooks, the Other Doesn't '83
For Love or Money '84
Dixie: Changing Habits '85
Kojak: The Belarus File '85
Alone in the Neon Jungle '87
The Queen of Mean '90
Battling for Baby '92

George Plimpton
Rio Lobo '70
Reds '81
Volunteers '85
A Fool and His Money '88
Easy Wheels '89
Little Man Tate '91
Just Cause '94

Martha Plimpton
Rollover '81
The River Rat '84
The Goonies '85
The Mosquito Coast '86
Shy People '87
Another Woman '88
Running on Empty '88
Stars and Bars '88
Parenthood '89
Silence Like Glass '90
Stanley and Iris '90
Samantha '92
Chantilly Lace '93
Daybreak '93
Inside Monkey Zetterland '93
Josh and S.A.M. '93
Forbidden Choices '94
Mrs. Parker and the Vicious Circle '94
A Woman at War '94
Beautiful Girls '96
Last Summer In the Hamptons '96

Melinda Plowman
Home Town Story '51
Billy the Kid Versus Dracula '66

Joan Plowright
Time Without Pity '57
The Entertainer '60
School for Scandal '65
The Merchant of Venice '73
Equus '77
Brimstone & Treacle '82
Britannia Hospital '82
Revolution '85
A Dedicated Man '86
Drowning by Numbers '87
The Dressmaker '89
Avalon '90
I Love You to Death '90
And a Nightingale Sang '91
Enchanted April '92
Stalin '92
Dennis the Menace '93
A Place for Annie '94
The Return of the Native '94
The Summer House '94
Widow's Peak '94
Mr. Wrong '95
A Pyromaniac's Love Story '95
The Scarlet Letter '95
Sorrento Beach '95
Jane Eyre '96

Eve Plumb
The Brady Bunch '69
Alexander: The Other Side of Dawn '77
Force of Evil '77
Little Women '78
Secrets of Three Hungry Wives '78
I'm Gonna Git You Sucka '88
A Very Brady Christmas '88
...And God Spoke '94

Amanda Plummer
The World According to Garp '82
Daniel '83
The Dollmaker '84
The Hotel New Hampshire '84
Courtship '87
Made in Heaven '87
Static '87
Gryphon '88
Riders to the Sea '88
Prisoners of Inertia '89
Joe Versus the Volcano '90
The Fisher King '91
Freejack '92
Miss Rose White '92
Last Light '93
Needful Things '93
Nostradamus '93
So I Married an Axe Murderer '93
Butterfly Kiss '94
Pulp Fiction '94
The Prophecy '95
The Right to Remain Silent '95

Christopher Plummer
Stage Struck '57
A Doll's House '59
The Fall of the Roman Empire '64
Inside Daisy Clover '65
The Sound of Music '65
Night of the Generals '67
Triple Cross '67
Battle of Britain '69
Waterloo '71
The Pyx '73
Return of the Pink Panther '74
Conduct Unbecoming '75
The Man Who Would Be King '75
Spiral Staircase '75
The Assignment '78
The Day That Shook the World '78
International Velvet '78
The Silent Partner '78
Star Crash '78
Hanover Street '79
Murder by Decree '79
Riel '79
Highpoint '80
The Shadow Box '80
Somewhere in Time '80
Disappearance '81
Eyewitness '81
The Amateur '82
Prototype '83
The Scarlet & the Black '83
The Thorn Birds '83
Dreamscape '84
Little Gloria...Happy at Last '84
Ordeal by Innocence '84
Lily in Love '85
The Boss' Wife '86
Boy in Blue '86
Many Faces of Sherlock Holmes '86
Dragnet '87
I Love N.Y. '87
Shadow Dancing '88
Souvenir '88
Mindfield '89
Firehead '90
Red Blooded American Girl '90
Where the Heart Is '90
Star Trek 6: The Undiscovered Country '91
Young Catherine '91
Liar's Edge '92
Crackerjack '94
Dolores Claiborne '94
Wolf '94
Kurt Vonnegut's Harrison Bergeron '95
12 Monkeys '95

Glenn Plummer
Pastime '91
South Central '92
Menace II Society '93
Speed '94
Convict Cowboy '95
Showgirls '95
Strange Days '95
The Substitute '96
Up Close and Personal '96

Werner Pochat
Flatfoot '78
Thunder Warrior 3 '88
Laser Mission '90

Rick Podell
Lunch Wagon '81
World Gone Wild '88

Rossana Podesta
Ulysses '55
Helen of Troy '56
Alone Against Rome '62
Sodom and Gomorrah '62
The Virgin of Nuremberg '65
Homo Eroticus/Man of the Year '71
The Sensual Man '74

Ken Pogue
The Grey Fox '83
Keeping Track '86
Miracle at Moreaux '86
Crazy Moon '87
Dead of Winter '87
Blind Man's Bluff '91
The Hitman '91
Run '91
Still Not Quite Human '92
The Amy Fisher Story '93

Eric Pohlmann
Blackout '50
Moulin Rouge '52
The Belles of St. Trinian's '53
Three Stops to Murder '53
Terror Street '54
Glass Tomb '55
Tiffany Jones '75

Larry Poindexter
American Ninja 2: The Confrontation '87
Blue Movies '88
Sorceress '94
Body Chemistry 4: Full Exposure '95

Priscilla Pointer
The Competition '80
Honeysuckle Rose '80
Archer: The Fugitive from the Empire '81
Mysterious Two '82
The Falcon and the Snowman '85
Rumpelstiltskin '86
A Nightmare on Elm Street 3: Dream Warriors '87
Disturbed '90
The Magic Bubble '93
Carried Away '95

Jean Poiret
The Last Metro '80
The Elegant Criminal '92

Sidney Poitier
Cry, the Beloved Country '51
Red Ball Express '52
Blackboard Jungle '55
Goodbye, My Lady '56
Band of Angels '57
The Mark of the Hawk '57
Something of Value '57
The Defiant Ones '58
All the Young Men '60
Paris Blues '61
A Raisin in the Sun '61
Pressure Point '62
Lilies of the Field '63
Bedford Incident '65
The Greatest Story Ever Told '65
A Patch of Blue '65
The Slender Thread '65
Duel at Diablo '66
Guess Who's Coming to Dinner '67
In the Heat of the Night '67
To Sir, with Love '67
For Love of Ivy '68
Brother John '70
They Call Me Mr. Tibbs! '70
The Organization '71
Buck and the Preacher '72
Uptown Saturday Night '74
Let's Do It Again '75
The Wilby Conspiracy '75
Piece of the Action '77
Little Nikita '88
Shoot to Kill '88
Separate But Equal '91
Sneakers '92
A Good Day to Die '95

Roman Polanski
A Generation '54
Innocent Sorcerers '60
The Fearless Vampire Killers '67
Ciao Federico! Fellini Directs Satyricon '69
The Magic Christian '69
Diary of Forbidden Dreams '73
The Tenant '76
Back in the USSR '92
A Pure Formality '94

Jon Polito
Deadly Business '86
Fire with Fire '86
Highlander '86
The Equalizer: Memories of Manon '88
The Freshman '90
Leather Jackets '90
Miller's Crossing '90
Barton Fink '91
The Crow '93
Fallen Angels 2 '93
Blankman '94
Bushwhacked '95
Fluke '95
The Invaders '95

Lina Polito
All Screwed Up '74
Blood Brothers '74

Oscar Polk
Green Pastures '36
Gone with the Wind '39

Ben Pollack
The Glenn Miller Story '54
The Benny Goodman Story '55

Sydney Pollack
Tootsie '82
Death Becomes Her '92
Husbands and Wives '92
The Player '92

Cheryl Pollak
My Best Friend Is a Vampire '88
Swimsuit: The Movie '89
Night Life '90
Pump Up the Volume '90
Crossing the Bridge '92

Kevin Pollak
Willow '88
Avalon '90
Another You '91
L.A. Story '91
Ricochet '91
A Few Good Men '92
Grumpy Old Men '93
Indian Summer '93
The Opposite Sex and How to Live With Them '93
Wayne's World 2 '93
Canadian Bacon '94
Clean Slate '94
Casino '95
Chameleon '95
Grumpier Old Men '95
Miami Rhapsody '95
The Usual Suspects '95
House Arrest '96

Tracy Pollan
Baby It's You '82
Great Love Experiment '84
The Tender Age '84
The Abduction of Kari Swenson '87
Bright Lights, Big City '88
Promised Land '88
Fine Things '90
A Stranger Among Us '92

Daphne Pollard
Laurel & Hardy Comedy Classics, Vol. 7 '30s
Bonnie Scotland '35
Our Relations '36

Michael J. Pollard
The Wild Angels '66
Bonnie & Clyde '67
Enter Laughing '67
Legend of Frenchie King '71
Between the Lines '77
Melvin and Howard '80
Vengeance Is Mine '84
America '86
The Patriot '86
Heated Vengeance '87
Roxanne '87
American Gothic '88
Riders of the Storm '88
Scrooged '88
Fast Food '89
Next of Kin '89
Night Visitor '89
Season of Fear '89
Sleepaway Camp 3: Teenage Wasteland '89
Tango and Cash '89
The Arrival '90
The Art of Dying '90
Dick Tracy '90
I Come in Peace '90
Why Me? '90
Motorama '91
Split Second '92
Skeeter '93

Snub Pollard
Laughfest '10s
I'm on My Way/The Non-Stop Kid '18
Don't Shove/Two Gun Gussie '19
Silent Laugh Makers, No. 3 '19
The White Legion '36
Arizona Days '37
A Nation Aflame '37
Riders of the Rockies '37
The Errand Boy '61

Sarah Polley
The Adventures of Baron Munchausen '89
Lantern Hill '90
Tales from Avonlea, Vol. 1: The Journey Begins '90
Exotica '94

Dee Pollock
Beware, My Lovely '52
Legend of Tom Dooley '59

Eileen Pollock
Four Days in July '85
Far and Away '92

Teri Polo
The Phantom of the Opera '90
Born to Ride '91
Mystery Date '91
Passed Away '92
Aspen Extreme '93
Golden Gate '93
Quick '93
The Arrival '96

John Polson
Dangerous Game '90
Sirens '94
The Sum of Us '94

Max Pomeranc
Searching for Bobby Fischer '93
Fluke '95
Journey '95

Lily Pons
I Dream Too Much '35
That Girl from Paris '36

Yvan Ponton
Pouvoir Intime '87
Men of Steel '88
Scanners 2: The New Order '91

Iggy Pop
Cry-Baby '90
Hardware '90
Dead Man '95
The Crow 2: City of Angels '96

Marc Poppel
Damned River '89
Separate Lives '94

Johnny Popwell
Challenge '74
Manhunter '83

Jorge Porcel
Naked Is Better '73
Carlito's Way '93

Paulina Porizkova
Anna '87
Her Alibi '88
Portfolio '88
Arizona Dream '94

Louise Portal
The Klutz '73
The Decline of the American Empire '86

Don Porter
Night Monster '42
Who Done It? '42
Buck Privates Come Home '47
The Racket '51
Our Miss Brooks '56
Live a Little, Love a Little '68
Bachelor in Paradise '69
The Candidate '72
The Christmas Coal Mine Miracle '77

Eric Porter
The Fall of the Roman Empire '64
The Pumpkin Eater '64
Hands of the Ripper '71
Antony and Cleopatra '73
The Belstone Fox '73
Hennessy '75
Macbeth '76
The Thirty-Nine Steps '79
Little Lord Fauntleroy '80
Churchill and the Generals '81
Oliver Twist '85

Jean Porter
Bathing Beauty '44
G.I. Jane '51
Kentucky Jubilee '51

Robert Porter
The Jesus Trip '71
Deadly Fieldtrip '74

Eric Portman
The Crimes of Stephen Hawke '36
Murder in the Old Red Barn '36
Moonlight Sonata '38
The Forty-Ninth Parallel '41
One of Our Aircraft Is Missing '41
We Dive at Dawn '43
A Canterbury Tale '44
Great Day '46
Men of Two Worlds '46
Dear Murderer '47
The Colditz Story '55
Saturday Night Shockers, Vol. 2 '58
The Naked Edge '61
Bedford Incident '65

Natalie Portman
The Professional '94
Heat '95
Beautiful Girls '96

Richard Portnow
In Dangerous Company '88
Meet the Hollowheads '89
Say Anything '89
Kindergarten Cop '90
Barton Fink '91
Sister Act '92
S.F.W. '94
Trial by Jury '94
Donor Unknown '95
Man of the House '95

Parker Posey
Dazed and Confused '93
Party Girl '94
Sleep with Me '94
Flirt '95
Kicking and Screaming '95

Markie Post
Scene of the Crime '85
TripleCross '85
Glitz '88
Tricks of the Trade '88

Saskia Post
One Night Stand '84
Dogs in Space '87

William Post, Jr.
Sherlock Holmes and the Secret Weapon '42
Ship Ahoy '42
House on 92nd Street '45
Call Northside 777 '48

Pete Postlethwaite
Distant Voices, Still Lives '88
The Dressmaker '89
To Kill a Priest '89
Hamlet '90
Split Second '92
Waterland '92
In the Name of the Father '93
Sharpe's Company '94
Sharpe's Enemy '94
Suite 16 '94
The Usual Suspects '95
Dragonheart '96
James and the Giant Peach '96

Laurens C. Postma
Heroes Three '84
To Live and Die in Hong Kong '89

Tom Poston
Zotz! '62
Soldier in the Rain '63
The Tempest '63
Cold Turkey '71
Up the Academy '80
Carbon Copy '81
A Perfect Little Murder '90

Victor Potel
Anna Christie '23
Captain Swagger '25
Doughboys '30
Paradise Island '30
Thunder Over Texas '34
Miracle of Morgan's Creek '44

Madeleine Potter
The Bostonians '84
Hello Again '87
The Suicide Club '88
Bloodhounds of Broadway '89
Slaves of New York '89
Two Evil Eyes '90

Martin Potter
Ciao Federico! Fellini Directs Satyricon '69
Fellini Satyricon '69
The Only Way '70
Twinsanity '70
Gunpowder '84

Annie Potts
Corvette Summer '78
King of the Gypsies '78
Flatbed Annie and Sweetiepie: Lady Truckers '79
Heartaches '82
Crimes of Passion '84
Ghostbusters '84
It Came Upon a Midnight Clear '84
Bayou Romance '86
Jumpin' Jack Flash '86
Pretty in Pink '86
Pass the Ammo '88
Ghostbusters 2 '89
Who's Harry Crumb? '89
Texasville '90
Breaking the Rules '92

Cliff Potts
Silent Running '71
The Groundstar Conspiracy '72
Little Women '78
The Last Ride of the Dalton Gang '79
Sahara '83

Ely Pouget
Cool Blue '88
Endless Descent '90
Silent Victim '92
Death Machine '95
Lawnmower Man 2: Beyond Cyberspace '95
Red Shoe Diaries 5: Weekend Pass '95
Tall, Dark and Deadly '95

Georges Poujouly
Forbidden Games '52
Frantic '58

CCH Pounder
Prizzi's Honor '85
Bagdad Cafe '88
Psycho 4: The Beginning '90
RoboCop 3 '91
Benny & Joon '93
The Disappearance of Christina '93
The Ernest Green Story '93
Lifepod '93
Question of Faith '93
Return to Lonesome Dove '93
Sliver '93
Tales from the Crypt Presents Demon Knight '94
White Dwarf '95
Zooman '95

Henri Poupon
Angele '34
Harvest '37

Jason Rai Pow
Black Dragon '74
Black Dragon's Revenge '75

Brittney Powell
Airborne '93
To Be the Best '93
Dragonworld '94

Charles Powell
Cheyenne Warrior '94
Screamers '96

Dick Powell
Blessed Event '32
Footlight Parade '33
42nd Street '33
Gold Diggers of 1933 '33
Dames '34
Flirtation Walk '34
Gold Diggers of 1935 '35
A Midsummer Night's Dream '35
On the Avenue '37
Christmas in July '40
In the Navy '41
Star Spangled Rhythm '42
Murder, My Sweet '44
Cornered '45
Pitfall '48
Station West '48
Cry Danger '51
The Bad and the Beautiful '52
Susan Slept Here '54

Eleanor Powell
Broadway Melody of 1936 '35
Born to Dance '36
Broadway Melody of 1938 '37
Rosalie '38
Honolulu '39
Broadway Melody of 1940 '40
Lady Be Good '41
Ship Ahoy '42
I Dood It '43
Thousands Cheer '43
Sensations of 1945 '44
The Duchess of Idaho '50

Jane Powell
Delightfully Dangerous '45
Holiday in Mexico '46
A Date with Judy '48
Three Daring Daughters '48
Nancy Goes to Rio '50
Two Weeks with Love '50
Rich, Young and Pretty '51
Royal Wedding '51
Small Town Girl '53
Athena '54
Deep in My Heart '54
Seven Brides for Seven Brothers '54
Hit the Deck '55
The Girl Most Likely '57
Enchanted Island '58

Lee Powell
Fighting Devil Dogs '38
The Lone Ranger '38
Trigger Pals '39
Along the Sundown Trail '42
Prairie Pals '42
Tumbleweed Trail '42

Robert Powell
Jude the Obscure '71
Secrets '71
The Asphyx '72
Mahler '74
Tommy '75
Jesus of Nazareth '77
The Four Feathers '78
The Thirty-Nine Steps '79
Jane Austen in Manhattan '80
Survivor '80
Frankenstein '82
The Hunchback of Notre Dame '82
Dark Forces '83
Shaka Zulu '83
What Waits Below '83
The Jigsaw Man '84
The Mystery of Edwin Drood '93

William Powell
Romola '25
Nevada '27
Feel My Pulse '28
Last Command '28
The Kennel Murder Case '33
Evelyn Prentice '34
Fashions of 1934 '34
Manhattan Melodrama '34
The Thin Man '34
Reckless '35
Star of Midnight '35
After the Thin Man '36
Ex-Mrs. Bradford '36
The Great Ziegfeld '36
Libeled Lady '36
My Man Godfrey '36
Double Wedding '37
The Last of Mrs. Cheyney '37
Another Thin Man '39
I Love You Again '40
Love Crazy '41
Shadow of the Thin Man '41
The Thin Man Goes Home '44
Ziegfeld Follies '46
Life with Father '47
The Senator was Indiscreet '47
Song of the Thin Man '47
Mr. Peabody & the Mermaid '48
The Girl Who Had Everything '53
How to Marry a Millionaire '53
Mister Roberts '55

Chad Power
3 Ninjas '92
3 Ninjas Knuckle Up '92

Taryn Power
The Count of Monte Cristo '74
Tracks '76
Sinbad and the Eye of the Tiger '77

Tyrone Power
Lloyds of London '36
Thin Ice '37
Alexander's Ragtime Band '38
In Old Chicago '38
Marie Antoinette '38
Jesse James '39
The Rains Came '39
Rose of Washington Square '39
Second Fiddle '39
Brigham Young: Frontiersman '40
Johnny Apollo '40
The Mark of Zorro '40
Blood and Sand '41
A Yank in the R.A.F. '41
The Black Swan '42
Son of Fury '42
Crash Dive '43
The Razor's Edge '46
Rawhide '50
Diplomatic Courier '52
The Long Gray Line '55
The Eddy Duchin Story '56
Witness for the Prosecution '57

Tyrone Power, Sr.
Dream Street '21
Red Kimono '25
Test of Donald Norton '26
Big Trail '30

Tyrone Power, Jr.
Cocoon '85
California Casanova '89
Shag: The Movie '89

Alexandra Powers
Mask '85
Sonny Boy '87
Dangerous Pursuit '89
Cast a Deadly Spell '91
The Seventh Coin '92

Beverly Powers
Kissin' Cousins '64
Sixteen '72

Lucille Powers
Two Gun Man '31
Texas Bad Man '32

Mala Powers
Cyrano de Bergerac '50
City That Never Sleeps '53
Rage at Dawn '55
Storm Rider '57
Escape from Planet Earth '67
Daddy's Gone A-Hunting '69

Stefanie Powers
Experiment in Terror '62
The Interns '62
McLintock! '63
Palm Springs Weekend '63
Die! Die! My Darling! '65
Love Has Many Faces '65
The Boatniks '70
Paper Man '71
Gone with the West '72
No Place to Run '72
Herbie Rides Again '74
Manhunter '74
Sky Hei$t '75
The Invisible Strangler '76
The Man Inside '76
Return to Earth '76
Little Moon & Jud McGraw '78
Escape to Athena '79
Family Secrets '84
Mistral's Daughter '84
Shadow on the Sun '88
Scott Turow's The Burden of Proof '92

Tom Powers
Double Indemnity '44
The Blue Dahlia '46
Mexican Hayride '48
Station West '48
Destination Moon '50
The Nevadan '50
Lucky Me '54

Vicki Powers
The Meal '75
Deadly Encounter '78

Leon Pownall
Termini Station '89
Love and Hate: A Marriage Made in Hell '90
Hiroshima '95
How the West was Fun '95

Clare Powney
Operation Julie '85
The Girl '86

Lilia Prado
Mexican Bus Ride '51
The Illusion Travels by Streetcar '53
Wuthering Heights '53

Michael Praed
Robin Hood...The Legend: Robin Hood and the Sorcerer '83
Robin Hood...The Legend: The Swords of Wayland '83
Nightflyers '87
To Die for 2: Son of Darkness '91
Writer's Block '91

Joan Prather
Smile '75
The Deerslayer '78

Wolfgang Preiss
Mistress of the World '59
Mill of the Stone Women '60
The Thousand Eyes of Dr. Mabuse '60
The Return of Dr. Mabuse '61
The Invisible Dr. Mabuse '62
Testament of Dr. Mabuse '62
Cave of the Living Dead '65
The Mad Executioners '65
The Train '65
Raid on Rommel '71
Club Extinction '89

June Preisser
Babes in Arms '39
Strike Up the Band '40

Albert Prejean
The Crazy Ray '22
Italian Straw Hat '27
Under the Roofs of Paris '29
Princess Tam Tam '35

Otto Preminger
They Got Me Covered '43
Stalag 17 '53

Luis Prendes
Ursus in the Valley of the Lions '62
The Christmas Kid '68
Alien Predators '80

Paula Prentiss
Where the Boys Are '60
The Honeymoon Machine '61
The Horizontal Lieutenant '62
Man's Favorite Sport? '63
The World of Henry Orient '64
In Harm's Way '65
What's New Pussycat? '65
Bachelor in Paradise '69
Catch-22 '70
Born to Win '71
Last of the Red Hot Lovers '72
The Parallax View '74
No Room to Run '78
The Black Marble '79
Buddy Buddy '81
Saturday the 14th '81
M.A.D.D.: Mothers Against Drunk Driving '83
Packin' It In '83
Mrs. Winterbourne '96

Robert Prescott
Bachelor Party '84
Blue De Ville '86

Micheline Presle
The French Way '40
Devil in the Flesh '46
Adventures of Captain Fabian '51
The Bride Is Much Too Beautiful '58
Mistress of the World '59
Time Out for Love '61
The Prize '63
The King of Hearts '66
The Nun '66
Legend of Frenchie King '71

Elvis Presley
Love Me Tender '56
Jailhouse Rock '57
Loving You '57
King Creole '58
Flaming Star '60
G.I. Blues '60
Follow That Dream '61
Wild in the Country '61
Blue Hawaii '62
Girls! Girls! Girls! '62
Kid Galahad '62
Fun in Acapulco '63
It Happened at the World's Fair '63
Viva Las Vegas '63
Kissin' Cousins '64
Roustabout '64
Frankie and Johnny '65
Girl Happy '65
Harum Scarum '65
Tickle Me '65
Paradise, Hawaiian Style '66
Spinout '66
Clambake '67
Double Trouble '67
Easy Come, Easy Go '67
Live a Little, Love a Little '68
Speedway '68
Stay Away, Joe '68
Change of Habit '69
Charro! '69
The Trouble with Girls (and How To Get Into It) '69
This Is Elvis '81

Priscilla Presley
The Naked Gun: From the Files of Police Squad '88
The Adventures of Ford Fairlane '90
Naked Gun 2 1/2: The Smell of Fear '91
Naked Gun 33 1/3: The Final Insult '94

Harve Presnell
The Unsinkable Molly Brown '64
Paint Your Wagon '69
Fargo '96

Lawrence Pressman
The Hellstrom Chronicle '71
The Man in the Glass Booth '75
Rich Man, Poor Man '76
The Gathering '77
The Trial of Lee Harvey Oswald '77
The Gathering: Part 2 '79
Rehearsal for Murder '82
The Winds of War '83
For Love or Money '84
The Deliberate Stranger '86
On Wings of Eagles '86
Hanoi Hilton '87
Fire and Rain '89
White Hot: The Mysterious Murder of Thelma Todd '91
Angus '95
The Late Shift '96

Jason Presson
The Stone Boy '84
Explorers '85
The Lady in White '88
Saturday the 14th Strikes Back '88

Billy Preston
Let It Be '70
The Compleat Beatles '82
Blame It on the Night '84
Wired '89

Cyndy Preston
The Darkside '87
The Brain '88
Pin '88
Prom Night 3: The Last Kiss '89
Black Fox: The Price of Peace '94
Whale Music '94

J.A. Preston
The Spook Who Sat By the Door '73
Fire Birds '90
A Few Good Men '92

Kelly Preston
Metalstorm: The Destruction of Jared Syn '83
Christine '84
Mischief '85
Secret Admirer '85
52 Pick-Up '86
Amazon Women on the Moon '87
Love at Stake '87
A Tiger's Tale '87
The Spellbinder '88
Twins '88
The Experts '89
Tales from the Crypt, Vol. 3 '90
The Perfect Bride '91
Run '91
Only You '92
Cheyenne Warrior '94
Double Cross '94
Love Is a Gun '94
From Dusk Till Dawn '95
Mrs. Munck '95

Mike Preston
Surabaya Conspiracy '75
Metalstorm: The Destruction of Jared Syn '83
Hot Pursuit '84
Blade in Hong Kong '85

Robert Preston
Beau Geste '39
Union Pacific '39
Reap the Wild Wind '42
This Gun for Hire '42
Wake Island '42
Blood on the Moon '48
Tulsa '49
Best of the Badmen '50
My Outlaw Brother '51
Face to Face '52
Savage Wilderness '55
The Music Man '62
How the West Was Won '63
Junior Bonner '72
Mame '74
My Father's House '75
Semi-Tough '77
The Chisholms '79
S.O.B. '81
Rehearsal for Murder '82
Victor/Victoria '82
September Gun '83
Finnegan Begin Again '84
The Last Starfighter '84
Outrage! '86

Wayde Preston
Today We Kill, Tomorrow We Die '71
Smokey & the Judge '80

Francoise Prevost
Paris Belongs to Us '60
Time Out for Love '61
Spirits of the Dead '68

Marie Prevost
Yankee Doodle in Berlin '19
Eyes of Turpin Are Upon You! '21
The Marriage Circle '24
The Flying Fool '29
Party Girls '29
The Sin of Madelon Claudet '31
Hands Across the Table '35
Tango '36

Alan Price
O Lucky Man! '73
Oh, Alfie '75

Dennis Price
A Canterbury Tale '44
Echo Murders '45
Dear Murderer '47
Kind Hearts and Coronets '49
The Adventurers '51
The Naked Truth '58
The Millionairess '60
No Love for Johnnie '60
Tunes of Glory '60
Victim '62
What a Carve-Up! '62
Cool Mikado '63
The V.I.P.'s '63
The Wrong Arm of the Law '63
Murder Most Foul '65
The Horror of Frankenstein '70
Venus in Furs '70
Twins of Evil '71
Pulp '72
The Screaming Dead '72
Horror Hospital '73

Theatre of Blood '73

Hal Price
Cavalry '36
Desert Phantom '36
Melody of the Plains '37
Where Trails Divide '37
Across the Plains '39
Man from Texas '39
Trigger Men '41
Rustler's Hideout '44

Marc Price
Trick or Treat '86
The Rescue '88
Killer Tomatoes Eat France '91

Molly Price
Jersey Girl '92
Risk '94

Nancy Price
The Speckled Band '31
Secret Mission '42
The Three Weird Sisters '48

Stanley Price
The Singing Cowgirl '39
The Driftin' Kid '41
Dynamite Canyon '41
The Invisible Monster '50
Rangeland Empire '50
Sudden Death '50

Vincent Price
The Private Lives of Elizabeth & Essex '39
The Tower of London '39
Brigham Young: Frontiersman '40
The Invisible Man Returns '40
The Song of Bernadette '43
The Keys of the Kingdom '44
Laura '44
Wilson '44
Leave Her to Heaven '45
Shock! '46
The Three Musketeers '48
Champagne for Caesar '50
Adventures of Captain Fabian '51
Baron of Arizona '51
His Kind of Woman '51
The Las Vegas Story '52
House of Wax '53
Casanova's Big Night '54
Dangerous Mission '54
Son of Sinbad '55
The Ten Commandments '56
While the City Sleeps '56
The Fly '58
House on Haunted Hill '58
The Bat '59
Return of the Fly '59
The Fall of the House of Usher '60
Master of the World '61
The Pit and the Pendulum '61
Tales of Terror '62
Tower of London '62
Diary of a Madman '63
The Haunted Palace '63
The Raven '63
Twice-Told Tales '63
The Comedy of Terrors '64
The Last Man on Earth '64
Nefertiti, Queen of the Nile '64
Pirate Warrior '64
Tomb of Ligeia '64
Masque of the Red Death '65
Masque of the Red Death/ Premature Burial '65
Dr. Goldfoot and the Bikini Machine '66
The House of 1000 Dolls '67
The Conqueror Worm '68
The Oblong Box '69
The Trouble with Girls (and How To Get Into It) '69
Ruddigore '70s
Cry of the Banshee '70
Scream and Scream Again '70
The Abominable Dr. Phibes '71
Doctor Phibes Rises Again '72
Theatre of Blood '73
It's Not the Size That Counts '74
Journey into Fear '74
Madhouse '74
Scavenger Hunt '79
House of the Long Shadows '82
Snow White and the Seven Dwarfs '83
Bloodbath at the House of Death '85
The Monster Club '85
Escapes '86
The Offspring '87
The Whales of August '87
Dead Heat '88
Backtrack '89
Edward Scissorhands '90
The Horror of It All '91

Robert Prichard
Class of Nuke 'Em High '86
The Toxic Avenger '86
Alien Space Avenger '91

Dan Priest
Black Like Me '64
Rattlers '76

Martin Priest
Nothing But a Man '64
The Plot Against Harry '69
Zebrahead '92

Pat Priest
Easy Come, Easy Go '67
The Incredible Two-Headed Transplant '71
Some Call It Loving '73

Jason Priestley
The Boy Who Could Fly '86
Nowhere to Run '88
Beverly Hills 90210 '90
Beverly Hills 90210: The Graduation '93
Calendar Girl '93
Tombstone '93
Coldblooded '94

Paco Christian Prieto
Only the Strong '93
Street Law '95

Suzy Prim
The Lower Depths '36
Heart of a Nation '43

Barry Primus
New York, New York '77
Autopsy '78
Night Games '80
Absence of Malice '81
Heartland '81
Shooting '82
Brotherly Love '85
Talking Walls '85
Down and Out in Beverly Hills '86
The Stranger '87
Big Business '88
Cannibal Women in the Avocado Jungle of Death '89
Torn Apart '89
Denial: The Dark Side of Passion '91
Guilty by Suspicion '91
Night and the City '92
Trade Off '95

Prince
Purple Rain '84
Under the Cherry Moon '86
Graffiti Bridge '90

Faith Prince
The Last Dragon '85
Dave '93
My Father the Hero '93
Big Bully '95

Jonathan Prince
Pray TV '82
Private School '83

William Prince
Destination Tokyo '43
Objective, Burma! '45
Dead Reckoning '47
Lust for Gold '49
Cyrano de Bergerac '50
Justice '55
Johnny We Hardly Knew Ye '77
The Promise '78
City in Fear '80
Spies Like Us '85
Nuts '87
Vice Versa '88
Second Sight '89
Spontaneous Combustion '89
The Taking of Beverly Hills '91
The Portrait '93

Victoria Principal
Life & Times of Judge Roy Bean '72
Earthquake '74
Fantasy Island '76
I Will, I Will for Now '76
Pleasure Palace '80
Mistress '87
Blind Witness '89
Naked Lie '89
Scott Turow's The Burden of Proof '92

Andrew Prine
The Miracle Worker '62
Texas Across the River '66
Bandolero! '68
The Devil's Brigade '68
Generation '69
Simon, King of the Witches '71
Barn of the Naked Dead '73
Crypt of the Living Dead '73
One Little Indian '73
The Centerfold Girls '74
Grizzly '76
Riding with Death '76
Town that Dreaded Sundown '76
The Christmas Coal Mine Miracle '77
The Evil '78
Callie and Son '81
A Small Killing '81
Amityville 2: The Possession '82
V '83
Donner Pass: The Road to Survival '84
They're Playing with Fire '84
And the Children Shall Lead '85
The Last of the Mohicans '85
The Eliminators '86
Chill Factor '90
Mission of the Shark '91
Deadly Exposure '93
Gettysburg '93
Serial Killer '95

Aileen Pringle
Murder at Midnight '31
Convicted '32
Jane Eyre '34
Sons of Steel '35

Bryan Pringle
Haunted Honeymoon '86
Getting It Right '89

Sandra Prinsloo
African Rage '78
The Gods Must Be Crazy '84
The Outcast '84
Claws '85

Ted Prior
Sledgehammer '83
Killzone '85
Killer Workout '86
Deadly Prey '87
Hell on the Battleground '88
Born Killer '89
Final Sanction '89
Hardcase and Fist '89
Jungle Assault '89
Future Zone '90
Raw Nerve '91
Center of the Web '92
Possessed by the Night '93
Mutant Species '95
The P.A.C.K. '96

Michael Pritchard
Lightblast '85
Massive Retaliation '85

Lucien Prival
Party Girls '29
Hell's Angels '30
Panama Menace '41

Juergen Prochnow
The Lost Honor of Katharina Blum '75
Das Boot '81
The Keep '83
Dune '84
Forbidden '85
Killing Cars '85
My Sweet Victim '85
The Cop & the Girl '86
Beverly Hills Cop 2 '87
The Seventh Sign '88
A Dry White Season '89
The Fourth War '90
Kill Cruise '90
The Man Inside '90
Robin Hood '91
Body of Evidence '92
Hurricane Smith '92
Interceptor '92
The Fire Next Time '93
Lie Down with Lions '94
In the Mouth of Madness '95
Judge Dredd '95
The Other Side of the Law '95

Phil Proctor
J-Men Forever! '79
Firesign Theatre Presents Nick Danger in the Case of the Missing Yolks '83
Lobster Man from Mars '89

Melissa Prophet
Van Nuys Blvd. '79
Better Late Than Never '83
Invasion U.S.A. '85

Robert Prosky
Thief '81
The Keep '83
The Lords of Discipline '83
Christine '84
The Natural '84
Into Thin Air '85
World War III '86
Big Shots '87
Broadcast News '87
The Murder of Mary Phagan '87
Things Change '88
From the Dead of Night '89
Funny About Love '90
Green Card '90
Age Isn't Everything '91
Far and Away '92
Hoffa '92
Teamster Boss: The Jackie Presser Story '92
Hit Woman: The Double Edge '93
Last Action Hero '93
Mrs. Doubtfire '93
Rudy '93
Miracle on 34th Street '94
Dead Man Walking '95
The Scarlet Letter '95

Jed Prouty
Ella Cinders '26
Broadway Melody '29
100 Men and a Girl '37
Small Town Boy '37
Danger on the Air '38
Remedy for Riches '40

David Proval
Mean Streets '73
Vice Versa '88
Innocent Blood '92
Romeo Is Bleeding '93
Four Rooms '95
To the Limit '95
The Phantom '96

Dorothy Provine
The 30-Foot Bride of Candy Rock '59
It's a Mad, Mad, Mad, Mad World '63
Good Neighbor Sam '64
That Darn Cat '65
Who's Minding the Mint? '67
Never a Dull Moment '68

Jon Provost
All Mine to Give '56
Escapade in Japan '57
Lassie's Great Adventure '62
This Property is Condemned '66

David Prowse
The Horror of Frankenstein '70
A Clockwork Orange '71
Vampire Circus '71
Blacksnake! '73
Frankenstein and the Monster from Hell '74
Star Wars '77
The Empire Strikes Back '80
From "Star Wars" to "Jedi": The Making of a Saga '83
Return of the Jedi '83

Juliet Prowse
Can-Can '60
G.I. Blues '60
Dingaka '65

Harold Pruett
Summer Camp Nightmare '86
Spellcaster '91

Jonathan Pryce
Breaking Glass '80
Loophole '83
The Ploughman's Lunch '83
Praying Mantis '83
Something Wicked This Way Comes '83
Brazil '85
The Doctor and the Devils '85
Haunted Honeymoon '86
Jumpin' Jack Flash '86
Man on Fire '87
Consuming Passions '88
The Adventures of Baron Munchausen '89
The Man from the Pru '89
The Rachel Papers '89
Glengarry Glen Ross '92
The Age of Innocence '93
Barbarians at the Gate '93
A Business Affair '93
Deadly Advice '93
Thicker Than Water '93
Carrington '95

Nicholas Pryor
Force Five '75
The Happy Hooker '75
Smile '75
Gumball Rally '76
The Life and Assassination of the Kingfish '76
Night Terror '76
The Fish that Saved Pittsburgh '79
East of Eden '80
The $5.20 an Hour Dream '80
Last Song '80
Risky Business '83
The Falcon and the Snowman '85
Into Thin Air '85
Morgan Stewart's Coming Home '87
Brain Dead '89
Nightbreaker '89
Pacific Heights '90
Hoffa '92
Hail Caesar '94

Richard Pryor
Wild in the Streets '68
Black Brigade '69
Dynamite Chicken '70
Lady Sings the Blues '72
Hit! '73
Mack '73
Some Call It Loving '73
Uptown Saturday Night '74
Adios Amigo '75
Bingo Long Traveling All-Stars & Motor Kings '76
Car Wash '76
Silver Streak '76
Greased Lightning '77
Which Way Is Up? '77
Blue Collar '78
California Suite '78
The Wiz '78
Stir Crazy '80
Wholly Moses! '80
Bustin' Loose '81
Some Kind of Hero '82
The Toy '82
Superman 3 '83
Brewster's Millions '85
Critical Condition '86
Jo Jo Dancer, Your Life is Calling '86
Moving '88
Harlem Nights '89
See No Evil, Hear No Evil '89
Another You '91

Roger Pryor
Belle of the Nineties '34
Lady by Choice '34
Headline Woman '35
The Man They Could Not Hang '39
Panama Menace '41
Meet the Mob '42
Identity Unknown '45
Kid Sister '45

Wojciech Pszoniak
Land of Promise '74
Danton '82
Angry Harvest '85

Tito Puente
Radio Days '87
The Mambo Kings '92

Robert Pugh
Danger UXB '81
Thicker Than Water '93
Priest '94

Willard Pugh
The Color Purple '85
Native Son '86
Ambition '91
A Rage in Harlem '91

Pugh ▶cont.

CB4: The Movie '93
Puppet Master 5: The Final Chapter '94

Frank Puglia
Romola '25
Viva Villa! '34
Bulldog Drummond's Revenge '37
The Fatal Hour '40
Billy the Kid '41
Ali Baba and the Forty Thieves '43
Without Reservations '46
The Black Hand '50
20 Million Miles to Earth '57

Aldo Puglisi
Marriage Italian Style '64
Seduced and Abandoned '64

Bill Pullman
Ruthless People '86
The Serpent and the Rainbow '87
Spaceballs '87
The Accidental Tourist '88
Rocket Gibraltar '88
Brain Dead '89
Cold Feet '89
Sibling Rivalry '90
Bright Angel '91
Going Under '91
Liebestraum '91
Crazy in Love '92
The Favor '92
A League of Their Own '92
Newsies '92
Singles '92
Malice '93
Nervous Ticks '93
Sleepless in Seattle '93
Sommersby '93
The Last Seduction '94
Wyatt Earp '94
Casper '95
Mr. Wrong '95
While You Were Sleeping '95
Independence Day '96

Lilo (Liselotte) Pulver
A Time to Love & a Time to Die '58
A Global Affair '63
The Nun '66

Dick Purcell
The Abe Lincoln of Ninth Avenue '39
Heroes in Blue '39
Irish Luck '39
Tough Kid '39
King of the Zombies '41
Phantom Killer '42
X Marks the Spot '42
Captain America '44
Timber Queen '44

James Purcell
Playroom '90
White Light '90

Lee Purcell
Adam at 6 a.m. '70
The Witching '72
Mr. Majestyk '74
The Amazing Howard Hughes '77
Big Wednesday '78
Kenny Rogers as the Gambler '80
Stir Crazy '80
Killing at Hell's Gate '81
Homework '82
Eddie Macon's Run '83
Jailbait: Betrayed By Innocence '86
Space Rage '86
The Incredible Hulk Returns '88
To Heal a Nation '88
Long Road Home '91

Noel Purcell
Encore '52
Land of Fury '55
Lust for Life '56

Reginald Purdell
The Old Curiosity Shop '35
Candles at Nine '44
Brighton Rock '47

Edmund Purdom
Athena '54
The Egyptian '54
The Student Prince '54
The King's Thief '55
The Prodigal '55
Herod the Great '60
Nefertiti, Queen of the Nile '64
Rulers of the City '71
Dr. Frankenstein's Castle of Freaks '74
Big Boss '77
Mr. Scarface '77
Ator the Fighting Eagle '83
Don't Open Till Christmas '84
After the Fall of New York '85

Carolyn Purdy-Gordon
From Beyond '86
Dolls '87

Om Puri
City of Joy '92
In Custody '94
Wolf '94

Linda Purl
Crazy Mama '75
Eleanor & Franklin '76
Little Ladies of the Night '77
The Flame Is Love '79
Last Cry for Help '79
The Night the City Screamed '80
The Adventures of Nellie Bly '81
High Country '81
The Manions of America '81
Visiting Hours '82
Outrage! '86
Viper '88
Web of Deceit '90
Spies, Lies and Naked Thighs '91
Body Language '92
Accidental Meeting '93
In Self Defense '93
Incident at Deception Ridge '94
Natural Causes '94

Edna Purviance
Rink/Immigrant '10s
The Champion/His New Job '15
Chaplin Essanay Book 1 '15
Charlie Chaplin: Night at the Show '15
Charlie Chaplin...Our Hero! '15
The Floorwalker/By the Sea '15
His Prehistoric Past/The Bank '15
Tramp & a Woman '15
Burlesque of Carmen '16
Charlie Chaplin: The Early Years, Vol. 3 '16
Charlie Chaplin: The Early Years, Vol. 4 '16
The Fireman '16
The Vagabond '16
Work/Police '16
Charlie Chaplin: The Early Years, Vol. 1 '17
Charlie Chaplin: The Early Years, Vol. 2 '17
Count/Adventurer '17
The Cure '17
Three Charlies and One Phoney! '18
Triple Trouble/Easy Street '18
The Kid '21
The Kid/Idle Class '21
Woman of Paris/Sunnyside '23
The Chaplin Revue '58

John Putch
Impure Thoughts '86
Curfew '88
Fallen Angels 2 '93

Denver Pyle
Rim of the Canyon '49
Too Late for Tears '49
Dynamite Pass '50
Hills of Utah '51
Oklahoma Annie '51
Naked Hills '56
Seventh Cavalry '56
Geronimo '62
The Rounders '65
Bonnie & Clyde '67
The Legend of Hillbilly John '73
Life & Times of Grizzly Adams '74
Murder or Mercy '74
The Adventures of Frontier Fremont '75
Hawmps! '76
Blood Brothers '77
Mountain Man '77
Legend of the Northwest '78

John Pyper-Ferguson
Showdown at Williams Creek '91
Killer Image '92

John Quade
Night Terror '76
Peter Lundy and the Medicine Hat Stallion '77
Dirkham Detective Agency '83
Fury to Freedom: The Life Story of Raul Ries '85
Tigershark '87
The Tracker '88
And You Thought Your Parents Were Weird! '91

Stephen Quadros
Shock 'Em Dead '90
Auntie Lee's Meat Pies '92
C.I.A.: Code Name Alexa '92

Dennis Quaid
September 30, 1955 '77
The Seniors '78
Breaking Away '79
Gorp '80
The Long Riders '80
All Night Long '81
Bill '81
Caveman '81
The Night the Lights Went Out in Georgia '81
Johnny Belinda '82
Bill: On His Own '83
Jaws 3 '83
The Right Stuff '83
Tough Enough '83
Dreamscape '84
Enemy Mine '85
The Big Easy '87
Innerspace '87
Suspect '87
D.O.A. '88
Everybody's All American '88
Great Balls of Fire '89
Come See the Paradise '90
Postcards from the Edge '90
Flesh and Bone '93
Undercover Blues '93
Wilder Napalm '93
Wyatt Earp '94
Something to Talk About '95
Dragonheart '96

Randy Quaid
The Last Picture Show '71
What's Up, Doc? '72
The Last Detail '73
Paper Moon '73
The Apprenticeship of Duddy Kravitz '74
Breakout '75
Bound for Glory '76
Missouri Breaks '76
The Choirboys '77
Three Warriors '77
Midnight Express '78
The Last Ride of the Dalton Gang '79
Foxes '80
The Guyana Tragedy: The Story of Jim Jones '80
The Long Riders '80
To Race the Wind '80
Heartbeeps '81
Of Mice and Men '81
Inside the Third Reich '82
National Lampoon's Vacation '83
A Streetcar Named Desire '84
The Wild Life '84
The Slugger's Wife '85
Fool for Love '86
No Man's Land '87
Sweet Country '87
The Wraith '87
Caddyshack 2 '88
Dead Solid Perfect '88
LBJ: The Early Years '88
Moving '88
Bloodhounds of Broadway '89
National Lampoon's Christmas Vacation '89
Out Cold '89
Parents '89
Days of Thunder '90
Martians Go Home! '90
Quick Change '90
Texasville '90
Frankenstein '93
Freaked '93
Bye Bye, Love '94
Curse of the Starving Class '94
Next Door '94
The Paper '94
Larry McMurtry's Streets of Laredo '95
Legends of the North '95
Woman Undone '95
Independence Day '96
Kingpin '96
Last Dance '96
Moonshine Highway '96

John Qualen
Our Daily Bread '34
Black Fury '35
Charlie Chan in Paris '35
Angels Over Broadway '40
The Grapes of Wrath '40
His Girl Friday '40
Knute Rockne: All American '40
The Long Voyage Home '40
The Devil & Daniel Webster '41
Casablanca '42
The Jungle Book '42
Tortilla Flat '42
Dark Waters '44
Adventure '45
Captain Kidd '45
The Fugitive '48
The Scar '48
Passion '54
At Gunpoint '55
Sea Chase '55
The Searchers '56
The Man Who Shot Liberty Valance '62
7 Faces of Dr. Lao '63
Cheyenne Autumn '64
I'll Take Sweden '65
A Patch of Blue '65
Those Calloways '65

Jonathan Ke Quan
The Goonies '85
Breathing Fire '91

Robert Quarry
Soldier of Fortune '55
Count Yorga, Vampire '70
The Return of Count Yorga '71
Doctor Phibes Rises Again '72
Madhouse '74
Commando Squad '87
Cyclone '87
Phantom Empire '87
Warlords '88
Alienator '89
Spirits '90
Evil Spirits '91
Teenage Exorcist '93

Anna Quayle
Arrivederci, Baby! '66
Chitty Chitty Bang Bang '68
Naughty Knights '71
Mistress Pamela '74

Anthony Quayle
Hamlet '48
The Wrong Man '56
Pursuit of the Graf Spee '57
It Takes a Thief '59
The Guns of Navarone '61
Damn the Defiant '62
Lawrence of Arabia '62
The Fall of the Roman Empire '64
Operation Crossbow '65
Barefoot in Athens '66
A Study in Terror '66
Anne of the Thousand Days '69
MacKenna's Gold '69
Everything You Always Wanted to Know about Sex (But Were Afraid to Ask) '72
QB VII '74
The Tamarind Seed '74
Moses '76
The Story of David '76
21 Hours at Munich '76
The Chosen '77
The Eagle Has Landed '77
Murder by Decree '79
Masada '81
The Key to Rebecca '85
Misunderstood '87
The Bourne Identity '88
Buster '88
Magdalene '88
The Endless Game '89

Queen Latifah
House Party 2: The Pajama Jam '91
My Life '93

Valerie Quennessen
French Postcards '79
Conan the Barbarian '82
Summer Lovers '82

John Quentin
The Terrorists '74
Wittgenstein '93

Mae Questel
A Majority of One '56
National Lampoon's Christmas Vacation '89
New York Stories '89

Diana Quick
The Duellists '77
Brideshead Revisited '81
Ordeal by Innocence '84
The Misadventures of Mr. Wilt '90
Nostradamus '93

Charles Quigley
Saddle Buster '32
Charlie Chan's Secret '35
Lady from Nowhere '36
Daredevils of the Red Circle '38
Heroes in Blue '39
A Woman's Face '41
Cyclotrode "X" '46

Linnea Quigley
The Black Room '82
Savage Streets '83
Return of the Living Dead '85
Creepozoids '87
Nightmare Sisters '87
Sorority Babes in the Slimeball Bowl-A-Rama '87
Deadly Embrace '88
Hollywood Chainsaw Hookers '88
Night of the Demons '88
Vice Academy '88
Assault of the Party Nerds '89
WitchTrap '89
Vice Academy 2 '90
Virgin High '90
Beach Babes from Beyond Infinity '93
Pumpkinhead 2: Blood Wings '94
Assault of the Party Nerds 2: Heavy Petting Detective '95
Jack-O '95

Rita Quigley
Susan and God '40
Riot Squad '41

Tim Quill
Hamburger Hill '87
Hiding Out '87
Thou Shalt Not Kill...Except '87
Listen to Me '89
Staying Together '89
Army of Darkness '92
Endangered '94

Eddie Quillan
The Tip-Off '31
Mutiny on the Bounty '35
The Mandarin Mystery '37
Young Mr. Lincoln '39
The Grapes of Wrath '40
Here Comes Kelly '43
Dark Mountain '44
Mystery of the Riverboat '44

Marie Quillen
Campus Knights '29
Saddle Buster '32

Denis Quilley
Murder of a Moderate Man '70s
Privates on Parade '84
Foreign Body '86
The Shell Seekers '89
A Dangerous Man: Lawrence after Arabia '91
Mister Johnson '91

Barry Quin
Prisoner Cell Block H '80
Sara Dane '81

Richard Quine
Babes on Broadway '41
For Me and My Gal '42

Kathleen Quinlan
American Graffiti '73
Where Have All the People Gone? '74
Lifeguard '75

Giovanna Ralli
What Did You Do in the War, Daddy? '66
Caper of the Golden Bulls '67
Sex with a Smile '76

Jessie Ralph
Evelyn Prentice '34
One Night of Love '34
I Live My Life '35
Les Miserables '35
After the Thin Man '36
Little Lord Fauntleroy '36
San Francisco '36
Yellow Dust '36
Double Wedding '37
The Last of Mrs. Cheyney '37
Drums Along the Mohawk '39
The Bank Dick '40
The Blue Bird '40
They Met in Bombay '41

Sheryl Lee Ralph
Codename: Foxfire '85
The Mighty Quinn '89
To Sleep with Anger '90
Mistress '91
The Distinguished Gentleman '92
Sister Act 2: Back in the Habit '93
Witch Hunt '94
White Man's Burden '95

Esther Ralston
Oliver Twist '22
$50,000 Reward '25
Lucky Devil '25
Old Ironsides '26
Lonely Wives '31
To the Last Man '33
Shadows of the Orient '37
We're in the Legion Now '37
Tin Pan Alley '40

Jobyna Ralston
Girl Shy '24
The Freshman '25
Dr. Jack/For Heaven's Sake '26
For Heaven's Sake '26
The Kid Brother '27

Vera Ralston
Dakota '45
The Fighting Kentuckian '49
Hoodlum Empire '52
Jubilee Trail '54

Enrique Rambal
The Exterminating Angel '62
The Man and the Monster '65

Marjorie Rambeau
Min & Bill '30
Laughing Sinners '31
The Rains Came '39
Primrose Path '40
Santa Fe Marshal '40
Forever Female '53
Torch Song '53
A Man Called Peter '55
Man of a Thousand Faces '57

Dack Rambo
Hit Lady '74
Waikiki '80
The Spring '89
River of Diamonds '90
Ultra Warrior '92

Henry Ramer
My Pleasure Is My Business '74
Starship Invasions '77
Hockey Night '84
Reno and the Doc '84
The Big Slice '90

Carlos Ramirez
Bathing Beauty '44
Two Girls and a Sailor '44
Anchors Aweigh '45

Frank Ramirez
Smith! '69
Miracle in Rome '88

Harold Ramis
The Best of John Candy on SCTV '80s
Stripes '81
Ghostbusters '84
Baby Boom '87
Stealing Home '88
Ghostbusters 2 '89
Love Affair '94

Rudy Ramos
Open House '86
Quicksilver '86
Colors '88
Blindsided '93
The Spy Within '94

Charlotte Rampling
Georgy Girl '66
The Damned '69
'Tis a Pity She's a Whore '73
Zardoz '73
Caravan to Vaccares '74
The Night Porter '74
Farewell, My Lovely '75
Sardinia Kidnapped '75
Ski Bum '75
Foxtrot '76
Orca '77
The Purple Taxi '77
Stardust Memories '80
The Verdict '82
Max, Mon Amour '86
Angel Heart '87
Mascara '87
D.O.A. '88

Bruce Ramsay
Alive '93
Dead Beat '94
Killing Zoe '94
The New Age '94

Remak Ramsay
The Dining Room '86
Mr. & Mrs. Bridge '90

Anne Ramsey
The Boy in the Plastic Bubble '76
Goin' South '78
The Black Marble '79
Marilyn: The Untold Story '80
White Mama '80
A Small Killing '81
The Goonies '85
Deadly Friend '86
Throw Momma from the Train '87
Weeds '87
Another Chance '88
Dr. Hackenstein '88
Meet the Hollowheads '89
Perfect Alibi '94
The River Pirates '94

Logan Ramsey
The Hoodlum Priest '61
Fury on Wheels '71
Confessions of Tom Harris '72
Conspiracy of Terror '75
Say Yes! '86
Dr. Hackenstein '88

Marion Ramsey
Police Academy 3: Back in Training '86
Police Academy 5: Assignment Miami Beach '88
Police Academy 6: City Under Siege '89

Nick Ramus
Journey to Spirit Island '92
3 Ninjas Knuckle Up '92
Geronimo '93

John Rand
Charlie Chaplin: The Early Years, Vol. 1 '17
Charlie Chaplin: The Early Years, Vol. 2 '17

Addison Randall
Red Lights Ahead '36
Hollow Gate '88
Chance '89
Deadly Breed '89

Ethan Randall
All I Want for Christmas '91
Dutch '91
A Far Off Place '93
Evolver '94
Season of Change '94
Empire Records '95

Jack Randall
Gun Packer '38
Gunsmoke Trail '38
Man's Country '38
Across the Plains '39
Wild Horse Canyon '39
Covered Wagon Trails '40

Lexi Randall
Sarah, Plain and Tall '91
Heidi '93
Skylark '93
The Stars Fell on Henrietta '94
The War '94

Meg Randall
Ma and Pa Kettle '49
Ma and Pa Kettle Go to Town '50
Ma and Pa Kettle Back On the Farm '51

Monica Randall
Five Giants from Texas '66
Commando Attack '67
Witches' Mountain '71

Stacie Randall
Trancers 4: Jack of Swords '93
Dream a Little Dream 2 '94
Trancers 5: Sudden Deth '94
Excessive Force 2: Force on Force '95

Tony Randall
Will Success Spoil Rock Hunter? '57
The Mating Game '59
Pillow Talk '59
The Adventures of Huckleberry Finn '60
Let's Make Love '60
Lover Come Back '61
Boys' Night Out '62
7 Faces of Dr. Lao '63
Send Me No Flowers '64
The Alphabet Murders '65
The Littlest Angel '69
Everything You Always Wanted to Know about Sex (But Were Afraid to Ask) '72
Scavenger Hunt '79
Foolin' Around '80
King of Comedy '82
That's Adequate '90
Fatal Instinct '93

Ron Randell
The Loves of Carmen '48
Omoo Omoo, the Shark God '49
Girl in Black Stockings '57

Theresa Randle
Malcolm X '92
CB4: The Movie '93
Beverly Hills Cop 3 '94
Sugar Hill '94
Bad Boys '95
Girl 6 '96

Anders Randolf
The Idol Dancer '20
The Love Flower '20
Ranson's Folly '26
The Kiss '29

Jane Randolph
Cat People '42
The Falcon's Brother '42
Curse of the Cat People '44
Abbott and Costello Meet Frankenstein '48
Open Secret '48

John Randolph
Pretty Poison '68
There was a Crooked Man '70
Serpico '73
The Runaways '75
King Kong '76
Secrets '77
The Winds of Kitty Hawk '78
The Adventures of Nellie Bly '81
Lovely ... But Deadly '82
Prizzi's Honor '85
As Summers Die '86
The Wizard of Loneliness '88
National Lampoon's Christmas Vacation '89
Iron Maze '91
A Foreign Field '93

Ty Randolph
Deadly Embrace '88
Nudity Required '90

Robert Random
Danger Zone 2 '89
Danger Zone 3: Steel Horse War '90

Salvo Randone
10th Victim '65
Spirits of the Dead '68
Fellini Satyricon '69

Dan Ranger
Cop-Out '91
The Last Ride '91

Arthur Rankin
Walking Back '26
Below the Deadline '29
Fighting Fool '32
Terror Trail '33

Kenny Ransom
There Goes My Baby '92
Prison for Children '93

Tim Ransom
The Dressmaker '89
Vital Signs '90

Prunella Ransome
Far from the Madding Crowd '67
Man in the Wilderness '71

Michael Rapaport
Zebrahead '92
Hand Gun '93
Money for Nothing '93
True Romance '93
The Basketball Diaries '94
Higher Learning '94
Kiss of Death '94
The Scout '94
Mighty Aphrodite '95
The Pallbearer '95
Beautiful Girls '96

Anthony Rapp
Adventures in Babysitting '87
Far from Home '89
School Ties '92
Dazed and Confused '93
Six Degrees of Separation '93

David Rappaport
Mysteries '84
The Bride '85
Peter Gunn '89

Eva Ras
Man Is Not a Bird '65
The Love Affair, or The Case of the Missing Switchboard Operator '67

David Rasche
Manhattan '79
Sanctuary of Fear '79
Native Son '86
An Innocent Man '89
Wedding Band '89
Wicked Stepmother '89
The Masters of Menace '90
Bingo '91
Delirious '91
Silhouette '91
Twenty Bucks '93
Bigfoot: The Unforgettable Encounter '94
Dead Weekend '95
Out There '95

Phylicia Rashad
Uncle Tom's Cabin '87
False Witness '89
Once Upon a Time...When We Were Colored '95

Fritz Rasp
Metropolis '26
Spies '28
Diary of a Lost Girl '29
The Threepenny Opera '31

Julien Rassam
The Accompanist '93
Queen Margot '94

Ivan Rassimov
The Next Victim '71
Man from Deep River '77
Beyond the Door 2 '79

Thalmus Rasulala
Blacula '72
Adios Amigo '75
Bucktown '75
Friday Foster '75
Sophisticated Gents '81
Born American '86
Bulletproof '88
The Package '89
Blind Vengeance '90
New Jack City '91
Mom and Dad Save the World '92

Mikhail Rasumny
For Whom the Bell Tolls '43
Anna and the King of Siam '46

Sandy Ratcliff
Family Life '71
Yesterday's Hero '79

Basil Rathbone
Sin Takes a Holiday '30
Anna Karenina '35
Captain Blood '35
David Copperfield '35
Last Days of Pompeii '35
A Tale of Two Cities '35
The Garden of Allah '36
Romeo and Juliet '36
Love from a Stranger '37
Make a Wish '37
The Adventures of Marco Polo '38
The Adventures of Robin Hood '38
Dawn Patrol '38
The Adventures of Sherlock Holmes '39
The Hound of the Baskervilles '39
Son of Frankenstein '39
The Tower of London '39
The Mark of Zorro '40
Rhythm on the River '40
Sherlock Holmes and the Secret Weapon '42
Sherlock Holmes: The Voice of Terror '42
Above Suspicion '43
Sherlock Holmes Faces Death '43
Sherlock Holmes in Washington '43
Bathing Beauty '44
The Pearl of Death '44
Scarlet Claw '44
Spider Woman '44
House of Fear '45
Pursuit to Algiers '45
The Woman in Green '45
Dressed to Kill '46
Heartbeat '46
Terror by Night '46
Terror by Night/Meeting at Midnight '46
Casanova's Big Night '54
A Christmas Carol '54
We're No Angels '55
Court Jester '56
Last Hurrah '58
Victoria Regina '61
The Magic Sword '62
Tales of Terror '62
The Comedy of Terrors '64
Voyage to the Prehistoric Planet '65
Planet of Blood '66
Autopsy of a Ghost '67
Hillbillies in a Haunted House '67
Many Faces of Sherlock Holmes '86

Gregory Ratoff
Skyscraper Souls '32
I'm No Angel '33
All About Eve '50
Abdulla the Great '56
Exodus '60

Devin Ratray
Home Alone '90
Home Alone 2: Lost in New York '92
Spy Trap '92

Heather Rattray
Across the Great Divide '76
Further Adventures of the Wilderness Family, Part 2 '77
Sea Gypsies '78
Mountain Family Robinson '79
Basket Case 2 '90

John Ratzenberger
Twilight's Last Gleaming '77
The Bitch '78
The Empire Strikes Back '80
Combat Academy '86
House 2: The Second Story '87
Timestalkers '87
Camp Cucamonga: How I Spent My Summer Vacation '90

Andrea Rau
Daughters of Darkness '71
Beyond Erotica '79

Alida Rauffe
Fanny '32
Cesar '36

Mike Raven
Crucible of Terror '72
Disciple of Death '72

Adrian Rawlins
Woman in Black '89
Breaking the Waves '95

Herbert Rawlinson
The Tomboy '24
Confidential '35
Show Them No Mercy '35
Blake of Scotland Yard '36
Robinson Crusoe of Clipper Island '36
Robinson Crusoe of Mystery Island '36
Blind Fools '40
Gentleman from Dixie '41
Riot Squad '41
I Killed That Man '42
The Panther's Claw '42
Smart Alecks '42
Colt Comrades '43
Lost Canyon '43
Nabonga '44
Shake Hands with Murder '44
Jail Bait '54

Aldo Ray
Pat and Mike '52
Miss Sadie Thompson '53
Battle Cry '55
We're No Angels '55
Nightfall '56
Men in War '57
God's Little Acre '58
The Naked and the Dead '58
Johnny Nobody '61
Dead Heat on a Merry-Go-Round '66
What Did You Do in the War, Daddy? '66
The Green Berets '68
Black Eliminator '70s
Angel Unchained '70
And Hope to Die '72
Gone with the West '72
The Centerfold Girls '74
The Dynamite Brothers '74
Inside Out '75
The Man Who Would Not Die '75
Psychic Killer '75
Seven Alone '75
Bad Bunch '76
Haunts '77
The Glove '78
Kill Factor '78
Little Moon & Jud McGraw '78
The Lucifer Complex '78
The Haunted '79
Human Experiments '79
Nightstalker '79
Mission to Glory '80
Dark Sanity '82
The Great Skycopter Rescue '82
Frankenstein's Great Aunt Tillie '83
Mongrel '83
Bog '84
The Executioner, Part 2: Frozen Scream '84
To Kill a Stranger '84
Vultures '84
Bio Hazard '85
Evils of the Night '85
Terror on Alcatraz '86
Hollywood Cop '87
Star Slammer '87
Blood Red '88
Swift Justice '88
Shooters '89
Shock 'Em Dead '90

Andrew Ray
Escapade '55
The Young and the Guilty '58
Tarzana, the Wild Girl '72
Mission Phantom '79

Charles Ray
Clodhopper '17
The Busher '19
Homer Comes Home '20
Sweet Adeline '26
Dracula/Garden of Eden '28
The Garden of Eden '28

James Ray
Return Engagement '78
Mass Appeal '84
She's Having a Baby '88

Michel Ray
The Brave One '56
The Tin Star '57

Nicholas Ray
James Dean: The First American Teenager '76
The American Friend '77
Hair '79
Lightning Over Water '80

Rene Ray
The Passing of the Third Floor Back '36
Housemaster '38
The Vicious Circle '57

Martha Raye
Rhythm on the Range '36
Waikiki Wedding '37
The Big Broadcast of 1938 '38
College Swing '38
Give Me a Sailor '38
Keep 'Em Flying '41
Pin-Up Girl '44
Monsieur Verdoux '47
Billy Rose's Jumbo '62
The Concorde: Airport '79 '79
Pippin '81

Bill Raymond
Sudden Death '77
The Man Who Envied Women '85
City of Hope '91
My New Gun '92
The Crow '93
Where the Rivers Flow North '94

Candy Raymond
Don's Party '76
Money Movers '78
Freedom '81
Monkey Grip '82

Cyril Raymond
The Shadow '36
Spy in Black '39
Brief Encounter '46
Men of Two Worlds '46
Angels One Five '54

Gary Raymond
Look Back in Anger '58
The Moonraker '58
Playboy of the Western World '62
Jason and the Argonauts '63
The Two Faces of Evil '82
Scarlett '94

Gene Raymond
Red Dust '32
Ex-Lady '33
Flying Down to Rio '33
Sadie McKee '34
Transatlantic Merry-Go-Round '34
The Bride Walks Out '36
That Girl from Paris '36
Mexican Spitfire/Smartest Girl in Town '40
Mr. & Mrs. Smith '41
Smilin' Through '41
Hit the Deck '55
Plunder Road '57
The Best Man '64

Jack Raymond
Last Command '28
Shake Hands with Murder '44

Lina Raymond
The Gypsy Warriors '78
The Key to Rebecca '85

Paula Raymond
Adam's Rib '50
The Duchess of Idaho '50
Texas Carnival '51
The Beast from 20,000 Fathoms '53
City That Never Sleeps '53
King Richard and the Crusaders '54
Blood of Dracula's Castle '69

Richard Raymond
Rats '83
Days of Hell '84

Robin Raymond
Girls in Chains '43
Rogue's Gallery '44
High School Confidential '58

Peggy Rea
The Waltons: The Christmas Carol '80
In Country '89
Love Field '91
Made in America '93

Stephen Rea
Danny Boy '84
The Company of Wolves '85
The Doctor and the Devils '85
Four Days in July '85
Loose Connections '87
Life Is Sweet '90
Bad Behavior '92
The Crying Game '92
Angie '94
Interview with the Vampire '94
Princess Caraboo '94
Ready to Wear '94
Citizen X '95

Barbara Read
Three Smart Girls '36
Behind the Mask '46

James Read
Remington Steele, Vol. 1: License to Steele '82
The Initiation '84
North and South Book 1 '85
North and South Book 2 '86
Poor Little Rich Girl: The Barbara Hutton Story '87
Beaches '88
Web of Deceit '90
Love Crimes '92
When the Dark Man Calls '95

Ronald Reagan
Boy Meets Girl '38
Dark Victory '39
Knute Rockne: All American '40
Santa Fe Trail '40
Kings Row '41
Desperate Journey '42
This Is the Army '43
It's a Great Feeling '49
Hollywood Bloopers '50s
Bedtime for Bonzo '51
Cavalry Charge '51
The Winning Team '52
Cattle Queen of Montana '54
The Jungle Trap '54
Tennessee's Partner '55
Hellcats of the Navy '57
The Killers '64
Death Valley Days: No Gun Behind His Badge '65
Hollywood Outtakes & Rare Footage '83

Rex Reason
This Island Earth '55
The Creature Walks Among Us '56
Band of Angels '57

Sady Rebbot
My Life to Live '62
Friends '71

James Rebhorn
Will: G. Gordon Liddy '82
Deadly Business '86
Lorenzo's Oil '92
Scent of a Woman '92
White Sands '92
Carlito's Way '93
JFK: Reckless Youth '93
Skylark '93
8 Seconds '94
I Love Trouble '94
The Buccaneers '95
If Lucy Fell '95
Up Close and Personal '96

Winston Reckert
Agnes of God '85
Glory! Glory! '90
The World's Oldest Living Bridesmaid '92

Mary-Robin Redd
The Group '66
Mirrors '78

Helen Reddy
Airport '75 '75
Pete's Dragon '77

Quinn Redeker
The Three Stooges Meet Hercules '61
Coast to Coast '80

Dennis Redfield
Private Duty Nurses '71
The Annihilators '85
Pulse '88

William Redfield
Conquest of Space '55
The Connection '61
Morituri '65
Fantastic Voyage '66
The Hot Rock '70
A New Leaf '71
Death Wish '74
For Pete's Sake '74
One Flew Over the Cuckoo's Nest '75

Robert Redford
The Twilight Zone '61
Inside Daisy Clover '65
The Chase '66
This Property is Condemned '66
Barefoot in the Park '67
Butch Cassidy and the Sundance Kid '69
Downhill Racer '69
Tell Them Willie Boy Is Here '69
The Hot Rock '70
The Candidate '72
Jeremiah Johnson '72
The Sting '73
The Way We Were '73
The Great Gatsby '74
The Great Waldo Pepper '75
Three Days of the Condor '75
All the President's Men '76
A Bridge Too Far '77
The Electric Horseman '79
Brubaker '80
The Natural '84
Out of Africa '85
Legal Eagles '86
Havana '90
Sneakers '92
Indecent Proposal '93
Up Close and Personal '96

Rockets Redglare
Down by Law '86
Salvation! '87
Shakedown '88
Cookie '89
Mystery Train '89
In the Soup '92

Corin Redgrave
The Charge of the Light Brigade '68
Between Wars '74
Excalibur '81
In the Name of the Father '93
Four Weddings and a Funeral '94
Persuasion '95

Jemma Redgrave
Dream Demon '88
Howard's End '92
Diana: Her True Story '93

Lynn Redgrave
Tom Jones '63
Georgy Girl '66
The Virgin Soldiers '69
Everything You Always Wanted to Know about Sex (But Were Afraid to Ask) '72
The Turn of the Screw '74
The Happy Hooker '75
The Big Bus '76
Sooner or Later '78
To Love Again '80
Rehearsal for Murder '82
Shooting '82
The Bad Seed '85
Morgan Stewart's Coming Home '87
Walking on Air '87
Getting It Right '89
Midnight '89
What Ever Happened To... '93
The Great American Sex Scandal '94

Michael Redgrave
The Lady Vanishes '38
Lady in Distress '39
The Stars Look Down '39
Kipps '41
Dead of Night '45
Captive Heart '47
Fame Is the Spur '47
Secret Beyond the Door '48
The Browning Version '51
Importance of Being Earnest '52
Dam Busters '55
Mr. Arkadin '55
The Sea Shall Not Have Them '55
Time Without Pity '57
Shake Hands with the Devil '59
The Wreck of the Mary Deare '59
The Innocents '61
The Loneliness of the Long Distance Runner '62
Heidi '67
Battle of Britain '69
Goodbye, Mr. Chips '69
Twinsanity '70
The Go-Between '71
Nicholas and Alexandra '71
Dr. Jekyll and Mr. Hyde '73
Hitchcock Collection '87

Vanessa Redgrave
Blow-Up '66
A Man for All Seasons '66
Morgan! '66
Camelot '67
The Charge of the Light Brigade '68
Isadora '68
The Devils '71
Trojan Women '71
Murder on the Orient Express '74
Out of Season '75
The Seven-Per-Cent Solution '76
Julia '77
Agatha '79
Yanks '79
Bear Island '80
Playing for Time '80
Snow White and the Seven Dwarfs '83
The Bostonians '84
Three Sovereigns for Sarah '85
Wagner: The Complete Epic '85
Wagner: The Movie '85
Wetherby '85
Peter the Great '86
Steaming '86
Prick Up Your Ears '87
Consuming Passions '88
A Man for All Seasons '88
The Ballad of the Sad Cafe '91
Orpheus Descending '91
Young Catherine '91
Howard's End '92
The House of the Spirits '93
They Watch '93
What Ever Happened To... '93
Down Came a Blackbird '94
Little Odessa '94
Mother's Boys '94
A Month by the Lake '95
Mission: Impossible '96

Juli Reding
Mission in Morocco '59
Tormented '60

Joyce Redman
Tom Jones '63
A Different Kind of Love '85
The Rector's Wife '94
Prime Suspect: The Scent of Darkness '95

Liam Redmond
Devil on Horseback '54
The Ghost and Mr. Chicken '66
The Last Safari '67

Siobhan Redmond
Look Back in Anger '89
Captives '94

Joe Redner
Thundering Ninja '80s
Clash of the Ninja '86

Alan Reed
Days of Glory '43
The Postman Always Rings Twice '46
Actors and Sin '52
A Woman's World '54
Tarnished Angels '57

Alan Reed, Jr.
Rock, Pretty Baby '56
Peyton Place '57

Alyson Reed
A Chorus Line '85
Skin Deep '89

Donna Reed
Shadow of the Thin Man '41
The Human Comedy '43
Thousands Cheer '43
Picture of Dorian Gray '45
They Were Expendable '45
It's a Wonderful Life '46
Green Dolphin Street '47
Hangman's Knot '52
The Caddy '53
From Here to Eternity '53
Gun Fury '53
Trouble Along the Way '53
The Last Time I Saw Paris '54
The Benny Goodman Story '55

George Reed
Green Pastures '36

Reed ▶cont.

Strange Illusion '45

Hal Reed
The Zodiac Killer '71
The Doberman Gang '72

James Reed
Tarzana, the Wild Girl '72
Eight Men Out '88

Jerry Reed
Gator '76
Smokey and the Bandit '77
High Ballin' '78
The Concrete Cowboys '79
Hot Stuff '80
Smokey and the Bandit, Part 2 '80
Smokey and the Bandit, Part 3 '83
Survivors '83
What Comes Around '85
Bat 21 '88

Lady Reed
Avenging Disco Godfather '76
Dolemite 2: Human Tornado '76

Lou Reed
One Trick Pony '80
Get Crazy '83
Faraway, So Close! '93
Blue In the Face '95

Maxwell Reed
Dear Murderer '47
Night Beat '48
Blackout '50
The Clouded Yellow '51
Roadhouse Girl '53
Sea Devils '53

Oliver Reed
Beat Girl '60
No Love for Johnnie '60
Sword of Sherwood Forest '60
The Curse of the Werewolf '61
Paranoiac '62
Trap '66
Blood Island '68
Oliver! '68
The Assassination Bureau '69
Dante's Inferno: Life of Dante Gabriel Rossetti '69
Women in Love '70
The Devils '71
Zero Population Growth '72
Blue Blood '73
One Russian Summer '73
The Three Musketeers '74
The Four Musketeers '75
Royal Flash '75
Ten Little Indians '75
Tommy '75
Burnt Offerings '76
Great Scout & Cathouse Thursday '76
Sell Out '76
Maniac '77
Tomorrow Never Comes '77
Triple Echo '77
The Big Sleep '78
The Class of Miss MacMichael '78
The Prince and the Pauper '78
The Brood '79
Dr. Heckyl and Mr. Hype '80
Condorman '81
Lion of the Desert '81
Spasms '82
Venom '82
Fanny Hill '83
The Sting 2 '83
Two of a Kind '83
The Black Arrow '84
Christopher Columbus '85
Captive '87
Castaway '87
The Misfit Brigade '87
Captive Rage '88
Dragonard '88
Gor '88
The House of Usher '88
Rage to Kill '88
The Adventures of Baron Munchausen '89
Master of Dragonard Hill '89
The Return of the Musketeers '89
Skeleton Coast '89
Treasure Island '89
The Revenger '90
Hired to Kill '91
The Pit & the Pendulum '91
Prisoner of Honor '91
Severed Ties '92
Return to Lonesome Dove '93
Funny Bones '94

Pamela Reed
The Long Riders '80
Melvin and Howard '80
Eyewitness '81
Young Doctors in Love '82
The Goodbye People '83
The Right Stuff '83
The Best of Times '86
The Clan of the Cave Bear '86
Rachel River '87
Tanner '88 '88
Chattahoochee '89
Cadillac Man '90
Caroline? '90
Kindergarten Cop '90
Passed Away '92
Woman With a Past '92
Junior '94

Penelope Reed
Amazons '86
Hired to Kill '91

Philip Reed
Female '33
Klondike Annie '36
Madame X '37
Big Town '47
Big Town After Dark '47
Song of the Thin Man '47
Underworld Scandal '47
Unknown Island '48
Bandit Queen '51

Robert Reed
Bloodlust '59
The Love Bug '68
Star! '68
The Brady Bunch '69
Haunts of the Very Rich '72
Snatched '72
The Boy in the Plastic Bubble '76
Nightmare in Badham County '76
Rich Man, Poor Man '76
The Hunted Lady '77
Bud and Lou '78
No Prince for My Cinderella '78
Love's Savage Fury '79
The Seekers '79
Casino '80
Nurse '80
Death of a Centerfold '81
A Very Brady Christmas '88
Prime Target '91

Shanna Reed
Legs '83
The Banker '89
Don't Talk to Strangers '94
The Sister-in-Law '95
Rattled '96

Suzanne Reed
Beyond the Bermuda Triangle '75
Up from the Depths '79

Tracy Reed
No Way Back '74
Piece of the Action '77

Walter Reed
Seven Days' Leave '42
The Torch '50
Government Agents vs. Phantom Legion '51
How to Make a Monster '58
Macumba Love '60

Harry Reems
Deadly Weapons '70
R.S.V.P. '84

Angharad Rees
Hands of the Ripper '71
Poldark '75
Poldark 2 '75

Donough Rees
Starship '87
Crush '93

Roger Rees
The Life and Adventures of Nicholas Nickleby '81
Star 80 '83
Ebony Tower '86
Mountains of the Moon '90
If Looks Could Kill '91
Stop! or My Mom Will Shoot '92
Charles & Diana: A Palace Divided '93
Robin Hood: Men in Tights '93

Della Reese
The Voyage of the Yes '72
Psychic Killer '75
Nightmare in Badham County '76
Harlem Nights '89
The Kid Who Loved Christmas '90
A Thin Line Between Love and Hate '96

Christopher Reeve
Gray Lady Down '77
Superman: The Movie '78
Somewhere in Time '80
Superman 2 '80
Deathtrap '82
Monsignor '82
Sleeping Beauty '83
Superman 3 '83
The Bostonians '84
Anna Karenina '85
The Aviator '85
Street Smart '87
Superman 4: The Quest for Peace '87
The Great Escape 2: The Untold Story '88
Switching Channels '88
The Rose and the Jackal '90
Death Dreams '92
Mortal Sins '92
Noises Off '92
Morning Glory '93
The Remains of the Day '93
The Sea Wolf '93
Black Fox: The Price of Peace '94
Blood Horse '94
Good Men and Bad '94
Speechless '94
Above Suspicion '95
Village of the Damned '95

George Reeves
Gone with the Wind '39
The Fighting 69th '40
Blood and Sand '41
Lydia '41
Strawberry Blonde '41
Bar-20 '43
Border Patrol '43
Colt Comrades '43
Hoppy Serves a Writ '43
Leather Burners '43
So Proudly We Hail '43
The Great Lover '49
Jungle Goddess '49
Pirate Ship '49
Thunder in the Pines '49
Superman & the Mole Men '51
TV's Best Adventures of Superman '51
Bugles in the Afternoon '52
Rancho Notorious '52
Forever Female '53
From Here to Eternity '53
Stamp Day for Superman '53
Westward Ho, the Wagons! '56

Keanu Reeves
Dream to Believe '85
Act of Vengeance '86
Babes in Toyland '86
Brotherhood of Justice '86
Youngblood '86
River's Edge '87
Dangerous Liaisons '88
The Night Before '88
Permanent Record '88
Prince of Pennsylvania '88
Bill & Ted's Excellent Adventure '89
Parenthood '89
I Love You to Death '90
Tune in Tomorrow '90
Bill & Ted's Bogus Journey '91
My Own Private Idaho '91
Point Break '91
Bram Stoker's Dracula '92
Little Buddha '93
Much Ado about Nothing '93
Even Cowgirls Get the Blues '94
Speed '94
Johnny Mnemonic '95
A Walk in the Clouds '95
Chain Reaction '96

Lisa Reeves
Pom Pom Girls '76
The Chicken Chronicles '77
Snowblind '78

Saskia Reeves
Antonia and Jane '91
Close My Eyes '91
December Bride '91
Traps '93
Butterfly Kiss '94

Scott Reeves
Friday the 13th, Part 8: Jason Takes Manhattan '89
Edge of Honor '91

Steve Reeves
Athena '54
Jail Bait '54
Hercules '58
Hercules Unchained '59
The Giant of Marathon '60
Goliath and the Barbarians '60
The Last Days of Pompeii '60
Morgan the Pirate '60
Thief of Baghdad '61
The Avenger '62
Pirates of the Seven Seas '62

Steve Reevis
The Last of the Dogmen '95
Fargo '96

Joe Regalbuto
Missing '82
Invitation to Hell '84
Lassiter '84
The Queen of Mean '90
Writer's Block '91
Bodily Harm '95

Jayne Regan
The Silver Bullet '34
Texas Jack '35

Mary Regan
Heart of the Stag '84
Sylvia '86
Midnight Dancer '87
Fever '88

Phil Regan
Manhattan Merry-Go-Round '37
Sweet Rosie O'Grady '43
Swing Parade of 1946 '46

George Regas
Sixteen Fathoms Deep '34
Hell-Ship Morgan '36
The Rains Came '39

Duncan Regehr
My Wicked, Wicked Ways '84
The Monster Squad '87
The Banker '89
Gore Vidal's Billy the Kid '89
The Last Samurai '90
Timemaster '95

Benoit Regent
Club Extinction '89
Trois Couleurs: Bleu '93

Serge Reggiani
Manon '50
La Ronde '51
Casque d'Or '52
Les Miserables '57
Le Doulos '61
Cat and Mouse '78

Nadja Regin
From Russia with Love '63
Goldfinger '64

Paul Regina
A Long Way Home '81
Adam '83
It's My Party '95
Sharon's Secret '95

Regine
Marry Me, Marry Me '69
The Seven-Per-Cent Solution '76
My New Partner '84

Frank Reicher
Scarlet Dawn '32
King Kong '33

Wolfgang Reichmann
The Nun '66
Signs of Life '68
Woyzeck '78
Beethoven's Nephew '88

Beryl Reid
The Belles of St. Trinian's '53
Star! '68
The Assassination Bureau '69
The Killing of Sister George '69
Beast in the Cellar '70
Entertaining Mr. Sloane '70
Doctor Phibes Rises Again '72
Psychomania '73
Joseph Andrews '77
Carry On Emmanuelle '78
The Doctor and the Devils '85
Duel of Hearts '92
The Best of Cracker Mysteries '93

Carl Benton Reid
The Fuller Brush Girl '50
In a Lonely Place '50
Indian Uprising '51
Escape from Fort Bravo '53
The Egyptian '54
Battle Hymn '57
The Trap '59
The Bramble Bush '60
Pressure Point '62

Christopher Reid
House Party '90
Class Act '91
House Party 2: The Pajama Jam '91
House Party 3 '94

Elliott Reid
The Story of Dr. Wassell '44
Gentlemen Prefer Blondes '53
A Woman's World '54
The Thrill of It All! '63
Follow Me, Boys! '66

Fiona Reid
Accident '83
Heaven on Earth '89
Mark Twain and Me '91
Beethoven Lives Upstairs '92

Kate Reid
One Plus One '61
Invincible Mr. Disraeli '63
Holy Terror '65
This Property is Condemned '66
The Andromeda Strain '71
The Rainbow Gang '73
Crossbar '79
Circle of Two '80
Death Ship '80
The Double Negative '80
Highpoint '80
Atlantic City '81
The Blood of Others '84
Execution of Raymond Graham '85
Heaven Help Us '85
Death of a Salesman '86
Fire with Fire '86
Control '87
Bye Bye Blues '89
Signs of Life '89
The Last Best Year '90
Deceived '91
Teamster Boss: The Jackie Presser Story '92

Tim Reid
WKRP in Cincinnati, Vol. 1 '78
Dead Bang '89
You Must Remember This '90s
The Fourth War '90
Stephen King's It '90

Wallace Reid
The Birth of a Nation '15
Hawthorne of the USA '19
The Roaring Road '19

Charles Nelson Reilly
Cannonball Run 2 '84
Body Slam '87

Hugh Reilly
Lassie's Great Adventure '62
Chuka '67

John C. Reilly
Missing Pieces '83
Touch and Go '86
Casualties of War '89
We're No Angels '89
Days of Thunder '90
State of Grace '90
Hoffa '92
Out on a Limb '92
Fallen Angels 1 '93
What's Eating Gilbert Grape '93
Dolores Claiborne '94
The River Wild '94
Boys '95
Georgia '95

Luke Reilly
Bye Bye Blues '89
Zebrahead '92

Tom Reilly
Kiss and Be Killed '91
Mirror Images 2 '93

Carl Reiner
The Gazebo '59
Gidget Goes Hawaiian '61
It's a Mad, Mad, Mad, Mad World '63
The Thrill of It All! '63
The Russians are Coming, the Russians are Coming '66
Generation '69
The End '78
Dead Men Don't Wear Plaid '82
Pinocchio '83
Spirit of '76 '91
The Right to Remain Silent '95

Rob Reiner
Enter Laughing '67
Where's Poppa? '70
How Come Nobody's On Our Side? '73
Thursday's Game '74
This Is Spinal Tap '84
Johnny Appleseed '86
Throw Momma from the Train '87
Postcards from the Edge '90
Spirit of '76 '91
Sleepless in Seattle '93
Bullets Over Broadway '94
Bye Bye, Love '94
Mixed Nuts '94

Tracy Reiner
Nothing in Common '86
Masque of the Red Death '89
New Year's Day '89
Frankie and Johnny '91
A League of Their Own '92
Apollo 13 '95

Judge Reinhold
On the Edge: The Survival of Dana '79
Running Scared '79
Stripes '81
Fast Times at Ridgemont High '82
Pandemonium '82
The Lords of Discipline '83
Beverly Hills Cop '84
Gremlins '84
Roadhouse 66 '84
Head Office '86
Off Beat '86
Ruthless People '86
Beverly Hills Cop 2 '87
Promised a Miracle '88
Vice Versa '88
Rosalie Goes Shopping '89
Daddy's Dyin'...Who's Got the Will? '90
Enid Is Sleeping '90
Near Misses '91
A Soldier's Tale '91
Zandalee '91
Baby on Board '92
Black Magic '92
Bank Robber '93
Four Eyes and Six Guns '93
Beverly Hills Cop 3 '94
The Santa Clause '94
As Good as Dead '95
The Right to Remain Silent '95
The Wharf Rat '95

Ann Reinking
All That Jazz '79
Annie '82
Micki & Maude '84

Paul Reiser
Diner '82
Sunset Limousine '83
Beverly Hills Cop '84
From Here to Maternity '85
Odd Jobs '85
Aliens '86
Beverly Hills Cop 2 '87
Cross My Heart '88
Crazy People '90
Family Prayers '91
The Marrying Man '91
Mr. Write '92
Bye Bye, Love '94

Winston Rekert
Heartaches '82
Dead Wrong '83
Eternal Evil '87
Toby McTeague '87

Maria Therese Relin
Quo Vadis '85
Secret Places '85

James Remar
The Warriors '79
Windwalker '81
48 Hrs. '82
The Cotton Club '84
The Clan of the Cave Bear '86
Quiet Cool '86
Rent-A-Cop '88
The Dream Team '89
Drugstore Cowboy '89
Silence Like Glass '90
Tales from the Darkside: The Movie '90
Deadlock '91
White Fang '91
Fatal Charm '92
Indecency '92
Blink '93
Fatal Instinct '93
The Tigress '93
Across the Moon '94
Boys on the Side '94
Confessions of a Hit Man '94
Miracle on 34th Street '94
Renaissance Man '94
The Surgeon '94
The Phantom '96
The Quest '96

Erika Remberg
Circus of Horrors '60
Cave of the Living Dead '65

Lee Remick
A Face in the Crowd '57
The Long, Hot Summer '58
Anatomy of a Murder '59
Days of Wine and Roses '62
Experiment in Terror '62
The Tempest '63
The Wheeler Dealers '63
Baby, the Rain Must Fall '64
The Hallelujah Trail '65
The Detective '68
No Way to Treat a Lady '68
Loot...Give Me Money, Honey! '70
Sometimes a Great Notion '71
QB VII '74
Touch Me Not '74
Hennessy '75
Hustling '75
The Omen '76
Telefon '77
Breaking Up '78
The Medusa Touch '78
The Europeans '79
Ike '79
Torn Between Two Lovers '79
The Competition '80
Tribute '80
The Snow Queen '83
I Do! I Do! '84
Mistral's Daughter '84
Follies in Concert '85
Toughlove '85
The Vision '87
Jesse '88
Around the World in 80 Days '89
Bridge to Silence '89

Bert Remsen
Pork Chop Hill '59
McCabe & Mrs. Miller '71
The Death Squad '73
Thieves Like Us '74
Nashville '75
Sweet Hostage '75
Tarantulas: The Deadly Cargo '77
Joni '79
Lies '83
M.A.D.D.: Mothers Against Drunk Driving '83
Policewoman Centerfold '83
Burning Rage '84
I Married a Centerfold '84
Code of Silence '85
Eye of the Tiger '86
Tai-Pan '86
Terrorvision '86
South of Reno '87
Curfew '88
Miss Firecracker '89
Daddy's Dyin'...Who's Got the Will? '90
Payback '90
Peacemaker '90
Evil Spirits '91
Only the Lonely '91

Kerry Remsen
Ghoulies 2 '87
Pumpkinhead '88

Albert Remy
Children of Paradise '44
The 400 Blows '59
Shoot the Piano Player '62
The Train '65

Ronald Remy
The Vampire People '66
Revenge of Doctor X '80s

Duncan Renaldo
Trader Horn '31
The Painted Stallion '37
Roaring Speedboats '37
Zorro Rides Again '37
Rose of Rio Grande '38
Cowboys from Texas '39
The Kansas Terrors '39
Rough Riders' Roundup '39
Don Amigo/Stage to Chino '40s
Covered Wagon Days '40
Rocky Mountain Rangers '40
Down Mexico Way '41
Outlaws of the Desert '41
Panama Menace '41
Border Patrol '43
Tiger Fangs '43
Perils of the Darkest Jungle '44
Western Double Feature 12 '44
Guns of Fury '45
In Old New Mexico '45
South of the Rio Grande '45
The Capture '50
The Cisco Kid '50
Manhunt in the African Jungle '54

Simone Renant
Jenny Lamour '47
Dangerous Liaisons '60
That Man from Rio '64
Dear Detective '77

Madeleine Renaud
Maria Chapdelaine '34
Stormy Waters '41

Liz Renay
The Thrill Killers '65
Blackenstein '73
Desperate Living '77

Brad Renfro
The Client '94
The Cure '95
Tom and Huck '95

Patrick Renna
The Sandlot '93
Son-in-Law '93
Beanstalk '94
The Big Green '95
Blue River '95

Deborah Rennard
Land of Doom '84
Lionheart '90

Michael Rennie
Tower of Terror '42
The Wicked Lady '45
Uneasy Terms '48
Trio '50
The Day the Earth Stood Still '51
Five Fingers '52
Phone Call from a Stranger '52
The Robe '53
Demetrius and the Gladiators '54
Desiree '54
Mambo '55
Seven Cities of Gold '55
Soldier of Fortune '55
Omar Khayyam '57
Third Man on the Mountain '59
Commando Attack '67
Hotel '67
The Battle of El Alamein '68
The Devil's Brigade '68
Dracula vs. Frankenstein '69
Die Screaming, Marianne '73
Surabaya Conspiracy '75

Jean Reno
Le Dernier Combat '84
Subway '85
The Big Blue '88
La Femme Nikita '91
The Professional '94
French Kiss '95

John Reno
Bloodspell '87
Mirror of Death '87

Kelly Reno
The Black Stallion '79
The Black Stallion Returns '83
Brady's Escape '84

Jean Renoir
The Rules of the Game '39
The Little Theatre of Jean Renoir '71

Pierre Renoir
Madame Bovary '34
La Marseillaise '37
Children of Paradise '44

Eva Renzi
Funeral in Berlin '66
The Bird with the Crystal Plumage '70
Night of the Assassin '77

Maggie Renzi
The Brother from Another Planet '84
Eight Men Out '88
City of Hope '91
Passion Fish '92

Tommy Rettig
The 5000 Fingers of Dr. T '53
River of No Return '54
The Cobweb '55

Gloria Reuben
Percy & Thunder '93
Dead Air '94
Timecop '94
Johnny's Girl '95
Nick of Time '95

Paul (Pee Wee Herman) Reubens
Cheech and Chong's Next Movie '80
Cheech and Chong's Nice Dreams '81
Pandemonium '82
The Pee Wee Herman Show '82
Pinocchio '83
Meatballs 2 '84
Pee Wee's Big Adventure '85
Back to the Beach '87
Big Top Pee Wee '88
Pee Wee's Playhouse Festival of Fun '88
Batman Returns '92
Buffy the Vampire Slayer '92
Dunston Checks In '95

Anne Revere
The Howards of Virginia '40
The Song of Bernadette '43
The Keys of the Kingdom '44
National Velvet '44
The Thin Man Goes Home '44
Body and Soul '47
Forever Amber '47
Gentleman's Agreement '47
Secret Beyond the Door '48
The Falcon Takes Over/Strange Bargain '49
A Place in the Sun '51

Dorothy Revier
The Dropkick '27
Dance of Life '29
The King Murder '32
The Secrets of Wu Sin '32
Green Eyes '34
When a Man Sees Red '34
Circumstantial Evidence '35

Clive Revill
A Fine Madness '66
The Assassination Bureau '69
The Private Life of Sherlock Holmes '70
Avanti! '72
Escape to the Sun '72
The Legend of Hell House '73
The Black Windmill '74
Ghost in the Noonday Sun '74
One of Our Dinosaurs Is Missing '75
Matilda '78
The Empire Strikes Back '80
George Washington '84
Rumpelstiltskin '86
Cannon Movie Tales: The Emperor's New Clothes '89
Mack the Knife '89
The Sea Wolf '93

Rex
King of the Wild Horses '24
Robinson Crusoe of Clipper Island '36
Robinson Crusoe of Mystery Island '36

Alejandro Rey
Solomon and Sheba '59
Fun in Acapulco '63
The Stepmother '71
The Ninth Configuration '79
The Grace Kelly Story '83
Rita Hayworth: The Love Goddess '83
Moscow on the Hudson '84
Terrorvision '86
Stickfighter '89

Fernando Rey
Pantaloons '57
Viridiana '61
The Castilian '63
Goliath Against the Giants '63
Attack of the Robots '66
Chimes at Midnight '67
Navajo Joe '67
Guns of the Magnificent Seven '69
Autopsy '70s
Cold Eyes of Fear '70s
Great Leaders of the Bibles '70s
The Adventurers '70
Tristana '70
The French Connection '71
The Discreet Charm of the Bourgeoisie '72
A Town Called Hell '72
Antony and Cleopatra '73
High Crime '73
La Grande Bourgeoise '74
French Connection 2 '75
Seven Beauties '76
Elisa, Vida Mia '77
That Obscure Object of Desire '77
The Assignment '78
Quintet '79
Cabo Blanco '81
Honey '81
Insanity '82
Monsignor '82
The Hit '85
Padre Nuestro '85
Angel of Death '86
Saving Grace '86
Moon over Parador '88
The Tunnel '89
1492: Conquest of Paradise '92

Mony Rey
Mademoiselle '66
Not Without My Daughter '90

Ernie Reyes, Jr.
Teenage Mutant Ninja Turtles 2: The Secret of the Ooze '91
Surf Ninjas '93
White Wolves 2: Legend of the Wild '94

Julian Reyes
Point Break '91
Mi Vida Loca '94

Kamar Reyes
East L.A. Warriors '89
Coldfire '90

Janine Reynaud
Castle of the Creeping Flesh '68
The Sensuous Teenager '70
The Scorpion's Tail '71

Burt Reynolds
Angel Baby '61
Armored Command '61
Operation C.I.A. '65
Navajo Joe '67
Iron Cowboy '68
Shark! '68
100 Rifles '69
Hard Frame '70
Savage Run '70
Skullduggery '70
Deliverance '72
Everything You Always Wanted to Know about Sex (But Were Afraid to Ask) '72
Fuzz '72
Man Who Loved Cat Dancing '73
Shamus '73
White Lightning '73

Reynolds ▶cont.

The Longest Yard '74
The Hustle '75
Gator '76
Silent Movie '76
Semi-Tough '77
Smokey and the Bandit '77
The End '78
Hooper '78
Starting Over '79
Rough Cut '80
Smokey and the Bandit, Part 2 '80
Cannonball Run '81
Paternity '81
Sharky's Machine '81
Best Friends '82
The Best Little Whorehouse in Texas '82
The Man Who Loved Women '83
Stroker Ace '83
Cannonball Run 2 '84
City Heat '84
Stick '85
Uphill All the Way '85
Heat '87
Malone '87
Rent-A-Cop '88
Switching Channels '88
Breaking In '89
Physical Evidence '89
Modern Love '90
Cop and a Half '93
The Man from Left Field '93
The Maddening '95
Striptease '96

Craig Reynolds
I Take This Oath '40
Nevada '44

Debbie Reynolds
Three Little Words '50
Two Weeks with Love '50
Singin' in the Rain '52
Skirts Ahoy! '52
The Affairs of Dobie Gillis '53
Give a Girl a Break '53
I Love Melvin '53
Athena '54
Susan Slept Here '54
Hit the Deck '55
The Tender Trap '55
Bundle of Joy '56
The Catered Affair '56
Tammy and the Bachelor '57
This Happy Feeling '58
The Gazebo '59
It Started with a Kiss '59
The Mating Game '59
The Rat Race '60
How the West Was Won '63
The Unsinkable Molly Brown '64
The Singing Nun '66
Divorce American Style '67
How Sweet It Is! '68
What's the Matter with Helen? '71
Detective Sadie & Son '84
Battling for Baby '92
Heaven and Earth '93

Gene Reynolds
Boys Town '38
In Old Chicago '38
Love Finds Andy Hardy '38
They Shall Have Music '39
Andy Hardy's Private Secretary '41
Life Begins for Andy Hardy '41
The Tuttles of Tahiti '42
Jungle Patrol '48
Country Girl '54

Marjorie Reynolds
Man's Country '38
Six Shootin' Sheriff '38
Western Trails '38
The Abe Lincoln of Ninth Avenue '39
Gone with the Wind '39
Mr. Wong in Chinatown '39
Mystery Plane '39
Racketeers of the Range '39
Stunt Pilot '39
Doomed to Die '40
The Fatal Hour '40
Midnight Limited '40
Up in the Air '40
Robin Hood of the Pecos '41
Holiday Inn '42
Monsieur Beaucaire '46
The Time of Their Lives '46
Home Town Story '51

Peter Reynolds
Devil Girl from Mars '54
It Takes a Thief '59
The Great Armored Car Swindle '64

Robert Reynolds
Daughter of Darkness '89
Traps '93
Tunnel Vision '95

Ryan Reynolds
Ordinary Magic '93
Sabrina the Teenage Witch '96

Vera Reynolds
The Night Club '25
The Road to Yesterday '25
Road to Yesterday/The Yankee Clipper '27
Risky Business '28
Sunny Side Up '28
The Monster Walks '32
Tangled Destinies '32

William Reynolds
Carrie '52
Francis Goes to West Point '52
Son of Ali Baba '52
Cult of the Cobra '55
The Land Unknown '57

Ving Rhames
Patty Hearst '88
The Long Walk Home '89
Jacob's Ladder '90
Rising Son '90
Homicide '91
The People Under the Stairs '91
Dave '93
The Saint of Fort Washington '93
DROP Squad '94
Kiss of Death '94
Pulp Fiction '94
Mission: Impossible '96
Striptease '96

Phillip Rhee
Ninja Turf '86
Silent Assassins '88
Best of the Best '89
Best of the Best 2 '93
Best of the Best 3: No Turning Back '95

Simon Rhee
Furious '83
Best of the Best '89
Best of the Best 2 '93

Ashlie Rhey
Bikini Drive-In '94
Midnight Tease '94

Barbara Rhoades
The Shakiest Gun in the West '68
Up the Sandbox '72
Hunter '73
Scream Blacula Scream '73
Conspiracy of Terror '75
The Choirboys '77
The Goodbye Girl '77
The Day the Women Got Even '80
Serial '80
Sex and the Single Parent '82

Bobby Rhodes
The Last Hunter '80
Endgame '85
Demons 2 '87

Cynthia Rhodes
Flashdance '83
Staying Alive '83
Runaway '84
Dirty Dancing '87
Curse of the Crystal Eye '93

Donnelly Rhodes
Goldenrod '77
Hard Part Begins '80s
After the Promise '87
Showdown at Williams Creek '91
Dirty Work '92
The Penthouse '92
Guitarman '95

Erik Rhodes
The Gay Divorcee '34
Charlie Chan in Paris '35
Top Hat '35
Special Investigator '36

Hari Rhodes
Shock Corridor '63
Conquest of the Planet of the Apes '72
Detroit 9000 '73
A Dream for Christmas '73
Coma '78
A Woman Called Moses '78

Marjorie Rhodes
Great Day '46
Decameron Nights '53

Madlyn Rhue
A Majority of One '56
The Cary Grant Collection '90

Paul Rhys
Vincent & Theo '90
Becoming Colette '92
Chaplin '92
Nina Takes a Lover '94
Gallowglass '95

John Rhys-Davies
Nativity '78
Shogun '80
Raiders of the Lost Ark '81
Sphinx '81
Ivanhoe '82
Victor/Victoria '82
Best Revenge '83
Sadat '83
Sahara '83
Sword of the Valiant '83
Kim '84
King Solomon's Mines '85
In the Shadow of Kilimanjaro '86
The Living Daylights '87
Nairobi Affair '88
Noble House '88
War & Remembrance, Part 1 '88
Great Expectations '89
Indiana Jones and the Last Crusade '89
The Trial of the Incredible Hulk '89
Tusks '89
War & Remembrance: The Final Chapter, Part 8 '89
Rebel Storm '90
Secret Weapon '90
Journey of Honor '91
Canvas: The Fine Art of Crime '92
The Double O Kid '92
The Lost World '92
The Seventh Coin '92
Sunset Grill '92
The Unnamable 2: The Statement of Randolph Carter '92
Cyborg Cop '93
Return to the Lost World '93
Ring of the Musketeers '93
Beyond Forgiveness '94
Robot in the Family '94
The Great White Hype '96

Candice Rialson
Candy Stripe Nurses '74
Mama's Dirty Girls '74
Summer School Teachers '75
Chatterbox '76
Hollywood Boulevard '76
Moonshine County Express '77

Alfonso Ribeiro
The Mighty Pawns '87
Ticks '93

Christina Ricci
Mermaids '90
The Addams Family '91
The Hard Way '91
Addams Family Values '93
The Cemetery Club '93
Casper '95
Gold Diggers: The Secret of Bear Mountain '95
Now and Then '95

Bill Rice
Vortex '81
Doomed Love '83
Landlord Blues '87

Florence Rice
Double Wedding '37
Navy Blue and Gold '37
Sweethearts '38
At the Circus '39
Boss of Big Town '43
The Ghost and the Guest '43

Frank Rice
Dynamite Dan '24
Red Signals '27
The Fighting Legion '30
Border Law '31
Hello Trouble '32
The Fiddlin' Buckaroo '33
Phantom Thunderbolt '33
Somewhere in Sonora '33

Joan Rice
The Story of Robin Hood & His Merrie Men '52
His Majesty O'Keefe '53

Adam Rich
The Devil & Max Devlin '81
Zertigo Diamond Caper '82

Allen Rich
The Seekers '79
Archer: The Fugitive from the Empire '81
Matters of the Heart '90

Christopher Rich
Prisoners of Inertia '89
Midnight Murders '91
The Joy Luck Club '93

Claude Rich
The Elusive Corporal '62
The Bride Wore Black '68
Is Paris Burning? '68
Le Crabe Tambour '77
Maria Chapdelaine '84

Eli Rich
Murderlust '86
Nudity Required '90
Deadly Diamonds '91

Irene Rich
The Trap '22
Beau Brummel '24
The Champ '31
Held for Murder '32
The Lady in Question '40
The Mortal Storm '40
Angel and the Badman '47

Emily Richard
The Life and Adventures of Nicholas Nickleby '81
Empire of the Sun '87

Jean Richard
Seven Deadly Sins '53
Elena and Her Men '56

Jean-Louis Richard
It Means That to Me '63
The Last Metro '80

Pierre Richard
Johnny Frenchman '46
Suicide Patrol '70s
The Tall Blond Man with One Black Shoe '72
Return of the Tall Blond Man With One Black Shoe '74
The Daydreamer '75
La Chevre '81
Too Shy to Try '82
Les Comperes '83

Addison Richards
Our Daily Bread '34
Bad Lands '39
The Fighting Sullivans '42
The Man with Two Lives '42
Ridin' Down the Canyon '42
Betrayal from the East '44
Bells of Rosarita '45
Criminal Court '46
Call Northside 777 '48
A Southern Yankee '48

Ann Richards
Badman's Territory '46
Lost Honeymoon '47
Love from a Stranger '47
Sorry, Wrong Number '48
Breakdown '53

Ariana Richards
Prancer '89
Spaced Invaders '90
Switched at Birth '91
Grand Tour: Disaster in Time '92
Jurassic Park '93
Angus '95

Beah Richards
The Miracle Worker '62
Gone are the Days '63
A Dream for Christmas '73
Roots: The Next Generation '79
A Christmas Without Snow '80
Acceptable Risks '86
As Summers Die '86
Drugstore Cowboy '89
Inside Out '91

Evan Richards
Down and Out in Beverly Hills '86
Dream Machine '91
Rock 'n' Roll High School Forever '91
Society '92
Mute Witness '95

Jeff Richards
Angels in the Outfield '51
Seven Brides for Seven Brothers '54
It's a Dog's Life '55
Born Reckless '59

Keith Richards
Gimme Shelter '70
Chuck Berry: Hail! Hail! Rock 'n' Roll '87

Kim Richards
Escape to Witch Mountain '75
Assault on Precinct 13 '76
Devil Dog: The Hound of Hell '78
Return from Witch Mountain '78
Meatballs 2 '84
Tuff Turf '85
Escape '90

Lisa Richards
The Prince of Central Park '77
Return '88
Eating '90

Michael Richards
Whoops Apocalypse '88
UHF '89
Problem Child '90
Coneheads '93
Airheads '94
Unstrung Heroes '95

Michele Lamar Richards
The Bodyguard '92
Top Dog '95

Tom Richards
Plunge Into Darkness '77
Dawn! '83
The Cursed Mountain Mystery '93

Ian Richardson
Marat/Sade '66
A Midsummer Night's Dream '68
The Hound of the Baskervilles '83
The Sign of Four '83
Whoops Apocalypse '83
Brazil '85
Cry Freedom '87
The Fourth Protocol '87
Burning Secret '89
House of Cards '90
The Phantom of the Opera '90
Monsignor Quixote '91
Year of the Comet '92
Foreign Affairs '93
M. Butterfly '93
To Play the King '93
The Final Cut '95

Jack Richardson
Toll Gate '20
Dynamite Dan '24
Marked Money '28
Trigger Tricks '30

Jay Richardson
The Newlydeads '87
Death Row Diner '88
Hollywood Chainsaw Hookers '88
Alienator '89
The Channeler '89
Slashdance '89
Bad Girls from Mars '90
Vice Academy 2 '90
Original Intent '91
Vice Academy 3 '91
Mind, Body & Soul '92
Sins of Desire '92
Teenage Exorcist '93

Joely Richardson
Wetherby '85
Drowning by Numbers '87
King Ralph '91
Shining Through '92
I'll Do Anything '93
Sister My Sister '94

John Richardson
Black Sunday '60
One Million Years B.C. '66
Torso '73
Eyeball '78
Frankenstein '80 '79
Cosmos: War of the Planets '80

Latanya Richardson
Losing Isaiah '94
When a Man Loves a Woman '94

Lee Richardson
Prizzi's Honor '85
The Believers '87
Sweet Lorraine '87
Tiger Warsaw '87
The Fly 2 '89
Q & A '90
A Stranger Among Us '92
Skylark '93

Miranda Richardson
Dance with a Stranger '85
Transmutations '85
Empire of the Sun '87
After Pilkington '88
Twisted Obsession '90
The Crying Game '92
Damage '92
Enchanted April '92
The Bachelor '93
Century '94
Fatherland '94
Tom & Viv '94

Natasha Richardson
Gothic '87
A Month in the Country '87
Patty Hearst '88
Fat Man and Little Boy '89
The Handmaid's Tale '90
The Comfort of Strangers '91
The Favor, the Watch, & the Very Big Fish '92
Past Midnight '92
Hostages '93
Nell '94
Widow's Peak '94

Ralph Richardson
The Ghoul '34
Bulldog Jack '35
Java Head '35
Things to Come '36
Amazing Adventure '37
The Man Who Could Work Miracles '37
Thunder in the City '37
The Citadel '38
The Divorce of Lady X '38
Clouds Over Europe '39
The Four Feathers '39
The Lion Has Wings '40
The Day Will Dawn '42
Anna Karenina '48
The Fallen Idol '49
The Heiress '49
Richard III '55
Exodus '60
Long Day's Journey into Night '62
Doctor Zhivago '65
Khartoum '66
The Wrong Box '66
Battle of Britain '69
The Looking Glass War '69
Who Slew Auntie Roo? '71
Alice's Adventures in Wonderland '72
Tales from the Crypt '72
Invitation to the Wedding '73
Lady Caroline Lamb '73
O Lucky Man! '73
The Man in the Iron Mask '77
Dragonslayer '81
Early Days '81
Time Bandits '81
Give My Regards to Broad Street '84
Greystoke: The Legend of Tarzan, Lord of the Apes '84
Wagner: The Complete Epic '85
A Doll's House '89

Regina Richardson
Tightrope '84
Nine Deaths of the Ninja '85

Salli Richardson
Up Against the Wall '91
How U Like Me Now? '92
Posse '93
Lily in Winter '94
A Low Down Dirty Shame '94
Sioux City '94
The Great White Hype '96

Sy Richardson
Fairy Tales '76
Repo Man '83
Straight to Hell '87
Dead Man Walking '88
They Live '88
Backtrack '89
Street Asylum '90
Ring of Fire 2: Blood and Steel '92
Floundering '94

Peter Mark Richman
Black Orchid '59
PSI Factor '80
Dempsey '83
City Killer '87
Judgment Day '88
Friday the 13th, Part 8: Jason Takes Manhattan '89
Naked Gun 2 1/2: The Smell of Fear '91

Anthony Richmond
Devil Girl from Mars '54
One Wish Too Many '55

Branscombe Richmond
The Taking of Beverly Hills '91
Christopher Columbus: The Discovery '92
DaVinci's War '92
Inside Edge '92
Jericho Fever '93
To the Limit '95

Fiona Richmond
The House on Straw Hill '76
Eat the Rich '87

Kane Richmond
Cavalier of the West '31
The Lost City '34
The Adventures of Rex & Rinty '35
Confidential '35
East Side Kids/The Lost City '35
The Reckless Way '36
Anything for a Thrill '37
Devil Diamond '37
Motorcycle Squad '37
Tough to Handle '37
Spy Smasher '42
Spy Smasher Returns '42
Haunted Harbor '44
Behind the Mask '46

Warner Richmond
The Speed Spook '24
Big News '29
The Lost Jungle '34
The New Frontier '35
Rainbow's End '35
Headin' for the Rio Grande '36
Song of the Gringo '36
Doomed at Sundown '37
A Lawman Is Born '37
Where Trails Divide '37
Wild Horse Canyon '39
Colorado Serenade '46
Wild West '46

Deborah Richter
The Rebels '79
Swap Meet '79
Twirl '81
Hot Moves '84
Square Dance '87
Promised Land '88
The Banker '89
Cyborg '89

Jason James Richter
Free Willy '93
Cops and Robbersons '94
The Neverending Story 3 '94
Free Willy 2: The Adventure Home '95

Paul Richter
Dr. Mabuse, Parts 1 & 2 '22
Kriemhilde's Revenge '24
Siegfried '24

Tony Rickards
Waterfront '83
Great Gold Swindle '84
Robbery '85
Castaway '87

Don Rickles
Run Silent, Run Deep '58
The Rat Race '60
X: The Man with X-Ray Eyes '63
Bikini Beach '64
Muscle Beach Party '64
Beach Blanket Bingo '65
Enter Laughing '67
Kelly's Heroes '70
For the Love of It '80
Keaton's Cop '90
Innocent Blood '92
Casino '95

Alan Rickman
Die Hard '88
The January Man '89
Closet Land '90
Quigley Down Under '90
Close My Eyes '91
Robin Hood: Prince of Thieves '91
Truly, Madly, Deeply '91
Bob Roberts '92
Fallen Angels 1 '93
An Awfully Big Adventure '94
Sense and Sensibility '95

Allen Rickman
I Was a Teenage Zombie '87
Shock! Shock! Shock! '87

John Ridgely
Air Force '43
Destination Tokyo '43
Arsenic and Old Lace '44
The Big Sleep '46
The Man I Love '46
Cry Wolf '47
The Possessed '47
Task Force '49
Cavalry Charge '51

Robert Ridgely
Rosie: The Rosemary Clooney Story '82
Who Am I This Time? '82
Philadelphia '93

Stanley Ridges
Internes Can't Take Money '37
Each Dawn I Die '39
Union Pacific '39
Black Friday '40
The Sea Wolf '41
Sergeant York '41
The Lady is Willing '42
Master Race '44
The Story of Dr. Wassell '44
Wilson '44
Mr. Ace '46
The Possessed '47
Task Force '49

Leni Riefenstahl
Sacred Mountain/White Flame '31
The Blue Light '32
Tiefland '44

Peter Riegert
National Lampoon's Animal House '78
Americathon '79
Chilly Scenes of Winter '79
National Lampoon Goes to the Movies '81
Local Hero '83
News at Eleven '86
A Man in Love '87
The Stranger '87
Crossing Delancey '88
A Shock to the System '90
That's Adequate '90
The Object of Beauty '91
Oscar '91
The Runestone '91
Passed Away '92
Barbarians at the Gate '93
Gypsy '93
Utz '93
Coldblooded '94
The Mask '94
The Infiltrator '95

Richard Riehle
Body of Evidence '92
Hero '92
Of Mice and Men '92
The Public Eye '92
A Dangerous Woman '93
Lone Justice 2 '93
Dominion '94
Holy Matrimony '94
Lightning Jack '94

Ron Rifkin
Silent Running '71
Mrs. R's Daughter '79
The Chosen '81
Courage '86
Manhattan Murder Mystery '93
Wolf '94
Last Summer In the Hamptons '96

Jorge Rigaud
Quatorze Juliet '32
The Castilian '63
Black Box Affair '66

Cathy Rigby
The Great Wallendas '78
Challenge of a Lifetime '85

Edward Rigby
Lorna Doone '34
Convoy '40
The Happiest Days of Your Life '50

Diana Rigg
A Midsummer Night's Dream '68
The Assassination Bureau '69
On Her Majesty's Secret Service '69
Julius Caesar '70
The Hospital '71
Theatre of Blood '73
In This House of Brede '75
A Little Night Music '77
The Great Muppet Caper '81
Evil under the Sun '82
Bleak House '85
The Worst Witch '86
Snow White '89
Unexplained Laughter '89
Mrs. 'Arris Goes to Paris '92
Genghis Cohn '93
Running Delilah '93
A Good Man in Africa '94

Rebecca Rigg
Doctors and Nurses '82
Fortress '85
The Efficiency Expert '92
The Hunting '92
Tunnel Vision '95

Brad Rijn
Perfect Strangers '84
Special Effects '85

Robin Riker
Alligator '80
Body Chemistry 2: Voice of a Stranger '91
Stepmonster '92

Elaine Riley
Hopalong Cassidy: The Devil's Playground '46
Hopalong Cassidy: Borrowed Trouble '48
Rider from Tucson '50
Clipped Wings '53

Jack Riley
McCabe & Mrs. Miller '71
Attack of the Killer Tomatoes '77
Night Patrol '85
Portrait of a White Marriage '88

Jeannine Riley
Big Mouth '67
The Comic '69
Electra Glide in Blue '73
Wackiest Wagon Train in the West '77

Larry Riley
Crackers '84
A Soldier's Story '84
Dead Solid Perfect '88

Michael Riley
Perfectly Normal '91
To Catch a Killer '92
...And God Spoke '94
Race to Freedom: The Story of the Underground Railroad '94
French Kiss '95
Heck's Way Home '95

Walter Rilla
Black Eyes '39
House of Mystery '41
Mr. Emmanuel '44
The Golden Salamander '51
The Gamma People '56
Frozen Alive '64

Shane Rimmer
S*P*Y*S '74
The People That Time Forgot '77
Dreamchild '85
Out of Africa '85
Crusoe '89

Molly Ringwald
The Tempest '82
Packin' It In '83
Spacehunter: Adventures in the Forbidden Zone '83
Sixteen Candles '84
The Breakfast Club '85
P.K. and the Kid '85
Johnny Appleseed '86
Pretty in Pink '86
King Lear '87
The Pick-Up Artist '87
For Keeps '88
Fresh Horses '88
Betsy's Wedding '90
Strike It Rich '90
Women & Men: Stories of Seduction '90
Face the Music '92
Stephen King's The Stand '94
Baja '95
Malicious '95

David Rintoul
Legend of the Werewolf '75
Pride and Prejudice '85

Nicole Rio
Sorority House Massacre '86
Zero Boys '86
Visitants '87

Marjorie Riordan
Stage Door Canteen '43
Pursuit to Algiers '45
South of Monterey '47
The Hoodlum '51

Michael Ripper
Eye Witness '49
Quatermass 2 '57
Dead Lucky '60
The Curse of the Werewolf '61
Where the Bullets Fly '66
Dracula Has Risen from the Grave '68
Girly '70
The Scars of Dracula '70
No Surrender '86

Leon Rippy
Jesse '88
Track 29 '88
The Hot Spot '90
Moon 44 '90
Eye of the Storm '91
Beyond the Law '92
Kuffs '92
Stargate '94

Elisabeth Risdon
Crime and Punishment '35
Theodora Goes Wild '36
Mannequin '37
The Great Man Votes '38
The Lady is Willing '42
Mexican Spitfire at Sea '42
Reap the Wild Wind '42
Down Dakota Way '49
Guilty of Treason '50
Hills of Oklahoma '50
Scaramouche '52

Miriam Riselle
The Singing Blacksmith '38
Tevye '39

Michael Rispoli
Household Saints '93
While You Were Sleeping '95
Homeward Bound 2: Lost in San Francisco '96

Robbie Rist
He is My Brother '75
Iron Eagle '86

Lazar Ristovski
Tito and Me '92
Underground '95

Cyril Ritchard
Blackmail '29
Peter Pan '60
Half a Sixpence '67
Hans Brinker '69

Clint Ritchie
The St. Valentine's Day Massacre '67

Ritchie ▶cont.

Peacekillers '71
Against A Crooked Sky '75

June Ritchie
A Kind of Loving '62
The Three Penny Opera '62

Martin Ritt
Conrack '74
The Slugger's Wife '85

John Ritter
The Barefoot Executive '71
Scandalous John '71
The Other '72
The Stone Killer '73
Americathon '79
Comeback Kid '80
Hero at Large '80
Wholly Moses! '80
They All Laughed '81
In Love with an Older Woman '82
Pray TV '82
Sunset Limousine '83
Letting Go '85
The Last Fling '86
A Smoky Mountain Christmas '86
Unnatural Causes '86
Real Men '87
Tricks of the Trade '88
My Brother's Wife '89
Skin Deep '89
Problem Child '90
Stephen King's It '90
Problem Child 2 '91
Noises Off '92
Stay Tuned '92
Danielle Steel's Heartbeat '93
Prison for Children '93
North '94
The Colony '95

Tex Ritter
Singing Cowboys, Vol. 2 '30s
Headin' for the Rio Grande '36
Song of the Gringo '36
Arizona Days '37
Hittin' the Trail '37
Mystery of the Hooded Horseman '37
Riders of the Rockies '37
Sing, Cowboy, Sing '37
Tex Rides with the Boy Scouts '37
Trouble in Texas '37
Rollin' Plains '38
Utah Trail '38
Down the Wyoming Trail '39
Man from Texas '39
Roll, Wagons, Roll '39
Take Me Back to Oklahoma '40
Dead or Alive '41
The Pioneers '41
Gangsters of the Frontier '44
Enemy of the Law '45
Frontier Fugitives '45
Marked for Murder '45
Three in the Saddle '45
Holiday Rhythm '50
The Marshal's Daughter '53
The Girl from Tobacco Row '66
Cowboys of the Saturday Matinee '84

Thelma Ritter
Miracle on 34th Street '47
Father Was a Fullback '49
A Letter to Three Wives '49
All About Eve '50
As Young As You Feel '51
The Farmer Takes a Wife '53
Pickup on South Street '53
Titanic '53
Rear Window '54
Daddy Long Legs '55
A Hole in the Head '59
Pillow Talk '59
The Misfits '61
Birdman of Alcatraz '62
For Love or Money '63
How the West Was Won '63
A New Kind of Love '63
Boeing Boeing '65
The Incident '67

The Ritz Brothers
One in a Million '36
On the Avenue '37
The Goldwyn Follies '38
The Gorilla '39
The Three Musketeers '39

Harry Ritz
Texas Layover '75
Silent Movie '76

Emmanuelle Riva
Hiroshima, Mon Amour '59
Kapo '59
Leon Morin, Priest '61

Carlos Rivas
The King and I '56
The Black Scorpion '57

Chita Rivera
Sweet Charity '69
Once Upon a Brothers Grimm '77
Pippin '81
Mayflower Madam '87

George Rivero
Bordello '79
Target Eagle '84
Counterforce '87
Fist Fighter '88

Jorge Rivero
Rio Lobo '70
Soldier Blue '70
Sin of Adam & Eve '72
Day of the Assassin '81
Priest of Love '81
Conquest '83
Ice '93

Julian Rivero
Beyond the Rockies '32
Man from Hell's Edges '32
Phantom Patrol '36
Heroes of the Alamo '37
Ridin' the Lone Trail '37
Arizona Gangbusters '40
Death Rides the Range '40

Joan Rivers
Spaceballs '87
Les Patterson Saves the World '90

Victor Rivers
Black Magic Woman '91
Blood In...Blood Out: Bound by Honor '93
A Million to Juan '94

George Riviere
Journey Beneath the Desert '61
Castle of Blood '64
The Virgin of Nuremberg '65

Marie Riviere
Summer '86
Four Adventures of Reinette and Mirabelle '89
A Tale of Winter '92

Gianni Rizzo
Desert Commandos '60s
Mission Stardust '68

Bert Roach
Smouldering Fires '25
The Crowd '28
The Great Waltz '38

Adam Roarke
Women of the Prehistoric Planet '66
Hell's Angels on Wheels '67
The Savage Seven '68
Hell's Belles '69
The Losers '70
Frogs '72
How Come Nobody's On Our Side? '73
Dirty Mary Crazy Larry '74
Four Deuces '75
This Is a Hijack '75
Hughes & Harlow: Angels in Hell '77
The Stunt Man '80
Beach Girls '82
Trespasses '86
Sioux City '94

Jason Robards, Sr.
White Eagle '32
Crimson Romance '34
The Miracle Rider '35
Fighting Marines '36
Sweetheart of the Navy '37
Wayne Murder Case '38
Stunt Pilot '39
The Fatal Hour '40
Mademoiselle Fifi '44
Bedlam '45
Desperate '47
Riff-Raff '47
Trail Street '47
Return of the Bad Men '48
Rimfire '49

Jason Robards, Jr.
A Doll's House '59
By Love Possessed '61
Long Day's Journey into Night '62
A Thousand Clowns '65
Any Wednesday '66
A Big Hand for the Little Lady '66
Divorce American Style '67
Hour of the Gun '67
The St. Valentine's Day Massacre '67
Isadora '68
Once Upon a Time in the West '68
The Night They Raided Minsky's '69
Ballad of Cable Hogue '70
Fools '70
Julius Caesar '70
Tora! Tora! Tora! '70
Johnny Got His Gun '71
Murders in the Rue Morgue '71
A House Without a Christmas Tree '72
Mr. Sycamore '74
A Boy and His Dog '75
All the President's Men '76
Julia '77
A Christmas to Remember '78
Comes a Horseman '78
Hurricane '79
Melvin and Howard '80
Raise the Titanic '80
Cabo Blanco '81
Legend of the Lone Ranger '81
Burden of Dreams '82
The Day After '83
Max Dugan Returns '83
Something Wicked This Way Comes '83
Sakharov '84
You Can't Take It with You '84
The Long, Hot Summer '86
Breaking Home Ties '87
Laguna Heat '87
Square Dance '87
Bright Lights, Big City '88
The Christmas Wife '88
The Good Mother '88
Reunion '88
Dream a Little Dream '89
Parenthood '89
Final Warning '90
Quick Change '90
Black Rainbow '91
An Inconvenient Woman '91
Mark Twain and Me '91
Storyville '92
The Adventures of Huck Finn '93
Heidi '93
Philadelphia '93
The Trial '93
The Enemy Within '94
Little Big League '94
My Antonia '94
The Paper '94
Journey '95

Sam Robards
The Tempest '82
Fandango '85
Into Thin Air '85
Not Quite Paradise '86
Pancho Barnes '88
Casualties of War '89
The Ballad of Little Jo '93
Mrs. Parker and the Vicious Circle '94
Ready to Wear '94
Donor Unknown '95
Beautiful Girls '96

Brian Robbins
Cellar Dweller '87
C.H.U.D. 2: Bud the Chud '89

Gale Robbins
My Girl Tisa '48
The Barkleys of Broadway '49
The Fuller Brush Girl '50
Three Little Words '50
The Belle of New York '52
Parasite '82

Marty Robbins
Ballad of a Gunfighter '64
Hell on Wheels '67
Road to Nashville '67

Oliver Robbins
Poltergeist '82
Poltergeist 2: The Other Side '86

Skeeter Bill Robbins
Hard Hombre '31
Man's Land '32
Fighting Parson '35

Tim Robbins
No Small Affair '84
Toy Soldiers '84
Fraternity Vacation '85
The Sure Thing '85
Howard the Duck '86
Top Gun '86
Bull Durham '88
Five Corners '88
Erik the Viking '89
Miss Firecracker '89
Tapeheads '89
Cadillac Man '90
Jacob's Ladder '90
Jungle Fever '91
Bob Roberts '92
The Player '92
The Hudsucker Proxy '93
Short Cuts '93
I.Q. '94
Ready to Wear '94
The Shawshank Redemption '94

Richard Rober
Call Northside 777 '48
Task Force '49
Man in the Saddle '51
The Well '51
Jet Pilot '57

Allene Roberts
The Red House '47
Union Station '50
The Hoodlum '51

Arthur Roberts
Deadly Vengeance '81
Revenge of the Ninja '83
Not of This Earth '88
Illegal Entry: Formula for Fear '93
Femme Fontaine: Killer Babe for the C.I.A. '95

Christian Roberts
To Sir, with Love '67
The Anniversary '68
Desperados '69
The Adventurers '70

Conrad Roberts
The Mosquito Coast '86
The Serpent and the Rainbow '87

Des Roberts
Black Bikers from Hell '70
The Outlaw Bikers—Gang Wars '70

Doris Roberts
Honeymoon Killers '70
The Taking of Pelham One Two Three '74
Hester Street '75
Ordinary Heroes '85
The Fig Tree '87
National Lampoon's Christmas Vacation '89
Simple Justice '89
Used People '92
The Night We Never Met '93

Edith Roberts
The Taxi Mystery '26
Man from Headquarters '28

Eric Roberts
King of the Gypsies '78
Raggedy Man '81
Star 80 '83
The Coca-Cola Kid '84
The Pope of Greenwich Village '84
Runaway Train '85
Nobody's Fool '86
Slow Burn '86
Blood Red '88
To Heal a Nation '88
Best of the Best '89
Rude Awakening '89
The Ambulance '90
Descending Angel '90
The Lost Capone '90
A Family Matter '91
Lonely Hearts '91
Final Analysis '92
Fugitive Among Us '92
Best of the Best 2 '93
By the Sword '93
Love, Cheat & Steal '93
Voyage '93
Babyfever '94
Firefall '94
The Hard Truth '94
Love Is a Gun '94
Nature of the Beast '94
Sensation '94
The Specialist '94
Heaven's Prisoners '95
The Immortals '95
It's My Party '95
Doctor Who '96

Florence Roberts
Kept Husbands '31
Harmony Lane '35
Sons of Steel '35

Francesca Roberts
The Heart of Dixie '89
Prison Stories: Women on the Inside '91

Jay Roberts, Jr.
White Phantom: Enemy of Darkness '87
Aftershock '88
Warlords 3000 '93

J.H. Roberts
The Courageous Mr. Penn '41
Spitfire '42

Julia Roberts
Baja Oklahoma '87
Blood Red '88
Mystic Pizza '88
Satisfaction '88
Steel Magnolias '89
Flatliners '90
Pretty Woman '90
Dying Young '91
Hook '91
Sleeping with the Enemy '91
The Pelican Brief '93
I Love Trouble '94
Ready to Wear '94
Mary Reilly '95
Something to Talk About '95

Ken Roberts
The Great Land of Small '86
Fatal Pulse '88

Lynn (Mary Hart) Roberts
Heart of the Rockies '37
Billy the Kid Returns '38
Hollywood Stadium Mystery '38
Shine on, Harvest Moon '38
In Old Caliente '39
Rough Riders' Roundup '39
Frolics on Ice '40
Sioux City Sue '46
Robin Hood of Texas '47
Eyes of Texas '48
Dynamite Pass '50
Hunt the Man Down '50
Hunt the Man Down/Smashing the Rackets '50

Mariwin Roberts
Jokes My Folks Never Told Me '77
Enforcer from Death Row '78

Michael D. Roberts
Heartbreaker '83
Ice Pirates '84
Rain Man '88
Live! From Death Row '92

Pascale Roberts
The Peking Blond '68
Friends '71
Le Grand Chemin '87

Pernell Roberts
Ride Lonesome '59
The Errand Boy '61
Bonanza '64
Four Rode Out '69
Kashmiri Run '69
Paco '75
Sniper '75
Magic of Lassie '78
Hot Rod '79
High Noon: Part 2 '80
The Night Train to Kathmandu '88
Around the World in 80 Days '89

Rachel Roberts
This Sporting Life '63
Doctors' Wives '70
Wild Rovers '71
Baffled '72
Alpha Beta '73
The Belstone Fox '73
O Lucky Man! '73
Murder on the Orient Express '74
Picnic at Hanging Rock '75
Foul Play '78
Sorrows of Gin '79
When a Stranger Calls '79
Yanks '79
The Hostage Tower '80
Charlie Chan and the Curse of the Dragon Queen '81

Roy Roberts
The Fighting Sullivans '42
Guadalcanal Diary '43
He Walked by Night '48
Force of Evil '49
Borderline '50
The Enforcer '51
Santa Fe '51
Second Chance '53
The King and Four Queens '56
I'll Take Sweden '65

Tanya Roberts
Forced Entry '75
Fingers '78
The Yum-Yum Girls '78
California Dreaming '79
Racquet '79
Tourist Trap '79
Beastmaster '82
Hearts & Armour '83
Sheena '84
A View to a Kill '85
Body Slam '87
Purgatory '89
Legal Tender '90
Night Eyes '90
Almost Pregnant '91
Inner Sanctum '91
Sins of Desire '92
Deep Down '94

Ted Jan Roberts
Magic Kid '92
A Dangerous Place '94
Magic Kid 2 '94
The Power Within '95
Tiger Heart '96

Theodore Roberts
The Roaring Road '19
Suds '20
The Ten Commandments '23

Tony Roberts
Million Dollar Duck '71
Star Spangled Girl '71
Play It Again, Sam '72
Serpico '73
The Taking of Pelham One Two Three '74
Lovers Like Us '75
The Lindbergh Kidnapping Case '76
Annie Hall '77
If Things Were Different '79
Just Tell Me What You Want '80
Question of Honor '80
Stardust Memories '80
A Midsummer Night's Sex Comedy '82
Amityville 3: The Demon '83
Packin' It In '83
Key Exchange '85
Hannah and Her Sisters '86
Seize the Day '86
Radio Days '87
18 Again! '88
Popcorn '89
Our Sons '91
Switch '91

Tracey Roberts
Queen for a Day '51
Actors and Sin '52
The Prodigal '55

Wink Roberts
The First Time '69
The Day It Came to Earth '77

Cliff Robertson
Picnic '55
Autumn Leaves '56
The Girl Most Likely '57
Days of Wine and Roses '58
The Naked and the Dead '58
Gidget '59
Underworld, U.S.A. '60
All in a Night's Work '61
The Interns '62
The Outer Limits: Galaxy Being '63
PT 109 '63
The Best Man '64
633 Squadron '64
Love Has Many Faces '65
The Honey Pot '67
Charly '68
The Devil's Brigade '68
Too Late the Hero '70
The Great Northfield Minnesota Raid '72
My Father's House '75
Out of Season '75
Three Days of the Condor '75
Midway '76
Obsession '76
Return to Earth '76
Danger in the Skies '79
Dominique is Dead '79
Two of a Kind '82
Brainstorm '83
Class '83
Star 80 '83
The Key to Rebecca '85
Shaker Run '85
Shoot '85
Ford: The Man & the Machine '87
Malone '87
Dead Reckoning '89
Wild Hearts Can't Be Broken '91
Wind '92
Escape from L.A. '96

Dale Robertson
Devil's Canyon '53
The Farmer Takes a Wife '53
Son of Sinbad '55
Dakota Incident '56
One-Eyed Soldiers '67
Melvin Purvis: G-Man '74
Kansas City Massacre '75
The Last Ride of the Dalton Gang '79

Jenny Robertson
Bull Durham '88
Jacob Have I Loved '88
The Nightman '93
Danger of Love '95
The Boys Next Door '96

Robbie Robertson
Carny '80
The Crossing Guard '94

Willard Robertson
Supernatural '33
Park Avenue Logger '37
Remember the Night '40

Paul Robeson
Body and Soul '24
Emperor Jones '33
Emperor Jones/Paul Robeson: Tribute to an Artist '33
Sanders of the River '35
Show Boat '36
King Solomon's Mines '37
Jericho '38
Song of Freedom '38
Tales of Manhattan '42

George Robey
Don Quixote '35
Henry V '44

Kim Robillard
Rain Man '88
Chrome Soldiers '92

Laila Robins
Planes, Trains & Automobiles '87
An Innocent Man '89
Welcome Home, Roxy Carmichael '90
Live Nude Girls '95

Andrew (Andy) Robinson
Dirty Harry '71
Charley Varrick '73
Someone I Touched '75
Mask '85
Not My Kid '85
Cobra '86
Hellraiser '87
Shoot to Kill '88
Child's Play 3 '91
Prime Target '91
Fatal Charm '92
Into the Badlands '92
There Goes My Baby '92
Trancers 3: Deth Lives '92
Pumpkinhead 2: Blood Wings '94

Ann Robinson
The War of the Worlds '53
Dragnet '54
Midnight Movie Massacre '88

Bill Robinson
Dixiana '30
The Little Colonel '35
The Littlest Rebel '35
Just Around the Corner '38
Rebecca of Sunnybrook Farm '38
Stormy Weather '43

Charles Robinson
The Brotherhood of Satan '71
Daring Dobermans '73
Black Gestapo '75
Fatal Chase '77

Chris Robinson
Darker than Amber '70
Stanley '72
Thunder County '74
Sunshine Run '79
Amy '81
Savannah Smiles '82
Ace of Hearts '85
Viper '88
Women's Prison Escape

Claudia Robinson
Back in the USSR '92
Wide Sargasso Sea '92

Dar Robinson
Stick '85
Cyclone '87

Edward G. Robinson
Kings, Queens, Jokers '30s
Little Caesar '30
Barbary Coast '35
Kid Galahad '37
Thunder in the City '37
Bullets or Ballots '38
I Am the Law '38
Brother Orchid '40
The Sea Wolf '41
Tales of Manhattan '42
Destroyer '43
Double Indemnity '44
Mr. Winkle Goes to War '44
Woman In the Window '44
Our Vines Have Tender Grapes '45
Scarlet Street '45
The Stranger '46
The Red House '47
Key Largo '48
House of Strangers '49
It's a Great Feeling '49
Actors and Sin '52
Hell on Frisco Bay '55
Illegal '55
The Violent Men '55
A Hole in the Head '59
Seven Thieves '60
My Geisha '62
Two Weeks in Another Town '62
The Prize '63
Cheyenne Autumn '64
Good Neighbor Sam '64
The Cincinnati Kid '65
Never a Dull Moment '68
The Peking Blond '68
MacKenna's Gold '69
Song of Norway '70
Soylent Green '73

Frances Robinson
Tim Tyler's Luck '37
Red Barry '38
Riders of Pasco Basin '40
Smilin' Through '41

Jay Robinson
The Robe '53
Demetrius and the Gladiators '54
The Virgin Queen '55
My Man Godfrey '57
Everything You Always Wanted to Know about Sex (But Were Afraid to Ask) '72
Three the Hard Way '74
This Is a Hijack '75
Partners '82
Malibu Bikini Shop '86
Transylvania Twist '89
Sinatra '92
Dying to Remember '93

Joe Robinson
Thor and the Amazon Women '60
The Invaders '63
Tor '64
Diamonds Are Forever '71

Leon Robinson
Streetwalkin' '85
Band of the Hand '86
The Father Clements Story '87

Madeleine Robinson
Mission to Venice '63
Camille Claudel '89

German Robles
The Vampire '57
The Vampire's Coffin '58
The Living Head '59
Genie of Darkness '60
The Monster Demolisher '60

Flora Robson
Catherine the Great '34
Fire Over England '37
Wuthering Heights '39
The Lion Has Wings '40
The Sea Hawk '40
Bahama Passage '42
Saratoga Trunk '45
Caesar and Cleopatra '46
Great Day '46
Black Narcissus '47
Frieda '47
Malta Story '53
Romeo and Juliet '54
55 Days at Peking '63
Murder at the Gallop '63
Guns at Batasi '64
Those Magnificent Men in Their Flying Machines '65
Blood Island '68
Beast in the Cellar '70
Alice's Adventures in Wonderland '72
Restless '72
Les Miserables '78
A Tale of Two Cities '80

Greer Robson
Smash Palace '82
Starlight Hotel '90

May Robson
Little Orphan Annie '32
Red Headed Woman '32
Strange Interlude '32
Dinner at Eight '33
Lady for a Day '33
Lady by Choice '34
Anna Karenina '35
Reckless '35
It Happened in New Orleans '36
Wife Versus Secretary '36
A Star is Born '37
The Adventures of Tom Sawyer '38
Bringing Up Baby '38
Four Daughters '38
The Texans '38
Nurse Edith Cavell '39
The Texas Rangers Ride Again '40
Playmates '41
Joan of Paris '42

Wayne Robson
Mania '80s
The Grey Fox '83
And Then You Die '88
Bye Bye Blues '89
Love & Murder '91
Two If by Sea '95

Patricia Roc
The Wicked Lady '45
Johnny Frenchman '46
Man on the Eiffel Tower '48
Captain Blackjack '51

Pascale Rocard
Police '85
Field of Honor '87

Daniela Rocca
The Giant of Marathon '60
Divorce—Italian Style '62

Alex Rocco
Motor Psycho '65
Blood Mania '70
Wild Riders '71
The Godfather '72
Stanley '72
Bonnie's Kids '73
Detroit 9000 '73
Slither '73
Three the Hard Way '74
The Blue Knight '75
Hustling '75
The Grass is Always Greener Over the Septic Tank '78
A Question of Guilt '78
Rabbit Test '78
Herbie Goes Bananas '80
The Stunt Man '80
The Godfather 1902-1959: The Complete Epic '81
The Entity '83
Badge of the Assassin '85
Gotcha! '85
P.K. and the Kid '85
Return to Horror High '87
Scenes from the Goldmine '87
The Lady in White '88
Dream a Little Dream '89
Wired '89
A Perfect Little Murder '90
The Pope Must Diet '91
Boris and Natasha: The Movie '92
The Spy Within '94

Eugene Roche
Cotton Comes to Harlem '70
They Might Be Giants '71
Slaughterhouse Five '72
Newman's Law '74
W '74
The Late Show '77
The Possessed '77
Corvette Summer '78
Foul Play '78
The Winds of Kitty Hawk '78
Rape and Marriage: The Rideout Case '80
Oh, God! You Devil '84
Eternity '90
When a Man Loves a Woman '94

Suzzy Roche
Almost You '85
Crossing Delancey '88

Jean Rochefort
The Tall Blond Man with One Black Shoe '72
Le Complot '73
Return of the Tall Blond Man With One Black Shoe '74
Salut l'Artiste '74
Till Marriage Do Us Part '74
Mean Frank and Crazy Tony '75
The Clockmaker '76
Dirty Hands '76
Pardon Mon Affaire '76
Le Crabe Tambour '77
Pardon Mon Affaire, Too! '77
Le Cavaleur '78
Who Is Killing the Great Chefs of Europe? '78
I Sent a Letter to My Love '81
Birgitt Haas Must Be Killed '83
My Wonderful Life '90
The Hairdresser's Husband '92
Ready to Wear '94

Claire Rochelle
Boothill Brigade '37
Guns in the Dark '37
Ridin' the Lone Trail '37
Two-Gun Troubador '37
Code of the Fearless '39
Texas Justice '42
Harvest Melody '43
Shake Hands with Murder '44

Lela Rochon
Waiting to Exhale '95
Mr. & Mrs. Loving '96

Chris Rock
I'm Gonna Git You Sucka '88
New Jack City '91
Boomerang '92
CB4: The Movie '93
Coneheads '93
The Immortals '95

Charles Rocket
Fraternity Vacation '85
Miracles '86
Down Twisted '89
Earth Girls Are Easy '89
How I Got into College '89
Dances with Wolves '90
Delirious '91
Hocus Pocus '93
Wild Palms '93
Dumb & Dumber '94

Rocket ▶cont.

It's Pat: The Movie *'94*
Steal Big, Steal Little *'95*
Tom and Huck *'95*

Jack Rockwell
The Fiddlin' Buckaroo *'33*
The Man from Hell *'34*
The Tonto Kid *'35*
Brand of the Outlaws *'36*
Outlaw Rule *'36*
The Rangers Step In *'37*
Hopalong Cassidy: Renegade Trail *'39*
Renegade Trail *'39*
Twilight on the Trail *'41*
Tumbleweed Trail *'42*
Raiders of Sunset Pass *'43*

Robert Rockwell
The Red Menace *'49*
Lassie: Adventures of Neeka *'68*

Sam Rockwell
Clown House *'88*
Jack and His Friends *'92*

Ziva Rodann
Last Train from Gun Hill *'59*
The Giants of Thessaly *'60*
Macumba Love *'60*
Samar *'62*

Marcia Rodd
Little Murders *'71*
How to Break Up a Happy Divorce *'76*
Citizens Band *'77*
Keeping On *'81*

Gene Roddenberry
Star Trek: The Cage *'65*
Star Trek 25th Anniversary Special *'91*

Ebbe Rode
Gertrud *'64*
Topsy Turvy *'84*
Babette's Feast *'87*

Anton Rodgers
Lillie *'79*
Pictures *'80s*
Dirty Rotten Scoundrels *'88*
Impromptu *'90*

Estelita Rodriguez
The Gay Ranchero *'42*
The Golden Stallion *'49*
Susanna Pass *'49*
Twilight in the Sierras *'50*

Freddy Rodriguez
Dead Presidents *'95*
A Walk in the Clouds *'95*

Marco Rodriguez
Internal Affairs *'90*
The Rookie *'90*
The Crow *'93*
Serial Killer *'95*

Paul Rodriguez
Miracles *'86*
Quicksilver *'86*
The Whoopee Boys *'86*
Born in East L.A. *'87*
Made in America *'93*
A Million to Juan *'94*

Norman Rodway
Chimes at Midnight *'67*
The Bretts *'88*
Coming Through *'90*

Channon Roe
Soldier Boyz *'95*
Marshal Law *'96*

Paul Roebling
End of August *'82*
Carolina Skeletons *'92*

Daniel Roebuck
Cave Girl *'85*
Dudes *'87*
River's Edge *'87*
Terror Eyes *'87*
Miles from Home *'88*
Disorganized Crime *'89*
The Killing Mind *'90*
The Fugitive *'93*
The Late Shift *'96*

William Roerick
The Wasp Woman *'59*
The Love Machine *'71*
A Separate Peace *'73*

Maurice Roeves
Ulysses *'67*
Danger UXB *'81*
Hidden Agenda *'90*
The Big Man: Crossing the Line *'91*
The Last of the Mohicans *'92*

Michael Rogan
Doom Asylum *'88*
Punch the Clock *'90*

Bill Rogers
The Girl, the Body and the Pill *'67*
Shanty Tramp *'67*

Charles "Buddy" Rogers
My Best Girl *'27*
Wings *'27*
Mexican Spitfire at Sea *'42*

Ginger Rogers
The Tip-Off *'31*
13th Guest *'32*
Finishing School *'33*
Flying Down to Rio *'33*
42nd Street *'33*
Gold Diggers of 1933 *'33*
Shriek in the Night *'33*
The Gay Divorcee *'34*
Romance in Manhattan *'34*
In Person *'35*
Roberta *'35*
Star of Midnight *'35*
Top Hat *'35*
Follow the Fleet *'36*
Swing Time *'36*
Shall We Dance *'37*
Stage Door *'37*
Carefree *'38*
Having Wonderful Time *'38*
Having Wonderful Time/Carnival Boat *'38*
Vivacious Lady *'38*
Bachelor Mother *'39*
Fifth Avenue Girl *'39*
The Story of Vernon and Irene Castle *'39*
Kitty Foyle *'40*
Lucky Partners *'40*
Primrose Path *'40*
Tom, Dick, and Harry *'41*
Once Upon a Honeymoon *'42*
Roxie Hart *'42*
Tales of Manhattan *'42*
Tender Comrade *'43*
Weekend at the Waldorf *'45*
Heartbeat *'46*
The Barkleys of Broadway *'49*
Monkey Business *'52*
We're Not Married *'52*
Forever Female *'53*
Cinderella *'64*
Quick, Let's Get Married *'71*
Gotta Dance, Gotta Sing *'84*
That's Dancing! *'85*
Irving Berlin's America *'86*

Ivan Rogers
Crazed Cop *'88*
Two Wrongs Make a Right *'89*
Slow Burn *'90*
Ballbuster

Jean Rogers
Ace Drummond *'36*
Flash Gordon: Rocketship *'36*
Rocketship *'36*
Flash Gordon: Mars Attacks the World *'38*
Brigham Young: Frontiersman *'40*
Whistling in Brooklyn *'43*

Jimmy Rogers
False Colors *'43*
Hopalong Cassidy: Riders of the Deadline *'43*
Mystery Man *'44*
Texas Masquerade *'44*

Kenny Rogers
Kenny Rogers as the Gambler *'80*
Coward of the County *'81*
Six Pack *'82*
Kenny Rogers as the Gambler, Part 2: The Adventure Continues *'83*
Wild Horses *'84*
Kenny Rogers as the Gambler, Part 3: The Legend Continues *'87*
The Gambler Returns: The Luck of the Draw *'93*
Rio Diablo *'93*

Mimi Rogers
Blue Skies Again *'83*
Embassy *'85*
Gung Ho *'85*
Someone to Watch Over Me *'87*
Street Smart *'87*
The Mighty Quinn *'89*
Desperate Hours *'90*
Fourth Story *'90*
Hider in the House *'90*
The Rousters *'90*
Deadlock *'91*
The Doors *'91*
The Palermo Connection *'91*
The Rapture *'91*
Dark Horse *'92*
Ladykiller *'92*
Shooting Elizabeth *'92*
White Sands *'92*
Far from Home: The Adventures of Yellow Dog *'94*
Monkey Trouble *'94*
Reflections in the Dark *'94*
Bulletproof Heart *'95*
Full Body Massage *'95*

Paul Rogers
Beau Brummel *'54*
Svengali *'55*
The Trials of Oscar Wilde *'60*
The Mark *'61*
Billy Budd *'62*
Stolen Hours *'63*
A Midsummer Night's Dream *'68*
The Tenth Man *'88*
The Return of the Native *'94*

Roxanne Rogers
Slow Moves *'84*
Punk Vacation *'90*

Roy Rogers
Singing Cowboys, Vol. 2 *'30s*
Old Corral *'36*
Western Double Feature 4 *'37*
Western Double Feature 5: Rogers & Autry *'37*
Billy the Kid Returns *'38*
Come On Rangers *'38*
Old Barn Dance *'38*
Shine on, Harvest Moon *'38*
Western Double Feature 1 *'38*
Arizona Kid *'39*
Frontier Pony Express *'39*
In Old Caliente *'39*
Rough Riders' Roundup *'39*
Saga of Death Valley *'39*
Southward Ho! *'39*
Wall Street Cowboy *'39*
The Great American Western Collection: Roy Rogers *'40s*
Western Double Feature 4: Rogers & Evans *'40s*
Western Double Feature 8: Hale & Carradine *'40s*
Western Double Feature 17 *'40s*
Western Double Feature 18 *'40s*
Western Double Feature 21 *'40s*
Western Double Feature 22 *'40s*
Western Double Feature 24 *'40s*
The Border Legion *'40*
Carson City Kid *'40*
Colorado *'40*
Dark Command *'40*
Ranger and the Lady *'40*
Young Bill Hickok *'40*
Young Buffalo Bill *'40*
Bad Man of Deadwood *'41*
In Old Cheyenne *'41*
Jesse James at Bay *'41*
Nevada City *'41*
Robin Hood of the Pecos *'41*
Sheriff of Tombstone *'41*
The Gay Ranchero *'42*
Heart of the Golden West *'42*
Man from Cheyenne *'42*
Ridin' Down the Canyon *'42*
Romance on the Range *'42*
Sons of the Pioneers *'42*
South of Santa Fe *'42*
Sunset on the Desert *'42*
Sunset Serenade *'42*
Hands Across the Border *'43*
Idaho *'43*
King of the Cowboys *'43*
Silver Spurs *'43*
Song of Texas *'43*
Texas Legionnaires *'43*
Cowboy & the Senorita *'44*
San Fernando Valley *'44*
Song of Nevada *'44*
The Yellow Rose of Texas *'44*
Bells of Rosarita *'45*
Sunset in El Dorado *'45*
Under Western Stars *'45*
Utah *'45*
Western Double Feature 19 *'45*
Helldorado *'46*
My Pal Trigger *'46*
Roll on Texas Moon *'46*
Song of Arizona *'46*
Under Nevada Skies *'46*
Western Double Feature 16 *'46*
Apache Rose *'47*
Bells of San Angelo *'47*
Home in Oklahoma *'47*
Lights of Old Santa Fe *'47*
On the Old Spanish Trail *'47*
Springtime in the Sierras *'47*
Eyes of Texas *'48*
Far Frontier *'48*
Grand Canyon Trail *'48*
Night Time in Nevada *'48*
Under California Stars *'48*
Down Dakota Way *'49*
The Golden Stallion *'49*
Susanna Pass *'49*
Bells of Coronado *'50*
North of the Great Divide *'50*
Trail of Robin Hood *'50*
Trigger, Jr. *'50*
Twilight in the Sierras *'50*
Western Double Feature 3: Rogers & Allen *'50*
Western Double Feature 6: Rogers & Trigger *'50*
Western Double Feature 11 *'50*
Western Double Feature 15 *'50*
Heart of the Rockies *'51*
Son of Paleface *'52*
Salute to the "King of the Cowboys," Roy Rogers *'70s*
Western Double Feature 10: Roy, Dale, & Trigger *'80s*
Cowboys of the Saturday Matinee *'84*

Steve Rogers
Trident Force *'88*
Triple Impact *'92*

Tristan Rogers
Flesh and Blood Show *'73*
Night Eyes 3 *'93*

Wayne Rogers
Cool Hand Luke *'67*
M*A*S*H: The Collector's Edition *'72*
Pocket Money *'72*
Once in Paris... *'79*
Hot Touch *'80s*
Chiefs *'83*
The Gig *'85*
Lady from Yesterday *'85*
The Girl Who Spelled Freedom *'86*
The Killing Time *'87*
Drop-Out Mother *'88*
Passion in Paradise *'89*
The Goodbye Bird *'93*

Will Rogers
Mack Sennett Comedies: Vol. 2 *'16*
Going to Congress/Don't Park There *'24*
Ambassador Bill *'31*
A Connecticut Yankee *'31*
Mr. Skitch *'33*
Judge Priest *'34*
Doubting Thomas *'35*
Golden Age of Comedy *'58*

Maria Rohm
The House of 1000 Dolls *'67*
Kiss and Kill *'68*
Venus in Furs *'70*
Count Dracula *'71*

Clayton Rohner
Just One of the Guys *'85*
April Fool's Day *'86*
Private Investigations *'87*
Bat 21 *'88*
I, Madman *'89*
Caroline at Midnight *'93*
Naked Souls *'95*

Gustavo Rojo
It Started with a Kiss *'59*
No Survivors, Please *'63*
The Christmas Kid *'68*
A Witch Without a Broom *'68*

Helena Rojo
Aguirre, the Wrath of God *'72*
Mary, Mary, Bloody Mary *'76*

Maria Rojo
Candy Stripe Nurses *'74*
Danzon *'91*

Ruben Rojo
Samson in the Wax Museum *'63*
Cauldron of Blood *'67*

Gilbert Roland
She Done Him Wrong *'33*
Thunder Pass *'37*
Thunder Trail *'37*
The Sea Hawk *'40*
Captain Kidd *'45*
Ridin' the California Trail *'47*
South of Monterey *'47*
Malaya *'49*
Bullfighter & the Lady *'50*
The Torch *'50*
The Bad and the Beautiful *'52*
Miracle of Our Lady of Fatima *'52*
Beneath the 12-Mile Reef *'53*
Thunder Bay *'53*
The French Line *'54*
The Racers *'55*
Treasure of Pancho Villa *'55*
Underwater! *'55*
Three Violent People *'57*
Samar *'62*
Cheyenne Autumn *'64*
The Poppy Is Also a Flower *'66*
Any Gun Can Play *'67*
Go Kill and Come Back *'68*
The Ruthless Four *'70*
Between God, the Devil & a Winchester *'72*
Running Wild *'73*
Islands in the Stream *'77*
The Sacketts *'79*
Cabo Blanco *'81*
Barbarosa *'82*

Gylian Roland
Barn of the Naked Dead *'73*
Deadly Sunday *'82*

Tutta Rolf
Swedenhielms *'35*
Dollar *'38*

Guy Rolfe
Young Bess *'53*
The Alphabet Murders *'65*
And Now the Screaming Starts *'73*
Dolls *'87*
Puppet Master 3: Toulon's Revenge *'90*
The Dark Angel *'91*
Puppet Master 4 *'93*
Puppet Master 5: The Final Chapter *'94*

Kirsten Rolffes
Sofie *'92*
The Kingdom *'95*

Esther Rolle
The Summer of My German Soldier *'78*
I Know Why the Caged Bird Sings *'79*
P.K. and the Kid *'85*
Age Old Friends *'89*
Driving Miss Daisy *'89*
The Mighty Quinn *'89*
A Raisin in the Sun *'89*
The Kid Who Loved Christmas *'90*
House of Cards *'92*
To Dance with the White Dog *'93*
Scarlett *'94*
How to Make an American Quilt *'95*

Henry Rollins
The Chase *'93*
Heat *'95*
Johnny Mnemonic *'95*

Howard E. Rollins, Jr.
King *'78*
Ragtime *'81*
The Member of the Wedding *'83*
A Soldier's Story *'84*
The Children of Times Square *'86*
Johnnie Gibson F.B.I. *'87*
For Us, the Living *'88*

The House of Dies Drear '88

Mark Rolston
Weeds '87
Prancer '89
A Sinful Life '89
Survival Quest '89
Body of Evidence '92
The Comrades of Summer '92
Scanner Cop '94
The Shawshank Redemption '94
Eraser '96

Yvonne Romain
The Curse of the Werewolf '61
Double Trouble '67

Candice Roman
The Big Bird Cage '72
Unholy Rollers '72

Leticia Roman
G.I. Blues '60
Fanny Hill: Memoirs of a Woman of Pleasure '64

Ruth Roman
Since You Went Away '44
Good Sam '48
Beyond the Forest '49
Champion '49
The Window '49
Three Secrets '50
Strangers on a Train '51
Blowing Wild '54
Far Country '55
Great Day in the Morning '56
Love Has Many Faces '65
The Baby '72
The Killing Kind '73
Impulse '74
Day of the Animals '77
The Sacketts '79
Echoes '83

Viviane Romance
Princess Tam Tam '35
Panique '47
The Big Grab '63
Melodie en Sous-Sol '63

Beatrice Romand
Claire's Knee '71
Le Beau Mariage '82
House of the Yellow Carpet '84
Summer '86
Four Adventures of Reinette and Mirabelle '89

Andy Romano
Get Christie Love! '74
Pump Up the Volume '90
Afterburn '92
Unlawful Entry '92
Drop Zone '94
Tryst '94
Under Siege 2: Dark Territory '95
Eraser '96
Two Bits '96

Anna Romantowska
A Woman and a Woman '80
The Interrogation '82

Richard Romanus
Mean Streets '73
Night Terror '76
Sitting Ducks '80
Strangers Kiss '83
Protocol '84
Murphy's Law '86
The Couch Trip '87
Hollywood Heartbreak '89
Oscar '91
To Protect and Serve '92
Point of No Return '93
Cops and Robbersons '94

Robert Romanus
Fast Times at Ridgemont High '82
Bad Medicine '85
Pulse '88

Lina Romay
Adventure '45
Love Laughs at Andy Hardy '46
The Perverse Countess '73
Ilsa, the Wicked Warden '78
Sex Is Crazy '79
The Loves of Irina '80s

Sindi Rome
Swift Justice '88
Knock Outs '92

Sydne Rome
Diary of Forbidden Dreams '73
Order to Kill '73
That Lucky Touch '75
Wanted: Babysitter '75
Twist '76
Just a Gigolo '79
The Puma Man '80

Rachel Romen
The Girl from Tobacco Row '66
Ransom Money '88

Cesar Romero
The Thin Man '34
Show Them No Mercy '35
Wee Willie Winkie '37
Happy Landing '38
My Lucky Star '38
The Little Princess '39
Lucky Cisco Kid '40
Dance Hall '41
The Great American Broadcast '41
Week-End In Havana '41
Orchestra Wives '42
Springtime in the Rockies '42
Tales of Manhattan '42
Wintertime '43
Julia Misbehaves '48
The Beautiful Blonde from Bashful Bend '49
Happy Go Lovely '51
The Lost Continent '51
FBI Girl '52
Jungle '52
Scotland Yard Inspector '52
The Shadow Man '53
Vera Cruz '53
Americano '55
The Racers '55
The Castilian '63
Donovan's Reef '63
The Man from U.N.C.L.E. '64
Batman '66
Madigan's Millions '67
Hot Millions '68
The Computer Wore Tennis Shoes '69
Crooks & Coronets '69
Gun Crazy '69
Now You See Him, Now You Don't '72
The Proud and the Damned '72
The Spectre of Edgar Allen Poe '73
The Big Push '75
Mission to Glory '80
Lust in the Dust '85
Judgment Day '88
Simple Justice '89
Mortuary Academy '91

Chanda Romero
The Last Reunion '80
Olongape: The American Dream '89

Joanelle Romero
Lost Legacy: A Girl Called Hatter Fox '77
Miracle in the Wilderness '91

Ned Romero
I Will Fight No More Forever '75
The Deerslayer '78
The Last of the Mohicans '85
House 4: Home Deadly Home '91
Children of the Corn 2: The Final Sacrifice '92

Maurice Ronet
Without Warning '52
Frantic '58
Time Out for Love '61
The Fire Within '64
L'Odeur des Fauves '66
The Lost Command '66
Scandal Man '67
How Sweet It Is! '68
Swimming Pool '70
The Deadly Trap '71
Sidney Sheldon's Bloodline '79
Beau Pere '81
Sphinx '81

Linda Ronstadt
FM '78
The Pirates of Penzance '83
Chuck Berry: Hail! Hail! Rock 'n' Roll '87

Michael Rooker
Light of Day '87
Eight Men Out '88
Mississippi Burning '88
Music Box '89
Sea of Love '89
Days of Thunder '90
Henry: Portrait of a Serial Killer '90
The Dark Half '91
JFK '91
Afterburn '92
Cliffhanger '93
Tombstone '93
The Hard Truth '94
Mallrats '95
The Trigger Effect '96

Mickey Rooney
My Pal, The King '32
Hide-Out '34
Manhattan Melodrama '34
Ah, Wilderness! '35
A Midsummer Night's Dream '35
Riff Raff '35
Healer '36
Little Lord Fauntleroy '36
Captains Courageous '37
Thoroughbreds Don't Cry '37
Boys Town '38
Love Finds Andy Hardy '38
The Adventures of Huckleberry Finn '39
Andy Hardy Gets Spring Fever '39
Babes in Arms '39
Mickey the Great '39
Andy Hardy Meets Debutante '40
Strike Up the Band '40
Young Tom Edison '40
Andy Hardy's Private Secretary '41
Babes on Broadway '41
Life Begins for Andy Hardy '41
Men of Boys Town '41
Andy Hardy's Double Life '42
Girl Crazy '43
The Human Comedy '43
Thousands Cheer '43
National Velvet '44
Love Laughs at Andy Hardy '46
Summer Holiday '48
Words and Music '48
The Big Wheel '49
Quicksand '50
My Outlaw Brother '51
Off Limits '53
The Atomic Kid '54
The Bridges at Toko-Ri '55
Francis in the Haunted House '56
Postmark for Danger/Quicksand '56
Platinum High School '60
Breakfast at Tiffany's '61
The King of the Roaring '20s: The Story of Arnold Rothstein '61
It's a Mad, Mad, Mad, Mad World '63
How to Stuff a Wild Bikini '65
The Comic '69
Manipulator '71
Pulp '72
Thunder County '74
Find the Lady '75
Rachel's Man '75
The Domino Principle '77
Pete's Dragon '77
Magic of Lassie '78
The Black Stallion '79
The Dark Side of Love '79
Bill '81
Leave 'Em Laughing '81
Senior Trip '81
The Odyssey of the Pacific '82
Bill: On His Own '83
It Came Upon a Midnight Clear '84
Ace of Hearts '85
Lightning: The White Stallion '86
Erik the Viking '89
Home for Christmas '90
My Heroes Have Always Been Cowboys '91
Silent Night, Deadly Night 5: The Toymaker '91
The Legend of Wolf Mountain '92
Maximum Force '92
The Gambler Returns: The Luck of the Draw '93
Revenge of the Red Baron '93
The Road Home '95
Women's Prison Escape

Buddy Roosevelt
Circle Canyon '33
Lightning Range '33
Boss Cowboy '35
Powdersmoke Range '35
Range Riders '35
Tribute to a Bad Man '56

Amanda Root
The Man Who Cried '93
Persuasion '95
Jane Eyre '96

Stephen Root
Monkey Shines '88
Bed & Breakfast '92
Till Murder Do Us Part '92
Night of the Scarecrow '95
The Road to Galveston '96

Hayden Rorke
Francis Goes to the Races '51
Spencer's Mountain '63
The Night Walker '64

Bert Rosario
Cold Justice '89
A Million to Juan '94

Tony Rosato
Hog Wild '80
Busted Up '86
City of Shadows '86
Switching Channels '88
The Good Fight '92
Rent-A-Kid '95

Francoise Rosay
Carnival in Flanders '35
Bizarre Bizarre '39
Johnny Frenchman '46
September Affair '50
The Red Inn '51
Seven Deadly Sins '53
Me and the Colonel '58
The Pedestrian '73

Gabrielle Rose
Family Viewing '87
Speaking Parts '89
The Adjuster '91
Timecop '94

George Rose
A Night to Remember '58
The Devil's Disciple '59
Jack the Ripper '60
Mania '60
A New Leaf '71
The Hideaways '73
The Pirates of Penzance '83
You Can't Take It with You '84

Jamie Rose
Twirl '81
In Love with an Older Woman '82
Heartbreakers '84
Tightrope '84
Rebel Love '85
Playroom '90
Chopper Chicks in Zombietown '91
To Die Standing '91

Laurie Rose
Hot Box '72
Woman Hunt '72
Working Girls '75
Blood Voyage '77

Rose Marie
Dead Heat on a Merry-Go-Round '66
Memory of Us '74
Bruce's Deadly Fingers '80
Cheaper to Keep Her '80
Witchboard '87
Ghetto Blaster '89

Sherrie Rose
Martial Law 2: Undercover '91
Double Threat '92
Maximum Force '92
New Crime City: Los Angeles 2020 '94

Roseanne
She-Devil '89
Backfield in Motion '91
Freddy's Dead: The Final Nightmare '91
Blue In the Face '95

Alan Rosenberg
Happy Birthday, Gemini '80
White of the Eye '88
After Midnight '89
Impulse '90
In a Stranger's Hand '92
Witch Hunt '94

Michael Rosenberg
His Wife's Lover '31
The Two Sisters '37
Mirele Efros '38

Maxie "Slapsie" Rosenbloom
Kelly the Second '36
Each Dawn I Die '39
Louisiana Purchase '41
To the Shores of Tripoli '42
Here Comes Kelly '43
Cooking Up Trouble '44
Ghost Crazy '44
Abbott and Costello Meet the Keystone Kops '54
Hollywood or Bust '56
I Married a Monster from Outer Space '58

Rosette
Pauline at the Beach '83
Summer '86
A Tale of Winter '92

Caroline Rosi
The Palermo Connection '91
Abraham '94

Annie Ross
Dressed for Death '74
Yanks '79
Funny Money '82
Superman 3 '83
Basket Case 2 '90
Pump Up the Volume '90
Basket Case 3: The Progeny '92
Short Cuts '93

Betsy King Ross
Fighting with Kit Carson '33
The Phantom Empire '35

Beverly Ross
Crazed '82
Bloodshed '83
Slipping into Darkness '88

Charlotte Ross
Foreign Student '94
Savage Land '94

Chelcie Ross
Keep My Grave Open '80
Bill & Ted's Bogus Journey '91
Basic Instinct '92
Legacy of Lies '92
Amos and Andrew '93
Rudy '93

Diana Ross
Lady Sings the Blues '72
Mahogany '75
The Wiz '78

Gene Ross
Don't Look in the Basement '73
Don't Open the Door! '74
Encounter with the Unknown '75
Poor White Trash 2 '75
Keep My Grave Open '80

Herbert Ross
Goodbye, Mr. Chips '69
Play It Again, Sam '72

Joe E. Ross
Car 54, Where Are You? '61
Slumber Party '57 '76

Katharine Ross
Shenandoah '65
The Singing Nun '66
The Graduate '67
Hellfighters '68
Butch Cassidy and the Sundance Kid '69
Tell Them Willie Boy Is Here '69
Fools '70
They Only Kill Their Masters '72
Pigs '73
Voyage of the Damned '76
The Betsy '78
The Swarm '78
The Legacy '79
Murder by Natural Causes '79
The Final Countdown '80
Rodeo Girl '80
Murder in Texas '81
The Shadow Riders '82
Wrong is Right '82
Red Headed Stranger '87
A Climate for Killing '91
Conagher '91

Kimberly Ross
The Last Starfighter '84

Ross ▶cont.

Nightmare at Noon '87
Pumpkinhead '88

Marion Ross
Forever Female '53
Grand Theft Auto '77
On the Edge: The Survival of Dana '79

Merrie Lynn Ross
Way He Was '76
The Lucifer Complex '78
Class of 1984 '82

Milton Ross
Narrow Trail '17
False Faces '18

Shavar Ross
Friday the 13th, Part 5: A New Beginning '85
The House of Dies Drear '88

Shirley Ross
Waikiki Wedding '37
The Big Braodcast of 1938 '38

Shirley Ross
Mindkiller '87
Night Vision '87

Ted Ross
The Wiz '78
Arthur 2: On the Rocks '88
Stealing Home '88

Isabella Rossellini
A Matter of Time '76
White Nights '85
Blue Velvet '86
Siesta '87
Tough Guys Don't Dance '87
Red Riding Hood '88
Zelly & Me '88
Cannon Movie Tales: Red Riding Hood '89
Cousins '89
Ivory Hunters '90
Wild at Heart '90
Lies of the Twins '91
Death Becomes Her '92
Fallen Angels 1 '93
Fearless '93
The Innocent '93
Immortal Beloved '94
Wyatt Earp '94
Big Night '95

Leo Rossi
Heart Like a Wheel '83
River's Edge '87
The Accused '88
The Hit List '88
Relentless '89
Maniac Cop 2 '90
Fast Getaway '91
Relentless 2: Dead On '91
We're Talkin' Serious Money '92
Where the Day Takes You '92
Raw Justice '93
Relentless 3 '93
Beyond Desire '94
Fast Getaway 2 '94
Relentless 4 '94
Felony '95
Mutant Species '95
Rave Review '95

Giacomo "Jack" Rossi-Stuart
The Avenger '62
Gun Fight at Red Sands '63
The Last Man on Earth '64
Planet on the Prowl '65
Kill, Baby, Kill '66
Hornet's Nest '70
The Night Evelyn Came Out of the Grave '71
Macabre '77

Norman Rossington
The Charge of the Light Brigade '68
Negatives '68
Man in the Wilderness '71

Leonard Rossiter
The Pink Panther Strikes Again '76
Fall and Rise of Reginald Perrin 1 '78
Fall and Rise of Reginald Perrin 2 '78

Britannia Hospital '82
Water '85

Angelo Rossitto
The Corpse Vanishes '42
Mesa of Lost Women '52
Invasion of the Saucer Men '57
Brain of Blood '71
Dracula vs. Frankenstein '71
Mad Max: Beyond Thunderdome '85
The Offspring '87

Rick Rossovich
The Lords of Discipline '83
Streets of Fire '84
The Terminator '84
Warning Sign '85
The Morning After '86
Top Gun '86
Let's Get Harry '87
Roxanne '87
The Spellbinder '88
Paint It Black '89
Navy SEALS '90
Tales from the Crypt, Vol. 3 '90
Secret Ingredient '92
The Gambler Returns: The Luck of the Draw '93
Tropical Heat '93
New Crime City: Los Angeles 2020 '94
Black Scorpion '95
Cover Me '95
Fatally Yours '95

Andrea Roth
The Good Fight '92
Seedpeople '92
The Club '94
RoboCop the Series: The Future of Law Enforcement '94

Cecilia Roth
Labyrinth of Passion '82
The Stranger '87
A Place in the World '95

Gene Roth
Pirates of the High Seas '50
Earth vs. the Spider '58
Attack of the Giant Leeches '59

Lillian Roth
Animal Crackers '30
Madam Satan '30
Ladies They Talk About '33

Louis Roth
Clash of the Ninja '86
Ninja Connection '90

Tim Roth
The Hit '85
A World Apart '88
To Kill a Priest '89
The Cook, the Thief, His Wife & Her Lover '90
Rosencrantz & Guildenstern Are Dead '90
Vincent & Theo '90
Jumpin' at the Boneyard '92
Reservoir Dogs '92
Bodies, Rest & Motion '93
Heart of Darkness '93
Captives '94
Little Odessa '94
Pulp Fiction '94
Four Rooms '95
Rob Roy '95

John Rothman
The Boost '88
Copycat '95

Cynthia Rothrock
China O'Brien '88
China O'Brien 2 '89
No Retreat, No Surrender 2 '89
The Deadliest Art: The Best of the Martial Arts Films '90
Martial Law '90
Fast Getaway '91
Martial Law 2: Undercover '91
Tiger Claws '91
Honor and Glory '92
Lady Dragon '92
Rage and Honor '92
24 Hours to Midnight '92
Angel of Fury '93
Lady Dragon 2 '93
Rage and Honor 2: Hostile Takeover '93
Fast Getaway 2 '94
Guardian Angel '94
Undefeatable '94

Yella Rottlaender
The Scarlet Letter '73
Alice in the Cities '74

Brigitte Rouan
Overseas: Three Women with Man Trouble '90
Olivier, Olivier '92

Richard Roundtree
Shaft '71
Diamonds '72
Embassy '72
Firehouse '72
Shaft's Big Score '72
Shaft in Africa '73
Earthquake '74
Man Friday '75
Portrait of a Hitman '77
Escape to Athena '79
Day of the Assassin '81
An Eye for an Eye '81
One Down, Two to Go! '82
Q (The Winged Serpent) '82
Big Score '83
Young Warriors '83
The Baron and the Kid '84
City Heat '84
Killpoint '84
Game for Vultures '86
The Last Contract '86
Jocks '87
Opposing Force '87
Angel 3: The Final Chapter '88
Maniac Cop '88
Party Line '88
Bad Jim '89
The Banker '89
Crack House '89
Miami Cops '89
Night Visitor '89
A Time to Die '91
Bloodfist 3: Forced to Fight '92
Christmas in Connecticut '92
Deadly Rivals '92
Getting Even '92
Amityville: A New Generation '93
Body of Influence '93
Bonanza: The Return '93
Mind Twister '93
Ballistic '94
Gypsy Angels '94
Once Upon a Time...When We Were Colored '95
Seven '95
Theodore Rex '95
Original Gangstas '96

Robert Rounseville
The Tales of Hoffmann '51
Carousel '56

Mickey Rourke
1941 '79
City in Fear '80
Fade to Black '80
Rape and Marriage: The Rideout Case '80
Body Heat '81
Eureka! '81
Heaven's Gate '81
Diner '82
Rumble Fish '83
The Pope of Greenwich Village '84
Year of the Dragon '85
9 1/2 Weeks '86
Angel Heart '87
Barfly '87
Prayer for the Dying '87
Homeboy '88
Johnny Handsome '89
Desperate Hours '90
Wild Orchid '90
Harley Davidson and the Marlboro Man '91
White Sands '92
Francesco '93
The Last Outlaw '93
Fall Time '94
The Last Ride '94

Graham Rouse
Ride a Wild Pony '75
Weekend of Shadows '77

Myriem Roussel
First Name: Carmen '83
Hail Mary '85
Sacrilege '86

Nathalie Roussel
My Father's Glory '91
My Mother's Castle '91

Alison Routledge
The Quiet Earth '85
The Bridge to Nowhere '86

Catherine Rouvel
Picnic on the Grass '59
Borsalino '70
La Rupture '70
Les Assassins de L'Ordre '71
Black and White in Color '76
Sand and Blood '87

Kelly Rowan
Adrift '93
Candyman 2: Farewell to the Flesh '94

Misty Rowe
Hitchhikers '72
Goodbye, Norma Jean '75
A Pleasure Doing Business '79
Loose Shoes '80
The Man with Bogart's Face '80
Meatballs 2 '84
Goodnight, Sweet Marilyn '89

Nevan Rowe
Sleeping Dogs '82
Nutcase '83

Nicholas Rowe
The Lawrenceville Stories '80s
Young Sherlock Holmes '85
Sharpe's Enemy '94

Victoria Rowell
The Distinguished Gentleman '92
Dumb & Dumber '94
Barb Wire '96

Steve Rowland
Gun Glory '57
Naked Youth '59

Gena Rowlands
Lonely Are the Brave '62
A Child is Waiting '63
Tony Rome '67
Faces '68
A Woman Under the Influence '74
Two Minute Warning '76
Opening Night '77
Brink's Job '78
A Question of Love '78
Strangers: The Story of a Mother and Daughter '79
Gloria '80
Rapunzel '82
The Tempest '82
Love Streams '84
An Early Frost '85
Light of Day '87
Another Woman '88
Montana '90
Night on Earth '91
Once Around '91
Crazy in Love '92
Parallel Lives '94
The Neon Bible '95
Something to Talk About '95

Polly Rowles
Springtime in the Rockies '37
Power '86

Lionel Royce
Panama Menace '41
The Road to Zanzibar '41
My Favorite Blonde '42
White Pongo '45

Roselyn Royce
Malibu Hot Summer '74
Retrievers '82

Virginia Roye
Pace That Kills '28
The Road to Ruin '28

Selena Royle
The Fighting Sullivans '42
Mrs. Parkington '44
Courage of Lassie '46
The Harvey Girls '46
Cass Timberlane '47
A Date with Judy '48
Moonrise '48
Summer Holiday '48
My Dream Is Yours '49
The Big Hangover '50
Robot Monster '53

William Royle
Mr. Wong in Chinatown '39
Mutiny in the Big House '39
The Rains Came '39

Gregory Rozakis
Abduction '75
Five Corners '88

Katt Shea Ruben
Preppies '82
Hollywood Hot Tubs '84
Barbarian Queen '85
Devastator '85

Alma Rubens
The Americano '17
Mystery of the Leaping Fish/Chess Fever '25
She Goes to War '29

Jan Rubes
Charlie Grant's War '80
Blood Relations '87
Dead of Winter '87
The Kiss '88
Blind Fear '89
Courage Mountain '89
The Amityville Curse '90
Descending Angel '90
Class Action '91
Deceived '91
The Birds 2: Land's End '94
D2: The Mighty Ducks '94

Benny Rubin
Sunny Skies '30
Sunny '41
The Bashful Bachelor '42
Mr. Wise Guy '42
Zis Boom Bah '42
The Noose Hangs High '48
Torch Song '53
The Tender Trap '55

Jennifer Rubin
Bad Dreams '88
Blueberry Hill '88
Permanent Record '88
Delusion '91
Victim of Beauty '91
The Fear Inside '92
A Woman, Her Men and Her Futon '92
Bitter Harvest '93
The Crush '93
Playmaker '94
Red Scorpion 2 '94
Stranger by Night '94
Saints and Sinners '95
Screamers '96

Saul Rubinek
Death Ship '80
Highpoint '80
The Agency '81
Ticket to Heaven '81
Soup for One '82
Young Doctors in Love '82
Against All Odds '84
Half a Lifetime '86
Wall Street '87
Obsessed '88
Outside Chance of Maximillian Glick '88
The Bonfire of the Vanities '90
Man Trouble '92
Unforgiven '92
And the Band Played On '93
The Quarrel '93
True Romance '93
Undercover Blues '93
Getting Even with Dad '94
I Love Trouble '94
The Android Affair '95
Hiroshima '95
Nixon '95
Synapse '95

Giulia Rubini
Journey Beneath the Desert '61
Adios, Hombre '68
Stranger in Paso Bravo '73

Sergio Rubini
Intervista '87
A Pure Formality '94

John Rubinstein
The Trouble with Girls (and How To Get Into It) '69
Defiant '70
Getting Straight '70
Zachariah '70
She's Dressed to Kill '79
Killjoy '81
Happily Ever After '82
Someone to Watch Over Me '87
Shadow on the Sun '88
Another Stakeout '93

RoboCop the Series: The Future of Law Enforcement '94

Zelda Rubinstein
Under the Rainbow '81
Poltergeist '82
Sixteen Candles '84
Poltergeist 2: The Other Side '86
Anguish '88
Poltergeist 3 '88
Teen Witch '89

Alan Ruck
Hard Knox '83
Ferris Bueller's Day Off '86
Three for the Road '87
Three Fugitives '89
Young Guns 2 '90
Speed '94
Star Trek Generations '94
Twister '96

Paul Rudd
Johnny We Hardly Knew Ye '77
Beulah Land '80
Last Song '80
Clueless '95

Michael Rudder
Blindside '88
Buying Time '89

Herbert Rudley
Abe Lincoln in Illinois '40
The Seventh Cross '44
Rhapsody in Blue '45
The Scar '48
Artists and Models '55
Beloved Infidel '59
The Jayhawkers '59

Joshua Rudoy
Harry and the Hendersons '87
Flatliners '90

Reed Rudy
Free Ride '86
Zapped Again '89

Mercedes Ruehl
84 Charing Cross Road '86
Heartburn '86
Leader of the Band '87
Radio Days '87
Big '88
Married to the Mob '88
Slaves of New York '89
Crazy People '90
Another You '91
The Fisher King '91
Last Action Hero '93
Lost in Yonkers '93
Indictment: The McMartin Trial '95

Heinz Ruehmann
The Captain from Koepenick '56
Ship of Fools '65

Leonora Ruffo
Goliath and the Dragon '61
Hercules in the Haunted World '64

Rufus
Jonah Who Will Be 25 in the Year 2000 '76
Erendira '83
Les Miserables '95

Charlie Ruggles
Melody Cruise '32
Murders in the Zoo '33
Goodbye Love '34
Ruggles of Red Gap '35
Breaking the Ice '38
Bringing Up Baby '38
Balalaika '39
The Invisible Woman '40
The Perfect Marriage '46
A Stolen Life '46
Ramrod '47
Look for the Silver Lining '49
The Lovable Cheat '49
All in a Night's Work '61
The Parent Trap '61
Papa's Delicate Condition '63
Son of Flubber '63
The Ugly Dachshund '65
Follow Me, Boys! '66

Vyto Ruginis
Descending Angel '90
Clean Slate '94

Barbara Ruick
The Affairs of Dobie Gillis '53
Carousel '56

Anthony Michael Ruivivar
White Fang 2: The Myth of the White Wolf '94
Race the Sun '96

Janice Rule
Battle Shock '56
Invitation to a Gunfighter '64
Alvarez Kelly '66
The Chase '66
The Ambushers '67
The Swimmer '68
Doctors' Wives '70
Gumshoe '72
The Word '78
Missing '82
American Flyers '85
L.A. Bad '85

Sig Rumann
Marie Galante '34
A Night at the Opera '35
The Bold Caballero '36
The Princess Comes Across '36
A Day at the Races '37
Nothing Sacred '37
On the Avenue '37
Thin Ice '37
The Great Waltz '38
Ninotchka '39
Only Angels Have Wings '39
Bitter Sweet '40
Comrade X '40
Love Crazy '41
That Uncertain Feeling '41
To Be or Not to Be '42
Sweet Rosie O'Grady '43
House of Frankenstein '44
The Dolly Sisters '45
A Night in Casablanca '46
Emperor Waltz '48
Houdini '53
Ma and Pa Kettle on Vacation '53
Stalag 17 '53
Wings of Eagles '57
The Errand Boy '61

Jenny Runacre
The Canterbury Tales '71
The Final Programme '73
The Passenger '75
Hussy '80

Joseph Runningfox
Geronimo '93
Lakota Woman: Siege at Wounded Knee '94

Jennifer Runyon
To All a Goodnight '80
Up the Creek '84
The Falcon and the Snowman '85
Blue De Ville '86
18 Again! '88
The In Crowd '88
A Very Brady Christmas '88
A Man Called Sarge '90
Carnosaur '93

Ying Ruocheng
The Last Emperor '87
Little Buddha '93

RuPaul
The Brady Bunch Movie '95
A Mother's Prayer '95

Al Ruscio
Deadly Force '83
The Cage '89
Romero '89

Elizabeth Ruscio
Hider in the House '90
The Positively True Adventures of the Alleged Texas Cheerleader-Murdering Mom '93

Barbara Rush
First Legion '51
When Worlds Collide '51
It Came From Outer Space '53
Magnificent Obsession '54
Harry Black and the Tiger '58
The Young Lions '58
The Young Philadelphians '59
The Bramble Bush '60
Strangers When We Meet '60
Come Blow Your Horn '63
Robin and the 7 Hoods '64
Hombre '67
Moon of the Wolf '72
Superdad '73
Portrait of Grandpa Doc '77
The Seekers '79
Web of Deceit '90

Deborah Rush
The Purple Rose of Cairo '85
Family Business '89
Parents '89
Unnatural Pursuits '91
Reckless '95

Jared Rushton
Big '88
The Lady in White '88
Honey, I Shrunk the Kids '89
A Cry in the Wild '90
Pet Sematary 2 '92

Joseph Ruskin
The Gypsy Warriors '78
Captain America '79
Prizzi's Honor '85
The Criminal Mind '93
Cyber-Tracker '93
Firepower '93

Robert Rusler
Thrashin' '86
Vamp '86
Shag: The Movie '89
The Game of Love '90
Sometimes They Come Back '91
Final Embrace '92

Tim Russ
Night Eyes 2 '91
Bitter Vengeance '94
Star Trek Voyager: Caretaker '95

William Russ
The Right Stuff '83
Beer '85
The Long, Hot Summer '86
Wanted Dead or Alive '86
Dead of Winter '87
The Unholy '88
Disorganized Crime '89
Crazy from the Heart '91
Pastime '91
Traces of Red '92
Aspen Extreme '93

Andy Russell
The Stork Club '45
Copacabana '47

Betsy Russell
Private School '83
Avenging Angel '85
Out of Control '85
Tomboy '85
Cheerleader Camp '88
The Prize Pulitzer '89
Trapper County War '89
Delta Heat '92
Amore! '93

Bing Russell
Suicide Battalion/Hell Squad '58
Stakeout '62
Billy the Kid Versus Dracula '66
Elvis: The Movie '79

Elizabeth Russell
Cat People '42
The Corpse Vanishes '42
Meet the Mob '42
Curse of the Cat People '44

Gail Russell
The Uninvited '44
Angel and the Badman '47
Moonrise '48
Great Dan Patch '49
Wake of the Red Witch '49

Jane Russell
The Outlaw '43
The Paleface '48
Double Dynamite '51
His Kind of Woman '51
The Las Vegas Story '52
Macao '52
Montana Belle '52
Son of Paleface '52
Gentlemen Prefer Blondes '53
The Road to Bali '53
The French Line '54
The Tall Men '55
Underwater! '55
Johnny Reno '66
Born Losers '67
Darker than Amber '70

John Russell
The Blue Bird '40
Forever Amber '47
Man in the Saddle '51
Oklahoma Annie '51
Hoodlum Empire '52
The Sun Shines Bright '53
Jubilee Trail '54
Rio Bravo '59
Apache Uprising '66
Hostile Guns '67
Buckskin '68
Noon Sunday '71
Blood Legacy '73
Smoke in the Wind '75
The Changeling '80
Runaways '84
Pale Rider '85
Under the Gun '88

Karen Russell
Vice Academy '88
Easy Wheels '89
Lethal Games '90
Wilding '90
Dead Certain '92

Kimberly Russell
Hangin' with the Homeboys '91
The O.J. Simpson Story '94

Kurt Russell
It Happened at the World's Fair '63
Guns of Diablo '64
The Adventures of Bullwhip Griffin '66
Follow Me, Boys! '66
Mosby's Marauders '66
The Horse in the Gray Flannel Suit '68
The One and Only, Genuine, Original Family Band '68
The Computer Wore Tennis Shoes '69
The Barefoot Executive '71
Now You See Him, Now You Don't '72
Charley and the Angel '73
Superdad '73
Search for the Gods '75
Sniper '75
The Captive: The Longest Drive 2 '76
The Longest Drive '76
The Christmas Coal Mine Miracle '77
Elvis: The Movie '79
Used Cars '80
Escape from New York '81
Amber Waves '82
The Thing '82
Silkwood '83
Swing Shift '84
Mean Season '85
The Best of Times '86
Big Trouble in Little China '86
Overboard '87
Tequila Sunrise '88
Tango and Cash '89
Winter People '89
Backdraft '91
Captain Ron '92
Unlawful Entry '92
Tombstone '93
Stargate '94
Escape from L.A. '96
Executive Decision '96

Monte Russell
Laurel Avenue '93
Lily in Winter '94

Nipsey Russell
Car 54, Where Are You? '61
The Wiz '78
Car 54, Where Are You? '94

Reb Russell
The Man from Hell '34
Arizona Badman '35
Border Vengeance '35
Outlaw Rule '36

Rosalind Russell
Evelyn Prentice '34
China Seas '35
Forsaking All Others '35
Reckless '35
Craig's Wife '36
The Citadel '38
The Women '39
His Girl Friday '40
They Met in Bombay '41
Sister Kenny '46
Velvet Touch '48
Tell It to the Judge '49
Hollywood Bloopers '50s
A Woman of Distinction '50
Never Wave at a WAC '52
Picnic '55
A Majority of One '56
Auntie Mame '58
Gypsy '62
The Trouble with Angels '66
Oh Dad, Poor Dad (Momma's Hung You in the Closet & I'm Feeling So Sad) '67
Where Angels Go, Trouble Follows '68

Theresa Russell
The Last Tycoon '76
Straight Time '78
Eureka! '81
The Razor's Edge '84
Insignificance '85
Black Widow '87
Aria '88
Track 29 '88
Physical Evidence '89
Impulse '90
Kafka '91
Whore '91
Cold Heaven '92
Thicker Than Water '93
A Woman's Guide to Adultery '93
Being Human '94
The Spy Within '94
Trade Off '95

Tony Russell
Wild, Wild Planet '65
The Hard Ride '71

James Russo
Vortex '81
Fast Times at Ridgemont High '82
Beverly Hills Cop '84
Extremities '86
China Girl '87
Blue Iguana '88
Freeway '88
We're No Angels '89
Illicit Behavior '91
Intimate Stranger '91
A Kiss Before Dying '91
My Own Private Idaho '91
Cold Heaven '92
Dangerous Game '93
Dario Argento's Trauma '93
Bad Girls '94
The Secretary '94
Condition Red '95
Panther '95
The Set Up '95

Michael Russo
Nitti: The Enforcer '88
Demonic Toys '90

Rene Russo
Major League '89
Mr. Destiny '90
One Good Cop '91
Freejack '92
Lethal Weapon 3 '92
In the Line of Fire '93
Outbreak '94
Get Shorty '95
Tin Cup '96

Leon Russom
Long Road Home '91
A Private Matter '92

Richard Rust
Legend of Tom Dooley '59
The Naked Angels '69
The Student Nurses '70
The Great Gundown '75
Double Revenge '89

Babe Ruth
Heading Home '24
The Pride of the Yankees '42

Mary Ruth
Gentleman from Dixie '41
Riot Squad '41

Ann Rutherford
Ghost City '32
Melody Trail '35
Doughnuts & Society '36
Fighting Marines '36
The Lawless Nineties '36
A Christmas Carol '38
Love Finds Andy Hardy '38
Of Human Hearts '38
Andy Hardy Gets Spring Fever '39

My Antonia '94

Lili St. Cyr
Son of Sinbad '55
The Naked and the Dead '58

Michael St. Gerard
Hairspray '88
Senior Week '88
Great Balls of Fire '89
Star Time '92
Replikator: Cloned to Kill '94

Raymond St. Jacques
The Comedians '67
Dead Right '68
The Green Berets '68
Cotton Comes to Harlem '70
Final Comedown '72
Search for the Gods '75
The Private Files of J. Edgar Hoover '77
Kill Castro '80
The Mercenaries '80
Sophisticated Gents '81
The Evil That Men Do '84
The Wild Pair '87
They Live '88
Glory '89
Voodoo Dawn '89
Timebomb '91

Susan St. James
Where Angels Go, Trouble Follows '68
Outlaw Blues '77
Desperate Women '78
Night Cries '78
Love at First Bite '79
S.O.S. Titanic '79
How to Beat the High Cost of Living '80
Carbon Copy '81
Don't Cry, It's Only Thunder '82
Sex and the Single Parent '82

Al "Fuzzy" St. John
Fatty and Mabel Adrift/Mabel, Fatty and the Law '16
Mabel & Fatty '16
Silent Movies...Just For the Fun of It! '26
Dance of Life '29
She Goes to War '29
Oklahoma Cyclone '30
His Private Secretary '33
Riders of Destiny '33
A Face in the Fog '36
West of Nevada '36
Melody of the Plains '37
The Roamin' Cowboy '37
Gunsmoke Trail '38
Ranger's Roundup '38
Songs and Bullets '38
Trigger Pals '39
Border Roundup '41
The Lone Rider in Ghost Town '41
Rangeland Racket '41
Trigger Men '41
Billy the Kid Trapped '42
Law and Order '42
The Lone Rider in Cheyenne '42
The Mysterious Rider '42
Prairie Pals '42
Texas Justice '42
Dead Men Walk '43
Raiders of Red Gap '43
Death Rides the Plains '44
Devil Riders '44
Frontier Outlaws '44
Oath of Vengeance '44
Rustler's Hideout '44
Wild Horse Phantom '44
Gangster's Den '45
His Brother's Ghost '45
Lightning Raiders '45
Shadows of Death '45
Outlaw of the Plains '46
Border Feud '47
Cheyenne Takes Over '47
Fighting Vigilantes '47
Ghost Town Renegades '47
Law of the Lash '47
Return of the Lash '47
Stage to Mesa City '48
Outlaw Country '49
King of the Bullwhip '51
Thundering Trail '51
The Black Lash '52

Betta St. John
All the Brothers Were Valiant '53
The Student Prince '54
Alias John Preston '56
Corridors of Blood '58
Horror Hotel '60

Howard St. John
I Died a Thousand Times '55
Illegal '55
The Tender Trap '55
Li'l Abner '59
Lover Come Back '61
Strange Bedfellows '65

Jill St. John
Roman Spring of Mrs. Stone '61
Come Blow Your Horn '63
The Oscar '66
Tony Rome '67
Diamonds Are Forever '71
The Act '82
The Concrete Jungle '82
Around the World in 80 Days '89
Out There '95

Michelle St. John
Where the Spirit Lives '89
Geronimo '93
Spirit Rider '93

John St. Polis
The Untamable '23
The Unknown '27
Coquette '29
Party Girls '29
Terror Trail '33
Death from a Distance '36
Phantom Ranger '38
Rocky Mountain Rangers '40

Marin Sais
Frontier Outlaws '44
Lightning Raiders '45
The Fighting Redhead '50

Frankie Sakai
Mothra '62
Last War '68
Master Mind '73

S.Z. Sakall
It's a Date '40
Ball of Fire '41
The Devil & Miss Jones '41
Casablanca '42
Yankee Doodle Dandy '42
Wintertime '43
Hollywood Canteen '44
Christmas in Connecticut '45
The Dolly Sisters '45
San Antonio '45
Wonder Man '45
Never Say Goodbye '46
Romance on the High Seas '48
In the Good Old Summertime '49
Look for the Silver Lining '49
My Dream Is Yours '49
Tea for Two '50
Lullaby of Broadway '51
Small Town Girl '53
The Student Prince '54

Sumiko Sakamota
The Pornographers '66
The Ballad of Narayama '83

Ryuichi Sakamoto
Merry Christmas, Mr. Lawrence '83
The Last Emperor '87

Amy Sakasitz
Dennis the Menace '93
A Home of Our Own '93
Mad Love '95

Harold Sakata
Goldfinger '64
Black Eliminator '70s
The Wrestler '73
Impulse '74
Jaws of Death '76
Goin' Coconuts '78
Kill Factor '78

Gene Saks
A Thousand Clowns '65
Prisoner of Second Avenue '74
The One and Only '78
A Fine Romance '92
I.Q. '94
Nobody's Fool '94

Renato Sala
Full Metal Ninja '89
Ninja of the Magnificence '89

Abel Salazar
The Vampire '57
The Vampire's Coffin '58
The Living Head '59
The Brainiac '61
The Curse of the Crying Woman '61
The Man and the Monster '65

Theresa Saldana
I Wanna Hold Your Hand '78
Defiance '79
Raging Bull '80
The Evil That Men Do '84
The Night Before '88
Angel Town '89
Double Revenge '89

Chic Sale
Treasure Island '34
The Fighting Westerner '35

Kario Salem
Triumph of the Spirit '89
1492: Conquest of Paradise '92
Killing Zoe '94

Pamela Salem
Never Say Never Again '83
After Darkness '85
Salome '85

Meredith Salenger
The Journey of Natty Gann '85
The Kiss '88
A Night in the Life of Jimmy Reardon '88
Dream a Little Dream '89
Edge of Honor '91
Dead Beat '94
Village of the Damned '95

Diane Salinger
Creature '85
Pee Wee's Big Adventure '85
The Morning After '86
The Butcher's Wife '91
The Magic Bubble '93
One Night Stand '95
The Scarlet Letter '95
Last Summer In the Hamptons '96

Matt Salinger
Manhunt for Claude Dallas '86
Power '86
Options '88
Captain America '89
Firehawk '92
Babyfever '94
Fortunes of War '94

Pascale Salkin
The Eighties '83
Window Shopping '86
Akermania, Vol. 1 '92

Albert Salmi
Bang the Drum Slowly '56
The Bravados '58
The Unforgiven '60
The Ambushers '67
Hour of the Gun '67
Menace on the Mountain '70
Lawman '71
The Meanest Men in the West '76
Black Oak Conspiracy '77
Empire of the Ants '77
Moonshine County Express '77
Viva Knievel '77
Kill Castro '80
The Mercenaries '80
Steel '80
Dragonslayer '81
Love Child '82
St. Helen's, Killer Volcano '82
Superstition '82
Sweet Creek County War '82
The Guns and the Fury '83
Hard to Hold '84
Born American '86
Jesse '88
Breaking In '89
Gore Vidal's Billy the Kid '89

Colin Salmon
Prime Suspect 2 '93
Captives '94

Frank S. Salsedo
Creepshow 2 '87
Magic in the Water '95

Jennifer Salt
Hi, Mom! '70
Play It Again, Sam '72
Out of the Darkness '85

Renato Salvatori
Rocco and His Brothers '60
RoGoPaG '62
Burn! '70
State of Siege '73
La Cicada '83

Aldo Sambrel
Navajo Joe '67
Hot Blood '89
Voodoo Black Exorcist '89

Emma Samms
Goliath Awaits '81
A Connecticut Yankee in King Arthur's Court '89
The Shrimp on the Barbie '90
Delirious '91
Illusions '91
Star Quest '94

Robert Sampson
Ethan '71
The Grass is Always Greener Over the Septic Tank '78
Gates of Hell '83
Re-Animator '84
The Arrival '90
Dark Side of the Moon '90
Robot Jox '90

Will Sampson
One Flew Over the Cuckoo's Nest '75
Buffalo Bill & the Indians '76
The Hunted Lady '77
Orca '77
The White Buffalo '77
Standing Tall '78
Vegas '78
Fish Hawk '79
From Here to Eternity '79
Insignificance '85
Poltergeist 2: The Other Side '86
Roanoak '86

Jeffrey D. Sams
Fly by Night '93
Waiting to Exhale '95

Joanne Samuel
Alison's Birthday '79
Mad Max '80
Queen of the Road '84
Gallagher's Travels '87

Laura San Giacomo
Miles from Home '88
sex, lies and videotape '89
Pretty Woman '90
Quigley Down Under '90
Vital Signs '90
Once Around '91
Under Suspicion '92
Nina Takes a Lover '94
Stephen King's The Stand '94
Stuart Saves His Family '94
The Right to Remain Silent '95

Olga San Juan
Blue Skies '46
One Touch of Venus '48
The Beautiful Blonde from Bashful Bend '49

Jaime Sanchez
The Pawnbroker '65
The Wild Bunch '69

Pedro Sanchez
Any Gun Can Play '67
White Fang and the Hunter '85
Night and the City '92

Aitana Sanchez-Gijon
Mouth to Mouth '95
A Walk in the Clouds '95

Fernando Sancho
Blood at Sundown '88
Voodoo Black Exorcist '89

Paul Sand
Once Upon a Brothers Grimm '77
Great Bank Hoax '78
The Legend of Sleepy Hollow '79
Can't Stop the Music '80
Wholly Moses! '80
The Last Fling '86
Teen Wolf Too '87
Frozen Assets '92
Getting Up and Going Home '92

Dominique Sanda
A Gentle Woman '69
First Love '70
The Conformist '71
The Garden of the Finzi-Continis '71
Mackintosh Man '73
The Story of a Love Story '73
Steppenwolf '74
The Inheritance '76
1900 '76
Damnation Alley '77
Cabo Blanco '81
Voyage en Douce '81
I, the Worst of All '90
Voyage of Terror: The Achille Lauro Affair '90
Joseph '95

Walter Sande
Don Winslow of the Navy '43
Nocturne '46
Rim of the Canyon '49
I'll Take Sweden '65

Otto Sander
Rosa Luxemburg '86
Wings of Desire '88
Faraway, So Close! '93
The Promise '95

John Sanderford
The Alchemist '81
Leprechaun '93

Dirk Sanders
Black Tights '60
Pierrot le Fou '65

George Sanders
Lloyds of London '36
Allegheny Uprising '39
Mr. Moto's Last Warning '39
Nurse Edith Cavell '39
The Saint in London '39
The Saint Strikes Back '39
Bitter Sweet '40
Foreign Correspondent '40
Rebecca '40
The Saint Takes Over '40
The Saint's Double Trouble '40
The Son of Monte Cristo '41
Sundown '41
The Black Swan '42
The Falcon's Brother '42
Son of Fury '42
Tales of Manhattan '42
The Moon and Sixpence '43
This Land is Mine '43
Action in Arabia '44
Picture of Dorian Gray '45
The Strange Affair of Uncle Harry '45
The Saint Strikes Back: Criminal Court '46
The Strange Woman '46
Forever Amber '47
The Ghost and Mrs. Muir '47
The Private Affairs of Bel Ami '47
The Falcon Takes Over/Strange Bargain '49
All About Eve '50
Samson and Delilah '50
Captain Blackjack '51
Ivanhoe '52
Voyage to Italy '53
King Richard and the Crusaders '54
Jupiter's Darling '55
The King's Thief '55
Moonfleet '55
Death of a Scoundrel '56
While the City Sleeps '56
From the Earth to the Moon '58
Outcasts of the City '58
Solomon and Sheba '59
The Last Voyage '60
Village of the Damned '60
In Search of the Castaways '62
A Shot in the Dark '64
The Amorous Adventures of Moll Flanders '65
The Quiller Memorandum '66
One Step to Hell '68
Invasion of the Body Stealers '69
Endless Night '71
Doomwatch '72
Psychomania '73

Henry Sanders
Boss' Son '79
Deadly Sunday '82

Hugh Sanders
The Magnificent Yankee '50
The Fighter '52
Pride of St. Louis '52

Jay O. Sanders
Mr. Destiny '90
JFK '91
Meeting Venus '91
V.I. Warshawski '91
Hostages '93
My Boyfriend's Back '93
Angels in the Outfield '94
Down Came a Blackbird '94
The Big Green '95
Three Wishes '95

Richard Sanders
WKRP in Cincinnati, Vol. 1 '78
Neon City '91
Forbidden Choices '94

Martyn Sanderson
Solo '77
Beyond Reasonable Doubt '80
An Angel at My Table '89

William Sanderson
Fight for Your Life '79
Raggedy Man '81
Blade Runner '82
Ballad of Gregorio Cortez '83
City Heat '84
Circle Man '87
Last Man Standing '87
Mirror, Mirror '90
Return to Lonesome Dove '93
Mirror, Mirror 2: Raven Dance '94
Wagons East '94
Andersonville '95
Hologram Man '95
Phoenix '95

Tiny Sandford
Laurel & Hardy Comedy Classics, Vol. 2 '30
Laurel & Hardy Comedy Classics, Vol. 3 '34

Elizabeth Sandifer
Animal Instincts 2 '94
Indecent Behavior 2 '94

Adam Sandler
Going Overboard '89
Shakes the Clown '92
Coneheads '93
Airheads '94
Billy Madison '94
Mixed Nuts '94
Happy Gilmore '96

Debra Sandlund
Tough Guys Don't Dance '87
Murder by Numbers '89
Victimless Crimes '90

Steve Sandor
The Only Way Home '72
Stryker '83

Miguel Sandoval
Walker '87
El Diablo '90
White Sands '92
Dancing with Danger '93
Lone Justice '93
Clear and Present Danger '94
Breach of Trust '95
Fair Game '95
Mrs. Winterbourne '96
Up Close and Personal '96

Stefania Sandrelli
Seduced and Abandoned '64
Partner '68
The Conformist '71
Alfredo, Alfredo '72
1900 '76
We All Loved Each Other So Much '77
The Family '87
The Sleazy Uncle '89
Jamon, Jamon '93
Of Love and Shadows '94
Stealing Beauty '96

Diana Sands
A Raisin in the Sun '61
Doctors' Wives '70
Georgia, Georgia '72
Honeybaby '74
Three Days in Beirut '83

Julian Sands
The Killing Fields '84
Oxford Blues '84
Privates on Parade '84
After Darkness '85
The Doctor and the Devils '85
Harem '86
A Room with a View '86
Gothic '87
The Room '87
Siesta '87
Vibes '88
Arachnophobia '90
Impromptu '90
Husbands and Lovers '91
Murder by Moonlight '91
Naked Lunch '91
Warlock '91
Crazy in Love '92
Grand Isle '92
Tale of a Vampire '92
The Turn of the Screw '92
Boxing Helena '93
Warlock: The Armageddon '93
Black Water '94
The Browning Version '94
Witch Hunt '94
The Great Elephant Escape '95
Leaving Las Vegas '95

Tommy Sands
Babes in Toyland '61
None But the Brave '65

Gary Sandy
Hail '73
WKRP in Cincinnati, Vol. 1 '78
Troll '86

Erskine Sanford
Citizen Kane '41
The Magnificent Ambersons '42
Crack-Up '46
The Lady from Shanghai '48

Garwin Sanford
Quarantine '89
Unforgettable '96

Isabel Sanford
Love at First Bite '79
Desperate Moves '86

Ralph Sanford
A Night for Crime '42
There Goes Kelly '45

Renoly Santiago
Dangerous Minds '95
Hackers '95

Saundra Santiago
Beat Street '84
Miami Vice '84

Santo
Invasion of the Zombies '61
Samson vs. the Vampire Women '61
Samson in the Wax Museum '63

Espartaco Santoni
The Castilian '63
Exorcism's Daughter '74

Reni Santoni
Enter Laughing '67
Anzio '68
Guns of the Magnificent Seven '69
The Student Nurses '70
Dirty Harry '71
Dead Men Don't Wear Plaid '82
Bad Boys '83
Cobra '86
The Package '89
The Late Shift '96

Gaston Santos
Black Pit of Dr. M '47
The Living Coffin '58
Swamp of the Lost Monster '65

Joe Santos
Shaft's Big Score '72
The Rockford Files: Backlash of the Hunter '74
Zandy's Bride '74
Fear City '85
Revenge '90
Deadly Desire '91
Mo' Money '92
Sinatra '92
Trial by Jury '94
Tyson '95

Thomas Santschi
The Spoilers '14
Little Orphan Annie '18
Paths to Paradise '25
Paradise Island '30
Phantom of the West '31
Ten Nights in a Bar-Room '31

Michael Sanville
First Turn On '83
Dreams Come True '84

Jorge Sanz
Lovers: A True Story '90
Belle Epoque '92

Al Sapienza
Animal Instincts 2 '94
The Voyeur '94

Mia Sara
Ferris Bueller's Day Off '86
Legend '86
Queenie '87
Apprentice to Murder '88
Shadows in the Storm '88
Daughter of Darkness '89
Any Man's Death '90
A Climate for Killing '91
A Stranger Among Us '92
Blindsided '93
By the Sword '93
Call of the Wild '93
Caroline at Midnight '93
Timecop '94
The Maddening '95
The Set Up '95
Undertow '95

Richard Sarafian
Bugsy '91
Ruby '92

Chris Sarandon
Dog Day Afternoon '75
Lipstick '76
The Sentinel '76
Cuba '79
A Tale of Two Cities '80
The Osterman Weekend '83
Protocol '84
Fright Night '85
Mayflower Madam '87
The Princess Bride '87
Child's Play '88
Goodbye, Miss 4th of July '88
Collision Course '89
Slaves of New York '89
Tailspin: Behind the Korean Airline Tragedy '89
Whispers '89
Forced March '90
The Resurrected '91
Dark Tide '93
Just Cause '94
Temptress '95
When the Dark Man Calls '95
Tales from the Crypt Presents Bordello of Blood '96

Susan Sarandon
Joe '70
The Front Page '74
The Great Waldo Pepper '75
The Rocky Horror Picture Show '75
Great Smokey Roadblock '76
One Summer Love '76
The Other Side of Midnight '77
King of the Gypsies '78
Pretty Baby '78
Something Short of Paradise '79
Loving Couples '80
Atlantic City '81
The Tempest '82
Who Am I This Time? '82
Beauty and the Beast '83
The Buddy System '83
The Hunger '83
Compromising Positions '85
Mussolini & I '85
Women of Valor '86
The Witches of Eastwick '87
Bull Durham '88
Sweet Hearts Dance '88
A Dry White Season '89
The January Man '89
White Palace '90
Thelma & Louise '91
Light Sleeper '92
Lorenzo's Oil '92
The Client '94
Little Women '94
Safe Passage '94
Dead Man Walking '95

Martine Sarcey
Pardon Mon Affaire '76
One Wild Moment '78

Fernand Sardou
Picnic on the Grass '59
The Little Theatre of Jean Renoir '71

Dick Sargent
That Touch of Mink '62
For Love or Money '63
Billie '65
The Ghost and Mr. Chicken '66
Live a Little, Love a Little '68
Melvin Purvis: G-Man '74
Fantasy Island '76
The Clonus Horror '79
Hardcore '79
Tanya's Island '81
Body Count '87
Murder by Numbers '89
Teen Witch '89
Frame Up '91
Twenty Dollar Star '91

Michael Sarne
Seaside Swingers '65
Head Over Heels '67
Cult People '89

Michael Sarrazin
The Doomsday Flight '66
Flim-Flam Man '67
They Shoot Horses, Don't They? '69
The Pursuit of Happiness '70
Sometimes a Great Notion '71
The Groundstar Conspiracy '72
For Pete's Sake '74
The Reincarnation of Peter Proud '75
Gumball Rally '76
Loves & Times of Scaramouche '76
Beulah Land '80
The Double Negative '80
Fighting Back '82
The Seduction '82
The Train Killer '83
Joshua Then and Now '85
Keeping Track '86
Captive Hearts '87
Mascara '87
Malarek '89
The Phone Call '89
Lena's Holiday '90

Gailard Sartain
Roadie '80
Hard Country '81
Ernest Goes to Camp '87
Leader of the Band '87
Mississippi Burning '88
Blaze '89
Ernest Goes to Jail '90
The Grifters '90
Fried Green Tomatoes '91
Guilty by Suspicion '91
Stop! or My Mom Will Shoot '92
Equinox '93
The Real McCoy '93
Walker: Texas Ranger: One Riot, One Ranger '93
Wishman '93
Getting Even with Dad '94
Speechless '94
Wagons East '94
The Spitfire Grill '95

Katsuhiko Sasakai
Godzilla vs. Megalon '76
Terror of Mechagodzilla '78

Jacqueline Sassard
Pirates of the Seven Seas '62
Accident '67
Les Biches '68

Catya Sassoon
Tuff Turf '85
Dance with Death '91
Bloodfist 4: Die Trying '92

Lina Sastri
Where's Piccone '84
The Inquiry '87
Goodnight, Michelangelo '89

Tura Satana
Faster Pussycat! Kill! Kill! '66
The Astro-Zombies '67
The Doll Squad '73

Kei Sato
Onibaba '64
Zatoichi: The Blind Swordsman's Vengeance '66

Jennifer Saunders
Supergrass '87
A Midwinter's Tale '95
Muppet Treasure Island '96

Ann Savage
The More the Merrier '43
Treasure of Fear '45
Detour '46
Renegade Girl '46
Pier 23 '51

Ben Savage
Little Monsters '89
Big Girls Don't Cry...They Get Even '92
Wild Palms '93

Fred Savage
The Boy Who Could Fly '86
Convicted: A Mother's Story '87
The Princess Bride '87
Vice Versa '88
Little Monsters '89
The Wizard '89

John Savage
Soldier's Revenge '70s
Bad Company '72
The Killing Kind '73
Steelyard Blues '73
All the Kind Strangers '74
The Sister-in-Law '74
Eric '75
The Deer Hunter '78
Hair '79
The Onion Field '79
Inside Moves '80
The Amateur '82
Coming Out of the Ice '82
Brady's Escape '84
Maria's Lovers '84
The Tender Age '84
Silent Witness '85
Salvador '86
Caribe '87
The Beat '88
Hotel Colonial '88
Nairobi Affair '88
Do the Right Thing '89
Any Man's Death '90
The Godfather, Part 3 '90
The Hunting '92
Primary Motive '92
Daybreak '93
Shattered Image '93
Carnosaur 2 '94
C.I.A. 2: Target Alexa '94
The Crossing Guard '94
Killing Obsession '94
Red Scorpion 2 '94
The Takeover '94
The Dangerous '95
White Squall '96

Rick Savage
Sensations '87
Ex-Cop '93

Dany Saval
Moon Pilot '62
Boeing Boeing '65

Telly Savalas
Cape Fear '61
Birdman of Alcatraz '62
The Interns '62
Battle of the Bulge '65
The Greatest Story Ever Told '65
The Slender Thread '65
The Dirty Dozen '67
Buona Sera, Mrs. Campbell '68
The Scalphunters '68
The Assassination Bureau '69
Crooks & Coronets '69
Land Raiders '69
MacKenna's Gold '69
On Her Majesty's Secret Service '69
Kelly's Heroes '70
Horror Express '72
New Mafia Boss '72
Pancho Villa '72
Scenes from a Murder '72
A Town Called Hell '72
The Family '73
A Reason to Live, A Reason to Die '73
Redneck '73
Sonny and Jed '73
Inside Out '75
Killer Force '75
Lisa and the Devil '75
Beyond Reason '77
Capricorn One '78
Beyond the Poseidon Adventure '79
Escape to Athena '79

Fake Out '82
Silent Rebellion '82
Cannonball Run 2 '84
Cartier Affair '84
Kojak: The Belarus File '85
The Dirty Dozen: The Deadly Mission '87
The Dirty Dozen: The Fatal Mission '88
The Hollywood Detective '89
Mind Twister '93

Doug Savant
Masquerade '88
Paint It Black '89
Red Surf '90
Shaking the Tree '92
Maniac Cop 3: Badge of Silence '93

Lyudmila Savelyeva
War and Peace '68
The Seagull '71

John Savident
Mountains of the Moon '90
Brain Donors '92
Mrs. 'Arris Goes to Paris '92
Middlemarch '93
Othello '95

Tom Savini
Maniac '80
Knightriders '81
Creepshow 2 '87
Heartstopper '92
From Dusk Till Dawn '95

Camille Saviola
Nightlife '90
Sunset Park '96

Suzanne Savoy
The Cellar '90
The Man with the Perfect Swing '95

Devon Sawa
Little Giants '94
Night of the Twisters '95
Robin of Locksley '95

Julia Sawalha
A Midwinter's Tale '95
Pride and Prejudice '95

Joseph Sawyer
Ace of Aces '33
The Informer '35
Special Investigator '36
The Border Legion '40
Lucky Cisco Kid '40
Melody Ranch '40
Tanks a Million '41
The Naughty Nineties '45
Fighting Father Dunne '48
As You Were '51
Comin' Round the Mountain '51
Indian Uprising '51
Mr. Walkie Talkie '52
The Kettles in the Ozarks '56
The Killing '56

John Saxon
Rock, Pretty Baby '56
The Reluctant Debutante '58
This Happy Feeling '58
The Unforgiven '60
Mr. Hobbs Takes a Vacation '62
The Cardinal '63
The Appaloosa '66
The Doomsday Flight '66
Night Caller from Outer Space '66
Planet of Blood '66
Death of a Gunfighter '69
Mr. Kingstreet's War '71
Joe Kidd '72
Snatched '72
Enter the Dragon '73
Planet Earth '74
Black Christmas '75
Mitchell '75
Strange New World '75
Strange Shadows in an Empty Room '76
Moonshine County Express '77
Raid on Entebbe '77
The Bees '78
Deadly Thief '78
Fast Company '78
The Glove '78
The Electric Horseman '79
Running Scared '79
Battle Beyond the Stars '80
Beyond Evil '80
Blood Beach '81
Invasion of the Flesh Hunters '82
Scorpion with Two Tails '82
Unsane '82
Wrong is Right '82
Big Score '83
A Nightmare on Elm Street '84
Prisoners of the Lost Universe '84
Fever Pitch '85
Half Slave, Half Free '85
Hands of Steel '86
A Nightmare on Elm Street 3: Dream Warriors '87
Aftershock '88
Criminal Act '88
Death House '88
Welcome to Spring Break '88
The Final Alliance '89
My Mom's a Werewolf '89
The Arrival '90
Blood Salvage '90
Crossing the Line '90
The Last Samurai '90
Blackmail '91
Deadly Conspiracy '91
Payoff '91
Animal Instincts '92
The Baby Doll Murders '92
Hellmaster '92
Maximum Force '92
No Escape, No Return '93
Beverly Hills Cop 3 '94
Killing Obsession '94
Wes Craven's New Nightmare '94
From Dusk Till Dawn '95

Philip Sayer
Green Horizon '83
Xtro '83
Slayground '84

Alexei Sayle
Whoops Apocalypse '83
Siesta '87
The Young Ones '88
Deadly Currents '93
Reckless Kelly '93

John Sayles
Hard Choices '84
Unnatural Causes '86
Eight Men Out '88
Little Vegas '90
City of Hope '91
Matinee '92
Straight Talk '92

Syd Saylor
The Light of Western Stars '30
The Lost Jungle '34
When a Man Sees Red '34
Headin' for the Rio Grande '36
Kelly of the Secret Service '36
Kelly the Second '36
Prison Shadows '36
Arizona Days '37
Forlorn River '37
Sea Racketeers '37
Harvest Melody '43
Ambush Trail '46

Raphael Sbarge
Risky Business '83
My Science Project '85
My Man Adam '86
Billionaire Boys Club '87
Back to Hannibal: The Return of Tom Sawyer and Huckleberry Finn '90
Murder 101 '91
Carnosaur '93
Prison for Children '93
The Hidden 2 '94

Mattia Sbragia
Dial Help '88
Year of the Gun '91

Greta Scacchi
Heat and Dust '82
Waterfront '83
The Coca-Cola Kid '84
Burke & Wills '85
Defense of the Realm '85
Ebony Tower '86
Good Morning, Babylon '87
A Man in Love '87
White Mischief '88
Presumed Innocent '90
Fires Within '91
Shattered '91
The Killing Beach '92
The Player '92
Desire '93
The Browning Version '94
Jefferson in Paris '94
Country Life '95
Emma '96

Gia Scala
Don't Go Near the Water '57
The Tunnel of Love '58

Prunella Scales
Fawlty Towers '77
The Wicked Lady '83
The Lonely Passion of Judith Hearne '87
Consuming Passions '88
A Chorus of Disapproval '89
A Question of Attribution '91
Howard's End '92
My Friend Walter '93
An Awfully Big Adventure '94
The Rector's Wife '94
Second Best '94
Wolf '94

Jack Scalia
The Devlin Connection '82
The Amazons '84
Fear City '85
After the Shock '90
Endless Descent '90
Deadly Desire '91
Illicit Behavior '91
Runaway Father '91
Amore! '93
Casualties of Love: The "Long Island Lolita" Story '93
Shattered Image '93
T-Force '94
The Silencers '95
Storybook '95
Tall, Dark and Deadly '95

Carlo Scandiuzzi
Shredder Orpheus '89
Red Snow '91
Killing Zoe '94

Kevin Scannell
Shoot to Kill '88
Backfield in Motion '91

Michelle Scarabelli
Perfect Timing '84
Age Old Friends '89
SnakeEater 2: The Drug Buster '89
Deadbolt '92
Alien Nation: Dark Horizon '94
The Colony '95

Don Scardino
Squirm '76
He Knows You're Alone '80

Alan Scarfe
Cathy's Curse '77
The Deserters '80s
The Bay Boy '85
Joshua Then and Now '85
Keeping Track '86
Iron Eagle 2 '88
Python Wolf '88
Heart of Darkness '93
Jericho Fever '93

Renato Scarpa
The Icicle Thief '89
Volere Volare '92
The Postman '94

Diana Scarwid
The Possessed '77
Forever '78
Pretty Baby '78
Inside Moves '80
Mommie Dearest '81
Desperate Lives '82
Rumble Fish '83
Silkwood '83
Strange Invaders '83
A Bunny's Tale '85
Brenda Starr '86
Extremities '86
The Ladies Club '86
Psycho 3 '86
After the Promise '87
JFK: Reckless Youth '93
The Cure '95
Gold Diggers: The Secret of Bear Mountain '95
The Neon Bible '95
Truman '95

Wendy Schaal
Where the Boys Are '84 '84
Creature '85
Innerspace '87
Going Under '91
When the Time Comes '91
Out There '95

Sam Schacht
A Secret Space '88
Heart of Midnight '89

Johnathon Schaech
The Doom Generation '95
How to Make an American Quilt '95
Poison Ivy 2: Lily '95

Laura Schaefer
Ghost Town '88
Catacombs '89
Curse 4: The Ultimate Sacrifice '90

Eric Schaeffer
My Life's In Turnaround '94
If Lucy Fell '95

Rebecca Schaeffer
Scenes from the Class Struggle in Beverly Hills '89
The End of Innocence '90
Voyage of Terror: The Achille Lauro Affair '90

Natalie Schafer
The Time of Your Life '48
Caught '49
Forever Darling '56
Gilligan's Island: Meet the Crew '64

William Schallert
Sword of Venus '53
Tarnished Angels '57
Speedway '68
The Computer Wore Tennis Shoes '69
Colossus: The Forbin Project '70
Man on a String '71
Trial of the Catonsville Nine '72
Death Sentence '74
The Grace Kelly Story '83
Twilight Zone: The Movie '83
Innerspace '87
War & Remembrance, Part 1 '88
The Incident '89
War & Remembrance: The Final Chapter, Part 8 '89
Held Hostage '91
House Party 2: The Pajama Jam '91

Sabrina Scharf
Hell's Angels on Wheels '67
Hunter '73

Roy Scheider
Curse of the Living Corpse '64
Paper Lion '68
Stiletto '69
The French Connection '71
Klute '71
The Outside Man '73
The Seven-Ups '73
Jaws '75
Marathon Man '76
Sorcerer '77
Jaws 2 '78
All That Jazz '79
Last Embrace '79
Still of the Night '82
Blue Thunder '83
Tiger Town '83
2010: The Year We Make Contact '84
52 Pick-Up '86
The Men's Club '86
Cohen and Tate '88
Listen to Me '89
Night Game '89
The Fourth War '90
The Russia House '90
Somebody Has to Shoot the Picture '90
Naked Lunch '91
Romeo Is Bleeding '93
Covert Assassin '94

Carl Schell
Werewolf in a Girl's Dormitory '61
Quick, Let's Get Married '71

Catherine Schell
On Her Majesty's Secret Service '69
Return of the Pink Panther '74
Gulliver's Travels '77
On the Third Day '83

Maria Schell
Angel with the Trumpet '50
Napoleon '55
Gervaise '56
White Nights '57
The Brothers Karamazov '58
The Hanging Tree '59
Cimarron '60
The Mark '61
End of Desire '62
99 Women '69
The Odessa File '74
Twist '76
Voyage of the Damned '76
Just a Gigolo '79
Inside the Third Reich '82
La Passante '83
Christmas Lilies of the Field '84
Samson and Delilah '84

Maximilian Schell
The Young Lions '58
Judgment at Nuremberg '61
Topkapi '64
Heidi '67
The Castle '68
Simon Bolivar '69
First Love '70
The Pedestrian '73
The Odessa File '74
The Man in the Glass Booth '75
Cross of Iron '76
St. Ives '76
Julia '77
The Day That Shook the World '78
Avalanche Express '79
The Black Hole '79
Players '79
Together? '79
The Chosen '81
The Assisi Underground '84
Peter the Great '86
The Rose Garden '89
The Freshman '90
Young Catherine '91
Miss Rose White '92
Stalin '92
A Far Off Place '93
Abraham '94
Little Odessa '94

August Schellenberg
Mark of Cain '84
Confidential '86
Striker's Mountain '87
Tramp at the Door '87
Black Robe '91
Free Willy '93
Geronimo '93
Iron Will '93
Getting Gotti '94
Lakota Woman: Siege at Wounded Knee '94
Free Willy 2: The Adventure Home '95
Tecumseh: The Last Warrior '95

Mary Kate Schellhardt
What's Eating Gilbert Grape '93
Apollo 13 '95

Robert Schenkkan
Sanctuary of Fear '79
Act of Vengeance '86
The Manhattan Project '86

Rosanna Schiaffino
RoGoPaG '62
Two Weeks in Another Town '62
Arrivederci, Baby! '66
The Witch '66
Code Name Alpha '67
Simon Bolivar '69

Vincent Schiavelli
One Flew Over the Cuckoo's Nest '75
The Return '80
Fast Times at Ridgemont High '82
The Adventures of Buckaroo Banzai Across the Eighth Dimension '84
Amadeus '84
Better Off Dead '85
Lots of Luck '85
Cold Feet '89
Valmont '89

Schiavelli ▶cont.

Ghost '90
Playroom '90
Waiting for the Light '90
Batman Returns '92
Miracle Beach '92
3 Ninjas Knuckle Up '92
Lurking Fear '94
Lord of Illusions '95
Prince Brat and the Whipping Boy '95
Two Much '96

Richard Schiff
City Hall '95
The Trigger Effect '96

Joseph Schildkraut
Wandering Jew '20
Orphans of the Storm '21
The Road to Yesterday '25
King of Kings '27
Road to Yesterday/The Yankee Clipper '27
Cleopatra '34
Viva Villa! '34
The Crusades '35
The Garden of Allah '36
The Life of Emile Zola '37
Marie Antoinette '38
Idiot's Delight '39
The Man in the Iron Mask '39
The Rains Came '39
The Three Musketeers '39
The Shop Around the Corner '40
Flame of the Barbary Coast '45
Monsieur Beaucaire '46
The Diary of Anne Frank '59

Gus Schilling
Citizen Kane '41
A Thousand and One Nights '45
The Lady from Shanghai '48

Vivian Schilling
Terror Eyes '87
Soultaker '90
Project: Eliminator '91
The Legend of Wolf Mountain '92
Future Shock '93
In a Moment of Passion '93
Savage Land '94

Tom Schioler
Storm '87
Maniac Warriors '90s

Sharon Schlarth
Dead as a Doorman '85
Eat and Run '86

Charlie Schlatter
Bright Lights, Big City '88
18 Again! '88
Heartbreak Hotel '88
All-American Murder '91
Sunset Heat '92
Police Academy: Mission to Moscow '94
Ed '96

Walter Schmidinger
From the Life of the Marionettes '80
Hanussen '88

Marlene Schmidt
The Stepmother '71
Scorchy '76

Christianne Schmidtmer
Boeing Boeing '65
The Big Doll House '71
The Giant Spider Invasion '75

Sybille Schmitz
Diary of a Lost Girl '29
Vampyr '31
F.P. 1 Doesn't Answer '33

Stefan Schnabel
Houdini '53
The 27 Day '57
Two Weeks in Another Town '62
Anna '87

Monika Schnarre
The Death Merchant '91
Waxwork 2: Lost in Time '91
Fearless Tiger '94
Bulletproof Heart '95

Bonnie Schneider
Mama Dracula '80
Murderlust '86

Dan Schneider
Better Off Dead '85
The Big Picture '89
Happy Together '89

Helmut Schneider
Captain Sinbad '63
Fifth Day of Peace '72

John Schneider
Eddie Macon's Run '83
Cocaine Wars '86
Stagecoach '86
Christmas Comes to Willow Creek '87
The Curse '87
Speed Zone '88
Ministry of Vengeance '89
Texas '94
Night of the Twisters '95

Maria Schneider
Last Tango in Paris '73
The Passenger '75
Wanted: Babysitter '75
Mama Dracula '80
Crime of Honor '85
Les Nuits Fauves '92

Rob Schneider
Home Alone 2: Lost in New York '92
The Beverly Hillbillies '93
Surf Ninjas '93
Judge Dredd '95
The Adventures of Pinocchio '96

Romy Schneider
Boccaccio '70 '62
The Trial '63
Good Neighbor Sam '64
What's New Pussycat? '65
Triple Cross '67
Swimming Pool '70
The Things of Life '70
The Hero '71
Assassination of Trotsky '72
Cesar & Rosalie '72
Infernal Trio '74
The Last Train '74
Dirty Hands '76
Mado '76
Old Gun '76
A Woman at Her Window '77
Sidney Sheldon's Bloodline '79
A Simple Story '79
Death Watch '80
La Passante '83

Andrea Schober
The Merchant of Four Seasons '71
Chinese Roulette '86

Michael Schoeffling
Sixteen Candles '84
Sylvester '85
Vision Quest '85
Belizaire the Cajun '86
Let's Get Harry '87
Longtime Companion '90
Mermaids '90
Wild Hearts Can't Be Broken '91

Jill Schoelen
D.C. Cab '84
Hot Moves '84
That Was Then...This Is Now '85
Thunder Alley '85
Babes in Toyland '86
Billionaire Boys Club '87
The Stepfather '87
Curse 2: The Bite '88
Cutting Class '89
The Phantom of the Opera '89
Popcorn '89
Rich Girl '91
Adventures in Spying '92
There Goes My Baby '92
When a Stranger Calls Back '93

Ingrid Schoeller
Psychopath '68
They Paid with Bullets: Chicago 1929 '70s

Margareta Schoen
Kriemhilde's Revenge '24
Siegfried '24

Ingeborg Schoener
Cold Steel for Tortuga '65
Mark of the Devil '69
Mr. Superinvisible '73

Dietmar Schoenherr
The Monster of London City '64
Journey of Hope '90

Annabel Schofield
Dragonard '88
Solar Crisis '92

Jason Schombing
3 Ninjas Kick Back '94
Timecop '94

Bob Schott
Future Hunters '88
Out for Blood '93

Lisa Schrage
Hello Mary Lou: Prom Night 2 '87
Food of the Gods: Part 2 '88
China White '91

Bitty Schram
A League of Their Own '92
My Family Treasure '93

Max Schreck
Nosferatu '22
Dracula/Garden of Eden '28

Avery Schreiber
Galaxina '80
Silent Scream '80
Hunk '87
Saturday the 14th Strikes Back '88

Liev Schreiber
Mixed Nuts '94
Party Girl '94
Buffalo Girls '95
Denise Calls Up '95

Rick Schroder
The Champ '79
Earthling '80
The Last Flight of Noah's Ark '80
Little Lord Fauntleroy '80
Hansel and Gretel '82
Two Kinds of Love '85
Across the Tracks '89
Lonesome Dove '89
There Goes My Baby '92
Call of the Wild '93
Return to Lonesome Dove '93
Texas '94
Crimson Tide '95

Karin Schubert
Cold Eyes of Fear '70s
Till Marriage Do Us Part '74
Delusions of Grandeur '76

John Schuck
Brewster McCloud '70
M*A*S*H '70
McCabe & Mrs. Miller '71
Blade '72
Hammersmith is Out '72
Thieves Like Us '74
Butch and Sundance: The Early Days '79
Finders Keepers '84
The New Adventures of Pippi Longstocking '88
My Mom's a Werewolf '89
Second Sight '89
Star Trek 6: The Undiscovered Country '91
Holy Matrimony '94
Tales from the Crypt Presents Demon Knight '94

Dwight Schultz
Alone in the Dark '82
When Your Lover Leaves '83
Fat Man and Little Boy '89
The Long Walk Home '89
Woman With a Past '92
The Temp '93

Paul Schulzie
Laws of Gravity '92
Hand Gun '93

Hans Schumm
Spy Smasher '42
Spy Smasher Returns '42

Reinhold Schunzel
Fortune's Fool '21
The Threepenny Opera '31
Notorious '46
Golden Earrings '47
Woman in Brown '48

Maurice Schwartz
Uncle Moses '32
Tevye '39
Salome '53

Scott Schwartz
Kidco '83
A Time to Live '85

Arnold Schwarzenegger
Hercules in New York '70
Pumping Iron '76
Stay Hungry '76
The Villain '79
The Jayne Mansfield Story '80
Conan the Barbarian '82
Conan the Destroyer '84
The Terminator '84
Commando '85
Red Sonja '85
Raw Deal '86
Predator '87
The Running Man '87
Red Heat '88
Twins '88
Kindergarten Cop '90
Total Recall '90
Terminator 2: Judgment Day '91
Last Action Hero '93
Junior '94
True Lies '94
Eraser '96

Eric Schweig
The Last of the Mohicans '92
The Broken Chain '93
Pontiac Moon '94
Squanto: A Warrior's Tale '94
Follow the River '95
Tom and Huck '95

Rusty Schwimmer
Jason Goes to Hell: The Final Friday '93
Lone Justice 2 '93
A Little Princess '95

Hanna Schygulla
Gods of the Plague '69
Why Does Herr R. Run Amok? '69
Beware of a Holy Whore '70
The Merchant of Four Seasons '71
The Bitter Tears of Petra von Kant '72
Effi Briest '74
The Wrong Move '78
The Marriage of Maria Braun '79
Berlin Alexanderplatz '80
La Nuit de Varennes '82
A Love in Germany '84
Sheer Madness '84
Barnum '86
Delta Force '86
Casanova '87
Forever, Lulu '87
The Summer of Miss Forbes '88
Dead Again '91

Annabella Sciorra
True Love '89
Cadillac Man '90
Internal Affairs '90
Reversal of Fortune '90
The Hard Way '91
Jungle Fever '91
Prison Stories: Women on the Inside '91
The Hand that Rocks the Cradle '92
Whispers in the Dark '92
Mr. Wonderful '93
The Night We Never Met '93
Romeo Is Bleeding '93
The Addiction '95
The Cure '95
National Lampoon's Favorite Deadly Sins '95

Edith Scob
The Horror Chamber of Dr. Faustus '59
The Burning Court '62
The Milky Way '68

Dean Scofield
Eden 3 '93
Eden 4 '93
Prehysteria 2 '94

Paul Scofield
Carve Her Name with Pride '58
The Train '65
A Man for All Seasons '66
Bartleby '70
King Lear '71
Scorpio '73
Anna Karenina '85
The Attic: The Hiding of Anne Frank '88
Henry V '89
When the Whales Came '89
Hamlet '90
Mr. Corbett's Ghost '90
Utz '93
Quiz Show '94

Tracy Scoggins
Twirl '81
Toy Soldiers '84
In Dangerous Company '88
The Gumshoe Kid '89
One Last Run '89
Beyond the Silhouette '90
Demonic Toys '90
The Red Raven Kiss-Off '90
Watchers 2 '90
Play Murder for Me '91
Timebomb '91
Ultimate Desires '91
Alien Intruder '93
Dead On '93
Dollman vs Demonic Toys '93
The Great American Sex Scandal '94

Peter Scolari
Bosom Buddies '80
Rosebud Beach Hotel '85
Mr. Bill's Real Life Adventures '86
Corporate Affairs '90
Perfect Harmony '91
Fallen Angels 2 '93
Ticks '93
Camp Nowhere '94

Zvee Scooler
Uncle Moses '32
Trumps '83

Martin Scorsese
Round Midnight '86
Akira Kurosawa's Dreams '90
Guilty by Suspicion '91
Quiz Show '94

Nicolette Scorsese
Aspen Extreme '93
Boxing Helena '93

Alex Scott
The Abominable Dr. Phibes '71
The Persuaders '71
The Asphyx '72
Space: 1999 '75
Next of Kin '82
Peter's Friends '92

Bainbridge Scott
Hell Squad '85
Death Chase '87

Brenda Scott
Johnny Tiger '66
Simon, King of the Witches '71

Campbell Scott
The Ghost of Fletcher Ridge '80s
Longtime Companion '90
The Sheltering Sky '90
Dead Again '91
Dying Young '91
Singles '92
The Innocent '93
Mrs. Parker and the Vicious Circle '94
Big Night '95

Carey Scott
Making the Grade '84
Diving In '90

Debralee Scott
Our Time '74
Deathmoon '78
Just Tell Me You Love Me '80
Police Academy '84

Donovan Scott
Savannah Smiles '82
Goldilocks & the Three Bears '83
Sheena '84

Eric Scott
The Waltons: A Thanksgiving Story '73
The Waltons: The Christmas Carol '80
A Day for Thanks on Walton's Mountain '82

Fred Scott
Melody of the Plains '37
The Roamin' Cowboy '37
Singing Buckaroo '37

Two-Gun Troubador '37
Ranger's Roundup '38
Songs and Bullets '38
Code of the Fearless '39
In Old Montana '39
Ridin' the Trail '40

Geoffrey Scott
First & Ten '85
First & Ten: The Team Scores Again '85
The Morning After '86

George C. Scott
Anatomy of a Murder '59
The Hanging Tree '59
The Hustler '61
The List of Adrian Messenger '63
Dr. Strangelove, or: How I Learned to Stop Worrying and Love the Bomb '64
The Bible...In the Beginning '66
Flim-Flam Man '67
Petulia '68
Patton '70
The Hospital '71
They Might Be Giants '71
The New Centurions '72
Rage '72
The Day of the Dolphin '73
Oklahoma Crude '73
Bank Shot '74
Savage Is Loose '74
The Hindenburg '75
Islands in the Stream '77
Movie, Movie '78
The Prince and the Pauper '78
Hardcore '79
The Changeling '80
The Formula '80
Taps '81
Oliver Twist '82
Firestarter '84
Choices '86
The Last Days of Patton '86
The Murders in the Rue Morgue '86
Pals '87
Descending Angel '90
Exorcist 3: Legion '90
Deadly Currents '93
Malice '93
Angus '95
Prince Brat and the Whipping Boy '95
Tyson '95

Gordon Scott
Tarzan and the Trappers '58
Samson and the 7 Miracles of the World '62
Conquest of Mycene '63
Gladiator of Rome '63
Hero of Rome '63
Tyrant of Lydia Against the Son of Hercules '63
Coriolanus, Man without a Country '64
Hercules and the Princess of Troy '65
Marauder '65
Tramplers '66
Death Ray

Jacqueline Scott
The Outer Limits: Galaxy Being '63
Empire of the Ants '77

Janet Scott
The Devil's Disciple '59
Day of the Triffids '63

Janette Scott
Helen of Troy '56
Paranoiac '62

Jay Scott
Grave of the Vampire '72
All the Lovin' Kinfolk '89
The Cut Throats '89

John Scott
The Tell-Tale Heart '62
Horror of Party Beach '64

Kathryn Leigh Scott
Dark Shadows '67
House of Dark Shadows '70
Witches' Brew '79
Visitor from the Grave '81
The Last Days of Patton '86
Murrow '86

Kimberly Scott
The Abyss '89
Flatliners '90

Larry B. Scott
A Hero Ain't Nothin' But a Sandwich '78
Revenge of the Nerds '84
That Was Then...This Is Now '85
The Children of Times Square '86
Iron Eagle '86
My Man Adam '86
Revenge of the Nerds 2: Nerds in Paradise '87
SnakeEater 2: The Drug Buster '89
Super Force '90
Fear of a Black Hat '94
Revenge of the Nerds 4: Nerds in Love '94

Lizabeth Scott
The Strange Love of Martha Ivers '46
Dead Reckoning '47
Pitfall '48
Easy Living '49
Killer Bait '49
Too Late for Tears '49
The Racket '51
A Stolen Face '52
Scared Stiff '53
Silver Lode '54
Loving You '57
Pulp '72

Margaretta Scott
Things to Come '36
Action for Slander '38
Calling Paul Temple '48
Counterblast '48
Man of Evil '48

Martha Scott
The Howards of Virginia '40
Our Town '40
Cheers for Miss Bishop '41
Hi Diddle Diddle '43
War of the Wildcats '43
The Falcon Takes Over/Strange Bargain '49
Desperate Hours '55
The Ten Commandments '56
Sayonara '57
Ben-Hur '59
The Turning Point '77
Father Figure '80
Adam '83

Pippa Scott
Petulia '68
Cold Turkey '71
Bad Ronald '74

Randolph Scott
When the West Was Young '32
Buffalo Stampede '33
Heritage of the Desert '33
Man of the Forest '33
Murders in the Zoo '33
Supernatural '33
To the Last Man '33
Wagon Wheels '34
The Fighting Westerner '35
Roberta '35
She '35
Follow the Fleet '36
Go West, Young Man '36
The Last of the Mohicans '36
Rebecca of Sunnybrook Farm '38
The Texans '38
Jesse James '39
Susannah of the Mounties '39
My Favorite Wife '40
Virginia City '40
Western Union '41
Pittsburgh '42
The Spoilers '42
To the Shores of Tripoli '42
Bombardier '43
Gung Ho! '43
China Sky '44
Captain Kidd '45
Abilene Town '46
Badman's Territory '46
Trail Street '47
Coroner Creek '48
Return of the Bad Men '48
The Doolins of Oklahoma '49
The Cariboo Trail '50
The Nevadan '50
Man in the Saddle '51
Santa Fe '51
Hangman's Knot '52
The Stranger Wore a Gun '53
Ten Wanted Men '54
A Lawless Street '55
Rage at Dawn '55
Seventh Cavalry '56
The Tall T '57
Ride Lonesome '59
Ride the High Country '62

Susan Scott
The Slasher '74
Day of the Maniac '77
Trap Them & Kill Them '84
Student Confidential '87

Timothy Scott
Love Me Deadly '76
Fried Green Tomatoes '91
Inside Out '91
Lone Justice '93
Return to Lonesome Dove '93

Zachary Scott
Mildred Pierce '45
The Southerner '45
Cass Timberlane '47
South of St. Louis '48
Flamingo Road '49
Born to Be Bad '50
Let's Make It Legal '51
Wings of Danger '52
Appointment in Honduras '53
Flame of the Islands '55
Shotgun '55
The Young One '61

Kristin Scott Thomas
Under the Cherry Moon '86
A Handful of Dust '88
The Tenth Man '88
The Endless Game '89
Framed '90
Spymaker: The Secret Life of Ian Fleming '90
Bitter Moon '92
The Bachelor '93
Weep No More My Lady '93
Four Weddings and a Funeral '94
An Unforgettable Summer '94
Angels and Insects '95
The Confessional '95
Gulliver's Travels '95
Richard III '95

Vito Scotti
Two Weeks in Another Town '62
Von Ryan's Express '65
What Did You Do in the War, Daddy? '66
Caper of the Golden Bulls '67
I Wonder Who's Killing Her Now? '76

Alexander Scourby
Affair in Trinidad '52
The Big Heat '53
The Redhead from Wyoming '53
Me and the Colonel '58

Angus Scrimm
Phantasm '79
The Lost Empire '83
Phantasm II '88
Transylvania Twist '89
Subspecies '90
Mindwarp '91
Phantasm III: Lord of the Dead '94

Sandra Seacat
Promised Land '88
The New Age '94

Susan Seaforth Hayes
Billie '65
Dream Machine '91

Steven Seagal
Above the Law '88
Hard to Kill '89
Marked for Death '90
Out for Justice '91
Under Siege '92
On Deadly Ground '94
Under Siege 2: Dark Territory '95
Executive Decision '96

Jenny Seagrove
Local Hero '83
Nate and Hayes '83
A Woman of Substance, Episode 1: Nest of Vipers '84
A Woman of Substance, Episode 2: The Secret is Revealed '84
A Woman of Substance, Episode 3: Fighting for the Dream '84
Hold the Dream '85
Appointment with Death '88
A Chorus of Disapproval '89
Magic Moments '90s
Bullseye! '90
The Guardian '90
Deadly Game '91
Sherlock Holmes and the Incident at Victoria Falls '91

Douglas Seale
Ernest Saves Christmas '88
Mr. Destiny '90

Franklyn Seales
The Onion Field '79
Southern Comfort '81

Jackie Searl
Hearts of Humanity '32
High Gear '33
Topaze '33
Peck's Bad Boy '34
The Return of Casey Jones '34

Heather Sears
Room at the Top '59
The Phantom of the Opera '62
Estate of Insanity '70

James Seay
In Old Colorado '41
Ridin' Down the Canyon '42
Turf Boy '42
Heartaches '47
Phantom from Space '53
The Amazing Colossal Man '57
Beginning of the End '57

Dorothy Sebastian
Our Dancing Daughters '28
A Woman of Affairs '28
His First Command '29
The Single Standard '29
Spite Marriage '29
They Never Come Back '32
Rough Riders' Roundup '39

Tracy Sebastian
On the Air Live with Captain Midnight '79
Running Cool '93

Jean Seberg
Bonjour Tristesse '57
Saint Joan '57
Breathless '59
The Mouse That Roared '59
Time Out for Love '61
Lilith '64
A Fine Madness '66
Paint Your Wagon '69
Pendulum '69
Airport '70
Macho Callahan '70

Harry Secombe
Down Among the Z Men '52
Goon Movie '53
Song of Norway '70

Kyle Secor
The Heart of Dixie '89
City Slickers '91
Delusion '91
Sleeping with the Enemy '91
Silent Victim '92
Untamed Heart '93
Children of Fury '94
Drop Zone '94

John Seda
Gladiator '92
I Like It Like That '94
12 Monkeys '95
Primal Fear '96

Margaret Seddon
Little Church Around the Corner '23
Smilin' Through '32
The Return of Casey Jones '34
Mr. Deeds Goes to Town '36

Kyra Sedgwick
War & Love '84
Tai-Pan '86
Kansas '88
Born on the Fourth of July '89
Mr. & Mrs. Bridge '90
Pyrates '91
Women & Men: In Love There Are No Rules '91
Miss Rose White '92
Singles '92
Family Pictures '93
Heart and Souls '93
Murder In the First '95
Something to Talk About '95
Phenomenon '96

Robert Sedgwick
Morgan Stewart's Coming Home '87
Nasty Hero '89
Tune in Tomorrow '90

Miriam Seegar
Seven Keys to Baldplate '29
Strangers of the Evening '32

George Segal
Invitation to a Gunfighter '64
King Rat '65
Ship of Fools '65
The Lost Command '66
The Quiller Memorandum '66
Who's Afraid of Virginia Woolf? '66
The St. Valentine's Day Massacre '67
No Way to Treat a Lady '68
The Bridge at Remagen '69
The Hot Rock '70
The Owl and the Pussycat '70
Where's Poppa? '70
Born to Win '71
Blume in Love '73
A Touch of Class '73
The Terminal Man '74
Black Bird '75
Russian Roulette '75
The Duchess and the Dirtwater Fox '76
Fun with Dick and Jane '77
Rollercoaster '77
Who Is Killing the Great Chefs of Europe? '78
Lost and Found '79
The Last Married Couple in America '80
Carbon Copy '81
Deadly Game '82
Cold Room '84
The Zany Adventures of Robin Hood '84
Killing 'em Softly '85
Not My Kid '85
Stick '85
All's Fair '89
The Endless Game '89
Look Who's Talking '89
For the Boys '91
Me, Myself & I '92
Direct Hit '93
Look Who's Talking Now '93
Taking the Heat '93
Army of One '94
Deep Down '94
The Babysitter '95
Flirting with Disaster '95
It's My Party '95
The Cable Guy '96

Zohra Segal
The Courtesans of Bombay '85
Masala '91

Jonathan Segall
Hot Bubblegum '81
Young Love—Lemon Popsicle 7 '87

Pamela Segall
Bad Manners '84
Something Special '86
After Midnight '89
Say Anything '89
Gate 2 '92
Bed of Roses '95
Sgt. Bilko '95

Emmanuelle Seigner
Frantic '88
Bitter Moon '92

Louis Seigner
Seven Deadly Sins '53
The Would-Be Gentleman '58
The Eclipse '66
This Special Friendship '67

John Seitz
The Prowler '81
Hard Choices '84
Five Corners '88
Forced March '90
Out of the Rain '90

Johnny Sekka
Khartoum '66
The Last Safari '67
Mohammed: Messenger of God '77

David Selby
Dark Shadows '67
Night of Dark Shadows '71
Up the Sandbox '72
The Girl in Blue '74
Rich Kids '79
Rich and Famous '81
Dying Young '91
Grave Secrets: The Legacy of Hilltop Drive '92
Intersection '93
Headless Body in Topless Bar '96
White Squall '96

Nicholas Selby
A Midsummer Night's Dream '68
Macbeth '71

Sarah Selby
An Affair to Remember '57
Huckleberry Finn '75

Marian Seldes
Fingers '78
Tom and Huck '95
Truman '95

Elizabeth Sellars
Desiree '54
Three Cases of Murder '55
Never Let Go '60
The Chalk Garden '64
A Voyage' Round My Father '89

Connie Sellecca
Captain America 2: Death Too Soon '79
She's Dressed to Kill '79
The Last Fling '86
The Brotherhood of the Rose '89

Tom Selleck
Myra Breckinridge '70
Daughters of Satan '72
Terminal Island '73
Midway '76
Most Wanted '76
Washington Affair '77
Coma '78
The Gypsy Warriors '78
The Concrete Cowboys '79
The Sacketts '79
Magnum P.I.: Don't Eat the Snow in Hawaii '80
The Shadow Riders '82
Bunco '83
High Road to China '83
Lassiter '84
Runaway '84
Three Men and a Baby '87
Her Alibi '88
An Innocent Man '89
Quigley Down Under '90
Three Men and a Little Lady '90
Christopher Columbus: The Discovery '92
Folks! '92
Mr. Baseball '92
Broken Trust '95

Peter Sellers
Down Among the Z Men '52
Goon Movie '53
The Ladykillers '55
The Case of the Mukkinese Battle Horn '56
The Smallest Show on Earth '57
The Naked Truth '58
Tom Thumb '58
Up the Creek '58
Carlton Browne of the F.O. '59
I'm All Right Jack '59
The Mouse That Roared '59
The Battle of the Sexes '60
The Millionairess '60
Never Let Go '60
Two-Way Stretch '60
Lolita '62
Only Two Can Play '62
The Road to Hong Kong '62
Waltz of the Toreadors '62
Heavens Above '63
The Wrong Arm of the Law '63
Dr. Strangelove, or: How I Learned to Stop Worrying and Love the Bomb '64
The Pink Panther '64
A Shot in the Dark '64
The World of Henry Orient '64
What's New Pussycat? '65
After the Fox '66
The Wrong Box '66
Bobo '67
Casino Royale '67
Woman Times Seven '67
I Love You, Alice B. Toklas! '68
The Party '68
The Magic Christian '69
There's a Girl in My Soup '70
Alice's Adventures in Wonderland '72
Blockhouse '73
Ghost in the Noonday Sun '74
Return of the Pink Panther '74
Great McGonagall '75
America at the Movies '76
Murder by Death '76
The Pink Panther Strikes Again '76
Revenge of the Pink Panther '78
Being There '79
Prisoner of Zenda '79
The Fiendish Plot of Dr. Fu Manchu '80
To See Such Fun '81
Trail of the Pink Panther '82
King Lear '87

Charles Sellon
The Monster '25
The Prairie King '27
Behind Office Doors '31
Ride Him, Cowboy '32

Milton Selzer
The Triangle Factory Fire Scandal '79
Miss Rose White '92

Harry Semels
Ghost Valley '32
Texas Buddies '32

Larry Semon
Bakery/Grocery Clerk '21
Sawmill/The Dome Doctor '22
The Wizard of Oz '25
Underworld '27

Aparna Sen
Bombay Talkie '70
Hullabaloo Over Georgie & Bonnie's Pictures '78

Joe Seneca
Wilma '77
Half Slave, Half Free '85
Crossroads '86
Samaritan: The Mitch Snyder Story '86
The Blob '88
School Daze '88
Mo' Better Blues '90
Murder on the Bayou '91
Mississippi Masala '92
The Saint of Fort Washington '93

Mack Sennett
Charlie Chaplin's Keystone Comedies #2 '14
Charlie Chaplin...Our Hero! '15
Abbott and Costello Meet the Keystone Kops '54
Man in the Silk Hat '83

Massimo Serato
The Love of Three Queens '54
The Naked Maja '59
Battle of Valiant '63
Tyrant of Lydia Against the Son of Hercules '63
10th Victim '65
Wild, Wild Planet '65

Serena
Jive Turkey '76
Dracula Sucks '79

Yahoo Serious
Young Einstein '89
Reckless Kelly '93

Assumpta Serna
Matador '86
I, the Worst of All '90
Wild Orchid '90
Revolver '92
Chain of Desire '93
Nostradamus '93
Sharpe's Eagle '93
Sharpe's Rifles '93
Sharpe's Company '94
Sharpe's Enemy '94
The Shooter '94
The Craft '96

Pepe Serna
The Student Nurses '70
Sniper '75
Ballad of Gregorio Cortez '83
The Adventures of Buckaroo Banzai Across the Eighth Dimension '84
Fandango '85
Bad Jim '89
The Forgotten '89
The Rookie '90
American Me '92
A Million to Juan '94

Jacques Sernas
The Golden Salamander '51
Helen of Troy '56
La Dolce Vita '60
55 Days at Peking '63
Hornet's Nest '70
Superfly T.N.T. '73
Blue Country '77

Raymond Serra
Hooch '76
Hardhat & Legs '80
Alphabet City '84
Splitz '84
Marilyn & Bobby: Her Final Affair '94
Sugar Hill '94

Julieta Serrano
Dark Habits '84
Matador '86
Women on the Verge of a Nervous Breakdown '88
Tie Me Up! Tie Me Down! '90

Nestor Serrano
Brenda Starr '86
Hangin' with the Homeboys '91
City Hall '95

Michel Serrault
Diabolique '55
La Cage aux Folles '78
Buffet Froid '79
La Cage aux Folles 2 '81
The Associate '82
La Cage aux Folles 3: The Wedding '86
Dr. Petiot '90
The Old Lady Who Walked in the Sea '91
Nelly et Monsieur Arnaud '95

Jean Servais
Rififi '54
Fever Mounts at El Pao '59
Tamango '59
The Liars '64
That Man from Rio '64
Murder at 45 R.P.M. '65
The Devil's Nightmare '71

Almira Sessions
The Heat's On '43
Miracle of Morgan's Creek '44
Diary of a Chambermaid '46
Oklahoma Annie '51

John Sessions
Sweet Revenge '90
Princess Caraboo '94
A Midwinter's Tale '95

Roshan Seth
Gandhi '82
My Beautiful Laundrette '85
Little Dorrit, Film 1: Nobody's Fault '88
Little Dorrit, Film 2: Little Dorrit's Story '88
Mountains of the Moon '90
Not Without My Daughter '90
London Kills Me '91
Mississippi Masala '92
Stalin '92
Street Fighter '94

Bruce Seton
Demon Barber of Fleet Street '36
Love from a Stranger '37
The Blue Lamp '49
Gorgo '61

Gerard Sety
Modigliani '58
Van Gogh '92

Joan Severance
No Holds Barred '89
See No Evil, Hear No Evil '89
Almost Pregnant '91
Another Pair of Aces: Three of a Kind '91
Illicit Behavior '91
The Runestone '91
Write to Kill '91
Lake Consequence '92
Red Shoe Diaries 2: Double Dare '92
Dangerous Indiscretion '94
Hard Evidence '94
Payback '94
Black Scorpion '95

William Severn
Journey for Margaret '42
Son of Lassie '45

Carmen Sevilla
Pantaloons '57
The Boldest Job in the West '71

Billie Seward
Branded a Coward '35
The Revenge Rider '35
The Man from Gun Town '36

Rufus Sewell
Twenty-One '91
Middlemarch '93
Cold Comfort Farm '94
A Man of No Importance '94
Carrington '95

Andrzej Seweryn
Land of Promise '74
Without Anesthesia '78
The Conductor '80

Athene Seyler
Private Life of Don Juan '34
Sailing Along '38
The Franchise Affair '52

Anne Seymour
All the King's Men '49
Portrait of Grandpa Doc '77
Gemini Affair '80s

Carolyn Seymour
Gumshoe '72
The Assignment '78
The Bitch '78
Midnight Cabaret '90

Dan Seymour
To Have & Have Not '44
A Night in Casablanca '46
Hard-Boiled Mahoney '47
Abbott and Costello Meet the Mummy '55
Return of the Fly '59

Jane Seymour
The Only Way '70
Young Winston '72
Live and Let Die '73
The Story of David '76
Killer on Board '77
Sinbad and the Eye of the Tiger '77
Battlestar Galactica '78
The Four Feathers '78
East of Eden '80
Oh, Heavenly Dog! '80
Somewhere in Time '80
Jamaica Inn '82
The Scarlet Pimpernel '82
The Haunting Passion '83
Lassiter '84
Head Office '86
Jack the Ripper '88
Onassis '88
War & Remembrance, Part 1 '88
War & Remembrance, Part 3 '88
War & Remembrance, Part 4 '88
War & Remembrance, Part 5 '88
War & Remembrance, Part 6 '88
War & Remembrance, Part 7 '88
The Woman He Loved '88
The Tunnel '89
War & Remembrance, Part 2 '89
War & Remembrance: The Final Chapter, Part 8 '89
War & Remembrance: The Final Chapter, Part 9 '89
War & Remembrance: The Final Chapter, Part 10 '89
War & Remembrance: The Final Chapter, Part 11 '89
War & Remembrance: The Final Chapter, Part 12 '89
Matters of the Heart '90
Are You Lonesome Tonight '92
Doctor Quinn, Medicine Woman '92
Sunstroke '92
Heidi '93
Praying Mantis '93

Ralph Seymour
Meatballs 2 '84
Killer Party '86
Rain Man '88

Delphine Seyrig
Last Year at Marienbad '61
Muriel '63
Accident '67
The Milky Way '68
Stolen Kisses '68
Donkey Skin '70
Daughters of Darkness '71
Dos Cruces en Danger Pass '71
The Discreet Charm of the Bourgeoisie '72
A Doll's House '73
The Black Windmill '74
I Sent a Letter to My Love '81
Grain of Sand '84
Window Shopping '86

Ted Shackleford
Summer Fantasy '84
Sweet Revenge '87
Baby of the Bride '91
Dying to Remember '93
The Spider and the Fly '94

Glenn Shadix
The Applegates '89
Heathers '89
Nightlife '90
Bingo '91
Demolition Man '93
Dark Side of Genius '94
Love Affair '94
My Summer Story '94
Dunston Checks In '95

Bobby Ray Shafer
Psycho Cop '88
Psycho Cop 2 '94

Jamal Shah
Traffik '90
K2: The Ultimate High '92

Tupac Shakur
Juice '92
Poetic Justice '93
Above the Rim '94

Victoria Shalet
The Maid '90
Haunted '95

Tony Shalhoub
Barton Fink '91
Honeymoon in Vegas '92
I.Q. '94
Big Night '95

Chuck Shamata
Death Weekend '76
Joshua Then and Now '85
Mafia Princess '86
Night Friend '87
Unfinished Business '89
Princes in Exile '90

Chang Shan
Shaolin Temple Strikes Back '72
Empire of the Dragon '80s

Garry Shandling
Mother Goose Rock 'n' Rhyme '90
The Night We Never Met '93
Love Affair '94
Mixed Nuts '94

Michael Shaner
Crime Zone '88
Bloodfist '89
The Expert '95

Amelia Shankley
Dreamchild '85
The Little Princess '87

Don Shanks
Life & Times of Grizzly Adams '74
Blood Brothers '77
Mountain Man '77
The Last of the Mohicans '85
Halloween 5: The Revenge of Michael Myers '89
Spirit of the Eagle '90
The Legend of Wolf Mountain '92
3 Ninjas Knuckle Up '92

Al Shannon
The Drifter '88
Out of the Rain '90

Frank Shannon
Flash Gordon: Rocketship '36
Flash Gordon Conquers the Universe '40

Harry Shannon
Citizen Kane '41
The Lady is Willing '42
Idaho '43
Song of Texas '43
The Yellow Rose of Texas '44
Fighting Father Dunne '48
Cow Town '50
The Jackie Robinson Story '50
The Underworld Story '50
Written on the Wind '56
Man or Gun '58
Summer and Smoke '61

Michael J. Shannon
Future Cop '76
Afterward '85
Smart-Aleck Kill '85
Detonator 2: Night Watch '95

Peggy Shannon
False Faces '32
Deluge '33
The Case of the Lucky Legs '35

Omar Sharif
Lawrence of Arabia '62
Behold a Pale Horse '64
The Fall of the Roman Empire '64
Doctor Zhivago '65
Night of the Generals '67
Funny Girl '68
Mayerling '68
MacKenna's Gold '69
The Horsemen '70
The Last Valley '71
Juggernaut '74
The Tamarind Seed '74
Crime & Passion '75
Funny Lady '75
Ashanti, Land of No Mercy '79
Sidney Sheldon's Bloodline '79
The Baltimore Bullet '80
Oh, Heavenly Dog! '80
Pleasure Palace '80
Green Ice '81
The Far Pavilions '84
Top Secret! '84
Anastasia: The Mystery of Anna '86
Harem '86
Peter the Great '86
Beyond Justice '92
Grand Larceny '92
Mrs. 'Arris Goes to Paris '92
Lie Down with Lions '94
Gulliver's Travels '95

David Shark
Invasion Force '90
Soultaker '90
Dark Rider '91
The Legend of Wolf Mountain '92
Femme Fontaine: Killer Babe for the C.I.A. '95

Ray Sharkey
Who'll Stop the Rain? '78
Heart Beat '80
Idolmaker '80
Willie & Phil '80
Some Kind of Hero '82
Regina '83
Body Rock '84
Dubeat-E-O '84
Behind Enemy Lines '85
Hellhole '85
No Mercy '86
Wise Guys '86
Private Investigations '87
Act of Piracy '89
Capone '89
The Neon Empire '89
Scenes from the Class Struggle in Beverly Hills '89
Wired '89
The Rain Killer '90
The Take '90
Relentless 2: Dead On '91
Caged Fear '92
Chrome Soldiers '92
Round Trip to Heaven '92
Zebrahead '92
Cop and a Half '93
Urban Crossfire '94

Lesley Sharp
Rita, Sue & Bob Too '87
The Rachel Papers '89
Naked '93
Priest '94
Prime Suspect: The Lost Child '94

Cornelia Sharpe
Serpico '73
Busting '74
The Reincarnation of Peter Proud '75
The Arab Conspiracy '76
S*H*E '79
Venom '82

David Sharpe
The Adventurous Knights '35
Roaring Roads '35
Social Error '35
Gun Grit '36
Doomed at Sundown '37
Melody of the Plains '37
Where Trails Divide '37
Covered Wagon Trails '40
Silver Stallion '41
Texas to Bataan '42
Trail Riders '42
Haunted Ranch '43
Two-Fisted Justice '43
Colorado Serenade '46

Melanie Shatner
Syngenor '90
Cthulhu Mansion '91

William Shatner
The Defender '57
The Brothers Karamazov '58
Judgment at Nuremberg '61
Shame '61
The Man from U.N.C.L.E. '64
White Comanche '67
Star Trek Bloopers '69
The Andersonville Trial '70
The People '71
Pioneer Woman '73
The Barbary Coast '74
Big Bad Mama '74
Impulse '74
Pray for the Wildcats '74
Devil's Rain '75
Whale of a Tale '76
Kingdom of the Spiders '77
The Bastard '78
The Crash of Flight 401 '78
Little Women '78
Riel '79
Third Walker '79
The Babysitter '80
The Kidnapping of the President '80
Star Trek: The Motion Picture '80
Airplane 2: The Sequel '82
Star Trek 2: The Wrath of Khan '82
Visiting Hours '82
Secrets of a Married Man '84
Star Trek 3: The Search for Spock '84
Star Trek 4: The Voyage Home '86
Broken Angel '88
Star Trek 5: The Final Frontier '89
Bill & Ted's Bogus Journey '91
Star Trek 6: The Undiscovered Country '91
National Lampoon's Loaded Weapon 1 '93
Star Trek Generations '94
TekWar '94

Shari Shattuck
Naked Cage '86
Hot Child in the City '87
Desert Warrior '88
Tainted '88
The Uninvited '88
Arena '89
The Spring '89
Mad About You '90
Body Chemistry 3: Point of Seduction '93
Dead On '93
Out for Blood '93

Grant Shaud
Wall Street '87
The Distinguished Gentleman '92

Mickey Shaughnessy
Last of the Comanches '52
From Here to Eternity '53
Conquest of Space '55
Designing Woman '57
Jailhouse Rock '57
The Adventures of Huckleberry Finn '60
The King of the Roaring '20s: The Story of Arnold Rothstein '61
Pocketful of Miracles '61
A Global Affair '63
My Dog, the Thief '69
Primal Scream '87

Helen Shaver
Outrageous! '77
Starship Invasions '77
Who Has Seen the Wind? '77
High Ballin' '78
In Praise of Older Women '78
The Amityville Horror '79
Off Your Rocker '80
Gas '81
Harry Tracy '83
The Osterman Weekend '83
Best Defense '84
Coming Out Alive '84
The Park is Mine '85
Shoot '85
The War Boy '85
The Color of Money '86
Desert Hearts '86
Lost '86
The Believers '87
Dr. Bethune '90
Innocent Victim '90
Pair of Aces '90
Trial and Error '92
Zebrahead '92
Morning Glory '93
Murder So Sweet '93
That Night '93
Born to be Wild '95
The Outer Limits: Sandkings '95
The Craft '96
Tremors 2: Aftershocks '96

Anabel Shaw
Shock! '46
Gun Crazy '49

Bobbi Shaw
Pajama Party '64
Beach Blanket Bingo '65
How to Stuff a Wild Bikini '65

Crystal Shaw
Hardbodies '84
Laser Moon '92

Fiona Shaw
My Left Foot '89
Mountains of the Moon '90
Three Men and a Little Lady '90
London Kills Me '91
Maria's Child '93
Super Mario Bros. '93
Undercover Blues '93
Persuasion '95
Jane Eyre '96

Huang Hsing Shaw
Renegade Monk '82
Shaolin Ex-Monk '82

Martin Shaw
Macbeth '71
Golden Voyage of Sinbad '73
Professionals '76
The Hound of the Baskervilles '83
Intrigue '90
The Last Place on Earth '94

Montague Shaw
Square Shoulders '29
The Rains Came '39
Holt of the Secret Service '42

Oscar Shaw
The Cocoanuts '29
Rhythm on the River '40

Reta Shaw
Picnic '55
All Mine to Give '56
The Pajama Game '57
The Ghost and Mr. Chicken '66

Robert Shaw
From Russia with Love '63
Battle of the Bulge '65
A Man for All Seasons '66
Battle of Britain '69
Diamonds '72
A Reflection of Fear '72
A Town Called Hell '72
Young Winston '72
The Sting '73
The Taking of Pelham One Two Three '74
Jaws '75
Robin and Marian '76
Swashbuckler '76
Black Sunday '77
The Deep '77
Force 10 from Navarone '78
Avalanche Express '79

Sebastian Shaw
Department Store '35
The Squeaker '37
Spy in Black '39
A Midsummer Night's Dream '68
Reilly: Ace of Spies '87
High Season '88

Stan Shaw
Bingo Long Traveling All-Stars & Motor Kings '76
The Boys in Company C '77
Roots: The Next Generation '79
Dirkham Detective Agency '83
Tough Enough '83
Runaway '84
D.P. '85
Busted Up '86
The Gladiator '86
Samaritan: The Mitch Snyder Story '86
Billionaire Boys Club '87
The Court Martial of Jackie Robinson '90
Fear '90
Fried Green Tomatoes '91
Body of Evidence '92
Lifepod '93
Houseguest '94
Cutthroat Island '95

Susan Shaw
Train of Events '49
Fire Maidens from Outer Space '56
Blonde Blackmailer '58

Susan Damante Shaw
The Student Teachers '73
The Adventures of the Wilderness Family '76
Further Adventures of the Wilderness Family, Part 2 '77
Mountain Family Robinson '79
Image of Passion '86

Vinessa Shaw
Ladybugs '92
Fallen Angels 2 '93
Hocus Pocus '93

Joan Shawlee
House of Horrors '46
Buck Privates Come Home '47
Prehistoric Women '50
Francis Joins the WACs '54
Some Like It Hot '59
The Apartment '60
The Reluctant Astronaut '67

Dick Shawn
It's a Mad, Mad, Mad, Mad World '63
What Did You Do in the War, Daddy? '66
The Producers '68
The Happy Ending '69
Love at First Bite '79
Goodbye Cruel World '82
Young Warriors '83
Angel '84
The Emperor's New Clothes '84
The Secret Diary of Sigmund Freud '84
Beer '85
Check Is in the Mail '85
Maid to Order '87
Rented Lips '88

Wallace Shawn
All That Jazz '79
Manhattan '79
Simon '80
My Dinner with Andre '81
First Time '82
A Little Sex '82
Deal of the Century '83
Strange Invaders '83
The Bostonians '84
Crackers '84
The Hotel New Hampshire '84
How to Be a Perfect Person in Just Three Days '84
Micki & Maude '84
Strong Medicine '84
Heaven Help Us '85
The Bedroom Window '87
Nice Girls Don't Explode '87
Prick Up Your Ears '87
The Princess Bride '87
Radio Days '87
The Moderns '88
Scenes from the Class Struggle in Beverly Hills '89
She's Out of Control '89
We're No Angels '89
The Double O Kid '92
Mom and Dad Save the World '92
Nickel & Dime '92
Shadows and Fog '92
The Cemetery Club '93
The Magic Bubble '93
Mrs. Parker and the Vicious Circle '94
Vanya on 42nd Street '94
Clueless '95
House Arrest '96

Robert Shayne
Christmas in Connecticut '45
Rhapsody in Blue '45
Behind the Mask '46
The Spirit of West Point '47
Welcome Stranger '47
TV's Best Adventures of Superman '51
Marshal of Cedar Rock '53
Stamp Day for Superman '53
The Giant Claw '57

Tamara Shayne
Somewhere I'll Find You '42
The Jolson Story '46

Gloria Shea
Dude Bandit '32
The Fiddlin' Buckaroo '33
Phantom of the Air '33
Last Days of Pompeii '35

John Shea
Nativity '78
Hussy '80
Missing '82
Kennedy '83
Windy City '84
A Case of Deadly Force '86
The Dining Room '86
Honeymoon '87
The Impossible Spy '87
A New Life '88
Stealing Home '88
Unsettled Land '88
Small Sacrifices '89
Magic Moments '90s
Freejack '92
Honey, I Blew Up the Kid '92
Ladykiller '92
Backstreet Justice '93

Al Shear
San Francisco '36
It Could Happen to You '37
Tim Tyler's Luck '37
The Great Waltz '38
Ziegfeld Girl '41

Harry Shearer
One Trick Pony '80
The Right Stuff '83
This Is Spinal Tap '84
Portrait of a White Marriage '88
The Fisher King '91
Pure Luck '91
The Return of Spinal Tap '92

Moira Shearer
The Red Shoes '48
The Tales of Hoffmann '51
Black Tights '60
Peeping Tom '63

Norma Shearer
He Who Gets Slapped '24
The Student Prince in Old Heidelberg '27
The Divorcee '30
A Free Soul '31
Private Lives '31
Smilin' Through '32
Strange Interlude '32
The Barretts of Wimpole Street '34
Riptide '34
Romeo and Juliet '36
Marie Antoinette '38
Idiot's Delight '39
The Women '39

Alan Shearman
Bullshot '83
Footlight Frenzy '84

Ally Sheedy
The Best Little Girl in the World '81
Bad Boys '83

Sheedy ▶cont.

WarGames '83
Oxford Blues '84
The Breakfast Club '85
St. Elmo's Fire '85
Twice in a Lifetime '85
Blue City '86
Short Circuit '86
Maid to Order '87
We are the Children '87
The Heart of Dixie '89
Betsy's Wedding '90
Fear '90
The Lost Capone '90
Only the Lonely '91
Tattle Tale '92
Chantilly Lace '93
Man's Best Friend '93
Red Shoe Diaries 4: Auto Erotica '93
The Haunting of Seacliff Inn '94
Parallel Lives '94
One Night Stand '95
The Tin Soldier '95

Charlie Sheen
Red Dawn '84
Silence of the Heart '84
The Boys Next Door '85
Ferris Bueller's Day Off '86
Lucas '86
Platoon '86
No Man's Land '87
Three for the Road '87
Wall Street '87
The Wraith '87
Eight Men Out '88
Young Guns '88
Cadence '89
Courage Mountain '89
Major League '89
Men at Work '90
Navy SEALS '90
The Rookie '90
Hot Shots! '91
Beyond the Law '92
The Chase '93
Deadfall '93
Hot Shots! Part Deux '93
The Three Musketeers '93
Major League 2 '94
Terminal Velocity '94
The Arrival '96

Martin Sheen
The Incident '67
The Andersonville Trial '70
Catch-22 '70
No Drums, No Bugles '71
When the Line Goes Through '71
Pursuit '72
Rage '72
Where the Eagle Flies '72
Catholics '73
Badlands '74
The Execution of Private Slovik '74
Legend of Earl Durand '74
Missiles of October '74
Sweet Hostage '75
The Cassandra Crossing '76
The Little Girl Who Lives Down the Lane '76
Apocalypse Now '79
Eagle's Wing '79
The Final Countdown '80
Blind Ambition '82
Enigma '82
Gandhi '82
In the Custody of Strangers '82
That Championship Season '82
Dead Zone '83
In the King of Prussia '83
Kennedy '83
Loophole '83
Man, Woman & Child '83
Firestarter '84
The Guardian '84
Consenting Adult '85
Fourth Wise Man '85
Out of the Darkness '85
News at Eleven '86
Samaritan: The Mitch Snyder Story '86
The Believers '87
Conspiracy: The Trial of the Chicago Eight '87
Siesta '87
Wall Street '87
Da '88
Judgment in Berlin '88
Beverly Hills Brats '89
Beyond the Stars '89
Cadence '89
Cold Front '89
Nightbreaker '89
The Maid '90
Hearts of Darkness: A Filmmaker's Apocalypse '91
Shattered Spirits '91
Gettysburg '93
The Ghost Brigade '93
Hear No Evil '93
When the Bough Breaks '93
Boca '94
Fortunes of War '94
Gospa '94
Roswell: The U.F.O. Cover-Up '94
The American President '95
Born Wild '95
The Break '95
Captain Nuke and the Bomber Boys '95
Dillinger and Capone '95

Michael Sheen
Gallowglass '95
Mary Reilly '95
Othello '95

Ruth Sheen
High Hopes '88
The Young Poisoner's Handbook '94

Chad Sheets
Dirt Bike Kid '86
Lone Star Kid '88

Craig Sheffer
That Was Then...This Is Now '85
Fire with Fire '86
Some Kind of Wonderful '87
Voyage of the Rock Aliens '87
Split Decisions '88
Babycakes '89
Instant Karma '90
Night Breed '90
Blue Desert '91
Eye of the Storm '91
A River Runs Through It '92
Fire in the Sky '93
The Program '93
The Desperate Trail '94
Sleep with Me '94
Bloodknot '95
In Pursuit of Honor '95
The Road Killers '95

Johnny Sheffield
Tarzan Finds a Son '39
Tarzan's Secret Treasure '41
Tarzan's New York Adventure '42

Maceo B. Sheffield
Harlem on the Prairie '38
Gang War '40
Look Out Sister '48

Sheila E
Krush Groove '85
The Adventures of Ford Fairlane '90

Gene Sheldon
The Dolly Sisters '45
Toby Tyler '59
The Sign of Zorro '60

Tom Shell
Surf Nazis Must Die '87
Dinosaur Island '93
Teenage Exorcist '93

Stephen Shellan
Gimme an F '85
Talking Walls '85
The Stepfather '87
Casual Sex? '88
Murder One '88
Damned River '89
Victim of Beauty '91
A River Runs Through It '92
Still Life '92
Model by Day '94
Dr. Jekyll and Ms. Hyde '95

Barbara Shelley
Cat Girl '57
Blood of the Vampire '58
Village of the Damned '60
The Gorgon '64
Madhouse Mansion '74
The Dark Angel '91

Adrienne Shelly
The Unbelievable Truth '90
Trust '91
Big Girls Don't Cry...They Get Even '92
Hexed '93
Hold Me, Thrill Me, Kiss Me '93
Sleep with Me '94
Sleeping with Strangers '94
Teresa's Tattoo '94
The Road Killers '95

Deborah Shelton
Mysterious Island of Beautiful Women '79
Body Double '84
Hunk '87
Perfect Victims '87
Blind Vision '91
Sins of the Night '93
Plughead Rewired: Circuitry Man 2 '94
Silk Degrees '94
Desire '95

John Shelton
Ghost City '32
The Time of Their Lives '46

Joy Shelton
Uneasy Terms '48
Norman Conquest '53
Impulse '55

Marla Shelton
The Phantom Rider '37
Stand-In '37
Escape to Paradise '39

Reid Shelton
Breakin' Through '84
First & Ten '85
First & Ten: The Team Scores Again '85

Paul Shenar
Deadly Force '83
Scarface '83
Brass '85
Dream Lover '85
Raw Deal '86
The Bedroom Window '87
Best Seller '87
Man on Fire '87
The Big Blue '88

Hilary Shepard
Peacemaker '90
Scanner Cop '94

Jewel Shepard
My Tutor '82
Hollywood Hot Tubs '84
Return of the Living Dead '85
Scenes from the Goldmine '87
Hollywood Hot Tubs 2: Educating Crystal '89
Caged Heat 2: Stripped of Freedom '94
Scanners: The Showdown '94

Patty Shepard
Dracula vs. Frankenstein '69
Surprise Attack '70s
The Werewolf vs. the Vampire Woman '70
Witches' Mountain '71
Crypt of the Living Dead '73
Curse of the Devil '73
The Stranger and the Gunfighter '76

Sam Shepard
Days of Heaven '78
Resurrection '80
Raggedy Man '81
Frances '82
The Right Stuff '83
Country '84
Crimes of the Heart '86
Fool for Love '86
Baby Boom '87
Steel Magnolias '89
Bright Angel '91
Defenseless '91
Voyager '91
Thunderheart '92
The Pelican Brief '93
Safe Passage '94
The Good Old Boys '95
Larry McMurtry's Streets of Laredo '95

Cybill Shepherd
The Last Picture Show '71
The Heartbreak Kid '72
Daisy Miller '74
Special Delivery '76
Taxi Driver '76
A Guide for the Married Woman '78
Silver Bears '78
The Lady Vanishes '79
The Return '80
Secrets of a Married Man '84
Moonlighting '85
Seduced '85
The Long, Hot Summer '86
Chances Are '89
Alice '90
Texasville '90
Which Way Home '90
Memphis '91
Once Upon a Crime '92
Married to It '93

Elizabeth Shepherd
Tomb of Ligeia '64
Invitation to the Wedding '73
The Double Negative '80
Phoenix Team '80

Jack Shepherd
The Virgin Soldiers '69
Escape from Sobibor '87
Murderers among Us: The Simon Wiesenthal Story '89
Twenty-One '91
No Escape '94

John Shepherd
Friday the 13th, Part 5: A New Beginning '85
Banzai Runner '86
Thunder Run '86

Simon Shepherd
Murder on Line One '90
Fire, Ice and Dynamite '91

Michael Shepley
A Shot in the Dark '33
The Private Secretary '35
Housemaster '38
Mine Own Executioner '47

Delia Sheppard
Witchcraft 2: The Temptress '90
Mirror Images '91
Roots of Evil '91
Animal Instincts '92
Night Rhythms '92
Secret Games '92
Sins of Desire '92
Dead Boyz Can't Fly '93

Paula Sheppard
Alice Sweet Alice '76
Liquid Sky '83

Anthony Sher
Shadey '87
Erik the Viking '89
Tartuffe '90
Genghis Cohn '93
The Young Poisoner's Handbook '94

Ann Sheridan
The Fighting Westerner '35
Angels with Dirty Faces '38
Letter of Introduction '38
Dodge City '39
They Made Me a Criminal '39
City for Conquest '40
They Drive by Night '40
Kings Row '41
The Man Who Came to Dinner '41
George Washington Slept Here '42
Edge of Darkness '43
Thank Your Lucky Stars '43
Good Sam '48
Silver River '48
I Was a Male War Bride '49
Appointment in Honduras '53
The Opposite Sex '56

Dinah Sheridan
Salute John Citizen '42
Calling Paul Temple '48
Blackout '50
No Trace '50
Genevieve '53
The Railway Children '70
Thirteenth Reunion '81

Jamey Sheridan
Quick Change '90
Stanley and Iris '90
All I Want for Christmas '91
Talent for the Game '91
A Stranger Among Us '92
Whispers in the Dark '92
Stephen King's The Stand '94

Jim Sheridan
Way of the West '35
Moll Flanders '96

Margaret Sheridan
The Thing '51
One Minute to Zero '52

Nicolette Sheridan
The Sure Thing '85
Deceptions '90
Noises Off '92
Silver Strand '95
Spy Hard '96

Lowell Sherman
Way Down East '20
Monsieur Beaucaire '24
The Garden of Eden '28
Bachelor Apartment '31
The Royal Bed '31
False Faces '32
Three Broadway Girls '32
What Price Hollywood? '32

David Sherwood
River of Diamonds '90
Curse of the Crystal Eye '93

Madeline Sherwood
Parrish '61
Sweet Bird of Youth '62
Pendulum '69
Teachers '84
Broken Vows '87

Robin Sherwood
Tourist Trap '79
Love Butcher '82

Vladek Sheybal
The Boy Friend '71
Scorpio '73
S*P*Y*S '74

Arthur Shields
Drums Along the Mohawk '39
How Green Was My Valley '41
Gentleman Jim '42
The Keys of the Kingdom '44
The White Cliffs of Dover '44
The Corn is Green '45
The Fabulous Dorseys '47
Fighting Father Dunne '48
The River '51
The Quiet Man '52
The King and Four Queens '56
The Daughter of Dr. Jekyll '57
Enchanted Island '58

Brooke Shields
Alice Sweet Alice '76
The Prince of Central Park '77
King of the Gypsies '78
Pretty Baby '78
Tilt '78
Wanda Nevada '79
The Blue Lagoon '80
Endless Love '81
Sahara '83
Wet Gold '84
Brenda Starr '86
Speed Zone '88
Backstreet Dreams '90
The Diamond Trap '91
Freaked '93
The Seventh Floor '93
Stalking Laura '93
Born Wild '95

Nicholas Shields
Princes in Exile '90
Lost in the Barrens '91
Liar's Edge '92

James Shigeta
Flower Drum Song '61
Paradise, Hawaiian Style '66
Enola Gay: The Men, the Mission, the Atomic Bomb '80
Tomorrow's Child '82
Die Hard '88
The Cage '89
China Cry '91
Blood for Blood '95

Marion Shilling
Man's Land '32
Shop Angel '32
Inside Information '34
Thunder Over Texas '34
Captured in Chinatown '35

Rio Rattler '35
A Shot in the Dark '35
Cavalcade of the West '36
Gun Play '36
I'll Name the Murderer '36

Shmuel Shilo
Noa at Seventeen '82
Goodbye, New York '85
Double Edge '92

Yoseph Shiloah
I Love You Rosa '72
Private Manoeuvres '83

Joseph Shiloal
Eagles Attack at Dawn '74
The Lion of Africa '87

Yoko Shimada
Shogun '80
My Champion '84
The Hunted '94

Armin Shimerman
Arena '89
Star Trek Deep Space Nine: Emissary '93

Joanna Shimkus
Six in Paris '68
The Virgin and the Gypsy '70
Les Aventuriers '77

Sab Shimono
Gung Ho '85
The Wash '88
Come See the Paradise '90
Hiroshima: Out of the Ashes '90
Presumed Innocent '90
Suture '93
Teenage Mutant Ninja Turtles 3 '93
3 Ninjas Kick Back '94

Takashi Shimura
Sanshiro Sugata '43
Drunken Angel '48
A Quiet Duel '49
Stray Dog '49
Scandal '50
The Idiot '51
Rashomon '51
Ikiru '52
Seven Samurai '54
I Live in Fear '55
Godzilla, King of the Monsters '56
Throne of Blood '57
The Mysterians '58
The Bad Sleep Well '60
Kwaidan '64
Last Days of Planet Earth '74
Love and Faith '78

Sofia Shinas
The Crow '93
Hourglass '95

Eitaro Shindo
A Geisha '53
The Crucified Lovers '54
Sansho the Bailiff '54

Chen Shing
The Amsterdam Connection '70s
The Two Great Cavaliers '73
Snake in the Eagle's Shadow 2 '83

Sue Shiomi
Dragon Princess '70s
The Street Fighter's Last Revenge '79
Shogun's Ninja '83

Toshi Shioya
Prisoners of the Sun '91
Mr. Baseball '92

John Wesley Shipp
The Flash '90
Baby of the Bride '91
The Flash 2: Revenge of the Trickster '91
NeverEnding Story 2: The Next Chapter '91
Soft Deceit '94

Yumi Shirakawa
Rodan '56
The Mysterians '58
H-Man '59
The Secret of the Telegian '61

Talia Shire
Gas-s-s-s! '70
The Godfather '72
The Godfather, Part 2 '74
Rich Man, Poor Man '76
Rocky '76
Old Boyfriends '79
Prophecy '79
Rocky 2 '79
Windows '80
The Godfather 1902-1959: The Complete Epic '81
Rocky 3 '82
Rip van Winkle '85
Rocky 4 '85
Hyper-Sapien: People from Another Star '86
Rad '86
Blood Vows: The Story of a Mafia Wife '87
Lionheart '87
Murderer's Keep '88
New York Stories '89
The Godfather, Part 3 '90
Rocky 5 '90
Mark Twain and Me '91
Bed & Breakfast '92
Cold Heaven '92
For Richer, For Poorer '92
Chantilly Lace '93
A Century of Women '94

Bill Shirk
Escapist '83
Ballbuster

Anne Shirley
Rasputin and the Empress '32
Anne of Green Gables '34
Stella Dallas '37
Law of the Underworld '38
The Devil & Daniel Webster '41
Four Jacks and a Jill '41
Bombardier '43
Murder, My Sweet '44

Bill Shirley
Abbott and Costello Meet Captain Kidd '52
I Dream of Jeannie '52

Cathie Shirriff
Covergirl '83
Star Trek 3: The Search for Spock '84

William Shockley
Howling 5: The Rebirth '89
Dream Lover '93
Girl in the Cadillac '94

Dan Shor
A Rumor of War '80
Strange Behavior '81
Tron '82
Strangers Kiss '83
Mesmerized '84
Mike's Murder '84
Daddy's Boys '87
Bill & Ted's Excellent Adventure '89
Red Rock West '93

Dinah Shore
Thank Your Lucky Stars '43
Up in Arms '44
Till the Clouds Roll By '46
Till the Clouds Roll By/A Star Is Born '46
Hollywood Goes to War '54
Oh, God! '77

Pauly Shore
Encino Man '92
Dream Date '93
Son-in-Law '93
In the Army Now '94
Jury Duty '95
Bio-Dome '96

Bobby Short
Hardhat & Legs '80
For Love or Money '93

Dorothy Short
Savage Fury '33
Brothers of the West '37
Reefer Madness '38
Camp Double Feature '39
Daughter of the Tong '39
Wild Horse Canyon '39
Pony Post '40
Trail of the Silver Spurs '41

Martin Short
The Family Man '79
Lost and Found '79
The Best of John Candy on SCTV '80s
Sunset Limousine '83
Johnny Appleseed '86
Really Weird Tales '86
Three Amigos '86
Innerspace '87
Cross My Heart '88
The Big Picture '89
Three Fugitives '89
Father of the Bride '91
Pure Luck '91
Captain Ron '92
Clifford '92
Father of the Bride Part II '95

Grant Show
Treacherous Crossing '92
A Woman, Her Men and Her Futon '92
Texas '94

Max Casey Adams Showalter
Niagara '52
What Price Glory? '52
Bus Stop '56
The Indestructible Man '56
The Monster That Challenged the World '57
Summer and Smoke '61
Racing with the Moon '84
Sixteen Candles '84

Kathy Shower
Commando Squad '87
Frankenstein General Hospital '88
The Further Adventures of Tennessee Buck '88
Bedroom Eyes 2 '89
Out on Bail '89
Robo-Chic '89
L.A. Goddess '92
Wild Cactus '92
American Kickboxer 2: To the Death '93
Sexual Malice '93
Improper Conduct '94
Married People, Single Sex 2: For Better or Worse '94
To the Limit '95

John Shrapnel
How to Get Ahead in Advertising '89
Tragedy of Flight 103: The Inside Story '91
Fatherland '94

Kin Shriner
Obsessive Love '84
Vendetta '85
Angel 3: The Final Chapter '88
Escape '90

Elisabeth Shue
Call to Glory '84
The Karate Kid '84
Link '86
Adventures in Babysitting '87
Cocktail '88
Back to the Future, Part 2 '89
Back to the Future, Part 3 '90
The Marrying Man '91
Soapdish '91
Heart and Souls '93
Twenty Bucks '93
Blind Justice '94
Radio Inside '94
Leaving Las Vegas '95
The Underneath '95
The Trigger Effect '96

Richard B. Shull
Hail '73
Slither '73
Cockfighter '74
The Big Bus '76
The Pack '77
Dreamer '79
Splash '84
Unfaithfully Yours '84
Housesitter '92
Trapped In Paradise '94

Antonina Shuranova
War and Peace '68
Tchaikovsky '71
An Unfinished Piece for a Player Piano '77

Sabrina Siani
Throne of Fire '82
Ator the Fighting Eagle '83
Conquest '83

Jane Sibbett
The Resurrected '91
It Takes Two '95

Alexander Siddig
A Dangerous Man: Lawrence after Arabia '91
Star Trek Deep Space Nine: Emissary '93

Sylvia Sidney
Street Scene '31
Fury '36
Sabotage '36
Dead End '37
You Only Live Once '37
One Third of a Nation '39
Blood on the Sun '45
Mr. Ace '46
Love from a Stranger '47
Summer Wishes, Winter Dreams '73
Death at Love House '75
God Told Me To '76
I Never Promised You a Rose Garden '77
Raid on Entebbe '77
Snowbeast '77
Damien: Omen 2 '78
The Shadow Box '80
A Small Killing '81
Hammett '82
Having It All '82
Come Along with Me '84
Corrupt '84
Finnegan Begin Again '84
An Early Frost '85
Pals '87
Beetlejuice '88
Used People '92

Charles Siebert
Tarantulas: The Deadly Cargo '77
Blue Sunshine '78
A Cry for Love '80

Jim Siedow
The Texas Chainsaw Massacre '74
Texas Chainsaw Massacre, Part 2 '86

Donald Siegel
Invasion of the Body Snatchers '56
Invasion of the Body Snatchers '78

George Siegmann
The Three Musketeers '21
Oliver Twist '22
Anna Christie '23
Hotel Imperial '27
The Man Who Laughs '27

Casey Siemaszko
Class '83
Amazing Stories '85
Back to the Future '85
Secret Admirer '85
Miracle of the Heart: A Boys Town Story '86
Stand By Me '86
Gardens of Stone '87
Three O'Clock High '87
Biloxi Blues '88
Young Guns '88
Back to the Future, Part 2 '89
Breaking In '89
The Big Slice '90
The Chase '91
Near Misses '91
Of Mice and Men '92
Milk Money '94
Teresa's Tattoo '94
Black Scorpion '95

Nina Siemaszko
Tucker: The Man and His Dream '88
Bed & Breakfast '92
Sinatra '92
Wild Orchid 2: Two Shades of Blue '92
Red Shoe Diaries 3: Another Woman's Lipstick '93
The Saint of Fort Washington '93
Airheads '94
Power of Attorney '94
The American President '95
Sawbones '95

Gregory Sierra
Pocket Money '72
The Clones '73
The Thief Who Came to Dinner '73
Mean Dog Blues '78
Miami Vice '84
Code Name: Dancer '87
Let's Get Harry '87
Dynamite and Gold '88
Deep Cover '92
Honey, I Blew Up the Kid '92
Hot Shots! Part Deux '93

Tom Signorelli
The Last Porno Flick '74
Crossover Dreams '85
Robot in the Family '94

Simone Signoret
Against the Wind '48
Dedee d'Anvers '49
La Ronde '51
Casque d'Or '52
Diabolique '55
Death in the Garden '56
The Crucible '57
Room at the Top '59
The Day and the Hour '63
Ship of Fools '65
Is Paris Burning? '68
Widow Couderc '74
Le Chat '75
Madame Rosa '77
I Sent a Letter to My Love '81

Caroline Sihol
Confidentially Yours '83
Tous les Matins du Monde '92

Cynthia Sikes
Goodbye Cruel World '82
The Man Who Loved Women '83
Oceans of Fire '86
Love Hurts '91

James B. Sikking
The Strangler '64
Von Ryan's Express '65
Point Blank '67
Charro! '69
Daddy's Gone A-Hunting '69
The New Centurions '72
Scorpio '73
Man on the Run '74
The Terminal Man '74
Black Force 2 '78
The Electric Horseman '79
The Night God Screamed '80s
The Competition '80
Ordinary People '80
Hill Street Blues, Vol. 1: Hill Street Station '81
Outland '81
The Star Chamber '83
Star Trek 3: The Search for Spock '84
Up the Creek '84
Morons from Outer Space '85
Dress Gray '86
Ollie Hopnoodle's Haven of Bliss '88
Around the World in 80 Days '89
The Brotherhood of the Rose '89
Narrow Margin '90
Final Approach '91
The Pelican Brief '93
Dead Badge '94
Seduced by Evil '94
In Pursuit of Honor '95
Tyson '95

Tusse Silberg
The Company of Wolves '85
Hidden City '87

Vira Silenti
Maciste in Hell '60
Atlas in the Land of the Cyclops '61
Son of Samson '62

Karen Sillas
Simple Men '92
Risk '94
What Happened Was... '94

David Silva
Senora Tentacion '49
Sisters of Satan '75

Geno Silva
Night Eyes 2 '91
Drug Wars 2: The Cocaine Cartel '92
Geronimo '93

Henry Silva
The Tall T '57

Silva ▶cont.

The Bravados '58
The Law and Jake Wade '58
Green Mansions '59
The Jayhawkers '59
Cinderfella '60
The Manchurian Candidate '62
A Gathering of Eagles '63
Never a Dull Moment '68
Killer '70s
Man & Boy '71
Cry of a Prostitute: Love Kills '72
Hired to Kill '73
Hit Men '73
Manhunt '73
Almost Human '79
Buck Rogers in the 25th Century '79
Crimebusters '79
Love and Bullets '79
The Desperados '80s
Alligator '80
Day of the Assassin '81
Sharky's Machine '81
Deadly Sting '82
Megaforce '82
Wrong is Right '82
Chained Heat '83
Violent Breed '83
Code of Silence '85
Escape from the Bronx '85
Lust in the Dust '85
Shoot '85
Thirst '87
Above the Law '88
Bulletproof '88
Trained to Kill '88
The Colombian Connection '91
Three Days to a Kill '91
The Harvest '92
Possessed by the Night '93
Killing in the Sun

Maria Silva
Curse of the Devil '73
The Mummy's Revenge '73

Simone Silva
The Shadow Man '53
Big Deadly Game '54

Trinidad Silva
Crackers '84
Colors '88
The Night Before '88

Fawn Silver
Orgy of the Dead '65
Terror in the Jungle '68

Joe Silver
The Apprenticeship of Duddy Kravitz '74
They Came from Within '75
Rabid '77
Almost You '85
The Gig '85
Mr. Nice Guy '86
Switching Channels '88

Ron Silver
Tunnelvision '76
Semi-Tough '77
Betrayal '78
Best Friends '82
Silent Rage '82
The Entity '83
The Goodbye People '83
Lovesick '83
Silkwood '83
Garbo Talks '84
Oh, God! You Devil '84
Romancing the Stone '84
Eat and Run '86
Billionaire Boys Club '87
A Father's Revenge '88
Enemies, a Love Story '89
Fellow Traveler '89
Blue Steel '90
Forgotten Prisoners '90
Reversal of Fortune '90
Live Wire '92
Mr. Saturday Night '92
Blind Side '93
Lifepod '93
Married to It '93
Timecop '94
The Arrival '96
Girl 6 '96
Kissinger and Nixon '96

Veronique Silver
The Woman Next Door '81
Toute Une Nuit '82

Frank Silvera
The Fighter '52
Miracle of Our Lady of Fatima '52
White Mane '52
Killer's Kiss '55
Death Tide '58
Toys in the Attic '63
Valdez is Coming '71

Jay Silverheels
Lust for Gold '49
Broken Arrow '50
War Arrow '53
Lone Ranger '56
Lone Ranger and the Lost City of Gold '58
Justice of the West '61
Indian Paint '64
Man Who Loved Cat Dancing '73
Santee '73

Jonathan Silverman
Challenge of a Lifetime '85
Brighton Beach Memoirs '86
Caddyshack 2 '88
Stealing Home '88
Traveling Man '89
Weekend at Bernie's '89
Age Isn't Everything '91
Class Action '91
Breaking the Rules '92
Broadway Bound '92
Death Becomes Her '92
For Richer, For Poorer '92
Little Sister '92
12:01 '93
Weekend at Bernie's 2 '93
Little Big League '94
Sketch Artist 2: Hands That See '94
Teresa's Tattoo '94
At First Sight '95

Phil Silvers
Lady Be Good '41
Tom, Dick, and Harry '41
All Through the Night '42
Footlight Serenade '42
Roxie Hart '42
Lady Takes a Chance '43
Cover Girl '44
A Thousand and One Nights '45
Summer Stock '50
Lucky Me '54
The Beverly Hillbillies '62
40 Pounds of Trouble '62
It's a Mad, Mad, Mad, Mad World '63
A Funny Thing Happened on the Way to the Forum '66
Follow That Camel '67
Buona Sera, Mrs. Campbell '68
The Boatniks '70
The Chicken Chronicles '77
The Cheap Detective '78
Racquet '79
The Happy Hooker Goes Hollywood '80

Sid Silvers
Broadway Melody of 1936 '35
Born to Dance '36

Alicia Silverstone
The Crush '93
Hideaway '94
The Babysitter '95
Clueless '95
True Crime '95

Armando Silvestre
The White Orchid '54
Wrestling Women vs. the Aztec Mummy '59
Neutron and the Black Mask '61
Neutron vs. the Amazing Dr. Caronte '61
Geronimo '62
Neutron vs. the Death Robots '62
Wrestling Women vs. the Aztec Ape '62
Night of the Bloody Apes '68
The Killing Zone '90
The Last Riders '90

Alastair Sim
Late Extra '35
The Private Secretary '35
Gangway '37
The Terror '38
Inspector Hornleigh '39
Cottage to Let '41
Green for Danger '47
Hue and Cry '47
The Happiest Days of Your Life '50
Stage Fright '50
A Christmas Carol '51
The Belles of St. Trinian's '53
Innocents in Paris '53
Escapade '55
Blue Murder at St. Trinian's '56
The Millionairess '60
The Ruling Class '72
Royal Flash '75
The Littlest Horse Thieves '76
Rogue Male '76

Gerald Sim
Dr. Jekyll and Sister Hyde '71
Long Ago Tomorrow '71

Sheila Sim
A Canterbury Tale '44
Great Day '46
The Guinea Pig '48
Pandora and the Flying Dutchman '51

Gene Simmons
KISS Meets the Phantom of the Park '78
Runaway '84
Never Too Young to Die '86
Trick or Treat '86
Wanted Dead or Alive '86
Decline of Western Civilization 2: The Metal Years '88
Red Surf '90

Jean Simmons
Mr. Emmanuel '44
Great Expectations '46
Black Narcissus '47
Inheritance '47
Hamlet '48
Trio '50
The Clouded Yellow '51
Androcles and the Lion '52
She Couldn't Say No '52
The Robe '53
Young Bess '53
A Bullet Is Waiting '54
Desiree '54
The Egyptian '54
Guys and Dolls '55
This Could Be the Night '57
Until They Sail '57
The Big Country '58
Elmer Gantry '60
Spartacus '60
The Grass is Greener '61
Divorce American Style '67
Heidi '67
Rough Night in Jericho '67
Soldier in Love '67
The Happy Ending '69
Say Hello to Yesterday '71
Mr. Sycamore '74
The Dain Curse '78
Dominique is Dead '79
A Small Killing '81
The Thorn Birds '83
Moment in Time '84
North and South Book 1 '85
North and South Book 2 '86
Perry Mason: The Case of the Lost Love '87
The Dawning '88
Going Undercover '88
Great Expectations '89
Dark Shadows: Episode 1 '91
How to Make an American Quilt '95
December Flower

Pat Simmons
The Giant Gila Monster '59
My Science Project '85

Ginny Simms
Playmates '41
Seven Days' Leave '42
Around the World '43
Hit the Ice '43
Broadway Rhythm '44
Night and Day '46

Larry Simms
Blondie '38
Blondie Takes a Vacation '39
Blondie Has Trouble '40
Blondie in Society '41
Blondie's Blessed Event '42
It's a Great Life '43
Blondie Knows Best '46
Blondie Hits the Jackpot '49

Michel Simon
La Chienne '31
Boudu Saved from Drowning '32
L'Atalante '34
Circonstances Attenuantes '36
Bizarre Bizarre '39
Panique '47
Fabiola '48
Beauty and the Devil '50
The Head '59
The Train '65
The Two of Us '68

Paul Simon
Annie Hall '77
All You Need Is Cash '78
One Trick Pony '80
Steve Martin Live '85
Mother Goose Rock 'n' Rhyme '90

Robert Simon
The Court Martial of Billy Mitchell '55
The Catered Affair '56
The Nine Lives of Elfego Baca '58
Compulsion '59

Robert F. Simon
Chinese Web '78
Spiderman: The Deadly Dust '78

Simone Simon
La Bete Humaine '38
The Devil & Daniel Webster '41
Cat People '42
Curse of the Cat People '44
Mademoiselle Fifi '44
Women in Prison '49
La Ronde '51
Le Plaisir '52

David Simonds
The Refrigerator '93
Amateur '94

O.J. Simpson
The Klansman '74
The Towering Inferno '74
The Cassandra Crossing '76
Roots '77
Capricorn One '78
Firepower '79
Hambone & Hillie '84
The Naked Gun: From the Files of Police Squad '88
Naked Gun 2 1/2: The Smell of Fear '91
C.I.A.: Code Name Alexa '92
No Place to Hide '93
Naked Gun 33 1/3: The Final Insult '94

Russell Simpson
Human Hearts '22
Peg O' My Heart '22
The Virginian '23
Abraham Lincoln '30
The Lone Star Ranger '30
The Riding Tornado '32
Sixteen Fathoms Deep '34
The Grapes of Wrath '40
Three Faces West '40
Border Patrol '43
Texas Masquerade '44
Ma and Pa Kettle at the Fair '52
The Sun Shines Bright '53
The Horse Soldiers '59

Joan Sims
Carry On Admiral '57
Carry On Cleo '65
Carry On Screaming '66
Carry On at Your Convenience '71
Carry On Camping '71
Carry On Henry VIII '71
Carry On Behind '75
Carry On Dick '75
One of Our Dinosaurs Is Missing '75
The Canterville Ghost '96

Mike Sims
The Bus Is Coming '72
Ghetto Revenge

Robin Sims
The Channeler '89
Shooters '89

Frank Sinatra
Higher and Higher '44
Step Lively '44
Strictly G.I. '44
Anchors Aweigh '45
Till the Clouds Roll By '46
Till the Clouds Roll By/A Star Is Born '46
It Happened in Brooklyn '47
The Miracle of the Bells '48
On the Town '49
Take Me Out to the Ball Game '49
Double Dynamite '51
Meet Danny Wilson '52
From Here to Eternity '53
Hollywood Goes to War '54
Suddenly '54
Young at Heart '54
Guys and Dolls '55
The Man with the Golden Arm '55
Not as a Stranger '55
The Tender Trap '55
High Society '56
Pal Joey '57
The Pride and the Passion '57
Kings Go Forth '58
Some Came Running '58
A Hole in the Head '59
Never So Few '59
Can-Can '60
Ocean's 11 '60
The Devil at 4 O'Clock '61
The Manchurian Candidate '62
Come Blow Your Horn '63
Four for Texas '63
The List of Adrian Messenger '63
Paris When It Sizzles '64
Robin and the 7 Hoods '64
None But the Brave '65
Von Ryan's Express '65
Assault on a Queen '66
Cast a Giant Shadow '66
The Oscar '66
Tony Rome '67
The Detective '68
Lady in Cement '68
That's Entertainment '74
The First Deadly Sin '80
Cannonball Run 2 '84

Frank Sinatra, Jr.
A Man Called Adam '66
Pepper and His Wacky Taxi '72
Code Name: Zebra '84
Cool World '92

Nancy Sinatra
The Wild Angels '66
Speedway '68

Sinbad
Necessary Roughness '91
Coneheads '93
Houseguest '94

Gordon John Sinclair
Gregory's Girl '80
Erik the Viking '89

Hugh Sinclair
The Secret Four '40
The Gay Lady '49
The Rocking Horse Winner '49
No Trace '50
The Saint's Vacation/The Narrow Margin '52

Madge Sinclair
Conrack '74
Cornbread, Earl & Me '75
Convoy '78
One in a Million: The Ron LeFlore Story '78
Coming to America '88
The End of Innocence '90
A Century of Women '94

Donald Sinden
Doctor in the House '53
Simba '55
Above Us the Waves '56
Doctor at Large '57
The Captain's Table '60
Rentadick '72
The Island at the Top of the World '74
The Children '90
The Canterville Ghost '96

Jeremy Sinden
Danger UXB '81
Fortunes of War '87
The Innocent '93

Chen Sing
Bruce Li in New Guinea '80

Bruce Li the Invincible *'80*
Invincible *'80*
Shaolin Vengence *'82*

Linda Singer
Junior *'86*
Zombie Nightmare *'86*

Lori Singer
Born Beautiful *'82*
Footloose *'84*
The Falcon and the Snowman *'85*
The Man with One Red Shoe *'85*
Trouble in Mind *'86*
Summer Heat *'87*
Made in USA *'88*
Storm and Sorrow *'90*
Warlock *'91*
Sunset Grill *'92*
Equinox *'93*
Short Cuts *'93*
The Last Ride *'94*

Marc Singer
Things in Their Season *'74*
Go Tell the Spartans *'78*
Sergeant Matlovich vs. the U.S. Air Force *'78*
Roots: The Next Generation *'79*
The Two Worlds of Jenny Logan *'79*
For Ladies Only *'81*
Beastmaster *'82*
If You Could See What I Hear *'82*
Her Life as a Man *'83*
V *'83*
V: The Final Battle *'84*
Born to Race *'88*
In the Cold of the Night *'89*
Beyond the Silhouette *'90*
Body Chemistry *'90*
Dead Space *'90*
High Desert Kill *'90*
A Man Called Sarge *'90*
The Red Raven Kiss-Off *'90*
Watchers 2 *'90*
Beastmaster 2: Through the Portal of Time *'91*
The Berlin Conspiracy *'91*
Deadly Game *'91*
Ultimate Desires *'91*
Sweet Justice *'92*
Silk Degrees *'94*
Beastmaster 3: The Eye of Braxus *'95*
Cyberzone *'95*
The Fighter *'95*

Joseph Singleton
Reggie Mixes In *'16*
Toll Gate *'20*
The Mad Whirl *'25*

Penny Singleton
Vogues of 1938 *'37*
Blondie *'38*
Boy Meets Girl *'38*
Blondie Takes a Vacation *'39*
Blondie Has Trouble *'40*
Blondie in Society *'41*
Blondie's Blessed Event *'42*
It's a Great Life *'43*
Blondie Knows Best *'46*
Blondie Hits the Jackpot *'49*

Gary Sinise
True West *'86*
A Midnight Clear *'92*
Of Mice and Men *'92*
Jack the Bear *'93*
Forrest Gump *'94*
Stephen King's The Stand *'94*
Apollo 13 *'95*
Truman *'95*

Sir Lancelot
I Walked with a Zombie *'43*
Zombies on Broadway *'44*

G. Anthony Sirico
Backtrack *'89*
Cookie *'89*

Marina Sirtis
Blind Date *'84*
Death Wish 3 *'85*
Star Trek the Next Generation: Encounter at Farpoint *'87*
Star Trek Generations *'94*
Star Trek the Next Generation, the Final Episode: All Good Things... *'94*

Noble Sissle
Junction 88 *'40*
Murder with Music *'45*

Jeremy Sisto
Grand Canyon *'91*
Hideaway *'94*
Clueless *'95*
The Crew *'95*
Moonlight and Valentino *'95*
White Squall *'96*

Rocco Sisto
Truth or Die *'86*
Red Riding Hood *'88*
Innocent Blood *'92*

Emil Sitka
Three Stooges in Orbit *'62*
The Outlaws is Coming! *'65*

Frank Sivero
Goodfellas *'90*
Fist of Honor *'92*
Cop and a Half *'93*

Tom Sizemore
Blue Steel *'90*
Flight of the Intruder *'90*
A Matter of Degrees *'90*
Harley Davidson and the Marlboro Man *'91*
Where Sleeping Dogs Lie *'91*
An American Story *'92*
Passenger 57 *'92*
Heart and Souls *'93*
Striking Distance *'93*
True Romance *'93*
Watch It *'93*
Natural Born Killers *'94*
Wyatt Earp *'94*
Bad Love *'95*
Devil in a Blue Dress *'95*
Heat *'95*
Strange Days *'95*

Gunnar Sjoberg
June Night *'40*
Brink of Life *'57*

Victor Sjostrom
The Outlaw and His Wife *'17*
Thomas Graal's Best Film *'17*
Thomas Graal's First Child *'18*
Walpurgis Night *'41*
Wild Strawberries *'57*

George Skaff
Man Beast *'55*
The Incredible Petrified World *'58*
Frogs *'72*

Jimmie F. Skaggs
Ghost Town *'88*
Puppet Master *'89*
The Lost Capone *'90*
Thousand Pieces of Gold *'91*
Backlash: Oblivion 2 *'95*
Tecumseh: The Last Warrior *'95*

Norman Skaggs
Chrome Soldiers *'92*
Getting Out *'94*

Lilia Skala
Lilies of the Field *'63*
Charly *'68*
Probe *'72*
Deadly Hero *'75*
Heartland *'81*
Flashdance *'83*
House of Games *'87*

Stellan Skarsgard
Noon Wine *'84*
The Unbearable Lightness of Being *'88*
The Ox *'91*
Wind *'92*
Good Evening, Mr. Wallenberg *'93*
The Slingshot *'93*
Breaking the Waves *'95*

Jackie Skarvellis
The Body Beneath *'70*
The Rats are Coming! The Werewolves are Here! *'72*

Red Skelton
Having Wonderful Time *'38*
Having Wonderful Time/Carnival Boat *'38*
Lady Be Good *'41*
Whistling in the Dark *'41*
Panama Hattie *'42*
Ship Ahoy *'42*
Whistling in Dixie *'42*
DuBarry Was a Lady *'43*
I Dood It *'43*
Thousands Cheer *'43*
Whistling in Brooklyn *'43*
Bathing Beauty *'44*
The Show-Off *'46*
Ziegfeld Follies *'46*
Merton of the Movies *'47*
The Fuller Brush Man *'48*
A Southern Yankee *'48*
Neptune's Daughter *'49*
Three Little Words *'50*
Watch the Birdie *'50*
The Yellow Cab Man *'50*
Texas Carnival *'51*
Lovely to Look At *'52*
Clown *'53*
Hollywood Goes to War *'54*
Those Magnificent Men in Their Flying Machines *'65*
Hollywood Clowns *'85*

Tom Skerritt
M*A*S*H *'70*
Wild Rovers *'71*
Fuzz *'72*
Big Bad Mama *'74*
Thieves Like Us *'74*
Devil's Rain *'75*
The Turning Point *'77*
Alien *'79*
Cheech and Chong's Up in Smoke *'79*
Ice Castles *'79*
Silence of the North *'81*
Dangerous Summer *'82*
Fighting Back *'82*
Dead Zone *'83*
Calendar Girl Murders *'84*
Miles to Go *'86*
Top Gun *'86*
Big Town *'87*
Hitchhiker 3 *'87*
Maid to Order *'87*
Opposing Force *'87*
Poker Alice *'87*
Wisdom *'87*
Poltergeist 3 *'88*
Big Man on Campus *'89*
The Heist *'89*
Red King, White Knight *'89*
Steel Magnolias *'89*
Child in the Night *'90*
The China Lake Murders *'90*
The Rookie *'90*
Nightmare at Bittercreek *'91*
Getting Up and Going Home *'92*
Poison Ivy *'92*
A River Runs Through It *'92*
Wild Orchid 2: Two Shades of Blue *'92*
Knight Moves *'93*

Anita Skinner
Girlfriends *'78*
Sole Survivor *'84*

Claire Skinner
Life Is Sweet *'90*
Naked *'93*
The Return of the Native *'94*

Pat Skipper
Dancing with Danger *'93*
Trade Off *'95*

Alison Skipworth
Dubarry *'30*
Night After Night *'32*
Dangerous *'35*
Doubting Thomas *'35*
The Princess Comes Across *'36*
Satan Met a Lady *'36*
Wide Open Faces *'38*

Jerzy Skolimowski
Innocent Sorcerers *'60*
White Nights *'85*
Big Shots *'87*

Ione Skye
River's Edge *'87*
Stranded *'87*
A Night in the Life of Jimmy Reardon *'88*
Carmilla *'89*
The Rachel Papers *'89*
Say Anything *'89*
Mindwalk: A Film for Passionate Thinkers *'91*
Gas Food Lodging *'92*
Guncrazy *'92*
Samantha *'92*
The Color of Evening *'95*
Four Rooms *'95*

Max Elliott Slade
3 Ninjas *'92*
3 Ninjas Knuckle Up *'92*
3 Ninjas Kick Back *'94*
Apollo 13 *'95*

Jeremy Slate
G.I. Blues *'60*
Girls! Girls! Girls! *'62*
I'll Take Sweden *'65*
Born Losers *'67*
The Devil's Brigade *'68*
Hell's Angels '69 *'69*
Hell's Belles *'69*
The Hooked Generation *'69*
Alligator Alley *'72*
The Centerfold Girls *'74*
Mr. Horn *'79*
Dead Pit *'89*
Goodnight, Sweet Marilyn *'89*
Dream Machine *'91*
The Lawnmower Man *'92*

Christian Slater
Living Proof: The Hank Williams Jr. Story *'83*
Legend of Billie Jean *'85*
The Name of the Rose *'86*
Twisted *'86*
Tucker: The Man and His Dream *'88*
Beyond the Stars *'89*
Gleaming the Cube *'89*
Heathers *'89*
The Wizard *'89*
Pump Up the Volume *'90*
Tales from the Darkside: The Movie *'90*
Young Guns 2 *'90*
Mobsters *'91*
Robin Hood: Prince of Thieves *'91*
Kuffs *'92*
Where the Day Takes You *'92*
True Romance *'93*
Untamed Heart *'93*
Interview with the Vampire *'94*
Jimmy Hollywood *'94*
Bed of Roses *'95*
Broken Arrow *'95*
Murder In the First *'95*

Helen Slater
Supergirl *'84*
Legend of Billie Jean *'85*
Ruthless People *'86*
The Secret of My Success *'87*
Sticky Fingers *'88*
Happy Together *'89*
City Slickers *'91*
Betrayal of the Dove *'92*
Chantilly Lace *'93*
A House In The Hills *'93*
12:01 *'93*
Lassie *'94*
Parallel Lives *'94*

Tony Slattery
Peter's Friends *'92*
Heaven's a Drag *'94*

Tod Slaughter
The Crimes of Stephen Hawke *'36*
Demon Barber of Fleet Street *'36*
Murder in the Old Red Barn *'36*
Never Too Late to Mend *'37*
Ticket of Leave Man *'37*
The Hooded Terror *'38*
Sexton Blake and the Hooded Terror *'38*
Crimes at the Dark House *'39*
The Face at the Window *'39*
The Greed of William Hart *'48*
Saturday Night Shockers, Vol. 2 *'58*

Darla Slavens
Red Snow *'91*
Married People, Single Sex *'93*

Millie Slavin
The People vs. Jean Harris *'81*
One Night Stand *'95*

Tommy Sledge
Lobster Man from Mars *'89*
Movie ... In Your Face *'90*

Victor Slezak
Bed & Breakfast *'92*
Beyond Rangoon *'95*
The Bridges of Madison County *'95*

Walter Slezak
Once Upon a Honeymoon *'42*
The Fallen Sparrow *'43*
This Land is Mine *'43*
Lifeboat *'44*
The Princess and the Pirate *'44*
Step Lively *'44*
Cornered *'45*
Salome, Where She Danced *'45*
The Spanish Main *'45*
Born to Kill *'47*
Riff-Raff *'47*
Sinbad, the Sailor *'47*
The Pirate *'48*
The Inspector General *'49*
Abbott and Costello in the Foreign Legion *'50*
The Yellow Cab Man *'50*
Bedtime for Bonzo *'51*
People Will Talk *'51*
Come September *'61*
The Wonderful World of the Brothers Grimm *'62*
Emil and the Detectives *'64*
Caper of the Golden Bulls *'67*
Black Beauty *'71*
Treasure Island *'72*

Everett Sloane
Citizen Kane *'41*
The Lady from Shanghai *'48*
The Men *'50*
The Enforcer *'51*
Sirocco *'51*
The Big Knife *'55*
Lust for Life *'56*
Patterns *'56*
Somebody Up There Likes Me *'56*
Marjorie Morningstar *'58*
Home from the Hill *'60*
Disorderly Orderly *'64*
The Patsy *'64*
Hercules and the Princess of Troy *'65*

James Sloyan
The Disappearance of Aimee *'76*
Callie and Son *'81*
Prime Suspect *'82*
Amos *'85*
Billionaire Boys Club *'87*
Deadline Assault *'90*
Danielle Steel's Changes *'91*

Errol Slue
Murder One *'88*
Baby on Board *'92*

Jean Smart
Fire with Fire *'86*
Maximum Security *'87*
Project X *'87*
A Fight for Jenny *'90*
Mistress *'91*
Homeward Bound: The Incredible Journey *'93*
Scarlett *'94*
The Yearling *'94*
The Brady Bunch Movie *'95*

Richard Smedley
The Abductors *'72*
A Place Called Today *'72*

Ron Smerczak
Hunted *'88*
Return of the Family Man *'89*

Yakov Smirnoff
The Adventures of Buckaroo Banzai Across the Eighth Dimension *'84*
Heartburn *'86*
Up Your Alley *'89*

Alexis Smith
Dive Bomber *'41*
Gentleman Jim *'42*
The Adventures of Mark Twain *'44*
Hollywood Canteen *'44*
Conflict *'45*
The Horn Blows at Midnight *'45*
Rhapsody in Blue *'45*
San Antonio *'45*
Night and Day *'46*
The Two Mrs. Carrolls *'47*
South of St. Louis *'48*
Any Number Can Play *'49*
Here Comes the Groom *'51*
Split Second *'53*
The Sleeping Tiger *'54*
This Happy Feeling *'58*
The Young Philadelphians *'59*
Once is Not Enough *'75*
The Little Girl Who Lives Down the Lane *'76*

Smith ▶cont.

Casey's Shadow '78
La Truite '83
Dress Gray '86
Tough Guys '86
The Age of Innocence '93

Allison Smith
At First Sight '95
A Reason to Believe '95

Anna Deavere Smith
Dave '93
Philadelphia '93
The American President '95

Anna Nicole Smith
To the Limit '95
Skyscraper '96

Art Smith
Letter from an Unknown Woman '48
Mr. Peabody & the Mermaid '48
Caught '49
In a Lonely Place '50
The Next Voice You Hear '50
The Painted Hills '51

Bill Smith
Atlantis, the Lost Continent '61
Spirit of the Eagle '90

Britta Smith
In the Name of the Father '93
The Summer House '94
Moll Flanders '96

Brooke Smith
The Silence of the Lambs '91
The Night We Never Met '93
A Century of Women '94
Vanya on 42nd Street '94
Last Summer In the Hamptons '96

Bubba Smith
Escape from DS-3 '80s
Stroker Ace '83
Police Academy '84
Police Academy 2: Their First Assignment '85
Police Academy 3: Back in Training '86
Police Academy 4: Citizens on Patrol '87
The Wild Pair '87
Police Academy 5: Assignment Miami Beach '88
Police Academy 6: City Under Siege '89
Fist of Honor '92
My Samurai '92

Sir C. Aubrey Smith
Trader Horn '31
Bombshell '33
Queen Christina '33
Cleopatra '34
Scarlet Empress '34
China Seas '35
The Crusades '35
The Lives of a Bengal Lancer '35
Transatlantic Tunnel '35
The Charge of the Light Brigade '36
The Garden of Allah '36
Little Lord Fauntleroy '36
Lloyds of London '36
The Hurricane '37
Prisoner of Zenda '37
Thoroughbreds Don't Cry '37
Wee Willie Winkie '37
Another Thin Man '39
Balalaika '39
Eternally Yours '39
Five Came Back '39
The Four Feathers '39
Beyond Tomorrow '40
Rebecca '40
Waterloo Bridge '40
Forever and a Day '43
Madame Curie '43
The Adventures of Mark Twain '44
Sensations of 1945 '44
The White Cliffs of Dover '44
And Then There Were None '45
Unconquered '47

Cedric Smith
Love and Hate: A Marriage Made in Hell '90
The Penthouse '92
Witchboard 3: The Possession '95

Charles Martin Smith
Culpepper Cattle Co. '72
Fuzz '72
American Graffiti '73
Pat Garrett & Billy the Kid '73
Rafferty & the Gold Dust Twins '75
Law of the Land '76
No Deposit, No Return '76
The Campus Corpse '77
The Buddy Holly Story '78
More American Graffiti '79
Herbie Goes Bananas '80
Cotton Candy '82
Never Cry Wolf '83
Starman '84
Strange Tales/Ray Bradbury Theatre '86
The Untouchables '87
The Experts '89
The Hot Spot '90
Deep Cover '92
And the Band Played On '93
Fifty/Fifty '93
Roswell: The U.F.O. Cover-Up '94
Speechless '94
Larry McMurtry's Streets of Laredo '95
The Road Home '95

Cheryl "Rainbeaux" Smith
Lemora, Lady Dracula '73
Caged Heat '74
The Swinging Cheerleaders '74
Farewell, My Lovely '75
Drum '76
Pom Pom Girls '76
Revenge of the Cheerleaders '76
Slumber Party '57 '76
Incredible Melting Man '77
Laserblast '78
Cheech and Chong's Up in Smoke '79
Melvin and Howard '80
Parasite '82
Vice Squad '82
Independence Day '83

Connie Smith
Room to Let '49
Treasure of the Golden Condor '53
Hell on Wheels '67
Road to Nashville '67

Cotter Smith
Broken Badge '85
A Bunny's Tale '85
Lady Beware '87
Cameron's Closet '89
K-9 '89
The Last Prostitute '91
Midnight's Child '93

Cynthia Smith
Benji '74
For the Love of Benji '77

David Anthony Smith
Judgment Day '88
Terror in Paradise '90

Garnett Smith
Laboratory '80
Whitcomb's War '87

Geraldine Smith
Flesh '68
Mixed Blood '84
Spike of Bensonhurst '88

Gregory Edward Smith
Leapin' Leprechauns '95
Harriet the Spy '96

Howard Smith
Call Northside 777 '48
State of the Union '48

Jaclyn Smith
Goodbye Columbus '69
The Adventurers '70
Probe '72
Users '78
Nightkill '80
Jacqueline Bouvier Kennedy '81
Rage of Angels '83
Deja Vu '84
George Washington '84
Rage of Angels: The Story Continues '86
The Night They Saved Christmas '87
The Bourne Identity '88
Windmills of the Gods '88
Danielle Steel's Kaleidoscope '92
Lies Before Kisses '92

John W. Smith
Hot Rod Girl '56
Star Crystal '85

Kate Smith
This Is the Army '43
Irving Berlin's America '86

Kent Smith
Back Door to Heaven '39
Cat People '42
Curse of the Cat People '44
The Spiral Staircase '46
Magic Town '47
The Badlanders '58
Party Girl '58
Strangers When We Meet '60
The Balcony '63
The Invaders '67
Pete 'n' Tillie '72
Probe '72
The Affair '73
Die Sister, Die! '74

Kurtwood Smith
RoboCop '87
Rambo 3 '88
Dead Poets Society '89
The Heart of Dixie '89
The Nightmare Years '89
True Believer '89
Quick Change '90
Company Business '91
Star Trek 6: The Undiscovered Country '91
Shadows and Fog '92
Boxing Helena '93
The Crush '93
Fortress '93
Dead on Sight '94
The Last of the Dogmen '95
To Die For '95

Lane Smith
Prime Suspect '82
The Solitary Man '82
Dress Gray '86
Weeds '87
Prison '88
The Final Days '89
Night Game '89
Air America '90
Blind Vengeance '90
The Distinguished Gentleman '92
Duplicates '92
False Arrest '92
The Mighty Ducks '92
My Cousin Vinny '92
Son-in-Law '93
The Scout '94
The Spy Within '94

Lewis Smith
The Final Terror '83
The Adventures of Buckaroo Banzai Across the Eighth Dimension '84
The Heavenly Kid '85
North and South Book 2 '86
Fulfillment '89
Diary of a Hitman '91

Liz Smith
A Private Function '84
Apartment Zero '88
We Think the World of You '88

Lois Smith
Five Easy Pieces '70
Reuben, Reuben '83
Reckless '84
Twisted '86
Black Widow '87
Green Card '90
Fried Green Tomatoes '91
Switched at Birth '91
Hard Promises '92
Keep the Change '92
Falling Down '93
Skylark '93
Holy Matrimony '94
Dead Man Walking '95
How to Make an American Quilt '95
Truman '95
Twister '96

Loring Smith
Shadow of the Thin Man '41
Ma and Pa Kettle at Waikiki '55

Madeleine Smith
The Vampire Lovers '70
Live and Let Die '73
Frankenstein and the Monster from Hell '74

Madolyn Smith
Urban Cowboy '80
Pray TV '82
Rehearsal for Murder '82
Sadat '83
All of Me '84
Ernie Kovacs: Between the Laughter '84
2010: The Year We Make Contact '84
The Caller '87
Funny Farm '88
The Rose and the Jackal '90
Final Approach '91
The Super '91

Maggie Smith
The V.I.P.'s '63
The Pumpkin Eater '64
The Honey Pot '67
Hot Millions '68
The Prime of Miss Jean Brodie '69
Travels with My Aunt '72
Murder by Death '76
California Suite '78
Death on the Nile '78
Clash of the Titans '81
Quartet '81
Evil under the Sun '82
The Missionary '82
Better Late Than Never '83
A Private Function '84
Lily in Love '85
Mrs. Silly '85
A Room with a View '86
The Lonely Passion of Judith Hearne '87
Hook '91
Sister Act '92
The Secret Garden '93
Sister Act 2: Back in the Habit '93
Richard III '95

Maurice Smith
Bloodfist 2 '90
Fist of Glory '95

Mel Smith
Slayground '84
Morons from Outer Space '85
The Princess Bride '87
The Misadventures of Mr. Wilt '90
Brain Donors '92

Melanie Smith
The Baby Doll Murders '92
Trancers 3: Deth Lives '92
Night Hunter '95

Oliver Smith
Hellraiser '87
Hellbound: Hellraiser 2 '88

Patricia Smith
Spirit of St. Louis '57
Save the Tiger '73

Paul Smith
Madron '70
Raiders in Action '71
Midnight Express '78
Return of the Tiger '78
Popeye '80
Mortuary '81
The Salamander '82
Pieces '83
Dune '84
Jungle Warriors '84
Crimewave '85
The Fire in the Stone '85
Red Sonja '85
Sno-Line '85
Haunted Honeymoon '86
Platypus Cove '86
Death Chase '87
Outlaw Force '87
Sonny Boy '87
Gor '88
Caged Fury '90
Crossing the Line '90
Desert Kickboxer '92
Maverick '94

Pete Smith
A Few Moments with Buster Keaton and Laurel and Hardy '63
Once Were Warriors '94

Rex Smith
Sooner or Later '78
The Pirates of Penzance '83
Snow White and the Seven Dwarfs '83
Street Hawk '84
Transformations '88
The Trial of the Incredible Hulk '89
A Passion to Kill '94

Robin Smith
Bopha! '93
Never Say Die '94

Roger Smith
Man of a Thousand Faces '57
Auntie Mame '58

Savannah Smith
The Long Riders '80
Code of Honor '84
Everybody's All American '88

Shawn Smith
The Land Unknown '57
It! The Terror from Beyond Space '58

Shawnee Smith
Summer School '87
The Blob '88
Who's Harry Crumb? '89
Desperate Hours '90
Stephen King's The Stand '94

Shelley Smith
The Night the City Screamed '80
National Lampoon's Class Reunion '82
The Fantastic World of D.C. Collins '84

Stuart Smith
Ninja Destroyer '70s
Ninja Hunt '80s

Will Smith
Where the Day Takes You '92
Made in America '93
Six Degrees of Separation '93
Bad Boys '95
Independence Day '96

William Smith
Run, Angel, Run! '69
Chrome Hearts '70
Darker than Amber '70
The Losers '70
Chrome and Hot Leather '71
Grave of the Vampire '72
The Deadly Trackers '73
Gentle Savage '73
Invasion of the Bee Girls '73
A Taste of Hell '73
Boss '74
The Rockford Files: Backlash of the Hunter '74
The Ultimate Warrior '75
Hollywood Man '76
Scorchy '76
Twilight's Last Gleaming '77
Blackjack '78
Fast Company '78
The Frisco Kid '79
The Rebels '79
Seven '79
Conan the Barbarian '82
Angels Die Hard '84
Red Dawn '84
Fever Pitch '85
Mean Season '85
Eye of the Tiger '86
Moon in Scorpio '86
Commando Squad '87
Platoon Leader '87
B.O.R.N. '88
Hell on the Battleground '88
Maniac Cop '88
Memorial Valley Massacre '88
Action U.S.A. '89
Deadly Breed '89
East L.A. Warriors '89
Emperor of the Bronx '89
Evil Altar '89
Jungle Assault '89
L.A. Vice '89
The Last Riders '90
Slow Burn '90

Terror in Beverly Hills '90

Yeardley Smith
Heaven Help Us '85
Legend of Billie Jean '85
Maximum Overdrive '86
Ginger Ale Afternoon '89
City Slickers '91

Jamie Smith-Jackson
Satan's School for Girls '73
Bug '75

Jan Smithers
Where the Lilies Bloom '74
WKRP in Cincinnati, Vol. 1 '78
Mr. Nice Guy '86

William Smithers
Scorpio '73
Death Sport '78

Bill Smitrovich
A Killing Affair '85
Crime Story: The Complete Saga '86
Renegades '89
Crazy People '90
Bodily Harm '95
Nick of Time '95
The Trigger Effect '96

Jimmy Smits
L.A. Law '86
Running Scared '86
The Believers '87
Stamp of a Killer '87
Glitz '88
Old Gringo '89
Vital Signs '90
Fires Within '91
Switch '91
Gross Misconduct '93
Stephen King's The Tommyknockers '93
The Cisco Kid '94
My Family '94
Marshal Law '96

Sonja Smits
War Brides '80s
The Pit '81
Videodrome '83
Hitchhiker 4 '87
That's My Baby! '88

Dick Smothers
Speed Zone '88
Tales of the Unexpected '91
Casino '95

Tom Smothers
Alice Through the Looking Glass '66
Silver Bears '78
A Pleasure Doing Business '79
Serial '80
Pandemonium '82
Speed Zone '88

Ann Smyrner
The House of 1000 Dolls '67
Beyond the Law '68

Wesley Snipes
Streets of Gold '86
Wildcats '86
Vietnam War Story 2 '88
Major League '89
King of New York '90
Mo' Better Blues '90
Jungle Fever '91
New Jack City '91
The Waterdance '91
Passenger 57 '92
White Men Can't Jump '92
Boiling Point '93
Demolition Man '93
Rising Sun '93
Drop Zone '94
Sugar Hill '94
America's Dream '95
Money Train '95
To Wong Foo, Thanks for Everything, Julie Newmar '95
The Fan '96

Carrie Snodgress
Silent Night, Lonely Night '69
Diary of a Mad Housewife '70
The Fury '78
The Attic '80
The Solitary Man '82
Trick or Treats '82
A Night in Heaven '83
Nadia '84
L.A. Bad '85
Pale Rider '85
Murphy's Law '86
Blueberry Hill '88
Across the Tracks '89
Chill Factor '90
The Rose and the Jackal '90
Blue Sky '91
Mission of the Shark '91
Woman With a Past '92
The Ballad of Little Jo '93
8 Seconds '94
White Man's Burden '95

Victoria Snow
Buffalo Jump '90
Love and Hate: A Marriage Made in Hell '90

Arlen Dean Snyder
Scalpel '76
Dear Detective '78
Yanks '79
Young Love, First Love '79
No Place to Hide '81
Red Flag: The Ultimate Game '81
Deadly Force '83
Night Partners '83
Heartbreak Ridge '86
Marked for Death '90
Wheels of Terror '90
Running Cool '93

Drew Snyder
Night School '81
Firestarter '84
Izzy & Moe '85
Dance with Death '91
Project: Eliminator '91
Blindfold: Acts of Obsession '94
Separate Lives '94

Suzanne Snyder
Prettykill '87
Killer Klowns from Outer Space '88
The Night Before '88
Retribution '88

Barry Sobel
Punchline '88
Martians Go Home! '90
Doc Hollywood '91

Maria Socas
The Warrior & the Sorceress '84
Deathstalker 2: Duel of the Titans '87

Kristina Soderbaum
Jud Suess '40
Kolberg '45
Night Train to Venice '93

Camilla Soeberg
Twist & Shout '84
A Night of Love '87

Abraham Sofaer
Dual Alibi '47
Calling Paul Temple '48
Quo Vadis '51
Elephant Walk '54
Naked Jungle '54
Bhowani Junction '56
Captain Sinbad '63
Demon with a Glass Hand '64

Hans Sohnker
For the First Time '59
Sherlock Holmes and the Deadly Necklace '62
The Phantom of Soho '64

Marilyn Sokol
The Goodbye Girl '77
Something Short of Paradise '79

Vladimir Sokoloff
The Lower Depths '36
Conquest '37
Comrade X '40
The Road to Morocco '42
For Whom the Bell Tolls '43
Cloak and Dagger '46
Baron of Arizona '51
I Was a Teenage Werewolf '57
Beyond the Time Barrier '60
Taras Bulba '62

Miguel Angel Sola
Funny, Dirty Little War '83
Mayalunta '86

Silvia Solar
As If It Were Raining '63
Finger on the Trigger '65
Night of the Howling Beast '75
The Gentleman Killer '78

Fernando Soler
The Great Madcap '49
Susana '51

Paul Soles
The Gunrunner '84
Beethoven Lives Upstairs '92
The Lotus Eaters '93

P.J. Soles
The Possessed '77
Halloween '78
Rock 'n' Roll High School '79
Stripes '81
B.O.R.N. '88
Innocent Prey '88
Saigon Commandos '88
Alienator '89
Soldier's Fortune '91
Out There '95

Bruce Solomon
Children Shouldn't Play with Dead Things '72
Foul Play '78

Charles Solomon
The Channeler '89
Witchcraft 2: The Temptress '90
Witchcraft 3: The Kiss of Death '90
Witchcraft 4: Virgin Heart '92

Anatoli Solonitzin
Andrei Rublev '66
Stalker '79

Elena Solovei
An Unfinished Piece for a Player Piano '77
A Slave of Love '78
Oblomov '81

Yanti Somer
Cosmos: War of the Planets '80
Reactor '85

Kristi Somers
Hardbodies '84
Tomboy '85

Suzanne Somers
American Graffiti '73
Sky Hei$t '75
Ants '77
Yesterday's Hero '79
Nothing Personal '80
Happily Ever After '82
Seduced by Evil '94

Geraldine Somerville
The Black Velvet Gown '92
Haunted '95

Julie Sommars
I'm the Girl He Wants to Kill '74
Herbie Goes to Monte Carlo '77
Sex and the Single Parent '82

Elke Sommer
Sweet Ecstasy '62
The Prize '63
A Shot in the Dark '64
Boy, Did I Get a Wrong Number! '66
The Oscar '66
The Corrupt Ones '67
The Invincible Six '68
Zeppelin '71
Probe '72
Torture Chamber of Baron Blood '72
It's Not the Size That Counts '74
Carry On Behind '75
Lisa and the Devil '75
Ten Little Indians '75
The Invisible Strangler '76
Left for Dead '78
The Big Scam '79
The Double McGuffin '79
Prisoner of Zenda '79
The Treasure Seekers '79
One Away '80
Fantastic Seven '82
Inside the Third Reich '82
Jenny's War '85
Lily in Love '85
No One Cries Forever '85
Anastasia: The Mystery of Anna '86
Adventures Beyond Belief '87
Severed Ties '92

Josef Sommer
Hide in Plain Sight '80
Absence of Malice '81
Reds '81
Rollover '81
Still of the Night '82
Independence Day '83
Silkwood '83
Iceman '84
Execution of Raymond Graham '85
Target '85
Witness '85
Yuri Nosenko, KGB '86
The Rosary Murders '87
Dracula's Widow '88
Bloodhounds of Broadway '89
Bridge to Silence '89
Chances Are '89
Forced March '90
A Woman Named Jackie '91
An American Story '92
The Mighty Ducks '92
Shadows and Fog '92
Hostages '93
Malice '93
The Enemy Within '94
Nobody's Fool '94
Letter to My Killer '95
Moonlight and Valentino '95
Strange Days '95

Helga Sommerfeld
The Phantom of Soho '64
Code Name Alpha '67

Gale Sondergaard
Anthony Adverse '36
The Life of Emile Zola '37
Juarez '39
The Blue Bird '40
The Letter '40
The Mark of Zorro '40
My Favorite Blonde '42
A Night to Remember '42
Isle of Forgotten Sins '43
The Invisible Man's Revenge '44
Spider Woman '44
Anna and the King of Siam '46
The Time of Their Lives '46
The Road to Rio '47
East Side, West Side '49
Savage Intruder '68
The Return of a Man Called Horse '76
Echoes '83

Jack Soo
Flower Drum Song '61
Return from Witch Mountain '78

Michael Sopkiw
After the Fall of New York '85
Blastfighter '85
Massacre in Dinosaur Valley '85

Agnes Soral
One Wild Moment '78
Tchao Pantin '84
Killing Cars '85
Window to Paris '95

Alberto Sordi
The White Sheik '52
I Vitelloni '53
Two Nights with Cleopatra '54
The Great War '59
Those Magnificent Men in Their Flying Machines '65

Jean Sorel
Sandra of a Thousand Delights '65
Belle de Jour '67
Paralyzed '70s

Louise Sorel
Plaza Suite '71
The President's Plane is Missing '71
Get Christie Love! '74
When Every Day was the Fourth of July '78
Mazes and Monsters '82

Ted Sorel
From Beyond '86
Basket Case 2 '90
Me and the Mob '94

Linda Sorensen
Stone Cold Dead '80
Kavik the Wolf Dog '84
Joshua Then and Now '85
Family Reunion '88
Relative Fear '95

Charo Soriano
The Garden of Delights '70
Dracula's Great Love '72
Orgy of the Vampires '73

Arleen Sorkin
From Here to Maternity '85
I Don't Buy Kisses Anymore '92
It's Pat: The Movie '94

Mira Sorvino
Amongst Friends '93
Barcelona '94
New York Cop '94
Parallel Lives '94
Quiz Show '94
Blue In the Face '95
The Buccaneers '95
Mighty Aphrodite '95
Beautiful Girls '96

Paul Sorvino
Cry Uncle '71
Fury on Wheels '71
The Day of the Dolphin '73
A Touch of Class '73
The Gambler '74
Tell Me Where It Hurts '74
Panic in Needle Park '75
I Will, I Will for Now '76
Oh, God! '77
Bloodbrothers '78
Brink's Job '78
Lost and Found '79
Cruising '80
Question of Honor '80
Reds '81
I, the Jury '82
Melanie '82
Off the Wall '82
That Championship Season '82
Chiefs '83
My Mother's Secret Life '84
Very Close Quarters '84
The Stuff '85
Turk 182! '85
A Fine Mess '86
Jailbait: Betrayed By Innocence '86
Vasectomy: A Delicate Matter '86
Almost Partners '87
Dick Tracy '90
Goodfellas '90
Age Isn't Everything '91
The Rocketeer '91
Backstreet Justice '93
Parallel Lives '94
Cover Me '95
Nixon '95

Ann Sothern
Kid Millions '34
Hell-Ship Morgan '36
Brother Orchid '40
Mexican Spitfire/Smartest Girl in Town '40
Lady Be Good '41
Panama Hattie '42
Words and Music '48
The Judge Steps Out '49
A Letter to Three Wives '49
Nancy Goes to Rio '50
The Best Man '64
Lady in a Cage '64
The Killing Kind '73
Crazy Mama '75
The Manitou '78
Little Dragons '80
The Whales of August '87

Fernando Soto
Boom in the Moon '46
The Illusion Travels by Streetcar '53
Invasion of the Vampires '61

Hugo Soto
Times to Come '81
Man Facing Southeast '86

Talisa Soto
Spike of Bensonhurst '88
License to Kill '89
Prison Stories: Women on the Inside '91
Silhouette '91
Hostage '92
The Mambo Kings '92
Don Juan DeMarco '94
Mortal Kombat: The Movie '95

David Soul
Magnum Force '73
Dog Pound Shuffle '75
Little Ladies of the Night '77
The Stick-Up '77
Salem's Lot '79
Homeward Bound '80

Soul ▶cont.

Rage *'80*
The Manions of America *'81*
The Key to Rebecca *'85*
World War III *'86*
Hanoi Hilton *'87*
Through Naked Eyes *'87*
Appointment with Death *'88*
The FBI Murders *'88*
In the Cold of the Night *'89*
Tides of War *'90*
Grave Secrets: The Legacy of Hilltop Drive *'92*
Pentathlon *'94*

Renee Soutendijk
The 4th Man *'79*
Spetters *'80*
Inside the Third Reich *'82*
Cold Room *'84*
Out of Order *'84*
Second Victory *'87*
Grave Secrets *'89*
Murderers among Us: The Simon Wiesenthal Story *'89*
Eve of Destruction *'90*
Forced March *'90*
Keeper of the City *'92*

Charles Southwood
Sartana's Here...Trade Your Pistol for a Coffin *'70*
Guns for Dollars *'73*

Ben Soutten
The Crimes of Stephen Hawke *'36*
The Mutiny of the Elsinore *'39*

Catherine Spaak
The Easy Life *'63*
Circle of Love *'64*
Empty Canvas *'64*
Hotel *'67*
The Cat o' Nine Tails *'71*
Counter Punch *'71*
Honey *'81*

Arthur Space
Riot Squad *'41*
A Southern Yankee *'48*
Miss Grant Takes Richmond *'49*
The Vanishing Westerner *'50*
Canadian Mounties vs. Atomic Invaders *'53*
Terror at Red Wolf Inn *'72*

Sissy Spacek
Prime Cut *'72*
Ginger in the Morning *'73*
The Girls of Huntington House *'73*
Badlands *'74*
The Migrants *'74*
Katherine *'75*
Carrie *'76*
Welcome to L.A. *'77*
Coal Miner's Daughter *'80*
Heart Beat *'80*
Raggedy Man *'81*
Missing *'82*
The Man with Two Brains *'83*
The River *'84*
Marie *'85*
Crimes of the Heart *'86*
'night, Mother *'86*
Violets Are Blue *'86*
The Long Walk Home *'89*
JFK *'91*
Hard Promises *'92*
A Private Matter *'92*
A Place for Annie *'94*
Trading Mom *'94*
The Good Old Boys *'95*
Larry McMurtry's Streets of Laredo *'95*

Kevin Spacey
The Murder of Mary Phagan *'87*
Long Day's Journey into Night *'88*
Rocket Gibraltar *'88*
Working Girl *'88*
Dad *'89*
Henry & June *'90*
Consenting Adults *'92*
Glengarry Glen Ross *'92*
Iron Will *'93*
The Ref *'93*
Doomsday Gun *'94*
Outbreak *'94*
Swimming with Sharks *'94*
Seven *'95*
The Usual Suspects *'95*
A Time to Kill *'96*

David Spade
Coneheads *'93*
P.C.U. *'94*
Tommy Boy *'95*
Black Sheep *'96*

James Spader
Endless Love *'81*
Family Secrets *'84*
The New Kids *'85*
Tuff Turf *'85*
Pretty in Pink *'86*
Baby Boom *'87*
Jack's Back *'87*
Less Than Zero *'87*
Mannequin *'87*
Wall Street *'87*
The Rachel Papers *'89*
sex, lies and videotape *'89*
Bad Influence *'90*
White Palace *'90*
True Colors *'91*
Storyville *'92*
Dream Lover *'93*
The Music of Chance *'93*
Stargate *'94*
Wolf *'94*
Crash *'95*

Fay Spain
Dragstrip Girl *'57*
God's Little Acre *'58*
Al Capone *'59*
Hercules and the Captive Women *'63*
Flight to Fury *'66*
The Godfather, Part 2 *'74*

Timothy Spall
Home Sweet Home *'82*
Dutch Girls *'87*
Gothic *'87*
Dream Demon *'88*
Crusoe *'89*
Life Is Sweet *'90*
The Sheltering Sky *'90*
White Hunter, Black Heart *'90*
Secrets and Lies *'95*

Joe Spano
American Graffiti *'73*
Warlock Moon *'73*
Northern Lights *'79*
Hill Street Blues, Vol. 1: Hill Street Station *'81*
The Dunera Boys *'85*
Terminal Choice *'85*
Brotherhood of Justice *'86*
Disaster at Silo 7 *'88*
Cast the First Stone *'89*
Fever *'91*
Rave Review *'95*
Primal Fear *'96*

Vincent Spano
The Double McGuffin *'79*
Over the Edge *'79*
Senior Trip *'81*
Baby It's You *'82*
The Black Stallion Returns *'83*
Rumble Fish *'83*
Alphabet City *'84*
Maria's Lovers *'84*
Creator *'85*
Blood Ties *'87*
Good Morning, Babylon *'87*
And God Created Woman *'88*
High Frequency *'88*
City of Hope *'91*
Oscar *'91*
Afterburn *'92*
Alive *'93*
Indian Summer *'93*
The Ascent *'94*
The Tie That Binds *'95*

Adrian Sparks
Roanoak *'86*
My Stepmother Is an Alien *'88*

Ned Sparks
Corsair *'31*
Kept Husbands *'31*
42nd Street *'33*
Going Hollywood *'33*
Gold Diggers of 1933 *'33*
Lady for a Day *'33*
Marie Galante *'34*
Sweet Adeline *'35*
The Bride Walks Out *'36*
One in a Million *'36*
Hawaii Calls *'38*

Camilla Sparv
Dead Heat on a Merry-Go-Round *'66*
Downhill Racer *'69*
Survival Zone *'84*

Tracy Spaulding
The Deadly Secret *'94*
Striking Point *'94*

Jeff Speakman
The Perfect Weapon *'91*
Street Knight *'93*
The Expert *'95*

Carol Speed
The Big Bird Cage *'72*
Bummer *'73*
Mack *'73*
Savage! *'73*
Avenging Disco Godfather *'76*

Hermann Speelmanns
F.P. 1 Doesn't Answer *'33*
Baron Munchausen *'43*

Martin Speer
The Hills Have Eyes *'77*
The Dark Ride *'84*

Dona Speir
Hard Ticket to Hawaii *'87*
Picasso Trigger *'89*
Savage Beach *'89*
Guns *'90*
Do or Die *'91*
Hard Hunted *'92*
Fit to Kill *'93*

George Spell
Man & Boy *'71*
A Dream for Christmas *'73*
All God's Children *'80*

Tori Spelling
Beverly Hills 90210 *'90*
Beverly Hills 90210: The Graduation *'93*

Peter Spellos
Dinosaur Island *'93*
Bound *'96*

Georgina Spelvin
Honkytonk Nights *'70s*
I Spit on Your Corpse *'74*
Police Academy *'84*

Bruce Spence
The Road Warrior *'82*
Where the Green Ants Dream *'84*
Mad Max: Beyond Thunderdome *'85*
Midnite Spares *'85*
Rikky and Pete *'88*
...Almost *'90*
The Shrimp on the Barbie *'90*
Sweet Talker *'91*

Peter Spence
Crazy Moon *'87*
Unfinished Business *'89*

Bud Spencer
Ace High *'68*
Beyond the Law *'68*
Boot Hill *'69*
Today We Kill, Tomorrow We Die *'71*
They Call Me Trinity *'72*
All the Way, Boys *'73*
A Reason to Live, A Reason to Die *'73*
Trinity is Still My Name *'75*
Crime Busters *'78*
Flatfoot *'78*
Odds and Evens *'78*
Go for It *'83*
Miami Supercops *'85*
Aladdin *'86*
Troublemakers *'94*

Douglas Spencer
Trouble Along the Way *'53*
River of No Return *'54*

John Spencer
Echoes *'83*
Black Rain *'89*
Simple Justice *'89*
Presumed Innocent *'90*
Forget Paris *'95*
The Rock *'96*

Volker Spengler
Satan's Brew *'76*
The Stationmaster's Wife *'77*
Despair *'78*
In a Year of 13 Moons *'78*
Veronika Voss *'82*
Chinese Roulette *'86*

Jeremy Spenser
Devil on Horseback *'54*
Escapade *'55*
The Prince and the Showgirl *'57*

Wendie Jo Sperber
I Wanna Hold Your Hand *'78*
Bosom Buddies *'80*
First Time *'82*
Bachelor Party *'84*
Back to the Future *'85*
Moving Violations *'85*
Stewardess School *'86*
Back to the Future, Part 3 *'90*
Mr. Write *'92*

Scott Spiegel
The Dead Next Door *'89*
Skinned Alive *'89*

David Spielberg
Force Five *'75*
Sergeant Matlovich vs. the U.S. Air Force *'78*
The Henderson Monster *'80*
Prime Time *'80*
The Best Little Girl in the World *'81*
Policewoman Centerfold *'83*
The Stranger *'87*
Alice *'90*

Riva Spier
Ghost Keeper *'80*
Syngenor *'90*

Jacques Spiesser
Black and White in Color *'76*
La Truite *'83*
Baxter *'89*

Mickey Spillane
Girl Hunters *'63*
Mommy *'95*

Grazia Maria Spina
Tiger of the Seven Seas *'62*
Revolt of the Barbarians *'64*

Joe Spinell
Cops and Robbers *'73*
The Godfather, Part 2 *'74*
One Man Jury *'78*
Star Crash *'78*
Winter Kills *'79*
Little Dragons *'80*
Maniac *'80*
The Godfather 1902-1959: The Complete Epic *'81*
Nighthawks *'81*
The Last Fight *'82*
The Last Horror Film *'82*
Big Score *'83*
Walking the Edge *'83*
Hollywood Harry *'86*
The Pick-Up Artist *'87*
Operation War Zone *'89*
Rapid Fire *'89*

Brent Spiner
Family Sins *'87*
Star Trek the Next Generation: Encounter at Farpoint *'87*
Crazy from the Heart *'91*
Star Trek Generations *'94*
Star Trek the Next Generation, the Final Episode: All Good Things... *'94*
Independence Day *'96*
Phenomenon *'96*

Victor Spinetti
Magical Mystery Tour *'67*
Start the Revolution Without Me *'70*
Return of the Pink Panther *'74*

Gregory Sporleder
The Rock *'96*
Twister *'96*

G.D. Spradlin
Zabriskie Point *'70*
The Only Way Home *'72*
The Godfather, Part 2 *'74*
One on One *'77*
And I Alone Survived *'78*
Apocalypse Now *'79*
North Dallas Forty *'79*
The Formula *'80*
The Jayne Mansfield Story *'80*
The Godfather 1902-1959: The Complete Epic *'81*
Wrong is Right *'82*
The Lords of Discipline *'83*
Tank *'83*
Call to Glory *'84*
The War of the Roses *'89*
Carolina Skeletons *'92*
Canadian Bacon *'94*
Nick of Time *'95*
Riders of the Purple Sage *'96*

Charlie Spradling
Puppet Master 2 *'90*
Bad Channels *'92*
To Sleep with a Vampire *'92*
Angel of Destruction *'94*

Rick Springfield
Nick Knight *'80s*
Hard to Hold *'84*
Dead Reckoning *'89*
Silent Motive *'91*

Pamela Springsteen
Fast Times at Ridgemont High *'82*
Reckless *'84*
My Science Project *'85*
Dixie Lanes *'88*
Sleepaway Camp 2: Unhappy Campers *'88*
The Gumshoe Kid *'89*
Sleepaway Camp 3: Teenage Wasteland *'89*

Ronald Squire
Action for Slander *'38*
No Highway in the Sky *'51*
Encore *'52*

Robert Stack
First Love *'39*
The Mortal Storm *'40*
To Be or Not to Be *'42*
A Date with Judy *'48*
Bullfighter & the Lady *'50*
Mr. Music *'50*
My Outlaw Brother *'51*
Conquest of Cochise *'53*
Sabre Jet *'53*
Great Day in the Morning *'56*
Written on the Wind *'56*
Tarnished Angels *'57*
John Paul Jones *'59*
The Last Voyage *'60*
Scarface Mob *'62*
The Corrupt Ones *'67*
Is Paris Burning? *'68*
A Strange and Deadly Occurence *'74*
Murder on Flight 502 *'75*
Most Wanted *'76*
1941 *'79*
Airplane! *'80*
Strike Force *'81*
Uncommon Valor *'83*
George Washington *'84*
Big Trouble *'86*
Caddyshack 2 *'88*
Dangerous Curves *'88*
Plain Clothes *'88*
Joe Versus the Volcano *'90*
The Return of Eliot Ness *'91*

James Stacy
A Swingin' Summer *'65*
Paper Man *'71*
Posse *'75*
The Dark Side of Love *'79*
Double Exposure *'82*
Something Wicked This Way Comes *'83*
Matters of the Heart *'90*

Lewis J. Stadlen
Savages *'72*
Between the Lines *'77*
Windy City *'84*

Ann Stafford
Poor White Trash 2 *'75*
Keep My Grave Open *'80*

Frederick Stafford
The Battle of El Alamein *'68*
Topaz *'69*

Jim Stafford
E.S.P. *'83*
Kid Colter *'85*

Nick Stahl
The Man Without a Face *'93*

Safe Passage '94
Blue River '95
Tall Tale: The Unbelievable Adventures of Pecos Bill '95

Richard Stahl
The Student Nurses '70
Private School '83

Brent Stait
Born to Run '93
Call of the Wild '93

James Staley
American Dreamer '84
Protocol '84
Robot Wars '93

Joan Staley
Roustabout '64
The Ghost and Mr. Chicken '66

Frank Stallone
The Pink Chiquitas '86
Barfly '87
Death Blow '87
Outlaw Force '87
Take Two '87
Fear '88
Midnight Cop '88
Prime Suspect '88
Death Feud '89
Easy Kill '89
Heart of Midnight '89
Order of the Eagle '89
Ten Little Indians '89
Lethal Games '90
Masque of the Red Death '90
Terror in Beverly Hills '90
Hudson Hawk '91

Sage Stallone
Rocky 5 '90
Fatally Yours '95

Sylvester Stallone
The Italian Stallion '73
Rebel '73
The Lords of Flatbush '74
Prisoner of Second Avenue '74
Death Race 2000 '75
Farewell, My Lovely '75
Cannonball '76
Rocky '76
F.I.S.T. '78
Paradise Alley '78
Rocky 2 '79
Nighthawks '81
Victory '81
First Blood '82
Rocky 3 '82
Rhinestone '84
Rambo: First Blood, Part 2 '85
Rocky 4 '85
Cobra '86
Over the Top '86
Rambo 3 '88
Lock Up '89
Tango and Cash '89
Rocky 5 '90
Oscar '91
Stop! or My Mom Will Shoot '92
Cliffhanger '93
Demolition Man '93
The Specialist '94
Assassins '95
Judge Dredd '95

Anne Stallybrass
Six Wives of Henry VIII '70s
Diana: Her True Story '93

John Stamos
Never Too Young to Die '86
Born to Ride '91
The Disappearance of Christina '93

Terence Stamp
Billy Budd '62
The Collector '65
Far from the Madding Crowd '67
Blue '68
Iron Cowboy '68
Spirits of the Dead '68
Teorema '68
Divine Nymph '71
Superman: The Movie '78
The Thief of Baghdad '78
Meetings with Remarkable Men '79
Together? '79
Superman 2 '80
Vatican Conspiracy '81
Insanity '82
The Hit '85
Alamut Ambush '86
Cold War Killers '86
Deadly Recruits '86
Legal Eagles '86
Link '86
The Sicilian '87
Wall Street '87
Alien Nation '88
Young Guns '88
Genuine Risk '89
The Real McCoy '93
The Adventures of Priscilla, Queen of the Desert '94

Wadeck Stanczak
Rendez-vous '85
Scene of the Crime '87

Lionel Stander
I Live My Life '35
Mr. Deeds Goes to Town '36
A Star is Born '37
Guadalcanal Diary '43
Spectre of the Rose '46
Till the Clouds Roll By/A Star Is Born '46
The Sin of Harold Diddlebock '47
Call Northside 777 '48
Unfaithfully Yours '48
St. Benny the Dip '51
The Loved One '65
Cul de Sac '66
Promise Her Anything '66
Beyond the Law '68
Dandy in Aspic '68
Once Upon a Time in the West '68
Boot Hill '69
1931: Once Upon a Time in New York '72
Pulp '72
Treasure Island '72
The Sensual Man '74
Black Bird '75
Black Hand '76
The Cassandra Crossing '76
Sting of the West '76
New York, New York '77
The Squeeze '80
The Heist '88
Cookie '89
Wicked Stepmother '89
The Last Good Time '94

Guy Standing
The Lives of a Bengal Lancer '35
I'd Give My Life '36
Lloyds of London '36
Bulldog Drummond Comes Back '37
Bulldog Drummond Escapes '37

John Standing
Walk, Don't Run '66
Rogue Male '76
The Legacy '79
To Catch a King '84
Nightflyers '87
The Endless Game '89
Chaplin '92
Gulliver's Travels '95

Arnold Stang
Seven Days' Leave '42
The Man with the Golden Arm '55
The Wonderful World of the Brothers Grimm '62
Hercules in New York '70
Ghost Dad '90
Dennis the Menace '93

Florence Stanley
A Perfect Little Murder '90
Trouble Bound '92
Trapped In Paradise '94

Forrest Stanley
Bare Knees '28
Outlaws of the Desert '41

Helene Stanley
Bandit King of Texas '49
The Snows of Kilimanjaro '52

Kim Stanley
The Goddess '58
Seance on a Wet Afternoon '64
Frances '82
The Right Stuff '83

Louise Stanley
Gun Lords of Stirrup Basin '37
Riders of the Rockies '37
Danger on the Air '38
Gun Packer '38
Thunder in the Desert '38
Pinto Canyon '40
Sky Bandits '40

Paul Stanley
I Heard the Owl Call My Name '73
KISS Meets the Phantom of the Park '78

Rebecca Stanley
Body Double '84
Eyes of Fire '84

Don Stannard
Dick Barton, Special Agent '48
Dick Barton Strikes Back '48
The Temptress '49

Claire Stansfield
The Swordsman '92
Best of the Best 2 '93
Drop Zone '94
Sensation '94
Red Shoe Diaries 5: Weekend Pass '95
Wes Craven Presents Mind Ripper '95

Harry Dean Stanton
Proud Rebel '58
The Adventures of Huckleberry Finn '60
Cool Hand Luke '67
The Hostage '67
Ride in the Whirlwind '67
Rebel Rousers '69
Kelly's Heroes '70
Dillinger '73
Pat Garrett & Billy the Kid '73
Cockfighter '74
The Godfather, Part 2 '74
Where the Lilies Bloom '74
Zandy's Bride '74
Farewell, My Lovely '75
Rafferty & the Gold Dust Twins '75
Rancho Deluxe '75
Missouri Breaks '76
92 in the Shade '76
Straight Time '78
Alien '79
The Black Marble '79
Flatbed Annie and Sweetiepie: Lady Truckers '79
The Rose '79
Wise Blood '79
Death Watch '80
Private Benjamin '80
Escape from New York '81
The Godfather 1902-1959: The Complete Epic '81
Uforia '81
Oldest Living Graduate '82
One from the Heart '82
Young Doctors in Love '82
Paris, Texas '83
Repo Man '83
Christine '84
Red Dawn '84
One Magic Christmas '85
Rip van Winkle '85
Fool for Love '86
Pretty in Pink '86
Slamdance '87
The Last Temptation of Christ '88
Mr. North '88
Stars and Bars '88
Dream a Little Dream '89
Twister '89
The Fourth War '90
Wild at Heart '90
Payoff '91
Man Trouble '92
Hostages '93
Hotel Room '93
Against the Wall '94
Blue Tiger '94
Never Talk to Strangers '95
Playback '95
Down Periscope '96

John Stanton
Bellamy '80
Dusty '85
The Naked Country '85
Tai-Pan '86
Great Expectations: The Untold Story '87
Day of the Panther '88
Rent-A-Cop '88

Paul Stanton
Stanley and Livingstone '39
Whistling in the Dark '41

Robert Stanton
Bob Roberts '92
Dennis the Menace '93

Barbara Stanwyck
Illicit '31
Night Nurse '31
The Purchase Price '32
Baby Face '33
The Bitter Tea of General Yen '33
Ladies They Talk About '33
Annie Oakley '35
The Bride Walks Out '36
Internes Can't Take Money '37
Stella Dallas '37
Mad Miss Manton '38
Golden Boy '39
Union Pacific '39
Remember the Night '40
Ball of Fire '41
The Lady Eve '41
Meet John Doe '41
The Great Man's Lady '42
Lady of Burlesque '43
Double Indemnity '44
Hollywood Canteen '44
Christmas in Connecticut '45
The Strange Love of Martha Ivers '46
Cry Wolf '47
The Two Mrs. Carrolls '47
Sorry, Wrong Number '48
East Side, West Side '49
Hollywood Bloopers '50s
To Please a Lady '50
Clash by Night '52
All I Desire '53
Titanic '53
Blowing Wild '54
Cattle Queen of Montana '54
Executive Suite '54
Escape to Burma '55
The Maverick Queen '55
The Violent Men '55
Crime of Passion '57
Walk on the Wild Side '62
The Night Walker '64
Roustabout '64
Big Valley '68
The Thorn Birds '83

Huub Stapel
The Lift '85
Amsterdamned '88
The Attic: The Hiding of Anne Frank '88

Jean Stapleton
Damn Yankees '58
Bells are Ringing '60
Up the Down Staircase '67
Cold Turkey '71
Klute '71
Eleanor: First Lady of the World '82
The Buddy System '83
Jack & the Beanstalk '83
Cinderella '84
Grown Ups '86
Mother Goose Rock 'n' Rhyme '90
The Habitation of Dragons '91

Maureen Stapleton
Lonelyhearts '58
The Fugitive Kind '60
Bye, Bye, Birdie '63
Airport '70
Plaza Suite '71
Tell Me Where It Hurts '74
Queen of the Stardust Ballroom '75
The Gathering '77
Interiors '78
The Gathering: Part 2 '79
Lost and Found '79
The Runner Stumbles '79
The Fan '81
On the Right Track '81
Reds '81
Family Secrets '84
Johnny Dangerously '84
Little Gloria...Happy at Last '84
Cocoon '85
Heartburn '86
The Money Pit '86
Made in Heaven '87
Nuts '87
Sweet Lorraine '87
Cocoon: The Return '88
Doin' Time on Planet Earth '88
Miss Rose White '92
Passed Away '92
The Last Good Time '94
Trading Mom '94

Don Stark
Evilspeak '82
Bloodfist 5: Human Target '93

Graham Stark
Adventures Beyond Belief '87
Blind Date '87

Jonathan Stark
Fright Night '85
House 2: The Second Story '87
Project X '87

Koo Stark
Emily '77
Electric Dreams '84

Anthony Starke
Return of the Killer Tomatoes! '88
Repossessed '90

Pauline Starke
Until They Get Me '18
Little Church Around the Corner '23
Dante's Inferno '24

Beau Starr
Manhunt for Claude Dallas '86
Dead Air '94
Never Talk to Strangers '95

Mike Starr
Nasty Hero '89
Goodfellas '90
Billy Bathgate '91
The Bodyguard '92
Mad Dog and Glory '93
Mardi Gras for the Devil '93
Dumb & Dumber '94
Two If by Sea '95

Ringo Starr
A Hard Day's Night '64
Help! '65
Magical Mystery Tour '67
The Magic Christian '69
Let It Be '70
200 Motels '71
Born to Boogie '72
That'll Be the Day '73
Lisztomania '75
Sextette '78
Caveman '81
The Compleat Beatles '82
Princess Daisy '83
Give My Regards to Broad Street '84

Charles Starrett
The Mask of Fu Manchu '32
Jungle Bride '33
Mr. Skitch '33
Dangerous Appointment '34
Green Eyes '34
The Return of Casey Jones '34
The Silver Streak '34
Make a Million '35
A Shot in the Dark '35
Sons of Steel '35

Jack Starrett
Angels from Hell '68
Mr. Horn '79
First Blood '82
Death Chase '87
Brothers in Arms '88
Nightwish '89

Imelda Staunton
Antonia and Jane '91
Peter's Friends '92
Deadly Advice '93
Much Ado about Nothing '93
Citizen X '95
Sense and Sensibility '95

Mary Stavin
House '86
Open House '86
The Opponent '89

Eddie Stazak
Fists of Blood '87
Day of the Panther '88

Alison Steadman
Hard Labour '73
Nuts in May '76
Abigail's Party '77
Kipperbang '82
Champions '84
Clockwise '86
The Adventures of Baron Munchausen '89

Steadman ▶cont.

Shirley Valentine '89
Coming Through '90
Life Is Sweet '90
The Misadventures of Mr. Wilt '90
Tartuffe '90
Blame It on the Bellboy '92
Pride and Prejudice '95

John Steadman
The Hills Have Eyes '77
Poco '77

Red Steagall
Benji the Hunted '87
Dark Before Dawn '89

Michael Stearns
Chrome and Hot Leather '71
Chain Gang Women '72

Myrtle Stedman
In the Days of the Thundering Herd & the Law & the Outlaw '14
Sex '20
The Mad Whirl '25

Alan Steel
The Fury of Hercules '61
Samson '61
Hercules Against the Moon Men '64
Samson and His Mighty Challenge '64

Amy Steel
Friday the 13th, Part 2 '81
April Fool's Day '86
Walk Like a Man '87
What Ever Happened To... '93

Anthony Steel
Wooden Horse '50
Malta Story '53
The Master of Ballantrae '53
Harry Black and the Tiger '58
48 Hours to Live '60
Tiger of the Seven Seas '62
Massacre in Rome '73
I'm the Girl He Wants to Kill '74
The Story of O '75
Perfect Crime '78

Barbara Steele
Black Sunday '60
La Dolce Vita '60
The Pit and the Pendulum '61
The Horrible Dr. Hichcock '62
8 1/2 '63
The Ghost '63
Castle of Blood '64
The Monocle '64
Nightmare Castle '65
The She-Beast '65
An Angel for Satan '66
Terror Creatures from the Grave '66
The Crimson Cult '68
Caged Heat '74
They Came from Within '75
Piranha '78
Pretty Baby '78
Silent Scream '80
The Winds of War '83
Dark Shadows: Episode 1 '91

Bob Steele
Texas Trouble '30s
Near the Rainbow's End '30
Oklahoma Cyclone '30
Sunrise Trail '31
Hidden Valley '32
Man from Hell's Edges '32
Riders of the Desert '32
South of Santa Fe '32
Texas Buddies '32
Breed of the Border '33
Fighting Champ '33
The Gallant Fool '33
Galloping Romeo '33
Mystery Squadron '33
Young Blood '33
Brand of Hate '34
Demon for Trouble '34
The Gun Ranger '34
Tombstone Terror '34
Alias John Law '35
Big Calibre '35
Kid Courageous '35
No Man's Range '35
Powdersmoke Range '35
Rider of the Law '35
Trail of Terror '35
Western Justice '35
Brand of the Outlaws '36
Cavalry '36
Kid Ranger '36
Last of the Warrens '36
The Law Rides '36
Smokey Smith '36
Sundown Saunders '36
Arizona Gunfighter '37
Border Phantom '37
Doomed at Sundown '37
Gun Lords of Stirrup Basin '37
Lightning Bill Crandall '37
Paroled to Die '37
The Red Rope '37
Ridin' the Lone Trail '37
Durango Valley Raiders '38
Feud Maker '38
Thunder in the Desert '38
El Diablo Rides '39
Mesquite Buckaroo '39
Of Mice and Men '39
Battling Outlaws '40s
Trails West '40s
Billy the Kid in Texas '40
City for Conquest '40
Pinto Canyon '40
Trigger Men '41
Twilight on the Rio Grande '41
Arizona Whirlwind '44
Death Valley Rangers '44
Marked Trails '44
Outlaw Trail '44
Sonora Stagecoach '44
Wildfire '45
Ambush Trail '46
The Big Sleep '46
Northwest Trail '46
Rio Grande Raiders '46
Western Double Feature 6: Rogers & Trigger '50
The Enforcer '51
Pardners '56
Giant from the Unknown '58
Atomic Submarine '59
Pork Chop Hill '59
Rio Bravo '59

Jadrien Steele
The Mosquito Coast '86
The Secret Garden '87

Karen Steele
Marty '55
Bail Out at 43,000 '57
Ride Lonesome '59
The Rise and Fall of Legs Diamond '60
Trap on Cougar Mountain '72

Marjorie Steele
Tough Assignment '49
Face to Face '52

Pippa Steele
The Vampire Lovers '70
Lust for a Vampire '71

Tommy Steele
G-Men Never Forget '48
Half a Sixpence '67
The Happiest Millionaire '67
Finian's Rainbow '68

Jessica Steen
John and the Missus '87
Sing '89
Still Life '92

Mary Steenburgen
Goin' South '78
Time After Time '79
Melvin and Howard '80
Ragtime '81
A Midsummer Night's Sex Comedy '82
Cross Creek '83
Little Red Riding Hood '83
Romantic Comedy '83
One Magic Christmas '85
Dead of Winter '87
The Whales of August '87
The Attic: The Hiding of Anne Frank '88
End of the Line '88
Miss Firecracker '89
Parenthood '89
Back to the Future, Part 3 '90
The Butcher's Wife '91
Clifford '92
Philadelphia '93
What's Eating Gilbert Grape '93
My Summer Story '94
Pontiac Moon '94
Gulliver's Travels '95
Nixon '95
Powder '95

Anthony Steffen
The Last Tomahawk '65
An Angel for Satan '66
Garringo '69
The Night Evelyn Came Out of the Grave '71
Stranger in Paso Bravo '73
The Gentleman Killer '78
On the Edge '82
Savage Island '85
Escape from Hell '89

Bernice Stegers
Frozen Terror '80
City of Women '81
Xtro '83
The Girl '86
A Dark Adapted Eye '93
To Play the King '93

Rod Steiger
On the Waterfront '54
The Big Knife '55
The Court Martial of Billy Mitchell '55
Oklahoma! '55
Back from Eternity '56
The Harder They Fall '56
Jubal '56
Run of the Arrow '56
Across the Bridge '57
Unholy Wife '57
Al Capone '59
Seven Thieves '60
The Mark '61
The Longest Day '62
Time of Indifference '64
Doctor Zhivago '65
The Loved One '65
The Pawnbroker '65
In the Heat of the Night '67
No Way to Treat a Lady '68
The Illustrated Man '69
Waterloo '71
A Fistful of Dynamite '72
Lucky Luciano '74
Hennessy '75
Dirty Hands '76
Last Four Days '77
Portrait of a Hitman '77
Breakthrough '78
F.I.S.T. '78
The Amityville Horror '79
Klondike Fever '79
Love and Bullets '79
Wolf Lake '79
The Chosen '81
Lion of the Desert '81
The Glory Boys '84
The Naked Face '84
The Last Contract '86
Sword of Gideon '86
Catch the Heat '87
The Kindred '87
American Gothic '88
The January Man '89
Passion in Paradise '89
That Summer of White Roses '90
The Ballad of the Sad Cafe '91
Midnight Murders '91
Guilty as Charged '92
Sinatra '92
The Neighbor '93
Black Water '94
The Specialist '94
Captain Nuke and the Bomber Boys '95
Dalva '95
In Pursuit of Honor '95
Out There '95

Margaret Sophie Stein
Enemies, a Love Story '89
Sarah, Plain and Tall '91
Skylark '93

David Steinberg
The End '78
Something Short of Paradise '79
The Marx Brothers in a Nutshell '90

John Steiner
Massacre in Rome '73
Beyond the Door 2 '79
Blood and Guns '79
Dagger Eyes '80s
The Last Hunter '80
Ark of the Sun God '82
Hunters of the Golden Cobra '82
Yor, the Hunter from the Future '83
Operation 'Nam '85
The Lone Runner '88
Sinbad of the Seven Seas '89

Sherry Steiner
Asylum of Satan '72
Three on a Meathook '72
Heaven Help Us '85

Robert J. Steinmiller, Jr.
Bingo '91
Jack the Bear '93
The Ref '93

William Steis
Equalizer 2000 '86
Demon of Paradise '87
Eye of the Eagle '87
Raiders of the Sun '92

Anna Sten
The Girl with the Hat Box '27
So Ends Our Night '41
Soldier of Fortune '55

Yutte Stensgaard
Alien Women '69
The Love Factor '69
Scream and Scream Again '70
Lust for a Vampire '71

Karel Stepanek
Secret Mission '42
Counterblast '48
Never Let Me Go '53
Sink the Bismarck '60
Second Best Secret Agent in the Whole Wide World '65

Daniel Stephen
2020 Texas Gladiators '85
Warbus '85

Susan Stephen
A Stolen Face '52
Heat Wave '54
White Huntress '57

Harvey Stephens
Evelyn Prentice '34
Let 'Em Have It '35
Forlorn River '37
The Texans '38
Oklahoma Kid '39
Abe Lincoln in Illinois '40
The Texas Rangers Ride Again '40
The Lady is Willing '42

James Stephens
First Monday in October '81
Mysterious Two '82
Pancho Barnes '88

Martin Stephens
Village of the Damned '60
The Innocents '61

Robert Stephens
A Taste of Honey '61
Morgan! '66
The Prime of Miss Jean Brodie '69
The Private Life of Sherlock Holmes '70
The Asphyx '72
Travels with My Aunt '72
Luther '74
Empire of the Sun '87
Fortunes of War '87
American Roulette '88
High Season '88
Wonderland '88
Henry V '89
The Bonfire of the Vanities '90
The Children '90
Afraid of the Dark '92
Chaplin '92
Searching for Bobby Fischer '93
Century '94
The Secret Rapture '94

Henry Stephenson
The Animal Kingdom '32
A Bill of Divorcement '32
Red Headed Woman '32
Tomorrow at Seven '33
Mutiny on the Bounty '35
The Charge of the Light Brigade '36
Conquest '37
The Prince and the Pauper '37
Marie Antoinette '38
The Old Maid '39
Tarzan Finds a Son '39
Down Argentine Way '40
It's a Date '40
Lady from Louisiana '42
Mr. Lucky '43
Heartbeat '46
Oliver Twist '48
Challenge to Lassie '49

James Stephenson
Boy Meets Girl '38
Beau Geste '39
The Letter '40
The Sea Hawk '40

Mark Kinsey Stephenson
The Unnamable '88
The Unnamable 2: The Statement of Randolph Carter '92

Michael Stephenson
Beyond Darkness '92
Troll 2 '92

Pamela Stephenson
The Comeback '77
History of the World: Part 1 '81
Finders Keepers '84
Scandalous '84
Bloodbath at the House of Death '85
Ghosts Can Do It '90
Les Patterson Saves the World '90

Craig Stepp
Indecent Behavior 2 '94
Married People, Single Sex 2: For Better or Worse '94
Play Time '94

Ford Sterling
Yankee Doodle in Berlin '19
Mack Sennett Comedies: Vol. 1 '21
Desperate Scoundrel/The Pride of Pikeville '22
He Who Gets Slapped '24
Headline Woman '35

Jan Sterling
Union Station '50
Pony Express '53
Split Second '53
The Harder They Fall '56
High School Confidential '58
The Incident '67
The Dark Side of Love '79
First Monday in October '81

Robert Sterling
Two-Faced Woman '41
Johnny Eager '42
Somewhere I'll Find You '42
Return to Peyton Place '61
Voyage to the Bottom of the Sea '61
A Global Affair '63

Tisha Sterling
Coogan's Bluff '68
Defiant '70
Powder Keg '70
Snatched '72
Betrayal '74
Killer Inside Me '76

Daniel Stern
Breaking Away '79
Starting Over '79
It's My Turn '80
One Trick Pony '80
Stardust Memories '80
Diner '82
I'm Dancing as Fast as I Can '82
Blue Thunder '83
Get Crazy '83
C.H.U.D. '84
Frankenweenie '84
Key Exchange '85
The Boss' Wife '86
Hannah and Her Sisters '86
Born in East L.A. '87
D.O.A. '88
The Milagro Beanfield War '88
Weekend War '88
Friends, Lovers & Lunatics '89
Leviathan '89
Little Monsters '89

Coupe de Ville '90
The Court Martial of Jackie Robinson '90
Home Alone '90
My Blue Heaven '90
City Slickers '91
Home Alone 2: Lost in New York '92
Rookie of the Year '93
City Slickers 2: The Legend of Curly's Gold '94
Bushwhacked '95
Celtic Pride '96

Tom Stern
Angels from Hell '68
The Devil's Brigade '68
Hell's Angels '69 '69

Wes Stern
The First Time '69
Three in the Cellar '70

Frances Sternhagen
Starting Over '79
Mother & Daughter: A Loving War '80
Outland '81
Who'll Save Our Children? '82
Independence Day '83
Prototype '83
Romantic Comedy '83
The Dining Room '86
Bright Lights, Big City '88
Communion '89
See You in the Morning '89
Misery '90
Sibling Rivalry '90
Doc Hollywood '91
Stephen King's Golden Years '91
Raising Cain '92

Robyn Stevan
Bye Bye Blues '89
Stepping Out '91

Jean-Francois Stevenin
Small Change '76
Olivier, Olivier '92

Andrew Stevens
Las Vegas Lady '76
Massacre at Central High '76
The Boys in Company C '77
Day of the Animals '77
Secrets '77
The Bastard '78
The Fury '78
The Rebels '79
Death Hunt '81
Miracle on Ice '81
Forbidden Love '82
The Seduction '82
Ten to Midnight '83
Counterforce '87
Scared Stiff '87
Deadly Innocence '88
Fine Gold '88
The Ranch '88
The Terror Within '88
Down the Drain '89
Tusks '89
Night Eyes '90
Red Blooded American Girl '90
Night Eyes 2 '91
The Terror Within 2 '91
Deadly Rivals '92
Double Threat '92
Munchie '92
Body Chemistry 3: Point of Seduction '93
Eyewitness to Murder '93
Night Eyes 3 '93
Scorned '93
Illicit Dreams '94
Night Eyes 4: Fatal Passion '95

Brinke Stevens
The Slumber Party Massacre '82
Nightmare Sisters '87
Slave Girls from Beyond Infinity '87
Sorority Babes in the Slimeball Bowl-A-Rama '87
Grandma's House '88
Warlords '88
Transylvania Twist '89
Bad Girls from Mars '90
Spirits '90
Haunting Fear '91
Teenage Exorcist '93
Mommy '95

Charles Stevens
The Three Musketeers '21
Aces and Eights '36
Border Bandits '46
Buffalo Bill Rides Again '47

Connie Stevens
Parrish '61
Palm Springs Weekend '63
The Littlest Angel '69
The Grissom Gang '71
Playmates '72
Scorchy '76
Love's Savage Fury '79
Scruples '80
Side Show '84
Back to the Beach '87
Tapeheads '89

Craig Stevens
Dive Bomber '41
Since You Went Away '44
Humoresque '46
The Man I Love '46
Blues Busters '50
Drums in the Deep South '51
Abbott and Costello Meet Dr. Jekyll and Mr. Hyde '52
Phone Call from a Stranger '52
The French Line '54
The Deadly Mantis '57
Secrets of Three Hungry Wives '78
S.O.B. '81
La Truite '83

Fisher Stevens
The Flamingo Kid '84
My Science Project '85
Short Circuit '86
Short Circuit 2 '88
Reversal of Fortune '90
The Marrying Man '91
Mystery Date '91
When the Party's Over '91
Super Mario Bros. '93
Nina Takes a Lover '94
Only You '94
Hackers '95
The Right to Remain Silent '95

Inger Stevens
The Buccaneer '58
A Guide for the Married Man '67
Hang 'Em High '67
Firecreek '68
Five Card Stud '68
Madigan '68
A Dream of Kings '69
Savage Run '70

K.T. Stevens
Port of New York '49
Harriet Craig '50
Jungle Hell '55
Missile to the Moon '59
They're Playing with Fire '84

Mark Stevens
Objective, Burma! '45
Dark Corner '46
The Snake Pit '48
The Street with No Name '48
Mutiny '52
Torpedo Alley '53
Cry Vengeance '54
Frozen Alive '64

Morgan Stevens
Up River '79
Survival Zone '84

Onslow Stevens
I Can't Escape '34
The Three Musketeers '35
Yellow Dust '36
Flight from Glory '37
The Monster and the Girl '41
Hands Across the Border '43
Seven Miles from Alcatraz/Flight from Glory '43
House of Dracula '45
Angel on My Shoulder '46
The Creeper '48
One Too Many '51
A Lion Is in the Streets '53
Fangs of the Wild '54
Them! '54
Tribute to a Bad Man '56

Paul Stevens
Exodus '60
The Mask '61
Hercules and the Princess of Troy '65
Get Christie Love! '74

Rise Stevens
The Chocolate Soldier '41
Going My Way '44

Stella Stevens
Li'l Abner '59
The Courtship of Eddie's Father '62
Girls! Girls! Girls! '62
The Nutty Professor '63
Where Angels Go, Trouble Follows '68
Ballad of Cable Hogue '70
Slaughter '72
A Town Called Hell '72
Arnold '73
Cleopatra Jones & the Casino of Gold '75
Las Vegas Lady '76
Cruise into Terror '78
The Manitou '78
Express to Terror '79
Make Me an Offer '80
Twirl '81
Chained Heat '83
Power, Passion & Murder '83
Wacko '83
The Amazons '84
The Longshot '86
Monster in the Closet '86
Adventures Beyond Belief '87
Down the Drain '89
Mom '89
Exiled in America '90
Last Call '90
The Terror Within 2 '91
Eye of the Stranger '93
The Granny '94
Hard Drive '94
Molly and Gina '94
National Lampoon's Attack of the 5 Ft. 2 Women '94
Virtual Combat '95

Warren Stevens
Shark River '53
Forbidden Planet '56
Man or Gun '58

Cynthia Stevenson
The Player '92
Watch It '93
Forget Paris '95
Home for the Holidays '95
Live Nude Girls '95
The Reluctant Agent '95

Juliet Stevenson
Drowning by Numbers '87
Truly, Madly, Deeply '91
The Trial '93
The Secret Rapture '94
Emma '96

McLean Stevenson
M*A*S*H: The Collector's Edition '72
Win, Place, or Steal '72
The Cat from Outer Space '78

Parker Stevenson
A Separate Peace '73
Our Time '74
Lifeguard '75
Stroker Ace '83
Shooting Stars '85
Stitches '85
North and South Book 2 '86
Are You Lonesome Tonight '92
Official Denial '93

Robert Stevenson
Fangs of the Wild '54
One of Our Dinosaurs Is Missing '75

Venetia Stevenson
Darby's Rangers '58
Horror Hotel '60

Joe Stewardson
Follow That Rainbow '66
Flatfoot '78
City of Blood '88

Alexandra Stewart
Exodus '60
RoGoPaG '62
Mickey One '65
Zeppelin '71
Day for Night '73
Because of the Cats '74
The Destructors '74
In Praise of Older Women '78
The Agency '81
Last Chase '81
Kemek '88

Athole Stewart
The Speckled Band '31
Accused '36

Byron Stewart
The White Shadow, Vol. 1 '78
Grambling's White Tiger '81
How U Like Me Now? '92

Catherine Mary Stewart
The Apple '80
Nighthawks '81
The Last Starfighter '84
Night of the Comet '84
Mischief '85
Sins '85
Dudes '87
Murder by the Book '87
Nightflyers '87
Scenes from the Goldmine '87
World Gone Wild '88
Passion in Paradise '89
Weekend at Bernie's '89
Cafe Romeo '91
Perfect Harmony '91
Psychic '91
Samurai Cowboy '93
The Sea Wolf '93
Number One Fan '94
Out of Annie's Past '94

Charlotte Stewart
Eraserhead '78
Tremors '89
Dark Angel: The Ascent '94

Don Stewart
The Doomsday Flight '66
Lost '83

Elaine Stewart
Riders of the Timberline '41
The Rise and Fall of Legs Diamond '60

Eleanor Stewart
The Gun Ranger '34
Headin' for the Rio Grande '36
Arizona Days '37
The Rangers Step In '37
Where Trails Divide '37
Flaming Lead '39
Mystery Man '44

Evelyn Stewart
Adios Gringo '65
Blood for a Silver Dollar '66
Murder Mansion '70
The Scorpion's Tail '71
Django Shoots First '74
The Psychic '78

Frank Stewart
Galactic Gigolo '87
Psychos in Love '87
Sensations '87
Sexpot '88
Cemetery High '89

James Stewart
After the Thin Man '36
Born to Dance '36
The Gorgeous Hussy '36
Rose Marie '36
Wife Versus Secretary '36
Navy Blue and Gold '37
Of Human Hearts '38
Shopworn Angel '38
Vivacious Lady '38
You Can't Take It with You '38
Destry Rides Again '39
Made for Each Other '39
Mr. Smith Goes to Washington '39
The Mortal Storm '40
The Philadelphia Story '40
The Shop Around the Corner '40
Pot O' Gold '41
Ziegfeld Girl '41
It's a Wonderful Life '46
Magic Town '47
Call Northside 777 '48
Rope '48
Malaya '49
The Stratton Story '49
Hollywood Bloopers '50s
Broken Arrow '50
Harvey '50
The Jackpot '50
Winchester '73 '50
No Highway in the Sky '51
Bend of the River '52
The Greatest Show on Earth '52
The Naked Spur '53
Thunder Bay '53
The Glenn Miller Story '54
Rear Window '54
Far Country '55
The Man from Laramie '55
Strategic Air Command '55
The Man Who Knew Too Much '56
Spirit of St. Louis '57
Bell, Book and Candle '58
Vertigo '58
Anatomy of a Murder '59
The FBI Story '59
The Mountain Road '60
Two Rode Together '61
The Man Who Shot Liberty Valance '62
Mr. Hobbs Takes a Vacation '62
How the West Was Won '63
Dear Brigitte '65
The Flight of the Phoenix '65
Shenandoah '65
The Rare Breed '66
Bandolero! '68
Firecreek '68
The Cheyenne Social Club '70
The Shootist '76
Airport '77 '77
The Big Sleep '78
Magic of Lassie '78
Green Horizon '83
Right of Way '84
North and South Book 2 '86

John Stewart
Boots Malone '52
Last of the Comanches '52

Kate McGregor Stewart
Father of the Bride '91
Father of the Bride Part II '95
Safe '95

Melvin Stewart
A Session with the Committee '69
Scorpio '73

Patrick Stewart
Hedda '75
Excalibur '81
Code Name: Emerald '85
The Doctor and the Devils '85
Lady Jane '85
Lifeforce '85
Star Trek the Next Generation: Encounter at Farpoint '87
L.A. Story '91
Detonator '93
Gunmen '93
Star Trek Generations '94
Star Trek the Next Generation, the Final Episode: All Good Things... '94
Jeffrey '95
The Canterville Ghost '96

Paul Stewart
Citizen Kane '41
Mr. Lucky '43
Easy Living '49
Twelve O'Clock High '49
Walk Softly, Stranger '50
The Joe Louis Story '53
The Cobweb '55
Kiss Me Deadly '55
King Creole '58
How to Commit Marriage '69
Bite the Bullet '75
Murph the Surf '75
Opening Night '77
The Tempest '82
Seduced '85

Peggy Stewart
Rough Riders of Cheyenne '45
The Vampire's Ghost '45
The Phantom Rider '46
Stagecoach to Denver '46
Vigilantes of Boom Town '46
Son of Zorro '47
The Fighting Redhead '50
The Black Lash '52

Penelope Stewart
Vigil '84
Boulevard of Broken Dreams '88

Richard Stewart
Terror Ship '54
Watch Me When I Kill '81

Robert Stewart
Annie O '95
Someone to Die For '95

Roy Stewart
With Kit Carson Over the Great Divide '25
Sparrows '26
Rustler's Roundup '33

Sophie Stewart
Murder in the Old Red Barn '36
Devil Girl from Mars '54

Trish Stewart
Breaking Up Is Hard to Do '79
Wild Times '79

Phyllis Stickney
Talkin' Dirty After Dark '91
What's Love Got to Do with It? '93
The Inkwell '94

David Ogden Stiers
Oh, God! '77
Sergeant Matlovich vs. the U.S. Air Force '78
Breaking Up Is Hard to Do '79
Damien: The Leper Priest '80
Oldest Living Graduate '82
M*A*S*H: Goodbye, Farewell & Amen '83
The First Olympics: Athens 1896 '84
Harry's War '84
The Innocents Abroad '84
The Bad Seed '85
Better Off Dead '85
Creator '85
The Man with One Red Shoe '85
North and South Book 1 '85
J. Edgar Hoover '87
Perry Mason: The Case of the Lost Love '87
The Accidental Tourist '88
Another Woman '88
Day One '89
The Final Days '89
Final Notice '89
The Kissing Place '90
Doc Hollywood '91
The Last of His Tribe '92
Shadows and Fog '92
Iron Will '93
Bad Company '94
Past Tense '94
Mighty Aphrodite '95
Steal Big, Steal Little '95

Hugo Stiglitz
Night of a Thousand Cats '72
Robinson Crusoe & the Tiger '72
Fantastic Balloon Voyage '80s
City of the Walking Dead '83
Counterforce '87

Robin Stille
The Slumber Party Massacre '82
American Ninja 4: The Annihilation '91

Ben Stiller
Empire of the Sun '87
Fresh Horses '88
Elvis Stories '89
Next of Kin '89
Stella '89
Heavyweights '94
Reality Bites '94
Flirting with Disaster '95
If Lucy Fell '95
Happy Gilmore '96

Jerry Stiller
The Taking of Pelham One Two Three '74
The Ritz '76
Nasty Habits '77
Those Lips, Those Eyes '80
The McGuffin '85
Seize the Day '86
Hot Pursuit '87
Nadine '87
Hairspray '88
Little Vegas '90
That's Adequate '90
Women & Men: In Love There Are No Rules '91
The Pickle '93
Heavyweights '94

Sting
Quadrophenia '79
Brimstone & Treacle '82
The Secret Policeman's Other Ball '82
Dune '84
The Bride '85
Plenty '85
Julia and Julia '87
Stormy Monday '88
The Adventures of Baron Munchausen '89

Linda Stirling
Perils of the Darkest Jungle '44
Zorro's Black Whip '44
D-Day on Mars '45
Manhunt of Mystery Island '45
The Purple Monster Strikes '45
The Topeka Terror '45
Cyclotrode "X" '46
Rio Grande Raiders '46
Jesse James Rides Again '47

Brian Stirner
All Creatures Great and Small '74
Poldark 2 '75

Barbara Stock
Long Time Gone '86
Verne Miller '88

Nigel Stock
Brighton Rock '47
The Silent Enemy '58
The Lion in Winter '68

Amy Stock-Poynton
Bill & Ted's Excellent Adventure '89
Bill & Ted's Bogus Journey '91
Beanstalk '94

Carl Stockdale
The Americano '17
The Greatest Question '19
Get That Girl '32
Condemned to Live '35
The Crimson Trail '35

Dean Stockwell
Anchors Aweigh '45
Gentleman's Agreement '47
Song of the Thin Man '47
The Boy with the Green Hair '48
The Secret Garden '49
Kim '50
Stars in My Crown '50
Compulsion '59
Long Day's Journey into Night '62
Psych-Out '68
The Dunwich Horror '70
Paper Man '71
Loners '72
Win, Place, or Steal '72
Werewolf of Washington '73
Tracks '76
She Came to the Valley '77
One Away '80
Alsino and the Condor '82
Wrong is Right '82
Paris, Texas '83
Dune '84
To Kill a Stranger '84
Legend of Billie Jean '85
To Live & Die in L.A. '85
Banzai Runner '86
Blue Velvet '86
Beverly Hills Cop 2 '87
Gardens of Stone '87
Kenny Rogers as the Gambler, Part 3: The Legend Continues '87
The Time Guardian '87
Blue Iguana '88
Married to the Mob '88
Palais Royale '88
Tucker: The Man and His Dream '88
Backtrack '89
Buying Time '89
Limit Up '89
Stickfighter '89
Smokescreen '90
Son of the Morning Star '91
The Player '92
Shame '92
Bonanza: The Return '93
Madonna: Innocence Lost '95
Mr. Wrong '95
Stephen King's The Langoliers '95

Guy Stockwell
The War Lord '65
And Now Miguel '66
Tobruk '66
The Gatling Gun '72
It's Alive '74
Grotesque '87
Santa Sangre '90

John Stockwell
Losin' It '82
Christine '84
City Limits '85
My Science Project '85
Quarterback Princess '85
Dangerously Close '86
Radioactive Dreams '86
Top Gun '86
Billionaire Boys Club '87
Eyes of the Panther '90
Born to Ride '91

Malcolm Stoddard
The Godsend '79
The Assassination Run '84

Austin Stoker
Twisted Brain '74
Sheba, Baby '75
Assault on Precinct 13 '76
The Uninvited '88

Barry Stokes
Space: 1999 '75
Spaced Out '80
Alien Prey '83

Susan Stokey
The Power '80
Phantom Empire '87

Mink Stole
Mondo Trasho '69
Multiple Maniacs '70
Pink Flamingos '72
Female Trouble '74
Desperate Living '77
Polyester '81
Cry-Baby '90
Liquid Dreams '92
Serial Mom '94

Shirley Stoler
Honeymoon Killers '70
Seven Beauties '76
The Deer Hunter '78
Splitz '84
Shakedown '88
Malcolm X '92

Eric Stoltz
The Grass is Always Greener Over the Septic Tank '78
The Seekers '79
Fast Times at Ridgemont High '82
Running Hot '83
Surf 2 '84
The Wild Life '84
Code Name: Emerald '85
Mask '85
The New Kids '85
Lionheart '87
A Night of Love '87
Sister, Sister '87
Some Kind of Wonderful '87
Haunted Summer '88
The Fly 2 '89
Our Town '89
Say Anything '89
Memphis Belle '90
The Waterdance '91
Bodies, Rest & Motion '93
Foreign Affairs '93
Naked in New York '93
Killing Zoe '94
Little Women '94
Pulp Fiction '94
Sleep with Me '94
A Woman at War '94
Fluke '95
Kicking and Screaming '95
The Prophecy '95
Rob Roy '95

Lena Stolze
The Last Five Days '82
The White Rose '83
The Nasty Girl '90

Christopher Stone
The Passing of Evil '70
Prisoner in the Middle '74
Love Me Deadly '76
The Howling '81
The Junkman '82
Cujo '83
The Annihilators '85
Dying to Remember '93

Danton Stone
Crazy People '90
He Said, She Said '91
Once Around '91

George E. Stone
Cimarron '30
Medicine Man '30
The Last Mile '32
The Vampire Bat '32
42nd Street '33
Viva Villa! '34
Broadway Limited '41
Road Show '41
Timber Queen '44
Jungle Hell '55

Harold J. Stone
The Invisible Boy '57
X: The Man with X-Ray Eyes '63
Girl Happy '65
Big Mouth '67
Legend of Valentino '75
Mitchell '75

Lewis Stone
Nomads of the North '20
Beau Revel '21
The Lost World '25
The Notorious Lady '27
Wild Orchids '28
A Woman of Affairs '28
The Big House '30
Romance '30
The Sin of Madelon Claudet '31
Grand Hotel '32
The Mask of Fu Manchu '32
Mata Hari '32
Red Headed Woman '32
Bureau of Missing Persons '33
Queen Christina '33
The Girl from Missouri '34
Treasure Island '34
China Seas '35
David Copperfield '35
Suzy '36
Love Finds Andy Hardy '38
Andy Hardy Gets Spring Fever '39
Andy Hardy Meets Debutante '40
Andy Hardy's Private Secretary '41
Life Begins for Andy Hardy '41
Andy Hardy's Double Life '42
Love Laughs at Andy Hardy '46
State of the Union '48
Any Number Can Play '49
The Sun Comes Up '49
Key to the City '50
Stars in My Crown '50
Angels in the Outfield '51
Prisoner of Zenda '52
Scaramouche '52
All the Brothers Were Valiant '53

Mike Stone
Warrior Within '80
Tigershark '87

Milburn Stone
Swing It, Professor '37
The Thirteenth Man '37
Mr. Boggs Steps Out '38
The Port of Missing Girls '38
Sinners in Paradise '38
Fighting Mad '39
Mystery Plane '39
Stunt Pilot '39
Colorado '40
Captive Wild Woman '43
The Mad Ghoul '43
Sherlock Holmes Faces Death '43
Master Key '44
Strange Confession '45
Heading for Heaven '47
Killer Dill '47
The Judge '49
Branded '50
The Atomic City '52
Arrowhead '53
Pickup on South Street '53
The Sun Shines Bright '53

Oliver Stone
Midnight Express '78
Scarface '83

Paula Stone
Hopalong Cassidy '35
Red Lights Ahead '36
Swing It, Professor '37
Convicts at Large '38

Philip Stone
The Unearthly Stranger '64
Monsignor Quixote '91

Sharon Stone
Deadly Blessing '81
Calendar Girl Murders '84
Irreconcilable Differences '84
The Vegas Strip Wars '84
King Solomon's Mines '85
Allan Quatermain and the Lost City of Gold '86
Cold Steel '87
Police Academy 4: Citizens on Patrol '87
Above the Law '88
Action Jackson '88
Tears in the Rain '88
War & Remembrance, Part 1 '88
Beyond the Stars '89
Blood and Sand '89
War & Remembrance: The Final Chapter, Part 8 '89
Total Recall '90
Diary of a Hitman '91
He Said, She Said '91
Scissors '91
Where Sleeping Dogs Lie '91
Year of the Gun '91
Basic Instinct '92
Intersection '93
Sliver '93
The Quick and the Dead '94
The Specialist '94
Casino '95
Diabolique '96
Last Dance '96

Sherri Stoner
Impulse '84
Lovelines '84
Reform School Girls '86

Paolo Stoppa
Beauty and the Devil '50
Miracle in Milan '51
Beauties of the Night '52
Seven Deadly Sins '53
The Gold of Naples '54
Where the Hot Wind Blows '59

Larry Storch
40 Pounds of Trouble '62
Captain Newman, M.D. '63
Sex and the Single Girl '64
Hard Frame '70
The Woman Hunter '72
The Incredible Rocky Mountain Race '77
The Adventures of Huckleberry Finn '78
Better Late Than Never '79
S.O.B. '81
Sweet 16 '81
Adventures Beyond Belief '87
I Don't Buy Kisses Anymore '92

June Storey
First Love '39
Dance Hall '41
The Strange Woman '46

Adam Storke
Mystic Pizza '88
The Phantom of the Opera '90
Death Becomes Her '92
Highway to Hell '92
Lifepod '93
National Lampoon's Attack of the 5 Ft. 2 Women '94
Stephen King's The Stand '94

Gale Storm
Let's Go Collegiate '41
Lure of the Islands '42
Man from Cheyenne '42
Smart Alecks '42
Revenge of the Zombies '43
Rhythm Parade '43
Swing Parade of 1946 '46
The Underworld Story '50
The Texas Rangers '51

James Storm
Night of Dark Shadows '71
Ants '77

Peter Stormare
Damage '92
Fargo '96

Ludwig Stossel
Pittsburgh '42
House of Dracula '45
Cloak and Dagger '46
G.I. Blues '60

George Stover
Fiend '83
Deadly Neighbor '91

Madeleine Stowe
Nativity '78
Gangster Wars '81
The Amazons '84
Stakeout '87
Tropical Snow '88
Worth Winning '89
Closet Land '90
Revenge '90
The Two Jakes '90
China Moon '91
The Last of the Mohicans '92
Unlawful Entry '92
Another Stakeout '93
Blink '93
Short Cuts '93
Bad Girls '94
12 Monkeys '95

Beatrice Straight
Patterns '56
The Nun's Story '59
Network '76
Killer on Board '77
The Dain Curse '78
The Promise '78
Sidney Sheldon's Bloodline '79
The Formula '80
Endless Love '81
Poltergeist '82
The Princess and the Pea '83
Two of a Kind '83
Power '86
Robert Kennedy and His Times '90
Deceived '91

Julie Strain
Mirror Images '91
Night Rhythms '92
The Unnamable 2: The Statement of Randolph Carter '92
Witchcraft 4: Virgin Heart '92
Enemy Gold '93
Fit to Kill '93
The Dallas Connection '94
Money to Burn '94
Psycho Cop 2 '94
Sorceress '94
Victim of Desire '94
Dark Secrets '95
Midnight Confessions '95
Virtual Desire '95

Harry Strang
Phantom Ranger '38
The Fighting Sullivans '42

Glenn Strange
Border Law '31
Hard Hombre '31
Border Vengeance '35
Ghost Town Riders '38
Gun Packer '38
Across the Plains '39
Law of the Pampas '39
Covered Wagon Trails '40
The Driftin' Kid '41
Fugitive Valley '41
Billy the Kid Trapped '42
Boot Hill Bandits '42
The Mad Monster '42
Sunset on the Desert '42
The Black Raven '43
House of Frankenstein '44
Sonora Stagecoach '44
House of Dracula '45
The Wistful Widow of Wagon Gap '47
Abbott and Costello Meet Frankenstein '48
Master Minds '49
Comin' Round the Mountain '51
Jailhouse Rock '57

Lee Strasberg
The Godfather, Part 2 '74
The Cassandra Crossing '76
And Justice for All '79
Going in Style '79
The Godfather 1902-1959: The Complete Epic '81

Susan Strasberg
The Cobweb '55
Picnic '55
Stage Struck '57
Kapo '59
Scream of Fear '61
The Trip '67
The Brotherhood '68
Psych-Out '68
The Sibling '72
Frankenstein '73
The Legend of Hillbilly John '73
Rollercoaster '77
In Praise of Older Women '78
The Manitou '78
Bloody Birthday '80
Sweet 16 '81
Mazes and Monsters '82
Delta Force '86
Prime Suspect '88
The Runnin' Kind '89
The Light in the Jungle '91

Marcia Strassman
Changes '69
Soup for One '82
The Aviator '85
Honey, I Shrunk the Kids '89
And You Thought Your Parents Were Weird! '91
Fast Getaway '91
Honey, I Blew Up the Kid '92
Another Stakeout '93

David Strathairn
Return of the Secaucus 7 '80
Enormous Changes '83
Silkwood '83
Trumps '83
The Brother from Another Planet '84
Iceman '84
At Close Range '86
Broken Vows '87
Matewan '87
Dominick & Eugene '88
Eight Men Out '88
Day One '89
The Feud '90
Heat Wave '90
Judgment '90
Memphis Belle '90
City of Hope '91
O Pioneers! '91
Son of the Morning Star '91
Without Warning: The James Brady Story '91
Big Girls Don't Cry...They Get Even '92
Bob Roberts '92
A League of Their Own '92
Passion Fish '92
Sneakers '92
A Dangerous Woman '93
The Firm '93
Lost in Yonkers '93
Dolores Claiborne '94
Losing Isaiah '94
The River Wild '94

Dorothy Stratten
Autumn Born '79
Galaxina '80
They All Laughed '81

Charles Stratton
Summer Camp Nightmare '86
Munchies '87

Peter Strauss
Hail, Hero! '69
Soldier Blue '70
Man of Legend '71
Trial of the Catonsville Nine '72
The Last Tycoon '76
Rich Man, Poor Man '76
The Jericho Mile '79
Angel on My Shoulder '80
Masada '81
Whale for the Killing '81
Spacehunter: Adventures in the Forbidden Zone '83
Penalty Phase '86
Proud Men '87
The Brotherhood of the Rose '89
Peter Gunn '89
Flight of Black Angel '91
Fugitive Among Us '92
The Yearling '94
Nick of Time '95

Robert Strauss
Jumping Jacks '52
Here Come the Girls '53
The Redhead from Wyoming '53
Stalag 17 '53
The Atomic Kid '54
The Bridges at Toko-Ri '55
The Man with the Golden Arm '55
The Seven Year Itch '55
I, Mobster '58
The 4D Man '59
Girls! Girls! Girls! '62
Family Jewels '65
Frankie and Johnny '65

Meryl Streep
Julia '77
The Deer Hunter '78
Holocaust '78
Kramer vs. Kramer '79
Manhattan '79
The Seduction of Joe Tynan '79
The French Lieutenant's Woman '81
Sophie's Choice '82
Still of the Night '82
Silkwood '83
Falling in Love '84
Out of Africa '85
Plenty '85
Heartburn '86
Ironweed '87
A Cry in the Dark '88
She-Devil '89
Postcards from the Edge '90
Defending Your Life '91
Death Becomes Her '92
The House of the Spirits '93
The River Wild '94
Before and After '95
The Bridges of Madison County '95

Elliot Street
Paper Man '71
Harrad Experiment '73
Melvin Purvis: G-Man '74

Barbra Streisand
Funny Girl '68
Hello, Dolly! '69
On a Clear Day You Can See Forever '70
The Owl and the Pussycat '70
Up the Sandbox '72
What's Up, Doc? '72
The Way We Were '73
For Pete's Sake '74
Funny Lady '75
A Star is Born '76
The Main Event '79
All Night Long '81
Yentl '83
Nuts '87
The Prince of Tides '91

Melissa Stribling
Crow Hollow '52
The Horror of Dracula '58

Connie Strickland
Bummer '73
Act of Vengeance '74

Gail Strickland
The Gathering '77
One on One '77
Snowblind '78
Who'll Stop the Rain? '78
The Gathering: Part 2 '79
Rape and Marriage: The Rideout Case '80
A Matter of Life and Death '81
Eleanor: First Lady of the World '82
Lies '83
Oxford Blues '84
Protocol '84
Hyper-Sapien: People from Another Star '86
The Man in the Moon '91
Scott Turow's The Burden of Proof '92
Three of Hearts '93
Last Time Out '94

Anita Strindberg
The Scorpion's Tail '71
The Tempter '74
Women in Cell Block 7 '77

Elaine Stritch
Three Violent People '57
Perfect Furlough '59
Providence '77
Follies in Concert '85
September '88

Woody Strode
Pork Chop Hill '59
The Last Voyage '60
Sergeant Rutledge '60
Spartacus '60
The Man Who Shot Liberty Valance '62
The Professionals '66
Once Upon a Time in the West '68
Shalako '68
Boot Hill '69
Ride to Glory '71
The Gatling Gun '72
Hired to Kill '73
Hit Men '73
Manhunt '73
Loaded Guns '75
Kingdom of the Spiders '77
Oil '78
Jaguar Lives '79
Kill Castro '80
The Mercenaries '80
The Final Executioner '83
Scream '83
Violent Breed '83
Jungle Warriors '84
Lust in the Dust '85
Super Brother '90
Murder on the Bayou '91
Storyville '92

Michael Strong
Point Blank '67
Patton '70
Queen of the Stardust Ballroom '75

Don Stroud
Coogan's Bluff '68
Madigan '68
Explosion '69
Angel Unchained '70
Bloody Mama '70
Joe Kidd '72
Slaughter's Big Ripoff '73
Murph the Surf '75
Death Weekend '76
Hollywood Man '76
Killer Inside Me '76
The Choirboys '77
Sudden Death '77
The Buddy Holly Story '78
The Amityville Horror '79
Express to Terror '79
The Night the Lights Went Out in Georgia '81
Search and Destroy '81
Sweet 16 '81
Armed and Dangerous '86
Two to Tango '88
Down the Drain '89
Twisted Justice '89
The Divine Enforcer '91
The King of the Kickboxers '91
Prime Target '91
Dillinger and Capone '95

Shepperd Strudwick
The Loves of Edgar Allen Poe '42
All the King's Men '49
The Red Pony '49
Let's Dance '50
Three Husbands '50
Beyond a Reasonable Doubt '56
Psychomania '63
Cops and Robbers '73

Joe Strummer
Straight to Hell '87
Mystery Train '89

Sally Struthers
Five Easy Pieces '70
The Getaway '72
Intimate Strangers '77
A Gun in the House '81

Carel Struycken
The Ewoks: Battle for Endor '85
The Witches of Eastwick '87
The Addams Family '91
Servants of Twilight '91
Addams Family Values '93
Oblivion '94
Backlash: Oblivion 2 '95
Out There '95
Under the Hula Moon '95

Cassie Stuart
Dolls '87
Hidden City '87

Gloria Stuart
The Old Dark House '32
The Invisible Man '33
Roman Scandals '33
Gold Diggers of 1935 '35
The Poor Little Rich Girl '36
Rebecca of Sunnybrook Farm '38
It Could Happen to You '39
The Three Musketeers '39
Enemy of Women '44
The Two Worlds of Jenny Logan '79
My Favorite Year '82

James R. Stuart
War of the Robots '78
Reactor '85

John Stuart
No. 17 '32
Old Mother Riley's Ghosts '41
Candles at Nine '44
Man on the Run '49
The Temptress '49
The Gilded Cage '54
Alias John Preston '56

Maxine Stuart
Coast to Coast '80
The Rousters '90
The Haunting of Seacliff Inn '94

Randy Stuart
I Was a Male War Bride '49
The Incredible Shrinking Man '57

Imogen Stubbs
A Summer Story '88
Erik the Viking '89
Fellow Traveler '89
True Colors '91
Sense and Sensibility '95
Jack and Sarah '96

Stephen Stucker
Airplane! '80
Airplane 2: The Sequel '82
Delinquent School Girls '84

Wes Studi
Dances with Wolves '90
The Doors '91
The Last of the Mohicans '92
The Broken Chain '93
Geronimo: An American Legend '93
Lone Justice 2 '93
Street Fighter '94
Heat '95
Larry McMurtry's Streets of Laredo '95

Jerzy Stuhr
Camera Buff '79
Provincial Actors '79
Deja Vu '89
Trois Couleurs: Blanc '94

Johnny Stumper
Covert Action '88
Mob War '88

Preston Sturges
Star Spangled Rhythm '42
Paris Holiday '57

Shannon Sturges
Pre-Madonnas: Rebels Without a Clue '95
Tornado! '96

Trudie Styler
Poldark 2 '75
Fair Game '89

David Suchet
Crime of Honor '85
The Falcon and the Snowman '85
Gulag '85
Iron Eagle '86
Murrow '86
Harry and the Hendersons '87
The Last Innocent Man '87
A World Apart '88
To Kill a Priest '89
When the Whales Came '89
Don't Hang Up '90
Executive Decision '96

Ichiro Sugai
Early Summer '51
Sansho the Bailiff '54

Bunta Sugawara
Tattooed Hit Man '76
Distant Justice '92

Haruko Sugimura
Late Spring '49

Sugimura ▶cont.

Early Summer '51
Tokyo Story '53
Late Chrysanthemums '54
Drifting Weeds '59

Barbara Sukowa
Berlin Alexanderplatz '80
Marianne and Juliane '82
Deadly Game '83
Rosa Luxemburg '86
The Sicilian '87
Voyager '91
Zentropa '92
M. Butterfly '93
Johnny Mnemonic '95

Margaret Sullavan
The Moon's Our Home '36
The Shining Hour '38
Shopworn Angel '38
Three Comrades '38
The Mortal Storm '40
The Shop Around the Corner '40
So Ends Our Night '41

Barry Sullivan
The Woman of the Town '44
The Gangster '47
Any Number Can Play '49
A Life of Her Own '50
Nancy Goes to Rio '50
Cause for Alarm '51
Three Guys Named Mike '51
The Bad and the Beautiful '52
Skirts Ahoy! '52
The Maverick Queen '55
Queen Bee '55
Strategic Air Command '55
Texas Lady '56
Another Time, Another Place '58
The Legend of the Sea Wolf '58
A Gathering of Eagles '63
Planet of the Vampires '65
Buckskin '68
Shark! '68
Night Gallery '69
Tell Them Willie Boy Is Here '69
Yuma '70
Kung Fu '72
Earthquake '74
Hurricane '74
The Human Factor '75
Take a Hard Ride '75
Oh, God! '77
Washington Affair '77
The Bastard '78
No Room to Run '78
Casino '80

Billy L. Sullivan
Little Big League '94
The Big Green '95

Brad Sullivan
Funny Farm '88
Guilty by Suspicion '91
Orpheus Descending '91
The Prince of Tides '91
Sister Act 2: Back in the Habit '93
Bushwhacked '95
The Jerky Boys '95

Don Sullivan
Teenage Zombies '58
The Giant Gila Monster '59
The Rebel Set '59

Ed Sullivan
Bye, Bye, Birdie '63
A Few Moments with Buster Keaton and Laurel and Hardy '63

Francis L. Sullivan
Power '34
Spy of Napoleon '36
Non-Stop New York '37
21 Days '37
Action for Slander '38
The Secret Four '40
The Day Will Dawn '42
Pimpernel Smith '42
Butler's Dilemma '43
Caesar and Cleopatra '46
Great Expectations '46
Oliver Twist '48
Christopher Columbus '49
Night and the City '50
Behave Yourself! '52
The Prodigal '55

Jean Sullivan
Uncertain Glory '44
Squirm '76

Susan Sullivan
The Incredible Hulk '77
Deadman's Curve '78
City in Fear '80
Marriage Is Alive and Well '80
The Ordeal of Dr. Mudd '80
The Dark Ride '84
Rage of Angels: The Story Continues '86

Frank Sully
Inside the Law '42
The Tender Trap '55

Diane Summerfield
Black Godfather '74
Blackjack '78

Eleanor Summerfield
Man on the Run '49
Black Glove '54

Roy Summerset
Overkill '86
Cold Heat '90

Slim Summerville
Charlie Chaplin's Keystone Comedies #4 '14
The Beloved Rogue '27
King of the Rodeo '28
All Quiet on the Western Front '30
Under Montana Skies '30
The Farmer Takes a Wife '35
Captain January '36
Rebecca of Sunnybrook Farm '38
Western Union '41
I'm from Arkansas '44

Bart Sumner
Video Violence '87
Video Violence Part 2...The Exploitation! '87

Clinton Sundberg
Mr. Peabody & the Mermaid '48
In the Good Old Summertime '49
Two Weeks with Love '50
As Young As You Feel '51
The Belle of New York '52
Main Street to Broadway '53

Bjorn Sundquist
The Dive '89
Shipwrecked '90

Gerry Sundquist
Great Expectations '81
Don't Open Till Christmas '84

Nicolas Surovy
The Act '82
Stark '85
Anastasia: The Mystery of Anna '86
Forever Young '92
12:01 '93

Todd Susman
Star Spangled Girl '71
Only the Strong '93
Bodily Harm '95
The Invaders '95

Paul Sutera
Problem Child 2 '91
The Brady Bunch Movie '95
A Very Brady Sequel '96

Donald Sutherland
Castle of the Living Dead '64
Bedford Incident '65
Die! Die! My Darling! '65
Dr. Terror's House of Horrors '65
The Dirty Dozen '67
Sebastian '68
Alex in Wonderland '70
Kelly's Heroes '70
M*A*S*H '70
Start the Revolution Without Me '70
Johnny Got His Gun '71
Klute '71
Little Murders '71
Dan Candy's Law '73
Don't Look Now '73
Lady Ice '73
Steelyard Blues '73
S*P*Y*S '74
The Day of the Locust '75
1900 '76
Bethune '77
Blood Relatives '77
The Eagle Has Landed '77
Kentucky Fried Movie '77
Invasion of the Body Snatchers '78
National Lampoon's Animal House '78
The Great Train Robbery '79
A Man, a Woman, and a Bank '79
Murder by Decree '79
Bear Island '80
Nothing Personal '80
Ordinary People '80
Disappearance '81
Eye of the Needle '81
Gas '81
Max Dugan Returns '83
Threshold '83
Crackers '84
Ordeal by Innocence '84
Heaven Help Us '85
Revolution '85
The Rosary Murders '87
The Trouble with Spies '87
The Wolf at the Door '87
Apprentice to Murder '88
A Dry White Season '89
Lock Up '89
Lost Angels '89
Dr. Bethune '90
Backdraft '91
Eminent Domain '91
JFK '91
Long Road Home '91
Quicksand: No Escape '91
Buffy the Vampire Slayer '92
The Railway Station Man '92
Shadow of the Wolf '92
Benefit of the Doubt '93
Six Degrees of Separation '93
Disclosure '94
Outbreak '94
The Puppet Masters '94
Younger & Younger '94
Citizen X '95
Oldest Confederate Widow Tells All '95
Red Hot '95
A Time to Kill '96

Kiefer Sutherland
Max Dugan Returns '83
Amazing Stories '85
The Bay Boy '85
At Close Range '86
Brotherhood of Justice '86
Stand By Me '86
Trapped in Silence '86
Crazy Moon '87
The Killing Time '87
The Lost Boys '87
Bright Lights, Big City '88
Promised Land '88
Young Guns '88
Flashback '89
1969 '89
Renegades '89
Chicago Joe & the Showgirl '90
Flatliners '90
Young Guns 2 '90
Article 99 '92
A Few Good Men '92
Twin Peaks: Fire Walk with Me '92
Last Light '93
The Three Musketeers '93
The Vanishing '93
The Cowboy Way '94
An Eye for an Eye '95

James Sutorius
A Question of Love '78
Prototype '83
My Mother's Secret Life '84
Windy City '84
On Wings of Eagles '86

Dolores Sutton
Where Angels Go, Trouble Follows '68
F. Scott Fitzgerald in Hollywood '76

Dudley Sutton
Leather Boys '63
Cry of the Penguins '71
The Devils '71
Edward II '92
Orlando '92
The Best of Lovejoy Mysteries '93

Grady Sutton
Pharmacist '32
Dangerous Holiday '37
Waikiki Wedding '37
The Bank Dick '40
The Bashful Bachelor '42
The More the Merrier '43
Going to Town '44
Paradise, Hawaiian Style '66

John Sutton
Arrest Bulldog Drummond '38
The Tower of London '39
The Invisible Man Returns '40
A Yank in the R.A.F. '41
Jane Eyre '44
Mickey '48
David and Bathsheba '51
Second Woman '51
The Bat '59
Beloved Infidel '59
Return of the Fly '59

Janet Suzman
A Day in the Death of Joe Egg '71
Nicholas and Alexandra '71
The Black Windmill '74
Macbeth '76
Voyage of the Damned '76
The House on Garibaldi Street '79
Nijinsky '80
Priest of Love '81
The Draughtsman's Contract '82
And the Ship Sails On '83
The Zany Adventures of Robin Hood '84
Bright Smiler '85
A Dry White Season '89
Nuns on the Run '90
Leon the Pig Farmer '93

Semyon Svashenko
Zvenigora '28
Arsenal '29
Earth '30

Bo Svenson
Big Mo '73
Frankenstein '73
The Great Waldo Pepper '75
Walking Tall: Part 2 '75
Special Delivery '76
Portrait of a Hitman '77
Snowbeast '77
Walking Tall: The Final Chapter '77
Deadly Mission '78
Gold of the Amazon Women '79
North Dallas Forty '79
Night Warning '82
Virus '82
Deadly Impact '84
Jealousy '84
Thunder Warrior '85
Thunder Warrior 2 '85
Wizards of the Lost Kingdom '85
Choke Canyon '86
Delta Force '86
Heartbreak Ridge '86
The Last Contract '86
The Manhunt '86
Deep Space '87
Delta Force Commando '87
The Dirty Dozen: The Deadly Mission '87
White Phantom: Enemy of Darkness '87
Curse 2: The Bite '88
Andy and the Airwave Rangers '89
The Kill Reflex '89
Primal Rage '90
Tides of War '90
Beyond the Door 3 '91
Steele's Law '91
Three Days to a Kill '91
Private Obsession '94
Savage Land '94
Steel Frontier '94

Howard Swain
Jon Jost's Frameup '93
Night of the Scarecrow '95

Mack Swain
Rink/Immigrant '10s
Charlie Chaplin's Keystone Comedies #1 '14
Charlie Chaplin's Keystone Comedies #2 '14
Charlie Chaplin's Keystone Comedies #3 '14
Charlie Chaplin's Keystone Comedies #4 '14
Tillie's Punctured Romance '14
The Champion/His New Job '15
His Prehistoric Past/The Bank '15
Kid's Auto Race/Mabel's Married Life '15
The Lizzies of Mack Sennett '15
Three Charlies and One Phoney! '18
Early Cinema Vol. 1 '19
The Gold Rush '25
Gold Rush/Payday '25
Hands Up '26
The Nervous Wreck '26
The Beloved Rogue '27
The Chaplin Revue '58

Darwyn Swalve
Take Two '87
Deadly Reactor '89

Hilary Swank
Buffy the Vampire Slayer '92
The Next Karate Kid '94

Brenda Swanson
Prototype X29A '92
Scanners: The Showdown '94
Secret Games 3 '94

Gary Swanson
Vice Squad '82
TripleCross '85
Witchfire '86
Coldfire '90

Gloria Swanson
The Champion/His New Job '15
A Hash House Fraud/The Sultan's Wife '15
Teddy at the Throttle '16
Teddy at the Throttle/Speeding Along '17
Shifting Sands '18
Male and Female '19
Why Change Your Wife? '20
Manhandled '24
Sadie Thompson '28
Queen Kelly '29
Indiscreet '31
Hedda Hopper's Hollywood '42
Sunset Boulevard '50
Three for Bedroom C '52
The Love Goddesses '65
Airport '75 '75

Kristy Swanson
Deadly Friend '86
Flowers in the Attic '87
Diving In '90
Dream Trap '90
Hot Shots! '91
Mannequin 2: On the Move '91
Buffy the Vampire Slayer '92
Highway to Hell '92
The Chase '93
The Program '93
Getting In '94
Higher Learning '94
Marshal Law '96
The Phantom '96

Maureen Swanson
Robbery Under Arms '57
The Spanish Gardener '57

Rochelle Swanson
Hard Bounty '94
Indecent Behavior 2 '94
Night Fire '94
Secret Games 3 '94

Don Swayze
Death Blow '87
Shy People '87
Driving Force '88
The Tracker '88
Trapper County War '89
Payback '90
Edge of Honor '91
Beach Babes from Beyond Infinity '93
Body of Influence '93
Broken Trust '93
Death Ring '93
Eye of the Stranger '93
Forced to Kill '93
Sexual Malice '93
Money to Burn '94

Patrick Swayze
Return of the Rebels '81
The Outsiders '83
Uncommon Valor '83
Grandview U.S.A. '84

Red Dawn '84
North and South Book 1 '85
North and South Book 2 '86
Youngblood '86
Dirty Dancing '87
Steel Dawn '87
Tiger Warsaw '87
Next of Kin '89
Road House '89
Ghost '90
Point Break '91
City of Joy '92
Father Hood '93
Tall Tale: The Unbelievable Adventures of Pecos Bill '95
Three Wishes '95
To Wong Foo, Thanks for Everything, Julie Newmar '95

Heidi Swedberg
Hot Shots! '91
Father and Scout '95

Bob Sweeney
A Christmas Carol '54
Toby Tyler '59

D.B. Sweeney
Fire with Fire '86
Gardens of Stone '87
No Man's Land '87
Eight Men Out '88
Lonesome Dove '89
Leather Jackets '90
Memphis Belle '90
Blue Desert '91
Heaven is a Playground '91
The Cutting Edge '92
A Day in October '92
Miss Rose White '92
Fire in the Sky '93
Hear No Evil '93
Roommates '95

Dominic Sweeney
In Too Deep '90
Jigsaw '90

Joseph Sweeney
The Man in the Gray Flannel Suit '56
Twelve Angry Men '57

Julia Sweeney
Honey, I Blew Up the Kid '92
Coneheads '93
It's Pat: The Movie '94

Blanche Sweet
Griffith Biograph Program '09
D.W. Griffith Triple Feature '13
Avenging Conscience '14
Home Sweet Home '14
Judith of Bethulia '14
Anna Christie '23
The Silver Horde '30

Dolph Sweet
Finian's Rainbow '68
Cops and Robbers '73
Amazing Grace '74
The Migrants '74
Deathmoon '78
Jacqueline Bouvier Kennedy '81
Reds '81
Acorn People '82

Gary Sweet
Stage Fright '83
An Indecent Obsession '85
Fever '88

Vonte Sweet
Laurel Avenue '93
The Walking Dead '94
Marshal Law '96

Rod Sweitzer
The Invisible Maniac '90
The Malibu Beach Vampires '91

Inga Swenson
The Miracle Worker '62
North and South Book 1 '85

Karl Swenson
The Hanging Tree '59
The Gallant Hours '60
Brighty of the Grand Canyon '67

Tommy Swerdlow
Hamburger Hill '87
Child's Play '88

Josef Swickard
The Four Horsemen of the Apocalypse '21
Dante's Inferno '24
The Wizard of Oz '25

The Night Patrol '26
The Lone Defender '32
Custer's Last Stand '36

Nora Swinburne
Man of Evil '48
Quo Vadis '51
The River '51
Betrayed '54
Helen of Troy '56
Strange Awakening '58

Tilda Swinton
Caravaggio '86
The Last of England '87
The Garden '90
Edward II '92
Orlando '92
Wittgenstein '93

Loretta Swit
M*A*S*H: The Collector's Edition '72
Freebie & the Bean '74
Race with the Devil '75
S.O.B. '81
First Affair '83
M*A*S*H: Goodbye, Farewell & Amen '83
Beer '85
The Execution '85
Miracle at Moreaux '86
Whoops Apocalypse '88

Carl "Alfalfa" Switzer
Little Rascals, Vol. 1 '29
Little Rascals, Book 1 '30s
Little Rascals, Vol. 2 '30
General Spanky '36
Our Gang Comedies '40s
Reg'lar Fellers '41
The Great Mike '44
Redwood Forest Trail '50
Cause for Alarm '51
Pat and Mike '52
Motorcycle Gang '57

Ken Swofford
Bless the Beasts and Children '71
Sky Hei$t '75
All God's Children '80
Black Roses '88
The Taking of Beverly Hills '91

Topo Swope
The Hot Rock '70
My Old Man's Place '71

Tracy Brooks Swope
The Big Picture '89
The Power of One '92
Inner Sanctum 2 '94

Basil Sydney
Accused '36
Rhodes '36
The Secret Four '40
Hamlet '48
Angel with the Trumpet '50
Treasure Island '50
Salome '53
Dam Busters '55
The Devil's Disciple '59
John Paul Jones '59
The Three Worlds of Gulliver '59
The Hands of Orlac '60

Brenda Sykes
Honky '71
Cleopatra Jones '73
Mandingo '75

Eric Sykes
Heavens Above '63
Those Daring Young Men in Their Jaunty Jalopies '69

Harold Sylvester
Fast Break '79
Uncommon Valor '83
Innerspace '87
In the Deep Woods '91
The Reluctant Agent '95

William Sylvester
Unholy Four '54
Postmark for Danger '56
Gorgo '61
Devil Doll '64
Beast of Morocco '66
2001: A Space Odyssey '68

Robert Symonds
Ice Pirates '84
Rumpelstiltskin '86

Mandroid '93

Sylvia Syms
Bachelor of Hearts '58
The Moonraker '58
Ferry to Hong Kong '59
Teenage Bad Girl '59
Conspiracy of Hearts '60
The World of Suzie Wong '60
Victim '62
Fiction Makers '67
Desperados '69
The Tamarind Seed '74
Nancy Astor '82
Murders at Lynch Cross '85
Intimate Contact '87
A Chorus of Disapproval '89
Shirley Valentine '89
Shining Through '92

Clancy Syrko
Black Bikers from Hell '70
The Outlaw Bikers—Gang Wars '70

Laszlo Szabo
Bad Guys '79
Nice Neighbor '79

Grazyna Szapolowska
Another Way '82
No End '84

Keith Szarabajka
Protocol '84
Marie '85
Billy Galvin '86
The Misfit Brigade '87
The Equalizer: Memories of Manon '88
Nightlife '90
Stephen King's Golden Years '91
Unnatural Pursuits '91
A Perfect World '93
Andre '94

Oleg Tabakov
An Unfinished Piece for a Player Piano '77
Oblomov '81

Eron Tabor
I Spit on Your Grave '77
Krush Groove '85

Kristopher Tabori
The Glass House '72
Marilyn & Bobby: Her Final Affair '94
Last Summer In the Hamptons '96

Sydney Tafler
Fire Maidens from Outer Space '56
The Way Out '56
The Adventurers '70

Cary-Hiroyuki Tagawa
The Last Warrior '89
Showdown in Little Tokyo '91
American Me '92
Nemesis '93
Rising Sun '93
Natural Causes '94
Picture Bride '94
Mortal Kombat: The Movie '95
Soldier Boyz '95
White Tiger '95
The Phantom '96

Rita Taggart
Torchlight '85
Weeds '87
The Horror Show '89
Coupe de Ville '90
At Home with the Webbers '94

Sharon Taggart
The Last Picture Show '71
Harrad Experiment '73

Sharmila Tagore
The World of Apu '59
Devi '60
Mississippi Masala '92

Taj Mahal
Sounder '72
Bill & Ted's Bogus Journey '91

Miiko Taka
A Global Affair '63
Walk, Don't Run '66

Koji Takahashi
Professional Killers 1 '73
Hiroshima '95

Ken Takakura
The Yakuza '75
Station '81
Antarctica '84
Black Rain '89
Mr. Baseball '92

Hideko Takamine
Mistress '53
Twenty-Four Eyes '54
When a Woman Ascends the Stairs '60

Akira Takarada
Half Human '58
Godzilla vs. Mothra '64
Last War '68
Minbo—Or the Gentle Art of Japanese Extortion '92

Tadao Takashima
King Kong vs. Godzilla '63
Son of Godzilla '66

George Takei
Ice Palace '60
Red Line 7000 '65
The Green Berets '68
Star Trek Bloopers '69
Star Trek: The Motion Picture '80
Star Trek 2: The Wrath of Khan '82
Star Trek 3: The Search for Spock '84
Star Trek 4: The Voyage Home '86
Star Trek 5: The Final Frontier '89
Prisoners of the Sun '91
Star Trek 6: The Undiscovered Country '91
Oblivion '94
Backlash: Oblivion 2 '95
Kissinger and Nixon '96

Takeshi
Merry Christmas, Mr. Lawrence '83
Johnny Mnemonic '95

Osamu Takizawa
Fires on the Plain '59
Zatoichi vs. Yojimbo '70

Helen Talbot
California Joe '43
Federal Operator 99 '45
King of the Forest Rangers '46

Lyle Talbot
The Purchase Price '32
13th Guest '32
Three on a Match '32
Ladies They Talk About '33
Shriek in the Night '33
One Night of Love '34
The Case of the Lucky Legs '35
Our Little Girl '35
Go West, Young Man '36
Three Legionnaires '37
Vengeance '37
Second Fiddle '39
Torture Ship '39
A Night for Crime '42
Gambler's Choice '44
Mystery of the Riverboat '44
One Body Too Many '44
Sensations of 1945 '44
Up in Arms '44
North of the Border '46
Song of Arizona '46
The Devil's Cargo '48
Highway 13 '48
Parole, Inc. '49
Pirate Ship '49
Thunder in the Pines '49
Wild Weed '49
Border Rangers '50
Gold Raiders '51
One Too Many '51
Mesa of Lost Women '52
Clipped Wings '53
Glen or Glenda: Confessions of Ed Wood '53
Jail Bait '54
Trader Tom of the China Seas '54
Plan 9 from Outer Space '56
High School Confidential '58
Sunrise at Campobello '60

Nita Talbot
I Married a Woman '56

Who's Got the Action? '63
Girl Happy '65
The Rockford Files: Backlash of the Hunter '74
Frightmare '81
The Concrete Jungle '82
Night Shift '82
Sweet Creek County War '82
Chained Heat '83
Fraternity Vacation '85
Take Two '87
Puppet Master 2 '90
Amityville 1992: It's About Time '92

Gloria Talbott
Cyclops '56
The Oklahoman '56
The Daughter of Dr. Jekyll '57
The Kettles on Old MacDonald's Farm '57
I Married a Monster from Outer Space '58
Girls' Town '59
Arizona Raiders '65

Michael Talbott
Miami Vice '84
Racing with the Moon '84

Hal Taliaferro
The Unknown Ranger '36
The Rangers Step In '37
Phantom Gold '38
Border Vigilantes '41
Riders of the Timberline '41
Frontier Law '43
Hoppy Serves a Writ '43
Leather Burners '43

Margaret Tallichet
Stranger on the Third Floor '40
It Started with Eve '41

Patricia Tallman
Night of the Living Dead '90
Army of Darkness '92

Constance Talmadge
The Babylon Story from "Intolerance" '16
Intolerance '16
Matrimaniac '16
The Primitive Lover '16
America/The Fall of Babylon '24

Norma Talmadge
Tale of Two Cities/In the Switch Tower '15
The Social Secretary '16
The Forbidden City '18
Dubarry '30

Richard Talmadge
Let's Go! '23
Laughing at Danger '24
The Night Patrol '26
Get That Girl '32
The Live Wire '34
Fighting Pilot '35
Speed Reporter '36

William Talman
Armored Car Robbery '50
The Falcon's Adventure/Armored Car Robbery '50
One Minute to Zero '52
The Hitch-Hiker '53
Crashout '55

Tetsuro Tamba
One-Eyed Swordsman '63
You Only Live Twice '67
Last Days of Planet Earth '74
Hunter in the Dark '80
Zero '84
The Imperial Japanese Empire '85
A Taxing Woman's Return '88
Tokyo Pop '88

Russ Tamblyn
Gun Crazy '49
Father of the Bride '50
Father's Little Dividend '51
Retreat, Hell! '52
The Winning Team '52
Seven Brides for Seven Brothers '54
Hit the Deck '55
Fastest Gun Alive '56
The Last Hunt '56
Don't Go Near the Water '57
Peyton Place '57
High School Confidential '58
Tom Thumb '58

Tamblyn ▶cont.

Cimarron '60
West Side Story '61
The Wonderful World of the Brothers Grimm '62
The Haunting '63
How the West Was Won '63
The Female Bunch '69
Free Grass '69
Satan's Sadists '69
War of the Gargantuas '70
Dracula vs. Frankenstein '71
The Last Movie '71
Commando Squad '87
Cyclone '87
Phantom Empire '87
Aftershock '88
B.O.R.N. '88
Necromancer: Satan's Servant '88
Twin Peaks '90
Twin Peaks '90
Running Mates '92
Cabin Boy '94
Desert Steel '94

Jeffrey Tambor
A Gun in the House '81
Take Your Best Shot '82
The Man Who Wasn't There '83
Mr. Mom '83
Sadat '83
Brenda Starr '86
Desert Hearts '86
Three O'Clock High '87
Lisa '90
A Perfect Little Murder '90
Tales from the Crypt, Vol. 3 '90
City Slickers '91
Life Stinks '91
Pastime '91
Article 99 '92
Crossing the Bridge '92
Scott Turow's The Burden of Proof '92
At Home with the Webbers '94
Heavyweights '94
Radioland Murders '94
Big Bully '95

Jenny Tamburi
Women in Cell Block 7 '77
Bloody Avenger '80s

Zoe Tamerlis
Ms. 45 '81
Special Effects '85

Akim Tamiroff
The Merry Widow '34
The Lives of a Bengal Lancer '35
Desire '36
The General Died at Dawn '36
The Story of Louis Pasteur '36
Union Pacific '39
The Great McGinty '40
The Texas Rangers Ride Again '40
The Corsican Brothers '42
Tortilla Flat '42
For Whom the Bell Tolls '43
His Butler's Sister '43
The Bridge of San Luis Rey '44
Dragon Seed '44
Miracle of Morgan's Creek '44
The Gangster '47
My Girl Tisa '48
Black Magic '49
Outpost in Morocco '49
Mr. Arkadin '55
Anastasia '56
Battle Hell '56
Me and the Colonel '58
Touch of Evil '58
Panic Button '62
The Bacchantes '63
The Trial '63
Topkapi '64
Alphaville '65
Lord Jim '65
Hotel Paradiso '66
Lt. Robin Crusoe, U.S.N. '66
Vulture '67
Deadly Sanctuary '68

Jiro Tamiya
Professional Killers 1 '73
Sword of Fury II '73

Mary Tamm
Tales That Witness Madness '73
The Odessa File '74
The Assassination Run '84

Takahiro Tamura
The Empire of Passion '76
In the Realm of Passion '80
The Silk Road '92

Haruo Tanaka
Snow Country '57
The Pornographers '66

Kinuyo Tanaka
Utamaro and His Five Women '46
Life of Oharu '52
Mother '52
Ugetsu '53
Sansho the Bailiff '54
Equinox Flower '58
Sandakan No. 8 '74

Toru Tanaka
Tax Season '90
3 Ninjas '92

Jessica Tandy
The Seventh Cross '44
The Valley of Decision '45
Forever Amber '47
September Affair '50
The Desert Fox '51
The Light in the Forest '58
The Birds '63
Best Friends '82
Still of the Night '82
The World According to Garp '82
The Bostonians '84
Gin Game '84
Cocoon '85
*batteries not included '87
Foxfire '87
Cocoon: The Return '88
The House on Carroll Street '88
Driving Miss Daisy '89
Fried Green Tomatoes '91
Used People '92
The Story Lady '93
To Dance with the White Dog '93
Camilla '94
Nobody's Fool '94

Mark Tandy
Maurice '87
The Railway Station Man '92
The Buccaneers '95

Alan Tang
The Bloody Fight '70s
The Dynamite Brothers '74

Yoko Tani
First Spaceship on Venus '60
Samson and the 7 Miracles of the World '62
Invasion '65
Koroshi '67

William Tannen
Whistling in the Dark '41
Jupiter's Darling '55

Warhawk Tanzania
Black Force '75
Gang Wars '75

Wang Tao
The Hot, the Cool, and the Vicious '80s
Ten Brothers of Shao-lin '80s
Two Assassins in the Dark '80s
Snake in the Eagle's Shadow 2 '83

Quentin Tarantino
Reservoir Dogs '92
Pulp Fiction '94
Sleep with Me '94
Destiny Turns on the Radio '95
Four Rooms '95
From Dusk Till Dawn '95
Girl 6 '96

Fran Tarkenton
First & Ten '85
First & Ten: The Team Scores Again '85

Rockne Tarkington
Clarence, the Cross-eyed Lion '65
Black Starlet '74
Zebra Force '76
Trained to Kill, U.S.A. '83

Lilyan Tashman
Manhandled '24
So This is Paris '26
Millie '31
Scarlet Dawn '32
Riptide '34

Coralina Cataldi Tassoni
Demons 2 '87
Terror at the Opera '88
Evil Clutch '89

Larenz Tate
Menace II Society '93
The Inkwell '94
Dead Presidents '95

Laura Tate
Dead Space '90
Subspecies '90

Nick Tate
Space: 1999 '75
The Devil's Playground '76
Space: 1999—Alien Attack '79
A Cry in the Dark '88

Reginald Tate
Immortal Battalion '44
The King's Rhapsody '55

Sharon Tate
The Fearless Vampire Killers '67
Valley of the Dolls '67
Ciao Federico! Fellini Directs Satyricon '69
12 Plus 1 '70

Jacques Tati
Sylvia and the Phantom '45
Jour de Fete '48
Mr. Hulot's Holiday '53
Mon Oncle '58
Playtime '67
Traffic '71
Parade '74

Bradford Tatum
Powder '95
Down Periscope '96

Sven-Bertil Taube
Puppet on a Chain '72
Codename Kyril '91

Nils Tavernier
Beatrice '88
The Story of Women '88
L.627 '92
Mina Tannenbaum '94

Vic Tayback
Door to Door Maniac '61
With Six You Get Eggroll '68
Alice Doesn't Live Here Anymore '74
Lepke '75
Special Delivery '76
The Choirboys '77
The Cheap Detective '78
Portrait of a Stripper '79
Great American Traffic Jam '80
The Night the City Screamed '80
Rage '80
Mysterious Two '82
Tut & Tuttle '82
Weekend Warriors '86
Criminal Act '88
Murderer's Keep '88
The Underachievers '88
Beverly Hills Bodysnatchers '89
The Horseplayer '91

Benedict Taylor
The Black Arrow '84
The Far Pavilions '84
Every Time We Say Goodbye '86
A Perfect Spy '88
Duel of Hearts '92
Charles & Diana: A Palace Divided '93

Buck Taylor
And Now Miguel '66
Pony Express Rider '76
Gunsmoke: Return to Dodge '87
Conagher '91
Tombstone '93

Christine Taylor
Night of the Demons 2 '94
The Brady Bunch Movie '95
Breaking Free '95
The Craft '96
A Very Brady Sequel '96

Courtney Taylor
Prom Night 3: The Last Kiss '89
Cover Me '95
Tracks of a Killer '95

Delores Taylor
Billy Jack '71
The Trial of Billy Jack '74

Don Taylor
Song of the Thin Man '47
The Naked City '48
Battleground '49
Father of the Bride '50
Father's Little Dividend '51
Stalag 17 '53
I'll Cry Tomorrow '55
Men of Sherwood Forest '57

Dub Taylor
You Can't Take It with You '38
Range Renegades '48
Brand of Fear '49
Riding High '50
Parrish '61
Spencer's Mountain '63
Bonnie & Clyde '67
The Wild Bunch '69
A Man Called Horse '70
Support Your Local Gunfighter '71
The Getaway '72
Poor Pretty Eddie '73
Flash & Firecat '75
This Is a Hijack '75
Creature from Black Lake '76
Gator '76
Pony Express Rider '76
Moonshine County Express '77
Soggy Bottom U.S.A. '84
On the Run '85
Back to the Future, Part 3 '90
Texas Guns '90
Conagher '91
My Heroes Have Always Been Cowboys '91
Falling from Grace '92

Elizabeth Taylor
Lassie, Come Home '43
Jane Eyre '44
National Velvet '44
The White Cliffs of Dover '44
Courage of Lassie '46
Life with Father '47
A Date with Judy '48
Julia Misbehaves '48
Conspirator '49
Little Women '49
The Big Hangover '50
Father of the Bride '50
Father's Little Dividend '51
A Place in the Sun '51
Ivanhoe '52
Love Is Better Than Ever '52
The Girl Who Had Everything '53
Beau Brummel '54
Elephant Walk '54
The Last Time I Saw Paris '54
Rhapsody '54
Giant '56
Raintree County '57
Cat on a Hot Tin Roof '58
Suddenly, Last Summer '59
Butterfield 8 '60
Cleopatra '63
The V.I.P.'s '63
The Love Goddesses '65
The Sandpiper '65
Who's Afraid of Virginia Woolf? '66
The Comedians '67
Reflections in a Golden Eye '67
The Taming of the Shrew '67
Doctor Faustus '68
Secret Ceremony '69
Divorce His, Divorce Hers '72
Hammersmith is Out '72
Night Watch '72
X, Y & Zee '72
Ash Wednesday '73
Driver's Seat '73
Under Milk Wood '73
James Dean: The First American Teenager '76
A Little Night Music '77
Return Engagement '78
Winter Kills '79
The Mirror Crack'd '80
Between Friends '83
North and South Book 1 '85
The Rumor Mill '86
Poker Alice '87
Sweet Bird of Youth '89
The Flintstones '94

Estelle Taylor
Don Juan '26
Where East Is East '29
Cimarron '30
Street Scene '31
The Southerner '45

Forrest Taylor
Riders of Destiny '33
Trail of Terror '35
A Face in the Fog '36
Kelly of the Secret Service '36
Prison Shadows '36
The Red Rope '37
The Roamin' Cowboy '37
Ghost Town Riders '38
Lightnin' Carson Rides Again '38
The Phantom of the Range '38
Outlaw's Paradise '39
Arizona Gangbusters '40
Trigger Men '41
Sons of the Pioneers '42
Trail Riders '42
Mystery Man '44
Shake Hands with Murder '44
Colorado Serenade '46
Driftin' River '46

Grant Taylor
Forty Thousand Horsemen '41
His Majesty O'Keefe '53
Long John Silver '53

Holland Taylor
Bosom Buddies '80
The Jewel of the Nile '85
She's Having a Baby '88
Alice '90
The Favor '92
Cop and a Half '93
Steal Big, Steal Little '95
To Die For '95
Last Summer In the Hamptons '96

Jack Taylor
Night of the Sorcerers '70
Dr. Jekyll and the Wolfman '71
Dr. Jekyll vs. the Werewolf '71
The Mummy's Revenge '73
Orgy of the Vampires '73
Horror of the Zombies '74
Where Time Began '77
Icebox Murders '80s
The Loves of Irina '80s

Jana Taylor
Hell's Angels on Wheels '67
Dreamscape '84

Joan Taylor
Rose Marie '54
Apache Woman '55
Earth vs. the Flying Saucers '56
Girls in Prison '56
Omar Khayyam '57
20 Million Miles to Earth '57

John Taylor
Foxstyle '73
The Seventh Sign '88

Kent Taylor
Badmen of Nevada '33
I'm No Angel '33
The Mysterious Rider '33
Gangbusters '38
Escape to Paradise '39
Five Came Back '39
Western Pacific Agent '51
The Phantom from 10,000 Leagues '56
Slightly Scarlet '56
The Crawling Hand '63
Brides of the Beast '68
Satan's Sadists '69
Brain of Blood '71
Angels' Wild Women '72
Blood of Ghastly Horror '72
I Spit on Your Corpse '74

Kimberly Taylor
Party Incorporated '89
Beauty School '93

Kit Taylor
Long John Silver '53
Cassandra '87
Innocent Prey '88

Lili Taylor
Mystic Pizza '88
Say Anything '89
Bright Angel '91
Dogfight '91
Household Saints '93

Rudy '93
Short Cuts '93
Watch It '93
Arizona Dream '94
Ready to Wear '94
The Addiction '95
Four Rooms '95
Girls Town '95

Marjorie Taylor
The Crimes of Stephen Hawke '36
Never Too Late to Mend '37
Ticket of Leave Man '37
The Face at the Window '39

Meshach Taylor
Explorers '85
House of Games '87
Mannequin '87
Class Act '91
Inside Out '91
Mannequin 2: On the Move '91
Ultra Warrior '92
Double Double Toil and Trouble '94

Noah Taylor
The Year My Voice Broke '87
Flirting '89
The Nostradamus Kid '92
One Crazy Night '93

Ray Taylor
Robinson Crusoe of Mystery Island '36
Man from Montana '41

Regina Taylor
Lean on Me '89
A Good Day to Die '95
Courage Under Fire '96
A Family Thing '96

Renee Taylor
The Errand Boy '61
Last of the Red Hot Lovers '72
The End of Innocence '90
That's Adequate '90
White Palace '90
Delirious '91
Forever: A Ghost of a Love Story '92

Rip Taylor
Cheech and Chong: Things Are Tough All Over '82
Minsky's Follies '83
Indecent Proposal '93
Private Obsession '94

Robert Taylor
Broadway Melody of 1936 '35
Camille '36
The Gorgeous Hussy '36
Broadway Melody of 1938 '37
Personal Property '37
Three Comrades '38
Waterloo Bridge '40
Billy the Kid '41
When Ladies Meet '41
Johnny Eager '42
Bataan '43
Conspirator '49
Quo Vadis '51
Westward the Women '51
Ivanhoe '52
Above and Beyond '53
All the Brothers Were Valiant '53
I Love Melvin '53
Knights of the Round Table '53
D-Day, the Sixth of June '56
The Last Hunt '56
The Law and Jake Wade '58
Party Girl '58
The Miracle of the White Stallions '63
The Night Walker '64
Death Valley Days: No Gun Behind His Badge '65
Johnny Tiger '66
The Hot Line '69

Rod Taylor
Long John Silver '53
The Catered Affair '56
Giant '56
Raintree County '57
Separate Tables '58
Ask Any Girl '59
The Time Machine '60
The Birds '63
A Gathering of Eagles '63
The V.I.P.'s '63
Colossus and the Amazon Queen '64
The Glass Bottom Boat '66
Chuka '67
Hotel '67
Dark of the Sun '68
Darker than Amber '70
Man Who Had Power Over Women '70
Powder Keg '70
Zabriskie Point '70
The Deadly Trackers '73
Train Robbers '73
Germicide '74
Hell River '75
The Treasure Seekers '79
Cry of the Innocent '80
Jacqueline Bouvier Kennedy '81
Time to Die '83
Marbella '85
Danielle Steel's Palomino '91
Nowhere to Hide

Tammy Taylor
Lovelines '84
Meatballs 2 '84

Vaughn Taylor
Francis Goes to the Races '51
Meet Danny Wilson '52
Jailhouse Rock '57
The Invaders '67

Wally Taylor
Shaft's Big Score '72
Hidden Fears '93

Leigh Taylor-Young
I Love You, Alice B. Toklas! '68
The Adventurers '70
The Horsemen '70
Soylent Green '73
Can't Stop the Music '80
Marathon '80
Looker '81
The Devlin Connection '82
The Jagged Edge '85
Secret Admirer '85
Accidents '89
Honeymoon Academy '90

Zack Taylor
Group Marriage '72
The Young Nurses '73

Ludmila Tcherina
The Red Shoes '48
Sins of Rome '54

Phil Tead
Music in My Heart '40
Fangs of the Wild '54

Anthony Teague
How to Succeed in Business without Really Trying '67
The Trouble with Girls (and How To Get Into It) '69

Marshall Teague
The Shadow Riders '82
Trained to Kill '88
Road House '89
Super Force '90
Fists of Iron '94
Guardian Angel '94
The Colony '95

Ray Teal
Hollywood Canteen '44
Rusty's Birthday '49
Distant Drums '51
Carrie '52
Jumping Jacks '52
Montana Belle '52
Ambush at Tomahawk Gap '53
Lucky Me '54
Band of Angels '57

Owen Teale
The Fifteen Streets '90
Robin Hood '91
The Hawk '93

Conway Tearle
Stella Maris '18
Dancing Mothers '26
Lost Zeppelin '29
Morals for Women '31
Pleasure '31
Held for Murder '32
Hurricane Express '32
The King Murder '32
Vanity Fair '32
Headline Woman '35
Sing Sing Nights '35
Desert Guns/Six-Shootin' Sheriff '36
Klondike Annie '36

Godfrey Tearle
The 39 Steps '35
One of Our Aircraft Is Missing '41

Verree Teasdale
Skyscraper Souls '32
Goodbye Love '34
Milky Way '36

Irene Tedrow
Special Olympics '78
The Two Worlds of Jenny Logan '79

Maureen Teefy
Fame '80
Legs '83
Supergirl '84
Star Time '92

Blair Tefkin
A Sinful Life '89
Dream Lover '93

Aaron Teich
Bloodspell '87
Darkroom '90

Shirley Temple
Kid 'n' Hollywood and Polly Tix in Washington '33
Shirley Temple Festival '33
To the Last Man '33
Baby, Take a Bow '34
Bright Eyes '34
Little Miss Marker '34
Stand Up and Cheer '34
Curly Top '35
The Little Colonel '35
The Littlest Rebel '35
Our Little Girl '35
Captain January '36
Dimples '36
The Poor Little Rich Girl '36
Stowaway '36
Heidi '37
Wee Willie Winkie '37
Just Around the Corner '38
Little Miss Broadway '38
Rebecca of Sunnybrook Farm '38
The Little Princess '39
Susannah of the Mounties '39
The Blue Bird '40
Young People '40
Miss Annie Rooney '42
Since You Went Away '44
The Bachelor and the Bobby-Soxer '47
Fort Apache '48
The Story of Seabiscuit '49
Gotta Dance, Gotta Sing '84

Victoria Tennant
Horror Planet '80
Little Lord Fauntleroy '80
The Dogs of War '81
Chiefs '83
Dempsey '83
Strangers Kiss '83
The Winds of War '83
All of Me '84
The Holcroft Covenant '85
Best Seller '87
Flowers in the Attic '87
War & Remembrance, Part 1 '88
War & Remembrance, Part 3 '88
War & Remembrance, Part 4 '88
War & Remembrance, Part 5 '88
War & Remembrance, Part 6 '88
War & Remembrance, Part 7 '88
War & Remembrance, Part 2 '89
War & Remembrance: The Final Chapter, Part 8 '89
War & Remembrance: The Final Chapter, Part 9 '89
War & Remembrance: The Final Chapter, Part 10 '89
War & Remembrance: The Final Chapter, Part 11 '89
War & Remembrance: The Final Chapter, Part 12 '89
Whispers '89
The Handmaid's Tale '90
L.A. Story '91

Jon Tenney
Tombstone '93
Watch It '93
Lassie '94
Free Willy 2: The Adventure Home '95
The Phantom '96

Julius Tennon
Riverbend '89
Lone Justice 2 '93

William Tepper
Miss Right '81
Bachelor Party '84

Johanna Ter Steege
The Vanishing '88
Vincent & Theo '90
Meeting Venus '91
Immortal Beloved '94

Akira Terao
Ran '85
Akira Kurosawa's Dreams '90

Max Terhune
Ghost Town Gold '36
Ride, Ranger, Ride '36
Heart of the Rockies '37
Hit the Saddle '37
Riders of the Whistling Skull '37
Roarin' Lead '37
The Trigger Trio '37
Heroes of the Hills '38
Outlaws of Sonora '38
Overland Stage Raiders '38
Pals of the Saddle '38
Purple Vigilantes '38
Santa Fe Stampede '38
Three Texas Steers '39
Range Busters '40
Trailing Double Trouble '40
West of Pinto Basin '40
Fugitive Valley '41
Kid's Last Ride '41
Saddle Mountain Round-Up '41
Tonto Basin Outlaws '41
Trail of the Silver Spurs '41
Tumbledown Ranch in Arizona '41
Underground Rustlers '41
Arizona Stagecoach '42
Boot Hill Bandits '42
Texas to Bataan '42
Thunder River Feud '42
Trail Riders '42
Black Market Rustlers '43
Cowboy Commandos '43
Haunted Ranch '43
Land of Hunted Men '43
Two-Fisted Justice '43

Studs Terkel
Long Shadows '86
Eight Men Out '88

John Terlesky
The Allnighter '87
Deathstalker 2: Duel of the Titans '87
Damned River '89
When He's Not a Stranger '89
Battling for Baby '92

Leonard Termo
Year of the Dragon '85
Midnight Cabaret '90

Steven Terrell
Dragstrip Girl '57
Invasion of the Saucer Men '57
Motorcycle Gang '57

Bob Terry
Brothers of the West '37
Down the Wyoming Trail '39
Outlaw's Paradise '39
Danger Ahead '40

Don Terry
Border Romance '30
Don Winslow of the Coast Guard '43
Don Winslow of the Navy '43

Harry Terry
Broken Melody '34
The Face at the Window '39

John Terry
Hawk the Slayer '81
In Country '89
A Killing in a Small Town '90
The Resurrected '91
Silhouette '91
Of Mice and Men '92
A Dangerous Woman '93
Iron Will '93
Reflections in the Dark '94
The Big Green '95

Nigel Terry
The Lion in Winter '68
Excalibur '81
Deja Vu '84
Caravaggio '86
Sylvia '86
Christopher Columbus: The Discovery '92
Edward II '92

Phillip Terry
The Monster and the Girl '41
George White's Scandals '45
The Lost Weekend '45
The Leech Woman '59

Ruth Terry
Alexander's Ragtime Band '38
Call of the Canyon '42
Heart of the Golden West '42
Hands Across the Border '43
Texas Legionnaires '43

Sheila Terry
Haunted Gold '32
Scarlet Dawn '32
The Sphinx '33
The Sphinx '33
'Neath the Arizona Skies '34
Go-Get-'Em-Haines '35
Lawless Frontier '35

Terry-Thomas
Blue Murder at St. Trinian's '56
Brothers in Law '57
Lucky Jim '58
The Naked Truth '58
Tom Thumb '58
Carlton Browne of the F.O. '59
I'm All Right Jack '59
Too Many Crooks '59
Make Mine Mink '60
A Matter of WHO '62
The Wonderful World of the Brothers Grimm '62
It's a Mad, Mad, Mad, Mad World '63
How to Murder Your Wife '64
How to Kill 400 Duponts '65
Strange Bedfellows '65
Those Magnificent Men in Their Flying Machines '65
La Grande Vadrouille '66
Those Fantastic Flying Fools '67
Danger: Diabolik '68
Don't Raise the Bridge, Lower the River '68
How Sweet It Is! '68
Where Were You When the Lights Went Out? '68
Those Daring Young Men in Their Jaunty Jalopies '69
12 Plus 1 '70
The Abominable Dr. Phibes '71
Doctor Phibes Rises Again '72
Vault of Horror '73
The Bawdy Adventures of Tom Jones '76

Laurent Terzieff
Kapo '59
Vanina Vanini '61
A Coeur Joie '67
Head Over Heels '67
The Milky Way '68
Medea '70
Red Kiss '85
Germinal '93

Robert Tessier
Born Losers '67
The Glory Stompers '67
The Velvet Vampire '71
Star Crash '78
The Villain '79
Sword & the Sorcerer '82
The Lost Empire '83
The Fix '84
Avenging Angel '85
The Last of the Mohicans '85
No Safe Haven '87
Future Force '89
Nightwish '89

Fabio Testi
The Garden of the Finzi-Continis '71
'Tis a Pity She's a Whore '73
Stateline Motel '75
The Inheritance '76
Gunfire '78
The Uranium Conspiracy '78
The Ambassador '84
Mussolini & I '85
Contraband '86

Lauren Tewes
The Love Boat '70s
Eyes of a Stranger '81
Camp Cucamonga: How I Spent My Summer Vacation '90
The China Lake Murders '90
Magic Kid '92
National Lampoon's Attack of the 5 Ft. 2 Women '94

Eric Thal
The Gun in Betty Lou's Handbag '92
A Stranger Among Us '92
Six Degrees of Separation '93
The Puppet Masters '94

Katharina Thalbach
The Tin Drum '79
Good Evening, Mr. Wallenberg '93

Byron Thames
Blame It on the Night '84
Seven Minutes in Heaven '86
84 Charlie Mopic '89

Heather Thatcher
Son of Fury '42
The Undying Monster '42
The Moon and Sixpence '43

Torin Thatcher
Great Expectations '46
Affair in Trinidad '52
Crimson Pirate '52
The Snows of Kilimanjaro '52
The Desert Rats '53
Houdini '53
Diane '55
Love Is a Many-Splendored Thing '55
Helen of Troy '56
Band of Angels '57
Istanbul '57
Darby's Rangers '58
The Seventh Voyage of Sinbad '58
Jack the Giant Killer '62
From Hell to Borneo '64
Holy Terror '65

John Thaw
Killing Heat '84
Cry Freedom '87
Business as Usual '88
A Year in Provence '89
Chaplin '92

Phyllis Thaxter
Thirty Seconds Over Tokyo '44
Weekend at the Waldorf '45
Jim Thorpe: All American '51
Springfield Rifle '52
Superman: The Movie '78
Three Sovereigns for Sarah '85

Brynn Thayer
Hero and the Terror '88
The Tracker '88
The Game of Love '90

Max Thayer
Retrievers '82
The Dolls '83
No Dead Heroes '87
No Retreat, No Surrender 2 '89

Tina Thayer
Jive Junction '43
The Payoff '43

Rosemary Theby
W.C. Fields: Flask of Fields '30
The Fatal Glass of Beer '33

Brother Theodore
The Invisible Kid '88
The 'Burbs '89
That's Adequate '90

Ernest Thesiger
The Old Dark House '32
The Ghoul '34
The Bride of Frankenstein '35
Henry V '44
Beware of Pity '46
A Christmas Carol '51
The Robe '53

David Thewlis
The Life and Adventures of Nicholas Nickleby '81
Life Is Sweet '90
Naked '93
Prime Suspect 3 '93
Black Beauty '94
Restoration '94
Total Eclipse '95
Dragonheart '96
The Island of Dr. Moreau '96

Debi Thibeault
Galactic Gigolo '87
Psychos in Love '87
Cemetery High '89

Alan Thicke
Club Med '83
Scene of the Crime '85
Not Quite Human '87
Obsessed '88
Not Quite Human 2 '89
Betrayal of the Dove '92
Stepmonster '92
Still Not Quite Human '92
Rubdown '93
The Great American Sex Scandal '94

Lynne Thigpen
Streets of Fire '84
Lean on Me '89
Impulse '90
Separate But Equal '91
Article 99 '92
Naked in New York '93
Just Cause '94
The Paper '94
The Boys Next Door '96

Roy Thinnes
The Invaders '67
Journey to the Far Side of the Sun '69
Satan's School for Girls '73
The Hindenburg '75
Code Name: Diamond Head '77
Secrets '77
From Here to Eternity '79
Sizzle '81
Rush Week '88
Dark Shadows: Episode 1 '91
The Invaders '95

Betty Thomas
Hill Street Blues, Vol. 1: Hill Street Station '81
Homework '82
When Your Lover Leaves '83
Troop Beverly Hills '89
Prison for Children '93

Billie "Buckwheat" Thomas
General Spanky '36
Our Gang Comedies '40s

Damien Thomas
Twins of Evil '71
Mohammed: Messenger of God '77
Shogun '80
Pirates '86

Danny Thomas
I'll See You in My Dreams '51
The Road to Lebanon '60
Side By Side '88

Dave Thomas
Stripes '81
Strange Brew '83
Sesame Street Presents: Follow That Bird '85
My Man Adam '86
Love at Stake '87
Moving '88
Boris and Natasha: The Movie '92
Cold Sweat '93
Coneheads '93

Frank M. Thomas, Sr.
Law of the Underworld '38
Sunset on the Desert '42

Frankie Thomas, Jr.
Tim Tyler's Luck '37
Boys Town '38
Nancy Drew, Reporter '39

Gareth Thomas
Blake's Seven '78
Visitor from the Grave '81
Super Bitch '89

Heather Thomas
Zapped! '82
Cyclone '87
Ford: The Man & the Machine '87
The Dirty Dozen: The Fatal Mission '88
Red Blooded American Girl '90
Hidden Obsession '92

Henry Thomas
Raggedy Man '81
E.T.: The Extra-Terrestrial '82
Cloak & Dagger '84
Misunderstood '84
The Quest '86
Murder One '88
Valmont '89
Psycho 4: The Beginning '90
A Taste for Killing '92
Fire in the Sky '93
Curse of the Starving Class '94
Legends of the Fall '94
Indictment: The McMartin Trial '95
Riders of the Purple Sage '96

Jameson Thomas
The Farmer's Wife '28
Night Birds '31
Night Life in Reno '31
Convicted '32
Beggars in Ermine '34
Jane Eyre '34
Sing Sing Nights '35

Jay Thomas
The Gig '85
Little Vegas '90
Straight Talk '92
Mr. Holland's Opus '95

Jonathan Taylor Thomas
Man of the House '95
Tom and Huck '95
The Adventures of Pinocchio '96

Marlo Thomas
Jenny '70
Act of Passion: The Lost Honor of Kathryn Beck '83
Consenting Adult '85
In the Spirit '90
Held Hostage '91

Philip Michael Thomas
Stigma '73
Streetfight '75
Sparkle '76
Homeboy '80s
Death Drug '83
Miami Vice '84
Miami Vice 2: The Prodigal Son '85
The Wizard of Speed and Time '88
False Witness '89
A Fight for Jenny '90

Richard Thomas
A Doll's House '59
Last Summer '69
Winning '69
Homecoming: A Christmas Story '71
The Todd Killings '71
Cactus in the Snow '72
The Waltons: A Thanksgiving Story '73
September 30, 1955 '77
All Quiet on the Western Front '79
Roots: The Next Generation '79
Battle Beyond the Stars '80
Berlin Tunnel 21 '81
Johnny Belinda '82
Hobson's Choice '83
Living Proof: The Hank Williams Jr. Story '83
Andy and the Airwave Rangers '89
Glory! Glory! '90
Stephen King's It '90
Mission of the Shark '91
Linda '93
Stalking Laura '93
A Thousand Heroes '94
Down, Out and Dangerous '95
The Invaders '95

Robin Thomas
About Last Night... '86
Summer School '87
From the Dead of Night '89
Memories of Murder '90
Personals '90

Ron Thomas
The Big Bet '85
Night Screams '87

Tim Thomerson
Terraces '77
Fade to Black '80
Jekyll & Hyde...Together Again '82
Metalstorm: The Destruction of Jared Syn '83
Uncommon Valor '83
Rhinestone '84
Trancers '84
Zone Troopers '84
Volunteers '85
Iron Eagle '86
The Legend of Sleepy Hollow '86
Glory Years '87
Near Dark '87
A Tiger's Tale '87
Cherry 2000 '88
The Wrong Guys '88
Who's Harry Crumb? '89
Air America '90
Dollman '90
Trancers 2: The Return of Jack Deth '90
Vietnam, Texas '90
Intimate Stranger '91
Bad Channels '92
The Harvest '92
Prime Time Murder '92
Trancers 3: Deth Lives '92
Die Watching '93
Dollman vs Demonic Toys '93
Nemesis '93
Trancers 4: Jack of Swords '93
The Cisco Kid '94
Dominion '94
Fleshtone '94
Hong Kong '97 '94
Natural Causes '94
Spitfire '94
Trancers 5: Sudden Deth '94
Nemesis 3: Time Lapse '96

Alina Thompson
Seduce Me: Pamela Principle 2 '94
Dead Cold '96

Brian Thompson
Commando Squad '87
Doctor Mordrid: Master of the Unknown '90
Lionheart '90
Moon 44 '90
Hired to Kill '91
Rage and Honor '92
Dragonheart '96

Derek Thompson
The Long Good Friday '79
Belfast Assassin '84

Emma Thompson
Fortunes of War '87
Henry V '89
Look Back in Anger '89
The Tall Guy '89
Impromptu '90
Dead Again '91
Howard's End '92
Peter's Friends '92
In the Name of the Father '93
Much Ado about Nothing '93
The Remains of the Day '93
Junior '94
Carrington '95
Sense and Sensibility '95

Fred Dalton Thompson
Marie '85
No Way Out '87
Feds '88
Days of Thunder '90
Die Hard 2: Die Harder '90
The Hunt for Red October '90
Cape Fear '91
Class Action '91
Curly Sue '91
Aces: Iron Eagle 3 '92
Keep the Change '92
Thunderheart '92
Barbarians at the Gate '93
Born Yesterday '93
In the Line of Fire '93
Baby's Day Out '94

Hal Thompson
Animal Crackers '30
Lassie from Lancashire '38

Jack Thompson
Jock Petersen '74
Sunday Too Far Away '74
Breaker Morant '80
Earthling '80
Caddie '81
The Club '81
The Man from Snowy River '82
Merry Christmas, Mr. Lawrence '83
Waterfront '83
Burke & Wills '85
Flesh and Blood '85
Bad Blood '87
Ground Zero '88
Shadow on the Sun '88
Trouble in Paradise '88
Deception '92
The Killing Beach '92
Wind '92
A Far Off Place '93
The Sum of Us '94
Last Dance '96

Kay Thompson
Manhattan Merry-Go-Round '37
Funny Face '57

Kenan Thompson
D2: The Mighty Ducks '94
Heavyweights '94

Lea Thompson
All the Right Moves '83
Jaws 3 '83
Red Dawn '84
The Wild Life '84
Back to the Future '85
Howard the Duck '86
Some Kind of Wonderful '87
Casual Sex? '88
Going Undercover '88
The Wizard of Loneliness '88
Back to the Future, Part 2 '89
Nightbreaker '89
Back to the Future, Part 3 '90
Montana '90
Article 99 '92
The Beverly Hillbillies '93
Dennis the Menace '93
The Substitute Wife '94
The Right to Remain Silent '95

Marshall Thompson
The Purple Heart '44
The Clock '45
They Were Expendable '45
The Show-Off '46
Words and Music '48
Battleground '49
The Caddy '53
Crashout '55
Cult of the Cobra '55
To Hell and Back '55
East of Kilimanjaro '57
Fiend Without a Face '58
It! The Terror from Beyond Space '58
First Man into Space '59
Mighty Jungle '64
Clarence, the Cross-eyed Lion '65
To the Shores of Hell '65
George! '70
The Turning Point '77
Bog '84

Peter Thompson
The Wistful Widow of Wagon Gap '47
Santa Fe '51

Rex Thompson
Young Bess '53
All Mine to Give '56
The Eddy Duchin Story '56
The King and I '56

Sada Thompson
Desperate Characters '71
Our Town '77
The Adventures of Huckleberry Finn '85
Indictment: The McMartin Trial '95

Scott Thompson
The Best of the Kids in the Hall '93
Kids In the Hall Brain Candy '96

Shawn Thompson
Hairspray '88
Sleeping with Strangers '94

Sophie Thompson
Twenty-One '91
Persuasion '95

Emma '96

Susanna Thompson
Little Giants '94
America's Dream '95

Teri Thompson
Married People, Single Sex '93
Breakaway '95

Victoria Thompson
Harrad Experiment '73
Harrad Summer '74

Anna Thomson
Unforgiven '92
The Crow '93
Angela '94
Outside the Law '95

Gordon Thomson
Explosion '69
The Donor '94

Kenneth Thomson
White Gold '28
Broadway Melody '29
Held for Murder '32
In Old Santa Fe '34
Hopalong Cassidy '35

Kim Thomson
Stealing Heaven '88
The Tall Guy '89
Hands of a Murderer '90
Jekyll and Hyde '90
Murder 101 '91

R.H. Thomson
Charlie Grant's War '80
Ticket to Heaven '81
If You Could See What I Hear '82
Surfacing '84
Ford: The Man & the Machine '87
And Then You Die '88
Heaven on Earth '89
Love and Hate: A Marriage Made in Hell '90
Mark Twain and Me '91
Glory Enough for All: The Discovery of Insulin '92
The Lotus Eaters '93
The Quarrel '93

Scott Thomson
Fast Times at Ridgemont High '82
Ghoulies '84

Jon Mikl Thor
Rock 'n' Roll Nightmare '85
Zombie Nightmare '86

Frankie Thorn
Bad Lieutenant '92
Liquid Dreams '92
Bad Blood '94

Bill Thornbury
Phantasm '79
Phantasm III: Lord of the Dead '94

Sybil Thorndike
Nine Days a Queen '34
Major Barbara '41
Nicholas Nickleby '46
Stage Fright '50
The Prince and the Showgirl '57
Shake Hands with the Devil '59

Angela Thorne
Poor Girl, A Ghost Story '74
The Lady's Not for Burning '95

Dyanne Thorne
Point of Terror '71
Ilsa, She-Wolf of the SS '74
Ilsa, Harem Keeper of the Oil Sheiks '76
Ilsa, the Wicked Warden '78
Ilsa, the Tigress of Siberia '79
Hellhole '85

Courtney Thorne-Smith
Lucas '86
Revenge of the Nerds 2: Nerds in Paradise '87
Summer School '87
Welcome to 18 '87
Side Out '90
Breach of Conduct '94

Billy Bob Thornton
One False Move '91
Indecent Proposal '93
Tombstone '93
Dead Man '95
Out There '95

Noley Thornton
Fine Things '90
Heidi '93

Sigrid Thornton
The Man from Snowy River '82
The Night After Halloween '83
All the Rivers Run '84
Street Hero '84
Nevil Shute's The Far Country '85
Best Enemies '86
Great Expectations: The Untold Story '87
The Lighthorsemen '87
Slate, Wyn & Me '87
Return to Snowy River '88
Over the Hill '93
Trapped in Space '94

Jim Thorpe
My Pal, The King '32
White Eagle '32

William Thourlby
Creeping Terror '64
Castle of Evil '66

David Threlfall
Kiss of Death '77
When the Whales Came '89
A Casualty of War '90
The Russia House '90
Diana: Her True Story '93
The Summer House '94

Frank Thring, Jr.
Alvin Rides Again '74
Mad Max: Beyond Thunderdome '85
Howling 3: The Marsupials '87

Luc Thuillier
Monsieur Hire '89
The Old Lady Who Walked in the Sea '91

Ingrid Thulin
Brink of Life '57
Wild Strawberries '57
The Magician '58
The Winter Light '62
The Silence '63
Hour of the Wolf '68
The Damned '69
The Rite '69
Paralyzed '70s
Cries and Whispers '72
The Cassandra Crossing '76
Moses '76
After the Rehearsal '84
Control '87

Chief Thundercloud
Rustlers of Red Dog '35
Ride, Ranger, Ride '36
King of the Stallions '42
Outlaw Trail '44
Sonora Stagecoach '44
The Phantom Rider '46
Call of the Forest '49

Bill Thurman
Curse of the Swamp Creature '66
It's Alive! '68
Gator Bait '73
Creature from Black Lake '76
Slumber Party '57 '76
Mountaintop Motel Massacre '86

Uma Thurman
Kiss Daddy Goodnight '87
Dangerous Liaisons '88
Johnny Be Good '88
The Adventures of Baron Munchausen '89
Henry & June '90
Where the Heart Is '90
Robin Hood '91
Final Analysis '92
Jennifer 8 '92
Mad Dog and Glory '93
Even Cowgirls Get the Blues '94
Pulp Fiction '94
A Month by the Lake '95
Beautiful Girls '96
The Truth About Cats and Dogs '96

Carol Thurston
China Sky '44
The Story of Dr. Wassell '44
Swamp Fire '46
Apache Chief '50

Gerard Tichy
Gladiators 7 '62
The Hot Line '69
Hatchet for the Honeymoon '70
The Hanging Woman '72
Ricco '74

Rachel Ticotin
Fort Apache, the Bronx '81
Critical Condition '86
When the Bough Breaks '86
Total Recall '90
F/X 2: The Deadly Art of Illusion '91
One Good Cop '91
Prison Stories: Women on the Inside '91
Spies, Lies and Naked Thighs '91
Keep the Change '92
Where the Day Takes You '92
Falling Down '93
Deconstructing Sarah '94
Don Juan DeMarco '94
Natural Born Killers '94
Steal Big, Steal Little '95
The Wharf Rat '95

Andrew Tiernan
Edward II '92
The Best of Cracker Mysteries '93

Gene Tierney
Return of Frank James '40
Sundown '41
The Shanghai Gesture '42
Son of Fury '42
Heaven Can Wait '43
Laura '44
Leave Her to Heaven '45
The Razor's Edge '46
The Ghost and Mrs. Muir '47
Night and the City '50
Never Let Me Go '53
The Egyptian '54
The Left Hand of God '55
Advise and Consent '62
Toys in the Attic '63
Scruples '80

Jacob Tierney
Josh and S.A.M. '93
The Neon Bible '95

Lawrence Tierney
Back to Bataan '45
Dillinger '45
Those Endearing Young Charms '45
Born to Kill '47
The Devil Thumbs a Ride '47
The Devil Thumbs a Ride/Having Wonderful Crime '47
Best of the Badmen '50
The Hoodlum '51
The Bushwackers '52
The Greatest Show on Earth '52
The Female Jungle '56
Abduction '75
Never Pick Up a Stranger '79
Midnight '81
The Prowler '81
Prizzi's Honor '85
Murphy's Law '86
The Offspring '87
Tough Guys Don't Dance '87
Why Me? '90
City of Hope '91
The Death Merchant '91
Reservoir Dogs '92
Casualties of Love: The "Long Island Lolita" Story '93
A Kiss Goodnight '94

Maura Tierney
Dead Women in Lingerie '90
White Sands '92
The Temp '93
Primal Fear '96

Angelo Tiffe
Sword of Honor '94
3 Ninjas Kick Back '94

Jerry Tiffe
Hollywood in Trouble '87
Sword of Honor '94

Pamela Tiffin
Summer and Smoke '61
State Fair '62
The Hallelujah Trail '65
Viva Max '69

Marie Tifo
Les Bons Debarras '81
Pouvoir Intime '87

Kevin Tighe
Matewan '87
Eight Men Out '88
K-9 '89
Lost Angels '89
Road House '89
Another 48 Hrs. '90
Tales from the Crypt, Vol. 3 '90
Bright Angel '91
City of Hope '91
Newsies '92
School Ties '92
Caught in the Act '93
Geronimo: An American Legend '93
A Man in Uniform '93
What's Eating Gilbert Grape '93
Double Cross '94
Men of War '94
The Avenging Angel '95
Race the Sun '96

Zeffie Tilbury
The Single Standard '29
The Grapes of Wrath '40

Nadja Tiller
The Burning Court '62
Tonio Kroger '65
Wanted: Babysitter '75

Mel Tillis
The Villain '79
Uphill All the Way '85

Grant Tilly
Beyond Reasonable Doubt '80
Carry Me Back '82
Treasure of the Yankee Zephyr '83

Jennifer Tilly
No Small Affair '84
Moving Violations '85
He's My Girl '87
High Spirits '88
Remote Control '88
Rented Lips '88
The Fabulous Baker Boys '89
Far from Home '89
Let It Ride '89
Inside Out '91
Scorchers '92
Shadow of the Wolf '92
The Getaway '93
Heads '93
Made in America '93
At Home with the Webbers '94
Bullets Over Broadway '94
Double Cross '94
Man with a Gun '95
Bound '96
House Arrest '96

Meg Tilly
One Dark Night '82
Tex '82
The Big Chill '83
Psycho 2 '83
Impulse '84
Agnes of God '85
Off Beat '86
Masquerade '88
Carmilla '89
The Girl in a Swing '89
Valmont '89
The Two Jakes '90
Leaving Normal '92
Body Snatchers '93
Fallen Angels 2 '93
Primal Secrets '94
Sleep with Me '94
Journey '95

Charlene Tilton
Sweater Girls '78
The Fall of the House of Usher '80
Diary of a Teenage Hitchhiker '82
Border Shootout '90
Ragin' Cajun '90
Deadly Bet '91
Problem Child 2 '91
Center of the Web '92
Silence of the Hams '93

Martha Tilton
Sunny '41
The Benny Goodman Story '55

Cali Timmins
Hard Evidence '94
The Takeover '94

Charles Tingwell
The Desert Rats '53
Murder She Said '62
Murder at the Gallop '63
Murder Ahoy '64
Murder Most Foul '65
Endplay '75
Gone to Ground '76
Money Movers '78
All the Rivers Run '84
Malcolm '86
Windrider '86
Miracle Down Under '87
A Cry in the Dark '88

Gabriele Tinti
Journey Beneath the Desert '61
Web of Deception '71
Delusions of Grandeur '76
Love Camp '76
Emmanuelle's Daughter '79
Caged Women '84
Trap Them & Kill Them '84

Kenneth Tobey
I Was a Male War Bride '49
The Thing '51
The Beast from 20,000 Fathoms '53
The Bigamist '53
Davy Crockett, King of the Wild Frontier '55
It Came from Beneath the Sea '55
The Great Locomotive Chase '56
The Man in the Gray Flannel Suit '56
The Search for Bridey Murphy '56
Gunfight at the O.K. Corral '57
Wings of Eagles '57
Rage '72
The Lost Empire '83
Strange Invaders '83
Innerspace '87
Freeway '88
Honey, I Blew Up the Kid '92
Single White Female '92

George Tobias
The Hunchback of Notre Dame '39
City for Conquest '40
Music in My Heart '40
The Bride Came C.O.D. '41
Sergeant York '41
Strawberry Blonde '41
Captains of the Clouds '42
Yankee Doodle Dandy '42
Air Force '43
This Is the Army '43
Passage to Marseilles '44
Objective, Burma! '45
Sinbad, the Sailor '47
The Judge Steps Out '49
The Set-Up '49
Rawhide '50
The Seven Little Foys '55
Silk Stockings '57
A New Kind of Love '63

Oliver Tobias
Romance of a Horsethief '71
'Tis a Pity She's a Whore '73
King Arthur, the Young Warlord '75
Young Warlord '75
The Stud '78
The Big Scam '79
The Wicked Lady '83
Mata Hari '85
Operation 'Nam '85

Dan Tobin
Black Limelight '38
Woman of the Year '42
Velvet Touch '48
The Last Angry Man '59

Vivian Tobin
The World Accuses '35
The Flustered Comedy of Leon Errol '39

Stephen Tobolowsky
Keep My Grave Open '80
Spaceballs '87
Mississippi Burning '88
Breaking In '89
Great Balls of Fire '89
Roe vs. Wade '89

Tobolowsky ▶cont.

Bird on a Wire *'90*
Funny About Love *'90*
Tagget *'90*
Deadlock *'91*
Thelma & Louise *'91*
Basic Instinct *'92*
Hero *'92*
Memoirs of an Invisible Man *'92*
Single White Female *'92*
Sneakers *'92*
Where the Day Takes You *'92*
Calendar Girl *'93*
Groundhog Day *'93*
Josh and S.A.M. *'93*
Radioland Murders *'94*
Dr. Jekyll and Ms. Hyde *'95*
Murder In the First *'95*

Brian Tochi
Revenge of the Nerds *'84*
Stitches *'85*

Ann Todd
Intermezzo *'39*
How Green Was My Valley *'41*
Three Daring Daughters *'48*
The Trouble with Father *'50*

Ann Todd
Action for Slander *'38*
The Seventh Veil *'46*
The Paradine Case *'47*
Madeleine *'50*
Time Without Pity *'57*
Scream of Fear *'61*
Son of Captain Blood *'62*
The Fiend *'71*
The Human Factor *'79*

Beverly Todd
Brother John *'70*
Don't Look Back: The Story of Leroy "Satchel" Paige *'81*
The Ladies Club *'86*
Clara's Heart *'88*
Lean on Me *'89*
Class of '61 *'92*

James Todd
Trapped *'49*
High School Confidential *'58*

Lisa Todd
Woman Hunt *'72*
Imposters *'84*
Blood Hook *'86*

Mabel Todd
The Cowboy and the Lady *'38*
The Ghost and the Guest *'43*

Richard Todd
Interrupted Journey *'49*
The Story of Robin Hood & His Merrie Men *'52*
Rob Roy—The Highland Rogue *'53*
The Sword & the Rose *'53*
Dam Busters *'55*
A Man Called Peter *'55*
The Virgin Queen *'55*
Battle Hell *'56*
D-Day, the Sixth of June *'56*
Saint Joan *'57*
Never Let Go *'60*
The Longest Day *'62*
The Very Edge *'63*
Subterfuge *'68*
Dorian Gray *'70*
Number 1 of the Secret Service *'77*
The Big Sleep *'78*
House of the Long Shadows *'82*
Bloodbath

Russell Todd
Chopping Mall *'86*
One Last Run *'89*
Border Shootout *'90*
Sweet Murder *'93*

Thelma Todd
Nevada *'27*
Corsair *'31*
The Maltese Falcon *'31*
Monkey Business *'31*
Horse Feathers *'32*
Laurel & Hardy Comedy Classics, Vol. 4 *'32*
Speak Easily *'32*
The Devil's Brother *'33*
Cockeyed Cavaliers *'34*
Hips, Hips, Hooray *'34*
Palooka *'34*
Bohemian Girl *'36*
Way Out West *'37*
Swiss Miss *'38*

Tony Todd
Voodoo Dawn *'89*
Criminal Justice *'90*
Ivory Hunters *'90*
Night of the Living Dead *'90*
Candyman *'92*
Keeper of the City *'92*
The Crow *'93*
Excessive Force *'93*
Black Fox: The Price of Peace *'94*
Blood Horse *'94*
Candyman 2: Farewell to the Flesh *'94*
Good Men and Bad *'94*
Beastmaster 3: The Eye of Braxus *'95*
The Rock *'96*

Ugo Tognazzi
Love in the City *'53*
RoGoPaG *'62*
Porcile *'69*
Head of the Family *'71*
L'Udienza *'71*
La Grande Bouffe *'73*
La Cage aux Folles *'78*
La Cage aux Folles 2 *'81*
The Tragedy of a Ridiculous Man *'81*
A Joke of Destiny, Lying in Wait Around the Corner Like a Bandit *'84*
La Cage aux Folles 3: The Wedding *'86*

Niall Toibin
Lovespell *'79*
Eat the Peach *'86*
Frankie Starlight *'95*

Marilyn Tokuda
My Tutor *'82*
The Jitters *'88*
The Cage *'89*
Farewell to the King *'89*

Henriette Tol
Question of Silence *'83*
Broken Mirrors *'85*

Michael Tolan
Night Terror *'76*
Half Slave, Half Free *'85*
Presumed Innocent *'90*

Sidney Toler
Blonde Venus *'32*
Speak Easily *'32*
Spitfire *'34*
Champagne for Breakfast *'35*
Our Relations *'36*
Double Wedding *'37*
The Mysterious Rider *'38*
Wide Open Faces *'38*
Law of the Pampas *'39*
Charlie Chan at the Wax Museum *'40*
Murder over New York *'40*
Charlie Chan in Rio *'41*
Castle in the Desert *'42*
A Night to Remember *'42*
Adventures of Smilin' Jack *'43*
Isle of Forgotten Sins *'43*
Charlie Chan in the Secret Service *'44*
The Chinese Cat *'44*
Meeting at Midnight *'44*
Mr. Moto's Last Warning/Meeting at Midnight *'44*
The Jade Mask *'45*
The Scarlet Clue *'45*
The Shanghai Cobra *'45*
Terror by Night/Meeting at Midnight *'46*

John Toles-Bey
Weeds *'87*
A Rage in Harlem *'91*
Leap of Faith *'92*

James Tolkan
Back to the Future *'85*
Off Beat *'86*
Split Decisions *'88*
Viper *'88*
Weekend War *'88*
Back to the Future, Part 2 *'89*
Family Business *'89*
The Hillside Strangler *'89*
Ministry of Vengeance *'89*
Second Sight *'89*
Back to the Future, Part 3 *'90*
Dick Tracy *'90*
Opportunity Knocks *'90*
Problem Child 2 *'91*
Bloodfist 4: Die Trying *'92*
Sketch Artist *'92*
Boiling Point *'93*
Question of Faith *'93*
Sketch Artist 2: Hands That See *'94*

Marilu Tolo
Marriage Italian Style *'64*
Messalina vs. the Son of Hercules *'64*
Terror of Rome Against the Son of Hercules *'64*
Confessions of a Police Captain *'72*
Killer Likes Candy *'78*
Sleep of Death *'79*

David Tom
Stay Tuned *'92*
Swing Kids *'93*

Lauren Tom
The Joy Luck Club *'93*
Mr. Jones *'93*
When a Man Loves a Woman *'94*

Nicholle Tom
Beethoven *'92*
Beethoven's 2nd *'93*
Season of Change *'94*

Jeana Tomasina
Beach Girls *'82*
Up the Creek *'84*

Concetta Tomei
China Beach *'88*
Don't Tell Mom the Babysitter's Dead *'91*
In Love and War *'91*
Scott Turow's The Burden of Proof *'92*
The Goodbye Bird *'93*

Marisa Tomei
Oscar *'91*
Zandalee *'91*
Chaplin *'92*
My Cousin Vinny *'92*
Equinox *'93*
Untamed Heart *'93*
Only You *'94*
The Paper *'94*
The Perez Family *'94*
Four Rooms *'95*

Frances Tomelty
Bullshot *'83*
Blue Money *'84*
Footlight Frenzy *'84*
Lamb *'85*
Bellman and True *'88*
A Perfect Spy *'88*
The Field *'90*

Joseph Tomelty
Devil Girl from Mars *'54*
The Atomic Man *'56*

Akihiro Tomikawa
Baby Cart 1: Lend a Child...Lend an Arm *'72*
Baby Cart 4: Heart of a Parent...Heart of a Child *'72*
Baby Cart at the River Styx *'72*
Baby Cart to Hades *'72*

Tamlyn Tomita
The Karate Kid: Part 2 *'86*
Hiroshima Maiden *'88*
Come See the Paradise *'90*
Hiroshima: Out of the Ashes *'90*
Vietnam, Texas *'90*
The Joy Luck Club *'93*
Picture Bride *'94*
Four Rooms *'95*

Lily Tomlin
Nashville *'75*
The Late Show *'77*
9 to 5 *'80*
The Incredible Shrinking Woman *'81*
All of Me *'84*
Big Business *'88*
Search for Signs of Intelligent Life in the Universe *'91*
Shadows and Fog *'92*
And the Band Played On *'93*
The Beverly Hillbillies *'93*
Short Cuts *'93*
Blue In the Face *'95*
Flirting with Disaster *'95*
Getting Away With Murder *'96*

David Tomlinson
Pimpernel Smith *'42*
Sleeping Car to Trieste *'45*
Fame Is the Spur *'47*
Wooden Horse *'50*
Made in Heaven *'52*
Carry On Admiral *'57*
Up the Creek *'58*
Tom Jones *'63*
Mary Poppins *'64*
Bedknobs and Broomsticks *'71*
Wombling Free *'77*
Water Babies *'79*
The Fiendish Plot of Dr. Fu Manchu *'80*

Ricky Tomlinson
Riff Raff *'92*
Raining Stones *'93*
Butterfly Kiss *'94*

Angel Tompkins
I Love My...Wife *'70*
Prime Cut *'72*
Probe *'72*
The Don is Dead *'73*
The Teacher *'74*
Walking Tall: Part 2 *'75*
The Bees *'78*
Murphy's Law *'86*
Naked Cage *'86*
A Tiger's Tale *'87*
Crack House *'89*
Relentless *'89*

Kate Toncray
The Lamb *'15*
The Country Kid *'23*

Franchot Tone
Bombshell *'33*
Dancing Lady *'33*
Gabriel Over the White House *'33*
Today We Live *'33*
The Girl from Missouri *'34*
Sadie McKee *'34*
Dangerous *'35*
The Lives of a Bengal Lancer *'35*
Mutiny on the Bounty *'35*
Reckless *'35*
The Gorgeous Hussy *'36*
Love on the Run *'36*
Suzy *'36*
The Bride Wore Red *'37*
Quality Street *'37*
Three Comrades *'38*
His Butler's Sister *'43*
Dark Waters *'44*
Her Husband's Affairs *'47*
Lost Honeymoon *'47*
Every Girl Should Be Married *'48*
Man on the Eiffel Tower *'48*
Jigsaw *'49*
Here Comes the Groom *'51*
Advise and Consent *'62*
In Harm's Way *'65*
Mickey One *'65*

Tone Loc
The Adventures of Ford Fairlane *'90*
Ace Ventura: Pet Detective *'93*
Blank Check *'93*
Posse *'93*
Surf Ninjas *'93*

Eijiro Tono
The Human Condition: No Greater Love *'58*
Yojimbo *'61*

Taiji Tonoyama
The Island *'61*
Tokyo Pop *'88*

Regis Toomey
The Light of Western Stars *'30*
They Never Come Back *'32*
Laughing at Life *'33*
"G" Men *'35*
Skull & Crown *'35*
Bulldog Edition *'36*
Shadows of the Orient *'37*
Wayne Murder Case *'38*
The Phantom Creeps *'39*
Union Pacific *'39*
Arizona *'40*
Dive Bomber *'41*
Meet John Doe *'41*
They Died with Their Boots On *'41*
Destroyer *'43*
The Adventures of the Flying Cadets *'44*
Betrayal from the East *'44*
Dark Mountain *'44*
Raiders of Ghost City *'44*
Spellbound *'45*
Strange Illusion *'45*
The Big Sleep *'46*
The Bishop's Wife *'47*
Magic Town *'47*
Beyond the Forest *'49*
Come to the Stable *'49*
Dynamite Pass *'50*
Never Wave at a WAC *'52*
Great Day in the Morning *'56*
The Curfew Breakers *'57*
Warlock *'59*
Change of Habit *'69*

Gordon Tootoosis
Dan Candy's Law *'73*
Stone Fox *'87*
Call of the Wild *'93*
Spirit Rider *'93*
Legends of the Fall *'94*
Pocahontas: The Legend *'95*

Chaim Topol
Sallah *'63*
Cast a Giant Shadow *'66*
Gun Crazy *'69*
Fiddler on the Roof *'71*
The House on Garibaldi Street *'79*
Flash Gordon *'80*
For Your Eyes Only *'81*
The Winds of War *'83*
Queenie *'87*
War & Remembrance, Part 1 *'88*
War & Remembrance: The Final Chapter, Part 8 *'89*

Peta Toppano
Echoes of Paradise *'86*
Which Way Home *'90*

Hal Torey
Earth vs. the Spider *'58*
Invisible Invaders *'59*

Sarah Torgov
Drying Up the Streets *'76*
If You Could See What I Hear *'82*
American Gothic *'88*

Mel Torme
Good News *'47*
Words and Music *'48*
Girls' Town *'59*
A Man Called Adam *'66*

Rip Torn
Baby Doll *'56*
Pork Chop Hill *'59*
The King of Kings *'61*
24 Hours in a Woman's Life *'61*
Sweet Bird of Youth *'62*
The Cincinnati Kid *'65*
You're a Big Boy Now *'66*
Tropic of Cancer *'70*
The President's Plane is Missing *'71*
Cotter *'72*
Payday *'72*
Slaughter *'72*
The Man Who Fell to Earth *'76*
Nasty Habits *'77*
The Private Files of J. Edgar Hoover *'77*
Betrayal *'78*
The Birch Interval *'78*
Coma *'78*
Steel Cowboy *'78*
The Seduction of Joe Tynan *'79*
A Shining Season *'79*
One Trick Pony *'80*
Rape and Marriage: The Rideout Case *'80*
Heartland *'81*
Airplane 2: The Sequel *'82*
Beastmaster *'82*
Blind Ambition *'82*
Jinxed *'82*
A Stranger is Watching *'82*
Cross Creek *'83*
Cat on a Hot Tin Roof *'84*
City Heat *'84*
Flashpoint *'84*
Misunderstood *'84*
Songwriter *'84*
Beer *'85*

The Execution '85
Summer Rental '85
Manhunt for Claude Dallas '86
Extreme Prejudice '87
J. Edgar Hoover '87
Laguna Heat '87
Nadine '87
The Hit List '88
By Dawn's Early Light '89
Cold Feet '89
Sweet Bird of Youth '89
Pair of Aces '90
Silence Like Glass '90
Another Pair of Aces: Three of a Kind '91
Defending Your Life '91
RoboCop 3 '91
Beautiful Dreamers '92
Beyond the Law '92
Dead Ahead: The Exxon Valdez Disaster '92
Dolly Dearest '92
Hard Promises '92
Canadian Bacon '94
Where the Rivers Flow North '94
How to Make an American Quilt '95
Letter to My Killer '95
Down Periscope '96

Mari Torocsik
Love '71
The Bachelor '93

David Torrence
Disraeli '29
The Mask of Fu Manchu '32
Jane Eyre '34

Ernest Torrence
Tol'able David '21
The Covered Wagon '23
The Hunchback of Notre Dame '23
The Pony Express '25
Mantrap '26
King of Kings '27
Steamboat Bill, Jr. '28
Fighting Caravans '31
I Cover the Waterfront '33

Pip Torrens
A Handful of Dust '88
A Dark Adapted Eye '93

Ana Torrent
Spirit of the Beehive '73
Cria '76
The Nest '80
Blood and Sand '89

Fernanda Torres
One Man's War '90
Savage Capitalism '93

Liz Torres
America '86
Lena's Holiday '90
Bloodfist 4: Die Trying '92
National Lampoon's Attack of the 5 Ft. 2 Women '94

Raquel Torres
White Shadows in the South Seas '28
Duck Soup '33

Joe Torry
Poetic Justice '93
Tales from the Hood '95

Jose Torvay
Borderline '50
My Outlaw Brother '51
The Hitch-Hiker '53
Green Fire '55

Leslie Toth
Buying Time '89
Unfinished Business '89

Merle Tottenham
Cavalcade '33
Room to Let '49

Audrey Totter
Lady in the Lake '46
The Postman Always Rings Twice '46
Any Number Can Play '49
The Set-Up '49
FBI Girl '52
Jet Attack/Paratroop Command '58
Man or Gun '58
The Carpetbaggers '64

George Touliatos
Firebird 2015 A.D. '81
Robbers of the Sacred Mountain '83
Red Scorpion 2 '94
Tracks of a Killer '95

Tamara Toumanova
Days of Glory '43
Invitation to the Dance '56

Sheila Tousey
Silent Tongue '92
Thunderheart '92
Slaughter of the Innocents '93
Medicine River '94

Beth Toussaint
Blackmail '91
Breach of Conduct '94
Night Siege Project: Shadowchaser 2 '94

Lorraine Toussaint
A Case of Deadly Force '86
Breaking In '89
Point of No Return '93
Mother's Boys '94
America's Dream '95
Dangerous Minds '95

Roland Toutain
Liliom '35
The Rules of the Game '39

Lupita Tovar
Border Law '31
Dracula (Spanish Version) '31
Old Spanish Custom '36

Constance Towers
Sergeant Rutledge '60
Shock Corridor '63
Naked Kiss '64
Sylvester '85
On Wings of Eagles '86

Tom Towles
The Borrower '89
Henry: Portrait of a Serial Killer '90
Night of the Living Dead '90
The Pit & the Pendulum '91
Blood In...Blood Out: Bound by Honor '93
Mad Dog and Glory '93
Normal Life '96

Aline Towne
The Invisible Monster '50
The Vanishing Westerner '50
Don Daredevil Rides Again '51
Radar Men from the Moon '52
Zombies of the Stratosphere '52
Trader Tom of the China Seas '54

Robert Towne
Villa Rides '68
The Pick-Up Artist '87

Jill Townsend
Oh, Alfie '75
Poldark '75
Poldark 2 '75

Patrice Townsend
Sitting Ducks '80
Always '85

Robert Townsend
A Soldier's Story '84
Streets of Fire '84
American Flyers '85
Odd Jobs '85
Ratboy '86
Hollywood Shuffle '87
The Mighty Quinn '89
That's Adequate '90
The Five Heartbeats '91
The Meteor Man '93

Pete Townshend
Tommy '75
Secret Policeman's Private Parts '81
The Secret Policeman's Other Ball '82
Pete Townshend: White City '85

Fausto Tozzi
East of Kilimanjaro '57
The Return of Dr. Mabuse '61
Sicilian Connection '74

Ian Tracey
The Comrades of Summer '92
Incident at Deception Ridge '94
Timecop '94
Man with a Gun '95

Lee Tracy
Blessed Event '32
Doctor X '32
The Strange Love of Molly Louvain '32
Bombshell '33
Dinner at Eight '33
The Payoff '43
Betrayal from the East '44
The Best Man '64

Spencer Tracy
Marie Galante '34
Riff Raff '35
Fury '36
Libeled Lady '36
San Francisco '36
Captains Courageous '37
Mannequin '37
Boys Town '38
Test Pilot '38
Stanley and Livingstone '39
Boom Town '40
Edison the Man '40
Northwest Passage '40
Dr. Jekyll and Mr. Hyde '41
Men of Boys Town '41
Keeper of the Flame '42
Tortilla Flat '42
Woman of the Year '42
A Guy Named Joe '44
The Seventh Cross '44
Thirty Seconds Over Tokyo '44
Without Love '45
Cass Timberlane '47
State of the Union '48
Malaya '49
Adam's Rib '50
Father of the Bride '50
Father's Little Dividend '51
Pat and Mike '52
Bad Day at Black Rock '54
Broken Lance '54
The Mountain '56
Desk Set '57
Last Hurrah '58
Inherit the Wind '60
The Devil at 4 O'Clock '61
Judgment at Nuremberg '61
How the West Was Won '63
It's a Mad, Mad, Mad, Mad World '63
Guess Who's Coming to Dinner '67
Hepburn & Tracy '84

William Tracy
Angels with Dirty Faces '38
Strike Up the Band '40
Tanks a Million '41
George Washington Slept Here '42
To the Shores of Tripoli '42
As You Were '51
Mr. Walkie Talkie '52

Mary Ellen Trainor
The Goonies '85
Die Hard '88
Lethal Weapon 2 '89
Tales from the Crypt '89
Fire Birds '90
Grand Canyon '91
Ricochet '91
Little Giants '94

Cordula Trantow
Hitler '62
The Castle '68

Helen Traubel
Deep in My Heart '54
The Ladies' Man '61

Daniel J. Travanti
St. Ives '76
Hill Street Blues, Vol. 1: Hill Street Station '81
Adam '83
A Case of Libel '83
Murrow '86
Midnight Crossing '87
Fellow Traveler '89
Millenium '89
Skin '89
Tagget '90
Megaville '91
Weep No More My Lady '93
Eyes of a Witness '94
Just Cause '94

Bill Travers
Trio '50
The Browning Version '51
Romeo and Juliet '54
Bhowani Junction '56
The Smallest Show on Earth '57
Gorgo '61
Born Free '66
Duel at Diablo '66
A Midsummer Night's Dream '68
Ring of Bright Water '69
Christian the Lion '76
The First Olympics: Athens 1896 '84

Henry Travers
The Sisters '38
Dark Victory '39
Dodge City '39
On Borrowed Time '39
The Rains Came '39
Stanley and Livingstone '39
Edison the Man '40
Primrose Path '40
Ball of Fire '41
A Girl, a Guy and a Gob '41
High Sierra '41
Mrs. Miniver '42
Random Harvest '42
Madame Curie '43
Shadow of a Doubt '43
Dragon Seed '44
The Bells of St. Mary's '45
The Naughty Nineties '45
Thrill of a Romance '45
It's a Wonderful Life '46
The Yearling '46

Linden Travers
The Lady Vanishes '38
The Terror '38

Susan Travers
The Snake Woman '61
Peeping Tom '63
The Abominable Dr. Phibes '71

June Travis
Ceiling Zero '35
Earthworm Tractors '36
Exiled to Shanghai '37
The Gladiator '38
Monster a Go-Go! '65

Nancy Travis
Harem '86
Three Men and a Baby '87
Married to the Mob '88
Air America '90
Internal Affairs '90
Loose Cannons '90
Three Men and a Little Lady '90
Chaplin '92
Passed Away '92
Fallen Angels 1 '93
So I Married an Axe Murderer '93
The Vanishing '93
Greedy '94
Body Language '95
Destiny Turns on the Radio '95
Fluke '95

Randy Travis
Dead Man's Revenge '93
Frank and Jesse '94
Texas '94

Richard Travis
The Man Who Came to Dinner '41
Big Town After Dark '47
Sky Liner '49
Danger Zone '51
Fingerprints Don't Lie '51
Mask of the Dragon '51
One Too Many '51
Roaring City '51
Mesa of Lost Women '52
Missile to the Moon '59

Stacy Travis
Dr. Hackenstein '88
Hardware '90
Dracula Rising '93
Only the Strong '93
Suspect Device '95

Tony Travis
The Beatniks '60
Flesh Gordon 2: Flesh Gordon Meets the Cosmic Cheerleaders '90

Joey Travolta
Sunnyside '79
Rosie: The Rosemary Clooney Story '82
The Prodigal '83
American Born '89
Ghost Writer '89
Sinners '89
Wilding '90
DaVinci's War '92
Beach Babes from Beyond Infinity '93
To the Limit '95
Car Crash

John Travolta
Devil's Rain '75
The Boy in the Plastic Bubble '76
Carrie '76
Saturday Night Fever '77
Grease '78
Urban Cowboy '80
Blow Out '81
Staying Alive '83
Two of a Kind '83
Perfect '85
Dumb Waiter '87
The Experts '89
Look Who's Talking '89
Look Who's Talking, Too '90
Eyes of an Angel '91
Shout '91
Chains of Gold '92
Look Who's Talking Now '93
Pulp Fiction '94
Broken Arrow '95
Get Shorty '95
White Man's Burden '95
Phenomenon '96

Susan Traylor
The New Age '94
Sleep with Me '94
To Die For '95

Arthur Treacher
Curly Top '35
David Copperfield '35
I Live My Life '35
A Midsummer Night's Dream '35
Satan Met a Lady '36
Stowaway '36
Heidi '37
Thin Ice '37
Mad About Music '38
My Lucky Star '38
The Little Princess '39
Star Spangled Rhythm '42
In Society '44
National Velvet '44
Delightfully Dangerous '45

Emerson Treacy
Champagne for Breakfast '35
Give Me a Sailor '38
A Star is Born '54

Michael Treanor
3 Ninjas '92
3 Ninjas Knuckle Up '92

Terri Treas
The Nest '88
The Terror Within '88
Deathstalker 3 '89
House 4: Home Deadly Home '91
Rage and Honor '92
Alien Nation: Dark Horizon '94
Yankee Zulu '95

Robert Trebor
Out of the Darkness '85
52 Pick-Up '86

Dorothy Tree
Mystery of Mr. Wong '39
Abe Lincoln in Illinois '40
Hitler: Dead or Alive '43

Mary Treen
Swing It, Sailor! '37
First Love '39
Hands Across the Border '43
Casanova Brown '44
It's a Wonderful Life '46
Clipped Wings '53
The Sad Sack '57
I Married a Monster from Outer Space '58
Paradise, Hawaiian Style '66

Danny Trejo
Undercover Cop '94
From Dusk Till Dawn '95

Les Tremayne
Francis Goes to West Point '52
I Love Melvin '53
The War of the Worlds '53
A Man Called Peter '55
The Monolith Monsters '57

Tremayne ▶*cont.*

The Monster of Piedras Blancas '57
The Angry Red Planet '59
The Gallant Hours '60
The Slime People '63
Creature of Destruction '67
Fangs '75

Johanne-Marie Tremblay
Straight for the Heart '88
Jesus of Montreal '89

John Trent
Mystery Plane '39
Stunt Pilot '39

Adam Trese
The Good Fight '92
Laws of Gravity '92
The Underneath '95

Frederick Treves
Flame to the Phoenix '85
Paper Mask '91

Leonardo Treviglio
Sebastiane '79
Stealing Beauty '96

Roger Treville
Mr. Peek-A-Boo '50
The Green Glove '52

Vic Trevino
Born in East L.A. '87
Firehawk '92

Austin Trevor
Broken Melody '34
Mimi '35
The Silent Passenger '35

Claire Trevor
Baby, Take a Bow '34
Dead End '37
Allegheny Uprising '39
Stagecoach '39
Dark Command '40
Honky Tonk '41
Texas '41
Murder, My Sweet '44
The Woman of the Town '44
Johnny Angel '45
Crack-Up '46
Born to Kill '47
Babe Ruth Story '48
Key Largo '48
Velvet Touch '48
Best of the Badmen '50
Borderline '50
Hoodlum Empire '52
The Stranger Wore a Gun '53
Man Without a Star '55
The Mountain '56
Marjorie Morningstar '58
Two Weeks in Another Town '62
The Stripper '63
How to Murder Your Wife '64
Kiss Me Goodbye '82
Breaking Home Ties '87

Jack Trevor
Secrets of a Soul '25
Champagne '28

Paula Trickey
Carnal Crimes '91
A Kiss Goodnight '94

Ivan Triesault
Cry of the Werewolf '44
Golden Earrings '47
Five Fingers '52
Jet Pilot '57
The Amazing Transparent Man '60

Leopoldo Trieste
The White Sheik '52
I Vitelloni '53
Divorce—Italian Style '62
Henry IV '85
Quo Vadis '85
Cinema Paradiso '88

Sarah Trigger
El Diablo '90
Kid '90
Bill & Ted's Bogus Journey '91
Paradise '91
Pet Sematary 2 '92
Deadfall '93
Sleepless in Seattle '93

P.C.U. '94

Jerry Trimble
Breathing Fire '91
Full Contact '93
One Man Army '93
Stranglehold '94

Jean-Louis Trintignant
And God Created Woman '57
Dangerous Liaisons '60
Journey Beneath the Desert '61
The Easy Life '63
Il Sorpasso '63
A Man and a Woman '66
Is Paris Burning? '68
Les Biches '68
My Night at Maud's '69
Z '69
The Conformist '71
And Hope to Die '72
Act of Aggression '73
The Outside Man '73
The Last Train '74
Le Secret '74
Les Violons du Bal '74
Intruder '77
Passion of Love '82
Confidentially Yours '83
I Love All of You '83
Under Fire '83
Next Summer '84
Rendez-vous '85
A Man and a Woman: 20 Years Later '86
Trois Couleurs: Rouge '94

Marie Trintignant
Next Summer '84
The Story of Women '88
Alberto Express '92
Betty '92

Louis Tripp
The Gate '87
Gate 2 '92

Jeanne Tripplehorn
Basic Instinct '92
The Firm '93
The Night We Never Met '93
Waterworld '95

Jan Triska
My Antonia '94
Andersonville '95

Elisabeth Trissenaar
The Stationmaster's Wife '77
In a Year of 13 Moons '78
Berlin Alexanderplatz '80
A Love in Germany '84
Angry Harvest '85

Dorothy Tristan
End of the Road '70
Griffin and Phoenix: A Love Story '76
Down and Out in Beverly Hills '86

Massimo Troisi
Hotel Colonial '88
The Postman '94

Laura Trotter
City of the Walking Dead '83
Rush '84
Miami Horror '87

David Troughton
Sharpe's Eagle '93
Sharpe's Rifles '93

Patrick Troughton
The Franchise Affair '52
The Moonraker '58
The Gorgon '64
The Scars of Dracula '70

Charles Trowbridge
Libeled Lady '36
Sea Racketeers '37
Gang Bullets '38
The Fatal Hour '40
The Mummy's Hand '40

Phillip Troy
Ice '93
To Be the Best '93

Isabelle Truchon
Backstab '90
Deadbolt '92

Jim True
Singles '92
The Hudsucker Proxy '93
Normal Life '96

Ernest Truex
The Adventures of Marco Polo '38
His Girl Friday '40
Club Havana '46
All Mine to Give '56

Francois Truffaut
The 400 Blows '59
Day for Night '73
Close Encounters of the Third Kind '77
The Green Room '78

Raoul Trujillo
The Adjuster '91
Scanners 2: The New Order '91
Black Fox: The Price of Peace '94
Blood Horse '94
Good Men and Bad '94
Medicine River '94
Paris, France '94
The Invaders '95

Ralph Truman
The Silent Passenger '35
Henry V '44
Treasure Island '50
The Man Who Knew Too Much '56
The Spaniard's Curse '58

Natalie Trundy
Beneath the Planet of the Apes '70
Escape from the Planet of the Apes '71
Conquest of the Planet of the Apes '72
Battle for the Planet of the Apes '73
Huckleberry Finn '74

Glenn Tryon
Battling Orioles '24
Dames Ahoy '30
Tangled Destinies '32

Tom Tryon
Three Violent People '57
Unholy Wife '57
I Married a Monster from Outer Space '58
Gunfight at Sandoval '59
Geronimo's Revenge '60
The Story of Ruth '60
Texas John Slaughter: Geronimo's Revenge '60
The Longest Day '62
Moon Pilot '62
Texas John Slaughter: Stampede at Bitter Creek '62
The Cardinal '63
In Harm's Way '65
Color Me Dead '69

Ludmila Tselikovskaya
Ivan the Terrible, Part 1 '44
Ivan the Terrible, Part 2 '46

Irene Tsu
How to Stuff a Wild Bikini '65
Paradise, Hawaiian Style '66
Women of the Prehistoric Planet '66

Yoshio Tsuchiya
Attack of the Mushroom People '63
Red Beard '65
Destroy All Monsters '68
Yog, Monster from Space '71

Masahiko Tsugawa
The Sun's Burial '60
A Taxing Woman's Return '88
Heaven & Earth '90

Koji Tsurata
Samurai 3: Duel at Ganryu Island '56
The Secret of the Telegian '61

Barry Tubb
Consenting Adult '85
Mask '85
Top Gun '86
Billionaire Boys Club '87
Valentino Returns '88
Warm Summer Rain '89
Guilty by Suspicion '91
Return to Lonesome Dove '93

William Tubbs
Paisan '46
Wages of Fear '55

Maria Tucci
Enormous Changes '83
Trumps '83
Touch and Go '86
To Die For '95

Stanley Tucci
Monkey Shines '88
Fear, Anxiety and Depression '89
Billy Bathgate '91
Men of Respect '91
Beethoven '92
In the Soup '92
Prelude to a Kiss '92
The Public Eye '92
The Pelican Brief '93
Undercover Blues '93
It Could Happen to You '94
Kiss of Death '94
Big Night '95
Jury Duty '95

Jessica Tuck
Mr. Write '92
Lifepod '93
The O.J. Simpson Story '94
Revenge of the Nerds 4: Nerds in Love '94

Chris Tucker
House Party 3 '94
Dead Presidents '95
Friday '95

Forrest Tucker
The Westerner '40
Robot Pilot '41
Keeper of the Flame '42
Never Say Goodbye '46
The Yearling '46
Coroner Creek '48
Hellfire '48
The Big Cat '49
Sands of Iwo Jima '49
The Nevadan '50
Bugles in the Afternoon '52
Hoodlum Empire '52
Montana Belle '52
Pony Express '53
Jubilee Trail '54
Trouble in the Glen '54
The Finger Man '55
Rage at Dawn '55
Three Violent People '57
Auntie Mame '58
The Cosmic Monsters '58
The Crawling Eye '58
Chisum '70
Cancel My Reservation '72
The Incredible Rocky Mountain Race '77
Wackiest Wagon Train in the West '77
Walking Tall: The Final Chapter '77
The Adventures of Huckleberry Finn '78
A Real American Hero '78
The Rebels '79
A Rare Breed '81
Outtakes '85
Thunder Run '86
Timestalkers '87

Martin Tucker
House of Death '82
Death Screams '83

Michael Tucker
Eyes of Laura Mars '78
Diner '82
The Purple Rose of Cairo '85
L.A. Law '86
Assault and Matrimony '87
Radio Days '87
Tin Men '87
Checking Out '89
Day One '89
Spy '89
Too Young to Die '90
For Love or Money '93
D2: The Mighty Ducks '94

Richard Tucker
The Worldly Madonna '22
Captain Swagger '25
King of the Kongo '29
The Bat Whispers '30
Convicted '32
Delinquent Parents '38

Rocky Tucker
Lunatic '91
Steps from Hell '92

Sophie Tucker
Broadway Melody of 1938 '37
Thoroughbreds Don't Cry '37
Sensations of 1945 '44

Tanya Tucker
The Rebels '79
Follow That Car '80
Hard Country '81

Sonny Tufts
So Proudly We Hail '43
Here Come the Waves '44
The Virginian '46
Easy Living '49
The Gift Horse '52
Cat Women of the Moon '53
Serpent Island '54
The Seven Year Itch '55

Tom Tully
Destination Tokyo '43
Northern Pursuit '43
Adventure '45
Lady in the Lake '46
Till the End of Time '46
The Virginian '46
June Bride '48
Texas Carnival '51
Love Is Better Than Ever '52
The Moon Is Blue '53
Trouble Along the Way '53
The Caine Mutiny '54
Love Me or Leave Me '55
Soldier of Fortune '55
Ten North Frederick '58
Coogan's Bluff '68

Frans Tumbuan
Rage and Honor 2: Hostile Takeover '93
Without Mercy '95

Tommy Tune
Hello, Dolly! '69
The Boy Friend '71

Bill Tung
Jackie Chan's Police Force '85
Rumble in the Bronx '96

Robin Tunney
Encino Man '92
JFK: Reckless Youth '93
Empire Records '95
The Craft '96
Riders of the Purple Sage '96

Paige Turco
Teenage Mutant Ninja Turtles 2: The Secret of the Ooze '91
Teenage Mutant Ninja Turtles 3 '93
Dead Funny '94
Vibrations '94

Ann Turkel
Paper Lion '68
99 & 44/100 Dead '74
The Cassandra Crossing '76
Golden Rendezvous '77
Portrait of a Hitman '77
Humanoids from the Deep '80
Death Ray 2000 '81
The Last Contract '86
Deep Space '87
The Fear '94

Joe Turkel
Cycle Psycho '72
The Desperados '80s
The Shining '80
Blade Runner '82
Dark Side of the Moon '90

Glynn Turman
The Blue Knight '75
Cooley High '75
J.D.'s Revenge '76
The River Niger '76
A Hero Ain't Nothin' But a Sandwich '78
Penitentiary 2 '82
Secrets of a Married Man '84
Charlotte Forten's Mission: Experiment in Freedom '85
Deep Cover '92
Race to Freedom: The Story of the Underground Railroad '94

John Turnbull
The Passing of the Third Floor Back '36
Make-Up '37
Man of Evil '48

The Happiest Days of Your Life '50

Elizabeth Turner
Invasion of the Flesh Hunters '82
Truck Stop

Florence Turner
Tale of Two Cities/In the Switch Tower '15
Walking Back '26
Pace That Kills '28

George Turner
Vigilantes of Boom Town '46
Son of Zorro '47

Janine Turner
Knights of the City '85
Monkey Shines '88
Steel Magnolias '89
The Ambulance '90
Cliffhanger '93

Jim Turner
Kid Colter '85
My Samurai '92
Joe's Apartment '96

Kathleen Turner
Body Heat '81
The Man with Two Brains '83
A Breed Apart '84
Crimes of Passion '84
Romancing the Stone '84
The Jewel of the Nile '85
Prizzi's Honor '85
Peggy Sue Got Married '86
Julia and Julia '87
The Accidental Tourist '88
Switching Channels '88
The War of the Roses '89
V.I. Warshawski '91
House of Cards '92
Naked in New York '93
Undercover Blues '93
Serial Mom '94
Moonlight and Valentino '95

Lana Turner
They Won't Forget '37
Love Finds Andy Hardy '38
Dr. Jekyll and Mr. Hyde '41
Honky Tonk '41
Ziegfeld Girl '41
Johnny Eager '42
Somewhere I'll Find You '42
Weekend at the Waldorf '45
The Postman Always Rings Twice '46
Cass Timberlane '47
Green Dolphin Street '47
Homecoming '48
The Three Musketeers '48
A Life of Her Own '50
The Bad and the Beautiful '52
The Merry Widow '52
Latin Lovers '53
Betrayed '54
Diane '55
The Prodigal '55
Sea Chase '55
Peyton Place '57
Another Time, Another Place '58
Imitation of Life '59
By Love Possessed '61
Who's Got the Action? '63
Love Has Many Faces '65
Madame X '66
Bachelor in Paradise '69
The Graveyard '74
Bittersweet Love '76
Witches' Brew '79

Tina Turner
Tommy '75
Mad Max: Beyond Thunderdome '85

Tyrin Turner
Menace II Society '93
Soldier Boyz '95

Ben Turpin
Laughfest '10s
Cannon Ball/Eyes Have It '15
The Champion/His New Job '15
Chaplin Essanay Book 1 '15
Silent Laugh Makers, No. 1 '15
Burlesque of Carmen '16
Yankee Doodle in Berlin '19
Charlie Chase and Ben Turpin '21
Eyes of Turpin Are Upon You! '21
Mack Sennett Comedies: Vol. 1 '21
Desperate Scoundrel/The Pride of Pikeville '22
Ben Turpin: An Eye for an Eye '24
Slapstick '30s
Law of the Wild '34
Chasing Those Depression Blues '35
Laurel & Hardy Comedy Classics, Vol. 6 '35
Saps at Sea '40
Golden Age of Comedy '58
When Comedy was King '59

Aida Turturro
True Love '89
Jersey Girl '92
Angie '94
Junior '94
Denise Calls Up '95

John Turturro
Desperately Seeking Susan '85
Gung Ho '85
To Live & Die in L.A. '85
The Color of Money '86
Hannah and Her Sisters '86
Off Beat '86
The Sicilian '87
Five Corners '88
Backtrack '89
Do the Right Thing '89
Miller's Crossing '90
Mo' Better Blues '90
State of Grace '90
Barton Fink '91
Jungle Fever '91
Men of Respect '91
Brain Donors '92
Fearless '93
Mac '93
Being Human '94
Quiz Show '94
Search and Destroy '94
Clockers '95
Sugartime '95
Unstrung Heroes '95
Girl 6 '96

Nicholas Turturro
Mo' Better Blues '90
Mac '93
Cosmic Slop '94
Federal Hill '94

Rita Tushingham
A Taste of Honey '61
Leather Boys '63
Doctor Zhivago '65
The Knack '65
Trap '66
Dressed for Death '74
The Human Factor '75
Rachel's Man '75
Green Eyes '76
Slaughterday '77
Loose in New York '80s
Spaghetti House '82
Mysteries '84
Dream to Believe '85
The Housekeeper '86
Paper Marriage '93
An Awfully Big Adventure '94

Dorothy Tutin
A Tale of Two Cities '58
Six Wives of Henry VIII '70s
Savage Messiah '72
Sister Dora '77
The Shooting Party '85
Scarlett '94

Lurene Tuttle
Homecoming '48
Don't Bother to Knock '52
The Affairs of Dobie Gillis '53
The Glass Slipper '55
Ma Barker's Killer Brood '60
The Fortune Cookie '66
The Ghost and Mr. Chicken '66
White Mama '80

Shannon Tweed
Hot Dog...The Movie! '83
Of Unknown Origin '83
The Last Fling '86
Codename: Vengeance '87
Hitchhiker 4 '87
Meatballs 3 '87
Lethal Woman '88
Surrogate '88
Cannibal Women in the Avocado Jungle of Death '89
In the Cold of the Night '89
Night Visitor '89
Twisted Justice '89
Last Call '90
The Firing Line '91
The Last Hour '91
Night Eyes 2 '91
Liar's Edge '92
Sexual Response '92
Cold Sweat '93
Indecent Behavior '93
Night Eyes 3 '93
Possessed by the Night '93
Scorned '93
Hard Vice '94
Illicit Dreams '94
Indecent Behavior 2 '94
Model by Day '94
Night Fire '94
No Contest '94
Victim of Desire '94
Body Chemistry 4: Full Exposure '95
The Dark Dancer '95
Indecent Behavior 3 '95

Terry Tweed
The Reincarnate '71
Night Rhythms '92

Helen Twelvetrees
Millie '31
Painted Desert '31
State's Attorney '31

Twiggy
The Boy Friend '71
W '74
Butterfly Ball '76
The Doctor and the Devils '85
Club Paradise '86
The Little Match Girl '87
Madame Sousatzka '88
Young Charlie Chaplin '88
Istanbul '90
The Diamond Trap '91
Body Bags '93

Anne Twomey
Behind Enemy Lines '85
Deadly Friend '86
Last Rites '88
Orpheus Descending '91
The Scout '94

Liv Tyler
Heavy '94
Silent Fall '94
Empire Records '95
Stealing Beauty '96

Tom Tyler
Battling with Buffalo Bill '31
Phantom of the West '31
Two Fisted Justice '31
The Forty-Niners '32
Deadwood Pass '33
Phantom of the Air '33
When a Man Rides Alone '33
The Silver Bullet '34
Coyote Trails '35
Laramie Kid '35
Powdersmoke Range '35
Ridin' Thru '35
Rio Rattler '35
Silent Code '35
Silent Valley '35
Last Outlaw '36
Pinto Rustlers '36
Rip Roarin' Buckaroo '36
Roamin' Wild '36
Brothers of the West '37
Feud of the Trail '37
Riding On '37
Santa Fe Bound '37
Cheyenne Rides Again '38
The Phantom of the Range '38
Stagecoach '39
The Mummy's Hand '40
The Adventures of Captain Marvel '41
Riders of the Timberline '41
Valley of the Sun '42
Fast Bullets '44
Guns of Justice '50

George Tyne
Call Northside 777 '48
Open Secret '48

Charles Tyner
Harold and Maude '71
Planes, Trains & Automobiles '87
Pulse '88

Susan Tyrrell
Fat City '72
Zandy's Bride '74
Killer Inside Me '76
Andy Warhol's Bad '77
Another Man, Another Chance '77
Islands in the Stream '77
September 30, 1955 '77
Lady of the House '78
Forbidden Zone '80
Loose Shoes '80
Fast Walking '82
Liar's Moon '82
Night Warning '82
Tales of Ordinary Madness '83
Angel '84
Avenging Angel '85
Flesh and Blood '85
The Offspring '87
Poker Alice '87
Big Top Pee Wee '88
The Underachievers '88
Windmills of the Gods '88
Far from Home '89
Tapeheads '89
Cry-Baby '90
Rockula '90
Thompson's Last Run '90
Motorama '91
The Demolitionist '95
Powder '95

Cathy Tyson
Mona Lisa '86
The Serpent and the Rainbow '87
Business as Usual '88
The Lost Language of Cranes '92
Priest '94

Cicely Tyson
A Man Called Adam '66
The Heart is a Lonely Hunter '68
Sounder '72
The Autobiography of Miss Jane Pittman '74
The River Niger '76
Roots '77
Wilma '77
A Hero Ain't Nothin' But a Sandwich '78
King '78
A Woman Called Moses '78
The Concorde: Airport '79 '79
Bustin' Loose '81
Acceptable Risks '86
Samaritan: The Mitch Snyder Story '86
The Women of Brewster Place '89
Heat Wave '90
The Kid Who Loved Christmas '90
Fried Green Tomatoes '91
Duplicates '92
Oldest Confederate Widow Tells All '95
The Road to Galveston '96

Pamela Tyson
What's Love Got to Do with It? '93
Last Dance '96

Richard Tyson
Three O'Clock High '87
Two Moon Junction '88
Kindergarten Cop '90
The Babe '92
Dark Tide '93
Red Shoe Diaries 3: Another Woman's Lipstick '93
Pharoah's Army '95

Margaret Tyzack
Quatermass Conclusion '79
Mr. Love '86
The King's Whore '90

Fabiana Udenio
Hardbodies 2 '86
Bride of Re-Animator '89

Claudia Udy
Out of Control '85
The Pink Chiquitas '86
Captive Rage '88

Helene Udy
The Hollywood Detective '89
Sweet Murder '93

Bob Uecker
Major League '89
Major League 2 '94

Kenjiro Uemura
A Quiet Duel '49
The Human Condition: Road to Eternity '59

Leslie Uggams
Two Weeks in Another Town '62
Poor Pretty Eddie '73
Sizzle '81
Sugar Hill '94

Gisela Uhlen
The Indian Scarf '63
The Marriage of Maria Braun '79
Toto le Heros '91

Tracey Ullman
Give My Regards to Broad Street '84
Plenty '85
I Love You to Death '90
Household Saints '93
I'll Do Anything '93
Robin Hood: Men in Tights '93
Bullets Over Broadway '94
Ready to Wear '94

Liv Ullmann
Persona '66
Hour of the Wolf '68
The Shame '68
The Night Visitor '70
The Passion of Anna '70
Cries and Whispers '72
The Emigrants '72
Forty Carats '73
The New Land '73
Scenes from a Marriage '73
Cold Sweat '74
Zandy's Bride '74
Leonor '75
Face to Face '76
A Bridge Too Far '77
Autumn Sonata '78
The Serpent's Egg '78
Richard's Things '80
Dangerous Moves '84
The Wild Duck '84
The Bay Boy '85
Gaby: A True Story '87
The Rose Garden '89
Mindwalk: A Film for Passionate Thinkers '91
The Ox '91

Lenore Ulric
Camille '36
Northwest Outpost '47

Skeet Ulrich
Boys '95
The Craft '96
Last Dance '96

Mikhail Ulyanov
The Theme '79
Private Life '82

Margaret Umbers
Death Warmed Up '85
The Bridge to Nowhere '86

Miyoshi Umeki
Sayonara '57
Flower Drum Song '61
The Horizontal Lieutenant '62

Yoko Umemura
Sisters of Gion '36
The Story of the Late Chrysanthemum '39

Edward Underdown
Inspector Hornleigh '39
Man on the Run '49
The Shadow Man '53
Pattern for Plunder '62

Blair Underwood
Krush Groove '85
Heat Wave '90
Dangerous Relations '93
Posse '93
Just Cause '94

Jay Underwood
The Boy Who Could Fly '86
Desert Bloom '86
Not Quite Human '87
The Invisible Kid '88
Promised Land '88
The Gumshoe Kid '89
Not Quite Human 2 '89
Uncle Buck '89
To Die for 2: Son of Darkness '91
Still Not Quite Human '92
The Raffle '94

Underwood ▶cont.

Sleepstalker: The Sandman's Last Rites *'94*
Stalked *'94*
Wyatt Earp: Return to Tombstone *'94*
A Reason to Believe *'95*

Deborah Unger
Prisoners of the Sun *'91*
Till There was You *'91*
Whispers in the Dark *'92*
Hotel Room *'93*
Highlander: The Final Dimension *'94*
Crash *'95*

Mary Ure
Windom's Way *'57*
Look Back in Anger *'58*
Where Eagles Dare *'68*
A Reflection of Fear *'72*

Fabio Urena
The Bronx War *'90*
Return of the Living Dead 3 *'93*

Robert Urich
Magnum Force *'73*
The Best of Soap: Who Killed Peter? *'77*
Vegas *'78*
The Shadow Box *'80*
Killing at Hell's Gate *'81*
Endangered Species *'82*
Take Your Best Shot *'82*
Bunco *'83*
Ice Pirates *'84*
Invitation to Hell *'84*
Mistral's Daughter *'84*
Turk 182! *'85*
Lonesome Dove *'89*
Murder by Night *'89*
A Perfect Little Murder *'90*
Blind Man's Bluff *'91*
In a Stranger's Hand *'92*
Revolver *'92*
Hit Woman: The Double Edge *'93*
Spenser: Ceremony *'93*
Spenser: Pale Kings & Princes *'94*
A Horse for Danny *'95*

Robert Urquhart
The House of the Arrow *'53*
The Curse of Frankenstein *'57*
White Huntress *'57*
Children of the Full Moon *'84*
Sharma & Beyond *'84*
The Kitchen Toto *'87*
Playing Away *'87*

Benny "The Jet" Urquidez
Down the Drain *'89*
Bloodmatch *'91*
The Kick Fighter *'91*

Susan Ursitti
Teen Wolf *'85*
Defense Play *'88*

Peter Ustinov
One of Our Aircraft Is Missing *'41*
Immortal Battalion *'44*
Quo Vadis *'51*
Beau Brummel *'54*
The Egyptian *'54*
Lola Montes *'55*
We're No Angels *'55*
The Man Who Wagged His Tail *'57*
Spartacus *'60*
The Sundowners *'60*
Billy Budd *'62*
Topkapi *'64*
Barefoot in Athens *'66*
Blackbeard's Ghost *'67*
The Comedians *'67*
Hot Millions *'68*
Viva Max *'69*
Hammersmith is Out *'72*
One of Our Dinosaurs Is Missing *'75*
Logan's Run *'76*
The Treasure of Matecumbe *'76*
The Last Remake of Beau Geste *'77*
The Purple Taxi *'77*
Death on the Nile *'78*
The Thief of Baghdad *'78*
Ashanti, Land of No Mercy *'79*
Charlie Chan and the Curse of the Dragon Queen *'81*
Evil under the Sun *'82*
Appointment with Death *'88*
Around the World in 80 Days *'89*
Lorenzo's Oil *'92*
The Old Curiosity Shop *'94*
The Phoenix and the Magic Carpet *'95*

Kari Vaananen
Leningrad Cowboys Go America *'89*
Amazon *'90*
Night on Earth *'91*
La Vie de Boheme *'93*

Brenda Vaccaro
Midnight Cowboy *'69*
I Love My...Wife *'70*
Summertree *'71*
Honor Thy Father *'73*
Once is Not Enough *'75*
Death Weekend *'76*
Airport '77 *'77*
Capricorn One *'78*
Dear Detective *'78*
The First Deadly Sin *'80*
The Guyana Tragedy: The Story of Jim Jones *'80*
A Long Way Home *'81*
Pride of Jesse Hallum *'81*
Zorro, the Gay Blade *'81*
Supergirl *'84*
Water *'85*
Cookie *'89*
Heart of Midnight *'89*
Ten Little Indians *'89*
Lethal Games *'90*
Masque of the Red Death *'90*
Love Affair *'94*

Annette Vadim
Dangerous Liaisons *'60*
Blood and Roses *'61*

Roger Vadim
Edie in Ciao! Manhattan *'72*
Into the Night *'85*

Dan Vadis
Sons of Hercules in the Land of Darkness *'55*
Bronco Billy *'80*
Seven Magnificent Gladiators *'84*

Lester Vail
Consolation Marriage *'31*
Dance Fools Dance *'31*

Charlotte Valandrey
Red Kiss *'85*
Orlando *'92*

Brigitta Valberg
The Virgin Spring *'59*
The Shame *'68*

Virginia Vale
The Flustered Comedy of Leon Errol *'39*
Bullet Code *'40*
Legion of the Lawless *'40*
Panama Menace *'41*

Anthony Valentine
The Carpathian Eagle *'81*
Robin Hood...The Legend: Robin Hood and the Sorcerer *'83*

Karen Valentine
Return to Fantasy Island *'77*
Hot Lead & Cold Feet *'78*
The North Avenue Irregulars *'79*
Skeezer *'82*
Jane Doe *'83*
Children in the Crossfire *'84*
The Power Within *'95*

Scott Valentine
Deadtime Stories *'86*
My Demon Lover *'87*
Dangerous Pursuit *'89*
After the Shock *'90*
Write to Kill *'91*
Homicidal Impulse *'92*
The Secret Passion of Robert Clayton *'92*
To Sleep with a Vampire *'92*
Double Obsession *'93*
Out of Annie's Past *'94*
Till the End of the Night *'94*
The Unborn 2 *'94*
Object of Obsession *'95*

Rudolph Valentino
The Eyes of Youth *'19*
Camille *'21*
The Four Horsemen of the Apocalypse *'21*
The Sheik *'21*
Blood and Sand *'22*
Moran of the Lady Letty *'22*
Monsieur Beaucaire *'24*
Cobra *'25*
The Eagle *'25*
Blood and Sand/Son of the Sheik *'26*
Son of the Sheik *'26*
The Tempest/The Eagle *'27*

Tasia Valenza
Crackers *'84*
Rappin' *'85*
The Hillside Strangler *'89*

Jeanne Valeri
Desert Commandos *'60s*
Dangerous Liaisons *'60*

Frederick Valk
Dangerous Moonlight *'41*
Hotel Reserve *'44*
Dead of Night *'45*
Frenzy *'46*

Kitty Vallacher
Grave of the Vampire *'72*
The Legend of Frank Woods *'77*

Marcel Vallee
The Crazy Ray *'22*
Topaze *'33*

Rudy Vallee
Vagabond Lover *'29*
Glorifying the American Girl *'30*
International House *'33*
Second Fiddle *'39*
The Palm Beach Story *'42*
People Are Funny *'46*
The Bachelor and the Bobby-Soxer *'47*
The Sin of Harold Diddlebock *'47*
I Remember Mama *'48*
Unfaithfully Yours *'48*
The Beautiful Blonde from Bashful Bend *'49*
Father Was a Fullback *'49*
My Dear Secretary *'49*
The Admiral Was a Lady *'50*
How to Succeed in Business without Really Trying *'67*
Live a Little, Love a Little *'68*
Slashed Dreams *'74*

Alida Valli
We the Living *'42*
The Paradine Case *'47*
The Miracle of the Bells *'48*
The Third Man *'49*
Walk Softly, Stranger *'50*
Senso *'54*
Il Grido *'57*
The Horror Chamber of Dr. Faustus *'59*
The Castilian *'63*
Oedipus Rex *'67*
The Spider's Stratagem *'70*
The Tempter *'74*
The Cassandra Crossing *'76*
1900 *'76*
Suspiria *'77*
Beyond Erotica *'79*
A Month by the Lake *'95*

Frankie Valli
Dirty Laundry *'87*
Eternity *'90*
Modern Love *'90*

Romolo Valli
The Garden of the Finzi-Continis *'71*
A Fistful of Dynamite *'72*
Bobby Deerfield *'77*

Virginia Valli
The Shock *'23*
Lost Zeppelin *'29*
Night Life in Reno *'31*

Rick Vallin
King of the Stallions *'42*
The Panther's Claw *'42*
Corregidor *'43*
The Last of the Redmen *'47*

Raf Vallone
Bitter Rice *'49*
Anna *'51*
El Cid *'61*
Phaedra *'61*
Two Women *'61*
Harlow *'65*
Nevada Smith *'66*
The Italian Job *'69*
A Gunfight *'71*
Honor Thy Father *'73*
Ricco *'74*
The Human Factor *'75*
Rosebud *'75*
That Lucky Touch *'75*
The Girl in Room 2A *'76*
The Other Side of Midnight *'77*
The Greek Tycoon *'78*
An Almost Perfect Affair *'79*
Lion of the Desert *'81*
The Scarlet & the Black *'83*
Time to Die *'83*
Christopher Columbus *'85*
The Godfather, Part 3 *'90*

Bobby Van
The Affairs of Dobie Gillis *'53*
Kiss Me Kate *'53*
Small Town Girl *'53*
Navy vs. the Night Monsters *'66*
Escape from Planet Earth *'67*

Willeke Van Ammelrooy
Fatal Error *'83*
The Lift *'85*
Antonia's Line *'95*

Joan Van Ark
Frogs *'72*
Red Flag: The Ultimate Game *'81*
Tainted Blood *'93*
When the Dark Man Calls *'95*

Lee Van Atta
Dick Tracy: The Original Serial, Vol. 1 *'37*
Dick Tracy: The Original Serial, Vol. 2 *'37*

Lewis Van Bergen
Overthrow *'82*
Rage of Honor *'87*
South of Reno *'87*
Bugsy *'91*
False Arrest *'92*
Street Knight *'93*

Lee Van Cleef
High Noon *'52*
Kansas City Confidential *'52*
The Beast from 20,000 Fathoms *'53*
Gypsy Colt *'54*
Big Combo *'55*
A Man Alone *'55*
The Conqueror *'56*
It Conquered the World *'56*
Pardners *'56*
Tribute to a Bad Man *'56*
China Gate *'57*
Gunfight at the O.K. Corral *'57*
The Tin Star *'57*
The Bravados *'58*
The Young Lions *'58*
Ride Lonesome *'59*
The Man Who Shot Liberty Valance *'62*
For a Few Dollars More *'65*
The Good, the Bad and the Ugly *'67*
Beyond the Law *'68*
El Condor *'70*
Captain Apache *'71*
Bad Man's River *'72*
New Mafia Boss *'72*
Commandos *'73*
The Grand Duel *'73*
God's Gun *'75*
Kid Vengeance *'75*
Mean Frank and Crazy Tony *'75*
Take a Hard Ride *'75*
Escape from Death Row *'76*
The Stranger and the Gunfighter *'76*
Fatal Chase *'77*
Perfect Killer *'77*
Master Ninja *'78*
The Rip Off *'78*
Hard Way *'80*
Octagon *'80*
The Squeeze *'80*
Escape from New York *'81*
Codename: Wildgeese *'84*
Jungle Raiders *'85*
Armed Response *'86*
The Heist *'88*
Speed Zone *'88*
Thieves of Fortune *'89*

Ron Van Cliff
Black Dragon *'74*
Black Dragon's Revenge *'75*
Fist of Fear, Touch of Death *'77*
Way of the Black Dragon *'81*
Fight to the Death *'83*

Jean-Claude Van Damme
Monaco Forever *'83*
No Retreat, No Surrender *'86*
Black Eagle *'88*
Bloodsport *'88*
Cyborg *'89*
Kickboxer *'89*
Death Warrant *'90*
Lionheart *'90*
Double Impact *'91*
Universal Soldier *'92*
Hard Target *'93*
Nowhere to Run *'93*
Street Fighter *'94*
Timecop *'94*
Sudden Death *'95*
The Quest *'96*

Monique Van De Ven
Turkish Delights *'73*
Keetje Tippel *'75*
The Assault *'86*
Amsterdamned *'88*
Paint It Black *'89*
The Man Inside *'90*

Sylvie van den Elsen
L'Argent *'83*
La Vie de Boheme *'93*

Nadine Van Der Velde
Critters *'86*
Munchies *'87*
Shadow Dancing *'88*
After Midnight *'89*

Diana Van Der Vlis
Girl in Black Stockings *'57*
X: The Man with X-Ray Eyes *'63*
Lovespell *'79*

Trish Van Devere
Where's Poppa? *'70*
The Day of the Dolphin *'73*
Savage Is Loose *'74*
Stalk the Wild Child *'76*
Movie, Movie *'78*
All God's Children *'80*
The Changeling *'80*
The Hearse *'80*
Uphill All the Way *'85*
Hollywood Vice Sqaud *'86*
Messenger of Death *'88*
Deadly Currents *'93*

Mamie Van Doren
Francis Joins the WACs *'54*
Girl in Black Stockings *'57*
High School Confidential *'58*
Teacher's Pet *'58*
Born Reckless *'59*
Girls' Town *'59*
Three Nuts in Search of a Bolt *'64*
Las Vegas Hillbillys *'66*
Navy vs. the Night Monsters *'66*
Voyage to the Planet of Prehistoric Women *'68*

Granville Van Dusen
War Between the Tates *'76*
Breaking Up *'78*
The Wild and the Free *'80*
Hotline *'82*
The Rose and the Jackal *'90*

Barry Van Dyke
Ants *'77*
Foxfire Light *'84*

Conny Van Dyke
Hell's Angels '69 *'69*
Framed *'75*

Dick Van Dyke
Bye, Bye, Birdie *'63*
Mary Poppins *'64*
Lt. Robin Crusoe, U.S.N. *'66*
Divorce American Style *'67*
Chitty Chitty Bang Bang *'68*
Never a Dull Moment *'68*
The Comic *'69*
Cold Turkey *'71*
The Runner Stumbles *'79*

Country Girl '82
Dick Tracy '90

Jerry Van Dyke
The Courtship of Eddie's Father '62
McLintock! '63
Death Blow '87
Run If You Can '87

Peter Van Eyck
Wages of Fear '55
The Thousand Eyes of Dr. Mabuse '60
The Brain '62
Dr. Mabuse vs. Scotland Yard '64
The Spy Who Came in from the Cold '65

John Van Eyssen
Four Sided Triangle '53
Men of Sherwood Forest '57
Quatermass 2 '57
The Horror of Dracula '58

Jo Van Fleet
East of Eden '54
I'll Cry Tomorrow '55
The Rose Tattoo '55
The King and Four Queens '56
Gunfight at the O.K. Corral '57
Cool Hand Luke '67
I Love You, Alice B. Toklas! '68
Satan's School for Girls '73
The Tenant '76

Kevin Van Hentenryck
Basket Case '82
Basket Case 2 '90
Basket Case 3: The Progeny '92

Merete Van Kamp
Princess Daisy '83
Lethal Woman '88

Peter Van Norden
The Accused '88
Scandal in a Small Town '88
Casualties of Love: The "Long Island Lolita" Story '93

Nina Van Pallandt
The Long Goodbye '73
Assault on Agathon '75
A Wedding '78
Diary of a Young Comic '79
Quintet '79
Cutter's Way '81
Sword & the Sorcerer '82
Jungle Warriors '84

Dick Van Patten
Psychomania '63
Charly '68
Zachariah '70
Joe Kidd '72
Son of Blob '72
Superdad '73
Westworld '73
Freaky Friday '76
Gus '76
High Anxiety '77
Diary of a Teenage Hitchhiker '82
The Hoboken Chicken Emergency '84
The Midnight Hour '86
Spaceballs '87
The New Adventures of Pippi Longstocking '88
Body Trouble '92
Final Embrace '92
Robin Hood: Men in Tights '93
A Dangerous Place '94

James Van Patten
Tennessee Stallion '78
Roller Boogie '79
Young Warriors '83
Nightforce '86
The Dirty Dozen: The Deadly Mission '87
Twisted Justice '89

Joyce Van Patten
I Love You, Alice B. Toklas! '68
The Trouble with Girls (and How To Get Into It) '69
Housewife '72
Thumb Tripping '72
Mame '74
The Stranger Within '74
The Bad News Bears '76
Eleanor: First Lady of the World '82
The Falcon and the Snowman '85
St. Elmo's Fire '85
Billy Galvin '86
Crawlspace '86
The Rumor Mill '86
Monkey Shines '88
Trust Me '89
Breathing Lessons '94

Nels Van Patten
Grotesque '87
Summer School '87
One Last Run '89
Mirror Images '91

Timothy Van Patten
Master Ninja '78
The White Shadow, Vol. 1 '78
Class of 1984 '82
Escape from El Diablo '83
Zone Troopers '84
Dress Gray '86
The Wrong Guys '88
Catacombs '89
Curse 4: The Ultimate Sacrifice '90

Vincent Van Patten
Charley and the Angel '73
Chino '75
Rock 'n' Roll High School '79
Survival Run '80
Hell Night '81
Rooster: Spurs of Death! '83
The Dirty Dozen: The Deadly Mission '87
The Victory '88
Payback '90
The Break '95

Mario Van Peebles
Delivery Boys '84
Exterminator 2 '84
Rappin' '85
South Bronx Heroes '85
Heartbreak Ridge '86
Hot Shot '86
Jaws: The Revenge '87
Identity Crisis '90
New Jack City '91
Full Eclipse '93
Gunmen '93
Posse '93
Highlander: The Final Dimension '94
Urban Crossfire '94
Panther '95

Melvin Van Peebles
Sweet Sweetback's Baadasssss Song '71
Sophisticated Gents '81
O.C. and Stiggs '87
Boomerang '92
Terminal Velocity '94

Edward Van Sloan
Dracula '31
Frankenstein '31
The Mummy '32
The Death Kiss '33
Deluge '33
Manhattan Melodrama '34
A Shot in the Dark '35
Dracula's Daughter '36
Danger on the Air '38
Before I Hang '40
The Mask of Dijon '46

Deborah Van Valkenburgh
The Warriors '79
King of the Mountain '81
Streets of Fire '84
A Bunny's Tale '85
Going for the Gold: The Bill Johnson Story '85
Rampage '87
Phantom of the Ritz '88
Python Wolf '88
One Man Out '89
Erik '90

Monique Van Vooren
Ash Wednesday '73
Andy Warhol's Frankenstein '74
Sugar Cookies '77

Philip Van Zandt
Citizen Kane '41
Sherlock Holmes and the Secret Weapon '42
A Thousand and One Nights '45
Woman in Brown '48
Ghost Chasers '51
Clipped Wings '53

Courtney B. Vance
Hamburger Hill '87
The Hunt for Red October '90
Beyond the Law '92
The Adventures of Huck Finn '93
Percy & Thunder '93
Holy Matrimony '94
The Piano Lesson '94
Race to Freedom: The Story of the Underground Railroad '94
The Affair '95
Dangerous Minds '95
Panther '95
The Tuskegee Airmen '95
The Boys Next Door '96
The Last Supper '96

Danitra Vance
Sticky Fingers '88
Limit Up '89
The War of the Roses '89
Little Man Tate '91
Jumpin' at the Boneyard '92

Jim Vance
Young Eagles '34
How to Make a Doll '68
Blood Cult '85

Joe Vance
L.A. Crackdown 2 '88
Deadly Breed '89

Musetta Vander
Backlash: Oblivion 2 '95
Project Shadowchaser 3000 '95
Under the Hula Moon '95

Alexandra Vandernoot
Highlander: The Gathering '93
Blood of the Hunter '94

Titos Vandis
Never on Sunday '60
Once Upon a Scoundrel '73
Piece of the Action '77

Pierre Vaneck
Is Paris Burning? '68
Sweet Country '87
Othello '95

Charles Vanel
Diabolique '55
To Catch a Thief '55
Wages of Fear '55
Death in the Garden '56
Three Brothers '80

Vanilla Ice
Cool As Ice '91
Teenage Mutant Ninja Turtles 2: The Secret of the Ooze '91

Vanity
Terror Train '80
Tanya's Island '81
The Last Dragon '85
52 Pick-Up '86
Never Too Young to Die '86
Deadly Illusion '87
Action Jackson '88
Memories of Murder '90
Neon City '91
DaVinci's War '92
South Beach '92
Highlander: The Gathering '93

Renata Vanni
Westward the Women '51
The Lady in White '88
Wait Until Spring, Bandini '90

Joanne Vannicola
Love and Human Remains '93
Iron Eagle 4 '95

Luigi Vannucchi
Red Tent '69
Lovers Like Us '75

Victor Varconi
King of Kings '27
Dancing Pirate '36
My Favorite Blonde '42
For Whom the Bell Tolls '43
Unconquered '47

Evelyn Varden
Athena '54
The Night of the Hunter '55
The Bad Seed '56

Norma Varden
National Velvet '44
The White Cliffs of Dover '44
Forever Amber '47
Fancy Pants '50
Jupiter's Darling '55
The Sound of Music '65

Antonio Vargas
Whore '91
Strictly Ballroom '92

Jacob Vargas
Gas Food Lodging '92
Mi Vida Loca '94
My Family '94

John Vargas
Unnatural Causes '86
Seduced by Evil '94

Valentina Vargas
Dirty Games '93
The Tigress '93
Hellraiser 4: Bloodline '95

Beatrice Varley
Great Day '46
Death Goes to School '53

Jim Varney
Dr. Otto & the Riddle of the Gloom Beam '86
Ernest Goes to Camp '87
Ernest Saves Christmas '88
Fast Food '89
Ernest Goes to Jail '90
The Rousters '90
Ernest Scared Stupid '91
The Beverly Hillbillies '93
Ernest Rides Again '93
Wilder Napalm '93
Ernest Goes to School '94
The Expert '95
Slam Dunk Ernest '95

Diane Varsi
Peyton Place '57
Ten North Frederick '58
Compulsion '59
Sweet Love, Bitter '67
Wild in the Streets '68
Bloody Mama '70
Johnny Got His Gun '71
The People '71
I Never Promised You a Rose Garden '77

Michael Vartan
Fiorile '93
The Pallbearer '95

Razvan Vasilescu
The Oak '93
Trahir '93

Roberta Vasquez
Easy Wheels '89
Picasso Trigger '89
The Rookie '90
Street Asylum '90
Do or Die '91
Hard Hunted '92
Fit to Kill '93

Robert Vattier
The Baker's Wife '33
Letters from My Windmill '54

Frankie Vaughan
Dangerous Youth '58
Let's Make Love '60

Paris Vaughan
Heat Wave '90
Buffy the Vampire Slayer '92

Peter Vaughan
Die! Die! My Darling! '65
The Man Outside '68
Savage Messiah '72
Straw Dogs '72
Blockhouse '73
Mackintosh Man '73
Valentino '77
Time Bandits '81
Coming Out of the Ice '82
The Razor's Edge '84
Bleak House '85
Brazil '85
Forbidden '85
Haunted Honeymoon '86
Mountains of the Moon '90
Codename Kyril '91
Porridge '91
Prisoner of Honor '91
Heart of Darkness '93
The Remains of the Day '93
Circle of Deceit '94
Fatherland '94

Alberta Vaughn
All Night Long/Smile Please '24
The Dropkick '27
Wild Horse '31
Daring Danger '32
The Live Wire '34
Randy Rides Alone '34
Laramie Kid '35

Heidi Vaughn
Trained to Kill, U.S.A. '83
Heaven's Heroes '87

Ned Vaughn
Chips, the War Dog '90
Wind '92

Robert Vaughn
Teenage Caveman '58
The Young Philadelphians '59
The Magnificent Seven '60
The Man from U.N.C.L.E. '64
Bullitt '68
The Bridge at Remagen '69
Julius Caesar '70
The Shaming '71
The Statue '71
The Woman Hunter '72
The Towering Inferno '74
Wanted: Babysitter '75
Starship Invasions '77
Brass Target '78
The Lucifer Complex '78
The Rebels '79
Blue Jeans and Dynamite '80s
Battle Beyond the Stars '80
City in Fear '80
Hangar 18 '80
Kill Castro '80
The Mercenaries '80
Question of Honor '80
S.O.B. '81
Inside the Third Reich '82
Virus '82
Return of the Man from U.N.C.L.E. '83
Superman 3 '83
The Last Bastion '84
Black Moon Rising '86
Delta Force '86
Hour of the Assassin '86
Murrow '86
Hitchhiker 4 '87
Nightstick '87
Prince of Bel Air '87
Captive Rage '88
Brutal Glory '89
Buried Alive '89
C.H.U.D. 2: Bud the Chud '89
Emissary '89
Skeleton Coast '89
Transylvania Twist '89
Nobody's Perfect '90
River of Death '90
That's Adequate '90
Blind Vision '91
Going Under '91
Joe's Apartment '96

Ron Vawter
Sudden Death '77
sex, lies and videotape '89
Internal Affairs '90
Swoon '91
King of the Hill '93
Philadelphia '93

Bruno Ve Sota
Daughter of Horror '55
The Gunslinger '56
Attack of the Giant Leeches '59
The Wasp Woman '59
Creature of the Walking Dead '60
The Choppers '61

Isela Vega
Bring Me the Head of Alfredo Garcia '74
Drum '76
Joshua '76
Bordello '79
Barbarosa '82

Conrad Veidt
The Cabinet of Dr. Caligari '19
Cesare Borgia '23
Waxworks '24
The Hands of Orlac '25
The Beloved Rogue '27
The Man Who Laughs '27
Congress Dances '31
F.P. 1 '33
Power '34
King of the Damned '36
The Passing of the Third Floor Back '36

Veidt ▶cont.

Under the Red Robe '36
Dark Journey '37
Spy in Black '39
The Thief of Bagdad '40
Whistling in the Dark '41
A Woman's Face '41
All Through the Night '42
Casablanca '42
Above Suspicion '43

Lorena Velasquez
Wrestling Women vs. the Aztec Mummy '59
Samson vs. the Vampire Women '61
Wrestling Women vs. the Aztec Ape '62

Eddie Velez
Doin' Time '85
Women's Club '87
Split Decisions '88
Romero '89
Rooftops '89
Bitter Vengeance '94

Lupe Velez
Stand and Deliver '28
Where East Is East '29
Hell Harbor '30
Mad About Money '30
Hollywood Party '34
Palooka '34
Mexican Spitfire/Smartest Girl in Town '40
Playmates '41
Mexican Spitfire at Sea '42

Evelyn Venable
Alice Adams '35
Harmony Lane '35
The Little Colonel '35
The Frontiersmen '38
Hollywood Stadium Mystery '38
Lucky Cisco Kid '40
Mrs. Wiggs of the Cabbage Patch '42

Chick Vennera
Thank God It's Friday '78
Yanks '79
Kidnapped '87
Last Rites '88
The Milagro Beanfield War '88
The Terror Within 2 '91
Double Threat '92

Diane Venora
Wolfen '81
The Cotton Club '84
Terminal Choice '85
F/X '86
Ironweed '87
Bird '88
Heat '95
Three Wishes '95
The Substitute '96

Wanda Ventham
Blood Beast Terror '67
Captain Kronos: Vampire Hunter '74

Clyde Ventura
Bury Me an Angel '71
Gator Bait '73

Jesse Ventura
Predator '87
The Running Man '87
Thunderground '89
Abraxas: Guardian of the Universe '90
Boxcar Blues '90
Repossessed '90
Ricochet '91

Lino Ventura
Grisbi '53
Modigliani '58
Mistress of the World '59
The Three Penny Opera '62
Jailbird's Vacation '65
Les Grandes Gueules '65
Happy New Year '74
The French Detective '75
The Slap '76
Les Aventuriers '77
Pain in the A— '77
The Medusa Touch '78
Sword of Gideon '86

Richard Venture
The Effect of Gamma Rays on Man-in-the-Moon Marigolds '73
Missing '82
Street Hawk '84
Scent of a Woman '92
Truman '95

Massimo Venturiello
Rorret '87
My Wonderful Life '90

Billy Vera
Finish Line '89
The Doors '91

Victoria Vera
Monster Dog '82
A Man of Passion '90s

Vera-Ellen
Wonder Man '45
Words and Music '48
On the Town '49
Love Happy '50
Three Little Words '50
Happy Go Lovely '51
The Belle of New York '52
White Christmas '54

Gwen Verdon
Damn Yankees '58
Legs '83
The Cotton Club '84
Cocoon '85
Nadine '87
Cocoon: The Return '88
Alice '90
Oldest Confederate Widow Tells All '95

Maribel Verdu
Lovers: A True Story '90
Belle Epoque '92

Elena Verdugo
The Moon and Sixpence '43
House of Frankenstein '44
Little Giant '46
The Big Sombrero '49
Cyrano de Bergerac '50
Boss' Son '79

Ben Vereen
Gas-s-s-s! '70
Funny Lady '75
Roots '77
All That Jazz '79
Pippin '81
Breakin' Through '84
The Jesse Owens Story '84
Puss 'n Boots '84
The Zoo Gang '85
Buy & Cell '89
The Kid Who Loved Christmas '90
Mother Goose Rock 'n' Rhyme '90
Intruders '92

Tom Verica
Die Hard 2: Die Harder '90
800 Leagues Down the Amazon '93
Breach of Conduct '94

Bernard Verley
The Milky Way '68
Chloe in the Afternoon '72
Helas Pour Moi '94

Harold Vermilyea
Emperor Waltz '48
Sorry, Wrong Number '48

Denise Vernac
The Mask of Dijon '46
Unnatural '52

Karen Verne
Kings Row '41
All Through the Night '42
Sherlock Holmes and the Secret Weapon '42
The Seventh Cross '44

Guy Verney
Fame Is the Spur '47
Martin Luther '53

Pierre Vernier
Mama, There's a Man in Your Bed '89
Betty '92

Anne Vernon
Umbrellas of Cherbourg '64
Therese & Isabelle '68

Bobby Vernon
A Hash House Fraud/The Sultan's Wife '15
Teddy at the Throttle '16
Teddy at the Throttle/Speeding Along '17

Glenn Vernon
Bedlam '45
Hollywood Varieties '50

Howard Vernon
The Awful Dr. Orlof '62
The Diabolical Dr. Z '65
Triple Cross '67
Castle of the Creeping Flesh '68
The Invisible Dead '70
Virgin Among the Living Dead '71
Dr. Orloff's Invisible Horror '72
The Screaming Dead '72
The Perverse Countess '73
Revenge in the House of Usher '82
Zombie Lake '84

John Vernon
Justine '69
Tell Them Willie Boy Is Here '69
Dirty Harry '71
Charley Varrick '73
Hunter '73
The Barbary Coast '74
The Black Windmill '74
W '74
Brannigan '75
The Outlaw Josey Wales '76
The Virginia Hill Story '76
Angela '77
Golden Rendezvous '77
Journey '77
National Lampoon's Animal House '78
Herbie Goes Bananas '80
Chained Heat '83
Curtains '83
Savage Streets '83
The Blood of Others '84
Jungle Warriors '84
Doin' Time '85
Fraternity Vacation '85
Blue Monkey '87
Ernest Goes to Camp '87
Nightstick '87
Deadly Stranger '88
Dixie Lanes '88
I'm Gonna Git You Sucka '88
Killer Klowns from Outer Space '88
Terminal Exposure '89
War Bus Commando '89
Bail Out '90
Mob Story '90
Hostage for a Day '94
Sodbusters '94
Malicious '95

Kate Vernon
Alphabet City '84
Roadhouse 66 '84
The Last of Philip Banter '87
Hostile Takeover '88
Mob Story '90
Malcolm X '92
Dangerous Touch '94
Soft Deceit '94
Bloodknot '95
Probable Cause '95
The Sister-in-Law '95

Richard Vernon
The Satanic Rites of Dracula '73
The Human Factor '79

Wally Vernon
Happy Landing '38
Broadway Serenade '39
Gunfire '50
Square Dance Jubilee '51

Christine Veronica
Love Notes '88
Party Incorporated '89

Cec Verrell
Silk '86
Eye of the Eagle '87
Mad at the Moon '92
Three of Hearts '93

Odile Versois
To Paris with Love '55
Cartouche '62
Le Crabe Tambour '77

Veruschka
Blow-Up '66
The Bride '85

Charlotte Very
A Tale of Winter '92
Trois Couleurs: Bleu '93

Victoria Vetri
When Dinosaurs Ruled the Earth '70
Group Marriage '72
Invasion of the Bee Girls '73

Karin Viard
Delicatessen '92
The Separation '94

Martha Vickers
The Big Sleep '46
The Man I Love '46
Big Bluff '55

Yvette Vickers
Attack of the Giant Leeches '59
Beach Party '63
Evil Spirits '91

John Vickery
Rapid Fire '92
Deconstructing Sarah '94

Charles Victor
Seven Days' Leave '42
San Demetrio, London '47
Motor Patrol '50

Henry Victor
The Beloved Rogue '27
King of the Zombies '41
Sherlock Holmes and the Secret Weapon '42

Katherine Victor
Mesa of Lost Women '52
Teenage Zombies '58
Curse of the Stone Hand '64
House of the Black Death '65
The Wild World of Batwoman '66

Gil Vidal
Night of the Howling Beast '75
Rape '80s

Gore Vidal
Bob Roberts '92
With Honors '94

Henri Vidal
Fabiola '48
Just Another Pretty Face '58
Sois Belle et Tais-Toi '58
Voulez-Vous Danser Avec Moi? '59

Steven Vidler
The Dunera Boys '85
Three's Trouble '85
The Good Wife '86
Encounter at Raven's Gate '88
Wrangler '88

Florence Vidor
Beau Revel '21
The Virginian '23
The Marriage Circle '24
Are Parents People? '25
The Coming of Amos '25
The Grand Duchess and the Waiter '26
Doomsday '28

Asia Vieira
The Good Mother '88
Omen 4: The Awakening '91

Abe Vigoda
The Godfather '72
The Godfather, Part 2 '74
Newman's Law '74
The Cheap Detective '78
How to Pick Up Girls '78
Great American Traffic Jam '80
The Godfather 1902-1959: The Complete Epic '81
Vasectomy: A Delicate Matter '86
Plain Clothes '88
Look Who's Talking '89
Prancer '89
Joe Versus the Volcano '90
Keaton's Cop '90
Fist of Honor '92
Home of Angels '94
North '94
Sugar Hill '94
Jury Duty '95

Robert Viharo
Valley of the Dolls '67
Bare Knuckles '77
Kid from Not-So-Big '78
Happy Birthday, Gemini '80
Hide in Plain Sight '80
Night Stalker '87
Romero '89
Coldfire '90

Antonio Vilar
Gunslinger '70s
Stranger's Gold '71

Henri Vilbert
Manon '50
Ali Baba and the 40 Thieves '54

Tom Villard
One Crazy Summer '86
Weekend Warriors '86
The Trouble with Dick '88
Popcorn '89
Swimsuit: The Movie '89
My Girl '91

Daniel Villarreal
American Me '92
Speed '94

Astrid Villaume
Famous Five Get into Trouble '87
Pelle the Conqueror '88

Herve Villechaize
The Man with the Golden Gun '74
Seizure '74
Return to Fantasy Island '77
The One and Only '78
Forbidden Zone '80
Rumpelstiltskin '82
Two Moon Junction '88

James Villemaire
Gate 2 '92
Matinee '92

Jacques Villeret
Robert et Robert '79
Bolero '82
Edith & Marcel '83
The Favor, the Watch, & the Very Big Fish '92

Christopher Villiers
Top Secret! '84
First Knight '95

James Villiers
The Nanny '65
Repulsion '65
Nice Girl Like Me '69
The Scarlet Pimpernel '82
Mrs. Silly '85
Fortunes of War '87
Mountains of the Moon '90
Wavelength '96

Pruitt Taylor Vince
Shy People '87
Mississippi Burning '88
Come See the Paradise '90
Jacob's Ladder '90
City Slickers 2: The Legend of Curly's Gold '94
Heavy '94
Natural Born Killers '94
Nobody's Fool '94
Under the Hula Moon '95
Beautiful Girls '96

Alex Vincent
Child's Play '88
Child's Play 2 '90
Wait Until Spring, Bandini '90
My Family Treasure '93

Allen Vincent
After Midnight '33
Carnival Lady '33

Frank Vincent
Raging Bull '80
Goodfellas '90
Street Hunter '90
Jungle Fever '91
Federal Hill '94

Jan-Michael Vincent
Crossfire '67
The Undefeated '69
Tribes '70
The Mechanic '72
Bandits '73
The World's Greatest Athlete '73
Buster and Billie '74
Bite the Bullet '75
White Line Fever '75
Damnation Alley '77
Big Wednesday '78

Hooper '78
Defiance '79
The Return '80
Hard Country '81
Last Plane Out '83
The Winds of War '83
Born in East L.A. '87
Enemy Territory '87
Deadly Embrace '88
The Hit List '88
Alienator '89
Demonstone '89
The Divine Enforcer '91
Hangfire '91
Haunting Fear '91
In Gold We Trust '91
Raw Nerve '91
Xtro 2: The Second Encounter '91
Animal Instincts '92
Beyond the Call of Duty '92
Hidden Obsession '92
Sins of Desire '92
Dirty Games '93
Indecent Behavior '93
Midnight Witness '93
Abducted 2: The Reunion '94
Ice Cream Man '95

June Vincent
Here Come the Co-Eds '45
The Creeper '48
Colorado Sundown '52
Clipped Wings '53

Russ Vincent
Heading for Heaven '47
Twilight in the Sierras '50

Lee Ving
Flashdance '83
Streets of Fire '84
The Wild Life '84
Clue '85
Dudes '87
Scenes from the Goldmine '87
Grave Secrets '89

Helen Vinson
I Am a Fugitive from a Chain Gang '32
They Call It Sin '32
Broadway Bill '34
Transatlantic Tunnel '35
King of the Damned '36
Vogues of 1938 '37
The Thin Man Goes Home '44

Alan Vint
The McMasters '70
Unholy Rollers '72
Macon County Line '74
Panic in Needle Park '75
Sniper '75
Ballad of Gregorio Cortez '83

Bill Vint
Summertree '71
Marilyn: The Untold Story '80

Jesse Vint
Pigs '73
Macon County Line '74
Bug '75
Bobbie Jo and the Outlaw '76
Black Oak Conspiracy '77
Death Sport '78
Forbidden World '82
Dempsey '83
On the Line '83
I Come in Peace '90
Merchants of War '90

Gustav Vintas
Welcome Back Mr. Fox '83
Vampire at Midnight '88
Midnight '89
Tales from the Crypt '89
And You Thought Your Parents Were Weird! '91
Drug Wars 2: The Cocaine Cartel '92

Bobby Vinton
Surf Party '64
Big Jake '71
Train Robbers '73

Michael Visaroff
Last Command '28
Charlie Chan at the Wax Museum '40

Sal Viscuso
The Taking of Pelham One Two Three '74
Spaceballs '87

Alex Vitale
Urban Warriors '75
Beyond the Door 3 '91

Joseph Vitale
Zombies on Broadway '44
The Stranger Wore a Gun '53

Keith Vitali
Revenge of the Ninja '83
American Kickboxer 1 '91
No Retreat, No Surrender 3: Blood Brothers '91

Joe Viterelli
Bullets Over Broadway '94
Heaven's Prisoners '95
Machine Gun Blues '95

Ray Vitte
Sky Hei$t '75
Grambling's White Tiger '81

Monica Vitti
L'Avventura '60
The Red Desert '64
The Eclipse '66
Phantom of Liberty '68
Blonde in Black Leather '77
An Almost Perfect Affair '79
Immortal Bachelor '80
Tigers in Lipstick '80
Bellissimo: Images of the Italian Cinema '87

Viva
Edie in Ciao! Manhattan '72
Play It Again, Sam '72
Forbidden Zone '80
State of Things '82

Sal Viviano
Black Roses '88
The Jitters '88

Floyd Vivino
Good Morning, Vietnam '87
Crazy People '90

Marina Vlady
Double Agents '59
Chimes at Midnight '67

Emmett Vogan
Robot Pilot '41
The Lady Confesses '45
Down Dakota Way '49

Darlene Vogel
Back to the Future, Part 2 '89
Ring of Steel '94
Decoy '95

Jack Vogel
Lock 'n' Load '90
Presumed Guilty '91

Nikolas Vogel
Dangerous Liaisons '60
The Inheritors '85

Ruediger Vogler
Alice in the Cities '74
Kings of the Road—In the Course of Time '76
The Wrong Move '78
Marianne and Juliane '82
Until The End of The World '91
Faraway, So Close! '93

Joan Vohs
As You Were '51
Cry Vengeance '54

Jon Voight
Hour of the Gun '67
Midnight Cowboy '69
Catch-22 '70
Deliverance '72
Conrack '74
The Odessa File '74
Coming Home '78
The Champ '79
Lookin' to Get Out '82
Table for Five '83
Runaway Train '85
Desert Bloom '86
Eternity '90
Final Warning '90
The Last of His Tribe '92
Return to Lonesome Dove '93
Rainbow Warrior '94
Convict Cowboy '95
Heat '95
The Tin Soldier '95
Mission: Impossible '96

Vicki Volante
Blood of Dracula's Castle '69
Horror of the Blood Monsters '70
Brain of Blood '71
Angels' Wild Women '72

Gian Marie Volonte
Journey Beneath the Desert '61
A Fistful of Dollars '64
For a Few Dollars More '65
The Witch '66
A Bullet for the General '68
Sacco & Vanzetti '71
Lucky Luciano '74
Christ Stopped at Eboli '79
Open Doors '89

Phillipe Volter
The Music Teacher '88
Cyrano de Bergerac '90
The Double Life of Veronique '91

Daniel von Bargen
Philadelphia '93
Before and After '95
Lord of Illusions '95
Truman '95

William von Brinken
King Kelly of the U.S.A. '34
International Crime '37
Hidden Enemy '40

Lenny Von Dohlen
Electric Dreams '84
Under the Biltmore Clock '85
Billy Galvin '86
Dracula's Widow '88
Blind Vision '91
Love Kills '91
Eyes of the Beholder '92
Leaving Normal '92
Tollbooth '94

Theodore von Eltz
No Man's Law '27
Drifting Souls '32
Strangers of the Evening '32
High Gear '33
Confidential '35

Rik von Nutter
Assignment Outer Space '61
Thunderball '65
Tharus Son of Attila '87

Joel von Ornsteiner
Robot Holocaust '87
Slashdance '89

Heidi von Palleske
Dead Ringers '88
Blind Fear '89
White Light '90

Gustav von Seyffertitz
Down to Earth '17
Don Juan '26
Sparrows '26
The Mysterious Lady '28
Dishonored '31
Rasputin and the Empress '32
Mystery Liner '34
She '35

Erich von Stroheim
The Birth of a Nation '15
Intolerance '16
Heart of Humanity '18
Hearts of the World '18
Blind Husbands '19
Foolish Wives '22
The Wedding March '28
The Great Gabbo '29
As You Desire Me '32
Lost Squadron '32
Crimson Romance '34
Fugitive Road '34
The Crime of Dr. Crespi '35
Grand Illusion '37
So Ends Our Night '41
The North Star '43
Great Flamarion '45
The Mask of Dijon '46
Sunset Boulevard '50
Unnatural '52
Napoleon '55
The Worst of Hollywood: Vol. 2 '90

Max von Sydow
The Seventh Seal '56
Brink of Life '57
Wild Strawberries '57
The Magician '58
The Virgin Spring '59
Through a Glass Darkly '61
The Winter Light '62
The Greatest Story Ever Told '65
Hawaii '66
The Quiller Memorandum '66
Hour of the Wolf '68
The Shame '68
The Night Visitor '70
The Passion of Anna '70
The Touch '71
Embassy '72
The Emigrants '72
The Exorcist '73
The New Land '73
Steppenwolf '74
Three Days of the Condor '75
The Ultimate Warrior '75
Foxtrot '76
Voyage of the Damned '76
The Exorcist 2: The Heretic '77
March or Die '77
Brass Target '78
Hurricane '79
Death Watch '80
Flash Gordon '80
Victory '81
Conan the Barbarian '82
Flight of the Eagle '82
Never Say Never Again '83
Strange Brew '83
Dreamscape '84
Dune '84
Samson and Delilah '84
Target Eagle '84
Christopher Columbus '85
Code Name: Emerald '85
Kojak: The Belarus File '85
Quo Vadis '85
Duet for One '86
Hannah and Her Sisters '86
Second Victory '87
The Wolf at the Door '87
Pelle the Conqueror '88
Red King, White Knight '89
Awakenings '90
Father '90
Hiroshima: Out of the Ashes '90
A Kiss Before Dying '91
The Ox '91
Until The End of The World '91
The Best Intentions '92
The Bachelor '93
Needful Things '93
The Last Place on Earth '94
The Silent Touch '94
Citizen X '95
Judge Dredd '95

Margarethe von Trotta
An Occurrence at Owl Creek Bridge/Coup de Grace '62
Beware of a Holy Whore '70
Coup de Grace '78

Gustav von Wagenheim
Nosferatu '22
Woman in the Moon '29

Harry von Zell
The Strange Affair of Uncle Harry '45
Son of Paleface '52

Danielle von Zerneck
My Science Project '85
La Bamba '87
Dangerous Curves '88
Under the Boardwalk '89
Living in Oblivion '94

Zandor Vorkov
Brain of Blood '71
Dracula vs. Frankenstein '71

George Voskovec
Twelve Angry Men '57
The 27 Day '57
The Bravados '58
The Boston Strangler '68

Arnold Vosloo
Reason to Die '90
The Rutanga Tapes '90
Living to Die '91
The Finishing Touch '92
Red Shoe Diaries 2: Double Dare '92
Hard Target '93
Darkman 2: The Return of Durant '94
Darkman 3: Die Darkman Die '95

Yorgo Voyagis
The Adventurers '70
The Little Drummer Girl '84
The Bourne Identity '88
Frantic '88
Courage Mountain '89

Vlasta Vrana
Keeping Track '86
Deadly Surveillance '91
Scanners 2: The New Order '91

Ron Vreeken
Deathfight '93
Rage and Honor 2: Hostile Takeover '93

Spencer Vrooman
Pet Shop '94
Man of the House '95

Murvyn Vye
A Connecticut Yankee in King Arthur's Court '49
Pickup on South Street '53
The Road to Bali '53
River of No Return '54
Green Fire '55
Al Capone '59

Steven Waddington
Edward II '92
1492: Conquest of Paradise '92
The Last of the Mohicans '92
Carrington '95

Russell Wade
The Iron Major '43
The Body Snatcher '45
Shoot to Kill '47
Sundown Riders '48

Stuart Wade
Monster from the Ocean Floor '54
Meteor Monster '57

Julian Wadham
Middlemarch '93
The Madness of King George '94

Henry Wadsworth
Applause '29
Evelyn Prentice '34
Ceiling Zero '35

Michael Wager
Hill 24 Doesn't Answer '55
Exodus '60
Jane Austen in Manhattan '80

Lyle Waggoner
Women of the Prehistoric Planet '66
Journey to the Center of Time '67
Love Me Deadly '76
Surf 2 '84
Robo-Chic '89
Dead Women in Lingerie '90
Mind Trap '91

Chuck Wagner
America 3000 '86
The Sisterhood '88

Fernando Wagner
The Pearl '48
Virgin Sacrifice '59

Jack Wagner
Swimsuit: The Movie '89
Play Murder for Me '91
Trapped in Space '94

Lindsay Wagner
The Paper Chase '73
The Rockford Files: Backlash of the Hunter '74
The Bionic Woman '75
High Risk '76
The Incredible Journey of Dr. Meg Laurel '79
The Two Worlds of Jenny Logan '79
Scruples '80
Callie and Son '81
Nighthawks '81
Princess Daisy '83
Martin's Day '85
Two Kinds of Love '85
Convicted '86
The Taking of Flight 847: The Uli Derickson Story '88
The Flight '89
From the Dead of Night '89
Second Wind '90
Nightmare at Bittercreek '91
Ricochet '91

Wagner ▶cont.

Treacherous Crossing '92
Shattered Dreams '94

Natasha Gregson Wagner
Buffy the Vampire Slayer '92
Fathers and Sons '92
The Substitute '93
Tainted Blood '93
Dead Beat '94
Molly and Gina '94
Wes Craven Presents Mind Ripper '95

Robert Wagner
The Halls of Montezuma '50
Let's Make It Legal '51
Stars and Stripes Forever '52
What Price Glory? '52
Beneath the 12-Mile Reef '53
Titanic '53
Broken Lance '54
Prince Valiant '54
Between Heaven and Hell '56
The Mountain '56
Stopover Tokyo '57
The Hunters '58
The Longest Day '62
War Lover '62
The Pink Panther '64
Harper '66
Winning '69
Madame Sin '71
The Streets of San Francisco '72
The Affair '73
The Towering Inferno '74
Abduction of St. Anne '75
Death at Love House '75
Midway '76
The Concorde: Airport '79 '79
Trail of the Pink Panther '82
Curse of the Pink Panther '83
I Am the Cheese '83
To Catch a King '84
Indiscreet '88
Windmills of the Gods '88
Around the World in 80 Days '89
This Gun for Hire '90
Delirious '91
False Arrest '92
Dragon: The Bruce Lee Story '93
Parallel Lives '94

Thomas Wagner
The Drifter '88
Dead On '93
Marilyn & Bobby: Her Final Affair '94

Ken Wahl
Running Scared '79
Wanderers '79
Fort Apache, the Bronx '81
Jinxed '82
The Soldier '82
Treasure of the Yankee Zephyr '83
Purple Hearts '84
The Dirty Dozen: The Next Mission '85
The Gladiator '86
Omega Syndrome '87
The Taking of Beverly Hills '91
The Favor '92

Mark Wahlberg
The Substitute '93
The Basketball Diaries '94
Renaissance Man '94
Fear '96

Edward Wain
Creature from the Haunted Sea '60
The Last Woman on Earth '61

James Wainwright
Jigsaw '71
The President's Plane is Missing '71
Joe Kidd '72
A Woman Called Moses '78
Warlords of the 21st Century '82

Loudon Wainwright, III
The Slugger's Wife '85
Jacknife '89

Ralph Waite
Cool Hand Luke '67
Five Easy Pieces '70
Chato's Land '71
The Grissom Gang '71
Lawman '71
The Sporting Club '72
Girls on the Road '73
The Stone Killer '73
The Waltons: A Thanksgiving Story '73
Red Alert '77
Angel City '80
On the Nickel '80
Gentleman Bandit '81
A Day for Thanks on Walton's Mountain '82
Crash and Burn '90
The Bodyguard '92
Cliffhanger '93
Sioux City '94

Thomas G. Waites
And Justice for All '79
On the Yard '79
The Warriors '79
The Thing '82
The Clan of the Cave Bear '86
Verne Miller '88
McBain '91

Tom Waits
The Outsiders '83
Rumble Fish '83
The Cotton Club '84
Down by Law '86
Candy Mountain '87
Ironweed '87
Shakedown '88
Cold Feet '89
At Play in the Fields of the Lord '91
Queens Logic '91
Bram Stoker's Dracula '92
Short Cuts '93

Akiko Wakabayashi
Dagora, the Space Monster '65
What's Up, Tiger Lily? '66
You Only Live Twice '67

Ayako Wakao
A Geisha '53
Drifting Weeds '59
An Actor's Revenge '63

Tomisaburo Wakayama
Baby Cart 1: Lend a Child...Lend an Arm '72
Baby Cart 4: Heart of a Parent...Heart of a Child '72
Baby Cart at the River Styx '72
Baby Cart to Hades '72
The Bad News Bears Go to Japan '78
Phoenix '78
Shogun Assassin '80

Deborah Wakeham
Middle Age Crazy '80
Covergirl '83
House of the Rising Sun '87

Jimmy Wakely
Range Renegades '48
Brand of Fear '49
Lonesome Trail '55
Silver Star '55

Anton Walbrook
Gaslight '39
Dangerous Moonlight '41
The Forty-Ninth Parallel '41
The Life and Death of Colonel Blimp '43
The Red Shoes '48
The Queen of Spades '49
La Ronde '51
Lola Montes '55
Saint Joan '57

Raymond Walburn
The Count of Monte Cristo '34
Lady by Choice '34
Born to Dance '36
Mr. Deeds Goes to Town '36
Thin Ice '37
It Could Happen to You '39
Let Freedom Ring '39
Christmas in July '40
Louisiana Purchase '41
Hail the Conquering Hero '44
Key to the City '50
Riding High '50

Gregory Walcott
Plan 9 from Outer Space '56
Texas Lady '56
Jet Attack/Paratroop Command '58
Joe Kidd '72
Prime Cut '72

John Walcutt
Return '88
Roseanne: An Unauthorized Biography '94

Lynette Walden
The Silencer '92
Almost Blue '93

Robert Walden
Bloody Mama '70
Everything You Always Wanted to Know about Sex (But Were Afraid to Ask) '72
Larry '74
Our Time '74
Kansas City Massacre '75
Blue Sunshine '78
Enola Gay: The Men, the Mission, the Atomic Bomb '80
Memorial Day '83
Perry Mason: The Case of the Lost Love '87
Murderer's Keep '88

Shawna Waldron
Little Giants '94
The American President '95

Ethel Wales
Made for Love '26
Under Montana Skies '30
The Gladiator '38
Border Vigilantes '41

Wally Wales
Desert of the Lost '27
Deadwood Pass '33
Lone Bandit '33
Sagebrush Trail '33
Danger Trails '35
The Miracle Rider '35
Powdersmoke Range '35
Rustlers of Red Dog '35
Way of the West '35
Gun Play '36
The Trigger Trio '37

Christopher Walken
The Anderson Tapes '71
Mind Snatchers '72
Next Stop, Greenwich Village '76
Annie Hall '77
Roseland '77
The Deer Hunter '78
Last Embrace '79
The Dogs of War '81
Heaven's Gate '81
Pennies From Heaven '81
Shoot the Sun Down '81
Who Am I This Time? '82
Brainstorm '83
Dead Zone '83
A View to a Kill '85
At Close Range '86
Deadline '87
Biloxi Blues '88
Homeboy '88
The Milagro Beanfield War '88
Communion '89
King of New York '90
All-American Murder '91
The Comfort of Strangers '91
McBain '91
Sarah, Plain and Tall '91
Batman Returns '92
A Business Affair '93
Day of Atonement '93
Scam '93
Skylark '93
True Romance '93
Wayne's World 2 '93
Pulp Fiction '94
Search and Destroy '94
The Addiction '95
Nick of Time '95
The Prophecy '95
Things to Do In Denver When You're Dead '95
Wild Side '95

Ally Walker
The Seventh Coin '92
Singles '92
Universal Soldier '92
When the Bough Breaks '93
Bed of Roses '95
Someone to Die For '95
While You Were Sleeping '95
Kazaam '96

Arnetia Walker
The Wizard of Speed and Time '88
Scenes from the Class Struggle in Beverly Hills '89
Love Crimes '92

Bill Walker
No Time for Romance '48
The Mask '61

Cheryl Walker
Stage Door Canteen '43
Identity Unknown '45

Clint Walker
None But the Brave '65
Maya '66
Night of the Grizzly '66
The Dirty Dozen '67
Yuma '70
The Bounty Man '72
Deadly Harvest '72
Pancho Villa '72
Baker's Hawk '76
Snowbeast '77
The White Buffalo '77
Mysterious Island of Beautiful Women '79
The Gambler Returns: The Luck of the Draw '93

Eric Walker
The Ewok Adventure '84
The Ewoks: Battle for Endor '85
And You Thought Your Parents Were Weird! '91

Fiona Walker
Jude the Obscure '71
The Asphyx '72

Helen Walker
Abroad with Two Yanks '44
Brewster's Millions '45
People Are Funny '46
Call Northside 777 '48
Big Combo '55

Jimmie Walker
Let's Do It Again '75
The Concorde: Airport '79 '79
B.A.D. Cats '80
Doin' Time '85
Water '85
My African Adventure '87
Going Bananas '88
Frankenstein Sings...The Movie '95

Kathryn Walker
Blade '72
The Winds of Kitty Hawk '78
Rich Kids '79
Neighbors '81
Whale for the Killing '81
Private Contentment '83
Special Bulletin '83
The Murder of Mary Phagan '87
Uncle Tom's Cabin '87
Dangerous Game '90

Kim Walker
Deadly Weapon '88
Heathers '89

Liza Walker
Twisted Obsession '90
Wavelength '96

Marcy Walker
Midnight's Child '93
Talking About Sex '94

Nancy Walker
Best Foot Forward '43
Girl Crazy '43
Broadway Rhythm '44
Lucky Me '54
Forty Carats '73
Thursday's Game '74
Death Scream '75
Murder by Death '76

Polly Walker
Lorna Doone '90
A Dangerous Man: Lawrence after Arabia '91
Enchanted April '92
Patriot Games '92
Sliver '93
The Trial '93
Restoration '94
Emma '96

Ray Walker
Goodbye Love '34
Bulldog Edition '36
The Dark Hour '36
House of Errors '42
Rogue's Gallery '44

Robert Walker
The Crimson Trail '35
Bataan '43
Madame Curie '43
Since You Went Away '44
Thirty Seconds Over Tokyo '44
The Clock '45
Till the Clouds Roll By '46
Till the Clouds Roll By/A Star Is Born '46
One Touch of Venus '48
Strangers on a Train '51
Vengeance Valley '51

Robert Walker, Jr.
Ensign Pulver '64
The War Wagon '67
Road to Salina '68
The Savage Seven '68
Easy Rider '69
Son of Blob '72
The Shrieking '73
The Spectre of Edgar Allen Poe '73
AngKor: Cambodia Express '81
Devonsville Terror '83
Olivia '83
Hambone & Hillie '84
Evil Town '87

Sarah Walker
Man of Flowers '84
Housekeeping '87

Terry Walker
23 1/2 Hours Leave '37
Delinquent Parents '38
Renfrew on the Great White Trail '38
Take Me Back to Oklahoma '40

Tippy Walker
The World of Henry Orient '64
The Jesus Trip '71

Max Wall
A Killer in Every Corner '74
Jabberwocky '77
Little Dorrit, Film 1: Nobody's Fault '88
Little Dorrit, Film 2: Little Dorrit's Story '88
We Think the World of You '88
Strike It Rich '90

Basil Wallace
Marked for Death '90
Deadlock '91
Return of the Living Dead 3 '93

Beryl Wallace
Rough Ridin' Rhythm '37
Sunset on the Desert '42

Bill Wallace
Force of One '79
Manchurian Avenger '84
Ninja Turf '86

David Wallace
The Babysitter '80
Humongous '82
Mazes and Monsters '82
Money to Burn '83

George Wallace
Radar Men from the Moon '52
Forbidden Planet '56
Defending Your Life '91
A Rage in Harlem '91
Diggstown '92

Jack Wallace
Things Change '88
The Bear '89

Jean Wallace
Jigsaw '49
Native Son '51
Big Combo '55
Sword of Lancelot '63

Marcia Wallace
Pray TV '80
My Mom's a Werewolf '89

Morgan Wallace
Confidential '35
The House of Secrets '37

Delinquent Parents '38
Gang Bullets '38
Star Reporter '39
Honky Tonk '41
In Old Colorado '41

Dee Wallace Stone
The Hills Have Eyes '77
10 '79
The Five of Me '81
The Howling '81
Whale for the Killing '81
E.T.: The Extra-Terrestrial '82
Jimmy the Kid '82
Skeezer '82
Cujo '83
Wait Till Your Mother Gets Home '83
Secret Admirer '85
Club Life '86
Critters '86
Shadow Play '86
Miracle Down Under '87
Popcorn '89
Alligator 2: The Mutation '90
I'm Dangerous Tonight '90
Discretion Assured '93
Huck and the King of Hearts '93
My Family Treasure '93
Rescue Me '93
The Phoenix and the Magic Carpet '95
The Road Home '95
Temptress '95
The Frighteners '96

Eli Wallach
Baby Doll '56
The Magnificent Seven '60
Seven Thieves '60
The Misfits '61
How the West Was Won '63
Kisses for My President '64
The Moon-Spinners '64
Lord Jim '65
How to Steal a Million '66
The Poppy Is Also a Flower '66
The Good, the Bad and the Ugly '67
Ace High '68
The Brain '69
MacKenna's Gold '69
The People Next Door '70
Romance of a Horsethief '71
Cinderella Liberty '73
Stateline Motel '75
Independence '76
The Deep '77
The Domino Principle '77
Nasty Habits '77
Circle of Iron '78
Girlfriends '78
Movie, Movie '78
Winter Kills '79
The Hunter '80
Pride of Jesse Hallum '81
The Executioner's Song '82
The Salamander '82
Sam's Son '84
Christopher Columbus '85
Embassy '85
Rocket to the Moon '86
Something in Common '86
Tough Guys '86
The Impossible Spy '87
Nuts '87
The Godfather, Part 3 '90
The Two Jakes '90
A Family Matter '91
Mistress '91
Article 99 '92
Legacy of Lies '92
Night and the City '92
Teamster Boss: The Jackie Presser Story '92
Two Much '96

Sigurd Wallen
The Count of the Old Town '34
Swedenhielms '35

Eddy Waller
Bandit King of Texas '49
El Paso Stampede '53
Marshal of Cedar Rock '53

Deborah Walley
Gidget Goes Hawaiian '61
Bon Voyage! '62
Summer Magic '63
Beach Blanket Bingo '65
Dr. Goldfoot and the Bikini Machine '66
Spinout '66
The Severed Arm '73
Benji '74

William Walling
Great K & A Train Robbery '26
Range Feud '31

Shani Wallis
Oliver! '68
Arnold '73
Round Numbers '91

Tom Walls
Johnny Frenchman '46
While I Live '47
Maytime in Mayfair '52

Jon Walmsley
The Waltons: A Thanksgiving Story '73
The Waltons: The Christmas Carol '80
A Day for Thanks on Walton's Mountain '82

Angela Walsh
Distant Voices, Still Lives '88
The Man Who Cried '93

Dermot Walsh
Murder on the Campus '52
Ghost Ship '53
Mania '60
The Tell-Tale Heart '62
The Great Armored Car Swindle '64

Dylan Walsh
Betsy's Wedding '90
Arctic Blue '93
Nobody's Fool '94
Radio Inside '94
Congo '95

George Walsh
American Pluck '25
Test of Donald Norton '26
The Broadway Drifter '27
The Live Wire '34

Gwynyth Walsh
Blue Monkey '87
The Challengers '93
The Crush '93
Soft Deceit '94

Johnny Walsh
Wild Women of Wongo '59
Body Parts '91

J.T. Walsh
Hard Choices '84
Power '86
Good Morning, Vietnam '87
House of Games '87
Tin Men '87
Tequila Sunrise '88
Things Change '88
The Big Picture '89
Dad '89
Wired '89
Crazy People '90
The Grifters '90
Narrow Margin '90
The Russia House '90
Why Me? '90
Backdraft '91
Defenseless '91
Iron Maze '91
A Few Good Men '92
Hoffa '92
Sniper '92
Morning Glory '93
Needful Things '93
Red Rock West '93
Blue Chips '94
The Client '94
The Last Seduction '94
Miracle on 34th Street '94
Outbreak '94
Silent Fall '94
The Babysitter '95
Nixon '95
Executive Decision '96

Kay Walsh
In Which We Serve '43
This Happy Breed '47
The October Man '48
Oliver Twist '48
Last Holiday '50
Stage Fright '50
Encore '52
Young Bess '53
Cast a Dark Shadow '55
The Horse's Mouth '58
Tunes of Glory '60
Tunes of Glory/Horse's Mouth '60
Greyfriars Bobby '61

Ken Walsh
Reno and the Doc '84
Love and Hate: A Marriage Made in Hell '90
Love, Lies and Murder '91
Dead Ahead: The Exxon Valdez Disaster '92

M. Emmet Walsh
Stiletto '69
They Might Be Giants '71
Dear Detective '78
Straight Time '78
Brubaker '80
East of Eden '80
Ordinary People '80
Reds '81
Blade Runner '82
Cannery Row '82
Fast Walking '82
Night Partners '83
Grandview U.S.A. '84
Missing in Action '84
The Pope of Greenwich Village '84
Raw Courage '84
Scandalous '84
Blood Simple '85
Fletch '85
Back to School '86
The Best of Times '86
Critters '86
The Deliberate Stranger '86
Rich Hall's Vanishing America '86
Wildcats '86
The Abduction of Kari Swenson '87
Broken Vows '87
Harry and the Hendersons '87
Murder Ordained '87
Raising Arizona '87
Clean and Sober '88
The Milagro Beanfield War '88
Sunset '88
The Brotherhood of the Rose '89
Catch Me...If You Can '89
Chattahoochee '89
The Mighty Quinn '89
Red Scorpion '89
Thunderground '89
War Party '89
Boxcar Blues '90
Fourth Story '90
Narrow Margin '90
Killer Image '92
White Sands '92
Wildcard '92
Bitter Harvest '93
Equinox '93
Four Eyes and Six Guns '93
The Music of Chance '93
Wilder Napalm '93
Camp Nowhere '94
Dead Badge '94
Criminal Hearts '95
The Glass Shield '95
Panther '95
Portraits of a Killer '95
Probable Cause '95
Relative Fear '95

Percy Walsh
King of the Damned '36
Secret Mission '42
The Golden Salamander '51

Raoul Walsh
The Birth of a Nation '15
Sadie Thompson '28

Sydney Walsh
To Die for '89
Three Men and a Little Lady '90
Point Break '91
Homewrecker '92
A Kiss Goodnight '94

Ray Walston
Damn Yankees '58
South Pacific '58
The Apartment '60
Tall Story '60
Kiss Me, Stupid! '64
The Sting '73
Silver Streak '76
The Happy Hooker Goes to Washington '77
The Fall of the House of Usher '80
Popeye '80
Galaxy of Terror '81
Fast Times at Ridgemont High '82
The Kid with the Broken Halo '82
O'Hara's Wife '82
Private School '83
For Love or Money '84
Johnny Dangerously '84
Amos '85
From the Hip '86
Blood Relations '87
O.C. and Stiggs '87
Fine Gold '88
Paramedics '88
Saturday the 14th Strikes Back '88
Popcorn '89
Ski Patrol '89
A Man of Passion '90s
Blood Salvage '90
Of Mice and Men '92
Stephen King's The Stand '94
House Arrest '96

Harriet Walter
The Good Father '87
May Fools '90
The Advocate '93
Sense and Sensibility '95

Jessica Walter
The Group '66
Play Misty for Me '71
Home for the Holidays '72
Hurricane '74
Dr. Strange '78
Secrets of Three Hungry Wives '78
Wild & Wooly '78
Goldengirl '79
She's Dressed to Kill '79
Going Ape! '81
Miracle on Ice '81
The Flamingo Kid '84
The Execution '85
Tapeheads '89
Ghost in the Machine '93
P.C.U. '94
Temptress '95

Tracey Walter
Mad Bull '77
Raggedy Man '81
Repo Man '83
Timerider '83
At Close Range '86
Something Wild '86
Married to the Mob '88
Out of the Dark '88
Batman '89
Under the Boardwalk '89
The Two Jakes '90
Young Guns 2 '90
City Slickers '91
Delusion '91
Mortuary Academy '91
Liquid Dreams '92
Philadelphia '93
Buffalo Girls '95
Destiny Turns on the Radio '95

Julie Walters
Educating Rita '83
She'll Be Wearing Pink Pajamas '84
Car Trouble '86
Personal Services '87
Prick Up Your Ears '87
Buster '88
Happy Since I Met You '89
Mack the Knife '89
Stepping Out '91
The Wedding Gift '93
Sister My Sister '94
The Summer House '94
Just Like a Woman '95

Laurie Walters
Harrad Experiment '73
Warlock Moon '73
Harrad Summer '74
The Taking of Flight 847: The Uli Derickson Story '88

Luana Walters
Fighting Texans '33
Assassin of Youth '35
Aces and Eights '36
Speed Reporter '36
Arizona Bound '41
Kid's Last Ride '41
Misbehaving Husbands '41
The Corpse Vanishes '42
Dick Tracy, Detective/The Corpse Vanishes '42
Inside the Law '42

Melora Walters
America's Deadliest Home Video '91
Twenty Bucks '93

Susan Walters
Shoot to Kill '47
Elvis and Me '88
Galaxies are Colliding '92

Thorley Walters
Blue Murder at St. Trinian's '56
The Pure Hell of St. Trinian's '61
Murder She Said '62
The Phantom of the Opera '62
Sherlock Holmes and the Deadly Necklace '62
Bartleby '70
Cry of the Penguins '71
Vampire Circus '71
The People That Time Forgot '77
The Adventures of Sherlock Holmes' Smarter Brother '78
The Sign of Four '83
The Little Drummer Girl '84
In the Secret State

Henry B. Walthall
Avenging Conscience '14
Home Sweet Home '14
Judith of Bethulia '14
The Birth of a Nation '15
The Raven '15
False Faces '18
The Confession '20
With Kit Carson Over the Great Divide '25
The Phantom in the House '29
Abraham Lincoln '30
The Cabin in the Cotton '32
Chandu the Magician '32
Ride Him, Cowboy '32
Strange Interlude '32
Flaming Signal '33
Laughing at Life '33
Somewhere in Sonora '33
Beggars in Ermine '34
Judge Priest '34
The Scarlet Letter '34
Viva Villa! '34
A Tale of Two Cities '35
Last Outlaw '36
Police Court '37

Douglas Walton
The Bride of Frankenstein '35
I Conquer the Sea '36
Mary of Scotland '36
Wallaby Jim of the Islands '37
Bad Lands '39

John Walton
Kangaroo '86
The Lighthorsemen '87

Lisa Waltz
Brighton Beach Memoirs '86
Pet Sematary 2 '92

Sam Wanamaker
My Girl Tisa '48
Taras Bulba '62
The Spy Who Came in from the Cold '65
Those Magnificent Men in Their Flying Machines '65
Spiral Staircase '75
Sell Out '76
Voyage of the Damned '76
From Hell to Victory '79
The Competition '80
Private Benjamin '80
Our Family Business '81
Detective Sadie & Son '84
Ghostwriter '84
Irreconcilable Differences '84
The Aviator '85
Embassy '85
Raw Deal '86
Baby Boom '87
Superman 4: The Quest for Peace '87
Judgment in Berlin '88
The Shell Seekers '89
Running Against Time '90
Guilty by Suspicion '91
Pure Luck '91
Secret Ingredient '92
Covert Assassin '94

Zoe Wanamaker
Poor Little Rich Girl: The Barbara Hutton Story '87
The Raggedy Rawney '90
Tales of the Unexpected '91
Prime Suspect '92

Peter Wang
Chan is Missing '82
A Great Wall '86
The Laserman '90

David Warbeck
Twins of Evil '71
Blacksnake! '73
The Last Hunter '80
The Black Cat '81
Ark of the Sun God '82
Hunters of the Golden Cobra '82
Seven Doors of Death '82
Panic '83
Formula for a Murder '85
Tiger Joe '85
Miami Horror '87

John Warburton
Cavalcade '33
Nothing But Trouble '44
The White Cliffs of Dover '44
Saratoga Trunk '45
Secret File of Hollywood '62

Burt Ward
Batman '66
Killcrazy '89
Robo-Chic '89
Smooth Talker '90
Virgin High '90
Beach Babes from Beyond Infinity '93
Assault of the Party Nerds 2: Heavy Petting Detective '95

Fred Ward
Escape from Alcatraz '79
Southern Comfort '81
Uforia '81
The Right Stuff '83
Silkwood '83
Timerider '83
Uncommon Valor '83
Noon Wine '84
Swing Shift '84
Remo Williams: The Adventure Begins '85
Secret Admirer '85
Florida Straits '87
Off Limits '87
Big Business '88
Prince of Pennsylvania '88
Backtrack '89
Tremors '89
Henry & June '90
Miami Blues '90
Cast a Deadly Spell '91
The Player '92
Thunderheart '92
Equinox '93
Four Eyes and Six Guns '93
Short Cuts '93
Two Small Bodies '93
Naked Gun 33 1/3: The Final Insult '94
Chain Reaction '96
Tremors 2: Aftershocks '96

John Ward
Robinson Crusoe of Clipper Island '36
Ridin' the Trail '40
Holt of the Secret Service '42

Jonathan Ward
White Water Summer '87
Mac and Me '88

Larry Ward
Deathhead Virgin '74
Macabre '77

Lyman Ward
Creature '85
Perfect Victims '87
The Taking of Beverly Hills '91
Mikey '92
Sleepwalkers '92
Serial Killer '95

Mary Ward
Prisoner Cell Block H '80
Smoke '95

Mary B. Ward
Hangin' with the Homeboys '91
Surviving Desire '91

Megan Ward
Trancers 2: The Return of Jack Deth '90
Amityville 1992: It's About Time '92
Encino Man '92
Trancers 3: Deth Lives '92
Arcade '93
Freaked '93
P.C.U. '94
Joe's Apartment '96

Penelope Dudley Ward
I Stand Condemned '36
The Citadel '38
The Case of the Frightened Lady '39
The Demi-Paradise '43

Rachel Ward
Night School '81
Sharky's Machine '81
Dead Men Don't Wear Plaid '82
The Final Terror '83
The Thorn Birds '83
Against All Odds '84
Fortress '85
The Good Wife '86
Hotel Colonial '88
How to Get Ahead in Advertising '89
After Dark, My Sweet '90
Black Magic '92
Christopher Columbus: The Discovery '92
Double Jeopardy '92
Wide Sargasso Sea '92
The Ascent '94

Richard Ward
Across 110th Street '72
Mandingo '75

Robin Ward
When Angels Fly '82
Mark of Cain '84
Thrillkill '84

Roger Ward
Mad Max '80
Quigley Down Under '90

Sandy Ward
The Velvet Vampire '71
Tank '83
Blue Desert '91
Delta Force 3: The Killing Game '91

Sela Ward
Nothing in Common '86
Hello Again '87
Steele Justice '87
Haunting of Sarah Hardy '89
Rainbow Drive '90
Child of Darkness, Child of Light '91
Double Jeopardy '92
The Fugitive '93

Simon Ward
If... '69
Young Winston '72
Dracula '73
Hitler: The Last Ten Days '73
All Creatures Great and Small '74
The Three Musketeers '74
Children of Rage '75
The Four Musketeers '75
The Chosen '77
The Four Feathers '78
Dominique is Dead '79
Zulu Dawn '79
Deadly Strangers '82
Supergirl '84
The Monster Club '85

Sophie Ward
Young Sherlock Holmes '85
Casanova '87
Little Dorrit, Film 1: Nobody's Fault '88
Little Dorrit, Film 2: Little Dorrit's Story '88
A Summer Story '88
The Shell Seekers '89
Class of '61 '92
A Demon in My View '92
A Dark Adapted Eye '93

Wally Ward
Thunder Run '86
The Chocolate War '88
The Invisible Kid '88

Warwick Ward
Variety '25
The Informer '29

Zack Ward
The Club '94
Ed '96

Jennifer Ward-Lealand
Dangerous Orphans '86
Desperate Remedies '93

Anthony Warde
There Goes Kelly '45
King of the Forest Rangers '46
The Black Widow '47

Jack Warden
From Here to Eternity '53
Justice '55
Twelve Angry Men '57
Darby's Rangers '58
Run Silent, Run Deep '58
Donovan's Reef '63
Brian's Song '71
Man on a String '71
Summertree '71
The Sporting Club '72
Man Who Loved Cat Dancing '73
The Apprenticeship of Duddy Kravitz '74
Shampoo '75
Raid on Entebbe '77
The White Buffalo '77
Death on the Nile '78
Heaven Can Wait '78
And Justice for All '79
Being There '79
Beyond the Poseidon Adventure '79
The Champ '79
Dreamer '79
Used Cars '80
Carbon Copy '81
Chu Chu & the Philly Flash '81
So Fine '81
The Verdict '82
Hobson's Choice '83
Crackers '84
The Aviator '85
Dead Solid Perfect '88
The Presidio '88
September '88
Everybody Wins '90
Judgment '90
Problem Child '90
Robert Kennedy and His Times '90
Problem Child 2 '91
Night and the City '92
Passed Away '92
Guilty as Sin '93
Bullets Over Broadway '94
Mighty Aphrodite '95
Things to Do In Denver When You're Dead '95
While You Were Sleeping '95
Ed '96

Herta Ware
Cocoon '85
Dakota '88
Crazy in Love '92
Top Dog '95

Irene Ware
Chandu the Magician '32
King Kelly of the U.S.A. '34
The Raven '35
The Dark Hour '36
Federal Agent '36

Chris Warfield
Dangerous Charter '62
Diary of a Madman '63

Emily Warfield
Pair of Aces '90
The Man in the Moon '91
Bonanza: The Return '93
Calendar Girl '93

Marsha Warfield
D.C. Cab '84
Mask '85

William Warfield
Show Boat '51
Old Explorers '90

Andy Warhol
Driver's Seat '73
Cocaine Cowboys '79

Todd Waring
Love & Murder '91
Sinatra '92

Billy Warlock
Hot Shot '86
Swimsuit: The Movie '89
Society '92
Honor Thy Father and Mother: The True Story of the Menendez Brothers '94

Gordon Warnecke
My Beautiful Laundrette '85
London Kills Me '91

David Warner
Tom Jones '63
Morgan! '66
The Fixer '68
A Midsummer Night's Dream '68
Ballad of Cable Hogue '70
Straw Dogs '72
A Doll's House '73
From Beyond the Grave '73
The Old Curiosity Shop '75
Cross of Iron '76
The Omen '76
Providence '77
Holocaust '78
Silver Bears '78
The Concorde: Airport '79 '79
Nightwing '79
S.O.S. Titanic '79
The Thirty-Nine Steps '79
Time After Time '79
The Island '80
The Boy Who Left Home to Find Out About the Shivers '81
Disappearance '81
Masada '81
Time Bandits '81
Frankenstein '82
Tron '82
The Man with Two Brains '83
The Company of Wolves '85
Hanna's War '88
Hostile Takeover '88
Magdalene '88
Mr. North '88
My Best Friend Is a Vampire '88
Waxwork '88
Grave Secrets '89
Star Trek 5: The Final Frontier '89
Tripwire '89
Blue Tornado '90
Code Name: Chaos '90
Mortal Passions '90
Spymaker: The Secret Life of Ian Fleming '90
Cast a Deadly Spell '91
Star Trek 6: The Undiscovered Country '91
Teenage Mutant Ninja Turtles 2: The Secret of the Ooze '91
The Lost World '92
The Unnamable 2: The Statement of Randolph Carter '92
Body Bags '93
Quest of the Delta Knights '93
Return to the Lost World '93
Wild Palms '93
Inner Sanctum 2 '94
Tryst '94
Beastmaster 3: The Eye of Braxus '95
Final Equinox '95
Ice Cream Man '95
In the Mouth of Madness '95
Naked Souls '95

H.B. Warner
Big Stakes '22
King of Kings '27
Cross Examination '32
Supernatural '33
A Tale of Two Cities '35
Mr. Deeds Goes to Town '36
Lost Horizon '37
The Adventures of Marco Polo '38
Arrest Bulldog Drummond '38
Bulldog Drummond in Africa/Arrest Bulldog Drummond '38
You Can't Take It with You '38
Bulldog Drummond's Bride '39
Bulldog Drummond's Secret Police '39
Let Freedom Ring '39
Mr. Smith Goes to Washington '39
The Rains Came '39
The Devil & Daniel Webster '41
Topper Returns '41
The Corsican Brothers '42
Yank in Libya '42
Boss of Big Town '43
Hitler's Children '43
Action in Arabia '44
Enemy of Women '44
Rogue's Gallery '44
It's a Wonderful Life '46
The Judge Steps Out '49
The Ten Commandments '56

Jack Warner
The Dummy Talks '43
Captive Heart '47
Dear Murderer '47
Hue and Cry '47
Against the Wind '48
The Blue Lamp '49
Train of Events '49
A Christmas Carol '51
Valley of the Eagles '51
The Quatermass Experiment '56

Julie Warner
Doc Hollywood '91
Mr. Saturday Night '92
Indian Summer '93
The Puppet Masters '94
Tommy Boy '95

Malcolm Jamal Warner
The Father Clements Story '87
Drop Zone '94
The Tuskegee Airmen '95
Tyson '95

E. Alyn Warren
Abraham Lincoln '30
Medicine Man '30
Tarzan the Fearless '33
Get That Man '35

Jennifer Warren
The Swap '71
Night Moves '75
Another Man, Another Chance '77
Slap Shot '77
Steel Cowboy '78
Ice Castles '79
Angel City '80
The Choice '81
Intruder Within '81
Mutant '83
The Amazons '84

Lesley Ann Warren
Cinderella '64
The Happiest Millionaire '67
The One and Only, Genuine, Original Family Band '68
Where the Eagle Flies '72
Legend of Valentino '75
Harry & Walter Go to New York '76
Betrayal '78
Portrait of a Stripper '79
Beulah Land '80
Portrait of a Showgirl '82
Victor/Victoria '82
A Night in Heaven '83
Treasure of the Yankee Zephyr '83
Choose Me '84
The Dancing Princesses '84
Songwriter '84
Clue '85
Apology '86
Baja Oklahoma '87
Burglar '87
Cop '88
Worth Winning '89
A Fight for Jenny '90
Life Stinks '91
Pure Country '92
Color of Night '94
Joseph '95

Michael Warren
Norman, Is That You? '76
Hill Street Blues, Vol. 1: Hill Street Station '81
The Kid Who Loved Christmas '90
Heaven is a Playground '91
Storyville '92
A Passion to Kill '94

Harold Warrender
Mimi '35

Conspirator '49
Pandora and the Flying Dutchman '51

Ruth Warrick
Citizen Kane '41
The Corsican Brothers '42
The Iron Major '43
China Sky '44
Mr. Winkle Goes to War '44
Guest in the House '45
Great Dan Patch '49
Let's Dance '50
Three Husbands '50
One Too Many '51
Deathmask '69

David Warrilow
Strong Medicine '84
Barton Fink '91

James Warwick
The Case of the Missing Lady '83
The Man in the Mist '83
The Secret Adversary '83
The Unbreakable Alibi '83
The Affair of the Pink Pearl '84
The Clergyman's Daughter '84
The Crackler '84
Finessing the King '84
The House of Lurking Death '84

John Warwick
Ticket of Leave Man '37
The Face at the Window '39
While I Live '47

Robert Warwick
A Girl's Folly '17
The Royal Bed '31
The Secrets of Wu Sin '32
Whispering Shadow '33
Hopalong Cassidy '35
A Shot in the Dark '35
The Bold Caballero '36
Bulldog Edition '36
The Awful Truth '37
The Trigger Trio '37
Sullivan's Travels '41
A Woman's Face '41
It Started with a Kiss '59

Mona Washbourne
Cast a Dark Shadow '55
Stranger in Town '57
The Brides of Dracula '60
My Fair Lady '64
The Collector '65
Mrs. Brown, You've Got a Lovely Daughter '68
If... '69
Driver's Seat '73
O Lucky Man! '73
Stevie '78
Brideshead Revisited '81
December Flower

Beverly Washburn
Old Yeller '57
When the Line Goes Through '71

Bryant Washburn
The Wizard of Oz '25
Kept Husbands '31
Drifting Souls '32
The Throwback '35

Rick Washburne
Hangmen '87
Covert Action '88
Comrades in Arms '91
The Outfit '93

Denzel Washington
Carbon Copy '81
License to Kill '84
A Soldier's Story '84
The George McKenna Story '86
Power '86
Cry Freedom '87
Glory '89
The Mighty Quinn '89
Heart Condition '90
Mo' Better Blues '90
Ricochet '91
Malcolm X '92
Mississippi Masala '92
Much Ado about Nothing '93
The Pelican Brief '93
Philadelphia '93
Crimson Tide '95
Devil In a Blue Dress '95
Virtuosity '95
Courage Under Fire '96

Gene Washington
The Black Six '74
Lady Cocoa '75

Isaiah Washington
Crooklyn '94
Clockers '95
Girl 6 '96
Mr. & Mrs. Loving '96

Shirley Washington
The Deadly and the Beautiful '73
Darktown Strutters '74

Ted Wass
The Best of Soap: Who Killed Peter? '77
The Triangle Factory Fire Scandal '79
Curse of the Pink Panther '83
Oh, God! You Devil '84
Sheena '84
TripleCross '85
The Longshot '86
Fine Gold '88
Pancho Barnes '88
Danielle Steel's Star '93

Craig Wasson
The Boys in Company C '77
Go Tell the Spartans '78
Skag '79
Carny '80
Schizoid '80
Four Friends '81
Ghost Story '81
Second Thoughts '83
Body Double '84
The Innocents Abroad '84
The Men's Club '86
A Nightmare on Elm Street 3: Dream Warriors '87
Midnight Fear '90
Malcolm X '92
Strapped '93
Trapped in Space '94
The Sister-in-Law '95

Gedde Watanabe
Sixteen Candles '84
Gung Ho '85
Volunteers '85
Vamp '86
The Spring '89

Ken Watanabe
Bruce's Fists of Vengeance '84
MacArthur's Children '85
Tampopo '86
Commando Invasion '87
Karate Warrior '88

Tsunehiko Watase
Tattooed Hit Man '76
Heaven & Earth '90
The Silk Road '92

Nick Wateres
The Big Hurt '87
The Lighthorsemen '87

Dennis Waterman
The Scars of Dracula '70
Fright '71
Man in the Wilderness '71
Cold Justice '89
Circle of Deceit '94

Felicity Waterman
Lena's Holiday '90
Miracle Beach '92
Hard Bounty '94

Willard Waterman
Hollywood or Bust '56
Hail '73

Cheryl Waters
Macon County Line '74
Image of Death '77
Didn't You Hear? '83

Ethel Waters
Cairo '42
Tales of Manhattan '42
Cabin in the Sky '43
Stage Door Canteen '43
Pinky '49
The Member of the Wedding '52

Harry Waters, Jr.
Back to the Future '85
Back to the Future, Part 2 '89

John Waters
Endplay '75
Demolition '77
The Getting of Wisdom '77
Scalp Merchant '77
Weekend of Shadows '77
Cass '78
Breaker Morant '80
All the Rivers Run '84
Attack Force Z '84
Three's Trouble '85
Alice to Nowhere '86
Miracle Down Under '87
True Colors '87
Boulevard of Broken Dreams '88
Grievous Bodily Harm '89
Which Way Home '90
Heaven Tonight '93

Sam Waterston
Generation '69
Who Killed Mary What's 'Er Name? '71
Savages '72
The Great Gatsby '74
Journey into Fear '74
Reflections of Murder '74
Rancho Deluxe '75
Capricorn One '78
Interiors '78
Eagle's Wing '79
Friendly Fire '79
Sweet William '79
Hopscotch '80
Heaven's Gate '81
Dempsey '83
The Boy Who Loved Trolls '84
Finnegan Begin Again '84
The Killing Fields '84
Warning Sign '85
Hannah and Her Sisters '86
Just Between Friends '86
Gore Vidal's Lincoln '88
September '88
Crimes & Misdemeanors '89
The Nightmare Years '89
Welcome Home '89
Trade Secrets '90s
Lantern Hill '90
A Captive in the Land '91
The Man in the Moon '91
Mindwalk: A Film for Passionate Thinkers '91
Assault at West Point: The Court-Martial of Johnson Whittaker '94
The Enemy Within '94
Serial Mom '94
The Journey of August King '95

Gwen Watford
The Fall of the House of Usher '49
Taste the Blood of Dracula '70
Ripping Yarns '75

Ian Watkin
Beyond Reasonable Doubt '80
Nutcase '83
Dead Alive '93

Pierre Watkin
Country Gentlemen '36
The Road to Singapore '40
The Magnificent Dope '42
The Great Mike '44
Little Giant '46
Swamp Fire '46
Superman: The Serial, Vol. 1 '48
Redwood Forest Trail '50
The Stranger Wore a Gun '53

Joanne Watkins
The Big Sweat '90
Cold Heat '90

Jack Watling
The Courtney Affair '47
Under Capricorn '49
The Nanny '65

Alberta Watson
Best Revenge '83
The Keep '83
Women of Valor '86
White of the Eye '88
The Hitman '91
Spanking the Monkey '94
Hackers '95

Bob Watson
In Hot Pursuit '82
Tough Enough '83

Bobby Watson
Captains Courageous '37
Hitler: Dead or Alive '43
The Band Wagon '53

Bobs Watson
Show Boat '36
In Old Chicago '38
On Borrowed Time '39
The Story of Alexander Graham Bell '39
Dreaming Out Loud '40

Jack Watson
Peeping Tom '63
Night Caller from Outer Space '66
The Devil's Brigade '68
McKenzie Break '70
Tower of Evil '72
King Arthur, the Young Warlord '75
Young Warlord '75

James A. Watson, Jr.
Sex Through a Window '72
Killings at Cutpost Zeta '80

Lucile Watson
Rhythm on the Range '36
Made for Each Other '39
The Women '39
Waterloo Bridge '40
Footsteps in the Dark '41
The Great Lie '41
Mr. & Mrs. Smith '41
The Thin Man Goes Home '44
Uncertain Glory '44
Never Say Goodbye '46
Tomorrow Is Forever '46
Emperor Waltz '48
Julia Misbehaves '48
Harriet Craig '50
Let's Dance '50

Mills Watson
The Migrants '74
Kansas City Massacre '75
Heated Vengeance '87

Minor Watson
Charlie Chan in Paris '35
Navy Blue and Gold '37
That Certain Woman '37
Abe Lincoln in Illinois '40
Western Union '41
To the Shores of Tripoli '42
Woman of the Year '42
Crash Dive '43
Guadalcanal Diary '43
A Southern Yankee '48
Beyond the Forest '49
The Jackie Robinson Story '50
As Young As You Feel '51
Face to Face '52
The Ambassador's Daughter '56

Tom Watson
Another Time, Another Place '83
Prime Suspect 2 '93

William Watson
Girl on a Chain Gang '65
Force of Evil '77

Woody Watson
All-American Murder '91
The Last Prostitute '91
Skylark '93
Texas '94

Wylie Watson
The 39 Steps '35
A Girl in a Million '46
Brighton Rock '47
Things Happen at Night '48
The Sundowners '60

Vernee Watson-Johnson
Norman, Is That You? '76
Death Drug '83

Richard Wattis
The Happiest Days of Your Life '50
My Son, the Vampire '52
Doctor in the House '53
Norman Conquest '53
Three Stops to Murder '53
The Prince and the Showgirl '57

Naomi Watts
Brides of Christ '91
Gross Misconduct '93
The Custodian '94
Tank Girl '94

Victoria Wauchope
Bluffing It '87
Cop '88

Love and Hate: A Marriage Made in Hell '90

Al Waxman
Wild Horse Hank '79
The Double Negative '80
Class of 1984 '82
Clown Murders '83
Meatballs 3 '87
Switching Channels '88
Collision Course '89
Malarek '89
Millenium '89
Mob Story '90
The Hitman '91
Teamster Boss: The Jackie Presser Story '92
Operation Golden Phoenix '94
Iron Eagle 4 '95

Eileen Way
Three Stops to Murder '53
Queen of Hearts '89

Damon Wayans
Beverly Hills Cop '84
Hollywood Shuffle '87
Roxanne '87
I'm Gonna Git You Sucka '88
Punchline '88
Earth Girls Are Easy '89
The Last Boy Scout '91
Mo' Money '92
Blankman '94
Major Payne '95
Celtic Pride '96
The Great White Hype '96

Keenen Ivory Wayans
Hollywood Shuffle '87
I'm Gonna Git You Sucka '88
A Low Down Dirty Shame '94

Kim Wayans
I'm Gonna Git You Sucka '88
Talking About Sex '94

Marlon Wayans
Mo' Money '92
Above the Rim '94

Carol Wayne
The Party '68
Heartbreakers '84
Surf 2 '84

David Wayne
Portrait of Jennie '48
Adam's Rib '50
As Young As You Feel '51
We're Not Married '52
How to Marry a Millionaire '53
The Tender Trap '55
Naked Hills '56
The Sad Sack '57
The Three Faces of Eve '57
The Last Angry Man '59
Lamp at Midnight '66
The Andromeda Strain '71
Huckleberry Finn '74
The Apple Dumpling Gang '75
An American Christmas Carol '79
Finders Keepers '84
Poker Alice '87
The Survivalist '87
The Gift of Love '90

John Wayne
Big Trail '30
Range Feud '31
The Range Feud/Two Fisted Law '31
The Big Stampede '32
Haunted Gold '32
Hurricane Express '32
Ride Him, Cowboy '32
Shadow of the Eagle '32
Texas Cyclone '32
Two-Fisted Law '32
Baby Face '33
His Private Secretary '33
Man from Monterey '33
Riders of Destiny '33
Sagebrush Trail '33
Somewhere in Sonora '33
Telegraph Trail '33
The Three Musketeers '33
Western Double Feature 2 '33
Blue Steel '34
John Wayne Anthology: Star Packer/Lawless Range '34
Lucky Texan '34
Man from Utah '34
'Neath the Arizona Skies '34

Secret of the Ice Cave '89
Midnight Cabaret '90
Arcade '93
Deceit '93
My Antonia '94
The Road to Wellville '94
Heatseeker '95
Nemesis 3: Time Lapse '96
Riders of the Purple Sage '96

Jeffrey Weissman
Back to the Future, Part 2 '89
Back to the Future, Part 3 '90

Johnny Weissmuller
Tarzan, the Ape Man '32
Tarzan and His Mate '34
Tarzan Escapes '36
Tarzan Finds a Son '39
Tarzan's Secret Treasure '41
Tarzan's New York Adventure '42
Swamp Fire '46

Lucinda Weist
The Haunting of Seacliff Inn '94
The Silencers '95

Bruce Weitz
Death of a Centerfold '81
Hill Street Blues, Vol. 1: Hill Street Station '81
The Queen of Mean '90
Rainbow Drive '90
The Liar's Club '93
No Place to Hide '93
Molly and Gina '94
The O.J. Simpson Story '94
Windrunner '94
Prehysteria 3 '95

Raquel Welch
Roustabout '64
A Swingin' Summer '65
Fantastic Voyage '66
One Million Years B.C. '66
Shoot Loud, Louder, I Don't Understand! '66
Oldest Profession '67
Bandolero! '68
Bedazzled '68
Lady in Cement '68
The Magic Christian '69
100 Rifles '69
Myra Breckinridge '70
Bluebeard '72
Fuzz '72
Hannie Caulder '72
Restless '72
The Last of Sheila '73
The Three Musketeers '74
Wild Party '74
The Four Musketeers '75
Mother, Jugs and Speed '76
The Prince and the Pauper '78
Stuntwoman '81
Legend of Walks Far Woman '82
Scandal in a Small Town '88
Trouble in Paradise '88
Tainted Blood '93
Naked Gun 33 1/3: The Final Insult '94

Tahnee Welch
Cocoon '85
Lethal Obsession '87
Cocoon: The Return '88
Sleeping Beauty '89
The Criminal Mind '93
Night Train to Venice '93
Improper Conduct '94

Tuesday Weld
Rock, Rock, Rock '56
The Five Pennies '59
Return to Peyton Place '61
Wild in the Country '61
Soldier in the Rain '63
The Cincinnati Kid '65
I'll Take Sweden '65
Pretty Poison '68
Reflections of Murder '74
F. Scott Fitzgerald in Hollywood '76
Looking for Mr. Goodbar '77
A Question of Guilt '78
Who'll Stop the Rain? '78
Mother & Daughter: A Loving War '80
Serial '80
Thief '81
Author! Author! '82
Once Upon a Time in America '84
Something in Common '86

Heartbreak Hotel '88
Mistress '91
Falling Down '93

Mary Louise Weller
National Lampoon's Animal House '78
Forced Vengeance '82

Peter Weller
Butch and Sundance: The Early Days '79
Shoot the Moon '82
Of Unknown Origin '83
The Adventures of Buckaroo Banzai Across the Eighth Dimension '84
The Dancing Princesses '84
First Born '84
A Killing Affair '85
Two Kinds of Love '85
Apology '86
RoboCop '87
Shakedown '88
Leviathan '89
The Tunnel '89
Cat Chaser '90
Rainbow Drive '90
RoboCop 2 '90
Women & Men: Stories of Seduction '90
Naked Lunch '91
Road to Ruin '91
Sunset Grill '92
Fifty/Fifty '93
The New Age '94
The Substitute Wife '94
Decoy '95
Mighty Aphrodite '95
Screamers '96

Gwen Welles
Hit! '73
Nashville '75
Desert Hearts '86
The Men's Club '86
Sticky Fingers '88
New Year's Day '89
Eating '90
Boys Life '94

Mel Welles
Abbott and Costello Meet the Mummy '55
The Undead '57
Little Shop of Horrors '60
The She-Beast '65
Joy Ride to Nowhere '78
Dr. Heckyl and Mr. Hype '80
Commando Squad '87
Rented Lips '88
Wizards of the Lost Kingdom 2 '89

Orson Welles
Citizen Kane '41
Journey into Fear '42
Jane Eyre '44
The Stranger '46
Tomorrow Is Forever '46
The Lady from Shanghai '48
Macbeth '48
Black Magic '49
The Third Man '49
Othello '52
Trouble in the Glen '54
Mr. Arkadin '55
Napoleon '55
Three Cases of Murder '55
Moby Dick '56
The Long, Hot Summer '58
Touch of Evil '58
Compulsion '59
Ferry to Hong Kong '59
The Battle of Austerlitz '60
RoGoPaG '62
The Trial '63
The V.I.P.'s '63
A Man for All Seasons '66
Casino Royale '67
Chimes at Midnight '67
Is Paris Burning? '68
Battle of Neretva '69
Catch-22 '70
Start the Revolution Without Me '70
12 Plus 1 '70
Waterloo '71
Ten Days Wonder '72
Treasure Island '72
The Witching '72
Inspiration of Mr. Budd '75
Ten Little Indians '75

America at the Movies '76
Voyage of the Damned '76
Blood and Guns '79
Hot Money '79
Butterfly '82
Slapstick of Another Kind '84
Someone to Love '87

Virginia Welles
Dynamite '49
Francis in the Haunted House '56

Titus Welliver
The Lost Capone '90
Zero Tolerance '93

William Wellman, Jr.
High School Confidential '58
Lafayette Escadrille '58
Macumba Love '60
A Swingin' Summer '65
Born Losers '67
The Trial of Billy Jack '74
Curfew '88
The Prodigal Planet '88

Carole Wells
The House of Seven Corpses '73
Funny Lady '75

Dawn Wells
Gilligan's Island: Meet the Crew '64
Town that Dreaded Sundown '76
Return to Boggy Creek '77

Dolores Wells
Beach Party '63
Bikini Beach '64
Muscle Beach Party '64
The Time Travelers '64

Jacqueline Wells
Laurel & Hardy Comedy Classics, Vol. 4 '32
Tarzan the Fearless '33
The Black Cat '34
Bohemian Girl '36
The Kansas Terrors '39
Torture Ship '39
Her First Romance '40
Riders of the Range/Storm Over Wyoming '50

Vernon Wells
The Losers '70
The Road Warrior '82
Commando '85
Innerspace '87
Last Man Standing '87
Nam Angels '88
Circle of Fear '89
American Eagle '90
Circuitry Man '90
Crossing the Line '90
The Shrimp on the Barbie '90
Enemy Unseen '91
Undeclared War '91
Sexual Response '92
Bounty Hunter 2002 '94
Plughead Rewired: Circuitry Man 2 '94
Stranglehold '94
Hard Justice '95

Kenneth Welsh
Of Unknown Origin '83
The War Boy '85
Lost '86
Loyalties '86
Screwball Academy '86
The Climb '87
And Then You Die '88
Another Woman '88
Crocodile Dundee 2 '88
The Big Slice '90
The Last Best Year '90
Perfectly Normal '91
The Good Fight '92
Adrift '93
Death Wish 5: The Face of Death '94
Getting Gotti '94
Legends of the Fall '94
The Spider and the Fly '94
Timecop '94
Whale Music '94
Hiroshima '95
Margaret's Museum '95
Portraits of a Killer '95
Kissinger and Nixon '96

Margaret Welsh
Mr. & Mrs. Bridge '90
American Heart '92

William Welsh
Traffic in Souls '13
20,000 Leagues Under the Sea '16

Ariadne Welter
The Criminal Life of Archibaldo de la Cruz '55
The Vampire '57
The Vampire's Coffin '58
The Brainiac '61
The Devil's Hand '61

Ming-Na Wen
The Joy Luck Club '93
Hong Kong '97 '94
Star Quest '94
Street Fighter '94

Lara Wendell
Intervista '87
Ghosthouse '88

Wim Wenders
The American Friend '77
Lightning Over Water '80

George Wendt
Dreamscape '84
No Small Affair '84
Thief of Hearts '84
Fletch '85
Gung Ho '85
House '86
Plain Clothes '88
The Masters of Menace '90
Never Say Die '90
Guilty by Suspicion '91
Forever Young '92
Hostage for a Day '94
Man of the House '95

John Wengraf
U-Boat Prisoner '44
Five Fingers '52

Martha Wentworth
Stagecoach to Denver '46
The Stranger '46
Vigilantes of Boom Town '46
Jupiter's Darling '55

Fritz Wepper
The Bridge '59
Le Dernier Combat '84

Jan Werich
Fabulous Adventures of Baron Munchausen '61
The Original Fabulous Adventures of Baron Munchausen '61

Oskar Werner
Angel with the Trumpet '50
Lola Montes '55
The Life and Loves of Mozart '59
Jules and Jim '62
Ship of Fools '65
The Spy Who Came in from the Cold '65
Fahrenheit 451 '66
The Shoes of the Fisherman '68
Voyage of the Damned '76

Otto Wernicke
Crimes of Dr. Mabuse '32
Das Testament des Dr. Mabuse '33

Doug Wert
Haunted Symphony '94
Roswell: The U.F.O. Cover-Up '94

Massimo Wertmuller
Sotto, Sotto '85
Summer Night '87

Dick Wessel
Tanks a Million '41
Bowery at Midnight/Dick Tracy vs. Cueball '42
X Marks the Spot '42

Dick Wesson
Destination Moon '50
Jim Thorpe: All American '51
The Desert Song '53
The Errand Boy '61

Adam West
Geronimo '62
Robinson Crusoe on Mars '64
The Outlaws is Coming! '65
Batman '66
Hell River '75
The Specialist '75
Hooper '78
For the Love of It '80

The Happy Hooker Goes Hollywood '80
One Dark Night '82
Hellriders '84
Young Lady Chatterly 2 '85
Zombie Nightmare '86
Doin' Time on Planet Earth '88
Mad About You '90
Omega Cop '90
Maxim Xul '91
Night of the Kickfighters '91
Return Fire '91
The New Age '94

Chandra West
Puppet Master 4 '93
Puppet Master 5: The Final Chapter '94

Gregory West
Class of 1999 2: The Substitute '93
The Surgeon '94

Jeremy West
Catacombs '89
Curse 4: The Ultimate Sacrifice '90

Mae West
Night After Night '32
I'm No Angel '33
She Done Him Wrong '33
Belle of the Nineties '34
Goin' to Town '35
Go West, Young Man '36
Klondike Annie '36
Every Day's a Holiday '38
My Little Chickadee '40
The Heat's On '43
The Love Goddesses '65
Myra Breckinridge '70
Sextette '78

Martin West
A Swingin' Summer '65
Assault on Precinct 13 '76

Red West
Will: G. Gordon Liddy '82
Hard Knox '83
Proud Men '87
Grizzly Adams: The Legend Continues '90
The Expert '95
The P.A.C.K. '96

Sam West
Reunion '88
Howard's End '92
Carrington '95
Persuasion '95

Sonny West
Hellcats '68
Outlaw Riders '72

Timothy West
Hedda '75
Agatha '79
Death by Prescription '80s
Rough Cut '80
Churchill and the Generals '81
Oliver Twist '82
The Last Bastion '84
Cry Freedom '87
Tragedy of Flight 103: The Inside Story '91
Hiroshima '95

Helen Westcott
Thunder Over Texas '34
The Gunfighter '50
Abbott and Costello Meet Dr. Jekyll and Mr. Hyde '52
The Invisible Avenger '58

Hakan Westergren
Swedenhielms '35
Dollar '38

Floyd "Red Crow" Westerman
Dances with Wolves '90
Clearcut '92
The Broken Chain '93
Walker: Texas Ranger: One Riot, One Ranger '93
Lakota Woman: Siege at Wounded Knee '94
Buffalo Girls '95

Dr. Ruth Westheimer
One Woman or Two '85
Forever, Lulu '87

Helen Westley
Dimples '36

Westley ▶cont.

Stowaway '36
Heidi '37
Alexander's Ragtime Band '38
Rebecca of Sunnybrook Farm '38
All This and Heaven Too '40
Sunny '41
Lady from Louisiana '42

Nydia Westman
One Night of Love '34
Bulldog Drummond's Revenge '37
The Chocolate Soldier '41
Velvet Touch '48

James Westmoreland
Stacey '73
Don't Answer the Phone '80

Celia Weston
Lost Angels '89
Little Man Tate '91
Dead Man Walking '95
Flirting with Disaster '95

Doris Weston
Born to Be Wild '38
Delinquent Parents '38

Jack Weston
Please Don't Eat the Daisies '60
The Honeymoon Machine '61
Palm Springs Weekend '63
The Incredible Mr. Limpet '64
The Cincinnati Kid '65
Mirage '66
Wait Until Dark '67
The Thomas Crown Affair '68
Cactus Flower '69
A New Leaf '71
Fuzz '72
Marco '73
Gator '76
The Ritz '76
Cuba '79
The Four Seasons '81
High Road to China '83
The Longshot '86
Rad '86
Dirty Dancing '87
Short Circuit 2 '88

Jeff Weston
Demonic Toys '90
Puppet Master 2 '90

Virginia Wetherell
The Crimson Cult '68
The Big Switch '70
Demons of the Mind '72
Disciple of Death '72

Patricia Wettig
City Slickers '91
Guilty by Suspicion '91
Silent Motive '91
Me & Veronica '93
City Slickers 2: The Legend of Curly's Gold '94
Parallel Lives '94
Stephen King's The Langoliers '95

Marius Weyers
African Rage '78
The Gods Must Be Crazy '84
Deepstar Six '89
Farewell to the King '89
Happy Together '89
The Power of One '92
Bopha! '93

Michael Whalen
The Poor Little Rich Girl '36
Wee Willie Winkie '37
Dawn Express '42
Highway 13 '48
Omoo Omoo, the Shark God '49
Thunder in the Pines '49
G.I. Jane '51
King of the Bullwhip '51
The Phantom from 10,000 Leagues '56
Missile to the Moon '59

Sean Whalen
The People Under the Stairs '91
Twister '96

Frank Whaley
Ironweed '87
Born on the Fourth of July '89
Field of Dreams '89
Little Monsters '89
The Freshman '90
Career Opportunities '91
The Doors '91
Back in the USSR '92
Hoffa '92
A Midnight Clear '92
Swing Kids '93
To Dance with the White Dog '93
The Desperate Trail '94
I.Q. '94
Pulp Fiction '94
Swimming with Sharks '94
Broken Arrow '95

Justin Whalin
Child's Play 3 '91
Perfect Harmony '91
The Fire Next Time '93
White Wolves 2: Legend of the Wild '94

Joanne Whalley
Dance with a Stranger '85
Edge of Darkness '86
No Surrender '86
The Good Father '87
Willow '88
Kill Me Again '89
Scandal '89
To Kill a Priest '89
Navy SEALS '90
The Big Man: Crossing the Line '91
Shattered '91
Storyville '92
A Good Man in Africa '94
Mother's Boys '94
Scarlett '94
The Secret Rapture '94
Trial by Jury '94

Liem Whatley
The Iron Triangle '89
Heaven and Earth '93

Alan Wheatley
Appointment with Crime '45
Brighton Rock '47
Calling Paul Temple '48
Counterblast '48
The Limping Man '53
Robin Hood: The Movie '55

Wil Wheaton
The Buddy System '83
The Last Starfighter '84
Long Time Gone '86
Stand By Me '86
The Curse '87
Star Trek the Next Generation: Encounter at Farpoint '87
December '91
The Last Prostitute '91
Toy Soldiers '91
The Liar's Club '93
Mr. Stitch '95

Bert Wheeler
Dixiana '30
Half-Shot at Sunrise '30
Hook, Line and Sinker '30
Hold 'Em Jail '32
Diplomaniacs '33
Cockeyed Cavaliers '34
Hips, Hips, Hooray '34
Kentucky Kernels '34

Dave Wheeler
Ninja Squad '80s
Ninja Commandments '87

John Wheeler
Bad Georgia Road '77
Lucy and Desi: Before the Laughter '91

Dana Wheeler-Nicholson
Mrs. Soffel '84
Fletch '85
Circuitry Man '90
The Night We Never Met '93
Tombstone '93
My Life's In Turnaround '94
Denise Calls Up '95

Arleen Whelan
Young Mr. Lincoln '39
Young People '40
Castle in the Desert '42
Ramrod '47
Never Wave at a WAC '52
The Sun Shines Bright '53

Lisa Whelchel
The Double McGuffin '79
Twirl '81
Where the Red Fern Grows: Part 2 '92

Manning Whiley
The Dummy Talks '43
Meet Sexton Blake '44

Barbara Whinnery
Crawlspace '86
Hot to Trot! '88

Shannon Whirry
Animal Instincts '92
Body of Influence '93
Mirror Images 2 '93
Animal Instincts 2 '94
The Granny '94
Lady in Waiting '94
Private Obsession '94
Dangerous Prey '95
Exit '95
Playback '95

Charles "Slim" Whitaker
Desert of the Lost '27
Ghost Valley '32
Saddle Buster '32
Deadwood Pass '33
The Fiddlin' Buckaroo '33
Man from Monterey '33
The Man from Hell '34
The Silver Bullet '34
Border Vengeance '35
Melody of the Plains '37
Santa Fe Bound '37
Cheyenne Rides Again '38
Phantom Gold '38
Bullet Code '40
The Mysterious Rider '42
Outlaw of the Plains '46

Christina Whitaker
Naked Cage '86
Assault of the Killer Bimbos '88
Vampire at Midnight '88

Damon Whitaker
Bird '88
Saints and Sinners '95

Forest Whitaker
Fast Times at Ridgemont High '82
The Color of Money '86
Platoon '86
Good Morning, Vietnam '87
Stakeout '87
Bird '88
Bloodsport '88
Downtown '89
Johnny Handsome '89
Criminal Justice '90
Diary of a Hitman '91
A Rage in Harlem '91
Article 99 '92
Consenting Adults '92
The Crying Game '92
Bank Robber '93
Body Snatchers '93
Last Light '93
Blown Away '94
The Enemy Within '94
Jason's Lyric '94
Lush Life '94
Ready to Wear '94
Smoke '95
Species '95
Phenomenon '96

Johnny Whitaker
The Littlest Angel '69
Napoleon and Samantha '72
Tom Sawyer '73

Alice White
Murder at Midnight '31
Employees' Entrance '33
Annabel Takes a Tour/Maid's Night Out '38
Flamingo Road '49

Bernie White
The Ghost of Fletcher Ridge '80s
Body Count '87
Twenty Dollar Star '91
The Abduction of Allison Tate '92
Killing Obsession '94

Carol White
Never Let Go '60
A Matter of WHO '62
The Fixer '68
Daddy's Gone A-Hunting '69
Man Who Had Power Over Women '70
Some Call It Loving '73
The Squeeze '77

Dan White
Outlaw Country '49
The Last Hunt '56

David White
The Tender Trap '55
The Amazing Spider-Man '77

Diz White
Bullshot '83
Footlight Frenzy '84

Harriet White
Paisan '46
The Ghost '63

Jacqueline White
Air Raid Wardens '43
The Show-Off '46
Return of the Bad Men '48
The Capture '50
The Narrow Margin '52
The Saint's Vacation/The Narrow Margin '52

Jesse White
Harvey '50
Bedtime for Bonzo '51
Francis Goes to the Races '51
Million Dollar Mermaid '52
Forever Female '53
Designing Woman '57
Tomboy & the Champ '58
The Rise and Fall of Legs Diamond '60
Pajama Party '64
The Reluctant Astronaut '67
Togetherness '70
Bless the Beasts and Children '71
Music Shoppe '82
Monster in the Closet '86
Matinee '92

Lee White
Red Rock Outlaw '47
Lonesome Trail '55

Patricia White
Cry Wolf '47
Riders of the Whistling Pines '49

Ron White
Cowboys Don't Cry '88
Love & Murder '91
Guilty as Sin '93
Race to Freedom: The Story of the Underground Railroad '94
Johnny's Girl '95
Kissinger and Nixon '96
Screamers '96

Slappy (Melvin) White
Amazing Grace '74
Mr. Saturday Night '92

Vanna White
Graduation Day '81
Gypsy Angels '94

O.Z. Whitehead
The Grapes of Wrath '40
Road House '48
Beware, My Lovely '52

Paxton Whitehead
Back to School '86
Baby Boom '87
Chips, the War Dog '90
Child of Darkness, Child of Light '91
Boris and Natasha: The Movie '92
The Adventures of Huck Finn '93
My Boyfriend's Back '93

Billie Whitelaw
Small Hotel '57
Make Mine Mink '60
Mania '60
No Love for Johnnie '60
Strange Case of Dr. Jekyll & Mr. Hyde '68
Start the Revolution Without Me '70
Frenzy '72
Gumshoe '72
Night Watch '72
The Omen '76
Leopard in the Snow '78
Water Babies '79
A Tale of Two Cities '80
Unsuitable Job for a Woman '82
Slayground '84
Murder Elite '86
Maurice '87
The Secret Garden '87
Shadey '87
The Dressmaker '89
The Fifteen Streets '90
The Krays '90
Lorna Doone '90
Duel of Hearts '92

Arkie Whiteley
Razorback '84
Princess Caraboo '94
Gallowglass '95

Jon Whiteley
Moonfleet '55
The Spanish Gardener '57

Paul Whiteman
King of Jazz '30
Strike Up the Band '40
The Fabulous Dorseys '47

Lynn Whitfield
Doctor Detroit '83
The Slugger's Wife '85
The George McKenna Story '86
Jaws: The Revenge '87
Johnnie Gibson F.B.I. '87
The Josephine Baker Story '90
Taking the Heat '93
State of Emergency '94
A Thin Line Between Love and Hate '96

Mitchell Whitfield
Dogfight '91
My Cousin Vinny '92

Bradley Whitford
Dead as a Doorman '85
Vital Signs '90
Scent of a Woman '92
My Life '93
A Perfect World '93
Philadelphia '93
Billy Madison '94
The Client '94

Peter Whitford
Dead End Drive-In '86
Warm Nights on a Slow-Moving Train '87
Strictly Ballroom '92

Jack Whiting
Give Me a Sailor '38
Sailing Along '38

Leonard Whiting
Romeo and Juliet '68
Say Hello to Yesterday '71
Rachel's Man '75

Margaret Whiting
Sinbad and the Eye of the Tiger '77
Trespasser '85

Ray Whitley
Hittin' the Trail '37
Renegade Ranger/Scarlet River '38
Racketeers of the Range '39

Lloyd Whitlock
The Prairie Pirate '25
The Michigan Kid '28
Tangled Destinies '32
Diamond Trail '33
West of the Divide '34

Jill Whitlow
Night of the Creeps '86
Thunder Run '86
Adventures Beyond Belief '87
Ghost Chase '88
Twice Dead '88

Kari Whitman
Phantom of the Mall: Eric's Revenge '89
Chained Heat 2 '92
Forced to Kill '93

Stuart Whitman
Silver Lode '54
Darby's Rangers '58
Ten North Frederick '58
The Story of Ruth '60
The Comancheros '61
The Mark '61
The Longest Day '62
The Day and the Hour '63
Rio Conchos '64

Those Magnificent Men in Their Flying Machines '65
The Invincible Six '68
Captain Apache '71
The Woman Hunter '72
Call Him Mr. Shatter '74
Crazy Mama '75
Mean Johnny Barrows '75
Eaten Alive '76
Las Vegas Lady '76
Strange Shadows in an Empty Room '76
Delta Fox '77
Maniac '77
Ruby '77
The White Buffalo '77
Oil '78
Run for the Roses '78
Hostages '79
The Seekers '79
The Treasure Seekers '79
Fury '80s
Kill Castro '80
The Mercenaries '80
Demonoid, Messenger of Death '81
Butterfly '82
The Treasure of the Amazon '84
Vultures '84
First Strike '85
The Monster Club '85
Deadly Reactor '89
Moving Target '89
Mob Boss '90
Omega Cop '90
Smooth Talker '90
Private Wars '93
Improper Conduct '94
Trial by Jury '94
Walker: Texas Ranger: Deadly Reunion '94

James Whitmore
Battleground '49
The Asphalt Jungle '50
The Next Voice You Hear '50
Because You're Mine '52
Above and Beyond '53
All the Brothers Were Valiant '53
The Girl Who Had Everything '53
Kiss Me Kate '53
Them! '54
Battle Cry '55
The McConnell Story '55
Oklahoma! '55
Savage Wilderness '55
The Eddy Duchin Story '56
Deep Six '58
Black Like Me '64
Chuka '67
Waterhole #3 '67
Madigan '68
Planet of the Apes '68
Guns of the Magnificent Seven '69
Tora! Tora! Tora! '70
Chato's Land '71
Harrad Experiment '73
High Crime '73
Where the Red Fern Grows '74
Give 'Em Hell, Harry! '75
I Will Fight No More Forever '75
The Serpent's Egg '78
The Word '78
The First Deadly Sin '80
Rage '80
Don't Cry, It's Only Thunder '82
All My Sons '86
Nuts '87
Target: Favorite Son '87
Glory! Glory! '90
Old Explorers '90
The Shawshank Redemption '94

James Whitmore, Jr.
The Boys in Company C '77
The Gypsy Warriors '78
The Long Riders '80
The Five of Me '81
Tricks of the Trade '88

Grace Lee Whitney
Star Trek 3: The Search for Spock '84
Star Trek 6: The Undiscovered Country '91

Peter Whitney
Rio Rita '42
Valley of the Sun '42
Whistling in Dixie '42
Destination Tokyo '43
All the Brothers Were Valiant '53
Savage Wilderness '55

Marguerite Whitten
Two-Gun Man from Harlem '38
Mystery in Swing '40

Margaret Whitton
The Best of Times '86
9 1/2 Weeks '86
Ironweed '87
The Secret of My Success '87
Little Monsters '89
Major League '89
Big Girls Don't Cry...They Get Even '92
The Man Without a Face '93
Major League 2 '94
Trial by Jury '94

May Whitty
Conquest '37
The Lady Vanishes '38
Suspicion '41
Mrs. Miniver '42
Crash Dive '43
Lassie, Come Home '43
Madame Curie '43
Gaslight '44
The White Cliffs of Dover '44

James Whitworth
Black Bikers from Hell '70
The Hills Have Eyes '77
357 Magnum '77
Planet of Dinosaurs '80
Bye Bye, Love '94

Richard Whorf
Midnight '34
Keeper of the Flame '42
Yankee Doodle Dandy '42
Chain Lightning '50

Anna Wiazemsky
Teorema '68
Porcile '69

Mary Wickes
The Man Who Came to Dinner '41
Blondie's Blessed Event '42
Private Buckaroo '42
Who Done It? '42
June Bride '48
I'll See You in My Dreams '51
On Moonlight Bay '51
By the Light of the Silvery Moon '53
Ma and Pa Kettle at Home '54
Dance with Me, Henry '56
How to Murder Your Wife '64
Where Angels Go, Trouble Follows '68
Almost Partners '87
Postcards from the Edge '90
The Canterville Ghost '91
Sister Act '92
Sister Act 2: Back in the Habit '93
Little Women '94

Bernhard Wicki
The Eternal Waltz '54
Crime & Passion '75

Kathleen Widdoes
The Group '66
Petulia '68
The Mephisto Waltz '71
Savages '72
Mafia Princess '86

Richard Widmark
Kiss of Death '47
Road House '48
The Street with No Name '48
The Halls of Montezuma '50
Night and the City '50
Panic in the Streets '50
Don't Bother to Knock '52
Pickup on South Street '53
Broken Lance '54
The Cobweb '55
Saint Joan '57
The Law and Jake Wade '58
The Tunnel of Love '58
The Trap '59
Warlock '59
The Alamo '60
Judgment at Nuremberg '61
Two Rode Together '61
How the West Was Won '63
Cheyenne Autumn '64
Bedford Incident '65
Alvarez Kelly '66
The Way West '67
Madigan '68
Death of a Gunfighter '69
Gun Crazy '69
When the Legends Die '72
Murder on the Orient Express '74
Sell Out '76
To the Devil, A Daughter '76
The Domino Principle '77
Rollercoaster '77
Twilight's Last Gleaming '77
Coma '78
The Swarm '78
Mr. Horn '79
All God's Children '80
Bear Island '80
National Lampoon Goes to the Movies '81
Whale for the Killing '81
The Final Option '82
Hanky Panky '82
Against All Odds '84
Blackout '85
Cold Sassy Tree '89
Texas Guns '90
Murder on the Bayou '91
True Colors '91

Lynda Wiesmeier
Preppies '82
R.S.V.P. '84
Wheels of Fire '84

Dianne Wiest
It's My Turn '80
Independence Day '83
Falling in Love '84
Footloose '84
The Purple Rose of Cairo '85
Hannah and Her Sisters '86
The Lost Boys '87
Radio Days '87
Bright Lights, Big City '88
September '88
Cookie '89
Parenthood '89
Edward Scissorhands '90
Little Man Tate '91
Bullets Over Broadway '94
Cops and Robbersons '94
The Scout '94
The Birdcage '95

Naima Wifstrand
Night Is My Future '47
The Magician '58

Chris Wiggins
King of the Grizzlies '69
Why Shoot the Teacher '79
Kavik the Wolf Dog '84
The Bay Boy '85
Ford: The Man & the Machine '87
Mark Twain and Me '91
Black Fox: The Price of Peace '94

Robert Wightman
A Day for Thanks on Walton's Mountain '82
Opposing Force '87
Stepfather 3: Father's Day '92
Living in Oblivion '94

Carlton Wilborn
Dance '90
Grief '94

James Wilby
Dreamchild '85
Maurice '87
A Handful of Dust '88
A Summer Story '88
Conspiracy '89
A Tale of Two Cities '91
Howard's End '92

Frank Wilcox
Infamous Crimes '47
Abbott and Costello Meet the Keystone Kops '54
A Majority of One '56
Seventh Cavalry '56

Larry Wilcox
Sky Heist '75
The Last Ride of the Dalton Gang '79
The Dirty Dozen: The Next Mission '85
Mission Manila '87

Lisa Wilcox
A Nightmare on Elm Street 4: Dream Master '88
A Nightmare on Elm Street 5: Dream Child '89

Mary Wilcox
Beast of the Yellow Night '70
Love Me Deadly '76

Robert Wilcox
Blondie Takes a Vacation '39
Buried Alive '39
The Man They Could Not Hang '39
Doctor Satan's Robot '40
Dreaming Out Loud '40
Mysterious Doctor Satan '40

Shannon Wilcox
When Your Lover Leaves '83
Hollywood Harry '86

Toyah Wilcox
Murder: Ultimate Grounds for Divorce '85
Ebony Tower '86

Collin Wilcox-Horne
The Baby Maker '70
Fury on Wheels '71

Henry Wilcoxon
Cleopatra '34
The Crusades '35
The Last of the Mohicans '36
The President's Mystery '36
Jericho '38
Tarzan Finds a Son '39
That Hamilton Woman '41
The Corsican Brothers '42
Mrs. Miniver '42
Unconquered '47
A Connecticut Yankee in King Arthur's Court '49
Samson and Delilah '50
Scaramouche '52
The Ten Commandments '56
The War Lord '65
Escape from Planet Earth '67
Man in the Wilderness '71
Pony Express Rider '76
When Every Day was the Fourth of July '78
The Two Worlds of Jenny Logan '79
Enola Gay: The Men, the Mission, the Atomic Bomb '80

Jack Wild
Oliver! '68
Melody '71
Robin Hood: Prince of Thieves '91

Andrew Wilde
1984 '84
Pete Townshend: White City '85
Murder on Line One '90

Cornel Wilde
High Sierra '41
Wintertime '43
Leave Her to Heaven '45
A Song to Remember '45
A Thousand and One Nights '45
Forever Amber '47
Road House '48
At Sword's Point '51
The Greatest Show on Earth '52
Treasure of the Golden Condor '53
Passion '54
A Woman's World '54
Big Combo '55
Omar Khayyam '57
Sword of Lancelot '63
The Naked Prey '66
The Comic '69
Sharks' Treasure '75
Norseman '78
The Fifth Musketeer '79

Gene Wilder
Bonnie & Clyde '67
The Producers '68
Quackser Fortune Has a Cousin in the Bronx '70
Start the Revolution Without Me '70
Willy Wonka & the Chocolate Factory '71
Everything You Always Wanted to Know about Sex (But Were Afraid to Ask) '72
Blazing Saddles '74
The Little Prince '74
Thursday's Game '74
Young Frankenstein '74
Silver Streak '76
World's Greatest Lover '77
The Adventures of Sherlock Holmes' Smarter Brother '78
The Frisco Kid '79
Stir Crazy '80
Hanky Panky '82
The Woman in Red '84
Haunted Honeymoon '86
See No Evil, Hear No Evil '89
Funny About Love '90
Another You '91

James Wilder
Zombie High '87
Murder One '88
Prey of the Chameleon '91
Scorchers '92
Tollbooth '94

Yvonne Wilder
The Return of Count Yorga '71
Bloodbrothers '78
Honeyboy '82

Michael Wilding
Late Extra '35
Convoy '40
Cottage to Let '41
Kipps '41
Secret Mission '42
The Courtney Affair '47
Under Capricorn '49
Stage Fright '50
Maytime in Mayfair '52
Torch Song '53
The Egyptian '54
The Glass Slipper '55
The World of Suzie Wong '60
The Naked Edge '61
Waterloo '71

John Wildman
My American Cousin '85
Sorority Babes in the Slimeball Bowl-A-Rama '87
Lethal Pursuit '88
American Boyfriends '89

Valerie Wildman
Inner Sanctum '91
Neon City '91

Dawn Wildsmith
Cyclone '87
Evil Spawn '87
Phantom Empire '87
Surf Nazis Must Die '87
Terminal Force '88
Warlords '88
Alienator '89

Jason Wiles
Higher Learning '94
Windrunner '94
Kicking and Screaming '95

Mike Wiles
Terror at Tenkiller '86
Cole Justice '89

Ed Wiley
Class of '61 '92
The Canterville Ghost '96

Jan Wiley
Tonto Basin Outlaws '41
Dawn on the Great Divide '42
Jive Junction '43
Rhythm Parade '43
The Underdog '43
Master Key '44
There Goes Kelly '45

John Wilford
Ninja Death Squad '87
Ninja: American Warrior '90

Kathleen Wilhoite
Private School '83
The Morning After '86
Murphy's Law '86
Angel Heart '87
Campus Man '87
Undercover '87
Witchboard '87
Dream Demon '88
Bad Influence '90
Everybody Wins '90
Lorenzo's Oil '92
Color of Night '94
Getting Even with Dad '94

Robert J. Wilke
High Noon '52
20,000 Leagues Under the Sea '54
Tarnished Angels '57

Jose Wilker
Xica '76
Dona Flor and Her Two Husbands '78
Bye Bye Brazil '79
Medicine Man '92

Guy Wilkerson
Dead or Alive '41
Fighting Valley '43
Guns of the Law '44
Outlaw Roundup '44
Frontier Fugitives '45
Marked for Murder '45
Comin' Round the Mountain '51
Man of the West '58

Donna Wilkes
Fyre '78
Blood Song '82
Angel '84
Grotesque '87
Hard Knocks

Elaine Wilkes
Roommate '84
Killer Party '86

Barbara Wilkin
The Flesh Eaters '64
Six in Paris '68

June Wilkinson
Macumba Love '60
The Bellboy and the Playgirls '62
The Florida Connection '74
Frankenstein's Great Aunt Tillie '83
Sno-Line '85
Vasectomy: A Delicate Matter '86

Tom Wilkinson
Sylvia '86
Paper Mask '91
Prime Suspect '92
Priest '94

Fred Willard
Chesty Anderson USN '76
Americathon '79
Salem's Lot '79
How to Beat the High Cost of Living '80
The History of White People in America '85
Lots of Luck '85
Moving Violations '85
Roxanne '87
Portrait of a White Marriage '88
High Strung '91
Sodbusters '94
Prehysteria 3 '95

Warren William
Skyscraper Souls '32
Three on a Match '32
Employees' Entrance '33
Gold Diggers of 1933 '33
Lady for a Day '33
Cleopatra '34
The Case of the Lucky Legs '35
Go West, Young Man '36
Satan Met a Lady '36
The Firefly '37
Madame X '37
Wives Under Suspicion '38
The Man in the Iron Mask '39
Arizona '40
The Wolf Man '41
Strange Illusion '45
Fear '46
The Private Affairs of Bel Ami '47
Black Tower '50

Adam Williams
Queen for a Day '51
Without Warning '52
Fear Strikes Out '57
The Badlanders '58
North by Northwest '59

Allen Williams
The Two Worlds of Jenny Logan '79
Scorpion '86

Barbara Williams
Tell Me That You Love Me '84
Thief of Hearts '84
Jo Jo Dancer, Your Life is Calling '86
Tiger Warsaw '87
Watchers '88
Peter Gunn '89
City of Hope '91
Indecency '92
Oh, What a Night '92
Spenser: Ceremony '93
Digger '94
Spenser: Pale Kings & Princes '94

Barry Williams
The Brady Bunch '69
A Very Brady Christmas '88

Bill Williams
Deadline at Dawn '46
Till the End of Time '46
The Clay Pigeon '49
The Stratton Story '49
A Woman's Secret '49
The Cariboo Trail '50
Operation Haylift '50
Adventures of Kit Carson '51
Cavalry Charge '51
Son of Paleface '52
Torpedo Alley '53
Storm Rider '57
Buckskin '68
The Giant Spider Invasion '75
Flight of the Grey Wolf '76

Billy Dee Williams
Black Brigade '69
The Out-of-Towners '70
Brian's Song '71
Final Comedown '72
The Glass House '72
Lady Sings the Blues '72
Hit! '73
Mahogany '75
Bingo Long Traveling All-Stars & Motor Kings '76
Children of Divorce '80
The Empire Strikes Back '80
The Hostage Tower '80
Nighthawks '81
Chiefs '83
From "Star Wars" to "Jedi": The Making of a Saga '83
Return of the Jedi '83
Christmas Lilies of the Field '84
The Imposter '84
Marvin & Tige '84
Fear City '85
Shooting Stars '85
Courage '86
Oceans of Fire '86
Deadly Illusion '87
Number One with a Bullet '87
Batman '89
Secret Agent 00-Soul '89
Driving Me Crazy '91
The Jacksons: An American Dream '92
Alien Intruder '93
Percy & Thunder '93
Dangerous Passion '95
Machine Gun Blues '95
Triplecross '95
Giant Steps

Billy "Sly" Williams
Voodoo Dawn '89
Mission of Justice '92

Cara Williams
Boomerang '47
Meet Me in Las Vegas '56
The Defiant Ones '58
Never Steal Anything Small '59
The White Buffalo '77

Caroline Williams
Texas Chainsaw Massacre, Part 2 '86
Stepfather 2: Make Room for Daddy '89
Leprechaun 3 '95

Charles Williams
Born to Be Wild '38
Hollywood Stadium Mystery '38

Chuck Williams
Soultaker '90
Dark Rider '91

Cindy Williams
Gas-s-s-s! '70
Travels with My Aunt '72
American Graffiti '73
The Killing Kind '73
The Conversation '74
The Migrants '74
The First Nudie Musical '75
More American Graffiti '79
Spaceship '81
Uforia '81
Tricks of the Trade '88
Big Man on Campus '89
Rude Awakening '89
Bingo '91

Clara Williams
Italian '15
Hell's Hinges '16

Clarence Williams, III
The Mod Squad '68
Purple Rain '84
52 Pick-Up '86
The Last Innocent Man '87
Perfect Victims '87
Tough Guys Don't Dance '87
The House of Dies Drear '88
I'm Gonna Git You Sucka '88
Maniac Cop 2 '90
My Heroes Have Always Been Cowboys '91
Deep Cover '92
Dangerous Relations '93
Against the Wall '94
Sugar Hill '94
The Immortals '95
The Silencers '95
Tales from the Hood '95
The Road to Galveston '96

Cynda Williams
Mo' Better Blues '90
One False Move '91
Armistead Maupin's Tales of the City '93
The Ghost Brigade '93
Condition Red '95
Machine Gun Blues '95
The Sweeper '95
The Tie That Binds '95

Dick Anthony Williams
A Woman Called Moses '78
An Almost Perfect Affair '79
The Night the City Screamed '80
Keeping On '81
Sophisticated Gents '81
For Us, the Living '88
Tap '89
Edward Scissorhands '90
Mo' Better Blues '90

D.J. Williams
The Crimes of Stephen Hawke '36
Murder in the Old Red Barn '36
The Courageous Mr. Penn '41

Edy Williams
Secret Life of an American Wife '68
Beyond the Valley of the Dolls '70
Bad Manners '84
Hollywood Hot Tubs '84
Hellhole '85
Mankillers '87
Rented Lips '88
Bad Girls from Mars '90

Emlyn Williams
The Iron Duke '34
The Citadel '38
The Stars Look Down '39
This England '42
The Last Days of Dolwyn '49
The Wreck of the Mary Deare '59
Deadly Game '82

Esther Williams
Andy Hardy's Double Life '42
Bathing Beauty '44
A Guy Named Joe '44
Thrill of a Romance '45
Ziegfeld Follies '46
On an Island with You '48
Neptune's Daughter '49
Take Me Out to the Ball Game '49
The Duchess of Idaho '50
Pagan Love Song '50
Texas Carnival '51
Million Dollar Mermaid '52
Skirts Ahoy! '52
Dangerous When Wet '53
Easy to Love '53
Jupiter's Darling '55
That's Entertainment '74

Grant Williams
Written on the Wind '56
The Incredible Shrinking Man '57
The Monolith Monsters '57
The Leech Woman '59
Escape from Planet Earth '67
Brain of Blood '71

Guinn "Big Boy" Williams
Rounding Up the Law '22
Wolfheart's Revenge '25
The Phantom '31
When the West Was Young '32
Heritage of the Desert '33
Mystery Squadron '33
The Phantom Broadcast '33
Danger Trails '35
Powdersmoke Range '35
Gun Play '36
Kelly the Second '36
The Vigilantes are Coming '36
Dangerous Holiday '37
Feud of the Trail '37
Bad Lands '39
The Fighting 69th '40
Virginia City '40
Wagon's Westward '40
Billy the Kid '41
Lure of the Islands '42
Mr. Wise Guy '42
Hands Across the Border '43
Nevada '44
Springfield Rifle '52
Hidden Guns '56

Guy Williams
Savage Wilderness '55
I Was a Teenage Werewolf '57
The Secret of El Zorro '57
The Sign of Zorro '60
The Prince and the Pauper '62
Captain Sinbad '63

Hal Williams
On the Nickel '80
Don't Look Back: The Story of Leroy "Satchel" Paige '81
Down Periscope '96

Heathcote Williams
Orlando '92
Cold Light of Day '95

Hugh Williams
Bitter Sweet '33
The Human Monster '39
Inspector Hornleigh '39
Wuthering Heights '39
One of Our Aircraft Is Missing '41
The Day Will Dawn '42
Secret Mission '42
A Girl in a Million '46
Elizabeth of Ladymead '48
Khartoum '66

Ian Patrick Williams
Dolls '87
Bloodmoon '90
Bad Channels '92

Jason Williams
Flesh Gordon '72
Copkillers '77
Cheerleaders' Wild Weekend '85
Danger Zone '87
Vampire at Midnight '88
Danger Zone 2 '89
Danger Zone 3: Steel Horse War '90

Jim Williams
The Executioner '78
Island of Blood '86
The Newlydeads '87
Living to Die '91
Ex-Cop '93

JoBeth Williams
Kramer vs. Kramer '79
Stir Crazy '80
The Dogs of War '81
Endangered Species '82
Poltergeist '82
Adam '83
The Big Chill '83
The Day After '83
American Dreamer '84
Teachers '84
Desert Bloom '86
Poltergeist 2: The Other Side '86
Murder Ordained '87
Memories of Me '88
Welcome Home '89
Child in the Night '90
Dutch '91
Switch '91
Victim of Love '91
Me, Myself & I '92
Stop! or My Mom Will Shoot '92
Chantilly Lace '93
Final Appeal '93
Sex, Love and Cold Hard Cash '93
Parallel Lives '94
Wyatt Earp '94

John Williams
Dial "M" for Murder '54
Sabrina '54
To Catch a Thief '55
D-Day, the Sixth of June '56
Island in the Sun '57
Witness for the Prosecution '57
The Young Philadelphians '59
24 Hours in a Woman's Life '61
Dear Brigitte '65
Double Trouble '67
The Secret War of Harry Frigg '68

Kelli Williams
Zapped Again '89
There Goes My Baby '92
Till Murder Do Us Part '92
Lifepod '93
Wavelength '96

Kenneth Williams
Carry On Cruising '62
Carry On Cleo '65
Carry On Cowboy '66
Carry On Screaming '66
Follow That Camel '67
Carry On Doctor '68
Carry On at Your Convenience '71
Carry On Camping '71
Carry On Henry VIII '71
Carry On 'Round the Bend '72
Carry On Behind '75
Carry On Emmanuelle '78

Kimberly Williams
Father of the Bride '91
Indian Summer '93
Coldblooded '94
Father of the Bride Part II '95

Malinda Williams
Laurel Avenue '93
A Thin Line Between Love and Hate '96

Michael Williams
Marat/Sade '66
Educating Rita '83
Murder by Night '89

Paul Williams
Battle for the Planet of the Apes '73
Phantom of the Paradise '74
Smokey and the Bandit '77
The Cheap Detective '78
Smokey and the Bandit, Part 2 '80
Stone Cold Dead '80
Smokey and the Bandit, Part 3 '83
Best Enemies '86
The Night They Saved Christmas '87
Zombie High '87
Frog '89
Frogs! '90s
Chill Factor '90
The Doors '91
A Million to Juan '94
Headless Body in Topless Bar '96

Peter Williams
Destroy All Planets '68
Robin Hood...The Legend: Robin Hood and the Sorcerer '83
Jungleground '95

Rhys Williams
How Green Was My Valley '41
Mrs. Miniver '42
The Corn is Green '45
Kiss Tomorrow Goodbye '50
The Showdown '50
Fastest Gun Alive '56
The Restless Breed '58
Skullduggery '70

Robert Williams
Devotion '31
Platinum Blonde '31

Robin Williams
Can I Do It...Till I Need Glasses? '77
Mork & Mindy '78

Popeye '80
The World According to Garp '82
An Evening with Robin Williams '83
Survivors '83
The Tale of the Frog Prince '83
Moscow on the Hudson '84
The Best of Times '86
Club Paradise '86
Seize the Day '86
Good Morning, Vietnam '87
Dead Poets Society '89
Awakenings '90
Cadillac Man '90
The Fisher King '91
Hook '91
Toys '92
Mrs. Doubtfire '93
Being Human '94
The Birdcage '95
Jumanji '95
Jack '96

Roger Williams
Toll of the Desert '35
Gun Grit '36
Phantom Patrol '36
Aces Wild '37
Heroes of the Alamo '37
The Roamin' Cowboy '37
Cheyenne Rides Again '38
Feud Maker '38
Valley of Terror '38
Code of the Fearless '39

Samm-Art Williams
The Adventures of Huckleberry Finn '85
A Rage in Harlem '91

Spencer Williams, Jr.
Cord & Dischords/Naughty Nurse '28
Bronze Buckaroo '39
Harlem Rides the Range '39
Son of Ingagi '40
Blood of Jesus '41
Go Down Death '41
Dirty Gertie from Harlem U.S.A. '46
Juke Joint '47

Steven Williams
Missing in Action 2: The Beginning '85
Silent Witness '85
Revolver '92
Jason Goes to Hell: The Final Friday '93

Treat Williams
Deadly Hero '75
The Ritz '76
The Eagle Has Landed '77
Hair '79
1941 '79
Prince of the City '81
The Pursuit of D.B. Cooper '81
Dempsey '83
Flashpoint '84
The Little Mermaid '84
Once Upon a Time in America '84
A Streetcar Named Desire '84
Smooth Talk '85
The Men's Club '86
Echoes in the Darkness '87
J. Edgar Hoover '87
Dead Heat '88
Sweet Lies '88
The Heart of Dixie '89
Night of the Sharks '89
Third Degree Burn '89
Third Solution '89
Max and Helen '90
Final Verdict '91
Till Death Do Us Part '92
The Water Engine '92
Hand Gun '93
Parallel Lives '94
Johnny's Girl '95
Mulholland Falls '95
Things to Do In Denver When You're Dead '95
The Late Shift '96
The Phantom '96

Vanessa Williams
Another You '91
Harley Davidson and the Marlboro Man '91
New Jack City '91
Candyman '92
DROP Squad '94
Eraser '96

Vanessa Williams
The Pick-Up Artist '87
Under the Gun '88
Full Exposure: The Sex Tape Scandals '89
The Kid Who Loved Christmas '90
The Jacksons: An American Dream '92

Clayton Williamson
Clowning Around '92
Clowning Around 2 '93

Fred Williamson
M*A*S*H '70
Black Caesar '73
Hell Up in Harlem '73
Boss '74
No Way Back '74
Three the Hard Way '74
Adios Amigo '75
Bucktown '75
Mean Johnny Barrows '75
Take a Hard Ride '75
Death Journey '76
Joshua '76
Fist of Fear, Touch of Death '77
Mister Mean '77
Blind Rage '78
Deadly Mission '78
Express to Terror '79
Jornada de Muerte '80s
Fear in the City '81
The Last Fight '82
New York Ripper '82
One Down, Two to Go! '82
Big Score '83
1990: The Bronx Warriors '83
Warriors of the Wasteland '83
White Fire '83
Deadly Impact '84
Foxtrap '85
The Black Cobra '87
Delta Force Commando '87
The Messenger '87
The New Gladiators '87
Deadly Intent '88
Black Cobra 2 '89
The Kill Reflex '89
Black Cobra 3: The Manila Connection '90
Delta Force Commando 2 '90
Steele's Law '91
Three Days to a Kill '91
South Beach '92
Silent Hunter '94
From Dusk Till Dawn '95
Original Gangstas '96

Mykelti Williamson
Streets of Fire '84
The First Power '89
Miracle Mile '89
Forrest Gump '94
Heat '95
How to Make an American Quilt '95
Waiting to Exhale '95

Nicol Williamson
Hamlet '69
The Wilby Conspiracy '75
Robin and Marian '76
The Seven-Per-Cent Solution '76
The Cheap Detective '78
The Word '78
The Human Factor '79
Excalibur '81
I'm Dancing as Fast as I Can '82
Venom '82
Christopher Columbus '85
Return to Oz '85
Passion Flower '86
Black Widow '87
Exorcist 3: Legion '90
The Advocate '93

Noble Willingham
My Sweet Charlie '70
Big Bad Mama '74
Kenny Rogers as the Gambler '80
Coward of the County '81
Good Morning, Vietnam '87
Blind Fury '90
Career Opportunities '91
City Slickers '91
The Last Boy Scout '91
Pastime '91
Article 99 '92
City Slickers 2: The Legend of Curly's Gold '94
Walker: Texas Ranger: Deadly Reunion '94
Up Close and Personal '96

Bruce Willis
Moonlighting '85
Blind Date '87
Die Hard '88
Sunset '88
In Country '89
The Bonfire of the Vanities '90
Die Hard 2: Die Harder '90
That's Adequate '90
Billy Bathgate '91
Hudson Hawk '91
The Last Boy Scout '91
Mortal Thoughts '91
Death Becomes Her '92
Striking Distance '93
Color of Night '94
Nobody's Fool '94
North '94
Pulp Fiction '94
Die Hard: With a Vengeance '95
Four Rooms '95
12 Monkeys '95

Matt Willis
Behind Prison Walls '43
Return of the Vampire '43
Blonde Savage '47
The Noose Hangs High '48

Noel Willman
Beau Brummel '54
The Warriors '55
Kiss of the Vampire '62
21 Hours at Munich '76

Chill Wills
Allegheny Uprising '39
Racketeers of the Range '39
Boom Town '40
Billy the Kid '41
Honky Tonk '41
Western Union '41
Tarzan's New York Adventure '42
The Harvey Girls '46
The Yearling '46
Heartaches '47
Tulsa '49
High Lonesome '50
Rio Grande '50
City That Never Sleeps '53
Man from the Alamo '53
Ride the Man Down '53
Small Town Girl '53
Francis Joins the WACs '54
Kentucky Rifle '55
Giant '56
Gun Glory '57
The Alamo '60
Deadly Companions '61
McLintock! '63
The Wheeler Dealers '63
The Rounders '65
Pat Garrett & Billy the Kid '73
Mr. Billion '77
Poco '77

Maury Wills
The Black Six '74
The Sandlot '93

Douglas Wilmer
Men of Sherwood Forest '57
Golden Voyage of Sinbad '73
The Incredible Sarah '76
The Adventures of Sherlock Holmes' Smarter Brother '78

Andre Wilms
Life Is a Long Quiet River '88
Monsieur Hire '89
La Vie de Boheme '93
L'Enfer '93

Ajita Wilson
Savage Island '85
Escape from Hell '89

Barbara Wilson
Lost, Lonely, and Vicious '59
Invasion of the Animal People '62

Brigitte Wilson
Last Action Hero '93
Billy Madison '94
Mortal Kombat: The Movie '95

Dana Wilson
The Body Vanished '39
Wild Women '53

David Wilson
Hometown U.S.A. '79
The Inside Man '84

Don Wilson
The Chase '46
Niagara '52

Don "The Dragon" Wilson
Bloodfist '89
Bloodfist 2 '90
Futurekick '91
Ring of Fire '91
Black Belt '92
Bloodfist 3: Forced to Fight '92
Bloodfist 4: Die Trying '92
Magic Kid '92
Ring of Fire 2: Blood and Steel '92
Bloodfist 5: Human Target '93
Cyber-Tracker '93
Out for Blood '93
Bloodfist 6: Ground Zero '94
Red Sun Rising '94
Ring of Fire 3: Lion Strike '94
Cyber-Tracker 2 '95
Manhunt '95
Night Hunter '95
Virtual Combat '95

Dooley Wilson
Casablanca '42
Stormy Weather '43
Seven Days Ashore/Hurry, Charlie, Hurry '44

Dorothy Wilson
Dangerous Appointment '34
Last Days of Pompeii '35
The Brighton Strangler/Before Dawn '45

Earl Wilson
Copacabana '47
Beach Blanket Bingo '65

Elizabeth Wilson
Patterns '56
The Tunnel of Love '58
The Graduate '67
Jenny '70
Little Murders '71
Miles to Go before I Sleep '74
Prisoner of Second Avenue '74
Sanctuary of Fear '79
Grace Quigley '84
You Can't Take It with You '84
Where Are the Children? '85
The Believers '87
A Conspiracy of Love '87
The Addams Family '91
Regarding Henry '91
Skylark '93
Quiz Show '94
Scarlett '94
The Boys Next Door '96

Flip Wilson
Cancel My Reservation '72
Uptown Saturday Night '74
The Fish that Saved Pittsburgh '79

Frank Wilson
Girl from Chicago '32
Emperor Jones '33
Emperor Jones/Paul Robeson: Tribute to an Artist '33
Green Pastures '36
Paradise in Harlem '40
Beware '46

George Wilson
Attack of the Killer Tomatoes '77
Make Room for Tomorrow '81
Nudo di Donna '83

Kristen Wilson
Tyson '95
Girl 6 '96

Lambert Wilson
Five Days One Summer '82
Sahara '83
The Blood of Others '84
Red Kiss '85
Rendez-vous '85
The Belly of an Architect '91
Frankenstein '93

Lewis Wilson
The Body Vanished '39
Wild Women '53

Lois Wilson
The Covered Wagon '23
Monsieur Beaucaire '24
Drifting Souls '32
The Secrets of Wu Sin '32
Female '33
Laughing at Life '33
Bright Eyes '34
In the Money '34

Mara Wilson
Mrs. Doubtfire '93
Miracle on 34th Street '94
Matilda '96

Marie Wilson
March of the Wooden Soldiers '34
Satan Met a Lady '36
Boy Meets Girl '38
Waterfront '39
Flying Blind '41
Fabulous Joe '47
The Private Affairs of Bel Ami '47
My Friend Irma '49
A Girl in Every Port '52
Never Wave at a WAC '52
Mr. Hobbs Takes a Vacation '62

Mary Louise Wilson
Green Card '90
Cheap Shots '91
The Adventures of Huck Finn '93

Paul Wilson
Devonsville Terror '83
My Best Friend Is a Vampire '88

Perry Wilson
Fear Strikes Out '57
The Matchmaker '58

Richard Wilson
How to Get Ahead in Advertising '89
Unnatural Pursuits '91

Rita Wilson
The Day It Came to Earth '77
Volunteers '85
Sleepless in Seattle '93
Mixed Nuts '94
Now and Then '95

Robert Wilson
I Beheld His Glory '53
Day of Triumph '54

Rod Wilson
Darkman 2: The Return of Durant '94
Madonna: Innocence Lost '95

Roger Wilson
Overthrow '82
Porky's '82
Porky's 2: The Next Day '83
Second Time Lucky '84
Thunder Alley '85
The Ghost Brigade '93

Scott Wilson
In Cold Blood '67
The Grissom Gang '71
The New Centurions '72
The Passover Plot '75
The Ninth Configuration '79
On the Line '83
The Right Stuff '83
Year of the Quiet Sun '84
The Aviator '85
Blue City '86
Malone '87
Jesse '88
The Tracker '88
Johnny Handsome '89
Exorcist 3: Legion '90
Femme Fatale '90
Pure Luck '91
Flesh and Bone '93

Sheree J. Wilson
Crimewave '85
Fraternity Vacation '85
News at Eleven '86
Walker: Texas Ranger: One Riot, One Ranger '93
Hellbound '94
Past Tense '94
Walker: Texas Ranger: Deadly Reunion '94

Stuart Wilson
Running Blind '70s
The Highest Honor '84
Romance on the Orient Express '89
Secret Weapon '90
Lethal Weapon 3 '92

Wilson ▶cont.

The Age of Innocence '93
Teenage Mutant Ninja Turtles 3 '93
Death and the Maiden '94
Exit to Eden '94
No Escape '94
Prime Suspect: The Lost Child '94
Prime Suspect: The Scent of Darkness '95

Teddy Wilson
The Benny Goodman Story '55
Cotton Comes to Harlem '70
The Ambush Murders '82
The Mighty Pawns '87
Kiss Shot '89
Life Stinks '91
Bottle Rocket '95

Thomas F. Wilson
Back to the Future '85
April Fool's Day '86
Back to the Future, Part 2 '89
Back to the Future, Part 3 '90
High Strung '91

Tom Wilson
Let's Get Harry '87
Mr. Write '92
Camp Nowhere '94

Tom Wilson
The Americano '17
California Straight Ahead '25
Battling Butler '26

Trey Wilson
The Vampire Hookers '78
Raising Arizona '87
Bull Durham '88
End of the Line '88
Married to the Mob '88
Twins '88
Great Balls of Fire '89
Miss Firecracker '89
Welcome Home '89

Penelope Wilton
Singleton's Pluck '84
Clockwise '86
Cry Freedom '87
Blame It on the Bellboy '92
The Borrowers '93
The Secret Rapture '94
Carrington '95

Brian Wimmer
China Beach '88
Dangerous Pursuit '89
Late for Dinner '91
The World's Oldest Living Bridesmaid '92
Blue Flame '93
Kiss of a Killer '93
Lipstick Camera '93
Dead Badge '94
Tank Girl '94
The Maddening '95

Jeff Wincott
Deadly Bet '91
Martial Law 2: Undercover '91
Mission of Justice '92
Martial Outlaw '93
The Donor '94
The Killing Man '94
Open Fire '94
Last Man Standing '95
Street Law '95

Michael Wincott
Wild Horse Hank '79
Talk Radio '88
The Doors '91
Robin Hood: Prince of Thieves '91
Tragedy of Flight 103: The Inside Story '91
1492: Conquest of Paradise '92
The Crow '93
Romeo Is Bleeding '93
The Three Musketeers '93
Dead Man '95
Strange Days '95

William Windom
To Kill a Mockingbird '62
For Love or Money '63
One Man's Way '63
Columbo: Prescription Murder '67
The Detective '68
Brewster McCloud '70
Escape from the Planet of the Apes '71
The Mephisto Waltz '71
Pursuit '72
The Girls of Huntington House '73
Abduction of St. Anne '75
Mean Dog Blues '78
Leave 'Em Laughing '81
Desperate Lives '82
Last Plane Out '83
Grandview U.S.A. '84
Planes, Trains & Automobiles '87
She's Having a Baby '88
Funland '89
Street Justice '89
Back to Hannibal: The Return of Tom Sawyer and Huckleberry Finn '90
Committed '91
Attack of the 50 Ft. Woman '93
Dennis the Menace: Dinosaur Hunter '93
Sommersby '93
Miracle on 34th Street '94

Barbara Windsor
Carry On Doctor '68
Carry On Camping '71
Carry On Henry VIII '71

Claire Windsor
The Blot '21
Too Wise Wives '21
The Claw '27

Marie Windsor
Smart Alecks '42
Hellfire '48
The Fighting Kentuckian '49
Force of Evil '49
Outpost in Morocco '49
Double Deal '50
The Showdown '50
Little Big Horn '51
Jungle '52
The Narrow Margin '52
Outlaw Women '52
The Saint's Vacation/The Narrow Margin '52
Cat Women of the Moon '53
City That Never Sleeps '53
Tall Texan '53
Trouble Along the Way '53
Abbott and Costello Meet the Mummy '55
Silver Star '55
Swamp Women '55
The Killing '56
Girl in Black Stockings '57
Unholy Wife '57
Bedtime Story '63
Wild Women '70
Cahill: United States Marshal '73
Salem's Lot '79
Commando Squad '87

Romy Windsor
The House of Usher '88
Howling 4: The Original Nightmare '88
Big Bad John '90

Paul Winfield
Brother John '70
R.P.M.* (*Revolutions Per Minute) '70
Sounder '72
Gordon's War '73
Conrack '74
Huckleberry Finn '74
It's Good to Be Alive '74
Green Eyes '76
High Velocity '76
Damnation Alley '77
The Greatest '77
Twilight's Last Gleaming '77
A Hero Ain't Nothin' But a Sandwich '78
King '78
Roots: The Next Generation '79
Angel City '80
Carbon Copy '81
Sophisticated Gents '81
Star Trek 2: The Wrath of Khan '82
Go Tell It On the Mountain '84
Mike's Murder '84
The Terminator '84
Blue City '86
Big Shots '87
Death Before Dishonor '87
Guilty of Innocence '87
The Mighty Pawns '87
The Serpent and the Rainbow '87
For Us, the Living '88
The Women of Brewster Place '89
Back to Hannibal: The Return of Tom Sawyer and Huckleberry Finn '90
Presumed Innocent '90
Cliffhanger '93
Dennis the Menace '93
Breathing Lessons '94
In the Kingdom of the Blind the Man with One Eye is King '94
Scarlett '94
Tyson '95
White Dwarf '95
Original Gangstas '96
Nowhere to Hide

Oprah Winfrey
The Color Purple '85
Native Son '86
The Women of Brewster Place '89

Leslie Wing
Dungeonmaster '83
The Cowboy & the Ballerina '84
Retribution '88

Debra Winger
Slumber Party '57 '76
Special Olympics '78
Thank God It's Friday '78
French Postcards '79
Urban Cowboy '80
Cannery Row '82
An Officer and a Gentleman '82
Terms of Endearment '83
Mike's Murder '84
Legal Eagles '86
Black Widow '87
Betrayed '88
Everybody Wins '90
The Sheltering Sky '90
Leap of Faith '92
A Dangerous Woman '93
Shadowlands '93
Wilder Napalm '93
Forget Paris '95

Angela Winkler
The Lost Honor of Katharina Blum '75
Knife in the Head '78
The Tin Drum '79
Danton '82
Sheer Madness '84

Henry Winkler
The Lords of Flatbush '74
Katherine '75
Heroes '77
The One and Only '78
An American Christmas Carol '79
Night Shift '82

Mel Winkler
Laurel Avenue '93
City Hall '95
Devil In a Blue Dress '95

Kitty Winn
Man on a String '71
They Might Be Giants '71
The Exorcist '73
Miles to Go before I Sleep '74
Panic in Needle Park '75
The Exorcist 2: The Heretic '77
Mirrors '78

Vic Winner
Horror Rises from the Tomb '72
The Rue Morgue Massacres '73

Lucyna Winnicka
First Spaceship on Venus '60
Mother Joan of the Angels '60
25 Fireman's Street '73

Charles Winninger
Night Nurse '31
The Sin of Madelon Claudet '31
Show Boat '36
Three Smart Girls '36
Nothing Sacred '37
Every Day's a Holiday '38
Babes in Arms '39
Destry Rides Again '39
Three Smart Girls Grow Up '39
Beyond Tomorrow '40
Little Nellie Kelly '40
Pot O' Gold '41
Ziegfeld Girl '41
Lady Takes a Chance '43
Broadway Rhythm '44
State Fair '45
The Sun Shines Bright '53
Torpedo Alley '53

Mare Winningham
Special Olympics '78
One Trick Pony '80
The Thorn Birds '83
Threshold '83
Single Bars, Single Women '84
St. Elmo's Fire '85
Nobody's Fool '86
A Winner Never Quits '86
Made in Heaven '87
Shy People '87
God Bless the Child '88
Miracle Mile '89
Turner and Hooch '89
Eye on the Sparrow '91
Fatal Exposure '91
Hard Promises '92
Intruders '92
Better Off Dead '94
The War '94
Wyatt Earp '94
Georgia '95
Letter to My Killer '95
The Boys Next Door '96

Kate Winslet
Heavenly Creatures '94
A Kid in King Arthur's Court '95
Sense and Sensibility '95

George Winslow
Monkey Business '52
Gentlemen Prefer Blondes '53
Artists and Models '55

Michael Winslow
Tag: The Assassination Game '82
Alphabet City '84
Lovelines '84
Police Academy '84
Police Academy 2: Their First Assignment '85
Police Academy 3: Back in Training '86
Police Academy 4: Citizens on Patrol '87
Spaceballs '87
Police Academy 5: Assignment Miami Beach '88
Buy & Cell '89
Far Out Man '89
Police Academy 6: City Under Siege '89
Going Under '91
Police Academy: Mission to Moscow '94

Ray Winstone
Scum '79
Ladybird, Ladybird '93

Alex Winter
Death Wish 3 '85
Haunted Summer '88
Bill & Ted's Excellent Adventure '89
Rosalie Goes Shopping '89
Bill & Ted's Bogus Journey '91
Freaked '93

Ed Winter
Mother & Daughter: A Loving War '80
The Buddy System '83
Held Hostage '91

Vincent Winter
Time Lock '57
Gorgo '61
Almost Angels '62
The Horse Without a Head '63

Deborah Winters
Hail, Hero! '69
The People Next Door '70
Kotch '71
Class of '44 '73
Tarantulas: The Deadly Cargo '77
Blue Sunshine '78
The Outing '87

Jonathan Winters
It's a Mad, Mad, Mad, Mad World '63
The Loved One '65
The Russians are Coming, the Russians are Coming '66
Oh Dad, Poor Dad (Momma's Hung You in the Closet & I'm Feeling So Sad) '67
Viva Max '69
The Fish that Saved Pittsburgh '79
More Wild, Wild West '80
The Longshot '86
Say Yes! '86
Moon over Parador '88
The Flintstones '94
The Shadow '94

Roland Winters
Riders of the Whistling Skull '37
Abbott and Costello Meet the Killer, Boris Karloff '49
Malaya '49
Guilty of Treason '50
To Please a Lady '50
The Underworld Story '50
The West Point Story '50
Jet Pilot '57
Cash McCall '60
Blue Hawaii '62

Shelley Winters
A Double Life '47
The Gangster '47
Winchester '73 '50
A Place in the Sun '51
Behave Yourself! '52
Meet Danny Wilson '52
Phone Call from a Stranger '52
Executive Suite '54
The Big Knife '55
I Am a Camera '55
I Died a Thousand Times '55
Mambo '55
The Night of the Hunter '55
Treasure of Pancho Villa '55
The Diary of Anne Frank '59
Lolita '62
The Balcony '63
Time of Indifference '64
The Greatest Story Ever Told '65
A Patch of Blue '65
Alfie '66
Harper '66
Enter Laughing '67
Buona Sera, Mrs. Campbell '68
The Scalphunters '68
Wild in the Streets '68
Bloody Mama '70
What's the Matter with Helen? '71
Who Slew Auntie Roo? '71
Diamonds '72
The Poseidon Adventure '72
Shattered '72
Blume in Love '73
Cleopatra Jones '73
Poor Pretty Eddie '73
Journey into Fear '74
That Lucky Touch '75
Next Stop, Greenwich Village '76
The Tenant '76
Pete's Dragon '77
Tentacles '77
City on Fire '78
Initiation of Sarah '78
King of the Gypsies '78
Elvis: The Movie '79
The Magician of Lublin '79
The Visitor '80
S.O.B. '81
Fanny Hill '83
Over the Brooklyn Bridge '83
Deja Vu '84
Ellie '84
Very Close Quarters '84
Delta Force '86
Witchfire '86
Purple People Eater '88
An Unremarkable Life '89
Stepping Out '91
The Pickle '93
Weep No More My Lady '93
Backfire! '94
Heavy '94
Jury Duty '95
Mrs. Munck '95
Raging Angels '95

Estelle Winwood
Quality Street '37
The Glass Slipper '55
The Swan '56
This Happy Feeling '58
Darby O'Gill & the Little People '59
The Misfits '61

The Magic Sword '62
The Producers '68
Murder by Death '76

Billy Wirth
The Lost Boys '87
War Party '89
Red Shoe Diaries '92
Body Snatchers '93
Final Mission '93
The Fence '94
Judicial Consent '94
A Good Day to Die '95
Venus Rising '95

Robert Wisden
Blood Clan '91
Glory Enough for All: The Discovery of Insulin '92

Norman Wisdom
Trouble in Store '53
The Night They Raided Minsky's '69
What's Good for the Goose '69

Greg Wise
The Buccaneers '95
Feast of July '95
Sense and Sensibility '95

Ray Wise
Swamp Thing '82
The Journey of Natty Gann '85
Beauty and the Beast, Episode 1: Once Upon a Time in New York '87
RoboCop '87
The Taking of Flight 847: The Uli Derickson Story '88
Season of Fear '89
Endless Descent '90
Twin Peaks '90
Twin Peaks '90
Write to Kill '91
Bob Roberts '92
Sunstroke '92
Twin Peaks: Fire Walk with Me '92
The Chase '93
The Ghost Brigade '93
Rising Sun '93
Powder '95

Joseph Wiseman
Detective Story '51
Viva Zapata! '52
The Silver Chalice '54
The Prodigal '55
The Unforgiven '60
Dr. No '62
Stiletto '69
Lawman '71
Pursuit '72
Zalmen or the Madness of God '75
Jaguar Lives '79
Ghostwriter '84
Seize the Day '86
Lady Mobster '88

Googie Withers
Accused '36
Action for Slander '38
The Lady Vanishes '38
One of Our Aircraft Is Missing '41
On Approval '44
Dead of Night '45
Pink Strings and Sealing Wax '45
Night and the City '50
Devil on Horseback '54
Hotel du Lac '86
Northanger Abbey '87
Country Life '95

Grant Withers
Final Extra '27
The Road to Ruin '28
The Secrets of Wu Sin '32
Tailspin Tommy '34
Fighting Marines '36
Let's Sing Again '36
Radio Patrol '37
Mr. Wong, Detective '38
Boy's Reformatory '39
Daughter of the Tong '39
Irish Luck '39
Mr. Wong in Chinatown '39
Mystery of Mr. Wong '39
Doomed to Die '40
The Fatal Hour '40
Phantom of Chinatown '40
Billy the Kid '41
The Masked Rider '41
The Yellow Rose of Texas '44
Bells of Rosarita '45
Night Time in Nevada '48
The Fighting Kentuckian '49
Bells of Coronado '50
Trigger, Jr. '50
Oklahoma Annie '51
Hoodlum Empire '52

Jane Withers
Bright Eyes '34
The Farmer Takes a Wife '35
Giant '56
Captain Newman, M.D. '63

Cora Witherspoon
Libeled Lady '36
On the Avenue '37
Personal Property '37
Quality Street '37
Just Around the Corner '38
Marie Antoinette '38
The Bank Dick '40
Just for You '52

Jimmy Witherspoon
Black Godfather '74
Georgia '95

John Witherspoon
Killer Tomatoes Strike Back '90
Boomerang '92
Friday '95
Vampire in Brooklyn '95

Reese Witherspoon
The Man in the Moon '91
Wildflower '91
A Far Off Place '93
Jack the Bear '93
Return to Lonesome Dove '93
S.F.W. '94
Fear '96

Glenn Withrow
Dudes '87
Pass the Ammo '88
Naked Lie '89

Michael Witney
The Way West '67
Darling Lili '70

Alicia Witt
Hotel Room '93
Four Rooms '95
Mr. Holland's Opus '95

Kathryn Witt
Cocaine Wars '86
Demon of Paradise '87
Philadelphia '93

Karen Witter
Perfect Match '88
Buried Alive '89
Midnight '89
The Vineyard '89

Stefan Wodoslowsky
90 Days '86
Mindfield '89

David Wohl
Armed and Dangerous '86
Chillers '88

Hillary Wolf
Big Girls Don't Cry...They Get Even '92
Home Alone 2: Lost in New York '92

Kelly Wolf
Great Love Experiment '84
Triumph of the Spirit '89
Graveyard Shift '90
A Day in October '92

Scott Wolf
Teenage Bonnie & Klepto Clyde '93
Double Dragon '94
White Squall '96

Sheldon Peters Wolfchild
Miracle in the Wilderness '91
The Scarlet Letter '95

David Wolfe
Five Fingers '52
Salt of the Earth '54

Ian Wolfe
The Barretts of Wimpole Street '34
Mutiny on the Bounty '35
Zombies on Broadway '44
Bedlam '45
The Judge Steps Out '49
The Magnificent Yankee '50
Houdini '53
Moonfleet '55
Diary of a Madman '63
One Man's Way '63

Jim Wolfe
Chillers '88
Invasion of the Space Preachers '90

Traci Wolfe
Lethal Weapon '87
Lethal Weapon 2 '89
Lethal Weapon 3 '92

Frank Wolff
The King's Rhapsody '55
The Wasp Woman '59
Atlas '60
The Beast from Haunted Cave '60
Ski Troop Attack '60
The Awful Dr. Orlof '62
When Women Had Tails '70

Donald Wolfit
Late Extra '35
The Silent Passenger '35
Svengali '55
Blood of the Vampire '58
Room at the Top '59
The Hands of Orlac '60
The Mark '61
Becket '64
The Charge of the Light Brigade '68

Wolfman Jack
The Committee '68
American Graffiti '73
Deadman's Curve '78
Hanging on a Star '78
Motel Hell '80
Midnight '89
Mortuary Academy '91

Louis Wolheim
The Tempest '28
Square Shoulders '29
All Quiet on the Western Front '30
Danger Lights '30
The Silver Horde '30

Sven Wollter
The Sacrifice '86
House of Angels '92

Stevie Wonder
Bikini Beach '64
Muscle Beach Party '64

Anna May Wong
The Thief of Baghdad '24
Daughter of the Dragon '31
Shanghai Express '32
A Study in Scarlet '33
Java Head '35

Anthony Wong
Hard-Boiled '92
The Heroic Trio '93
Organized Crime & Triad Bureau '93

B.D. Wong
The Freshman '90
Father of the Bride '91
Mystery Date '91
Jurassic Park '93
Men of War '94
Father of the Bride Part II '95
Executive Decision '96

Carter Wong
Born Invincible '76
Shaolin Traitor '82
Story of the Dragon '82
The Ninja Pirates '90

Russell Wong
Tai-Pan '86
China Girl '87
Eat a Bowl of Tea '89
China Cry '91
China White '91
New Jack City '91
The Joy Luck Club '93

Victor Wong
Dim Sum: A Little Bit of Heart '85
Big Trouble in Little China '86
The Golden Child '86
The Last Emperor '87
Prince of Darkness '87
Eat a Bowl of Tea '89
Tremors '89
3 Ninjas '92
3 Ninjas Knuckle Up '92
The Ice Runner '93
The Joy Luck Club '93
3 Ninjas Kick Back '94

Arthur Wontner
The Triumph of Sherlock Holmes '35
Murder at the Baskervilles '37
The Terror '38
Sherlock Holmes: The Silver Blaze '41

Andy Wood
The Annihilators '85
Ghostwarrior '86
Eye of the Eagle 2 '89

Britt Wood
Knights of the Range '40
The Showdown '40
Detour to Danger '45

Clive Wood
Treasure Island '89
The Crucifer of Blood '91

David Wood
If... '69
Tales That Witness Madness '73

Elijah Wood
Avalon '90
Child in the Night '90
Paradise '91
Forever Young '92
Radio Flyer '92
The Adventures of Huck Finn '93
The Good Son '93
North '94
The War '94
Flipper '96

G. Wood
M*A*S*H '70
Bank Shot '74

Gary Wood
Hardbodies '84
Martial Outlaw '93

Gordon Wood
Mother and Son '31
The Forty-Niners '32

Harley Wood
Marihuana '36
Border Phantom '37
Valley of Terror '38
Camp Double Feature '39

Janet Wood
G.I. Executioner '71
Terror at Red Wolf Inn '72
Fangs '75
Slumber Party '57 '76

John Wood
U-Boat Prisoner '44
The Lady Says No '51
Revenge of the Creature '55
The Club '81
Maniac Warriors '90s
Ultimate Desires '91

John Wood
WarGames '83
Ladyhawke '85
The Purple Rose of Cairo '85
Jumpin' Jack Flash '86
Orlando '92
Shadowlands '93
The Young Americans '93
The Madness of King George '94
The Summer House '94
Citizen X '95
Sabrina '95
Jane Eyre '96
Richard III '95

Karen Wood
Scalps '83
Loose Screws '85

Lana Wood
The Searchers '56
Black Water Gold '69
Free Grass '69
Diamonds Are Forever '71
A Place Called Today '72
Grayeagle '77
A Question of Guilt '78
Captain America 2: Death Too Soon '79
Justin Morgan Had a Horse '81
Demon Rage '82

Mary Laura Wood
Hour of Decision '57
Stranger in Town '57

Montgomery Wood
Adios Gringo '65
Blood for a Silver Dollar '66

Natalie Wood
Tomorrow Is Forever '46
The Ghost and Mrs. Muir '47
Miracle on 34th Street '47
Father Was a Fullback '49
The Green Promise '49
The Jackpot '50
Never a Dull Moment '50
Just for You '52
The Silver Chalice '54
Rebel Without a Cause '55
The Burning Hills '56
The Searchers '56
Kings Go Forth '58
Marjorie Morningstar '58
Cash McCall '60
Splendor in the Grass '61
West Side Story '61
Gypsy '62
Love with the Proper Stranger '63
Sex and the Single Girl '64
The Great Race '65
Inside Daisy Clover '65
This Property is Condemned '66
Bob & Carol & Ted & Alice '69
The Affair '73
James Dean: The First American Teenager '76
The Cracker Factory '79
From Here to Eternity '79
Meteor '79
The Last Married Couple in America '80
Willie & Phil '80
Brainstorm '83

Peggy Wood
The Story of Ruth '60
The Sound of Music '65

Robert Wood
How to Make a Doll '68
Belle Starr '79
White Fang and the Hunter '85

Thomas Wood
Blood Feast '63
2000 Maniacs '64
Bushwhacked '95

Alfre Woodard
Freedom Road '79
Sophisticated Gents '81
The Ambush Murders '82
Cross Creek '83
Code of Honor '84
Go Tell It On the Mountain '84
Words by Heart '84
Killing Floor '85
Extremities '86
Unnatural Causes '86
Mandela '87
Scrooged '88
Miss Firecracker '89
Grand Canyon '91
The Gun in Betty Lou's Handbag '92
Passion Fish '92
Bopha! '93
Heart and Souls '93
Rich in Love '93
Blue Chips '94
Crooklyn '94
The Piano Lesson '94
Gulliver's Travels '95
How to Make an American Quilt '95
Primal Fear '96

Charlaine Woodard
Crackers '84
God Bless the Child '88
He Said, She Said '91
One Good Cop '91
Buffalo Girls '95

Bokeem Woodbine
Strapped '93
Jason's Lyric '94
Dead Presidents '95
Panther '95
The Rock '96

Joan Woodbury
Bulldog Courage '35
Rogue's Tavern '36

Woodbury ▶cont.

Song of the Gringo '36
Gangs, Inc. '41
King of the Zombies '41
I Killed That Man '42
Phantom Killer '42
Yank in Libya '42
Here Comes Kelly '43
The Chinese Cat '44
Northwest Trail '46
The Time Travelers '64

Margo Woode
Bullfighters '45
Iron Angel '64

Pat Woodell
The Big Doll House '71
Twilight People '72

Holly Woodlawn
Trash '70
Is There Sex After Death? '71

Bert Woodruff
Paths to Paradise '25
Marked Money '28
Speedy '28

Kurt Woodruff
Moving Target '89
Party Incorporated '89

Largo Woodruff
Bill '81
The Choice '81
Coward of the County '81
The Funhouse '81
Bill: On His Own '83

Barbara Alyn Woods
Circuitry Man '90
Eden '92
Eden 2 '93
Eden 3 '93
Eden 4 '93
Ghoulies 4 '93

Bill Woods
Maniac '34
The Worst of Hollywood: Vol. 1 '90

Donald Woods
Sweet Adeline '35
A Tale of Two Cities '35
The Story of Louis Pasteur '36
Sea Devils '37
Danger on the Air '38
Beauty for the Asking '39
Mexican Spitfire/Smartest Girl in Town '40
Corregidor '43
Watch on the Rhine '43
The Bridge of San Luis Rey '44
Enemy of Women '44
Never Say Goodbye '46
Bells of San Fernando '47
Mr. Music '50
The Beast from 20,000 Fathoms '53
Glen or Glenda: Confessions of Ed Wood '53
13 Ghosts '60
Door to Door Maniac '61
Kissin' Cousins '64

Edward Woods
Public Enemy '31
Tarzan the Fearless '33
Shadows Over Shanghai '38

Harry Woods
Dynamite Dan '24
Pardon My Gun '30
Monkey Business '31
Range Feud '31
Haunted Gold '32
Belle of the Nineties '34
The Adventures of Rex & Rinty '35
Rustlers of Red Dog '35
Last Outlaw '36
The Lawless Nineties '36
The Unknown Ranger '36
Hawaiian Buckaroo '38
Bullet Code '40
Winners of the West '40
Boss of Bullion City '41
Dawn on the Great Divide '42
Riders of the West '42
Today I Hang '42
Nevada '44

West of the Pecos '45

James Woods
The Way We Were '73
The Gambler '74
Night Moves '75
The Disappearance of Aimee '76
F. Scott Fitzgerald in Hollywood '76
The Choirboys '77
Holocaust '78
The Black Marble '79
The Incredible Journey of Dr. Meg Laurel '79
The Onion Field '79
Eyewitness '81
Fast Walking '82
Split Image '82
Videodrome '83
Against All Odds '84
Once Upon a Time in America '84
Badge of the Assassin '85
Cat's Eye '85
Joshua Then and Now '85
Salvador '86
Best Seller '87
The Boost '88
Cop '88
Immediate Family '89
True Believer '89
The Gift of Love '90
Women & Men: Stories of Seduction '90
The Hard Way '91
In Love and War '91
Chaplin '92
Citizen Cohn '92
Diggstown '92
Straight Talk '92
Fallen Angels 1 '93
The Getaway '93
Curse of the Starving Class '94
Next Door '94
The Specialist '94
Casino '95
For Better or Worse '95
Indictment: The McMartin Trial '95
Nixon '95

Michael Woods
Lady Beware '87
War & Remembrance, Part 1 '88
War & Remembrance, Part 3 '88
War & Remembrance, Part 4 '88
War & Remembrance, Part 5 '88
War & Remembrance, Part 6 '88
War & Remembrance, Part 7 '88
Haunting of Sarah Hardy '89
War & Remembrance, Part 2 '89
War & Remembrance: The Final Chapter, Part 8 '89
War & Remembrance: The Final Chapter, Part 9 '89
War & Remembrance: The Final Chapter, Part 10 '89
War & Remembrance: The Final Chapter, Part 11 '89
War & Remembrance: The Final Chapter, Part 12 '89
Omen 4: The Awakening '91
Hit Woman: The Double Edge '93
Blindfold: Acts of Obsession '94

Nan Woods
One More Saturday Night '86
China Beach '88

Robert Woods
The Perverse Countess '73
Challenge of McKenna '83
Chase '85

Kate Woodville
Sex Through a Window '72
Posse '75
Computer Wizard '77
Where's Willie? '77

John Woodvine
Assault on Agathon '75
The Life and Adventures of Nicholas Nickleby '81
Edge of Darkness '86
And a Nightingale Sang '91
Glory Enough for All: The Discovery of Insulin '92
Dragonworld '94
Fatherland '94
Persuasion '95

Edward Woodward
The Bloodsuckers '70
Young Winston '72
The Wicker Man '75
Breaker Morant '80
The Appointment '82
The Final Option '82
Champions '84
King David '85
Merlin and the Sword '85
Uncle Tom's Cabin '87
The Equalizer: Memories of Manon '88
Hands of a Murderer '90
Codename Kyril '91
Mister Johnson '91
Gulliver's Travels '95

Joanne Woodward
The Three Faces of Eve '57
The Long, Hot Summer '58
From the Terrace '60
The Fugitive Kind '60
Paris Blues '61
A New Kind of Love '63
The Stripper '63
A Big Hand for the Little Lady '66
A Fine Madness '66
Rachel, Rachel '68
Winning '69
They Might Be Giants '71
The Effect of Gamma Rays on Man-in-the-Moon Marigolds '73
Summer Wishes, Winter Dreams '73
The Drowning Pool '75
Sybil '76
A Christmas to Remember '78
The End '78
See How She Runs '78
The Streets of L.A. '79
Crisis at Central High '80
The Shadow Box '80
Harry & Son '84
The Glass Menagerie '87
Mr. & Mrs. Bridge '90
Blind Spot '93
Foreign Affairs '93
Philadelphia '93
Breathing Lessons '94

Morgan Woodward
Running Wild '73
Ride in a Pink Car '74
The Killing of a Chinese Bookie '76
The Longest Drive '76
Moonshine County Express '77
Walking Tall: The Final Chapter '77
Which Way Is Up? '77
Speedtrap '78
Girls Just Want to Have Fun '85
Dark Before Dawn '89

Tim Woodward
The Europeans '79
Personal Services '87
Piece of Cake '90
The Dark Angel '91
Prime Suspect: The Scent of Darkness '95
The Scarlet Letter '95

Marjorie Woodworth
Broadway Limited '41
Road Show '41

Norman Wooland
Angel with the Trumpet '50
Teenage Bad Girl '59
Saul and David '68

Susan Wooldridge
The Jewel in the Crown '84
Loyalties '86
Hope and Glory '87
How to Get Ahead in Advertising '89
Twenty-One '91
The Last Place on Earth '94
Just Like a Woman '95

Sheb Wooley
High Noon '52
Hoosiers '86

Charles Woolf
Private Parts '72
No Way Back '74

Monty Woolley
Everybody Sing '38
Three Comrades '38
The Man Who Came to Dinner '41
Since You Went Away '44
Night and Day '46
The Bishop's Wife '47
As Young As You Feel '51

Robert Woolsey
Dixiana '30
Half-Shot at Sunrise '30
Hook, Line and Sinker '30
Hold 'Em Jail '32
Diplomaniacs '33
Cockeyed Cavaliers '34
Hips, Hips, Hooray '34
Kentucky Kernels '34

Jaimz Woolvett
Unforgiven '92
The Dark '94

Tom Wopat
Burning Rage '84
Christmas Comes to Willow Creek '87

Hank Worden
Ghost Town Riders '38
Red River '48
The Searchers '56
Scream '83

Richard Wordsworth
The Quatermass Experiment '56
Time Without Pity '57

Jimmy Workman
The Addams Family '91
Addams Family Values '93

Frederick Worlock
Strange Cargo '40
The Woman in Green '45
The Last of the Redmen '47

Mary Woronov
Silent Night, Bloody Night '73
Cover Girl Models '75
Death Race 2000 '75
Hollywood Boulevard '76
Hollywood Man '76
Jackson County Jail '76
Sugar Cookies '77
The Movie House Massacre '78
Rock 'n' Roll High School '79
Angel of H.E.A.T. '82
Eating Raoul '82
Night of the Comet '84
The Princess Who Never Laughed '84
Challenge of a Lifetime '85
Hellhole '85
Chopping Mall '86
Nomads '86
Terrorvision '86
Black Widow '87
Kemek '88
Let It Ride '89
Scenes from the Class Struggle in Beverly Hills '89
Club Fed '90
Mortuary Academy '91
Motorama '91
Rock 'n' Roll High School Forever '91
Warlock '91
Good Girls Don't '95

Barbara Worth
The Prairie King '27
Below the Deadline '29
Racing Luck '35

Constance Worth
Windjammer '37
Criminals Within '41
Dawn Express '42
G-Men vs. the Black Dragon '43
Kid Sister '45

Irene Worth
King Lear '71
Eyewitness '81
Deathtrap '82
Separate Tables '83
Forbidden '85
The Shell Seekers '89
Lost in Yonkers '93

Lilian Worth
Tarzan the Tiger '29
The Fighting Sheriff '31

Mike Worth
Final Impact '91
Street Crimes '92
To Be the Best '93
Fists of Iron '94

Nicholas Worth
Doin' Time '85
Dirty Laundry '87
The Red Raven Kiss-Off '90
Fist of Honor '92
Dark Angel: The Ascent '94
Plughead Rewired: Circuitry Man 2 '94

Fay Wray
Blind Husbands '19
The Coast Patrol '25
The Wedding March '28
Doctor X '32
The Most Dangerous Game '32
The Vampire Bat '32
King Kong '33
Mystery of the Wax Museum '33
The Evil Mind '34
Viva Villa! '34
Woman in the Shadows '34
Bulldog Jack '35
When Knights were Bold '36
Adam Had Four Sons '41
Melody for Three '41
Small Town Girl '53
Treasure of the Golden Condor '53
The Cobweb '55
Hell on Frisco Bay '55
Queen Bee '55
Rock, Pretty Baby '56
Crime of Passion '57
Tammy and the Bachelor '57
Gideon's Trumpet '80

John Wray
All Quiet on the Western Front '30
Green Eyes '34

Clare Wren
Season of Fear '89
Steel and Lace '90
Midnight Edition '93

Amy Wright
The Deer Hunter '78
Girlfriends '78
The Amityville Horror '79
Breaking Away '79
Wise Blood '79
Inside Moves '80
Stardust Memories '80
Off Beat '86
Trapped in Silence '86
The Telephone '87
The Accidental Tourist '88
Crossing Delancey '88
Miss Firecracker '89
Daddy's Dyin'...Who's Got the Will? '90
Deceived '91
Final Verdict '91
Love Hurts '91
Hard Promises '92
To Dance with the White Dog '93
Robot in the Family '94
Where the Rivers Flow North '94
The Scarlet Letter '95
Tom and Huck '95

Cobina Wright, Jr.
Charlie Chan in Rio '41
Week-End In Havana '41

Jenny Wright
The Executioner's Song '82
The Wild Life '84
St. Elmo's Fire '85
Out of Bounds '86
Near Dark '87
The Chocolate War '88
Valentino Returns '88
I, Madman '89
Twister '89
A Shock to the System '90
Young Guns 2 '90
The Lawnmower Man '92

Ken Wright
Opposing Force '87
Hollywood Boulevard 2 '89
Eye of the Eagle 3 '91

Max Wright
Fraternity Vacation '85
Touch and Go '86
Konrad '90s
White Mile '94

Michael Wright
Streamers '83
The Principal '87
The Five Heartbeats '91
Confessions of a Hit Man '94
Sugar Hill '94

N'Bushe Wright

Patrick Wright

Robin Wright

Steven Wright

Teresa Wright

Tom Wright

Tony Wright

Whittni Wright

William Wright

Maris Wrixon

Vivian Wu

Robert Wuhl

Kari Wuhrer

Kai Wulff

Shelley Wyant

Jane Wyatt

Margaret Wycherly

Katya Wyeth

Noah Wyle

Gretchen Wyler

John Wylie

Meg Wyllie

Jane Wyman

John Wyman

Patrick Wymark

Patrice Wymore

George Wyner

Peter Wyngarde

Ed Wynn

Keenan Wynn

May Wynn

Dana Wynter

Charlotte Wynters

Diana Wynyard

Amanda Wyss

Nelson Xavier

Frank Yaconelli

Raghubir Yadav

Jeff Yagher

Simon Yam

Isuzu Yamada

Fujiko Yamamoto

So Yamamura

Al Yamanouchi

Tadashi Yamashita

Tsutomu Yamazaki

Nancy Yan

Oleg Yankovsky

Jean Yanne

Rossana Yanni

Celeste Yarnall

Amy Yasbeck

Cassie Yates

Biff Yeager

Sally Yeh

Michelle Yeoh

Don Yesso

Bolo Yeung

Chang Yi

Yi ▶cont.

Bells of Death '90

Mao Ying
The Two Great Cavaliers '73
Dance of Death '84

Pai Ying
The Bloody Fight '70s
Dynasty '77
Ninja Massacre '84

Richard Yniguez
Sniper '75
Boulevard Nights '79
World War III '86
Stalking Laura '93

Dwight Yoakam
Red Rock West '93
Roswell: The U.F.O. Cover-Up '94
Painted Hero '95

Erica Yohn
A Streetcar Named Desire '84
Corrina, Corrina '94

Dick York
My Sister Eileen '55
Cowboy '58
They Came to Cordura '59
Inherit the Wind '60

Francine York
Secret File of Hollywood '62
Wild Ones on Wheels '62
Curse of the Swamp Creature '66
The Doll Squad '73
The Centerfold Girls '74
Flood! '76

Jeff York
The Yearling '46
The Lady Says No '51
Davy Crockett and the River Pirates '56
Westward Ho, the Wagons! '56
Old Yeller '57
Savage Sam '63

Kathleen York
Winners Take All '87
Checking Out '89
Cold Feet '89
Thompson's Last Run '90
Wild Hearts Can't Be Broken '91
Dream Lover '93

Michael York
Accident '67
The Taming of the Shrew '67
Romeo and Juliet '68
Justine '69
Something for Everyone '70
Zeppelin '71
Cabaret '72
Murder on the Orient Express '74
The Three Musketeers '74
Conduct Unbecoming '75
The Four Musketeers '75
Logan's Run '76
Island of Dr. Moreau '77
The Last Remake of Beau Geste '77
The Riddle of the Sands '79
Final Assignment '80
Success is the Best Revenge '84
Weather in the Streets '84
Nevil Shute's The Far Country '85
Sword of Gideon '86
Lethal Obsession '87
Phantom of Death '87
Midnight Cop '88
The Return of the Musketeers '89
Night of the Fox '90
The Heat of the Day '91
Duel of Hearts '92
Wide Sargasso Sea '92
Discretion Assured '93
Fall from Grace '94
Gospa '94

Rachel York
Killer Instinct '92
Dead Center '94

Susannah York
Tunes of Glory '60
Tom Jones '63
A Man for All Seasons '66
Sebastian '68
Battle of Britain '69
The Killing of Sister George '69
They Shoot Horses, Don't They? '69
X, Y & Zee '72
Conduct Unbecoming '75
That Lucky Touch '75
Adventures of Eliza Fraser '76
Sky Riders '76
The Shout '78
The Silent Partner '78
Superman: The Movie '78
The Awakening '80
Falling in Love Again '80
Second Chance '80
Superman 2 '80
Loophole '83
Yellowbeard '83
Alice '86
The Land of Faraway '87
Prettykill '87
American Roulette '88
Diamond's Edge '88
A Summer Story '88
The Man from the Pru '89
Fate '90
Devices and Desires '94

Yitsuko Yoshimura
The Insect Woman '63
Onibaba '64

Kazuko Yoshiyuki
The Empire of Passion '76
In the Realm of Passion '80

Ge You
Farewell My Concubine '93
To Live '94

Aden Young
Black Robe '91
Sniper '92

Alan Young
Androcles and the Lion '52
The Time Machine '60
Beverly Hills Cop 3 '94

Artie Young
Bronze Buckaroo '39
Harlem Rides the Range '39

Bruce A. Young
Basic Instinct '92
Blink '93
What Ever Happened To... '93
The War '94
Normal Life '96

Burt Young
Carnival of Blood '71
Cinderella Liberty '73
Chinatown '74
The Gambler '74
The Killer Elite '75
Harry & Walter Go to New York '76
Rocky '76
The Choirboys '77
Twilight's Last Gleaming '77
Convoy '78
Rocky 2 '79
...All the Marbles '81
Blood Beach '81
Amityville 2: The Possession '82
Lookin' to Get Out '82
Rocky 3 '82
Over the Brooklyn Bridge '83
Once Upon a Time in America '84
The Pope of Greenwich Village '84
A Summer to Remember '84
Rocky 4 '85
Back to School '86
Blood Red '88
Beverly Hills Brats '89
Going Overboard '89
Backstreet Dreams '90
Betsy's Wedding '90
Club Fed '90
Diving In '90
Last Exit to Brooklyn '90
Rocky 5 '90
Wait Until Spring, Bandini '90
Bright Angel '91
A Family Matter '91
Excessive Force '93

Carleton Young
Outlaw Express '38
Reefer Madness '38
El Diablo Rides '39
Up in the Air '40
Trigger Men '41
People Will Talk '51
20,000 Leagues Under the Sea '54
Sergeant Rutledge '60
Armored Command '61
The Man Who Shot Liberty Valance '62

Chris Young
The Great Outdoors '88
Book of Love '91
December '91
The Runestone '91
Warlock: The Armageddon '93
Deep Down '94
P.C.U. '94

Clara Kimball Young
Trilby '17
The Eyes of Youth '19
Mid-Channel '20
The Worldly Madonna '22
Kept Husbands '31
Mother and Son '31
Probation '32
Chandu on the Magic Island '34
I Can't Escape '34
Return of Chandu '34
Rogue's Tavern '36
The Frontiersmen '38
Oh Susannah '38

Dey Young
Rock 'n' Roll High School '79
Strange Invaders '83
Doin' Time '85
Frankie and Johnny '91
Murder 101 '91
Back in the USSR '92
Conflict of Interest '92
No Place to Hide '93
Letter to My Killer '95

Faron Young
Daniel Boone: Trail Blazer '56
Hidden Guns '56

Gig Young
Air Force '43
Escape Me Never '47
The Three Musketeers '48
Lust for Gold '49
Tell It to the Judge '49
Wake of the Red Witch '49
Hunt the Man Down '50
Hunt the Man Down/Smashing the Rackets '50
Only the Valiant '50
Slaughter Trail '51
City That Never Sleeps '53
The Girl Who Had Everything '53
Torch Song '53
Young at Heart '54
Desperate Hours '55
Desk Set '57
Teacher's Pet '58
The Tunnel of Love '58
Ask Any Girl '59
Kid Galahad '62
That Touch of Mink '62
For Love or Money '63
Strange Bedfellows '65
Blood Island '68
They Shoot Horses, Don't They? '69
Lovers and Other Strangers '70
Bring Me the Head of Alfredo Garcia '74
The Hindenburg '75
The Killer Elite '75

Karen Young
Deep in the Heart '83
Birdy '84
Maria's Lovers '84
Almost You '85
9 1/2 Weeks '86
Heat '87
Jaws: The Revenge '87
Torch Song Trilogy '88
Criminal Law '89
Night Game '89
Little Sweetheart '90
The Ten Million Dollar Getaway '91
Drug Wars 2: The Cocaine Cartel '92
Hoffa '92

Loretta Young
Big Business Girl '31
Platinum Blonde '31
They Call It Sin '32
Employees' Entrance '33
Heroes for Sale '33
The Crusades '35
Eternally Yours '39
The Story of Alexander Graham Bell '39
Doctor Takes a Wife '40
A Night to Remember '42
Along Came Jones '45
The Perfect Marriage '46
The Stranger '46
The Bishop's Wife '47
The Farmer's Daughter '47
The Accused '48
Rachel and the Stranger '48
Come to the Stable '49
Key to the City '50
Cause for Alarm '51
The Loretta Young Show '54

Nedrick Young
Dead Men Walk '43
Gun Crazy '49
Captain Scarlett '53

Neil Young
'68 '87
Love at Large '89

Noah Young
Don't Shove/Two Gun Gussie '19
Battling Orioles '24
For Heaven's Sake '26

Otis Young
The Last Detail '73
The Capture of Bigfoot '79
Blood Beach '81

Paul Young
Another Time, Another Place '83
The Girl in the Picture '86

Polly Ann Young
Man from Utah '34
The Crimson Trail '35
Sons of Steel '35
Western Double Feature 5 '35
Mystery Plane '39
The Story of Alexander Graham Bell '39
Murder on the Yukon '40
The Invisible Ghost '41
Road Show '41

Ray Young
Blood of Dracula's Castle '69
Blue Sunshine '78

Ric Young
Drachenfutter '87
The Last Emperor '87
Ping Pong '87
Dragon: The Bruce Lee Story '93

Richard Young
Night Call Nurses '72
Final Mission '84
Friday the 13th, Part 5: A New Beginning '85
Ninja Masters of Death '85
Assassin '86
Love at the Top '86
Inferno in Paradise '88
Saigon Commandos '88
An Innocent Man '89

Robert Young
The Sin of Madelon Claudet '31
Strange Interlude '32
Today We Live '33
Hollywood Party '34
Spitfire '34
The Bride Walks Out '36
It's Love Again '36
The Secret Agent '36
Stowaway '36
The Bride Wore Red '37
Navy Blue and Gold '37
The Shining Hour '38
Three Comrades '38
Honolulu '39
The Mortal Storm '40
Northwest Passage '40
Lady Be Good '41
Western Union '41
Cairo '42
Journey for Margaret '42
Sweet Rosie O'Grady '43
The Canterville Ghost '44
The Enchanted Cottage '45
Those Endearing Young Charms '45
Crossfire '47
They Won't Believe Me '47
That Forsyte Woman '50
The Half-Breed '51
Second Woman '51
Little Women '78
A Conspiracy of Love '87

Roland Young
Madam Satan '30
The Guardsman '31
Wedding Rehearsal '32
His Double Life '33
David Copperfield '35
Ruggles of Red Gap '35
One Rainy Afternoon '36
King Solomon's Mines '37
The Man Who Could Work Miracles '37
Topper '37
Sailing Along '38
The Young in Heart '38
Topper Takes a Trip '39
No, No Nanette '40
The Philadelphia Story '40
Topper Returns '41
Two-Faced Woman '41
Forever and a Day '43
And Then There Were None '45
The Great Lover '49
Let's Dance '50
St. Benny the Dip '51

Sean Young
Jane Austen in Manhattan '80
Stripes '81
Blade Runner '82
Young Doctors in Love '82
Dune '84
Baby ... Secret of the Lost Legend '85
Under the Biltmore Clock '85
No Way Out '87
Wall Street '87
The Boost '88
Cousins '89
Fire Birds '90
A Kiss Before Dying '91
Blue Ice '92
Forever: A Ghost of a Love Story '92
Love Crimes '92
Once Upon a Crime '92
Sketch Artist '92
Ace Ventura: Pet Detective '93
Fatal Instinct '93
Hold Me, Thrill Me, Kiss Me '93
Mirage '94
Model by Day '94
Witness to the Execution '94
Dr. Jekyll and Ms. Hyde '95

Stephen Young
Patton '70
Lifeguard '75
Deadline '82
Who's Harry Crumb? '89
Scorned '93

Tony Young
Chrome and Hot Leather '71
Policewomen '73

William Allen Young
Outrage! '86
Johnnie Gibson F.B.I. '87
Stalking Laura '93

Jack Youngblood
Stalking Danger '86
Python Wolf '88

Barrie Youngfellow
Nightmare in Blood '75
It Came Upon a Midnight Clear '84
Lady from Yesterday '85

Henny Youngman
The Unkissed Bride '66
National Lampoon Goes to the Movies '81
Amazon Women on the Moon '87
Goodfellas '90

Gail Youngs
Hockey Night '84
Belizaire the Cajun '86
Last Days of Frank & Jesse James '86
Timestalkers '87

Jim Youngs
Hot Shot '86
Nobody's Fool '86
You Talkin' to Me? '87
Skeeter '93

Chief Yowlachie
King of the Stallions '42
Wild West '46

Zutaut ▶*cont.*

Knock Outs *'92*

Noam Zylberman
Outside Chance of Maximillian Glick *'88*
Love and Hate: A Marriage Made in Hell *'90*

Elsa Zylberstein
Farinelli *'94*
Mina Tannenbaum *'94*

The Director Index provides a complete videography for any director with a video credit. The listings for the director names follow an alphabetical sort by last name (although the names appear in a first name last name format). The videographies are listed chronologically, from oldest film to the most recent. If a director helmed more than one film in the same year, these movies are listed alphabetically within the year. Use this index in conjunction with the **Cast** (immediately preceding this index), **Writer**, and **Cinematographer** indexes (immediately following) to see where some of today's hottest directors got their starts.

Paul Aaron
Different Story *'78*
Force of One *'79*
The Miracle Worker *'79*
Imperial Navy *'80s*
Deadly Force *'83*
Maxie *'85*
In Love and War *'91*

Dodo Abashidze
Ashik Kerib *'88*

Charles Abbott
The Adventures of the Masked Phantom *'38*

George Abbott
Too Many Girls *'40*
The Pajama Game *'57*
Damn Yankees *'58*

Alan Abel
Is There Sex After Death? *'71*

Jeanne Abel
Is There Sex After Death? *'71*

Lewis Abernathy
House 4: Home Deadly Home *'91*

Derwin Abrahams
Border Vigilantes *'41*
Northwest Trail *'46*

Jim Abrahams
Airplane! *'80*
Police Squad! Help Wanted! *'82*
Top Secret! *'84*
Ruthless People *'86*
Big Business *'88*
Welcome Home, Roxy Carmichael *'90*
Hot Shots! *'91*
Hot Shots! Part Deux *'93*

Tengiz Abuladze
Repentance *'87*

Jon Acevski
Freddie the Frog *'92*

Jovan Acin
Hey, Babu Riba *'88*

Robert Ackerman
Safe Passage *'94*

Rodney Ackland
Thursday's Child *'43*

David Acomba
Night Life *'90*

Catlin Adams
Sticky Fingers *'88*

Daniel Adams
A Fool and His Money *'88*
Primary Motive *'92*

Doug Adams
Blackout *'88*

Al Adamson
Blood of Dracula's Castle *'69*
The Female Bunch *'69*
Gun Riders *'69*
Satan's Sadists *'69*
Horror of the Blood Monsters *'70*
Brain of Blood *'71*
Dracula vs. Frankenstein *'71*
Angels' Wild Women *'72*
Blood of Ghastly Horror *'72*
The Dynamite Brothers *'74*
I Spit on Your Corpse *'74*
Blazing Stewardesses *'75*
Jessie's Girls *'75*
Texas Layover *'75*
Black Samurai *'77*
Cinderella 2000 *'78*
Hospital of Terror *'78*
Kill Factor *'78*

Victor Adamson
Fighting Cowboy *'33*
Rawhide Romance *'34*
Boss Cowboy *'35*

Gilbert Adler
Tales from the Crypt Presents Bordello of Blood *'96*

Joseph Adler
Sex and the College Girl *'64*
Scream, Baby, Scream *'69*

Lou Adler
Cheech and Chong's Up in Smoke *'79*

Percy Adlon
Celeste *'81*
The Last Five Days *'82*
Sugarbaby *'85*
Bagdad Cafe *'88*
Rosalie Goes Shopping *'89*
Salmonberries *'91*
Younger & Younger *'94*

Ed Adlum
Invasion of the Blood Farmers *'72*

Edvin Adolphson
The Count of the Old Town *'34*

Frank Agrama
Dawn of the Mummy *'82*

Joseph Louis Agraz
Treasure of the Moon Goddess *'88*

Javier Aguirre
Dracula's Great Love *'72*
The Rue Morgue Massacres *'73*

Agust Agustsson
Maya *'82*

Charlie Ahearn
Wild Style *'83*

Mac Ahlberg
Gangsters *'79*

Faruque Ahmed
Warlords 3000 *'93*

John Ainsworth
Pattern for Plunder *'62*

Chantal Akerman
Je Tu Il Elle *'74*
News from Home *'76*
Les Rendez-vous D'Anna *'78*
Toute Une Nuit *'82*
The Eighties *'83*
Window Shopping *'86*
Night and Day *'91*
Akermania, Vol. 1 *'92*

Moustapha Akkad
Mohammed: Messenger of God *'77*
Lion of the Desert *'81*

Benito Alazraki
Invasion of the Zombies *'61*
Spiritism *'61*

Rafael Morena Alba
Exorcism's Daughter *'74*

Jean-Gabriel Albicocco
The Wanderer *'67*

Hans Albin
No Survivors, Please *'63*

Carlton J. Albright
Luther the Geek *'90*

Alan Alda
The Four Seasons *'81*
Sweet Liberty *'86*
A New Life *'88*
Betsy's Wedding *'90*

Thomas Alderman
The Severed Arm *'73*

Will Aldis
Stealing Home *'88*

Adell Aldrich
The Kid from Left Field *'79*

Robert Aldrich
Vera Cruz *'53*
Apache *'54*
The Big Knife *'55*
Kiss Me Deadly *'55*
Autumn Leaves *'56*
Sodom and Gomorrah *'62*
What Ever Happened to Baby Jane? *'62*
Four for Texas *'63*
The Flight of the Phoenix *'65*
Hush, Hush, Sweet Charlotte *'65*
The Dirty Dozen *'67*
The Killing of Sister George *'69*
Too Late the Hero *'70*
The Grissom Gang *'71*
Ulzana's Raid *'72*
The Longest Yard *'74*
The Hustle *'75*
The Choirboys *'77*
Twilight's Last Gleaming *'77*
The Frisco Kid *'79*
...All the Marbles *'81*

Goffredo Alessandrini
We the Living *'42*

Ottavio Alessi
The Seducers *'70*

Bill Alexander
Tartuffe *'90*

Jason Alexander
For Better or Worse *'95*

Tom Alexander
The Dark Dealer *'95*

Grigori Alexandrov
Ten Days That Shook the World *'27*
Que Viva Mexico *'32*

James Algar
The Adventures of Ichabod and Mr. Toad *'49*
The Legend of Sleepy Hollow *'49*
Vanishing Prairie *'54*

Sidney Algier
Wild Horse *'31*

Dan Algrant
Naked in New York *'93*

Marcello Aliprandi
Vatican Conspiracy *'81*

Howard Alk
Janis: A Film *'74*

Don Allan
Jungleground *'95*

Marc Allegret
Fanny *'32*
Zou Zou *'34*
The Love of Three Queens *'54*
Lady Chatterley's Lover *'55*
Mademoiselle Striptease *'57*
Sois Belle et Tais-Toi *'58*

Yves Allegret
Johnny Apollo *'40*
Dedee d'Anvers *'49*
The Proud Ones *'53*
Seven Deadly Sins *'53*

A.K. Allen
The Ladies Club *'86*

Corey Allen
Thunder and Lightning *'77*
Avalanche *'78*
The Man in the Santa Claus Suit *'79*
Return of Frank Cannon *'80*
Brass *'85*
Codename: Foxfire *'85*
The Last Fling *'86*
The Ann Jillian Story *'88*

David Allen
Dungeonmaster *'83*

Allen ▶*cont.*

Puppet Master 2 '90

Debbie Allen
Out of Sync '95

Fred Allen
Beyond the Rockies '32
Ghost Valley '32
Ride Him, Cowboy '32
Saddle Buster '32
The Mysterious Rider '33

Irving Allen
Slaughter Trail '51

Irwin Allen
Voyage to the Bottom of the Sea '61
Five Weeks in a Balloon '62
The Towering Inferno '74
The Swarm '78
Beyond the Poseidon Adventure '79

James Allen
Burndown '89

Jordan Allen
Terminal Bliss '91

Lewis Allen
The Uninvited '44
Those Endearing Young Charms '45
The Perfect Marriage '46
At Sword's Point '51
Suddenly '54
Illegal '55
Another Time, Another Place '58

Patrick Allen
Shootfighter: Fight to the Death '93

Woody Allen
What's Up, Tiger Lily? '66
Take the Money and Run '69
Bananas '71
Everything You Always Wanted to Know about Sex (But Were Afraid to Ask) '72
Sleeper '73
Love and Death '75
Annie Hall '77
Interiors '78
Manhattan '79
Stardust Memories '80
A Midsummer Night's Sex Comedy '82
Zelig '83
Broadway Danny Rose '84
The Purple Rose of Cairo '85
Hannah and Her Sisters '86
Radio Days '87
Another Woman '88
September '88
Crimes & Misdemeanors '89
New York Stories '89
Alice '90
Husbands and Wives '92
Shadows and Fog '92
Manhattan Murder Mystery '93
Bullets Over Broadway '94
Mighty Aphrodite '95

Roger Allers
The Lion King '94

Michael Almereyda
Twister '89
Nadja '95

Pedro Almodovar
Pepi, Luci, Bom and Other Girls on the Heap '80
Labyrinth of Passion '82
Dark Habits '84
What Have I Done to Deserve This? '85
Law of Desire '86
Matador '86
Women on the Verge of a Nervous Breakdown '88
Tie Me Up! Tie Me Down! '90
High Heels '91
Kika '94
The Flower of My Secret '95

Paul Almond
Journey '77
Final Assignment '80
Prep School '81
Captive Hearts '87
The Dance Goes On '92

Rami Alon
Choices '81

John Alonzo
Portrait of a Stripper '79
Blinded by the Light '82

Emmett Alston
New Year's Evil '78
Three Way Weekend '81
Nine Deaths of the Ninja '85
Tigershark '87
Little Ninjas '92

Robert Altman
Countdown '68
That Cold Day in the Park '69
Brewster McCloud '70
M*A*S*H '70
McCabe & Mrs. Miller '71
The Long Goodbye '73
Thieves Like Us '74
Nashville '75
Buffalo Bill & the Indians '76
A Wedding '78
Quintet '79
Popeye '80
Come Back to the Five & Dime Jimmy Dean, Jimmy Dean '82
Streamers '83
Secret Honor '85
Beyond Therapy '86
Fool for Love '86
Dumb Waiter '87
O.C. and Stiggs '87
The Room '87
Aria '88
The Caine Mutiny Court Martial '88
Tanner '88 '88
Vincent & Theo '90
The Player '92
Short Cuts '93
Ready to Wear '94

Robert Alton
Merton of the Movies '47
Pagan Love Song '50

Joe Alves
Jaws 3 '83

Denis Amar
L'Addition '85

Suzana Amaral
The Hour of the Star '85

Rod Amateau
The Bushwackers '52
The Statue '71
Drive-In '76
The Seniors '78
High School USA '84
Lovelines '84
The Garbage Pail Kids Movie '87

Gianni Amelio
Open Doors '89
The Stolen Children '92
Lamerica '95

Keita Amemiya
Zeram '91

Pino Amenta
Bellamy '80
All the Rivers Run '84
True Colors '87
Boulevard of Broken Dreams '88
What the Moon Saw '90
Heaven Tonight '93

Lem Amero
R.S.V.P. '84

Jon Amiel
Queen of Hearts '89
Tune in Tomorrow '90
Sommersby '93
Copycat '95

Gideon Amir
The P.O.W. Escape '86
Accidents '89

James Amonte
The Alchemist '81

Franco Amurri
Flashback '89
Monkey Trouble '94

Julian Amyes
The Lady's Not for Burning '95

Allison Anders
Border Radio '88
Gas Food Lodging '92
Mi Vida Loca '94
Four Rooms '95

Andy Anderson
Positive I.D. '87

"Broncho" Billy Anderson
The First Movie Cowboy '13

Clyde Anderson
Monster Dog '82
Beyond Darkness '92

John Murray Anderson
King of Jazz '30

Kurt Anderson
Martial Law 2: Undercover '91
Martial Outlaw '93
Dead Cold '96

Lindsay Anderson
This Sporting Life '63
If... '69
O Lucky Man! '73
In Celebration '75
Britannia Hospital '82
The Whales of August '87
Glory! Glory! '90

Michael Anderson, Sr.
The House of the Arrow '53
Dam Busters '55
Around the World in 80 Days '56
Battle Hell '56
Shake Hands with the Devil '59
The Wreck of the Mary Deare '59
The Naked Edge '61
Operation Crossbow '65
The Quiller Memorandum '66
The Shoes of the Fisherman '68
Conduct Unbecoming '75
Doc Savage '75
Logan's Run '76
Orca '77
Dominique is Dead '79
The Martian Chronicles: Part 1 '79
The Martian Chronicles: Part 2 '79
The Martian Chronicles: Part 3 '79
Murder by Phone '82
Second Time Lucky '84
Separate Vacations '86
Sword of Gideon '86
Millenium '89
Young Catherine '91
The Sea Wolf '93

Paul Anderson
Mortal Kombat: The Movie '95

Robert Anderson
The Young Graduates '71

Sarah Pia Anderson
Prime Suspect: Inner Circles '95

Steve Anderson
South Central '92

Wes Anderson
Bottle Rocket '95

Mario Andreacchio
Fair Game '85

George Andrews
Hero Bunker '71

Stephen M. Andrews
Striker '88

Roger Andrieux
L'Amour en Herbe '77
La Petite Sirene '80

Mikel Angel
Love Butcher '82

Edmond Angelo
Breakdown '53

Yves Angelo
Colonel Chabert '94

Theo Angelopoulos
Landscape in the Mist '88
Ulysses' Gaze '95

Gianfranco Angelucci
Honey '81

Philippe Angers
Red Shoe Diaries 6: How I Met My Husband '95

Erik Anjou
The Cool Surface '92

Ken Annakin
Trio '50
The Story of Robin Hood & His Merrie Men '52
The Sword & the Rose '53
Land of Fury '55
Across the Bridge '57
Third Man on the Mountain '59
The Swiss Family Robinson '60
The Longest Day '62
Battle of the Bulge '65
Those Magnificent Men in Their Flying Machines '65
Those Daring Young Men in Their Jaunty Jalopies '69
Call of the Wild '72
Paper Tiger '74
The Fifth Musketeer '79
Cheaper to Keep Her '80
Pirate Movie '82
The New Adventures of Pippi Longstocking '88

Jean-Jacques Annaud
Black and White in Color '76
Hothead '78
Quest for Fire '82
The Name of the Rose '86
The Bear '89
The Lover '92

Paul Annett
Black Werewolf '75
Poldark '75
Tales of the Unexpected '91
The Witching of Ben Wagner '95

David Anspaugh
Hoosiers '86
Fresh Horses '88
Rudy '93
Moonlight and Valentino '95

Jerzy Antczak
Nights and Days '76

Joseph Anthony
The Rainmaker '56
The Matchmaker '58
Career '59
All in a Night's Work '61
Tomorrow '72

Len Anthony
Fright House '89

Robert Anthony
Without Mercy '95

Manuel Antin
Don Segundo Sombra '69
Far Away and Long Ago '74

Karl Anton
The Avenger '60

Lou Antonio
Someone I Touched '75
The Gypsy Warriors '78
A Real American Hero '78
Breaking Up Is Hard to Do '79
Silent Victory: The Kitty O'Neil Story '79
Between Friends '83
Mayflower Madam '87
Pals '87
This Gun for Hire '90
The Last Prostitute '91
Lies Before Kisses '92
A Taste for Killing '92

Michelangelo Antonioni
Love in the City '53
Il Grido '57
L'Avventura '60
The Red Desert '64
Blow-Up '66
The Eclipse '66
Zabriskie Point '70
The Passenger '75

Ackyl Anwary
Angel of Fury '93

Daniel Appleby
Bound and Gagged: A Love Story '93

Norman Apstein
Ice Cream Man '95

Michael Apted
Poor Girl, A Ghost Story '74
The Squeeze '77
Triple Echo '77
Agatha '79
Coal Miner's Daughter '80
Continental Divide '81
Kipperbang '82
Gorky Park '83
First Born '84
Critical Condition '86
Gorillas in the Mist '88
Class Action '91
Incident at Oglala: The Leonard Peltier Story '92
Thunderheart '92
Blink '93
Nell '94

Manuel Gutierrez Aragon
Demons in the Garden '82
Half of Heaven '86

Gregg Araki
The Living End '92
Totally F***ed Up '94
The Doom Generation '95

Vicente Aranda
The Blood Spattered Bride '72
Lovers: A True Story '90

Alfonso Arau
Like Water for Chocolate '93
A Walk in the Clouds '95

Denys Arcand
The Decline of the American Empire '86
Jesus of Montreal '89
Love and Human Remains '93

George Archainbaud
The Silver Horde '30
The Lady Refuses '31
State's Attorney '31
Lost Squadron '32
False Colors '43
Hoppy Serves a Writ '43
The Kansan '43
Mystery Man '44
Texas Masquerade '44
The Woman of the Town '44
Hopalong Cassidy: The Devil's Playground '46
Hopalong Cassidy: Hoppy's Holiday '47
Hopalong Cassidy: The Marauders '47
Hopalong Cassidy: Unexpected Guest '47
Hopalong Cassidy: Borrowed Trouble '48
Hopalong Cassidy: False Paradise '48
Hopalong Cassidy: Silent Conflict '48
Hopalong Cassidy: Sinister Journey '48
Hopalong Cassidy: The Dead Don't Dream '48
Hunt the Man Down '50
Hunt the Man Down/Smashing the Rackets '50
Blue Canadian Rockies '52
Night Stage to Galveston '52
Gene Autry Matinee Double Feature #1 '53
Gene Autry Matinee Double Feature #2 '53
Gene Autry Matinee Double Feature #3 '53
Last of the Pony Riders '53
On Top of Old Smoky '53
Winning of the West '53

Cesar Ardavin
Lazarillo '59

Emile Ardolino
The Rise & Rise of Daniel Rocket '86
Dirty Dancing '87
Chances Are '89
Three Men and a Little Lady '90
Sister Act '92
George Balanchine's The Nutcracker '93
Gypsy '93

Mats Arehn
The Assignment '78
Istanbul '90

Dario Argento
The Bird with the Crystal Plumage '70
The Cat o' Nine Tails '71
Deep Red: Hatchet Murders '75
Suspiria '77
Inferno '78
Unsane '82
Creepers '85
Terror at the Opera '88
Two Evil Eyes '90
Dario Argento's Trauma '93

Adolfo Aristarain
Time for Revenge '82
The Stranger '87
A Place in the World '95

Alan Arkin
Little Murders '71

Robert Arkless
The Man Who Would Not Die '75

Allan Arkush
Hollywood Boulevard '76
Death Sport '78
Rock 'n' Roll High School '79
Heartbeeps '81
Get Crazy '83
Caddyshack 2 '88

Leslie Arliss
The Night Has Eyes '42
The Man in Grey '45
The Wicked Lady '45
A Man About the House '47

George Armitage
Private Duty Nurses '71
Hot Rod '79
Miami Blues '90

Andy Armstrong
Moonshine Highway '96

Gillian Armstrong
My Brilliant Career '79
Starstruck '82
Mrs. Soffel '84
High Tide '87
Fires Within '91
The Last Days of Chez Nous '92
Little Women '94

Karl Armstrong
Ninja Vengeance '93

Michael Armstrong
Mark of the Devil '69

Moira Armstrong
How Many Miles to Babylon? '82

Robin B. Armstrong
Pastime '91

Vic Armstrong
Army of One '94

Gwen Arner
A Matter of Principle '83
Necessary Parties '88

Eddie Arno
Murder Story '89

Frank Arnold
A Waltz Through the Hills '88
Josh Kirby...Time Warrior: Chapter 2, The Human Pets '95
Josh Kirby...Time Warrior: Chapter 3, Trapped on Toyworld '95
Josh Kirby...Time Warrior: Chapter 6, Last Battle for the Universe '96

Jack Arnold
It Came From Outer Space '53
Creature from the Black Lagoon '54
Revenge of the Creature '55
Tarantula '55
The Incredible Shrinking Man '57
High School Confidential '58
Monster on the Campus '59
The Mouse That Roared '59
A Global Affair '63
Bachelor in Paradise '69
Boss '74
Games Girls Play '75
Swiss Conspiracy '77
Marilyn: The Untold Story '80

Newton Arnold
Hands of a Stranger '62
Bloodsport '88

Fernando Arrabal
The Odyssey of the Pacific '82

Karen Arthur
My Sister, My Love '78
Broken Badge '85
A Bunny's Tale '85
Lady Beware '87
Bridge to Silence '89
The Jacksons: An American Dream '92
The Disappearance of Christina '93
The Secret '93

Raul Artigot
Witches' Mountain '71

Ami Artzi
Purgatory '89

Dorothy Arzner
Christopher Strong '33
Craig's Wife '36
The Bride Wore Red '37
Dance, Girl, Dance '40

Anthony Ascot
Gunslinger '70s
Guns for Dollars '73

Hal Ashby
Harold and Maude '71
The Last Detail '73
Shampoo '75
Bound for Glory '76
Coming Home '78
Being There '79
Lookin' to Get Out '82
8 Million Ways to Die '85
The Slugger's Wife '85

Ronnie Ashcroft
The Astounding She-Monster '58

Richard Ashe
Track of the Moonbeast '76

Robert Asher
Make Mine Mink '60

William Asher
Beach Party '63
Bikini Beach '64
Muscle Beach Party '64
Beach Blanket Bingo '65
How to Stuff a Wild Bikini '65
Night Warning '82
Movers and Shakers '85

Melvin Ashford
Mondo Magic '76

Christopher Ashley
Jeffrey '95

Alexander Askoldov
Commissar '68

Samson Aslanian
Torment '85

Anthony Asquith
I Stand Condemned '36
Pygmalion '38
Cottage to Let '41
The Demi-Paradise '43
We Dive at Dawn '43
Man of Evil '48
The Winslow Boy '48
The Browning Version '51
Importance of Being Earnest '52
Carrington, V.C. '54
The Millionairess '60
The V.I.P.'s '63

Ovidio G. Assonitis
Madhouse '87

Patti Astor
Assault of the Killer Bimbos '88

Alexandre Astruc
End of Desire '62

Thomas Atcheson
Deadly Diamonds '91

Thomas Atkins
The Silver Streak '34

Richard Attenborough
Young Winston '72
A Bridge Too Far '77
Magic '78
Gandhi '82
A Chorus Line '85
Cry Freedom '87
Chaplin '92
Shadowlands '93

Daniel Attias
Silver Bullet '85

David Attwood
Wild West '93

Bobby A. Auarez
One Armed Executioner '80

Pascal Aubier
Death of the Rat '75

Guillaume Martin Aucion
Oh! Calcutta! '72

Michael Audley
The Mark of the Hawk '57

John H. Auer
The Crime of Dr. Crespi '35
Wheel of Fortune '41
City That Never Sleeps '53

Bille August
Twist & Shout '84
Pelle the Conqueror '88
The Best Intentions '92
The House of the Spirits '93

Carlos Aured
Horror Rises from the Tomb '72
Curse of the Devil '73
House of Psychotic Women '73
The Mummy's Revenge '73

Bernard Auroux
Red Shoe Diaries 6: How I Met My Husband '95

Carl Ausino
Don't Look in the Attic '81

Paul Auster
Blue In the Face '95

Sam Auster
Screen Test '85
Bounty Hunter 2002 '94

Albert Austin
My Boy '21

Michael Austin
Princess Caraboo '94

Ray Austin
The Virgin Witch '70
House of the Living Dead '73
Return of the Man from U.N.C.L.E. '83
The Zany Adventures of Robin Hood '84
Highlander: The Gathering '93

Claude Autant-Lara
Sylvia and the Phantom '45
Devil in the Flesh '46
The Red Inn '51
Seven Deadly Sins '53
Four Bags Full '56
The Red and the Black '57
Oldest Profession '67

Igor Auzins
High Rolling in a Hot Corvette '77
Night Nurse '77
Death Train '79
We of the Never Never '82

Aram Avakian
End of the Road '70
Cops and Robbers '73
11 Harrowhouse '74

Marcello Avallone
Specters '87

Walter Avancini
Boca '94

Roger Roberts Avary
Killing Zoe '94
Mr. Stitch '95

Pupi Avati
Revenge of the Dead '84
Bix '90
The Story of Boys & Girls '91

Howard (Hikmet) Avedis
The Stepmother '71
The Teacher '74
The Specialist '75
Scorchy '76
Texas Detour '77
The Fifth Floor '80
Mortuary '81
Separate Ways '82
They're Playing with Fire '84
Kidnapped '87

Jose Mari Avellano
Fist of Glory '95

Hy Averback
I Love You, Alice B. Toklas! '68
Where Were You When the Lights Went Out? '68
Suppose They Gave a War and Nobody Came? '70
A Guide for the Married Woman '78
She's in the Army Now '81
Where the Boys Are '84 '84

Rick Avery
The Expert '95

Tex Avery
Bugs Bunny Superstar '75

John G. Avildsen
Guess What We Learned in School Today? '70
Joe '70
Cry Uncle '71
Save the Tiger '73
Foreplay '75
Rocky '76
The Formula '80
Neighbors '81
A Night in Heaven '83
The Karate Kid '84
The Karate Kid: Part 2 '86
Happy New Year '87
For Keeps '88
The Karate Kid: Part 3 '89
Lean on Me '89
Rocky 5 '90
The Power of One '92
8 Seconds '94

Tom Avildsen
Cheech and Chong: Things Are Tough All Over '82

Meiert Avis
Far from Home '89

Jon Avnet
Between Two Women '86
Fried Green Tomatoes '91
The War '94
Up Close and Personal '96

Gabriel Axel
Babette's Feast '87

George Axelrod
Secret Life of an American Wife '68

Dan Aykroyd
Nothing But Trouble '91

Julian Aymes
Jane Eyre '83

Carlos Azpurua
Shoot to Kill '90

Mario Azzopardi
Deadline '82
Nowhere to Hide '87

Beth B
Vortex '81
Salvation! '87
Two Small Bodies '93

Scott B
Vortex '81

Hector Babenco
Pixote '81
Kiss of the Spider Woman '85
Ironweed '87
At Play in the Fields of the Lord '91

Gideon Bachmann
Ciao Federico! Fellini Directs Satyricon '69

Lloyd Bacon
Kept Husbands '31
Footlight Parade '33
42nd Street '33
Devil Dogs of the Air '35
Marked Woman '37
Boy Meets Girl '38
Oklahoma Kid '39
Brother Orchid '40
Knute Rockne: All American '40
Footsteps in the Dark '41
The Fighting Sullivans '42
Silver Queen '42
Action in the North Atlantic '43
It Happens Every Spring '49
Miss Grant Takes Richmond '49
The Fuller Brush Girl '50

She Couldn't Say No '52
The French Line '54

Peter Bacso
Oh, Bloody Life! '88

Randall Badat
Surf 2 '84

Clarence Badger
Teddy at the Throttle '16
Paths to Paradise '25
Hands Up '26
It '27

Phillip Badger
The Forgotten One '89

John Badham
Reflections of Murder '74
Bingo Long Traveling All-Stars & Motor Kings '76
Saturday Night Fever '77
Dracula '79
Whose Life Is It Anyway? '81
Blue Thunder '83
WarGames '83
American Flyers '85
Short Circuit '86
Stakeout '87
Bird on a Wire '90
The Hard Way '91
Another Stakeout '93
Point of No Return '93
Drop Zone '94
Nick of Time '95

Reza Badiyi
Of Mice and Men '81
Policewoman Centerfold '83
Blade in Hong Kong '85

Max Baer, Jr.
Ode to Billy Joe '76
Hometown U.S.A. '79

Milton Bagby, Jr.
Rebel Love '85

King Baggot
Tumbleweeds '25
The Notorious Lady '27

James Bagle
Stones of Death '88

Fax Bahr
Hearts of Darkness: A Filmmaker's Apocalypse '91

Chuck Bail
Cleopatra Jones & the Casino of Gold '75
Gumball Rally '76
Choke Canyon '86

John Bailey
China Moon '91
Search for Signs of Intelligent Life in the Universe '91

Patrick Bailey
Door to Door '84

Richard Bailey
Win, Place, or Steal '72

Paule Baillargeon
Le Sexe des Etoiles '93

Whitney Bain
That Darn Sorceress '88

Stuart Baird
Executive Decision '96

David Baker
Air Hawk '84
Best Enemies '86

Graham Baker
The Final Conflict '81
Impulse '84
Alien Nation '88
Born to Ride '91

Michael Baker
An Affair in Mind '89

Robert S. Baker
Blackout '50
Jack the Ripper '60
The Hellfire Club '61

Roy Ward Baker
The October Man '48
The Weaker Sex '49
Don't Bother to Knock '52
One That Got Away '57
A Night to Remember '58
The Anniversary '68
The Scars of Dracula '70
The Vampire Lovers '70

Baker ▶cont.

Dr. Jekyll and Sister Hyde '71
Asylum '72
And Now the Screaming Starts '73
The 7 Brothers Meet Dracula '73
Vault of Horror '73
Mission: Monte Carlo '75
The Monster Club '85
Masks of Death '86

Ralph Bakshi
Fritz the Cat '72
Heavy Traffic '73
Streetfight '75
Wizards '77
The Lord of the Rings '78
Hey Good Lookin' '82
Fire and Ice '83
Cool World '92

Walter Bal
Jacko & Lise '82

Bob Balaban
Parents '89
My Boyfriend's Back '93
The Last Good Time '94

Josiane Balasko
French Twist '95

Antony Balch
Horror Hospital '73

Jim Balden
Gamble on Love '86

Ferdinando Baldi
Duel of Champions '61
Treasure of the Four Crowns '82

Armenia Balducci
Together? '79

Richard Balducci
L'Odeur des Fauves '66
Scandal Man '67
Too Pretty to Be Honest '72

Peter Baldwin
The Hoboken Chicken Emergency '84
Lots of Luck '85
A Very Brady Christmas '88

Paul Trevor Bale
The Littlest Viking '94

Rafael Baledon
The Man and the Monster '65
Swamp of the Lost Monster '65

Carroll Ballard
The Black Stallion '79
Never Cry Wolf '83
Nutcracker: The Motion Picture '86
Wind '92

John Ballard
The Orphan '79

Robert E. Balzer
It's Three Strikes, Charlie Brown '86

Anne Bancroft
Fatso '80

Albert Band
I Bury the Living '58
Tramplers '66
Zoltan...Hound of Dracula '78
Ghoulies 2 '87
Doctor Mordrid: Master of the Unknown '90
Prehysteria '93
Robot Wars '93
Prehysteria 2 '94

Charles Band
Parasite '82
Dungeonmaster '83
Metalstorm: The Destruction of Jared Syn '83
Trancers '84
Crash and Burn '90
Doctor Mordrid: Master of the Unknown '90
Meridian: Kiss of the Beast '90
Trancers 2: The Return of Jack Deth '90
Dollman vs Demonic Toys '93
Prehysteria '93

Mirra Bank
Enormous Changes '83
Trumps '83

Montague Banks
Great Guns '41

Walter Bannert
The Inheritors '85

Yoshimitu Banno
Godzilla vs. the Smog Monster '72

Richard Bansbach
Claws '77

Jack Baran
Destiny Turns on the Radio '95

Norberto Barba
Blue Tiger '94

Uri Barbash
Beyond the Walls '84
Unsettled Land '88

Peter Barber-Fleming
Coming Through '90

Joseph Barbera
Jetsons: The Movie '90

Paris Barclay
America's Dream '95

Juan Antonio Bardem
Last Day of the War '69

Leora Barish
Venus Rising '95

Geoffrey Barkas
Q Ships '28

Clive Barker
Hellraiser '87
Night Breed '90
Lord of Illusions '95

Reginald Barker
On the Night Stage '15
Civilization '16
Seven Keys to Baldplate '29
Healer '36

Christopher Barnard
Conspiracy '89

Boris Barnet
The Girl with the Hat Box '27
The Patriots '33

Ivan Barnett
The Fall of the House of Usher '49

Ken Barnett
Dark Tower '87

Steve Barnett
Emmanuelle 5 '87
Hollywood Boulevard 2 '89
Mindwarp '91
Mission of Justice '92
Scanners: The Showdown '94

M. Neema Barnette
Better Off Dead '94

Allen Baron
Foxfire Light '84

Douglas Barr
Frame by Frame '95

Bruno Barreto
Dona Flor and Her Two Husbands '78
Amor Bandido '79
Gabriela '84
Happily Ever After '86
The Story of Fausta '88
A Show of Force '90
Carried Away '95

Fabio Barreto
Luzia '88
O Quatrilho '95

Lezli-Ann Barrett
Business as Usual '88

Michael Barringer
Q Ships '28

Steven Barron
Electric Dreams '84
Teenage Mutant Ninja Turtles: The Movie '90
Coneheads '93
The Adventures of Pinocchio '96

Zelda Barron
Secret Places '85
Bulldance '88
Forbidden Sun '89
Shag: The Movie '89

Christopher Barry
Poldark '75

Ian Barry
Chain Reaction '80
Wrangler '88
The Seventh Floor '93
Crime Broker '94

Michael Barry
Second Coming of Suzanne '80

Wesley E. Barry
The Creation of the Humanoids '62

Roger J. Barski
Chains '89

Bud Barsky
The Coast Patrol '25

Paul Bartel
Paul Bartel's The Secret Cinema '69
Private Parts '72
Death Race 2000 '75
Cannonball '76
The Secret Cinema '78
Eating Raoul '82
Not for Publication '84
Lust in the Dust '85
The Longshot '86
Scenes from the Class Struggle in Beverly Hills '89

Carl Bartholomew
Cole Justice '89

Charles Bartlett
Sands of Sacrifice '21

Dick Bartlett
Ollie Hopnoodle's Haven of Bliss '88

Hall Bartlett
All the Young Men '60
Changes '69
Defiant '70
Jonathan Livingston Seagull '73
Children of Sanchez '79

Richard Bartlett
Lonesome Trail '55
Rock, Pretty Baby '56

William S. Bartman
O'Hara's Wife '82

Charles T. Barton
Wagon Wheels '34
Desert Gold '36
Western Double Feature 3 '36
Forlorn River '37
Thunder Pass '37
Thunder Trail '37
Helltown '38
Harmon of Michigan '41
The Time of Their Lives '46
Buck Privates Come Home '47
The Wistful Widow of Wagon Gap '47
Abbott and Costello Meet Frankenstein '48
Mexican Hayride '48
The Noose Hangs High '48
Abbott and Costello Meet the Killer, Boris Karloff '49
Africa Screams '49
Ma and Pa Kettle at the Fair '52
Dance with Me, Henry '56
The Shaggy Dog '59
Toby Tyler '59

Earl Barton
Deadly Fieldtrip '74

Sean Barton
Curse 3: Blood Sacrifice '90

Hal Barwood
Warning Sign '85

Nick Barwood
Nasty Hero '89

Juliet Bashore
Kamikaze Hearts '91

Richard Baskin
Sing '89

Jules Bass
Mad Monster Party '68
Santa Claus Is Coming to Town '70
The Ballad of Paul Bunyan '72
The Hobbit '78
The Return of the King '80
Flight of Dragons '82
The Last Unicorn '82

Kim Bass
Ballistic '94

Saul Bass
Phase 4 '74

Lawrence Bassoff
Weekend Pass '84
Hunk '87

William Bast
James Dean '76

Michal Bat-Adam
Boy Takes Girl '83

Alexei Batalov
The Overcoat '59

Joy Batchelor
Animal Farm '55

Kent Bateman
Headless Eyes '83

Bradley Battersby
Blue Desert '91

Roy Battersby
Winter Flight '84
Mr. Love '86

Giacomo Battiato
Hearts & Armour '83
Blood Ties '87

Evgenii Bauer
Early Russian Cinema, Vol. 6: Class Distinctions '14
Early Russian Cinema, Vol. 7: Evgenii Bauer '15
Early Russian Cinema, Vol. 10: The End of an Era '17
Early Russian Cinema, Vol. 9: High Society '19

L. Frank Baum
His Majesty, the Scarecrow of Oz/The Magic Cloak of Oz '14
Patchwork Girl of Oz '14

Noah Baumbach
Kicking and Screaming '95

Lamberto Bava
Frozen Terror '80
A Blade in the Dark '83
Devilfish '84
Blastfighter '85
Demons '86
Demons 2 '87

Mario Bava
Black Sunday '60
The Wonders of Aladdin '61
The Invaders '63
Black Sabbath '64
Blood and Black Lace '64
Hercules in the Haunted World '64
Planet of the Vampires '65
Kill, Baby, Kill '66
Danger: Diabolik '68
Hatchet for the Honeymoon '70
Twitch of the Death Nerve '71
Torture Chamber of Baron Blood '72
Lisa and the Devil '75
Beyond the Door 2 '79

Craig R. Baxley
Action Jackson '88
I Come in Peace '90
Stone Cold '91
Deconstructing Sarah '94
Deep Red '94
The Avenging Angel '95

John Baxter
Love on the Dole '41
Old Mother Riley's Ghosts '41

Michael Bay
Bad Boys '95
The Rock '96

Rolf Bayer
Pacific Inferno '85

Stephen Bayly
Coming Up Roses '87
Diamond's Edge '88

Camillo Bazzoni
Black Lemons '80s

David Beaird
Octavia '82
Party Animal '83
My Chauffeur '86
It Takes Two '88
Pass the Ammo '88
Scorchers '92

Rick Beairsto
Close to Home '86

Chris Bearde
Hysterical '83

Alan Beattie
Delusion '84
Stand Alone '85

Warren Beatty
Reds '81
Dick Tracy '90

William Beaudine
The Country Kid '23
Little Annie Rooney '25
Sparrows '26
Misbehaving Husbands '41
Robot Pilot '41
Miracle Kid '42
The Panther's Claw '42
Phantom Killer '42
Turf Boy '42
The Ape Man '43
Ghost on the Loose '43
Here Comes Kelly '43
Spotlight Scandals '43
Follow the Leader '44
Bowery Buckaroos '47
Hard-Boiled Mahoney '47
Infamous Crimes '47
Mom & Dad '47
Smugglers' Cove '48
Spook Busters '48
Blues Busters '50
Ghost Chasers '51
Bela Lugosi Meets a Brooklyn Gorilla '52
Here Come the Marines '52
Westward Ho, the Wagons! '56
Ten Who Dared '60
Lassie's Great Adventure '62
Jesse James Meets Frankenstein's Daughter '65
Billy the Kid Versus Dracula '66

Gabrielle Beaumont
The Godsend '79
Death of a Centerfold '81
Gone are the Days '84
He's My Girl '87
Carmilla '89
Beastmaster 3: The Eye of Braxus '95

Harry Beaumont
Beau Brummel '24
Our Dancing Daughters '28
Broadway Melody '29
Dance Fools Dance '31
Laughing Sinners '31
When's Your Birthday? '37
The Show-Off '46

Gorman Bechard
Galactic Gigolo '87
Psychos in Love '87
Cemetery High '89

George Beck
Behave Yourself! '52

Josh Beck
Lunatics: A Love Story '92

Martin Beck
Challenge '74
Last Game '80

Reginald Beck
The Long Dark Hall '51

Harold Becker
The Black Marble '79
The Onion Field '79
Taps '81
Vision Quest '85
The Boost '88
Sea of Love '89
Malice '93
City Hall '95

Jacques Becker
Casque d'Or '52
Grisbi '53
Ali Baba and the 40 Thieves '54
Modigliani '58

Jean Becker
One Deadly Summer '83

Terry Becker
The Thirsty Dead '74

Vernon Becker
A Man with a Maid '73

James Becket
Ulterior Motives '92
Natural Causes '94

Ron Beckstrom
Sarah's Child '96

Terry Bedford
Slayground '84

Ford Beebe
The Last of the Mohicans '32
Shadow of the Eagle '32
Laughing at Life '33
The Adventures of Rex & Rinty '35
Ace Drummond '36
The Man from Gun Town '36
Radio Patrol '37
Tim Tyler's Luck '37
Flash Gordon: Mars Attacks the World '38
Red Barry '38
Buck Rogers Conquers the Universe '39
Destination Saturn '39
Oregon Trail '39
The Phantom Creeps '39
Winners of the West '40
The Masked Rider '41
Riders of Death Valley '41
Night Monster '42
Don Winslow of the Coast Guard '43
Don Winslow of the Navy '43
The Invisible Man's Revenge '44
My Dog Shep '46

Greg Beeman
License to Drive '88
Mom and Dad Save the World '92
Bushwhacked '95

Tom Beeman
The Legend of Black Thunder Mountain '79

Jean-Jacques Beineix
Diva '82
Moon in the Gutter '83
Betty Blue '86

Jean-Pierre Bekolo
Quartier Mozart '92

Arnold Belgard
East of Kilimanjaro '57

A. Dean Bell
Backfire! '94

Alan Bell
Ripping Yarns '75
The Hitchhiker's Guide to the Galaxy '81

Jeffrey Bell
Radio Inside '94

Martin Bell
Streetwise '85
American Heart '92

Earl Bellamy
Justice of the West '61
The Trackers '71
Against A Crooked Sky '75
Seven Alone '75
Walking Tall: Part 2 '75
Flood! '76
Fire '77
Sidewinder One '77
Desperate Women '78
Speedtrap '78
Magic on Love Island '80

Donald P. Bellisario
Last Rites '88
JAG '95

Marco Bellochio
The Eyes, the Mouth '83
Henry IV '85
Devil in the Flesh '87

Yannick Bellon
Rape of Love '79

Vera Belmont
Red Kiss '85

Jerry Belson
Jekyll & Hyde...Together Again '82
Surrender '87

Remy Belvaux
Man Bites Dog '91

Maria-Luisa Bemberg
Camila '84
Miss Mary '86
I, the Worst of All '90
I Don't Want to Talk About It '94

Jacob Ben-Ami
Green Fields '37

Don Bendell
The Instructor '83

Jack Bender
In Love with an Older Woman '82
Shattered Vows '84
Letting Go '85
Two Kinds of Love '85
The Midnight Hour '86
Side By Side '88
Tricks of the Trade '88
My Brother's Wife '89
Child's Play 3 '91
Lone Justice 2 '93

Joel Bender
Gas Pump Girls '79
The Immortalizer '89
Rich Girl '91
Midnight Kiss '93

Laslo Benedek
Port of New York '49
The Wild One '54
Namu, the Killer Whale '66
Daring Game '68
The Night Visitor '70
Assault on Agathon '75

Terry Benedict
Painted Hero '95

Roberto Benigni
Johnny Stecchino '92

Richard Benjamin
My Favorite Year '82
City Heat '84
Racing with the Moon '84
The Money Pit '86
Little Nikita '88
My Stepmother Is an Alien '88
Downtown '89
Mermaids '90
Made in America '93
Milk Money '94
Mrs. Winterbourne '96

Richard Benner
Outrageous! '77
Happy Birthday, Gemini '80

Spencer Gordon Bennet
Marked Money '28
Last Frontier '32
Midnight Warning '32
The Fighting Rookie '34
Get That Man '35
The Unknown Ranger '36
The Rangers Step In '37
Across the Plains '39
Western Double Feature 1: Wild Bill & Sunset Carson '40s
Arizona Bound '41
Gunman from Bodie '41
The Secret Code '42
Calling Wild Bill Elliott '43
The Masked Marvel '43
Perils of the Darkest Jungle '44
Zorro's Black Whip '44
D-Day on Mars '45
Manhunt of Mystery Island '45
The Purple Monster Strikes '45
The Black Widow '47
Superman: The Serial, Vol. 1 '48
Pirates of the High Seas '50
King of the Congo '52
Atomic Submarine '59
Submarine Seahawk '59

Bill Bennett
Backlash '86
Two If by Sea '95

Compton Bennett
The Seventh Veil '46
King Solomon's Mines '50
That Forsyte Woman '50
The Gift Horse '52

Edward Bennett
A Woman at War '94

Gary Bennett
Rain Without Thunder '93

Richard Bennett
Harper Valley P.T.A. '78

Rodney Bennett
Sense & Sensibility '85
Monsignor Quixote '91

Wallace C. Bennett
George! '70

Walter Bennett
Young Love—Lemon Popsicle 7 '87

Leon Benson
Flipper's New Adventure '64

Richard Benson
The Day the Sky Exploded '57
Werewolf in a Girl's Dormitory '61

Robby Benson
White Hot '88
Modern Love '90

Steve Benson
Endgame '85

Thomas Bentley
The Old Curiosity Shop '35
Murder at the Baskervilles '37

Robert Benton
Bad Company '72
The Late Show '77
Kramer vs. Kramer '79
Still of the Night '82
Places in the Heart '84
Nadine '87
Billy Bathgate '91
Nobody's Fool '94

Yakov Bentsvi
Legion of Iron '90

Obie Benz
Heavy Petting '89

Luc Beraud
Heat of Desire '84

Luca Bercovici
Ghoulies '84
Rockula '90
The Granny '94

Geza Beremenyi
The Midas Touch '89

Al Beresford
Screamtime '83

Bruce Beresford
Barry McKenzie Holds His Own '74
Don's Party '76
The Getting of Wisdom '77
Money Movers '78
Breaker Morant '80
The Club '81
Puberty Blues '81
Tender Mercies '83
King David '85
Crimes of the Heart '86
The Fringe Dwellers '86
Aria '88
Her Alibi '88
Driving Miss Daisy '89
Black Robe '91
Mister Johnson '91
Rich in Love '93
A Good Man in Africa '94
Silent Fall '94
Last Dance '96

Phyllis Berg-Pigorsch
The Islander '88

Ludwig Berger
The Thief of Bagdad '40

Pamela Berger
The Imported Bridegroom '89

Andrew Bergman
So Fine '81
The Freshman '90
Honeymoon in Vegas '92
It Could Happen to You '94
Striptease '96

Daniel Bergman
Sunday's Children '94

Ingmar Bergman
Night Is My Future '47
Port of Call '48
Devil's Wanton '49
Three Strange Loves '49
Summer Interlude '50
To Joy '50
Monika '52
Secrets of Women '52
Sawdust & Tinsel '53
Lesson in Love '54
Dreams '55
Smiles of a Summer Night '55
The Seventh Seal '56
Brink of Life '57
Wild Strawberries '57
The Magician '58
The Virgin Spring '59
The Devil's Eye '60
Through a Glass Darkly '61
The Winter Light '62
The Silence '63
Persona '66
Hour of the Wolf '68
The Shame '68
The Rite '69
The Passion of Anna '70
The Touch '71
Cries and Whispers '72
The Magic Flute '73
Scenes from a Marriage '73
Face to Face '76
Autumn Sonata '78
The Serpent's Egg '78
From the Life of the Marionettes '80
Fanny and Alexander '83
After the Rehearsal '84

Robert Bergman
Skull: A Night of Terror '88
A Whisper to a Scream '88

William (Lester Williams) Berke
Toll of the Desert '35
Gun Grit '36
Dick Tracy, Detective/The Corpse Vanishes '42
Betrayal from the East '44
Dangerous Passage '44
Dark Mountain '44
The Falcon in Mexico '44
Navy Way '44
Dick Tracy, Detective '45
Renegade Girl '46
Shoot to Kill '47
Highway 13 '48
Border Rangers '50
The Falcon's Adventure/Armored Car Robbery '50
Gunfire '50
I Shot Billy the Kid '50
Operation Haylift '50
Treasure of Monte Cristo '50
Bandit Queen '51
Roaring City '51
Savage Drums '51
FBI Girl '52
Jungle '52
The Marshal's Daughter '53
The Lost Missile '58

Busby Berkeley
Gold Diggers of 1935 '35
Babes in Arms '39
They Made Me a Criminal '39
Strike Up the Band '40
Babes on Broadway '41
For Me and My Gal '42
Take Me Out to the Ball Game '49

Abby Berlin
Blondie Knows Best '46
Double Deal '50

Joe Berlinger
Brother's Keeper '92

Harvey Berman
The Wild Ride '60

Monty Berman
Jack the Ripper '60
The Hellfire Club '61

Ted Berman
The Fox and the Hound '81

Chris Bernard
Letter to Brezhnev '86

John Bernard
Stay Awake '87

Michael Bernard
Nights in White Satin '87

Edward L. Bernds
Blondie Hits the Jackpot '49
Gold Raiders '51
Clipped Wings '53
Bowery Boys Meet the Monsters '54
Reform School Girl '57
Storm Rider '57
Queen of Outer Space '58
Return of the Fly '59
The Three Stooges Meet Hercules '61
Three Stooges in Orbit '62

Joseph Berne
Mirele Efros '38

Peter Berneis
No Survivors, Please '63

Jack Bernhard
Unknown Island '48

Curtis Bernhardt
Conflict '45
A Stolen Life '46
The Possessed '47
Sirocco '51
The Merry Widow '52
Miss Sadie Thompson '53
Beau Brummel '54
Interrupted Melody '55
Kisses for My President '64

Adam Bernstein
It's Pat: The Movie '94

Armyan Bernstein
Windy City '84
Cross My Heart '88

Walter Bernstein
Little Miss Marker '80
Women & Men: In Love There Are No Rules '91

Claude Berri
The Two of Us '68
Marry Me, Marry Me '69
Le Sex Shop '73
One Wild Moment '78
I Love All of You '83
Tchao Pantin '84
Jean de Florette '87
Manon of the Spring '87
Uranus '91
Germinal '93

Bill Berry
Brotherhood of Death '76
Off the Mark '87

John Berry
Pantaloons '57
Tamango '59
Maya '66
The Bad News Bears Go to Japan '78
Angel on My Shoulder '80
Honeyboy '82
A Captive in the Land '91

Robert Berry
House of Dreams '64

Tom Berry
Blind Fear '89
The Amityville Curse '90

Bernardo Bertolucci
The Grim Reaper '62
Before the Revolution '65
Partner '68
The Spider's Stratagem '70
The Conformist '71
Last Tango in Paris '73
1900 '76
The Tragedy of a Ridiculous Man '81
The Last Emperor '87
The Sheltering Sky '90
Little Buddha '93
Stealing Beauty '96

Kenneth Berton
Devil's Gift '84

Jean-Louis Bertucelli
Ramparts of Clay '71

Irvin Berwick
The Monster of Piedras Blancas '57
The 7th Commandment '61
Malibu High '79

Wayne Berwick
Microwave Massacre '83

Michael Berz
Snow White '89

James Beshears
Homework '82

Milad Bessada
Quiet Day In Belfast '74

Dan Bessie
Hard Traveling '85

Luc Besson
Le Dernier Combat '84
Subway '85
The Big Blue '88
La Femme Nikita '91
The Professional '94

Bruce Best
Queen of the Road '84

Gil Bettman
Never Too Young to Die '86
Crystal Heart '87

Jonathan Betuel
My Science Project '85
Theodore Rex '95

Eddie Beverly, Jr.
Escapist '83
Ballbuster

Radha Bharadwaj
Closet Land '90

Andrew Bianchi
Cry of a Prostitute: Love Kills '72
Burial Ground '85

Edward Bianchi
The Fan '81

Herbert Biberman
Master Race '44
Salt of the Earth '54

Robert Bierman
Apology '86
Vampire's Kiss '88

Edward A. Biery
How to Succeed with Girls '64

Kathryn Bigelow
Loveless '83
Near Dark '87
Blue Steel '90
Point Break '91
Wild Palms '93
Strange Days '95

Joseph Bigwood
Never Pick Up a Stranger '79

David Bilcock
Alvin Rides Again '74

Tony Bill
My Bodyguard '80
Six Weeks '82
The Princess and the Pea '83
Five Corners '88
Crazy People '90
A Home of Our Own '93
Untamed Heart '93
Next Door '94

Kevin Billington
Light at the Edge of the World '71

Pierre Billon
Ruyblas '48

Bruce Bilson
The North Avenue Irregulars '79
Chattanooga Choo Choo '84

Danny Bilson
Zone Troopers '84
The Wrong Guys '88

John Binder
Uforia '81

Mike Binder
Crossing the Bridge '92
Indian Summer '93
Blankman '94

Steve Binder
Give 'Em Hell, Harry! '75

William Bindley
Freeze Frame '92
Judicial Consent '94

Steve Bing
Every Breath '93

Josh Binney
Hi-De-Ho '35
Boardinghouse Blues '48
Killer Diller '48

Claude Binyon
Here Come the Girls '53

Dudley Birch
Flight from Singapore '62

Patricia Birch
Grease 2 '82

Antonia Bird
Priest '94
Mad Love '95

Richard Bird
Men of Ireland '38
The Terror '38

Stuart Bird
Home Free All '84

Andrew Birkin
Burning Secret '89
Desire '93

Alan Birkinshaw
The House of Usher '88
Ten Little Indians '89
Masque of the Red Death '90

Fernando Birri
A Very Old Man with Enormous Wings '88

Daniel Birt
The Three Weird Sisters '48
Interrupted Journey '49
Robin Hood: The Movie '55

Sam Bischoff
The Last Mile '32

Terry Bishop
The Unstoppable Man '59

Shem Bitterman
Peephole '93

Lauren Bivens
Trespasses '86

Bill Bixby
The Barbary Coast '74
The Trial of the Incredible Hulk '89
Death of the Incredible Hulk '90
Another Pair of Aces: Three of a Kind '91
Baby of the Bride '91

Stig Bjorkman
Georgia, Georgia '72

Herbert Blache
The Saphead '21
The Untamable '23

Noel Black
Pretty Poison '68
Mirrors '78
A Man, a Woman, and a Bank '79
Prime Suspect '82
Private School '83
Quarterback Princess '85
A Conspiracy of Love '87
Eyes of the Panther '90

Richard Blackburn
Lemora, Lady Dracula '73

Cullen Blaine
R.O.T.O.R. '88

David Blair
Wax, or the Discovery of Television Among the Bees '93

George Blair
Silver City Bonanza '51

Les Blair
Bad Behavior '92

Mark Blair
Confessions of a Serial Killer '87

Alfonso Corona Blake
Samson vs. the Vampire Women '61
Samson in the Wax Museum '63

T.C. Blake
Nightflyers '87

Michael Blakemore
Privates on Parade '84
Country Life '95

Michel Blanc
Grosse Fatigue '94

Ken Blancato
Stewardess School '86

John Blanchard
The Last Polka '84

Harrod Blank
In the Land of the Owl Turds '87

Les Blank
Burden of Dreams '82

Alessandro Blasetti
1860 '33
The Iron Crown '41
Fabiola '48

William Peter Blatty
The Ninth Configuration '79
Exorcist 3: Legion '90

Jeff Bleckner
When Your Lover Leaves '83
Brotherly Love '85
White Water Summer '87

Bertrand Blier
Going Places '74
Get Out Your Handkerchiefs '78
Buffet Froid '79
Beau Pere '81
My Best Friend's Girl '84
Menage '86
Too Beautiful for You '88

Bob Blizz
Vengeance '80

Bruce Block
Princess Academy '87

George J. Bloom, III
Brothers in Arms '88

Jason Bloom
Bio-Dome '96

Jeffrey Bloom
Dog Pound Shuffle '75
The Stick-Up '77
Blood Beach '81
Jealousy '84
Flowers in the Attic '87

George Bloomfield
Jenny '70
To Kill a Clown '72
Riel '79
The Double Negative '80
Nothing Personal '80

Philippe Blot
Hot Blood '89
Running Wild '94

Pavel Blumenfeld
Tereza '61

Mort Blumenstock
Morals for Women '31

Andy Blumenthal
Bloodfist 2 '90

Ralph Blumke
Robby '68

Don Bluth
The Secret of NIMH '82
An American Tail '86
The Land Before Time '88
All Dogs Go to Heaven '89
Rock-a-Doodle '92
Thumbelina '94
A Troll in Central Park '94

John Blystone
Our Hospitality '23
Dick Turpin '25
Great Guy '36
23 1/2 Hours Leave '37
Block-heads '38
Swiss Miss '38

David Blyth
Death Warmed Up '85
Red Blooded American Girl '90
My Grandpa is a Vampire '92

Jeff Blyth
Cheetah '89

Kam Bo
Blind Fists of Bruce '70s

Hart Bochner
P.C.U. '94
High School High '96

Jean Bodon
Hidden Fears '93

Sergei Bodrov
Freedom Is Paradise '89

Budd Boetticher
Behind Locked Doors '48
Bullfighter & the Lady '50
Horizons West '52
Red Ball Express '52
Man from the Alamo '53
The Magnificent Matador '55
The Tall T '57
Ride Lonesome '59
The Rise and Fall of Legs Diamond '60

Paul Bogart
Marlowe '69
Skin Game '71
Cancel My Reservation '72
A House Without a Christmas Tree '72
Class of '44 '73
Tell Me Where It Hurts '74
Power, Passion & Murder '83
Oh, God! You Devil '84
Torch Song Trilogy '88
Broadway Bound '92
The Heidi Chronicles '95

Yurek Bogayevicz
Anna '87
Three of Hearts '93

Peter Bogdanovich
Targets '68
Voyage to the Planet of Prehistoric Women '68
The Last Picture Show '71
What's Up, Doc? '72
Paper Moon '73
Daisy Miller '74
Saint Jack '79
They All Laughed '81
Mask '85
Illegally Yours '87
Texasville '90
Noises Off '92
The Thing Called Love '93

Willy Bogner
Fire and Ice '87
Fire, Ice and Dynamite '91

Michael Derek Bohusz
Uninvited '93

Michel Boisrond
That Naughty Girl '58
Voulez-Vous Danser Avec Moi? '59
Catherine & Co. '76

Yves Boisset
Cobra '71
Dupont Lajoie '74
The Purple Taxi '77
Dog Day '83
Prize of Peril '84
Double Identity '89

Johanne Boisvert
Being at Home with Claude '92

Jerome Boivin
Baxter '89
Barjo '93

Jose Antonio Bolanos
Born in America '90

Richard Boleslawski
Rasputin and the Empress '32
The Painted Veil '34
Les Miserables '35
The Garden of Allah '36
Theodora Goes Wild '36
The Last of Mrs. Cheyney '37

Heinrich Boll
Germany in Autumn '78

Mauro Bolognini
Il Bell'Antonio '60
Oldest Profession '67
La Grande Bourgeoise '74
The Inheritance '76
Husbands and Lovers '91

Craig Bolotin
That Night '93

William T. Bolson
Sleeping with Strangers '94

Ben Bolt
Big Town '87

Robert Bolt
Lady Caroline Lamb '73

Jack Bond
It Couldn't Happen Here '88

James Bond, III
Def by Temptation '90

Timothy Bond
Deadly Harvest '72
One Night Only '84
The Lost World '92
Return to the Lost World '93

Sergei Bondarchuk
War and Peace '68
Waterloo '71

Peter Bonerz
Nobody's Perfekt '79
Police Academy 6: City Under Siege '89

Mike Bonifer
Lipstick Camera '93

Mario Bonnard
The Last Days of Pompeii '60

Lee Bonner
Adventure of the Action Hunters '87

Rene Bonniere
Perfect Timing '84
Dream Man '94
The Halfback of Notre Dame '96

Andre Bonzel
Man Bites Dog '91

John Boorman
Point Blank '67
Hell in the Pacific '69
Deliverance '72
Zardoz '73
The Exorcist 2: The Heretic '77
Excalibur '81
The Emerald Forest '85
Hope and Glory '87
Where the Heart Is '90
Beyond Rangoon '95
Picture Windows '95

H. Gordon Boos
Red Surf '90

Walter Boos
Train Station Pickups '70s

Jose Luis Borau
On the Line '83

Donald P. Borchers
Grave Secrets '89

Lizzie Borden
Born in Flames '83
Working Girls '87
Love Crimes '92

Bernard Borderie
Your Turn Darling '63

Michael Bordon
The Ghost of Fletcher Ridge '80s

Robert Boris
Oxford Blues '84
Steele Justice '87
Buy & Cell '89
Frank and Jesse '94

Arthur Borman
...And God Spoke '94

Walerian Borowczyk
Emmanuelle 5 '87

Clay Borris
Quiet Cool '86
The Gunfighters '87
Prom Night 4: Deliver Us From Evil '91
Suspicious Agenda '94
Someone to Die For '95

Phillip Borsos
The Grey Fox '83
Mean Season '85
One Magic Christmas '85
Dr. Bethune '90
Far from Home: The Adventures of Yellow Dog '94

Michael Bortman
Crooked Hearts '91

Frank Borzage
Song O' My Heart '29
A Farewell to Arms '32
Flirtation Walk '34
Desire '36
History is Made at Night '37
Mannequin '37
The Shining Hour '38
Three Comrades '38
The Mortal Storm '40
Strange Cargo '40
Smilin' Through '41

His Butler's Sister '43
Stage Door Canteen '43
The Spanish Main '45
I've Always Loved You '46
Moonrise '48
Journey Beneath the Desert '61

Juan Bosch
Exorcism '74

Mark Steven Bosko
Bride of Killer Nerd '91

Fritz Bottger
Horrors of Spider Island '59

John Boulting
Brighton Rock '47
Lucky Jim '58
I'm All Right Jack '59
Heavens Above '63

Roy Boulting
Fame Is the Spur '47
The Guinea Pig '48
Brothers in Law '57
Carlton Browne of the F.O. '59
Heavens Above '63
There's a Girl in My Soup '70

Serge Bourguignon
Sundays & Cybele '62
A Coeur Joie '67
Head Over Heels '67

Robert Bouvier
City in Panic '86

Haim Bouzaglo
Fictitious Marriage '88

John Bowab
Love at the Top '86

Jenny Bowen
Street Music '81
The Wizard of Loneliness '88
Animal Behavior '89

John Bowen
Lethal Games '90
Knock Outs '92

Dallas Bower
Alice in Wonderland '50

Anthony Bowers
Shame, Shame on the Bixby Boys '82

Geoffrey G. Bowers
Danger Zone 2 '89

George Bowers
The Hearse '80
Body & Soul '81
My Tutor '82
Private Resort '84

John R. Bowey
Mutator '90

Rob Bowman
Airborne '93

John Bown
Nudity Required '90

Kenneth Bowser
In a Shallow Grave '88

Muriel Box
Truth About Women '58
Rattle of a Simple Man '64

Daniel Boyd
Chillers '88
Paradise Park '90s
Invasion of the Space Preachers '90

Don Boyd
East of Elephant Rock '76
Twenty-One '91

Julianne Boyd
Eubie! '82

Jean Boyer
Circonstances Attenuantes '36
Mr. Peek-A-Boo '50
The French Touch '54
Dressmaker '56
Fernandel the Dressmaker '57

Pat Boyette
Dungeon of Harrow '64

Danny Boyle
Shallow Grave '94
Trainspotting '95

Bruno Bozzetto
Allegro Non Troppo '76
VIP, My Brother Superman '90

Charles Brabant
The Respectful Prostitute '52

Charles Brabin
The Raven '15
The Mask of Fu Manchu '32

Bertram Bracken
The Confession '20

Robert North Bradbury
Hidden Valley '32
Man from Hell's Edges '32
Texas Buddies '32
Breed of the Border '33
The Gallant Fool '33
Galloping Romeo '33
Riders of Destiny '33
Western Double Feature 2 '33
Blue Steel '34
The Gun Ranger '34
John Wayne Anthology: Star Packer/Lawless Range '34
Lucky Texan '34
Man from Utah '34
The Star Packer '34
Trail Beyond '34
West of the Divide '34
Alias John Law '35
Between Men '35
Big Calibre '35
Dawn Rider '35
Desert Trail '35
Lawless Frontier '35
Lawless Range '35
Trail of Terror '35
Western Double Feature 5 '35
Western Justice '35
Westward Ho '35
Brand of the Outlaws '36
Cavalry '36
Headin' for the Rio Grande '36
Kid Ranger '36
Last of the Warrens '36
Smokey Smith '36
Sundown Saunders '36
Valley of the Lawless '36
God's Country and the Man '37
Hittin' the Trail '37
Riders of the Rockies '37
Trouble in Texas '37
Where Trails Divide '37
Dawn Rider/Frontier Horizon '39
Forbidden Trails '41

Samuel Bradford
Teen Vamp '88

Al Bradley
Captive Planet '78
Bloody Avenger '80s
Cosmos: War of the Planets '80
Metallica '85
Iron Warrior '87
Cross Mission '89
Miami Cops '89

David Bradley
They Saved Hitler's Brain '64

John Bradshaw
That's My Baby! '88
The Big Slice '90

Randy Bradshaw
Blades of Courage '88
Song Spinner '95

Carlo L. Bragaglia
The Sword and the Cross '58
The Loves of Hercules '60

John Brahm
The Undying Monster '42
Wintertime '43
Guest in the House '45
Singapore '47
Face to Face '52
Miracle of Our Lady of Fatima '52

Stan Brakhage
Dog Star Man '64

Robert Bralver
Midnight Ride '92

Marco Brambilla
Demolition Man '93

Bill Brame
Miss Melody Jones '73
Jive Turkey '76
Ebony Dreams '80

Kenneth Branagh
Henry V '89
Dead Again '91
Peter's Friends '92
Much Ado about Nothing '93
Mary Shelley's Frankenstein '94
A Midwinter's Tale '95

Joshua Brand
A Pyromaniac's Love Story '95

Larry Brand
The Drifter '88
Masque of the Red Death '89
Overexposed '90
Till the End of the Night '94

Timothy Brand
Till Death Do Us Part '72

Richard Brander
Malibu Hot Summer '74

Marlon Brando
One-Eyed Jacks '61

Clark Brandon
Skeeter '93

Michael Brandon
Queen of the Stardust Ballroom '75

Charlotte Brandstrom
Sweet Revenge '90
Road to Ruin '91
A Business Affair '93

Fred Brannon
D-Day on Mars '45
Cyclotrode "X" '46
Jesse James Rides Again '47
G-Men Never Forget '48
Bandit King of Texas '49
Federal Agents vs. Underworld, Inc. '49
King of the Rocketmen '49
Lost Planet Airmen '49
The Invisible Monster '50
Radar Men from the Moon '52
Zombies of the Stratosphere '52
Jungle Drums of Africa '53

Dominick Brascia
Evil Laugh '86

Enrique Braso
In Memoriam '76

Tinto Brass
Caligula '80

Keefe Brasselle
If You Don't Stop It...You'll Go Blind '77

Michel Brault
A Paper Wedding '89

Franklyn Brauner
Wild Side '95

Joseph Braunstein
Rest In Pieces '87
Edge of the Axe '89

Charles Braverman
Hit & Run '82
Brotherhood of Justice '86
Prince of Bel Air '87

Bob Bravler
Rush Week '88

John Bravman
Zombie Nightmare '86

William Brayne
Flame to the Phoenix '85
Cold War Killers '86

Rossano Brazzi
The Christmas That Almost Wasn't '66

George Breakston
Geisha Girl '52
Scarlet Spear '54
White Huntress '57
The Manster '59

Gil Brealey
A Test of Love '84

Julian Breen
Prehysteria 3 '95

Richard L. Breen
Stopover Tokyo '57

Catherine Breillat
36 Fillete '88

Valerie Breiman
Going Overboard '89

Jacques Brel
Franz '72

Tia Brelis
Trading Mom '94

Milton Bren
Three for Bedroom C '52

Herbert Brenon
Dancing Mothers '26
Housemaster '38
Black Eyes '39

Alfonso Brescia
White Fang and the Hunter '85

Robert Bresson
The Ladies of the Bois de Bologne '44
Diary of a Country Priest '50
A Man Escaped '57
Pickpocket '59
Mouchette '67
A Gentle Woman '69
Lancelot of the Lake '74
L'Argent '83

Martin Brest
Going in Style '79
Beverly Hills Cop '84
Midnight Run '88
Scent of a Woman '92

Howard Bretherton
Ladies They Talk About '33
Hopalong Cassidy '35
Western Gold '37
Boy's Reformatory '39
Irish Luck '39
Star Reporter '39
Tough Kid '39
Hidden Enemy '40
Midnight Limited '40
The Showdown '40
Up in the Air '40
In Old Colorado '41
Outlaws of the Desert '41
Below the Border '42
Dawn on the Great Divide '42
Down Texas Way '42
Ghost Town Law '42
Riders of the West '42
West of the Law '42
Rhythm Parade '43
The Topeka Terror '45
The Prince of Thieves '48

Salome Breziner
Tollbooth '94

Michael E. Briant
Blake's Seven '78

Jules Bricken
Explosion '69

Marshall Brickman
Simon '80
Lovesick '83
The Manhattan Project '86

Paul Brickman
Risky Business '83
Men Don't Leave '89

Alan Bridges
Invasion '65
Out of Season '75
Return of the Soldier '82
The Shooting Party '85
Pudd'nhead Wilson '87

Beau Bridges
The Wild Pair '87
Seven Hours to Judgment '88

James Bridges
The Baby Maker '70
The Paper Chase '73
September 30, 1955 '77
The China Syndrome '79
Urban Cowboy '80
Mike's Murder '84
Perfect '85
Bright Lights, Big City '88

Steven Brill
Heavyweights '94

Burt Brinckerhoff
Can You Hear the Laughter? The Story of Freddie Prinze '79
The Cracker Factory '79
The Day the Women Got Even '80
Mother & Daughter: A Loving War '80

Bo Brinkman
Ice House '89

Jean Brismee
The Devil's Nightmare '71

Donald Britlain
Accident '83

Lawrence Britten
Whose Child Am I? '75

Tracy Lynch Britton
Maximum Breakout '91

Deborah Brock
Slumber Party Massacre 2 '87
Andy and the Airwave Rangers '89
Rock 'n' Roll High School Forever '91

John Broderick
Bad Georgia Road '77
The Warrior & the Sorceress '84

Kevin Brodie
Mugsy's Girls '85

Rex Bromfield
Love at First Sight '76
Melanie '82
Home Is Where the Hart Is '88
Cafe Romeo '91

Douglas Bronco
Danger Zone 3: Steel Horse War '90

Clive Brook
On Approval '44

Peter Brook
Lord of the Flies '63
Marat/Sade '66
King Lear '71
Meetings with Remarkable Men '79
The Mahabharata '89

Ralph Brooke
Bloodlust '59

Dorothea Brooking
The Moon Stallion '85

Howard Brookner
Bloodhounds of Broadway '89

Adam Brooks
Almost You '85
Cannon Movie Tales: Red Riding Hood '89

Albert Brooks
Real Life '79
Modern Romance '81
Lost in America '85
Defending Your Life '91

Bob Brooks
Tattoo '81

James L. Brooks
Thursday's Game '74
Terms of Endearment '83
Broadcast News '87
I'll Do Anything '93

Joseph Brooks
Invitation to the Wedding '73
You Light Up My Life '77
If Ever I See You Again '78

Mel Brooks
The Producers '68
Twelve Chairs '70
Blazing Saddles '74
Young Frankenstein '74
Silent Movie '76
High Anxiety '77
History of the World: Part 1 '81
Spaceballs '87
Life Stinks '91
Robin Hood: Men in Tights '93
Dracula: Dead and Loving It '95

Richard Brooks
Battle Circus '53
The Last Time I Saw Paris '54
Blackboard Jungle '55
The Catered Affair '56
The Last Hunt '56
Something of Value '57
The Brothers Karamazov '58
Cat on a Hot Tin Roof '58
Elmer Gantry '60
Sweet Bird of Youth '62
Lord Jim '65
The Professionals '66
In Cold Blood '67
The Happy Ending '69
Dollars '71
Bite the Bullet '75

Brooks ►cont.

Looking for Mr. Goodbar '77
Wrong is Right '82
Fever Pitch '85

Robert Brooks
Who Shot Pat? '92

Nick Broomfield
Dark Obsession '90
Monster in a Box '92

Philip Brophy
Body Melt '93

James Broughton
Dreamwood '72

Otto Brower
The Light of Western Stars '30
Clearing the Range '31
Fighting Caravans '31
Hard Hombre '31
Devil Horse '32
Spirit of the West '32
I Can't Escape '34
Mystery Mountain '34
The Outlaw Deputy '35
The Phantom Empire '35
Postal Inspector '36

Arvin Brown
Diary of the Dead '80s

Barry Brown
Cloud Dancer '80
Lonely in America '90

Bruce Brown
The Endless Summer '66
The Endless Summer 2 '94

Clarence Brown
The Last of the Mohicans '20
The Light of Faith '22
The Eagle '25
Smouldering Fires '25
The Flesh and the Devil '27
The Tempest/The Eagle '27
A Woman of Affairs '28
Anna Christie '30
Romance '30
A Free Soul '31
Possessed '31
Chained '34
Sadie McKee '34
Ah, Wilderness! '35
Anna Karenina '35
The Gorgeous Hussy '36
Wife Versus Secretary '36
Conquest '37
Of Human Hearts '38
Idiot's Delight '39
The Rains Came '39
Edison the Man '40
They Met in Bombay '41
The Human Comedy '43
National Velvet '44
The White Cliffs of Dover '44
The Yearling '46
Intruder in the Dust '49
To Please a Lady '50
Angels in the Outfield '51

Curtis Brown
The Game '89

Edwin Scott Brown
The Prey '80

Ewing Miles Brown
Whale of a Tale '76
Killers '88

Georg Stanford Brown
Grambling's White Tiger '81
Miracle of the Heart: A Boys Town Story '86
Alone in the Neon Jungle '87

Gregory Brown
Dead Man Walking '88
Street Asylum '90
Stranger by Night '94

Gwen Brown
Emergency '68

Harry Joe Brown
One-Punch O'Day '26
The Fighting Legion '30
Mountain Justice '30

Julie Brown
National Lampoon's Attack of the 5 Ft. 2 Women '94

Karl Brown
The White Legion '36
Fire Alarm '38
The Port of Missing Girls '38

Larry G. Brown
Psychopath '73
Final Cut '88

Melville Brown
Check & Double Check '30
Mad About Money '30
Behind Office Doors '31
Champagne for Breakfast '35

Mitch Brown
Death Shot '73

Robert Brown
Two Wrongs Make a Right '89

William O. Brown
The Witchmaker '69

Ricou Browning
Salty '73

Tod Browning
Outside the Law '21
White Tiger '23
The Unholy Three '25
The Unknown '27
West of Zanzibar '28
Dracula '31
Freaks '32
Mark of the Vampire '35
Devil Doll '36

S.F. Brownrigg
Don't Look in the Basement '73
Don't Open the Door! '74
Poor White Trash 2 '75
Keep My Grave Open '80
Thinkin' Big '87

James Bruce
The Suicide Club '88
Headless Body in Topless Bar '96

Clyde Bruckman
The General '27
Feet First '30

Adrian Brunel
Old Spanish Custom '36

Franco Brusati
Bread and Chocolate '74
To Forget Venice '79
The Sleazy Uncle '89

Alf Brustellin
Germany in Autumn '78

Charles Bryant
Salome '22
Salome/Queen Elizabeth '23

James Bryant
The Executioner, Part 2: Frozen Scream '84

Bill Bryden
Aria '88

Zbynek Brynych
Transport from Paradise '65

Larry Buchanan
Free, White, and 21 '62
The Eye Creatures '65
Curse of the Swamp Creature '66
Mars Needs Women '66
Zontar, the Thing from Venus '66
Creature of Destruction '67
Hell Raiders '68
It's Alive! '68
Goodbye, Norma Jean '75
Hughes & Harlow: Angels in Hell '77
Mistress of the Apes '79
The Loch Ness Horror '82
Goodnight, Sweet Marilyn '89

Dimitri Buchowetzki
Othello '22
The Swan '25

Julio Buchs
Bullet for Sandoval '70

Chris Buck
Family Dog: Complete Series '92

Bethel Buckalew
My Boys Are Good Boys '78

Allan A. Buckhantz
Portrait of a Hitman '77
The Last Contract '86

Colin Bucksey
Blue Money '84
The McGuffin '85
Dealers '89
Curiosity Kills '90
Midnight's Child '93

Harold Bucquet
On Borrowed Time '39
Dr. Kildare's Strange Case '40
The Adventures of Tartu '43
Without Love '45

Colin Budds
Hurricane Smith '92

John Carl Buechler
Dungeonmaster '83
Troll '86
Cellar Dweller '87
Friday the 13th, Part 7: The New Blood '88
Ghoulies 3: Ghoulies Go to College '91

Peter Bufa
Ghost Dance '83

Richard Bugajski
A Woman and a Woman '80
The Interrogation '82
Clearcut '92

Penelope Buitenhuis
Boulevard '94

Veljko Bulajic
Battle of Neretva '69
The Day That Shook the World '78

Alan Bunce
Babar: The Movie '88

Mark Buntzman
Exterminator 2 '84

Joyce Bunuel
Dirty Dishes '82

Juan Bunuel
Leonor '75

Luis Bunuel
Un Chien Andalou '28
L'Age D'Or '30
The Great Madcap '49
Los Olvidados '50
Mexican Bus Ride '51
Susana '51
A Woman Without Love '51
El Bruto '52
El: This Strange Passion '52
The Illusion Travels by Streetcar '53
Wuthering Heights '53
The Criminal Life of Archibaldo de la Cruz '55
Death in the Garden '56
Nazarin '58
Fever Mounts at El Pao '59
Viridiana '61
The Young One '61
The Exterminating Angel '62
Diary of a Chambermaid '64
Simon of the Desert '66
Belle de Jour '67
The Milky Way '68
Phantom of Liberty '68
Tristana '70
The Discreet Charm of the Bourgeoisie '72
That Obscure Object of Desire '77

Jacob Burckhardt
Landlord Blues '87

Robert Burge
Vasectomy: A Delicate Matter '86
Keaton's Cop '90

Stuart Burge
Julius Caesar '70

Martyn Burke
Last Chase '81
Power Play '81
Clown Murders '83

Terry Burke
Inn of the Damned '74

Tom Burman
Meet the Hollowheads '89

Charles Burnett
To Sleep with Anger '90
The Glass Shield '95

Paul Burnford
The Adventures of Rusty '45

Allan Burns
Just Between Friends '86

Edward Burns
The Brothers McMullen '94

Ken Burns
The Civil War, Episode 1: The Cause—1861 '90
The Civil War, Episode 2: A Very Bloody Affair—1862 '90
The Civil War, Episode 3: Forever Free—1862 '90
The Civil War, Episode 4: Simply Murder—1863 '90
The Civil War, Episode 5: The Universe of Battle—1863 '90
The Civil War, Episode 6: Valley of the Shadow of Death—1864 '90
The Civil War, Episode 7: Most Hallowed Ground—1864 '90
The Civil War, Episode 8: War is All Hell—1865 '90
The Civil War, Episode 9: The Better Angels of Our Nature—1865 '90
Baseball '94

Robert Burns
Mongrel '83

Jeff Burr
The Offspring '87
Leatherface: The Texas Chainsaw Massacre 3 '89
Stepfather 2: Make Room for Daddy '89
Puppet Master 4 '93
Pumpkinhead 2: Blood Wings '94
Puppet Master 5: The Final Chapter '94
Night of the Scarecrow '95

Robert L. Burrill
The Milpitas Monster '75

Geoff Burrowes
Return to Snowy River '88
Run '91

James Burrows
Partners '82

Tim Burstall
Alvin Purple '73
Jock Petersen '74
Endplay '75
Adventures of Eliza Fraser '76
Attack Force Z '84
The Naked Country '85
Kangaroo '86
Great Expectations: The Untold Story '87
Nightmare at Bittercreek '91

David Burton
Fighting Caravans '31
Lady by Choice '34

Geoff Burton
The Sum of Us '94

Richard Burton
Doctor Faustus '68

Tim Burton
Aladdin and His Wonderful Lamp '84
Frankenweenie '84
Pee Wee's Big Adventure '85
Beetlejuice '88
Batman '89
Edward Scissorhands '90
Batman Returns '92
Ed Wood '94

Leszek Burzynski
Trapped Alive '93

Anthony Bushell
Angel with the Trumpet '50
The Long Dark Hall '51

John Bushelman
L.A. Gangs Rising '89

Christel Bushmann
Comeback '83

William H. Bushnell, Jr.
Four Deuces '75

Tom Bussmann
Whoops Apocalypse '83

David Butler
A Connecticut Yankee '31
Bright Eyes '34
Doubting Thomas '35
The Little Colonel '35
The Littlest Rebel '35
Captain January '36
You'll Find Out '40
Caught in the Draft '41
Playmates '41
The Road to Morocco '42
Thank Your Lucky Stars '43
They Got Me Covered '43
The Princess and the Pirate '44
San Antonio '45
It's a Great Feeling '49
Look for the Silver Lining '49
The Story of Seabiscuit '49
Tea for Two '50
Lullaby of Broadway '51
April In Paris '52
By the Light of the Silvery Moon '53
Calamity Jane '53
King Richard and the Crusaders '54
Glory '56

George Butler
Pumping Iron '76
Pumping Iron 2: The Women '85

Robert Butler
Star Trek: The Cage '65
The Computer Wore Tennis Shoes '69
The Barefoot Executive '71
Scandalous John '71
Now You See Him, Now You Don't '72
The Ultimate Thrill '74
Strange New World '75
James Dean '76
Hot Lead & Cold Feet '78
A Question of Guilt '78
Night of the Juggler '80
Underground Aces '80
Concrete Beat '84
Up the Creek '84
Moonlighting '85
Long Time Gone '86
Out on a Limb '87
White Mile '94

Hendel Butoy
The Rescuers Down Under '90

Bernard Buys
Demon Lust

Zane Buzby
Last Resort '86

Edward Buzzell
At the Circus '39
Honolulu '39
Go West '40
Ship Ahoy '42
Best Foot Forward '43
Song of the Thin Man '47
Neptune's Daughter '49
A Woman of Distinction '50

Mark Byers
Criminal Act '88
Digging Up Business '91

Caruth C. Byrd
Hollywood High, Part 2 '81

David Byrne
True Stories '86

John Byrum
Inserts '76
Heart Beat '80
The Razor's Edge '84
The Whoopee Boys '86

James Caan
Hide in Plain Sight '80

Richard Caan
War of the Wizards '81

Christy Cabanne
The Lamb '15
Flirting with Fate '16
Reggie Mixes In '16
The Average Woman '24
Annapolis '28
Convicted '32
Hearts of Humanity '32
The World Gone Mad '33
Jane Eyre '34

One Frightened Night '35
Last Outlaw '36
The Mummy's Hand '40
Dixie Jamboree '44
Scared to Death '47

Ellen Cabot
Deadly Embrace '88
Beach Babes from Beyond Infinity '93
Test Tube Teens from the Year 2000 '93

Sergio Cabrera
Details of a Duel: A Question of Honor '89

Nick Cacas
Forgotten Warrior '86

Michael Cacoyannis
Stella '55
Girl in Black '56
A Matter of Dignity '57
Zorba the Greek '64
Trojan Women '71
The Story of Jacob & Joseph '74
Iphigenia '77
Sweet Country '87

Michael Caffey
The Hanged Man '74

Edward L. Cahn
Confidential '35
Girls in Prison '56
Dragstrip Girl '57
Flesh and the Spur '57
Invasion of the Saucer Men '57
Motorcycle Gang '57
Shake, Rattle and Rock '57
Voodoo Woman '57
Zombies of Moratau '57
It! The Terror from Beyond Space '58
Jet Attack/Paratroop Command '58
Suicide Battalion/Hell Squad '58
Invisible Invaders '59
Frontier Uprising '61

Mario Caiano
Adios, Hombre '68

Barry Caillier
To Cross the Rubicon '95

Christopher Cain
Elmer '76
The Stone Boy '84
That Was Then...This Is Now '85
Where the River Runs Black '86
The Principal '87
Young Guns '88
Wheels of Terror '90
Pure Country '92
The Next Karate Kid '94
The Amazing Panda Adventure '95

Thomas Calabrese
Even Angels Fall '90

Stephen Calamari
The Satan Killer '93

Antonio Calenda
One Russian Summer '73

Mark Callan
Hector's Bunyip '86

John Callas
Lone Wolf '88

Simon Callow
The Ballad of the Sad Cafe '91

Art Camacho
The Power Within '95

Mario Camerini
Ulysses '55

James Cameron
Piranha 2: The Spawning '82
The Spawning '82
The Terminator '84
Aliens '86
The Abyss '89
Terminator 2: Judgment Day '91
True Lies '94

Ken Cameron
Monkey Grip '82
Fast Talking '86
The Good Wife '86
Wild Thing '87
Brides of Christ '91
Oldest Confederate Widow Tells All '95

Ray Cameron
Bloodbath at the House of Death '85

Douglas Camfield
Ivanhoe '82

Donald Cammell
Performance '70
Demon Seed '77
White of the Eye '88

Joe Camp
Benji '74
Hawmps! '76
For the Love of Benji '77
The Double McGuffin '79
Oh, Heavenly Dog! '80
Benji the Hunted '87

Pasquale Festa Campanile
When Women Had Tails '70
When Women Lost Their Tails '75

Colin Campbell
In the Days of the Thundering Herd & the Law & the Outlaw '14
The Spoilers '14
Little Orphan Annie '18

Douglas Campbell
Season of Fear '89
Zapped Again '89

Graeme Campbell
Blood Relations '87
Into the Fire '88
Murder One '88
Still Life '92
Deadlock 2 '94
The Man in the Attic '94

Martin Campbell
Edge of Darkness '86
Criminal Law '89
Cast a Deadly Spell '91
Defenseless '91
No Escape '94
Goldeneye '95

Anna Campion
Loaded '96

Jane Campion
An Angel at My Table '89
Sweetie '89
The Piano '93

Carlo Campogalliani
Goliath and the Barbarians '60
Son of Samson '62
Ursus in the Valley of the Lions '62

Michael Campus
Zero Population Growth '72
Mack '73
The Education of Sonny Carson '74
The Passover Plot '75

Marcel Camus
Black Orpheus '58
Where the Sky Begins '84

Mario Camus
The Holy Innocents '84

John Candy
Hostage for a Day '94

Richard Cannistraro
Violated '84

Danny Cannon
The Young Americans '93
Judge Dredd '95

Dyan Cannon
The End of Innocence '90

Raymond Cannon
Swing It, Sailor! '37

Yakima Canutt
The Adventures of Frank and Jesse James '48
G-Men Never Forget '48
Oklahoma Badlands '48

Louis Capauno
Executioner of Venice '63

Giorgio Capitani
The Ruthless Four '70
Lobster for Breakfast '82
I Hate Blondes '83

Frank Cappello
American Yakuza '94

Bernt Capra
Mindwalk: A Film for Passionate Thinkers '91

Frank Capra
Strong Man '26
That Certain Thing '28
Platinum Blonde '31
The Bitter Tea of General Yen '33
Lady for a Day '33
Broadway Bill '34
It Happened One Night '34
Mr. Deeds Goes to Town '36
Lost Horizon '37
You Can't Take It with You '38
Mr. Smith Goes to Washington '39
Meet John Doe '41
Prelude to War '42
Arsenic and Old Lace '44
Battle of China '44
The Battle of Russia '44
It's a Wonderful Life '46
State of the Union '48
Riding High '50
Here Comes the Groom '51
A Hole in the Head '59
Pocketful of Miracles '61

Luigi Capuano
Tiger of the Seven Seas '62
Cold Steel for Tortuga '65
Marauder '65
The Snake Hunter Strangler '66

Leos Carax
Boy Meets Girl '84

Costa Carayiannis
The Brave Bunch '70
Land of the Minotaur '77

Lamar Card
The Clones '73

Hernan Cardenas
Island Claw '80

Jack Cardiff
My Geisha '62
Dark of the Sun '68
The Girl on a Motorcycle '68
The Freakmaker '73

Roger Cardinal
Malarek '89

Rene Cardona, Sr.
Santa Claus '59
Wrestling Women vs. the Aztec Mummy '59
Wrestling Women vs. the Aztec Ape '62

Rene Cardona, Jr.
Night of the Bloody Apes '68
Night of a Thousand Cats '72
Robinson Crusoe & the Tiger '72
Tintorera...Tiger Shark '78
The Treasure of the Amazon '84
Beaks: The Movie '87

J.S. Cardone
The Slayer '82
The Slayer/The Scalps '82
Thunder Alley '85
Shadowzone '89
A Climate for Killing '91
Shadowhunter '93

John Cardos
The Female Bunch '69
Kingdom of the Spiders '77
The Dark '79
Day Time Ended '80
Mutant '83
Outlaw of Gor '87
Skeleton Coast '89

Topper Carew
Talkin' Dirty After Dark '91

Edwin Carewe
Evangeline '29

Gilles Carle
In Trouble '67
The Red Half-Breed '70
Maria Chapdelaine '84
Blood of the Hunter '94
The Other Side of the Law '95

Carlo Carlei
Flight of the Innocent '93
Fluke '95

Lewis John Carlino
The Sailor Who Fell from Grace with the Sea '76

The Great Santini '80
Class '83

Henning Carlsen
A World of Strangers '62
Hunger '66
The Wolf at the Door '87

Don Carmody
Surrogate '88

Marcel Carne
Bizarre Bizarre '39
Le Jour Se Leve '39
Les Visiteurs du Soir '42
Children of Paradise '44
Les Assassins de L'Ordre '71
La Merveilleuse Visite '74

Marc Caro
Delicatessen '92
The City of Lost Children '95

Glenn Gordon Caron
Clean and Sober '88
Wilder Napalm '93
Love Affair '94

John Carpenter
Dark Star '74
Assault on Precinct 13 '76
The Fog '78
Halloween '78
Elvis: The Movie '79
Escape from New York '81
The Thing '82
Christine '84
Starman '84
Big Trouble in Little China '86
Prince of Darkness '87
They Live '88
Memoirs of an Invisible Man '92
Body Bags '93
In the Mouth of Madness '95
Village of the Damned '95
Escape from L.A. '96

Stephen Carpenter
The Power '80
Dorm That Dripped Blood '82
The Kindred '87

Fabio Carpi
Basileus Quartet '82

Adrian Carr
Now and Forever '82

Bernard Carr
Curley '47

John Carr
Death Wish Club '83

Terry Carr
Welcome to 18 '87

Thomas Carr
Jesse James Rides Again '47
Guns of Justice '50
Marshal of Heldorado '50
Pirates of the High Seas '50
Captain Scarlett '53
Dino '57
Wanted: Dead or Alive '59

David Carradine
Americana '81

Anthony Carras
Fearmaker '89

Michael Carreras
Maniac '63
Call Him Mr. Shatter '74

Rick Carrier
Strangers in the City '62

Frank G. Carroll
Death Ray

Larry Carroll
Ghostwarrior '86

Robert Martin Carroll
Sonny Boy '87

Willard Carroll
The Runestone '91

David Carson
Star Trek Generations '94

John Paddy Carstairs
The Saint in London '39
Sleeping Car to Trieste '45
Tony Draws a Horse '51
Made in Heaven '52
Trouble in Store '53

Michael Cartel
Runaway Nightmare '84

Bruce Carter
Laser Moon '92

John N. Carter
Zombie Island Massacre '84

Karen Carter
The Big Bust Out '73

Peter Carter
High Ballin' '78
Klondike Fever '79
Rituals '79
Highpoint '80
Intruder Within '81
Kavik the Wolf Dog '84

Thomas Carter
Miami Vice '84
Swing Kids '93

Steve Carver
Naked Warriors '73
Big Bad Mama '74
Drum '76
Steel '80
An Eye for an Eye '81
Lone Wolf McQuade '83
Oceans of Fire '86
Jocks '87
Bulletproof '88
River of Death '90
Dead Center '94

Ron Casden
Campus Man '87

George Case
Body Language '95

Kimberly Casey
Born Killer '89
Deadly Dancer '90

Richard Casey
Horror House on Highway 5 '86
Hellbent '90

George S. Casorati
Summer Affair '79

Henry Cass
Last Holiday '50
Blood of the Vampire '58
The Hand '60

John Cassavetes
Shadows '60
A Child is Waiting '63
Faces '68
A Woman Under the Influence '74
The Killing of a Chinese Bookie '76
Opening Night '77
Gloria '80
Love Streams '84
Big Trouble '86

Richard Cassidy
Crazed '82
Bloodshed '83

Alexander Cassini
Star Time '92

Renato Castellani
Romeo and Juliet '54

Enzo G. Castellari
Any Gun Can Play '67
Go Kill and Come Back '68
Cold Eyes of Fear '70s
High Crime '73
Loves & Times of Scaramouche '76
1990: The Bronx Warriors '83
Warriors of the Wasteland '83
Day of the Cobra '84
Escape from the Bronx '85
Lightblast '85
Sinbad of the Seven Seas '89

Nardo Castillo
The Gunrunner '84

Alien Castle
Desire and Hell at Sunset Motel '92

Nick Castle
Tag: The Assassination Game '82
The Last Starfighter '84
The Boy Who Could Fly '86
Tap '89
Dennis the Menace '93
Major Payne '95

Castle ▶cont.

Mr. Wrong '95

William Castle
The Law Rides Again '43
Conquest of Cochise '53
Americano '55
House on Haunted Hill '58
13 Ghosts '60
The Night Walker '64
Strait-Jacket '64

William Allen Castleman
Bummer '73
Johnny Firecloud '75

Hoite C. Caston
Dirt Bike Kid '86

Claude Castravelli
Evil Judgement '85

Joe Catalanotto
French Quarter Undercover '85
Terror in the Swamp '85

Gilbert Cates
I Never Sang For My Father '70
To All My Friends on Shore '71
The Affair '73
Summer Wishes, Winter Dreams '73
One Summer Love '76
Johnny We Hardly Knew Ye '77
The Promise '78
The Last Married Couple in America '80
Oh, God! Book 2 '80
Goldilocks & the Three Bears '83
Hobson's Choice '83
Burning Rage '84
Consenting Adult '85
Backfire '88

Don Cato
Dixie Lanes '88

Michael Caton-Jones
Scandal '89
Memphis Belle '90
Doc Hollywood '91
This Boy's Life '93
Rob Roy '95

Joe Cauley
Silk n' Sabotage '94

Michael Caulfield
Gallagher's Travels '87

Kelley Cauthen
Indecent Behavior 3 '95

Alberto Cavalcanti
Dead of Night '45
Nicholas Nickleby '46

Alain Cavalier
Therese '86

Liliana Cavani
The Night Porter '74
Beyond Obsession '82
The Berlin Affair '85
Francesco '93

Vladimir Cech
New Pastures '62

Jeff Celentano
Under the Hula Moon '95

Fernando Cerchio
Nefertiti, Queen of the Nile '64

Norman A. Cerf
Jungle Hell '55

Tonino Cervi
Today We Kill, Tomorrow We Die '71

Gerban Ceth
Counter Measures '80s

Claude Chabrol
Le Beau Serge '58
The Cousins '59
Les Bonnes Femmes '60
Bluebeard '63
Les Biches '68
Six in Paris '68
Le Boucher '69
La Rupture '70
A Piece of Pleasure '70
This Man Must Die '70
High Heels '72
Ten Days Wonder '72
Wedding in Blood '74
Dirty Hands '76
Twist '76
Blood Relatives '77
Violette '78
The Horse of Pride '80
The Blood of Others '84
The Story of Women '88
Club Extinction '89
Madame Bovary '91
Betty '92
The Cry of the Owl '92
L'Enfer '93
La Ceremonie '95

Gurinder Chadha
Bhaji on the Beach '94

Don Chaffey
Greyfriars Bobby '61
A Matter of WHO '62
The Horse Without a Head '63
Jason and the Argonauts '63
The Three Lives of Thomasina '63
Secret Agent '64
One Million Years B.C. '66
The Prisoner: Arrival '68
Creatures the World Forgot '70
The Graveyard '74
Fourth Wish '75
Ride a Wild Pony '75
Pete's Dragon '77
Magic of Lassie '78
C.H.O.M.P.S. '79
Casino '80
The Gift of Love '90

Karen Chakhnazarov
Jazzman '84

P. Chalong
H-Bomb '71
In Gold We Trust '91

Gower Champion
Bank Shot '74

Gregg Champion
Short Time '90
The Cowboy Way '94

Jackie Chan
Jackie Chan's Police Force '85
New Fist of Fury '85
The Armour of God '86

Pauline Chan
Traps '93

Philip Chan
Tongs: An American Nightmare '88

Tony Chan
Combination Platter '93

Wallace Chan
Clash of the Ninja '86

Tom Chaney
Frostbiter: Wrath of the Wendigo '94

Cheung Wo Chang
The Association '80s

Li Chao
Cantonen Iron Kung Fu '70s

Charlie Chaplin
Charlie Chaplin's Keystone Comedies #3 '14
Charlie Chaplin's Keystone Comedies #5 '14
The Knockout/Dough and Dynamite '14
The Champion/His New Job '15
Charlie Chaplin: Night at the Show '15
Charlie Chaplin...Our Hero! '15
The Floorwalker/By the Sea '15
His Prehistoric Past/The Bank '15
Burlesque of Carmen '16
The Count '16
Easy Street '16
The Fireman '16
The Rink '16
The Vagabond '16
Work/Police '16
The Adventurer '17
Count/Adventurer '17
The Cure '17
The Floorwalker '17
The Immigrant '17
The Best of Chaplin '18
Three Charlies and One Phoney! '18
The Circus '19
The Kid '21
The Kid/Idle Class '21
Woman of Paris/Sunnyside '23
The Gold Rush '25
Gold Rush/Payday '25
City Lights '31
Modern Times '36
The Great Dictator '40
Monsieur Verdoux '47
Limelight '52
A King in New York '57
The Chaplin Revue '58
A Countess from Hong Kong '67

Sydney Chaplin
The Knockout/Dough and Dynamite '14

Matthew Chapman
Hussy '80
Strangers Kiss '83
Slow Burn '86
Heart of Midnight '89

Michael Chapman
All the Right Moves '83
The Clan of the Cave Bear '86

Robert Chappell
Diamond Run '90

Joe Chappelle
Halloween 6: The Curse of Michael Myers '95

Petr Chardynin
Early Russian Cinema, Vol. 5: Chardynin's Pushkin '13

Erik Charell
Congress Dances '31

Robert Charlton
No Big Deal '83

Henri Charr
Illegal Entry: Formula for Fear '93
Caged Hearts '95

Richard Chase
Hell's Angels Forever '83

Etienne Chatiliez
Life Is a Long Quiet River '88
Tatie Danielle '91

Louis Chaudet
Fighting Jack '26
Tentacles of the North '26

Amin Q. Chaudhri
Tiger Warsaw '87
An Unremarkable Life '89

Jaime Chavarri
I'm the One You're Looking For '88

Jeremiah S. Chechik
National Lampoon's Christmas Vacation '89
Benny & Joon '93
Tall Tale: The Unbelievable Adventures of Pecos Bill '95
Diabolique '96

Douglas Cheek
C.H.U.D. '84

Ara Chekmayan
Forever James Dean '88

Peter Chelsom
Hear My Song '91
Funny Bones '94

Chen Chen
The Chinatown Kid '78

Yeung Ching Chen
The Two Great Cavaliers '73

Pierre Chenal
Crime and Punishment '35
Man from Nowhere '37
Native Son '51

Tommy Cheng
Ninja Death Squad '87
Ninja: American Warrior '90

Patrice Chereau
L'Homme Blesse '83
Queen Margot '94

John R. Cherry, III
Dr. Otto & the Riddle of the Gloom Beam '86
Ernest Goes to Camp '87
Ernest Saves Christmas '88
Ernest Goes to Jail '90
Ernest Scared Stupid '91
Ernest Rides Again '93
Slam Dunk Ernest '95

George Chesebro
Wolf Blood '25

Lionel Chetwynd
Hanoi Hilton '87

Alfred Cheung
Paper Marriage '88

Alton Cheung
Kickboxer the Champion '91

Lu Chia-Liang
Shaolin Executioner '80s
Challenge of the Masters '89

Andrew Chiaramonte
Twogether '94

Yvan Chiffre
President's Target '93

Stephen Chiodo
Killer Klowns from Outer Space '88

Mel Chionglo
Midnight Dancers '94

Marvin J. Chomsky
The Shaming '71
Evel Knievel '72
Fireball Forward '72
Murph the Surf '75
Little Ladies of the Night '77
Holocaust '78
Attica '80
Inside the Third Reich '82
Tank '83
Anastasia: The Mystery of Anna '86
The Deliberate Stranger '86
Billionaire Boys Club '87
Nairobi Affair '88
The Brotherhood of the Rose '89
Robert Kennedy and His Times '90

Thomas Chong
Cheech and Chong's Next Movie '80
Cheech and Chong's Nice Dreams '81
Cheech and Chong: Still Smokin' '83
Cheech and Chong's The Corsican Brothers '84
Far Out Man '89

Joyce Chopra
Smooth Talk '85
The Lemon Sisters '90
Murder in New Hampshire: The Pamela Smart Story '91
Danger of Love '95

Elie Chouraqui
Love Songs '85
Man on Fire '87

Raymond Chow
When Taekwondo Strikes '83

Nathaniel Christian
California Casanova '89
Club Fed '90

Roger Christian
The Sender '82
Starship '87
Nostradamus '93

Christian-Jaque
Legend of Frenchie King '71

Benjamin Christiansen
Witchcraft Through the Ages '22
Mockery '27

Jean Christopher
One-Eyed Soldiers '67

Yeh Yung Chu
Fists of Dragons '69

Lyndon Chubbuck
Naked Souls '95

Byron Ross Chudnow
The Doberman Gang '72
Daring Dobermans '73
The Amazing Dobermans '76

Grigori Chukrai
Ballad of a Soldier '60

Mario Ciano
Terror of Rome Against the Son of Hercules '64
Fighting Fists of Shanghai Joe '65

Gerard Ciccoritti
Psycho Girls '86
Graveyard Shift '87
Understudy: The Graveyard Shift 2 '88
Paris, France '94

Matt Cimber
Single Room Furnished '68
The Black Six '74
Candy Tangerine Man '75
Lady Cocoa '75
Witch Who Came from the Sea '76
Butterfly '82
Fake Out '82
Time to Die '83
Yellow Hair & the Fortress of Gold '84
Hundra '85

Michael Cimino
Thunderbolt & Lightfoot '74
The Deer Hunter '78
Heaven's Gate '81
Year of the Dragon '85
The Sicilian '87
Desperate Hours '90

Grigorij Ciukhrai
Life Is Beautiful '79

Rene Clair
The Crazy Ray '22
Entr'acte '24
Italian Straw Hat '27
Under the Roofs of Paris '29
A Nous la Liberte '31
Le Million '31
Quatorze Juliet '32
The Ghost Goes West '36
I Married a Witch '42
Forever and a Day '43
And Then There Were None '45
Beauty and the Devil '50
Beauties of the Night '52
Les Grandes Manoeuvres '55

Bob Clampett
Bugs Bunny Superstar '75
Looney Looney Looney Bugs Bunny Movie '81

Barry Clark
Bimini Code '84

B.D. Clark
Galaxy of Terror '81

Bob (Benjamin) Clark
Children Shouldn't Play with Dead Things '72
Deathdream '72
Black Christmas '75
Murder by Decree '79
Tribute '80
Porky's '82
A Christmas Story '83
Porky's 2: The Next Day '83
Rhinestone '84
Turk 182! '85
From the Hip '86
Loose Cannons '90
My Summer Story '94

Bruce Clark
The Naked Angels '69
Ski Bum '75

Colbert Clark
Fighting with Kit Carson '33
Mystery Squadron '33
Whispering Shadow '33
Wolf Dog '33

Duane Clark
Shaking the Tree '92
Bitter Harvest '93

Greydon Clark
Bad Bunch '76
Black Shampoo '76
Hi-Riders '77
Satan's Cheerleaders '77
Angel's Brigade '79
The Return '80
Joy Sticks '83
Wacko '83
Final Justice '84
Skinheads: The Second Coming of Hate '88
The Uninvited '88
The Forbidden Dance '90
Dance Macabre '91
Killer Instinct '92

Russian Roulette '93

James B. Clark
A Dog of Flanders '59
Misty '61
Flipper '63
Island of the Blue Dolphins '64
And Now Miguel '66
My Side of the Mountain '69

Jim Clark
Think Dirty '70
Rentadick '72
Madhouse '74

Larry Clark
Kids '95

Lawrence Gordon Clark
Jamaica Inn '82
Romance on the Orient Express '89
Monkey Boy '90

Les Clark
Sleeping Beauty '59

Matt Clark
Da '88

Richard Clark
Dr. Hackenstein '88

Ron Clark
The Funny Farm '82

Warren Clark
Inside Edge '92

William Clark
The Goodbye Bird '93
Windrunner '94

Alan Clarke
Scum '79
Rita, Sue & Bob Too '87

James Kenelm Clarke
The House on Straw Hill '76
Funny Money '82
Going Undercover '88

Robert Clarke
Hideous Sun Demon '59

Shirley Clarke
The Connection '61

Stephen Clarkson
Death Goes to School '53

James Clavell
To Sir, with Love '67
The Last Valley '71

Bob Claver
Jaws of Satan '81

William Claxton
Fangs of the Wild '54

Jack Clayton
Room at the Top '59
The Innocents '61
The Pumpkin Eater '64
The Great Gatsby '74
Something Wicked This Way Comes '83
The Lonely Passion of Judith Hearne '87

John Clayton
Summerdog '78

Tom Clegg
McVicar '80
Children of the Full Moon '84
The Inside Man '84
Any Man's Death '90
A Casualty of War '90
Stroke of Midnight '90
Sharpe's Eagle '93
Sharpe's Rifles '93
Sharpe's Battle '94
Sharpe's Company '94
Sharpe's Enemy '94
Sharpe's Gold '94
Sharpe's Honour '94
Sharpe's Sword '94

John Clein
Keep Punching '39

Brian Clemens
Captain Kronos: Vampire Hunter '74

William Clemens
Nancy Drew, Reporter '39

Dick Clement
Catch Me a Spy '71
Bullshot '83
Water '85
Porridge '91

Rene Clement
The Walls of Malapaga '49
Forbidden Games '52
Gervaise '56
The Day and the Hour '63
Joy House '64
Is Paris Burning? '68
Rider on the Rain '70
The Deadly Trap '71
And Hope to Die '72
Wanted: Babysitter '75

Ron Clements
The Great Mouse Detective '86
The Little Mermaid '89
Aladdin '92

Max Cleven
Night Stalker '87

Graeme Clifford
The Boy Who Left Home to Find Out About the Shivers '81
Frances '82
Little Red Riding Hood '83
Burke & Wills '85
Gleaming the Cube '89
The Turn of the Screw '89
Deception '92
Past Tense '94

Elmer Clifton
Down to the Sea in Ships '22
Let 'er Go Gallegher '28
Assassin of Youth '35
Captured in Chinatown '35
Cyclone of the Saddle '35
Fighting Caballero '35
Custer's Last Stand '36
Roaring Speedboats '37
Law of the Texan '38
Dead or Alive '41
Frontier Law '43
Gangsters of the Frontier '44
Guns of the Law '44
Seven Doors to Death '44
Marked for Murder '45
The Judge '49
Streets of Sin '49
Youth Aflame '59

Paul E. Clinco
Death Magic '92

Eddie Cline
Cops/One Week '22
Three Ages '23
Hook, Line and Sinker '30
Dude Ranger '34
Peck's Bad Boy '34
Cowboy Millionaire '35
Hawaii Calls '38
Peck's Bad Boy with the Circus '38
The Bank Dick '40
My Little Chickadee '40
Never Give a Sucker an Even Break '41
The Villain Still Pursued Her '41
Private Buckaroo '42
Snuffy Smith, Yard Bird '42

Maurice Cloche
Monsieur Vincent '48

Art Clokey
Gumby: The Movie '95

Hans Peter Cloos
Germany in Autumn '78

Robert Clouse
Darker than Amber '70
Enter the Dragon '73
Black Belt Jones '74
The Ultimate Warrior '75
The Pack '77
The Amsterdam Kill '78
Game of Death '79
The Big Brawl '80
Force: Five '81
Deadly Eyes '82
Gymkata '85
China O'Brien '88
China O'Brien 2 '89
Ironheart '92

Henri-Georges Clouzot
Le Corbeau '43
Jenny Lamour '47
Manon '50
Diabolique '55
Wages of Fear '55

E.B. Clucher
They Call Me Trinity '72
Trinity is Still My Name '75
Crime Busters '78
Go for It '83
The Odd Squad '86

Rick Cluchey
The Cage '90

Harold Clurman
Deadline at Dawn '46

Craig Clyde
Little Heroes '91
The Legend of Wolf Mountain '92

Franklin Coates
Jesse James Under the Black Flag '21

Lewis (Luigi Cozzi) Coates
Star Crash '78
Alien Contamination '81
Hercules '83
Hercules 2 '85
Black Cat '90

David Cobham
Tales of the Klondike: Race for Number One '87
Woof! '90

Glenn Coburn
Bloodsuckers from Outer Space '83

Stacy Cochran
My New Gun '92
Boys '95

Jean Cocteau
The Blood of a Poet '30
Beauty and the Beast '46
The Eagle Has Two Heads '48
The Storm Within '48
Orpheus '49
The Testament of Orpheus '59

Fred Coe
A Thousand Clowns '65

Wayne Coe
Grim Prairie Tales '89

Joel Coen
Blood Simple '85
Raising Arizona '87
Miller's Crossing '90
Barton Fink '91
The Hudsucker Proxy '93
Fargo '96

Nevill Coghill
Doctor Faustus '68

Dan Cohen
Madman '79

David M. Cohen
Hollywood Zap '86

Eli Cohen
The Quarrel '93
The Soft Kill '94

Gary P. Cohen
Video Violence '87
Video Violence Part 2...The Exploitation! '87

Gerry Cohen
It's a Bundyful Life '92

Herman Cohen
Crocodile '81

Howard R. Cohen
Saturday the 14th '81
Space Raiders '83
Saturday the 14th Strikes Back '88
Time Trackers '88
Deathstalker 4: Match of Titans '92

Joel Cohen
Frankenstein Sings...The Movie '95

Larry Cohen
Housewife '72
Black Caesar '73
Hell Up in Harlem '73
It's Alive '74
God Told Me To '76
The Private Files of J. Edgar Hoover '77
It's Alive 2: It Lives Again '78
Q (The Winged Serpent) '82
Perfect Strangers '84
Special Effects '85
The Stuff '85
Deadly Illusion '87
It's Alive 3: Island of the Alive '87
Return to Salem's Lot '87
Wicked Stepmother '89
The Ambulance '90
As Good as Dead '95
Original Gangstas '96

Martin B. Cohen
Rebel Rousers '69

Rob Cohen
A Small Circle of Friends '80
Scandalous '84
Dragon: The Bruce Lee Story '93
Dragonheart '96

S.E. Cohen
Martial Law '90

Thomas A. Cohen
Massive Retaliation '85

Randolph Cohlan
Night Shadow '90

Michael Cohn
Interceptor '92
When the Bough Breaks '93

Cyril Coke
Pride and Prejudice '85

Harley Cokliss
Warlords of the 21st Century '82
Black Moon Rising '86
Malone '87
Dream Demon '88

Marcus Cole
From the Mixed-Up Files of Mrs. Basil E. Frankweiler '95

Sidney Cole
Train of Events '49

Tristan De Vere Cole
The Dive '89

William Cole
Unveiled '94

John David Coles
Signs of Life '89
Rising Son '90
The Good Fight '92

Duilio Coletti
Lure of the Sila '49

Giuseppe Colizzi
Ace High '68
Boot Hill '69
All the Way, Boys '73

Richard A. Colla
Fuzz '72
Battlestar Galactica '78
Olly Olly Oxen Free '78
Don't Look Back: The Story of Leroy "Satchel" Paige '81
Blind Witness '89
Naked Lie '89
The Prize Pulitzer '89

Jeanne Collachia
Odd Birds '85

Cyril Collard
Les Nuits Fauves '92

Robert Collector
Red Heat '85

James F. Collier
The Hiding Place '75
Joni '79
A Cry from the Mountain '85
Beyond the Next Mountain '87
China Cry '91

Bob Collins
The Bronx Executioner '86

Boon Collins
Abducted '86
Spirit of the Eagle '90
Abducted 2: The Reunion '94

Edward Collins
Evil Town '87

Gunther Collins
Jud '71

Lewis D. Collins
Gun Law '33
Trouble Busters '33
Brand of Hate '34
The Man from Hell '34
Sing Sing Nights '35
The Adventures of the Flying Cadets '44
Master Key '44
Mystery of the Riverboat '44
Lost City of the Jungle '45
Heading for Heaven '47
Killer Dill '47
Jungle Goddess '49
The Fighting Redhead '50

Max Allan Collins
Mommy '95

Robert Collins
The Life and Assassination of the Kingfish '76
Gideon's Trumpet '80
Our Family Business '81
Mafia Princess '86
J. Edgar Hoover '87

Peter Collinson
The Italian Job '69
Fright '71
Dressed for Death '74
Spiral Staircase '75
Ten Little Indians '75
Sell Out '76
Tomorrow Never Comes '77
African Rage '78
The House on Garibaldi Street '79
Earthling '80

Walter Colmes
Identity Unknown '45
The Woman Who Came Back '45
Accomplice '46

Fernando Colombo
Skyline '84

Carl Colpaert
In the Aftermath: Angels Never Sleep '87
Delusion '91
The Crew '95

Chris Columbus
Adventures in Babysitting '87
Heartbreak Hotel '88
Home Alone '90
Only the Lonely '91
Home Alone 2: Lost in New York '92
Mrs. Doubtfire '93
Nine Months '95

Luigi Comencini
Heidi '52
Till Marriage Do Us Part '74
Misunderstood '87

Lance Comfort
The Courageous Mr. Penn '41
Hotel Reserve '44
Great Day '46
The Great Armored Car Swindle '64

Don Como
Aliens from Spaceship Earth '77
Unknown Powers '80

J.C. Compton
Buckeye and Blue '87

Richard Compton
Macon County Line '74
Return to Macon County '75
Maniac '77
Deadman's Curve '78
Wild Times '79
Angels Die Hard '84
Super Force '90

Jeff Conaway
Bikini Summer 2 '92

Bill Condon
Sister, Sister '87
Dead in the Water '91
Murder 101 '91
White Lie '91
Candyman 2: Farewell to the Flesh '94

John Coney
Sun Ra & His Intergalactic Solar Arkestra: Space is the Place '74

Stijn Coninx
Daens '92

Nicole Conn
Claire of the Moon '92

W. Merle Connell
Test Tube Babies '48
The Devil's Sleep '51

Marc Connelly
Green Pastures '36

Carey Connor
Fall from Innocence '88

Kevin Connor
From Beyond the Grave '73
The Land That Time Forgot '75
At the Earth's Core '76
Choice of Weapons '76
The People That Time Forgot '77
Motel Hell '80
Goliath Awaits '81
House Where Evil Dwells '82
The Lion of Africa '87
Great Expectations '89
The Hollywood Detective '89
Iran: Days of Crisis '91
Sunset Grill '92
Diana: Her True Story '93
The Old Curiosity Shop '94

Claude Conrad
Birthday Boy '85

Mikel Conrad
The Flying Saucer '50

Patrick Conrad
Mascara '87

Robert Conrad
Crossfire '67
Bandits '73

William Conrad
Side Show '84

Richard Conte
Operation Cross Eagles '69

Therese Conte
Chasing Dreams '81

James A. Contner
Hitler's Daughter '90
The Return of Eliot Ness '91
The Ten Million Dollar Getaway '91
The Cover Girl Murders '93

Bert Convy
Weekend Warriors '86

Gary Conway
Sara Dane '81

Jack Conway
Our Modern Maidens '29
The Unholy Three '30
Red Headed Woman '32
The Girl from Missouri '34
Tarzan and His Mate '34
Viva Villa! '34
A Tale of Two Cities '35
Libeled Lady '36
Saratoga '37
Too Hot to Handle '38
Let Freedom Ring '39
Boom Town '40
Honky Tonk '41
Love Crazy '41
Dragon Seed '44
The Hucksters '47
Julia Misbehaves '48

James L. Conway
The Incredible Rocky Mountain Race '77
The Fall of the House of Usher '80
Hangar 18 '80
Donner Pass: The Road to Survival '84
The Last of the Mohicans '85

Rif Coogan
The Invisible Maniac '90
Psycho Cop 2 '94

Bruce Cook, Jr.
Husbands, Wives, Money, and Murder '86
Nightwish '89

Fielder Cook
Patterns '56
A Big Hand for the Little Lady '66
Homecoming: A Christmas Story '71
The Hideaways '73
Miles to Go before I Sleep '74
Judge Horton and the Scottsboro Boys '76
Love Affair: The Eleanor & Lou Gehrig Story '77
I Know Why the Caged Bird Sings '79
Seize the Day '86

Phillip Cook
Star Quest '89
Invader '91

Troy Cook
The Takeover '94

Alan Cooke
Nadia '84

William Cooke
Freakshow '95

Tony Cookson
And You Thought Your Parents Were Weird! '91

Martha Coolidge
Valley Girl '83
Joy of Sex '84
Real Genius '85
Plain Clothes '88
Bare Essentials '91
Rambling Rose '91
Crazy in Love '92
Lost in Yonkers '93
Angie '94
Three Wishes '95

Buddy Cooper
The Mutilator '85

George Cooper
The Shadow '36

Jackie Cooper
Rainbow '78
Marathon '80
Rodeo Girl '80
White Mama '80
Leave 'Em Laughing '81
Rosie: The Rosemary Clooney Story '82
Sex and the Single Parent '82
Izzy & Moe '85
The Night They Saved Christmas '87

Peter H. Cooper
Ordinary Heroes '85

Stuart Cooper
Disappearance '81
The Long, Hot Summer '86
Payoff '91
Dancing with Danger '93
Rubdown '93
Bitter Vengeance '94

Christopher Coppola
Dracula's Widow '88
Deadfall '93

Francis Ford Coppola
Tonight for Sure '61
The Bellboy and the Playgirls '62
Battle Beyond the Sun '63
Dementia 13 '63
You're a Big Boy Now '66
Finian's Rainbow '68
The Rain People '69
The Godfather '72
The Conversation '74
The Godfather, Part 2 '74
Apocalypse Now '79
The Godfather 1902-1959: The Complete Epic '81
One from the Heart '82
The Outsiders '83
Rumble Fish '83
The Cotton Club '84
Rip van Winkle '85
Peggy Sue Got Married '86
Gardens of Stone '87
Tucker: The Man and His Dream '88
New York Stories '89
The Godfather, Part 3 '90
Bram Stoker's Dracula '92
Jack '96

Joe Coppoletta
Death Match '94

Frank Coraci
Murdered Innocence '94

Gregory Corarito
Wanda, The Sadistic Hypnotist '67
Delinquent School Girls '84

Gerard Corbiau
The Music Teacher '88
Farinelli '94

Bruno Corbucci
Cop in Blue Jeans '78
Miami Supercops '85
Aladdin '86

Sergio Corbucci
Minnesota Clay '65
Hellbenders '67
Navajo Joe '67
Django '68
Sonny and Jed '73
Odds and Evens '78
The Con Artists '80
Super Fuzz '81

Bill Corcoran
Sherlock Holmes and the Incident at Victoria Falls '91
Portraits of a Killer '95

Nick Corea
Archer: The Fugitive from the Empire '81
The Incredible Hulk Returns '88

Roger Corman
Apache Woman '55
Day the World Ended '55
Swamp Women '55
The Gunslinger '56
It Conquered the World '56
She Gods of Shark Reef '56
Carnival Rock '57
Rock All Night '57
Sorority Girl '57
The Undead '57
I, Mobster '58
Machine Gun Kelly '58
Teenage Caveman '58
A Bucket of Blood '59
The Wasp Woman '59
Atlas '60
Creature from the Haunted Sea '60
The Fall of the House of Usher '60
Little Shop of Horrors '60
The Last Woman on Earth '61
The Pit and the Pendulum '61
Shame '61
Premature Burial '62
Tales of Terror '62
Tower of London '62
The Haunted Palace '63
The Raven '63
The Terror '63
X: The Man with X-Ray Eyes '63
Tomb of Ligeia '64
Masque of the Red Death '65
Masque of the Red Death/ Premature Burial '65
The Wild Angels '66
The St. Valentine's Day Massacre '67
The Trip '67
Bloody Mama '70
Gas-s-s-s! '70
Frankenstein Unbound '90
Little Miss Millions '93

Alain Corneau
Choice of Arms '83
Fort Saganne '84
Tous les Matins du Monde '92

Henry Cornelius
Passport to Pimlico '49
Genevieve '53
I Am a Camera '55

John Cornell
Crocodile Dundee 2 '88
Almost an Angel '90

Hubert Cornfield
Plunder Road '57
Angel Baby '61
Pressure Point '62
The Night of the Following Day '69

Stephen Cornwell
Killing Streets '91
Philadelphia Experiment 2 '93
Marshal Law '96

Alfonso Corona
Deathstalker 3 '89

Eugene Corr
Desert Bloom '86

Charles Correll
Deadly Desire '91
In the Deep Woods '91
Writer's Block '91

Richard Correll
Ski Patrol '89

Michael Corrente
Federal Hill '94

Lloyd Corrigan
Daughter of the Dragon '31
Dancing Pirate '36

Ian Corson
Malicious '95

Bud Cort
Ted & Venus '93

Michael Cort
Alien Women '69

Frederic Corte
Creature of the Walking Dead '60

Don A. Coscarelli
Phantasm '79
Beastmaster '82
Phantasm II '88
Survival Quest '89
Phantasm III: Lord of the Dead '94

George P. Cosmatos
Restless '72
Massacre in Rome '73
The Cassandra Crossing '76
Escape to Athena '79
Of Unknown Origin '83
Rambo: First Blood, Part 2 '85
Cobra '86
Leviathan '89
Tombstone '93

Mario Costa
Gladiator of Rome '63
Rough Justice '87

Mary Costa
Pirate Warrior '64

Constantin Costa-Gavras
Z '69
State of Siege '73
Missing '82
Hanna K. '83
Betrayed '88
Music Box '89

Kevin Costner
Dances with Wolves '90

Peter Cotes
The Young and the Guilty '58

Manny Coto
Playroom '90
Cover-Up '91
Dr. Giggles '92

Vittorio Cottafavi
Goliath and the Dragon '61
Hercules and the Captive Women '63

John Cotter
Mountain Family Robinson '79

Jack Couffer
Nikki, the Wild Dog of the North '61
Ring of Bright Water '69
Living Free '72

Ian Coughlan
Alison's Birthday '79

Bill Couturie
Dear America: Letters Home from Vietnam '88
Ed '96

Hil Covington
Adventures in Spying '92

Noel Coward
In Which We Serve '43

William J. Cowen
Oliver Twist '33

Alex Cox
Repo Man '83
Sid & Nancy '86
Straight to Hell '87
Walker '87

Mitchell Cox
Rule #3 '93

Neil Cox
Roommate '84
Konrad '90s
Once Upon a Midnight Scary '90

Paul Cox
Kostas '79
Lonely Hearts '82
Man of Flowers '84
My First Wife '84
Cactus '86
Vincent: The Life and Death of Vincent van Gogh '87
A Woman's Tale '92

Arthur Crabtree
Dear Murderer '47
Fiend Without a Face '58

William James Craft
Dames Ahoy '30

William Crain
Blacula '72
Dr. Black, Mr. Hyde '76
Kid from Not-So-Big '78
Midnight Fear '90

Massey Cramer
Demon Hunter '88

Ross Cramer
Riding High '78

Barry Crane
Charlotte Forten's Mission: Experiment in Freedom '85

Kenneth Crane
Monster from Green Hell '58
When Hell Broke Loose '58
The Manster '59

Jay Craven
Where the Rivers Flow North '94

Wes Craven
Last House on the Left '72
The Hills Have Eyes '77
Summer of Fear '78
Deadly Blessing '81
Swamp Thing '82
The Hills Have Eyes, Part 2 '84
Invitation to Hell '84
A Nightmare on Elm Street '84
Deadly Friend '86
The Serpent and the Rainbow '87
Shocker '89
The People Under the Stairs '91
Wes Craven's New Nightmare '94
Vampire in Brooklyn '95

Wayne Crawford
Crime Lords '91
American Cop '94

Francis Creighton
The Malibu Beach Vampires '91

Lol Creme
The Lunatic '92

Kevin G. Cremin
Siringo '94

Richard Crenna
Better Late Than Never '79

Alfredo B. Crevenna
The New Invisible Man '58

Charles Crichton
Dead of Night '45
Hue and Cry '47
Against the Wind '48
Train of Events '49
The Lavender Hill Mob '51
The Battle of the Sexes '60
A Fish Called Wanda '88

Michael Crichton
Pursuit '72
Westworld '73
Coma '78
The Great Train Robbery '79
Looker '81
Runaway '84
Physical Evidence '89

Donald Crisp
The Navigator '24
Stand and Deliver '28
Sunny Side Up '28

Armando Crispino
Commandos '73
Autopsy '78

George Cristallini
You're Jinxed, Friend, You've Met Sacramento '70

Donald Crombie
The Irishman '78
Caddie '81
Killing of Angel Street '81
Kitty and the Bagman '82

John Cromwell
Dance of Life '29
Tom Sawyer '30
Vice Squad '31
Ann Vickers '33
Of Human Bondage '34
Spitfire '34
I Dream Too Much '35
Little Lord Fauntleroy '36
Prisoner of Zenda '37
Algiers '38
In Name Only '39
Made for Each Other '39
Abe Lincoln in Illinois '40
So Ends Our Night '41
Son of Fury '42
Since You Went Away '44
The Enchanted Cottage '45
Anna and the King of Siam '46
Dead Reckoning '47
The Racket '51
The Goddess '58

George Crone
Get That Girl '32

David Cronenberg
They Came from Within '75
Rabid '77
Fast Company '78
The Brood '79
Scanners '81
Dead Zone '83
Videodrome '83
The Fly '86
Dead Ringers '88
Naked Lunch '91
M. Butterfly '93
Crash '95

Alan Crosland
Don Juan '26
The Beloved Rogue '27
The Jazz Singer '27

William Forest Crouch
Reet, Petite and Gone '47

Avery Crounse
Eyes of Fire '84
The Invisible Kid '88

Dean Crow
Backwoods '87

Cameron Crowe
Say Anything '89
Singles '92

Christopher Crowe
Off Limits '87
Whispers in the Dark '92

Tom Cruise
Fallen Angels 1 '93

James Cruze
Hawthorne of the USA '19
The Roaring Road '19
The Covered Wagon '23
The Pony Express '25
Old Ironsides '26
The Great Gabbo '29
I Cover the Waterfront '33
Mr. Skitch '33
The Wrong Road '37

Billy Crystal
Mr. Saturday Night '92
Forget Paris '95

Alfonso Cuaron
Fallen Angels 1 '93
A Little Princess '95

George Cukor
A Bill of Divorcement '32
What Price Hollywood? '32
Dinner at Eight '33
Little Women '33
David Copperfield '35
Sylvia Scarlett '35
Camille '36
Romeo and Juliet '36
Holiday '38
The Women '39
The Philadelphia Story '40
Susan and God '40
Two-Faced Woman '41
A Woman's Face '41
Keeper of the Flame '42
Gaslight '44
A Double Life '47
Adam's Rib '50
Born Yesterday '50
A Life of Her Own '50
Pat and Mike '52
It Should Happen to You '54
A Star is Born '54
Bhowani Junction '56
Les Girls '57
Heller in Pink Tights '60
Let's Make Love '60
Song Without End '60
My Fair Lady '64
Justine '69
Travels with My Aunt '72
Love Among the Ruins '75
Rich and Famous '81

Mark Cullingham
Cinderella '84
Gryphon '88
Dead on the Money '91

Bill Cummings
Bad Attitude '93

Howard Cummings
Courtship '87

Irving Cummings
Flesh and Blood '22
Broken Hearts of Broadway '23
Curly Top '35
The Poor Little Rich Girl '36
Vogues of 1938 '37
Just Around the Corner '38
Little Miss Broadway '38
Everything Happens at Night '39
The Story of Alexander Graham Bell '39
Down Argentine Way '40
Louisiana Purchase '41
Springtime in the Rockies '42
Sweet Rosie O'Grady '43
The Dolly Sisters '45
Double Dynamite '51

James Cummins
The Bone Yard '90

Rusty Cundieff
Fear of a Black Hat '94
Tales from the Hood '95

Richard Cunha
Frankenstein's Daughter '58
Giant from the Unknown '58
She Demons '58
Missile to the Moon '59

Curtis Cunningham
Mata Hari '85

Sean S. Cunningham
Manny's Orphans '78
Friday the 13th '80
A Stranger is Watching '82
Spring Break '83
The New Kids '85
Deepstar Six '89

Frederick Curiel
Genie of Darkness '60
The Monster Demolisher '60
Neutron and the Black Mask '61
Neutron vs. the Amazing Dr. Caronte '61
Neutron vs. the Death Robots '62

William Curran
Love, Cheat & Steal '93

Anthony Currie
The Pink Chiquitas '86

Dan Curtis
House of Dark Shadows '70
Night of Dark Shadows '71
Dracula '73
Melvin Purvis: G-Man '74
The Turn of the Screw '74
Kansas City Massacre '75
Trilogy of Terror '75
Burnt Offerings '76
Curse of the Black Widow '77
Dead of Night '77
When Every Day was the Fourth of July '78
Express to Terror '79
The Last Ride of the Dalton Gang '79
Mrs. R's Daughter '79
The Long Days of Summer '80
The Winds of War '83
War & Remembrance, Part 1 '88
War & Remembrance, Part 3 '88
War & Remembrance, Part 4 '88
War & Remembrance, Part 5 '88
War & Remembrance, Part 6 '88
War & Remembrance, Part 7 '88
War & Remembrance, Part 2 '89
War & Remembrance: The Final Chapter, Part 8 '89
War & Remembrance: The Final Chapter, Part 9 '89
War & Remembrance: The Final Chapter, Part 10 '89
War & Remembrance: The Final Chapter, Part 11 '89
War & Remembrance: The Final Chapter, Part 12 '89
Dark Shadows: Episode 1 '91
Intruders '92
Me and the Kid '93

Douglas Curtis
The Campus Corpse '77
The Sleeping Car '90

Jack Curtis
The Flesh Eaters '64

Michael Curtiz
The Cabin in the Cotton '32
Doctor X '32
The Strange Love of Molly Louvain '32
Female '33
The Kennel Murder Case '33
Mystery of the Wax Museum '33
Black Fury '35
Captain Blood '35
The Charge of the Light Brigade '36
Kid Galahad '37
The Adventures of Robin Hood '38
Angels with Dirty Faces '38
Four Daughters '38
Dodge City '39
The Private Lives of Elizabeth & Essex '39
Santa Fe Trail '40
The Sea Hawk '40
Virginia City '40
Dive Bomber '41
The Sea Wolf '41
Captains of the Clouds '42
Casablanca '42
Yankee Doodle Dandy '42
This Is the Army '43
Passage to Marseilles '44
Mildred Pierce '45
Night and Day '46
Life with Father '47
Romance on the High Seas '48
Flamingo Road '49
My Dream Is Yours '49
Young Man with a Horn '50
I'll See You in My Dreams '51
Jim Thorpe: All American '51
Trouble Along the Way '53
The Egyptian '54
White Christmas '54
We're No Angels '55
King Creole '58
Proud Rebel '58
The Adventures of Huckleberry Finn '60
Breath of Scandal '60
The Comancheros '61

Ralph Cushman
Secret File of Hollywood '62

Michael Custance
The Little Match Girl '87

Rudolph Cusumano
Wild Ones on Wheels '62

Julie Cypher
Teresa's Tattoo '94

Catherine Cyran
In the Heat of Passion 2: Unfaithful '94
Hostile Intentions '95

Paul Czinner
Catherine the Great '34
As You Like It '36
Dreaming Lips '37

Renee Daalder
Massacre at Central High '76

Morton DaCosta
Auntie Mame '58
The Music Man '62

Dimis Dadiras
The Mediterranean in Flames '72

John Dahl
Kill Me Again '89
Red Rock West '93
The Last Seduction '94
Unforgettable '96

Bob Dahlin
Monster in the Closet '86

Reno Dakota
American Fabulous '92

Tom Daley
The Outing '87

Salvador Dali
Un Chien Andalou '28

Massimo Dallamano
A Black Veil for Lisa '68
Dorian Gray '70
Super Bitch '89

Neville D'Almedia
Lady on the Bus '78

Robert Dalva
The Black Stallion Returns '83

William Robert Daly
Uncle Tom's Cabin '14

Joe D'Amato
Buried Alive '81
Grim Reaper '81
Passion '92

Damiano Damiani
Empty Canvas '64
The Witch '66
A Bullet for the General '68
Confessions of a Police Captain '72
The Warning '80
Amityville 2: The Possession '82
The Inquiry '87

Charles Damic
Bomb at 10:10 '67

Mel Damski
Long Journey Back '78
American Dream '81
For Ladies Only '81
Legend of Walks Far Woman '82
Yellowbeard '83
Badge of the Assassin '85
Mischief '85
A Winner Never Quits '86
Murder by the Book '87
A Connecticut Yankee in King Arthur's Court '89
Happy Together '89
Wildcard '92

Anthony D'Andrea
Thrillkill '84

Lawrence Dane
Heavenly Bodies '84

Rod Daniel
Teen Wolf '85
Like Father, Like Son '87
K-9 '89
The Super '91
Beethoven's 2nd '93

Georgi Daniela
Autumn Marathon '79

Godfrey Daniels
Cassie '87

Harold Daniels
Sword of Venus '53
Poor White Trash '57
Terror in the Haunted House '58
House of the Black Death '65

Marc Daniels
Planet Earth '74
Vengeance '89

Tage Danielsson
The Adventures of Picasso '80

Claude D'Anna
Salome '85

Danniel Danniel
Egg '88

Herbert Danska
Sweet Love, Bitter '67

Joe Dante
Hollywood Boulevard '76
Piranha '78
The Howling '81
Twilight Zone: The Movie '83
Gremlins '84
Explorers '85
Amazon Women on the Moon '87
Innerspace '87
The 'Burbs '89
Gremlins 2: The New Batch '90
Matinee '92
Picture Windows '95

Maria Dante
The Dangerous '95

Ray Danton
Crypt of the Living Dead '73
Psychic Killer '75
Tales of the Unexpected '91

Phil D'Antoni
The Seven-Ups '73

Richard Danus
No Place to Hide '93

Frank Darabont
Buried Alive '90
The Shawshank Redemption '94

Jonathan Darby
The Enemy Within '94

Joan Darling
First Love '77
Willa '79
Check Is in the Mail '85
Hiroshima Maiden '88

David Darlow
Tailspin: Behind the Korean Airline Tragedy '89

Harry D'Abbadie D'Arrast
Topaze '33

Mark D'Aruia
Smoke '93

Julie Dash
Daughters of the Dust '91

Sean Dash
Breakaway '95

Jules Dassin
Reunion in France '42
The Canterville Ghost '44
The Naked City '48
Night and the City '50
Rififi '54
Where the Hot Wind Blows '59
Never on Sunday '60
Phaedra '61
Topkapi '64
A Dream of Passion '78
Circle of Two '80

Tony Zarin Dast
Cat in the Cage '68

Herschel Daugherty
The Light in the Forest '58

Darrell Davenport
Shadow Force '92

Harry Davenport
Tillie Wakes Up '17

Harry Bromley Davenport
Xtro '83
Xtro 2: The Second Encounter '91
Xtro 3: Watch the Skies '95

Delmer Daves
Destination Tokyo '43
Hollywood Canteen '44
Dark Passage '47
The Red House '47
Task Force '49
Broken Arrow '50
Never Let Me Go '53
Treasure of the Golden Condor '53
Demetrius and the Gladiators '54
Drum Beat '54
Jubal '56
3:10 to Yuma '57
The Badlanders '58
Cowboy '58
Kings Go Forth '58
The Hanging Tree '59
A Summer Place '59
Parrish '61
Rome Adventure '62
Spencer's Mountain '63

Allan David
The Magic Fountain '61

Charles David
Lady On a Train '45

Hugh David
Jude the Obscure '71

Pierce David
Scanner Cop '94
Serial Killer '95

Boaz Davidson
Hospital Massacre '81
Last American Virgin '82
Dutch Treat '86
Going Bananas '88
Salsa '88
American Cyborg: Steel Warrior '94
Solar Force '94
Outside the Law '95

Gordon Davidson
Trial of the Catonsville Nine '72
The Trial of Lee Harvey Oswald '77

John Davidson
The Hanging Woman '72

Martin Davidson
The Lords of Flatbush '74
Hero at Large '80
Eddie and the Cruisers '83
Long Gone '87
The Heart of Dixie '89
Hard Promises '92
Follow the River '95

Howard Davies
The Secret Rapture '94

John Davies
Kim '84
A Married Man '84

Terence Davies
Distant Voices, Still Lives '88
The Long Day Closes '92
The Neon Bible '95

Valentine Davies
The Benny Goodman Story '55

Andrew Davis
The Final Terror '83
Code of Silence '85
Above the Law '88
The Package '89
Under Siege '92
The Fugitive '93
Chain Reaction '96

Andy Davis
Steal Big, Steal Little '95

Beau Davis
Laser Mission '90

B.J. Davis
White Ghost '88

Charles Davis
Die Watching '93

Desmond Davis
Nice Girl Like Me '69
Clash of the Titans '81
The Sign of Four '83
Ordeal by Innocence '84

Eddie Davis
Color Me Dead '69

Gary Davis
Conflict of Interest '92

Julie Davis
Witchcraft 6: The Devil's Mistress '94

Michael Paul Davis
Beanstalk '94

Ossie Davis
Cotton Comes to Harlem '70
Gordon's War '73

Roy Davis
Surabaya Conspiracy '75

Tamra Davis
Guncrazy '92
CB4: The Movie '93
Billy Madison '94

Norman Dawn
Tundra '36
Orphans of the North '40
Two Lost Worlds '50

Vincent Dawn
Rats '83
Caged Women '84
Strike Commando '87

Anthony (Antonio Margheriti) Dawson
Assignment Outer Space '61
Battle of the Worlds '61
Castle of Blood '64
Hercules, Prisoner of Evil '64
Planet on the Prowl '65
The Virgin of Nuremberg '65
Wild, Wild Planet '65
Lightning Bolt '67
Web of the Spider '70
Seven Deaths in the Cat's Eye '72
Mr. Superinvisible '73
Take a Hard Ride '75
The Stranger and the Gunfighter '76
Death Rage '77
The Rip Off '78
Killer Fish '79
The Last Hunter '80
The Squeeze '80
Ark of the Sun God '82
Hunters of the Golden Cobra '82
Invasion of the Flesh Hunters '82
Tornado '83
Yor, the Hunter from the Future '83
Codename: Wildgeese '84
Jungle Raiders '85
Tiger Joe '85
Indio '90

Ernest Day
Green Ice '81
Waltz Across Texas '83

Robert Day
Corridors of Blood '58
The Haunted Strangler '58
First Man into Space '59
Two-Way Stretch '60
Death Stalk '74
The Grass is Always Greener Over the Septic Tank '78
Initiation of Sarah '78
Murder by Natural Causes '79
The Man with Bogart's Face '80
Walking Through the Fire '80
Your Place or Mine '83
Lady from Yesterday '85
The Quick and the Dead '87

Lyman Dayton
Baker's Hawk '76
Dream Machine '91

Jaime de Arminan
The Nest '80

Jacques de Baroncelli
The French Way '40

Jan De Bont
Speed '94
Twister '96

Philippe de Broca
Cartouche '62
That Man from Rio '64
The King of Hearts '66
Oldest Profession '67
Dear Detective '77
Le Cavaleur '78
Jupiter's Thigh '81
Louisiana '87

Pierre de Celles
Pound Puppies and the Legend of Big Paw '88

Ennio de Concini
Hitler: The Last Ten Days '73

Fred de Cordova
Bedtime for Bonzo '51
Frankie and Johnny '65
I'll Take Sweden '65

Paul de Cruccio
Desert Snow '89

Frank de Felitta
The Two Worlds of Jenny Logan '79
Dark Night of the Scarecrow '81
Scissors '91

Eduardo de Filippo
Seven Deadly Sins '53
Shoot Loud, Louder, I Don't Understand! '66

Michael de Gaetano
UFO: Target Earth '74
The Haunted '79

Rolf de Heer
Encounter at Raven's Gate '88
Bad Boy Bubby '93

Ate De Jong
A Flight of Rainbirds '81
Drop Dead Fred '91
Highway to Hell '92

Paula de Koenigsberg
Rate It X '86

Hubert de la Bouillerie
The Right to Remain Silent '95

Eloy De La Iglesia
El Diputado '78

Jose Antonio De La Loma
The Barcelona Kill '77
Street Warriors '87
Street Warriors, Part 2 '87

Robert De Lacy
Pardon My Gun '30

Charles De Latour
The Limping Man '53
Impulse '55

Gerardo (Gerry) De Leon
Terror Is a Man '59
The Vampire People '66
Brides of the Beast '68
Mad Doctor of Blood Island '69

Marcus De Leon
Kiss Me a Killer '91

Paul de Lussanet
Dear Boys '80
Mysteries '84

Alberto De Martino
Secret Agent 00 '67
Dirty Heroes '71
New Mafia Boss '72
Scenes from a Murder '72
The Tempter '74
The Chosen '77
The Puma Man '80
Bloodlink '86

Pierre De Moro
Savannah Smiles '82
Hellhole '85

Robert De Niro
A Bronx Tale '93

Oswald De Oliveira
Amazon Jail '85

Armando de Ossorio
Fangs of the Living Dead '68
Night of the Sorcerers '70
Tombs of the Blind Dead '72
When the Screaming Stops '73
Horror of the Zombies '74
Night of the Death Cult '75
People Who Own the Dark '75
Return of the Evil Dead '75

Frank De Palma
Private War '90

Guiseppe de Santis
Bitter Rice '49

Vittorio de Seta
Bandits of Orgosolo '61

Vittorio De Sica
Teresa Venerdi '41
The Children Are Watching Us '44
Shoeshine '47
The Bicycle Thief '48
Miracle in Milan '51
The Gold of Naples '54
Indiscretion of an American Wife '54
Umberto D '55
It Happened in the Park '56
The Roof '56
Two Women '61
Boccaccio '70 '62
Marriage Italian Style '64
Yesterday, Today and Tomorrow '64
After the Fox '66
Woman Times Seven '67
The Garden of the Finzi-Continis '71

Tom De Simone
Terror in the Jungle '68
Chatterbox '76
Hell Night '81
The Concrete Jungle '82
Reform School Girls '86
Angel 3: The Final Chapter '88

Steven E. de Souza
Street Fighter '94

Andre de Toth
Dark Waters '44
Ramrod '47
Pitfall '48
Man in the Saddle '51
Last of the Comanches '52
Springfield Rifle '52
House of Wax '53
The Stranger Wore a Gun '53
The Indian Fighter '55
The Mongols '60
Morgan the Pirate '60

Ralph De Vito
Family Enforcer '76

Elmo De Witt
Enemy Unseen '91

Basil Dean
Lorna Doone '34
21 Days '37

Charles Deane
Blonde Blackmailer '58

William Dear
Timerider '83
Harry and the Hendersons '87
If Looks Could Kill '91
Angels in the Outfield '94

Basil Dearden
Dead of Night '45
Captive Heart '47
Frieda '47
The Blue Lamp '49
Train of Events '49
The Smallest Show on Earth '57
Sapphire '59
The League of Gentlemen '60
Victim '62
Khartoum '66
The Assassination Bureau '69
The Man Who Haunted Himself '70
The Persuaders '71
Mission: Monte Carlo '75

James Dearden
Cold Room '84
Pascali's Island '88
A Kiss Before Dying '91

Frank Deasy
The Courier '88

John DeBello
Attack of the Killer Tomatoes '77
Happy Hour '87
Return of the Killer Tomatoes! '88
Killer Tomatoes Strike Back '90
Killer Tomatoes Eat France '91

Gianfranco DeBosio
Moses '76

Tom DeCerchio
Celtic Pride '96

Henri Decoin
License to Kill '64

David DeCoteau
Creepozoids '87
Nightmare Sisters '87
Sorority Babes in the Slimeball Bowl-A-Rama '87
Dr. Alien '88
Puppet Master 3: Toulon's Revenge '90

Miles Deem
Jungle Master '56

Allessandro DeGaetano
Bloodbath in Psycho Town '89
Project Metalbeast: DNA Overload '94

Andre Degas
American Autobahn '84

Joseph DeGrasse
The Scarlet Car '17

Philip DeGuere
Dr. Strange '78
Misfits of Science '85

Jamil Dehlavi
Born of Fire '87

Mark Deimel
Perfect Match '88

Edward Dein
Shack Out on 101 '55
The Leech Woman '59

Donna Deitch
Desert Hearts '86
The Women of Brewster Place '89
Prison Stories: Women on the Inside '91

Steve DeJarnatt
Cherry 2000 '88
Miracle Mile '89

Fred Dekker
Night of the Creeps '86
The Monster Squad '87
RoboCop 3 '91

Jack Del
The Committee '68
A Session with the Committee '69

Peter Del Monte
Invitation au Voyage '82
Julia and Julia '87

Deborah Del Prete
Simple Justice '89

Roy Del Ruth
Blonde Crazy '31
The Maltese Falcon '31
Blessed Event '32
Bureau of Missing Persons '33
Employees' Entrance '33
Lady Killer '33
Kid Millions '34
Broadway Melody of 1936 '35
Born to Dance '36
Broadway Melody of 1938 '37
On the Avenue '37
Happy Landing '38
My Lucky Star '38
The Chocolate Soldier '41
Topper Returns '41
DuBarry Was a Lady '43
Broadway Rhythm '44
Babe Ruth Story '48
The West Point Story '50
On Moonlight Bay '51

Guillermo del Toro
Cronos '94

Jean Delannoy
Eternal Return '43
La Symphonie Pastorale '46
Love and the Frenchwoman '60
This Special Friendship '67
Imperial Venus '71
Bernadette '90

Leslie Delano
Deadly Lessons '94

Bill D'Elia
The Feud '90

Francis Delia
Freeway '88

Bert Deling
Dead Easy '82

Jeffrey Dell
Carlton Browne of the F.O. '59

Jeffrey Delman
Deadtime Stories '86

Nathalie Delon
Sweet Lies '88

Robert Deltano
Gun Girls '56

Rudy DeLuca
Transylvania 6-5000 '85

Dom DeLuise
Hot Stuff '80

Michael DeLuise
Almost Pregnant '91

Richard Dembo
Dangerous Moves '84

Eames Demetrios
Mind Trap '91

Tulio Demicheli
Son of Captain Blood '62
Dracula vs. Frankenstein '69

Jacques Dorfman
Shadow of the Wolf '92

Robert Dornhelm
The Children of Theatre Street '77
Echo Park '86
Cold Feet '89
Requiem for Dominic '91

Doris Dorrie
Men... '85
Me and Him '89

Nelson Pereira dos Santos
How Tasty Was My Little Frenchman '71

Shimon Dotan
The Finest Hour '91
Warriors '94

Jean Douchet
Six in Paris '68

Russell S. Doughten, Jr.
The Hostage '67
Whitcomb's War '87

Gordon Douglas
Saps at Sea '40
Broadway Limited '41
The Great Gildersleeve '43
The Falcon in Hollywood '44
Girl Rush '44
Zombies on Broadway '44
First Yank into Tokyo '45
Dick Tracy vs. Cueball '46
Black Arrow '48
If You Knew Susie '48
The Doolins of Oklahoma '49
Kiss Tomorrow Goodbye '50
The Nevadan '50
Only the Valiant '50
Great Missouri Raid '51
Them! '54
Young at Heart '54
The McConnell Story '55
Sincerely Yours '56
Up Periscope '59
Follow That Dream '61
Call Me Bwana '63
Rio Conchos '64
Robin and the 7 Hoods '64
Harlow '65
Chuka '67
In Like Flint '67
Tony Rome '67
The Detective '68
Lady in Cement '68
Skullduggery '70
They Call Me Mr. Tibbs! '70
Slaughter's Big Ripoff '73
Viva Knievel '77

Kirk Douglas
Posse '75

Neil Douglas
Sinner's Blood '70

Peter Douglas
A Tiger's Tale '87

Lorenzo Doumani
Mad About You '90
Amore! '93
Storybook '95

Alexander Dovzhenko
Zvenigora '28
Arsenal '29
Earth '30

Kathleen Dowdey
Blue Heaven '84

Kevin Dowling
The Sum of Us '94

Robert Downey
Putney Swope '69
Greaser's Palace '72
Up the Academy '80
America '86
Rented Lips '88
Too Much Sun '90

Michael Drach
Les Violons du Bal '74

Mircea Dragan
Oil '78

Bert L. Dragin
Summer Camp Nightmare '86
Twice Dead '88

Stan Dragoti
Love at First Bite '79
Mr. Mom '83
The Man with One Red Shoe '85
She's Out of Control '89
Necessary Roughness '91

Jim Drake
Mr. Bill's Real Life Adventures '86
Police Academy 4: Citizens on Patrol '87
Speed Zone '88
Based on an Untrue Story '93

Oliver Drake
Today I Hang '42
Fighting Valley '43
Battling Marshal '48
Brand of Fear '49
Mummy & Curse of the Jackal '67

Tom Drake
Keeper '84

Tony Drazan
Zebrahead '92
Imaginary Crimes '94

Arthur Dreifuss
Double Deal '39
Mystery in Swing '40
Reg'lar Fellers '41
Baby Face Morgan '42
Boss of Big Town '43
The Payoff '43

Fred Dresch
My Samurai '92

Jean Dreville
Seven Deadly Sins '53
Sputnik '61

Di Drew
The Right Hand Man '87
Trouble in Paradise '88

Sidney Drew
Playing Dead '15

Carl Theodor Dreyer
Leaves from Satan's Book '19
Master of the House '25
The Passion of Joan of Arc '28
Vampyr '31
Day of Wrath '43
Ordet '55
Gertrud '64

Richard Driscoll
The Comic '85

Sara Driver
Sleepwalk '88

Antonio Drove
The Tunnel '89

David Drury
Defense of the Realm '85
Forever Young '85
Split Decisions '88
Intrigue '90
Prime Suspect 3 '93

Mihael Dryhurst
Hard Way '80

Lee Drysdale
Leather Jackets '90

Charles S. Dubin
Cinderella '64
Murder Once Removed '71
Moving Violation '76
The Gathering: Part 2 '79
The Manions of America '81
Drop-Out Mother '88

Jean-Claude Dubois
The Evil Below '87

Adam Dubov
Dead Beat '94

Arthur Dubs
Vanishing Wilderness '73

Remy Duchemin
A la Mode '94

Roger Duchonwny
Camp Cucamonga: How I Spent My Summer Vacation '90

Philip Dudley
Poldark 2 '75

Peter Duffell
The House that Dripped Blood '71
Inside Out '75
Experience Preferred... But Not Essential '83
The Far Pavilions '84
Letters to an Unknown Lover '84

Dennis Dugan
Problem Child '90
Brain Donors '92
Happy Gilmore '96

Michael Dugan
Super Seal '77
Mausoleum '83

George Dugdale
Slaughter High '86

Martine Dugowson
Mina Tannenbaum '94

Christian Duguay
Scanners 2: The New Order '91
Live Wire '92
Scanners 3: The Takeover '92
Adrift '93
Model by Day '94
Screamers '96

John Duigan
The Winter of Our Dreams '82
One Night Stand '84
Far East '85
The Year My Voice Broke '87
Flirting '89
Romero '89
Wide Sargasso Sea '92
Sirens '94
The Journey of August King '95

Bill Duke
Johnnie Gibson F.B.I. '87
Maximum Security '87
A Raisin in the Sun '89
A Rage in Harlem '91
Deep Cover '92
The Cemetery Club '93
Sister Act 2: Back in the Habit '93
America's Dream '95

Daryl Duke
The President's Plane is Missing '71
Payday '72
I Heard the Owl Call My Name '73
Griffin and Phoenix: A Love Story '76
The Silent Partner '78
The Thorn Birds '83
Tai-Pan '86

William Duke
Killing Floor '85

Germaine Dulac
Smiling Madame Beudet/The Seashell and the Clergyman '28

Georges Dumoulin
Nous N'Irons Plus au Bois '69
We Will Not Enter the Forest '79

Patrick Duncan
84 Charlie Mopic '89
Live! From Death Row '92

Duwayne Dunham
Homeward Bound: The Incredible Journey '93
Little Giants '94

George Duning
Yellow Submarine '68

Philip Dunne
Ten North Frederick '58
Wild in the Country '61

E.A. Dupont
The Americano/Variety '25
Variety '25

Michael DuPont
Ethan '71

William Duprey
Uncaged '91

Ciro Duran
Tropical Snow '88

Rudy Durand
Tilt '78

Alberto Durant
Alias, La Gringa '91

John Durst
One Wish Too Many '55

David E. Durston
I Drink Your Blood '71
Stigma '73

Robert Duvall
Angelo My Love '83

Julien Duvivier
Poil de Carotte '31
Maria Chapdelaine '34
Pepe Le Moko '37
The Great Waltz '38
Lydia '41
Tales of Manhattan '42
Heart of a Nation '43
Panique '47
Anna Karenina '48
Captain Blackjack '51
Little World of Don Camillo '51
The Man in the Raincoat '57
Diabolically Yours '67

Allan Dwan
Robin Hood '22
Manhandled '24
The Iron Mask '29
Hollywood Party '34
Heidi '37
Rebecca of Sunnybrook Farm '38
The Gorilla '39
The Three Musketeers '39
Young People '40
Look Who's Laughing '41
Here We Go Again! '42
Around the World '43
Abroad with Two Yanks '44
Brewster's Millions '45
Northwest Outpost '47
Sands of Iwo Jima '49
I Dream of Jeannie '52
Montana Belle '52
Cattle Queen of Montana '54
Passion '54
Silver Lode '54
Escape to Burma '55
Pearl of the South Pacific '55
Tennessee's Partner '55
Slightly Scarlet '56
Enchanted Island '58
The Restless Breed '58

H. Kaye Dyal
Memory of Us '74
Trained to Kill '88
Project: Eliminator '91

Robert Dyke
Moontrap '89

David Eady
Three Cases of Murder '55

Boris Eagle
The Tormentors '80s

B. Reeves Eason
Test of Donald Norton '26
Roaring Ranch '30
Spurs '30
Trigger Tricks '30
The Galloping Ghost '31
Vanishing Legion '31
Cornered '32
The Last of the Mohicans '32
Hollywood Mystery '34
Law of the Wild '34
Mystery Mountain '34
The Adventures of Rex & Rinty '35
The Miracle Rider '35
The Phantom Empire '35
Darkest Africa '36
Fighting Marines '36
Red River Valley '36
Undersea Kingdom '36
North of the Border '46
Rimfire '49

Walter B. Eason
Sea Hound '47

Allan Eastman
The War Boy '85
Crazy Moon '87
Ford: The Man & the Machine '87

G.L. Eastman
Metamorphosis '90

Clint Eastwood
Play Misty for Me '71
High Plains Drifter '73
The Eiger Sanction '75
The Outlaw Josey Wales '76
The Gauntlet '77
Bronco Billy '80
Firefox '82
Honkytonk Man '82
Sudden Impact '83
Pale Rider '85
Heartbreak Ridge '86
Bird '88
The Rookie '90
White Hunter, Black Heart '90
Unforgiven '92
A Perfect World '93
The Bridges of Madison County '95

Thom Eberhardt
Night of the Comet '84
Sole Survivor '84
The Night Before '88
Without a Clue '88
Gross Anatomy '89
Captain Ron '92

Ghasem Ebrahimian
The Suitors '88

Desire Ecare
Faces of Women '85

Nicolas Echevarria
Cabeza de Vaca '90

Uli Edel
Christiane F. '82
Last Exit to Brooklyn '90
Body of Evidence '92
Tyson '95

Gustaf Edgren
Walpurgis Night '41

Don Edmunds
Tender Loving Care '73
Ilsa, She-Wolf of the SS '74
Bare Knuckles '77
Terror on Tour '83

Blake Edwards
This Happy Feeling '58
Operation Petticoat '59
Perfect Furlough '59
Breakfast at Tiffany's '61
Days of Wine and Roses '62
Experiment in Terror '62
The Pink Panther '64
A Shot in the Dark '64
The Great Race '65
What Did You Do in the War, Daddy? '66
The Party '68
Darling Lili '70
Wild Rovers '71
Return of the Pink Panther '74
The Tamarind Seed '74
The Pink Panther Strikes Again '76
Revenge of the Pink Panther '78
10 '79
S.O.B. '81
Trail of the Pink Panther '82
Victor/Victoria '82
Curse of the Pink Panther '83
The Man Who Loved Women '83
Micki & Maude '84
A Fine Mess '86
That's Life! '86
Blind Date '87
Sunset '88
Peter Gunn '89
Skin Deep '89
The Cary Grant Collection '90
Switch '91
Son of the Pink Panther '93

Charles Edwards
The Flaming Teen-Age '56

Don Edwards
Black Cobra 3: The Manila Connection '90

George Edwards
The Attic '80

Harry Edwards
Baby Face Harry Langdon '26

Henry Edwards
The Private Secretary '35
Scrooge '35

Peter Edwards
A Mind to Kill '95

Robert Edwards
Thunder in the Pines '49

Christine Edzard
Little Dorrit, Film 1: Nobody's Fault '88

Little Dorrit, Film 2: Little Dorrit's Story '88
Arthur Egeli
Maxim Xul '91
Mark Egerton
The Winds of Jarrah '83
Colin Eggleston
Bellamy '80
Cassandra '87
Sky Pirates '87
Innocent Prey '88
The Wicked '89
Jan Egleson
The Tender Age '84
Roanoak '86
A Shock to the System '90
The Last Hit '93
Oleg Egorov
Osa '85
Atom Egoyan
Next of Kin '84
Family Viewing '87
Speaking Parts '89
The Adjuster '91
Calendar '93
Exotica '94
Richard Eichberg
Night Birds '31
Franz Eichhorn
The Violent Years '56
Rafael Eisenman
Lake Consequence '92
Red Shoe Diaries 3: Another Woman's Lipstick '93
Sergei Eisenstein
Strike '24
The Battleship Potemkin '25
Ten Days That Shook the World '27
The General Line '29
Que Viva Mexico '32
Alexander Nevsky '38
Ivan the Terrible, Part 1 '44
Ivan the Terrible, Part 2 '46
Nicolai Ekk
The Road to Life '31
George Elanjian, Jr.
Syngenor '90
Judit Elek
Maria's Day '84
Clifford S. Elfelt
Big Stakes '22
Richard Elfman
Forbidden Zone '80
Shrunken Heads '94
Michael Elias
Lush Life '94
Jan Eliasberg
Past Midnight '92
Larry Elikann
The Great Wallendas '78
Charlie and the Great Balloon Chase '82
Spraggue '84
Poison Ivy '85
Hands of a Stranger '87
Stamp of a Killer '87
Disaster at Silo 7 '88
God Bless the Child '88
Fever '91
The Great Los Angeles Earthquake '91
One Against the Wind '91
Kiss of a Killer '93
The Story Lady '93
Blue River '95
A Mother's Prayer '95
Tecumseh: The Last Warrior '95
Harrison Ellenshaw
Dead Silence '90
B. Ron Elliott
The Acid Eaters '67
Lang Elliott
The Private Eyes '80
Cage 2: The Arena of Death '94
Stephan Elliott
The Adventures of Priscilla, Queen of the Desert '94
Paul Elliotts
Great Adventure '75

Bob Ellis
Warm Nights on a Slow-Moving Train '87
The Nostradamus Kid '92
David R. Ellis
Homeward Bound 2: Lost in San Francisco '96
Joseph Ellison
Don't Go in the House '80
Javier Elorrieta
Blood and Sand '89
Maurice Elvey
The Evil Mind '34
Lily of Killarney '34
Phantom Fiend '35
Transatlantic Tunnel '35
Beware of Pity '46
The Obsessed '51
Cassian Elwes
Blue Flame '93
Tony Elwood
Road Kill USA '93
John Emerson
His Picture in the Papers '16
The Social Secretary '16
The Americano '17
Down to Earth '17
Reaching for the Moon '17
The Americano/Variety '25
Mystery of the Leaping Fish/ Chess Fever '25
Dick Emery
Yellow Submarine '68
Robert Emery
Scream Bloody Murder '72
Ride in a Pink Car '74
Ian Emes
Knights & Emeralds '87
Roland Emmerich
Making Contact '86
Ghost Chase '88
Moon 44 '90
Universal Soldier '92
Stargate '94
Independence Day '96
Robert Enders
Stevie '78
Cy Endfield
Try and Get Me '50
The Underworld Story '50
Mysterious Island '61
Zulu '64
Erich Engel
The Blum Affair '48
David Engelbach
America 3000 '86
Harrison Engle
Indomitable Teddy Roosevelt '83
John English
Whistling Bullets '36
Arizona Days '37
Dick Tracy '37
Zorro Rides Again '37
Daredevils of the Red Circle '38
Fighting Devil Dogs '38
The Lone Ranger '38
Zorro's Fighting Legion '39
Doctor Satan's Robot '40
Drums of Fu Manchu '40
King of the Texas Rangers '41
Death Valley Manhunt '43
Man from Thunder River '43
Raiders of Sunset Pass '43
Captain America '44
Utah '45
Loaded Pistols '48
Riders of the Whistling Pines '49
Rim of the Canyon '49
Cow Town '50
Hills of Utah '51
Valley of Fire '51
George Englund
The Ugly American '63
Zachariah '70
A Christmas to Remember '78
The Vegas Strip Wars '84
Dixie: Changing Habits '85
Robert Englund
976-EVIL '88

Robert Enrico
An Occurrence at Owl Creek Bridge/Coup de Grace '62
Red Balloon/Occurrence at Owl Creek Bridge '62
Jailbird's Vacation '65
Les Grandes Gueules '65
Le Secret '74
Old Gun '76
Ray Enright
Tomorrow at Seven '33
Dames '34
Earthworm Tractors '36
The Spoilers '42
Gung Ho! '43
The Iron Major '43
China Sky '44
Trail Street '47
Coroner Creek '48
Return of the Bad Men '48
South of St. Louis '48
Man from Cairo '54
Ildiko Enyedi
My Twentieth Century '90
Nora Ephron
This Is My Life '92
Sleepless in Seattle '93
Mixed Nuts '94
Jean Epstein
La Chute de la Maison Usher '28
Marcelo Epstein
Body Rock '84
Robert Epstein
Times of Harvey Milk '83
Common Threads: Stories from the Quilt '89
The Celluloid Closet '95
Rene Eram
Voodoo '95
Richard Erdman
Brothers O'Toole '73
Victor Erice
Spirit of the Beehive '73
A.F. Erickson
The Lone Star Ranger '30
Gordon Eriksen
The Big Dis '89
Charles Erman
Just Me & You '78
John Erman
Green Eyes '76
Alexander: The Other Side of Dawn '77
Child of Glass '78
My Old Man '79
Eleanor: First Lady of the World '82
A Streetcar Named Desire '84
An Early Frost '85
The Attic: The Hiding of Anne Frank '88
Stella '89
The Last Best Year '90
Our Sons '91
When the Time Comes '91
Carolina Skeletons '92
Breathing Lessons '94
Scarlett '94
The Boys Next Door '96
Frederic Ermler
No Greater Love '43
George Erschbamer
SnakeEater '89
SnakeEater 2: The Drug Buster '89
SnakeEater 3: His Law '92
Final Round '93
Flinch '94
Jack Ersgard
Invisible: The Chronicles of Benjamin Knight '93
Joakim Ersgard
The Visitors '89
Mandroid '93
Chester Erskine
Midnight '34
Frankie and Johnny '36
Egg and I '47
Androcles and the Lion '52
A Girl in Every Port '52
Dwain Esper
Maniac '34

Marihuana '36
The Worst of Hollywood: Vol. 1 '90
Jett C. Espirtu
P.O.W. Deathcamp '89
Harry Essex
Octaman '71
The Cremators '72
Emilio Estevez
Wisdom '87
Men at Work '90
Ray Etheridge
The Vernonia Incident '89
Corey Michael Eubanks
Bigfoot: The Unforgettable Encounter '94
Two Bits & Pepper '95
Bruce A. Evans
Kuffs '92
David Mickey Evans
The Sandlot '93
John Evans
Black Godfather '74
Blackjack '78
Marc Evans
Thicker Than Water '93
Roger Evans
Jet Benny Show '86
D.S. Everett
Running Brave '83
Tim Everitt
Fatally Yours '95
Valie Export
Invisible Adversaries '77
Menschenfrauen '80
The Practice of Love '84
Richard Eyre
The Ploughman's Lunch '83
Singleton's Pluck '84
Loose Connections '87
John Eyres
Project: Shadowchaser '92
Monolith '93
Night Siege Project: Shadowchaser 2 '94
Project Shadowchaser 3000 '95
Mark Ezra
Savage Hearts '95
Christian Faber
Bail Jumper '89
Zoltan Fabri
The Fifth Seal '76
Roberto Faenza
Corrupt '84
The Bachelor '93
Peter Faiman
Crocodile Dundee '86
Dutch '91
William Fairchild
The Silent Enemy '58
Horsemasters '61
Ferdinand Fairfax
Nate and Hayes '83
The Rescue '88
Spymaker: The Secret Life of Ian Fleming '90
Feliks Falk
Hero of the Year '85
Harry Falk
The Death Squad '73
Abduction of St. Anne '75
Beulah Land '80
The Night the City Screamed '80
Sophisticated Gents '81
High Desert Kill '90
Jamaa Fanaka
Soul Vengeance '75
Black Sister's Revenge '76
Penitentiary '79
Penitentiary 2 '82
Penitentiary 3 '87
Street Wars '91
Jacques Fansten
Cross My Heart '91
James Fargo
The Enforcer '76
Every Which Way But Loose '78

Forced Vengeance '82
Game for Vultures '86
Voyage of the Rock Aliens '87
Born to Race '88
Ernest Farino
Steel and Lace '90
Josh Kirby...Time Warrior: Chapter 1, Planet of the Dino-Knights '95
Josh Kirby...Time Warrior: Chapter 5, Journey to the Magic Cavern '96
W. Farkas
Prime Risk '84
Donald Farmer
Demon Queen '80s
Scream Dream '89
Anthony Farrar
Sin You Sinners '63
Bobby Farrelly
Kingpin '96
Peter Farrelly
Dumb & Dumber '94
Kingpin '96
John Farris
Dear Dead Delilah '72
John Farrow
Five Came Back '39
The Saint Strikes Back '39
Wake Island '42
Commandos Strike at Dawn '43
The Saint Strikes Back: Criminal Court '46
Copper Canyon '50
His Kind of Woman '51
Botany Bay '53
Hondo '53
A Bullet Is Waiting '54
Sea Chase '55
Back from Eternity '56
Unholy Wife '57
John Paul Jones '59
Andre Farwagi
Boarding School '83
John Fasano
Rock 'n' Roll Nightmare '85
Black Roses '88
The Jitters '88
Rainer Werner Fassbinder
Gods of the Plague '69
Why Does Herr R. Run Amok? '69
The American Soldier '70
Beware of a Holy Whore '70
The Merchant of Four Seasons '71
The Bitter Tears of Petra von Kant '72
Ali: Fear Eats the Soul '74
Effi Briest '74
Fox and His Friends '75
I Only Want You to Love Me '76
Mother Kusters Goes to Heaven '76
Satan's Brew '76
The Stationmaster's Wife '77
Despair '78
Germany in Autumn '78
In a Year of 13 Moons '78
The Marriage of Maria Braun '79
The Tin Drum '79
Berlin Alexanderplatz '80
Veronika Voss '82
Querelle '83
Chinese Roulette '86
William C. Faure
Shaka Zulu '83
Neill Fearnley
Black Ice '92
Linda Feferman
Seven Minutes in Heaven '86
Xie Fei
Girl from Hunan '86
A Mongolian Tale '94
Women From the Lake of Scented Souls '94
Beda Ocampo Feijoo
Under the Earth '86
Felix Feist
Deluge '33
George White's Scandals '45

Feist ▶cont.

The Devil Thumbs a Ride *'47*
The Devil Thumbs a Ride/Having Wonderful Crime *'47*
Threat *'49*
Guilty of Treason *'50*
Big Trees *'52*
Donovan's Brain *'53*

Dennis Feldman
Real Men *'87*

Gene Feldman
Danny *'79*

John Feldman
Alligator Eyes *'90*
Dead Funny *'94*

Marty Feldman
The Last Remake of Beau Geste *'77*

Federico Fellini
Variety Lights *'51*
The White Sheik *'52*
I Vitelloni *'53*
Love in the City *'53*
La Strada *'54*
The Swindle *'55*
Nights of Cabiria *'57*
La Dolce Vita *'60*
Boccaccio '70 *'62*
8 1/2 *'63*
Juliet of the Spirits *'65*
Spirits of the Dead *'68*
Fellini Satyricon *'69*
The Clowns *'71*
Fellini's Roma *'72*
Amarcord *'74*
City of Women *'81*
And the Ship Sails On *'83*
Ginger & Fred *'86*
Intervista *'87*

Georg Fenady
Arnold *'73*
Terror in the Wax Museum *'73*

Huang Feng
Sting of the Dragon Masters *'74*

Michael Fengler
Why Does Herr R. Run Amok? *'69*

Philip Fently
The Baron *'88*

Claude Feraldo
Trade Secrets *'90s*

Rene Feret
The Mystery of Alexina *'86*

Larry Ferguson
Beyond the Law *'92*

Michael Ferguson
The Glory Boys *'84*

Norman Ferguson
The Three Caballeros *'45*

Guy Ferland
The Babysitter *'95*

Emilio Fernandez
Maria Candelaria *'46*
The Pearl *'48*
The Torch *'50*
Flor Silvestre *'58*

Pablo Fero
Me, Myself & I *'92*

Abel Ferrara
Driller Killer *'74*
Ms. 45 *'81*
Fear City *'85*
The Gladiator *'86*
China Girl *'87*
Cat Chaser *'90*
King of New York *'90*
Bad Lieutenant *'92*
Body Snatchers *'93*
Dangerous Game *'93*
The Addiction *'95*

Romano Ferrara
Planets Against Us *'61*

Jeff Ferrell
Revenge of the Teenage Vixens from Outer Space *'86*

Jose Ferrer
Return to Peyton Place *'61*
State Fair *'62*

Mel Ferrer
Green Mansions *'59*

Marco Ferreri
El Cochecito *'60*
L'Udienza *'71*
La Grande Bouffe *'73*
Tales of Ordinary Madness *'83*

Robert A. Ferretti
Fear *'88*

Frank Ferrin
Sabaka *'55*

Stan Ferris
Tulips *'81*

George Ferron
The Scalawag Bunch *'75*

Giorgio Ferroni
Mill of the Stone Women *'60*
The Bacchantes *'63*
Conquest of Mycene *'63*

Jacques Feyder
Crainquebille *'23*
The Kiss *'29*
Carnival in Flanders *'35*
Knight Without Armour *'37*

Leonard Fields
King Kelly of the U.S.A. *'34*

Michael Fields
Noon Wine *'84*
Bright Angel *'91*

Steven Fierberg
Voodoo Dawn *'89*

Douglas Fifthian
Touch Me Not *'74*

Mike Figgis
Stormy Monday *'88*
Internal Affairs *'90*
Liebestraum *'91*
Women & Men: In Love There Are No Rules *'91*
Mr. Jones *'93*
The Browning Version *'94*
Leaving Las Vegas *'95*

Charles Finch
Priceless Beauty *'90*
Where Sleeping Dogs Lie *'91*

Nigel Finch
The Lost Language of Cranes *'92*

David Fincher
Alien 3 *'92*
Seven *'95*

Michael Findlay
Shriek of the Mutilated *'74*

Roberta Findlay
The Oracle *'85*
Blood Sisters *'86*
Lurkers *'88*
Prime Evil *'88*

John P. Finegan
Girls School Screamers *'86*

Janace Fink
Velvet Smooth *'76*

Kenneth Fink
Tall, Dark and Deadly *'95*

Michael Fink
Black Force *'75*

Ken Finkleman
Airplane 2: The Sequel *'82*
Head Office *'86*

Joe Finley
Barbarian Queen 2: The Empress Strikes Back *'89*

Edward Finney
Riot Squad *'41*
Silver Stallion *'41*
King of the Stallions *'42*

Rex Firlin
The Death of Adolf Hitler *'84*

Sam Firstenberg
Revenge of the Ninja *'83*
Breakin' 2: Electric Boogaloo *'84*
Ninja 3: The Domination *'84*
American Ninja *'85*
Avenging Force *'86*
American Ninja 2: The Confrontation *'87*
My African Adventure *'87*
Riverbend *'89*
One More Chance *'90*
Delta Force 3: The Killing Game *'91*
American Samurai *'92*
Blood Warriors *'93*
Cyborg Soldier *'94*

Michael Firth
Heart of the Stag *'84*
Sylvia *'86*

Michael Fischa
Death Spa *'87*
Crack House *'89*
My Mom's a Werewolf *'89*

Max Fischer
Killing 'em Softly *'85*
Entangled *'93*

Deirdre Fishel
Risk *'94*

David Fisher
Liar's Moon *'82*
Toy Soldiers *'84*

Jack Fisher
Torn Apart *'89*

Mary Ann Fisher
Lords of the Deep *'89*

Terence Fisher
Man Bait *'52*
A Stolen Face *'52*
Four Sided Triangle *'53*
Spaceways *'53*
Three Stops to Murder *'53*
Blackout *'54*
Unholy Four *'54*
Race for Life *'55*
Robin Hood: The Movie *'55*
The Curse of Frankenstein *'57*
The Horror of Dracula *'58*
The Revenge of Frankenstein *'58*
The Hound of the Baskervilles *'59*
The Mummy *'59*
The Brides of Dracula *'60*
Sword of Sherwood Forest *'60*
The Two Faces of Dr. Jekyll *'60*
The Curse of the Werewolf *'61*
The Phantom of the Opera *'62*
Sherlock Holmes and the Deadly Necklace *'62*
The Gorgon *'64*
Island of Terror *'66*
Island of the Burning Doomed *'67*
Frankenstein and the Monster from Hell *'74*

Tom Fisher
Cannibal Campout *'88*

Bill Fishman
Tapeheads *'89*
Car 54, Where Are You? *'94*

Jack Fisk
Raggedy Man *'81*
Violets Are Blue *'86*
Daddy's Dyin'...Who's Got the Will? *'90*
Final Verdict *'91*

Christopher Fitchett
Blood Money *'80*
Fair Game *'82*

Jon FitzGerald
Apart from Hugh *'94*

George Fitzmaurice
Son of the Sheik *'26*
As You Desire Me *'32*
Mata Hari *'32*
Suzy *'36*
The Last of Mrs. Cheyney *'37*

James A. Fitzpatrick
Lady of the Lake *'28*

Robert S. Fiveson
The Clonus Horror *'79*

Paul Flaherty
18 Again! *'88*
Who's Harry Crumb? *'89*
Clifford *'92*

Robert Flaherty
Moana, a Romance of the Golden Age *'26*
Tabu: A Story of the South Seas *'31*
Man of Aran *'34*
Elephant Boy *'37*
Louisiana Story *'48*

Freddie Fleck
The Magnificent Ambersons *'42*

Gary Fleder
The Companion *'94*
Things to Do In Denver When You're Dead *'95*

Dave Fleischer
Gulliver's Travels *'39*
Hoppity Goes to Town *'41*

Max Fleischer
Max Fleischer's Documentary Features *'23*

Richard Fleischer
The Clay Pigeon *'49*
Follow Me Quietly *'49*
Trapped *'49*
Armored Car Robbery *'50*
The Narrow Margin *'52*
20,000 Leagues Under the Sea *'54*
Between Heaven and Hell *'56*
The Vikings *'58*
Compulsion *'59*
Barabbas *'62*
Fantastic Voyage *'66*
Doctor Dolittle *'67*
The Boston Strangler *'68*
Tora! Tora! Tora! *'70*
See No Evil *'71*
10 Rillington Place *'71*
The New Centurions *'72*
The Don is Dead *'73*
Soylent Green *'73*
Mr. Majestyk *'74*
Mandingo *'75*
The Incredible Sarah *'76*
The Prince and the Pauper *'78*
Ashanti, Land of No Mercy *'79*
The Jazz Singer *'80*
Amityville 3: The Demon *'83*
Tough Enough *'83*
Conan the Destroyer *'84*
Red Sonja *'85*
Million Dollar Mystery *'87*

Andrew Fleming
Bad Dreams *'88*
Threesome *'94*
The Craft *'96*

Edward Fleming
Topsy Turvy *'84*

Erik Fleming
Cyber Bandits *'94*

Victor Fleming
When the Clouds Roll By *'19*
Mantrap *'26*
Hula *'28*
The Virginian *'29*
Red Dust *'32*
Bombshell *'33*
Treasure Island *'34*
The Farmer Takes a Wife *'35*
Reckless *'35*
Captains Courageous *'37*
Test Pilot *'38*
Gone with the Wind *'39*
The Wizard of Oz *'39*
Dr. Jekyll and Mr. Hyde *'41*
Tortilla Flat *'42*
A Guy Named Joe *'44*
Adventure *'45*
Joan of Arc *'48*

Gordon Flemyng
Doctor Who and the Daleks *'65*
Daleks—Invasion Earth 2150 A.D. *'66*
Philby, Burgess and MacLean: Spy Scandal of the Century *'84*
Cloud Waltzing *'87*

Rodman Flender
In the Heat of Passion *'91*
The Unborn *'91*
Leprechaun 2 *'94*

Mandie Fletcher
Deadly Advice *'93*

Clive Fleury
Fatal Past *'94*
Tunnel Vision *'95*

Theodore J. Flicker
The President's Analyst *'67*
Three in the Cellar *'70*
Playmates *'72*
Soggy Bottom U.S.A. *'84*

James T. Flocker
The Secret of Navajo Cave *'76*
Ghosts That Still Walk *'77*
Ground Zero *'88*

John Florea
Island of the Lost *'68*
Where the Eagle Flies *'72*
The Invisible Strangler *'76*
Computer Wizard *'77*
Where's Willie? *'77*
Hot Child in the City *'87*

Isaac Florentine
Desert Kickboxer *'92*
The Fighter *'95*

Robert Florey
The Cocoanuts *'29*
Murders in the Rue Morgue *'32*
Ex-Lady *'33*
The Beast with Five Fingers *'46*
Outpost in Morocco *'49*

Aldo Florio
Five Giants from Texas *'66*

Calvin Floyd
Sleep of Death *'79*

Drago Floyd
Troll 2 *'92*

John Flynn
Rolling Thunder *'77*
Defiance *'79*
Marilyn: The Untold Story *'80*
Touched *'82*
Best Seller *'87*
Lock Up *'89*
Nails *'92*
Scam *'93*
Brainscan *'94*

Peter Flynn
Project Vampire *'93*

Tom Flynn
Watch It *'93*

Helmut Foernbacher
What a Way to Die *'70*

Lawrence Foldes
The Great Skycopter Rescue *'82*
Young Warriors *'83*
Nightforce *'86*
Curse of the Living Dead *'89*
Pre-Madonnas: Rebels Without a Clue *'95*

Peter Foldy
Midnight Witness *'93*
Tryst *'94*
Widow's Kiss *'96*

Peter Foleg
The Unseen *'80*

James Foley
Reckless *'84*
At Close Range *'86*
Who's That Girl? *'87*
After Dark, My Sweet *'90*
Glengarry Glen Ross *'92*
Fear *'96*
Two Bits *'96*

Peter Fonda
Hired Hand *'71*
Idaho Transfer *'73*
Wanda Nevada *'79*

Marcello Fondato
Immortal Bachelor *'80*

Allen Fong
Just Like Weather *'86*

Leo Fong
Hawkeye *'88*
24 Hours to Midnight *'92*
Showdown *'93*

Jorge Fons
Jory *'72*

Anne Fontaine
Augustin *'95*

Lloyd Fonvielle
Gotham *'88*

Bryan Forbes
Whistle Down the Wind *'62*
Seance on a Wet Afternoon *'64*
King Rat *'65*
The Wrong Box *'66*
The Madwoman of Chaillot *'69*
Long Ago Tomorrow *'71*
International Velvet *'78*
Better Late Than Never *'83*
The Naked Face *'84*

Francis Ford
Custer's Last Fight *'12*

Greg Ford
Daffy Duck's Quackbusters '89

John Ford
Straight Shootin' '17
Arrowsmith '31
Judge Priest '34
The Lost Patrol '34
The Informer '35
Mary of Scotland '36
The Hurricane '37
Wee Willie Winkie '37
Drums Along the Mohawk '39
Stagecoach '39
Young Mr. Lincoln '39
The Grapes of Wrath '40
The Long Voyage Home '40
How Green Was My Valley '41
They Were Expendable '45
My Darling Clementine '46
Fort Apache '48
The Fugitive '48
Three Godfathers '48
She Wore a Yellow Ribbon '49
Rio Grande '50
Wagon Master '50
The Quiet Man '52
What Price Glory? '52
Mogambo '53
The Sun Shines Bright '53
The Long Gray Line '55
Mister Roberts '55
The Searchers '56
Wings of Eagles '57
Last Hurrah '58
The Horse Soldiers '59
Sergeant Rutledge '60
Two Rode Together '61
The Man Who Shot Liberty Valance '62
Donovan's Reef '63
How the West Was Won '63
Cheyenne Autumn '64
December 7th: The Movie '91

Philip Ford
The Inner Circle '46
Redwood Forest Trail '50
The Vanishing Westerner '50

Phillip R. Ford
Vegas in Space '94

Stephen Ford
Dungeonmaster '83

Eugene Forde
Inspector Hornleigh '39

Walter Forde
Bulldog Jack '35
King of the Damned '36
The Secret Four '40
The Ghost Train '41

Timothy Forder
The Mystery of Edwin Drood '93

Richard Foreman
Sudden Death '77

Milos Forman
Loves of a Blonde '65
The Firemen's Ball '68
One Flew Over the Cuckoo's Nest '75
Hair '79
Ragtime '81
Amadeus '84
Valmont '89

Tom Forman
Shadows '22
The Virginian '23
The Fighting American '24

Rolf Forsberg
Beyond the Next Mountain '87

Robert Forster
Hollywood Harry '86

Bill Forsyth
That Sinking Feeling '79
Gregory's Girl '80
Local Hero '83
Comfort and Joy '84
Housekeeping '87
Breaking In '89
Being Human '94

Ed Forsyth
Superchick '71
Chesty Anderson USN '76
Inferno in Paradise '88

John Fortenberry
Jury Duty '95

Bob Fosse
Sweet Charity '69
Cabaret '72
Lenny '74
All That Jazz '79
Star 80 '83

Giles Foster
Silas Marner '85
Hotel du Lac '86
Dutch Girls '87
Consuming Passions '88
Innocent Victim '90
The Rector's Wife '94

Harve Foster
Fabulous Joe '47

Jodie Foster
Little Man Tate '91
Home for the Holidays '95

Lewis R. Foster
Cavalry Charge '51
Crashout '55
Dakota Incident '56
Tonka '58
The Sign of Zorro '60

Norman Foster
Mr. Moto's Last Warning '39
Journey into Fear '42
Rachel and the Stranger '48
Tell It to the Judge '49
Davy Crockett, King of the Wild Frontier '55
Davy Crockett and the River Pirates '56
The Nine Lives of Elfego Baca '58
The Sign of Zorro '60
Indian Paint '64
Brighty of the Grand Canyon '67

Claude Fournier
Dan Candy's Law '73
Tales of the Klondike: The Scorn of Women '87

Gene Fowler, Jr.
I Was a Teenage Werewolf '57
I Married a Monster from Outer Space '58
Showdown at Boot Hill '58
The Rebel Set '59

Robert Fowler
Below the Belt '80

Douglas Fowley
Macumba Love '60

Emerson Fox
Shocking Asia '75

Erika Fox
Dead Women in Lingerie '90

Marilyn Fox
Codename: Icarus '85

Wallace Fox
Powdersmoke Range '35
Yellow Dust '36
Gun Packer '38
Bowery Blitzkrieg '41
Bowery at Midnight '42
The Corpse Vanishes '42
Let's Get Tough '42
'Neath Brooklyn Bridge '42
Smart Alecks '42
Ghost Rider '43
Kid Dynamite '43
The Great Mike '44
Million Dollar Kid '44
Bad Men of the Border '45

William A. Fraker
Monte Walsh '70
A Reflection of Fear '72
Legend of the Lone Ranger '81

Gianni Franciolini
Pardon My Trunk '52

Coleman Francis
The Beast of Yucca Flats '61

Freddie Francis
The Brain '62
Paranoiac '62
Day of the Triffids '63
Nightmare '63
The Evil of Frankenstein '64
Hysteria '64
Dr. Terror's House of Horrors '65
The Skull '65
They Came from Beyond Space '67
Torture Garden '67
Dracula Has Risen from the Grave '68
Girly '70
The Vampire Happening '71
The Creeping Flesh '72
Tales from the Crypt '72
Tales That Witness Madness '73
Craze '74
The Ghoul '75
Legend of the Werewolf '75
The Doctor and the Devils '85

Karl Francis
And Nothing But the Truth '82

Pietro Francisci
Hercules '58
Hercules Unchained '59

Jess (Jesus) Franco
The Awful Dr. Orlof '62
Dr. Orloff's Monster '64
The Diabolical Dr. Z '65
Attack of the Robots '66
The Castle of Fu Manchu '68
Deadly Sanctuary '68
Kiss and Kill '68
99 Women '69
The Invisible Dead '70
Venus in Furs '70
Count Dracula '71
Virgin Among the Living Dead '71
The Screaming Dead '72
The Perverse Countess '73
Ilsa, the Wicked Warden '78
Sex Is Crazy '79
The Loves of Irina '80s
Jack the Ripper '80
Revenge in the House of Usher '82
Bloody Moon '83
Angel of Death '86

Richardo Franco
Berlin Blues '89

Georges Franju
The Horror Chamber of Dr. Faustus '59
Judex '64

A.M. Frank
Oasis of the Zombies '82

Carol Frank
Sorority House Massacre '86

Charles Frank
Inheritance '47

Christopher Frank
Josepha '82
L'Annee des Meduses '86

Hubert Frank
Melody in Love '78
The Dolls '83

Melvin Frank
Above and Beyond '53
Court Jester '56
The Jayhawkers '59
Li'l Abner '59
Strange Bedfellows '65
Buona Sera, Mrs. Campbell '68
A Touch of Class '73
Prisoner of Second Avenue '74
The Duchess and the Dirtwater Fox '76
Lost and Found '79
Walk Like a Man '87

Robert Frank
Candy Mountain '87

Cyril Frankel
Devil on Horseback '54
Make Me an Offer '55
The Very Edge '63
Permission To Kill '75

David Frankel
Miami Rhapsody '95

John Frankenheimer
Days of Wine and Roses '58
All Fall Down '62
Birdman of Alcatraz '62
The Manchurian Candidate '62
Seven Days in May '64
The Train '65
Grand Prix '66
The Fixer '68
The Horsemen '70
The Story of a Love Story '73
99 & 44/100 Dead '74
French Connection 2 '75
Black Sunday '77
Prophecy '79
The Challenge '82
The Holcroft Covenant '85
52 Pick-Up '86
Dead Bang '89
The Fourth War '90
Year of the Gun '91
Against the Wall '94
The Burning Season '94
Andersonville '95
The Island of Dr. Moreau '96

Carl Franklin
Nowhere to Run '88
Eye of the Eagle 2 '89
Full Fathom Five '90
One False Move '91
Laurel Avenue '93
Devil In a Blue Dress '95

Chester M. Franklin
Vanity Fair '32

Howard Franklin
Quick Change '90
The Public Eye '92

Jeff Franklin
Double Double Toil and Trouble '94
To Grandmother's House We Go '94

Jimmy Franklin
Ripping Yarns '75

Richard Franklin
Patrick '78
Road Games '81
Psycho 2 '83
Cloak & Dagger '84
Link '86
F/X 2: The Deadly Art of Illusion '91
Sorrento Beach '95

Roger Franklin
Raiders of Atlantis '83

Sidney Franklin
The Primitive Lover '16
The Forbidden City '18
Wild Orchids '28
The Guardsman '31
Private Lives '31
Smilin' Through '32
The Barretts of Wimpole Street '34
The Good Earth '37

Harry Fraser
Broadway to Cheyenne '32
Ghost City '32
Mason of the Mounted '32
The Savage Girl '32
Diamond Trail '33
Rainbow Ranch '33
Wolf Dog '33
'Neath the Arizona Skies '34
Randy Rides Alone '34
Feud of the West '35
Fighting Parson '35
Rustler's Paradise '35
The Tonto Kid '35
Wagon Trail '35
Wild Mustang '35
Cavalcade of the West '36
The Riding Avenger '36
Aces Wild '37
Galloping Dynamite '37
Ghost Town '37
Heroes of the Alamo '37
Six Shootin' Sheriff '38
Outlaw Roundup '44
Enemy of the Law '45
Frontier Fugitives '45
Three in the Saddle '45
Ambush Trail '46
Chained for Life '51

James Frawley
The Big Bus '76
The Muppet Movie '79
Great American Traffic Jam '80
Hansel and Gretel '82
Fraternity Vacation '85
Assault and Matrimony '87
Spies, Lies and Naked Thighs '91

Stephen Frears
Gumshoe '72
The Hit '85
My Beautiful Laundrette '85
Prick Up Your Ears '87
Saigon: Year of the Cat '87
Sammy & Rosie Get Laid '87
Dangerous Liaisons '88
The Grifters '90
Hero '92
The Snapper '93
Mary Reilly '95
The Van '95

Riccardo (Robert Hampton) Freda
Les Miserables '52
Sins of Rome '54
The Devil's Commandment '56
Evil's Commandment '56
The Giants of Thessaly '60
Maciste in Hell '60
The Mongols '60
Devil of the Desert Against the Son of Hercules '62
The Horrible Dr. Hichcock '62
Samson and the 7 Miracles of the World '62
The Ghost '63

Herb Freed
Haunts '77
Beyond Evil '80
Graduation Day '81
Tomboy '85
Survival Game '87

Mark Freed
Shock 'Em Dead '90

Jerrold Freedman
He Who Walks Alone '78
The Streets of L.A. '79
Borderline '80
Legs '83
Seduced '85
Native Son '86
Family Sins '87
Best Kept Secrets '88
Thompson's Last Run '90

Thornton Freeland
Whoopee! '30
They Call It Sin '32
Flying Down to Rio '33
Accused '36
Jericho '38

Hal Freeman
Blood Frenzy '87

Joan Freeman
Streetwalkin' '85
Satisfaction '88

Morgan Freeman
Bopha! '93

Warwick Freeman
Demonstrator '71

Paul Frees
The Beatniks '60

Hugo Fregonese
Decameron Nights '53
Blowing Wild '54
Harry Black and the Tiger '58
Dracula vs. Frankenstein '69

Isadore "Friz" Freleng
Best of Bugs Bunny & Friends '40
Bugs & Daffy: The Wartime Cartoons '45
Starring Bugs Bunny! '48
Bugs Bunny Superstar '75
Looney Looney Looney Bugs Bunny Movie '81
Daffy Duck's Movie: Fantastic Island '83

Harold French
The Day Will Dawn '42
Secret Mission '42
Trio '50
Encore '52
Paris Express '53
Rob Roy—The Highland Rogue '53

Charles Frend
The Foreman Went to France '42
Johnny Frenchman '46
San Demetrio, London '47
Scott of the Antarctic '48
Cruel Sea '53
The Third Key '57

Robert M. Fresco
Small Kill '93

Karl Freund
The Mummy '32
Mad Love '35

Ron Fricke
Baraka '93

Fridrik Thor Fridriksson
Children of Nature '91

Randall Fried
Heaven is a Playground '91

Rick Friedberg
Pray TV '80
Off the Wall '82
Spy Hard '96

Richard Friedenberg
Life & Times of Grizzly Adams '74
The Adventures of Frontier Fremont '75
The Deerslayer '78
Mr. & Mrs. Loving '96

Bud Friedgen
That's Entertainment, Part 3 '93

William Friedkin
The Night They Raided Minsky's '69
The Boys in the Band '70
The French Connection '71
The Exorcist '73
Sorcerer '77
Brink's Job '78
Cruising '80
Deal of the Century '83
To Live & Die in L.A. '85
Stalking Danger '86
Rampage '87
Python Wolf '88
The Guardian '90
Blue Chips '94
Jade '95

Adam Friedman
To Sleep with a Vampire '92

Anthony Friedman
Bartleby '70

David Friedman
The Defilers '65

Jeffrey Friedman
Common Threads: Stories from the Quilt '89
The Celluloid Closet '95

Ken Friedman
Made in USA '88

Richard S. Friedman
Deathmask '69
Scared Stiff '87
Doom Asylum '88
Phantom of the Mall: Eric's Revenge '89

Seymour Friedman
Rusty's Birthday '49
Loan Shark '52
I'll Get You '53

Gunther Fritsch
Stolen Identity '53

Bill Froelich
Return to Horror High '87

David Frost
Ring of Steel '94

Harvey Frost
Midnight Heat '95
Tracks of a Killer '95

Lee Frost
Chrome and Hot Leather '71
Chain Gang Women '72
Policewomen '73
Dixie Dynamite '76
Private Obsession '94

Mark Frost
Storyville '92

William Fruet
Wedding in White '72
Death Weekend '76
Search and Destroy '81
Funeral Home '82
Spasms '82
Bedroom Eyes '86
Killer Party '86
Blue Monkey '87

Boris Frumin
The Errors of Youth '78

Benjamin Fry
Wavelength '96

E. Max Frye
Amos and Andrew '93

Robert Fuest
And Soon the Darkness '70
Wuthering Heights '70
The Abominable Dr. Phibes '71
Doctor Phibes Rises Again '72
The Final Programme '73
Devil's Rain '75
A Movie Star's Daughter '79
Revenge of the Stepford Wives '80

Kinji Fukasaku
Black Lizard '68
The Green Slime '68
Tora! Tora! Tora! '70
Samurai Reincarnation '81
Virus '82

Jun Fukuda
The Secret of the Telegian '61
Godzilla vs. the Sea Monster '66
Son of Godzilla '66
Godzilla on Monster Island '72
Godzilla vs. the Cosmic Monster '74
Godzilla vs. Megalon '76

Lucio Fulci
The Psychic '78
Zombie '80
The Black Cat '81
Manhattan Baby '82
New York Ripper '82
Conquest '83
Gates of Hell '83
The House by the Cemetery '83
Challenge to White Fang '86
Contraband '86
The New Gladiators '87
Dangerous Obsession '88

Fleming Fuller
Prey of the Chameleon '91

Louis Fuller
Seven Doors of Death '82

Samuel Fuller
I Shot Jesse James '49
Baron of Arizona '51
The Steel Helmet '51
Pickup on South Street '53
Run of the Arrow '56
China Gate '57
Verboten! '59
Underworld, U.S.A. '60
Merrill's Marauders '62
Shock Corridor '63
Naked Kiss '64
Shark! '68
Dead Pigeon on Beethoven Street '72
The Meanest Men in the West '76
The Big Red One '80

Tex Fuller
Stranded '87

Jill Fullerton-Smith
Alive: 20 Years Later '93

Yueh Fung
Bells of Death '90

Allen Funt
What Do You Say to a Naked Lady? '70

John Furey
Shadow Dancing '88

Sidney J. Furie
The Snake Woman '61
Doctor Blood's Coffin '62
Leather Boys '63
The Ipcress File '65
The Appaloosa '66
Lady Sings the Blues '72
Hit! '73
The Boys in Company C '77
The Entity '83
Purple Hearts '84
Iron Eagle '86
Superman 4: The Quest for Peace '87
Iron Eagle 2 '88
The Taking of Beverly Hills '91
Ladybugs '92
Iron Eagle 4 '95

Stephen Furst
Magic Kid 2 '94

Yasuo Furuhata
Station '81

Tim Fywell
A Dark Adapted Eye '93
Gallowglass '95

Richard Gabai
Assault of the Party Nerds '89
Virgin High '90
Hot Under the Collar '91

Martin Gabel
Lost Moment '47

Pal Gabor
Brady's Escape '84

Mitchell Gabourie
Buying Time '89

Radu Gabrea
A Man Like Eva '83
Secret of the Ice Cave '89

Mike Gabriel
The Rescuers Down Under '90
Pocahontas '95

Frederic Gadette
This Is Not a Test '62

Robert Gaffney
Frankenstein Meets the Space Monster '65

George Gage
Fleshburn '84

John Gage
Velvet Touch '48

Rene Gainville
Le Complot '73
The Associate '82

Pierre-Dominique Gaisseau
The Sky Above, the Mud Below '61

Richard Galbreath
Night of Evil '62

John Gale
Commando Invasion '87
Slash '87
The Firing Line '91

Ricardo Jacques Gale
Alien Intruder '93

Timothy Galfas
Sunnyside '79

John A. Gallagher
Street Hunter '90

Andy Galler
Bums '93

Fred Gallo
Dead Space '90
The Finishing Touch '92
Dracula Rising '93
Lady in Waiting '94
Machine Gun Blues '95

George Gallo
29th Street '91
Trapped In Paradise '94

Carmine Gallone
Carthage in Flames '60

Samuel Gallu
Theatre of Death '67
The Man Outside '68

Abel Gance
The Torture of Silence '17
Napoleon '27
J'Accuse '37
The Battle of Austerlitz '60

Albert C. Gannaway
Daniel Boone: Trail Blazer '56
Hidden Guns '56
Man or Gun '58

Armand Garabidian
Silk Degrees '94

David Garcia
Sex Crimes '92

Michael Garcia
Armageddon: The Final Challenge '94

Nicole Garcia
The Favorite Son '94

Bud Gardner
Model Behavior '82

Herb Gardner
The Goodbye People '83

Richard Harding Gardner
Sherlock: Undercover Dog '94

Leo Garen
The Shrieking '73

Patrick Garland
A Doll's House '89

Lee Garmes
Dreaming Lips '37
Angels Over Broadway '40
Actors and Sin '52

Tay Garnett
The Flying Fool '29
China Seas '35
Stand-In '37
Joy of Living '38
Eternally Yours '39
Seven Sinners '40
Slightly Honorable '40
Cheers for Miss Bishop '41
Bataan '43
Mrs. Parkington '44
The Valley of Decision '45
The Postman Always Rings Twice '46
A Connecticut Yankee in King Arthur's Court '49
Cause for Alarm '51
One Minute to Zero '52
Main Street to Broadway '53
The Big Push '75
Challenge To Be Free '76

Tony Garnett
Deep in the Heart '83

Lila Garrett
Terraces '77

Otis Garrett
Danger on the Air '38

Roy Garrett
Eyes Behind the Stars '72
White Slave '86

Mick Garris
Critters 2: The Main Course '88
Psycho 4: The Beginning '90
Sleepwalkers '92
Stephen King's The Stand '94

Andrew Garroni
Body of Influence '93

Harry Garson
Mid-Channel '20
The Worldly Madonna '22

John Garwood
Violent Zone '89

Jerome Gary
Stripper '86
Traxx '87

Louis Gasnier
Kismet '20
Topaze '33
Reefer Madness '38
Murder on the Yukon '40

Mark Gasper
An Empty Bed '90

Mae Gaston
Seven Keys to Baldplate '17

Nils Gaup
Pathfinder '87
Shipwrecked '90

Roberto Gavaldon
The Littlest Outlaw '54

Eleanor Gaver
Slipping into Darkness '88

Victor Gaviria
Rodrigo D.: No Future '91

Joe Gayton
Warm Summer Rain '89
Wes Craven Presents Mind Ripper '95

Armand Gazarian
Game of Survival '89
Prison Planet '92

Gyula Gazdag
A Hungarian Fairy Tale '87
Stand Off '89

Glenn Gebhard
One Last Run '89
Desert Steel '94

Dieter Geissler
Deadly Game '83

Bruce Geller
The Savage Bees '76

Augusto Genina
Cyrano de Bergerac '25
Prix de Beaute '30

Arnaldo Genoino
Herod the Great '60

John Gentil
Battle of Valiant '63

Giacomo Gentilomo
Hercules Against the Moon Men '64

George W. George
James Dean Story '57

Jim George
Rover Dangerfield '91

Matthew George
Under the Gun '95

Peter George
Surf Nazis Must Die '87

Maurice Geraghty
Sword of Monte Cristo '51

Fred Gerber
Rent-A-Kid '95

Haile Gerima
Bush Mama '76
Ashes and Embers '82

Marion Gering
Thunder in the City '37

Pietro Germi
Four Ways Out '57
Divorce—Italian Style '62
Seduced and Abandoned '64
Alfredo, Alfredo '72

Chris Gerolmo
Citizen X '95

Clyde Geronomi
The Adventures of Ichabod and Mr. Toad '49
The Legend of Sleepy Hollow '49
Alice in Wonderland '51
Sleeping Beauty '59
101 Dalmatians '61

Peter Gerretsen
Night Friend '87

Theodore Gershuny
Silent Night, Bloody Night '73

Nicolas Gessner
The Peking Blond '68
12 Plus 1 '70
Someone Behind the Door '71
The Little Girl Who Lives Down the Lane '76
It Rained All Night the Day I Left '78
Quicker Than the Eye '88
Black Water '94

Steven Gethers
Billy: Portrait of a Street Kid '77
Damien: The Leper Priest '80
Jacqueline Bouvier Kennedy '81
Jenny's War '85
The Hillside Strangler '89

Francis Giacobetti
Emmanuelle, the Joys of a Woman '76
Emmanuelle 4 '84

David Giancola
Time Chasers '95

Alfredo Gianelli
Mother Doesn't Always Know Best '60s

Duncan Gibbins
Fire with Fire '86
Eve of Destruction '90
A Case for Murder '93

Pamela Gibbons
Midnight Dancer '87

Rodney Gibbons
The Neighbor '93

Alan Gibson
Twinsanity '70
The Satanic Rites of Dracula '73
The Two Faces of Evil '82
A Woman Called Golda '82
Silent Scream '84
Martin's Day '85
The Charmer '89

Brian Gibson
Breaking Glass '80
Poltergeist 2: The Other Side '86
Murderers among Us: The Simon Wiesenthal Story '89
The Josephine Baker Story '90
What's Love Got to Do with It? '93
The Juror '96

Mel Gibson
The Man Without a Face '93
Braveheart '95

Robert Gibson
Snow: The Movie '83

Tom Gibson
Singing Buckaroo '37

Gregory Gieras
The Whispering '94

Brian Gilbert
Sharma & Beyond '84
The French Lesson '86
Vice Versa '88
Not Without My Daughter '90
Tom & Viv '94

Lewis Gilbert
Tough Guy '53
Cast a Dark Shadow '55
The Sea Shall Not Have Them '55
Reach for the Sky '56
A Cry from the Streets '57
Ferry to Hong Kong '59
Sink the Bismarck '60
Damn the Defiant '62
Alfie '66
You Only Live Twice '67
The Adventurers '70
Friends '71
Paul and Michelle '74
The Spy Who Loved Me '77
Moonraker '79
Educating Rita '83
Not Quite Paradise '86
Shirley Valentine '89
Stepping Out '91
Haunted '95

David Giler
Black Bird '75

David Giles
Mansfield Park '85
A Murder Is Announced '87

Tom Giles
Journey Through Rosebud '72

Joseph Gilford
Max '79

Mark Gilhuis
Bloody Wednesday '87

Tony Jiti Gill
Murder-in-Law '92

Stuart Gillard
Paradise '82
A Man Called Sarge '90
Teenage Mutant Ninja Turtles 3 '93
The Outer Limits: Sandkings '95

Jeff Gillen
Deranged '74

Terry Gilliam
Monty Python and the Holy Grail '75
Jabberwocky '77
Time Bandits '81
Brazil '85
The Adventures of Baron Munchausen '89
The Fisher King '91
12 Monkeys '95

Sidney Gilliat
Green for Danger '47
Only Two Can Play '62
The Great St. Trinian's Train Robbery '66
Endless Night '71

John Gilling
No Trace '50
My Son, the Vampire '52
White Fire '53
The Gilded Cage '54
The Gamma People '56
It Takes a Thief '59
Mania '60
Night Caller from Outer Space '66

Where the Bullets Fly '66

Stuart Gilmore
The Virginian '46
The Half-Breed '51
Hot Lead '51

Frank D. Gilroy
Desperate Characters '71
From Noon Till Three '76
Once in Paris... '79
The Gig '85

Milton Moses Ginsberg
Werewolf of Washington '73

Brad F. Ginter
Flesh Feast '69

Robert Ginty
Bounty Hunters '89
Vietnam, Texas '90

Christian Gion
Here Comes Santa Claus '84

Jose Giovanni
Gypsy '75
Boomerang '76

Marita Giovanni
Bar Girls '95

Buddy Giovnazzo
Combat Shock '84

Bob Giraldi
Club Med '83
Hiding Out '87

Franco Giraldi
A Minute to Pray, A Second to Die '67

Andre Girard
Qui Etes Vous, Mr. Sorge? '61

Bernard Girard
Dead Heat on a Merry-Go-Round '66
Hard Frame '70
A Name for Evil '70
Mind Snatchers '72
Little Moon & Jud McGraw '78

Francois Girard
32 Short Films about Glenn Gould '93

Michael Paul Girard
Witchcraft 7: Judgement Hour '95

Bernard Giraudeau
Gone with the West '72

William Girdler
Asylum of Satan '72
Three on a Meathook '72
Sheba, Baby '75
Grizzly '76
Day of the Animals '77
The Manitou '78

Francois Girod
Infernal Trio '74
L'Etat Sauvage '78
The Elegant Criminal '92

Marcel Gisler
The Blue Hour '91

Wyndham Gittens
Tim Tyler's Luck '37

Paul Michael Glaser
The Amazons '84
Band of the Hand '86
The Running Man '87
The Cutting Edge '92
The Air Up There '94
Kazaam '96

Arnold Glassman
Visions of Light: The Art of Cinematography '93

Lesli Linka Glatter
Into the Homeland '87
State of Emergency '94
Now and Then '95

Richard Glatzer
Grief '94

Michie Gleason
Summer Heat '87

John Glen
For Your Eyes Only '81
Octopussy '83
A View to a Kill '85
The Living Daylights '87
License to Kill '89

Aces: Iron Eagle 3 '92
Christopher Columbus: The Discovery '92

John Glenister
After Julius '78

Bert Glennon
Paradise Island '30
South of Santa Fe '32

Peter Glenville
The Prisoner '55
Me and the Colonel '58
Summer and Smoke '61
Becket '64
Hotel Paradiso '66
The Comedians '67

James Glickenhaus
Exterminator '80
The Soldier '82
Protector '85
Shakedown '88
McBain '91
Slaughter of the Innocents '93
Timemaster '95

Paul Glickler
The Cheerleaders '72
Running Scared '79

Arne Glimcher
The Mambo Kings '92
Just Cause '94

Greg Glionna
Meet the Parents '91

Wolfgang Gluck
'38: Vienna Before the Fall '88

Tom Gniazdowski
Death Collector '89

Constantine S. Gochis
The Redeemer '76

Jean-Luc Godard
Godard/Truffaut Shorts '58
Breathless '59
A Woman is a Woman '60
My Life to Live '62
RoGoPaG '62
Les Carabiniers '63
Band of Outsiders '64
Contempt '64
Alphaville '65
The Joy of Knowledge '65
A Married Woman '65
Pierrot le Fou '65
Masculine Feminine '66
Oldest Profession '67
Weekend '67
Six in Paris '68
Here and Elsewhere '70s
Sympathy for the Devil '70
Numero Deux '75
Comment Ca Va? '76
Six Fois Deux/Sur et Sous la Communication '76
France/Tour/Detour/Deux/Enfants '78
Scenario du Film Passion '82
First Name: Carmen '83
Hail Mary '85
Soft and Hard '85
King Lear '87
Aria '88
Nouvelle Vague '90
Helas Pour Moi '94

Gary Goddard
Masters of the Universe '87

Jim Goddard
A Tale of Two Cities '80
The Life and Adventures of Nicholas Nickleby '81
Shanghai Surprise '86
The Impossible Spy '87
Reilly: Ace of Spies '87
Lie Down with Lions '94

Peter Godfrey
Christmas in Connecticut '45
Cry Wolf '47
Escape Me Never '47
The Two Mrs. Carrolls '47

Jill Godmilow
Waiting for the Moon '87

Alex E. Goiten
Cherry Hill High '76

Menahem Golan
What's Good for the Goose '69

Lupo '70
Diamonds '72
Escape to the Sun '72
Lepke '75
Operation Thunderbolt '77
The Magician of Lublin '79
The Apple '80
Enter the Ninja '81
Over the Brooklyn Bridge '83
Delta Force '86
Over the Top '86
Hanna's War '88
Mack the Knife '89
Hit the Dutchman '92
Silent Victim '92

Greg Gold
House of the Rising Sun '87

Jack Gold
Catholics '73
Man Friday '75
The Naked Civil Servant '75
Roboman '75
The Medusa Touch '78
Little Lord Fauntleroy '80
Praying Mantis '83
Sakharov '84
Murrow '86
Escape from Sobibor '87
The Tenth Man '88
The Rose and the Jackal '90
The Return of the Native '94

Myron G. Gold
Frankenstein's Great Aunt Tillie '83

Willis Goldbeck
Love Laughs at Andy Hardy '46

Dan Goldberg
Feds '88

Eric Goldberg
Pocahontas '95

Gary David Goldberg
Dad '89

Mark Goldblatt
Dead Heat '88
The Punisher '90

Dan Golden
Naked Obsession '91
Saturday Night Special '92
Stripteaser '95

John Golden
Fat Guy Goes Nutzoid '86

Murray Golden
Haunting of Harrington House '82

Michael Goldenberg
Bed of Roses '95

Sidney Goldin
East and West '23
His Wife's Lover '31
Uncle Moses '32

Paul Golding
Pulse '88

Gary Goldman
Thumbelina '94
A Troll in Central Park '94

Jill Goldman
Bad Love '95

Jim Goldman
Desert Warrior '88

Martin Goldman
Dark August '76

Stuart Goldman
Senior Week '88

John Goldschmidt
She'll Be Wearing Pink Pajamas '84
Crime of Honor '85

Allan Goldstein
The Dining Room '86
True West '86
The House of Dies Drear '88
Outside Chance of Maximillian Glick '88
Cold Front '89
The Phone Call '89
Common Bonds '91
Death Wish 5: The Face of Death '94
Synapse '95

Amy Goldstein
The Silencer '92

Scott Goldstein
Walls of Glass '85
Ambition '91

James Goldstone
Winning '69
Brother John '70
They Only Kill Their Masters '72
Cry Panic '74
Things in Their Season '74
Eric '75
Swashbuckler '76
Rollercoaster '77
When Time Ran Out '80
Kent State '81
Calamity Jane '82
Rita Hayworth: The Love Goddess '83

Bob(cat) Goldthwait
Shakes the Clown '92

Steve Gomer
Sweet Lorraine '87
Fly by Night '93
Sunset Park '96

Nick Gomez
Laws of Gravity '92
New Jersey Drive '95

Manuel Gomez Pereira
Mouth to Mouth '95

Vasilii Goncharov
Early Russian Cinema, Vol. 2: Folklore & Legend '12
Early Russian Cinema, Vol. 6: Class Distinctions '14

Regelio A. Gonzalez, Jr.
The Oval Portrait '88

Servando Gonzalez
The Fool Killer '65

Gregory Goodell
Human Experiments '79

Saul Goodkind
Buck Rogers Conquers the Universe '39
The Phantom Creeps '39

Fred Goodwin
Curse 2: The Bite '88

Leslie Goodwins
Anything for a Thrill '37
Day the Bookies Wept '39
Pop Always Pays '40
Mexican Spitfire at Sea '42
The Mummy's Curse '44

Bert I. Gordon
Cyclops '56
The Amazing Colossal Man '57
Beginning of the End '57
Earth vs. the Spider '58
The War of the Colossal Beast '58
Tormented '60
The Magic Sword '62
Village of the Giants '65
Picture Mommy Dead '66
The Mad Bomber '72
The Witching '72
Food of the Gods '76
Empire of the Ants '77
The Big Bet '85
Satan's Princess '90

Bette Gordon
Variety '83

Bryan Gordon
Career Opportunities '91

Keith Gordon
The Chocolate War '88
A Midnight Clear '92
Wild Palms '93

Michael Gordon
Cyrano de Bergerac '50
Pillow Talk '59
Boys' Night Out '62
For Love or Money '63
Texas Across the River '66
The Impossible Years '68

Robert Gordon
It Came from Beneath the Sea '55
The Gatling Gun '72
Revenge of the Red Baron '93

Steve Gordon
Arthur '81
Stuart Gordon
Re-Animator '84
From Beyond '86
Dolls '87
Daughter of Darkness '89
Robot Jox '90
The Pit & the Pendulum '91
Fortress '93
Castle Freak '95
Berry Gordy
Mahogany '75
Serif Goren
Yol '82
Claude Goretta
The Lacemaker '77
Vladimir Gorikker
The Tsar's Bride '66
Jean-Pierre Gorin
Here and Elsewhere '70s
Charles Gormley
The Gospel According to Vic '87
Michael Gornick
Creepshow 2 '87
Marleen Gorris
Question of Silence '83
Broken Mirrors '85
Antonia's Line '95
Ron Gorton, Sr.
Whispers of White '93
Rene Goscinny
Lucky Luke: The Ballad of the Daltons '78
Hideo Gosha
Hunter in the Dark '80
The Wolves '82
Jurgen Goslar
Albino '76
Slavers '77
Peter Gothar
Time Stands Still '82
Toshio Goto
Forest of Little Bear '79
Carl Gottlieb
Caveman '81
Amazon Women on the Moon '87
Franz Gottlieb
The Black Abbot '63
Curse of the Yellow Snake '63
The Phantom of Soho '64
Lisa Gottlieb
Just One of the Guys '85
Across the Moon '94
Michael Gottlieb
Mannequin '87
Mr. Nanny '93
A Kid in King Arthur's Court '95
Robert Gottschalk
Dangerous Charter '62
Heywood Gould
One Good Cop '91
Trial by Jury '94
Alfred Goulding
A Chump at Oxford '40
Dick Barton, Special Agent '48
Edmund Goulding
Reaching for the Moon '31
Grand Hotel '32
Riptide '34
That Certain Woman '37
Dawn Patrol '38
Dark Victory '39
The Old Maid '39
The Great Lie '41
Forever and a Day '43
The Razor's Edge '46
We're Not Married '52
Anne Goursaud
Embrace of the Vampire '95
Poison Ivy 2: Lily '95
Red Shoe Diaries 6: How I Met My Husband '95
Richard Governor
Ghost Town '88
William Grace
Tomb of Torture '65

Marc Gracie
A Kink in the Picasso '90
Roger Graef
Secret Policeman's Private Parts '81
Tom Graeff
Teenagers from Outer Space '59
Anders Grafstrom
The Long Island Four '80
Bob Graham
End of August '82
David C. Graham
The Undertaker and His Pals '67
Roderick Graham
Elizabeth R '72
S. Edwin Graham
Devil Monster '46
William A. Graham
The Doomsday Flight '66
Waterhole #3 '67
Change of Habit '69
Honky '71
Jigsaw '71
Thief '71
Birds of Prey '72
Deadly Encounter '72
Get Christie Love! '74
Larry '74
Mr. Inside, Mr. Outside '74
Where the Lilies Bloom '74
Beyond the Bermuda Triangle '75
21 Hours at Munich '76
The Amazing Howard Hughes '77
And I Alone Survived '78
One in a Million: The Ron LeFlore Story '78
Orphan Train '79
The Guyana Tragedy: The Story of Jim Jones '80
Rage '80
Harry Tracy '83
M.A.D.D.: Mothers Against Drunk Driving '83
Calendar Girl Murders '84
Secrets of a Married Man '84
George Washington: The Forging of a Nation '86
Last Days of Frank & Jesse James '86
Proud Men '87
Gore Vidal's Billy the Kid '89
Montana '90
Return to the Blue Lagoon '91
Vladimir Grammatikov
The Land of Faraway '87
Richard Grand
Fyre '78
Gilles Grangier
Duke of the Derby '62
Pierre Granier-Deferre
Widow Couderc '74
The French Detective '75
Le Chat '75
A Woman at Her Window '77
Brian Grant
Love Kills '91
Sweet Poison '91
Sensation '94
The Immortals '95
James Edward Grant
Angel and the Badman '47
Lee Grant
Tell Me a Riddle '80
Staying Together '89
Michael Grant
Fatal Attraction '80
Alex Grasshof
Pepper and His Wacky Taxi '72
A Billion for Boris '90
Jorge Grau
The Legend of Blood Castle '72
Walter Grauman
Lady in a Cage '64
633 Squadron '64
Paper Man '71
The Streets of San Francisco '72
Manhunter '74
Force Five '75

Most Wanted '76
Are You in the House Alone? '78
Pleasure Palace '80
To Race the Wind '80
Scene of the Crime '85
Outrage! '86
Nightmare on the 13th Floor '90
Gary Graver
Trick or Treats '82
Moon in Scorpio '86
Party Camp '87
Crossing the Line '90
Evil Spirits '91
Roots of Evil '91
Alex Graves
The Crude Oasis '95
F. Gary Gray
Friday '95
James Gray
Little Odessa '94
John Gray
Billy Galvin '86
When He's Not a Stranger '89
The Lost Capone '90
An American Story '92
A Place for Annie '94
Born to Be Wild '95
Mike Gray
Wavelength '83
Godfrey Grayson
Dick Barton Strikes Back '48
Room to Let '49
Kjell Grede
Good Evening, Mr. Wallenberg '93
Janet Greek
The Spellbinder '88
Alfred E. Green
Ella Cinders '26
Disraeli '29
Baby Face '33
Dangerous '35
Thoroughbreds Don't Cry '37
South of Pago Pago '40
Mr. Winkle Goes to War '44
A Thousand and One Nights '45
The Jolson Story '46
Copacabana '47
The Fabulous Dorseys '47
Four Faces West '48
The Jackie Robinson Story '50
Invasion U.S.A. '52
Bruce Seth Green
Running Against Time '90
The Hunt for the Night Stalker '91
In Self Defense '93
David Green
Code of Honor '84
Car Trouble '86
Buster '88
Fire Birds '90
Guy Green
River Beat '54
Postmark for Danger '56
Postmark for Danger/Quicksand '56
Sea of Sand '58
S.O.S. Pacific '60
The Mark '61
Diamond Head '62
A Patch of Blue '65
Walk in the Spring Rain '70
Luther '74
Once is Not Enough '75
The Incredible Journey of Dr. Meg Laurel '79
Strong Medicine '84
Joseph Green
Yidl Mitn Fidl '36
Der Purimshpiler '37
A Brivele der Mamen '38
Mamele '38
The Brain That Wouldn't Die '63
Sparky Green
Savage Hunger '84
Terry Green
Cold Justice '89
Walon Green
The Hellstrom Chronicle '71
Peter Greenaway
The Draughtsman's Contract '82
Drowning by Numbers '87

A Zed & Two Noughts '88
The Cook, the Thief, His Wife & Her Lover '90
The Belly of an Architect '91
Prospero's Books '91
Richard Alan Greenberg
Little Monsters '89
Danford B. Greene
The Secret Diary of Sigmund Freud '84
David Greene
Blood Island '68
Sebastian '68
The People Next Door '70
Madame Sin '71
The Count of Monte Cristo '74
Gray Lady Down '77
Roots '77
Friendly Fire '79
The Choice '81
Hard Country '81
Rehearsal for Murder '82
Take Your Best Shot '82
Prototype '83
Fatal Vision '84
The Guardian '84
TripleCross '85
Miles to Go '86
World War III '86
After the Promise '87
Vanishing Act '88
Small Sacrifices '89
In a Stranger's Hand '92
The Penthouse '92
What Ever Happened To... '93
A Good Day to Die '95
Don Fox Greene
Last Time Out '94
Herbert Greene
The Cosmic Man '59
Martin Greene
Dark Sanity '82
Undercover Cop '94
Max Greene
Hotel Reserve '44
Gregory Greens
The Sea Serpent '85
Bud Greenspan
Wilma '77
Maggie Greenwald
Home Remedy '88
The Ballad of Little Jo '93
Robert Greenwald
Flatbed Annie and Sweetiepie: Lady Truckers '79
Xanadu '80
In the Custody of Strangers '82
The Burning Bed '85
Sweet Hearts Dance '88
Forgotten Prisoners '90
Hear No Evil '93
David Greenwalt
Secret Admirer '85
Rude Awakening '89
William Grefe
The Checkered Flag '63
Wild Rebels '71
Alligator Alley '72
Stanley '72
Impulse '74
Jaws of Death '76
Whiskey Mountain '77
Colin Gregg
Lamb '85
We Think the World of You '88
Ezio Greggio
Silence of the Hams '93
Ugo Gregoretti
RoGoPaG '62
Frank Gregory
The Invincible Gladiator '63
Jean Gremillon
Stormy Waters '41
Pattes Blanches '49
Wolf Gremm
Kamikaze '89 '83
Edmond T. Greville
Princess Tam Tam '35
Beat Girl '60
The Hands of Orlac '60

The Liars '64
John Greyson
Zero Patience '94
Sharon Greytak
Hearing Voices '90
Sergio Grieco
Man of Legend '71
Mad Dog '84
Tom Gries
Will Penny '67
100 Rifles '69
Fools '70
The Glass House '72
The Connection '73
Lady Ice '73
The Migrants '74
QB VII '74
Breakout '75
Breakheart Pass '76
Helter Skelter '76
The Greatest '77
Andrew Grieve
Suspicion '87
Lorna Doone '90
Ken Grieve
Alamut Ambush '86
Giuseppe Patroni Griffi
Divine Nymph '71
Driver's Seat '73
'Tis a Pity She's a Whore '73
Collector's Item '89
Charles B. Griffith
Eat My Dust '76
Up from the Depths '79
Dr. Heckyl and Mr. Hype '80
Smokey Bites the Dust '81
Wizards of the Lost Kingdom 2 '89
D.W. Griffith
Griffith Biograph Program '09
Battle of Elderbush Gulch '13
D.W. Griffith Triple Feature '13
Avenging Conscience '14
Home Sweet Home '14
Judith of Bethulia '14
The Birth of a Nation '15
The Babylon Story from "Intolerance" '16
Intolerance '16
Hearts of the World '18
Broken Blossoms '19
The Greatest Question '19
True Heart Susie '19
The Idol Dancer '20
The Love Flower '20
Way Down East '20
Dream Street '21
Orphans of the Storm '21
The White Rose '23
Isn't Life Wonderful '24
Sally of the Sawdust '25
The Sorrows of Satan '26
Abraham Lincoln '30
Edward H. Griffith
Captain Swagger '25
The Animal Kingdom '32
My Love For Yours '39
Bahama Passage '42
Young & Willing '42
The Sky's the Limit '43
Mark Griffiths
Running Hot '83
Hardbodies '84
Hardbodies 2 '86
Heroes Stand Alone '89
A Cry in the Wild '90
Cheyenne Warrior '94
Max is Missing '95
Gary Grillo
American Justice '86
Aurelio Grimaldi
Acla's Descent into Floristella '87
Hugo Grimaldi
The Human Duplicators '64
Nick Grinde
Exiled to Shanghai '37
Delinquent Parents '38
The Man They Could Not Hang '39
Before I Hang '40
Hitler: Dead or Alive '43

Brad Grinter
Blood Freak '72
Wallace Grissell
King of the Congo '52
John Grissmer
Scalpel '76
Blood Rage '87
Rajko Grlic
That Summer of White Roses '90
Ferde Grofe, Jr.
Satan's Harvest '65
Warkill '65
The Proud and the Damned '72
Judgment Day '88
Ulu Grosbard
Straight Time '78
True Confessions '81
Falling in Love '84
Georgia '95
Jerry Gross
Girl on a Chain Gang '65
Teenage Mother '67
Larry Gross
3:15—The Moment of Truth '86
Yoram Gross
Camel Boy '84
Douglas Grossman
Hell High '86
Sam Grossman
The Van '77
Charles Grosvenor
Once Upon a Forest '93
Krzysztof Gruber
Greta '86
David Grubin
LBJ: A Biography '91
Karl Grune
The Street '23
Allan Grunewald
Nightmare Castle '65
Enrico Guazzoni
Quo Vadis '12
Nikolai Gubenko
Orphans '83
Robert Guenette
Here's Looking at You, Warner Bros. '93
James W. Guercio
Electra Glide in Blue '73
Ruy Guerra
Erendira '83
Opera do Malandro '87
The Fable of the Beautiful Pigeon Fancier '88
Romolo Guerrieri
The Final Executioner '83
Mino Guerrini
Mines of Kilimanjaro '87
Christopher Guest
The Big Picture '89
Attack of the 50 Ft. Woman '93
Cliff Guest
Disturbance '89
Robert Guest
Fatal Confinement '64
Val Guest
Just William's Luck '47
The Runaway Bus '54
The Quatermass Experiment '56
Carry On Admiral '57
Men of Sherwood Forest '57
Quatermass 2 '57
Up the Creek '58
The Day the Earth Caught Fire '61
Casino Royale '67
When Dinosaurs Ruled the Earth '70
Killer Force '75
Charles Guggenheim
The Great St. Louis Bank Robbery '59
John Guillermin
Never Let Go '60
Waltz of the Toreadors '62
Guns at Batasi '64
The Blue Max '66
The Bridge at Remagen '69
El Condor '70
Shaft in Africa '73
The Towering Inferno '74
King Kong '76
Death on the Nile '78
Crossover '82
Sheena '84
King Kong Lives '86
The Tracker '88
Fred Guiol
Battling Orioles '24
Tanks a Million '41
Mr. Walkie Talkie '52
Sacha Guitry
The Story of a Cheat '36
Napoleon '55
Yilmaz Guney
Baba '73
The Wall '83
Bill Gunn
Black Vampire '73
Gilbert Gunn
The Cosmic Monsters '58
Hrafn Gunnlaugsson
Revenge of the Barbarians '85
Carlo Gustaff
Indecent Behavior 2 '94
Thomas Gutierrez Alea
Death of a Bureaucrat '66
Memories of Underdevelopment '68
The Last Supper '76
Up to a Certain Point '83
Letters from the Park '88
Strawberry and Chocolate '93
Nathaniel Gutman
Deadline '87
Linda '93
When the Dark Man Calls '95
Andre Guttfreund
Femme Fatale '90
Amos Guttman
Drifting '82
Claudio Guzman
Antonio '73
Willa '79
The Hostage Tower '80
Stephen Gyllenhaal
Certain Fury '85
The Abduction of Kari Swenson '87
Promised a Miracle '88
A Killing in a Small Town '90
Paris Trout '91
Waterland '92
A Dangerous Woman '93
Question of Faith '93
Losing Isaiah '94
Imre Gyongyossy
The Revolt of Job '84
Charles Haas
Girls' Town '59
Platinum High School '60
Philip Haas
The Music of Chance '93
Angels and Insects '95
Herve Hachuel
The Last of Philip Banter '87
Taylor Hackford
Idolmaker '80
An Officer and a Gentleman '82
Against All Odds '84
White Nights '85
Chuck Berry: Hail! Hail! Rock 'n' Roll '87
Everybody's All American '88
Blood In...Blood Out: Bound by Honor '93
Dolores Claiborne '94
Rolf Haedrich
Among the Cinders '83
Petra Hafter
A Demon in My View '92
Ross Hagen
The Glove '78
B.O.R.N. '88
Mark Haggard
The First Nudie Musical '75
Piers Haggard
The Blood on Satan's Claw '71
Quatermass Conclusion '79
The Fiendish Plot of Dr. Fu Manchu '80
Venom '82
A Summer Story '88
Fulfillment '89
Back Home '90
Four Eyes and Six Guns '93
Paul Haggis
Red Hot '95
Larry Hagman
Son of Blob '72
Stuart Hagmann
The Strawberry Statement '70
Tarantulas: The Deadly Cargo '77
Steven Hahn
Starchaser: The Legend of Orin '85
Weng Yao Hai
Crack Shadow Boxers '70s
Charles Haid
Cooperstown '93
Iron Will '93
The Nightman '93
Children of Fury '94
Riders of the Purple Sage '96
Fred Haines
Steppenwolf '74
Randa Haines
Children of a Lesser God '86
The Doctor '91
Wrestling Ernest Hemingway '93
Richard W. Haines
Splatter University '84
Class of Nuke 'Em High '86
Alien Space Avenger '91
John Halas
Animal Farm '55
Don Haldane
Nikki, the Wild Dog of the North '61
The Reincarnate '71
Alan Hale
Braveheart '25
Risky Business '28
Billy Hale
Red Alert '77
S.O.S. Titanic '79
Harem '86
The Murder of Mary Phagan '87
Sonnie Hale
Gangway '37
Sailing Along '38
William Hale
Stalk the Wild Child '76
Murder in Texas '81
One Shoe Makes It Murder '82
Jack Haley, Jr.
The Love Machine '71
That's Entertainment '74
That's Dancing! '85
H.B. Halicki
Gone in 60 Seconds '74
The Junkman '82
Deadline Auto Theft '83
Alexander Hall
Little Miss Marker '34
Goin' to Town '35
I Am the Law '38
Doctor Takes a Wife '40
Here Comes Mr. Jordan '41
Down to Earth '47
The Great Lover '49
Because You're Mine '52
Forever Darling '56
Anthony Michael Hall
Hail Caesar '94
Gary Skeen Hall
Prime Time Murder '92
Godfrey Hall
Honor and Glory '92
Undefeatable '94
Ivan Hall
Funeral for an Assassin '77
Kill or Be Killed '80
Kill and Kill Again '81
Jon Hall
The Beach Girls and the Monster '65
Kenneth J. Hall
Evil Spawn '87
Ghost Writer '89
Peter Hall
A Midsummer Night's Dream '68
Orpheus Descending '91
Jacob '94
Never Talk to Strangers '95
Daniel Haller
Die, Monster, Die! '65
Devil's Angels '67
The Dunwich Horror '70
Paddy '70
Buck Rogers in the 25th Century '79
Follow That Car '80
Margin for Murder '81
Todd Hallowell
Love or Money? '88
Lasse Hallstrom
My Life as a Dog '85
Once Around '91
What's Eating Gilbert Grape '93
Something to Talk About '95
Victor Halperin
Party Girls '29
The White Zombie '32
Supernatural '33
I Conquer the Sea '36
Revolt of the Zombies '36
A Nation Aflame '37
Buried Alive '39
Torture Ship '39
Glenda Hambly
Fran '85
Robert Hamer
Dead of Night '45
Pink Strings and Sealing Wax '45
Kind Hearts and Coronets '49
The Detective '54
To Paris with Love '55
David Hamilton
Bilitis '77
Dean Hamilton
Strike a Pose '93
The Road Home '95
Guy Hamilton
The Colditz Story '55
The Devil's Disciple '59
Goldfinger '64
Funeral in Berlin '66
Battle of Britain '69
Diamonds Are Forever '71
Live and Let Die '73
The Man with the Golden Gun '74
Force 10 from Navarone '78
The Mirror Crack'd '80
Evil under the Sun '82
Remo Williams: The Adventure Begins '85
Strathford Hamilton
Blueberry Hill '88
Diving In '90
Betrayal of the Dove '92
Temptation '94
The Set Up '95
William Hamilton
Call Out the Marines '42
Robert Hammer
Don't Answer the Phone '80
Jason Hammond
The Deadly Secret '94
Peter Hammond
The Dark Angel '91
Benjamin B. Hampton
Heart's Haven '22
Christopher Hampton
Carrington '95
Victor Hanbury
The Avenging Hand '43
Hotel Reserve '44
John Hancock
Let's Scare Jessica to Death '71
Bang the Drum Slowly '73
California Dreaming '79
Weeds '87
Steal the Sky '88
Prancer '89
David Hand
Snow White and the Seven Dwarfs '37
Bambi '42
Richard Handford
Second Chance '80
Alan Handley
Alice Through the Looking Glass '66
Ken Handley
Delivery Boys '84
Susumu Hani
She and He '63
Tom Hanks
Fallen Angels 2 '93
William Hanna
Hey There, It's Yogi Bear '64
Jetsons: The Movie '90
Ken Hannam
Sunday Too Far Away '74
The Assassination Run '84
Brian Hannant
The Time Guardian '87
Izhak Hanooka
Red Nights '87
Marion Hansel
Dust '85
Between Heaven and Earth '93
Ed Hansen
Takin' It All Off '87
Party Favors '89
Robo-Chic '89
The Bikini Car Wash Company '90
Party Plane '90
Rolf Hansen
The Devil in Silk '56
Curtis Hanson
The Arousers '70
Little Dragons '80
Losin' It '82
The Children of Times Square '86
The Bedroom Window '87
Bad Influence '90
The Hand that Rocks the Cradle '92
The River Wild '94
David W. Hanson
Night of the Bloody Transplant '86
John Hanson
Northern Lights '79
Wildrose '85
Tom Hanson
The Zodiac Killer '71
Richard Harbinger
T-Bird Gang '59
Cedric Hardwicke
Forever and a Day '43
Joseph Hardy
Return Engagement '78
Users '78
Love's Savage Fury '79
To Love Again '80
Robin Hardy
The Wicker Man '75
The Fantasist '89
Rod Hardy
Sara Dane '81
Under Capricorn '82
Thirst '87
The Yearling '94
Buffalo Girls '95
David Hare
Wetherby '85
Strapless '90
Dean Hargrove
Dear Detective '78
Veit Harlan
Jud Suess '40
Kolberg '45
Renny Harlin
Born American '86
A Nightmare on Elm Street 4: Dream Master '88

Harlin ▶cont.

Prison '88
The Adventures of Ford Fairlane '90
Die Hard 2: Die Harder '90
Cliffhanger '93
Cutthroat Island '95

John Harlow
Spellbound '41
Candles at Nine '44
Meet Sexton Blake '44
Appointment with Crime '45
While I Live '47

Robert Harmon
The Hitcher '86
Eyes of an Angel '91
Nowhere to Run '93

Curtis Harrington
Night Tide '63
Voyage to the Prehistoric Planet '65
Planet of Blood '66
What's the Matter with Helen? '71
Who Slew Auntie Roo? '71
The Killing Kind '73
The Dead Don't Die '75
Ruby '77
Devil Dog: The Hound of Hell '78

Damian Harris
The Rachel Papers '89
Deceived '91
Bad Company '94

Denny Harris
Silent Scream '80

Frank Harris
Killpoint '84
Low Blow '85
The Patriot '86
Aftershock '88

Harry Harris
The Runaways '75
A Day for Thanks on Walton's Mountain '82

Jack H. Harris
The Unkissed Bride '66

James B. Harris
Bedford Incident '65
Some Call It Loving '73
Fast Walking '82
Cop '88
Boiling Point '93

Leslie Harris
Just Another Girl on the I.R.T. '93

Richard Harris
The Hero '71

Steven Harris
At Gunpoint '90

Trent Harris
Rubin & Ed '92
Plan 10 from Outer Space '95

Wendell B. Harris, Jr.
Chameleon Street '89

John Harrison
Tales from the Darkside: The Movie '90
Donor Unknown '95

John Kent Harrison
Beautiful Dreamers '92
City Boy '93
The Sound and the Silence '93
Hole in the Sky '95
Johnny's Girl '95

Jules Harrison
Exterminators of the Year 3000 '83

Ken Harrison
1918 '85
On Valentine's Day '86

Matthew Harrison
Rhythm Thief '94

Paul Harrison
The House of Seven Corpses '73

Sam Harrison
Sex and Buttered Popcorn '91

Lee Harry
Silent Night, Deadly Night 2 '87
Street Soldiers '91

Bruce Hart
Sooner or Later '78

Christopher Hart
Eat and Run '86

Harvey Hart
Fortune and Men's Eyes '71
The Pyx '73
Murder or Mercy '74
Panic on the 5:22 '74
The City '76
Goldenrod '77
The Prince of Central Park '77
Standing Tall '78
Aliens Are Coming '80
East of Eden '80
High Country '81
Born Beautiful '82
Utilities '83
Reckless Disregard '84
Shoot '85
Beverly Hills Madam '86
Stone Fox '87
Passion in Paradise '89

Jacobsen Hart
Steel Frontier '94

William S. Hart
The Disciple '15
Hell's Hinges '16
Return of Draw Egan '16
Narrow Trail '17

David M. Hartford
Nomads of the North '20

Kenneth Hartford
The Lucifer Complex '78
Hell Squad '85

Robert Hartford-Davis
The Bloodsuckers '70
Estate of Insanity '70
The Fiend '71

Karl Hartl
F.P. 1 Doesn't Answer '33
The Mozart Story '48
The Life and Loves of Mozart '59

Hal Hartley
The Unbelievable Truth '90
Surviving Desire '91
Trust '91
Simple Men '92
Amateur '94
Flirt '95

Richard Hartley
Kennedy '83

Don Hartman
Every Girl Should Be Married '48
Holiday Affair '49

David Hartwell
Love Is a Gun '94

Anthony Harvey
Dutchman '67
The Lion in Winter '68
They Might Be Giants '71
Eagle's Wing '79
Players '79
Richard's Things '80
Svengali '83
Grace Quigley '84

Gail Harvey
Cold Sweat '93

Harold (Herk) Harvey
Carnival of Souls '62

Rupert Harvey
Critters 4 '91

Wojciech Has
The Saragossa Manuscript '65

Patrick Hasburgh
Aspen Extreme '93

Kohji Hashimoto
Godzilla 1985 '85

Byron Haskin
Killer Bait '49
Too Late for Tears '49
Treasure Island '50
The Denver & Rio Grande '51
His Majesty O'Keefe '53
Long John Silver '53
The War of the Worlds '53
Naked Jungle '54
Conquest of Space '55
From the Earth to the Moon '58
Jet Over the Atlantic '59
Armored Command '61
Captain Sinbad '63
Robinson Crusoe on Mars '64

Linda Hassani
Dark Angel: The Ascent '94

Masami Hata
Little Nemo: Adventures in Slumberland '92

Masanori Hata
The Adventures of Milo & Otis '89

Henry Hathaway
When the West Was Young '32
Heritage of the Desert '33
Man of the Forest '33
To the Last Man '33
The Lives of a Bengal Lancer '35
Go West, Young Man '36
The Real Glory '39
Brigham Young: Frontiersman '40
Sundown '41
A Wing and a Prayer '44
House on 92nd Street '45
Dark Corner '46
13 Rue Madeleine '46
Kiss of Death '47
Call Northside 777 '48
Rawhide '50
The Desert Fox '51
Diplomatic Courier '52
Niagara '52
Prince Valiant '54
The Racers '55
Legend of the Lost '57
North to Alaska '60
Seven Thieves '60
How the West Was Won '63
Circus World '64
Of Human Bondage '64
Sons of Katie Elder '65
Nevada Smith '66
The Last Safari '67
Five Card Stud '68
True Grit '69
Raid on Rommel '71

Bob Hathcock
DuckTales the Movie: Treasure of the Lost Lamp '90

Jeff Hathcock
Night Ripper '86

Kayo Hatta
Picture Bride '94

Maurice Hatton
American Roulette '88

Didier Haudepin
Elsa, Elsa '85

Reinhard Hauff
Knife in the Head '78

Wings Hauser
The Art of Dying '90
Coldfire '90
Living to Die '91

Steve Hawkes
Blood Freak '72

Tara Hawkins Moore
Tusks '89

Don Hawks
Hush Little Baby, Don't You Cry '86

Howard Hawks
Criminal Code '31
Scarface '31
Today We Live '33
Twentieth Century '34
Barbary Coast '35
Ceiling Zero '35
Come and Get It '36
Bringing Up Baby '38
Only Angels Have Wings '39
His Girl Friday '40
Ball of Fire '41
Sergeant York '41
Air Force '43
To Have & Have Not '44
The Big Sleep '46
Red River '48
A Song is Born '48
I Was a Male War Bride '49
The Thing '51
The Big Sky '52
Monkey Business '52
Gentlemen Prefer Blondes '53
Land of the Pharaohs '55
Rio Bravo '59
Hatari! '62
Man's Favorite Sport? '63
Red Line 7000 '65
El Dorado '67
Rio Lobo '70

Peter Hawley
Victimless Crimes '90

Rod Hay
Breaking Loose '90

Richard Haydn
Dear Wife '49
Mr. Music '50

Sidney Hayers
Circus of Horrors '60
Burn Witch, Burn! '62
Trap '66
Assault '70
Revenge '71
King Arthur, the Young Warlord '75
Bananas Boat '78
The Seekers '79
Deadly Strangers '82

Bill Hayes
King Kung Fu '87

John Hayes
Five Minutes to Love '63
Grave of the Vampire '72
Tomb of the Undead '72
Mama's Dirty Girls '74
Dream No Evil '75
End of the World '76
Shell Shock '80s
All the Lovin' Kinfolk '89
The Cut Throats '89
Sweet Trash '89

John Patrick Hayes
The Farmer's Other Daughter '65

Robert Hayes
Phoenix the Warrior '88

David Hayman
The Hawk '93
A Woman's Guide to Adultery '93

Todd Haynes
Poison '91
Safe '95

Jonathan Heap
Benefit of the Doubt '93

Howard Heard
Shadows Run Black '84

Robert Heath
Hugh Hefner: Once Upon a Time '92

David Heavener
Outlaw Force '87
Deadly Reactor '89
Killcrazy '89
Twisted Justice '89
Prime Target '91
Eye of the Stranger '93
Dragon Fury '95

Ben Hecht
Angels Over Broadway '40
Spectre of the Rose '46
Actors and Sin '52

Amy Heckerling
Fast Times at Ridgemont High '82
Johnny Dangerously '84
National Lampoon's European Vacation '85
Look Who's Talking '89
Look Who's Talking, Too '90
Clueless '95

Rob Hedden
Friday the 13th, Part 8: Jason Takes Manhattan '89
The Colony '95

Trine Hedman
Famous Five Get into Trouble '87

Victor Heerman
Animal Crackers '30

Avram Heffner
But Where Is Daniel Wax? '74

Richard T. Heffron
Newman's Law '74
The Rockford Files: Backlash of the Hunter '74
Death Scream '75
I Will Fight No More Forever '75
Futureworld '76
Outlaw Blues '77
See How She Runs '78
Foolin' Around '80
A Rumor of War '80
Whale for the Killing '81
I, the Jury '82
V: The Final Battle '84
Samaritan: The Mitch Snyder Story '86
Convicted: A Mother's Story '87
Guilty of Innocence '87
Broken Angel '88
Pancho Barnes '88
Tagget '90

Chris Hegedus
The War Room '93

Robert Hegyes
E. Nick: A Legend in His Own Mind '84

Yosif Heifitz
Baltic Deputy '37
The Lady with the Dog '59

Ray Heinz
Border Vengeance '35

Stuart Heisler
The Monster and the Girl '41
The Glass Key '42
Along Came Jones '45
Blue Skies '46
Smash-Up: The Story of a Woman '47
Tokyo Joe '49
Tulsa '49
Chain Lightning '50
Island of Desire '52
I Died a Thousand Times '55
The Burning Hills '56
Lone Ranger '56
Hitler '62

Mats Helge
Ninja Mission '84
The Russian Terminator '90

Olle Hellbron
Pippi Longstocking '73
Pippi in the South Seas '74
Pippi Goes on Board '75
Brothers Lionheart '85

Jerome Hellman
Promises in the Dark '79

Monte Hellman
The Beast from Haunted Cave '60
Creature from the Haunted Sea '60
Flight to Fury '66
The Shooting '66
Ride in the Whirlwind '67
Cockfighter '74
Gunfire '78
Iguana '89
Silent Night, Deadly Night 3: Better Watch Out! '89

Oliver Hellman
Beyond the Door '75
Tentacles '77
Desperate Moves '86

Paul Helmick
Hard Drivin' '60

David Helpern
Something Short of Paradise '79

Ralph Hemecker
Dead On '93

David Hemmings
Just a Gigolo '79
Survivor '80
Treasure of the Yankee Zephyr '83
The Key to Rebecca '85
Dark Horse '92

Joseph Henabery
The Man from Painted Post '17
His Majesty, the American '19
Cobra '25
Leather Burners '43

Clark Henderson
Warlords from Hell '87
Saigon Commandos '88
Circle of Fear '89

Primary Target '89

Don Henderson
The Touch of Satan '70
Weekend with the Babysitter '70

John Henderson
The Borrowers '93

Frank Henenlotter
Basket Case '82
Brain Damage '88
Basket Case 2 '90
Frankenhooker '90
Basket Case 3: The Progeny '92

Peter Henkel
Three Bullets for a Long Gun '73

Paul Henreid
Tall Lie '53
Battle Shock '56
Ballad in Blue '66

Buck Henry
Heaven Can Wait '78
First Family '80

Brian Henson
The Muppet Christmas Carol '92
Muppet Treasure Island '96

Jim Henson
The Great Muppet Caper '81
The Dark Crystal '82
Labyrinth '86

Robby Henson
Pharoah's Army '95

Stefan Christian Henszelman
Friends Forever '86

Perry Henzell
The Harder They Come '72

Bill Herbert
Warlock Moon '73

Henry Herbert
Emily '77

Martin Herbert
Strange Shadows in an Empty Room '76
Miami Horror '87

Stephen Herek
Critters '86
Bill & Ted's Excellent Adventure '89
Don't Tell Mom the Babysitter's Dead '91
The Mighty Ducks '92
The Three Musketeers '93
Mr. Holland's Opus '95

Al(bert) Herman
Beyond the Trail '26
Whispering Shadow '33
Cowboy & the Bandit '35
Western Frontier '35
Gun Play '36
Outlaws of the Range '36
Renfrew of the Royal Mounted '37
Renfrew on the Great White Trail '38
Rollin' Plains '38
Utah Trail '38
Valley of Terror '38
Down the Wyoming Trail '39
Man from Texas '39
Roll, Wagons, Roll '39
Take Me Back to Oklahoma '40
Gentleman from Dixie '41
Dawn Express '42
Delinquent Daughters '44
Rogue's Gallery '44
Shake Hands with Murder '44
The Missing Corpse '45
The Phantom of 42nd Street '45

Jean Herman
Honor Among Thieves '68
Butterfly Affair '71

Mark Herman
Blame It on the Bellboy '92

Jaime Humberto Hermosillo
Dona Herlinda & Her Son '86
The Summer of Miss Forbes '88

Miguel Hermoso
Marbella '85

Tibor Hernadi
Felix the Cat: The Movie '91

Denis Heroux
The Uncanny '78
Naked Massacre '80s

Mark Herrier
Popcorn '89

Rowdy Herrington
Jack's Back '87
Road House '89
Gladiator '92
Striking Distance '93

W. Blake Herron
Skin Art '93

Joel Hershman
Hold Me, Thrill Me, Kiss Me '93

Marshall Herskovitz
Jack the Bear '93

Michael Herz
Sugar Cookies '77
First Turn On '83
Stuck on You '84
The Toxic Avenger '86
Troma's War '88
The Toxic Avenger, Part 2 '89
The Toxic Avenger, Part 3: The Last Temptation of Toxie '89

John Herzfeld
Two of a Kind '83
A Father's Revenge '88
The Preppie Murder '89
Casualties of Love: The "Long Island Lolita" Story '93

Werner Herzog
Signs of Life '68
Aguirre, the Wrath of God '72
Heart of Glass '74
Every Man for Himself & God Against All '75
Stroszek '77
Woyzeck '78
Fitzcarraldo '82
Where the Green Ants Dream '84

David Hess
To All a Goodnight '80

Eugene Hess
Don't Do It '94

Jon Hess
The Lawless Land '88
Watchers '88
Assassin '89
Excessive Force '93

Gordon Hessler
The Oblong Box '69
Cry of the Banshee '70
Scream and Scream Again '70
Murders in the Rue Morgue '71
Embassy '72
Golden Voyage of Sinbad '73
Betrayal '74
Medusa '74
KISS Meets the Phantom of the Park '78
Puzzle '78
Secrets of Three Hungry Wives '78
Escape from El Diablo '83
Pray for Death '85
The Misfit Brigade '87
Rage of Honor '87
The Girl in a Swing '89
Out on Bail '89
Journey of Honor '91
Tales of the Unexpected '91

Charlton Heston
Antony and Cleopatra '73
Mother Lode '82
A Man for All Seasons '88

Fraser Heston
Treasure Island '89
The Crucifer of Blood '91
Needful Things '93
Alaska '96

Neil Hetherington
Black Terrorist '85

David L. Hewitt
Horrors of the Red Planet '64
Monsters Crash the Pajama Party '65
Alien Massacre '67
Journey to the Center of Time '67
The Lucifer Complex '78

Jean Hewitt
Blood of Dracula's Castle '69

Pete Hewitt
Bill & Ted's Bogus Journey '91
Wild Palms '93
Tom and Huck '95

Rod Hewitt
Verne Miller '88
The Dangerous '95

Douglas Heyes
Powder Keg '70

Laurent Heynemann
Birgitt Haas Must Be Killed '83
The Old Lady Who Walked in the Sea '91

Jesse Hibbs
To Hell and Back '55

Winston Hibler
Charlie, the Lonesome Cougar '67

Jochen Hick
Via Appia '92

George Hickenlooper
Hearts of Darkness: A Filmmaker's Apocalypse '91
The Ghost Brigade '93

Anthony Hickox
Waxwork '88
Sundown '91
Waxwork 2: Lost in Time '91
Hellraiser 3: Hell on Earth '92
Full Eclipse '93
Warlock: The Armageddon '93
Payback '94

Douglas Hickox
Entertaining Mr. Sloane '70
Theatre of Blood '73
Brannigan '75
Sky Riders '76
Zulu Dawn '79
The Hound of the Baskervilles '83
Mistral's Daughter '84
Blackout '85
Sins '85

James D.R. Hickox
Children of the Corn 3: Urban Harvest '95

Howard Higgin
Power '28
High Voltage '29
The Racketeer '29
Painted Desert '31
Hell's House '32

Colin Higgins
Foul Play '78
9 to 5 '80
The Best Little Whorehouse in Texas '82

Nat Hiken
Car 54, Where Are You? '61
The Love God? '70

Claudio Guerin Hill
Bell from Hell '74

George Hill
The Big House '30

George Roy Hill
Min & Bill '30
Period of Adjustment '62
Toys in the Attic '63
The World of Henry Orient '64
Hawaii '66
Thoroughly Modern Millie '67
Butch Cassidy and the Sundance Kid '69
Slaughterhouse Five '72
The Sting '73
The Great Waldo Pepper '75
Slap Shot '77
A Little Romance '79
The World According to Garp '82
The Little Drummer Girl '84
Funny Farm '88

Jack Hill
Spider Baby '64
Portrait in Terror '66
Track of the Vampire '66
The Fear Chamber '68
The Big Doll House '71
The Big Bird Cage '72
Coffy '73
Foxy Brown '74
The Swinging Cheerleaders '74
Switchblade Sisters '75

James Hill
Seaside Swingers '65
Born Free '66
A Study in Terror '66
The Corrupt Ones '67
Black Beauty '71
The Belstone Fox '73
The Wild and the Free '80

Robert F. "Bob" Hill
Come On Danger! '32
Tarzan the Fearless '33
Danger Trails '35
Queen of the Jungle '35
Blake of Scotland Yard '36
A Face in the Fog '36
Kelly of the Secret Service '36
Prison Shadows '36
Rip Roarin' Buckaroo '36
Rogue's Tavern '36
Feud of the Trail '37
The Roamin' Cowboy '37
Cheyenne Rides Again '38
Flash Gordon: Mars Attacks the World '38
Man's Country '38
The Phantom of the Range '38
Whirlwind Horseman '38
Wild Horse Canyon '39
East Side Kids '40

Sinclair Hill
Greek Street '30

Terence Hill
Lucky Luke '94

Walter Hill
Hard Times '75
The Driver '78
The Warriors '79
The Long Riders '80
Southern Comfort '81
48 Hrs. '82
Streets of Fire '84
Brewster's Millions '85
Crossroads '86
Extreme Prejudice '87
Red Heat '88
Johnny Handsome '89
Tales from the Crypt '89
Another 48 Hrs. '90
Tales from the Crypt, Vol. 3 '90
Trespass '92
Geronimo: An American Legend '93
Wild Bill '95

Arthur Hiller
The Miracle of the White Stallions '63
The Wheeler Dealers '63
The Americanization of Emily '64
Promise Her Anything '66
Tobruk '66
Popi '69
Love Story '70
The Out-of-Towners '70
The Hospital '71
Plaza Suite '71
Man of La Mancha '72
The Man in the Glass Booth '75
Silver Streak '76
The In-Laws '79
Nightwing '79
Author! Author! '82
Making Love '82
Romantic Comedy '83
The Lonely Guy '84
Teachers '84
Outrageous Fortune '87
See No Evil, Hear No Evil '89
Taking Care of Business '90
The Babe '92
Married to It '93

Richard Hilliard
Psychomania '63

David Michael Hillman
The Strangeness '85

William B. Hillman
Photographer '75
Double Exposure '82
Ragin' Cajun '90

David Hills
Ator the Fighting Eagle '83
Blade Master '84
Quest for the Mighty Sword '90

Lambert Hillyer
Wagon Tracks '19
Toll Gate '20
Three Word Brand '21
The Shock '23
Fighting Fool '32
Hello Trouble '32
White Eagle '32
Dracula's Daughter '36
The Invisible Ray '36
Gang Bullets '38
Six Gun Gospel '43
Texas Kid '43
Partners of the Trail '44
Range Law '44
South of the Rio Grande '45
The Stranger from Pecos '45
Border Bandits '46
Gentleman from Texas '46
Hat Box Mystery '47
Land of the Lawless '47
Range Renegades '48
Sundown Riders '48

Arthur Hilton
Return of Jesse James '50
Cat Women of the Moon '53

Howard Himelstein
Power of Attorney '94

Charles Hines
The Speed Spook '24

Bill Hinzman
Revenge of the Living Zombies '88

Alexander Gregory Hippolyte
Carnal Crimes '91
Mirror Images '91
Animal Instincts '92
Night Rhythms '92
Secret Games '92
Mirror Images 2 '93
Secret Games 2: The Escort '93
Animal Instincts 2 '94
Secret Games 3 '94
Undercover '94
Animal Instincts 3: The Seductress '95
Object of Obsession '95

Bettina Hirsch
Munchies '87

Ray Hirschman
Plutonium Baby '87

Leslie Hiscott
Department Store '35
The Triumph of Sherlock Holmes '35

Alfred Hitchcock
The Lodger '26
Easy Virtue '27
The Ring '27
Champagne '28
The Farmer's Wife '28
Three by Hitchcock '28
Blackmail '29
The Manxman '29
Juno and the Paycock '30
Murder '30
Skin Game '31
No. 17 '32
Rich and Strange '32
The Man Who Knew Too Much '34
The 39 Steps '35
Sabotage '36
The Secret Agent '36
Young and Innocent '37
The Lady Vanishes '38
Jamaica Inn '39
Foreign Correspondent '40
Rebecca '40
Mr. & Mrs. Smith '41
Suspicion '41
Saboteur '42
Shadow of a Doubt '43
Alfred Hitchcock's Aventure Malgache '44
Alfred Hitchcock's Bon Voyage '44
Lifeboat '44
Spellbound '45
Notorious '46
The Paradine Case '47
Rope '48
Under Capricorn '49
Stage Fright '50
Strangers on a Train '51
I Confess '53
Dial "M" for Murder '54

Hitchcock ▶cont.

Rear Window '54
To Catch a Thief '55
The Trouble with Harry '55
The Man Who Knew Too Much '56
The Wrong Man '56
Vertigo '58
North by Northwest '59
Psycho '60
The Birds '63
Marnie '64
Torn Curtain '66
Topaz '69
Frenzy '72
Family Plot '76
Hitchcock Classics Collection: Trailers on Tape '85
Hitchcock Collection '87

Carl K. Hittleman
Kentucky Rifle '55

Rupert Hitzig
Night Visitor '89
Backstreet Dreams '90

Jack B. Hively
Lassie: Adventures of Neeka '68
Starbird and Sweet William '73
The Adventures of Huckleberry Finn '78
California Gold Rush '81

Jack Hively
The Saint Takes Over '40
The Saint's Double Trouble '40
Four Jacks and a Jill '41

A.J. Hixon
Little Marines '90

Godfrey Ho
Ninja Destroyer '70s
Ninja Champion '80s
The Dragon's Showdown '83
Hands of Death '88

Yim Ho
The Day the Sun Turned Cold '94

Fredric Hobbs
Alabama's Ghost '72

Lyndall Hobbs
Back to the Beach '87

Gregory Hoblit
L.A. Law '86
Roe vs. Wade '89
Class of '61 '92
Primal Fear '96

Victoria Hochberg
Jacob Have I Loved '88
Sweet 15 '90

Roberta Hodes
A Secret Space '88

Mike Hodges
Pulp '72
The Terminal Man '74
Flash Gordon '80
Missing Pieces '83
Morons from Outer Space '85
Florida Straits '87
Prayer for the Dying '87
Black Rainbow '91

Jeno Hodl
Deadly Obsession '88
American Kickboxer 2: To the Death '93
Triplecross '95

Mark Hoeger
The Little Match Girl '84

Jeremy Hoenack
The Dark Ride '84

Arthur Hoerl
Drums O'Voodoo '34

Michael Hoey
Navy vs. the Night Monsters '66

Ernest Hofbauer
Code Name Alpha '67

Herman Hoffman
It's a Dog's Life '55
The Invisible Boy '57

Jerzy Hoffman
Colonel Wolodyjowski '69
Leper '76

Jon Hoffman
Strange Confession '45

Julian Hoffman
The Bloody Brood '59

Michael Hoffman
Promised Land '88
Some Girls '88
Soapdish '91
Restoration '94

Peter Hoffman
Valentino Returns '88

Tamar Simon Hoffs
The Allnighter '87

Gray Hofmeyr
The Light in the Jungle '91
Dirty Games '93
Yankee Zulu '95

Jack Hofsiss
I'm Dancing as Fast as I Can '82
Cat on a Hot Tin Roof '84
Family Secrets '84

David Hogan
Barb Wire '96

James Hogan
The Broken Mask '28
Arizona Mahoney '36
Bulldog Drummond Escapes '37
Arrest Bulldog Drummond '38
Bulldog Drummond's Peril '38
The Texans '38
Bulldog Drummond's Bride '39
Bulldog Drummond's Secret Police '39
The Texas Rangers Ride Again '40
The Mad Ghoul '43

P.J. Hogan
Muriel's Wedding '94

Michael Hohensee
Mad Wax: The Surf Movie '90

Rod Holcomb
Captain America '79
Cartier Affair '84
The Red Light Sting '84
Chase '85
Stark '85
Two Fathers' Justice '85
Blind Justice '86
China Beach '88
Chains of Gold '92
Dead to Rights '93
Royce '93
Convict Cowboy '95

John Hold
Viking Massacre '65

Anton Holden
Aroused '66

Lansing C. Holden
She '35

William Hole, Jr.
The Devil's Hand '61

Adam Holender
Twisted '86

Agnieszka Holland
Provincial Actors '79
Fever '81
Angry Harvest '85
To Kill a Priest '89
Europa, Europa '91
Olivier, Olivier '92
The Secret Garden '93
Total Eclipse '95

Steve Holland
Better Off Dead '85
One Crazy Summer '86
How I Got into College '89

Todd Holland
The Wizard '89

Tom Holland
Fright Night '85
Fatal Beauty '87
Child's Play '88
The Temp '93
Stephen King's The Langoliers '95

Eli Hollander
Out '88

Allan Holleb
Candy Stripe Nurses '74
School Spirit '85

Doug Holloway
Fast Money '83

Ben Holmes
Maid's Night Out '38
The Saint in New York '38

Fred Holmes
Dakota '88
Harley '90

Jason Holt
Wager of Love '90
Swindle '92

Seth Holt
Scream of Fear '61
The Nanny '65

Allen Holubar
Heart of Humanity '18

Roger Holzberg
Midnight Crossing '87

Allan Holzman
Forbidden World '82
Grunt! The Wrestling Movie '85
Out of Control '85
Programmed to Kill '86
Intimate Stranger '91

Edward Holzman
Seduce Me: Pamela Principle 2 '94

Lau Shing Hon
To Live and Die in Hong Kong '89

Inoshiro Honda
Rodan '56
Half Human '58
The Mysterians '58
H-Man '59
Varan the Unbelievable '61
Mothra '62
Attack of the Mushroom People '63
Godzilla vs. Mothra '64
Gorath '64
Dagora, the Space Monster '65
Ghidrah the Three Headed Monster '65
Destroy All Monsters '68
Godzilla vs. Monster Zero '68
Godzilla's Revenge '69
Yog, Monster from Space '71

Elliot Hong
Kill the Golden Goose '79
They Call Me Bruce? '82

James Hong
Girls Next Door '79
The Vineyard '89

Ron Honthaner
The House on Skull Mountain '74

Randall Hood
Die Sister, Die! '74

Harry Hook
The Kitchen Toto '87
Lord of the Flies '90
The Last of His Tribe '92

Kevin Hooks
Roots: The Gift '88
Strictly Business '91
Murder without Motive '92
Passenger 57 '92
Fled '96

Lance Hool
Missing in Action 2: The Beginning '85
Steel Dawn '87

Tobe Hooper
The Texas Chainsaw Massacre '74
Eaten Alive '76
Salem's Lot '79
The Funhouse '81
Poltergeist '82
Lifeforce '85
Invaders from Mars '86
Texas Chainsaw Massacre, Part 2 '86
Spontaneous Combustion '89
I'm Dangerous Tonight '90
Body Bags '93
The Mangler '94

Claudia Hoover
Double Exposure '93

Harry Hope
Swift Justice '88

Margot Hope
Femme Fontaine: Killer Babe for the C.I.A. '95

Anthony Hopkins
August '95

Arthur Hopkins
His Double Life '33

John Hopkins
Torment '85

Stephen Hopkins
A Nightmare on Elm Street 5: Dream Child '89
Dangerous Game '90
Predator 2 '90
Judgment Night '93
Blown Away '94

Dennis Hopper
Easy Rider '69
The Last Movie '71
Out of the Blue '80
Colors '88
Backtrack '89
The Hot Spot '90
Chasers '94

E. Mason Hopper
Square Shoulders '29
Held for Murder '32
Shop Angel '32
Hong Kong Nights '35

Jerry Hopper
The Atomic City '52
Pony Express '53
Madron '70

Russell Hopton
Black Gold '36
Song of the Trail '36

Richard Horian
Student Confidential '87

Andrew Horn
Doomed Love '83

Leonard Horn
Hunter '73

Jeffrey Hornaday
Shout '91

James W. Horne
Laughing at Danger '24
College '27
Bonnie Scotland '35
Bohemian Girl '36
All Over Town '37
Way Out West '37
Green Archer '40
Holt of the Secret Service '42

Harry Horner
Beware, My Lovely '52
Red Planet Mars '52
New Faces of 1952 '54

Robert J. Horner
The Walloping Kid '26

Peter Horton
Amazon Women on the Moon '87
The Cure '95

Bob Hoskins
The Raggedy Rawney '90

Dan Hoskins
Chopper Chicks in Zombietown '91

Robert Hossein
I Killed Rasputin '67

Joy Houck, Jr.
Mind Warp '72
Night of the Strangler '73
Creature from Black Lake '76
The St. Tammany Miracle '94

John Hough
Sudden Terror '70
Twins of Evil '71
Treasure Island '72
The Legend of Hell House '73
Dirty Mary Crazy Larry '74
Escape to Witch Mountain '75
Brass Target '78
Return from Witch Mountain '78
The Watcher in the Woods '81
Incubus '82
Triumphs of a Man Called Horse '83
The Black Arrow '84
Biggles '85
American Gothic '88

Howling 4: The Original Nightmare '88
The Dying Truth '91
Duel of Hearts '92

Bobby Houston
Bad Manners '84
Trust Me '89
Caged Fear '92

Clyde Houston
Foxstyle '73

Robert Houston
Shogun Assassin '80

Tony Houston
Outlaw Riders '72

Ellen Hovde
Trumps '83

Adrian Hoven
Mark of the Devil 2 '72
Dandelions '74

Michael Hovis
The Man with the Perfect Swing '95

Cy Howard
Lovers and Other Strangers '70

David Howard
Crimson Romance '34
Daniel Boone '34
In Old Santa Fe '34
The Lost Jungle '34
Mystery Ranch '34
Park Avenue Logger '37
Hollywood Stadium Mystery '38
Renegade Ranger/Scarlet River '38
Bullet Code '40

Leslie Howard
Pygmalion '38
Pimpernel Smith '42
Spitfire '42

Paul Howard
Night Terror '89

Ron Howard
Grand Theft Auto '77
Cotton Candy '82
Night Shift '82
Splash '84
Cocoon '85
Gung Ho '85
Willow '88
Parenthood '89
Backdraft '91
Far and Away '92
The Paper '94
Apollo 13 '95

William K. Howard
Let's Go! '23
White Gold '28
Evelyn Prentice '34
The Princess Comes Across '36
Fire Over England '37
Back Door to Heaven '39
Johnny Come Lately '43

C. Thomas Howell
Hourglass '95

John Howley
Happily Ever After '93

Frank Howson
The Hunting '92

Harry Hoyt
The Lost World '25
The Return of Boston Blackie '27

Robert Hoyt
Gunners & Guns '34

Hou Hsaio-hsien
A Time to Live and a Time to Die '85

Talun Hsu
Witchcraft 5: Dance with the Devil '92
Body Count '95

VV Dachin Hsu
Pale Blood '91

Hua-Shan
Infra-Man '76

George Huang
Swimming with Sharks '94

Daniel Hubenbecker
Wardogs '87

Jean-Loup Hubert
Next Year If All Goes Well '83
Le Grand Chemin '87
Faith Hubley
The Cosmic Eye '71
John Huckert
The Passing '88
Reginald Hudlin
House Party '90
Boomerang '92
Cosmic Slop '94
The Great White Hype '96
Warrington Hudlin
Cosmic Slop '94
Gary Hudson
Thunder Run '86
Hugh Hudson
Chariots of Fire '81
Greystoke: The Legend of Tarzan, Lord of the Apes '84
Revolution '85
Lost Angels '89
P.I. Huemer
Kiss Daddy Goodnight '87
Marc Huestis
Men in Love '90
Roy Huggins
Hangman's Knot '52
R. John Hugh
Yellowneck '55
Naked in the Sun '57
The Meal '75
Deadly Encounter '78
Albert Hughes
Menace II Society '93
Dead Presidents '95
Allen Hughes
Menace II Society '93
Dead Presidents '95
Bronwen Hughes
Harriet the Spy '96
David Hughes
Missing Link '88
Howard Hughes
Hell's Angels '30
The Outlaw '43
John Hughes
Sixteen Candles '84
The Breakfast Club '85
Weird Science '85
Ferris Bueller's Day Off '86
Planes, Trains & Automobiles '87
She's Having a Baby '88
Uncle Buck '89
Curly Sue '91
Ken Hughes
Heat Wave '54
The Atomic Man '56
The Long Haul '57
The Trials of Oscar Wilde '60
Of Human Bondage '64
Arrivederci, Baby! '66
Casino Royale '67
Chitty Chitty Bang Bang '68
Cromwell '70
Internecine Project '73
Oh, Alfie '75
Sextette '78
Night School '81
Kris Hughes
Dying Game '94
Robert C. Hughes
Hunter's Blood '87
Memorial Valley Massacre '88
Down the Drain '89
Terry Hughes
Ripping Yarns '75
Monty Python Live at the Hollywood Bowl '82
Sunset Limousine '83
For Love or Money '84
The Butcher's Wife '91
Ann Hui
Song of the Exile '90
Summer Snow '94
Don Hulette
Breaker! Breaker! '77
Great Ride '78
Steven A. Hull
Devil Wears White '86

Ron Hulme
Fearless Tiger '94
H. Bruce Humberstone
The Crooked Circle '32
Strangers of the Evening '32
Charlie Chan at the Opera '36
Lucky Cisco Kid '40
I Wake Up Screaming '41
Sun Valley Serenade '41
Iceland '42
To the Shores of Tripoli '42
Hello, Frisco, Hello '43
Pin-Up Girl '44
Wonder Man '45
Happy Go Lovely '51
The Desert Song '53
Ten Wanted Men '54
Tarzan and the Trappers '58
Humphrey Humbert
Ghosthouse '88
Chieng Hung
Tough Guy '70s
Tran Anh Hung
The Scent of Green Papaya '93
Jackson Hunsicker
Oddball Hall '91
David Hunt
Triple Impact '92
Edward Hunt
Starship Invasions '77
Bloody Birthday '80
Alien Warrior '85
The Brain '88
Maurice Hunt
The Pagemaster '94
Paul Hunt
The Clones '73
The Great Gundown '75
Twisted Nightmare '87
Merlin '92
Peter Hunt
On Her Majesty's Secret Service '69
Shout at the Devil '76
Gulliver's Travels '77
Death Hunt '81
Smart-Aleck Kill '85
Wild Geese 2 '85
Hyper-Sapien: People from Another Star '86
Assassination '87
Peter H. Hunt
1776 '72
The Mysterious Stranger '82
Skeezer '82
It Came Upon a Midnight Clear '84
The Adventures of Huckleberry Finn '85
Max (Massimo Pupillo) Hunter
The Bloody Pit of Horror '65
Ross Hunter
Son of Ali Baba '52
T. Hayes Hunter
The Ghoul '34
Tim Hunter
Tex '82
Sylvester '85
River's Edge '87
Paint It Black '89
Lies of the Twins '91
The Saint of Fort Washington '93
Lawrence Huntington
Tower of Terror '42
Man on the Run '49
The Franchise Affair '52
Vulture '67
Caroline Huppert
Sincerely Charlotte '86
Brian Desmond Hurst
The Lion Has Wings '40
Dangerous Moonlight '41
The Gay Lady '49
A Christmas Carol '51
Malta Story '53
Simba '55

Playboy of the Western World '62
Paul Hurst
Branded a Bandit '24
William T. Hurtz
Little Nemo: Adventures in Slumberland '92
Harry Hurwitz
The Projectionist '71
Safari 3000 '82
Rosebud Beach Hotel '85
That's Adequate '90
Fleshtone '94
Waris Hussein
Doctor Who: An Unearthly Child '63
Quackser Fortune Has a Cousin in the Bronx '70
Melody '71
Divorce His, Divorce Hers '72
The Possession of Joel Delaney '72
And Baby Makes Six '79
Edward and Mrs. Simpson '80
The Henderson Monster '80
Callie and Son '81
Coming Out of the Ice '82
Princess Daisy '83
Little Gloria...Happy at Last '84
Arch of Triumph '85
When the Bough Breaks '86
Intimate Contact '87
Onassis '88
The Shell Seekers '89
Switched at Birth '91
Fall from Grace '94
The Summer House '94
Danny Huston
Mr. North '88
Becoming Colette '92
The Maddening '95
Jimmy Huston
Death Driver '78
Final Exam '81
My Best Friend Is a Vampire '88
The Wharf Rat '95
John Huston
The Maltese Falcon '41
Across the Pacific '42
In This Our Life '42
Key Largo '48
Treasure of the Sierra Madre '48
The Asphalt Jungle '50
The African Queen '51
The Red Badge of Courage '51
Moulin Rouge '52
Beat the Devil '53
Moby Dick '56
Barbarian and the Geisha '58
The Unforgiven '60
The Misfits '61
The List of Adrian Messenger '63
The Night of the Iguana '64
The Bible...In the Beginning '66
Casino Royale '67
Reflections in a Golden Eye '67
Fat City '72
Life & Times of Judge Roy Bean '72
Mackintosh Man '73
The Man Who Would Be King '75
Independence '76
Wise Blood '79
Phobia '80
Victory '81
Annie '82
Under the Volcano '84
Prizzi's Honor '85
The Dead '87
Zoltan Huszarik
Sinbad '71
Charles Hutchinson
Found Alive '34
Phantom Patrol '36
Harold Huth
Night Beat '48
Brian G. Hutton
Where Eagles Dare '68
Kelly's Heroes '70
Night Watch '72
X, Y & Zee '72
The First Deadly Sin '80
High Road to China '83
Robert Hutton
The Slime People '63

Willard Huyck
Messiah of Evil '74
French Postcards '79
Best Defense '84
Howard the Duck '86
Jacky Hwong
Ninja vs. the Shaolin '84
Nessa Hyams
Leader of the Band '87
Peter Hyams
Busting '74
Our Time '74
Capricorn One '78
Hanover Street '79
Outland '81
Death Target '83
The Star Chamber '83
2010: The Year We Make Contact '84
Running Scared '86
The Presidio '88
Narrow Margin '90
Stay Tuned '92
Timecop '94
Sudden Death '95
Nicholas Hytner
The Madness of King George '94
Chang Shinn I
Snake in the Eagle's Shadow 2 '83
Juan Ibanez
Dance of Death '68
The Fear Chamber '68
The Sinister Invasion '68
Leon Ichaso
El Super '79
Power, Passion & Murder '83
Crossover Dreams '85
The Take '90
Sugar Hill '94
Zooman '95
Kon Ichikawa
The Burmese Harp '56
Enjo '58
Fires on the Plain '59
Odd Obsession '60
Being Two Isn't Easy '62
An Actor's Revenge '63
Revenge of a Kabuki Actor '63
Tokyo Olympiad '66
The Makioka Sisters '83
Eric Idle
All You Need Is Cash '78
The Tale of the Frog Prince '83
Miguel Iglesias
The Sword of El Cid '62
Night of the Howling Beast '75
Kazuo Ikehiro
Zatoichi: Master Ichi and a Chest of Gold '64
Zatoichi: Zatoichi's Flashing Sword '64
Shohei Imamura
The Insect Woman '63
The Pornographers '66
Vengeance Is Mine '79
Eijanaika '81
The Ballad of Narayama '83
Black Rain '88
Shmuel Imberman
I Don't Give a Damn '88
Markus Imhoof
The Boat is Full '81
Hiroshi Inagaki
Samurai 1: Musashi Miyamoto '55
Samurai 2: Duel at Ichijoji Temple '55
Samurai 3: Duel at Ganryu Island '56
Rikisha-Man '58
Kojiro '67
Thomas Ince
Civilization '16
Franco Indovina
Oldest Profession '67
Catch as Catch Can '68
Lloyd Ingraham
American Aristocracy '17
Eyes of Julia Deep '18
Rex Ingram
The Four Horsemen of the Apocalypse '21

Boris Ingster
Stranger on the Third Floor '40
The Judge Steps Out '49
J. Christian Ingvordsen
Firehouse '87
Hangmen '87
Covert Action '88
Mob War '88
Search and Destroy '88
Comrades in Arms '91
The Outfit '93
Markus Innocenti
Murder Story '89
Jerald Intrator
Satan in High Heels '62
Otar Iosseliani
Chasing Butterflies '94
John Ireland
The Fast and the Furious '54
O'Dale Ireland
High School Caesar '56
Date Bait '60
Matthew Irmas
When the Party's Over '91
John Irvin
Haunted: The Ferryman '74
The Dogs of War '81
Ghost Story '81
Champions '84
Raw Deal '86
Turtle Diary '86
Hamburger Hill '87
Next of Kin '89
Eminent Domain '91
Robin Hood '91
Firefall '94
Widow's Peak '94
A Month by the Lake '95
Sam Irvin
Guilty as Charged '92
Oblivion '94
Backlash: Oblivion 2 '95
Magic Island '95
Out There '95
Kevin Irvine
Greenstone '85
David Irving
Goodbye Cruel World '82
Rumpelstiltskin '86
Cannon Movie Tales: Sleeping Beauty '89
Cannon Movie Tales: The Emperor's New Clothes '89
C.H.U.D. 2: Bud the Chud '89
Night of the Cyclone '90
Richard Irving
Columbo: Prescription Murder '67
The Art of Crime '75
The Jesse Owens Story '84
James Isaac
The Horror Show '89
Ronnie Isaacs
Warriors from Hell '90
Antonio Isasi
Ricco '74
Vengeance '86
Robert Iscove
The Lawrenceville Stories '80s
The Little Mermaid '84
Puss 'n Boots '84
Mission of the Shark '91
Gerald I. Isenberg
Seizure: The Story of Kathy Morris '82
Wayne Isham
For Those About to Rock: Monsters in Moscow '91
Neal Israel
Tunnelvision '76
Americathon '79
Bachelor Party '84
Moving Violations '85
Combat Academy '86
Breaking the Rules '92
Surf Ninjas '93
Peter Israelson
Side Out '90
Juzo Itami
The Funeral '84

Itami ▶cont.

Tampopo '86
A Taxing Woman '87
A Taxing Woman's Return '88
Minbo—Or the Gentle Art of Japanese Extortion '92

Kenneth Ives
Poldark '75

James Ivory
The Householder '63
Shakespeare Wallah '65
Bombay Talkie '70
Savages '72
Wild Party '74
Autobiography of a Princess '75
Roseland '77
Hullabaloo Over Georgie & Bonnie's Pictures '78
The Europeans '79
Jane Austen in Manhattan '80
Quartet '81
Heat and Dust '82
The Bostonians '84
The Courtesans of Bombay '85
A Room with a View '86
Maurice '87
Slaves of New York '89
Mr. & Mrs. Bridge '90
Howard's End '92
The Remains of the Day '93
Jefferson in Paris '94

David Jablin
National Lampoon's Favorite Deadly Sins '95

Arnaldo Jabor
I Love You '81

Fred Jackman
King of the Wild Horses '24
No Man's Law '27

David S. Jackson
Detonator '93
Detonator 2: Night Watch '95

Donald G. Jackson
The Demon Lover '77
Roller Blade '85

Douglas Jackson
Whispers '89
Deadbolt '92
The Paperboy '94
Stalked '94

G. Philip Jackson
Replikator: Cloned to Kill '94

George Jackson
House Party 2: The Pajama Jam '91

Horace Jackson
The Bus Is Coming '72

Jalil Jackson
Lady Terminator '89

Larry Jackson
Bugs Bunny Superstar '75

Lewis Jackson
Terror in Toyland '85

Mick Jackson
Threads '85
Yuri Nosenko, KGB '86
Chattahoochee '89
L.A. Story '91
The Bodyguard '92
Clean Slate '94
Indictment: The McMartin Trial '95

Mike Jackson
Blood Tracks '86

Pat Jackson
Encore '52
What a Carve-Up! '62
King Arthur, the Young Warlord '75

Peter Jackson
Bad Taste '88
Meet the Feebles '89
Dead Alive '93
Heavenly Creatures '94
The Frighteners '96

Philip Jackson
Project: Genesis '93

Wilfred Jackson
Cinderella '50

Alan Jacobs
Nina Takes a Lover '94

Harry Jacobs
Rebel High '88

Jerry P. Jacobs
A Dangerous Place '94

John Jacobs
Rocket to the Moon '86

Jon Jacobs
The Girl with the Hungry Eyes '94

Lawrence-Hilton Jacobs
Angels of the City '89
Quiet Fire '91

Nicholas A.E. Jacobs
The Refrigerator '93

Werner Jacobs
Heidi '65

Rick Jacobson
Full Contact '93
Bloodfist 6: Ground Zero '94
Ring of Fire 3: Lion Strike '94
Star Quest '94
The Unborn 2 '94
Night Hunter '95
Suspect Device '95

Irving Jacoby
Snow Treasure '67

Joseph Jacoby
Hurry Up or I'll Be Thirty '73
Great Bank Hoax '78

Gualtiero Jacopetti
Mondo Cane '63
Mondo Cane 2 '64

Just Jaeckin
Emmanuelle '74
The Story of O '75
The French Woman '79
Lady Chatterley's Lover '81
The Perils of Gwendoline '84

Stanley R. Jaffe
Without a Trace '83

Henry Jaglom
Tracks '76
Sitting Ducks '80
National Lampoon Goes to the Movies '81
Can She Bake a Cherry Pie? '83
Always '85
Someone to Love '87
New Year's Day '89
Eating '90
Babyfever '94
Last Summer In the Hamptons '96

Sam Jaimes
Happy New Year, Charlie Brown '82
Good Grief, Charlie Brown '83

Patrick Jamain
Honeymoon '87

Alan James
Backfire '22
The Phantom '31
Fargo Express '32
Phantom Thunderbolt '33
When a Man Sees Red '34
Lucky Terror '36
Red Barry '38

Bob James
Alien Seed '89

Steve James
Hoop Dreams '94

Jerry Jameson
Dirt Gang '71
The Bat People '74
Hurricane '74
Terror on the 40th Floor '74
Sniper '75
High Noon: Part 2 '80
Raise the Titanic '80
Killing at Hell's Gate '81
Hotline '82
Starflight One '83
The Cowboy & the Ballerina '84
Fire and Rain '89

Miklos Jancso
The Round Up '66
The Red and the White '68
Hungarian Rhapsody '78

Gerhard Janda
Tea For Three '84

Annabel Jankel
D.O.A. '88
Super Mario Bros. '93

Stole Jankovic
Hell River '75

Victor Janos
Last House on Dead End Street '77

Derek Jarman
Sebastiane '79
Caravaggio '86
The Last of England '87
Aria '88
The Garden '90
Edward II '92
Blue '93
Wittgenstein '93

Jim Jarmusch
Permanent Vacation '84
Stranger than Paradise '84
Down by Law '86
Mystery Train '89
Night on Earth '91
Dead Man '95

Charles Jarrott
Strange Case of Dr. Jekyll & Mr. Hyde '68
Anne of the Thousand Days '69
The Dove '74
The Littlest Horse Thieves '76
The Other Side of Midnight '77
The Last Flight of Noah's Ark '80
Condorman '81
The Amateur '82
Boy in Blue '86
Poor Little Rich Girl: The Barbara Hutton Story '87
The Woman He Loved '88
Night of the Fox '90
Danielle Steel's Changes '91
Lucy and Desi: Before the Laughter '91

Vojtech Jasny
All My Good Countrymen '68
The Great Land of Small '86

Leigh Jason
High Gear '33
The Bride Walks Out '36
That Girl from Paris '36
Mad Miss Manton '38
Lady for a Night '42
Lost Honeymoon '47
Out of the Blue '47
The Choppers '61

Will Jason
Everybody's Dancin' '50

Vadim Jean
Leon the Pig Farmer '93
Nightscare '93

Roland S. Jefferson
Perfume '91

Tom Jeffrey
Weekend of Shadows '77
The Odd Angry Shot '79

Herbert Jeffries
World of the Depraved '67

Lionel Jeffries
The Railway Children '70
Amazing Mr. Blunden '72
Wombling Free '77
Water Babies '79

Richard Jeffries
Blood Tide '82

Andras Jeles
The Little Valentino '79

Bunker Jenkins
Space Ninja: Sword of the Space Ark '81

Michael Jenkins
Rebel '85
Sweet Talker '91

Patrick Jenkins
The Gambler & the Lady '52

Roger Jenkins
Poldark 2 '75

Astrid Henning Jensen
Boy of Two Worlds '70

Leopold Jessner
Backstairs '21

Alain Jessua
The Killing Game '67

Jean-Marie Jeunet
Delicatessen '92
The City of Lost Children '95

Norman Jewison
40 Pounds of Trouble '62
The Thrill of It All! '63
Send Me No Flowers '64
The Cincinnati Kid '65
The Russians are Coming, the Russians are Coming '66
In the Heat of the Night '67
The Thomas Crown Affair '68
Fiddler on the Roof '71
Jesus Christ, Superstar '73
Rollerball '75
F.I.S.T. '78
And Justice for All '79
Best Friends '82
A Soldier's Story '84
Agnes of God '85
Moonstruck '87
In Country '89
Other People's Money '91
Only You '94

Ruth Prawer Jhabvala
The Courtesans of Bombay '85

Huang Jianxin
The Wooden Man's Bride '94

Neal Jimenez
The Waterdance '91

Robert Jiras
I Am the Cheese '83

Duan Jishun
The Go-Masters '82

Mike Jittlov
The Wizard of Speed and Time '88

Leo Joannon
Utopia '51

Phil Joanou
Three O'Clock High '87
State of Grace '90
Final Analysis '92
Fallen Angels 2 '93
Wild Palms '93
Heaven's Prisoners '95

Dickie Jobson
Countryman '83

Alejandro Jodorowsky
Santa Sangre '90

Steve Jodrell
Shame '87

Michael Joens
My Little Pony: The Movie '86

Arthur Joffe
Harem '85
Alberto Express '92

Mark Joffe
Night Master '87
Grievous Bodily Harm '89
The Efficiency Expert '92

Roland Joffe
The Killing Fields '84
The Mission '86
Fat Man and Little Boy '89
City of Joy '92
The Scarlet Letter '95

Sande Johnsen
Teenage Gang Debs '66

Alan Johnson
To Be or Not to Be '83
Solarbabies '86

Cindy Lou Johnson
Trusting Beatrice '92

David Johnson
DROP Squad '94

Emory Johnson
Phantom Express '32

Irvin Johnson
Blood Ring '93
Fist of Steel '93

Jed Johnson
Andy Warhol's Bad '77

John H. Johnson
Curse of the Blue Lights '88

Kenneth Johnson
The Incredible Hulk '77
Senior Trip '81
V '83
Short Circuit 2 '88
Alien Nation: Dark Horizon '94

Lamont Johnson
The Twilight Zone '61
McKenzie Break '70
My Sweet Charlie '70
A Gunfight '71
The Groundstar Conspiracy '72
The Last American Hero '73
The Execution of Private Slovik '74
Lipstick '76
One on One '77
FM '78
Crisis at Central High '80
Jack & the Beanstalk '83
Spacehunter: Adventures in the Forbidden Zone '83
Ernie Kovacs: Between the Laughter '84
Unnatural Causes '86
Gore Vidal's Lincoln '88
Escape '90
The Broken Chain '93

Nunnally Johnson
The Man in the Gray Flannel Suit '56
The Three Faces of Eve '57

Patrick Read Johnson
Spaced Invaders '90
Baby's Day Out '94
Angus '95

Raymond K. Johnson
I'll Name the Murderer '36
The Reckless Way '36
Code of the Fearless '39
Daughter of the Tong '39
In Old Montana '39
Covered Wagon Trails '40
Pinto Canyon '40
Ridin' the Trail '40

Tucker Johnson
Blood Salvage '90

Aaron Kim Johnston
The Last Winter '89
For the Moment '94

Jim Johnston
Blue De Ville '86

Joe Johnston
Honey, I Shrunk the Kids '89
The Rocketeer '91
The Pagemaster '94
Jumanji '95

Oskar Jonasson
Remote Control '94

Amy Holden Jones
The Slumber Party Massacre '82
Love Letters '83
Maid to Order '87

Brian Thomas Jones
Ocean Drive Weekend '85
Escape from Safehaven '88
The Rejuvenator '88
Posed For Murder '89

Chuck Jones
Best of Bugs Bunny & Friends '40
Bugs & Daffy: The Wartime Cartoons '45
Starring Bugs Bunny! '48
Phantom Tollbooth '69
The Bugs Bunny/Road Runner Movie '79
Looney Looney Looney Bugs Bunny Movie '81

David Jones
Betrayal '83
84 Charing Cross Road '86
The Christmas Wife '88
Jacknife '89
Look Back in Anger '89
The Trial '93
Is There Life Out There? '94

Donald M. Jones
Sweater Girls '78
Deadly Sunday '82
Love Butcher '82
The Forest '83
Project: Nightmare '85
Murderlust '86
Lethal Pursuit '88

Eugene S. Jones
High Ice '80

F. Richard Jones
Extra Girl '23
Bulldog Drummond '29

Gary Jones
Stay Tuned for Murder '88
Mosquito '95

Harmon Jones
As Young As You Feel '51
Pride of St. Louis '52
Bullwhip '58
The Legend of the Sea Wolf '58

James Cellan Jones
Fortunes of War '87

Lee Jones
Invasion of the Girl Snatchers '73

L.Q. Jones
A Boy and His Dog '75

Mark Jones
Leprechaun '93

Philip Jones
Cause of Death '90
Wish Me Luck '95

Terry Jones
Monty Python and the Holy Grail '75
Monty Python's Life of Brian '79
Monty Python's The Meaning of Life '83
Personal Services '87
Erik the Viking '89

Tommy Lee Jones
The Good Old Boys '95

Andrew Jordan
Things '80s

Glenn Jordan
Frankenstein '73
Picture of Dorian Gray '74
One of My Wives Is Missing '76
Les Miserables '78
The Family Man '79
Only When I Laugh '81
Lois Gibbs and the Love Canal '82
The Buddy System '83
Mass Appeal '84
Toughlove '85
Dress Gray '86
Something in Common '86
Echoes in the Darkness '87
Jesse '88
O Pioneers! '91
Sarah, Plain and Tall '91
Barbarians at the Gate '93
To Dance with the White Dog '93
A Streetcar Named Desire '95

Neil Jordan
Danny Boy '84
The Company of Wolves '85
Mona Lisa '86
High Spirits '88
We're No Angels '89
The Miracle '91
The Crying Game '92
Interview with the Vampire '94

Knut W. Jorfald
The Littlest Viking '94

George Joseph
Horror of the Blood Monsters '70

Jon Jost
Bell Diamond '81
Chameleon '81
Angel City '84
Slow Moves '84
Sure Fire '90
All the Vermeers in New York '91
Jon Jost's Frameup '93

Pierre Jourdan
Phedre '68

Ron Joy
The Desperados '80s

C. Courtney Joyner
Trancers 3: Deth Lives '92
Lurking Fear '94

Rupert Julian
Merry-Go-Round '23
The Phantom of the Opera '25
Walking Back '26
Yankee Clipper '27

Zheng Junli
Crows and Sparrows '49

Nathan (Hertz) Juran
The Black Castle '52
The Brain from Planet Arous '57
The Deadly Mantis '57
Hellcats of the Navy '57
20 Million Miles to Earth '57
Attack of the 50 Foot Woman '58
The Seventh Voyage of Sinbad '58
Jack the Giant Killer '62
First Men in the Moon '64
Land Raiders '69

Juan Jose Jusid
Made in Argentina '86

Paul Justman
Gimme an F '85

Claude Jutra
Mon Oncle Antoine '71
By Design '82
Surfacing '84

Barna Kabay
The Revolt of Job '84

Gaston Kabore
Wend Kuuni '82

Karel Kachyna
The Last Butterfly '92

George Kaczender
The Girl in Blue '74
In Praise of Older Women '78
The Agency '81
Chanel Solitaire '81
Your Ticket Is No Longer Valid '84
Prettykill '87

Jan Kadar
Death is Called Engelchen '63
The Shop on Main Street '65
Lies My Father Told Me '75
Freedom Road '79

Ellis Kadisan
Git! '65
The Cat '66

Helmut Kaeutner
The Captain from Koepenick '56

Jeremy Paul Kagan
Katherine '75
Heroes '77
The Big Fix '78
The Chosen '81
The Sting 2 '83
The Journey of Natty Gann '85
Courage '86
Conspiracy: The Trial of the Chicago Eight '87
Big Man on Campus '89
Descending Angel '90
By the Sword '93
Roswell: The U.F.O. Cover-Up '94

Jeff Kahn
Revolution! A Red Comedy '91

Richard C. Kahn
Two-Gun Man from Harlem '38
Bronze Buckaroo '39
Harlem Rides the Range '39
Son of Ingagi '40

Chen Kaige
Yellow Earth '89
Life on a String '90
Farewell My Concubine '93

Connie Kaiserman
My Little Girl '87

Mikhail Kalatozov
The Cranes are Flying '57
I Am Cuba '64
Red Tent '69

Tom Kalin
Swoon '91

Max Kalmanowicz
The Children '80
Dreams Come True '84

Scott Kalvert
The Basketball Diaries '94

Jay Kamen
Transformations '88

Steven Kampmann
Stealing Home '88

Yu Kan-Ping
The Outcasts '86

Tony Kandah
L.A. Wars '94

Dennis Kane
French Quarter '78

Joseph Kane
In Old Santa Fe '34
Melody Trail '35
Darkest Africa '36
Fighting Marines '36
Ghost Town Gold '36
King of the Pecos '36
The Lawless Nineties '36
Old Corral '36
Ride, Ranger, Ride '36
Boots & Saddles '37
Git Along Little Dogies '37
Heart of the Rockies '37
Round-Up Time in Texas '37
Springtime in the Rockies '37
Western Double Feature 4 '37
Yodelin' Kid From Pine Ridge '37
Billy the Kid Returns '38
Born to Be Wild '38
Oh Susannah '38
Old Barn Dance '38
Shine on, Harvest Moon '38
Western Double Feature 1 '38
Arizona Kid '39
Frontier Pony Express '39
Rough Riders' Roundup '39
Saga of Death Valley '39
The Border Legion '40
Colorado '40
Ranger and the Lady '40
Young Buffalo Bill '40
Jesse James at Bay '41
Robin Hood of the Pecos '41
Heart of the Golden West '42
Ridin' Down the Canyon '42
Sons of the Pioneers '42
South of Santa Fe '42
Sunset on the Desert '42
Sunset Serenade '42
Hands Across the Border '43
Idaho '43
Silver Spurs '43
Song of Texas '43
Texas Legionnaires '43
Song of Nevada '44
The Yellow Rose of Texas '44
Dakota '45
Flame of the Barbary Coast '45
Hoodlum Empire '52
Gene Autry Matinee Double Feature #2 '53
Ride the Man Down '53
Jubilee Trail '54
The Maverick Queen '55
Smoke in the Wind '75

Rolfe Kanefsky
There's Nothing Out There '90
My Family Treasure '93

Shusuke Kaneko
Summer Vacation: 1999 '88

Vitaly Kanevski
Freeze-Die-Come to Life '90

Jeff Kanew
Natural Enemies '79
Eddie Macon's Run '83
Revenge of the Nerds '84
Gotcha! '85
Tough Guys '86
Troop Beverly Hills '89
V.I. Warshawski '91

Charles Kanganis
Chance '89
Deadly Breed '89
Sinners '89
A Time to Die '91
No Escape, No Return '93
3 Ninjas Kick Back '94
Race the Sun '96

Marek Kanievska
Another Country '84
Less Than Zero '87

Garson Kanin
The Great Man Votes '38
Next Time I Marry '38
Bachelor Mother '39
My Favorite Wife '40
They Knew What They Wanted '40
Tom, Dick, and Harry '41

Alexis Kanner
Kings and Desperate Men '83

Hal Kanter
I Married a Woman '56
Loving You '57
For the Love of It '80

Richard Kanter
Wild Riders '71

Betty Kaplan
Of Love and Shadows '94

Ed Kaplan
Walking on Air '87
Chips, the War Dog '90
Primal Secrets '94

Jonathan Kaplan
Night Call Nurses '72
The Student Teachers '73
Truck Turner '74
White Line Fever '75
Mr. Billion '77
Over the Edge '79
Gentleman Bandit '81
Heart Like a Wheel '83
Girls of the White Orchid '85
Project X '87
The Accused '88
Immediate Family '89
Love Field '91
Unlawful Entry '92
Fallen Angels 1 '93
Bad Girls '94

Nelly Kaplan
A Very Curious Girl '69
Nea '78
Charles et Lucie '79

Ted Kaplan
Warbus '85

Shekhar Kapur
Bandit Queen '94

Wong Kar-Wai
Chungking Express '95

Yuri Karasik
The Seagull '71

Michael Karbelnikoff
Mobsters '91
The Last Ride '94

Leslie Kardos
Small Town Girl '53

Phil Karlson
The Shanghai Cobra '45
There Goes Kelly '45
Behind the Mask '46
Swing Parade of 1946 '46
The Big Cat '49
Ladies of the Chorus '49
The Texas Rangers '51
Kansas City Confidential '52
Hell to Eternity '60
Kid Galahad '62
Scarface Mob '62
Hornet's Nest '70
Ben '72
Walking Tall '73
Framed '75

Janice Karman
The Chipmunk Adventure '87

Bill Karn
Gang Busters '55
Ma Barker's Killer Brood '60
Door to Door Maniac '61

Eric Karson
Octagon '80
Opposing Force '87
Black Eagle '88
Angel Town '89

Y. Kasancki
The Amphibian Man '61

Lawrence Kasdan
Body Heat '81
The Big Chill '83
Silverado '85
The Accidental Tourist '88
I Love You to Death '90
Grand Canyon '91
Wyatt Earp '94
French Kiss '95

Mathieu Kassovitz
Cafe au Lait '94
Hate '95

Peter Kassovitz
Make Room for Tomorrow '81

Pierre Kast
Girl in His Pocket '57

Leonard Kastle
Honeymoon Killers '70

Michael Katleman
The Spider and the Fly '94

Milton Katselas
Butterflies Are Free '72
Forty Carats '73
Report to the Commissioner '74
Strangers: The Story of a Mother and Daughter '79

Gloria Katz
Messiah of Evil '74

Lee H. Katzin
Whatever Happened to Aunt Alice? '69
Le Mans '71
The Salzburg Connection '72
The Voyage of the Yes '72
The Stranger '73
Savages '75
Sky Hei$t '75
The Longest Drive '76
The Man from Atlantis '77
The Bastard '78
Terror Out of the Sky '78
Space: 1999—Alien Attack '79
Death Ray 2000 '81
The Dirty Dozen: The Deadly Mission '87
The Dirty Dozen: The Fatal Mission '88
World Gone Wild '88

Jonathan Kaufer
Soup for One '82

Charles Kaufman
Mother's Day '80
When Nature Calls '85
Jakarta '88

George S. Kaufman
The Senator was Indiscreet '47

Jim Kaufman
Backstab '90

Lloyd (Samuel Weil) Kaufman
Squeeze Play '79
Waitress '81
First Turn On '83
Stuck on You '84
Class of Nuke 'Em High '86
The Toxic Avenger '86
Troma's War '88
The Toxic Avenger, Part 2 '89
The Toxic Avenger, Part 3: The Last Temptation of Toxie '89

Philip Kaufman
The Great Northfield Minnesota Raid '72
The White Dawn '75
Invasion of the Body Snatchers '78
Wanderers '79
The Right Stuff '83
The Unbearable Lightness of Being '88
Henry & June '90
Rising Sun '93

Aki Kaurismaki
Ariel '89
Leningrad Cowboys Go America '89
The Match Factory Girl '90
La Vie de Boheme '93

Mika Kaurismaki
Amazon '90
Condition Red '95

Brian Kavanagh
Double Deal '84

Anwar Kawadri
Nutcracker Sweet '84
Claudia '85

Jerzy Kawalerowicz
Mother Joan of the Angels '60
Pharaoh '66

Gilbert Kay
White Comanche '67

James H. Kay
Seeds of Evil '76

Robert Kaylor
Derby '71
Carny '80
Nobody's Perfect '90

Elia Kazan
A Tree Grows in Brooklyn '45
Boomerang '47
Gentleman's Agreement '47
Pinky '49
Panic in the Streets '50
A Streetcar Named Desire '51
Viva Zapata! '52
East of Eden '54
On the Waterfront '54
Baby Doll '56
A Face in the Crowd '57
Splendor in the Grass '61
The Arrangement '69
The Last Tycoon '76

Nicholas Kazan
Dream Lover '93

Fran Rubel Kazui
Tokyo Pop '88
Buffy the Vampire Slayer '92

Lo Ke
The Amsterdam Connection '70s

James Keach
The Forgotten '89
False Identity '90
Sunstroke '92
Praying Mantis '93
The Stars Fell on Henrietta '94

Buster Keaton
Cops/One Week '22
The Balloonatic/One Week '23
The Blacksmith/The Balloonatic '23
Our Hospitality '23
Three Ages '23
The Navigator '24
Seven Chances '25
Battling Butler '26
The General '27

Diane Keaton
Heaven '87
Wildflower '91
Unstrung Heroes '95

Zsolt Kedzi-Kovacs
Nice Neighbor '79

Nietzchka Keene
The Juniper Tree '87

Worth Keeter
Lady Grey '82
The Wolfman '82
Dogs of Hell '83
Unmasking the Idol '86
Order of the Black Eagle '87
L.A. Bounty '89
Trapper County War '89
Illicit Behavior '91
Snapdragon '93

Douglas Keeve
Unzipped '94

Peter Keglevic
The Cop & the Girl '86
Kill Cruise '90

Michael Kehoe
Dominion '94

William Keighley
Ladies They Talk About '33
"G" Men '35
Green Pastures '36
The Prince and the Pauper '37
Bullets or Ballots '38
Each Dawn I Die '39
The Fighting 69th '40
The Bride Came C.O.D. '41
The Man Who Came to Dinner '41
George Washington Slept Here '42
The Street with No Name '48
The Master of Ballantrae '53

George Keil
2069: A Sex Odyssey '78

David Keith
The Curse '87
The Further Adventures of Tennessee Buck '88

Harvey Keith
Jezebel's Kiss '90

Frederick King Keller
The Eyes of the Amaryllis '82
Vamping '84

Harry Keller
El Paso Stampede '53
Marshal of Cedar Rock '53
Geronimo's Revenge '60
Texas John Slaughter: Geronimo's Revenge '60
Texas John Slaughter: Stampede at Bitter Creek '62
Tammy and the Doctor '63

Bob Kellett
Naughty Knights '71
Space: 1999 '75

Hugh Kelley
The Cage '89

Roy Kellino
I Met a Murderer '39
Charade '53

Nick Kellis
Endangered '94

Bob Kelljan
Count Yorga, Vampire '70
The Return of Count Yorga '71
Scream Blacula Scream '73
Act of Vengeance '74
Black Oak Conspiracy '77

Barnet Kellman
Key Exchange '85
Straight Talk '92

David Kellogg
Cool As Ice '91

Ray Kellogg
The Giant Gila Monster '59
The Killer Shrews '59

Albert Kelly
Campus Knights '29

Gene Kelly
On the Town '49
Singin' in the Rain '52
Invitation to the Dance '56
The Tunnel of Love '58
A Guide for the Married Man '67
Hello, Dolly! '69
The Cheyenne Social Club '70

James Kelly
Beast in the Cellar '70

Nancy Kelly
Thousand Pieces of Gold '91

Patrick Kelly
Beer '85

Peter Kelly
The Dawson Patrol '78

Ron Kelly
King of the Grizzlies '69

Rory Kelly
Sleep with Me '94

Jack Kemp
Miracle in Harlem '48

Ralph Kemplen
The Spaniard's Curse '58

David Kendall
Luggage of the Gods '87

James Kennaway
Tunes of Glory/Horse's Mouth '60

Arthur Kennedy
Assault with a Deadly Weapon '82

Burt Kennedy
The Rounders '65
Return of the Seven '66
The War Wagon '67
The Good Guys and the Bad Guys '69
Support Your Local Sheriff '69
Ride to Glory '71
Support Your Local Gunfighter '71
Hannie Caulder '72
Train Robbers '73
All the Kind Strangers '74
Killer Inside Me '76
The Concrete Cowboys '79
Wild, Wild West Revisited '79
Wolf Lake '79
More Wild, Wild West '80
The Trouble with Spies '87
Dynamite and Gold '88
Suburban Commando '91

Ken Kennedy
Iron Angel '64
Mission to Glory '80
Grizzly Adams: The Legend Continues '90

Leon Isaac Kennedy
Knights of the City '85

Lou Kennedy
Breathing Fire '91

Michael Kennedy
Caribe '87
One Man Out '89
The Swordsman '92
Talons of the Eagle '92
Hard Evidence '94
Red Scorpion 2 '94
Robin of Locksley '95

Tom Kennedy
Time Walker '82

Larry Kent
The Victory '88

Eric Kenton
Fight for the Title '57

Erle C. Kenton
Bare Knees '28
Island of Lost Souls '32
Escape to Paradise '39
Remedy for Riches '40
Melody for Three '41
They Meet Again '41
The Ghost of Frankenstein '42
Pardon My Sarong '42
Who Done It? '42
House of Frankenstein '44
House of Dracula '45

Roeland Kerbosch
For a Lost Soldier '93

Patrick Kerby
Ex-Cop '93

James V. Kern
Never Say Goodbye '46
Second Woman '51
Two Tickets to Broadway '51

Russell Kern
Spittin' Image '83

Sarah Kernochan
Marjoe '72

Lodge Kerrigan
Clean, Shaven '93

Irvin Kershner
The Hoodlum Priest '61
A Fine Madness '66
Flim-Flam Man '67
Up the Sandbox '72
S*P*Y*S '74
The Return of a Man Called Horse '76
Raid on Entebbe '77
Eyes of Laura Mars '78
The Empire Strikes Back '80
Never Say Never Again '83
Traveling Man '89
RoboCop 2 '90

Emmanuel Kervyn
Rabid Grannies '89

Harry Kerwin
Cheering Section '73
God's Bloody Acre '75
Barracuda '78

Alek Keshishian
Truth or Dare '91
With Honors '94

Bruce Kessler
Angels from Hell '68
Simon, King of the Witches '71
Cruise into Terror '78
Deathmoon '78

Kliff Keuhl
Murder Rap '87

Michael Keusch
Lena's Holiday '90
Huck and the King of Hearts '93
Just One of the Girls '93
Samurai Cowboy '93

Riffat A. Khan
Feelin' Screwy '90

Michel Khleifi
A Wedding in Galilee '87

Kim Ki-dak
Yongkari Monster of the Deep '67

Abbas Kiarostami
Through the Olive Trees '94

Beeban Kidron
Antonia and Jane '91
Used People '92
To Wong Foo, Thanks for Everything, Julie Newmar '95

Fritz Kiersch
Children of the Corn '84
Tuff Turf '85
Winners Take All '87
Gor '88
Under the Boardwalk '89
Into the Sun '92
Shattered Image '93
The Stranger '95

Krzysztof Kieslowski
Camera Buff '79
No End '84
The Double Life of Veronique '91
Trois Couleurs: Bleu '93
Trois Couleurs: Blanc '94
Trois Couleurs: Rouge '94

Gerard Kikione
Dragonard '88
Buried Alive '89
Edge of Sanity '89

Jon Killough
Skinned Alive '89

Edward Killy
Don Amigo/Stage to Chino '40s
Nevada '44
West of the Pecos '45

Richard H. Kim
Kill Line '91

Clinton Kimbrough
The Young Nurses '73

Bruce Kimmel
Spaceship '81

Anthony Kimmins
Mine Own Executioner '47
Bonnie Prince Charlie '48
Captain's Paradise '53

John Kincade
Terminal Entry '87
Back to Back '90

Tim Kincaid
Bad Girls Dormitory '84
Mutant Hunt '87
Necropolis '87
Robot Holocaust '87
Maximum Thrust '88
She's Back '88
The Occultist '89

Allan Winton King
Silence of the North '81

Allen King
Termini Station '89

Burton King
The Man from Beyond '22
The Adorable Cheat '28

George King
The Crimes of Stephen Hawke '36
Demon Barber of Fleet Street '36
Sexton Blake and the Hooded Terror '38
The Case of the Frightened Lady '39
Crimes at the Dark House '39
The Face at the Window '39

Henry King
Tol'able David '21
The White Sister '23
Romola '25
She Goes to War '29
Hell Harbor '30
Marie Galante '34
Lloyds of London '36
Alexander's Ragtime Band '38
In Old Chicago '38
Jesse James '39
Stanley and Livingstone '39
A Yank in the R.A.F. '41
The Black Swan '42
The Song of Bernadette '43
Wilson '44
Twelve O'Clock High '49
The Gunfighter '50
David and Bathsheba '51
I'd Climb the Highest Mountain '51
The Snows of Kilimanjaro '52
Love Is a Many-Splendored Thing '55
Carousel '56
The Bravados '58
Beloved Infidel '59

Louis King
Border Law '31
The Fighting Sheriff '31
Drifting Souls '32
Special Investigator '36
Bulldog Drummond Comes Back '37
Bulldog Drummond's Revenge '37
Sabre Jet '53
Dangerous Mission '54

Rick King
Hard Choices '84
Hot Shot '86
The Killing Time '87
Forced March '90
Prayer of the Rollerboys '91
Kickboxer 3: The Art of War '92
Quick '93
A Passion to Kill '94

Robert Lee King
Boys Life '94

Stephen King
Maximum Overdrive '86

Zalman King
Two Moon Junction '88
Wildfire '88
Wild Orchid '90
Red Shoe Diaries '92
Red Shoe Diaries 2: Double Dare '92
Wild Orchid 2: Two Shades of Blue '92
Red Shoe Diaries 3: Another Woman's Lipstick '93
Red Shoe Diaries 4: Auto Erotica '93
Delta of Venus '95

Alan Kingsberg
Almost Partners '87

Jack Kinney
The Legend of Sleepy Hollow '49
1001 Arabian Nights '59

Keisuke Kinoshita
Twenty-Four Eyes '54

Teinosuke Kinugasa
Gate of Hell '54

Alex Kirby
The Chronicles of Narnia '89

Robert Kirk
Destroyer '88

David Kirkland
The Tomboy '24

John Kirkland
Curse of the Headless Horseman '72

Klaus Kirschner
Mozart: A Childhood Chronicle '76

John Kirsh
Jesus '79

Ephraim Kishon
Sallah '63

Lek Kitiparaporn
AngKor: Cambodia Express '81

Carl Kitt
Up River '79

Robert J. Kizer
Godzilla 1985 '85
Hell Comes to Frogtown '88
Death Ring '93

Alf Kjellin
The McMasters '70
The Girls of Huntington House '73

Robert Klane
Thank God It's Friday '78
Weekend at Bernie's 2 '93

Damian Klaus
Futurekick '91

Dennis Klein
One More Saturday Night '86

Randal Kleiser
The Boy in the Plastic Bubble '76
The Gathering '77
Grease '78
The Blue Lagoon '80
Summer Lovers '82
Grandview U.S.A. '84
Flight of the Navigator '86
Big Top Pee Wee '88
Getting It Right '89
White Fang '91
Honey, I Blew Up the Kid '92
It's My Party '95

Walter Klenhard
The Haunting of Seacliff Inn '94

Richard Kletter
Dangerous Indiscretion '94
The Android Affair '95

Max Kleven
Ruckus '81
Deadly Stranger '88
Bail Out '90

Roland Klick
Let It Rock '86

Elem Klimov
Come and See '85
Rasputin '85

Leon Klimovsky
The Werewolf vs. the Vampire Woman '70
Dr. Jekyll and the Wolfman '71
The Saga of the Draculas '72
Vengeance of the Zombies '72
Orgy of the Vampires '73
The Devil's Possessed '74

Ben Kline
Lightning Warrior '31

Herbert Kline
The Fighter '52

Tony Klinger
Butterfly Ball '76

Werner Klinger
Secret of the Black Trunk '62

Elmar Klos
Death is Called Engelchen '63
The Shop on Main Street '65

Andre Klotzel
Savage Capitalism '93

Steven Kloves
The Fabulous Baker Boys '89
Flesh and Bone '93

Alexander Kluge
Germany in Autumn '78

Pavel Klushantsev
Planet Burg '62

Castleton Knight
The Flying Scotsman '29

Robert Knights
Lovers of Their Time '85
A Dedicated Man '86
Ebony Tower '86
The Dawning '88
Double Vision '92

Edwin H. Knopf
The Light of Western Stars '30

Bernard Knowles
Norman Conquest '53
Murder on Approval '56
Frozen Alive '64

Werner Knox
Scalps '83

Philip Ko
Platoon the Warriors '88

Masaki Kobayashi
The Human Condition: No Greater Love '58
The Human Condition: Road to Eternity '59
The Human Condition: A Soldier's Prayer '61
Kwaidan '64

Howard W. Koch
Girl in Black Stockings '57
Born Reckless '59
Badge 373 '73

Philip Koch
Pink Nights '87

David Koepp
The Trigger Effect '96

Manfred Kohler
Target for Killing '66

Pancho Kohner
Mr. Sycamore '74

Marja Kok
In for Treatment '82

Ana Kokkinos
Only the Brave '94

Winrich Kolbe
Star Trek the Next Generation, the Final Episode: All Good Things... '94
Star Trek Voyager: Caretaker '95

Amos Kollek
Goodbye, New York '85
Forever, Lulu '87
High Stakes '89
Double Edge '92
Whore 2 '94

Xavier Koller
Journey of Hope '90
Squanto: A Warrior's Tale '94

James Komack
Porky's Revenge '85

Sergei Komarov
A Kiss for Mary Pickford '27

Andrei Konchalovsky
Siberiade '79
Maria's Lovers '84
Runaway Train '85
Duet for One '86
Shy People '87
Homer and Eddie '89
Tango and Cash '89
The Inner Circle '91

Jackie Kong
The Being '83
Night Patrol '85
Blood Diner '87
The Underachievers '88

Joseph Kong
Thundering Ninja '80s
Clones of Bruce Lee '80

Barbara Kopple
Harlan County, U.S.A. '76
Keeping On '81
Fallen Champ: The Untold Story of Mike Tyson '93

Alexander Korda
Marius '31
Wedding Rehearsal '32
The Private Life of Henry VIII '33
Private Life of Don Juan '34
Rembrandt '36
That Hamilton Woman '41

Zoltan Korda
If I Were Rich '33
Sanders of the River '35
Elephant Boy '37
Drums '38
The Four Feathers '39
The Jungle Book '42
Sahara '43
Cry, the Beloved Country '51

John Korty
The People '71
Class of '63 '73
Silence '73
The Autobiography of Miss Jane Pittman '74
Forever '78
Oliver's Story '78
A Christmas Without Snow '80
The Haunting Passion '83
The Ewok Adventure '84
Deadly Business '86
Baby Girl Scott '87
Cast the First Stone '89
Eye on the Sparrow '91
Long Road Home '91
They Watch '93
Getting Out '94
Redwood Curtain '95

Waldemar Korzenioswsky
The Chair '87

Grigori Kosintsev
Don Quixote '57

Henry Koster
Three Smart Girls '36
100 Men and a Girl '37
The Rage of Paris '38
First Love '39
Three Smart Girls Grow Up '39
It Started with Eve '41
The Bishop's Wife '47
Come to the Stable '49
The Inspector General '49
Harvey '50
No Highway in the Sky '51
Stars and Stripes Forever '52
The Robe '53
Desiree '54
A Man Called Peter '55
The Virgin Queen '55
D-Day, the Sixth of June '56
My Man Godfrey '57
The Naked Maja '59
The Story of Ruth '60
Flower Drum Song '61
Mr. Hobbs Takes a Vacation '62
Dear Brigitte '65
The Singing Nun '66

Tom Kotani
The Bushido Blade '80

Ted Kotcheff
Tiara Tahiti '62
The Apprenticeship of Duddy Kravitz '74
Fun with Dick and Jane '77
Who Is Killing the Great Chefs of Europe? '78
North Dallas Forty '79
First Blood '82
Split Image '82
Uncommon Valor '83
Joshua Then and Now '85
Switching Channels '88
Weekend at Bernie's '89
Winter People '89
Folks! '92
Red Shoe Diaries 3: Another Woman's Lipstick '93
The Shooter '94
Red Shoe Diaries 5: Weekend Pass '95

Jerzy Kotkowski
In an Old Manor House '84

Jim Kouf
Miracles '86
Disorganized Crime '89

Nikos Koundouros
Young Aphrodites '63

Steven Kovacks
'68 '87

Andras Kovacs
Cold Days '66

Paul Koval
Blue Movies '88

Bernard L. Kowalski
Night of the Blood Beast '58
Attack of the Giant Leeches '59
Stiletto '69
Macho Callahan '70
The Woman Hunter '72
Nativity '78
Marciano '79
B.A.D. Cats '80
Nashville Beat '89

Soeren Kragh-Jacobsen
Emma's Shadow '88

Frank Kramer
Five for Hell '67
God's Gun '75
This Time I'll Make You Rich '75

Jerry Kramer
Modern Girls '86

Remi Kramer
High Velocity '76

Stanley Kramer
Not as a Stranger '55
The Pride and the Passion '57
The Defiant Ones '58
On the Beach '59
Inherit the Wind '60
Judgment at Nuremberg '61
It's a Mad, Mad, Mad, Mad World '63
Ship of Fools '65
Guess Who's Coming to Dinner '67
R.P.M.* (*Revolutions Per Minute) '70
Bless the Beasts and Children '71
Oklahoma Crude '73
The Domino Principle '77
The Runner Stumbles '79

Norman Krasna
The Big Hangover '50
The Ambassador's Daughter '56

Paul Krasny
Christina '74
Joe Panther '76
When Hell Was in Session '82
Back to Hannibal: The Return of Tom Sawyer and Huckleberry Finn '90
Drug Wars 2: The Cocaine Cartel '92

Lee Kresel
Alakazam the Great! '61

Harold F. Kress
The Painted Hills '51

John Krish
The Unearthly Stranger '64
Man Who Had Power Over Women '70

Srinivas Krishna
Masala '91

Suri Krishnamma
A Man of No Importance '94

Allen Kroeker
Tramp at the Door '87
Age Old Friends '89
Heaven on Earth '89
Showdown at Williams Creek '91

Bill Krohn
It's All True '93

Jon Kroll
Amanda and the Alien '95

Frank Krom
To Play or To Die '91

Jeremy Joe Kronsberg
Going Ape! '81

Steve Kroschel
Running Free '94

Bill Kroyer
Ferngully: The Last Rain Forest '92

Michael Krueger
Mindkiller '87
Night Vision '87

Stanley Kubrick
Killer's Kiss '55
The Killing '56
Paths of Glory '57
Spartacus '60
Lolita '62
Dr. Strangelove, or: How I Learned to Stop Worrying and Love the Bomb '64
2001: A Space Odyssey '68
A Clockwork Orange '71
Barry Lyndon '75
The Shining '80
Full Metal Jacket '87

Andrew J. Kuehn
Flush '81

Steven Kuether
Demons of Ludlow '75

Lev Kuleshov
The Extraordinary Adventures of Mr. West in the Land of the Bolsheviks '24

Lev Kulijanov
Crime and Punishment '70

Buzz Kulik
Sergeant Ryker '68
Villa Rides '68
Riot '69
Brian's Song '71
Pioneer Woman '73
Shamus '73
Bad Ronald '74
Babe! '75
The Lindbergh Kidnapping Case '76
From Here to Eternity '79
The Hunter '80
Rage of Angels '83
Women of Valor '86
Around the World in 80 Days '89

Edward Kull
The New Adventures of Tarzan '35
Tarzan and the Green Goddess '38

Victor Kulle
Illusions '91

Kei Kumai
Sandakan No. 8 '74
Love and Faith '78

Harry Kumel
Daughters of Darkness '71

Joseph Kuo
Shaolin Temple Strikes Back '72
Born Invincible '76
Dragon's Claw '80s
The Unbeaten 28 '80s

Koreyoshi Kurahara
Antarctica '84
Hiroshima '95

Hanif Kureishi
London Kills Me '91

Akira Kurosawa
Sanshiro Sugata '43
The Men Who Tread on the Tiger's Tail '45
No Regrets for Our Youth '46
Drunken Angel '48
A Quiet Duel '49
Stray Dog '49
Scandal '50
The Idiot '51
Rashomon '51
Ikiru '52
Seven Samurai '54
I Live in Fear '55
The Lower Depths '57
Throne of Blood '57
The Hidden Fortress '58
The Bad Sleep Well '60
Yojimbo '61
High & Low '62
Sanjuro '62
Red Beard '65
Dodes 'ka-den '70
Dersu Uzala '75
Kagemusha '80
Ran '85
Akira Kurosawa's Dreams '90
Rhapsody in August '91

Mitsuo Kurotsuchi
Traffic Jam '91

Robert Kurtzman
The Demolitionist '95

Diane Kurys
Peppermint Soda '77
Entre-Nous '83
A Man in Love '87
Love After Love '94

Donald Kushner
First & Ten '85

Emir Kusturica
When Father was Away on Business '85
Time of the Gypsies '90
Arizona Dream '94
Underground '95

Ken Kwapis
The Beniker Gang '83
Sesame Street Presents: Follow That Bird '85
Vibes '88
He Said, She Said '91
Dunston Checks In '95

Jeff Kwitny
Iced '88
Beyond the Door 3 '91

Paul Kyriazi
Death Machines '76
Crazed Cop '88
Omega Cop '90

Gregory La Cava
Running Wild '27
Feel My Pulse '28
Big News '29
His First Command '29
Gabriel Over the White House '33
My Man Godfrey '36

La Cava ▶cont.

Stage Door '37
Fifth Avenue Girl '39
Primrose Path '40

Steven La Rocque
Samantha '92

Jeanne Labrune
Sand and Blood '87

Harry Lachman
Baby, Take a Bow '34
Our Relations '36
Murder over New York '40
Charlie Chan in Rio '41
Castle in the Desert '42
The Loves of Edgar Allen Poe '42

Georges Lacombe
Seven Deadly Sins '53

Joe Lacy
A Witch Without a Broom '68

Diane Ladd
Mrs. Munck '95

Aldo Lado
Paralyzed '70s

Edward Laemmle
Texas Bad Man '32

John Lafia
Blue Iguana '88
Child's Play 2 '90
Man's Best Friend '93

Jean LaFleur
Ilsa, the Tigress of Siberia '79
Mystery of the Million Dollar Hockey Puck '80s

Ron Lagomarsino
Dinner at Eight '89

Craig Lahiff
Deadly Possession '88
Fever '88
Strangers '90
Ebbtide '94

Joseph Lai
Ninja Hunt '80s
Cobra Against Ninja '87
Ninja Commandments '87
Ninja Operation: Licensed to Terminate '87
Ninja Strike Force '88
The Power of the Ninjitsu '88
Ninja Powerforce '90
Ninja Showdown '90

Harvey Laidman
Steel Cowboy '78
The Boy Who Loved Trolls '84

John Laing
Beyond Reasonable Doubt '80
Dangerous Orphans '86
The Lost Tribe '89
Absent Without Leave '95

Frank Laloggia
Fear No Evil '80
The Lady in White '88
Mother '94

Rene Laloux
Fantastic Planet '73

Ringo Lam
Undeclared War '91

York Lam
Ninja Connection '90

Fernando Lamas
Violent Ones '68

Lorenzo Lamas
C.I.A. 2: Target Alexa '94

John Lamb
The Mermaids of Tiburon '62

Gregory Lamberson
Slime City '89

Bruce Lambert
Ninja Masters of Death '85
Ninja Fantasy '86
Ninja, the Violent Sorcerer '86
Ninja Phantom Heroes '87
Vampire Raiders—Ninja Queen '89

Mary Lambert
Siesta '87
Pet Sematary '89
Grand Isle '92
Pet Sematary 2 '92

Susan Lambert
Talk '94

John Lamond
Breakfast in Paris '81

Charles Lamont
Circumstantial Evidence '35
A Shot in the Dark '35
Sons of Steel '35
The World Accuses '35
Bulldog Edition '36
The Dark Hour '36
International Crime '37
Wallaby Jim of the Islands '37
Shadows Over Shanghai '38
Panama Patrol '39
Hit the Ice '43
Salome, Where She Danced '45
Ma and Pa Kettle '49
Abbott and Costello in the Foreign Legion '50
Ma and Pa Kettle Go to Town '50
Abbott and Costello Meet the Invisible Man '51
Comin' Round the Mountain '51
Abbott and Costello Meet Captain Kidd '52
Abbott and Costello Meet Dr. Jekyll and Mr. Hyde '52
Abbott and Costello Go to Mars '53
Ma and Pa Kettle on Vacation '53
Abbott and Costello Meet the Keystone Kops '54
Ma and Pa Kettle at Home '54
Abbott and Costello Meet the Mummy '55
Francis in the Haunted House '56
The Kettles in the Ozarks '56

Albert Lamorisse
White Mane '52
The Red Balloon '56
Voyage en Balloon '59
Red Balloon/Occurrence at Owl Creek Bridge '62
Circus Angel '65

Georges Lampin
L'Idiot '46

Bernard Lamy
La Vie est Belle '87

Burt Lancaster
The Kentuckian '55

Lew (Louis Friedlander) Landers
Tailspin Tommy '34
The Raven '35
Rustlers of Red Dog '35
Flight from Glory '37
Annabel Takes a Tour/Maid's Night Out '38
Law of the Underworld '38
Bad Lands '39
Wagon's Westward '40
Ridin' on a Rainbow '41
Return of the Vampire '43
I'm from Arkansas '44
U-Boat Prisoner '44
The Enchanted Forest '45
Death Valley '46
The Mask of Dijon '46
The Adventures of Gallant Bess '48
Inner Sanctum '48
Dynamite Pass '50
Torpedo Alley '53

James Landis
Stakeout '62
The Sadist '63
Nasty Rabbit '64
Deadwood '65

John Landis
Schlock '73
Kentucky Fried Movie '77
National Lampoon's Animal House '78
The Blues Brothers '80
An American Werewolf in London '81
Trading Places '83
Twilight Zone: The Movie '83
Into the Night '85
Spies Like Us '85
Three Amigos '86
Amazon Women on the Moon '87
Coming to America '88
Oscar '91
Innocent Blood '92
Beverly Hills Cop 3 '94
The Stupids '95

Michael Landon
It's Good to Be Alive '74
Little House on the Prairie '74
The Loneliest Runner '76
Killing Stone '78
Sam's Son '84

Paul Landres
Square Dance Jubilee '51
Return of Dracula '58
Go, Johnny Go! '59
Flipper's Odyssey '66

Alan Landsburg
Black Water Gold '69

Andrew Lane
Jake Speed '86
Mortal Passions '90
Desperate Motives '92
The Secretary '94
Trade Off '95

Charles Lane
True Identity '91

Rocky Lane
All's Fair '89

Eric Laneuville
The George McKenna Story '86
The Mighty Pawns '87
The Ernest Green Story '93

Sidney Lanfield
One in a Million '36
Thin Ice '37
The Hound of the Baskervilles '39
Second Fiddle '39
You'll Never Get Rich '41
My Favorite Blonde '42
Where There's Life '47
Station West '48
Sorrowful Jones '49
The Lemon Drop Kid '51
Skirts Ahoy! '52

Fritz Lang
Spiders '18
Dr. Mabuse, Parts 1 & 2 '22
Kriemhilde's Revenge '24
Siegfried '24
Metropolis '26
Spies '28
Woman in the Moon '29
M '31
Crimes of Dr. Mabuse '32
Das Testament des Dr. Mabuse '33
Liliom '35
Fury '36
You Only Live Once '37
Return of Frank James '40
Western Union '41
Woman In the Window '44
Scarlet Street '45
Cloak and Dagger '46
Secret Beyond the Door '48
Clash by Night '52
Rancho Notorious '52
The Big Heat '53
Human Desire '54
Moonfleet '55
Beyond a Reasonable Doubt '56
While the City Sleeps '56
Journey to the Lost City '58
The Thousand Eyes of Dr. Mabuse '60

Krzysztof Lang
Paper Marriage '93

Michael Lang
Holiday Hotel '77
The Gift '82

Perry Lang
Little Vegas '90
Men of War '94

Richard Lang
Fantasy Island '76
Force of Evil '77
The Hunted Lady '77
Night Cries '78
Vegas '78
The Word '78
A Change of Seasons '80
The Mountain Men '80
Strike Force '81
Don't Go to Sleep '82
Shooting Stars '85
Kung Fu: The Movie '86
Christmas Comes to Willow Creek '87
Texas '94

Rocky Lang
Race for Glory '89
Nervous Ticks '93

Walter Lang
Red Kimono '25
The Little Princess '39
The Blue Bird '40
Tin Pan Alley '40
Moon over Miami '41
Week-End In Havana '41
The Magnificent Dope '42
Song of the Islands '42
State Fair '45
Cheaper by the Dozen '50
The Jackpot '50
There's No Business Like Show Business '54
The King and I '56
Desk Set '57
But Not for Me '59
Can-Can '60
Snow White and the Three Stooges '61

Declan Langan
Erotic Images '85

Noel Langley
The Pickwick Papers '54
The Adventures of Sadie '55
Svengali '55
The Search for Bridey Murphy '56

Chris Langman
Moving Targets '87

Murray Langston
Wishful Thinking '92

Simon Langton
Act of Passion: The Lost Honor of Kathryn Beck '83
Anna Karenina '85
Casanova '87
Laguna Heat '87
The Whistle Blower '87
The Cinder Path '94
Pride and Prejudice '95

Lawrence Lanoff
Indecent Behavior '93
Temptress '95

Anthony M. Lanza
The Glory Stompers '67
The Incredible Two-Headed Transplant '71

James Lapine
Sunday in the Park with George '86
Impromptu '90
Life with Mikey '93

Christopher Larkin
A Very Natural Thing '73

Joseph Larraz
The House that Vanished '73
Vampyres '74
Golden Lady '79

Sheldon Larry
Behind Enemy Lines '85
Terminal Choice '85

Keith Larsen
Mission Batangas '69
Trap on Cougar Mountain '72
Whitewater Sam '78
Young & Free '78

Robert W. Larsen
The Narcotics Story '58

Eric Larson
Sleeping Beauty '59

Larry Larson
Deadly Passion '85

J.A. Laser
Zombie Lake '84

John Lasseter
Toy Story '95

Stan Lathan
Amazing Grace '74
Beat Street '84
Go Tell It On the Mountain '84
Uncle Tom's Cabin '87

John Latos
The Voyage of Tanai '75

Steve Latshaw
Dark Universe '93
Biohazard: The Alien Force '95
Jack-O '95

David Michael Latt
Sorority House Party '92

Alberto Lattuada
Anna '51
Variety Lights '51
Love in the City '53
Stay As You Are '78
La Cicada '83
Christopher Columbus '85

S.H. Lau
Heroes Three '84

Frank Laughlin
The Trial of Billy Jack '74

Michael Laughlin
Strange Behavior '81
Strange Invaders '83
Mesmerized '84

Tom Laughlin
Born Losers '67
Billy Jack '71

Charles Laughton
The Night of the Hunter '55

Frank Launder
I See a Dark Stranger '46
The Happiest Days of Your Life '50
The Belles of St. Trinian's '53
Blue Murder at St. Trinian's '56
The Pure Hell of St. Trinian's '61
The Great St. Trinian's Train Robbery '66

Dale Launer
Love Potion #9 '92

Fabrizio Laurenti
Witchery '88

George Lauris
Buffalo Rider '78

Fernand Lauterier
Nais '45

Georges Lautner
Road to Salina '68
Icy Breasts '75
My Other Husband '85
La Cage aux Folles 3: The Wedding '86

Linda Lautrec
My Breakfast with Blassie '83

Gerard Lauzier
Petit Con '84

Jean-Claude Lauzon
Night Zoo '87
Leolo '92

Arnold Laven
Without Warning '52
The Monster That Challenged the World '57
Geronimo '62
Rough Night in Jericho '67

Julianna Lavin
Live Nude Girls '95

Martin Lavut
Palais Royale '88
Smokescreen '90

Clara Law
The Reincarnation of Golden Lotus '89
Autumn Moon '92
Temptation of a Monk '94

George Law
Torpedo Attack '72

Tom Law
Tax Season '90

Denny Lawrence
Archer's Adventure '85

John Lawrence
Cycle Psycho '72
Savage Abduction '73

Marc Lawrence
Pigs '73

Martin Lawrence
A Thin Line Between Love and Hate '96

Quentin Lawrence
The Crawling Eye '58

Ray Lawrence
Bliss '85

J.F. Lawton
Cannibal Women in the Avocado Jungle of Death '89
Pizza Man '91

Jonathan Lawton
The Hunted '94

Jennifer Lax
Max '79

Pedro Lazaga
Gladiators 7 '62

Ashley Lazarus
Golden Rendezvous '77

Julius Le Flore
Secret Agent 00-Soul '89

Wilford Leach
The Wedding Party '69
The Pirates of Penzance '83

Philip Leacock
Escapade '55
The Spanish Gardener '57
War Lover '62
Shattered Silence '71
Baffled '72
Dying Room Only '73
The Waltons: A Thanksgiving Story '73
Killer on Board '77
Wild & Wooly '78
Angel City '80
The Curse of King Tut's Tomb '80
Three Sovereigns for Sarah '85

Anton Leader
Children of the Damned '63

Paul Leaf
Sergeant Matlovich vs. the U.S. Air Force '78

Louis Leahman
South of Hell Mountain '70

Larry Leahy
Confessions of a Hit Man '94

David Lean
In Which We Serve '43
Blithe Spirit '45
Brief Encounter '46
Great Expectations '46
This Happy Breed '47
Oliver Twist '48
Madeleine '50
Hobson's Choice '53
Summertime '55
The Bridge on the River Kwai '57
Lawrence of Arabia '62
Doctor Zhivago '65
Ryan's Daughter '70
A Passage to India '84

Norman Lear
Cold Turkey '71

Denis Leary
National Lampoon's Favorite Deadly Sins '95

Timothy Leary
Cheech and Chong's Nice Dreams '81

Maria Lease
Dolly Dearest '92

Don Leaver
Witching Time '84

Reginald LeBorg
The Mummy's Ghost '44
Great Jesse James Raid '49
G.I. Jane '51
Sins of Jezebel '54
The White Orchid '54
Diary of a Madman '63
House of the Black Death '65
The Sibling '72

Jean-Paul LeChanois
Passion for Life '48
L'Ecole Buisoniere '51
Le Cas du Dr. Laurent '57
Les Miserables '57

Patrice Leconte
French Fried Vacation '79
Monsieur Hire '89
The Hairdresser's Husband '92

Mimi Leder
Woman With a Past '92

Paul Leder
I Dismember Mama '74
A*P*E* '76
Sketches of a Strangler '78
Vultures '84
Body Count '87
Murder by Numbers '89
Exiled in America '90
Deadly Conspiracy '91
Frame Up '91
Twenty Dollar Star '91
The Abduction of Allison Tate '92
The Baby Doll Murders '92
Killing Obsession '94
Molly and Gina '94

Charles Lederer
Never Steal Anything Small '59

David Ross Lederman
Phantom of the West '31
Range Feud '31
The Range Feud/Two Fisted Law '31
Daring Danger '32
The Fighting Marshal '32
The Riding Tornado '32
Texas Cyclone '32
Two-Fisted Law '32
Hell-Ship Morgan '36
Tarzan's Revenge '38
Racketeers of the Range '39
Shadows on the Stairs '41

Paul Leduc
Frida '84

Ang Lee
Pushing Hands '92
The Wedding Banquet '93
Eat Drink Man Woman '94
Sense and Sensibility '95

Bruce Lee
Return of the Dragon '73

Charles Lee
Full Metal Ninja '89
Ninja of the Magnificence '89

Damian Lee
Last Man Standing '87
Food of the Gods: Part 2 '88
Boxcar Blues '90
Ski School '91
The Donor '94

DeWitt Lee
The Legend of Jedediah Carver '70s
Ransom Money '88

Jack Lee
Wooden Horse '50
Robbery Under Arms '57
The Captain's Table '60

Joanna Lee
Children of Divorce '80

Joe Lee
The Courier '88

Norman Lee
Bulldog Drummond at Bay '37
Chamber of Horrors '40

Robert Lee
Virtual Assassin '95

Rowland V. Lee
Doomsday '28
The Count of Monte Cristo '34
The Three Musketeers '35
One Rainy Afternoon '36
Love from a Stranger '37
Toast of New York '37
Son of Frankenstein '39
The Tower of London '39
The Son of Monte Cristo '41
The Bridge of San Luis Rey '44
Captain Kidd '45

Spike Lee
Joe's Bed-Stuy Barbershop: We Cut Heads '83
She's Gotta Have It '86
School Daze '88
Do the Right Thing '89
Mo' Better Blues '90
Jungle Fever '91
Malcolm X '92
Crooklyn '94
Clockers '95
Girl 6 '96

David Leeds
Shoot the Sun Down '81

Abraham Leff
Where Is My Child? '37

Johnny Legend
My Breakfast with Blassie '83

Gary Legon
My Therapist '84

Francosis Legrand
Sex on the Run '78

Ernest Lehman
Portnoy's Complaint '72

Lew Lehman
The Pit '81

Michael Lehmann
The Applegates '89
Heathers '89
Hudson Hawk '91
Airheads '94
The Truth About Cats and Dogs '96

Peter Lehner
Megaville '91

Arnold Leibovit
The Puppetoon Movie '87

Neil Leifer
Yesterday's Hero '79
Trading Hearts '87

Mike Leigh
Hard Labour '73
Nuts in May '76
Abigail's Party '77
Kiss of Death '77
Who's Who '78
Grown Ups '80
Home Sweet Home '82
Four Days in July '85
High Hopes '88
Life Is Sweet '90
Naked '93
Secrets and Lies '95

Warren Leight
The Night We Never Met '93

Mitchell Leisen
Murder at the Vanities '34
Hands Across the Table '35
Swing High, Swing Low '37
The Big Braodcast of 1938 '38
Midnight '39
Remember the Night '40
The Lady is Willing '42
The Girl Most Likely '57

Erwin Leiser
Mein Kampf: Hitler's Rise and Fall '60

Christopher Leitch
The Hitter '79
Teen Wolf Too '87
Courage Mountain '89

Larry Leker
All Dogs Go to Heaven 2 '95

David Leland
Wish You Were Here '87
Checking Out '89
The Big Man: Crossing the Line '91

Claude Lelouch
A Man and a Woman '66
And Now My Love '74
Happy New Year '74
Another Man, Another Chance '77
Cat and Mouse '78
Robert et Robert '79
Bolero '82
Edith & Marcel '83
Bandits '86
A Man and a Woman: 20 Years Later '86
Les Miserables '95

Alan LeMay
High Lonesome '50

James Lemmo
Heart '87
Tripwire '89
We're Talkin' Serious Money '92
Relentless 3 '93
Bodily Harm '95

Jack Lemmon
Kotch '71

Rusty Lemorande
Journey to the Center of the Earth '88
The Turn of the Screw '92

Paul Leni
Waxworks '24
The Cat and the Canary '27
The Man Who Laughs '27

Terry Lennon
Daffy Duck's Quackbusters '89

Miklos Lente
Oddballs '84

Umberto Lenzi
Pirates of the Seven Seas '62
Messalina vs. the Son of Hercules '64
Paranoia '69
Battle of the Commandos '71
Bruce Lee Fights Back From the Grave '76
Man from Deep River '77
Battleforce '78
Eyeball '78
Almost Human '79
From Hell to Victory '79
Emerald Jungle '80
City of the Walking Dead '83
Bridge to Hell '87

Malcolm Leo
This Is Elvis '81
It Came from Hollywood '82

Arthur Leonard
Boy! What a Girl '45

Brett Leonard
Dead Pit '89
The Lawnmower Man '92
Hideaway '94
Virtuosity '95

Leo Leonard
Omoo Omoo, the Shark God '49

Robert Z. Leonard
A Mormon Maid '17
The Divorcee '30
Susan Lenox: Her Fall and Rise '31
Strange Interlude '32
Dancing Lady '33
The Great Ziegfeld '36
The Firefly '37
Maytime '37
Girl of the Golden West '38
Broadway Serenade '39
New Moon '40
Pride and Prejudice '40
When Ladies Meet '41
Ziegfeld Girl '41
Weekend at the Waldorf '45
In the Good Old Summertime '49
The Duchess of Idaho '50
Nancy Goes to Rio '50
Clown '53
The King's Thief '55

Terry J. Leonard
Death Before Dishonor '87

Jordan Leondopoulos
The Swap '71

John Leone
Great Smokey Roadblock '76

Sergio Leone
A Fistful of Dollars '64
For a Few Dollars More '65
The Good, the Bad and the Ugly '67
Once Upon a Time in the West '68
A Fistful of Dynamite '72
Once Upon a Time in America '84

Po Chich Leong
Ping Pong '87

Antonio Leonuiola
Atlas in the Land of the Cyclops '61
Tor '64

Robert Lepage
The Confessional '95

Reymond LePlont
La Balance '82

Carl Lerner
Black Like Me '64

Dan Lerner
Shame '92

Irving Lerner
Studs Lonigan '60
Cry of Battle '63

Joseph Lerner
The C-Man '49

Richard Lerner
Revenge of the Cheerleaders '76

Mervyn LeRoy
Little Caesar '30
I Am a Fugitive from a Chain Gang '32
Three on a Match '32
Gold Diggers of 1933 '33
Sweet Adeline '35
Anthony Adverse '36
Three Men on a Horse '36
They Won't Forget '37
Waterloo Bridge '40
Blossoms in the Dust '41
Johnny Eager '42
Random Harvest '42
Madame Curie '43
Thirty Seconds Over Tokyo '44
Without Reservations '46
Homecoming '48
Any Number Can Play '49
East Side, West Side '49
Little Women '49
Quo Vadis '51
Lovely to Look At '52
Million Dollar Mermaid '52
Latin Lovers '53
Rose Marie '54
Mister Roberts '55
The Bad Seed '56
A Majority of One '56
No Time for Sergeants '58
The FBI Story '59
The Devil at 4 O'Clock '61
Gypsy '62

Bill Lesley
Nail Gun Massacre '86

Michael Lessac
House of Cards '92

Mark L. Lester
Steel Arena '72
Truck Stop Women '74
Bobbie Jo and the Outlaw '76
Stunts '77
Gold of the Amazon Women '79
Roller Boogie '79
Class of 1984 '82
Firestarter '84
Commando '85
Armed and Dangerous '86
Class of 1999 '90
Showdown in Little Tokyo '91
Night of the Running Man '94

Richard Lester
A Hard Day's Night '64
Help! '65
The Knack '65
A Funny Thing Happened on the Way to the Forum '66
How I Won the War '67
Petulia '68
Juggernaut '74
The Three Musketeers '74
The Four Musketeers '75
Royal Flash '75
The Ritz '76
Robin and Marian '76
Butch and Sundance: The Early Days '79
Cuba '79
Superman 2 '80
Superman 3 '83
Finders Keepers '84
The Return of the Musketeers '89

Gil Letourneau
The Hound of London '93

Sheldon Lettich
Lionheart '90
Double Impact '91
Only the Strong '93

Clarence Fok Yiu Leung
Naked Killer '92

Brian Levant
Problem Child 2 '91
Beethoven '92
The Flintstones '94

Jeremy Leven
Don Juan DeMarco '94

Joseph Levering
Defenders of the Law '31
Sea Devils '31
Phantom Gold '38

Michel Levesque
Werewolves on Wheels '71
Sweet Sugar '72

Jay Levey
UHF '89

William A. Levey
Blackenstein '73
Slumber Party '57 '76
The Happy Hooker Goes to Washington '77
Monaco Forever '83
Lightning: The White Stallion '86
Hellgate '89
Committed '91

Alan J. Levi
Riding with Death '76
Last Song '80
Blood Song '82
Dead Man's Revenge '93

Henry Levin
Cry of the Werewolf '44
Jolson Sings Again '49
Man from Colorado '49
The Farmer Takes a Wife '53
The Warriors '55
Lonely Man '57
Journey to the Center of the Earth '59
Where the Boys Are '60
The Wonders of Aladdin '61
The Wonderful World of the Brothers Grimm '62
Murderers' Row '66
The Ambushers '67
Desperados '69
Run for the Roses '78
Scout's Honor '80

Peter Levin
Comeback Kid '80
Rape and Marriage: The Rideout Case '80
Washington Mistress '81

Jack Levine
Ghost Rider '35

Paul Levine
Operation Intercept '95

Barry Levinson
Diner '82
The Natural '84
Young Sherlock Holmes '85
Good Morning, Vietnam '87
Tin Men '87
Rain Man '88
Avalon '90
Bugsy '91
Toys '92
Disclosure '94
Jimmy Hollywood '94

Fred Levinson
Hail '73

Israeli Nadav Levitan
Intimate Story '81
The Seventeenth Bride '84

Abe Levitow
Gay Purr-ee '62

Gene Levitt
Magee and the Lady '78

Edmond Levy
Mom, the Wolfman and Me '80

Eugene Levy
Once Upon a Crime '92
Sodbusters '94

Gerry Levy
Invasion of the Body Stealers '69

I. Robert Levy
Can I Do It...Till I Need Glasses? '77
If You Don't Stop It...You'll Go Blind '77

Jefery Levy
Inside Monkey Zetterland '93
S.F.W. '94

Ralph Levy
Bedtime Story '63

Scott Levy
Midnight Tease '94

Shuki Levy
Perfect Victims '87
Blind Vision '91

Stephen Lewicki
Certain Sacrifice '80

Albert Lewin
The Moon and Sixpence '43
Picture of Dorian Gray '45
The Private Affairs of Bel Ami '47
Pandora and the Flying Dutchman '51

Ben Lewin
Georgia '87
The Favor, the Watch, & the Very Big Fish '92

Sam Lewin
The Dunera Boys '85

Al Lewis
Our Miss Brooks '56

Christopher Lewis
Blood Cult '85
Revenge '86
The Ripper '86
The Red Raven Kiss-Off '90

David Lewis
Dangerous Curves '88

Everet Lewis
The Natural History of Parking Lots '94

Herschell Gordon Lewis
The Prime Time '60
Nature's Playmates '62
Blood Feast '63
Color Me Blood Red '64
Moonshine Mountain '64
2000 Maniacs '64
Monster a Go-Go! '65
Jimmy, the Boy Wonder '66
Blast-Off Girls '67
The Girl, the Body and the Pill '67
Gruesome Twosome '67
Suburban Roulette '67
How to Make a Doll '68
Just for the Hell of It '68
The Psychic '68
She-Devils on Wheels '68
Something Weird '68
The Wizard of Gore '70
This Stuff'll Kill Ya! '71
The Gore-Gore Girls '72

Jay Lewis
The Baby and the Battleship '56

Jerry Lewis
The Bellboy '60
The Errand Boy '61
The Ladies' Man '61
The Nutty Professor '63
The Patsy '64
Family Jewels '65
Big Mouth '67
Which Way to the Front? '70
Hardly Working '81
Cracking Up '83

Joseph H. Lewis
Boys of the City '40
That Gang of Mine '40
Criminals Within '41
The Invisible Ghost '41
Pride of the Bowery '41
Gun Crazy '49
Retreat, Hell! '52
Big Combo '55
A Lawless Street '55
Seventh Cavalry '56

Mark Lewis
Gordy '95

Richard J. Lewis
Whale Music '94

Robert Lewis
Pray for the Wildcats '74
No Room to Run '78
If Things Were Different '79
S*H*E '79
Child Bride of Short Creek '81
Fallen Angel '81
Desperate Lives '82
A Summer to Remember '84
Embassy '85
City Killer '87
Ladykillers '88
Dead Reckoning '89
Memories of Murder '90
Don't Talk to Strangers '94
Circumstances Unknown '95

Stanley Lewis
Punk Vacation '90

Denis Lewiston
Hot Target '85

Bruce Li
Counter Attack '84

Liu Chia Liang
Master Killer '84

Howard Libov
Midnight Edition '93

Carlo Liconti
Goodnight, Michelangelo '89

Jeff Lieberman
Squirm '76
Blue Sunshine '78
Just Before Dawn '80
Remote Control '88

Ron Lieberman
All I Want for Christmas '91

Robert Liebmann
Will: G. Gordon Liddy '82
Table for Five '83
Fire in the Sky '93

Jimmy Lifton
Mirror, Mirror 2: Raven Dance '94

Mike Light
Flesh Gordon '72

Peter Lilienthal
David '79
The Uprising '81

Kevin Lima
A Goofy Movie '94

Walter Lima, Jr.
The Dolphin '87

Doug Liman
Getting In '94

Fred J. Lincoln
Wild Man '89

Per Lindberg
June Night '40

Mitchell Linden
The American Scream '80s

Maud Linder
Man in the Silk Hat '15

Max Linder
Early Cinema Vol. 1 '19

Lance Lindsay
Star Crystal '85
Real Bullets '90

Michael Lindsay-Hogg
Let It Be '70
Nasty Habits '77
Brideshead Revisited '81
Thumbelina '82
Master Harold and the Boys '84
Annie Oakley '85
As Is '85
Strange Case of Dr. Jekyll & Mr. Hyde '89
The Habitation of Dragons '91
Murder by Moonlight '91
The Object of Beauty '91
Running Mates '92
Frankie Starlight '95

Jon Lindstrom
Dreaming of Rita '94

Leopold Lindtberg
The Last Chance '45
Four in a Jeep '51

John F. Link
The Devil's Cargo '48
Call of the Forest '49

Ron Link
Zombie High '87

Richard Linklater
Slacker '91
Dazed and Confused '93
Before Sunrise '94

Art Linson
Where the Buffalo Roam '80
The Wild Life '84

Aaron Lipstadt
Android '82
The Slumber Party Massacre '82
City Limits '85
Pair of Aces '90

Steven Lisberger
Tron '82
Hot Pursuit '87
Slipstream '89

David Lister
Hunted '88
The Rutanga Tapes '90

Peter MacKenzie Litten
Heaven's a Drag '94

Miguel Littin
Alsino and the Condor '82

Dwight Little
Getting Even '86
Bloodstone '88
Halloween 4: The Return of Michael Myers '88
The Phantom of the Opera '89
Marked for Death '90
Rapid Fire '92
Free Willy 2: The Adventure Home '95

Lynne Littman
Testament '83

Anatole Litvak
Mayerling '36
The Sisters '38
All This and Heaven Too '40
City for Conquest '40
The Snake Pit '48
Sorry, Wrong Number '48
Anastasia '56
Goodbye Again '61
Night of the Generals '67

Gerry Lively
Body Moves '90

Jennie Livingston
Paris is Burning '91

Carlo Lizzani
Love in the City '53
Last Four Days '77
House of the Yellow Carpet '84

Luis Llosa
Hour of the Assassin '86
Crime Zone '88
Sniper '92
800 Leagues Down the Amazon '93
The Specialist '94

Frank Lloyd
Oliver Twist '22
Cavalcade '33
Mutiny on the Bounty '35
The Howards of Virginia '40
Forever and a Day '43
Blood on the Sun '45
The Last Command '55

Harold Lloyd
I'm on My Way/The Non-Stop Kid '18
Early Cinema Vol. 1 '19
His Royal Slyness/Haunted Spooks '20

Norman Lloyd
Tales of the Unexpected '91

Ken Loach
Family Life '71
Singing the Blues in Red '87
Hidden Agenda '90
Riff Raff '92
Ladybird, Ladybird '93
Raining Stones '93
Land and Freedom '95

Tony LoBianco
Too Scared to Scream '85

Victor Lobl
Eden '92
Eden 3 '93

Sondra Locke
Ratboy '86
Impulse '90

Roy Lockwood
The Mutiny of the Elsinore '39

Norman Loftis
Small Time '91

Bob Logan
Up Your Alley '89
Repossessed '90
Meatballs 4 '92

Bruce Logan
Vendetta '85

Joshua Logan
Picnic '55
Bus Stop '56
Sayonara '57
South Pacific '58
Tall Story '60
Fanny '61
Ensign Pulver '64
Camelot '67
Paint Your Wagon '69

Stanley Logan
The Falcon's Brother '42

Tom Logan
Dream Trap '90
The Night Brings Charlie '90

Dimitri Logothetis
Pretty Smart '87
Slaughterhouse Rock '88
The Closer '91
Body Shot '93

J. Anthony Loma
Target Eagle '84
Counterforce '87
Fine Gold '88
A Man of Passion '90s

Joseph Loman
Surprise Attack '70s
The Boldest Job in the West '71

Francisco J. Lombardi
La Boca del Lobo '89

Lou Lombardo
Russian Roulette '75
P.K. and the Kid '85

Ulli Lommel
Cocaine Cowboys '79
The Boogey Man '80
Brainwaves '82
Devonsville Terror '83
Olivia '83
Overkill '86
Strangers in Paradise '86
Warbirds '88
The Big Sweat '90
Cold Heat '90

Richard Loncraine
Full Circle '77
Brimstone & Treacle '82
The Missionary '82
Bellman and True '88
Deep Cover '88
The Wedding Gift '93
Richard III '95

Jerry London
Father Figure '80
Shogun '80
Chiefs '83
The Scarlet & the Black '83
Manhunt for Claude Dallas '86
Rent-A-Cop '88
Haunting of Sarah Hardy '89
Kiss Shot '89
Victim of Love '91

Roy London
Diary of a Hitman '91

Stanley Long
Adventures of a Taxi Driver '76
Adventures of a Private Eye '87

Robert Longo
Johnny Mnemonic '95

Harry S. Longstreet
Sex, Love and Cold Hard Cash '93
A Vow to Kill '94

Temistocles Lopez
Exquisite Corpses '88
Chain of Desire '93

Del Lord
Vengeance '37

Jean-Claude Lord
Visiting Hours '82
Covergirl '83
The Vindicator '85
Toby McTeague '87

Eddie and the Cruisers 2: Eddie Lives! '89
Mindfield '89
Landslide '92

Ken Loring
Combat Killers '80

Peter Lorre
The Lost One '51

Vere Lorrimer
Blake's Seven '78

Joseph Losey
The Boy with the Green Hair '48
Prowler '51
The Sleeping Tiger '54
Time Without Pity '57
The Servant '63
Accident '67
Secret Ceremony '69
The Go-Between '71
Assassination of Trotsky '72
A Doll's House '73
Mr. Klein '75
Romantic Englishwoman '75
Roads to the South '78
La Truite '83
Steaming '86

Emil Loteanu
The Shooting Party '77

Eb Lottimer
Love Matters '93
Twisted Love '95

Patrick Loubert
125 Rooms of Comfort '83

Pavel Lounguine
Taxi Blues '90
Luna Park '91

John Lounsbery
The Rescuers '77

Eugene Lourie
The Beast from 20,000 Fathoms '53
Gorgo '61

Eric Louzil
Lust for Freedom '87
Wilding '90
Class of Nuke 'Em High 2: Subhumanoid Meltdown '91
Class of Nuke 'Em High 3: The Good, the Bad and the Subhumanoid '94

Horace Love
Playing Away '87

Charles Loventhal
First Time '82
My Demon Lover '87
Mr. Write '92

Otho Lovering
Drift Fence '36

Bert Lovitt
Prince Jack '83

Robert Lovy
Plughead Rewired: Circuitry Man 2 '94

Steven Lovy
Circuitry Man '90
Plughead Rewired: Circuitry Man 2 '94

Lucas Lowe
The King of the Kickboxers '91
American Shaolin: King of the Kickboxers 2 '92

William Lowe
Slaughter in San Francisco '81

Richard Lowenstein
Pete Townshend: White City '85
Dogs in Space '87

Dick Lowry
The Jayne Mansfield Story '80
Kenny Rogers as the Gambler '80
Coward of the County '81
Kenny Rogers as the Gambler, Part 2: The Adventure Continues '83
Living Proof: The Hank Williams Jr. Story '83
Smokey and the Bandit, Part 3 '83
Wet Gold '84
Wild Horses '84
Kenny Rogers as the Gambler, Part 3: The Legend Continues '87
The FBI Murders '88
Midnight Murders '91
Till Murder Do Us Part '92
The Gambler Returns: The Luck of the Draw '93
In the Line of Duty: Ambush in Waco '93
Urban Crossfire '94
A Horse for Danny '95

David Loxton
Lathe of Heaven '80

Nanni Loy
Head of the Family '71
Cafe Express '83
Where's Piccone '84

Arthur Lubin
Yellowstone '36
Black Friday '40
Buck Privates '41
Hold That Ghost '41
In the Navy '41
Keep 'Em Flying '41
Ride 'Em Cowboy '42
Ali Baba and the Forty Thieves '43
The Phantom of the Opera '43
Delightfully Dangerous '45
Francis the Talking Mule '49
Impact '49
Francis Goes to the Races '51
Queen for a Day '51
Francis Goes to West Point '52
Francis Covers the Big Town '53
Francis Joins the WACs '54
Francis in the Navy '55
Escapade in Japan '57
Thief of Baghdad '61
The Incredible Mr. Limpet '64

Ernst Lubitsch
Gypsy Blood '18
Passion '19
One Arabian Night '21
The Marriage Circle '24
Lady Windermere's Fan '26
So This is Paris '26
The Student Prince in Old Heidelberg '27
The Merry Widow '34
Angel '37
Bluebeard's Eighth Wife '38
Ninotchka '39
The Shop Around the Corner '40
That Uncertain Feeling '41
To Be or Not to Be '42
Heaven Can Wait '43

S. Roy Luby
Arizona Badman '35
Desert Phantom '36
Outlaw Rule '36
Border Phantom '37
The Red Rope '37
Tough to Handle '37
Fugitive Valley '41
Kid's Last Ride '41
Tonto Basin Outlaws '41
Trail of the Silver Spurs '41
Tumbledown Ranch in Arizona '41
Underground Rustlers '41
Arizona Stagecoach '42
Boot Hill Bandits '42
Black Market Rustlers '43
Cowboy Commandos '43

George Lucas
THX 1138 '71
American Graffiti '73
Star Wars '77
From "Star Wars" to "Jedi": The Making of a Saga '83

Leandro Lucchetti
Getting Even '92

Francesco Lucente
Virgin Queen of St. Francis High '88

Maurizio Lucidi
Stateline Motel '75
Street People '76

William Lucking
Humanoid Defender '85

Larry Ludman
Overthrow '82
Deadly Impact '84
Operation 'Nam '85
Thunder Warrior '85
Thunder Warrior 2 '85
The Manhunt '86
Thunder Warrior 3 '88

Edward Ludwig
Fighting Seabees '44
The Big Wheel '49
Wake of the Red Witch '49
Big Jim McLain '52
Flame of the Islands '55
The Black Scorpion '57

Laszlo Lugossy
Flowers of Reverie '84

Baz Luhrmann
Strictly Ballroom '92

Eric Luke
Not Quite Human 2 '89
Still Not Quite Human '92

Sidney Lumet
Stage Struck '57
Twelve Angry Men '57
The Fugitive Kind '60
Long Day's Journey into Night '62
Fail-Safe '64
The Pawnbroker '65
The Group '66
The Anderson Tapes '71
The Offence '73
Serpico '73
Murder on the Orient Express '74
Dog Day Afternoon '75
Network '76
Equus '77
The Wiz '78
Just Tell Me What You Want '80
Prince of the City '81
Deathtrap '82
The Verdict '82
Daniel '83
Garbo Talks '84
The Morning After '86
Power '86
Running on Empty '88
Family Business '89
Q & A '90
A Stranger Among Us '92
Guilty as Sin '93

Auguste Lumiere
The Great Train Robbery: Cinema Begins '03

Bigas Luna
Anguish '88
Jamon, Jamon '93

Ida Lupino
The Bigamist '53
The Hitch-Hiker '53
The Trouble with Angels '66

Michele Lupo
Goliath and the Sins of Babylon '64
Master Touch '74
Mean Frank and Crazy Tony '75

Hamilton Luske
Peter Pan '53
Lady and the Tramp '55
101 Dalmatians '61

William Lustig
Maniac '80
Vigilante '83
The Hit List '88
Maniac Cop '88
Relentless '89
Maniac Cop 2 '90
Maniac Cop 3: Badge of Silence '93

Salvo Luther
Forget Mozart '85

David Lynch
Eraserhead '78
The Elephant Man '80
Dune '84
Blue Velvet '86
Twin Peaks '90
Twin Peaks '90
Wild at Heart '90
Twin Peaks: Fire Walk with Me '92
Hotel Room '93

Jennifer Lynch
Boxing Helena '93

Paul Lynch
Prom Night '80
Humongous '82
Cross Country '83
Dream to Believe '85
Bullies '86
Blindside '88
Murder by Night '89
Victim of Beauty '91
Spenser: Ceremony '93
No Contest '94
The Reluctant Agent '95

Adrian Lyne
Foxes '80
9 1/2 Weeks '86
Fatal Attraction '87
Jacob's Ladder '90
Indecent Proposal '93

Harry Lynn
Where Is My Child? '37

Jonathan Lynn
Clue '85
Nuns on the Run '90
The Distinguished Gentleman '92
My Cousin Vinny '92
Greedy '94
Sgt. Bilko '95

Francis D. Lyon
Cult of the Cobra '55
The Great Locomotive Chase '56
The Oklahoman '56
Bail Out at 43,000 '57
Tomboy & the Champ '58
Castle of Evil '66

Dick Maas
The Lift '85
Amsterdamned '88

Byron Mabe
She-Freak '67

Syd Macartney
Prince Brat and the Whipping Boy '95
The Canterville Ghost '96

Kurt MacCarley
Rock & the Money-Hungry Party Girls '89
Sexual Intent '94

David MacDonald
Never Too Late to Mend '37
This England '42
Christopher Columbus '49
The Adventurers '51
Devil Girl from Mars '54
Alias John Preston '56
Small Hotel '57
The Moonraker '58

Peter Macdonald
Mo' Money '92
The Neverending Story 3 '94

Ranald MacDougall
Queen Bee '55

Hamilton MacFadden
Stand Up and Cheer '34
Legion of Missing Men '37
Sea Racketeers '37
Inside the Law '42

Mike MacFarland
Hanging on a Star '78
Pink Motel '82

Gustav Machaty
Ecstasy '33

Juliusz Machulski
Deja Vu '89

Brice Mack
Jennifer '78
Swap Meet '79

Earle Mack
The Children of Theatre Street '77

Roy Mack
Hillbilly Blitzkrieg '42

Russell Mack
Lonely Wives '31

Yvonne Mackay
The Silent One '86

Alexander MacKendrick
Whiskey Galore '48
The Man in the White Suit '51
Mandy '53
The Ladykillers '55
Sweet Smell of Success '57

John MacKenzie
One Brief Summer '70
A Sense of Freedom '78
The Long Good Friday '79
Beyond the Limit '83
Act of Vengeance '86
The Fourth Protocol '87
The Last of the Finest '90
Ruby '92
Voyage '93
The Infiltrator '95

Peter M. MacKenzie
Merchants of War '90

Will MacKenzie
Hobo's Christmas '87
Worth Winning '89
Perfect Harmony '91

Gilles Mackinnon
The Playboys '92
A Simple Twist of Fate '94

Alison Maclean
Crush '93

Stephen MacLean
Around the World in 80 Ways '86

Hugh MacMullen
Footsteps in the Dark '41

Ian MacNaughton
Monty Python's Flying Circus '71

Henry MacRae
King of the Rodeo '28
Tarzan the Tiger '29
Rustler's Roundup '33

William H. Macy
Lip Service '88

David Madden
Separate Lives '94

John Madden
Grown Ups '86
Ethan Frome '92
Golden Gate '93
Prime Suspect: The Lost Child '94

Lee Madden
Hell's Angels '69 '69
Angel Unchained '70
The Manhandlers '73
Night Creature '79
The Night God Screamed '80s

Guy Maddin
Tales from the Gimli Hospital '88
Careful '94

Miguel Madrid
Graveyard of Horror '71

Kenneth Madsen
A Day in October '92

Jose Maesso
Order to Kill '73

Kurt Maetzig
First Spaceship on Venus '60

Guy Magar
Retribution '88
Stepfather 3: Father's Day '92

Maria Maggenti
The Incredibly True Adventure of Two Girls in Love '95

Constantino Magnatta
The Darkside '87

Luigi Magni
In the Name of the Pope-King '85

Albert Magnoli
Atom Age Vampire '61
Purple Rain '84
American Anthem '86
Born to Run '93
Street Knight '93

Dezso Magyar
King of America '80
No Secrets '91

Redge Mahaffey
Life 101 '95

Anthony Maharaj
Crossfire '89
The Kick Fighter '91
Deathfight '93

Barry Mahon
Rocket Attack U.S.A. '58

Mahon ▶cont.

Assault of the Rebel Girls '59
Violent Women '59
Pagan Island '60
The Beast that Killed Women '65

Bob Mahoney
Operation Julie '85

Norman Mailer
Tough Guys Don't Dance '87

Stewart Main
Desperate Remedies '93

Maximiliane Mainka
Germany in Autumn '78

Beate Mainka-Jellinghaus
Germany in Autumn '78

George Maitland
Invasion Earth: The Aliens Are Here! '87

Lech Majewski
Prisoner of Rio '89

Peter Mak
Wicked City '92

Dusan Makavejev
Man Is Not a Bird '65
The Love Affair, or The Case of the Missing Switchboard Operator '67
Innocence Unprotected '68
WR: Mysteries of the Organism '71
Sweet Movie '75
Montenegro '81
The Coca-Cola Kid '84
A Night of Love '87

Kelly Makin
National Lampoon's Senior Trip '95
Kids In the Hall Brain Candy '96

Karoly Makk
Love '71
Cat's Play '74
Another Way '82
Deadly Game '83
Lily in Love '85

Guido Malatesta
Goliath Against the Giants '63

Roberto Malenotti
Slave Trade in the World Today '64

Terence Malick
Badlands '74
Days of Heaven '78

Louis Malle
Frantic '58
The Lovers '59
A Very Private Affair '62
The Fire Within '64
Viva Maria! '65
Spirits of the Dead '68
Murmur of the Heart '71
Pretty Baby '78
Atlantic City '81
My Dinner with Andre '81
Crackers '84
Alamo Bay '85
Au Revoir Les Enfants '87
May Fools '90
Damage '92
Vanya on 42nd Street '94

Matthew Mallinson
Fist of Fear, Touch of Death '77

James Mallon
Blood Hook '86
Mystery Science Theater 3000: The Movie '96

Bruce Malmuth
Foreplay '75
Nighthawks '81
The Man Who Wasn't There '83
Where Are the Children? '85
Hard to Kill '89
Pentathlon '94

Mark Malone
Bulletproof Heart '95

William Malone
Scared to Death '80
Creature '85

Paul Maloney
I Live with Me Dad '86

Djibril Diop Mambety
Touki Bouki '73

David Mamet
House of Games '87
Things Change '88
Homicide '91
Oleanna '94

Yuri Mamin
Sideburns '91
Window to Paris '95

Oshii Mamoru
Urusei Yatsura Movie 2: Beautiful Dreamer '92

Rouben Mamoulian
Applause '29
Dr. Jekyll and Mr. Hyde '31
Queen Christina '33
Becky Sharp '35
Golden Boy '39
The Mark of Zorro '40
Blood and Sand '41
Summer Holiday '48
Silk Stockings '57

Janine Manatis
Tales of the Klondike: In a Far Country '87

Milcho Manchevski
Before the Rain '94

Mario Mancini
Frankenstein '80 '79

Kevin Mancuso
2020 Texas Gladiators '85

Jeffrey Mandel
Elves '89
Robo-Chic '89

Robert Mandel
Independence Day '83
F/X '86
Touch and Go '86
Big Shots '87
Perfect Witness '89
School Ties '92
The X-Files: Pilot Episode/Deep Throat '93
The Substitute '96

Luis Mandoki
Gaby: A True Story '87
White Palace '90
Born Yesterday '93
When a Man Loves a Woman '94

Dharan Mandrayar
Ele, My Friend '93

Joseph Manduke
Cornbread, Earl & Me '75
Kid Vengeance '75
Beatlemania! The Movie '81
Omega Syndrome '87
The Gumshoe Kid '89

Gianni Manera
Fear in the City '81

Nino Manfredi
Nudo di Donna '83

Joseph Mangine
Neon Maniacs '86

James Mangold
Heavy '94

Francis Mankiewicz
Les Bons Debarras '81
And Then You Die '88
Love and Hate: A Marriage Made in Hell '90

Joseph L. Mankiewicz
The Ghost and Mrs. Muir '47
House of Strangers '49
A Letter to Three Wives '49
All About Eve '50
People Will Talk '51
Five Fingers '52
Julius Caesar '53
The Barefoot Contessa '54
Guys and Dolls '55
Suddenly, Last Summer '59
Cleopatra '63
The Honey Pot '67
There was a Crooked Man '70
Sleuth '72

Tom Mankiewicz
Dragnet '87
Delirious '91
Taking the Heat '93

Henry Mankiewirk
Hell's Brigade: The Final Assault '80

Abby Mann
King '78

Anthony Mann
Great Flamarion '45
Desperate '47
Railroaded '47
T-Men '47
He Walked by Night '48
Reign of Terror '49
Winchester '73 '50
Bend of the River '52
The Naked Spur '53
Thunder Bay '53
The Glenn Miller Story '54
Far Country '55
The Man from Laramie '55
Savage Wilderness '55
Strategic Air Command '55
Men in War '57
The Tin Star '57
God's Little Acre '58
Man of the West '58
Cimarron '60
El Cid '61
The Fall of the Roman Empire '64
Dandy in Aspic '68

Daniel Mann
Come Back, Little Sheba '52
I'll Cry Tomorrow '55
The Rose Tattoo '55
The Teahouse of the August Moon '56
Hot Spell '58
The Last Angry Man '59
Butterfield 8 '60
The Mountain Road '60
Who's Got the Action? '63
Our Man Flint '66
For Love of Ivy '68
A Dream of Kings '69
Willard '71
Big Mo '73
Interval '73
Journey into Fear '74
Matilda '78
Playing for Time '80
The Man Who Broke 1,000 Chains '87

Delbert Mann
Marty '55
Desire Under the Elms '58
Separate Tables '58
Lover Come Back '61
That Touch of Mink '62
A Gathering of Eagles '63
Heidi '67
David Copperfield '70
She Waits '71
No Place to Run '72
Francis Gary Powers: The True Story of the U-2 Spy '76
The Birch Interval '78
Breaking Up '78
All Quiet on the Western Front '79
Home to Stay '79
Torn Between Two Lovers '79
Night Crossing '81
The Member of the Wedding '83
Love Leads the Way '84
The Last Days of Patton '86
Ironclads '90
Lily in Winter '94

Edward Mann
Cauldron of Blood '67
Hallucination '67
Hooch '76

Farhad Mann
Return to Two Moon Junction '93
Lawnmower Man 2: Beyond Cyberspace '95

Michael Mann
The Jericho Mile '79
Thief '81
The Keep '83
Manhunter '86
The Last of the Mohicans '92
Heat '95

Kim Manners
K-9000 '89

Michelle Manning
Blue City '86

Peter Manoogian
Dungeonmaster '83
The Eliminators '86
Enemy Territory '87
Arena '89
Demonic Toys '90
Seedpeople '92

Mark Manos
Liquid Dreams '92
Josh Kirby...Time Warrior: Chapter 4, Eggs from 70 Million B.C. '95

Manoussos Manoussakis
The Enchantress '85

Duncan Mansfield
Sweetheart of the Navy '37

Scott Mansfield
Deadly Games '80

Guido Manuli
Volere Volare '92

Ray Manzarek
The Doors: Soft Parade, a Retrospective '69

Rene Manzor
Warrior Spirit '94

Robert Marcarelli
Original Intent '91
I Don't Buy Kisses Anymore '92

Terry Marcel
Hawk the Slayer '81
Prisoners of the Lost Universe '84
Jane & the Lost City '87

Siro Marcellini
Gangster's Law '86

Alex March
Paper Lion '68
Firehouse '72
Master Mind '73

Rafael Romero Marchent
Garringo '69

David Marconi
The Harvest '92

Adam Marcus
Jason Goes to Hell: The Final Friday '93

James Marcus
Double Cross '92

Mitch Marcus
A Boy Called Hate '95

Paul Marcus
Prime Suspect: The Scent of Darkness '95

Philip Marcus
Terror on Alcatraz '86

Andreas Marfori
Evil Clutch '89
Desperate Crimes '93

Stuart Margolin
A Shining Season '79
The Glitter Dome '84
Paramedics '88
Medicine River '94
How the West was Fun '95

Jeff Margolis
Oscar's Greatest Moments: 1971-1991 '92

Edwin L. Marin
The Death Kiss '33
A Study in Scarlet '33
I'd Give My Life '36
A Christmas Carol '38
Everybody Sing '38
Listen, Darling '38
Invisible Agent '42
Miss Annie Rooney '42
Show Business '44
Tall in the Saddle '44
Johnny Angel '45
Abilene Town '46
Mr. Ace '46
Nocturne '46
The Cariboo Trail '50

Richard "Cheech" Marin
Born in East L.A. '87

Lex Marinos
An Indecent Obsession '85
Remember Me '85

Peter Maris
Delirium '77
Land of Doom '84
Terror Squad '87
Viper '88
True Blood '89
Diplomatic Immunity '91
Hangfire '91

Chris Marker
Le Joli Mai '62
Sans Soleil '82

Russ Marker
The Yesterday Machine '63

Anthony Markes
Bikini Island '91
Last Dance '91

David Markey
Desperate Teenage Lovedolls '84
1991: The Year Punk Broke '92

Monte Markham
Defense Play '88
Neon City '91

Kelly Markin
Tiger Claws '91

Gabriel Markiw
Mob Story '90

Jancarlo Markiw
Mob Story '90

Fletcher Markle
Jigsaw '49
The Incredible Journey '63

Peter Markle
Hot Dog...The Movie! '83
The Personals '83
Youngblood '86
Bat 21 '88
Nightbreaker '89
El Diablo '90
Through the Eyes of a Killer '92
Wagons East '94
White Dwarf '95

Goran Markovic
Tito and Me '92

Murray Markowitz
Left for Dead '78

Robert Markowitz
A Long Way Home '81
Pray TV '82
My Mother's Secret Life '84
Kojak: The Belarus File '85
Decoration Day '90
Too Young to Die '90
Love, Lies and Murder '91
Afterburn '92
The Tuskegee Airmen '95

Arthur Marks
Togetherness '70
Bonnie's Kids '73
Detroit 9000 '73
Bucktown '75
Friday Foster '75
J.D.'s Revenge '76
Monkey Hustle '77

Morley Markson
Off Your Rocker '80

Brad Marlowe
At Home with the Webbers '94

Malcolm Marmorstein
Dead Men Don't Die '91

Richard Marquand
The Legacy '79
Eye of the Needle '81
Return of the Jedi '83
Until September '84
The Jagged Edge '85
Hearts of Fire '87

Jacques Marquette
Meteor Monster '57

Leon Marr
Dancing in the Dark '86

Roberto Marrtero
Thirty-Six Hours of Hell '77

David Marsh
Lords of Magick '88
Stormswept '95

Ray Marsh
The Last Porno Flick '74

Philip Marshak
Dracula Sucks '79
Cataclysm '81

Frank Marshall
Arachnophobia '90
Alive '93
Congo '95

Garry Marshall
Young Doctors in Love '82
The Flamingo Kid '84
Nothing in Common '86
Overboard '87
Beaches '88
Pretty Woman '90
Frankie and Johnny '91
Exit to Eden '94

George Marshall
Pack Up Your Troubles '32
Show Them No Mercy '35
The Goldwyn Follies '38
Destry Rides Again '39
You Can't Cheat an Honest Man '39
The Ghost Breakers '40
Pot O' Gold '41
Texas '41
Star Spangled Rhythm '42
Valley of the Sun '42
The Blue Dahlia '46
Monsieur Beaucaire '46
The Perils of Pauline '47
My Friend Irma '49
Fancy Pants '50
Never a Dull Moment '50
Houdini '53
Off Limits '53
Scared Stiff '53
Red Garters '54
The Sad Sack '57
The Gazebo '59
It Started with a Kiss '59
The Mating Game '59
How the West Was Won '63
Papa's Delicate Condition '63
Boy, Did I Get a Wrong Number! '66

Penny Marshall
Jumpin' Jack Flash '86
Big '88
Awakenings '90
A League of Their Own '92
Renaissance Man '94

William Marshall
Adventures of Captain Fabian '51
The Phantom Planet '61

Charles Martin
My Dear Secretary '49
Death of a Scoundrel '56
One Man Jury '78

Darnell Martin
I Like It Like That '94

D'Urville Martin
Dolemite '75
Fass Black '77

Eugenio Martin
It Happened at Nightmare Inn '70
Pancho Villa '72

Frank Martin
Doctor Butcher M.D. '80
Elvis in Hollywood '93

Gene Martin
Bad Man's River '72
Horror Express '72

James Aviles Martin
Flesh Eating Mothers '89

Richard Martin
Elizabeth R '72
White Tiger '95

Steven M. Martin
Theremin: An Electronic Odyssey '95

Vince Martin
The Cursed Mountain Mystery '93

Wyre Martin
The Unearthing '93

Chuck Martinez
Nice Girls Don't Explode '87

Rene Martinez, Jr.
The Guy from Harlem '77

Richard Martini
You Can't Hurry Love '88
Limit Up '89

Raymond Martino
American Born '89
DaVinci's War '92
To the Limit '95

Sergio Martino
The Next Victim '71
The Scorpion's Tail '71
Torso '73
Violent Professionals '73
The Cheaters '76
Sex with a Smile '76
Day of the Maniac '77
Slave of the Cannibal God '79
Screamers '80
The Great Alligator '81
Casablanca Express '89
The Opponent '89

Leslie Martinson
The Atomic Kid '54
Hot Rod Girl '56
PT 109 '63
Batman '66
The Kid with the Broken Halo '82
The Kid with the 200 I.Q. '83
The Fantastic World of D.C. Collins '84
Return to Africa '89

Andrew Marton
Gypsy Colt '54
Men of the Fighting Lady '54
Green Fire '55
Around the World Under the Sea '65
Clarence, the Cross-eyed Lion '65
Africa Texas Style '67

Mike Marvin
Hamburger...The Motion Picture '86
The Wraith '87
Wishman '93

Joseph Mascelli
The Atomic Brain '64

Francesco Maselli
Love in the City '53
Time of Indifference '64

Claudio Masenza
James Dean '85
Marlon Brando '85

Giuseppe Masini
Journey Beneath the Desert '61

Herbert Mason
Lady in Distress '39

Noel Mason Smith
The Night Patrol '26
Fighting Pilot '35

Francesco Massaro
Private Affairs '89

Ivana Massetti
Domino '88

Joe Massot
Wonderwall: The Movie '69
Space Riders '83

Quentin Masters
Thumb Tripping '72
The Stud '78
Dangerous Summer '82

Peter Masterson
The Trip to Bountiful '85
Blood Red '88
Full Moon in Blue Water '88
Night Game '89
Arctic Blue '93

Nico Mastorakis
Blind Date '84
Next One '84
Sky High '84
Zero Boys '86
Nightmare at Noon '87
The Wind '87
Glitch! '88
In the Cold of the Night '89
Terminal Exposure '89
Ninja Academy '90
Hired to Kill '91

Camillo Mastrocinque
Full Hearts & Empty Pockets '63

Armand Mastroianni
He Knows You're Alone '80
Killing Hour '84
The Supernaturals '86
Distortions '87
Cameron's Closet '89
Double Revenge '89

Toshio Masuda
Tora! Tora! Tora! '70
Last Days of Planet Earth '74
Zero '84

Orestes Matacena
Tainted '88

Eddy Matalon
Cathy's Curse '77
Blackout '78
Sweet Killing '93

Vivian Matalon
Private Contentment '83

Rudolph Mate
The Dark Past '49
D.O.A. '49
Branded '50
Union Station '50
When Worlds Collide '51
The Green Glove '52
Second Chance '53
The Violent Men '55
Three Violent People '57
Deep Six '58
For the First Time '59

Tim Matheson
Breach of Conduct '94
Tails You Live, Heads You're Dead '95

Shue Matsubayashi
Last War '68

Bruno Mattei
Night of the Zombies '83
Seven Magnificent Gladiators '84

Marius Mattei
Moving Target '89

Charles Matthau
Doin' Time on Planet Earth '88

Paul Matthews
Grim '95

Burny Mattinson
The Great Mouse Detective '86

Frank S. Mattison
With Kit Carson Over the Great Divide '25

Sally Mattison
Slumber Party Massacre 3 '90

Mario Mattoli
Two Nights with Cleopatra '54

Arne Mattson
The Doll '62
The Girl '86

Norman Maurer
Around the World in a Daze '63
The Outlaws is Coming! '65

Robert Mauri
The Slaughter of the Vampires '62
Invincible Gladiators '64

Garth Maxwell
Jack Be Nimble '94

John Maxwell
The Man I Love '46

Paul Maxwell
Superargo '67

Peter Maxwell
Plunge Into Darkness '77
Touch & Go '80
Run, Rebecca, Run '81
The Highest Honor '84
Platypus Cove '86

Ronald F. Maxwell
Little Darlings '80
The Night the Lights Went Out in Georgia '81
Kidco '83
Gettysburg '93

Bradford May
Lethal Lolita—Amy Fisher: My Story '92
Mortal Sins '92
Darkman 2: The Return of Durant '94
Marilyn & Bobby: Her Final Affair '94
Darkman 3: Die Darkman Die '95
Madonna: Innocence Lost '95

Elaine May
A New Leaf '71
The Heartbreak Kid '72
Mikey & Nicky '76
Ishtar '87

Joe May
Homecoming '28
The Invisible Man Returns '40

Paul May
Dr. Mabuse vs. Scotland Yard '64

Russ Mayberry
The Jesus Trip '71
Probe '72
Fer-De-Lance '74
The Rebels '79
Unidentified Flying Oddball '79
The $5.20 an Hour Dream '80
Marriage Is Alive and Well '80
A Matter of Life and Death '81
Challenge of a Lifetime '85

Daisy von Scherler Mayer
Party Girl '94

Gerald Mayer
The Man Inside '76

Paul Mayersberg
Captive '87
Nightfall '88
The Last Samurai '90

Les Mayfield
Encino Man '92
Miracle on 34th Street '94

Tony Maylam
The Riddle of the Sands '79
The Burning '82
The Sins of Dorian Gray '82
Split Second '92

Ken Maynard
The Fiddlin' Buckaroo '33
Strawberry Roan '33
Honor of the Range '34

Archie Mayo
Illicit '31
Svengali '31
Night After Night '32
The Case of the Lucky Legs '35
Petrified Forest '36
The Adventures of Marco Polo '38
They Shall Have Music '39
House Across the Bay '40
The Great American Broadcast '41
Orchestra Wives '42
Crash Dive '43
Angel on My Shoulder '46
A Night in Casablanca '46

Melanie Mayron
The Baby-Sitters Club '95

David Maysles
Gimme Shelter '70

Michael Mazo
Possession: Until Death Do You Part '90
Time Runner '92
Crackerjack '94

Paul Mazursky
Bob & Carol & Ted & Alice '69
Alex in Wonderland '70
Blume in Love '73
Harry and Tonto '74
Next Stop, Greenwich Village '76
An Unmarried Woman '78
Willie & Phil '80
The Tempest '82
Moscow on the Hudson '84
Down and Out in Beverly Hills '86
Moon over Parador '88
Enemies, a Love Story '89
Scenes from a Mall '91
The Pickle '93
Faithful '95

Joseph Mazzuca
Sisters of Death '76

Don McBrearty
American Nightmare '81
Child's Christmas in Wales '88
Race to Freedom: The Story of the Underground Railroad '94

Jim McBride
David Holzman's Diary '67
Glen and Randa '71
Hot Times '74
Breathless '83
The Big Easy '87
Great Balls of Fire '89
Blood Ties '92
The Wrong Man '93

Jon McBride
Cannibal Campout '88
Woodchipper Massacre '89

Gene McCabe
Follow Me '69

Robert McCahon
Running Wild '73

Howard McCain
No Dessert Dad, 'Til You Mow the Lawn '94

Rod McCall
Cheatin' Hearts '93

James McCalmont
Escape from Safehaven '88
Underground Terror '88

Leo McCarey
Indiscreet '31
Duck Soup '33
Belle of the Nineties '34
Ruggles of Red Gap '35
Milky Way '36
The Awful Truth '37
Love Affair '39
Once Upon a Honeymoon '42
Going My Way '44
The Bells of St. Mary's '45
Good Sam '48
An Affair to Remember '57

Ray McCarey
The Mystery Man '35
Devil's Party '38
You Can't Fool Your Wife '40

John P. McCarthy
Oklahoma Cyclone '30
Cavalier of the West '31
Mother and Son '31
Sunrise Trail '31
The Forty-Niners '32
Fighting Champ '33
The Return of Casey Jones '34
Song of the Gringo '36

Michael McCarthy
Crow Hollow '52
Operation Amsterdam '60

Peter McCarthy
Floundering '94

Todd McCarthy
Visions of Light: The Art of Cinematography '93

John McCauley
Rattlers '76

Michael McClary
Curse of the Starving Class '94
Annie O '95

Gregory McClatchy
Vampire at Midnight '88

Arn McConnell
Shock! Shock! Shock! '87

Bret McCormick
Tabloid! '88
Blood on the Badge '92

George McCowan
Savage Run '70
Frogs '72
Murder on Flight 502 '75
Return to Fantasy Island '77

Peter McCubbin
Home for Christmas '90

Jim McCullough
Charge of the Model T's '76
The Aurora Encounter '85
Mountaintop Motel Massacre '86
Where the Red Fern Grows: Part 2 '92

Bruce McDonald
Roadkill '89

McDonald ►cont.

Highway 61 '91
Dance Me Outside '95

Frank McDonald
Twilight on the Rio Grande '41
Wildcat '42
Gambler's Choice '44
One Body Too Many '44
Take It Big '44
Timber Queen '44
Bells of Rosarita '45
Sunset in El Dorado '45
Treasure of Fear '45
My Pal Trigger '46
Song of Arizona '46
Under Nevada Skies '46
The Big Sombrero '49
Apache Chief '50
Thunder Pass '54

Michael James McDonald
The Crazysitter '94

Peter McDonald
Rambo 3 '88

Rodney McDonald
Night Eyes 2 '91
Night Eyes 4: Fatal Passion '95

Donald McDougall
Chinese Web '78

Ross McElwee
Sherman's March: An Improbable Search for Love '86
Time Indefinite '93

Bernard McEveety, Sr.
The Broadway Drifter '27

Bernard McEveety
The Brotherhood of Satan '71
Napoleon and Samantha '72
One Little Indian '73
The Bears & I '74
Roughnecks '80

Vincent McEveety
Firecreek '68
Menace on the Mountain '70
Smoke '70
Million Dollar Duck '71
Charley and the Angel '73
Superdad '73
The Castaway Cowboy '74
Gus '76
The Treasure of Matecumbe '76
Herbie Goes to Monte Carlo '77
The Apple Dumpling Gang Rides Again '79
Herbie Goes Bananas '80
Amy '81
Gunsmoke: Return to Dodge '87

Bruce McFarlane
Kill Slade '89

William F. McGaha
The Speed Lovers '68
Iron Horsemen '71

William McGann
Dr. Christian Meets the Women '40
American Empire '42
In Old California '42

Darren McGavin
Run, Stranger, Run '73

Scott McGehee
Suture '93

Robert McGinley
Shredder Orpheus '89

Scott McGinnis
Caroline at Midnight '93

Dorrell McGowan
The Showdown '50

J.P. McGowan
Blood and Steel '25
Road Agent '26
Red Signals '27
Below the Deadline '29
Near the Rainbow's End '30
Hurricane Express '32
Mark of the Spur '32
Deadwood Pass '33
Drum Taps '33
Lone Bandit '33
The Outlaw Tamer '33
When a Man Rides Alone '33
Rough Ridin' Rhythm '37

Robert McGowan
Frontier Justice '35
Old Swimmin' Hole '40

Stuart E. McGowan
The Showdown '50
The Billion Dollar Hobo '78

Tom McGowan
Cataclysm '81
Savage Journey '83

Douglas McGrath
Emma '96

Joseph McGrath
Casino Royale '67
The Bliss of Mrs. Blossom '68
30 Is a Dangerous Age, Cynthia '68
The Magic Christian '69
Digby, the Biggest Dog in the World '73
Great McGonagall '75

Sean McGregor
Gentle Savage '73
Devil Times Five '74

Thomas McGuane
92 in the Shade '76

Don McGuire
The Delicate Delinquent '56

Doug McHenry
House Party 2: The Pajama Jam '91
Jason's Lyric '94

Chris McIntyre
Backstreet Justice '93

C.T. McIntyre
Border Shootout '90

Thom McIntyre
The Rutherford County Line '87

Cole McKay
The Secret of the Golden Eagle '91

Jim McKay
Girls Town '95

Malcolm McKay
Maria's Child '93

Douglas McKeown
Return of the Aliens: The Deadly Spawn '83

Robert McKimson
Best of Bugs Bunny & Friends '40
Bugs & Daffy: The Wartime Cartoons '45
Starring Bugs Bunny! '48

Duncan McLachlan
Scavengers '87
The Double O Kid '92
Born Wild '95

Andrew V. McLaglen
McLintock! '63
Shenandoah '65
Monkeys, Go Home! '66
The Rare Breed '66
The Way West '67
Bandolero! '68
The Devil's Brigade '68
Hellfighters '68
The Undefeated '69
Chisum '70
Cahill: United States Marshal '73
Mitchell '75
Breakthrough '78
Wild Geese '78
ffolkes '80
Sea Wolves '81
The Shadow Riders '82
Sahara '83
The Blue and the Gray '85
The Dirty Dozen: The Next Mission '85
On Wings of Eagles '86

Norman McLaren
Scherzo '39

Sheila McLaughlin
She Must Be Seeing Things '87

Steve McLean
Postcards from America '95

Don McLennan
Hard Knocks '80
Slate, Wyn & Me '87

Norman Z. McLeod
Monkey Business '31
Horse Feathers '32
It's A Gift '34
Topper '37
Topper Takes a Trip '39
Little Men '40
Lady Be Good '41
Panama Hattie '42
Kid from Brooklyn '46
The Road to Rio '47
The Secret Life of Walter Mitty '47
The Paleface '48
Let's Dance '50
Never Wave at a WAC '52
Casanova's Big Night '54

Tom McLoughlin
One Dark Night '82
Friday the 13th, Part 6: Jason Lives '86
Date with an Angel '87
The Fire Next Time '93
Journey '95

Marshall McLuhan
Third Walker '79

Robert McMahon
Night of the Assassin '77

Sean McNamara
Hollywood Chaos '89

Ian McNaughton
And Now for Something Completely Different '72

John McNaughton
The Borrower '89
Henry: Portrait of a Serial Killer '90
Sex, Drugs, Rock & Roll: Eric Bogosian '91
Mad Dog and Glory '93
Normal Life '96

John McPherson
Strays '91
Dirty Work '92
Fade to Black '93
Incident at Deception Ridge '94
Incident at Deception Ridge '94

John McTiernan
Nomads '86
Predator '87
Die Hard '88
The Hunt for Red October '90
Medicine Man '92
Last Action Hero '93
Die Hard: With a Vengeance '95

Nick Mead
Bank Robber '93

John Meagher
Fantasy Man '84

Nancy Meckler
Sister My Sister '94

Peter Medak
Negatives '68
A Day in the Death of Joe Egg '71
The Ruling Class '72
Ghost in the Noonday Sun '74
The Odd Job '78
The Babysitter '80
The Changeling '80
Zorro, the Gay Blade '81
Pinocchio '83
The Snow Queen '83
Snow White and the Seven Dwarfs '83
Breakin' Through '84
The Dancing Princesses '84
The Emperor's New Clothes '84
The Men's Club '86
The Krays '90
Let Him Have It '91
Romeo Is Bleeding '93
Pontiac Moon '94

Don Medford
The Organization '71
Sizzle '81

Cary Medoway
Paradise Motel '84
The Heavenly Kid '85

Alexander Medvedkin
Happiness '34

Jeanine Meerapfel
Malou '83

Pomme Meffre
Grain of Sand '84

Leslie Megahey
The Advocate '93

Francis Megahy
The Great Riviera Bank Robbery '79
The Carpathian Eagle '81
Taffin '88
Con Man '92
Red Sun Rising '94

Alan Mehrez
Bloodsport 2: The Next Kumite '95

Deepa Mehta
Camilla '94

Ketan Mehta
Spices '86

Zhang Meijun
Dynasty '77

Gus Meins
March of the Wooden Soldiers '34
Kelly the Second '36
The Gentleman from California '37
Roll Along Cowboy '37

Myron Meise
It's All True '93

Norbert Meisel
The Adultress '77
Walking the Edge '83
Night Children '89

John Mekas
The Brig '64

Andre Melancon
The Dog Who Stopped the War '84

Ib Melchior
The Angry Red Planet '59
The Time Travelers '64

Arthur N. Mele
Soldier's Fortune '91

Bill Melendez
A Charlie Brown Christmas '65
Charlie Brown's All-Stars '66
It Was a Short Summer, Charlie Brown '69
A Boy Named Charlie Brown '70
Snoopy, Come Home '72
Race for Your Life, Charlie Brown '77
Bon Voyage, Charlie Brown '80
A Charlie Brown Thanksgiving '81
Happy New Year, Charlie Brown '82
Good Grief, Charlie Brown '83
It's an Adventure, Charlie Brown! '83
A Charlie Brown Celebration '84
It's Flashbeagle, Charlie Brown/ She's a Good Skate, Charlie Brown '84
It's Three Strikes, Charlie Brown '86

George Melford
The Sheik '21
Moran of the Lady Letty '22
Dracula (Spanish Version) '31
East of Borneo '31
Man of Action '33

Georges Melies
Early Cinema Vol. 1 '19

James Melkonian
The Stoned Age '94
The Jerky Boys '95

John Cougar Mellencamp
Falling from Grace '92

Jean-Pierre Melville
Les Enfants Terrible '50
Bob le Flambeur '55
Le Doulos '61
Leon Morin, Priest '61
Godson '72

John Melville
Confessions of a Vice Baron '42

Robert Menard
L'Enfant d'Eau '95

Christopher Menaul
A Dangerous Man: Lawrence after Arabia '91
Prime Suspect '92
Fatherland '94
Feast of July '95

Lee Mendelson
Bon Voyage, Charlie Brown '80

George Mendeluk
The Kidnapping of the President '80
Stone Cold Dead '80
Doin' Time '85
Meatballs 3 '87

Lothar Mendes
Power '34
The Man Who Could Work Miracles '37
Moonlight Sonata '38

Odorico Mendes
Discretion Assured '93

Fernando Mendez
Black Pit of Dr. M '47
The Vampire '57
The Living Coffin '58
The Vampire's Coffin '58

Ramon Menendez
Stand and Deliver '88
Money for Nothing '93

Chris Menges
A World Apart '88
Crisscross '92
Second Best '94

Nina Menkes
Queen of Diamonds '91

Gian-Carlo Menotti
The Medium '51

Barnard Menoud
Scenario du Film Passion '82

Vladimir Menshov
Moscow Does Not Believe in Tears '80

Jiri Menzel
Closely Watched Trains '66
Larks on a String '68
My Sweet Little Village '86

William Cameron Menzies
Chandu the Magician '32
Things to Come '36
Drums in the Deep South '51
Invaders from Mars '53

Louis Mercanton
Salome/Queen Elizabeth '23

Antonio Mercero
Don Juan, My Love '90

Ismail Merchant
The Courtesans of Bombay '85
In Custody '94

Burgess Meredith
Man on the Eiffel Tower '48
Yin & Yang of Mr. Go '71

James Merendino
Witchcraft 4: Virgin Heart '92
Hard Drive '94

Jalal Merhi
Operation Golden Phoenix '94

Joseph Merhi
Epitaph '87
Fresh Kill '87
Heat Street '87
The Killing Game '87
L.A. Crackdown '87
The Newlydeads '87
The Glass Jungle '88
L.A. Crackdown 2 '88
L.A. Heat '88
L.A. Vice '89
Midnight Warrior '89
The Last Riders '90
Night of the Wilding '90
Final Impact '91
C.I.A.: Code Name Alexa '92
Magic Kid '92
Maximum Force '92

Direct Hit '93
To Be the Best '93
Zero Tolerance '93
Last Man Standing '95
The Sweeper '95

J.L. Merino
Hell Commandos '69
Scream of the Demon Lover '71

Ron Merk
Pinocchio's Storybook Adventures '79

Agnes Merlet
The Son of the Shark '93

Ian Merrick
Black Panther '77

Lawrence Merrick
Black Bikers from Hell '70
The Outlaw Bikers—Gang Wars '70

Keith Merrill
Take Down '79
Windwalker '81
Harry's War '84

George Merriweather
Blondes Have More Guns '95

William Mesa
Galaxis '95

Matthew Meshekoff
The Opposite Sex and How to Live With Them '93

Jason Meshover-Iorg
Legacy of Lies '92

Philip Frank Messina
Spy '89

Marta Meszaros
The Girl '68
Riddance '73
Adoption '75

Alan Metter
Girls Just Want to Have Fun '85
Back to School '86
Moving '88
Police Academy: Mission to Moscow '94

Alan Metzger
The China Lake Murders '90
Fatal Exposure '91
Red Wind '91
New Eden '94

Radley Metzger
Therese & Isabelle '68
The Cat and the Canary '79
The Princess & the Call Girl '84

Andrew Meyer
Night of the Cobra Woman '72
Tidal Wave '75

Kevin Meyer
Invasion of Privacy '92
Under Investigation '93
Perfect Alibi '94

Nicholas Meyer
Time After Time '79
Star Trek 2: The Wrath of Khan '82
The Day After '83
The Pied Piper of Hamelin '84
Volunteers '85
The Deceivers '88
Company Business '91
Star Trek 6: The Undiscovered Country '91

Russ Meyer
Fanny Hill: Memoirs of a Woman of Pleasure '64
Motor Psycho '65
Faster Pussycat! Kill! Kill! '66
Beyond the Valley of the Dolls '70
Blacksnake! '73
Supervixens '75
Beneath the Valley of the Ultra-Vixens '79

Turi Meyer
Sleepstalker: The Sandman's Last Rites '94

Janet Meyers
Letter to My Killer '95

Eric Meza
House Party 3 '94

Richard Michaels
Homeward Bound '80
Berlin Tunnel 21 '81
Plutonium Incident '82
Blue Skies Again '83
One Cooks, the Other Doesn't '83
Sadat '83
Silence of the Heart '84
Heart of a Champion: The Ray Mancini Story '85
Indiscreet '88
The Queen of Mean '90
Backfield in Motion '91
Father and Scout '95

John E. Michalakis
I Was a Teenage Zombie '87

Oscar Micheaux
Body and Soul '24
Girl from Chicago '32
Lying Lips '39

Dave Michener
The Great Mouse Detective '86

Paulmichel Miekhe
Murderer's Keep '88

Anne-Marie Mieville
Six Fois Deux/Sur et Sous la Communication '76
France/Tour/Detour/Deux/Enfants '78
Scenario du Film Passion '82
Soft and Hard '85

Radu Mihaileanu
Trahir '93

George Mihalka
Pick-Up Summer '79
My Bloody Valentine '81
Eternal Evil '87
Hostile Takeover '88
Relative Fear '95

Ted V. Mikels
The Black Klansman '66
The Astro-Zombies '67
Girl in Gold Boots '69
The Corpse Grinders '71
The Doll Squad '73
Hustler Squad '76
Cruise Missile '78
10 Violent Women '79
Aftermath '85
WarCat '88

Elfi Mikesch
Seduction: The Cruel Woman '89

Nikita Mikhalkov
An Unfinished Piece for a Player Piano '77
A Slave of Love '78
Oblomov '81
Dark Eyes '87
Close to Eden '90
Burnt by the Sun '94

Christopher Miles
The Virgin and the Gypsy '70
That Lucky Touch '75
Priest of Love '81

Lewis Milestone
The Garden of Eden '28
All Quiet on the Western Front '30
The Front Page '31
Rain '32
Hallelujah, I'm a Bum '33
The General Died at Dawn '36
Of Mice and Men '39
Lucky Partners '40
Edge of Darkness '43
The North Star '43
The Purple Heart '44
The Strange Love of Martha Ivers '46
A Walk in the Sun '46
Arch of Triumph '48
The Red Pony '49
The Halls of Montezuma '50
Pork Chop Hill '59
Ocean's 11 '60
Mutiny on the Bounty '62

John Milius
Dillinger '73
The Wind and the Lion '75
Big Wednesday '78
Conan the Barbarian '82
Red Dawn '84
Farewell to the King '89

Flight of the Intruder '90

Gerry Mill
Second Chance '80

Ray Milland
A Man Alone '55
Lisbon '56
Panic in the Year Zero! '62

Gavin Millar
Secrets '82
Dreamchild '85
Tidy Endings '88
My Friend Walter '93

Stuart Millar
When the Legends Die '72
Rooster Cogburn '75

Claude Miller
This Sweet Sickness '77
The Best Way '82
The Little Thief '89
The Accompanist '93

Dan T. Miller
Screamers '80

David Miller
Billy the Kid '41
Flying Tigers '42
Love Happy '50
Sudden Fear '52
Diane '55
The Opposite Sex '56
Midnight Lace '60
Back Street '61
Lonely Are the Brave '62
Captain Newman, M.D. '63
Hail, Hero! '69
Executive Action '73
Bittersweet Love '76

George Miller
The Man from Snowy River '82
All the Rivers Run '84
Anzacs: The War Down Under '85
The Aviator '85
Nevil Shute's The Far Country '85
Goodbye, Miss 4th of July '88
Les Patterson Saves the World '90
NeverEnding Story 2: The Next Chapter '91
Frozen Assets '92
Gross Misconduct '93
Over the Hill '93
Andre '94
The Great Elephant Escape '95

George Miller
Mad Max '80
The Road Warrior '82
Twilight Zone: The Movie '83
Mad Max: Beyond Thunderdome '85
Miracle Down Under '87
The Witches of Eastwick '87
Lorenzo's Oil '92
Silver Strand '95

Harvey Miller
Bad Medicine '85
Getting Away With Murder '96

Ira Miller
Loose Shoes '80

Jason Miller
That Championship Season '82

J.C. Miller
No Dead Heroes '87

Jonathan Miller
Long Day's Journey into Night '88

Mark Miller
Sister Dora '77

Michael Miller
Street Girls '75
Jackson County Jail '76
Outside Chance '78
National Lampoon's Class Reunion '82
Silent Rage '82
Can You Feel Me Dancing? '85
Silent Witness '85
A Case of Deadly Force '86
Blown Away '90
Danielle Steel's "Daddy" '92
Danielle Steel's Heartbeat '93
Danielle Steel's Star '93
Dangerous Passion '95

Neal Miller
Under the Biltmore Clock '85

Randall Miller
Class Act '91
Houseguest '94

Rebecca Miller
Angela '94

Robert Ellis Miller
Any Wednesday '66
The Heart is a Lonely Hunter '68
The Girl from Petrovka '74
The Baltimore Bullet '80
Her Life as a Man '83
Reuben, Reuben '83
Brenda Starr '86
Hawks '89
Bed & Breakfast '92

Sharron Miller
The Woman Who Willed a Miracle '83

Sidney Miller
The 30-Foot Bride of Candy Rock '59

Stephen E. Miller
Visions '90

Andy Milligan
The Naked Witch '64
The Ghastly Ones '68
The Body Beneath '70
Torture Dungeon '70
Fleshpot on 42nd Street '71
Man with Two Heads '72
The Rats are Coming! The Werewolves are Here! '72
Legacy of Horror '78
Carnage '84
The Weirdo '89

Bill Milling
Lauderdale '89
Caged Fury '90
Body Trouble '92

Alec Mills
Bloodmoon '90
Dead Sleep '91

Reginald Mills
Tales of Beatrix Potter '71

Dan Milner
The Phantom from 10,000 Leagues '56

Tom Milo
Smooth Talker '90
Kiss and Be Killed '91

Elia Milonakos
Operation Orient

Robert Milton
Devotion '31

Chai Yang Min
Kick of Death: The Prodigal Boxer '80s

Michael Miner
Deadly Weapon '88

Steve Miner
Friday the 13th, Part 2 '81
Friday the 13th, Part 3 '82
House '86
Soul Man '86
Warlock '91
Wild Hearts Can't Be Broken '91
Forever Young '92
My Father the Hero '93
Big Bully '95

Anthony Minghella
Truly, Madly, Deeply '91
Mr. Wonderful '93

Gianfranco Mingozzi
Sardinia Kidnapped '75
Bellissimo: Images of the Italian Cinema '87

Joe Minion
Daddy's Boys '87

Rob Minkoff
Honey, I Shrunk the Kids '89
The Lion King '94

Vincente Minnelli
Cabin in the Sky '43
I Dood It '43
Meet Me in St. Louis '44
The Clock '45
Yolanda and the Thief '45
Ziegfeld Follies '46
The Pirate '48
Madame Bovary '49
Father of the Bride '50
An American in Paris '51
Father's Little Dividend '51
The Bad and the Beautiful '52
The Band Wagon '53
Brigadoon '54
The Long, Long Trailer '54
The Cobweb '55
Kismet '55
Lust for Life '56
Tea and Sympathy '56
Designing Woman '57
Gigi '58
The Reluctant Debutante '58
Some Came Running '58
Bells are Ringing '60
Home from the Hill '60
The Courtship of Eddie's Father '62
The Four Horsemen of the Apocalypse '62
Two Weeks in Another Town '62
The Sandpiper '65
On a Clear Day You Can See Forever '70
A Matter of Time '76

Murray Mintz
Cardiac Arrest '74

Emilio P. Miraglio
The Night Evelyn Came Out of the Grave '71
Halloween Night '90
Night Eyes '90

Bob Misiorowski
Beyond Forgiveness '94

Kenji Misumi
Zatoichi: The Life and Opinion of Masseur Ichi '62
Zatoichi: The Blind Swordsman and the Chess Expert '65
Baby Cart 1: Lend a Child...Lend an Arm '72
Baby Cart at the River Styx '72
Baby Cart to Hades '72
Shogun Assassin '80

Bruce Mitchell
Dynamite Dan '24

David Mitchell
Club Med '83
City of Shadows '86
Thunderground '89
Ski School 2 '94

Duke Mitchell
The Executioner '78

Eric Mitchell
Underground U.S.A. '84

Frank Mitchell
Blood Voyage '77

George Mitchell
Wolf Blood '25

Oswald Mitchell
The Dummy Talks '43
The Greed of William Hart '48
The Temptress '49

Roger Mitchell
Persuasion '95

Sollace Mitchell
Call Me '88

Roberto Mitrotti
Little Girl ... Big Tease '75

Hayao Miyazaki
My Neighbor Totoro '93

Kenji Mizoguchi
Osaka Elegy '36
Sisters of Gion '36
The Story of the Late Chrysanthemum '39
47 Ronin, Part 1 '42
47 Ronin, Part 2 '42
Utamaro and His Five Women '46
Life of Oharu '52
A Geisha '53
Ugetsu '53
The Crucified Lovers '54
Sansho the Bailiff '54
Princess Yang Kwei Fei '55
Shin Heike Monogatari '55
Street of Shame '56

Moshe Mizrahi
I Love You Rosa '72

Mizrahi ▶cont.

The House on Chelouche Street '73
Rachel's Man '75
Madame Rosa '77
I Sent a Letter to My Love '81
La Vie Continue '82
War & Love '84
Every Time We Say Goodbye '86

Luke Moberly
Little Laura & Big John '73

Juan Lopez Moctezuma
Sisters of Satan '75
Mary, Mary, Bloody Mary '76

Richard Moder
Lassie: Adventures of Neeka '68
The Bionic Woman '75

Philip Moeller
Break of Hearts '35

John Moffitt
Love at Stake '87

Flavio Mogherini
Lunatics & Lovers '76

Leonide Moguy
Action in Arabia '44
Whistle Stop '46

Hanro Mohr
Hostage '87

Jose Mojica Marins
At Midnight, I'll Take Your Soul '63
Awakenings of the Beast '68
Strange World of Coffin Joe '68
Hallucinations of a Deranged Mind '70

Gustaf Molander
Swedenhielms '35
Intermezzo '36
Dollar '38
A Woman's Face '38
Only One Night '42

Jack Molina
The Craving '80

Edouard Molinaro
Back to the Wall '56
Ravishing Idiot '64
Dracula & Son '76
Pain in the A— '77
La Cage aux Folles '78
La Cage aux Folles 2 '81
Just the Way You Are '84

Paul Mones
Fathers and Sons '92
Saints and Sinners '95

Peter Mones
The Beat '88

Christopher Monger
Waiting for the Light '90
The Englishman Who Went Up a Hill But Came Down a Mountain '95
Just Like a Woman '95

Mario Monicelli
Joyful Laughter '54
Big Deal on Madonna Street '58
The Great War '59
Passionate Thief '60
Casanova '70 '65
Lovers and Liars '81

Egon Monk
The Oppermann Family '82

Noel Monkman
Typhoon Treasure '39

Phil Monroe
The Bugs Bunny/Road Runner Movie '79

Carl Monson
Please Don't Eat My Mother '72
Blood Legacy '73

Edward Montagne
The Reluctant Astronaut '67
They Went That-a-Way & That-a-Way '78

Guiliano Montaldo
Sacco & Vanzetti '71
Fifth Day of Peace '72
Control '87
Time to Kill '89

Jose Monter
As If It Were Raining '63

Robert Montero
Island Monster '53
Mondo Balardo '64
Tharus Son of Attila '87

Eduardo Montes
Double Obsession '93

Jorge Montesi
Omen 4: The Awakening '91
Soft Deceit '94
Bloodknot '95

George Montgomery
The Steel Claw '61
Samar '62
From Hell to Borneo '64

Jennifer Montgomery
Art for Teachers of Children '95

Patrick Montgomery
The Compleat Beatles '82

Robert Montgomery
Lady in the Lake '46
Eye Witness '49
The Gallant Hours '60

Thomas Montgomery
King Kong vs. Godzilla '63

Vincent Monton
Windrider '86
Fatal Bond '91

Charles Philip Moore
Demon Wind '90
Dance with Death '91
Black Belt '92
Angel of Destruction '94

Michael Moore
Paradise, Hawaiian Style '66
Talion '66
Buckskin '68
Fastest Guitar Alive '68

Michael Moore
Roger & Me '89
Canadian Bacon '94

Richard Moore
Circle of Iron '78

Robert Moore
Murder by Death '76
The Cheap Detective '78
Chapter Two '79

Ronald W. Moore
Future Kill '85

Rudy Ray Moore
Avenging Disco Godfather '76

Simon Moore
Under Suspicion '92

Tom Moore
Return to Boggy Creek '77
'night, Mother '86
Fine Things '90

Jocelyn Moorhouse
Proof '91
How to Make an American Quilt '95

Philippe Mora
Mad Dog Morgan '76
The Beast Within '82
Return of Captain Invincible '83
A Breed Apart '84
Death of a Soldier '85
Howling 2: Your Sister is a Werewolf '85
Howling 3: The Marsupials '87
Communion '89

Andrew Morahan
Highlander: The Final Dimension '94

Christopher Morahan
The Jewel in the Crown '84
Clockwise '86
After Pilkington '88
Paper Mask '91

Rick Moranis
Strange Brew '83

Miguel Morayta
Invasion of the Vampires '61

Tony Mordente
Just Tell Me You Love Me '80

Gerard Mordillat
My Life and Times with Antonin Artaud '93

Jeanne Moreau
Lumiere '76

Nanni Moretti
Palombella Rossa '89
Caro Diario '93

Robert W. Morgan
Bloodstalkers '76

William M. Morgan
Heart of the Rio Grande '42

W.T. Morgan
A Matter of Degrees '90

Yoshimitsu Morita
The Family Game '83

Louis Morneau
To Die Standing '91
Final Judgement '92
Quake '92
Carnosaur 2 '94
Soldier Boyz '95

David Burton Morris
Patti Rocks '88
Jersey Girl '92
Hometown Boy Makes Good '93

Ernest Morris
The Tell-Tale Heart '62

Errol Morris
The Thin Blue Line '88
The Dark Wind '91
A Brief History of Time '92

Howard Morris
Who's Minding the Mint? '67
With Six You Get Eggroll '68
Don't Drink the Water '69
Goin' Coconuts '78

Martin Morris
L.A. Wars '94

Robert Morris
King of Kong Island '78

Bruce Morrison
Shaker Run '85
Tearaway '87

Paul Morrissey
Flesh '68
Trash '70
Heat '72
Andy Warhol's Dracula '74
Andy Warhol's Frankenstein '74
The Hound of the Baskervilles '77
Mixed Blood '84
Beethoven's Nephew '88
Spike of Bensonhurst '88

Vic Morrow
A Man Called Sledge '71

Hollingsworth Morse
Daughters of Satan '72
Justin Morgan Had a Horse '81

Terry Morse
Waterfront '39
British Intelligence '40
Fog Island '45
Bells of San Fernando '47
Unknown World '51
Godzilla, King of the Monsters '56

Edmund Mortimer
The Prairie Pirate '25

Derek Morton
Wild Horses '82

Rocky Morton
D.O.A. '88
Super Mario Bros. '93

Lawrence Mortorff
Deadly Exposure '93

Ben Moses
Nickel & Dime '92

Gilbert Moses
The Fish that Saved Pittsburgh '79
Runaway '89
A Fight for Jenny '90

Harry Moses
Assault at West Point: The Court-Martial of Johnson Whittaker '94

Han Moshenson
The Wooden Gun '79

Gregory Mosher
Our Town '89
A Life in the Theater '93

Elijah Moshinsky
The Green Man '91
Genghis Cohn '93

George Moskov
Married Too Young '62

Gustavo Mosquera
Times to Come '81

Jon Mostow
Beverly Hills Bodysnatchers '89
Flight of Black Angel '91

Ilya Motyleff
The Cantor's Son '37

Malcolm Mowbray
A Private Function '84
Out Cold '89
Don't Tell Her It's Me '90

John Llewellyn Moxey
Horror Hotel '60
Circus of Fear '67
The Bounty Man '72
Home for the Holidays '72
A Strange and Deadly Occurence '74
Where Have All the People Gone? '74
Conspiracy of Terror '75
Nightmare in Badham County '76
Intimate Strangers '77
Panic in Echo Park '77
President's Mistress '78
The Power Within '79
Sanctuary of Fear '79
Killjoy '81
Mating Season '81
No Place to Hide '81
The Solitary Man '82
The Cradle Will Fall '83
Through Naked Eyes '87
Lady Mobster '88

Allan Moyle
Times Square '80
Pump Up the Volume '90
The Gun in Betty Lou's Handbag '92
Empire Records '95

Russell Mulcahy
Razorback '84
Highlander '86
Highlander 2: The Quickening '91
Ricochet '91
Blue Ice '92
The Real McCoy '93
The Shadow '94

Edward Muller
Savage Island '85
Escape from Hell '89

Ray Muller
The Wonderful, Horrible Life of Leni Riefenstahl '93

Robert Mulligan
Fear Strikes Out '57
The Rat Race '60
Come September '61
The Great Impostor '61
To Kill a Mockingbird '62
Love with the Proper Stranger '63
Baby, the Rain Must Fall '64
Inside Daisy Clover '65
Up the Down Staircase '67
The Stalking Moon '69
The Pursuit of Happiness '70
Summer of '42 '71
The Other '72
Bloodbrothers '78
Same Time, Next Year '78
Kiss Me Goodbye '82
Clara's Heart '88
The Man in the Moon '91

Mark Mullin
Cool Blue '88

Claude Mulot
Black Venus '83

Christopher Munch
The Hours and Times '92
Color of a Brisk and Leaping Day '95

Richard W. Munchkin
Dance or Die '87
Deadly Bet '91
Ring of Fire '91
Ring of Fire 2: Blood and Steel '92
Out for Blood '93
Guardian Angel '94
Texas Payback '95

Jag Mundhra
Open House '86
Hack O'Lantern '87
Jigsaw Murders '89
Last Call '90
Legal Tender '90
L.A. Goddess '92
Wild Cactus '92
Eyewitness to Murder '93
Sexual Malice '93
Tropical Heat '93
Improper Conduct '94

Ian Mune
Came a Hot Friday '85
The Bridge to Nowhere '86

Chris Munger
Black Starlet '74
Kiss of the Tarantula '75

Cynthia Munroe
The Wedding Party '69

Jimmy T. Murakami
Battle Beyond the Stars '80
When the Wind Blows '86

Ryu Murakami
Tokyo Decadence '91

Toru Murakawa
Distant Justice '92
New York Cop '94

Walter Murch
Return to Oz '85

Fredi M. Murer
Alpine Fire '89

John Murlowski
Return of the Family Man '89
Amityville: A New Generation '93
Automatic '94

F.W. Murnau
The Haunted Castle '21
Nosferatu '22
The Last Laugh '24
Faust '26
Sunrise '27
City Girl '30
Tabu: A Story of the South Seas '31

Jim Muro
Street Trash '87

Brianne Murphy
Mortal Danger '94

Dudley Murphy
Emperor Jones '33
Emperor Jones/Paul Robeson: Tribute to an Artist '33
One Third of a Nation '39

Eddie Murphy
Harlem Nights '89

Edward Murphy
Raw Force '81
Heated Vengeance '87

Geoff Murphy
Goodbye Pork Pie '81
Utu '83
The Quiet Earth '85
Red King, White Knight '89
Never Say Die '90
Young Guns 2 '90
Freejack '92
Blind Side '93
The Last Outlaw '93
Under Siege 2: Dark Territory '95

Maurice Murphy
Doctors and Nurses '82
Fatty Finn '84
Wet and Wild Summer '92

Ralph Murphy
The Spirit of West Point '47
Mickey '48
The Black Devils of Kali '55

Richard Murphy
Wackiest Ship in the Army '61
Tab Murphy
The Last of the Dogmen '95
Bill Murray
Quick Change '90
Don Murray
The Cross & the Switchblade '72
Katrina Murray
The Secret Garden '84
Robin Murray
Dance '90
Season of Change '94
Scott Murray
Beyond Innocence '87
William Murray
Primal Scream '87
John Musker
The Great Mouse Detective '86
The Little Mermaid '89
Aladdin '92
Floyd Mutrux
Aloha, Bobby and Rose '74
There Goes My Baby '92
Nagangura Mweze
La Vie est Belle '87
Frank Myers
Lost, Lonely, and Vicious '59
Zion Myers
Sidewalks of New York '31
Alan Myerson
Steelyard Blues '73
Private Lessons '81
Police Academy 5: Assignment Miami Beach '88
John Myhers
Terror in Beverly Hills '90
Bruce Myles
Ground Zero '88
Arthur Nadel
Clambake '67
Michael Nader
The Great Escape 2: The Untold Story '88
Ivan Nagy
Bad Charleston Charlie '73
Deadly Hero '75
Captain America 2: Death Too Soon '79
A Gun in the House '81
Jane Doe '83
Skinner '93
Philippe Nahoun
A Girl on Her Own '76
Mira Nair
Salaam Bombay! '88
Mississippi Masala '92
The Perez Family '94
Sadao Nakajima
Renegade Ninja '83
Takehiro Nakajima
Okoge '93
Novuru Nakamuru
Shiokari Pass '77
Desmond Nakano
White Man's Burden '95
Key-Nam Nam
Dragon Force '82
Lisandro Duque Naranjo
Miracle in Rome '88
Don Nardo
In Deadly Heat '87
Stuff Stephanie in the Incinerator '89
James Nares
Rome '78 '78
Silvio Narizzano
24 Hours in a Woman's Life '61
Die! Die! My Darling! '65
Georgy Girl '66
Blue '68
Loot...Give Me Money, Honey! '70
Redneck '73
The Class of Miss MacMichael '78
Why Shoot the Teacher '79
The Body in the Library '87
Bloodbath
Mikio Naruse
Mother '52
Late Chrysanthemums '54
When a Woman Ascends the Stairs '60
Paul Naschy
Inquisition '76
Human Beasts '80
Alan Nathanson
Playing with Fire '70s
Bill Naud
Whodunit '82
Ricky 1 '88
Gregory Nava
El Norte '83
A Time of Destiny '88
My Family '94
Tony Navarro
Widow's Nest '77
Erastheo J. Navda
The Boy God '86
Ray Nazarro
Indian Uprising '51
Kansas Pacific '53
Dog Eat Dog '64
Ronald Neame
The Golden Salamander '51
The Promoter '52
The Man Who Never Was '55
Windom's Way '57
The Horse's Mouth '58
Tunes of Glory '60
Tunes of Glory/Horse's Mouth '60
I Could Go on Singing '63
The Chalk Garden '64
Gambit '66
The Prime of Miss Jean Brodie '69
Scrooge '70
The Poseidon Adventure '72
The Odessa File '74
Meteor '79
Hopscotch '80
First Monday in October '81
Foreign Body '86
Hal Needham
Smokey and the Bandit '77
Hooper '78
The Villain '79
Smokey and the Bandit, Part 2 '80
Cannonball Run '81
Megaforce '82
Stroker Ace '83
Cannonball Run 2 '84
Rad '86
Body Slam '87
Thomas L. Neff
Running Mates '86
Alberto Negrin
Mussolini & I '85
Voyage of Terror: The Achille Lauro Affair '90
Jean Negulesco
Humoresque '46
Johnny Belinda '48
Road House '48
Three Came Home '50
Phone Call from a Stranger '52
How to Marry a Millionaire '53
Titanic '53
Three Coins in the Fountain '54
A Woman's World '54
Daddy Long Legs '55
The Best of Everything '59
The Invincible Six '68
Marshall Neilan
Rebecca of Sunnybrook Farm '17
Stella Maris '18
Vagabond Lover '29
Swing It, Professor '37
Roy William Neill
The Black Room '35
Dr. Syn '37
Frankenstein Meets the Wolfman '42
Sherlock Holmes and the Secret Weapon '42
Sherlock Holmes Faces Death '43
Sherlock Holmes in Washington '43
The Pearl of Death '44
Scarlet Claw '44
Spider Woman '44
House of Fear '45
Pursuit to Algiers '45
The Woman in Green '45
Dressed to Kill '46
Terror by Night '46
Terror by Night/Meeting at Midnight '46
James Neilson
Bon Voyage! '62
Moon Pilot '62
Mooncussers '62
Johnny Shiloh '63
Summer Magic '63
Dr. Syn, Alias the Scarecrow '64
The Moon-Spinners '64
The Adventures of Bullwhip Griffin '66
Gentle Giant '67
Where Angels Go, Trouble Follows '68
The First Time '69
L.E. Neiman
Time Troopers '89
Daniel Neira
Immortal Combat '94
Frans Nel
Lights! Camera! Murder! '89
American Kickboxer 1 '91
David Nelson
Confessions of Tom Harris '72
A Rare Breed '81
Last Plane Out '83
Dusty Nelson
White Phantom: Enemy of Darkness '87
Necromancer: Satan's Servant '88
Gary Nelson
Molly & Lawless John '72
Santee '73
Freaky Friday '76
The Black Hole '79
Pride of Jesse Hallum '81
Jimmy the Kid '82
Murder in Coweta County '83
The Baron and the Kid '84
Allan Quatermain and the Lost City of Gold '86
Get Smart, Again! '89
The Lookalike '90
Revolver '92
Gene Nelson
Kissin' Cousins '64
Harum Scarum '65
Jessie Nelson
Corrina, Corrina '94
Ozzie Nelson
The Adventures of Ozzie & Harriet '50s
Ralph Nelson
Requiem for a Heavyweight '56
Lilies of the Field '63
Soldier in the Rain '63
Father Goose '64
Duel at Diablo '66
Charly '68
Soldier Blue '70
The Wilby Conspiracy '75
Embryo '76
A Hero Ain't Nothin' But a Sandwich '78
Lady of the House '78
Christmas Lilies of the Field '84
The Cary Grant Collection '90
Sam Nelson
Sagebrush Law '43
Jan Nemec
Diamonds of the Night '64
The Report on the Party and the Guests '66
Luis Nepomuceno
Stickfighter '89
Efrain Lopez Neris
A Life of Sin '92
Avi Nesher
She '83
Doppelganger: The Evil Within '90
Timebomb '91
Michael Nesmith
Doctor Duck's Super Secret All-Purpose Sauce '85
Max Neufeld
An Orphan Boy of Vienna '37
Kurt Neumann
My Pal, The King '32
Let's Sing Again '36
Make a Wish '37
Wide Open Faces '38
Bad Boy '39
Return of the Vampire '43
Rocketship X-M '50
The Ring '52
Carnival Story '54
They Were So Young '55
Mohawk '56
Kronos '57
The Fly '58
Peter Newbrook
The Asphyx '72
Mike Newell
The Man in the Iron Mask '77
The Awakening '80
Dance with a Stranger '85
Amazing Grace & Chuck '87
Bad Blood '87
The Good Father '87
Enchanted April '92
Into the West '92
An Awfully Big Adventure '94
Four Weddings and a Funeral '94
Sam Newfield
Frontier Days '34
Branded a Coward '35
Bulldog Courage '35
Go-Get-'Em-Haines '35
Racing Luck '35
Aces and Eights '36
Border Caballero '36
Federal Agent '36
Ghost Patrol '36
Roaring Guns '36
The Traitor '36
Arizona Gunfighter '37
Boothill Brigade '37
Doomed at Sundown '37
The Gambling Terror '37
Gun Lords of Stirrup Basin '37
Guns in the Dark '37
A Lawman Is Born '37
Lightning Bill Crandall '37
Melody of the Plains '37
Ridin' the Lone Trail '37
Windjammer '37
Durango Valley Raiders '38
Feud Maker '38
Frontier Scout '38
Harlem on the Prairie '38
Lightnin' Carson Rides Again '38
Phantom Ranger '38
Songs and Bullets '38
Terror of Tiny Town '38
Thunder in the Desert '38
Fighting Mad '39
Fighting Renegade '39
Flaming Lead '39
Outlaw's Paradise '39
Trigger Pals '39
Arizona Gangbusters '40
Death Rides the Range '40
Gun Code '40
I Take This Oath '40
The Invisible Killer '40
Border Roundup '41
The Lone Rider in Ghost Town '41
Trigger Men '41
Along the Sundown Trail '42
Billy the Kid Trapped '42
Jungle Siren '42
The Lone Rider in Cheyenne '42
The Mad Monster '42
The Mysterious Rider '42
Prairie Pals '42
Texas Justice '42
Tumbleweed Trail '42
The Black Raven '43
Dead Men Walk '43
Harvest Melody '43
Tiger Fangs '43
Death Rides the Plains '44
Devil Riders '44
Frontier Outlaws '44
The Monster Maker '44
Nabonga '44
Oath of Vengeance '44
Rustler's Hideout '44
Wild Horse Phantom '44
Border Badmen '45
Gangster's Den '45
His Brother's Ghost '45
The Lady Confesses '45
Lightning Raiders '45
White Pongo '45
Outlaw of the Plains '46
Adventure Island '47
State Department File 649 '49
Wild Weed '49
Three Desperate Men '50
Fingerprints Don't Lie '51
The Lost Continent '51
Western Pacific Agent '51
Outlaw Women '52
Scotland Yard Inspector '52
John Newland
One Step Beyond '59
Don't Be Afraid of the Dark '73
The Legend of Hillbilly John '73
Anthony Newley
Summertree '71
Martin Newlin
The Crawlers '93
Joseph M. Newman
Jungle Patrol '48
Great Dan Patch '49
Love Nest '51
This Island Earth '55
The King of the Roaring '20s: The Story of Arnold Rothstein '61
Paul Newman
Rachel, Rachel '68
Sometimes a Great Notion '71
The Effect of Gamma Rays on Man-in-the-Moon Marigolds '73
The Shadow Box '80
Harry & Son '84
The Glass Menagerie '87
Fred Newmeyer
Girl Shy '24
The Freshman '25
General Spanky '36
Ted Newsom
Dracula: A Cinematic Scrapbook '91
Frankenstein: A Cinematic Scrapbook '91
Chan Wui Ngai
Way of the Black Dragon '81
Phil Nibbelink
An American Tail: Fievel Goes West '91
We're Back! A Dinosaur's Story '93
Fred Niblo
Dangerous Hours '19
Mark of Zorro '20
Sex '20
Camille '21
The Three Musketeers '21
Blood and Sand '22
Ben-Hur '26
Maurizio Nichetti
The Icicle Thief '89
Volere Volare '92
Stephano Quantestorie '93
Paul Nicholas
Daughter of Death '82
Chained Heat '83
Naked Cage '86
George Nicholls, Jr.
Finishing School '33
Anne of Green Gables '34
The Return of Peter Grimm '35
Charles A. Nichols
Charlotte's Web '79
Dudley Nichols
Sister Kenny '46
Mike Nichols
Who's Afraid of Virginia Woolf? '66
The Graduate '67
Catch-22 '70
Carnal Knowledge '71
The Day of the Dolphin '73
Silkwood '83
Gin Game '84
Heartburn '86
Biloxi Blues '88
Working Girl '88

Nichols ▶cont.

Postcards from the Edge '90
Regarding Henry '91
Wolf '94
The Birdcage '95

Arch Nicholson
Fortress '85
Dark Age '88

Jack Nicholson
Goin' South '78
The Two Jakes '90

Martin Nicholson
The Day My Parents Ran Away '93

Sam Nicholson
It's Three Strikes, Charlie Brown '86

Alex Nicol
The Screaming Skull '58
Point of Terror '71

Ted Nicolaou
Dungeonmaster '83
Terrorvision '86
Subspecies '90
Bad Channels '92
Bloodstone: Subspecies 2 '92
Bloodlust: Subspecies 3 '93
Remote '93
Dragonworld '94
Leapin' Leprechauns '95

John Nicolella
Finish Line '89
Runaway Father '91
Sunset Heat '92

Douglas C. Nicolle
Ladies of the Lotus '87

Jose Antonio Nieves-Conde
Sound of Horror '64

William Nigh
Fighting Thru '30
Border Devils '32
Without Honors '32
House of Mystery '34
Monte Carlo Nights '34
Mystery Liner '34
Headline Woman '35
Mysterious Mr. Wong '35
The Thirteenth Man '37
Mr. Wong, Detective '38
Rose of Rio Grande '38
The Abe Lincoln of Ninth Avenue '39
Mr. Wong in Chinatown '39
Mutiny in the Big House '39
Mystery of Mr. Wong '39
The Ape '40
Doomed to Die '40
The Fatal Hour '40
The Black Dragons '42
Mr. Wise Guy '42
Corregidor '43
The Ghost and the Guest '43
The Underdog '43
South of Monterey '47

Nazui Nihonmatsu
X from Outer Space '67

Rob Nilsson
Northern Lights '79
Signal 7 '83
On the Edge '86
Heat and Sunlight '87

Leonard Nimoy
Star Trek 3: The Search for Spock '84
Star Trek 4: The Voyage Home '86
Three Men and a Baby '87
The Good Mother '88
Funny About Love '90
Holy Matrimony '94

Charles Nizet
Commando Squad '76

Rudolf Noelte
The Castle '68

Chris Noonan
Babe '95

Tom Noonan
What Happened Was... '94

Tommy Noonan
Three Nuts in Search of a Bolt '64

Lindsay Norgard
Homeboys '92

Mabel Normand
Early Cinema Vol. 1 '19

Stephen Norrington
Death Machine '95

Aaron Norris
Platoon Leader '87
Braddock: Missing in Action 3 '88
Delta Force 2: Operation Stranglehold '90
The Hitman '91
Sidekicks '93
Hellbound '94
Top Dog '95

Guy Norris
Rage and Honor 2: Hostile Takeover '93

Bill W.L. Norton
More American Graffiti '79
Baby ... Secret of the Lost Legend '85
Three for the Road '87
Tour of Duty '87
Hard Rain-The Tet 1968 '89
False Arrest '92

Max Nosseck
Brighton Strangler '45
Dillinger '45
Black Beauty '46
The Hoodlum '51
Black Beauty/Courage of Black Beauty '57

Noel Nosseck
Las Vegas Lady '76
Dreamer '79
King of the Mountain '81
Return of the Rebels '81
Night Partners '83
Summer Fantasy '84
Full Exposure: The Sex Tape Scandals '89
French Silk '94
Down, Out and Dangerous '95
The Sister-in-Law '95
Tornado! '96

Thierry Notz
The Terror Within '88
Watchers 2 '90
Fortunes of War '94

Blaine Novak
Short Fuse '88

Maria Novaro
Danzon '91

Phillip Noyce
Newsfront '78
Heatwave '83
Echoes of Paradise '86
Dead Calm '89
Blind Fury '90
Patriot Games '92
Sliver '93
Clear and Present Danger '94

Simon Nuchtern
New York Nights '84
Savage Dawn '84
Silent Madness '84

Elliott Nugent
Give Me a Sailor '38
Up in Arms '44
My Favorite Brunette '47
Welcome Stranger '47
My Girl Tisa '48
My Outlaw Brother '51
Just for You '52

Victor Nunez
Gal Young 'Un '79
A Flash of Green '85
Ruby in Paradise '93

Trevor Nunn
Hedda '75
Lady Jane '85

Deland Nuse
The Chilling '89

Raphael Nussbaum
Sinai Commandos '68
Death Blow '87
Private Road: No Trespassing '87

Colin Nutley
House of Angels '92

David Nutter
Cease Fire '85
Trancers 5: Sudden Deth '94

Bruno Nuytten
Camille Claudel '89

Christian Nyby
The Thing '51
Operation C.I.A. '65
The Devlin Connection '82

Sven Nykvist
Gorilla '56
The Ox '91

Ron Nyswaner
Prince of Pennsylvania '88

Joe Oaks
Deadly Twins '85

Dan O'Bannon
Return of the Living Dead '85
The Resurrected '91

Rockne S. O'Bannon
Fear '90

Stefan Oblowsky
Other Hell '85

Arch Oboler
One Plus One '61

Edmund Oboler
Bewitched '85

Jim O'Brien
The Jewel in the Crown '84
The Dressmaker '89
Foreign Affairs '93

John O'Brien
The Big Dis '89
Vermont Is for Lovers '92

Jeffrey Obrow
Dorm That Dripped Blood '82
The Kindred '87
Servants of Twilight '91

Maurice O'Callaghan
Broken Harvest '95

Jack O'Connell
Revolution '69

Raoul O'Connell
Boys Life '94

John O'Conner
Prisoner in the Middle '74

James O'Connolly
Berserk! '67
Vendetta for the Saint '68
Crooks & Coronets '69
The Valley of Gwangi '69
Tower of Evil '72

Frank O'Connor
Free to Love '25
Spangles '26
Mystic Circle Murder '39

Jim O'Connor
Mistress Pamela '74

Pat O'Connor
Cal '84
A Month in the Country '87
Stars and Bars '88
The January Man '89
Fools of Fortune '90
Circle of Friends '94

Terry O'Connor
Early Frost '84

William O'Connor
Ten Nights in a Bar-Room '31
Cocaine Fiends '36

David Odell
Martians Go Home! '90

Sias Odendal
Nukie '93

Clifford Odets
None But the Lonely Heart '44

Luciano Odorisio
Sacrilege '86

Steve Oedekerk
Ace Ventura: When Nature Calls '95

George More O'Ferrell
Three Cases of Murder '55

George Ogilvie
Mad Max: Beyond Thunderdome '85

Gerry O'Hara
Maroc 7 '67
The Bitch '78
Leopard in the Snow '78

Terrence O'Hara
Darkroom '90
The Perfect Bride '91

Michael O'Herlihy
The Fighting Prince of Donegal '66
Mosby's Marauders '66
The One and Only, Genuine, Original Family Band '68
Smith! '69
Peter Lundy and the Medicine Hat Stallion '77
The Flame Is Love '79
Cry of the Innocent '80
A Time for Miracles '80

Don Ohlmeyer
The Heroes of Desert Storm '91

Kazuki Ohmori
Godzilla vs. Biollante '89

Tom O'Horgan
Futz '69

Kihachi Okamoto
Sword of Doom '67
Red Lion '69
Zatoichi vs. Yojimbo '70

Steven Okazaki
Living on Tokyo Time '87

Kazuyoshi Okuyama
The Mystery of Rampo '94

Sidney Olcott
From the Manger to the Cross '15
Monsieur Beaucaire '24
Ranson's Folly '26
The Claw '27

Enrico Oldoini
Bye Bye Baby '88

Ronan O'Leary
Riders to the Sea '88

Joel Oliansky
The Competition '80

Ken Olin
White Fang 2: The Myth of the White Wolf '94
In Pursuit of Honor '95

David Oliver
Cave Girl '85

Richard Oliver
A Girl to Kill For '90

Robert Oliver
Dr. Frankenstein's Castle of Freaks '74

Ron Oliver
Prom Night 3: The Last Kiss '89
Liar's Edge '92

Ruby L. Oliver
Love Your Mama '89

Hector Olivera
El Muerto '75
Fridays of Eternity '81
Funny, Dirty Little War '83
Barbarian Queen '85
Wizards of the Lost Kingdom '85
Cocaine Wars '86
Two to Tango '88
Play Murder for Me '91

Laurence Olivier
Henry V '44
Hamlet '48
Richard III '55
The Prince and the Showgirl '57

Marty Ollstein
Dangerous Love '87

Ermanno Olmi
Fiances '63
The Tree of Wooden Clogs '78

Edward James Olmos
American Me '92

William Olsen
Getting It On '83
Return to Eden '89

David O'Malley
Mountain Man '77
Kid Colter '85
Easy Wheels '89

Carlo Ombra
Dracula Blows His Cool '82

Ron O'Neal
Superfly T.N.T. '73
Up Against the Wall '91

Douglas F. Oneans
Sno-Line '85

Robert Vincent O'Neil
Blood Mania '70
The Deadly and the Beautiful '73
Paco '75
Angel '84
Avenging Angel '85

Marcel Ophuls
The Sorrow and the Pity '71

Max Ophuls
La Signora di Tutti '34
Letter from an Unknown Woman '48
Caught '49
Reckless Moment '49
La Ronde '51
Le Plaisir '52
The Earrings of Madame De... '54
Lola Montes '55

Peer J. Oppenheimer
Terror in Paradise '90

Charlie Ordonez
Forgotten Warrior '86
Wolf '86

Wyott Ordung
Monster from the Ocean Floor '54

Mario Orfini
Fair Game '89

Valery Orgorodnikov
Burglar '87

Dominic Orlando
Knights of the City '85

Susan Orlikoff-Simon
Image of Passion '86

Stuart Orme
The Heist '89
Hands of a Murderer '90
The Puppet Masters '94

James Ormerod
Next Victim '74
Frankenstein '82

Ron Ormond
King of the Bullwhip '51
Yes, Sir, Mr. Bones '51
The Black Lash '52
Mesa of Lost Women '52
The Girl from Tobacco Row '66

Peter Ormrod
Eat the Peach '86

Alan Ormsby
Deranged '74

Bruce Ornstein
Jack and His Friends '92

Gary Orona
The Bikini Car Wash Company 2 '92
Great Bikini Off-Road Adventure '94
Stripshow '95

James Orr
Breaking All the Rules '85
Mr. Destiny '90
Man of the House '95

Valintino Orsini
Smugglers '75

Kenny Ortega
Newsies '92
Hocus Pocus '93

Aaron Osborne
Zarkorr! The Invader '96

Kent Osborne
Women Unchained '70s

Nagisa Oshima
The Cruel Story of Youth '60
The Sun's Burial '60
Violence at Noon '66
The Empire of Passion '76
In the Realm of the Senses '76
In the Realm of Passion '80

Merry Christmas, Mr. Lawrence '83
Max, Mon Amour '86

Cliff Osmond
The Penitent '88

Jaime Osorio Gomez
Confessing to Laura '90

Sam O'Steen
Brand New Life '72
Sparkle '76
The Best Little Girl in the World '81

Suzanne Osten
The Mozart Brothers '86

Thaddeus O'Sullivan
December Bride '91

Gerd Oswald
Crime of Passion '57
Paris Holiday '57

Richard Oswald
Cesare Borgia '23
My Song Goes Round the World '34
The Lovable Cheat '49

Dominique Othenin-Girard
After Darkness '85
Halloween 5: The Revenge of Michael Myers '89
Night Angel '90
Omen 4: The Awakening '91
Beyond Desire '94
Private Lessons, Another Story '94

Katsuhiro Otomo
Akira '89

Matteo Ottaviano
Single Room Furnished '68

Henry Otto
Dante's Inferno '24

Filippo Ottoni
Detective School Dropouts '85

Lar Henrik Ottoson
Gorilla '56

Idrissa Ouedraogo
Tilai '90

Jean-Paul Ouellette
The Unnamable '88
Chinatown Connection '90
The Unnamable 2: The Statement of Randolph Carter '92

Gerard Oury
The Sucker '65
La Grande Vadrouille '66
The Brain '69
Delusions of Grandeur '76

Cliff Owen
The Wrong Arm of the Law '63
The Bawdy Adventures of Tom Jones '76

Don Owen
Unfinished Business '89

Richard Owens
Killer Likes Candy '78

Earl Owensby
Manhunter '83

Jan Oxenberg
Thank You & Good Night '91

Frank Oz
The Dark Crystal '82
The Muppets Take Manhattan '84
Little Shop of Horrors '86
Dirty Rotten Scoundrels '88
What About Bob? '91
Housesitter '92
The Indian in the Cupboard '95

Sakae Ozawa
The Street Fighter '75
The Street Fighter's Last Revenge '79

Fedor Ozep
Whispering City '47

Ali Ozgenturk
The Horse '82

Yasujiro Ozu
Record of a Tenement Gentleman '47
Late Spring '49
Early Summer '51
Tokyo Story '53
Equinox Flower '58
Drifting Weeds '59
An Autumn Afternoon '62

G.W. Pabst
Joyless Street '25
Secrets of a Soul '25
Pandora's Box '28
Diary of a Lost Girl '29
Westfront 1918 '30
Kameradschaft '31
The Threepenny Opera '31
Don Quixote '35

Frank Packard
In Your Face '77

Calvin Jackson Padget
Secret Agent Super Dragon '66
The Battle of El Alamein '68

Anthony Page
Alpha Beta '73
Pueblo Affair '73
Missiles of October '74
F. Scott Fitzgerald in Hollywood '76
I Never Promised You a Rose Garden '77
The Lady Vanishes '79
Absolution '81
Bill '81
Johnny Belinda '82
Bill: On His Own '83
The Grace Kelly Story '83
Forbidden '85
Heartbreak House '86
Monte Carlo '86
Scandal in a Small Town '88
The Nightmare Years '89
Final Warning '90
Middlemarch '93

Teddy Page
Blood Debts '83

Marcel Pagliero
The Respectful Prostitute '52

Marcel Pagnol
The Baker's Wife '33
Angele '34
Cesar '36
Harvest '37
Le Schpountz '38
Well-Digger's Daughter '46
Topaze '51
Letters from My Windmill '54

John Paizs
The Big Crimewave '86

Alan J. Pakula
The Sterile Cuckoo '69
Klute '71
The Parallax View '74
All the President's Men '76
Comes a Horseman '78
Starting Over '79
Rollover '81
Sophie's Choice '82
Dream Lover '85
Orphans '87
See You in the Morning '89
Presumed Innocent '90
Consenting Adults '92
The Pelican Brief '93

George Pal
Tom Thumb '58
The Time Machine '60
Atlantis, the Lost Continent '61
The Wonderful World of the Brothers Grimm '62
7 Faces of Dr. Lao '63

Laszlo Pal
Journey to Spirit Island '92

Tom Palazzolo
Caligari's Cure '82

Euzhan Palcy
Sugar Cane Alley '83
A Dry White Season '89

Larry Pall
Off Your Rocker '80

Jean Marie Pallardy
Truck Stop

Rospo Pallenberg
Cutting Class '89

Anders Palm
Unmasked Part 25 '88
Murder on Line One '90
Dead Certain '92

Thomas Palmer, Jr.
Forever: A Ghost of a Love Story '92

Tony Palmer
Wagner: The Complete Epic '85
Wagner: The Movie '85
The Children '90

Conrad Palmisano
Busted Up '86
Space Rage '86

Bruce Paltrow
A Little Sex '82

Herve Palud
Little Indian, Big City '95

Rick Pamplin
Provoked '89

George Pan-Andreas
Crime Killer '85

Jafar Panahi
The White Balloon '95

Norman Panama
Above and Beyond '53
Court Jester '56
The Trap '59
The Road to Hong Kong '62
How to Commit Marriage '69
I Will, I Will for Now '76
Barnaby and Me '77

Gleb Panfilov
The Theme '79

Domenico Paolella
Pirates of the Coast '61

Deno Paoli
The Legend of Frank Woods '77

Phedon Papamichael
Sketch Artist '92
Dark Side of Genius '94

Michael Papas
The Lifetaker '89

Lakis Papastathis
When the Greeks '81

Giullo Paradisi
The Visitor '80
Spaghetti House '82

Sergei Paradjanov
Shadows of Forgotten Ancestors '64
The Color of Pomegranates '69
The Legend of Suram Fortress '85
Ashik Kerib '88

John Paragon
Double Trouble '91
Ring of the Musketeers '93
Twinsitters '95

Paul S. Parco
Deadly Alliance '78
Pucker Up and Bark Like a Dog '89

Domonic Paris
Dracula's Last Rites '79
Splitz '84

Jerry Paris
Don't Raise the Bridge, Lower the River '68
How Sweet It Is! '68
Never a Dull Moment '68
Viva Max '69
The Passing of Evil '70
Star Spangled Girl '71
Only with Married Men '74
How to Break Up a Happy Divorce '76
Make Me an Offer '80
Police Academy 2: Their First Assignment '85
Police Academy 3: Back in Training '86

Dean Parisot
Framed '90

Chul-Soo Park
301, 302 '94

Richard W. Park
Gang Justice '94

Alan Parker
Bugsy Malone '76
Midnight Express '78
Fame '80
Pink Floyd: The Wall '82
Shoot the Moon '82
Birdy '84
Angel Heart '87
Mississippi Burning '88
Come See the Paradise '90
The Commitments '91
The Road to Wellville '94

Albert Parker
The Black Pirate '26
Late Extra '35

Ben Parker
The Invisible Avenger '58

Cary Parker
The Girl in the Picture '86

John Parker
Daughter of Horror '55

Norton S. Parker
The Road to Ruin '28

Oliver Parker
Othello '95

Percy G. Parker
Castle of the Creeping Flesh '68

Rocky Parker
Ava's Magical Adventure '94

Eric Parkinson
Future Shock '93

Tom Parkinson
Disciple of Death '72

Gordon Parks
The Learning Tree '69
Shaft '71
Shaft's Big Score '72
Three the Hard Way '74
Half Slave, Half Free '85

Gordon Parks, Jr.
Superfly '72
Aaron Loves Angela '75

Hugh Parks
Deadly Innocence '88
Shakma '89
Dream Trap '90
King's Ransom '91
Shoot '92

Michael Parks
The Return of Josey Wales '86

Billy Parolini
Igor & the Lunatics '85

Gianfranco Parolini
The Fury of Hercules '61
Samson '61

John H. Parr
Pursuit '90
Prey for the Hunter '92

Larry Parr
A Soldier's Tale '91

James D. Parriott
Heart Condition '90

Robert Parrish
Cry Danger '51
Fire Down Below '57
Bobo '67
Casino Royale '67
Journey to the Far Side of the Sun '69
A Town Called Hell '72
The Destructors '74

James Parrott
Pardon Us '31

Gordon Parry
Tom Brown's School Days '51
Innocents in Paris '53

John Parsons
Watched '73

Gabriel Pascal
Major Barbara '41
Caesar and Cleopatra '46

Michael Paseornek
Vibrations '94

Pier Paolo Pasolini
Accatone! '61
Mamma Roma '62
RoGoPaG '62
The Gospel According to St. Matthew '64
Love Meetings '64
The Hawks & the Sparrows '67
Oedipus Rex '67
Teorema '68
Porcile '69
The Decameron '70
Medea '70
Notes for an African Orestes '70
The Canterbury Tales '71
Arabian Nights '74
Salo, or the 120 Days of Sodom '75

John Pasquin
The Santa Clause '94

Ivan Passer
Born to Win '71
Law and Disorder '74
Crime & Passion '75
Silver Bears '78
Cutter's Way '81
The Nightingale '83
Creator '85
Haunted Summer '88
Fourth Story '90
Stalin '92

Giovanni Pastrone
Cabiria '14
Salammbo '14

Franca Pasut
Flashdance '83

Tom Patchett
Best Legs in the 8th Grade '84

Michael Pate
Tim '79

Raju Patel
In the Shadow of Kilimanjaro '86

Sharad Patel
Amin: The Rise and Fall '82

Stuart Paton
20,000 Leagues Under the Sea '16
Chinatown After Dark '31

Matthew Patrick
Tainted Blood '93

Michael Patrick
Hider in the House '90

Nigel Patrick
Johnny Nobody '61

Robert Patrick
Road to Nashville '67

Frank Patterson
Black Snow '93

John D. Patterson
Legend of Earl Durand '74
Deadly Innocence '88
The Spring '89
Taken Away '89
Grave Secrets: The Legacy of Hilltop Drive '92

Pat Patterson
The Body Shop '72

Ray Patterson
The Good, the Bad, and Huckleberry Hound '88

Richard Patterson
J-Men Forever! '79

Willi Patterson
Dreams Lost, Dreams Found '87

Michael Pattinson
Moving Out '83
Ground Zero '88
...Almost '90
One Crazy Night '93

Peter Patzak
Slaughterday '77
Lethal Obsession '87
Midnight Cop '88

Byron Paul
Lt. Robin Crusoe, U.S.N. '66

Steven Paul
Falling in Love Again '80
Slapstick of Another Kind '84
Eternity '90

Stuart Paul
Emanon '86
Fate '90

David Paulsen
Schizoid '80

George Pavlou
Transmutations '85
Rawhead Rex '87
Yuri Pavlov
Creation of Adam '93
Michael Pavone
Chameleon '95
Clark Paylow
Ring of Terror '62
Dave Payne
Concealed Weapon '94
Alien Terminator '95
Criminal Hearts '95
John Payson
Joe's Apartment '96
Barry Peak
The Big Hurt '87
Michael Pearce
James Joyce's Women '85
Richard Pearce
Heartland '81
Sessions '83
Threshold '83
Country '84
No Mercy '86
Dead Man Out '89
The Final Days '89
The Long Walk Home '89
Leap of Faith '92
A Family Thing '96
Steven Pearl
At First Sight '95
Robert E. Pearso
Devil & Leroy Basset '73
George Pearson
A Shot in the Dark '33
Midnight at the Wax Museum '36
Peter Pearson
Paperback Hero '73
Tales of the Klondike: The Unexpected '87
Max Pecas
Sweet Ecstasy '62
Erotic Touch of Hot Skin '65
The Sensuous Teenager '70
Brian Peck
The Willies '90
Ron Peck
Empire State '87
Sam Peckinpah
Deadly Companions '61
Ride the High Country '62
Major Dundee '65
The Wild Bunch '69
Ballad of Cable Hogue '70
The Getaway '72
Junior Bonner '72
Straw Dogs '72
Pat Garrett & Billy the Kid '73
Bring Me the Head of Alfredo Garcia '74
The Killer Elite '75
Cross of Iron '76
Convoy '78
The Osterman Weekend '83
Larry Peerce
The Incident '67
Goodbye Columbus '69
The Sporting Club '72
Ash Wednesday '73
A Separate Peace '73
The Stranger Who Looks Like Me '74
The Other Side of the Mountain '75
Two Minute Warning '76
The Other Side of the Mountain, Part 2 '78
The Bell Jar '79
Love Child '82
Hard to Hold '84
Queenie '87
Elvis and Me '88
The Neon Empire '89
Wired '89
The Court Martial of Jackie Robinson '90
A Woman Named Jackie '91
Prison for Children '93
Barbara Peeters
Bury Me an Angel '71
Summer School Teachers '75
Starhops '78
Humanoids from the Deep '80
Antonio Pelaez
Crystalstone '88
Anthony Pelissier
The Rocking Horse Winner '49
Encore '52
Scott Pembroke
Medicine Man '30
Nettie Pena
Home Sweet Home '80
Maurice Penczner
I Was a Zombie for the FBI '82
Sze Ma Peng
Venus the Ninja '80s
Chang Peng-I
Shaolin Kung Fu Mystagogue '84
Arthur Penn
The Left-Handed Gun '58
The Miracle Worker '62
Mickey One '65
The Chase '66
Bonnie & Clyde '67
Alice's Restaurant '69
Little Big Man '70
Night Moves '75
Missouri Breaks '76
Four Friends '81
Target '85
Dead of Winter '87
Penn and Teller Get Killed '90
The Portrait '93
Leonard Penn
A Man Called Adam '66
The Dark Secret of Harvest Home '78
Judgment in Berlin '88
Sean Penn
The Indian Runner '91
The Crossing Guard '94
D.A. Pennebaker
Bob Dylan: Don't Look Back '91
The War Room '93
Eagle Pennell
The Whole Shootin' Match '79
Last Night at the Alamo '83
Ice House '89
C.M. Pennington-Richards
Hour of Decision '57
Ladies Who Do '63
David Peoples
The Blood of Heroes '89
Richard Pepin
Fist of Honor '92
Cyber-Tracker '93
T-Force '94
Hologram Man '95
The Silencers '95
Clare Peploe
High Season '88
Mark Peploe
Afraid of the Dark '92
Frank Peregini
Scar of Shame '27
Miguel Pereira
Veronico Cruz '87
Hope Perello
Howling 6: The Freaks '90
Pet Shop '94
Antonio Perez
The 13th Mission '91
Jack Perez
America's Deadliest Home Video '91
Etienne Perier
Murder at 45 R.P.M. '65
The Hot Line '69
Zeppelin '71
Investigation '79
Paco Perinan
Against the Wind '90
Zoran Perisic
The Phoenix and the Magic Carpet '95
Anthony Perkins
Psycho 3 '86
Lucky Stiff '88
Harold Perkins
Help Wanted Female '68
Paul Perri
Revenge of the Virgins '62
Frank Perry
David and Lisa '62
ABC Stage 67: Truman Capote's A Christmas Memory '66
The Swimmer '68
Last Summer '69
Diary of a Mad Housewife '70
Rancho Deluxe '75
Skag '79
Mommie Dearest '81
Monsignor '82
Compromising Positions '85
Hello Again '87
Peter Perry
Cycle Vixens '79
Bill Persky
How to Pick Up Girls '78
Serial '80
Wait Till Your Mother Gets Home '83
Francisco J. Lombardi Pery
The City and the Dogs '85
P.J. Pesce
Body Waves '92
The Desperate Trail '94
Brooke L. Peters
The Unearthly '57
Anatomy of a Psycho '61
Charlie Peters
Passed Away '92
Daniel Peters
Masseuse '95
Wolfgang Petersen
For Your Love Only '79
Das Boot '81
The NeverEnding Story '84
Enemy Mine '85
Shattered '91
In the Line of Fire '93
Outbreak '94
Daniel M. Peterson
Girlfriend from Hell '89
Kristine Peterson
Deadly Dreams '88
Body Chemistry '90
Critters 3 '91
Lower Level '91
Eden 2 '93
Eden 4 '93
The Hard Truth '94
Christopher Petit
Unsuitable Job for a Woman '82
Chinese Boxes '84
Elio Petri
10th Victim '65
Dan Petrie, Jr.
Toy Soldiers '91
In the Army Now '94
Daniel Petrie
The Bramble Bush '60
A Raisin in the Sun '61
Stolen Hours '63
Spy with a Cold Nose '66
Silent Night, Lonely Night '69
Moon of the Wolf '72
Neptune Factor '73
Buster and Billie '74
Lifeguard '75
Eleanor & Franklin '76
Sybil '76
The Betsy '78
Resurrection '80
Fort Apache, the Bronx '81
Six Pack '82
The Dollmaker '84
The Bay Boy '85
Execution of Raymond Graham '85
Square Dance '87
Cocoon: The Return '88
Rocket Gibraltar '88
Mark Twain and Me '91
Lassie '94
Kissinger and Nixon '96
Donald Petrie
Mystic Pizza '88
Opportunity Knocks '90
The Favor '92
Grumpy Old Men '93
Richie Rich '94
Boris L. Petroff
Hats Off '37
Outcasts of the City '58
Giulio Petroni
Blood and Guns '79
Vladimir Petrov
Peter the First: Part 1 '37
Peter the First: Part 2 '38
The Inspector General '54
Joseph Pevney
Meet Danny Wilson '52
Away All Boats '56
Istanbul '57
Man of a Thousand Faces '57
Tammy and the Bachelor '57
Torpedo Run '58
Cash McCall '60
Night of the Grizzly '66
Who Is the Black Dahlia? '75
Mysterious Island of Beautiful Women '79
John Peyser
Four Rode Out '69
Kashmiri Run '69
The Centerfold Girls '74
Scott Pfeiffer
Firefight '87
Michael Pfleghar
Oldest Profession '67
Will Phelps
North Shore '87
Lee Philips
The Stranger Within '74
Sweet Hostage '75
War Between the Tates '76
The Spell '77
Special Olympics '78
Hardhat & Legs '80
On the Right Track '81
Mae West '84
Samson and Delilah '84
Barnum '86
The Blue Lightning '86
Windmills of the Gods '88
Blind Vengeance '90
Silent Motive '91
Harald Phillipe
Escape from the KGB '87
Bill Phillips
There Goes the Neighborhood '92
Lou Diamond Phillips
Dangerous Touch '94
Sioux City '94
Maurice Phillips
Riders of the Storm '88
Enid Is Sleeping '90
Another You '91
Nick Phillips
Criminally Insane '75
Crazy Fat Ethel II '85
Death Nurse '87
Toby Phillips
The Pamela Principle '91
Killer Looks '94
Maurice Pialat
Loulou '80
A Nos Amours '84
Police '85
Under Satan's Sun '87
Van Gogh '92
Miguel Picazo
Extramuros '85
Picha
Shame of the Jungle '90
Irving Pichel
The Most Dangerous Game '32
She '35
Dance Hall '41
The Great Commandment '41
Colonel Effingham's Raid '45
Tomorrow Is Forever '46
They Won't Believe Me '47
The Miracle of the Bells '48
Mr. Peabody & the Mermaid '48
Destination Moon '50
The Great Rupert '50
Quicksand '50
Santa Fe '51
Day of Triumph '54
Lupu Pick
Shattered '21
Rex Pickett
From Hollywood to Deadwood '89
Arthur C. Pierce
Las Vegas Hillbillys '66
Women of the Prehistoric Planet '66
Charles B. Pierce
Legend of Boggy Creek '75
Town that Dreaded Sundown '76
Grayeagle '77
Norseman '78
The Evictors '79
Boggy Creek II '83
Sacred Ground '83
Hawken's Breed '87
Arthur Pierson
Home Town Story '51
Carl Pierson
The New Frontier '35
Frank Pierson
The Looking Glass War '69
A Star is Born '76
King of the Gypsies '78
Somebody Has to Shoot the Picture '90
Citizen Cohn '92
Lakota Woman: Siege at Wounded Knee '94
Truman '95
R.E. Pierson
Claws '77
Sam Pillsbury
Starlight Hotel '90
Zandalee '91
Into the Badlands '92
Phillip Pine
Pot, Parents, and Police '71
William H. Pine
Swamp Fire '46
Dynamite '49
He Ping
Red Firecracker, Green Firecracker '93
Yuen Woo Ping
Eagle's Shadow '84
Wing Chun '94
Sidney Pink
Finger on the Trigger '65
The Christmas Kid '68
Efren C. Pinon
Blind Rage '78
Claude Pinoteau
The Slap '76
La Boum '81
Gordon Pinsent
John and the Missus '87
Seth Pinsker
The Hidden 2 '94
Lucian Pintilie
The Oak '93
An Unforgettable Summer '94
Ward Six
Ernie Pintoff
Dynamite Chicken '70
Who Killed Mary What's 'Er Name? '71
Blade '72
Jaguar Lives '79
Lunch Wagon '81
St. Helen's, Killer Volcano '82
Mario Pinzauti
Mandinga '77
Bret Piper
They Bite '95
Robert Pirosh
Go for Broke! '51
Massimo Pirri
Could It Happen Here? '80s
Fatal Fix '80s
Mark Pirro
A Polish Vampire in Burbank '80
Curse of the Queerwolf '87
Deathrow Gameshow '88
Buford's Beach Bunnies '92

Peter Pistor
The Fence '94

Vassili Pitchul
Little Vera '88

Glen Pitre
Belizaire the Cajun '86

Arthur Pitt
Sundance and the Kid '76

Walter W. Pitt, III
Welcome Back Mr. Fox '83

Bruce Pittman
Mark of Cain '84
Confidential '86
Hello Mary Lou: Prom Night 2 '87
Where the Spirit Lives '89
Kurt Vonnegut's Harrison Bergeron '95

Radoslaw Piwowarski
Train to Hollywood '86

Lou Place
Daddy-O '59

Lucas Platt
Girl in the Cadillac '94

Allen Plone
Night Screams '87
Phantom of the Ritz '88
Sweet Justice '92

Bill Plympton
The Tune '92

Amos Poe
The Foreigner '78
Alphabet City '84
Dead Weekend '95

Rudiger Poe
Monster High '89

Benoit Poelvoorde
Man Bites Dog '91

Sidney Poitier
Buck and the Preacher '72
Uptown Saturday Night '74
Let's Do It Again '75
Piece of the Action '77
Stir Crazy '80
Hanky Panky '82
Fast Forward '84
Ghost Dad '90

James Polakof
Slashed Dreams '74
Midnight Auto Supply '78
Swim Team '79
Balboa '82
Demon Rage '82
The Vals '85

Roman Polanski
Two Men & a Wardrobe '58
Fat and the Lean '61
Knife in the Water '62
Repulsion '65
Cul de Sac '66
The Fearless Vampire Killers '67
Rosemary's Baby '68
Macbeth '71
Diary of Forbidden Dreams '73
Chinatown '74
The Tenant '76
Tess '80
Pirates '86
Frantic '88
Bitter Moon '92
Death and the Maiden '94

Stephen Poliakoff
Hidden City '87
Close My Eyes '91
Century '94

Gian Polidoro
Loose in New York '80s

Jeff Pollack
Above the Rim '94

Sydney Pollack
The Slender Thread '65
This Property is Condemned '66
The Scalphunters '68
They Shoot Horses, Don't They? '69
Jeremiah Johnson '72
The Way We Were '73
Three Days of the Condor '75
The Yakuza '75
Bobby Deerfield '77
The Electric Horseman '79
Absence of Malice '81
Tootsie '82
Out of Africa '85
Havana '90
The Firm '93
Sabrina '95

Bud Pollard
The Black King '32
Beware '46
Tall, Tan and Terrific '46
Look Out Sister '48

Harry Pollard
California Straight Ahead '25

Jean-Daniel Pollet
Six in Paris '68

Jack Pollexfen
The Indestructible Man '56

George Pollock
Stranger in Town '57
Broth of a Boy '59
Murder She Said '62
Murder at the Gallop '63
Murder Ahoy '64
Murder Most Foul '65

Abraham Polonsky
Force of Evil '49
Tell Them Willie Boy Is Here '69
Romance of a Horsethief '71

Francisco Lara Polop
Murder Mansion '70

Barry Poltermann
The Unearthing '93

Erich Pommer
Beachcomber '38

Gillo Pontecorvo
Kapo '59
The Battle of Algiers '66
Burn! '70

Maurizio Ponzi
Pool Hustlers '83

Lea Pool
Straight for the Heart '88
The Savage Woman '91

Patrick C. Poole
Oklahoma Bound '81

Angela Pope
Captives '94

Tim Pope
The Crow 2: City of Angels '96

Petru Popescu
Death of an Angel '86

Leo Popkin
Gang War '40
The Well '51

Edwin S. Porter
The Great Train Robbery: Cinema Begins '03
The Count of Monte Cristo '12

Eric Porter
Marco Polo, Jr. '72

Jeffrey Porter
The Liar's Club '93

Rafael Portillo
The Curse of the Aztec Mummy '59
Curse of the Aztec Mummy/ Robot vs. the Aztec Mummy '59
The Robot vs. the Aztec Mummy '59
Broken Trust '93

Ralph Portillo
Hollywood Dreams '94

Bill Posner
Teenage Strangler '64

Geoffrey Posner
The Young Ones '88

Ted Post
Legend of Tom Dooley '59
Hang 'Em High '67
Beneath the Planet of the Apes '70
Yuma '70
The Baby '72
Harrad Experiment '73
Magnum Force '73
Whiffs '75
Go Tell the Spartans '78
Good Guys Wear Black '78
Nightkill '80
Diary of a Teenage Hitchhiker '82
Stagecoach '86
The Human Shield '92

George Potter
Seven Sixgunners '87

H.C. Potter
Beloved Enemy '36
The Cowboy and the Lady '38
Shopworn Angel '38
The Story of Vernon and Irene Castle '39
Second Chorus '40
Mr. Lucky '43
The Farmer's Daughter '47
Mr. Blandings Builds His Dream House '48
The Time of Your Life '48
The Miniver Story '50

Sally Potter
Orlando '92

Gerald Potterton
Heavy Metal '81

Richard Pottier
The Rape of the Sabines '61

Wallace Potts
Psycho Cop '88

Mansour Pourmand
Zipperface '92

Dick Powell
Split Second '53
The Conqueror '56
Enemy Below '57
The Hunters '58

Frank Powell
A Fool There Was '14

Michael Powell
The Phantom Light '35
Edge of the World '37
Spy in Black '39
The Lion Has Wings '40
The Thief of Bagdad '40
The Forty-Ninth Parallel '41
One of Our Aircraft Is Missing '41
The Life and Death of Colonel Blimp '43
A Canterbury Tale '44
I Know Where I'm Going '45
Black Narcissus '47
The Red Shoes '48
The Small Back Room '49
The Elusive Pimpernel '50
The Tales of Hoffmann '51
Night Ambush '57
Pursuit of the Graf Spee '57
Peeping Tom '63

Tristam Powell
Ghostwriter '84
American Friends '91

John Power
Alice to Nowhere '86
All My Sons '86
Father '90
Charles & Diana: A Palace Divided '93
Stephen King's The Tommyknockers '93

Stanley Prager
Car 54, Where Are You? '61
Bang Bang Kid '67
Madigan's Millions '67

Jean-Yves Prate
Regina '83

Michael Preece
Prize Fighter '79

Otto Preminger
Laura '44
Forever Amber '47
The Moon Is Blue '53
Carmen Jones '54
River of No Return '54
The Court Martial of Billy Mitchell '55
The Man with the Golden Arm '55
Bonjour Tristesse '57
Saint Joan '57
Anatomy of a Murder '59
Exodus '60
Advise and Consent '62
The Cardinal '63
In Harm's Way '65
Rosebud '75
The Human Factor '79

John Prescott
Bootleg '89

Emeric Pressburger
One of Our Aircraft Is Missing '41
The Life and Death of Colonel Blimp '43
A Canterbury Tale '44
Black Narcissus '47
The Red Shoes '48
The Small Back Room '49
The Tales of Hoffmann '51
Night Ambush '57

Michael Pressman
The Great Texas Dynamite Chase '76
The Bad News Bears in Breaking Training '77
Secret Passions '78
Boulevard Nights '79
Those Lips, Those Eyes '80
Some Kind of Hero '82
Doctor Detroit '83
The Imposter '84
And the Children Shall Lead '85
To Heal a Nation '88
Quicksand: No Escape '91
Teenage Mutant Ninja Turtles 2: The Secret of the Ooze '91

Gaylene Preston
Dark of the Night '85

Ruben Preuss
In Dangerous Company '88
Blackmail '91
Write to Kill '91
Almost Dead '94
Dead on Sight '94

Pierre Prevert
Voyage-Suprise '46

Steve Previn
Almost Angels '62
Escapade in Florence '62
Waltz King '63

B. Lawrence Price
Teenage Devil Dolls '53

David F. Price
To Die for 2: Son of Darkness '91
Children of the Corn 2: The Final Sacrifice '92
Dr. Jekyll and Ms. Hyde '95

Will Price
Rock, Rock, Rock '56

Joseph Prieto
Shanty Tramp '67
Savages from Hell '68

Barry Primus
Mistress '91

Prince
Under the Cherry Moon '86
Graffiti Bridge '90

Harold Prince
Something for Everyone '70
A Little Night Music '77
Sweeney Todd: The Demon Barber of Fleet Street '84

Jonathan Prince
Camp Nowhere '94

Ian Pringle
Panic Station '82

David A. Prior
Killzone '85
Killer Workout '86
Deadly Prey '87
Death Chase '87
Mankillers '87
Hell on the Battleground '88
Night Wars '88
Final Sanction '89
Jungle Assault '89
The Lost Platoon '89
Rapid Fire '89
Future Zone '90
Invasion Force '90
Lock 'n' Load '90
White Fury '90
Center of the Web '92
Double Threat '92
Mardi Gras for the Devil '93
Raw Justice '93
Felony '95
Mutant Species '95

Vincent J. Privitera
Witchfire '86

Elaine Proctor
Friends '95

Franco Prosperi
Counter Punch '71
Throne of Fire '82
The Wild Beasts '85

Yakov Protazanov
Early Russian Cinema, Vol. 8: Iakov Protazanov '16
Aelita: Queen of Mars '24

A.J. Prowse
Driving Force '88

Andrew Prowse
Demonstone '89

Alex Proyas
The Crow '93

Craig Pryce
Revenge of the Radioactive Reporter '91
The Dark '94

Richard Pryor
Jo Jo Dancer, Your Life is Calling '86

Alexander Ptushko
The Magic Voyage of Sinbad '52
Sword & the Dragon '56

Vsevolod Pudovkin
Mystery of the Leaping Fish/ Chess Fever '25
Mother '26
The End of St. Petersburg '27
Storm Over Asia '28

Luis Puenzo
The Official Story '85
Old Gringo '89
The Plague '92

Evelyn Purcell
Nobody's Fool '86
Woman Undone '95

Joseph Purcell
Delos Adventure '86

Edmund Purdom
Don't Open Till Christmas '84

Jon Purdy
Reflections in the Dark '94
Dillinger and Capone '95

Manfred Purzer
Girls Riot '88

Dorothy Ann Puzo
Cold Steel '87

Joe Pytka
Let It Ride '89

Albert Pyun
Sword & the Sorcerer '82
Dangerously Close '86
Radioactive Dreams '86
Alien from L.A. '87
Captain America '89
Cyborg '89
Down Twisted '89
Dollman '90
Kickboxer 2: The Road Back '90
Bloodmatch '91
Arcade '93
Brain Smasher...A Love Story '93
Deceit '93
Knights '93
Nemesis '93
Hong Kong '97 '94
Kickboxer 4: The Aggressor '94
Spitfire '94
Heatseeker '95
Nemesis 3: Time Lapse '96

Mohy Quandour
The Spectre of Edgar Allen Poe '73

John Quested
Loophole '83

George P. Quigley
Murder with Music '45

Thomas Quillen
Apache Blood '75

Richard Quine
My Sister Eileen '55
Full of Life '56
Solid Gold Cadillac '56
Bell, Book and Candle '58
Strangers When We Meet '60
The World of Suzie Wong '60
How to Murder Your Wife '64

Quine ▶cont.

Paris When It Sizzles '64
Sex and the Single Girl '64
Hotel '67
Oh Dad, Poor Dad (Momma's Hung You in the Closet & I'm Feeling So Sad) '67
Gun Crazy '69
W '74
Prisoner of Zenda '79

Anthony Quinn
The Buccaneer '58

James Quinn
Blind Man's Bluff '91

John Quinn
Cheerleader Camp '88
Total Exposure '91
The Magic of the Golden Bear: Goldy 3 '94

Gene Quintano
Honeymoon Academy '90
Why Me? '90
National Lampoon's Loaded Weapon 1 '93

Carlo U. Quinterio
Night Train to Venice '93

Jose Quintero
Medea '59
Roman Spring of Mrs. Stone '61

Byron Quisenberry
Scream '83

Ellis Raab
You Can't Take It with You '84

Arthur Maria Rabenalt
Unnatural '52

Al Raboch
The Crimson Trail '35

Fons Rademakers
Because of the Cats '74
The Assault '86
The Rose Garden '89

Peter Rader
Grandma's House '88
Hired to Kill '91

Michael Radford
Another Time, Another Place '83
1984 '84
White Mischief '88
The Postman '94

Robert Radler
Best of the Best '89
Best of the Best 2 '93
Showdown '93

Eric Radomski
Batman: Mask of the Phantasm '93

Geza Radvanyi
Women in Prison '49

Michael Raeburn
Laserblast '78
Killing Heat '84
Jit '94

Bob Rafelson
Head '68
Five Easy Pieces '70
The King of Marvin Gardens '72
Stay Hungry '76
The Postman Always Rings Twice '81
Black Widow '87
Mountains of the Moon '90
Man Trouble '92
Picture Windows '95

Piccio Raffanini
Obsession: A Taste for Fear '89

Kevin Rafferty
The Atomic Cafe '82

Stewart Raffill
The Tender Warrior '71
When the North Wind Blows '74
Across the Great Divide '76
The Adventures of the Wilderness Family '76
High Risk '76
Sea Gypsies '78
Ice Pirates '84
The Philadelphia Experiment '84
Mac and Me '88
Mannequin 2: On the Move '91
Tammy and the T-Rex '94

Alan Rafkin
The Ghost and Mr. Chicken '66
The Shakiest Gun in the West '68

Ubaldo Ragona
The Last Man on Earth '64

Ed Ragozzini
Sasquatch '76

Ken Raich
Hollywood Hot Tubs 2: Educating Crystal '89

Steve Railsback
The Spy Within '94

Sam Raimi
Evil Dead '83
Crimewave '85
Evil Dead 2: Dead by Dawn '87
Darkman '90
Army of Darkness '92
The Quick and the Dead '94

Paul Raimondi
Crosscut '96

Yvonne Rainer
The Man Who Envied Women '85

Frank Rainone
Me and the Mob '94

Alvin Rakoff
Room 43 '58
Say Hello to Yesterday '71
King Solomon's Treasure '76
City on Fire '78
Death Ship '80
Dirty Tricks '81
Mister Halpren & Mister Johnson '83
The First Olympics: Athens 1896 '84
A Voyage' Round My Father '89

Alexander Ramati
The Assisi Underground '84

Victor Rambaldi
Decoy '95

Vittoria Rambaldi
Primal Rage '90

Harold Ramis
Caddyshack '80
National Lampoon's Vacation '83
Club Paradise '86
Groundhog Day '93
Stuart Saves His Family '94
Multiplicity '96

Patrick Rand
Mom '89

Addison Randall
Chance '89
East L.A. Warriors '89
The Killing Zone '90

Tony Randel
Hellbound: Hellraiser 2 '88
Amityville 1992: It's About Time '92
Children of the Night '92
Ticks '93
Rattled '96

Arthur Rankin, Jr.
Santa Claus Is Coming to Town '70
The Ballad of Paul Bunyan '72
The Hobbit '78
The Return of the King '80
Flight of Dragons '82

Lazlo Ranody
Nobody's Daughter '76

Mort Ransen
Margaret's Museum '95

Whitney Ransick
Hand Gun '93

Frederic Raphael
Women & Men: Stories of Seduction '90

Joel Rapp
The Battle of Blood Island '60

Mark Rappaport
Rock Hudson's Home Movies '92

Jean-Paul Rappeneau
Lovers Like Us '75
Swashbuckler '84
Cyrano de Bergerac '90
The Horseman on the Roof '95

Irving Rapper
Now, Voyager '42
The Adventures of Mark Twain '44
The Corn is Green '45
Rhapsody in Blue '45
Deception '46
Forever Female '53
The Brave One '56
Marjorie Morningstar '58
Joseph & His Brethren '60
Born Again '78

Steve Rash
The Buddy Holly Story '78
Under the Rainbow '81
Rich Hall's Vanishing America '86
Can't Buy Me Love '87
Queens Logic '91
Son-in-Law '93
Eddie '96

Jay Raskin
I Married a Vampire '87

Daniel Raskov
Wedding Band '89
The Masters of Menace '90
A Kiss Goodnight '94

Lars Rasmussen
The Littlest Viking '94

Tina Rathborne
Zelly & Me '88

Gregory Ratoff
Intermezzo '39
Rose of Washington Square '39
Adam Had Four Sons '41
The Corsican Brothers '42
Footlight Serenade '42
The Heat's On '43
Black Magic '49
Abdulla the Great '56

Jans Rautenbach
No One Cries Forever '85

Max Raven
The Abomination '88

Ousama Rawi
The Housekeeper '86

John Rawlins
Arabian Nights '42
Sherlock Holmes: The Voice of Terror '42
Dick Tracy Meets Gruesome '47
Dick Tracy's Dilemma '47
Shark River '53

Albert Ray
13th Guest '32
Dancing Man '33
Shriek in the Night '33
Undercover Man '36

Bernard B. Ray
The Silver Bullet '34
Texas Jack '35
Roamin' Wild '36
Speed Reporter '36
Broken Strings '40
House of Errors '42
Buffalo Bill Rides Again '47
Movie Stuntmen '53

Fred Olen Ray
Alien Dead '85
Bio Hazard '85
Armed Response '86
Tomb '86
Commando Squad '87
Cyclone '87
Deep Space '87
Phantom Empire '87
Star Slammer '87
Beverly Hills Vamp '88
Hollywood Chainsaw Hookers '88
Terminal Force '88
Warlords '88
Alienator '89
Bad Girls from Mars '90
Evil Toons '90
Mob Boss '90
Spirits '90
Haunting Fear '91
Inner Sanctum '91
Dinosaur Island '93
Mind Twister '93
Possessed by the Night '93
Bikini Drive-In '94
Inner Sanctum 2 '94
Attack of the 60-Foot Centerfold '95

Nicholas Ray
Knock on Any Door '49
They Live by Night '49
A Woman's Secret '49
Born to Be Bad '50
In a Lonely Place '50
Flying Leathernecks '51
On Dangerous Ground '51
The Lusty Men '52
Johnny Guitar '53
Rebel Without a Cause '55
Party Girl '58
The King of Kings '61
55 Days at Peking '63

Satyajit Ray
Pather Panchali '54
Aparajito '58
The World of Apu '59
Devi '60
Two Daughters '61
Days and Nights in the Forest '70
The Adversary '71
Distant Thunder '73
The Home and the World '84

Herman C. Raymaker
The Night Cry '26

Jack Raymond
The Speckled Band '31

Tom Raymonth
Battle of the Eagles '81

Spiro Razatos
Fast Getaway '91
Class of 1999 2: The Substitute '93

Bill Rebane
The Giant Spider Invasion '75
The Alpha Incident '76
The Capture of Bigfoot '79

Ito Rebane
They '77

Robert Rector
Don't Change My World '83

Eric Red
Cohen and Tate '88
Body Parts '91
Undertow '95

Robert Redford
Ordinary People '80
The Milagro Beanfield War '88
A River Runs Through It '92
Quiz Show '94

Carol Reed
The Stars Look Down '39
Night Train to Munich '40
Kipps '41
Immortal Battalion '44
Odd Man Out '47
The Fallen Idol '49
The Third Man '49
Trapeze '56
The Key '58
The Agony and the Ecstasy '65
Oliver! '68
Unicorn '83

James Reed
Mission Phantom '79

Jerry Reed
What Comes Around '85

Joel M. Reed
G.I. Executioner '71
Bloodsucking Freaks '75
Night of the Zombies '81

Luther Reed
Dixiana '30

Roland D. Reed
Red Lights Ahead '36
The House of Secrets '37

Theodore Reed
The Nut '21

William Reed
Scorpion '86

Clive Rees
Blockhouse '73
When the Whales Came '89

Jerry Rees
The Marrying Man '91

Geoffrey Reeve
Puppet on a Chain '72
Caravan to Vaccares '74
Souvenir '88

Matt Reeves
Future Shock '93
The Pallbearer '95

Michael Reeves
The She-Beast '65
The Conqueror Worm '68

Thomas G. Reeves
Angry Joe Bass '76

Patrick Regan
Kiss Daddy Goodbye '81

Godfrey Reggio
Koyaanisqatsi '83
Powaqqatsi: Life in Transformation '88

Francisco Regueiro
Padre Nuestro '85

Mark Reichart
Union City '81

Alastair Reid
Baby Love '69
Shattered '72
Traffik '90
Teamster Boss: The Jackie Presser Story '92
Armistead Maupin's Tales of the City '93

Dorothy Davenport Reid
Linda '29
Sucker Money '34

Max Reid
Wild Thing '87

Tim Reid
The Little Mermaid '78
Once Upon a Time...When We Were Colored '95

William Reilly
Men of Respect '91

Carl Reiner
Enter Laughing '67
The Comic '69
Where's Poppa? '70
Oh, God! '77
The One and Only '78
The Jerk '79
Dead Men Don't Wear Plaid '82
The Man with Two Brains '83
All of Me '84
Summer Rental '85
Summer School '87
Bert Rigby, You're a Fool '89
Sibling Rivalry '90
Fatal Instinct '93

Jeff Reiner
Blood & Concrete: A Love Story '90
Trouble Bound '92

Lucas Reiner
Spirit of '76 '91

Rob Reiner
This Is Spinal Tap '84
The Sure Thing '85
Stand By Me '86
The Princess Bride '87
When Harry Met Sally... '89
Misery '90
A Few Good Men '92
North '94
The American President '95

Gottfried Reinhardt
Betrayed '54

John Reinhardt
Open Secret '48

Max Reinhardt
A Midsummer Night's Dream '35

Deborah Reinisch
Caught in the Act '93

Harald Reinl
Forger of London '61
The Return of Dr. Mabuse '61
The Invisible Dr. Mabuse '62
The Torture Chamber of Dr. Sadism '69
Hell Hounds of Alaska '73
Fight for Gold '86

Irving Reis
Big Street '42
Crack-Up '46
The Bachelor and the Bobby-Soxer '47
The Falcon Takes Over/Strange Bargain '49
Three Husbands '50

Walter Reisch
Men Are Not Gods '37

Allen Reisner
All Mine to Give '56

Charles F. Reisner
The Man on the Box '25
The Cobra Strikes '48
Train to Tombstone '50

Karel Reisz
Morgan! '66
Isadora '68
The Gambler '74
Who'll Stop the Rain? '78
The French Lieutenant's Woman '81
Sweet Dreams '85
Everybody Wins '90

Wolfgang Reitherman
Sleeping Beauty '59
101 Dalmatians '61
The Sword in the Stone '63
The Jungle Book '67
The Aristocats '70
Robin Hood '73
The Rescuers '77

Ivan Reitman
Meatballs '79
Stripes '81
Ghostbusters '84
Legal Eagles '86
Twins '88
Ghostbusters 2 '89
Kindergarten Cop '90
Dave '93
Junior '94

Edgar Reitz
Germany in Autumn '78

Sheldon Renan
Akira '89

Norman Rene
Longtime Companion '90
Prelude to a Kiss '92
Reckless '95

Jean Renoir
Charleston '26
Renoir Shorts '27
Tournament '29
La Chienne '31
Boudu Saved from Drowning '32
Madame Bovary '34
Toni '34
The Crime of Monsieur Lange '36
The Lower Depths '36
Grand Illusion '37
La Marseillaise '37
La Bete Humaine '38
The Rules of the Game '39
This Land is Mine '43
The Southerner '45
A Day in the Country '46
Diary of a Chambermaid '46
The River '51
The Golden Coach '52
French Can-Can '55
Elena and Her Men '56
Picnic on the Grass '59
The Testament of Dr. Cordelier '59
The Elusive Corporal '62
The Little Theatre of Jean Renoir '71
Zero for Conduct/Taris/A Propos de Nice '91

Alain Resnais
Hiroshima, Mon Amour '59
Last Year at Marienbad '61
Muriel '63
Stavisky '74
Providence '77
Mon Oncle D'Amerique '80
Smoking/No Smoking '94

Adam Resnick
Cabin Boy '94

Robert Resnikoff
The First Power '89

Harry Revier
The Lost City '34

Bernard Revon
The Rascals '81

Buddy Reyes
Night of the Kickfighters '91

Burt Reynolds
Gator '76
The End '78
Sharky's Machine '81
Stick '85
The Man from Left Field '93

C.D.H. Reynolds
Day of Judgment '81

Christopher Reynolds
Offerings '89

Don Reynolds
His Name was King '85

Gene Reynolds
Truth or Die '86

Kevin Reynolds
Fandango '85
The Beast '88
Robin Hood: Prince of Thieves '91
Rapa Nui '93
Waterworld '95

Lynn F. Reynolds
Trailin' '21
Sky High '22
Riders of the Purple Sage '25

Ursi Reynolds
Ganjasaurus Rex '87

Peter Reynolds-Long
The Hound of London '93

Mark Rezyka
South of Reno '87

Phillip Rhee
Best of the Best 3: No Turning Back '95

Michael Rhodes
The Killing Mind '90
Matters of the Heart '90
Heidi '93
Christy '94

Tonino Ricci
Great Treasure Hunt '70s
Rush '84

Bill Rice
The Vineyard '89

David Rice
Quiet Thunder '87

David Lowell Rich
Have Rocket Will Travel '59
Madame X '66
Northeast of Seoul '72
Satan's School for Girls '73
Family Upside Down '78
Little Women '78
The Concorde: Airport '79 '79
Enola Gay: The Men, the Mission, the Atomic Bomb '80
Nurse '80
Chu Chu & the Philly Flash '81
The Hearst and Davies Affair '85
Choices '86
Convicted '86

John Rich
Roustabout '64
Boeing Boeing '65
Easy Come, Easy Go '67
Clarence Darrow '78

Matty Rich
Straight Out of Brooklyn '91
The Inkwell '94

Richard Rich
The Fox and the Hound '81
The Swan Princess '94

Jef Richard
Berserker '87

Jefferson Richard
In Search of a Golden Sky '84

Pierre Richard
The Daydreamer '75
Too Shy to Try '82

Dick Richards
Culpepper Cattle Co. '72
Farewell, My Lovely '75
Rafferty & the Gold Dust Twins '75
March or Die '77
Death Valley '81
Man, Woman & Child '83

Lloyd Richards
Paul Robeson '70s
The Piano Lesson '94

R.M. Richards
Heat '87

John Richardson
Dusty '85

Mark Richardson
Robot in the Family '94

Peter Richardson
Eat the Rich '87
Supergrass '87
The Pope Must Diet '91

Tony Richardson
Look Back in Anger '58
The Entertainer '60
A Taste of Honey '61
The Loneliness of the Long Distance Runner '62
Tom Jones '63
The Loved One '65
Mademoiselle '66
The Charge of the Light Brigade '68
Hamlet '69
Ned Kelly '70
Joseph Andrews '77
The Border '82
The Hotel New Hampshire '84
Penalty Phase '86
Shadow on the Sun '88
The Phantom of the Opera '90
Women & Men: Stories of Seduction '90
Blue Sky '91

William Richert
Winter Kills '79
A Night in the Life of Jimmy Reardon '88

Anthony Richmond
Days of Hell '84
Deja Vu '84
A Man Called Rage '84
Night of the Sharks '89

Ota Richter
Skullduggery '79

W.D. Richter
The Adventures of Buckaroo Banzai Across the Eighth Dimension '84
Late for Dinner '91

James Ricketson
Kiss the Night '87

Tom Rickman
The River Rat '84

Philip Ridley
The Reflecting Skin '91

Leni Riefenstahl
The Blue Light '32
Triumph of the Will '34
Tiefland '44

Charles Riesner
Steamboat Bill, Jr. '28
Manhattan Merry-Go-Round '37
Big Store '41
Lost in a Harem '44

Dean Riesner
Bill and Coo '47

Vladmir Rif
Very Close Quarters '84

J. Riffel
The House on Tombstone Hill '92

Adam Rifkin
Never on Tuesday '88
The Dark Backward '91
The Chase '93
The Nutt House '95

Gennaro Righelli
Peddlin' in Society '47

Eran Riklis
Cup Final '92

Wolf Rilla
Roadhouse Girl '53
Bachelor of Hearts '58
Village of the Damned '60

Carlo Rim
Seven Deadly Sins '53

Alfredo Ringel
The Magic Bubble '93

Deborah Taper Ringel
The Magic Bubble '93

Arthur Ripley
The Chase '46
Thunder Road '58

Frank Ripploh
Taxi zum Klo '81

Arturo Ripstein
Foxtrot '76

Michael Rischa
Delta Heat '92

Dino Risi
Love in the City '53
The Easy Life '63
Il Sorpasso '63
Tiger and the Pussycat '67
The Scent of a Woman '75
How Funny Can Sex Be? '76
Running Away '89

Marco Risi
Forever Mary '89

Michael Rissi
Soultaker '90

Michael Ritchie
Downhill Racer '69
The Candidate '72
Prime Cut '72
Smile '75
The Bad News Bears '76
Semi-Tough '77
An Almost Perfect Affair '79
Divine Madness '80
The Island '80
Survivors '83
Fletch '85
The Golden Child '86
Wildcats '86
The Couch Trip '87
Fletch Lives '89
Diggstown '92
The Positively True Adventures of the Alleged Texas Cheerleader-Murdering Mom '93
Cops and Robbersons '94
The Scout '94

Viktors Ritelis
Crucible of Horror '69

Martin Ritt
The Long, Hot Summer '58
Black Orchid '59
Paris Blues '61
Hud '63
The Spy Who Came in from the Cold '65
Hombre '67
The Brotherhood '68
The Great White Hope '70
Molly Maguires '70
Pete 'n' Tillie '72
Sounder '72
Conrack '74
The Front '76
Casey's Shadow '78
Norma Rae '79
Back Roads '81
Cross Creek '83
Murphy's Romance '85
Nuts '87
Stanley and Iris '90

Giorgio Rivalta
The Avenger '62

Joan Rivers
Rabbit Test '78

Jacques Rivette
Paris Belongs to Us '60
The Nun '66
La Belle Noiseuse '90

Chris Roach
The 13th Floor '88

Frank Roach
Nomad Riders '81

Hal Roach
The Devil's Brother '33
One Million B.C. '40
Road Show '41

Hal Roach, Jr.
One Million B.C. '40

Alain Robak
The Evil Within '94

Seymour Robbie
Chrome Hearts '70
Marco '73

Brian Robbins
The Show '95

Jerome Robbins
West Side Story '61

Matthew Robbins
Corvette Summer '78
Dragonslayer '81
Legend of Billie Jean '85
*batteries not included '87
Bingo '91

Tim Robbins
Bob Roberts '92
Dead Man Walking '95

Mike Robe
Urge to Kill '84
News at Eleven '86
Murder Ordained '87
Child in the Night '90
Son of the Morning Star '91
Scott Turow's The Burden of Proof '92
Return to Lonesome Dove '93

Jim Roberson
Legend of Alfred Packer '80

Syd Roberson
Robin Hood...The Legend: The Time of the Wolf '85

Genevieve Robert
Casual Sex? '88

Vincent Robert
The Fear '94

Yves Robert
The Tall Blond Man with One Black Shoe '72
Return of the Tall Blond Man With One Black Shoe '74
Salut l'Artiste '74
Pardon Mon Affaire '76
Pardon Mon Affaire, Too! '77
My Father's Glory '91
My Mother's Castle '91

Alan Roberts
The Happy Hooker Goes Hollywood '80
Young Lady Chatterly 2 '85
Round Trip to Heaven '92
Karate Cop '93
Save Me '93

Daryll Roberts
How U Like Me Now? '92

Deborah Roberts
Frankenstein General Hospital '88

Edward Roberts
The Adventurous Knights '35

John Roberts
War of the Buttons '95

Stephen Roberts
Romance in Manhattan '34
Star of Midnight '35
Ex-Mrs. Bradford '36

Cliff Robertson
Danger in the Skies '79

David Robertson
Firebird 2015 A.D. '81

Doug Robertson
HauntedWeen '91

James Robertson
Superstition '82

John S. Robertson
Dr. Jekyll and Mr. Hyde '20
Shore Leave '25
Soul-Fire '25
The Single Standard '29
Little Orphan Annie '32
Our Little Girl '35

Joseph F. Robertson
Auntie Lee's Meat Pies '92

Tom G. Robertson
The River Pirates '94

Herb Robins
The Worm Eaters '77

John Robins
Hot Resort '85

Bruce Robinson
Withnail and I '87
How to Get Ahead in Advertising '89
Jennifer 8 '92

Chris Robinson
Sunshine Run '79
Women's Prison Escape

John Mark Robinson
Roadhouse 66 '84
Kid '90
All Tied Up '92

Lee Robinson
Walk into Hell '57

Paul D. Robinson
Last Flight to Hell

Phil Alden Robinson
In the Mood '87
Field of Dreams '89
Sneakers '92

Richard Robinson
Bloody Trail '72
Poor Pretty Eddie '73

Arthur Robison
Warning Shadows '23
The Informer '29

Michael Robison
Deadly Sins '95

Armando Robles Godoy
The Green Wall '70

Mark Robson
The Seventh Victim '43
Bedlam '45
Isle of the Dead '45
Champion '49
Home of the Brave '49
Return to Paradise '53
Phffft! '54
The Bridges at Toko-Ri '55
The Harder They Fall '56
Peyton Place '57
The Inn of the Sixth Happiness '58
From the Terrace '60
The Prize '63
Von Ryan's Express '65
The Lost Command '66
Valley of the Dolls '67
Daddy's Gone A-Hunting '69
Earthquake '74
Avalanche Express '79

Marc Rocco
Scenes from the Goldmine '87
Dream a Little Dream '89
Where the Day Takes You '92
Murder In the First '95

Glauce Rocha
Black God & White Devil '64
Earth Entranced '66
Antonio Das Mortes '68

Eric Rochant
The Fifth Monkey '90
Love Without Pity '91

Sean Roche
Chasing Dreams '81

Sheldon Rochlin
Signals Through the Flames '83

Alexandre Rockwell
Sons '91
In the Soup '92
Four Rooms '95

Franc Roddam
Quadrophenia '79
The Lords of Discipline '83
The Bride '85
Aria '88
War Party '89
K2: The Ultimate High '92

Serge Rodnunsky
Lovers' Lovers '94

Ismael Rodriguez
Daniel Boone: Trail Blazer '56

Paul Rodriguez
A Million to Juan '94

Robert Rodriguez
El Mariachi '93
Desperado '95
Four Rooms '95
From Dusk Till Dawn '95

Nicolas Roeg
Performance '70
Don't Look Now '73
The Man Who Fell to Earth '76
Eureka! '81
Insignificance '85
Castaway '87
Aria '88
Track 29 '88
Sweet Bird of Youth '89
The Witches '90
Cold Heaven '92
Heart of Darkness '93
Full Body Massage '95

Larry Roemer
Rudolph the Red-Nosed Reindeer '64

Michael Roemer
Nothing But a Man '64
The Plot Against Harry '69
Pilgrim, Farewell '82

Rick Roessler
Slaughterhouse '87

Koos Roets
Brutal Glory '89

Julian Roffman
The Mask '61

Albert Rogell
Cyclone Cavalier '25
The Tip-Off '31
Li'l Abner '40
War of the Wildcats '43
The Admiral Was a Lady '50

Charles R. Rogers
The Devil's Brother '33
March of the Wooden Soldiers '34

Maclean Rogers
Calling Paul Temple '48
Down Among the Z Men '52

Cliff Roguemore
Devil's Son-in-Law '77

Eric Rohmer
La Collectionneuse '67
Six in Paris '68
My Night at Maud's '69
Claire's Knee '71
Chloe in the Afternoon '72
Le Beau Mariage '82
Pauline at the Beach '83
Full Moon in Paris '84
Summer '86
Boyfriends & Girlfriends '88
Four Adventures of Reinette and Mirabelle '89
A Tale of Springtime '92
A Tale of Winter '92

Rob Rohrer
The Man from the Pru '89

Sutton Roley
Loners '72
Snatched '72

Bernie Rollins
Getting Over '81

Phil Roman
Be My Valentine, Charlie Brown '75
It's Your First Kiss, Charlie Brown/Someday You'll Find Her, Charlie Brown '77
Race for Your Life, Charlie Brown '77
Life is a Circus, Charlie Brown/You're the Greatest, Charlie Brown '80
She's a Good Skate, Charlie Brown '80
A Charlie Brown Thanksgiving '81
It's Magic, Charlie Brown/Charlie Brown's All Star '81
Good Grief, Charlie Brown '83
It's Three Strikes, Charlie Brown '86
It's a Mystery, Charlie Brown '87
Tom and Jerry: The Movie '93

Mark Romanek
Static '87

Eddie Romero
Cavalry Command '63
Brides of the Beast '68
Beast of the Yellow Night '70
Twilight People '72
Woman Hunt '72
Beyond Atlantis '73
WhiteForce '88

George A. Romero
Night of the Living Dead '68
The Crazies '73
Season of the Witch '73
Martin '77
Dawn of the Dead '78
Knightriders '81
Creepshow '82
Day of the Dead '85
Monkey Shines '88
Two Evil Eyes '90
The Dark Half '91

Joanelle Romero
Powwow Highway '89

Charles R. Rondeau
The Devil's Partner '58
The Girl in Lover's Lane '60

Ronnie Rondell
No Safe Haven '87

Chito Rono
Olongape: The American Dream '89

Darrell Roodt
Place of Weeping '86
City of Blood '88
Sarafina! '92
Father Hood '93
To the Death '93
Cry, the Beloved Country '95

Abram Room
Bed and Sofa '27

Wells Root
The Bold Caballero '36

Tom Ropelewski
Madhouse '90
Look Who's Talking Now '93

Mark Roper
Live Wire: Human Timebomb '95

Faliero Rosati
High Frequency '88

Nello Rosatti
The Sensuous Nurse '76

Bernard Rose
Paperhouse '89
Chicago Joe & the Showgirl '90
Candyman '92
Immortal Beloved '94

Les Rose
Hog Wild '80
Gas '81
Title Shot '81

Mickey Rose
Student Bodies '81

Pierre Rose
The Klutz '73

Reuben Rose
Screwball Academy '86

Barry Rosen
Gang Wars '75
The Yum-Yum Girls '78

Martin Rosen
Watership Down '78
The Plague Dogs '82
Stacking '87

Phil Rosen
The Phantom in the House '29
Branded Men '31
The Pocatello Kid '31
Two Gun Man '31
Man's Land '32
Whistlin' Dan '32
The Phantom Broadcast '33
The Sphinx '33
The Sphinx '33
Young Blood '33
Beggars in Ermine '34
Mistaken Identity '36
The President's Mystery '36
Tango '36
It Could Happen to You '37
Phantom of Chinatown '40
Gangs, Inc. '41
Spooks Run Wild '41
I Killed That Man '42
Wings Over the Pacific '43
Charlie Chan in the Secret Service '44
The Chinese Cat '44
Meeting at Midnight '44
Return of the Ape Man '44
The Jade Mask '45
The Scarlet Clue '45

Robert L. Rosen
Raw Courage '84

Rick Rosenberg
Distant Thunder '88

Stuart Rosenberg
Cool Hand Luke '67
April Fools '69
Pocket Money '72
The Laughing Policeman '74
The Drowning Pool '75
Voyage of the Damned '76
The Amityville Horror '79
Love and Bullets '79
Brubaker '80
The Pope of Greenwich Village '84
My Heroes Have Always Been Cowboys '91

Tanya Rosenberg
Blood Games '90

Ralph Rosenblum
Summer Solstice '81

Keva Rosenfeld
Twenty Bucks '93

Scott Rosenfelt
Family Prayers '91

Dan Rosenthal
Sloane '84

Mark Rosenthal
The In Crowd '88

Rick Rosenthal
Halloween 2: The Nightmare Isn't Over! '81
Bad Boys '83
American Dreamer '84
Russkies '87
Devlin '92
The Birds 2: Land's End '94

Robert J. Rosenthal
Malibu Beach '78
Zapped! '82

Francesco Rosi
Lucky Luciano '74
Christ Stopped at Eboli '79
Three Brothers '80
The Palermo Connection '91

Mark Rosman
The House on Sorority Row '83
The Blue Yonder '86
Evolver '94

Milton Rosmer
The Secret of the Loch '34
Murder in the Old Red Barn '36

Benjamin Ross
The Young Poisoner's Handbook '94

Frank Ross
The Lady Says No '51

Herbert Ross
Goodbye Love '34
Goodbye, Mr. Chips '69
The Owl and the Pussycat '70
Play It Again, Sam '72
The Last of Sheila '73
Funny Lady '75
The Sunshine Boys '75
The Seven-Per-Cent Solution '76
The Goodbye Girl '77
The Turning Point '77
California Suite '78
Nijinsky '80
Pennies From Heaven '81
I Ought to Be in Pictures '82
Max Dugan Returns '83
Footloose '84
Protocol '84
Dancers '87
The Secret of My Success '87
Steel Magnolias '89
My Blue Heaven '90
True Colors '91
Undercover Blues '93
Boys on the Side '94

Nat Ross
April Fool '26

Neil Rossati
Tides of War '90

Roberto Rossellini
Man with a Cross '43
Open City '45
Paisan '46
Deutschland im Jahre Null '47
Amore '48
Machine to Kill Bad People '48
The Miracle '48
The Flowers of St. Francis '50
Stromboli '50
Europa '51 '52
Seven Deadly Sins '53
Voyage to Italy '53
Era Notte a Roma '60
Generale Della Rovere '60
Vanina Vanini '61
RoGoPaG '62
The Rise of Louis XIV '66
Blaise Pascal '71
Augustine of Hippo '72
The Messiah '75

Robert Rossen
Body and Soul '47
All the King's Men '49
Alexander the Great '55
Mambo '55
Island in the Sun '57
They Came to Cordura '59
The Hustler '61
Lilith '64

Franco Rossi
Quo Vadis '85

Arthur Rosson
The Last Outlaw '27
The Concentratin' Kid '30
Trailing Trouble '30
Hidden Gold '33
Boots of Destiny '37

Kaspar Rostrup
Memories of a Marriage '90

Bobby Roth
Boss' Son '79
Circle of Power '83
Heartbreakers '84
Baja Oklahoma '87
Dead Solid Perfect '88
The Game of Love '90
The Man Inside '90
Rainbow Drive '90
Keeper of the City '92

Cy Roth
Fire Maidens from Outer Space '56

Joe Roth
Streets of Gold '86
Revenge of the Nerds 2: Nerds in Paradise '87
Coupe de Ville '90

Phillip J. Roth
Red Snow '91
Prototype X29A '92
A.P.E.X. '94
Digital Man '94

Stephanie Rothman
Track of the Vampire '66
The Student Nurses '70
The Velvet Vampire '71
Group Marriage '72
Terminal Island '73
Working Girls '75

William Rotsler
Mantis in Lace '68
Psychedelic Fever '90

Brigitte Rouan
Overseas: Three Women with Man Trouble '90

Jean Rouch
Jaguar '56
Six in Paris '68

Jacques Rouffio
La Passante '83

Raymond Rouleau
The Crucible '57

Dominique Roulet
Tiger Heart '96

Russel Rouse
The Well '51
The Thief '52
Fastest Gun Alive '56
The Oscar '66
Caper of the Golden Bulls '67

Gilbert Roussel
Women's Prison Massacre '85
George Rowe
Fatal Mission '89
Peter Rowe
Lost '86
Take Two '87
Personal Exemptions '88
Tom Rowe
Get Rita '75
Roy Rowland
Our Vines Have Tender Grapes '45
Two Weeks with Love '50
Bugles in the Afternoon '52
The 5000 Fingers of Dr. T '53
Hit the Deck '55
Meet Me in Las Vegas '56
Gun Glory '57
The Seven Hills of Rome '58
Girl Hunters '63
William Rowland
Follies Girl '43
Flight to Nowhere '46
Christopher Rowley
Soul Patrol '80
Jean-Claude Roy
Deadly Sting '82
Fanchon Royer
Bell Ringer of Antigua '46
Patricia Rozema
I've Heard the Mermaids Singing '87
When Night is Falling '95
Janosz Rozsa
Sunday Daughters '80
John Ruane
Death in Brunswick '90
That Eye, The Sky '94
Michael Rubbo
The Peanut Butter Solution '85
Andy Ruben
Streets '90
J. Walter Ruben
Ace of Aces '33
Java Head '35
Riff Raff '35
Joseph Ruben
Pom Pom Girls '76
Joyride '77
Gorp '80
Dreamscape '84
The Stepfather '87
True Believer '89
Sleeping with the Enemy '91
The Good Son '93
Money Train '95
Katt Shea Ruben
Stripped to Kill '87
Dance of the Damned '88
Stripped to Kill II: Live Girls '89
Streets '90
Poison Ivy '92
Nik Rubenfeld
Alien Private Eye '87
Percival Rubens
Mr. Kingstreet's War '71
Survival Zone '84
Wild Zone '89
Sweet Murder '93
Harold Rubie
Island Trader '71
Howard Rubie
Scalp Merchant '77
Bruce Joel Rubin
My Life '93
Joseph Rubin
The Sister-in-Law '74
Rick Rubin
Tougher than Leather '88
Sergio Rubini
The Station '92
Alan Rudolph
Premonition '71
Barn of the Naked Dead '73
Welcome to L.A. '77
Roadie '80
Endangered Species '82
Choose Me '84
Songwriter '84
Trouble in Mind '86
Made in Heaven '87
The Moderns '88
Love at Large '89
Mortal Thoughts '91
Equinox '93
Mrs. Parker and the Vicious Circle '94
Louis Rudolph
Double Standard '88
Wesley Ruggles
Cimarron '30
No Man of Her Own '32
I'm No Angel '33
Arizona '40
Somewhere I'll Find You '42
Raul Ruiz
The Hypothesis of the Stolen Painting '78
On Top of the Whale '82
Craig T. Rumar
Instant Justice '86
Robert Rundle
The Divine Enforcer '91
Katja Rupe
Germany in Autumn '78
Richard Rush
Hell's Angels on Wheels '67
Psych-Out '68
The Savage Seven '68
Getting Straight '70
Freebie & the Bean '74
The Stunt Man '80
Color of Night '94
Chuck Russell
A Nightmare on Elm Street 3: Dream Warriors '87
The Blob '88
The Mask '94
Eraser '96
David O. Russell
Spanking the Monkey '94
Flirting with Disaster '95
Jay Russell
End of the Line '88
Ken Russell
Dante's Inferno: Life of Dante Gabriel Rossetti '69
Women in Love '70
The Boy Friend '71
The Devils '71
The Music Lovers '71
Savage Messiah '72
Mahler '74
Lisztomania '75
Tommy '75
Valentino '77
Altered States '80
Crimes of Passion '84
Gothic '87
Aria '88
The Lair of the White Worm '88
Salome's Last Dance '88
The Rainbow '89
Women & Men: Stories of Seduction '90
Prisoner of Honor '91
Whore '91
Ray Russell
Zotz! '62
William D. Russell
The Green Promise '49
Best of the Badmen '50
Aaron Russo
Rude Awakening '89
John Russo
Midnight '81
The Majorettes '87
Midnight 2: Sex, Death, and Videotape '93
Mario Russo
The Naked Maja '59
Mardi Rustam
Evils of the Night '85
Mark Rutland
Prime Suspect '88
Todd Rutt
Shock! Shock! Shock! '87
Frank Ryan
Call Out the Marines '42
Edgar Ryazanov
Private Life '82
A Forgotten Tune for the Flute '88
Mark Rydell
The Reivers '69
The Cowboys '72
Cinderella Liberty '73
Harry & Walter Go to New York '76
The Rose '79
On Golden Pond '81
The River '84
For the Boys '91
Intersection '93
Renny Rye
Lipstick On Your Collar '94
Stellan Rye
Student of Prague '13
John Ryman
Galaxies are Colliding '92
Judy Rymer
Who Killed Baby Azaria? '83
Michael Rymer
Angel Baby '95
Paul Sabella
All Dogs Go to Heaven 2 '95
William Sachs
South of Hell Mountain '70
Incredible Melting Man '77
Van Nuys Blvd. '79
Galaxina '80
The Last Hour '91
Daniel Sackheim
The X-Files: Pilot Episode/Deep Throat '93
Alan Sacks
Dubeat-E-O '84
James Sadwith
Bluffing It '87
Sinatra '92
Eddie Saeta
Dr. Death, Seeker of Souls '73
Henri Safran
Norman Loves Rose '82
The Wild Duck '84
Boris Sagal
Guns of Diablo '64
Girl Happy '65
Night Gallery '69
Omega Man '71
The Runaway Barge '75
Angela '77
Masada '81
Leontine Sagan
Maedchen in Uniform '31
Malcolm St. Clair
The Grand Duchess and the Waiter '26
The Bashful Bachelor '42
Bullfighters '45
Christopher St. John
Top of the Heap '72
Gene Saks
Barefoot in the Park '67
The Odd Couple '68
Cactus Flower '69
Last of the Red Hot Lovers '72
Mame '74
Brighton Beach Memoirs '86
Henry Sala
Nightmare Weekend '86
Richard Sale
Ticket to Tomahawk '50
Let's Make It Legal '51
Leander Sales
Don't Let Your Meat Loaf '95
Sidney Salkow
City Without Men '43
Twice-Told Tales '63
The Last Man on Earth '64
David Salle
Search and Destroy '94
Mikael Salomon
A Far Off Place '93
Victor Salva
Clown House '88
Nature of the Beast '94
Powder '95
Jaime Salvador
Boom in the Moon '46
Gabriele Salvatores
Mediterraneo '91
Emmimo Salvi
Vulcan God of Fire '62
Hal Salwen
Denise Calls Up '95
Glen Salzman
Rubberface '81
Salvatore Samperi
Malicious '74
Submission '77
Ernesto '79
Edwards Sampson
The Fast and the Furious '54
Coke Sams
Ernest Goes to School '94
Barry Samson
Ice Pawn '92
The Ice Runner '93
Stuart Samuels
Visions of Light: The Art of Cinematography '93
Fang Mui San
The Amsterdam Connection '70s
Denis Sanders
One Man's Way '63
Invasion of the Bee Girls '73
Ake Sandgren
The Slingshot '93
Jay Sandrich
Seems Like Old Times '80
For Richer, For Poorer '92
Mark Sandrich
Melody Cruise '32
Aggie Appleby, Maker of Men '33
Cockeyed Cavaliers '34
The Gay Divorcee '34
Hips, Hips, Hooray '34
Top Hat '35
Follow the Fleet '36
A Woman Rebels '36
Shall We Dance '37
Carefree '38
Holiday Inn '42
So Proudly We Hail '43
Here Come the Waves '44
Arlene Sanford
A Very Brady Sequel '96
Helen Sanford
Angel of H.E.A.T. '82
Clifford Sanforth
Murder by Television '35
Luk Pak Sang
Tattoo Connection '78
Jonathan Sanger
Code Name: Emerald '85
Down Came a Blackbird '94
Jimmy Sangster
The Horror of Frankenstein '70
Lust for a Vampire '71
Dynasty of Fear '72
Erick Santamaria
Playgirl Killer '66
Alfred Santell
Winterset '36
Internes Can't Take Money '37
Having Wonderful Time '38
The Hairy Ape '44
Jack London '44
That Brennan Girl '46
Cirio H. Santiago
Firecracker '71
Savage! '73
Cover Girl Models '75
TNT Jackson '75
The Muthers '76
Fighting Mad '77
Death Force '78
The Vampire Hookers '78
Caged Fury '80
Stryker '83
Final Mission '84
Wheels of Fire '84
Devastator '85
Naked Vengeance '85
Equalizer 2000 '86
Silk '86
Demon of Paradise '87
Eye of the Eagle '87
Future Hunters '88
Nam Angels '88
The Sisterhood '88
The Expendables '89
Silk 2 '89
Dune Warriors '91
Eye of the Eagle 3 '91
Beyond the Call of Duty '92
Field of Fire '92
Firehawk '92
Raiders of the Sun '92
One Man Army '93
Caged Heat 2: Stripped of Freedom '94
Stranglehold '94
She Devils in Chains
Pablo Santiago
South Seas Massacre
Joseph Santley
The Cocoanuts '29
Harmony Lane '35
Melody Ranch '40
Music in My Heart '40
Down Mexico Way '41
Call of the Canyon '42
Damon Santostefano
Severed Ties '92
David Saperstein
A Killing Affair '85
Beyond the Stars '89
Deran Sarafian
Alien Predators '80
Interzone '88
To Die for '89
Death Warrant '90
Back in the USSR '92
Gunmen '93
Terminal Velocity '94
The Road Killers '95
Richard Sarafian
Man in the Wilderness '71
Vanishing Point '71
Man Who Loved Cat Dancing '73
The Arab Conspiracy '76
Sunburn '79
Gangster Wars '81
Eye of the Tiger '86
Street Justice '89
Solar Crisis '92
Joseph Sargent
The Invaders '67
Colossus: The Forbin Project '70
Maybe I'll Be Home in the Spring '70
Tribes '70
Man on a String '71
White Lightning '73
The Taking of Pelham One Two Three '74
Hustling '75
MacArthur '77
Goldengirl '79
Coast to Coast '80
The Manions of America '81
Amber Waves '82
Tomorrow's Child '82
Memorial Day '83
Nightmares '83
Passion Flower '86
Jaws: The Revenge '87
Day One '89
The Incident '89
Caroline? '90
Ivory Hunters '90
Never Forget '91
Miss Rose White '92
Skylark '93
Abraham '94
My Antonia '94
World War II: When Lions Roared '94
Larry McMurtry's Streets of Laredo '95
Marina Sargenti
Mirror, Mirror '90
Child of Darkness, Child of Light '91
Dick Sarin
Family Reunion '88
Vic Sarin
Cold Comfort '90
Maurice Sarli
The Bodyguard '76

Michael Sarne
Myra Breckinridge '70
Jonathan Sarno
The Kirlian Witness '78
Peter Sasdy
Taste the Blood of Dracula '70
Hands of the Ripper '71
Doomwatch '72
Nothing But the Night '72
The Devil's Undead '75
I Don't Want to Be Born '75
King Arthur, the Young Warlord '75
Young Warlord '75
Rude Awakening '81
Thirteenth Reunion '81
The Two Faces of Evil '82
The Lonely Lady '83
Barbara Sass
Without Love '80
Oley Sassone
Bloodfist 3: Forced to Fight '92
Final Embrace '92
Future Shock '93
Fast Getaway 2 '94
Relentless 4 '94
Playback '95
Ron Satlof
Spiderman: The Deadly Dust '78
Waikiki '80
Perry Mason Returns '85
Perry Mason: The Case of the Lost Love '87
Buichi Sato
Baby Cart 4: Heart of a Parent...Heart of a Child '72
Hajime Sato
Terror Beneath the Sea '66
Body Snatcher from Hell '69
Junya Sato
The Go-Masters '82
The Silk Road '92
Shimako Sato
Tale of a Vampire '92
Ernest G. Sauer
Beauty School '93
Bikini Bistro '94
Carlos Saura
The Hunt '67
The Garden of Delights '70
Cria '76
Elisa, Vida Mia '77
Mama Turns a Hundred '79
Blood Wedding '81
Carmen '83
The Stilts '84
El Amor Brujo '86
Ay, Carmela! '90
Outrage '93
Claude Sautet
The Things of Life '70
Cesar & Rosalie '72
Mado '76
Vincent, Francois, Paul and the Others '76
A Simple Story '79
Un Coeur en Hiver '93
Nelly et Monsieur Arnaud '95
Derek Savage
The Meateater '79
Telly Savalas
Beyond Reason '77
Igor Savchenko
Guerilla Brigade '39
Brian Savegar
The Inheritor '90
Philip Saville
Secrets '71
Those Glory, Glory Days '83
Mandela '87
Shadey '87
Wonderland '88
Fellow Traveler '89
Max and Helen '90
Family Pictures '93
The Buccaneers '95
Victor Saville
Evergreen '34
The Iron Duke '34
It's Love Again '36
Dark Journey '37
Storm in a Teacup '37
Forever and a Day '43
Tonight and Every Night '45
Green Dolphin Street '47
Conspirator '49
Kim '50
The Silver Chalice '54
Tom Savini
Night of the Living Dead '90
Nancy Savoca
True Love '89
Dogfight '91
Household Saints '93
Leopoldo Savona
The Mongols '60
Geoffrey Sax
Broken Trust '95
Doctor Who '96
John Saxon
Death House '88
Stephen Sayadian
Dr. Caligari '89
Eric Sayers
Common Law Wife '63
John Sayles
Return of the Secaucus 7 '80
Baby It's You '82
Lianna '83
The Brother from Another Planet '84
Matewan '87
Eight Men Out '88
City of Hope '91
Passion Fish '92
The Secret of Roan Inish '94
Lone Star '95
James Sbardellati
Under the Gun '88
Joseph L. Scanlan
Spring Fever '81
Nightstick '87
The World's Oldest Living Bridesmaid '92
Don Scardino
Me & Veronica '93
Umberto Scarpelli
The Giant of Metropolis '61
Romano Scavolini
Nightmare '82
Steven Schachter
Getting Up and Going Home '92
The Water Engine '92
Above Suspicion '95
Armand Schaefer
Lightning Warrior '31
Hurricane Express '32
Outlaw Justice '32
Fighting Texans '33
Fighting with Kit Carson '33
Sagebrush Trail '33
Terror Trail '33
Law of the Wild '34
The Lost Jungle '34
Sixteen Fathoms Deep '34
The Miracle Rider '35
George Schaefer
Victoria Regina '61
Invincible Mr. Disraeli '63
The Tempest '63
Holy Terror '65
Barefoot in Athens '66
Lamp at Midnight '66
Soldier in Love '67
Elizabeth, the Queen '68
Generation '69
Pendulum '69
Doctors' Wives '70
Once Upon a Scoundrel '73
In This House of Brede '75
Lost Legacy: A Girl Called Hatter Fox '77
The People vs. Jean Harris '81
Deadly Game '82
A Piano for Mrs. Cimino '82
Who'll Save Our Children? '82
Children in the Crossfire '84
Right of Way '84
The Man Upstairs '93
Eric Schaeffer
My Life's In Turnaround '94
If Lucy Fell '95
Francis Schaeffer
Wired to Kill '86
Headhunter '89
Rebel Storm '90
Baby on Board '92
Marianne Schafer
Traenen in Florenz '84
Franklin J. Schaffner
The Stripper '63
The Best Man '64
The War Lord '65
Planet of the Apes '68
Patton '70
Nicholas and Alexandra '71
Papillon '73
Islands in the Stream '77
Our Town '77
The Boys from Brazil '78
Sphinx '81
Yes, Giorgio '82
Lionheart '87
Welcome Home '89
Don Schain
The Abductors '72
Ginger '72
A Place Called Today '72
Girls Are for Loving '73
Too Hot to Handle '76
Peter Schamoni
Spring Symphony '86
Jerry Schatzberg
Scarecrow '73
Panic in Needle Park '75
The Seduction of Joe Tynan '79
Honeysuckle Rose '80
Misunderstood '84
No Small Affair '84
Street Smart '87
Blood Money: The Story of Clinton and Nadine '88
Reunion '88
Hans Scheepmaker
Field of Honor '86
Robert Scheerer
Hans Brinker '69
Adam at 6 a.m. '70
The World's Greatest Athlete '73
Ants '77
How to Beat the High Cost of Living '80
Happily Ever After '82
Andrew Scheinman
Little Big League '94
Maximilian Schell
First Love '70
The Pedestrian '73
Henning Schellerup
Time Machine '78
The Adventures of Nellie Bly '81
Carl Schenkel
Strike Back '80
Out of Order '84
Eye of the Demon '87
The Mighty Quinn '89
Silence Like Glass '90
Silhouette '91
Knight Moves '93
The Surgeon '94
Fred Schepisi
The Devil's Playground '76
Barbarosa '82
Iceman '84
Plenty '85
Roxanne '87
A Cry in the Dark '88
The Russia House '90
Mr. Baseball '92
Six Degrees of Separation '93
I.Q. '94
Victor Schertzinger
Clodhopper '17
What Happened to Rosa? '21
Uptown New York '32
One Night of Love '34
Something to Sing About '36
Rhythm on the River '40
The Road to Singapore '40
Birth of the Blues '41
The Road to Zanzibar '41
Paul Schibli
The Nutcracker Prince '91
Suzanne Schiffman
Sorceress '88
Lawrence Schiller
Marilyn: The Untold Story '80
The Executioner's Song '82
Double Exposure: The Story of Margaret Bourke-White '89
Double Jeopardy '92
Vittorio Schiraldi
Fangs '75
Heinz Schirk
The Wannsee Conference '84
Eric L. Schlagman
Punch the Clock '90
Thomas Schlamme
Spalding Gray: Terrors of Pleasure '88
Miss Firecracker '89
Crazy from the Heart '91
So I Married an Axe Murderer '93
You So Crazy '94
Kingfish: A Story of Huey P. Long '95
George Schlatter
Norman, Is That You? '76
John Schlesinger
A Kind of Loving '62
Billy Liar '63
Darling '65
Far from the Madding Crowd '67
Midnight Cowboy '69
Sunday, Bloody Sunday '71
The Day of the Locust '75
Marathon Man '76
Yanks '79
Honky Tonk Freeway '81
An Englishman Abroad '83
Separate Tables '83
The Falcon and the Snowman '85
The Believers '87
Madame Sousatzka '88
Pacific Heights '90
A Question of Attribution '91
The Innocent '93
Cold Comfort Farm '94
An Eye for an Eye '95
Volker Schlondorff
An Occurrence at Owl Creek Bridge/Coup de Grace '62
The Lost Honor of Katharina Blum '75
Coup de Grace '78
Germany in Autumn '78
The Tin Drum '79
Swann in Love '84
Death of a Salesman '86
The Handmaid's Tale '90
Murder on the Bayou '91
Voyager '91
Jay Schlossberg-Cohen
Night Train to Terror '84
Daniel Schmid
Shadow of Angels '76
Rick Schmidt
A Man, a Woman and a Killer
Thomas J. Schmidt
Girls on the Road '73
David Schmoeller
Tourist Trap '79
The Seduction '82
Crawlspace '86
Catacombs '89
Puppet Master '89
The Arrival '90
Curse 4: The Ultimate Sacrifice '90
Netherworld '90
Paul Schneider
Something Special '86
Babycakes '89
Daniel and the Towers '90s
Honor Thy Father and Mother: The True Story of the Menendez Brothers '94
Robert Allen Schnitzer
The Premonition '75
Kandyland '87
Ernest B. Schoedsack
Chang: A Drama of the Wilderness '27
The Most Dangerous Game '32
King Kong '33
Son of Kong '33
Last Days of Pompeii '35
Dr. Cyclops '40
Mighty Joe Young '49
Pierre Schoendoerffer
The 317th Platoon '65
Le Crabe Tambour '77
Jan Scholtz
Emissary '89
Skip Schoolnik
Hide and Go Shriek '87
Renen Schorr
Late Summer Blues '87
Dale Schott
The Care Bears Movie 2: A New Generation '86
Paul Schrader
Blue Collar '78
American Gigolo '79
Hardcore '79
Cat People '82
Mishima: A Life in Four Chapters '85
Light of Day '87
Patty Hearst '88
The Comfort of Strangers '91
Light Sleeper '92
Witch Hunt '94
Myrl A. Schreibman
Angel of H.E.A.T. '82
Liberty & Bash '90
William Schreiner
A Sinful Life '89
John F. Schreyer
Naked Youth '59
Barbet Schroeder
More '69
The Valley Obscured by the Clouds '72
Maitresse '76
Tricheurs '84
Barfly '87
Reversal of Fortune '90
Single White Female '92
Kiss of Death '94
Before and After '95
Frank C. Schroeder
Pistol: The Birth of a Legend '90
Michael Schroeder
Out of the Dark '88
Damned River '89
Mortuary Academy '91
Relentless 2: Dead On '91
Cover Me '95
Cyborg 3: The Recycler '95
Peter Schubert
Germany in Autumn '78
Patrick Schulmann
Rendez-Moi Ma Peau '81
Et La Tenoresse?...Bordel! '84
Carl Schultz
Blue Fin '78
Careful, He Might Hear You '84
Travelling North '87
The Seventh Sign '88
Which Way Home '90
Deadly Currents '93
Michael A. Schultz
Honeybaby '74
Cooley High '75
Car Wash '76
Greased Lightning '77
Which Way Is Up? '77
Sgt. Pepper's Lonely Hearts Club Band '78
Scavenger Hunt '79
Carbon Copy '81
Three Days in Beirut '83
Krush Groove '85
The Last Dragon '85
Disorderlies '87
Timestalkers '87
For Us, the Living '88
Livin' Large '91
The Great American Sex Scandal '94
Bob Schulz
Robbers of the Sacred Mountain '83
Douglas Schulze
Hellmaster '92
Joel Schumacher
The Virginia Hill Story '76

The Incredible Shrinking Woman '81
D.C. Cab '84
St. Elmo's Fire '85
The Lost Boys '87
Cousins '89
Flatliners '90
Dying Young '91
Falling Down '93
The Client '94
Batman Forever '95
A Time to Kill '96

Phillip Schuman
Jailbird Rock '88

Reinhold Schunzel
Fortune's Fool '21
Balalaika '39

Harold Schuster
Dinner at the Ritz '37
Marine Raiders '43
My Friend Flicka '43
Breakfast in Hollywood '46
The Tender Years '47
So Dear to My Heart '49
The Finger Man '55
Black Beauty/Courage of Black Beauty '57
Courage of Black Beauty '57

Jan Schutte
Drachenfutter '87

Douglas Schwartz
Peacekillers '71
Thunder in Paradise '93
Thunder in Paradise 2 '94
Baywatch the Movie: Forbidden Paradise '95

Maurice Schwartz
Tevye '39

Arnold Schwarzenegger
Tales from the Crypt, Vol. 3 '90
Christmas in Connecticut '92

David Scmidlapp
Not Quite Love '88

Ettore Scola
Down & Dirty '76
A Special Day '77
We All Loved Each Other So Much '77
La Nuit de Varennes '82
Le Bal '82
Passion of Love '82
Macaroni '85
The Family '87

Martin Scorsese
Who's That Knocking at My Door? '68
Boxcar Bertha '72
Mean Streets '73
Alice Doesn't Live Here Anymore '74
Taxi Driver '76
New York, New York '77
The Last Waltz '78
Raging Bull '80
King of Comedy '82
After Hours '85
The Color of Money '86
The Last Temptation of Christ '88
New York Stories '89
Goodfellas '90
Cape Fear '91
The Age of Innocence '93
Casino '95
Italianamerican/The Big Shave

Campbell Scott
Big Night '95

Cynthia Scott
Strangers in Good Company '91

George C. Scott
The Andersonville Trial '70
Rage '72
Savage Is Loose '74
Don't Look Back: The Story of Leroy "Satchel" Paige '81
Descending Angel '90

James Scott
Strike It Rich '90

Michael Scott
Ladykiller '92
Dangerous Heart '93
Heck's Way Home '95
Sharon's Secret '95

Oz Scott
Bustin' Loose '81

Peter Graham Scott
Subterfuge '68

Ridley Scott
The Duellists '77
Alien '79
Blade Runner '82
Legend '86
Someone to Watch Over Me '87
Black Rain '89
Thelma & Louise '91
1492: Conquest of Paradise '92
White Squall '96

Robert Scott
The Video Dead '87

T.J. Scott
TC 2000 '93

Tony Scott
The Hunger '83
Top Gun '86
Beverly Hills Cop 2 '87
Days of Thunder '90
Revenge '90
The Last Boy Scout '91
True Romance '93
Crimson Tide '95
The Fan '96

Aubrey Scotto
Uncle Moses '32

George Scribner
Oliver & Company '88

Sandra Seacat
In the Spirit '90

Steven Seagal
On Deadly Ground '94

John Seale
Till There was You '91

Francis Searle
A Girl in a Million '46
Things Happen at Night '48
Someone at the Door '50
Profile '54

Fred F. Sears
Ambush at Tomahawk Gap '53
Teenage Crime Wave '55
Earth vs. the Flying Saucers '56
The Giant Claw '57

Victor Sears
Ninja the Battalion '90
Ninja's Extreme Weapons '90

George Seaton
Miracle on 34th Street '47
The Big Lift '50
Country Girl '54
Teacher's Pet '58
The Counterfeit Traitor '62
Airport '70
Showdown '73

Beverly Sebastian
Gator Bait '73
Delta Fox '77
Gator Bait 2: Cajun Justice '88
The American Angels: Baptism of Blood '89
Running Cool '93

Ferd Sebastian
Hitchhikers '72
Gator Bait '73
Flash & Firecat '75
Delta Fox '77
On the Air Live with Captain Midnight '79
Rocktober Blood '85
Gator Bait 2: Cajun Justice '88
The American Angels: Baptism of Blood '89
Running Cool '93

Gregg Sebelious
The Day the Earth Froze '59

David Secter
Feelin' Up '76

Mike Sedan
Married People, Single Sex '93
Married People, Single Sex 2: For Better or Worse '94
Night Fire '94
Lap Dancing '95

Edward Sedgwick
The Cameraman '28
Spite Marriage '29
Doughboys '30
Free and Easy '30
Parlor, Bedroom and Bath '31
Speak Easily '32
What! No Beer? '33
Fit for a King '37
Pick a Star '37
Riding on Air '37
The Gladiator '38
Air Raid Wardens '43
A Southern Yankee '48
Ma and Pa Kettle Back On the Farm '51

Jakov Sedlar
Gospa '94

John Sedwick
Dark Shadows '67

Paul Seed
Dead Ahead: The Exxon Valdez Disaster '92
To Play the King '93
The Affair '95

Charles Seeling
Rounding Up the Law '22

Steven Seemayer
Miami Vendetta '87

Alex Segal
The Story of David '76

Peter Segal
Naked Gun 33 1/3: The Final Insult '94
Tommy Boy '95

Stu Segall
Illegal in Blue '95

Arthur Seidelman
Hercules in New York '70
Children of Rage '75
Echoes '83
The Caller '87
Glory Years '87
Poker Alice '87
A Friendship in Vienna '88
False Witness '89
Body Language '92
Dying to Remember '93
Rescue Me '93
Trapped in Space '94

Susan Seidelman
Smithereens '82
Desperately Seeking Susan '85
Making Mr. Right '86
Cookie '89
She-Devil '89

Joseph Seiden
Eli Eli '40
Paradise in Harlem '40
God, Man and Devil '49

Lewis Seiler
Great K & A Train Robbery '26
Charlie Chan in Paris '35
Pittsburgh '42
Guadalcanal Diary '43
Doll Face '46
The Winning Team '52

William A. Seiter
Little Church Around the Corner '23
The White Sin '24
Skinner's Dress Suit '26
The Cheerful Fraud '27
Big Business Girl '31
Way Back Home '32
Diplomaniacs '33
Sons of the Desert '33
In Person '35
Roberta '35
Dimples '36
The Moon's Our Home '36
Stowaway '36
Room Service '38
Allegheny Uprising '39
Susannah of the Mounties '39
It's a Date '40
You Were Never Lovelier '42
Destroyer '43
Lady Takes a Chance '43
Little Giant '46
One Touch of Venus '48
Borderline '50
Make Haste to Live '54

George B. Seitz
The Ice Flood '26
Vanishing American '26
Danger Lights '30
Drums of Jeopardy '31
The Last of the Mohicans '36
Love Finds Andy Hardy '38
Andy Hardy Meets Debutante '40
Kit Carson '40
Andy Hardy's Private Secretary '41
Life Begins for Andy Hardy '41
Andy Hardy's Double Life '42

Steve Sekely
Behind Prison Walls '43
Revenge of the Zombies '43
Waterfront '44
Blonde Savage '47
The Scar '48
Day of the Triffids '63

Lesley Selander
Sandflow '37
The Frontiersmen '38
The Mysterious Rider '38
Hopalong Cassidy: Renegade Trail '39
Renegade Trail '39
Knights of the Range '40
The Light of Western Stars '40
Santa Fe Marshal '40
Doomed Caravan '41
Riders of the Timberline '41
Bar-20 '43
Border Patrol '43
Buckskin Frontier '43
Colt Comrades '43
Hopalong Cassidy: Riders of the Deadline '43
Lost Canyon '43
The Vampire's Ghost '45
The Red Stallion '47
Robin Hood of Texas '47
Rider from Tucson '50
Flat Top '52
Flight to Mars '52
Fighter Attack '53
Dragonfly Squadron '54
Shotgun '55
Lone Ranger and the Lost City of Gold '58
Arizona Bushwackers '67

Jay Noyles Seles
Prisoners of Inertia '89

Henry Selick
The Nightmare Before Christmas '93
James and the Giant Peach '96

Jack M. Sell
Outtakes '85
Deadly Spygames '89
The Psychotronic Man '91

Charles E. Sellier
Silent Night, Deadly Night '84
The Annihilators '85

David Selman
Fighting Shadows '35
The Revenge Rider '35
Prescott Kid '36

Herbert Selpin
Geheimakte WB1 '42

David Seltzer
Lucas '86
Punchline '88
Shining Through '92

Edgar Selwyn
The Sin of Madelon Claudet '31
Skyscraper Souls '32

Arna Selznick
The Care Bears Movie '84

Larry Semon
Bakery/Grocery Clerk '21
The Wizard of Oz '25

Dominic Sena
Kalifornia '93

Peter Senelka
Teen Alien '88

Ralph Senensky
A Dream for Christmas '73
Death Cruise '74

Ron Senkowski
Let's Kill All the Lawyers '93

Mack Sennett
Tillie's Punctured Romance '14
Kid's Auto Race/Mabel's Married Life '15
The Lizzies of Mack Sennett '15
Cannonball/Dizzy Heights and Daring Hearts '16
Mack Sennett Comedies: Vol. 2 '16
Mickey '17
Early Cinema Vol. 1 '19
Mack Sennett Comedies: Vol. 1 '21

Mario Sequi
Tramplers '66
The Cobra '68

Eva Sereny
Foreign Student '94

Michael Seresin
Homeboy '88

Yahoo Serious
Young Einstein '89
Reckless Kelly '93

Coline Serreau
Three Men and a Cradle '85
Mama, There's a Man in Your Bed '89

Juan Carlos Sesanzo
Deadly Revenge '83

Alex Sessa
Amazons '86
Stormquest '87

Phillip Setbon
Mr. Frost '89

Javier Seto
The Castilian '63

Vernon Sewell
Frenzy '46
Ghosts of Berkeley Square '47
The World Owes Me a Living '47
Uneasy Terms '48
Ghost Ship '53
Terror Ship '54
Rogue's Yarn '56
Blood Beast Terror '67
The Crimson Cult '68
Horrors of Burke & Hare '71
Ghost Keeper '80

Jeff Seymour
Rave Review '95

Nicholas Sgarro
The Happy Hooker '75
Fortune Dane '86

Michael Shackleton
Survivor '87

Susan Shadburne
Shadow Play '86

Tom Shadyac
Ace Ventura: Pet Detective '93
The Nutty Professor '96

Matt Shaffen
Tabloid! '88

Josef Shaftel
Naked Hills '56

Krishna Shah
Rivals '72
The River Niger '76
Deadly Thief '78
Hard Rock Zombies '85

Deborah Shames
The Voyeur '94

Franklin Shamray
Rio Rattler '35

Maxwell Shane
Fear in the Night '47

John Patrick Shanley
Joe Versus the Volcano '90

Joy Shannon
Uptown Angel '90

Jack Shaoul
Robot in the Family '94

Alan Shapiro
Tiger Town '83
The Crush '93
Flipper '96

Ken Shapiro
The Groove Tube '72
Modern Problems '81

Mike Shapiro
Fireballs '90

Paul Shapiro
Hockey Night '84
Miracle at Moreaux '86

Shapiro ▶cont.

Heads '93
The Lotus Eaters '93
The Invaders '95

Jim Sharman
The Rocky Horror Picture Show '75
Shock Treatment '81

Alan Sharp
Little Treasure '85

Don Sharp
Kiss of the Vampire '62
Those Fantastic Flying Fools '67
Dark Places '73
Psychomania '73
Hennessy '75
The Four Feathers '78
The Thirty-Nine Steps '79
Bear Island '80
Guardian of the Abyss '82
What Waits Below '83
A Woman of Substance, Episode 1: Nest of Vipers '84
A Woman of Substance, Episode 2: The Secret is Revealed '84
A Woman of Substance, Episode 3: Fighting for the Dream '84
Hold the Dream '85
Tears in the Rain '88

Ian Sharp
The Final Option '82
Robin Hood...The Legend: Robin Hood and the Sorcerer '83
Secret Weapon '90
Codename Kyril '91

Ben Sharpsteen
Pinocchio '40
Dumbo '41

William Shatner
Star Trek 5: The Final Frontier '89
TekWar '94

Alfred Shaughnessy
Suspended Alibi '56
Cat Girl '57

Melville Shavelson
The Seven Little Foys '55
Houseboat '58
The Five Pennies '59
It Started in Naples '60
A New Kind of Love '63
Cast a Giant Shadow '66
Yours, Mine & Ours '68
Legend of Valentino '75
Ike '79

Chris Shaw
Split '90

Jimmy Shaw
Return of the Tiger '78

Tom Shaw
Courier of Death '84

Robert Shaye
Book of Love '91

Linda Shayne
Purple People Eater '88

Bashar Shbib
Julia Has Two Lovers '91

Jack Shea
Dayton's Devils '68

James K. Shea
Planet of Dinosaurs '80

Barry Shear
Wild in the Streets '68
The Todd Killings '71
Across 110th Street '72
The Deadly Trackers '73
Strike Force '75
The Crash of Flight 401 '78

Harry Shearer
The History of White People in America '85
The History of White People in America: Vol. 2 '85
Portrait of a White Marriage '88

Donald Shebib
Fish Hawk '79
Heartaches '82
The Climb '87
Men of Steel '88
The Little Kidnappers '90
The Ascent '94

Martin Sheen
Cadence '89

Simon S. Sheen
3 Ninjas Knuckle Up '92

Riki Shelach
The Last Winter '84
Mercenary Fighters '88

David Sheldon
Lovely ... But Deadly '82

Forrest Sheldon
Between Fighting Men '32
Hell Fire Austin '32

Ron Shelton
Bull Durham '88
Blaze '89
White Men Can't Jump '92
Cobb '94
Tin Cup '96

Richard Shepard
Cool Blue '88
The Linguini Incident '92

Sam Shepard
Far North '88
Silent Tongue '92

Gordon Sheppard
Eliza's Horoscope '70

John Sheppard
Higher Education '88

Jack Sher
The Three Worlds of Gulliver '59

Jim Sheridan
My Left Foot '89
The Field '90
In the Name of the Father '93

Michael J. Sheridan
That's Entertainment, Part 3 '93

Edwin Sherin
My Old Man's Place '71
Valdez is Coming '71
The Father Clements Story '87

Arthur Sherman
Spy Trap '92

Gary Sherman
Dead and Buried '81
Mysterious Two '82
Vice Squad '82
Wanted Dead or Alive '86
Poltergeist 3 '88
After the Shock '90
Lisa '90
Murderous Vision '91

George Sherman
Outlaws of Sonora '38
Overland Stage Raiders '38
Pals of the Saddle '38
Santa Fe Stampede '38
Dawn Rider/Frontier Horizon '39
Frontier Horizon '39
The Kansas Terrors '39
Lonely Trail/Three Texas Steers '39
Three Texas Steers '39
Wyoming Outlaw '39
Covered Wagon Days '40
Rocky Mountain Rangers '40
The Sombrero Kid '42
X Marks the Spot '42
The Last of the Redmen '47
Comanche Territory '50
Against All Flags '52
War Arrow '53
Treasure of Pancho Villa '55
Panic Button '62
Big Jake '71
Western Double Feature 2: Wayne & Hale '80s

Lowell Sherman
Bachelor Apartment '31
The Royal Bed '31
False Faces '32
Three Broadway Girls '32
Morning Glory '33
She Done Him Wrong '33

Vincent Sherman
All Through the Night '42
Mr. Skeffington '44
Adventures of Don Juan '49
Harriet Craig '50
Affair in Trinidad '52
Lone Star '52
The Young Philadelphians '59
Ice Palace '60
Bogie: The Last Hero '80

Amir Shervan
Hollywood Cop '87

Bill Sherwood
Parting Glances '86

John Sherwood
The Creature Walks Among Us '56
The Monolith Monsters '57
Creeping Terror '64

Frank Shields
Savage Attraction '83
Project: Alien '89

Pat Shields
Frasier the Sensuous Lion '73

Stanley Shiff
Lobster Man from Mars '89

Slobodan Shijan
Secret Ingredient '92

Barry Shils
Motorama '91
Wigstock: The Movie '95

Koji Shima
Golden Demon '53
Warning from Space '56

Nelson Shin
Transformers: The Movie '86

Kaneto Shindo
The Island '61
Onibaba '64

Masahiro Shinoda
Double Suicide '69
MacArthur's Children '85
Gonza the Spearman '86

Talia Shire
One Night Stand '95

Jack Sholder
Alone in the Dark '82
A Nightmare on Elm Street 2: Freddy's Revenge '85
The Hidden '87
By Dawn's Early Light '89
Renegades '89
12:01 '93
Sketch Artist 2: Hands That See '94

Lee Sholem
Superman & the Mole Men '51
The Redhead from Wyoming '53
Tobor the Great '54
Ma and Pa Kettle at Waikiki '55
Hell Ship Mutiny '57
Escape from Planet Earth '67

Roger Sholes
The Tale of Ruby Rose '87

Lindsay Shonteff
Devil Doll '64
Second Best Secret Agent in the Whole Wide World '65
Big Zapper '73
Fast Kill '73
Number 1 of the Secret Service '77
The Killing Edge '86

Sig Shore
Shining Star '75
The Act '82
Sudden Death '85
The Survivalist '87

Lynn Shores
The Glory Trail '36
A Million to One '37
Charlie Chan at the Wax Museum '40

Richard Shorr
Witches' Brew '79

Ko Shu-How
Five Fighters from Shaolin '70s

Irene Shubik
Staying On '80

Mina Shum
Double Happiness '94

Herman Shumlin
Watch on the Rhine '43

Charles Shyer
Irreconcilable Differences '84
Baby Boom '87
Father of the Bride '91
I Love Trouble '94
Father of the Bride Part II '95

Melville Shyer
Mad Youth '40

James Shyman
Hollywood's New Blood '88
Slashdance '89

Mussef Sibay
A Woman, Her Men and Her Futon '92

Andy Sidaris
Stacey '73
Seven '79
Malibu Express '85
Hard Ticket to Hawaii '87
Picasso Trigger '89
Savage Beach '89
Guns '90
Do or Die '91
Hard Hunted '92
Fit to Kill '93

Drew Sidaris
Enemy Gold '93
The Dallas Connection '94

George Sidney
Thousands Cheer '43
Bathing Beauty '44
Anchors Aweigh '45
The Harvey Girls '46
Holiday in Mexico '46
Cass Timberlane '47
The Three Musketeers '48
Key to the City '50
Show Boat '51
Scaramouche '52
Kiss Me Kate '53
Young Bess '53
Jupiter's Darling '55
The Eddy Duchin Story '56
Pal Joey '57
Bye, Bye, Birdie '63
Viva Las Vegas '63
Half a Sixpence '67

Scott Sidney
Tarzan of the Apes '17
Charley's Aunt '25
The Nervous Wreck '26

David Siegel
Suture '93

Donald Siegel
Big Steal '49
Private Hell 36 '54
Riot in Cell Block 11 '54
The Annapolis Story '55
Invasion of the Body Snatchers '56
Flaming Star '60
Hell is for Heroes '62
The Killers '64
Coogan's Bluff '68
Madigan '68
Death of a Gunfighter '69
The Beguiled '70
Two Mules for Sister Sara '70
Dirty Harry '71
Charley Varrick '73
The Black Windmill '74
The Shootist '76
Telefon '77
Escape from Alcatraz '79
Rough Cut '80
Jinxed '82

Robert Siegel
The Line '80

James Signorelli
Easy Money '83
Elvira, Mistress of the Dark '88
Hotel Room '93

Dai Sijie
China, My Sorrow '89

Joel Silberg
Breakin' '84
Rappin' '85
Bad Guys '86
Catch the Heat '87
Lambada '89

Yoel Silberg
Kuni Lemel in Tel Aviv '77

Brad Silberling
Casper '95

Andrew Silver
Return '88

Joan Micklin Silver
Hester Street '75
Between the Lines '77
Chilly Scenes of Winter '79
Finnegan Begin Again '84
Crossing Delancey '88
Loverboy '89
Prison Stories: Women on the Inside '91
Big Girls Don't Cry...They Get Even '92
A Private Matter '92

Lynn Silver
Ghost Stories: Graveyard Thriller '86

Marisa Silver
Old Enough '84
Permanent Record '88
Vital Signs '90
He Said, She Said '91
Indecency '92

Raphael D. Silver
The Legend of the Wolf Woman '77
On the Yard '79

Ron Silver
Lifepod '93

Elliot Silverstein
Cat Ballou '65
A Man Called Horse '70
Jailbait: Betrayed By Innocence '86
Flashfire '94

Dario Silvester
Between God, the Devil & a Winchester '72

Lloyd A. Simanol
Ladies of the Lotus '87
Beyond the Silhouette '90
Possession: Until Death Do You Part '90
Ultimate Desires '91
Chained Heat 2 '92
Dangerous Prey '95

Marc Simenon
By the Blood of Others '73

Lawrence L. Simeone
Cop-Out '91
Presumed Guilty '91
Eyes of the Beholder '92
Blindfold: Acts of Obsession '94

Allen Simmonds
Striker's Mountain '87

Anthony Simmons
Little Sweetheart '90

Sandor Simo
The Train Killer '83

Adam Simon
Brain Dead '89
Body Chemistry 2: Voice of a Stranger '91
Carnosaur '93

Francis Simon
The Chicken Chronicles '77

J. Piquer Simon
Where Time Began '77
Supersonic Man '78
Pieces '83
Slugs '87
Endless Descent '90
Cthulhu Mansion '91

Roger L. Simon
My Man Adam '86

Sylvan Simon
Whistling in the Dark '41
Rio Rita '42
Whistling in Dixie '42
Whistling in Brooklyn '43
Abbott and Costello in Hollywood '45
Son of Lassie '45
Her Husband's Affairs '47
Lust for Gold '49

Yves Simoneau
Pouvoir Intime '87
Memphis '91
Perfectly Normal '91
Till Death Do Us Part '92
Amelia Earhart: The Final Flight '94
Mother's Boys '94

Gregory Simpson
Rogue '76
Jane Simpson
Number One Fan '94
Megan Simpson
Alex '92
Michael A. Simpson
Impure Thoughts '86
Sleepaway Camp 2: Unhappy Campers '88
Fast Food '89
Funland '89
Sleepaway Camp 3: Teenage Wasteland '89
Peter Simpson
Prom Night 3: The Last Kiss '89
Frank Sinatra
None But the Brave '65
Andrew Sinclair
Blue Blood '73
Under Milk Wood '73
Tuxedo Warrior '82
Gerald Seth Sindell
Teenager '74
H.O.T.S. '79
Alexander Singer
Love Has Many Faces '65
Captain Apache '71
Bryan Singer
Public Access '93
The Usual Suspects '95
Gail Singer
Wisecracks '93
Stanford Singer
I Was a Teenage TV Terrorist '87
John Singleton
Boyz N the Hood '91
Poetic Justice '93
Higher Learning '94
Ralph S. Singleton
Graveyard Shift '90
Gary Sinise
Miles from Home '88
Of Mice and Men '92
Bernhard Sinkel
Germany in Autumn '78
Bruce Sinofsky
Brother's Keeper '92
Gary Sinyor
Leon the Pig Farmer '93
Curt Siodmak
Bride of the Gorilla '51
Robert Siodmak
Son of Dracula '43
Cobra Woman '44
The Strange Affair of Uncle Harry '45
Dark Mirror '46
The Spiral Staircase '46
Criss Cross '48
Crimson Pirate '52
Andrew Sipes
Fair Game '95
Douglas Sirk
First Legion '51
All I Desire '53
Magnificent Obsession '54
Written on the Wind '56
Battle Hymn '57
Tarnished Angels '57
A Time to Love & a Time to Die '58
Imitation of Life '59
Marlon Sirko
Perfect Killer '77
Hal Sitowitz
Last Cry for Help '79
Yuri Sivo
Mortal Sins '90
Alf Sjoberg
Torment '44
Miss Julie '50
John Sjogren
Money to Burn '94
The Mosaic Project '95
Vilgot Sjoman
I Am Curious (Yellow) '67

Victor Sjostrom
The Outlaw and His Wife '17
The Phantom Chariot '20
He Who Gets Slapped '24
The Wind '28
Under the Red Robe '36
Calvin Skaggs
The Fig Tree '87
Jerzy Skolimowski
Deep End '70
King, Queen, Knave '72
The Shout '78
Hands Up '81
Moonlighting '82
Success is the Best Revenge '84
The Lightship '86
Torrents of Spring '90
Guy Slater
A Pocketful of Rye '87
Bob Slatzer
Hellcats '68
Big Foot '72
John Sledge
The Invisible Avenger '58
New Orleans After Dark '58
Wladyslaw Slesicki
In Desert and Wilderness '73
Brian Sloan
Boys Life '94
Holly Goldberg Sloan
The Big Green '95
Paul Sloane
The Coming of Amos '25
Made for Love '26
Half-Shot at Sunrise '30
Consolation Marriage '31
Rick Sloane
Hobgoblins '80s
Visitants '87
Vice Academy '88
Marked for Murder '89
Vice Academy 2 '90
Vice Academy 3 '91
Mind, Body & Soul '92
Edward Sloman
Lost Zeppelin '29
George Sluizer
Red Desert Penitentiary '83
The Vanishing '88
Utz '93
The Vanishing '93
John Smallcombe
An African Dream '90
Ralph Smart
Curtain Up '53
Robin Hood: The Movie '55
Robert J. Smawley
Murphy's Fault '88
American Eagle '90
River of Diamonds '90
Jack Smight
Harper '66
No Way to Treat a Lady '68
The Secret War of Harry Frigg '68
The Illustrated Man '69
Airport '75 '75
Midway '76
Airport '77 '77
Damnation Alley '77
Roll of Thunder, Hear My Cry '78
Fast Break '79
Loving Couples '80
Holocaust Survivors...Remembrance of Love '83
Number One with a Bullet '87
Intimate Power '89
Bruce Smith
Bebe's Kids '92
Bud Smith
Johnny Be Good '88
Charles Martin Smith
Trick or Treat '86
Boris and Natasha: The Movie '92
Fifty/Fifty '93
Cliff Smith
Radio Patrol '37
Clive A. Smith
Rock & Rule '83

Howard Smith
Marjoe '72
John N. Smith
The Boys of St. Vincent '93
Dangerous Minds '95
Sugartime '95
Kent Smith
Forever and a Day '43
Kevin Smith
Clerks '94
Mallrats '95
Mel Smith
The Tall Guy '89
Radioland Murders '94
Peter Smith
No Surrender '86
Richard Smith
Trident Force '88
Roy Allen Smith
The Land Before Time 3: The Time of the Great Giving '95
Alan Smithee
Iron Cowboy '68
City in Fear '80
Appointment with Fear '85
Stitches '85
Ghost Fever '87
I Love N.Y. '87
Let's Get Harry '87
Morgan Stewart's Coming Home '87
Bloodsucking Pharoahs of Pittsburgh '90
The Shrimp on the Barbie '90
Fatal Charm '92
Gypsy Angels '94
The O.J. Simpson Story '94
Hellraiser 4: Bloodline '95
Raging Angels '95
Stephen Smoke
Final Impact '91
Street Crimes '92
Sandy Smolan
Rachel River '87
Phil Smoot
The Dark Power '85
Skott Snider
Miracle Beach '92
Michael Snyder
Caged in Paradiso '89
Michele (Michael) Soavi
Stagefright '87
The Church '90
The Devil's Daughter '91
Cemetery Man '95
Mark Sobel
Access Code '84
Sweet Revenge '87
Trial and Error '92
Steven Soderbergh
sex, lies and videotape '89
Kafka '91
Fallen Angels 2 '93
King of the Hill '93
The Underneath '95
Iain Softley
Backbeat '94
Hackers '95
Joel Soisson
Maniac Cop 3: Badge of Silence '93
Alec Sokolow
Frankenstein Sings...The Movie '95
Peter Solan
The Boxer and Death '63
Gilberto Martinez Solares
Face of the Screaming Werewolf '59
Russell Solberg
Payback '90
Forced to Kill '93
Mario Soldati
The Wayward Wife '52
Alfred Sole
Alice Sweet Alice '76
Tanya's Island '81

Pandemonium '82
Sergio Sollima
The Family '73
Peter J. Solmo
Jack & the Beanstalk '76
Todd Solondz
Fear, Anxiety and Depression '89
Welcome to the Dollhouse '95
Andrew Solt
This Is Elvis '81
Ola Solum
Turnaround '87
The Polar Bear King '94
Paul Solvay
Devil's Wedding Night '73
Josef Sommer
Thoughts are Free '84
Stephen Sommers
Catch Me...If You Can '89
The Adventures of Huck Finn '93
Rudyard Kipling's The Jungle Book '94
Barry Sonnenfeld
The Addams Family '91
Addams Family Values '93
For Love or Money '93
Get Shorty '95
Dror Soref
The Seventh Coin '92
Carlos Sorin
Eversmile New Jersey '89
Dimitri Sotirakis
Beverly Hills Brats '89
Jim Sotos
Forced Entry '75
Sweet 16 '81
Hot Moves '84
Colin South
In Too Deep '90
Larry Spangler
Joshua '76
Hans A. Spanuth
The Great Train Robbery: Cinema Begins '03
Teresa Sparks
Over the Summer '85
Robert Sparr
A Swingin' Summer '65
Shane Spaulding
Armed for Action '92
Martin Speer
The Hasty Heart '86
Aaron Speiser
Talking About Sex '94
Michael Spence
Edge of Honor '91
Richard Spence
Blind Justice '94
Alan Spencer
Hexed '93
Benton Spencer
The Club '94
Jane Spencer
Little Noises '91
Josh Spencer
Easy Kill '89
Norman Spencer
Rainbow's End '35
Robert Spera
Witchcraft '88
Penelope Spheeris
Decline of Western Civilization 1 '81
Suburbia '83
The Boys Next Door '85
Hollywood Vice Sqaud '86
Dudes '87
Decline of Western Civilization 2: The Metal Years '88
Thunder & Mud '89
Prison Stories: Women on the Inside '91
Wayne's World '92
The Beverly Hillbillies '93
The Little Rascals '94
Black Sheep '96

Bryan Spicer
Mighty Morphin Power Rangers: The Movie '95
Larry Spiegel
Survival Run '80
Scott Spiegel
Intruder '88
Steven Spielberg
Night Gallery '69
Columbo: Murder By the Book '71
Duel '71
The Sugarland Express '74
Jaws '75
Close Encounters of the Third Kind '77
1941 '79
Raiders of the Lost Ark '81
E.T.: The Extra-Terrestrial '82
Twilight Zone: The Movie '83
Indiana Jones and the Temple of Doom '84
Amazing Stories '85
The Color Purple '85
Empire of the Sun '87
Always '89
Indiana Jones and the Last Crusade '89
Hook '91
Jurassic Park '93
Schindler's List '93
Martin J. Spinelli
Sourdough '77
Alan Spires
Little Boy Lost '78
Tony Spiridakis
The Last Word '95
Murray Douglas Sporup
Rock, Baby, Rock It '57
Roger Spottiswoode
Terror Train '80
The Pursuit of D.B. Cooper '81
Under Fire '83
The Best of Times '86
The Last Innocent Man '87
Shoot to Kill '88
Third Degree Burn '89
Time Flies When You're Alive '89
Turner and Hooch '89
Air America '90
Stop! or My Mom Will Shoot '92
And the Band Played On '93
Hiroshima '95
G.D. Spradlin
The Only Way Home '72
Tim Spring
Reason to Die '90
R.G. Springsteen
Stagecoach to Denver '46
Vigilantes of Boom Town '46
Hellfire '48
Arizona Cowboy '49
The Red Menace '49
Hills of Oklahoma '50
Oklahoma Annie '51
When Gangland Strikes '56
Apache Uprising '66
Johnny Reno '66
Hostile Guns '67
Robin Spry
Drying Up the Streets '76
Keeping Track '86
Obsessed '88
A Cry in the Night '93
Pasquale Squitieri
Blood Brothers '74
Corleone '79
Third Solution '89
Stephen Stafford
I Posed for Playboy '91
Nick Stagliano
Home of Angels '94
Juan Bautista Stagnaro
Under the Earth '86
C. Ray Stahl
Geisha Girl '52
Eric Steven Stahl
Final Approach '91

John M. Stahl
Letter of Introduction '38
Immortal Sergeant '43
The Keys of the Kingdom '44
Leave Her to Heaven '45
Father Was a Fullback '49

Sylvester Stallone
Paradise Alley '78
Rocky 2 '79
Rocky 3 '82
Staying Alive '83
Rocky 4 '85

Jeremy Stanford
Watchers 3 '94

John Stanley
Nightmare in Blood '75

Michael Stanley
Attack of the Beast Creatures '85

Paul Stanley
Cotter '72
The Ultimate Imposter '79

Richard Stanley
Hardware '90
Dust Devil '93

David L. Stanton
Chill Factor '90

Richard Stanton
American Pluck '25

Jeff Stanzler
Jumpin' at the Boneyard '92

George Stapleford
Mountain Charlie '80

Wladislaw Starewicz
Early Russian Cinema, Vol. 3: Starewicz's Fantasies '15

Edward Staroselsky
My Family Treasure '93

Bruce Starr
Boogey Man 2 '83

Ringo Starr
Born to Boogie '72

Steven Starr
Joey Breaker '93

Jack Starrett
Run, Angel, Run! '69
The Losers '70
Slaughter '72
Cleopatra Jones '73
Race with the Devil '75
Hollywood Man '76
A Small Town in Texas '76
Fatal Chase '77
Walking Tall: The Final Chapter '77
Mr. Horn '79
On the Edge: The Survival of Dana '79
Kiss My Grits '82

Ralph Staub
Country Gentlemen '36
The Mandarin Mystery '37
Danger Ahead '40
Gene Autry Matinee Double Feature #3 '53

Ray Dennis Steckler
Eegah! '62
Wild Guitar '62
Incredibly Strange Creatures Who Stopped Living and Became Mixed-Up Zombies '63
The Thrill Killers '65
Rat Pfink a Boo-Boo '66
Sinthia: The Devil's Doll '70
The Hollywood Strangler Meets the Skid Row Slasher '79

David Steensland
Escapes '86

Giorgio Stegani
Beyond the Law '68

Herbert Stein
Escape to Love '82

Ken Stein
The Rain Killer '90
Killer Instinct '92

Paul Stein
Lottery Bride '30
Sin Takes a Holiday '30
Mimi '35
Heart's Desire '37
Black Limelight '38
Counterblast '48

David Steinberg
Paternity '81
Going Berserk '83
Casey at the Bat '85

David Max Steinberg
Severance '88

Michael Steinberg
The Waterdance '91
Bodies, Rest & Motion '93

Ziggy Steinberg
The Boss' Wife '86

Danny Steinmann
Savage Streets '83
Friday the 13th, Part 5: A New Beginning '85

Jos Stelling
Rembrandt—1669 '77
The Pointsman '86

Steno
Flatfoot '78

Frederick Stephani
Flash Gordon: Rocketship '36

A.C. Stephen
Orgy of the Dead '65
Saturday Night Sleazies, Vol. 1 '66
Lady Godiva Rides '68

William Sterling
Alice's Adventures in Wonderland '72

Daniel Stern
Rookie of the Year '93

David Hillard Stern
Morning Glory '93

Noah Stern
Pyrates '91

Sandor Stern
John & Yoko: A Love Story '85
Assassin '86
Glitz '88
Pin '88
Amityville 4 '89
Dangerous Pursuit '89
Web of Deceit '90
Duplicates '92
Jericho Fever '93

Steven Hilliard Stern
Harrad Summer '74
I Wonder Who's Killing Her Now? '76
Anatomy of a Seduction '79
Young Love, First Love '79
The Devil & Max Devlin '81
Draw! '81
Miracle on Ice '81
A Small Killing '81
The Ambush Murders '82
Forbidden Love '82
Mazes and Monsters '82
Portrait of a Showgirl '82
Getting Physical '84
Obsessive Love '84
Murder in Space '85
The Park is Mine '85
Undergrads '85
Not Quite Human '87
Rolling Vengeance '87
Weekend War '88
Final Notice '89
Personals '90
Love & Murder '91
Black Fox: The Price of Peace '94
Blood Horse '94
Good Men and Bad '94
Kill My Wife...Please!

Tom Stern
Freaked '93

Andrew Stevens
The Terror Within 2 '91
Night Eyes 3 '93
Scorned '93
Virtual Combat '95

Arnold Stevens
Attack of the Swamp Creature '75

Art Stevens
The Fox and the Hound '81

David Stevens
Roses Bloom Twice '77
A Town Like Alice '85
Kansas '88

George Stevens
Kentucky Kernels '34
Alice Adams '35
Annie Oakley '35
Swing Time '36
A Damsel in Distress '37
Quality Street '37
Vivacious Lady '38
Gunga Din '39
Penny Serenade '41
Talk of the Town '42
Woman of the Year '42
The More the Merrier '43
I Remember Mama '48
A Place in the Sun '51
Shane '53
Giant '56
The Diary of Anne Frank '59
The Greatest Story Ever Told '65

George Stevens, Jr.
Separate But Equal '91

Leslie Stevens
The Outer Limits: Galaxy Being '63
Three Kinds of Heat '87

Mark Stevens
Cry Vengeance '54

Robert Stevens
Never Love a Stranger '58

Stella Stevens
The Ranch '88

Rick Stevenson
Magic in the Water '95

Robert Stevenson
Nine Days a Queen '34
The Man Who Lived Again '36
King Solomon's Mines '37
Non-Stop New York '37
Tom Brown's School Days '40
Joan of Paris '42
Forever and a Day '43
Jane Eyre '44
Dishonored Lady '47
Walk Softly, Stranger '50
My Forbidden Past '51
The Las Vegas Story '52
Old Yeller '57
Johnny Tremain & the Sons of Liberty '58
Darby O'Gill & the Little People '59
Kidnapped '60
The Absent-Minded Professor '61
In Search of the Castaways '62
The Misadventures of Merlin Jones '63
Son of Flubber '63
Mary Poppins '64
Monkey's Uncle '65
That Darn Cat '65
Blackbeard's Ghost '67
The Gnome-Mobile '67
The Love Bug '68
My Dog, the Thief '69
Bedknobs and Broomsticks '71
Herbie Rides Again '74
The Island at the Top of the World '74
One of Our Dinosaurs Is Missing '75
The Shaggy D.A. '76

Alan L. Stewart
Ghostriders '87
Ghetto Blaster '89

Douglas Day Stewart
Thief of Hearts '84
Listen to Me '89

John Stewart
Action U.S.A. '89
Hidden Obsession '92

Larry Stewart
The Initiation '84

Robert Stewart
Rock & Roll Cowboys '92
Mark of the Beast

Roger Stigliano
Fun Down There '88

Ben Stiller
Reality Bites '94
The Cable Guy '96

Mauritz Stiller
Thomas Graal's Best Film '17
Thomas Graal's First Child '18
Treasure of Arne '19
The Atonement of Gosta Berling '24
Hotel Imperial '27

Whit Stillman
Metropolitan '90
Barcelona '94

Alexander Stitt
Grendel, Grendel, Grendel '82

Mark Stock
Midnight Movie Massacre '88

John Stockwell
Undercover '87

Ben Stoloff
Night of Terror '33
Palooka '34
Transatlantic Merry-Go-Round '34
Sea Devils '37
The Affairs of Annabel '38
It's a Joke, Son! '47

Victor Stoloff
Washington Affair '77

Andrew L. Stone
Hell's Headquarters '32
The Girl Said No '37
Hi Diddle Diddle '43
Stormy Weather '43
Sensations of 1945 '44
The Last Voyage '60
Song of Norway '70

Norman Stone
Shadowlands '85
The Vision '87
The Black Velvet Gown '92

Oliver Stone
Seizure '74
The Hand '81
Platoon '86
Salvador '86
Wall Street '87
Talk Radio '88
Born on the Fourth of July '89
The Doors '91
JFK '91
Heaven and Earth '93
Natural Born Killers '94
Nixon '95

Virginia Lively Stone
The Treasure of Jamaica Reef '74
Money to Burn '83
Run If You Can '87

Tom Stoppard
Rosencrantz & Guildenstern Are Dead '90

Esben Storm
In Search of Anna '79

Howard Storm
The Three Little Pigs '84
Once Bitten '85

Jerome Storm
Sweet Adeline '26
Courtin' Wildcats '29

Mark Story
Odd Jobs '85

Thomas L. Story
Last Frontier '32

Larry N. Stouffer
Twisted Brain '74

Mark Stouffer
Man Outside '88

Louis Clyde Stouman
Operation Dames '59

Walter Strate
Violated '53

Joe Straw
Kill or Be Killed '93

Frank Strayer
Murder at Midnight '31
The Monster Walks '32
Tangled Destinies '32
The Vampire Bat '32
Fugitive Road '34
The Ghost Walks '34
In the Money '34
Condemned to Live '35
Death from a Distance '36
Blondie '38
Blondie Takes a Vacation '39
Blondie Has Trouble '40
Blondie in Society '41
Blondie's Blessed Event '42
It's a Great Life '43

Barbra Streisand
Yentl '83
The Prince of Tides '91

Joseph Strick
The Balcony '63
Ulysses '67
Tropic of Cancer '70

Wesley Strick
The Tie That Binds '95

John Strickland
Prime Suspect 2 '93

Herbert L. Strock
Blood of Dracula '57
How to Make a Monster '58
Teenage Frankenstein '58
The Crawling Hand '63
Man on the Run '74
Monster '78
Witches' Brew '79

William R. Stromberg
The Crater Lake Monster '77

Jonathan Stryker
Curtains '83

Brian Stuart
Sorceress '82

Mel Stuart
If It's Tuesday, This Must Be Belgium '69
I Love My...Wife '70
Willy Wonka & the Chocolate Factory '71
Mean Dog Blues '78
The Chisholms '79
The Triangle Factory Fire Scandal '79
Sophia Loren: Her Own Story '80
Happy Anniversary 007: 25 Years of James Bond '87

John Sturges
The Capture '50
The Magnificent Yankee '50
Escape from Fort Bravo '53
Bad Day at Black Rock '54
Underwater! '55
Gunfight at the O.K. Corral '57
The Law and Jake Wade '58
Last Train from Gun Hill '59
Never So Few '59
The Magnificent Seven '60
By Love Possessed '61
The Great Escape '63
The Hallelujah Trail '65
Hour of the Gun '67
Ice Station Zebra '68
Marooned '69
Joe Kidd '72
McQ '74
Chino '75
The Eagle Has Landed '77

Preston Sturges
Christmas in July '40
The Great McGinty '40
The Lady Eve '41
Sullivan's Travels '41
The Palm Beach Story '42
The Great Moment '44
Hail the Conquering Hero '44
Miracle of Morgan's Creek '44
The Sin of Harold Diddlebock '47
Unfaithfully Yours '48
The Beautiful Blonde from Bashful Bend '49

Charles Sturridge
Brideshead Revisited '81
Aria '88
A Handful of Dust '88
Where Angels Fear to Tread '91
A Foreign Field '93
Gulliver's Travels '95

Richard Styles
Shallow Grave '87
Escape '90
Midnight Tease 2 '95

Bobby Suarez
Pay or Die '83
American Commandos '84
Warriors of the Apocalypse '85

Gonzolo Suarez
House of the Damned '71

Eliseo Subiela
Man Facing Southeast *'86*

Arne Sucksdorff
The Great Adventure *'53*

L. Sudjio
Black Magic Terror *'79*

Andrew Sugarman
Basic Training *'86*

Toshio Sugie
Saga of the Vagabond *'59*

Daniele Suissa
Pocahontas: The Legend *'95*

Terrence Sul
Wonsan Operation *'78*

Fred G. Sullivan
Cold River *'81*

Kevin Sullivan
Wild Pony *'83*
Anne of Green Gables *'85*
Anne of Avonlea *'87*
Lantern Hill *'90*
Cosmic Slop *'94*

Kevin Rodney Sullivan
America's Dream *'95*

Tim Sullivan
Jack and Sarah *'96*

Dirk Summers
Survival of Spaceship Earth *'90*

Jeremy Summers
Five Golden Dragons *'67*
The House of 1000 Dolls *'67*

Walter Summers
The Human Monster *'39*
House of Mystery *'41*

Shirley Sun
Iron & Silk *'91*

Cedric Sundstrom
Captive Rage *'88*
American Ninja 3: Blood Hunt *'89*
The Revenger *'90*
American Ninja 4: The Annihilation *'91*

Neal Sundstrom
Howling 5: The Rebirth *'89*

Jack A. Sunseri
The Chilling *'89*

Fred Surin
The Bride Is Much Too Beautiful *'58*

Stephen Surjik
Wayne's World 2 *'93*

Henry Suso
Death Sport *'78*

Edward Sutherland
Behind the Front *'26*
It's the Old Army Game *'26*
Mr. Robinson Crusoe *'32*
International House *'33*
Murders in the Zoo *'33*
Every Day's a Holiday *'38*
The Flying Deuces *'39*
Beyond Tomorrow *'40*
The Invisible Woman *'40*
One Night in the Tropics *'40*
The Navy Comes Through *'42*
Sing Your Worries Away *'42*
Follow the Boys *'44*
Having Wonderful Crime *'45*
The Devil Thumbs a Ride/Having Wonderful Crime *'47*

Kiefer Sutherland
Last Light *'93*

Noribumi Suzuki
Shogun's Ninja *'83*

Jan Svankmajer
Alice *'88*

Peter Svatek
Mystery of the Million Dollar Hockey Puck *'80s*
Witchboard 3: The Possession *'95*

E.W. Swackhamer
Man & Boy *'71*
Death Sentence *'74*
Death at Love House *'75*
Night Terror *'76*
The Amazing Spider-Man *'77*
The Dain Curse *'78*
The Winds of Kitty Hawk *'78*
Terror at London Bridge *'85*
The Rousters *'90*
Are You Lonesome Tonight *'92*
Perfect Family *'92*
The Secret Passion of Robert Clayton *'92*

Bob Swaim
Half Moon Street *'86*
Masquerade *'88*

Don Swan
Gore-Met Zombie Chef From Hell *'87*

Bob Sweeney
Return to Mayberry *'85*

Bruce Sweeney
Live Bait *'95*

Charles Swenson
Little Rascals Christmas Special *'79*

Arthur Swerdloff
Road Racers *'59*

Larry Swerdlove
The Skateboard Kid *'93*

Charles Swickard
The Three Musketeers *'16*

David Swift
Pollyanna *'60*
The Parent Trap *'61*
The Interns *'62*
Good Neighbor Sam *'64*
How to Succeed in Business without Really Trying *'67*

Saul Swimmer
Mrs. Brown, You've Got a Lovely Daughter *'68*

Michael Switzer
Nitti: The Enforcer *'88*
The Lightning Incident *'91*
Fergie & Andrew: Behind Palace Doors *'93*
Past the Bleachers *'95*

Ron Switzer
Science Crazed *'90*

Peter Sykes
Demons of the Mind *'72*
Night of the Laughing Dead *'75*
To the Devil, A Daughter *'76*
Jesus *'79*

Paul Sylbert
The Steagle *'71*

Istvan Szabo
Father *'67*
Love Film *'70*
25 Fireman's Street *'73*
Mephisto *'81*
Hanussen *'88*
Meeting Venus *'91*

Laszlo Szabo
Colonel Redl *'84*

William Szarka
South Bronx Heroes *'85*
Phantom Brother *'88*

Andras Szirtes
After the Revolution *'90*

Samy Szlingerbaum
Brussels Transit *'80*

Gyorgy Szomjas
Bad Guys *'79*

Reszo Szoreny
A Happy New Year! *'79*

Boris Szulzinger
Mama Dracula *'80*
Shame of the Jungle *'90*

Jeannot Szwarc
Sex Through a Window *'72*
Bug *'75*
Code Name: Diamond Head *'77*
Jaws 2 *'78*
Somewhere in Time *'80*
Enigma *'82*
Supergirl *'84*
Santa Claus: The Movie *'85*
The Murders in the Rue Morgue *'86*
Grand Larceny *'92*

Micheal Taav
The Paint Job *'93*

Sylvio Tabet
Beastmaster 2: Through the Portal of Time *'91*

Juan Carlos Tabio
Strawberry and Chocolate *'93*

Jean-Charles Tacchella
The Last Winters *'71*
Cousin, Cousine *'76*

Gene Taft
Blame It on the Night *'84*

Kidlat Tahimik
Turumba *'84*
Perfumed Nightmare *'89*

Robert Taicher
Inside Out *'91*

Tibor Takacs
984: Prisoner of the Future *'84*
The Gate *'87*
I, Madman *'89*
Gate 2 *'92*
Red Shoe Diaries 2: Double Dare *'92*
Bad Blood *'94*
Sabrina the Teenage Witch *'96*

Isao Takahata
Grave of the Fireflies *'88*

Glen Takakjian
Metamorphosis: The Alien Factor *'93*

Rachel Talalay
Freddy's Dead: The Final Nightmare *'91*
Ghost in the Machine *'93*
Tank Girl *'94*

Igor Talankin
Tchaikovsky *'71*

Paul Talbot
Freakshow *'95*

C.M. Talkington
Love and a .45 *'94*

Greg Tallas
Prehistoric Women *'50*
Assignment Skybolt *'80s*
Cataclysm *'81*

Richard Talmadge
Devil Horse *'32*
Detour to Danger *'45*
Project Moon Base *'53*

Lee Tamahori
Once Were Warriors *'94*
Mulholland Falls *'95*

Harry Tampa
Fairy Tales *'76*
Nocturna *'79*

Shigeo Tanaka
Gamera vs. Barugon *'66*

Tokuzo Tanaka
Zatoichi: The Blind Swordsman's Vengeance *'66*

Senkichi Taniguhi
The Gambling Samurai *'60*
What's Up, Tiger Lily? *'66*

Terrell Tannen
A Minor Miracle *'83*
Shadows in the Storm *'88*

William Tannen
Flashpoint *'84*
Deadly Illusion *'87*
Hero and the Terror *'88*

Alain Tanner
La Salamandre *'71*
Jonah Who Will Be 25 in the Year 2000 *'76*
Messidor *'77*
In the White City *'83*

Robert Tanos
Fly with the Hawk

Robert Emmett Tansey
Way of the West *'35*
The Driftin' Kid *'41*
Dynamite Canyon *'41*
Riding the Sunset Trail *'41*
Arizona Roundup *'42*
Lone Star Law Men *'42*
Texas to Bataan *'42*
Western Mail *'42*
Where Trails End *'42*
Haunted Ranch *'43*
Death Valley Rangers *'44*
Outlaw Trail *'44*
Sonora Stagecoach *'44*
Song of Old Wyoming *'45*
Wildfire *'45*
The Caravan Trail *'46*
Colorado Serenade *'46*
Driftin' River *'46*
God's Country *'46*
Wild West *'46*

Daniel Taplitz
Nightlife *'90*
Black Magic *'92*

Michael Tarantini
Crimebusters *'79*

Quentin Tarantino
Reservoir Dogs *'92*
Pulp Fiction *'94*
Four Rooms *'95*

Andrei Tarkovsky
My Name is Ivan *'62*
Andrei Rublev *'66*
Solaris *'72*
The Mirror *'75*
Stalker *'79*
The Sacrifice *'86*

Bela Tarr
Almanac of Fall

Max Tash
The Runnin' Kind *'89*

Frank Tashlin
The Fuller Brush Man *'48*
Son of Paleface *'52*
Susan Slept Here *'54*
Artists and Models *'55*
The Girl Can't Help It *'56*
Hollywood or Bust *'56*
Will Success Spoil Rock Hunter? *'57*
The Geisha Boy *'58*
Cinderfella *'60*
Disorderly Orderly *'64*
The Alphabet Murders *'65*
The Glass Bottom Boat *'66*

Nadia Tass
Malcolm *'86*
Rikky and Pete *'88*
Pure Luck *'91*

Paul Tassie
A Pig's Tale *'94*

Jacques Tati
Jour de Fete *'48*
Mr. Hulot's Holiday *'53*
Mon Oncle *'58*
Playtime *'67*
Traffic *'71*
Parade *'74*

John Tatoulis
The Silver Stallion: King of the Wild Brumbies *'93*

Norman Taurog
Sunny Skies *'30*
Hold 'Em Jail *'32*
We're Not Dressing *'34*
Rhythm on the Range *'36*
The Adventures of Tom Sawyer *'38*
Boys Town *'38*
Mad About Music *'38*
Broadway Melody of 1940 *'40*
Little Nellie Kelly *'40*
Young Tom Edison *'40*
Men of Boys Town *'41*
Mrs. Wiggs of the Cabbage Patch *'42*
Girl Crazy *'43*
Presenting Lily Mars *'43*
Words and Music *'48*
That Midnight Kiss *'49*
The Toast of New Orleans *'50*
Rich, Young and Pretty *'51*
The Stooge *'51*
Jumping Jacks *'52*
The Caddy *'53*
Birds & the Bees *'56*
Bundle of Joy *'56*
Pardners *'56*
G.I. Blues *'60*
Blue Hawaii *'62*
Girls! Girls! Girls! *'62*
It Happened at the World's Fair *'63*
Palm Springs Weekend *'63*
Tickle Me *'65*
Dr. Goldfoot and the Bikini Machine *'66*
Spinout *'66*
Double Trouble *'67*
Live a Little, Love a Little *'68*
Speedway *'68*

David Tausik
Haunted Symphony *'94*

Bertrand Tavernier
The Judge and the Assassin *'75*
The Clockmaker *'76*
Spoiled Children *'77*
Death Watch *'80*
Coup de Torchon *'81*
A Sunday in the Country *'84*
Round Midnight *'86*
Beatrice *'88*
Life and Nothing But *'89*
Daddy Nostalgia *'90*
L.627 *'92*
L'Appat *'94*

Paolo Taviani
Allonsanfan *'73*
Padre Padrone *'77*
The Night of the Shooting Stars *'82*
Kaos *'85*
Good Morning, Babylon *'87*
Fiorile *'93*

Vittorio Taviani
Padre Padrone *'77*
The Night of the Shooting Stars *'82*
Kaos *'85*
Good Morning, Babylon *'87*
Fiorile *'93*

Baz Taylor
Happy Since I Met You *'89*
Near Misses *'91*
Shooting Elizabeth *'92*
Tattle Tale *'92*

Don Taylor
Ride the Wild Surf *'64*
Wild Women *'70*
Escape from the Planet of the Apes *'71*
Tom Sawyer *'73*
Great Scout & Cathouse Thursday *'76*
Island of Dr. Moreau *'77*
Damien: Omen 2 *'78*
The Final Countdown *'80*
Red Flag: The Ultimate Game *'81*
Listen to Your Heart *'83*
September Gun *'83*
My Wicked, Wicked Ways *'84*
Going for the Gold: The Bill Johnson Story *'85*
Secret Weapons *'85*
The Diamond Trap *'91*

Jud Taylor
Say Goodbye, Maggie Cole *'72*
Search for the Gods *'75*
Future Cop *'76*
Return to Earth *'76*
The Christmas Coal Mine Miracle *'77*
Mary White *'77*
Question of Honor *'80*
Lovey: A Circle of Children 2 *'82*
Packin' It In *'83*
License to Kill *'84*
Out of the Darkness *'85*
Broken Vows *'87*
Foxfire *'87*
The Old Man and the Sea *'90*
Danielle Steel's Kaleidoscope *'92*

Ray Taylor
Phantom of the Air *'33*
The Perils of Pauline *'34*
Return of Chandu *'34*
The Throwback *'35*
The Vigilantes are Coming *'36*
Dick Tracy: The Original Serial, Vol. 1 *'37*
Dick Tracy: The Original Serial, Vol. 2 *'37*
Mystery of the Hooded Horseman *'37*
The Painted Stallion *'37*
Flaming Frontiers *'38*
Hawaiian Buckaroo *'38*
Panamint's Bad Man *'38*
Rawhide *'38*
Pony Post *'40*
Riders of Pasco Basin *'40*
Winners of the West *'40*

Taylor ▶cont.

Boss of Bullion City '41
Bury Me Not On the Lone Prairie '41
Riders of Death Valley '41
Adventures of Smilin' Jack '43
Don Winslow of the Coast Guard '43
Don Winslow of the Navy '43
The Adventures of the Flying Cadets '44
Master Key '44
Mystery of the Riverboat '44
Lost City of the Jungle '45
Border Feud '47
Cheyenne Takes Over '47
Fighting Vigilantes '47
Ghost Town Renegades '47
Return of the Lash '47
West to Glory '47
Wild Country '47
Black Hills '48
Check Your Guns '48
The Hawk of Powder River '48
Stage to Mesa City '48
The Tioga Kid '48
Outlaw Country '49

Richard Taylor
Stingray '78

Robert Taylor
Nine Lives of Fritz the Cat '74

Roderick Taylor
Instant Karma '90

Sam Taylor
The Freshman '25
Dr. Jack/For Heaven's Sake '26
For Heaven's Sake '26
My Best Girl '27
The Tempest/The Eagle '27
The Tempest '28
Coquette '29
The Taming of the Shrew '29
Dubarry '30
Ambassador Bill '31
Nothing But Trouble '44

Ron Teachworth
Going Back '83

Lewis Teague
Lady in Red '79
Alligator '80
Fighting Back '82
Cujo '83
Cat's Eye '85
The Jewel of the Nile '85
Collision Course '89
Navy SEALS '90
Deadlock '91

Andre Techine
Rendez-vous '85
Scene of the Crime '87
Wild Reeds '94

Frank Telford
The Bamboo Saucer '68

Julien Temple
The Secret Policeman's Other Ball '82
Absolute Beginners '86
Running Out of Luck '86
Aria '88
Earth Girls Are Easy '89

Andy Tennant
Keep the Change '92
The Amy Fisher Story '93
It Takes Two '95

Del Tenney
Curse of the Living Corpse '64
Horror of Party Beach '64
I Eat Your Skin '64

Kevin S. Tenney
Witchboard '87
Night of the Demons '88
WitchTrap '89
The Cellar '90
Peacemaker '90
Witchboard 2: The Devil's Doorway '93

Pen Tennyson
Convoy '40

John Tenorio
Grad Night '81

George Terwilliger
Married? '26

Hiroshi Teshigahara
Woman in the Dunes '64
Face of Another '66
Rikyu '90

Duccio Tessari
Blood at Sundown '88

Ted Tetzlaff
Riff-Raff '47
Fighting Father Dunne '48
The Window '49
The White Tower '50
Son of Sinbad '55
The Young Land '59

Monica Teuber
Magdalene '88

Akiva Tevet
Atalia '85

Herbert Tevos
Mesa of Lost Women '52

Joan Tewkesbury
Old Boyfriends '79
Tenth Month '79
Acorn People '82
Cold Sassy Tree '89
Sudie & Simpson '90
Strangers '91

Peter Tewkesbury
Emil and the Detectives '64
Stay Away, Joe '68
The Trouble with Girls (and How To Get Into It) '69

Leon Thau
Save the Lady '82

Otis Thayer
Riders of the Range '24

Graham Theakston
Tripods: The White Mountains '84
Brother Cadfael '94

Rolf Thiele
Tonio Kroger '65

Albie Thomas
Palm Beach '79

Antony Thomas
Code Name: Chaos '90

Betty Thomas
The Brady Bunch Movie '95
The Late Shift '96

Dave Thomas
Strange Brew '83
The Experts '89

Gerald Thomas
Time Lock '57
The Vicious Circle '57
Carry On Nurse '59
Carry On Cruising '62
Carry On Cleo '65
Carry On Screaming '66
Follow That Camel '67
Carry On Doctor '68
Carry On at Your Convenience '71
Carry On Camping '71
Carry On Henry VIII '71
Carry On 'Round the Bend '72
Carry On Behind '75
Carry On Dick '75
Carry On England '76
Carry On Emmanuelle '78
Second Victory '87

John G. Thomas
Tin Man '83
Banzai Runner '86
Arizona Heat '87

Ralph Thomas
The Clouded Yellow '51
Doctor in the House '53
Above Us the Waves '56
Doctor at Sea '56
Doctor at Large '57
A Tale of Two Cities '58
Conspiracy of Hearts '60
No Love for Johnnie '60
Doctor in Distress '63
Quest for Love '71
It's Not the Size That Counts '74
The Big Scam '79

Ralph L. Thomas
Ticket to Heaven '81
The Terry Fox Story '83
Apprentice to Murder '88

Scott Thomas
Silent Assassins '88

Theodore Thomas
Frank and Ollie '95

William C. Thomas
Dark Mountain '44
Navy Way '44
Big Town '47
Big Town After Dark '47

Harry Z. Thomason
Encounter with the Unknown '75
Hootch Country Boys '75
The Day It Came to Earth '77

Brett Thompson
Adventures in Dinosaur City '92

Caroline Thompson
Black Beauty '94

Donald W. Thompson
Heaven's Heroes '87
Blood on the Mountain '88
The Prodigal Planet '88

Ernest Thompson
1969 '89

J. Lee Thompson
Tiger Bay '59
Flame Over India '60
Cape Fear '61
The Guns of Navarone '61
Taras Bulba '62
MacKenna's Gold '69
Conquest of the Planet of the Apes '72
Battle for the Planet of the Apes '73
Huckleberry Finn '74
The Blue Knight '75
The Reincarnation of Peter Proud '75
St. Ives '76
The Widow '76
The White Buffalo '77
The Greek Tycoon '78
Cabo Blanco '81
Happy Birthday to Me '81
Ten to Midnight '83
The Ambassador '84
The Evil That Men Do '84
King Solomon's Mines '85
Firewalker '86
Murphy's Law '86
Death Wish 4: The Crackdown '87
Messenger of Death '88
Kinjite: Forbidden Subjects '89

Marcus Thompson
Adventures Beyond Belief '87

Peter Thompson
Films by Peter Thompson '87

Robert C. Thompson
Bud and Lou '78

Robert Thompson
Words by Heart '84

Christian Braad Thomsen
Ladies on the Rocks '83

Chris Thomson
Waterfront '83
The Empty Beach '85
Three's Trouble '85
Swimsuit: The Movie '89

Michael Thornhill
Between Wars '74
Robbery '85
The Everlasting Secret Family '88

Jerry Thorpe
Kung Fu '72
Smile, Jenny, You're Dead '74
Wonderland Cove '75
The Possessed '77
A Question of Love '78
All God's Children '80

Richard Thorpe
Desert of the Lost '27
King of the Kongo '29
Under Montana Skies '30
Wild Horse '31
The King Murder '32
The Lone Defender '32
Probation '32
The Secrets of Wu Sin '32
After Midnight '33
Rainbow Over Broadway '33
Green Eyes '34
Tarzan Escapes '36
Double Wedding '37
The Adventures of Huckleberry Finn '39
Tarzan Finds a Son '39
Tarzan's Secret Treasure '41
Tarzan's New York Adventure '42
White Cargo '42
Above Suspicion '43
The Thin Man Goes Home '44
Two Girls and a Sailor '44
Thrill of a Romance '45
Fiesta '47
A Date with Judy '48
On an Island with You '48
Challenge to Lassie '49
Malaya '49
The Sun Comes Up '49
The Black Hand '50
Three Little Words '50
The Great Caruso '51
Vengeance Valley '51
Ivanhoe '52
Prisoner of Zenda '52
All the Brothers Were Valiant '53
The Girl Who Had Everything '53
Knights of the Round Table '53
Athena '54
The Student Prince '54
The Prodigal '55
Jailhouse Rock '57
The Honeymoon Machine '61
The Horizontal Lieutenant '62
Fun in Acapulco '63

Alexis Thurn-Taxis
A Night for Crime '42

N.G. Tien Tsu
The Bloody Fight '70s

Robert Tiffe
Sword of Honor '94

Eric Till
Hot Millions '68
Bethune '77
An American Christmas Carol '79
Mary and Joseph: A Story of Faith '79
Wild Horse Hank '79
If You Could See What I Hear '82
Improper Channels '82
A Case of Libel '83
Bridge to Terabithia '85
Buffalo Jump '90
Clarence '91
Glory Enough for All: The Discovery of Insulin '92
Oh, What a Night '92
To Catch a Killer '92

R.L. Tillmanns
Witchcraft 3: The Kiss of Death '90

Bruce W. Timm
Batman: Mask of the Phantasm '93

James Tinling
Tales of Robin Hood '52

George Tirl
Pay Off '89

Douglas Tirola
A Reason to Believe '95

Stacy Title
The Last Supper '96

Johnny To
The Heroic Trio '93

James Toback
Fingers '78
Exposed '83
The Pick-Up Artist '87

Marice Tobias
Pulsebeat '85

Ricardo Tognazzi
La Scorta '94

Norman Tokar
Big Red '62
Sammy, the Way-Out Seal '62
Savage Sam '63
A Tiger Walks '64
Those Calloways '65
The Ugly Dachshund '65
Follow Me, Boys! '66
The Happiest Millionaire '67
The Horse in the Gray Flannel Suit '68
The Boatniks '70
Snowball Express '72
Where the Red Fern Grows '74
The Apple Dumpling Gang '75
No Deposit, No Return '76
Candleshoe '78
The Cat from Outer Space '78

Sergio Toledo
One Man's War '90

Michael Tolkin
The Rapture '91
The New Age '94

Stephen Tolkin
Daybreak '93

Stanley Tong
Rumble in the Bronx '96

Wilson Tong
Two Wondrous Tigers '79

Tom Topor
Judgment '90

Ralph Toporoff
American Blue Note '89

Burt Topper
Hell Squad '58
Suicide Battalion/Hell Squad '58
Tank Commando '59
The Strangler '64
The Hard Ride '71
Soul Hustler '76

Rip Torn
The Telephone '87

Giuseppe Tornatore
Cinema Paradiso '88
Everybody's Fine '90
A Pure Formality '94
The Star Maker '95

Joe Tornatore
Zebra Force '76
Code Name: Zebra '84
Grotesque '87
Curse of the Crystal Eye '93

Robert Torrance
Mutant on the Bounty '89

Fina Torres
Oriane '85

Gabe Torres
December '91

Miguel Contreras Torres
Pancho Villa Returns '50

Cinzia Torrini
Hotel Colonial '88

Ivan Tors
Zebra in the Kitchen '65

Bruce Toscano
The Jar '84

Robert Totten
The Wild Country '71
Huckleberry Finn '75
Pony Express Rider '76
The Red Pony '76
The Sacketts '79
Dark Before Dawn '89

Mikhail Toumanichulli
Solo Voyage: The Revenge '90

Jacques Tourneur
Cat People '42
Days of Glory '43
I Walked with a Zombie '43
The Leopard Man '43
Experiment Perilous '45
Out of the Past '47
Berlin Express '48
Easy Living '49
The Flame & the Arrow '50
Stars in My Crown '50
Appointment in Honduras '53
Great Day in the Morning '56
Nightfall '56
Curse of the Demon '57
The Giant of Marathon '60
The Comedy of Terrors '64

Maurice Tourneur
The Wishing Ring '14
A Girl's Folly '17
A Poor Little Rich Girl '17
Trilby '17

Pride of the Clan '18
The Last of the Mohicans '20
Lorna Doone '22
Volpone '39

Robert Towne
Personal Best '82
Tequila Sunrise '88

Bud Townsend
Nightmare in Wax '69
Terror at Red Wolf Inn '72
Coach '78

Patrice Townsend
Beach Girls '82

Robert Townsend
Eddie Murphy: Raw '87
Hollywood Shuffle '87
The Five Heartbeats '91
The Meteor Man '93

Wendy Toye
Three Cases of Murder '55

Ian Toynton
The Maid '90

Shiro Toyoda
Mistress '53
Snow Country '57

Benno Trachtmann
The Jumper '85

Jean-Claude Tramont
All Night Long '81
As Summers Die '86

Alfred Travers
Dual Alibi '47

Bill Travers
Christian the Lion '76

Joey Travolta
Hard Vice '94

Stephen Traxler
Slithis '78

Peter S. Traynor
Seducers '77

Brian Trenchard-Smith
Deathcheaters '76
Day of the Assassin '81
Escape 2000 '81
BMX Bandits '83
Dead End Drive-In '86
The Quest '86
Fists of Blood '87
Day of the Panther '88
Out of the Body '88
The Siege of Firebase Gloria '89
Official Denial '93
Night of the Demons 2 '94
Leprechaun 3 '95

John Trent
The Bushbaby '70
Find the Lady '75
Crossbar '79
Middle Age Crazy '80
Best Revenge '83
Vengeance Is Mine '84

Georg Tressler
Teenage Wolfpack '57

Monika Treut
Seduction: The Cruel Woman '89
My Father Is Coming '91

Dale Trevillion
Las Vegas Weekend '85
One Man Force '89

Gus Trikonis
Nashville Girl '76
Moonshine County Express '77
The Evil '78
She's Dressed to Kill '79
Touched by Love '80
Take This Job & Shove It '81
Twirl '81
Miss All-American Beauty '82
Dempsey '83
First Affair '83
Jungle Heat '84
Love on the Run '85
The Rumor Mill '86

Nadine Trintignant
Next Summer '84

Victor Trivas
The Head '59

Bryan Trizers
PSI Factor '80

Rose Troche
Go Fish '94

Jan Troell
The Emigrants '72
The New Land '73
Zandy's Bride '74
Hurricane '79
Flight of the Eagle '82

Tzipi Trope
Tell Me That You Love Me '84

Gary Trousdale
Beauty and the Beast '91
The Hunchback of Notre Dame '96

Gary A. Troy
Computer Beach Party '88

Fernando Trueba
Twisted Obsession '90
Belle Epoque '92
Two Much '96

Francois Truffaut
Les Mistons '57
Godard/Truffaut Shorts '58
The 400 Blows '59
Jules and Jim '62
Shoot the Piano Player '62
The Soft Skin '64
Fahrenheit 451 '66
The Bride Wore Black '68
Stolen Kisses '68
Mississippi Mermaid '69
The Wild Child '70
Two English Girls '72
Day for Night '73
Story of Adele H. '75
Small Change '76
The Man Who Loved Women '77
The Green Room '78
Love on the Run '78
The Last Metro '80
The Woman Next Door '81
Confidentially Yours '83

Michael Truman
Koroshi '67

Dalton Trumbo
Johnny Got His Gun '71

Douglas Trumbull
Silent Running '71
Brainstorm '83

Glenn Tryon
Small Town Boy '37
Law West of Tombstone '38
Beauty for the Asking '39

Manolis Tsafos
Rip-Off '77

Chan Tsi-liang
Lai Shi: China's Last Eunuch '88

Shinya Tsukamoto
Tetsuo: The Iron Man '92

Slava Tsukerman
Liquid Sky '83

Stanley Tucci
Big Night '95

Michael Tuchner
The Old Curiosity Shop '75
The Summer of My German Soldier '78
The Hunchback of Notre Dame '82
Adam '83
Trenchcoat '83
Amos '85
Not My Kid '85
Trapped in Silence '86
Mistress '87
The Misadventures of Mr. Wilt '90
Firestorm: 72 Hours in Oakland '93
Rainbow Warrior '94

David Tucker
A Year in Provence '89

George Tucker
Traffic in Souls '13

James Tucker
Lunatic '91
Steps from Hell '92

Phil Tucker
Robot Monster '53
Dance Hall Racket '58

Roger Tucker
Deadly Recruits '86

Richard Tuggle
Tightrope '84
Out of Bounds '86

Montgomery Tully
Paid to Kill '54
Glass Tomb '55
The Way Out '56
The Electronic Monster '57
The Key Man '57
Strange Awakening '58
Dead Lucky '60
The House in Marsh Road '60
The Terrornauts '67
Battle Beneath the Earth '68

Ching Siu Tung
The Heroic Trio '93

Sandy Tung
Across the Tracks '89

Saul J. Turell
The Love Goddesses '65

Sophia Turkiewicz
Silver City '84

Rosemarie Turko
Dungeonmaster '83
Scarred '84

Zygmund Turkow
The Jolly Paupers '38

Lawrence Turman
Second Thoughts '83

Ann Turner
Celia: Child Of Terror '89

Chester Turner
Black Devil Doll from Hell '84

Clive Turner
The Howling: New Moon Rising '95

Paul Turner
Hedd Wyn '92

Robert Turner
Digger '94

Jon Turteltaub
Driving Me Crazy '91
3 Ninjas '92
Cool Runnings '93
While You Were Sleeping '95
Phenomenon '96

John Turturro
Mac '93

Frank Tuttle
Lucky Devil '25
Love 'Em and Leave 'Em '26
Roman Scandals '33
Waikiki Wedding '37
This Gun for Hire '42
Hell on Frisco Bay '55

Derek Twist
Green Grow the Rushes '51

David N. Twohy
Grand Tour: Disaster in Time '92
The Arrival '96

Tomu Uchida
Swords of Death '71

Seiichiro Uchikawa
One-Eyed Swordsman '63

Liv Ullmann
Sofie '92

Juanma Bajo Ulloa
Butterfly Wings '91

Edgar G. Ulmer
The Black Cat '34
Thunder Over Texas '34
The Singing Blacksmith '38
The Light Ahead '39
Moon over Harlem '39
Girls in Chains '43
Isle of Forgotten Sins '43
Jive Junction '43
Bluebeard '44
Strange Illusion '45
Club Havana '46
Detour '46
The Strange Woman '46
St. Benny the Dip '51
The Daughter of Dr. Jekyll '57
Naked Venus '58
The Amazing Transparent Man '60

Beyond the Time Barrier '60
Journey Beneath the Desert '61

Ron Underwood
Tremors '89
City Slickers '91
Heart and Souls '93
Speechless '94

Lawrence Unger
Novel Desires '92

Michael Toshiyuki Uno
The Wash '88
Without Warning: The James Brady Story '91
Blind Spot '93
The Road to Galveston '96

Jeff Ureles
Cheap Shots '91

Frank Urson
The Night Club '25

Chano Urueto
The Living Head '59
The Witch's Mirror '60

Peter Ustinov
Billy Budd '62
Lady L '65
Hammersmith is Out '72

Jamie Uys
Dingaka '65
The Gods Must Be Crazy '84
The Gods Must Be Crazy 2 '89

Jack Vacek
Rock House '92

Roger Vadim
And God Created Woman '57
Dangerous Liaisons '60
Blood and Roses '61
Le Repos du Guerrier '62
Circle of Love '64
The Game is Over '66
Barbarella '68
Spirits of the Dead '68
Night Games '80
Beauty and the Beast '83
Game of Seduction '86
And God Created Woman '88

Steve Vagnino
A Pleasure Doing Business '79

Ladislao Vajda
The Man Who Wagged His Tail '57

Luis Valdez
Zoot Suit '81
La Bamba '87
The Cisco Kid '94

Frank Valenti
War Bus Commando '89
Delta Force Commando 2 '90

Jon Valentine
Night of the Living Babes '87

Jean Valere
Time Out for Love '61

Tonino Valerii
A Reason to Live, A Reason to Die '73
My Name is Nobody '74

Nick Vallelonga
A Brilliant Disguise '93
In the Kingdom of the Blind the Man with One Eye is King '94

Robert Van Ackeren
A Woman in Flames '84

Jean-Claude Van Damme
The Quest '96

Rudolf Van Den Berg
Cold Light of Day '95

Jaco Van Dormael
Toto le Heros '91
The Eighth Day '95

Bruce Van Dusen
Cold Feet '84

Woodbridge S. Van Dyke
White Shadows in the South Seas '28
Trader Horn '31
Tarzan, the Ape Man '32
Penthouse '33

The Prizefighter and the Lady '33
Hide-Out '34
Manhattan Melodrama '34
The Thin Man '34
Forsaking All Others '35
I Live My Life '35
Naughty Marietta '35
After the Thin Man '36
Love on the Run '36
Rose Marie '36
San Francisco '36
Personal Property '37
Marie Antoinette '38
Rosalie '38
Sweethearts '38
Andy Hardy Gets Spring Fever '39
Another Thin Man '39
Bitter Sweet '40
I Love You Again '40
Shadow of the Thin Man '41
Cairo '42
I Married an Angel '42
Journey for Margaret '42

Ruud Van Hemert
Army Brats '84

Buddy Van Horn
Any Which Way You Can '80
The Dead Pool '88
Pink Cadillac '89

Mario Van Peebles
New Jack City '91
Posse '93
Panther '95

Melvin Van Peebles
The Story of a Three Day Pass '68
Watermelon Man '70
Sweet Sweetback's Baadasssss Song '71
Identity Crisis '90

Gus Van Sant
Drugstore Cowboy '89
My Own Private Idaho '91
Even Cowgirls Get the Blues '94
To Die For '95

Sterling Van Wagenen
Alan & Naomi '92

Joseph Van Winkle
The Woman Inside '83

Eric Van Zuylen
In for Treatment '82

Florestano Vancini
That Long Night in '43 '60

William Vanderkloot
Dead Aim '87

Norman Thaddeus Vane
Frightmare '81
The Black Room '82
Club Life '86
Midnight '89
Taxi Dancers '93

Carlo Vanzina
Dagger Eyes '80s
Nothing Underneath '85
The Gamble '88
Millions '90
My Wonderful Life '90

Agnes Varda
Cleo from 5 to 7 '61
Le Bonheur '65
One Sings, the Other Doesn't '77
Vagabond '85
Le Petit Amour '87
Jacquot '91

Mike Vardy
The Final Cut '95

Marcel Varnel
Chandu the Magician '32
Oh, Mr. Porter '37

Henri Vart
Secret Obsession '88

Gregory Vasiliev
Chapayev '34

Sergei Vasiliev
Chapayev '34

Joseph B. Vasquez
The Bronx War '90
Hangin' with the Homeboys '91

Vasquez ▶cont.

Street Hitz '92

Bruno Ve Sota
The Female Jungle '56
The Brain Eaters '58

Francis Veber
La Chevre '81
Les Comperes '83
Three Fugitives '89
Out on a Limb '92

Pastor Vega
Portrait of Teresa '79

Carlos Velo
Torero '56

Itsvan Ventilla
Nicole '72

Ben Verbong
Lily Was Here '89

Carlo Verdone
Acqua e Sapone '83

Pat Verducci
True Crime '95

Enrique Vergara
The Snake People '68

Michael Verhoeven
The White Rose '83
Killing Cars '85
The Nasty Girl '90

Paul Verhoeven
The Eternal Waltz '54
Turkish Delights '73
Keetje Tippel '75
Soldier of Orange '78
The 4th Man '79
Spetters '80
Flesh and Blood '85
RoboCop '87
Total Recall '90
Basic Instinct '92
Showgirls '95

Henri Verneuil
Forbidden Fruit '52
The Sheep Has Five Legs '54
Just Another Pretty Face '58
Un Singe en Hiver '62
The Big Grab '63
Melodie en Sous-Sol '63
Night Flight from Moscow '73

Henry Vernon
Danger Zone '87

Richard Vernon
The Shadow Man '53

Stephen Verona
The Lords of Flatbush '74
Pipe Dreams '76
Talking Walls '85

Wim Verstappen
Fatal Error '83

Dziga Vertov
The Man with a Movie Camera '29
Kino Pravda/Enthusiasm '31

Robert Veze
Bikini Summer '91

Michael Vianey
Special Police '85

Marco Vicario
The Sensual Man '74
Wifemistress '79

Lindsey C. Vickers
The Appointment '82

Edward Victor
Alley Cat '84

Charles Vidor
The Lady in Question '40
The Tuttles of Tahiti '42
Cover Girl '44
A Song to Remember '45
Gilda '46
The Loves of Carmen '48
Hans Christian Andersen '52
Rhapsody '54
Love Me or Leave Me '55
The Swan '56
Song Without End '60

King Vidor
The Jack Knife Man '20
The Sky Pilot '21
Peg O' My Heart '22
The Big Parade '25
The Crowd '28
Show People '28
Hallelujah! '29
The Champ '31
Street Scene '31
Bird of Paradise '32
Our Daily Bread '34
The Texas Rangers '36
Stella Dallas '37
The Citadel '38
Comrade X '40
Northwest Passage '40
Duel in the Sun '46
Beyond the Forest '49
The Fountainhead '49
Ruby Gentry '52
Man Without a Star '55
War and Peace '56
Solomon and Sheba '59

Berthold Viertel
The Passing of the Third Floor Back '36
Rhodes '36

Emilio Vieyra
The Curious Dr. Humpp '70

Daniel Vigne
The Return of Martin Guerre '83
One Woman or Two '85

Robert G. Vignola
The Scarlet Letter '34

Jean Vigo
A Propos de Nice '29
Zero for Conduct '33
L'Atalante '34

Camilo Vila
Options '88
The Unholy '88

Felix Vilars
Devil Woman '76

Reynaldo Villalobos
Conagher '91

Agustin Villaronga
In a Glass Cage '86

Christian Vincent
La Discrete '90
The Separation '94

Chuck Vincent
American Tickler '76
A Matter of Love '78
Hot T-Shirts '79
Preppies '82
C.O.D. '83
Hollywood Hot Tubs '84
If Looks Could Kill '86
Deranged '87
New York's Finest '87
Sensations '87
Slammer Girls '87
Wimps '87
Sexpot '88
Student Affairs '88
Thrilled to Death '88
A Woman Obsessed '88
Bedroom Eyes 2 '89
Cleo/Leo '89
Party Incorporated '89
Young Nurses in Love '89
Enrapture '90
Wildest Dreams '90

Harry Vincent
She Came on the Bus '69

Jerry Vint
Another Chance '88

Will Vinton
The Adventures of Mark Twain '85

Albert T. Viola
Cry of the Penguins '71
Preacherman '83

Joe Viola
Angels Hard as They Come '71
Hot Box '72

Luchino Visconti
Ossessione '42
La Terra Trema '48
Bellissima '51
Senso '54
White Nights '57
Rocco and His Brothers '60
Boccaccio '70 '62
Sandra of a Thousand Delights '65
The Damned '69
Death in Venice '71
Conversation Piece '75
The Innocent '76

Laszlo Vitezy
Red Earth

Joseph Vittorie
The Criminal Mind '93

Piero Vivarelli
Satanik '69

Virgil W. Vogel
The Mole People '56
The Kettles on Old MacDonald's Farm '57
The Land Unknown '57
Invasion of the Animal People '62
Beulah Land '80
Portrait of a Rebel: Margaret Sanger '82
Walker: Texas Ranger: One Riot, One Ranger '93

Alfred Vohrer
Dead Eyes of London '61
Door with the Seven Locks '62
Inn on the River '62
The Indian Scarf '63
The Mysterious Magician '65
The Squeaker '65
Creature with the Blue Hand '70

Jon Voight
The Tin Soldier '95

Paul G. Volk
Sunset Strip '91
Steel Frontier '94

Josef von Baky
Baron Munchausen '43
The Strange Countess '61

Geza von Bolvary
Charm of La Boheme '36

Gunther Von Fritsch
Curse of the Cat People '44

Veith von Furstenberg
Fire and Sword '82

Rosa von Praunheim
Anita, Dances of Vice '87

Geza von Radvanyi
Uncle Tom's Cabin '69

Akos Von Rathony
Cave of the Living Dead '65

Josef von Sternberg
Underworld '27
Docks of New York '28
Last Command '28
The Blue Angel '30
Morocco '30
Dishonored '31
Blonde Venus '32
Shanghai Express '32
Scarlet Empress '34
Crime and Punishment '35
The Shanghai Gesture '42
Macao '52
Jet Pilot '57

Erich von Stroheim
Blind Husbands '19
Foolish Wives '22
Merry-Go-Round '23
Greed '24
The Wedding March '28
Queen Kelly '29
The Worst of Hollywood: Vol. 2 '90

Ernst R. von Theumer
Jungle Warriors '84

Lars von Trier
The Element of Crime '84
Zentropa '92
Breaking the Waves '95
The Kingdom '95

Margarethe von Trotta
The Lost Honor of Katharina Blum '75
Marianne and Juliane '82
Sheer Madness '84
Rosa Luxemburg '86
The Promise '95

Bernard Vorhaus
The Ghost Camera '33
Broken Melody '34
Cotton Queen '37
Fisherman's Wharf '39
Meet Dr. Christian '39
Way Down South '39
Courageous Dr. Christian '40
Three Faces West '40
Lady from Louisiana '42
The Amazing Mr. X '48

Kurt Voss
Border Radio '88
Genuine Risk '89
The Horseplayer '91
Baja '95

Otakar Votocek
Wings of Fame '93

Andy Wachowski
Bound '96

Larry Wachowski
Bound '96

Daniel Wachsmann
Hamsin '83

Jonathan Wacks
Powwow Highway '89
Mystery Date '91
Ed and His Dead Mother '93

Michael Wadleigh
Woodstock '70
Wolfen '81

George Waggner
Ghost Town Riders '38
Outlaw Express '38
Western Trails '38
Mystery Plane '39
Stunt Pilot '39
Wolf Call '39
Man Made Monster '41
The Wolf Man '41
The Fighting Kentuckian '49
The Commies are Coming, the Commies are Coming '57

Fernando Wagner
Virgin Sacrifice '59

Rupert Wainwright
Dillinger '91
Blank Check '93

Ralph Waite
On the Nickel '80

Andrzej Wajda
A Generation '54
Kanal '56
Ashes and Diamonds '58
Innocent Sorcerers '60
Fury is a Woman '61
Lotna '64
Land of Promise '74
Man of Marble '76
Without Anesthesia '78
Maids of Wilko '79
The Conductor '80
Man of Iron '81
Danton '82
A Love in Germany '84
Korczak '90

Chris Walas
The Fly 2 '89
The Vagrant '92

Grant Austin Waldman
The Channeler '89
Teenage Exorcist '93

Dorian Walker
Making the Grade '84
Teen Witch '89

Giles Walker
90 Days '86
Princes in Exile '90
Ordinary Magic '93

Hal Walker
The Stork Club '45
The Road to Utopia '46
At War with the Army '50
The Road to Bali '53

Nancy Walker
Can't Stop the Music '80

Pete Walker
The Big Switch '70
Man of Violence '71
Die Screaming, Marianne '73
Flesh and Blood Show '73
Frightmare '74
The Confessional '75
House of Whipcord '75
Tiffany Jones '75
The Comeback '77
Schizo '77
House of the Long Shadows '82
Home Before Midnight '84

Stuart Walker
Werewolf of London '35

Gary Walkow
The Trouble with Dick '88

Richard Wallace
Little Minister '34
The Young in Heart '38
Captain Caution '40
A Girl, a Guy and a Gob '41
A Night to Remember '42
Bombardier '43
The Fallen Sparrow '43
It's in the Bag '45
Sinbad, the Sailor '47
Tycoon '47

Rick Wallace
California Girls '84
A Time to Live '85
Acceptable Risks '86

Stephen Wallace
For Love Alone '86
Prisoners of the Sun '91
The Killing Beach '92

Tommy Lee Wallace
Halloween 3: Season of the Witch '82
Aloha Summer '88
Fright Night 2 '88
Stephen King's It '90
The Comrades of Summer '92
Witness to the Execution '94

Sigurd Wallen
The Count of the Old Town '34

Anthony Waller
Mute Witness '95

Herb Wallerstein
Snowbeast '77

Raoul Walsh
Regeneration '15
The Thief of Baghdad '24
Sadie Thompson '28
Big Trail '30
Going Hollywood '33
Klondike Annie '36
O.H.M.S. '37
When Thief Meets Thief '37
College Swing '38
The Roaring Twenties '39
Dark Command '40
They Drive by Night '40
High Sierra '41
Strawberry Blonde '41
They Died with Their Boots On '41
Desperate Journey '42
Gentleman Jim '42
Background to Danger '43
Northern Pursuit '43
Uncertain Glory '44
The Horn Blows at Midnight '45
Objective, Burma! '45
The Man I Love '46
Pursued '47
Silver River '48
White Heat '49
Along the Great Divide '51
Captain Horatio Hornblower '51
Distant Drums '51
The Enforcer '51
Blackbeard the Pirate '52
Gun Fury '53
A Lion Is in the Streets '53
Sea Devils '53
Battle Cry '55
The Tall Men '55
The King and Four Queens '56
Band of Angels '57
The Naked and the Dead '58
Esther and the King '60

Charles Walters
Good News '47
Easter Parade '48
The Barkleys of Broadway '49
Summer Stock '50
Texas Carnival '51
Three Guys Named Mike '51

The Belle of New York '52
Dangerous When Wet '53
Easy to Love '53
Lili '53
Torch Song '53
The Glass Slipper '55
The Tender Trap '55
High Society '56
Don't Go Near the Water '57
Ask Any Girl '59
Please Don't Eat the Daisies '60
Billy Rose's Jumbo '62
The Unsinkable Molly Brown '64
Walk, Don't Run '66

Fred Walton
When a Stranger Calls '79
Hadley's Rebellion '84
April Fool's Day '86
The Rosary Murders '87
Trapped '89
Homewrecker '92
When a Stranger Calls Back '93
Dead Air '94

Sam Wanamaker
The Executioner '70
Catlow '71
Sinbad and the Eye of the Tiger '77
Killing of Randy Webster '81

Peter Wang
A Great Wall '86
The Laserman '90

Steve Wang
The Guyver '91
Guyver 2: Dark Hero '94

Wayne Wang
Chan is Missing '82
Dim Sum: A Little Bit of Heart '85
Slamdance '87
Eat a Bowl of Tea '89
The Joy Luck Club '93
Blue In the Face '95
Smoke '95
A Man, a Woman and a Killer

Orville Wanzer
The Devil's Mistress '68

Grzegorz Warchol
I Like Bats '85

Bill Ward
Ballad of a Gunfighter '64

David S. Ward
Cannery Row '82
Major League '89
King Ralph '91
The Program '93
Major League 2 '94
Down Periscope '96

Donal Lardner Ward
My Life's In Turnaround '94

Richard Ward
Sakura Killers '86

Vincent Ward
Vigil '84
The Navigator '88
Map of the Human Heart '93

Clyde Ware
No Drums, No Bugles '71
The Hatfields & the McCoys '75
Bad Jim '89

Chris Warfield
Little Miss Innocence '73

Regis Wargnier
Indochine '92

Paul Warner
Fall Time '94

Ed Warnick
Manchurian Avenger '84

Charles Marquis Warren
Red Desert '50
Little Big Horn '51
Arrowhead '53
Tension at Table Rock '56
Charro! '69

Deryn Warren
Bloodspell '87
Black Magic Woman '91

Hal P. Warren
Manos, the Hands of Fate '66

Jennifer Warren
Forbidden Choices '94

Jerry Warren
Man Beast '55
The Incredible Petrified World '58
Teenage Zombies '58
Face of the Screaming Werewolf '59
Creature of the Walking Dead '60
Invasion of the Animal People '62
Terror of the Bloodhunters '62
Attack of the Mayan Mummy '63
Curse of the Stone Hand '64
The Wild World of Batwoman '66
Frankenstein Island '81

Joseph Warren
Urban Warriors '75

Norman J. Warren
The Terror '79
Horror Planet '80
Spaced Out '80
Alien Prey '83
Bloody New Year '87

Darrell Wasyk
H '90

Michal Waszynski
The Dybbuk '37

John Waters
Mondo Trasho '69
Multiple Maniacs '70
Pink Flamingos '72
Female Trouble '74
Desperate Living '77
Polyester '81
Hairspray '88
Cry-Baby '90
Divine '90
Serial Mom '94

John Waters
Nevada '27

Frederick P. Watkins
Brutal Fury '92
A Matter of Honor '95

Greg Watkins
A Little Stiff '91

Peter Watkins
The Gladiators '70
Edvard Munch '74

James C. Watson
Night of the Demon '80

John Watson
Deathstalker '83
The Zoo Gang '85

William Watson
Heroes in Blue '39

Harry Watt
Overlanders '46
Eureka Stockade '49

Nate Watt
Rustler's Valley '37
Law of the Pampas '39

Roy Watts
Hambone & Hillie '84

Ric Roman Waugh
Exit '95

Al Waxman
My Pleasure Is My Business '74
White Light '90
Diamond Fleece '92

Keoni Waxman
Almost Blue '93

Ron Way
Frenchman's Farm '87

Keenen Ivory Wayans
I'm Gonna Git You Sucka '88
A Low Down Dirty Shame '94

John Wayne
The Alamo '60
The Green Berets '68

Michael Weaver
Night Terror '89

Harry S. Webb
The Live Wire '34
Laramie Kid '35
Ridin' Thru '35
Riding On '37
Santa Fe Bound '37
Mesquite Buckaroo '39

Jack Webb
Dragnet '54
Pete Kelly's Blues '55
D.I. '57

Kenneth Webb
Just Suppose '26

Millard Webb
The Dropkick '27
Glorifying the American Girl '30

Peter Webb
Give My Regards to Broad Street '84

Robert D. Webb
Beneath the 12-Mile Reef '53
Seven Cities of Gold '55
Love Me Tender '56

William Webb
Dirty Laundry '87
Party Line '88
The Banker '89
The Hit List '93

Billy Weber
Josh and S.A.M. '93

Bruce Weber
Let's Get Lost '88

Lois Weber
Discontent '16
The Blot '21
Too Wise Wives '21
Chapter in Her Life '23

Christopher Webster
Demon Possessed '93

D.J. Webster
Dark Side of the Moon '90

Nicholas Webster
Gone are the Days '63
Purlie Victorious '63
Santa Claus Conquers the Martians '64
Mission Mars '67

David Wechter
Midnight Madness '80
Malibu Bikini Shop '86

Stephen Weeks
Madhouse Mansion '74
Sword of the Valiant '83

Paul Wegener
Student of Prague '13
The Golem '20

Bob Wehling
What's Up Front '63

Lo Wei
Chinese Connection '73
Fists of Fury '73

Alfred Weidenmann
Adorable Julia '62

John Weidner
Private Wars '93
Blood for Blood '95

Paul Weiland
Leonard Part 6 '87
Bernard and the Genie '90s
City Slickers 2: The Legend of Curly's Gold '94

Claudia Weill
Girlfriends '78
It's My Turn '80
Once a Hero '88

Chuck Wein
Rainbow Bridge '71

Yossi Wein
Never Say Die '94

Bob Weinstein
Playing for Keeps '86

Harvey Weinstein
Light Years '88

Sandra Weintraub
Women's Club '87
The Deadliest Art: The Best of the Martial Arts Films '90

Peter Weir
The Cars That Ate Paris '74
Picnic at Hanging Rock '75
The Last Wave '77
Plumber '79
Gallipoli '81
The Year of Living Dangerously '82
Witness '85
The Mosquito Coast '86
Dead Poets Society '89
Green Card '90
Fearless '93

Bob Weis
The Wacky World of Wills & Burke '85

Don Weis
The Affairs of Dobie Gillis '53
I Love Melvin '53
The Gene Krupa Story '59
Pajama Party '64
Billie '65
Zero to Sixty '78
The Munsters' Revenge '81

Gary Weis
All You Need Is Cash '78
Diary of a Young Comic '79
Wholly Moses! '80

Jack Weis
Storyville '74
Crypt of Dark Secrets '76
Mardi Gras Massacre '78

Sam Weisman
Bye Bye, Love '94
D2: The Mighty Ducks '94

Straw Weisman
Dead Mate '88

Adrian Weiss
The Bride & the Beast '58

Helmut Weiss
Tromba, the Tiger Man '52

Jiri Weiss
Sweet Light in a Dark Room '60
Martha and I '91

Rob Weiss
Amongst Friends '93

Robert Weiss
Amazon Women on the Moon '87

Mel Welles
Lady Frankenstein '72

Orson Welles
Citizen Kane '41
The Magnificent Ambersons '42
The Stranger '46
The Lady from Shanghai '48
Macbeth '48
Othello '52
Mr. Arkadin '55
Touch of Evil '58
The Trial '63
Chimes at Midnight '67
It's All True '93

David Wellington
The Carpenter '89
A Man in Uniform '93

William A. Wellman
Wings '27
Night Nurse '31
Public Enemy '31
The Purchase Price '32
Heroes for Sale '33
Nothing Sacred '37
A Star is Born '37
Beau Geste '39
The Great Man's Lady '42
Roxie Hart '42
Lady of Burlesque '43
The Ox-Bow Incident '43
Buffalo Bill '44
Till the Clouds Roll By/A Star Is Born '46
Magic Town '47
Battleground '49
The Next Voice You Hear '50
Across the Wide Missouri '51
Westward the Women '51
Blood Alley '55
Goodbye, My Lady '56
Darby's Rangers '58
Lafayette Escadrille '58

Alex Wells
The Curfew Breakers '57

Peter Wells
Desperate Remedies '93

Simon Wells
An American Tail: Fievel Goes West '91
We're Back! A Dinosaur's Story '93
Balto '95

Li Wen-Hua
Breaking with Old Ideas '75

Wim Wenders
The Goalie's Anxiety at the Penalty Kick '71
The Scarlet Letter '73
Alice in the Cities '74
Kings of the Road—In the Course of Time '76
The American Friend '77
The Wrong Move '78
Lightning Over Water '80
Hammett '82
State of Things '82
Paris, Texas '83
Tokyo-Ga '85
Wings of Desire '88
Until The End of The World '91
Faraway, So Close! '93

Paul Wendkos
Gidget '59
Angel Baby '61
Gidget Goes Hawaiian '61
Gidget Goes to Rome '63
Johnny Tiger '66
Guns of the Magnificent Seven '69
The Mephisto Waltz '71
The Tattered Web '71
Haunts of the Very Rich '72
Honor Thy Father '73
The Death of Richie '76
Special Delivery '76
Secrets '77
Betrayal '78
A Woman Called Moses '78
A Cry for Love '80
The Ordeal of Dr. Mudd '80
Awakening of Candra '81
The Five of Me '81
Cocaine: One Man's Seduction '83
The Bad Seed '85
Celebrity '85
The Execution '85
Rage of Angels: The Story Continues '86
Blood Vows: The Story of a Mafia Wife '87
The Great Escape 2: The Untold Story '88
The Taking of Flight 847: The Uli Derickson Story '88
The Flight '89
From the Dead of Night '89
Deadline Assault '90
White Hot: The Mysterious Murder of Thelma Todd '91

Richard Wenk
Vamp '86
National Lampoon's Attack of the 5 Ft. 2 Women '94

Alfred Werker
The Adventures of Sherlock Holmes '39
It Could Happen to You '39
The Reluctant Dragon '41
Shock! '46
He Walked by Night '48
Lost Boundaries '49
Devil's Canyon '53
At Gunpoint '55

Sandra Werneck
Boca '94

Jeff Werner
Die Laughing '80
Cheerleaders' Wild Weekend '85

Peter Werner
In the Region of Ice '76
Don't Cry, It's Only Thunder '82
Hard Knox '83
I Married a Centerfold '84
The Alamo: Thirteen Days to Glory '87
No Man's Land '87
LBJ: The Early Years '88
The Image '89
Hiroshima: Out of the Ashes '90
Lone Justice '93
The Substitute Wife '94

Lina Wertmuller
Seduction of Mimi '72
Love and Anarchy '73
All Screwed Up '74
Swept Away... '75
Seven Beauties '76
A Night Full of Rain '78
Belle Starr '79
Blood Feud '79

Wertmuller ▶cont.

A Joke of Destiny, Lying in Wait Around the Corner Like a Bandit '84
Camorra: The Naples Connection '85
Sotto, Sotto '85
Summer Night '87
Summer Night with Greek Profile, Almond Eyes & Scent of Basil '87
Ciao, Professore! '94

Jay Wertz
The Last Reunion '80

Raymond B. West
Civilization '16

Roland West
The Monster '25
The Bat '26
The Bat Whispers '30
Corsair '31

William West
Flying Wild '41

Armand Weston
The Nesting '80

Eric Weston
Evilspeak '82
Marvin & Tige '84
The Iron Triangle '89
To Protect and Serve '92

Sam Weston
It's Called Murder, Baby '82

Fulvio Wetzl
Rorret '87

Haskell Wexler
Medium Cool '69
Latino '85

James Whale
Frankenstein '31
The Old Dark House '32
The Invisible Man '33
The Bride of Frankenstein '35
Show Boat '36
Sinners in Paradise '38
Wives Under Suspicion '38
The Man in the Iron Mask '39

George Whaley
Clowning Around 2 '93

Tom Wharmby
Bouquet of Barbed Wire '76

Tony Wharmby
The Equalizer: Memories of Manon '88
Sorry, Wrong Number '89
The Kissing Place '90
Treacherous Crossing '92
Covert Assassin '94
Seduced by Evil '94

Claude Whatham
Elizabeth R '72
That'll Be the Day '73
All Creatures Great and Small '74
Sweet William '79
Murder Elite '86

Donald Whatham
Elizabeth R '72

Jim Wheat
Lies '83
The Ewoks: Battle for Endor '85
After Midnight '89

Ken Wheat
Lies '83
The Ewoks: Battle for Endor '85

David Wheatley
The Fifteen Streets '90
Hostages '93

Anne Wheeler
Loyalties '86
Bye Bye Blues '89
Angel Square '92

Tim Whelan
The Mill on the Floss '37
Action for Slander '38
The Divorce of Lady X '38
Clouds Over Europe '39
Sidewalks of London '40
The Thief of Bagdad '40
Seven Days' Leave '42
Higher and Higher '44
Step Lively '44
Badman's Territory '46
Rage at Dawn '55
Texas Lady '56

Forest Whitaker
Strapped '93
Waiting to Exhale '95

Jules White
Sidewalks of New York '31
Stop! Look! and Laugh! '60

Nathan J. White
The Carrier '87

Sam White
People Are Funny '46

Wally White
Lie Down with Dogs '95

Alexander Whitelaw
Lifespan '75

John Whitesell
Calendar Girl '93

Philip H. Whitman
Girl from Calgary '32
His Private Secretary '33

Preston A. Whitmore, II
The Walking Dead '94

Richard Whorf
Till the Clouds Roll By '46
Till the Clouds Roll By/A Star Is Born '46
It Happened in Brooklyn '47
Love from a Stranger '47
Champagne for Caesar '50

Michael Whyte
The Railway Station Man '92

William Wiard
Snowblind '78
Tom Horn '80
Help Wanted: Male '82
Kicks '85

David Wickes
Silver Dream Racer '83
Jack the Ripper '88
Jekyll and Hyde '90
Frankenstein '93

Bernhard Wicki
The Bridge '59
Morituri '65

Gregory Widen
The Prophecy '95

Bo Widerberg
Elvira Madigan '67
All Things Fair '95

Ken Wiederhorn
Shock Waves '77
Eyes of a Stranger '81
Meatballs 2 '84
Return of the Living Dead 2 '88

Robert Wiemer
Anna to the Infinite Power '84
Somewhere Tomorrow '85
The Night Train to Kathmandu '88

Robert Wiene
The Cabinet of Dr. Caligari '19
The Hands of Orlac '25

Hal Wiener
Imagemaker '86

Crane Wilbur
Tomorrow's Children '34
Yellow Cargo '36
The Bat '59

Fred M. Wilcox
Lassie, Come Home '43
Courage of Lassie '46
The Hills of Home '48
Three Daring Daughters '48
The Secret Garden '49
Forbidden Planet '56

Herbert Wilcox
Bitter Sweet '33
London Melody '37
Nurse Edith Cavell '39
No, No Nanette '40
Sunny '41
Forever and a Day '43
I Live in Grosvenor Square '46
The Courtney Affair '47
Elizabeth of Ladymead '48
Maytime in Mayfair '52
Trouble in the Glen '54
The King's Rhapsody '55
Let's Make Up '55
Dangerous Youth '58
Teenage Bad Girl '59

Cornel Wilde
Sword of Lancelot '63
The Naked Prey '66
Sharks' Treasure '75

Ted Wilde
Battling Orioles '24
The Kid Brother '27
Speedy '28

Billy Wilder
Double Indemnity '44
The Lost Weekend '45
Emperor Waltz '48
Sunset Boulevard '50
Stalag 17 '53
Sabrina '54
The Seven Year Itch '55
Love in the Afternoon '57
Spirit of St. Louis '57
Witness for the Prosecution '57
Some Like It Hot '59
The Apartment '60
One, Two, Three '61
Irma La Douce '63
Kiss Me, Stupid! '64
The Fortune Cookie '66
The Private Life of Sherlock Holmes '70
Avanti! '72
The Front Page '74
Buddy Buddy '81

Gene Wilder
World's Greatest Lover '77
The Adventures of Sherlock Holmes' Smarter Brother '78
The Woman in Red '84
Haunted Honeymoon '86

Glenn Wilder
Master Blaster '85

John Wilder
Breaking Home Ties '87

W. Lee Wilder
Woman in Brown '48
Phantom from Space '53
Killers from Space '54
The Snow Creature '54
Big Bluff '55
Fright '56
Manfish '56

Gavin Wilding
The Raffle '94

Gordon Wiles
Charlie Chan's Secret '35
Lady from Nowhere '36
Mr. Boggs Steps Out '38
Prison Train '38
The Gangster '47
Ginger in the Morning '73

Ethan Wiley
House 2: The Second Story '87

Charles Wilkinson
Quarantine '89
Blood Clan '91
Breach of Trust '95

Irvin Willat
False Faces '18
The Michigan Kid '28

Anson Williams
Little White Lies '89
A Perfect Little Murder '90
All-American Murder '91
Dream Date '93

Douglas Williams
Overdrawn at the Memory Bank '83

Elmo Williams
Tall Texan '53
Hell Ship Mutiny '57

Emlyn Williams
The Last Days of Dolwyn '49

Oscar Williams
Final Comedown '72
Hot Potato '76
Death Drug '83

Paul Williams
Miss Right '81

Paul W. Williams
Mirage '94

Richard Williams
Raggedy Ann and Andy: A Musical Adventure '77

Spencer Williams, Jr.
Blood of Jesus '41
Go Down Death '41
Juke Joint '47

Tony Williams
Solo '77
Next of Kin '82

Fred Williamson
No Way Back '74
Adios Amigo '75
Mean Johnny Barrows '75
Death Journey '76
Mister Mean '77
The Last Fight '82
One Down, Two to Go! '82
Big Score '83
Foxtrap '85
The Kill Reflex '89
Steele's Law '91
Three Days to a Kill '91
South Beach '92
Silent Hunter '94

Gordon Willis
Windows '80

J. Elder Wills
Song of Freedom '38

Bruce Wilson
Bombs Away! '86

Dean Wilson
Clayton County Line '80s
Blind Faith '89
Free Amerika Broadcasting '89

Hugh Wilson
Police Academy '84
Rustler's Rhapsody '85
Burglar '87
Guarding Tess '94

Jim Wilson
Stacy's Knights '83
Movie Maker '86

John D. Wilson
Shinbone Alley '70

Richard Wilson
Al Capone '59
Invitation to a Gunfighter '64
Three in the Attic '68
It's All True '93

Sandy Wilson
My American Cousin '85
American Boyfriends '89

S.S. Wilson
Tremors 2: Aftershocks '96

Yale Wilson
Truth or Dare? '86

Kurt Wimmer
One Man's Justice '95

James R. Winburn
Evil Altar '89
The Death Merchant '91
Miami Beach Cops '93

Simon Wincer
Dark Forces '83
Phar Lap '84
D.A.R.Y.L. '85
The Girl Who Spelled Freedom '86
The Lighthorsemen '87
Quigley Down Under '90
Harley Davidson and the Marlboro Man '91
Free Willy '93
Lightning Jack '94
Operation Dumbo Drop '95
The Phantom '96

Fred Windermere
The Taxi Mystery '26

Chris Windsor
Big Meat Eater '85

Simon Windsor
Lonesome Dove '89

Bretaigne Windust
June Bride '48
Winter Meeting '48
The Enforcer '51
The Pied Piper of Hamelin '57

Harry Winer
Single Bars, Single Women '84
Mirrors '85
JFK: Reckless Youth '93
House Arrest '96

Lucy Winer
Rate It X '86

Jonathan Winfrey
Black Scorpion '95
Excessive Force 2: Force on Force '95

Gary Winick
Curfew '88
Out of the Rain '90

Charles Winkler
You Talkin' to Me? '87
Disturbed '90

Henry Winkler
A Smoky Mountain Christmas '86
Memories of Me '88
Cop and a Half '93

Irwin Winkler
Guilty by Suspicion '91
Night and the City '92
The Net '95

Terence H. Winkless
The Nest '88
Bloodfist '89
Corporate Affairs '90
The Berlin Conspiracy '91
Rage and Honor '92
White Wolves 2: Legend of the Wild '94

Michael Winner
Murder on the Campus '52
Cool Mikado '63
Chato's Land '71
Lawman '71
The Mechanic '72
The Nightcomers '72
Scorpio '73
The Stone Killer '73
Death Wish '74
The Sentinel '76
The Big Sleep '78
Firepower '79
Death Wish 2 '82
The Wicked Lady '83
Death Wish 3 '85
Scream for Help '86
Appointment with Death '88
A Chorus of Disapproval '89
Bullseye! '90

David Winning
Storm '87
Killer Image '92

Peter Winograd
Flicks '85
One Last Run '89

Stan Winston
Pumpkinhead '88
The Adventures of a Gnome Named Gnorm '93

Alex Winter
Freaked '93

Michael Winterbottom
Butterfly Kiss '94

John Wintergate
Boarding House '83

David Winters
Dr. Jekyll and Mr. Hyde '73
Racquet '79
The Last Horror Film '82
Mission to Kill '85
Thrashin' '86
Codename: Vengeance '87
Rage to Kill '88
Space Mutiny '88

Donovan Winters
The Seducer '82

Howard Winters
Dead Boyz Can't Fly '93

Paul Winters
The Freeway Maniac '88

Frank Wisbar
The Devil Bat's Daughter '46
Strangler of the Swamp '46

Herbert Wise
Alone Against Rome '62
Castle of the Living Dead '64
Elizabeth R '72
The Gathering Storm '74

I, Claudius, Vol. 2: Waiting in the Wings/What Shall We Do With Claudius? '80
I, Claudius, Vol. 3: Poison is Queen/Some Justice '80
I, Claudius, Vol. 5: Zeus, By Jove!/Hail Who? '80
I, Claudius, Vol. 6: Fool's Luck/A God in Colchester '80
I, Claudius, Vol. 7: Old King Log '80
Pope John Paul II '84
Woman in Black '89
Strange Interlude '90
I, Claudius, Vol. 1: A Touch of Murder/Family Affairs '91

Kirk Wise
Beauty and the Beast '91
The Hunchback of Notre Dame '96

Robert Wise
The Magnificent Ambersons '42
Curse of the Cat People '44
Mademoiselle Fifi '44
The Body Snatcher '45
Criminal Court '46
Born to Kill '47
Blood on the Moon '48
The Set-Up '49
Three Secrets '50
The Day the Earth Stood Still '51
The Desert Rats '53
Executive Suite '54
Helen of Troy '56
Somebody Up There Likes Me '56
Tribute to a Bad Man '56
This Could Be the Night '57
Until They Sail '57
I Want to Live! '58
Run Silent, Run Deep '58
West Side Story '61
Two for the Seesaw '62
The Haunting '63
The Sound of Music '65
The Sand Pebbles '66
Star! '68
The Andromeda Strain '71
The Hindenburg '75
Audrey Rose '77
Star Trek: The Motion Picture '80
Rooftops '89

Carol Wiseman
The Little Princess '87
Does This Mean We're Married? '90

Doris Wishman
Nude on the Moon '61
Bad Girls Go to Hell '65
The Amazing Transplant '70
Deadly Weapons '70

Stephen Withrow
Friends, Lovers & Lunatics '89

William Witney
The Painted Stallion '37
The Trigger Trio '37
Western Double Feature 5: Rogers & Autry '37
Zorro Rides Again '37
Daredevils of the Red Circle '38
Dick Tracy Returns '38
Fighting Devil Dogs '38
Hawk of the Wilderness '38
The Lone Ranger '38
Zorro's Fighting Legion '39
Western Double Feature 17 '40s
Western Double Feature 18 '40s
Western Double Feature 21 '40s
Western Double Feature 22 '40s
Adventures of Red Ryder '40
Doctor Satan's Robot '40
Drums of Fu Manchu '40
Mysterious Doctor Satan '40
The Adventures of Captain Marvel '41
Dick Tracy vs. Crime Inc. '41
King of the Texas Rangers '41
The Gay Ranchero '42
Nyoka and the Tigermen '42
Spy Smasher '42
Spy Smasher Returns '42
G-Men vs. the Black Dragon '43
Cyclotrode "X" '46
Helldorado '46
Roll on Texas Moon '46
Apache Rose '47
Bells of San Angelo '47
Home in Oklahoma '47
On the Old Spanish Trail '47
Springtime in the Sierras '47
Eyes of Texas '48
Grand Canyon Trail '48
Night Time in Nevada '48
Under California Stars '48
Down Dakota Way '49
The Golden Stallion '49
Susanna Pass '49
Bells of Coronado '50
North of the Great Divide '50
Trail of Robin Hood '50
Trigger, Jr. '50
Twilight in the Sierras '50
Western Double Feature 3: Rogers & Allen '50
Western Double Feature 6: Rogers & Trigger '50
Heart of the Rockies '51
Colorado Sundown '52
The Outcast '54
Jet Attack/Paratroop Command '58
Master of the World '61
Arizona Raiders '65
Darktown Strutters '74
Western Double Feature 10: Roy, Dale, & Trigger '80s

William D. Wittliff
Red Headed Stranger '87

Peter Wittman
Play Dead '81
Ellie '84

Jay Woelfel
Beyond Dream's Door '88
Things '93

Jerzy Wojcik
Karate Polish Style '82

James L. Wolcott
Wild Women of Wongo '59

Fred Wolf
The Point '71
Mouse and His Child '77
Little Rascals Christmas Special '79

Donald Wolfe
Savage Intruder '68

Art Wolff
Battling for Baby '92

Andy Wolk
Criminal Justice '90
Traces of Red '92

Dan Wolman
My Michael '75
Hide and Seek '80
Nana '82
Soldier of the Night '84

M. Wallace Wolodarsky
Coldblooded '94

James Wolpaw
Complex World '92

Kirk Wong
Organized Crime & Triad Bureau '93

John Woo
A Better Tomorrow '86
A Better Tomorrow, Part 2 '88
A Bullet in the Head '90
The Killer '90
Hard-Boiled '92
Hard Target '93
Broken Arrow '95

Raymond Woo
Ninja Brothers of Blood '89

Edward D. Wood, Jr.
Glen or Glenda: Confessions of Ed Wood '53
Jail Bait '54
Bride of the Monster '56
Plan 9 from Outer Space '56
The Violent Years '56
Night of the Ghouls '59
The Sinister Urge '60

James Wood
Dr. Jekyll's Dungeon of Death '82

Sam Wood
Peck's Bad Boy '21
Hold Your Man '33
Let 'Em Have It '35
A Night at the Opera '35
A Day at the Races '37
Madame X '37
Navy Blue and Gold '37
Goodbye, Mr. Chips '39
Kitty Foyle '40
Our Town '40
The Devil & Miss Jones '41
Kings Row '41
The Pride of the Yankees '42
For Whom the Bell Tolls '43
Casanova Brown '44
Guest Wife '45
Saratoga Trunk '45
Heartbeat '46
Command Decision '48
The Stratton Story '49

Leslie Woodhead
Tragedy of Flight 103: The Inside Story '91

Frank Woodruff
Lady Scarface '41
Lady Scarface/The Threat '49

Jack Woods
Equinox '71

Mark Woods
Witchcraft 2: The Temptress '90

Joanne Woodward
Come Along with Me '84

Abbe Wool
Roadside Prophets '92

Gerry Woolery
Jokes My Folks Never Told Me '77

Chuck Workman
The Money '75
Kill Castro '80
The Mercenaries '80
Stoogemania '85
Superstar: The Life and Times of Andy Warhol '90

Mary Woronov
Eating Raoul '82

Wallace Worsley
The Penalty '20
The Hunchback of Notre Dame '23

Clark Worswick
Agent on Ice '86

Aaron Worth
9 1/2 Ninjas '90

David Worth
Warrior of the Lost World '84
Lady Dragon '92
Lady Dragon 2 '93

William Worthington
The Tong Man '19

Soenke Wortmann
Maybe...Maybe Not '94

Martin Wragge
The Last Warrior '89

John Wray
Beau Revel '21
Anna Christie '23

Caspar Wrede
One Day in the Life of Ivan Denisovich '71
The Terrorists '74

Geoffrey Wright
Romper Stomper '92

Mack V. Wright
Haunted Gold '32
Man from Monterey '33
Somewhere in Sonora '33
Robinson Crusoe of Clipper Island '36
Robinson Crusoe of Mystery Island '36
The Vigilantes are Coming '36
Western Double Feature 3 '36
Winds of the Wasteland '36
Big Show '37
Hit the Saddle '37
Riders of the Whistling Skull '37
Western Double Feature 5: Rogers & Autry '37
Rootin' Tootin' Rhythm '38
Sea Hound '47

Patrick Wright
Hollywood High '77

Tenny Wright
The Big Stampede '32
Telegraph Trail '33

Thomas J. Wright
Torchlight '85
No Holds Barred '89
The Fatal Image '90
Snow Kill '90
Chrome Soldiers '92
Highlander: The Gathering '93

Tom Wright
Deadly Game '91

Donald Wrye
Born Innocent '74
Death Be Not Proud '75
Ice Castles '79

James Wu
Ninja Condors '87

Richard Wulicher
House of Shadows '83

William Wyler
Come and Get It '36
Dodsworth '36
These Three '36
Dead End '37
Jezebel '38
Wuthering Heights '39
The Letter '40
The Westerner '40
The Little Foxes '41
Mrs. Miniver '42
The Best Years of Our Lives '46
The Heiress '49
Detective Story '51
Carrie '52
Roman Holiday '53
Desperate Hours '55
Friendly Persuasion '56
The Big Country '58
Ben-Hur '59
The Children's Hour '61
The Collector '65
How to Steal a Million '66
Funny Girl '68
The Liberation of L.B. Jones '70
War in the Sky '82

David Wyles
Man with a Gun '95

Bob Wynn
Resurrection of Zachary Wheeler '71

Tracy Keenan Wynn
Hit Lady '74

Jim Wynorski
The Lost Empire '83
Chopping Mall '86
Big Bad Mama 2 '87
Deathstalker 2: Duel of the Titans '87
Not of This Earth '88
The Return of Swamp Thing '89
Transylvania Twist '89
Hard to Die '90
The Haunting of Morella '91
976-EVIL 2: The Astral Factor '91
Munchie '92
Sins of Desire '92
Sorority House Massacre 2: Nighty Nightmare '92
Body Chemistry 3: Point of Seduction '93
Dinosaur Island '93
Ghoulies 4 '93
Hard Bounty '94
Sorceress '94

Yabo Yablonsky
Manipulator '71

Greg Yaitanes
Hard Justice '95

Boaz Yakin
Fresh '94

Kazuo Yakmazaki
A Wind Named Amnesia '93

Michael Yakub
The Shaman '87

Kazuhiko Yamaguchi
Sister Street Fighter '76

Tetsuya Yamauchi
Magic Serpent '66

Mitsuo Yanagimachi
Himatsuri '85
Shadow of China '91

C.Y. Yang
Bruce Li in New Guinea '80

Jean Yarbrough
The Gang's All Here '40
The Devil Bat '41
King of the Zombies '41
Let's Go Collegiate '41
Panama Menace '41
Law of the Jungle '42
Lure of the Islands '42
Meet the Mob '42
In Society '44
Here Come the Co-Eds '45
The Naughty Nineties '45
Under Western Stars '45
The Brute Man '46
House of Horrors '46
The Creeper '48
Holiday in Havana '49
Master Minds '49
Pirate Ship '49
Jack & the Beanstalk '52
Lost in Alaska '52
Hillbillies in a Haunted House '67

Bob Yari
Mind Games '89

Kimiyoshi Yasuda
Zatoichi: The Blind Swordsman and the Fugitives '68

Peter Yates
Koroshi '67
Robbery '67
Bullitt '68
Murphy's War '71
For Pete's Sake '74
Mother, Jugs and Speed '76
The Deep '77
Breaking Away '79
Eyewitness '81
The Dresser '83
Krull '83
Eleni '85
Suspect '87
The House on Carroll Street '88
An Innocent Man '89
Year of the Comet '92
Roommates '95
The Run of the Country '95

Rebecca Yates
Rubberface '81

Brook Yeaton
Ice '93

Irvin S. Yeaworth, Jr.
The Flaming Teen-Age '56
The Blob '58
The 4D Man '59
Dinosaurus! '60

Linda Yellen
Chantilly Lace '93
Parallel Lives '94

Isaac Yeshurun
Noa at Seventeen '82

Yevgeny Yevtushenko
Kindergarten '84

Zhang Yimou
Red Sorghum '87
Ju Dou '90
Raise the Red Lantern '91
The Story of Qui Ju '91
To Live '94
Shanghai Triad '95

Edie Yolles
That's My Baby! '88

Jeff Yonis
Bloodfist 5: Human Target '93

Bud Yorkin
Come Blow Your Horn '63
Divorce American Style '67
Start the Revolution Without Me '70
The Thief Who Came to Dinner '73
Twice in a Lifetime '85
Arthur 2: On the Rocks '88
Love Hurts '91

Yaky Yosha
Sexual Response '92

Hiroaki Yoshida
Twilight of the Cockroaches '90
Iron Maze '91

Frederick A. (Freddie) Young
Arthur's Hallowed Ground '84

Harold Young
The Scarlet Pimpernel '34
Little Tough Guys '38
Dreaming Out Loud '40
The Mummy's Tomb '42

James Young
The Unchastened Woman '25

Karen Young
Deadly Darling '85

Robert M. Young
Trauma '62
Romance with a Double Bass '74
Rich Kids '79
Short Eyes '79
One Trick Pony '80
Charlie Boy '81
Ballad of Gregorio Cortez '83
Robin Hood...The Legend: The Swords of Wayland '83
Robin Hood...The Legend: Herne's Son '85
Extremities '86
Saving Grace '86
The Worst Witch '86
We are the Children '87
Dominick & Eugene '88
Triumph of the Spirit '89
Talent for the Game '91
Splitting Heirs '93
Doomsday Gun '94
Roosters '95

Robert W. Young
Vampire Circus '71
The World is Full of Married Men '80
Scandalous '88
Hostage '92

Roger Young
Magnum P.I.: Don't Eat the Snow in Hawaii '80
Bitter Harvest '81
Two of a Kind '82
Lassiter '84
Gulag '85
Into Thin Air '85
The Squeeze '87
The Bourne Identity '88
Held Hostage '91
Geronimo '93
Mercy Mission '93
Getting Gotti '94
Joseph '95

Terence Young
Valley of the Eagles '51
Black Tights '60
Dr. No '62
From Russia with Love '63
The Amorous Adventures of Moll Flanders '65
Thunderball '65
The Poppy Is Also a Flower '66
Triple Cross '67
Wait Until Dark '67
Mayerling '68
When Wolves Cry '69
Red Sun '71
Cold Sweat '74
The Klansman '74
Sidney Sheldon's Bloodline '79
The Jigsaw Man '84

Bae Young-kyun
Why Has Bodhi-Darma Left for the East '89

Gary Youngman
Dead as a Doorman '85

Robert Youngson
When Comedy was King '59
Days of Thrills and Laughter '61

Jerry Younkins
The Demon Lover '77

Albert Yu
Devil Woman '76

Ronny Yu
China White '91

Noriaki Yuasa
Gamera, the Invincible '66
Gamera vs. Gaos '67
Destroy All Planets '68
Gamera vs. Guiron '69
Gamera vs. Zigra '71

Corey Yuen
No Retreat, No Surrender '86
No Retreat, No Surrender 2 '89

Jim Yukich
Double Dragon '94

Johnny Yune
They Still Call Me Bruce '86

Larry Yust
Homebodies '74
Say Yes! '86

Peter Yuval
Dead End City '88
Firehead '90

Brian Yuzna
Bride of Re-Animator '89
Silent Night, Deadly Night 4: Initiation '90
Society '92
Return of the Living Dead 3 '93

Jose Maria Zabalza
The Fury of the Wolfman '70

Gabor Zabo
Where '94

Alfredo Zacharias
Crossfire '67
Bandits '73
The Bees '78
Demonoid, Messenger of Death '81

Steve Zacharias
Revenge of the Nerds 4: Nerds in Love '94

Michael Zachary
Sin of Adam & Eve '72

Robert Zagone
Stand-In '85

Caveh Zahedi
A Little Stiff '91

Raja Zahr
The Last Season '87

Steven Zaillian
Searching for Bobby Fischer '93

Nancy Zala
Round Numbers '91

Alain Zaloum
Canvas: The Fine Art of Crime '92

Luigi Zampa
A Woman of Rome '56
Tigers in Lipstick '80

Mario Zampi
The Naked Truth '58
Too Many Crooks '59

Susanne Zanke
The Scorpion Woman '89

Lili Fini Zanuck
Rush '91

Krzysztof Zanussi
The Structure of Crystals '69
Family Life '71
Illumination '73
The Catamount Killing '74
The Unapproachable '82
Year of the Quiet Sun '84
The Silent Touch '94

Janusz Zaorski
Baritone '85

Fabrice A. Zaphiratos
Bloodbeat '85

Frank Zappa
200 Motels '71
Baby Snakes: The Complete Version '79

Mier Zarchi
I Spit on Your Grave '77
Don't Mess with My Sister! '85

Tony Zarindast
The Guns and the Fury '83
Treasure of the Lost Desert '83
Hardcase and Fist '89

Cesare Zavattini
Love in the City '53

Edwin Zbonek
The Monster of London City '64
The Mad Executioners '65

Kristi Zea
Women & Men: In Love There Are No Rules '91

Nick Zedd
Geek Maggot Bingo '83

Franco Zeffirelli
The Taming of the Shrew '67
Romeo and Juliet '68
Brother Sun, Sister Moon '73
Jesus of Nazareth '77
The Champ '79
Endless Love '81
Otello '86
Hamlet '90
Jane Eyre '96

Primo Zeglio
Mission Stardust '68

Paul Zehrer
Blessing '94

Rafal Zeilinski
Screwballs '83
Loose Screws '85
Recruits '86
Ginger Ale Afternoon '89
Spellcaster '91

Alfred Zeisler
Amazing Adventure '37
Make-Up '37
Enemy of Women '44
Fear '46
Parole, Inc. '49

Yuri Zeltser
Eye of the Storm '91
Playmaker '94

Karel Zeman
Fabulous Adventures of Baron Munchausen '61
The Original Fabulous Adventures of Baron Munchausen '61
On the Comet '68

Robert Zemeckis
I Wanna Hold Your Hand '78
Used Cars '80
Romancing the Stone '84
Back to the Future '85
Who Framed Roger Rabbit '88
Back to the Future, Part 2 '89
Tales from the Crypt '89
Back to the Future, Part 3 '90
Death Becomes Her '92
Forrest Gump '94

Will Zens
Hell on Wheels '67
Hot Summer in Barefoot County '74
Trucker's Woman '83
The Fix '84

Barry Zetlin
The Dogfighters '95

Mai Zetterling
Scrubbers '82

V. Zhalakyavichus
Adomas Nori Buti Zmogumi '59

Arunas Zhebrunas
Grazuole '69

Yuri Zhelyabuzhsky
The Cigarette Girl of Mosselprom '24

Tian Zhuangzhuang
The Horse Thief '87
The Blue Kite '93

Claude Zidi
Stuntwoman '81
My New Partner '84

Howard Zieff
Slither '73
Hearts of the West '75
House Calls '78
The Main Event '79
Private Benjamin '80
Unfaithfully Yours '84
The Dream Team '89
My Girl '91
My Girl 2 '94

Howard Ziehm
Flesh Gordon 2: Flesh Gordon Meets the Cosmic Cheerleaders '90

Rafal Zielinksi
Jailbait '93
National Lampoon's Last Resort '94

Paul Ziller
Pledge Night '90
Deadly Surveillance '91
Bloodfist 4: Die Trying '92
Back in Action '94
Breaking Point '94
Probable Cause '95

Vernon Zimmerman
Unholy Rollers '72
Fade to Black '80

Michael Zinberg
Accidental Meeting '93

Fred Zinnemann
The Seventh Cross '44
The Search '48
The Men '50
High Noon '52
The Member of the Wedding '52
From Here to Eternity '53
Oklahoma! '55
The Nun's Story '59
The Sundowners '60
Behold a Pale Horse '64
A Man for All Seasons '66
The Day of the Jackal '73
Julia '77
Five Days One Summer '82

Peter Zinner
The Salamander '82

Joseph Zito
Abduction '75
The Prowler '81
Friday the 13th, Part 4: The Final Chapter '84
Missing in Action '84
Invasion U.S.A. '85
Red Scorpion '89

Milan Zivkovich
Concealed Weapon '94

Lee David Zlotoff
The Spitfire Grill '95

Dick Zondag
We're Back! A Dinosaur's Story '93

Ralph Zondag
We're Back! A Dinosaur's Story '93

David Zucker
Airplane! '80
Police Squad! Help Wanted! '82
Top Secret! '84
Ruthless People '86
The Naked Gun: From the Files of Police Squad '88
Naked Gun 2 1/2: The Smell of Fear '91

Jerry Zucker
Airplane! '80
Police Squad! Help Wanted! '82
Top Secret! '84
Ruthless People '86
Ghost '90
First Knight '95

Ralph Zucker
Terror Creatures from the Grave '66

Andrzej Zulawski
Possession '81

Frank Zuniga
Further Adventures of the Wilderness Family, Part 2 '77
The Golden Seal '83
Heartbreaker '83
Fist Fighter '88

Marcos Zurinaga
Tango Bar '88

Guido Zurli
Psychopath '68

John Zuru
The Mad Butcher '72

Martin Zweiback
Cactus in the Snow '72

Edward Zwick
Having It All '82
Special Bulletin '83
About Last Night... '86
Glory '89
Leaving Normal '92
Legends of the Fall '94
Courage Under Fire '96

Joel Zwick
Second Sight '89

Karl Zwicky
Contagion '87
Vicious '88

Terry Zwigoff
Crumb '94

The **Writer Index** provides a videography for any writer with a video credit. The listings for the writer names follow an alphabetical sort by last name (although the names appear in a first name last name format). The videographies are listed chronologically, from oldest film to the most recent. If a writer wrote (or script doctored) more than one film in the same year, these movies are listed alphabetically within the year. Used in conjunction with the **Cast** index, this index will let you find actors and actresses who wrote themselves juicy parts (with varying degrees of success). Directors also tend to show up here, either before their directorial ambitions surfaced, or after they'd gained enough clout to get one of their scripts to the screen.

Dough Aarniokoski
- Puppet Master 4 *'93*

Paul Aaron
- Octagon *'80*
- Laurel Avenue *'93*

Scott Abbott
- Breach of Conduct *'94*

Shepard Abbott
- C.H.U.D. *'84*

Lewis Abernathy
- Deepstar Six *'89*

Anthony Able
- Project: Alien *'89*

Jim Abrahams
- Kentucky Fried Movie *'77*
- Airplane! *'80*
- Police Squad! Help Wanted! *'82*
- Top Secret! *'84*
- The Naked Gun: From the Files of Police Squad *'88*
- Hot Shots! *'91*
- Hot Shots! Part Deux *'93*

Jerry Abrahamson
- Wagons East *'94*

Jack Abramoff
- Red Scorpion *'89*

Robert Abramoff
- Red Scorpion *'89*

Celia Abrams
- Easy Wheels *'89*

Ian Abrams
- Undercover Blues *'93*

Jeffrey Abrams
- Taking Care of Business *'90*
- Regarding Henry *'91*
- Forever Young *'92*

Tom Abrams
- The Desperate Trail *'94*

Jon Acevski
- Freddie the Frog *'92*

Jovan Acin
- Hey, Babu Riba *'88*

Rodney Ackland
- The Forty-Ninth Parallel *'41*

Allen Actor
- Dungeonmaster *'83*

Alfred Adam
- Belle Americaine *'61*

Catlin Adams
- Sticky Fingers *'88*

Daniel Adams
- Primary Motive *'92*

Ewart Adamson
- Circumstantial Evidence *'35*

Richard Adcock
- Hyper-Sapien: People from Another Star *'86*

Alan J. Adler
- The Alchemist *'81*
- The Concrete Jungle *'82*
- Parasite *'82*
- Metalstorm: The Destruction of Jared Syn *'83*

Gilbert Adler
- Children of the Corn 2: The Final Sacrifice *'92*
- Tales from the Crypt Presents Bordello of Blood *'96*

Eleonore Adlon
- Bagdad Cafe *'88*
- Rosalie Goes Shopping *'89*

Felix Adlon
- Salmonberries *'91*
- Younger & Younger *'94*

Percy Adlon
- Celeste *'81*
- Sugarbaby *'85*
- Bagdad Cafe *'88*
- Rosalie Goes Shopping *'89*
- Salmonberries *'91*
- Younger & Younger *'94*

Nelly Adnil
- Silent Victim *'92*

Gilles Adrien
- Delicatessen *'92*
- The City of Lost Children *'95*

James Agee
- The African Queen *'51*
- The Night of the Hunter *'55*

Faruque Ahmed
- Warlords 3000 *'93*

Kamal Ahmed
- The Jerky Boys *'95*

Chantal Akerman
- News from Home *'76*
- Les Rendez-vous D'Anna *'78*
- The Eighties *'83*
- Window Shopping *'86*
- Night and Day *'91*

Andra Akers
- Toute Une Nuit *'82*

William M. Akers
- Ernest Rides Again *'93*

Norman Aladjem
- Firewalker *'86*

Jeff Albert
- Never Say Die *'94*
- Live Wire: Human Timebomb *'95*

Marvin H. Albert
- Rough Night in Jericho *'67*

Luis Alcoriza
- Death in the Garden *'56*

Alan Alda
- The Seduction of Joe Tynan *'79*
- The Four Seasons *'81*
- Sweet Liberty *'86*
- A New Life *'88*
- Betsy's Wedding *'90*

Robert Alden
- Streetwalkin' *'85*
- Uncaged *'91*

Steve Alden
- Fall Time *'94*

Phillip Alderton
- The Expendables *'89*

Will Aldis
- Back to School *'86*
- The Couch Trip *'87*
- Stealing Home *'88*
- Clifford *'92*

Ronald Alexander
- Billie *'65*

Scott Alexander
- Problem Child *'90*
- Problem Child 2 *'91*
- Ed Wood *'94*

Scott Lawrence Alexander
- Spaced Invaders *'90*

Michel Alexandre
- L.627 *'92*

Richard Alfieri
- Children of Rage *'75*
- Echoes *'83*
- A Friendship in Vienna *'88*

Dan Algrant
- Naked in New York *'93*

Ranald Allan
- The Crossing *'92*

Ted Allan
- Lies My Father Told Me *'75*
- Falling in Love Again *'80*
- Love Streams *'84*
- Dr. Bethune *'90*

Pat Allee
- Bums *'93*

Chris Allen
- The Last Remake of Beau Geste *'77*

Corey Allen
- Avalanche *'78*

Curt Allen
- Walking the Edge *'83*
- Hollywood Harry *'86*
- Bloodstone *'88*
- Alligator 2: The Mutation *'90*
- Blind Vengeance *'90*

Irwin Allen
- Voyage to the Bottom of the Sea *'61*
- Five Weeks in a Balloon *'62*

Janis Allen
- Meatballs *'79*
- The Double Negative *'80*

Jay Presson Allen
- Marnie *'64*
- The Prime of Miss Jean Brodie *'69*
- Cabaret *'72*
- Travels with My Aunt *'72*
- Forty Carats *'73*
- Funny Lady *'75*
- Just Tell Me What You Want *'80*
- Prince of the City *'81*
- Deathtrap *'82*
- Year of the Gun *'91*

Jim Allen
- Hidden Agenda *'90*
- Raining Stones *'93*
- Land and Freedom *'95*

Jordan Allen
- Terminal Bliss *'91*

J.T. Allen
- Geronimo *'93*
- The Good Old Boys *'95*

Woody Allen
- What's New Pussycat? *'65*
- Take the Money and Run *'69*
- Bananas *'71*
- Everything You Always Wanted to Know about Sex (But Were Afraid to Ask) *'72*
- Play It Again, Sam *'72*
- Sleeper *'73*
- Love and Death *'75*
- Annie Hall *'77*
- Interiors *'78*
- Manhattan *'79*
- Stardust Memories *'80*
- A Midsummer Night's Sex Comedy *'82*
- Zelig *'83*
- Broadway Danny Rose *'84*
- The Purple Rose of Cairo *'85*
- Hannah and Her Sisters *'86*
- Radio Days *'87*
- Another Woman *'88*
- September *'88*
- Crimes & Misdemeanors *'89*
- New York Stories *'89*
- Alice *'90*
- Husbands and Wives *'92*
- Shadows and Fog *'92*
- Manhattan Murder Mystery *'93*
- Bullets Over Broadway *'94*
- Mighty Aphrodite *'95*

Michael Almereyda
- Cherry 2000 *'88*
- Twister *'89*
- Search and Destroy *'94*
- Nadja *'95*

Pedro Almodovar
Pepi, Luci, Bom and Other Girls on the Heap '80
Labyrinth of Passion '82
Dark Habits '84
What Have I Done to Deserve This? '85
Law of Desire '86
Matador '86
Women on the Verge of a Nervous Breakdown '88
Tie Me Up! Tie Me Down! '90
High Heels '91
Kika '94
The Flower of My Secret '95

Paul Almond
The Dance Goes On '92

Arthur Alsberg
Gus '76
No Deposit, No Return '76
Herbie Goes to Monte Carlo '77
Hot Lead & Cold Feet '78

John Alsop
Brides of Christ '91

Emmett Alston
New Year's Evil '78
Nine Deaths of the Ninja '85
Hunter's Blood '87

Greg Alt
Zorro, the Gay Blade '81

Richard Altabef
The Kissing Place '90

Eric Alter
Hardbodies '84
Hardbodies 2 '86
The Experts '89

Sergio D. Altieri
Blind Fear '89
Little Sister '92

Robert Altman
McCabe & Mrs. Miller '71
Thieves Like Us '74
Buffalo Bill & the Indians '76
A Wedding '78
Quintet '79
Beyond Therapy '86
Short Cuts '93
Ready to Wear '94

Shelly Altman
Sweet Lorraine '87

David Amann
Dead Air '94

Marino Amaruso
Beach House '82

Rod Amateau
Hook, Line and Sinker '30
The Wilby Conspiracy '75
The Garbage Pail Kids Movie '87
Sunset '88

Eric Ambler
Immortal Battalion '44
The Clouded Yellow '51
A Night to Remember '58

David Ambrose
The Fifth Musketeer '79
The Final Countdown '80
Survivor '80
Dangerous Summer '82
Amityville 3: The Demon '83
Blackout '85
D.A.R.Y.L. '85
Taffin '88
Year of the Gun '91

Gianni Amelio
Open Doors '89
The Stolen Children '92
Lamerica '95

Deborah Amelon
Exit to Eden '94

Nicholas Amendolare
Hard Justice '95

Christopher Ames
Class Action '91

Taylor Ames
He's My Girl '87

Sergio Amidei
Open City '45
Shoeshine '47

Gideon Amir
American Ninja '85

Martin Amis
Saturn 3 '80

Morey Amsterdam
The Ghost and the Guest '43

Franco Amurri
Monkey Trouble '94

Allison Anders
Border Radio '88
Gas Food Lodging '92
Mi Vida Loca '94
Four Rooms '95

Andy Anderson
Positive I.D. '87

Clyde Anderson
Troll 2 '92

Doris Anderson
Give Me a Sailor '38

Elizabeth Anderson
Lassie '94
Three Wishes '95

Gerry Anderson
Journey to the Far Side of the Sun '69

Hesper Anderson
Touched by Love '80
Children of a Lesser God '86
Grand Isle '92

Jane Anderson
The Positively True Adventures of the Alleged Texas Cheerleader-Murdering Mom '93
It Could Happen to You '94
How to Make an American Quilt '95

Robert Anderson
Tea and Sympathy '56
Until They Sail '57
The Nun's Story '59
The Sand Pebbles '66
I Never Sang For My Father '70

Steve Anderson
South Central '92

Wes Anderson
Bottle Rocket '95

William C. Anderson
Bat 21 '88

Lucette Andrei
My Father's Glory '91

Guy Andrews
Lie Down with Lions '94
The Infiltrator '95

Roger Andrieux
La Petite Sirene '80

James Andronica
Mirage '94

Mark Andrus
Late for Dinner '91

Dan Angel
Body Bags '93

Mikel Angel
Evil Spirits '91

Michael Angeli
Conflict of Interest '92
Sketch Artist '92
Sketch Artist 2: Hands That See '94

Yves Angelo
Colonel Chabert '94

Theo Angelopoulos
Landscape in the Mist '88
Ulysses' Gaze '95

Maya Angelou
Georgia, Georgia '72

Gianfranco Angelucci
Intervista '87

Carole Angier
Wide Sargasso Sea '92

Edward Anhalt
Panic in the Streets '50
The Member of the Wedding '52
Not as a Stranger '55
The Pride and the Passion '57
The Young Lions '58
Girls! Girls! Girls! '62
Becket '64
Boeing Boeing '65
Hour of the Gun '67
The Boston Strangler '68
The Madwoman of Chaillot '69
Jeremiah Johnson '72
Luther '74
The Man in the Glass Booth '75
Fatal Chase '77
Escape to Athena '79
Green Ice '81
The Holcroft Covenant '85
The Take '90

Erik Anjou
The Road to Ruin '28
976-EVIL 2: The Astral Factor '91
The Cool Surface '92

Ken Annakin
Those Magnificent Men in Their Flying Machines '65
Those Daring Young Men in Their Jaunty Jalopies '69
The New Adventures of Pippi Longstocking '88

Jean-Jacques Annaud
Black and White in Color '76
The Lover '92

Jean Anouilh
Circle of Love '64

Joseph Anthony
Crime and Punishment '35

Richard J. Anthony
Echoes '83

Robert Anthony
Without Mercy '95

Stuart Anthony
Border Law '31
The Fighting Sheriff '31
Arizona Mahoney '36
Drift Fence '36
The Monster and the Girl '41

Steve Antin
Inside Monkey Zetterland '93

Michelangelo Antonioni
Il Grido '57
L'Avventura '60
The Red Desert '64
Blow-Up '66
The Eclipse '66
Zabriskie Point '70
The Passenger '75

Bill Apablasa
Airborne '93

Judd Apatow
Heavyweights '94
The Cable Guy '96
Celtic Pride '96

Leah Appet
Every Time We Say Goodbye '86

Max Apple
Smokey Bites the Dust '81
The Air Up There '94
Roommates '95

Daniel Appleby
Bound and Gagged: A Love Story '93

A.L. Appling
Running Mates '92

Igor Aptekman
Little Indian, Big City '95

Gregg Araki
The Living End '92
Totally F***ed Up '94
The Doom Generation '95

Ivan Aralica
Gospa '94

Shimon Arama
Triumph of the Spirit '89

Paul Aratow
Purgatory '89

Denys Arcand
The Decline of the American Empire '86
Jesus of Montreal '89

Manuel Arce
El Super '79
Crossover Dreams '85

Jeffrey Arch
Iron Will '93
Sleepless in Seattle '93

Evan P. Archerd
American Anthem '86

William Archibald
The Innocents '61

Cesar Ardavin
Lazarillo '59

Claudio Argento
Santa Sangre '90

Dario Argento
Once Upon a Time in the West '68
The Bird with the Crystal Plumage '70
The Cat o' Nine Tails '71
Suspiria '77
Inferno '78
Unsane '82
Creepers '85
Demons 2 '87
Terror at the Opera '88
The Church '90
Two Evil Eyes '90
The Devil's Daughter '91
Dario Argento's Trauma '93

Adolfo Aristarain
A Place in the World '95

Adam Arkin
Improper Channels '82

Alice Arlen
Silkwood '83
Alamo Bay '85
Cookie '89

George Armitage
Gas-s-s-s! '70
Private Duty Nurses '71
Night Call Nurses '72
The Last of the Finest '90
Miami Blues '90
The Late Shift '96

Andy Armstrong
Moonshine Highway '96

Carrie Armstrong
Ninja Vengeance '93

Karl Armstrong
Ninja Vengeance '93

Michael Armstrong
Black Panther '77
House of the Long Shadows '82
Two If by Sea '95

Robin B. Armstrong
Pastime '91

Eddie Arno
Murder Story '89

Danny Arnold
The Caddy '53

Frank Arnold
Humanoids from the Deep '80

David Arnott
The Adventures of Ford Fairlane '90
Last Action Hero '93

Alexandre Arnoux
Don Quixote '35

Antonin Artaud
Smiling Madame Beudet/The Seashell and the Clergyman '28

Art Arthur
Everything Happens at Night '39

Victor Arthur
Hills of Oklahoma '50

Morris Asgar
Project: Eliminator '91

William Asher
Bikini Beach '64
Muscle Beach Party '64
Beach Blanket Bingo '65
How to Stuff a Wild Bikini '65

David Ashton
Freddie the Frog '92

Piers Ashworth
Nostradamus '93

Isaac Asimov
Light Years '88

Peter Askin
Smithereens '82

Samson Aslanian
Torment '85

Olivier Assayas
Rendez-vous '85
Scene of the Crime '87

Patti Astor
Assault of the Killer Bimbos '88

David Atkins
Arizona Dream '94

Peter Atkins
Hellbound: Hellraiser 2 '88
Hellraiser 3: Hell on Earth '92
Hellraiser 4: Bloodline '95

Larry Atlas
Sleepless in Seattle '93

Paul Attanasio
Rapid Fire '92
Disclosure '94
Quiz Show '94

Margaret Atwood
Heaven on Earth '89

Ronald Atwood
Cry, the Beloved Country '95

Jacques Audiard
Baxter '89
Barjo '93

Michel Audiard
Dear Detective '77

John P. Auerbach
Stepfather 2: Make Room for Daddy '89

Michael Auerbach
The Tie That Binds '95

Bille August
Twist & Shout '84
Pelle the Conqueror '88
The House of the Spirits '93

Joe Augustyn
Night of the Demons '88
Night Angel '90
Night of the Demons 2 '94

Carlos Aured
Triumphs of a Man Called Horse '83

Jean Aurenche
The Walls of Malapaga '49
The Red Inn '51

Robert Alan Aurthur
Warlock '59

Paul Auster
Smoke '70
Blue In the Face '95
Smoke '95

Sam Auster
Screen Test '85
Bounty Hunter 2002 '94

Carl Austin
Wild Cactus '92
Sexual Malice '93
Improper Conduct '94

Irving Austin
Warlords of the 21st Century '82

Michael Austin
The Shout '78
Five Days One Summer '82
Greystoke: The Legend of Tarzan, Lord of the Apes '84
Princess Caraboo '94

Phillip Avalon
Fatal Bond '91

Roger Roberts Avary
Killing Zoe '94
Pulp Fiction '94

Antonio Avati
Bix '90

Pupi Avati
Bix '90
The Story of Boys & Girls '91

Howard (Hikmet) Avedis
Scorchy '76
The Fifth Floor '80
Mortuary '81
They're Playing with Fire '84
Kidnapped '87

Ruth Avergon
Night School '81
Robert J. Avrech
Body Double '84
Dark Tower '87
A Stranger Among Us '92
Barry Avrich
Scorned '93
Gabriel Axel
Babette's Feast '87
David Axelrod
Charlie Chan and the Curse of the Dragon Queen '81
George Axelrod
Phffft! '54
The Seven Year Itch '55
Bus Stop '56
Breakfast at Tiffany's '61
The Manchurian Candidate '62
How to Murder Your Wife '64
Paris When It Sizzles '64
Secret Life of an American Wife '68
The Lady Vanishes '79
The Holcroft Covenant '85
The Fourth Protocol '87
Alan Ayckbourn
A Chorus of Disapproval '89
Clay Ayers
Sword of Honor '94
Dan Aykroyd
The Blues Brothers '80
Ghostbusters '84
Spies Like Us '85
Dragnet '87
Ghostbusters 2 '89
Nothing But Trouble '91
Coneheads '93
Peter Aykroyd
Nothing But Trouble '91
Marcel Ayme
Crime and Punishment '35
John Ayre
Surf Nazis Must Die '87
Gerald Ayres
Foxes '80
Rich and Famous '81
Crazy in Love '92
Rafael Azcona
La Grande Bouffe '73
Ay, Carmela! '90
Belle Epoque '92
Beth B
Vortex '81
Salvation! '87
Two Small Bodies '93
Scott B
Vortex '81
Thom Babbes
Deadly Dreams '88
Body Chemistry '90
Hector Babenco
Pixote '81
At Play in the Fields of the Lord '91
Jimmy Santiago Baca
Blood In...Blood Out: Bound by Honor '93
Daniel F. Bacaner
Scared Stiff '87
Danilo Bach
Beverly Hills Cop '84
April Fool's Day '86
Michael Backes
Rising Sun '93
Jean-Pierre Bacri
Smoking/No Smoking '94
Peter Bacso
Oh, Bloody Life! '88
Tom Badal
Out on Bail '89
Vietnam, Texas '90
Randall Badat
Surf 2 '84
Born to Run '93
Hear No Evil '93
Giya Badridze
Ashik Kerib '88

Bill Baer
The Quiet Earth '85
Meredith Baer
The Magic Bubble '93
Geoffrey Baere
School Spirit '85
Campus Man '87
Corporate Affairs '90
Michael Bafaro
Crackerjack '94
Milton Bagby, Jr.
Rebel Love '85
Ross Bagdasarian
The Chipmunk Adventure '87
Fax Bahr
Hearts of Darkness: A Filmmaker's Apocalypse '91
Son-in-Law '93
In the Army Now '94
Jury Duty '95
Frederick Bailey
Desert Warrior '88
Quick '93
Robert Bailey
Yor, the Hunter from the Future '83
Sandra K. Bailey
Hambone & Hillie '84
The KGB: The Secret War '86
Prettykill '87
False Identity '90
Gary L. Bain
Ice Castles '79
Beryl Bainbridge
Sweet William '79
John Baines
Dead of Night '45
Harwant Bains
Wild West '93
Jon Robin Baitz
Fallen Angels 1 '93
Bart Baker
Baby of the Bride '91
Live Wire '92
Edwin Baker
Combination Platter '93
Herbert Baker
Artists and Models '55
Kyle Baker
Cosmic Slop '94
Michael Baker
Dead Ahead: The Exxon Valdez Disaster '92
Ralph Bakshi
Fritz the Cat '72
Heavy Traffic '73
Streetfight '75
Wizards '77
Hey Good Lookin' '82
Fire and Ice '83
Bob Balaban
The Last Good Time '94
Josiane Balasko
French Twist '95
John Balderston
Frankenstein '31
The Lives of a Bengal Lancer '35
Prisoner of Zenda '37
Red Planet Mars '52
James Baldwin
Malcolm X '92
David Ball
Hard Rock Zombies '85
Peter Baloff
Near Misses '91
Quicksand: No Escape '91
Anne Bancroft
Fatso '80
Jonathan Banks
Saturday Night Special '92
Walter Bannert
The Inheritors '85
Jack Baran
Band of the Hand '86
Great Balls of Fire '89
Steve Barancik
The Last Seduction '94

Dana Baratta
Andre '94
Benny Barbash
Beyond the Walls '84
Neal Barbera
The Prowler '81
P.K. and the Kid '85
Too Scared to Scream '85
Franco Barbieri
Beyond the Door 2 '79
Malcolm Barbour
The P.O.W. Escape '86
Deadly Sins '95
Ann Louise Bardach
Backtrack '89
Sorry, Wrong Number '89
Ronda Barendse
Bodily Harm '95
Frank Barhydt
Quintet '79
Short Cuts '93
Leora Barish
Desperately Seeking Susan '85
Venus Rising '95
Clive Barker
Transmutations '85
Hellraiser '87
Rawhead Rex '87
Night Breed '90
Lord of Illusions '95
Ira Barmak
Hotel Colonial '88
Jeff Barmash
Power of Attorney '94
Peter Barnes
Enchanted April '92
Enrique Pineda Barnet
I Am Cuba '64
Alexander Baron
Poldark 2 '75
Willie Baronet
Adventures in Dinosaur City '92
Douglas Barr
The Cover Girl Murders '93
Fade to Black '93
Jackson Barr
Body Chemistry '90
Bad Channels '92
Seedpeople '92
800 Leagues Down the Amazon '93
Mandroid '93
Matthew F. Barr
Deadly Blessing '81
Earl Barret
See No Evil, Hear No Evil '89
Bruno Barreto
Dona Flor and Her Two Husbands '78
Gabriela '84
James Lee Barrett
Angel City '80
Poker Alice '87
Lezli-Ann Barrett
Business as Usual '88
J.M. Barrie
As You Like It '36
Quality Street '37
Michael Barrie
Ratings Game '84
Amazon Women on the Moon '87
Oscar '91
Bad Boys '95
National Lampoon's Favorite Deadly Sins '95
Fred Barron
Between the Lines '77
Something Short of Paradise '79
Steven Barron
The Adventures of Pinocchio '96
Zelda Barron
Secret Places '85
Julian Barry
Lenny '74
The River '84
Me, Myself & I '92

Odile Barski
The Cry of the Owl '92
Peter Barsocchini
Drop Zone '94
Paul Bartel
Cannonball '76
Eating Raoul '82
Not for Publication '84
Basil Bartlett
Secret Mission '42
Hall Bartlett
All the Young Men '60
Children of Sanchez '79
Sy Bartlett
Beloved Infidel '59
William S. Bartman
O'Hara's Wife '82
Jim Barton
That Eye, The Sky '94
Hal Barwood
The Sugarland Express '74
Bingo Long Traveling All-Stars & Motor Kings '76
MacArthur '77
Corvette Summer '78
Dragonslayer '81
Warning Sign '85
Ben Barzman
Time Without Pity '57
Ron Base
Heavenly Bodies '84
Gordon Basichis
Breach of Trust '95
Kim Bass
A Thin Line Between Love and Hate '96
Ronald Bass
Code Name: Emerald '85
Black Widow '87
Gardens of Stone '87
Rain Man '88
Sleeping with the Enemy '91
The Joy Luck Club '93
The Enemy Within '94
When a Man Loves a Woman '94
Dangerous Minds '95
Waiting to Exhale '95
Lawrence Bassoff
Weekend Pass '84
Hunk '87
William Bast
The Valley of Gwangi '69
James Dean '76
The Betsy '78
Janet Scott Batchler
Batman Forever '95
Lee Batchler
Batman Forever '95
Kent Bateman
Headless Eyes '83
Alan Bates
The Story of a Love Story '73
Cary Bates
Christopher Columbus: The Discovery '92
Djalma Batista
Savage Capitalism '93
Joe Batteer
Curiosity Kills '90
Blown Away '94
Chasers '94
Bradley Battersby
Blue Desert '91
Lloyd Battista
Treasure of the Four Crowns '82
Fred Bauer
Under the Rainbow '81
Thomas Baum
Hugo the Hippo '76
Carny '80
Simon '80
The Sender '82
The Manhattan Project '86
Witness to the Execution '94
Noah Baumbach
Kicking and Screaming '95
Lamberto Bava
Beyond the Door 2 '79

Demons 2 '87
George L. Baxt
Circus of Horrors '60
Horror Hotel '60
John Baxter
The Time Guardian '87
Sergio Bazzini
Husbands and Lovers '91
Peter S. Beagle
The Dove '74
The Lord of the Rings '78
The Last Unicorn '82
David Beaird
Octavia '82
Party Animal '83
My Chauffeur '86
Scorchers '92
Henry Bean
Running Brave '83
Internal Affairs '90
Deep Cover '92
Douglas Carter Beane
To Wong Foo, Thanks for Everything, Julie Newmar '95
Winston Beard
Cyber Bandits '94
Nicholas Beardsley
Savage Island '85
Richard Beattie
Cold Sweat '93
Warren Beatty
Shampoo '75
Heaven Can Wait '78
Reds '81
Reds '81
Love Affair '94
D.D. Beauchamp
Abbott and Costello Go to Mars '53
Marcel Beaulieu
Farinelli '94
Trace Beaulieu
Mystery Science Theater 3000: The Movie '96
Gorman Bechard
Cemetery High '89
Josh Beck
Lunatics: A Love Story '92
Jacques Becker
Casque d'Or '52
Grisbi '53
Ali Baba and the 40 Thieves '54
Modigliani '58
Barry Beckerman
Shamus '73
St. Ives '76
Michael Frost Beckner
Sniper '92
Dick Beebe
Prison Stories: Women on the Inside '91
Into the Badlands '92
Ford Beebe
Fighting Shadows '35
Prescott Kid '36
Riders of Pasco Basin '40
John Beech
Warlords of the 21st Century '82
Jeff Begun
Saturday the 14th '81
Marc Behm
Help! '65
The Peking Blond '68
Hospital Massacre '81
Nana '82
Harry Behn
Hell's Angels '30
Jack Behr
Birdy '84
S.N. Behrman
Hallelujah, I'm a Bum '33
A Tale of Two Cities '35
Me and the Colonel '58
Jean-Jacques Beineix
Diva '82

Beineix ▶cont.
Moon in the Gutter '83
Betty Blue '86

William Bekkala
Silent Motive '91

Elisa Bell
Writer's Block '91
Treacherous Crossing '92
Dancing with Danger '93

Jeffrey Bell
Radio Inside '94

Neal Bell
Terminal Choice '85
Two Small Bodies '93

Robert Bell
Free Ride '86

Ross Bell
To Die Standing '91

James Warner Bellah
Sergeant Rutledge '60

Bruce Belland
Weekend Warriors '86

Michelle Bellerose
Replikator: Cloned to Kill '94

Donald P. Bellisario
Magnum P.I.: Don't Eat the Snow in Hawaii '80
Last Rites '88
JAG '95

Stephen F. Bello
Circle of Power '83

Marco Bellochio
The Eyes, the Mouth '83
Henry IV '85
Devil in the Flesh '87

Peter Bellwood
Phobia '80
Highlander '86
Highlander 2: The Quickening '91

Vera Belmont
Red Kiss '85

Edmund Beloin
Lady On a Train '45

Jerry Belson
How Sweet It Is! '68
Smile '75
Fun with Dick and Jane '77
The End '78
Smokey and the Bandit, Part 2 '80
Jekyll & Hyde...Together Again '82
Surrender '87
Always '89

James Belushi
Birthday Boy '85
Number One with a Bullet '87

Remy Belvaux
Man Bites Dog '91

Maria-Luisa Bemberg
Miss Mary '86
I, the Worst of All '90
I Don't Want to Talk About It '94

Peter Benchley
Jaws '75
The Deep '77
The Island '80

Robert Benchley
Foreign Correspondent '40

Alessandro Bencivenni
Ciao, Professore! '94

Lawrence Bender
Intruder '88

Barbara Benedek
The Big Chill '83
Immediate Family '89
Men Don't Leave '89
Sabrina '95

Tom Benedek
Cocoon '85
The Adventures of Pinocchio '96

Robert Benedetto
Aloha Summer '88
The Canterville Ghost '96

Glenn Benest
Deadly Blessing '81

Roberto Benigni
Johnny Stecchino '92

Tomas Benitez
Salsa '88

Jeff Benjamin
American Anthem '86

Richard Benner
Happy Birthday, Gemini '80

Alan Bennett
An Englishman Abroad '83
A Private Function '84
Prick Up Your Ears '87
A Question of Attribution '91
The Madness of King George '94

Bill Bennett
Backlash '86

Charles Bennett
Blackmail '29
The Evil Mind '34
The Man Who Knew Too Much '34
The 39 Steps '35
King of the Damned '36
Sabotage '36
The Secret Agent '36
The Young in Heart '38
Balalaika '39
Foreign Correspondent '40
Joan of Paris '42
Forever and a Day '43
The Story of Dr. Wassell '44
Unconquered '47
Black Magic '49
The Green Glove '52
Dangerous Mission '54
Curse of the Demon '57
Voyage to the Bottom of the Sea '61
Five Weeks in a Balloon '62

Gary Bennett
Rain Without Thunder '93

Harve Bennett
Star Trek 3: The Search for Spock '84
Star Trek 4: The Voyage Home '86

Parker Bennett
Mystery Date '91
Super Mario Bros. '93

Valerie Bennett
The Companion '94

Wallace C. Bennett
George! '70
Silent Scream '80
Rage of Honor '87

Robby Benson
One on One '77
Die Laughing '80
Modern Love '90
Betrayal of the Dove '92

Sally Benson
Shadow of a Doubt '43
Anna and the King of Siam '46
Come to the Stable '49
Conspirator '49

Trevor Bentham
A Month by the Lake '95

Robert Bentley
Shanghai Surprise '86

Robert Benton
Bonnie & Clyde '67
There was a Crooked Man '70
Bad Company '72
What's Up, Doc? '72
The Late Show '77
Superman: The Movie '78
Kramer vs. Kramer '79
Still of the Night '82
Places in the Heart '84
Nadine '87
Nobody's Fool '94

Leo Benvenuti
Ciao, Professore! '94
The Santa Clause '94

Luc Beraud
This Sweet Sickness '77
The Accompanist '93

Luca Bercovici
Ghoulies '84
Rockula '90
The Granny '94

Geza Beremenyi
The Midas Touch '89

Bruce Beresford
Barry McKenzie Holds His Own '74
Money Movers '78
Breaker Morant '80
The Fringe Dwellers '86
Mister Johnson '91
Curse of the Starving Class '94

Rhoisin Beresford
The Fringe Dwellers '86

James Berg
A Very Brady Sequel '96

John Berger
La Salamandre '71

Pamela Berger
Sorceress '88
The Imported Bridegroom '89

Robert Berger
Final Analysis '92

Andrew Bergman
Blazing Saddles '74
The In-Laws '79
So Fine '81
Oh, God! You Devil '84
Fletch '85
Big Trouble '86
The Freshman '90
Soapdish '91
Honeymoon in Vegas '92
It Could Happen to You '94
The Scout '94
Striptease '96

Ingmar Bergman
Torment '44
Devil's Wanton '49
Summer Interlude '50
Monika '52
Secrets of Women '52
Sawdust & Tinsel '53
Lesson in Love '54
Dreams '55
Smiles of a Summer Night '55
The Seventh Seal '56
Wild Strawberries '57
The Magician '58
The Devil's Eye '60
Through a Glass Darkly '61
The Winter Light '62
The Silence '63
Persona '66
Hour of the Wolf '68
The Shame '68
The Rite '69
The Passion of Anna '70
The Touch '71
Cries and Whispers '72
Scenes from a Marriage '73
Face to Face '76
Autumn Sonata '78
The Serpent's Egg '78
From the Life of the Marionettes '80
Fanny and Alexander '83
After the Rehearsal '84
The Best Intentions '92
Sunday's Children '94

Linda J. Bergman
The Lookalike '90
Matters of the Heart '90

Martin Bergman
Peter's Friends '92

Robert Bergman
Skull: A Night of Terror '88
A Whisper to a Scream '88

Eric Bergren
The Elephant Man '80
Frances '82
The Dark Wind '91

Eleanor Bergstein
It's My Turn '80
Dirty Dancing '87

Howard Berk
Target '85

Martin Berkeley
Revenge of the Creature '55
Tarantula '55
The Deadly Mantis '57

Oliver Berkman
Kicking and Screaming '95

Jeannie Berlin
In the Spirit '90

Barry Berman
Benny & Joon '93

Judd Bernard
The Destructors '74
The Class of Miss MacMichael '78
Enter the Ninja '81

Sam Bernard
Rad '86
3:15—The Moment of Truth '86
Warlock: The Armageddon '93

Paul Bernbaum
Royce '93
Rent-A-Kid '95

Edward L. Bernds
Blondie Knows Best '46
Reform School Girl '57
Storm Rider '57

Peter Berneis
My Man Godfrey '57

Kevin Bernhardt
The Immortals '95

Gisella Bernice
Parallel Lives '94

Armyan Bernstein
Thank God It's Friday '78
One from the Heart '82
Windy City '84
Cross My Heart '88

Jack Bernstein
Ace Ventura: Pet Detective '93

Jane Bernstein
Seven Minutes in Heaven '86

Nat Bernstein
Opportunity Knocks '90

Walter Bernstein
Heller in Pink Tights '60
Paris Blues '61
Fail-Safe '64
The Train '65
Molly Maguires '70
The Front '76
Semi-Tough '77
The Betsy '78
An Almost Perfect Affair '79
Yanks '79
Little Miss Marker '80
The House on Carroll Street '88
Doomsday Gun '94

Eric Bernt
Surviving the Game '94
Virtuosity '95

Claude Berri
One Wild Moment '78
Jean de Florette '87
Manon of the Spring '87
Uranus '91
Germinal '93

Gina Berriault
The Stone Boy '84

David Berry
The Whales of August '87

Michael Berry
Short Time '90

Tom Berry
Crazy Moon '87

Bernardo Bertolucci
Before the Revolution '65
Once Upon a Time in the West '68
The Spider's Stratagem '70
The Conformist '71
Last Tango in Paris '73
1900 '76
The Tragedy of a Ridiculous Man '81
The Last Emperor '87
The Sheltering Sky '90
Stealing Beauty '96

Giuseppe Bertolucci
1900 '76

Dan Bessie
Hard Traveling '85

Luc Besson
Le Dernier Combat '84
Subway '85
The Big Blue '88
La Femme Nikita '91
The Professional '94

Pete Best
Accidental Meeting '93

Rob Bettinson
The Fifteen Streets '90

Gil Bettman
Never Too Young to Die '86

Jonathan Betuel
The Last Starfighter '84
My Science Project '85
Theodore Rex '95

Eddie Beverly, Jr.
Ballbuster

Radha Bharadwaj
Closet Land '90

Grace Cary Bickley
The Gun in Betty Lou's Handbag '92

William Bickley
Hawmps! '76

Ann Biderman
Copycat '95
Primal Fear '96

Kathryn Bigelow
Loveless '83
Near Dark '87
Blue Steel '90
Undertow '95

Paul Billing
Prime Suspect: The Lost Child '94

Danny Bilson
Future Cop '76
Trancers '84
Zone Troopers '84
The Eliminators '86
The Wrong Guys '88
Arena '89
The Rocketeer '91

Carl Binder
Pocahontas '95

John Binder
Honeysuckle Rose '80
Uforia '81
Endangered Species '82

Mike Binder
Coupe de Ville '90
Crossing the Bridge '92
Indian Summer '93

William Bindley
Freeze Frame '92
Judicial Consent '94

Steve Bing
Missing in Action 2: The Beginning '85
Every Breath '93

Edfrid Bingham
Riders of the Purple Sage '25

Claude Binyon
Arizona '40
A Woman's World '54

Lee Biondi
National Lampoon's Favorite Deadly Sins '95

Dudley Birch
Flight from Singapore '62

Harry Birckmayer
Party Girl '94

Brad Bird
*batteries not included '87

Brian Bird
Bopha! '93

Sarah Bird
Don't Tell Her It's Me '90

David Birke
The Fear Inside '92

Andrew Birkin
The Final Conflict '81
King David '85
The Name of the Rose '86
Burning Secret '89

Stuart Birnbaum
Smokey and the Bandit, Part 3 '83

Lajos Biro
The Private Life of Henry VIII '33

Louise Birt
The Three Weird Sisters '48

Larry J. Bischof
Dreamer '79

John Bishop
The Package '89
Drop Zone '94

Mark Bishop
Tales from the Crypt Presents Demon Knight '94

Rod Bishop
Body Melt '93

Shem Bitterman
Halloween 5: The Revenge of Michael Myers '89
Out of the Rain '90
Peephole '93

Chris Bittler
Raging Angels '95

Rick Bitzelberger
Embrace of the Vampire '95

Emerson Bixby
Disturbed '90
Bikini Island '91

Carol Black
Soul Man '86

David Black
Legacy of Lies '92

John D.F. Black
Shaft '71

Noel Black
Mischief '85

Shane Black
Lethal Weapon '87
The Monster Squad '87
The Last Boy Scout '91
Last Action Hero '93

Stephen Black
Eden '92
Eden 2 '93

Susan Black
State of Emergency '94

Terry Black
Dead Heat '88

Richard Blackburn
Eating Raoul '82

Kenneth G. Blackwell
Triumphs of a Man Called Horse '83
Dark Tower '87

Ruben Blades
Crossover Dreams '85

David Blair
Wax, or the Discovery of Television Among the Bees '93

Dennis Blair
Easy Money '83

Jeanne Blake
Steal Big, Steal Little '95

Michael Blake
Stacy's Knights '83
Dances with Wolves '90

Michael Blakemore
Country Life '95

Beverly Blakenship
Shame '87

Michel Blanc
Grosse Fatigue '94

Ken Blancato
Stewardess School '86

Dorothy Blank
Snow White and the Seven Dwarfs '37

Michael Blankfort
Tribute to a Bad Man '56

Jerry Blatt
Divine Madness '80

William Peter Blatty
A Shot in the Dark '64
Promise Her Anything '66
What Did You Do in the War, Daddy? '66
Darling Lili '70
The Exorcist '73
The Ninth Configuration '79
Exorcist 3: Legion '90

Raphael David Blau
Fear Strikes Out '57

Barry W. Blaustein
Police Academy 2: Their First Assignment '85
Coming to America '88
Boomerang '92
The Nutty Professor '96

Alan Bleasdale
No Surrender '86

Corey Blechman
Dominick & Eugene '88
Max and Helen '90
Free Willy '93
Free Willy 2: The Adventure Home '95

Robert Blees
All I Desire '53
Cattle Queen of Montana '54
Magnificent Obsession '54
Autumn Leaves '56
Slightly Scarlet '56
The Black Scorpion '57
From the Earth to the Moon '58
Who Slew Auntie Roo? '71
Doctor Phibes Rises Again '72
Frogs '72

William Bleich
The Hearse '80

Lee Blessing
Cooperstown '93
Steal Big, Steal Little '95

Bertrand Blier
Going Places '74
Get Out Your Handkerchiefs '78
Buffet Froid '79
Beau Pere '81
My Best Friend's Girl '84
Menage '86
Too Beautiful for You '88

William Blinn
Purple Rain '84
The Boys Next Door '96

John W. Bloch
One Man's Way '63

Robert Bloch
The Night Walker '64
Strait-Jacket '64
Torture Garden '67
The House that Dripped Blood '71

Joel Block
Nobody's Perfect '90

Larry Block
The Funhouse '81

Michael Blodgett
Hero and the Terror '88
Rent-A-Cop '88
Turner and Hooch '89
Run '91

Eric L. Bloom
Eyes of a Stranger '81

George Arthur Bloom
The Last Flight of Noah's Ark '80

Harold Jack Bloom
Land of the Pharaohs '55
A Gunfight '71

Jeffrey Bloom
11 Harrowhouse '74
Dog Pound Shuffle '75
Swashbuckler '76
The Stick-Up '77
Blood Beach '81
Nightmares '83
Flowers in the Attic '87

Max Bloom
Fist Fighter '88

Steven L. Bloom
The Sure Thing '85
Like Father, Like Son '87
Tall Tale: The Unbelievable Adventures of Pecos Bill '95

Oola Bloome
Undercover '94

Noah Blough
Crossfire '89

Christopher Blue
Hyper-Sapien: People from Another Star '86

Edwin Blum
The Adventures of Sherlock Holmes '39
Young People '40
The Canterville Ghost '44
Down to Earth '47
Stalag 17 '53
Pearl of the South Pacific '55

Len Blum
Meatballs '79
Heavy Metal '81
Stripes '81
Spacehunter: Adventures in the Forbidden Zone '83
Feds '88
Beethoven's 2nd '93

John Blumenthal
Short Time '90

Don Bluth
The Secret of NIMH '82
All Dogs Go to Heaven '89
Thumbelina '94

Jeffrey Boam
Straight Time '78
Dead Zone '83
Innerspace '87
The Lost Boys '87
Funny Farm '88
Indiana Jones and the Last Crusade '89
Lethal Weapon 2 '89
Lethal Weapon 3 '92
The Phantom '96

Al Boasberg
A Night at the Opera '35

Sam Bobrick
Norman, Is That You? '76
Jimmy the Kid '82

Steven Bochco
Columbo: Murder By the Book '71
Silent Running '71

Sally Bochner
Strangers in Good Company '91

Sydney Boehm
Rough Night in Jericho '67

Michael Boekner
Psycho Girls '86

Knut Boeser
Nostradamus '93

Yurek Bogayevicz
Anna '87

Peter Bogdanovich
The Wild Angels '66
Targets '68
The Last Picture Show '71
Saint Jack '79
They All Laughed '81
Texasville '90

Michael Bogert
Dead End City '88

Willy Bogner
Fire and Ice '83

Eric Bogosian
Talk Radio '88
Sex, Drugs, Rock & Roll: Eric Bogosian '91

Endre Bohem
Twenty Bucks '93

Leslie Bohem
The Horror Show '89
A Nightmare on Elm Street 5: Dream Child '89
Nowhere to Run '93
Twenty Bucks '93

Charles F. Bohl
He's My Girl '87

Dan Bohlinger
The Killing Time '87

Michael Derek Bohusz
Uninvited '93

Jerome Boivin
Baxter '89
Barjo '93

Chris Bold
Hard Justice '95

Heinrich Boll
Germany in Autumn '78

Joseph Bologna
Lovers and Other Strangers '70

Craig Bolotin
Black Rain '89
Straight Talk '92
That Night '93

Troy Bolotnick
Red Scorpion 2 '94
Cyborg 3: The Recycler '95

Max Bolt
The Big Sweat '90

Robert Bolt
Lawrence of Arabia '62
Doctor Zhivago '65
A Man for All Seasons '66
Ryan's Daughter '70
Lady Caroline Lamb '73
The Bounty '84
The Mission '86
Without Warning: The James Brady Story '91

Guy Bolton
Angel '37
Weekend at the Waldorf '45

James Bond, III
Def by Temptation '90

Julian Bond
Choice of Weapons '76
The Shooting Party '85
The Whistle Blower '87
Lie Down with Lions '94

Timothy Bond
Happy Birthday to Me '81

Sergei Bondarchuk
Waterloo '71

Vittorio Bonicelli
Moses '76

Mike Bonifer
Lipstick Camera '93

Pascal Bonitzer
Night and Day '91

Bob Bonney
The Night the Lights Went Out in Georgia '81

Andre Bonzel
Man Bites Dog '91

J.R. Bookwalter
The Dead Next Door '89

John Boorman
Zardoz '73
Excalibur '81
Hope and Glory '87
Where the Heart Is '90

Telsche Boorman
Where the Heart Is '90
French Twist '95

Jon Boorstin
Dream Lover '85

Paul Boorstin
Fire with Fire '86

Sharon Boorstin
Fire with Fire '86

Charles G. Booth
House on 92nd Street '45

Connie Booth
Fawlty Towers '77

James Booth
Sunburn '79
Pray for Death '85
Avenging Force '86
American Ninja 2: The Confrontation '87

Jason Booth
Out on Bail '89

Jose Luis Borau
On the Line '83

Ethel B. Borden
I Live My Life '35

Lizzie Borden
Born in Flames '83
Working Girls '87

Allen Boretz
Where There's Life '47

Alvin Boretz
Brass Target '78

Robert Boris
Electra Glide in Blue '73
Some Kind of Hero '82
Doctor Detroit '83
Oxford Blues '84
Steele Justice '87
Extreme Justice '93
Frank and Jesse '94

Herb Borkland
Honor and Glory '92

Jim Borrelli
Cat Chaser '90

Clay Borris
Quiet Cool '86

Phillip Borsos
Far from Home: The Adventures of Yellow Dog '94

Terry Borst
Private War '90

Chris Borthwick
A Test of Love '84

Michael Bortman
The Good Mother '88
Crooked Hearts '91

Aida Bortnik
The Official Story '85
Old Gringo '89

Roselyne Bosch
1492: Conquest of Paradise '92

Pierre Bost
The Walls of Malapaga '49
The Red Inn '51

Nancy Trite Botkin
Race to Freedom: The Story of the Underground Railroad '94

Jean Boudin
Being at Home with Claude '92

Roy Boulting
The Guinea Pig '48
Brothers in Law '57
Carlton Browne of the F.O. '59

Susan Bowen
The Power Within '95
Storybook '95

William Bowers
Split Second '53
My Man Godfrey '57
Support Your Local Sheriff '69

Douglas Bowie
Boy in Blue '86

Mike Bowler
Things '93

Craig Bowlsby
The Hound of London '93

Alan Bowne
Spike of Bensonhurst '88

Kenneth Bowser
In a Shallow Grave '88

Frank Cottrell Boyce
A Woman's Guide to Adultery '93
Butterfly Kiss '94

Daniel Boyd
Chillers '88
Invasion of the Space Preachers '90

Don Boyd
East of Elephant Rock '76
Twenty-One '91

William Boyd
Stars and Bars '88
Tune in Tomorrow '90
Mister Johnson '91
Chaplin '92
A Good Man in Africa '94

Richard Boyle
Salvador '86

Bill Bozzone
Full Moon in Blue Water '88
Ivory Hunters '90

Gerard Brach
Repulsion '65
Cul de Sac '66
The Fearless Vampire Killers '67

Brach ▶cont.
Diary of Forbidden Dreams '73
The Tenant '76
Tess '80
I Sent a Letter to My Love '81
Quest for Fire '82
Maria's Lovers '84
My Best Friend's Girl '84
The Name of the Rose '86
Pirates '86
Jean de Florette '87
Manon of the Spring '87
Shy People '87
Frantic '88
The Bear '89
Bitter Moon '92
The Lover '92

Charles Brackett
Bluebeard's Eighth Wife '38
Midnight '39
Ball of Fire '41
The Lost Weekend '45
Emperor Waltz '48
Sunset Boulevard '50
Titanic '53

Leigh Brackett
The Big Sleep '46
The Long Goodbye '73
The Empire Strikes Back '80

Jacob Brackman
The King of Marvin Gardens '72
Times Square '80

Malcolm Bradbury
The Green Man '91
Cold Comfort Farm '94

Ray Bradbury
It Came From Outer Space '53
Moby Dick '56
Something Wicked This Way Comes '83

Robert North Bradbury
Texas Buddies '32
The Gallant Fool '33
Valley of the Lawless '36

Al Bradley
Iron Warrior '87

Pat Bradley
Under the Rainbow '81

John Bradshaw
The Big Slice '90

Jim Brady
Boy Meets Girl '84

Brannon Braga
Star Trek Generations '94
Star Trek the Next Generation, the Final Episode: All Good Things... '94

Melvin Bragg
Isadora '68
The Music Lovers '71
Jesus Christ, Superstar '73

Diana Braithwaite
Race to Freedom: The Story of the Underground Railroad '94

Malcolm Braly
On the Yard '79

Bill Brame
Miss Melody Jones '73

Kenneth Branagh
Henry V '89
Much Ado about Nothing '93

John Brancato
Femme Fatale '90
Interceptor '92
Into the Sun '92
The Net '95

Larry Brand
Backfire '88
The Drifter '88
Masque of the Red Death '89
Overexposed '90
Till the End of the Night '94

Max Brand
Uncertain Glory '44

Millen Brand
The Snake Pit '48

David Brandes
Dirt Bike Kid '86
The Quarrel '93

Richard Brandes
Party Line '88
Martial Law '90
Martial Law 2: Undercover '91
Dead Cold '96

Gary Brandner
Howling 2: Your Sister is a Werewolf '85
Cameron's Closet '89

Clark Brandon
Fast Food '89
Skeeter '93

John F. Brascia
The Baltimore Bullet '80

Caliope Brattlestreet
Showdown in Little Tokyo '91

Asher Brauner
Deadly Exposure '93

Irving Brecher
Ship Ahoy '42
Best Foot Forward '43
DuBarry Was a Lady '43
Bye, Bye, Birdie '63

Andy Breckman
Arthur 2: On the Rocks '88
Moving '88
True Identity '91
I.Q. '94
Sgt. Bilko '95

Don Bredos
Where the Rivers Flow North '94

Philip M. Breen
Sword of the Valiant '83

Richard L. Breen
Titanic '53

Catherine Breillat
Police '85

Stephen Breimer
Night Warning '82

Tia Brelis
Trading Mom '94

Frederick Hazlitt Brennan
Adventure '45

Johnny Brennan
The Jerky Boys '95

Richard Brennan
Bloodmoon '90

Terrence (Terry) Brennan
Rooftops '89

Lou Breslow
Follow the Boys '44
Merton of the Movies '47

Robert Bresson
The Ladies of the Bois de Bologne '44
Diary of a Country Priest '50
A Gentle Woman '69
Lancelot of the Lake '74
L'Argent '83

Martin Brest
Going in Style '79

Jameson Brewer
The Incredible Mr. Limpet '64
Arnold '73
Terror in the Wax Museum '73

E. Kim Brewster
Food of the Gods: Part 2 '88

Salome Breziner
Tollbooth '94

George Bricker
House of Horrors '46

Marshall Brickman
Sleeper '73
Annie Hall '77
Manhattan '79
Simon '80
Lovesick '83
The Manhattan Project '86
For the Boys '91
Intersection '93
Manhattan Murder Mystery '93

Paul Brickman
The Bad News Bears in Breaking Training '77
Citizens Band '77
Deal of the Century '83
Risky Business '83
Men Don't Leave '89

Leslie Bricusse
Bachelor of Hearts '58
Doctor Dolittle '67
Scrooge '70
Bullseye! '90

James Bridges
The Appaloosa '66
The Baby Maker '70
Colossus: The Forbin Project '70
The Paper Chase '73
September 30, 1955 '77
The China Syndrome '79
Urban Cowboy '80
Mike's Murder '84
Perfect '85
White Hunter, Black Heart '90

Matthew Bright
Forbidden Zone '80
Wildfire '88
Guncrazy '92
Dark Angel: The Ascent '94
Shrunken Heads '94

John Briley
Children of the Damned '63
That Lucky Touch '75
The Medusa Touch '78
Eagle's Wing '79
Enigma '82
Gandhi '82
Marie '85
Tai-Pan '86
Cry Freedom '87
Christopher Columbus: The Discovery '92

Steven Brill
The Mighty Ducks '92
D2: The Mighty Ducks '94
Heavyweights '94

Max Brindle
Prince Brat and the Whipping Boy '95

Michael Brindley
Shame '87

Bo Brinkman
Ice House '89

Mort Briskin
Walking Tall '73
Framed '75

Deborah Brock
Slumber Party Massacre 2 '87
Rock 'n' Roll High School Forever '91

John Broderick
The Warrior & the Sorceress '84

Oscar Brodney
Mexican Hayride '48
Comanche Territory '50
Harvey '50
Francis Goes to the Races '51
Francis Goes to West Point '52
Francis Covers the Big Town '53
The Glenn Miller Story '54
Tammy and the Bachelor '57
When Hell Broke Loose '58
Tammy and the Doctor '63
Ghost Fever '87

Larry Brody
The Night the City Screamed '80

Rex Bromfield
Home Is Where the Hart Is '88

Dan Bronson
The Last Innocent Man '87
A Taste for Killing '92

Peter Brook
Lord of the Flies '63
Swann in Love '84

Ralph Brooke
Bloodlust '59

Howard Brookner
Bloodhounds of Broadway '89

Adam Brooks
Heads '93
French Kiss '95

Albert Brooks
Real Life '79
Modern Romance '81
Lost in America '85
Defending Your Life '91
The Scout '94

Carlos Brooks
American Cop '94

Halle Brooks
Who Shot Pat? '92

James L. Brooks
Thursday's Game '74
Starting Over '79
Terms of Endearment '83
Broadcast News '87
I'll Do Anything '93

Joseph Brooks
You Light Up My Life '77
If Ever I See You Again '78

Mel Brooks
The Producers '68
Twelve Chairs '70
Blazing Saddles '74
Young Frankenstein '74
Silent Movie '76
High Anxiety '77
History of the World: Part 1 '81
Spaceballs '87
Life Stinks '91
Robin Hood: Men in Tights '93
Dracula: Dead and Loving It '95

Richard Brooks
Cobra Woman '44
Key Largo '48
Any Number Can Play '49
Battle Circus '53
The Last Time I Saw Paris '54
Blackboard Jungle '55
The Last Hunt '56
Something of Value '57
The Brothers Karamazov '58
Cat on a Hot Tin Roof '58
Elmer Gantry '60
Sweet Bird of Youth '62
Lord Jim '65
The Professionals '66
In Cold Blood '67
The Happy Ending '69
Dollars '71
Bite the Bullet '75
Looking for Mr. Goodbar '77
Wrong is Right '82
Fever Pitch '85

Robert Brooks
Who Shot Pat? '92

Stephen Brooks
The Mangler '94

Philip Brophy
Body Melt '93

Peter Brosnan
The Hit List '88

Larry Brothers
An Innocent Man '89
Fever '91

Tamar Brott
The Linguini Incident '92

Walter Brough
Desperados '69

Barry Brown
Lonely in America '90

Billy Brown
Body Bags '93

Bruce Brown
The Endless Summer '66
The Endless Summer 2 '94

Curtis Brown
The Game '89

Dana Brown
The Endless Summer 2 '94

Edwin Scott Brown
The Prey '80

Gerard Brown
Juice '92

Harry Brown
Arch of Triumph '48
All the Brothers Were Valiant '53

Jamie Brown
Toby McTeague '87

Jeffrey Brown
Pontiac Moon '94

Julie Brown
Earth Girls Are Easy '89
National Lampoon's Attack of the 5 Ft. 2 Women '94

Leigh Brown
A Christmas Story '83
My Summer Story '94

Michael Henry Brown
Laurel Avenue '93
Dead Presidents '95

Mitch Brown
In Dangerous Company '88

Paul Brown
Thrashin' '86

Rita Mae Brown
The Slumber Party Massacre '82

Riwia Brown
Once Were Warriors '94

Steve Brown
Second Thoughts '83

Summer Brown
The Prey '80

William O. Brown
The Witchmaker '69

Woody Brown
Dominion '94

L. Virginia Browne
Sioux City '94

Janet Brownell
Sweet Revenge '90
Christmas in Connecticut '92
The Amy Fisher Story '93

Rod Browning
Oh, Heavenly Dog! '80

Tod Browning
Mystery of the Leaping Fish/Chess Fever '25
Devil Doll '36

John Brownjohn
Bitter Moon '92

William Broyles, Jr.
JFK: Reckless Youth '93
Apollo 13 '95

George Bruce
Navy Blue and Gold '37

Glenn A. Bruce
Kickboxer '89
Cyborg Cop '93
Undercover Cop '94

Philippe Bruneau
Little Indian, Big City '95

James Bruner
An Eye for an Eye '81
Missing in Action '84
Invasion U.S.A. '85
Delta Force '86
The P.O.W. Escape '86
Braddock: Missing in Action 3 '88

Bob Brunner
Exit to Eden '94

Franco Brusati
Bread and Chocolate '74

Chris Bryant
Man Who Had Power Over Women '70
Don't Look Now '73
The Girl from Petrovka '74
Spiral Staircase '75
Joseph Andrews '77
The Awakening '80
Martin's Day '85
Sword of Gideon '86
Stealing Heaven '88
Young Catherine '91
Foreign Affairs '93

John Bryant
Mission of Justice '92
Scanner Cop '94

James Bryce
Treasure of the Four Crowns '82

Bill Bryden
The Long Riders '80

James David Buchanan
Brenda Starr '86
Deadly Currents '93

Larry Buchanan
Mars Needs Women '66
Zontar, the Thing from Venus '66
It's Alive! '68
Mistress of the Apes '79

Sidney Buchman
The Sign of the Cross '32
Theodora Goes Wild '36
Holiday '38
Mr. Smith Goes to Washington '39
Here Comes Mr. Jordan '41

Andrea Buck
The Double O Kid '92
Born Wild '95

Peter Buckman
Appointment with Death '88

Robert Buckner
Dive Bomber '41
Yankee Doodle Dandy '42

Victor Buell
Silhouette '91

Adele Buffington
Haunted Gold '32
Bad Men of the Border '45

Takashi Bufford
House Party 3 '94

Kenny Buford
A Thin Line Between Love and Hate '96

Jeff Buhai
Revenge of the Nerds '84
Last Resort '86
The Whoopee Boys '86
Jocks '87
Johnny Be Good '88
Eddie '96

Steve Buhai
Revenge of the Nerds 4: Nerds in Love '94

Charles Bukowski
Barfly '87

Harvey Bulloch
Girl Happy '65

Vicangelo Bullock
Out of Control '85

Alan Bunce
Babar: The Movie '88

Edward Bunker
Straight Time '78
Runaway Train '85

Mark Buntzman
Exterminator 2 '84

Joyce Bunuel
Tattoo '81

Luis Bunuel
L'Age D'Or '30
Death in the Garden '56
Viridiana '61
The Young One '61
Diary of a Chambermaid '64
Simon of the Desert '66
Belle de Jour '67
Tristana '70
The Discreet Charm of the Bourgeoisie '72
That Obscure Object of Desire '77

John Bunzel
Born to Be Wild '95

Curtis Burch
Ladybugs '92

Andy Burg
Alaska '96

Robert Burge
Vasectomy: A Delicate Matter '86

Anthony Burgess
Moses '76

David Burke
The Taking of Beverly Hills '91

Martyn Burke
Last Chase '81
Power Play '81
Top Secret! '84
Sugartime '95

Jeff Burkhart
Where the Boys Are '84 '84

Steven H. Burkow
Body Slam '87

Tom Burman
Meet the Hollowheads '89

Johnny Burne
To Die For '95

Alan Burnett
DuckTales the Movie: Treasure of the Lost Lamp '90
Batman: Mask of the Phantasm '93

Allison Burnett
Bloodfist 3: Forced to Fight '92

Charles Burnett
To Sleep with Anger '90
The Glass Shield '95

W.R. Burnett
High Sierra '41
This Gun for Hire '42
Dangerous Mission '54
I Died a Thousand Times '55
The Great Escape '63

Allan Burns
Butch and Sundance: The Early Days '79
A Little Romance '79
Just the Way You Are '84
Just Between Friends '86

Edward Burns
The Brothers McMullen '94

Jack Burns
The Muppet Movie '79

Ken Burns
The Civil War, Episode 1: The Cause—1861 '90
The Civil War, Episode 2: A Very Bloody Affair—1862 '90
The Civil War, Episode 3: Forever Free—1862 '90
The Civil War, Episode 4: Simply Murder—1863 '90
The Civil War, Episode 5: The Universe of Battle—1863 '90
The Civil War, Episode 6: Valley of the Shadow of Death—1864 '90
The Civil War, Episode 7: Most Hallowed Ground—1864 '90
The Civil War, Episode 8: War is All Hell—1865 '90
The Civil War, Episode 9: The Better Angels of Our Nature—1865 '90

Mark Burns
Married to the Mob '88
She-Devil '89

Stanley Burns
Charlie Chan and the Curse of the Dragon Queen '81

Tim Burns
Freaked '93

Jim Burnstein
Renaissance Man '94

Jeff Burr
The Offspring '87

Richard Burridge
Absolute Beginners '86
The Fourth Protocol '87

Geoff Burrowes
Return to Snowy River '88

Abe Burrows
Solid Gold Cadillac '56
How to Succeed in Business without Really Trying '67

Tim Burstall
Alvin Purple '73
Alvin Rides Again '74

Michael Burton
Flight of the Navigator '86
Shoot to Kill '88

Tim Burton
Frankenweenie '84
Edward Scissorhands '90
The Nightmare Before Christmas '93

Leszek Burzynski
Trapped Alive '93

Niven Busch
Scarlet Dawn '32

John Bushelman
The Iron Triangle '89
Violent Zone '89

Oliver Butcher
Dr. Jekyll and Ms. Hyde '95

Daniel Butler
Slam Dunk Ernest '95

Frank Butler
The Princess Comes Across '36
Waikiki Wedding '37
Give Me a Sailor '38
My Favorite Blonde '42
Going My Way '44
Golden Earrings '47

Hugo Butler
Young Tom Edison '40
The Southerner '45

Ken Butler
Wittgenstein '93

Michael Butler
The Don is Dead '73
Brannigan '75
The Gauntlet '77
Murder by Phone '82
Flashpoint '84
Code of Silence '85
Pale Rider '85
Fifty/Fifty '93
White Mile '94

Floyd Byars
Making Mr. Right '86
Mindwalk: A Film for Passionate Thinkers '91

Danny Byers
Bushwhacked '95

David Byrne
True Stories '86

Johnny Byrne
Heaven's a Drag '94

Jim Byrnes
Miracle in the Wilderness '91
Dead Man's Revenge '93

John Byrum
Mahogany '75
Harry & Walter Go to New York '76
Inserts '76
Valentino '77
Heart Beat '80
Sphinx '81
The Razor's Edge '84
Scandalous '84

Cheri Caffaro
H.O.T.S. '79

Gerard M. Cahill
Survival Run '80

Hy Cahl
Teenage Gang Debs '66

Alan Cailou
Clarence, the Cross-eyed Lion '65
Kingdom of the Spiders '77

Jeffrey Caine
Goldeneye '95

Joseph M. Cala
Angel '84
Avenging Angel '85

David Callaway
The Sister-in-Law '95

Paul Callisi
Josh Kirby...Time Warrior: Chapter 1, Planet of the Dino-Knights '95
Josh Kirby...Time Warrior: Chapter 2, The Human Pets '95

Anne Cameron
Ticket to Heaven '81

James Cameron
The Terminator '84
Rambo: First Blood, Part 2 '85
Aliens '86
The Abyss '89
Terminator 2: Judgment Day '91
True Lies '94
Strange Days '95

Ken Cameron
Monkey Grip '82
Fast Talking '86

Lorne Cameron
Like Father, Like Son '87
Clarence '91

China Cammell
White of the Eye '88

Donald Cammell
Performance '70
Tilt '78
White of the Eye '88

Joe Camp
Benji '74
For the Love of Benji '77
Oh, Heavenly Dog! '80
Benji the Hunted '87

Alan Campbell
Tales of Manhattan '42

Darrel A. Campbell
Pistol: The Birth of a Legend '90

Douglas Campbell
Season of Fear '89

Kevin Campbell
The Return of Jafar '94

Anna Campion
Loaded '96

Jane Campion
Sweetie '89
The Piano '93

John Camps
Mighty Morphin Power Rangers: The Movie '95

Christopher Canaan
The Ten Million Dollar Getaway '91
The Great Elephant Escape '95

Cuca Canals
Jamon, Jamon '93

Stephen J. Cannell
The Rockford Files: Backlash of the Hunter '74
The Rousters '90

Danny Cannon
The Young Americans '93

Doran William Cannon
Brewster McCloud '70

Dyan Cannon
The End of Innocence '90

Donald Cantrell
O.C. and Stiggs '87

Leon Capetanos
Gumball Rally '76
Greased Lightning '77
The Tempest '82
Moscow on the Hudson '84
Down and Out in Beverly Hills '86
Moon over Parador '88
Fletch Lives '89

James Caplin
Transmutations '85

Carmine Capobianco
Cemetery High '89

Truman Capote
Indiscretion of an American Wife '54
The Innocents '61

James Cappe
The Adventures of Ford Fairlane '90

Frank Cappello
Suburban Commando '91

Frank Capra
Baby Face Harry Langdon '26
His First Flame '26

Fritjof Capra
Mindwalk: A Film for Passionate Thinkers '91

Jim Carabatsos
Heroes '77
Underground Aces '80
Heartbreak Ridge '86
No Mercy '86
Hamburger Hill '87

Steven W. Carabatsos
El Condor '70
Tentacles '77
The Last Flight of Noah's Ark '80
Hot Pursuit '87

Walter Carbone
Something Special '86

Frank Cardea
Dying to Remember '93

J.S. Cardone
The Slayer '82
Thunder Alley '85
Shadowzone '89
Crash and Burn '90
A Climate for Killing '91
Shadowhunter '93

Mark Patrick Carducci
Pumpkinhead '88
Buried Alive '90
Flying Saucers Over Hollywood: The Plan 9 Companion '93

Topper Carew
D.C. Cab '84
Talkin' Dirty After Dark '91

Peter Carey
Bliss '85
Until The End of The World '91

Carlo Carlei
Flight of the Innocent '93
Fluke '95

John Carlen
Blind Side '93

Clancy Carlile
Honkytonk Man '82

Lewis John Carlino
The Brotherhood '68
The Mechanic '72
A Reflection of Fear '72
The Sailor Who Fell from Grace with the Sea '76
I Never Promised You a Rose Garden '77
The Great Santini '80
Resurrection '80
Haunted Summer '88

Anne Carlisle
Liquid Sky '83

Henning Carlsen
Hunger '66

Jim Carlson
Pound Puppies and the Legend of Big Paw '88

Matthew Carlson
Wagons East '94

Roy Carlson
Stand Alone '85
China Moon '91

Don Carmody
Whispers '89

Marcel Carne
La Merveilleuse Visite '74

Charles Robert Carner
Gymkata '85
Let's Get Harry '87
Blind Fury '90

Marc Caro
The City of Lost Children '95

Glenn Gordon Caron
Condorman '81

A.J. Carothers
The Miracle of the White Stallions '63
Emil and the Detectives '64
The Happiest Millionaire '67
Never a Dull Moment '68
Hero at Large '80
The Secret of My Success '87

Fred Carpenter
Small Kill '93

John Carpenter
Dark Star '74
Assault on Precinct 13 '76
Eyes of Laura Mars '78
The Fog '78
Halloween '78
Escape from New York '81
Halloween 2: The Nightmare Isn't Over! '81
Black Moon Rising '86
Prince of Darkness '87
They Live '88
El Diablo '90

High Anxiety '77
Revenge of the Pink Panther '78
The Funny Farm '82

Arthur C. Clarke
2001: A Space Odyssey '68

Frank Clarke
Letter to Brezhnev '86
Wonderland '88

John Clarke
Lonely Hearts '82

Mary Ruth Clarke
Meet the Parents '91

Roy Clarke
Pictures '80s
Hawks '89
A Foreign Field '93

T.E.B. Clarke
Dead of Night '45
The Lavender Hill Mob '51

James Clavell
The Fly '58
The Great Escape '63
633 Squadron '64
To Sir, with Love '67
The Last Valley '71

Tim Clawson
They Call Me Bruce? '82

Thomas McKelvey Cleaver
The Terror Within '88
Heroes Stand Alone '89
Immortal Sins '91
Field of Fire '92

John Cleese
And Now for Something Completely Different '72
Rentadick '72
Monty Python and the Holy Grail '75
Fawlty Towers '77
Monty Python's Life of Brian '79
Monty Python Live at the Hollywood Bowl '82
Monty Python's The Meaning of Life '83
A Fish Called Wanda '88

Tom Clegg
McVicar '80

Brian Clemens
The Tell-Tale Heart '62
The Corrupt Ones '67
And Soon the Darkness '70
Dr. Jekyll and Sister Hyde '71
See No Evil '71
Golden Voyage of Sinbad '73
Captain Kronos: Vampire Hunter '74
The Watcher in the Woods '81

Dick Clement
Catch Me a Spy '71
Prisoner of Zenda '79
Water '85
Vice Versa '88
The Commitments '91

Rene Clement
Joy House '64

Dulany Ross Clements
Danger Zone 2 '89

Ron Clements
The Great Mouse Detective '86
The Little Mermaid '89
Aladdin '92

Laury Clemmons
The Fox and the Hound '81

Jake Clesi
Buried Alive '90

Elmer Clifton
Frontier Law '43
Captain America '44
Gangsters of the Frontier '44
Guns of the Law '44
Lightning Raiders '45
Marked for Murder '45
Youth Aflame '59

Paul E. Clinco
Death Magic '92

Edward Clinton
Honky Tonk Freeway '81

Art Clokey
Gumby: The Movie '95

Harry Clork
Ship Ahoy '42
Broadway Rhythm '44
Ma and Pa Kettle at Waikiki '55

Daniel Clough
Ninja, the Violent Sorcerer '86

Robert Clouse
The Ultimate Warrior '75
The Pack '77
The Amsterdam Kill '78
The Big Brawl '80
Force: Five '81

Henri-Georges Clouzot
Wages of Fear '55
L'Enfer '93

Rick Cluchey
The Cage '90

Raphael Cluzel
Light Years '88

Craig Clyde
Little Heroes '91
The Legend of Wolf Mountain '92

Nicole Coady
Embrace of the Vampire '95

Lewis (Luigi Cozzi) Coates
Star Crash '78
Alien Contamination '81
Hercules '83
Black Cat '90

Henry Cobbold
Lake Consequence '92

Arthur Coburn
Triumph of the Spirit '89

James Coburn
Circle of Iron '78

Randy Sue Coburn
Mrs. Parker and the Vicious Circle '94

Rudolph Coburn
Mrs. Parker and the Vicious Circle '94

Stacy Cochran
My New Gun '92
Boys '95

Jay Cocks
The Age of Innocence '93
Strange Days '95

Jean Cocteau
Eternal Return '43
The Ladies of the Bois de Bologne '44
The Eagle Has Two Heads '48
Ruyblas '48
The Storm Within '48
Les Enfants Terrible '50

Fred Coe
This Property is Condemned '66

Wayne Coe
Grim Prairie Tales '89

Ethan Coen
Blood Simple '85
Crimewave '85
Raising Arizona '87
Miller's Crossing '90
Barton Fink '91
The Hudsucker Proxy '93
Fargo '96

Joel Coen
Blood Simple '85
Crimewave '85
Raising Arizona '87
Miller's Crossing '90
Barton Fink '91
The Hudsucker Proxy '93
Fargo '96

Joseph Coencas
A Very Natural Thing '73

Lenore Coffee
Evelyn Prentice '34
Sudden Fear '52
Cash McCall '60

Charlie Coffey
Earth Girls Are Easy '89
National Lampoon's Attack of the 5 Ft. 2 Women '94

Barney Cohen
Friday the 13th, Part 4: The Final Chapter '84
Killer Party '86
Next Door '94
Sabrina the Teenage Witch '96

Bennett Cohen
Come On Danger! '32
Melody of the Plains '37
Sagebrush Law '43
Rainbow Drive '90

Catherine Cohen
Indochine '92

Charles Cohen
Beyond Forgiveness '94

Charles Zev Cohen
Lady Beware '87
Eddie and the Cruisers 2: Eddie Lives! '89

Charlie Cohen
Ernest Goes to Jail '90

David Aaron Cohen
V.I. Warshawski '91

David M. Cohen
Friday the 13th, Part 5: A New Beginning '85
Hollywood Zap '86

David Steven Cohen
Balto '95

Howard R. Cohen
Saturday the 14th '81
Deathstalker '83
Space Raiders '83
Stryker '83
Saturday the 14th Strikes Back '88
Deathstalker 3 '89
Lords of the Deep '89

Joel Cohen
Sister, Sister '87
Pass the Ammo '88
Toy Story '95

Larry Cohen
Return of the Seven '66
Daddy's Gone A-Hunting '69
El Condor '70
Hell Up in Harlem '73
It's Alive '74
God Told Me To '76
The Private Files of J. Edgar Hoover '77
I, the Jury '82
Q (The Winged Serpent) '82
Perfect Strangers '84
Scandalous '84
Into Thin Air '85
Special Effects '85
The Stuff '85
Best Seller '87
Deadly Illusion '87
It's Alive 3: Island of the Alive '87
Return to Salem's Lot '87
Maniac Cop '88
Wicked Stepmother '89
The Ambulance '90
Maniac Cop 2 '90
Guilty as Sin '93
Maniac Cop 3: Badge of Silence '93
As Good as Dead '95

Lawrence D. Cohen
Carrie '76
Ghost Story '81
Stephen King's The Tommyknockers '93

Lawrence J. Cohen
Start the Revolution Without Me '70
S*P*Y*S '74
The Big Bus '76
Delirious '91

Neil Cohen
Pass the Ammo '88

Rob Cohen
Scandalous '84
Dragon: The Bruce Lee Story '93

Ronald M. Cohen
Blue '68
The Good Guys and the Bad Guys '69
Twilight's Last Gleaming '77

Randolph Cohlan
Night Shadow '90

Art Cohn
The Seven Hills of Rome '58

Jeff Cohn
The Reluctant Agent '95

Michael Cohn
When the Bough Breaks '93

Harley Cokliss
Warlords of the 21st Century '82

Mirith J.S. Colao
The Return of Jafar '94

Brandon Cole
Sons '91
Mac '93

Lester Cole
Footsteps in the Dark '41
Objective, Burma! '45

Tom Cole
Smooth Talk '85
Streets of Gold '86

Clifford Coleman
The Ice Runner '93

David Coleman
Endless Descent '90

Christine Colfer
Double Exposure '93

Russell W. Colgin
Young Warriors '83

Lewis Colick
Dirt Bike Kid '86
Unlawful Entry '92
Judgment Night '93

Jeanne Collachia
Odd Birds '85

Cyril Collard
Les Nuits Fauves '92

Robert Collector
Memoirs of an Invisible Man '92

John Collee
Paper Mask '91

Peter Colley
Mark of Cain '84
Illusions '91

John Collier
The War Lord '65

Boon Collins
Spirit of the Eagle '90

Jackie Collins
The Stud '78
Yesterday's Hero '79
The World is Full of Married Men '80

Max Allan Collins
The Expert '95
Mommy '95

Arthur Collis
Blue Desert '91

Harry Colomby
Johnny Dangerously '84
Touch and Go '86

Carl Colpaert
Delusion '91
The Crew '95

Chris Columbus
Gremlins '84
Reckless '84
The Goonies '85
Young Sherlock Holmes '85
Heartbreak Hotel '88
Only the Lonely '91
Little Nemo: Adventures in Slumberland '92
Nine Months '95

Adele Comandini
Three Smart Girls '36
Her First Romance '40

Betty Comden
Good News '47
The Barkleys of Broadway '49
On the Town '49
Singin' in the Rain '52
The Band Wagon '53
It's Always Fair Weather '55
Auntie Mame '58
Bells are Ringing '60

Bob Comfort
Dogfight '91

Jacques Companeez
Casque d'Or '52
Forbidden Fruit '52

Nina Companeez
The Horseman on the Roof '95

Richard Compton
Return to Macon County '75

George Conchon
Black and White in Color '76
The Elegant Criminal '92

Bill Condon
Strange Behavior '81
Strange Invaders '83
Sister, Sister '87
F/X 2: The Deadly Art of Illusion '91
Murder 101 '91

Richard Condon
Prizzi's Honor '85

Stijn Coninx
Daens '92

Heather Conkie
Beethoven Lives Upstairs '92

J.C. (Chris) Conkling
The Lord of the Rings '78

Nicole Conn
Claire of the Moon '92

Shane Connaughton
My Left Foot '89
The Playboys '92
The Run of the Country '95

Ray Connelly
That'll Be the Day '73
Forever Young '85

Jon Connolly
The Dream Team '89
Eddie '96

Phillip D. Connors
Evils of the Night '85

Chris Conrad
Junior '94

Steve Conrad
Wrestling Ernest Hemingway '93

Pat Conroy
The Prince of Tides '91

John Considine
A Wedding '78

Robert Conte
Odd Jobs '85
Who's Harry Crumb? '89

Ernie Contreras
The Pagemaster '94

Gary Conway
Over the Top '86
American Ninja 2: The Confrontation '87
American Ninja 3: Blood Hunt '89

Gerry Conway
Fire and Ice '83

Tim Conway
They Went That-a-Way & That-a-Way '78
Prize Fighter '79
The Private Eyes '80
The Longshot '86

Rif Coogan
The Invisible Maniac '90

David Cook
Second Best '94

Douglas S. Cook
Payoff '91
Holy Matrimony '94

Peter Cook
Bedazzled '68
The Hound of the Baskervilles '77
Yellowbeard '83

T.S. Cook
The China Syndrome '79
Out of the Darkness '85
Nightbreaker '89
High Desert Kill '90

Tony Cookson
And You Thought Your Parents Were Weird! '91

Michael Cooney
Tracks of a Killer *'95*
Barry Michael Cooper
New Jack City *'91*
Above the Rim *'94*
Sugar Hill *'94*
Dorothy Cooper
Rich, Young and Pretty *'51*
Merian C. Cooper
Chang: A Drama of the Wilderness *'27*
Natalie Cooper
Desert Hearts *'86*
Olive Cooper
The Border Legion *'40*
Bandit King of Texas *'49*
Hills of Oklahoma *'50*
Paul Cooper
Once Upon a Time...When We Were Colored *'95*
Robert Cooper
The Club *'94*
No Contest *'94*
Susan Cooper
George Balanchine's The Nutcracker *'93*
To Dance with the White Dog *'93*
Ken Copel
At First Sight *'95*
Martin Copeland
The Heavenly Kid *'85*
Rick Copp
The Brady Bunch Movie *'95*
Christopher Coppola
Deadfall *'93*
Francis Ford Coppola
The Magic Voyage of Sinbad *'52*
Tonight for Sure *'61*
The Bellboy and the Playgirls *'62*
Dementia 13 *'63*
This Property is Condemned *'66*
You're a Big Boy Now *'66*
Is Paris Burning? *'68*
The Rain People *'69*
Patton *'70*
The Godfather *'72*
The Conversation *'74*
The Godfather, Part 2 *'74*
The Great Gatsby *'74*
Apocalypse Now *'79*
The Godfather 1902-1959: The Complete Epic *'81*
One from the Heart *'82*
Rumble Fish *'83*
The Cotton Club *'84*
New York Stories *'89*
The Godfather, Part 3 *'90*
Sofia Coppola
New York Stories *'89*
Jane Corbett
Tale of a Vampire *'92*
Andree Corbiau
Farinelli *'94*
Gerard Corbiau
Farinelli *'94*
Sergio Corbucci
Super Fuzz *'81*
John Corcoran
American Samurai *'92*
John Cork
The Long Walk Home *'89*
Roger Corman
Frankenstein Unbound *'90*
The Skateboard Kid *'93*
Jan Cornall
Talk *'94*
Alain Corneau
Fort Saganne *'84*
Tous les Matins du Monde *'92*
John Cornell
Crocodile Dundee *'86*
Hubert Cornfield
The Night of the Following Day *'69*
Stephen Cornwell
Killing Streets *'91*

Marshal Law *'96*
Eugene Corr
Wildrose *'85*
Desert Bloom *'86*
Getting Out *'94*
Charles Correll
Fortune Dane *'86*
Michael Corrente
Federal Hill *'94*
John W. Corrington
Boxcar Bertha *'72*
Battle for the Planet of the Apes *'73*
Joyce H. Corrington
Boxcar Bertha *'72*
Battle for the Planet of the Apes *'73*
Bud Cort
Ted & Venus *'93*
Norman Corwin
The Naked Maja *'59*
Michael Cory
Loose Screws *'85*
Bill Cosby
Leonard Part 6 *'87*
Christopher Cosby
Bloodsport *'88*
Don A. Coscarelli
Phantasm *'79*
Beastmaster *'82*
Phantasm II *'88*
Survival Quest *'89*
Phantasm III: Lord of the Dead *'94*
George P. Cosmatos
Massacre in Rome *'73*
The Cassandra Crossing *'76*
Jean Cosmos
Colonel Chabert *'94*
Constantin Costa-Gavras
Z *'69*
Missing *'82*
James Costigan
King David *'85*
Mr. North *'88*
Lanny Cotler
Earthling *'80*
Manny Coto
Dr. Giggles *'92*
John Cotter
Cheetah *'89*
Suzette Couture
Love and Hate: A Marriage Made in Hell *'90*
Bill Couturie
Dear America: Letters Home from Vietnam *'88*
Michael Cove
Deathcheaters *'76*
Hil Covington
Adventures in Spying *'92*
Gil Cowan
Opposing Force *'87*
Noel Coward
Bitter Sweet *'33*
Bitter Sweet *'40*
In Which We Serve *'43*
Brief Encounter *'46*
Alex Cox
Repo Man *'83*
Sid & Nancy *'86*
Straight to Hell *'87*
Brian Cox
Deadly Obsession *'88*
Jim Cox
Oliver & Company *'88*
The Rescuers Down Under *'90*
Ferngully: The Last Rain Forest *'92*
Paul Cox
Lonely Hearts *'82*
Man of Flowers *'84*
My First Wife *'84*
Cactus *'86*
Vincent: The Life and Death of Vincent van Gogh *'87*
A Woman's Tale *'92*

Kerry Crabbe
The Playboys *'92*
Innocent Lies *'95*
Peter Crabbe
Car 54, Where Are You? *'94*
H.A.L. Craig
Waterloo *'71*
Lion of the Desert *'81*
Laurie Craig
Modern Girls *'86*
Robert Crane
Hostage for a Day *'94*
Jay Craven
Where the Rivers Flow North *'94*
Jonathan Craven
Wes Craven Presents Mind Ripper *'95*
Wes Craven
The Hills Have Eyes *'77*
Deadly Blessing *'81*
Swamp Thing *'82*
The Hills Have Eyes, Part 2 *'84*
A Nightmare on Elm Street *'84*
A Nightmare on Elm Street 3: Dream Warriors *'87*
Shocker *'89*
The People Under the Stairs *'91*
Wes Craven's New Nightmare *'94*
Darlene Craviotto
Squanto: A Warrior's Tale *'94*
Bobby Crawford
A Rage in Harlem *'91*
Joanna Crawford
The Birch Interval *'78*
Sophia Loren: Her Own Story *'80*
Nancy Voyles Crawford
Sidewinder One *'77*
Wayne Crawford
Valley Girl *'83*
Jake Speed *'86*
Richard Creedon
Snow White and the Seven Dwarfs *'37*
James Cresson
The Morning After *'86*
Chattahoochee *'89*
Defenseless *'91*
John Cresswell
Cast a Dark Shadow *'55*
Charles Crichton
A Fish Called Wanda *'88*
Michael Crichton
Sex Through a Window *'72*
Westworld *'73*
Coma *'78*
The Great Train Robbery *'79*
Looker *'81*
Runaway *'84*
Jurassic Park *'93*
Rising Sun *'93*
Twister *'96*
Arthur Crimm
Kurt Vonnegut's Harrison Bergeron *'95*
Michael Cristofer
Falling in Love *'84*
The Witches of Eastwick *'87*
The Bonfire of the Vanities *'90*
Mr. Jones *'93*
Keith Critchlow
Night Life *'90*
New Jack City *'91*
David Cronenberg
They Came from Within *'75*
Rabid *'77*
Fast Company *'78*
The Brood *'79*
Scanners *'81*
Videodrome *'83*
The Fly *'86*
Dead Ringers *'88*
Naked Lunch *'91*
Crash *'95*
Isaac Cronin
Chan is Missing *'82*
Andrew Cross
Shock 'Em Dead *'90*

Beverley Cross
Jason and the Argonauts *'63*
Half a Sixpence *'67*
Sinbad and the Eye of the Tiger *'77*
Clash of the Titans *'81*
Paul Cross
Ice Pawn *'92*
Avery Crounse
Eyes of Fire *'84*
The Invisible Kid *'88*
Bill Crounse
9 1/2 Ninjas *'90*
American Cyborg: Steel Warrior *'94*
Russel Crouse
A Woman's World *'54*
Cameron Crowe
Fast Times at Ridgemont High *'82*
The Wild Life *'84*
Say Anything *'89*
Singles *'92*
Christopher Crowe
Last Chase *'81*
Nightmares *'83*
Mean Season *'85*
Off Limits *'87*
The Last of the Mohicans *'92*
Whispers in the Dark *'92*
Fear *'96*
Matt Crowley
The Boys in the Band *'70*
John Crowther
Kill and Kill Again *'81*
The Evil That Men Do *'84*
Damned River *'89*
Jim Cruickshank
Breaking All the Rules *'85*
Tough Guys *'86*
Three Men and a Baby *'87*
Mr. Destiny *'90*
Sister Act 2: Back in the Habit *'93*
Man of the House *'95*
Tom Cruise
Days of Thunder *'90*
Robert Riley Crutcher
Key to the City *'50*
Billy Crystal
Memories of Me *'88*
Mr. Saturday Night *'92*
City Slickers 2: The Legend of Curly's Gold *'94*
Forget Paris *'95*
Allan Cubitt
Prime Suspect 2 *'93*
Frank Cucci
Lily in Love *'85*
Serge Cukier
The Evil Within *'94*
Alma Cullen
Intimate Contact *'87*
Robert Cullen
As You Like It *'36*
Carmen Culver
The Last Prostitute *'91*
Hugh Cummings
Pardon My Gun *'30*
James Cummins
The Bone Yard *'90*
Rusty Cundieff
House Party 2: The Pajama Jam *'91*
Fear of a Black Hat *'94*
Tales from the Hood *'95*
Ray Cunneff
The Rain Killer *'90*
Jere P. Cunningham
The Last of the Finest *'90*
Tim Curnen
Forbidden World *'82*
Ghostwarrior *'86*
William Curran
Love, Cheat & Steal *'93*
Jean Curtelin
L'Addition *'85*

Valerie Curtin
And Justice for All *'79*
Inside Moves *'80*
Best Friends *'82*
Unfaithfully Yours *'84*
Toys *'92*
Dan Curtis
Burnt Offerings *'76*
John Vincent Curtis
Trapped in Space *'94*
Michael Curtis
...And God Spoke *'94*
Richard Curtis
The Tall Guy *'89*
Four Weddings and a Funeral *'94*
Stephen J. Curwick
Police Academy 5: Assignment Miami Beach *'88*
Police Academy 6: City Under Siege *'89*
Neil Cuthbert
Hocus Pocus *'93*
Ron Cutler
Blood Red *'88*
Article 99 *'92*
Catherine Cyran
A Cry in the Wild *'90*
Slumber Party Massacre 3 *'90*
Uncaged *'91*
Hostile Intentions *'95*
Bohdan Czeszko
A Generation *'54*
Renee Daalder
Massacre at Central High *'76*
John Dahl
Private Investigations *'87*
Kill Me Again *'89*
Red Rock West *'93*
Rick Dahl
Red Rock West *'93*
Roald Dahl
Chitty Chitty Bang Bang *'68*
Bob Dahlin
Monster in the Closet *'86*
Salvador Dali
L'Age D'Or *'30*
Walter Dallenbach
Las Vegas Lady *'76*
Herbert Dalmas
The Last of the Redmen *'47*
Ian Dalrymple
Three Cases of Murder *'55*
Darren Dalton
Hourglass *'95*
Deborah Dalton
Whore *'91*
Gerry Daly
Black Magic Woman *'91*
Suso Cecchi D'Amico
Bellissima *'51*
Sandra of a Thousand Delights *'65*
Zhao Dan
Crows and Sparrows *'49*
Barbara Dana
Chu Chu & the Philly Flash *'81*
Bill Dana
The Nude Bomb *'80*
Lawrence Dane
Heavenly Bodies *'84*
Logan N. Danforth
Cross Country *'83*
Rodney Dangerfield
Easy Money *'83*
R.E. Daniels
Lonely Hearts *'91*
Stan Daniels
The Lonely Guy *'84*
Glory! Glory! *'90*
For Richer, For Poorer *'92*
The Substitute Wife *'94*
Max Dann
The Efficiency Expert *'92*
Leslie Danon
The Whispering *'94*

Herbert Danska
Sweet Love, Bitter '67
Maria Dante
Space Mutiny '88
Richard Danus
Xanadu '80
No Place to Hide '93
Frank Darabont
A Nightmare on Elm Street 3: Dream Warriors '87
The Blob '88
The Fly 2 '89
Mary Shelley's Frankenstein '94
The Shawshank Redemption '94
Jack Darcus
The Portrait '93
Istvan Darday
Red Earth
W. Scott Darling
King of the Sierras '38
The Ghost of Frankenstein '42
Julie Dash
Daughters of the Dust '91
Sean Dash
Ice '93
Breakaway '95
David Dashev
Smokey and the Bandit, Part 3 '83
Jules Dassin
Rififi '54
Where the Hot Wind Blows '59
Never on Sunday '60
Phaedra '61
A Dream of Passion '78
Delmer Daves
Dames '34
Flirtation Walk '34
Love Affair '39
Hollywood Canteen '44
Task Force '49
An Affair to Remember '57
Parrish '61
Rome Adventure '62
Spencer's Mountain '63
Marjorie David
Maria's Lovers '84
Shy People '87
Into the Badlands '92
Peter David
Trancers 4: Jack of Swords '93
Oblivion '94
Trancers 5: Sudden Deth '94
Backlash: Oblivion 2 '95
Paul Davids
Roswell: The U.F.O. Cover-Up '94
Arlene Davidson
Eddie and the Cruisers '83
Bill Davidson
The Art of Crime '75
Boaz Davidson
Last American Virgin '82
Hot Resort '85
Salsa '88
Delta Force 3: The Killing Game '91
Martin Davidson
Eddie and the Cruisers '83
Ronald Davidson
Range Renegades '48
Andrew Davies
Private Life '82
Consuming Passions '88
Middlemarch '93
To Play the King '93
Circle of Friends '94
The Final Cut '95
Pride and Prejudice '95
Jack Davies
Curtain Up '53
Doctor at Sea '56
Those Magnificent Men in Their Flying Machines '65
Gambit '66
Those Daring Young Men in Their Jaunty Jalopies '69
Paper Tiger '74
Ron Davies
Blood Ring '93

Terence Davies
Distant Voices, Still Lives '88
The Long Day Closes '92
The Neon Bible '95
Valentine Davies
It Happens Every Spring '49
The Bridges at Toko-Ri '55
Bachelor in Paradise '69
William Davies
Twins '88
Stop! or My Mom Will Shoot '92
Ghost in the Machine '93
The Real McCoy '93
Dr. Jekyll and Ms. Hyde '95
Almer John Davis
Under the Gun '88
Andrew Davis
Beat Street '84
Above the Law '88
Andy Davis
Steal Big, Steal Little '95
Bart Davis
Impulse '84
Love or Money? '88
Full Fathom Five '90
Bill Davis
Mass Appeal '84
Carlos Davis
Drop Dead Fred '91
Charles Davis
Thunder Run '86
Christopher Davis
Pattern for Plunder '62
Deborah Dean Davis
It Takes Two '95
Fitzroy Davis
The Heat's On '43
Frank Davis
The Train '65
Ian Davis
The Hunger '83
Jerry Davis
Cult of the Cobra '55
Pardners '56
L.A. Goddess '92
Julie Davis
Witchcraft 6: The Devil's Mistress '94
Luther Davis
Kismet '55
Lady in a Cage '64
Across 110th Street '72
Michael Paul Davis
Beanstalk '94
Double Dragon '94
Prehysteria 2 '94
Prehysteria 3 '95
Mitch Davis
Windrunner '94
Nick Davis
Night Siege Project: Shadowchaser 2 '94
Project Shadowchaser 3000 '95
Ossie Davis
Gone are the Days '63
Cotton Comes to Harlem '70
Randolph Davis
Police Academy: Mission to Moscow '94
Regina Davis
Alien from L.A. '87
Sidney Davis
The Dove '68
Stephen Davis
Ruby '92
Tom Davis
One More Saturday Night '86
Coneheads '93
Walter Halsey Davis
Seven Hours to Judgment '88
Zach Davis
Liquid Dreams '92
Anthony (Antonio Margheriti) Dawson
Invasion of the Flesh Hunters '82
Yor, the Hunter from the Future '83

Gordon Dawson
Bring Me the Head of Alfredo Garcia '74
Into the Badlands '92
John Dawson
Replikator: Cloned to Kill '94
Gerry Day
The Black Hole '79
Piero De Bernardi
Ciao, Professore! '94
Philippe de Broca
Cartouche '62
That Man from Rio '64
Dear Detective '77
Christian de Chalonge
Dr. Petiot '90
Ennio de Concini
Il Grido '57
Divorce—Italian Style '62
The Bachelor '93
Frank de Felitta
Zero Population Growth '72
Audrey Rose '77
The Entity '83
Scissors '91
Anatole de Grunwald
Secret Mission '42
Rolf de Heer
Bad Boy Bubby '93
Furland de Kay
Lost Boundaries '49
Robert De Laurentis
Green Ice '81
A Little Sex '82
Marcus De Leon
Kiss Me a Killer '91
Michael De Luca
Freddy's Dead: The Final Nightmare '91
In the Mouth of Madness '95
Judge Dredd '95
Merrill De Maris
Snow White and the Seven Dwarfs '37
Albert De Mond
Ridin' Down the Canyon '42
Giuliani G. De Negri
The Night of the Shooting Stars '82
Armando de Ossorio
Fangs of the Living Dead '68
Horror of the Zombies '74
People Who Own the Dark '75
Frank De Palma
Private War '90
Vittorio De Sica
The Children Are Watching Us '44
Umberto D '55
Two Women '61
Steven E. de Souza
48 Hrs. '82
Return of Captain Invincible '83
Commando '85
The Running Man '87
Bad Dreams '88
Die Hard '88
Seven Hours to Judgment '88
Die Hard 2: Die Harder '90
Hudson Hawk '91
Ricochet '91
Beverly Hills Cop 3 '94
The Flintstones '94
Street Fighter '94
Judge Dredd '95
Gary De Vore
Back Roads '81
The Dogs of War '81
Raw Deal '86
Running Scared '86
Traxx '87
Timecop '94
Nicole De Wilde
The Raggedy Rawney '90
Karen De Wolf
Blondie in Society '41
Blondie's Blessed Event '42
It's a Great Life '43

Eric Deacon
Prime Suspect: Inner Circles '95
Basil Dean
21 Days '37
Charles Deane
Blonde Blackmailer '58
Nick Dear
Persuasion '95
William Dear
Northville Cemetery Massacre '76
Timerider '83
Harry and the Hendersons '87
James Dearden
Fatal Attraction '87
Pascali's Island '88
A Kiss Before Dying '91
Frank Deasy
Captives '94
John DeBello
Attack of the Killer Tomatoes '77
Happy Hour '87
Return of the Killer Tomatoes! '88
Allen N. DeBevoise
Breakin' '84
Marge Decker
To Please a Lady '50
Denise DeClue
About Last Night... '86
For Keeps '88
Edward Decter
Options '88
Frank Deese
The Principal '87
Josh and S.A.M. '93
Christopher DeFaria
Amityville: A New Generation '93
James DeFelice
Why Shoot the Teacher '79
Out of the Dark '88
Angel Square '92
Frank Deford
Trading Hearts '87
Allessandro DeGaetano
Bloodbath in Psycho Town '89
Michael deGuzman
Jaws: The Revenge '87
Steve DeJarnatt
Strange Brew '83
Miracle Mile '89
Colman DeKay
Bloodhounds of Broadway '89
Fred Dekker
Night of the Creeps '86
The Monster Squad '87
If Looks Could Kill '91
RoboCop 3 '91
John deKlein
Babar: The Movie '88
Peter Del Monte
Julia and Julia '87
Guillermo del Toro
Cronos '94
Shelagh Delaney
A Taste of Honey '61
Dance with a Stranger '85
The Railway Station Man '92
Walter DeLeon
Ruggles of Red Gap '35
The Princess Comes Across '36
Rhythm on the Range '36
Waikiki Wedding '37
The Big Broadcast of 1938 '38
Union Pacific '39
Birth of the Blues '41
Little Giant '46
Bill D'Elia
The Feud '90
Francis Delia
Freeway '88
Trouble Bound '92
Wanda Dell
Marvin & Tige '84
Duane Dell'Amico
Sleep with Me '94

William F. Delligan
Praying Mantis '93
A Passion to Kill '94
Jeffrey Delman
Voodoo Dawn '89
Double Obsession '93
Vina Delmar
The Awful Truth '37
Rudy DeLuca
Silent Movie '76
High Anxiety '77
Caveman '81
Transylvania 6-5000 '85
Million Dollar Mystery '87
Life Stinks '91
Dracula: Dead and Loving It '95
John DeMarco
Impulse '90
Richard Dembo
Dangerous Moves '84
Paul DeMeo
Future Cop '76
Zone Troopers '84
The Eliminators '86
The Wrong Guys '88
Arena '89
The Rocketeer '91
Gloria Demers
Strangers in Good Company '91
Paul DeMielche
American Ninja 3: Blood Hunt '89
Jonathan Demme
Angels Hard as They Come '71
Hot Box '72
Caged Heat '74
Fighting Mad '76
Jacques Demy
Umbrellas of Cherbourg '64
Claire Denis
Chocolat '88
No Fear, No Die '90
I Can't Sleep '93
Susan Denis
Orphans of the North '40
Dennis Dimster Denk
Outside the Law '95
Gill Dennis
Riders of the Purple Sage '96
Pen Densham
The Zoo Gang '85
Robin Hood: Prince of Thieves '91
Lifepod '93
Moll Flanders '96
Alan Dent
Henry V '44
Hamlet '48
Brian DePalma
Greetings '68
The Wedding Party '69
Hi, Mom! '70
Sisters '73
Phantom of the Paradise '74
Home Movies '79
Dressed to Kill '80
Blow Out '81
Body Double '84
Raising Cain '92
Jacques Deray
Borsalino '70
John Derek
Bolero '84
Anita Desai
In Custody '94
Lorain Despres
Highlander: The Gathering '93
David Deutsch
A Day in the Death of Joe Egg '71
Helen Deutsch
National Velvet '44
Golden Earrings '47
Valley of the Dolls '67
Jacques Deval
Balalaika '39
Claire Devers
Noir et Blanc '86
Michel DeVille
Peril '85

DeVille ▶cont.
La Lectrice '88

Rosalinde DeVille
La Lectrice '88

Dennis Devine
Things '93

Barry Devlin
A Man of No Importance '94

Dean Devlin
Stargate '94
Independence Day '96

Christopher DeVore
The Elephant Man '80
Frances '82
Hamlet '90

Jack DeWitt
Bells of San Fernando '47
The Legend of the Sea Wolf '58
A Man Called Horse '70
Man in the Wilderness '71
Neptune Factor '73
The Return of a Man Called Horse '76
Sky Riders '76
Triumphs of a Man Called Horse '83

Patrick Dewolf
Innocent Lies '95

Pete Dexter
Paris Trout '91
Rush '91
Mulholland Falls '95

Robert Dhery
Belle Americaine '61

Michael J. Di Gaetano
Houseguest '94

Gerald Di Pega
Keeper of the City '92

I.A.L. Diamond
Never Say Goodbye '46
Monkey Business '52
Love in the Afternoon '57
The Apartment '60
One, Two, Three '61
Irma La Douce '63
Kiss Me, Stupid! '64
The Fortune Cookie '66
The Private Life of Sherlock Holmes '70
Avanti! '72
The Front Page '74
Buddy Buddy '81

Michael Diamond
Unveiled '94

Graziano Diana
La Scorta '94

Tom DiCillo
Johnny Suede '92
Living in Oblivion '94

Ernest R. Dickerson
Juice '92

Basil Dickey
Brand of Fear '49

James Dickey
Deliverance '72

Joan Didion
Panic in Needle Park '75
A Star is Born '76
True Confessions '81
Broken Trust '95
Up Close and Personal '96

Carlos Diegues
Bye Bye Brazil '79
Quilombo '84

Frank Dietz
Naked Souls '95

John Dighton
The Happiest Days of Your Life '50

Eric Dignam
Denial: The Dark Side of Passion '91

Flint Dille
An American Tail: Fievel Goes West '91

Robert Dillon
The Last of the Mohicans '20
The Old Dark House '32
X: The Man with X-Ray Eyes '63
Bikini Beach '64
Muscle Beach Party '64
Prime Cut '72
99 & 44/100 Dead '74
French Connection 2 '75
The River '84
Revolution '85
The Survivalist '87
Flight of the Intruder '90
Deception '92

Brian DiMuccio
Voodoo '95

Greg Dinallo
Ladykillers '88

Pece Dingo
Midnight Cabaret '90

Paul Dini
Batman: Mask of the Phantasm '93

Gerald DiPego
Phenomenon '96

Mark DiSalle
Kickboxer '89

James Dixon
Return to Salem's Lot '87

Leslie Dixon
Outrageous Fortune '87
Overboard '87
Loverboy '89
Look Who's Talking Now '93
Mrs. Doubtfire '93

Peter Dixon
Down the Wyoming Trail '39

Lem Dobbs
The Hard Way '91
Kafka '91

Neal Dobrofsky
The Donor '94

Tippi Dobrofsky
The Donor '94

Jacques Doillon
La Vengeance d'une Femme '89

Bob Dolman
Willow '88
Far and Away '92

Henry Dominick
Flight of Black Angel '91
Mindwarp '91

James Donadio
By the Sword '93

Tom Donnelly
Defiance '79
Quicksilver '86
Talent for the Game '91

Mary Agnes Donoghue
The Buddy System '83
Beaches '88
Deceived '91
Paradise '91

Martin Donovan
Apartment Zero '88
Death Becomes Her '92
Mad at the Moon '92

Anita Doohan
Whispers '89

Ariel Dorfman
Death and the Maiden '94

Phoebe Dorin
Perfect Family '92

Robert E. Dorn
Out of Sync '95

Shimon Dotan
The Finest Hour '91

James Dott
The Invaders '95

Jean Douchet
Six in Paris '68

Michael Feit Dougan
Public Access '93

Joseph Dougherty
Steel and Lace '90
Cast a Deadly Spell '91
Attack of the 50 Ft. Woman '93
Witch Hunt '94

Nathan E. Douglas
The Defiant Ones '58

Lorenzo Doumani
Amore! '93
Storybook '95

Sir Arthur Conan Doyle
Tales from the Darkside: The Movie '90

Roddy Doyle
The Commitments '91
The Snapper '93
The Van '95

Brian Doyle-Murray
Caddyshack '80
Club Paradise '86

Diane Drake
Only You '94

Oliver Drake
Fighting Valley '43

Tom Drake
Keeper '84

William A. Drake
The Three Musketeers '39

Peter Draper
Poldark '75

Tony Drazan
Zebrahead '92

Carl Theodor Dreyer
Vampyr '31
Day of Wrath '43
Gertrud '64

Kevin Droney
Down Came a Blackbird '94

Michael B. Druxman
Cheyenne Warrior '94
Dillinger and Capone '95

Lee Drysdale
Leather Jackets '90

Charles S. Dubin
The Meanest Men in the West '76

David DuBos
Playback '95

Adam Dubov
Dead Beat '94

Charlotte Dubreuil
Spoiled Children '77

Remy Duchemin
A la Mode '94

Warren Duff
Last Command '28
Angels with Dirty Faces '38

Jo Duffy
Puppet Master 4 '93

Martine Dugowson
Mina Tannenbaum '94

John Duigan
The Year My Voice Broke '87
Flirting '89
Wide Sargasso Sea '92
Sirens '94

Andrea Dunbar
Rita, Sue & Bob Too '87

David Duncan
The Leech Woman '59
Monster on the Campus '59

Patrick Duncan
84 Charlie Mopic '89
Live! From Death Row '92
A Home of Our Own '93
Nick of Time '95

Patrick Sheane Duncan
Mr. Holland's Opus '95
Courage Under Fire '96

Winifred Dunn
The Dropkick '27

John Gregory Dunne
Panic in Needle Park '75
A Star is Born '76
True Confessions '81
Broken Trust '95
Up Close and Personal '96

Philip Dunne
The Rains Came '39
How Green Was My Valley '41
Son of Fury '42
Forever Amber '47
The Ghost and Mrs. Muir '47
Pinky '49
David and Bathsheba '51
Demetrius and the Gladiators '54
The Egyptian '54
Ten North Frederick '58
The Agony and the Ecstasy '65

John Dunning
SnakeEater 3: His Law '92

Rudy Durand
Tilt '78

Marguerite Duras
Hiroshima, Mon Amour '59

Laurence Dworet
Outbreak '94

H. Kaye Dyal
Lone Wolf McQuade '83
Trained to Kill '88
Project: Eliminator '91

Terry Eagleton
Wittgenstein '93

B. Reeves Eason
Roaring Ranch '30

James Eastwood
Devil Girl from Mars '54

Halle Eaton
Embrace of the Vampire '95

Thom Eberhardt
Night of the Comet '84
The Night Before '88
All I Want for Christmas '91
Captain Ron '92
Honey, I Blew Up the Kid '92

Roger Ebert
Beyond the Valley of the Dolls '70
Beneath the Valley of the Ultra-Vixens '79

Nicolas Echevarria
Cabeza de Vaca '90

David Edgar
The Life and Adventures of Nicholas Nickleby '81

Patrick Edgeworth
BMX Bandits '83
Raw Deal '86
Driving Force '88

Dave Edison
Steel and Lace '90
Cast a Deadly Spell '91

Blake Edwards
The Atomic Kid '54
My Sister Eileen '55
This Happy Feeling '58
Soldier in the Rain '63
The Pink Panther '64
A Shot in the Dark '64
What Did You Do in the War, Daddy? '66
The Party '68
Darling Lili '70
Wild Rovers '71
Return of the Pink Panther '74
The Tamarind Seed '74
Revenge of the Pink Panther '78
10 '79
S.O.B. '81
Trail of the Pink Panther '82
Victor/Victoria '82
Curse of the Pink Panther '83
The Man Who Loved Women '83
City Heat '84
A Fine Mess '86
That's Life! '86
Sunset '88
Skin Deep '89
Switch '91
Son of the Pink Panther '93

Paul F. Edwards
High Ballin' '78
Fire Birds '90
Tecumseh: The Last Warrior '95

Christine Edzard
Little Dorrit, Film 1: Nobody's Fault '88
Little Dorrit, Film 2: Little Dorrit's Story '88

Fred Eggers
Thunder Pass '54

Jan Egleson
The Tender Age '84

Atom Egoyan
Next of Kin '84
Family Viewing '87
Speaking Parts '89
The Adjuster '91
Calendar '93
Exotica '94

John Ehle
The Journey of August King '95

Kerry Ehrin
Mr. Wrong '95

Max Ehrlich
Zero Population Growth '72
The Reincarnation of Peter Proud '75

Rosanne Ehrlich
Chantilly Lace '93

Robert Eisele
Lily in Winter '94

Sergei Eisenstein
Ivan the Terrible, Part 1 '44

Jo Eisinger
Night and the City '50
Crime of Passion '57

Nicolai Ekk
The Road to Life '31

Lonne Elder, III
Sounder '72
A Woman Called Moses '78
Bustin' Loose '81

Kevin Elders
Iron Eagle '86
Iron Eagle 2 '88

Laurice Elehwany
My Girl '91
The Amazing Panda Adventure '95
The Brady Bunch Movie '95

Richard Elfman
Forbidden Zone '80

Harry Elfont
A Very Brady Sequel '96

Caroline Eliacheff
La Ceremonie '95

Michael Elias
The Frisco Kid '79
The Jerk '79
Serial '80
Young Doctors in Love '82
Lush Life '94

Joyce Eliason
Tell Me a Riddle '80
Small Sacrifices '89
A Good Day to Die '95
Oldest Confederate Widow Tells All '95

Irving Elinson
By the Light of the Silvery Moon '53

Michael Elkins
Esther and the King '60

Mercer Ellington
Avenging Force '86

Ted Elliot
Little Monsters '89
Aladdin '92

B. Ron Elliott
The Acid Eaters '67

Stephan Elliott
The Adventures of Priscilla, Queen of the Desert '94

Ted Elliott
The Puppet Masters '94

Anderson Ellis
The Mortal Storm '40

Aunjanue Ellis
Girls Town '95

Bob Ellis
Man of Flowers '84
My First Wife '84
Cactus '86
Warm Nights on a Slow-Moving Train '87

Flaiano ▶cont.

The Swindle '55
Nights of Cabiria '57
La Dolce Vita '60
8 1/2 '63
Juliet of the Spirits '65

Fionnula Flanagan
James Joyce's Women '85

Peter Flannery
Funny Bones '94

Harvey Flaxman
Preacherman '83

Gregory Fleeman
F/X '86

Hugh Fleetwood
The Bachelor '93

A.S. Fleischman
Lafayette Escadrille '58

Andrew Fleming
Bad Dreams '88
Every Breath '93
Threesome '94
The Craft '96

Peter Fleming
Witchcraft 7: Judgement Hour '95

Bill Flemming
Northern Extremes '93

Rodman Flender
In the Heat of Passion '91

Charlie Fletcher
Fair Game '95

Theodore J. Flicker
The President's Analyst '67

Ruth Brooks Flippen
Love Is Better Than Ever '52

Robert Florey
Frankenstein '31

Richard Flournoy
Blondie '38
Blondie Takes a Vacation '39
Blondie Has Trouble '40
Blondie's Blessed Event '42

Errol Flynn
Assault of the Rebel Girls '59

Tom Flynn
Watch It '93

Lawrence Foldes
Young Warriors '83

Peter Foldy
Midnight Witness '93
Tryst '94

James Foley
After Dark, My Sweet '90
S.F.W. '94

Naomi Foner
Violets Are Blue '86
Running on Empty '88
A Dangerous Woman '93
Losing Isaiah '94

Leo Fong
Showdown '93

Anne Fontaine
Augustin '95

Randall Fontana
Bitter Harvest '93

Bradbury Foote
Of Human Hearts '38
Young Tom Edison '40

Horton Foote
To Kill a Mockingbird '62
Baby, the Rain Must Fall '64
The Chase '66
Tomorrow '72
Tender Mercies '83
1918 '85
The Trip to Bountiful '85
On Valentine's Day '86
The Habitation of Dragons '91
Of Mice and Men '92

John Taintor Foote
The Mark of Zorro '40

Bryan Forbes
Of Human Bondage '64
Chaplin '92

Christian Ford
Kazaam '96

Phillip R. Ford
Vegas in Space '94

Richard Ford
Bright Angel '91

Ron Ford
The Fear '94

Timothy Forder
The Mystery of Edwin Drood '93

Carl Foreman
Spooks Run Wild '41
Cyrano de Bergerac '50
High Noon '52
The Bridge on the River Kwai '57
The Key '58

Susan Forman
Dream a Little Dream 2 '94

Brent Forrester
The Stupids '95

Bengt Forslund
The Emigrants '72
The New Land '73

Bill Forsyth
That Sinking Feeling '79
Gregory's Girl '80
Local Hero '83
Housekeeping '87
Being Human '94

Frederick Forsyth
The Fourth Protocol '87
A Casualty of War '90

Garrett Fort
Dracula (Spanish Version) '31
Frankenstein '31

Lewis R. Foster
Never Say Goodbye '46

Robert Foster
Dead Bang '89

Tony Foster
The Sound and the Silence '93

Gene Fowler, Jr.
Billy the Kid '41

Florence Fox
The Phoenix and the Magic Carpet '95

Robbie Fox
So I Married an Axe Murderer '93

Terry Curtis Fox
Fortress '93

Victoria Foyt
Babyfever '94
Last Summer In the Hamptons '96

Michael France
Cliffhanger '93
Goldeneye '95

Adolfo Franci
Shoeshine '47

Coleman Francis
The Beast of Yucca Flats '61

Dan Franck
The Separation '94

Bruno Frank
The Hunchback of Notre Dame '39

Frederic M. Frank
Unconquered '47

Harriet Frank, Jr.
Silver River '48
Ten Wanted Men '54
The Long, Hot Summer '58
Home from the Hill '60
Hud '63
Hombre '67
The Reivers '69
The Cowboys '72
Conrack '74
Norma Rae '79
Murphy's Romance '85
Stanley and Iris '90

Melvin Frank
Monsieur Beaucaire '46
Above and Beyond '53
Strange Bedfellows '65

Scott Frank
Dead Again '91
Little Man Tate '91
Fallen Angels 2 '93
Malice '93
Get Shorty '95
Heaven's Prisoners '95

David Frankel
Funny About Love '90
Nervous Ticks '93
Miami Rhapsody '95

Al Franken
One More Saturday Night '86
Stuart Saves His Family '94
When a Man Loves a Woman '94

John Frankenheimer
The Manchurian Candidate '62

Carl Franklin
Eye of the Eagle 3 '91
Devil In a Blue Dress '95

Dean Franklin
The Fighting 69th '40

Howard Franklin
The Name of the Rose '86
Someone to Watch Over Me '87
Quick Change '90
The Public Eye '92

Jeff Franklin
Summer School '87
Double Double Toil and Trouble '94
To Grandmother's House We Go '94

Paul Franklin
The Fighting Redhead '50

Richard Franklin
Sorrento Beach '95

David Franzoni
Jumpin' Jack Flash '86
Citizen Cohn '92

Brad Fraser
Love and Human Remains '93

George MacDonald Fraser
Royal Flash '75
Casanova '87
The Return of the Musketeers '89

Harry Fraser
Galloping Romeo '33

Michael Frayn
Clockwise '86

Donald Freed
Of Love and Shadows '94

Herb Freed
Beyond Evil '80

Robert Freedman
Taken Away '89

David Freeman
Street Smart '87

Everett Freeman
My Man Godfrey '57
The Glass Bottom Boat '66

Joan Freeman
Streetwalkin' '85
Uncaged '91

Fred Freiberger
The Beast from 20,000 Fathoms '53

Robert M. Fresco
Tarantula '55
The Monolith Monsters '57

Bill Freut
125 Rooms of Comfort '83

Ron Fricke
Baraka '93

Fridrik Thor Fridriksson
Children of Nature '91

Randall Fried
Heaven is a Playground '91

Jason Friedberg
Spy Hard '96

Rick Friedberg
Spy Hard '96

Richard Friedenberg
Dying Young '91
A River Runs Through It '92
Mr. & Mrs. Loving '96

Bud Friedgen
That's Entertainment, Part 3 '93

William Friedkin
Cruising '80
To Live & Die in L.A. '85
Rampage '87
The Guardian '90

Brent Friedman
Pet Shop '94
Prehysteria 2 '94
Magic Island '95

Ken Friedman
White Line Fever '75
Mr. Billion '77
Heart Like a Wheel '83
Made in USA '88
Johnny Handsome '89
Cadillac Man '90
Bad Girls '94

Merrill Friedman
Beauty School '93

Richard S. Friedman
Scared Stiff '87

James Fritzell
The Ghost and Mr. Chicken '66
The Reluctant Astronaut '67

John Frizzell
Dance Me Outside '95

George Froeschel
The Mortal Storm '40
Mrs. Miniver '42
The Miniver Story '50
Never Let Me Go '53
Me and the Colonel '58

Clayton Frohman
Under Fire '83

Diane Frolov
Alien Nation: Dark Horizon '94

Seth Front
Nickel & Dime '92

Mark Frost
The Believers '87
Scared Stiff '87
Storyville '92

Roy Frumkes
The Substitute '96

Benjamin Fry
Wavelength '96

Christopher Fry
The Lady's Not for Burning '95

E. Max Frye
Something Wild '86
Amos and Andrew '93

Carol Fuchs
Alaska '96

Daniel Fuchs
Criss Cross '48
The Underneath '95

Lucio Fulci
The Black Cat '81

Charles Fuller
Zooman '95

Samuel Fuller
I Shot Jesse James '49
Baron of Arizona '51
The Steel Helmet '51
Pickup on South Street '53
Run of the Arrow '56
China Gate '57
Underworld, U.S.A. '60
Merrill's Marauders '62
Shock Corridor '63
Shark! '68
Dead Pigeon on Beethoven Street '72
The Klansman '74
The Big Red One '80
Let's Get Harry '87

Sidney J. Furie
The Boys in Company C '77
Purple Hearts '84
Iron Eagle '86
Iron Eagle 2 '88
The Taking of Beverly Hills '91

Jules Furthman
Shanghai Express '32
Mutiny on the Bounty '35
Only Angels Have Wings '39
The Big Sleep '46

John Fusco
Crossroads '86
Young Guns '88
Young Guns 2 '90
The Babe '92
Thunderheart '92

Richard Gabai
Virgin High '90

Bob Gale
1941 '79
Back to the Future '85
Back to the Future, Part 2 '89
Back to the Future, Part 3 '90
Trespass '92

Henrik Galeen
Waxworks '24

Chris Gallagher
White Phantom: Enemy of Darkness '87

Carlos Gallardo
El Mariachi '93

George Gallo
Midnight Run '88
29th Street '91
Trapped In Paradise '94

Kenneth Gamet
Pittsburgh '42
Man in the Saddle '51
Santa Fe '51
A Lawless Street '55

Abel Gance
Beethoven '36

Paul Gangelin
The Mad Ghoul '43

Lowell Ganz
Night Shift '82
Splash '84
Gung Ho '85
Spies Like Us '85
Vibes '88
Parenthood '89
City Slickers '91
A League of Their Own '92
Mr. Saturday Night '92
City Slickers 2: The Legend of Curly's Gold '94
Greedy '94
Forget Paris '95
Multiplicity '96

George Garcia
Armageddon: The Final Challenge '94

Michael Garcia
Armageddon: The Final Challenge '94

Nicole Garcia
The Favorite Son '94

Louis Gardel
Fort Saganne '84
Indochine '92

Fred Gardner
Zabriskie Point '70

Herb Gardner
A Thousand Clowns '65
The Goodbye People '83

Richard Harding Gardner
Sherlock: Undercover Dog '94

Leo Garen
Band of the Hand '86

Robert Garland
No Way Out '87

Helen Garner
The Last Days of Chez Nous '92

Tony Garnett
Deep in the Heart '83
Fat Man and Little Boy '89

Dominique Garnier
Dr. Petiot '90

George Garret
Frankenstein Meets the Space Monster '65

Mick Garris
Critters 2: The Main Course '88
The Fly 2 '89
Hocus Pocus '93

Jacek Gasiorowski
Danton '82

Mark Gasper
An Empty Bed '90

Howard Gast
A Woman Called Golda '82

Ernesto Gastaldi
The Scorpion's Tail '71
Torso '73

Nate Gatzert
The Fiddlin' Buckaroo '33

Nils Gaup
Pathfinder '87
Shipwrecked '90

Gene Gauthier
From the Manger to the Cross '15

Eleanor Gaver
Dead in the Water '91

John Gay
Run Silent, Run Deep '58
Separate Tables '58
The Courtship of Eddie's Father '62
The Four Horsemen of the Apocalypse '62
The Hallelujah Trail '65
The Last Safari '67
No Way to Treat a Lady '68
Soldier Blue '70
Sometimes a Great Notion '71
Hennessy '75
A Tale of Two Cities '80
Manhunt for Claude Dallas '86
Windmills of the Gods '88
Final Notice '89

Laurence Gay
Houseguest '94

Armand Gazarian
Prison Planet '92

Glenn Gebhard
One Last Run '89

Bill Geddie
Unforgettable '96

David Geeves
American Ninja 4: The Annihilation '91

Theodore "Dr. Seuss" Geisel
The 5000 Fingers of Dr. T '53

Larry Gelbart
The Wrong Box '66
Oh, God! '77
Movie, Movie '78
Rough Cut '80
Neighbors '81
Tootsie '82
Blame It on Rio '84
Barbarians at the Gate '93

Erwin Gelsey
Scarlet Dawn '32
The Strange Love of Molly Louvain '32

Jean Genet
Mademoiselle '66

Dr. Lance Gentile
State of Emergency '94

Paul Geoauff
Les Bonnes Femmes '60

George S. George
The Heat's On '43

Jon George
Don't Talk to Strangers '94

Nelson George
CB4: The Movie '93

Peter George
Dr. Strangelove, or: How I Learned to Stop Worrying and Love the Bomb '64

Terry George
In the Name of the Father '93

Gerald Geraghty
Trigger, Jr. '50

Gary Gerani
Pumpkinhead '88

Pietro Germi
Divorce—Italian Style '62

Chris Gerolmo
Miles from Home '88
Mississippi Burning '88
Citizen X '95

Vance Gerry
The Fox and the Hound '81

Nicolas Gessner
The Peking Blond '68
Black Water '94

Robert Getchell
Alice Doesn't Live Here Anymore '74
Bound for Glory '76
Mommie Dearest '81
Sweet Dreams '85
Stella '89
Point of No Return '93
This Boy's Life '93
The Client '94

Steven Gethers
A Woman Called Golda '82
Jenny's War '85

Earl Ghaffari
The Kindred '87

Alfredo Giannetti
Divorce—Italian Style '62

Duncan Gibbins
Eve of Destruction '90
A Case for Murder '93

Rodney Gibbons
Digger '94

Stuart Gibbs
Silk Degrees '94

Tom Gibson
Covered Wagon Trails '40

William Gibson
Johnny Mnemonic '95

Raynold Gideon
A Man, a Woman, and a Bank '79
Starman '84
Stand By Me '86
Made in Heaven '87
Kuffs '92
The River Wild '94

Barry Gifford
Hotel Room '93

Lewis Gilbert
Haunted '95

David Giler
Fun with Dick and Jane '77
Southern Comfort '81

Stuart Gillard
Teenage Mutant Ninja Turtles 3 '93

Terry Gilliam
And Now for Something Completely Different '72
Monty Python and the Holy Grail '75
Jabberwocky '77
Monty Python's Life of Brian '79
Time Bandits '81
Monty Python Live at the Hollywood Bowl '82
Monty Python's The Meaning of Life '83
Brazil '85
The Adventures of Baron Munchausen '89

Sidney Gilliat
King of the Damned '36
The Lady Vanishes '38

Vince Gilligan
Wilder Napalm '93

Dan Gilroy
Freejack '92
Chasers '94

Frank D. Gilroy
Fastest Gun Alive '56
The Gallant Hours '60
Desperate Characters '71
From Noon Till Three '76
Once in Paris... '79
Jinxed '82
The Gig '85

Tony Gilroy
The Cutting Edge '92
Dolores Claiborne '94

Steven Ginsburg
Family Prayers '91

George Gipe
The Man with Two Brains '83

Andre Girard
La Chienne '31

Francois Girard
32 Short Films about Glenn Gould '93

William Girdler
Asylum of Satan '72
Three on a Meathook '72

Gilbert Girion
American Blue Note '89

Francois Girod
The Elegant Criminal '92

Tomas Gislason
The Kingdom '95

Robert Glass
Running Against Time '90
Death Dreams '92

Handel Glassberg
The Take '90
The Day My Parents Ran Away '93

Barry Glasser
Gold Diggers: The Secret of Bear Mountain '95

Richard Glatzer
Grief '94

Mitch Glazer
Moon over Miami '41
Mr. Mike's Mondo Video '79
Scrooged '88

James Gleason
The Flying Fool '29

Peter Glenville
Hotel Paradiso '66

James Glickenhaus
Shakedown '88
McBain '91
Slaughter of the Innocents '93
Timemaster '95

Jean-Luc Godard
Breathless '59
My Life to Live '62
RoGoPaG '62
Band of Outsiders '64
Contempt '64
Alphaville '65
The Joy of Knowledge '65
A Married Woman '65
Oldest Profession '67
Weekend '67
Six in Paris '68
Numero Deux '75
Hail Mary '85
Nouvelle Vague '90
Helas Pour Moi '94

Peter Godfrey
Forever and a Day '43

Ivan Goff
Captain Horatio Hornblower '51
Green Fire '55
Band of Angels '57
Man of a Thousand Faces '57
Shake Hands with the Devil '59
Midnight Lace '60
Legend of the Lone Ranger '81

Menahem Golan
What's Good for the Goose '69
Hanna's War '88

Jack Gold
The Medusa Touch '78

Myron G. Gold
Frankenstein's Great Aunt Tillie '83

Willis Goldbeck
Sergeant Rutledge '60

Dan Goldberg
Heavy Metal '81
Feds '88

Gary David Goldberg
Dad '89
Bye Bye, Love '94

Michael Goldberg
Cool Runnings '93
Little Giants '94
Bushwhacked '95

John Golden
Samantha '92

Jorge Goldenberg
Miss Mary '86

Eversmile New Jersey '89
I Don't Want to Talk About It '94

Michael Goldenberg
Bed of Roses '95

Marilyn Goldin
Camille Claudel '89

Bo Goldman
One Flew Over the Cuckoo's Nest '75
Melvin and Howard '80
Shoot the Moon '82
Swing Shift '84
Little Nikita '88
Scent of a Woman '92
City Hall '95

Gary Goldman
Big Trouble in Little China '86
Navy SEALS '90
Total Recall '90

James Goldman
The Lion in Winter '68
Oliver Twist '82
Anastasia: The Mystery of Anna '86

William Goldman
Butch Cassidy and the Sundance Kid '69
The Great Waldo Pepper '75
All the President's Men '76
Marathon Man '76
A Bridge Too Far '77
Magic '78
Heat '87
The Princess Bride '87
Misery '90
Chaplin '92
Year of the Comet '92
Maverick '94

Akiva Goldsman
The Client '94
Silent Fall '94
Batman Forever '95
A Time to Kill '96

Joel Goldsmith
Army of One '94

John Goldsmith
The Old Curiosity Shop '94

Allan Goldstein
Rooftops '89
Death Wish 5: The Face of Death '94

Amy Goldstein
The Silencer '92

Josh Goldstein
18 Again! '88

Mark Goldstein
Prehysteria '93
Pet Shop '94

Deena Goldstone
Safe Passage '94

Peter Goldsworthy
Ebbtide '94

Bob(cat) Goldthwait
Shakes the Clown '92

Bryan Goluboff
The Basketball Diaries '94
The Affair '95

Nick Gomez
Laws of Gravity '92
New Jersey Drive '95

Manuel Gomez Pereira
Mouth to Mouth '95

William Goodhart
Generation '69
Cloud Dancer '80

David Zelag Goodman
Lovers and Other Strangers '70
Monte Walsh '70
Straw Dogs '72
Farewell, My Lovely '75
Logan's Run '76
March or Die '77
Eyes of Laura Mars '78
Fighting Back '82

Frances Goodrich
It's a Wonderful Life '46
The Virginian '46
Father of the Bride '50

Father's Little Dividend '51

Garry Goodrow
Honey, I Blew Up the Kid '92

Bert I. Gordon
Empire of the Ants '77

Dan Gordon
Gotcha! '85
Passenger 57 '92
Highlander: The Gathering '93
Surf Ninjas '93
Taking the Heat '93
New Eden '94
Wyatt Earp '94
Murder In the First '95

Jill Gordon
Angus '95

Keith Gordon
Static '87
The Chocolate War '88
A Midnight Clear '92

Leo Gordon
Attack of the Giant Leeches '59

Leon Gordon
Balalaika '39
They Met in Bombay '41
White Cargo '42

Ruth Gordon
A Double Life '47
Adam's Rib '50
Pat and Mike '52
It Should Happen to You '54
Hardhat & Legs '80

Stuart Gordon
Re-Animator '84
Honey, I Shrunk the Kids '89
Body Snatchers '93

Laszlo Gorog
The Mole People '56
The Land Unknown '57
Earth vs. the Spider '58

Marleen Gorris
Broken Mirrors '85
Antonia's Line '95

Ron Gorton, Sr.
Whispers of White '93

Carl Gottlieb
Jaws '75
Which Way Is Up? '77
Jaws 2 '78
The Jerk '79
Caveman '81
Doctor Detroit '83
Jaws 3 '83

Michael Gottlieb
Mr. Nanny '93

Robert Gottlieb
Silk Degrees '94

Heywood Gould
Rolling Thunder '77
The Boys from Brazil '78
Fort Apache, the Bronx '81
Streets of Gold '86
Cocktail '88
One Good Cop '91
Trial by Jury '94

Peter Gould
Double Dragon '94

Edmund Goulding
Riptide '34
That Certain Woman '37

David S. Goyer
Arcade '93
The Puppet Masters '94
The Crow 2: City of Angels '96

Jean-Francois Goyet
La Vengeance d'une Femme '89

Anna Grace
Girls Town '95

Todd Graff
Used People '92
Fly by Night '93
The Vanishing '93
Angie '94

Bruce Graham
Dunston Checks In '95

Norman Graham
Lost, Lonely, and Vicious '59

Ronny Graham
To Be or Not to Be '83

Never Cry Wolf '83
The Bedroom Window '87

John Hanson
Wildrose '85

Robert Harari
Everything Happens at Night '39

Jonathon Hardy
Breaker Morant '80

David Hare
Plenty '85
Wetherby '85
Saigon: Year of the Cat '87
Strapless '90
Damage '92
The Secret Rapture '94

Marion Hargrove
Cash McCall '60
40 Pounds of Trouble '62
The Music Man '62

Eric Harlacher
Homewrecker '92

Robert Harling
Steel Magnolias '89
Soapdish '91

John Harlow
Meet Sexton Blake '44
Appointment with Crime '45

Patricia Harper
The Topeka Terror '45

Sam Harper
Rookie of the Year '93

Stephen Harrigan
The O.J. Simpson Story '94

Bruklin Harris
Girls Town '95

Damian Harris
The Rachel Papers '89

Eoghan Harris
Sharpe's Eagle '93
Sharpe's Rifles '93
Sharpe's Enemy '94
Sharpe's Sword '94

James B. Harris
Cop '88
Boiling Point '93

Leslie Harris
Just Another Girl on the I.R.T. '93

Owen Harris
Frontier Uprising '61

Richard Harris
Stepping Out '91

Steven Harris
At Gunpoint '90

Timothy Harris
Cheaper to Keep Her '80
Trading Places '83
Brewster's Millions '85
My Stepmother Is an Alien '88
Twins '88
Kindergarten Cop '90
Pure Luck '91

Trent Harris
Rubin & Ed '92
Plan 10 from Outer Space '95

Wendell B. Harris, Jr.
Chameleon Street '89

Jim Harrison
Cold Feet '89
Revenge '90
Wolf '94

Joan Harrison
Foreign Correspondent '40
Rebecca '40

John Harrison
Donor Unknown '95

John Kent Harrison
Murder by Phone '82
Memories of Murder '90
Beautiful Dreamers '92
City Boy '93
The Sound and the Silence '93

Matthew Harrison
Rhythm Thief '94

Bruce Hart
Question of Faith '93

Jacobsen Hart
Direct Hit '93
Zero Tolerance '93
Steel Frontier '94
The Power Within '95

Jim V. Hart
Bram Stoker's Dracula '92
Muppet Treasure Island '96

Moss Hart
Gentleman's Agreement '47
Hans Christian Andersen '52

Kenneth Hartford
Hell Squad '85

Hal Hartley
The Unbelievable Truth '90
Trust '91
Simple Men '92
Amateur '94
Flirt '95

Don Hartman
The Princess Comes Across '36
Waikiki Wedding '37
My Favorite Blonde '42

Phil Hartman
Pee Wee's Big Adventure '85

Edmund Hartmann
Ali Baba and the Forty Thieves '43
In Society '44
The Lemon Drop Kid '51
Casanova's Big Night '54

Anthony Harvey
The Disappearance of Aimee '76

Johanna Harwood
Call Me Bwana '63

Ronald Harwood
One Day in the Life of Ivan Denisovich '71
The Dresser '83
The Doctor and the Devils '85
A Fine Romance '92
The Browning Version '94

Patrick Hasburgh
Aspen Extreme '93

Keiji Hasebe
Enjo '58

Gustav Hasford
Full Metal Jacket '87

Izo Hashimoto
Akira '89

Shinobu Hashimoto
Throne of Blood '57
Yojimbo '61

Michael Hastings
Tom & Viv '94

Richard Hatem
Under Siege 2: Dark Territory '95

Kayo Hatta
Picture Bride '94

Mari Hatta
Picture Bride '94

Chris Hauty
Homeward Bound 2: Lost in San Francisco '96

Stephen Hawking
A Brief History of Time '92

Richard Hawley
Mother's Boys '94

Christopher Hawthorne
Parents '89

Helen Haxton
Night Fire '94

Carey Hayes
Down, Out and Dangerous '95

Chad Hayes
Down, Out and Dangerous '95

Clyde Allen Hayes
Rubdown '93

John Hayes
The Cut Throats '89

John Michael Hayes
Red Ball Express '52
Thunder Bay '53
War Arrow '53
Rear Window '54
It's a Dog's Life '55
To Catch a Thief '55
The Trouble with Harry '55
The Man Who Knew Too Much '56
Peyton Place '57
The Matchmaker '58
But Not for Me '59
Butterfield 8 '60
The Children's Hour '61
The Carpetbaggers '64
The Chalk Garden '64
Where Love Has Gone '64
Harlow '65
Nevada Smith '66
Pancho Barnes '88
Iron Will '93

Joseph Hayes
Stolen Hours '63

Raphael Hayes
Have Rocket Will Travel '59

Terry Hayes
Mad Max: Beyond Thunderdome '85
Dead Calm '89

Todd Haynes
Poison '91
Safe '95

Lillie Hayward
They Call It Sin '32
Lady Killer '33

Lawrence Hazard
Mannequin '37

Laurence Heath
Triumph of the Spirit '89

David Heavener
Killcrazy '89
Twisted Justice '89
Prime Target '91
Eye of the Stranger '93

Ben Hecht
Hallelujah, I'm a Bum '33
Twentieth Century '34
Viva Villa! '34
Nothing Sacred '37
Let Freedom Ring '39
Wuthering Heights '39
Comrade X '40
The Black Swan '42
Tales of Manhattan '42
Notorious '46
Spectre of the Rose '46
Monkey Business '52
The Indian Fighter '55
Circus World '64

Amy Heckerling
Look Who's Talking '89
Clueless '95

Rob Hedden
Friday the 13th, Part 8: Jason Takes Manhattan '89
The Colony '95

Roger Hedden
Bodies, Rest & Motion '93
Sleep with Me '94

Peter Hedges
What's Eating Gilbert Grape '93

Victor Heerman
Little Women '33
Golden Boy '39

Carol Heikkinen
The Thing Called Love '93
Empire Records '95

Jo Heims
Double Trouble '67
Play Misty for Me '71

Mats Helge
The Russian Terminator '90

Brian Helgeland
A Nightmare on Elm Street 4: Dream Master '88
Assassins '95

Lukas Heller
Damnation Alley '77
Blue City '86

Lillian Hellman
Watch on the Rhine '43
The Chase '66

Sam Hellman
The Three Musketeers '39

John Hemphill
Sodbusters '94

Tony Hendra
The Great White Hype '96

Frank Henenlotter
Basket Case 2 '90
Basket Case 3: The Progeny '92

James Henerson
The Fire Next Time '93
Getting Gotti '94

Liu Heng
The Story of Qui Ju '91

Paul Hengge
The Rose Garden '89

Ken Henkel
The Texas Chainsaw Massacre '74
Last Night at the Alamo '83

Hilary Henkin
Romeo Is Bleeding '93

Beth Henley
Crimes of the Heart '86
Nobody's Fool '86
True Stories '86
Miss Firecracker '89

Jack Henley
A Thousand and One Nights '45
Blondie Hits the Jackpot '49
Ma and Pa Kettle Back On the Farm '51
Ma and Pa Kettle on Vacation '53
Ma and Pa Kettle at Waikiki '55

Richard P. Henrick
Crimson Tide '95

Buck Henry
The Graduate '67
Catch-22 '70
The Owl and the Pussycat '70
What's Up, Doc? '72
The Day of the Dolphin '73
First Family '80
Protocol '84
To Die For '95

Todd Henschell
Puppet Master 4 '93

Jonathan Hensleigh
A Far Off Place '93
Die Hard: With a Vengeance '95
Jumanji '95
The Rock '96

J. Miyoko Hensley
Can You Feel Me Dancing? '85

Steven Hensley
Can You Feel Me Dancing? '85

Robby Henson
Pharoah's Army '95

F. Hugh Herbert
Let's Make It Legal '51

John Herbert
Fortune and Men's Eyes '71

Ron Herbst
Deadly Diamonds '91
Warlords 3000 '93

Stephen Herek
Critters '86

Tim Herlihy
Happy Gilmore '96

Mark Herman
Blame It on the Bellboy '92

Gyula Hernadi
The Round Up '66

Denise Hernandez
Girls Town '95

Michael Herr
Full Metal Jacket '87

Rowdy Herrington
Striking Distance '93

W. Blake Herron
Skin Art '93

Joel Hershman
Hold Me, Thrill Me, Kiss Me '93

Marshall Herskovitz
Special Bulletin '83

John Herzfeld
Casualties of Love: The "Long Island Lolita" Story '93

Werner Herzog
Signs of Life '68
Aguirre, the Wrath of God '72
Every Man for Himself & God Against All '75
Woyzeck '78
Fitzcarraldo '82

Kit Hesketh-Harvey
Maurice '87

Eugene Hess
Don't Do It '94

Fraser Heston
Treasure Island '89

Rod Hewitt
The Dangerous '95

Louis M. Heyward
Pajama Party '64

Stephen Hibbert
It's Pat: The Movie '94

Jochen Hick
Via Appia '92

George Hickenlooper
Hearts of Darkness: A Filmmaker's Apocalypse '91

Neill D. Hicks
Don't Talk to Strangers '94

Seymour Hicks
Scrooge '35

Julie Hickson
Homeward Bound 2: Lost in San Francisco '96

Howard Higgin
Revolt of the Zombies '36

Colin Higgins
Harold and Maude '71
Silver Streak '76

John C. Higgins
Robinson Crusoe on Mars '64

Lynn Rose Higgins
Mutator '90

Patrick Highsmith
Automatic '94

Charles Higson
Suite 16 '94

Nat Hiken
The Love God? '70

Kari Hildebrand
Hostage for a Day '94

David Hill
Promised a Miracle '88

Debra Hill
Halloween '78
Halloween 2: The Nightmare Isn't Over! '81
Escape from L.A. '96

Gladys Hill
The Man Who Would Be King '75

John Hill
Quigley Down Under '90

Walter Hill
The Getaway '72
Mackintosh Man '73
The Thief Who Came to Dinner '73
The Drowning Pool '75
Hard Times '75
The Driver '78
The Warriors '79
Southern Comfort '81
48 Hrs. '82
Streets of Fire '84
Aliens '86
Blue City '86
Red Heat '88
The Getaway '93
Wild Bill '95

Shirley Hillard
Season of Change '94

David Hilton
The Young Americans '93

James Hilton
Foreign Correspondent '40
Mrs. Miniver '42

David Himmelstein
Power '86
Talent for the Game '91
Village of the Damned '95

Anthony John Elder Hinds
Kiss of the Vampire '62
The Phantom of the Opera '62

Alan Hines
Square Dance '87

Nigel Hinton
Buddy's Song '91

James G. Hirsch
Broken Badge '85

Roger O. Hirson
The Old Man and the Sea '90
A Woman Named Jackie '91

Michael Hirst
Fools of Fortune '90
The Ballad of the Sad Cafe '91
Meeting Venus '91

Toni Hirtreiter
Night Train to Venice '93

Norm Hiscock
Kids In the Hall Brain Candy '96

Alfred Hitchcock
The Lodger '26
The Ring '27
Champagne '28
The Farmer's Wife '28
Blackmail '29
Juno and the Paycock '30
Murder '30
Skin Game '31
No. 17 '32
Rich and Strange '32
Saboteur '42

Michael Hitchcock
Where the Day Takes You '92
House Arrest '96

Ken Hixon
Caught in the Act '93
Incident at Deception Ridge '94

Godfrey Ho
Ninja Destroyer '70s
Ninja Champion '80s

Yim Ho
The Day the Sun Turned Cold '94

John Hodge
Shallow Grave '94
Trainspotting '95

Steve Hodge
Mosquito '95

Adrian Hodges
Tom & Viv '94

Mike Hodges
Pulp '72
The Terminal Man '74
Damien: Omen 2 '78
Black Rainbow '91

Arthur Hoerl
The Singing Cowgirl '39

Michael Hoey
Navy vs. the Night Monsters '66

Samuel Hoffenstein
Tales of Manhattan '42
His Butler's Sister '43

Bridget Hoffman
Double Exposure '93

Charles Hoffman
The West Point Story '50

Lauran Hoffman
Bar Girls '95

Michael Hoffman
Promised Land '88

Ota Hofman
The Last Butterfly '92

Gray Hofmeyr
Yankee Zulu '95

Michael Hogan
Arabian Nights '42
Forever and a Day '43

Paul Hogan
Crocodile Dundee '86
Crocodile Dundee 2 '88
Almost an Angel '90
Lightning Jack '94

P.J. Hogan
Muriel's Wedding '94

Brian Hohlfield
He Said, She Said '91
The Mighty Ducks '92

Agnieszka Holland
Without Anesthesia '78
Danton '82
A Love in Germany '84
Angry Harvest '85
Anna '87
To Kill a Priest '89
Korczak '90
Europa, Europa '91
Olivier, Olivier '92

Steve Holland
Better Off Dead '85
One Crazy Summer '86

Tom Holland
The Beast Within '82
Class of 1984 '82
Psycho 2 '83
Cloak & Dagger '84
Fright Night '85
Scream for Help '86
Child's Play '88
Stephen King's The Langoliers '95

Eli Hollander
Out '88

Don Holley
National Lampoon's Loaded Weapon 1 '93

Kari Holman
The Death Merchant '91

Brown Holmes
The Strange Love of Molly Louvain '32

Rita Holst
Dreaming of Rita '94

Lou Holtz, Jr.
The Cable Guy '96

Mark Homer
Sharon's Secret '95

Geoffrey Homes
Out of the Past '47
Cavalry Charge '51

Kirk Honeycutt
Final Judgement '92

Thomas Hood
Circumstances Unknown '95

Harry Hook
The Kitchen Toto '87

Tobe Hooper
The Texas Chainsaw Massacre '74
The Mangler '94

Claudia Hoover
Double Exposure '93

Arthur Hopcraft
A Perfect Spy '88

Margot Hope
Femme Fontaine: Killer Babe for the C.I.A. '95

Alan Hopgood
Alvin Purple '73
Alvin Rides Again '74

John Hopkins
Thunderball '65
The Virgin Soldiers '69
The Offence '73
Murder by Decree '79
The Holcroft Covenant '85
Torment '85
Codename Kyril '91
Dunston Checks In '95
Hiroshima '95

Robert Hopkins
Saratoga '37

Arthur T. Horman
Here Come the Co-Eds '45

Lanny Horn
Skeeter '93

Christopher Horner
Accidental Meeting '93

Israel Horovitz
The Strawberry Statement '70
Author! Author! '82
A Man in Love '87

Anthony Horowitz
Diamond's Edge '88

Ed Horowitz
On Deadly Ground '94

Jordan Horowitz
Alan & Naomi '92

Bob Hoskins
The Raggedy Rawney '90

Dan Hoskins
Chopper Chicks in Zombietown '91

John Houseman
Jane Eyre '44

Lionel Houser
First Love '39

Bobby Houston
Caged Fear '92

Michael Hovis
The Man with the Perfect Swing '95

Clint Howard
Cotton Candy '82

Elizabeth Jane Howard
Getting It Right '89

Joseph Howard
Sister Act '92

Ron Howard
Grand Theft Auto '77
Cotton Candy '82
Parenthood '89

Sidney Howard
Gone with the Wind '39

C. Thomas Howell
Hourglass '95

Dorothy Howell
Platinum Blonde '31

Frank Howson
The Hunting '92

Perry Howze
Maid to Order '87
Mystic Pizza '88
Chances Are '89

Randy Howze
Chances Are '89

Yu Hua
To Live '94

George Huang
Swimming with Sharks '94

Tom Hubbard
Thunder Pass '54
Daniel Boone: Trail Blazer '56

Jean-Loup Hubert
Le Grand Chemin '87

Tom Huckabee
Deathfight '93

Reginald Hudlin
House Party '90
Bebe's Kids '92

Warrington Hudlin
Cosmic Slop '94

Dick Huemer
Dumbo '41

Chuck Hughes
Ed and His Dead Mother '93

John Hughes
National Lampoon's Class Reunion '82
Mr. Mom '83
National Lampoon's Vacation '83
Sixteen Candles '84
The Breakfast Club '85
National Lampoon's European Vacation '85
Weird Science '85
Ferris Bueller's Day Off '86
Pretty in Pink '86
Planes, Trains & Automobiles '87
Some Kind of Wonderful '87
The Great Outdoors '88
She's Having a Baby '88
National Lampoon's Christmas Vacation '89
Uncle Buck '89
Home Alone '90
Career Opportunities '91
Curly Sue '91
Dutch '91
Beethoven '92
Home Alone 2: Lost in New York '92
Dennis the Menace '93
Baby's Day Out '94
Miracle on 34th Street '94

Ken Hughes
Heat Wave '54
The Trials of Oscar Wilde '60
Arrivederci, Baby! '66
Chitty Chitty Bang Bang '68
Cromwell '70
Oh, Alfie '75

Langston Hughes
Way Down South '39

Russell S. Hughes
Savage Wilderness '55

Jay Huguely-Cass
Jason Goes to Hell: The Final Friday '93

Steve Hulett
The Fox and the Hound '81

Ron Hulme
Fearless Tiger '94

Cyril Hume
Trader Horn '31
The Invisible Boy '57

Joel Don Humphreys
My Heroes Have Always Been Cowboys '91

Barry Humphries
Barry McKenzie Holds His Own '74

Tran Anh Hung
The Scent of Green Papaya '93

Jackson Hunsicker
Oddball Hall '91

Bob Hunt
The Hidden '87

Edward Hunt
Starship Invasions '77

Thomas Hunter
The Final Countdown '80

Georgie Huntington
Teresa's Tattoo '94

Lawrence Huntington
Man on the Run '49

Earl Hurd
Snow White and the Seven Dwarfs '37

Gladys Hurlbut
Love on the Run '36

Ben Hurst
Bums '93

Harry Hurwitz
The Projectionist '71
Under the Rainbow '81
That's Adequate '90
Fleshtone '94

Shahrukh Husain
In Custody '94

Rich Husky
Children of Fury '94

Jimmy Huston
The Wharf Rat '95

John Huston
High Sierra '41
The Maltese Falcon '41
Sergeant York '41
Key Largo '48
Treasure of the Sierra Madre '48
The African Queen '51
Moby Dick '56
The Man Who Would Be King '75
Mr. North '88

Ron Hutchinson
Blue Ice '92
Against the Wall '94
The Burning Season '94
Fatherland '94
The Tuskegee Airmen '95

Aldous Huxley
Jane Eyre '44

Willard Huyck
American Graffiti '73
Messiah of Evil '74
French Postcards '79
Best Defense '84
Indiana Jones and the Temple of Doom '84
Howard the Duck '86
Radioland Murders '94

David Henry Hwang
Golden Gate '93
M. Butterfly '93

Peter Hyams
Busting '74
Telefon '77
Capricorn One '78
Hanover Street '79
The Hunter '80
Outland '81
The Star Chamber '83
2010: The Year We Make Contact '84
Narrow Margin '90

Chris Hyde
Chained Heat 2 '92

Noel Hynd
Illegal in Blue '95

Jeremy Iacone
Blood In...Blood Out: Bound by Honor '93

Juan Luis Iborra
Mouth to Mouth '95

Rustam Ibragimbekov
Close to Eden '90
Burnt by the Sun '94

Ice Cube
Friday '95

Leon Ichaso
El Super '79
Crossover Dreams '85

Masato Ide
Ran '85

Eric Idle
Monty Python and the Holy Grail '75
Monty Python's Life of Brian '79
Monty Python's The Meaning of Life '83
The Tale of the Frog Prince '83
National Lampoon's European Vacation '85
Splitting Heirs '93

W. Peter Iliff
Point Break '91
Patriot Games '92

Lou Illar
Sidekicks '93

Shohei Imamura
The Ballad of Narayama '83

Thomas Ince
The Disciple '15

William Inge
Splendor in the Grass '61
All Fall Down '62

Raul Inglis
Breach of Trust '95

Boris Ingster
Thin Ice '37
Happy Landing '38

J. Christian Ingvordsen
Comrades in Arms '91
The Outfit '93

Tino Insana
The Masters of Menace '90

Otar Iosseliani
Chasing Butterflies '94

Ronnie Isaacs
Warriors from Hell '90

Bjorn Isfalt
The Slingshot '93

Christopher Isherwood
Forever and a Day '43
Diane '55
The Loved One '65

Toshiro Ishido
Hiroshima '95

Charles Israel
Arch of Triumph '85

Neal Israel
Police Academy '84
Real Genius '85
All I Want for Christmas '91

Juzo Itami
A Taxing Woman '87
A Taxing Woman's Return '88
Minbo—Or the Gentle Art of Japanese Extortion '92

Daisuke Ito
An Actor's Revenge '63

James Ivory
Shakespeare Wallah '65
Maurice '87

Bob Ivy
Dark Rider '91

Simona Izzo
La Scorta '94

David S. Jackson
Detonator '93
Detonator 2: Night Watch '95

Donald G. Jackson
The Demon Lover '77

Felix Jackson
Mad About Music '38
Destry Rides Again '39
Three Smart Girls Grow Up '39

Horace Jackson
The Animal Kingdom '32
We're Not Dressing '34

Peter Jackson
Meet the Feebles '89
Dead Alive '93
Heavenly Creatures '94
The Frighteners '96

Philip Jackson
Project: Genesis '93

Alan Jacobs
Nina Takes a Lover '94

Jon Jacobs
The Girl with the Hungry Eyes '94

Lawrence-Hilton Jacobs
Angels of the City '89

Lewis Jacobs
Sweet Love, Bitter '67

Matthew Jacobs
Paperhouse '89
Lorna Doone '90
Lassie '94
Doctor Who '96

Nicholas A.E. Jacobs
The Refrigerator '93

Rick Jaffa
An Eye for an Eye '95

Henry Jaglom
Tracks '76
Sitting Ducks '80
Can She Bake a Cherry Pie? '83
Always '85
Someone to Love '87
New Year's Day '89
Eating '90
Babyfever '94
Last Summer In the Hamptons '96

Don Jakoby
Blue Thunder '83
The Philadelphia Experiment '84
Lifeforce '85
Invaders from Mars '86
Arachnophobia '90

Alan James
Dick Tracy: The Original Serial, Vol. 1 '37
Dick Tracy: The Original Serial, Vol. 2 '37

Polly James
Mrs. Parkington '44
The Redhead from Wyoming '53

Rian James
42nd Street '33
Internes Can't Take Money '37

Tama Janowitz
Slaves of New York '89

Michael January
To Be the Best '93
C.I.A. 2: Target Alexa '94

Agnes Jaoui
Smoking/No Smoking '94

Derek Jarman
Caravaggio '86
The Garden '90
Edward II '92
Blue '93
Wittgenstein '93

Jim Jarmusch
Permanent Vacation '84
Stranger than Paradise '84
Down by Law '86
Mystery Train '89
Night on Earth '91

Kevin Jarre
Glory '89
Tombstone '93

Paul Jarrice
Messenger of Death '88

Charles Jarrott
Morning Glory '93

Steve Jarvis
Things '93

Griffin Jay
The Mummy's Tomb '42
Captive Wild Woman '43
The Mummy's Ghost '44

Vadim Jean
Nightscare '93

Henri Jeanson
Modigliani '58

Brian D. Jeffries
Hangfire '91

Herbert Jeffries
World of the Depraved '67

Dan Jenkins
Dead Solid Perfect '88

John Jenkins
Patti Rocks '88

Jim Jennewein
The Flintstones '94
Getting Even with Dad '94
Richie Rich '94

Talbot Jennings
Mutiny on the Bounty '35
Anna and the King of Siam '46

Bill Jesse
Riff Raff '92

Anthony Jesu
Fist of Steel '93

Jean-Marie Jeunet
The City of Lost Children '95

Jack Jevne
Wintertime '43

Ruth Prawer Jhabvala
The Householder '63
Shakespeare Wallah '65
Bombay Talkie '70
Autobiography of a Princess '75
Roseland '77
Hullabaloo Over Georgie & Bonnie's Pictures '78
The Europeans '79
Jane Austen in Manhattan '80
Quartet '81
Heat and Dust '82
The Bostonians '84
A Room with a View '86
Madame Sousatzka '88
Mr. & Mrs. Bridge '90
Howard's End '92
The Remains of the Day '93
Jefferson in Paris '94

Neal Jimenez
River's Edge '87
For the Boys '91
The Waterdance '91
Hideaway '94
Sleep with Me '94

Mike Jittlov
The Wizard of Speed and Time '88

Alejandro Jodorowsky
Santa Sangre '90

Arthur Joffe
Alberto Express '92

Roland Joffe
Fat Man and Little Boy '89

Tim John
Dr. Jekyll and Ms. Hyde '95

Charles Eric Johnson
The George McKenna Story '86

Cindy Lou Johnson
Trusting Beatrice '92

David Johnson
DROP Squad '94

George Clayton Johnson
The Twilight Zone '61

J. Randall Johnson
The Doors '91

Kenneth Johnson
V '83

Kristine Johnson
Imaginary Crimes '94

Mark Steven Johnson
Grumpy Old Men '93
Big Bully '95
Grumpier Old Men '95

Monica Johnson
Americathon '79
Real Life '79
Modern Romance '81
Jekyll & Hyde...Together Again '82
Lost in America '85
The Scout '94

Nora Johnson
The World of Henry Orient '64

Nunnally Johnson
Rose of Washington Square '39
The Grapes of Wrath '40
Roxie Hart '42
Casanova Brown '44
The Keys of the Kingdom '44
Woman In the Window '44
Along Came Jones '45
Mr. Peabody & the Mermaid '48
Phone Call from a Stranger '52
We're Not Married '52
How to Marry a Millionaire '53
The World of Henry Orient '64

Randy Johnson
The Doors '91

Robert Johnson
Tyson '95

Steve Johnson
Cover Me '95

Terry Johnson
Insignificance '85

Aaron Kim Johnston
The Last Winter '89
For the Moment '94

Becky Johnston
The Prince of Tides '91

Tony Johnston
Replikator: Cloned to Kill '94

Norman Jolley
The Monolith Monsters '57

Oskar Jonasson
Remote Control '94

Amy Holden Jones
Mystic Pizza '88
Beethoven '92
Indecency '92
The Getaway '93
Indecent Proposal '93

Bridget Jones
Mystery Science Theater 3000: The Movie '96

Charles Reed Jones
The King Murder '32

Chuck Jones
Gay Purr-ee '62

Ed Jones
Carried Away '95

Evan Jones
Funeral in Berlin '66
Killing of Angel Street '81
Champions '84
Kangaroo '86
A Show of Force '90
Shadow of the Wolf '92

Gary Jones
Mosquito '95

Ian Jones
Ned Kelly '70
The Lighthorsemen '87

Laura Jones
High Tide '87
An Angel at My Table '89

Laurie Jones
In the Spirit '90

Mark Jones
Leprechaun '93

Robert C. Jones
Coming Home '78

Terry Jones
And Now for Something Completely Different '72
Monty Python and the Holy Grail '75
Ripping Yarns '75
Monty Python's Life of Brian '79
Monty Python's The Meaning of Life '83
Labyrinth '86
Erik the Viking '89

Tommy Lee Jones
The Good Old Boys '95

Glenn Jordan
O Pioneers! '91

John Jordan
Bushwhacked '95

Neil Jordan
Danny Boy '84
The Company of Wolves '85
Mona Lisa '86
High Spirits '88
The Miracle '91
The Crying Game '92

Robert L. Joseph
World War III '86

Julien Josephson
The Rains Came '39

Jon Jost
Sure Fire '90
All the Vermeers in New York '91
Jon Jost's Frameup '93

Adrien (Carole Eastman) Joyce
Five Easy Pieces '70
Man Trouble '92

C. Courtney Joyner
The Offspring '87
Prison '88
Catacombs '89
Class of 1999 '90
Vietnam, Texas '90
Desperate Motives '92
Trancers 3: Deth Lives '92
Lurking Fear '94

Jerry Juhl
Muppet Treasure Island '96

Aaron Julien
Dirty Work '92

Zheng Junli
Crows and Sparrows '49

Karel Kachyna
The Last Butterfly '92

Jeremy Paul Kagan
Roswell: The U.F.O. Cover-Up '94

Marcy Kahan
Antonia and Jane '91

Jeff Kahn
Revolution! A Red Comedy '91

Richard C. Kahn
Bronze Buckaroo '39

Terry Kahn
Steal Big, Steal Little '95

Tom Kalin
Swoon '91

Stanley Kallis
Road Racers '59

Bert Kalmar
Duck Soup '33
A Night at the Opera '35

Steven Kaman
The Outfit '93

Robert Mark Kamen
Taps '81
Split Image '82
The Karate Kid '84
The Karate Kid: Part 2 '86
The Karate Kid: Part 3 '89
Lethal Weapon 3 '92
The Power of One '92
A Walk in the Clouds '95

Zbigniew Kaminski
Maids of Wilko '79

Stuart Kaminsky
Hidden Fears '93

Steven Kampmann
Back to School '86
The Couch Trip '87
Stealing Home '88
Clifford '92

Aben Kandel
They Won't Forget '37

Stephen Kandel
Living Proof: The Hank Williams Jr. Story '83

Kristi Kane
The Reluctant Agent '95

Michael Kane
Foolin' Around '80
Hot Stuff '80
Smokey and the Bandit, Part 2 '80
Hard Country '81
Legend of the Lone Ranger '81
Southern Comfort '81
All the Right Moves '83
The Bear '89
The Cisco Kid '94

Rolfe Kanefsky
There's Nothing Out There '90

Jeff Kanew
Natural Enemies '79

Charles Kanganis
A Time to Die '91
Fist of Honor '92
No Escape, No Return '93

Fay Kanin
Rhapsody '54
The Opposite Sex '56
Teacher's Pet '58

Garson Kanin
A Double Life '47
Adam's Rib '50
Pat and Mike '52
It Should Happen to You '54

Michael Kanin
Woman of the Year '42
Rhapsody '54
The Opposite Sex '56
Teacher's Pet '58
How to Commit Marriage '69

Hal Kanter
Here Come the Girls '53
Casanova's Big Night '54
Artists and Models '55
The Rose Tattoo '55
Loving You '57
Blue Hawaii '62
Dear Brigitte '65
Bachelor in Paradise '69

Deborah Kaplan
A Very Brady Sequel '96

Jonathan Kaplan
White Line Fever '75
Mr. Billion '77

Marty Kaplan
The Distinguished Gentleman '92
Noises Off '92
Striking Distance '93

Wong Kar-Wai
Chungking Express '95

Larry Karaszewski
Problem Child '90
Problem Child 2 '91
Ed Wood '94

Janice Karman
The Chipmunk Adventure '87

Tom Kartozian
Frozen Assets '92

Lawrence Kasdan
The Empire Strikes Back '80
Body Heat '81
Continental Divide '81
The Big Chill '83
Return of the Jedi '83
Silverado '85
The Accidental Tourist '88
Grand Canyon '91
The Bodyguard '92
Wyatt Earp '94

Meg Kasdan
Grand Canyon '91
MaryAnne Kasica
Tall, Dark and Deadly '95
Mathieu Kassovitz
Cafe au Lait '94
Hate '95
Jason Katims
The Pallbearer '95
Mitchel Katlin
Opportunity Knocks '90
A.L. Katz
Children of the Corn 2: The Final Sacrifice '92
Tales from the Crypt Presents Bordello of Blood '96
Douglas Katz
Age Isn't Everything '91
Gloria Katz
American Graffiti '73
Messiah of Evil '74
French Postcards '79
Best Defense '84
Indiana Jones and the Temple of Doom '84
Howard the Duck '86
Radioland Murders '94
Lee Katz
Waterfront '39
Steven Katz
Fallen Angels 1 '93
Charles Kaufman
Return to Paradise '53
Mother's Day '80
George S. Kaufman
The Cocoanuts '29
A Night at the Opera '35
Ken Kaufman
In the Army Now '94
Lloyd (Samuel Weil) Kaufman
The Toxic Avenger, Part 2 '89
The Toxic Avenger, Part 3: The Last Temptation of Toxie '89
Class of Nuke 'Em High 3: The Good, the Bad and the Subhumanoid '94
Millard Kaufman
The War Lord '65
Philip Kaufman
The Great Northfield Minnesota Raid '72
The Outlaw Josey Wales '76
Wanderers '79
Raiders of the Lost Ark '81
The Right Stuff '83
The Unbearable Lightness of Being '88
Henry & June '90
Rising Sun '93
Aki Kaurismaki
Ariel '89
Leningrad Cowboys Go America '89
The Match Factory Girl '90
La Vie de Boheme '93
Gina Kaus
All I Desire '53
Frances Kavanaugh
The Driftin' Kid '41
Dynamite Canyon '41
Riding the Sunset Trail '41
Driftin' River '46
Jerzy Kawalerowicz
Mother Joan of the Angels '60
Sandra Kay
Working Girls '87
Tony Kayden
Slipstream '89
Norman Kaye
Cactus '86
Richard Kaye
The Wizard of Speed and Time '88
Nicholas Kazan
Frances '82
At Close Range '86
Patty Hearst '88
Reversal of Fortune '90
Mobsters '91
Dream Lover '93
Matilda '96
Fran Rubel Kazui
Tokyo Pop '88
Tim Kazurinsky
About Last Night... '86
For Keeps '88
James Keach
Slashed Dreams '74
The Long Riders '80
Armed and Dangerous '86
The Forgotten '89
Stacy Keach
The Long Riders '80
Robert Keats
The Closer '91
Joe Keenan
Sleep with Me '94
Peter Keglevic
Kill Cruise '90
Michael Kehoe
Dominion '94
Harvey Keith
Jezebel's Kiss '90
John Kelleher
Eat the Peach '86
Wendy Kellelman
Sister My Sister '94
George Keller
Six in Paris '68
Bob Kellett
Haunted '95
Nick Kellis
Endangered '94
Bob Kelljan
The Return of Count Yorga '71
Marjorie Kellogg
Rosebud '75
David Kelly
From the Hip '86
Mark Kelly
One in a Million '36
Rory Kelly
Sleep with Me '94
Kurt Kempler
The Big Stampede '32
Telegraph Trail '33
Anne Kennedy
Crush '93
Burt Kennedy
The Tall T '57
Ride Lonesome '59
The Rounders '65
Hannie Caulder '72
Train Robbers '73
The Trouble with Spies '87
Dynamite and Gold '88
White Hunter, Black Heart '90
Ken Kennedy
Iron Angel '64
Leon Isaac Kennedy
Knights of the City '85
Michael Kennedy
The Swordsman '92
William Kennedy
The Cotton Club '84
Ironweed '87
Doug Kenney
Caddyshack '80
Willis Kent
Mad Youth '40
Earl Kenton
Invisible: The Chronicles of Benjamin Knight '93
Mandroid '93
Roeland Kerbosch
For a Lost Soldier '93
Bill Kerby
Lakota Woman: Siege at Wounded Knee '94
James V. Kern
Never Say Goodbye '46
Sarah Kernochan
Impromptu '90
Sommersby '93
Lodge Kerrigan
Clean, Shaven '93
Claude Kerven
Mortal Thoughts '91
Emmanuel Kervyn
Rabid Grannies '89
Ken Kesey
One Flew Over the Cuckoo's Nest '75
Lyle Kessler
Orphans '87
The Saint of Fort Washington '93
Larry Ketron
Freeway '88
Permanent Record '88
Michael Keusch
Samurai Cowboy '93
Christopher Keyser
Benefit of the Doubt '93
Riffat A. Khan
Feelin' Screwy '90
Edward Khmara
Enemy Mine '85
Ladyhawke '85
Dragon: The Bruce Lee Story '93
Callie Khouri
Thelma & Louise '91
Something to Talk About '95
Abbas Kiarostami
Through the Olive Trees '94
The White Balloon '95
Roland Kibbee
The Desert Song '53
Krzysztof Kieslowski
Camera Buff '79
No End '84
The Double Life of Veronique '91
Trois Couleurs: Bleu '93
Trois Couleurs: Rouge '94
Andrzej Kijowski
The Conductor '80
Hideyuki Kikuchi
A Wind Named Amnesia '93
Riyuzo Kikushima
Scandal '50
Throne of Blood '57
Jon Killough
Skinned Alive '89
Tom Kilpatrick
Dr. Cyclops '40
Alex S. Kim
3 Ninjas Knuckle Up '92
Richard H. Kim
Kill Line '91
Tim Kincaid
Mutant Hunt '87
Robot Holocaust '87
The Occultist '89
Chloe King
Red Shoe Diaries 3: Another Woman's Lipstick '93
Poison Ivy 2: Lily '95
I. Marlene King
National Lampoon's Senior Trip '95
Now and Then '95
Rick King
Hard Choices '84
Robert King
The Nest '88
Clean Slate '94
Speechless '94
Cutthroat Island '95
Robert Lee King
Boys Life '94
Stephen King
Creepshow '82
Cat's Eye '85
Silver Bullet '85
Maximum Overdrive '86
Pet Sematary '89
Graveyard Shift '90
Stephen King's It '90
Tales from the Darkside: The Movie '90
Sleepwalkers '92
Stephen King's The Stand '94
Zalman King
9 1/2 Weeks '86
Two Moon Junction '88
Wildfire '88
Wild Orchid '90
Lake Consequence '92
Wild Orchid 2: Two Shades of Blue '92
Red Shoe Diaries 3: Another Woman's Lipstick '93
Dorothy Kingsley
Broadway Rhythm '44
Angels in the Outfield '51
Don't Go Near the Water '57
Green Mansions '59
Valley of the Dolls '67
Ernest Kinoy
The Story of Jacob & Joseph '74
The Story of David '76
Murrow '86
Gore Vidal's Lincoln '88
Teinosuke Kinugasa
An Actor's Revenge '63
Karey Kirkpatrick
The Rescuers Down Under '90
David Kirschner
The Pagemaster '94
Leonard Kirtman
Carnival of Blood '71
Tim Kissell
In the Soup '92
Robert Klane
Unfaithfully Yours '84
National Lampoon's European Vacation '85
Weekend at Bernie's '89
Weekend at Bernie's 2 '93
Damian Klaus
Futurekick '91
Andrew Klavan
A Shock to the System '90
Dena Kleiman
Strapped '93
Dennis Klein
Family Dog: Complete Series '92
Don Klein
Frozen Assets '92
Stuart Klein
The Quest '96
Ted Klein
Dario Argento's Trauma '93
Randal Kleiser
It's My Party '95
Walter Klenhard
Dead in the Water '91
The Last Hit '93
The Haunting of Seacliff Inn '94
Richard Kletter
Dangerous Indiscretion '94
The Android Affair '95
Andre Klotzel
Savage Capitalism '93
Steven Kloves
Racing with the Moon '84
The Fabulous Baker Boys '89
Flesh and Bone '93
Nigel Kneale
First Men in the Moon '64
Sharpe's Gold '94
Andrew Knight
The Efficiency Expert '92
Patricia Louisianna Knop
9 1/2 Weeks '86
Siesta '87
Delta of Venus '95
Christopher Knopf
The King's Thief '55
Not My Kid '85
Bernard Knowles
Norman Conquest '53
Herman Koch
Wings of Fame '93
Howard Koch
The Letter '40
The Sea Hawk '40
Sergeant York '41
Casablanca '42
Rhapsody in Blue '45
War Lover '62
Laird Koeing
Black Water '94
Kip Koenig
Bio-Dome '96
David Koepp
Apartment Zero '88
Death Becomes Her '92
Carlito's Way '93
Jurassic Park '93
The Paper '94
The Shadow '94
Mission: Impossible '96
The Trigger Effect '96
Steven Koepp
The Paper '94
Frederick Kohner
Three Daring Daughters '48
Ana Kokkinos
Only the Brave '94
Kenneth Kolb
The Seventh Voyage of Sinbad '58
Emil Kolbe
American Kickboxer 1 '91
Amos Kollek
Double Edge '92
Whore 2 '94
Xavier Koller
Journey of Hope '90
Manuel Komroff
Scarlet Empress '34
Andrei Konchalovsky
Andrei Rublev '66
Siberiade '79
Maria's Lovers '84
Runaway Train '85
The Inner Circle '91
Larry Konner
The Jewel of the Nile '85
The Beverly Hillbillies '93
For Love or Money '93
Tadeusz Konwicki
Mother Joan of the Angels '60
Peter Koper
Headless Body in Topless Bar '96
Arthur Kopit
Hands of a Stranger '87
The Phantom of the Opera '90
Roswell: The U.F.O. Cover-Up '94
Rachel Koretsky
The Pebble and the Penguin '94
Harmony Korine
Kids '95
Randy Kornfield
Incident at Deception Ridge '94
Bloodknot '95
Mari Kornhauser
Zandalee '91
The Last Ride '94
Ken Koser
Sudie & Simpson '90
Ron Koslow
Into the Night '85
Last Dance '96
John Kostmayer
I Love You to Death '90
William Kotzwinkle
Book of Love '91
Jim Kouf
Stakeout '87
Another Stakeout '93
Operation Dumbo Drop '95
Dusan Kovacevic
Underground '95
Janet Kovalcik
Married to It '93
My Girl 2 '94
Scott Kraft
The Silencer '92
Andrzej Krakowski
Triumph of the Spirit '89
Eminent Domain '91

Martin Lynch
Prayer for the Dying '87

Barre Lyndon
House on 92nd Street '45
To Please a Lady '50

Jonathan Lynn
Clue '85
Nuns on the Run '90

Judd B. Lynn
Shootfighter: Fight to the Death '93

Fibe Ma
Rumble in the Bronx '96

Charles MacArthur
Rasputin and the Empress '32
Twentieth Century '34
Wuthering Heights '39

Nino Maccari
Two Nights with Cleopatra '54

Ruggero Maccari
The Family '87

Kurt MacCarley
Sexual Intent '94

Colin MacDonald
Sharpe's Honour '94

Mike MacDonald
Beauty School '93

Ranald MacDougall
Mildred Pierce '45
Objective, Burma! '45
June Bride '48
Queen Bee '55

Roger MacDougall
The Mouse That Roared '59

Patricia MacLachlan
Skylark '93
Journey '95

Bernard MacLaverty
Cal '84
Lamb '85
Hostages '93

Alison Maclean
Crush '93

Stephen MacLean
Around the World in 80 Ways '86

Matt MacManus
Flight of the Navigator '86

Angus MacPhail
Dead of Night '45

Don MacPherson
Absolute Beginners '86
The Big Man: Crossing the Line '91

Malcolm MacRury
The Man Without a Face '93

Guy Maddin
Careful '94

Brent Maddock
Short Circuit '86
*batteries not included '87
Short Circuit 2 '88
Tremors '89
Ghost Dad '90
Heart and Souls '93
Tremors 2: Aftershocks '96

Ben Maddow
The Asphalt Jungle '50

Robert Madero
All Tied Up '92

David Madsen
Copycat '95

Doug Magee
Somebody Has to Shoot the Picture '90

Maria Maggenti
The Incredibly True Adventure of Two Girls in Love '95

Mark Magidson
Baraka '93

Jymn Magon
A Goofy Movie '94

Gerard Maguire
Gross Misconduct '93

Jeff Maguire
Victory '81
In the Line of Fire '93

Redge Mahaffey
Deadly Rivals '92

John Lee Mahin
Love on the Run '36
Johnny Eager '42

Anthony Mahon
The Premonition '75

Clelle Mahon
Pagan Island '60

Richard Maibaum
Thunderball '65
S*H*E '79
The Living Daylights '87
License to Kill '89

Norman Mailer
King Lear '87
Tough Guys Don't Dance '87

Stewart Main
Desperate Remedies '93

Dusan Makavejev
Man Is Not a Bird '65
The Love Affair, or The Case of the Missing Switchboard Operator '67
Innocence Unprotected '68
WR: Mysteries of the Organism '71
Sweet Movie '75
Montenegro '81

Anne Makepeace
Thousand Pieces of Gold '91

Terence Malick
Pocket Money '72
Badlands '74
Days of Heaven '78

Gregory S. Malins
...And God Spoke '94

Louis Malle
The Lovers '59
Zazie dans le Metro '61
The Fire Within '64
Viva Maria! '65
Murmur of the Heart '71
Au Revoir Les Enfants '87
May Fools '90

Miles Malleson
Night Birds '31
Lorna Doone '34

James Mallon
Mystery Science Theater 3000: The Movie '96

Mark Malone
Dead of Winter '87
Signs of Life '89
Bulletproof Heart '95

Albert Maltz
This Gun for Hire '42
Cloak and Dagger '46
Broken Arrow '50
Two Mules for Sister Sara '70

David Mamet
The Postman Always Rings Twice '81
The Verdict '82
House of Games '87
The Untouchables '87
Things Change '88
We're No Angels '89
Homicide '91
Glengarry Glen Ross '92
Hoffa '92
The Water Engine '92
A Life in the Theater '93
Oleanna '94
Vanya on 42nd Street '94

Yuri Mamin
Window to Paris '95

Chan Man-keung
Summer Snow '94

Milcho Manchevski
Before the Rain '94

Don Mancini
Child's Play '88
Child's Play 2 '90
Child's Play 3 '91

Babaloo Mandel
Night Shift '82
Splash '84
Gung Ho '85
Spies Like Us '85
Vibes '88
Parenthood '89
City Slickers '91
A League of Their Own '92
Mr. Saturday Night '92
City Slickers 2: The Legend of Curly's Gold '94
Greedy '94
Forget Paris '95
Multiplicity '96

Cynthia Mandelberg
The Grace Kelly Story '83

Dharan Mandrayar
Ele, My Friend '93

Nino Manfredi
Bread and Chocolate '74

James Mangold
Oliver & Company '88
Heavy '94

Herman J. Mankiewicz
Dinner at Eight '33
Citizen Kane '41
A Woman's Secret '49
Pride of St. Louis '52

Joseph L. Mankiewicz
Diplomaniacs '33
Forsaking All Others '35
I Live My Life '35
The Keys of the Kingdom '44
A Letter to Three Wives '49
All About Eve '50
People Will Talk '51
Julius Caesar '53
The Barefoot Contessa '54
Guys and Dolls '55
Cleopatra '63
The Honey Pot '67

Tom Mankiewicz
Diamonds Are Forever '71
Live and Let Die '73
The Man with the Golden Gun '74
The Cassandra Crossing '76
Mother, Jugs and Speed '76
The Eagle Has Landed '77
Ladyhawke '85
Dragnet '87

Wolf Mankowitz
The Day the Earth Caught Fire '61

Abby Mann
Judgment at Nuremberg '61
A Child is Waiting '63
Ship of Fools '65
The Detective '68
Report to the Commissioner '74
King '78
Murderers among Us: The Simon Wiesenthal Story '89
Indictment: The McMartin Trial '95

Edward Mann
Cauldron of Blood '67

Farhad Mann
Lawnmower Man 2: Beyond Cyberspace '95

Michael Mann
Vegas '78
Thief '81
The Keep '83
Manhunter '86
The Last of the Mohicans '92
Heat '95

Myra Mann
Indictment: The McMartin Trial '95

Stanley Mann
The Mouse That Roared '59

K. Mannah
Bloodmatch '91

Albert Mannheimer
Three Daring Daughters '48

Bruce Manning
Mad About Music '38
First Love '39
Three Smart Girls Grow Up '39

Mark Manos
Liquid Dreams '92

Jean Manse
Forbidden Fruit '52

Michael Mansfield
The Bridge '59

Guido Manuli
Volere Volare '92

Xiao Mao
The Blue Kite '93

Scott Marcano
Bio-Dome '96

Robert Marcarelli
Original Intent '91

Joseph Moncure March
Hell's Angels '30

David Marconi
The Harvest '92

Lawrence B. Marcus
Petulia '68
Justine '69
The Stunt Man '80

Mitch Marcus
A Boy Called Hate '95

Andreas Marfori
Evil Clutch '89

Herbert Margolis
Ma and Pa Kettle '49
Francis in the Haunted House '56
The Kettles on Old MacDonald's Farm '57

Richard "Cheech" Marin
Cheech and Chong's Up in Smoke '79
Cheech and Chong's Next Movie '80
Cheech and Chong's Nice Dreams '81
Cheech and Chong: Things Are Tough All Over '82
Cheech and Chong: Still Smokin' '83
Cheech and Chong's The Corsican Brothers '84

Frances Marion
Tillie Wakes Up '17
The Wind '28
The Big House '30
The Champ '31
Dinner at Eight '33

Petros Markaris
Ulysses' Gaze '95

Chris Marker
Sans Soleil '82

Gene Markey
Female '33
On the Avenue '37

David Markov
Raging Angels '95

Goran Markovic
Tito and Me '92

Mitch Markowitz
Good Morning, Vietnam '87
Crazy People '90

Dennis Marks
Tom and Jerry: The Movie '93

Megan Marks
The Sister-in-Law '95

Ben Markson
Lady Killer '33

Brian Marlow
Supernatural '33

Brad Marlowe
At Home with the Webbers '94

Malia Scotch Marmo
Once Around '91

Malcolm Marmorstein
S*P*Y*S '74
Whiffs '75
Pete's Dragon '77
Return from Witch Mountain '78
Konrad '90s
Dead Men Don't Die '91

Gabriel Garcia Marquez
Letters from the Park '88
Miracle in Rome '88

Leon Marr
Dancing in the Dark '86

Andrew Marshall
Whoops Apocalypse '83

D.M. Marshman, Jr.
Sunset Boulevard '50

William Martel
Hard Evidence '94

Al Martin
Kelly of the Secret Service '36
Prison Shadows '36
Blondie Knows Best '46

Anne-Marie Martin
Twister '96

Charles Martin
My Dear Secretary '49

Darnell Martin
I Like It Like That '94

Francis Martin
We're Not Dressing '34
The Princess Comes Across '36
Rhythm on the Range '36
Waikiki Wedding '37
The Big Braodcast of 1938 '38
One Night in the Tropics '40

Mardik Martin
Mean Streets '73
New York, New York '77
Valentino '77
Raging Bull '80

Robert Martin
Basket Case 3: The Progeny '92

Steve Martin
The Jerk '79
Dead Men Don't Wear Plaid '82
The Man with Two Brains '83
Three Amigos '86
Roxanne '87
L.A. Story '91
A Simple Twist of Fate '94

Steven M. Martin
Theremin: An Electronic Odyssey '95

William E. Martin
Harry and the Hendersons '87

Wyre Martin
The Unearthing '93

Yves Andre Martin
The Shooter '94

Denny Martin Flinn
Star Trek 6: The Undiscovered Country '91

Raymond Martino
American Born '89
Angels of the City '89
DaVinci's War '92
To the Limit '95

Sergio Martino
Torso '73

Mike Marvin
Wishman '93

Arthur Marx
A Global Affair '63
I'll Take Sweden '65
Cancel My Reservation '72

R.J. Marx
C.O.D. '83
Outlaw of Gor '87
Platoon Leader '87
Dead Man Walking '88
Dragonard '88
Gor '88
Master of Dragonard Hill '89
Double Obsession '93

Judi Ann Mason
Sister Act 2: Back in the Habit '93

Lesley Mason
Man from Monterey '33

Sarah Y. Mason
Little Women '33
Golden Boy '39

Scott Mason
Ride Him, Cowboy '32

Olivier Massart
Wild Reeds '94

Icel Dobell Massey
Magic in the Water '95

Quentin Masters
PSI Factor '80

Nico Mastorakis
Blood Tide '82
Blind Date '84
Bloodstone '88
Glitch! '88
Hired to Kill '91

William Mastrosimone
Extremities '86
The Beast '88
Sinatra '92
The Burning Season '94
With Honors '94

Eddy Matalon
Sweet Killing '93

Diego Matamoros
Murdered Innocence '94

John C. Mather
Devil Girl from Mars '54

Chris Matheson
Bill & Ted's Excellent Adventure '89
Bill & Ted's Bogus Journey '91
A Goofy Movie '94
Mr. Wrong '95

Richard Matheson
The Incredible Shrinking Man '57
The Fall of the House of Usher '60
Master of the World '61
The Pit and the Pendulum '61
The Twilight Zone '61
Burn Witch, Burn! '62
Tales of Terror '62
The Raven '63
The Comedy of Terrors '64
Die! Die! My Darling! '65
Duel '71
Dying Room Only '73
The Legend of Hell House '73
Trilogy of Terror '75
Somewhere in Time '80
Jaws 3 '83
Young Warriors '83
Loose Cannons '90

Richard Christian Matheson
Three O'Clock High '87

Melissa Mathison
The Black Stallion '79
The Escape Artist '82
E.T.: The Extra-Terrestrial '82
The Indian in the Cupboard '95

Francisca Matos
A Million to Juan '94

Hajime Matsumoto
Zeram '91

Burny Mattinson
The Fox and the Hound '81

John Mattson
Milk Money '94
Free Willy 2: The Adventure Home '95

Ned Mauldin
Renaissance Man '94

J. Stephen Maunder
Talons of the Eagle '92

Armistead Maupin
The Celluloid Closet '95

Michael Maurer
Red Hot '95

Robert Mauri
The Slaughter of the Vampires '62

Garth Maxwell
Jack Be Nimble '94

Richard Maxwell
The Challenge '82
The Serpent and the Rainbow '87
Shadow of China '91

Ronald F. Maxwell
Gettysburg '93

Elaine May
A New Leaf '71
Mikey & Nicky '76
Heaven Can Wait '78
Ishtar '87
The Birdcage '95

Toshiro Mayazumi
Enjo '58

Bernard Maybeck
The Cover Girl Murders '93

Carl Mayer
Shattered '21

Daisy von Scherler Mayer
Party Girl '94

Edwin Justus Mayer
Desire '36
They Met in Bombay '41

Lise Mayer
Suite 16 '94

Wendell Mayes
Spirit of St. Louis '57
The Hunters '58
Anatomy of a Murder '59
The Hanging Tree '59
Advise and Consent '62
In Harm's Way '65
Von Ryan's Express '65
Hotel '67
The Poseidon Adventure '72
Bank Shot '74
Death Wish '74
Go Tell the Spartans '78
Love and Bullets '79
Monsignor '82

Melanie Mayron
Sticky Fingers '88

Dan Mazur
Night of the Scarecrow '95

Steve Mazur
The Little Rascals '94

Paul Mazursky
I Love You, Alice B. Toklas! '68
Bob & Carol & Ted & Alice '69
Alex in Wonderland '70
Blume in Love '73
Harry and Tonto '74
Next Stop, Greenwich Village '76
An Unmarried Woman '78
Willie & Phil '80
The Tempest '82
Moscow on the Hudson '84
Down and Out in Beverly Hills '86
Moon over Parador '88
Enemies, a Love Story '89
Scenes from a Mall '91
The Pickle '93

Jim McBride
David Holzman's Diary '67
Glen and Randa '71
Hot Times '74
Breathless '83
Great Balls of Fire '89

Robert McCahon
Running Wild '73

Leo McCarey
Love Affair '39
My Favorite Wife '40
Going My Way '44
An Affair to Remember '57

Louise McCarn
Walker: Texas Ranger: One Riot, One Ranger '93

John P. McCarthy
Beyond the Rockies '32

Peter McCarthy
Car 54, Where Are You? '94
Floundering '94

Todd McCarthy
Visions of Light: The Art of Cinematography '93

Nick McCarty
Merlin '92

John McClain
Cairo '42

Albert McCleery
The Lady is Willing '42

Jonas McCord
Class of '61 '92

John McCormick
Living on Tokyo Time '87

Pat McCormick
Under the Rainbow '81

Horace McCoy
The Texas Rangers Ride Again '40

Bruce McCulloch
Kids In the Hall Brain Candy '96

Jim McCullough, Jr.
The St. Tammany Miracle '94

Bruce McDonald
Dance Me Outside '95

John McDonald
By the Sword '93

Kevin McDonald
Kids In the Hall Brain Candy '96

Michael James McDonald
Revenge of the Red Baron '93

Kevin McDonough
I Was a Teenage TV Terrorist '87

Michael McDowell
Beetlejuice '88
Tales from the Darkside: The Movie '90

Maureen McElheron
The Tune '92

Alan B. McElroy
Rapid Fire '92

Ross McElwee
Sherman's March: An Improbable Search for Love '86
Time Indefinite '93

Ian McEwan
The Good Son '93
The Innocent '93

William F. McGaha
The Speed Lovers '68

Michael McGann
Leapin' Leprechauns '95

Mark Thomas McGee
Bad Girls from Mars '90
Sins of Desire '92

Rex McGee
Pure Country '92

Scott McGehee
Suture '93

Kathleen McGhee-Anderson
Sunset Park '96

Josann McGibbon
Worth Winning '89
Three Men and a Little Lady '90
The Favor '92

Jimmy McGovern
The Best of Cracker Mysteries '93
Priest '94

Dorrell McGowan
The Showdown '50

Stuart E. McGowan
The Showdown '50

Douglas McGrath
Born Yesterday '93
Bullets Over Broadway '94
Emma '96

John McGreevey
Hot Rod Girl '56
Night Crossing '81
Consenting Adult '85

Thomas McGuane
Rancho Deluxe '75
Missouri Breaks '76
92 in the Shade '76
Tom Horn '80
Cold Feet '89

Don McGuire
Meet Danny Wilson '52
The Delicate Delinquent '56
Suppose They Gave a War and Nobody Came? '70
Tootsie '82

William Anthony McGuire
The Great Ziegfeld '36

Jay McInerney
Hotel Room '93

Douglas Lloyd McIntosh
Disaster at Silo 7 '88

Chris McIntyre
Backstreet Justice '93

Dennis McIntyre
State of Grace '90

Jim McKay
Girls Town '95

Malcolm McKay
Maria's Child '93

Steven McKay
Diggstown '92
Darkman 2: The Return of Durant '94

Michael McKean
The Big Picture '89
The Return of Spinal Tap '92

Don McKellar
Roadkill '89
Highway 61 '91
32 Short Films about Glenn Gould '93
Dance Me Outside '95

Ian McKellen
Richard III '95

Bernard McKenna
Yellowbeard '83

Mark McKinney
Kids In the Hall Brain Candy '96

Duncan McLachlan
The Double O Kid '92
Born Wild '95

John McLaughlin
The Last Good Time '94

Sheila McLaughlin
She Must Be Seeing Things '87

Steve McLean
Postcards from America '95

Victor McLeod
Boss of Bullion City '41
Bury Me Not On the Lone Prairie '41
The Masked Rider '41

Robert McMullen
Hell's Belles '69

Larry McMurtry
The Last Picture Show '71
Montana '90
Memphis '91
Falling from Grace '92
Larry McMurtry's Streets of Laredo '95

Terrance McNally
Earth Girls Are Easy '89
Frankie and Johnny '91

John McNaughton
Henry: Portrait of a Serial Killer '90

Christopher McQuarrie
Public Access '93
The Usual Suspects '95

James McTernan
Small Kill '93

Kathy McWorter
The War '94

Nick Mead
Bank Robber '93

Herb Meadow
The Redhead from Wyoming '53

John Meagher
Fantasy Man '84

Irene Mecchi
The Lion King '94

Russell Medcroft
Angel '37

Mark Medoff
Good Guys Wear Black '78
Apology '86
Children of a Lesser God '86
Off Beat '86
Clara's Heart '88
City of Joy '92

Cary Medoway
The Heavenly Kid '85

John Meehan
Madame X '37
The Valley of Decision '45
Three Daring Daughters '48

Thomas Meehan
Annie '82
One Magic Christmas '85
Spaceballs '87

Leslie Megahey
The Advocate '93

Robert T. Megginson
F/X '86

Myron Meise
It's All True '93

Gordon Melbourne
Bulletproof Heart '95
White Tiger '95

Ib Melchior
Robinson Crusoe on Mars '64

James Melkonian
The Jerky Boys '95

Lewis Meltzer
Comanche Territory '50

Jean-Pierre Melville
Les Enfants Terrible '50

Ivan Menchell
The Cemetery Club '93

George Mendeluk
Stone Cold Dead '80

Ramon Menendez
Stand and Deliver '88
Money for Nothing '93

Robin Menken
Teen Witch '89

Nina Menkes
Queen of Diamonds '91

Tina "Tigr" Mennett
Kamikaze Hearts '91

Gian-Carlo Menotti
The Medium '51

Jiri Menzel
Closely Watched Trains '66
Larks on a String '68

Burgess Meredith
Yin & Yang of Mr. Go '71

Sean Meredith
Texas '94

James Merendino
Hard Drive '94

Joseph Merhi
Angels of the City '89
Last Man Standing '95

Agnes Merlet
The Son of the Shark '93

William Mernit
Private Lessons, Another Story '94

Lawrence Merrick
Black Bikers from Hell '70

Monte Merrick
Staying Together '89
Memphis Belle '90
Mr. Baseball '92
8 Seconds '94

Norman Merrill
The Taking of Flight 847: The Uli Derickson Story '88

Roger Merton
Down the Wyoming Trail '39

Stephen Metcalfe
Florida Straits '87
Cousins '89
Jacknife '89
Roommates '95

Tim Metcalfe
Revenge of the Nerds '84
Million Dollar Mystery '87
Three for the Road '87
Fright Night 2 '88
Iron Maze '91
Kalifornia '93

Andrew Meyer
Night of the Cobra Woman '72

Kevin Meyer
Invasion of Privacy '92
Under Investigation '93

Marlane X. Meyer
Better Off Dead '94
Nicholas Meyer
Invasion of the Bee Girls '73
The Seven-Per-Cent Solution '76
Time After Time '79
Star Trek 4: The Voyage Home '86
Company Business '91
Star Trek 6: The Undiscovered Country '91
Sommersby '93
Russ Meyer
Faster Pussycat! Kill! Kill! '66
Supervixens '75
Turi Meyer
Leprechaun 2 '94
Nancy Meyers
Private Benjamin '80
Irreconcilable Differences '84
Protocol '84
Baby Boom '87
Father of the Bride '91
Patrick Meyers
K2: The Ultimate High '92
Menno Meyjes
Foreign Student '94
Lorne Michaels
Three Amigos '86
Boleslaw Michalek
Danton '82
A Love in Germany '84
Dave Michener
The Fox and the Hound '81
The Great Mouse Detective '86
William Mickelberry
Woman Undone '95
Bette Midler
Divine Madness '80
Anne-Marie Mieville
Numero Deux '75
First Name: Carmen '83
Radu Mihaileanu
Trahir '93
Ted V. Mikels
The Astro-Zombies '67
The Corpse Grinders '71
Elfi Mikesch
Seduction: The Cruel Woman '89
Nikita Mikhalkov
Burnt by the Sun '94
Bernard Miles
The Guinea Pig '48
Lewis Milestone
Arch of Triumph '48
Djordje Milicevic
Victory '81
Runaway Train '85
Toby McTeague '87
Iron Will '93
John Milius
Evel Knievel '72
Jeremiah Johnson '72
Life & Times of Judge Roy Bean '72
Dillinger '73
Magnum Force '73
The Wind and the Lion '75
Big Wednesday '78
Apocalypse Now '79
Conan the Barbarian '82
Red Dawn '84
Farewell to the King '89
Geronimo: An American Legend '93
Clear and Present Danger '94
Ronald Millar
The Miniver Story '50
Never Let Me Go '53
Oscar Millard
Come to the Stable '49
No Highway in the Sky '51
The Conqueror '56
Annie Miller
The Little Thief '89
Arthur Miller
The Misfits '61
Everybody Wins '90

Chris Miller
Multiplicity '96
Claude Miller
This Sweet Sickness '77
The Little Thief '89
The Accompanist '93
F.E. Miller
Harlem Rides the Range '39
Frank Miller
RoboCop 3 '91
George Miller
Mad Max '80
The Road Warrior '82
Mad Max: Beyond Thunderdome '85
Lorenzo's Oil '92
Babe '95
Gregory Miller
Conflict of Interest '92
Harvey Miller
Private Benjamin '80
Jekyll & Hyde...Together Again '82
Cannonball Run 2 '84
Protocol '84
Bad Medicine '85
Getting Away With Murder '96
Jennifer Miller
Family Pictures '93
Michael Alexander Miller
Dream Man '94
Rebecca Miller
Angela '94
Seton I. Miller
Murders in the Zoo '33
Kid Galahad '37
The Adventures of Robin Hood '38
Here Comes Mr. Jordan '41
The Black Swan '42
Singapore '47
Istanbul '57
Winston Miller
Cavalry Charge '51
Bertram Millhauser
The Texans '38
The Invisible Man's Revenge '44
Andy Milligan
Man with Two Heads '72
The Rats are Coming! The Werewolves are Here! '72
Bill Milling
Body Trouble '92
Hugh Mills
Personal Property '37
Sherry Mills
The Adventures of Pinocchio '96
Paula Milne
Mad Love '95
Michael Miner
RoboCop '87
Deadly Weapon '88
Anthony Minghella
Truly, Madly, Deeply '91
Joe Minion
Motorama '91
Susan Minot
Stealing Beauty '96
Brad Mirman
Body of Evidence '92
Knight Moves '93
Yukio Mishima
Black Lizard '68
C. Gaby Mitchell
Fallen Angels 2 '93
Duke Mitchell
The Executioner '78
Gene Mitchell
The Takeover '94
Julian Mitchell
Elizabeth R '72
August '95
Keith Mitchell
Eddie '96
Melissa Mitchell
Temptress '95

Robert Mitchum
Thunder Road '58
Robert Mittenthal
Hail Caesar '94
Phil Mittleman
Wes Craven Presents Mind Ripper '95
Hayao Miyazaki
My Neighbor Totoro '93
Wilson Mizner
Heroes for Sale '33
Moshe Mizrahi
I Love You Rosa '72
I Sent a Letter to My Love '81
La Vie Continue '82
Every Time We Say Goodbye '86
Peter Modos
A Happy New Year! '79
David Moessinger
Daddy-O '59
John Moffitt
Rhythm on the Range '36
Clifford Mohr
Lady Dragon 2 '93
Edouard Molinaro
Pain in the A— '77
Ferenc Molnar
Tales of Manhattan '42
Paul Monash
Bail Out at 43,000 '57
Scarface Mob '62
Stalin '92
Kingfish: A Story of Huey P. Long '95
Nate Monaster
Call Me Bwana '63
Paul Mones
Fathers and Sons '92
Saints and Sinners '95
The Quest '96
Peter Mones
The Beat '88
Christopher Monger
Waiting for the Light '90
The Englishman Who Went Up a Hill But Came Down a Mountain '95
John Monks, Jr.
House on 92nd Street '45
Knock on Any Door '49
The West Point Story '50
Carl Monson
The Acid Eaters '67
Eric Monte
Cooley High '75
Enzo Monteleone
Hotel Colonial '88
Eduardo Montes
Double Obsession '93
Jorge Montesi
Soft Deceit '94
Jennifer Montgomery
Art for Teachers of Children '95
Mark Montgomery
South Beach '92
Brian Moore
Torn Curtain '66
The Blood of Others '84
Black Robe '91
Charles Philip Moore
Black Belt '92
Dudley Moore
Bedazzled '68
30 Is a Dangerous Age, Cynthia '68
The Hound of the Baskervilles '77
Michael Moore
Roger & Me '89
Canadian Bacon '94
Ronald D. Moore
Star Trek Generations '94
Star Trek the Next Generation, the Final Episode: All Good Things... '94
Ronald W. Moore
Future Kill '85

Simon Moore
Under Suspicion '92
The Quick and the Dead '94
Gulliver's Travels '95
Wesley Moore
Apprentice to Murder '88
Are You Lonesome Tonight '92
Jocelyn Moorhouse
Proof '91
E. Edwin Moran
Wintertime '43
Jack Moran
Faster Pussycat! Kill! Kill! '66
Martha Moran
Happily Ever After '93
Patrick Moran
Dark Universe '93
Paul Morand
Don Quixote '35
Rick Moranis
Strange Brew '83
Miguel Morayta
Invasion of the Vampires '61
Gerard Mordillat
My Life and Times with Antonin Artaud '93
Nanni Moretti
Caro Diario '93
Rafael Moreu
Hackers '95
Larry Morey
Bambi '42
Denise Morgan
An Indecent Obsession '85
Glen Morgan
The Boys Next Door '85
Peter Morgan
The Silent Touch '94
Richard Morgieve
A la Mode '94
Joe Morhaim
Doc Savage '75
Louis Morheim
Ma and Pa Kettle '49
The Beast from 20,000 Fathoms '53
Yoshimitsu Morita
The Family Game '83
Louis Morneau
Final Judgement '92
Tony Morphett
Sweet Talker '91
Crime Broker '94
Michael Morpugo
When the Whales Came '89
David Burton Morris
Patti Rocks '88
Howard J. Morris
Mr. Write '92
Richard Morris
Ma and Pa Kettle at the Fair '52
Thoroughly Modern Millie '67
Paul Morrissey
Andy Warhol's Dracula '74
Andy Warhol's Frankenstein '74
The Hound of the Baskervilles '77
Mixed Blood '84
Beethoven's Nephew '88
Spike of Bensonhurst '88
Barry Morrow
Rain Man '88
Race the Sun '96
Douglas S. Morrow
The Stratton Story '49
Jim Thorpe: All American '51
Beyond a Reasonable Doubt '56
John Mortimer
24 Hours in a Woman's Life '61
Penelope Mortimer
A Summer Story '88
Lisa Morton
Adventures in Dinosaur City '92
Ben Moses
Nickel & Dime '92

Harry Moses
Assault at West Point: The Court-Martial of Johnson Whittaker '94
D. Brent Mote
Deep Red '94
Mark Mothersbaugh
The New Age '94
Laurent Moussard
Trahir '93
Marcel Moussey
The 400 Blows '59
Shoot the Piano Player '62
Allan Moyle
Pump Up the Volume '90
The Thing Called Love '93
Danny Mulheron
Meet the Feebles '89
Jim Mulholland
Ratings Game '84
Amazon Women on the Moon '87
Oscar '91
Bad Boys '95
National Lampoon's Favorite Deadly Sins '95
Chris Mulkey
Patti Rocks '88
Christopher Munch
The Hours and Times '92
Color of a Brisk and Leaping Day '95
Rona Munro
Ladybird, Ladybird '93
Craig Munson
Mr. Wrong '95
Ryu Murakami
Tokyo Decadence '91
John Murdy
Sorority House Party '92
Jane Murfin
The Shining Hour '38
Charles Murphy
Vampire in Brooklyn '95
Gary Murphy
Without a Clue '88
Geoff Murphy
Dark of the Night '85
Kevin Murphy
Mystery Science Theater 3000: The Movie '96
Richard Murphy
Boomerang '47
Compulsion '59
Tab Murphy
The Last of the Dogmen '95
Don Murray
The Hoodlum Priest '61
Confessions of Tom Harris '72
Michael J. Murray
The House of Usher '88
The Lightning Incident '91
Honor Thy Father and Mother: The True Story of the Menendez Brothers '94
Madonna: Innocence Lost '95
Tom Musca
Stand and Deliver '88
Money for Nothing '93
Clarence Muse
Way Down South '39
John Musker
The Little Mermaid '89
Aladdin '92
M.M. Musselman
The Three Musketeers '39
Floyd Mutrux
American Me '92
There Goes My Baby '92
Blood In...Blood Out: Bound by Honor '93
Cindy Myers
Bed & Breakfast '92
Henry Myers
Diplomaniacs '33
Destry Rides Again '39
Mike Myers
Wayne's World '92

Myers ▶cont.

So I Married an Axe Murderer '93
Wayne's World 2 '93

Nancy Myers
I Love Trouble '94
Father of the Bride Part II '95

Scott Myers
K-9 '89

Stanley Myers
Middlemarch '93

Zion Myers
April Fool '26
Here Come the Waves '44

John Myhers
The Private Eyes '80
The Longshot '86
Terror in Beverly Hills '90

Ed Naha
Dolls '87
Honey, I Shrunk the Kids '89

Suzanne Glazener Naha
Dragonworld '94

Kenji Nakagami
Himatsuri '85

Takehiro Nakajima
Okoge '93

Desmond Nakano
American Me '92
White Man's Burden '95

Ed Namzug
Redwood Curtain '95

Michael Nankin
Gate 2 '92

Jay Naples
Ski School 2 '94

Lisandro Duque Naranjo
Miracle in Rome '88

Paul Naschy
Dracula vs. Frankenstein '69
The Fury of the Wolfman '70
Curse of the Devil '73
House of Psychotic Women '73
The Mummy's Revenge '73
Inquisition '76
Human Beasts '80

N. Richard Nash
Helen of Troy '56
The Rainmaker '56
One Summer Love '76

Ogden Nash
The Shining Hour '38

Mort Nathan
Kingpin '96

Robert Nathan
In the Deep Woods '91

Jeff Nathanson
For Better or Worse '95

Maria Nation
Blue River '95

Jack Natteford
The Crimson Trail '35

Gregory Nava
End of August '82
El Norte '83
A Time of Destiny '88
My Family '94

Jeff Neal
Virgin High '90

Christopher Neame
Feast of July '95

Hal Needham
Stroker Ace '83

Jake Raymond Needham
Natural Causes '94

William Neff
I Was a Male War Bride '49

Troy Neighbors
Fortress '93

B.J. Nelson
Scanners 2: The New Order '91

Carl Nelson
Talking About Sex '94

Davia Nelson
Imaginary Crimes '94

Jessie Nelson
Corrina, Corrina '94

John Allen Nelson
Best of the Best 2 '93
American Yakuza '94

Judd Nelson
Every Breath '93

Michael J. Nelson
Mystery Science Theater 3000: The Movie '96

Peter Nelson
The Lonely Passion of Judith Hearne '87
Getting Up and Going Home '92

Richard Nelson
Ethan Frome '92

Dennis Nemec
God Bless the Child '88
The Avenging Angel '95

Jan Nemec
Diamonds of the Night '64
The Report on the Party and the Guests '66

Avi Nesher
Doppelganger: The Evil Within '90
Timebomb '91

Edward Neumeier
RoboCop '87

John Thomas Neville
Trader Horn '31

Martin Newlin
The Crawlers '93

David Newman
Bonnie & Clyde '67
There was a Crooked Man '70
Bad Company '72
What's Up, Doc? '72
Superman: The Movie '78
Superman 2 '80
Jinxed '82
Still of the Night '82
Superman 3 '83
Sheena '84
Santa Claus: The Movie '85

Randy Newman
Three Amigos '86

Samuel Newman
Invisible Invaders '59

Ted Newsom
Dracula: A Cinematic Scrapbook '91
Frankenstein: A Cinematic Scrapbook '91

Mbongeni Ngema
Sarafina! '92

Sloan Nibley
Hostile Guns '67

Fred Niblo
The Fighting 69th '40

Maurizio Nichetti
Volere Volare '92
Stephano Quantestorie '93

Allan Nicholls
A Wedding '78

Dudley Nichols
The Crusades '35
The Informer '35
She '35
Bringing Up Baby '38
For Whom the Bell Tolls '43
The Fugitive '48
Pinky '49
Prince Valiant '54

Jack Nicholson
Flight to Fury '66
Ride in the Whirlwind '67
The Trip '67
Head '68

William Nicholson
A Private Matter '92
Sarafina! '92
Shadowlands '93
Nell '94
First Knight '95

Nicholas Niciphor
Fatal Charm '92

Daryl G. Nickens
House Party 2: The Pajama Jam '91

Ted Nicolaou
Terrorvision '86
Bloodstone: Subspecies 2 '92
Bloodlust: Subspecies 3 '93
Dragonworld '94
Leapin' Leprechauns '95

Alison Nigh
Out There '95

Rob Nilsson
Northern Lights '79
Signal 7 '83
On the Edge '86
Heat and Sunlight '87

Susan D. Nimm
Ava's Magical Adventure '94

Brian Nissen
The Swan Princess '94

Chris Noonan
Babe '95

Tom Noonan
What Happened Was... '94

Michael Norell
Diamond Fleece '92

Marc Norman
Oklahoma Crude '73
Zandy's Bride '74
The Killer Elite '75
The Aviator '85
Bat 21 '88
Cutthroat Island '95
Waterworld '95

Marsha Norman
'night, Mother '86

Michael Normand
Leon the Pig Farmer '93

Chuck Norris
Braddock: Missing in Action 3 '88

Pamela Norris
Troop Beverly Hills '89

William J. Norris
Re-Animator '84

Edmund H. North
Flamingo Road '49
The Day the Earth Stood Still '51
Cowboy '58
Patton '70

William W. Norton, Sr.
The Scalphunters '68
McKenzie Break '70
White Lightning '73
Big Bad Mama '74
Brannigan '75
Gator '76
Moving Violation '76
A Small Town in Texas '76
Day of the Animals '77
Night of the Juggler '80
Dirty Tricks '81

Frank Norwood
Past Midnight '92

Blaine Novak
Strangers Kiss '83

Betriz Novaro
Danzon '91

Maria Novaro
Danzon '91

Louis Nowra
Map of the Human Heart '93

Simon Nuchtern
The Rejuvenator '88

Frank Nugent
The Quiet Man '52
Mister Roberts '55
The Searchers '56

Victor Nunez
A Flash of Green '85
Ruby in Paradise '93

Ilya Nusinov
Rasputin '85

Bruno Nuytten
Camille Claudel '89

Joseph Nuzzolo
Kill or Be Killed '93

Nelson Nye
Seven Sixgunners '87

Sven Nykvist
The Ox '91

Ron Nyswaner
Smithereens '82
Mrs. Soffel '84
Purple Hearts '84
Swing Shift '84
Prince of Pennsylvania '88
Gross Anatomy '89
Love Hurts '91
Philadelphia '93

Dan O'Bannon
Dark Star '74
Alien '79
Dead and Buried '81
Blue Thunder '83
Lifeforce '85
Invaders from Mars '86
Total Recall '90
Screamers '96

Rockne S. O'Bannon
Alien Nation '88

Margaret Grieco Oberman
Troop Beverly Hills '89

Arch Oboler
One Plus One '61

Raymond Obon
Black Pit of Dr. M '47

Edna O'Brien
X, Y & Zee '72

Liam O'Brien
Young at Heart '54

Robert O'Brien
Lady On a Train '45
The Lemon Drop Kid '51
By the Light of the Silvery Moon '53

Jeffrey Obrow
The Kindred '87

Maurice O'Callaghan
Broken Harvest '95

Raoul O'Connell
Boys Life '94

Pat O'Connor
The January Man '89

David Odell
Cry Uncle '71
The Dark Crystal '82

Clifford Odets
The General Died at Dawn '36
None But the Lonely Heart '44
Deadline at Dawn '46
Sweet Smell of Success '57
Wild in the Country '61

Joseph O'Donnell
Border Caballero '36

Michael O'Donoghue
Scrooged '88

Steve Oedekerk
Ace Ventura: When Nature Calls '95
The Nutty Professor '96

Hideo Oguni
Throne of Blood '57
Yojimbo '61
Ran '85

Colo Tavernier O'Hagan
A Sunday in the Country '84
Beatrice '88
The Story of Women '88
Daddy Nostalgia '90
L'Appat '94

Paul Ohl
Highlander: The Final Dimension '94

Kazuki Ohmori
Godzilla vs. Biollante '89

Steven Okazaki
Living on Tokyo Time '87

Kazuyoshi Okuyama
The Mystery of Rampo '94

Sidney Olcott
From the Manger to the Cross '15

Ronan O'Leary
Frankie Starlight '95

Joel Oliansky
The Todd Killings '71
Bird '88

David Oliver
Cave Girl '85

Deanna Oliver
Casper '95

Ron Oliver
Hello Mary Lou: Prom Night 2 '87
Liar's Edge '92

Ruby L. Oliver
Love Your Mama '89

Laurence Olivier
Henry V '44

Ermanno Olmi
Fiances '63
The Tree of Wooden Clogs '78

Arne Olsen
Red Scorpion '89
Cop and a Half '93
Final Round '93
All Dogs Go to Heaven 2 '95
Mighty Morphin Power Rangers: The Movie '95

David O'Malley
Mountain Man '77
Hangar 18 '80
Kid Colter '85
Easy Wheels '89
Edge of Honor '91
Fatal Instinct '93

Carlo Ombra
Dracula Blows His Cool '82

Robert Vincent O'Neil
The Baltimore Bullet '80
Vice Squad '82
Deadly Force '83
Jailbait '93

Eugene O'Neill
Long Day's Journey into Night '62

Max Ophuls
Lola Montes '55
Modigliani '58

Joaquin Oristrell
Mouth to Mouth '95

Ron Ormond
Yes, Sir, Mr. Bones '51

Peter Ormrod
Eat the Peach '86

Alan Ormsby
Children Shouldn't Play with Dead Things '72
Deathdream '72
Little Dragons '80
My Bodyguard '80
Touch & Go '80
Cat People '82
Porky's 2: The Next Day '83
Popcorn '89
Indecency '92
The Substitute '96

Gary Orona
Stripshow '95

James Orr
Breaking All the Rules '85
Tough Guys '86
Three Men and a Baby '87
Mr. Destiny '90
Sister Act 2: Back in the Habit '93
Man of the House '95

Erik Orsenna
Indochine '92

Paul Osborn
The Young in Heart '38
Homecoming '48
East of Eden '54

Ron Osborn
Radioland Murders '94

John Osborne
Look Back in Anger '58
The Entertainer '60

Robert Pirosh
Battleground '49
Hell is for Heroes '62

Mark Pirro
Deathrow Gameshow '88
My Mom's a Werewolf '89
Buford's Beach Bunnies '92

Glen Pitre
Belizaire the Cajun '86

C. William Pitt
Monaco Forever '83

Angelo Pizzo
Hoosiers '86
Rudy '93

Alan Plater
The Virgin and the Gypsy '70
Priest of Love '81
Fortunes of War '87
Coming Through '90

Jonathan Platnick
Silent Victim '92

Allen Plone
Sweet Justice '92

Terry Plumeri
Relentless 4 '94

Bill Plympton
The Tune '92

George Plympton
Doomed at Sundown '37
Feud Maker '38

Rick Podell
Nothing in Common '86

Amos Poe
The Foreigner '78
Alphabet City '84
Rocket Gibraltar '88

James Poe
Around the World in 80 Days '56
Cat on a Hot Tin Roof '58
Toys in the Attic '63
Riot '69
The Nightman '93

Benoit Poelvoorde
Man Bites Dog '91

Charles Edward Pogue
The Fly '86
Psycho 3 '86
D.O.A. '88
Hands of a Murderer '90
Dragonheart '96

Gregory Poirier
The Stranger '95

Roman Polanski
Knife in the Water '62
Repulsion '65
Cul de Sac '66
The Fearless Vampire Killers '67
Rosemary's Baby '68
Diary of Forbidden Dreams '73
The Tenant '76
Tess '80
Pirates '86
Frantic '88
Bitter Moon '92

Stephen Poliakoff
Century '94

Jeff Pollack
Above the Rim '94

Jean-Daniel Pollet
Six in Paris '68

Jeffrey Polman
Benefit of the Doubt '93

Eddy Polon
Nickel & Dime '92

Vicki Polon
Girlfriends '78
Mr. Wonderful '93

Abraham Polonsky
Body and Soul '47
Golden Earrings '47
Force of Evil '49
Madigan '68
Tell Them Willie Boy Is Here '69
Avalanche Express '79
Monsignor '82

Barry Poltermann
The Unearthing '93

Darryl Ponicsan
Cinderella Liberty '73
Taps '81
Vision Quest '85
Nuts '87
The Boost '88
School Ties '92
The Enemy Within '94

Gillo Pontecorvo
Kapo '59

DJ Pooh
Friday '95

Robert Roy Pool
Outbreak '94

Duane Poole
Sunstroke '92
Praying Mantis '93
The Man in the Attic '94

Eric Poppen
Virtual Assassin '95

Andrea Porporati
Lamerica '95

Joel Posner
Getting In '94

P.J. Posner
Getting In '94

Dennis Potter
Pennies From Heaven '81
Brimstone & Treacle '82
Gorky Park '83
Dreamchild '85
Track 29 '88
Christabel '89
Lipstick On Your Collar '94

Sally Potter
Orlando '92

Michael W. Potts
Night Eyes 3 '93
Tropical Heat '93

Peter Poulsen
Sofie '92

Michael Powell
Edge of the World '37
The Red Shoes '48
The Elusive Pimpernel '50

Tristam Powell
American Friends '91

Udana Power
The Voyeur '94

Tim Prager
Haunted '95

Leonard Praskins
One in a Million '36

John Prebble
Elizabeth R '72

Burt Prelutsky
A Winner Never Quits '86

Eric Lee Preminger
Rosebud '75

Robert Presnell
Employees' Entrance '33

Emeric Pressburger
The Forty-Ninth Parallel '41
The Red Shoes '48
The Elusive Pimpernel '50

Steven Pressfield
King Kong Lives '86
Above the Law '88
Freejack '92
Army of One '94
Separate Lives '94

Kenneth Pressman
Diary of a Hitman '91

Gaylene Preston
Dark of the Night '85

Trevor Preston
Thicker Than Water '93

Jacques Prevert
The Crime of Monsieur Lange '36
Les Visiteurs du Soir '42
Children of Paradise '44

Dan Price
The Crawlers '93

Jeffrey Price
Trenchcoat '83
Who Framed Roger Rabbit '88
Doc Hollywood '91

Richard Price
The Color of Money '86
Streets of Gold '86
New York Stories '89
Sea of Love '89
Night and the City '92
Mad Dog and Glory '93
Kiss of Death '94
Clockers '95

Stanley Price
Genghis Cohn '93

Tim Rose Price
Dark Obsession '90
A Dangerous Man: Lawrence after Arabia '91
Rapa Nui '93

James Prideaux
The Man Upstairs '93

J.B. Priestley
Last Holiday '50

Joseph Prieto
Savages from Hell '68

Jerome Prieur
My Life and Times with Antonin Artaud '93

Barry Primus
Mistress '91

Prince
Graffiti Bridge '90

Jonathan Prince
18 Again! '88

Peter Prince
The Hit '85
Waterland '92

Allan Prior
The Charmer '89

David A. Prior
Deadly Prey '87
Hell on the Battleground '88
Final Sanction '89
Deadly Dancer '90
Raw Nerve '91
Mardi Gras for the Devil '93
Raw Justice '93
Felony '95
Mutant Species '95

David Pritchard
Slashed Dreams '74
Violent Zone '89

Vincent J. Privitera
Witchfire '86

Leon Prochnik
Four Eyes and Six Guns '93

Elaine Proctor
Friends '95

Pat Proft
Bachelor Party '84
Police Academy '84
Moving Violations '85
Real Genius '85
Lucky Stiff '88
The Naked Gun: From the Files of Police Squad '88
Hot Shots! '91
Naked Gun 2 1/2: The Smell of Fear '91
Brain Donors '92
Hot Shots! Part Deux '93
Naked Gun 33 1/3: The Final Insult '94

Chip Proser
Iceman '84
Innerspace '87

Giorgio Prosperi
The Seven Hills of Rome '58
The Naked Maja '59

Monique Proulx
Le Sexe des Etoiles '93

Richard Pryor
Blazing Saddles '74
Bustin' Loose '81
Jo Jo Dancer, Your Life is Calling '86

Geof Pryssir
The Magic Bubble '93

Robert Pucci
The Spider and the Fly '94

Luis Puenzo
The Official Story '85
Old Gringo '89

Jack Pulman
Poldark '75

Gertrude Purcell
Destry Rides Again '39
The Invisible Woman '40
One Night in the Tropics '40
Follow the Boys '44

Jon Purdy
Reflections in the Dark '94

Charles Purpura
Heaven Help Us '85
Satisfaction '88

Tony Puryear
Eraser '96

Mario Puzo
The Godfather '72
Earthquake '74
The Godfather, Part 2 '74
Superman: The Movie '78
Superman 2 '80
The Godfather 1902-1959: The Complete Epic '81
The Cotton Club '84
The Godfather, Part 3 '90
Christopher Columbus: The Discovery '92

Daniel Pyne
Pacific Heights '90
Doc Hollywood '91
The Hard Way '91
White Sands '92

Albert Pyun
Sword & the Sorcerer '82
Radioactive Dreams '86
Alien from L.A. '87
Down Twisted '89
Knights '93
Nemesis 3: Time Lapse '96

Paris Qualles
The Inkwell '94
The Tuskegee Airmen '95

Darryl Quarles
Soldier Boyz '95

Paul Quarrington
Perfectly Normal '91
Camilla '94
Whale Music '94

Jonas Quastel
Crackerjack '94

Raymond Queneau
Death in the Garden '56

Florence Quentin
Life Is a Long Quiet River '88

Pascal Quignard
Tous les Matins du Monde '92
A Pure Formality '94

Richard Quine
My Sister Eileen '55

Gene Quintano
Making the Grade '84
King Solomon's Mines '85
Allan Quatermain and the Lost City of Gold '86
Police Academy 3: Back in Training '86
Police Academy 4: Citizens on Patrol '87
Honeymoon Academy '90
National Lampoon's Loaded Weapon 1 '93
Operation Dumbo Drop '95
Sudden Death '95

David Rabe
I'm Dancing as Fast as I Can '82
Streamers '83
Casualties of War '89

Martin Rackin
The Enforcer '51
The Stooge '51

Peter Rader
Waterworld '95

Michael Radford
The Postman '94

Geza Radvanyi
Women in Prison '49

Bob Rafelson
Head '68
Five Easy Pieces '70
Stay Hungry '76
Mountains of the Moon '90

Stewart Raffill
Napoleon and Samantha '72
Across the Great Divide '76
The Adventures of the Wilderness Family '76
Sea Gypsies '78
Ice Pirates '84
Mac and Me '88

Deborah Raffin
Morning Glory '93

John Raffo
Dragon: The Bruce Lee Story '93

Martin Ragaway
Abbott and Costello in the Foreign Legion '50
Ma and Pa Kettle Go to Town '50
Lost in Alaska '52

Wess Rahn
Enemy Gold '93

Philip Railsback
The Stars Fell on Henrietta '94

Steve Railsback
The Forgotten '89

Ivan Raimi
Easy Wheels '89
Darkman '90
Army of Darkness '92

Sam Raimi
Evil Dead '83
Crimewave '85
Evil Dead 2: Dead by Dawn '87
Darkman '90
Army of Darkness '92
The Hudsucker Proxy '93

Norman Reilly Raine
The Adventures of Robin Hood '38
The Fighting 69th '40

Yvonne Rainer
The Man Who Envied Women '85

Frank Rainone
Me and the Mob '94

Harold Ramis
National Lampoon's Animal House '78
Meatballs '79
Caddyshack '80
Stripes '81
National Lampoon's Vacation '83
Ghostbusters '84
Armed and Dangerous '86
Back to School '86
Club Paradise '86
Caddyshack 2 '88
Ghostbusters 2 '89
Rover Dangerfield '91
Groundhog Day '93
Multiplicity '96

Robert Ramsey
Destiny Turns on the Radio '95

Nick Randall
Chrome Soldiers '92

Joe Ranft
The Rescuers Down Under '90

Mort Ransen
Margaret's Museum '95

Whitney Ransick
Hand Gun '93
The Outfit '93

Peter Ransley
The Hawk '93

Frederic Raphael
Bachelor of Hearts '58
Darling '65
Far from the Madding Crowd '67
Two for the Road '67
Daisy Miller '74
Rogue Male '76
Richard's Things '80
The King's Whore '90

Samson Raphaelson
Angel '37

I.C. Rapoport
Living Proof: The Hank Williams Jr. Story '83
Jericho Fever '93

Ezra D. Rappaport
Deja Vu '84
Harry and the Hendersons '87

Mark Rappaport
Rock Hudson's Home Movies '92

Elisabeth Rappeneau
One Woman or Two '85

Jean-Paul Rappeneau
That Man from Rio '64
Lovers Like Us '75
Cyrano de Bergerac '90
The Horseman on the Roof '95

Judith Rascoe
Who'll Stop the Rain? '78
Endless Love '81
Eat a Bowl of Tea '89
Havana '90

Daniel Raskov
A Kiss Goodnight '94

Tina Rathborne
Zelly & Me '88

Aubrey Rattan
Original Gangstas '96

Terence Rattigan
The Day Will Dawn '42
The Winslow Boy '48
The Prince and the Showgirl '57
The V.I.P.'s '63

Irving Ravetch
Ten Wanted Men '54
The Long, Hot Summer '58
Home from the Hill '60
Hud '63
Hombre '67
The Reivers '69
The Cowboys '72
Conrack '74
Norma Rae '79
Murphy's Romance '85
Stanley and Iris '90

Rand Ravich
Candyman 2: Farewell to the Flesh '94

Jeff Rawle
The Young Poisoner's Handbook '94

Billy Ray
Color of Night '94
The Shooter '94

Satyajit Ray
Pather Panchali '54
The World of Apu '59
Two Daughters '61
The Adversary '71

David Rayfiel
Valdez is Coming '71
Three Days of the Condor '75
Lipstick '76
Death Watch '80
Round Midnight '86
Havana '90
The Firm '93
Intersection '93
Sabrina '95

Chet Raymo
Frankie Starlight '95

William Raynor
Francis in the Haunted House '56
The Kettles on Old MacDonald's Farm '57

Jan Read
Jason and the Argonauts '63
First Men in the Moon '64

Theresa Rebeck
Harriet the Spy '96

Eric Red
The Hitcher '86
Near Dark '87
Cohen and Tate '88
Blue Steel '90
Body Parts '91
The Last Outlaw '93
Undertow '95

Robert Redlin
After Dark, My Sweet '90

Joel M. Reed
Night of the Zombies '81

Tom Reed
Pittsburgh '42

Matt Reeves
The Pallbearer '95

Michael Reeves
Batman: Mask of the Phantasm '93

Theodore Reeves
Internes Can't Take Money '37
National Velvet '44

Steven Reich
Rage and Honor 2: Hostile Takeover '93

Ethan Reiff
Men of War '94
Tales from the Crypt Presents Demon Knight '94
Josh Kirby...Time Warrior: Chapter 1, Planet of the Dino-Knights '95
Josh Kirby...Time Warrior: Chapter 2, The Human Pets '95
Josh Kirby...Time Warrior: Chapter 5, Journey to the Magic Cavern '96
Josh Kirby...Time Warrior: Chapter 6, Last Battle for the Universe '96

William Reilly
Men of Respect '91
Mortal Thoughts '91

Carl Reiner
The Thrill of It All! '63
Enter Laughing '67
The Comic '69
Dead Men Don't Wear Plaid '82
The Man with Two Brains '83
Bert Rigby, You're a Fool '89

Jeff Reiner
Blood & Concrete: A Love Story '90

Lucas Reiner
Spirit of '76 '91

Al Reinert
Apollo 13 '95

Bety Reinhardt
His Butler's Sister '43

Gottfried Reinhardt
I Live My Life '35

Walter Reisch
Somewhere I'll Find You '42
Titanic '53

Richard Reitinger
Faraway, So Close! '93

Duncan Renaldo
Bells of San Fernando '47

Robert Reneau
Action Jackson '88
Demolition Man '93

Jeff Reno
Radioland Murders '94

Jean Renoir
La Chienne '31
La Marseillaise '37
The Rules of the Game '39
The Southerner '45
The River '51
The Little Theatre of Jean Renoir '71

David Renwick
Whoops Apocalypse '83

Ed Earl Repp
The Tioga Kid '48

David Reskin
Action U.S.A. '89
Hidden Obsession '92

Adam Resnick
Cabin Boy '94

Patricia Resnick
A Wedding '78
Quintet '79
9 to 5 '80
Maxie '85
Second Sight '89
Straight Talk '92

Robert Resnikoff
The First Power '89

Paul (Pee Wee Herman) Reubens
Pee Wee's Big Adventure '85
Big Top Pee Wee '88

Alma Reville
The 39 Steps '35
Shadow of a Doubt '43

Jonathan Reynolds
Micki & Maude '84
Leonard Part 6 '87
My Stepmother Is an Alien '88
Switching Channels '88

Kevin Reynolds
Red Dawn '84
Fandango '85
Rapa Nui '93

Lee Reynolds
Allan Quatermain and the Lost City of Gold '86
Delta Force 2: Operation Stranglehold '90
Storyville '92

Lynn F. Reynolds
Sky High '22

Don Rhymer
Past the Bleachers '95

Debra Ricci
Alien from L.A. '87

Anne Rice
Interview with the Vampire '94

John Rice
Curiosity Kills '90
Blown Away '94
Chasers '94

Susan Rice
Trumps '83
Something in Common '86
Animal Behavior '89

Matty Rich
Straight Out of Brooklyn '91

Richard Rich
The Swan Princess '94

Dick Richard
Snow White and the Seven Dwarfs '37

Jean-Louis Richard
Day for Night '73

Pierre Richard
The Daydreamer '75

Doug Richardson
Die Hard 2: Die Harder '90
Money Train '95

Scobie Richardson
Wildcard '92

Sy Richardson
Posse '93

Tony Richardson
A Taste of Honey '61
Ned Kelly '70
The Hotel New Hampshire '84

Mordecai Richler
No Love for Johnnie '60
The Apprenticeship of Duddy Kravitz '74
Fun with Dick and Jane '77
Joshua Then and Now '85

Maurice Richlin
Come September '61

W.D. Richter
Slither '73
Invasion of the Body Snatchers '78
Dracula '79
Brubaker '80
All Night Long '81
Big Trouble in Little China '86
Needful Things '93
Home for the Holidays '95

Tom Rickman
Truman '95

Tom Ricostronza
The Inkwell '94

Philip Ridley
The Krays '90
The Reflecting Skin '91

Leni Riefenstahl
The Blue Light '32

Dean Riesner
Play Misty for Me '71

J. Riffel
The House on Tombstone Hill '92

Adam Rifkin
Never on Tuesday '88
The Dark Backward '91
The Chase '93

Lawrence Riggins
Ironheart '92

Sharon Riis
Loyalties '86

Rob Riley
Number One with a Bullet '87

Wolf Rilla
Roadhouse Girl '53

Fred Rinaldo
The Invisible Woman '40
Comin' Round the Mountain '51

Fabio Rinaudo
The Star Maker '95

David W. Rintels
Day One '89
The Last Best Year '90
World War II: When Lions Roared '94
Andersonville '95

Arthur Ripley
Baby Face Harry Langdon '26
Waterfront '39

Robert Riskin
It Happened One Night '34
Mr. Deeds Goes to Town '36
Lost Horizon '37
You Can't Take It with You '38
Riding High '50

J. William Ritchie
George's Island '91

Joe Ritter
The Toxic Avenger '86

Thomas Ritz
Martial Outlaw '93

Stephen J. Rivele
Nixon '95

W.L. Rivers
The Great Man's Lady '42

Jacques Rivette
Paris Belongs to Us '60

Janet Roach
Prizzi's Honor '85
Mr. North '88

Joe Roach
Somewhere in Sonora '33

M. Jay Roach
Lifepod '93

Alain Robak
The Evil Within '94

Matthew Robbins
The Sugarland Express '74
Bingo Long Traveling All-Stars & Motor Kings '76
MacArthur '77
Corvette Summer '78
Dragonslayer '81
Warning Sign '85
*batteries not included '87

Tim Robbins
Bob Roberts '92
Dead Man Walking '95

Ben Roberts
Green Fire '55

Daryll Roberts
How U Like Me Now? '92

Jonathan Roberts
Once Bitten '85
The Sure Thing '85
The Lion King '94

June Roberts
Experience Preferred... But Not Essential '83
Mermaids '90

Marguerite Roberts
Somewhere I'll Find You '42

Scott Roberts
Riders of the Storm '88
K2: The Ultimate High '92

Stanley Roberts
The Caine Mutiny '54

William Roberts
Easy to Love '53
The Mating Game '59
The Magnificent Seven '60
The Wonderful World of the Brothers Grimm '62
The Devil's Brigade '68
The Bridge at Remagen '69
Red Sun '71
The Last American Hero '73
Posse '75
Legend of the Lone Ranger '81
Ten to Midnight '83

Mira Robertson
Only the Brave '94

R.J. Robertson
Forbidden World '82
Big Bad Mama 2 '87
Not of This Earth '88
Transylvania Twist '89
Think Big '90
The Haunting of Morella '91
Final Embrace '92

Robbie Robertson
Carny '80

Herb Robins
The Worm Eaters '77

John Robins
Hot Resort '85

Bruce Robinson
The Killing Fields '84
Withnail and I '87
Fat Man and Little Boy '89
How to Get Ahead in Advertising '89
Jennifer 8 '92

Butch Robinson
DROP Squad '94

Casey Robinson
Saratoga Trunk '45
The Snows of Kilimanjaro '52
The Egyptian '54

James Robinson
Cyber Bandits '94

Phil Alden Robinson
All of Me '84
Rhinestone '84
In the Mood '87
Field of Dreams '89
Sneakers '92

Sally Robinson
A Far Off Place '93

Todd Robinson
White Squall '96

Armando Robles Godoy
The Green Wall '70

Marc Rocco
Dream a Little Dream '89
Where the Day Takes You '92

Glauce Rocha
Earth Entranced '66
Antonio Das Mortes '68

Eric Rochant
The Fifth Monkey '90
Love Without Pity '91

Chris Rock
CB4: The Movie '93

Jay Dee Rock
Clifford '92

Kevin Rock
Philadelphia Experiment 2 '93
Warlock: The Armageddon '93
Suspicious Agenda '94
Raging Angels '95

Alexandre Rockwell
Sons '91
In the Soup '92
Four Rooms '95

Lisa-Marie Rodano
Mrs. Winterbourne '96

Robert Rodat
The Comrades of Summer '92
Tall Tale: The Unbelievable Adventures of Pecos Bill '95

Gene Roddenberry
Star Trek the Next Generation: Encounter at Farpoint '87

Ian Rodger
Elizabeth R '72

Howard A. Rodman
Fallen Angels 1 '93

Rodman ▶cont.

Fallen Angels 2 '93

Serge Rodnunsky
Lovers' Lovers '94

Robert Rodriguez
El Mariachi '93
Desperado '95
Four Rooms '95

Michael Roemer
Nothing But a Man '64
The Plot Against Harry '69

Howard Emmett Rogers
Hold Your Man '33

Ivan Rogers
Tigershark '87

Mary Rogers
A Billion for Boris '90

Steve Rogers
Triple Impact '92

Wayne Rogers
The Astro-Zombies '67

Will Rogers
Stand Up and Cheer '34

Eric Rohmer
La Collectionneuse '67
Six in Paris '68
My Night at Maud's '69
Claire's Knee '71
Chloe in the Afternoon '72
Le Beau Mariage '82
Pauline at the Beach '83
Full Moon in Paris '84
Summer '86
Boyfriends & Girlfriends '88
Four Adventures of Reinette and Mirabelle '89
A Tale of Springtime '92
A Tale of Winter '92

Bernie Rollins
Getting Over '81

Mark Romanek
Static '87

Eddie Romero
Cavalry Command '63

George A. Romero
The Crazies '73
Season of the Witch '73
Martin '77
Dawn of the Dead '78
Knightriders '81
Day of the Dead '85
Creepshow 2 '87
Monkey Shines '88
Night of the Living Dead '90
The Dark Half '91

Gianni Romoli
Cemetery Man '95

Neil Ronco
Save Me '93

Brunello Rondi
La Strada '54
La Dolce Vita '60
8 1/2 '63
Juliet of the Spirits '65

Jean-Pierre Ronssin
La Discrete '90

Don Roos
Love Field '91
Single White Female '92
Boys on the Side '94
Diabolique '96

Wells Root
Prisoner of Zenda '37
Texas Across the River '66

Tom Ropelewski
The Kiss '88
Loverboy '89
Madhouse '90
Look Who's Talking Now '93

Bradford Ropes
Redwood Forest Trail '50

Bernard Rose
Candyman '92
Immortal Beloved '94

Jack Rose
The Road to Rio '47
Sorrowful Jones '49
Riding High '50
I'll See You in My Dreams '51
On Moonlight Bay '51
April In Paris '52
Trouble Along the Way '53
The Seven Little Foys '55
Houseboat '58
The Five Pennies '59
It Started in Naples '60
Papa's Delicate Condition '63
Who's Got the Action? '63
A Touch of Class '73
Lost and Found '79
The Great Muppet Caper '81

Joel Rose
Dead Weekend '95

Lee Rose
Deconstructing Sarah '94
A Mother's Prayer '95

Reginald Rose
Twelve Angry Men '57
Man of the West '58
Wild Geese '78
Sea Wolves '81
Whose Life Is It Anyway? '81
The Final Option '82
Wild Geese 2 '85

Ruth Rose
She '35

William Rose
The Ladykillers '55
Guess Who's Coming to Dinner '67

Gualtiero Rosella
Flight of the Innocent '93

Dan Rosen
The Last Supper '96

Gary Rosen
Major Payne '95

Martin Rosen
Watership Down '78
The Plague Dogs '82

Robert Rosenbaum
In the Deep Woods '91

Anita Rosenberg
Assault of the Killer Bimbos '88

C.A. Rosenberg
Maniac '80

Jeanne Rosenberg
The Black Stallion '79
The Journey of Natty Gann '85
White Fang '91
Heidi '93

Scott Rosenberg
Things to Do In Denver When You're Dead '95
Beautiful Girls '96

Seth Zvi Rosenfeld
Sunset Park '96

Jack Rosenthal
The Wedding Gift '93

Mark Rosenthal
The Jewel of the Nile '85
Legend of Billie Jean '85
Superman 4: The Quest for Peace '87
The In Crowd '88
Desperate Hours '90
The Beverly Hillbillies '93
For Love or Money '93

Francesco Rosi
Bellissima '51
Christ Stopped at Eboli '79
Three Brothers '80

Arthur Ross
Creature from the Black Lagoon '54
The Creature Walks Among Us '56
The Three Worlds of Gulliver '59
Brubaker '80

Benjamin Ross
The Young Poisoner's Handbook '94

Brian Ross
Body Language '92
The Secret Passion of Robert Clayton '92
Dying to Remember '93

Gary Ross
Big '88
Mr. Baseball '92
Dave '93
Lassie '94

Roberto Rossellini
Paisan '46
Machine to Kill Bad People '48
Era Notte a Roma '60
RoGoPaG '62

Robert Rossen
They Won't Forget '37
The Sea Wolf '41
Edge of Darkness '43
A Walk in the Sun '46
All the King's Men '49
The Hustler '61
Billy Budd '62

Leo Rossi
We're Talkin' Serious Money '92

Terry Rossio
Little Monsters '89
Aladdin '92
The Puppet Masters '94

Arthur Rosson
Boots of Destiny '37

Rick Rossovich
New Crime City: Los Angeles 2020 '94

Leo Rosten
Velvet Touch '48

Bobby Roth
Boss' Son '79
Heartbreakers '84
Baja Oklahoma '87
Dead Solid Perfect '88
The Man Inside '90

Cy Roth
Fire Maidens from Outer Space '56

Eric Roth
The Concorde: Airport '79 '79
Suspect '87
Memories of Me '88
Mr. Jones '93
Forrest Gump '94

Lynn Roth
The Portrait '93

Phillip J. Roth
Ghostwriter '84
Prototype X29A '92
A.P.E.X. '94
Digital Man '94

Jeff Rothberg
The Amazing Panda Adventure '95

Stephanie Rothman
Starhops '78

Elisa Rothstein
Delta of Venus '95

Talbot Rothwell
Carry On Camping '71
Carry On Henry VIII '71

Brigitte Rouan
Overseas: Three Women with Man Trouble '90

Jean Rouch
Six in Paris '68

Dominique Roulet
The Old Lady Who Walked in the Sea '91

Russel Rouse
Fastest Gun Alive '56

Kathleen Rowell
The Outsiders '83
Joy of Sex '84
Hear No Evil '93
Tainted Blood '93

Charles Francis Royal
Ridin' the Lone Trail '37

Fanchon Royer
Bell Ringer of Antigua '46

Patricia Rozema
When Night is Falling '95

John Ruane
Death in Brunswick '90
That Eye, The Sky '94

Michael Rubbo
The Peanut Butter Solution '85

Andy Ruben
The Patriot '86
Stripped to Kill '87
Dance of the Damned '88
Streets '90
Poison Ivy '92

Katt Shea Ruben
The Patriot '86
Stripped to Kill '87
Dance of the Damned '88
Stripped to Kill II: Live Girls '89
Poison Ivy '92

Bill Rubenstein
Beyond Rangoon '95

Bruce Joel Rubin
Brainstorm '83
Deadly Friend '86
Ghost '90
Jacob's Ladder '90
My Life '93

Daniel F. Rubin
Groundhog Day '93

Daniel N. Rubin
Dishonored '31

Mann Rubin
The Best of Everything '59

Sergio Rubini
The Station '92

George Rubio
Into Thin Air '85

Cliff Ruby
Balto '95

Harry Ruby
Duck Soup '33
A Night at the Opera '35

Allen Rucker
Hometown Boy Makes Good '93

David Rudkin
December Bride '91

Rita Rudner
Peter's Friends '92

Paul Rudnick
Addams Family Values '93
Jeffrey '95

Steve Rudnick
The Santa Clause '94

Alan Rudolph
Premonition '71
Buffalo Bill & the Indians '76
Welcome to L.A. '77
Roadie '80
Endangered Species '82
Choose Me '84
Trouble in Mind '86
The Moderns '88
Love at Large '89
Equinox '93

Ed Rugoff
Mannequin '87
Mannequin 2: On the Move '91
Mr. Nanny '93

Raul Ruiz
The Hypothesis of the Stolen Painting '78

Stefano Rulli
The Stolen Children '92

Terry Runte
Mystery Date '91
Super Mario Bros. '93

Jordan Rush
Never Talk to Strangers '95

Richard Rush
Psych-Out '68
The Stunt Man '80
Air America '90
Color of Night '94

Lou Rusoff
Day the World Ended '55
Motorcycle Gang '57
Shake, Rattle and Rock '57
Beach Party '63

Chuck Russell
Dreamscape '84
A Nightmare on Elm Street 3: Dream Warriors '87
The Blob '88

David O. Russell
Spanking the Monkey '94
Flirting with Disaster '95

Jack Russell
Poldark '75

Ken Russell
The Boy Friend '71
The Devils '71
Mahler '74
Lisztomania '75
Tommy '75
Valentino '77
The Lair of the White Worm '88
Salome's Last Dance '88
The Rainbow '89
Whore '91

Kurt Russell
Escape from L.A. '96

Ray Russell
Zotz! '62
X: The Man with X-Ray Eyes '63

Vivian Russell
The Rainbow '89

Willy Russell
Educating Rita '83
Shirley Valentine '89

John Russo
Voodoo Dawn '89

Neil Ruttenberg
Magic Island '95
Prehysteria 3 '95

Richard Ryan
Fatal Past '94

John Ryman
Galaxies are Colliding '92

Michael Rymer
Angel Baby '95

Morrie Ryskind
The Cocoanuts '29
Animal Crackers '30
A Night at the Opera '35
My Man Godfrey '36

Timothy E. Sabo
Project Metalbeast: DNA Overload '94

Michael Sadler
A Year in Provence '89

Arthur St. Claire
Boss of Bullion City '41

Adela Rogers St. John
The Great Man's Lady '42

Nicholas St. John
Fear City '85
China Girl '87
King of New York '90
Body Snatchers '93
Dangerous Game '93
The Addiction '95

Armand Salacrou
Beauty and the Devil '50

Alfredo Salazar
The Robot vs. the Aztec Mummy '59

Richard Sale
A Woman's World '54

Murray Salem
Kindergarten Cop '90

Martin Salinas
Gaby: A True Story '87

Sidney Salkow
Rhythm on the Range '36

Waldo Salt
Shopworn Angel '38
Midnight Cowboy '69

Mark Saltzman
The Adventures of Milo & Otis '89
Iron & Silk '91
3 Ninjas Kick Back '94

Victor Salva
Nature of the Beast '94
Powder '95

Hal Salwen
Denise Calls Up '95
Probable Cause '95

Daniel S. Sample
Ex-Cop '93

Jeremy Sams
Persuasion '95

Jon Robert Samsel
Carnal Crimes '91

Lesser Samuels
Gangway '37
Bitter Sweet '40

Milcha Sanchez-Scott
Roosters '95

Duke Sandefur
Ghost Town '88

Ake Sandgren
The Slingshot '93

Adam Sandler
Billy Madison '94
Happy Gilmore '96

Barry Sandler
Loners '72
The Duchess and the Dirtwater Fox '76
The Mirror Crack'd '80
Making Love '82
Crimes of Passion '84
All-American Murder '91

Susan Sandler
Crossing Delancey '88

Anna Sandor
Miss Rose White '92
Amelia Earhart: The Final Flight '94

Jimmy Sangster
The Curse of Frankenstein '57
Blood of the Vampire '58
The Crawling Eye '58
The Horror of Dracula '58
The Revenge of Frankenstein '58
The Mummy '59
The Hellfire Club '61
Scream of Fear '61
Paranoiac '62
Maniac '63
Nightmare '63
Hysteria '64
The Nanny '65
The Anniversary '68
The Horror of Frankenstein '70
Dynasty of Fear '72
Phobia '80
The Devil & Max Devlin '81

Tedi Sarafian
Tank Girl '94
The Road Killers '95

Alvin Sargent
Gambit '66
The Stalking Moon '69
The Sterile Cuckoo '69
Paper Moon '73
Bobby Deerfield '77
Julia '77
Straight Time '78
Ordinary People '80
Nuts '87
Dominick & Eugene '88
White Palace '90
Other People's Money '91
What About Bob? '91

Arlene Sarner
Peggy Sue Got Married '86
Blue Sky '91

Robert Sarno
Decoy '95

William Saroyan
The Human Comedy '43

Jean-Paul Sartre
The Respectful Prostitute '52
The Crucible '57

Oley Sassone
Wild Hearts Can't Be Broken '91
Playback '95

Shimako Sato
Tale of a Vampire '92

Stephen Saul
Ninja Hunt '80s

Derek Saunders
Deceived '91

George Saunders
Scanner Cop '94
Malicious '95

Carlos Saura
Elisa, Vida Mia '77

Claude Sautet
Borsalino '70
Nelly et Monsieur Arnaud '95

Domenico Saverni
Ciao, Professore! '94

Nancy Savoca
True Love '89
Household Saints '93

Linwood Sawyer
Alien Space Avenger '91

John Sayles
Piranha '78
Lady in Red '79
Alligator '80
Battle Beyond the Stars '80
Return of the Secaucus 7 '80
The Howling '81
Baby It's You '82
The Challenge '82
Enormous Changes '83
Lianna '83
Trumps '83
The Brother from Another Planet '84
The Clan of the Cave Bear '86
Unnatural Causes '86
Matewan '87
Wild Thing '87
Eight Men Out '88
Breaking In '89
City of Hope '91
Passion Fish '92
Men of War '94
The Secret of Roan Inish '94
Lone Star '95

George Wallace Sayre
Wings Over the Pacific '43

Joel Sayre
Gunga Din '39

James Sbardellati
Under the Gun '88

Dario Scardapane
Posse '93

Furio Scarpelli
The Family '87
Time to Kill '89
The Postman '94

Giacomo Scarpelli
The Postman '94

Romano Scavolini
Nightmare '82

Sauro Scavolini
The Scorpion's Tail '71

Eric Schaeffer
My Life's In Turnaround '94
If Lucy Fell '95

James Schamus
The Wedding Banquet '93
Eat Drink Man Woman '94

Larry Schanker
American Blue Note '89

Dore Schary
Young Tom Edison '40
Sunrise at Campobello '60

Oliver Schatzky
A Man in Love '87

Richard Schayer
Trader Horn '31

Michael Scheff
Tall, Dark and Deadly '95

Adam Scheinman
Little Big League '94

Andrew Scheinman
North '94

George Schenck
Futureworld '76
Escape 2000 '81
Dying to Remember '93

Fred Schepisi
The Devil's Playground '76
A Cry in the Dark '88

Shawn Schepps
Encino Man '92
Son-in-Law '93

Gregory Scherick
The Night Before '88

Roberto Scheuer
Eversmile New Jersey '89

Laura Schiff
800 Leagues Down the Amazon '93

Robert Schiff
Swimsuit: The Movie '89

Michael Schiffer
Colors '88
Lean on Me '89
Crimson Tide '95

Karl Schiffman
Back in Action '94

Suzanne Schiffman
Day for Night '73
Story of Adele H. '75
Small Change '76
The Man Who Loved Women '77
The Last Metro '80
The Woman Next Door '81
Confidentially Yours '83
Sorceress '88

Fred Schiller
The Heat's On '43

Vivian Schilling
Soultaker '90

Murray Schisgal
Luv '67
Tootsie '82

George Schlatter
Norman, Is That You? '76
Fire and Ice '87

John Schlesinger
Madame Sousatzka '88

Volker Schlondorff
The Tin Drum '79
Voyager '91

Daniel Schmid
Shadow of Angels '76

Ronald Schmidt
A.P.E.X. '94
Digital Man '94

William Schmidt
The Sound and the Silence '93

David Schmoeller
Tourist Trap '79
Day Time Ended '80
The Seduction '82
Crawlspace '86
The Arrival '90

Charles Schnee
Red River '48
Westward the Women '51
Butterfield 8 '60

Andrew Schneider
Alien Nation: Dark Horizon '94

Barry Schneider
Ruby '77
Harper Valley P.T.A. '78
Roller Boogie '79
Take This Job & Shove It '81
Deadly Force '83
Mother's Boys '94

Bob Schneider
Normal Life '96

Peter Schneider
Knife in the Head '78
The Promise '95

Ernest B. Schoedsack
Chang: A Drama of the Wilderness '27

Pierre Schoendoerffer
The 317th Platoon '65

Amy Schor
Mr. Wonderful '93

David J. Schow
Leatherface: The Texas Chainsaw Massacre 3 '89
Critters 3 '91
Critters 4 '91
The Crow '93

Leonard Schrader
The Yakuza '75
Blue Collar '78
Old Boyfriends '79
Kiss of the Spider Woman '85
Mishima: A Life in Four Chapters '85

Paul Schrader
The Yakuza '75
Obsession '76
Taxi Driver '76
Rolling Thunder '77
Blue Collar '78
American Gigolo '79
Hardcore '79
Old Boyfriends '79
Raging Bull '80
Mishima: A Life in Four Chapters '85
The Mosquito Coast '86
Light of Day '87
The Last Temptation of Christ '88
Light Sleeper '92
City Hall '95

Carol Schreder
In Love and War '91

David Schreiber
Body of Influence '93

Nevin Schreiner
The China Lake Murders '90
Memories of Murder '90
Linda '93
Don't Talk to Strangers '94

Doris Schroeder
Bullet Code '40

Bernard Schubert
The Mummy's Curse '44

Budd Schulberg
On the Waterfront '54
A Face in the Crowd '57
Question of Honor '80

Arnold Schulman
A Hole in the Head '59
Cimarron '60
Love with the Proper Stranger '63
The Night They Raided Minsky's '69
Funny Lady '75
Players '79
A Chorus Line '85
Tucker: The Man and His Dream '88
And the Band Played On '93

Roger S.H. Schulman
Balto '95

Tom Schulman
Dead Poets Society '89
Honey, I Shrunk the Kids '89
Second Sight '89
What About Bob? '91

Charles M. Schulz
A Boy Named Charlie Brown '70
Snoopy, Come Home '72
Race for Your Life, Charlie Brown '77
Bon Voyage, Charlie Brown '80

Douglas Schulze
Hellmaster '92

Joel Schumacher
Car Wash '76
Sparkle '76
The Wiz '78
D.C. Cab '84
St. Elmo's Fire '85

Leon Schuster
Yankee Zulu '95

Marjorie Schwartz
The Butcher's Wife '91

Mark Evan Schwartz
Quake '92

S.S. Schweitzer
Hornet's Nest '70

Aleksander Scibor-Rylski
Man of Marble '76
Man of Iron '81

Ettore Scola
Two Nights with Cleopatra '54
Down & Dirty '76
A Special Day '77
La Nuit de Varennes '82
Passion of Love '82
Macaroni '85
The Family '87

Kathryn Scola
Night After Night '32
Female '33
Alexander's Ragtime Band '38
One Night in the Tropics '40

Martin Scorsese
Mean Streets '73
Goodfellas '90
The Age of Innocence '93
Casino '95

Allan Scott
Top Hat '35
So Proudly We Hail '43
The 5000 Fingers of Dr. T '53
Man Who Had Power Over Women '70
Don't Look Now '73
The Girl from Petrovka '74
Spiral Staircase '75
Joseph Andrews '77
The Awakening '80
D.A.R.Y.L. '85
Martin's Day '85
Castaway '87
Apprentice to Murder '88
The Witches '90
Cold Heaven '92

Cynthia Scott
Strangers in Good Company '91

Darin Scott
Tales from the Hood '95

George C. Scott
Descending Angel '90

Kevin Scott
Key Exchange '85

Sherman Scott
Bad Girls from Mars '90
Haunting Fear '91
Inner Sanctum 2 '94

T.J. Scott
TC 2000 '93

Sam A. Scribner
The Criminal Mind '93

Peter S. Seaman
Trenchcoat '83
Who Framed Roger Rabbit '88
Doc Hollywood '91

Ted Sears
Snow White and the Seven Dwarfs '37

George Seaton
Doctor Takes a Wife '40
Miracle on 34th Street '47
Country Girl '54
The Counterfeit Traitor '62
Airport '70
Miracle on 34th Street '94

Beverly Sebastian
Gator Bait '73
Gator Bait 2: Cajun Justice '88
Running Cool '93

Ferd Sebastian
Gator Bait '73
Gator Bait 2: Cajun Justice '88
Running Cool '93

Ian Seeberg
The Companion '94

Manuel Seff
Love on the Run '36

Erich Segal
Yellow Submarine '68
Love Story '70
R.P.M.* (*Revolutions Per Minute) '70
Oliver's Story '78
A Change of Seasons '80
Man, Woman & Child '83

Harry Segall
Angel on My Shoulder '46

Robert Seidenberg
Dead in the Water '91

David Seidler
The Rumor Mill '86
Tucker: The Man and His Dream '88

Shinichi Sekizawa
Dagora, the Space Monster '65

Jack M. Sell
Deadly Spygames '89

Steven Selling
One Man's Justice '95

Aaron Seltzer
Spy Hard '96

David Seltzer
The Hellstrom Chronicle '71
King, Queen, Knave '72
The Other Side of the Mountain '75
The Omen '76
Prophecy '79
Table for Five '83
Lucas '86
Punchline '88
Bird on a Wire '90
Shining Through '92

Terrel Seltzer
Chan is Missing '82
Dim Sum: A Little Bit of Heart '85
How I Got into College '89

David O. Selznick
A Star is Born '37
Since You Went Away '44

Jorge Semprun
A Woman at Her Window '77

Mala Sen
Bandit Queen '94

Ron Senkowski
Let's Kill All the Lawyers '93

Mack Sennett
Extra Girl '23

Al Septien
Leprechaun 2 '94

Yahoo Serious
Young Einstein '89
Reckless Kelly '93

Rod Serling
Patterns '56
Requiem for a Heavyweight '56
Seven Days in May '64
Assault on a Queen '66
The Doomsday Flight '66
Planet of the Apes '68

Alessandro Sermoneta
Lamerica '95

Alexandra Seros
Point of No Return '93
The Specialist '94

Leopoldo Serran
O Quatrilho '95

Coline Serreau
Three Men and a Cradle '85
Mama, There's a Man in Your Bed '89

Phillip Setbon
Honeymoon '87
Mr. Frost '89

Mark Sevi
Class of 1999 2: The Substitute '93
Ghoulies 4 '93
Fast Getaway 2 '94
Relentless 4 '94
Scanners: The Showdown '94
Excessive Force 2: Force on Force '95

Vernon Sewell
Frenzy '46
The World Owes Me a Living '47

John Sexton
Wrangler '88

Alan Seymour
The Cinder Path '94

James Seymour
42nd Street '33

Jeff Seymour
Rave Review '95

Samantha Shad
Class Action '91

Susan Shadburne
The Adventures of Mark Twain '85
Shadow Play '86

Tom Shadyac
Ace Ventura: Pet Detective '93
The Nutty Professor '96

Anthony Shaffer
Cry of the Penguins '71
Frenzy '72
Sleuth '72
The Wicker Man '75
Death on the Nile '78
Evil under the Sun '82
Whodunit '82
Appointment with Death '88

Peter Shaffer
Equus '77
Amadeus '84

Josef Shaftel
Naked Hills '56

Steve Shagan
Primal Fear '96

Virginia Shaler
Lost Boundaries '49

Robert Shallcross
Little Giants '94

Peter Shaner
Shootfighter: Fight to the Death '93

John Patrick Shanley
Moonstruck '87
Five Corners '88
The January Man '89
Joe Versus the Volcano '90
Alive '93
We're Back! A Dinosaur's Story '93
Congo '95

Joy Shannon
Uptown Angel '90

Jack Shaoul
Robot in the Family '94

Alan Shapiro
The Crush '93
Flipper '96

J. David Shapiro
Robin Hood: Men in Tights '93

Paul Shapiro
Breaking the Rules '92
Calendar Girl '93

Richard Shapiro
Blood Ties '92

Ruth Shapiro
Getting Out '94

Stanley Shapiro
Come September '61
Carbon Copy '81
Dirty Rotten Scoundrels '88

Alan Sharp
Damnation Alley '77
Little Treasure '85
The Last Hit '93
Rob Roy '95

Jan Sharp
Wide Sargasso Sea '92

William Shatner
Star Trek 5: The Final Frontier '89

Melville Shavelson
Where There's Life '47
Sorrowful Jones '49
Riding High '50
Double Dynamite '51
I'll See You in My Dreams '51
On Moonlight Bay '51
April In Paris '52
Trouble Along the Way '53
The Seven Little Foys '55
Houseboat '58
The Five Pennies '59
It Started in Naples '60
A New Kind of Love '63
Cast a Giant Shadow '66
Yours, Mine & Ours '68

Irwin Shaw
Commandos Strike at Dawn '43

Philip Shaw
Tarzana, the Wild Girl '72

Harry Shearer
Real Life '79
The Return of Spinal Tap '92

Donald Shebib
The Climb '87

Arthur Sheekman
Duck Soup '33
Blue Skies '46
Welcome Stranger '47

David Sheffield
Coming to America '88
Boomerang '92
The Nutty Professor '96

Sidney Sheldon
The Bachelor and the Bobby-Soxer '47
Easter Parade '48
Nancy Goes to Rio '50
Rich, Young and Pretty '51
Three Guys Named Mike '51
Birds & the Bees '56
Pardners '56
All in a Night's Work '61
Billy Rose's Jumbo '62

Ron Shelton
Under Fire '83
The Best of Times '86
Bull Durham '88
Blaze '89
White Men Can't Jump '92
Blue Chips '94
Cobb '94
The Great White Hype '96
Tin Cup '96

Nina Shengold
Blind Spot '93

Richard Shepard
The Linguini Incident '92

Sam Shepard
Zabriskie Point '70
Paris, Texas '83
Fool for Love '86
Far North '88
Silent Tongue '92

Cybill Shepherd
Memphis '91

Jean Shepherd
A Christmas Story '83
My Summer Story '94

Jack Sher
Shane '53
The Three Worlds of Gulliver '59
Paris Blues '61

Bob Sheridan
Dinosaur Island '93

Guillermo Sheridan
Cabeza de Vaca '90

Jim Sheridan
My Left Foot '89
The Field '90
Into the West '92
In the Name of the Father '93

Michael J. Sheridan
That's Entertainment, Part 3 '93

Gary Sherman
Phobia '80
Fire and Rain '89
After the Shock '90

Martin Sherman
The Summer House '94

R.C. Sherriff
The Invisible Man '33
The Four Feathers '39
No Highway in the Sky '51

Bill Sherwood
Parting Glances '86

Robert Sherwood
The Ghost Goes West '36
The Adventures of Marco Polo '38
Abe Lincoln in Illinois '40
Rebecca '40
The Best Years of Our Lives '46

Susan Shilliday
Legends of the Fall '94

John Shirley
The Crow '93

Mark Shmuger
Dead of Winter '87

Emily Shoemaker
Circumstances Unknown '95

Roger Sholes
The Tale of Ruby Rose '87

Del Shores
Daddy's Dyin'...Who's Got the Will? '90

Dennis Shryack
Pale Rider '85
Fifty/Fifty '93

Barbara Shulgasser
Ready to Wear '94

Max Shulman
The Affairs of Dobie Gillis '53

Mina Shum
Double Happiness '94

Ronald Shusett
Phobia '80
Freejack '92

Charles Shyer
Smokey and the Bandit '77
Goin' South '78
House Calls '78
Private Benjamin '80
Irreconcilable Differences '84
Protocol '84
Baby Boom '87
Father of the Bride '91
I Love Trouble '94
Father of the Bride Part II '95

Melville Shyer
Green Eyes '34

James Shyman
Slashdance '89

Mussef Sibay
A Woman, Her Men and Her Futon '92

Andy Sidaris
Guns '90
Do or Die '91
Hard Hunted '92
Fit to Kill '93

Christian Sidaris
Enemy Gold '93

Lynn Siefert
Cool Runnings '93

David Siegel
Suture '93

Steven Siegel
K-9 '89

Mark Siegler
Galaxy of Terror '81

Tom Sierchio
Untamed Heart '93

Dai Sijie
China, My Sorrow '89

Sean Silas
A Vow to Kill '94

James R. Silke
Revenge of the Ninja '83
Sahara '83
Ninja 3: The Domination '84

Stirling Silliphant
Nightfall '56
Village of the Damned '60
The Slender Thread '65
In the Heat of the Night '67
Charly '68
Marlowe '69
The Liberation of L.B. Jones '70
Walk in the Spring Rain '70
Murphy's War '71
The New Centurions '72
The Poseidon Adventure '72
Shaft in Africa '73
The Towering Inferno '74
Death Scream '75
The Killer Elite '75
The Enforcer '76
Telefon '77
Circle of Iron '78
The Swarm '78
When Time Ran Out '80
Over the Top '86
Catch the Heat '87

Amanda Silver
The Hand that Rocks the Cradle '92
Fallen Angels 1 '93
An Eye for an Eye '95

Joan Micklin Silver
Chilly Scenes of Winter '79

Marisa Silver
Old Enough '84

Stu Silver
Throw Momma from the Train '87

Peter Silverman
American Heart '92

Nancy Silvers
Battling for Baby '92

Ed Silverstein
Boca '94

Shel Silverstein
Things Change '88

Lawrence L. Simeone
Cop-Out '91
Presumed Guilty '91
Eyes of the Beholder '92
Blindfold: Acts of Obsession '94

David Simkins
Adventures in Babysitting '87

Posy S. Simmonds
The French Lesson '86

Redbeard Simmons
The Applegates '89

Adam Simon
Carnosaur '93

Alex Simon
Suspect Device '95

Ellen Simon
Moonlight and Valentino '95

J. Piquer Simon
Cthulhu Mansion '91

Neil Simon
After the Fox '66
Barefoot in the Park '67
The Odd Couple '68
The Out-of-Towners '70
Plaza Suite '71
Star Spangled Girl '71
The Heartbreak Kid '72
Last of the Red Hot Lovers '72
Prisoner of Second Avenue '74
The Sunshine Boys '75
Murder by Death '76
The Goodbye Girl '77
California Suite '78
The Cheap Detective '78
Chapter Two '79
Seems Like Old Times '80
Only When I Laugh '81
I Ought to Be in Pictures '82
Max Dugan Returns '83
The Slugger's Wife '85
Brighton Beach Memoirs '86
Biloxi Blues '88
The Marrying Man '91
Broadway Bound '92
Lost in Yonkers '93

Rocco Simonelli
The Substitute '96

Henri Simoun
Blind Vengeance '90

Byron Simpson
The Rescuers Down Under '90

Joshua Sinclair
Judgment in Berlin '88

Bryan Singer
Public Access '93

Randi Mayem Singer
Mrs. Doubtfire '93

John Singleton
Boyz N the Hood '91
Poetic Justice '93
Higher Learning '94

Gary Sinyor
Leon the Pig Farmer '93

Curt Siodmak
Black Friday '40
Invisible Agent '42
Bride of the Gorilla '51
Earth vs. the Flying Saucers '56

Rosemary Anne Sisson
Elizabeth R '72
The Bretts '88

John Sjogren
Money to Burn '94

Victor Sjostrom
He Who Gets Slapped '24

Warren Skaaren
Beverly Hills Cop 2 '87
Beetlejuice '88
Batman '89

Vance Skarstedt
Man or Gun '58

Paul Skemp
Fall Time '94

Thomas Strittmatter
Drachenfutter '87

Max Strom
Best of the Best 2 '93
American Yakuza '94

Fred Stroppel
Almost Pregnant '91
Dark Side of Genius '94

Jeffrey Strouth
American Fabulous '92

Barry Strugatz
Married to the Mob '88
She-Devil '89

Norman Strum
Letter to My Killer '95

Jeb Stuart
Die Hard '88
Leviathan '89
Lock Up '89
Another 48 Hrs. '90
Vital Signs '90
The Fugitive '93
Just Cause '94

Jerzy Stuhr
Camera Buff '79

Christopher Sturgeon
Huck and the King of Hearts '93

Preston Sturges
The Great McGinty '40
Remember the Night '40
The Lady Eve '41
Sullivan's Travels '41
Miracle of Morgan's Creek '44

Charles Sturridge
A Handful of Dust '88

Hel Styverson
Indecent Behavior 3 '95

Milton Subotsky
Vault of Horror '73

Henry Sucher
The Mummy's Tomb '42
Captive Wild Woman '43
The Mummy's Ghost '44

Arne Sucksdorff
The Great Adventure '53

Greg Suddeth
Prehysteria '93
Pet Shop '94

Daniele Suissa
Pocahontas: The Legend '95

C. Gardner Sullivan
Union Pacific '39

Daniel G. Sullivan
While You Were Sleeping '95

Kevin Sullivan
Anne of Green Gables '85
Anne of Avonlea '87

Tim Sullivan
A Handful of Dust '88
Jack and Sarah '96

Arne Sultan
See No Evil, Hear No Evil '89

Lasse Summanen
The Ox '91

Dirk Summers
Survival of Spaceship Earth '90

Walter Summers
Black Limelight '38
The Human Monster '39

Louis Sun
Rage and Honor 2: Hostile Takeover '93

Shirley Sun
A Great Wall '86
Iron & Silk '91

Alan M. Surgal
Mickey One '65

Joel Surnow
Ring of the Musketeers '93

Phoef Sutton
The Fan '96
Mrs. Winterbourne '96

Bill Svanoe
Seduced by Evil '94

Zdenek Sverak
My Sweet Little Village '86

E.W. Swackhamer
The Rousters '90

Tom Swale
The Man in the Attic '94

Ron Swanson
Top Dog '95

Alfred Sweeney
Up from the Depths '79

Bruce Sweeney
Live Bait '95

Julia Sweeney
It's Pat: The Movie '94

Terry Sweeney
Shag: The Movie '89

John Sweet
The Great Elephant Escape '95

Edithe Swensen
They Watch '93

Tommy Swerdlow
Cool Runnings '93
Little Giants '94
Bushwhacked '95

Jo Swerling
Platinum Blonde '31
Lady by Choice '34
Double Wedding '37
I Am the Law '38
Blood and Sand '41
Crash Dive '43
Leave Her to Heaven '45
It's a Wonderful Life '46

Robin Swicord
Shag: The Movie '89
Little Women '94
The Perez Family '94
Matilda '96

David Swift
How to Succeed in Business without Really Trying '67

Meera Syal
Bhaji on the Beach '94

Istvan Szabo
Father '67
Meeting Venus '91

Thomas Szollosi
Three O'Clock High '87

Reszo Szoreny
A Happy New Year! '79

Micheal Taav
The Paint Job '93

Jim Tabilio
Sweet Justice '92

Brian Taggert
Visiting Hours '82
Of Unknown Origin '83
The New Kids '85
Wanted Dead or Alive '86
Poltergeist 3 '88
Child of Darkness, Child of Light '91
What Ever Happened To... '93

Robert Taicher
Inside Out '91

Isao Takahata
Grave of the Fireflies '88

C.M. Talkington
Love and a .45 '94

Ted Tally
White Palace '90
The Silence of the Lambs '91

Ted Tally
Before and After '95
The Juror '96

Takeski Tamura
MacArthur's Children '85

Amy Tan
The Joy Luck Club '93

Edward Tang
Rumble in the Bronx '96

Senkichi Taniguhi
A Quiet Duel '49

William Tannen
Inside Edge '92

Alain Tanner
La Salamandre '71

Jonah Who Will Be 25 in the Year 2000 '76
Messidor '77

Robert Emmett Tansey
The Driftin' Kid '41
Dynamite Canyon '41

Daniel Taplitz
Black Magic '92

Daniel Taradash
Golden Boy '39
Knock on Any Door '49
Don't Bother to Knock '52
Rancho Notorious '52
From Here to Eternity '53
Desiree '54
Picnic '55
Bell, Book and Candle '58
Morituri '65
Hawaii '66
Doctors' Wives '70
The Other Side of Midnight '77

Quentin Tarantino
Reservoir Dogs '92
True Romance '93
Pulp Fiction '94
Four Rooms '95
From Dusk Till Dawn '95

Sooni Taraporevala
Salaam Bombay! '88
Mississippi Masala '92

Andrei Tarkovsky
Andrei Rublev '66

Erik Tarloff
Car 54, Where Are You? '94

Frank Tarloff
Father Goose '64
A Guide for the Married Man '67

Jack Tarpon
Dangerous Indiscretion '94

Bela Tarr
Almanac of Fall

Frank Tashlin
The Fuller Brush Girl '50
The Lemon Drop Kid '51
Artists and Models '55
Will Success Spoil Rock Hunter? '57
Cinderfella '60

Jacques Tati
Parade '74

John Tatoulis
The Silver Stallion: King of the Wild Brumbies '93

Gilles Taurand
Wild Reeds '94

Catherine Tavel
Married People, Single Sex '93
Night Fire '94

Bertrand Tavernier
The Judge and the Assassin '75
Spoiled Children '77
Death Watch '80
Coup de Torchon '81
A Sunday in the Country '84
Round Midnight '86
Life and Nothing But '89
L.627 '92
L'Appat '94

Paolo Taviani
Padre Padrone '77
The Night of the Shooting Stars '82
Kaos '85
Good Morning, Babylon '87
Fiorile '93

Vittorio Taviani
Padre Padrone '77
The Night of the Shooting Stars '82
Kaos '85
Good Morning, Babylon '87
Fiorile '93

Vincent Tavier
Man Bites Dog '91

David Taylor
DROP Squad '94

Dwight Taylor
Today We Live '33
Top Hat '35
Rhythm on the River '40

We're Not Married '52

Eric Taylor
Black Friday '40

Finn Taylor
Pontiac Moon '94

Lili Taylor
Girls Town '95

Philip John Taylor
Lust in the Dust '85

Renee Taylor
Lovers and Other Strangers '70

Roderick Taylor
The Star Chamber '83

Sam Taylor
Girl Shy '24
The Freshman '25
Vertigo '58

Steve Taylor
Sorority House Party '92

Theodore Taylor
Showdown '73

Pierre Tchernia
Belle Americaine '61

Andre Techine
Wild Reeds '94

Miguel Tejada-Flores
Tails You Live, Heads You're Dead '95
Screamers '96

Kevin S. Tenney
Witchboard '87
Peacemaker '90
Witchboard 2: The Devil's Doorway '93
Witchboard 3: The Possession '95

Gay Partington Terry
The Toxic Avenger, Part 2 '89
The Toxic Avenger, Part 3: The Last Temptation of Toxie '89

Steve Tesich
Breaking Away '79
Eyewitness '81
Four Friends '81
The World According to Garp '82
American Flyers '85
Eleni '85

Graham Tetley
Dark of the Night '85

Herbert Tevos
Mesa of Lost Women '52

Joan Tewkesbury
Thieves Like Us '74
Nashville '75
A Night in Heaven '83
Cold Sassy Tree '89

Kirk R. Thatcher
Muppet Treasure Island '96

Meg Thayer
The Shooter '94

Harvey Thew
Illicit '31
Supernatural '33

Jack Thibeau
Off Limits '87

Nick Thiel
The Experts '89
Fire Birds '90
Shipwrecked '90
V.I. Warshawski '91
White Fang '91

Robert Thoeren
Mrs. Parkington '44
Singapore '47

Robert Thom
Death Race 2000 '75

Michael Thoma
The Set Up '95

Anna Thomas
End of August '82
El Norte '83
A Time of Destiny '88
My Family '94

Dave Thomas
Strange Brew '83

Dylan Thomas
The Three Weird Sisters '48

Jerry Thomas
The Fighting Redhead '50

Jim Thomas
Predator '87
The Rescue '88
Predator 2 '90
Executive Decision '96

John Thomas
Predator '87
The Rescue '88
Predator 2 '90
Executive Decision '96

Michael Thomas
The Hunger '83
Burke & Wills '85
Ladyhawke '85
Scandal '89
Deception '92
Backbeat '94

Muffy Mead Thomas
Sarah's Child '96

Ralph Thomas
The Doors '91

Ross Thomas
Bad Company '94

Theodore Thomas
Frank and Ollie '95

Camille Thomasson
The Disappearance of Christina '93

Caroline Thompson
Edward Scissorhands '90
The Addams Family '91
The Nightmare Before Christmas '93
The Secret Garden '93
Black Beauty '94

Carolyn Thompson
Homeward Bound: The Incredible Journey '93

Daniele Thompson
Queen Margot '94

Donald W. Thompson
Sidekicks '93

Emma Thompson
Sense and Sensibility '95

Ernest Thompson
On Golden Pond '81
Sweet Hearts Dance '88

Larry Thompson
The Addams Family '91

Peggy Thompson
The Lotus Eaters '93

Rob Thompson
Hearts of the West '75
Ratboy '86
The Cowboy Way '94

Ron Stacker Thompson
America's Dream '95

Scott Thompson
Kids In the Hall Brain Candy '96

Selma Thomson
Taken Away '89

Billy Bob Thornton
One False Move '91
A Family Thing '96

Ralph Thornton
I Was a Teenage Werewolf '57

Roderick Thorp
Rainbow Drive '90

Leo Tichat
Night Train to Venice '93

Ernest Tidyman
Shaft's Big Score '72
Stark '85

Robert Tiffe
Sword of Honor '94

Arkadi Tigai
Window to Paris '95

Douglas Tirola
A Reason to Believe '95

James Toback
The Gambler '74
Fingers '78
Exposed '83
The Pick-Up Artist '87
Bugsy '91

Stephen Tobolowsky
True Stories '86

George Toles
Careful '94

John Toles-Bey
A Rage in Harlem '91

Michael Tolkin
Gleaming the Cube '89
The Rapture '91
Deep Cover '92
The Player '92
The Burning Season '94
The New Age '94

Stephen Tolkin
Captain America '89
Daybreak '93

Jerome Tonnerre
Un Coeur en Hiver '93

Tom Topor
Nuts '87
The Accused '88
Judgment '90

Burt Topper
Suicide Battalion/Hell Squad '58
Tank Commando '59
The Hard Ride '71

Tracy Torme
The Spellbinder '88
Fire in the Sky '93

Giuseppe Tornatore
Cinema Paradiso '88
Everybody's Fine '90
A Pure Formality '94
The Star Maker '95

Antonio Toro
Amityville: A New Generation '93

Peter Torokvei
Real Genius '85
Armed and Dangerous '86
Back to School '86
Caddyshack 2 '88
Guarding Tess '94
Hostage for a Day '94

Gabe Torres
December '91

Miguel Contreras Torres
Pancho Villa Returns '50

Wellyn Totman
Fighting Champ '33

Robert Totten
Death of a Gunfighter '69

Maurice Tourneur
The Wishing Ring '14

Robert Towne
The Last Woman on Earth '61
Tomb of Ligeia '64
Villa Rides '68
The Last Detail '73
Chinatown '74
Shampoo '75
The Yakuza '75
Personal Best '82
Tequila Sunrise '88
Days of Thunder '90
The Two Jakes '90
The Firm '93
Love Affair '94
Mission: Impossible '96

Jack Townley
All Over Town '37

Leo Townsend
It Started with Eve '41
Bikini Beach '64
Beach Blanket Bingo '65
How to Stuff a Wild Bikini '65

Robert Townsend
Hollywood Shuffle '87
The Five Heartbeats '91
The Meteor Man '93

Sher Townsend
Beach Blanket Bingo '65

Mark Trafficante
The Halfback of Notre Dame '96

Joey Travolta
Hard Vice '94
To the Limit '95

Stephen Traxler
Slithis '78

Monika Treut
Seduction: The Cruel Woman '89
My Father Is Coming '91

Dale Trevillion
Las Vegas Weekend '85
One Man Force '89

Dorothy Tristan
Weeds '87

Victor Trivas
The Head '59

Rose Troche
Go Fish '94

Jan Troell
The Emigrants '72
The New Land '73

Massimo Troisi
The Postman '94

Joseph Tropiano
Big Night '95

Guy Trosper
The Stratton Story '49
Darby's Rangers '58

Lamar Trotti
Alexander's Ragtime Band '38
In Old Chicago '38
The Story of Alexander Graham Bell '39
Young Mr. Lincoln '39
Brigham Young: Frontiersman '40
Immortal Sergeant '43
The Ox-Bow Incident '43
Wilson '44
Cheaper by the Dozen '50
I'd Climb the Highest Mountain '51

David Trueba
Two Much '96

Fernando Trueba
Two Much '96

Francois Truffaut
The 400 Blows '59
Shoot the Piano Player '62
Mississippi Mermaid '69
Day for Night '73

Dalton Trumbo
A Guy Named Joe '44
Thirty Seconds Over Tokyo '44
Our Vines Have Tender Grapes '45
Gun Crazy '49
Roman Holiday '53
The Brave One '56
Exodus '60
Spartacus '60
Hawaii '66
The Fixer '68
The Horsemen '70

Alan R. Trustman
Bullitt '68
The Thomas Crown Affair '68
They Call Me Mr. Tibbs! '70
Hit! '73
Lady Ice '73
The Arab Conspiracy '76

Glenn Tryon
Small Town Boy '37

Dean Tschetter
Bloodsucking Pharoahs of Pittsburgh '90

Shinya Tsukamoto
Tetsuo: The Iron Man '92

Stanley Tucci
Big Night '95

Fred Tuch
The Speed Lovers '68

James Tucker
Lunatic '91
Steps from Hell '92

Larry Tucker
Bob & Carol & Ted & Alice '69
Alex in Wonderland '70

Harry Tugend
My Lucky Star '38
Second Fiddle '39
Birth of the Blues '41
Caught in the Draft '41

Karl Tunberg
Week-End In Havana '41
Beau Brummel '54
Ben-Hur '59

Sandy Tung
Across the Tracks '89

Rosemarie Turko
Scarred '84

Ann Turner
The Killing Beach '92

Barbara Turner
Georgia '95

Bonnie Turner
Wayne's World '92
Coneheads '93
Wayne's World 2 '93
The Brady Bunch Movie '95
Tommy Boy '95

Clive Turner
The Howling: New Moon Rising '95

Dennis Turner
Poor Little Rich Girl: The Barbara Hutton Story '87

Guinevere Turner
Go Fish '94

Terry Turner
Wayne's World '92
Coneheads '93
Wayne's World 2 '93
The Brady Bunch Movie '95
Tommy Boy '95

Catherine Turney
The Man I Love '46
Cry Wolf '47

John Turturro
Mac '93

John Twist
Pittsburgh '42
King Richard and the Crusaders '54
Helen of Troy '56
Band of Angels '57

David N. Twohy
Critters 2: The Main Course '88
Warlock '91
Grand Tour: Disaster in Time '92
The Fugitive '93
Terminal Velocity '94
Waterworld '95
The Arrival '96

Jonathan Tydor
The Hard Truth '94

Ashley Tyler
America's Dream '95

Nona Tyson
The Hot Spot '90

Alfred Uhry
Mystic Pizza '88
Driving Miss Daisy '89
Rich in Love '93

Elwood Ullman
The Stooge '51
Ma and Pa Kettle at Waikiki '55

Liv Ullmann
Sofie '92

Yves Ulmann
Un Coeur en Hiver '93

Matt Unger
Bikini Bistro '94

Tara Untiedt
Provoked '89

Rocco Urbisci
Jo Jo Dancer, Your Life is Calling '86

Jeff Ureles
Cheap Shots '91

Leon Uris
Gunfight at the O.K. Corral '57

Anatoli Usov
The Inner Circle '91

Peter Ustinov
Immortal Battalion '44
Billy Budd '62
Lady L '65
Hot Millions '68

Pierre Uytterhoeven
Bandits '86

Jack Vacek
Rock House '92

Roger Vadim
And God Created Woman '57
Dangerous Liaisons '60
Blood and Roses '61

Laszlo Vadnay
Uncertain Glory '44

Emilio Diaz Valcarcel
A Life of Sin '92

Luis Valdez
Zoot Suit '81
La Bamba '87
The Cisco Kid '94

Nick Vallelonga
A Brilliant Disguise '93
In the Kingdom of the Blind the Man with One Eye is King '94

Thanassis Valtinos
Landscape in the Mist '88

Jean-Claude Van Damme
Kickboxer '89
Lionheart '90
Double Impact '91

Anne Van De Putte
To Play or To Die '91

Sytze Van Der Laan
Lily Was Here '89

Keith Van Der Wat
Three Bullets for a Long Gun '73

Jaco Van Dormael
Toto le Heros '91
The Eighth Day '95

Dale Van Every
Trader Horn '31

Melvin Van Peebles
The Story of a Three Day Pass '68
Sweet Sweetback's Baadasssss Song '71
Greased Lightning '77
Sophisticated Gents '81
Panther '95

Gus Van Sant
Drugstore Cowboy '89
My Own Private Idaho '91
Even Cowgirls Get the Blues '94

Virginia Van Upp
Young & Willing '42

Norman Thaddeus Vane
Taxi Dancers '93

Rolfe E. Vanlo
The Informer '29

Agnes Varda
Cleo from 5 to 7 '61
Le Bonheur '65
One Sings, the Other Doesn't '77
Vagabond '85
Jacquot '91

Michael Varhol
The Last Word '80
Pee Wee's Big Adventure '85
The Big Picture '89

John Varley
Millenium '89

Joseph B. Vasquez
Hangin' with the Homeboys '91

Francis Veber
The Tall Blond Man with One Black Shoe '72
Return of the Tall Blond Man With One Black Shoe '74
Le Magnifique '76
Pain in the A— '77
Hothead '78
La Cage aux Folles '78
La Cage aux Folles 2 '81
Partners '82
Les Comperes '83
Three Fugitives '89
My Father the Hero '93

Anthony Veiller
Red Planet Mars '52

Michael Ventura
Roadie '80
Echo Park '86

Ben Verbong
Lily Was Here '89

Mark Verheiden
Timecop '94

Michael Verhoeven
The Nasty Girl '90

Paul Verhoeven
Soldier of Orange '78
Flesh and Blood '85

Cynthia Verlaine
The Substitute '93

Henri Verneuil
Forbidden Fruit '52

Robert Veze
Bikini Summer '91

Michael Vianey
Special Police '85

Barry Victor
Red Scorpion 2 '94
Cyborg 3: The Recycler '95

Mark Victor
Death Hunt '81
Poltergeist '82
Poltergeist 2: The Other Side '86
Marked for Death '90

Gore Vidal
The Catered Affair '56
Suddenly, Last Summer '59
The Best Man '64
Is Paris Burning? '68
Caligula '80
Dress Gray '86
The Palermo Connection '91

King Vidor
Our Daily Bread '34

Peter Viertel
Saboteur '42
White Hunter, Black Heart '90

William Vigil
Mutant Species '95

Daniel Vigne
The Return of Martin Guerre '83
One Woman or Two '85
The King's Whore '90

Jean Vigo
Zero for Conduct '33

Agustin Villaronga
In a Glass Cage '86

Christian Vincent
La Discrete '90
The Separation '94

Dino Vindeni
Voodoo '95

Albert T. Viola
Mondo Balardo '64
Preacherman '83

C.G. Viola
Shoeshine '47

Joe Viola
Hot Box '72

Luchino Visconti
Bellissima '51
Sandra of a Thousand Delights '65

Randal Viscovich
Night Visitor '89

Gino Vissentini
Il Bell'Antonio '60

Karl-Wilhelm Vivier
The Bridge '59

John Vlahos
Tonto Basin Outlaws '41

Stephen Volk
Gothic '87

Karl Vollmoller
The Blue Angel '30

Alexander Volodin
Autumn Marathon '79

Bobby Von Hayes
Clifford '92

Josef von Sternberg
Dishonored '31

Erich von Stroheim
Devil Doll '36

Lars von Trier
Zentropa '92
Breaking the Waves '95
The Kingdom '95

Margarethe von Trotta
Coup de Grace '78
Sheer Madness '84
Rosa Luxemburg '86
The Promise '95

Cyrus Voris
Men of War '94
Tales from the Crypt Presents Demon Knight '94
Josh Kirby...Time Warrior: Chapter 1, Planet of the Dino-Knights '95
Josh Kirby...Time Warrior: Chapter 2, The Human Pets '95
Josh Kirby...Time Warrior: Chapter 5, Journey to the Magic Cavern '96
Josh Kirby...Time Warrior: Chapter 6, Last Battle for the Universe '96

Niels Vorsel
Zentropa '92

Kurt Voss
Border Radio '88
Genuine Risk '89
Delusion '91
Where the Day Takes You '92
Baja '95

Otakar Votocek
Wings of Fame '93

Andy Wachowski
Assassins '95
Bound '96

Larry Wachowski
Assassins '95
Bound '96

Natto Wada
Enjo '58
An Actor's Revenge '63

Kevin Wade
Working Girl '88
Mr. Baseball '92
Junior '94

Maggie Wadey
The Buccaneers '95

Mark Wadlow
The Silent Touch '94

Bruce Wagner
A Nightmare on Elm Street 3: Dream Warriors '87
Scenes from the Class Struggle in Beverly Hills '89
Wild Palms '93
White Dwarf '95

Jane Wagner
The Incredible Shrinking Woman '81
Search for Signs of Intelligent Life in the Universe '91

Michael Waite
Fun Down There '88

Ralph Waite
On the Nickel '80

Andrzej Wajda
Innocent Sorcerers '60
Lotna '64
Land of Promise '74
Without Anesthesia '78
Danton '82
A Love in Germany '84

Eliot Wald
See No Evil, Hear No Evil '89
Camp Nowhere '94
Down Periscope '96

Edwards Waldman
The Pink Panther Strikes Again '76

Frank Waldman
Return of the Pink Panther '74
The Pink Panther Strikes Again '76
Revenge of the Pink Panther '78
Trail of the Pink Panther '82

Andrew Kevin Walker
Brainscan '94
Hideaway '94
Seven '95

Keith A. Walker
Free Willy '93

Tom Walla
The Haunting of Seacliff Inn '94

Doug Wallace
Sensation '94

Earl W. Wallace
The Broken Chain '93

Irving Wallace
The West Point Story '50
Split Second '53
Sincerely Yours '56

Randall Wallace
Braveheart '95

Tommy Lee Wallace
Fright Night 2 '88

Ira Wallach
Boys' Night Out '62
Hot Millions '68

Kathryn Wallack
Sabrina the Teenage Witch '96

Anthony Waller
Mute Witness '95

Tom Walmsley
Paris, France '94

Hugh Walpole
David Copperfield '35

Des Walsh
The Boys of St. Vincent '93

Frances Walsh
Meet the Feebles '89
Heavenly Creatures '94
The Frighteners '96

Raoul Walsh
Esther and the King '60

Rupert Walters
Restoration '94

Fred Walton
Hadley's Rebellion '84
The Rosary Murders '87
Trapped '89
When a Stranger Calls Back '93

Hui-Ling Wang
Eat Drink Man Woman '94

Peter Wang
A Great Wall '86
The Laserman '90

Wayne Wang
Blue in the Face '95

Orville Wanzer
The Devil's Mistress '68

David S. Ward
Steelyard Blues '73
The Sting '73
Cannery Row '82
The Sting 2 '83
Saving Grace '86
The Milagro Beanfield War '88
Major League '89
King Ralph '91
The Program '93
Sleepless in Seattle '93

Donal Lardner Ward
My Life's In Turnaround '94

Edmund Ward
Twinsanity '70
Prayer for the Dying '87

Kelly Ward
Once Upon a Forest '93
All Dogs Go to Heaven 2 '95

Morgan Ward
A Pyromaniac's Love Story '95

Stephen Ward
Backbeat '94

Vincent Ward
Vigil '84
The Navigator '88
Map of the Human Heart '93

David Warfield
Private Investigations '87
Kill Me Again '89
Kiss of a Killer '93

Regis Wargnier
Indochine '92

Charles Marquis Warren
Charro! '69

Hal P. Warren
Manos, the Hands of Fate '66

Jerry Warren
Terror of the Bloodhunters '62

John Warren
Naked in New York '93
Flashfire '94
Girl in the Cadillac '94

Joyce Warren
The Ice Runner '93

Deric Washburn
Silent Running '71
The Deer Hunter '78
The Border '82
Extreme Prejudice '87

Art Washington
Percy & Thunder '93

Wendy Wasserstein
The Heidi Chronicles '95

Daniel Waters
The Adventures of Ford Fairlane '90
Hudson Hawk '91
Batman Returns '92
Demolition Man '93

John Waters
Mondo Trasho '69
Pink Flamingos '72
Female Trouble '74
Desperate Living '77
Polyester '81
Hairspray '88
Cry-Baby '90
Serial Mom '94

Peter Watkins
Edvard Munch '74

John Watson
The Zoo Gang '85
Robin Hood: Prince of Thieves '91

Damon Wayans
Mo' Money '92
Blankman '94
Major Payne '95

Keenen Ivory Wayans
Hollywood Shuffle '87
I'm Gonna Git You Sucka '88
The Five Heartbeats '91
A Low Down Dirty Shame '94

April Wayne
Dead On '93

Frank Wead
Ceiling Zero '35
Dive Bomber '41

Julian Weaver
Demon Possessed '93

Arthur Webb
Trained to Kill '88

James R. Webb
How the West Was Won '63

Weaver Webb
Courage Mountain '89

David Wechter
Midnight Madness '80
Malibu Bikini Shop '86

Lu Wei
Farewell My Concubine '93
To Live '94

John Weidner
Midnight Kiss '93
Private Wars '93

Herschel Weingrod
Cheaper to Keep Her '80
Trading Places '83
Brewster's Millions '85
My Stepmother Is an Alien '88
Twins '88
Kindergarten Cop '90
Pure Luck '91

Sandra Weintraub
The Deadliest Art: The Best of the Martial Arts Films '90

Peter Weir
The Cars That Ate Paris '74
The Last Wave '77
Plumber '79
Gallipoli '81
The Year of Living Dangerously '82
Green Card '90

Brenda Weisberg
The Mad Ghoul '43
The Mummy's Ghost '44
Rusty's Birthday '49

David Weisberg
Holy Matrimony '94

Joe Weisenfeld
Anne of Green Gables '85

Stanley Weiser
Project X '87
Wall Street '87
Fatherland '94

David A. Weiss
All Dogs Go to Heaven '89
Rock-a-Doodle '92

Jiri Weiss
Martha and I '91

Marie Weiss
The Ref '93

Rob Weiss
Amongst Friends '93

David Weissman
Dream a Little Dream 2 '94

Peter Welbeck
The Mangler '94

Sandy Welch
A Dark Adapted Eye '93

Colin Welland
Yanks '79
Chariots of Fire '81
Twice in a Lifetime '85
A Dry White Season '89
War of the Buttons '95

Michael Weller
Hair '79
Ragtime '81
Lost Angels '89

Halsted Welles
The Hanging Tree '59

Orson Welles
Citizen Kane '41
The Magnificent Ambersons '42
The Lady from Shanghai '48
Touch of Evil '58
Chimes at Midnight '67
Treasure Island '72

David Wellington
A Man in Uniform '93

William A. Wellman
A Star is Born '37

George Wells
The Show-Off '46
Merton of the Movies '47
Angels in the Outfield '51
Designing Woman '57
Don't Go Near the Water '57
The Gazebo '59
The Horizontal Lieutenant '62
The Impossible Years '68

John Wells
Princess Caraboo '94

Peter Wells
Desperate Remedies '93

Wim Wenders
Alice in the Cities '74
Kings of the Road—In the Course of Time '76
The American Friend '77
Lightning Over Water '80
Tokyo-Ga '85
Wings of Desire '88
Until The End of The World '91
Faraway, So Close! '93

Gina Wendkos
Ginger Ale Afternoon '89
Jersey Girl '92

Mike Werb
Machine Gun Kelly '58
The Mask '94
Darkman 3: Die Darkman Die '95

Lina Wertmuller
Seduction of Mimi '72
Love and Anarchy '73
All Screwed Up '74
Swept Away... '75
Seven Beauties '76
A Night Full of Rain '78
Blood Feud '79
A Joke of Destiny, Lying in Wait Around the Corner Like a Bandit '84
Camorra: The Naples Connection '85
Sotto, Sotto '85
Summer Night with Greek Profile, Almond Eyes & Scent of Basil '87
Ciao, Professore! '94

Quentin Werty
Dark of the Sun '68

Richard Wesley
Uptown Saturday Night '74
Let's Do It Again '75
Fast Forward '84
Native Son '86

Claudine West
The Mortal Storm '40
Mrs. Miniver '42

Jessamyn West
Stolen Hours '63

Joseph West
Man Made Monster '41

Mae West
Night After Night '32
I'm No Angel '33
Belle of the Nineties '34
Goin' to Town '35
Go West, Young Man '36
Klondike Annie '36
Every Day's a Holiday '38

Roland West
The Bat '26
The Bat Whispers '30

Robert Westerby
Sea of Sand '58

Donald E. Westlake
Cops and Robbers '73
Hot Stuff '80
The Stepfather '87
The Grifters '90
Why Me? '90

Ellen Weston
Lies Before Kisses '92

Eric Weston
Marvin & Tige '84

Fulvio Wetzl
Rorret '87

Gerald Wexler
Margaret's Museum '95

Haskell Wexler
Medium Cool '69
Latino '85

John Wexley
Angels with Dirty Faces '38
Footsteps in the Dark '41

Joseph Whaley
Bodily Harm '95

Jim Wheat
Silent Scream '80
The Fly 2 '89
The Birds 2: Land's End '94
Rattled '96

Ken Wheat
Silent Scream '80
The Fly 2 '89
The Birds 2: Land's End '94
Rattled '96

Joss Whedon
Buffy the Vampire Slayer '92
Toy Story '95

Anne Wheeler
Bye Bye Blues '89

Paul Wheeler
Poldark '75

Graeme Whifler
Sonny Boy '87

Dr. Giggles '92
Denis Whitburn
The Cursed Mountain Mystery '93
Cynthia Whitcomb
Buffalo Girls '95
Garry Michael White
Sky Riders '76
The Promise '78
James Gordon White
Hell's Belles '69
Wally White
Lie Down with Dogs '95
Hugh Whitemore
Elizabeth R '72
The Rector's Wife '94
Jane Eyre '96
Steve Whitestone
The Pebble and the Penguin '94
Preston A. Whitmore, II
The Walking Dead '94
Fled '96
David Wickes
Jack the Ripper '88
Jekyll and Hyde '90
Frankenstein '93
Bernhard Wicki
The Longest Day '62
Gregory Widen
Highlander '86
Backdraft '91
The Prophecy '95
Bo Widerberg
Elvira Madigan '67
All Things Fair '95
John Wierick
Bopha! '93
Joe Wiesenfeld
The Yearling '94
Crane Wilbur
Yellow Cargo '36
Billy Wilder
Bluebeard's Eighth Wife '38
Midnight '39
Ninotchka '39
Ball of Fire '41
Double Indemnity '44
The Lost Weekend '45
Emperor Waltz '48
Sunset Boulevard '50
Stalag 17 '53
Sabrina '54
The Seven Year Itch '55
Love in the Afternoon '57
Spirit of St. Louis '57
Witness for the Prosecution '57
Some Like It Hot '59
The Apartment '60
One, Two, Three '61
Irma La Douce '63
Kiss Me, Stupid! '64
The Fortune Cookie '66
The Private Life of Sherlock Holmes '70
Avanti! '72
The Front Page '74
Buddy Buddy '81
Gene Wilder
Young Frankenstein '74
World's Greatest Lover '77
The Adventures of Sherlock Holmes' Smarter Brother '78
The Woman in Red '84
Haunted Honeymoon '86
See No Evil, Hear No Evil '89
John Wilder
Breaking Home Ties '87
Return to Lonesome Dove '93
Robert Wilder
Flamingo Road '49
Thorton Wilder
Shadow of a Doubt '43
Yvonne Wilder
The Return of Count Yorga '71
John Wiles
Poldark 2 '75
Ethan Wiley
House '86
House 2: The Second Story '87

Elaine Wilkerson
The Speed Lovers '68
Rich Wilkes
Airheads '94
The Jerky Boys '95
Charles Wilkinson
Quarantine '89
Christopher Wilkinson
Nixon '95
Barbara Williams
Jury Duty '95
Bob Williams
Silver City Bonanza '51
Charles Williams
The Hot Spot '90
Chuck Williams
Dark Rider '91
Emlyn Williams
The Man Who Knew Too Much '34
The Last Days of Dolwyn '49
Samm-Art Williams
Charlotte Forten's Mission: Experiment in Freedom '85
Spencer Williams, Jr.
Harlem Rides the Range '39
Son of Ingagi '40
Blood of Jesus '41
Tennessee Williams
A Streetcar Named Desire '51
The Rose Tattoo '55
Baby Doll '56
The Glass Menagerie '87
Orpheus Descending '91
Tyger Williams
Menace II Society '93
David Williamson
Don's Party '76
The Club '81
Gallipoli '81
The Year of Living Dangerously '82
Phar Lap '84
Travelling North '87
Dangerous Life '89
Fred Williamson
Boss '74
Adios Amigo '75
Thomas Williamson
Escape Me Never '47
Calder Willingham
Paths of Glory '57
The Vikings '58
One-Eyed Jacks '61
The Graduate '67
Little Big Man '70
Thieves Like Us '74
Rambling Rose '91
Constance Willis
A Man for All Seasons '66
Alice Wilson
I'm Dangerous Tonight '90
August Wilson
The Piano Lesson '94
Carey Wilson
He Who Gets Slapped '24
Mutiny on the Bounty '35
David Wilson
The Perfect Weapon '91
Strangers in Good Company '91
Dean Wilson
Blind Faith '89
Donald Wilson
Three Cases of Murder '55
Gerald Wilson
Lawman '71
Hugh Wilson
Stroker Ace '83
Police Academy '84
Rustler's Rhapsody '85
Burglar '87
Guarding Tess '94
Down Periscope '96
Lanford Wilson
The Migrants '74
Michael Wilson
Five Fingers '52

The Bridge on the River Kwai '57
Lawrence of Arabia '62
Michael G. Wilson
Planet of the Apes '68
For Your Eyes Only '81
Octopussy '83
A View to a Kill '85
The Living Daylights '87
License to Kill '89
Owen C. Wilson
Bottle Rocket '95
Richard Wilson
It's All True '93
Sandy Wilson
My American Cousin '85
American Boyfriends '89
Snoo Wilson
Shadey '87
S.S. Wilson
Short Circuit '86
*batteries not included '87
Short Circuit 2 '88
Tremors '89
Ghost Dad '90
Heart and Souls '93
Tremors 2: Aftershocks '96
Kurt Wimmer
The Neighbor '93
Relative Fear '95
Arthur Wimperis
The Private Life of Henry VIII '33
Mrs. Miniver '42
Young Bess '53
Charles Winkler
You Talkin' to Me? '87
Disturbed '90
Irwin Winkler
Guilty by Suspicion '91
Terence H. Winkless
The Howling '81
He's My Girl '87
Corporate Affairs '90
Rage and Honor '92
Michael Winner
Murder on the Campus '52
The Sentinel '76
The Big Sleep '78
Firepower '79
The Wicked Lady '83
Appointment with Death '88
A Chorus of Disapproval '89
Bullseye! '90
Peter Winograd
One Last Run '89
Alex Winter
Freaked '93
Aubrey Wisberg
The Adventures of Rusty '45
Norman Wisdom
What's Good for the Goose '69
David Wise
Beastmaster 3: The Eye of Braxus '95
Naomi Wise
Mouth to Mouth '95
Thomas Wiseman
Romantic Englishwoman '75
William Wisher
Judge Dredd '95
Doris Wishman
Bad Girls Go to Hell '65
William D. Wittliff
The Black Stallion '79
Honeysuckle Rose '80
Raggedy Man '81
Country '84
Red Headed Stranger '87
Lonesome Dove '89
Lone Justice '93
Lone Justice 2 '93
The Cowboy Way '94
Legends of the Fall '94
Stefan Wodoslowsky
Crazy Moon '87
John Wohlbruck
End of the Line '88
Claire Wojas
L'Enfant d'Eau '95

David M. Wolf
Hit! '73
Dick Wolf
Skateboard '77
Gas '81
No Man's Land '87
Masquerade '88
School Ties '92
Fred Wolf
Black Sheep '96
Lalo Wolf
Undercover '94
Andy Wolk
Criminal Justice '90
Dave Wollert
Near Misses '91
Quicksand: No Escape '91
M. Wallace Wolodarsky
Coldblooded '94
James Wolpaw
Complex World '92
Barry Wong
Hard-Boiled '92
James Wong
The Boys Next Door '85
John Woo
The Killer '90
Charles Wood
Help! '65
The Knack '65
How I Won the War '67
The Charge of the Light Brigade '68
Cuba '79
An Awfully Big Adventure '94
Sharpe's Company '94
Edward D. Wood, Jr.
The Violent Years '56
The Bride & the Beast '58
Orgy of the Dead '65
Victoria Wood
Happy Since I Met You '89
Christopher Wooden
Dinosaur Island '93
Grahame Woods
Glory Enough for All: The Discovery of Insulin '92
Walter Woods
The Pony Express '25
Abbe Wool
Roadside Prophets '92
Linda Woolverton
Homeward Bound: The Incredible Journey '93
David Worth
Lady Dragon '92
Martin Worth
Poldark 2 '75
Jan Worthington
Danielle Steel's Heartbeat '93
Soenke Wortmann
Maybe...Maybe Not '94
Geoffrey Wright
Romper Stomper '92
Donald Wrye
Ice Castles '79
Rudy Wurlitzer
Glen and Randa '71
Pat Garrett & Billy the Kid '73
Candy Mountain '87
Walker '87
Voyager '91
Shadow of the Wolf '92
Wind '92
Little Buddha '93
Robert Wyler
Detective Story '51
Philip Wylie
Island of Lost Souls '32
Murders in the Zoo '33
Ned Wynn
Don't Go to Sleep '82
Tracy Keenan Wynn
The Longest Yard '74
The Drowning Pool '75
The Deep '77

The FBI Murders '88
Carolina Skeletons '92
Jim Wynorski
Forbidden World '82
Sorceress '82
The Lost Empire '83
Screwballs '83
Chopping Mall '86
Big Bad Mama 2 '87
Deathstalker 2: Duel of the Titans '87
Not of This Earth '88
Think Big '90
The Haunting of Morella '91
Final Embrace '92
Boaz Yakin
Fresh '94
David Yallop
Beyond Reasonable Doubt '80
Mitsuo Yanagimachi
Shadow of China '91
George Worthing Yates
Cavalry Charge '51
Earth vs. the Spider '58
Jack Yellen
My Lucky Star '38
Linda Yellen
Chantilly Lace '93
Bennett Yellin
Dumb & Dumber '94
Yevgeny Yevtushenko
I Am Cuba '64
Valentin Yezhov
Siberiade '79
Rafael Yglesias
Fearless '93
Death and the Maiden '94
Da Ying
Red Firecracker, Green Firecracker '93
Yoshikata Yoda
Utamaro and His Five Women '46
A Geisha '53
Sansho the Bailiff '54
Jeff Yonis
Firehawk '92
Bloodfist 5: Human Target '93
Philip Yordan
Dillinger '45
The Chase '46
Whistle Stop '46
House of Strangers '49
Reign of Terror '49
Detective Story '51
Drums in the Deep South '51
Mutiny '52
Houdini '53
Johnny Guitar '53
Blowing Wild '54
Broken Lance '54
Naked Jungle '54
Big Combo '55
The Man from Laramie '55
Savage Wilderness '55
The Harder They Fall '56
Men in War '57
The Bravados '58
God's Little Acre '58
The Bramble Bush '60
Studs Lonigan '60
El Cid '61
The King of Kings '61
Day of the Triffids '63
55 Days at Peking '63
The Fall of the Roman Empire '64
Battle of the Bulge '65
Captain Apache '71
Bad Man's River '72
Bloody Wednesday '87
The Unholy '88
Dan York
Flashfire '94
Daniel Yost
Drugstore Cowboy '89
Graham Yost
Speed '94
Broken Arrow '95
Robert Yost
Arizona Mahoney '36

Cinematographer Index

The **Cinematographer Index** provides a videography for any cinematographer, or Director of Photography, as they are also known, with a video credit. The listings for the cinematographer names follow an alphabetical sort by last name (although the names appear in a first name last name format). The videographies are listed chronologically, from oldest film to the most recent. If a cinematographer lensed more than one film in the same year, these movies are listed alphabetically within the year. Many of today's top directors started as cinematographers, the people responsible for the "look" of a movie.

Thomas Ackerman
Jumanji *'95*

Barry Ackroyd
Land and Freedom *'95*

Remi Adefarasin
Captives *'94*

Lloyd Ahern
Trespass *'92*
Geronimo: An American Legend *'93*
Wild Bill *'95*

Mac Ahlberg
The Late Shift *'96*

Pierre Aim
Cafe au Lait *'94*
Hate *'95*

Robert Alazraki
The Old Lady Who Walked in the Sea *'91*

Arthur Albert
One Night Stand *'95*
Happy Gilmore *'96*

Jose Luis Alcaine
Two Much *'96*

John Alcott
Zontar, the Thing from Venus *'66*
Beastmaster *'82*

Henri Alekan
Forbidden Fruit *'52*
Mayerling *'68*

Nestor Almendros
La Collectionneuse *'67*
Six in Paris *'68*
More *'69*
My Night at Maud's *'69*
The Wild Child *'70*
Claire's Knee *'71*
Chloe in the Afternoon *'72*
Two English Girls *'72*
Cockfighter *'74*
Story of Adele H. *'75*
Maitresse *'76*
Madame Rosa *'77*
The Man Who Loved Women *'77*
Days of Heaven *'78*
The Green Room *'78*
Love on the Run *'78*
Kramer vs. Kramer *'79*
The Blue Lagoon *'80*
The Last Metro *'80*
Sophie's Choice *'82*
Confidentially Yours *'83*
Pauline at the Beach *'83*
Places in the Heart *'84*
Heartburn *'86*
Nadine *'87*
New York Stories *'89*

Alan Almond
Loaded *'96*

John A. Alonzo
Bloody Mama *'70*
Harold and Maude *'71*
Vanishing Point *'71*
Lady Sings the Blues *'72*
Pete 'n' Tillie *'72*
Sounder *'72*
Chinatown *'74*
Conrack *'74*
Farewell, My Lovely *'75*
Once is Not Enough *'75*
The Bad News Bears *'76*
I Will, I Will for Now *'76*
Black Sunday *'77*
Casey's Shadow *'78*
The Cheap Detective *'78*
Norma Rae *'79*
Tom Horn *'80*
Back Roads *'81*
Zorro, the Gay Blade *'81*
Blue Thunder *'83*
Cross Creek *'83*
Scarface *'83*
Out of Control *'85*
Nothing in Common *'86*
Overboard *'87*
Physical Evidence *'89*
Steel Magnolias *'89*
Internal Affairs *'90*
Navy SEALS *'90*
Housesitter *'92*
The Meteor Man *'93*
World War II: When Lions Roared *'94*

John Alton
Courageous Dr. Christian *'40*
T-Men *'47*
He Walked by Night *'48*
Reign of Terror *'49*
Father of the Bride *'50*
An American in Paris *'51*
Battle Circus *'53*
Big Combo *'55*
The Catered Affair *'56*
Tea and Sympathy *'56*
The Teahouse of the August Moon *'56*
Designing Woman *'57*
The Brothers Karamazov *'58*
Elmer Gantry *'60*

Juan Amoros
Mouth to Mouth *'95*

Jamie Anderson
Man of the House *'95*
The Juror *'96*

Shohei Ando
Hiroshima *'95*

Yves Angelo
Tous les Matins du Monde *'92*
Germinal *'93*

Gregg Araki
Totally F***ed Up *'94*

Thierry Arbogast
La Femme Nikita *'91*
The Professional *'94*
The Horseman on the Roof *'95*

Fernando Arguelles
The Shooter *'94*
Wes Craven Presents Mind Ripper *'95*

John Aronson
Suspect Device *'95*

Yorgos Arvanitis
Total Eclipse *'95*
Ulysses' Gaze *'95*

Howard Atherton
Bad Boys *'95*
Gulliver's Travels *'95*

John G. Avildsen
Cry Uncle *'71*

Andre Bac
The Red Inn *'51*

Hanania Baer
Last Summer In the Hamptons *'96*

John Bailey
Premonition *'71*
American Gigolo *'79*
Boulevard Nights *'79*
Ordinary People *'80*
Honky Tonk Freeway *'81*
Cat People *'82*
End of August *'82*
That Championship Season *'82*
The Big Chill *'83*
Without a Trace *'83*
The Pope of Greenwich Village *'84*
Racing with the Moon *'84*
Mishima: A Life in Four Chapters *'85*
Silverado *'85*
Brighton Beach Memoirs *'86*
Light of Day *'87*
Swimming to Cambodia *'87*
The Accidental Tourist *'88*
Vibes *'88*
My Blue Heaven *'90*
A Brief History of Time *'92*
In the Line of Fire *'93*

Ian Baker
Roxanne *'87*
The Russia House *'90*
Mr. Baseball *'92*
Six Degrees of Separation *'93*

Lucien Ballard
Ride the High Country *'62*
The Wild Bunch *'69*
Ballad of Cable Hogue *'70*
The Getaway *'72*
Junior Bonner *'72*

Michael Ballhaus
Beware of a Holy Whore *'70*
The Bitter Tears of Petra von Kant *'72*
Fox and His Friends *'75*
Mother Kusters Goes to Heaven *'76*
The Stationmaster's Wife *'77*
Despair *'78*
The Marriage of Maria Braun *'79*
Baby It's You *'82*
Heartbreakers *'84*
Sheer Madness *'84*
After Hours *'85*
Chinese Roulette *'86*
The Color of Money *'86*
Death of a Salesman *'86*
Broadcast News *'87*
Dirty Rotten Scoundrels *'88*
The Last Temptation of Christ *'88*
Working Girl *'88*
The Fabulous Baker Boys *'89*
Goodfellas *'90*
Postcards from the Edge *'90*
Guilty by Suspicion *'91*
What About Bob? *'91*
Bram Stoker's Dracula *'92*
The Mambo Kings *'92*
The Age of Innocence *'93*
Outbreak *'94*

Larry Banks
The Show *'95*

Jim Barham
The Man with the Perfect Swing *'95*

George Barnes
Dangerous Hours *'19*
Peg O' My Heart *'22*
The Eagle *'25*
Son of the Sheik *'26*
Our Dancing Daughters *'28*
Street Scene *'31*
Footlight Parade *'33*
Dames *'34*
Gold Diggers of 1935 *'35*
Marked Woman *'37*
Stanley and Livingstone *'39*
Rebecca *'40*
Meet John Doe *'41*
That Uncertain Feeling *'41*
Once Upon a Honeymoon *'42*
Mr. Lucky *'43*
Jane Eyre *'44*
None But the Lonely Heart *'44*
The Bells of St. Mary's *'45*
The Spanish Main *'45*
Spellbound *'45*
Sister Kenny *'46*
Sinbad, the Sailor *'47*
Emperor Waltz *'48*
Force of Evil *'49*
Riding High *'50*
Samson and Delilah *'50*
The War of the Worlds *'53*

Andrzej Bartkowiak
Losing Isaiah *'94*

Bartkowiak ▶cont.

Jade '95
Species '95

Adolfo Bartoli
Forbidden Zone: Alien Abduction '96

Bojan Bazelli
The Rapture '91
Deep Cover '92
Body Snatchers '93
Kalifornia '93

Alfonso Beato
The Flower of My Secret '95

Steven Bernsein
Like Water for Chocolate '93
Kicking and Screaming '95

Eduardo Berra
Funny Bones '94

Ross Berryman
The Hard Truth '94
Playmaker '94
Chameleon '95
Gold Diggers: The Secret of Bear Mountain '95

Renato Berta
Messidor '77

Kent Beyda
Forget Paris '95

Luca Bigazzi
Lamerica '95

Joseph Biroc
Magic Town '47
Cry Danger '51
Donovan's Brain '53
Tall Texan '53
The Amazing Colossal Man '57
The FBI Story '59
Ice Palace '60
The Devil at 4 O'Clock '61
Bye, Bye, Birdie '63
Toys in the Attic '63
Viva Las Vegas '63
The Flight of the Phoenix '65
Hush, Hush, Sweet Charlotte '65
The Russians are Coming, the Russians are Coming '66
Enter Laughing '67
Who's Minding the Mint? '67
The Detective '68
Lady in Cement '68
The Killing of Sister George '69
Whatever Happened to Aunt Alice? '69
Too Late the Hero '70
Escape from the Planet of the Apes '71
The Grissom Gang '71
The Organization '71
Ulzana's Raid '72
Blazing Saddles '74
The Longest Yard '74
The Towering Inferno '74
The Hustle '75
The Duchess and the Dirtwater Fox '76
The Choirboys '77
Beyond the Poseidon Adventure '79
Airplane! '80
...All the Marbles '81
Airplane 2: The Sequel '82
Hammett '82

Peter Biziou
Mississippi Burning '88
Richard III '95

Patrick Blossier
Innocent Lies '95

Ralf Bode
Foreplay '75
Saturday Night Fever '77
Rich Kids '79
Coal Miner's Daughter '80
Dressed to Kill '80
A Long Way Home '81
Raggedy Man '81
A Little Sex '82
Gorky Park '83
Critical Condition '86
Violets Are Blue '86
Big Town '87
The Accused '88
Distant Thunder '88
Cousins '89
Uncle Buck '89
One Good Cop '91
Gypsy '93
The Big Green '95
A Streetcar Named Desire '95

Alun Bollinger
The Frighteners '96

Michael Bonvillain
Amongst Friends '93
The Desperate Trail '94
Saints and Sinners '95

Rick Bota
Barb Wire '96

Jean Bourgoin
La Marseillaise '37
Voyage-Suprise '46
Dedee d'Anvers '49
Mr. Arkadin '55
Black Orpheus '58
Mon Oncle '58
The Counterfeit Traitor '62

Richard Bowen
Fair Game '95

Russell Boyd
Operation Dumbo Drop '95

Russ Brandt
Excessive Force 2: Force on Force '95

Woody Bredell
His Butler's Sister '43
Lady On a Train '45

Brian J. Breheny
The Adventures of Priscilla, Queen of the Desert '94

Robert Brinkmann
The Cable Guy '96

Norbert Brodine
House on 92nd Street '45
Boomerang '47

Morten Bruus
All Things Fair '95

John Buck
The Frighteners '96

Bobby Bukowski
Search and Destroy '94
The Tie That Binds '95
Tom and Huck '95

Don Burgess
Mo' Money '92
Josh and S.A.M. '93
Forrest Gump '94
Richie Rich '94

Robert Burks
Beyond the Forest '49
The Fountainhead '49
The Enforcer '51
Strangers on a Train '51
The Desert Song '53
Hondo '53
I Confess '53
Dial "M" for Murder '54
Rear Window '54
To Catch a Thief '55
The Trouble with Harry '55
The Man Who Knew Too Much '56
The Wrong Man '56
Vertigo '58
Black Orchid '59
But Not for Me '59
North by Northwest '59
The Rat Race '60
The Great Impostor '61
The Music Man '62
The Birds '63
Marnie '64
A Patch of Blue '65
Waterhole #3 '67
The Glass Menagerie '87

David Burr
The Phantom '96
Race the Sun '96

Dan Burstall
Crime Broker '94

Thomas Burstyn
The Surgeon '94
Magic in the Water '95

Geoff Burton
Sorrento Beach '95

Stephen Burum
The Escape Artist '82
The Entity '83
The Outsiders '83
Rumble Fish '83
Something Wicked This Way Comes '83
Uncommon Valor '83
Body Double '84
The Bride '85
St. Elmo's Fire '85
The Untouchables '87
Arthur 2: On the Rocks '88
Casualties of War '89
The War of the Roses '89
Hoffa '92
Raising Cain '92
Carlito's Way '93
The Shadow '94
Mission: Impossible '96

Bill Butler
Flipper '96

Lamberto Caimi
Fiances '63

Thomas Callaway
Assault of the Killer Bimbos '88

Tom Calloway
Night of the Scarecrow '95

Maurizio Calvesi
Acla's Descent into Floristella '87

Paul Cameron
The Last Supper '96

John Campbell
Even Cowgirls Get the Blues '94

Jack Cardiff
Black Narcissus '47
The Red Shoes '48
The African Queen '51
Pandora and the Flying Dutchman '51
The Master of Ballantrae '53
The Barefoot Contessa '54
The Brave One '56
Legend of the Lost '57
The Prince and the Showgirl '57
The Vikings '58
Fanny '61
Death on the Nile '78
The Prince and the Pauper '78
Avalanche Express '79
The Fifth Musketeer '79
The Awakening '80
The Dogs of War '81
Ghost Story '81
The Wicked Lady '83
Conan the Destroyer '84
Rambo: First Blood, Part 2 '85
Tai-Pan '86
Million Dollar Mystery '87

Russell Carpenter
The Lady in White '88
The Lawnmower Man '92
Solar Crisis '92
Hard Target '93
True Lies '94
The Indian in the Cupboard '95

James L. Carter
Destiny Turns on the Radio '95

Alan Caso
Ed '96

Francois Catonne
My Life and Times with Antonin Artaud '93

Sarah Cawley
A Reason to Believe '95

Caroline Champtier
Helas Pour Moi '94

Tom Chaney
Mosquito '95

Gu Changwei
Red Sorghum '87
Ju Dou '90
Life on a String '90
Farewell My Concubine '93

Michael Chapman
The Last Detail '73
The White Dawn '75
The Arab Conspiracy '76
The Front '76
Taxi Driver '76
Fingers '78
Invasion of the Body Snatchers '78
The Last Waltz '78
Hardcore '79
Wanderers '79
Raging Bull '80
Dead Men Don't Wear Plaid '82
Personal Best '82
The Man with Two Brains '83
Scrooged '88
Shoot to Kill '88
Ghostbusters 2 '89
Kindergarten Cop '90
Quick Change '90
The Fugitive '93
Primal Fear '96

Dominique Chapuis
Mina Tannenbaum '94

Richard Clabaugh
The Prophecy '95

Barbara Claman
Beastmaster 3: The Eye of Braxus '95

Ghislan Cloquet
Girl in His Pocket '57
Belle Americaine '61
The Fire Within '64
Mickey One '65
Mouchette '67
A Gentle Woman '69
Marry Me, Marry Me '69
Donkey Skin '70
Love and Death '75
Tess '80
Four Friends '81
I Sent a Letter to My Love '81

William Clothier
Phantom from Space '53
Blood Alley '55
Sea Chase '55
Darby's Rangers '58
Lafayette Escadrille '58
The Horse Soldiers '59
The Alamo '60
The Comancheros '61
Deadly Companions '61
The Man Who Shot Liberty Valance '62
Merrill's Marauders '62
Donovan's Reef '63
McLintock! '63
Cheyenne Autumn '64
Shenandoah '65
The Rare Breed '66
The War Wagon '67
The Way West '67
Bandolero! '68
The Devil's Brigade '68
Firecreek '68
Hellfighters '68
The Undefeated '69
The Cheyenne Social Club '70
Chisum '70
Rio Lobo '70
Big Jake '71
Train Robbers '73

Peter Collister
Dunston Checks In '95

Edward Colman
The Shaggy Dog '59
The Absent-Minded Professor '61
Babes in Toyland '61
Big Red '62
The Misadventures of Merlin Jones '63
Savage Sam '63
Son of Flubber '63
Mary Poppins '64
Monkey's Uncle '65
That Darn Cat '65
Those Calloways '65
The Ugly Dachshund '65
The Adventures of Bullwhip Griffin '66
Blackbeard's Ghost '67
The Gnome-Mobile '67
The Happiest Millionaire '67
The Love Bug '68

David Connell
Buffalo Girls '95
Silver Strand '95

Jack Conroy
The Hunted '94
Broken Harvest '95
Homeward Bound 2: Lost in San Francisco '96

Steven Consentino
The Show '95

Fabio Conversi
Love After Love '94

Wilkie Cooper
Sea of Sand '58

Ericson Core
The Show '95

Michael Coulter
The Neon Bible '95
Sense and Sensibility '95

Raoul Coutard
The Bride Wore Black '68

Jordan Cronenweth
Altered States '80
Blade Runner '82

Floyd Crosby
Tabu: A Story of the South Seas '31
High Noon '52
I, Mobster '58
Machine Gun Kelly '58
The Fall of the House of Usher '60
The Pit and the Pendulum '61
Premature Burial '62
Tales of Terror '62
The Raven '63
Sallah '63
X: The Man with X-Ray Eyes '63
Bikini Beach '64
The Comedy of Terrors '64
Pajama Party '64
How to Stuff a Wild Bikini '65

Richard Crudo
Federal Hill '94

Dean Cundey
Where the Red Fern Grows '74
The Fog '78
Halloween '78
Rock 'n' Roll High School '79
Escape from New York '81
The Thing '82
Psycho 2 '83
Romancing the Stone '84
Back to the Future '85
Big Trouble in Little China '86
Project X '87
Big Business '88
Who Framed Roger Rabbit '88
Back to the Future, Part 2 '89
Road House '89
Back to the Future, Part 3 '90
Hook '91
Death Becomes Her '92
Jurassic Park '93
Apollo 13 '95
Casper '95

Erik Daarstad
Frank and Ollie '95

John Daly
Persuasion '95

Lee Daniel
Before Sunrise '94

William H. Daniels
The Flesh and the Devil '27
The Mysterious Lady '28
Wild Orchids '28
The Kiss '29
Anna Christie '30
Romance '30
A Free Soul '31
Susan Lenox: Her Fall and Rise '31
Grand Hotel '32
Mata Hari '32
Rasputin and the Empress '32
Dinner at Eight '33
Queen Christina '33
The Barretts of Wimpole Street '34
The Painted Veil '34
Anna Karenina '35
Naughty Marietta '35
Camille '36
Romeo and Juliet '36
Rose Marie '36
Broadway Melody of 1938 '37
Marie Antoinette '38
Idiot's Delight '39
Ninotchka '39
The Mortal Storm '40
The Shop Around the Corner '40
So Ends Our Night '41

Keeper of the Flame '42
Girl Crazy '43
The Naked City '48
Harvey '50
Winchester '73 '50
Pat and Mike '52
Thunder Bay '53
The Glenn Miller Story '54
Far Country '55
Strategic Air Command '55
Istanbul '57
My Man Godfrey '57
Cat on a Hot Tin Roof '58
Some Came Running '58
A Hole in the Head '59
Never So Few '59
Can-Can '60
Ocean's 11 '60
Back Street '61
Come September '61
Come Blow Your Horn '63
The Prize '63
Von Ryan's Express '65
Assault on a Queen '66
In Like Flint '67
Valley of the Dolls '67
Marlowe '69

Allen Daviau
E.T.: The Extra-Terrestrial '82
The Color Purple '85
Empire of the Sun '87
Avalon '90
Bugsy '91
Fearless '93
Congo '95

Elliot Davis
Love at Large '89
Mortal Thoughts '91
Equinox '93
The Glass Shield '95
Things to Do In Denver When You're Dead '95
The Underneath '95

Ricardo De Angelis
A Place in the World '95

Gerard de Battista
French Twist '95

Jan De Bont
Turkish Delights '73
Keetje Tippel '75
Soldier of Orange '78
The 4th Man '79
Spetters '80
Private Lessons '81
I'm Dancing as Fast as I Can '82
All the Right Moves '83
Cujo '83
Flesh and Blood '85
The Jewel of the Nile '85
Ruthless People '86
RoboCop '87
Die Hard '88
Black Rain '89
The Hunt for Red October '90
Total Recall '90
Basic Instinct '92

Bruno de Keyzer
December Bride '91
War of the Buttons '95

Pasquale De Santis
Romeo and Juliet '68
Death in Venice '71
Assassination of Trotsky '72
Lancelot of the Lake '74
Lucky Luciano '74
Conversation Piece '75
The Innocent '76
A Special Day '77
Christ Stopped at Eboli '79
Three Brothers '80
L'Argent '83
Misunderstood '84
A Month by the Lake '95

Jean De Segonzac
Normal Life '96

Clyde De Vinna
Ben-Hur '26
White Shadows in the South Seas '28
Trader Horn '31
Tarzan, the Ape Man '32
Tarzan and His Mate '34
Treasure Island '34
Ah, Wilderness! '35
Of Human Hearts '38
Immortal Sergeant '43
Jungle '52

Roger Deakins
Another Time, Another Place '83
1984 '84
White Mischief '88
Mountains of the Moon '90
Barton Fink '91
Homicide '91
Passion Fish '92
Thunderheart '92
The Hudsucker Proxy '93
The Secret Garden '93
Nobody's Fool '94
The Shawshank Redemption '94
Dead Man Walking '95
Courage Under Fire '96
Fargo '96

Henri Decae
Les Bonnes Femmes '60

Tonino Delli Colli
Accatone! '61
Mamma Roma '62
The Gospel According to St. Matthew '64
The Good, the Bad and the Ugly '67
Once Upon a Time in the West '68
Porcile '69
The Decameron '70
Salo, or the 120 Days of Sodom '75
Seven Beauties '76
Tales of Ordinary Madness '83
Once Upon a Time in America '84
Ginger & Fred '86
The Name of the Rose '86
Intervista '87
Bitter Moon '92
Death and the Maiden '94

John Demps
The Show '95

John L. Demps, Jr.
The Walking Dead '94

Jim Denault
Nadja '95

Joe DeSalvo
What Happened Was... '94

Caleb Deschanel
Being There '79
The Black Stallion '79
More American Graffiti '79
The Right Stuff '83
The Natural '84
The Slugger's Wife '85
It Could Happen to You '94

Franco Di Giacomo
The Postman '94

Georges Diane
Hate '95

Billy Dickson
Halloween 6: The Curse of Michael Myers '95

Phillip W. Dingeldein
Mommy '95

Andrew Dintenfass
The Cure '95

Carlo DiPalma
The Red Desert '64
Blow-Up '66
The Eclipse '66
The Tragedy of a Ridiculous Man '81
The Appointment '82
Hannah and Her Sisters '86
September '88
Husbands and Wives '92
Shadows and Fog '92
Bullets Over Broadway '94
Mighty Aphrodite '95

Todd A. Dos Reis
The Show '95

Alan Dostie
The Confessional '95

Christopher Doyle
Chungking Express '95

Rob Draper
The Spitfire Grill '95

Jean-Marie Dreujou
Augustin '95

Randy Drummond
Welcome to the Dollhouse '95

Stuart Dryburgh
An Angel at My Table '89
The Piano '93
The Perez Family '94
Lone Star '95

Bryan Duggan
Plan 10 from Outer Space '95

Rick Dupree
I Was a Zombie for the FBI '82

Charles Durnham
Splendor in the Grass '61

Eric Alan Edwards
Even Cowgirls Get the Blues '94
Flirting with Disaster '95
Kids '95
To Die For '95

David Eggby
Dragonheart '96

Eagle Egilsson
Delta of Venus '95

Ian Elkin
For the Moment '94

Paul Elliott
Citizen Cohn '92
And the Band Played On '93
Truman '95

Frederick Elmes
Blue Velvet '86
Reckless '95

Robert Elswit
Boys '95
The Pallbearer '95

Bryan England
Raging Angels '95

Jean-Yves Escoffier
Jack and Sarah '96

Daniel F. Fapp
Golden Earrings '47
Sorrowful Jones '49
Union Station '50
The Lemon Drop Kid '51
The Stooge '51
Jumping Jacks '52
Artists and Models '55
Desire Under the Elms '58
Kings Go Forth '58
The Five Pennies '59
Li'l Abner '59
On the Beach '59
All the Young Men '60
Let's Make Love '60
One, Two, Three '61
West Side Story '61
Fun in Acapulco '63
The Great Escape '63
A New Kind of Love '63
Send Me No Flowers '64
The Unsinkable Molly Brown '64
I'll Take Sweden '65
Our Man Flint '66
Ice Station Zebra '68
Marooned '69

Jim Fealy
The Doom Generation '95

John Fenner
Muppet Treasure Island '96

Joao Fernandes
Top Dog '95

Michael Ferris
Bar Girls '95

Vilko Filac
Underground '95

Russell Fine
Girls Town '95

Steven Firestone
Swimming with Sharks '94

Ron Fortunato
If Lucy Fell '95

Robert Fraisse
L'Addition '85
The Lover '92
Citizen X '95

Graham Frake
A Woman's Guide to Adultery '93

William A. Fraker
Bullitt '68
Rosemary's Baby '68
Looking for Mr. Goodbar '77
Heaven Can Wait '78
1941 '79
Father of the Bride Part II '95

Freddie Francis
Time Without Pity '57
The Innocents '61
Glory '89

Tom Fraser
Alien from L.A. '87

Ellsworth Fredericks
At Gunpoint '55
Shotgun '55
Friendly Persuasion '56
Invasion of the Body Snatchers '56
Sayonara '57
The Light in the Forest '58
Tall Story '60
Picture Mommy Dead '66

Karl Freund
Dracula '31
Murders in the Rue Morgue '32
Conquest '37
The Good Earth '37
Letter of Introduction '38
Balalaika '39
Rose of Washington Square '39
Pride and Prejudice '40
The Chocolate Soldier '41
Tortilla Flat '42
DuBarry Was a Lady '43
A Guy Named Joe '44
The Seventh Cross '44
Without Love '45
Key Largo '48
South of St. Louis '48

Ron Fricke
Baraka '93

Tak Fujimoto
Swing Shift '84
Ferris Bueller's Day Off '86
Pretty in Pink '86
Something Wild '86
Cocoon: The Return '88
Married to the Mob '88
The Silence of the Lambs '91
Night and the City '92
Philadelphia '93
Devil In a Blue Dress '95
Grumpier Old Men '95

Rodrigo Garcia
Four Rooms '95
Indictment: The McMartin Trial '95

Ron Garcia
The Great White Hype '96

Greg Gardiner
Suture '93

Mike Garfath
Lamb '85

Lee Garmes
Disraeli '29
Morocco '30
Dishonored '31
Scarface '31
Shanghai Express '32
Smilin' Through '32
Strange Interlude '32
Dreaming Lips '37
Angels Over Broadway '40
Lydia '41
Footlight Serenade '42
The Jungle Book '42
Guest in the House '45
The Paradine Case '47
The Secret Life of Walter Mitty '47
Caught '49
Detective Story '51
The Lusty Men '52
Desperate Hours '55
Land of the Pharaohs '55
D-Day, the Sixth of June '56
A Big Hand for the Little Lady '66

Gaetano Antonio "Tony" Gaudio
Kismet '20
The Notorious Lady '27
Little Caesar '30
The Mask of Fu Manchu '32
Anthony Adverse '36
The Story of Louis Pasteur '36
Kid Galahad '37
The Life of Emile Zola '37
Dawn Patrol '38
Juarez '39
The Old Maid '39
Brother Orchid '40
The Fighting 69th '40
The Letter '40
The Great Lie '41
High Sierra '41
The Man Who Came to Dinner '41
Days of Glory '43
A Song to Remember '45
I've Always Loved You '46
The Red Pony '49

Eric Gautier
The Favorite Son '94

David Geddes
Incident at Deception Ridge '94

Maury Gertsman
Singapore '47
Red Ball Express '52
Invisible Invaders '59

Calin Ghibu
An Unforgettable Summer '94

Rodney Gibbons
Screamers '96

Paul Gilpin
Cry, the Beloved Country '95

Basco Giurato
A Pure Formality '94

Irving Glassberg
Tarnished Angels '57

Bert Glennon
Lloyds of London '36

James Glennon
In the Deep Woods '91
Mrs. Munck '95

Agnes Godard
I Can't Sleep '93

Stephen Goldblatt
The Pelican Brief '93
Batman Forever '95

Eric Goldstein
Naked Souls '95

Carlos Gonzalez
Mutant Species '95
Original Gangstas '96

Mark J. Gordon
Fall Time '94

Arthur Grant
Paranoiac '62
The Phantom of the Opera '62

Barry Gravelle
Witchboard 3: The Possession '95

Gary Graver
Femme Fontaine: Killer Babe for the C.I.A. '95
Night Eyes 4: Fatal Passion '95

Guy Green
Immortal Battalion '44
Great Expectations '46
Oliver Twist '48
Madeleine '50
Captain Horatio Hornblower '51
I Am a Camera '55

Jack N. Green
Heartbreak Ridge '86
Bird '88
White Hunter, Black Heart '90
Deceived '91
Unforgiven '92
A Perfect World '93
Rookie of the Year '93
Bad Company '94
The Amazing Panda Adventure '95
The Bridges of Madison County '95
The Net '95
Twister '96

Adam Greenberg
First Knight '95
Eraser '96

Robbie Greenberg
Creator '85
Sweet Dreams '85
Far North '88
The Milagro Beanfield War '88
All I Want for Christmas '91

Greenberg ►cont.
Free Willy '93
Under Siege 2: Dark Territory '95
Sunset Park '96

William Howard Greene
The Garden of Allah '36
Nothing Sacred '37
A Star is Born '37
Ali Baba and the Forty Thieves '43
Cobra Woman '44
Salome, Where She Danced '45
The Big Cat '49
When Worlds Collide '51

David Gribble
The Quest '96

Loyal Griggs
Cavalry Charge '51
Shane '53
Elephant Walk '54
White Christmas '54
The Bridges at Toko-Ri '55
We're No Angels '55
The Ten Commandments '56
The Sad Sack '57
Three Violent People '57
The Tin Star '57
The Buccaneer '58
Hot Spell '58
G.I. Blues '60
Girls! Girls! Girls! '62
Papa's Delicate Condition '63
The Greatest Story Ever Told '65
In Harm's Way '65
The Slender Thread '65

Alexander Grusynski
Angus '95
The Craft '96

Burnett Guffey
All the King's Men '49
Knock on Any Door '49
Reckless Moment '49
In a Lonely Place '50
Sirocco '51
From Here to Eternity '53
Human Desire '54
The Violent Men '55
The Harder They Fall '56
Me and the Colonel '58
Gidget '59
Birdman of Alcatraz '62
Kid Galahad '62
King Rat '65
Bonnie & Clyde '67
How to Succeed in Business without Really Trying '67
The Learning Tree '69
The Great White Hope '70

Carl Guthrie
Francis Goes to West Point '52
Francis Covers the Big Town '53

Ron Hagen
Talk '94

Jacques Haitkin
Silence of the Hams '93
Two Bits & Pepper '95

Conrad Hall
Morituri '65
Harper '66
The Professionals '66
Cool Hand Luke '67
Divorce American Style '67
In Cold Blood '67
Butch Cassidy and the Sundance Kid '69
The Happy Ending '69
Hell in the Pacific '69
Tell Them Willie Boy Is Here '69
Fat City '72
Electra Glide in Blue '73
The Day of the Locust '75
Smile '75
Marathon Man '76
Incubus '82
Black Widow '87
Tequila Sunrise '88
Searching for Bobby Fischer '93

Harry Hallenberger
The Virginian '46

Ernest Haller
Saratoga Trunk '45

Victor Hammer
Heavyweights '94
Down Periscope '96

Robert B. Hauser
The Odd Couple '68
Hail, Hero! '69
A Man Called Horse '70
Soldier Blue '70
Le Mans '71
Willard '71
Twilight's Last Gleaming '77
Walking Tall: The Final Chapter '77
Mean Dog Blues '78
The Frisco Kid '79

Kevin Hayward
Traps '93

Bernd Heinl
Younger & Younger '94
It's My Party '95

Karl Herrmann
America's Dream '95

Jack Hildyard
Hobson's Choice '53
Summertime '55
Anastasia '56
The Bridge on the River Kwai '57
Another Time, Another Place '58
The Devil's Disciple '59
Suddenly, Last Summer '59
The Millionairess '60
The Sundowners '60
The Road to Hong Kong '62
55 Days at Peking '63
The V.I.P.'s '63
Circus World '64
Battle of the Bulge '65
Casino Royale '67
Villa Rides '68
Topaz '69
Puppet on a Chain '72
Emily '77
Mohammed: Messenger of God '77
Lion of the Desert '81

Winton C. Hoch
Dr. Cyclops '40
Three Godfathers '48
She Wore a Yellow Ribbon '49
Tulsa '49
Mister Roberts '55
The Searchers '56
Jet Pilot '57
Darby O'Gill & the Little People '59
The Young Land '59
Voyage to the Bottom of the Sea '61
Five Weeks in a Balloon '62
Robinson Crusoe on Mars '64
The Green Berets '68
The Witching '72

Paul Holahan
A Boy Called Hate '95

Adam Holender
Midnight Cowboy '69
Panic in Needle Park '75
Idolmaker '80
Street Smart '87
To Kill a Priest '89
Fresh '94
Smoke '95

James Wong Howe
Chandu the Magician '32
Manhattan Melodrama '34
The Thin Man '34
Mark of the Vampire '35
Under the Red Robe '36
Fire Over England '37
Prisoner of Zenda '37
The Adventures of Tom Sawyer '38
Algiers '38
Oklahoma Kid '39
They Made Me a Criminal '39
Abe Lincoln in Illinois '40
City for Conquest '40
Kings Row '41
Strawberry Blonde '41
Yankee Doodle Dandy '42
Air Force '43
Passage to Marseilles '44
Objective, Burma! '45
Body and Soul '47
Pursued '47
Baron of Arizona '51
Come Back, Little Sheba '52
Picnic '55
The Rose Tattoo '55
Sweet Smell of Success '57
Bell, Book and Candle '58
The Last Angry Man '59
Song Without End '60
Hud '63
Hombre '67
The Heart is a Lonely Hunter '68
Molly Maguires '70
Funny Lady '75
The Old Man and the Sea '90

Michel Hugo
Bug '75

Alan Hume
Kiss of the Vampire '62
Just Like a Woman '95

J. Roy Hunt
She '35

Peter Hyams
Sudden Death '95

Arthur Ibbetson
A Countess from Hong Kong '67

Slawomir Idziak
The Double Life of Veronique '91
Trois Couleurs: Bleu '93
The Journey of August King '95

Mark Irwin
Vampire in Brooklyn '95
Kingpin '96

Levie Isaacks
The Dogfighters '95
The Expert '95
The Wharf Rat '95
Marshal Law '96

Hossein Jafarian
Through the Olive Trees '94

Peter James
Alive '93
Diabolique '96
Last Dance '96

Maris Jansons
The Halfback of Notre Dame '96

Johnny E. Jensen
An American Story '92
Three Wishes '95

Bruce Douglas Johnson
Public Access '93
The Prophecy '95

David Johnson
Othello '95

Hugh Johnson
White Squall '96

Farzad Jowdat
The White Balloon '95

Mario Garcia Joya
Strawberry and Chocolate '93

Jeffrey Jur
Unforgettable '96

Janusz Kaminski
Grim Prairie Tales '89
Cool As Ice '91
Class of '61 '92
The Adventures of Huck Finn '93
Schindler's List '93
Little Giants '94
How to Make an American Quilt '95
Tall Tale: The Unbelievable Adventures of Pecos Bill '95

Avi Karpik
The Seventh Coin '92
Solar Force '94
Outside the Law '95

Norayr Kasper
Calendar '93

Stephen M. Katz
My Summer Story '94
Letter to My Killer '95

Boris Kaufman
Zero for Conduct '33
On the Waterfront '54
Baby Doll '56
Patterns '56
Twelve Angry Men '57
The Fugitive Kind '60
Long Day's Journey into Night '62
Gone are the Days '63
The World of Henry Orient '64
The Pawnbroker '65
The Group '66
The Brotherhood '68

Stephen Kazmierski
Blessing '94

Wayne Keenan
For Better or Worse '95

Michel Kelber
Beauty and the Devil '50

Ken Kelsch
Big Night '95

Victor Kemper
Eddie '96

Francis Kenny
A Thin Line Between Love and Hate '96

John Kenway
Bhaji on the Beach '94
Pride and Prejudice '95

Glenn Kershaw
A Kiss Goodnight '94
At First Sight '95

Darius Khondji
The City of Lost Children '95
Seven '95
Stealing Beauty '96

Gary B. Kibbe
Village of the Damned '95

Jan Kiesser
Clean and Sober '88
Mrs. Parker and the Vicious Circle '94
Georgia '95
Man with a Gun '95

Adam Kimmel
Bed of Roses '95
New Jersey Drive '95
Beautiful Girls '96

Alan Kivilo
The Invaders '95

David Klein
Mallrats '95

Edward Klosinski
Illumination '73

Thomas Kloss
Fear '96

Bernard Knowles
Secret Mission '42

Cyril Knowles
Secret Mission '42

Douglas Koch
When Night is Falling '95

Fred W. Koenekamp
Patton '70
Rage '72
Papillon '73
The Towering Inferno '74
Uptown Saturday Night '74
Doc Savage '75
White Line Fever '75
Embryo '76
The Domino Principle '77
Fun with Dick and Jane '77
Islands in the Stream '77
The Other Side of Midnight '77
The Swarm '78
The Amityville Horror '79
The Champ '79
Love and Bullets '79
The Hunter '80
When Time Ran Out '80
First Monday in October '81
Wrong is Right '82
Two of a Kind '83
The Adventures of Buckaroo Banzai Across the Eighth Dimension '84
Listen to Me '89
Welcome Home '89
Flight of the Intruder '90

Hajime Koizumi
Dagora, the Space Monster '65

Erich Kollmar
Shadows '60

Lajos Koltai
Mephisto '81
Colonel Redl '84
Gaby: A True Story '87
Hanussen '88
Homer and Eddie '89
White Palace '90
Meeting Venus '91
Mobsters '91
Born Yesterday '93
Wrestling Ernest Hemingway '93
Just Cause '94
Home for the Holidays '95

Laszlo Kovacs
Copycat '95
Free Willy 2: The Adventure Home '95

Pete Kozachik
James and the Giant Peach '96

Jon Kranhouse
Decoy '95

Robert Krasker
Henry V '44
Brief Encounter '46
Caesar and Cleopatra '46
Odd Man Out '47
The Third Man '49
Cry, the Beloved Country '51
Romeo and Juliet '54
Senso '54
Alexander the Great '55
Trapeze '56
El Cid '61
Billy Budd '62
Birdman of Alcatraz '62
The Fall of the Roman Empire '64
The Collector '65
Trap '66

Milton Krasner
You Can't Cheat an Honest Man '39
The Bank Dick '40
The Invisible Man Returns '40
Buck Privates '41
Arabian Nights '42
The Ghost of Frankenstein '42
Pardon My Sarong '42
The Spoilers '42
Gung Ho! '43
The Invisible Man's Revenge '44
Woman In the Window '44
Along Came Jones '45
Scarlet Street '45
Dark Mirror '46
Without Reservations '46
A Double Life '47
Egg and I '47
The Farmer's Daughter '47
The Accused '48
House of Strangers '49
The Set-Up '49
All About Eve '50
Rawhide '50
People Will Talk '51
Monkey Business '52
Phone Call from a Stranger '52
Demetrius and the Gladiators '54
Desiree '54
Three Coins in the Fountain '54
The Seven Year Itch '55
Bus Stop '56
An Affair to Remember '57
Bells are Ringing '60
Home from the Hill '60
The King of Kings '61
The Courtship of Eddie's Father '62
The Four Horsemen of the Apocalypse '62
Sweet Bird of Youth '62
Two Weeks in Another Town '62
How the West Was Won '63
Love with the Proper Stranger '63
Red Line 7000 '65
The Sandpiper '65
The Singing Nun '66
The St. Valentine's Day Massacre '67
The Sterile Cuckoo '69
Beneath the Planet of the Apes '70

Eric Kress
The Kingdom '95

Howard Krupa
Rhythm Thief '94

Willy Kurant
A Business Affair '93
The Baby-Sitters Club '95
White Man's Burden '95

Ellen Kuras
Postcards from America '95

Toyomichi Kurita
Woman Undone '95

Edward Lachman
My Family '94
Theremin: An Electronic Odyssey '95

Kjell Lagerros
Dreaming of Rita '94

John Lambert
Hourglass '95

Charles B(ryant) Lang
Tom Sawyer '30
Vice Squad '31
A Farewell to Arms '32
She Done Him Wrong '33
The Lives of a Bengal Lancer '35
Angel '37
Midnight '39
The Ghost Breakers '40
Sundown '41
The Uninvited '44
Blue Skies '46
The Ghost and Mrs. Muir '47
Fancy Pants '50
September Affair '50
Sudden Fear '52
The Big Heat '53
Salome '53
It Should Happen to You '54
Phffft! '54
Sabrina '54
The Man from Laramie '55
Queen Bee '55
Autumn Leaves '56
The Rainmaker '56
Solid Gold Cadillac '56
Gunfight at the O.K. Corral '57
The Matchmaker '58
Separate Tables '58
Last Train from Gun Hill '59
Some Like It Hot '59
The Magnificent Seven '60
Strangers When We Meet '60
One-Eyed Jacks '61
Summer and Smoke '61
Charade '63
How the West Was Won '63
Father Goose '64
Sex and the Single Girl '64
Inside Daisy Clover '65
How to Steal a Million '66
Flim-Flam Man '67
Hotel '67
Wait Until Dark '67
Bob & Carol & Ted & Alice '69
Cactus Flower '69
Doctors' Wives '70
Walk in the Spring Rain '70
The Love Machine '71
Butterflies Are Free '72
Forty Carats '73

Roger Lanser
A Midwinter's Tale '95

Jeanne Lapoirie
Wild Reeds '94

Joseph LaShelle
Laura '44
Come to the Stable '49
The Jackpot '50
Les Miserables '52
River of No Return '54
Marty '55
The Conqueror '56
The Long, Hot Summer '58
The Naked and the Dead '58
Career '59
The Apartment '60
Kiss Me, Stupid! '64
The Fortune Cookie '66
Barefoot in the Park '67

Walter Lassally
A Taste of Honey '61
The Loneliness of the Long Distance Runner '62
Tom Jones '63
Zorba the Greek '64
Something for Everyone '70
Savages '72
Run, Stranger, Run '73
Wild Party '74
Great Bank Hoax '78
Hullabaloo Over Georgie & Bonnie's Pictures '78
Danger in the Skies '79
Heat and Dust '82
Private School '83
The Bostonians '84
The Deceivers '88
The Ballad of the Sad Cafe '91

Andrew Laszlo
The Owl and the Pussycat '70

Ernest Laszlo
The Road to Rio '47
D.O.A. '49
The Well '51
The Moon Is Blue '53
Stalag 17 '53
Vera Cruz '53
Apache '54
Naked Jungle '54
The Big Knife '55
The Kentuckian '55
Kiss Me Deadly '55
While the City Sleeps '56
Inherit the Wind '60
Judgment at Nuremberg '61
Four for Texas '63
It's a Mad, Mad, Mad, Mad World '63
Baby, the Rain Must Fall '64
Ship of Fools '65
Fantastic Voyage '66
Luv '67
Star! '68
Daddy's Gone A-Hunting '69
Airport '70
Showdown '73
Logan's Run '76

Paul Laufer
Frankie Starlight '95

Charles Lawton, Jr.
Cowboy '58

Vernon Layton
The Englishman Who Went Up a Hill But Came Down a Mountain '95

Robert Le Febvre
Casque d'Or '52

Sam Leavitt
The Thief '52
Carmen Jones '54
A Star is Born '54
The Court Martial of Billy Mitchell '55
The Man with the Golden Arm '55
The Defiant Ones '58
Anatomy of a Murder '59
Pork Chop Hill '59
Seven Thieves '60
Cape Fear '61
Advise and Consent '62
Diamond Head '62
Major Dundee '65
Guess Who's Coming to Dinner '67
Desperados '69
The Passing of Evil '70
Star Spangled Girl '71
The Man in the Glass Booth '75

Philip Lee
Galaxies are Colliding '92

Claude Lelouch
Les Miserables '95

Denis Lenoir
The Separation '94
Carrington '95

John R. Leonetti
Spy Hard '96

Matthew F. Leonetti
Weird Science '85
Strange Days '95
Fled '96

Andrew Lesnie
Temptation of a Monk '94
Babe '95
Two If by Sea '95

Pierre Letarte
The Boys of St. Vincent '93
Dangerous Minds '95
Sugartime '95

Moshe Levin
Hard Justice '95

Peter Levy
Broken Arrow '95
Cutthroat Island '95

David Lewis
The Set Up '95

Denis Lewiston
The Canterville Ghost '96

Jong Lin
Pushing Hands '92
Eat Drink Man Woman '94

Karl Walter Lindenlaub
The Last of the Dogmen '95
Rob Roy '95
Independence Day '96
Up Close and Personal '96

John Lindley
Father of the Bride '91
Sneakers '92
The Good Son '93
I Love Trouble '94
Money Train '95

Lionel Lindon
Going My Way '44
The Blue Dahlia '46
Monsieur Beaucaire '46
The Road to Utopia '46
My Favorite Brunette '47
Welcome Stranger '47
Destination Moon '50
Only the Valiant '50
Casanova's Big Night '54
Conquest of Space '55
A Man Alone '55
Around the World in 80 Days '56
Lonely Man '57
I Want to Live! '58
All Fall Down '62
The Manchurian Candidate '62
Dead Heat on a Merry-Go-Round '66
Grand Prix '66
The Trouble with Angels '66
Generation '69
Pendulum '69

Philip Linzey
Bloodknot '95

Jerzy Lipman
Lotna '64

Gerry Lively
Children of the Corn 3: Urban Harvest '95
Friday '95
Hellraiser 4: Bloodline '95
Without Mercy '95

Walt Lloyd
Dangerously Close '86
The Wash '88
Down Twisted '89
sex, lies and videotape '89
To Sleep with Anger '90
Kafka '91
Short Cuts '93
Empire Records '95

Chris Lombardi
Theremin: An Electronic Odyssey '95

Pierre Lorraine
Little Indian, Big City '95

Emmanuel Lubezki
The Birdcage '95
A Little Princess '95
A Walk in the Clouds '95

Yang Lun
Red Firecracker, Green Firecracker '93

Bernard Lutic
Colonel Chabert '94

Jingle Ma
Rumble in the Bronx '96

Julio Macat
Moonlight and Valentino '95
The Nutty Professor '96

Joe MacDonald
Will Success Spoil Rock Hunter? '57

Kenneth Macmillan
Mr. & Mrs. Loving '96

Glen MacPherson
Doctor Who '96

Yonezo Maeda
Minbo—Or the Gentle Art of Japanese Extortion '92

Paul Maibaum
Stephen King's The Langoliers '95
Tornado! '96

David Makin
Kids In the Hall Brain Candy '96

Denis Maloney
Natural Causes '94
Baja '95
Witchcraft 7: Judgement Hour '95

Teodoro Maniaci
Clean, Shaven '93

Isidore Mankofsky
The Heidi Chronicles '95

Mauro Marchetti
Cemetery Man '95

William Margulies
The Ghost and Mr. Chicken '66
The Love God? '70

Jack Marta
Earth vs. the Spider '58

Otello Martelli
Anna '51

Arthur Martinelli
Supernatural '33

Christian Matras
L'Idiot '46

Thomas Mauch
Signs of Life '68

Joe C. Maxwell
Zarkorr! The Invader '96

Mike Mayers
Denise Calls Up '95

Donald McAlpine
Nine Months '95

Gregory McClatchy
Blown Away '94

Seamus McGarvey
Butterfly Kiss '94

Phil Meheux
The Long Good Friday '79
The Final Conflict '81
The Final Option '82
Beyond the Limit '83
Experience Preferred... But Not Essential '83
Morons from Outer Space '85
The Fourth Protocol '87
Renegades '89
Highlander 2: The Quickening '91
Ruby '92
Goldeneye '95

Ashok Mehta
Bandit Queen '94

William Mellor
The Great McGinty '40
The Road to Singapore '40
Birth of the Blues '41
The Great Man's Lady '42
My Favorite Blonde '42
The Road to Morocco '42
Commandos Strike at Dawn '43
The Senator was Indiscreet '47
Love Happy '50
Across the Wide Missouri '51
A Place in the Sun '51
Westward the Women '51
The Affairs of Dobie Gillis '53
The Naked Spur '53
Bad Day at Black Rock '54
Back from Eternity '56
Giant '56
Love in the Afternoon '57
Peyton Place '57
The Best of Everything '59
Compulsion '59
The Diary of Anne Frank '59
Wild in the Country '61
State Fair '62
The Greatest Story Ever Told '65

Chris Menges
Black Beauty '71
Gumshoe '72
Warlords of the 21st Century '82
Local Hero '83
Comfort and Joy '84
The Killing Fields '84
Marie '85
The Mission '86
Shy People '87
High Season '88

Peter Menzies, Jr.
A Time to Kill '96

Raffaele Mertes
Fluke '95
Joseph '95

Russell Metty
Sylvia Scarlett '35
Bringing Up Baby '38
The Great Man Votes '38
No, No Nanette '40
Master Race '44
West of the Pecos '45
The Stranger '46
Arch of Triumph '48
Magnificent Obsession '54
Written on the Wind '56
Battle Hymn '57
Man of a Thousand Faces '57
Touch of Evil '58
Imitation of Life '59
Midnight Lace '60
Spartacus '60
By Love Possessed '61
Flower Drum Song '61
The Misfits '61
That Touch of Mink '62
The Thrill of It All! '63
The War Lord '65
The Appaloosa '66
Madame X '66
Texas Across the River '66
Thoroughly Modern Millie '67
Madigan '68
The Secret War of Harry Frigg '68
Change of Habit '69
Omega Man '71
Ben '72
Cancel My Reservation '72

Richard Michalak
Gordy '95

Chris Middleton
Wavelength '96

Saul Midwall
Frankenstein Meets the Space Monster '65

Pierre Mignot
Hiroshima '95

Arthur C. Miller
The Little Colonel '35
Stowaway '36
Heidi '37
Wee Willie Winkie '37
Little Miss Broadway '38
Rebecca of Sunnybrook Farm '38
The Little Princess '39
The Rains Came '39
Susannah of the Mounties '39
The Blue Bird '40
Brigham Young: Frontiersman '40
Johnny Apollo '40
The Mark of Zorro '40
How Green Was My Valley '41
The Ox-Bow Incident '43
The Song of Bernadette '43
The Keys of the Kingdom '44
The Purple Heart '44
Anna and the King of Siam '46
The Razor's Edge '46
Gentleman's Agreement '47
A Letter to Three Wives '49
The Gunfighter '50
Prowler '51

William J. Miller
Lost Boundaries '49

Charles Mills
Lily in Winter '94

Victor Milner
Cleopatra '34
The Crusades '35
The General Died at Dawn '36
The Plainsman '37
Union Pacific '39
The Lady Eve '41
The Monster and the Girl '41
The Palm Beach Story '42
Reap the Wild Wind '42
The Great Moment '44
The Princess and the Pirate '44
The Story of Dr. Wassell '44
Wonder Man '45
The Strange Love of Martha Ivers '46
Unfaithfully Yours '48
Carrie '52

Doug Milsome
The Old Curiosity Shop '94

Katsuji Misawa
Akira '89

George Mitas
Lie Down with Dogs '95

Hal Mohr
The Jazz Singer '27
The Wedding March '28
The Front Page '31
Captain Blood '35
A Midsummer Night's Dream '35
Green Pastures '36
Bullets or Ballots '38
Destry Rides Again '39
The Phantom of the Opera '43
Watch on the Rhine '43
Salome, Where She Danced '45
Lost Moment '47
The Member of the Wedding '52
Rancho Notorious '52
The Wild One '54
The Last Voyage '60
Underworld, U.S.A. '60

Amir M. Mokri
An Eye for an Eye '95

Jennifer Montgomery
Art for Teachers of Children '95

Felix Monti
I, the Worst of All '90
Of Love and Shadows '94
O Quatrilho '95

George Mooradian
Nemesis 3: Time Lapse '96

Ted Moore
The Gamma People '56
The Trials of Oscar Wilde '60
Dr. No '62
From Russia with Love '63
Goldfinger '64
The Amorous Adventures of Moll Flanders '65
Thunderball '65
A Man for All Seasons '66
The Last Safari '67
Shalako '68
The Prime of Miss Jean Brodie '69
Diamonds Are Forever '71
Golden Voyage of Sinbad '73
Live and Let Die '73
The Man with the Golden Gun '74
Orca '77
Sinbad and the Eye of the Tiger '77
Clash of the Titans '81
Priest of Love '81

Donald M. Morgan
Christine '84
Starman '84
Dillinger '91
Double-Crossed '91
Excessive Force '93
Born to Be Wild '95

Mark Morris
Texas Payback '95

Oswald Morris
The Golden Salamander '51
Moulin Rouge '52
Beat the Devil '53
Beau Brummel '54
Indiscretion of an American Wife '54
The Man Who Never Was '55
Moby Dick '56
The Key '58
Look Back in Anger '58
The Entertainer '60
The Guns of Navarone '61
Lolita '62
Of Human Bondage '64
The Pumpkin Eater '64
The Spy Who Came in from the Cold '65
Reflections in a Golden Eye '67
The Taming of the Shrew '67
Oliver! '68
Goodbye, Mr. Chips '69
Scrooge '70
Fiddler on the Roof '71
Sleuth '72
Lady Caroline Lamb '73
The Odessa File '74
The Man Who Would Be King '75
The Seven-Per-Cent Solution '76
Equus '77
The Wiz '78
Just Tell Me What You Want '80
The Great Muppet Caper '81
The Dark Crystal '82

Reginald Morris
Empire of the Ants '77

Kevin Morrisey
Headless Body in Topless Bar '96

Robby Muller
Breaking the Waves '95

Fred Murphy
Eddie and the Cruisers '83
The Trip to Bountiful '85
Hoosiers '86
The Dead '87
Five Corners '88
Enemies, a Love Story '89
Scenes from a Mall '91
Jack the Bear '93
Faithful '95
Murder in the First '95
A Family Thing '96

Paul Murphy
Mighty Morphin Power Rangers: The Movie '95

Leon Narbey
Desperate Remedies '93

Hiro Narita
The Arrival '96
James and the Giant Peach '96

Guillermo Navarro
Desperado '95
Four Rooms '95
From Dusk Till Dawn '95

Alex Nepomniaschy
Safe '95
Mrs. Winterbourne '96

Yuri Neyman
Liquid Sky '83
Back in the USSR '92

John M. Nickolaus, Jr.
Attack of the Giant Leeches '59

Eric Van Haren Noman
Blue River '95

Danny Nowak
Probable Cause '95

Sven Nykvist
The Virgin Spring '59
Through a Glass Darkly '61
The Winter Light '62
The Silence '63
Persona '66
Hour of the Wolf '68
The Shame '68
The Rite '69
First Love '70
The Passion of Anna '70
One Day in the Life of Ivan Denisovich '71
The Touch '71
Cries and Whispers '72
Scenes from a Marriage '73
The Dove '74
Face to Face '76
The Tenant '76
Autumn Sonata '78
King of the Gypsies '78
Pretty Baby '78
The Serpent's Egg '78
Hurricane '79
Starting Over '79
From the Life of the Marionettes '80
Willie & Phil '80
The Postman Always Rings Twice '81
Cannery Row '82
Fanny and Alexander '83
Star 80 '83
After the Rehearsal '84
Swann in Love '84
Agnes of God '85
Dream Lover '85
The Sacrifice '86
Another Woman '88
The Unbearable Lightness of Being '88
Crimes & Misdemeanors '89
New York Stories '89
Chaplin '92
Sleepless in Seattle '93
Something to Talk About '95

John O'Brien
Vermont Is for Lovers '92

David Odd
Prime Suspect: Inner Circles '95

Rene Ohashi
Rent-A-Kid '95

Daryn Okada
Big Bully '95
Black Sheep '96

Jeff Okun
Stargate '94

Ronald Orieux
The Tuskegee Airmen '95

Ray Orton
Hedd Wyn '92

Michael D. O'Shea
Dracula: Dead and Loving It '95

Luc Pages
A Tale of Winter '92

Ernest Palmer
Cavalcade '33
Stand Up and Cheer '34
Blood and Sand '41
Springtime in the Rockies '42
Sweet Rosie O'Grady '43
Pin-Up Girl '44
The Dolly Sisters '45
Broken Arrow '50

Phedon Papamichael
Body Chemistry '90
Love Crimes '92
Poison Ivy '92
Cool Runnings '93
Wild Palms '93
Dark Side of Genius '94
Unstrung Heroes '95
While You Were Sleeping '95
Bio-Dome '96
Phenomenon '96

Phil Parmet
Harlan County, U.S.A. '76
Fatal Mission '89
Street Hunter '90
In the Soup '92
Nina Takes a Lover '94
Four Rooms '95
Under the Hula Moon '95

Peter Pearce
Risk '94

Eddie Pei
Stephen King's The Stand '94
Larry McMurtry's Streets of Laredo '95
Panther '95

David Pelletier
Live Bait '95

Georges Perinal
Under the Roofs of Paris '29
The Blood of a Poet '30
A Nous la Liberte '31
The Private Life of Henry VIII '33
Catherine the Great '34
Private Life of Don Juan '34
Sanders of the River '35
Rembrandt '36
Things to Come '36
The Four Feathers '39
The Thief of Bagdad '40
Spitfire '42
The Life and Death of Colonel Blimp '43
Nicholas Nickleby '46
The Fallen Idol '49
Three Cases of Murder '55
Bonjour Tristesse '57
A King in New York '57
Saint Joan '57
Tom Thumb '58

Don Peterman
Get Shorty '95

Curtis Petersen
Iron Eagle 4 '95

David Phillips
The Basketball Diaries '94

Tony Pierce-Roberts
Moonlighting '82
A Private Function '84
A Room with a View '86
A Tiger's Tale '87
Mr. & Mrs. Bridge '90
White Fang '91
Howard's End '92
The Remains of the Day '93
Haunted '95

Lee Ping-bing
Summer Snow '94

Larry Pizer
In Custody '94

Gene Polito
Colossus: The Forbin Project '70

Bill Pope
Clueless '95
Bound '96

Dick Pope
An Awfully Big Adventure '94
Secrets and Lies '95

Gideon Porath
Breach of Conduct '94

Steven Poster
The Boy Who Could Fly '86
Someone to Watch Over Me '87
Big Top Pee Wee '88
Next of Kin '89
Rocky 5 '90
Life Stinks '91
The Cemetery Club '93
Roswell: The U.F.O. Cover-Up '94

Jack Priestley
A Man Called Adam '66
No Way to Treat a Lady '68
Stiletto '69
Where's Poppa? '70
Born to Win '71
Across 110th Street '72
The First Deadly Sin '80
Rage of Angels: The Story Continues '86

Tom Priestley
Dr. Jekyll and Ms. Hyde '95

Robert Primes
Bird on a Wire '90
The Hard Way '91
My Antonia '94

Frank Prinzi
Living in Oblivion '94

Francois Protat
Johnny Mnemonic '95

Ian Punter
The Final Cut '95

Steven Quale
The Crude Oasis '95

Dick Quinlan
Moonshine Highway '96

Declan Quinn
Vanya on 42nd Street '94
Carried Away '95
Leaving Las Vegas '95

Elemer Ragaly
A Kid in King Arthur's Court '95
Never Talk to Strangers '95

Claudia Rashke
Thank You & Good Night '91
The Last Good Time '94

Franz Rath
The Promise '95

Ray Rennahan
Mystery of the Wax Museum '33
Becky Sharp '35
Drums Along the Mohawk '39
Gone with the Wind '39
Blood and Sand '41
For Whom the Bell Tolls '43
Up in Arms '44
A Thousand and One Nights '45
Duel in the Sun '46
The Perils of Pauline '47
Unconquered '47
The Paleface '48
A Connecticut Yankee in King Arthur's Court '49
Great Missouri Raid '51
Arrowhead '53
Pony Express '53
A Lawless Street '55
Seventh Cavalry '56

Claude Renoir
Barbarella '68

Brian Reynolds
Guarding Tess '94

Robert Richardson
Platoon '86
Salvador '86
Wall Street '87
Eight Men Out '88
Talk Radio '88
Born on the Fourth of July '89
City of Hope '91
The Doors '91
JFK '91
A Few Good Men '92
Heaven and Earth '93
Natural Born Killers '94
Casino '95
Nixon '95

Anthony Richmond
Tales from the Hood '95
Full Body Massage '95

Tom Richmond
Killing Zoe '94

Lisa Rinzler
Dead Presidents '95

Neil Roach
To Dance with the White Dog '93

Jean-Francois Robin
Suite 16 '94
Nelly et Monsieur Arnaud '95

George Robinson
Abbott and Costello Meet the Invisible Man '51
Francis in the Haunted House '56

Owen Roizman
The French Connection '71
The Heartbreak Kid '72
Play It Again, Sam '72
The Exorcist '73
The Taking of Pelham One Two Three '74
Three Days of the Condor '75
Network '76
The Return of a Man Called Horse '76
Straight Time '78
Absence of Malice '81
True Confessions '81
Tootsie '82
Havana '90
I Love You to Death '90
The Addams Family '91
Grand Canyon '91
Wyatt Earp '94
French Kiss '95

Gernot Roll
Maybe...Maybe Not '94

Ashley Ropwe
Sister My Sister '94

Charles Rosher
Pollyanna '20
Little Annie Rooney '25
Sparrows '26
My Best Girl '27
Sunrise '27
The Tempest '28
Dance Fools Dance '31
Laughing Sinners '31
What Price Hollywood? '32
Broadway Melody of 1936 '35
Little Lord Fauntleroy '36
Yolanda and the Thief '45
The Yearling '46
Ziegfeld Follies '46
Fiesta '47
Song of the Thin Man '47
East Side, West Side '49
Neptune's Daughter '49
Show Boat '51
Scaramouche '52
Kiss Me Kate '53
Young Bess '53
Jupiter's Darling '55

Ann T. Rossetti
Go Fish '94

Giuseppe Rotunno
The Bible...In the Beginning '66
Fellini Satyricon '69
Carnal Knowledge '71
All That Jazz '79
City of Women '81
Casanova '87

The Adventures of Baron Munchausen '89
Regarding Henry '91
Wolf '94
Sabrina '95

Philippe Rousselot
Peppermint Soda '77
Diva '82
Moon in the Gutter '83
The Emerald Forest '85
Hope and Glory '87
Dangerous Liaisons '88
The Bear '89
We're No Angels '89
Henry & June '90
The Miracle '91
A River Runs Through It '92
Interview with the Vampire '94
Mary Reilly '95

Al Ruban
Faces '68

Juan Ruiz-Anchia
Maria's Lovers '84
The Stone Boy '84
At Close Range '86
Where the River Runs Black '86
House of Games '87
Surrender '87
Dying Young '91
Glengarry Glen Ross '92
A Far Off Place '93
Two Bits '96

Ward Russell
Lawnmower Man 2: Beyond Cyberspace '95

Joseph Ruttenberg
Fury '36
A Day at the Races '37
The Great Waltz '38
Shopworn Angel '38
Three Comrades '38
On Borrowed Time '39
The Women '39
The Philadelphia Story '40
Waterloo Bridge '40
Dr. Jekyll and Mr. Hyde '41
Two-Faced Woman '41
Mrs. Miniver '42
Random Harvest '42
Woman of the Year '42
Madame Curie '43
Presenting Lily Mars '43
Gaslight '44
Mrs. Parkington '44
Adventure '45
The Valley of Decision '45
The Miniver Story '50
That Forsyte Woman '50
The Great Caruso '51
Prisoner of Zenda '52
Julius Caesar '53
Brigadoon '54
The Last Time I Saw Paris '54
Kismet '55
The Prodigal '55
Somebody Up There Likes Me '56
The Swan '56
Gigi '58
The Reluctant Debutante '58
Green Mansions '59
Butterfield 8 '60
A Global Affair '63
Harlow '65
The Oscar '66
Speedway '68

Viktor Ruzicka
Martha and I '91

Ellery Ryan
That Eye, The Sky '94
Angel Baby '95

Farhad Saba
Through the Olive Trees '94

Amnon Salomon
The Mangler '94

Mikael Salomon
Torch Song Trilogy '88
Zelly & Me '88
The Abyss '89
Always '89
Arachnophobia '90
Backdraft '91
Far and Away '92

Vic Sarin
Whale Music '94

Margaret's Museum '95

Paul Sarossy
The Adjuster '91
Love and Human Remains '93

Yasushi Sasakibara
The Mystery of Rampo '94

Harris Savides
Heaven's Prisoners '95

Malik Hassan Sayeed
Clockers '95
Girl 6 '96

Doron Schlair
Pharoah's Army '95

Tobias Schliessler
Candyman 2: Farewell to the Flesh '94
Bulletproof Heart '95

Ronn Schmidt
Men of War '94
Lord of Illusions '95

Nancy Schreiber
Girl in the Cadillac '94
The Celluloid Closet '95

John Schwartzman
Mr. Wrong '95
A Pyromaniac's Love Story '95
The Rock '96

Chris Seager
Cold Comfort Farm '94

John Seale
Picnic at Hanging Rock '75
The Last Wave '77
Gallipoli '81
The Year of Living Dangerously '82
Witness '85
Children of a Lesser God '86
The Mosquito Coast '86
Gorillas in the Mist '88
Rain Man '88
Dead Poets Society '89
The Doctor '91
Lorenzo's Oil '92
The Firm '93
The American President '95
Beyond Rangoon '95

Christian Sebaldt
Revenge of the Red Baron '93

Andrzej Sekula
Across the Moon '94
Pulp Fiction '94
Four Rooms '95
Hackers '95

Dean Semler
The Road Warrior '82
Cocktail '88
Dead Calm '89
Farewell to the King '89
Dances with Wolves '90
City Slickers '91
Last Action Hero '93
Waterworld '95

Michael Seresin
City Hall '95

Eduardo Serra
Grosse Fatigue '94

Leon Shamroy
The Adventures of Sherlock Holmes '39
Made for Each Other '39
The Story of Alexander Graham Bell '39
Down Argentine Way '40
Tin Pan Alley '40
The Great American Broadcast '41
Moon over Miami '41
The Black Swan '42
Roxie Hart '42
Crash Dive '43
Stormy Weather '43
Buffalo Bill '44
Wilson '44
Leave Her to Heaven '45
State Fair '45
A Tree Grows in Brooklyn '45
Forever Amber '47
Twelve O'Clock High '49
Cheaper by the Dozen '50
David and Bathsheba '51
The Snows of Kilimanjaro '52
The Robe '53
The Egyptian '54

Daddy Long Legs '55
Love Is a Many-Splendored Thing '55
Desk Set '57
The Bravados '58
South Pacific '58
Beloved Infidel '59
North to Alaska '60
The Cardinal '63
Cleopatra '63
The Agony and the Ecstasy '65
The Glass Bottom Boat '66
Planet of the Apes '68
Justine '69

Henry Sharp
Dr. Cyclops '40
The Young Land '59

Eugene Shlugleit
3 Ninjas Knuckle Up '92
Twogether '94

Eugene Eugen Shufftan Shuftan
The Horror Chamber of Dr. Faustus '59
The Hustler '61
Lilith '64

Newton Thomas Sigel
The Usual Suspects '95
The Trigger Effect '96

Johnny Simmons
Once Upon a Time...When We Were Colored '95

Gerard Simon
The Son of the Shark '93

Geoffrey Simpson
Little Women '94

Sandi Sissel
Salaam Bombay! '88
The People Under the Stairs '91
Camp Nowhere '94

Michael Slovis
Party Girl '94
Breach of Trust '95

Piotr Sobocinski
Trois Couleurs: Rouge '94

Jaromir Sofr
My Sweet Little Village '86

Mike Southon
Roommates '95
The Run of the Country '95

Peter Sova
Diner '82
Good Morning, Vietnam '87
Tin Men '87
Fatherland '94
Jimmy Hollywood '94
Feast of July '95
Sgt. Bilko '95

Thomas E. Spalding
The Blob '58

Theodor Sparkuhl
Internes Can't Take Money '37

James Lawrence Spencer
Magic Island '95

Michael Spiller
Search and Destroy '94
Flirt '95

Dante Spinotti
Crimes of the Heart '86
Beaches '88
The Comfort of Strangers '91
Frankie and Johnny '91
The Last of the Mohicans '92
Blink '93
The Quick and the Dead '94
Heat '95
The Star Maker '95

Jorge Stahl, Jr.
Death in the Garden '56

Oliver Stapleton
Restoration '94
The Van '95

Willy Stassen
Antonia's Line '95

Robert Steadman
Executive Action '73
Above the Law '88
Return to the Blue Lagoon '91

Ueli Steiger
Now and Then '95

Rod Stewart
Live Wire: Human Timebomb '95

Witold Stok
Century '94

Robert Stone
Theremin: An Electronic Odyssey '95

Jeff Stonehouse
Mystery Science Theater 3000: The Movie '96

Vittorio Storaro
The Conformist '71
Last Tango in Paris '73
1900 '76
The Last Emperor '87
The Sheltering Sky '90
Little Buddha '93

Gregg Stouffer
Sarah's Child '96

Archie Stout
The Ten Commandments '23
Captain Kidd '45
Angel and the Badman '47
Fort Apache '48
Big Jim McLain '52
The Quiet Man '52
Hondo '53
The Sun Shines Bright '53

Harry Stradling
Carnival in Flanders '35
Knight Without Armour '37
The Citadel '38
The Divorce of Lady X '38
Pygmalion '38
Clouds Over Europe '39
Jamaica Inn '39
The Lion Has Wings '40
They Knew What They Wanted '40
The Devil & Miss Jones '41
Suspicion '41
The Corsican Brothers '42
The Human Comedy '43
Bathing Beauty '44
Picture of Dorian Gray '45
Holiday in Mexico '46
Till the Clouds Roll By '46
Easter Parade '48
The Pirate '48
The Barkleys of Broadway '49
In the Good Old Summertime '49
A Streetcar Named Desire '51
Androcles and the Lion '52
Johnny Guitar '53
Guys and Dolls '55
The Eddy Duchin Story '56
Helen of Troy '56
A Face in the Crowd '57
The Pajama Game '57
Auntie Mame '58
Marjorie Morningstar '58
A Summer Place '59
The Young Philadelphians '59
Parrish '61
Gypsy '62
How to Murder Your Wife '64
My Fair Lady '64
Funny Girl '68
Hello, Dolly! '69
On a Clear Day You Can See Forever '70
The Owl and the Pussycat '70

Harry Stradling, Jr.
With Six You Get Eggroll '68
The Good Guys and the Bad Guys '69
Support Your Local Sheriff '69
Little Big Man '70
There was a Crooked Man '70
1776 '72
Man Who Loved Cat Dancing '73
The Way We Were '73
Bank Shot '74
McQ '74
Bite the Bullet '75
Rooster Cogburn '75
The Big Bus '76
Midway '76
Special Delivery '76
Damnation Alley '77
The Greatest '77
Born Again '78
Convoy '78
Go Tell the Spartans '78

Prophecy '79
Carny '80
Buddy Buddy '81
The Pursuit of D.B. Cooper '81
S.O.B. '81
Micki & Maude '84
A Fine Mess '86
Blind Date '87
Caddyshack 2 '88

Ivan Strasburg
The Affair '95

Karl Struss
Sunrise '27
Coquette '29
The Taming of the Shrew '29
Abraham Lincoln '30
Dr. Jekyll and Mr. Hyde '31
Island of Lost Souls '32
Belle of the Nineties '34
Goin' to Town '35
Go West, Young Man '36
Rhythm on the Range '36
Waikiki Wedding '37
The Great Dictator '40
Journey into Fear '42
Limelight '52
Mesa of Lost Women '52
Mohawk '56
The Fly '58
The Rebel Set '59

Bruce Surtees
The Beguiled '70
Dirty Harry '71
Play Misty for Me '71
Conquest of the Planet of the Apes '72
The Great Northfield Minnesota Raid '72
Joe Kidd '72
Blume in Love '73
Lenny '74
Night Moves '75
The Outlaw Josey Wales '76
The Shootist '76
Escape from Alcatraz '79
Firefox '82
Honkytonk Man '82
Sudden Impact '83
Beverly Hills Cop '84
Tightrope '84
Pale Rider '85
Out of Bounds '86
Psycho 3 '86
Ratboy '86
Back to the Beach '87
License to Drive '88
Men Don't Leave '89
Run '91
The Super '91
The Stars Fell on Henrietta '94
The Substitute '96

Robert L. Surtees
Thirty Seconds Over Tokyo '44
Two Girls and a Sailor '44
Our Vines Have Tender Grapes '45
A Date with Judy '48
Intruder in the Dust '49
That Midnight Kiss '49
King Solomon's Mines '50
Quo Vadis '51
The Bad and the Beautiful '52
The Merry Widow '52
Escape from Fort Bravo '53
Mogambo '53
Oklahoma! '55
The Swan '56
Les Girls '57
Raintree County '57
Ben-Hur '59
Mutiny on the Bounty '62
The Collector '65
The Hallelujah Trail '65
The Lost Command '66
Doctor Dolittle '67
The Graduate '67
The Arrangement '69
Sweet Charity '69
The Last Picture Show '71
Summer of '42 '71
The Cowboys '72
The Other '72
Oklahoma Crude '73
The Sting '73
The Great Waldo Pepper '75
The Hindenburg '75
A Star is Born '76
The Turning Point '77

Surtees ▶cont.

Bloodbrothers *'78*
Same Time, Next Year *'78*

Peter Suschitzsky
The Empire Strikes Back *'80*
Crash *'95*

Rob Sweeney
Color of a Brisk and Leaping Day *'95*

Hubert Taczanowski
The Young Poisoner's Handbook *'94*

Fred Tammes
Priest *'94*
Mad Love *'95*

David Tattersall
Radioland Murders *'94*
Theodore Rex *'95*
Moll Flanders *'96*

Gale Tattersall
Hideaway *'94*
Virtuosity *'95*

Christopher Taylor
Live Nude Girls *'95*

Manuel Teran
Before the Rain *'94*

Ted Tetzlaff
Hands Across the Table *'35*
The Princess Comes Across *'36*
Remember the Night *'40*

Armand Thirard
Beauties of the Night *'52*

Alex Thomson
Cliffhanger *'93*
The Scarlet Letter *'95*
Executive Decision *'96*

Donald E. Thorin
Thief *'81*
An Officer and a Gentleman *'82*
Bad Boys *'83*
Against All Odds *'84*
Purple Rain *'84*
Midnight Run *'88*
Scent of a Woman *'92*
Boys on the Side *'94*
Ace Ventura: When Nature Calls *'95*

Frank Tidy
Steal Big, Steal Little *'95*
The Boys Next Door *'96*
Chain Reaction *'96*
Getting Away With Murder *'96*

Gary Tieche
Out There *'95*

Gregg Toland
Roman Scandals *'33*
Les Miserables *'35*
Beloved Enemy *'36*
These Three *'36*
Dead End *'37*
History is Made at Night *'37*
The Cowboy and the Lady *'38*
The Goldwyn Follies *'38*
Intermezzo *'39*
Wuthering Heights *'39*
The Grapes of Wrath *'40*
The Long Voyage Home *'40*
The Westerner *'40*
Ball of Fire *'41*
Citizen Kane *'41*
The Best Years of Our Lives *'46*
Kid from Brooklyn *'46*
The Bishop's Wife *'47*
A Song is Born *'48*

John Toll
Wind *'92*
Legends of the Fall *'94*
Braveheart *'95*

Leo Tover
The Day the Earth Stood Still *'51*
Strange Bedfellows *'65*

Luciano Tovoli
Bread and Chocolate *'74*
Before and After *'95*

Brian Tufano
Middlemarch *'93*
Trainspotting *'95*

Jeffery Tufano
Jeffrey *'95*

George Tutanes
Midnight Dancers *'94*

Geoffrey Unsworth
Scott of the Antarctic *'48*
The Clouded Yellow *'51*
The Sword & the Rose *'53*
Simba *'55*
A Night to Remember *'58*
Flame Over India *'60*
The World of Suzie Wong *'60*
Becket *'64*
Half a Sixpence *'67*
2001: A Space Odyssey *'68*
The Assassination Bureau *'69*
The Magic Christian *'69*
Cromwell *'70*
Alice's Adventures in Wonderland *'72*
Cabaret *'72*
Internecine Project *'73*
Murder on the Orient Express *'74*
Return of the Pink Panther *'74*
Royal Flash *'75*
A Matter of Time *'76*
A Bridge Too Far *'77*
Superman: The Movie *'78*
The Great Train Robbery *'79*
Tess *'80*

Sergei Urusevsky
I Am Cuba *'64*

Jost Vacano
Showgirls *'95*

Joseph Valentine
Night of Terror *'33*
The Moon's Our Home *'36*
Three Smart Girls *'36*
100 Men and a Girl *'37*
Mad About Music *'38*
The Rage of Paris *'38*
First Love *'39*
It's a Date *'40*
My Little Chickadee *'40*
In the Navy *'41*
The Wolf Man *'41*
Saboteur *'42*
Shadow of a Doubt *'43*
Guest Wife *'45*
Heartbeat *'46*
Tomorrow Is Forever *'46*
The Possessed *'47*
Joan of Arc *'48*

Eddy van der Enden
Lie Down with Lions *'94*

Kees Van Oostrum
Scott Turow's The Burden of Proof *'92*
Down Came a Blackbird *'94*
Journey *'95*

Walther Vanden Ende
The Eighth Day *'95*
Farinelli *'94*

Henry Vargas
Tollbooth *'94*

Robin Vidgeon
August *'95*

Reynaldo Villalobos
9 to 5 *'80*
Urban Cowboy *'80*
Ballad of Gregorio Cortez *'83*
Risky Business *'83*
Desert Bloom *'86*
Punchline *'88*
Major League *'89*
American Me *'92*
Sinatra *'92*
Roosters *'95*

Paul Vogel
Fit for a King *'37*
Wide Open Faces *'38*
Lady in the Lake *'46*
Battleground *'49*
The Black Hand *'50*
Angels in the Outfield *'51*
Go for Broke! *'51*
Clown *'53*
Rose Marie *'54*
The Student Prince *'54*
Interrupted Melody *'55*
The Tender Trap *'55*
High Society *'56*
Wings of Eagles *'57*
The Time Machine *'60*
The Wonderful World of the Brothers Grimm *'62*
The Rounders *'65*
Return of the Seven *'66*

Gerd Von Bonen
The Bridge *'59*

Vjekoslav Vrdoljak
Gospa *'94*

Mario Vulpiani
La Grande Bouffe *'73*
Castle Freak *'95*

Maggie Wadey
The Buccaneers *'95*

William Wages
Riders of the Purple Sage *'96*

Roy Wagner
A Nightmare on Elm Street 3: Dream Warriors *'87*
Witchboard *'87*
Disaster at Silo 7 *'88*
Another Stakeout *'93*
Nick of Time *'95*

Lau Wai-Keung
Chungking Express *'95*

Ric Waite
Andersonville *'95*

Joseph Walker
Theodora Goes Wild *'36*
Tales of Manhattan *'42*
Harriet Craig *'50*

Jack Wallner
Miami Rhapsody *'95*

John Ward
Heaven's a Drag *'94*

Gilbert Warrenton
Mesa of Lost Women *'52*
Atomic Submarine *'59*

David Watkin
Help! *'65*
The Knack *'65*
Marat/Sade *'66*
How I Won the War *'67*
The Charge of the Light Brigade *'68*
Catch-22 *'70*
The Boy Friend *'71*
The Devils *'71*
The Three Musketeers *'74*
Mahogany *'75*
Robin and Marian *'76*
To the Devil, A Daughter *'76*
Joseph Andrews *'77*
Cuba *'79*
Hanover Street *'79*
Chariots of Fire *'81*
Endless Love *'81*
Yentl *'83*
The Hotel New Hampshire *'84*
Out of Africa *'85*
Return to Oz *'85*
White Nights *'85*
Moonstruck *'87*
The Good Mother *'88*
Last Rites *'88*
Masquerade *'88*
Hamlet *'90*
Memphis Belle *'90*
The Object of Beauty *'91*
This Boy's Life *'93*
Jane Eyre *'96*

Michael Watkins
Point of No Return *'93*

Henry Waxman
The Nanny *'65*
The Anniversary *'68*

Egon Werdin
Mute Witness *'95*

Haskell Wexler
Angel Baby *'61*
The Hoodlum Priest *'61*
The Best Man *'64*
The Loved One *'65*
In the Heat of the Night *'67*
The Thomas Crown Affair *'68*
Medium Cool *'69*
Gimme Shelter *'70*
One Flew Over the Cuckoo's Nest *'75*
Bound for Glory *'76*
Coming Home *'78*
Matewan *'87*
Colors *'88*
Blaze *'89*
Three Fugitives *'89*
Other People's Money *'91*
The Babe *'92*
Canadian Bacon *'94*
The Secret of Roan Inish *'94*
Mulholland Falls *'95*

John Wilcox
Nightmare *'63*

Billy Williams
Women in Love *'70*
Night Watch *'72*
X, Y & Zee *'72*
The Wind and the Lion *'75*
Voyage of the Damned *'76*
The Silent Partner *'78*
Eagle's Wing *'79*
Saturn 3 *'80*
On Golden Pond *'81*
Gandhi *'82*
Monsignor *'82*
Survivors *'83*
Ordeal by Innocence *'84*
Dreamchild *'85*
Eleni *'85*
The Manhattan Project *'86*
Suspect *'87*
The Rainbow *'89*
Stella *'89*

Gordon Willis
End of the Road *'70*
Klute *'71*
Little Murders *'71*
Bad Company *'72*
The Godfather *'72*
Up the Sandbox *'72*
The Paper Chase *'73*
The Godfather, Part 2 *'74*
The Parallax View *'74*
The Drowning Pool *'75*
All the President's Men *'76*
Annie Hall *'77*
Comes a Horseman *'78*
Interiors *'78*
Manhattan *'79*
Stardust Memories *'80*
Windows *'80*
Pennies From Heaven *'81*
A Midsummer Night's Sex Comedy *'82*
Zelig *'83*
Broadway Danny Rose *'84*
Perfect *'85*
The Purple Rose of Cairo *'85*
The Money Pit *'86*
The Pick-Up Artist *'87*
Bright Lights, Big City *'88*
The Godfather, Part 3 *'90*
Presumed Innocent *'90*
Malice *'93*

Willy
Le Schpountz *'38*

Ian Wilson
The Secret Rapture *'94*
Emma *'96*

Rexford Wimpy
The Reluctant Astronaut *'67*

Stephen Windon
Country Life *'95*
In Pursuit of Honor *'95*

Dariusz Wolski
Crimson Tide *'95*

Oliver Wood
Mr. Holland's Opus *'95*
Celtic Pride *'96*

Bruce Worrall
Hard Evidence *'94*
Tracks of a Killer *'95*

Peter Wunstorf
Double Happiness *'94*

Bao Xianran
Women From the Lake of Scented Souls *'94*

Zhang Xiaoguang
The Wooden Man's Bride *'94*

Robert Yeoman
Coldblooded *'94*
Bottle Rocket *'95*

Hou Yong
The Day the Sun Turned Cold *'94*

Frederick A. (Freddie) Young
The Speckled Band *'31*
When Knights were Bold *'36*
Goodbye, Mr. Chips *'39*
While I Live *'47*
The Winslow Boy *'48*
Conspirator *'49*
Treasure Island *'50*
Ivanhoe *'52*
Knights of the Round Table *'53*
Betrayed *'54*
Bhowani Junction *'56*
Island in the Sun *'57*
Indiscreet *'58*
The Inn of the Sixth Happiness *'58*
Solomon and Sheba *'59*
Gorgo *'61*
Lawrence of Arabia *'62*
Doctor Zhivago *'65*
Lord Jim *'65*
You Only Live Twice *'67*
Battle of Britain *'69*
Ryan's Daughter *'70*
Nicholas and Alexandra *'71*
The Asphyx *'72*
Luther *'74*
The Tamarind Seed *'74*
Permission To Kill *'75*
Stevie *'78*
Sidney Sheldon's Bloodline *'79*
Richard's Things *'80*
Rough Cut *'80*
Sword of the Valiant *'83*

Bae Young-kyun
Why Has Bodhi-Darma Left for the East *'89*

Lu Yue
Shanghai Triad *'95*

Hu Zhenhua
Crows and Sparrows *'49*

Miao Zhenhua
Crows and Sparrows *'49*

Jerzy Zielinski
Houseguest *'94*
Powder *'95*

Bernard Zitzermann
The Music of Chance *'93*
Angels and Insects *'95*

Vilmos Zsigmond
McCabe & Mrs. Miller *'71*
Deliverance *'72*
Cinderella Liberty *'73*
The Long Goodbye *'73*
Scarecrow *'73*
The Sugarland Express *'74*
Close Encounters of the Third Kind *'77*
The Deer Hunter *'78*
The Rose *'79*
Blow Out *'81*
Heaven's Gate *'81*
The River *'84*
The Witches of Eastwick *'87*
The Bonfire of the Vanities *'90*
The Two Jakes *'90*
Stalin *'92*
Intersection *'93*
Sliver *'93*
The Crossing Guard *'94*
Maverick *'94*
Assassins *'95*

Kenneth Zunder
It Takes Two *'95*

Composer Index

The **Composer Index** provides a videography for any composer, arranger, lyricist, or band that has provided an original music score for a film now on video. The listings for the composer names follow an alphabetical sort by last name (although the names appear in a first name last name format). The videographies are listed chronologically, from oldest film to the most recent. If a composer provided music for more than one film in the same year, these movies are listed alphabetically within the year.

Michael Abene
Goodbye, New York '85

Barron Abramovitch
Hard Evidence '94
Tracks of a Killer '95

Jack Ackerman
Faces '68

Barry Adamson
Delusion '91
Gas Food Lodging '92

Richard Addinsell
A Christmas Carol '51

John Addison
Reach for the Sky '56
Look Back in Anger '58
Lucky Jim '58
Carlton Browne of the F.O. '59
The Entertainer '60
A Taste of Honey '61
The Loneliness of the Long Distance Runner '62
Tom Jones '63
Guns at Batasi '64
The Amorous Adventures of Moll Flanders '65
The Loved One '65
A Fine Madness '66
Torn Curtain '66
The Honey Pot '67
The Charge of the Light Brigade '68
Start the Revolution Without Me '70
Cry of the Penguins '71
Sleuth '72
Luther '74
Ride a Wild Pony '75
The Seven-Per-Cent Solution '76
Swashbuckler '76
A Bridge Too Far '77
Joseph Andrews '77
The Bastard '78
Love's Savage Fury '79
Eleanor: First Lady of the World '82
Grace Quigley '84
Code Name: Emerald '85
Something in Common '86
The Phantom of the Opera '90

Larry Adler
Genevieve '53
A Cry from the Streets '57
Great Chase '63

Mark Adler
Eat a Bowl of Tea '89
Slam Dunk Ernest '95

Yashushi Akutagawa
An Actor's Revenge '63

Robert Alcivar
Butterflies Are Free '72
Olly Olly Oxen Free '78
One from the Heart '82
Hysterical '83
Blind Witness '89
Naked Lie '89

Jeff Alexander
Westward the Women '51
Gun Glory '57

Van Alexander
The Atomic Kid '54
Jaguar '56
When Gangland Strikes '56
Girls' Town '59
Platinum High School '60
Strait-Jacket '64

Eric Allaman
The Battleship Potemkin '25
Angel 3: The Final Chapter '88
Down Twisted '89

Cameron Allan
Midnite Spares '85
The Good Wife '86
Jericho Fever '93
JFK: Reckless Youth '93

Billy Allen
The Acid Eaters '67

Dave Allen
The Harvest '92

Peter Allen
Crackerjack '94

Woody Allen
Sleeper '73

Byron Allred
Don't Answer the Phone '80

Gerald Alters
Your Place or Mine '83

John Altman
Hear My Song '91
Bad Behavior '92
Bhaji on the Beach '94
Funny Bones '94

Ed Alton
My Demon Lover '87

Minette Alton
Children of Divorce '80
Devlin '92

Dave Alvin
Border Radio '88

Daniele Amfitheatrof
The Virginian '46
Singapore '47
The Last Hunt '56

David Amram
Splendor in the Grass '61
The Manchurian Candidate '62
The Arrangement '69

Anastasia
Before the Rain '94

Laurie Anderson
Something Wild '86
Swimming to Cambodia '87
Monster in a Box '92

Pete Anderson
Chasers '94

Dwight Andrews
The Piano Lesson '94

Gerard Anfosso
Cousin, Cousine '76
Blue Country '77

Antonio Ramirez Angel
The Awful Dr. Orlof '62

Scott Angley
Clerks '94

Paul Antonelli
Avenging Angel '85
Princess Academy '87
Women's Club '87
China O'Brien '88
Out of the Dark '88

Louis Applebaum
Lost Boundaries '49

Philip Appleby
Maria's Child '93

Shimon Arama
Bigfoot: The Unforgettable Encounter '94

Sebastian Argol
Yol '82

Eddie Arkin
Hardbodies 2 '86
Modern Girls '86
Pretty Smart '87

Harold Arlen
Cabin in the Sky '43
Gay Purr-ee '62
Last Summer In the Hamptons '96

Martin Armiger
Sweetie '89
Young Einstein '89
The Crossing '92

Michael Armstrong
Silent Night, Deadly Night 2 '87

David Arnold
The Young Americans '93
The Last of the Dogmen '95
Independence Day '96

Malcolm Arnold
Eye Witness '49
No Highway in the Sky '51
A Stolen Face '52
Wings of Danger '52
The Belles of St. Trinian's '53
Captain's Paradise '53
Curtain Up '53
Four Sided Triangle '53
Hobson's Choice '53
Devil on Horseback '54
The Sleeping Tiger '54
I Am a Camera '55
The Sea Shall Not Have Them '55
Blue Murder at St. Trinian's '56
Trapeze '56
The Bridge on the River Kwai '57
Island in the Sun '57
The Inn of the Sixth Happiness '58
The Key '58
Solomon and Sheba '59
Suddenly, Last Summer '59
No Love for Johnnie '60
Tunes of Glory '60
The Pure Hell of St. Trinian's '61
Whistle Down the Wind '62
The Chalk Garden '64
The Great St. Trinian's Train Robbery '66
Africa Texas Style '67
David Copperfield '70

Peter Arnow
Torn Apart '89

Bruce Arntson
Ernest Goes to Jail '90
Ernest Scared Stupid '91
Ernest Rides Again '93

Leon Aronson
Eddie and the Cruisers 2: Eddie Lives! '89

Jorge Arriagada
It's All True '93

Eduard Artemyev
Solaris '72
A Slave of Love '78
Siberiade '79
Stalker '79
Homer and Eddie '89
Close to Eden '90
The Inner Circle '91
Double Jeopardy '92
Burnt by the Sun '94

Howard Ashman
Little Shop of Horrors '86
The Little Mermaid '89
Beauty and the Beast '91
Aladdin '92

Edwin Astley
To Paris with Love '55
The Case of the Mukkinese Battle Horn '56
The Mouse That Roared '59
A Matter of WHO '62
The Phantom of the Opera '62
Digby, the Biggest Dog in the World '73

Paul Aston
Joey Breaker '93

Chet Atkins
Stroszek '77
Michael Atkinson
Backlash '86
Murray Attaway
Midnight Edition '93
Georges Auric
Dead of Night '45
Lola Montes '55
Wages of Fear '55
Gervaise '56
The Innocents '61
Gene Austin
Follow the Leader '44
Pepe Avila
My Family '94
David A. Axelrod
Cannonball '76
Roy Ayers
Coffy '73
Pedro Aznar
Man Facing Southeast '86
Babyface
Waiting to Exhale '95
Luis Bacalov
Empty Canvas '64
The Gospel According to St. Matthew '64
A Bullet for the General '68
Catch as Catch Can '68
City of Women '81
Entre-Nous '83
The Postman '94
Burt Bacharach
The Sad Sack '57
What's New Pussycat? '65
After the Fox '66
Casino Royale '67
Butch Cassidy and the Sundance Kid '69
Together? '79
Arthur '81
Night Shift '82
Arthur 2: On the Rocks '88
Pierre Bachelet
Emmanuelle '74
Black and White in Color '76
The Perils of Gwendoline '84
Emmanuelle 5 '87
Brian Backus
Young Guns '88
Angelo Badalamenti
Gordon's War '73
Law and Disorder '74
Across the Great Divide '76
Blue Velvet '86
A Nightmare on Elm Street 3: Dream Warriors '87
Tough Guys Don't Dance '87
Weeds '87
Cousins '89
National Lampoon's Christmas Vacation '89
Parents '89
Twin Peaks '90
Twin Peaks '90
Wait Until Spring, Bandini '90
Wild at Heart '90
The Comfort of Strangers '91
Twin Peaks: Fire Walk with Me '92
Hotel Room '93
Naked in New York '93
Witch Hunt '94
The City of Lost Children '95
Wally Badarou
Kiss of the Spider Woman '85
The Lunatic '92
Don Bagley
Mama's Dirty Girls '74
Tom Bahler
Mary, Mary, Bloody Mary '76
Fast Forward '84
Cold Feet '89
The Object of Beauty '91
Gordy '95
Tadeusz Baird
Lotna '64
Buddy Baker
The Misadventures of Merlin Jones '63
Summer Magic '63
A Tiger Walks '64
Monkey's Uncle '65
The Gnome-Mobile '67
Million Dollar Duck '71
Napoleon and Samantha '72
Superdad '73
The Bears & I '74
The Apple Dumpling Gang '75
No Deposit, No Return '76
The Shaggy D.A. '76
The Treasure of Matecumbe '76
Hot Lead & Cold Feet '78
The Apple Dumpling Gang Rides Again '79
The Devil & Max Devlin '81
The Fox and the Hound '81
The Puppetoon Movie '87
Michael Conway Baker
The Deserters '80s
Silence of the North '81
The Grey Fox '83
One Magic Christmas '85
Loyalties '86
Showdown at Williams Creek '91
The Portrait '93
Alexander Balanescu
Angels and Insects '95
Jim Ball
Sarah's Child '96
Richard Band
Laserblast '78
Day Time Ended '80
Dr. Heckyl and Mr. Hype '80
The Alchemist '81
Parasite '82
Time Walker '82
Dungeonmaster '83
The House on Sorority Row '83
Metalstorm: The Destruction of Jared Syn '83
Mutant '83
Ghoulies '84
Re-Animator '84
Zone Troopers '84
The Eliminators '86
From Beyond '86
Terrorvision '86
Troll '86
The Caller '87
Dolls '87
Prison '88
Arena '89
Bride of Re-Animator '89
Puppet Master '89
The Arrival '90
Crash and Burn '90
Doctor Mordrid: Master of the Unknown '90
Puppet Master 2 '90
Puppet Master 3: Toulon's Revenge '90
The Pit & the Pendulum '91
The Resurrected '91
Trancers 3: Deth Lives '92
Dollman vs Demonic Toys '93
Puppet Master 4 '93
Remote '93
Dragonworld '94
Prehysteria 2 '94
Puppet Master 5: The Final Chapter '94
Shrunken Heads '94
Castle Freak '95
Magic Island '95
Zarkorr! The Invader '96
Brian Banks
Nice Girls Don't Explode '87
Young Guns '88
Graveyard Shift '90
Internal Affairs '90
Don Banks
Nightmare '63
The Evil of Frankenstein '64
Hysteria '64
Die, Monster, Die! '65
I Killed Rasputin '67
Torture Garden '67
Tony Banks
The Shout '78
The Wicked Lady '83
Quicksilver '86
Claus Bantzer
Drachenfutter '87
Jack Baran
Great Balls of Fire '89
Billy Barber
Mystery Science Theater 3000: The Movie '96
John Barber
The Incredible Two-Headed Transplant '71
Lesley Barber
When Night is Falling '95
Samuel Barber
The Elephant Man '80
Stephen Barber
Galaxies are Colliding '92
Denis Barbier
A la Mode '94
Gato Barbieri
Before the Revolution '65
Notes for an African Orestes '70
Last Tango in Paris '73
Firepower '79
Strangers Kiss '83
Louis Barlow
Kids '95
John Barnes
Daughters of the Dust '91
Bebe's Kids '92
CB4: The Movie '93
Charles P. Barnett
Hell Squad '85
Busted Up '86
Headless Body in Topless Bar '96
George Barrie
Fingers '78
Bebe Barron
Forbidden Planet '56
Louis Barron
Forbidden Planet '56
Daemion Barry
A Woman's Guide to Adultery '93
Jeff Barry
Idolmaker '80
John Barry
Beat Girl '60
Never Let Go '60
Dr. No '62
From Russia with Love '63
Goldfinger '64
Seance on a Wet Afternoon '64
Zulu '64
The Ipcress File '65
King Rat '65
The Knack '65
Thunderball '65
Born Free '66
The Chase '66
The Quiller Memorandum '66
The Wrong Box '66
Dutchman '67
You Only Live Twice '67
The Dove '68
The Lion in Winter '68
Petulia '68
Midnight Cowboy '69
On Her Majesty's Secret Service '69
Monte Walsh '70
Diamonds Are Forever '71
The Last Valley '71
Murphy's War '71
They Might Be Giants '71
Alice's Adventures in Wonderland '72
A Doll's House '73
The Man with the Golden Gun '74
The Tamarind Seed '74
The Day of the Locust '75
Love Among the Ruins '75
The Rocky Horror Picture Show '75
Shampoo '75
Eleanor & Franklin '76
King Kong '76
Robin and Marian '76
War Between the Tates '76
The Deep '77
First Love '77
The Gathering '77
The White Buffalo '77
The Betsy '78
Star Crash '78
The Black Hole '79
Game of Death '79
Hanover Street '79
Moonraker '79
Willa '79
Inside Moves '80
Night Games '80
Raise the Titanic '80
Somewhere in Time '80
Touched by Love '80
Body Heat '81
Legend of the Lone Ranger '81
Frances '82
Hammett '82
Murder by Phone '82
The Golden Seal '83
High Road to China '83
Octopussy '83
Svengali '83
The Cotton Club '84
Mike's Murder '84
Until September '84
The Jagged Edge '85
A Killing Affair '85
Out of Africa '85
A View to a Kill '85
Howard the Duck '86
Peggy Sue Got Married '86
Hearts of Fire '87
The Living Daylights '87
Masquerade '88
Dances with Wolves '90
Chaplin '92
Deception '92
The Public Eye '92
Indecent Proposal '93
My Life '93
The Specialist '94
Cry, the Beloved Country '95
The Scarlet Letter '95
Lionel Bart
Black Beauty '71
Steve Bartek
Guilty as Charged '92
Past Midnight '92
Cabin Boy '94
Coldblooded '94
Dee Barton
Play Misty for Me '71
High Plains Drifter '73
Thunderbolt & Lightfoot '74
Richard Baskin
Nashville '75
Buffalo Bill & the Indians '76
Welcome to L.A. '77
Honeysuckle Rose '80
Uforia '81
Kevin Bassinson
Cyborg '89
Beanstalk '94
George Bassman
A Damsel in Distress '37
A Day at the Races '37
Everybody Sing '38
Babes in Arms '39
Go West '40
Too Many Girls '40
Babes on Broadway '41
Big Store '41
Lady Be Good '41
For Me and My Gal '42
Panama Hattie '42
Best Foot Forward '43
Cabin in the Sky '43
Whistling in Brooklyn '43
The Canterville Ghost '44
Abbott and Costello in Hollywood '45
The Clock '45
The Postman Always Rings Twice '46
The Joe Louis Story '53
Ride the High Country '62
Wombling Free '77
Les Baxter
Monika '52
Battle Shock '56
Girl in Black Stockings '57
The Invisible Boy '57
The Key Man '57
Storm Rider '57
The Bride & the Beast '58
Lone Ranger and the Lost City of Gold '58
Black Sunday '60
The Fall of the House of Usher '60
Goliath and the Barbarians '60
Alakazam the Great! '61
Goliath and the Dragon '61
Master of the World '61
The Pit and the Pendulum '61
Panic in the Year Zero! '62
Samson and the 7 Miracles of the World '62
Tales of Terror '62
Battle Beyond the Sun '63
Beach Party '63
The Invaders '63
The Raven '63
X: The Man with X-Ray Eyes '63
Bikini Beach '64
Black Sabbath '64
The Comedy of Terrors '64
Muscle Beach Party '64
Pajama Party '64
Beach Blanket Bingo '65
How to Stuff a Wild Bikini '65
Dr. Goldfoot and the Bikini Machine '66
Terror in the Jungle '68
Wild in the Streets '68
Hell's Belles '69
Cry of the Banshee '70
The Dunwich Horror '70
The Big Doll House '71
Frogs '72
Torture Chamber of Baron Blood '72
Devil & Leroy Basset '73
Switchblade Sisters '75
Born Again '78
The Beast Within '82
Irwin Bazelon
Wilma '77
David Beal
The Take '90
Jeff Beal
Cheap Shots '91
The Fence '94
Ring of Steel '94
John Beal
Zero to Sixty '78
Defiance '79
The Man with Bogart's Face '80
The Funhouse '81
Lookin' to Get Out '82
The Stone Boy '84
Under the Volcano '84
Killer Party '86
The Offspring '87
Michael Bearden
DROP Squad '94
The Beatles
Let It Be '70
Jeff Beck
Blue Chips '94
Joe Beck
Goodbye, Norma Jean '75
Frank Becker
American Kickboxer 1 '91
Terminal Bliss '91
Danny Beckerman
Fortress '85
Hal Beckett
Power of Attorney '94
Stephen Bedell
Jersey Girl '92
Michael Been
Light Sleeper '92
Daniel Bell
Fanny and Alexander '83
David Bell
Killing at Hell's Gate '81
Final Justice '84
Memphis '91
There Goes the Neighborhood '92
Thom Bell
The Fish that Saved Pittsburgh '79
Wayne Bell
The Texas Chainsaw Massacre '74
Eaten Alive '76
Last Night at the Alamo '83
Andrew Belling
The Killing Kind '73
End of the World '76
Wizards '77
The Deerslayer '78

Zoltan...Hound of Dracula '78
Starchaser: The Legend of Orin '85

Richard Bellis
Breaking Up Is Hard to Do '79
A Shining Season '79
Fallen Angel '81
Stephen King's It '90
Blind Man's Bluff '91
Double-Crossed '91
The Spider and the Fly '94
How the West was Fun '95

Roger Bellon
Princess Academy '87
The Unholy '88
Waxwork '88

Vassal Benford
Class Act '91
House Party 2: The Pajama Jam '91

James Bennett
Poison '91
Swoon '91

Richard Rodney Bennett
Indiscreet '58
The Devil's Disciple '59
The Mark '61
Only Two Can Play '62
Billy Liar '63
Heavens Above '63
The Wrong Arm of the Law '63
The Nanny '65
Far from the Madding Crowd '67
Secret Ceremony '69
Nicholas and Alexandra '71
Lady Caroline Lamb '73
Murder on the Orient Express '74
Permission To Kill '75
Equus '77
Brink's Job '78
Yanks '79
Return of the Soldier '82
Ebony Tower '86
Poor Little Rich Girl: The Barbara Hutton Story '87
The Attic: The Hiding of Anne Frank '88
Enchanted April '92
Four Weddings and a Funeral '94

David Benoit
Captive Hearts '87
The Stars Fell on Henrietta '94

Robby Benson
Die Laughing '80

David Bergeaud
Twice Dead '88

Cary Berger
Suture '93

Alan Bergman
Yentl '83

Marilyn Bergman
Yentl '83

Michael Berkeley
Twenty-One '91

Irving Berlin
The Cocoanuts '29
Hallelujah! '29
Top Hat '35
Follow the Fleet '36
On the Avenue '37
Alexander's Ragtime Band '38
Carefree '38
Second Fiddle '39
Easter Parade '48
Le Bal '82

James Bernard
The Quatermass Experiment '56
Across the Bridge '57
The Curse of Frankenstein '57
Quatermass 2 '57
The Horror of Dracula '58
The Hound of the Baskervilles '59
Kiss of the Vampire '62
The Gorgon '64
Torture Garden '67
Dracula Has Risen from the Grave '68
The Scars of Dracula '70
Taste the Blood of Dracula '70
The 7 Brothers Meet Dracula '73
Frankenstein and the Monster from Hell '74

Marie Bernard
Strangers in Good Company '91

Charles Bernstein
Invasion of the Bee Girls '73
Pigs '73
The Shrieking '73
White Lightning '73
Mr. Majestyk '74
Gator '76
Nightmare in Badham County '76
A Small Town in Texas '76
Outlaw Blues '77
Viva Knievel '77
Are You in the House Alone? '78
Steel Cowboy '78
Wild & Wooly '78
The Winds of Kitty Hawk '78
The House on Garibaldi Street '79
Love at First Bite '79
Bogie: The Last Hero '80
Coast to Coast '80
Foolin' Around '80
The Hunter '80
Scruples '80
Cujo '83
The Entity '83
Independence Day '83
Sadat '83
A Nightmare on Elm Street '84
Chase '85
Secret Weapons '85
April Fool's Day '86
Deadly Friend '86
The Last Fling '86
The Long, Hot Summer '86
The Rumor Mill '86
The Allnighter '87
Dudes '87
The Man Who Broke 1,000 Chains '87
Caroline? '90
Ivory Hunters '90
Too Young to Die '90
Payoff '91
Excessive Force '93
Final Appeal '93
The Sea Wolf '93

Elmer Bernstein
Boots Malone '52
Never Wave at a WAC '52
Sudden Fear '52
Cat Women of the Moon '53
Robot Monster '53
Make Haste to Live '54
Silent Raiders '54
It's a Dog's Life '55
The Man with the Golden Arm '55
The Ten Commandments '56
Fear Strikes Out '57
Men in War '57
Sweet Smell of Success '57
The Tin Star '57
The Buccaneer '58
Desire Under the Elms '58
God's Little Acre '58
Kings Go Forth '58
Some Came Running '58
From the Terrace '60
The Magnificent Seven '60
The Rat Race '60
By Love Possessed '61
The Comancheros '61
Summer and Smoke '61
Birdman of Alcatraz '62
To Kill a Mockingbird '62
Walk on the Wild Side '62
The Great Escape '63
Hud '63
Love with the Proper Stranger '63
Baby, the Rain Must Fall '64
The Carpetbaggers '64
The World of Henry Orient '64
The Hallelujah Trail '65
Sons of Katie Elder '65
Cast a Giant Shadow '66
Hawaii '66
Return of the Seven '66
Thoroughly Modern Millie '67
Will Penny '67
I Love You, Alice B. Toklas! '68
The Scalphunters '68
The Bridge at Remagen '69
Guns of the Magnificent Seven '69
True Grit '69
Doctors' Wives '70
The Liberation of L.B. Jones '70
Walk in the Spring Rain '70
Big Jake '71
See No Evil '71
Amazing Mr. Blunden '72
Cahill: United States Marshal '73
McQ '74
Report to the Commissioner '74
The Trial of Billy Jack '74
The Old Curiosity Shop '75
From Noon Till Three '76
The Incredible Sarah '76
The Shootist '76
Slap Shot '77
Bloodbrothers '78
Little Women '78
National Lampoon's Animal House '78
The Chisholms '79
Meatballs '79
Zulu Dawn '79
Airplane! '80
The Great Santini '80
The Guyana Tragedy: The Story of Jim Jones '80
Saturn 3 '80
An American Werewolf in London '81
The Chosen '81
Going Ape! '81
Heavy Metal '81
Honky Tonk Freeway '81
Stripes '81
Airplane 2: The Sequel '82
Five Days One Summer '82
Class '83
Prince Jack '83
Spacehunter: Adventures in the Forbidden Zone '83
Trading Places '83
Bolero '84
The Ewok Adventure '84
Ghostbusters '84
Gulag '85
Spies Like Us '85
Hamburger...The Motion Picture '86
Legal Eagles '86
Three Amigos '86
Amazing Grace & Chuck '87
Leonard Part 6 '87
Da '88
Funny Farm '88
The Good Mother '88
A Night in the Life of Jimmy Reardon '88
My Left Foot '89
Slipstream '89
The Grifters '90
Cape Fear '91
Oscar '91
A Rage in Harlem '91
Rambling Rose '91
The Babe '92
The Age of Innocence '93
The Cemetery Club '93
Fallen Angels 1 '93
The Good Son '93
Lost in Yonkers '93
Mad Dog and Glory '93
Canadian Bacon '94
Search and Destroy '94
Devil In a Blue Dress '95
Frankie Starlight '95
Roommates '95

Leonard Bernstein
On the Waterfront '54
West Side Story '61
On the Town '91

Peter Bernstein
National Lampoon's Class Reunion '82
Silent Rage '82
Club Med '83
Hot Dog...The Movie! '83
Bolero '84
The Ewok Adventure '84
Summer Fantasy '84
Surf 2 '84
Broken Badge '85
The Ewoks: Battle for Endor '85
Kicks '85
My Science Project '85
Miracles '86
The Alamo: Thirteen Days to Glory '87
Morgan Stewart's Coming Home '87
Remote Control '88
Nightbreaker '89
Fifty/Fifty '93

Peter Best
Crocodile Dundee '86
High Tide '87
Crocodile Dundee 2 '88
Muriel's Wedding '94
Country Life '95

Harry Betts
Big Mouth '67
Cheech and Chong's Nice Dreams '81

Amin Bhatia
Storm '87
Iron Eagle 2 '88
Black Ice '92
Just One of the Girls '93

Nick Bicat
Oliver Twist '82
The Scarlet Pimpernel '82
To Catch a King '84
Wetherby '85
Stealing Heaven '88
Strapless '90
The Reflecting Skin '91
The Hawk '93

Arnold Bieber
Small Time '91
Smoke '93

Keith Bilderbeck
Voodoo '95

Rene Marc Bini
Grosse Fatigue '94

Nathan Birnbaum
Chain of Desire '93

Johnny Bishop
The Gods Must Be Crazy '84

Karen Black
Can She Bake a Cherry Pie? '83

Stanley Black
The Crawling Eye '58
Jack the Ripper '60
Mania '60
Maniac '63

Wendy Blackstone
Eddie Macon's Run '83
Only You '92
New Jersey Drive '95

Ruben Blades
The Story of Fausta '88
Q & A '90

Howard Blake
The Odd Job '78
The Riddle of the Sands '79
S.O.S. Titanic '79
Flash Gordon '80
Amityville 2: The Possession '82
Amityville 3: The Demon '83
The Lords of Discipline '83
A Month in the Country '87

Ronee Blakley
Lightning Over Water '80

Terence Blanchard
Jungle Fever '91
Malcolm X '92
Assault at West Point: The Court-Martial of Johnson Whittaker '94
Crooklyn '94
The Inkwell '94
Sugar Hill '94
Trial by Jury '94
Clockers '95

Ralph Blane
Athena '54

Larry Blank
Taxi Dancers '93

George Blondheim
Bye Bye Blues '89
Gate 2 '92
Red Scorpion 2 '94
Whale Music '94
Man with a Gun '95
The Halfback of Notre Dame '96

John Bloom
Nobody's Fool '94

Kath Bloom
A Little Stiff '91

Frankie Blue
Out There '95

Chris Boardman
The Color Purple '85
Prime Target '91

Jerry Bock
A Stranger Among Us '92

Roland Bocquet
La Balance '82

Michael Boddicker
Get Crazy '83
The Adventures of Buckaroo Banzai Across the Eighth Dimension '84
White Water Summer '87
The Adventures of Milo & Otis '89
F/X 2: The Deadly Art of Illusion '91
Freejack '92

Todd Boekelheide
Dim Sum: A Little Bit of Heart '85
Dear America: Letters Home from Vietnam '88
The Blood of Heroes '89
Exposure '91
Hearts of Darkness: A Filmmaker's Apocalypse '91
Digger '94
Nina Takes a Lover '94

Ed Bogas
Fritz the Cat '72
Heavy Traffic '73
Race for Your Life, Charlie Brown '77
Bon Voyage, Charlie Brown '80
A Christmas Without Snow '80

William Bolcom
Hester Street '75

Martin D. Bolin
Forced to Kill '93

Claude Bolling
The Hands of Orlac '60
The Day and the Hour '63
Borsalino '70
Catch Me a Spy '71
The Passenger '75
Le Magnifique '76
California Suite '78
Silver Bears '78
The Awakening '80
Willie & Phil '80
The Bay Boy '85

Bernardo Bonazzi
Matador '86
Women on the Verge of a Nervous Breakdown '88
Don Juan, My Love '90
All Tied Up '92
Mouth to Mouth '95

Luis Bonfa
Black Orpheus '58

Bono
In the Name of the Father '93

John Boshoff
The Gods Must Be Crazy '84

Rick Boston
The Harvest '92

Simon Boswell
Creepers '85
Demons 2 '87
Dangerous Obsession '88
Hardware '90
Santa Sangre '90
The Turn of the Screw '92
Dust Devil '93
Love Matters '93
Second Best '94
Shallow Grave '94
Hackers '95
Jack and Sarah '96

Perry Botkin
R.P.M.* (*Revolutions Per Minute) '70
Bless the Beasts and Children '71
They Only Kill Their Masters '72
Lady Ice '73
Goin' South '78
Tarzan, the Ape Man '81
Silent Night, Deadly Night '84
Weekend Warriors '86
Windmills of the Gods '88

Jean Bouchety
The Game is Over '66

Hubert Bougis
Sweet Revenge '90

Lili Boulanger
Beatrice '88

Roger Bourland
The Wolf at the Door '87
The Trouble with Dick '88
Night Life '90
New Jack City '91
The Rescue '88
Jacknife '89
Sorry, Wrong Number '89
Betsy's Wedding '90
Narrow Margin '90
The Old Man and the Sea '90
The Rescuers Down Under '90
All I Want for Christmas '91
Honey, I Blew Up the Kid '92
Stay Tuned '92
For Love or Money '93
Homeward Bound: The Incredible Journey '93
So I Married an Axe Murderer '93
Tombstone '93
Baby's Day Out '94
Holy Matrimony '94
Miracle on 34th Street '94
Carried Away '95
JAG '95

David Bowie
Christiane F. '82
Party! Party! '83
Labyrinth '86

Euel Box
Benji '74
Hawmps! '76
For the Love of Benji '77
The Double McGuffin '79
Benji the Hunted '87

Michael Boyd
Breakin' '84

Charles Bradshaw
Miracle of Morgan's Creek '44

Fred Brathwaite
Wild Style '83

David Bravo
Federal Hill '94

Goran Bregovic
Queen Margot '94
Underground '95

Torsten Breuer
Maybe...Maybe Not '94

Alan Brewer
Tokyo Pop '88

Peter Brewis
Morons from Outer Space '85
The Tall Guy '89

Leslie Bricusse
Doctor Dolittle '67
Goodbye, Mr. Chips '69
Scrooge '70
Willy Wonka & the Chocolate Factory '71
Babes in Toyland '86
Tom and Jerry: The Movie '93

David Bridie
That Eye, The Sky '94

Tony Britten
Pirate Movie '82

Nicholas Brodszky
Rich, Young and Pretty '51

David Broeckman
Frankenstein '31

Richard Bronskill
The Perfect Bride '91

Joseph Brooks
Invitation to the Wedding '73
The Lords of Flatbush '74
You Light Up My Life '77
If Ever I See You Again '78

Philip Brophy
Body Melt '93

Dirk Brosse
Daens '92

Bruce Broughton
Return of Frank Cannon '80
Killjoy '81
Desperate Lives '82
One Shoe Makes It Murder '82
M.A.D.D.: Mothers Against Drunk Driving '83
The Prodigal '83
The Cowboy & the Ballerina '84
The First Olympics: Athens 1896 '84
Ice Pirates '84
The Blue and the Gray '85
Silverado '85
Young Sherlock Holmes '85
The Boy Who Could Fly '86
George Washington: The Forging of a Nation '86
Sweet Liberty '86
Big Shots '87
Harry and the Hendersons '87
The Monster Squad '87
Square Dance '87
Cross My Heart '88
Last Rites '88
The Presidio '88

Leo Brower
Up to a Certain Point '83
Like Water for Chocolate '93
A Walk in the Clouds '95

Earl Brown, Jr.
Americathon '79

James Brown
Black Caesar '73

Larry Brown
Rio Diablo '93

Nacio Herb Brown
Broadway Melody '29
Broadway Melody of 1936 '35
Broadway Melody of 1938 '37

Jackson Browne
Incident at Oglala: The Leonard Peltier Story '92

Tom Bruner
School Spirit '85

Robert F. Brunner
That Darn Cat '65
Lt. Robin Crusoe, U.S.N. '66
Monkeys, Go Home! '66
Blackbeard's Ghost '67
Never a Dull Moment '68
The Computer Wore Tennis Shoes '69
Smith! '69
The Boatniks '70
The Barefoot Executive '71
The Wild Country '71
Now You See Him, Now You Don't '72
Snowball Express '72
The Castaway Cowboy '74
Gus '76
The North Avenue Irregulars '79
Amy '81

George Bruns
Davy Crockett, King of the Wild Frontier '55
Davy Crockett and the River Pirates '56
Westward Ho, the Wagons! '56
Sleeping Beauty '59
The Absent-Minded Professor '61
Babes in Toyland '61
101 Dalmatians '61
Son of Flubber '63
The Sword in the Stone '63
Man from Button Willow '65
The Adventures of Bullwhip Griffin '66
The Fighting Prince of Donegal '66
Follow Me, Boys! '66
The Jungle Book '67
Daring Game '68
The Horse in the Gray Flannel Suit '68
Island of the Lost '68
The Love Bug '68
The Aristocats '70
Robin Hood '73
Herbie Rides Again '74

Joanne Bruzdowicz
Jacquot '91

Chico Buarque
Dona Flor and Her Two Husbands '78

Alexander Bubenheim
Night Train to Venice '93

Paul Buckmaster
The Spy Who Loved Me '77
Diving In '90
12 Monkeys '95

Nonong Buenoamino
Midnight Dancers '94

Jimmy Buffett
Rancho Deluxe '75

Eric Burdon
Comeback '83

Geoffrey Burgon
Monty Python's Life of Brian '79
Brideshead Revisited '81
The Dogs of War '81
Bleak House '85
Turtle Diary '86
Robin Hood '91
A Foreign Field '93

Chris Burke
Splatter University '84

Johnny Burke
Welcome Stranger '47

Sonny Burke
Lady and the Tramp '55

Billy Burnette
Saturday Night Special '92

Ralph Burns
Cabaret '72
Lenny '74
New York, New York '77
Movie, Movie '78
All That Jazz '79
First Family '80
Make Me an Offer '80
Urban Cowboy '80
Pennies From Heaven '81
Annie '82
Kiss Me Goodbye '82
My Favorite Year '82
National Lampoon's Vacation '83
Star 80 '83
Ernie Kovacs: Between the Laughter '84
The Muppets Take Manhattan '84
Side Show '84
A Chorus Line '85
Moving Violations '85
Perfect '85
Penalty Phase '86
After the Promise '87
In the Mood '87
All Dogs Go to Heaven '89
Bert Rigby, You're a Fool '89
Sweet Bird of Youth '89
The Josephine Baker Story '90

George Burt
Secret Honor '85
Fool for Love '86

Carter Burwell
Blood Simple '85
Psycho 3 '86
Raising Arizona '87
The Beat '88
It Takes Two '88
Pass the Ammo '88
Checking Out '89
Miller's Crossing '90
Barton Fink '91
Doc Hollywood '91
Buffy the Vampire Slayer '92
Storyville '92
Waterland '92
And the Band Played On '93
A Dangerous Woman '93
The Hudsucker Proxy '93
Kalifornia '93
This Boy's Life '93
Wayne's World 2 '93
Airheads '94
Bad Company '94
The Celluloid Closet '95
Fargo '96
Fear '96

Cobb Bussinger
I Don't Buy Kisses Anymore '92

Artie Butler
The Love Machine '71
What's Up, Doc? '72
Harrad Experiment '73
For Pete's Sake '74
Rafferty & the Gold Dust Twins '75
The Rescuers '77
Sextette '78
Angel on My Shoulder '80
American Dream '81
She's in the Army Now '81
Sizzle '81
Grease 2 '82
O'Hara's Wife '82

David Buttolph
Crash Dive '43
House on 92nd Street '45
Boomerang '47

Donald Byrd
Cornbread, Earl & Me '75

David Byrne
True Stories '86
The Last Emperor '87
Married to the Mob '88

Sammy Cahn
Anchors Aweigh '45
The West Point Story '50
Rich, Young and Pretty '51

John Cale
Something Wild '86
Primary Motive '92

Gerard Calvi
Belle Americaine '61

Michel Camilo
Two Much '96

Claudio Capponi
Jane Eyre '96

Tony Carey
Lethal Obsession '87

Antonio Carlos
Gabriela '84

Larry Carlton
Against All Odds '84

Hoagy Carmichael
Hoppity Goes to Town '41

John Carpenter
Dark Star '74
Assault on Precinct 13 '76
The Fog '78
Halloween '78
Escape from New York '81
Halloween 2: The Nightmare Isn't Over! '81
Halloween 3: Season of the Witch '82
Christine '84
Big Trouble in Little China '86
Prince of Darkness '87
They Live '88
Body Bags '93
In the Mouth of Madness '95
Village of the Damned '95

Gaylord Carter
Rebecca of Sunnybrook Farm '17
Spiders '18
The Ten Commandments '23
Old Ironsides '26
My Best Girl '27
Running Wild '27
Docks of New York '28
Last Command '28
The Wedding March '28

Doreen Carwithen
Three Cases of Murder '55

Tristram Cary
The Ladykillers '55
Time Without Pity '57

Del Casher
Tropical Heat '93

Patrick Cassidy
Broken Harvest '95

Exene Cervenka
Across the Moon '94

Matthieu Chabrol
The Story of Women '88
Madame Bovary '91
Betty '92
The Cry of the Owl '92

Frankie Chan
Chungking Express '95

Gary Chang
The Breakfast Club '85
52 Pick-Up '86
Firewalker '86
3:15—The Moment of Truth '86
The House of Usher '88
Sticky Fingers '88
Dead Bang '89
Miami Blues '90
A Shock to the System '90
Murder in New Hampshire: The Pamela Smart Story '91
The Perfect Weapon '91
Sniper '92
Under Siege '92
The Last Hit '93
The Nightman '93
Against the Wall '94
The Burning Season '94
Fatherland '94
The Last Ride '94
The Walking Dead '94
Andersonville '95
The Substitute '96

Charlie Chaplin
Modern Times '36
A Countess from Hong Kong '67

John Charles
Utu '83
The Quiet Earth '85
A Soldier's Tale '91
The Sound and the Silence '93

Tom Chase
Scared to Death '80
Creature '85
Catch the Heat '87
And God Created Woman '88
976-EVIL '88
Syngenor '90
Little Nemo: Adventures in Slumberland '92

Yves Chicha
Street Wars '91

Frederic Chopin
Le Bal '82

Bob Christianson
Vibrations '94

Frank Churchill
Snow White and the Seven Dwarfs '37
Dumbo '41
Bambi '42

Chuck Cirino
Inner Sanctum 2 '94

Eric Clapton
Wonderwall: The Movie '69
The Hit '85
Edge of Darkness '86
Lethal Weapon '87
Homeboy '88
Communion '89
Lethal Weapon 2 '89
Rush '91
Lethal Weapon 3 '92
The Van '95

Stanley Clarke
Book of Love '91
Boyz N the Hood '91
Cool As Ice '91
The Five Heartbeats '91
Passenger 57 '92
Poetic Justice '93
Watch It '93
What's Love Got to Do with It? '93
Panther '95
Eddie '96
The Road to Galveston '96

George S. Clinton
Cheech and Chong: Still Smokin' '83
The Boys Next Door '85
Avenging Force '86
The Lion of Africa '87
Platoon Leader '87
Wild Thing '87
Gotham '88
American Ninja 3: Blood Hunt '89
Hard Promises '92
Lake Consequence '92
Through the Eyes of a Killer '92
Amelia Earhart: The Final Flight '94
Brainscan '94
Mother's Boys '94
Delta of Venus '95

Rene Cloerec
The Red Inn '51

Tom Cochrane
Skier's Dream '88

Harvey R. Cohen
Ghost Town '88

Delerue ▸cont.

Mister Johnson '91
Man Trouble '92
Rich in Love '93

Joe Delia
Driller Killer '74
China Girl '87
Freeway '88
King of New York '90
Bad Lieutenant '92
Body Snatchers '93
The Addiction '95

Alexandre Desplat
Innocent Lies '95

Adolph Deutsch
The Maltese Falcon '41
Little Women '49
Stars in My Crown '50
Some Like It Hot '59

Orlando Di Lasso
Every Man for Himself & God Against All '75

Neil Diamond
Jonathan Livingston Seagull '73

Andrew Dickson
Naked '93
Secrets and Lies '95

Howard Dietz
The Band Wagon '53

Loek Dikker
The 4th Man '79
Slow Burn '86
Pascali's Island '88
Body Parts '91
The Babysitter '95

Andrew Dixon
High Hopes '88

Willie Dixon
Ginger Ale Afternoon '89

Brendan Dolan
Go Fish '94

Robert Emmett Dolan
Birth of the Blues '41

Thomas Dolby
Fever Pitch '85
Gothic '87

Klaus Doldinger
Das Boot '81
The NeverEnding Story '84
A Father's Revenge '88
Me and Him '89

Pino Donaggio
Don't Look Now '73
Carrie '76
Haunts '77
Gunfire '78
Piranha '78
Home Movies '79
Tourist Trap '79
Beyond Evil '80
Dressed to Kill '80
The Black Cat '81
Blow Out '81
The Fan '81
The Howling '81
Tex '82
Hercules '83
Over the Brooklyn Bridge '83
The Assisi Underground '84
Body Double '84
Deja Vu '84
Ordeal by Innocence '84
The Berlin Affair '85
Hercules 2 '85
Crawlspace '86
The Barbarians '87
Dancers '87
Phantom of Death '87
Appointment with Death '88
Hotel Colonial '88
Kansas '88
Zelly & Me '88
Catacombs '89
Night Game '89
Meridian: Kiss of the Beast '90
Two Evil Eyes '90
The Devil's Daughter '91
A Fine Romance '92
Indio 2: The Revolt '92
Raising Cain '92
Oblivion '94
Backlash: Oblivion 2 '95
Never Talk to Strangers '95

Mark Donohue
Murphy's Law '86
Opposing Force '87

Donovan
Brother Sun, Sister Moon '73
84 Charlie Mopic '89

Stephen Dorff
The Defiant Ones '58
Every Which Way But Loose '78
Bronco Billy '80
Honky Tonk Freeway '81
Honkytonk Man '82
Waltz Across Texas '83
Cannonball Run 2 '84
Rustler's Rhapsody '85
Stick '85
Convicted '86
Manhunt for Claude Dallas '86
Back to the Beach '87
The Quick and the Dead '87
My Best Friend Is a Vampire '88
Kiss Shot '89
Pink Cadillac '89
Pure Country '92

Michael Doucet
Belizaire the Cajun '86

Patrick Doyle
Henry V '89
Shipwrecked '90
Dead Again '91
Indochine '92
Into the West '92
Carlito's Way '93
Much Ado about Nothing '93
Needful Things '93
Exit to Eden '94
Mary Shelley's Frankenstein '94
A Little Princess '95
Sense and Sensibility '95
Mrs. Winterbourne '96

Daryl Dragon
Payback '90

George Dreyfus
Tender Mercies '83
The Fringe Dwellers '86

John Du Prez
Monty Python Live at the Hollywood Bowl '82
Bullshot '83
Monty Python's The Meaning of Life '83
Oxford Blues '84
A Private Function '84
She'll Be Wearing Pink Pajamas '84
Once Bitten '85
Love with a Perfect Stranger '86
Personal Services '87
A Fish Called Wanda '88
A Chorus of Disapproval '89
UHF '89
Bullseye! '90
Teenage Mutant Ninja Turtles: The Movie '90
Mystery Date '91
Teenage Mutant Ninja Turtles 3 '93

Al Dubin
42nd Street '33

Anne Dudley
Disorderlies '87
Hiding Out '87
Buster '88
The Mighty Quinn '89
Say Anything '89
The Misadventures of Mr. Wilt '90
Silence Like Glass '90
The Miracle '91
The Pope Must Diet '91
The Crying Game '92
Knight Moves '93

Antoine Duhamel
Pierrot le Fou '65
Weekend '67
Stolen Kisses '68
Mississippi Mermaid '69
The Wild Child '70
Daddy Nostalgia '90
Twisted Obsession '90

David Dundas
Withnail and I '87
How to Get Ahead in Advertising '89

George Duning
Down to Earth '47
Her Husband's Affairs '47
The Dark Past '49
The Doolins of Oklahoma '49
Jolson Sings Again '49
Lust for Gold '49
Man from Colorado '49
Harriet Craig '50
From Here to Eternity '53
Salome '53
Picnic '55
Queen Bee '55
The Eddy Duchin Story '56
3:10 to Yuma '57
Bell, Book and Candle '58
Cowboy '58
Houseboat '58
Me and the Colonel '58
1001 Arabian Nights '59
The Devil at 4 O'Clock '61
Any Wednesday '66
Yuma '70
Arnold '73
Honor Thy Father '73
Pat Garrett & Billy the Kid '73
Terror in the Wax Museum '73
Abduction of St. Anne '75
The Man with Bogart's Face '80
Goliath Awaits '81

Michael Dunlap
Street Wars '91

Paul Durand
Forbidden Fruit '52

Arie Dzierlatka
Messidor '77

Charles Earland
The Dynamite Brothers '74

Randy Edelman
Snatched '72
Executive Action '73
When Your Lover Leaves '83
The Chipmunk Adventure '87
Feds '88
Twins '88
Ghostbusters 2 '89
Troop Beverly Hills '89
Come See the Paradise '90
Kindergarten Cop '90
Quick Change '90
Drop Dead Fred '91
Shout '91
V.I. Warshawski '91
The Distinguished Gentleman '92
The Last of the Mohicans '92
My Cousin Vinny '92
Beethoven's 2nd '93
Dragon: The Bruce Lee Story '93
Gettysburg '93
Billy Madison '94
Greedy '94
The Mask '94
Pontiac Moon '94
The Big Green '95
Citizen X '95
While You Were Sleeping '95
Diabolique '96
Down Periscope '96
Dragonheart '96
The Quest '96

Steve Edwards
Night Siege Project: Shadowchaser 2 '94
Illegal in Blue '95
Project Shadowchaser 3000 '95

Seamus Egan
The Brothers McMullen '94

Cliff Eidelman
Animal Behavior '89
Dead Man Out '89
To Die for '89
Triumph of the Spirit '89
Crazy People '90
Strike It Rich '90
Delirious '91
Star Trek 6: The Undiscovered Country '91
Christopher Columbus: The Discovery '92
Leap of Faith '92
Untamed Heart '93
My Girl 2 '94
A Simple Twist of Fate '94
Now and Then '95

Richard Einhorn
Shock Waves '77
Don't Go in the House '80
Eyes of a Stranger '81
The Prowler '81
Blood Rage '87
Dead of Winter '87
Sister, Sister '87
Closet Land '90

Kahil El Zabar
How U Like Me Now? '92

Danny Elfman
Forbidden Zone '80
Pee Wee's Big Adventure '85
Back to School '86
Summer School '87
Wisdom '87
Beetlejuice '88
Big Top Pee Wee '88
Hot to Trot! '88
Midnight Run '88
Scrooged '88
Batman '89
Darkman '90
Dick Tracy '90
Edward Scissorhands '90
The Flash '90
Army of Darkness '92
Article 99 '92
Batman Returns '92
The Nightmare Before Christmas '93
Sommersby '93
Dolores Claiborne '94
Dead Presidents '95
To Die For '95
The Frighteners '96
Mission: Impossible '96

Jonathan Elias
Children of the Corn '84
Almost You '85
Key Exchange '85
Tuff Turf '85
Vamp '86
Shakedown '88
Two Moon Junction '88
Far from Home '89
Parents '89
Rude Awakening '89
Morning Glory '93
Leprechaun 2 '94

Duke Ellington
Cabin in the Sky '43
Anatomy of a Murder '59
Paris Blues '61

Marc Ellis
Assault of the Killer Bimbos '88

Keith Emerson
Inferno '78
Nighthawks '81
Best Revenge '83
The Church '90

Stephen Endelman
The Desperate Trail '94
Imaginary Crimes '94
The Englishman Who Went Up a Hill But Came Down a Mountain '95
Flirting with Disaster '95
Jeffrey '95
The Journey of August King '95
Postcards from America '95
Reckless '95
Tom and Huck '95
Ed '96

Paul English
The Man with the Perfect Swing '95

Charles Engstrom
A Flash of Green '85
Ruby in Paradise '93

Brian Eno
Land of the Minotaur '77
Sebastiane '79
Dune '84

Sebastien Erms
A Tale of Winter '92

Bengt Ernryd
The New Land '73

Esquivel
Four Rooms '95

David Essex
Silver Dream Racer '83

Melissa Etheridge
Teresa's Tattoo '94

Ray Evans
Red Garters '54

Sammy Fain
Calamity Jane '53

Harold Faltermeyer
Beverly Hills Cop '84
Thief of Hearts '84
Fletch '85
Top Gun '86
Beverly Hills Cop 2 '87
Fatal Beauty '87
Fire and Ice '87
The Running Man '87
Fletch Lives '89
Tango and Cash '89
Kuffs '92

Carlos Farinas
I Am Cuba '64

Jim Farmer
Johnny Suede '92
Living in Oblivion '94

Ricky Fataar
High Tide '87
The Efficiency Expert '92

Dave Faulkner
The Sum of Us '94

Louis Febre
Last Man Standing '95
Two Bits & Pepper '95

Jack Feldman
Newsies '92
Thumbelina '94

Jose Feliciano
Aaron Loves Angela '75

Rick Fenn
White of the Eye '88

George Fenton
Hussy '80
Gandhi '82
An Englishman Abroad '83
The Jewel in the Crown '84
The Company of Wolves '85
Clockwise '86
84 Charing Cross Road '86
Cry Freedom '87
Saigon: Year of the Cat '87
Dangerous Liaisons '88
A Handful of Dust '88
High Spirits '88
White Mischief '88
White of the Eye '88
The Dressmaker '89
The Long Walk Home '89
We're No Angels '89
Memphis Belle '90
White Palace '90
China Moon '91
Final Analysis '92
Hero '92
Born Yesterday '93
Groundhog Day '93
Shadowlands '93
The Madness of King George '94
Mixed Nuts '94
Heaven's Prisoners '95
Land and Freedom '95
Mary Reilly '95

David Ferguson
Tailspin: Behind the Korean Airline Tragedy '89
Dead Ahead: The Exxon Valdez Disaster '92
A Dark Adapted Eye '93

Jay Michael Ferguson
Death of an Angel '86
The Patriot '86
Quiet Cool '86
Best Seller '87
Bad Dreams '88
Johnny Be Good '88
License to Drive '88
Pulse '88
Gleaming the Cube '89
A Nightmare on Elm Street 5: Dream Child '89
Race for Glory '89
Double Dragon '94

Gianni Ferrio
Fiances '63

Bryan Ferry
House of the Rising Sun '87

Brad Fiedel
Deadly Hero '75
The Day the Women Got Even '80
Hardhat & Legs '80
Just Before Dawn '80
Playing for Time '80
Night School '81
The People vs. Jean Harris '81
Born Beautiful '82
Hit & Run '82
Cocaine: One Man's Seduction '83
Murder in Coweta County '83
The Baron and the Kid '84
Calendar Girl Murders '84
Children in the Crossfire '84
Eyes of Fire '84
Mae West '84
My Mother's Secret Life '84
Right of Way '84
The Terminator '84
Compromising Positions '85
Fraternity Vacation '85
Fright Night '85
Girls of the White Orchid '85
Into Thin Air '85
Brotherhood of Justice '86
Desert Bloom '86
The Midnight Hour '86
The Big Easy '87
Bluffing It '87
Hostage '87
The Last Innocent Man '87
Let's Get Harry '87
Nowhere to Hide '87
The Serpent and the Rainbow '87
The Accused '88
Fright Night 2 '88
Weekend War '88
Cold Sassy Tree '89
Immediate Family '89
Perfect Witness '89
True Believer '89
Blue Steel '90
Forgotten Prisoners '90
Terminator 2: Judgment Day '91
Straight Talk '92
Blink '93
Striking Distance '93
Johnny Mnemonic '95

Dorothy Fields
Swing Time '36
Joy of Living '38

Mike Figgis
Stormy Monday '88
Internal Affairs '90
Leaving Las Vegas '95

Peter Filleul
Sweet Talker '91

Richard Fiocca
Alien Space Avenger '91

Jeff Fishman
Carnal Crimes '91

Frank Fitzpatrick
Friday '95

Robert Folk
The Slayer '82
Bachelor Party '84
Police Academy '84
Purple Hearts '84
Odd Jobs '85
Police Academy 3: Back in Training '86
Stewardess School '86
Can't Buy Me Love '87
Police Academy 4: Citizens on Patrol '87
Prince of Bel Air '87
Miles from Home '88
Police Academy 5: Assignment Miami Beach '88
Happy Together '89
Police Academy 6: City Under Siege '89
Wicked Stepmother '89
Honeymoon Academy '90
Beastmaster 2: Through the Portal of Time '91
A Climate for Killing '91
NeverEnding Story 2: The Next Chapter '91
Toy Soldiers '91
Rock-a-Doodle '92
In the Army Now '94
Police Academy: Mission to Moscow '94
Trapped In Paradise '94
A Troll in Central Park '94
Ace Ventura: When Nature Calls '95
Lawnmower Man 2: Beyond Cyberspace '95
Theodore Rex '95

Ray Foote
It Takes Two '95

Sherman Foote
It Takes Two '95

Lou Forestieri
Crazy Moon '87
Sherlock: Undercover Dog '94

Chet Forrest
Music in My Heart '40

Keith Forsey
The Breakfast Club '85

David Foster
St. Elmo's Fire '85
The Secret of My Success '87
Fresh Horses '88
Stealing Home '88
Listen to Me '89
If Looks Could Kill '91
The Little Rascals '94

Charles Fox
The Incident '67
Barbarella '68
Goodbye Columbus '69
Star Spangled Girl '71
Dying Room Only '73
The Last American Hero '73
A Separate Peace '73
The Laughing Policeman '74
The Stranger Within '74
Bug '75
The Drowning Pool '75
The Other Side of the Mountain '75
The Duchess and the Dirtwater Fox '76
Two Minute Warning '76
One on One '77
Foul Play '78
Rainbow '78
Better Late Than Never '79
The Last Married Couple in America '80
Little Darlings '80
9 to 5 '80
Oh, God! Book 2 '80
Love Child '82
Six Pack '82
Zapped! '82
Strange Brew '83
Trenchcoat '83
A Summer to Remember '84
Doin' Time '85
National Lampoon's European Vacation '85
The Longshot '86
Unnatural Causes '86
Christmas Comes to Willow Creek '87
Love at Stake '87
Short Circuit 2 '88
False Witness '89
The Gods Must Be Crazy 2 '89
Hard to Kill '89
One Man Force '89
Repossessed '90
The Broken Chain '93

Cesar Franck
Sandra of a Thousand Delights '65

David Michael Frank
I'm Gonna Git You Sucka '88
Best of the Best 2 '93
Linda '93
The Baby-Sitters Club '95

Christopher Franke
The Surgeon '94

Michael Franks
Cockfighter '74
Zandy's Bride '74

Carlos Franzetti
The Mambo Kings '92

Arthur Freed
Broadway Melody '29
Broadway Melody of 1936 '35
Broadway Melody of 1938 '37
Yolanda and the Thief '45

Hugo Friedhofer
The Adventures of Marco Polo '38
The Best Years of Our Lives '46
An Affair to Remember '57
Barbarian and the Geisha '58

Rudolf Friml
Rose Marie '36

Marco Frisina
Jacob '94
Joseph '95

John Frizzell
Undertow '95

Dominic Frontiere
The Stunt Man '80
Color of Night '94

Gary Fry
Cease Fire '85
Trancers 4: Jack of Swords '93
Trancers 5: Sudden Deth '94

Lewis Furey
The Agency '81
American Dreamer '84
The Peanut Butter Solution '85

Giovanni Fusco
Il Grido '57
Hiroshima, Mon Amour '59

Peter Gabriel
Birdy '84
The Last Temptation of Christ '88

Serge Gainsbourg
Too Pretty to Be Honest '72
Le Sex Shop '73
The French Woman '79
Menage '86

Chen Qi Gang
China, My Sorrow '89

Ge Ganru
A Great Wall '86

Roel A. Garcia
Chungking Express '95

Art Garfunkel
The Graduate '67

Robert Garrett
Eye of the Stranger '93

Raviv Gazil
Cup Final '92

Kay Gee
Sunset Park '96

Lynne Geller
Denise Calls Up '95

Papo Gely
Robot in the Family '94

Sergio George
I Like It Like That '94

Joseph Gershenson
Francis Goes to West Point '52
All I Desire '53
Francis Covers the Big Town '53
The Creature Walks Among Us '56
Francis in the Haunted House '56
The Monolith Monsters '57

George Gershwin
A Damsel in Distress '37
Shall We Dance '37
The Goldwyn Follies '38
Lady Be Good '41
Girl Crazy '43
Rhapsody in Blue '45
An American in Paris '51
Funny Face '57
Manhattan '79

Ira Gershwin
A Damsel in Distress '37
Shall We Dance '37
The Goldwyn Follies '38
Lady Be Good '41
Girl Crazy '43
Cover Girl '44
Rhapsody in Blue '45
The Barkleys of Broadway '49
An American in Paris '51
Funny Face '57

Michael Gibbs
Madame Sin '71
Secrets '71
Heat '87
Housekeeping '87
American Roulette '88
Breaking In '89
Iron & Silk '91
Hard-Boiled '92
Being Human '94
Century '94

Richard Gibbs
Sweet Hearts Dance '88
Say Anything '89
A Killing in a Small Town '90
Bingo '91
Clifford '92
The Gun in Betty Lou's Handbag '92
Ladybugs '92
Once Upon a Crime '92
Passed Away '92
Amos and Andrew '93
Barbarians at the Gate '93
The Chase '93
Fatal Instinct '93
Son-in-Law '93
Three of Hearts '93
Dangerous Indiscretion '94
At First Sight '95

Alan Gill
Letter to Brezhnev '86

Philip Glass
Koyaanisqatsi '83
Mishima: A Life in Four Chapters '85
Hamburger Hill '87
Powaqqatsi: Life in Transformation '88
The Thin Blue Line '88
Mindwalk: A Film for Passionate Thinkers '91
A Brief History of Time '92
Candyman '92
Candyman 2: Farewell to the Flesh '94

Patrick Gleeson
The Plague Dogs '82
The Zoo Gang '85
The Children of Times Square '86
The Bedroom Window '87
Deadly Illusion '87
Stacking '87
In Self Defense '93

Nick Glennie-Smith
The Rock '96

Ernest Gold
Unknown World '51
The Screaming Skull '58
On the Beach '59
The Young Philadelphians '59
Exodus '60
Inherit the Wind '60
Judgment at Nuremberg '61
Pressure Point '62
A Child is Waiting '63
It's a Mad, Mad, Mad, Mad World '63
Ship of Fools '65
Betrayal '74
Cross of Iron '76
Fun with Dick and Jane '77
Marciano '79
The Runner Stumbles '79
Tom Horn '80
Safari 3000 '82
Gore Vidal's Lincoln '88

Lee Gold
A Captive in the Land '91

Barry Goldberg
The Trip '67
Thrashin' '86
Three for the Road '87
Beverly Hills Brats '89
Flashback '89
Powwow Highway '89
Hometown Boy Makes Good '93
Return of the Living Dead 3 '93

Billy Goldenberg
Change of Habit '69
Silent Night, Lonely Night '69
The Passing of Evil '70
Duel '71
Brand New Life '72
The Glass House '72
Play It Again, Sam '72
Up the Sandbox '72
The Last of Sheila '73
Busting '74
Reflections of Murder '74
Queen of the Stardust Ballroom '75
Helter Skelter '76
James Dean '76
The Lindbergh Kidnapping Case '76
The Domino Principle '77
King '78
A Question of Love '78
The Cracker Factory '79
The Family Man '79
The Miracle Worker '79
Scavenger Hunt '79
All God's Children '80
Crisis at Central High '80
Father Figure '80
The Best Little Girl in the World '81
Callie and Son '81
Jacqueline Bouvier Kennedy '81
Rehearsal for Murder '82
Dempsey '83
Memorial Day '83
Prototype '83
Rage of Angels '83
Reuben, Reuben '83
For Love or Money '84
Love on the Run '85
Dress Gray '86
Rage of Angels: The Story Continues '86
Johnnie Gibson F.B.I. '87
18 Again! '88

Elliot Goldenthal
Drugstore Cowboy '89
Pet Sematary '89
Alien 3 '92
Demolition Man '93
Golden Gate '93
Interview with the Vampire '94
Roswell: The U.F.O. Cover-Up '94
Batman Forever '95
Heat '95
A Time to Kill '96

Peter Goldfoot
Judgment in Berlin '88

Bobby Goldsboro
The Man from Left Field '93

Jerry Goldsmith
The Detective '54
Studs Lonigan '60
Lonely Are the Brave '62
A Gathering of Eagles '63
Lilies of the Field '63
The List of Adrian Messenger '63
The Prize '63
The Stripper '63
Rio Conchos '64
Seven Days in May '64
The Agony and the Ecstasy '65
In Harm's Way '65
Morituri '65
A Patch of Blue '65
Von Ryan's Express '65
The Blue Max '66
Our Man Flint '66
The Sand Pebbles '66
The Trouble with Angels '66
Flim-Flam Man '67
Hour of the Gun '67
In Like Flint '67
Bandolero! '68
Planet of the Apes '68
Sebastian '68
The Illustrated Man '69
Justine '69
100 Rifles '69
Ballad of Cable Hogue '70
Patton '70
Rio Lobo '70
Tora! Tora! Tora! '70
Escape from the Planet of the Apes '71
The Mephisto Waltz '71
Wild Rovers '71
Culpepper Cattle Co. '72
The Other '72
Pursuit '72
The Don is Dead '73
One Little Indian '73
Papillon '73
Shamus '73
Chinatown '74
QB VII '74
S*P*Y*S '74
The Terrorists '74
Babe! '75
Breakout '75

Goldsmith ▶cont.

The Reincarnation of Peter Proud '75
Take a Hard Ride '75
The Wind and the Lion '75
Breakheart Pass '76
The Cassandra Crossing '76
High Velocity '76
Logan's Run '76
The Omen '76
Damnation Alley '77
Islands in the Stream '77
MacArthur '77
Twilight's Last Gleaming '77
The Boys from Brazil '78
Capricorn One '78
Coma '78
Damien: Omen 2 '78
Magic '78
The Swarm '78
Alien '79
The Great Train Robbery '79
Players '79
Star Trek: The Motion Picture '80
Cabo Blanco '81
The Final Conflict '81
Masada '81
Night Crossing '81
Outland '81
Raggedy Man '81
The Challenge '82
First Blood '82
Poltergeist '82
The Salamander '82
The Secret of NIMH '82
Psycho 2 '83
Twilight Zone: The Movie '83
Under Fire '83
Gremlins '84
The Lonely Guy '84
Runaway '84
Supergirl '84
Explorers '85
King Solomon's Mines '85
Rambo: First Blood, Part 2 '85
Hoosiers '86
Legend '86
Link '86
Poltergeist 2: The Other Side '86
Extreme Prejudice '87
Innerspace '87
Lionheart '87
Rambo 3 '88
Rent-A-Cop '88
The 'Burbs '89
Criminal Law '89
Leviathan '89
Star Trek 5: The Final Frontier '89
Gremlins 2: The New Batch '90
The Russia House '90
Total Recall '90
Blue Desert '91
Love Field '91
Sleeping with the Enemy '91
Warlock '91
Basic Instinct '92
Forever Young '92
Matinee '92
Medicine Man '92
Mr. Baseball '92
Mom and Dad Save the World '92
Dennis the Menace '93
Malice '93
Maniac Cop 3: Badge of Silence '93
Rudy '93
Six Degrees of Separation '93
The Vanishing '93
Bad Girls '94
I.Q. '94
The River Wild '94
City Hall '95
Congo '95
First Knight '95
Powder '95
Executive Decision '96

Joel Goldsmith
Laserblast '78
The Man with Two Brains '83
Banzai Runner '86
Crystal Heart '87
No Safe Haven '87
Ricky 1 '88
Watchers '88
Across the Tracks '89
A Woman, Her Men and Her Futon '92
Man's Best Friend '93
Blood for Blood '95

William Goldstein
Bingo Long Traveling All-Stars & Motor Kings '76
Norman, Is That You? '76
Terror Out of the Sky '78
Aliens Are Coming '80
Marilyn: The Untold Story '80
An Eye for an Eye '81
Force: Five '81
A Long Way Home '81
Forced Vengeance '82
Holocaust Survivors...Remembrance of Love '83
Getting Physical '84
Up the Creek '84
Lots of Luck '85
Bad Guys '86
Saving Grace '86
Blood Vows: The Story of a Mafia Wife '87
Hello Again '87
Shocker '89
The Quarrel '93

Vinnie Golia
Trouble Bound '92

John Gonzalez
Bikini Summer '91
Final Impact '91
Sunset Strip '91
Street Crimes '92
Hologram Man '95

Jerry Goodman
Search for Signs of Intelligent Life in the Universe '91

Miles Goodman
Slumber Party '57 '76
Last Cry for Help '79
Having It All '82
Jinxed '82
Lookin' to Get Out '82
The Man Who Wasn't There '83
Table for Five '83
Footloose '84
High School USA '84
Poison Ivy '85
Teen Wolf '85
About Last Night... '86
Blind Justice '86
Little Shop of Horrors '86
Passion Flower '86
La Bamba '87
Like Father, Like Son '87
Real Men '87
The Squeeze '87
Dirty Rotten Scoundrels '88
K-9 '89
Staying Together '89
Traveling Man '89
Opportunity Knocks '90
Problem Child '90
Thompson's Last Run '90
Vital Signs '90
He Said, She Said '91
What About Bob? '91
Housesitter '92
The Muppet Christmas Carol '92
Indian Summer '93
Sister Act 2: Back in the Habit '93
Dunston Checks In '95
For Better or Worse '95
The Indian in the Cupboard '95
Sunset Park '96

Jim Goodwin
A.P.E.X. '94

Ron Goodwin
The Trials of Oscar Wilde '60

Mack Gordon
We're Not Dressing '34

Michael Gore
Fame '80
Terms of Endearment '83
Pretty in Pink '86
Broadcast News '87
Don't Tell Her It's Me '90
The Butcher's Wife '91
Defending Your Life '91
Mr. Wonderful '93

Adam Gorgoni
Tollbooth '94

Jay Gottlieb
La Discrete '90

Gerald Gouriet
Madame Sousatzka '88
The Innocent '93
Philadelphia Experiment 2 '93
Rubdown '93
The Substitute '93
They Watch '93
Men of War '94

Paul Grabowsky
The Last Days of Chez Nous '92

Georges Granier
Le Grand Chemin '87

Stephane Grappelli
May Fools '90

Adolph Green
It's Always Fair Weather '55
On the Town '91

Harry Griegson-Williams
Full Body Massage '95

Murray Grindlay
Once Were Warriors '94

Francis Gromon
Marius '31

Andrew Gross
Bio-Dome '96

Guy Gross
The Adventures of Priscilla, Queen of the Desert '94

Dave Grusin
Divorce American Style '67
The Graduate '67
Waterhole #3 '67
The Heart is a Lonely Hunter '68
Generation '69
Tell Them Willie Boy Is Here '69
Winning '69
Fuzz '72
The Great Northfield Minnesota Raid '72
Eric '75
Three Days of the Condor '75
The Yakuza '75
The Front '76
Murder by Death '76
Bobby Deerfield '77
The Goodbye Girl '77
Mr. Billion '77
Heaven Can Wait '78
And Justice for All '79
The Champ '79
The Electric Horseman '79
My Bodyguard '80
Absence of Malice '81
On Golden Pond '81
Reds '81
Author! Author! '82
Tootsie '82
Falling in Love '84
The Little Drummer Girl '84
The Pope of Greenwich Village '84
Racing with the Moon '84
Scandalous '84
The Goonies '85
Lucas '86
Ishtar '87
Clara's Heart '88
The Milagro Beanfield War '88
Tequila Sunrise '88
A Dry White Season '89
The Fabulous Baker Boys '89
The Bonfire of the Vanities '90
Havana '90
For the Boys '91
The Firm '93
The Cure '95
Mulholland Falls '95

Scott Grusin
We're Talkin' Serious Money '92

Jay Gruska
The Principal '87
Traxx '87
Shadow Dancing '88
Sing '89
Wheels of Terror '90
Mo' Money '92
Trapped in Space '94

Zhang Guangtain
Shanghai Triad '95

Vince Guaraldi
A Boy Named Charlie Brown '70

Christopher Gunning
Twinsanity '70
Hands of the Ripper '71
When the Whales Came '89
Under Suspicion '92
The Affair '95

Jonas Gwangwa
Cry Freedom '87

Itai Haber
Live Wire: Human Timebomb '95

Shifi Hadi
Shadows '60

Manos Hadjidakis
Stella '55
Never on Sunday '60
Topkapi '64
Blue '68
The Pedestrian '73
Sweet Movie '75

Philippe Haim
L'Appat '94

Jim Halfpenny
Bikini Summer 2 '92
Magic Kid '92
No Escape, No Return '93
The Power Within '95
Texas Payback '95
To the Limit '95

Marvin Hamlisch
The Swimmer '68
April Fools '69
Take the Money and Run '69
Bananas '71
Kotch '71
Fat City '72
Save the Tiger '73
The Sting '73
The Way We Were '73
The World's Greatest Athlete '73
Prisoner of Second Avenue '74
The Spy Who Loved Me '77
Same Time, Next Year '78
Ice Castles '79
Starting Over '79
Ordinary People '80
Seems Like Old Times '80
The Devil & Max Devlin '81
Pennies From Heaven '81
I Ought to Be in Pictures '82
Sophie's Choice '82
Romantic Comedy '83
A Streetcar Named Desire '84
A Chorus Line '85
D.A.R.Y.L. '85
Three Men and a Baby '87
Little Nikita '88
The Experts '89
The January Man '89
Frankie and Johnny '91
When the Time Comes '91

Jan Hammer
K-9000 '89
I Come in Peace '90
Beastmaster 3: The Eye of Braxus '95

Oscar Hammerstein
Sweet Adeline '35
Show Boat '36
Lady Be Good '41
State Fair '45
Show Boat '51
Oklahoma! '55
Carousel '56
The King and I '56
South Pacific '58
Flower Drum Song '61
Cinderella '64
The Sound of Music '65

Herbie Hancock
Blow-Up '66
The Spook Who Sat By the Door '73
Death Wish '74
A Soldier's Story '84
The George McKenna Story '86
Jo Jo Dancer, Your Life is Calling '86
Round Midnight '86
Action Jackson '88
Colors '88
Harlem Nights '89
Livin' Large '91

Jonathan Hannah
Beauty School '93

Erik Hansen
The Deadly Secret '94

E.Y. Harburg
Cabin in the Sky '43

John Wesley Harding
The Paint Job '93

Hagood Hardy
An American Christmas Carol '79
Anatomy of a Seduction '79
Home to Stay '79
Klondike Fever '79
Dirty Tricks '81
Forbidden Love '82
Mazes and Monsters '82
Wild Pony '83
Anne of Green Gables '85
Anne of Avonlea '87

John E.R. Hardy
Hedd Wyn '92

John Harle
Butterfly Kiss '94

Leigh Harline
Snow White and the Seven Dwarfs '37
It Happens Every Spring '49
Savage Wilderness '55
Strange Bedfellows '65

Udi Harpaz
Hollywood Shuffle '87

Johnny Harris
Man in the Wilderness '71

Max Harris
Dreamchild '85

George Harrison
Wonderwall: The Movie '69
Shanghai Surprise '86

Michael Allen Harrison
Claire of the Moon '92

Deborah Harry
Polyester '81
Rock & Rule '83

Lorenz Hart
Hallelujah, I'm a Bum '33
Evergreen '34
The Merry Widow '34
Babes in Arms '39
Too Many Girls '40
I Married an Angel '42
Words and Music '48
Pal Joey '57

Hal Hartley
Simple Men '92

Richard Hartley
The Good Father '87
An Awfully Big Adventure '94
Princess Caraboo '94
The Rector's Wife '94
The Secret Rapture '94
The Van '95
Stealing Beauty '96

Richard Harvey
Paper Mask '91

Jimmie Haskell
The Dogfighters '95

Greg Hawkes
Anna '87

Fumio Hayasaka
Scandal '50
Sansho the Bailiff '54
Seven Samurai '54

Isaac Hayes
Truck Turner '74

Reed Hays
My Life's In Turnaround '94

Randall Kent Heddon
Undercover Cop '94

Neal Hefti
Sex and the Single Girl '64

Bob Held
Federal Hill '94

Jimi Hendrix
Skier's Dream '88

Nona Hendryx
Gospa '94

Jerry Herman
Hello, Dolly! '69

Marc Herouet
Night and Day '91

Bernard Herrmann
Citizen Kane '41
The Magnificent Ambersons '42
Jane Eyre '44
Anna and the King of Siam '46
The Ghost and Mrs. Muir '47
The Day the Earth Stood Still '51
On Dangerous Ground '51
Five Fingers '52
The Trouble with Harry '55
The Seventh Voyage of Sinbad '58
Vertigo '58
North by Northwest '59
The Three Worlds of Gulliver '59
Psycho '60
Mysterious Island '61
The Bride Wore Black '68
Sisters '73
Obsession '76
Psycho 4: The Beginning '90
Cape Fear '91

Tom Hiel
Dark Side of Genius '94

Jack Hildyard
Black Werewolf '75

Marc Hillman
Baxter '89

Graydon Hillock
Midnight Witness '93

Hilmar Orn Hilmarsson
Children of Nature '91

Rupert Hine
Better Off Dead '85

Wilbert Hirsch
Mute Witness '95

Joel Hirschhorn
Rescue Me '93

David Hirshfelder
Strictly Ballroom '92

Joachim Holbek
Breaking the Waves '95
The Kingdom '95

Mark Holden
Ava's Magical Adventure '94

Lee Holdridge
Old Gringo '89
Back to Hannibal: The Return of Tom Sawyer and Huckleberry Finn '90
Heidi '93
Texas '94
The Yearling '94
Buffalo Girls '95
Prince Brat and the Whipping Boy '95
The Tuskegee Airmen '95

Deborah Holland
Circuitry Man '90
Out There '95

Friedrich Hollander
The Blue Angel '30
Desire '36
Angel '37
Remember the Night '40
Here Comes Mr. Jordan '41

Rupert Holmes
No Small Affair '84

Nigel Holton
South of Reno '87
Bloodfist 3: Forced to Fight '92
Carnosaur '93
Twogether '94
Naked Souls '95

Toshiyuki Honda
Minbo—Or the Gentle Art of Japanese Extortion '92

Arthur Honegger
Crime and Punishment '35
Harvest '37

Anthony Hopkins
August '95

James Horner
Lady in Red '79
Up from the Depths '79
Battle Beyond the Stars '80
Humanoids from the Deep '80
Deadly Blessing '81
The Hand '81
The Pursuit of D.B. Cooper '81
Wolfen '81
48 Hrs. '82
A Piano for Mrs. Cimino '82
Star Trek 2: The Wrath of Khan '82
Between Friends '83
Brainstorm '83
The Dresser '83
Gorky Park '83
Krull '83
Something Wicked This Way Comes '83
Testament '83
Uncommon Valor '83
Star Trek 3: The Search for Spock '84
The Stone Boy '84
Cocoon '85
Commando '85
Heaven Help Us '85
The Journey of Natty Gann '85
P.K. and the Kid '85
Volunteers '85
Aliens '86
An American Tail '86
The Name of the Rose '86
Off Beat '86
Where the River Runs Black '86
*batteries not included '87
Project X '87
Cocoon: The Return '88
The Land Before Time '88
Red Heat '88
Vibes '88
Willow '88
Dad '89
Field of Dreams '89
Glory '89
Honey, I Shrunk the Kids '89
In Country '89
Another 48 Hrs. '90
I Love You to Death '90
An American Tail: Fievel Goes West '91
Class Action '91
My Heroes Have Always Been Cowboys '91
Once Around '91
The Rocketeer '91
Patriot Games '92
Sneakers '92
Thunderheart '92
Unlawful Entry '92
Bopha! '93
A Far Off Place '93
Jack the Bear '93
The Man Without a Face '93
The Pelican Brief '93
Searching for Bobby Fischer '93
Swing Kids '93
Legends of the Fall '94
The Pagemaster '94
Apollo 13 '95
Balto '95
Braveheart '95
Casper '95
Jade '95
Jumanji '95
Courage Under Fire '96

Richard Horowitz
The Sheltering Sky '90
Lakota Woman: Siege at Wounded Knee '94
Broken Trust '95

Vladimir Horunzhy
Stephen King's The Langoliers '95
Original Gangstas '96

James Newton Howard
8 Million Ways to Die '85
Head Office '86
Never Too Young to Die '86
Nobody's Fool '86
Tough Guys '86
Wildcats '86
Campus Man '87
Off Limits '87
Russkies '87
Everybody's All American '88
Five Corners '88
Promised Land '88
Some Girls '88
The Image '89
Major League '89
The Package '89
Tap '89
Coupe de Ville '90
Flatliners '90
Pretty Woman '90
Three Men and a Little Lady '90
Grand Canyon '91
Guilty by Suspicion '91
King Ralph '91
My Girl '91
The Prince of Tides '91
American Heart '92
Diggstown '92
Glengarry Glen Ross '92
Night and the City '92
Alive '93
Dave '93
Falling Down '93
The Fugitive '93
Intersection '93
The Saint of Fort Washington '93
Junior '94
Just Cause '94
Outbreak '94
Restoration '94
Wyatt Earp '94
An Eye for an Eye '95
French Kiss '95
Waterworld '95
The Juror '96
Primal Fear '96
The Trigger Effect '96

Ken Howard
Foreign Body '86

Tom Howard
Tryst '94

Alan Howarth
Christine '84
Big Trouble in Little China '86
They Live '88
Arcade '93
Halloween 6: The Curse of Michael Myers '95

Walter Hus
Suite 16 '94

Zakir Hussain
In Custody '94

Dick Hyman
The Purple Rose of Cairo '85
Leader of the Band '87
Alan & Naomi '92
Mighty Aphrodite '95

Jacques Ibert
Don Quixote '35

Abdullah Ibrahim
No Fear, No Die '90

Ice-T
Return of Superfly '90

Akira Ifukube
A Quiet Duel '49

Shinichiro Ikebe
Akira Kurosawa's Dreams '90

Paul Inder
The Girl with the Hungry Eyes '94

Alberto Inglesias
The Flower of My Secret '95

Tassos Ioannides
The Silver Stallion: King of the Wild Brumbies '93

Ashley Irwin
Deadly Rivals '92
Secret Games 2: The Escort '93
Stranger by Night '94
The Expert '95

Pat Irwin
My New Gun '92

Bjorn Isfalt
What's Eating Gilbert Grape '93

Mark Isham
Mrs. Soffel '84
The Hitcher '86
Made in Heaven '87
The Beast '88
The Moderns '88
Billy Bathgate '91
Little Man Tate '91
Mortal Thoughts '91
Point Break '91
A Midnight Clear '92
A River Runs Through It '92
Fire in the Sky '93
The Getaway '93
Made in America '93
Nowhere to Run '93
Romeo Is Bleeding '93
Short Cuts '93
The Browning Version '94
Losing Isaiah '94
Quiz Show '94
Safe Passage '94
Home for the Holidays '95
Miami Rhapsody '95
The Net '95
Last Dance '96

Howard Jackson
Sergeant Rutledge '60
Merrill's Marauders '62

Joe Jackson
Party! Party! '83
Tucker: The Man and His Dream '88
Queens Logic '91

Chaz Jankel
D.O.A. '88
The Rachel Papers '89

Alaric Jans
House of Games '87
Things Change '88

Pierre Jansen
Les Bonnes Femmes '60
La Rupture '70

Maurice Jarre
The Horror Chamber of Dr. Faustus '59
Lawrence of Arabia '62
The Longest Day '62
Sundays & Cybele '62
Behold a Pale Horse '64
Judex '64
The Collector '65
Doctor Zhivago '65
The Train '65
Gambit '66
Grand Prix '66
The Professionals '66
Night of the Generals '67
Five Card Stud '68
The Fixer '68
Is Paris Burning? '68
Isadora '68
Villa Rides '68
The Damned '69
Topaz '69
El Condor '70
Ryan's Daughter '70
Plaza Suite '71
Red Sun '71
Life & Times of Judge Roy Bean '72
Ash Wednesday '73
Mackintosh Man '73
The Island at the Top of the World '74
Mr. Sycamore '74
The Man Who Would Be King '75
Mandingo '75
Posse '75
The Last Tycoon '76
Shout at the Devil '76
Jesus of Nazareth '77
March or Die '77
Mohammed: Messenger of God '77
The Prince and the Pauper '78
Users '78
The Black Marble '79
The Magician of Lublin '79
The Tin Drum '79
Winter Kills '79
Enola Gay: The Men, the Mission, the Atomic Bomb '80
The Last Flight of Noah's Ark '80
Resurrection '80
Shogun '80
Lion of the Desert '81
Taps '81
Coming Out of the Ice '82
Don't Cry, It's Only Thunder '82
Firefox '82
The Year of Living Dangerously '82
Young Doctors in Love '82
Dreamscape '84
A Passage to India '84
Samson and Delilah '84
Top Secret! '84
The Bride '85
Enemy Mine '85
Mad Max: Beyond Thunderdome '85
Witness '85
Apology '86
The Mosquito Coast '86
Solarbabies '86
Tai-Pan '86
Fatal Attraction '87
Gaby: A True Story '87
Julia and Julia '87
The Murder of Mary Phagan '87
No Way Out '87
Distant Thunder '88
Gorillas in the Mist '88
Moon over Parador '88
Wildfire '88
Chances Are '89
Dead Poets Society '89
Enemies, a Love Story '89
Prancer '89
After Dark, My Sweet '90
Ghost '90
Jacob's Ladder '90
Only the Lonely '91
School Ties '92
Solar Crisis '92
Fearless '93
Mr. Jones '93

Simon Jeffes
Malcolm '86

Peter Jermyn
The Climb '87

Zhao Jiping
Farewell My Concubine '93
To Live '94

Antonio Carlos Jobim
Black Orpheus '58

David Johansen
Mr. Nanny '93

Elton John
Friends '71
The Lion King '94

Laurie Johnson
Dr. Strangelove, or: How I Learned to Stop Worrying and Love the Bomb '64

Freedy Johnston
Kingpin '96

Philip Johnston
The Music of Chance '93

Alain Jomy
The Little Thief '89
The Accompanist '93

David Allen Jones
House Party 3 '94

John Paul Jones
Risk '94

Mick Jones
Amongst Friends '93

Quincy Jones
The Pawnbroker '65
The Slender Thread '65
Mirage '66
Walk, Don't Run '66
Enter Laughing '67
In Cold Blood '67
In the Heat of the Night '67
Dandy in Aspic '68
For Love of Ivy '68
Bob & Carol & Ted & Alice '69
Cactus Flower '69
The Italian Job '69
MacKenna's Gold '69
Brother John '70
The Hot Rock '70
They Call Me Mr. Tibbs! '70
The Anderson Tapes '71
Dollars '71
Honky '71
Man & Boy '71
The Getaway '72
The New Centurions '72
Roots '77
The Wiz '78
The Color Purple '85

Trevor Jones
Excalibur '81
The Dark Crystal '82

William Murphy
Bound and Gagged: A Love Story '93

Bill Murray
Polyester '81

Jane Musky
Two Bits '96

Stanley Myers
Dreamchild '85
Castaway '87
Prick Up Your Ears '87
Sammy & Rosie Get Laid '87
Wish You Were Here '87
Paperhouse '89
Scenes from the Class Struggle in Beverly Hills '89
The Witches '90
Sarafina! '92
Heart of Darkness '93
The Summer House '94

Fred Myrow
Plan 10 from Outer Space '95

Ogden Nash
One Touch of Venus '48

Lou Natale
The Man in the Attic '94

Chris Neal
Around the World in 80 Ways '86
Jack Be Nimble '94

Willie Nelson
Honeysuckle Rose '80
1918 '85
Stagecoach '86

John Neschling
Pixote '81
Kiss of the Spider Woman '85

Ira Newborn
The Blues Brothers '80
All Night Long '81
Sixteen Candles '84
Into the Night '85
Weird Science '85
Ferris Bueller's Day Off '86
Wise Guys '86
Amazon Women on the Moon '87
Dragnet '87
Planes, Trains & Automobiles '87
Caddyshack 2 '88
The Naked Gun: From the Files of Police Squad '88
Cast the First Stone '89
Uncle Buck '89
My Blue Heaven '90
Short Time '90
Naked Gun 2 1/2: The Smell of Fear '91
Brain Donors '92
Innocent Blood '92
Ace Ventura: Pet Detective '93
The Opposite Sex and How to Live With Them '93
Naked Gun 33 1/3: The Final Insult '94
Mallrats '95
The Late Shift '96

Alfred Newman
Street Scene '31
Mr. Robinson Crusoe '32
Les Miserables '35
Gunga Din '39
The Hunchback of Notre Dame '39
The Rains Came '39
Stanley and Livingstone '39
Wuthering Heights '39
Foreign Correspondent '40
The Mark of Zorro '40
Tin Pan Alley '40
Blood and Sand '41
How Green Was My Valley '41
Week-End In Havana '41
The Black Swan '42
Roxie Hart '42
Son of Fury '42
The Song of Bernadette '43
Wilson '44
Leave Her to Heaven '45
A Tree Grows in Brooklyn '45
Call Northside 777 '48
The Snake Pit '48
A Letter to Three Wives '49
Pinky '49
How to Marry a Millionaire '53
Love Is a Many-Splendored Thing '55
The Best of Everything '59

David Newman
Vendetta '85
Critters '86
The Kindred '87
Malone '87
My Demon Lover '87
Throw Momma from the Train '87
Bill & Ted's Excellent Adventure '89
Disorganized Crime '89
Gross Anatomy '89
Heathers '89
Little Monsters '89
The War of the Roses '89
DuckTales the Movie: Treasure of the Lost Lamp '90
Fire Birds '90
The Freshman '90
Madhouse '90
Bill & Ted's Bogus Journey '91
The Marrying Man '91
Other People's Money '91
Paradise '91
Rover Dangerfield '91
The Runestone '91
Talent for the Game '91
Hoffa '92
Honeymoon in Vegas '92
The Mighty Ducks '92
My Father the Hero '93
The Sandlot '93
Undercover Blues '93
The Air Up There '94
The Cowboy Way '94
The Flintstones '94
Big Bully '95
Operation Dumbo Drop '95
Tommy Boy '95
The Nutty Professor '96
The Phantom '96

Randy Newman
Cold Turkey '71
Ragtime '81
The Natural '84
Parenthood '89
Avalon '90
Awakenings '90
Maverick '94
The Paper '94
Toy Story '95
James and the Giant Peach '96

Thomas Newman
Grandview U.S.A. '84
Reckless '84
Revenge of the Nerds '84
Desperately Seeking Susan '85
Girls Just Want to Have Fun '85
Gung Ho '85
The Man with One Red Shoe '85
Real Genius '85
Jumpin' Jack Flash '86
Less Than Zero '87
Light of Day '87
The Lost Boys '87
The Great Outdoors '88
Prince of Pennsylvania '88
Cookie '89
Men Don't Leave '89
Career Opportunities '91
Deceived '91
Fried Green Tomatoes '91
The Favor '92
The Linguini Incident '92
The Player '92
Scent of a Woman '92
Whispers in the Dark '92
Flesh and Bone '93
Josh and S.A.M. '93
Little Women '94
Threesome '94
How to Make an American Quilt '95
Unstrung Heroes '95
Phenomenon '96
Up Close and Personal '96

David Nichtern
The Big Picture '89

Bruno Nicolai
The Scorpion's Tail '71

Lennie Niehaus
City Heat '84
Tightrope '84
Pale Rider '85
Sesame Street Presents: Follow That Bird '85
Heartbreak Ridge '86
Never Too Young to Die '86
Ratboy '86
Bird '88
White Hunter, Black Heart '90
Unforgiven '92
A Perfect World '93
The Bridges of Madison County '95

Jose Nieto
Of Love and Shadows '94

Harry Nilsson
The Point '71
Popeye '80

Jack Nitzsche
Village of the Giants '65
Performance '70
Greaser's Palace '72
The Exorcist '73
One Flew Over the Cuckoo's Nest '75
Heroes '77
Blue Collar '78
Hardcore '79
Cruising '80
Heart Beat '80
Cutter's Way '81
Cannery Row '82
An Officer and a Gentleman '82
Personal Best '82
Breathless '83
Without a Trace '83
The Razor's Edge '84
Starman '84
Windy City '84
The Jewel of the Nile '85
9 1/2 Weeks '86
Stand By Me '86
Streets of Gold '86
Stripper '86
The Whoopee Boys '86
The Seventh Sign '88
Next of Kin '89
The Hot Spot '90
The Last of the Finest '90
Mermaids '90
Revenge '90
Blue Sky '91
The Crossing Guard '94

Matt Noble
Jason's Lyric '94

Erik Nordgren
The Seventh Seal '56
The Emigrants '72

Alex North
A Streetcar Named Desire '51
Les Miserables '52
The Member of the Wedding '52
Viva Zapata! '52
Desiree '54
Daddy Long Legs '55
I'll Cry Tomorrow '55
The Racers '55
The Rose Tattoo '55
The Bad Seed '56
The King and Four Queens '56
The Rainmaker '56
Stage Struck '57
Hot Spell '58
The Long, Hot Summer '58
Spartacus '60
The Children's Hour '61
The Misfits '61
All Fall Down '62
Cleopatra '63
Cheyenne Autumn '64
The Agony and the Ecstasy '65
Who's Afraid of Virginia Woolf? '66
The Devil's Brigade '68
The Shoes of the Fisherman '68
A Dream of Kings '69
Willard '71
Pocket Money '72
Once Upon a Scoundrel '73
Journey into Fear '74
Bite the Bullet '75
The Passover Plot '75
Rich Man, Poor Man '76
The Word '78
Wise Blood '79
Carny '80
Dragonslayer '81
Under the Volcano '84
Prizzi's Honor '85
Death of a Salesman '86
The Dead '87
Good Morning, Vietnam '87
The Penitent '88
The Last Butterfly '92

Craig Northey
Kids In the Hall Brain Candy '96

Julian Nott
A Man of No Importance '94

Michael Nyman
The Draughtsman's Contract '82
Cold Room '84
Drowning by Numbers '87
A Zed & Two Noughts '88
The Cook, the Thief, His Wife & Her Lover '90
Prospero's Books '91
The Hairdresser's Husband '92
The Piano '93
Carrington '95

Casimir Oberfeld
Le Schpountz '38

Sinead O'Connor
In the Name of the Father '93

George Oddner
The New Land '73

Jacques Offenbach
Peter's Friends '92

Patrick O'Hearn
Silent Tongue '92
White Sands '92

Wendy Oldfield
Never Say Die '94

Stephen Oliver
The Life and Adventures of Nicholas Nickleby '81

William Olvis
29th Street '91
The Comrades of Summer '92
Red Rock West '93
Separate Lives '94
Steal Big, Steal Little '95

Riz Ortolani
The Story of Boys & Girls '91

Jason Osborn
High Season '88

Yoshihide Otomo
The Day the Sun Turned Cold '94
Summer Snow '94

John Ottman
Public Access '93
The Usual Suspects '95
The Cable Guy '96

Albinoni Pachelbel
Every Man for Himself & God Against All '75

J.M. Pagan
Anguish '88

Jose Pagan
The Awful Dr. Orlof '62

Jimmy Page
Death Wish 2 '82
Death Wish 3 '85

Christopher Palmer
Valmont '89

George Papadakis
When the Greeks '81

Alan Parker
What's Eating Gilbert Grape '93
The Phoenix and the Magic Carpet '95

Clifton Parker
Sea of Sand '58

Jim Parker
The Final Cut '95

Gordon Parks
Shaft's Big Score '72

Van Dyke Parks
Club Paradise '86
The Two Jakes '90
Wild Bill '95

Arvo Part
Rachel River '87

Daniele Patrucchi
Bread and Chocolate '74

Rosemary Paul
Something Wild '86

Don Peake
The People Under the Stairs '91
Solar Force '94
Hard Justice '95

Krzysztof Penderecki
The Saragossa Manuscript '65

Serge Perathone
Love After Love '94

Giovanni Pergolese
Cactus '86

William Perry
Sparrows '26

Jean-Claude Petit
L'Addition '85
Uranus '91
The Playboys '92
My Life and Times with Antonin Artaud '93
Foreign Student '94
The Horseman on the Roof '95

Laurent Petitgrand
Faraway, So Close! '93

Charles Pettis
If Lucy Fell '95

Barrington Pheloung
The Cinder Path '94
The Mangler '94

Barry Phillips
Ele, My Friend '93

Stu Phillips
Jud '71

Rebecca Pidgeon
Oleanna '94

Franco Piersanti
The Stolen Children '92
Lamerica '95

Nicholas Pike
Perfect Family '92
Attack of the 50 Ft. Woman '93
Blank Check '93

Pink Floyd
The Valley Obscured by the Clouds '72

Nicola Piovani
The Night of the Shooting Stars '82
Ginger & Fred '86
Good Morning, Babylon '87
Intervista '87
Caro Diario '93
Fiorile '93
Jamon, Jamon '93
A Month by the Lake '95

Edward Plumb
Bambi '42

Terry Plumer
Death Wish 5: The Face of Death '94
Raging Angels '95

Basil Poledouris
Big Wednesday '78
Defiance '79
The Blue Lagoon '80
Whale for the Killing '81
Conan the Barbarian '82
Summer Lovers '82
The Amazons '84
Conan the Destroyer '84
Making the Grade '84
Protocol '84
Red Dawn '84
Single Bars, Single Women '84
Flesh and Blood '85
Iron Eagle '86
No Man's Land '87
RoboCop '87
Cherry 2000 '88
The Spellbinder '88
Split Decisions '88
Farewell to the King '89
Lonesome Dove '89
Wired '89
Flight of the Intruder '90
The Hunt for Red October '90
Quigley Down Under '90
RoboCop 3 '91
White Fang '91
Wind '92
Free Willy '93
Hot Shots! Part Deux '93
Lone Justice '93
On Deadly Ground '94
Serial Mom '94

Free Willy 2: The Adventure Home '95
It's My Party '95
Under Siege 2: Dark Territory '95
Celtic Pride '96

Iggy Pop
Rock & Rule '83

Temistocle Popa
Trahir '93

Conrad Pope
Project Metalbeast: DNA Overload '94
The Set Up '95

Roland Pope
Preacherman '83

Michel Portal
Max, Mon Amour '86

Cole Porter
Born to Dance '36
Rosalie '38
Panama Hattie '42
High Society '56

Rachel Portman
Sharma & Beyond '84
Young Charlie Chaplin '88
Antonia and Jane '91
Where Angels Fear to Tread '91
Used People '92
Benny & Joon '93
The Road to Wellville '94
Sirens '94
A Pyromaniac's Love Story '95
Smoke '95
To Wong Foo, Thanks for Everything, Julie Newmar '95
War of the Buttons '95
Emma '96

Andrew Powell
Ladyhawke '85
Rocket Gibraltar '88

Reg Powell
Test Tube Teens from the Year 2000 '93
Pet Shop '94
Baja '95
Forbidden Zone: Alien Abduction '96

Pray For Rain
Car 54, Where Are You? '94

Zbigniew Preisner
At Play in the Fields of the Lord '91
Eminent Domain '91
Damage '92
The Secret Garden '93
Trois Couleurs: Rouge '94
When a Man Loves a Woman '94
Feast of July '95

Craig Preuss
Bhaji on the Beach '94

Andre Previn
Challenge to Lassie '49
The Sun Comes Up '49
Kim '50
Three Little Words '50
Cause for Alarm '51
The Girl Who Had Everything '53
Give a Girl a Break '53
Kiss Me Kate '53
Small Town Girl '53
Bad Day at Black Rock '54
It's Always Fair Weather '55
Kismet '55
The Catered Affair '56
Fastest Gun Alive '56
Designing Woman '57
Silk Stockings '57
Bells are Ringing '60
Elmer Gantry '60
All in a Night's Work '61
One, Two, Three '61
The Four Horsemen of the Apocalypse '62
Long Day's Journey into Night '62
Two for the Seesaw '62
Irma La Douce '63
Kiss Me, Stupid! '64
Inside Daisy Clover '65
The Fortune Cookie '66
Paint Your Wagon '69
Rollerball '75

Alan Price
O Lucky Man! '73

Prince
J.D.'s Revenge '76
Batman '89
Girl 6 '96

Sergei Prokofiev
Alexander Nevsky '38
Ivan the Terrible, Part 1 '44

Sacha Puttnam
The Confessional '95

Xiao-Song Qu
Pushing Hands '92

Peer Raben
The American Soldier '70
Beware of a Holy Whore '70
Satan's Brew '76
The Stationmaster's Wife '77
Despair '78
In a Year of 13 Moons '78
The Marriage of Maria Braun '79
Veronika Voss '82
Querelle '83

Douglas Stephen Rae
Traps '93

Robert O. Ragland
Messenger of Death '88
The Raffle '94

Ralph Rainger
Ruggles of Red Gap '35
Waikiki Wedding '37

David Raksin
Laura '44
Forever Amber '47

Ron Ramin
Christy '94
Rent-A-Kid '95

Alan Rawsthorne
Pandora and the Flying Dutchman '51

J.A.C. Redford
Bye Bye, Love '94
D2: The Mighty Ducks '94
Heavyweights '94
A Kid in King Arthur's Court '95

Joshua Redman
Vanya on 42nd Street '94

Lou Reed
Rock & Rule '83

Alan Reeves
Dr. Bethune '90

Ruth Rennie
When the Whales Came '89

Joe Renzetti
The Buddy Holly Story '78
Child's Play '88
Basket Case 2 '90
Basket Case 3: The Progeny '92
South Beach '92

Harry Revel
We're Not Dressing '34

Graeme Revell
Dead Calm '89
Spontaneous Combustion '89
Child's Play 2 '90
Till There was You '91
Until The End of The World '91
Body of Evidence '92
The Hand that Rocks the Cradle '92
Love Crimes '92
Traces of Red '92
Boxing Helena '93
The Crow '93
The Crush '93
Ghost in the Machine '93
Hard Target '93
Hear No Evil '93
The Basketball Diaries '94
Down Came a Blackbird '94
No Escape '94
Street Fighter '94
Tank Girl '94
From Dusk Till Dawn '95
Mighty Morphin Power Rangers: The Movie '95
Strange Days '95
The Tie That Binds '95
The Craft '96
The Crow 2: City of Angels '96
Fled '96
Race the Sun '96

Trent Reznor
Natural Born Killers '94

Tim Rice
Aladdin '92
The Lion King '94

David Rickets
Echo Park '86

Nelson Riddle
The Great Gatsby '74

Ned Rifle
Amateur '94
Flirt '95

Tony Riparetti
Bloodmatch '91
Nemesis 3: Time Lapse '96

Carlo Ristichelli
RoGoPaG '62

Lee Ritenour
American Flyers '85

Nicholas Rivera
Saturday Night Special '92

David Robbins
Bob Roberts '92
Twenty Bucks '93
Fast Getaway 2 '94
Dead Man Walking '95

Richard Robbins
Maurice '87
Sweet Lorraine '87
The Ballad of the Sad Cafe '91
The Remains of the Day '93
Jefferson in Paris '94

Andy Roberts
Priest '94

Eric N. Robertson
Millenium '89

Harry Robertson
Jane & the Lost City '87

Robbie Robertson
Jimmy Hollywood '94

Leo Robin
Waikiki Wedding '37
Two Tickets to Broadway '51

J. Peter Robinson
The Believers '87
Cocktail '88
Blind Fury '90
Wayne's World '92
The Day My Parents Ran Away '93
Highlander: The Final Dimension '94
Wes Craven's New Nightmare '94
Vampire in Brooklyn '95
Wes Craven Presents Mind Ripper '95
Rumble in the Bronx '96

Milan Roder
The Lives of a Bengal Lancer '35

Nile Rodgers
Coming to America '88
Earth Girls Are Easy '89
Beverly Hills Cop 3 '94
Blue Chips '94

Richard Rodgers
Hallelujah, I'm a Bum '33
Evergreen '34
Babes in Arms '39
Too Many Girls '40
I Married an Angel '42
State Fair '45
Words and Music '48
Oklahoma! '55
Carousel '56
The King and I '56
Pal Joey '57
South Pacific '58
Flower Drum Song '61
Cinderella '64
The Sound of Music '65

Pierre Rodnunsky
Lovers' Lovers '94

Patrick Roffe
Baxter '89

Michael Rohatyn
Angela '94

Jeff Rona
White Squall '96

Jean-Louis Roques
Germinal '93

Joel Rosenbaum
Billy Galvin '86

Leonard Rosenman
East of Eden '54
Rebel Without a Cause '55
Lafayette Escadrille '58
Ambition '91
Mrs. Munck '95

John Ross
Easy Wheels '89

Matthew Ross
Carnal Crimes '91

William Ross
One Good Cop '91
Look Who's Talking Now '93
Cops and Robbersons '94
Thumbelina '94
The Amazing Panda Adventure '95
Black Sheep '96

Nino Rota
The Hidden Room '49
Anna '51
Valley of the Eagles '51
The White Sheik '52
I Vitelloni '53
La Strada '54
Mambo '55
The Swindle '55
War and Peace '56
Nights of Cabiria '57
White Nights '57
The Great War '59
La Dolce Vita '60
Rocco and His Brothers '60
Boccaccio '70 '62
8 1/2 '63
Juliet of the Spirits '65
Shoot Loud, Louder, I Don't Understand! '66
The Taming of the Shrew '67
Romeo and Juliet '68
Spirits of the Dead '68
Fellini Satyricon '69
The Clowns '71
Waterloo '71
Fellini's Roma '72
The Godfather '72
Love and Anarchy '73
Amarcord '74
The Godfather, Part 2 '74
Death on the Nile '78
Hurricane '79
The Godfather 1902-1959: The Complete Epic '81
The Godfather, Part 3 '90

Christopher Rousset
Farinelli '94

Hahn Rowe
Clean, Shaven '93

Bruce Rowland
Andre '94
Lightning Jack '94

Miklos Rozsa
Knight Without Armour '37
The Squeaker '37
Thunder in the City '37
The Divorce of Lady X '38
The Four Feathers '39
Spy in Black '39
The Thief of Bagdad '40
Lydia '41
Melody Master '41
Sundown '41
That Hamilton Woman '41
Jacare '42
The Jungle Book '42
So Proudly We Hail '43
Dark Waters '44
Double Indemnity '44
The Woman of the Town '44
Blood on the Sun '45
Lady On a Train '45
The Lost Weekend '45
A Song to Remember '45
Spellbound '45
The Strange Love of Martha Ivers '46
A Double Life '47
The Red House '47
Command Decision '48
Criss Cross '48
The Naked City '48
Secret Beyond the Door '48
East Side, West Side '49
Madame Bovary '49
Adam's Rib '50
The Asphalt Jungle '50
The Miniver Story '50
Quo Vadis '51
Ivanhoe '52
All the Brothers Were Valiant '53
Julius Caesar '53
Knights of the Round Table '53
Young Bess '53
Men of the Fighting Lady '54
Diane '55
Green Fire '55
The King's Thief '55
Moonfleet '55
Bhowani Junction '56
Lust for Life '56
Tribute to a Bad Man '56
Something of Value '57
A Time to Love & a Time to Die '58
Ben-Hur '59
El Cid '61
The King of Kings '61
Sodom and Gomorrah '62
The V.I.P.'s '63
The Green Berets '68
The Private Life of Sherlock Holmes '70
Golden Voyage of Sinbad '73
Providence '77
Last Embrace '79
Time After Time '79
Eye of the Needle '81
Dead Men Don't Wear Plaid '82

Michael Rubini
Nemesis '93

Arthur B. Rubinstein
Lost in America '85
Stakeout '87
The Hard Way '91
Nick of Time '95

David Rubinstein
Sword of Honor '94

Harry Ruby
Duck Soup '33

Steve Rucker
Creature '85
Catch the Heat '87
And God Created Woman '88
976-EVIL '88
Syngenor '90
Little Nemo: Adventures in Slumberland '92

Todd Rundgren
Dumb & Dumber '94

Daryl Runswick
No Surrender '86

Patrice Rushen
Hollywood Shuffle '87
America's Dream '95

Willy Russell
Mr. Love '86
Shirley Valentine '89

David E. Russo
Shaking the Tree '92
Angus '95

John Clifford Ryan
Angel Baby '95

Craig Safan
The Stranger '87
A Nightmare on Elm Street 4: Dream Master '88
Stand and Deliver '88
Money for Nothing '93
Mr. Wrong '95

Martin St. Pierre
Dust '85

Camille Saint-Saens
Au Revoir Les Enfants '87

Ichiro Saito
A Geisha '53

Ryuichi Sakamoto
The Last Emperor '87
The Sheltering Sky '90
High Heels '91
Tokyo Decadence '91
Little Buddha '93
Wild Palms '93

Hans J. Salter
His Butler's Sister '43
Creature from the Black Lagoon '54
Come September '61

David Sanborn
Lethal Weapon 2 '89
Lethal Weapon 3 '92

Anton Sanko
Girl in the Cadillac '94
Party Girl '94
Live Nude Girls '95

Carlos Santana
La Bamba '87

Chris Saranec
Huck and the King of Hearts '93
Hourglass '95

Philippe Sarde
La Grande Bouffe '73
Lancelot of the Lake '74
Spoiled Children '77
Fort Saganne '84
Joshua Then and Now '85
Every Time We Say Goodbye '86
Lost Angels '89
Music Box '89
The Old Lady Who Walked in the Sea '91
L.627 '92
The Favorite Son '94
Nelly et Monsieur Arnaud '95

Erik Satie
Elisa, Vida Mia '77
Dancing in the Dark '86

Masaru Sato
Throne of Blood '57
Yojimbo '61
The Silk Road '92

Eddie Sauter
Mickey One '65

Jordi Savall
Tous les Matins du Monde '92

Walter Scharf
Three Violent People '57

Glenn Schellenberg
Zero Patience '94

Prof. Peter Schickele
Silent Running '71

Poul Schierbeck
Day of Wrath '43

Lalo Schifrin
The Cincinnati Kid '65
Murderers' Row '66
Cool Hand Luke '67
The President's Analyst '67
The Brotherhood '68
Bullitt '68
Coogan's Bluff '68
Hell in the Pacific '69
The Beguiled '70
Kelly's Heroes '70
Dirty Harry '71
THX 1138 '71
Joe Kidd '72
Prime Cut '72
Charley Varrick '73
Enter the Dragon '73
Hit! '73
Magnum Force '73
The Four Musketeers '75
St. Ives '76
Sky Riders '76
Special Delivery '76
Voyage of the Damned '76
The Eagle Has Landed '77
Rollercoaster '77
Telefon '77
The Manitou '78
The Amityville Horror '79
Boulevard Nights '79
The Concorde: Airport '79 '79
Escape to Athena '79
Love and Bullets '79
The Big Brawl '80
Brubaker '80
The Competition '80
The Nude Bomb '80
When Time Ran Out '80
Buddy Buddy '81
Caveman '81
Class of 1984 '82
The Seduction '82
Doctor Detroit '83
The Osterman Weekend '83
The Sting 2 '83
Sudden Impact '83
Tank '83
Mean Season '85
Black Moon Rising '86
The Fourth Protocol '87
The Dead Pool '88
F/X 2: The Deadly Art of Illusion '91
The Beverly Hillbillies '93

Peter Scholes
Desperate Remedies '93

Franz Schubert
Au Revoir Les Enfants '87

Paul Schutze
The Tale of Ruby Rose '87

Arthur Schwartz
The Band Wagon '53
Dangerous When Wet '53

David Schwartz
Magic in the Water '95

Stephen Schwartz
Pocahontas '95
The Hunchback of Notre Dame '96

Garry Schyman
Tornado! '96

Gary Stevan Scott
3 Ninjas Knuckle Up '92

John Scott
The Whistle Blower '87
Shoot to Kill '88
Winter People '89
Becoming Colette '92
Ruby '92
Detonator 2: Night Watch '95

Tom Scott
Final Notice '89
Percy & Thunder '93
Deconstructing Sarah '94

Vincent Scotto
Fanny '32
Cesar '36

Peter Sculthorpe
Burke & Wills '85

John Sebastian
The Act '82

Ilona Seckaz
Antonia's Line '95

Sholom Secunda
Eli Eli '40

Dov Seltzer
Hanna's War '88

Al Sendry
Bloody Wednesday '87

Akira Senju
The Mystery of Rampo '94

Eric Serra
La Femme Nikita '91
The Professional '94
Goldeneye '95

Luis Maria Serra
I, the Worst of All '90

Patrick Seymour
Chantilly Lace '93
Parallel Lives '94
Night Eyes 4: Fatal Passion '95

Marc Shaiman
When Harry Met Sally... '89
Misery '90
The Addams Family '91
City Slickers '91
A Few Good Men '92
Mr. Saturday Night '92
Sister Act '92
Addams Family Values '93
Heart and Souls '93
Sleepless in Seattle '93
That's Entertainment, Part 3 '93
City Slickers 2: The Legend of Curly's Gold '94
North '94
Speechless '94
Stuart Saves His Family '94
The American President '95
Forget Paris '95

Jack Shaindlin
Mickey One '65

Leon Shamroy
The King and I '56

Ravi Shankar
Pather Panchali '54
The World of Apu '59
Wonderwall: The Movie '69

Jennifer Sharpe
Go Fish '94

Francis Shaw
The Fourth Protocol '87

Ed Shearmur
Tales from the Crypt Presents Demon Knight '94

Jonathan Sheffer
On Valentine's Day '86
Bloodhounds of Broadway '89

Kirby Shelstad
Ernest Rides Again '93

David Shire
Skin Game '71
Summertree '71
Class of '44 '73
Showdown '73
Steelyard Blues '73
The Conversation '74
The Taking of Pelham One Two Three '74
Tell Me Where It Hurts '74
Farewell, My Lovely '75
The Hindenburg '75
All the President's Men '76
The Big Bus '76
Harry & Walter Go to New York '76
Raid on Entebbe '77
Saturday Night Fever '77
The Promise '78
Straight Time '78
Fast Break '79
Norma Rae '79
Old Boyfriends '79
The Night the Lights Went Out in Georgia '81
Only When I Laugh '81
Paternity '81
The World According to Garp '82
Max Dugan Returns '83
Oh, God! You Devil '84
2010: The Year We Make Contact '84
Return to Oz '85
'night, Mother '86
Short Circuit '86
Convicted: A Mother's Story '87
Mayflower Madam '87
Backfire '88
God Bless the Child '88
Jesse '88
Monkey Shines '88
Vice Versa '88
The Women of Brewster Place '89
The Habitation of Dragons '91
Bed & Breakfast '92
Sidekicks '93
Lily in Winter '94
The Heidi Chronicles '95
Larry McMurtry's Streets of Laredo '95
One Night Stand '95
Tecumseh: The Last Warrior '95

Alfred Shnitke
Rasputin '85

Howard Shore
The Brood '79
Scanners '81
Videodrome '83
Places in the Heart '84
After Hours '85
Belizaire the Cajun '86
Fire with Fire '86
The Fly '86
Heaven '87
Nadine '87
Big '88
Dead Ringers '88
Moving '88
An Innocent Man '89
She-Devil '89
Signs of Life '89
Quick Change '90
Naked Lunch '91
The Silence of the Lambs '91
Prelude to a Kiss '92
Single White Female '92
M. Butterfly '93
Mrs. Doubtfire '93
Philadelphia '93
Sliver '93
Before and After '95
Crash '95
Moonlight and Valentino '95
Seven '95
White Man's Burden '95

Dimitri Shostakovich
Ten Days That Shook the World '27

Lawrence Shragge
Blue River '95
Redwood Curtain '95

Michael Shrieve
The Bedroom Window '87

Leo Shuken
Miracle of Morgan's Creek '44

Tony Silbert
Vermont Is for Lovers '92

Carlo Siliotto
Fluke '95

Sheila Silver
Alligator Eyes '90
Dead Funny '94

Shel Silverstein
Ned Kelly '70

Alan Silvestri
The Amazing Dobermans '76
Las Vegas Lady '76
Romancing the Stone '84
Back to the Future '85
Cat's Eye '85
Fandango '85
Summer Rental '85
American Anthem '86
The Clan of the Cave Bear '86
Critical Condition '86
Delta Force '86
Flight of the Navigator '86
No Mercy '86
Outrageous Fortune '87
Overboard '87
Predator '87
Mac and Me '88
My Stepmother Is an Alien '88
Who Framed Roger Rabbit '88
The Abyss '89
Back to the Future, Part 2 '89
Downtown '89
She's Out of Control '89
Tales from the Crypt '89
Back to the Future, Part 3 '90
Young Guns 2 '90
Father of the Bride '91
Ricochet '91
Soapdish '91
The Bodyguard '92
Death Becomes Her '92
Ferngully: The Last Rain Forest '92
Stop! or My Mom Will Shoot '92
Cop and a Half '93
Grumpy Old Men '93
Judgment Night '93
Sidekicks '93
Super Mario Bros. '93
Clean Slate '94
The Perez Family '94
Richie Rich '94
Father of the Bride Part II '95
Grumpier Old Men '95
Judge Dredd '95
Sgt. Bilko '95
Eraser '96

Carly Simon
Heartburn '86
Working Girl '88

Lucy Simon
The Positively True Adventures of the Alleged Texas Cheerleader-Murdering Mom '93

Marty Simon
George's Island '91
Scanners 2: The New Order '91

Paul Simon
The Graduate '67

Yves Simon
Love After Love '94

Claudio Simonetti
Conquest '83

Frank Sinatra, Jr.
The Beach Girls and the Monster '65

Marlin Skiles
A Thousand and One Nights '45

Frank Skinner
Destry Rides Again '39
First Love '39
Francis the Talking Mule '49
Francis Goes to the Races '51
Battle Hymn '57
Tarnished Angels '57

Michael Small
Brighton Beach Memoirs '86
Black Widow '87
Orphans '87

Bruce Smeaton
Picnic at Hanging Rock '75
The Devil's Playground '76
Circle of Iron '78
Barbarosa '82
Grendel, Grendel, Grendel '82
The Winds of Jarrah '83
Iceman '84
Eleni '85
The Naked Country '85
Plenty '85
Roxanne '87
Undercover '87
A Cry in the Dark '88

Mauricio Smith
Crossover Dreams '85

Michael Smith
The Bikini Car Wash Company 2 '92

Paul Smith
Snow White and the Seven Dwarfs '37

W. Henry Smith
Preacherman '83

Neil Smolar
The Boys of St. Vincent '93

David Snell
Billy the Kid '41

Mark Snow
Playmaker '94
The Substitute Wife '94
A Good Day to Die '95
Oldest Confederate Widow Tells All '95

Curt Sobel
Alien Nation '88

Steven Soles
Destiny Turns on the Radio '95

Stephen Sondheim
West Side Story '61
Stavisky '74
Reds '81
Sweeney Todd: The Demon Barber of Fleet Street '84
Sunday in the Park with George '86
Dick Tracy '90
Gypsy '93

Lodovico Sorret
What Happened Was... '94

Michael Spicer
Backlash '86

Mischa Spoliansky
Secret Mission '42
The Happiest Days of Your Life '50

Robert Sprayberry
Quick '93
Bodily Harm '95

Frank Stallone
Staying Alive '83

Michael Stearns
Baraka '93
Temptress '95

David Steele
Tin Men '87

Herman Stein
It Came From Outer Space '53
This Island Earth '55

Ronald Stein
Invasion of the Saucer Men '57
Legend of Tom Dooley '59

Max Steiner
Last Command '28
Check & Double Check '30
Cimarron '30
Dixiana '30
Half-Shot at Sunrise '30
Kept Husbands '31
State's Attorney '31
A Bill of Divorcement '32
Bird of Paradise '32

Dana Walden
Molly and Gina '94
W.G. Snuffy Walden
The Good Fight '92
Mal Waldron
Sweet Love, Bitter '67
Shirley Walker
Batman: Mask of the Phantasm '93
Oliver Wallace
Dumbo '41
Karl Wallinger
Reality Bites '94
Rob Walsh
Revenge of the Ninja '83
William Walton
Spitfire '42
Henry V '44
Hamlet '48
Nathan Wang
Natural Causes '94
Stephen Warbeck
Prime Suspect 3 '93
Prime Suspect: The Lost Child '94
Sister My Sister '94
Prime Suspect: Inner Circles '95
Edward Ward
Cheers for Miss Bishop '41
Harry Warren
42nd Street '33
Yolanda and the Thief '45
The Harvey Girls '46
The Barkleys of Broadway '49
Mervyn Warren
The Wharf Rat '95
Don Was
Backbeat '94
David Waters
Rescue Me '93
Mark Watters
The Pebble and the Penguin '94
All Dogs Go to Heaven 2 '95
Franz Waxman
Three Comrades '38
Honolulu '39
The Philadelphia Story '40
Rebecca '40
Woman of the Year '42
Objective, Burma! '45
Night and the City '50
A Place in the Sun '51
Stalag 17 '53
Rear Window '54
The Silver Chalice '54
Mister Roberts '55
Spirit of St. Louis '57
Beloved Infidel '59
Cimarron '60
Chuck Webb
How U Like Me Now? '92
Jim Webb
The Last Unicorn '82
Roy Webb
The Magnificent Ambersons '42
Andrew Lloyd Webber
Gumshoe '72
The Odessa File '74
Paul Francis Webster
Calamity Jane '53
Jay Weigel
The St. Tammany Miracle '94
Cynthia Weil
All Dogs Go to Heaven 2 '95
Kurt Weill
One Touch of Venus '48
Eric Weissburg
Deliverance '72
Rick Wentworth
How to Get Ahead in Advertising '89
Jim West
Lady Dragon 2 '93
Paul Westerberg
Singles '92
Nigel Westlake
Babe '95
John Clifford White
Talk '94
Jean Wiener
Grisbi '53
A Gentle Woman '69
Scott Wilk
Plain Clothes '88
Brooks Williams
Wax, or the Discovery of Television Among the Bees '93
David Williams
The Prophecy '95
John Williams
Diamond Head '62
Gidget Goes to Rome '63
The Killers '64
None But the Brave '65
How to Steal a Million '66
The Rare Breed '66
A Guide for the Married Man '67
Heidi '67
Valley of the Dolls '67
Sergeant Ryker '68
Daddy's Gone A-Hunting '69
Goodbye, Mr. Chips '69
The Reivers '69
Fiddler on the Roof '71
The Cowboys '72
Pete 'n' Tillie '72
The Poseidon Adventure '72
Cinderella Liberty '73
The Long Goodbye '73
Man Who Loved Cat Dancing '73
The Paper Chase '73
Psychopath '73
Tom Sawyer '73
Conrack '74
Earthquake '74
The Sugarland Express '74
The Towering Inferno '74
The Eiger Sanction '75
Jaws '75
Family Plot '76
Midway '76
Missouri Breaks '76
Black Sunday '77
Close Encounters of the Third Kind '77
Star Wars '77
The Deer Hunter '78
The Fury '78
Jaws 2 '78
Superman: The Movie '78
The Swarm '78
Dracula '79
1941 '79
The Empire Strikes Back '80
Superman 2 '80
Heartbeeps '81
Raiders of the Lost Ark '81
E.T.: The Extra-Terrestrial '82
Monsignor '82
Yes, Giorgio '82
Jaws 3 '83
Return of the Jedi '83
Superman 3 '83
Indiana Jones and the Temple of Doom '84
The River '84
Empire of the Sun '87
Superman 4: The Quest for Peace '87
The Witches of Eastwick '87
The Accidental Tourist '88
Always '89
Born on the Fourth of July '89
Indiana Jones and the Last Crusade '89
Home Alone '90
Presumed Innocent '90
Stanley and Iris '90
Hook '91
JFK '91
Far and Away '92
Home Alone 2: Lost in New York '92
Jurassic Park '93
Schindler's List '93
Nixon '95
Sabrina '95
Joseph Williams
Embrace of the Vampire '95
Poison Ivy 2: Lily '95
Patrick Williams
Violets Are Blue '86
Cry-Baby '90
In the Spirit '90
The Cutting Edge '92
Blind Spot '93
Geronimo '93
Getting Gotti '94
Kingfish: A Story of Huey P. Long '95
Paul Williams
Phantom of the Paradise '74
Bugsy Malone '76
A Star is Born '76
The End '78
The Muppet Movie '79
The Muppet Christmas Carol '92
Meredith Willson
The Unsinkable Molly Brown '64
Hal Wilner
Theremin: An Electronic Odyssey '95
Nancy Wilson
Say Anything '89
Edgar Winter
Netherworld '90
Debbie Wiseman
Tom & Viv '94
Haunted '95
Jill Wisoff
Welcome to the Dollhouse '95
Peter Wolf
Weekend at Bernie's 2 '93
Larry Wolff
Silk Degrees '94
Michael Wolff
Who's the Man? '93
Christine Woodruff
The Year My Voice Broke '87
Harry Woods
Evergreen '34
Glenn Workman
Sarah's Child '96
Bernie Worrell
Car 54, Where Are You? '94
Robert Wright
Music in My Heart '40
Stavros Xarchakos
Signs of Life '68
Motofumi Yamaguchi
The Hunted '94
Yanni
Heart of Midnight '89
Gabriel Yared
Betty Blue '86
Light Years '88
Camille Claudel '89
Romero '89
Black Water '94
Dwight Yoakam
Chasers '94
Vincent Youmans
Flying Down to Rio '33
Hit the Deck '55
Christopher Young
Hellraiser '87
Bright Angel '91
The Dark Half '91
Rapid Fire '92
Dream Lover '93
Judicial Consent '94
Copycat '95
Murder In the First '95
Species '95
Tales from the Hood '95
Virtuosity '95
Unforgettable '96
Neil Young
Where the Buffalo Roam '80
Dead Man '95
Victor Young
Arizona '40
Rhythm on the River '40
The Great Man's Lady '42
For Whom the Bell Tolls '43
The Story of Dr. Wassell '44
The Blue Dahlia '46
Unconquered '47
Emperor Waltz '48
The Quiet Man '52
Shane '53
Around the World in 80 Days '56
Jimmy Yuill
A Midwinter's Tale '95
Wang Yunjie
Crows and Sparrows '49
Aleksei Zalivalov
Window to Paris '95
Paul Zaza
The Club '94
My Summer Story '94
Iron Eagle 4 '95
Wolfgang Zeller
Vampyr '31
Hans Zimmer
Moonlighting '82
Success is the Best Revenge '84
Insignificance '85
Rain Man '88
Wonderland '88
A World Apart '88
Black Rain '89
Burning Secret '89
Driving Miss Daisy '89
Paperhouse '89
Prisoner of Rio '89
Twister '89
Bird on a Wire '90
Chicago Joe & the Showgirl '90
Dark Obsession '90
Days of Thunder '90
Fools of Fortune '90
Green Card '90
Pacific Heights '90
Backdraft '91
Regarding Henry '91
Thelma & Louise '91
A League of Their Own '92
Calendar Girl '93
Cool Runnings '93
The House of the Spirits '93
I'll Do Anything '93
Point of No Return '93
True Romance '93
Drop Zone '94
The Lion King '94
Renaissance Man '94
Younger & Younger '94
Beyond Rangoon '95
Broken Arrow '95
Crimson Tide '95
Nine Months '95
Something to Talk About '95
Muppet Treasure Island '96

Song Title Index

The **Song Title Index** lists songs from major movie musicals, ranging from Elvis movies to **State Fair**. They are arranged alphabetically by song, each title referenced to the movie in which it appears. In some cases, the same song has been used in more than one movie. These songs will have separate citations for each film.

The A-stairable Rag *See* You'll Never Get Rich (1941)

A-Tisket-A-Tasket *See* Two Girls and a Sailor (1944)

Aba Daba Honeymoon *See* Two Weeks with Love (1950)

About A Quarter To Nine *See* The Jolson Story (1946)

About a Quarter to Nine *See* Jolson Sings Again (1949)

Above the Stars *See* The Wonderful World of the Brothers Grimm (1962)

Abraham *See* White Christmas (1954)

Abraham, Abraham *See* Holiday Inn (1942)

Absolute Beginners *See* Absolute Beginners (1986)

Absolute Perfection *See* Back to the Beach (1987)

Ac-cent-tchu-ate the Positive *See* Here Come the Waves (1944)

Accidents Will Happen *See* Mr. Music (1950)

The Acid Queen *See* Tommy (1975)

Action *See* Breakin' 2: Electric Boogaloo (1984)

Adam and Eve *See* Spinout (1966)

Adelaide's Lament *See* Guys and Dolls (1955)

Adios *See* The Glenn Miller Story (1954)

Afraid to Fall in Love *See* Summer Holiday (1948)

African Etude *See* The Road to Zanzibar (1941)

After All This Time *See* Swing Parade of 1946 (1946)

After Dark *See* Thank God It's Friday (1978)

After Sundown *See* Going Hollywood (1933)

After the Ball *See* The Jolson Story (1946)

After the Ball *See* Show Boat (1936)

After the Ball *See* Show Boat (1951)

After the Ball *See* Strike Up the Band (1940)

After the Party *See* How to Stuff a Wild Bikini (1965)

After Today *See* Doctor Dolittle (1967)

After You Get What You Want You Don't Want It *See* There's No Business Like Show Business (1954)

After You've Gone *See* All That Jazz (1979)

After You've Gone *See* For Me and My Gal (1942)

After You've Gone *See* Jolson Sings Again (1949)

Ah Che a Voi Perdoni Iddio *See* A Damsel in Distress (1937)

Ah, Love *See* Meet Me in St. Louis (1944)

Ah-Oom *See* The Wonderful World of the Brothers Grimm (1962)

Ah Still Suits Me *See* Show Boat (1936)

Ah, Sweet Mystery of Life *See* Naughty Marietta (1935)

Ah, the Moon is Here *See* Footlight Parade (1933)

Ah Yes, I Remember It Well *See* Gigi (1958)

Ain't Got a Dime to My Name *See* The Road to Morocco (1942)

Ain't It a Shame About Mame? *See* Rhythm on the River (1940)

Ain't Misbehavin' *See* Stormy Weather (1943)

Ain't Nature Grand *See* Dangerous When Wet (1953)

Ain't There Anyone Here For Love? *See* Gentlemen Prefer Blondes (1953)

Ain't We Got Fun *See* By the Light of the Silvery Moon (1953)

Ain't We Got Fun *See* I'll See You in My Dreams (1951)

Air des Bijoux *See* San Francisco (1936)

Alabamy Bound *See* Show Business (1944)

Albany Bound *See* The Great American Broadcast (1941)

Aldonza *See* Man of La Mancha (1972)

Alexander's Ragtime Band *See* Alexander's Ragtime Band (1938)

Alexander's Ragtime Band *See* There's No Business Like Show Business (1954)

Ali Baba Be My Baby *See* Here Come the Girls (1953)

Alice in Wonderland *See* Alice in Wonderland (1951)

Alive and Kicking *See* Best Foot Forward (1943)

All About Love *See* Bundle of Joy (1956)

All Alone *See* Alexander's Ragtime Band (1938)

All Alone Monday *See* Three Little Words (1950)

The All-American Swing *See* My Lucky Star (1938)

All By Myself *See* Blue Skies (1946)

All 'Er Nuthin' *See* Oklahoma! (1955)

All God's Chillun Got Rhythm *See* A Day at the Races (1937)

All Hail, Danville High *See* Summer Holiday (1948)

All Hallow's Eve *See* Meet Me in St. Louis (1944)

All I Do Is Dream of You *See* The Affairs of Dobie Gillis (1953)

All I Do Is Dream Of You *See* The Boy Friend (1971)

All I Do Is Dream of You *See* Broadway Melody of 1936 (1935)

All I Do is Dream of You *See* Singin' in the Rain (1952)

All I Need is the Girl *See* Gypsy (1962)

All I Need Is the Girl *See* Gypsy (1993)

All I Owe Iowa *See* State Fair (1945)

All I Want Is You *See* Seaside Swingers (1965)

All I Want to Do Play the Drums *See* Follow the Leader (1944)

All In Fun *See* Broadway Rhythm (1944)

All In The Cause Of Economy *See* Half a Sixpence (1967)

All My Loving *See* A Hard Day's Night (1964)

All My Tomorrows *See* A Hole in the Head (1959)

All of a Sudden My Heart Sings *See* Anchors Aweigh (1945)

All Of Me *See* Lady Sings the Blues (1972)

All of Me *See* Meet Danny Wilson (1952)

All of You *See* Silk Stockings (1957)

All Out for Freedom *See* Up in Arms (1944)

All Over the World *See* Xanadu (1980)

All That I Am *See* Spinout (1966)

All the Colors of the Rainbow *See* The Girl Most Likely (1957)

All the Things You Are *See* Because You're Mine (1952)

All the Things You Are *See* Broadway Rhythm (1944)

All the Things You Are *See* Till the Clouds Roll By (1946)

All Together Now *See* Yellow Submarine (1968)

Be a Clown *See* The Pirate (1948)

Be a Lion *See* The Wiz (1978)

Be Back Soon *See* Oliver! (1968)

Be Careful, It's My Heart *See* Holiday Inn (1942)

The Be-Gat *See* Finian's Rainbow (1968)

Be Happy *See* The Little Prince (1974)

Be My Baby *See* Dirty Dancing (1987)

Be My Little Baby Bumble Bee *See* By the Light of the Silvery Moon (1953)

Be My Love *See* Because You're Mine (1952)

Be My Love *See* The Toast of New Orleans (1950)

Be Optimistic *See* Little Miss Broadway (1938)

Be Our Guest *See* Beauty and the Beast (1991)

Be Prepared *See* The Lion King (1994)

Beach Ball *See* Pajama Party (1964)

Beach Blanket Bingo *See* Beach Blanket Bingo (1965)

Beach Party *See* Beach Party (1963)

Beach Shack *See* Spinout (1966)

Beale Street Blues *See* Stormy Weather (1943)

Beat Out Dat Rhythm on a Drum *See* Carmen Jones (1954)

Beat Street Breakdown *See* Beat Street (1984)

Beat Street Strut *See* Beat Street (1984)

Beautiful Changes *See* Glorifying the American Girl (1930)

The Beautiful Day *See* Scrooge (1970)

Beautiful Dreamer *See* Harmony Lane (1935)

Beautiful Face, Have a Heart *See* Funny Lady (1975)

Beautiful Faces Need Beautiful Clothes *See* Easter Parade (1948)

Beautiful Girl *See* Going Hollywood (1933)

Beautiful Girl *See* Singin' in the Rain (1952)

Beautiful Lady *See* Two Weeks with Love (1950)

The Beautiful People of Denver *See* The Unsinkable Molly Brown (1964)

Beautiful Spring *See* Easy to Love (1953)

Beautiful Things *See* Doctor Dolittle (1967)

Beauty and the Beast *See* Beauty and the Beast (1991)

Beauty School Dropout *See* Grease (1978)

Because *See* The Great Caruso (1951)

Because *See* Sgt. Pepper's Lonely Hearts Club Band (1978)

Because of You *See* Girls! Girls! Girls! (1962)

Because You're Mine *See* Because You're Mine (1952)

Because You're You *See* Bikini Beach (1964)

Bed of Ashes *See* Knights of the City (1985)

Bedelia *See* Hello, Frisco, Hello (1943)

The Bee *See* Hollywood Canteen (1944)

Been A Long Day *See* How to Succeed in Business without Really Trying (1967)

Before the Parade Passes By *See* Hello, Dolly! (1969)

Begin the Beguine *See* Broadway Melody of 1940 (1940)

Begin the Beguine *See* Night and Day (1946)

Beginner's Luck *See* Frankie and Johnny (1965)

Beginner's Luck *See* Shall We Dance (1937)

Being for the Benefit of Mr. Kite *See* Sgt. Pepper's Lonely Hearts Club Band (1978)

Being in Love *See* The Music Man (1962)

Believe in Yourself *See* The Wiz (1978)

Bell Song *See* I Dream Too Much (1935)

Bella Notte *See* Lady and the Tramp (1955)

Belle *See* Beauty and the Beast (1991)

Belly Up to the Bar, Boys *See* The Unsinkable Molly Brown (1964)

Beloved *See* The Student Prince (1954)

A Bench in the Park *See* King of Jazz (1930)

Berceuse In D Flat, Opus 57 *See* A Song to Remember (1945)

Berry Me Not *See* Panama Hattie (1942)

Besame Mucho *See* Club Havana (1946)

Beside the Rio Tonto *See* Ride 'Em Cowboy (1942)

Best Things *See* Paint Your Wagon (1969)

The Best Things Happen While You're Dancing *See* White Christmas (1954)

The Best Things in Life Are Free *See* Good News (1947)

Betrothal Hymn *See* Song of Norway (1970)

Better Be Ready *See* How to Stuff a Wild Bikini (1965)

Better Git It In Your Soul (The Hot and the Cool) *See* Absolute Beginners (1986)

Better Luck Next Time *See* Easter Parade (1948)

Better Than a Dream *See* Bells are Ringing (1960)

Between You and Me *See* Broadway Melody of 1940 (1940)

Beware *See* Call Out the Marines (1942)

Bewitched, Bothered and Bewildered *See* Pal Joey (1957)

Beyond the Bend *See* It Happened at the World's Fair (1963)

Beyond the Blue Horizon *See* Follow the Boys (1944)

Bibbidy-Bobbidi-Boo *See* Cinderella (1950)

Bidin' My Time *See* Girl Crazy (1943)

Bidin' My Time *See* The Glenn Miller Story (1954)

Bidin' My Time *See* Rhapsody in Blue (1945)

Big Boots *See* G.I. Blues (1960)

Big Chief Hole in the Ground *See* Two Tickets to Broadway (1951)

Big Girls Don't Cry *See* Dirty Dancing (1987)

Big Love, Big Heartache *See* Roustabout (1964)

Big Stuff *See* Dixie Jamboree (1944)

The Bigger the Army and the Navy *See* Follow the Boys (1944)

Bikini Drag *See* Bikini Beach (1964)

Bill *See* The Man I Love (1946)

Bill *See* Show Boat (1936)

Bill *See* Show Boat (1951)

Bill Bailey, Won't You Please Come Home? *See* Papa's Delicate Condition (1963)

Bill Bailey, Won't You Please Come Home? *See* Paradise, Hawaiian Style (1966)

Billie *See* Yankee Doodle Dandy (1942)

Billy-A-Dick *See* For the Boys (1991)

Billy Boy *See* So Dear to My Heart (1949)

Bim, Bam, Boom *See* Bathing Beauty (1944)

The Binge *See* It's Always Fair Weather (1955)

Birds of a Feather *See* The Road to Zanzibar (1941)

Birth of the Blues *See* Birth of the Blues (1941)

Black Bottom *See* A Star is Born (1954)

The Black Hills of Dakota *See* Calamity Jane (1953)

A Blarney from Killarney *See* The Naughty Nineties (1945)

Bless Your Beautiful Hide *See* Seven Brides for Seven Brothers (1954)

Blind Barnabas *See* A Song is Born (1948)

Blind Date *See* Funny Lady (1975)

Blood Money *See* Jesus Christ, Superstar (1973)

Bloody Mary *See* South Pacific (1958)

Bluddle-Uddle-Um-Dum *See* Snow White and the Seven Dwarfs (1937)

Blue Bell *See* The Jolson Story (1946)

The Blue Danube *See* The Great Waltz (1938)

The Blue Danube *See* That Girl from Paris (1936)

Blue Hawaii *See* Waikiki Wedding (1937)

Blue Jay Way *See* Magical Mystery Tour (1967)

Blue Jean Polka *See* Summer Stock (1950)

Blue Monday Blues *See* Rhapsody in Blue (1945)

Blue Moon *See* Arthur (1981)

Blue Moon *See* At the Circus (1939)

Blue Moon *See* Grease (1978)

Blue Moon *See* New York, New York (1977)

Blue Moon *See* This Could Be the Night (1957)

Blue Moon of Kentucky *See* Sweet Dreams (1985)

Blue Skies *See* Alexander's Ragtime Band (1938)

Blue Skies *See* Blue Skies (1946)

Blue Skies *See* Glorifying the American Girl (1930)

Blue Skies *See* The Jazz Singer (1927)

Blue Skies *See* White Christmas (1954)

Blue Skies, Grey Skies *See* Yankee Doodle Dandy (1942)

Blue Suede Shoes *See* G.I. Blues (1960)

Bluebells of Broadway *See* Lucky Me (1954)

Bluebird *See* Nashville (1975)

Blues in the Night *See* Thank Your Lucky Stars (1943)

Bobby's Dream *See* New York, New York (1977)

Boccherini's Minuet in Boogie *See* Higher and Higher (1944)

Body and Soul *See* The Man I Love (1946)

Body Rock *See* Body Rock (1984)

Bojangles of Harlem *See* Swing Time (1936)

Bolero in the Jungle *See* George White's Scandals (1945)

Bombshell From Brooklyn *See* Stage Door Canteen (1943)

Bongo Rock *See* Absolute Beginners (1986)

Bonjour Paris *See* Funny Face (1957)

Bonne Nuit, Good Night *See* Here Comes the Groom (1951)

Boogie Barcarolle *See* You'll Never Get Rich (1941)

Boogie Stop Shuffle (The Rough and the Smooth) *See* Absolute Beginners (1986)

Boogie Woogie Conga *See* Four Jacks and a Jill (1941)

Boom Biddy Boom Boom *See* The Toast of New Orleans (1950)

Bored *See* Kismet (1955)

Born Free *See* Born Free (1966)

Born Reckless *See* Born Reckless (1959)

Born to Hand-Jive *See* Grease (1978)

Born to Love *See* Rappin' (1985)

Bosom Buddies *See* Mame (1974)

Boston Beguine *See* New Faces of 1952 (1954)

Bounce *See* Knights of the City (1985)

Bouncin' the Blues *See* The Barkleys of Broadway (1949)

Bouquet and Lace *See* George White's Scandals (1945)

The Bowery *See* Stars and Stripes Forever (1952)

Boy For Sale *See* Oliver! (1968)

The Boy Friend *See* The Boy Friend (1971)

The Boy Friend *See* Broadway Melody (1929)

The Boy I Left Behind *See* Tonight and Every Night (1945)

A Boy Like Me, A Girl Like You *See* Girls! Girls! Girls! (1962)

A Boy Like That *See* West Side Story (1961)

A Boy Needs a Girl *See* Muscle Beach Party (1964)

The Boy Next Door *See* Meet Me in St. Louis (1944)

Boy, What Love Has Done to Me *See* Girl Crazy (1943)

Brand New Day *See* The Wiz (1978)

Brass Buttons and Epaulets *See* Just Around the Corner (1938)

Brazil *See* The Road to Rio (1947)

Brazilian Boogie *See* Broadway Rhythm (1944)

Breakers Revenge *See* Beat Street (1984)

Breakin...There's No Stopping Us *See* Breakin' (1984)

Breakout *See* Staying Alive (1983)

The Breeze Kissed Your Hair *See* The Cat and the Fiddle (1934)

The Simple Joys of Maidenhood *See* Camelot (1967)

Sin *See* Girl in Gold Boots (1969)

Sin Fe *See* Crossover Dreams (1985)

Since I Kissed My Baby Goodbye *See* You'll Never Get Rich (1941)

Since You've Gone *See* Nashville (1975)

Sincere *See* The Music Man (1962)

Sing a Rainbow *See* Pete Kelly's Blues (1955)

Sing a Song *See* Nashville (1975)

Sing Before Breakfast *See* Broadway Melody of 1936 (1935)

Sing Me a Song That Sells *See* Let's Make Love (1960)

Sing of Spring *See* A Damsel in Distress (1937)

Sing, Sing, Sing *See* The Benny Goodman Story (1955)

Sing to Your Senorita *See* Down Argentine Way (1940)

Sing, You Children *See* Easy Come, Easy Go (1967)

Sing You Sinners *See* I'll Cry Tomorrow (1955)

Sing Your Worries Away *See* Sing Your Worries Away (1942)

Singin' in the Rain *See* Singin' in the Rain (1952)

Singing in the Rain *See* Little Nellie Kelly (1940)

Singing in the Sun *See* Pagan Love Song (1950)

Singlefoot Serenade *See* The Duchess of Idaho (1950)

Sister Suffragette *See* Mary Poppins (1964)

Sisters *See* White Christmas (1954)

Sit Down John *See* 1776 (1972)

Sit Down, You're Rocking the Boat *See* Guys and Dolls (1955)

Sittin' on a Backyard Fence *See* Footlight Parade (1933)

Situation Wise *See* It's Always Fair Weather (1955)

Six Jerks in a Jeep *See* Private Buckaroo (1942)

Six Months Out of Every Year *See* Damn Yankees (1958)

Sixteen, Going on Seventeen *See* The Sound of Music (1965)

Skip to My Lou *See* Meet Me in St. Louis (1944)

Skirts Ahoy! *See* Skirts Ahoy! (1952)

Slap Polka *See* Hit the Ice (1943)

Slap That Bass *See* Shall We Dance (1937)

Sleep, Baby, Sleep in Your Jeep *See* Stage Door Canteen (1943)

Sleep Lagoon *See* Absolute Beginners (1986)

Sleeping Beauty Ballet *See* Meet Me in Las Vegas (1956)

Sleepy Lagoon *See* DuBarry Was a Lady (1943)

Slide Some Oil to Me *See* The Wiz (1978)

Slipped Disc *See* The Benny Goodman Story (1955)

Slow Ride *See* FM (1978)

Slowly but Surely *See* Tickle Me (1965)

Sluefoot *See* Daddy Long Legs (1955)

Slumming on Park Avenue *See* On the Avenue (1937)

The Small House of Uncle Thomas *See* The King and I (1956)

Small Talk *See* The Pajama Game (1957)

Small Towns Are Smile Towns *See* Small Town Girl (1953)

Small World *See* Gypsy (1962)

Smash the Mirror *See* Tommy (1975)

Smile Away Each Rainy Day *See* Darling Lili (1970)

Smiles *See* For Me and My Gal (1942)

Smoke Gets in Your Eyes *See* Lovely to Look At (1952)

Smoke Gets in Your Eyes *See* Roberta (1935)

Smoke Gets in Your Eyes *See* Till the Clouds Roll By (1946)

Smorgasbord *See* Spinout (1966)

Snack Attack *See* Rappin' (1985)

Snookey Ookums *See* Easter Parade (1948)

Snooks *See* Everybody Sing (1938)

Snow *See* White Christmas (1954)

So Am I *See* Lady Be Good (1941)

So Dear To My Heart *See* So Dear to My Heart (1949)

So In Love *See* Kiss Me Kate (1953)

So In Love *See* Wonder Man (1945)

So Long, Dearie *See* Hello, Dolly! (1969)

So Long, Farewell *See* The Sound of Music (1965)

So Long, Honey Lamb *See* Funny Lady (1975)

So Long Mary *See* Yankee Doodle Dandy (1942)

So-Long, Oo-Long *See* Three Little Words (1950)

So Long Sarah Jane *See* I Dood It (1943)

So Near and Yet So Far *See* You'll Never Get Rich (1941)

So the Bluebirds and the Blackbirds Got Together *See* King of Jazz (1930)

So This Is Love *See* Cinderella (1950)

So What? *See* Absolute Beginners (1986)

So You Wanted to See the Wizard *See* The Wiz (1978)

Sobbin' Women *See* Seven Brides for Seven Brothers (1954)

Softly as in a Morning Sunrise *See* New Moon (1940)

Softly, as in a Morning Sunrise *See* Deep in My Heart (1954)

Sold My Soul To Rock 'n' Roll *See* The Rose (1979)

Soldier's Chorus *See* Maytime (1937)

Soldiers of Fortune *See* Girl of the Golden West (1938)

Soldiers of Fortune Reprise *See* Girl of the Golden West (1938)

Solid Potato Salad *See* Broadway Rhythm (1944)

Soliloquies *See* South Pacific (1958)

Soliloquy *See* Carousel (1956)

Soliloquy For Three Heads *See* The Inspector General (1949)

Solitary Seminole *See* Moon over Miami (1941)

The Solitary Wanderer *See* Song of Norway (1970)

Solvejg's Song—Norwegian National Anthem *See* Song of Norway (1970)

Sombody Loves Me *See* Pete Kelly's Blues (1955)

Some Day My Prince Will Come *See* Snow White and the Seven Dwarfs (1937)

Some Enchanted Evening *See* South Pacific (1958)

Some Fun Now *See* Little Shop of Horrors (1986)

Some Kind-a Wonderful *See* Dirty Dancing (1987)

Some Like You *See* My Dream Is Yours (1949)

Some of These Days *See* All That Jazz (1979)

Some of These Days *See* Broadway Melody of 1938 (1937)

Some of These Days *See* Follow the Boys (1944)

Some of These Days *See* Rose Marie (1936)

Some Other Time *See* Step Lively (1944)

Some People *See* Gypsy (1962)

Some People *See* Gypsy (1993)

Somebody Loves Me *See* Broadway Rhythm (1944)

Somebody Loves Me *See* Lullaby of Broadway (1951)

Somebody Loves Me *See* Rhapsody in Blue (1945)

Somebody Super Like You *See* Phantom of the Paradise (1974)

Somebody's Eyes *See* Footloose (1984)

Somebody's Walkin' In My Dreams *See* Doll Face (1946)

Someday I'll Find You *See* Star! (1968)

Someday Soon *See* Bundle of Joy (1956)

Someone Belonging to Someone *See* Staying Alive (1983)

Someone Loves You After All *See* The Great Ziegfeld (1936)

Someone to Care for Me *See* Three Smart Girls (1936)

Someone to Love *See* Follies Girl (1943)

Someone to Love *See* Holiday in Mexico (1946)

Someone To Watch Over Me *See* Rhapsody in Blue (1945)

Someone to Watch Over Me *See* Star! (1968)

Someone to Watch Over Me *See* Young at Heart (1954)

Someplace on Anywhere Road *See* Riding High (1950)

Somethin' Real Special *See* The Farmer Takes a Wife (1953)

Something Better *See* The Muppet Movie (1979)

Something Good *See* The Sound of Music (1965)

Something in Your Smile *See* Doctor Dolittle (1967)

Something Sort of Grandish *See* Finian's Rainbow (1968)

Something There *See* Beauty and the Beast (1991)

Something to Dream About *See* Born Reckless (1959)

Something to Remember You By *See* The Band Wagon (1953)

Something to Sing About *See* Something to Sing About (1936)

Something Wonderful *See* The King and I (1956)

Something's Coming *See* West Side Story (1961)

Something's Got To Give *See* Daddy Long Legs (1955)

Sometimes I Feel Like a Motherless Child *See* Way Down South (1939)

Sometimes I'm Happy *See* Hit the Deck (1955)

Sometimes in the Night *See* Thunder Alley (1985)

Somewhere *See* The Old Curiosity Shop (1975)

Somewhere *See* West Side Story (1961)

(Somewhere) Over the Rainbow *See* The Wizard of Oz (1939)

Somewhere There's Someone *See* A Star is Born (1954)

The Son of a Gun Who Pick on Uncle Sam *See* Panama Hattie (1942)

Sonata In B Minor *See* Song Without End (1960)

The Song Angels Sing *See* Because You're Mine (1952)

A Song is Born *See* A Song is Born (1948)

Song O' My Heart *See* Song O' My Heart (1929)

Song of Freedom *See* Holiday Inn (1942)

Song of India *See* New York, New York (1977)

The Song of Norway *See* Song of Norway (1970)

Song of the Bandoleros *See* Rogue of the Rio Grande (1930)

Song of the Bayou *See* The Toast of New Orleans (1950)

Song of the Dawn *See* King of Jazz (1930)

Song of the Enchilada Man *See* Scared Stiff (1953)

Song of the King *See* The King and I (1956)

Song of the Metronome *See* Second Fiddle (1939)

Song of the Musketeers *See* The Three Musketeers (1939)

Song of the Rodeo *See* Born Reckless (1959)

The Song of the Setting Sun *See* Whoopee! (1930)

Song of the Shrimp *See* Girls! Girls! Girls! (1962)

Songs of Life *See* The Jazz Singer (1980)

Songwriter *See* Songwriter (1984)

Sonny Boy *See* Jolson Sings Again (1949)

Soon as I Get Home *See* The Wiz (1978)

Sooner or Later *See* Dick Tracy (1990)

Sophistication *See* Can't Stop the Music (1980)

The Sorcerer's Apprentice *See* Fantasia (1940)

A Sorry Phoney *See* The Wiz (1978)

The Sound of Music *See* The Sound of Music (1965)

The Sound of the City *See* Can't Stop the Music (1980)

Sourwood Mountain *See* So Dear to My Heart (1949)

South America, Take It Away *See* New York, New York (1977)

South American Way *See* Down Argentine Way (1940)

Southland *See* Yes, Sir, Mr. Bones (1951)

Spaghetti *See* Marco (1973)

The Spaniard Who Blighted My Life *See* The Jolson Story (1946)

Alternate Formats Index

The **Alternate Formats Index** lists videos that are available in formats that either enhance the popular VHS format (letterbox, captioned) or provide an alternative to it (Beta, 8mm, Laserdisc, CD-I). Two of these formats, Laserdisc (with CD-I) and captioned, used to have their own indexes within these pages. They have been combined with each other and previously non-indexed formats to provide a complete list of alternative and new technologies. Many laserdiscs provide bonuses such as extra footage, interviews with cast members, or the original theater trailer. The Letterbox format is designed to give the panoramic view of a theater viewing. Beta was on the losing end of the format wars (won by VHS) at the beginning of the video era. Many older titles are available in Beta, but new releases generally aren't.

Beta

All-American Murder
All Creatures Great and Small
All Dogs Go to Heaven
All God's Children
All in a Night's Work
All Mine to Give
All My Good Countrymen
All My Sons
All Night Long
All Night Long/Smile Please
All of Me
All Over Town
All Quiet on the Western Front
All Screwed Up
All That Jazz
All the Kind Strangers
All the King's Men
...All the Marbles
All the President's Men
All the Right Moves
All the Way, Boys
All the Young Men
All This and Heaven Too
All You Need Is Cash
Allan Quatermain and the Lost City of Gold
Allegheny Uprising
Alley Cat
Alligator
Alligator Alley
The Allnighter
Allonsanfan
All's Fair
Almost Angels
Almost Human
An Almost Perfect Affair
Almost Royal Family
Almost You
Aloha, Bobby and Rose
Aloha Summer
Alone Against Rome
Alone in the Dark
Alone in the T-Shirt Zone
Along Came Jones
Along the Great Divide
Along the Sundown Trail
Alpha Beta
The Alpha Incident
Alphabet City
The Alphabet Murders
Alphaville
Alpine Fire
Alsino and the Condor
Altered States
Alternative
Alvarez Kelly
Alvin Purple
Alvin Rides Again
Always
Amadeus
The Amateur
Amateur Night
Amazing Adventure
The Amazing Dobermans
Amazing Grace & Chuck
The Amazing Howard Hughes
Amazing Mr. Blunden
The Amazing Mr. X
The Amazing Spider-Man
The Amazing Transplant
Amazon Jail
Amazon Women on the Moon
The Amazons
Amazons
The Ambassador
Amber Waves
Ambition
Ambush at Tomahawk Gap
The Ambush Murders
The Ambushers
America at the Movies
America First
America/The Fall of Babylon
America 3000
The American Angels: Baptism of Blood
American Anthem
American Aristocracy
American Autobahn
American Boyfriends
An American Christmas Carol
American Commandos
American Dream
American Dreamer
American Empire
American Flyers
The American Friend
American Gigolo
American Gothic
American Graffiti
An American in Paris
American Justice
American Kickboxer 1
American Nightmare
American Ninja
American Ninja 2: The Confrontation
American Ninja 3: Blood Hunt
American Ninja 4: The Annihilation
American Pluck
The American Scream
An American Tail
An American Tail: Fievel Goes West
American Tickler
An American Werewolf in London
Americana
The Americano
The Americano/Variety
Americathon
Amin: The Rise and Fall
The Amityville Horror
Amityville 2: The Possession
Amityville 3: The Demon
Among the Cinders
The Amsterdam Connection
The Amsterdam Kill
Amsterdamned
Amy
Anatomy of a Murder
Anatomy of a Psycho
Anatomy of Terror
Anchors Aweigh
And God Created Woman
And God Said to Cain
And Hope to Die
And I Alone Survived
And Justice for All
And Nothing But the Truth
And Now for Something Completely Different
And Now My Love
And Now the Screaming Starts
And Soon the Darkness
And the Ship Sails On
And Then There Were None
And Then You Die
The Anderson Tapes
The Andersonville Trial
Andre
Androcles and the Lion
Android
The Andromeda Strain
Andy Griffith Show
Andy Hardy Gets Spring Fever
Andy Hardy Meets Debutante
Andy Hardy's Double Life
Andy Hardy's Private Secretary
Andy Warhol's Bad
Andy Warhol's Dracula
Andy Warhol's Frankenstein
Angel
Angel 3: The Final Chapter
Angel City
Angel Heart
Angel in a Taxi
Angel of Death
Angel of H.E.A.T.
Angel on My Shoulder
Angel Town
Angela
Angelo My Love
Angel's Brigade
Angels Die Hard
Angels Hard as They Come
Angels of the City
Angels Over Broadway
Angels with Dirty Faces
AngKor: Cambodia Express
Angry Harvest
Angry Joe Bass
The Angry Red Planet
Anguish
Animal Behavior
Animal Called Man
Animal Crackers
Animal Farm
Animal Instincts 2
Anita, Dances of Vice
The Ann Jillian Story
Ann Vickers
Anna
Anna Christie
Anna Karenina
Anna to the Infinite Power
Annabel Takes a Tour/Maid's Night Out
Annapolis
The Annapolis Story
Anne of Avonlea
Anne of Green Gables
Annie
Annie Hall
Annie Oakley
The Annihilators
Another Country
Another 48 Hrs.
Another Man, Another Chance
Another Time, Another Place
Another Way
Another Woman
Antarctica
Anthony Adverse
Antonia and Jane
Antonio
Antony and Cleopatra
Ants
Any Man's Death
Any Wednesday
Any Which Way You Can
Anzacs: The War Down Under
Anzio
Apache
Apache Chief
Apache Kid's Escape
Apache Rose
Aparajito
The Apartment
Apartment Zero
The Ape
A*P*E*
The Ape Man
Apocalypse Now
The Appaloosa
The Apple
The Apple Dumpling Gang
The Apple Dumpling Gang Rides Again
The Applegates
The Appointment
Appointment in Honduras
Appointment with Crime
Appointment with Death
Appointment with Fear
Apprentice to Murder
The Apprenticeship of Duddy Kravitz
April Fools
April Fool's Day
Arabesque
Arabian Nights
Arachnophobia
Arcade
Archer: The Fugitive from the Empire
Archer's Adventure
Are You in the House Alone?
Are You Lonesome Tonight
Aria
Arizona
Arizona Badman
Arizona Bound
Arizona Cowboy
Arizona Days
Arizona Gunfighter
Arizona Kid
Arizona Raiders
Arizona Roundup
Arizona Stagecoach
Arizona Terror
Arizona Whirlwind
Ark of the Sun God
Armed and Dangerous
Armed Response
Armored Command
Army Brats
Army of Darkness
Arnold
Around the World
Around the World in 80 Days
Around the World Under the Sea
The Arousers
The Arrangement
Arrest Bulldog Drummond
Arrowhead
Arrowsmith
Arsenal
Arsenic and Old Lace
Arthur
Arthur 2: On the Rocks
Arthur's Hallowed Ground
Artist's Studio Secrets
As Good as Dead
As Is
As Summers Die
As You Desire Me
As You Like It
As You Were
Ashanti, Land of No Mercy
Ashes and Diamonds
Aspen Extreme
The Asphalt Jungle
The Asphyx
Assassin
Assassin of Youth
Assassination
Assassination of Trotsky
The Assassination Run
Assault
The Assault
Assault and Matrimony
Assault of the Killer Bimbos
Assault of the Party Nerds
Assault of the Rebel Girls
Assault on Agathon
Assault on Precinct 13
Assault with a Deadly Weapon
The Assignment
Assignment Skybolt
The Assisi Underground
The Associate
The Association
Assunta Spina
The Astro-Zombies
Asylum
Asylum of Satan
At Close Range
At Gunpoint
At Play in the Fields of the Lord
At Sword's Point
At the Circus
At the Earth's Core
At War with the Army
Atlantic City
Atom Age Vampire
The Atomic Cafe
Atomic Submarine
Ator the Fighting Eagle
Attack Force Z
Attack of the Beast Creatures
Attack of the 50 Foot Woman
Attack of the Robots
Attack of the Swamp Creature
Attack Squadron
The Attic
Attica
Au Revoir Les Enfants
Audrey Rose
Augustine of Hippo
Auntie
Auntie Mame
The Aurora Encounter
Author! Author!
The Autobiography of Miss Jane Pittman
Autopsy
Autumn Born
Autumn Leaves
Autumn Sonata
Avalanche
Avalon
Avenging Angel
Avenging Conscience
Avenging Disco Godfather
Avenging Force
The Average Woman
The Aviator
The Awakening
Awakening of Candra
Awakenings
Away All Boats
The Awful Truth
Babar: The Movie
Babe Ruth Story
Babes in Arms
Babes in Toyland
Babes on Broadway
Babette's Feast
The Baby
Baby Boom
Baby Doll
Baby Face
Baby Face Harry Langdon
Baby It's You
Baby Love
Baby on Board
Baby ... Secret of the Lost Legend
Baby Snakes: The Complete Version
Baby, Take a Bow
Baby, the Rain Must Fall
The Babylon Story from "Intolerance"
The Babysitter
The Bachelor and the Bobby-Soxer
Bachelor Bait
Bachelor Mother
Bachelor Party
Back from Eternity
Back Roads
Back Street
Back to Back
Back to Bataan
Back to School
Back to the Beach
Back to the Future
Back to the Future, Part 2
Back to the Future, Part 3
Backdraft
Backfield in Motion
Backfire
Backlash
Backstairs
Backwoods
Bad Blood
Bad Boy
Bad Boys
Bad Bunch
B.A.D. Cats
Bad Channels
Bad Company
Bad Dreams
Bad Georgia Road
Bad Girls Dormitory
Bad Girls in the Movies

Bad Influence
Bad Jim
Bad Lands
Bad Man of Deadwood
Bad Manners
Bad Man's River
Bad Medicine
The Bad News Bears
The Bad News Bears Go to Japan
The Bad News Bears in Breaking Training
The Bad Seed
The Bad Sleep Well
Badge of the Assassin
Badge 373
Badlands
Badman's Territory
Badmen of Nevada
Bagdad Cafe
Bail Jumper
Bail Out
Baja Oklahoma
Baker's Hawk
The Baker's Wife
Bakery/Grocery Clerk
Balboa
The Balcony
Ball of Fire
Ballad in Blue
Ballad of a Gunfighter
Ballad of a Soldier
Ballad of Cable Hogue
Ballad of Gregorio Cortez
The Balloonatic/One Week
Baltic Deputy
The Baltimore Bullet
Bambi
Bananas
Band of Outsiders
Band of the Hand
The Band Wagon
Bandit Queen
Bandits
Bandits of Orgosolo
Bandolero!
Bang Bang Kid
Bang the Drum Slowly
The Bank Dick
The Banker
Banzai Runner
Bar-20
Barabbas
Barbarella
Barbarian and the Geisha
Barbarian Queen
The Barbarians
Barbarosa
Barbary Coast
The Barber Shop
The Barcelona Kill
Bare Hunt
Bare Knees
Bare Knuckles
The Barefoot Contessa
The Barefoot Executive
Barefoot in Athens
Barefoot in the Park
Barfly
The Bargain
The Barkleys of Broadway
Barnaby and Me
Barnum
The Baron and the Kid
Baron Munchausen
Baron of Arizona
Barracuda
Barry Lyndon
Barry McKenzie Holds His Own
Basic Instinct
Basic Training
Basket Case
Basket Case 2
The Bat
The Bat People
Bat 21
Bataan
Batman
*batteries not included
Battle Beneath the Earth
Battle Beyond the Stars
Battle Cry
Battle for the Planet of the Apes
Battle Hell
The Battle of Algiers
The Battle of Blood Island
Battle of Britain
Battle of China
The Battle of El Alamein
Battle of Elderbush Gulch
The Battle of Russia
The Battle of San Pietro
Battle of the Bulge
Battle of the Bullies
Battle of the Eagles
The Battle of the Japan Sea
The Battle of the Sexes
Battle of Valiant
Battleforce
Battleground
The Battleship Potemkin
Battlestar Galactica
Battling Bunyon
Battling Marshal
Battling Orioles
Battling Outlaws
Battling with Buffalo Bill
The Bawdy Adventures of Tom Jones
The Bay Boy
Bayou Romance
Be My Valentine, Charlie Brown
Beach Blanket Bingo
Beach Girls
Beach House
Beach Party
Beachcomber
Beaches
Beaks: The Movie
Beanstalk
The Bear
Bear Island
The Beast
The Beast from 20,000 Fathoms
Beast in the Cellar
Beast of the Yellow Night
The Beast Within
Beastmaster
Beasts
The Beat
Beat Street
Beat the Devil
Beatlemania! The Movie
Beatrice
Beau Brummel
Beau Geste
Beau Pere
Beau Revel
Beauty and the Beast
Beauty on the Beach
Bebe's Kids
Because of the Cats
Becket
Becky Sharp
Bed and Sofa
Bedazzled
Bedford Incident
Bedknobs and Broomsticks
Bedlam
Bedroom Eyes
The Bedroom Window
Bedtime for Bonzo
Bedtime Story
Beer
The Bees
Beethoven's Nephew
Beetlejuice
Before I Hang
Before Morning
Beggars in Ermine
The Beguiled
Behave Yourself!
Behind Enemy Lines
Behind the Rising Sun
Behold a Pale Horse
The Being
Being There
Bela Lugosi Meets a Brooklyn Gorilla
Bela Lugosi Scrapbook
Belfast Assassin
The Believers
Belizaire the Cajun
Bell, Book and Candle
Bell Diamond
Bell from Hell
The Bell Jar
Bellamy
The Bellboy
The Belle of New York
Belle Starr
The Belles of St. Trinian's
Bellhop/The Noon Whistle
Bellissimo: Images of the Italian Cinema
Bellman and True
Bells are Ringing
Bells of Rosarita
The Bells of St. Mary's
Bells of San Angelo
Beloved Enemy
The Beloved Rogue
Below the Belt
Below the Border
The Belstone Fox
Ben
Ben-Hur
Ben Turpin: An Eye for an Eye
Bend of the River
Beneath Arizona Skies/Paradise Canyon
Beneath the Planet of the Apes
Beneath the 12-Mile Reef
Benefit of the Doubt
The Beniker Gang
Benji
Benji the Hunted
Benji's Very Own Christmas Story
Benny & Joon
The Benny Goodman Story
Benny Hill's Crazy World
Bergonzi Hand
The Berlin Affair
Berlin Alexanderplatz
Berlin Express
Berlin Tunnel 21
Bernadette
Berserk!
Berserker
Bert Rigby, You're a Fool
Best Defense
Best Enemies
Best Foot Forward
Best Friends
Best Kept Secrets
Best Legs in the 8th Grade
The Best Little Girl in the World
The Best Little Whorehouse in Texas
The Best Man
The Best of Abbott & Costello Live
The Best of Bogart
Best of Bugs Bunny & Friends
Best of Eddie Murphy
Best of Ernie Kovacs
Best of the Badmen
Best of the Best
The Best of the Kenny Everett Video Show
The Best of the Two Ronnies
The Best of Times
Best Revenge
Best Seller
The Best Way
The Best Years of Our Lives
Bethune
Betrayal
Betrayal from the East
Betrayed
The Betsy
Betsy's Wedding
Better Late Than Never
Better Off Dead
Betty Blue
Between Friends
Between God, the Devil & a Winchester
Between Men
Between the Lines
Between Two Women
Between Wars
Beulah Land
Beverly Hills Brats
Beverly Hills Cop
Beverly Hills Cop 2
Beverly Hills Cop 3
Beverly Hills Knockouts
Beverly Hills Madam
Beverly Hills Vamp
Bewitched
Beyond Atlantis
Beyond Dream's Door
Beyond Evil
Beyond Fear
Beyond Innocence
Beyond Reason
Beyond Reasonable Doubt
Beyond the Door
Beyond the Door 2
Beyond the Limit
Beyond the Next Mountain
Beyond the Poseidon Adventure
Beyond the Silhouette
Beyond the Stars
Beyond the Time Barrier
Beyond the Valley of the Dolls
Beyond the Walls
Beyond Therapy
Beyond Tomorrow
The Bible...In the Beginning
The Bicycle Thief
Big
Big Bad John
Big Bad Mama
Big Bad Mama 2
The Big Bet
The Big Bird Cage
The Big Blue
Big Boss
The Big Brawl
The Big Bus
Big Business
The Big Bust Out
Big Calibre
The Big Cat
Big Chase
The Big Chill
Big Combo
The Big Country
The Big Crimewave
Big Deadly Game
Big Deal on Madonna Street
The Big Doll House
The Big Easy
The Big Fix
Big Foot
The Big Gag
The Big Grab
A Big Hand for the Little Lady
The Big Heat
The Big Hurt
Big Jake
The Big Lift
Big Man on Campus
Big Meat Eater
Big Mo
Big Mouth
The Big Picture
The Big Push
Big Red
The Big Red One
Big Score
Big Shots
Big Show
The Big Sky
The Big Sleep
Big Steal
Big Store
Big Street
The Big Switch
Big Top Pee Wee
Big Town
Big Trail
Big Trees
Big Trouble
Big Trouble in Little China
Big Valley
Big Wednesday
Biggles
Bikini Beach
Bikini Island
Bilitis
Bill
Bill and Coo
Bill & Ted's Excellent Adventure
A Bill of Divorcement
Billie
The Billion Dollar Hobo
A Billion for Boris
Billy Bathgate
Billy Budd
Billy Galvin
Billy Jack
Billy Liar
Billy: Portrait of a Street Kid
Billy the Kid in Texas
Billy the Kid Returns
Billy the Kid Versus Dracula
Billyboy
Biloxi Blues
Bim/Dream of the Wild Horses
Bimini Code
Bingo Inferno
Bingo Long Traveling All-Stars & Motor Kings
Bio Hazard
The Bionic Woman
The Birch Interval
Bird
Bird of Paradise
Bird on a Wire
The Bird with the Crystal Plumage
The Birds
Birds & the Bees
Birds of Paradise
Birds of Prey
Birdy
Birgitt Haas Must Be Killed
Birthday Boy
The Bishop's Wife
The Bitch
Bite the Bullet
Bits and Pieces
Bitter Harvest
Bitter Sweet
Bitter Vengeance
Bittersweet Love
Bizarre
Bizarre Bizarre
Black and White in Color
Black Arrow
The Black Arrow
Black Beauty
Black Beauty/Courage of Black Beauty
Black Belt Jones
Black Bikers from Hell
Black Bird
Black Box Affair
Black Caesar
Black Cat
Black Christmas
Black Cobra
The Black Cobra
The Black Coin
Black Devil Doll from Hell

The Black Dragons
Black Eagle
Black Eliminator
Black Force
Black Fury
Black Gestapo
Black Glove
Black Godfather
Black Hand
The Black Hole
Black Ice
The Black Klansman
The Black Lash
Black Lemons
Black Like Me
Black Magic
Black Magic Terror
The Black Maid
The Black Marble
Black Market Rustlers
Black Moon Rising
Black Narcissus
Black Oak Conspiracy
Black Orchid
Black Orpheus
Black Panther
The Black Pirate
Black Pit of Dr. M
Black Rain
Black Rainbow
The Black Raven
The Black Room
Black Roses
Black Sabbath
Black Samurai
Black Shampoo
Black Sheep
Black Sister's Revenge
The Black Six
The Black Stallion
The Black Stallion Returns
Black Sunday
Black Terrorist
Black Tights
Black Tower
Black Vampire
Black Venus
Black Werewolf
Black Widow
The Black Windmill
Blackbeard the Pirate
Blackbeard's Ghost
Blackboard Jungle
Blackenstein
Blackmail
Blackout
The Blacksmith/The Balloonatic
The Blacksmith/The Cops
Blacula
Blade
A Blade in the Dark
Blade Master
Blade of the Ripper
Blade Runner
Blades
Blades of Courage
Bladestorm
Blaise Pascal
Blake of Scotland Yard
Blame It on Rio
Blame It on the Bellboy
Blame It on the Night
The Blasphemer
Blastfighter
Blaze
Blazing Guns
Blazing Saddles
Bleak House
Bless the Beasts and Children
Blind Ambition
Blind Date
Blind Fear
Blind Fists of Bruce
Blind Fools
Blind Fury
Blind Husbands
Blind Justice
Blind Man's Bluff
Blind Rage
Blinded by the Light
Blindside
Bliss
The Blob
Block-heads
Blockhouse
Blonde Cobra/The Doctor's Dream
Blonde in Black Leather
Blonde Savage
Blonde Venus
Blood Alley
Blood and Black Lace
Blood and Guns
Blood and Sand
Blood and Sand/Son of the Sheik
Blood and Steel
Blood at Sundown
Blood Beach
Blood Beast Terror
Blood Bride
Blood Brothers
Blood Cult
Blood Debts
Blood Diner
Blood Feast
Blood Feud
Blood for a Silver Dollar
Blood Freak
Blood Frenzy
Blood Hook
Blood In...Blood Out: Bound by Honor
Blood Legacy
Blood Lust
Blood Mania
Blood Money
Blood Money: The Story of Clinton and Nadine
The Blood of a Poet
Blood of Dracula's Castle
The Blood of Heroes
The Blood of Others
Blood of the Vampire
The Blood on Satan's Claw
Blood on the Moon
Blood Orgy of the She-Devils
Blood Rage
Blood Red
Blood Relations
Blood Salvage
Blood Screams
Blood Simple
Blood Sisters
Blood Song
The Blood Spattered Bride
Blood Tide
Blood Ties
Blood Tracks
Blood Voyage
Blood Wedding
Bloodbath
Bloodbath at the House of Death
Bloodbeat
Bloodfist
Bloodfist 2
Bloodhounds of Broadway
Bloodknot
Bloodlink
Bloodlust: Subspecies 3
Bloodmoon
Bloodshed
Bloodspell
Bloodsport
Bloodstalkers
Bloodstone
The Bloodsuckers
Bloodsuckers from Outer Space
Bloodsucking Freaks
Bloodsucking Pharoahs of Pittsburgh
Bloody Avenger
Bloody Birthday
The Bloody Fight
Bloody Mama
Bloody Moon
Bloody New Year
Bloody Wednesday
Blossoms in the Dust
The Blot
Blow Out
Blow-Up
Blown Away
The Blue and the Gray
The Blue Angel
The Blue Bird
Blue Blazes Rawden
Blue Blood
Blue Canadian Rockies
Blue Chips
Blue City
Blue Collar
Blue Country
Blue Fin
Blue Fire Lady
Blue Hawaii
Blue Heaven
Blue Iguana
Blue Jeans
The Blue Lagoon
The Blue Light
The Blue Max
Blue Money
Blue Monkey
Blue Movies
Blue Paradise
Blue Ribbon Babes
Blue Skies Again
Blue Steel
Blue Sunshine
Blue Thunder
Blue Velvet
The Blue Yonder
Bluebeard
Blueberry Hill
The Blues Brothers
The Blum Affair
Blume in Love
Boarding House
Boarding School
The Boat is Full
The Boatniks
Bob & Carol & Ted & Alice
Bob Dylan: Don't Look Back
Bob le Flambeur
Bobbie Jo and the Outlaw
Bobby Deerfield
Bobo
Boccaccio '70
Body & Soul
Body Beat
The Body Beneath
Body Chemistry
Body Count
Body Double
Body Heat
The Body in the Library
Body Language
Body Moves
Body of Evidence
Body Parts
Body Rock
Body Slam
The Body Snatcher
The Bodyguard
Bog
Boggy Creek II
Bogie: The Last Hero
Bohemian Girl
Boiling Point
The Bold Caballero
The Boldest Job in the West
Bolero
Bomb at 10:10
Bombardier
Bombay Talkie
Bombs Away!
Bombshell
Bon Voyage!
Bon Voyage, Charlie Brown
The Bone Yard
The Bonfire of the Vanities
Bonjour Tristesse
Bonnie & Clyde
Bonnie Scotland
Bonnie's Kids
The Boogey Man
Boogey Man 2
Boom Town
Boomerang
The Boost
Boot Hill
Boots & Saddles
Bopha!
Bordello
The Border
Border Badmen
Border Devils
Border Feud
Border Rangers
Border Romance
Border Roundup
Border Saddlemates
Border Shootout
Border Street
Borderline
Bordertown Gunfighters
B.O.R.N.
Born Again
Born American
Born Free
Born in East L.A.
Born Innocent
Born Invincible
Born Killer
Born Losers
Born of Fire
Born on the Fourth of July
Born to Be Bad
Born to Be Wild
Born to Dance
Born to Kill
Born to Race
Born to Ride
Born to Run
Born Yesterday
Boss Cowboy
Boss Foreman
The Boss Is Served
Boss of Big Town
Boss of Rawhide
Boss' Son
The Boss' Wife
The Boston Strangler
The Bostonians
Botany Bay
Bottoms Up
Boudu Saved from Drowning
Boulevard Nights
Bound for Glory
The Bounty
Bounty Hunters
The Bounty Man
Bowery at Midnight
Bowery at Midnight/Dick Tracy vs. Cueball
Boxcar Bertha
The Boxer and Death
A Boy and His Dog
A Boy Called Hate
Boy, Did I Get a Wrong Number!
The Boy God
Boy in Blue
The Boy in the Plastic Bubble
A Boy Named Charlie Brown
Boy of Two Worlds
Boy Takes Girl
Boy! What a Girl
The Boy Who Could Fly
The Boy Who Left Home to Find Out About the Shivers
The Boy with the Green Hair
Boyfriends & Girlfriends
The Boys from Brazil
The Boys in Company C
The Boys in the Band
The Boys Next Door
Boys of the City
Boys Town
Boyz N the Hood
Braddock: Missing in Action 3
The Brady Bunch Movie
Brady's Escape
The Brain
Brain Damage
Brain Dead
Brain Donors
The Brain from Planet Arous
Brain of Blood
The Brain That Wouldn't Die
The Brainiac
Brainstorm
Brainwaves
Bram Stoker's Dracula
Brand New Life
Brand of Hate
Brand of the Outlaws
Branded a Coward
Brannigan
Brass Target
The Bravados
The Brave Bunch
The Brave One
Braveheart
Brazil
Break of Hearts
Breakdown
Breaker! Breaker!
Breaker Morant
Breakfast at Tiffany's
The Breakfast Club
Breakfast in Hollywood
Breakfast in Paris
Breakheart Pass
Breakin'
Breakin' 2: Electric Boogaloo
Breakin' Through
Breaking All the Rules
Breaking Away
Breaking Glass
Breaking In
Breaking the Ice
Breaking Up
Breaking Up Is Hard to Do
Breaking with Old Ideas
Breakout
Breakthrough
Breathless
A Breed Apart
Breed of the Border
Brewster McCloud
Brewster's Millions
Brian's Song
The Bride
The Bride & the Beast
The Bride Is Much Too Beautiful
The Bride of Frankenstein
Bride of Re-Animator
Bride of the Monster
The Bride Walks Out
Brides of the Beast
The Brides Wore Blood
Brideshead Revisited
The Bridge at Remagen
The Bridge of San Luis Rey
The Bridge on the River Kwai
The Bridge to Nowhere
A Bridge Too Far
The Bridges at Toko-Ri
Brief Encounter
A Brief History of Time
The Brig
Brigadoon
Bright Eyes
Bright Lights, Big City
Bright Smiler
Brighton Beach Memoirs
Brighton Strangler

The Brighton Strangler/Before Dawn
Brighty of the Grand Canyon
Brimstone & Treacle
Bringing Up Baby
Brink of Life
Brink's Job
Britannia Hospital
A Brivele der Mamen
Broadcast News
Broadway Bill
Broadway Danny Rose
The Broadway Drifter
Broadway Melody
Broadway Melody of 1936
Broadway Melody of 1938
Broadway Melody of 1940
Broadway to Cheyenne
Broken Arrow
Broken Blossoms
Broken Lance
The Broken Mask
Broken Strings
Bronco Billy
Bronson Lee, Champion
The Bronx Executioner
The Brood
The Brother from Another Planet
Brother John
Brother Orchid
Brother Sun, Sister Moon
The Brotherhood
Brotherhood of Death
The Brotherhood of Satan
Brotherly Love
The Brothers Karamazov
Brothers Lionheart
Brothers of the West
Brothers O'Toole
The Browning Version
Brubaker
Bruce Lee: Curse of the Dragon
Bruce Lee Fights Back From the Grave
Bruce Lee's Ways of Kung Fu
Bruce Le's Greatest Revenge
Bruce Li in New Guinea
Bruce the Superhero
Bruce's Deadly Fingers
Bruce's Fists of Vengeance
The Brute Man
The Buccaneer
Buck and the Preacher
Buck Privates
Buck Rogers Conquers the Universe
Buck Rogers in the 25th Century
A Bucket of Blood
Buckeye and Blue
Buckskin Frontier
Bucktown
Bud and Lou
Buddha Assassinator
Buddy Buddy
The Buddy Holly Story
The Buddy System
Buffalo Bill
Buffalo Bill & the Indians
Buffalo Bill Rides Again
Buffalo Rider
Buffalo Stampede
Bug
Bugs & Daffy: The Wartime Cartoons
The Bugs Bunny/Road Runner Movie
Bugsy
Bugsy Malone
Bull Durham
Bulldance
Bulldog Courage
Bulldog Drummond
Bulldog Drummond Comes Back
Bulldog Drummond Escapes
Bulldog Drummond in Africa/ Arrest Bulldog Drummond
Bulldog Drummond's Bride
Bulldog Drummond's Peril
Bulldog Drummond's Revenge/ Bulldog Drummond's Peril
Bulldog Drummond's Secret Police
Bulldog Edition
Bulldog Jack
Bullet for Sandoval
A Bullet for the General
A Bullet Is Waiting
Bulletproof
Bullets or Ballots
Bullfighters
Bullies
Bullitt
Bullshot
Bummer
Bunco
Bundle of Joy
A Bunny's Tale
The 'Burbs
Burden of Dreams
Burglar
Burial Ground
Buried Alive
Burke & Wills
Burlesque of Carmen
The Burmese Harp
Burn!
Burn 'Em Up Barnes
Burndown
The Burning
The Burning Bed
Burning Secret
Burning Vengeance
The Burns and Allen Show
Burnt Offerings
Bury Me an Angel
The Bus Is Coming
Bus Stop
The Busher
The Bushido Blade
Business as Usual
Busted Up
Buster
Buster and Billie
Buster Keaton Rides Again/The Railrodder
Bustin' Loose
But Where Is Daniel Wax?
Butch and Sundance: The Early Days
Butch Cassidy and the Sundance Kid
The Butcher's Wife
Butler's Dilemma
Butterfield 8
Butterflies Are Free
Butterfly
Butterfly Affair
Butterfly Ball
Buying Time
By Dawn's Early Light
By Design
By the Blood of Others
Bye Bye Baby
Bye, Bye, Birdie
Bye Bye Brazil
Cabaret
Cabin in the Sky
The Cabinet of Dr. Caligari
Cabiria
Cabo Blanco
Cactus
Cactus Flower
Cactus in the Snow
Caddie
The Caddy
Caddyshack
Caddyshack 2
Cadillac Man
Caesar and Cleopatra
Cafe Express
The Cage
Caged Fury
Caged in Paradiso
Caged Terror
Caged Women
Cahill: United States Marshal
The Caine Mutiny
Cain's Cutthroats
Cajon Pass
Cal
Calamity Jane
California Dreaming
California Girls
California Gold Rush
California Joe
California Straight Ahead
California Suite
Caligari's Cure
Caligula
Call Him Mr. Shatter
Call Me
Call of the Canyon
Call of the Wild
Call Out the Marines
Call to Glory
The Caller
Callie and Son
Calling Paul Temple
Came a Hot Friday
Camel Boy
Camelot
Camila
Camille
Camille Claudel
Camorra: The Naples Connection
Camp Classics 1
Camp Double Feature
Campaign in Poland
The Campus Corpse
Campus Knights
Campus Man
Can-Can
Can I Do It...Till I Need Glasses?
Can She Bake a Cherry Pie?
Can You Hear the Laughter? The Story of Freddie Prinze
Canada's Sweetheart: The Saga of Hal C. Banks
Cancel My Reservation
The Candidate
Candles at Nine
Candleshoe
Candy Stripe Nurses
Candy Tangerine Man
Candyman
Cannery Row
Cannibal Campout
Cannibal Women in the Avocado Jungle of Death
Cannon Ball/Eyes Have It
Cannonball
Cannonball/Dizzy Heights and Daring Hearts
Cannonball Run
Cannonball Run 2
The Canon Operation
Can't Buy Me Love
Can't Stop the Music
The Canterbury Tales
The Canterville Ghost
Cantonen Iron Kung Fu
The Cantor's Son
Cape Fear
Caper of the Golden Bulls
Capricorn One
Captain America
Captain America 2: Death Too Soon
Captain Apache
Captain Blood
Captain Caution
The Captain from Koepenick
Captain Horatio Hornblower
Captain Kidd
Captain Kronos: Vampire Hunter
Captain Newman, M.D.
Captain Ron
Captain Scarlett
Captain Swagger
Captains Courageous
Captain's Paradise
Captive
Captive Heart
Captive Hearts
Captive Planet
Captive Rage
The Capture of Bigfoot
Captured in Chinatown
Car Trouble
Car Wash
Caravaggio
Caravan to Vaccares
Carbon Copy
Cardiac Arrest
The Cardinal
The Care Bears Movie
The Care Bears Movie 2: A New Generation
Carefree
Careful, He Might Hear You
Caribe
Carlton Browne of the F.O.
Carmen
Carmilla
Carnage
Carnal Knowledge
Carnival in Flanders
Carnival Lady
Carnival of Blood
Carnival of Souls
Carnival Rock
Carnival Story
The Carnivores
Carny
Carousel
The Carpathian Eagle
The Carpetbaggers
Carrie
The Carrier
Carrington, V.C.
Carry Me Back
Carry On at Your Convenience
Carry On Behind
Carry On Cleo
Carry On Cowboy
Carry On Cruising
Carry On Emmanuelle
Carry On Nurse
The Cars That Ate Paris
Carson City Kid
Carthage in Flames
Cartier Affair
Carve Her Name with Pride
The Cary Grant Collection
Casablanca
Casablanca Express
Casanova
Casanova Brown
A Case of Libel
Case of the Baby Sitter
The Case of the Frightened Lady
The Case of the Lucky Legs
The Case of the Missing Lady
The Case of the Mukkinese Battle Horn
Casey at the Bat
Casey Jones and Fury (Brave Stallion)
Casey's Shadow
Casino
Casino Royale
Cass
Cassandra
The Cassandra Crossing
Cassie
Cast a Giant Shadow
Castaway
The Castaway Cowboy
Casting Call
The Castle
Castle of the Creeping Flesh
Casual Sex?
Casualties of War
The Cat
Cat and Mouse
The Cat and the Canary
Cat Ballou
The Cat from Outer Space
Cat in the Cage
Cat on a Hot Tin Roof
Cat People
Cat Women of the Moon
Cataclysm
Catacombs
The Catamount Killing
Catch as Catch Can
Catch Me a Spy
Catch the Heat
Catch-22
Catherine & Co.
Catherine the Great
Catholic Hour
Catholics
Cathy's Curse
Cat's Eye
Cattle Queen of Montana
Cavalcade of the West
The Cavalier
Cavalier of the West
Cavalry
Cavalry Command
Cave Girl
Cave of the Living Dead
Caveman
Cease Fire
Celebrity
Celia: Child Of Terror
Cellar Dweller
The Cemetery Club
Cemetery High
The Centerfold Girls
Certain Fury
Certain Sacrifice
Cesar
Cesar & Rosalie
Chain Gang Killings
Chain of Desire
Chain Reaction
Chained
Chained for Life
Chained Heat
The Chalk Garden
The Challenge
Challenge the Ninja
Challenge To Be Free
Challenge to Lassie
Challenge to White Fang
Chamber of Horrors
Chameleon
The Champ
Champagne for Caesar
The Champion/His New Job
Champions
Chances Are
Chandu on the Magic Island
Chandu the Magician
Chanel Solitaire
Change of Habit
A Change of Seasons
The Changeling
Changes
The Channeler
Chapayev
Chaplin: A Character Is Born
Chaplin Essanay Book 1
The Chaplin Revue
Chapter in Her Life
Chapter Two
Charade
The Charge of the Light Brigade
Charge of the Model T's
Chariots of Fire
Charles et Lucie
Charleston

Charley Chase Festival, Vol. 1
Charley Varrick
Charley's Aunt
Charlie and the Great Balloon Chase
Charlie Boy
Charlie Bravo
A Charlie Brown Celebration
A Charlie Brown Christmas
A Charlie Brown Thanksgiving
Charlie Chan and the Curse of the Dragon Queen
Charlie Chaplin: Night at the Show
Charlie Chaplin: The Early Years, Vol. 4
Charlie Chaplin...Our Hero!
Charlie Chaplin's Keystone Comedies 1
Charlie Chaplin's Keystone Comedies 2
Charlie Chaplin's Keystone Comedies 3
Charlie Chaplin's Keystone Comedies 4
Charlie Chase and Ben Turpin
Charlie Grant's War
Charlie, the Lonesome Cougar
Charlotte's Web
Charly
Charm of La Boheme
The Chase
Chase
Chasing Dreams
Chasing Those Depression Blues
Chato's Land
Chattanooga Choo Choo
Chatterbox
Cheaper to Keep Her
The Cheat
The Cheaters
Cheaters
Check & Double Check
Check Is in the Mail
Checking Out
Cheech and Chong: Still Smokin'
Cheech and Chong: Things Are Tough All Over
Cheech and Chong's Next Movie
Cheech and Chong's Nice Dreams
Cheech and Chong's Up in Smoke
The Cheerful Fraud
Cheerleader Camp
The Cheerleaders
Cheerleaders' Wild Weekend
Cheers for Miss Bishop
Cherry Hill High
Cherry 2000
Chesty Anderson USN
Cheyenne Autumn
Cheyenne Kid
Cheyenne Rides Again
Cheyenne Takes Over
The Chicken Chronicles
Chiefs
Child Bride of Short Creek
Child in the Night
A Child is Waiting
Child of Darkness, Child of Light
Child of Glass
Child of the Prairie
The Children
The Children Are Watching Us
Children of a Lesser God
The Children of An Lac
Children of Divorce
Children of Rage
Children of Sanchez
Children of the Corn
Children of the Full Moon
The Children of Theatre Street
The Children of Times Square
Children Shouldn't Play with Dead Things
Children's Island
Child's Christmas in Wales
Child's Play
Child's Play 2
Child's Play 3
Chillers
Chilly Scenes of Winter
Chimes at Midnight
China Beach
China Girl
The China Lake Murders
China Seas
China Sky
The China Syndrome
Chinatown
Chinese Boxes
Chinese Connection
Chinese Connection 2
Chinese Roulette
Chinese Web
Chino
The Chipmunk Adventure
The Chisholms
Chisum
Chitty Chitty Bang Bang
Chloe in the Afternoon
Chocolat
The Chocolate War
The Choice
Choice of Arms
Choice of Weapons
Choices
The Choirboys
Choke Canyon
C.H.O.M.P.S.
Choose Me
The Choppers
Chopping Mall
A Chorus Line
A Chorus of Disapproval
The Chosen
Christ Stopped at Eboli
Christabel
Christian the Lion
Christiane F.
Christina
Christine
A Christmas Carol
The Christmas Coal Mine Miracle
Christmas Comes to Willow Creek
Christmas in Connecticut
Christmas in July
Christmas Lilies of the Field
A Christmas Story
The Christmas That Almost Wasn't
A Christmas to Remember
The Christmas Wife
A Christmas Without Snow
Christopher Columbus: The Discovery
Christopher Strong
Chrome Hearts
Chrome Soldiers
Chu Chu & the Philly Flash
Chuck Berry: Hail! Hail! Rock 'n' Roll
C.H.U.D.
C.H.U.D. 2: Bud the Chud
A Chump at Oxford
Churchill and the Generals
Ciao Federico! Fellini Directs Satyricon
Cimarron
The Cincinnati Kid
Cinderella
Cinderella Liberty
Cinderfella
Cinema Shrapnel
Cinemagic
Circle Canyon
Circle Man
Circle of Death
Circle of Fear
Circle of Iron
Circle of Love
Circle of Two
Circumstances Unknown
Circus Angel
Circus of Fear
Circus of Horrors
Circus World
The Citadel
Citizen Kane
Citizens Band
The City
The City and the Dogs
City for Conquest
City Girl
City Heat
City in Fear
City in Panic
City Killer
City Lights
City Limits
City of Blood
City of Shadows
City of Women
City on Fire
City Slickers
The City's Edge
Civilization
Claire's Knee
Clambake
The Clan of the Cave Bear
Clara's Heart
Clarence Darrow
Clark & McCullough
Clash of the Ninja
Clash of the Titans
Class
Class Action
Class of '44
The Class of Miss MacMichael
Class of 1984
Class of 1999
Class of Nuke 'Em High
Class of Nuke 'Em High 2: Subhumanoid Meltdown
Class of '63
Class Reunion
Class Reunion Massacre
The Claw
Claws
The Clay Pigeon
Clean and Sober
Clean Slate
Clear and Present Danger
Clearing the Range
Cleo from 5 to 7
Cleopatra
Cleopatra Jones
Cleopatra Jones & the Casino of Gold
The Clergyman's Daughter
Cliffhanger
A Climate for Killing
The Climb
Cloak & Dagger
The Clockmaker
A Clockwork Orange
Clodhopper
The Clones
Clones of Bruce Lee
The Clonus Horror
Close Encounters of the Third Kind
Close to Eden
Close to Home
Closely Watched Trains
Closet Cases of the Nerd Kind
Closet Land
Cloud Dancer
Cloud Waltzing
Clouds Over Europe
Clown
Clown House
Clown Murders
The Clowns
The Club
Club Extinction
Club Fed
Club Havana
Club Life
Club Med
Club Paradise
Clue
The Clutching Hand
Coach
Coal Miner's Daughter
The Coast Patrol
Coast to Coast
Cobra
The Coca-Cola Kid
Cocaine Cowboys
Cocaine Fiends
Cocaine: One Man's Seduction
Cocaine Wars
Cockeyed Cavaliers
Cockfighter
Cocktail
The Cocoanuts
Cocoon
Cocoon: The Return
C.O.D.
Code Name: Diamond Head
Code Name: Emerald
Code Name: Zebra
Code of Silence
Codename: Foxfire
Codename: Icarus
Cody
A Coeur Joie
Coffy
Cohen and Tate
Cold Blood
Cold Eyes of Fear
Cold Feet
Cold Front
Cold Heat
Cold River
Cold Room
Cold Steel
Cold Steel for Tortuga
Cold Sweat
Cold Turkey
Cold War Killers
The Colditz Story
Cole Justice
The Collector
Collector's Item
College
Collision Course
The Colombian Connection
Colonel Effingham's Raid
Colonel Redl
Color Me Blood Red
The Color of Money
The Color Purple
Colorado
Colors
Colossus and the Amazon Queen
Colossus: The Forbin Project
Columbo: Murder By the Book
Columbo: Prescription Murder
Coma
The Comancheros
Combat!
Combat Killers
Combat Shock
Come Along with Me
Come and Get It
Come Back, Africa
Come Back Little Reba
Come Back, Little Sheba
Come Back to the Five & Dime Jimmy Dean, Jimmy Dean
Come Blow Your Horn
Come On, Cowboys
Come On Rangers
Come On Tarzan
Come See the Paradise
The Comeback
Comeback
Comeback Kid
Comes a Horseman
Comfort and Joy
The Comfort of Strangers
The Comic
Comic Book Kids
Comic Cabby
Coming Home
The Coming of Amos
Coming Out Alive
Coming Out of the Ice
Coming to America
Coming Up Roses
Commando
Commando Attack
Commando Squad
Commandos
Commandos Strike at Dawn
The Commies are Coming, the Commies are Coming
The Commitments
The Committee
Common Bonds
Common Threads: Stories from the Quilt
Communion
Company Limited
The Company of Wolves
The Competition
The Compleat Beatles
Complex
Compromising Positions
Computer Beach Party
Computer Wizard
The Computer Wore Tennis Shoes
The Con Artists
Conagher
Conan the Barbarian
Conan the Destroyer
The Concentratin' Kid
The Concorde: Airport '79
Concrete Angels
Concrete Beat
The Concrete Jungle
Condemned to Hell
Condorman
Coneheads
The Confessional
Confessions of a Police Captain
Confessions of a Vice Baron
Confessions of Tom Harris
Confidential
Confidentially Yours
The Conformist
Congo
Congress Dances
A Connecticut Yankee in King Arthur's Court
The Connection
The Conqueror
Conqueror & the Empress
Conqueror of the World
Conquest
Conquest of Cochise
Conquest of the Normans
Conquest of the Planet of the Apes
Conrack
Consenting Adults
Consolation Marriage
Conspiracy
Conspiracy of Hearts
Conspiracy: The Trial of the Chicago Eight
Consuming Passions
Contagion
Contempt
Continental Divide
Contra Company
Contraband
Control
The Conversation
Conversation Piece

Convicted
Convicted: A Mother's Story
Convicts at Large
Convoy
Coogan's Bluff
Cookie
Cool As Ice
Cool Blue
Cool Hand Luke
Cool Mikado
Cool World
Cop
The Cop & the Girl
Cop in Blue Jeans
Cop-Out
Copkillers
Copperhead
Cops/One Week
Cord & Dischords/Naughty Nurse
Cordelia
Coriolanus, Man without a Country
Corleone
The Corn is Green
Cornbread, Earl & Me
Cornered
The Corpse Grinders
The Corpse Vanishes
Corrida Interdite
The Corridor: Death
Corridors of Blood
Corrupt
The Corrupt Ones
Corsair
The Corsican Brothers
Corvette Summer
Cosh Boy
The Cosmic Eye
The Cosmic Man
The Cosmic Monsters
Cosmos: War of the Planets
Cottage to Let
Cotter
Cotton Candy
The Cotton Club
Cotton Queen
The Couch Trip
Could It Happen Here?
The Count
Count/Adventurer
The Count of Monte Cristo
The Count of the Old Town
Count Yorga, Vampire
Countdown
Counter Attack
Counter Measures
Counter Punch
Counterblast
The Counterfeit Traitor
Counterforce
Country
Country Gentlemen
Country Girl
The Country Kid
Country Lovers, City Lovers
Countryman
County Fair
Coup de Grace
Coupe de Ville
Couples and Robbers
Courage
Courage Mountain
Courage of Black Beauty
Courage of Rin Tin Tin
Courage of the North
Courageous Avenger
Courageous Dr. Christian
The Courageous Mr. Penn
The Courier
Courier of Death
Court Jester
The Court Martial of Jackie Robinson
The Courtesans of Bombay
Courtship

Cousin, Cousine
Cousins
Cover Girl
Cover Girl Models
The Cover Girl Murders
Cover Me
Covergirl
Covert Action
Cow Town
Coward of the County
Cowboy
The Cowboy & the Ballerina
Cowboy & the Bandit
Cowboy & the Senorita
Cowboy Counselor
The Cowboys
Cowboys Don't Cry
Cowboys from Texas
Cowboys of the Saturday Matinee
Coyote Trails
Crack House
Crack Shadow Boxers
Crack-Up
The Cracker Factory
Crackers
Cracking Up
The Crackler
The Cradle Will Fall
Craig's Wife
Crainquebille
The Cranes are Flying
Crash and Burn
The Crash of Flight 401
The Crater Lake Monster
The Craving
The Crawling Eye
The Crawling Hand
Crawlspace
Craze
Crazed
Crazed Cop
The Crazies
Crazy Fat Ethel II
Crazy for Love
Crazy from the Heart
Crazy Mama
Crazy Moon
Crazy People
The Crazy Ray
The Creation of the Humanoids
Creator
Creature
Creature from Black Lake
Creature from the Black Lagoon
Creature from the Haunted Sea
Creature with the Blue Hand
Creatures the World Forgot
The Creeper
Creepers
The Creeping Flesh
Creeping Terror
Creepozoids
Creepshow
Creepshow 2
The Cremators
Cria
Cricket on the Hearth
Cries and Whispers
Crime & Passion
Crime Busters
Crime Killer
The Crime of Dr. Crespi
Crime of Honor
The Crime of Monsieur Lange
Crimebusters
Crimes & Misdemeanors
Crimes of Passion
The Crimes of Stephen Hawke
Crimes of the Heart
Crimewave
Criminal Act
Criminal Code
Criminal Court
Criminal Law

The Criminal Life of Archibaldo de la Cruz
Criminally Insane
Criminals Within
Crimson Pirate
Crimson Romance
Crisis at Central High
Criss Cross
Critical Condition
Critters
Critters 2: The Main Course
Crocodile
Crocodile Dundee
Crocodile Dundee 2
Cromwell
Crooked Hearts
Crooked Trail
Crooks & Coronets
The Cross & the Switchblade
Cross Country
Cross Creek
Cross Examination
Cross My Heart
Cross of Iron
Crossbar
Crossfire
Crossing Delancey
Crossing the Bridge
Crossing the Line
Crossover
Crossover Dreams
Crossroads
Crow Hollow
The Crowd
Crucible of Horror
Crucible of Terror
The Crucifer of Blood
The Crude Oasis
Cruel Sea
Cruise into Terror
Cruise Missile
Cruisin' High
Cruising
The Crush
Crusoe
Cry-Baby
A Cry for Love
Cry Freedom
A Cry from the Mountain
A Cry in the Dark
Cry of a Prostitute: Love Kills
Cry of Battle
Cry of the Banshee
Cry of the Black Wolves
Cry of the Innocent
Cry Panic
Cry Terror
Cry Vengeance
Crypt of Dark Secrets
Crypt of the Living Dead
Crystal Heart
Crystalstone
Cuba
Cujo
Culpepper Cattle Co.
The Cure
Curfew
Curley
Curly Sue
Curly Top
The Curse
Curse 2: The Bite
The Curse of Frankenstein
The Curse of King Tut's Tomb
Curse of the Alpha Stone
Curse of the Aztec Mummy/Robot vs. the Aztec Mummy
Curse of the Black Widow
Curse of the Blue Lights
Curse of the Cat People
The Curse of the Crying Woman
Curse of the Demon
Curse of the Living Corpse
Curse of the Living Dead
Curse of the Pink Panther
Curse of the Screaming Dead

The Curse of the Werewolf
Curse of the Yellow Snake
Curtain Up
Curtains
Custer's Last Fight
Custer's Last Stand
Cut and Run
Cutter's Way
Cyborg
Cycle Psycho
Cyclone
Cyclone Cavalier
Cyclone of the Saddle
Cyclops
Cyclotrode "X"
D-Day, the Sixth of June
Da
Dad
Daddy's Boys
Daddy's Dyin'...Who's Got the Will?
Daffy Duck's Movie: Fantastic Island
Daffy Duck's Quackbusters
Dagger Eyes
Dagora, the Space Monster
The Dain Curse
Daisy Miller
Dakota
Daleks—Invasion Earth 2150 A.D.
Dam Busters
Dames
Damien: Omen 2
Damien: The Leper Priest
Damn the Defiant
Damn Yankees
Damnation Alley
The Damned
Damned River
A Damsel in Distress
Dan Candy's Law
Dance
Dance Fools Dance
Dance, Girl, Dance
Dance Hall
Dance Hall Racket
Dance of Death
Dance of the Damned
Dance or Die
Dance with a Stranger
Dancers
Dances with Wolves
Dancing in the Dark
Dancing Lady
Dancing Man
Dancing Mothers
The Dancing Princesses
Dancing with Danger
Dandelions
Dandy in Aspic
Danger in the Skies
Danger Lights
Danger on the Air
Danger Zone
Danger Zone 3: Steel Horse War
Dangerous
Dangerous Charter
Dangerous Curves
Dangerous Game
Dangerous Holiday
Dangerous Hours
Dangerous Liaisons
Dangerous Life
Dangerous Love
Dangerous Mission
Dangerous Moonlight
Dangerous Moves
Dangerous Orphans
Dangerous Passage
Dangerous Pursuit
Dangerous Summer
Dangerous When Wet
Dangerously Close
Daniel

Daniel Boone
Danny
Danny Boy
Danton
Darby O'Gill & the Little People
Daring Dobermans
Daring Game
The Dark
Dark Age
Dark Angel: The Ascent
Dark August
Dark Before Dawn
Dark Command
Dark Corner
The Dark Crystal
Dark Eyes
Dark Forces
Dark Habits
The Dark Hour
Dark Journey
Dark Night of the Scarecrow
Dark Obsession
Dark of the Night
Dark Passage
The Dark Past
Dark Places
The Dark Power
The Dark Ride
Dark Sanity
The Dark Secret of Harvest Home
Dark Side of Genius
The Dark Side of Love
Dark Side of Midnight
Dark Star
Dark Tower
Dark Universe
Dark Victory
Dark Waters
Darkman
Darktown Strutters
Darling
D.A.R.Y.L.
Das Boot
Das Testament des Dr. Mabuse
Date Bait
Date with an Angel
A Date with Judy
The Daughter of Dr. Jekyll
Daughter of the Tong
Daughters of Darkness
Daughters of Satan
Dave
David
David and Lisa
David Copperfield
Davy Crockett and the River Pirates
Davy Crockett, King of the Wild Frontier
Dawn!
Dawn Express
Dawn of the Dead
Dawn of the Mummy
Dawn on the Great Divide
Dawn Patrol
Dawn Rider/Frontier Horizon
The Dawson Patrol
The Day After
The Day and the Hour
A Day at the Races
Day for Night
A Day in the Country
A Day in the Death of Joe Egg
The Day It Came to Earth
Day of Judgment
Day of the Assassin
Day of the Cobra
Day of the Dead
The Day of the Dolphin
The Day of the Jackal
The Day of the Locust
Day of the Maniac
Day of the Panther
Day of the Triffids
Day the Bookies Wept

The Day the Earth Caught Fire
The Day the Earth Stood Still
The Day the Women Got Even
Day Time Ended
The Day Will Dawn
Day with Conrad Green
The Daydreamer
Days of Glory
Days of Heaven
Days of Hell
Days of Thrills and Laughter
Days of Thunder
Days of Wine and Roses
Dayton's Devils
D.C. Cab
The Dead
Dead and Buried
Dead as a Doorman
Dead Bang
Dead Calm
The Dead Don't Die
Dead Easy
Dead End
Dead End City
Dead End Drive-In
Dead End Street
Dead for a Dollar
Dead Heat
Dead Heat on a Merry-Go-Round
Dead in the Water
Dead Lucky
Dead Man Out
Dead Mate
Dead Men Don't Wear Plaid
Dead Men Walk
Dead of Night
Dead of Winter
Dead on the Money
Dead or Alive
Dead Pit
Dead Poets Society
The Dead Pool
Dead Reckoning
Dead Right
Dead Ringers
Dead Solid Perfect
Dead Wrong
Dead Zone
Deadline
Deadline at Dawn
Deadline Auto Theft
Deadlock
Deadly Alliance
The Deadly and the Beautiful
Deadly Blessing
Deadly Business
Deadly Companions
Deadly Darling
Deadly Diamonds
Deadly Dreams
Deadly Embrace
Deadly Encounter
Deadly Eyes
Deadly Fieldtrip
Deadly Force
Deadly Friend
Deadly Game
Deadly Games
Deadly Harvest
Deadly Hero
Deadly Illusion
Deadly Impact
Deadly Intruder
Deadly Mission
Deadly Passion
Deadly Possession
Deadly Prey
Deadly Reactor
Deadly Recruits
Deadly Revenge
Deadly Sanctuary
Deadly Sting
Deadly Strangers
Deadly Sunday
Deadly Thief
Deadly Twins
Deadly Vengeance
Deadtime Stories
Deadwood
Deal of the Century
Dealers
Dear America: Letters Home from Vietnam
Dear Brigitte
Dear Dead Delilah
Dear Murderer
Dear Wife
Death at Love House
Death Be Not Proud
Death Becomes Her
Death Before Dishonor
Death Blow
Death by Dialogue
Death by Prescription
Death Challenge
Death Chase
Death Collector
Death Cruise
The Death Curse of Tartu
Death Driver
Death Drug
Death Feud
Death Force
Death from a Distance
Death Games
Death Goes to School
Death Hunt
Death in Deep Water
Death in Venice
Death is Called Engelchen
Death Journey
The Death Kiss
Death Kiss
Death Machines
Death Mask of the Ninja
Death of a Bureaucrat
Death of a Centerfold
Death of a Gunfighter
Death of a Salesman
Death of a Scoundrel
Death of a Soldier
The Death of Adolf Hitler
Death of an Angel
The Death of Richie
Death of the Rat
Death on the Nile
Death Promise
Death Race 2000
Death Rage
Death Ray
Death Ray 2000
Death Rides the Plains
Death Row Diner
Death Screams
Death Sentence
Death Ship
Death Sport
The Death Squad
Death Stalk
Death Target
Death Train
Death Valley
Death Valley Manhunt
Death Warmed Up
Death Weekend
Death Wish
Death Wish 2
Death Wish 3
Death Wish 4: The Crackdown
Death Wish Club
Deathcheaters
Deathdream
Deathhead Virgin
Deathmask
Deathmoon
Deathrow Gameshow
Deathstalker
Deathstalker 2: Duel of the Titans
Deathstalker 3
Deathtrap
The Decameron
Decameron Nights
Deceived
The Deceivers
Deception
The Decline of the American Empire
Decline of Western Civilization 1
Decline of Western Civilization 2: The Metal Years
Dedee d'Anvers
The Deep
Deep Cover
Deep in My Heart
Deep in the Heart
Deep Red: Hatchet Murders
Deep Six
Deep Space
Deepstar Six
The Deer Hunter
The Deerslayer
Def by Temptation
Def-Con 4
The Defender
The Defense Never Rests
Defense of the Realm
Defense Play
Defiance
Defiant
The Defiant Ones
Deja Vu
The Deliberate Stranger
The Delicate Delinquent
Delicatessen
Delinquent Daughters
Delinquent School Girls
Delirious
Delirium
Deliverance
Delivery Boys
Delos Adventure
Delta Force
Delta Force 2: Operation Stranglehold
Delta Fox
Deluge
Delusion
Delusions of Grandeur
Demented
Dementia 13
Demetrius and the Gladiators
The Demi-Paradise
Demolition
Demolition Man
The Demon
Demon Barber of Fleet Street
Demon for Trouble
Demon Hunter
The Demon Lover
Demon Lust
Demon of Paradise
Demon Queen
Demon Rage
Demon Seed
Demon Wind
Demon Witch Child
Demon with a Glass Hand
Demonic Toys
Demonoid, Messenger of Death
The Demons
Demons
Demons of Ludlow
Demons of the Mind
Demonstone
Demonwarp
Dempsey
Dennis the Menace
The Dentist
Deputy Marshall
Der Purimshpiler
Derby
Dersu Uzala
Desert Bloom
The Desert Fox
Desert Gold
Desert Hearts
The Desert of the Tartars
Desert Phantom
The Desert Rats
Desert Snow
Desert Trail
Desert Warrior
The Deserters
Designing Woman
Desire and Hell at Sunset Motel
Desire Under the Elms
Desiree
Desk Set
Despair
Desperados
Desperate
Desperate Cargo
Desperate Hours
Desperate Journey
Desperate Lives
Desperate Living
Desperate Moves
Desperate Remedies
Desperate Scoundrel/The Pride of Pikeville
Desperate Target
Desperate Teenage Lovedolls
Desperate Women
Desperately Seeking Susan
Destination Moon
Destination Moonbase Alpha
Destination Saturn
Destination Tokyo
Destroyer
The Destructors
Destry Rides Again
The Detective
Detective Sadie & Son
Detective School Dropouts
Detour
Detour to Danger
Detroit 9000
Deutschland im Jahre Null
Devastator
Devi
The Devil
The Devil & Daniel Webster
Devil & Leroy Basset
The Devil & Max Devlin
The Devil at 4 O'Clock
The Devil Bat
The Devil Bat's Daughter
Devil Dog: The Hound of Hell
Devil Doll
Devil Girl from Mars
Devil Horse
The Devil in Silk
Devil in the Flesh
Devil Kiss
Devil Monster
Devil of the Desert Against the Son of Hercules
Devil on Horseback
The Devil Thumbs a Ride
The Devil Thumbs a Ride/Having Wonderful Crime
Devil Times Five
Devil Wears White
Devilfish
The Devils
The Devil's Brigade
Devil's Canyon
The Devil's Cargo
The Devil's Commandment
Devil's Crude
The Devil's Daughter
The Devil's Eye
Devil's Gift
The Devil's Harvest
The Devil's Nightmare
Devil's Party
The Devil's Playground
The Devil's Possessed
Devil's Rain
The Devil's Sleep
Devil's Son-in-Law
The Devil's Undead
Devil's Wanton
The Devil's Web
Devil's Wedding Night
Devlin
The Devlin Connection
Devonsville Terror
D.I.
Diabolically Yours
Diabolique
Dial Help
Dial "M" for Murder
Diamond Head
Diamond Ninja Force
Diamond Run
Diamond Trail
Diamonds
Diamonds Are Forever
Diamond's Edge
Diamonds of the Night
Diamonds on Wheels
Diary of a Chambermaid
Diary of a Country Priest
Diary of a Lost Girl
Diary of a Mad Housewife
Diary of a Mad Old Man
Diary of a Madman
Diary of a Rebel
Diary of a Teenage Hitchhiker
Diary of a Young Comic
The Diary of Anne Frank
Diary of Forbidden Dreams
Diary of the Dead
Dick Barton, Special Agent
Dick Barton Strikes Back
Dick Tracy
Dick Tracy, Detective
Dick Tracy, Detective/The Corpse Vanishes
Dick Tracy Double Feature 1
Dick Tracy Double Feature 2
Dick Tracy Meets Gruesome
Dick Tracy Returns
Dick Tracy: The Original Serial, Vol. 1
Dick Tracy: The Original Serial, Vol. 2
Dick Tracy: The Spider Strikes
Dick Tracy vs. Crime Inc.
Dick Tracy vs. Cueball
Dick Tracy's Dilemma
Dick Turpin
Didn't You Hear?
Die! Die! My Darling!
Die Grosse Freiheit Nr. 7
Die Hard
Die Laughing
Die Screaming, Marianne
Die Sister, Die!
A Different Kind of Love
Different Story
Digby, the Biggest Dog in the World
Diggstown
Dillinger
Dim Sum: A Little Bit of Heart
Dimples
Diner
Dingaka
The Dining Room
Dinner at Eight
Dinner at the Ritz
Dino
Dinosaurus!
Diplomaniacs
Diplomatic Immunity
Dirkham Detective Agency
Dirt Bike Kid
Dirt Gang
Dirty Dancing
Dirty Dishes
The Dirty Dozen
The Dirty Dozen: The Next Mission
Dirty Gertie from Harlem U.S.A.
Dirty Harry
Dirty Heroes

Dirty Laundry
Dirty Mary Crazy Larry
Dirty Mind of Young Sally
Dirty Rotten Scoundrels
Dirty Tricks
Dirty Work
Disappearance
The Disappearance of Aimee
The Disciple
Disciple of Death
Disconnected
Discontent
The Discovery Program
The Discreet Charm of the Bourgeoisie
Dishonored Lady
Disney's Storybook Classics
Disorderlies
Disorderly Orderly
Disorganized Crime
Distant Thunder
Distant Voices, Still Lives
Distortions
Disturbance
Diva
The Dive
The Divine Enforcer
Divine Madness
Divine Nymph
Diving In
Divorce His, Divorce Hers
The Divorce of Lady X
Dixiana
Dixie Dynamite
Dixie Jamboree
Dixie Lanes
Django
Django Shoots First
Do the Right Thing
D.O.A.
The Doberman Gang
Doc Hollywood
Doc Savage
Docks of New York
The Doctor
Dr. Alien
The Doctor and the Devils
Doctor at Large
Doctor at Sea
Dr. Black, Mr. Hyde
Doctor Butcher M.D.
Dr. Christian Meets the Women
Dr. Cyclops
Dr. Death, Seeker of Souls
Doctor Detroit
Doctor Dolittle
Doctor Duck's Super Secret All-Purpose Sauce
Doctor Faustus
Dr. Frankenstein's Castle of Freaks
Dr. Giggles
Dr. Hackenstein
Dr. Heckyl and Mr. Hype
Doctor in Distress
Dr. Jack/For Heaven's Sake
Dr. Jekyll and Mr. Hyde
Dr. Jekyll and Sister Hyde
Dr. Jekyll's Dungeon of Death
Dr. Kildare's Strange Case
Dr. Mabuse, Parts 1 & 2
Dr. Mabuse vs. Scotland Yard
Doctor Mordrid: Master of the Unknown
Dr. No
Dr. Otto & the Riddle of the Gloom Beam
Doctor Phibes Rises Again
Dr. Strange
Dr. Strangelove, or: How I Learned to Stop Worrying and Love the Bomb
Dr. Syn
Dr. Syn, Alias the Scarecrow
Doctor Takes a Wife
Dr. Tarr's Torture Dungeon

Doctor Who and the Daleks
Doctor X
Doctor Zhivago
Doctors and Nurses
Doctors' Wives
Dodes 'ka-den
Dodge City
Dodsworth
Dog Day
Dog Day Afternoon
Dog Eat Dog
A Dog of Flanders
Dog Pound Shuffle
The Dog Soldier
Dog Star Man
The Dog Who Stopped the War
Dogfight
Dogs in Space
Dogs of Hell
The Dogs of War
Doin' Time
Doin' Time on Planet Earth
Doll Face
The Doll Squad
Dollar
Dollars
The Dollmaker
Dollman
Dollman vs Demonic Toys
The Dolls
Dolls
A Doll's House
Dominick & Eugene
Dominique is Dead
Domino
The Domino Principle
Don Amigo/Stage to Chino
Don Daredevil Rides Again
The Don is Dead
Don Q., Son of Zorro
Don Quixote
Don Segundo Sombra
Don Winslow of the Coast Guard
Don Winslow of the Navy
Dona Flor and Her Two Husbands
Dona Herlinda & Her Son
Donkey Skin
Donner Pass: The Road to Survival
Donovan's Brain
Donovan's Reef
Don's Party
Don't Answer the Phone
Don't Be Afraid of the Dark
Don't Change My World
Don't Cry, It's Only Thunder
Don't Drink the Water
Don't Go in the House
Don't Go in the Woods
Don't Look in the Attic
Don't Look in the Basement
Don't Look Now
Don't Mess with My Sister!
Don't Open the Door!
Don't Open Till Christmas
Don't Raise the Bridge, Lower the River
Don't Shove/Two Gun Gussie
Don't Tell Her It's Me
Don't Tell Mom the Babysitter's Dead
The Doolins of Oklahoma
Doom Asylum
Doomed to Die
The Doomsday Flight
Doomwatch
Door to Door
Door to Door Maniac
Dope Mania
Dorm That Dripped Blood
Dos Cruces en Danger Pass
Double Agents
Double Deal
Double Dynamite

Double Edge
Double Exposure
Double Face
Double Impact
Double Indemnity
Double Jeopardy
The Double Life of Veronique
The Double McGuffin
The Double Negative
The Double O Kid
Double Suicide
Double Trouble
Doughnuts & Society
The Dove
Down Among the Z Men
Down & Dirty
Down and Out in Beverly Hills
Down Argentine Way
Down by Law
Down Mexico Way
Down, Out and Dangerous
Down Texas Way
Down the Drain
Down to Earth
Down to the Sea in Ships
Down Twisted
Down Under
Downhill Racer
Downtown
Drachenfutter
Dracula
Dracula: A Cinematic Scrapbook
Dracula & Son
Dracula Blows His Cool
Dracula/Garden of Eden
Dracula Sucks
Dracula: Up in Harlem
Dracula's Great Love
Dracula's Last Rites
Dracula's Widow
Dragnet
Dragon Force
Dragon Princess
Dragon Seed
Dragon the Odds
Dragon vs. Needles of Death
Dragonard
Dragonfight
Dragon's Claw
The Dragon's Showdown
Dragonslayer
Dragonworld
The Drake Case
Draw!
Dreadnaught Rivals
Dream a Little Dream
Dream Chasers
Dream Lover
Dream No Evil
A Dream of Passion
Dream Street
The Dream Team
Dream to Believe
Dreamchild
The Dreaming
Dreaming Lips
Dreaming Out Loud
Dreams
Dreams Come True
Dreams of Desire
Dreamscape
Dreamwood
Dress Gray
Dressed for Death
Dressed to Kill
The Dresser
Dressmaker
The Drifter
Drifting
Drifting Souls
Drifting Weeds
Driller Killer
Drive-In
Drive-In Massacre
The Driver

Driver's Seat
Driving Force
Driving Miss Daisy
Drop Zone
The Dropkick
The Drowning Pool
Drugstore Cowboy
Drum
Drum Beat
Drum Taps
Drums
Drums Along the Mohawk
Drums in the Deep South
Drums of Fu Manchu
Drums O'Voodoo
Drunken Angel
A Dry White Season
Drying Up the Streets
Dual Alibi
Dual Flying Kicks
Dubarry
DuBarry Was a Lady
Dubeat-E-O
The Duchess and the Dirtwater Fox
Duck Soup
DuckTales the Movie: Treasure of the Lost Lamp
Dude Bandit
Dude Ranger
Dudes
Duel
Duel in the Sun
Duel of Champions
Duel of Fists
Duel of Hearts
Duel of the Iron Fist
Duel of the Seven Tigers
The Duellists
Duet for One
The Duke is Tops
Duke of the Derby
Dumb Waiter
Dumbo
The Dummy Talks
Dune
The Dunera Boys
Dungeonmaster
The Dunwich Horror
Duplicates
Durango Valley Raiders
Dust
Dust Devil
Dust to Dust
Dusty
Dutch Girls
Dutch Treat
D.W. Griffith Triple Feature
The Dybbuk
Dying to Remember
Dynamite
Dynamite Chicken
Dynamite Dan
Dynamite Pass
Dynamite Ranch
Dynamo
Dynasty
Dynasty of Fear
E. Nick: A Legend in His Own Mind
Each Dawn I Die
The Eagle
Eagle Claws Champion
The Eagle Has Landed
Eagles Attack at Dawn
Eagle's Shadow
Eagle's Wing
Early Cinema Vol. 1
Early Days
Early Frost
An Early Frost
Early Sound Films
Early Summer
The Earrings of Madame De...
Earth
Earth Girls Are Easy

Earth vs. the Flying Saucers
Earthling
Earthquake
East End Hustle
East L.A. Warriors
East of Borneo
East of Eden
East of Elephant Rock
East Side Kids
East Side Kids/The Lost City
Easter Parade
Easy Come, Easy Go
Easy Kill
Easy Living
Easy Money
Easy Rider
Easy Street
Easy Virtue
Easy Wheels
Eat a Bowl of Tea
Eat and Run
Eat My Dust
Eat the Peach
Eat the Rich
Eaten Alive
Eating
Eating Raoul
Ebony Tower
Echo Murders
Echo Park
Echoes
Echoes of Paradise
The Eclipse
Ecstasy
Eddie and the Cruisers
Eddie and the Cruisers 2: Eddie Lives!
Eddie Macon's Run
Eddie Murphy: Raw
Edge of Darkness
Edge of Sanity
Edge of the Axe
Edie in Ciao! Manhattan
Edison the Man
Edith & Marcel
Educating Rita
The Education of Sonny Carson
Edward and Mrs. Simpson
Edward Scissorhands
Eegah!
The Efficiency Expert
Egg and I
The Egyptian
The Eiger Sanction
8 1/2
Eight Men Out
8 Million Ways to Die
18 Again!
Eighteen Jade Arhats
84 Charing Cross Road
84 Charlie Mopic
El Amor Brujo
El Barbaro
El Bruto
El Cid
El Cochecito
El Diablo Rides
El Dorado
El Mariachi
El Muerto
El Norte
El Paso Stampede
Eleanor & Franklin
Electric Dreams
The Electric Horseman
The Element of Crime
Elena and Her Men
Eleni
Elephant Boy
The Elephant Man
11 Harrowhouse
Eli Eli
The Eliminators
Elizabeth of Ladymead
Elizabeth, the Queen
Eliza's Horoscope

Ella Cinders
Ellie
Elmer
Elmer Gantry
The Elusive Corporal
The Elusive Pimpernel
Elves
Elvira Madigan
Elvira, Mistress of the Dark
Elvis and Me
Elvis Stories
Elvis: The Movie
Emanon
Embassy
Embryo
The Emerald Forest
Emerald Jungle
Emergency
Emil and the Detectives
Emily
Emissary
Emmanuelle
Emmanuelle 4
Emmanuelle & Joanna
Emmanuelle in Bangkok
Emmanuelle in Soho
Emmanuelle in the Country
Emmanuelle on Taboo Island
Emmanuelle, the Joys of a Woman
Emmanuelle, the Queen
Emmanuelle's Daughter
Emperor Jones
Emperor Jones/Paul Robeson: Tribute to an Artist
Emperor of the Bronx
The Emperor's New Clothes
Empire of the Ants
Empire of the Dragon
Empire of the Sun
Empire State
The Empire Strikes Back
The Empty Beach
Empty Canvas
Enchanted April
The Enchanted Cottage
The Enchanted Forest
Enchanted Island
The Enchantress
Encino Man
Encore
Encounter at Raven's Gate
Encounter with the Unknown
The End
End of August
The End of Innocence
The End of St. Petersburg
End of the Line
End of the Road
End of the World
Endangered Species
Endgame
Endless Descent
Endless Love
Endless Night
The Endless Summer
Enemies, a Love Story
Enemy Below
Enemy Gold
Enemy Mine
Enemy of the Law
Enemy of Women
Enemy Territory
The Enforcer
Enforcer from Death Row
Enigma
Enola Gay: The Men, the Mission, the Atomic Bomb
Enormous Changes
Ensign Pulver
Enter Laughing
Enter the Dragon
Enter the Ninja
Enter the Panther
Entertaining Mr. Sloane
The Entity
Entr'acte
Entre-Nous
Epitaph
The Equalizer: Memories of Manon
Equalizer 2000
Equus
Eraserhead
Erendira
Eric
Erik
Erik, the Viking
Erik the Viking
Ernest Goes to Camp
Ernest Saves Christmas
Ernest Scared Stupid
Ernesto
Ernie Kovacs: Between the Laughter
Erotic Dreams
Erotic Escape
Erotic Images
Erotic Touch of Hot Skin
The Errand Boy
Escapade in Florence
Escapade in Japan
The Escape Artist
Escape from Alcatraz
Escape from Cell Block 3
Escape from Death Row
Escape from El Diablo
Escape from Fort Bravo
Escape from Galaxy Three
Escape from New York
Escape from Safehaven
Escape from the Bronx
Escape from the KGB
Escape from the Planet of the Apes
Escape to Athena
Escape to Burma
Escape to Love
Escape to the Sun
Escape to Witch Mountain
Escape 2000
Escapes
Escapist
E.S.P.
Estate of Insanity
Et La Tenoresse?...Bordel!
E.T.: The Extra-Terrestrial
Eternal Evil
Eternal Return
Eternally Yours
Ethan
Ethan Frome
Eubie!
Eureka!
Eureka Stockade
Europa '51
The Europeans
Eve of Destruction
Evel Knievel
An Evening with Robin Williams
Evergreen
Eversmile New Jersey
Every Girl Should Be Married
Every Girl Should Have One
Every Man for Himself & God Against All
Every Man's Law
Every Time We Say Goodbye
Every Which Way But Loose
Everybody Wins
Everybody's All American
Everybody's Dancin'
Everything You Always Wanted to Know about Sex (But Were Afraid to Ask)
The Evictors
The Evil
The Evil Below
Evil Dead
Evil Dead 2: Dead by Dawn
Evil Judgement
The Evil Mind
The Evil of Frankenstein
Evil Spawn
Evil Spirits
The Evil That Men Do
Evil Toons
Evil Town
Evil under the Sun
Evils of the Night
Evilspeak
The Ewok Adventure
The Ewoks: Battle for Endor
Ex-Mrs. Bradford
Excalibur
The Execution
Execution of Raymond Graham
The Executioner
Executioner of Venice
The Executioner, Part 2: Frozen Scream
The Executioner's Song
Executive Action
Executive Suite
Exit the Dragon, Enter the Tiger
Exodus
Exorcism
The Exorcist
The Exorcist 2: The Heretic
Exorcist 3: Legion
The Expendables
Experience Preferred... But Not Essential
Experiment in Terror
Experiment Perilous
The Experts
Explorers
Explosion
Exposed
Express to Terror
The Exterminating Angel
Exterminator
Exterminator 2
Exterminators of the Year 3000
Extra Girl
The Extraordinary Adventures of Mr. West in the Land of the Bolsheviks
Extreme Prejudice
Extremities
An Eye for an Eye
Eye of the Eagle
Eye of the Eagle 2
Eye of the Needle
Eye of the Octopus
Eye of the Tiger
Eyeball
Eyes Behind the Stars
Eyes of a Stranger
Eyes of Fire
Eyes of Laura Mars
Eyes of Texas
The Eyes of the Amaryllis
Eyes of the Panther
Eyes of Turpin Are Upon You!
The Eyes of Youth
Eyes Right!
The Eyes, the Mouth
Eyewitness
F. Scott Fitzgerald in Hollywood
F/X
Fabulous Adventures of Baron Munchausen
The Fabulous Baker Boys
Fabulous Joe
A Face in the Crowd
A Face in the Fog
Face of Another
Fade to Black
Fahrenheit 451
Fail-Safe
Fair Game
Fairy Tales
Fake Out
Falcon
The Falcon and the Snowman
The Falcon in Mexico
The Falcon Takes Over/Strange Bargain
The Falcon's Adventure/Armored Car Robbery
The Falcon's Brother
The Fall of the House of Usher
The Fall of the Roman Empire
Fallen Angel
The Fallen Idol
The Fallen Sparrow
Falling in Love
Falling in Love Again
False Arrest
False Colors
False Faces
False Identity
False Note
Fame
The Family
Family Business
Family Enforcer
The Family Game
Family Life
The Family Man
Family Plot
Family Reunion
Family Secrets
Family Upside Down
Famous Five Get into Trouble
The Fan
Fancy Pants
Fandango
Fangoria's Weekend of Horrors
Fangs
Fangs of Fate
Fanny
Fanny and Alexander
Fanny Hill
Fanny Hill: Memoirs of a Woman of Pleasure
Fantasies
Fantastic Balloon Voyage
Fantastic Planet
Fantastic Seven
Fantastic Voyage
Fantasy Island
Fantasy Man
Far and Away
Far Country
Far Cry from Home
Far East
Far from the Madding Crowd
Far North
A Far Off Place
Far Out Man
The Far Pavilions
Farewell, My Lovely
A Farewell to Arms
Farewell to the King
Fargo Express
The Farmer Takes a Wife
The Farmer's Daughter
Fashions of 1934
Fast Break
Fast Bullets
Fast Company
Fast Food
Fast Forward
Fast Kill
Fast Lane Fever
Fast Money
Fast Talking
Fast Times at Ridgemont High
Fast Walking
Fastest Guitar Alive
Fat and the Lean
Fat City
Fat Guy Goes Nutzoid
Fat Man and Little Boy
Fatal Attraction
Fatal Beauty
Fatal Error
Fatal Exposure
Fatal Fix
Fatal Games
The Fatal Glass of Beer
The Fatal Hour
Fatal Images
Fatal Mission
Fatal Past
Fatal Pulse
Fatal Skies
Fatal Vision
Father
Father Figure
Father of the Bride
Father's Little Dividend
Fatso
Fatty and Mabel Adrift/Mabel, Fatty and the Law
Fatty Finn
Faust
FBI Girl
Fear
Fear, Anxiety and Depression
Fear City
Fear in the City
The Fear Inside
Fear No Evil
Fear Strikes Out
Fearless
The Fearless Vampire Killers
Fearmaker
Feast for the Devil
Federal Agent
Feds
Feel My Pulse
Feel the Motion
Feelin' Up
Feet First
Feet Foremost
Felix the Cat: The Movie
Fellini Satyricon
Fellini's Roma
Fellow Traveler
Female Trouble
Femmes de Paris
Fer-De-Lance
Fergie & Andrew: Behind Palace Doors
Fernandel the Dressmaker
Ferocious Female Freedom Fighters
Ferris Bueller's Day Off
Ferry to Hong Kong
Feud of the Trail
Feud of the West
Fever
Fever Mounts at El Pao
Fever Pitch
A Few Good Men
A Few Moments with Buster Keaton and Laurel and Hardy
ffolkes
Fiction Makers
Fiddler on the Roof
Field of Dreams
Field of Honor
The Fiend
Fiend
The Fiendish Plot of Dr. Fu Manchu
Fiesta
Fifth Avenue Girl
Fifth Day of Peace
The Fifth Floor
The Fifth Musketeer
$50,000 Reward
52 Pick-Up
55 Days at Peking
Fight for Survival
Fight for Us
Fight for Your Life
Fightin' Ranch
The Fighting American
Fighting Back
Fighting Black Kings
Fighting Caballero
Fighting Caravans
Fighting Cowboy
Fighting Father Dunne
Fighting Fists of Shanghai Joe

The Fringe Dwellers
The Frisco Kid
Fritz the Cat
Frog
Frogs
Frolics on Ice
From Beyond
From Beyond the Grave
From Hell to Borneo
From Hell to Victory
From Here to Eternity
From Here to Maternity
From Hollywood to Deadwood
From Russia with Love
From "Star Wars" to "Jedi": The Making of a Saga
From the Earth to the Moon
From the Hip
From the Life of the Marionettes
From the Terrace
The Front
The Front Page
Frontier Days
Frontier Horizon
Frontier Justice
Frontier Pony Express
Frontier Scout
Frontier Vengeance
Frozen Terror
Fu Manchu
The Fugitive
Fugitive Alien
The Fugitive Kind
The Fugitive: Taking of Luke McVane
Full Circle
Full Fathom Five
Full Hearts & Empty Pockets
Full Metal Jacket
Full Metal Ninja
Full Moon in Blue Water
Full Moon in Paris
The Fuller Brush Man
Fun in Acapulco
Fun with Dick and Jane
Funeral for an Assassin
Funeral Home
Funeral in Berlin
The Funhouse
Funny About Love
Funny, Dirty Little War
Funny Face
The Funny Farm
Funny Girl
Funny Lady
Funny Money
A Funny Thing Happened on the Way to the Forum
Furious
The Furious Avenger
The Further Adventures of Tennessee Buck
Further Adventures of the Wilderness Family, Part 2
Fury
The Fury
Fury
The Fury of the Wolfman
Fury on Wheels
Future Force
Future Hunters
Future Kill
Futureworld
Futz
Fuzz
Fyre
"G" Men
Gabriela
Gaby: A True Story
Gaiety
Gal Young 'Un
Galactic Gigolo
Galaxina
Galaxy Invader
Galaxy of Terror
Gallagher's Travels
Gallipoli
Galloping Dynamite
The Galloping Ghost
Galyon
Gambit
The Gamble
Gamble on Love
The Gambler
The Gambler & the Lady
The Gambling Samurai
The Gambling Terror
The Game
Game for Vultures
The Game is Over
Game of Death
Game of Seduction
Game of Survival
Gamera vs. Barugon
Gamera vs. Gaos
Gamera vs. Guiron
Gamera vs. Zigra
Games Girls Play
The Gamma People
Gandhi
Gang Bullets
Gangbusters
Gangs, Inc.
Gangster Wars
Gangsters
Gangster's Den
Gangster's Law
Gangsters of the Frontier
Ganjasaurus Rex
Gappa the Trifibian Monster
The Garbage Pail Kids Movie
Garbo Talks
The Garden of Delights
The Garden of Eden
The Garden of the Finzi-Continis
Gardens of Stone
Garringo
Gas
Gas Pump Girls
Gas-s-s-s!
Gaslight
The Gate
Gate of Hell
Gates of Hell
The Gathering
The Gathering Storm
Gator
Gator Bait
Gator Bait 2: Cajun Justice
The Gauntlet
The Gay Divorcee
The Gay Ranchero
Geheimakte WB1
Gemini Affair
Gene Autry Matinee Double Feature 2
Gene Autry Matinee Double Feature 3
The Gene Krupa Story
The General
The General Died at Dawn
The General Line
Generale Della Rovere
Generation
Generations: Mind Control-From the Future
Genevieve
Gentleman Bandit
The Gentleman from California
Gentleman Jim
The Gentleman Killer
Gentlemen Prefer Blondes
George!
George Washington
George White's Scandals
Georgia, Georgia
Georgy Girl
Germicide
Geronimo's Revenge
Gertrud
Gervaise
Get Crazy
Get Out Your Handkerchiefs
Get Rita
Get That Man
The Getaway
Getting Even
Getting It On
Getting It Right
The Getting of Wisdom
Getting Over
Getting Physical
Getting Straight
Getting Up and Going Home
Getting Wasted
The Ghastly Ones
Ghetto Blaster
Ghidrah the Three Headed Monster
The Ghost
Ghost
The Ghost and Mrs. Muir
The Ghost and the Guest
Ghost Chase
Ghost Dad
Ghost Dance
Ghost Fever
The Ghost Goes West
Ghost in the Noonday Sun
Ghost Keeper
The Ghost of Rashmon Hall
The Ghost of Yatsuya
Ghost Patrol
Ghost Rider
Ghost Ship
Ghost Stories: Graveyard Thriller
Ghost Story
Ghost Town
Ghost Town Gold
Ghost Town Law
Ghost Town Renegades
The Ghost Train
Ghost Writer
Ghostbusters
Ghostbusters 2
Ghosthouse
Ghostriders
Ghosts Can't Do It
Ghosts of Berkeley Square
The Ghosts of Hanley House
Ghosts That Still Walk
Ghostwarrior
Ghostwriter
The Ghoul
Ghoulies
Ghoulies 2
G.I. Blues
G.I. Executioner
G.I. Jane
Giant
Giant from the Unknown
Giants of Rome
Gideon's Trumpet
Gidget
Gidget Goes Hawaiian
Gidget Goes to Rome
The Gift
The Gift Horse
The Gig
Gigi
Gilda
The Gilded Cage
Gimme an F
Gimme Shelter
Gin Game
Ginger
Ginger Ale Afternoon
Ginger & Fred
Ginger in the Morning
The Girl
A Girl, a Guy and a Gob
The Girl Can't Help It
Girl Crazy
Girl from Calgary
The Girl from Petrovka
The Girl from Tobacco Row
Girl Happy
Girl Hunters
The Girl in a Swing
Girl in Black
The Girl in Blue
A Girl in Every Port
Girl in Gold Boots
The Girl in Lover's Lane
The Girl in Room 2A
The Girl in the Picture
The Girl Most Likely
Girl of the Golden West
Girl on a Chain Gang
The Girl on a Motorcycle
Girl Rush
The Girl Said No
Girl Shy
A Girl to Kill For
Girl Under the Sheet
The Girl Who Spelled Freedom
Girlfriend from Hell
Girlfriends
Girls Are for Loving
A Girl's Folly
Girls! Girls! Girls!
Girls in Chains
Girls Just Want to Have Fun
Girls Next Door
Girls Night Out
Girls of the White Orchid
Girls on the Road
Girls Riot
Girls School Screamers
Girly
Git!
Git Along Little Dogies
Give 'Em Hell, Harry!
Give My Regards to Broad Street
The Gladiator
The Gladiators
Gladiators 7
The Glass Bottom Boat
The Glass House
The Glass Jungle
The Glass Key
The Glass Menagerie
The Glass Slipper
Glass Tomb
Gleaming the Cube
Glen and Randa
Glen or Glenda: Confessions of Ed Wood
The Glenn Miller Story
Glitch!
The Glitter Dome
Glitz
A Global Affair
Gloria
Glorifying the American Girl
Glory
The Glory Boys
Glory! Glory!
Glory Years
The Glove
The Gnome-Mobile
Go Down Death
Go for Broke!
Go for It
Go for the Gold
Go, Johnny Go!
Go Kill and Come Back
The Go-Masters
Go Tell the Spartans
Go West
The Goalie's Anxiety at the Penalty Kick
God Told Me To
Godard/Truffaut Shorts
The Goddess
The Godfather
The Godfather 1902-1959: The Complete Epic
The Godfather, Part 2
The Godfather, Part 3
God's Bloody Acre
God's Country
God's Gun
God's Little Acre
The Gods Must Be Crazy
The Gods Must Be Crazy 2
The Godsend
Godzilla, King of the Monsters
Godzilla 1985
Godzilla vs. Monster Zero
Godzilla vs. Mothra
Godzilla vs. the Sea Monster
Godzilla vs. the Smog Monster
Goetz von Berlichingen
Goin' South
Going Ape!
Going Back
Going Bananas
Going Berserk
Going in Style
Going My Way
Going Places
Going to Congress/Don't Park There
Going to Town
Going Under
Going Undercover
The Gold & Glory
Gold Diggers of 1933
Gold Diggers of 1935
The Gold of Naples
Gold of the Amazon Women
Gold Raiders
The Gold Rush
Gold Rush/Payday
Golden Age of Comedy
Golden Age of Hollywood
Golden Boy
The Golden Child
The Golden Coach
Golden Demon
Golden Exterminators
Golden Lady
Golden Ninja Warrior
Golden Rendezvous
The Golden Seal
Golden Sun
The Golden Triangle
Golden Voyage of Sinbad
Goldengirl
Goldenrod
Goldfinger
Goldilocks & the Three Bears
The Goldwyn Follies
Goldy: The Last of the Golden Bears
Goldy 2: The Saga of the Golden Bear
The Golem
Goliath Against the Giants
Goliath and the Barbarians
Goliath and the Dragon
Gone are the Days
Gone in 60 Seconds
Gone to Ground
Gone with the West
Gone with the Wind
The Good Earth
The Good Father
The Good Fight
Good Guys Wear Black
Good Morning, Babylon
Good Morning, Vietnam
The Good Mother
Good Neighbor Sam
Good News
The Good, the Bad, and Huckleberry Hound
The Good, the Bad and the Ugly
Good Time with a Bad Girl
The Good Wife
Goodbye Columbus
Goodbye Cruel World
Goodbye Emmanuelle
The Goodbye Girl
Goodbye, Mr. Chips
Goodbye, My Lady
Goodbye, New York
Goodbye, Norma Jean

The Goodbye People
Goodbye Pork Pie
Goodfellas
Goodnight God Bless
Goodnight, Sweet Marilyn
Goof Balls
Goon Movie
The Goonies
Gor
Gorath
Gordon's War
Gore-Met Zombie Chef From Hell
Gorgo
The Gorgon
The Gorilla
Gorilla
Gorillas in the Mist
Gorky Park
Gorp
The Gospel According to St. Matthew
The Gospel According to Vic
Gotcha!
Gothic
Gotta Dance, Gotta Sing
Government Agents vs. Phantom Legion
Grace Quigley
Grad Night
The Graduate
Graduation Day
Graffiti Bridge
Grain of Sand
Grambling's White Tiger
Grampa's Monster Movies
Grampa's Sci-Fi Hits
Grand Canyon Trail
The Grand Duchess and the Waiter
Grand Hotel
Grand Illusion
Grand Prix
Grand Theft Auto
Grandes Amigos
Grandma's House
Grandview U.S.A.
The Grapes of Wrath
The Grass is Always Greener Over the Septic Tank
Grave of the Vampire
The Graveyard
Graveyard of Horror
Graveyard Shift
Gray Lady Down
Grayeagle
Grazuole
Grease
Grease 2
Greased Lightning
Greaser's Palace
The Great Adventure
Great Adventure
The Great Alligator
Great American Traffic Jam
The Great Armored Car Swindle
Great Balls of Fire
Great Bank Hoax
The Great Caruso
Great Chase
Great Dan Patch
Great Day
Great Day in the Morning
The Great Dictator
The Great Escape
Great Expectations
Great Flamarion
The Great Gabbo
The Great Gatsby
Great Gold Swindle
The Great Gundown
Great Guns
Great Guy
The Great Hunter
The Great Impostor
Great Jesse James Raid
Great K & A Train Robbery
The Great Land of Small
Great Leaders of the Bibles
The Great Lie
The Great Locomotive Chase
Great Love Experiment
The Great Lover
The Great Man Votes
The Great McGinty
Great Missouri Raid
The Great Moment
The Great Mouse Detective
Great Movie Stunts & the Making of Raiders of the Lost Ark
The Great Muppet Caper
The Great Northfield Minnesota Raid
The Great Outdoors
Great Ride
The Great Riviera Bank Robbery
The Great Rupert
The Great St. Trinian's Train Robbery
The Great Santini
Great Scout & Cathouse Thursday
The Great Skycopter Rescue
Great Smokey Roadblock
The Great Texas Dynamite Chase
The Great Train Robbery
The Great Train Robbery: Cinema Begins
Great Treasure Hunt
The Great Waldo Pepper
A Great Wall
The Great Wallendas
The Great White Hope
The Great Ziegfeld
The Greatest
The Greatest Show on Earth
The Greatest Story Ever Told
Greedy Terror
Greek Street
The Greek Tycoon
Green Archer
The Green Berets
Green Card
Green Dolphin Street
Green Dragon Inn
Green Fields
Green for Danger
Green Horizon
The Green Hornet
Green Ice
Green Inferno
Green Pastures
The Green Promise
The Green Room
The Green Slime
Greenstone
Greetings
Gregory's Girl
Gremlins
Gremlins 2: The New Batch
Grendel, Grendel, Grendel
Greta
The Grey Fox
Greystoke: The Legend of Tarzan, Lord of the Apes
Grievous Bodily Harm
Griffith Biograph Program
The Grifters
Grim Reaper
Grit of the Girl Telegrapher/In the Switch Tower
Grizzly
The Groove Tube
Gross Anatomy
Grotesque
Ground Zero
The Group
Group Marriage
Growing Pains
Grown Ups
Gruesome Twosome
Grunt! The Wrestling Movie
Guadalcanal Diary
The Guardian
Guardian of the Abyss
Guerilla Brigade
Guess What We Learned in School Today?
Guess Who's Coming to Dinner
Guest in the House
A Guide for the Married Man
A Guide for the Married Woman
Guilty as Sin
Gulag
Gulliver's Travels
Gumball Rally
Gumshoe
The Gumshoe Kid
Gun Cargo
Gun Code
Gun Fury
The Gun in Betty Lou's Handbag
A Gun in the House
Gun Law
The Gun Ranger
Gun Riders
Gun Smugglers/Hot Lead
Gunblast
Guncrazy
A Gunfight
Gunfight at Sandoval
Gunfight at the O.K. Corral
The Gunfighter
Gunfire
Gung Ho!
Gung Ho
Gunga Din
Gunman from Bodie
Gunners & Guns
Gunplay
Gunpowder
The Guns and the Fury
Guns in the Dark
Guns of Fury
Guns of Justice
The Guns of Navarone
Guns of War
Gunslinger
Gus
A Guy Named Joe
The Guyana Tragedy: The Story of Jim Jones
Guys and Dolls
Gymkata
Gypsy
Gypsy Blood
The Gypsy Warriors
H-Bomb
H-Man
Hack O'Lantern
Hadley's Rebellion
Hail
Hail Caesar
Hail, Hero!
Hail Mary
Hair
Hairspray
Half a Lifetime
Half a Loaf of Kung Fu
Half a Soldier
The Half-Breed
Half Moon Street
Half of Heaven
Half-Shot at Sunrise
Half Slave, Half Free
Hallelujah, I'm a Bum
Halloween
Halloween 2: The Nightmare Isn't Over!
Halloween 3: Season of the Witch
Halloween 4: The Return of Michael Myers
Halloween 5: The Revenge of Michael Myers
Halloween with the Addams Family
The Halls of Montezuma
Hallucination
Hambone & Hillie
Hamburger Hill
Hamburger...The Motion Picture
Hamlet
Hammersmith is Out
Hammett
Hamsin
The Hand
The Hand that Rocks the Cradle
A Handful of Dust
The Handmaid's Tale
Hands of Death
Hands of Steel
Hands of the Ripper
Hands Up
Hang 'Em High
Hangar 18
Hanging on a Star
The Hanging Woman
Hangman's Knot
Hangmen
Hanky Panky
Hanna K.
Hannah and Her Sisters
Hanna's War
Hanoi Hilton
Hanover Street
Hans Brinker
Hans Christian Andersen
Hansel and Gretel
Hanussen
The Happiest Millionaire
Happily Ever After
Happy Anniversary 007: 25 Years of James Bond
Happy Birthday to Me
Happy Go Lovely
The Happy Hooker
The Happy Hooker Goes Hollywood
The Happy Hooker Goes to Washington
Happy Hour
Happy New Year
Happy New Year, Charlie Brown
Happy Since I Met You
Happy Together
Hard Choices
A Hard Day's Night
Hard Drivin'
Hard Hombre
Hard Knocks
Hard Knox
Hard Part Begins
Hard Rock Zombies
Hard Ticket to Hawaii
Hard Times
Hard to Hold
Hard to Kill
Hard Traveling
Hard Way
The Hard Way
Hardbodies
Hardbodies 2
Hardcase and Fist
Hardcore
The Harder They Come
The Harder They Fall
Hardhat & Legs
Hardly Working
Hardware
Hardware Wars & Other Film Farces
Harem
Harlan County, U.S.A.
Harlem Nights
Harley Davidson and the Marlboro Man
Harlow
Harmony Trail
Harold and Maude
Harper
Harper Valley P.T.A.
Harrad Experiment
Harry & Son
Harry and the Hendersons
Harry and Tonto
Harry & Walter Go to New York
Harry Tracy
Harry's War
Harum Scarum
Harvest
Harvey
The Harvey Girls
A Hash House Fraud/The Sultan's Wife
The Hasty Heart
Hat Box Mystery
Hatari!
Hatchet for the Honeymoon
The Hatfields & the McCoys
The Haunted
The Haunted Castle
Haunted Honeymoon
The Haunted Palace
Haunted Ranch
The Haunted Strangler
Haunted Summer
Haunted: The Ferryman
The Haunting
Haunting of Harrington House
Haunting of Sarah Hardy
The Haunting Passion
Haunts
Haunts of the Very Rich
Havana
Having It All
Having Wonderful Time
Having Wonderful Time/Carnival Boat
Hawaii
Hawk and Castile
Hawk the Slayer
Hawken's Breed
Hawkeye
Hawks
Hawmps!
Hawthorne of the USA
Hazel's People
He is My Brother
He Kills Night After Night After Night
He Knows You're Alone
He Lives: The Search for the Evil One
He Walked by Night
He Who Walks Alone
Head
Head of the Family
Head Office
Head Over Heels
Head Winds
Headhunter
Headin' for the Rio Grande
Heading Home
Headline Woman
Healer
Hear My Song
The Hearse
Heart
Heart Beat
Heart Condition
The Heart is a Lonely Hunter
Heart Like a Wheel
Heart of a Champion: The Ray Mancini Story
The Heart of Dixie
Heart of Humanity
Heart of Midnight
Heart of Texas Ryan
Heart of the Golden West
Heart of the Rio Grande
Heart of the Rockies
Heart of the Stag
Heartaches
Heartbeeps
Heartbreak Hotel
Heartbreak House

The Heartbreak Kid
Heartbreak Ridge
Heartbreaker
Heartbreakers
Heartburn
Heartland
Hearts & Armour
Heart's Desire
Heart's Haven
Hearts of Darkness: A Filmmaker's Apocalypse
Hearts of Fire
Hearts of the West
Hearts of the World
Heat
Heat and Dust
Heat and Sunlight
Heat of Desire
Heat of the Flame
Heat Street
Heat Wave
Heated Vengeance
Heathers
Heatwave
Heaven
Heaven Can Wait
Heaven Help Us
Heaven on Earth
Heavenly Bodies
The Heavenly Kid
Heavens Above
Heaven's Gate
Heaven's Heroes
Heavy Petting
Heavy Traffic
Hedda
Heidi
The Heiress
The Heist
Held for Murder
Hell Comes to Frogtown
Hell Commandos
Hell Fire Austin
Hell Harbor
Hell High
Hell Hounds of Alaska
Hell Hunters
Hell in the Pacific
Hell is for Heroes
Hell Night
Hell on Frisco Bay
Hell on the Battleground
Hell on Wheels
Hell Raiders
Hell River
Hell Ship Mutiny
Hell Squad
Hell to Eternity
Hell Up in Harlem
Hellbenders
Hellbent
Hellbound: Hellraiser 2
Hellcats
Hellcats of the Navy
Helldorado
Heller in Pink Tights
Hellfighters
The Hellfire Club
Hellhole
Hello Again
Hello, Dolly!
Hello Mary Lou: Prom Night 2
Hellraiser
Hellriders
Hell's Angels Forever
Hell's Angels on Wheels
Hell's Angels '69
Hell's Brigade: The Final Assault
Hell's Hinges
Hell's House
Hell's Wind Staff
The Hellstrom Chronicle
Helltown
Help!
Help Wanted: Male
Helter Skelter

The Henderson Monster
Henry IV
Henry V
Henry: Portrait of a Serial Killer
Hepburn & Tracy
Her Alibi
Her Life as a Man
Her Silent Sacrifice
Herbie Goes Bananas
Herbie Goes to Monte Carlo
Herbie Rides Again
Hercules
Hercules Against the Moon Men
Hercules and the Captive Women
Hercules and the Princess of Troy
Hercules in New York
Hercules in the Haunted World
Hercules Unchained
Here Come the Littles: The Movie
Here Comes Kelly
Here Comes Mr. Jordan
Here Comes Santa Claus
Here Comes the Groom
Here We Go Again!
The Hereafter
Heritage of the Desert
The Hero
A Hero Ain't Nothin' But a Sandwich
Hero and the Terror
Hero at Large
Hero Bunker
Hero of Rome
Heroes
Heroes Die Young
Heroes in Blue
Heroes in Hell
The Heroes of Desert Storm
Heroes of the Alamo
Heroes of the Hills
Heroes of the West
Heroes Stand Alone
Heroes Three
He's My Girl
He's Your Dog, Charlie Brown!
Hester Street
Hey, Babu Riba
Hey Good Lookin'
Hey There, It's Yogi Bear
Hi-De-Ho
Hi-Di-Hi
Hi Diddle Diddle
Hi-Jacked
Hi-Riders
The Hidden
Hidden City
Hidden Enemy
Hidden Fears
The Hidden Fortress
Hidden Gold
The Hidden Room
Hide and Go Shriek
Hide and Seek
Hide in Plain Sight
The Hideaways
Hideous Sun Demon
Hider in the House
Hiding Out
High & Low
High Anxiety
High Ballin'
High Command
High Country
High Country Calling
High Crime
High Desert Kill
High Heels
High Hopes
High Ice
High Noon: Part 2
High Plains Drifter
High Risk
High Road to China

High Rolling in a Hot Corvette
High School Caesar
High School Confidential
High School USA
High Season
High Sierra
High Society
High Spirits
High Tide
High Velocity
High Voltage
Higher and Higher
The Highest Honor
Highlander
Highpoint
Highway 13
Hijazo de Mi Vidaza
Hill Number One
Hill 24 Doesn't Answer
Hillbillies in a Haunted House
The Hills Have Eyes
The Hills Have Eyes, Part 2
Hills of Utah
The Hillside Strangler
Himatsuri
The Hindenburg
Hips, Hips, Hooray
Hired Hand
Hired to Kill
Hiroshima, Mon Amour
His Double Life
His Fighting Blood
His First Command
His First Flame
His Girl Friday
His Kind of Woman
His Majesty O'Keefe
His Majesty, the Scarecrow of Oz/The Magic Cloak of Oz
His Name was King
His Picture in the Papers
His Prehistoric Past/The Bank
His Private Secretary
His Royal Slyness/Haunted Spooks
His Wife's Lover
History is Made at Night
History of the World: Part 1
The History of White People in America
The History of White People in America: Vol. 2
The Hit
Hit & Run
Hit Lady
The Hit List
The Hit Man
Hit Men
Hit the Deck
Hit the Ice
Hit the Saddle
Hitchcock Classics Collection: Trailers on Tape
Hitchcock Collection
The Hitcher
The Hitchhiker
Hitchhiker 2
Hitchhiker 3
Hitchhiker 4
Hitchhikers
Hitler
Hitler: Dead or Alive
Hitler: The Last Ten Days
Hitler's Children
Hitler's Daughter
Hittin' the Trail
The Hobbit
Hobgoblins
Hobo's Christmas
Hobson's Choice
Hockey Night
Hocus Pocus
Hog Wild
The Holcroft Covenant
Hold 'Em Jail
Hold That Ghost

Hold the Dream
A Hole in the Head
The Holes
Holiday
Holiday Affair
Holiday Hotel
Holiday Inn
Holiday Rhythm
Hollow Gate
Hollywood Bloopers
Hollywood Boulevard
Hollywood Boulevard 2
Hollywood Chainsaw Hookers
Hollywood Clowns
Hollywood Come Home
Hollywood Confidential
Hollywood Cop
Hollywood Crime Wave
The Hollywood Detective
Hollywood Erotic Film Festival
Hollywood Ghost Stories
Hollywood Goes to War
Hollywood Harry
Hollywood High
Hollywood High, Part 2
Hollywood Home Movies
Hollywood Hot Tubs
Hollywood Hot Tubs 2: Educating Crystal
Hollywood in Trouble
Hollywood Man
Hollywood Outtakes & Rare Footage
Hollywood Scandals and Tragedies
Hollywood Shuffle
Hollywood Stadium Mystery
Hollywood Uncensored
Hollywood Varieties
Hollywood without Makeup
Hollywood Zap
Hollywood's New Blood
Holocaust
Holocaust Survivors...Remembrance of Love
The Holy Innocents
Holy Terror
Hombre
Home Alone
The Home and the World
Home Before Midnight
Home for the Holidays
Home Free All
Home from the Hill
Home in Oklahoma
Home Is Where the Hart Is
Home Movies
A Home of Our Own
Home of the Brave
Home Remedy
Home Sweet Home
Home to Stay
Homebodies
Homeboy
Homecoming
Homecoming: A Christmas Story
Homer and Eddie
Homer Comes Home
Homesteaders of Paradise Valley
Hometown U.S.A.
Homeward Bound
Homework
Homewrecker
Homo Eroticus/Man of the Year
Honey
Honey, I Blew Up the Kid
Honey, I Shrunk the Kids
Honeyboy
Honeymoon
Honeymoon Horror
Honeymoon Killers
Honeymooners Hidden Episodes, Vol. 1

Honeysuckle Rose
Hong Kong Nights
Honky
Honky Tonk
Honky Tonk Freeway
Honkytonk Man
Honkytonk Nights
Honor Among Thieves
Honor Thy Father
Hooch
The Hoodlum
The Hoodlum Priest
Hoodoo Ann
Hook
Hooper
Hoosiers
Hootch Country Boys
Hopalong Cassidy: Dangerous Venture
Hopalong Cassidy: False Paradise
Hopalong Cassidy: Hoppy's Holiday
Hopalong Cassidy: Renegade Trail
Hopalong Cassidy: Riders of the Deadline
Hopalong Cassidy: Silent Conflict
Hopalong Cassidy: Sinister Journey
Hopalong Cassidy: The Dead Don't Dream
Hopalong Cassidy: The Devil's Playground
Hopalong Cassidy: The Marauders
Hopalong Cassidy: Unexpected Guest
Hope and Glory
Hopscotch
The Horror Chamber of Dr. Faustus
Horror Express
Horror Hospital
Horror House on Highway 5
The Horror of Dracula
The Horror of Frankenstein
Horror of Party Beach
Horror of the Blood Monsters
Horror Planet
Horror Rises from the Tomb
The Horror Show
Horrors of Burke & Hare
Horrors of the Red Planet
The Horse
Horse Feathers
The Horse in the Gray Flannel Suit
The Horse of Pride
The Horse Soldiers
The Horse Without a Head
Horsemasters
The Horsemen
The Horse's Mouth
The Hospital
Hospital Massacre
Hostage
The Hostage Tower
Hostages
Hostile Takeover
Hot Blood
Hot Box
Hot Bubblegum
Hot Child in the City
Hot Dog...The Movie!
Hot Foot/A Happy Married Couple
Hot Lead & Cold Feet
Hot Money
Hot Moves
Hot Potato
Hot Pursuit
Hot Resort
The Hot Rock
Hot Rod

Hot Shot
Hot Spell
Hot Stuff
Hot Summer in Barefoot County
Hot T-Shirts
Hot Target
Hot Times
Hot to Trot!
Hot Touch
Hot Water/Safety Last
Hot Wire
Hotel
Hotel Colonial
Hotel du Lac
The Hotel New Hampshire
Hotel Reserve
Hothead
H.O.T.S.
The Hound of the Baskervilles
Hour of Decision
Hour of the Assassin
The Hour of the Star
Hour of the Wolf
House
House 2: The Second Story
House Across the Bay
The House by the Cemetery
House Calls
House of Dark Shadows
House of Death
House of Fear
House of Games
The House of Lurking Death
The House of 1000 Dolls
House of Psychotic Women
The House of Secrets
House of Shadows
House of Terror
The House of the Arrow
House of the Damned
House of the Living Dead
House of the Long Shadows
House of the Rising Sun
House of the Yellow Carpet
House of Wax
House of Whipcord
The House on Carroll Street
The House on Chelouche Street
The House on Garibaldi Street
House on Haunted Hill
The House on Skull Mountain
The House on Sorority Row
The House on Straw Hill
House on the Edge of the Park
House Party
The House that Bled to Death
The House that Dripped Blood
The House that Vanished
House Where Evil Dwells
A House Without a Christmas Tree
Houseboat
The Housekeeper
Housekeeping
Housesitter
Housewife
How Come Nobody's On Our Side?
How Funny Can Sex Be?
How Green Was My Valley
How I Got into College
How I Learned to Love Women
How I Won the War
How Many Miles to Babylon?
How the Grinch Stole Christmas
How the West Was Won
How to Beat the High Cost of Living
How to Break Up a Happy Divorce
How to Get Ahead in Advertising
How to Kill 400 Duponts
How to Marry a Millionaire
How to Murder Your Wife
How to Pick Up Girls

How to Seduce a Woman
How to Stuff a Wild Bikini
Howard the Duck
The Howards of Virginia
The Howling
Howling 2: Your Sister is a Werewolf
Howling 3: The Marsupials
Howling 4: The Original Nightmare
Howling 5: The Rebirth
Huck and the King of Hearts
Huckleberry Finn
The Hucksters
Hud
Hudson Hawk
Hughes & Harlow: Angels in Hell
Hugo the Hippo
Hula
Hullabaloo Over Georgie & Bonnie's Pictures
Human Beasts
The Human Comedy
The Human Condition: A Soldier's Prayer
The Human Condition: No Greater Love
The Human Condition: Road to Eternity
The Human Duplicators
Human Experiments
The Human Factor
Human Gorilla
Human Hearts
The Human Monster
The Human Vapor
Humanoid Defender
Humanoids from the Deep
Humongous
The Hunchback of Notre Dame
Hundra
Hungarian Rhapsody
The Hunger
Hunk
The Hunt for Red October
Hunt the Man Down
Hunt the Man Down/Smashing the Rackets
Hunted!
Hunter
The Hunter
Hunter's Blood
Hunters of the Golden Cobra
The Hunting
The Hurricane
Hurricane
Hurricane Express
Hurricane Sword
Hurry, Charlie, Hurry
Hurry Up or I'll Be Thirty
Husband Hunting
Husbands, Wives, Money, and Murder
Hush, Hush, Sweet Charlotte
Hush Little Baby, Don't You Cry
Hussy
The Hustle
The Hustler
Hustler Squad
Hustling
Hyper-Sapien: People from Another Star
Hysteria
Hysterical
I Accuse My Parents
I Am a Camera
I Am a Fugitive from a Chain Gang
I Am the Cheese
I Am the Law
I Can't Escape
I Come in Peace
I Confess
I Conquer the Sea
I Could Go on Singing
I Cover the Waterfront

I Dismember Mama
I Do! I Do!
I Don't Buy Kisses Anymore
I Don't Give a Damn
I Dream Too Much
I Hate Blondes
I Heard the Owl Call My Name
I Killed Rasputin
I Killed That Man
I Know Where I'm Going
I Know Why the Caged Bird Sings
I Live with Me Dad
I Love All of You
I Love My...Wife
I Love N.Y.
I Love You
I Love You, Alice B. Toklas!
I Love You ... Goodbye
I Love You to Death
I, Madman
I Married a Centerfold
I Married a Monster from Outer Space
I Married a Vampire
I Married a Witch
I Married a Woman
I Married an Angel
I Never Promised You a Rose Garden
I Never Sang For My Father
I Ought to Be in Pictures
I Remember Mama
I See a Dark Stranger
I Sent a Letter to My Love
I Shot Billy the Kid
I Shot Jesse James
I Spit on Your Corpse
I Spit on Your Grave
I Stand Condemned
I Take This Oath
I, the Jury
I Wake Up Screaming
I Walked with a Zombie
I Wanna Be a Beauty Queen
I Wanna Hold Your Hand
I Want to Live!
I Want What I Want
I Was a Teenage TV Terrorist
I Was a Teenage Zombie
I Was a Zombie for the FBI
I Will Fight No More Forever
I Will, I Will for Now
Ice Castles
The Ice Flood
Ice House
Ice Palace
Ice Pirates
Ice Station Zebra
Icebox Murders
Iced
Iceman
Icy Breasts
I'd Give My Life
Idaho
Idaho Transfer
Identity Unknown
Idiot's Delight
Idolmaker
If...
If Ever I See You Again
If I Were Rich
If It's a Man, Hang Up
If Looks Could Kill
If Things Were Different
If You Could See What I Hear
If You Don't Stop It...You'll Go Blind
If You Knew Susie
Igor & the Lunatics
Ike
Ikiru
I'll Cry Tomorrow
I'll Get You
I'll Take Sweden
Illegally Yours

Illusions
The Illustrated Man
I'm All Right Jack
I'm Dancing as Fast as I Can
I'm from Arkansas
I'm Gonna Git You Sucka
I'm on My Way/The Non-Stop Kid
I'm the Girl He Wants to Kill
Image of Bruce Lee
Image of Death
Image of Passion
Imagemaker
Imitation of Life
Immediate Family
The Immigrant
Immortal Bachelor
Immortal Battalion
Immortal Sergeant
The Immortalizer
Impact
The Imperial Japanese Empire
Imperial Navy
Imperial Venus
Importance of Being Earnest
The Imposter
Imposters
Improper Channels
Impulse
Impure Thoughts
In a Lonely Place
In Cold Blood
In Country
The In Crowd
In Deadly Heat
In for Treatment
In Harm's Way
In Hot Pursuit
The In-Laws
In Like Flint
In Love with an Older Woman
In 'n Out
In Name Only
In Old Caliente
In Old Cheyenne
In Old Montana
In Old New Mexico
In Old Santa Fe
In Person
In Praise of Older Women
In Search of a Golden Sky
In Search of Anna
In Search of the Castaways
In the Aftermath: Angels Never Sleep
In the Days of the Thundering Herd & the Law & the Outlaw
In the Good Old Summertime
In the Heat of the Night
In the King of Prussia
In the Land of the Owl Turds
In the Mood
In the Name of the Pope-King
In the Region of Ice
In the Shadow of Kilimanjaro
In the Spirit
In the Steps of a Dead Man
In This House of Brede
In This Our Life
In Too Deep
In Trouble
In Which We Serve
The Incident
Incident at Channel Q
An Inconvenient Woman
The Incredible Hulk
The Incredible Journey
The Incredible Journey of Dr. Meg Laurel
Incredible Master Beggars
Incredible Melting Man
The Incredible Mr. Limpet
The Incredible Rocky Mountain Race
The Incredible Sarah
The Incredible Shrinking Man

The Incredible Shrinking Woman
Incredibly Strange Creatures Who Stopped Living and Became Mixed-Up Zombies
Incubus
An Indecent Obsession
Indecent Proposal
Independence
Independence Day
Indian Paint
Indian Summer
Indian Uprising
Indiana Jones and the Last Crusade
Indiana Jones and the Temple of Doom
Indio
Indiscreet
Indiscretion of an American Wife
Indomitable Teddy Roosevelt
Infamous Crimes
Inferno
The Informer
Infra-Man
Inga
Inherit the Wind
Inheritance
The Inheritance
The Inheritors
Inhibition
The Initiation
Initiation of Sarah
Inn of Temptation
Inn of the Damned
The Inn of the Sixth Happiness
The Inner Circle
Innerspace
The Innocent
Innocent Blood
An Innocent Man
Innocents in Paris
Inquisition
Insanity
Inside Information
The Inside Man
Inside Moves
Inside Out
Inside the Lines
Inside the Third Reich
Insignificance
The Inspector General
Inspector Hornleigh
Inspiration of Mr. Budd
Instant Justice
Instant Karma
Instant Kung-Fu Man
The Instructor
Interface
Interiors
Intermezzo
Internal Affairs
International Crime
International House
International Velvet
Internecine Project
The Interns
Intersection
Interval
Interzone
Intimate Contact
Intimate Power
Intimate Story
Intimate Stranger
Intimate Strangers
Into the Darkness
Into the Fire
Into the Homeland
Into the Night
Into Thin Air
Intruder
Intruder Within
The Invaders
Invaders from Mars
Invasion Earth: The Aliens Are Here!
The Invasion of Carol Enders

Invasion of the Blood Farmers
Invasion of the Body Snatchers
Invasion of the Body Stealers
Invasion of the Flesh Hunters
Invasion of the Girl Snatchers
Invasion of the Space Preachers
Invasion U.S.A.
Investigation
Invincible
Invincible Armor
Invincible Barbarian
Invincible Gladiators
Invincible Mr. Disraeli
The Invincible Six
Invisible Adversaries
The Invisible Avenger
The Invisible Dr. Mabuse
The Invisible Ghost
The Invisible Kid
The Invisible Killer
The Invisible Man
The Invisible Ray
The Invisible Strangler
Invisible: The Chronicles of Benjamin Knight
Invitation au Voyage
Invitation to a Gunfighter
Invitation to Hell
Invitation to the Dance
Invitation to the Wedding
The Ipcress File
Iphigenia
I.Q.
Irezumi
Iris
Irish Cinderella
The Irishman
Irma La Douce
Iron Dragon Strikes Back
The Iron Duke
Iron Eagle
Iron Eagle 2
Iron Horsemen
The Iron Major
The Iron Mask
The Iron Triangle
Iron Warrior
Ironmaster
Ironweed
Irreconcilable Differences
Irving Berlin's America
Is There Sex After Death?
Isadora
Ishtar
The Island
The Island at the Top of the World
Island Claw
Island Monster
Island of Adventure
Island of Desire
Island of Dr. Moreau
Island of Lost Girls
The Island of Nevawuz
Island of the Blue Dolphins
Island Trader
The Islander
Islands
Islands in the Stream
Isle of Forgotten Sins
Isle of Secret Passion
Isle of the Dead
Isn't Life Wonderful
Istanbul
It
It Came from Beneath the Sea
It Came from Hollywood
It Came Upon a Midnight Clear
It Could Happen to You
It Happened at the World's Fair
It Happened in New Orleans
It Happened in the Park
It Happened One Night
It Rained All Night the Day I Left
It Should Happen to You
It Takes Two
It! The Terror from Beyond Space
Italian
The Italian Stallion
Italian Straw Hat
It's A Gift
It's a Mad, Mad, Mad, Mad World
It's a Mystery, Charlie Brown
It's Alive
It's Alive 2: It Lives Again
It's Alive 3: Island of the Alive
It's Always Fair Weather
It's an Adventure, Charlie Brown!
It's Arbor Day, Charlie Brown
It's Called Murder, Baby
It's Flashbeagle, Charlie Brown/ She's a Good Skate, Charlie Brown
It's Good to Be Alive
It's Love Again
It's Magic, Charlie Brown/ Charlie Brown's All Star
It's My Turn
It's the Great Pumpkin, Charlie Brown
It's the Old Army Game
It's Three Strikes, Charlie Brown
It's Your First Kiss, Charlie Brown/Someday You'll Find Her, Charlie Brown
Ivan the Terrible, Part 1
Ivan the Terrible, Part 2
Ivanhoe
I've Heard the Mermaids Singing
Ivory Hunters
Izzy & Moe
J. Edgar Hoover
J-Men Forever!
Jabberwalk
Jabberwocky
Jack & the Beanstalk
Jack Frost
The Jack Knife Man
Jack London
Jack the Giant Killer
Jack the Ripper
The Jackie Robinson Story
Jacknife
Jacko & Lise
Jack's Back
Jackson County Jail
Jacob's Ladder
Jacqueline Bouvier Kennedy
The Jagged Edge
Jaguar Lives
Jail Bait
Jailbait: Betrayed By Innocence
Jailbird Rock
Jailbird's Vacation
Jailbreakin'
Jailhouse Rock
Jakarta
Jake Speed
Jamaica Inn
James Dean
James Dean Story
James Dean: The First American Teenager
James Joyce's Women
James Stewart: A Wonderful Life
Jane & the Lost City
Jane Austen in Manhattan
Jane Doe
Jane Eyre
Janis: A Film
The January Man
Japanese Connection
The Jar
Jason and the Argonauts
Java Head
Jaws
Jaws 2
Jaws 3
Jaws of Death
Jaws of Justice
Jaws: The Revenge
The Jayne Mansfield Story
The Jazz Singer
Jealousy
Jean de Florette
Jekyll & Hyde...Together Again
Jennifer
Jennifer 8
Jenny
Jenny Lamour
Jeremiah Johnson
Jericho
Jericho Fever
The Jericho Mile
The Jerk
Jesse James
Jesse James at Bay
Jesse James Meets Frankenstein's Daughter
Jesse James Under the Black Flag
The Jesse Owens Story
Jessie's Girls
Jesus
Jesus Christ, Superstar
Jesus of Nazareth
The Jesus Trip
Jet Benny Show
Jet Over the Atlantic
The Jetsons Meet the Flintstones
Jetsons: The Movie
The Jewel in the Crown
The Jewel of the Nile
Jezebel
JFK
JFK Remembered
The Jigsaw Man
Jigsaw Murders
Jim Thorpe: All American
Jimmy Hollywood
Jimmy the Kid
Jinxed
The Jitters
Jive Junction
Jo Jo Dancer, Your Life is Calling
Joan of Arc
Joan of Paris
Jock Petersen
Jocks
Joe
Joe Kidd
The Joe Louis Story
Joe Versus the Volcano
Joe's Bed-Stuy Barbershop: We Cut Heads
Joey
Joey Breaker
John and the Missus
John & Yoko: A Love Story
Johnnie Gibson F.B.I.
Johnny Angel
Johnny Apollo
Johnny Be Good
Johnny Belinda
Johnny Dangerously
Johnny Firecloud
Johnny Got His Gun
Johnny Handsome
Johnny Nobody
Johnny Shiloh
Johnny Tiger
Johnny Tremain & the Sons of Liberty
Johnny We Hardly Knew Ye
A Joke of Destiny, Lying in Wait Around the Corner Like a Bandit
Jokes My Folks Never Told Me
Jolson Sings Again
The Jolson Story
Jonathan Livingston Seagull
Joni
Jornada de Muerte
Jory
Joseph & His Brethren
Joseph Andrews
Josepha
Josh Kirby...Time Warrior: Chapter 1, Planet of the Dino-Knights
Josh Kirby...Time Warrior: Chapter 2, The Human Pets
Josh Kirby...Time Warrior: Chapter 3, Trapped on Toyworld
Josh Kirby...Time Warrior: Chapter 4, Eggs from 70 Million B.C.
Josh Kirby...Time Warrior: Chapter 5, Journey to the Magic Cavern
Josh Kirby...Time Warrior: Chapter 6, Last Battle for the Universe
Joshua Then and Now
Jour de Fete
Journey
Journey Back to Oz
Journey Beneath the Desert
Journey into Fear
Journey into the Beyond
Journey of Honor
The Journey of Natty Gann
Journey Through Rosebud
Journey to the Center of the Earth
Journey to the Center of Time
Journey to the Far Side of the Sun
Journey to the Lost City
Journeys from Berlin/1971
Joy House
Joy of Living
Joy of Sex
Joy Ride to Nowhere
Joy Sticks
Joyless Street
Joyride
Juarez
Jubal
Jud
Jud Suess
Judex
The Judge and the Assassin
Judge Priest
Judge Roy Bean
Judgment at Nuremberg
Judgment Day
Judgment in Berlin
Juggernaut
The Juggler of Notre Dame
Juke Joint
Jules and Jim
Julia
Julia and Julia
Juliet of the Spirits
Julius Caesar
July Group
The Jumper
Jumpin' Jack Flash
Junction 88
June Night
Jungle
Jungle Assault
The Jungle Book
Jungle Bride
Jungle Fever
Jungle Goddess
Jungle Heat
Jungle Hell
Jungle Holocaust
Jungle Inferno
Jungle Master
Jungle Patrol
Jungle Raiders
Jungle Siren
Jungle Warriors
Junior
Junior Bonner
Junior G-Men
Junior G-Men of the Air
Junior High School
The Junkman
Jupiter's Thigh
Just Another Pretty Face
Just Before Dawn
Just Between Friends
Just Me & You
Just One of the Guys
Just Suppose
Just Tell Me What You Want
Just Tell Me You Love Me
Just the Way You Are
Just William's Luck
Justice
Justice of the West
Justice Rides Again
Justin Morgan Had a Horse
Justine
K-9
Kafka
Kagemusha
Kameradschaft
Kamikaze
Kamikaze '89
Kanal
Kandyland
Kangaroo
The Kansan
Kansas
Kansas City Massacre
Kansas Pacific
The Karate Kid
The Karate Kid: Part 2
The Karate Kid: Part 3
Karate Warrior
Karate Warriors
Katherine
Kavik the Wolf Dog
Keaton's Cop
The Keep
Keep My Grave Open
Keeper
Keeper of the City
Keeping Track
Keetje Tippel
Kelly's Heroes
Kemek
Kennedy
The Kennedys Don't Cry
The Kennel Murder Case
Kenny Rogers as the Gambler, Part 2: The Adventure Continues
Kenny Rogers as the Gambler, Part 3: The Legend Continues
Kent State
The Kentuckian
Kentucky Blue Streak
Kentucky Fried Movie
Kentucky Jubilee
Kentucky Rifle
The Key
Key Exchange
Key Largo
The Key Man
The Keys of the Kingdom
Khartoum
Kick of Death: The Prodigal Boxer
Kickboxer
Kicks
Kid
Kid and the Killers
The Kid Brother
Kid Colter
Kid Courageous
Kid from Brooklyn
Kid from Gower Gulch
The Kid from Left Field
Kid from Not-So-Big
Kid Galahad

The Kid/Idle Class
Kid Millions
Kid 'n' Hollywood and Polly Tix in Washington
Kid Ranger
Kid Sister
Kid Vengeance
The Kid with the 200 I.Q.
Kidco
Kidnap Syndicate
Kidnapped
Kidnapping of Baby John Doe
The Kidnapping of the President
Kid's Auto Race/Mabel's Married Life
Kids In the Hall Brain Candy
The Kill
Kill Alex Kill
Kill and Go Hide
Kill and Kill Again
Kill Castro
Kill Cruise
Kill Factor
Kill Me Again
Kill or Be Killed
The Kill Reflex
Kill Slade
Kill Squad
Kill the Golden Goose
Killer
Killer Diller
Killer Elephants
The Killer Elite
Killer Fish
Killer Force
Killer Image
A Killer in Every Corner
Killer Inside Me
Killer Klowns from Outer Space
Killer Likes Candy
Killer on Board
Killer Party
Killer with Two Faces
Killer Workout
The Killers
Killers
Killers from Space
Killer's Moon
The Killing
A Killing Affair
Killing at Hell's Gate
Killing Cars
Killing 'em Softly
The Killing Fields
Killing Floor
The Killing Game
Killing Heat
Killing Hour
The Killing of a Chinese Bookie
Killing of Angel Street
Killing of Randy Webster
The Killing of Sister George
Killing Stone
The Killing Time
Killings at Outpost Zeta
Killjoy
Killpoint
Killzone
Kilma, Queen of the Amazons
Kim
Kind Hearts and Coronets
A Kind of Loving
Kindergarten Cop
The Kindred
King
The King and Four Queens
The King and I
King Arthur, the Young Warlord
King Boxers
King Creole
King David
King Dinosaur
A King in New York
King Kong
King Kong Lives
King of America
King of Comedy
The King of Hearts
King of Jazz
King of Kings
The King of Kings
King of Kong Island
King of the Bullwhip
King of the Forest Rangers
King of the Grizzlies
King of the Gypsies
King of the Kongo
King of the Mountain
The King of the Roaring '20s: The Story of Arnold Rothstein
King of the Rodeo
King of the Wild Horses
King of the Zombies
The King on Main Street
King, Queen, Knave
King Ralph
King Rat
King Solomon's Mines
King Solomon's Treasure
Kingdom of the Spiders
Kingfisher Caper
Kingfisher the Killer
Kings Go Forth
Kings of the Road—In the Course of Time
Kings, Queens, Jokers
Kings Row
Kinjite: Forbidden Subjects
Kino Pravda/Enthusiasm
Kipperbang
Kipps
The Kirlian Witness
Kismet
The Kiss
Kiss and Be Killed
A Kiss Before Dying
Kiss Daddy Goodbye
Kiss Daddy Goodnight
A Kiss for Mary Pickford
Kiss Me Deadly
Kiss Me Goodbye
Kiss Me Kate
Kiss Me, Kill Me
Kiss Me, Stupid!
KISS Meets the Phantom of the Park
Kiss My Grits
Kiss of the Spider Woman
Kiss of the Tarantula
Kiss Shot
Kisses
Kissin' Cousins
The Kissing Place
Kit Carson
The Kitchen Toto
Kitty and the Bagman
Kitty Foyle
Klondike Fever
Klute
The Klutz
Knife in the Water
Knight Without Armour
Knightriders
Knights
Knights & Emeralds
Knights of the City
Knights of the Range
Knights of the Round Table
Knock on Any Door
The Knockout/Dough and Dynamite
Knute Rockne: All American
Kojak: The Belarus File
Kojiro
Kolberg
Koroshi
Kostas
Kowloon Assignment
Koyaanisqatsi
Kramer vs. Kramer
Kronos
Krull
Krush Groove
K2: The Ultimate High
Kuffs
Kung Fu
Kung Fu Avengers
Kung Fu Commandos
Kung Fu Massacre
Kung Fu Rebels
Kung Fu: The Movie
Kwaidan
L.A. Bad
La Balance
La Bamba
La Bete Humaine
La Boum
L.A. Bounty
La Cage aux Folles
La Cage aux Folles 2
La Cage aux Folles 3: The Wedding
La Chevre
La Chienne
La Chute de la Maison Usher
La Cicada
L.A. Crackdown
L.A. Crackdown 2
L.A. Gangs Rising
La Grande Bourgeoise
L.A. Heat
L.A. Law
La Lectrice
La Marseillaise
La Nuit de Varennes
La Passante
La Ronde
La Signora di Tutti
L.A. Story
La Strada
La Terra Trema
La Truite
L.A. Vice
La Vie Continue
Laboratory
Labyrinth
Labyrinth of Passion
L'Addition
The Ladies Club
The Ladies' Man
Ladies of the Lotus
Lady and the Tramp
Lady Avenger
Lady Beware
Lady Caroline Lamb
Lady Chatterley's Lover
Lady Cocoa
The Lady Eve
Lady for a Day
Lady Frankenstein
Lady from Nowhere
The Lady from Shanghai
Lady from Yesterday
Lady Grey
Lady Ice
Lady in a Cage
Lady in Cement
Lady in Distress
The Lady in Question
Lady in Red
Lady in the Death House
Lady in the Lake
The Lady in White
Lady Jane
Lady L
Lady Mobster
Lady of Burlesque
Lady of the Evening
Lady of the House
Lady on the Bus
The Lady Refuses
Lady Scarface
Lady Scarface/The Threat
Lady Sings the Blues
Lady Stay Dead
Lady Street Fighter
Lady Takes a Chance
Lady Terminator
The Lady Vanishes
Lady Windermere's Fan
The Lady with the Dog
The Lady Without Camelias
Ladybugs
Ladyhawke
The Ladykillers
Ladykillers
The Lady's Maid's Bell
L'Age D'Or
Laguna Heat
The Lair of the White Worm
The Lamb
Lambada
Lamp at Midnight
Lana in Love
Land of Doom
The Land of Faraway
Land of Hunted Men
Land of the Minotaur
Land Raiders
The Land That Time Forgot
Landlord Blues
L'Annee des Meduses
Laramie Kid
Larry
Las Vegas Hillbillys
Las Vegas Lady
Las Vegas Serial Killer
The Las Vegas Story
Las Vegas Weekend
Laserblast
The Lash of the Penitents
Lassie
Lassie: Adventures of Neeka
Lassie, Come Home
Lassie from Lancashire
Lassie: The Miracle
Lassie: Well of Love
Lassie's Great Adventure
Lassiter
Last Action Hero
The Last American Hero
Last American Virgin
The Last Angry Man
The Last Bastion
Last Bullet
Last Call
Last Chase
Last Command
Last Cry for Help
Last Dance
Last Day of the War
Last Days of Frank & Jesse James
The Last Days of Patton
Last Days of Pompeii
The Last Detail
The Last Dragon
Last Embrace
The Last Emperor
The Last Fight
The Last Flight of Noah's Ark
Last Four Days
Last Frontier
Last Game
Last Gun
Last Holiday
The Last Horror Film
The Last Hour
Last House on the Left
The Last Hunter
Last Hurrah
The Last Innocent Man
The Last Laugh
Last Man Standing
The Last Married Couple in America
Last Mercenary
The Last Metro
The Last Mile
The Last of England
The Last of Mrs. Lincoln
The Last of Sheila
Last of the Clintons
Last of the Comanches
The Last of the Finest
The Last of the Mohicans
Last of the Pony Riders
Last of the Red Hot Lovers
Last of the Warrens
Last of the Wild Horses
The Last Outlaw
Last Outlaw
Last Plane Out
The Last Polka
The Last Radio Station
The Last Remake of Beau Geste
Last Resort
The Last Ride of the Dalton Gang
Last Rites
The Last Slumber Party
Last Song
The Last Starfighter
Last Summer
The Last Supper
Last Tango in Paris
The Last Temptation of Christ
The Last Time I Saw Paris
The Last Train
The Last Tycoon
The Last Unicorn
The Last Waltz
Last War
The Last Warrior
The Last Wave
The Last Winter
The Last Winters
Last Witness
The Last Word
Last Year at Marienbad
L'Atalante
Late Extra
The Late Show
Late Spring
Lathe of Heaven
Latino
Lauderdale
Laugh with Linder!
Laughfest
The Laughing Policeman
Laura
Laurel & Hardy Comedy Classics, Vol. 1
Laurel & Hardy Comedy Classics, Vol. 2
Laurel & Hardy Comedy Classics, Vol. 3
Laurel & Hardy Comedy Classics, Vol. 4
Laurel & Hardy Comedy Classics, Vol. 5
Laurel & Hardy Comedy Classics, Vol. 6
Laurel & Hardy Comedy Classics, Vol. 7
Laurel & Hardy Comedy Classics, Vol. 8
Laurel & Hardy Comedy Classics, Vol. 9
Laurel & Hardy Special
The Lavender Hill Mob
L'Avventura
Law and Lawless
Law and Order
Law of Desire
Law of the Jungle
Law of the Land
Law of the Lash
Law of the Saddle
Law of the Sea
Law of the Underworld
The Law Rides
Law West of Tombstone
Lawless Frontier
The Lawless Land
A Lawman Is Born
Lawmen
Lawrence of Arabia
The Lazarus Syndrome

LBJ: The Early Years
Le Beau Mariage
Le Beau Serge
Le Bourgeois Gentilhomme
Le Cas du Dr. Laurent
Le Cavaleur
Le Chat
Le Corbeau
Le Dernier Combat
Le Doulos
Le Gentleman D'Epsom
Le Grand Chemin
Le Joli Mai
Le Magnifique
Le Million
Le Petit Amour
Le Plaisir
Le Repos du Guerrier
Le Secret
Le Sex Shop
Leader of the Band
The League of Gentlemen
A League of Their Own
Lean on Me
Leap of Faith
Leap Year
Leapin' Leprechauns
The Learning Tree
Leather Boys
Leatherface: The Texas Chainsaw Massacre 3
The Leatherneck
Leave 'Em Laughing
Leave It to the Marines
Leaves from Satan's Book
Left for Dead
The Left Hand of God
The Left-Handed Gun
The Legacy
A Legacy for Leonette
Legacy of Horror
Legal Eagles
Legal Tender
Legend
Legend of Alfred Packer
Legend of Big Foot
Legend of Billie Jean
The Legend of Black Thunder Mountain
The Legend of Blood Castle
Legend of Boggy Creek
Legend of Frenchie King
The Legend of Hell House
The Legend of Hillbilly John
Legend of Lobo
The Legend of Sea Wolf
The Legend of Sleepy Hollow
Legend of the Dinosaurs
Legend of the Lone Ranger
Legend of the Northwest
Legend of the Werewolf
The Legend of the Wolf Woman
Legend of Valentino
The Legend of Valentino
Legend of Walks Far Woman
Legion of Iron
Legion of Missing Men
Legion of the Lawless
Legs
The Lemon Drop Kid
Lena's Holiday
Lenny
Lenny Bruce Performance Film
Leonard Part 6
Leonor
Leopard Fist Ninja
Leopard in the Snow
The Leopard Man
The Leopard Woman
Lepke
Les Assassins de L'Ordre
Les Bons Debarras
Les Carabiniers
Les Comperes
Les Enfants Terrible
Les Girls
Les Grandes Gueules
Les Miserables
Les Mistons
Less Than Zero
Lesson in Love
Let 'er Go Gallegher
Let It Be
Let It Ride
Let It Rock
L'Etat Sauvage
Lethal Obsession
Lethal Pursuit
Lethal Weapon
Lethal Weapon 2
Lethal Woman
Let's Dance
Let's Do It Again
Let's Get Harry
Let's Get Married
Let's Get Tough
Let's Go!
Let's Make Love
Let's Scare Jessica to Death
The Letter
Letter of Introduction
Letter to Brezhnev
A Letter to Three Wives
Letters to an Unknown Lover
Letting Go
Leviathan
L'Homme Blesse
Lianna
Liar's Moon
Libeled Lady
The Liberation of L.B. Jones
Liberators
Liberty & Bash
License to Drive
License to Kill
Lies
Lies Before Kisses
Lt. Robin Crusoe, U.S.N.
The Life and Assassination of the Kingfish
The Life and Death of Colonel Blimp
Life and Nothing But
Life & Times of Grizzly Adams
Life & Times of Judge Roy Bean
Life Begins for Andy Hardy
Life is a Circus, Charlie Brown/ You're the Greatest, Charlie Brown
Life Is Beautiful
The Life of Emile Zola
Life of Oharu
Life of Verdi
Life Stinks
Life with Father
Life with Mikey
Lifeboat
Lifeforce
Lifeguard
Lifepod
Lifespan
The Lift
Light at the Edge of the World
The Light in the Forest
Light of Day
The Light of Faith
Light Years
Lightblast
The Lighthorsemen
Lightnin' Carson Rides Again
Lightning Bill
The Lightning Incident
Lightning Over Water
Lightning Range
Lightning Strikes West
Lightning: The White Stallion
Lightning Warrior
Lights of Old Santa Fe
The Lightship
Like Father, Like Son
Li'l Abner
Lili
Lilies of the Field
Liliom
Lilith
Lily in Love
Lily of Killarney
Limelight
Limit Up
The Limping Man
Lincoln County Incident
Linda
The Lindbergh Kidnapping Case
The Line
Link
The Lion Has Wings
Lion Man
The Lion of Africa
Lion of the Desert
The Lion of Thebes
The Lion of Venice
Lionheart
Lion's Den
The Lion's Share
Lip Service
Lipstick
Liquid Dreams
Liquid Sky
Lisbon
The List of Adrian Messenger
Listen to Me
Listen to Your Heart
Lisztomania
The Little American
Little Annie Rooney
Little Ballerina
Little Big Horn
Little Big Man
Little Boy Lost
Little Caesar
Little Church Around the Corner
The Little Colonel
Little Darlings
Little Dorrit, Film 1: Nobody's Fault
Little Dorrit, Film 2: Little Dorrit's Story
Little Dragons
The Little Drummer Girl
The Little Foxes
Little Girl ... Big Tease
The Little Girl Who Lives Down the Lane
Little Gloria...Happy at Last
Little Heroes of Shaolin Temple
Little House on the Prairie
Little Johnny Jones
Little Ladies of the Night
Little Laura & Big John
Little Lord Fauntleroy
The Little Match Girl
Little Men
The Little Mermaid
Little Minister
Little Miss Broadway
Little Miss Innocence
Little Miss Marker
Little Monsters
Little Moon & Jud McGraw
Little Murders
A Little Night Music
Little Nikita
Little Noises
Little Orphan Annie
The Little Prince
The Little Princess
Little Rascals, Book 1
Little Rascals Christmas Special
Little Red Riding Hood
Little Red Schoolhouse
A Little Romance
A Little Sex
Little Shop of Horrors
Little Sweetheart
The Little Theatre of Jean Renoir
The Little Thief
Little Tough Guys
Little Treasure
Little Vera
Little Women
Little World of Don Camillo
The Littlest Angel
The Littlest Horse Thieves
The Littlest Outlaw
The Littlest Rebel
Live a Little, Love a Little
Live and Let Die
The Live Wire
The Lives of a Bengal Lancer
The Living Daylights
The Living Dead
Living Free
The Living Head
Living on Tokyo Time
The Lizzies of Mack Sennett
Loaded Guns
Loaded Pistols
Loan Shark
Lobster for Breakfast
Lobster Man from Mars
Local Badman
Local Hero
The Loch Ness Horror
Lock Up
L'Odeur des Fauves
The Lodger
Logan's Run
Lola Montes
Lolita
London Melody
The Lone Avenger
Lone Bandit
The Lone Defender
The Lone Ranger
Lone Ranger
The Lone Runner
Lone Wolf
Lone Wolf McQuade
The Loneliest Runner
The Loneliness of the Long Distance Runner
Lonely Are the Brave
The Lonely Guy
Lonely Hearts
The Lonely Lady
Lonely Man
Lonely Wives
Loners
Lonesome Trail
Long Ago Tomorrow
The Long Dark Hall
Long Day's Journey into Night
Long Gone
The Long Good Friday
The Long Goodbye
The Long, Hot Summer
Long John Silver
The Long Riders
Long Shadows
Long Shot
Long Time Gone
The Long Voyage Home
A Long Way Home
The Long Weekend
The Longest Day
The Longest Yard
The Longshot
Look Back in Anger
Look for the Silver Lining
Look Who's Laughing
Look Who's Talking
Looker
Lookin' to Get Out
Looking for Mr. Goodbar
The Looking Glass War
Looney Looney Looney Bugs Bunny Movie
Loophole
Loose Cannons
Loose Connections
Loose in New York
Loose Screws
Loose Shoes
Loot...Give Me Money, Honey!
Lord Jim
Lord of the Flies
The Lord of the Rings
The Lords of Discipline
The Lords of Flatbush
Lords of Magick
Lords of the Deep
Lorenzo's Oil
The Loretta Young Show
Lorna Doone
Los Olvidados
The Losers
Losin' It
Losing Isaiah
Lost
Lost and Found
Lost Angels
The Lost Boys
The Lost Capone
The Lost City
Lost City of the Jungle
The Lost Command
The Lost Continent
Lost Diamond
The Lost Empire
Lost Honeymoon
The Lost Honor of Katharina Blum
Lost Horizon
Lost in America
The Lost Jungle
The Lost Patrol
Lost Planet Airmen
The Lost Platoon
Lost Squadron
The Lost Stooges
The Lost Tribe
The Lost Weekend
The Lost World
Lost Zeppelin
Lots of Luck
Lottery Bride
Louisiana
Louisiana Story
Loulou
The Love Affair, or The Case of the Missing Switchboard Operator
Love Affair: The Eleanor & Lou Gehrig Story
Love Among the Ruins
Love and Anarchy
Love and Bullets
Love and Death
Love and Faith
Love and Hate: A Marriage Made in Hell
Love and the Frenchwoman
Love at First Bite
Love at First Sight
Love at Large
Love at the Top
The Love Bug
Love Butcher
Love by Appointment
Love Camp
Love Child
Love Desperados
Love 'Em and Leave 'Em
Love Finds Andy Hardy
The Love Flower
Love from a Stranger
The Love Goddesses
Love Has Many Faces
A Love in Germany
Love in the Afternoon
Love in the City
Love in the Present Tense
Love Is a Many-Splendored Thing
Love Kills
Love Laughs at Andy Hardy
Love Leads the Way
Love Letters

The Love Machine
Love Me Deadly
Love Me or Leave Me
Love Me Tender
Love Notes
The Love of Three Queens
Love on the Dole
Love on the Run
Love or Money?
Love Songs
Love Story
Love Strange Love
Love Streams
Love Thrill Murders
Love with a Perfect Stranger
Love with the Proper Stranger
The Loved One
Loveless
Lovelines
Lovely ... But Deadly
The Lover
Lover Come Back
Loverboy
Lovers and Liars
Lovers Like Us
Lovers of Their Time
Loves & Times of Scaramouche
Loves of a Blonde
The Loves of Carmen
The Loves of Irina
Love's Savage Fury
Lovesick
Lovey: A Circle of Children 2
Loving
Loving Couples
Loving You
Low Blow
The Lower Depths
Lucas
The Lucifer Complex
Lucky Devil
Lucky Jim
Lucky Luciano
Lucky Luke: The Ballad of the Daltons
Lucky Partners
Lucky Stiff
Lucky Terror
Lucky Texan
L'Udienza
Luggage of the Gods
Lumiere
The Lunatic
Lunatics & Lovers
Lunch Wagon
Lupo
Lure of the Islands
Lure of the Sila
Lurking Fear
Lust for a Vampire
Lust for Gold
Lust for Life
Lust in the Dust
The Lusty Men
Luv
Lydia
Lying Lips
M
M. Butterfly
Ma Barker's Killer Brood
Mabel & Fatty
Mac and Me
Macabre
Macao
Macaroni
MacArthur
MacArthur's Children
Macbeth
Macho Callahan
Machoman
Mack
Mack & Carole
Mack the Knife
MacKenna's Gold
Mackintosh Man
Macon County Line
Mad About Money
Mad About You
The Mad Bomber
Mad Bull
The Mad Butcher
Mad Doctor of Blood Island
Mad Dog
Mad Dog Morgan
Mad Max
Mad Max: Beyond Thunderdome
Mad Miss Manton
Mad Mission 3
Mad Monster Party
Mad Wax: The Surf Movie
The Mad Whirl
Mad Youth
Madame Bovary
Madame Rosa
Madame Sin
Madame Sousatzka
Madame X
M.A.D.D.: Mothers Against Drunk Driving
Made for Each Other
Made for Love
Made in America
Made in Argentina
Made in Heaven
Made in USA
Madeleine
Mademoiselle Striptease
Madhouse
Madigan
Madigan's Millions
Madman
Mado
Madron
Mae West
Maedchen in Uniform
Mafia vs. Ninja
Magdalene
Magee and the Lady
Magic
The Magic Christian
The Magic Flute
The Magic Legend of the Golden Goose
Magic of Lassie
Magic on Love Island
The Magic Sword
The Magic Voyage of Sinbad
Magical Mystery Tour
Magical Wonderland
The Magician
The Magician of Lublin
Magnificent Adventurer
The Magnificent Ambersons
The Magnificent Matador
Magnificent Obsession
The Magnificent Seven
The Magnificent Yankee
Magnum Force
Magnum Killers
Mahler
Mahogany
The Maid
Maid to Order
The Main Event
Main Street to Broadway
Major Barbara
Major Dundee
Major League
The Majorettes
Make a Million
Make a Wish
Make Me an Offer
Make Mine Mink
Make Room for Tomorrow
Making Contact
Making Love
Making Mr. Right
Making the Grade
Malarek
Malcolm
Malcolm X
Male and Female
Malibu Beach
Malibu Bikini Shop
Malibu Express
Malibu High
Malicious
Malone
Malou
Malta Story
The Maltese Falcon
Mama, There's a Man in Your Bed
Mama Turns a Hundred
Mama's Dirty Girls
Mame
Mamele
A Man, a Woman, and a Bank
A Man and a Woman
A Man and a Woman: 20 Years Later
Man & Boy
Man Bait
Man Beast
A Man Called Adam
A Man Called Horse
A Man Called Peter
A Man Called Rage
A Man Called Sarge
Man Facing Southeast
A Man for All Seasons
The Man from Atlantis
The Man from Beyond
Man from Button Willow
Man from Cairo
Man from Cheyenne
Man from Colorado
Man from Deep River
Man from Hell's Edges
The Man from Laramie
The Man from Music Mountain
Man from Nowhere
The Man from Snowy River
Man from Texas
Man from Thunder River
The Man from U.N.C.L.E.
Man from Utah
The Man in Grey
A Man in Love
The Man in the Attic
The Man in the Gray Flannel Suit
The Man in the Iron Mask
The Man in the Mist
The Man in the Raincoat
The Man in the Santa Claus Suit
Man in the Silk Hat
The Man in the White Suit
The Man Inside
Man Is Not a Bird
A Man Like Eva
Man of Destiny
Man of Flowers
Man of La Mancha
Man of Legend
Man of the West
Man of Violence
Man on Fire
Man on the Eiffel Tower
Man on the Run
The Man They Could Not Hang
The Man Who Broke 1,000 Chains
The Man Who Came to Dinner
The Man Who Could Work Miracles
The Man Who Envied Women
The Man Who Fell to Earth
Man Who Had Power Over Women
The Man Who Haunted Himself
The Man Who Knew Too Much
The Man Who Lived Again
Man Who Loved Cat Dancing
The Man Who Loved Women
The Man Who Never Was
The Man Who Shot Liberty Valance
The Man Who Wasn't There
The Man Who Would Be King
The Man Who Would Not Die
The Man with a Movie Camera
The Man with Bogart's Face
The Man with One Red Shoe
The Man with the Golden Arm
The Man with the Golden Gun
The Man with Two Brains
The Man Without a Face
Man Without a Star
Man, Woman & Child
Manchurian Avenger
The Manchurian Candidate
The Mandarin Mystery
Mandela
Mandinga
Mandingo
Mandroid
Mandy
The Mango Tree
The Manhandlers
Manhattan
Manhattan Baby
Manhattan Melodrama
Manhattan Merry-Go-Round
The Manhattan Project
Manhunt
The Manhunt
Manhunt for Claude Dallas
Manhunt of Mystery Island
Manhunter
Mania
Maniac
Maniac Cop
The Manions of America
Manipulator
The Manitou
Mankillers
Mannequin
Manny's Orphans
Manon of the Spring
Man's Country
Man's Favorite Sport?
Man's Land
Mansfield Park
Mantrap
The Manxman
Many Faces of Sherlock Holmes
Marathon Man
Marauder
Marbella
Marciano
Marco
Marco Polo, Jr.
Mardi Gras for the Devil
Mardi Gras Massacre
Margin for Murder
Maria Candelaria
Maria Chapdelaine
Maria's Day
Maria's Lovers
Marie
Marie Antoinette
Marie Galante
Marihuana
Marine Raiders
Marius
Marjoe
The Mark
Mark of Cain
Mark of the Devil
Mark of the Spur
Mark of the Vampire
Marked for Murder
Marked Money
Marked Trails
Marked Woman
Marlon Brando
Marlowe
Marnie
Marooned
The Marriage of Maria Braun
Married?
A Married Man
Married to the Mob
A Married Woman
The Martian Chronicles: Part 1
The Martian Chronicles: Part 2
The Martian Chronicles: Part 3
Martians Go Home!
Martin
Martin Luther
Martin's Day
Marty
Marvelous Stunts of Kung Fu
Marvin & Tige
Mary and Joseph: A Story of Faith
Mary, Mary, Bloody Mary
Mary of Scotland
Mary Poppins
Mary White
Masada
Mascara
Masculine Feminine
M*A*S*H
M*A*S*H: Goodbye, Farewell & Amen
The Mask
Mask
Mask of the Dragon
Masks of Death
Masque of the Red Death
Masquerade
Mass Appeal
Massacre in Dinosaur Valley
Massacre in Rome
Massive Retaliation
Master Harold and the Boys
Master Key
Master Killer
Master Mind
Master Ninja
The Master of Ballantrae
Master of Dragonard Hill
Master of Kung Fu
Master of the House
Master of the World
Master Race
Master Touch
Masters of the Universe
Masters of Venus
Mata Hari
Matador
The Matchmaker
Matewan
Matilda
Matinee
Mating Season
Matrimaniac
A Matter of Degrees
A Matter of Dignity
A Matter of Love
A Matter of Principle
A Matter of Time
A Matter of WHO
Maurice
Mausoleum
Max
Max and Helen
Max Dugan Returns
Max Fleischer's Documentary Features
Max Headroom, the Original Story
Maxie
Maximum Overdrive
Maximum Thrust
Maya
Mayerling
Mayflower Madam
Mayhem
The Maze
Mazes and Monsters
McCabe & Mrs. Miller
The McConnell Story
McQ
McVicar
Mean Dog Blues
Mean Frank and Crazy Tony
Mean Johnny Barrows

Mean Machine
Mean Season
Mean Streets
The Meanest Men in the West
Meatballs
Meatballs 2
Meatballs 3
The Meateater
The Mechanic
Medea
Medicine Man
The Mediterranean in Flames
Mediterraneo
The Medium
Medium Cool
Medusa
Medusa Against the Son of Hercules
Meet Dr. Christian
Meet Me in St. Louis
Meet Sexton Blake
Meet the Navy
Meeting at Midnight
Meeting Venus
Meetings with Remarkable Men
Megaforce
Mein Kampf: Hitler's Rise and Fall
Melanie
Melodie en Sous-Sol
Melody
Melody Cruise
Melody for Three
Melody in Love
Melody Master
Melody Ranch
Melody Trail
Melvin and Howard
The Member of the Wedding
Memorial Valley Massacre
Memories of Hell
Memories of Me
Memories of Murder
Memphis
Memphis Belle
Memphis Belle: A Story of a Flying Fortress
Men Are Not Gods
Men at Work
Men Don't Leave
Men in War
Men of Ireland
Men of Steel
Men of the Fighting Lady
Men of Two Worlds
The Men Who Tread on the Tiger's Tail
Menace on the Mountain
The Men's Club
Menschenfrauen
Mephisto
The Mercenaries
Mercenary Fighters
The Merchant of Four Seasons
Meridian: Kiss of the Beast
Merlin and the Sword
Mermaids
Merry Christmas, Mr. Lawrence
The Merry Widow
Merton of the Movies
Mesmerized
Mesquite Buckaroo
Messalina, Empress of Rome
Messalina vs. the Son of Hercules
The Messenger
Messenger of Death
The Messiah
Messiah of Evil
Metallica
Metalstorm: The Destruction of Jared Syn
Metamorphosis
Meteor
Meteor Monster
Metropolis
Mexican Bus Ride
Mexican Spitfire/Smartest Girl in Town
Miami Blues
Miami Cops
Miami Horror
Miami Supercops
Miami Vendetta
Miami Vice
Miami Vice 2: The Prodigal Son
The Michigan Kid
Mickey
Mickey the Great
Mickey's Christmas Carol
Micki & Maude
Mid-Channel
Mid Knight Rider
The Midas Touch
Midnight
Midnight Cabaret
Midnight Cop
Midnight Cowboy
Midnight Crossing
Midnight Dancer
Midnight Express
Midnight Faces
Midnight Girl
Midnight Lace
Midnight Limited
Midnight Madness
Midnight Run
Midnight Warrior
Midnight's Child
Midnite Spares
A Midsummer Night's Dream
A Midsummer Night's Sex Comedy
Midway
The Mighty Ducks
Mighty Joe Young
Mighty Jungle
The Mighty Quinn
Mike's Murder
Mikey & Nicky
The Milagro Beanfield War
Mildred Pierce
Miles from Home
Miles to Go
Miles to Go before I Sleep
Milk Money
Milky Way
The Milky Way
The Mill on the Floss
Millenium
Miller's Crossing
Million Dollar Duck
Million Dollar Haul
Million Dollar Mermaid
Millions
Milo Milo
The Milpitas Monster
Min & Bill
Mind Games
Mind Snatchers
Mind Warp
Mindfield
Mindkiller
Mindwalk: A Film for Passionate Thinkers
Mines of Kilimanjaro
Ministry of Vengeance
Minnesota Clay
A Minor Miracle
Minsky's Follies
A Minute to Pray, A Second to Die
The Miracle
Miracle Down Under
Miracle in Milan
Miracle Mile
Miracle of Morgan's Creek
Miracle of Our Lady of Fatima
The Miracle of the Bells
Miracle of the Heart: A Boys Town Story
The Miracle of the White Stallions
Miracle on Ice
Miracle on 34th Street
The Miracle Worker
Miracles
Mirage
Mirele Efros
The Mirror Crack'd
Mirror of Death
Mirrors
The Misadventures of Merlin Jones
Mischief
Misery
The Misfit Brigade
The Misfits
Misfits of Science
Mishima: A Life in Four Chapters
Miss All-American Beauty
Miss Annie Rooney
Miss Firecracker
Ms. 45
Miss Julie
Miss Mary
Miss Sadie Thompson
Missile to the Moon
Missiles of October
Missing
Missing in Action
Missing in Action 2: The Beginning
Missing Link
The Mission
Mission Batangas
Mission Corbari
Mission Galactica: The Cylon Attack
Mission Inferno
Mission Manila
Mission Mars
Mission: Monte Carlo
Mission Phantom
Mission Stardust
Mission to Glory
Mission to Kill
The Missionary
Mississippi Burning
Missouri Breaks
Missouri Traveler
Missourians
Mrs. Brown, You've Got a Lovely Daughter
Mrs. Miniver
Mrs. R's Daughter
Mrs. Silly
Mrs. Soffel
Mistaken Identity
Mr. Ace
Mr. & Mrs. Smith
Mr. Arkadin
Mr. Baseball
Mr. Billion
Mr. Bill's Real Life Adventures
Mr. Blandings Builds His Dream House
Mr. Deeds Goes to Town
Mr. Destiny
Mr. Emmanuel
Mister Halpren & Mister Johnson
Mr. Hobbs Takes a Vacation
Mr. Hulot's Holiday
Mr. Inside, Mr. Outside
Mr. Kingstreet's War
Mr. Klein
Mr. Love
Mr. Lucky
Mr. Majestyk
Mister Mean
Mr. Mike's Mondo Video
Mr. Mom
Mr. Moto's Last Warning
Mr. Moto's Last Warning/ Meeting at Midnight
Mr. Nice Guy
Mr. North
Mr. Peek-A-Boo
Mr. Reeder in Room 13
Mister Roberts
Mr. Robinson Crusoe
Mr. Scarface
Mr. Skeffington
Mr. Smith Goes to Washington
Mr. Superinvisible
Mr. Sycamore
Mr. Walkie Talkie
Mr. Winkle Goes to War
Mr. Wise Guy
Mr. Wonderful
Mr. Wong, Detective
Mistral's Daughter
Mistress
Mistress of the Apes
Mistress of the World
Mistress Pamela
Misunderstood
Mixed Blood
M'Lady's Court
Mo' Better Blues
Mo' Money
Mob Story
Mob War
Mobsters
Moby Dick
Model Behavior
Model by Day
Modern Girls
Modern Love
Modern Problems
Modern Romance
Modern Times
The Moderns
Mogambo
Mohawk
Mole Men against the Son of Hercules
Molly & Lawless John
Molly Maguires
Mom & Dad
Mom, the Wolfman and Me
Moment in Time
Mommie Dearest
Mon Oncle
Mon Oncle D'Amerique
Mona Lisa
Mondo Cane
Mondo Cane 2
Mondo Magic
Mondo Trasho
The Money Pit
Money to Burn
Mongrel
Monique
Monkey Boy
Monkey Business
Monkey Shines
Monkeys, Go Home!
Monkey's Uncle
Monsieur Beaucaire
Monsieur Verdoux
Monsieur Vincent
Monsignor
Monster
Monster a Go-Go!
The Monster and the Stripper
The Monster Club
Monster Dog
Monster from Green Hell
Monster from the Ocean Floor
Monster High
Monster in the Closet
The Monster Maker
The Monster of London City
The Monster Squad
The Monster Walks
Montana
Montana Belle
Monte Carlo
Monte Carlo Nights
Monte Walsh
Montenegro
Monterey Pop
A Month in the Country
Monty Python and the Holy Grail
Monty Python Live at the Hollywood Bowl
Monty Python's Flying Circus
Monty Python's Life of Brian
Monty Python's The Meaning of Life
Moon in Scorpio
Moon in the Gutter
The Moon Is Blue
Moon of the Wolf
Moon over Harlem
Moon over Miami
Moon over Parador
Moon Pilot
The Moon-Spinners
Mooncussers
Moonlighting
Moonraker
The Moon's Our Home
Moonshine County Express
Moonshine Highway
Moonshine Mountain
Moonstruck
Moran of the Lady Letty
More
More! Police Squad
The More the Merrier
More Wild, Wild West
Morgan!
Morgan Stewart's Coming Home
Morgan the Pirate
Morituri
A Mormon Maid
The Morning After
Morning Glory
Morocco
Mortal Passions
Mortal Thoughts
Mortuary
Mosby's Marauders
Moscow Does Not Believe in Tears
Moscow on the Hudson
Moses
The Mosquito Coast
The Most Dangerous Game
Most Wanted
Motel Hell
Mother
Mother & Daughter: A Loving War
Mother Doesn't Always Know Best
Mother Goose Rock 'n' Rhyme
Mother Lode
Mother's Day
Mothra
Motor Patrol
Mouchette
Moulin Rouge
The Mountain
Mountain Charlie
Mountain Family Robinson
Mountain Man
The Mountain Men
Mountains of the Moon
Mountaintop Motel Massacre
Mouse and His Child
The Mouse That Roared
Movers and Shakers
The Movie House Massacre
Movie Maker
A Movie Star's Daughter
Moving
Moving Out
Moving Target
Moving Targets
Moving Violation
Moving Violations
Mozart: A Childhood Chronicle
The Mozart Story

Mugsy's Girls
The Mummy
The Mummy's Revenge
Munchies
The Munsters' Revenge
The Muppet Christmas Carol
The Muppet Movie
The Muppets Take Manhattan
Murder
Murder Ahoy
Murder at Midnight
Murder at the Baskervilles
Murder at the Gallop
Murder at the Vanities
Murder by Death
Murder by Decree
Murder by Natural Causes
Murder by Night
Murder by Numbers
Murder by Phone
Murder by Television
Murder by the Book
Murder Elite
Murder for Sale
Murder in Coweta County
Murder in New Hampshire: The Pamela Smart Story
Murder in Space
Murder in Texas
Murder in the Doll House
Murder in the Old Red Barn
A Murder Is Announced
Murder Mansion
Murder Most Foul
Murder Motel
Murder, My Sweet
Murder on Flight 502
Murder on Line One
Murder on the Campus
Murder on the Midnight Express
Murder on the Orient Express
Murder on the Yukon
Murder Once Removed
Murder One
Murder over New York
Murder Rap
Murder She Said
Murder Story
Murder: Ultimate Grounds for Divorce
Murder with Music
Murderer's Keep
Murderers' Row
Murderlust
Murders at Lynch Cross
Murders in the Rue Morgue
Muriel
Murmur of the Heart
Murph the Surf
Murphy's Fault
Murphy's Law
Murphy's Romance
Murphy's War
Murrow
Muscle Beach Party
Music Box
Music Box/Helpmates
The Music Man
Music Shoppe
The Music Teacher
Musica Proibita
Mussolini & I
Mutant
Mutant Hunt
Mutant Video
Mutants In Paradise
Mutator
The Muthers
The Mutilator
Mutiny
Mutiny in the Big House
Mutiny on the Bounty
Mutual Respect
My African Adventure
My American Cousin
My Antonia

My Beautiful Laundrette
My Best Friend's Girl
My Best Girl
My Bloody Valentine
My Blue Heaven
My Bodyguard
My Boy
My Boys Are Good Boys
My Breakfast with Blassie
My Brilliant Career
My Champion
My Chauffeur
My Darling Clementine
My Dear Secretary
My Demon Lover
My Dinner with Andre
My Dog Shep
My Dog, the Thief
My Fair Lady
My Father, My Rival
My Father's House
My Father's Nurse
My Favorite Brunette
My Favorite Wife
My Favorite Year
My Forbidden Past
My Friend Flicka
My Heroes Have Always Been Cowboys
My Lady of Whims
My Left Foot
My Life as a Dog
My Life to Live
My Little Chickadee
My Little Girl
My Little Pony: The Movie
My Love For Yours
My Man Adam
My Man Godfrey
My Michael
My Mom's a Werewolf
My Mother's Secret Life
My Name Called Bruce
My Name is Ivan
My Name is Nobody
My Neighborhood
My New Partner
My Night at Maud's
My Old Man
My Old Man's Place
My Other Husband
My Pal Trigger
My Science Project
My Side of the Mountain
My Stepmother Is an Alien
My Sweet Charlie
My Therapist
My Tutor
My Wicked, Wicked Ways
My Wonderful Life
Myra Breckinridge
The Mysterians
Mysteries
Mysterious Desperado
Mysterious Desperado/Rider From Tucson
Mysterious Island
Mysterious Jane
Mysterious Mr. Wong
Mysterious Planet
Mysterious Two
Mystery at Castle House
Mystery at Fire Island
Mystery in Swing
Mystery Island
Mystery Liner
The Mystery Man
Mystery Mansion
Mystery Mountain
The Mystery of Alexina
Mystery of the Hooded Horseman
Mystery of the Leaping Fish/ Chess Fever
The Mystery of the Mary Celeste

Mystery of the Million Dollar Hockey Puck
Mystery of the Riverboat
Mystery of the Wax Museum
Mystery Plane
Mystery Ranch
Mystery Squadron
Mystery Trooper
Mystic Pizza
Nadia
Nadine
Nail Gun Massacre
Nails
Nairobi Affair
Nais
The Naked and the Dead
The Naked Angels
Naked Cage
The Naked Civil Servant
The Naked Face
The Naked Gun: From the Files of Police Squad
Naked Gun 33 1/3: The Final Insult
Naked Gun 2 1/2: The Smell of Fear
Naked Is Better
Naked Jungle
Naked Massacre
Naked Paradise
The Naked Prey
The Naked Spur
The Naked Truth
Naked Vengeance
Naked Venus
Naked Warriors
Naked Youth
Nam Angels
A Name for Evil
The Name of the Rose
Nana
Nancy Astor
Napoleon
Napoleon and Samantha
Narrow Trail
Nashville
Nashville Girl
Nasty Habits
Nasty Hero
Nasty Rabbit
Natas...The Reflection
Nate and Hayes
A Nation Aflame
National Lampoon's Animal House
National Lampoon's Christmas Vacation
National Lampoon's Class of '86
National Lampoon's Class Reunion
National Lampoon's European Vacation
National Lampoon's Vacation
Native Son
Nativity
The Natural
Natural Enemies
Naughty Knights
Naughty Marietta
The Naughty Nineties
Navy SEALS
Navy vs. the Night Monsters
Nazarin
Nea
Near Dark
Near Misses
'Neath Canadian Skies
Necessary Roughness
Necromancer: Satan's Servant
Necropolis
Neighbors
The Neon Empire
Neon Maniacs
Neptune Factor
Neptune's Daughter

The Nervous Wreck
The Nest
The Nesting
Network
Nevada City
Nevada Smith
The Nevadan
Never a Dull Moment
Never Cry Wolf
Never Forget
Never Give a Sucker an Even Break
Never Let Go
Never on Sunday
Never on Tuesday
Never Pick Up a Stranger
Never Say Die
Never Say Never Again
Never Steal Anything Small
Never Too Late to Mend
Never Too Young to Die
Never Weaken/Why Worry?
The NeverEnding Story
Nevil Shute's The Far Country
The New Adventures of Pippi Longstocking
The New Adventures of Tarzan
The New Centurions
New Faces of 1952
New Fist of Fury
The New Gladiators
The New Kids
A New Kind of Love
A New Life
New Mafia Boss
New Moon
New Pastures
New Year's Day
New Year's Evil
New York, New York
New York Nights
New York Ripper
New York Stories
New York's Finest
The Newlydeads
Newman's Law
News at Eleven
Newsies
Next of Kin
Next One
Next Summer
The Next Victim
Next Victim
The Next Voice You Hear
Next Year If All Goes Well
Niagara
Nice Girl Like Me
Nice Girls Don't Explode
Nice Neighbor
Nicholas and Alexandra
Nicholas Nickleby
Nick of Time
Nickel Mountain
Nicole
The Night After Halloween
Night and Day
Night Angel
A Night at the Opera
Night Beast
The Night Before
Night Breed
Night Call Nurses
Night Caller from Outer Space
Night Children
The Night Club
Night Creature
Night Cries
Night Crossing
The Night Cry
Night Eyes
Night Eyes 2
Night Eyes 3
Night Flight from Moscow
Night Friend
Night Gallery
Night Game

Night Games
The Night God Screamed
The Night Has Eyes
A Night in Casablanca
A Night in Heaven
A Night in the Life of Jimmy Reardon
Night Is My Future
Night Life in Reno
Night Master
'night, Mother
Night Moves
Night Nurse
Night of a Thousand Cats
Night of Bloody Horror
Night of Dark Shadows
Night of Evil
Night of Horror
Night of the Assassin
Night of the Bloody Apes
Night of the Bloody Transplant
Night of the Cobra Woman
Night of the Comet
Night of the Creeps
Night of the Death Cult
Night of the Demon
Night of the Generals
Night of the Ghouls
Night of the Grizzly
Night of the Howling Beast
The Night of the Hunter
The Night of the Iguana
Night of the Juggler
Night of the Sharks
The Night of the Shooting Stars
Night of the Sorcerers
Night of the Strangler
Night of the Wilding
Night of the Zombies
Night Partners
Night Patrol
The Night Porter
Night Rider
Night Riders of Montana
Night Ripper
Night School
Night Screams
Night Shift
Night Slasher
Night Stage to Galveston
Night Stalker
The Night Stalker: Two Tales of Terror
Night Terror
The Night the Lights Went Out in Georgia
The Night They Raided Minsky's
The Night They Robbed Big Bertha's
The Night They Saved Christmas
Night Time in Nevada
A Night to Remember
The Night Train to Kathmandu
Night Train to Munich
Night Train to Terror
Night Vision
The Night Visitor
Night Visitor
Night Warning
Night Wars
Night Watch
Night Zoo
The Nightcomers
Nightfall
Nightflyers
Nightforce
Nighthawks
The Nightingale
Nightkill
Nightlife
Nightmare
Nightmare at 43 Hillcrest
Nightmare Castle
Nightmare in Badham County
Nightmare in Blood

Nightmare in Red China
Nightmare in Wax
A Nightmare on Elm Street
A Nightmare on Elm Street 2: Freddy's Revenge
A Nightmare on Elm Street 3: Dream Warriors
A Nightmare on Elm Street 4: Dream Master
A Nightmare on Elm Street 5: Dream Child
Nightmare on the 13th Floor
Nightmare Sisters
Nightmare Weekend
The Nightmare Years
Nightmares
Nights in White Satin
Nights of Cabiria
Nightstalker
Nightstick
Nightwing
Nijinsky
Nikki, the Wild Dog of the North
Nine Ages of Nakedness
9 1/2 Ninjas
9 1/2 Weeks
Nine Days a Queen
Nine Deaths of the Ninja
The Nine Lives of Elfego Baca
9 to 5
976-EVIL
984: Prisoner of the Future
1900
1918
1931: Once Upon a Time in New York
1941
1969
1984
1990: The Bronx Warriors
90 Days
92 in the Shade
99 Women
Ninja 3: The Domination
Ninja: American Warrior
Ninja Brothers of Blood
Ninja Champion
Ninja Checkmate
Ninja Commandments
Ninja Condors
Ninja Connection
Ninja Death Squad
Ninja Demon's Massacre
Ninja Destroyer
Ninja Dragon
Ninja Exterminators
Ninja Fantasy
Ninja Hunt
Ninja Massacre
Ninja Masters of Death
Ninja Mission
Ninja Nightmare
Ninja of the Magnificence
Ninja Operation: Licensed to Terminate
Ninja Phantom Heroes
The Ninja Pirates
Ninja Powerforce
Ninja Showdown
Ninja Squad
Ninja Strike Force
Ninja Supremo
Ninja Swords of Death
Ninja the Battalion
Ninja the Protector
Ninja, the Violent Sorcerer
Ninja Turf
Ninja vs. Ninja
Ninja vs. the Shaolin
Ninja Wars
Ninja's Extreme Weapons
Ninotchka
The Ninth Configuration
No Comebacks
No Dead Heroes
No Deposit, No Return

No Drums, No Bugles
No Greater Love
No Grumps Allowed!
No Holds Barred
No Love for Johnnie
No Man of Her Own
No Man's Land
No Man's Range
No Mercy
No One Cries Forever
No Place to Hide
No Place to Run
No Prince for My Cinderella
No Problem
No Retreat, No Surrender
No Retreat, No Surrender 2
No Room to Run
No Safe Haven
No Small Affair
No Surrender
No Time for Sergeants
No Time to Die
No Trace
No Way Back
No Way Out
No Way to Treat a Lady
Noa at Seventeen
The Noble Ninja
Nobody's Fool
Nobody's Perfect
Nobody's Perfekt
Nocturna
Nocturne
Noises Off
Nomad Riders
Nomads
Nomads of the North
Nomugi Pass
None But the Brave
None But the Lonely Heart
Noon Sunday
Noon Wine
Norma Rae
The Norman Conquests, Part 1: Table Manners
The Norman Conquests, Part 2: Living Together
The Norman Conquests, Part 3: Round and Round the Garden
Norman Loves Rose
Norman's Awesome Experience
Norseman
North and South Book 1
North by Northwest
North Dallas Forty
North of the Border
North Shore
The North Star
North to Alaska
Northeast of Seoul
Northern Lights
Northern Pursuit
Northville Cemetery Massacre
Northwest Passage
Northwest Trail
Nosferatu
Not for Publication
Not My Kid
Not of This Earth
Not Quite Human
Not Quite Human 2
Not Quite Paradise
Not Tonight Darling
Not Without My Daughter
Nothing But Trouble
Nothing in Common
Nothing Personal
Nothing Sacred
Nothing Underneath
Notorious
Nous N'Irons Plus au Bois
Now and Forever
Now, Voyager
Now You See Him, Now You Don't

Nowhere to Hide
Nowhere to Run
Nuclear Conspiracy
Nudo di Donna
Number 1 of the Secret Service
Number One with a Bullet
No. 17
Nuns on the Run
The Nun's Story
Nurse
Nurse Edith Cavell
Nurse on Call
Nutcase
Nutcracker, A Fantasy on Ice
Nutcracker Sweet
Nutcracker: The Motion Picture
Nuts
The Nutty Professor
O Lucky Man!
Oasis of the Zombies
Oath of Vengeance
Objective, Burma!
Oblivion
Oblomov
The Oblong Box
Obsessed
Obsession
Obsession: A Taste for Fear
O.C. and Stiggs
The Occultist
An Occurrence at Owl Creek Bridge/Coup de Grace
Ocean Drive Weekend
Ocean's 11
Oceans of Fire
Octagon
Octaman
Octavia
Octopussy
The Odd Angry Shot
The Odd Couple
The Odd Job
Odd Jobs
Odd Man Out
Odd Obsession
The Odd Squad
Oddballs
Odds and Evens
Ode to Billy Joe
The Odessa File
The Odyssey of the Pacific
Of Cooks and Kung-Fu
Of Human Bondage
Of Mice and Men
Of Unknown Origin
Off Beat
Off Limits
Off on a Comet
Off the Mark
Off the Wall
Off Your Rocker
Offerings
Office Romances
An Officer and a Gentleman
Official Denial
The Official Story
Offnight
The Offspring
Oh, Alfie
Oh! Calcutta!
Oh Dad, Poor Dad (Momma's Hung You in the Closet & I'm Feeling So Sad)
Oh, God!
Oh, God! Book 2
Oh, God! You Devil
Oh, Heavenly Dog!
Oh Susannah
O'Hara's Wife
Oil
Oklahoma!
Oklahoma Annie
Oklahoma Badlands
Oklahoma Bound
Oklahoma Kid
The Oklahoman

Old Barn Dance
Old Boyfriends
Old Corral
The Old Curiosity Shop
Old Enough
Old Gringo
Old Gun
Old Ironsides
The Old Maid
Old Mother Riley's Ghosts
Old Spanish Custom
Old Swimmin' Hole
Old Yeller
Oldest Living Graduate
Oldest Profession
Oliver!
Oliver Twist
Oliver's Story
Olivia
Ollie Hopnoodle's Haven of Bliss
Olly Olly Oxen Free
Olongape: The American Dream
Omega Man
Omega Syndrome
The Omen
On a Clear Day You Can See Forever
On Approval
On Dangerous Ground
On Golden Pond
On Her Majesty's Secret Service
On the Air Live with Captain Midnight
On the Beach
On the Comet
On the Edge
On the Edge: The Survival of Dana
On the Line
On the Nickel
On the Night Stage
On the Old Spanish Trail
On the Right Track
On the Run
On the Third Day
On the Town
On the Waterfront
On the Yard
On Top of Old Smoky
On Valentine's Day
Once Around
Once Bitten
Once in Paris...
Once is Not Enough
Once Upon a Brothers Grimm
Once Upon a Honeymoon
Once Upon a Scoundrel
Once Upon a Time
Once Upon a Time in America
Once Upon a Time in the West
Once Upon a Time in Vietnam
One A.M.
The One and Only
The One and Only, Genuine, Original Family Band
One Arabian Night
The One Arm Swordsmen
One Armed Executioner
One Away
One Body Too Many
One Cooks, the Other Doesn't
One Crazy Summer
One Dark Night
One Deadly Owner
One Deadly Summer
One Down, Two to Go!
One-Eyed Jacks
One-Eyed Swordsman
One Flew Over the Cuckoo's Nest
One Frightened Night
One from the Heart
One Good Cop
100 Rifles
101 Dalmatians

125 Rooms of Comfort
One in a Million: The Ron LeFlore Story
One Last Run
One Little Indian
One Magic Christmas
One Man Force
One Man Jury
One Man Out
One Man's Way
One Million B.C.
One Minute Before Death
One Minute to Zero
One More Chance
One More Saturday Night
One Night of Love
One Night Only
One Night Stand
One of My Wives Is Missing
One of Our Dinosaurs Is Missing
One on One
One Plus One
One-Punch O'Day
One Rainy Afternoon
One Russian Summer
One Shoe Makes It Murder
One Sings, the Other Doesn't
One Step to Hell
One That Got Away
1001 Arabian Nights
One Trick Pony
One, Two, Three
One Wild Moment
One Wish Too Many
One Woman or Two
Onibaba
The Onion Field
Only Angels Have Wings
Only Once in a Lifetime
Only One Night
Only the Lonely
Only Two Can Play
The Only Way
The Only Way Home
Only When I Laugh
Only with Married Men
Open All Hours
Open City
Open House
Open Secret
Opening Night
Opera do Malandro
Operation Amsterdam
Operation C.I.A.
Operation Haylift
Operation Inchon
Operation Julie
Operation Orient
Operation Thunderbolt
Operation War Zone
The Oppermann Family
Opportunity Knocks
Opposing Force
The Oracle
Orca
Orchestra Wives
Ordeal by Innocence
The Ordeal of Dr. Mudd
Order of the Black Eagle
Order of the Eagle
Order to Kill
Ordet
Ordinary People
Oregon Trail
The Organization
Orgy of the Dead
Original Intent
Orion's Belt
The Orphan
An Orphan Boy of Vienna
Orphans
Orphans of the North
Orpheus
The Oscar
Ossessione
The Osterman Weekend

Otello
Othello
The Other
Other Hell
The Other Side of Midnight
The Other Side of the Mountain
The Other Side of the Mountain, Part 2
Oubliette
Our Daily Bread
Our Dancing Daughters
Our Gang
Our Gang Comedies
Our Little Girl
Our Man Flint
Our Relations
Our Town
Out Cold
Out for Justice
Out of Africa
Out of Bounds
Out of Control
Out of Order
Out of Season
Out of Sight, Out of Her Mind
Out of the Blue
Out of the Dark
Out of the Darkness
Out of the Past
Out of the Rain
The Out-of-Towners
Out on a Limb
Out on Bail
Out There
The Outcasts
The Outer Limits: Galaxy Being
The Outing
Outland
The Outlaw
The Outlaw and His Wife
The Outlaw Bikers—Gang Wars
Outlaw Blues
Outlaw Express
Outlaw Force
Outlaw Fury
Outlaw Gang
The Outlaw Josey Wales
Outlaw Justice
Outlaw of Gor
Outlaw Riders
Outlaw Roundup
Outlaw Rule
The Outlaw Tamer
Outlaw Trail
Outlaw Women
Outlaws of the Range
Outrageous!
Outrageous Fortune
Outside Chance
Outside Chance of Maximillian Glick
The Outsiders
Outtakes
The Oval Portrait
Over Indulgence
Over the Brooklyn Bridge
Over the Edge
Over the Summer
Over the Top
Overboard
The Overcoat
Overdrawn at the Memory Bank
Overkill
Overland Mail
Overlanders
The Overlanders
Overnight Sensation
Overthrow
Overture to Glory
The Owl and the Pussycat
The Ox-Bow Incident
Oxford Blues
Pace That Kills
Pacific Inferno
The Pack
Pack Up Your Troubles
The Package
Packin' It In
Paco
Paddy
Padre Padrone
Paid to Kill
Pain in the A—
Paint It Black
Paint Your Wagon
Painted Desert
The Painted Hills
The Painted Veil
Paisan
The Pajama Game
Pal Joey
Pale Rider
The Paleface
Palm Beach
The Palm Beach Story
Palm Springs Weekend
Palooka
Pals of the Range
Panama Lady
Panama Menace
Panama Patrol
Panamint's Bad Man
Pandemonium
Pandora's Box
Panic
Panic on the 5:22
Panique
Papa's Delicate Condition
The Paper Chase
Paper Lion
Paper Moon
Paper Tiger
Paperhouse
Papillon
The Paradine Case
Paradise
Paradise Alley
Paradise, Hawaiian Style
Paradise in Harlem
Paradise Motel
Paradisio
The Parallax View
Parallel Corpse
Parallel Lives
Paralyzed
Paramedics
Paranoia
Parasite
Pardon Mon Affaire
Pardon Mon Affaire, Too!
Pardon My Trunk
Pardon Us
The Parent Trap
Parenthood
Parents
Paris Blues
Paris Express
Paris Holiday
Paris, Texas
Paris Trout
Paris When It Sizzles
The Park is Mine
Parker
Parlor, Bedroom and Bath
Paroled to Die
Parting Glances
Partners
Party Animal
Party Camp
Party Favors
Party Girl
Party Girls
Party Line
Party Plane
Pascali's Island
Pass the Ammo
A Passage to India
Passage to Marseilles
Passed Away
The Passenger
The Passing of the Third Floor Back
Passion
Passion for Life
The Passion of Joan of Arc
Passion of Love
Passionate Thief
The Passover Plot
Passport to Pimlico
Pat and Mike
Pat Garrett & Billy the Kid
A Patch of Blue
Patchwork Girl of Oz
Paternity
Pather Panchali
Paths of Glory
Paths to Paradise
Patrick
The Patriot
Patriot Games
The Patriots
The Patsy
Patti Rocks
Patton
Patty Hearst
Paul Bartel's The Secret Cinema
Paul Robeson
Pauline at the Beach
Pawnshop
Pay Off
Pay or Die
Payback
Payday
Payoff
Peacekillers
Peacemaker
The Peacock Fan
The Peanut Butter Solution
The Pearl of Death
Pearl of the South Pacific
Peck's Bad Boy
Peck's Bad Boy with the Circus
Pecos Kid
The Pedestrian
Pee Wee's Big Adventure
Pee Wee's Playhouse Festival of Fun
Peeping Tom
Peggy Sue Got Married
Pelle the Conqueror
Penalty Phase
Pendulum
The Penitent
Penitentiary
Penitentiary 2
Penitentiary 3
Penn and Teller Get Killed
Pennies From Heaven
The People
People Are Funny
The People That Time Forgot
The People Under the Stairs
The People vs. Jean Harris
People's Choice
Pepe Le Moko
Pepper and His Wacky Taxi
Perfect
The Perfect Bride
Perfect Crime
Perfect Family
Perfect Furlough
Perfect Harmony
Perfect Killer
Perfect Match
Perfect Strangers
Perfect Timing
Perfect Victims
The Perfect Weapon
Perfect Witness
Perfectly Normal
Performance
Peril
The Perils of Gwendoline
The Perils of Pauline
Permanent Record
Permanent Vacation
Permission To Kill
Perry Mason Returns
Persona
Personal Best
Personal Exemptions
Personal Services
The Personals
Personals
The Persuaders
Pet Sematary
Pet Sematary 2
Pet Shop
Pete Kelly's Blues
Pete 'n' Tillie
Pete Townshend: White City
Peter Lundy and the Medicine Hat Stallion
Peter Pan
Peter the First: Part 1
Peter the First: Part 2
Pete's Dragon
Petit Con
Petrified Forest
Petulia
Phantasm
Phantasm II
The Phantom Broadcast
Phantom Brother
The Phantom Bullet
The Phantom Chariot
The Phantom Creeps
The Phantom Empire
Phantom Empire
Phantom Express
The Phantom Flyer
Phantom from Space
The Phantom in the House
Phantom of Death
Phantom of Liberty
The Phantom of Soho
Phantom of the Mall: Eric's Revenge
The Phantom of the Opera
Phantom of the Paradise
Phantom of the Ritz
Phantom of the West
Phantom Patrol
The Phantom Planet
Phantom Rancher
The Phantom Rider
Phantom Thunderbolt
Phantom Tollbooth
Phar Lap
Pharaoh
Pharmacist
Phase 4
Phedre
The Philadelphia Experiment
The Philadelphia Story
Philby, Burgess and MacLean: Spy Scandal of the Century
Phobia
Phoenix
Phoenix Team
Phoenix the Ninja
Phone Call from a Stranger
Photographer
Physical Evidence
P.I. Private Investigations
Piaf
A Piano for Mrs. Cimino
The Pick-Up Artist
Pick-Up Summer
Pickpocket
Pickup on South Street
The Pickwick Papers
Picnic
Picnic at Hanging Rock
Picnic on the Grass
Picture Mommy Dead
Picture of Dorian Gray
A Piece of Pleasure
Piece of the Action
Pieces
The Pied Piper of Hamelin
Pier 23
Pigs
Pilgrim, Farewell
Pillow Talk
Pilot
Pimpernel Smith
Pin
The Pinchcliffe Grand Prix
Ping Pong
Pink Cadillac
The Pink Chiquitas
Pink Flamingos
Pink Floyd: The Wall
Pink Motel
Pink Nights
The Pink Panther
The Pink Panther Strikes Again
Pink Strings and Sealing Wax
Pinocchio
Pinocchio's Storybook Adventures
Pinto Rustlers
Pioneer Marshal
Pioneer Woman
The Pioneers
Pipe Dreams
Pippi Goes on Board
Pippi in the South Seas
Pippi Longstocking
Pippi on the Run
Pippin
Piranha
Piranha 2: The Spawning
The Pirate
Pirate Movie
Pirate Warrior
Pirates
The Pirates of Penzance
Pirates of the Coast
Pirates of the Seven Seas
Pistol: The Birth of a Legend
Pistoleros Asesinos
The Pit
The Pit and the Pendulum
Pixote
P.K. and the Kid
A Place Called Today
Place in Hell
A Place in the Sun
Place of Weeping
Places in the Heart
The Plague Dogs
Plain Clothes
The Plainsman
Plan 9 from Outer Space
Planes, Trains & Automobiles
Planet Burg
Planet of Dinosaurs
Planet of the Apes
Planet of the Vampires
Planet on the Prowl
Platoon
Platoon Leader
Platoon the Warriors
Platypus Cove
Play It Again, Charlie Brown
Play It Again, Sam
Play Misty for Me
Playback
Playboy of the Western World
Players
Playgirl Killer
Playing Away
Playing for Keeps
Playing for Time
Playing with Fire
Playmates
Playtime
Plaza Suite
Please Don't Eat the Daisies
Pleasure
A Pleasure Doing Business
Pleasure Palace
Plenty
The Ploughman's Lunch
Plumber
Plunge Into Darkness
Plutonium Baby
Plutonium Incident

The Pocatello Kid
Pocket Money
Pocketful of Miracles
A Pocketful of Rye
Poco
Pogo for President: "I Go Pogo"
Poil de Carotte
The Point
Point Blank
Point of No Return
Point of Terror
The Pointsman
Poison Ivy
Poker Alice
Police Academy
Police Academy 2: Their First Assignment
Police Academy 3: Back in Training
Police Academy 4: Citizens on Patrol
Police Academy 5: Assignment Miami Beach
Police Court
Police Squad! Help Wanted!
Policewoman Centerfold
Policewomen
A Polish Vampire in Burbank
Pollyanna
Poltergeist
Poltergeist 2: The Other Side
Poltergeist 3
Polyester
Pom Pom Girls
Pontiac Moon
Pony Express
Pool Hustlers
Pool Sharks
Poor Girl, A Ghost Story
A Poor Little Rich Girl
The Poor Little Rich Girl
Poor Pretty Eddie
Poor White Trash
Poor White Trash 2
Pop Always Pays
Pop Goes the Cork
Pope John Paul II
The Pope Must Diet
The Pope of Greenwich Village
Popeye
Popi
The Poppy Is Also a Flower
Pork Chop Hill
Porky's
Porky's 2: The Next Day
Porky's Revenge
Port Arthur
Port of Call
The Port of Missing Girls
Port of New York
Portnoy's Complaint
Portrait of a Hitman
Portrait of a Rebel: Margaret Sanger
Portrait of a Showgirl
Portrait of a Stripper
Portrait of a White Marriage
Portrait of Grandpa Doc
Portrait of Jennie
Posed For Murder
The Poseidon Adventure
Positive I.D.
Posse
Possessed
The Possessed
Possession
Postcards from the Edge
The Postman Always Rings Twice
Postmark for Danger
Postmark for Danger/Quicksand
Pot O' Gold
The P.O.W. Escape
Powaqqatsi: Life in Transformation
Powder Keg
Powdersmoke Range
Power
The Power of the Ninjitsu
Power, Passion & Murder
Power Play
The Power Within
Powwow Highway
Prairie Badmen
The Prairie King
Prairie Moon
Prairie Pals
Prancer
Pray for Death
Pray for the Wildcats
Pray TV
Prayer for the Dying
Praying Mantis
Predator
Predator 2
Prehistoric Women
Prehysteria
Prehysteria 2
Prelude to War
Premature Burial
Premonition
The Premonition
Prep School
Preppies
Presenting Lily Mars
President's Mistress
The President's Mystery
The Presidio
Presumed Innocent
Pretty Baby
Pretty in Pink
Pretty Smart
Pretty Woman
Prettykill
The Prey
Prey of the Chameleon
Prick Up Your Ears
Pride and Prejudice
The Pride and the Passion
Pride of Jesse Hallum
Pride of St. Louis
Pride of the Bowery
Pride of the Clan
The Pride of the Yankees
Priest of Love
Primal Impulse
Primal Rage
Primary Motive
Primary Target
Prime Cut
The Prime of Miss Jean Brodie
Prime Risk
Prime Suspect
Prime Time
The Primitive Lover
Primrose Path
Prince and the Great Race
The Prince and the Pauper
The Prince and the Showgirl
Prince Jack
Prince of Bel Air
The Prince of Central Park
Prince of Darkness
Prince of Pennsylvania
Prince of the City
The Prince of Tides
Prince Valiant
Princes in Exile
Princess Academy
The Princess & the Call Girl
The Princess and the Pea
The Princess and the Pirate
The Princess and the Swineherd
The Princess Bride
Princess Cinderella
Princess Daisy
Princess Tam Tam
The Princess Who Never Laughed
The Principal
Prison
Prison Break
Prison Stories: Women on the Inside
The Prisoner: Arrival
Prisoner in the Middle
Prisoner of Rio
Prisoner of Second Avenue
Prisoner of Zenda
Prisoners of the Lost Universe
Prisoners of the Sun
Private Affairs
Private Benjamin
Private Buckaroo
Private Contentment
Private Duty Nurses
The Private Eyes
A Private Function
The Private History of a Campaign That Failed
Private Investigations
Private Lessons
Private Life of Don Juan
The Private Life of Henry VIII
The Private Lives of Elizabeth & Essex
Private Manoeuvres
Private Passions
Private Resort
Private Road: No Trespassing
Private School
Privates on Parade
Prix de Beaute
Prize Fighter
Prize of Peril
Prizzi's Honor
Probation
Problem Child 2
The Prodigal
Prodigal Boxer: The Kick of Death
The Prodigal Planet
The Producers
Professional Killers 1
The Professionals
Professionals
Profile
The Program
Programmed to Kill
Project: Kill!
Project Moon Base
Project X
The Projectionist
Prom Night
Prom Night 3: The Last Kiss
Promise to Murder
Promised Land
Promises in the Dark
Promises! Promises!
The Promoter
Proof of the Man
Prophecy
A Propos de Nice
Prospero's Books
Protector
Protocol
The Proud and the Damned
Proud Rebel
Providence
Provoked
Prowler
Prudential Family Playhouse
Prurient Interest
Psych-Out
The Psychic
Psychic Killer
Psycho
Psycho 2
Psycho 3
Psycho Cop
Psycho from Texas
Psycho Girls
Psychomania
Psychopath
Psychos in Love
PT 109
Puberty Blues
A Public Affair
Public Cowboy No. 1
Public Enemy
The Public Eye
Pudd'nhead Wilson
Pueblo Affair
Pulp
Pulse
Pulsebeat
The Puma Man
Pumping Iron
Pumping Iron 2: The Women
Pumpkinhead
Punchline
The Punisher
Punk Rock Movie
Punk Vacation
Puppet Master
Puppet Master 2
Puppet Master 4
Puppet Master 5: The Final Chapter
Puppet on a Chain
The Puppetoon Movie
Pure Country
Pure Luck
Purgatory
Purlie Victorious
The Purple Heart
Purple Hearts
Purple People Eater
Purple Rain
The Purple Rose of Cairo
The Purple Taxi
Purple Vigilantes
Pursuit
The Pursuit of D.B. Cooper
The Pursuit of Happiness
Pursuit of the Graf Spee
Pursuit to Algiers
Puss 'n Boots
Putney Swope
Pygmalion
Q & A
Q Ships
Q (The Winged Serpent)
QB VII
Quackser Fortune Has a Cousin in the Bronx
Quadrophenia
Quarterback Princess
Quartet
Quatermass 2
Quatermass Conclusion
Que Viva Mexico
Queen Boxer
Queen Christina
Queen Kelly
Queen of Diamonds
Queen of Hearts
Queen of Outer Space
Queen of the Amazons
Queen of the Jungle
Queen of the Road
Queen of the Stardust Ballroom
Querelle
The Quest
Quest for Fire
Quest for Love
Quest for the Mighty Sword
Question of Honor
Question of Silence
Question 7
Qui Etes Vous, Mr. Sorge?
The Quick and the Dead
Quick Change
Quick, Let's Get Married
Quicker Than the Eye
Quicksand
Quicksand: No Escape
Quicksilver
Quiet Cool
Quiet Day In Belfast
The Quiet Earth
Quiet Thunder
Quigley Down Under
The Quiller Memorandum
Quintet
Quo Vadis
Rabbit Test
Rabid
Rabid Grannies
Race for Glory
Race for Life
Race for Your Life, Charlie Brown
Race with the Devil
Rachel and the Stranger
The Rachel Papers
Rachel, Rachel
Rachel's Man
Racing Luck
Racing with the Moon
The Racket
The Racketeer
Racketeers of the Range
Racquet
Rad
Radar Secret Service
Radio Days
Radio Patrol
Radioactive Dreams
Rafferty & the Gold Dust Twins
Rage
Rage of Angels
Rage of Honor
The Rage of Paris
Rage of Wind
Rage to Kill
Raggedy Ann and Andy: A Musical Adventure
Raggedy Man
Raging Bull
Rags to Riches
Ragtime
Raid on Entebbe
Raid on Rommel
Raiders in Action
Raiders of Atlantis
Raiders of Red Gap
Raiders of the Border
Raiders of the Lost Ark
Railroaded
Railrodder
The Railway Children
The Railway Station Man
Rain
Rain Man
The Rain People
Rainbow
Rainbow Bridge
The Rainbow Gang
Raintree County
Rainy Day
Raise the Titanic
A Raisin in the Sun
Raising Arizona
Raising Cain
Rambo: First Blood, Part 2
Rambo 3
Rampage
Ramparts of Clay
The Ramrodder
Ran
Rana: The Legend of Shadow Lake
The Ranch
Rancho Notorious
Random Harvest
Randy Rides Alone
Range Busters
Range Law
Range Rider
Range Riders
Rangeland Empire
Rangeland Racket
Ranger and the Lady
Ranger's Roundup
Rangers Take Over
Ransom Money
Ranson's Folly
Rape

Rape and Marriage: The Rideout Case
Rape of Love
The Rape of the Sabines
Rapid Fire
Rappin'
Rapunzel
The Rare Breed
A Rare Breed
Rascal Dazzle
The Rascals
Rashomon
Rasputin
Rat Pfink a Boo-Boo
Ratboy
Rate It X
Ratings Game
Rats
The Rats are Coming! The Werewolves are Here!
Rattle of a Simple Man
Rattler Kid
Rattlers
The Raven
Ravishing Idiot
Raw Courage
Raw Deal
Raw Force
Raw Nerve
Rawhead Rex
Rawhide
Rawhide Romance
Razorback
The Razor's Edge
Re-Animator
Reach for the Sky
Reaching for the Moon
Reactor
A Real American Hero
Real Bruce Lee
The Real Buddy Holly Story
Real Bullets
Real Genius
Real Life
Real Men
Really Weird Tales
Reap the Wild Wind
Rear Window
A Reason to Live, A Reason to Die
Rebecca
Rebecca of Sunnybrook Farm
Rebel
Rebel High
Rebel Love
Rebel Rousers
The Rebel Set
Rebel Storm
Rebel Vixens
Rebel Without a Cause
Reborn
Reckless
Reckless Disregard
Reckless Moment
The Reckless Way
Recruits
Red Alert
The Red and the Black
The Red Badge of Courage
The Red Balloon
Red Balloon/Occurrence at Owl Creek Bridge
Red Beard
Red Blooded American Girl
Red Dawn
Red Desert
The Red Desert
Red Desert Penitentiary
Red Dust
Red Flag: The Ultimate Game
The Red Half-Breed
Red Headed Stranger
Red Headed Woman
Red Heat
The Red House
Red Kimono
Red King, White Knight
The Red Light Sting
Red Lion
Red Nightmare
Red Nights
The Red Pony
The Red Raven Kiss-Off
Red Riding Hood
Red River
Red Rock Outlaw
The Red Shoes
Red Signals
Red Sonja
Red Sun
Red Surf
Red Tent
Red, White & Busted
The Redeemer
Redneck
Redneck Zombies
Reds
Reefer Madness
Reet, Petite and Gone
A Reflection of Fear
Reflections in a Golden Eye
Reform School Girls
Refuge of Fear
Regarding Henry
Reggie Mixes In
Regina
Rehearsal for Murder
Reilly: Ace of Spies
The Reincarnate
The Reincarnation of Peter Proud
The Reivers
Relentless
The Reluctant Debutante
The Reluctant Dragon
Rembrandt
Remedy for Riches
Remember Me
Remo Williams: The Adventure Begins
Remolina de Pasiones
Remote
Remote Control
Rendez-Moi Ma Peau
Renegade Girl
Renegade Monk
Renegade Ninja
Renegade Ranger/Scarlet River
Renegades
Renfrew of the Royal Mounted
Reno and the Doc
Renoir Shorts
Rent-A-Cop
Rented Lips
Repentance
Repo Man
The Report on the Party and the Guests
Report to the Commissioner
Repulsion
Requiem for a Heavyweight
The Rescue
The Rescuers Down Under
Rest In Pieces
Restless
Resurrection
Resurrection of Zachary Wheeler
Retribution
Retrievers
The Return
Return
Return Engagement
Return from Witch Mountain
The Return of a Man Called Horse
The Return of Boston Blackie
Return of Captain Invincible
Return of Chandu
The Return of Dr. Mabuse
Return of Draw Egan
Return of Frank Cannon
Return of Frank James
The Return of Grey Wolf
Return of Jesse James
The Return of Martin Guerre
The Return of Our Gang
The Return of Swamp Thing
Return of the Bad Men
Return of the Chinese Boxer
Return of the Dinosaurs
Return of the Dragon
Return of the Fly
Return of the Jedi
Return of the Killer Tomatoes!
Return of the Lash
Return of the Living Dead
Return of the Living Dead 2
Return of the Man from U.N.C.L.E.
Return of the Pink Panther
Return of the Scorpion
Return of the Secaucus 7
Return of the Seven
Return of the Soldier
Return of the Tall Blond Man With One Black Shoe
Return of the Tiger
Return of the Vampire
Return of Wildfire
Return to Africa
Return to Boggy Creek
Return to Earth
Return to Fantasy Island
Return to Horror High
Return to Macon County
Return to Mayberry
Return to Oz
Return to Paradise
Return to Salem's Lot
Return to Snowy River
Reuben, Reuben
Reunion
Reunion in France
Revenge
Revenge of Doctor X
Revenge of the Barbarians
Revenge of the Cheerleaders
Revenge of the Dead
Revenge of the Living Zombies
Revenge of the Nerds
Revenge of the Nerds 2: Nerds in Paradise
Revenge of the Ninja
Revenge of the Pink Panther
Revenge of the Stepford Wives
Revenge of the Teenage Vixens from Outer Space
The Revenger
Reversal of Fortune
The Revolt of Job
Revolt of the Barbarians
Revolt of the Dragon
Revolt of the Zombies
Revolution
Rhinestone
Ricco
Rich and Famous
Rich Hall's Vanishing America
Rich Kids
Richard III
Richard Petty Story
Richard's Things
Riddance
The Riddle of the Sands
Ride a Wild Pony
Ride in a Pink Car
Ride in the Whirlwind
Ride, Ranger, Ride
Ride the High Country
Ride the Wind
Rider from Tucson
Rider of the Law
Rider on the Rain
Riders of Death Valley
Riders of the Desert
Riders of the Range
Riders of the Range/Storm Over Wyoming
Riders of the Rockies
Riders of the Storm
Riders of the Whistling Pines
Riders of the Whistling Skull
Riders to the Sea
Ridin' on a Rainbow
Ridin' the California Trail
Ridin' the Trail
Ridin' Thru
The Riding Avenger
Riding High
Riding on Air
Riding Speed
Riding with Death
Riel
Riff-Raff
Rififi
The Right Hand Man
Right of Way
The Right Stuff
Rikisha-Man
Rikky and Pete
Rim of the Canyon
Rimfire
Rin Tin Tin, Hero of the West
Ring of Bright Water
Ring of Death
Ringside
The Rink
Rink/Immigrant
Rio Bravo
Rio Conchos
Rio Grande Raiders
Rio Lobo
Rio Rattler
Riot in Cell Block 11
Riot Squad
Rip-Off
The Rip Off
Rip Roarin' Buckaroo
Rip van Winkle
The Ripper
Ripping Yarns
The Rise & Rise of Daniel Rocket
Rising Son
Risky Business
Rita Hayworth: The Love Goddess
Rita, Sue & Bob Too
Rituals
The Ritz
Rivals
Rivals of the Silver Fox
The River
River Beat
River of Death
River of Diamonds
River of No Return
River of Unrest
The River Rat
Riverbend
River's Edge
Road Agent
Road Games
Road House
The Road to Bali
The Road to Galveston
The Road to Lebanon
Road to Nashville
The Road to Rio
The Road to Ruin
Road to Salina
The Road to Utopia
The Road to Yesterday
Road to Yesterday/The Yankee Clipper
The Road Warrior
Roadhouse Girl
Roadhouse 66
Roamin' Wild
Roanoak
Roarin' Lead
Roaring City
Roaring Guns
The Roaring Road
Roaring Roads
Roaring Six Guns
Roaring Speedboats
The Roaring Twenties
Rob Roy—The Highland Rogue
Robbers of the Sacred Mountain
Robbery
Robby
The Robe
Robert et Robert
Roberta
Robin and Marian
Robin and the 7 Hoods
Robin Hood
Robin Hood of Texas
Robin Hood of the Pecos
Robin Hood...The Legend: Herne's Son
Robin Hood...The Legend: The Swords of Wayland
Robin Hood...The Legend: The Time of the Wolf
Robinson Crusoe
Robinson Crusoe & the Tiger
Robinson Crusoe of Mystery Island
Robo-Chic
RoboCop
RoboCop 2
Robot Holocaust
Robot Monster
Robot Pilot
The Robot vs. the Aztec Mummy
Robot Wars
Rock & Rule
Rock & the Money-Hungry Party Girls
Rock, Baby, Rock It
Rock 'n' Roll High School
Rock 'n' Roll High School Forever
Rock 'n' Roll Nightmare
Rock, Pretty Baby
Rock River Renegades
Rock, Rock, Rock
Rocket Attack U.S.A.
Rocket Gibraltar
Rocket to the Moon
The Rocketeer
Rocketship X-M
Rockin' Road Trip
Rocktober Blood
Rockula
Rocky
Rocky 2
Rocky 3
Rocky 4
Rocky 5
Rocky Jones, Space Ranger
Rodan
Rodeo Girl
Roe vs. Wade
Roger & Me
Rogue
Rogue Lion
Rogue of the Range
Rogue of the Rio Grande
Rogue's Gallery
Rogue's Tavern
Rogue's Yarn
Roland the Mighty
Roll Along Cowboy
Roll of Thunder, Hear My Cry
Roll, Wagons, Roll
Roller Blade
Rollerball
Rollercoaster
Rollin' Plains
Rolling Home
Rolling Thunder
Rolling Vengeance
Rollover

Roman Holiday
Roman Scandals
Roman Spring of Mrs. Stone
Romance on the Orient Express
Romance with a Double Bass
Romancing the Stone
Romantic Comedy
Romantic Englishwoman
Romeo and Juliet
Romero
Romola
The Roof
Rooftops
The Rookie
The Room
Room 43
Room Service
Room to Let
A Room with a View
Roommate
Rooster Cogburn
Rooster: Spurs of Death!
Rootin' Tootin' Rhythm
Roots
Rope
Rosalie
The Rosary Murders
The Rose
The Rose and the Jackal
The Rose Garden
Rose Marie
Rose of Rio Grande
The Rose Tattoo
Rosebud Beach Hotel
Roseland
Rosemary's Baby
Rosencrantz & Guildenstern Are Dead
Roses Bloom Twice
Rosie: The Rosemary Clooney Story
Rough Cut
Rough Justice
Rough Riders of Cheyenne
Rough Riders' Roundup
Rough Riding Rangers
Roughnecks
Round Midnight
Round-Up Time in Texas
Rounding Up the Law
Roustabout
Roxanne
The Royal Bed
Royal Wedding
R.P.M.* (*Revolutions Per Minute)
R.S.V.P.
Rubdown
Ruby
Ruby Gentry
Ruckus
Ruddigore
Rude Awakening
Rudolph & Frosty's Christmas in July
Rudolph the Red-Nosed Reindeer
Rudyard Kipling's Classic Stories
The Rue Morgue Massacres
Ruggles of Red Gap
Rulers of the City
The Rules of the Game
The Ruling Class
Rumble Fish
The Rumor Mill
A Rumor of War
Rumpelstiltskin
Run
Run, Angel, Run!
Run for the Roses
Run If You Can
Run of the Arrow
Run, Rebecca, Run
Run Silent, Run Deep
Runaway
The Runaway Bus
Runaway Train
The Runaways
Runaways
The Runner Stumbles
The Runnin' Kind
Running Brave
Running Cool
Running Hot
The Running Man
Running Mates
Running on Empty
Running Out of Luck
Running Scared
Running Wild
Rush It
Russian Roulette
The Russians are Coming, the Russians are Coming
Russkies
Rustler's Hideout
Rustler's Paradise
Rustler's Rhapsody
Rustler's Valley
The Rutherford County Line
The Ruthless Four
Ruthless People
Ryan's Daughter
Ryder P.I.
Sabotage
Saboteur
Sabre Jet
Sabrina
Sacco & Vanzetti
The Sacketts
Sacred Ground
Sacred Mountain/White Flame
The Sacrifice
Sacrilege
Saddle Mountain Round-Up
The Sadist
Safari 3000
Saga of Death Valley
Saga of the Vagabond
Sahara
Saigon Commandos
Saigon: Year of the Cat
Sailor-Made Man/Grandma's Boy
The Sailor Who Fell from Grace with the Sea
St. Elmo's Fire
St. Helen's, Killer Volcano
The Saint in London
The Saint in New York
St. Ives
Saint Jack
Saint Joan
The Saint of Fort Washington
The Saint Strikes Back: Criminal Court
The St. Valentine's Day Massacre
The Saint's Vacation/The Narrow Margin
Sakharov
Sakura Killers
Salaam Bombay!
The Salamander
Salammbo
Salem's Lot
Sallah
Sally of the Sawdust
Salome
Salome/Queen Elizabeth
Salome, Where She Danced
Salome's Last Dance
Salsa
Salt of the Earth
Salty
Salute John Citizen
Salute to the "King of the Cowboys," Roy Rogers
Salvador
Salvation!
The Salzburg Connection
Samantha
Samar
Samaritan: The Mitch Snyder Story
Same Time, Next Year
Sammy & Rosie Get Laid
Sammy, the Way-Out Seal
Sam's Son
Samson Against the Sheik
Samson and Delilah
Samson and His Mighty Challenge
Samson and the 7 Miracles of the World
Samson vs. the Vampire Women
Samurai 1: Musashi Miyamoto
Samurai 2: Duel at Ichijoji Temple
Samurai 3: Duel at Ganryu Island
San Antonio
San Fernando Valley
San Francisco
Sanctuary of Fear
Sand and Blood
The Sand Pebbles
Sandakan No. 8
Sanders of the River
The Sandpiper
Sanjuro
Sansho the Bailiff
Santa Claus
Santa Claus Conquers the Martians
Santa Claus Is Coming to Town
Santa Claus: The Movie
Santa Fe Trail
Santa Fe Uprising
Santee
Sapphire
Saps at Sea
Sara Dane
Sarafina!
Sardinia Kidnapped
Sartana's Here...Trade Your Pistol for a Coffin
S.A.S. San Salvador
Sasquatch
Satan's Black Wedding
Satan's Blade
Satan's Cheerleaders
Satan's Harvest
Satan's Princess
Satan's School for Girls
Satan's Touch
Satanwar
Satisfaction
Saturday Night Fever
Saturday Night Live
Saturday Night Serials
Saturday Night Shockers
Saturday Night Shockers, Vol. 2
Saturday Night Sleazies, Vol. 1
Saturday the 14th
Saturday the 14th Strikes Back
Saturn 3
Saul and David
Savage!
Savage Abduction
Savage Attraction
Savage Beach
The Savage Bees
Savage Dawn
Savage Drums
Savage Fury
Savage Guns
Savage Hunger
Savage Is Loose
Savage Journey
Savage Justice
Savage Sam
Savage Streets
Savage Weekend
Savages
Savannah Smiles
Save the Lady
Save the Tiger
Saving Grace
Sawdust & Tinsel
Sawmill/The Dome Doctor
Say Anything
Say Goodbye, Maggie Cole
Say Hello to Yesterday
Say Yes!
Sayonara
The Scalawag Bunch
Scalp Merchant
Scalpel
The Scalphunters
Scalps
Scandal
Scandal Man
Scandalous
Scandalous John
Scanners
Scanners 2: The New Order
Scarecrow
Scared to Death
Scared to Death/Dick Tracy's Dilemma
Scarface
Scarface Mob
The Scarlet & the Black
The Scarlet Car
Scarlet Claw
The Scarlet Letter
The Scarlet Pimpernel
Scarlet Spear
Scarlet Street
Scarred
The Scars of Dracula
Scavenger Hunt
Scavengers
Scenario du Film Passion
Scene of the Crime
Scenes from a Mall
Scenes from a Marriage
Scenes from a Murder
Scenes from the Class Struggle in Beverly Hills
Scenes from the Goldmine
Scherzo
Schizo
Schizoid
Schnelles Geld
School Daze
School for Scandal
School Spirit
School Ties
Science Crazed
Scissors
Scorchers
Scorchy
Scorpion
The Scorpion Woman
Scotland Yard Inspector
Scott of the Antarctic
Scoumoune
Scout's Honor
Scrambled Feet
Scream
Scream and Scream Again
Scream, Baby, Scream
Scream Bloody Murder
Scream for Help
Scream of Fear
Scream of the Demon Lover
Screamer
Screamers
Screams of a Winter Night
Screamtime
Screen Test
Screwball Academy
Screwballs
Scrooge
Scrooged
Scrubbers
Scruffy
Scruples
Scum
Sea Chase
Sea Devils
Sea Gypsies
The Sea Hawk
Sea Lion
Sea of Dreams
Sea of Love
Sea Prince and the Fire Child
Sea Racketeers
The Sea Serpent
Sea Wolves
The Seagull
Seance on a Wet Afternoon
Search and Destroy
The Searchers
Searching for Bobby Fischer
Seaside Swingers
Season for Assassins
Season of Fear
Season of the Witch
Sebastiane
Second Best Secret Agent in the Whole Wide World
Second Chance
Second Chorus
Second Coming of Suzanne
Second Sight
Second Thoughts
Second Time Lucky
Second Woman
Secret Admirer
The Secret Adversary
The Secret Agent
Secret Agent
Secret Agent Super Dragon
Secret Ceremony
The Secret Diary of Sigmund Freud
The Secret Four
The Secret Garden
Secret Honor
Secret Life of an American Wife
The Secret Life of Walter Mitty
Secret Obsession
The Secret of El Zorro
The Secret of My Success
The Secret of NIMH
Secret of the Ice Cave
Secret of Yolanda
Secret Passions
Secret Places
The Secret Policeman's Other Ball
Secret Policeman's Private Parts
A Secret Space
The Secret War of Harry Frigg
Secret Weapon
Secrets
Secrets of a Married Man
Secrets of a Soul
Secrets of Sweet Sixteen
Secrets of Women
Seduced and Abandoned
Seduced by Evil
Seducers
The Seduction
The Seduction of Joe Tynan
Seduction of Mimi
See How She Runs
See No Evil
See No Evil, Hear No Evil
See You in the Morning
Seedpeople
Seeds of Evil
Seems Like Old Times
Seize the Day
Seizure
Seizure: The Story of Kathy Morris
Self-Defense
Sell Out
Semi-Tough
Send Me No Flowers
The Sender
Senior Trip
Senior Week
The Seniors

Senora Tentacion
Sensations
Sensations of 1945
Sense & Sensibility
A Sense of Freedom
The Sensual Man
Sensual Partners
The Sensuous Nurse
The Sentinel
A Separate Peace
Separate Tables
Separate Vacations
Separate Ways
Sepia Cinderella
September
September Gun
Sgt. Pepper's Lonely Hearts Club Band
Sergeant York
Serial
The Serpent and the Rainbow
Serpent Island
The Serpent of Death
The Serpent's Egg
Serpico
The Servant
Sesame Street Presents: Follow That Bird
Sessions
The Set-Up
Seven
Seven Alone
Seven Beauties
Seven Blows of the Dragon
Seven Brides for Seven Brothers
Seven Cities of Gold
Seven Days Ashore/Hurry, Charlie, Hurry
Seven Days in May
Seven Days' Leave
Seven Deaths in the Cat's Eye
Seven Doors of Death
Seven Doors to Death
7 Faces of Dr. Lao
Seven Hours to Judgment
The Seven Little Foys
Seven Magnificent Gladiators
Seven Miles from Alcatraz/Flight from Glory
Seven Minutes in Heaven
The Seven-Per-Cent Solution
Seven Samurai
Seven Sinners
The Seven-Ups
The Seven Year Itch
Seven Years Bad Luck
1776
The Seventh Seal
The Seventh Sign
The Seventh Veil
The Seventh Victim
The Seventh Voyage of Sinbad
Severance
The Severed Arm
Sex
Sex Adventures of the Three Musketeers
Sex and the Single Parent
Sex, Drugs, and Rock-n-Roll
sex, lies and videotape
The Sex Machine
Sex on the Run
Sex Through a Window
Sex with a Smile
Sexpot
Sextette
Sexton Blake and the Hooded Terror
Shadey
The Shadow
The Shadow Box
Shadow Dancing
Shadow Killers
The Shadow Man
Shadow Man
Shadow of a Doubt
Shadow of Chikara
Shadow of the Chinatown
Shadow of the Thin Man
Shadow Play
The Shadow Strikes
Shadows of Death
Shadows of Forgotten Ancestors
Shadows on the Stairs
Shadows Run Black
Shadowzone
Shaft
Shag: The Movie
The Shaggy D.A.
The Shaggy Dog
Shaka Zulu
Shake Hands with Murder
Shakedown
Shaker Run
Shakespeare Wallah
Shalako
Shall We Dance
Shallow Grave
The Shaman
Shame
Shame, Shame on the Bixby Boys
The Shaming
Shampoo
Shamus
Shane
The Shanghai Gesture
Shanghai Surprise
Shaolin Ex-Monk
Shaolin Executioner
Shaolin Kids
Shaolin Kung Fu Mystagogue
Shaolin Temple Strikes Back
Shaolin Traitor
Shark!
Shark Hunter
Shark River
Shark's Paradise
Sharks' Treasure
Sharky's Machine
Sharma & Beyond
Shattered
Shattered Vows
She
S*H*E
She
The She-Beast
She Came to the Valley
She Couldn't Say No
She Demons
She-Devil
She-Devils on Wheels
She Done Him Wrong
She-Freak
She Goes to War
She Likes You, Charlie Brown
She Shall Have Music
She Waits
She Wore a Yellow Ribbon
Sheba, Baby
Sheena
The Sheep Has Five Legs
Sheer Madness
The Sheik
She'll Be Wearing Pink Pajamas
Shell Shock
The Sheltering Sky
Shenandoah
Shep Comes Home
Sheriff of Tombstone
Sherlock Holmes Faces Death
Sherlock Holmes in Washington
Sherlock Holmes: The Sign of Four
Sherlock Holmes: The Silver Blaze
Sherlock Holmes: The Voice of Terror
Sherlock Hound: Tales of Mystery
Sherlock's Rivals & Where's My Wife
She's a Good Skate, Charlie Brown
She's Back
She's Gotta Have It
She's Having a Baby
She's in the Army Now
She's Out of Control
Shifting Sands
Shin Heike Monogatari
Shinbone Alley
Shine on, Harvest Moon
The Shining
A Shining Season
Shinobi Ninja
Ship of Fools
Ships in the Night
Shirley Temple Festival
The Shock
Shock!
Shock! Shock! Shock!
A Shock to the System
Shock Treatment
Shock Waves
Shocker
Shocking Asia
The Shoes of the Fisherman
Shoeshine
Shogun
Shogun Assassin
Shogun's Ninja
Shoot
Shoot It Black, Shoot It Blue
Shoot Loud, Louder, I Don't Understand!
Shoot the Living, Pray for the Dead
Shoot the Moon
Shoot the Piano Player
Shoot the Sun Down
Shoot to Kill
Shooters
The Shooting
Shooting
The Shooting Party
Shooting Stars
The Shootist
Shop Angel
The Shop on Main Street
Short Circuit
Short Circuit 2
Short Eyes
Short Fuse
A Shot in the Dark
The Shout
Shout
Shout at the Devil
Show Boat
Show Business
A Show of Force
The Show-Off
Showdown at the Equator
Showdown in Little Tokyo
Shredder Orpheus
Shriek in the Night
Shriek of the Mutilated
The Shrieking
The Shrimp on the Barbie
Shrunken Heads
Shy People
The Sibling
Sibling Rivalry
The Sicilian
Sicilian Connection
The Sicilian Connection
Sid & Nancy
Side By Side
Side Out
Side Show
Sidewalks of London
Sidewalks of New York
Sidewinder One
Sidney Sheldon's Bloodline
The Siege of Firebase Gloria
Siesta
The Sign of Four
The Sign of Zorro
Signal 7
Signals Through the Flames
Signs of Life
Silas Marner
The Silence
Silence
Silence Like Glass
The Silence of the Lambs
Silence of the North
Silent Code
The Silent Enemy
Silent Laugh Makers, No. 1
Silent Laugh Makers, No. 2
Silent Laugh Makers, No. 3
Silent Madness
Silent Movie
Silent Movies...Just For the Fun of It!
Silent Night, Deadly Night
Silent Night, Deadly Night 2
Silent Night, Deadly Night 3: Better Watch Out!
Silent Night, Lonely Night
The Silent One
The Silent Partner
The Silent Passenger
Silent Rage
Silent Raiders
Silent Rebellion
Silent Running
Silent Scream
Silent Valley
Silent Victory: The Kitty O'Neil Story
Silent Witness
Silk
Silk 2
Silk n' Sabotage
Silk Stockings
Silkwood
Silver Bandit
Silver Bears
The Silver Chalice
Silver City
Silver City Kid
Silver Dream Racer
Silver Lode
Silver Queen
Silver Spurs
Silver Stallion
The Silver Stallion: King of the Wild Brumbies
Silver Star
The Silver Streak
Silver Streak
Silverado
Simba
Simon
Simon Bolivar
Simon, King of the Witches
Simon of the Desert
A Simple Story
The Simple Truth
Sin of Adam & Eve
The Sin of Harold Diddlebock
Sinatra
Sinbad
Sinbad and the Eye of the Tiger
Sinbad of the Seven Seas
Sinbad, the Sailor
Since You Went Away
Sincerely Charlotte
Sincerely Yours
A Sinful Life
Sing
Sing, Cowboy, Sing
Sing Your Worries Away
Singin' in the Rain
Singing Buckaroo
Singing the Blues in Red
Single Bars, Single Women
Single Room Furnished
Single White Female
Singles
Singleton's Pluck
The Sinister Invasion
The Sinister Urge
Sink the Bismarck
Sinners
Sinner's Blood
Sinners in Paradise
Sins
The Sins of Dorian Gray
Sins of Jezebel
Sioux City Sue
Sirocco
Sister Act
The Sister-in-Law
Sister Kenny
Sister, Sister
The Sisterhood
Sisters
Sisters of Death
Sisters of Gion
Sisters of Satan
Sitting Ducks
Six Fois Deux/Sur et Sous la Communication
Six Gun Rhythm
633 Squadron
Six Pack
Six Shootin' Sheriff
Six Weeks
Sixteen
Sixteen Candles
'68
Sizzle
Skag
Skateboard
Sketch Artist
Sketches of a Strangler
Ski Bum
Ski Patrol
Ski Troop Attack
Skin Deep
Skin Game
Skinned Alive
Skinner's Dress Suit
Skull: A Night of Terror
Skull & Crown
Skullduggery
The Sky Above, the Mud Below
Sky Bandits
Sky High
Sky Liner
The Sky Pilot
Sky Pirates
Skyline
The Sky's the Limit
Slamdance
Slammer Girls
Slap Shot
Slapstick
Slapstick of Another Kind
Slash
Slashdance
The Slasher
Slate, Wyn & Me
Slaughter
Slaughter High
Slaughter Hotel
Slaughter in San Francisco
The Slaughter of the Vampires
Slaughter Trail
Slaughterday
Slaughterhouse
Slaughterhouse Five
Slaughterhouse Rock
Slaughter's Big Ripoff
Slave Girls from Beyond Infinity
A Slave of Love
Slave of the Cannibal God
Slave Trade in the World Today
Slavers
Slaves of New York
The Slayer
The Slayer/The Scalps
Slayground
Sleazemania

Sleazemania III: The Good, the Bad & the Sleazy
The Sleazy Uncle
Sledgehammer
Sleep of Death
Sleepaway Camp
Sleepaway Camp 2: Unhappy Campers
Sleepaway Camp 3: Teenage Wasteland
Sleeper
Sleeping Beauty
Sleeping Car to Trieste
Sleeping Dogs
Sleeping with the Enemy
Sleepwalk
Sleuth
Slightly Honorable
A Slightly Pregnant Man
Slightly Scarlet
Slime City
The Slime People
Slipping into Darkness
Slipstream
Slither
Slithis
Sliver
Sloane
Slow Burn
Slow Moves
The Slugger's Wife
Slugs
Slumber Party '57
The Slumber Party Massacre
Slumber Party Massacre 2
Slumber Party Massacre 3
Small Change
A Small Circle of Friends
A Small Killing
Small Sacrifices
Small Town Girl
A Small Town in Texas
Smart-Aleck Kill
Smash Palace
Smash-Up: The Story of a Woman
Smile
Smiles of a Summer Night
Smilin' Through
Smiling Madame Beudet/The Seashell and the Clergyman
Smith!
Smithereens
Smoke
Smoke in the Wind
Smokey and the Bandit
Smokey and the Bandit, Part 2
Smokey and the Bandit, Part 3
Smokey & the Hotwire Gang
Smokey Bites the Dust
Smokey Smith
A Smoky Mountain Christmas
Smooth Talk
Smouldering Fires
Smugglers
Smuggler's Cove
The Snake Hunter Strangler
Snake in the Eagle's Shadow 2
The Snake People
SnakeEater
SnakeEater 2: The Drug Buster
SnakeEater 3: His Law
Snapdragon
Snapshot
Sneakers
The Sniper
Sno-Line
Snoopy, Come Home
Snoopy's Getting Married, Charlie Brown
Snow Country
The Snow Creature
Snow Kill
The Snow Queen
Snow: The Movie
Snow Treasure
Snow White and the Seven Dwarfs
Snow White and the Three Stooges
Snowball Express
Snowballin'
Snowballing
Snowbeast
The Snows of Kilimanjaro
Snuff-Bottle Connection
So Dear to My Heart
So Fine
So This is Paris
So This is Washington
Soapdish
S.O.B.
Social Error
The Social Secretary
Sodom and Gomorrah
Soft and Hard
The Soft Skin
Soggy Bottom U.S.A.
Sois Belle et Tais-Toi
Solarbabies
Soldat Duroc...Ca Va Etre Ta Fete!
The Soldier
Soldier Blue
Soldier in Love
Soldier in the Rain
Soldier of Fortune
Soldier of Orange
Soldier of the Night
Soldier's Revenge
A Soldier's Story
Sole Survivor
The Solitary Man
Solo
Solomon and Sheba
The Sombrero Kid
Some Came Running
Some Girls
Some Kind of Hero
Some Like It Hot
Somebody Has to Shoot the Picture
Somebody Up There Likes Me
Someone at the Door
Someone Behind the Door
Someone I Touched
Someone to Love
Someone to Watch Over Me
Something for Everyone
Something in Common
Something of Value
Something Short of Paradise
Something to Sing About
Something Weird
Something Wicked This Way Comes
Something Wild
Sometimes a Great Notion
Sometimes Aunt Martha Does Dreadful Things
Sometimes It Works, Sometimes It Doesn't
Somewhere in Time
Somewhere Tomorrow
Sommersby
Son-in-Law
Son of a Gun
Son of Blob
Son of Captain Blood
Son of Dracula
Son of Flubber
Son of Frankenstein
Son of God's Country
Son of Godzilla
Son of Kong
The Son of Monte Cristo
Son of Paleface
Son of Sinbad
Son of the Sheik
Song O' My Heart
Song of Arizona
The Song of Bernadette
Song of Freedom
Song of Nevada
Song of Norway
Song of Texas
Song of the Gringo
Song of the Islands
Song of the Thin Man
Song of the Trail
A Song to Remember
Songwriter
Sonny and Jed
Sonny Boy
Sons of Hercules in the Land of Darkness
Sons of Katie Elder
Sons of the Desert
Sooner or Later
Sophia Loren: Her Own Story
Sophie's Choice
Sorceress
Sorority Babes in the Slimeball Bowl-A-Rama
Sorority House Massacre
The Sorrow and the Pity
Sorrowful Jones
Sorrows of Gin
The Sorrows of Satan
Sorry, Wrong Number
S.O.S. Titanic
Sotto, Sotto
Soul-Fire
Soul Hustler
Soul Man
Soul of the Beast
Soul Patrol
Sound of Love
Sound of Murder
The Sound of Music
Sounder
Sounds of Silence
Soup for One
Sourdough
South Bronx Heroes
South Central
South of Hell Mountain
South of Monterey
South of Pago Pago
South of Santa Fe
South of the Border
South of the Rio Grande
South Pacific
South Seas Massacre
Southern Comfort
A Southern Yankee
The Southerner
Southward Ho!
Souvenir
Soviet Spy
Soylent Green
Space Mutiny
Space: 1999—Alien Attack
Space Ninja: Sword of the Space Ark
Space Patrol
Space Rage
Space Raiders
Space Riders
Space Soldiers Conquer the Universe
Spaceballs
Spaced Invaders
Spaced Out
Spacehunter: Adventures in the Forbidden Zone
Spaceways
Spaghetti House
Spaghetti Western
Spalding Gray: Terrors of Pleasure
Spangles
The Spaniard's Curse
Spare Parts
Sparkle
Sparrows
Spartacus
Spasms
The Spawning
Special Bulletin
A Special Day
Special Delivery
Special Effects
Special Forces
Special Olympics
The Specialist
The Speckled Band
Specters
The Spectre of Edgar Allen Poe
The Speed Spook
Speed Zone
Speeding Up Time
Speedtrap
Speedway
Speedy
The Spell
The Spellbinder
Spellbound
Spetters
Sphinx
The Spider and the Fly
Spider Baby
Spider Woman
Spiderman: The Deadly Dust
Spiders
Spies
Spies Like Us
Spike of Bensonhurst
Spinout
Spiral Staircase
Spirit of St. Louis
Spirit of the Beehive
Spirit of the West
The Spirit of West Point
The Spirit of Youth
Spite Marriage
Spitfire
Spittin' Image
Splash
Splatter University
Splendor in the Grass
Split Image
Split Second
Splitz
The Spoilers
Spontaneous Combustion
The Spook Who Sat By the Door
Spookies
Spooks Run Wild
The Sporting Club
Spring Break
Spring Fever
Spring Symphony
Springhill
Springtime in the Rockies
Springtime in the Sierras
The Sprinter
Sputnik
Spy
Spy in Black
Spy of Napoleon
Spy Story
The Spy Who Came in from the Cold
The Spy Who Loved Me
Spy with a Cold Nose
S*P*Y*S
Square Dance
Square Dance Jubilee
Square Shoulders
The Squeeze
Squeeze Play
Squirm
Squizzy Taylor
S.S. Experiment Camp 2
SS Girls
S.S. Love Camp No. 27
Stacey
Stacking
Stacy's Knights
Stage Door
Stage Door Canteen
Stage Fright
Stage Struck
Stage to Mesa City
Stagecoach
Stagecoach to Denver
Stagefright
Stakeout
Stalag 17
Stalking Danger
Stamp Day for Superman
Stan Without Ollie, Vol. 1
Stan Without Ollie, Vol. 2
Stan Without Ollie, Vol. 3
Stan Without Ollie, Vol. 4
Stand Alone
Stand and Deliver
Stand By Me
Stand-In
Stand Up and Cheer
Stanley
Stanley and Iris
Stanley and Livingstone
The Star Chamber
Star Crash
Star Crystal
Star 80
A Star is Born
Star of Midnight
The Star Packer
Star Quest
Star Reporter
Star Slammer
Star Trek: The Motion Picture
Star Trek 2: The Wrath of Khan
Star Trek 3: The Search for Spock
Star Trek 4: The Voyage Home
Star Trek 5: The Final Frontier
Star Trek 6: The Undiscovered Country
Star Trek Bloopers
Star Trek Deep Space Nine: Emissary
Star Trek Generations
Star Trek: The Cage
Star Trek the Next Generation, the Final Episode: All Good Things...
Star Trek 25th Anniversary Special
Star Wars
Starchaser: The Legend of Orin
Stardust Memories
The Starfighters
Starflight One
Stark
Starman
Stars and Bars
The Stars Look Down
Starship
Start the Revolution Without Me
Starting Over
Starvengers
State Department File 649
State Fair
State of Siege
State of the Union
State of Things
Stateline Motel
State's Attorney
Static
Station
Station West
The Statue
Stay As You Are
Stay Awake
Stay Away, Joe
Stay Hungry
Stay Tuned for Murder
Staying Alive
Staying On
Staying Together
The Steagle
Steal the Sky
Stealing Heaven
Steamboat Bill, Jr.
Steaming

Steel
Steel and Lace
Steel Arena
The Steel Claw
Steel Cowboy
Steel Dawn
Steel Fisted Dragon
The Steel Helmet
Steel Magnolias
Steele Justice
Steelyard Blues
Stella
Stella Dallas
Stella Maris
Step Lively
The Stepfather
Stepfather 2: Make Room for Daddy
Stephen King's It
Steppenwolf
Stepping Out
Stepsisters
The Sterile Cuckoo
Steve Martin Live
Stewardess School
Stick
The Stick-Up
Sticky Fingers
Stigma
Stiletto
Still Not Quite Human
Still of the Night
The Stilts
The Sting
The Sting 2
Sting of the Dragon Masters
Sting of the West
Stingray
Stir Crazy
Stitches
Stocks and Blondes
A Stolen Face
Stolen Identity
Stolen Kisses
A Stolen Life
Stolen Painting
The Stone Boy
Stone Cold
Stone Cold Dead
The Stone Killer
Stones of Death
Stoogemania
The Stoogephile Trivia Movie
Stooges Shorts Festival
Stop Making Sense
Stop! or My Mom Will Shoot
Stop That Cab
Stopover Tokyo
Storm in a Teacup
Storm Over Asia
Storm Over Wyoming
Stormy Monday
Stormy Trails
Stormy Waters
Stormy Weather
Story of a Cowboy Angel
The Story of a Three Day Pass
Story of Adele H.
The Story of Louis Pasteur
The Story of O
The Story of O, Part 2
The Story of Robin Hood & His Merrie Men
The Story of Ruth
Story of the Dragon
The Story of the Late Chrysanthemum
The Story of Vernon and Irene Castle
Story of William S. Hart/Sad Clowns
Storytime Classics
Storyville
Stowaway
Straight Shooter
Straight Shootin'
Straight Talk
Straight Time
Straight to Hell
Straight Up
Strait-Jacket
Stranded
A Strange and Deadly Occurence
Strange Behavior
Strange Brew
Strange Cargo
Strange Case of Dr. Jekyll & Mr. Hyde
Strange Fruit
Strange Illusion
Strange Invaders
The Strange Love of Martha Ivers
Strange Shadows in an Empty Room
Strange Tales
Strange Tales/Ray Bradbury Theatre
The Strangeness
The Stranger
A Stranger Among Us
The Stranger and the Gunfighter
The Stranger from Venus
Stranger in Paso Bravo
Stranger in Town
A Stranger is Watching
Stranger on the Third Floor
Stranger than Paradise
The Stranger Who Looks Like Me
The Stranger Within
Stranger's Gold
Strangers in Good Company
Strangers in Paradise
Strangers in the City
Strangers Kiss
Strangers on a Train
Strangers: The Story of a Mother and Daughter
Strangers When We Meet
The Strangler
Strangler of the Swamp
Strapless
Strategic Air Command
The Stratton Story
Straw Dogs
Strawberry Blonde
The Strawberry Statement
Stray Dog
Streamers
The Street
Street Asylum
Street Girls
Street Hawk
Street Hero
Street Justice
Street Knight
Street Law
Street Music
Street of Shame
Street People
Street Scene
Street Smart
Street Soldiers
Street Trash
Street War
Street Warriors
Street Warriors, Part 2
A Streetcar Named Desire
Streetfight
Streets
Streets of Fire
Streets of Gold
The Streets of L.A.
The Streets of San Francisco
Streetwalkin'
Streetwise
Strictly G.I.
Strike
Strike Back
Strike Commando
Strike Force
Strike It Rich
Strike Up the Band
Strikeback
Striker
Stripes
Stripped to Kill
Stripped to Kill II: Live Girls
The Stripper
Stripper
Striptease
Stroke of Midnight
Stroker Ace
Stromboli
Strong Man
Strong Medicine
Stryker
Stuart Saves His Family
Stuck on You
Stuckey's Last Stand
The Stud
Student Affairs
Student Bodies
Student Confidential
The Student Nurses
Student of Prague
The Student Teachers
Studs Lonigan
A Study in Scarlet
A Study in Terror
The Stuff
Stuff Stephanie in the Incinerator
The Stunt Man
Stunt Rock
Stunts
Submission
The Substitute
Subterfuge
Suburbia
Subway
Sucker Money
Sudden Death
Sudden Impact
Sudden Terror
Suddenly
Suddenly, Last Summer
Suds
Sugar Cookies
Sugarbaby
The Sugarland Express
The Suicide Club
Suicide Cult
Suicide Patrol
Sullivan's Travels
Summer
Summer Affair
Summer and Smoke
Summer Camp Nightmare
Summer City
Summer Fantasy
Summer Heat
Summer Interlude
Summer Lovers
Summer Magic
Summer Night
Summer Night with Greek Profile, Almond Eyes & Scent of Basil
Summer of Fear
Summer of '42
The Summer of My German Soldier
Summer of Secrets
A Summer Place
Summer Rental
Summer School
Summer School Teachers
Summer Solstice
Summer Stock
A Summer Story
A Summer to Remember
Summer Vacation: 1999
Summer Wishes, Winter Dreams
Summerdog
Summer's Children
Summer's Games
Summertime
Summertree
Sunburn
Sundance
Sundance and the Kid
Sunday Daughters
A Sunday in the Country
Sunday in the Park with George
Sunday Too Far Away
Sundays & Cybele
Sundown
Sundown Fury
Sundown Kid
Sundown Riders
Sundown Saunders
The Sundowners
Sunny Side Up
Sunrise at Campobello
Sunset
Sunset Boulevard
Sunset in El Dorado
Sunset Limousine
Sunset on the Desert
Sunset Range
Sunset Serenade
Sunset Strip
Sunset Trail
The Sunshine Boys
Sunshine Run
Sunstroke
Super Brother
Super Fuzz
Super Mario Bros.
Super Ninjas
Super Seal
Superargo
Superbug Super Agent
Superchick
Superdad
Superfly
Supergirl
Supergrass
Superman: The Movie
Superman 2
Superman 3
Superman 4: The Quest for Peace
Superman & the Mole Men
Superman: The Serial, Vol. 1
The Supernaturals
Supersonic Man
Superstition
Support Your Local Sheriff
Surabaya Conspiracy
The Sure Thing
Surf Nazis Must Die
Surf 2
Surfacing
Surprise Attack
Surrender
Surrogate
Survival Game
Survival of a Dragon
Survival Quest
Survival Run
Survival Zone
The Survivalist
Survivor
Survivors
Susan Lenox: Her Fall and Rise
Susan Slept Here
Susana
Susannah of the Mounties
Suspect
Suspicion
Suspiria
Suzanne
Svengali
Swamp Fire
Swamp of the Lost Monster
Swamp Thing
The Swan
Swann in Love
The Swarm
Sweater Girls
Swedenhielms
Sweeney Todd: The Demon Barber of Fleet Street
Sweet Adeline
Sweet Beat
Sweet Bird of Youth
Sweet Charity
Sweet Country
Sweet Country Road
Sweet Creek County War
Sweet Dreams
Sweet Hearts Dance
Sweet Killing
Sweet Liberty
Sweet Lies
Sweet Lorraine
Sweet Movie
Sweet Revenge
Sweet 16
Sweet Spirits
Sweet Sweetback's Baadasssss Song
Sweet William
Sweet Young Thing
Sweetie
Sweetwater
Swept Away...
Swift Justice
Swifty
Swim Team
The Swimmer
Swimming Pool
Swimming to Cambodia
Swing
Swing High, Swing Low
Swing It, Sailor!
Swing Kids
Swing Shift
Swing Time
The Swinging Cheerleaders
Swinging Wives
Swiss Conspiracy
The Swiss Family Robinson
Swiss Miss
Switchblade Sisters
Switching Channels
The Sword and the Cross
Sword & the Dragon
The Sword & the Rose
Sword & the Sorcerer
The Sword in the Stone
Sword of Doom
The Sword of El Cid
Sword of Fury II
Sword of Lancelot
Sword of Monte Cristo
Sword of the Valiant
Swords of Death
Sybil
Sylvester
Sylvia
Sylvia and the Phantom
Sylvia Scarlett
Sympathy for the Devil
Symphony in the Mountains
Symphony of Living
T-Men
Table for Five
Table Settings
Tabu: A Story of the South Seas
Taffin
Tag: The Assassination Game
Tai-Pan
Tails You Live, Heads You're Dead
Tailspin: Behind the Korean Airline Tragedy
Tainted
Tainted Blood
Take a Hard Ride
Take Down
Take It Big
Take Me Back to Oklahoma
Take Me Out to the Ball Game
Take the Money and Run
Take This Job & Shove It

Take Two
Take Your Best Shot
Taking Care of Business
Taking My Turn
The Taking of Pelham One Two Three
The Tale of the Frog Prince
A Tale of Two Cities
Tale of Two Cities/In the Switch Tower
Talent for the Game
Tales from Avonlea, Vol. 1: The Journey Begins
Tales from the Crypt
Tales from the Crypt, Vol. 3
Tales from the Darkside
Tales from the Darkside: The Movie
Tales of Ordinary Madness
Tales of Robin Hood
Tales of Terror
Tales of the Klondike: In a Far Country
Tales of the Klondike: Race for Number One
Tales of the Klondike: The Scorn of Women
Tales of the Klondike: The Unexpected
Tales of the Unexpected
Talion
Talk of the Town
Talk Radio
Talk to Me
Talking Walls
The Tall Blond Man with One Black Shoe
Tall in the Saddle
Tall Lie
The Tall Men
Tall, Tan and Terrific
Tall Texan
The Tamarind Seed
The Taming of the Shrew
Tammy and the Bachelor
Tammy and the Doctor
Tango and Cash
Tango Bar
Tank
Tanya's Island
Tap
Tapeheads
Taps
Target
Target Eagle
Targets
Tarka the Otter
Tartuffe
Tarzan and the Green Goddess
Tarzan and the Trappers
Tarzan of the Apes
Tarzan, the Ape Man
Tarzan the Fearless
Tarzan's Revenge
Task Force
Taste of Death
A Taste of Hell
The Tattered Web
Tattoo
Tattoo Connection
Tattooed Hit Man
Tax Season
Taxi Driver
The Taxi Mystery
Taxi zum Klo
A Taxing Woman
Tchao Pantin
Tea For Three
The Teacher
Teachers
Teacher's Pet
The Teahouse of the August Moon
Tearaway
Teddy at the Throttle
Teddy at the Throttle/Speeding Along
Teen Alien
Teen Mothers
Teen Vamp
Teen Witch
Teen Wolf
Teen Wolf Too
Teenage Bad Girl
Teenage Crime Wave
Teenage Devil Dolls
Teenage Mother
Teenage Mutant Ninja Turtles: The Movie
Teenage Mutant Ninja Turtles 2: The Secret of the Ooze
Teenage Strangler
Teenage Zombies
Teenager
Telefon
The Telephone
Tell Me a Riddle
Tell Me That You Love Me
Tell Me Where It Hurts
Tell Them Willie Boy Is Here
The Temp
The Tempest
The Tempest/The Eagle
The Tempter
The Temptress
Temptress
10
Ten Brothers of Shao-lin
The Ten Commandments
Ten Days That Shook the World
Ten Little Indians
The Ten Million Dollar Getaway
Ten Nights in a Bar Room
Ten Nights in a Bar-Room
10 Rillington Place
Ten Speed
Ten to Midnight
10 Violent Women
Ten Wanted Men
Ten Who Dared
The Tenant
The Tender Age
Tender Is the Night
Tender Loving Care
Tender Mercies
The Tender Warrior
The Tender Years
Tenement
Tennessee Stallion
Tennessee's Partner
Tension at Table Rock
Tentacles
Tenth Month
10th Victim
Tequila Sunrise
Teresa Venerdi
Tereza
Terminal Choice
Terminal Entry
Terminal Exposure
Terminal Island
The Terminal Man
The Terminator
Terms of Endearment
Terraces
The Terror
Terror at London Bridge
Terror at Red Wolf Inn
Terror at Tenkiller
Terror Beach
Terror Beneath the Sea
Terror by Night/Meeting at Midnight
Terror Eyes
Terror in Beverly Hills
Terror in the Haunted House
Terror in the Swamp
Terror in the Wax Museum
Terror in Toyland
Terror of Mechagodzilla
Terror of Rome Against the Son of Hercules
Terror of the Bloodhunters
Terror of the Steppes
Terror of Tiny Town
Terror on the 40th Floor
Terror on Tour
Terror Out of the Sky
Terror Street
Terror Train
The Terror Within
The Terrorists
Terrorists
The Terrornauts
Terrorvision
The Terry Fox Story
Tess
Test of Donald Norton
A Test of Love
Test Pilot
Test Tube Babies
Test Tube Teens from the Year 2000
Testament
The Testament of Dr. Cordelier
The Testament of Orpheus
Tevye
Tex
Tex Rides with the Boy Scouts
Texas
Texas Chainsaw Massacre, Part 2
Texas Detour
Texas Gunfighter
Texas John Slaughter: Geronimo's Revenge
Texas John Slaughter: Stampede at Bitter Creek
Texas Justice
Texas Kid
Texas Lightning
Texas Pioneers
The Texas Rangers
Texas to Bataan
Texas Trouble
Texas Wildcats
Thank God It's Friday
Thank Your Lucky Stars
Tharus Son of Attila
That Certain Thing
That Championship Season
That Cold Day in the Park
That Darn Cat
That Darn Sorceress
That Gang of Mine
That Girl from Paris
That Hamilton Woman
That Long Night in '43
That Lucky Touch
That Man Is Pregnant
That Naughty Girl
That Night
That Obscure Object of Desire
That Sinking Feeling
That Summer of White Roses
That Uncertain Feeling
That Was Then...This Is Now
That'll Be the Day
That's Dancing!
That's Entertainment
That's Entertainment, Part 2
That's Entertainment, Part 3
That's Life!
That's My Baby!
That's Singing: The Best of Broadway
Theatre of Death
Thelma & Louise
Them!
There Goes the Neighborhood
There was a Crooked Man
There's a Girl in My Soup
There's No Business Like Show Business
There's No Time for Love, Charlie Brown
There's Nothing Out There
Therese
Therese & Isabelle
These Girls Won't Talk
These Three
They
They All Laughed
They Call Me Bruce?
They Call Me Mr. Tibbs!
They Call Me Trinity
They Came from Beyond Space
They Came from Within
They Came to Cordura
They Died with Their Boots On
They Drive by Night
They Got Me Covered
They Knew What They Wanted
They Live
They Live by Night
They Made Me a Criminal
They Meet Again
They Might Be Giants
They Never Come Back
They Paid with Bullets: Chicago 1929
They Saved Hitler's Brain
They Shall Have Music
They Still Call Me Bruce
They Went That-a-Way & That-a-Way
They Were Expendable
They Were So Young
They Were Ten
They Won't Believe Me
They're Playing with Fire
The Thief
Thief
The Thief of Bagdad
The Thief of Baghdad
Thief of Baghdad
The Thief of Baghdad
Thief of Hearts
The Thief Who Came to Dinner
Thieves of Fortune
The Thin Blue Line
The Thin Man
The Thin Man Goes Home
The Thing
The Thing Called Love
Things
Things Change
Things Happen at Night
Things in Their Season
The Things of Life
Things to Come
Think Big
Think Dirty
Thinkin' Big
Third Degree Burn
The Third Man
Third Man on the Mountain
Third Solution
Third Walker
Thirst
The Thirsty Dead
13 Ghosts
13 Rue Madeleine
Thirteenth Day of Christmas
The 13th Floor
13th Guest
The Thirteenth Man
Thirteenth Reunion
The 30-Foot Bride of Candy Rock
30 Is a Dangerous Age, Cynthia
The Thirty-Nine Steps
Thirty Seconds Over Tokyo
Thirty-Six Hours of Hell
The 39 Steps
This Boy's Life
This Gun for Hire
This Happy Feeling
This Is a Hijack
This Is Elvis
This Is Not a Test
This Is Spinal Tap
This Is the Army
This Island Earth
This Land is Mine
This Lightning Always Strikes Twice
This Man Must Die
This Property is Condemned
This Special Friendship
This Sporting Life
This Time I'll Make You Rich
The Thomas Crown Affair
Thomas Graal's Best Film
Thomas Graal's First Child
Thompson's Last Run
The Thorn
The Thorn Birds
Thoroughly Modern Millie
Those Calloways
Those Endearing Young Charms
Those Glory, Glory Days
Those Lips, Those Eyes
Those Magnificent Men in Their Flying Machines
Thou Shalt Not Kill...Except
Thoughts are Free
A Thousand Clowns
Thousands Cheer
Thrashin'
Threads
Threat
Three Ages
Three Amigos
Three Broadway Girls
Three Brothers
Three Bullets for a Long Gun
Three by Hitchcock
The Three Caballeros
Three Charlies and One Phoney!
Three Coins in the Fountain
Three Days in Beirut
Three Days of the Condor
Three Desperate Men
3:15—The Moment of Truth
Three for Bedroom C
Three for the Road
Three Fugitives
Three Godfathers
357 Magnum
Three in the Attic
Three in the Saddle
Three Kinds of Heat
Three Legionnaires
The Three Little Pigs
Three Little Words
The Three Lives of Thomasina
Three Men and a Baby
Three Men and a Little Lady
The Three Musketeers
3 Ninjas
Three Nuts in Search of a Bolt
Three O'Clock High
Three on a Match
Three on a Meathook
The Three Penny Opera
Three Sovereigns for Sarah
Three Stooges Comedy Capers: Vol. 1
Three Stooges Festival
The Three Stooges Meet Hercules
Three Stops to Murder
Three Strange Loves
3:10 to Yuma
Three Warriors
Three Way Weekend
Three Word Brand
The Three Worlds of Gulliver
Three's Trouble
Threshold
The Thrill Killers
The Thrill of It All!
Thrillkill
Throne of Blood
Throne of Fire
Through a Glass Darkly

Through Naked Eyes
Through the Breakers
Through the Eyes of a Killer
Throw Momma from the Train
Thumb Tripping
Thumbelina
Thunder Alley
Thunder and Lightning
Thunder & Mud
Thunder Bay
Thunder County
Thunder in God's Country
Thunder in the City
Thunder in the Desert
Thunder in the Pines
Thunder Mountain
Thunder Over Texas
Thunder River Feud
Thunder Road
Thunder Run
Thunder Warrior
Thunder Warrior 2
Thunderball
Thunderbolt & Lightfoot
Thundering Gunslingers
Thundering Ninja
Thundering Trail
Thundersquad
Thursday's Child
Thursday's Game
THX 1138
Tiara Tahiti
Ticket of Leave Man
Ticket to Heaven
Tickle Me
Tidy Endings
Tiefland
Tiffany Jones
Tiger and the Pussycat
Tiger Bay
Tiger Claws
Tiger Town
A Tiger Walks
Tiger Warsaw
Tigers in Lipstick
A Tiger's Tale
Tigershark
Tightrope
Till Death Do Us Part
Till Marriage Do Us Part
Till the Clouds Roll By
Till the Clouds Roll By/A Star Is Born
Till the End of Time
Tillie's Punctured Romance
Tim
Timber Terrors
Time After Time
Time Bandits
Time Burst: The Final Alliance
Time Fighters
Time Flies When You're Alive
A Time for Miracles
Time for Murder
Time for Revenge
The Time Guardian
Time Lock
The Time Machine
Time Machine
A Time of Destiny
Time of Tears
Time of the Apes
Time of the Gypsies
The Time of Their Lives
Time Stands Still
Time to Die
A Time to Live
A Time to Love & a Time to Die
Time Trackers
The Time Travelers
Time Troopers
Time Walker
Timebomb
Timepiece
Timerider
Times of Harvey Milk
Times Square
Timothy and the Angel
The Tin Drum
Tin Man
Tin Men
The Tin Star
Tintorera...Tiger Shark
Tiny Toon Adventures: How I Spent My Vacation
'Tis a Pity She's a Whore
Title Shot
TNT Jackson
To All a Goodnight
To All My Friends on Shore
To Be or Not to Be
To Catch a King
To Catch a Thief
To Die for
To Forget Venice
To Have & Have Not
To Hell and Back
To Joy
To Kill a Clown
To Kill a Mockingbird
To Kill a Priest
To Kill a Stranger
To Live & Die in L.A.
To Love Again
To Paris with Love
To Race the Wind
To See Such Fun
To Sir, with Love
To Sleep with Anger
To the Camp & Back
To the Devil, A Daughter
To the Last Man
To the Lighthouse
To the Shores of Hell
To the Shores of Tripoli
The Toast of New Orleans
Toast of New York
Tobruk
Toby McTeague
Toby Tyler
Today I Hang
Today We Kill, Tomorrow We Die
Today We Live
Toga Party
Together?
Togetherness
Tokyo-Ga
Tokyo Joe
Tokyo Olympiad
Tol'able David
Toll Gate
Toll of the Desert
Tom Brown's School Days
Tom, Dick, and Harry
Tom Horn
Tom Jones
Tom Mix Compilation 1
Tom Mix Compilation 2
Tom Sawyer
Tom Thumb
Tomb
Tomb of Ligeia
Tomb of the Undead
Tomb of Torture
The Tomboy
Tomboy
Tomboy & the Champ
Tombs of the Blind Dead
Tombstone Canyon
Tombstone Terror
Tommy
Tommy Boy
Tomorrow
Tomorrow at Seven
Tomorrow Never Comes
Tomorrow's Child
Tomorrow's Children
Tongs: An American Nightmare
Toni
Tonight and Every Night
Tonight for Sure
Tonio Kroger
Tonka
The Tonto Kid
Tony Rome
Too Hot to Handle
Too Late for Tears
Too Late the Hero
Too Many Crooks
Too Many Girls
Too Pretty to Be Honest
Too Scared to Scream
Too Shy to Try
Too Wise Wives
The Toolbox Murders
Tootsie
Top Gun
Top Hat
Top of the Heap
Top Secret!
Topaz
Topaze
Topkapi
Topper
Topper Returns
Topper Takes a Trip
Topsy Turvy
Tor
Tora! Tora! Tora!
Torch Song Trilogy
Torchlight
Torero
Torment
The Tormentors
Torn Allegiance
Torn Apart
Torn Curtain
Tornado
Torpedo Attack
Torpedo Run
Torrents of Spring
Torso
Torture Chamber of Baron Blood
The Torture Chamber of Dr. Sadism
Torture Garden
The Torture of Silence
Torture Train
Total Recall
Toto le Heros
The Touch
Touch & Go
Touch and Go
A Touch of Class
Touch of Evil
The Touch of Satan
Touched
Touched by Love
Tough Assignment
Tough Enough
Tough Guy
Tough Guys
Tough Guys Don't Dance
Tough Kid
Tougher than Leather
Toughlove
Tour of Duty
Tourist Trap
Tournament
Tower of Evil
Tower of London
Tower of Screaming Virgins
Tower of Terror
The Towering Inferno
A Town Called Hell
A Town Like Alice
Town that Dreaded Sundown
The Toxic Avenger
The Toxic Avenger, Part 2
Toxic Zombies
The Toy
Toy Soldiers
Track of the Moonbeast
The Tracker
The Trackers
Tracks
Trading Hearts
Trading Places
Traenen in Florenz
Traffic in Souls
Trail Drive
Trail of Terror
Trail of the Hawk
Trail of the Mounties
Trail of the Pink Panther
Trail Riders
Trail Street
Trailing Double Trouble
Trails West
The Train Killer
Train Robbers
Train to Tombstone
Trained to Kill, U.S.A.
The Traitor
Tramp & a Woman
Tramp at the Door
Tramplers
Trancers
Trancers 2: The Return of Jack Deth
Trancers 3: Deth Lives
Trancers 4: Jack of Swords
Trancers 5: Sudden Deth
Transatlantic Merry-Go-Round
Transatlantic Tunnel
Transformers: The Movie
Transmutations
Transport from Paradise
Transylvania 6-5000
Transylvania Twist
The Trap
Trap
Trap on Cougar Mountain
Trap Them & Kill Them
Trapeze
Trapped
Trapped by the Mormons
Trapped in Space
Trash
Trauma
Traveling Man
Travelling North
Traxx
Treacherous Crossing
Treasure Island
Treasure of Arne
Treasure of Fear
The Treasure of Jamaica Reef
The Treasure of Matecumbe
Treasure of Monte Cristo
Treasure of Pancho Villa
The Treasure of the Amazon
Treasure of the Four Crowns
Treasure of the Lost Desert
Treasure of the Moon Goddess
Treasure of the Sierra Madre
Treasure of the Yankee Zephyr
The Treasure Seekers
A Tree Grows in Brooklyn
The Tree of Wooden Clogs
Tremors
Trenchcoat
Trespass
Trespasser
Trespasses
The Trial
Trial and Error
The Trial of Lee Harvey Oswald
Trial of the Catonsville Nine
Tribes
Tribute
Tricheurs
Trick or Treat
Trick or Treats
Trident Force
Trifles
The Trigger Trio
Trilby
Trilogy of Terror
Trinity is Still My Name
Trio
The Trip
The Trip to Bountiful
Triple Cross
Triple Echo
Triple Trouble/Easy Street
TripleCross
Tripods: The White Mountains
Tripwire
The Triumph of Sherlock Holmes
Triumph of the Son of Hercules
Triumph of the Spirit
Triumph of the Will
Triumphs of a Man Called Horse
Trojan Women
Troll
Tromba, the Tiger Man
Tron
Troop Beverly Hills
Tropical Snow
Trouble Busters
Trouble in Mind
Trouble in Texas
The Trouble with Angels
The Trouble with Dick
The Trouble with Father
The Trouble with Girls (and How To Get Into It)
The Trouble with Harry
The Trouble with Spies
Truck Stop Women
Trucker's Woman
True Believer
True Blood
True Colors
True Confessions
The True Game of Death
True Grit
True Heart Susie
True Identity
True Love
True Romance
True Stories
True West
Trust Me
Truth About Women
Truth or Dare?
Tucker: The Man and His Dream
Tuff Turf
Tulips
Tulsa
Tumbleweed Trail
Tumbleweeds
Tunes of Glory
Tunes of Glory/Horse's Mouth
The Tunnel
Tunnelvision
Turk 182!
The Turn of the Screw
Turnaround
Turner and Hooch
The Turning Point
Turtle Diary
Turumba
Tusks
Tut & Tuttle
The Tuttles of Tahiti
Tuxedo Warrior
TV's Best Adventures of Superman
Twelve Angry Men
Twelve Chairs
Twelve O'Clock High
12 Plus 1
Twentieth Century
20,000 Leagues Under the Sea
Twenty-Four Eyes
25 Fireman's Street
Twice a Judas
Twice a Woman
Twice Dead
Twice in a Lifetime
Twice-Told Tales
Twilight on the Rio Grande
Twilight on the Trail
Twilight People
The Twilight Zone

Twilight Zone: The Movie
Twilight's Last Gleaming
Twins
Twins of Evil
Twinsanity
Twirl
Twist
Twist & Shout
Twisted Brain
Twisted Nightmare
Twisted Obsession
Twister
Twitch of the Death Nerve
Two Assassins in the Dark
Two by Forsyth
Two Daughters
Two English Girls
Two Evil Eyes
Two-Faced Woman
The Two Faces of Evil
Two Fisted Justice
Two-Fisted Justice
Two Girls and a Sailor
Two Graves to Kung-Fu
The Two Great Cavaliers
Two Gun Man
Two-Gun Troubador
200 Motels
The Two Jakes
Two Kinds of Love
Two Lost Worlds
Two Men & a Wardrobe
Two Moon Junction
Two Mules for Sister Sara
Two Nights with Cleopatra
Two of a Kind
Two Rode Together
2000 Maniacs
2001: A Space Odyssey
2010: The Year We Make Contact
2020 Texas Gladiators
2069: A Sex Odyssey
Two Tickets to Broadway
Two to Tango
Two-Way Stretch
Two Weeks to Live
Two Women
Two Wondrous Tigers
The Two Worlds of Jenny Logan
Two Wrongs Make a Right
Tycoon
Tyrant of Lydia Against the Son of Hercules
Uforia
Ugetsu
The Ugly American
The Ugly Dachshund
UHF
Ultimate Desires
The Ultimate Imposter
The Ultimate Thrill
The Ultimate Warrior
Ultra Flash
Ulysses
Ulzana's Raid
Umberto D
Umbrellas of Cherbourg
Un Chien Andalou
Un Singe en Hiver
The Unapproachable
The Unbearable Lightness of Being
The Unbeaten 28
The Unbreakable Alibi
The Uncanny
Uncensored
The Unchastened Woman
Uncle Buck
Uncle Tom's Cabin
Uncommon Valor
The Undefeated
Under California Stars
Under Capricorn
Under Fire
Under Milk Wood
Under Montana Skies
Under Siege
Under the Biltmore Clock
Under the Boardwalk
Under the Cherry Moon
Under the Earth
Under the Rainbow
Under the Red Robe
Under the Roofs of Paris
Under the Volcano
Under Western Stars
The Underachievers
The Underdog
Undergrads
Underground Aces
Underground Rustlers
Underground U.S.A.
Understudy: The Graveyard Shift 2
Underwater!
Underworld, U.S.A.
Une Jeunesse
The Unearthly
Uneasy Terms
Unfaithfully Yours
Unfinished Business
An Unfinished Piece for a Player Piano
The Unforgiven
Unforgiven
The Unholy
Unholy Four
Unholy Wife
Unicorn
Unidentified Flying Oddball
The Uninvited
Union City
Union Station
The Unkissed Bride
Unknown Powers
Unknown World
An Unmarried Woman
Unmasked Part 25
Unmasking the Idol
The Unnamable
Unnatural Causes
An Unremarkable Life
The Unseen
Unsettled Land
The Unsinkable Molly Brown
The Unstoppable Man
Unsuitable Job for a Woman
The Untamable
Untamed Heart
Until September
Until The End of The World
Until They Get Me
The Untouchables
Up from the Depths
Up in Arms
Up the Academy
Up the Creek
Up the Sandbox
Up Your Alley
Uphill All the Way
Upper Crust
The Uprising
Uptown New York
Uptown Saturday Night
The Uranium Conspiracy
Urban Cowboy
Urban Warriors
Urge to Kill
Used Cars
Users
Utah
Utah Trail
Utilities
Utopia
Utu
The Vagabond
Vagabond
Vagabond Lover
Valentino Returns
Valley Girl
Valley of Fire
The Valley of Gwangi
Valley of Terror
Valley of the Eagles
Valley of the Lawless
Valley of the Sun
Valley of Wanted Men
Valmont
The Vals
Vamp
Vamping
Vampire at Midnight
The Vampire Bat
The Vampire Happening
The Vampire Hookers
The Vampire Lovers
The Vampire People
Vampire's Kiss
Vampyr
Vampyres
The Van
Van Nuys Blvd.
Vanina Vanini
Vanishing Act
Vanishing American
Vanishing Legion
Vanishing Point
Vanishing Prairie
The Vanishing Westerner
Vanishing Wilderness
Varan the Unbelievable
Varieties on Parade
Variety
Variety Lights
Vasectomy: A Delicate Matter
Vatican Conspiracy
Vault of Horror
Vegas
The Vegas Strip Wars
Velnio Nuotaka
Velvet Touch
The Velvet Vampire
Vendetta
Vendetta for the Saint
Vengeance
Vengeance Is Mine
Vengeance of the Snowmaid
Vengeance of the Zombies
Vengeance Valley
Venom
Venus Against the Son of Hercules
Venus in Furs
Venus the Ninja
Vera Cruz
The Verdict
Verne Miller
The Vernonia Incident
Vertigo
Very Close Quarters
A Very Curious Girl
The Very Edge
A Very Private Affair
V.I. Warshawski
Vibes
Vice Academy
Vice Academy 2
Vice Academy 3
Vice Squad
Vice Versa
The Vicious Circle
Victim
Victim of Love
Victor/Victoria
Victoria Regina
Victory
The Victory
Video Americana
Video Baby
The Video Dead
Video Murders
Video Violence
Video Violence Part 2...The Exploitation!
Videodrome
Vietnam: Chronicle of a War
Vietnam, Texas
Vietnam War Story 2
Vietnam War Story 3
A View to a Kill
Vigil
Vigilante
The Vigilantes are Coming
Vigilantes of Boom Town
Viking Massacre
The Vikings
Villa Rides
Village of the Damned
Village of the Giants
The Villain Still Pursued Her
Vincent & Theo
Vincent, Francois, Paul and the Others
The Vindicator
The Vineyard
Violated
Violent Breed
Violent Ones
Violent Professionals
Violent Women
The Violent Years
Violets Are Blue
Virgin Among the Living Dead
The Virgin of Nuremberg
The Virgin Queen
Virgin Queen of St. Francis High
Virgin Sacrifice
The Virgin Soldiers
The Virgin Spring
The Virgin Witch
The Virginia Hill Story
The Virginian
Viridiana
Virtue's Revolt
Virtuosity
Virus
The Vision
Vision Quest
Visions of Evil
Visitants
Visiting Hours
Visitor from the Grave
The Visitors
Vital Signs
Viva Knievel
Viva Las Vegas
Viva Zapata!
Vivacious Lady
Vogues of 1938
Voice of Hollywood
Volpone
Volunteers
Von Ryan's Express
Voulez-Vous Danser Avec Moi?
A Vow to Kill
Voyage en Balloon
The Voyage of Tanai
Voyage of the Damned
Voyage of the Rock Aliens
A Voyage' Round My Father
Voyage-Suprise
Voyage to Italy
Voyage to the Bottom of the Sea
Vulcan God of Fire
Vulture
Vultures
W
Wackiest Ship in the Army
Wackiest Wagon Train in the West
Wacko
The Wacky World of Wills & Burke
Wages of Fear
Wagner: The Complete Epic
Wagner: The Movie
Wagon Master
Wagon Trail
Wagon Wheels
Waikiki
Wait Till Your Mother Gets Home
Wait Until Dark
Waiting for the Moon
Waitress
Wake Island
Wake of the Red Witch
Walk, Don't Run
Walk in the Spring Rain
A Walk in the Sun
Walk into Hell
Walk Like a Man
Walk on the Wild Side
Walk Softly, Stranger
Walker
Walking Back
Walking Tall
Walking Tall: Part 2
Walking Tall: The Final Chapter
Walking the Edge
Walking Through the Fire
The Wall
Wall Street
Wall Street Cowboy
The Walloping Kid
Walls of Glass
Walpurgis Night
The Waltons: The Christmas Carol
Waltz Across Texas
Waltz King
Waltz of the Toreadors
Wanda Nevada
Wanderers
Wandering Jew
The Wannsee Conference
Wanted: Babysitter
Wanted: Dead or Alive
Wanted Dead or Alive
War & Love
War and Peace
War & Remembrance, Part 1
War & Remembrance, Part 2
War & Remembrance, Part 3
War & Remembrance, Part 4
War & Remembrance, Part 5
War & Remembrance, Part 6
War & Remembrance, Part 7
War & Remembrance: The Final Chapter, Part 8
War & Remembrance: The Final Chapter, Part 9
War & Remembrance: The Final Chapter, Part 10
War & Remembrance: The Final Chapter, Part 11
War & Remembrance: The Final Chapter, Part 12
War Between the Tates
War Brides
War in Space
War in the Sky
The War Lord
War Lover
War of the Robots
The War of the Roses
War of the Wizards
The War of the Worlds
War Party
War Victims
The War Wagon
Warbirds
Warbus
Ward Six
Wardogs
WarGames
Warkill
Warlock
Warlock Moon
Warlords
Warlords from Hell
Warlords of the 21st Century
Warm Nights on a Slow-Moving Train
Warm Summer Rain
The Warning

Warning Shadows
Warning Sign
The Warrior & the Sorceress
Warrior of the Lost World
Warrior Within
The Warriors
Warriors of the Apocalypse
Warriors of the Wasteland
The Wash
Washington Affair
Watch Me When I Kill
Watch on the Rhine
Watch the Birdie
Watched
The Watcher in the Woods
Watchers
Watchers 2
Water
Water Babies
Water Rustlers
Waterfront
Waterloo Bridge
Watermelon Man
Watership Down
Wavelength
Waxwork
Waxworks
Way Back Home
Way Down East
Way He Was
Way of the Black Dragon
Way of the West
Way Out West
The Way We Were
Wayne Murder Case
Wayne's World 2
W.C. Fields Comedy Bag
W.C. Fields: Flask of Fields
We All Loved Each Other So Much
We are the Children
We Dive at Dawn
We of the Never Never
We the Living
We Think the World of You
We Will Not Enter the Forest
Weapons of Death
Weather in the Streets
Web of Deceit
Web of Deception
A Wedding
Wedding Band
Wedding in Blood
Wedding in White
The Wedding March
The Wedding Party
Wedding Rehearsal
Wee Willie Winkie
Weeds
Weekend at Bernie's
Weekend of Shadows
Weekend Pass
Weekend Warriors
Weekend with the Babysitter
Weird Science
The Weirdo
Welcome Back Mr. Fox
Welcome Home
Welcome Home, Roxy Carmichael
Welcome to Blood City
Welcome to 18
Welcome to L.A.
Welcome to Spring Break
The Well
Well-Digger's Daughter
We're in the Legion Now
We're in the Navy Now
We're No Angels
Werewolf of Washington
Werewolves on Wheels
West-Bound Limited
West of Nevada
West of Pinto Basin
West of the Divide
West of the Law
West Side Story
Western Double Feature 1
Western Double Feature 1: Wild Bill & Sunset Carson
Western Double Feature 2
Western Double Feature 2: Wayne & Hale
Western Double Feature 3
Western Double Feature 3: Rogers & Allen
Western Double Feature 4
Western Double Feature 4: Rogers & Evans
Western Double Feature 5
Western Double Feature 5: Rogers & Autry
Western Double Feature 6: Rogers & Trigger
Western Double Feature 7: Wild Bill & Crabbe
Western Double Feature 8: Hale & Carradine
Western Double Feature 9: LaRue & Beery
Western Double Feature 10: Roy, Dale, & Trigger
Western Double Feature 11
Western Double Feature 12
Western Double Feature 13
Western Double Feature 14
Western Double Feature 15
Western Double Feature 16
Western Double Feature 17
Western Double Feature 18
Western Double Feature 19
Western Double Feature 21
Western Double Feature 22
Western Double Feature 24
Western Frontier
Western Justice
Western Pacific Agent
Western Trails
Western Union
The Westerner
Westfront 1918
Westward Ho, the Wagons!
Westworld
Wet Gold
Wetherby
Whale for the Killing
Whale of a Tale
The Whales of August
What a Way to Die
What About Bob?
What Comes Around
What Do You Say to a Naked Lady?
What Ever Happened to Baby Jane?
What Have I Done to Deserve This?
What Price Glory?
What Price Hollywood?
What the Peeper Saw
What Waits Below
Whatever Happened to Aunt Alice?
Whatever Happened to Susan Jane?
What's Eating Gilbert Grape
What's New Pussycat?
What's Up, Doc?
What's Up Front
What's Up, Tiger Lily?
Wheels of Fire
Wheels of Terror
When a Stranger Calls
When Angels Fly
When Comedy was King
When Dinosaurs Ruled the Earth
When Every Day was the Fourth of July
When Harry Met Sally...
When Hell Was in Session
When Knights were Bold
When Lightning Strikes
When Nature Calls
When Taekwondo Strikes
When the Clouds Roll By
When the Legends Die
When the Line Goes Through
When the North Wind Blows
When the Screaming Stops
When the West Was Young
When the Whales Came
When the Wind Blows
When Thief Meets Thief
When Time Ran Out
When Wolves Cry
When Women Had Tails
When Women Lost Their Tails
When Worlds Collide
When's Your Birthday?
Where Are the Children?
Where Eagles Dare
Where Have All the People Gone?
Where the Boys Are
Where the Boys Are '84
Where the Buffalo Roam
Where the Green Ants Dream
Where the Hot Wind Blows
Where the North Begins
Where the Red Fern Grows
Where the River Runs Black
Where the Sky Begins
Where Time Began
Where Trails End
Where's Piccone
Where's Poppa?
Where's Willie?
Which Way Home
Which Way Is Up?
Which Way to the Front?
While I Live
While the City Sleeps
Whirlwind Horseman
Whiskey Galore
Whiskey Mountain
A Whisper to a Scream
Whispering City
Whispering Shadow
Whispers in the Dark
The Whistle Blower
Whistle Down the Wind
Whistle Stop
Whistlin' Dan
Whistling Bullets
Whistling in Dixie
White Apache
The White Buffalo
White Cannibal Queen
White Christmas
White Comanche
The White Dawn
White Fang and the Hunter
White Fire
White Ghost
White Gold
White Gorilla
White Heat
White Hot
White Hunter, Black Heart
White Huntress
The White Legion
White Lightning
White Line Fever
White Mama
White Mane
White Mischief
White Nights
White of the Eye
The White Orchid
White Phantom: Enemy of Darkness
White Pongo
The White Rose
White Sands
The White Sin
The White Sister
White Slave
The White Tower
White Water Summer
The White Zombie
WhiteForce
Whitewater Sam
Who Am I This Time?
Who Done It?
Who Framed Roger Rabbit
Who Has Seen the Wind?
Who Is the Black Dahlia?
Who Killed Baby Azaria?
Who Killed Doc Robbin?
Who Killed Mary What's 'Er Name?
Who Slew Auntie Roo?
Whodunit
Who'll Save Our Children?
Who'll Stop the Rain?
Wholly Moses!
Whoopee!
The Whoopee Boys
Whoops Apocalypse
Who's Afraid of Virginia Woolf?
Who's Harry Crumb?
Who's Minding the Mint?
Who's That Girl?
Who's That Knocking at My Door?
Whose Life Is It Anyway?
Why Change Your Wife?
Why Shoot the Teacher
The Wicked Lady
Wicked Stepmother
The Wicker Man
The Widow
Widow Couderc
Widow's Nest
Wifemistress
The Wild Aces
The Wild and the Free
Wild & Wooly
Wild at Heart
The Wild Beasts
The Wild Bunch
The Wild Country
The Wild Duck
Wild Engine/Mistaken Orders
Wild Frontier
Wild Geese
Wild Geese 2
Wild Guitar
Wild Gypsies
Wild Hearts Can't Be Broken
Wild Horse
Wild Horse Canyon
Wild Horse Hank
Wild Horse Phantom
Wild Horse Rodeo
Wild Horses
Wild in the Country
Wild in the Streets
The Wild Life
Wild Man
Wild Mustang
The Wild One
Wild Ones on Wheels
Wild Orchid
Wild Orchids
The Wild Pair
Wild Party
Wild Pony
Wild Rapture
Wild Rebels
The Wild Ride
Wild Riders
Wild Rovers
Wild Strawberries
Wild Style
Wild Thing
Wild Times
Wild West
Wild Wheels
Wild, Wild West Revisited
Wild, Wild World of Jayne Mansfield
Wild Women
Wild Women of Wongo
The Wild World of Batwoman
Wild Zone
Wildcats
Wildest Dreams
The Wildest Office Party
Wildfire
Wilding
Wildrose
Will Penny
Willa
Willard
Willow
Willy Wonka & the Chocolate Factory
Wilma
Wimps
Win, Place, or Steal
Winchester '73
The Wind
The Wind and the Lion
The Wind That Walks
Windom's Way
The Window
The Winds of Jarrah
The Winds of Kitty Hawk
The Winds of War
Windwalker
Windy City
Wings
Wings of Danger
Wings of Desire
Wings of Eagles
Wings of Fame
Winner Takes All
Winners Take All
Winning
Winning of the West
The Winslow Boy
Winter Flight
Winter Kills
The Winter Light
The Winter of Our Dreams
Winter People
Winterset
Wired
Wired to Kill
Wisdom
Wise Blood
Wise Guys
Wish You Were Here
The Wishing Ring
The Wishmaker
Witch Who Came from the Sea
Witchboard
Witchcraft
Witchcraft 2: The Temptress
Witchcraft Through the Ages
Witchery
The Witches
Witches' Brew
Witches' Mountain
The Witches of Eastwick
Witchfire
The Witching
Witching Time
The Witchmaker
The Witch's Mirror
WitchTrap
With Kit Carson Over the Great Divide
With Six You Get Eggroll
Withnail and I
Without a Clue
Without a Trace
Without Honors
Without Love
Without Reservations
Witness
Witness for the Prosecution
Wives Under Suspicion
The Wiz
The Wizard
The Wizard of Gore
The Wizard of Loneliness
The Wizard of Oz

Wizards
Wizards of the Lost Kingdom
Wizards of the Lost Kingdom 2
Wolf
The Wolf at the Door
Wolf Call
Wolf Dog
Wolf Lake
The Wolf Man
Wolfen
Wolfen Ninja
Wolfheart's Revenge
The Wolfman
A Woman Called Golda
Woman Condemned
Woman Hunt
The Woman Hunter
Woman in Brown
A Woman in Flames
Woman in Grey
The Woman in Red
Woman in the Dunes
Woman in the Moon
Woman in the Shadows
The Woman Inside
The Woman Next Door
A Woman Obsessed
A Woman of Distinction
Woman of Paris/Sunnyside
A Woman of Rome
A Woman of Substance, Episode 1: Nest of Vipers
A Woman of Substance, Episode 2: The Secret is Revealed
A Woman of Substance, Episode 3: Fighting for the Dream
The Woman of the Town
Woman of the Year
A Woman Rebels
Woman Times Seven
A Woman Under the Influence
The Woman Who Came Back
The Woman Who Willed a Miracle
A Woman Without Love
A Woman's Face
A Woman's Secret
Wombling Free
The Women
Women in Cell Block 7
Women in Fury
Women in Love
The Women of Brewster Place
Women of the Prehistoric Planet
Women of Valor
Women on the Verge of a Nervous Breakdown
Women Unchained
Women's Club
Women's Prison Massacre
Wonder Man
The Wonderful World of the Brothers Grimm
Wonderland Cove
The Wonders of Aladdin
Wonderwall: The Movie
Wonsan Operation
Woodchipper Massacre
The Wooden Gun
Wooden Horse
Woodstock
The Word
Words and Music
Work/Police
Workin' for Peanuts
Working Girl
Working Girls
Working Winnie/Oh So Simple
The World According to Garp
A World Apart
The World Gone Mad
World Gone Wild
The World is Full of Married Men
The World of Apu
The World of Henry Orient
The World of Suzie Wong
World War III
The World's Greatest Athlete
The Worm Eaters
The Worst of Faces of Death
The Worst of Hollywood: Vol. 1
The Worst of Hollywood: Vol. 2
The Worst of Hollywood: Vol. 3
The Worst Witch
Worth Winning
The Would-Be Gentleman
WR: Mysteries of the Organism
The Wraith
The Wrestler
Wrestling Racket Girls
Wrestling Women vs. the Aztec Ape
Wrestling Women vs. the Aztec Mummy
Writer's Block
Written on the Wind
The Wrong Arm of the Law
The Wrong Box
The Wrong Guys
Wrong is Right
The Wrong Man
The Wrong Move
The Wrong Road
Wuthering Heights
X from Outer Space
X Marks the Spot
X: The Man with X-Ray Eyes
X, Y & Zee
Xanadu
Xtro
The Yakuza
Yanco
A Yank in Australia
Yank in Libya
A Yank in the R.A.F.
Yankee Clipper
Yankee Doodle Dandy
Yankee Doodle in Berlin
The Year My Voice Broke
The Year of Living Dangerously
Year of the Dragon
Year of the Quiet Sun
The Yearling
Yellow Cargo
Yellow Hair & the Fortress of Gold
The Yellow Rose of Texas
Yellow Submarine
Yellowbeard
Yellowstone
Yentl
Yes, Giorgio
Yes, Sir, Mr. Bones
The Yesterday Machine
Yesterday's Hero
Yidl Mitn Fidl
Yin & Yang of Mr. Go
Yodelin' Kid From Pine Ridge
Yog, Monster from Space
Yojimbo
Yol
Yolanda and the Thief
Yongkari Monster of the Deep
Yor, the Hunter from the Future
You Are Not Alone
You Are Not I
You Can't Cheat an Honest Man
You Can't Fool Your Wife
You Can't Hurry Love
You Can't Take It with You
You Light Up My Life
You Only Live Once
You Only Live Twice
You Talkin' to Me?
You Were Never Lovelier
You'll Find Out
You'll Never Get Rich
Young & Free
Young and Innocent
Young & Willing
Young Aphrodites
Young Bill Hickok
Young Blood
The Young Bruce Lee
Young Buffalo Bill
Young Caruso
Young Catherine
Young Charlie Chaplin
Young Doctors in Love
Young Eagles
Young Einstein
Young Frankenstein
Young Guns
Young Lady Chatterly 2
The Young Lions
Young Love, First Love
Young Love—Lemon Popsicle 7
Young Man with a Horn
Young Mr. Lincoln
The Young Nurses
Young Nurses in Love
The Young Ones
The Young Philadelphians
Young Sherlock Holmes
The Young Teacher
Young Tiger
Young Tom Edison
Young Warlord
Young Warriors
Young Winston
Youngblood
Your Place or Mine
Your Show of Shows
Your Ticket Is No Longer Valid
You're a Big Boy Now
You're a Good Man, Charlie Brown
You're in Love, Charlie Brown
You're Jinxed, Friend, You've Met Sacramento
Yours, Mine & Ours
You've Got to Have Heart
Yukon Flight
The Yum-Yum Girls
Yuma
Z
Zabriskie Point
Zachariah
Zalmen or the Madness of God
The Zany Adventures of Robin Hood
Zapped!
Zapped Again
Zardoz
Zebra Force
A Zed & Two Noughts
Zelig
Zelly & Me
Zentropa
Zeppelin
Zero
Zero Boys
Zero for Conduct
Zero Pilot
Zero to Sixty
Zertigo Diamond Caper
Ziegfeld Follies
Ziegfeld Girl
Zis Boom Bah
The Zodiac Killer
Zoltan...Hound of Dracula
Zombie
Zombie High
Zombie Island Massacre
Zombie Nightmare
Zombies of Moratau
Zombies of the Stratosphere
Zombiethon
Zone of the Dead
Zone Troopers
The Zoo Gang
Zorba the Greek
Zorro Rides Again
Zorro, the Gay Blade
Zotz!
Zulu
Zulu Dawn
Zvenigora

8mm

A Nous la Liberte
ABC Stage 67: Truman Capote's A Christmas Memory
The Abe Lincoln of Ninth Avenue
Above the Law
The Accidental Tourist
The Accused
Ace Ventura: Pet Detective
Action for Slander
The Adorable Cheat
Adventures in Babysitting
The Adventures of Baron Munchausen
Against All Odds
The Age of Innocence
Airplane!
All Dogs Go to Heaven
An American in Paris
American Pluck
Anatomy of a Seduction
And Baby Makes Six
And Justice for All
Angel in a Taxi
Animal Farm
Annie
Another 48 Hrs.
Another You
The Appointment
Arthur
Arthur 2: On the Rocks
Avalon
Awakenings
Babar: The Movie
Baby Face Harry Langdon
The Bad News Bears
Barfly
Batman
Battling Orioles
Beaches
Beetlejuice
Ben Turpin: An Eye for an Eye
The Best of Times
Beverly Hills Cop
Beverly Hills Cop 2
Big Business
The Big Chill
Big Top Pee Wee
Bill and Coo
Bill & Ted's Excellent Adventure
Bird of Paradise
Black Rain
Blade Runner
Blood and Steel
Blood Red
The Blue Angel
Blue Blazes Rawden
Blue Steel
The Bonfire of the Vanities
Book of Love
Born on the Fourth of July
Boyz N the Hood
Bram Stoker's Dracula
Braveheart
Breaker Morant
Breakfast at Tiffany's
Brigadoon
The Broadway Drifter
Bugsy
Cabiria
Caddyshack 2
The Caine Mutiny
Calendar Girl
Candyman
Carnal Knowledge
Casablanca
The Case of the Mukkinese Battle Horn
Casualties of War
The Cat o' Nine Tails
The Champion/His New Job
Chances Are
Charlie Chaplin...Our Hero!
Charlie Chaplin's Keystone Comedies 4
Child of the Prairie
Children of a Lesser God
Chinatown
A Chorus Line
Christine
Cinema Paradiso
Citizen Kane
City of Hope
City Slickers
The Claw
Clean and Sober
The Client
Cliffhanger
Cocktail
Colossus and the Amazon Queen
Coming to America
Cookie
Cops and Robbersons
Cops/One Week
The Cotton Club
Cotton Queen
Crimson Romance
Crocodile Dundee
Crossing Delancey
A Cry in the Dark
Curly Sue
Dancing Man
Dangerous Hours
Dangerous Liaisons
Dangerous Passage
The Day Will Dawn
Dead Bang
Dead Calm
Dead Poets Society
The Dead Pool
The Death Kiss
Defending Your Life
Delirious
Demolition Man
Dennis the Menace
Desperado
Detour to Danger
Devil on Horseback
Diabolique
Dinner at Eight
Dirt Bike Kid
Dirty Harry
The Disciple
Doc Hollywood
Dr. Christian Meets the Women
Dr. Strangelove, or: How I Learned to Stop Worrying and Love the Bomb
Dog Eat Dog
Dogfight
Don't Tell Mom the Babysitter's Dead
The Doors
Double Impact
Driving Miss Daisy
Easy Rider
Ecstasy
Eddie and the Cruisers
Eddie Murphy: Raw
Educating Rita
El Mariachi
Eleni
The Emerald Forest
Emmanuelle, the Joys of a Woman
Empire of the Sun
Everybody's All American
The Evil That Men Do
The Experts
Extra Girl
Extremities

The Fabulous Baker Boys
Family Business
Fangs of Fate
Far North
Fast Getaway
Fat Man and Little Boy
Fatal Attraction
The Fatal Hour
Fernandel the Dressmaker
Ferris Bueller's Day Off
A Few Good Men
A Few Moments with Buster Keaton and Laurel and Hardy
The Fighting Rookie
The Fighting Stallion
The Fighting Westerner
Final Extra
First Knight
The First Movie Cowboy
The First Power
The Fisher King
Five Easy Pieces
Flashdance
Flatliners
Flesh and Blood
The Floorwalker/By the Sea
The Flustered Comedy of Leon Errol
The Fog
Footloose
Forever Young
Foul Play
Frantic
Free Willy
The Freshman
From Here to Eternity
Full Metal Jacket
Funny About Love
Funny Face
The Garden of Eden
Gate of Hell
The General
The Gentleman from California
George Balanchine's The Nutcracker
Geronimo: An American Legend
Ghost
Ghostbusters
Ghostbusters 2
Gigi
A Girl's Folly
Glory
The Godfather
The Godfather, Part 2
The Godfather, Part 3
Going to Congress/Don't Park There
The Gold Rush
The Golden Child
The Golden Seal
Good Morning, Vietnam
Goodfellas
The Gospel According to St. Matthew
The Graduate
Grand Illusion
The Great Santini
The Great Train Robbery: Cinema Begins
Gremlins
Gremlins 2: The New Batch
Grumpy Old Men
Guarding Tess
Guilty by Suspicion
Gun Cargo
Gung Ho
Half Moon Street
Hamlet
Hard Promises
Hard to Kill
Harley Davidson and the Marlboro Man
Harold and Maude
Hawks
Heart of Humanity
Heartbreak Ridge
Heartburn
Hearts of the World
Her Alibi
Hero
High Season
High Society
High Tide
Highlander 2: The Quickening
Hiroshima, Mon Amour
His First Command
His Picture in the Papers
The Hitman
The Hobbit
Hollywood Come Home
Hollywood without Makeup
Homicide
Hook
Hope and Glory
Hot Foot/A Happy Married Couple
Hotel Colonial
Howard's End
Hudson Hawk
Human Hearts
The Hunt for Red October
I Conquer the Sea
I Stand Condemned
Identity Unknown
If Looks Could Kill
I'll Do Anything
In Country
In the Line of Fire
The Indian in the Cupboard
Indiana Jones and the Last Crusade
Indiana Jones and the Temple of Doom
Indochine
Infamous Crimes
The Inner Circle
Innerspace
Internal Affairs
Irish Cinderella
The Island
Isle of Forgotten Sins
It Could Happen to You
Ivan the Terrible, Part 1
Ivan the Terrible, Part 2
Jack Frost
The Jagged Edge
Jason and the Argonauts
Java Head
Jaws of Justice
The Jazz Singer
Jesus of Nazareth
Joe Versus the Volcano
Johnny Mnemonic
The Juror
The Karate Kid
The Karate Kid: Part 2
The Karate Kid: Part 3
Kenny Rogers as the Gambler, Part 2: The Adventure Continues
King Kong
Kiss and Be Killed
Kiss of the Spider Woman
The Krays
La Bamba
La Bete Humaine
Labyrinth
Lady Windermere's Fan
Last Action Hero
The Last Emperor
Last Flight Out: A True Story
The Last Picture Show
Last Year at Marienbad
A League of Their Own
Lean on Me
Legends of the Fall
Let It Ride
Lethal Weapon
Lethal Weapon 2
Lethal Weapon 3
Let's Get Tough
Let's Go!
Lightnin' Carson Rides Again
Lily of Killarney
The Little Mermaid
Little Sweetheart
Little Women
Little World of Don Camillo
London Melody
Look Who's Talking Now
Look Who's Talking, Too
Lord of the Flies
Lorna Doone
Los Olvidados
The Lost Boys
Lost in Yonkers
Lure of the Sila
M
Mabel & Fatty
Mad Max: Beyond Thunderdome
Major League
Malcolm X
The Mambo Kings
The Man in the Raincoat
The Man Who Lived Again
Manhattan Murder Mystery
A Married Woman
Mary Shelley's Frankenstein
Meatballs 2
Meet Me in St. Louis
Melody for Three
Memphis Belle
Men Don't Leave
Men of Ireland
Men of Respect
Midnight Express
Midnight Faces
Midnight Girl
The Mission
Mr. Hulot's Holiday
Mo' Money
The Moderns
Mon Oncle
Money Train
Monterey Pop
Monty Python and the Holy Grail
Mortal Thoughts
Moscow on the Hudson
Moving
Murder at Midnight
Mutiny on the Bounty
My Girl
My Girl 2
My Life
Mystery of the Leaping Fish/ Chess Fever
Nais
The Naked Gun: From the Files of Police Squad
Naked Gun 2 1/2: The Smell of Fear
National Lampoon's Christmas Vacation
National Lampoon's European Vacation
'Neath Canadian Skies
The Net
Never Too Late to Mend
The NeverEnding Story
NeverEnding Story 2: The Next Chapter
Next of Kin
Night Time in Nevada
Ninotchka
Nomads of the North
Not Without My Daughter
Nothing But Trouble
Nowhere to Run
No. 17
The Nutcracker Prince
Nuts
An Officer and a Gentleman
Old Gringo
On the Night Stage
Open City
Orphans of the North
Orpheus
Oscar's Greatest Moments: 1971-1991
Other People's Money
Our Gang
Out for Justice
Pace That Kills
Paisan
Pale Rider
The Pelican Brief
Pepe Le Moko
Persona
Pet Sematary
The Phantom Broadcast
The Phantom Flyer
Philadelphia
Pink Cadillac
Planes, Trains & Automobiles
Play It Again, Sam
Poetic Justice
Police Academy
Popcorn
The Port of Missing Girls
Postcards from the Edge
Prancer
The Presidio
Presumed Innocent
Pretty in Pink
The Prince of Tides
The Princess Bride
Prisoner in the Middle
The Producers
Pump Up the Volume
Queen Kelly
Queen of the Jungle
The Quick and the Dead
Quick Change
Quigley Down Under
Raging Bull
Raiders of the Lost Ark
Rain Man
Reaching for the Moon
The Red Balloon
The Remains of the Day
Remedy for Riches
Return of Draw Egan
The Return of Grey Wolf
The Return of Our Gang
Revenge
Reversal of Fortune
Ricochet
Risky Business
A River Runs Through It
River's Edge
Road House
The Roaring Road
Roaring Speedboats
Robot Pilot
Rocky
Rocky 5
Roman Holiday
The Rookie
Rounding Up the Law
Rover Dangerfield
Roxanne
Rudolph the Red-Nosed Reindeer
Rudy
The Rules of the Game
Running on Empty
The Russia House
Sabotage
Salome/Queen Elizabeth
Saving Grace
Screamers
Scrooged
The Secret of NIMH
See No Evil, Hear No Evil
Sense and Sensibility
Seven Brides for Seven Brothers
The Seventh Seal
sex, lies and videotape
Shattered
She Goes to War
The Sheep Has Five Legs
She's Having a Baby
She's Out of Control
Shifting Sands
Shirley Valentine
Shop Angel
Showdown in Little Tokyo
Sibling Rivalry
Sidekicks
Silent Movies...Just For the Fun of It!
Silent Rage
Single White Female
Sky Bandits
Sleepless in Seattle
Sniper
So I Married an Axe Murderer
Soapdish
Sommersby
Soul of the Beast
The Southerner
The Speckled Band
Spitfire
Splash
Split Decisions
Stakeout
Stan Without Ollie, Vol. 4
Stand and Deliver
Stand By Me
Star Trek 2: The Wrath of Khan
Star Trek 3: The Search for Spock
Star Trek 4: The Voyage Home
Star Trek 5: The Final Frontier
Steel Magnolias
Stone Cold
Stormy Monday
The Stranger
Street Scene
Striking Distance
Subspecies
Sudden Impact
Summer Rental
The Sure Thing
Suspect
Tale of Two Cities/In the Switch Tower
The Tall Blond Man with One Black Shoe
Tango and Cash
Taxi Driver
Teen Wolf
Teenage Mutant Ninja Turtles: The Movie
Tequila Sunrise
Terminator 2: Judgment Day
Test of Donald Norton
Thelma & Louise
They Meet Again
They Saved Hitler's Brain
The Third Man
The 39 Steps
This Is Spinal Tap
Three Charlies and One Phoney!
Three Men and a Baby
The Three Musketeers
Threesome
The Time Guardian
A Time of Destiny
Tiny Toon Adventures: How I Spent My Vacation
To Die For
Top Gun
Top Hat
Total Recall
Tower of Screaming Virgins
The Toy
Toy Soldiers
Trading Places
Trapped by the Mormons
The Trip to Bountiful
Triple Trouble/Easy Street
Troop Beverly Hills
Trouble in Mind
Tucker: The Man and His Dream
Ugetsu
Umberto D
Uncommon Valor

Under Siege
Under the Biltmore Clock
The Underdog
Unforgiven
Unsettled Land
The Untouchables
Used Cars
Valley of Wanted Men
Waiting for the Light
A Walk in the Sun
The Walloping Kid
Warning Shadows
Watership Down
The Way We Were
W.C. Fields: Flask of Fields
Welcome Home, Roxy Carmichael
We're in the Legion Now
The Whales of August
When Harry Met Sally...
White Christmas
White Hunter, Black Heart
White Mischief
The White Sin
Who's That Girl?
Wild Strawberries
Willow
Wind
Winter People
The Witches
The Witches of Eastwick
With Kit Carson Over the Great Divide
Witness
The Wizard of Oz
Wolf
Wolf Call
Wolfheart's Revenge
Working Winnie/Oh So Simple
A Yank in Australia
Year of the Gun
Yellowstone
Yojimbo
Young Sherlock Holmes
Zapped Again
Zebrahead
Zelig

Laserdisc

A la Mode
A Nos Amours
Abbott and Costello Meet Captain Kidd
Abbott and Costello Meet Frankenstein
Abbott and Costello Meet the Killer, Boris Karloff
The Abominable Dr. Phibes
About Last Night...
Above the Law
Above the Rim
Abraham Lincoln
Absence of Malice
The Absent-Minded Professor
Absolute Beginners
Absolution
The Abyss
The Accidental Tourist
The Accused
Ace Ventura: Pet Detective
Ace Ventura: When Nature Calls
Aces: Iron Eagle 3
Aces Wild
Act of Piracy
Action Jackson
Actors and Sin
Adam's Rib
The Addams Family
Addams Family Values
Adios Amigo
Adventures in Babysitting
Adventures in Dinosaur City
The Adventures of Baron Munchausen
The Adventures of Buckaroo Banzai Across the Eighth Dimension
The Adventures of Captain Marvel
Adventures of Don Juan
Adventures of Eliza Fraser
The Adventures of Ford Fairlane
The Adventures of Huck Finn
The Adventures of Ichabod and Mr. Toad
The Adventures of Mark Twain
The Adventures of Milo & Otis
The Adventures of Priscilla, Queen of the Desert
The Adventures of Robin Hood
The Adventures of the Wilderness Family
The Adventures of Tom Sawyer
The Adventurous Knights
The Advocate
Aelita: Queen of Mars
Affair in Trinidad
An Affair to Remember
The Affairs of Annabel
Afraid of the Dark
Africa Screams
An African Dream
The African Queen
After Dark, My Sweet
After Hours
Afterburn
Against All Flags
Against All Odds
Against the Wall
The Age of Innocence
Agnes of God
The Agony and the Ecstasy
Air America
The Air Up There
Airborne
Airheads
Airplane!
Airplane 2: The Sequel
Airport
Airport '77
Akira
Akira Kurosawa's Dreams
Aladdin
The Alamo
Alamo Bay
Alan & Naomi
Alex
Alexander Nevsky
Alexander the Great
Alice
Alice Adams
Alice Doesn't Live Here Anymore
Alice in Wonderland
Alien
Alien 3
Alien from L.A.
Alien Intruder
Alien Nation
Alienator
Aliens
Alive
Alive: 20 Years Later
All About Eve
All-American Murder
All Dogs Go to Heaven
All Dogs Go to Heaven 2
All I Want for Christmas
All of Me
All Quiet on the Western Front
All That Jazz
All the King's Men
...All the Marbles
All the President's Men
All the Right Moves
All the Vermeers in New York
All You Need Is Cash
Allegheny Uprising
Allegro Non Troppo
Alligator 2: The Mutation
All's Fair
...Almost
Almost an Angel
Almost Blue
Almost Pregnant
Aloha Summer
Alpine Fire
Alsino and the Condor
Altered States
Alvin Purple
Always
Amadeus
Amateur
Amazing Grace & Chuck
The Amazing Panda Adventure
The Amazing Spider-Man
Amazing Stories
Amazon
Amazon Women on the Moon
Ambition
The Ambulance
The Ambushers
Amelia Earhart: The Final Flight
America at the Movies
The American Angels: Baptism of Blood
American Anthem
American Blue Note
American Boyfriends
American Cop
American Cyborg: Steel Warrior
American Eagle
American Flyers
The American Friend
American Friends
American Gigolo
American Gothic
American Graffiti
American Heart
An American in Paris
American Kickboxer 2: To the Death
American Me
American Ninja 2: The Confrontation
American Ninja 3: Blood Hunt
American Ninja 4: The Annihilation
The American President
American Roulette
American Samurai
An American Tail
An American Tail: Fievel Goes West
An American Werewolf in London
The Americanization of Emily
The Amityville Horror
Amityville 2: The Possession
Amityville 3: The Demon
Amityville: A New Generation
The Amityville Curse
Amityville 1992: It's About Time
Among the Cinders
Amongst Friends
Amor Bandido
Amore!
Amos and Andrew
The Amsterdam Kill
Amsterdamned
Anastasia
Anastasia: The Mystery of Anna
Anatomy of a Murder
Anchors Aweigh
And God Created Woman
And Justice for All
And Now for Something Completely Different
And the Band Played On
And the Ship Sails On
And Then There Were None
The Anderson Tapes
The Andersonville Trial
Andrei Rublev
Android
The Android Affair
The Andromeda Strain
Andy and the Airwave Rangers
Andy Hardy Meets Debutante
Andy Warhol's Bad
Angel 3: The Final Chapter
Angel and the Badman
Angel Heart
Angel of Destruction
Angel of Fury
Angel of H.E.A.T.
Angel Town
Angelo My Love
Angels Die Hard
Angels Over Broadway
Angels with Dirty Faces
Angie
Anguish
Animal Behavior
Animal Crackers
Animal Farm
Animal Instincts 2
Anna
Anna Karenina
Anne of Avonlea
Anne of Green Gables
Annie
Annie Hall
Another Chance
Another Country
Another 48 Hrs.
Another Stakeout
Another Time, Another Place
Another Woman
Another You
Any Man's Death
Any Which Way You Can
Apache Chief
Apache Rose
The Apartment
Apartment Zero
A.P.E.X.
Apocalypse Now
Apollo 13
The Appaloosa
The Applegates
Appointment with Death
Appointment with Fear
Apprentice to Murder
April Fool's Day
Arabian Nights
Arachnophobia
Arctic Blue
Arena
Arizona Bushwackers
Armed and Dangerous
Armed Response
Army of Darkness
Army of One
Around the World in 80 Days
Around the World in 80 Ways
The Arrival
Arrowhead
Arsenic and Old Lace
The Art of Dying
Arthur
Arthur 2: On the Rocks
Article 99
As You Like It
As You Were
Ashes and Diamonds
Aspen Extreme
The Asphalt Jungle
Assassin
Assassination
The Assassination Bureau
Assassination of Trotsky
Assault and Matrimony
Assault on Precinct 13
Asylum
At Close Range
At Home with the Webbers
At Play in the Fields of the Lord
At Sword's Point
At the Circus
Atlantic City
Attack of the 50 Foot Woman
Attack of the 50 Ft. Woman
The Attic: The Hiding of Anne Frank
Au Revoir Les Enfants
Auntie Lee's Meat Pies
Auntie Mame
Autobiography of a Princess
Automatic
Autumn Sonata
Avalon
Ava's Magical Adventure
Avenging Angel
Avenging Force
Awakenings
The Awful Truth
An Awfully Big Adventure
Babar: The Movie
The Babe
Babe
Babes in Arms
Babes in Toyland
Babes on Broadway
Babette's Feast
Baby Boom
Baby It's You
Baby on Board
Baby ... Secret of the Lost Legend
The Baby-Sitters Club
Baby, the Rain Must Fall
The Babysitter
The Bachelor and the Bobby-Soxer
Bachelor Mother
Bachelor Party
Back from Eternity
Back in Action
Back to Bataan
Back to School
Back to the Beach
Back to the Future
Back to the Future, Part 2
Back to the Future, Part 3
Backbeat
Backdraft
Backfire
Backlash: Oblivion 2
Backstab
Backstreet Dreams
Backstreet Justice
The Bad and the Beautiful
Bad Blood
Bad Boy
Bad Boys
B.A.D. Cats
Bad Company
Bad Day at Black Rock
Bad Dreams
Bad Girls
Bad Influence
Bad Jim
Bad Lieutenant
The Bad News Bears
The Bad News Bears Go to Japan
The Bad News Bears in Breaking Training
Bad Taste
Badge of the Assassin
Badlands
Bail Out
Baja
Baja Oklahoma
The Balcony
Ball of Fire
Ballad of Cable Hogue
Ballad of Gregorio Cortez
The Ballad of the Sad Cafe
Ballistic
Balto
Bambi
Bananas
Band of the Hand
The Band Wagon
Bandit Queen
Bang the Drum Slowly

The Bank Dick
Bank Robber
The Banker
Bar Girls
Barabbas
Baraka
Barb Wire
Barbarella
Barbarian Queen
The Barbarians
Barbarosa
Barbary Coast
Barcelona
Barefoot in the Park
Barfly
The Barkleys of Broadway
Barnum
The Barretts of Wimpole Street
Barry Lyndon
Bartleby
Basileus Quartet
Basket Case
Basket Case 2
Bat 21
The Bat Whispers
Bathing Beauty
Batman
Batman Forever
Batman: Mask of the Phantasm
*batteries not included
Battle Beyond the Stars
Battle Cry
The Battle of Algiers
Battle of Britain
Battle of the Bulge
Battleground
The Battleship Potemkin
Battlestar Galactica
Baxter
The Bay Boy
Beach Blanket Bingo
Beach Girls
Beaches
The Bear
The Beast from 20,000 Fathoms
Beastmaster
Beastmaster 2: Through the Portal of Time
Beastmaster 3: The Eye of Braxus
The Beat
Beat Street
Beat the Devil
Beatlemania! The Movie
Beatrice
The Beautiful Blonde from Bashful Bend
Beautiful Dreamers
Beauty and the Beast
Beauty and the Beast, Episode 1: Once Upon a Time in New York
Beauty and the Beast: Though Lovers Be Lost
Beauty School
Bebe's Kids
Becket
Bed & Breakfast
Bed of Roses
Bedazzled
Bedford Incident
Bedknobs and Broomsticks
Bedlam
Bedroom Eyes
Bedroom Eyes 2
The Bedroom Window
Beethoven
Beethoven's Nephew
Beethoven's 2nd
Beetlejuice
Before Morning
Before Sunrise
The Beguiled
Being Human
Being There
The Believers
Bell, Book and Candle
The Bellboy
Belle de Jour
Belle Epoque
Bells are Ringing
The Bells of St. Mary's
The Belly of an Architect
The Beloved Rogue
Ben
Ben-Hur
Beneath the Planet of the Apes
Beneath the 12-Mile Reef
Benji the Hunted
Benny & Joon
Berlin Blues
The Berlin Conspiracy
Berlin Express
Bert Rigby, You're a Fool
Best Buns on the Beach
Best Defense
Best Friends
The Best Little Whorehouse in Texas
The Best of John Candy on SCTV
Best of the Best
Best of the Best 2
Best of the Best 3: No Turning Back
The Best of Times
Best Seller
The Best Years of Our Lives
Betrayed
Betsy's Wedding
Better Off Dead
Betty Blue
Beulah Land
The Beverly Hillbillies
Beverly Hills Bodysnatchers
Beverly Hills Brats
Beverly Hills Cop
Beverly Hills Cop 2
Beverly Hills Madam
Beverly Hills 90210
Beware, My Lovely
Beyond Darkness
Beyond Forgiveness
Beyond Justice
Beyond Rangoon
Beyond the Call of Duty
Beyond the Door
Beyond the Door 3
Beyond the Law
Beyond the Stars
Beyond the Valley of the Dolls
Bhowani Junction
The Bible...In the Beginning
The Bicycle Thief
Big
Big Bad John
The Big Blue
Big Business
Big Chase
The Big Chill
Big Deadly Game
The Big Easy
Big Girls Don't Cry...They Get Even
The Big Green
The Big Heat
The Big Hurt
Big Jake
Big Jim McLain
The Big Knife
The Big Man: Crossing the Line
Big Man on Campus
The Big Parade
The Big Picture
The Big Red One
Big Shots
The Big Sleep
The Big Slice
Big Steal
Big Street
The Big Sweat
Big Top Pee Wee
Big Town
Big Trouble
Big Trouble in Little China
Big Wednesday
Biggles
The Bikini Car Wash Company 2
Bikini Summer
Bikini Summer 2
Bill & Ted's Excellent Adventure
A Bill of Divorcement
Billie
Billy Bathgate
Billy Budd
Billy Jack
Billy Madison
Billy Rose's Jumbo
Biloxi Blues
Bingo
Bio-Dome
Bird
Bird on a Wire
The Bird with the Crystal Plumage
The Birdcage
The Birds
The Birds 2: Land's End
Birds of Paradise
Birdy
The Birth of a Nation
The Bishop's Wife
Bite the Bullet
Bitter Moon
Black and White in Color
Black Beauty
Black Caesar
The Black Cat
The Black Coin
Black Eagle
Black Glove
The Black Hole
Black Magic
Black Moon Rising
Black Narcissus
Black Orpheus
The Black Pirate
Black Rain
Black Rainbow
Black Robe
The Black Room
Black Roses
Black Snow
The Black Stallion
The Black Stallion Returns
Black Sunday
Black Werewolf
Black Widow
Blackbeard the Pirate
Blackbeard's Ghost
Blackmail
Blackout
Blacula
Blade Runner
Blades
Blame It on Rio
Blank Check
Blankman
Blaze
Blazing Guns
Blazing Saddles
Blind Date
Blind Fear
Blind Fools
Blind Fury
Blind Vision
Blindside
Blindsided
Blink
Blink of an Eye
Bliss
The Bliss of Mrs. Blossom
The Blob
Blood Alley
Blood & Concrete: A Love Story
Blood and Sand
Blood for Blood
Blood Games
Blood In...Blood Out: Bound by Honor
The Blood of Heroes
Blood on the Moon
Blood on the Sun
Blood Red
Blood Relations
Blood Salvage
Blood Simple
Blood Warriors
Bloodfist 4: Die Trying
Bloodfist 6: Ground Zero
Bloodhounds of Broadway
Bloodlust: Subspecies 3
Bloodmatch
Bloodmoon
Bloodsport
Bloodstone: Subspecies 2
Bloody Mama
Blow Out
Blow-Up
Blowing Wild
Blown Away
The Blue and the Gray
Blue Chips
Blue City
Blue Collar
Blue Hawaii
Blue Ice
Blue Iguana
Blue In the Face
The Blue Lagoon
The Blue Max
Blue Skies
Blue Sky
Blue Steel
Blue Thunder
Blue Tiger
Blue Velvet
The Blues Brothers
Bob & Carol & Ted & Alice
Bob Dylan: Don't Look Back
Bob le Flambeur
Bob Roberts
Bobo
Bodies, Rest & Motion
Body and Soul
Body Bags
Body Chemistry
Body Chemistry 2: Voice of a Stranger
Body Chemistry 3: Point of Seduction
Body Chemistry 4: Full Exposure
Body Count
Body Double
Body Heat
Body Melt
Body of Evidence
Body Parts
Body Shot
The Body Snatcher
Body Snatchers
The Bodyguard
Boeing Boeing
Boggy Creek II
Boiling Point
Bon Voyage!
Bon Voyage, Charlie Brown
Bonanza: The Return
The Bonfire of the Vanities
Bonnie & Clyde
The Boogey Man
Book of Love
Boomerang
The Boost
Bopha!
The Border
Border Devils
Border Rangers
Born Free
Born in East L.A.
Born Losers
Born of Fire
Born on the Fourth of July
Born to Be Bad
Born to Be Wild
Born to Dance
Born to Run
Born Wild
Born Yesterday
The Borrower
The Bostonians
Boulevard
Bound and Gagged: A Love Story
Bound for Glory
The Bounty
Bounty Hunter 2002
Bounty Tracker
Boxcar Bertha
Boxing Helena
A Boy and His Dog
A Boy Named Charlie Brown
The Boy Who Could Fly
The Boy Who Left Home to Find Out About the Shivers
The Boy with the Green Hair
Boyfriends & Girlfriends
The Boys from Brazil
The Boys in Company C
The Boys in the Band
The Boys Next Door
Boys on the Side
Boys Town
Boyz N the Hood
Braddock: Missing in Action 3
Brady's Escape
The Brain
Brain Donors
The Brain from Planet Arous
Brain Smasher...A Love Story
Brainscan
Brainstorm
Bram Stoker's Dracula
Branded
Brass
Brass Target
The Brave One
Brazil
Breach of Conduct
Breach of Trust
Break of Hearts
Breaker Morant
Breakfast at Tiffany's
The Breakfast Club
Breakheart Pass
Breakin'
Breakin' 2: Electric Boogaloo
Breaking Away
Breaking In
Breaking Point
Breaking the Rules
Breaking Up Is Hard to Do
Breakout
Breathless
Brewster McCloud
Brewster's Millions
Brian's Song
The Bride
The Bride of Frankenstein
Bride of Re-Animator
The Bride Wore Black
The Brides of Dracula
The Bridge of San Luis Rey
The Bridge on the River Kwai
A Bridge Too Far
The Bridges at Toko-Ri
The Bridges of Madison County
Brigadoon
Bright Lights, Big City
Brighton Beach Memoirs
A Brilliant Disguise
Bringing Up Baby
Broadcast News
Broadway Bill
Broadway Danny Rose
Broadway Melody of 1940
Broken Blossoms
Broken Lance

Bronco Billy
A Bronx Tale
The Brood
The Brotherhood
The Brotherhood of Satan
Brothers in Arms
Brother's Keeper
Brubaker
Bruce Lee: Curse of the Dragon
The Brute Man
The Buccaneer
Buck Privates
Buck Rogers in the 25th Century
Buckskin
Bud and Lou
The Buddy Holly Story
Buddy's Song
Buffet Froid
Buffy the Vampire Slayer
Bugs & Daffy: The Wartime Cartoons
Bugs Bunny Superstar
Bugsy
Bugsy Malone
Bull Durham
Bulldog Drummond
Bulletproof
Bulletproof Heart
Bullets Over Broadway
Bullfighter & the Lady
Bullies
Bullitt
Bullseye!
Bundle of Joy
Buona Sera, Mrs. Campbell
The 'Burbs
Burden of Dreams
Burglar
Buried Alive
Burke & Wills
The Burmese Harp
Burn!
Burndown
Burning Rage
Burning Secret
The Burns and Allen Show
Burnt by the Sun
Bury Me an Angel
Bus Stop
The Busby Berkeley Disc
Buster
Buster Keaton Rides Again/The Railrodder
Bustin' Loose
Butch Cassidy and the Sundance Kid
The Butcher's Wife
Butterfield 8
Butterfly
Buy & Cell
By Dawn's Early Light
By the Light of the Silvery Moon
Bye Bye Baby
Bye, Bye, Birdie
Bye Bye Brazil
Bye Bye, Love
Cabaret
Cabin Boy
Cabin in the Sky
The Cabinet of Dr. Caligari
Cactus Flower
Cactus in the Snow
Caddyshack
Caddyshack 2
Cadence
Cadillac Man
Cafe Romeo
The Cage
Caged Fear
Caged Fury
Caged Heat
Caged Heat 2: Stripped of Freedom
Caged in Paradiso
Cahill: United States Marshal
The Caine Mutiny
The Caine Mutiny Court Martial
Calamity Jane
Calendar Girl
California Suite
Caligula
Call Me
Call to Glory
Camelot
The Cameraman
Cameron's Closet
Camilla
Camille Claudel
Camp Nowhere
Campus Man
Can-Can
The Candidate
Candyman
Cannibal Women in the Avocado Jungle of Death
Cannonball Run
Cannonball Run 2
Can't Buy Me Love
Cape Fear
Capone
Capricorn One
Captain America
Captain Horatio Hornblower
Captain Ron
The Captive: The Longest Drive 2
Captured in Chinatown
Car 54, Where Are You?
Car Trouble
Caravaggio
Carbon Copy
The Cardinal
Career
Career Opportunities
Carefree
Caribe
The Cariboo Trail
Carlito's Way
Carmen Jones
Carnal Knowledge
Carnival of Souls
Carnosaur 2
Caro Diario
Carolina Skeletons
Caroline?
Caroline at Midnight
Carousel
The Carpenter
Carrie
Carried Away
Carrington
Cartel
Casablanca
Casanova
Casanova's Big Night
A Case for Murder
A Case of Deadly Force
Case of the Baby Sitter
Casino
Casino Royale
Casper
Cassandra
Cast a Deadly Spell
Cast the First Stone
Castle Freak
Casual Sex?
Casualties of War
Cat on a Hot Tin Roof
Cat People
Catch Me...If You Can
Catch-22
Catherine the Great
Cat's Eye
Cattle Queen of Montana
Caught in the Act
Cavalier of the West
Cave Girl
CB4: The Movie
Cellar Dweller
The Cemetery Club
Center of the Web
Certain Fury
Cesar
Cesar & Rosalie
Chain of Desire
Chain Reaction
Chained Heat
Chained Heat 2
Chains
The Chair
Chameleon Street
The Champ
Champagne for Caesar
Champions
Chances Are
The Changeling
Chaplin
Chapter Two
The Charge of the Light Brigade
Chariots of Fire
Charlie Chan at the Opera
Charlie Chan at the Wax Museum
The Charlie Chan Collection
Charlie Chan in Paris
Charlie Chan in Rio
Charlie Chaplin: The Early Years, Vol. 1
Charlie Chaplin: The Early Years, Vol. 2
Charlie Chaplin: The Early Years, Vol. 3
Charlie Chaplin: The Early Years, Vol. 4
Charlotte's Web
Charly
The Chase
Chasers
Chattahoochee
Cheatin' Hearts
Check & Double Check
Checking Out
Cheech and Chong: Still Smokin'
Cheech and Chong's Next Movie
Cheech and Chong's Nice Dreams
Cheech and Chong's The Corsican Brothers
Cheech and Chong's Up in Smoke
The Cheerleaders
Cheetah
Cherry 2000
Cheyenne Warrior
Chicago Joe & the Showgirl
Children in the Crossfire
Children of a Lesser God
Children of Paradise
Children of the Corn
Children of the Corn 3: Urban Harvest
Children of the Damned
The Children's Hour
Child's Play
Child's Play 2
Child's Play 3
China Girl
China Moon
China Sky
The China Syndrome
Chinatown
Chinese Connection
Chinese Roulette
The Chipmunk Adventure
Chisum
Chitty Chitty Bang Bang
Chocolat
The Chocolate War
Choose Me
Chopper Chicks in Zombietown
A Chorus Line
Christine
A Christmas Carol
Christmas in Connecticut
Christmas in July
A Christmas Story
Christopher Columbus: The Discovery
Christopher Strong
C.H.U.D.
C.H.U.D. 2: Bud the Chud
A Chump at Oxford
C.I.A.: Code Name Alexa
C.I.A. 2: Target Alexa
Ciao, Professore!
The Cincinnati Kid
Cinderella
Cinema Paradiso
Circuitry Man
Circus World
The Cisco Kid
Citizen Cohn
Citizen Kane
City Hall
City Heat
City Lights
City Limits
City of Hope
City of Joy
The City of Lost Children
City Slickers
City Slickers 2: The Legend of Curly's Gold
Claire's Knee
The Clan of the Cave Bear
Clara's Heart
Clarence Darrow
Clash of the Titans
Class
Class Act
Class Action
Class of 1984
Class of 1999 2: The Substitute
Class of Nuke 'Em High 2: Subhumanoid Meltdown
Class Reunion
Clean and Sober
Clean Slate
Cleopatra
Clerks
The Client
Cliffhanger
Clifford
A Climate for Killing
The Climb
Cloak and Dagger
Cloak & Dagger
The Clock
Clockers
The Clockmaker
Clockwise
A Clockwork Orange
Close Encounters of the Third Kind
Closely Watched Trains
The Closer
Closet Land
Clouds Over Europe
Clown House
The Club
Club Paradise
Clue
Coal Miner's Daughter
Coast to Coast
Cobb
Cobra
The Cobweb
The Coca-Cola Kid
Cocktail
The Cocoanuts
Cocoon
Cocoon: The Return
Code Name: Emerald
Code of Silence
Coffy
Cohen and Tate
Cold Feet
Cold Front
Cold Heaven
Cold Justice
Cold Turkey
Coldfire
The Collector
College
Collision Course
Colonel Redl
The Color of Money
The Color Purple
Colors
Coma
The Comancheros
Combat Academy
Come Back Little Reba
Come Back, Little Sheba
Come Back to the Five & Dime Jimmy Dean, Jimmy Dean
Come See the Paradise
The Comedy of Terrors
The Comic
Coming Home
Coming to America
Commando
The Commitments
Common Threads: Stories from the Quilt
Communion
The Companion
The Company of Wolves
The Competition
The Compleat Beatles
Compromising Positions
The Comrades of Summer
Conan the Barbarian
Conan the Destroyer
Confessions of a Hit Man
Confidentially Yours
The Conformist
A Connecticut Yankee in King Arthur's Court
Conquest of the Planet of the Apes
Consenting Adults
Consuming Passions
Contempt
Continental Divide
The Conversation
Convicted
Convicts at Large
Coogan's Bluff
Cookie
Cool As Ice
Cool Blue
Cool Hand Luke
Cool Runnings
Cool World
Cooley High
Cop
Cop and a Half
Cop-Out
Copacabana
Cops and Robbersons
Cornered
Corrina, Corrina
The Corsican Brothers
The Cosmic Eye
The Cotton Club
The Couch Trip
Counterforce
Country
Country Life
Coupe de Ville
Courage Mountain
Courageous Avenger
The Courier
Court Jester
The Court Martial of Billy Mitchell
Cousin, Cousine
Cousins
Cover Girl
Cover-Up
The Covered Wagon
Cowboy
The Cowboy Way
The Cowboys
Crack House
Crack-Up
Crackerjack

Crackers
The Cranes are Flying
Crash and Burn
The Crawling Eye
The Crawling Hand
Crazy from the Heart
Crazy in Love
Crazy Moon
Crazy People
The Crazysitter
Creator
Creature
Creature from the Black Lagoon
The Creature Walks Among Us
The Creeping Flesh
Creepozoids
Creepshow
Creepshow 2
Cria
Cries and Whispers
Crimes & Misdemeanors
Crimes of Passion
Crimes of the Heart
Criminal Law
Crimson Pirate
Crimson Tide
Crisscross
Critical Condition
Critters
Critters 2: The Main Course
Critters 4
Crocodile Dundee
Crocodile Dundee 2
Cromwell
Cronos
Crooked Hearts
Crooked Trail
Crooklyn
Cross Country
Cross Examination
Crosscut
Crossfire
The Crossing
Crossing Delancey
The Crossing Guard
Crossing the Bridge
Crossing the Line
Crossroads
The Crow
The Crowd
Crumb
The Crush
Crusoe
Cry-Baby
Cry Freedom
A Cry from the Mountain
A Cry in the Dark
Cry, the Beloved Country
The Crying Game
Cujo
The Cure
Curfew
Curly Sue
The Curse
Curse 3: Blood Sacrifice
Curse 4: The Ultimate Sacrifice
Curse of the Cat People
Curse of the Demon
Curse of the Starving Class
The Custodian
Cutter's Way
Cutthroat Island
Cutting Class
The Cutting Edge
Cyber Bandits
Cyber-Tracker
Cyborg
Cyborg 2
Cyborg Cop
Cyborg Soldier
Cyclone
Cyrano de Bergerac
Da
Dad
Daddy Long Legs
Daddy's Boys
Daddy's Dyin'...Who's Got the Will?
Daffy Duck's Movie: Fantastic Island
Daffy Duck's Quackbusters
The Dagger of Kamui
Dakota
Damage
Dames
Damien: Omen 2
Damn the Defiant
Damn Yankees
A Damsel in Distress
Dance, Girl, Dance
Dance Macabre
Dance Me Outside
Dance of the Damned
Dance with a Stranger
Dance with Death
Dancers
Dances with Wolves
Dandy in Aspic
Danger Zone
Dangerous
The Dangerous
Dangerous Game
Dangerous Heart
Dangerous Liaisons
Dangerous Life
Dangerous Minds
Dangerous Moves
A Dangerous Place
Dangerous Pursuit
Dangerous Touch
Dangerous When Wet
A Dangerous Woman
Danton
Darby O'Gill & the Little People
The Dark
Dark Age
The Dark Backward
Dark Before Dawn
The Dark Crystal
Dark Habits
Dark Passage
Dark Side of the Moon
Dark Star
Dark Tide
Dark Tower
Dark Victory
Dark Waters
The Dark Wind
Darkest Africa
Darkman
Darkman 2: The Return of Durant
Darkman 3: Die Darkman Die
Darling
D.A.R.Y.L.
Das Boot
Date with an Angel
A Date with Judy
Dave
David and Bathsheba
David and Lisa
David Copperfield
David Holzman's Diary
Davy Crockett and the River Pirates
Dawn of the Dead
The Dawning
The Day After
A Day at the Races
The Day My Parents Ran Away
Day of Atonement
Day of the Dead
The Day of the Dolphin
The Day of the Jackal
The Day of the Locust
Day of the Triffids
The Day the Earth Stood Still
Day Time Ended
Days of Heaven
Days of Thunder
Days of Wine and Roses
Dazed and Confused
D.C. Cab
The Dead
Dead Again
Dead Aim
Dead Air
Dead Alive
Dead Bang
Dead Calm
Dead Center
Dead Cold
Dead End
Dead Funny
Dead Heat
Dead Man Out
Dead Man Walking
Dead Man's Revenge
Dead Men Don't Wear Plaid
Dead of Night
Dead of Winter
Dead On
Dead Poets Society
The Dead Pool
Dead Presidents
Dead Reckoning
Dead Ringers
Dead Space
Dead Zone
Deadbolt
Deadfall
Deadline
Deadlock
Deadly Bet
Deadly Companions
Deadly Daphne's Revenge
Deadly Dreams
Deadly Friend
Deadly Illusion
Deadly Possession
Deadly Rivals
The Deadly Trackers
Deadtime Stories
Deal of the Century
Dealers
Death and the Maiden
Death Becomes Her
Death Before Dishonor
Death Dreams
Death Hunt
Death Machine
Death of a Salesman
Death of a Scoundrel
Death of an Angel
Death on the Nile
Death Ring
Death Warrant
Death Watch
Death Wish
Death Wish 2
Death Wish 3
Death Wish 4: The Crackdown
Death Wish 5: The Face of Death
Deathrow Gameshow
Deathstalker
Deathstalker 2: Duel of the Titans
Deathstalker 3
The Decameron
The Deceivers
December
Deception
Deceptions
Decline of Western Civilization 1
Decoration Day
Decoy
The Deep
Deep Cover
Deep Red
Deepstar Six
The Deer Hunter
Def by Temptation
Defending Your Life
Defense of the Realm
Defenseless
Deja Vu
The Delicate Delinquent
Delicatessen
Delirious
Deliverance
Delta Force
Delta Force 2: Operation Stranglehold
Delta Force 3: The Killing Game
Delta of Venus
Delusion
Demetrius and the Gladiators
Demolition Man
The Demolitionist
Demon City Shinjuku
A Demon in My View
Demon Possessed
Demon Seed
Demon Wind
Demonic Toys
Demons
Demons 2
Demonstone
Denial: The Dark Side of Passion
Dennis the Menace
Dennis the Menace: Dinosaur Hunter
Descending Angel
Desert Bloom
The Desert Fox
Desert Hearts
Desert Kickboxer
Desert Phantom
Designing Woman
Desire and Hell at Sunset Motel
Desire Under the Elms
Desiree
Desk Set
Desperado
Desperate Hours
Desperate Motives
Desperately Seeking Susan
Destination Moon
Destroyer
Destry Rides Again
The Detective
Detonator 2: Night Watch
Detour
The Devil & Daniel Webster
The Devil at 4 O'Clock
Devil In a Blue Dress
Devil in the Flesh
Devil Monster
The Devil's Commandment
Devil's Rain
Devlin
Diabolique
Dial "M" for Murder
Diamond Head
Diamond Run
The Diamond Trap
Diamonds Are Forever
Diane
Diary of a Chambermaid
Diary of a Hitman
Diary of a Lost Girl
The Diary of Anne Frank
Dick Tracy
Dick Tracy Returns
Dick Tracy vs. Crime Inc.
Die Hard
Die Hard 2: Die Harder
Die Hard: With a Vengeance
Die, Monster, Die!
Diggstown
Dillinger
Dillinger and Capone
Dim Sum: A Little Bit of Heart
Diner
Dinner at Eight
Diplomaniacs
Diplomatic Immunity
Direct Hit
Dirt Bike Kid
Dirty Dancing
The Dirty Dozen
Dirty Harry
Dirty Mary Crazy Larry
Dirty Rotten Scoundrels
The Disappearance of Christina
Disclosure
The Discreet Charm of the Bourgeoisie
Disorderlies
Disorderly Orderly
Disorganized Crime
Distant Thunder
Distant Voices, Still Lives
The Distinguished Gentleman
Disturbed
Diva
The Dive
Divine Madness
The Divorce of Lady X
Do or Die
Do the Right Thing
D.O.A.
Doc Hollywood
The Doctor
Dr. Alien
Dr. Caligari
Dr. Cyclops
Doctor Detroit
Doctor Dolittle
Doctor Duck's Super Secret All-Purpose Sauce
Dr. Giggles
Dr. Jekyll and Mr. Hyde
Dr. No
Dr. Strangelove, or: How I Learned to Stop Worrying and Love the Bomb
Doctor X
Doctor Zhivago
Dodge City
Dodsworth
Does This Mean We're Married?
Dog Day Afternoon
Dogfight
The Dogfighters
The Dogs of War
Doll Face
Dollar
Dollars
Dollman
The Dolls
A Doll's House
Dolly Dearest
Dolores Claiborne
Dominick & Eugene
Domino
Don Juan
Don Juan DeMarco
Don Juan, My Love
Don Q., Son of Zorro
Dona Flor and Her Two Husbands
Dona Herlinda & Her Son
Donovan's Brain
Donovan's Reef
Don't Look Now
Don't Mess with My Sister!
Don't Talk to Strangers
Don't Tell Her It's Me
Don't Tell Mom the Babysitter's Dead
The Doors
The Doors: Soft Parade, a Retrospective
Doppelganger: The Evil Within
Double-Crossed
Double Dragon
Double Exposure
Double Exposure: The Story of Margaret Bourke-White
Double Happiness
Double Impact
Double Indemnity
Double Jeopardy
The Double Life of Veronique
Double Trouble
Down Among the Z Men
Down and Out in Beverly Hills

Down Argentine Way
Down Came a Blackbird
Down the Drain
Down to Earth
Downhill Racer
Downtown
Dracula
Dracula Blows His Cool
Dracula: Dead and Loving It
Dragnet
Dragon: The Bruce Lee Story
Dragonslayer
Dream a Little Dream
Dream Lover
Dream Machine
Dream Man
The Dream Team
Dreams
Dreamscape
Dressed to Kill
The Dresser
Dressmaker
The Drifter
Drifting Weeds
Drive-In Massacre
Driving Force
Driving Me Crazy
Driving Miss Daisy
Drop Dead Fred
DROP Squad
Drowning by Numbers
Drugstore Cowboy
Drums
Drums Along the Mohawk
A Dry White Season
D2: The Mighty Ducks
The Duchess and the Dirtwater Fox
Duck Soup
DuckTales the Movie: Treasure of the Lost Lamp
Dudes
Duel of Hearts
The Duellists
Dumb & Dumber
Dumbo
Dune
Dune Warriors
The Dunera Boys
Dungeonmaster
Dunston Checks In
Dynamite and Gold
The Eagle
Early Frost
An Early Frost
Earth Girls Are Easy
Earth vs. the Flying Saucers
Earthquake
East of Eden
Easter Parade
Easy Living
Easy Money
Easy Rider
Easy Wheels
Eat a Bowl of Tea
Eat Drink Man Woman
Eating
Echo Park
Echoes of Paradise
Ed
Ed and His Dead Mother
Ed Wood
Eddie and the Cruisers
Eddie and the Cruisers 2: Eddie Lives!
Eddie Macon's Run
Eddie Murphy: Raw
The Eddy Duchin Story
Edge of Sanity
Educating Rita
Edward Scissorhands
Edward II
Egg
Egg and I
The Egyptian
The Eiger Sanction

8 1/2
Eight Men Out
8 Million Ways to Die
8 Seconds
18 Again!
84 Charing Cross Road
84 Charlie Mopic
Eijanaika
El Amor Brujo
El Cid
El Dorado
El Mariachi
Electra Glide in Blue
Electric Dreams
The Electric Horseman
Elena and Her Men
Eleni
Elephant Boy
The Elephant Man
Elmer Gantry
The Elusive Corporal
Elvira Madigan
Elvira, Mistress of the Dark
Elvis in Hollywood
Embrace of the Vampire
The Emerald Forest
Emissary
Emmanuelle in the Country
Emmanuelle, the Joys of a Woman
Emperor Jones
Empire of the Sun
The Empire Strikes Back
Enchanted April
The Enchanted Cottage
The Enchanted Forest
Encounter at Raven's Gate
The End
End of the Line
Endless Descent
Endless Love
Endless Night
The Endless Summer
The Endless Summer 2
Enemies, a Love Story
Enemy Gold
Enemy Mine
The Enforcer
The Englishman Who Went Up a Hill But Came Down a Mountain
Enigma
Enormous Changes
Enrapture
Entangled
Enter the Dragon
Equinox
Equus
Eraserhead
Erik the Viking
Ernest Goes to Jail
Ernest Saves Christmas
The Errand Boy
The Escape Artist
Escape from Alcatraz
Escape from New York
Escape from the Planet of the Apes
Escape to Witch Mountain
E.T.: The Extra-Terrestrial
Eternal Evil
Ethan Frome
Eve of Destruction
Even Cowgirls Get the Blues
An Evening with Robin Williams
Evergreen
Eversmile New Jersey
Every Girl Should Be Married
Every Time We Say Goodbye
Every Which Way But Loose
Everybody Wins
Everybody's All American
Everybody's Dancin'
Everybody's Fine

Everything You Always Wanted to Know about Sex (But Were Afraid to Ask)
Evil Clutch
Evil Dead
Evil Dead 2: Dead by Dawn
Evil Spirits
The Evil That Men Do
Evil under the Sun
Evolver
The Ewok Adventure
The Ewoks: Battle for Endor
Ex-Mrs. Bradford
Excalibur
Excessive Force
Excessive Force 2: Force on Force
Executive Action
Executive Decision
Exodus
The Exorcist
Exorcist 3: Legion
Exotica
The Expendables
Experiment in Terror
The Experts
Explorers
Exquisite Corpses
Exterminator
Extra Girl
Extreme Justice
Extreme Prejudice
Extreme Vengeance
Extremities
Eyes of a Witness
Eyes of an Angel
Eyes of Fire
Eyes of Laura Mars
Eyes of the Beholder
Eyes of the Panther
Eyewitness
F/X
F/X 2: The Deadly Art of Illusion
The Fable of the Beautiful Pigeon Fancier
The Fabulous Baker Boys
The Fabulous Dorseys
Fahrenheit 451
Fail-Safe
Fair Game
Faith
Faithful
The Falcon and the Snowman
The Fall of the Roman Empire
Fall Time
The Fallen Idol
Falling Down
Falling from Grace
Falling in Love
False Identity
Fame
The Family
Family Business
Family Dog: Complete Series
A Family Matter
Family Plot
Family Viewing
The Fan
Fancy Pants
Fanny
Fanny and Alexander
Fantasia
Fantastic Voyage
Far and Away
Far from Home
Far from Home: The Adventures of Yellow Dog
Far from the Madding Crowd
Far North
A Far Off Place
Far Out Man
Faraway, So Close!
Farewell My Concubine
A Farewell to Arms
Farewell to the King
Farinelli

The Farmer Takes a Wife
Fast Food
Fast Forward
Fast Getaway
Fast Times at Ridgemont High
Fat Man and Little Boy
Fatal Attraction
Fatal Beauty
Fatal Exposure
Fatal Instinct
Fatal Mission
Fatal Vision
Father
Father and Scout
Father Hood
Father of the Bride
Father of the Bride Part II
Fathers and Sons
Father's Little Dividend
A Father's Revenge
The Favor
The Favor, the Watch, & the Very Big Fish
FBI Girl
The FBI Story
Fear
Fear City
The Fear Inside
Fear Strikes Out
Fearless
Fearless Tiger
The Fearless Vampire Killers
Feast of July
Federal Hill
Feds
Fellini Satyricon
Fellini's Roma
Femme Fatale
Ferocious Female Freedom Fighters
Ferris Bueller's Day Off
Fever
A Few Good Men
Fiddler on the Roof
The Field
Field of Dreams
Field of Fire
Field of Honor
Fiend Without a Face
The Fiendish Plot of Dr. Fu Manchu
Fifth Avenue Girl
The Fifth Monkey
Fifty/Fifty
52 Pick-Up
55 Days at Peking
Fight for Us
Fighting Cowboy
The Final Alliance
Final Analysis
Final Approach
The Final Conflict
The Final Countdown
Final Embrace
Final Mission
Final Notice
The Final Terror
A Fine Mess
The Finest Hour
Fingerprints Don't Lie
Finian's Rainbow
Fiorile
Fire Alarm
Fire and Ice
Fire and Rain
Fire Birds
Fire Down Below
Fire in the Sky
Firefall
Firefox
Firehawk
Firehead
Firepower
Firestarter
Firewalker
The Firing Line

The Firm
First Blood
First Born
The First Deadly Sin
First Knight
First Men in the Moon
First Monday in October
First Name: Carmen
The First Power
A Fish Called Wanda
The Fisher King
F.I.S.T.
Fist Fighter
Fist of Steel
A Fistful of Dollars
A Fistful of Dynamite
Fists of Iron
Five Came Back
Five Easy Pieces
The Five Heartbeats
The 5000 Fingers of Dr. T
Five Weeks in a Balloon
The Flame & the Arrow
Flaming Signal
The Flamingo Kid
Flamingo Road
The Flash
Flash Gordon
Flashback
Flashdance
Flashpoint
Flat Top
Flatliners
Flesh and Blood
Flesh and Bone
Flesh Gordon
Fleshtone
Fletch
Fletch Lives
The Flight
A Flight of Rainbirds
Flight of the Eagle
Flight of the Innocent
Flight of the Intruder
Flight of the Navigator
The Flight of the Phoenix
Flight to Mars
Flight to Nowhere
The Flintstones
Flirting
Florida Straits
Flower Drum Song
Flowers in the Attic
Fluke
The Fly
The Fly
The Fly 2
The Flying Deuces
Flying Leathernecks
Flying Tigers
FM
The Fog
Follies in Concert
Follow That Dream
Follow the Fleet
Food of the Gods: Part 2
Foolish Wives
Fools of Fortune
Footlight Parade
Footloose
For a Few Dollars More
For Better and For Worse
For Keeps
For Love or Money
For Me and My Gal
For Those About to Rock: Monsters in Moscow
For Your Eyes Only
Forbidden Choices
The Forbidden Dance
Forbidden Games
Forbidden Planet
Forbidden Sun
Forbidden World
The Force
Force of Evil

Force 10 from Navarone
Forced March
Forced to Kill
Foreign Affairs
Foreign Correspondent
Forever Emmanuelle
Forever, Lulu
Forever Young
Forget Paris
The Forgotten
The Forgotten One
A Forgotten Tune for the Flute
Fort Apache
Fort Apache, the Bronx
Fortress
The Fortune Cookie
Fortunes of War
The Forty-Ninth Parallel
42nd Street
48 Hrs.
Foul Play
The Four Feathers
Four for Texas
The 400 Blows
Four Rooms
The Four Seasons
Four Weddings and a Funeral
The 4D Man
1492: Conquest of Paradise
The 4th Man
The Fourth Protocol
Fourth Story
The Fourth War
Frame Up
Frances
Francesco
Francis the Talking Mule
Frank and Jesse
Frankenhooker
Frankenstein
Frankenstein General Hospital
Frankenstein Meets the Wolfman
Frankenstein Sings...The Movie
Frankenstein Unbound
Frankie and Johnny
Frankie Starlight
Frantic
Fraternity Vacation
Frauds
Freaked
Freaks
Freddy's Dead: The Final Nightmare
Free Grass
Free Ride
Free Willy
Free Willy 2: The Adventure Home
Freebie & the Bean
Freejack
Freeway
Freeze Frame
French Can-Can
The French Connection
French Connection 2
French Kiss
The French Lieutenant's Woman
French Silk
Frenzy
Fresh
Fresh Horses
The Freshman
Frida
Friday
Friday the 13th
Friday the 13th, Part 2
Friday the 13th, Part 3
Friday the 13th, Part 4: The Final Chapter
Friday the 13th, Part 5: A New Beginning
Friday the 13th, Part 6: Jason Lives
Friday the 13th, Part 7: The New Blood
Friday the 13th, Part 8: Jason Takes Manhattan
Fried Green Tomatoes
Friendly Persuasion
Friends, Lovers & Lunatics
Fright Night
Fright Night 2
The Fringe Dwellers
Frog
From Beyond
From Here to Eternity
From Hollywood to Deadwood
From Russia with Love
From the Earth to the Moon
From the Hip
From the Life of the Marionettes
From the Terrace
The Front
The Front Page
The Fugitive
Full Eclipse
Full Metal Jacket
Full Moon in Blue Water
The Fuller Brush Man
Funeral in Berlin
The Funhouse
Funland
Funny About Love
Funny Bones
Funny Face
Funny Farm
Funny Girl
Funny Lady
A Funny Thing Happened on the Way to the Forum
The Further Adventures of Tennessee Buck
Future Hunters
Future Kill
Future Zone
Futureworld
G-Men vs. the Black Dragon
Gaby: A True Story
Galaxina
Galaxy of Terror
Gallipoli
The Gamble
The Gambler
The Gambler & the Lady
The Game
Game of Death
The Game of Love
Gamera, the Invincible
Gamera vs. Gaos
Gamera vs. Zigra
Gandhi
Gang Justice
The Garbage Pail Kids Movie
The Garden of Allah
The Garden of the Finzi-Continis
Gardens of Stone
Gas Food Lodging
Gas Pump Girls
Gaslight
The Gate
Gate 2
Gator Bait
Gator Bait 2: Cajun Justice
The Gauntlet
The Gay Divorcee
Gay Purr-ee
The General
General Spanky
Gentleman Jim
Gentleman's Agreement
Gentlemen Prefer Blondes
Genuine Risk
George Balanchine's The Nutcracker
George's Island
Georgia
Georgy Girl
Germinal
Geronimo
Geronimo: An American Legend
Get Crazy
Get Out Your Handkerchiefs
Get Shorty
Get That Man
The Getaway
Getting Even with Dad
Getting In
Getting It Right
Getting Out
Ghost
The Ghost and Mrs. Muir
The Ghost Breakers
Ghost Chase
Ghost Dad
Ghost Fever
Ghost in the Machine
Ghost Story
Ghost Town
Ghostbusters
Ghostbusters 2
Ghosts Can't Do It
Ghoulies 2
G.I. Blues
G.I. Jane
Giant
Gidget
The Gig
Gigi
Gilda
Gimme Shelter
Ginger Ale Afternoon
The Girl Can't Help It
Girl Crazy
Girl from Calgary
The Girl in a Swing
A Girl in Every Port
The Girl Most Likely
A Girl to Kill For
Girlfriend from Hell
Girls Just Want to Have Fun
Girls Next Door
Give My Regards to Broad Street
The Gladiator
Gladiator
The Glass Bottom Boat
The Glass Key
The Glass Menagerie
The Glass Shield
Glass Tomb
Gleaming the Cube
Glen and Randa
Glengarry Glen Ross
The Glenn Miller Story
Glitch!
Gloria
Glory
Glory! Glory!
Go, Johnny Go!
Go Tell the Spartans
Go West
God Told Me To
The Goddess
The Godfather
The Godfather, Part 2
The Godfather, Part 3
God's Country
The Gods Must Be Crazy
The Gods Must Be Crazy 2
Godzilla, King of the Monsters
Godzilla 1985
Goin' South
Going Berserk
Going My Way
Going Places
Going Undercover
The Gold & Glory
Gold Diggers of 1933
Gold Diggers of 1935
Gold Diggers: The Secret of Bear Mountain
The Gold Rush
Golden Age of Comedy
Golden Boy
The Golden Child
The Golden Coach
Golden Gate
The Golden Seal
Golden Voyage of Sinbad
Goldeneye
Goldfinger
Goldilocks & the Three Bears
The Goldwyn Follies
Goliath Awaits
Gone with the Wind
Gonza the Spearman
Good Guys Wear Black
Good Morning, Babylon
Good Morning, Vietnam
The Good Mother
Good News
The Good Son
The Good, the Bad and the Ugly
The Good Wife
Goodbye Columbus
The Goodbye Girl
Goodbye, Mr. Chips
Goodbye, My Lady
Goodbye, New York
The Goodbye People
Goodfellas
The Goonies
Gorgo
The Gorgon
The Gorilla
Gorillas in the Mist
Gorky Park
The Gospel According to St. Matthew
Gotcha!
Gotham
Gothic
The Graduate
Graffiti Bridge
Grand Hotel
Grand Illusion
Grand Isle
Grand Prix
Grand Tour: Disaster in Time
Grandma's House
The Grapes of Wrath
The Grass is Greener
Grave of the Fireflies
Grave Secrets
Graveyard Shift
Grease
Grease 2
Great Balls of Fire
Great Bikini Off-Road Adventure
The Great Caruso
The Great Dictator
The Great Escape
Great Expectations
The Great Gatsby
The Great Lie
The Great McGinty
The Great Mouse Detective
Great Movie Stunts & the Making of Raiders of the Lost Ark
The Great Muppet Caper
The Great Outdoors
The Great Train Robbery
The Great Waldo Pepper
A Great Wall
The Great Waltz
The Great Ziegfeld
The Greatest Show on Earth
The Greatest Story Ever Told
Greed
Greedy
The Green Berets
Green Card
Green for Danger
Green Ice
Greetings
Gremlins
Gremlins 2: The New Batch
The Grey Fox
Greystoke: The Legend of Tarzan, Lord of the Apes
Griffith Biograph Program
The Grifters
Grim
Grim Prairie Tales
The Grim Reaper
Gross Anatomy
Grosse Fatigue
Grotesque
Ground Zero
Groundhog Day
Grumpier Old Men
Grumpy Old Men
Guadalcanal Diary
The Guardian
Guarding Tess
Guess Who's Coming to Dinner
Guilty as Charged
Guilty as Sin
Guilty by Suspicion
Gulliver's Travels
The Gumshoe Kid
Gun Fury
The Gun in Betty Lou's Handbag
Guncrazy
Gunfight at the O.K. Corral
The Gunfighter
The Gunfighters
Gunfire
Gung Ho
Gunga Din
Gunmen
The Gunrunner
Guns
Guns of Justice
The Guns of Navarone
Gus
Guys and Dolls
Guyver 2: Dark Hero
Gypsy
Hackers
Hail Caesar
Hail Mary
Hair
The Hairdresser's Husband
Hairspray
Half Moon Street
The Halfback of Notre Dame
The Hallelujah Trail
Halloween
Halloween 2: The Nightmare Isn't Over!
Halloween 3: Season of the Witch
Halloween 4: The Return of Michael Myers
Halloween 5: The Revenge of Michael Myers
Hamburger Hill
Hamburger...The Motion Picture
Hamlet
Hand Gun
The Handmaid's Tale
Hang 'Em High
Hangfire
Hangin' with the Homeboys
Hanky Panky
Hannah and Her Sisters
Hanna's War
Hanoi Hilton
Hanover Street
Hans Christian Andersen
Hansel and Gretel
Hanussen
Happy Birthday to Me
The Happy Hooker
The Happy Hooker Goes Hollywood
Happy Hour
Happy Together
Hard Country
A Hard Day's Night
Hard Drive
Hard Justice
Hard Promises
Hard Target

Hard Times
Hard to Hold
Hard to Kill
Hard Vice
The Hard Way
Hardbodies
Hardbodies 2
Hardcore
The Harder They Come
Hardware
Harem
Harlem Nights
Harley Davidson and the Marlboro Man
Harmagedon
Harold and Maude
Harper
Harry & Son
Harry and the Hendersons
Harry & Walter Go to New York
The Harvest
Harvey
The Harvey Girls
Hat Box Mystery
Hatari!
Haunted Honeymoon
The Haunted Palace
Haunted Summer
The Haunting
The Haunting of Morella
Haunting of Sarah Hardy
The Haunting of Seacliff Inn
Havana
Having It All
Having Wonderful Crime
Hawaii
Hawk the Slayer
Hawken's Breed
Hawks
The Hawks & the Sparrows
He Said, She Said
Head
Headhunter
Hear No Evil
Heart and Souls
Heart Condition
Heart Like a Wheel
Heart of Darkness
The Heart of Dixie
Heart of Midnight
Heart of the Stag
Heartaches
Heartbreak Hotel
The Heartbreak Kid
Heartbreak Ridge
Heartbreaker
Heartburn
Hearts of Fire
Hearts of the World
Heat
Heat and Sunlight
Heat of Desire
Heat Wave
Heathers
Heaven
Heaven & Earth
Heaven and Earth
Heaven Can Wait
Heaven Help Us
Heaven is a Playground
Heavenly Creatures
Heaven's Gate
Heavy Metal
Heavy Petting
Heavyweights
Heidi
The Heiress
Helen of Troy
Hell Comes to Frogtown
Hell in the Pacific
Hell is for Heroes
Hellbound: Hellraiser 2
Hellfighters
Hellgate
Hellhole
Hello Again
Hello, Dolly!
Hello Mary Lou: Prom Night 2
Hellraiser
Hellraiser 3: Hell on Earth
Help!
Henry V
Henry & June
Henry: Portrait of a Serial Killer
Her Alibi
Herbie Rides Again
Hercules
Hercules Unchained
Here Comes Mr. Jordan
Here Comes the Groom
Here's Looking at You, Warner Bros.
Hero
Hero and the Terror
The Heroic Trio
Hexed
Hey, Babu Riba
Hey There, It's Yogi Bear
Hi-Jacked
The Hidden
The Hidden 2
Hidden Agenda
The Hidden Fortress
Hidden Obsession
Hide and Go Shriek
Hideaway
Hider in the House
High & Low
High Anxiety
High Frequency
High Noon
High Plains Drifter
High Road to China
High Season
High Sierra
High Society
High Spirits
High Stakes
High Tide
Higher and Higher
Higher Learning
The Highest Honor
Highlander
Highlander 2: The Quickening
Highlander: The Final Dimension
Highpoint
Highway 13
The Hills Have Eyes
The Hindenburg
Hips, Hips, Hooray
His Majesty O'Keefe
History is Made at Night
History of the World: Part 1
The Hit
The Hit List
Hit the Deck
The Hitcher
The Hitchhiker
Hitchhiker 2
Hitchhiker 3
Hitchhiker 4
The Hitchhiker's Guide to the Galaxy
The Hitman
Hobson's Choice
Hocus Pocus
Hoffa
The Holcroft Covenant
A Hole in the Head
Holiday
Holiday Affair
Holiday Inn
Holiday Rhythm
Hollywood Hot Tubs 2: Educating Crystal
Hollywood Outtakes & Rare Footage
Hollywood Shuffle
Hollywood Varieties
Hollywood Vice Sqaud
Hologram Man
Holy Matrimony
Hombre
Home Alone
Home Alone 2: Lost in New York
Home for the Holidays
Home from the Hill
Home Is Where the Hart Is
Home Movies
A Home of Our Own
Home of the Brave
Homeboy
Homeboys
Homer and Eddie
Hometown Boy Makes Good
Homeward Bound: The Incredible Journey
Homework
Homicide
Honey, I Blew Up the Kid
Honey, I Shrunk the Kids
Honeymoon Academy
Honeymoon in Vegas
Honeymoon Killers
Honeysuckle Rose
Hong Kong '97
Honkytonk Man
Honor and Glory
Hook
Hook, Line and Sinker
Hoop Dreams
Hooper
Hoosiers
Hope and Glory
Hoppity Goes to Town
Hopscotch
The Horror Chamber of Dr. Faustus
Horror Hotel
The Horror of Dracula
Horror Planet
Horrors of Burke & Hare
Horse Feathers
The Horseplayer
The Horse's Mouth
Hostage for a Day
The Hostage Tower
Hostile Guns
Hostile Takeover
Hot Chocolate
Hot Pursuit
The Hot Rock
Hot Shots! Part Deux
The Hot Spot
Hot Stuff
Hot Target
Hot to Trot!
Hotel Colonial
The Hotel New Hampshire
The Hound of the Baskervilles
Hourglass
House
House 2: The Second Story
House 4: Home Deadly Home
House Calls
A House In The Hills
House of Cards
House of Dracula
House of Frankenstein
House of Games
The House of the Spirits
The House of Usher
House of Wax
The House on Carroll Street
House on Haunted Hill
The House on Sorority Row
House Party
House Party 2: The Pajama Jam
House Party 3
Houseboat
Houseguest
The Householder
The Housekeeper
Housesitter
How I Got into College
How I Won the War
How the West Was Won
How to Get Ahead in Advertising
How to Make an American Quilt
How to Marry a Millionaire
How to Murder Your Wife
How to Succeed in Business without Really Trying
How U Like Me Now?
Howard the Duck
Howard's End
The Howling
Howling 2: Your Sister is a Werewolf
Howling 3: The Marsupials
Howling 4: The Original Nightmare
Howling 5: The Rebirth
Howling 6: The Freaks
The Howling: New Moon Rising
Huck and the King of Hearts
Huckleberry Finn
Hud
Hudson Hawk
The Hudsucker Proxy
Hugh Hefner: Once Upon a Time
The Human Comedy
The Human Shield
Humoresque
The Hunchback of Notre Dame
The Hunger
Hunk
The Hunt for Red October
The Hunt for the Night Stalker
The Hunter
Hunter in the Dark
Hunter's Blood
The Hurricane
Husbands and Wives
Hush, Hush, Sweet Charlotte
Hussy
The Hustler
Hyper-Sapien: People from Another Star
Hysterical
I Am the Law
I Come in Peace
I Confess
I Could Go on Singing
I Died a Thousand Times
I Don't Want to Talk About It
I Know Where I'm Going
I Like It Like That
I Like to Play Games
I Love Lucy
I Love N.Y.
I Love Trouble
I Love You Again
I Love You, Alice B. Toklas!
I Love You to Death
I, Madman
I Married a Centerfold
I Married a Witch
I Married a Woman
I Never Sang For My Father
I Posed for Playboy
I Remember Mama
I Shot Billy the Kid
I Spit on Your Grave
I Vitelloni
I Walked with a Zombie
I Wanna Hold Your Hand
I Want to Live!
I Was a Teenage Zombie
Ice
Ice Pirates
Ice Station Zebra
Iceman
Identity Crisis
Idiot's Delight
Idolmaker
If...
If It's Tuesday, This Must Be Belgium
If Looks Could Kill
If You Could See What I Hear
Ike
Ikiru
I'll Cry Tomorrow
I'll Do Anything
I'll Get You
Illegal in Blue
Ilsa, Harem Keeper of the Oil Sheiks
Ilsa, She-Wolf of the SS
Ilsa, the Wicked Warden
I'm Dancing as Fast as I Can
I'm Gonna Git You Sucka
I'm the One You're Looking For
Imagemaker
Imaginary Crimes
Immediate Family
Immortal Beloved
Immortal Combat
The Immortalizer
Impromptu
Improper Channels
Impulse
In Cold Blood
In Country
The In Crowd
In Harm's Way
The In-Laws
In Like Flint
In Love and War
In Name Only
In Person
In Praise of Older Women
In the Army Now
In the Cold of the Night
In the Good Old Summertime
In the Heat of Passion
In the Heat of Passion 2: Unfaithful
In the Heat of the Night
In the Line of Fire
In the Mood
In the Mouth of Madness
In the Name of the Father
In the Navy
In the Soup
The Incident
Incident at Channel Q
Incident at Deception Ridge
The Incredible Hulk
The Incredible Hulk Returns
The Incredible Journey
The Incredible Mr. Limpet
The Incredible Sarah
The Incredible Shrinking Man
The Incredible Shrinking Woman
Incubus
Indecency
The Indian in the Cupboard
The Indian Runner
Indian Summer
Indiana Jones and the Last Crusade
Indiana Jones and the Temple of Doom
Indictment: The McMartin Trial
Indio
Indochine
The Informer
Inherit the Wind
The Inkwell
The Inner Circle
Inner Sanctum
Inner Sanctum 2
Innerspace
The Innocent
Innocent Blood
An Innocent Man
Inside Daisy Clover
Inside Information
Inside Monkey Zetterland
Inside Moves
Inside the Third Reich
Insignificance
Interceptor
Interiors
Intermezzo

Internal Affairs
International House
The Interns
Intersection
Interview with the Vampire
Intimate Power
Intimate Stranger
Into the Fire
Into the Homeland
Into the Night
Into the Sun
Into the West
Into Thin Air
Intolerance
Intrigue
Intruder
Invader
The Invaders
Invaders from Mars
Invasion Earth: The Aliens Are Here!
Invasion of the Body Snatchers
Invasion U.S.A.
The Invisible Kid
The Invisible Man
The Invisible Ray
Irezumi
Irma La Douce
Iron & Silk
Iron Eagle
Iron Eagle 2
Iron Eagle 4
The Iron Mask
Iron Maze
The Iron Triangle
Iron Will
Ironheart
Ironweed
Irreconcilable Differences
Ishtar
The Island
The Island at the Top of the World
Islands in the Stream
Isle of the Dead
Istanbul
It
It Came from Beneath the Sea
It Came from Hollywood
It Could Happen to You
It Couldn't Happen Here
It Happened One Night
It Should Happen to You
It Takes Two
The Italian Job
It's A Gift
It's a Great Feeling
It's a Mad, Mad, Mad, Mad World
It's a Wonderful Life
It's All True
It's Always Fair Weather
It's in the Bag
It's My Party
It's My Turn
I've Always Loved You
I've Heard the Mermaids Singing
Izzy & Moe
J. Edgar Hoover
Jabberwocky
Jack & the Beanstalk
Jack-O
Jack the Bear
Jack the Giant Killer
Jacknife
Jack's Back
Jacob's Ladder
The Jagged Edge
Jailhouse Rock
Jakarta
Jake Speed
James Dean Story
Jamon, Jamon
Jane Eyre
The January Man

Jason and the Argonauts
Jason Goes to Hell: The Final Friday
Jaws
Jaws 2
Jaws 3
Jaws: The Revenge
The Jazz Singer
Jean de Florette
Jefferson in Paris
Jeffrey
Jennifer 8
Jeremiah Johnson
The Jerk
The Jerky Boys
Jesse James
Jesus Christ, Superstar
Jesus of Montreal
Jet Pilot
The Jetsons Meet the Flintstones
Jetsons: The Movie
The Jewel of the Nile
Jezebel
Jezebel's Kiss
JFK
The JFK Conspiracy
The Jigsaw Man
Jimmy Hollywood
Jo Jo Dancer, Your Life is Calling
Joan of Arc
Joe
Joe Kidd
Joe Versus the Volcano
John & Yoko: A Love Story
Johnny Angel
Johnny Be Good
Johnny Come Lately
Johnny Got His Gun
Johnny Guitar
Johnny Handsome
Johnny Mnemonic
Johnny Stecchino
Johnny Suede
Jolson Sings Again
The Jolson Story
Josh and S.A.M.
Jour de Fete
Journey into Fear
The Journey of August King
Journey of Honor
Journey of Hope
The Journey of Natty Gann
Journey to the Center of the Earth
Journey to the Far Side of the Sun
The Joy Luck Club
Joy of Living
Joy Sticks
Joyless Street
Ju Dou
Jubal
The Judge and the Assassin
Judge Dredd
Judgment at Nuremberg
Judgment in Berlin
Judgment Night
Judith of Bethulia
Jules and Jim
Julia
Julia and Julia
Juliet of the Spirits
Julius Caesar
Jumanji
Jumpin' at the Boneyard
Jumpin' Jack Flash
Jumping Jacks
June Night
Jungle
The Jungle Book
Jungle Bride
Jungle Fever
Jungle Goddess
Jungleground

Junior
Jupiter's Darling
Jurassic Park
The Juror
Jury Duty
Just a Gigolo
Just Another Girl on the I.R.T.
Just Cause
Just One of the Girls
Just One of the Guys
K-9
Kafka
Kagemusha
Kalifornia
Kandyland
Kansas
Karate Cop
The Karate Kid
The Karate Kid: Part 2
The Karate Kid: Part 3
Katherine
Keaton's Cop
The Keep
Keep 'Em Flying
Keep the Change
Keeper of the City
Keeping Track
Keetje Tippel
Kelly's Heroes
Kentucky Fried Movie
Kentucky Jubilee
Kentucky Kernels
The Key
Key Largo
The Keys of the Kingdom
The KGB: The Secret War
Khartoum
Kickboxer
Kickboxer 2: The Road Back
Kickboxer 3: The Art of War
Kickboxer 4: The Aggressor
Kid
Kid from Brooklyn
Kid from Gower Gulch
Kid Galahad
Kidnapped
Kids
Kill Cruise
The Kill Reflex
Kill Slade
Killcrazy
The Killer Elite
Killer Image
Killer Instinct
Killer Klowns from Outer Space
Killer Looks
Killer Tomatoes Eat France
The Killer's Edge
The Killing
A Killing Affair
The Killing Fields
Killing Floor
A Killing in a Small Town
Killing Obsession
The Killing Time
Killing Zoe
Killpoint
Kind Hearts and Coronets
Kindergarten Cop
The Kindred
The King and I
King Creole
King David
King Dinosaur
King Kong
King Kong Lives
King of Comedy
The King of Hearts
The King of Kings
King of New York
King of the Gypsies
King of the Hill
King of the Rocketmen
King Ralph
The King's Whore
Kinjite: Forbidden Subjects

Kismet
The Kiss
A Kiss Before Dying
Kiss Me a Killer
Kiss Me Deadly
Kiss Me Kate
Kiss Me, Stupid!
Kiss of Death
Kiss of the Spider Woman
Kiss Tomorrow Goodbye
The Kitchen Toto
Klute
Knife in the Water
Knight Moves
Knightriders
Knights of the Round Table
Knock on Any Door
Koyaanisqatsi
Kramer vs. Kramer
The Krays
Kriemhilde's Revenge
Kronos
Krull
Krush Groove
Kuffs
Kwaidan
La Bamba
L.A. Bounty
La Cage aux Folles
La Cage aux Folles 2
La Cage aux Folles 3: The Wedding
La Chienne
La Dolce Vita
La Lectrice
La Nuit de Varennes
La Passante
L.A. Story
La Strada
Labyrinth
Labyrinth of Passion
The Lacemaker
The Ladies' Man
Lady and the Tramp
Lady Beware
Lady Chatterley's Lover
Lady Dragon
The Lady Eve
Lady for a Day
The Lady from Shanghai
The Lady in Question
The Lady in White
Lady Jane
Lady Mobster
Lady on the Bus
Lady Sings the Blues
The Lady Vanishes
Ladyhawke
Ladykiller
L'Age D'Or
Laguna Heat
The Lair of the White Worm
Lake Consequence
Lambada
The Land Before Time
The Land Before Time 2: The Great Valley Adventure
The Land Before Time 3: The Time of the Great Giving
Land of the Pharaohs
Landslide
Lantern Hill
Lap Dancing
Laser Mission
Laserblast
Lassie, Come Home
Lassiter
Last Action Hero
The Last Boy Scout
Last Bullet
The Last Butterfly
Last Dance
The Last Days of Chez Nous
Last Days of Pompeii
The Last Detail
The Last Emperor

Last Exit to Brooklyn
The Last Fling
The Last Hit
The Last Hour
Last House on the Left
Last Hurrah
Last Light
The Last Metro
The Last of England
The Last of His Tribe
Last of the Clintons
The Last of the Finest
The Last of the Mohicans
Last of the Red Hot Lovers
The Last Picture Show
The Last Radio Station
Last Resort
The Last Riders
Last Rites
The Last Seduction
The Last Starfighter
Last Tango in Paris
The Last Temptation of Christ
The Last Time I Saw Paris
Last Time Out
The Last Tycoon
The Last Unicorn
The Last Voyage
The Last Waltz
The Last Warrior
Late for Dinner
The Late Show
Latino
Lauderdale
Laura
The Lavender Hill Mob
L'Avventura
Law of Desire
Law of the Sea
The Lawnmower Man
Lawnmower Man 2: Beyond Cyberspace
Lawrence of Arabia
Le Boucher
Le Chat
Le Complot
Le Crabe Tambour
Le Grand Chemin
Le Mans
Leader of the Band
A League of Their Own
Lean on Me
Leap of Faith
Leather Jackets
Leatherface: The Texas Chainsaw Massacre 3
Leave It to the Marines
Leaving Las Vegas
Leaving Normal
Legacy of Lies
Legal Eagles
Legend
The Legend of Hell House
The Legend of Hillbilly John
The Legend of Sleepy Hollow
The Legend of Wolf Mountain
Legends of the Fall
Legion of Iron
The Lemon Drop Kid
The Lemon Sisters
Lena's Holiday
Leningrad Cowboys Go America
Lenny
Lensman
Leolo
Leonard Part 6
The Leopard Man
Leprechaun
Leprechaun 2
Leprechaun 3
Les Biches
Les Comperes
Les Girls
Les Miserables
Less Than Zero

Let Him Have It
Let It Be
Let It Ride
L'Etat Sauvage
Lethal Ninja
Lethal Weapon
Lethal Weapon 2
Lethal Weapon 3
Lethal Woman
Let's Dance
Let's Get Harry
The Letter
Letter from an Unknown Woman
Letter to Brezhnev
A Letter to Three Wives
Leviathan
Liar's Edge
Libeled Lady
License to Drive
License to Kill
Liebestraum
The Life and Death of Colonel Blimp
Life & Times of Judge Roy Bean
A Life in the Theater
Life Is Sweet
The Life of Emile Zola
Life Stinks
Life with Mikey
Lifeboat
Lifeforce
Lifepod
The Lift
The Light in the Jungle
Light of Day
Light Sleeper
Light Years
Lightning Bill
Lightning Jack
Lightning Over Water
Like Father, Like Son
Like Water for Chocolate
Lily in Love
Limelight
Limit Up
The Linguini Incident
The Lion Has Wings
The Lion in Winter
Lionheart
Lipstick
Lipstick Camera
Liquid Sky
Listen to Me
Lisztomania
Little Annie Rooney
Little Big League
Little Big Man
Little Buddha
Little Darlings
Little Dorrit, Film 1: Nobody's Fault
Little Dorrit, Film 2: Little Dorrit's Story
The Little Drummer Girl
The Little Foxes
Little Giants
The Little Girl Who Lives Down the Lane
The Little Mermaid
Little Monsters
Little Nemo: Adventures in Slumberland
A Little Night Music
Little Nikita
Little Ninjas
Little Odessa
The Little Prince
The Little Princess
A Little Princess
The Little Rascals
Little Red Riding Hood
A Little Romance
Little Shop of Horrors
Little Sweetheart
The Little Theatre of Jean Renoir
The Little Thief
Little Treasure
Little Vegas
Little Vera
Little Women
The Littlest Viking
Live and Let Die
Live Nude Girls
The Living Daylights
Living Free
Living in Oblivion
Loan Shark
Lobster Man from Mars
Local Hero
Lock 'n' Load
Logan's Run
Lola Montes
Lolita
London Kills Me
Lone Justice
The Lone Runner
Lone Wolf McQuade
Lonely Are the Brave
The Lonely Guy
The Lonely Lady
Lonesome Dove
Long Day's Journey into Night
Long Gone
The Long Goodbye
The Long, Long Trailer
The Long Riders
The Long Voyage Home
The Long Walk Home
The Longest Day
The Longest Drive
The Longest Yard
Look Back in Anger
Look Who's Laughing
Look Who's Talking
Look Who's Talking Now
Look Who's Talking, Too
Looker
Looking for Miracles
Looking for Mr. Goodbar
Loose Cannons
Lord of Illusions
Lord of the Flies
The Lords of Discipline
The Lords of Flatbush
Lorenzo's Oil
Losin' It
Lost Angels
The Lost Boys
The Lost Continent
Lost Horizon
Lost in America
Lost in Yonkers
The Lost Patrol
The Lost Platoon
Lost Squadron
The Lost Weekend
The Lost World
Love
Love Affair
Love Among the Ruins
Love and a .45
Love and Death
Love and Hate: A Marriage Made in Hell
Love and Human Remains
Love at First Bite
Love at Large
Love at Stake
The Love Bug
Love Crimes
Love Field
Love Finds Andy Hardy
Love from a Stranger
The Love Goddesses
Love Happy
Love Is a Gun
Love Is a Many-Splendored Thing
Love Kills
Love Letters
Love, Lies and Murder
Love Matters
Love Me or Leave Me
Love Meetings
Love or Money?
Love Potion 9
Love Story
Love with the Proper Stranger
The Loved One
Lovely to Look At
The Lover
Loverboy
Lovers' Lovers
Lovesick
Loving You
A Low Down Dirty Shame
Lower Level
Lucky Luke: The Ballad of the Daltons
Lucky Me
Lucky Stiff
Lucy and Desi: Before the Laughter
Lunatics: A Love Story
Lurking Fear
Lust for a Vampire
Lust for Life
Lust in the Dust
The Lusty Men
Luv
Lydia
M
M. Butterfly
Mac
Mac and Me
Macao
Macaroni
MacArthur
MacArthur's Children
Macbeth
Mack the Knife
MacKenna's Gold
Mad About You
Mad at the Moon
Mad Dog and Glory
Mad Love
Mad Max
Mad Max: Beyond Thunderdome
Mad Miss Manton
Madame Bovary
Madame Curie
Madame Sousatzka
The Maddening
Made in America
Made in Heaven
Made in USA
Mademoiselle Fifi
Madhouse
The Madness of King George
The Madwoman of Chaillot
Magdalene
Magic
The Magic Christian
The Magic Flute
Magic Kid
Magic Kid 2
The Magic Voyage
Magical Mystery Tour
The Magician
The Magnificent Ambersons
The Magnificent Seven
Magnum Force
The Mahabharata
Mahogany
The Maid
Maid to Order
Major League
Major League 2
Major Payne
Making Mr. Right
The Makioka Sisters
Malarek
Malcolm
Malcolm X
Malice
Malicious
Mallrats
Malone
The Maltese Falcon
Mama, There's a Man in Your Bed
The Mambo Kings
Mame
Man Bait
A Man Called Horse
A Man Called Sarge
Man Facing Southeast
A Man for All Seasons
Man from Cairo
The Man from Snowy River
Man from Utah
A Man in Love
The Man in the Gray Flannel Suit
The Man Inside
Man of a Thousand Faces
Man of Flowers
Man of La Mancha
A Man of No Importance
Man of the House
Man on Fire
Man Outside
Man Trouble
The Man Who Came to Dinner
The Man Who Could Work Miracles
The Man Who Fell to Earth
The Man Who Knew Too Much
The Man Who Loved Women
The Man Who Shot Liberty Valance
The Man Who Would Be King
The Man with the Golden Gun
The Man with Two Brains
The Man Without a Face
The Manchurian Candidate
Mandingo
The Mangler
Manhattan
Manhattan Melodrama
Manhattan Murder Mystery
The Manhattan Project
Manhunt
Manhunt in the African Jungle
Manhunt of Mystery Island
Manhunter
Maniac Cop 2
The Manitou
Mannequin
Mannequin 2: On the Move
Manon of the Spring
Man's Best Friend
Marat/Sade
Marathon Man
March of the Wooden Soldiers
Marie Antoinette
Marius
Mark of Zorro
Marked for Death
Marked for Murder
Marked Woman
Marnie
Marooned
Married to It
Married to the Mob
The Marrying Man
Martial Law 2: Undercover
Martial Outlaw
Martians Go Home!
Martin
Marty
The Marx Brothers in a Nutshell
Mary of Scotland
Mary Poppins
Mary Reilly
Mary Shelley's Frankenstein
M*A*S*H
M*A*S*H: Goodbye, Farewell & Amen
The Mask
Mask
Mask of the Dragon
Masks of Death
Masque of the Red Death
Masque of the Red Death/ Premature Burial
Masquerade
Mass Appeal
Massive Retaliation
The Master of Ballantrae
The Masters of Menace
Masters of the Universe
Matador
The Matchmaker
Matewan
Matinee
Maurice
Mausoleum
Maverick
Max Dugan Returns
Max Headroom, the Original Story
Maxie
Maximum Force
Maximum Overdrive
Maximum Security
May Fools
May Wine
Mayerling
Maytime
McCabe & Mrs. Miller
The McConnell Story
McLintock!
McQ
McVicar
Me and Him
Me and the Kid
Mean Season
Mean Streets
Meatballs
Meatballs 2
The Mechanic
Mediterraneo
Meet John Doe
Meet Me in Las Vegas
Meet Me in St. Louis
Meet the Hollowheads
Meeting Venus
Mein Kampf: Hitler's Rise and Fall
Melvin and Howard
Memoirs of an Invisible Man
Memorial Valley Massacre
Memories of Me
Memphis
Memphis Belle
Men Are Not Gods
Men at Work
Men Don't Leave
Men of Respect
Men of War
Menace II Society
The Men's Club
Mercenary Fighters
Meridian: Kiss of the Beast
Mermaids
The Merry Widow
Messenger of Death
Metalstorm: The Destruction of Jared Syn
Meteor
The Meteor Man
Metropolis
Metropolitan
MGM: When the Lion Roars
Miami Blues
Miami Rhapsody
Miami Vice
Miami Vice 2: The Prodigal Son
Mickey One
Mickey's Christmas Carol
Micki & Maude
Midnight
Midnight Cabaret
A Midnight Clear
Midnight Confessions
Midnight Cop

Midnight Cowboy
Midnight Crossing
Midnight Express
Midnight Run
Midnight Tease
Midway
Mighty Aphrodite
The Mighty Ducks
Mighty Joe Young
The Mighty Quinn
The Milagro Beanfield War
Mildred Pierce
Miles from Home
Milky Way
The Milky Way
Millenium
Miller's Crossing
Million Dollar Haul
Million Dollar Mystery
Mindfield
Mindwarp
Ministry of Vengeance
Minnesota Clay
A Minor Miracle
The Miracle
Miracle Beach
Miracle in Milan
Miracle in Rome
Miracle in the Wilderness
Miracle Mile
Miracle of Our Lady of Fatima
Miracle on 34th Street
Miracles
The Mirror Crack'd
Mirror, Mirror
Mirror, Mirror 2: Raven Dance
Mischief
Misery
The Misfits
Miss Firecracker
Ms. 45
Miss Right
Miss Sadie Thompson
Missing
Missing in Action
Missing in Action 2: The Beginning
The Mission
Mission Batangas
Mission Galactica: The Cylon Attack
Mission Manila
Mission of Justice
Mississippi Burning
Mississippi Masala
Mississippi Mermaid
Mrs. Doubtfire
Mrs. Miniver
Mrs. Parker and the Vicious Circle
Mrs. Soffel
Mr. Ace
Mr. & Mrs. Bridge
Mr. & Mrs. Loving
Mr. & Mrs. Smith
Mr. Arkadin
Mr. Baseball
Mr. Blandings Builds His Dream House
Mr. Deeds Goes to Town
Mr. Destiny
Mr. Holland's Opus
Mr. Hulot's Holiday
Mr. Jones
Mr. Lucky
Mr. Mom
Mr. North
Mr. Robinson Crusoe
Mr. Saturday Night
Mr. Skeffington
Mr. Smith Goes to Washington
Mr. Walkie Talkie
Mr. Wonderful
Mr. Write
Mistress
Mixed Nuts

Mo' Better Blues
Mo' Money
Mob Story
Mob War
Mobsters
Moby Dick
Model by Day
Modern Girls
Modern Romance
Modern Times
The Moderns
Mom
Mom and Dad Save the World
Mommie Dearest
Mon Oncle
Mona Lisa
Money for Nothing
The Money Pit
Money to Burn
Money Train
Monkey Business
Monkey Shines
Monkey Trouble
Monolith
Monsieur Hire
Monsieur Verdoux
The Monster Club
Monster High
Monster in a Box
The Monster Squad
Monterey Pop
A Month by the Lake
A Month in the Country
Monty Python and the Holy Grail
Monty Python Live at the Hollywood Bowl
Monty Python's Flying Circus
Monty Python's Life of Brian
Monty Python's Parrot Sketch Not Included
Monty Python's The Meaning of Life
Moon 44
The Moon Is Blue
Moon over Parador
Moonfleet
Moonlight and Valentino
Moonlighting
Moonraker
Moonrise
Moonstruck
Moontrap
More American Graffiti
More! Police Squad
The More the Merrier
Morgan!
Morgan Stewart's Coming Home
Morgan the Pirate
The Morning After
Morning Glory
Morocco
Mortal Danger
Mortal Sins
Mortal Thoughts
Mortuary Academy
Moscow Does Not Believe in Tears
Moscow on the Hudson
The Mosquito Coast
Motel Hell
Mother
Mother's Boys
Motor Patrol
Moulin Rouge
The Mountain Men
Mountains of the Moon
Moving
Moving Violation
Moving Violations
Mozart: A Childhood Chronicle
Much Ado about Nothing
Mulholland Falls
The Mummy
The Muppet Movie
The Muppets Take Manhattan

Murder by Death
Murder by Numbers
Murder In the First
Murder, My Sweet
Murder on the Bayou
Murder on the Orient Express
Murder One
Murder Story
Murderous Vision
Muriel's Wedding
Murmur of the Heart
Murphy's Fault
Murphy's Law
Murphy's Romance
Muscle Beach Party
Music Box
The Music Lovers
The Music Man
The Music of Chance
The Music Teacher
Mutant
Mutant Species
Mute Witness
The Mutilator
Mutiny on the Bounty
My American Cousin
My Beautiful Laundrette
My Best Girl
My Bloody Valentine
My Blue Heaven
My Boyfriend's Back
My Chauffeur
My Darling Clementine
My Demon Lover
My Dinner with Andre
My Dog Shep
My Fair Lady
My Family
My Father the Hero
My Favorite Brunette
My Favorite Wife
My Favorite Year
My Friend Irma
My Girl
My Girl 2
My Heroes Have Always Been Cowboys
My Left Foot
My Life
My Life as a Dog
My Little Chickadee
My Little Girl
My Mom's a Werewolf
My Name is Ivan
My Neighbor Totoro
My New Gun
My New Partner
My Night at Maud's
My Own Private Idaho
My Samurai
My Science Project
My Stepmother Is an Alien
My Summer Story
My Tutor
My Wonderful Life
Mysterious Island
Mystery of the Wax Museum
Mystery Science Theater 3000: The Movie
Mystery Train
Mystic Pizza
Nadine
Nails
Naked
The Naked Gun: From the Files of Police Squad
Naked Gun 33 1/3: The Final Insult
Naked Gun 2 1/2: The Smell of Fear
Naked in New York
Naked Jungle
Naked Kiss
The Naked Prey
The Name of the Rose
Napoleon

Narrow Margin
Nashville
Nasty Hero
Nate and Hayes
National Lampoon's Animal House
National Lampoon's Christmas Vacation
National Lampoon's Class Reunion
National Lampoon's European Vacation
National Lampoon's Last Resort
National Lampoon's Loaded Weapon 1
National Lampoon's Senior Trip
National Lampoon's Vacation
National Velvet
Native Son
The Natural
Natural Born Killers
Nature of the Beast
Naughty Marietta
Navy SEALS
Nazarin
Near Dark
Near Misses
'Neath Canadian Skies
Necessary Roughness
Necromancer: Satan's Servant
Needful Things
Neighbors
Nemesis
The Neon Empire
Neptune's Daughter
The Net
Netherworld
Network
Nevada Smith
Never a Dull Moment
Never Cry Wolf
Never Give a Sucker an Even Break
Never on Tuesday
Never Say Die
Never Say Never Again
Never So Few
Never Talk to Strangers
Never Too Young to Die
The NeverEnding Story
NeverEnding Story 2: The Next Chapter
The New Adventures of Pippi Longstocking
The New Age
The New Centurions
New Crime City: Los Angeles 2020
New Eden
New Jack City
New Jersey Drive
The New Kids
A New Life
New York, New York
New York Stories
News at Eleven
Newsfront
The Next Karate Kid
Next of Kin
Niagara
Nicholas and Alexandra
Night and the City
Night Angel
A Night at the Opera
Night Breed
Night Caller from Outer Space
Night Eyes
Night Game
Night Games
A Night in the Life of Jimmy Reardon
Night Life
Night Life in Reno
'night, Mother
Night Nurse
Night of the Creeps

Night of the Cyclone
Night of the Demons
Night of the Demons 2
Night of the Fox
Night of the Generals
The Night of the Hunter
The Night of the Iguana
Night of the Laughing Dead
Night of the Living Dead
Night of the Living Dead, 25th Anniversary Documentary
Night of the Running Man
Night of the Sharks
Night of the Warrior
Night of the Wilding
Night on Earth
Night Patrol
The Night Porter
Night Rhythms
Night Shift
Night Siege Project: Shadowchaser 2
A Night to Remember
The Night Train to Kathmandu
Night Train to Venice
Night Zoo
The Nightcomers
Nightflyers
Nighthawks
The Nightingale
Nightlife
The Nightman
The Nightmare Before Christmas
A Nightmare on Elm Street
A Nightmare on Elm Street 2: Freddy's Revenge
A Nightmare on Elm Street 3: Dream Warriors
A Nightmare on Elm Street 4: Dream Master
A Nightmare on Elm Street 5: Dream Child
Nightscare
Nightwing
Nightwish
Nina Takes a Lover
9 1/2 Ninjas
9 1/2 Weeks
Nine Lives of Fritz the Cat
Nine Months
9 to 5
976-EVIL
1900
1941
1969
1984
Ninja Brothers of Blood
Ninja Turf
Ninotchka
The Ninth Configuration
Nixon
No Escape
No Escape, No Return
No Holds Barred
No Man of Her Own
No Man's Land
No Mercy
No Retreat, No Surrender
No Secrets
No Small Affair
No Time for Sergeants
No Way Out
Nobody's Fool
Nobody's Perfect
Nocturna
Nocturne
Noises Off
Nomads
None But the Brave
Norma Rae
North
North by Northwest
North Dallas Forty
North of the Border
North to Alaska

Nosferatu
Nostradamus
Not Without My Daughter
Nothing But Trouble
Nothing in Common
Nothing Personal
Nothing Sacred
Notorious
Now and Forever
Now and Then
Now, Voyager
Nowhere to Run
The Nude Bomb
Nudo di Donna
Nukie
Nuns on the Run
The Nun's Story
The Nutcracker Prince
Nuts
The Nutt House
The Nutty Professor
Nyoka and the Tigermen
O Pioneers!
The Object of Beauty
Object of Obsession
The Obsessed
Obsessed
Obsession
The Occult Experience
Ocean's 11
Oceans of Fire
Octagon
Octopussy
The Odd Couple
Odd Man Out
The Odessa File
Of Human Bondage
Of Mice and Men
Off Beat
Off Limits
An Officer and a Gentleman
The Official Story
The Offspring
Oh, God!
Oh, God! You Devil
Oh, What a Night
Oklahoma!
Old Boyfriends
Old Explorers
Old Gringo
Old Yeller
Oldest Profession
Oleanna
Oliver!
Oliver Twist
Olivier, Olivier
Omega Man
The Omen
On a Clear Day You Can See Forever
On Dangerous Ground
On Deadly Ground
On Golden Pond
On Her Majesty's Secret Service
On Moonlight Bay
On the Beach
On the Town
On the Waterfront
Onassis
Once Around
Once Bitten
Once Upon a Forest
Once Upon a Honeymoon
Once Upon a Time in America
Once Upon a Time in the West
Once Were Warriors
The One and Only, Genuine, Original Family Band
One Crazy Summer
One Day in the Life of Ivan Denisovich
One-Eyed Jacks
One False Move
One Flew Over the Cuckoo's Nest
One from the Heart
One Good Cop
One Magic Christmas
One Man Force
One Man Out
One Man's Justice
One More Saturday Night
One Night of Love
One, Two, Three
The Onion Field
Only One Night
Only the Lonely
Only the Strong
Only the Valiant
Only When I Laugh
Only You
Open Fire
Opera do Malandro
Operation Dumbo Drop
Operation Golden Phoenix
Operation Haylift
Operation Petticoat
The Opponent
Opportunity Knocks
The Opposite Sex
Options
Orca
Orchestra Wives
Ordeal by Innocence
Ordinary People
Organized Crime & Triad Bureau
The Original Fabulous Adventures of Baron Munchausen
Orlando
Orphans
Orphans of the Storm
Oscar
Oscar's Greatest Moments: 1971-1991
The Osterman Weekend
Otello
Othello
Other People's Money
The Other Side of Midnight
Our Daily Bread
Our Gang Comedies
Our Hospitality
Our Man Flint
Our Town
Out Cold
Out for Justice
Out of Africa
Out of Bounds
Out of Control
Out of Sight, Out of Her Mind
Out of Sync
Out of the Blue
Out of the Body
Out of the Dark
Out of the Darkness
Out of the Past
Out of the Rain
The Out-of-Towners
Out on a Limb
Outbreak
The Outfit
Outland
The Outlaw
The Outlaw and His Wife
Outlaw Fury
Outlaw Gang
The Outlaw Josey Wales
Outrageous Fortune
Outside the Law
The Outsiders
Over the Hill
Over the Top
Overboard
The Owl and the Pussycat
The Ox-Bow Incident
Oxford Blues
Pacific Heights
The Package
The Pagemaster
Paid to Kill
Paint It Black
Paint Your Wagon
The Painted Stallion
The Pajama Game
Pajama Party
Pal Joey
Pale Blood
Pale Rider
The Paleface
The Palermo Connection
The Palm Beach Story
Palm Springs Weekend
The Pamela Principle
Panic in Needle Park
Panic in the Streets
The Paper
The Paper Chase
Paper Moon
A Paper Wedding
The Paperboy
Paperhouse
Papillon
Parade
The Paradine Case
Paradise
Paradise Alley
Paramedics
Parasite
Pardon Mon Affaire
The Parent Trap
Parenthood
Parents
Paris, Texas
Paris Trout
Party Girl
Party Incorporated
Party Plane
Pascali's Island
Pass the Ammo
A Passage to India
Passenger 57
Passion Fish
Passion in Paradise
Past Midnight
Past Tense
Past the Bleachers
Pastime
Pat and Mike
Pat Garrett & Billy the Kid
Paternity
Paths of Glory
The Patriot
Patti Rocks
Patton
Patty Hearst
Pauline at the Beach
The Pawnbroker
Payback
Payoff
P.C.U.
Peacemaker
The Pebble and the Penguin
Peck's Bad Boy
Pecos Kid
Pee Wee's Big Adventure
Peeping Tom
Peggy Sue Got Married
The Pelican Brief
Pelle the Conqueror
Pendulum
Penn and Teller Get Killed
Pennies From Heaven
Penny Serenade
Pentathlon
Penthouse
The People Under the Stairs
People's Choice
Perfect
The Perfect Bride
Perfect Victims
The Perfect Weapon
Perfect Witness
A Perfect World
Perfectly Normal
Performance
The Perils of Gwendoline
Perils of the Darkest Jungle
Permanent Record
Personal Services
Personals
Persuasion
Pet Sematary
Pet Sematary 2
Pete Kelly's Blues
Pete Townshend: White City
Peter Pan
Peter's Friends
Pete's Dragon
Peyton Place
Phantasm
Phantasm II
Phantasm III: Lord of the Dead
Phantom of Liberty
Phantom of the Mall: Eric's Revenge
The Phantom of the Opera
Phantom of the Paradise
Phase 4
Philadelphia
The Philadelphia Experiment
Philadelphia Experiment 2
The Philadelphia Story
Physical Evidence
The Piano
The Piano Lesson
The Pick-Up Artist
The Pickle
Picnic
Picture Bride
Picture of Dorian Gray
Pier 23
Pierrot le Fou
Pillow Talk
Pin
Pin-Up Girl
Ping Pong
Pink Cadillac
Pink Flamingos
Pink Floyd: The Wall
Pink Nights
The Pink Panther
The Pink Panther Strikes Again
Pinocchio
Pippin
Piranha 2: The Spawning
The Pirate
The Pirates of Penzance
The Pit & the Pendulum
Pitfall
P.K. and the Kid
A Place in the Sun
Places in the Heart
The Plainsman
Plan 9 from Outer Space
Planes, Trains & Automobiles
Planet of the Apes
Platoon
Platoon Leader
Play It Again, Sam
Play Misty for Me
The Player
Playing Away
Playing for Keeps
Playroom
Plaza Suite
Please Don't Eat the Daisies
Pleasure
Pledge Night
Plenty
Pocketful of Miracles
Poetic Justice
The Point
Point Break
Point of Impact
Point of No Return
The Pointsman
Poison Ivy 2: Lily
The Polar Bear King
Police Academy
Police Academy 2: Their First Assignment
Police Academy 3: Back in Training
Police Academy 4: Citizens on Patrol
Police Academy 5: Assignment Miami Beach
Police Academy 6: City Under Siege
Police Court
Police Squad! Help Wanted!
Pollyanna
Poltergeist
Poltergeist 2: The Other Side
Poltergeist 3
Polyester
Popcorn
The Pope Must Diet
The Pope of Greenwich Village
Popeye
Porcile
Pork Chop Hill
Porky's
Porky's 2: The Next Day
Porky's Revenge
Portfolio
The Portrait
Portrait of Jennie
Portraits of a Killer
The Poseidon Adventure
Posse
The Possessed
Possessed by the Night
Postcards from the Edge
The Postman Always Rings Twice
The P.O.W. Escape
Power
The Power of One
Power, Passion & Murder
Prancer
Pray TV
Prayer for the Dying
Prayer of the Rollerboys
Pre-Madonnas: Rebels Without a Clue
Predator
Predator 2
Prehysteria
Prelude to a Kiss
Premature Burial
The Presidio
Presumed Guilty
Presumed Innocent
Pretty Baby
Pretty in Pink
Pretty Woman
Prettykill
Priceless Beauty
Prick Up Your Ears
Pride and Prejudice
The Pride of the Yankees
Primary Motive
Prime Evil
The Prince and the Pauper
The Prince and the Showgirl
Prince Brat and the Whipping Boy
Prince of Bel Air
Prince of Darkness
Prince of Pennsylvania
Prince of the City
The Prince of Tides
Princes in Exile
The Princess and the Pea
The Princess and the Pirate
The Princess Bride
Princess Caraboo
Princess Tam Tam
The Principal
Prison
The Prisoner: Arrival
Prisoner in the Middle
Prisoner of Rio
Prisoner of Second Avenue
Prisoner of Zenda
Private Benjamin

The Private Eyes
Private Hell 36
Private Lessons
The Private Life of Henry VIII
The Private Life of Sherlock Holmes
Private Lives
A Private Matter
Private Resort
Private School
Private Wars
The Prizefighter and the Lady
Prizzi's Honor
Problem Child
Problem Child 2
The Prodigal
Prodigal Boxer: The Kick of Death
The Producers
The Professional
The Professionals
Professionals
The Program
Project A-ko
Project: Alien
Project: Genesis
Project Shadowchaser 3000
Project X
Prom Night
Prom Night 3: The Last Kiss
The Promise
Promised a Miracle
Promised Land
Proof
The Prophecy
Prospero's Books
Protector
Protocol
Prototype
Prototype X29A
Psych-Out
Psycho
Psycho 2
Psycho 3
Psycho 4: The Beginning
PT 109
Public Enemy
The Public Eye
Pulp Fiction
Pulse
Pump Up the Volume
Pumping Iron
Pumping Iron 2: The Women
Pumpkinhead
Pumpkinhead 2: Blood Wings
Punchline
The Punisher
Punk Vacation
Puppet Master
Puppet Master 2
Puppet Master 3: Toulon's Revenge
Puppet Master 5: The Final Chapter
The Puppet Masters
The Puppetoon Movie
Pure Country
A Pure Formality
Pure Luck
Purgatory
Purple People Eater
Purple Rain
The Purple Rose of Cairo
The Pursuit of D.B. Cooper
Pushed to the Limit
Pushing Hands
Pygmalion
A Pyromaniac's Love Story
Python Wolf
Q & A
QB VII
Quackser Fortune Has a Cousin in the Bronx
Quadrophenia
Quality Street
Quatermass 2
Queen Christina
Queen Kelly
Queen Margot
Queen of Hearts
The Queen of Spades
Queen of the Amazons
Queens Logic
The Quest
Quest for Fire
Quest for the Mighty Sword
The Quick and the Dead
Quick Change
Quick, Let's Get Married
Quicksand: No Escape
Quicksilver
Quiet Cool
The Quiet Earth
The Quiet Man
Quiet Thunder
Quigley Down Under
Quiz Show
Quo Vadis
Rabbit Test
Rabid Grannies
Race for Life
Race for Your Life, Charlie Brown
Rachel and the Stranger
Rachel River
Racing with the Moon
The Racket
Rad
Radar Men from the Moon
Radar Secret Service
Radio Days
Radio Flyer
Radio Inside
Radioactive Dreams
Radioland Murders
The Raffle
Rage and Honor
A Rage in Harlem
Raggedy Man
Raging Bull
Ragtime
Raiders of the Lost Ark
Railroaded
The Railway Station Man
The Rain Killer
Rain Man
Rainbow
The Rainbow
The Rainmaker
Raintree County
Raise the Red Lantern
Raise the Titanic
A Raisin in the Sun
Raising Arizona
Raising Cain
Rambling Rose
Rambo: First Blood, Part 2
Rambo 3
Rampage
Ran
Rancho Notorious
Rangeland Empire
Rapa Nui
Rapid Fire
The Rapture
Rapunzel
Rascal Dazzle
Rashomon
Ratings Game
The Raven
Raw Courage
Raw Deal
Raw Justice
Raw Nerve
Rawhead Rex
Rawhide Romance
The Razor's Edge
Re-Animator
Ready to Wear
The Real Buddy Holly Story
Real Bullets
Real Genius
The Real McCoy
Real Men
Reality Bites
Rear Window
Reason to Die
Rebecca
Rebecca of Sunnybrook Farm
Rebel
Rebel Storm
Rebel Without a Cause
Reckless
Recruits
The Red and the White
The Red Balloon
Red Beard
Red Blooded American Girl
Red Dawn
Red Desert
Red Headed Stranger
Red Heat
Red Hot
Red Kiss
Red Line 7000
The Red Menace
The Red Pony
Red River
Red Rock Outlaw
Red Rock West
Red Scorpion
Red Scorpion 2
Red Shoe Diaries
Red Shoe Diaries 2: Double Dare
Red Shoe Diaries 3: Another Woman's Lipstick
The Red Shoes
Red Sonja
Red Surf
Red Tent
Red, White & Busted
Reds
The Ref
The Reflecting Skin
Reflections in the Dark
Reform School Girls
Regarding Henry
Reilly: Ace of Spies
The Reincarnation of Peter Proud
The Rejuvenator
Relentless
Relentless 2: Dead On
Relentless 4
The Reluctant Debutante
The Remains of the Day
Rembrandt
Remo Williams: The Adventure Begins
Remote Control
Renaissance Man
Rendez-vous
Renegade Girl
Renegades
Rent-A-Cop
Rent-A-Kid
Rented Lips
Repentance
Repo Man
Repossessed
Repulsion
Requiem for Dominic
The Rescue
Rescue Me
The Rescuers
The Rescuers Down Under
Reservoir Dogs
The Restless Breed
Retribution
Return
Return of Captain Invincible
Return of Frank James
The Return of Jafar
The Return of Martin Guerre
The Return of Spinal Tap
The Return of Swamp Thing
Return of the Dragon
Return of the Fly
Return of the Jedi
Return of the Killer Tomatoes!
Return of the Living Dead
Return of the Living Dead 2
Return of the Living Dead 3
The Return of the Musketeers
Return of the Pink Panther
Return of the Vampire
Return to Lonesome Dove
Return to Oz
Return to Snowy River
Return to the Blue Lagoon
Return to Two Moon Junction
Reunion
Revenge
Revenge of the Creature
Revenge of the Nerds
Revenge of the Nerds 2: Nerds in Paradise
Revenge of the Pink Panther
Revenge of the Red Baron
Reversal of Fortune
Revolution
Rhapsody in August
Rhapsody in Blue
Rhinestone
Rich and Famous
Rich and Strange
Rich Girl
Rich in Love
Richard III
Richie Rich
Ricochet
Ride in the Whirlwind
Ride the High Country
Riders of the Storm
Riding Speed
Riding the Edge
Riff Raff
The Right Stuff
Rikky and Pete
Rikyu
Rimfire
Ring of Fire
Ring of Fire 3: Lion Strike
Ring of Steel
Ringside
Rio Grande
Rio Lobo
The Rise and Fall of Legs Diamond
Rising Sun
Risky Business
Rita, Sue & Bob Too
The Ritz
The River
River of Death
River of No Return
The River Pirates
The River Rat
A River Runs Through It
The River Wild
River's Edge
Road House
The Road Killers
The Road to Hong Kong
The Road to Morocco
The Road to Singapore
The Road to Utopia
The Road to Wellville
The Road to Zanzibar
The Road Warrior
Roads to the South
Roadside Prophets
Roaring City
Roaring Roads
The Roaring Twenties
Rob Roy
The Robe
Robin and Marian
Robin and the 7 Hoods
Robin Hood
Robin Hood: Prince of Thieves
Robinson Crusoe of Clipper Island
Robinson Crusoe on Mars
RoboCop
RoboCop 2
RoboCop 3
RoboCop the Series: The Future of Law Enforcement
Robot Jox
Robot Monster
Robot Wars
Rocco and His Brothers
Rock-a-Doodle
Rock & Rule
Rock 'n' Roll High School Forever
The Rocketeer
Rocketship X-M
Rockula
Rockwell: A Legend of the Wild West
Rocky
Rocky 2
Rocky 3
Rocky 4
Rocky 5
The Rocky Horror Picture Show
Rodan
Roe vs. Wade
Roger & Me
Rollerball
Rollercoaster
Rolling Home
Rolling Thunder
Rolling Vengeance
Roman Holiday
Romance on the High Seas
Romance with a Double Bass
Romancing the Stone
Rome Adventure
Romeo and Juliet
Romeo Is Bleeding
Romero
Rooftops
The Rookie
Rookie of the Year
Room Service
A Room with a View
Roommates
Rooster Cogburn
Rope
Rosalie Goes Shopping
The Rosary Murders
The Rose
The Rose Garden
Rose Marie
The Rose Tattoo
Rosebud Beach Hotel
Roseland
Rosemary's Baby
Rosencrantz & Guildenstern Are Dead
Roswell: The U.F.O. Cover-Up
R.O.T.O.R.
Rough Cut
Round Midnight
Round Trip to Heaven
The Rousters
Rover Dangerfield
Roxanne
Royal Wedding
R.S.V.P.
Rubin & Ed
Ruby
Ruby in Paradise
Rude Awakening
Rudolph the Red-Nosed Reindeer
Rudy
Rudyard Kipling's The Jungle Book
The Rules of the Game
The Ruling Class
Rumble Fish
Rumble in the Bronx
The Rumor Mill
Rumpelstiltskin
Run

Run of the Arrow
The Run of the Country
Runaway
Runaway Train
The Runestone
Running Away
Running Brave
Running Free
The Running Man
Running Mates
Running on Empty
Running Out of Luck
Running Scared
Running Wild
Rush Week
The Russia House
Russkies
Rustler's Paradise
Rustler's Rhapsody
Ruthless People
Ryan's Daughter
Sabotage
Saboteur
Sabrina
The Sacrifice
Sadie Thompson
Safe
Safe Passage
Sagebrush Trail
Sahara
Saigon Commandos
The Sailor Who Fell from Grace with the Sea
St. Elmo's Fire
The Saint of Fort Washington
Saints and Sinners
Salaam Bombay!
Salem's Lot
Salo, or the 120 Days of Sodom
Salome's Last Dance
Salsa
Salt of the Earth
Salvador
Same Time, Next Year
Sammy & Rosie Get Laid
Samson and Delilah
Samurai 1: Musashi Miyamoto
Samurai 2: Duel at Ichijoji Temple
Samurai 3: Duel at Ganryu Island
San Francisco
The Sand Pebbles
The Sandlot
Sands of Iwo Jima
Sanjuro
Sansho the Bailiff
Santa Claus Is Coming to Town
Santa Claus: The Movie
Santa Sangre
Saps at Sea
Sarafina!
Sarah, Plain and Tall
Satisfaction
Saturday Night Fever
Saturn 3
Savage Beach
Savage Drums
Savage Land
Savage Streets
Savannah Smiles
Save Me
Save the Tiger
Saving Grace
Sawdust & Tinsel
Say Anything
Say Yes!
Scandal
Scandal in a Small Town
Scandalous
Scanner Cop
Scanners
Scanners 2: The New Order
Scanners 3: The Takeover
Scaramouche
Scared Stiff
Scarface
The Scarlet Letter
The Scarlet Pimpernel
The Scars of Dracula
Scavengers
Scenes from a Mall
Scenes from the Class Struggle in Beverly Hills
Scenes from the Goldmine
Scent of a Woman
The Scent of Green Papaya
Schindler's List
School Daze
School Ties
Scorchers
Scorned
Scorpion
Scotland Yard Inspector
Scream for Help
Screamers
Screen Test
Scrooge
Scrooged
Sea Chase
The Sea Hawk
Sea of Love
Search and Destroy
The Searchers
Searching for Bobby Fischer
Second Best
Second Chance
Second Chorus
Second Sight
Second Victory
Secret Admirer
The Secret Agent
The Secret Garden
Secret Honor
The Secret Life of Walter Mitty
The Secret of My Success
The Secret of NIMH
The Secret of Roan Inish
The Secret Policeman's Other Ball
Secret Policeman's Private Parts
The Secret Rapture
The Secretary
The Seduction of Joe Tynan
See No Evil
See No Evil, Hear No Evil
See You in the Morning
Seems Like Old Times
Seize the Day
Self-Defense
Semi-Tough
The Sender
Sensation
Sense and Sensibility
Separate But Equal
Separate Ways
September
September Affair
Sgt. Bilko
Sgt. Pepper's Lonely Hearts Club Band
Serial
Serial Mom
The Serpent and the Rainbow
The Serpent of Death
Serpico
Sesame Street Presents: Follow That Bird
The Set-Up
Seven
Seven Beauties
Seven Brides for Seven Brothers
Seven Days in May
7 Faces of Dr. Lao
Seven Hours to Judgment
The Seven-Per-Cent Solution
Seven Samurai
Seven Sinners
The Seven-Ups
The Seven Year Itch
1776
The Seventh Coin
The Seventh Seal
The Seventh Sign
The Seventh Victim
The Seventh Voyage of Sinbad
Sex and the Single Girl
sex, lies and videotape
Sex on the Run
Sexual Response
The Shadow
Shadow Force
The Shadow Man
Shadow of a Doubt
Shadow of Chikara
Shadow of China
Shadow of the Wolf
Shadowhunter
Shadowlands
Shadows and Fog
Shadows in the Storm
Shadowzone
Shag: The Movie
The Shaggy Dog
Shakedown
Shaker Run
Shakes the Clown
The Shakiest Gun in the West
Shall We Dance
Shame
Shampoo
Shamus
Shane
The Shanghai Gesture
Shanghai Surprise
Shanghai Triad
Sharky's Machine
Shattered
Shattered Image
The Shawshank Redemption
She-Devil
She Done Him Wrong
She Wore a Yellow Ribbon
Sheena
Shelley Duvall's Bedtime Stories
The Sheltering Sky
Shenandoah
Shep Comes Home
Sherlock Holmes and the Secret Weapon
Sherlock Holmes Faces Death
Sherlock Holmes: The Voice of Terror
She's Back
She's Gotta Have It
She's Having a Baby
She's Out of Control
The Shining
Ship of Fools
Shipwrecked
Shirley Valentine
Shock Corridor
Shock 'Em Dead
A Shock to the System
Shocker
The Shoes of the Fisherman
Shogun
Shogun Assassin
Shoot the Moon
Shoot the Piano Player
Shoot to Kill
Shootfighter: Fight to the Death
The Shooting
Shooting Elizabeth
The Shootist
The Shop Around the Corner
The Shop on Main Street
Short Circuit
Short Circuit 2
Short Cuts
Short Time
A Shot in the Dark
Shout
Shout at the Devil
The Show
Show Boat
Show Business
A Show of Force
Showdown
Showdown in Little Tokyo
The Shrieking
The Shrimp on the Barbie
Shrunken Heads
Shy People
Sibling Rivalry
The Sicilian
Sid & Nancy
Side Out
Sidekicks
The Siege of Firebase Gloria
Siegfried
Siesta
Signs of Life
The Silence
Silence Like Glass
The Silence of the Lambs
Silent Fall
Silent Hunter
Silent Movie
Silent Night, Deadly Night
Silent Night, Deadly Night 2
Silent Night, Deadly Night 3: Better Watch Out!
Silent Night, Deadly Night 4: Initiation
The Silent Partner
Silent Rage
Silent Running
Silent Tongue
Silk Degrees
Silk n' Sabotage
The Silk Road
Silk Stockings
Silkwood
Silver Bandit
Silver Bullet
Silver Streak
Silverado
Simba
Simple Men
A Simple Twist of Fate
Sinatra
Sinbad and the Eye of the Tiger
Sinbad of the Seven Seas
Sinbad, the Sailor
Since You Went Away
Sincerely Charlotte
Sincerely Yours
A Sinful Life
Sing
Singin' in the Rain
Single White Female
Singles
Sins of Jezebel
Sirens
Sirocco
Sister Act
Sister Act 2: Back in the Habit
Sister Kenny
Sister, Sister
The Sisterhood
Six Degrees of Separation
Six Weeks
Sixteen Candles
'68
Skeeter
Skeleton Coast
Sketch Artist
Sketch Artist 2: Hands That See
Ski Patrol
Ski School
Skin Art
Skin Deep
Skinner
Sky High
Sky Liner
Skyline
Slam Dunk Ernest
Slamdance
Slammer Girls
Slap Shot
Slapstick of Another Kind
Slaughter
Slaughter of the Innocents
Slaughterhouse Five
Slave Girls from Beyond Infinity
Slaves of New York
Sleep with Me
Sleepaway Camp 3: Teenage Wasteland
Sleeper
Sleeping Beauty
The Sleeping Car
Sleeping with the Enemy
Sleepless in Seattle
Sleepwalk
Sleepwalkers
Sleuth
The Slingshot
Slipping into Darkness
Slipstream
Sliver
The Slugger's Wife
Slugs
Slumber Party '57
Slumber Party Massacre 2
Small Change
Small Sacrifices
Smash Palace
Smile
Smiles of a Summer Night
Smithereens
Smoke
Smokescreen
Smokey and the Bandit
Smokey and the Bandit, Part 2
Smokey and the Bandit, Part 3
Smooth Talk
The Snapper
Sneakers
Sniper
Snoopy, Come Home
Snow White and the Seven Dwarfs
So Dear to My Heart
So I Married an Axe Murderer
Soapdish
S.O.B.
Social Error
Sodom and Gomorrah
Soft Deceit
The Soft Skin
Solar Crisis
Solar Force
Solarbabies
Solaris
Soldier of Orange
A Soldier's Story
Solomon and Sheba
Some Came Running
Some Kind of Hero
Some Kind of Wonderful
Some Like It Hot
Somebody Has to Shoot the Picture
Someone Behind the Door
Someone to Love
Someone to Watch Over Me
Something Special
Something to Sing About
Something to Talk About
Something Wicked This Way Comes
Something Wild
Sometimes They Come Back
Somewhere in Time
Sommersby
Son-in-Law
Son of Dracula
Son of Frankenstein
Son of Kong
The Son of Monte Cristo
Son of Paleface
Son of the Morning Star
Son of the Pink Panther
Son of the Sheik
The Song of Bernadette
Song of the Islands
A Song to Remember

Song Without End
Songwriter
Sonny Boy
Sons of Katie Elder
Sophie's Choice
Sorcerer
Sorority Babes in the Slimeball Bowl-A-Rama
Sorry, Wrong Number
S.O.S. Coast Guard
Soul Man
Soultaker
The Sound of Music
Sounder
Sourdough
South Central
South of Reno
South Pacific
Southern Comfort
Souvenir
Soylent Green
Space: 1999
Spaceballs
Spaced Invaders
Spacehunter: Adventures in the Forbidden Zone
Spaceways
The Spanish Main
Spanking the Monkey
Sparrows
Spartacus
The Spawning
Speaking Parts
A Special Day
The Specialist
Species
Spectre of the Rose
Speechless
Speed
Speed Zone
Spellbound
Spellcaster
Spetters
Spiders
Spies
Spies, Lies and Naked Thighs
Spies Like Us
Spike of Bensonhurst
The Spiral Staircase
Spirit of '76
Spirit of the Beehive
Spirit of the Eagle
The Spirit of West Point
Spite Marriage
Splash
Splendor in the Grass
Split Decisions
Splitting Heirs
The Spoilers
Spontaneous Combustion
Spookies
Spring Break
Springtime in the Rockies
Spy
Spy in Black
The Spy Who Came in from the Cold
The Spy Who Loved Me
Squanto: A Warrior's Tale
Square Dance
Square Dance Jubilee
The Squeeze
Squeeze Play
Squirm
Stacking
Stage Door Canteen
Stage Fright
Stage Struck
Stagecoach
Stakeout
Stalag 17
Stalin
Stalked
Stalking Danger
Stand and Deliver
Stand By Me

Stanley and Iris
Star!
The Star Chamber
Star Crash
Star 80
A Star is Born
Star of Midnight
Star Quest
Star Slammer
Star Trek: The Motion Picture
Star Trek 2: The Wrath of Khan
Star Trek 3: The Search for Spock
Star Trek 4: The Voyage Home
Star Trek 5: The Final Frontier
Star Trek: The Cage
Star Trek the Next Generation: Encounter at Farpoint
Star Wars
Starchaser: The Legend of Orin
Stardust Memories
Stargate
Starlight Hotel
Starman
Stars and Bars
Starting Over
State of Emergency
State of Grace
State of Siege
State of the Union
State of Things
Static
Stay Awake
Stay Hungry
Stay Tuned
Staying Alive
Staying Together
Steal Big, Steal Little
Steal the Sky
Stealing Heaven
Stealing Home
Steamboat Bill, Jr.
Steel
Steel and Lace
Steel Dawn
Steel Frontier
The Steel Helmet
Steel Magnolias
Steele Justice
Steele's Law
Stella
Stella Dallas
Step Lively
The Stepfather
Stepfather 2: Make Room for Daddy
Stepfather 3: Father's Day
Stephen King's Golden Years
Stephen King's It
Stephen King's The Langoliers
Stephen King's The Stand
Stephen King's The Tommyknockers
Steppenwolf
Stepping Out
The Sterile Cuckoo
Steve Martin Live
Stewardess School
Stick
Sticky Fingers
Still of the Night
The Sting
The Sting 2
Stir Crazy
A Stolen Face
Stone Cold
The Stone Killer
Stop Making Sense
Stop! or My Mom Will Shoot
Stop That Cab
Stormy Monday
Stormy Weather
Story of Adele H.
The Story of Boys & Girls
The Story of O
The Story of O, Part 2

The Story of Qui Ju
The Story of Vernon and Irene Castle
Storyville
Stranded
The Strange Affair of Uncle Harry
Strange Brew
Strange Invaders
The Strange Love of Martha Ivers
A Stranger Among Us
The Stranger and the Gunfighter
Stranger on the Third Floor
Stranger than Paradise
Strangers
Strangers on a Train
Strapless
Strapped
Strategic Air Command
Straw Dogs
Strays
Streamers
Street Asylum
Street Crimes
The Street Fighter
Street Fighter
Street Hunter
Street Knight
Street Smart
Street Soldiers
Street Wars
A Streetcar Named Desire
Streets of Fire
Streets of Gold
Streetwalkin'
Streetwise
Strictly Ballroom
Strike a Pose
Strike It Rich
Strike Up the Band
Striking Distance
Stripes
Stroke of Midnight
Strong Man
Student Bodies
A Study in Terror
Stuff Stephanie in the Incinerator
The Stunt Man
Subspecies
The Substitute
Suburban Commando
Suburbia
Subway
Success is the Best Revenge
Sucker Money
Sudden Death
Sudden Impact
Suddenly, Last Summer
Suds
Sugar Cane Alley
Sugar Hill
The Sugarland Express
The Suicide Club
Sullivan's Travels
Summer
Summer and Smoke
Summer Camp Nightmare
Summer Heat
Summer Lovers
Summer of '42
The Summer of Miss Forbes
A Summer Place
Summer Rental
Summer School
Summer Stock
Summer's Games
Summertime
Sunday, Bloody Sunday
Sunday in the Park with George
Sundown Riders
The Sundowners
Sunset
Sunset Boulevard
Sunset Strip
The Sunshine Boys

Super Force
Super Mario Bros.
Supergirl
Superman: The Movie
Superman 2
Superman 3
Superman 4: The Quest for Peace
Support Your Local Sheriff
Suppose They Gave a War and Nobody Came?
The Sure Thing
Surf Ninjas
Surrender
The Survivalist
Surviving the Game
Survivor
Survivors
Susan Slept Here
Suspect
Suspicion
Suspiria
Swamp Thing
The Swan
Swashbuckler
Swedenhielms
Sweeney Todd: The Demon Barber of Fleet Street
Sweet Bird of Youth
Sweet Charity
Sweet Country
Sweet Dreams
Sweet Hearts Dance
Sweet Liberty
Sweet Smell of Success
Sweet Talker
Sweethearts
Sweetie
Swept Away...
The Swimmer
Swimming to Cambodia
Swimming with Sharks
The Swindle
Swing Kids
Swing Shift
Swing Time
The Swiss Family Robinson
Switch
Switching Channels
Swoon
The Sword & the Rose
Sword & the Sorcerer
The Sword in the Stone
Sword of Honor
The Swordsman
Sylvester
Sylvia Scarlett
T Bone N Weasel
T-Force
T-Men
Table for Five
Taffin
Tai-Pan
Tailspin: Behind the Korean Airline Tragedy
Take Me Out to the Ball Game
Take the Money and Run
Take Two
Taken Away
The Takeover
Taking Care of Business
The Taking of Beverly Hills
The Taking of Flight 847: The Uli Derickson Story
The Tale of the Frog Prince
Talent for the Game
Tales from the Crypt
Tales from the Crypt Presents Demon Knight
Tales from the Darkside
Tales from the Darkside: The Movie
The Tales of Hoffmann
Tales of Robin Hood
Tales of the Unexpected
Talk of the Town

Talk Radio
The Tall Guy
Tall in the Saddle
Tall Lie
Tall Story
Tall Tale: The Unbelievable Adventures of Pecos Bill
Tall Texan
Talons of the Eagle
The Taming of the Shrew
Tammy and the T-Rex
Tampopo
Tango and Cash
Tank
Tank Girl
Tanner '88
Tap
Tapeheads
Taras Bulba
Target
Tartuffe
Tarzan and His Mate
Tarzan, the Ape Man
A Taste for Killing
Tatie Danielle
Tattle Tale
Taxi Dancers
Taxi Driver
A Taxing Woman
A Taxing Woman's Return
TC 2000
Tea and Sympathy
The Teacher
Teachers
The Teahouse of the August Moon
Teamster Boss: The Jackie Presser Story
Teen Wolf
Teenage Exorcist
Teenage Mutant Ninja Turtles: The Movie
Teenage Mutant Ninja Turtles 3
The Telephone
Tell Them Willie Boy Is Here
The Temp
The Tempest
Temptation
10
The Ten Commandments
Ten Days That Shook the World
Ten Little Indians
10 Rillington Place
Ten to Midnight
Ten Wanted Men
Tender Mercies
The Tender Trap
The Tenth Man
Tequila Sunrise
Terminal Bliss
Terminal Exposure
Terminal Force
Terminal Impact
Terminal Velocity
The Terminator
Terminator 2: Judgment Day
Terms of Endearment
Terror by Night
Terror in Beverly Hills
Terror in the Swamp
Terror Street
Terror Train
Tess
Test Tube Teens from the Year 2000
Testament
Tex
Texas
Texas Across the River
The Texas Chainsaw Massacre
Texas Chainsaw Massacre, Part 2
Texas Guns
Texasville
Thank Your Lucky Stars
That Hamilton Woman

That Night
That Obscure Object of Desire
That Sinking Feeling
That Summer of White Roses
That Touch of Mink
That Was Then...This Is Now
That'll Be the Day
That's Dancing!
That's Entertainment
That's Entertainment, Part 2
That's Entertainment, Part 3
That's Life!
That's Singing: The Best of Broadway
Theatre of Blood
Thelma & Louise
Them!
Theodore Rex
There Goes My Baby
Theremin: An Electronic Odyssey
There's No Business Like Show Business
There's Nothing Out There
These Three
They All Laughed
They Came to Cordura
They Got Me Covered
They Live
They Live by Night
They Made Me a Criminal
They Never Come Back
They Shoot Horses, Don't They?
They Were So Young
They Won't Believe Me
The Thief
Thief
The Thief of Bagdad
The Thief of Baghdad
Thief of Hearts
Thieves of Fortune
The Thin Blue Line
The Thin Man
The Thing
The Thing Called Love
Things Change
The Things of Life
Think Big
Third Degree Burn
The Third Man
Third Solution
32 Short Films about Glenn Gould
'38: Vienna Before the Fall
The 39 Steps
This Boy's Life
This Could Be the Night
This Gun for Hire
This Is Spinal Tap
This Island Earth
This Land is Mine
This Property is Condemned
Thompson's Last Run
Thoroughly Modern Millie
Those Daring Young Men in Their Jaunty Jalopies
Those Magnificent Men in Their Flying Machines
A Thousand Heroes
Thousand Pieces of Gold
Thousands Cheer
Three Amigos
The Three Caballeros
Three Days of the Condor
Three Days to a Kill
The Three Faces of Eve
Three for the Road
Three Fugitives
The 317th Platoon
Three Legionnaires
Three Men and a Baby
Three Men and a Cradle
Three Men and a Little Lady
The Three Musketeers
3 Ninjas
3 Ninjas Kick Back
3 Ninjas Knuckle Up
Three O'Clock High
Three of Hearts
The Three Penny Opera
3:10 to Yuma
Three Wishes
The Three Worlds of Gulliver
Threesome
Throne of Blood
Throw Momma from the Train
Thumbelina
Thunder & Mud
Thunder in Paradise
Thunder in the Pines
Thunderball
Thunderbolt & Lightfoot
Thunderground
Thunderheart
Thursday's Game
THX 1138
Ticks
Tie Me Up! Tie Me Down!
The Tie That Binds
Tiger Claws
Tiger Warsaw
A Tiger's Tale
Tightrope
The Tigress
Till Marriage Do Us Part
Till the Clouds Roll By
Till the End of Time
Tillie's Punctured Romance
Time After Time
Time Bandits
The Time Guardian
The Time Machine
A Time of Destiny
Time of the Gypsies
Time Runner
A Time to Die
Time to Kill
Timebomb
Timecop
Timemaster
Timerider
Times of Harvey Milk
Tin Men
Tiny Toon Adventures: How I Spent My Vacation
To Be or Not to Be
To Catch a Killer
To Catch a Thief
To Die for
To Die For
To Die Standing
To Have & Have Not
To Joy
To Kill a Mockingbird
To Kill a Priest
To Live
To Live & Die in L.A.
To the Death
To Wong Foo, Thanks for Everything, Julie Newmar
Toast of New York
Tobor the Great
Toby McTeague
Togetherness
Tokyo Decadence
Tokyo Joe
Tokyo Olympiad
Tokyo Pop
Toll of the Desert
Tollbooth
Tom & Viv
Tom, Dick, and Harry
Tom Jones
Tom Sawyer
Tom Thumb
Tomb of Ligeia
Tombstone
Tomcat: Dangerous Desires
Tommy
Too Many Girls
Too Much Sun
Tootsie
Top Dog
Top Gun
Top Hat
Top Secret!
Topaz
Topaze
Topper Returns
Tora! Tora! Tora!
Torch Song
Torch Song Trilogy
Torchlight
Torn Curtain
Tornado!
Torrents of Spring
Torture Garden
Total Exposure
Total Recall
Toto le Heros
Touch and Go
Touch of Evil
Tough Assignment
Tough Guys
Tough Guys Don't Dance
Tour of Duty
Tourist Trap
Tous les Matins du Monde
The Towering Inferno
The Toxic Avenger
The Toxic Avenger, Part 2
The Toy
Toy Soldiers
Traces of Red
Tracks of a Killer
Trade Off
Trading Hearts
Trading Mom
Trading Places
Trail of Terror
Trail of the Mounties
Trail of the Pink Panther
The Train
Train Robbers
Train to Tombstone
Trained to Kill
Trancers
Trancers 2: The Return of Jack Deth
Trancers 3: Deth Lives
Transformations
Transmutations
Transylvania 6-5000
Trap on Cougar Mountain
Trapeze
Trapped In Paradise
Trapper County War
Travels with My Aunt
Treasure Island
Treasure of Monte Cristo
Treasure of the Sierra Madre
A Tree Grows in Brooklyn
The Tree of Wooden Clogs
Tremors
Tremors 2: Aftershocks
Trespass
The Trial
Trial by Jury
Tribute
Tricks of the Trade
Trinity is Still My Name
The Trip to Bountiful
Triple Impact
Tripods: The White Mountains
Tripwire
Triumph of the Spirit
Trois Couleurs: Bleu
Trois Couleurs: Rouge
Troll
A Troll in Central Park
Tron
Troop Beverly Hills
Tropical Snow
Trouble Bound
Trouble in Mind
The Trouble with Angels
The Trouble with Harry
True Believer
True Blood
True Colors
True Confessions
True Grit
True Lies
True Love
True Romance
True Stories
Trust
Trust Me
Truth or Dare
Truth or Die
Tucker: The Man and His Dream
Tuff Turf
Tumbleweeds
Tune in Tomorrow
Tunes of Glory
The Tunnel
The Tunnel of Love
The Turn of the Screw
Turner and Hooch
Turtle Diary
Tusks
The Tuttles of Tahiti
Twelve Angry Men
Twelve Chairs
12 Monkeys
Twelve O'Clock High
12:01
20 Million Miles to Earth
20,000 Leagues Under the Sea
Twenty-One
Twice Dead
Twice in a Lifetime
Twilight of the Cockroaches
The Twilight Zone
Twilight Zone: The Movie
Twilight's Last Gleaming
Twin Peaks
Twin Peaks: Fire Walk with Me
Twins
Twisted Obsession
Twister
Two Bits
Two English Girls
Two Evil Eyes
Two for the Road
Two for the Seesaw
Two Girls and a Sailor
Two If by Sea
The Two Jakes
Two Minute Warning
Two Moon Junction
Two Much
Two of a Kind
Two Rode Together
2001: A Space Odyssey
2010: The Year We Make Contact
Two Weeks in Another Town
Tycoon
Ugetsu
UHF
Ulysses
Ulzana's Raid
Umberto D
Un Coeur en Hiver
The Unbearable Lightness of Being
The Unbelievable Truth
The Unborn
The Unborn 2
Uncaged
Uncle Buck
Uncommon Valor
Undeclared War
The Undefeated
Under Capricorn
Under Fire
Under Siege
Under Siege 2: Dark Territory
Under Suspicion
Under the Biltmore Clock
Under the Boardwalk
Under the Cherry Moon
Under the Earth
Under the Gun
Under the Volcano
Undercover Blues
Undersea Kingdom
Understudy: The Graveyard Shift 2
Underwater!
The Unearthing
Unfaithfully Yours
Unforgettable
The Unforgiven
Unforgiven
The Unholy
Unholy Four
The Unholy Three
The Uninvited
Uninvited
Union City
Universal Soldier
Unlawful Entry
The Unnamable
The Unnamable 2: The Statement of Randolph Carter
Unnatural Causes
Unsettled Land
The Unsinkable Molly Brown
Unstrung Heroes
Untamed Heart
Until The End of The World
The Untouchables
Unveiled
Unzipped
Up in Arms
Up Periscope
Up the Creek
Up Your Alley
Uranus
Urban Cowboy
Urban Crossfire
Urusei Yatsura Movie 2: Beautiful Dreamer
Urusei Yatsura Movie 3: Remember My Love
Urusei Yatsura Movie 4: Lum the Forever
Urusei Yatsura Movie 5: The Final Chapter
Used Cars
Used People
The Usual Suspects
Utilities
Vagabond
Valentino Returns
Valley Girl
The Valley of Gwangi
Valley of the Lawless
Valmont
Vamp
Vampire's Kiss
Vanishing Point
Vanya on 42nd Street
Varieties on Parade
The Velvet Vampire
Vengeance
Vengeance Is Mine
Vera Cruz
The Verdict
Verne Miller
Vertigo
A Very Old Man with Enormous Wings
V.I. Warshawski
Vibrations
Vice Academy
Vice Squad
Vice Versa
Victim of Love
Victor/Victoria
Videodrome
Vietnam, Texas
A View to a Kill
The Vikings
Village of the Damned
Vincent & Theo

Vincent, Francois, Paul and the Others
Vincent: The Life and Death of Vincent van Gogh
The Vineyard
The Violent Men
Violets Are Blue
Virgin High
Virgin Queen of St. Francis High
Virgin Sacrifice
Virtual Assassin
Virtual Desire
Vision Quest
Visions of Light: The Art of Cinematography
The Visitors
Vital Signs
Viva Las Vegas
Viva Villa!
Viva Zapata!
Volere Volare
Volunteers
Von Ryan's Express
Voodoo
Voyage to the Bottom of the Sea
Voyager
Wackiest Ship in the Army
Wacko
Wages of Fear
Wagon Master
Wagons East
Wait Until Dark
Waiting for the Light
A Walk in the Sun
Walker: Texas Ranger: One Riot, One Ranger
Walking Tall
Walking Tall: Part 2
Walking Tall: The Final Chapter
Wall Street
The Wannsee Conference
Wanted Dead or Alive
The War
War and Peace
The War Lord
War Lover
War of the Gargantuas
War of the Robots
The War of the Roses
The War of the Worlds
War Party
The War Room
The War Wagon
WarGames
Warlords
Warm Nights on a Slow-Moving Train
Warm Summer Rain
The Warrior & the Sorceress
Warrior Queen
The Warriors
Warriors
The Wash
Watchers
Watchers 2
The Waterdance
Waterland
Waterloo Bridge
Watermelon Man
Watership Down
Waterworld
Wavelength
Waxwork
Way Down East
The Way We Were
Wayne's World
Wayne's World 2
We All Loved Each Other So Much
We the Living
We Think the World of You
Wedding Band
The Wedding Banquet
The Wedding Gift
A Wedding in Galilee
Wedding Rehearsal
Weeds
Weekend at Bernie's 2
Weekend Pass
Weird Science
Welcome Home
Welcome Home, Roxy Carmichael
Welcome to Spring Break
We're Back! A Dinosaur's Story
We're No Angels
We're Not Dressing
We're Talkin' Serious Money
Wes Craven's New Nightmare
West of Zanzibar
West Side Story
Western Pacific Agent
The Westerner
Westworld
Wet and Wild Summer
The Whales of August
What About Bob?
What Comes Around
What Ever Happened to Baby Jane?
What Have I Done to Deserve This?
What Price Hollywood?
What's Eating Gilbert Grape
What's Love Got to Do with It?
What's New Pussycat?
What's Up, Tiger Lily?
Wheels of Fire
When a Man Loves a Woman
When a Stranger Calls
When a Stranger Calls Back
When Comedy was King
When Dinosaurs Ruled the Earth
When Harry Met Sally...
When Nature Calls
When the Whales Came
When the Wind Blows
When Worlds Collide
Where Angels Fear to Tread
Where Eagles Dare
Where the Boys Are
Where the Day Takes You
Where the Heart Is
Where the North Begins
Where's Poppa?
While the City Sleeps
While You Were Sleeping
A Whisper to a Scream
Whispers
Whispers in the Dark
The Whistle Blower
White Christmas
The White Dawn
White Fang
White Fang 2: The Myth of the White Wolf
White Gorilla
White Heat
White Hot
White Hunter, Black Heart
White Light
White Line Fever
White Mane
White Mile
White Mischief
White Nights
White Palace
White Sands
White Squall
White Water Summer
Who Am I This Time?
Who Framed Roger Rabbit
Who'll Stop the Rain?
Wholly Moses!
The Whoopee Boys
Whore 2
Who's Afraid of Virginia Woolf?
Who's Harry Crumb?
Who's That Girl?
Why Me?
Wide Sargasso Sea
Widow's Peak
Wild at Heart
Wild Bill
The Wild Bunch
Wild Geese
Wild Gypsies
Wild in the Streets
The Wild Life
The Wild One
Wild Orchid
The Wild Pair
Wild Rovers
Wild Strawberries
Wild Thing
Wild Zone
Wildcard
Wildcats
Wilder Napalm
Wildest Dreams
Wildfire
Will Penny
Willard
Willie & Phil
The Willies
Willow
Willy Wonka & the Chocolate Factory
Winchester '73
Wind
The Wind and the Lion
The Window
Window to Paris
Windy City
Wing Chun
Wings
Wings of Danger
Wings of Desire
Winners Take All
Winning
The Winning Team
Winter Kills
The Winter Light
Winter People
Wired
Wisdom
Wish You Were Here
Witchboard
Witchboard 2: The Devil's Doorway
Witchcraft
Witchcraft 2: The Temptress
Witchcraft 4: Virgin Heart
The Witches
The Witches of Eastwick
WitchTrap
With Honors
Withnail and I
Without a Clue
Without Honors
Without Mercy
Without Reservations
Witness
Witness for the Prosecution
The Wiz
The Wizard
The Wizard of Loneliness
The Wizard of Oz
The Wizard of Speed and Time
Wizards
Wolf
The Wolf Man
Wolfen
The Wolves
Woman Condemned
The Woman in Green
The Woman in Red
A Woman Named Jackie
The Woman Next Door
Woman of Desire
A Woman of Distinction
Woman of the Year
Woman Undone
A Woman's Tale
The Women
Women & Men: In Love There Are No Rules
Women & Men: Stories of Seduction
Women in Love
Women on the Verge of a Nervous Breakdown
Wonder Man
The Wonderful World of the Brothers Grimm
Wonderland
Woodstock
The Word
Working Girl
The World According to Garp
A World Apart
World Gone Wild
The World of Henry Orient
The World of Suzie Wong
World's Greatest Lover
The Worst Witch
Worth Winning
The Wraith
Wrangler
The Wreck of the Mary Deare
Wrestling Ernest Hemingway
Write to Kill
The Wrong Guys
Wrong is Right
The Wrong Man
Wuthering Heights
Wyatt Earp
Wyatt Earp: Return to Tombstone
X: The Man with X-Ray Eyes
Xanadu
Xtro
Xtro 2: The Second Encounter
Xtro 3: Watch the Skies
The Yakuza
Yankee Doodle Dandy
Yanks
The Year My Voice Broke
The Year of Living Dangerously
Year of the Comet
Year of the Dragon
Year of the Gun
Year of the Quiet Sun
The Yearling
Yellow Submarine
Yellowbeard
Yentl
Yes, Giorgio
Yojimbo
Yor, the Hunter from the Future
You Can't Hurry Love
You Can't Take It with You
You Only Live Twice
You Were Never Lovelier
You'll Never Get Rich
The Young Americans
Young and Innocent
Young Doctors in Love
Young Einstein
Young Frankenstein
Young Guns
Young Guns 2
Young Lady Chatterly 2
The Young Lions
Young Man with a Horn
Young Mr. Lincoln
Young Nurses in Love
Young Sherlock Holmes
Youngblood
Younger & Younger
Yours, Mine & Ours
Z
Zabriskie Point
Zandalee
Zapped!
Zapped Again
Zardoz
Zarkorr! The Invader
Zebrahead
Zelig
Zelly & Me
Zentropa
Zeppelin
Zero Tolerance
Ziegfeld Follies
Ziegfeld Girl
Zipperface
Zombie
Zombies of the Stratosphere
Zombies on Broadway
Zoot Suit
Zora Is My Name!
Zorba the Greek
Zorro's Black Whip
Zorro's Fighting Legion
Zou Zou
Zulu
Zulu Dawn

CD-I

Apocalypse Now
The Firm
A Hard Day's Night
Indecent Proposal
Patriot Games
Salt of the Earth
Sliver
Star Trek 6: The Undiscovered Country

Letterbox

The Abyss
The Accidental Tourist
The Addams Family
Addams Family Values
The Adventures of Ford Fairlane
The Adventures of Huck Finn
The Adventures of Robin Hood
An Affair to Remember
After Hours
Against All Odds
The Age of Innocence
The Agony and the Ecstasy
Akira Kurosawa's Dreams
The Alamo
Alexander the Great
Alice Doesn't Live Here Anymore
Alien 3
Aliens
Alive
All That Jazz
All the President's Men
All the Vermeers in New York
Always
An American Tail: Fievel Goes West
The Americanization of Emily
Amsterdamned
Anastasia
The Andromeda Strain
Angie
Annie
Annie Hall
The Apartment
Apocalypse Now
Arabian Nights
Arachnophobia
Army of Darkness
Auntie Mame
Avalon
The Awful Dr. Orlof
Baby Cart to Hades
Back to the Future
Back to the Future, Part 2
Back to the Future, Part 3
Backbeat
Backdraft
Bad Day at Black Rock
Bad Girls
Baraka
Barbarella
Barry Lyndon

Batman
Batman: Mask of the Phantasm
Battle Cry
Battle of Britain
Battle of the Bulge
The Bear
Beautiful Dreamers
Beauty and the Beast
Becket
Bedazzled
Beethoven's 2nd
Being Human
The Bellboy
Bells are Ringing
Ben-Hur
Beneath the Planet of the Apes
Beneath the 12-Mile Reef
Benny & Joon
The Best Little Whorehouse in Texas
Best of the Best 2
Bhowani Junction
The Big Chill
Big Jake
Big Trouble in Little China
Big Wednesday
Billie
Billy Bathgate
Billy Rose's Jumbo
Bird on a Wire
Bitter Moon
Black Rain
Black Robe
Blade Runner
Blink
The Blob
Blood Alley
Blood & Concrete: A Love Story
Bloodhounds of Broadway
Blow-Up
Blown Away
Blue Chips
The Blue Max
Blue Thunder
Blue Velvet
Bobo
Body Double
Body of Evidence
Body Parts
Boiling Point
The Bonfire of the Vanities
Boomerang
Born on the Fourth of July
Born Yesterday
Boyz N the Hood
Brain Donors
Brainstorm
Bram Stoker's Dracula
Brazil
Brewster McCloud
The Bridge on the River Kwai
A Bridge Too Far
Brigadoon
Broken Lance
Buona Sera, Mrs. Campbell
Burn!
The Butcher's Wife
Butterfield 8
Bye, Bye, Birdie
Cahill: United States Marshal
Camelot
Can-Can
Candyman
Cape Fear
The Cardinal
Carlito's Way
Carmen Jones
Carnal Knowledge
Casualties of War
Cat People
CB4: The Movie
The Champ
Chaplin
The Chase
Chasers
Chinatown
Chinese Connection
Chinese Roulette
Chisum
Cimarron
Circuitry Man
Circus World
City of Joy
City Slickers
Clash of the Titans
Class Act
Clean and Sober
Cleopatra
The Client
Cliffhanger
A Clockwork Orange
Close Encounters of the Third Kind
The Color Purple
The Comancheros
Come See the Paradise
Conan the Barbarian
The Cook, the Thief, His Wife & Her Lover
Cop and a Half
The Court Martial of Billy Mitchell
The Cowboys
The Cranes are Flying
Cria
Crooklyn
The Crush
The Crying Game
Cyborg
Daddy Long Legs
Damage
Damien: Omen 2
Dances with Wolves
Dandy in Aspic
Dangerous Liaisons
The Dark Backward
Dark Habits
Dark Star
Darkman 2: The Return of Durant
Darkman 3: Die Darkman Die
Dave
Day of the Triffids
Day the World Ended
Days of Thunder
Dazed and Confused
Dead Again
Dead Calm
Death Becomes Her
The Decameron
The Deep
Deep Cover
The Deer Hunter
Defending Your Life
Deliverance
Delusion
Demolition Man
Dennis the Menace
Designing Woman
Desiree
The Detective
Diamonds Are Forever
Diane
The Diary of Anne Frank
Diary of Forbidden Dreams
Dick Tracy
Die Hard
Die Hard 2: Die Harder
Diner
The Dirty Dozen
Dirty Harry
Doc Hollywood
The Doctor
Doctor Dolittle
Dr. Giggles
Dr. No
Dr. Strangelove, or: How I Learned to Stop Worrying and Love the Bomb
Doctor Zhivago
The Doors
Dracula
Dragon: The Bruce Lee Story
Dressed to Kill
Driving Miss Daisy
DROP Squad
The Duellists
East of Eden
The Eddy Duchin Story
The Eiger Sanction
8 1/2
The Electric Horseman
Empire of the Sun
The Empire Strikes Back
Enter the Dragon
Equinox
The Errand Boy
Escape from the Planet of the Apes
E.T.: The Extra-Terrestrial
Excalibur
The Fall of the Roman Empire
Falling Down
Fantastic Voyage
Far and Away
Far from the Madding Crowd
A Far Off Place
Fatal Attraction
Father of the Bride
Fear
Fearless
The Fearless Vampire Killers
Fellini Satyricon
Fellini's Roma
A Few Good Men
Fiddler on the Roof
Field of Dreams
55 Days at Peking
Final Approach
The Final Conflict
Finian's Rainbow
Fire in the Sky
The Firm
First Blood
First Men in the Moon
The Fisher King
A Fistful of Dollars
A Fistful of Dynamite
Five Easy Pieces
Five Weeks in a Balloon
Flash Gordon
Flatliners
Flight of the Intruder
FM
Follow That Dream
For a Few Dollars More
For Your Eyes Only
Forbidden Planet
Forever Young
Fort Apache, the Bronx
The Fortune Cookie
The 400 Blows
Four Weddings and a Funeral
1492: Conquest of Paradise
Frankie and Johnny
Free Willy
Freebie & the Bean
Freejack
The Freshman
From Russia with Love
The Funhouse
Funny Face
Funny Girl
Funny Lady
Fury is a Woman
Game of Death
Gandhi
Gas Food Lodging
Geronimo
Gettysburg
Ghost
Ghostbusters
Ghostbusters 2
Gigi
The Glass Bottom Boat
Glengarry Glen Ross
Glory
Going Places
Goldfinger
Gonza the Spearman
The Good, the Bad and the Ugly
Goodbye, Mr. Chips
Goodfellas
The Goonies
The Gospel According to St. Matthew
The Graduate
Grand Prix
The Grass is Greener
Grave of the Fireflies
The Great Escape
The Greatest Story Ever Told
Greedy
The Green Berets
Gremlins
Gremlins 2: The New Batch
Greystoke: The Legend of Tarzan, Lord of the Apes
Grumpy Old Men
Guilty as Sin
Guilty by Suspicion
The Guns of Navarone
Gypsy
Hair
The Hallelujah Trail
Hamlet
Hard Target
The Hard Way
The Harder They Come
Harlem Nights
Harper
Hawaii
The Hawks & the Sparrows
He Said, She Said
Heart and Souls
Heaven and Earth
Heaven's Gate
Hellfighters
Henry V
Henry & June
Hercules
Hero
The Hidden Fortress
High & Low
High Plains Drifter
High Society
The Hindenburg
History of the World: Part 1
Hit the Deck
Hoffa
A Hole in the Head
Hombre
Home Alone
Home from the Hill
Homeward Bound: The Incredible Journey
Honey, I Blew Up the Kid
The Hot Rock
The House of the Spirits
How the West Was Won
How to Succeed in Business without Really Trying
Howard's End
Huckleberry Finn
The Hudsucker Proxy
The Hunger
The Hunt for Red October
Hunter in the Dark
Husbands and Wives
I Could Go on Singing
I Died a Thousand Times
I Love You to Death
Ice Station Zebra
Iceman
In Like Flint
In the Line of Fire
In the Name of the Father
In the Navy
The Indian Runner
Indiana Jones and the Last Crusade
Indochine
Innocent Blood
Inside Daisy Clover
Invasion of the Body Snatchers
Irma La Douce
Islands in the Stream
It's a Mad, Mad, Mad, Mad World
It's Always Fair Weather
Ivan the Terrible, Part 1
Ivan the Terrible, Part 2
Jack the Bear
The Jagged Edge
Jailhouse Rock
Jaws
Jaws 2
Jennifer 8
Jesus Christ, Superstar
JFK
Joe Kidd
Joe Versus the Volcano
Journey of Honor
Journey to the Far Side of the Sun
The Joy Luck Club
The Judge and the Assassin
Jules and Jim
Jupiter's Darling
Kafka
Kagemusha
Kalifornia
The Karate Kid: Part 3
The Keep
Kelly's Heroes
Khartoum
Kid Galahad
The Killing Fields
The King and I
The King of Hearts
The King of Kings
King of the Hill
Kismet
Kiss Me, Stupid!
Klute
Knights of the Round Table
Kramer vs. Kramer
The Krays
Kwaidan
La Dolce Vita
Labyrinth of Passion
The Lacemaker
Ladyhawke
Land of the Pharaohs
The Last Boy Scout
Last Exit to Brooklyn
The Last of the Mohicans
The Last Picture Show
Last Tango in Paris
L'Avventura
Lawrence of Arabia
Le Complot
Le Crabe Tambour
Le Mans
A League of Their Own
Leap of Faith
Leningrad Cowboys Go America
Les Girls
L'Etat Sauvage
Lethal Weapon
Lethal Weapon 2
Leviathan
License to Kill
Liebestraum
Life & Times of Judge Roy Bean
Life with Mikey
Lisztomania
Little Big Man
Little Nemo: Adventures in Slumberland
A Little Romance
Live and Let Die
The Living Daylights
Logan's Run
Lola Montes
Lolita
The Long Goodbye
The Longest Day
Lorenzo's Oil
The Lost Boys

Lost Horizon
Lost in America
Lost in Yonkers
Love Me or Leave Me
Love Meetings
The Lover
Lucky Me
Lust for Life
M. Butterfly
Mac
Mad Dog and Glory
Mad Max: Beyond Thunderdome
Made in America
The Madwoman of Chaillot
The Magnificent Seven
Major League 2
Malcolm X
Mame
A Man Called Horse
The Man from Snowy River
Man of a Thousand Faces
Man Trouble
The Man Who Fell to Earth
The Man Who Would Be King
The Man with the Golden Gun
Manhattan
Manhunter
Maniac Cop 2
Mary Poppins
M*A*S*H
Matador
Maverick
McCabe & Mrs. Miller
Meet Me in Las Vegas
Men of Respect
The Meteor Man
Midnight Cowboy
Midnight Express
Midway
The Mission
Mississippi Mermaid
Mrs. Soffel
Mr. Baseball
Mr. Jones
Mr. Wonderful
Mo' Money
Monty Python and the Holy Grail
Moonraker
Moonstruck
Mortal Thoughts
The Mosquito Coast
Music Box
The Music Lovers
The Music Man
Mutiny on the Bounty
My Fair Lady
My Favorite Year
My New Gun
My Own Private Idaho
Mystery Science Theater 3000: The Movie
Mystery Train
Naked Gun 2 1/2: The Smell of Fear
Naked Killer
Naked Kiss
Narrow Margin
The Natural
Necessary Roughness
Nemesis
Never So Few
The NeverEnding Story
NeverEnding Story 2: The Next Chapter
New York, New York
Nicholas and Alexandra
A Night at the Opera
The Night of the Iguana
Night on Earth
9 1/2 Weeks
Nixon
Noises Off
North by Northwest
North to Alaska
Ocean's 11
Octopussy
Oklahoma!
Old Gringo
Oliver!
The Omen
On Her Majesty's Secret Service
One, Two, Three
Only the Lonely
The Opposite Sex
Orlando
Other People's Money
The Other Side of Midnight
Our Man Flint
Out for Justice
Outland
The Outsiders
Overboard
The Paper
Party Girl
Passenger 57
Passion Fish
Past Midnight
Pat Garrett & Billy the Kid
Patton
The Pelican Brief
A Perfect World
Pete Kelly's Blues
Peyton Place
The Pickle
Picnic
Pierrot le Fou
Pillow Talk
Pink Floyd: The Wall
The Pink Panther
Planet of the Apes
The Player
Please Don't Eat the Daisies
Pocketful of Miracles
Point Blank
Point Break
Point of No Return
Poltergeist
Poltergeist 2: The Other Side
The Poseidon Adventure
Predator
Predator 2
Presumed Innocent
The Princess Bride
Prisoner of Second Avenue
The Producers
The Professionals
PT 109
The Public Eye
Pure Country
The Quest
Quest for Fire
Quigley Down Under
Rage and Honor
Raging Bull
Raintree County
Raising Cain
Ran
The Real McCoy
Reality Bites
Rebel Without a Cause
The Red and the White
Red Beard
Red Dawn
Regarding Henry
The Reluctant Debutante
The Remains of the Day
Reservoir Dogs
Return of the Dragon
Return of the Jedi
Revenge
Revenge of the Pink Panther
Rich in Love
Richard III
Ride the High Country
The Right Stuff
Rising Sun
Risky Business
A River Runs Through It
Road House
The Road Warrior
The Robe
Robin and the 7 Hoods
Robin Hood: Prince of Thieves
RoboCop
Rocco and His Brothers
The Rocketeer
Rollerball
Rollercoaster
Romancing the Stone
The Rookie
Rose Marie
Runaway Train
Running Scared
The Russia House
Ryan's Daughter
The Sacrifice
The Saint of Fort Washington
The Sandlot
Scarface
Scent of a Woman
Schindler's List
School Ties
Sea Chase
Sea of Love
The Searchers
Sgt. Bilko
Serial Mom
Seven Brides for Seven Brothers
7 Faces of Dr. Lao
1776
sex, lies and videotape
Shadow of the Wolf
The Shakiest Gun in the West
Shampoo
Shattered
The Sheltering Sky
Shipwrecked
Shock Corridor
The Shoes of the Fisherman
Shoot the Piano Player
A Shot in the Dark
The Silence of the Lambs
Silk Stockings
Silverado
Singles
Sister Act
Sleepless in Seattle
Sliver
Sneakers
Sniper
Soapdish
S.O.B.
Sofie
Solar Crisis
Solaris
Solomon and Sheba
Some Came Running
Some Like It Hot
Sommersby
The Sound of Music
South Central
South Pacific
Spartacus
A Special Day
The Specialist
The Spy Who Loved Me
Stanley and Iris
Star!
Star Trek 2: The Wrath of Khan
Star Trek 3: The Search for Spock
Star Trek 4: The Voyage Home
Star Trek 5: The Final Frontier
Star Wars
Starman
A Stranger Among Us
Street Fighter
Sudden Impact
The Sugarland Express
Summer and Smoke
Sunday, Bloody Sunday
Super Mario Bros.
Superman: The Movie
Suspiria
Swashbuckler
Sweet Bird of Youth
The Swiss Family Robinson
The Taking of Beverly Hills
Tampopo
Tango and Cash
Taras Bulba
Taxi Driver
Tea and Sympathy
The Teahouse of the August Moon
Teenage Mutant Ninja Turtles 3
Tell Them Willie Boy Is Here
The Temp
The Ten Commandments
The Tender Trap
The Terminator
Texas Across the River
That Obscure Object of Desire
That Touch of Mink
That's Entertainment
Thelma & Louise
There's No Business Like Show Business
The Thing
The Things of Life
Third Solution
This Boy's Life
This Could Be the Night
Those Magnificent Men in Their Flying Machines
Three Days of the Condor
Threesome
Thumbelina
Thunderball
Thunderbolt & Lightfoot
THX 1138
Tie Me Up! Tie Me Down!
The Time Machine
Tokyo Olympiad
Tom Sawyer
Tootsie
The Towering Inferno
Trading Places
The Train
Train Robbers
Trapeze
Travels with My Aunt
Trespass
Trois Couleurs: Bleu
Tucker: The Man and His Dream
The Tunnel of Love
20,000 Leagues Under the Sea
Twin Peaks: Fire Walk with Me
Two for the Road
Two for the Seesaw
The Two Jakes
2001: A Space Odyssey
2010: The Year We Make Contact
Two Weeks in Another Town
Ulysses
Umberto D
Under Siege
Undercover Blues
The Unforgiven
Unforgiven
Unlawful Entry
The Unsinkable Molly Brown
Untamed Heart
The Untouchables
Up Periscope
Used People
Victor/Victoria
A View to a Kill
The Vikings
Vincent, Francois, Paul and the Others
The Violent Men
Viva Las Vegas
Von Ryan's Express
Voyage to the Bottom of the Sea
The War Lord
The War of the Roses
The War Wagon
Waterland
The Way We Were
West Side Story
Westworld
What Ever Happened to Baby Jane?
What's New Pussycat?
When Harry Met Sally...
Where Eagles Dare
Where the Boys Are
Where the Day Takes You
Whispers in the Dark
White Christmas
White Nights
White Squall
Who Framed Roger Rabbit
Who's Afraid of Virginia Woolf?
Wild at Heart
Wild Rovers
Wilder Napalm
Wind
The Wind and the Lion
Winning
Witness for the Prosecution
The Wiz
Wolfen
The Wolves
Women on the Verge of a Nervous Breakdown
The Wonderful World of the Brothers Grimm
Woodstock
The World of Henry Orient
Wrangler
The Wreck of the Mary Deare
Wyatt Earp
The Yakuza
The Year of Living Dangerously
Yojimbo
You Only Live Twice
Young Guns 2
The Young Lions
Zardoz
Zulu

Closed Caption

Abbott and Costello Go to Mars
Abbott and Costello in the Foreign Legion
Abbott and Costello Meet the Keystone Kops
Abbott and Costello Meet the Killer, Boris Karloff
Above the Law
Above the Rim
The Abyss
Acceptable Risks
Accidental Meeting
The Accidental Tourist
The Accused
Ace Ventura: Pet Detective
Ace Ventura: When Nature Calls
Aces: Iron Eagle 3
Act of Vengeance
Action Jackson
Adam
The Addams Family
Addams Family Values
Adrift
The Adventurers
Adventures in Babysitting
Adventures in Dinosaur City
Adventures in Spying
The Adventures of Baron Munchausen
The Adventures of Buckaroo Banzai Across the Eighth Dimension
The Adventures of Ford Fairlane
The Adventures of Huck Finn
The Adventures of Milo & Otis
The Adventures of Robin Hood
The Adventures of Sherlock Holmes

The Advocate
An Affair in Mind
An Affair to Remember
Afraid of the Dark
African Journey
After Dark, My Sweet
After Hours
After Midnight
After Pilkington
After the Shock
Afterburn
Against All Odds
The Age of Innocence
Age Old Friends
Agnes of God
Air America
Air Force
The Air Up There
Airborne
Airheads
Aladdin
Aladdin and His Wonderful Lamp
Aladdin and the King of Thieves
The Alamo
Alamo Bay
The Alamo: Thirteen Days to Glory
Alfredo, Alfredo
Ali Baba and the Forty Thieves
Alias Billy the Kid
Alice
Alice in Wonderland
Alien 3
Alien Intruder
Alien Nation
Alien Nation: Dark Horizon
Aliens
Alive
Alive: 20 Years Later
All-American Murder
All Creatures Great and Small
All Dogs Go to Heaven
All Dogs Go to Heaven 2
All I Desire
All That Jazz
All the Kind Strangers
All the Right Moves
All Through the Night
Allan Quatermain and the Lost City of Gold
Allegheny Uprising
All's Fair
Almost an Angel
Almost Partners
Almost Pregnant
Almost You
Always
Amanda and the Alien
Amateur
Amazing Grace & Chuck
The Amazing Panda Adventure
The Amazing Spider-Man
Amazon
Ambition
The Ambulance
Amelia Earhart: The Final Flight
The American Angels: Baptism of Blood
American Anthem
American Dreamer
American Flyers
American Kickboxer 2: To the Death
American Me
American Ninja
American Ninja 2: The Confrontation
American Ninja 4: The Annihilation
The American President
American Samurai
American Shaolin: King of the Kickboxers 2
An American Story
An American Summer
An American Tail
An American Tail: Fievel Goes West
American Yakuza
Amityville: A New Generation
Amityville 1992: It's About Time
Amongst Friends
Amore!
Amos and Andrew
Anchors Aweigh
And a Nightingale Sang
And the Band Played On
And You Thought Your Parents Were Weird!
Andre
The Android Affair
Andy Hardy Meets Debutante
Angel of Fury
Angels in the Outfield
Angie
Anguish
Animal Instincts
Animal Instincts 2
Anna
Anne of Avonlea
Anne of Green Gables
Annie
Annie O
Annie Oakley
Another 48 Hrs.
Another Stakeout
Another Thin Man
Another Time, Another Place
Another Woman
Another You
Antarctica
Antonia and Jane
Apache Uprising
A.P.E.X.
Apollo 13
The Apple Dumpling Gang
The Applegates
Appointment with Death
Apprentice to Murder
April Fool's Day
Arabian Nights
Arachnophobia
Arcade
Arctic Blue
Are You Lonesome Tonight
Arena
Arizona Dream
Armed and Dangerous
Armed for Action
Army of Darkness
Around the World in 80 Days
Arrivederci, Baby!
Arrowhead
Arsenic and Old Lace
Arthur
Arthur 2: On the Rocks
Article 99
Artists and Models
As Good as Dead
The Ascent
Ash Wednesday
Aspen Extreme
Assassination
The Assassination Bureau
Assault and Matrimony
Assault at West Point: The Court-Martial of Johnson Whittaker
Assault on a Queen
At Close Range
At Home with the Webbers
At Play in the Fields of the Lord
The Atomic City
Attack of the Killer Tomatoes
The Attic: The Hiding of Anne Frank
Automatic
Avalon
Avenging Angel
Avenging Force
Awakenings
An Awfully Big Adventure
The Babe
Babe
Babe Ruth Story
Baby Boom
The Baby Doll Murders
Baby It's You
Baby of the Bride
Baby on Board
The Baby-Sitters Club
Baby, Take a Bow
Babycakes
Baby's Day Out
The Babysitter
Bachelor in Paradise
Bachelor Party
Back Home
Back in Action
Back to Bataan
Back to School
Back to the Beach
Back to the Future
Back to the Future, Part 2
Back to the Future, Part 3
Backbeat
Backdraft
Backfield in Motion
Backlash: Oblivion 2
Backstab
Backtrack
The Bad and the Beautiful
Bad Behavior
Bad Blood
Bad Boys
Bad Channels
Bad Company
Bad Dreams
Bad Girls
Bad Lieutenant
Bad Medicine
Bagdad Cafe
Baja
The Ballad of Little Jo
The Ballad of the Sad Cafe
Ballistic
Balto
Bambi
Bandolero!
Bank Robber
Bar Girls
Barb Wire
Barbarian and the Geisha
Barbarians at the Gate
Bare Essentials
Barfly
The Baron and the Kid
Based on an Untrue Story
Basic Instinct
Basket Case 2
Basket Case 3: The Progeny
The Bastard
Bat 21
Batman
Batman Forever
Batman: Mask of the Phantasm
Batman Returns
Battle Circus
Battle Cry
Battle for the Planet of the Apes
Battle Hymn
Battle of Britain
Battle of the Bulge
Battleground
Battling for Baby
The Bay Boy
Beach Babes from Beyond Infinity
Beanstalk
The Bear
The Beast
The Beast with Five Fingers
Beastmaster 2: Through the Portal of Time
Beastmaster 3: The Eye of Braxus
Beat the Devil
The Beautiful Blonde from Bashful Bend
Beautiful Dreamers
Beauty and the Beast
Beauty and the Beast: Though Lovers Be Lost
Bebe's Kids
Becoming Colette
Bed & Breakfast
Bed of Roses
The Bedroom Window
Beer
Beethoven
Beethoven Lives Upstairs
Beethoven's 2nd
Beetlejuice
Before Sunrise
Being Human
Being There
The Believers
Belizaire the Cajun
The Bells of St. Mary's
Ben-Hur
Beneath the Planet of the Apes
Benefit of the Doubt
Benji the Hunted
Benny & Joon
Bernard and the Genie
Bert Rigby, You're a Fool
Best Defense
Best of Eddie Murphy
The Best of Everything
Best of the Best 2
Best of the Best 3: No Turning Back
The Best of the Two Ronnies
The Best of Times
Betrayed
Betsy's Wedding
Better Off Dead
Betty Blue
The Beverly Hillbillies
Beverly Hills Brats
Beverly Hills Cop
Beverly Hills Cop 2
Beverly Hills Cop 3
Beyond Darkness
Beyond Desire
Beyond Forgiveness
Beyond Justice
Beyond Rangoon
Beyond the Door
Beyond the Door 3
Beyond Therapy
Bhaji on the Beach
The Big Blue
Big Business
The Big Chill
The Big Easy
Big Girls Don't Cry...They Get Even
The Big Green
Big Jake
Big Jim McLain
The Big Picture
Big Shots
The Big Sky
The Big Stampede
Big Top Pee Wee
Big Trail
Big Trouble in Little China
Bigfoot: The Unforgettable Encounter
Biggles
The Bikini Car Wash Company
The Bikini Car Wash Company 2
Bill & Ted's Bogus Journey
Bill & Ted's Excellent Adventure
A Bill of Divorcement
Billy Bathgate
Billy Madison
Billy the Kid
Bingo
Bio-Dome
Bird
Bird on a Wire
The Birdcage
The Birds 2: Land's End
Birdy
Birth of the Blues
Bitter Harvest
Bitter Vengeance
Black Beauty
Black Belt
The Black Castle
Black Fox: The Price of Peace
Black Friday
Black Ice
Black Magic
Black Magic Woman
Black Moon Rising
Black Rain
Black Rainbow
Black Sheep
The Black Stallion
The Black Stallion Returns
The Black Swan
Black Water
Black Widow
Blackboard Jungle
Blackmail
Blame It on the Bellboy
Blank Check
Blankman
Blaze
Bleak House
Blessed Event
Blind Fury
Blind Man's Bluff
Blind Spot
Blind Vision
Blind Witness
Blink
Blink of an Eye
The Bliss of Mrs. Blossom
The Blob
Blood Alley
Blood and Roses
Blood for Blood
Blood Games
Blood Horse
Blood In...Blood Out: Bound by Honor
The Blood of Heroes
Blood Simple
Blood Warriors
Bloodfist 2
Bloodhounds of Broadway
Bloodknot
Bloodlust: Subspecies 3
Bloodmatch
Bloodsport
Bloodstone: Subspecies 2
Bloodsucking Pharoahs of Pittsburgh
Blossoms in the Dust
Blown Away
Blue
The Blue Bird
Blue Chips
Blue City
The Blue Dahlia
Blue De Ville
Blue Flame
Blue Ice
Blue Iguana
Blue In the Face
Blue Skies
Blue Sky
Blue Steel
Blue Thunder
Blue Tiger
Blue Velvet
The Blue Yonder
Bluebeard's Eighth Wife
Bob Roberts
Boca
Bodies, Rest & Motion
Body Bags
Body Chemistry 2: Voice of a Stranger

Body Double
The Body in the Library
Body Language
Body of Evidence
Body of Influence
Body Parts
Body Snatchers
Body Waves
The Bodyguard
Boeing Boeing
Bonanza: The Return
The Bonfire of the Vanities
Bonnie & Clyde
Book of Love
Boom Town
Boomerang
Bopha!
Border Radio
Border Shootout
Borderline
Boris and Natasha: The Movie
Born on the Fourth of July
Born to Be Wild
Born to Ride
Born Wild
Born Yesterday
The Borrowers
Bosom Buddies
The Boss' Wife
The Boston Strangler
Boulevard
Bounty Tracker
Boxing Helena
A Boy Called Hate
Boy in Blue
A Boy Named Charlie Brown
The Boy Who Could Fly
The Boy Who Loved Trolls
Boys on the Side
Boys Town
Boyz N the Hood
Braddock: Missing in Action 3
The Brady Bunch
The Brady Bunch Movie
The Brain
Brain Damage
Brain Donors
Brain Smasher...A Love Story
Brainscan
Bram Stoker's Dracula
Branded
The Bravados
Braveheart
Brazil
Breach of Conduct
Breach of Trust
The Breakfast Club
Breakheart Pass
Breaking In
Breaking Point
Breaking the Rules
Breath of Scandal
Breathing Fire
Breathing Lessons
Brewster's Millions
Brian's Song
The Bride
Bride of Re-Animator
The Bride Wore Red
Brideshead Revisited
Bridge to Silence
Bridge to Terabithia
A Bridge Too Far
The Bridges of Madison County
A Brief History of Time
Bright Angel
Bright Eyes
Bright Lights, Big City
Brighton Beach Memoirs
Broadcast News
Broadway Bound
Broadway Melody of 1938
Broken Angel
Broken Arrow
The Broken Chain
Broken Lance
Broken Vows
A Bronx Tale
The Brother from Another Planet
The Brotherhood of the Rose
Brotherly Love
The Brothers McMullen
The Browning Version
The Buccaneer
Buckskin
The Buddy Holly Story
The Buddy System
Buddy's Song
Buffalo Bill
Buffalo Girls
Buford's Beach Bunnies
Bugsy
Bull Durham
The Bulldozer Brigade
Bulletproof Heart
Bullets Over Broadway
Bullies
A Bunny's Tale
Bureau of Missing Persons
Burglar
Burke & Wills
The Burning Bed
The Burning Season
The Burns and Allen Show
Bushwhacked
Business as Usual
Busted Up
Buster
But Not for Me
The Butcher's Wife
By the Sword
Bye Bye, Love
Cabaret
Cabin Boy
The Cabin in the Cotton
Caddyshack 2
Cadence
Cadillac Man
Cafe Romeo
The Cage
The Caine Mutiny
The Caine Mutiny Court Martial
Calendar Girl
Call Northside 777
Call of the Rockies
Call of the Wild
Came a Hot Friday
Camelot
Camilla
Camp Nowhere
Can-Can
Can She Bake a Cherry Pie?
Candleshoe
Candyman
Cannibal Women in the Avocado Jungle of Death
Cannonball Run 2
Can't Buy Me Love
The Canterville Ghost
Cape Fear
Capone
Captain Blood
Captain January
Captain Nuke and the Bomber Boys
Captain Ron
Captive Hearts
The Captive: The Longest Drive 2
Captive Wild Woman
Car 54, Where Are You?
The Care Bears Movie
The Care Bears Movie 2: A New Generation
Career
Career Opportunities
Careful, He Might Hear You
The Cariboo Trail
Carlito's Way
Carmen Jones
Caroline?
Carousel
Carrie
Carried Away
Casablanca
Casanova
A Case for Murder
Casey at the Bat
Casino
Casper
Cast a Deadly Spell
Cast a Giant Shadow
Castaway
Castle in the Desert
Casualties of War
Catch Me...If You Can
Catch the Heat
Cat's Eye
Caught in the Act
Caught in the Draft
CB4: The Movie
The Cemetery Club
Chained Heat 2
Chains of Gold
The Chair
Champion
Champions
Chances Are
Chantilly Lace
Chaplin
Chapter Two
The Charge of the Light Brigade
Charles & Diana: A Palace Divided
A Charlie Brown Christmas
Charlie Brown's All-Stars
Charlie Chan at the Opera
Charlie Chan at the Wax Museum
Charlie Chan in Paris
Charlie Chan in Rio
Charlie Chan's Secret
The Chase
Chasers
Chato's Land
Cheatin' Hearts
Cheetah
Cherry 2000
Chicago Joe & the Showgirl
Child of Darkness, Child of Light
Children of a Lesser God
Children of the Corn 2: The Final Sacrifice
Children of the Corn 3: Urban Harvest
The Children of Times Square
The Children's Hour
Child's Play
Child's Play 2
Child's Play 3
China Beach
The China Lake Murders
China Moon
China O'Brien
China O'Brien 2
The China Syndrome
China White
Chinatown
The Chinatown Murders: Man Against the Mob
Chinese Web
The Chipmunk Adventure
Chitty Chitty Bang Bang
The Chocolate War
Chopper Chicks in Zombietown
A Chorus Line
Christabel
Christine
A Christmas Carol
The Christmas Coal Mine Miracle
Christmas in Connecticut
The Christmas Wife
A Christmas Without Snow
Christopher Columbus: The Discovery
Chrome and Hot Leather
Chrome Soldiers
The Chronicles of Narnia
Chuka
C.I.A.: Code Name Alexa
Cinderella
Circumstances Unknown
The Circus
The Cisco Kid
Citizen Cohn
Citizen Kane
City Boy
City Hall
City Heat
City of Hope
The City of Lost Children
City Slickers
City Slickers 2: The Legend of Curly's Gold
The Civil War, Episode 1: The Cause—1861
The Civil War, Episode 2: A Very Bloody Affair—1862
The Civil War, Episode 3: Forever Free—1862
The Civil War, Episode 4: Simply Murder—1863
The Civil War, Episode 5: The Universe of Battle—1863
The Civil War, Episode 6: Valley of the Shadow of Death—1864
The Civil War, Episode 7: Most Hallowed Ground—1864
The Civil War, Episode 8: War is All Hell—1865
The Civil War, Episode 9: The Better Angels of Our Nature—1865
The Clan of the Cave Bear
Clara's Heart
Clarence
Class Action
The Class of Miss MacMichael
Class of 1999 2: The Substitute
Class of Nuke 'Em High 2: Subhumanoid Meltdown
Class of '61
Clean and Sober
Clean Slate
Clear and Present Danger
Cleopatra
Clerks
The Client
Cliffhanger
Clifford
A Climate for Killing
Cloak & Dagger
Clockers
Clockwise
A Clockwork Orange
Close Encounters of the Third Kind
Closet Land
Clown House
Club Paradise
Clue
Cobb
Cobra
The Coca-Cola Kid
Cocktail
Cocoon
Cocoon: The Return
Code Name: Emerald
Codename: Icarus
Cohen and Tate
Cold Feet
Cold Heaven
Cold Sweat
College Swing
Collision Course
The Colony
The Color Purple
Colors
Comanche Territory
The Comancheros
Come Back Little Reba
Come Back, Little Sheba
Come Blow Your Horn
Come See the Paradise
Come September
The Comfort of Strangers
Comin' Round the Mountain
Coming Home
Coming Out of the Ice
Coming to America
Commando
The Commitments
Committed
Common Bonds
Common Threads: Stories from the Quilt
The Companion
The Company of Wolves
Compromising Positions
Comrades in Arms
The Comrades of Summer
Conagher
Conan the Barbarian
Conan the Destroyer
Coneheads
Confessions of a Serial Killer
Congo
Conquest of Space
Conquest of the Planet of the Apes
Conrack
Consenting Adults
Cookie
Cool As Ice
Cool Blue
Cool Change
Cool Runnings
Cool World
Cop
Cop and a Half
Copper Canyon
Cops and Robbersons
Copycat
Corrina, Corrina
Cosmic Slop
The Cotton Club
The Couch Trip
The Counterfeit Traitor
A Countess from Hong Kong
Country Life
Coupe de Ville
Courage
Courage Mountain
The Court Martial of Jackie Robinson
The Courtyard
Cousins
The Cover Girl Murders
Cover Me
Cover-Up
Covergirl
The Cowboy Way
Crackerjack
Crash and Burn
The Crawlers
Crazy from the Heart
Crazy in Love
Crazy Moon
Crazy People
Creature
The Creature Walks Among Us
Creepshow
Creepshow 2
The Crew
Crime of Passion
Crimes & Misdemeanors
Crimes of Passion
Crimes of the Heart
Crimewave
Criminal Justice
The Criminal Mind
Crimson Tide
Crisscross
Critical Condition
Critters 2: The Main Course
Critters 3
Critters 4
Crocodile Dundee

Crocodile Dundee 2
Crooked Hearts
Crooklyn
The Crossing
Crossing Delancey
The Crossing Guard
Crossing the Bridge
Crossroads
The Crow
The Crucifer of Blood
The Crude Oasis
Crumb
The Crusades
The Crush
Cry-Baby
A Cry in the Dark
A Cry in the Night
A Cry in the Wild
Cry, the Beloved Country
The Crying Game
Cthulhu Mansion
Cult of the Cobra
The Cure
Curly Sue
Curly Top
The Curse
Curse 3: Blood Sacrifice
Curse 4: The Ultimate Sacrifice
Curse of the Pink Panther
Curse of the Starving Class
Cutthroat Island
The Cutting Edge
Cyber Bandits
Cyber-Tracker
Cyber-Tracker 2
Cyborg 2
Cyborg Cop
Cyborg Soldier
Da
Dad
Daddy Long Legs
Daddy's Dyin'...Who's Got the Will?
Daffy Duck's Quackbusters
Dakota
Damage
Damn Yankees
Damned River
Dance with a Stranger
Dance with Death
Dancers
Dances with Wolves
The Dancing Princesses
Dancing with Danger
Danger: Diabolik
The Dangerous
Dangerous Game
Dangerous Heart
Dangerous Indiscretion
Dangerous Liaisons
A Dangerous Man: Lawrence after Arabia
Dangerous Minds
A Dangerous Place
Dangerous Pursuit
Dangerous Touch
A Dangerous Woman
Dangerously Close
Danielle Steel's Changes
Danielle Steel's "Daddy"
Danielle Steel's Kaleidoscope
Daring Dobermans
Dario Argento's Trauma
The Dark
Dark Angel: The Ascent
Dark Corner
The Dark Half
Dark Night of the Scarecrow
Dark Secrets
Dark Side of Genius
Dark Victory
The Dark Wind
Darkman
Darkman 2: The Return of Durant
Darkman 3: Die Darkman Die

D.A.R.Y.L.
A Date with Judy
Dave
David and Bathsheba
David Copperfield
Davy Crockett, King of the Wild Frontier
A Day in October
The Day My Parents Ran Away
Day of Atonement
Day One
Days of Thunder
Dazed and Confused
D.C. Cab
The Dead
Dead Again
Dead Air
Dead Alive
Dead Badge
Dead Beat
Dead Calm
Dead Center
Dead Cold
Dead Connection
Dead End Drive-In
Dead Heat
Dead in the Water
Dead Man's Revenge
Dead of Winter
Dead On
Dead on Sight
Dead on the Money
The Dead Pool
Dead Presidents
Dead Reckoning
Dead Silence
Dead Weekend
Dead Wrong
Dead Wrong: The John Evans Story
Dead Zone
Deadfall
Deadlock
Deadly Conspiracy
Deadly Currents
Deadly Desire
Deadly Exposure
Deadly Friend
Deadly Game
Deadly Illusion
The Deadly Mantis
Deadly Rivals
Deadly Surveillance
The Deadly Trackers
Dear America: Letters Home from Vietnam
Dear Brigitte
Death and the Maiden
Death Becomes Her
Death Before Dishonor
Death Machine
Death of a Salesman
Death of a Soldier
Death Warrant
Death Wish 4: The Crackdown
Death Wish 5: The Face of Death
Deathfight
Deceived
The Deceivers
December
Deception
Deceptions
Decline of Western Civilization 2: The Metal Years
Decoration Day
Deep Cover
Deep Down
Deep Red
Defending Your Life
Defense of the Realm
Defenseless
The Defiant Ones
The Delicate Delinquent
Delicatessen
Delirious

Delta Force
Delta Force 2: Operation Stranglehold
Delta Heat
Delta of Venus
Demetrius and the Gladiators
Demolition Man
A Demon in My View
Demonic Toys
Denial: The Dark Side of Passion
Dennis the Menace
Dennis the Menace: Dinosaur Hunter
The Denver & Rio Grande
Descending Angel
Desert Kickboxer
Desire and Hell at Sunset Motel
Desire Under the Elms
Desiree
Desk Set
Desperado
Desperate Characters
Desperate Hours
Desperate Prey
Desperate Remedies
Destiny Turns on the Radio
Detonator
Detonator 2: Night Watch
Devil In a Blue Dress
The Devil's Daughter
The Devil's Disciple
The Diamond Trap
Diamonds Are Forever
Diamond's Edge
Diana: Her True Story
Diary of a Hitman
The Diary of Anne Frank
Dick Tracy
Die Hard
Die Hard 2: Die Harder
Die Hard: With a Vengeance
Digger
Diggstown
Digital Man
Dillinger
Dimples
Diplomatic Immunity
Direct Hit
Dirt Bike Kid
Dirty Dancing
The Dirty Dozen: The Next Mission
Dirty Rotten Scoundrels
Dirty Work
The Disappearance of Christina
Disclosure
Dishonored
Disorderlies
Disorganized Crime
Distant Thunder
The Distinguished Gentleman
The Dive
Dive Bomber
Diving In
Do the Right Thing
D.O.A.
The Doberman Gang
Doc Hollywood
The Doctor
Dr. Alien
Doctor Dolittle
Dr. Giggles
Doctor Mordrid: Master of the Unknown
Dr. No
Doctor Who and the Daleks
Doctor Zhivago
Dodge City
Dog Day Afternoon
Dog Pound Shuffle
The Dogfighters
Doin' Time on Planet Earth
The Dollmaker
Dollman
Dollman vs Demonic Toys

Dolly Dearest
The Dolly Sisters
Dolores Claiborne
Dominick & Eugene
Dominion
Don Juan DeMarco
Donor Unknown
Don't Talk to Strangers
Don't Tell Her It's Me
Don't Tell Mom the Babysitter's Dead
The Doors
The Doors: Soft Parade, a Retrospective
Doppelganger: The Evil Within
Double Cross
Double-Crossed
Double Double Toil and Trouble
Double Dragon
Double Happiness
Double Impact
A Double Life
The Double Life of Veronique
The Double O Kid
Double Vision
The Dove
Down & Dirty
Down Argentine Way
Down by Law
Down Came a Blackbird
Down, Out and Dangerous
Down Periscope
Down Twisted
Downtown
Dracula Blows His Cool
Dracula: Dead and Loving It
Dracula's Daughter
Dracula's Widow
Dragnet
Dragon: The Bruce Lee Story
Dragonard
Dragonworld
Dream a Little Dream
Dream a Little Dream 2
Dream Chasers
Dream Man
The Dream Team
Dressed to Kill
The Dresser
The Driver
Driving Miss Daisy
Drop Dead Fred
DROP Squad
Drop Zone
Drums Along the Mohawk
A Dry White Season
D2: The Mighty Ducks
DuckTales the Movie: Treasure of the Lost Lamp
Duel at Diablo
Duel of Hearts
Dumb & Dumber
Dumbo
Dune
Dunston Checks In
Duplicates
Dust Devil
Dutch
Dying to Remember
Dying Young
Earth Girls Are Easy
East of Eden
Eat a Bowl of Tea
Eat the Peach
Eating
Ebbtide
Ed
Ed and His Dead Mother
Ed Wood
Eddie and the Cruisers
Eddie Murphy: Raw
The Eddy Duchin Story
Edge of Darkness
Edge of Sanity
Educating Rita
Edward Scissorhands

The Efficiency Expert
The Egyptian
Eight Men Out
8 Million Ways to Die
8 Seconds
18 Again!
El Diablo
Eleni
Elephant Walk
11 Harrowhouse
The Eliminators
Elvira, Mistress of the Dark
Elvis and Me
Embrace of the Vampire
The Emerald Forest
Emperor Waltz
The Emperor's New Clothes
Empire of the Sun
Empire Records
The Empire Strikes Back
Employees' Entrance
Enchanted April
The Enchantress
Encino Man
Encounter at Raven's Gate
The End of Innocence
End of the Line
End of the Road
The Endless Game
The Endless Summer 2
Enemies, a Love Story
Enemy Mine
Enemy Territory
The Englishman Who Went Up a Hill But Came Down a Mountain
Entangled
Enter the Dragon
Equinox
Equinox Flower
ER
Erik the Viking
Ernest Goes to Jail
Ernest Goes to School
The Ernest Green Story
Ernest Scared Stupid
Escape from Fort Bravo
Escape from Planet Earth
Escape from the Planet of the Apes
Escape Me Never
E.T.: The Extra-Terrestrial
Ethan Frome
Eve of Destruction
Every Breath
Everybody Wins
Everybody's All American
Everybody's Fine
Evil Clutch
The Evil That Men Do
Evolver
The Ewok Adventure
The Ewoks: Battle for Endor
Ex-Lady
Excessive Force
Excessive Force 2: Force on Force
Executive Decision
Executive Suite
Exit
Exit to Eden
Exodus
Exorcist 3: Legion
Exotica
The Expert
The Experts
Explorers
Exposure
Extreme Justice
Extremities
An Eye for an Eye
Eye on the Sparrow
Eyes of an Angel
Eyes of Julia Deep
Eyes of Laura Mars
Eyes of the Beholder

F/X
F/X 2: The Deadly Art of Illusion
Fade to Black
Fail-Safe
Fair Game
Faith
Faithful
The Falcon and the Snowman
Fall Time
Fallen Angels 1
Fallen Angels 2
Fallen Champ: The Untold Story of Mike Tyson
Falling Down
Falling from Grace
Falling in Love
False Arrest
Family Business
Family Dog: Complete Series
Fancy Pants
Fanny and Alexander
Fantasia
Far and Away
Far from Home: The Adventures of Yellow Dog
Far North
A Far Off Place
Faraway, So Close!
Farewell to the King
The Farmer Takes a Wife
Fast Forward
Fastest Gun Alive
Fat Man and Little Boy
Fatal Attraction
Fatal Beauty
Fatal Charm
Fatal Exposure
Fatal Instinct
Fatal Mission
Fatal Past
Father and Scout
Father Goose
Father Hood
Father of the Bride
Father of the Bride Part II
Fatherland
Fatso
The Favor
The Favor, the Watch, & the Very Big Fish
Fawlty Towers
The FBI Murders
The FBI Story
Fear
Fear, Anxiety and Depression
The Fear Inside
Fear of a Black Hat
Fear Strikes Out
Fearless
Fearless Tiger
Feast of July
Federal Hill
Feds
Felix the Cat: The Movie
Felony
Female
Femme Fatale
Fergie & Andrew: Behind Palace Doors
Ferris Bueller's Day Off
Fever
Fever Pitch
A Few Good Men
Fiddler on the Roof
Field of Dreams
Field of Fire
Fifty/Fifty
52 Pick-Up
The Fig Tree
The Fighting Kentuckian
Fighting Seabees
The Final Alliance
Final Analysis
Final Appeal
Final Approach
The Final Days
Final Mission
Final Notice
Final Round
Final Verdict
Final Warning
Finders Keepers
A Fine Mess
Fine Things
The Finest Hour
The Finishing Touch
Fire and Ice
Fire and Rain
Fire Birds
Fire in the Sky
The Fire Next Time
Firefall
The Firefly
Firepower
Firestarter
Firewalker
The Firm
First Born
First Knight
First Love
The First Power
A Fish Called Wanda
The Fisher King
Fist of Honor
A Fistful of Dollars
Fists of Iron
The Five Heartbeats
The Five Pennies
The Flamingo Kid
Flamingo Road
The Flash
The Flash 2: Revenge of the Trickster
Flashback
Flashdance
Flashpoint
Flatliners
Flesh and Bone
Fletch
Fletch Lives
Flight of the Intruder
The Flight of the Phoenix
Flim-Flam Man
Flinch
The Flintstones
Flipper
Flirting
Florida Straits
Flowers in the Attic
Fluke
The Fly
Fly by Night
Flying Tigers
Folks!
Footlight Serenade
Footloose
For a Few Dollars More
For Love or Money
For Me and My Gal
For Richer, For Poorer
For the Boys
For the First Time
For Your Eyes Only
Forbidden
Forbidden Choices
The Forbidden Dance
The Force
Force of Evil
Foreign Correspondent
A Foreign Field
Forever Amber
Forever Female
Forever James Dean
Forever Young
Forget Paris
The Forgotten
Forgotten Prisoners
Forrest Gump
Forsaking All Others
Fortress
Fortunes of War
40 Pounds of Trouble
48 Hrs.
Four Eyes and Six Guns
Four for Texas
Four Rooms
1492: Conquest of Paradise
The Fourth War
The Fox and the Hound
Foxes
Foxfire
Frame by Frame
Frame Up
Framed
Francis Covers the Big Town
Francis Goes to West Point
Francis in the Haunted House
Frank and Jesse
Frankenhooker
Frankenstein
Frankenstein and the Monster from Hell
Frankenstein Unbound
Frankenweenie
Frankie and Johnny
Frankie Starlight
Frantic
Fraternity Vacation
Freaky Friday
Freddie the Frog
Freddy's Dead: The Final Nightmare
Free Willy
Free Willy 2: The Adventure Home
Freeway
Freeze Frame
French Connection 2
French Kiss
The French Lesson
Fresh
Fresh Horses
The Freshman
Friday
Friday the 13th
Friday the 13th, Part 4: The Final Chapter
Friday the 13th, Part 5: A New Beginning
Friday the 13th, Part 6: Jason Lives
Friday the 13th, Part 7: The New Blood
Friday the 13th, Part 8: Jason Takes Manhattan
Fried Green Tomatoes
Friendly Fire
Friendly Persuasion
Friends
A Friendship in Vienna
Fright Night
Frog
From Beyond
From Hollywood to Deadwood
From Russia with Love
From "Star Wars" to "Jedi": The Making of a Saga
From the Hip
Frozen Assets
The Fugitive
Fugitive Among Us
Fulfillment
Full Body Massage
Full Exposure: The Sex Tape Scandals
Full Metal Jacket
Funny About Love
Funny Bones
The Funny Farm
Funny Farm
Future Cop
The Gamble
The Gambler Returns: The Luck of the Draw
Garbo Talks
Gardens of Stone
Gargoyles, The Movie: The Heroes Awaken
Gas Food Lodging
Gate 2
Gator Bait 2: Cajun Justice
The Gauntlet
Gay Purr-ee
The Geisha Boy
Gentleman Jim
George Balanchine's The Nutcracker
George Washington
George Washington: The Forging of a Nation
Georgia
Geronimo: An American Legend
Get Shorty
Get Smart, Again!
The Getaway
Getting Even with Dad
Getting In
Getting Out
Getting Physical
Getting Up and Going Home
Gettysburg
Ghost
The Ghost and Mrs. Muir
The Ghost and Mr. Chicken
The Ghost Breakers
The Ghost Brigade
Ghost Dad
Ghost in the Machine
The Ghost of Frankenstein
Ghostbusters
Ghostbusters 2
Ghosts Can't Do It
Giant
Giants of Rome
The Gift of Love
The Gig
Gilda
The Girl from Missouri
The Girl Who Spelled Freedom
Girls Just Want to Have Fun
Give My Regards to Broad Street
The Gladiator
Gladiator
The Glass Shield
Gleaming the Cube
Glengarry Glen Ross
Glory
Glory Years
God Bless the Child
The Godfather 1902-1959: The Complete Epic
The Godfather, Part 3
The Gods Must Be Crazy
The Gods Must Be Crazy 2
Godzilla vs. Biollante
Going Bananas
Going Under
Gold Diggers: The Secret of Bear Mountain
The Golden Child
Golden Earrings
Golden Gate
Golden Voyage of Sinbad
Goldeneye
Goldfinger
Goldilocks & the Three Bears
Gone with the Wind
The Good Father
Good Men and Bad
Good Morning, Vietnam
The Good Mother
The Good Son
The Goodbye Bird
Goodbye, Miss 4th of July
Goodbye, Mr. Chips
The Goodbye People
Goodfellas
A Goofy Movie
The Goonies
Gor
Gordon's War
Gordy
The Gorgeous Hussy
The Gospel According to Vic
Gotcha!
The Grace Kelly Story
The Graduate
Graffiti Bridge
Grand Canyon
Grand Hotel
Grand Isle
Grand Prix
Grand Tour: Disaster in Time
Grandview U.S.A.
The Grapes of Wrath
Grave Secrets: The Legacy of Hilltop Drive
Graveyard Shift
Greased Lightning
Great American Traffic Jam
Great Balls of Fire
Great Bank Hoax
Great Bikini Off-Road Adventure
The Great Elephant Escape
The Great Escape
Great Expectations
The Great Gatsby
The Great Los Angeles Earthquake
The Great Man's Lady
The Great Moment
The Great Mouse Detective
The Great Outdoors
The Great Race
The Great White Hope
The Greatest Story Ever Told
Greedy
The Green Berets
Green Card
Green Ice
Gremlins
Gremlins 2: The New Batch
Greystoke: The Legend of Tarzan, Lord of the Apes
The Grifters
Gross Anatomy
Gross Misconduct
Groundhog Day
Grumpier Old Men
Grumpy Old Men
Gryphon
The Guardian
Guardian Angel
Guarding Tess
The Guardsman
Guess Who's Coming to Dinner
Guilty as Charged
Guilty as Sin
Guilty by Suspicion
Guilty of Innocence
Gulliver's Travels
Gun Glory
The Gun in Betty Lou's Handbag
Guncrazy
Gung Ho
Guys and Dolls
Guyver 2: Dark Hero
Gypsy
Gypsy Angels
Hackers
Hadley's Rebellion
Hail the Conquering Hero
The Hairdresser's Husband
Hairspray
Half a Sixpence
Half Moon Street
The Halfback of Notre Dame
Halloween 4: The Return of Michael Myers
Halloween 5: The Revenge of Michael Myers
Hamburger...The Motion Picture
Hamlet
The Hand that Rocks the Cradle
The Handmaid's Tale
Hands Across the Table
Hangin' with the Homeboys
Hanky Panky

Hannah and Her Sisters
Hannie Caulder
Hanoi Hilton
Hansel and Gretel
Happily Ever After
Happy Anniversary 007: 25 Years of James Bond
Happy Gilmore
Hard Hunted
Hard Justice
Hard Promises
Hard Target
Hard to Hold
Hard to Kill
The Hard Way
Hardbodies
Hardware
Harlem Nights
Harley Davidson and the Marlboro Man
Harry and the Hendersons
Harry and Tonto
The Harvest
Haunted Gold
Haunting of Sarah Hardy
The Haunting of Seacliff Inn
Havana
Hawks
He Said, She Said
Heads
Hear My Song
Hear No Evil
Heart and Souls
The Heart is a Lonely Hunter
Heart Like a Wheel
Heart of Darkness
The Heart of Dixie
Heartbreak Hotel
Heartbreak Ridge
Heartburn
Hearts of Darkness: A Filmmaker's Apocalypse
Hearts of Fire
Heat
The Heat of the Day
Heat Wave
Heathers
Heaven and Earth
Heaven Can Wait
Heaven is a Playground
Heavenly Creatures
Heavyweights
Hector's Bunyip
Heidi
Helen of Troy
Hell is for Heroes
Hellbound
Hellbound: Hellraiser 2
Heller in Pink Tights
Hellhole
Hello Again
Hello, Dolly!
Hello Mary Lou: Prom Night 2
Hellraiser
Hellraiser 3: Hell on Earth
Helter Skelter
Henry V
Henry & June
Her Alibi
Hercules
Here Come the Girls
Here Come the Littles: The Movie
Here Come the Waves
Here Comes the Groom
Hero
A Hero Ain't Nothin' But a Sandwich
Hero and the Terror
Heroes for Sale
He's Your Dog, Charlie Brown!
Hexed
Hey There, It's Yogi Bear
The Hidden
The Hidden 2
Hidden Agenda

Hidden Obsession
Hideaway
Hiding Out
High Anxiety
High Heels
High Noon
High Spirits
High Strung
Higher Learning
Highlander
Highlander 2: The Quickening
Highlander: The Final Dimension
Highway to Hell
The Hindenburg
Hired to Kill
His Butler's Sister
History of the World: Part 1
Hit!
The Hit List
Hit the Dutchman
The Hitcher
Hitler's Daughter
The Hitman
Hitz
Hobson's Choice
Hocus Pocus
Hoffa
The Holcroft Covenant
Hold Your Man
Hollywood Boulevard 2
Hologram Man
Holy Matrimony
Home Alone
Home Alone 2: Lost in New York
Home for the Holidays
A Home of Our Own
Homecoming: A Christmas Story
Hometown Boy Makes Good
Homewrecker
Homicide
Honey, I Blew Up the Kid
Honey, I Shrunk the Kids
Honeymoon Academy
Honeymoon in Vegas
Honeymooners Hidden Episodes, Vol. 1
Hong Kong '97
Honor and Glory
Hook
Hooper
Hoosiers
Hope and Glory
The Horse Soldiers
The Horseplayer
The Hospital
Hostage
Hostages
Hostile Guns
Hostile Intentions
Hot Dog...The Movie!
Hot Millions
Hot Shots!
Hot Shots! Part Deux
The Hot Spot
Hot to Trot!
Hotel Imperial
Hotel Room
Houdini
The Hound of the Baskervilles
Hourglass
House
House 2: The Second Story
House 4: Home Deadly Home
A House In The Hills
House of Cards
House of Dracula
House of Fear
House of Horrors
House of Strangers
The House of the Spirits
The House on Carroll Street
House on Haunted Hill
House on 92nd Street
The House on Skull Mountain

House Party 2: The Pajama Jam
House Party 3
Houseguest
Household Saints
The Housekeeper
Housekeeping
Housesitter
How I Got into College
How the West was Fun
How to Be a Perfect Person in Just Three Days
How to Make an American Quilt
How to Murder Your Wife
How to Steal a Million
How U Like Me Now?
Howard the Duck
Howard's End
The Howling: New Moon Rising
Huckleberry Finn
The Hucksters
Hudson Hawk
The Hudsucker Proxy
The Human Shield
The Hunt for Red October
Hunter's Blood
Hurricane Smith
Husbands and Lovers
Husbands and Wives
Hush, Hush, Sweet Charlotte
The Hustler
I Come in Peace
I Died a Thousand Times
I Don't Buy Kisses Anymore
I Like It Like That
I Live My Life
I Live with Me Dad
I Love Trouble
I Love You to Death
I Posed for Playboy
I Wake Up Screaming
I Wanna Hold Your Hand
Ice
If Looks Could Kill
I'll Do Anything
I'll Take Sweden
Illegally Yours
Illicit Behavior
Illicit Dreams
Illusions
Imaginary Crimes
Immediate Family
Immortal Beloved
Immortal Sergeant
The Immortals
Impulse
In a Moment of Passion
In a Stranger's Hand
The In Crowd
In Harm's Way
In Search of a Golden Sky
In Search of the Castaways
In Self Defense
In the Army Now
In the Cold of the Night
In the Line of Duty: Ambush in Waco
In the Line of Fire
In the Mood
In the Mouth of Madness
In the Name of the Father
In the Navy
In the Soup
The Incident
Incident at Deception Ridge
An Inconvenient Woman
The Incredible Mr. Limpet
Indecency
Indecent Proposal
The Indian in the Cupboard
The Indian Runner
Indian Summer
Indiana Jones and the Last Crusade
Indiana Jones and the Temple of Doom
Indictment: The McMartin Trial

Indio
Indiscreet
Indochine
The Inkwell
The Inner Circle
Inner Sanctum
Inner Sanctum 2
Innerspace
The Innocent
Innocent Blood
An Innocent Man
Innocent Prey
Instant Justice
Instant Karma
Interceptor
Internal Affairs
Internecine Project
Internes Can't Take Money
Intersection
Interview with the Vampire
Intimate Power
Intimate Stranger
Into the Night
Into the Sun
Into the West
Intruder
Intruders
The Invaders
Invaders from Mars
Invasion of Privacy
Invasion of the Body Snatchers
Invisible Agent
Invisible Invaders
The Invisible Man's Revenge
Invisible: The Chronicles of Benjamin Knight
The Invisible Woman
Invitation to a Gunfighter
I.Q.
Irma La Douce
Iron Eagle
Iron Warrior
Iron Will
Ironclads
Ironheart
Ironweed
Irreconcilable Differences
Is Paris Burning?
Ishtar
Island of Lost Souls
Island of Terror
Istanbul
It Came From Outer Space
It Came Upon a Midnight Clear
It Could Happen to You
It Happened One Night
It Started in Naples
It Takes Two
The Italian Job
It's a Wonderful Life
It's My Party
It's Pat: The Movie
Ivory Hunters
Jack & the Beanstalk
Jack the Bear
Jacknife
Jack's Back
Jacob's Ladder
Jade
JAG
The Jagged Edge
Jailbait
Jake Speed
Jane Eyre
The January Man
Jason Goes to Hell: The Final Friday
Jaws: The Revenge
The Jayhawkers
Jeeves & Wooster: Jeeves' Arrival
Jefferson in Paris
Jeffrey
Jennifer 8
Jericho Fever
The Jerky Boys

Jersey Girl
Jesse
Jet Pilot
Jetsons: The Movie
The Jewel of the Nile
JFK
JFK: Reckless Youth
Jimmy Hollywood
Jo Jo Dancer, Your Life is Calling
Joey Breaker
Johnny Appleseed
Johnny Be Good
Johnny Dangerously
Johnny Guitar
Johnny Handsome
Johnny Mnemonic
Johnny Suede
Joseph
The Josephine Baker Story
Josh and S.A.M.
Josh Kirby...Time Warrior: Chapter 1, Planet of the Dino-Knights
Josh Kirby...Time Warrior: Chapter 2, The Human Pets
Josh Kirby...Time Warrior: Chapter 3, Trapped on Toyworld
Josh Kirby...Time Warrior: Chapter 4, Eggs from 70 Million B.C.
Josh Kirby...Time Warrior: Chapter 5, Journey to the Magic Cavern
Josh Kirby...Time Warrior: Chapter 6, Last Battle for the Universe
Joshua Then and Now
The Journey of August King
Journey of Honor
Journey to the Center of the Earth
The Joy Luck Club
Judge Dredd
Judgment
Judgment Night
Juggernaut
Juice
Julia and Julia
Jumanji
Jumpin' Jack Flash
Jumping Jacks
June Bride
The Jungle Book
Jungle Fever
Junior
Jurassic Park
The Juror
Jury Duty
Just Around the Corner
Just Cause
Just for You
Just One of the Guys
Just the Way You Are
Justine
K-9
K-9000
Kafka
Kalifornia
Karate Cop
The Karate Kid
The Karate Kid: Part 2
The Karate Kid: Part 3
Keep 'Em Flying
Keep the Change
Keeper of the City
Keeping Track
The Kettles in the Ozarks
The Kettles on Old MacDonald's Farm
Key Exchange
The Keys of the Kingdom
Kickboxer 3: The Art of War
Kickboxer 4: The Aggressor
Kid

Kid Colter
Kid Galahad
A Kid in King Arthur's Court
The Kid Who Loved Christmas
Kidco
Kidnapped
Kids
Kids In the Hall Brain Candy
Kill Cruise
Kill Me Again
Killer Fish
Killer Image
Killer Instinct
Killer Klowns from Outer Space
Killer Looks
Killer Tomatoes Strike Back
Killing at Hell's Gate
The Killing Beach
The Killing Fields
Killing Hour
A Killing in a Small Town
The Killing of a Chinese Bookie
Kindergarten Cop
The King and I
King David
King Kong
King Kong Lives
King of New York
King of the Hill
The King of the Kickboxers
King of the Wind
King Ralph
Kings Row
The King's Whore
Kismet
A Kiss Before Dying
Kiss Me Deadly
Kiss of Death
Kiss of the Spider Woman
Kiss of the Vampire
Kiss Shot
The Kissing Place
The Kitchen Toto
The Klansman
Knight Moves
Knights
Knights & Emeralds
Kramer vs. Kramer
The Krays
Krull
Krush Groove
K2: The Ultimate High
Kuffs
Kurt Vonnegut's Harrison Bergeron
La Balance
La Bamba
L.A. Law
L.A. Story
Labyrinth
The Ladies' Man
Ladies of the Chorus
Ladies They Talk About
Lady by Choice
Lady Dragon
Lady Dragon 2
The Lady in White
Lady Jane
Lady Killer
Lady Mobster
Lady On a Train
Ladybugs
Ladyhawke
Ladykiller
Ladykillers
Lake Consequence
Lakota Woman: Siege at Wounded Knee
Lambada
The Land Before Time
The Land Before Time 2: The Great Valley Adventure
The Land Before Time 3: The Time of the Great Giving
Land of the Pharaohs
The Land Unknown

Landslide
Lantern Hill
Laser Mission
Lassie
Last Action Hero
The Last Boy Scout
The Last Days of Chez Nous
The Last Days of Patton
Last Days of Planet Earth
Last Days of Pompeii
The Last Dragon
The Last Emperor
The Last Hit
The Last Hunt
Last Light
Last Man Standing
The Last of His Tribe
The Last of Mrs. Cheyney
The Last of the Finest
The Last Picture Show
Last Plane Out
The Last Ride
Last Rites
The Last Safari
The Last Seduction
Last Song
Last Time Out
The Last Unicorn
The Last Voyage
The Last Waltz
The Last Winter
The Late Show
Latino
The Laughing Policeman
Laurel Avenue
The Law and Jake Wade
The Lawnmower Man
Lawnmower Man 2: Beyond Cyberspace
Lawrence of Arabia
Le Mans
A League of Their Own
Lean on Me
Leap of Faith
Leapin' Leprechauns
Leather Jackets
Leave 'Em Laughing
Leaving Las Vegas
Leaving Normal
The Leech Woman
Legacy of Lies
Legal Eagles
Legend
Legend of Billie Jean
The Legend of Hell House
The Legend of Sleepy Hollow
The Legend of Wolf Mountain
Legends of the Fall
The Lemon Sisters
Lenny
Leonard Part 6
Leprechaun 2
Leprechaun 3
Less Than Zero
Let Freedom Ring
Let It Ride
Lethal Lolita—Amy Fisher: My Story
Lethal Weapon
Lethal Weapon 2
Lethal Weapon 3
Let's Dance
Let's Get Harry
Let's Make It Legal
Letter to Brezhnev
Letter to My Killer
Leviathan
Liberty & Bash
License to Kill
Lies
Lies Before Kisses
A Life in the Theater
Life Is Sweet
A Life of Sin
Life Stinks
Life with Mikey

Lifeboat
The Lighthorsemen
The Lightning Incident
Lightning: The White Stallion
The Lightship
Li'l Abner
Lili
Lilies of the Field
Limit Up
Linda
The Linguini Incident
Link
The Lion King
Lionheart
Lisa
Listen to Me
Little Big League
Little Big Man
Little Buddha
The Little Colonel
Little Dorrit, Film 1: Nobody's Fault
Little Dorrit, Film 2: Little Dorrit's Story
The Little Drummer Girl
Little Lord Fauntleroy
Little Man Tate
The Little Match Girl
The Little Mermaid
Little Miss Broadway
Little Miss Millions
Little Monsters
Little Nikita
Little Odessa
The Little Princess
A Little Princess
The Little Rascals
Little Red Riding Hood
Little Shop of Horrors
Little Treasure
Little Women
The Littlest Rebel
Live Nude Girls
Live Wire
Live Wire: Human Timebomb
Livin' Large
The Living Daylights
Living in Oblivion
Living Proof: The Hank Williams Jr. Story
Local Hero
Lock Up
London Kills Me
Lone Justice
Lonely in America
Lonesome Dove
The Long Day Closes
The Long Gray Line
The Long, Hot Summer
The Long, Long Trailer
The Long Walk Home
Look Who's Talking
Look Who's Talking Now
Look Who's Talking, Too
The Lookalike
Looker
Looking for Miracles
Loose Cannons
Lord of Illusions
Lord of the Flies
Lorenzo's Oil
Lorna Doone
Losing Isaiah
Lost Angels
The Lost Boys
The Lost Capone
Lost in America
Lost in Yonkers
The Lost World
Love Affair
Love Among the Ruins
Love and a .45
Love and Bullets
Love at Large
The Love Bug
Love, Cheat & Steal

Love Field
Love Finds Andy Hardy
The Love God?
Love Hurts
A Love in Germany
Love in the Afternoon
Love Is a Gun
Love Is a Many-Splendored Thing
Love Kills
Love, Lies and Murder
Love Matters
Love Me or Leave Me
Love or Money?
Love Potion 9
Love with the Proper Stranger
Lovelines
The Lover
Loverboy
A Low Down Dirty Shame
Lower Level
Lucas
Lucy and Desi: Before the Laughter
Lush Life
Lust in the Dust
M. Butterfly
Ma and Pa Kettle
Ma and Pa Kettle at Home
Ma and Pa Kettle at the Fair
Ma and Pa Kettle at Waikiki
Ma and Pa Kettle Back On the Farm
Ma and Pa Kettle Go to Town
Ma and Pa Kettle on Vacation
Mac
Mac and Me
Macaroni
Mad About Music
Mad at the Moon
Mad Dog and Glory
The Mad Ghoul
Mad Love
Mad Max: Beyond Thunderdome
Madam Satan
The Maddening
Made for Each Other
Made in America
Made in Heaven
Madhouse
The Madness of King George
Madonna: Innocence Lost
Magic in the Water
Magic Island
Magic Kid
The Magic of the Golden Bear: Goldy 3
The Magnificent Ambersons
The Maid
Major League
Major League 2
Major Payne
Malcolm X
Malibu Bikini Shop
Malice
Malicious
Mallrats
Malone
The Maltese Falcon
The Mambo Kings
A Man and a Woman
A Man Called Horse
A Man Called Peter
A Man for All Seasons
The Man from Left Field
Man from Monterey
Man from the Alamo
The Man I Love
The Man in the Attic
The Man in the Gray Flannel Suit
The Man in the Iron Mask
The Man in the Moon
Man Made Monster
A Man of No Importance
Man of the House

Man of the West
Man Trouble
The Man Upstairs
The Man Who Loved Women
The Man Who Shot Liberty Valance
The Man Who Would Be King
Man with a Gun
The Man with One Red Shoe
The Man Without a Face
The Manchurian Candidate
Mandroid
The Mangler
Manhattan Murder Mystery
Manhunter
Maniac Cop 2
Maniac Cop 3: Badge of Silence
Mannequin
Man's Best Friend
Mansfield Park
The Many Adventures of Winnie the Pooh
Map of the Human Heart
Marie
Marked for Death
Marked Woman
Maroc 7
Married to It
Married to the Mob
The Marrying Man
Marshal Law
Martial Law 2: Undercover
Martial Outlaw
Martin's Day
Marty
Mary Poppins
Mary Shelley's Frankenstein
Mascara
Mask
The Mask
Masquerade
Mass Appeal
Masters of the Universe
The Matchmaker
Matewan
Matinee
Matters of the Heart
Maurice
Maverick
Max and Helen
Max Headroom, the Original Story
Max is Missing
May Wine
McBain
The McConnell Story
McQ
Me and Him
Me and the Kid
Mean Streets
Meatballs
Meatballs 2
Meatballs 4
Mediterraneo
Medium Cool
Meet Danny Wilson
Meet the Hollowheads
Melody in Love
Memoirs of an Invisible Man
Memories of Me
Memphis
Memphis Belle
Men at Work
Men Don't Leave
Men of Respect
Men of War
Menace II Society
Meridian: Kiss of the Beast
Mermaids
Merton of the Movies
Messenger of Death
The Meteor Man
Miami Blues
Miami Rhapsody
Micki & Maude
Middlemarch

Midnight
A Midnight Clear
Midnight Edition
Mighty Aphrodite
The Mighty Ducks
The Mighty Pawns
Mikey
Mildred Pierce
Miles from Home
Milk Money
Millenium
Miller's Crossing
Million Dollar Mystery
A Million to Juan
Millions
Milo & Otis
Mindwalk: A Film for Passionate Thinkers
Mindwarp
Miracle Down Under
Miracle Mile
Miracle on 34th Street
Mirrors
Mischief
Misery
Mishima: A Life in Four Chapters
Miss Firecracker
Miss Rose White
The Mission
Mission of Justice
Mississippi Burning
Mississippi Masala
Mrs. Doubtfire
Mrs. Munck
Mrs. Parker and the Vicious Circle
Mrs. Soffel
Mr. & Mrs. Bridge
Mr. Baseball
Mr. Billion
Mr. Corbett's Ghost
Mr. Destiny
Mr. Frost
Mr. Hobbs Takes a Vacation
Mr. Holland's Opus
Mister Johnson
Mr. Jones
Mr. Love
Mr. Lucky
Mr. Mom
Mr. Music
Mr. Nanny
Mr. North
Mr. Saturday Night
Mr. Wonderful
Mr. Write
Mistress
Misty
Mixed Nuts
Mo' Better Blues
Mobsters
Moby Dick
Model by Day
Modern Love
The Mole People
Mom
Mom and Dad Save the World
Money for Nothing
The Money Pit
Money Train
Monkey Shines
Monkey Trouble
Monolith
The Monolith Monsters
Monsieur Beaucaire
The Monster and the Girl
Monster in a Box
Monster in the Closet
Monster on the Campus
Montana
Monte Carlo
Monte Walsh
A Month by the Lake
Monty Python Live at the Hollywood Bowl
Monty Python's Life of Brian
Monty Python's Parrot Sketch Not Included
Moon 44
Moon over Miami
Moonlighting
Moonraker
Moonshine Highway
Moonstruck
More American Graffiti
Morituri
Mork & Mindy
The Morning After
Mortal Danger
Mortal Kombat: The Movie
Mortal Passions
Mortal Sins
Mortal Thoughts
Moscow on the Hudson
The Mosquito Coast
Mother Goose Rock 'n' Rhyme
Mother's Boys
A Mother's Prayer
The Mountain
Mountains of the Moon
Moving
Moving Violations
Much Ado about Nothing
Mulholland Falls
The Mummy's Curse
The Mummy's Ghost
The Mummy's Hand
The Mummy's Tomb
Munchie
The Muppet Christmas Carol
The Muppets Take Manhattan
Murder by Moonlight
Murder in New Hampshire: The Pamela Smart Story
Murder In the First
A Murder Is Announced
Murder 101
Murder Ordained
Murder over New York
Murdered Innocence
Murderers among Us: The Simon Wiesenthal Story
Murderous Vision
Murders in the Rue Morgue
Murders in the Zoo
Muriel's Wedding
Murphy's Law
Murphy's Romance
The Music Man
The Music of Chance
Mute Witness
My Antonia
My Beautiful Laundrette
My Best Friend Is a Vampire
My Blue Heaven
My Boyfriend's Back
My Cousin Vinny
My Darlin' Clementine
My Darling Clementine
My Fair Lady
My Family
My Father Is Coming
My Father the Hero
My Favorite Blonde
My Friend Irma
My Geisha
My Girl
My Girl 2
My Grandpa is a Vampire
My Heroes Have Always Been Cowboys
My Left Foot
My Life
My Little Pony: The Movie
My Man Adam
My New Gun
My Own Private Idaho
My Samurai
My Stepmother Is an Alien
My Summer Story
Mysterious Island
Mystery Date
Mystery Science Theater 3000: The Movie
Mystic Pizza
Nadine
Nails
The Naked Country
The Naked Edge
The Naked Gun: From the Files of Police Squad
Naked Gun 33 1/3: The Final Insult
Naked Gun 2 1/2: The Smell of Fear
Naked in New York
Naked Lunch
The Naked Maja
The Name of the Rose
The Nanny
Narrow Margin
National Lampoon's Attack of the 5 Ft. 2 Women
National Lampoon's Christmas Vacation
National Lampoon's European Vacation
National Lampoon's Favorite Deadly Sins
National Lampoon's Last Resort
National Lampoon's Senior Trip
National Velvet
Native Son
Nativity
The Natural
Natural Born Killers
Natural Causes
Nature of the Beast
Navy SEALS
Necessary Roughness
Needful Things
Nell
Nemesis
Neon City
Neptune Factor
Neptune's Daughter
Nervous Ticks
The Net
Netherworld
Never Forget
Never on Tuesday
Never Say Die
Never Say Never Again
Never Talk to Strangers
Never Too Young to Die
The NeverEnding Story
NeverEnding Story 2: The Next Chapter
The New Adventures of Pippi Longstocking
The New Age
New Eden
New Jersey Drive
The New Kids
A New Kind of Love
A New Life
New Year's Day
New York Cop
New York, New York
Newsies
The Next Karate Kid
Next of Kin
Next Stop, Greenwich Village
Nick of Time
Night and the City
The Night Before
Night Breed
Night Eyes 2
A Night in Heaven
A Night in the Life of Jimmy Reardon
Night Monster
'night, Mother
Night of Dark Shadows
Night of the Comet
Night of the Creeps
Night of the Cyclone
Night of the Demons 2
The Night of the Following Day
Night of the Running Man
Night of the Scarecrow
Night Patrol
Night Rhythms
Night Siege Project: Shadowchaser 2
The Night They Raided Minsky's
The Night Train to Kathmandu
Night Train to Venice
The Night Walker
Nighthawks
The Nightingale
Nightmare
The Nightmare Before Christmas
A Nightmare on Elm Street
A Nightmare on Elm Street 2: Freddy's Revenge
A Nightmare on Elm Street 3: Dream Warriors
A Nightmare on Elm Street 4: Dream Master
A Nightmare on Elm Street 5: Dream Child
Nightmare on the 13th Floor
Nightscare
Nijinsky
Nina Takes a Lover
9 1/2 Ninjas
Nine Months
976-EVIL
976-EVIL 2: The Astral Factor
1918
1969
90 Days
Ninja the Battalion
Ninja Vengeance
Nixon
No Contest
No Escape
No Escape, No Return
No Holds Barred
No Man's Land
No Retreat, No Surrender 3: Blood Brothers
No Small Affair
No Time for Sergeants
Nobody's Fool
Nobody's Perfect
None But the Brave
North
North to Alaska
Nostradamus
Not as a Stranger
Not Quite Human
Not Quite Human 2
Not Without My Daughter
Nothing But Trouble
Nothing in Common
Notorious
Now and Then
Nowhere to Hide
Nowhere to Run
Number One Fan
The Nutcracker Prince
Nuts
O Pioneers!
The Object of Beauty
Oblivion
O.C. and Stiggs
The Odessa File
Of Mice and Men
Off Limits
Official Denial
Oh, God! You Devil
Oh, Heavenly Dog!
Oh, What a Night
Oklahoma!
The Old Curiosity Shop
Old Gringo
Old Yeller
Oldest Confederate Widow Tells All
Oleanna
Oliver!
Oliver & Company
Oliver Twist
Ollie Hopnoodle's Haven of Bliss
Omar Khayyam
Omen 4: The Awakening
On Borrowed Time
On Deadly Ground
On the Line
On the Waterfront
Onassis
Once Around
Once Bitten
Once Upon a Crime
Once Upon a Forest
Once Upon a Time in America
Once Were Warriors
One Against the Wind
One Crazy Summer
One Deadly Summer
One False Move
One Good Cop
One Magic Christmas
One Man's Justice
One Man's War
One Million Years B.C.
One More Saturday Night
Only the Strong
Only You
Open Fire
Opening Night
Opera do Malandro
Operation C.I.A.
Operation Crossbow
Operation Dumbo Drop
Operation Golden Phoenix
Operation Petticoat
Opportunity Knocks
Orchestra Wives
The Organization
Original Intent
Orlando
Orphans
Orpheus Descending
Oscar
Oscar's Greatest Moments: 1971-1991
Othello
Other People's Money
Our Little Girl
Our Modern Maidens
Out for Blood
Out of Africa
Out of Bounds
Out of Sync
Out of the Dark
Out on a Limb
Out There
Outbreak
The Outer Limits: Sandkings
The Outfit
Outland
Outlaw of Gor
Outrageous Fortune
Outside the Law
Over the Hill
Over the Top
Overboard
The Ox-Bow Incident
Oxford Blues
Pacific Heights
The Package
Painted Hero
Pair of Aces
The Pajama Game
Pale Rider
The Palermo Connection
The Pamela Principle
Panic in the Streets
Papa's Delicate Condition
The Paper
A Paper Wedding
The Paperboy
The Paradine Case
Paradise

Paradise Motel
Parallel Lives
Paranoiac
Parasite
Pardners
The Parent Trap
Parenthood
Paris Blues
Paris, Texas
Paris Trout
The Park is Mine
Parting Glances
The Party
Party Girl
A Passage to India
Passed Away
Passenger 57
Passion Fish
Past Midnight
Past Tense
Past the Bleachers
Pat and Mike
Paths of Glory
Patriot Games
Paul and Michelle
The Pawnbroker
Payback
Payoff
P.C.U.
The Pearl of Death
The Pebble and the Penguin
Pecos Bill
Pee Wee's Big Adventure
Pee Wee's Playhouse Festival of Fun
Peggy Sue Got Married
The Pelican Brief
Penalty Phase
Penitentiary 3
Penn and Teller Get Killed
Pentathlon
The Penthouse
The People Under the Stairs
Percy & Thunder
The Perez Family
Perfect
The Perfect Bride
Perfect Family
Perfect Harmony
A Perfect Little Murder
The Perfect Marriage
The Perfect Weapon
A Perfect World
Permanent Record
Personal Property
Personals
Persuasion
Pet Sematary
Pet Sematary 2
Peter Pan
Peter's Friends
Pete's Dragon
Peyton Place
Phantasm III: Lord of the Dead
The Phantom of the Opera
Phantom of the Ritz
Phar Lap
Philadelphia
Philadelphia Experiment 2
Phobia
The Phoenix and the Magic Carpet
Phone Call from a Stranger
Physical Evidence
The Piano
The Piano Lesson
The Pick-Up Artist
The Pickle
Picture Bride
The Pied Piper of Hamelin
Pin-Up Girl
Pink Cadillac
Pinocchio
Pistol: The Birth of a Legend
The Pit & the Pendulum
Pittsburgh
A Place for Annie
Places in the Heart
The Plague
The Plague Dogs
Plain Clothes
Planes, Trains & Automobiles
Planet of the Apes
Platinum Blonde
Platoon
Playback
The Player
Playing for Keeps
Playroom
Pocahontas
Pocketful of Miracles
A Pocketful of Rye
Poetic Justice
Point Blank
Point Break
Point of Impact
Point of No Return
Poison Ivy 2: Lily
Poker Alice
Police Academy
Police Academy 2: Their First Assignment
Police Academy 3: Back in Training
Police Academy 4: Citizens on Patrol
Police Academy 5: Assignment Miami Beach
Police Academy 6: City Under Siege
Pollyanna
Poltergeist 2: The Other Side
Poltergeist 3
Pontiac Moon
A Poor Little Rich Girl
The Poor Little Rich Girl
The Pope Must Diet
Pork Chop Hill
Porky's Revenge
The Portrait
Portrait of Jennie
Portraits of a Killer
Posse
Possessed by the Night
The Possession of Joel Delaney
Postcards from the Edge
The Postman Always Rings Twice
Power
The Power of One
The Power Within
Prancer
Prayer for the Dying
Praying Mantis
Pre-Madonnas: Rebels Without a Clue
Predator
Predator 2
Prehysteria
Prehysteria 2
Prehysteria 3
Prelude to a Kiss
The Preppie Murder
President's Target
The Presidio
Pressure Point
Presumed Innocent
Pretty in Pink
Pretty Woman
Prey of the Chameleon
Priceless Beauty
Pride and Prejudice
Pride of Jesse Hallum
The Pride of the Yankees
Prime Cut
The Prime of Miss Jean Brodie
Prime Target
Primo Baby
Prince Brat and the Whipping Boy
The Prince of Tides
Princes in Exile
The Princess and the Pea
The Princess Bride
Princess Caraboo
The Princess Comes Across
The Princess Who Never Laughed
Prison
Prison Stories: Women on the Inside
Private Investigations
Private Lessons, Another Story
Private Lives
A Private Matter
Private Wars
Prizzi's Honor
Probable Cause
Problem Child
Problem Child 2
The Program
Programmed to Kill
Project: Shadowchaser
Project Shadowchaser 3000
Project X
Prom Night 4: Deliver Us From Evil
The Promise
Promised a Miracle
Proof
The Prophecy
Protector
Protocol
Prototype X29A
Proud Men
Psychic
Psycho 3
Pucker Up and Bark Like a Dog
Pulp Fiction
Pulse
Pump Up the Volume
Pumping Iron 2: The Women
The Pumpkin Eater
Pumpkinhead
Punchline
The Punisher
Puppet Master
Puppet Master 2
Puppet Master 3: Toulon's Revenge
Puppet Master 4
Puppet Master 5: The Final Chapter
The Puppet Masters
Pure Country
Pure Luck
Purple Rain
The Purple Rose of Cairo
Pursued
Pursuit
Pursuit to Algiers
Puss 'n Boots
A Pyromaniac's Love Story
Q & A
Quarterback Princess
Queen Bee
The Queen of Mean
Queens Logic
The Quest
Question of Faith
The Quick and the Dead
Quick Change
Quicksand: No Escape
Quicksilver
The Quiet Earth
The Quiet Man
Quigley Down Under
The Quiller Memorandum
Quiz Show
Quo Vadis
Race with the Devil
The Racers
The Rachel Papers
Racing with the Moon
Rad
Radio Flyer
Radio Inside
Radioland Murders
Rafferty & the Gold Dust Twins
Rage
Rage and Honor
A Rage in Harlem
Raggedy Ann and Andy: A Musical Adventure
Raging Angels
Raiders of the Lost Ark
Raiders of the Sun
The Railway Station Man
Rain Man
The Rainmaker
Raise the Red Lantern
A Raisin in the Sun
Raising Arizona
Raising Cain
Rambo: First Blood, Part 2
Rampage
Ran
Rancho Deluxe
Rapa Nui
Rapid Fire
Rapunzel
The Rare Breed
Ratboy
Ratings Game
Rattled
Raw Deal
Raw Justice
The Razor's Edge
Ready to Wear
Real Genius
The Real McCoy
Real Men
Reality Bites
Rebecca
Rebecca of Sunnybrook Farm
Rebel
Rebel Without a Cause
The Rebels
Reckless
Reckless Kelly
Red Ball Express
Red Garters
Red Headed Stranger
Red Line 7000
Red River
Red Rock West
Red Scorpion 2
Red Shoe Diaries
Red Shoe Diaries 2: Double Dare
Red Shoe Diaries 3: Another Woman's Lipstick
Red Shoe Diaries 4: Auto Erotica
Red Shoe Diaries 5: Weekend Pass
Red Shoe Diaries 6: How I Met My Husband
The Red Shoes
Red Sonja
Red Wind
The Redhead from Wyoming
Reds
Redwood Curtain
The Ref
Reflections in the Dark
Reform School Girl
Regarding Henry
Relative Fear
Relentless
Relentless 3
Relentless 4
The Reluctant Astronaut
The Remains of the Day
Remember the Night
Remote
Renaissance Man
Renegades
Rent-A-Cop
Rent-A-Kid
Replikator: Cloned to Kill
Repossessed
The Rescue
The Rescuers
The Rescuers Down Under
Reservoir Dogs
The Restless Breed
Return of Frank James
The Return of Jafar
Return of Superfly
The Return of Swamp Thing
Return of the Bad Men
Return of the Dragon
Return of the Jedi
Return of the Killer Tomatoes!
Return of the Living Dead 2
Return of the Living Dead 3
The Return of the Musketeers
The Return of the Native
Return to Lonesome Dove
Return to Peyton Place
Return to Salem's Lot
Return to the Blue Lagoon
Return to the Lost World
Return to Two Moon Junction
Reuben, Reuben
Reunion
Revenge of the Creature
Revenge of the Nerds
Revenge of the Nerds 2: Nerds in Paradise
Revenge of the Nerds 4: Nerds in Love
Reversal of Fortune
Revolution
Revolver
Rhinestone
Rhythm on the Range
Rhythm on the River
Rich Girl
Rich in Love
Richard III
Richie Rich
Ricochet
Ride Him, Cowboy
Ride the Wild Surf
Riding High
Riding the Edge
Riff Raff
The Right Stuff
The Right to Remain Silent
Rikky and Pete
Ring of Fire
Ring of Fire 2: Blood and Steel
Ring of Fire 3: Lion Strike
Ring of Steel
Ring of the Musketeers
Rio Grande
Rio Lobo
Rip van Winkle
Ripping Yarns
Rising Son
Rising Sun
The Ritz
The River
River of Death
River of Diamonds
The River Rat
A River Runs Through It
The River Wild
River's Edge
The Road Home
The Road Killers
The Road to Galveston
The Road to Wellville
Roadside Prophets
The Roaring Twenties
Rob Roy
Robin Hood
Robin Hood: Men in Tights
Robin Hood: Prince of Thieves
Robin Hood...The Legend: Herne's Son
Robin Hood...The Legend: Robin Hood and the Sorcerer
Robin Hood...The Legend: The Swords of Wayland
Robin Hood...The Legend: The Time of the Wolf
Robinson Crusoe & the Tiger

RoboCop
RoboCop 2
RoboCop 3
Robot Jox
Robot Wars
Rock 'n' Roll High School
Rock 'n' Roll High School Forever
Rocket Gibraltar
The Rocketeer
Rockula
Rockwell: A Legend of the Wild West
Rocky 4
Rocky 5
The Rocky Horror Picture Show
Roe vs. Wade
Roger & Me
Romancing the Stone
Romantic Comedy
Rome Adventure
Romeo Is Bleeding
Romero
The Rookie
Rookie of the Year
A Room with a View
Roommates
Roosters
The Rosary Murders
The Rose
The Rose and the Jackal
The Rose Tattoo
Rosencrantz & Guildenstern Are Dead
Roswell: The U.F.O. Cover-Up
Rough Night in Jericho
Round Midnight
Round Numbers
Round Trip to Heaven
The Rounders
Roxanne
Royce
Rubberface
Rubdown
Ruby
Ruby in Paradise
Rudolph the Red-Nosed Reindeer
Rudy
Rudyard Kipling's Classic Stories
Rudyard Kipling's The Jungle Book
Rumble in the Bronx
Rumpelstiltskin
Run
The Run of the Country
Runaway
Runaway Father
Runaway Train
The Runestone
The Runner Stumbles
Running Away
Running Cool
Running Delilah
Running Free
Running Mates
Running on Empty
Running Scared
The Russia House
The Russians are Coming, the Russians are Coming
Russkies
Rustler's Rhapsody
Sabrina
Sacred Ground
Safe
Safe Passage
St. Elmo's Fire
The Saint of Fort Washington
Saints and Sinners
Salvador
Samantha
Samaritan: The Mitch Snyder Story
San Antonio
The Sandlot
Sands of Iwo Jima
Santa Claus Is Coming to Town
Santa Claus: The Movie
The Santa Clause
Santa Sangre
Sarafina!
Sarah, Plain and Tall
Saratoga Trunk
Satan's Princess
Satisfaction
Save Me
Saving Grace
Say Anything
Scanner Cop
Scanners 2: The New Order
Scanners 3: The Takeover
Scanners: The Showdown
The Scarlet & the Black
Scarlet Claw
Scarlet Empress
The Scarlet Letter
Scarlett
Scenes from a Mall
Scent of a Woman
Schindler's List
School Daze
School Ties
Scissors
The Scout
Screamers
Scrooge
Scrooged
Scruples
Sea of Love
Sea Wolves
Search and Destroy
The Search for Bridey Murphy
Searching for Bobby Fischer
Second Best
Second Sight
Second Victory
The Secret
The Secret Diary of Sigmund Freud
Secret Games
Secret Games 2: The Escort
The Secret Garden
The Secret of My Success
The Secret of NIMH
The Secret of Roan Inish
Secret Places
Secret Weapon
The Secretary
Seduced by Evil
See No Evil, Hear No Evil
See You in the Morning
Seedpeople
The Seekers
Sensation
Sense & Sensibility
Sense and Sensibility
The Sensuous Nurse
Separate But Equal
September
September 30, 1955
Sgt. Bilko
Serial Killer
Serial Mom
The Serpent of Death
Servants of Twilight
Sesame Street Presents: Follow That Bird
The Set Up
Seven
Seven Minutes in Heaven
Seven Thieves
The Seven-Ups
The Seventh Sign
Sex and the Single Girl
Sex Crimes
sex, lies and videotape
Sexual Response
S.F.W.
Shadey
The Shadow
Shadow Force
Shadow of the Wolf
Shadowhunter
Shadowlands
Shadows and Fog
Shadowzone
Shampoo
Sharon's Secret
Shattered
Shattered Image
Shattered Vows
The Shawshank Redemption
She-Devil
Sheena
The Shell Seekers
Shelley Duvall's Bedtime Stories
The Sheltering Sky
Sherlock Holmes and the Secret Weapon
Sherlock Holmes Faces Death
Sherlock Holmes in Washington
Sherlock Holmes: The Voice of Terror
Sherlock: Undercover Dog
She's a Good Skate, Charlie Brown
She's Gotta Have It
She's Having a Baby
She's Out of Control
The Shining
The Shining Hour
Shining Through
Ship of Fools
Shipwrecked
Shirley Valentine
A Shock to the System
Shock Treatment
Shocker
Shoot to Kill
Shootfighter: Fight to the Death
The Shop Around the Corner
Short Circuit
Short Circuit 2
Short Cuts
Short Time
Shout
The Show
A Show of Force
Showdown
Showdown at Williams Creek
Showdown in Little Tokyo
Showgirls
The Shrimp on the Barbie
Shy People
Sibling Rivalry
Sid & Nancy
Side By Side
Side Out
Sidekicks
Siesta
The Sign of Four
The Sign of the Cross
Silas Marner
Silence Like Glass
Silence of the Hams
The Silence of the Lambs
The Silencer
Silent Fall
Silent Hunter
Silent Motive
Silent Tongue
Silent Victim
Silk Degrees
Silver Bullet
Silver River
The Silver Stallion: King of the Wild Brumbies
Silver Strand
Silverado
Simple Men
A Simple Twist of Fate
Sinatra
Since You Went Away
Sincerely Charlotte
Singapore
Singin' in the Rain
Single White Female
Singles
Sins of Desire
The Sins of Dorian Gray
Sioux City
Sirens
Sister Act
Sister Act 2: Back in the Habit
The Sister-in-Law
The Sisters
Six Degrees of Separation
Sketch Artist
Sketch Artist 2: Hands That See
Ski Patrol
Ski School
Skier's Dream
Skin Art
The Skull
Sky Pirates
Skylark
Skyscraper
Skyscraper Souls
Slam Dunk Ernest
Slamdance
Slaughter of the Innocents
Sleeper
Sleeping Beauty
Sleeping with Strangers
Sleeping with the Enemy
Sleepless in Seattle
Sleepwalkers
The Slender Thread
Sliver
Slow Burn
The Slugger's Wife
Slumber Party Massacre 2
Smoke
Smokescreen
A Smoky Mountain Christmas
Smooth Talker
SnakeEater 2: The Drug Buster
SnakeEater 3: His Law
The Snapper
Sneakers
Sniper
Snoopy, Come Home
Snow Kill
The Snow Queen
Snow White and the Seven Dwarfs
Snow White and the Three Stooges
So I Married an Axe Murderer
So Proudly We Hail
Soapdish
Society
Sodbusters
Sodom and Gomorrah
Solar Crisis
Solar Force
Solarbabies
The Soldier
Soldier in the Rain
Soldier of Fortune
Soldier's Fortune
A Soldier's Story
A Soldier's Tale
Solid Gold Cadillac
Some Kind of Wonderful
Some Like It Hot
Somebody Has to Shoot the Picture
Somebody Up There Likes Me
Someone to Love
Someone to Watch Over Me
Something to Talk About
Something Wild
Sometimes They Come Back
Somewhere in Sonora
Sommersby
Son-in-Law
Son of Ali Baba
Son of the Morning Star
Son of the Pink Panther
Song of the Islands
Song Spinner
Songwriter
Sorcerer
Sorority Girl
Sorry, Wrong Number
Soul Man
The Sound of Music
Sounder
Sourdough
South Central
South Pacific
Souvenir
Spaceballs
Spaced Invaders
Spacehunter: Adventures in the Forbidden Zone
Spartacus
The Specialist
Species
Speechless
Speed
The Spellbinder
Spellbound
Spellcaster
The Spider and the Fly
Spider Woman
Spiderman: The Deadly Dust
Spies Like Us
Spirit of '76
Spirits
Split Decisions
Split Second
Splitting Heirs
Springtime in the Rockies
Spy
The Spy Who Came in from the Cold
Spymaker: The Secret Life of Ian Fleming
Squanto: A Warrior's Tale
The Squeeze
Stakeout
Stalin
Stalked
Stand and Deliver
Stand By Me
Stand Up and Cheer
Stanley and Iris
Stanley and Livingstone
Star!
Star Spangled Girl
Star Trek: The Motion Picture
Star Trek 2: The Wrath of Khan
Star Trek 3: The Search for Spock
Star Trek 4: The Voyage Home
Star Trek 5: The Final Frontier
Star Trek 6: The Undiscovered Country
Star Trek Generations
Star Trek the Next Generation: Encounter at Farpoint
Star Trek the Next Generation, the Final Episode: All Good Things...
Star Trek 25th Anniversary Special
Star Trek Voyager: Caretaker
Star Wars
Stargate
Stark
Starman
Stars and Bars
Stars and Stripes Forever
Stars in My Crown
State Fair
State of Grace
Stay Tuned
Staying Alive
Steal the Sky
Stealing Home
Steaming
Steel and Lace
Steel Frontier
Steel Magnolias
Steele Justice
Stella

The Stepfather
Stepfather 3: Father's Day
Stephen King's Golden Years
Stephen King's The Langoliers
Stephen King's The Stand
Stephen King's The Tommyknockers
Stepmonster
Stepping Out
Stick
Still Not Quite Human
The Sting
Stolen Hours
The Stone Boy
Stone Cold
The Stooge
Stop! or My Mom Will Shoot
Storm
Storm and Sorrow
Stormy Monday
Stormy Weather
The Story of Dr. Wassell
The Story of Robin Hood & His Merrie Men
The Story of Ruth
Storybook
Storyville
Stowaway
Straight Talk
Straight to Hell
Stranded
Strange Bedfellows
Strange Days
Strange Interlude
The Stranger
A Stranger Among Us
The Stranger and the Gunfighter
Stranger than Paradise
Strangers
Strangers in Good Company
Strays
Street Fighter
Street Knight
Street Smart
A Streetcar Named Desire
Streets of Fire
Strictly Ballroom
Strike a Pose
Striking Distance
Stripes
Stuart Saves His Family
The Stuff
Subspecies
The Substitute
Suburban Commando
Subway
Sudden Death
Sudden Impact
Sudie & Simpson
Sugar Hill
Summer and Smoke
Summer Camp Nightmare
Summer of '42
Summer Rental
Summer School
A Summer Story
A Summer to Remember
Sun Valley Serenade
Sunset
Sunset Grill
Sunset Heat
Sunstroke
Super Mario Bros.
Superfly T.N.T.
Superman 4: The Quest for Peace
Supernatural
The Supernaturals
Support Your Local Gunfighter
Support Your Local Sheriff
The Sure Thing
Surf Nazis Must Die
Surf Ninjas
Surrender
Survival Quest
Surviving the Game
Survivors
Susan and God
Susannah of the Mounties
Suspect Device
Suspiria
Suzy
The Swan Princess
Sweet Hearts Dance
Sweet Killing
Sweet Liberty
Sweet Lies
Sweet Poison
Sweet Revenge
Sweet Talker
Swimming to Cambodia
Swimming with Sharks
Swing Kids
Switch
Switching Channels
Swoon
The Sword in the Stone
Sword of Gideon
Sword of Honor
Sylvester
Sylvia
T-Force
Tagget
Tai-Pan
Tails You Live, Heads You're Dead
Tainted Blood
Take This Job & Shove It
Taken Away
The Takeover
Taking Care of Business
The Taking of Beverly Hills
A Tale of Springtime
The Tale of the Frog Prince
A Tale of Two Cities
Talent for the Game
Tales from Avonlea, Vol. 1: The Journey Begins
Tales from the Crypt Presents Demon Knight
Tales from the Crypt, Vol. 3
Tales from the Darkside: The Movie
Tales from the Gimli Hospital
Tales of Manhattan
Tales That Witness Madness
Talk to Me
Talkin' Dirty After Dark
Tall, Dark and Deadly
Tall Tale: The Unbelievable Adventures of Pecos Bill
Talons of the Eagle
Tammy and the T-Rex
Tango and Cash
Tank
Tank Girl
Tap
Tarantula
Target
Target: Favorite Son
Tarnished Angels
A Taste for Killing
TC 2000
Tea and Sympathy
Teachers
Teamster Boss: The Jackie Presser Story
Teen Wolf
Teen Wolf Too
Teenage Mutant Ninja Turtles: The Movie
Teenage Mutant Ninja Turtles 2: The Secret of the Ooze
Telegraph Trail
The Telephone
The Temp
Temptation
Temptress
The Ten Million Dollar Getaway
The Tenth Man
Tequila Sunrise
Terminal Bliss
Terminal Impact
Terminal Velocity
Terminator 2: Judgment Day
Termini Station
Terms of Endearment
Terror by Night
Terror Stalks the Class Reunion
The Terrorists
Test Tube Teens from the Year 2000
Testament
The Texans
Texas
The Texas Chainsaw Massacre
Texas Chainsaw Massacre, Part 2
Texas Payback
The Texas Rangers
The Texas Rangers Ride Again
Texasville
That Certain Woman
That Night
That Summer of White Roses
That Was Then...This Is Now
That's Entertainment, Part 3
That's Life!
Thelma & Louise
Theodore Rex
There Goes My Baby
There Goes the Neighborhood
Theremin: An Electronic Odyssey
There's No Business Like Show Business
Thief of Hearts
The Thin Blue Line
The Thing Called Love
Things Change
Third Degree Burn
This Boy's Life
This Is My Life
This Property is Condemned
The Thorn Birds
Those Daring Young Men in Their Jaunty Jalopies
Thousand Pieces of Gold
Three Amigos
Three Daring Daughters
Three Days of the Condor
Three Days to a Kill
Three Fugitives
Three Kinds of Heat
The Three Little Pigs
The Three Lives of Thomasina
Three Men and a Baby
Three Men and a Little Lady
Three Men on a Horse
The Three Musketeers
3 Ninjas
3 Ninjas Kick Back
Three Violent People
Three Wishes
Threesome
Through the Eyes of a Killer
Throw Momma from the Train
Thumbelina
Thunder and Lightning
Thunder in Paradise 2
Ticks
The Tie That Binds
Tiger Claws
Tiger Heart
A Tiger's Tale
Tightrope
The Tigress
Till There was You
Time Bandits
Time Runner
Time to Kill
Timebomb
Timecop
Timemaster
Tin Men
The Tin Soldier
Tiny Toon Adventures: How I Spent My Vacation
To Be or Not to Be
To Be the Best
To Dance with the White Dog
To Die For
To Die for 2: Son of Darkness
To Grandmother's House We Go
To Kill a Priest
To Live & Die in L.A.
To Play the King
To Sleep with Anger
To the Death
To Wong Foo, Thanks for Everything, Julie Newmar
Tokyo Pop
Tollbooth
Tom and Huck
Tom and Jerry: The Movie
Tom & Viv
Tombstone
Tomcat: Dangerous Desires
Tommy Boy
Tomorrow's Child
Too Hot to Handle
Too Young to Die
Tootsie
Top Dog
Top Gun
Top Secret!
Topaze
Torch Song Trilogy
Total Eclipse
Total Exposure
Total Recall
Toto le Heros
Touch and Go
Tough Guys Don't Dance
Tourist Trap
The Towering Inferno
The Toxic Avenger, Part 2
Toy Soldiers
Toys in the Attic
Traces of Red
The Tracker
Tracks
Tracks of a Killer
Trade Off
Trading Mom
Trading Places
Trail of the Pink Panther
Trancers
Trancers 2: The Return of Jack Deth
Trancers 3: Deth Lives
Trancers 4: Jack of Swords
Trancers 5: Sudden Deth
Transylvania 6-5000
Trapped In Paradise
Trapped in Space
Treacherous Crossing
Treasure Island
A Tree Grows in Brooklyn
Tremors
Tremors 2: Aftershocks
Trial and Error
Trial by Jury
Tribute to a Bad Man
Trick or Treat
Trigger, Jr.
The Trip to Bountiful
TripleCross
Troll 2
A Troll in Central Park
Troop Beverly Hills
Tropical Snow
Trouble Bound
Trouble in Mind
True Believer
True Colors
True Identity
True Lies
True Love
True Romance
True Stories
Trust
Truth or Dare
Truth or Die
Tryst
Tucker: The Man and His Dream
Tuff Turf
Tune in Tomorrow
Turk 182!
The Turn of the Screw
Turtle Diary
Twelve Angry Men
12 Monkeys
12:01
Twenty Bucks
Twenty Dollar Star
20,000 Leagues Under the Sea
24 Hours to Midnight
29th Street
Twice in a Lifetime
Twin Peaks
Twin Peaks: Fire Walk with Me
Twinsitters
Two Bits
Two Bits & Pepper
The Two Faces of Dr. Jekyll
Two for the Seesaw
Two If by Sea
The Two Jakes
Two Kinds of Love
Two Much
Two of a Kind
2010: The Year We Make Contact
Two Weeks in Another Town
Twogether
UHF
Ulterior Motives
Ultimate Desires
Ulzana's Raid
The Unbearable Lightness of Being
Uncommon Valor
Unconquered
Undeclared War
The Undefeated
Under Siege
Under Siege 2: Dark Territory
Under Suspicion
Under the Cherry Moon
Undercover
Undercover Blues
Undertow
Unfaithfully Yours
Unforgettable
Unforgiven
Uninvited
Union Pacific
Universal Soldier
Unlawful Entry
The Unnamable 2: The Statement of Randolph Carter
Unstrung Heroes
Untamed Heart
Until September
Until The End of The World
Until They Sail
The Untouchables
Unveiled
Unzipped
Used People
The Usual Suspects
Utu
V: The Final Battle
The Vagrant
Valdez is Coming
Valmont
Vamp
Vampire at Midnight
The Vanishing
Venus Rising
A Very Brady Christmas
V.I. Warshawski
Vibes
Vibrations
Vice Versa
Victim of Beauty
Victory

Video Americana
Vietnam War Story 1
Vietnam War Story 2
A View to a Kill
Village of the Damned
The Vindicator
Violence at Noon
Violets Are Blue
The Virgin Queen
The Virginian
Virtuosity
Vision Quest
Vital Signs
Voodoo
A Vow to Kill
Voyage of Terror: The Achille Lauro Affair
Voyage to the Bottom of the Sea
Wager of Love
Wagon Master
Wagons East
Waikiki Wedding
Wait Until Spring, Bandini
Waiting for the Light
Waiting for the Moon
A Walk in the Clouds
Walker: Texas Ranger: Deadly Reunion
Walker: Texas Ranger: One Riot, One Ranger
Wall Street
The Waltons: The Christmas Carol
A Waltz Through the Hills
Wanted Dead or Alive
The War
War Arrow
War of the Gargantuas
The War of the Roses
War Party
The War Room
WarGames
Warlock
Warning Sign
Warriors
The Waterdance
Waterloo
Waterloo Bridge
Waterworld
Wavelength
Waxwork 2: Lost in Time
Way Out West
Wayne's World 2
Web of Deceit
The Wedding Banquet
The Wedding Gift
Wee Willie Winkie
Weekend at Bernie's 2
Weep No More My Lady
Weird Science
Welcome Home, Roxy Carmichael
Welcome Stranger
Welcome to L.A.
We're No Angels
We're Not Dressing
We're Not Married
Wes Craven's New Nightmare
West Side Story
Western Union
Westward the Women
Wetherby
Whale for the Killing
The Wharf Rat
What Comes Around
What Ever Happened to Baby Jane?
What the Moon Saw
What's Eating Gilbert Grape
What's Love Got to Do with It?
When a Man Loves a Woman
When a Stranger Calls Back
When Harry Met Sally...
When Ladies Meet
When the Bough Breaks
When the Dark Man Calls
When the Time Comes
When the Whales Came
Where Angels Fear to Tread
Where Angels Go, Trouble Follows
Where Are the Children?
Where Love Has Gone
Where Sleeping Dogs Lie
Where the Boys Are '84
Where the Day Takes You
Where the Heart Is
Where the Red Fern Grows: Part 2
Where the River Runs Black
Where's Poppa?
Which Way Home
While You Were Sleeping
Whispers in the Dark
The Whistle Blower
White Christmas
White Dwarf
White Fang
White Fang 2: The Myth of the White Wolf
White Heat
White Hunter, Black Heart
White Lie
White Man's Burden
White Nights
White of the Eye
White Palace
White Sands
White Squall
White Tiger
Who Has Seen the Wind?
Who Is Killing the Great Chefs of Europe?
Who Shot Pat?
Whore
Who's Harry Crumb?
Who's That Girl?
Who's the Man?
Why Me?
Wide Sargasso Sea
The Wilby Conspiracy
Wild at Heart
Wild Bill
Wild Cactus
Wild Hearts Can't Be Broken
The Wild Life
The Wild One
Wild Orchid
Wild Orchid 2: Two Shades of Blue
Wild Palms
Wild Side
Wildcats
Wilder Napalm
Wildfire
Wildflower
Will Penny
Willow
Willy Wonka & the Chocolate Factory
Wind
The Winds of War
Windy City
Wings of Fame
Winner Takes All
Winners Take All
The Winning Team
Winter Meeting
Winter People
Wisdom
Wise Guys
Witchboard 2: The Devil's Doorway
Witchboard 3: The Possession
Witchcraft 4: Virgin Heart
The Witches
The Witches of Eastwick
The Witching of Ben Wagner
Without a Clue
Without Mercy
Witness
The Wizard
The Wizard of Loneliness
The Wizard of Oz
The Wizard of Speed and Time
Wizards
Wolf
The Wolf at the Door
A Woman at War
A Woman, Her Men and Her Futon
The Woman in Green
Woman In the Window
Woman of Desire
A Woman Under the Influence
Woman Undone
A Woman's Tale
Wombling Free
Women & Men: In Love There Are No Rules
Women & Men: Stories of Seduction
Woodstock
Woof!
Words by Heart
Workin' for Peanuts
Working Girl
The World According to Garp
A World Apart
The World of Abbott & Costello
The World of Henry Orient
World War III
Worth Winning
The Wreck of the Mary Deare
Wrestling Ernest Hemingway
Writer's Block
The Wrong Guys
The Wrong Man
The Wrong Woman
Wyatt Earp
The X-Files: Pilot Episode/Deep Throat
Yankee Doodle Dandy
Yankee Zulu
Yanks
The Year of Living Dangerously
Year of the Comet
Year of the Dragon
Yentl
You Can't Take It with You
Young Catherine
The Young Detectives on Wheels
Young Einstein
Young Frankenstein
Young Guns
Young Guns 2
Young Mr. Lincoln
Young People
Young Sherlock Holmes
Younger & Younger
Yours, Mine & Ours
Zandalee
Zebrahead
Zelly & Me
Zentropa
Zeppelin
Zero Tolerance
Zoo Radio
Zooman
Zorro, the Gay Blade
Zulu

Distributor List

AAE—A & E Home Video
ABC—ABC Video
ACA—Academy Entertainment
ACD—Academy Videos
ACE—Ace Video
ACN—Acorn Video
ADL—Anti-Defamation League of B'nai B'rith
AEE—American Electronics & Entertainment Corporation
AEL—Atlantic Entertainment Ltd.
AFC—Capital Communications
AFE—Amazing Fantasy Entertainment
AFR—Afro-Am Distributing Company
AHV—Active Home Video
AIM—AIMS Media
AIP—A.I.P. Home Video, Inc.
ALD—Alden Films
ALL—Allied Artists
AMB—Ambrose Video Publishing, Inc.
ANI—AnimEigo Inc.
AOV—Admit One Video
APD—Applause Productions, Inc.
APP—Applause Theatre and Cinema
APX—A-PIX Entertainment Inc.
ATL—Atlas Entertainment Corporation
ATM—Atomic Pictures
ATS—Acorn Media Publishing
ATU—Atlantic Video
ATV—Atlantic Video
AUD—Audio-Forum
AVE—WarnerVision
AVI—Arrow Video, Inc.
BAR—Barr Films
BBE—Blockbuster Entertainment Corporation
BBF—Bonnie Business Forms
BFA—Phoenix/BFA Films
BFV—Best Film & Video Corporation
BIJ—Bijou Video
BMG—BMG
BMV—Bennett Marine Video
BPG—Bridgestone Multimedia
BRT—Britannica Films
BST—ETD
BSV—Bosko Video
BTV—Baker & Taylor Video
BUL—Bullfrog Films, Inc.
CAB—Cable Films & Video
CAF—Cabin Fever Entertainment
CAL—California Newsreel
CAN—Cannon Video
CAP—Capitol Video Communications, Inc.
CCB—Critics' Choice Video, Inc.
CCC—Cyclops Communications Corp.
CCN—Cinevista
CCP—Cambridge Educational
CDV—Television International
CEL—Celebrity Home Entertainment
CFV—Carousel Film & Video
CHF—Churchill Media
CHI—Center for Humanities, Inc.
CIC—Cinema International Canada
CIG—The Cinema Guild
CMB—Columbia House Video Library
CMR—Camera Three Productions, Inc.
CNG—Congress Entertainment, Ltd.
CNM—Cinemacabre Video
COL—Columbia Tristar Home Video
COV—Covenant Video
CPM—Central Park Media/U.S. Manga Corps
CRC—Criterion Collection
CRV—Crown Video
CRY—Crystal Productions
CSM—Coliseum Video
CTC—Coast to Coast Video
CTD—Coast to Coast Home Video
CTH—Corinth Video
CTL—Capitol Home Video
CVC—Connoisseur Video Collection
CVD—Consumer Video Distributers
DCL—Direct Cinema Ltd.
DIS—Walt Disney Home Video
DMP—Ariztical Entertainment
DSN—Disney Educational Productions
DVT—Discount Video Tapes, Inc.
EAI—Electronic Arts Intermix
ECU—EcuFilm
EDV—EDDE Entertainment
EHV—Enterprise Home Video
ELE—Electric Productions
ELV—Electric Video
EMI—EMI Video
EPC—Epic Records
ERG—Ergo Media Inc.
EVD—European Video Distributor
EXP—Expanded Entertainment
FAF—Fast Forward
FCT—Facets Multimedia, Inc.
FEI—FM Entertainment, Inc.
FFM—Flower Films
FGF—Military/Combat Stock Footage Library
FHE—Family Home Entertainment
FHS—Films for the Humanities & Sciences
FHV—Foothill Video
FLI—Films Inc. Video
FLL—Filmakers Library, Inc.
FLL—Full Moon Home Video
FMT—Format International
FOC—Focus on Animals
FOX—CBS/Fox Video
FRA—Video France
FRG—Fright Video
FRH—Fries Home Video
FRV—First Run Video
FST—Festival Films
FUS—Fusion Video
FXL—Fox/Lorber Home Video
FXV—FoxVideo
GEM—Video Gems
GFV—Vision Video/Gateway Films
GHV—Genesis Home Video
GKK—Goodtimes Entertainment
GLV—German Language Video Center
GNS—21st Genesis Home Video
GPV—Grapevine Video
GRG—Gorgon Video
GVV—Glenn Video Vistas, Ltd.
HBO—HBO Home Video
HCV—Henwood Cinema Video
HEG—Horizon Entertainment
HHE—Hollywood Home Entertainment
HHT—Hollywood Home Theatre
HMD—Hemdale Home Video
HMK—Hallmark Home Entertainment
HMV—Home Vision Cinema
HPH—Hollywood Pictures Home Video
HSE—High/Scope Educational Research Foundation
HTV—Hen's Tooth Video
HVL—Home Video Library
ICA—First Run Features/Icarus Films
IFB—International Film Bureau, Inc.
IGP—Ignatius Press
IHF—International Historic Films, Inc. (IHF)
IME—Image Entertainment
IMP—Imperial Entertainment Corp.
INC—Increase/SilverMine Video
ING—Ingram Entertainment
INJ—Ingram International Films
INT—Interama, Inc.
IPI—Intrepid Productions Inc.
ITC—ITC
IUF—Interurban Press Videos
IVY—Ivy Film/Video
JAF—James Agee Film Project
JCF—Judaica Captioned Film Center, Inc.
JEF—JEF Films, Inc.
JFK—Just for Kids Home Video
JHV—Jim Henson Productions
JOU—Journal Films, Inc.
JTC—J2 Communications
KAR—Karol Video
KEP—Keep the Faith Inc.
KID—Kid Vision
KIT—Kit Parker Video
KIV—Kino on Video
KUI—Knowledge Unlimited, Inc.
KUL—Kultur Video
LBD—LB Distributors, Inc.
LCA—Modern Curriculum Press - MCP
LEO—Leo Films
LIV—Live Entertainment
LME—Lucerne Media
LOO—Loonic Video
LRP—Light Rain Productions
LSV—LSVideo, Inc.
LTY—Lightyear Entertainment
LUM—Lumivision Corporation
MAD—Madera Cinevideo
MAS—Mastervision, Inc.
MAX—Miramax Pictures Home Video
MCA—MCA/Universal Home Video
MCG—Management Company Entertainment Group (MCEG), Inc.
MED—Media Home Entertainment
MFI—Meridian Films, Inc.
MFV—Mystic Fire Video
MGI—Monarich Group, Inc.
MGM—MGM/UA Home Entertainment
MHF—Magic Hour Films
MIL—Milestone Film & Video
MLB—Mike LeBell's Video
MLT—Music for Little People
MNC—Monarch Home Video
MON—Monterey Home Video
MOR—Morris Video

MOV—Movies Unlimited
MPI—MPI Home Video
MRV—Moore Video
MSP—Modern Sound Pictures, Inc.
MTH—MTI Home Video
MTI—Coronet/MTI Film & Video
MTM—MTM Home Video
MTP—Maryland Public Television
MTX—MNTEX Entertainment, Inc.
MVC—Moviecraft, Inc.
MVD—Music Video Distributors
MWF—Monday/Wednesday/Friday Video
MWP—Wade Williams Productions, Inc.
NCJ—National Center for Jewish Film
NEW—New Video Group
NFB—National Film Board of Canada
NHO—New Horizons Home Video
NJN—New Jersey Network
NLC—New Line Home Video
NMD—Neville Meyer Distribution (NMD)
NOS—Nostalgia Family Video
NWV—New World Entertainment
NYF—New Yorker Video
NYR—Not Yet Released
NYS—New York State Education Department
ORI—Orion Home Video
ORP—Orphan Entertainment
PAP—Pacific Arts Publishing
PAR—Paramount Home Video
PAU—Paulist Productions
PBC—Princeton Book Co. Publishers
PBS—PBS Home Video
PCV—Pacific Coast Video
PEN—Pentrex Video
PGV—Polygram Video (PV)
PIC—Videos.com, Inc.
PME—Public Media Video
PMH—PM Entertainment Group, Inc.
PMR—Premiere Home Video
PMS—Professional Media Service Corp.
PRD—Peter Pan Entertainment (PPI)
PRS—Proscenium Entertainment
PRV—Prime Video
PSM—Prism Entertainment
PSV—Power Sports Video
PTB—Proud To Be...A Black Video Collection
PYR—Pyramid Film & Video
QHV—Questar Video, Inc.
QVD—Quality Video
RAP—RAP Entertainment Inc.
RDG—Reader's Digest Home Video
REP—Republic Pictures Home Video
RHI—Rhino Home Video
RHP—Rhapsody Films
RHU—Random House Media
RHV—Regency Home Video
RMF—RM Films International, Inc.
RXM—Rex #Miller
SCH—Schoolmasters Video
SDE—Stardance Entertainment
SFR—Passport International Productions
SGE—SGE Entertainment Corp.
SHO—Shokus Video
SHR—Shanachie Entertainment
SHV—Snoopy's Home Video Library
SHV—Strand Home Video
SIG—Signals
SIM—Simitar Entertainment
SMV—Sony Music Video Enterprises
SMW—Something Weird Video
SNC—Sinister Cinema
SPW—Chordant Distribution Group
STP—Streamline Pictures
STS—Stagestep
STV—Studio Video Productions
SUN—Sun Video
SVE—Society for Visual Education, Inc. (SVE)
SWC—Simon Wiesenthal Center
SWI—ScreenWorks Inc.
TAI—Tai Seng Video Marketing Inc.
TCE—Third Coast Entertainment
TCF—20th Century Fox Film Corporation
TEM—Tempe Video
THA—3M Audio Visual Division
TIM—Timeless Video Inc.
TLF—Time-Life Video and Television
TOU—Buena Vista Home Video
TPI—Thomson Productions, Inc.
TPV—Tapeworm Video Distributors
TRI—Triboro Entertainment Group
TSR—Three Star Releasing
TTC—Turner Home Entertainment Company
TTV—Troma Team Video
TVC—The Video Catalog
TWE—Trans-World Entertainment
TWV—Time Warner Viewer's Edge
UAV—UAV Corporation
UND—Uni Distribution
UNI—Unicorn Video, Inc.
UNT—Unity Productions
UWA—University of Washington Educational Media Collection
VAI—Video Artists International, Inc.
VAN—Vantage Communications, Inc.
VBL—Video Bible Library, Inc.
VCD—Video City Productions/Distributing
VCI—Video Communications, Inc. (VCI)
VCN—Video Connection
VCO—Video Collectibles/BFS Video
VDA—Video Action
VDC—Vidcrest
VDM—Video Dimensions
VEC—Valencia Entertainment Corp.
VES—Vestron Video
VGR—Videograf
VHE—VCII Home Entertainment, Inc.
VIP—VIP Video
VLL—Video Learning Library
VMK—Vidmark Entertainment
VPL—Video Placement International
VRS—Video Resources
VSE—Vista Street Entertainment
VSM—Video Search of Miami
VTR—Anchor Bay
VYY—Video Yesteryear
WAC—World Artists Home Video
WAR—Warner Home Video, Inc.
WAX—Waxworks/Videoworks, Inc.
WBF—Water Bearer Films
WEA—Warner/Elektra/Atlantic (WEA) Corporation
WFV—Western Media Systems
WKV—Wood Knapp & Company, Inc.
WLA—Western L.A. Film Productions, Inc.
WLF—Wolfe Video
WME—Warren Miller Entertainment
WNE—WNET/Thirteen Non-Broadcast
WOM—Wombat Film and Video
WOV—Worldvision Home Video, Inc.
WRV—Warner Reprise Video
WSH—Wishing Well Distributing
WST—White Star
WVE—World Video Enterprises, Inc.
XVC—Xenon
YOC—Yankee-Oriole Co.
ZGI—Zeitgeist Films

Distributor Guide

The **Distributor Guide** provides full contact information, including address, phone, fax and toll-free numbers, for over 340 distributors. The distributors are listed alphabetically. Each video in the main section has at least one and as many as three distributor codes located at the end of the entry. The key to these codes, preceding this guide, will lead you to the appropriate distributor. Those reviews with the code **OM** are on moratorium, meaning that they were distributed at one time, but aren't currently. Since it was once available, an On Moratorium title may show up at your local video store. If the distributor for a movie is not known, the code **NO** will follow the review. New theatrical releases that haven't made it to video at press time have the designation **NYR** (not yet released). These are titles that we expect will be released on video before our next edition. **Warning!** From year to year, a small minority of distributors move without telling anyone, or just plain go out of business. **Warning!**

Warning! Studio distributors do not sell to the general public, they generally act as wholesalers, selling only to retail outlets. Many video stores provide an ordering service. If your local video store doesn't carry a video you're looking for, you can ask them to order it for you.

A-PIX ENTERTAINMENT INC.(*APX*)
500 5th Ave., 46th Fl.
New York, NY 10110
212-764-7171

A & E HOME VIDEO(*AAE*)
c/o New Video Group
126 5th Ave., 15th Fl.
New York, NY 10011
212-206-8600
800-423-1212
Fax: 212-206-9001

ABC VIDEO(*ABC*)
Capital Cities/ABC Video Enterprises
1200 High Ridge Rd.
Stamford, CT 06905
203-968-9100
Fax: 203-329-6464

ACADEMY ENTERTAINMENT(*ACA*)
9250 Wilshire Blvd., Ste. 400
Beverly Hills, CA 90212
Fax: 310-275-2195

ACADEMY VIDEOS(*ACD*)
Box 5224
Sherman Oaks, CA 91423-5224
818-788-6662
800-423-2397
Fax: 818-788-1580

ACE VIDEO(*ACE*)
19749 Dearborn St.
Chatsworth, CA 91311
818-718-1116
800-727-2229
Fax: 818-718-9109

ACORN MEDIA PUBLISHING(*ATS*)
7910 Woodmont Ave., Ste. 350
Bethesda, MD 20814
301-907-0030
800-999-0212
Fax: 301-907-9049

ACORN VIDEO(*ACN*)
c/o Academy Entertainment
9250 Wilshire Blvd., Ste. 400
Beverly Hills, CA 90212

ACTIVE HOME VIDEO(*AHV*)
12121 Wilshire Blvd., No. 401
Los Angeles, CA 90025
310-447-6131
800-824-6109
Fax: 310-207-0411

ADMIT ONE VIDEO(*AOV*)
PO Box 66, Sta. O
Toronto, ON, Canada M4A 2M8
416-463-5714
Fax: 416-463-5714

AFRO-AM DISTRIBUTING COMPANY(*AFR*)
1909 W. 95th St.
Chicago, IL 60643-1105
312-235-4504

AIMS MEDIA(*AIM*)
9710 DeSoto Ave.
Chatsworth, CA 91311-4409
818-773-4300
800-367-2467
Fax: 818-341-6700

A.I.P. HOME VIDEO, INC.(*AIP*)
10726 McCune Ave.
Los Angeles, CA 90034
Fax: 213-559-8849

ALDEN FILMS(*ALD*)
PO Box 449
Clarksburg, NJ 08510
908-462-3522
Fax: 908-294-0330

ALLIED ARTISTS(*ALL*)
3415 S. Sepulveda Blvd., Ste. 630
Los Angeles, CA 90034
310-390-6161
Fax: 310-390-6031

AMAZING FANTASY ENTERTAINMENT(*AFE*)
3061 Fletcher Dr.
Los Angeles, CA 90065
213-550-4530

AMBROSE VIDEO PUBLISHING, INC.(*AMB*)
1290 Avenue of the Americas, Ste. 2245
New York, NY 10104
212-265-7272
800-526-4663
Fax: 212-265-8088

AMERICAN ELECTRONICS & ENTERTAINMENT CORPORATION(*AEE*)
7074 Commerce Circle, Ste. D
Pleasanton, CA 94588
510-416-1259
Fax: 510-416-1279

ANCHOR BAY(*VTR*)
500 Kirts Blvd.
Troy, MI 48084
810-362-9660
800-786-8777
Fax: 810-362-4454

ANIMEIGO INC.(*ANI*)
PO Box 989
Wilmington, NC 28402-0989
910-251-1850
800-242-6463
Fax: 910-763-2376

ANTI-DEFAMATION LEAGUE OF B'NAI B'RITH(*ADL*)
Audio-Visual Dept.
823 United Nations Plaza
New York, NY 10017
212-490-2525
Fax: 212-867-0779

APPLAUSE PRODUCTIONS, INC.(*APD*)
85 Longview Rd.
Port Washington, NY 11050
516-883-2825
800-278-7326
Fax: 516-883-7460

APPLAUSE THEATRE AND CINEMA(*APP*)
211 W. 71st St.
New York, NY 10023
212-496-7511
Fax: 212-721-2856

ARIZTICAL ENTERTAINMENT(*DMP*)
405 E. Wetmore, Ste. 117-516
Tucson, AZ 85705
800-356-4386

ARROW VIDEO, INC.(*AVI*)
135 W. 50th St., Ste. 1925
New York, NY 10020
212-258-2200
Fax: 212-245-1252

ATLANTIC ENTERTAINMENT LTD.(*AEL*)
1111 Rte. 110, Ste. 324
E. Farmingdale, NY 11735
Fax: 516-249-1690

ATLANTIC VIDEO(*ATV*)
75 Rockefeller Plaza
New York, NY 10019
212-275-2000

ATLANTIC VIDEO(*ATU*)
150 S. Gordon St.
Alexandria, VA 22304
703-823-2800
Fax: 703-370-6748

ATLAS ENTERTAINMENT CORPORATION(*ATL*)
1 Jocama Blvd., Ste. 2E
Old Bridge, NJ 08857
908-591-1155
Fax: 908-591-0660

ATOMIC PICTURES(*ATM*)
PO Box 15824
North Hollywood, CA 91615-5824

AUDIO-FORUM(*AUD*)
96 Broad St.
Guilford, CT 06437
203-453-9794
800-243-1234
Fax: 203-453-9774

BAKER & TAYLOR VIDEO(*BTV*)
501 S. Gladiolus
Momence, IL 60954
815-472-2444
800-775-2300
Fax: 800-775-3500

BARR FILMS(*BAR*)
12801 Schabarum
Irwindale, CA 91706
818-338-7878
800-234-7878
Fax: 818-814-2672

BENNETT MARINE VIDEO(*BMV*)
8436 W. 3rd St., Ste. 740
Los Angeles, CA 90048
213-951-7570
800-733-8862
Fax: 213-957—595

BEST FILM & VIDEO CORPORATION(*BFV*)
108 New South Rd.
Hicksville, NY 11801-5223
516-931-6969
800-527-2189
Fax: 516-931-5959

BIJOU VIDEO(*BIJ*)
1349 N. Wells
Chicago, IL 60610
312-943-5397
800-932-7111
Fax: 312-337-1270

BLOCKBUSTER ENTERTAINMENT CORPORATION(*BBE*)
12655 N. Central Expwy., Ste. 600
Dallas, TX 75243
214-866-2200
800-733-1939
Fax: 214-866-2250

BMG(*BMG*)
6363 Sunset Blvd., 6th Fl.
Hollywood, CA 90028-7318

BONNIE BUSINESS FORMS(*BBF*)
2691 Freewood
Dallas, TX 75220

214-357-3956
Fax: 214-357-4512

BOSKO VIDEO*(BSV)*
3802 E. Cudahy Ave.
Cudahy, WI 53110-1234

BRIDGESTONE MULTIMEDIA*(BPG)*
300 N. McKemy Ave.
Chandler, AZ 85226
602-940-5771
800-523-0988
Fax: 602-940-8924

BRITANNICA FILMS*(BRT)*
310 S. Michigan Ave.
Chicago, IL 60604
312-347-7900
800-554-9862
Fax: 312-347-7966

BUENA VISTA HOME VIDEO*(TOU)*
350 S. Buena Vista St.
Burbank, CA 91521-7145
818-562-3568

BULLFROG FILMS, INC.*(BUL)*
PO Box 149
Oley, PA 19547
610-779-8226
800-543-3764
Fax: 610-370-1978

CABIN FEVER ENTERTAINMENT*(CAF)*
100 W. Putnam Ave.
Greenwich, CT 06830
203-661-1100
Fax: 203-863-5258

CABLE FILMS & VIDEO*(CAB)*
Country Club Sta.
PO Box 7171
Kansas City, MO 64113
816-362-2804
800-514-2804
Fax: 816-341-7365

CALIFORNIA NEWSREEL*(CAL)*
149 9th St., Ste. 420
San Francisco, CA 94103
415-621-6196
Fax: 415-621-6522

CAMBRIDGE EDUCATIONAL*(CCP)*
PO Box 2153
Charleston, WV 25328-2153
304-744-9323
800-468-4227
Fax: 304-744-9351

CAMERA THREE PRODUCTIONS, INC.*(CMR)*
PO Box 739
Kent, CT 06757
860-868-1771
Fax: 860-868-9999

CANNON VIDEO*(CAN)*
PO Box 17198
Beverly Hills, CA 90290
310-772-7765

CAPITAL COMMUNICATIONS*(AFC)*
2210 S. Tamiami Tr.
Venice, FL 34293
941-496-2040
800-822-5678
Fax: 941-496-4331

CAPITOL HOME VIDEO*(CTL)*
4818 Yuma St. NW
Washington, DC 20016
202-363-8800
Fax: 202-363-4680

CAPITOL VIDEO COMMUNICATIONS, INC.*(CAP)*
2121 Wisconsin Ave. NW
Washington, DC 20007
202-965-7800
Fax: 202-965-7815

CAROUSEL FILM & VIDEO*(CFV)*
260 5th Ave., Rm. 405
New York, NY 10001
212-683-1660
800-683-1660
Fax: 212-683-1662

CBS/FOX VIDEO*(FOX)*
PO Box 900
Beverly Hills, CA 90213
562-373-4800
800-800-2369
Fax: 562-373-4803

CELEBRITY HOME ENTERTAINMENT*(CEL)*
22025 Ventura Blvd., Ste. 200
PO Box 4112
Woodland Hills, CA 91365-4112
818-595-0666
Fax: 818-716-0168

CENTER FOR HUMANITIES, INC.*(CHI)*
Communications Park
Box 1000
Mount Kisco, NY 10549
914-666-4100
800-431-1242
Fax: 914-666-5319

CENTRAL PARK MEDIA/U.S. MANGA CORPS*(CPM)*
250 W. 57th St., Ste. 317
New York, NY 10107
212-977-7456
800-833-7456
Fax: 212-977-8709

CHORDANT DISTRIBUTION GROUP*(SPW)*
101 Winners Circle
Brentwood, TN 37027
615-371-6800
800-877-4443
Fax: 615-371-6980

CHURCHILL MEDIA*(CHF)*
6901 Woodley Ave.
Van Nuys, CA 91406
818-778-1978
800-334-7830
Fax: 818-778-1994

THE CINEMA GUILD*(CIG)*
1697 Broadway, Ste. 506
New York, NY 10019
212-246-5522
800—723-5522
Fax: 212-246-5525

CINEMA INTERNATIONAL CANADA*(CIC)*
8275 Mayrand
Montreal, PQ, Canada H4P 2C8
514-342-2340
Fax: 514-342-1922

CINEMACABRE VIDEO*(CNM)*
PO Box 10005-D
Baltimore, MD 21285-0005

CINEVISTA*(CCN)*
560 W. 43rd, No. 8J
New York, NY 10036
212-947-4373
800-341-CINE
Fax: 212-947-0644

COAST TO COAST HOME VIDEO*(CTD)*
1766 Griffith Park Blvd., Apt. 4
Los Angeles, CA 90226-1060

COAST TO COAST VIDEO*(CTC)*
148 Lafayette St., 5th Fl.
New York, NY 10013
212-431-3890
800-221-3420

COLISEUM VIDEO*(CSM)*
430 W. 54th St.
New York, NY 10019
212-489-8130
800-288-8130
Fax: 212-582-5690

COLUMBIA HOUSE VIDEO LIBRARY*(CMB)*
PO Box 1112
Terre Haute, IN 47811
812-262-2001
800-538-7766

COLUMBIA TRISTAR HOME VIDEO*(COL)*
Sony Pictures Plaza
10202 W. Washington Blvd.
Culver City, CA 90232
310-280-8000
Fax: 310-280-2485

CONGRESS ENTERTAINMENT, LTD.*(CNG)*
Learn Plaza, Ste. 6
PO Box 845
Tannersville, PA 18372-0845
717-620-9001
800-847-8273
Fax: 717-620-9278

CONNOISSEUR VIDEO COLLECTION*(CVC)*
1575 Westwood Blvd., Ste. 305
Los Angeles, CA 90024
310-231-1350
800-529-2300
Fax: 310-231-1359

CONSUMER VIDEO DISTRIBUTERS*(CVD)*
1427 Woodhurst St.
Bowling Green, KY 42104
502-843-8300
Fax: 502-843-8300

CORINTH VIDEO*(CTH)*
34 Gansevoort St.
New York, NY 10014
212-463-0305
800-221-4720
Fax: 212-929-0010

CORONET/MTI FILM & VIDEO*(MTI)*
4350 Equity Dr.
PO Box 2649
Columbus, OH 43216
614-876-0371
800-777-8100
Fax: 614-771-5841

COVENANT VIDEO*(COV)*
3200 W. Foster Ave.
Chicago, IL 60625
312-478-4676
800-621-1290
Fax: 312-478-2622

CRITERION COLLECTION*(CRC)*
c/o The Voyager Company
1 Bridge St.
Irvington, NY 10533-1543

CRITICS' CHOICE VIDEO, INC.*(CCB)*
PO Box 749
Itasca, IL 60143-0749
708-775-3300
800-367-7765
Fax: 708-775-3355

CROWN VIDEO*(CRV)*
225 Park Ave., S.
New York, NY 10003

CRYSTAL PRODUCTIONS*(CRY)*
1812 Johns Dr.
Box 2159
Glenview, IL 60025
708-657-8144
800-255-8629
Fax: 708-657-8149

CYCLOPS COMMUNICATIONS CORP.*(CCC)*
44 Gibson Ave.
Toronto, ON, Canada M5R 1T5
416-926-8981
Fax: 416-926-9878

DIRECT CINEMA LTD.*(DCL)*
PO Box 10003
Santa Monica, CA 90410
310-396-4774
800-525-0000
Fax: 310-396-3233

DISCOUNT VIDEO TAPES, INC.*(DVT)*
PO Box 7122
Burbank, CA 91510
818-843-3366
Fax: 818-843-3821

DISNEY EDUCATIONAL PRODUCTIONS*(DSN)*
4350 Equity
Columbus, OH 43228
800-621-2131
Fax: 614-771-7362

ECUFILM*(ECU)*
810 12th Ave. S.
Nashville, TN 37203
615-242-6277
800-251-4091
Fax: 615-742-5125

EDDE ENTERTAINMENT*(EDV)*
19749 Dearborn St.
Chatsworth, CA 91311
818-718-1116
800-727-2229
Fax: 818-718-9026

ELECTRIC PRODUCTIONS*(ELE)*
10010 Canoga Ave., No. B-8
Chatsworth, CA 91311-6734

ELECTRIC VIDEO*(ELV)*
PO Box 784
Tiffin, OH 44883
419-447-0110

ELECTRONIC ARTS INTERMIX*(EAI)*
536 Broadway, 9th Fl.
New York, NY 10012
212-966-4605
Fax: 212-941-6118

EMI VIDEO*(EMI)*
1290 Ave. of the Americas, 42nd Fl.
New York, NY 10104
212-492-1200

ENTERPRISE HOME VIDEO*(EHV)*
12551 Cluster Pines Rd.
Garden Grove, CA 92645
800-553-5011
Fax: 714-895-5190

EPIC RECORDS*(EPC)*
550 Madison Ave.
New York, NY 10022-3297
212-833-7442
Fax: 212-833-5719

ERGO MEDIA INC.*(ERG)*
668 American Legion Dr.
PO Box 2037
Teaneck, NJ 07666
201-692-0404
800-695-3746
Fax: 201-692-0663

ETD*(BST)*
1221 Profit Dr.
Dallas, TX 75247-3919
214-634-7883
800-541-1008
Fax: 214-634-9747

EUROPEAN VIDEO DISTRIBUTOR*(EVD)*
2402 W. Olive Ave.
Burbank, CA 91506
818-848-5902
800-423-6752
Fax: 818-848-1965

EXPANDED ENTERTAINMENT*(EXP)*
28024 Dorothy Dr.
Agoura Hills, CA 91301-2635
818-991-2884
800-996-TOON
Fax: 818-991-3773

FACETS MULTIMEDIA, INC.*(FCT)*
1517 W. Fullerton Ave.
Chicago, IL 60614
312-281-9075
800-331-6197
Fax: 312-929-5437

FAMILY HOME ENTERTAINMENT*(FHE)*
c/o Live Home Video
15400 Sherman Way
PO Box 10124
Van Nuys, CA 91410-0124
818-908-0303
800-677-0789
Fax: 818-778-3259

FAST FORWARD*(FAF)*
3420 Ocean Park Blvd., Ste. 3075
Santa Monica, CA 90405
310-396-4434
Fax: 310-396-2292

FESTIVAL FILMS*(FST)*
6115 Chestnut Terr.
Excelsior, MN 55331-8107
612-470-2172
800-798-6083
Fax: 612-470-2172

FILMAKERS LIBRARY, INC.*(FLL)*
124 E. 40th
New York, NY 10016
212-808-4980
800-555-9815
Fax: 212-808-4983

FILMS FOR THE HUMANITIES & SCIENCES*(FHS)*
PO Box 2053
Princeton, NJ 08543-2053
609-275-1400
800-257-5126
Fax: 609-275-3767

FILMS INC. VIDEO*(FLI)*
5547 N. Ravenswood Ave.
Chicago, IL 60640-1199
312-878-2600
800-323-4222
Fax: 312-878-0416

FIRST RUN FEATURES/ ICARUS FILMS*(ICA)*
153 Waverly Pl.
New York, NY 10014
212-727-1711
800-876-1710
Fax: 212-989-7649

FIRST RUN VIDEO*(FRV)*
622 N. Alpine Dr.
Beverly Hills, CA 90210-3304
Fax: 310-246-9606

FLOWER FILMS*(FFM)*
10341 San Pablo Ave.
El Cerrito, CA 94530
510-525-0942
800-572-7618
Fax: 510-525-1204

FM ENTERTAINMENT, INC.*(FEI)*
10551 W. Pico Blvd.
Los Angeles, CA 90064
310-441-4417
Fax: 310-446-9791

FOCUS ON ANIMALS*(FOC)*
Fay Spring Center-Humane Education Center
534 Red Bud Rd.
Winchester, VA 22603
703-665-2827

FOOTHILL VIDEO*(FHV)*
PO Box 547
Tujunga, CA 91043
818-353-8591
Fax: 818-353-7242

FORMAT INTERNATIONAL*(FMT)*
2421 E. Washington St.
Indianapolis, IN 46201-4123

FOX/LORBER HOME VIDEO*(FXL)*
419 Park Ave., S., 20th Fl.
New York, NY 10016
212-532-3392
Fax: 212-685-2625

FOXVIDEO(*FXV*)
2121 Avenue of the Stars, 25th Fl.
Los Angeles, CA 90067
310-369-3900
800-800-2FOX
Fax: 310-369-5811

FRIES HOME VIDEO(*FRH*)
6922 Hollywood Blvd., 12th Fl.
Hollywood, CA 90028
213-466-2266
Fax: 213-466-2126

FRIGHT VIDEO(*FRG*)
16 Kenmar Dr., Ste. 141
Billerica, MA 01821-4788

FULL MOON HOME VIDEO(*FLL*)
8721 Santa Monica Blvd., Ste. 526
W. Hollywood, CA 90069
213-341-5959

FUSION VIDEO(*FUS*)
100 Fusion Way
Country Club Hills, IL 60478
708-799-2073
Fax: 708-799-8375

GENESIS HOME VIDEO(*GHV*)
15820 Arminta St.
Van Nuys, CA 91406

GERMAN LANGUAGE VIDEO CENTER(*GLV*)
7625 Pendleton Pike
Indianapolis, IN 46226-5298
317-547-1257
800-252-1957
Fax: 317-547-1263

GLENN VIDEO VISTAS, LTD.(*GVV*)
6924 Canby Ave., Ste. 103
Reseda, CA 91335
818-881-8110
Fax: 818-981-5506

GOODTIMES ENTERTAINMENT(*GKK*)
16 E. 40th St., 8th Fl.
New York, NY 10016-0113
212-951-3000
Fax: 212-213-9319

GORGON VIDEO(*GRG*)
10750 W. 161st
Orland Park, IL 60462
708-873-3131
800-367-3845
Fax: 708-873-3135

GRAPEVINE VIDEO(*GPV*)
PO Box 46161
Phoenix, AZ 85063
602-973-3661
Fax: 602-973-0060

HALLMARK HOME ENTERTAINMENT(*HMK*)
6100 Wilshire Blvd., Ste. 1400
Los Angeles, CA 90048
213-549-3790
Fax: 213-549-3760

HBO HOME VIDEO(*HBO*)
1100 6th Ave.
New York, NY 10036
212-512-7400
Fax: 212-512-7498

HEMDALE HOME VIDEO(*HMD*)
7966 Beverly Blvd.
Los Angeles, CA 90048
213-966-3700
Fax: 213-653-5452

HEN'S TOOTH VIDEO(*HTV*)
2805 E. State Blvd.
Fort Wayne, IN 46805
219-471-4332
Fax: 219-471-4449

HENWOOD CINEMA VIDEO(*HCV*)
PO Box 376
Jamison, PA 18929-0376
215-552-8584
Fax: 215-788-7186

HIGH/SCOPE EDUCATIONAL RESEARCH FOUNDATION(*HSE*)
600 N. River St.
Ypsilanti, MI 48198-2898
313-485-2000
800-40-PRESS
Fax: 313-485-0704

HOLLYWOOD HOME ENTERTAINMENT(*HHE*)
6165 Crooked Creek Rd., Ste. B
Norcross, GA 30092-3105

HOLLYWOOD HOME THEATRE(*HHT*)
1540 N. Highland Ave., Ste. 110
Hollywood, CA 90028
213-466-0127

HOLLYWOOD PICTURES HOME VIDEO(*HPH*)
Fairmont Bldg. 526
500 S. Buena Vista St.
Burbank, CA 91505-9842

HOME VIDEO LIBRARY(*HVL*)
Better Homes & Gardens Books
PO Box 10670
Des Moines, IA 50336
800-678-2665
Fax: 515-237-4765

HOME VISION CINEMA(*HMV*)
5547 N. Ravenswood Ave.
Chicago, IL 60640-1199
312-878-2600
800-826-3456
Fax: 312-878-8648

HORIZON ENTERTAINMENT(*HEG*)
45030 Trevor Ave.
Lancaster, CA 93534
805-940-1040
800-323-2061
Fax: 805-940-8511

IGNATIUS PRESS(*IGP*)
33 Oakland Ave.
Harrison, NY 10528-9974
914-835-4216
Fax: 914-835-8406

IMAGE ENTERTAINMENT(*IME*)
9333 Oso Ave.
Chatsworth, CA 91311
818-407-9100
800-473-3475
Fax: 818-407-9111

IMPERIAL ENTERTAINMENT CORP.(*IMP*)
4640 Lankershim Blvd., Ste. 201
North Hollywood, CA 91602
818-762-0005
800-888-5826
Fax: 818-762-0006

INCREASE/SILVERMINE VIDEO(*INC*)
6860 Canby Ave., Ste. 118
Reseda, CA 91335
818-342-2880
800-233-2880
Fax: 818-342-4029

INGRAM ENTERTAINMENT(*ING*)
2 Ingram Blvd.
La Vergne, TN 37086-7006
615-287-4000
800-759-5000
Fax: 615-287-4992

INGRAM INTERNATIONAL FILMS(*INJ*)
7900 Hickman Rd.
Des Moines, IA 50322
515-254-7000
800-621-1333
Fax: 515-254-7021

INTERAMA, INC.(*INT*)
301 W. 53rd St., Ste. 19E
New York, NY 10019
212-977-4830
Fax: 212-581-6582

INTERNATIONAL FILM BUREAU, INC.(*IFB*)
332 S. Michigan Ave.
Chicago, IL 60604-4382
312-427-4545
800-432-2241
Fax: 312-427-4550

INTERNATIONAL HISTORIC FILMS, INC. (IHF)(*IHF*)
PO Box 29035
Chicago, IL 60629
312-927-2900
Fax: 312-927-9211

INTERURBAN PRESS VIDEOS(*IUF*)
PO Box 94911
Pasadena, CA 91109
818-793-3400
800-950-9333
Fax: 818-793-3797

INTREPID PRODUCTIONS INC.(*IPI*)
203 - 2130 W. 3rd Ave.
Vancouver, BC, Canada V6K 1L1
604-737-0530

ITC(*ITC*)
13515 Dulles Technology Dr.
Herndon, VA 22071-3416
703-713-3335
800-638-3757
Fax: 703-713-0065

IVY FILM/VIDEO(*IVY*)
PO Box 18376
Asheville, NC 28814
704-285-9995
800-669-4057
Fax: 704-285-9997

JAMES AGEE FILM PROJECT(*JAF*)
316 1/2 E. Main St.
Johnson City, TN 37601
615-926-8637
800-352-5111
Fax: 615-971-2921

JEF FILMS, INC.(*JEF*)
Film House
143 Hickory Hill Circle
Osterville, MA 02655-1322
508-428-7198
Fax: 508-428-7198

JIM HENSON PRODUCTIONS(*JHV*)
5358 Melroswe Ave., Ste. 300W
Los Angeles, CA 90038
818-953-3030

JOURNAL FILMS, INC.(*JOU*)
1560 Sherman Ave., Ste. 100
Evanston, IL 60201
708-328-6700
800-323-9084
Fax: 708-328-6706

J2 COMMUNICATIONS(*JTC*)
10850 Wilshire Blvd., Ste. 1000
Los Angeles, CA 90024
310-474-5252
800-521-8273
Fax: 310-474-1219

JUDAICA CAPTIONED FILM CENTER, INC.(*JCF*)
PO Box 21439
Baltimore, MD 21208-0439
410-655-6767

JUST FOR KIDS HOME VIDEO(*JFK*)
6320 Canoga Ave., Penthouse Ste.
PO Box 4112
Woodland Hills, CA 91365-4112
818-715-1980
800-445-8210
Fax: 818-716-0168

KAROL VIDEO(*KAR*)
PO Box 7600
Wilkes Barre, PA 18773
717-822-8899
Fax: 717-822-8226

KEEP THE FAITH INC.(*KEP*)
PO Box 10544
10 Audrey Pl.
Fairfield, NJ 07004
201-244-1990
Fax: 201-244-1990

KID VISION(*KID*)
75 Rockefeller Plaza
New York, NY 10019
212-275-2900
800-3KID-VID
Fax: 212-765-0899

KINO ON VIDEO(*KIV*)
333 W. 39th St., Ste. 503
New York, NY 10018
212-629-6880
800-562-3330
Fax: 212-714-0871

KIT PARKER VIDEO(*KIT*)
c/o Central Park Media
250 W, 57th St., Ste. 317
New York, NY 10107
212-977-7456
Fax: 212-977-8709

KNOWLEDGE UNLIMITED, INC.(*KUI*)
Box 52
Madison, WI 53701-0052
608-836-6660
800-356-2303
Fax: 608-831-1570

KULTUR VIDEO(*KUL*)
195 Hwy. No. 36
West Long Branch, NJ 07764
908-229-2343
800-458-5887
Fax: 908-229-0066

LB DISTRIBUTORS, INC.(*LBD*)
3200 Doolittle Dr.
Northbrook, IL 60062
708-564-8820
800-950-0255
Fax: 800-564-8656

LEO FILMS(*LEO*)
1509 N. Hoover, Ste. 1/2
Los Angeles, CA 90027
213-913-3038
800-888-5481
Fax: 800-888-5481

LIGHT RAIN PRODUCTIONS(*LRP*)
1927 NW Kearney
Portland, OR 97209
503-224-4080
Fax: 503-224-4180

LIGHTYEAR ENTERTAINMENT(*LTY*)
350 5th Ave., Ste. 5101
New York, NY 10118
212-563-4610
800-229-7867
Fax: 212-563-1932

LIVE ENTERTAINMENT(*LIV*)
15400 Sherman Way
PO Box 10124
Van Nuys, CA 91410-0124
818-988-5060

LOONIC VIDEO(*LOO*)
2022 Taraval St., Ste. 6427
San Francisco, CA 94116
510-526-5681

LSVIDEO, INC.(*LSV*)
PO Box 415
Carmel, IN 46032

LUCERNE MEDIA(*LME*)
37 Ground Pine Rd.
Morris Plains, NJ 07950
201-538-1401
800-341-2293
Fax: 201-538-0855

LUMIVISION CORPORATION(*LUM*)
877 Federal Blvd.
Denver, CO 80204-3212
303-446-0400
800-776-LUMI
Fax: 303-446-0101

MADERA CINEVIDEO(*MAD*)
525 E. Yosemite Ave.
Madera, CA 93638
209-661-6000
Fax: 209-674-3650

MAGIC HOUR FILMS(*MHF*)
55 Bell St., Ste. 202
Seattle, WA 98121
206-443-9818
Fax: 206-443-1453

MANAGEMENT COMPANY ENTERTAINMENT GROUP (MCEG), INC.(*MCG*)
1888 Century Park, E., Ste. 1777
Los Angeles, CA 90067-1721
310-282-0871
Fax: 310-282-8303

MARYLAND PUBLIC TELEVISION(*MTP*)
11767 Owings Mills Blvd.
Owings Mills, MD 21117-1499
410-356-5600
800-873-6154
Fax: 410-581-0980

MASTERVISION, INC.(*MAS*)
969 Park Ave.
New York, NY 10028
212-879-0448
Fax: 212-744-3560

MCA/UNIVERSAL HOME VIDEO(*MCA*)
100 Universal City Plaza
Universal City, CA 91608-9955
818-777-1000
Fax: 818-733-1483

MEDIA HOME ENTERTAINMENT(*MED*)
510 W. 6th St., Ste. 1032
Los Angeles, CA 90014
213-236-1336
Fax: 213-236-1346

MERIDIAN FILMS, INC.(*MFI*)
Box 5917
Columbia, SC 29250
803-988-1028
800-THE-FIRM
Fax: 803-988-1023

MGM/UA HOME ENTERTAINMENT(*MGM*)
2500 Broadway
Santa Monica, CA 90404-6061
310-449-3000
Fax: 310-449-3100

MIKE LEBELL'S VIDEO(*MLB*)
75 Freemont Pl.
Los Angeles, CA 90005
213-938-3333
Fax: 213-938-3334

MILESTONE FILM & VIDEO(*MIL*)
275 W. 96th St., Ste 28C
New York, NY 10025
212-865-7449
Fax: 212-222-8952

MILITARY/COMBAT STOCK FOOTAGE LIBRARY(*FGF*)
PO Box 399
Union Washington
Union, WA 98592
206-898-8080
Fax: 206-898-8081

REX #MILLER(*RXM*)
Rte. 1, Box 457-D
East Prairie, MO 63845
314-649-5048

MIRAMAX PICTURES HOME VIDEO(*MAX*)
500 S. Buena Vista St.
Burbank, CA 91521

MNTEX ENTERTAINMENT, INC.(*MTX*)
500 Kirts Dr.
Troy, MI 48084-5225

MODERN CURRICULUM PRESS - MCP(*LCA*)
PO Box 70935
108 Wilmot Rd.
Chicago, IL 60673-0933
800-777-8100

MODERN SOUND PICTURES, INC.(*MSP*)
1402 Howard St.
Omaha, NE 68102
402-341-8476
800-228-9584
Fax: 402-341-8487

MONARCH HOME VIDEO(*MNC*)
Two Ingram Blvd.
La Vergne, TN 37086-7006
615-287-4632
Fax: 615-287-4992

MONARICH GROUP, INC.(*MGI*)
2550 Corporate Pl., Ste. C103
Monterey Park, CA 91754
213-268-2288
800-700-8998
Fax: 213-268-2233

MONDAY/WEDNESDAY/ FRIDAY VIDEO(*MWF*)
123 Scribner Ave.
Staten Island, NY 10301
718-447-1347

MONTEREY HOME VIDEO(*MON*)
28038 Dorothy Dr., Ste. 1
Agoura Hills, CA 91301
818-597-0047
800-424-2593
Fax: 818-597-0105

MOORE VIDEO(*MRV*)
PO Box 5703
Richmond, VA 23220
804-745-9785
Fax: 804-745-9785

MORRIS VIDEO(*MOR*)
2707 Plaza Del Amo, Ste. 601
Torrance, CA 90503
310-533-4800
800-843-3606
Fax: 310-533-1993

MOVIECRAFT, INC.(*MVC*)
PO Box 438
Orland Park, IL 60462
708-460-9082
Fax: 708-460-9099

MOVIES UNLIMITED(*MOV*)
6736 Castor Ave.
Philadelphia, PA 19149
215-722-8298
800-466-8437
Fax: 215-725-3683

MPI HOME VIDEO(*MPI*)
16101 S. 108th Ave.
Orland Park, IL 60462
708-460-0555
Fax: 708-873-3177

MTI HOME VIDEO(*MTH*)
14216 SW 136th St.
Miami, FL 33186
305-255-8684
800-821-7461
Fax: 305-233-6943

MTM HOME VIDEO(*MTM*)
2200 Carolina Place
Fort Mill, SC 29715
803-548-7300
Fax: 803-548-3335

MUSIC FOR LITTLE PEOPLE(*MLT*)
Box 1460
Redway, CA 95560
707-923-3991
800-346-4445
Fax: 707-923-3241

MUSIC VIDEO DISTRIBUTORS(*MVD*)
O'Neill Industrial Center
1210 Standbridge St.
Norristown, PA 19401
610-272-7771
800-888-0486
Fax: 610-272-6074

MYSTIC FIRE VIDEO(*MFV*)
524 Broadway, Ste. 604
New York, NY 10012
212-941-0999
800-292-9001
Fax: 212-941-1443

NATIONAL CENTER FOR JEWISH FILM(*NCJ*)
Brandeis University
Lown Bldg. 102
Waltham, MA 02254-9110
617-899-7044
Fax: 617-736-2070

NATIONAL FILM BOARD OF CANADA(*NFB*)
1251 Avenue of the Americas, 16th Fl.
New York, NY 10020-1173
212-596-1770
800-542-2164
Fax: 212-596-1779

NEVILLE MEYER DISTRIBUTION (NMD)(*NMD*)
65 High Ridge Road, Ste. 304
Stamford, CT 06905
203-968-8905
Fax: 203-968-2953

NEW HORIZONS HOME VIDEO(*NHO*)
2951 Flowers Rd., S., Ste. 237
Atlanta, GA 30341
404-458-3488
800-854-3323
Fax: 404-458-2679

NEW JERSEY NETWORK(*NJN*)
CN-777
Trenton, NJ 08625-0777
609-777-5000
800-792-8645
Fax: 609-633-2920

NEW LINE HOME VIDEO(*NLC*)
116 N. Robertson Blvd.
Los Angeles, CA 90048
310-967-6670
Fax: 310-854-0602

NEW VIDEO GROUP(*NEW*)
126 5th Ave., 15th Fl.
New York, NY 10011
212-206-8600
800-423-1212
Fax: 212-206-9001

NEW WORLD ENTERTAINMENT(*NWV*)
1440 S. Sepulveda Blvd.
Los Angeles, CA 90025
310-444-8100
Fax: 310-444-8101

NEW YORK STATE EDUCATION DEPARTMENT(*NYS*)
Media Distribution Network
Rm. C-7 - CEC
Empire State Plaza
Albany, NY 12230
518-474-3168

NEW YORKER VIDEO(*NYF*)
16 W. 61st St., 11th Fl.
New York, NY 10023
212-247-6110
800-447-0196
Fax: 212-307-7855

NOSTALGIA FAMILY VIDEO(*NOS*)
PO Box 606
Baker City, OR 97814
503-523-9034
800-784-8362
Fax: 503-523-7115

ORION HOME VIDEO(*ORI*)
1888 Century Park E.
Los Angeles, CA 90067
310-282-0550
Fax: 310-282-9902

ORPHAN ENTERTAINMENT(*ORP*)
6930 Sunset Blvd.
Hollywood, CA 90028
213-962-6280

PACIFIC ARTS PUBLISHING(*PAP*)
11858 La Grange Ave.
Los Angeles, CA 90025
800-538-5856
Fax: 310-826-9351

PACIFIC COAST VIDEO(*PCV*)
635 1/2 Chapala St.
Santa Barbara, CA 93101
805-965-5015
Fax: 805-965-5015

PARAMOUNT HOME VIDEO(*PAR*)
Bluhdorn Bldg.
5555 Melrose Ave.
Los Angeles, CA 90038
213-956-8090
Fax: 213-862-1100

PASSPORT INTERNATIONAL PRODUCTIONS(*SFR*)
10520 Magnolia Blvd.
North Hollywood, CA 91601
818-505-0696

PAULIST PRODUCTIONS(*PAU*)
PO Box 1057
Pacific Palisades, CA 90272
310-454-0688
800-624-8613
Fax: 310-459-6549

PBS HOME VIDEO(*PBS*)
Catalog Fulfillment Center
PO Box 4030
Santa Monica, CA 90411
800-531-4727
800-645-4PBS

PENTREX VIDEO(*PEN*)
PO Box 94911
Pasadena, CA 91107
818-793-3400
800-950-9333
Fax: 818-793-3797

PETER PAN ENTERTAINMENT (PPI)(*PRD*)
88 St. Francis St.
Newark, NJ 07105
201-344-4214
Fax: 201-344-0465

PHOENIX/BFA FILMS(*BFA*)
2349 Chaffee Dr.
St. Louis, MO 63146
314-569-0211
800-221-1274
Fax: 314-569-2834

PM ENTERTAINMENT GROUP, INC.(*PMH*)
9450 Chivers Ave.
Sun Valley, CA 91352
818-504-6332
800-934-2111
Fax: 818-504-6380

POLYGRAM VIDEO (PV)(*PGV*)
825 8th Ave.
New York, NY 10019
212-333-8000
800-825-7781
Fax: 212-603-7960

POWER SPORTS VIDEO(*PSV*)
18226 Ventura Blvd., Ste. 102
Tarzana, CA 91356-4229
818-407-0590
Fax: 818-708-0598

PREMIERE HOME VIDEO(*PMR*)
755 N. Highland
Hollywood, CA 90038
213-934-8903
Fax: 213-934-8910

PRIME VIDEO(*PRV*)
19749 Dearborn St.
Chatsworth, CA 91311-6510
818-718-1116
800-727-2229
Fax: 818-718-9026

PRINCETON BOOK CO. PUBLISHERS(*PBC*)
PO Box 57
Pennington, NJ 08534
609-737-8177
800-220-7149
Fax: 609-737-1869

PRISM ENTERTAINMENT(*PSM*)
1888 Century Park, E., Ste. 350
Los Angeles, CA 90067
310-277-3270
Fax: 310-203-8036

PROFESSIONAL MEDIA SERVICE CORP.(*PMS*)
19122 S. Vermont Ave.
Gardena, CA 90248
310-532-9024
800-223-7672
Fax: 800-253-8853

PROSCENIUM ENTERTAINMENT(*PRS*)
PO Box 909
Hightstown, NJ 08520
800-222-6260
Fax: 609-448-9499

PROUD TO BE**A BLACK VIDEO COLLECTION**(*PTB*)
1235-E East Blvd., Ste. 209
Charlotte, NC 28203
704-523-2227

PUBLIC MEDIA VIDEO(*PME*)
5547 N. Ravenswood Ave.
Chicago, IL 60640-1199
312-878-2600
800-826-3456
Fax: 312-878-8406

PYRAMID FILM & VIDEO(*PYR*)
2801 Colorado Ave.
Santa Monica, CA 90404
310-828-7577
800-421-2304
Fax: 310-453-9083

QUALITY VIDEO(*QVD*)
7399 Bush Lake Rd.
Minneapolis, MN 55439-2027
612-893-0903
Fax: 612-893-1585

QUESTAR VIDEO, INC.(*QHV*)
PO Box 11345
Chicago, IL 60611
312-266-9400
800-544-8422
Fax: 312-266-9523

RANDOM HOUSE MEDIA(*RHU*)
400 Hahn Rd.
Westminster, MD 21157
410-848-1900
800-726-0600
Fax: 800-632-9242

RAP ENTERTAINMENT INC.(*RAP*)
100-707 15th Ave. SW
Calgary, AB, Canada T2R 0R8
403-244-7000
800-565-7777
Fax: 403-245-0511

READER'S DIGEST HOME VIDEO(*RDG*)
Reader's Digest Rd.
Pleasantville, NY 10570

REGENCY HOME VIDEO(*RHV*)
9911 W. Pico Blvd.
Los Angeles, CA 90035
310-552-2660
Fax: 310-552-9039

REPUBLIC PICTURES HOME VIDEO(*REP*)
5700 Wilshire Blvd., Ste. 525
Los Angeles, CA 90036
213-965-6900
Fax: 213-965-6963

RHAPSODY FILMS(*RHP*)
PO Box 179
New York, NY 10014
212-243-0152
Fax: 212-645-9250

RHINO HOME VIDEO(*RHI*)
10635 Santa Monica Blvd., 2nd Fl.
Los Angeles, CA 90025-4900
310-828-1980
800-843-3670
Fax: 310-453-5529

RM FILMS INTERNATIONAL, INC.(*RMF*)
PO Box 3748
Los Angeles, CA 90078
213-466-7791
Fax: 213-461-4152

SCHOOLMASTERS VIDEO(*SCH*)
745 State Circle
PO Box 1941
Ann Arbor, MI 48106
313-761-5175
800-521-2832
Fax: 313-761-8711

SCREENWORKS INC.(*SWI*)
8019 1/2 Melrose Ave., Ste. 6
Los Angeles, CA 90046
213-782-3865
Fax: 213-782-3868

SGE ENTERTAINMENT CORP.(*SGE*)
12001 Ventura Pl., 4th Fl., Ste. 404
Studio City, CA 91604
818-766-8500
Fax: 818-766-7873

SHANACHIE ENTERTAINMENT(*SHR*)
13 Laight St.
New York, NY 10013
212-334-0284
Fax: 212-334-5207

SHOKUS VIDEO(*SHO*)
PO Box 3125
Chatsworth, CA 91313
818-704-0400
Fax: 818-701-0560

SIGNALS(*SIG*)
PO Box 64428
St. Paul, MN 55164-0428
612-659-4738
800-669-5225
Fax: 612-659-4320

SIMITAR ENTERTAINMENT(*SIM*)
3850 Annapolis Ln., Ste. 140
Plymouth, MN 55447
612-559-6660
800-486-TAPE
Fax: 612-559-0210

SIMON WIESENTHAL CENTER(*SWC*)
9760 W. Pico Blvd.
Los Angeles, CA 90035-4792
310-553-9036
Fax: 310-553-8007

SINISTER CINEMA(*SNC*)
PO Box 4369
Medford, OR 97501-0168
503-773-6860
Fax: 503-779-8650

SNOOPY'S HOME VIDEO LIBRARY(*SHV*)
c/o Media Home Entertainment
510 W. 6th St., Ste. 1032
Los Angeles, CA 90014-1311
213-236-1336
Fax: 818-992-6520

SOCIETY FOR VISUAL EDUCATION, INC. (SVE)(*SVE*)
6677 N. NW Hwy.
Chicago, IL 60631

312-775-9550
800-829-1900
Fax: 312-775-5091

SOMETHING WEIRD VIDEO(*SMW*)
c/o Mike Vraney
PO Box 33664
Seattle, WA 98133
206-361-3759
Fax: 206-364-7526

SONY MUSIC VIDEO ENTERPRISES(*SMV*)
550 Madison Ave.
New York, NY 10022
212-833-7095

STAGESTEP(*STS*)
PO Box 328
Philadelphia, PA 19105
215-829-9800
800-523-0961
Fax: 215-829-0508

STARDANCE ENTERTAINMENT(*SDE*)
11101 Washington Blvd., Ste. 101
Culver, CA 90232
800-959-8985
Fax: 310-559-8987

STRAND HOME VIDEO(*SHV*)
225 Santa Monica Blvd., Ste. 810
Santa Monica, CA 90401
310-395-5002

STREAMLINE PICTURES(*STP*)
PO Box 691418
W. Hollywood, CA 90069
310-998-0070
Fax: 310-998-1145

STUDIO VIDEO PRODUCTIONS(*STV*)
793 Foothills Blvd., Ste. A
San Luis Obispo, CA 93405
805-543-0707
800-541-1843
Fax: 805-549-0352

SUN VIDEO(*SUN*)
15 Donnybrook
Demarest, NJ 07627
201-784-0662
Fax: 201-784-0665

TAI SENG VIDEO MARKETING INC.(*TAI*)
170 S. Spruce Ave., Ste. 200
San Francisco, CA 94080
415-871-8118
800-888-3836
Fax: 415-871-2392

TAPEWORM VIDEO DISTRIBUTORS(*TPV*)
27833 Hopkins Ave., Unit 6
Valencia, CA 91355
805-257-4904
Fax: 805-257-4820

TELEVISION INTERNATIONAL(*CDV*)
c/o Jason Films
2825 Wilcrest, Ste. 407
Houston, TX 77042
713-266-3097
Fax: 713-266-3148

TEMPE VIDEO(*TEM*)
Box 6573
Akron, OH 44312
216-628-1950
Fax: 216-628-4316

THIRD COAST ENTERTAINMENT(*TCE*)
12750 Ventura Blvd., Ste. 102
Studio City, CA 91604
818-769-9986

THOMSON PRODUCTIONS, INC.(*TPI*)
PO Box 1225
Orem, UT 84059
801-226-0155
Fax: 801-226-0166

THREE STAR RELEASING(*TSR*)
15745 Stagg St.
Van Nuys, CA 91406

3M AUDIO VISUAL DIVISION(*THA*)
6801 Riverplace Blvd.
Austin, TX 78726-9000
800-328-1371

TIME-LIFE VIDEO AND TELEVISION(*TLF*)
1450 E. Parham Rd.
Richmond, VA 23280
804-266-6330
800-621-7026

TIME WARNER VIEWER'S EDGE(*TWV*)
PO Box 85098
Richmond, VA 23285-5098
800-947-3928
Fax: 203-699-9586

TIMELESS VIDEO INC.(*TIM*)
9943 Canoga Ave., Ste. B2
Chatsworth, CA 91311
818-773-0284
800-478-6734
Fax: 818-773-0176

TRANS-WORLD ENTERTAINMENT(*TWE*)
8899 Beverly Blvd., 8th Fl.
Los Angeles, CA 90048-2412

TRIBORO ENTERTAINMENT GROUP(*TRI*)
12 W. 27th St., 15th Fl.
New York, NY 10001
212-686-6116
Fax: 212-686-6178

TROMA TEAM VIDEO(*TTV*)
1501 Broadway, Ste. 2605
New York, NY 10036
212-997-0595
Fax: 212-997-0968

TURNER HOME ENTERTAINMENT COMPANY(*TTC*)
Box 105366
Atlanta, GA 35366
404-827-3066
800-523-0823
Fax: 404-827-3266

20TH CENTURY FOX FILM CORPORATION(*TCF*)
PO Box 900
Beverly Hills, CA 90213
310-369-1000
Fax: 310-369-3318

21ST GENESIS HOME VIDEO(*GNS*)
15820 Arminta St.
Van Nuys, CA 91406

UAV CORPORATION(*UAV*)
PO Box 5497
Fort Mill, SC 29715
803-548-7300
800-486-6782
Fax: 803-548-3335

UNI DISTRIBUTION(*UND*)
60 Universal City Plaza
Universal City, CA 91608
818-777-4400
Fax: 818-766-5740

UNICORN VIDEO, INC.(*UNI*)
9025 Eton Ave., Ste. D.
Canoga Park, CA 91304
818-407-1333
800-528-4336
Fax: 818-407-8246

UNITY PRODUCTIONS(*UNT*)
4007 Willowwood Ln.
Aberdeen, SD 57401-9544

UNIVERSITY OF WASHINGTON EDUCATIONAL MEDIA COLLECTION(*UWA*)
Kane Hall
Box 353090
Seattle, WA 98195
206-543-9909
Fax: 206-685-7892

VALENCIA ENTERTAINMENT CORP.(*VEC*)
45030 Trevor Ave.
Lancaster, CA 93534-2648
805-940-1040
800-323-2061
Fax: 805-940-8511

VANTAGE COMMUNICATIONS, INC.(*VAN*)
PO Box 546-G
Nyack, NY 10960
914-268-0715
800-872-0068
Fax: 914-268-3429

VCII HOME ENTERTAINMENT, INC.(*VHE*)
13418 Wyandotte St.
North Hollywood, CA 91605
818-764-1777
800-350-1931
Fax: 818-764-0231

VESTRON VIDEO(*VES*)
c/o Live Home Video
15400 Sherman Way
PO Box 10124
Van Nuys, CA 91410-0124
818-988-5060
800-367-7765
Fax: 818-778-3125

VIDCREST(*VDC*)
PO Box 69642
Los Angeles, CA 90069
213-650-7310
Fax: 213-654-4810

VIDEO ACTION(*VDA*)
708 W. 1st St.
Los Angeles, CA 90012
213-687-8262
800-422-2241
Fax: 213-687-8425

VIDEO ARTISTS INTERNATIONAL, INC.(*VAI*)
158 Linwood Plaza, Ste. 301
Fort Lee, NJ 07024
201-944-0099
800-477-7146
Fax: 201-947-8850

VIDEO BIBLE LIBRARY, INC.(*VBL*)
Box 17515
Portland, OR 97217
360-892-7707
Fax: 360-254-8318

THE VIDEO CATALOG(*TVC*)
PO Box 64267
Saint Paul, MN 55164-0267
612-659-4312
800-733-6656
Fax: 612-659-4320

VIDEO CITY PRODUCTIONS/ DISTRIBUTING(*VCD*)
4266 Broadway
Oakland, CA 94611
510-428-0202
Fax: 510-654-7802

VIDEO COLLECTIBLES/BFS VIDEO(*VCO*)
1500 Clinton St.
Buffalo, NY 14206-9911
800-268-3891
Fax: 800-269-8877

VIDEO COMMUNICATIONS, INC. (VCI)(*VCI*)
11333 E. 60th Pl.
Tulsa, OK 74146
918-254-6337
800-331-4077
Fax: 918-254-6117

VIDEO CONNECTION(*VCN*)
3123 W. Sylvania Ave.
Toledo, OH 43613
419-472-7727
800-365-0449
Fax: 419-472-2655

VIDEO DIMENSIONS(*VDM*)
322 8th Ave., 4th Fl.
New York, NY 10001
212-929-6135
Fax: 212-929-6135

VIDEO FRANCE(*FRA*)
4822 St. Elmo Ave.
Bethesda, MD 20814
301-654-2224
Fax: 301-229-0621

VIDEO GEMS(*GEM*)
12228 Venice Blvd., No. 504
Los Angeles, CA 90066

VIDEO LEARNING LIBRARY(*VLL*)
15838 N. 62nd St., Ste. 100
Scottsdale, AZ 85254
602-596-9970
800-383-8811
Fax: 602-596-9973

VIDEO PLACEMENT INTERNATIONAL(*VPL*)
240 E. 27th St., Ste. 81
New York, NY 10016
212-696-9207

VIDEO RESOURCES(*VRS*)
220 W. 71st St.
New York, NY 10023
212-724-7055
800-442-7055
Fax: 212-595-0189

VIDEO SEARCH OF MIAMI(*VSM*)
PO Box 161917
Miami, FL 33116
305-279-9773
Fax: 305-598-2665

VIDEO YESTERYEAR(*VYY*)
Box C
Sandy Hook, CT 06482
203-426-2574
800-243-0987
Fax: 203-797-0819

VIDEOGRAF(*VGR*)
144 W. 27th St.
New York, NY 10001
212-242-7871
Fax: 212-206-6986

VIDEOS.COM, INC.(*PIC*)
1725 W. Catalpa Ave., 3rd Fl.
Chicago, IL 60640
312-878-9282
800-670-9282
Fax: 800-308-5003

VIDMARK ENTERTAINMENT(*VMK*)
2644 30th St.
Santa Monica, CA 90405-3009
310-314-2000
Fax: 310-392-0252

VIP VIDEO(*VIP*)
c/o JEF Films
Film House
143 Hickory Hill Circle
Osterville, MA 02655-1322
508-428-7198
Fax: 508-428-7198

VISION VIDEO/GATEWAY FILMS(*GFV*)
2030 Wentz Church Rd.
Box 540
Worcester, PA 19490-0540
610-584-1893
800-523-0226
Fax: 610-584-4610

VISTA STREET ENTERTAINMENT(*VSE*)
9911 W. Pico Blvd., Ste. PHP
Los Angeles, CA 90035
310-556-3074
Fax: 310-556-8815

WADE WILLIAMS PRODUCTIONS, INC.(*MWP*)
13001 Wornall Rd.
Kansas City, MO 64145-1211
Fax: 816-941-7055

WALT DISNEY HOME VIDEO(*DIS*)
500 S. Buena Vista St.
Burbank, CA 91521
818-562-3560

WARNER/ELEKTRA/ ATLANTIC (WEA) CORPORATION(*WEA*)
9451 LBJ Fwy., Ste. 107
Dallas, TX 75243
214-234-6200
Fax: 214-699-9343

WARNER HOME VIDEO, INC.(*WAR*)
4000 Warner Blvd.
Burbank, CA 91522
818-954-6000

WARNER REPRISE VIDEO(*WRV*)
3300 Warner Blvd.
Burbank, CA 91505-4694
818-846-9090
Fax: 818-953-3329

WARNERVISION(*AVE*)
A Time Warner Company
75 Rockefeller Plaza
New York, NY 10019
212-275-2900
800-95-WARNER
Fax: 212-765-0899

WARREN MILLER ENTERTAINMENT(*WME*)
2540 Frontier Ave., Ste. 104
Bouldeer, CO 80301
303-442-3430
800-523-7117
Fax: 303-442-3402

WATER BEARER FILMS(*WBF*)
205 West End Ave., Ste. 24H
New York, NY 10023
212-580-8185
800-551-8304
Fax: 212-787-5455

WAXWORKS/VIDEOWORKS, INC.(*WAX*)
325 E. 3rd St.
Owensboro, KY 42303
502-926-0008
800-825-8558
Fax: 502-685-0563

WESTERN L.A. FILM PRODUCTIONS, INC.(*WLA*)
7425 Clinton St.
Los Angeles, CA 90036-5703

WESTERN MEDIA SYSTEMS(*WFV*)
30941 W. Agoura Rd., Ste. 302
Westlake Village, CA 91361
818-889-7350
Fax: 818-889-7350

WHITE STAR(*WST*)
195 Hwy. 36
West Long Branch, NJ 07764
908-229-2343
800-458-5887
Fax: 908-229-0066

WISHING WELL DISTRIBUTING(*WSH*)
PO Box 1008
Silver Lake, WI 53170
414-889-8501
800-888-9355
Fax: 414-889-8591

WNET/THIRTEEN NON-BROADCAST(*WNE*)
356 W. 58th St.
New York, NY 10019
212-560-2000
Fax: 212-582-3297

WOLFE VIDEO(*WLF*)
PO Box 64
New Almaden, CA 95042
408-268-6782
800-438-9653
Fax: 408-268-9449

WOMBAT FILM AND VIDEO*(WOM)*
1560 Sherman Ave., Ste. 100
Evanston, IL 60201
708-328-6700
800-323-9084
Fax: 708-328-6706

WOOD KNAPP & COMPANY, INC.*(WKV)*
Knapp Press
5900 Wilshire Blvd.
Los Angeles, CA 90036
800-521-2666
Fax: 213-930-2742

WORLD ARTISTS HOME VIDEO*(WAC)*
5150 Wilshire Blvd., Ste. 506
Los Angeles, CA 90036
213-933-7057
800-821-1205
Fax: 213-933-2356

WORLD VIDEO ENTERPRISES, INC.*(WVE)*
150 Executive Park Blvd., No. 1600
San Francisco, CA 94134-3303
415-468-6218
Fax: 415-468-1381

WORLDVISION HOME VIDEO, INC.*(WOV)*
1700 Broadway
New York, NY 10019-5905
212-261-2700
Fax: 212-261-2950

XENON*(XVC)*
211 Arizona Ave.
Santa Monica, CA 90401

YANKEE-ORIOLE CO.*(YOC)*
398 Ogden Ave.
Jersey City, NJ 07307-1115
201-656-4348
Fax: 201-656-4348

ZEITGEIST FILMS*(ZGI)*
247 Centre St., 2nd Fl.
New York, NY 10013
212-274-1989
Fax: 212-274-1644

Web Site Guide

Welcome to the newest feature of the already informative *VideoHound's Golden Movie Retriever*, the all new **Web Site Guide.** Suddenly, the Internet has become an important resource for movie information, appreciation, and (especially) obsession. For your web surfing enjoyment, we have compiled a comprehensive list of many of the top entertainment websites that will expand your knowledge of either a particular movie, actor, director, or Hollywood studio. If you're looking for information on how to make your own film, there are sites for that, too. The guide is divided into six categories: actors and actresses (ranges from Cher to Elijah Wood); cult movie resources; film magazines; film studios; filmmaker resources; film reviews; general entertainment; individual movies; and video outlets. The sites are listed alphabetically within each category, and each site includes name and URL address information. Actors, directors, and movies may have more than one URL, as they are likely to have more than one site devoted to them. These sites have no description because the name of the website is self-explanatory. The general information websites briefly describe what you can expect to find. Just as you can spend hours flipping through *VideoHound*, you can spend hours cruising the web with the sites listed below since a majority of these homepages can link you to other sites on the web.

ACTORS AND ACTRESSES

Kevin Bacon (The Oracle of)
http://www.cs.virginia.edu/~bct7m/bacon.html

Alec Baldwin
http://qlink.queensu.ca/~4yrr/alec.htm

Stephen Baldwin
http://www.li.net/~yesnet/Opening_Page/Opening_page.htm

Antonio Banderas
http://www.sju.edu/~delvalle/antonio.html

Drew Barrymore
http://www.wfu.edu/~david/drew/

Halle Berry
http://www.contrib.andrew.cmu.edu/~jack/halle.html

Kenneth Branagh
http://sfbox.vt.edu:10021/T/tpower/ken.html

Matthew Broderick
http://www.ccn.cs.dal.ca/~ag249//matt.html

Pierce Bronson
http://www.mcs.net/~klast/www/brosnan.html

Sandra Bullock
http://user.aol.com/dsctexmex/web/sandra.htm

Nicholas Cage
http://members.aol.com/ToniGrrl/cage/main.htm

Bruce Campbell
http://spage.com/bruce/

Jim Carrey
http://www.inforamp.net/~petroff/

Cher
http://www.inch.com/~harbur/cher/index.html

Jackie Chan
http://www.pitt.edu/~oren/jackie/jackie.html

Jean Claude Van Damme
http://www.shef.ac.uk/uni/union/susoc/caa/homes/pm/pm933303/vandamme.html

George Clooney
http://www.hooked/net/users/cpatubo/clooney.html

Sean Connery
http://www.mcs.net/~Klast/www/connery.html
http://www.wsu.edu:8080/~dock/

Kevin Costner
http://www.hhs.nl/~v942549/kevin.htm

Courtney Cox
http://www.uidaho.edu/~hodge8931/friends/cox/cox.html

Tom Cruise
http://www.cyberhighway.net/~phlacin/cruise.html

Macaulay Culkin
http://www.onlink.com/culkin/index.html

Jamie Lee Curtis
http://sdcc8.uscsd.edu/~jelwell/jlc/

John Cusack
http://www.unm.edu/~matts/John_Cusack.html

Geena Davis
http://www.mv.com/users/dld/more/geena.html

Judy Davis
http://elycion.geology.ualberta.ca/~tpreston/judy.html

Daniel Day Lewis
http://www.well.com/user/dkscully/index.htm

James Dean
http://www.jdean.com/
http://www.americanlegends.com/jamesdean

Rebecca DeMornay
http://web-star.com/rebecca/rebecca.html

Robert De Niro
http://www.cs.bc.edu/~kawashim/deniro.html

Johnny Depp
http://mastrangelo.polito.it/jonydepp/index.htm

Cameron Diaz
http://www.cs.uit.no/~haakonb/diaz.html

Leonardo DiCaprio
http;//meadow.greenwing.com/leo/

Michael Douglas
http://www.texas/net/users/mikedoug/

Richard Dreyfuss
http://www.electriciti.com/namm/opus.transcript.html
An audio interview of the actor discussing his film Mr. Holland's Opus.

David Duchovny
http://duggy.extern.uscd.edu/~linny/David.html

Clint Eastwood
http://www.powernet.net/~cal/eastwood.html

Chris Farley
http://pantheon.cis.yale.edu/~odonnell/farley/farley.html

Ralph Fiennes
http;//student-www.uchicago.edu/users/cceccare/Fiennes.html

Linda Fiorentino
http://www.resus.univ-mrs.fr:2000/~mactyler/
Written in French.

Bridget Fonda
http://www.cs.utexas.edu/users/ddk/bridgetfonda/bridgetfonda.html

Harrison Ford
http://www.smartlink.net/~deej7/ford.html

Jodie Foster
http://www.tcp.com/~mary/foster.html

Mel Gibson
http://pages.prodigy.com/MelGibson/gibson.htm

Whoopi Goldberg
http;//www.tu-berlin.de/~gruhlke/forum/whoopi/index.html

Hugh Grant
http://ucsub.colorado.edu/~kritzber.new/hugh/hugh.html

Tom Hanks
http://www.wsu.edu:8080/~jtwillia/hanks.html

Ed Harris
http://www.fishnet.net/~decadent/edharris.html

Teri Hatcher
http://www.escape.ca/~hazlitt/teri/thind.htm

Dustin Hoffman
http://www.sky.net/~emily/dustin.html

Sir Anthony Hopkins
http://www.mit.edu:8001/people/douglas/sirtony.html

Helen Hunt
http://www.ltm.com/dinan/hhunt/html/hhunt/.html

Nicole Kidman
http://www-personal.umich.edu/~rkmead/kidman.html

Val Kilmer
http://www.eskimo.com/~kilmer

Stephen King
http://www.acs.appstate.edu/~pl17714/sking_html/

Brandon Lee
http://europa.cs.mun.ca/~loreilly/brandon.htm

Bruce Lee
http://www.yab.com/~streaker/brucel.html
http://www.infi.net/~danaj/bruce.html

Juliette Lewis
http://www.solace.mh.se/~alpha/jlwp/jl.htm

Steve Martin
http://qlink.queensu.ca/~4kgd/steve/

Bette Milder
http://www.interactive8.com/bette/

An interactive site.

Marilyn Monroe
http://www.ionet.net/~jellenc/marilyn.html
http://wwww2.int-evry.fr/~hug/marliyna.html
http;//www.uiuc.edu/ph/www.arch/m_index.html

Demi Moore
http://www.diskriter.com/demi/

Sam Neill
http://kevin.net/~erika/sn.html

Leonard Nimoy
http://www.grady.uga.edu/spock.html

Gary Oldman
http://pages/prodigy.com/oldman/oldman.html
http://www.csh.rit.edu/~halle/oldman.html

Julia Ormond
http://student.curtin.edu.au/~ekenwright/Ormond/Ormond.html
http://home.cc.umantioba.ca/~umloew33/julia.html

Al Pacino
http://pubweb.acns.nwu.edu/~apoorman/pacino.html

Bill Paxton
http://qlink.queensu.ca/~3bjw6/

Michelle Pfeiffer
http://www.geocities.com/Paris/1032/pfeiffer.html

River Pheonix
http://magna.com.au/~tpropert/pheonix.html

Brad Pitt
http://www.eis.or.jp/muse/junko003.bp.html

Bill Pullman
http://copper.ucs.indiana.edu/~mtsai/bill_pullman.html

Christopher Reeve
http://web.syr.edu/~ajgould/reeve.html

Keanu Reeves
http://www.empirenet.com/~jahvah/skc/skc.html

Christina Ricci
http;//www.ny.frontiercomm.net/~freeprny/crhp.html

Alan Rickman
http;//www.csh.rit.edu/~halle/rickman.html

Tim Robbins
http;//us.imdb.com/M/person-exact?Robbins,+Tim

Julia Roberts
http://studentweb.tulane.edu/~sbuckle/

Tim Roth
http://weber.u.washington.edu/~jenhwolf/

Meg Ryan
http://web.cs.ualberta.ca/~davidw/MegRyan/meg.cgi

Winona Ryder
http://www.duc.auburn.edu/~harshec/WWW/Winona.html

Susan Sarandon
http://zen.sunderland.ac.uk/~aa1gha/susan.html

William Shatner
http://www.fastlane.net.~hattan/hattan.html

Elisabeth Shue
http://orion.adnc.com/~websites/dapence/shue.html

Alicia Silverstone
http://www.duke.edu/~x12/alicia/index.html
http://www.unc.edu/~kchadn/alicia.index2.html

Christian Slater
http://www.magna.com.au/~hodge.cslater.html

Kevin Spacey
http://www.duke.edu/~jlg1/kevin-spacey.html

David Spade
http://www.cs.montana.edu/~ashworth/spade.html

Patrick Stewart
http://ourworld.compuserve.com/homepages/psas/

Sharon Stone
http://www.mdc.net/~oh2smooth/

Barbra Streisand
http://www.hhs.nl~v942549/barbra.htm

Jonathan Taylor-Thomas
http://home.aol.com/Temp4JTT

Emma Thompson
http://www.calvin.edu/~planting/et/emma.html

Uma Thurman
http://www.duke.edu/~x12uma/index.html

Marisa Tomei
http://www.vuse.vanderbilt.edu/~burketrd/tomei.htm

John Travolta
http://www.auburn.edu/~proppka/travolta.htm

Christopher Walken
http://www.ior.com/~cmohney/walken/walken.html

John Wayne
http://www.napanet.net~donc/

Sigourney Weaver
http://www.pt.hk-r.se/student/di94vno/ripley.html

Bruce Willis
http://www.accsyst.com/writers/bruno.htm

Kate Winslet
http://www.ioorg/~sdh/winslet.html
http://www2.cibola.net/~michaela/kate

Elijah Wood
http://www.elijahwood.com/

CULT MOVIE RESOURCES

Anime Resources and Info
http://www.best.com:80/~gaxiola/Anime/
Includes upcoming anime features and background information on the genre.

Captain Fly: A Guide to Blaxploitation
http://www.halcyon.com/zaguero/fly.blaxploit.html
Information on a film niche that has been ignored on the Web. "Captain Fly", a self-pronounced guru of Blaxploitation films, offers advice on how to purchase such forgotton gems as Hell Up From Harlem *and* Sheba Baby.

The Cult Shop
http://www.public.iastate.edu/~abormann
Gives the latest information on your favorite cult movie stars like Bruce Campbell and Steve Buscemi. Also offers links to other movie sites.

The Gamera Home Page
http://tswww.cc.emory.edu/~kgowen/gamera.html
A home page devoted to that giant nuclear Japanese turtle, Gamera. Showcases, in depth, all nine of his films.

Hong Kong Movies Home Page
http://www.mstud.chalmers.se/hkmovie
An interest in Hong Kong films has significantly increased due to the sudden rise of Jackie Chan and action director John Woo. This comprehensive site offers much information on the Hong Kong film industry. Includes an update of new Hong Kong films, filmographies, interviews, reviews, and a searchable database on Hong Kong actors and actresses.

Mad Prof. Mike's Headbanger Movie Reviews
http://www.dnai.com/~ochobbit
The lunatic rantings of Professor Headbanger dominate as he raves about such schlock classics as Teenagers from Outer Space *and* This Island Earth.

Mel's Godzilla Page
http://www.ama.caltech.edu/users/mrm/godzilla.html
Designed to give glory to Japan's most favorite export. Features updated reports on an upcoming Godzilla movie in the states, photos of Godzilla in action and a listing of FAQ's about this creature and its movies.

No Place for a Woman: The Family in Film Noir
http://www.obs.net:80/Noir/
Reports on the implications that film noir has had on society. The author, John Blaser, pinpoints the role that women and family have in this genre. Subtopics include,"Pro-family Messages in Film Noir" and "Women's Anti-Family Function in Film Noir."

Professor Neon's TV and Movie Mania
http://www.vortex.com/ProfNeon.html
Covers a gamut of information on film, television, radio and the cable industry. When it comes to films, the Professor leans more to sci-fi, cult and weird stuff.

Reel Talk
http://www.reellife.com/PFE/index.html
Allows you to talk amongst yourselves about recent or past cult film releases.

The Vampyres Movie List
http://www.netxs.com/~elmo/vamp-mov.html
A listing of most, not all, vampire films made, including the most obscure.

DIRECTORS

Woody Allen
http://www.idt.unit.no/~torp/woody

Allison Anders
http://home.earthlink.net/~kristinm/aahome.html

Roger Avary
http://www.avary.com/

Ingmar Bergman
www.voyagerco.com/CC/gh/featured/p.bergman.htm;
Not a homepage, but a Criterion Collection site for the famed director.

James Cameron
http://www.soton.ac.uk/~pdc194/cameron/

Joel and Ethan Coen
http://lasarto.cnde.iastate.edu/Movies/CultShop/Movies/coen.html

Frederico Fellini
http://www.conexis.es/ddc/

Terry Gilliam
http://www.ionsys.com/~gurney/terry.html
http://gladstone.uoregon.edu/~chrismcg/gilliam.html

Alfred Hitchcock
http://nextch.mty.itesm.mx/~plopezg/Kaplan/Hitchock.html
http://www.primenet.com/~mwc/

Stanley Kubrick
http://pages.prodigy.com/Other/kubrick/
http://www.lehigh.edu/~pj12/kubrick.html

Akira Kurosawa
http://www.voyagerco.com/CC/ghgraphics/kurosawa.html

David Lynch
http://web.city.ac.uk/~cb157/Dave.html
http://www.4w.com/pages/mdunn/dltp.htm

Rob Reiner
http://zen.sunderland.ac.uk/~aa4dhu/rob.html

Oliver Stone
http://www.geocities.com/Hollywood/2682

Quentin Tarantino
http://www.GANet.Net/~pg0/quentin/greatbig.htm
http://www.mind.net/nikko11/QT.html

http://osiris.sunderland.ac.uk/~ca5sli/home.htm
http://koganuts.com./Galleries/qt.home.html
http://rmd-www.mr.ic/ac.uk/~dan/tarantino/tarantino.html
http://www.xs4all.nl/~mrblond/
http://www.blarg.net/~kbilly/
http://www.calweb.com/~gerrit01/qtshrine/
http://www.tarantino.com/top.shtml

Francios Truffault
http://www.inxpress.net/~avatar/truffaut.html

John Waters
http://www.hotwired.com/retina.95/29/waters/index.html
http://www.reed.edu/~mfagan/dreamland.html
http://blackrock.sametz.com/dreamland/
http://www.northcoast.com/~shojo/Waters/

Orson Welles
http://www.voyagerc.com/CC/gh/welles/intro.html
Not a homepage. Part of the Criterion Collection series.

John Woo
http://koganuts.com./Galleries/jw.home.html

Ed Wood
http://garnet.acns.fsu.edu/~lflynn.edwood.html

FILM FESTIVALS

AFI Los Angeles International Film Festival (USA)
http://www.afionline.org/index/index.home.html
Features attractions from this huge film festival held every October. Also lists synposes of the films featured.

Berlin Film Festivals
http://www.b.shuttle.de/forum-ifb/
Lists production information on all the films featured in this festival.

Cannes Film Festival
http://www.mhm.fr/cannes/eng/index.html
Official site gives you a rundown of all the films running in the competition and an icon called "guest book" so that you can go starchasing in cyberspace.

Chicago International Film Festival
http://www.chicago.ddbn.com/filmfest/menu.html
Answers questions in the area of awards, entries, juries and transportation.

Chicago Lesbian and Gay International Film Festival
http://videos.com/gandl/index.htm
Offers a rundown of films featured in this alternative film festival.

Denver International Film Festival
http://www2.csn.net/DenverFilm/
Besides information on the entries, this site offers insight into the Denver Film Society, supporters, new media and workshops.

London Film Festival
http://www.ibmpcug.co.uk/lff.html
Lists the star attendees and has a program diary which records all the relevant action at the festival.

Montreal World Film Festival
http://www.ffm-montreal.org/home-f.htm
Offers a rundown of the festival in both English and French.

Santa Clarita International Film Festival
http://www.smartlink.net/~director/scviff
A site acknowledging the only film festival in Santa Clarita, California specializing in family films.

Seattle International Film Festival
http://www.seattlefilm.com/
Enables you to look at some photo stills from the festival, read audio speeches and check out some internet broadcasts.

Sundance Film Festival
http://www.sundancefilm.com
This official site includes a daily report, listings of films competing and a guide for getting around. Also has an archive for past festivals.

Toronto International Film Festival
http://www.bell.ca/toronto/filmfest/
Includes cine-bytes and a feature to browse the poster gallery and check out the paparazzi.

Venice Film Festival
http://www.portve.interbusiness.it/wetvenice/biennale/binfoe.html
Not only does it include information on the film festival, but news on other cultural activities happening in Venice.

FILM MAGAZINES

Box Office
http://www.boxoff.com
One of the first trade publications to go online, reporting on current films and films in production.

CinemaSpace
http://cinemaspace.berkeley.edu/
Journal dedicated to all aspects of cinema and new media. Covers such areas as film theory, criticism, multimedia lectures and the film program at UC Berkeley.

FilmMaker
http://found.cs.nyu.edu/CAT/affiliates/filmmaker/filmmaker.html
Quarterly publication that showcases independent film and filmmakers.

Millennium Film Journal
http://www.sva.edu/MFJ/
Includes published articles about independent, experimental, and avant-garde
cinema, video, and, more recently, works that use the newer technologies. Also has an archive for past issues.

Premiere
http://www.premieremag.com/
On-line version of the leading entertainment magazine with various segments including a chat circle called schmoozing and a trivia game.

Time Out
http://www.timeout.co.uk./
Provides a rundown of many cultural and art events happening around the world.

FILM STUDIOS

Fine Line Features
http://www.flf.com/
The leading studio of independent films presents information on upcoming releases and offers enlightenment to budding filmmakers.

Gramercy Pictures
http://spider.media.philips.com/polygram/PolyGram.html
A division of Polygram, you can jump to various sites dealing with their movies and music.

MCA/Universal Cyberwalk
http://www.mca.com
Take a stroll through MCA's family tree of entertainment companies which includes Universal Studios, MCA Home Video, MCA Records and Spencer's Gifts. Links to coming attractions and to a screening room with current video releases.

MGM Lion's Den
http://www.mgmua.com/
Home of the revamped ShowGirls *site, also has coverage on the huge distributor's large slate of theatrical releases. Divided into MGM's niches, such as MGM television and home video.*

The Miramax Cafe
http://www.miramax.com/
Walk into a smorgasbord of Miramax delectables. Includes chances to win a trip to premieres and Miramax clothing. Click on their week's specials and get a glimpse into their upcoming and current releases.

New Line Cinema
http://cybertimes.com/NewLine/Welcome.html
Displays their current and upcoming releases.

Paramount Pictures
http://www.paramount.com
Click on any icon from the movies shown and receive information on production and cast.

Sony Classics
http://www.spe.sony.com/Pictures/SonyClassics
Focuses on Sony's independent releases and offers links to other sites.

Sony Pictures Entertainment
http://www.spe.sony.com/Pictures/SonyMovies/index.html
Sony (which includes Columbia and TriStar) gives you the latest on their crop of films. Along with film and studio information, you can enter their contests to win movie t-shirts or trips to a Hollywood premiere.

Trimark Pictures
http://www.trimarkpictures.com/
Takes you behind the scenes of their latest releases and gives you a glimpse of future films.

Troma
http://www.troma.com/home
With its #1 citizen Toxie welcoming you, indulge in the trash-camp cinema in which Troma specializes. Features information on such classics as Toxic Avenger, Class of Nuke'em High *and their latest,* Sgt. Kabukiman NYPD.

Twentieth Century Fox Home Entertainment
http://www.tcfhe.com
Promotes the studio's library of films. Divided into a time line enabling you to browse through their collection beginning with the 1920's and ending with the 1990's.

United International Pictures
http://www.uip.com/
Comes in a variety of languages and has downloadable materials on their films.

Walt Disney Studios
http://www.disney.com
Divided into nine categories where you can find the latest on Disney books, home video, movies, music, shopping, software, television, theater and theme parks.

Warner Brothers
http://www.movies.warnerbros.com/
Get the latest on WB's films, tv programs, music, merchandise, DC comics and kid's programming.

FILMMAKER RESOURCES

American Film Institute
http://www.afionline.org/
The American Film Institute created this site to further its cause of finding talent that will prolong the life of art and film. The site reveals the various courses, study facilities and grants that this non-profit organziation offers.

Cyber Film School
http://www.cyberfilmschool.com/
Want to become the next Quentin or Spike, but can't afford film school? Try this informative and entertaining venue that teaches the tricks of the trade in areas such as screenwriting, cinematography and producing.

Film Finances
http://www.primenet.com/~ffi/ffihome.html
Check out this site provided by the world leader in information on film financing. Provides insights on financing film, television and CD-ROM productions.

Independent Film and Video Makers Internet Resource Guide
http://www.echonyc.com/~mvidal/Indi-Film+Video.html
Questions on funding and film festivals are answered, and changes in film and video production are documented in this site that should benefit any independent film or video maker.

Mandy's Film and Television Production Directory
http://www.mandy.com/
An international geographical listing of film technicans, facilities and producers. Helpful site for anyone looking for a film crew.

Screenwriter's Online
http://www.screenwriter.com/insider/news.html
Welcomes novice screenwriters to interact with those who are in the business.

Screenwriter's Resources Pages
http://www.teleport.com/~cdeemer/Screenwriters.html
A screenwriter's one-stop resource site. Learn about the format and structure of scripts, how to market your script, network among your peers, receive tips from the pros and become informed of the latest events and seminars.

FILM REVIEWS

Critics Roost
http://moviereviews.com/coc-roost.html
The home of a circle of film critics with their individual slant on film. Women's Lip, The Movie Avenger, The Movie Assassin and J-Man offer their personal perspective on film.

Film.com
http://www.film.com/film/
Bringing a casual spin on film criticism from self-made critics around the country. Also has a calendar noting upcoming film releases.

Mandel & Patrick's Movie Corner!
http://www.fyi.net/~andre/mand&pat.htm
Two teenaged boys, using a 4-star rating system, review current theatrical and video releases.

The Movie Mom's Guide to Movies and Videos for Families
http://pages.prodigy.com/VA/rcpj55a/moviemom.html
Created by movie critic and mother, Nell Minow, who gives critiques and advice on how to get children to watch movies that aren't doused in violence.

Movie Reviews by Ellis: The Art and Craft of Cultural Context
http://movie.infocom.net/
Film critic Joan Ellis puts her acerbic and astute observations on the Internet as she examines the cultural implications of current film.

Movie Reviews by Matt and Kenny
http://www.winternet.com/~nudnik/reviews/
Gives skeletal reviews of films but offers a link to information regarding Lucasfilm's THX sound system.

Movie Review Query Engine
http://www.cinema.pgh.pa.us/movie/reviews
Allows you to search on any movie and find all available reviews appearing in the Usernet group rec.arts.movies. reviews.

Out Magazine Movie Reviews
http://www.out.com/out/entertainment/movies.html
On-line version of the gay magazine that includes movie reviews and commentary on gay and lesbian cinema.

Skew
http://www.ot.com/skew/

Targeted for the teenage crowd, includes adolescent criticisms on films and popular culture.

Teen Movie Critic
http://www.dreamagic.com/roger/teencritic.html
A seventeen year old movie buff from Minnesota offers his thoughts on current theatrical releases. Also has a link to a listing of many video rental stores around America.

The Third Thumb
http://www.ganesa.com/ganesa/~pat/movies/movrev2.html
Gives brief film reviews and has a searchable database.

VideoHound
http://www.thomson.com/videhound.html
Offers reviews on current video releases, as well as videographies of highlighted personalities. You can also find information on the many fine VIP entertainment titles available. In all modesty, it is a very nice site.

Women Studies Film Reviews
http://www.ganesa.com/ganesa/~pat/movies/movrev2.html
Movie reviews with a feminist angle written by Florida radio personality Linda Lopez McAlister's and film scholar Cynthia Fuchs.

GENERAL ENTERTAINMENT

Academy of Motion Picture Arts and Sciences
http://www.oscars.org/ampas/
Site proves that the AMPAS does more than just hand out gold statuettes every year. This homepage reveals this organization's dedication to spreading the love of film around the world. Includes information on AMPAS's varous fellowships, educational and historical activities.

American Memory
http://lcweb2.loc.gov/papr/mpixhome.html
Collection of historical film stock that can be downloaded from the Library of Congress. Time frame is from 1897 to 1916 and includes such archival footage as President William McKinley's funeral and "actuality films" showing panoramic views of old San Francisco policemen and firemen in action.

Ashley Marcelline's Black Film & Video Guide
http://www.inforamp.net/ashleyma/blakcine.html
An on-line version of Marcelline's book dealing exclusively with Black cinema and documenting films that are virtually unknown to the public.

Big Bad Barbarian
http://pages.ripco.com:8080/~bbb/scripts.html
There are many popular scripts on the Internet, such as Star Wars *and* Alien, *and the barabarian can lead you to them.*

The Cabinet of Dr. Casey
http://www.cat.pdx.edu/~caseyh/horror/index.html
Immense site that includes interviews from artists and actors in horror films and graphics from famous horror movies. Links you to other horror sites such as "The Ooga Booga Page" and "The Page That Dripped Blood".

Cinemedia
http://www.gu.edu.au/gwis/cinemedia/CineMedia.cinema.html
An index which allows you to begin your own search for other entertainment web sites.

Crazy Movie Credits
http://www.cis.ohio-state.edu/hypertext/faq/usenet/movies/crazy-credits/faq.html
If you think that a movie ends when the credits roll, then you're wrong, at least for some movies. This site showcases the end credits of quirky movies that go out of their to leave the best for last.

Cybersleaze
http://metaverse.com/vibe/sleaze/index.html
Created by former MTV veejay Adam Curry, this site dishes out the dirt on the celebrities, but in a playful way.

Cyber Sightings
http://www.cyberpages.com/cybersightings
Create your own rumors for others to read and perhaps spread. Stumble onto this site, you may very well be convinced that Babe the pig actually can talk but the government is trying to cover it up.

The Darkside of the Web
http://www.cascade.net/darkweb.html
Specializes in shedding light on the bizarre and creepy.

The Drudge Report
http://www.lainet.com/~drudge
If you get pass the political reports and the weather forecasts that smother this site, you can find some interesting gossip from an anoynomous insider from Hollywood.

The Envelope Please
http://garbo.virtualize.com/
The official site for the Oscars which provides eye catching graphics, an expansive Oscar trivia game and information on production of the award show. Noteworthy feature involves video clips from nominated films which can be downloaded.

Film and Video Resources
http://http2.sils.umich.edu/Public/fvl/film.html
Created by the folks at the University of Michigan School of Information and Library Studies, this site leads you to many of the textual resources available that deal with film and video. Organized according to reviews, filmographies, discussions and other databases.

Film Forum
http://www.filmforum.com/
Showcases the latest releases in New York's leading independent movie house. Offers premiere information on independent features and reportory programming.

Filmzone
http://www.Filmzone.com/
Offers tons of information on independent films, including long lost gems and interviews with filmmakers and actors suchs as the Coen Brothers and Jackie Chan. Also gives visitors the current trends in mulitplexes.

Foresight New Media
http://www.foresight.co.uk/ents/
European company that makes web site pages has its own site that can link you up to other movie sites.

The Gigaplex
http://www.gigaplex.com/
This site has information divided into 15 plexes that include film, tv, music, theater, books, photos, art, golf, yoga, food, sex, love , travel, puzzles and top ten listings from every spectrum of popular culture.

The GRAFICS Server
http://grafics.histart.umontreal.ca/default-eng.html
Sponsored by a French-Canadian research group that specalizes in the early cinema of Quebec. Much of the information is in French, but you can dowload many documents and articles on this province's early cinema.

Hollywood Online
http://www.hollywood.com
Packaged like a row of slot machines in Vegas, try your luck at movie trailers, movie trivia, movie chat, vote on the latest contest or check out some real estate in California.

Hollywood Sign
http://www.rfx.com/hollywood/
Shows snapshots of the famous Hollywood sign from various angles.

The Internet Entertainment Network
http://www.hollywoodnetwork.com/dealmaking/index.html
Enables you to become a member of the Screenwriters, Producers or Writers Network. Divided into such sites as dealmaking, box office, in-production and script sales.

The Internet Movie Database
http://www.msstate.edu/Movies
The mother of all entertainment databases. Users can frequently update the information and submit their own film reviews. With thousands of movies stored in its database, you can search by title, actor, director, country and even by character name.

James Bond
http://www.mcs.net/~klast/www/bond.html
With the arrival and success of Goldeneye, *the phenomenon of Bond has invaded cyberspace with his own homepage. Includes a rundown of all Bond villains and their famous lines, and trivia on every Bond film ever made.*

Kino on Video
http://www.kino.com/
Kino International showcases a breadth of films from world cinema.

The Left-Wing Film Guide
http://ccme-mac4.bsd.uchicago.edu/DSADocs/Films.html
Helpful guide for any social and political group planning their next movie themed rally. Pick any movie from any of their categories that include feminism, race relations and anti-authoritian struggles.

Library of Congress Archive
http://lcweb2.loc.gov/papr/mpixhome.html
Allows you to download historical film images from the early 1900's.

Local Movie Listings
http://www.actwin.com/movies/other.html
Includes movie theater showtimes from Canada, England and South Africa as well as American cities.

Lucy Lipps
http://www.lucylipps.com/
Includes a Kiss & Tell section which brings you the latest scoop on celebrities and the buzz around Tinseltown.

Movies.com
http://www.movies.com/
Displays the latest films and allows celebrities to welcome visitors onto the site.

The Movie Cliches List
http://www.like.it/vertigo/cliches.html
A vast list of common stereotypes and movie occurrences that defy logic. Divided into over fifty topics including bodily functions, minorities, teenagers and wood. A growing site since people can submit their own materials.

MovieLink
http://www.movielink.com/?TP:National
On-line movie guide with listings of local movie theaters in the 22 most populated cities in the country. Features include a section for users to cast their votes for "The American Moviegoer Awards" and a place called the "cafe" for users to chit chat.

Movie Mania
http://www.movievan.com/
Find out what's new and what's hot on the video scene. Also keeps you informed of the latest free software available on the Web.

MovieNet
http://www.movienet.com/
A consulting firm used by Hollywood execs seeking information on the latest film projects in production, up and coming directors, acting talent and news on the acquistions of remakes.

The Movie Posters Archive
http://anubis.science.unitn.it/services/movies/index.html
An on-line vault of old movie posters from the sci-fi, horror, animation and classic genres.

Movie Poster Web Page
http://www.musicman.com/mp/mp.html
No you're not seeing double. This one is a catalog of movie posters available for sale. Includes foreign films.

Movie Snapshot
http://www.moviesnapshot.com/
Reviews, photographs, celebrity interviews, biographies, games and awards.

The Movie Sound Page
http://www.netaxs.com/~dgrash/sndir.html
Download various sound bites from famous flicks and link to other sites.

Movie Recommendation System
http://www.labs.bt.com/innovate/multimed/morse/morse.htm
Your votes count with this site that enables you to rate movies you have seen and based on your rating, will recommend movies you might like. This is not a game, but a service.

MovieWEB
http://movieweb.com/movie/movie.html
Dumps all film studios into one site and offers production information and still photos of their new releases. Also offers the latest box office statistics.

Mr. Showbiz
http://www.mrshowbiz.com/showbiz/
Bundles the latest entertainment gossip and news, movie reviews, and music reviews. Includes an in-depth volume of knowledge on the history of the Academy Awards.

The Muse
http://www.hyperlink.com/muse
Dedicated to the Greek mythology figure who spawned the arts. Among its links for books, music, theater and dance, includes one for cinema that showcases such directors as Roman Polanski and Martin Scorsese.

The Obituary Page
http://catless.ncl.ac.uk/Obituary/movies.html
A listing of the latest celebrity deaths in Hollywood.

OscarNet
http://www.dkdigital.com/Netties/
Encourages visitors to vote for nominees and for alternative nominations called the "Netty Awards" and you can cast your vote for the" Golden Raspberry Awards "for the year's worst performances.

Our Secret Century: Revelations from The Prelinger Archive
gopher://gopher.well.sf.ca.us:70/11/Art/Experimental.Film.and.Video/secret.century
Contains footage and information on films from The Prelinger Archives *which is a collection of instititutional films made from '30's to the early '60's. Some of these clips can been seen on* The Late Show with David Letterman.

Pathfinder
http://www.pathfinder.com
Created by Time Warner. Coincidentally, you can obtain access to their magazines, such as People, Vibe, Groove *and* Entertainment Weekly, *which check the pulse of popular culture.*

The Phantasmagoria Graveyard Web Page
http://libstaff.lib.lehigh.edu
An audio website that features the theme music from such horror films as Halloween *and* The Shining.

Planet Earth
http://www.demon.co.uk/elpasso/planet-earth/index.htm
If you're looking for film and tv memorablilia from such popular movies and series as Alien *or* Space 1999, *here's the place to be. An on-line catalog for costumes, model kits, back issues of specialized magazines and trading cards. You can even post descriptions of any items you might want to sell.*

Reel Talk
http://www.reellife.com/PFE/index.html
If you're a movie buff, then join the crowd as you talk amongst yourselves about the latest releases.

Science Fiction Contiuum
http://www.webcreations.com/sjvideo/

A guide to a diverse collection of sci-fi and horror films, as well as animation, television and UFO documentaries on video and laser discs.

ScreenSite
http://www.sa.ua.edu/TCF/welcome.htm
Primarily devoted to the teaching and researching of film and television.

Silent Movies
http://www.cs.monash.edu.au/~pringle/silent/
Information on silent films. Includes a listing for many silent film screenings and bios on many of the era's top stars such as Charlie Chaplin, Buster Keaton and Lillian Gish.

The Top 25
http://movieweb.com/movie/top25.html
Provides the box office ranking of all current releases; updated every Thursday.

U.C. Berkeley Film Studies Science Fiction Page
http://remarque.berkeley.edu:8001/~xcohen/Resources/localres.html
For avid SciFi film buffs, it has separate sites on such classics as Blade Runner, Star Trek, Alien, Star Wars *and other genre related sites.*

Wiretap Archive
gopher://wiretap.spies.com:70/11/Library/Media/Film
Very straightforward and diverse listing of special interest movies. Categories include: films with rape scenes, film noir listing, railway movies, Japanese monster guide, naval related movies and vampires in movies.

INDIVIDUAL MOVIE SITES

Ace Ventura: When Nature Call
http://www.aceventura.com

The Adventures of Buckaroo Banzai
http://bbs.annex.com/relayer/bbanzai.htm

Airplane
http://www.d.umn.edu/~elindsko/Airplane/airplane.html

Akira
http://www.voyagerco.com/CC/featured/akira/akiraintro.html

ALIEN Saga
http://found.cs.nyu.edu/michael/alien/

The American President
http://www.americanpresident.com

Apocalypse Now
http://www.luhsd.k12.ca.us/~nc670597/apocnow.html

Apollo 13
http://www.mca.com/universal_pictures/apollo13/index.html

Babe
http://www.mca.com/universal_pictures/babe/index.html

Batman Forever
http://www.batmanforever.com

Blade Runner
http://kzsu.stanford.edu/uwi/br/off-world.html

Braveheart
http://www.aloha.net/~brvhrt/index.html

Brazil
http://www.cis.ohio-state.edu/hypertext/faq/usenet/movies/brazil-faq.html

The Cable Guy
http://www.thecableguy.com

Casablanca
http://users.aol.com/VRVI/index.html

Casino
http://www.mca.com/universal_pictures/casino/index.html

A Christmas Story
http://www.easttexas.com/pdlg/c-story/

Citizen Kane
http://www/voyagerco.com/CC/gh/welles/p.makingkane,html

Clockers
http://www.mca.com/universal_pictures/clockers/index.html

A Clockwork Orange
http://www.lehigh.edu/~pj12/films/clockwork.html

Clueless
http://www.paramount.com/Clueless.html

Death Race 2000
http://www.mcn.net/~netrencher/dr2k.html

The Doom Generation
http://www.filmzone.com/doom

Dr. Strangelove
http://xis.com/~dainjeur/ds.html

Dragonheart
http://www.mca.com/universal_pictures/dragonheart/

Eraserhead
http://users.aol.com/RayWolf1/eraser.htm

The Evil Dead
http://www.daze.com/exit13/evil/

Fast Times at Ridgemont High
http://wizvax.net/tuegger/fast-times.html

From Dusk Till Dawn
http://www.hooked.net/users/cpatubo/fdtd.html

Get Shorty
http://www.uip.com/getshorty/

Ghost in the Shell
http://www.manga.com/manga/ghost/ghost.html

Ghostbusters
http://www.nwdc.com/~vostok/ghostbusters.html

The Godfather Trilogy
http://www.exit109.com/~jgeoff/godfathr.html

Goldeneye
http://www.mgmua.com/bond/index.html

Gone With the Wind
http://users.aol.com/axlrose75/gone.htm

Halloween
http://ourworld.compuserve.com/homepages/Garrick_Bernard/

Heathers
http://www.bestcom/~sirlou/heathers.shtml

Hellraiser
http://www-personal.umich.edu/~rexerm/hell/

Hudson Hawk
http://ourworld.compuserve.com/homepage/David_HudsonHawk/

Indiana Jones
http://www.smartlink.net/~deej7/indy3.html

Independence Day
http://www.id4.com/

Jade
http://www.paramount.com/jade/index.html

Jaws
http://www.winternet.com/~tandj04/jaws.html

The Jerk
http://www.hirons.com/~lburgess/jerk.html

Joe vs. the Volcano
http://sashimi.wwa.com/~shopnet/jvv/

Jurassic Park
http://uslink.net/~warrior/

Mission Impossible
http://www.missionimpossible.com.

Monty Python's Holy Grail
http://bucket.ualr.edu/echo/contents.html

The Nutty Professor
http://www.mca.com/universal_pictures/nutty/

The Phantom
http://www.thephantom.com/

Phantasm
http://www.phantasm.com/

Plan 9 From Outer Space
http://www.eng2.uconn.edu/~jstrip/plan9/

Psycho
http://www.geocities.com/Hollywood/1645/index.html

Pulp Fiction
http://www/columbia.edu/~gan3/pulp.html

Ranma
http://www.coe.uncc.edu/~tecardwe/ranma.html

Reservoir Dogs
http://www.foresight.co.uk/ents/dogs/

Return of the Texas Chainsaw Massacre
http://chainsaw.crimson.com/rtcm/

Rob Roy
http://www.mgmua.com/robroy/index.html

Rocky Horror Picture Show
http://www-scf.usc.edu/~proulx/RHPS.html
http://www.insv.com/rhps/

Scarface
http://pubweb.acns.nwu.edu/~apoorman/scarface.html

Seven
http://www.filmzone.com/seven

Shaft
http://users.aol.com/PizarroD/shaft.html
http://www.rapidcity.com

The Shining
http://pubweb.acns.nwu.edu/~mdk899/overlook.html

Showgirls
http://www.mgmua.com/showgirls/index.html

Silence of the Lambs
http://www.pitt.edu/~elkst2/silence.html

Star Trek (Trek Reviews Archive)
http://www.mcs.net/~forbes/trek-reviews/

Strange Days
http://www.strangedays.com/

Superfly
http://student-www.uchicago.edu/users/bra9/fly.html

Terminator (1 &2)
http://www.maths.tcd.ie/pub/films/terminator/

This Is Spinal Tap
http://www.spinaltap.com/

Toy Story
http://www.disney.com/ToyStory/?GL=H

Truck Turner
http://www.castle.net/~dcentury/truck.html

12 Monkeys
http://www.mca.com/universal_pictures/12/faq.html

Twister
http://www.indirect.com/www/storm5/twisterhomepage.html

2001: A Space Odyssey
http://www.lehigh.edu/~pj12/films/2001.html

The Usual Suspects
http://www.spectra.net/~funkman/spacey/usual/usual/html

Virtuosity
http://www.paramount.com/virtuosity/index.html

Waterworld
http://mca.com/universal_pictures/waterworld/index.html

Willy Wonka and the Chocolate Factory
http://www.fred.net/gregg/html/willy/willy.html#index
http://www.stcloud.msus.edu/~hazelc01/wonka//willy.html

VIDEO OUTLETS

Adventures in Video
http://www.tds.net/aiv/htm
Offers a wide assortment of video titles from self-help to study aides.

Art and Trash Video
http://www.io.org/~imp/athome.htm
An outlet of over 7,500 har-to-find titles in the art and trash genres.

Best Video
http://www.bestvideo.com
With over 24,000 titles, you can search their inventory via various topics and subject categories. Also includes brief monthly reviews of current releases.

Big Lizard Video
http://www.well.com/user/bigliz/
Mail-order house specializing in obscure and bizarre films.

Blockbuster
http://pwr.com/blockbuster/
Find video releases, movie merchandise, movie reviews and news here. Ordering is only done through e-mail.

Carpel Video
http;//www.peakcom.com/carpel/
If you're only interested in purchasing blank and recycled video tapes, then you've hit the jackpot with this site.

CINEVISTA Video
http://www.gayweb.com/112/112home.html
Deals mainly in the distribution of independent gay films and videos.

Family Home Video
http://www.iea.com/~fhv/
On-line ordering service for over 25,000 titles that are also linked to the Internet Movie Database.

Flicks on Disc
http://www.teleport.com/~gilbert/flicks/public_html/index.html
Exclusive to the laser disc market with an expansive list of titles and news of upcoming releases.

HBO Home Video Online
http://hbohomevideo.com/
Along with information of their productions released on video, this site includes sounds, video clips, and celebrity photos.

Ken Crane's Laser Disc Super Store
http://www.kencranes.com/laserdiscs/
Largest retailer of laser discs offers mail- or on-line ordering.

Picture Palace
http://www.ids.net/picpal/index.html
Enormous on-line catalog with a comprehensive and searchable database for its 36,000+ titles. Also has special features including a magazine rack and a section for international cinema.

Rocket Video
http://www.rocketvideo.com/
A "virtual video store" that carries over 12,000 VHS titles and 500 laser discs. Has features which include "staff picks" and "coming soon".

Video Oyster
http://www.VideoOyster.com
Specializes in hard-to-find and out-of-print titles

More Credits

Sales Enthusiast:
Lauri Taylor

Special Sales:
Roger Janecke

Best Boys:
Bill Hoar
Robert Ahlers
Ken Hill

Set Director:
Ted Wedel

Gaffers:
Moira Magargee
Randall M. Spurgin
Sara Sinclair

Casting:
Jerry Stroud

Photography:
Michael Gorley

Sound Mixer:
Don Sturtz

Location Scout:
Richard Detrano

Costumes:
Linda Ziegler
Bob Arnold

Driver:
Ken Proctor

Catering:
Britts Cafe
Eddie's Drive-In

Any resemblance to persons living or dead is purely intentional (this is a non-fiction work, after all). The entries you have just read are true. No names were changed to protect anybody, even when they tried to use Alan Smithee, which is an alias people use when they realize they've been involved in a piece of junk. No freelancers were seriously harmed during the making of this book.

A Cunning Canine Production™

VideoHound's VideoDiary

(Notes on Tracking the *Wild Video*)

VideoHound's VideoDiary

(Notes on Tracking the *Wild Video*)

VideoHound's VideoDiary

(Notes on Tracking the *Wild Video*)

VideoHound's VideoDiary

(Notes on Tracking the *Wild Video*)

VideoHound's VideoDiary

(Notes on Tracking the *Wild Video*)

VideoHound's VideoDiary

(Notes on Tracking the *Wild Video*)

VideoHound's VideoDiary

(Notes on Tracking the *Wild Video*)

VideoHound's VideoDiary

(Notes on Tracking the *Wild Video*)

VideoHound's VideoDiary

(Notes on Tracking the *Wild Video*)

VideoHound's VideoDiary

(Notes on Tracking the *Wild Video*)

VideoHound's VideoDiary

(Notes on Tracking the *Wild Video*)

VideoHound's VideoDiary

(Notes on Tracking the *Wild Video*)

VideoHound's VideoDiary

(Notes on Tracking the *Wild Video*)

VideoHound's VideoDiary

(Notes on Tracking the *Wild Video*)